This Bible is given to:

Haley Sue Kirk

in celebration of her Confirmation Day

by

St. Paul's Lutheran Church

April 29th, 2007

The Learning Bible

New International Version

THE LEARNING BIBLE

New International Version

AMERICAN BIBLE SOCIETY
NEW YORK

THE LEARNING BIBLE

New International Version

Consulting editors: Howard Clark Kee, David G. Burke, Steven W. Berneking, and Erroll F. Rhodes.
Development editors: Charles Houser and Scott Tunseth.
Art development editor: Carol Sailors.
Contributing editors: Mark A. Throntveit, Carol Throntveit, Celia Brewer Marshall, David A. Renwick, and J. Clinton McCann, Jr.
Cover design by Bill Smith Studio.
Text design by A Good Thing, Inc.
Composition and page make-up by The Livingstone Corporation.

Quotation rights for the New International Version

Quotation rights for Learning Bible notes, articles, and reader's helps

Policy concerning illustrations and photographs

ISBN 1-58516-681-2

Printed in the United States of America
Eng. Bible NIV053P-112707
ABS-2/04-15,000-35,000—QW2

CONTENTS

THE NEW TESTAMENT

Alphabetical Listing with Abbreviations

THE NEW INTERNATIONAL VERSION

The New International Version is a completely new translation of the Holy Bible made by over a hundred scholars working directly from the best available Hebrew, Aramaic and Greek texts. It had its beginning in 1965 when, after several years of exploratory study by committees from the Christian Reformed Church and the National Association of Evangelicals, a group of scholars met at Palos Heights, Illinois, and concurred in the need for a new translation of the Bible in contemporary English. This group, though not made up of official church representatives, was transdenominational. Its conclusion was endorsed by a large number of leaders from many denominations who met in Chicago in 1966.

Responsibility for the new version was delegated by the Palos Heights group to a self-governing body of fifteen, the Committee on Bible Translation, composed for the most part of biblical scholars from colleges, universities and seminaries. In 1967 the New York Bible Society (now the International Bible Society) generously undertook the financial sponsorship of the project—a sponsorship that made it possible to enlist the help of many distinguished scholars. The fact that participants from the United States, Great Britain, Canada, Australia and New Zealand worked together gave the project its international scope. That they were from many denominations—including Anglican, Assemblies of God, Baptist, Brethren, Christian Reformed, Church of Christ, Evangelical Free, Lutheran, Mennonite, Methodist, Nazarene, Presbyterian, Wesleyan and other churches—helped to safeguard the translation from sectarian bias.

How it was made helps to give the New International Version its distinctiveness. The translation of each book was assigned to a team of scholars. Next, one of the Intermediate Editorial Committees revised the initial translation, with constant reference to the Hebrew, Aramaic or Greek. Their work then went to one of the General Editorial Committees, which checked it in detail and made another thorough revision. This revision in turn was carefully reviewed by the Committee on Bible Translation, which made further changes and then released the final version for publication. In this way the entire Bible underwent three revisions, during each of which the translation was examined for its faithfulness to the original languages and for its English style.

All this involved many thousands of hours of research and discussion regarding the meaning of the texts and the precise way of putting them into English. It may well be that no other translation has been made by a more thorough process of review and revision from committee to committee than this one.

From the beginning of the project, the Committee on Bible Translation held to certain goals for the New International Version: that it would be an accurate translation and one that would have clarity and literary quality and so prove suitable for public and private reading, teaching, preaching, memorizing and liturgical use.

The Committee also sought to preserve some measure of continuity with the long tradition of translating the Scriptures into English.

In working toward these goals, the translators were united in their commitment to the authority and infallibility of the Bible as God's Word in written form. They believe that it contains the divine answer to the deepest needs of humanity, that it sheds unique light on our path in a dark world, and that it sets forth the way to our eternal well-being.

The first concern of the translators has been the accuracy of the translation and its fidelity to the thought of the biblical writers. They have weighed the significance of the lexical and grammatical details of the Hebrew, Aramaic and Greek texts. At the same time, they have striven for more than a word-for-word translation. Because thought patterns and syntax differ from language to language, faithful communication of the meaning of the writers of the Bible demands frequent modifications in sentence structure and constant regard for the contextual meanings of words.

A sensitive feeling for style does not always accompany scholarship. Accordingly the Committee on Bible Translation submitted the developing version to a number of stylistic consultants. Two of them read every book of both Old and New Testaments twice—once before and once after the last major revision—and made invaluable suggestions. Samples of the translation were tested for clarity and ease of reading by various kinds of people—young and old, highly educated and less well educated, ministers and laymen.

Concern for clear and natural English—that the New International Version should be idiomatic but not idiosyncratic, contemporary but not dated—motivated the translators and consultants. At the same time, they tried to reflect the differing styles of the biblical writers. In view of the international use of English, the translators sought to avoid obvious Americanisms on the one hand and obvious Anglicisms on the other. A British edition reflects the comparatively few differences of significant idiom and of spelling.

As for the traditional pronouns "thou," "thee" and "thine" in reference to the Deity, the translators judged that to use these archaisms (along with the old verb forms such as "doest," "wouldest" and "hadst") would violate accuracy in translation. Neither Hebrew, Aramaic nor Greek uses special pronouns for the persons of the Godhead. A present-day translation is not enhanced by forms that in the time of the King James Version were used in everyday speech, whether referring to God or man.

For the Old Testament the standard Hebrew text, the Masoretic Text as published in the latest editions of *Biblia Hebraica*, was used throughout. The Dead Sea Scrolls contain material bearing on an earlier stage of the Hebrew text. They were consulted, as were the Samaritan Pentateuch and the ancient scribal traditions relating to textual changes. Sometimes a variant Hebrew reading in the margin of the Masoretic Text was followed instead of the text itself. Such instances, being variants within the Masoretic tradition, are not specified by footnotes. In rare cases, words in the consonantal text were divided differently from the way they appear in the Masoretic Text. Footnotes indicate this. The translators also consulted the more important early versions—the Septuagint; Aquila, Symmachus and Theodotion; the Vulgate; the Syriac Peshitta; the Targums; and for the Psalms the *Juxta Hebraica* of Jerome. Readings from these versions were occasionally followed where the Masoretic Text seemed doubtful and where accepted principles of textual criticism showed that one or more of these textual witnesses appeared to provide the correct reading. Such instances are footnoted. Sometimes vowel letters and vowel signs did not, in the judgment of the translators, represent the correct vowels for the original consonantal text. Accordingly some words were read with a different set of vowels. These instances are usually not indicated by footnotes.

The Greek text used in translating the New Testament was an eclectic one. No other piece of ancient literature has such an abundance of manuscript witnesses as does the New Testament. Where existing manuscripts differ, the translators made their choice of readings according to accepted principles of New Testament textual criticism. Footnotes call attention to places where there was uncertainty about what the original text was. The best current printed texts of the Greek New Testament were used.

There is a sense in which the work of translation is never wholly finished. This applies to all great literature and uniquely so to the Bible. In 1973 the New Testament in the New International Version was published. Since then, suggestions for corrections and revisions have been received from various sources. The Committee on Bible Translation carefully considered the suggestions and adopted a number of them. These were incorporated in the first printing of the entire Bible in 1978. Additional revisions were made by the Committee on Bible Translation in 1983 and appear in printings after that date.

As in other ancient documents, the precise meaning of the biblical texts is sometimes uncertain. This is more often the case with the Hebrew and Aramaic texts than with the Greek text. Although archaeological and linguistic discoveries in this century aid in understanding difficult passages, some uncertainties remain. The more significant of these have been called to the reader's attention in the footnotes.

In regard to the divine name *YHWH*, commonly referred to as the *Tetragrammaton*, the translators adopted the device used in most English versions of rendering that name as "LORD" in capital letters to distinguish it from *Adonai*, another Hebrew word rendered "Lord," for which small letters are used. Wherever the two names stand together in the Old Testament as a compound name of God, they are rendered "Sovereign LORD."

Because for most readers today the phrases "The LORD of hosts" and "the God of hosts" have little meaning, this version renders them "the LORD Almighty" and "God Almighty." These renderings convey the sense of the Hebrew, namely, "he who is sovereign over all the 'hosts' (powers) in heaven and on earth, especially over the 'hosts' (armies) of Israel." For readers unacquainted with Hebrew this does not make clear the distinction between *Sabaoth* ("hosts" or "Almighty") and *Shaddai* (which can also be translated "Almighty"), but the latter occurs infrequently and is always footnoted. When *Adonai* and *YHWH Sabaoth* occur together, they are rendered "the Lord, the LORD Almighty."

As for other proper nouns, the familiar spellings of the King James Version are generally retained. Names traditionally spelled with "ch," except where it is final, are usually spelled in this translation with "k" or "c," since the biblical languages do not have the sound that "ch" frequently indicates in English—for example, in *chant*. For well-known names such as Zechariah, however, the traditional spelling has been retained. Variation in the spelling of names in the original languages has usually not been indicated. Where a person or place has two or more different names in the Hebrew, Aramaic or Greek texts, the more familiar one has generally been used, with footnotes where needed.

To achieve clarity the translators sometimes supplied words not in the original texts but required by the context. If there was uncertainty about such material, it is enclosed in brackets. Also for the sake of clarity or style, nouns, including some proper nouns, are sometimes substituted for pronouns, and vice versa. And though the Hebrew writers often shifted back and forth between first, second and third personal pronouns without change of antecedent, this translation often makes them uniform, in accordance with English style and without the use of footnotes.

Poetical passages are printed as poetry, that is, with indentation of lines with separate stanzas. These are generally designed to reflect the structure of Hebrew poetry.

This poetry is normally characterized by parallelism in balanced lines. Most of the poetry in the Bible is in the Old Testament, and scholars differ regarding the scansion of Hebrew lines. The translators determined the stanza divisions for the most part by analysis of the subject matter. The stanzas therefore serve as poetic paragraphs.

As an aid to the reader, italicized sectional headings are inserted in most of the books. They are not to be regarded as part of the NIV text, are not for oral reading, and are not intended to dictate the interpretation of the sections they head.

The footnotes in this version are of several kinds, most of which need no explanation. Those giving alternative translations begin with "Or" and generally introduce the alternative with the word preceding it in the text, except when it is a single-word alternative; in poetry quoted in a footnote a slant mark indicates a line division. Footnotes introduced by "Or" do not have uniform significance. In some cases two possible translations were considered to have about equal validity. In other cases, though the translators were convinced that the translation in the text was correct they judged that another interpretation was possible and of sufficient importance to be represented in a footnote.

In the New Testament, footnotes that refer to uncertainty regarding the original text are introduced by "Some manuscripts" or similar expressions. In the Old Testament, evidence for the reading chosen is given first and evidence for the alternative is added after a semicolon (for example: Septuagint; Hebrew *father*). In such notes the term "Hebrew" refers to the Masoretic Text.

It should be noted that minerals, flora and fauna, architectural details, articles of clothing and jewelry, musical instruments and other articles cannot always be identified with precision. Also measures of capacity in the biblical period are particularly uncertain (see the Table of Weights Measures on p. 2445).

Like all translations of the Bible, made as they are by imperfect man, this one undoubtedly falls short of its goals. Yet we are grateful to God for the extent to which he has enabled us to realize these goals and for the strength he has given us and our colleagues to complete our task. We offer this version of the Bible to him in whose name and for whose glory it has been made. We pray that it will lead many into a better understanding of the Holy Scriptures and a fuller knowledge of Jesus Christ the incarnate Word, of whom the Scriptures so faithfully testify.

The Committee on Bible Translation

June 1978
(Revised Aug 1983)

Names of the translators and editors may be secured from the International Bible Society, translation sponsors of the New International Version, 1820 Jet Stream Drive, Colorado Springs, Colorado 08921-3696

HOW TO USE THE LEARNING BIBLE

The Learning Bible is an easy and colorful way to discover God's Word. Whether you began reading the Bible as a child or whether you are taking on this challenge now for the first time, the *Learning Bible* will help you get the most out of the time you set aside for this important educational and spiritual experience. This short article will introduce you to the many features and tools that are built into *The Learning Bible*. Take a moment to locate them in the text and become familiar with how they work. Each feature is designed to help you in one of three ways: (1) Point you in the right direction; (2) Get you the information you need; and (3) Help you connect with the Bible's message.

Getting You Pointed in the Right Direction

When church members have been surveyed and asked why they don't read the Bible on their own more often, the most frequent replies are "I don't know where to begin" and "I began at the beginning with GENESIS, but couldn't get through LEVITICUS." The Bible is a difficult book to read and even a modern translation can be hard to understand, because the events and customs it describes happened "long ago and far away" (some of them thousands of years ago). Because the Bible is a collection of many books, it doesn't matter which book of the Bible you read first. Some people like to begin with GENESIS. Others want to learn about Jesus right away, and select one of the Gospels. Wherever you begin, *The Learning Bible* has a number of tools to help you find your footing and head you in the right direction on the path of discovery.

Introductions and Outlines

Each book of the Bible starts with an Introduction, which gives information about who may have written the book and when it may have been written. It also introduces the book's important themes and provides you with clues to understanding its structure, including an outline of the book's contents.

In addition, *The Learning Bible* has Introductions to the Old and New Testaments and to groups of books within each Testament. These Introductions will give you a quick overview of the books contained in these sections and can help you decide which ones you'll want to read first.

Section Headings and Summary Introductions

The Bible text, which runs in the wide columns on either side of the book's "gutter," is divided by headings that have been added to make it easy for the reader to follow the action or the framework of a book. The large purple Section Headings are followed by short summaries of key events or teachings that will be covered in the Scripture text to follow. Some of these large sections may be further divided by blue-green headings that are printed in all capital letters. Note that both types of headings are taken directly from the outlines in the book Introductions. Then there are smaller, black headings that divide the Bible text even further. You can find your place easily in the Bible because references are noted with the name of the book, the chapter number, and then the verse number. For help on how to look up Bible references, see the explanation in "How To Look Up a Scripture Reference" (shaded box on the next page).

Getting You the Information You Need

The Learning Bible is designed so that you won't have to leave your chair in order to get the information you need to understand what's going on in the Bible. Definitions of words and explanations of concepts and customs that may be unfamiliar are on the page near the Scripture text they refer to. Or, you can find them in clearly identified sections positioned throughout the *Learning Bible.*

The New International Version

The translators of the *New International Version (NIV)* did many things to make the Bible easy to read and understand. For instance, the text is written to clarify certain terms and to still be true to the Bible texts in Hebrew and Greek. Special care was taken to make sure that figures of speech and customs that ancient people would have understood have been phrased in ways that are clear and to the point.

Notes

The Learning Bible provides six different categories of notes, which appear in the narrow outside columns on each page. Each of these categories is marked with its own colored symbol:

Geography

People and Nations

Objects, Plants, and Animals

History and Culture

Ideas and Concepts

Cross references

Mini-Articles and Background Articles

Some important topics call for more information than can be given in a simple note in the margin. *The Learning Bible* has over

HOW TO LOOK UP A SCRIPTURE REFERENCE

Here's a helpful hint for those who are unfamiliar with looking up Bible passages. Like many books, the Bible is divided into units (here called "books" of the Bible); and each book is divided into chapters. However, unlike most books, chapters are divided into much smaller units called "verses" (usually consisting of a sentence or two). Both chapters and verses are numbered. This provides a very convenient and useful system for identifying specific verses in the Bible. References to Bible passages will be listed in the following way.

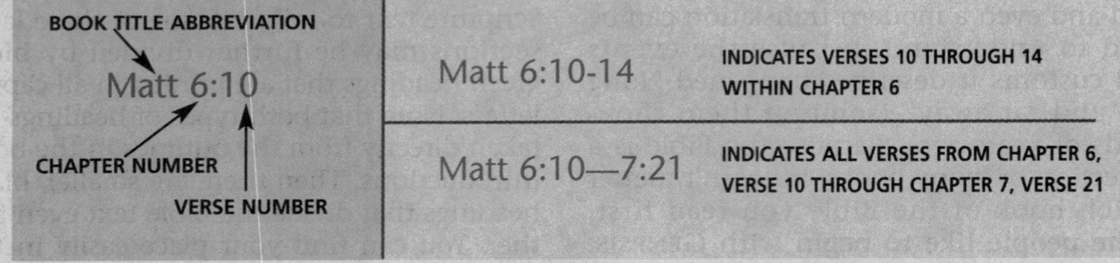

The more you look up Scripture references, the sooner you will become familiar with the abbreviations used and this system of notation. In the meantime, the "Alphabetical Listing with Abbreviations" located immediately after the "Contents" page will help you become familiar with any abbreviations you don't recognize.

one hundred mini-articles on such topics positioned at various places in the text. Like the marginal notes, they are keyed with one of the five color symbols to let you know if it is an article about Geography, People, an Object, History and Culture, or an Idea and Concept. *The Learning Bible* also includes fifteen longer background articles that give an overview of important topics. These are collected in three separate sections: (1) Articles on the Bible and how it came to be, (2) Articles on the ancient world and the religion of Israel, and (3) Articles on the world in the time of Jesus. A complete list of these articles is given on the contents page.

Cross References

Sometimes the author of one book of the Bible quotes another book of the Bible or makes a statement that is very similar to what another biblical author has written. Where this has happened, *The Learning Bible* lists a cross reference. Cross references are shown in one of two ways: (1) Listed within a note, footnote, or article; or (2) listed without text or comment after the orange symbol at the bottom of the narrow column on any page.

Footnotes

The *NIV* Bible was translated into English from ancient Greek and Hebrew manuscripts. These manuscripts are very old and were copied out by hand. Consequently, they do not always agree with one another word for word. When these differences occur, translators need to decide which manuscript to use in the translation. After making their decision, they often list other possible renderings in a footnote. They also use footnotes to identify when the original language text is unclear and to explain other decisions they had to make.

Charts and Bible Timeline

The Learning Bible provides throughout the book a number of charts that summarize detailed information and display it in a way that is easy for the reader to look up. At the back of *The Learning Bible* is a Bible Timeline that provides an easy-to-follow overview of the history of the ancient world from the earliest times through the time of the apostles.

Maps

The events described in the Bible occurred over a period of thousands of years and in places as far apart as Mesopotamia, Ethiopia, Greece, and Rome. To help the reader keep track of the way the "Bible Lands" changed from one era to the next, *The Learning Bible* provides a number of reference maps. Large, full-color, topographical maps keyed to specific periods of history are gathered together in the Mini-Atlas at the back of this volume. These provide a good overview of the Holy Land and include most of the place names you will encounter when reading the Bible. From time to time, one of the articles or marginal notes will direct you to one of these maps. In addition, there are a number of small spot maps positioned at various points within the text for quick reference or to provide specific information not found in the Mini-Atlas maps.

Illustrations and Photographs

The Learning Bible also provides illustrations, diagrams, and photographs to help you understand life in Bible times and to get a view of the way the Holy Land looks today.

Helping You Connect with the Bible's Message

Most people who read the Bible are looking for more than information about ancient people and customs. They believe (or hope) it contains truth, comfort, and spiritual insight that will provide them with guidance for their daily lives. *The Learning Bible* has a number of features that will help you understand and appreciate the impact God's Word has had and continues to have.

Art from Around the World

The events and stories in the Bible have touched people's hearts and lives throughout the world for many centuries. *The Learning Bible* includes reproductions of paintings, drawings, sculpture, and other powerful works of art from many cultures.

Questions about Each Book of the Bible

Sections of "Reflection Questions" are provided at various points within the Scripture books. These questions are intended to help you review the content of the book, discover what it means, and see how it relates to your life today. You can answer these questions silently to yourself, keep a "devotional journal" of your responses, or use the questions as a discussion guide for group Bible study.

Memory Verses

Many people find comfort and strength from memorizing Scripture verses. A number of important and inspirational verses have been highlighted in the top outside corners of the pages. These are by no means the *only* verses worth memorizing, but they do represent the kinds of messages that you'll discover each time you read the Bible.

Bible Reading Plans

At the back of *The Learning Bible* are two Bible reading plans. Select the one that best matches your needs and fits into your schedule. Most people who make a practice of reading the Bible say they benefit most from reading the Bible on a daily basis—regardless of how much or how little time they set aside to do this. The Reading Plans in *The Learning Bible* are:

1. *Read Through the Bible in a Year.* Many people have always wanted to read the Bible all the way through. This plan provides a scheme that allows you to read some Old Testament and some New Testament every day. Be prepared to spend about a half hour every day in order to complete your reading on schedule.

2. *A Moment with Scripture.* Many people feel pulled in a hundred different directions and complain about too many demands on their time. Reading the Bible is a wonderful way to "get one's bearings" before facing all these challenges. This plan only requires five minutes a day. And the passages selected are especially geared to people who are caught up in the "rush of life."

It's never too soon to begin discovering God's Word for yourself . . . or to rediscover it, if you set it aside because you found it too difficult to understand. *The Learning Bible* gives you the help you need to make Bible reading a consistent part of your life. Start reading it today!

Your statutes are wonderful;
therefore I obey them.
The unfolding of your words gives light;
it gives understanding to the simple.
I open my mouth and pant,
longing for your commands.
Psalm 119:129-131

The Old Testament

HOW THE BIBLE CAME TO US

The Bible is like a small library that contains many books written by many authors. The word "Bible" comes from the Greek word *biblia*, meaning "books." It took well over one thousand years for all of these books to be written down, and it was many more years before the list of books now known as the Bible came together in one large book.

Passing Stories Along

Before anything in the Bible was written down, people told stories about God and God's relationship with the people we now read about in the Bible. This stage of passing on stories by word of mouth is known as the "oral tradition." This stage of relating stories by word of mouth lasted for many years as families passed along the stories of their ancestors to each new generation. In the case of the Jewish Scriptures (Old Testament), some stories were told for centuries before they were written down in a final form.

Long before the Bible was ever written, its stories, teachings, lists of ancestors, and poems were passed along from one generation to the next by word of mouth in storytelling gatherings. This is known as "the oral tradition."

Writing Down the Bible Stories

Eventually, as human societies in the Near East began to develop forms of writing that were easy to learn and use (around 1800 B.C.), people began to write down the stories, songs (psalms), and prophecies that would one day become a part of the Bible. These were written on papyrus, a paper-like material made from reeds, or on vellum, which was made from dried animal skins. (See the mini-article called "Scrolls," p. 1491). But all the books found in the Old Testament were not written down at one time. This process took centuries. While some books were being written and collected, others were still being passed on in storytelling fashion.

The very first manuscripts of the books that make up the Old and New Testaments have never been found, and most likely wore out from continued use or were destroyed centuries ago. However, copies of these manuscripts were made by hand and became valued possessions of synagogues, churches, and monasteries. Before these copies wore out, new copies were made, and then eventually copies were made from these copies—and so on, from one generation to the next. Some very old copies of both the Old and New Testament writings have been preserved, and they are now stored in museums and libraries around the world in places like Jerusalem, London, Paris, Dublin, New York, Chicago, Philadelphia, and Ann Arbor, Michigan.

Collecting the Jewish Scriptures

It is not possible to know exactly when all the books of the Jewish Scriptures were finally collected. Some of the writings in the Jewish Scriptures may go back as far as 1300 B.C., but the process of bringing the books together may not have begun until

Once the stories of the Bible began to be written down, it became necessary to make new copies before the old ones wore out from repeated use and became unreadable. Sometimes several scribes made copies while another scribe read the text aloud.

around 400 B.C. The process of deciding which books would be part of the official Jewish Scriptures went on until almost A.D. 100. This work was often done by Jewish rabbis (teachers).

Preparing the Bible for a Changing World

It was during this time that the Jewish Scriptures were translated into Greek. This translation is called the Septuagint, which means "seventy," and is often identified by the Roman numeral for seventy (LXX). The legend of how the Septuagint came to be, and how it got its name is told in a document called the *Letter of Aristeas.* The legend says that seventy-two scholars began translating the Jewish Scriptures from Hebrew, all at the same time. The *Letter* goes on to say that they all finished at the same time, in seventy-two days, and that all seventy-two scholars discovered that their translations were exactly the same! All the seventy-some numbers in this story gave the translation its name. This Greek version of the Bible was used by Jewish people scattered throughout the Roman world, because most of them spoke Greek instead of Hebrew. The oldest copies of the Septuagint date from the second century B.C., more than one hundred years before Jesus was born. The Septuagint was also the main version of the Jewish Scriptures used by early Christians.

It is not exactly clear how it was decided which books should be considered holy enough to be included in the Jewish Scriptures. We do know that around A.D. 100, a group of Jewish scholars met at Jamnia, a center of Jewish learning west of Jerusalem. During this time, the scholars debated which books should be in the Jewish Scriptures. Probably these scholars' discussions were a large part of the Jewish community's decision that thirty-nine books should be on the holy list (canon). Seven books, sometimes called the "deuterocanonical" books (meaning "second list"), were not included on the list. Today, most Protestant churches follow the original list of thirty-nine books and call it the Old Testament. The Roman Catholic, Anglican (Episcopal), and Eastern Orthodox churches include the deuterocanonical books in their Old Testament. For more about this, see the article called "What Books Belong in the Bible?," p. 13.

The Stories of Christ and His First Followers

Jesus and most of his followers were Jewish, and so they used and quoted the Jewish Scriptures. After Jesus died and was raised to life around A.D. 30, the stories about Jesus, as well as his sayings, were passed on by word of mouth. It probably wasn't until about A.D. 65 that these stories and sayings began to be gathered and written down in books known as the Gospels, which make up about half of what Christians call the New Testament. The earliest writings of the New Testament, however, are probably some of the letters that the apostle Paul wrote to groups of Jesus' followers who were scattered throughout the Roman empire. The first of these letters, probably 1 THESSALONIANS, may have been written as early as A.D. 50. Some scholars feel that all the New Testament writings were written by the end of the first century A.D.; others feel that a portion of the New Testament was written early in the second century.

The New Testament books were written in Greek, an international language during this period of the Roman empire. They were often passed on and read as single books or letters. For nearly three hundred years (A.D. 100-400), the early church leaders and councils debated about which New Testament writings should be considered inspired by God and treated with the same respect given to the Jewish Scriptures. In A.D. 367, Athanasius, the bishop of Alexandria, wrote a letter that listed the twenty-seven books he said Christians should consider authoritative. His list included the books already in widest use in the Christian churches, and the writings he named are the same twenty-seven books that today we call the New Testament.

Translating the Bible

When the New Testament books were written, the Greek language was understood all over the Mediterranean world. But by the late second century A.D., local languages were becoming popular again, especially in local churches. Translations of the Bible were then made into Latin, the language of Rome; Coptic, a language of Egypt; and Syriac, a language of Syria. In A.D. 383, Pope Damasus I assigned a scholar priest named Jerome to create an official translation of the Bible into Latin. It took Jerome about twenty-seven years to translate the whole Bible. His translation came to be known as the Vulgate and served as the standard version of the Bible in Western Europe for the next thousand years. By the Middle Ages, only scholars could read and understand Latin. But by the time Johannes Guttenberg invented the modern printing press (around 1456), the use of vernacular (local or national) languages was becoming acceptable and widespread in official, educational, and religious settings. And as more people began to learn to read, there was a new demand for the Bible in vernacular languages. And so translators like Martin Luther, William Tyndale, Cassiodoro de Reina, and Giovanni Diodati began to translate the Bible into the languages that people spoke in their everyday lives.

The process of Bible translating continues today, and it has been helped by some recent discoveries. For example, many ancient Greek manuscripts of the New Testament have been found in the last 150 years. In 1947, some very old manuscripts of the Jewish Scriptures were found in caves at Qumran, Murabba'at, and other locations just west of the Dead Sea in Israel, and have become known as the Dead Sea Scrolls. These manuscripts, which date from between the third century B.C. and the first century A.D., have helped modern scholars to better understand the wording of certain texts and to make decisions about how to best translate specific verses or words. See the photograph on p. 933.

The Bible is a very old book that has come to us because many men and women have worked hard copying and studying manuscripts, examining important artifacts and ancient ruins, and translating ancient texts into modern languages. Their dedication has helped keep the story of God's people and the work of God's revelation alive.

INSPIRATION OF SCRIPTURE

Christians believe that the Bible is inspired by God. The apostle Paul wrote to his co-worker Timothy, "All Scripture is God-breathed and is useful for teaching, rebuking, correcting and training in righteousness" (2 Tim 3:16). Paul asserts God's active role in the writing of Scripture—a role so significant that what is written is the authoritative Word of God. God "breathed," as it were, on the authors of Scripture, and they were compelled to record the message God desired people to hear.

Of course, Paul would have been referring to the Jewish Scriptures (Old Testament), since some of the New Testament books had yet to be written at the time. But there are indications that, if Paul wrote 2 Timothy near the end of his life, some writings that would eventually be included in the New Testament were already being copied and circulated among the early churches throughout the Roman Empire. Since they reflected the teachings of Jesus' earliest disciples, they were cherished and considered equal in authority to the Old Testament Scriptures. For instance, in one letter Paul quotes Deuteronomy 25:4 and Luke 10:7—referring to both as "Scripture" (1 Tim 5:18). And 2 Peter reveals that, at the time this letter was written, Paul's letters were already considered Scripture: "[Paul's] letters contain some things that are hard to understand, which ignorant and unstable people distort, as they do the other Scriptures" (2 Pet 3:16).

Second Peter contains another important passage about the inspiration of Scripture. "Above all, you must understand that no prophecy of Scripture came about by the prophet's own interpretation. For prophecy never had its origin in the will of man, but men spoke from God as they were carried along by the Holy Spirit" (2 Pet 1:20, 21). This shows that both God and the human authors were actively involved in the production of Scripture. The writings of Scripture have their origin in God, not in the will of a human being. Therefore, what Scripture says is what God wished to communicate. But this wasn't a process of simple dictation; the human authors also actively spoke. The personalities and communication styles of the writers are evident—"as they were carried along by the Holy Spirit."

Luke said he "carefully investigated" his subject while writing his Gospel (Luke 1:3), showing that inspiration by the Holy Spirit did not exclude human effort. In addition, 1 Peter reveals that, although the Old Testament prophets produced Holy Scripture, inspiration did not bring them complete understanding (1 Pet 1:10-12). They did not necessarily comprehend the complete significance of all the words they spoke and wrote.

Because of the character of the God who inspired them, the writings of Scripture are totally trustworthy. Jesus succinctly testified to the authority of the Old Testament when he said, "The Scripture cannot be broken" (John 10:35). Regarding the gospel message of the New Testament, Paul wrote to the believers in Thessalonica: "We also thank God continually because, when you received the word of God, which you heard from us, you accepted it not as the word of men, but as it actually is, the word of God, which is at work in you who believe" (1 Thes 2:13). Since the word of God is "living and active" and "enduring" (Heb 4:12; 1 Pet 1:23), we can be sure that the Scriptures are at work in those who believe today as well.

WHAT BOOKS BELONG IN THE BIBLE?

The Bible as Christians know it today did not begin as one large volume—with Old and New Testaments. It came into being as part of a selection process called "canonization." The Greek word for "canon" can mean many things, such as "measuring rod" or "ruler." At first, the early church leaders used "canon" to mean a "standard," and later a "list" or "catalog" of authoritative writings. There were many books circulating among the churches throughout the Roman world that were read and studied by the early church. It was important for the church leaders at that time to go through a process of deciding which books were inspired by God and had authority for God's people. This process did not happen overnight. In some cases, it took hundreds of years from the time they were written to decide which of the many writings that were being read should be part of Holy Scripture, that is, the Bible.

The Hebrew Scriptures and the Old Testament

The books in the Old Testament section of *The Learning Bible* are translations of the Hebrew Scriptures still used by the Jewish people in their worship services today. These books were written by many different authors over a period of hundreds of years. The Introductions to the individual books of the Old Testament in *The Learning Bible* offer some suggestions about where and when these books may have been written, so this article will not try to deal with this issue.

It can be said that the Old Testament developed in stages and its books were collected in groups. Before the process of collecting books and putting them in some kind of order took place, individual manuscripts were copied by hand and passed among groups. The earliest literature of the Jewish people may date as far back as

BOOKS OF THE HEBREW SCRIPTURES, OR "TANAK"

TORAH (The Law)	NEVI'IM (The Prophets)	KETHUVIM (The Writings)
GENESIS	JOSHUA	PSALMS
EXODUS	JUDGES	JOB
LEVITICUS	SAMUEL (1 & 2 Sam)	PROVERBS
NUMBERS	KINGS (1 & 2 Kgs)	RUTH
DEUTERONOMY	ISAIAH	SONG OF SONGS
	JEREMIAH	ECCLESIASTES
	EZEKIEL	LAMENTATIONS
	BOOK OF THE TWELVE	ESTHER
	Hosea	DANIEL
	Joel	EZRA–NEHEMIAH
	Amos	CHRONICLES (1 & 2 Chr)
	Obadiah	
	Jonah	
	Micah	
	Nahum	
	Habakkuk	
	Zephaniah	
	Haggai	
	Zechariah	
	Malachi	

THE OLD TESTAMENT IN CHRISTIAN BIBLES

The Old Testament in Christian Bibles contains all of the books included in the Jewish Scriptures. Some Christian traditions, however, also include books that are not part of the Hebrew Bible. Most of these books were included in the Septuagint, a Greek translation of the Hebrew Bible that was used by the apostles and the early Christians.

The Protestant Old Testament contains only the books found in the Hebrew Bible, but arranges them in a different order. The Catholic Old Testament contains all of these books

PROTESTANT	CATHOLIC	ORTHODOX
GENESIS	GENESIS	GENESIS
EXODUS	EXODUS	EXODUS
LEVITICUS	LEVITICUS	LEVITICUS
NUMBERS	NUMBERS	NUMBERS
DEUTERONOMY	DEUTERONOMY	DEUTERONOMY
JOSHUA	JOSHUA	JOSHUA
JUDGES	JUDGES	JUDGES
RUTH	RUTH	RUTH
1 SAMUEL	1 SAMUEL	1 KINGDOMS (1 SAM)
2 SAMUEL	2 SAMUEL	2 KINGDOMS (2 SAM)
1 KINGS	1 KINGS	3 KINGDOMS (1 KGS)
2 KINGS	2 KINGS	4 KINGDOMS (2 KGS)
1 CHRONICLES	1 CHRONICLES	1 CHRONICLES
2 CHRONICLES	2 CHRONICLES	2 CHRONICLES
EZRA	EZRA	*1 ESDRAS*
NEHEMIAH	NEHEMIAH	*2 ESDRAS* (EZRA + NEH)
ESTHER	*TOBIT*	*ESTHER (with additions)*[1]
JOB	*JUDITH*	*JUDITH*
PSALMS	*ESTHER (with additions)*[1]	*TOBIT*
PROVERBS	*1 MACCABEES*	*1 MACCABEES*
ECCLESIASTES	*2 MACCABEES*	*2 MACCABEES*
SONG OF SONGS	JOB	*3 MACCABEES*
ISAIAH	PSALMS	PSALMS (plus *Ps 151*)
JEREMIAH	PROVERBS	*PRAYER OF MANASSEH*
LAMENTATIONS	ECCLESIASTES	JOB
EZEKIEL	SONG OF SONGS	PROVERBS
DANIEL	*WISDOM OF SOLOMON*	ECCLESIASTES

Books listed in the Catholic and Orthodox columns that are printed in *red italics* are part of the traditional Protestant Apocrypha. Books that are printed in *black italics* are traditionally included only in Orthodox Bibles.

[1]ESTHER in Catholic and Orthodox Bibles includes six additional passages that are found in the Septuagint version of ESTHER.

plus the other books that were part of the Septuagint. The Orthodox Old Testament includes all of these books, plus *3* and *4 Maccabees, Prayer of Manasseh, Psalm 151*, and *1 Esdras* which are included in the Orthodox Bible because they appear in some versions of the Septuagint. The list below shows the order in which these books usually appear in Bibles printed for each of these Christian communities.

PROTESTANT	CATHOLIC	ORTHODOX
HOSEA	*SIRACH*[2]	SONG OF SONGS
JOEL	ISAIAH	*WISDOM OF SOLOMON*
AMOS	JEREMIAH	*SIRACH*[2]
OBADIAH	LAMENTATIONS	HOSEA
JONAH	*BARUCH (with Letter of Jeremiah)*	AMOS
MICAH	EZEKIEL	MICAH
NAHUM	*DANIEL (with additions)*[3]	JOEL
HABAKKUK	HOSEA	OBADIAH
ZEPHANIAH	JOEL	JONAH
HAGGAI	AMOS	NAHUM
ZECHARIAH	OBADIAH	HABAKKUK
MALACHI	JONAH	ZEPHANIAH
	MICAH	HAGGAI
	NAHUM	ZECHARIAH
	HABAKKUK	MALACHI
	ZEPHANIAH	ISAIAH
	HAGGAI	JEREMIAH
	ZECHARIAH	*BARUCH*
	MALACHI	LAMENTATIONS
		LETTER OF JEREMIAH
		EZEKIEL
		DANIEL (with additions)[3]
		4 MACCABEES (in Appendix)

[2]*SIRACH* is also known as *Ecclesiasticus*.

[3]DANIEL in Catholic and Orthodox Bibles includes additional sections sometimes printed with the titles: "Prayer of Azariah and the Song of the Three Young Men," "Susanna," and "Bel and the Dragon."

the time of Moses or earlier (about 1300 B.C.), while other literature found in the Old Testament (for instance DANIEL) may have been written as late as the second century B.C. That would mean that the literature collected into the Old Testament was written over a period of 1000 years or more!

While the writing of Hebrew manuscripts was taking place, the process of collecting and editing was also going on. One important collection of books was called "The Law," which included the first five books of the Bible. "The Law" is also called by its Hebrew name, *Torah*, and by the name *Pentateuch,* which is the Greek term for a five-volume book. Another collection was called "The Prophets." In the Jewish Bible, this collection includes certain books that Christians would call "history books." The last major group of books to be collected was simply called "The Writings." They contain books of poetry and wise sayings, and books that Christians would consider prophetic or historical in nature. Because different religious traditions arrange these books differently, a chart has been provided for easy reference.

It is not known exactly how or when the books of the Old Testament were selected and approved for inclusion in the Hebrew Scriptures, but it is certain that the books of the *Torah* were accepted as authoritative almost from the time they were written. There is also some evidence that the list of authoritative books was not finalized until after A.D. 100. Only the books on this final list were considered to be Scripture by the Jewish people.

The chart on p. 13 shows the three main sections of the Hebrew Scriptures: The Law, The Prophets, and The Writings. If you compare this list to the chart on p. 14, you'll notice that all of these books are included in the Old Testaments of Christian Bibles, though they are grouped differently and placed in a slightly different order. The Hebrew word for Bible is *Tanak* (sometimes spelled *Tanakh*). This is an acronym, or a word made from the first letters of the Hebrew words for each of the three main sections: *Torah, Nevi'im,* and *Kethuvim*.

If you further examine the chart on p. 14, you'll notice that some Christian traditions include other books in their Old Testaments as well. These additional writings are known as "apocryphal" or "deuterocanonical" books. The term "apocrypha" comes from a Greek word meaning "hidden," and today suggests books that have been "set aside" or given secondary status. The term "deuterocanonical," a word that Catholics prefer to use when referring to many of these same books, means books that came into the canon at a later (secondary) date, in order to distinguish them from the Hebrew Scriptures discussed above. In the 1600s, some Protestant Christians began to use only the Jewish list of Old Testament books, while the Roman Catholic and Eastern Orthodox Christians continued to use some or all of the apocryphal/deuterocanonical books as well. Some of these books are discussed in the following section on Greek versions of the Jewish Scriptures.

Greek Versions of the Jewish Scriptures

In the third century B.C. Jewish scholars in Alexandria, Egypt, translated the Hebrew Scriptures into Greek, since many Jewish people lived in Greek-speaking areas of the Mediterranean world, and spoke Greek on an everyday basis. This Greek version of the Jewish Scriptures is known as the Septuagint (commonly abbreviated LXX). For an explanation of this name, see the article called "How the Bible Came to Us," p. 9.

Some of the Jewish scholars in Egypt did not agree on which books should be included in the official list of Scriptures, even though a canon was being agreed upon by another group of Jewish scholars in Palestine. For example, some of the Egyptian scholars would allow only documents written in Hebrew or Aramaic (a Semitic language similar to Hebrew). Other

Alexandria on the Nile Delta was one of the most important cultural centers in the Mediterranean world in the first century A.D. Its library had over four hundred thousand volumes and would have been used frequently by the large Jewish community that lived there. The Septuagint, a Greek translation of the Hebrew Bible, was made by Jewish scholars in Alexandria.

Greek-speaking Jews included documents originally written in Greek (some of them from as late as the first century A.D.). These Greek writings included:

Historical writings: *1 Esdras* (a Greek version of EZRA in the Hebrew Bible, with some additions); *Judith; Tobit; 1–4 Maccabees*; and

Poetic and prophetic writings, wisdom, and tales: *Sirach* (sometimes called *Ecclesiasticus*); *Wisdom of Solomon; Baruch; Letter of Jeremiah; Susanna; Prayer of Azariah and the Song of the Three Young Men;* and *Bel and the Dragon.*

Though most of these titles may not sound familiar to many Christians today, many of the early Christians seem to have accepted them as part of their Scriptures. Aside from these documents, there were also additions to the Greek translation of the Hebrew book of ESTHER that was made in the second and first centuries B.C. And, some of the tales listed above were added to the Greek translation of DANIEL (see the notes in the chart on p. 14-15).

The Roman Catholic Bible still includes many of these books, along with the fuller versions of the books of ESTHER and DANIEL. The Greek Orthodox Bible includes many of these books, plus a few others, such as the *Prayer of Manasseh* and an extra psalm (151). Although most Protestant Bibles now follow the list called "Hebrew Scriptures" shown in the chart on p. 13, and exclude the "extra" books, some editions include them but place them between the Old and New Testaments or at the end of the Bible.

The New Testament

Jesus and his disciples spoke Aramaic and used the Hebrew version of the Jewish Scriptures, but the apostle Paul and many other early Christians spoke Greek and used the Greek version of the Jewish Scriptures (Septuagint). Of the many Old Testament passages quoted or referred to in the New Testament, most are taken from the Septuagint. Though a small number of Christians, by the third and fourth centuries, thought that the Jewish Scriptures should not be part of the Christian Bible, most believed, as did the writers of the New Testament, that the Jewish Scriptures were the Word of God. They considered these writings to be inspired by God and authoritative, and to be suitable for instructing Christians about God and faith (see Mark 7:13; Rom 3:2; 2 Tim 3:16; Heb 1:1). After all, they would have argued, Jesus said that he did not come to do away with the Law and the Prophets, but to fulfill them (Matt 5:17-19).

The twenty-seven books that are included in the present New Testament were written by a number of different authors, the earliest ones being written as early as A.D. 50 and none being written any later than the early part of the second century. Exact dating is not possible, but certain books give clues about when they may have been written. The letters of Paul are probably the oldest writings included in the New Testament.

MATTHEW, MARK, LUKE, and JOHN (the Gospels) were probably written between A.D. 60, ten years before the temple was destroyed in Jerusalem, and A.D. 100. Most scholars agree that MARK was probably the first Gospel written, since MATTHEW and LUKE seem to take many of their details and the order of events directly from MARK. Some of the other letters and REVELATION were probably some of the last books to be written, since they seem to give a picture of the situations Christians faced at the end of the first century and in the early part of the second century A.D. See the Introduction to each New Testament book for an explanation of when they might have been written.

The books included in the present New Testament were not the only letters or Gospels written by Christians during the first and second centuries. It took many years of debate between church leaders and scholars to finally settle on an accepted list (canon) of New Testament books. Various church leaders proposed different lists in the three hundred years that followed the writing of the New Testament books, but the list proposed in A.D. 367 by Athanasius, a bishop of Alexandria, is the accepted list that nearly all Christian traditions use today.

How did the church leaders decide which books should become part of the accepted list of writings inspired by God? There were probably three "tests" they used to make their decision. First of all, a book had to have some connection with one of the early apostles. This meant that either an apostle or an immediate associate was judged to be the writer of the book, and the material was thought to capture the key teachings of the apostles. Second, the book or letter had to be in agreement with the Jewish Scriptures and other accepted New Testament writings. The third test had to do with usage. Was the book or letter accepted and being used by a majority of Christians? If so, the case for including it as part of the New Testament was stronger.

The Protestant, Roman Catholic, and Eastern Orthodox churches all generally consider the twenty-seven books of the New Testament to be "canonical" and usually list them in the same order in their Bibles. See the Contents page for the names of these books and the Introduction to the New Testament on p. 1843 for a description of how the New Testament is organized.

DIFFERENT KINDS OF LITERATURE IN THE BIBLE

Most books fall into one particular category of literature or another. An instruction booklet for making something uses technical language; a novel will probably use some kind of fictional narrative; a book of poetry may use rhymed or non-rhymed verse; and a book of history uses factual narrative writing. The type of book almost always determines the literary form used. The Bible is bound as one large book, but it is really made up of many different books using many different kinds of literature. This makes the Bible both challenging and exciting to read.

When studying the books of the Bible, it is important to look not only at the information a book contains but also at the literary form that the author has used. The kind of literature used can give clues about what the author was trying to say. For example, look at 1 Samuel 1:1-28 and compare it to 1 Samuel 2:1-10. These passages from the same book use two different kinds of writing. The first section is more like prose, or story, while the second section is a prayer or song in poetic form. Noticing the change from prose to poetry can give a reader more to think about regarding the text.

A brief example from the New Testament is the story of Jesus' birth. Luke 2:1-21 tells of the events of Jesus' birth and gives many details regarding the birth itself. In contrast, JOHN does not use a story to tell about Jesus' birth. Instead, it begins with a poem (1:1-14), which refers to Jesus as "the Word" and "the true light" that "became flesh." How do these different kinds of literature influence the way we think about who Jesus is? Why has the writer of each of these Gospels emphasized different aspects of Jesus' birth and identity? Looking at how a writer chooses to share information can open the way for new ways of understanding what the Bible has to say.

The Bible includes a great number of types of literature. Some forms of literature describe an entire book. In the Bible the most important of these forms are laws and rules, history, poetry and songs, wisdom sayings and proverbs, Gospels, letters, and apocalyptic writings. Other forms of literature describe sections within a book. The most important of these forms are prose narrative, prayers, parables, prophecies (oracles), and long family lists (genealogies). Regardless of literary type, Christians believe that the writings of Scripture are uniquely and powerfully inspired by God.

Literary Forms for Whole Books

Laws and rules. Many ancient Near Eastern cultures developed law codes. One of the most famous was the Code developed by the Babylonian leader named Hammurabi, who ruled from about 1792 to 1750 B.C. The first five books of the Jewish Scriptures (Old Testament) make up the section known as the Law, or *Torah.* Not all of the literature in these five books includes laws, but much does. These laws include both laws that forbid things ("Do not...") and laws that encourage things ("Do..."), and were given to the people of Israel in order to help them worship correctly and treat one another with respect and care. The most well-known law literature in the Bible is the Ten Commandments (Exod 20:1-17; Deut 5:6-21; see also the mini-article called "Ten Commandments," p. 354). Other examples are found in Exodus 21:1—23:19; Leviticus 1:1—7:36; Numbers 6:1-21; 35:6-34; Deuteronomy 14:3—17:7; James 4:11,12.

History. In the Old Testament, history writings tell the story of Israel's history from the settlement of Canaan in 1250 B.C. to the fall of Jerusalem in 587 B.C. These books describe the activities of such important figures as the prophets Elijah and Elisha, and the kings of Israel and Judah, including King David and King Solomon. These books also include information about the events of the two Israelite kingdoms after the split in 931 B.C. Examples of history books in the Old Testament are JOSHUA and 1 and 2 KINGS.

LES

PSEAVMES DE DAVID.

PSEAVME I. C. M.

Pſeaume de doctrine. Beatus vir qui non abiit in conſilio.

Qvi au conſeil des malins n'a eſté, Qui n'eſt au
train des pecheurs arreſté, Qui des moqueurs au
banc place n'a priſe, Mais nuict & jour la Loi contemple & priſe
De l'Eternel, & en eſt deſireux : Certainement celui-là eſt heureux.
Et ſemblera un arbre grand & beau,
Planté au long d'un clair courant ruiſſeau,
Et qui ſon fruict en ſa ſaiſon apporte,
Duquel auſſi la fueille ne chet morte.
Si qu'un tel homme & tout ce qu'il fera,
Toſjours heureux & proſpere ſera.

This French New Testament, printed in 1664, includes psalms marked with musical notation for singing. Although little is known about the exact way the psalms of the Bible were originally performed, the beautiful poetry of Psalms *has never ceased to inspire Jews and Christians to put them to music and to perform them as part of their worship.*

In the New Testament, Acts tells the history of the early church.

Poetry and songs. This is a large category that includes different forms. Poetry is used especially in Psalms, Job, and the Song of Songs. But poetry can be found in many books of the Bible. Some poems in the Bible are examples of old hymns or songs. Many of the psalms were meant for use in worship and prayer. The speeches of the prophets include poetic forms of language. Translating Hebrew poetry into English is not simple, and sometimes special techniques that are effective in the original language cannot be meaningfully carried over into English. One important feature of Hebrew poetry is the repeating of a single idea in two similar but different ways. This is called "parallelism" and an example is Psalm 22:9, 10. Other examples of poetry in the Old Testament include: Exodus 15:1-18; Job 22:21-30; Psalm 23; Isaiah 5:1-7; and Jonah 2:2-9. Poetry is also used in the New Testament. Some examples are Luke 1:46-55; Philippians 2:6-11; and Revelation 15:3,4.

Wisdom sayings and proverbs. The large division of the Old Testament called "Wisdom and Worship" literature includes poetry, psalms, stories, and more. Here, wisdom sayings and proverbs have a unique style which makes them read like common sense reflections about the world, God, and the place of human beings. Wisdom sayings fill a book like Proverbs, but they can also be found in other books. Books like Ecclesiastes and Job offer wisdom along with the kinds of philosophic reflections listed above. Wisdom writings usually do not give much direct information about Israel's history. Instead, they raise questions about moral issues, and ask hard questions about life. Some of these Wisdom writings are attributed to Solomon, who was known as Israel's wisest king. In addition to the books already mentioned, Psalm 1 and Psalm 37 are good examples of wisdom literature. Wisdom sayings are also an important part of the New Testament. Examples can be found in Jesus' "Sermon on the Mount" (Matt 5–7) and in James 3:2-8; and 4:13-17.

Gospels. Matthew, Mark, Luke, and John are the four books of the New Testament which tell about the life and teachings of Jesus. These books are called "Gospels." The word "gospel" comes from the Old English word *godspel,* which is a strict translation of the Greek word *euangelion*, meaning "good news." For more about this important and unique kind of literature see the Introduction to The Gospels and Acts, p. 1845.

Letters. A number of books in the New Testament are letters written by the apostle Paul or others. These letters are written in the formal Greek letter-writing style of the first century A.D. The person writing a letter is identified first (Rom 1:1-6). This is followed by the name of the persons being written to, and a greeting (Rom 1:7). In most of Paul's letters, a prayer of thanksgiving follows the greeting (Rom 1:8-15). The largest section of a letter is the "body"

Paul traveled to many parts of the Roman Empire preaching the Good News about Jesus Christ. As he moved from place to place he wrote to many of the churches he helped set up in different cities to give them encouragement and advice. These letters, an important part of the New Testament, are the only documents we have from this great "Apostle to the Gentiles."

(Rom 1:16—15:33). A final greeting and blessing closes the letter (Rom 16:1-27). Within each letter a number of different kinds of literature can be found, including prayers, instructions, teaching, wisdom, warnings, hymns or songs, and personal news.

Some writings in the New Testament that have also been called "letters" deal with more general questions that would be of concern to Christian communities almost anywhere. HEBREWS is an example of this type. Brief letters to the Seven Churches of Asia Minor appear in Revelation 2; 3. The Bible books that are letters or written in the style of letters can be found after ACTS and before REVELATION. For more about letters, see the Introduction to the Letters of Paul, p. 2171, and the Introduction to the General Letters and REVELATION, p. 2329.

Apocalyptic writings. "Apocalyptic" comes from the Greek word *apokalypsis*, meaning "a revealing or an unveiling." This type of literature is sometimes called prophecy (see p. 22 for more about prophecies). Like prophecy, apocalyptic writings deal with future events, but apocalyptic writings have certain other features that make them unique. For instance, apocalyptic literature contains visions from God, people appearing in the shape of animals or beasts, colors and numbers that have secret meanings, and predictions about a coming Day of the LORD. They were usually written during times of trouble and speak of a time when God will bring in a new creation, and everyone who has been faithful will live with God forever. DANIEL and REVELATION are two books most commonly identified as apocalyptic literature.

Literary Forms for Sections in Books

Prose narrative. Prose is a term that describes many forms of narrative and descriptive literature. Prose is often used when telling stories about people and historical events. It can include dialogue. Most of the Bible is written in prose. A very common form of prose in the Bible is the story. Some stories are short and are told in a few chapters within a book like the stories of Noah (Gen 6–10) and Joseph (Gen 37:1—47:27). Other stories take up a whole book, like RUTH, or ESTHER. As described earlier, the Gospels tell the story of Jesus' life, death, and resurrection. But the Gospels contain other stories as well, such as the story of John the Baptist (Matt 3:1-17; 11:1-19; 14:1-12). ACTS tells many stories about Peter, Paul, and other followers of Jesus who preached the good news about Jesus Christ.

Prayers. Prayers appear in the Bible in both prose and poetry. What makes "prayer" a unique category of literature is that it expresses direct communication between people and their God. PSALMS contains many prayers that are written in poetic form. Some psalm prayers were written for group worship when all the people came together to ask for God's help (Ps 79; 80), to give thanks to God at the time of harvest (Ps 126), or to celebrate the crowning of a new king (Ps 2). Other psalm prayers are more personal. They were used as individual prayers expressing sadness, asking for help, giving thanks, or asking for forgiveness (see Ps 12; 51; 120; 138). Prayers can be found throughout the Bible. (Some examples are Gen 18:27, 28; Exod 17:4; Judg 5:2-31; 1 Sam 2:1-10; 1 Kgs 3:6-9; Jonah 2:2-9; Luke 11:2-4; 22:42; John 17; Rom 16:25-27; and Heb 13:21.) Perhaps the most famous prayer in the Bible is the one Jesus taught his disciples (Matt 6:9-13).

Prophecies. Prophecies, or prophetic speeches, make up a large portion of the Old Testament. Many prophetic speeches (also called oracles) begin with the phrase "The LORD said" or "This is what the LORD says." This phrase makes it clear that the message given by the prophets is not their own, but comes from God. Prophetic speeches often look like Hebrew poetry and even use some of the features of poetry, such as parallelism. The books of prophecy in the Old Testament often combine a story giving information about the prophet and his work along with his prophetic messages from God. (Vivid examples of prophecies in the Old Testament include Isaiah 1:2-31; 10:24-27; Jeremiah 2; Ezekiel 36:22-32; Amos 5:4-27; and Zechariah 9.) The New Testament includes examples of prophetic speeches as well, especially when telling the stories of John the Baptist and Jesus (Matt 3:1-12; 24:1-31). See also 2 Peter 3:8-13. For more about this type of literature see the Introduction to the Prophetic Books, p. 1287.

Jesus' parables have been a rich source of inspiration for artists over the centuries. This nineteenth century engraving shows the different kinds of soil Jesus described in his parable of the farmer (Luke 8:4-15).

Parables. Parables are stories about familiar, everyday things that were told in order to teach an important truth about God and life in God's kingdom. The Gospels show that Jesus used parables frequently when talking to his disciples and to the crowd who came to hear him speak. Parables can be very short (Matthew 13:44-48 is made up of three very short parables); or they can be somewhat longer, involving several characters or images (Luke 10:30-37; 15:11-32). For more about parables and for some examples from the Old Testament see the mini-article called "Parables," p. 1876.

Long family lists (genealogies). A number of long family lists appear in the Bible. They trace the family background of important figures in Israel's history and show how people are related to one another. One particularly important list found at the beginning of MATTHEW traces Jesus' family line back to King David (Matt 1:1-17). MATTHEW includes this genealogy to show that Jesus was descended from King David and to affirm that he was the Messiah that the prophets said would come to save the people. Although it is not always clear why a list of a person's ancestors is given in the Bible, it is clear that for the people of Israel, and other people in the ancient Near East, family connections were important. Some other genealogies and lists of names are found in Genesis 5:1-32; 1 Chronicles 1–8; and Ezra 8:2-14.

TRANSLATING THE BIBLE

Translation is the process of communicating a message into a language that is different from the one in which the message was originally written. The message may be in a song, a poem, a story, directions, a telephone message, or a sermon. But if a person is not able to understand that message because it is written or told in an unfamiliar language, the message must be translated. Without the process of translation, that message will never be effectively communicated to a new audience (group of listeners). The message may be heard, but it will not be understood. This is especially important when the Bible is the message to be communicated.

The Bible is made up of several individual books that were written and told long ago in various languages quite unfamiliar to us today. These books came together over a period of more than a thousand years to form what we know as the Bible. None of these books were originally written in English (or Spanish or most other languages used throughout the world today). They were written in ancient Hebrew and Aramaic (for the Hebrew Scriptures/Old Testament) and in Greek (for the New Testament). Without Bible translation, people today would have to learn these three languages in order to read and understand the words of the Bible!

The Beginnings of Bible Translation

The work of translating the Bible began around 250 B.C. when a group of Jewish scholars translated the Hebrew Scriptures into Greek because many Jewish people were living in places where Greek was the everyday language. This translation is known as the Septuagint. The purpose of the Septuagint was clear: to communicate the Hebrew Scriptures in the language familiar to most of the Jewish people in these particular places.

Since that first Bible translation, the words of both the Hebrew Scriptures and the New Testament have been translated into hundreds of languages. These languages include ancient languages (like Coptic, Arabic, Latin, and Syriac), as well as more recent, modern languages (like Portuguese, Russian, Navajo, Danish, Spanish, and English). The purpose behind all these Bible translations is exactly the same as that behind the Septuagint: to put the words of the Bible into a language that people will understand.

How Is Bible Translation Done?

Until recently, most Bible translations were done according to an approach called "formal equivalence" (or "word-for-word translation"). The goal of the formal equivalence approach is to communicate both the words and the grammatical structure (the "form") of the original language (or source language) into the other language (or receptor language). Such an approach would suggest that the translation is truly accurate and precise. What sometimes happens, however, is that the translation looks and sounds unnatural in the receptor language because it does not follow the rules of grammar and sentence structure of that language.

In the 1960s, a new way of thinking about Bible translation developed based on recent theories in communication that focused more on the needs of the audience than on the form of the message. The result was another approach for Bible translation. This new approach is called "functional equivalence" translation and emphasizes the need to translate the *meaning* of the words in whole thought units (like phrases, sentences, and paragraphs), rather than translating the individual words themselves. This approach is more concerned about the "function" of the words which carry meaning than about their "form."

Whether using a formal equivalence approach or a functional equivalence approach, Bible translators are always concerned to use the best Hebrew and Greek manuscripts available for their work. Translators base their translations on "critical editions" (or standard editions) of the Hebrew Scriptures and the New Testament, which offer careful assessments of all available ancient biblical manuscripts. These critical editions ensure that the translations are based on the most accurate and reliable manuscripts available.

Translating the Bible into English

The story of the translation of the Bible into English is long and complex. The chart of the English Bible on p. 25 helps to sort through many of the difficulties in understanding this history. It is important to remember, though, that each of these English Bible translations set out to make versions of the Bible that were reliable and understandable to various audiences.

One of the most important Bible translators was the Englishman William Tyndale (1484-1536), often called "The Father of the English Bible." Tyndale wanted to make the Scriptures understandable to all people. But due to the political and religious tensions that existed throughout Europe during the Reformation (14th-17th centuries), he was unable to get permission to do his translation in England. So he went to Germany, where he published his New Testament in February, 1526. Though he experienced a great deal of opposition, he continued his work of translating the Old Testament from Hebrew, and he published the Pentateuch (GENESIS through DEUTERONOMY) in 1530. In 1536, Tyndale was found guilty of heresy, and in October of that same year, he was strangled and burned at the stake.

Tyndale's work and influence can still be seen in what is surely the most significant English Bible translation ever done, the King James Version of the Bible, published in 1611. The King James Version (also called the Authorized Version) was prepared at the request of King James I of England at a time when several sectarian versions of the English Bible were in use (most notably the Geneva Bible, favored by Puritans, and the Bishops' and Great Bibles used by the official Church of England; see the chart). Although there was resistance to the King James Version at first (since many people felt a loyalty to their own sectarian translations), it eventually won wide acceptance and became the standard English version of the Bible in the English-speaking world for three centuries. The style of the King James Version is at times unfamiliar to us today because of its very literal dependence on Hebrew and Greek sources (clearly, a "formal" equivalence approach). Still, it remains one of the most widely used English translations of the Bible today.

William Tyndale's English New Testament (1526) was translated directly from Greek sources and not from the Latin version that was read in the churches of his day. By the time he was burned at the stake on charges of heresy in 1536, he had also translated almost half of the Old Testament.

The Bible in English

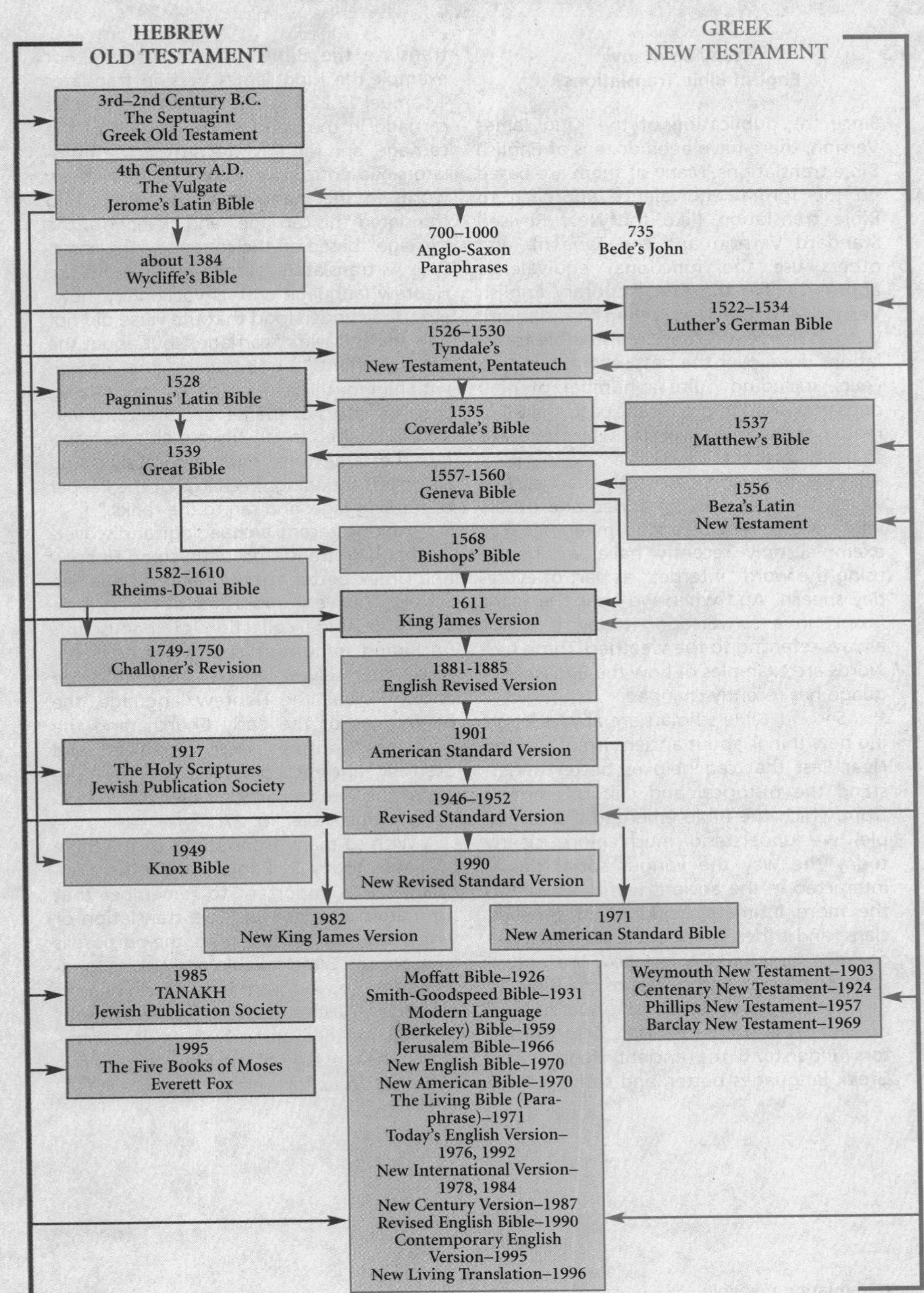

HEBREW OLD TESTAMENT
GREEK NEW TESTAMENT
3rd–2nd Century B.C. The Septuagint Greek Old Testament
4th Century A.D. The Vulgate Jerome's Latin Bible
700–1000 Anglo-Saxon Paraphrases
735 Bede's John
about 1384 Wycliffe's Bible
1522–1534 Luther's German Bible
1526–1530 Tyndale's New Testament, Pentateuch
1528 Pagninus' Latin Bible
1535 Coverdale's Bible
1537 Matthew's Bible
1539 Great Bible
1557-1560 Geneva Bible
1556 Beza's Latin New Testament
1568 Bishops' Bible
1582–1610 Rheims-Douai Bible
1611 King James Version
1749-1750 Challoner's Revision
1881–1885 English Revised Version
1901 American Standard Version
1917 The Holy Scriptures Jewish Publication Society
1946–1952 Revised Standard Version
1949 Knox Bible
1990 New Revised Standard Version
1982 New King James Version
1971 New American Standard Bible
1985 TANAKH Jewish Publication Society
1995 The Five Books of Moses Everett Fox
Moffatt Bible–1926
Smith-Goodspeed Bible–1931
Modern Language (Berkeley) Bible–1959
Jerusalem Bible–1966
New English Bible–1970
New American Bible–1970
The Living Bible (Paraphrase)–1971
Today's English Version–1976, 1992
New International Version–1978, 1984
New Century Version–1987
Revised English Bible–1990
Contemporary English Version–1995
New Living Translation–1996
Weymouth New Testament–1903
Centenary New Testament–1924
Phillips New Testament–1957
Barclay New Testament–1969

Why So Many English Bible Translations?

Since the publication of the King James Version, there have been dozens of English Bible translations. Many of them are based on the formal equivalence approach to Bible translation (like the New Revised Standard Version and the *Tanakh*), and others use the functional equivalence approach (like the Contemporary English Version and the New Living Translation). With so many different English Bible translations done over the past several hundred years, including quite a number of new ones published in the recent past, the Bible reader today must wonder why there are so many of them.

First, languages constantly change. New words are always being added and others take on different or added meanings. For example, only recently have we begun using the word "internet" as part of everyday speech. And when we hear the word "cool" in a conversation today, it is not always referring to the weather! These two words are examples of how the English language has recently changed.

Second, Bible scholars are always learning new things about ancient Israel and the Near East that can help us better understand the historical and cultural context from which the Bible emerged. For example, we understand much more clearly today the way the various social classes interacted in the ancient world, as well as the more intimate workings of families, clans, and tribes in ancient Israel. Such discoveries sometimes affect how we understand the words and stories of the Bible. In addition, archaeologists continue to find documents and libraries that help translators understand the ancient Hebrew and Greek languages better, and so help them translate the Bible more accurately. For example,the King James Version translates 1 Samuel 17:22 like this: "And David left his carriage in the hand of the keeper of the carriage, and ran into the army." The translators had difficulty with one of the Hebrew words in the manuscripts they used, and translated "his carriage" and "keeper of the carriage" based on the context of the narrative. As translators learned more about the Hebrew language and its vocabulary, however, they understood that the verse did not talk about David's "carriage," but about the "carried things" or "baggage" that he had with him for the soldiers in the army. And so, the translators of the Revised Standard Version (published in 1952) were able to translate the same verse more accurately: "And David left the things in charge of the keeper of the baggage, and ran to the ranks."

Among recent archaeological discoveries that help translators understand Hebrew and Greek better are the famous Dead Sea Scrolls. This very important discovery consists of a huge collection of manuscripts (including important copies of the Scriptures themselves) which shed light on ancient Israel, the Hebrew language, the beginnings of the early Church, and the way the Scriptures were organized and used by ancient communities. For more about this, see the article called "Archaeology and the Bible," p. 27.

With so many translations of the Bible available today in English and other languages, it is important to remember that no matter who does a Bible translation or which basic approach is used, the purpose is to make the Bible reliable and understandable to those who want to read and hear its message of justice, hope, and love. Without the skill, sacrifice, and efforts of Bible translators, the message of the Bible might have been lost to us forever.

ARCHAEOLOGY AND THE BIBLE

Archaeology studies past human cultures by examining the physical objects they have left behind. It includes excavating (digging) to recover objects that have been buried for long periods of time. Often, cities were built on top of the ruins of older cities. Sometimes archaeologists find huge mounds that are made of debris from layers upon layers of vanished civilizations. These mounds are called "tells." There are two basic types of artifacts that have been recovered from the "tells": (1) objects, such as buildings (houses, temples), statues, pottery, weapons, farming tools, and household utensils; and (2) the remains of written documents, including inscriptions and decaying documents consisting of little more than fragments of words.

How has archaeology affected the study of the Bible? The recovery of physical objects and written documents, especially, has greatly improved biblical understanding. Archaeology has provided much information about the history and culture of ancient Israel and its surrounding neighbors. Archaeology has also helped us to understand the history, culture, and religion of the people who lived in Bible lands long before the Israelites settled there. The objects found have taught much about how these previous cultures and religions influenced the new settlers. The phrase "biblical archaeology" refers to archaeology related to the study of the Bible. Although the Scriptures were inspired by God, the Bible writers were shaped by their cultural surroundings. It would be difficult to understand the Bible without some knowledge of the history and culture of the ancient Near East.

This tell at Beersheba is typical of mounds found throughout the Near East. By studying tells, archaeologists are able to learn many things about former civilizations. At least two city walls were discovered in the excavation of this tell.

What Ancient Writings Reveal

Bible translators sometimes have difficulty rendering accurate translations of certain Hebrew words until these words (or words similar to them) are discovered in other ancient writings. These writings can then be compared with biblical words, and the meaning of the Hebrew becomes clearer. Some of these ancient writings describe religious practices, government policies, history, and the cultures of nations that surrounded ancient Israel. Ancient documents were written on stone and clay tablets, broken pieces of pottery (called "ostraca"), or on parchment made from animal skins and papyrus. Papyrus is a writing material made from the plant of the same name. For more about these, see the mini-article called "Scrolls," p. 1491.

One important document discovered by archaeologists is the Cyrus Cylinder, a 10-inch long clay barrel. This was written in the Akkadian language in the 500s B.C. The inscription tells how King Cyrus of Persia defeated the kingdom of Babylonia. It also tells that Cyrus was generous toward his new subjects and allowed them to practice their own religions. Similarly, EZRA, tells that Cyrus allowed the people of Judah to return to their homeland with what remained of the treasures that the Babylonians had taken from the temple in Jerusalem (Ezra 1:1-11). See the photograph of the Cyrus Cylinder on p. 854.

ANCIENT TEXTS RELATED TO THE OLD TESTAMENT

ANCIENT DOCUMENT AND DATE	LANGUAGE	DESCRIPTION
Gilgamesh Epic around 1700 B.C.; some versions circulated as early as 2100 B.C.	Akkadian	Gilgamesh, the ruler of Uruk, has many adventures and meets Utnapishtim, the only survivor of a great flood.
Enuma Elish around 1200 B.C.	Akkadian	A story written on seven stone tablets which tells of the Babylonian god Marduk and how the world was created.
Code of Hammurabi around 1750 B.C.	Akkadian	A listing of laws for the people of the kingdom of Babylonia. It has many laws similar to the Law of Moses in the Bible. Moses lived about 400 years after Hammurabi.
Ras-Shamra Tablets around 1450 B.C.	Ugaritic	Tells of the adventures of Canaanite gods and rulers which helps biblical scholars to better understand Canaanite religion and Old Testament poetry.
Amarna Letters around 1350 B.C.	Canaanite Akkadian	Hundreds of letters written by Canaanite scribes give information about political, social, and religious relationships between Canaan and Egypt during the rule of Egyptian Pharaohs, Amenhotep III and Akhenaton.
Merneptah Stele around 1210 B.C.	Egyptian	Also known as the "Israel Stele," it describes the victory of Egyptian king Merneptah over peoples from the west, including "Israel." Shows that by this time a people known as "Israel" existed in Canaan.
Gezer Calendar around 925 B.C.	Hebrew	A student from Israel (northern kingdom) describes the seasons, the crops, and the yearly farm work done in Israel.
Moabite Stone around 850 B.C.	Moabite	Describes how Mesha, king of Moab, rebelled against one of the kings of Israel from King Omri's line (see 2 Kgs 3:4,5).
Clay Prism of Sennacherib around 690 B.C.	Akkadian	The Annals of Sennacherib describe how Sennacherib of Assyria surrounded Jerusalem and made King Hezekiah of Judah a prisoner in his own city.
Lachish Letters around 590 B.C.	Hebrew	Writings on pottery fragments tell about the difficult days in Jerusalem before the Babylonians surrounded the city.
Cyrus Cylinder around 539 B.C.	Akkadian	Describes how King Cyrus of Persia defeated the Babylonians, tells of his policies toward the peoples he ruled, and describes their gods.
Dead Sea Scrolls some as early as 250 B.C., others as late as A.D. 70	Hebrew Aramaic Greek	Hundreds of scrolls and scroll fragments, including the oldest existing copies of Old Testament books and passages. Some documents describe the religious community, possibly Essenes, who wrote and collected these documents.

Other ancient documents, which describe events reported in EZRA and NEHEMIAH, have also been discovered through archaeology.

In 927 B.C., King Shishak of Egypt attacked Jerusalem and looted the temple (1 Kgs 14:25,26; 2 Chr 12:2-4). Writings from the court of King Shishak found by archaeologists on the walls of the temple of Amun in Thebes (Egypt) tell of this event and about the other cities that Shishak destroyed in Palestine. His military campaign was waged against Israel after Solomon's death when Israel was weak and divided into northern (Israel) and southern (Judah) kingdoms.

One of the most exciting archaeological finds ever occurred in 1947 when a shepherd boy wandered into a cave searching for a lost sheep. He found many ancient clay jars containing scrolls. The cave was located just west of the Dead Sea, so these important documents have come to be known as the "Dead Sea Scrolls." These scrolls include a variety of writings about the Essene community that lived in the wilderness area near these caves from around 250 B.C. to A.D. 68. The Essenes were a group of very religious people who left Jerusalem for religious and political reasons and settled in the secluded location around Qumran. Perhaps the most interesting documents discovered there were the scrolls of Old Testament books, the oldest copies of Hebrew Scriptures currently in existence. Of these, the most precious find is the "Isaiah Scroll." It contains a complete copy of ISAIAH, which was copied around 150-50 B.C. The parchment is over 20-feet long and remarkably well preserved. See the photographs on p. 933.

Unearthing the Past

Archaeology has helped to confirm some of the events reported in the Bible. Although it cannot "prove" every detail found in the Bible (since the Bible was written thousands of years ago), many archaeological excavations have provided useful evidence that in some cases supports what the Bible says. For example, archaeological evidence shows that there were many Philistines in Palestine around 1000 B.C., and that they were most likely a threat to neighboring peoples, including the Israelites. This may be one reason why the people of Israel felt the need for a strong ruler (king) so that they could better defend themselves (1 Sam 8).

Also, archaeological studies of village sites in Judea dating from the sixth century B.C. show that many of them had been abandoned for a number of years before being used again. This supports the Bible's extensive description of how the Babylonians took many of the people away from Judah and into exile in Babylon. See the article called "From Joshua to the Exile: The People of Israel in the Promised Land," p. 924. The exile lasted from 586 B.C. to about 538 B.C. when Cyrus (see above) allowed the people of Judea to return home.

Other important archaeological finds are those uncovered at:

Jericho, where many layers of civilizations have been unearthed, the oldest dating from before 5000 B.C., several thousand years before the Israelites conquered it (Josh 5:13—6:27). Archaeologists also uncovered the ruins of a building near Jericho from a later period. It has been identified as the winter palace of Herod the Great.

Shechem, Mount Gerizim, and Samaria, all sites in central Palestine, which are important because they were centers of royal power and worship for the northern tribes of Israel.

Megiddo, where the famous "Stables of Solomon" were found (1 Kgs 9:19). The "tell" at Megiddo is about 70 feet deep, so several strata (layers) of material have been uncovered.

Jerusalem, where a tunnel known as "Hezekiah's Tunnel" was found. This tunnel was used to bring water into the city during the Assyrian siege in 701 B.C. (2 Kgs 20:20).

Capernaum, where an early synagogue (Jewish meeting place) was found that may relate to Mark 1:21. A fisherman's house which dates from the first century A.D. was also found nearby.

Ephesus, where the temple of Artemis was unearthed along with writings that mention the silver statues of this temple, possibly similar to those mentioned in Acts 19:24.

Learning about How People Lived

Some archaeological finds provide us with information on what life was like in biblical times. We have glimpses of how the royal and military rulers governed their countries; how people earned a living, produced food and goods; how buildings were built; how people worshiped, what they believed about how the world came into existence, and what they believed the future held for them.

Cultural information about the ancient world has come from many different sources. The Code of Hammurabi (see chart on p. 28) describes the practice of a woman asking her husband and her hand-maiden to have a baby together if the wife has not been able to get pregnant. This may have been the same custom as described in Genesis 16, where Sarah asks Abraham and Hagar to have a baby together because Sarah has not been able to have children.

Another important archaeological find that reflects biblical culture are coins such as those described in Ezra 2:69 and Nehemiah 7:70-72. They are especially useful in identifying local and regional authorities and helping scholars to establish dates.

Archaeological discoveries of ivory carvings, religious figurines, pottery, jewelry, and even animal and human bones have provided additional clues about the culture of biblical times. Skeletons found from the time of Jesus show that the average height of people was just over 5 feet. They also confirm that people were indeed nailed to crosses (crucified) as a form of capital punishment as described in the Gospels. See the mini-article called "Crucifixion," p. 1914, and accompanying illustrations. The foot bones of one male skeleton, for instance, had a nail in them and the lower leg of the man had been broken. JOHN describes both crucifixion in general and the practice of breaking a condemned person's legs (John 19:18,32).

Other archaeological discoveries reveal much about the types of architecture and building projects undertaken by the Romans who ruled over Palestine during the time of Jesus. Portions of the Jewish temple built by Herod the Great can still be seen, as can the ruins of ancient temples built to honor Greek and Roman gods. All of these are useful to people who want to understand the biblical world, because the early church developed from the Jewish religion but was influenced by other philosophies and religions as well. For more about this see the article, "Religions and Philosophies in Bible Times," p. 1832.

The History and Development of Archaeology

Serious study of the remains of the ancient Near East began around 1800 when Napoleon invaded Egypt, taking with him artists and scholars to study the culture of that ancient land. These specialists studied the ruins of temples, palaces, and burial places. During this expedition, they found many ancient writings and inscriptions. A very famous stone, called the "Rosetta Stone," was discovered by some of Napoleon's soldiers. The stone had an inscription in three different languages: two forms of Egyptian and one of Greek. The letters on the stone were in the form of "hieroglyphs" (pictures representing letters and words). After much hard work, a French scholar was able to decipher (translate) the inscriptions. Through his impor-

The study of pottery shapes, colors, and finishes provide archaeologists with a valuable way of establishing dates for the layers of an excavation. These restored pottery vessels from Tell es-Safi date from the tenth to seventh century B.C.

tant work, many inscriptions on the walls, tombs, and palaces in Egypt can be understood today. By the middle of the 1800s, ancient ruins in Mesopotamia, the land between the Tigris and Euphrates rivers, (modern Iraq and Iran), were also uncovered. These remains include cities, forts, palaces, and temples, as well as ordinary houses and shops.

Careful study has made it possible to decode and translate the ancient writings which have been found, and to determine the dates of many of the artifacts. Looking carefully at pottery has been one way to determine the dates of other items in a dig area. Since pottery was made in different shapes, using different techniques and finishes during different periods of history, archaeologists have gradually learned how to date the layers of their excavations by the kinds of pottery they find. For example, much pottery from the Iron Age (1225-539 B.C.) is thick and colored light gray, while pottery from the Roman Era (63 B.C. to A.D. 324) is often reddish in color, and fairly thin. Another example is the ability to tell the age of oil lamps based on their designs. Over the centuries people made lamps differently. Early lamps were much more open and bowl-like, while later ones, in the time of Jesus, were almost completely enclosed.

In addition to learning how to date certain areas and layers of a "tell" by looking at pottery, archaeologists have developed methods for uncovering these ancient sites one layer at a time. These methods give archaeologists a better picture of how people lived in each period. Usually a square area is marked off with stakes, and then each layer is carefully removed using shovels, picks, hoes, brooms and dustpans. When archaeologists reach layers where pottery or other objects are present, they work very carefully, using small picks and brushes. They collect all the material in buckets and sift through it in order to catch any small items like coins, bone fragments, or jewelry. Since a marked-off area is worked on for a period of time, a slice or cross-section of the layers can be viewed at the side of the

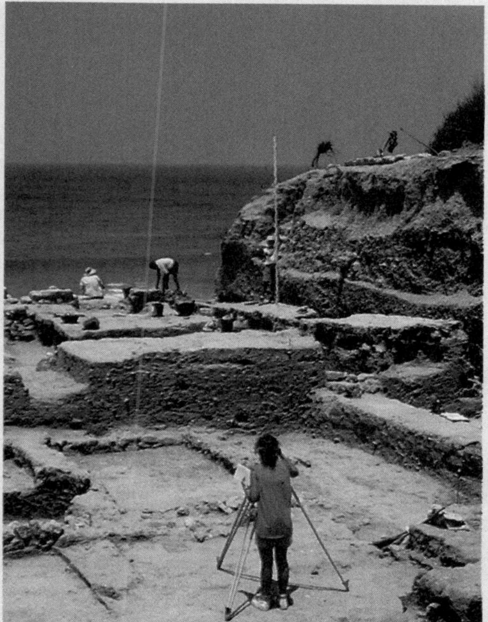

Archaeological workers at a dig in Ashkelon, Israel, by the Mediterranean Sea.

square as the archaeologists dig deeper and deeper. An example of an archaeological dig is shown on the previous page.

Many other specialists work on digs with archaeologists so that the maximum amount of information possible can be gathered. These include architects, geologists, soil specialists, photographers, language and script specialists, bone and animal specialists, pottery restorers, and aerial photographers, as well as many students and volunteers.

New archaeological discoveries related to the Bible require cooperation with other fields such as anthropology, ancient literature, linguistics, art, and sociology. The work of archaeology is often slow and tedious, but its results can be very rewarding. By putting the special interests of biblical archaeology in the context of the larger field of archaeology and its related fields, our knowledge about the peoples, places, and writings of the biblical world continues to increase.

THE OLD TESTAMENT

THE "OLD TESTAMENT" is the name Christians have given to the Jewish Scriptures and the first part of the Christian Bible. When the earliest Christians quoted from "Scripture," they quoted from the Jewish Scriptures. It was not until after the New Testament books were written in the first (and perhaps second) century A.D. that Christians started referring to the Jewish Scriptures as the "Old Testament." For the differences in the order of the books in the Jewish Scriptures and the Old Testament, see the chart on p. 14.

The Old Testament is actually many different books of various kinds written by many different writers during a period of at least a thousand years. In fact, some parts of the Old Testament date back as far as 1300 B.C. Many of the books that make up the Old Testament were originally stories that were told over and over from generation to generation. They were eventually written down and gathered together into longer collections (like the stories about Abraham in Genesis 12–24). The books of the Old Testament were originally written in Hebrew, the language of the people of Israel, though portions of a few books were written in Aramaic, a closely-related language.

The Old Testament is a record of Israel's experience of what God is like and what the people who worship God should be like (Lev 20:7, 8). It proclaims the LORD God as the creator of the world (Gen 1; Ps 104), and it describes God as one who promises to bless. God's "blessings" are described in the covenants (agreements) God made with the people of Israel, beginning with Abraham. God promised Abraham and Sarah that their descendants would become a great nation, that they would have a land they could call their own, and that other nations of the world would be blessed because of Israel's unique relationship with God (Gen 12:1-3; 15:5-7, 18-21; 17:8). God asked Abraham and his descendants to uphold this covenant by circumcising all the men and boys of the Israelite people as a sign of their devotion to God (Gen 17:9-14).

Many years later, God helped Moses lead the descendants of Abraham (the Israelites) out of slavery in Egypt. But before reaching the land God promised to give them (Canaan), the people of Israel wandered in the desert for forty years. It was during this time of wandering that God made a covenant with Moses and the people at Mount Sinai. This covenant contained the laws and instructions (Hebrew, *Torah*) that were to guide the people in how to live together and worship the LORD God. If the people obeyed the laws and remained faithful to God, the promises God made to their ancestor Abraham would be fulfilled. But if they did not obey, they would be in danger of losing their land and being punished by their enemies (Deut 7:6-16). Much of the Old Testament tells the story of how God's chosen people struggled to keep their part of this covenant with God, and how God continually offered guidance and forgiveness when they disobeyed. See also the Introductions to The Pentateuch, the Historical Books, the Books of Wisdom and Poetry, and the Prophetic Books.

The Old Testament is a book of faith, which means that both Jews and Christians view it as a sacred book that has meaning and authority for their lives. Much of it is read and sung in worship. Its laws and instructions reflect God's desire for people's behavior to stand out as holy and moral. The stories of the Old Testament teach and inspire by giving examples of ordinary people who struggled with issues of faith and obedience, and of how a loving God relates to them. The messages of its prophets emphasize the need for right living and proper worship of God, and reveal a God who cares deeply for the poor and is willing to forgive those who have been disobedient. The wisdom writings offer practical advice for living and explore difficult questions that people have struggled to answer since ancient times.

Not all Christian groups have the same number of Old Testament books in their Bibles (see the article called "What Books Belong in the Bible?" p. 13). But all agree that the Old Testament deals in a special way with the relationship between God and God's people, while it also provides a background for understanding the message of the New Testament (see the Introduction to the New Testament, p. 1843).

The Pentateuch

The "Pentateuch" is a term used to describe the first five books of the Old Testament (Genesis—Deuteronomy). In the Jewish Scriptures these books are referred to as the Law, or *Torah*, a Hebrew word that means "guide" or "instruction" (see also the article called "What Books Belong in the Bible?" p. 13). But the Pentateuch includes more than just laws. The great narratives of the Pentateuch tell the story of creation, of God's choosing of a special people (Israel), and of the person God chose to lead these people out of slavery in Egypt. This leader, Moses, receives from God the laws and instructions that were to guide Israel's life and worship. Along with these stories, several other important events are recorded in the Pentateuch, including the choosing of Abraham and Sarah to be Israel's earliest ancestors, the escape from slavery in Egypt, and the wandering of the people of Israel through the desert to the edge of the land God promised to give them.

The Pentateuch begins at the "beginning," with stories about how God created the world and its people (Gen 1–5). This is followed by the story of Noah and the great flood and a story explaining why there are different human languages (Gen 6–11). These stories are sometimes described as "pre-history." But in Genesis 12 the history of God's people, Israel, begins with God's choosing of Abraham and his wife Sarah to leave their home and go to a new land (Canaan). God promised Abraham that his descendants would become a great nation and would eventually make the land of Canaan their home (Gen 12:1-3; 17:1-8). The remainder of Genesis describes how the promises God made to Abraham and Sarah began to be worked out in their descendants, including Isaac, Jacob, and their families.

As Exodus begins, however, these promises are in question because Abraham and Sarah's descendants are living as slaves in Egypt. But God hears the people begging for help and chooses Moses to lead the people out of Egypt (Exod 3:4-12). This great event, known as the "exodus," is told about in exciting detail in Exodus. Israel's time of slavery in Egypt became a reminder to future generations. The Lord instructed each household to sacrifice a lamb and apply some of the blood to their doorframes, so that the Lord would "pass over" their homes while inflicting the final plague on the Egyptians. The Passover ceremony was to be a "lasting ordinance" for the Israelites (Exod 12).

Jesus and his followers applied the meaning of Passover to Jesus' sacrificial death (Matt 26:17-29; 1 Cor 5:7). And because God cared about the people of Israel and responded to them when they were suffering and oppressed, they were to treat others, especially the poor and powerless, with fairness and justice (Exod 23:6-9; Lev 25:35-38; Deut 5:6, 12-15).

The second major event in EXODUS is the covenant (agreement) that the LORD made with Moses and the people of Israel at Mount Sinai. In this covenant, God gives the laws and instructions that would guide how the people were to live and worship. God had chosen them and then brought them out of Egypt. At Sinai, God made it clear what the people of Israel must do in order to show that they were God's "holy" people. These laws and instructions are found in Exodus 20–40; LEVITICUS; selected portions of NUMBERS; and in Moses' sermons in DEUTERONOMY. The remainder of NUMBERS tells about the years the people spent wandering through the desert on their way to the promised land of Canaan. The narratives in this book focus on the way the LORD God continued to care for the people even in the terrible years they spent in the desert. The Pentateuch ends with the people of Israel camped in Moab just across the Jordan River from Canaan, ready to enter the land God had promised to their ancestors.

Because the main human figure of the Pentateuch is Moses, these books have traditionally been called the "Books of Moses." The question of what person or persons wrote these books is still discussed by historians and biblical scholars. But based on the manuscripts that currently exist, it is not likely that the question of authorship can be answered with any degree of certainty. Many scholars see evidence in the text itself that the Pentateuch took its final shape over a period of hundreds of years, long after the time of Moses. For further discussion of when each of these books was written, see the Introductions to GENESIS—DEUTERONOMY.

GENESIS

How did the world begin? Who were God's chosen people? Find the answers to these questions and more in Genesis.

What makes Genesis special?

The word *genesis* comes from a Greek word meaning "beginning." And this is a book about beginnings—the beginning of the world, the beginning of the human race, and the beginning of the people of Israel. Genesis is also a book of faith, which means that it is mainly concerned with who God is and how God has been involved in the lives of people from the time of creation.

Why was Genesis written?

The earliest ancestors of the Israelites did not write down their family history, but they told their stories. These stories were passed on for generations. Eventually, they were written down so that the people of Israel would have a record of how God created the world and how they became God's people. The book also describes how the first human beings broke the perfect relationship they had with God in the Garden of Eden. But God did not give up on human beings, and eventually chose Abram and Sarai (later called Abraham and Sarah) to leave their home in northern Mesopotamia and go to Canaan, a land God promised to give to Abram and his descendants. God also promised Abram that his descendants would be a great people who would bring God's blessings to all the other nations of the world (12:1-3).

Genesis includes a number of family lists (genealogies) to explain how the Israelite people are related to each other and to other peoples and nations in the ancient Near East, Middle East, and northeastern Africa.

What's the story behind the scene?

According to tradition, Moses was considered the author and collector of the first five books of the Bible, including Genesis. It is difficult to say for certain when Moses lived, but the Bible (1 Kgs 6:1) and other ancient documents seem to point to some time between 1450 and 1250 B.C. That would make Genesis over 3300 years old! However, in the past two centuries, some Bible scholars have suggested that Genesis actually reached its final form much later than the time of Moses, perhaps as late as the time of Israel's exile in Babylon (587-538 B.C.). They noted that the two descriptions of God's creation of the earth (Gen 1:1—2:4 and 2:4-25) differ slightly, and each uses a different name for God. They began to wonder if the book may be a collection of the writings of different authors, each having important stories and history to contribute to this "family album" of Israel's earliest ancestors. But no matter who wrote the book, its main message is clear: The God of Abraham, Sarah, and their descendants (the people of Israel) is the Creator of the world and acts in history to offer salvation to all people.

God created the heavens . . . the second day: Genesis describes God as the creator of everything that exists. In the opening verses of this book of beginnings, the phrase "the heavens and the earth" stands for the universe and all its galaxies, stars, and planets. The earth is described as a formless, water mass. Ancient peoples viewed the earth as a flat disc stretched over the oceans (Ps 136:6). The sky also was believed to be a great ocean that was kept from flooding the earth by a solid bowl or dome called "sky" (1:8). Before the earth was created, these two watery masses were mixed together, but on the second day God separated them, just as he separated the light from the darkness on the first day (1:3-5). A writer of some of the Psalms, like the author of Genesis, says one of the ways God creates is with words (Ps 33:6; 148:5). For example, God gave a command for light to shine, and it happened (1:3). And then, God commanded the lights (the sun and moon and stars) that separate day from night to appear (1:14-19). Ancient people feared the darkness and welcomed each new day as a reminder of God's victory over the dark chaos at creation.

1:1 *God:* The Hebrew name translated as "God" here and throughout 1:1—2:3 is *Elohim.* It is a plural form of *El,* and can refer to "gods," but here it means the one true God who creates.

1:1,2 *the heavens and the earth . . . formless and empty:* See the note on p. 37.

1:3,4 *God . . . separated the light from the darkness:* See the note on p. 37.

1:5 *evening . . . the first day:* The Jewish day began at sundown, so a full day was measured from evening to evening.

1:3 2 Cor 4:6.

How is Genesis constructed?

Genesis can be divided into two main parts: Chapters 1–11 cover the creation of the world and the earliest human families, as well as the Great Flood and the creation of different languages; chapters 12–50 tell the story of the ancestors of the people of Israel, beginning with the adventures of Abraham and Sarah and ending with their grandson Jacob's family living in Egypt. A broad outline of the book follows these two main parts:

The beginning of human history (1:1—11:32)
- God creates the universe and all living things (1:1—2:25)
- Sin in Eden (3:1—4:26)
- The first generations of human beings (5:1-32)
- Noah and his descendants (6:1—11:32)

The beginning of God's people, Israel (12:1—50:26)
- Abraham, Sarah, and Isaac (12:1—23:20)
- Isaac and his family (24:1—28:9)
- Jacob and Esau and their families (28:10—36:43)
- The story of Jacob's son, Joseph (37:1—50:26)

The Beginning of Human History

The first eleven chapters of Genesis tell how God creates the universe and human beings, and how those first humans disobey God and are sent from the Garden of Eden. Beginning with Cain's murder of his brother Abel, the first generations of people become so evil that God sends a great flood to destroy the earth and its people. Only Noah and his family, the living things Noah takes with them on the ark, and the fish in the waters are saved. Also, the generations of Noah's sons are named, and the story of the Tower of Babel explains why so many languages are spoken by the people on earth.

GOD CREATES THE UNIVERSE AND ALL LIVING THINGS

The Beginning

1 In the beginning God created the heavens and the earth.
2 Now the earth was[a] formless and empty, darkness was
over the surface of the deep, and the Spirit of God was
hovering over the waters.
3 And God said, "Let there be light," and there was light. 4 God saw that
the light was good, and he separated the light from the darkness. 5 God called the light "day," and the darkness he called
"night." And there was evening, and there was morning—the
first day.

[a]2 Or possibly *became*

The Andromeda Galaxy, telescope photograph. In the Bible the heavens are often used to symbolize the vastness of God's creation. Pictured here is the Andromeda galaxy, located 2.2 million light years from Earth. Genesis 1:1—2:4 is a familiar and beautiful account of how God created everything that exists and declared that "it was good."

6 And God said, "Let there be an expanse between the waters to
separate water from water." 7 So God made the expanse and
separated the water under the expanse from the water
above it. And it was so. 8 God called the expanse "sky." And
there was evening, and there was morning—the second
day.
9 And God said, "Let the water under the sky be gathered to one
place, and let dry ground appear." And it was so. 10 God
called the dry ground "land," and the gathered waters he
called "seas." And God saw that it was good.
11 Then God said, "Let the land produce vegetation:
seed-bearing plants and trees on the land that bear fruit
with seed in it, according to their various kinds." And it
was so. 12 The land produced vegetation: plants bearing
seed according to their kinds and trees bearing fruit with
seed in it according to their kinds. And God saw that it was
good. 13 And there was evening, and there was morning—
the third day.
14 And God said, "Let there be lights in the expanse of the sky to
separate the day from the night, and let them serve as signs
to mark seasons and days and years, 15 and let them be
lights in the expanse of the sky to give light on the earth."
And it was so. 16 God made two great lights—the greater
light to govern the day and the lesser light to govern the
night. He also made the stars. 17 God set them in the

1:6–8 *an expanse . . . "sky":* Ancient Hebrews understood the expanse of the sky to be like a solid dome set over the earth, and high mountains held up the sky like columns (Job 26:11). The sky had to be solid in order to hold back the flood of water above. They described rain and snow as coming through this dome when God opened windows or doors in the sky (Gen 7:11,12; Ps 78:23).

1:16 *the greater . . . the lesser:* This refers to the sun and the moon. They are not called by their names in this verse, because in the ancient world some people worshiped the sun and moon as gods. Here they are simply powerful lights created by God.

1:6–8 2 Pet 3:5.

expanse of the sky to give light on the earth, 18 to govern
the day and the night, and to separate light from darkness.
And God saw that it was good. 19 And there was evening,
and there was morning—the fourth day.
20 And God said, "Let the water teem with living creatures, and let
birds fly above the earth across the expanse of the sky."
21 So God created the great creatures of the sea and every
living and moving thing with which the water teems,
according to their kinds, and every winged bird according
to its kind. And God saw that it was good. 22 God blessed
them and said, "Be fruitful and increase in number and fill
the water in the seas, and let the birds increase on the
earth." 23 And there was evening, and there was morning—
the fifth day.
24 And God said, "Let the land produce living creatures according
to their kinds: livestock, creatures that move along the
ground, and wild animals, each according to its kind." And
it was so. 25 God made the wild animals according to their
kinds, the livestock according to their kinds, and all the
creatures that move along the ground according to their
kinds. And God saw that it was good.
26 Then God said, "Let us make man in our image, in our
likeness, and let them rule over the fish of the sea and the
birds of the air, over the livestock, over all the earth,[a] and
over all the creatures that move along the ground."

27 So God created man in his own image,
in the image of God he created him;
male and female he created them.

28 God blessed them and said to them, "Be fruitful
and increase in number; fill the earth and subdue it. Rule
over the fish of the sea and the birds of the air and over
every living creature that moves on the ground."
29 Then God said, "I give you every seed-bearing
plant on the face of the whole earth and every tree that has
fruit with seed in it. They will be yours for food. 30 And to
all the beasts of the earth and all the birds of the air and all
the creatures that move on the ground—everything that
has the breath of life in it—I give every green plant for
food." And it was so.
31 God saw all that he had made, and it was very
good. And there was evening, and there was morning—the
sixth day.

2 Thus the heavens and the earth were completed in all
their vast array.

[a]26 Hebrew; Syriac *all the wild animals*

1:21 *great creatures of the sea:* This refers to Leviathan or Rahab, familiar monsters in Canaanite mythology. Sometimes the opponents of God and God's people are described as sea monsters (Ps 89:10; Isa 51:9; Jer 51:34). Here the sea monster is important simply as a part of God's good creation.

1:26 *Let us make man in our image:* The plural (us, our) may refer to God and the heavenly beings that make up God's heavenly court (11:7; 1 Kgs 22:19; Isa 6:8). The Hebrew word for "man" here is *adam,* which is also the name of the first human created (3:20). Humans alone are made in God's image, which means they have a special relationship with God and represent God on earth by ruling over the other creatures. See also 5:1; Ps 8:5-8.

2:3 *God blessed the seventh day and . . . rested:* The Hebrew verb translated as "rested" is the basis for the word *sabbath,* which means "rest." God's rest is one reason given for the Sabbath Commandment in the Law of Moses (Exod 20:8-11; 31:12-17; see also Heb 4:10).

2:4 *LORD God:* In 1:1—2:4, the Hebrew name translated as "God" is *Elohim.* In a second description of creation beginning with 2:4, the name used for God combines the Hebrew words *Yahweh* and *Elohim.* In the NIV these are translated as "LORD God." While *Elohim* is a general name for God, *Yahweh* is a more particular name. It is the name God told Moses to use when telling the Hebrew people who it was who had sent Moses to speak to them (Exod 3:14,15). For more, see the mini-article called "LORD (YHWH)," p. 140.

1:27,28 Gen 5:1,2; Matt 19:4; Mark 10:6.

2 By the seventh day God had finished the work he had been doing;
so on the seventh day he rested[a] from all his work. 3 And God
blessed the seventh day and made it holy, because on it he
rested from all the work of creating that he had done.

Adam and Eve

4 This is the account of the heavens and the earth when they
were created.

When the LORD God made the earth and the heavens— 5 and
no shrub of the field had yet appeared on the earth[b] and no plant
of the field had yet sprung up, for the LORD God had not sent rain
on the earth[b] and there was no man to work the ground, 6 but
streams[c] came up from the earth and watered the whole surface of
the ground— 7 the LORD God formed the man[d] from the dust of
the ground and breathed into his nostrils the breath of life, and the
man became a living being.

8 Now the LORD God had planted a garden in the east, in
Eden; and there he put the man he had formed. 9 And the LORD
God made all kinds of trees grow out of the ground—trees that
were pleasing to the eye and good for food. In the middle of the
garden were the tree of life and the tree of the knowledge of good
and evil.

10 A river watering the garden flowed from Eden; from there
it was separated into four headwaters. 11 The name of the first is the
Pishon; it winds through the entire land of Havilah, where there is
gold. 12 (The gold of that land is good; aromatic resin[e] and onyx are
also there.) 13 The name of the second river is the Gihon; it winds
through the entire land of Cush.[f] 14 The name of the third river is
the Tigris; it runs along the east side of Asshur. And the fourth
river is the Euphrates.

15 The LORD God took the man and put him in the Garden of
Eden to work it and take care of it. 16 And the LORD God commanded the man, "You are free to eat from any tree in the garden;
17 but you must not eat from the tree of the knowledge of good and
evil, for when you eat of it you will surely die."

18 The LORD God said, "It is not good for the man to be alone.
I will make a helper suitable for him."

19 Now the LORD God had formed out of the ground all the
beasts of the field and all the birds of the air. He brought them to
the man to see what he would name them; and whatever the man
called each living creature, that was its name. 20 So the man gave
names to all the livestock, the birds of the air and all the beasts of
the field.

2:7 *dust . . . man:* In Hebrew "man" (*adam*) comes from the same word as "dust" or "ground" (*adamah*). People are true "earth"-lings.

2:10–14 *Eden . . . Euphrates:* In Hebrew, *Eden* means "pleasure" or "delight." The location of the Garden of Eden is described here as being somewhere in Mesopotamia (see the map on p. 2462). The Tigris and Euphrates Rivers formed the fertile river valleys in Mesopotamia. The land of Havilah is unknown, as are the Pishon River and Gihon River. They may be streams in southeastern Mesopotamia. Or, the Pishon may refer to the Persian Gulf, and the Gihon may refer to the Nile River that runs from Ethiopia through Egypt.

2:15 *man:* See the note at 1:26. As part of the "rule" over creation that God gave humans (1:26-29), man is expected to take care of the Garden of Eden.

2:18–23 *helper suitable . . . 'woman':* The animals and birds were not the right kind of partner for man, so woman was created. The woman is made from the man's rib, and not from the earth like the animals (2:19,20). Man and woman come from the same flesh (2:23) and together represent the human race. Here, the Hebrew words for "man" (*ish*) and "woman" (*ishah*) are similar. This is a different word for "man" than the word used in 1:26 and 3:20 ("adam").

2:7 1 Cor 15:45. **2:9** Rev 2:7; 22:2,14.

---

[a] **2** Or *ceased*; also in verse 3 [b] **5** Or *land*; also in verse 6 [c] **6** Or *mist* [d] **7** The Hebrew for *man (adam)* sounds like and may be related to the Hebrew for *ground (adamah)*; it is also the name *Adam* (see Gen. 2:20). [e] **12** Or *good; pearls*
[f] **13** Possibly southeast Mesopotamia

But for Adam[a] no suitable helper was found. 21So the LORD
God caused the man to fall into a deep sleep; and while he was
sleeping, he took one of the man's ribs[b] and closed up the place
with flesh. 22Then the LORD God made a woman from the rib[c] he
had taken out of the man, and he brought her to the man.
23The man said,

"This is now bone of my bones
 and flesh of my flesh;
she shall be called 'woman,[d]'
 for she was taken out of man."

24For this reason a man will leave his father and mother and be
united to his wife, and they will become one flesh.
25The man and his wife were both naked, and they felt no
shame.

SIN IN EDEN

The perfect life God has given to human beings in the Garden of Eden is destroyed when Adam and Eve disobey God's command not to eat fruit from the tree of the knowledge of good and evil. Their son Cain murders his brother Abel as an early result of sin entering human life.

The Fall of Man

3 Now the serpent was more crafty than any of the wild animals
the LORD God had made. He said to the woman, "Did God really
say, 'You must not eat from any tree in the garden'?"
2The woman said to the serpent, "We may eat fruit from the
trees in the garden, 3but God did say, 'You must not eat fruit from
the tree that is in the middle of the garden, and you must not
touch it, or you will die.' "
4"You will not surely die," the serpent said to the woman.
5"For God knows that when you eat of it your eyes will be opened,
and you will be like God, knowing good and evil."
6When the woman saw that the fruit of the tree was good for
food and pleasing to the eye, and also desirable for gaining wisdom, she took some and ate it. She also gave some to her husband,
who was with her, and he ate it. 7Then the eyes of both of them
were opened, and they realized they were naked; so they sewed fig
leaves together and made coverings for themselves.
8Then the man and his wife heard the sound of the LORD
God as he was walking in the garden in the cool of the day, and
they hid from the LORD God among the trees of the garden. 9But
the LORD God called to the man, "Where are you?"

---

[a]**20** Or *the man* [b]**21** Or *took part of the man's side* [c]**22** Or *part* [d]**23** The Hebrew for *woman* sounds like the Hebrew for *man.*

3:1 *serpent:* The serpent is one of the wild animals made as part of God's good creation (1:24,25). In the ancient world, most snakes were thought to be poisonous and so were both respected and feared. In the Jewish Scriptures (Old Testament), the snake came to represent the evil in the world that is able to tempt human beings to disobey God. In both the Old and New Testaments, an image of a snake is sometimes used to describe evil persons or nations or instruments of punishment (Deut 32:33; Ps 58:1-5; Isa 14:29; Jer 8:17; Matt 3:7; 23:33; Luke 3:7). In REVELATION Satan is also described as a serpent (Rev 12:9,13-15; 20:2). That is why the serpent in the Garden of Eden is sometimes referred to as Satan, even though GENESIS does not say this and also does not clearly say where evil came from. See also the mini-article called "Satan," p. 963.

3:5 *knowing good and evil:* The man and woman were tempted to eat so they could know what God knows. Perhaps they wondered: "If we have this special knowledge, maybe we will be like gods ourselves." But when they ate the fruit God told them not to eat, they not only became aware of the difference between good and evil, they also felt the pain of guilt and shame for the first time. They realized that they were naked (3:7) and tried to hide from God (3:10). The perfect relationship that existed in the beginning between God and human beings was now broken.

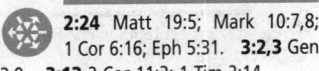

2:24 Matt 19:5; Mark 10:7,8; 1 Cor 6:16; Eph 5:31. **3:2,3** Gen 2:9. **3:13** 2 Cor 11:3; 1 Tim 2:14.

[10]He answered, "I heard you in the garden, and I was afraid
because I was naked; so I hid."
[11]And he said, "Who told you that you were naked? Have you
eaten from the tree that I commanded you not to eat from?"
[12]The man said, "The woman you put here with me—she
gave me some fruit from the tree, and I ate it."
[13]Then the LORD God said to the woman, "What is this you
have done?"
The woman said, "The serpent deceived me, and I ate."
[14]So the LORD God said to the serpent, "Because you have
done this,

God said, *"Have you eaten from the tree that I commanded you not to eat from?"*
Gen 3:11

The Expulsion from Paradise, page from the Hunterian Psalter, around 1170, England, artist unknown. God created the first man (Adam) and woman (Eve) to live in the beauty of the Garden of Eden. But they disobeyed God by eating from the one tree in the garden that God told them not to eat. For this they were expelled from the garden and forced to live lives of hardship (see 3:1-19).

"Cursed are you above all the livestock
and all the wild animals!
You will crawl on your belly
and you will eat dust
all the days of your life.
15 And I will put enmity
between you and the woman,
and between your offspring[a] and hers;
he will crush[b] your head,
and you will strike his heel."

16 To the woman he said,

"I will greatly increase your pains in
childbearing;
with pain you will give birth to children.
Your desire will be for your husband,
and he will rule over you."

17 To Adam he said, "Because you listened to your wife and
ate from the tree about which I commanded you, 'You must not
eat of it,'

"Cursed is the ground because of you;
through painful toil you will eat of it
all the days of your life.
18 It will produce thorns and thistles
for you,
and you will eat the plants of the field.
19 By the sweat of your brow
you will eat your food
until you return to the ground,
since from it you were taken;
for dust you are
and to dust you will return."

20 Adam[c] named his wife Eve,[d] because she would become the
mother of all the living.
21 The LORD God made garments of skin for Adam and his
wife and clothed them. 22 And the LORD God said, "The man has
now become like one of us, knowing good and evil. He must not
be allowed to reach out his hand and take also from the tree of life
and eat, and live forever." 23 So the LORD God banished him from
the Garden of Eden to work the ground from which he had been
taken. 24 After he drove the man out, he placed on the east side[e] of
the Garden of Eden cherubim and a flaming sword flashing back
and forth to guard the way to the tree of life.

3:16-18 *greatly increase your pains . . . ground . . . will produce thorns:* As punishment for disobeying God, the woman will have pain during childbirth and the man will have to work hard to grow food, since the ground will naturally produce weeds, thorns, and thistles. After a lifetime of work, human beings will die and return to the ground God made them from (see the note at 2:7).

3:20 *Adam . . . Eve:* In Hebrew "man" and "Adam" are the same (see the note at 1:26). In Hebrew "Eve" sounds like the word for "living."

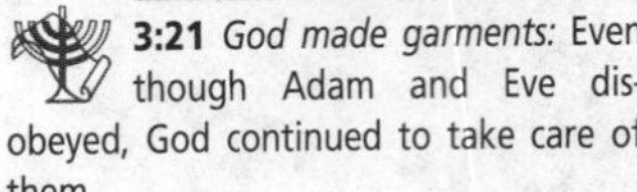

3:21 *God made garments:* Even though Adam and Eve disobeyed, God continued to take care of them.

3:22 *tree of life:* Adam and Eve did not eat fruit from the tree of life, probably meaning the tree that would let them live forever (2:9). To be near this tree meant being in the presence of God. But to be sent away from this tree (3:23) shows how their relationship with God was broken, and living forever with God was now impossible. The New Testament tells how God gives people new life, which includes one day being able to eat from the tree of life (Rev 22:14).

3:23 *Garden of Eden:* See the note at 2:10-14.

3:24 *cherubim . . . flaming sword:* These *cherubim* are mighty angels. In the Bible, they guard sacred areas (Exod 25:18-22; 1 Kgs 8:6, 7) and are often pictured as looking like the Sphinx of Egypt, having a human head and lion's body (Ezek 41:17-20) or like the human-headed bulls and lions that guarded ancient Mesopotamian temples. The sword is like the sword God used to defeat Israel's enemies (Isa 34:5,6; Jer 47:6,7). Flames, fire, and smoke are often used as symbols of God's presence (Exod 3:1-6; 19:16-18; Rev 1:12-16).

[a]**15** Or *seed* [b]**15** Or *strike* [c]**20** Or *The man* [d]**20** *Eve* probably means *living.*
[e]**24** Or *placed in front*

Cain and Abel

4 Adam[a] lay with his wife Eve, and she became pregnant and
gave birth to Cain.[b] She said, "With the help of the LORD I have
brought forth[c] a man." [2]Later she gave birth to his brother Abel.

Now Abel kept flocks, and Cain worked the soil. [3]In the
course of time Cain brought some of the fruits of the soil as an
offering to the LORD. [4]But Abel brought fat portions from some of
the firstborn of his flock. The LORD looked with favor on Abel and
his offering, [5]but on Cain and his offering he did not look with
favor. So Cain was very angry, and his face was downcast.

[6]Then the LORD said to Cain, "Why are you angry? Why is
your face downcast? [7]If you do what is right, will you not be
accepted? But if you do not do what is right, sin is crouching at
your door; it desires to have you, but you must master it."

[8]Now Cain said to his brother Abel, "Let's go out to the
field."[d] And while they were in the field, Cain attacked his brother
Abel and killed him.

[9]Then the LORD said to Cain, "Where is your brother Abel?"

"I don't know," he replied. "Am I my brother's keeper?"

[10]The LORD said, "What have you done? Listen! Your brother's blood cries out to me from the ground. [11]Now you are under
a curse and driven from the ground, which opened its mouth to
receive your brother's blood from your hand. [12]When you work
the ground, it will no longer yield its crops for you. You will be a
restless wanderer on the earth."

[13]Cain said to the LORD, "My punishment is more than I can
bear. [14]Today you are driving me from the land, and I will be hidden from your presence; I will be a restless wanderer on the earth,
and whoever finds me will kill me."

[15]But the LORD said to him, "Not so[e]; if anyone kills Cain, he
will suffer vengeance seven times over." Then the LORD put a mark
on Cain so that no one who found him would kill him. [16]So Cain
went out from the LORD's presence and lived in the land of Nod,[f]
east of Eden.

[17]Cain lay with his wife, and she became pregnant and gave
birth to Enoch. Cain was then building a city, and he named it
after his son Enoch. [18]To Enoch was born Irad, and Irad was the
father of Mehujael, and Mehujael was the father of Methushael,
and Methushael was the father of Lamech.

[19]Lamech married two women, one named Adah and the
other Zillah. [20]Adah gave birth to Jabal; he was the father of those
who live in tents and raise livestock. [21]His brother's name was
Jubal; he was the father of all who play the harp and flute. [22]Zillah

---

[a]1 Or *The man* [b]1 *Cain* sounds like the Hebrew for *brought forth* or *acquired.*
[c]1 Or *have acquired* [d]8 Samaritan Pentateuch, Septuagint, Vulgate and Syriac; Masoretic Text does not have *"Let's go out to the field."* [e]15 Septuagint, Vulgate and Syriac; Hebrew *Very well* [f]16 *Nod* means *wandering* (see verses 12 and 14).

4:1,2 *Adam . . . Eve . . . Cain . . . Abel:* See the note at 3:20. In Hebrew, "Cain" sounds like "got." Abel means "breath" or "temporary." Abel's sacrifice of a firstborn lamb was proper and pleasing to God (Exod 13:2,12,15; Lev 27:26; Heb 11:4). Although grain offerings were usually considered good, Cain may not have offered God the "first," or best, part of his harvest. See also the chart called "Sacrifices and Offerings," p. 219.

4:7 *sin is crouching at your door:* Here the word for "crouching" comes from the Babylonian word for a demon waiting by a door threatening to pounce on those inside. Sin turns Cain away from doing what is right. See also the mini-article called "Sin," p. 2181.

4:10,11 *blood . . . curse:* Blood was believed to be the life-source of animals and human beings (Lev 17:11, 14). Cain was cursed, just as the ground was earlier put under a curse (3:17). See also the mini-article called "Blood," p. 180.

4:14 *hidden from your presence:* Ancient peoples often believed that their gods lived or looked after particular places. This thinking is reflected in Cain's concern. Later, the Hebrew people would discover that their God was not limited to a particular place.

4:15 *mark:* Just what kind of mark is not clear. The mark was a sign of God's protection and mercy. See the note at 3:21.

4:17,18 *Cain . . . Lamech:* Counting Adam, the number of the first generations is seven, a number that symbolizes perfection. See also the chart called "Numbers in the Bible," p. 2405.

3:15 Rev 12:7. **3:17,18** Heb 6:8. **4:8** Matt 23:35; Luke 11:50, 51; 1 John 3:12. **4:10** Heb 12:24.

When God created man, he made him in the likeness of God. He created them male and female and blessed them. And when they were created, he called them "man."
Gen 5:1-2

4:23 *wives:* It was not unusual in ancient times for a man to have more than one wife (16:1-3; 29:16-30).

4:25 *Seth . . . granted:* In Hebrew, the words for "Seth" and "granted" sound alike.

5:1–4 *Adam . . . had a son in his own likeness . . . Seth:* See the notes at 1:26 and 3:20. The same phrase that describes how the first man (Adam) was created to be like God is now used to describe how Adam's son, Seth, was made like Adam. See the note at 4:25.

5:3–32 *Adam . . . Noah:* The number of generations from Adam to Noah is ten and equals about 8,400 years. Whether these years are meant to be taken as an exact number or a symbolic number has been debated, especially when compared to archaeological discoveries. For example, Enoch's years are 365 (5:23,24), the same number of days in a year, meaning he had a full life. See also the mini-article called "Genealogies in the Bible," p. 734 and the chart called "Numbers in the Bible," p. 2405.

In Hebrew the name Noah sounds like "comfort," which emphasizes Noah's part in how God delivered the human race from the flood and promised never to destroy humankind this way again (9:11-17).

5:1,2 Gen 1:27,28; Matt 19:4; Mark 10:6.

also had a son, Tubal-Cain, who forged all kinds of tools out of[a] bronze and iron. Tubal-Cain's sister was Naamah.

[23]Lamech said to his wives,

"Adah and Zillah, listen to me;
  wives of Lamech, hear my words.
I have killed[b] a man for wounding me,
  a young man for injuring me.
[24]If Cain is avenged seven times,
  then Lamech seventy-seven times."

[25]Adam lay with his wife again, and she gave birth to a son and named him Seth,[c] saying, "God has granted me another child in place of Abel, since Cain killed him." [26]Seth also had a son, and he named him Enosh.

At that time men began to call on[d] the name of the LORD.

THE FIRST GENERATIONS OF HUMAN BEINGS

The first of a number of family lists (genealogies) found in GENESIS *is given.*

From Adam to Noah

5 This is the written account of Adam's line.

When God created man, he made him in the likeness of God. [2]He created them male and female and blessed them. And when they were created, he called them "man.[e]"

[3]When Adam had lived 130 years, he had a son in his own likeness, in his own image; and he named him Seth. [4]After Seth was born, Adam lived 800 years and had other sons and daughters. [5]Altogether, Adam lived 930 years, and then he died.

[6]When Seth had lived 105 years, he became the father[f] of Enosh. [7]And after he became the father of Enosh, Seth lived 807 years and had other sons and daughters. [8]Altogether, Seth lived 912 years, and then he died.

[9]When Enosh had lived 90 years, he became the father of Kenan. [10]And after he became the father of Kenan, Enosh lived 815 years and had other sons and daughters. [11]Altogether, Enosh lived 905 years, and then he died.

[12]When Kenan had lived 70 years, he became the father of Mahalalel. [13]And after he became the father of Mahalalel, Kenan lived 840 years and had other sons and daughters. [14]Altogether, Kenan lived 910 years, and then he died.

[15]When Mahalalel had lived 65 years, he became the father of

[a]**22** Or *who instructed all who work in* [b]**23** Or *I will kill* [c]**25** *Seth* probably means *granted.* [d]**26** Or *to proclaim* [e]**2** Hebrew *adam* [f]**6** *Father* may mean *ancestor*; also in verses 7-26.

Jared. 16And after he became the father of Jared, Mahalalel lived
830 years and had other sons and daughters. 17Altogether, Mahalalel lived 895 years, and then he died.
18When Jared had lived 162 years, he became the father of
Enoch. 19And after he became the father of Enoch, Jared lived 800
years and had other sons and daughters. 20Altogether, Jared lived
962 years, and then he died.
21When Enoch had lived 65 years, he became the father of
Methuselah. 22And after he became the father of Methuselah,
Enoch walked with God 300 years and had other sons and daughters. 23Altogether, Enoch lived 365 years. 24Enoch walked with God;
then he was no more, because God took him away.
25When Methuselah had lived 187 years, he became the
father of Lamech. 26And after he became the father of Lamech,
Methuselah lived 782 years and had other sons and daughters.
27Altogether, Methuselah lived 969 years, and then he died.
28When Lamech had lived 182 years, he had a son. 29He
named him Noah[a] and said, "He will comfort us in the labor and
painful toil of our hands caused by the ground the LORD has
cursed." 30After Noah was born, Lamech lived 595 years and had
other sons and daughters. 31Altogether, Lamech lived 777 years,
and then he died.
32After Noah was 500 years old, he became the father of
Shem, Ham and Japheth.

NOAH AND HIS DESCENDANTS

This section tells how God saved Noah and his family from the great flood that destroyed the earth and its sinful people. It then lists the descendants of Noah and his sons and tells the story of the Tower of Babel, where God causes people to speak different languages and scatters them all over the world.

The Flood

6 When men began to increase in number on the earth and daughters were born to them, 2the sons of God saw that the daughters of
men were beautiful, and they married any of them they chose. 3Then
the LORD said, "My Spirit will not contend with[b] man forever, for he
is mortal[c]; his days will be a hundred and twenty years."
4The Nephilim were on the earth in those days—and also
afterward—when the sons of God went to the daughters of men and
had children by them. They were the heroes of old, men of renown.
5The LORD saw how great man's wickedness on the earth had
become, and that every inclination of the thoughts of his heart was
only evil all the time. 6The LORD was grieved that he had made

6:1-4 *sons of God . . . Nephilim:* The "sons of God" probably refer to angels or other divine beings in God's heavenly court (see the note at 1:26; see also Job 1:6; 2:1). The children born to the women who married these heavenly beings were called Nephilim, which means "fallen ones." They are also mentioned in Numbers 13:31-33 and as "Anakites" in Deuteronomy 2:10, 11; 9:2.

5:23,24 Heb 11:5; Jude 14. **6:5-8** Matt 24:37; Luke 17:26; 1 Pet 3:20.

[a]29 *Noah* sounds like the Hebrew for *comfort.* [b]3 Or *My spirit will not remain in* [c]3 Or *corrupt*

Noah's Ark, color print by Sadao Watanabe, 1980. God destroyed his own creation in a great flood because the human race had become so wicked. Only one man, Noah, pleased God. God told Noah to build an ark of cypress wood to save his whole family and to save pairs of every kind of animal. (See 6:1—8:22.)

6:8,9 *Noah found favor in the eyes of the* LORD: See the notes at 2:4 and 5:3-32. See also 2 Pet 2:5.

6:14 *an ark of cypress wood:* The Hebrew word used for "ark" is the same Hebrew word used for the floating basket that was used to save the baby Moses (Exod 2:3-5). The boat is about the length of one-and-a-half modern American football fields.

6:22 Heb 11:7.

man on the earth, and his heart was filled with pain. [7]So the LORD
said, "I will wipe mankind, whom I have created, from the face of
the earth—men and animals, and creatures that move along the
ground, and birds of the air—for I am grieved that I have made
them." [8]But Noah found favor in the eyes of the LORD.

[9]This is the account of Noah.

Noah was a righteous man, blameless among the people of
his time, and he walked with God. [10]Noah had three sons: Shem,
Ham and Japheth.

[11]Now the earth was corrupt in God's sight and was full of
violence. [12]God saw how corrupt the earth had become, for all the
people on earth had corrupted their ways. [13]So God said to Noah,
"I am going to put an end to all people, for the earth is filled with
violence because of them. I am surely going to destroy both them
and the earth. [14]So make yourself an ark of cypress[a] wood; make

[a]**14** The meaning of the Hebrew for this word is uncertain.

rooms in it and coat it with pitch inside and out. [15]This is how you
are to build it: The ark is to be 450 feet long, 75 feet wide and 45
feet high.[a] [16]Make a roof for it and finish[b] the ark to within 18
inches[c] of the top. Put a door in the side of the ark and make
lower, middle and upper decks. [17]I am going to bring floodwaters
on the earth to destroy all life under the heavens, every creature
that has the breath of life in it. Everything on earth will perish.
[18]But I will establish my covenant with you, and you will enter the
ark—you and your sons and your wife and your sons' wives with
you. [19]You are to bring into the ark two of all living creatures, male
and female, to keep them alive with you. [20]Two of every kind of
bird, of every kind of animal and of every kind of creature that
moves along the ground will come to you to be kept alive. [21]You
are to take every kind of food that is to be eaten and store it away
as food for you and for them."

[22]Noah did everything just as God commanded him.

Noah was a righteous man, blameless among the people of his time, and he walked with God.
Gen 6:9

a15 Hebrew *300 cubits long, 50 cubits wide and 30 cubits high* (about 140 meters long, 23 meters wide and 13.5 meters high) **b16** Or *Make an opening for light by finishing* **c16** Hebrew *a cubit* (about 0.5 meter)

AN ANCIENT FLOOD STORY

Many ancient Near Eastern stories describe a terrible flood that destroyed much of humankind. Ancient flood stories also are common in other parts of the world—from the Arctic to Indonesia. It is impossible to tell whether these stories all refer to the same flood. An ancient flood story from Babylonia called the *Gilgamesh Epic* has a number of similarities to the flood story in GENESIS. Since the earliest ancestors of Israel came from Babylonia, they may have known this story.

In the *Gilgamesh Epic,* the hero Utnapishtim is told in a dream by the god Ea to build a boat, because the other gods plan to send a flood to destroy the earth and all its people. The hero builds the boat in the shape of a cube and makes it waterproof by smearing the seams with sticky tree sap. Then he takes on board his family, his builders, and some animals. A storm comes and covers the earth with water in seven days. The boat eventually comes to rest on a mountain. After six days, Utnapishtim sends out a dove and later a swallow. Both return to the boat because they can't find a place to land. Then he sends out a raven, which does not return. Utnapishtim leaves the boat and makes a sacrifice to the gods, who promise that there will never again be a flood. Utnapishtim is then taken away by the gods to live as one of them.

The differences between the account of the flood in GENESIS and this ancient Babylonian story are important. The Babylonian story tells of a number of gods, who decide to destroy the earth simply because the humans are bothering them. The GENESIS story speaks of one all-powerful God, who is saddened by how evil human beings have become (6:5-7) and so uses a flood to wipe them out. Noah's offering is made to please the LORD, while Utnapishtim's offering is made to the gods who hover around the offering like flies because they are hungry.

The differences between these stories point out a key difference between Israel's religion and the religions of their neighbors. While most ancient cultures followed a number of gods, Israel followed one God, the all-powerful Creator of the world, who chose them and acted in history to save them.

7:2 *seven of every kind of clean animal:* Compare this verse to 6:19,20. The number seven is a sacred number. Animals that could be sacrificed according to the Law of Moses were called "clean" animals, and animals that could not be sacrificed were called "unclean." Extra "clean" animals would have been needed for the burnt offerings that Noah would later make (8:20) and for food (9:3). See also the article called "People of the Law: The Religion of Israel," p. 939, and the mini-article called "Purity (Clean and Unclean)," p. 2125.

7:4 *forty days and forty nights:* In the Bible, this length of time is often associated with a time of preparation. See Deut 9:11; Matt 4:1-11; and the chart called "Numbers in the Bible," p. 2405.

7:11,12 *the springs of the great deep . . . floodgates of the heavens:* The water did not simply fall as rain, but also came out of the ground like geysers gushing from underground oceans. See the note on p. 37 and the note at 1:6-8. This flood is described as the reversal of what God did to overcome the watery chaos at the time of creation, when he separated the dry ground (earth) from the water below and above the earth (1:7).

7:22,23 *Everything . . . that had the breath . . . died:* Except for the people and animals on the ark, the gift of breath, which God gave at creation (1:30; 2:7), was taken away.

8:1 *God . . . sent a wind over the earth:* Compare the order of events in chapters 8 and 9 to the order of events in chapter 1. This new beginning after the flood is like the beginning of creation: 8:1 (1:2); 8:2 (1:6,7); 8:5 (1:9); 8:17 (1:24); 9:1,2 (1:28).

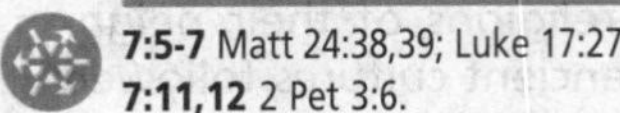

7:5-7 Matt 24:38,39; Luke 17:27.
7:11,12 2 Pet 3:6.

7 The LORD then said to Noah, "Go into the ark, you and your
whole family, because I have found you righteous in this generation. 2Take with you seven[a] of every kind of clean animal, a male
and its mate, and two of every kind of unclean animal, a male and
its mate, 3and also seven of every kind of bird, male and female, to
keep their various kinds alive throughout the earth. 4Seven days
from now I will send rain on the earth for forty days and forty
nights, and I will wipe from the face of the earth every living creature I have made."

5And Noah did all that the LORD commanded him.

6Noah was six hundred years old when the floodwaters came
on the earth. 7And Noah and his sons and his wife and his sons'
wives entered the ark to escape the waters of the flood. 8Pairs of
clean and unclean animals, of birds and of all creatures that move
along the ground, 9male and female, came to Noah and entered the
ark, as God had commanded Noah. 10And after the seven days the
floodwaters came on the earth.

11In the six hundredth year of Noah's life, on the seventeenth
day of the second month—on that day all the springs of the great
deep burst forth, and the floodgates of the heavens were opened.
12And rain fell on the earth forty days and forty nights.

13On that very day Noah and his sons, Shem, Ham and
Japheth, together with his wife and the wives of his three sons,
entered the ark. 14They had with them every wild animal according to its kind, all livestock according to their kinds, every creature
that moves along the ground according to its kind and every bird
according to its kind, everything with wings. 15Pairs of all creatures
that have the breath of life in them came to Noah and entered the
ark. 16The animals going in were male and female of every living
thing, as God had commanded Noah. Then the LORD shut him in.

17For forty days the flood kept coming on the earth, and as
the waters increased they lifted the ark high above the earth. 18The
waters rose and increased greatly on the earth, and the ark floated
on the surface of the water. 19They rose greatly on the earth, and all
the high mountains under the entire heavens were covered. 20The
waters rose and covered the mountains to a depth of more than
twenty feet.[b,c] 21Every living thing that moved on the earth perished—birds, livestock, wild animals, all the creatures that swarm
over the earth, and all mankind. 22Everything on dry land that had
the breath of life in its nostrils died. 23Every living thing on the
face of the earth was wiped out; men and animals and the creatures that move along the ground and the birds of the air were
wiped from the earth. Only Noah was left, and those with him in
the ark.

24The waters flooded the earth for a hundred and fifty days.

---

[a] **2** Or *seven pairs*; also in verse 3 [b] **20** Hebrew *fifteen cubits* (about 6.9 meters)
[c] **20** Or *rose more than twenty feet, and the mountains were covered*

8 But God remembered Noah and all the wild animals and the
livestock that were with him in the ark, and he sent a wind over
the earth, and the waters receded. 2Now the springs of the deep
and the floodgates of the heavens had been closed, and the rain
had stopped falling from the sky. 3The water receded steadily from
the earth. At the end of the hundred and fifty days the water had
gone down, 4and on the seventeenth day of the seventh month the
ark came to rest on the mountains of Ararat. 5The waters continued to recede until the tenth month, and on the first day of the
tenth month the tops of the mountains became visible.

6After forty days Noah opened the window he had made in
the ark 7and sent out a raven, and it kept flying back and forth
until the water had dried up from the earth. 8Then he sent out a
dove to see if the water had receded from the surface of the
ground. 9But the dove could find no place to set its feet because
there was water over all the surface of the earth; so it returned to
Noah in the ark. He reached out his hand and took the dove and
brought it back to himself in the ark. 10He waited seven more days
and again sent out the dove from the ark. 11When the dove
returned to him in the evening, there in its beak was a freshly
plucked olive leaf! Then Noah knew that the water had receded
from the earth. 12He waited seven more days and sent the dove out
again, but this time it did not return to him.

13By the first day of the first month of Noah's six hundred
and first year, the water had dried up from the earth. Noah then
removed the covering from the ark and saw that the surface of the
ground was dry. 14By the twenty-seventh day of the second month
the earth was completely dry.

15Then God said to Noah, 16"Come out of the ark, you and
your wife and your sons and their wives. 17Bring out every kind of
living creature that is with you—the birds, the animals, and all the
creatures that move along the ground—so they can multiply on
the earth and be fruitful and increase in number upon it."

18So Noah came out, together with his sons and his wife and
his sons' wives. 19All the animals and all the creatures that move
along the ground and all the birds—everything that moves on the
earth—came out of the ark, one kind after another.

20Then Noah built an altar to the LORD and, taking some of
all the clean animals and clean birds, he sacrificed burnt offerings
on it. 21The LORD smelled the pleasing aroma and said in his heart:
"Never again will I curse the ground because of man, even though[a]
every inclination of his heart is evil from childhood. And never
again will I destroy all living creatures, as I have done.

[a]21 Or *man, for*

8:4 *mountains of Ararat:* Probably refers to the area northwest of ancient Mesopotamia known as Urartu (modern-day northeast Turkey or Armenia). See the map on p. 2462.

8:6-8 *sent out a raven . . . a dove:* A raven is a black bird that can survive in difficult circumstances and can live easily on its own. They were considered "unclean" birds because according to the Law of Moses they were not acceptable for eating or as sacrifices for sin (see Deut 14:14).

Doves are "clean" birds, similar to pigeons. They could be easily trained to carry messages. According to the Law of Moses they were acceptable sacrifices for sin for poor people who couldn't afford to sacrifice a larger animal (see Lev 5:7).

8:20 *clean animals . . . sacrificed:* See the note at 7:2. The offerings Noah made were completely burned on the altar similar to the burnt offerings described in Leviticus 1.

8:21 *every inclination of his heart is evil from childhood:* The flood didn't destroy sin, which comes from within the human heart from the time we are young. But God promises not to destroy all living things because of sin. See also the note at 4:7.

God said, *"I have set my rainbow in the clouds, and it will be the sign of the covenant between me and the earth."*
Gen 9:13

9:3,4 *Everything that lives and moves will be food for you . . . But you must not eat meat that has its lifeblood still in it:* Meat is here added to the food God provided at the time of creation (1:29). But because blood was thought to carry life (see the note at 4:10,11), it was not to be eaten (Lev 17:10-14; Deut 12:23,24). See also the mini-article called "Blood," p. 180.

9:9 *covenant:* An agreement between two or more persons (or groups). Most ancient covenants stated what both parties would do to keep the terms of the agreement. But here, God alone is making an unconditional promise not to destroy the earth by a flood (9:11,15). The rainbow will be a sign of this promise. Noah's part of the covenant is not stated. See the mini-article called "Covenants (Agreements)," p. 386.

9:1 Gen 1:28. **9:5-7** Exod 20:13; Gen 1:26, 28. **9:11** Gen 8:21.

22 "As long as the earth endures,
seedtime and harvest,
cold and heat,
summer and winter,
day and night
will never cease."

God's Covenant With Noah

9 Then God blessed Noah and his sons, saying to them, "Be
fruitful and increase in number and fill the earth. 2 The fear and
dread of you will fall upon all the beasts of the earth and all the
birds of the air, upon every creature that moves along the ground,
and upon all the fish of the sea; they are given into your hands.
3 Everything that lives and moves will be food for you. Just as I gave
you the green plants, I now give you everything.
4 "But you must not eat meat that has its lifeblood still in it.
5 And for your lifeblood I will surely demand an accounting. I will
demand an accounting from every animal. And from each man,
too, I will demand an accounting for the life of his fellow man.

6 "Whoever sheds the blood of man,
by man shall his blood be shed;
for in the image of God
has God made man.

7 As for you, be fruitful and increase in number; multiply on the
earth and increase upon it."
8 Then God said to Noah and to his sons with him: 9 "I now
establish my covenant with you and with your descendants after
you 10 and with every living creature that was with you—the birds,
the livestock and all the wild animals, all those that came out
of the ark with you—every living creature on earth. 11 I establish
my covenant with you: Never again will all life be cut off by
the waters of a flood; never again will there be a flood to destroy
the earth."
12 And God said, "This is the sign of the covenant I am making between me and you and every living creature with you, a
covenant for all generations to come: 13 I have set my rainbow in
the clouds, and it will be the sign of the covenant between me and
the earth. 14 Whenever I bring clouds over the earth and the rainbow appears in the clouds, 15 I will remember my covenant
between me and you and all living creatures of every kind. Never
again will the waters become a flood to destroy all life. 16 Whenever the rainbow appears in the clouds, I will see it and remember
the everlasting covenant between God and all living creatures of
every kind on the earth."
17 So God said to Noah, "This is the sign of the covenant I
have established between me and all life on the earth."

The Sons of Noah

18 The sons of Noah who came out of the ark were Shem,
Ham and Japheth. (Ham was the father of Canaan.) 19 These were
the three sons of Noah, and from them came the people who were
scattered over the earth.

20 Noah, a man of the soil, proceeded[a] to plant a vineyard.
21 When he drank some of its wine, he became drunk and lay
uncovered inside his tent. 22 Ham, the father of Canaan, saw his
father's nakedness and told his two brothers outside. 23 But Shem
and Japheth took a garment and laid it across their shoulders; then
they walked in backward and covered their father's nakedness.
Their faces were turned the other way so that they would not see
their father's nakedness.

24 When Noah awoke from his wine and found out what his
youngest son had done to him, 25 he said,

"Cursed be Canaan!
The lowest of slaves
will he be to his brothers."

26 He also said,

"Blessed be the LORD, the God of Shem!
May Canaan be the slave of Shem.[b]
27 May God extend the territory of Japheth[c];
may Japheth live in the tents of Shem,
and may Canaan be his[d] slave."

28 After the flood Noah lived 350 years. 29 Altogether, Noah
lived 950 years, and then he died.

The Table of Nations

10 This is the account of Shem, Ham and Japheth, Noah's sons,
who themselves had sons after the flood.

THE JAPHETHITES

2 The sons[e] of Japheth:
Gomer, Magog, Madai, Javan, Tubal, Meshech and Tiras.
3 The sons of Gomer:
Ashkenaz, Riphath and Togarmah.
4 The sons of Javan:
Elishah, Tarshish, the Kittim and the Rodanim.[f] 5 (From these
the maritime peoples spread out into their territories by
their clans within their nations, each with its own language.)

[a]**20** Or *soil, was the first* [b]**26** Or *be his slave* [c]**27** *Japheth* sounds like the Hebrew for *extend.* [d]**27** Or *their* [e]**2** *Sons* may mean *descendants* or *successors* or *nations*; also in verses 3, 4, 6, 7, 20-23, 29 and 31. [f]**4** Some manuscripts of the Masoretic Text and Samaritan Pentateuch (see also Septuagint and 1 Chron. 1:7); most manuscripts of the Masoretic Text *Dodanim*

9:20 *plant a vineyard:* Grapes, unlike grains, can grow easily on hillsides. Also unlike grains, grapevines require a lot of attention and care from the farmer (vinedresser) in order to produce a tasty and bountiful crop. This is why cultures that practice vinedressing and winemaking are often seen as more advanced than those that practice simpler forms of agriculture. Grapes were eaten fresh or sun-dried (raisins), but more often were crushed to make wine. See also the mini-article called "Wine," p. 2047.

This verse seems to indicate that the misuse of wine (drunkenness) was a problem from the time when humans first began to make wine. See also Gen 19:30-35; Prov 20:1; 23:20,21; Gal 5:21.

9:22-27 *Ham . . . Canaan . . . Japheth:* Canaan is the son of Ham, Noah's youngest son. Because Noah curses Canaan, some have suggested that it was actually Canaan who saw Noah naked and told his uncles. Later, the Israelites, who were descendants of Shem, did enter and take over the land of the Canaanites, the descendants of Canaan. The curse could imply that the Canaanites became Israel's slaves because of their evil sexual actions (see Lev 18:24-30). For example, Canaanite worship included having sex with temple prostitutes who served the Canaanite fertility goddess. For more, see the mini-article called "Canaanite Gods and Goddesses," p. 469.

In Hebrew "Japheth" sounds like the word that means "more and more."

10:2-5 *sons of Japheth . . . maritime peoples:* These tribes and lands were centered mostly in Asia Minor and the upper Euphrates River region.

Elishah could refer to all or part of the island of Cyprus, whose ancient name was Alashia. Tarshish probably refers to southern Spain; Kittim most likely is Cyprus. The Rodanim may be the people who lived along the coasts in the land of Greece (see the map on p. 2462).

10:6-20 *sons of Ham:* These tribes and nations were mainly located in northeastern Africa and Canaan, but certain ancestors such as the warrior Nimrod ruled city-states in Shinar (Babylonia), another name for southern Mesopotamia, and Nineveh in Assyria, which was in the northern part of the Tigris and Euphrates River valleys.

The land of Cush has been identified with the region south of Egypt that included parts of the present countries of Ethiopia and Sudan.

The Philistines were from Caphtor (Jer 47:4; Amos 9:7), better known as Crete.

The Jebusites were located in and around Jerusalem, until King David drove them out and took over Jerusalem (2 Sam 5:6-9). The Amorites lived in the hill country of Canaan at the time the Israelites invaded (Num 21:21-35; Josh 2:10). The other Canaanite groups listed were located in city-states in Canaan. See the maps on p. 2462 and p. 2464. See also the article called "The Ancient World: Peoples, Powers, and Politics," p. 919.

10:21-31 *sons of Shem:* These descendants were "Shemites," a name later modified to Semites. The people known as Israel descended from the Hebrew people (children of Eber), one group of ancient Semitic peoples. Elam was an early name for Assyria, and Aram was an early name for Syria. In Hebrew "Peleg" means "divided."

Sheba was probably located in southwest Arabia. The queen of Sheba made a famous visit to King Solomon of Israel (1 Kgs 10:1-13). Ophir, in southern Arabia or in Africa, was an important source of gold for Solomon (1 Kgs 9:28; 10:11). See the map on p. 2462.

The Hamites

6 The sons of Ham:
Cush, Mizraim,[a] Put and Canaan.
7 The sons of Cush:
Seba, Havilah, Sabtah, Raamah and Sabteca.
The sons of Raamah:
Sheba and Dedan.

8 Cush was the father[b] of Nimrod, who grew to be a mighty
warrior on the earth. 9 He was a mighty hunter before the LORD;
that is why it is said, "Like Nimrod, a mighty hunter before the
LORD." 10 The first centers of his kingdom were Babylon, Erech,
Akkad and Calneh, in[c] Shinar.[d] 11 From that land he went to Assyria, where he built Nineveh, Rehoboth Ir,[e] Calah 12 and Resen,
which is between Nineveh and Calah; that is the great city.

13 Mizraim was the father of
the Ludites, Anamites, Lehabites, Naphtuhites, 14 Path-
rusites, Casluhites (from whom the Philistines came) and
Caphtorites.
15 Canaan was the father of
Sidon his firstborn,[f] and of the Hittites, 16 Jebusites, Amorites, Girgashites, 17 Hivites, Arkites, Sinites, 18 Arvadites,
Zemarites and Hamathites.

Later the Canaanite clans scattered 19 and the borders of
Canaan reached from Sidon toward Gerar as far as Gaza, and then
toward Sodom, Gomorrah, Admah and Zeboiim, as far as Lasha.
20 These are the sons of Ham by their clans and languages, in
their territories and nations.

The Semites

21 Sons were also born to Shem, whose older brother was[g]
Japheth; Shem was the ancestor of all the sons of Eber.

22 The sons of Shem:
Elam, Asshur, Arphaxad, Lud and Aram.
23 The sons of Aram:
Uz, Hul, Gether and Meshech.[h]
24 Arphaxad was the father of[i] Shelah,
and Shelah the father of Eber.
25 Two sons were born to Eber:
One was named Peleg,[j] because in his time the earth was
divided; his brother was named Joktan.

---

[a]6 That is, Egypt; also in verse 13 [b]8 *Father* may mean *ancestor* or *predecessor* or *founder*; also in verses 13, 15, 24 and 26. [c]10 Or *Erech and Akkad—all of them in* [d]10 That is, Babylonia [e]11 Or *Nineveh with its city squares* [f]15 Or *of the Sidonians, the foremost* [g]21 Or *Shem, the older brother of* [h]23 See Septuagint and 1 Chron. 1:17; Hebrew *Mash* [i]24 Hebrew; Septuagint *father of Cainan, and Cainan was the father of* [j]25 *Peleg* means *division.*

The Tower of Babel by Peter Breugel the Elder, 1563. The descendants of Noah all spoke one language. But after they attempted to build a tower to heaven, God confused their languages and scattered them all over the earth to punish them. This biblical story continues to be a lesson about the danger that comes to arrogant people who only want to glorify themselves. (See 11:1-9.)

26 Joktan was the father of
Almodad, Sheleph, Hazarmaveth, Jerah, 27 Hadoram, Uzal,
Diklah, 28 Obal, Abimael, Sheba, 29 Ophir, Havilah and
Jobab. All these were sons of Joktan.

30 The region where they lived stretched from Mesha toward
Sephar, in the eastern hill country.

31 These are the sons of Shem by their clans and languages,
in their territories and nations.

32 These are the clans of Noah's sons, according to their lines
of descent, within their nations. From these the nations spread out
over the earth after the flood.

The Tower of Babel

11 Now the whole world had one language and a common
speech. 2 As men moved eastward,[a] they found a plain in Shinar[b]
and settled there.
3 They said to each other, "Come, let's make bricks and bake
them thoroughly." They used brick instead of stone, and tar for
mortar. 4 Then they said, "Come, let us build ourselves a city, with
a tower that reaches to the heavens, so that we may make a name
for ourselves and not be scattered over the face of the whole earth."
5 But the LORD came down to see the city and the tower that

[a]2 Or *from the east*; or *in the east* [b]2 That is, Babylonia

11:2-4 *Shinar . . . tower:* Shinar is another name for Babylonia (see the note at 10:6-20). A number of tall temples (called ziggurats) were built in ancient Mesopotamia to honor the gods. They usually had a square base with sloping stepped sides leading up to an altar area at the top. These towers were meant to be stairways to heaven and had names such as "The House of the Link between Heaven and Earth" at Larsa and "The House of the Mountain of the Universe" at Asshur.

> The LORD said, *"Come, let us go down and confuse their language so they will not understand each other."*
> Gen 11:7

11:7 *let us go down:* The LORD is speaking. See the note at 1:26.

11:8,9 *Babel:* This means "the gate of God," but here the word is said to come from the Hebrew word for "confused" (*balal*).

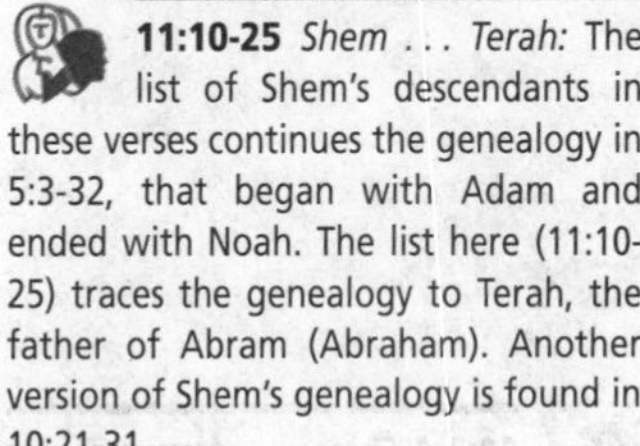

11:10-25 *Shem . . . Terah:* The list of Shem's descendants in these verses continues the genealogy in 5:3-32, that began with Adam and ended with Noah. The list here (11:10-25) traces the genealogy to Terah, the father of Abram (Abraham). Another version of Shem's genealogy is found in 10:21-31.

the men were building. [6]The LORD said, "If as one people speaking the same language they have begun to do this, then nothing they plan to do will be impossible for them. [7]Come, let us go down and confuse their language so they will not understand each other."

[8]So the LORD scattered them from there over all the earth, and they stopped building the city. [9]That is why it was called Babel[a]—because there the LORD confused the language of the whole world. From there the LORD scattered them over the face of the whole earth.

From Shem to Abram

[10]This is the account of Shem.

Two years after the flood, when Shem was 100 years old, he became the father[b] of Arphaxad. [11]And after he became the father of Arphaxad, Shem lived 500 years and had other sons and daughters.

[12]When Arphaxad had lived 35 years, he became the father of Shelah. [13]And after he became the father of Shelah, Arphaxad lived 403 years and had other sons and daughters.[c]

[14]When Shelah had lived 30 years, he became the father of Eber. [15]And after he became the father of Eber, Shelah lived 403 years and had other sons and daughters.

[16]When Eber had lived 34 years, he became the father of Peleg.

---

a9 That is, Babylon; *Babel* sounds like the Hebrew for *confused.* **b10** *Father* may mean *ancestor;* also in verses 11-25. **c12,13** Hebrew; Septuagint (see also Luke 3:35, 36 and note at Gen. 10:24) *35 years, he became the father of Cainan. [13]And after he became the father of Cainan, Arphaxad lived 430 years and had other sons and daughters, and then he died. When Cainan had lived 130 years, he became the father of Shelah. And after he became the father of Shelah, Cainan lived 330 years and had other sons and daughters*

QUESTIONS ABOUT GENESIS 1:1—11:32

1. Why do you think the first three chapters of GENESIS were written? What beliefs or perspectives are being passed on?
2. How does the Bible's description of creation fit with modern theories about how the world began? Do you see any conflicts? Why or why not?
3. From the story in chapter 3, what would you say "sin" is? What effects of human sin do you see in the world today?
4. How would you answer Cain's question in 4:9?
5. The first eleven chapters of GENESIS include a number of family lists (genealogies). Why do you think these lists are included?
6. Why did God send a flood to destroy the earth and its people? (6:1-13) Why was Noah chosen to build the ark? What promise did God make to Noah after the flood waters went down? (8:21,22; 9:9-17) What do you make of the existence of a flood story in the writings of a number of ancient peoples?
7. Why did the people try to build the tower at Babel? (11:1-4) How did God respond to their building of this tower? Why? If God created human beings "in his own image" (1:27), what was wrong with building a tower that got the people "closer" to God in the heavens?
8. What is your overall impression of the first eleven chapters of GENESIS? How would you describe the purpose of GENESIS so far?

17 And after he became the father of Peleg, Eber lived 430 years and
had other sons and daughters.
18 When Peleg had lived 30 years, he became the father of
Reu. 19 And after he became the father of Reu, Peleg lived 209 years
and had other sons and daughters.
20 When Reu had lived 32 years, he became the father of
Serug. 21 And after he became the father of Serug, Reu lived 207
years and had other sons and daughters.
22 When Serug had lived 30 years, he became the father of
Nahor. 23 And after he became the father of Nahor, Serug lived 200
years and had other sons and daughters.
24 When Nahor had lived 29 years, he became the father of
Terah. 25 And after he became the father of Terah, Nahor lived 119
years and had other sons and daughters.
26 After Terah had lived 70 years, he became the father of
Abram, Nahor and Haran.

27 This is the account of Terah.

Terah became the father of Abram, Nahor and Haran. And
Haran became the father of Lot. 28 While his father Terah was still
alive, Haran died in Ur of the Chaldeans, in the land of his birth.
29 Abram and Nahor both married. The name of Abram's wife was
Sarai, and the name of Nahor's wife was Milcah; she was the
daughter of Haran, the father of both Milcah and Iscah. 30 Now
Sarai was barren; she had no children.
31 Terah took his son Abram, his grandson Lot son of Haran,
and his daughter-in-law Sarai, the wife of his son Abram, and
together they set out from Ur of the Chaldeans to go to Canaan.
But when they came to Haran, they settled there.
32 Terah lived 205 years, and he died in Haran.

The Beginning of God's People, Israel

The story of God's people begins when God chooses Abram (Abraham), son of Terah, and tells him to go to Canaan. The last forty chapters of GENESIS tell how God's promises to Abraham and his wife Sarah begin to be worked out in the lives and adventures of their descendants, especially Isaac, Jacob, Joseph, and their families.

ABRAHAM, SARAH, AND ISAAC

Abram and Sarai (later, Abraham and Sarah) follow God's command to go to Canaan. When they are very old, God blesses them with a child named Isaac who will carry on God's promises. But Abram and Sarai run into some problems along the way. God's promises are often challenged, especially when Abram is told to sacrifice Isaac.

The Call of Abram

12 The LORD had said to Abram, "Leave your country, your people
and your father's household and go to the land I will show you.

11:26,27 *Terah . . . Haran:* These verses list the immediate family of Abram, whose descendants became the people of Israel. Haran is the name of one of Terah's sons, as well as the name of a place (11:31).

11:26-31 *Ur of the Chaldeans . . . Haran:* Chaldea was a region at the northern end of the Persian Gulf. Ur was on the main trade routes from Mesopotamia to the Mediterranean Sea. Terah wanted to go to Canaan, which was west of Chaldea, but traveling directly west meant traveling through the dangerous Arabian Desert. The safer route to Canaan was northwest along the Euphrates River Valley to Haran and then turning southwest toward Canaan. See the article called "Trade and Travel," p. 948 and the map on p. 2462.

12:1-3 *Abram:* The name Abram means "exalted father." His name later is changed to Abraham (17:4,5). See the mini-article called "Abraham," p. 2254. See also Gen 12:7; 15:5-21; 17:4-8; 18:18,19; 22:1-19; Acts 7:2,3; Heb 11:8.

[2]“I will make you into a great nation
and I will bless you;
I will make your name great,
and you will be a blessing.
[3]I will bless those who bless you,
and whoever curses you I will curse;
and all peoples on earth
will be blessed through you.”

[4]So Abram left, as the LORD had told him; and Lot went with him. Abram was seventy-five years old when he set out from Haran. [5]He took his wife Sarai, his nephew Lot, all the possessions they had accumulated and the people they had acquired in Haran, and they set out for the land of Canaan, and they arrived there.

[6]Abram traveled through the land as far as the site of the great tree of Moreh at Shechem. At that time the Canaanites were in the land. [7]The LORD appeared to Abram and said, “To your offspring[a] I will give this land.” So he built an altar there to the LORD, who had appeared to him.

[8]From there he went on toward the hills east of Bethel and pitched his tent, with Bethel on the west and Ai on the east. There he built an altar to the LORD and called on the name of the LORD. [9]Then Abram set out and continued toward the Negev.

Abram in Egypt

[10]Now there was a famine in the land, and Abram went down to Egypt to live there for a while because the famine was severe. [11]As he was about to enter Egypt, he said to his wife Sarai, “I know what a beautiful woman you are. [12]When the Egyptians see you, they will say, ‘This is his wife.’ Then they will kill me but will let you live. [13]Say you are my sister, so that I will be treated well for your sake and my life will be spared because of you.”

[14]When Abram came to Egypt, the Egyptians saw that she was a very beautiful woman. [15]And when Pharaoh’s officials saw her, they praised her to Pharaoh, and she was taken into his palace. [16]He treated Abram well for her sake, and Abram acquired sheep and cattle, male and female donkeys, menservants and maidservants, and camels.

[17]But the LORD inflicted serious diseases on Pharaoh and his household because of Abram’s wife Sarai. [18]So Pharaoh summoned Abram. “What have you done to me?” he said. “Why didn’t you tell me she was your wife? [19]Why did you say, ‘She is my sister,’ so that I took her to be my wife? Now then, here is your wife. Take her and go!” [20]Then Pharaoh gave orders about Abram to his men, and they sent him on his way, with his wife and everything he had.

[a]7 Or *seed*

12:4-6 *Haran . . . Shechem:* See the note at 11:26-31. Canaan included lands that today make up the states of Israel, Lebanon, and southern Syria. The Canaanites were descendants of Noah’s son, Ham (10:6-20).

Abram’s travels followed a main trade route between Mesopotamia, Canaan, and Egypt (see the map on p. 2462). Abram claimed this place for the LORD by building an altar there (12:7). Shechem was located in central Canaan. It became an important meeting place for the tribes of Israel after they entered Canaan (Josh 24:1).

12:6 *great tree:* This tree may have been a place where the Canaanites worshiped Asherah, the goddess of fertility. See Deut 11:30.

12:8,9 *Bethel . . . Negev:* Bethel became an important town in Israel’s history (Gen 28:10-22; 35:1-8; 1 Kgs 12:26-29). The city of Ai was one that the Israelites would destroy when they captured Canaan, about six hundred years after the time of Abram (Josh 8:1-29; 10:1).

The Negev was a desert area south and west of the Dead Sea, which formed a land bridge between Canaan, the Sinai Peninsula, and Egypt. For these locations, see the map on p. 2464.

12:10,11 *Egypt:* At the time of Abram, Egypt was an important power in the ancient Near East and played a significant role in the history of Israel (Gen 37–50; Exod 1–15). See also the article called “The Ancient World: Peoples, Powers, and Politics,” p. 919 and the mini-article called “Egypt,” p. 135.

12:15 *Pharaoh:* See the mini-article called “King of Egypt (Pharaoh),” p. 110.

12:19 *I took her to be my wife:* The king of Egypt took Sarai into his palace, where she was expected to be part of the community of women who were the king’s wives (a harem). By letting the king think that Sarai was his sister, Abram put the LORD’s promise (12:1-3) at risk.

Abram and Lot Separate

13 So Abram went up from Egypt to the Negev, with his wife and everything he had, and Lot went with him. [2]Abram had become very wealthy in livestock and in silver and gold.

[3]From the Negev he went from place to place until he came to Bethel, to the place between Bethel and Ai where his tent had been earlier [4]and where he had first built an altar. There Abram called on the name of the LORD.

[5]Now Lot, who was moving about with Abram, also had flocks and herds and tents. [6]But the land could not support them while they stayed together, for their possessions were so great that they were not able to stay together. [7]And quarreling arose between Abram's herdsmen and the herdsmen of Lot. The Canaanites and Perizzites were also living in the land at that time.

[8]So Abram said to Lot, "Let's not have any quarreling between you and me, or between your herdsmen and mine, for we are brothers. [9]Is not the whole land before you? Let's part company. If you go to the left, I'll go to the right; if you go to the right, I'll go to the left."

[10]Lot looked up and saw that the whole plain of the Jordan was well watered, like the garden of the LORD, like the land of Egypt, toward Zoar. (This was before the LORD destroyed Sodom and Gomorrah.) [11]So Lot chose for himself the whole plain of the Jordan and set out toward the east. The two men parted company: [12]Abram lived in the land of Canaan, while Lot lived among the cities of the plain and pitched his tents near Sodom. [13]Now the men of Sodom were wicked and were sinning greatly against the LORD.

[14]The LORD said to Abram after Lot had parted from him, "Lift up your eyes from where you are and look north and south, east and west. [15]All the land that you see I will give to you and your offspring[a] forever. [16]I will make your offspring like the dust of the earth, so that if anyone could count the dust, then your offspring could be counted. [17]Go, walk through the length and breadth of the land, for I am giving it to you."

[18]So Abram moved his tents and went to live near the great trees of Mamre at Hebron, where he built an altar to the LORD.

Abram Rescues Lot

14 At this time Amraphel king of Shinar,[b] Arioch king of Ellasar, Kedorlaomer king of Elam and Tidal king of Goiim [2]went to war against Bera king of Sodom, Birsha king of Gomorrah, Shinab king of Admah, Shemeber king of Zeboiim, and the king of Bela (that is, Zoar). [3]All these latter kings joined forces in the Valley of Siddim (the Salt Sea[c]). [4]For twelve years they had been subject to Kedorlaomer, but in the thirteenth year they rebelled.

[a]15 Or *seed*; also in verse 16 [b]1 That is, Babylonia; also in verse 9 [c]3 That is, the Dead Sea

13:1-4 *Negev . . . Bethel and Ai:* See the note at 12:8,9.

13:5-7 *Lot . . . Perizzites:* Lot is Abram's nephew (11:31). It is not clear who the Perizzites were. They may have been country dwellers as opposed to city dwellers.

13:10-12 *plain of the Jordan . . . Zoar . . . Sodom and Gomorrah:* The plain of the Jordan stretched from the Sea of Galilee in the north to Zoar, which was at the southern end of the present Dead Sea (see the map on p. 2464). The location of Sodom and Gomorrah is not certain, but they may have been in the Valley of Siddim (14:1-4), the area that is now covered by the southern part of the Dead Sea. The plain of the Jordan was like the Nile River Valley in Egypt with plenty of water for growing crops and rich vegetation for feeding flocks. Settling near Sodom was risky, since the people there were thought to be evil (13:13; 19:1-29).

13:18 *great trees of Mamre at Hebron:* See the note at 12:6. Mamre, a town named after one of Abram's Amorite friends (14:13), was near Hebron, located about twenty miles south of Jerusalem. It is where Sarah would later die (23:1). See the map on p. 2462.

14:1-4 *Amraphel king of Shinar . . . Salt Sea:* The kings named in 14:1 were from the lands to the east of Canaan. See the note at 10:6-20. The kings named in 14:2 were leaders of cities in southern Canaan (see the note at 13:10-12). They battled in the Valley of Siddim, an area that is now likely covered by the southern part of the Dead Sea, also known as the Salt Sea because it is ten times saltier than ocean water. It is located 1,300 feet below sea level (see the map on p. 2462).

12:7 Acts 7:5; Gal 3:16. **12:13** Gen 20:2; 26:7. **13:15** Gen 12:1; 17:7, 8; Acts 7:5.

14:5-7 *Ashteroth Karnaim ... Hazazon Tamar:* The places and the peoples who were attacked by the eastern king, Kedorlaomer, lived in the lands east and southwest of the Jordan River and Dead Sea. Seir (also called Edom) was south of the Dead Sea. Kadesh was located in the Negev (see the note at 12:8,9) and was later known as Kadesh Barnea (Num 32:8). The constant warfare in the area where Lot had chosen to live threatened his family and flocks.

14:13 *Abram the Hebrew ... Mamre the Amorite:* Abram is the first person in the Bible to be called a "Hebrew" (see the note at 10:21-31). Ancient sources other than the Bible speak of a people known as *Habiru* or *Apiru,* which may be related to the name Hebrew. These people were described as poor immigrants or nomads who did not own land or property in a specific place. For Mamre, see the note at 13:18.

14:14-17 *Dan ... Valley of Shaveh (that is, the King's Valley):* Dan was located north of the Sea of Galilee, and Hobah was north of the city of Damascus (see the map on p. 2465). Abram and his men chased Kedorlaomer's army at least 150 miles to rescue Lot (14:16) before returning to the Shaveh Valley, or King's Valley, which was probably the valley east of Jerusalem (2 Sam 18:18).

14:18 *Melchizedek king of Salem ... priest of God Most High:* Melchizedek means "king of justice," and "Salem" means "peace" (see Heb 7:2). Salem is a shortened form of Jerusalem. In ancient countries, a king often performed the religious duties of a priest. "God Most High" was the name of the highest Canaanite god in Jerusalem. Abram identifies God Most High with "the LORD" (14:22; see also Num 24:16; Ps 46:4) and gives Melchizedek a tenth of the spoils from the battle. A tenth was considered a king's share (1 Sam 8:15,17). See also Ps 110:4.

5 In the fourteenth year, Kedorlaomer and the kings allied
with him went out and defeated the Rephaites in Ashteroth Karnaim, the Zuzites in Ham, the Emites in Shaveh Kiriathaim 6 and
the Horites in the hill country of Seir, as far as El Paran near the
desert. 7 Then they turned back and went to En Mishpat (that is,
Kadesh), and they conquered the whole territory of the Amalekites, as well as the Amorites who were living in Hazazon Tamar.
8 Then the king of Sodom, the king of Gomorrah, the king of
Admah, the king of Zeboiim and the king of Bela (that is, Zoar)
marched out and drew up their battle lines in the Valley of Siddim
9 against Kedorlaomer king of Elam, Tidal king of Goiim,
Amraphel king of Shinar and Arioch king of Ellasar—four kings
against five. 10 Now the Valley of Siddim was full of tar pits, and
when the kings of Sodom and Gomorrah fled, some of the men
fell into them and the rest fled to the hills. 11 The four kings seized
all the goods of Sodom and Gomorrah and all their food; then
they went away. 12 They also carried off Abram's nephew Lot and
his possessions, since he was living in Sodom.
13 One who had escaped came and reported this to Abram
the Hebrew. Now Abram was living near the great trees of Mamre
the Amorite, a brother[a] of Eshcol and Aner, all of whom were
allied with Abram. 14 When Abram heard that his relative had been
taken captive, he called out the 318 trained men born in his household and went in pursuit as far as Dan. 15 During the night Abram
divided his men to attack them and he routed them, pursuing
them as far as Hobah, north of Damascus. 16 He recovered all the
goods and brought back his relative Lot and his possessions,
together with the women and the other people.
17 After Abram returned from defeating Kedorlaomer and the
kings allied with him, the king of Sodom came out to meet him in
the Valley of Shaveh (that is, the King's Valley).
18 Then Melchizedek king of Salem[b] brought out bread and
wine. He was priest of God Most High, 19 and he blessed Abram,
saying,

"Blessed be Abram by God Most High,
    Creator[c] of heaven and earth.
20 And blessed be[d] God Most High,
    who delivered your enemies into your hand."

Then Abram gave him a tenth of everything.
21 The king of Sodom said to Abram, "Give me the people
and keep the goods for yourself."
22 But Abram said to the king of Sodom, "I have raised my
hand to the LORD, God Most High, Creator of heaven and earth,
and have taken an oath 23 that I will accept nothing belonging to

[a]**13** Or *a relative;* or *an ally* [b]**18** That is, Jerusalem [c]**19** Or *Possessor;* also in verse 22 [d]**20** Or *And praise be to*

you, not even a thread or the thong of a sandal, so that you will never be able to say, 'I made Abram rich.' 24 I will accept nothing but what my men have eaten and the share that belongs to the men who went with me—to Aner, Eshcol and Mamre. Let them have their share."

God's Covenant With Abram

15 After this, the word of the LORD came to Abram in a vision:

"Do not be afraid, Abram.
I am your shield,[a]
your very great reward.[b]"

2 But Abram said, "O Sovereign LORD, what can you give me since I remain childless and the one who will inherit[c] my estate is Eliezer of Damascus?" 3 And Abram said, "You have given me no children; so a servant in my household will be my heir."

4 Then the word of the LORD came to him: "This man will not be your heir, but a son coming from your own body will be your heir." 5 He took him outside and said, "Look up at the heavens and count the stars—if indeed you can count them." Then he said to him, "So shall your offspring be."

6 Abram believed the LORD, and he credited it to him as righteousness.

7 He also said to him, "I am the LORD, who brought you out of Ur of the Chaldeans to give you this land to take possession of it."

8 But Abram said, "O Sovereign LORD, how can I know that I will gain possession of it?"

9 So the LORD said to him, "Bring me a heifer, a goat and a ram, each three years old, along with a dove and a young pigeon."

10 Abram brought all these to him, cut them in two and arranged the halves opposite each other; the birds, however, he did not cut in half. 11 Then birds of prey came down on the carcasses, but Abram drove them away.

12 As the sun was setting, Abram fell into a deep sleep, and a thick and dreadful darkness came over him. 13 Then the LORD said to him, "Know for certain that your descendants will be strangers in a country not their own, and they will be enslaved and mistreated four hundred years. 14 But I will punish the nation they serve as slaves, and afterward they will come out with great possessions. 15 You, however, will go to your fathers in peace and be buried at a good old age. 16 In the fourth generation your descendants will come back here, for the sin of the Amorites has not yet reached its full measure."

[a]1 Or *sovereign* [b]1 Or *shield; / your reward will be very great* [c]2 The meaning of the Hebrew for this phrase is uncertain.

The LORD said, *"Look up at the heavens and count the stars—if indeed you can count them. . . . So shall your offspring be."*
Gen 15:5

15:2 *Eliezer of Damascus:* Abram probably recruited Eliezer to be one of his servants as he traveled south from Haran to Canaan (see the note at 12:4-6). Eliezer may be the "chief servant" named in 24:2. A law found in writings from ancient Babylonia said that a slave could be adopted if a couple had no children. In such a case, the servant would inherit his master's (father's) wealth and property.

15:7 *Ur of the Chaldeans:* See the note at 11:26-31.

15:8-10 *how can I know . . . cut them in two:* In Hebrew "cut" sounds something like "agreement." These verses describe an ancient ceremony showing a covenant (agreement) being made (see the note at 9:9). Animals were cut in two, and the persons making the agreement walked between these parts (Jer 34:17-19). See the mini-article called "Covenants (Agreements)," p. 386.

15:13-16 *Know for certain:* See the note at 9:9. God's promise to Abram included the news that his descendants would live as slaves in Egypt (see Exod 1:1-14; 12:40,41; Acts 7:6,7) for four hundred years. "The fourth generation" (15:16) may refer to the "four hundred years" (15:13-15).

14:18-20 Ps 110:4; Heb 7:1-10. **14:24** Gen 14:13. **15:5** Gen 12:2; 17:4-6; Rom 4:18; Heb 11:12. **15:6** Rom 4:3; Gal 3:6; Jas 2:23. **15:12** Job 4:13,14.

15:17 *smoking firepot with a blazing torch:* The smoke and fire represent the presence of the LORD (see also the note at 3:24).

15:18 *river of Egypt . . . great river, the Euphrates:* The river of Egypt (also called the Shihor) was a brook in the wilderness area between Egypt and Canaan, and the Euphrates River was in Mesopotamia (see the note at 2:10-14 and the map on p. 2462). Only during the reign of King David did the people of Israel control this much land (see the map on p. 2465). See also Deut 11:24; Josh 13:2-7; 2 Sam 8:3.

15:19-21 *Kenites . . . Jebusites:* See the note at 10:6-20 (sons of Ham).

16:3 *Sarai . . . Egyptian maidservant Hagar . . . to be his wife:* When ten years had passed (compare 15:4 and 16:3), and Sarai still was not pregnant, she told Abram to take her slave Hagar as a wife. Ancient Assyrian marriage laws dating to the time before Abram allowed a man to sleep with his wife's slave if his wife could not get pregnant and have children. The children of the slave would belong to the husband's wife. Abram was eighty-five years old when he slept with Hagar (see 12:4; 16:15,16).

16:7 *Shur:* The exact location of Shur is not known, but it was east of Egypt (25:17,18; 1 Sam 15:7).

16:7 *angel of the LORD:* See the note at 32:1.

16:10-12 *Ishmael . . . wild donkey:* In Hebrew the word for "Ishmael" sounds like the word for "God hears." God's promise to Hagar is repeated in 17:20 and fulfilled in 25:13-16. Ishmael's descendants would be nomads living free in the desert like wild donkeys (see Job 24:5; Hos 8:9).

[17]When the sun had set and darkness had fallen, a smoking
firepot with a blazing torch appeared and passed between the
pieces. [18]On that day the LORD made a covenant with Abram and
said, "To your descendants I give this land, from the river[a] of Egypt
to the great river, the Euphrates— [19]the land of the Kenites,
Kenizzites, Kadmonites, [20]Hittites, Perizzites, Rephaites, [21]Amo-
rites, Canaanites, Girgashites and Jebusites."

Hagar and Ishmael

16 Now Sarai, Abram's wife, had borne him no children. But she
had an Egyptian maidservant named Hagar; [2]so she said to Abram,
"The LORD has kept me from having children. Go, sleep with my
maidservant; perhaps I can build a family through her."
Abram agreed to what Sarai said. [3]So after Abram had been
living in Canaan ten years, Sarai his wife took her Egyptian maidservant Hagar and gave her to her husband to be his wife. [4]He slept
with Hagar, and she conceived.
When she knew she was pregnant, she began to despise her
mistress. [5]Then Sarai said to Abram, "You are responsible for the
wrong I am suffering. I put my servant in your arms, and now that
she knows she is pregnant, she despises me. May the LORD judge
between you and me."
[6]"Your servant is in your hands," Abram said. "Do with her
whatever you think best." Then Sarai mistreated Hagar; so she fled
from her.
[7]The angel of the LORD found Hagar near a spring in the
desert; it was the spring that is beside the road to Shur. [8]And he
said, "Hagar, servant of Sarai, where have you come from, and
where are you going?"
"I'm running away from my mistress Sarai," she answered.
[9]Then the angel of the LORD told her, "Go back to your mistress and submit to her." [10]The angel added, "I will so increase your
descendants that they will be too numerous to count."
[11]The angel of the LORD also said to her:

"You are now with child
and you will have a son.
You shall name him Ishmael,[b]
for the LORD has heard of your misery.
[12]He will be a wild donkey of a man;
his hand will be against everyone
and everyone's hand against him,
and he will live in hostility
toward[c] all his brothers."

[13]She gave this name to the LORD who spoke to her: "You are

---

[a]**18** Or *Wadi* [b]**11** *Ishmael* means *God hears.* [c]**12** Or *live to the east / of*

the God who sees me," for she said, "I have now seen[a] the One who
sees me." [14]That is why the well was called Beer Lahai Roi[b]; it is still
there, between Kadesh and Bered.
[15]So Hagar bore Abram a son, and Abram gave the name
Ishmael to the son she had borne. [16]Abram was eighty-six years old
when Hagar bore him Ishmael.

The Covenant of Circumcision

17 When Abram was ninety-nine years old, the LORD appeared
to him and said, "I am God Almighty[c]; walk before me and be
blameless. [2]I will confirm my covenant between me and you and
will greatly increase your numbers."
[3]Abram fell facedown, and God said to him, [4]"As for me, this
is my covenant with you: You will be the father of many nations.
[5]No longer will you be called Abram[d]; your name will be Abraham,[e] for I have made you a father of many nations. [6]I will make
you very fruitful; I will make nations of you, and kings will come
from you. [7]I will establish my covenant as an everlasting covenant
between me and you and your descendants after you for the generations to come, to be your God and the God of your descendants
after you. [8]The whole land of Canaan, where you are now an alien,
I will give as an everlasting possession to you and your descendants after you; and I will be their God."
[9]Then God said to Abraham, "As for you, you must keep my
covenant, you and your descendants after you for the generations to
come. [10]This is my covenant with you and your descendants after
you, the covenant you are to keep: Every male among you shall be
circumcised. [11]You are to undergo circumcision, and it will be the
sign of the covenant between me and you. [12]For the generations to
come every male among you who is eight days old must be circumcised, including those born in your household or bought with money
from a foreigner—those who are not your offspring. [13]Whether born
in your household or bought with your money, they must be circumcised. My covenant in your flesh is to be an everlasting covenant.
[14]Any uncircumcised male, who has not been circumcised in the
flesh, will be cut off from his people; he has broken my covenant."
[15]God also said to Abraham, "As for Sarai your wife, you are
no longer to call her Sarai; her name will be Sarah. [16]I will bless her
and will surely give you a son by her. I will bless her so that she will
be the mother of nations; kings of peoples will come from her."
[17]Abraham fell facedown; he laughed and said to himself,
"Will a son be born to a man a hundred years old? Will Sarah bear
a child at the age of ninety?" [18]And Abraham said to God, "If only
Ishmael might live under your blessing!"

[a]13 Or *seen the back of* [b]14 *Beer Lahai Roi* means *well of the Living One who sees me.* [c]1 Hebrew *El-Shaddai* [d]5 *Abram* means *exalted father.*
[e]5 *Abraham* means *father of many.*

16:14 *Kadesh and Bered:* Probably located in the southwest part of the area called the Negev (see the map on p. 2464).

17:1 *God Almighty:* See the note at 43:14.

17:2 *covenant:* See the note at 9:9. Earlier promises of God to Abram (12:2,3; 13:14-16; 15:4,5) did not include any requirements, except that Abram go to Canaan. In this covenant (17:1-22), God tells Abraham to practice circumcision as a way to keep his part of the covenant (17:9-14). See the mini-article called "Covenants (Agreements)," p. 386.

17:4,5 *Abraham:* See the note at 12:1-3. The name "Abraham" is a form of Abram that is similar to the word meaning "father of many."

17:10,11 *circumcision:* "Circumcision" was the ceremony of cutting off the foreskin of a male's penis. This was a common rite among many people in the ancient Near East, though the reasons why are not clear. God commanded circumcision as a physical sign that Abraham's descendants were God's chosen people (17:12-14). Circumcision was a requirement in the Law of Moses (Gen 34:21-23; Lev 12:3). See also the mini-article called "Circumcision," p. 2251.

17:15 *Sarah:* Both "Sarai" and "Sarah" mean "princess." This name emphasizes that Sarah would be the mother of Israel's rulers (17:16).

17:18 *Ishmael:* The son of Abram and Hagar (see the note at 16:10-12).

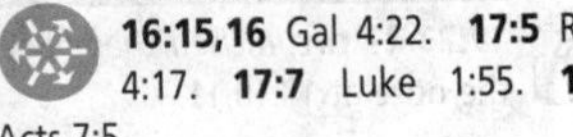

16:15,16 Gal 4:22. **17:5** Rom 4:17. **17:7** Luke 1:55. **17:8** Acts 7:5.

Abraham and the Three Angels, scene from a copper and enamel altar by Nicholas of Verdun (died around 1216). Abraham quickly offered hospitality to the three visitors who appeared before his tent near the great trees of Mamre. One of the visitors was the LORD, who told Abraham that, although both Abraham and his wife Sarah were very old, they would have a son within a year. (See 18:1-15.)

17:19 *Isaac:* In Hebrew the word "Isaac" sounds like the word for "laugh." See 17:17; 18:12-15; 21:6.

17:20 *father of twelve rulers:* See 25:13-16, which describes the fulfillment of this promise about Ishmael.

17:23-27 *circumcised them:* See the note at 17:10,11.

19 Then God said, "Yes, but your wife Sarah will bear you a
son, and you will call him Isaac.[a] I will establish my covenant with
him as an everlasting covenant for his descendants after him.
20 And as for Ishmael, I have heard you: I will surely bless him; I
will make him fruitful and will greatly increase his numbers. He
will be the father of twelve rulers, and I will make him into a great
nation. 21 But my covenant I will establish with Isaac, whom Sarah
will bear to you by this time next year." 22 When he had finished
speaking with Abraham, God went up from him.
23 On that very day Abraham took his son Ishmael and all
those born in his household or bought with his money, every male
in his household, and circumcised them, as God told him. 24 Abra-

[a]19 *Isaac* means *he laughs.*

ham was ninety-nine years old when he was circumcised, [25]and his
son Ishmael was thirteen; [26]Abraham and his son Ishmael were
both circumcised on that same day. [27]And every male in Abraham's
household, including those born in his household or bought from
a foreigner, was circumcised with him.

The Three Visitors

18 The LORD appeared to Abraham near the great trees of
Mamre while he was sitting at the entrance to his tent in the heat
of the day. [2]Abraham looked up and saw three men standing nearby. When he saw them, he hurried from the entrance of his tent to
meet them and bowed low to the ground.

[3]He said, "If I have found favor in your eyes, my lord,[a] do not
pass your servant by. [4]Let a little water be brought, and then you
may all wash your feet and rest under this tree. [5]Let me get you
something to eat, so you can be refreshed and then go on your
way—now that you have come to your servant."

"Very well," they answered, "do as you say."

[6]So Abraham hurried into the tent to Sarah. "Quick," he said,
"get three seahs[b] of fine flour and knead it and bake some bread."

[7]Then he ran to the herd and selected a choice, tender calf
and gave it to a servant, who hurried to prepare it. [8]He then
brought some curds and milk and the calf that had been prepared,
and set these before them. While they ate, he stood near them
under a tree.

[9]"Where is your wife Sarah?" they asked him.

"There, in the tent," he said.

[10]Then the LORD[c] said, "I will surely return to you about this
time next year, and Sarah your wife will have a son."

Now Sarah was listening at the entrance to the tent, which
was behind him. [11]Abraham and Sarah were already old and well
advanced in years, and Sarah was past the age of childbearing. [12]So
Sarah laughed to herself as she thought, "After I am worn out and
my master[d] is old, will I now have this pleasure?"

[13]Then the LORD said to Abraham, "Why did Sarah laugh
and say, 'Will I really have a child, now that I am old?' [14]Is anything
too hard for the LORD? I will return to you at the appointed time
next year and Sarah will have a son."

[15]Sarah was afraid, so she lied and said, "I did not laugh."

But he said, "Yes, you did laugh."

Abraham Pleads for Sodom

[16]When the men got up to leave, they looked down toward
Sodom, and Abraham walked along with them to see them on

[a]3 Or *O Lord* [b]6 That is, probably about 20 quarts (about 22 liters)
[c]10 Hebrew *Then he* [d]12 Or *husband*

18:1 *great trees of Mamre:* See the note at 13:18.

18:2-8 *three men . . . While they ate:* See the note at 18:16.

18:12 *have this pleasure:* This may refer to either the joy of making love or to the joy of having children.

18:16 *men:* It appears that these "men" were two angels and the LORD. See the note at 32:1 and the mini-article called "Angels," p. 88. Abraham greeted them with respect and invited them to his home. He prepared a meal, brought water for them to wash their feet (18:4), and stood nearby like a servant (18:8) as they ate. These are common examples of hospitality in the ancient Near East. See also the note at 24:31-33.

18:10 Rom 9:9. **18:14** Luke 1:37.

18:20 *Sodom and Gomorrah:* See the note at 13:10-12. The evil referred to in this verse appears to be some kind of sexual sin (see 19:4, 5).

18:23 *the righteous:* The word "righteous" refers to being right with God, or living according to God's Law. The ancient Israelites believed that the evil done by one or a few can spoil a whole community (Deut 21:1-9). Here Abraham argues the opposite: that a few good people could help save a whole community that was mostly evil.

18:33 *returned home:* To Mamre (see 18:1).

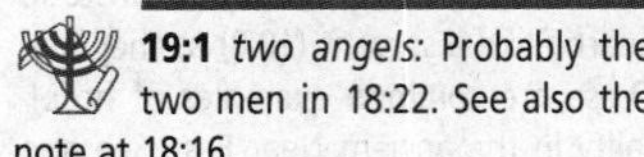

19:1 *two angels:* Probably the two men in 18:22. See also the note at 18:16.

19:1 *in the gateway of the city:* People would gather near the city gate to conduct community business and meet friends (see Ruth 4:1-12, for example).

18:18,19 Gen 12:1-3; 15:5; 17:1-10.

their way. [17]Then the LORD said, "Shall I hide from Abraham what
I am about to do? [18]Abraham will surely become a great and powerful nation, and all nations on earth will be blessed through him.
[19]For I have chosen him, so that he will direct his children and his
household after him to keep the way of the LORD by doing what is
right and just, so that the LORD will bring about for Abraham what
he has promised him."

[20]Then the LORD said, "The outcry against Sodom and
Gomorrah is so great and their sin so grievous [21]that I will go
down and see if what they have done is as bad as the outcry that
has reached me. If not, I will know."

[22]The men turned away and went toward Sodom, but Abraham remained standing before the LORD.[a] [23]Then Abraham
approached him and said: "Will you sweep away the righteous
with the wicked? [24]What if there are fifty righteous people in the
city? Will you really sweep it away and not spare[b] the place for the
sake of the fifty righteous people in it? [25]Far be it from you to do
such a thing—to kill the righteous with the wicked, treating the
righteous and the wicked alike. Far be it from you! Will not the
Judge[c] of all the earth do right?"

[26]The LORD said, "If I find fifty righteous people in the city of
Sodom, I will spare the whole place for their sake."

[27]Then Abraham spoke up again: "Now that I have been so
bold as to speak to the Lord, though I am nothing but dust and
ashes, [28]what if the number of the righteous is five less than fifty?
Will you destroy the whole city because of five people?"

"If I find forty-five there," he said, "I will not destroy it."

[29]Once again he spoke to him, "What if only forty are found
there?"

He said, "For the sake of forty, I will not do it."

[30]Then he said, "May the Lord not be angry, but let me
speak. What if only thirty can be found there?"

He answered, "I will not do it if I find thirty there."

[31]Abraham said, "Now that I have been so bold as to speak to
the Lord, what if only twenty can be found there?"

He said, "For the sake of twenty, I will not destroy it."

[32]Then he said, "May the Lord not be angry, but let me speak
just once more. What if only ten can be found there?"

He answered, "For the sake of ten, I will not destroy it."

[33]When the LORD had finished speaking with Abraham, he
left, and Abraham returned home.

Sodom and Gomorrah Destroyed

19 The two angels arrived at Sodom in the evening, and Lot was
sitting in the gateway of the city. When he saw them, he got up to

[a]**22** Masoretic Text; an ancient Hebrew scribal tradition *but the LORD remained standing before Abraham* [b]**24** Or *forgive*; also in verse 26 [c]**25** Or *Ruler*

meet them and bowed down with his face to the ground. 2 “My
lords,” he said, “please turn aside to your servant’s house. You can
wash your feet and spend the night and then go on your way early
in the morning.”

“No,” they answered, “we will spend the night in the square.”

3 But he insisted so strongly that they did go with him and
entered his house. He prepared a meal for them, baking bread
without yeast, and they ate. 4 Before they had gone to bed, all the
men from every part of the city of Sodom—both young and old—
surrounded the house. 5 They called to Lot, “Where are the men
who came to you tonight? Bring them out to us so that we can
have sex with them.”

6 Lot went outside to meet them and shut the door behind
him 7 and said, “No, my friends. Don’t do this wicked thing. 8 Look,
I have two daughters who have never slept with a man. Let me
bring them out to you, and you can do what you like with them.
But don’t do anything to these men, for they have come under the
protection of my roof.”

9 “Get out of our way,” they replied. And they said, “This fel-
low came here as an alien, and now he wants to play the judge!
We’ll treat you worse than them.” They kept bringing pressure on
Lot and moved forward to break down the door.

10 But the men inside reached out and pulled Lot back into
the house and shut the door. 11 Then they struck the men who were
at the door of the house, young and old, with blindness so that
they could not find the door.

12 The two men said to Lot, “Do you have anyone else here—
sons-in-law, sons or daughters, or anyone else in the city who
belongs to you? Get them out of here, 13 because we are going to
destroy this place. The outcry to the LORD against its people is so
great that he has sent us to destroy it.”

14 So Lot went out and spoke to his sons-in-law, who were
pledged to marry[a] his daughters. He said, “Hurry and get out of
this place, because the LORD is about to destroy the city!” But his
sons-in-law thought he was joking.

15 With the coming of dawn, the angels urged Lot, saying,
“Hurry! Take your wife and your two daughters who are here, or
you will be swept away when the city is punished.”

16 When he hesitated, the men grasped his hand and the
hands of his wife and of his two daughters and led them safely out
of the city, for the LORD was merciful to them. 17 As soon as they
had brought them out, one of them said, “Flee for your lives! Don’t
look back, and don’t stop anywhere in the plain! Flee to the mountains or you will be swept away!”

18 But Lot said to them, “No, my lords,[b] please! 19 Your[c] servant

[a] 14 Or *were married to* [b] 18 Or *No, Lord*; or *No, my lord* [c] 19 The Hebrew is singular.

The men grasped his hand and the hands of his wife and of his two daughters and led them safely out of the city, for the LORD was merciful to them.
Gen 19:16

19:3 *bread without yeast:* This kind of flat bread could be fixed quickly when guests came without warning. Bread with yeast has to rise for a period of time before it can be baked. Compare Lot’s hospitality to that of Abraham (see the note at 18:16).

19:8 *I have two daughters . . . don’t do anything to these men, for they have . . . protection:* According to the ancient customs of hospitality (see the note at 24:31-33), Lot was expected to make his two guests as comfortable and safe as possible. But by offering the men of Sodom his own daughters so that his guests would be protected, Lot actually put them, his daughters, and himself in greater danger. As it turned out, it was his guests (the angels) who ended up protecting Lot.

19:9 *an alien:* Lot had moved to the area around Sodom after parting with Abraham (13:8-13), making him an outsider (alien). Compare the hostility of the people of Sodom toward Lot with the Egyptian’s reaction to Moses (Exod 2:14; Acts 7:27).

19:17-23 *Flee to the mountains . . . Zoar:* This probably refers to the hills of Moab to the east (19:30,37). But first Lot and his family went to the small town of Zoar, a few miles south of the Dead Sea. In Hebrew “Zoar” sounds like the word for “small.” See the map on p. 2462.

19:5-8 Judg 19:22-30. **19:11** 2 Kgs 6:18. **19:16** 2 Pet 2:7.

has found favor in your[c] eyes, and you[c] have shown great kindness to me in sparing my life. But I can't flee to the mountains; this disaster will overtake me, and I'll die. 20 Look, here is a town near enough to run to, and it is small. Let me flee to it—it is very small, isn't it? Then my life will be spared."

21 He said to him, "Very well, I will grant this request too; I will not overthrow the town you speak of. 22 But flee there quickly, because I cannot do anything until you reach it." (That is why the town was called Zoar.[a])

23 By the time Lot reached Zoar, the sun had risen over the land. 24 Then the LORD rained down burning sulfur on Sodom and Gomorrah—from the LORD out of the heavens. 25 Thus he overthrew those cities and the entire plain, including all those living in the cities—and also the vegetation in the land. 26 But Lot's wife looked back, and she became a pillar of salt.

27 Early the next morning Abraham got up and returned to the place where he had stood before the LORD. 28 He looked down toward Sodom and Gomorrah, toward all the land of the plain, and he saw dense smoke rising from the land, like smoke from a furnace.

29 So when God destroyed the cities of the plain, he remembered Abraham, and he brought Lot out of the catastrophe that overthrew the cities where Lot had lived.

Lot and His Daughters

30 Lot and his two daughters left Zoar and settled in the mountains, for he was afraid to stay in Zoar. He and his two daughters lived in a cave. 31 One day the older daughter said to the younger, "Our father is old, and there is no man around here to lie with us, as is the custom all over the earth. 32 Let's get our father to drink wine and then lie with him and preserve our family line through our father."

33 That night they got their father to drink wine, and the older daughter went in and lay with him. He was not aware of it when she lay down or when she got up.

34 The next day the older daughter said to the younger, "Last night I lay with my father. Let's get him to drink wine again tonight, and you go in and lie with him so we can preserve our family line through our father." 35 So they got their father to drink wine that night also, and the younger daughter went and lay with him. Again he was not aware of it when she lay down or when she got up.

36 So both of Lot's daughters became pregnant by their father. 37 The older daughter had a son, and she named him Moab[b]; he is the father of the Moabites of today. 38 The younger daughter also had a son, and she named him Ben-Ammi[c]; he is the father of the Ammonites of today.

[a]22 *Zoar* means *small.* [b]37 *Moab* sounds like the Hebrew for *from father.*
[c]38 *Ben-Ammi* means *son of my people.*

19:26 *Lot's wife ... pillar of salt:* Salt formations can be seen near the southern end of the Dead Sea. The one shown here is known locally as "Lot's Wife."

19:30 *Zoar ... mountains:* See the note at 19:17-23.

19:30-38 *his two daughters ... father of the Moabites ... father of the Ammonites:* By telling how Lot's daughters deceived him into being the father of their children, these verses explain the shameful origin of two of Israel's closest neighbors (and later, their enemies). The daughters perhaps felt they had no other chance of having children.

19:37,38 *Moab ... Moabites ... Ben-Ammi ... Ammonites:* In Hebrew "Moab" sounds like the word for "from (my) father." Moab was located to the east of the Dead Sea. In Hebrew "Ben-Ammi" means "son of my people." Ammon was a land east of the Jordan River valley. The Moabites and Ammonites would later become enemies of Abraham's descendants, Israel (Judg 10:11-18; 1 Sam 14:47,48; 2 Kgs 3:21-27; 2 Chr 20:10,11). See also the map on p. 2464.

19:24,25 Matt 10:15; 11:23,24; Luke 10:12; 17:29; 2 Pet 2:6; Jude 7. **19:26** Luke 17:32.

Abraham and Abimelech

20 Now Abraham moved on from there into the region of the
Negev and lived between Kadesh and Shur. For a while he stayed
in Gerar, 2and there Abraham said of his wife Sarah, "She is
my sister." Then Abimelech king of Gerar sent for Sarah and
took her.

3But God came to Abimelech in a dream one night and said
to him, "You are as good as dead because of the woman you have
taken; she is a married woman."

4Now Abimelech had not gone near her, so he said, "Lord,
will you destroy an innocent nation? 5Did he not say to me, 'She is
my sister,' and didn't she also say, 'He is my brother'? I have done
this with a clear conscience and clean hands."

6Then God said to him in the dream, "Yes, I know you did
this with a clear conscience, and so I have kept you from sinning
against me. That is why I did not let you touch her. 7Now return
the man's wife, for he is a prophet, and he will pray for you and
you will live. But if you do not return her, you may be sure that
you and all yours will die."

8Early the next morning Abimelech summoned all his
officials, and when he told them all that had happened, they
were very much afraid. 9Then Abimelech called Abraham in
and said, "What have you done to us? How have I wronged you
that you have brought such great guilt upon me and my kingdom? You have done things to me that should not be done."
10And Abimelech asked Abraham, "What was your reason for
doing this?"

11Abraham replied, "I said to myself, 'There is surely no fear
of God in this place, and they will kill me because of my wife.'
12Besides, she really is my sister, the daughter of my father though
not of my mother; and she became my wife. 13And when God had
me wander from my father's household, I said to her, 'This is how
you can show your love to me: Everywhere we go, say of me, "He
is my brother." ' "

14Then Abimelech brought sheep and cattle and male and
female slaves and gave them to Abraham, and he returned Sarah
his wife to him. 15And Abimelech said, "My land is before you; live
wherever you like."

16To Sarah he said, "I am giving your brother a thousand
shekels[a] of silver. This is to cover the offense against you before all
who are with you; you are completely vindicated."

17Then Abraham prayed to God, and God healed Abimelech,
his wife and his slave girls so they could have children again, 18for
the LORD had closed up every womb in Abimelech's household
because of Abraham's wife Sarah.

20:1 *Negev . . . Gerar:* See the notes at 12:8,9 and 14:5-7. Gerar was located at the southern end of Philistine territory, about halfway between Gaza on the Mediterranean coast and Beersheba to the southeast. See the map on p. 2464.

20:4,5 *Abimelech:* Possibly the father or grandfather of the later king with the same name (26:1). In Hebrew the name means "my father is king."

20:7 *he is a prophet:* This refers to Abraham, whose role as a prophet was to pray to God (18:22-33) and to make sure his family obeyed God by following the rite of circumcision (17:7-14). Abraham was the first man to be called a prophet in the Bible. See also the article called "Prophets and Prophecy," p. 935.

20:12 *my sister:* Sarah was actually a half-sister. Marriage with a half-sister apparently was not unusual in ancient times (2 Sam 13:13). However, the Law of Moses would later forbid it (Lev 18:9,11; 20:17).

20:16 *shekels of silver:* These were not coins, but pieces of silver that likely weighed about a shekel each. The shekel was the common unit of weight in the ancient Near East.

20:1-18 Gen 12:10-20; 26:1-11.

[a]**16** That is, about 25 pounds (about 11.5 kilograms)

21:3,4 *Isaac . . . circumcised:* See the notes at 17:19 and 17:10,11. See also Gen 17:12,17; Acts 7:8.

21:6 *God has brought me laughter:* See the note at 17:19.

21:8 *Isaac was weaned:* In Sarah's day, mothers nursed their children until the children were about three years old. When the time of nursing was done and the child was weaned, the family had a celebration, perhaps as a sign of joy and thanksgiving that the child had survived these early years of life.

21:9,10 *that slave woman's son will never share in the inheritance with my son Isaac:* See the note at 16:10-12. See also Gen 16:1-6; Gal 4:21-31. When Abraham accepted Ishmael as his son, it gave Ishmael the right to inherit part of what Abraham owned. But slaves who were given their freedom lost the right to inherit such property. Sarah wanted her son Isaac to inherit everything that Abraham owned.

21:14 *Beersheba:* This town was located in southern Canaan (see the map on p. 2464). See also the note at 21:31.

21:20,21 *God was with the boy:* Compare to 16:6-12. Even though Sarah did not want Ishmael to inherit anything, God did bless Ishmael and promised to make his descendants a great nation (25:12-18).

21:20,21 *Desert of Paran:* This desert was located on the Sinai Peninsula between Canaan and Egypt. See the map on p. 2463.

21:1 Gen 17:16; Gal 4:22, 23, 28. **21:2** Heb 11:11. **21:12** Rom 9:7; Heb 11:18.

The Birth of Isaac

21 Now the LORD was gracious to Sarah as he had said, and the
LORD did for Sarah what he had promised. 2Sarah became pregnant and bore a son to Abraham in his old age, at the very time
God had promised him. 3Abraham gave the name Isaac[a] to the son
Sarah bore him. 4When his son Isaac was eight days old, Abraham
circumcised him, as God commanded him. 5Abraham was a hundred years old when his son Isaac was born to him.
6Sarah said, "God has brought me laughter, and everyone
who hears about this will laugh with me." 7And she added, "Who
would have said to Abraham that Sarah would nurse children? Yet
I have borne him a son in his old age."

Hagar and Ishmael Sent Away

8The child grew and was weaned, and on the day Isaac was
weaned Abraham held a great feast. 9But Sarah saw that the son
whom Hagar the Egyptian had borne to Abraham was mocking,
10and she said to Abraham, "Get rid of that slave woman and her
son, for that slave woman's son will never share in the inheritance
with my son Isaac."
11The matter distressed Abraham greatly because it concerned his son. 12But God said to him, "Do not be so distressed
about the boy and your maidservant. Listen to whatever Sarah tells
you, because it is through Isaac that your offspring[b] will be reckoned. 13I will make the son of the maidservant into a nation also,
because he is your offspring."
14Early the next morning Abraham took some food and a
skin of water and gave them to Hagar. He set them on her shoulders and then sent her off with the boy. She went on her way and
wandered in the desert of Beersheba.
15When the water in the skin was gone, she put the boy
under one of the bushes. 16Then she went off and sat down nearby, about a bowshot away, for she thought, "I cannot watch the boy
die." And as she sat there nearby, she[c] began to sob.
17God heard the boy crying, and the angel of God called to
Hagar from heaven and said to her, "What is the matter, Hagar?
Do not be afraid; God has heard the boy crying as he lies there.
18Lift the boy up and take him by the hand, for I will make him
into a great nation."
19Then God opened her eyes and she saw a well of water.
So she went and filled the skin with water and gave the boy a
drink.
20God was with the boy as he grew up. He lived in the desert
and became an archer. 21While he was living in the Desert of
Paran, his mother got a wife for him from Egypt.

---

[a]**3** *Isaac* means *he laughs.* [b]**12** Or *seed* [c]**16** Hebrew; Septuagint *the child*

The Treaty at Beersheba

22 At that time Abimelech and Phicol the commander of his
forces said to Abraham, "God is with you in everything you do. 23 Now
swear to me here before God that you will not deal falsely with me or
my children or my descendants. Show to me and the country where
you are living as an alien the same kindness I have shown to you."
24 Abraham said, "I swear it."
25 Then Abraham complained to Abimelech about a well of
water that Abimelech's servants had seized. 26 But Abimelech said,
"I don't know who has done this. You did not tell me, and I heard
about it only today."
27 So Abraham brought sheep and cattle and gave them to
Abimelech, and the two men made a treaty. 28 Abraham set apart
seven ewe lambs from the flock, 29 and Abimelech asked Abraham,
"What is the meaning of these seven ewe lambs you have set apart
by themselves?"
30 He replied, "Accept these seven lambs from my hand as a
witness that I dug this well."
31 So that place was called Beersheba,[a] because the two men
swore an oath there.
32 After the treaty had been made at Beersheba, Abimelech
and Phicol the commander of his forces returned to the land of the
Philistines. 33 Abraham planted a tamarisk tree in Beersheba, and
there he called upon the name of the LORD, the Eternal God. 34 And
Abraham stayed in the land of the Philistines for a long time.

Abraham Tested

22 Some time later God tested Abraham. He said to him,
"Abraham!"
"Here I am," he replied.
2 Then God said, "Take your son, your only son, Isaac, whom
you love, and go to the region of Moriah. Sacrifice him there as a
burnt offering on one of the mountains I will tell you about."
3 Early the next morning Abraham got up and saddled his
donkey. He took with him two of his servants and his son Isaac.
When he had cut enough wood for the burnt offering, he set out
for the place God had told him about. 4 On the third day Abraham
looked up and saw the place in the distance. 5 He said to his servants, "Stay here with the donkey while I and the boy go over there.
We will worship and then we will come back to you."
6 Abraham took the wood for the burnt offering and placed
it on his son Isaac, and he himself carried the fire and the knife. As
the two of them went on together, 7 Isaac spoke up and said to his
father Abraham, "Father?"
"Yes, my son?" Abraham replied.

---

[a] **31** *Beersheba* can mean *well of seven* or *well of the oath.*

21:22 *Abimelech . . . Phicol:* See the note at 20:4,5. Phicol may have been either the commander's family name or his title. See also 26:26.

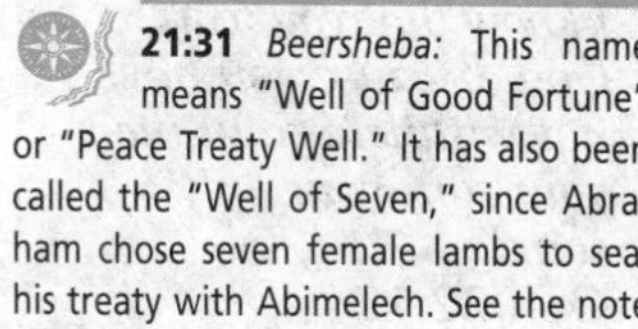

21:31 *Beersheba:* This name means "Well of Good Fortune" or "Peace Treaty Well." It has also been called the "Well of Seven," since Abraham chose seven female lambs to seal his treaty with Abimelech. See the note at 21:14.

21:32 *Philistines:* This group of people came from Caphtor (Jer 47:4; Amos 9:7), which may be Crete or the islands of the Aegean Sea. They were not part of the peoples that were related to Abraham's descendants. The land of the Philistines refers to the plains area along the Mediterranean Sea coast from Joppa to the area just south of Gaza. It had five main cities—Ashdod, Ashkelon, Ekron, Gath, and Gaza—whose rulers were often at war with Israel in the days of the judges and later during the time of Israel's kings. See the map on p. 2464.

21:33 *tamarisk tree:* This tall shade tree has deep roots and needs little water.

The LORD's angel said to Abraham, *"Do not lay a hand on the boy . . . Now I know that you fear God, because you have not withheld from me your son, your only son."*
Gen 22:12

22:7,8 *lamb for the burnt offering:* In ancient times, offering burned sacrifices was a way to worship God, and to maintain, restore, or celebrate the relationship between the giver and God. In this story, Abraham is prepared to offer his son, the child of God's promise. The death of Isaac would be a direct threat to the covenant God had made with Abraham and Sarah (15:5). Sacrifices were offered by the head of each family in the period before the Law of Moses, which commanded sacrifices to be done by Israel's priests (see especially Lev 2–6). See also the chart called "Sacrifices and Offerings," p. 219.

22:11 *angel of the LORD:* See the note at 32:1.

22:13 *a ram caught by its horns:* Rams are male sheep. Besides eating the meat they provided, people in Palestine used the skins of rams for making tents and the curved horns of rams for making trumpets (called "shofars") and containers for holding oil. Their long broad tails contained fat which was burned as an offering to the LORD (see Lev 3:9; 7:3; 8:25).

22:19 *Beersheba:* See the note at 21:14.

22:9 Jas 2:21.

Dome of the Rock, Jerusalem. Tradition holds that this is the rock on which Abraham was ordered to sacrifice Isaac. Because of Abraham's willingness to give up his only son, God blessed him. (See 22:1-19.) This rock continued to have religious importance through the ages. Solomon built a temple to the LORD here in the tenth century B.C. Today it is the site of a Muslim mosque, in a city that is home to three of the world's great religions.

"The fire and wood are here," Isaac said, "but where is the lamb for the burnt offering?"
[8]Abraham answered, "God himself will provide the lamb for the burnt offering, my son." And the two of them went on together.
[9]When they reached the place God had told him about, Abraham built an altar there and arranged the wood on it. He bound his son Isaac and laid him on the altar, on top of the wood.
[10]Then he reached out his hand and took the knife to slay his son.
[11]But the angel of the LORD called out to him from heaven, "Abraham! Abraham!"

"Here I am," he replied.

[12]"Do not lay a hand on the boy," he said. "Do not do anything to him. Now I know that you fear God, because you have not withheld from me your son, your only son."

[13]Abraham looked up and there in a thicket he saw a ram[a]

---

[a]**13** Many manuscripts of the Masoretic Text, Samaritan Pentateuch, Septuagint and Syriac; most manuscripts of the Masoretic Text *a ram behind* ⌊*him*⌋

caught by its horns. He went over and took the ram and sacrificed it as a burnt offering instead of his son. [14]So Abraham called that place The LORD Will Provide. And to this day it is said, "On the mountain of the LORD it will be provided."

[15]The angel of the LORD called to Abraham from heaven a second time [16]and said, "I swear by myself, declares the LORD, that because you have done this and have not withheld your son, your only son, [17]I will surely bless you and make your descendants as numerous as the stars in the sky and as the sand on the seashore. Your descendants will take possession of the cities of their enemies, [18]and through your offspring[a] all nations on earth will be blessed, because you have obeyed me."

[19]Then Abraham returned to his servants, and they set off together for Beersheba. And Abraham stayed in Beersheba.

Nahor's Sons

[20]Some time later Abraham was told, "Milcah is also a mother; she has borne sons to your brother Nahor: [21]Uz the firstborn, Buz his brother, Kemuel (the father of Aram), [22]Kesed, Hazo, Pildash, Jidlaph and Bethuel." [23]Bethuel became the father of Rebekah. Milcah bore these eight sons to Abraham's brother Nahor. [24]His concubine, whose name was Reumah, also had sons: Tebah, Gaham, Tahash and Maacah.

The Death of Sarah

23 Sarah lived to be a hundred and twenty-seven years old. [2]She died at Kiriath Arba (that is, Hebron) in the land of Canaan, and Abraham went to mourn for Sarah and to weep over her.

[3]Then Abraham rose from beside his dead wife and spoke to the Hittites.[b] He said, [4]"I am an alien and a stranger among you.

[a]18 Or *seed* [b]3 Or *the sons of Heth*; also in verses 5, 7, 10, 16, 18 and 20

22:20-24 *Nahor . . . Maacah:* Nahor (11:22-28) had twelve sons by two different wives. These sons became the ancestors of twelve Aramean tribes, just as Abraham's grandson Jacob would become the ancestor of the twelve tribes of Israel (49:28). Some of the sons' names correspond to place names in the area east of modern Lebanon and Jordan bordering the Arabian Desert.

The list introduces Bethuel, whose daughter Rebekah later marries Isaac (chapter 24). Reumah is called a concubine, which is a woman who was legally bound to a man, but without the full privileges of a wife.

23:1,2 *Kiriath Arba (that is, Hebron):* Kiriath Arba means "town of Arba" and was the older name of Hebron. See also Josh 14:15; 15:13; Judg 1:10.

23:3 *Hittites:* A powerful people who were descendants of Heth, grandson of Ham (10:6-20). They established an empire in Asia Minor and were a dominant force in Canaan from the time of Abraham to the twelfth century B.C. Isaac's son Esau married Hittite wives (26:34; 36:2). Israelites later looked down upon marriage to Hittites (1 Kgs 11:1,2; Ezra 9:1; but see 2 Sam 11,12).

22:16-18 Gen 12:1-3; 15:5; 17:1-11; Heb 6:13,14; 11:12. **23:4** Heb 11:9,13; Acts 7:16.

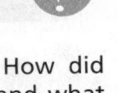

QUESTIONS ABOUT GENESIS 12:1—23:20

1. What are the three main promises God made to Abraham and his descendants? (12:1-3; 15:5-7; 17:1-8) What were Abraham and his descendants expected to do in order to hold up their part of the agreement with God? (17:9-14)
2. Who were Ishmael and Isaac? (16:1-16; 21:1-21) Why do you think Isaac was given a name similar to the word for laughter? (18:10-15; 21:1-7) Why is Isaac sometimes called "the child of the promise"?
3. How did God test Abraham? How did Abraham hold up to the test, and what happened as a result of Abraham's actions? (22:1-19) What might it be like to face such a test?
4. Why do you think the writer chose to focus on the story of Abraham right after finishing the accounts of the creation and the destruction of the flood?
5. See Romans 4:1-25; Hebrews 11:8-19; James 2:20-24. How do these New Testament writers interpret Abraham's actions?

23:9 *cave of Machpelah:* The cave provided a safe place to bury Sarah and was used later as a burial place for Abraham and some of his descendants (25:7-10; 49:29-31; 50:12, 13). According to tradition this cave is located beneath the Muslim Mosque of Abraham in Hebron. Abraham probably offered to pay full price for the cave in order to get legal title to the land (see 23:13). The important point is that Abraham now owned a piece of land in Canaan, the land God promised to give Abraham and his descendants.

23:10 *the gate of his city:* See the note at 19:1 (in the gateway of the city). It was important that Abraham's deal with Ephron was witnessed by others (23:11-13).

23:14,15 *four hundred shekels of silver:* See the note at 20:16. Though Ephron seems to make it sound like a small amount, it was actually an expensive price for the field.

24:2 *chief servant:* See the note at 15:2.

Sell me some property for a burial site here so I can bury my dead."
5 The Hittites replied to Abraham, 6 "Sir, listen to us. You are a
mighty prince among us. Bury your dead in the choicest of our
tombs. None of us will refuse you his tomb for burying your dead."
7 Then Abraham rose and bowed down before the people of
the land, the Hittites. 8 He said to them, "If you are willing to let
me bury my dead, then listen to me and intercede with Ephron
son of Zohar on my behalf 9 so he will sell me the cave of Machpelah, which belongs to him and is at the end of his field. Ask him
to sell it to me for the full price as a burial site among you."
10 Ephron the Hittite was sitting among his people and he
replied to Abraham in the hearing of all the Hittites who had come
to the gate of his city. 11 "No, my lord," he said. "Listen to me; I give[a]
you the field, and I give[a] you the cave that is in it. I give[a] it to you
in the presence of my people. Bury your dead."
12 Again Abraham bowed down before the people of the land
13 and he said to Ephron in their hearing, "Listen to me, if you will.
I will pay the price of the field. Accept it from me so I can bury my
dead there."
14 Ephron answered Abraham, 15 "Listen to me, my lord; the
land is worth four hundred shekels[b] of silver, but what is that
between me and you? Bury your dead."
16 Abraham agreed to Ephron's terms and weighed out for
him the price he had named in the hearing of the Hittites: four
hundred shekels of silver, according to the weight current among
the merchants.
17 So Ephron's field in Machpelah near Mamre—both the
field and the cave in it, and all the trees within the borders of the
field—was deeded 18 to Abraham as his property in the presence of
all the Hittites who had come to the gate of the city. 19 Afterward
Abraham buried his wife Sarah in the cave in the field of Machpelah near Mamre (which is at Hebron) in the land of Canaan.
20 So the field and the cave in it were deeded to Abraham by the
Hittites as a burial site.

ISAAC AND HIS FAMILY

Isaac marries Rebekah, daughter of his uncle Bethuel. She has twin sons, Esau and Jacob. Jacob tricks Esau out of his rights as the firstborn son and, with his mother's help, gets Isaac to give Jacob a special blessing. Jacob runs away from his angry brother.

Isaac and Rebekah

24 Abraham was now old and well advanced in years, and the
LORD had blessed him in every way. 2 He said to the chief[c] servant

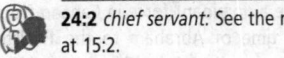

[a]11 Or *sell* [b]15 That is, about 10 pounds (about 4.5 kilograms) [c]2 Or *oldest*

in his household, the one in charge of all that he had, "Put your
hand under my thigh. [3]I want you to swear by the LORD, the God
of heaven and the God of earth, that you will not get a wife for my
son from the daughters of the Canaanites, among whom I am living, [4]but will go to my country and my own relatives and get a wife
for my son Isaac."
[5]The servant asked him, "What if the woman is unwilling to
come back with me to this land? Shall I then take your son back to
the country you came from?"
[6]"Make sure that you do not take my son back there," Abraham said. [7]"The LORD, the God of heaven, who brought me out of
my father's household and my native land and who spoke to me
and promised me on oath, saying, 'To your offspring[a] I will give
this land'—he will send his angel before you so that you can get a
wife for my son from there. [8]If the woman is unwilling to come
back with you, then you will be released from this oath of mine.
Only do not take my son back there." [9]So the servant put his hand
under the thigh of his master Abraham and swore an oath to him
concerning this matter.
[10]Then the servant took ten of his master's camels and left,
taking with him all kinds of good things from his master. He set
out for Aram Naharaim[b] and made his way to the town of Nahor.
[11]He had the camels kneel down near the well outside the town; it
was toward evening, the time the women go out to draw water.

[a]7 Or *seed* [b]10 That is, Northwest Mesopotamia

Rebekah and Eliezer by the Well, Ukrainian folk picture, nineteenth century. After Sarah died, Abraham sent a servant back to his homeland in northern Syria to find a suitable bride for their son Isaac. When the servant got to the city where Abraham's brother lived, he prayed and asked the LORD for help. When Rebekah, the beautiful daughter of Bethuel, offered to draw water from the well for Abraham's servant and camels, the servant knew she was the one God had chosen. (See 24:1-67.)

Abraham told his servant: *"Go to my country and my own relatives and get a wife for my son Isaac."* Gen 24:4

24:4 *my country and my own relatives:* Abraham was born in Mesopotamia (see the note at 11:26-31). He was living there when God told him to go to Canaan (11:31; 12:1). For a list of Abraham's relatives, Nahor's family, including Bethuel and his daughter Rebekah, see 22:20-23.

24:7 *his angel:* See the note at 32:1 and the mini-article called "Angels," p. 88.

24:10 *camels . . . good things:* Camels are stubborn animals, but they are very valuable as pack animals, because they can easily carry up to 350 pounds of goods long distances with little water and food (see also the article called "Trade and Travel," p. 948). The "good things" were gifts that included gold and silver jewelry and clothing (24:53), and may have included food.

24:10 *Aram Naharaim . . . town of Nahor:* This probably means a city near Haran. See the map on p. 2462.

24:11 *toward evening . . . women go out to draw water:* The women took water from the well at this time of day, because it was beginning to get cool.

24:22 *gold nose ring:* Nose rings were popular jewelry items, as were earrings.

24:29,30 *Laban:* Laban is Rebekah's brother. His daughters, Leah and Rachel, later would marry Isaac's son Jacob (Gen 29–31).

24:31-33 *went to the house . . . food was set before him:* Compare Laban's hospitality to that of Abraham (see the note at 18:16).

In the ancient Near East, the customs of hospitality required that the owner of a house take care of and protect any stranger he invited to stay in his house. Travelers who were not taken into someone's home would have no status or protection in the community. Once a host agreed to take in strangers, he was expected to treat his guests as if they were family members, to serve them the best meals, and to give them places of honor. Any host who did not meet these expectations brought shame to himself, his family, and the community. In addition, any disrespect shown to the guest by the community was considered an offense against the host. See also 18:1-15 and 19:1-11.

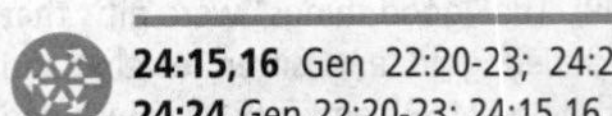

24:15,16 Gen 22:20-23; 24:24.
24:24 Gen 22:20-23; 24:15,16.

12 Then he prayed, "O LORD, God of my master Abraham,
give me success today, and show kindness to my master Abraham.
13 See, I am standing beside this spring, and the daughters of the
townspeople are coming out to draw water. 14 May it be that when
I say to a girl, 'Please let down your jar that I may have a drink,'
and she says, 'Drink, and I'll water your camels too'—let her be the
one you have chosen for your servant Isaac. By this I will know
that you have shown kindness to my master."

15 Before he had finished praying, Rebekah came out with her
jar on her shoulder. She was the daughter of Bethuel son of Milcah, who was the wife of Abraham's brother Nahor. 16 The girl was
very beautiful, a virgin; no man had ever lain with her. She went
down to the spring, filled her jar and came up again.

17 The servant hurried to meet her and said, "Please give me
a little water from your jar."

18 "Drink, my lord," she said, and quickly lowered the jar to
her hands and gave him a drink.

19 After she had given him a drink, she said, "I'll draw water
for your camels too, until they have finished drinking." 20 So she
quickly emptied her jar into the trough, ran back to the well to
draw more water, and drew enough for all his camels. 21 Without
saying a word, the man watched her closely to learn whether or
not the LORD had made his journey successful.

22 When the camels had finished drinking, the man took out
a gold nose ring weighing a beka[a] and two gold bracelets weighing
ten shekels.[b] 23 Then he asked, "Whose daughter are you? Please tell
me, is there room in your father's house for us to spend the night?"

24 She answered him, "I am the daughter of Bethuel, the son
that Milcah bore to Nahor." 25 And she added, "We have plenty of
straw and fodder, as well as room for you to spend the night."

26 Then the man bowed down and worshiped the LORD, 27 saying, "Praise be to the LORD, the God of my master Abraham, who
has not abandoned his kindness and faithfulness to my master. As
for me, the LORD has led me on the journey to the house of my
master's relatives."

28 The girl ran and told her mother's household about these
things. 29 Now Rebekah had a brother named Laban, and he hurried out to the man at the spring. 30 As soon as he had seen the
nose ring, and the bracelets on his sister's arms, and had heard
Rebekah tell what the man said to her, he went out to the man and
found him standing by the camels near the spring. 31 "Come, you
who are blessed by the LORD," he said. "Why are you standing out
here? I have prepared the house and a place for the camels."

32 So the man went to the house, and the camels were
unloaded. Straw and fodder were brought for the camels, and

[a]**22** That is, about 1/5 ounce (about 5.5 grams) [b]**22** That is, about 4 ounces (about 110 grams)

water for him and his men to wash their feet. 33Then food was set
before him, but he said, "I will not eat until I have told you what I
have to say."
"Then tell us," ⌊Laban⌋ said.
34So he said, "I am Abraham's servant. 35The LORD has
blessed my master abundantly, and he has become wealthy. He has
given him sheep and cattle, silver and gold, menservants and
maidservants, and camels and donkeys. 36My master's wife Sarah
has borne him a son in her[a] old age, and he has given him everything he owns. 37And my master made me swear an oath, and said,
'You must not get a wife for my son from the daughters of the
Canaanites, in whose land I live, 38but go to my father's family and
to my own clan, and get a wife for my son.'
39"Then I asked my master, 'What if the woman will not
come back with me?'
40"He replied, 'The LORD, before whom I have walked, will
send his angel with you and make your journey a success, so that
you can get a wife for my son from my own clan and from my
father's family. 41Then, when you go to my clan, you will be
released from my oath even if they refuse to give her to you—you
will be released from my oath.'
42"When I came to the spring today, I said, 'O LORD, God of
my master Abraham, if you will, please grant success to the journey on which I have come. 43See, I am standing beside this spring;
if a maiden comes out to draw water and I say to her, "Please let
me drink a little water from your jar," 44and if she says to me,
"Drink, and I'll draw water for your camels too," let her be the one
the LORD has chosen for my master's son.'
45"Before I finished praying in my heart, Rebekah came out,
with her jar on her shoulder. She went down to the spring and
drew water, and I said to her, 'Please give me a drink.'
46"She quickly lowered her jar from her shoulder and said,
'Drink, and I'll water your camels too.' So I drank, and she watered
the camels also.
47"I asked her, 'Whose daughter are you?'
"She said, 'The daughter of Bethuel son of Nahor, whom
Milcah bore to him.'
"Then I put the ring in her nose and the bracelets on her
arms, 48and I bowed down and worshiped the LORD. I praised the
LORD, the God of my master Abraham, who had led me on the
right road to get the granddaughter of my master's brother for his
son. 49Now if you will show kindness and faithfulness to my master, tell me; and if not, tell me, so I may know which way to turn."
50Laban and Bethuel answered, "This is from the LORD; we
can say nothing to you one way or the other. 51Here is Rebekah;

[a]**36** Or *his*

The servant prayed, *"O LORD, God of my master Abraham, if you will, please grant success to the journey on which I have come."* Gen 24:42

24:40 *his angel:* See 24:7 and the note at 32:1.

24:48 *worshiped the LORD. I praised the LORD:* See the note at 2:4; see also the mini-articles called "Names of God," p. 243 and "LORD (YHWH)," p. 140.

24:50 *This is from the LORD:* The story of finding a wife for Isaac often mentions that the LORD is guiding events (24:21,26,27,48,56).

24:37 Gen 24:2-4. **24:47** Gen 24:24.

24:59 *her nurse:* This probably refers to Deborah, who had taken care of Rebekah from the time she was born (35:8).

24:63-67 *took her veil and covered herself . . . Isaac brought her into the tent:* Since the veiling of a bride was part of the wedding ceremony, this means that she was willing to become the wife of Isaac. When Rebekah went into Isaac's tent, she became his wife and so took Sarah's place as the leading woman in the tribe.

25:1-4 *Keturah . . . Eldaah:* Abraham would have been close to one hundred forty years old by this time, if his marriage to Keturah happened after Sarah died. The descendants of Abraham and Keturah were the first ancestors of certain Arabic tribes, including the Midianites who were desert nomads. Moses' father-in-law Jethro was a Midianite priest (Exod 2:15-22).

24:62 Gen 16:14.

take her and go, and let her become the wife of your master's son,
as the LORD has directed."
52 When Abraham's servant heard what they said, he bowed
down to the ground before the LORD. 53 Then the servant brought
out gold and silver jewelry and articles of clothing and gave them
to Rebekah; he also gave costly gifts to her brother and to her
mother. 54 Then he and the men who were with him ate and drank
and spent the night there.

When they got up the next morning, he said, "Send me on
my way to my master."
55 But her brother and her mother replied, "Let the girl
remain with us ten days or so; then you[a] may go."
56 But he said to them, "Do not detain me, now that the LORD
has granted success to my journey. Send me on my way so I may
go to my master."
57 Then they said, "Let's call the girl and ask her about it." 58 So
they called Rebekah and asked her, "Will you go with this man?"

"I will go," she said.
59 So they sent their sister Rebekah on her way, along with her
nurse and Abraham's servant and his men. 60 And they blessed
Rebekah and said to her,

"Our sister, may you increase
to thousands upon thousands;
may your offspring possess
the gates of their enemies."

61 Then Rebekah and her maids got ready and mounted their
camels and went back with the man. So the servant took Rebekah
and left.
62 Now Isaac had come from Beer Lahai Roi, for he was living
in the Negev. 63 He went out to the field one evening to meditate,[b]
and as he looked up, he saw camels approaching. 64 Rebekah also
looked up and saw Isaac. She got down from her camel 65 and asked
the servant, "Who is that man in the field coming to meet us?"

"He is my master," the servant answered. So she took her veil
and covered herself.
66 Then the servant told Isaac all he had done. 67 Isaac brought
her into the tent of his mother Sarah, and he married Rebekah. So
she became his wife, and he loved her; and Isaac was comforted
after his mother's death.

The Death of Abraham

25 Abraham took[c] another wife, whose name was Keturah. 2 She
bore him Zimran, Jokshan, Medan, Midian, Ishbak and Shuah.
3 Jokshan was the father of Sheba and Dedan; the descendants of

[a]55 Or *she* [b]63 The meaning of the Hebrew for this word is uncertain.
[c]1 Or *had taken*

Dedan were the Asshurites, the Letushites and the Leummites. [4]The sons of Midian were Ephah, Epher, Hanoch, Abida and Eldaah. All these were descendants of Keturah.

[5]Abraham left everything he owned to Isaac. [6]But while he was still living, he gave gifts to the sons of his concubines and sent them away from his son Isaac to the land of the east.

[7]Altogether, Abraham lived a hundred and seventy-five years. [8]Then Abraham breathed his last and died at a good old age, an old man and full of years; and he was gathered to his people. [9]His sons Isaac and Ishmael buried him in the cave of Machpelah near Mamre, in the field of Ephron son of Zohar the Hittite, [10]the field Abraham had bought from the Hittites.[a] There Abraham was buried with his wife Sarah. [11]After Abraham's death, God blessed his son Isaac, who then lived near Beer Lahai Roi.

Ishmael's Sons

[12]This is the account of Abraham's son Ishmael, whom Sarah's maidservant, Hagar the Egyptian, bore to Abraham.

[13]These are the names of the sons of Ishmael, listed in the order of their birth: Nebaioth the firstborn of Ishmael, Kedar, Adbeel, Mibsam, [14]Mishma, Dumah, Massa, [15]Hadad, Tema, Jetur, Naphish and Kedemah. [16]These were the sons of Ishmael, and these are the names of the twelve tribal rulers according to their settlements and camps. [17]Altogether, Ishmael lived a hundred and thirty-seven years. He breathed his last and died, and he was gathered to his people. [18]His descendants settled in the area from Havilah to Shur, near the border of Egypt, as you go toward Asshur. And they lived in hostility toward[b] all their brothers.

Jacob and Esau

[19]This is the account of Abraham's son Isaac.

Abraham became the father of Isaac, [20]and Isaac was forty years old when he married Rebekah daughter of Bethuel the Aramean from Paddan Aram[c] and sister of Laban the Aramean.

[21]Isaac prayed to the LORD on behalf of his wife, because she was barren. The LORD answered his prayer, and his wife Rebekah became pregnant. [22]The babies jostled each other within her, and she said, "Why is this happening to me?" So she went to inquire of the LORD.

[23]The LORD said to her,

"Two nations are in your womb,
and two peoples from within you will be separated;

25:5,6 *left everything he owned to Isaac:* Ancient laws allowed for a man to give a greater share of his property to his oldest son. The Law of Moses later said that at least a double share of a father's property should be given to the firstborn son when the father died (Deut 21:15-17). Technically, Hagar's son Ishmael was Abraham's firstborn. Abraham gave Ishmael and his other sons gifts, but reserved the bulk of his property for Isaac, the son of God's promise (18:1-15). See the mini-article called "Birthright," p. 80.

25:9-11 *cave of Machpelah near Mamre:* See the note at 23:9.

25:13-16 *names of the sons of Ishmael . . . twelve tribal rulers:* Many of the names in this list are of Arabic origin. The Jewish historian Josephus names Ishmael as "the father of the Arabs." Ishmael's sons were the ancestors of twelve tribes (as predicted in 17:20), just as Jacob was the ancestor of the twelve tribes of Israel (Gen 49:1-28; Josh 13:14—19:51).

25:17,18 *Havilah . . . Asshur:* The location of Havilah, meaning "sand land," is not certain (Gen 2:11,12; 1 Sam 15:7), but it may be in the Negev or farther south on the Sinai Peninsula. See the note at 16:7 (Shur). Asshur is unknown, though it has sometimes been thought to refer to Assyria.

25:20 *Paddan Aram:* See the note at 24:10 (Aram Naharaim).

25:10 Gen 23:3-20. **25:12** Gen 16:1-16; 21:9-21. **25:19,20** Gen 24:15,16,62-67.

[a]**10** Or *the sons of Heth* [b]**18** Or *lived to the east of* [c]**20** That is, Northwest Mesopotamia

25:23 *the older will serve the younger:* According to ancient customs, younger sons ranked below the oldest son. Here, the LORD is telling Rebekah that the expected order will be reversed. God's actions overrule human laws and customs. See also Rom 9:11,12.

25:25,26 *Esau . . . Jacob:* In Hebrew the word "Esau" sounds like the word for "hairy," and the word for "Jacob" sounds like the word for "heel" or "he takes by the heel" (see also Hos 12:3).

25:30 *red stew . . . Edom:* In Hebrew the word "Edom" sounds like the word for "red." The land of Edom, or Seir, was south and southeast of the Dead Sea (see the map on p. 2463). The Edomites were descended from Esau (36:1-43). The descendants of Jacob (the Israelites) often battled with the Edomites (Num 20:14-21; Obad 9,10).

25:31 *birthright:* See the note at 25:5,6 and the mini-article below. In addition to a double-share of the property, the older son inherited leadership of the family.

one people will be stronger than the other,
and the older will serve the younger."

24 When the time came for her to give birth, there were twin boys
in her womb. 25 The first to come out was red, and his whole body was
like a hairy garment; so they named him Esau.[a] 26 After this, his brother came out, with his hand grasping Esau's heel; so he was named
Jacob.[b] Isaac was sixty years old when Rebekah gave birth to them.
27 The boys grew up, and Esau became a skillful hunter, a man
of the open country, while Jacob was a quiet man, staying among the
tents. 28 Isaac, who had a taste for wild game, loved Esau, but Rebekah
loved Jacob.
29 Once when Jacob was cooking some stew, Esau came in
from the open country, famished. 30 He said to Jacob, "Quick, let
me have some of that red stew! I'm famished!" (That is why he was
also called Edom.[c])
31 Jacob replied, "First sell me your birthright."
32 "Look, I am about to die," Esau said. "What good is the
birthright to me?"
33 But Jacob said, "Swear to me first." So he swore an oath to
him, selling his birthright to Jacob.
34 Then Jacob gave Esau some bread and some lentil stew. He
ate and drank, and then got up and left.
So Esau despised his birthright.

[a]25 *Esau* may mean *hairy*; he was also called Edom, which means *red*. [b]26 *Jacob* means *he grasps the heel* (figuratively, *he deceives*). [c]30 *Edom* means *red*.

BIRTHRIGHT

Israel and other cultures of the ancient Near East gave special honor and privileges to the oldest son in every family. This "birthright" also included a special share in the family inheritance and leadership of the family after the father died (Deut 21:15-17). But these special rights could be transferred, as when Esau (the firstborn son of Isaac) sold his birthright to Jacob (Gen 25:29-34). The twelve tribes of Israel were named for the twelve sons of Jacob, whose name was later changed to Israel (Gen 32:22-28).

When Reuben, Jacob's oldest son, slept with one of his father's wives (Gen 35:22), he lost his place as head of the family (Gen 49:3,4). When Israel was ruled by kings, it was the oldest son of the king who was expected to take the place of the king when he died (2 Chr 21:3; Ps 89:27).

In some cases, however, the notion of the birthright was ignored, and the oldest son was passed over or rejected. The best-known example of this reversal is the LORD's choosing of David, the youngest of Jesse's eight sons, to be the king of Israel (1 Sam 16:1-13).

God treated the whole people of Israel as a firstborn, and is pictured in the Scriptures as being happy over this special relationship with them. God gave them special attention and favors (Exod 4:22, 23). Later, the prophet Jeremiah describes God as rejoicing when Israel, the disobedient son, returns and the close relationship is restored (Jer 31:8,9).

Isaac and Abimelech

26 Now there was a famine in the land—besides the earlier
famine of Abraham's time—and Isaac went to Abimelech king of
the Philistines in Gerar. 2The LORD appeared to Isaac and said, "Do
not go down to Egypt; live in the land where I tell you to live. 3Stay
in this land for a while, and I will be with you and will bless you.
For to you and your descendants I will give all these lands and will
confirm the oath I swore to your father Abraham. 4I will make
your descendants as numerous as the stars in the sky and will give
them all these lands, and through your offspring[a] all nations on
earth will be blessed, 5because Abraham obeyed me and kept my
requirements, my commands, my decrees and my laws." 6So Isaac
stayed in Gerar.

7When the men of that place asked him about his wife, he
said, "She is my sister," because he was afraid to say, "She is my
wife." He thought, "The men of this place might kill me on
account of Rebekah, because she is beautiful."

8When Isaac had been there a long time, Abimelech king of
the Philistines looked down from a window and saw Isaac caress-
ing his wife Rebekah. 9So Abimelech summoned Isaac and said,
"She is really your wife! Why did you say, 'She is my sister'?"

Isaac answered him, "Because I thought I might lose my life
on account of her."

10Then Abimelech said, "What is this you have done to us?
One of the men might well have slept with your wife, and you
would have brought guilt upon us."

11So Abimelech gave orders to all the people: "Anyone who
molests this man or his wife shall surely be put to death."

12Isaac planted crops in that land and the same year reaped
a hundredfold, because the LORD blessed him. 13The man became
rich, and his wealth continued to grow until he became very
wealthy. 14He had so many flocks and herds and servants that the
Philistines envied him. 15So all the wells that his father's servants
had dug in the time of his father Abraham, the Philistines stopped
up, filling them with earth.

16Then Abimelech said to Isaac, "Move away from us; you
have become too powerful for us."

17So Isaac moved away from there and encamped in the Valley of Gerar and settled there. 18Isaac reopened the wells that had
been dug in the time of his father Abraham, which the Philistines
had stopped up after Abraham died, and he gave them the same
names his father had given them.

19Isaac's servants dug in the valley and discovered a well of
fresh water there. 20But the herdsmen of Gerar quarreled with
Isaac's herdsmen and said, "The water is ours!" So he named the
well Esek,[b] because they disputed with him. 21Then they dug

[a]**4** Or *seed* [b]**20** *Esek* means *dispute.*

26:1 *Abimelech king of the Philistines:* See the notes at 20:4, 5 (Abimelech), 21:32 (Philistines), and 20:1 (Negev . . . Gerar).

26:5 *Abraham obeyed me:* Even though God gave the Law to Moses many years after Abraham died (Exod 19,20), Abraham's faithful obedience in the past (17:9-14, 23-27; 22:9-18) was to be an example of how the people should be loyal to God's commands.

26:15-22 *stopped up, filling them with earth:* Apparently the Philistines threw dirt into the wells that Isaac used (26:17). But Isaac cleaned them out and called them by the names his father had given them, which meant that he claimed ownership of the wells. Disputes over wells and water rights were common in the ancient Near East and continue to be so today, because the land is dry most of the year (see also 13:6-11; 21:25; 36:7). The Hebrew names for the wells mentioned are *Esek* ("Quarrel"), *Sitnah* ("Jealousy" or "Hostility"), and *Rehoboth* ("Lots of Room").

25:33 Heb 12:16. **26:3,4** Gen 22:16-18; 12:3. **26:7-11** Gen 12:10-20; 20:1-18.

26:23 *Beersheba:* See the note at 21:31.

26:26 *Phicol:* See the note at 21:22.

26:30 *feast:* Important agreements were often celebrated with a feast (Gen 31:54; Exod 24:11). For more about agreements, see the notes at 9:9 and 15:8-10.

26:33 *Shibah . . . Beersheba:* In Hebrew "Shibah" sounds something like the words for "good luck" and "promise." For more about Beersheba, see the note at 21:31.

26:34 *Esau . . . Hittite:* Esau was Isaac and Rebekah's oldest son and the twin of Jacob (25:19-33). Esau also married Ishmael's daughter Mahalath (28:9). Compare this list with 36:2, 3. Why the names are different is not clear. Perhaps Esau married more than three different women.

For more about Hittites, see the note at 23:3.

27:4 *give you my blessing:* Spoken promises and deathbed blessings were important in the lives of ancient peoples (Gen 48:8-20; 49:1-28; Deut 33; Josh 23). What was said by the person giving these blessings was considered as valid as any written law. In fact, such blessings were considered so powerful, they could not be taken back (27:33).

27:3 Gen 25:27.

another well, but they quarreled over that one also; so he named it
Sitnah.[a] 22He moved on from there and dug another well, and no
one quarreled over it. He named it Rehoboth,[b] saying, "Now the
LORD has given us room and we will flourish in the land."
23From there he went up to Beersheba. 24That night the LORD
appeared to him and said, "I am the God of your father Abraham.
Do not be afraid, for I am with you; I will bless you and will
increase the number of your descendants for the sake of my servant Abraham."
25Isaac built an altar there and called on the name of the
LORD. There he pitched his tent, and there his servants dug a well.
26Meanwhile, Abimelech had come to him from Gerar, with
Ahuzzath his personal adviser and Phicol the commander of his
forces. 27Isaac asked them, "Why have you come to me, since you
were hostile to me and sent me away?"
28They answered, "We saw clearly that the LORD was with
you; so we said, 'There ought to be a sworn agreement between
us'—between us and you. Let us make a treaty with you 29that you
will do us no harm, just as we did not molest you but always treated you well and sent you away in peace. And now you are blessed
by the LORD."
30Isaac then made a feast for them, and they ate and drank.
31Early the next morning the men swore an oath to each other.
Then Isaac sent them on their way, and they left him in peace.
32That day Isaac's servants came and told him about the well
they had dug. They said, "We've found water!" 33He called it
Shibah,[c] and to this day the name of the town has been Beersheba.[d]
34When Esau was forty years old, he married Judith daughter of Beeri the Hittite, and also Basemath daughter of Elon the
Hittite. 35They were a source of grief to Isaac and Rebekah.

Jacob Gets Isaac's Blessing

27 When Isaac was old and his eyes were so weak that he could
no longer see, he called for Esau his older son and said to him,
"My son."

"Here I am," he answered.

2Isaac said, "I am now an old man and don't know the day of
my death. 3Now then, get your weapons—your quiver and bow—
and go out to the open country to hunt some wild game for me.
4Prepare me the kind of tasty food I like and bring it to me to eat,
so that I may give you my blessing before I die."
5Now Rebekah was listening as Isaac spoke to his son Esau.
When Esau left for the open country to hunt game and bring it
back, 6Rebekah said to her son Jacob, "Look, I overheard your
father say to your brother Esau, 7'Bring me some game and pre-

[a]21 *Sitnah* means *opposition.* [b]22 *Rehoboth* means *room.* [c]33 *Shibah* can mean *oath* or *seven.* [d]33 *Beersheba* can mean *well of the oath* or *well of seven.*

pare me some tasty food to eat, so that I may give you my blessing
in the presence of the LORD before I die.' 8Now, my son, listen carefully and do what I tell you: 9Go out to the flock and bring me two
choice young goats, so I can prepare some tasty food for your
father, just the way he likes it. 10Then take it to your father to eat,
so that he may give you his blessing before he dies."
11Jacob said to Rebekah his mother, "But my brother Esau is
a hairy man, and I'm a man with smooth skin. 12What if my father
touches me? I would appear to be tricking him and would bring
down a curse on myself rather than a blessing."
13His mother said to him, "My son, let the curse fall on me.
Just do what I say; go and get them for me."
14So he went and got them and brought them to his mother,
and she prepared some tasty food, just the way his father liked it.
15Then Rebekah took the best clothes of Esau her older son, which
she had in the house, and put them on her younger son Jacob.
16She also covered his hands and the smooth part of his neck with
the goatskins. 17Then she handed to her son Jacob the tasty food
and the bread she had made.
18He went to his father and said, "My father."
"Yes, my son," he answered. "Who is it?"
19Jacob said to his father, "I am Esau your firstborn. I have
done as you told me. Please sit up and eat some of my game so
that you may give me your blessing."
20Isaac asked his son, "How did you find it so quickly, my
son?"
"The LORD your God gave me success," he replied.
21Then Isaac said to Jacob, "Come near so I can touch you,
my son, to know whether you really are my son Esau or not."
22Jacob went close to his father Isaac, who touched him and
said, "The voice is the voice of Jacob, but the hands are the hands
of Esau." 23He did not recognize him, for his hands were hairy like
those of his brother Esau; so he blessed him. 24"Are you really my
son Esau?" he asked.
"I am," he replied.
25Then he said, "My son, bring me some of your game to eat,
so that I may give you my blessing."
Jacob brought it to him and he ate; and he brought some
wine and he drank. 26Then his father Isaac said to him, "Come
here, my son, and kiss me."
27So he went to him and kissed him. When Isaac caught the
smell of his clothes, he blessed him and said,

"Ah, the smell of my son
is like the smell of a field
that the LORD has blessed.
28May God give you of heaven's dew
and of earth's richness—
an abundance of grain and new wine.

Isaac blessed Jacob and said, *"May God give you of heaven's dew, and of earth's richness—an abundance of grain and new wine."* Gen 27:28

27:19 *your firstborn:* See the note at 25:5,6 and the mini-article called "Birthright," p. 80. See also 25:27-33.

27:27-29 Heb 11:20.

29 May nations serve you
and peoples bow down to you.
Be lord over your brothers,
and may the sons of your mother bow down to you.
May those who curse you be cursed
and those who bless you be blessed."

30 After Isaac finished blessing him and Jacob had scarcely left
his father's presence, his brother Esau came in from hunting. 31 He
too prepared some tasty food and brought it to his father. Then he
said to him, "My father, sit up and eat some of my game, so that
you may give me your blessing."
32 His father Isaac asked him, "Who are you?"
"I am your son," he answered, "your firstborn, Esau."
33 Isaac trembled violently and said, "Who was it, then, that
hunted game and brought it to me? I ate it just before you came
and I blessed him—and indeed he will be blessed!"
34 When Esau heard his father's words, he burst out with a
loud and bitter cry and said to his father, "Bless me—me too, my
father!"
35 But he said, "Your brother came deceitfully and took your
blessing."
36 Esau said, "Isn't he rightly named Jacob[a]? He has deceived
me these two times: He took my birthright, and now he's taken my
blessing!" Then he asked, "Haven't you reserved any blessing for
me?"
37 Isaac answered Esau, "I have made him lord over you and
have made all his relatives his servants, and I have sustained him with
grain and new wine. So what can I possibly do for you, my son?"
38 Esau said to his father, "Do you have only one blessing, my
father? Bless me too, my father!" Then Esau wept aloud.
39 His father Isaac answered him,

"Your dwelling will be
away from the earth's richness,
away from the dew of heaven above.
40 You will live by the sword
and you will serve your brother.
But when you grow restless,
you will throw his yoke
from off your neck."

Jacob Flees to Laban

41 Esau held a grudge against Jacob because of the blessing
his father had given him. He said to himself, "The days of mourning for my father are near; then I will kill my brother Jacob."

---

[a]**36** *Jacob* means *he grasps the heel* (figuratively, *he deceives*).

When Esau heard his father's words, he burst out with a loud and bitter cry and said to his father, "Bless me—me too, my father!"
Gen 27:34

27:29 *Be lord over your brothers:* Isaac's blessing fulfilled what God had told Rebekah (25:23). See also Gen 12:3; Num 24:9.

27:33 *I blessed him:* See the note at 27:4. The spoken blessing was like an arrow shot at a target. Once it was released, it could not be taken back. Esau also wanted a blessing, but Isaac could not undo the blessing he had already given Jacob, which gave Jacob the right to rule over Esau (27:29). The blessing was to be the birthright of the firstborn, but Esau had earlier sold his birthright to Jacob (25:27-33). See also the note at 25:5,6.

27:36 *Jacob:* In Hebrew "Jacob" sounds like the word for "cheat." See also 25:29-34.

27:39,40 *Your dwelling . . . live by the sword . . . throw his yoke from off your neck:* See the note at 25:30. Edom was a mostly dry, hilly area, not fertile and green like the Jordan Valley in Canaan (36:6-8). Living by the sword is a reference to Edom's disputes with Israel (Amos 1:11,12; Joel 3:19; Obad 1-21; Ezek 25:12-14). But the people of Israel did recognize the Edomites as their "brothers" (Deut 23:7,8). King Jehoshaphat of Judah controlled Edom at a time when Edom had no king (1 Kgs 22:47). When Jehoram was king of Judah, the Edomites broke free (2 Kgs 8:20-22).

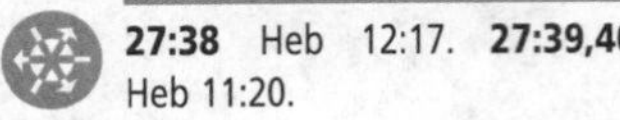
27:38 Heb 12:17. **27:39,40** Heb 11:20.

42When Rebekah was told what her older son Esau had said,
she sent for her younger son Jacob and said to him, "Your brother
Esau is consoling himself with the thought of killing you. 43Now
then, my son, do what I say: Flee at once to my brother Laban in
Haran. 44Stay with him for a while until your brother's fury sub-
sides. 45When your brother is no longer angry with you and forgets
what you did to him, I'll send word for you to come back from
there. Why should I lose both of you in one day?"
46Then Rebekah said to Isaac, "I'm disgusted with living
because of these Hittite women. If Jacob takes a wife from among
the women of this land, from Hittite women like these, my life will
not be worth living."
28 So Isaac called for Jacob and blessed[a] him and commanded
him: "Do not marry a Canaanite woman. 2Go at once to Paddan
Aram,[b] to the house of your mother's father Bethuel. Take a wife
for yourself there, from among the daughters of Laban, your
mother's brother. 3May God Almighty[c] bless you and make you
fruitful and increase your numbers until you become a community of peoples. 4May he give you and your descendants the blessing
given to Abraham, so that you may take possession of the land
where you now live as an alien, the land God gave to Abraham."
5Then Isaac sent Jacob on his way, and he went to Paddan Aram, to
Laban son of Bethuel the Aramean, the brother of Rebekah, who
was the mother of Jacob and Esau.
6Now Esau learned that Isaac had blessed Jacob and had sent
him to Paddan Aram to take a wife from there, and that when he
blessed him he commanded him, "Do not marry a Canaanite
woman," 7and that Jacob had obeyed his father and mother and
had gone to Paddan Aram. 8Esau then realized how displeasing the
Canaanite women were to his father Isaac; 9so he went to Ishmael
and married Mahalath, the sister of Nebaioth and daughter of Ishmael son of Abraham, in addition to the wives he already had.

27:43 *Laban in Haran:* See the notes at 24:29,30 (Laban) and 11:26-31 (Haran).

27:45 *lose both of you:* Esau would be hunted down as a murderer if he killed Jacob, and so Rebekah would lose both her sons.

27:46 *Hittite women:* See 26:34, 35 and the note at 23:3.

28:1,2 *Canaanite woman . . . Bethuel . . . Laban:* Isaac's wish for Jacob is similar to Abraham's wish for Isaac (24:3). Isaac wanted the family line to continue and not be mixed with the Canaanites, who worshiped a number of gods but not the God he and Abraham worshiped. See the notes at 22:20-24 and 28:5 (Bethuel); 24:29,30 (Laban).

28:3,4 *God Almighty:* See the note at 43:14. For the blessing of many descendants and land, see 12:1-3; 17:1-8.

28:5 *Bethuel the Aramean:* The Arameans were said to be descendants of Aram, son of Noah's son Shem (Gen 10:21-31; 1 Chr 1:17). They came out of Arabia before the time of Abraham and settled in Aram, also called Syria. See also Deut 26:4,5. The language of the Arameans was known as Aramaic. At least 1,500 years after the time of Jacob, many people in the land of Israel, including Jesus, continued to speak a form of Aramaic.

28:9 *Nebaioth:* Ishmael's oldest son (see 25:13).

28:10 *Beersheba . . . Haran:* See the notes at 21:31 (Beersheba); 11:26-31 (Haran); and the map on p. 2462.

JACOB AND ESAU AND THEIR FAMILIES

The next chapters of GENESIS mainly follow the travels and adventures of Jacob, whose sons would become the ancestors of the twelve tribes of Israel. Jacob marries Leah and Rachel, the daughters of his uncle Laban, who tricks Jacob into working for him an extra seven years. Jacob finally leaves Laban with his large family and flocks and later is reunited with his brother Esau.

Jacob's Dream at Bethel

10Jacob left Beersheba and set out for Haran. 11When he
reached a certain place, he stopped for the night because the sun had

[a]1 Or *greeted* [b]2 That is, Northwest Mesopotamia; also in verses 5, 6 and 7
[c]3 Hebrew *El-Shaddai*

Jacob's Ladder, by Zeev Raban, 1963. Jacob (later called Israel) went to Haran to visit his uncle Laban. He rested on the way at Bethel and had a dream. He saw a ladder or stairway that reached from the earth to heaven with angels going up and down on it. The LORD was standing above the stairway and blessed Jacob, promising Jacob and his descendants the land on which Jacob was sleeping. (See 28:10-22.)

28:12 *stairway:* This was probably like a stairway that went up the side of a Mesopotamian temple or ziggurat (see the note at 11:2-4). In Jacob's dream, the LORD stands above the stairway (28:13), just as a place of worship was located at the top of each Mesopotamian ziggurat.

28:15 *wherever you go . . . I will not leave you:* The gods of certain peoples, such as the ancient Mesopotamians, were connected to particular places, and they only gave protection within that area. But the LORD God of Abraham and Isaac promised to be with Jacob no matter where he went.

28:12 John 1:51. **28:13** Gen 13:14,15.

set. Taking one of the stones there, he put it under his head and lay
down to sleep. 12 He had a dream in which he saw a stairway[a] resting
on the earth, with its top reaching to heaven, and the angels of God
were ascending and descending on it. 13 There above it[b] stood the
LORD, and he said: "I am the LORD, the God of your father Abraham
and the God of Isaac. I will give you and your descendants the land
on which you are lying. 14 Your descendants will be like the dust of
the earth, and you will spread out to the west and to the east, to the
north and to the south. All peoples on earth will be blessed through
you and your offspring. 15 I am with you and will watch over you
wherever you go, and I will bring you back to this land. I will not
leave you until I have done what I have promised you."

---

[a]12 Or *ladder* [b]13 Or *There beside him*

[16]When Jacob awoke from his sleep, he thought, "Surely the
LORD is in this place, and I was not aware of it." [17]He was afraid
and said, "How awesome is this place! This is none other than the
house of God; this is the gate of heaven."
[18]Early the next morning Jacob took the stone he had placed
under his head and set it up as a pillar and poured oil on top of it.
[19]He called that place Bethel,[a] though the city used to be called
Luz.
[20]Then Jacob made a vow, saying, "If God will be with me
and will watch over me on this journey I am taking and will give
me food to eat and clothes to wear [21]so that I return safely to my
father's house, then the LORD[b] will be my God [22]and[c] this stone
that I have set up as a pillar will be God's house, and of all that you
give me I will give you a tenth."

Jacob Arrives in Paddan Aram

29 Then Jacob continued on his journey and came to the land
of the eastern peoples. [2]There he saw a well in the field, with three
flocks of sheep lying near it because the flocks were watered from
that well. The stone over the mouth of the well was large. [3]When
all the flocks were gathered there, the shepherds would roll the
stone away from the well's mouth and water the sheep. Then they
would return the stone to its place over the mouth of the well.
[4]Jacob asked the shepherds, "My brothers, where are you
from?"
"We're from Haran," they replied.
[5]He said to them, "Do you know Laban, Nahor's grandson?"
"Yes, we know him," they answered.
[6]Then Jacob asked them, "Is he well?"
"Yes, he is," they said, "and here comes his daughter Rachel
with the sheep."
[7]"Look," he said, "the sun is still high; it is not time for the
flocks to be gathered. Water the sheep and take them back to
pasture."
[8]"We can't," they replied, "until all the flocks are gathered
and the stone has been rolled away from the mouth of the well.
Then we will water the sheep."
[9]While he was still talking with them, Rachel came with her
father's sheep, for she was a shepherdess. [10]When Jacob saw Rachel
daughter of Laban, his mother's brother, and Laban's sheep, he
went over and rolled the stone away from the mouth of the well
and watered his uncle's sheep. [11]Then Jacob kissed Rachel and
began to weep aloud. [12]He had told Rachel that he was a relative of
her father and a son of Rebekah. So she ran and told her father.
[13]As soon as Laban heard the news about Jacob, his sister's

28:18 *took the stone . . . poured oil on top of it:* In ancient times stones were often used at places set apart to honor a god (Josh 24:26). Olive oil was poured on objects like these marker stones to dedicate them to God. This was called "anointing" (Gen 35:14; Exod 30:25-31; 1 Sam 10:1).

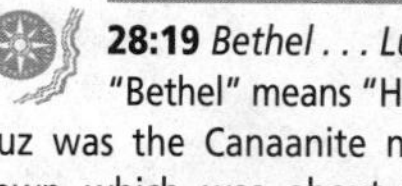

28:19 *Bethel . . . Luz:* In Hebrew "Bethel" means "House of God." Luz was the Canaanite name for this town which was about twelve miles north of Jerusalem. See the map on p. 2464.

28:22 *a tenth:* Jacob's promise to give one-tenth may refer to his offering part of his flock of sheep or goats as a sacrifice to God. Some years later, Jacob did have his own flocks (31:1-18,38-42). Giving a tenth (tithe) of one's crops or animal herds later became a requirement for all the people of Israel according to the Law of Moses (Num 18:21-24).

29:5 *Laban, Nahor's grandson:* See the notes at 24:29,30 (Laban) and 22:20-24 (Nahor).

---

[a]**19** *Bethel* means *house of God.* [b]**20,21** Or *Since God . . . father's house, the* LORD [c]**21,22** Or *house, and the* LORD *will be my God,* [22]*then*

son, he hurried to meet him. He embraced him and kissed him and brought him to his home, and there Jacob told him all these things. [14]Then Laban said to him, "You are my own flesh and blood."

Jacob Marries Leah and Rachel

After Jacob had stayed with him for a whole month,
[15]Laban said to him, "Just because you are a relative of mine, should you work for me for nothing? Tell me what your wages should be."

ANGELS

The word "angel" in English is based on the Greek word *angelos*, which means "messenger." Most often in the Bible, this is exactly what angels do—bring messages from God to people. Sometimes angels deliver messages or give orders in a personal meeting (Num 22:22-35; Luke 1:11-20,26-38). At other times they bring messages to people in their dreams (Gen 31:10-13; Matt 1:20,21). Angels often are present in visions. Angels may guide human beings to a vision and they may interpret the meaning of a vision (Zech 1:7-17; 5:5-11; Acts 10:3-23; Rev 10:1-11). In some instances, the angel is designated as "the angel of the LORD" (as in Gen 16:7-12) and was probably a special messenger or a preincarnate manifestation of Christ.

But angels are more than messengers. They carry out God's will by acting as God's agents. They protect God's people (Exod 14:19; 23:23; Ps 34:7; Dan 6:22) or punish them when they have sinned against God (2 Sam 24:11-17). God's angels also punish the enemies of God's people or punish other evil forces (Exod 12:23,29,30; Isa 37:36; Matt 13:49,50; Rev 14:14-20; 20:1-3). Angels are said to be part of a council that surrounds God in heaven (Job 1:6; Zech 3:1). Angels came to help Jesus after his time of being tested by the devil in the wilderness (Matt 4:11), and one rolled back the stone of Jesus' tomb so Jesus' disciples could enter and see that Jesus had risen (Matt 28:2).

Angels are often pictured in art as beings in long robes with wings. But in the Bible they appear in many forms. Moses saw the angel of the LORD in a burning bush (Exod 3:2). Jacob saw angels going up and down a stairway between heaven and earth (Gen 28:12). Two of the three "men" who ate with Abraham and told him that he would have a son apparently were angels, while the third was actually the LORD (Gen 18:1-10; 19:1). The being who appeared in the fiery furnace to protect Daniel's friends was said to "look like a son of the gods," and may have been an angel (Dan 3:21-25,28). The winged guardians (seraphim or cherubim) of the Most Holy Place in the temple (Isa 6:1-7; Ezek 10:1-5) were angelic beings. The angel who helped Peter escape from prison appeared in a flash of light and somehow made Peter invisible to the prison guards (Acts 12:6-10).

Some angels in the Bible have names. DANIEL mentions Gabriel (Dan 9:21), who also later appears to Mary (Luke 1:26-28), and Michael, who is called a protector of God's people (Dan 10:13; 12:1). It is possible that Satan may have been part of God's council of angels (Job 1:6; Zech 3:1). In the New Testament period, angels became known more and more as spiritual beings who helped God battle against and defeat Satan and his helpers, the demons. See also the mini-article called "Satan," p. 963.

16Now Laban had two daughters; the name of the older was Leah, and the name of the younger was Rachel. 17Leah had weak[a] eyes, but Rachel was lovely in form, and beautiful. 18Jacob was in love with Rachel and said, "I'll work for you seven years in return for your younger daughter Rachel."

19Laban said, "It's better that I give her to you than to some other man. Stay here with me." 20So Jacob served seven years to get Rachel, but they seemed like only a few days to him because of his love for her.

21Then Jacob said to Laban, "Give me my wife. My time is completed, and I want to lie with her."

22So Laban brought together all the people of the place and gave a feast. 23But when evening came, he took his daughter Leah and gave her to Jacob, and Jacob lay with her. 24And Laban gave his servant girl Zilpah to his daughter as her maidservant.

25When morning came, there was Leah! So Jacob said to Laban, "What is this you have done to me? I served you for Rachel, didn't I? Why have you deceived me?"

26Laban replied, "It is not our custom here to give the younger daughter in marriage before the older one. 27Finish this daughter's bridal week; then we will give you the younger one also, in return for another seven years of work."

28And Jacob did so. He finished the week with Leah, and then Laban gave him his daughter Rachel to be his wife. 29Laban gave his servant girl Bilhah to his daughter Rachel as her maidservant. 30Jacob lay with Rachel also, and he loved Rachel more than Leah. And he worked for Laban another seven years.

Jacob's Children

31When the LORD saw that Leah was not loved, he opened her womb, but Rachel was barren. 32Leah became pregnant and gave birth to a son. She named him Reuben,[b] for she said, "It is because the LORD has seen my misery. Surely my husband will love me now."

33She conceived again, and when she gave birth to a son she said, "Because the LORD heard that I am not loved, he gave me this one too." So she named him Simeon.[c]

34Again she conceived, and when she gave birth to a son she said, "Now at last my husband will become attached to me, because I have borne him three sons." So he was named Levi.[d]

35She conceived again, and when she gave birth to a son she said, "This time I will praise the LORD." So she named him Judah.[e] Then she stopped having children.

29:18 *seven years:* Seven was considered a perfect or complete number in ancient times. See the chart called "Numbers in the Bible," p. 2405.

29:23-30 *lay with her . . . Laban gave his servant girl Zilpah . . . Bilhah:* In ancient Palestine marriages were important family events even though couples did not exchange vows as in modern weddings. Instead, a couple was considered married if they slept together. Laban brought Leah to Jacob's tent at night, and Leah was probably wearing a veil over her face (see the note at 24:63-67). The festivities celebrating the couple's union often lasted as long as a week (29:27; see also Judg 14:12,17).

Giving a servant was a wedding custom taken from old Babylonian wedding contracts (see also 29:28-30).

29:27 *bridal week:* The wedding feast lasted for seven days.

29:28-30 *gave . . . Bilhah:* See the note at 29:23-30.

29:32-35 *Leah . . . gave birth to . . . Reuben . . . Simeon . . . Levi . . . Judah:* In Hebrew these names sound like words that mean the following: Reuben ("Look, a son!"), Simeon ("someone who hears"), Levi ("hold close"), and Judah ("praise"). Levi was the ancestor of Aaron, whose descendants were Israel's priests. Judah was the ancestor of Israel's King David. See also the chart called "Jacob's Children and Their Mothers," p. 99.

---

[a]17 Or *delicate* [b]32 *Reuben* sounds like the Hebrew for *he has seen my misery;* the name means *see, a son.* [c]33 *Simeon* probably means *one who hears.*
[d]34 *Levi* sounds like and may be derived from the Hebrew for *attached.*
[e]35 *Judah* sounds like and may be derived from the Hebrew for *praise.*

30:3 *she can bear children for me:* Most likely this phrase was meant to express the concept of adoption.

30:4-8 *Bilhah . . . Dan . . . Naphtali:* In Hebrew these names sound like words that mean the following: Dan ("judge"), Naphtali ("struggle" or "contest").

30:9-13 *Zilpah . . . Gad . . . Asher:* In Hebrew these names sound like words that mean the following: Gad ("lucky"), Asher ("happy").

30:14 *mandrakes:* The roots of this flowering plant were thought to give sexual powers and induce pregnancy. See the illustration, p. 1270.

30:18-21 *Leah . . . Issachar . . . Zebulun . . . Dinah:* In Hebrew Leah's sons' names sound like words that mean the following: Issachar ("reward"), Zebulun ("give" and "praise"). No explanation is given for the meaning of Dinah's name. For more about Dinah, see 34:1-24.

30:22-24 *Rachel . . . Joseph:* In Hebrew "Joseph" sounds like the words for "take away" and "add." For more about Joseph, see chapters 39–50. See also the chart called "Jacob's Children and Their Mothers," p. 99.

30 When Rachel saw that she was not bearing Jacob any children, she became jealous of her sister. So she said to Jacob, "Give me children, or I'll die!"

2 Jacob became angry with her and said, "Am I in the place of God, who has kept you from having children?"

3 Then she said, "Here is Bilhah, my maidservant. Sleep with her so that she can bear children for me and that through her I too can build a family."

4 So she gave him her servant Bilhah as a wife. Jacob slept with her, 5 and she became pregnant and bore him a son. 6 Then Rachel said, "God has vindicated me; he has listened to my plea and given me a son." Because of this she named him Dan.[a]

7 Rachel's servant Bilhah conceived again and bore Jacob a second son. 8 Then Rachel said, "I have had a great struggle with my sister, and I have won." So she named him Naphtali.[b]

9 When Leah saw that she had stopped having children, she took her maidservant Zilpah and gave her to Jacob as a wife. 10 Leah's servant Zilpah bore Jacob a son. 11 Then Leah said, "What good fortune!"[c] So she named him Gad.[d]

12 Leah's servant Zilpah bore Jacob a second son. 13 Then Leah said, "How happy I am! The women will call me happy." So she named him Asher.[e]

14 During wheat harvest, Reuben went out into the fields and found some mandrake plants, which he brought to his mother Leah. Rachel said to Leah, "Please give me some of your son's mandrakes."

15 But she said to her, "Wasn't it enough that you took away my husband? Will you take my son's mandrakes too?"

"Very well," Rachel said, "he can sleep with you tonight in return for your son's mandrakes."

16 So when Jacob came in from the fields that evening, Leah went out to meet him. "You must sleep with me," she said. "I have hired you with my son's mandrakes." So he slept with her that night.

17 God listened to Leah, and she became pregnant and bore Jacob a fifth son. 18 Then Leah said, "God has rewarded me for giving my maidservant to my husband." So she named him Issachar.[f]

19 Leah conceived again and bore Jacob a sixth son. 20 Then Leah said, "God has presented me with a precious gift. This time my husband will treat me with honor, because I have borne him six sons." So she named him Zebulun.[g]

21 Some time later she gave birth to a daughter and named her Dinah.

---

[a] **6** *Dan* here means *he has vindicated.* [b] **8** *Naphtali* means *my struggle.* [c] **11** Or *"A troop is coming!"* [d] **11** *Gad* can mean *good fortune* or *a troop.* [e] **13** *Asher* means *happy.* [f] **18** *Issachar* sounds like the Hebrew for *reward.* [g] **20** *Zebulun* probably means *honor.*

[22]Then God remembered Rachel; he listened to her and opened her womb. [23]She became pregnant and gave birth to a son and said, "God has taken away my disgrace." [24]She named him Joseph,[a] and said, "May the LORD add to me another son."

Jacob's Flocks Increase

[25]After Rachel gave birth to Joseph, Jacob said to Laban, "Send me on my way so I can go back to my own homeland. [26]Give me my wives and children, for whom I have served you, and I will be on my way. You know how much work I've done for you."

[27]But Laban said to him, "If I have found favor in your eyes, please stay. I have learned by divination that[b] the LORD has blessed me because of you." [28]He added, "Name your wages, and I will pay them."

[29]Jacob said to him, "You know how I have worked for you and how your livestock has fared under my care. [30]The little you had before I came has increased greatly, and the LORD has blessed you wherever I have been. But now, when may I do something for my own household?"

[31]"What shall I give you?" he asked.

"Don't give me anything," Jacob replied. "But if you will do this one thing for me, I will go on tending your flocks and watching over them: [32]Let me go through all your flocks today and remove from them every speckled or spotted sheep, every dark-colored lamb and every spotted or speckled goat. They will be my wages. [33]And my honesty will testify for me in the future, whenever you check on the wages you have paid me. Any goat in my possession that is not speckled or spotted, or any lamb that is not dark-colored, will be considered stolen."

[34]"Agreed," said Laban. "Let it be as you have said." [35]That same day he removed all the male goats that were streaked or spotted, and all the speckled or spotted female goats (all that had white on them) and all the dark-colored lambs, and he placed them in the care of his sons. [36]Then he put a three-day journey between himself and Jacob, while Jacob continued to tend the rest of Laban's flocks.

[37]Jacob, however, took fresh-cut branches from poplar, almond and plane trees and made white stripes on them by peeling the bark and exposing the white inner wood of the branches. [38]Then he placed the peeled branches in all the watering troughs, so that they would be directly in front of the flocks when they came to drink. When the flocks were in heat and came to drink, [39]they mated in front of the branches. And they bore young that were streaked or speckled or spotted. [40]Jacob set apart the young of the flock by themselves, but made the rest face the streaked and dark-colored animals that belonged to Laban. Thus he made separate flocks for himself and did not put them with Laban's

[a]24 *Joseph* means *may he add.* [b]27 Or possibly *have become rich and*

Then God remembered Rachel; he listened to her and opened her womb. She became pregnant and gave birth to a son and said, "God has taken away my disgrace." She named him Joseph.
Gen 30:22-24

30:25 *Send me on my way:* Jacob had agreed to work seven years for each of Laban's two daughters (see 29:18).

30:27,28 *learned by divination:* The Hebrew text here refers to knowledge received by some form of divination, which means trying to discover the wishes of the gods by the use of such means as magic, fortune-telling, reading fluids in a cup (44:5), communicating with the dead (1 Sam 28:3-25), inspecting the liver and other organs of dead animals, interpreting dreams (41:1-32), and casting lots (drawing objects out of a container). Later the Law of Moses would ban most of these things in Israel (Lev 19:26; Deut 18:10-14).

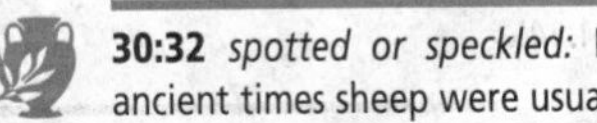

30:32 *spotted or speckled:* In ancient times sheep were usually white, and goats were usually black or dark brown. Only a few sheep and goats would have had spots, and only a few sheep would have been black.

30:38 *peeled branches . . . directly in front of the flocks:* It was believed by some that what sheep and goats saw at the time of breeding would determine the coloring of their young.

30:25,26 Gen 29:18,27.

31:3 *land of your fathers:* This means Canaan (see 31:17, 18).

31:4 *Jacob sent word to Rachel and Leah:* According to legal customs, Rachel and Leah belonged to their father's house and were considered part of his property (see Ruth 4:5, 10), so Jacob asked their opinion about what to do.

31:9 *God has . . . given them to me:* Jacob gives credit to God for helping him gain large flocks, rather than his own idea to use speckled branches (30:37-42). This is a common theme in these stories of Israel's ancestors: God is at work in the common events of people's lives and in their actions.

31:13 *Bethel:* The place where Jacob had seen angels in a dream (see 28:18-22 and the notes at 12:8,9 and 28:19).

31:15 *what was paid for us:* Usually the husband-to-be paid a "bride price" to the father of the bride. But Jacob didn't pay Laban for either Leah or Rachel. Instead he was tricked into working fourteen years to get the bride he loved. So there was no money for either of Laban's daughters (31:14).

31:18 *Paddan Aram:* In northern Syria. See the map on p. 2462.

animals. 41Whenever the stronger females were in heat, Jacob
would place the branches in the troughs in front of the animals so
they would mate near the branches, 42but if the animals were weak,
he would not place them there. So the weak animals went to Laban
and the strong ones to Jacob. 43In this way the man grew exceedingly prosperous and came to own large flocks, and maidservants
and menservants, and camels and donkeys.

Jacob Flees From Laban

31 Jacob heard that Laban's sons were saying, "Jacob has taken
everything our father owned and has gained all this wealth from
what belonged to our father." 2And Jacob noticed that Laban's attitude toward him was not what it had been.

3Then the LORD said to Jacob, "Go back to the land of your
fathers and to your relatives, and I will be with you."

4So Jacob sent word to Rachel and Leah to come out to the
fields where his flocks were. 5He said to them, "I see that your
father's attitude toward me is not what it was before, but the God
of my father has been with me. 6You know that I've worked for
your father with all my strength, 7yet your father has cheated me
by changing my wages ten times. However, God has not allowed
him to harm me. 8If he said, 'The speckled ones will be your
wages,' then all the flocks gave birth to speckled young; and if he
said, 'The streaked ones will be your wages,' then all the flocks bore
streaked young. 9So God has taken away your father's livestock and
has given them to me.

10"In breeding season I once had a dream in which I looked
up and saw that the male goats mating with the flock were
streaked, speckled or spotted. 11The angel of God said to me in the
dream, 'Jacob.' I answered, 'Here I am.' 12And he said, 'Look up and
see that all the male goats mating with the flock are streaked,
speckled or spotted, for I have seen all that Laban has been doing
to you. 13I am the God of Bethel, where you anointed a pillar and
where you made a vow to me. Now leave this land at once and go
back to your native land.' "

14Then Rachel and Leah replied, "Do we still have any share in
the inheritance of our father's estate? 15Does he not regard us as foreigners? Not only has he sold us, but he has used up what was paid
for us. 16Surely all the wealth that God took away from our father
belongs to us and our children. So do whatever God has told you."

17Then Jacob put his children and his wives on camels, 18and
he drove all his livestock ahead of him, along with all the goods he
had accumulated in Paddan Aram,[a] to go to his father Isaac in the
land of Canaan.

19When Laban had gone to shear his sheep, Rachel stole her

---

[a]**18** That is, Northwest Mesopotamia

father's household gods. [20]Moreover, Jacob deceived Laban the
Aramean by not telling him he was running away. [21]So he fled with
all he had, and crossing the River,[a] he headed for the hill country
of Gilead.

Laban Pursues Jacob

[22]On the third day Laban was told that Jacob had fled. [23]Tak-
ing his relatives with him, he pursued Jacob for seven days and
caught up with him in the hill country of Gilead. [24]Then God
came to Laban the Aramean in a dream at night and said to him,
"Be careful not to say anything to Jacob, either good or bad."

[25]Jacob had pitched his tent in the hill country of Gilead
when Laban overtook him, and Laban and his relatives camped
there too. [26]Then Laban said to Jacob, "What have you done? You've
deceived me, and you've carried off my daughters like captives in
war. [27]Why did you run off secretly and deceive me? Why didn't you
tell me, so I could send you away with joy and singing to the music
of tambourines and harps? [28]You didn't even let me kiss my grandchildren and my daughters good-by. You have done a foolish thing.
[29]I have the power to harm you; but last night the God of your
father said to me, 'Be careful not to say anything to Jacob, either
good or bad.' [30]Now you have gone off because you longed to
return to your father's house. But why did you steal my gods?"

[31]Jacob answered Laban, "I was afraid, because I thought you
would take your daughters away from me by force. [32]But if you
find anyone who has your gods, he shall not live. In the presence of
our relatives, see for yourself whether there is anything of yours
here with me; and if so, take it." Now Jacob did not know that
Rachel had stolen the gods.

[33]So Laban went into Jacob's tent and into Leah's tent and
into the tent of the two maidservants, but he found nothing. After
he came out of Leah's tent, he entered Rachel's tent. [34]Now Rachel
had taken the household gods and put them inside her camel's
saddle and was sitting on them. Laban searched through everything in the tent but found nothing.

[35]Rachel said to her father, "Don't be angry, my lord, that I
cannot stand up in your presence; I'm having my period." So he
searched but could not find the household gods.

[36]Jacob was angry and took Laban to task. "What is my crime?"
he asked Laban. "What sin have I committed that you hunt me
down? [37]Now that you have searched through all my goods, what
have you found that belongs to your household? Put it here in front
of your relatives and mine, and let them judge between the two of us.

[38]"I have been with you for twenty years now. Your sheep and
goats have not miscarried, nor have I eaten rams from your flocks.

---

[a]**21** That is, the Euphrates

31:19 *household gods*: These small statues representing gods were thought to protect the house from danger. It is also possible that the person who had them would inherit the family property.

31:20 *Aramean:* See the note at 28:5.

31:21 *the River . . . hill country of Gilead:* The Euphrates River (see the note at 2:10-14). Gilead was the area east of the Jordan River between the Sea of Galilee and the Dead Sea. It had high pasturelands and fertile lowlands where grain was grown. See the maps on p. 2462 and p. 2467.

31:26 *You've deceived me:* See the note at 27:36.

31:27 *tambourines and harps:* A tambourine is a circular frame with metal disks attached that jingle when the frame is shaken or hit. The harp here was probably a lyre, a stringed musical instrument that could be held by hand. See the illustration on p. 1190.

31:30 *gods:* See the note at 31:19. See also the mini-article called "Canaanite Gods and Goddesses," p. 469.

31:33 *two maidservants:* Bilhah and Zilpah (see 30:3-10).

31:35 *my period:* In ancient times, anything a woman sat on while having her period was considered ritually unclean (Lev 15:19-23).

31:39 *you demanded . . . night:* A shepherd was not responsible for sheep and goats killed by wild animals, if the shepherd could supply proof of how they were killed.

31:43 *the children are my children:* See the note at 31:4.

31:47-49 *called it Jegar Sahadutha . . . Galeed . . . Mizpah:* Making a pile of rocks was a way to leave evidence of a covenant between people, or between people and God (Gen 28:18-22; Josh 4:4-7). In Aramaic "Jegar Sahadutha" means "a pile of rocks to remind us." In Hebrew "Galeed" means "a pile of rocks to remind us," and "Mizpah" sounds like the word for "a place from which to watch."

31:54 *sacrifice . . . meal:* See the notes at 22:7,8 and 26:30.

32:1 *angels of God:* In Hebrew the word for "angel" means "messenger." In the Bible, angels act both as messengers and servants of God. See the mini-article called "Angels," p. 88.

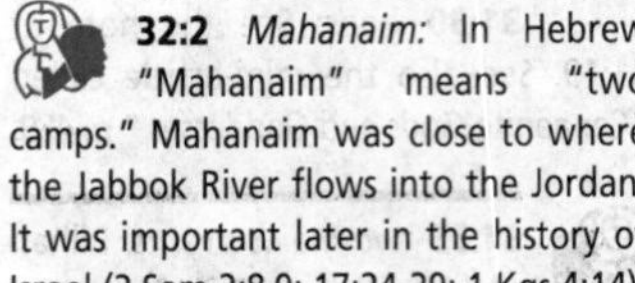

32:2 *Mahanaim:* In Hebrew "Mahanaim" means "two camps." Mahanaim was close to where the Jabbok River flows into the Jordan. It was important later in the history of Israel (2 Sam 2:8,9; 17:24-29; 1 Kgs 4:14).

32:3 *Esau . . . Seir . . . Edom:* The story of Jacob's relationship with his brother Esau is taken up once again (see 25:19-33; 26:34—28:9). For more about Edom, see the note at 25:30 and the map on p. 2464.

31:53 Gen 22:20-24.

[39]I did not bring you animals torn by wild beasts; I bore the loss
myself. And you demanded payment from me for whatever was
stolen by day or night. [40]This was my situation: The heat consumed me in the daytime and the cold at night, and sleep fled
from my eyes. [41]It was like this for the twenty years I was in your
household. I worked for you fourteen years for your two daughters
and six years for your flocks, and you changed my wages ten times.
[42]If the God of my father, the God of Abraham and the Fear of
Isaac, had not been with me, you would surely have sent me away
empty-handed. But God has seen my hardship and the toil of my
hands, and last night he rebuked you."

[43]Laban answered Jacob, "The women are my daughters, the
children are my children, and the flocks are my flocks. All you see
is mine. Yet what can I do today about these daughters of mine, or
about the children they have borne? [44]Come now, let's make a
covenant, you and I, and let it serve as a witness between us."

[45]So Jacob took a stone and set it up as a pillar. [46]He said to
his relatives, "Gather some stones." So they took stones and piled
them in a heap, and they ate there by the heap. [47]Laban called it
Jegar Sahadutha,[a] and Jacob called it Galeed.[b]

[48]Laban said, "This heap is a witness between you and me
today." That is why it was called Galeed. [49]It was also called Mizpah,[c]
because he said, "May the LORD keep watch between you and me
when we are away from each other. [50]If you mistreat my daughters
or if you take any wives besides my daughters, even though no one
is with us, remember that God is a witness between you and me."

[51]Laban also said to Jacob, "Here is this heap, and here is this
pillar I have set up between you and me. [52]This heap is a witness,
and this pillar is a witness, that I will not go past this heap to your
side to harm you and that you will not go past this heap and pillar to my side to harm me. [53]May the God of Abraham and the
God of Nahor, the God of their father, judge between us."

So Jacob took an oath in the name of the Fear of his father
Isaac. [54]He offered a sacrifice there in the hill country and invited his
relatives to a meal. After they had eaten, they spent the night there.

[55]Early the next morning Laban kissed his grandchildren and
his daughters and blessed them. Then he left and returned home.

Jacob Prepares to Meet Esau

32 Jacob also went on his way, and the angels of God met him.
[2]When Jacob saw them, he said, "This is the camp of God!" So he
named that place Mahanaim.[d]

[3]Jacob sent messengers ahead of him to his brother Esau in
the land of Seir, the country of Edom. [4]He instructed them: "This

[a]47 The Aramaic *Jegar Sahadutha* means *witness heap.* [b]47 The Hebrew *Galeed* means *witness heap.* [c]49 *Mizpah* means *watchtower.* [d]2 *Mahanaim* means *two camps.*

is what you are to say to my master Esau: 'Your servant Jacob says,
I have been staying with Laban and have remained there till now.
5 I have cattle and donkeys, sheep and goats, menservants and
maidservants. Now I am sending this message to my lord, that I
may find favor in your eyes.' "

6 When the messengers returned to Jacob, they said, "We
went to your brother Esau, and now he is coming to meet you, and
four hundred men are with him."

7 In great fear and distress Jacob divided the people who were
with him into two groups,[a] and the flocks and herds and camels as
well. 8 He thought, "If Esau comes and attacks one group,[b] the
group[b] that is left may escape."

9 Then Jacob prayed, "O God of my father Abraham, God of my
father Isaac, O LORD, who said to me, 'Go back to your country and
your relatives, and I will make you prosper,' 10 I am unworthy of all the
kindness and faithfulness you have shown your servant. I had only my
staff when I crossed this Jordan, but now I have become two groups.
11 Save me, I pray, from the hand of my brother Esau, for I am afraid
he will come and attack me, and also the mothers with their children.
12 But you have said, 'I will surely make you prosper and will make
your descendants like the sand of the sea, which cannot be counted.' "

13 He spent the night there, and from what he had with him
he selected a gift for his brother Esau: 14 two hundred female goats
and twenty male goats, two hundred ewes and twenty rams, 15 thirty
female camels with their young, forty cows and ten bulls, and
twenty female donkeys and ten male donkeys. 16 He put them in
the care of his servants, each herd by itself, and said to his servants, "Go ahead of me, and keep some space between the herds."

17 He instructed the one in the lead: "When my brother Esau
meets you and asks, 'To whom do you belong, and where are you
going, and who owns all these animals in front of you?' 18 then you
are to say, 'They belong to your servant Jacob. They are a gift sent
to my lord Esau, and he is coming behind us.' "

19 He also instructed the second, the third and all the others
who followed the herds: "You are to say the same thing to Esau
when you meet him. 20 And be sure to say, 'Your servant Jacob is
coming behind us.' " For he thought, "I will pacify him with these
gifts I am sending on ahead; later, when I see him, perhaps he will
receive me." 21 So Jacob's gifts went on ahead of him, but he himself
spent the night in the camp.

Jacob Wrestles With God

22 That night Jacob got up and took his two wives, his two
maidservants and his eleven sons and crossed the ford of the
Jabbok. 23 After he had sent them across the stream, he sent over all

[a]**7** Or *camps*; also in verse 10 [b]**8** Or *camp*

Jacob prayed, "O God of my Father Abraham, . . . I am unworthy of all the kindness and faithfulness you have shown your servant. . . . Save me, I pray."
Gen 32:9-11

32:4 *Your servant Jacob:* Jacob shows his humility toward Esau.

32:9 *LORD:* See the note at 2:4. See also 24:12; 28:13.

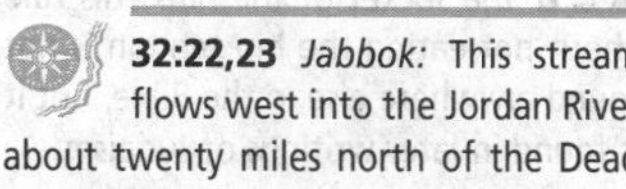
32:22,23 *Jabbok:* This stream flows west into the Jordan River about twenty miles north of the Dead Sea. See the map on p. 2464.

32:12 Gen 22:17.

his possessions. [24]So Jacob was left alone, and a man wrestled with him till daybreak. [25]When the man saw that he could not overpower him, he touched the socket of Jacob's hip so that his hip was wrenched as he wrestled with the man. [26]Then the man said, "Let me go, for it is daybreak."

But Jacob replied, "I will not let you go unless you bless me."

[27]The man asked him, "What is your name?"

"Jacob," he answered.

[28]Then the man said, "Your name will no longer be Jacob, but Israel,[a] because you have struggled with God and with men and have overcome."

[29]Jacob said, "Please tell me your name."

But he replied, "Why do you ask my name?" Then he blessed him there.

[30]So Jacob called the place Peniel,[b] saying, "It is because I saw God face to face, and yet my life was spared."

[31]The sun rose above him as he passed Peniel,[c] and he was limping because of his hip. [32]Therefore to this day the Israelites do not eat the tendon attached to the socket of the hip, because the socket of Jacob's hip was touched near the tendon.

Jacob Meets Esau

33 Jacob looked up and there was Esau, coming with his four hundred men; so he divided the children among Leah, Rachel and the two maidservants. [2]He put the maid-servants and their children in front, Leah and her children next, and Rachel and Joseph in the rear. [3]He himself went on ahead and bowed down to the ground seven times as he approached his brother.

[4]But Esau ran to meet Jacob and embraced him; he threw his arms around his neck and kissed him. And they wept. [5]Then Esau looked up and saw the women and children. "Who are these with you?" he asked.

Jacob answered, "They are the children God has graciously given your servant."

[6]Then the maidservants and their children approached and bowed down. [7]Next, Leah and her children came and bowed down. Last of all came Joseph and Rachel, and they too bowed down.

[8]Esau asked, "What do you mean by all these droves I met?"

"To find favor in your eyes, my lord," he said.

[9]But Esau said, "I already have plenty, my brother. Keep what you have for yourself."

[10]"No, please!" said Jacob. "If I have found favor in your eyes, accept this gift from me. For to see your face is like seeing the face of God, now that you have received me favorably. [11]Please accept

[a]28 *Israel* means *he struggles with God.* [b]30 *Peniel* means *face of God.*
[c]31 Hebrew *Penuel*, a variant of *Peniel*

32:24 *man:* This means God or the "angel of the LORD" (32:28-30). See also the note at 18:16.

32:28 *Israel:* In Hebrew one meaning of "Israel" is "a man who wrestles with God." Abraham's descendants eventually were known as the people of Israel and Israelites. In the Bible, Israel is the nation made up of the twelve tribes descended from Jacob. See also the mini-article called "Israel," p. 264.

32:30 *Peniel:* In Hebrew "Peniel" means "face of God." Seeing God's face was believed to bring death (Exod 33:20), but Jacob survived.

32:32 *the tendon attached to the socket of the hip:* This rule about not eating the hip tendon is not found anywhere else in the Bible, but it is found in later writings of Judaism.

33:2 *maidservants and their children . . . Leah and her children . . . Rachel and Joseph:* See the chart called "Jacob's Children and Their Mothers," p. 99. Jacob had his favorite wife (Rachel) and her son (Joseph) walk at the rear, where it was safest.

33:3 *bowed . . . seven times:* This ancient act of showing honor and humility toward another is also described in writings found at Tell el-Amarna in Egypt and dating to the fourteenth century B.C.

33:11 *the present:* In Hebrew, the word for "present" can also mean "blessing." This may be Jacob's attempt to return at least a part of the "blessing" he tricked his brother out of (27:1-40).

32:24-26 Hos 12:4. **32:28** Gen 35:9-11. **32:29** Judg 13:17,18.

the present that was brought to you, for God has been gracious
to me and I have all I need." And because Jacob insisted, Esau
accepted it.

12Then Esau said, "Let us be on our way; I'll accompany
you."

13But Jacob said to him, "My lord knows that the children
are tender and that I must care for the ewes and cows that are
nursing their young. If they are driven hard just one day, all the
animals will die. 14So let my lord go on ahead of his servant, while
I move along slowly at the pace of the droves before me and that
of the children, until I come to my lord in Seir."

15Esau said, "Then let me leave some of my men with you."

"But why do that?" Jacob asked. "Just let me find favor in the
eyes of my lord."

16So that day Esau started on his way back to Seir. 17Jacob, however, went to Succoth, where he built a place for himself and made
shelters for his livestock. That is why the place is called Succoth.[a]

18After Jacob came from Paddan Aram,[b] he arrived safely at
the[c] city of Shechem in Canaan and camped within sight of the
city. 19For a hundred pieces of silver,[d] he bought from the sons of
Hamor, the father of Shechem, the plot of ground where he pitched
his tent. 20There he set up an altar and called it El Elohe Israel.[e]

Dinah and the Shechemites

34 Now Dinah, the daughter Leah had borne to Jacob, went out
to visit the women of the land. 2When Shechem son of Hamor the
Hivite, the ruler of that area, saw her, he took her and violated her.
3His heart was drawn to Dinah daughter of Jacob, and he loved the
girl and spoke tenderly to her. 4And Shechem said to his father
Hamor, "Get me this girl as my wife."

5When Jacob heard that his daughter Dinah had been
defiled, his sons were in the fields with his livestock; so he kept
quiet about it until they came home.

6Then Shechem's father Hamor went out to talk with Jacob.
7Now Jacob's sons had come in from the fields as soon as they
heard what had happened. They were filled with grief and fury,
because Shechem had done a disgraceful thing in[f] Israel by lying
with Jacob's daughter—a thing that should not be done.

8But Hamor said to them, "My son Shechem has his heart
set on your daughter. Please give her to him as his wife. 9Inter-
marry with us; give us your daughters and take our daughters for
yourselves. 10You can settle among us; the land is open to you. Live
in it, trade[g] in it, and acquire property in it."

33:13 *If they are driven hard:* Jacob's family and flocks had traveled over three hundred miles by foot in a short time since leaving Haran (31:21-23). See the map on p. 2462.

33:16,17 *Seir . . . Succoth:* For more about Seir, see the note at 25:30. In Hebrew "Succoth" means "shelters." It is thought to have been a few miles west of Mahanaim, just north of where the Jabbok River flows into the Jordan. See the map on p. 2464.

33:18 *Shechem:* See the note at 12:4-6.

33:19—34:2 *Hamor, the father of Shechem . . . Dinah . . . Hivite:* The Bible also refers to Hamor as the founder of the town of Shechem (Josh 24:32; Judg 9:28). He apparently named his son after the town. For Dinah, see also 30:21 and 46:8-15. The Hivites may also be the people known as the Horites, who may have settled in the area around Mount Seir but were later pushed out by the descendants of Esau, the Edomites.

34:7 *a disgraceful thing:* In ancient Israel rape was not seen just as an act of violence against the victim, it was also seen as something that insulted and brought shame to the entire tribe and nation. Compare this story to the rape and murder of the Levite's wife in Judges 19.

---

a17 *Succoth* means *shelters.* b18 That is, Northwest Mesopotamia c18 Or *arrived at Shalem, a* d19 Hebrew *hundred kesitahs*; a kesitah was a unit of money of unknown weight and value. e20 *El Elohe Israel* can mean *God, the God of Israel* or *mighty is the God of Israel.* f7 Or *against* g10 Or *move about freely*; also in verse 21

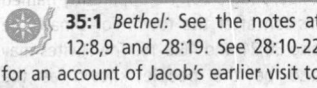

34:14 *circumcised:* See the note at 17:10,11. If Hamor's son and other Hivite men were circumcised, they could be part of the people of Israel. In addition to the possibility of gaining the wife he desired, Shechem saw a chance to gain part of the property of Jacob's family (34:22,23).

34:25 *Simeon and Levi:* Dinah's full brothers, whose mother was Leah (29:33,34; 30:21). Later, Simeon and Levi's own descendants were to be scattered because of the violent revenge they took on the men of Shechem (49:5-7). Their action caused Jacob to leave the area around Shechem and move on to Bethel (34:30; 35:1).

34:30 *Canaanites and Perizzites:* See the notes at 12:4-6 and 13:5-7.

35:1 *Bethel:* See the notes at 12:8,9 and 28:19. See 28:10-22 for an account of Jacob's earlier visit to Bethel.

35:2-4 *foreign gods . . . rings in their ears:* The gods were probably the small household gods mentioned in 31:19, but Jacob's family members might have collected small statues of Canaanite gods, such as Baal. The earrings likely had symbols of foreign gods on them. The earrings shown here, from the fifteenth century B.C., possibly represent the goddess Ashtoreth. See Exod 32:2,3; Judg 8:24; and the mini-article called "Canaanite Gods and Goddesses," p. 469.

[11]Then Shechem said to Dinah's father and brothers, "Let me
find favor in your eyes, and I will give you whatever you ask. [12]Make
the price for the bride and the gift I am to bring as great as you like,
and I'll pay whatever you ask me. Only give me the girl as my wife."
[13]Because their sister Dinah had been defiled, Jacob's sons
replied deceitfully as they spoke to Shechem and his father Hamor.
[14]They said to them, "We can't do such a thing; we can't give our
sister to a man who is not circumcised. That would be a disgrace to
us. [15]We will give our consent to you on one condition only: that
you become like us by circumcising all your males. [16]Then we will
give you our daughters and take your daughters for ourselves. We'll
settle among you and become one people with you. [17]But
if you will not agree to be circumcised, we'll take our sister[a] and go."
[18]Their proposal seemed good to Hamor and his son
Shechem. [19]The young man, who was the most honored of all his
father's household, lost no time in doing what they said, because
he was delighted with Jacob's daughter. [20]So Hamor and his son
Shechem went to the gate of their city to speak to their fellow
townsmen. [21]"These men are friendly toward us," they said. "Let
them live in our land and trade in it; the land has plenty of room
for them. We can marry their daughters and they can marry ours.
[22]But the men will consent to live with us as one people only on
the condition that our males be circumcised, as they themselves
are. [23]Won't their livestock, their property and all their other animals
become ours? So let us give our consent to them, and they
will settle among us."
[24]All the men who went out of the city gate agreed with
Hamor and his son Shechem, and every male in the city was circumcised.
[25]Three days later, while all of them were still in pain, two of
Jacob's sons, Simeon and Levi, Dinah's brothers, took their swords
and attacked the unsuspecting city, killing every male. [26]They put
Hamor and his son Shechem to the sword and took Dinah from
Shechem's house and left. [27]The sons of Jacob came upon the dead
bodies and looted the city where[b] their sister had been defiled.
[28]They seized their flocks and herds and donkeys and everything
else of theirs in the city and out in the fields. [29]They carried off all
their wealth and all their women and children, taking as plunder
everything in the houses.
[30]Then Jacob said to Simeon and Levi, "You have brought
trouble on me by making me a stench to the Canaanites and Perizzites,
the people living in this land. We are few in number, and if
they join forces against me and attack me, I and my household will
be destroyed."
[31]But they replied, "Should he have treated our sister like a
prostitute?"

[a]17 Hebrew *daughter* [b]27 Or *because*

Jacob Returns to Bethel

35 Then God said to Jacob, "Go up to Bethel and settle there,
and build an altar there to God, who appeared to you when you
were fleeing from your brother Esau."
[2]So Jacob said to his household and to all who were with
him, "Get rid of the foreign gods you have with you, and purify
yourselves and change your clothes. [3]Then come, let us go up to
Bethel, where I will build an altar to God, who answered me in the
day of my distress and who has been with me wherever I have
gone." [4]So they gave Jacob all the foreign gods they had and the
rings in their ears, and Jacob buried them under the oak at
Shechem. [5]Then they set out, and the terror of God fell upon the
towns all around them so that no one pursued them.
[6]Jacob and all the people with him came to Luz (that is,
Bethel) in the land of Canaan. [7]There he built an altar, and he
called the place El Bethel,[a] because it was there that God revealed
himself to him when he was fleeing from his brother.
[8]Now Deborah, Rebekah's nurse, died and was buried under
the oak below Bethel. So it was named Allon Bacuth.[b]
[9]After Jacob returned from Paddan Aram,[c] God appeared to
him again and blessed him. [10]God said to him, "Your name is
Jacob,[d] but you will no longer be called Jacob; your name will be
Israel.[e]" So he named him Israel.
[11]And God said to him, "I am God Almighty[f]; be fruitful and
increase in number. A nation and a community of nations will
come from you, and kings will come from your body. [12]The land I
gave to Abraham and Isaac I also give to you, and I will give this

[a]7 *El Bethel* means *God of Bethel.* [b]8 *Allon Bacuth* means *oak of weeping.* [c]9 That is, Northwest Mesopotamia; also in verse 26 [d]10 *Jacob* means *he grasps the heel* (figuratively, *he deceives*). [e]10 *Israel* means *he struggles with God.* [f]11 Hebrew *El-Shaddai*

God said, *"Your name is Jacob, but you will no longer be called Jacob; your name will be Israel."*
Gen 35:10

35:2 *purify yourselves and change your clothes:* Those who wanted to worship God or come into God's presence needed to become ritually "clean" first (see Exod 19:10-14). Specific instructions for this kind of cleansing were later given in the Law of Moses (Lev 16:1-4; Num 8:5-8).

35:4 *oak at Shechem:* This may be the great tree mentioned in 12:6. See also the note at 13:18.

35:8 *Deborah:* See the note at 24:59.

35:9-11 *you will no longer be called Jacob; your name will be Israel:* This appears to be another version of Jacob's name being changed (32:24-30), of God's promises to his family (17:4-8; 28:13-15), and of his dedicating the rock at Bethel (28:18-22).

35:9-11 *Israel . . . God Almighty:* See the notes at 32:28 and 43:14.

35:7 Gen 28:10-22.

JACOB'S CHILDREN AND THEIR MOTHERS

LEAH	ZILPAH (Leah's servant)	BILHAH (Rachel's servant)	RACHEL
Reuben (1)	Gad (7)	Dan (5)	Joseph (12)
Simeon (2)	Asher (8)	Naphtali (6)	Benjamin (13)
Levi (3)			
Judah (4)			
Issachar (9)			
Zebulun (10)			
Dinah (11)			

Note: The numbers after Jacob's children's names indicate their birth order as given in Genesis 29–30; 35:16-26. See the mini-article called "Israel" on p. 264 for more about how the tribes of Israel are identified with Jacob's twelve sons.

35:14 *poured out a drink offering . . . poured oil:* Wine, like oil, was sometimes used to dedicate an object to God. See also Exod 29:38-41 and the note at 28:18.

35:15-19 *Bethel . . . Ephrath:* For Bethel, see the notes at 12:8,9 and 28:19. Ephrath is identified with Bethlehem (35:19; 48:7; see also Ruth 4:11; Mic 5:2). Bethlehem is located a few miles south of Jerusalem. In other passages, Rachel's grave is said to be in the territory of the tribe of Benjamin, which was north of Jerusalem (1 Sam 10:2; Jer 31:15).

35:18 *Ben-Oni . . . Benjamin:* In Hebrew "Ben-Oni" means "Son of my Sorrow," "Benjamin" can mean "Son at my Right Hand," which was considered the place of power in ancient times, or it can mean "Son of the South," since his other brothers were born in the north (29:28—30:23).

35:21 *Migdal Eder:* This means "tower of the flock," probably referring to a watchtower built to keep watch over flocks of sheep and goats and protect them from robbers and wild animals.

35:22 *his father's concubine Bilhah:* See the note at 22:20-24. Reuben later paid for what he did by losing his rights as the oldest son (1 Chr 5:1). See also 49:4.

35:22 *Jacob had twelve sons:* See 29:31—30:24.

35:27 *Mamre, near Kiriath Arba (that is, Hebron):* See the notes at 13:8 and 23:1,2.

36:1 *Esau (that is, Edom):* See the notes at 25:25,26 and 25:30.

36:2,3 *the women of Canaan:* See 26:34 and 28:9. See also the notes at 23:3 and 33:19—34:2.

land to your descendants after you." [13]Then God went up from
him at the place where he had talked with him.

[14]Jacob set up a stone pillar at the place where God had
talked with him, and he poured out a drink offering on it; he also
poured oil on it. [15]Jacob called the place where God had talked
with him Bethel.[a]

The Deaths of Rachel and Isaac

[16]Then they moved on from Bethel. While they were still
some distance from Ephrath, Rachel began to give birth and had
great difficulty. [17]And as she was having great difficulty in childbirth, the midwife said to her, "Don't be afraid, for you have
another son." [18]As she breathed her last—for she was dying—she
named her son Ben-Oni.[b] But his father named him Benjamin.[c]

[19]So Rachel died and was buried on the way to Ephrath (that
is, Bethlehem). [20]Over her tomb Jacob set up a pillar, and to this
day that pillar marks Rachel's tomb.

[21]Israel moved on again and pitched his tent beyond Migdal
Eder. [22]While Israel was living in that region, Reuben went in and
slept with his father's concubine Bilhah, and Israel heard of it.

Jacob had twelve sons:

[23]The sons of Leah:
Reuben the firstborn of Jacob,
Simeon, Levi, Judah, Issachar and Zebulun.

[24]The sons of Rachel:
Joseph and Benjamin.

[25]The sons of Rachel's maidservant Bilhah:
Dan and Naphtali.

[26]The sons of Leah's maidservant Zilpah:
Gad and Asher.

These were the sons of Jacob, who were born to him in Paddan Aram.

[27]Jacob came home to his father Isaac in Mamre, near
Kiriath Arba (that is, Hebron), where Abraham and Isaac had
stayed. [28]Isaac lived a hundred and eighty years. [29]Then he
breathed his last and died and was gathered to his people, old and
full of years. And his sons Esau and Jacob buried him.

Esau's Descendants

36 This is the account of Esau (that is, Edom).

[2]Esau took his wives from the women of Canaan: Adah
daughter of Elon the Hittite, and Oholibamah daughter of
Anah and granddaughter of Zibeon the Hivite— [3]also Basemath daughter of Ishmael and sister of Nebaioth.

---

[a]**15** *Bethel* means *house of God.* [b]**18** *Ben-Oni* means *son of my trouble.*
[c]**18** *Benjamin* means *son of my right hand.*

4Adah bore Eliphaz to Esau, Basemath bore Reuel, 5and
Oholibamah bore Jeush, Jalam and Korah. These were the
sons of Esau, who were born to him in Canaan.

6Esau took his wives and sons and daughters and all the
members of his household, as well as his livestock and all his
other animals and all the goods he had acquired in Canaan,
and moved to a land some distance from his brother Jacob.
7Their possessions were too great for them to remain together; the land where they were staying could not support them
both because of their livestock. 8So Esau (that is, Edom) settled in the hill country of Seir.

9This is the account of Esau the father of the Edomites in the
hill country of Seir.

10These are the names of Esau's sons:
Eliphaz, the son of Esau's wife Adah, and Reuel, the son of Esau's wife Basemath.

11The sons of Eliphaz:
Teman, Omar, Zepho, Gatam and Kenaz.
12Esau's son Eliphaz also had a concubine named Timna, who bore him Amalek. These were grandsons of Esau's wife Adah.

13The sons of Reuel:
Nahath, Zerah, Shammah and Mizzah. These were grandsons of Esau's wife Basemath.

14The sons of Esau's wife Oholibamah daughter of Anah and granddaughter of Zibeon, whom she bore to Esau:
Jeush, Jalam and Korah.

15These were the chiefs among Esau's descendants:
The sons of Eliphaz the firstborn of Esau:
Chiefs Teman, Omar, Zepho, Kenaz, 16Korah,[a] Gatam and
Amalek. These were the chiefs descended from Eliphaz in Edom; they were grandsons of Adah.

17The sons of Esau's son Reuel:
Chiefs Nahath, Zerah, Shammah and Mizzah. These were the chiefs descended from Reuel in Edom; they were grandsons of Esau's wife Basemath.

18The sons of Esau's wife Oholibamah:
Chiefs Jeush, Jalam and Korah. These were the chiefs descended from Esau's wife Oholibamah daughter of Anah.
19These were the sons of Esau (that is, Edom), and these
were their chiefs.

20These were the sons of Seir the Horite, who were living in
the region:

36:4,5,9-14 *the sons of Esau:* Compare the list in 36:4, 5 to the list in 36:9-14, which also includes Esau's grandchildren. Esau's descendants were the people of Edom, or Seir (see the note at 25:30).

Timna is called "a concubine" of Eliphaz. This translates a Hebrew word for a woman who was legally bound to a man, but without the full privileges of a wife.

36:15-19 *chiefs:* These are the common ancestors of a clan. The list of chiefs given here is another way of identifying the descendants of Esau. Compare this list with the previous one (36:9-14) and the list found in 1 Chronicles 1:35-37.

36:20 *the Horite:* See the note at 33:19—34:2.

[a]**16** Masoretic Text; Samaritan Pentateuch (see also Gen. 36:11 and 1 Chron. 1:36) does not have *Korah*.

Lotan, Shobal, Zibeon, Anah, 21 Dishon, Ezer and Dishan.
These sons of Seir in Edom were Horite chiefs.

22 The sons of Lotan:
Hori and Homam.[a] Timna was Lotan's sister.

23 The sons of Shobal:
Alvan, Manahath, Ebal, Shepho and Onam.

24 The sons of Zibeon:
Aiah and Anah. This is the Anah who discovered the hot
springs[b] in the desert while he was grazing the donkeys of
his father Zibeon.

25 The children of Anah:
Dishon and Oholibamah daughter of Anah.

26 The sons of Dishon[c]:
Hemdan, Eshban, Ithran and Keran.

27 The sons of Ezer:
Bilhan, Zaavan and Akan.

28 The sons of Dishan:
Uz and Aran.

29 These were the Horite chiefs:
Lotan, Shobal, Zibeon, Anah, 30 Dishon, Ezer and Dishan.
These were the Horite chiefs, according to their divisions,
in the land of Seir.

---

[a]**22** Hebrew *Hemam,* a variant of *Homam* (see 1 Chron. 1:39) [b]**24** Vulgate; Syriac *discovered water;* the meaning of the Hebrew for this word is uncertain.
[c]**26** Hebrew *Dishan,* a variant of *Dishon*

QUESTIONS ABOUT GENESIS 24:1—36:43

1. According to the Abraham's servant, why was the servant successful in finding a wife for Isaac? (Gen 24, especially 24:42-48) What can we learn about faith from the story?
2. From the time they were in their mother's womb, Isaac's sons, Esau and Jacob, were rivals. What were the main reasons for this rivalry? (25:19-34) What role did Rebekah play in their rivalry? (27:5-13) Name instances where this rivalry was played out.
3. Why couldn't Isaac take back the blessing of the firstborn that he mistakenly gave to Jacob? (27:30-40) In your opinion, do spoken promises have such power today? Why or why not?
4. What promise did Jacob receive at Bethel while he was dreaming? (28:10-15; see also 35:9-15) What did Jacob promise God in return? (28:20-22)
5. Who was Laban and how did he trick Jacob? (29:1-30) How did Jacob trick Laban in return? (30:25-43)
6. Jacob's name was changed to what? Where did this happen? (32:22-30; 35:9-11) Why is this important for the history of God's people, the descendants of Abraham?
7. Do you agree or disagree with the following statement: "God's purposes are carried out by people who sometimes act in sneaky and dishonorable ways." Explain, using examples from GENESIS.
8. These chapters show us much about personal, family, social, business, and religious life at the time of Abraham and Isaac. What strikes you as most different from our own life and culture? Do you think people lived "closer" to God then? Explain.

The Rulers of Edom

31 These were the kings who reigned in Edom before any Israelite king reigned[a]:

32 Bela son of Beor became king of Edom. His city was named Dinhabah.
33 When Bela died, Jobab son of Zerah from Bozrah succeeded him as king.
34 When Jobab died, Husham from the land of the Temanites succeeded him as king.
35 When Husham died, Hadad son of Bedad, who defeated Midian in the country of Moab, succeeded him as king. His city was named Avith.
36 When Hadad died, Samlah from Masrekah succeeded him as king.
37 When Samlah died, Shaul from Rehoboth on the river[b] succeeded him as king.
38 When Shaul died, Baal-Hanan son of Acbor succeeded him as king.
39 When Baal-Hanan son of Acbor died, Hadad[c] succeeded him as king. His city was named Pau, and his wife's name was Mehetabel daughter of Matred, the daughter of Me-Zahab.

40 These were the chiefs descended from Esau, by name, according to their clans and regions:
Timna, Alvah, Jetheth, 41 Oholibamah, Elah, Pinon, 42 Kenaz, Teman, Mibzar, 43 Magdiel and Iram. These were the chiefs of Edom, according to their settlements in the land they occupied.

This was Esau the father of the Edomites.

THE STORY OF JACOB'S SON, JOSEPH

With the exception of chapter 38, the final chapters focus on the story of Jacob and Rachel's son, Joseph. Near the end of this section, Jacob's descendants are settled in Egypt, setting the stage for the events in Exodus.

Joseph's Dreams

37 Jacob lived in the land where his father had stayed, the land of Canaan.

2 This is the account of Jacob.

Joseph, a young man of seventeen, was tending the flocks with his brothers, the sons of Bilhah and the sons of Zilpah, his father's wives, and he brought their father a bad report about them.

---

[a]**31** Or *before an Israelite king reigned over them* [b]**37** Possibly the Euphrates [c]**39** Many manuscripts of the Masoretic Text, Samaritan Pentateuch and Syriac (see also 1 Chron. 1:50); most manuscripts of the Masoretic Text *Hadar*

36:31-39 *before any Israelite king reigned:* The land of Edom was ruled by kings long before Israel was (Num 20:14).

36:40-43 Gen 25:12-16. **37:2** Gen 30:3,9,22-24.

The Story of Joseph, by John August Swanson, 1986. Joseph was the eleventh son of Jacob (Israel) and the first one to be born to his favorite wife, Rachel. Jacob was very fond of Joseph and even had a richly ornamented robe made for him. Joseph's brothers were jealous and sold him to a caravan of merchants who were on their way to Egypt. (See 37:1-36.) Eventually, Joseph would become one of the Egyptian pharaoh's most trusted officials (see 41:37-43).

37:3 *richly ornamented robe:* The robe probably was long with sleeves as would normally be worn by wealthy men, and not the more common sleeveless robe (like a long open vest) worn for everyday work (2 Sam 13:18).

37:9 *eleven stars:* Often in the ancient world the positions of the sun, the moon, and the stars were studied for signs of God's purpose, but their appearance in Joseph's dream had a specific meaning that his father and brothers seemed to understand.

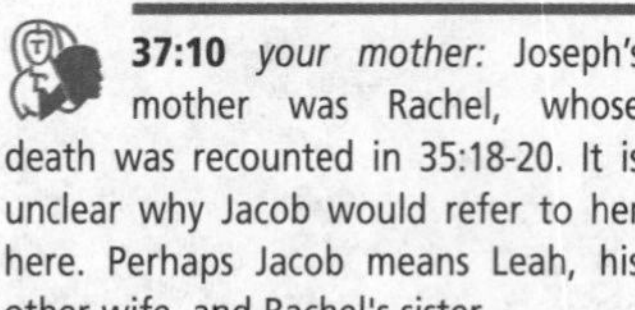

37:10 *your mother:* Joseph's mother was Rachel, whose death was recounted in 35:18-20. It is unclear why Jacob would refer to her here. Perhaps Jacob means Leah, his other wife, and Rachel's sister.

37:5-11 Gen 42:6; 43:26; 44:14; 50:18; Deut 33:16; Acts 7:9.

3 Now Israel loved Joseph more than any of his other sons,
because he had been born to him in his old age; and he made a
richly ornamented[a] robe for him. 4 When his brothers saw that
their father loved him more than any of them, they hated him and
could not speak a kind word to him.

5 Joseph had a dream, and when he told it to his brothers,
they hated him all the more. 6 He said to them, "Listen to this
dream I had: 7 We were binding sheaves of grain out in the field
when suddenly my sheaf rose and stood upright, while your
sheaves gathered around mine and bowed down to it."

8 His brothers said to him, "Do you intend to reign over us?
Will you actually rule us?" And they hated him all the more
because of his dream and what he had said.

9 Then he had another dream, and he told it to his brothers.
"Listen," he said, "I had another dream, and this time the sun and
moon and eleven stars were bowing down to me."

10 When he told his father as well as his brothers, his father
rebuked him and said, "What is this dream you had? Will your
mother and I and your brothers actually come and bow down to
the ground before you?" 11 His brothers were jealous of him, but
his father kept the matter in mind.

---

[a]3 The meaning of the Hebrew for *richly ornamented* is uncertain; also in verses 23 and 32.

Joseph Sold by His Brothers

12Now his brothers had gone to graze their father's flocks near Shechem, 13and Israel said to Joseph, "As you know, your brothers are grazing the flocks near Shechem. Come, I am going to send you to them."

"Very well," he replied.

14So he said to him, "Go and see if all is well with your brothers and with the flocks, and bring word back to me." Then he sent him off from the Valley of Hebron.

When Joseph arrived at Shechem, 15a man found him wandering around in the fields and asked him, "What are you looking for?"

16He replied, "I'm looking for my brothers. Can you tell me where they are grazing their flocks?"

17"They have moved on from here," the man answered. "I heard them say, 'Let's go to Dothan.' "

So Joseph went after his brothers and found them near Dothan. 18But they saw him in the distance, and before he reached them, they plotted to kill him.

19"Here comes that dreamer!" they said to each other. 20"Come now, let's kill him and throw him into one of these cisterns and say that a ferocious animal devoured him. Then we'll see what comes of his dreams."

21When Reuben heard this, he tried to rescue him from their hands. "Let's not take his life," he said. 22"Don't shed any blood. Throw him into this cistern here in the desert, but don't lay a hand on him." Reuben said this to rescue him from them and take him back to his father.

23So when Joseph came to his brothers, they stripped him of his robe—the richly ornamented robe he was wearing— 24and they took him and threw him into the cistern. Now the cistern was empty; there was no water in it.

25As they sat down to eat their meal, they looked up and saw a caravan of Ishmaelites coming from Gilead. Their camels were loaded with spices, balm and myrrh, and they were on their way to take them down to Egypt.

26Judah said to his brothers, "What will we gain if we kill our brother and cover up his blood? 27Come, let's sell him to the Ishmaelites and not lay our hands on him; after all, he is our brother, our own flesh and blood." His brothers agreed.

28So when the Midianite merchants came by, his brothers pulled Joseph up out of the cistern and sold him for twenty shekels[a] of silver to the Ishmaelites, who took him to Egypt.

29When Reuben returned to the cistern and saw that Joseph was not there, he tore his clothes. 30He went back to his brothers and said, "The boy isn't there! Where can I turn now?"

[a]**28** That is, about 8 ounces (about 0.2 kilogram)

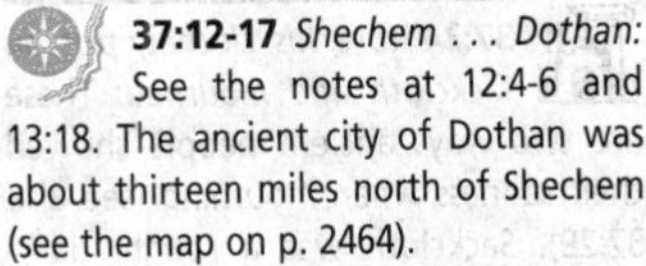

37:12-17 *Shechem . . . Dothan:* See the notes at 12:4-6 and 13:18. The ancient city of Dothan was about thirteen miles north of Shechem (see the map on p. 2464).

37:20 *one of these cisterns:* This probably was an open well used to store rain water.

37:21 *Reuben:* Jacob's oldest son (29:31,32).

37:25 *Ishmaelites . . . Gilead . . . Egypt:* The Ishmaelites were descendants of Ishmael, the son of Abraham and the Egyptian slave woman Hagar (16:1-16; 25:12-18). The Ishmaelites were generally known as nomads and caravan traders. See also the note at 31:21 and the mini-article called "Egypt," p. 135.

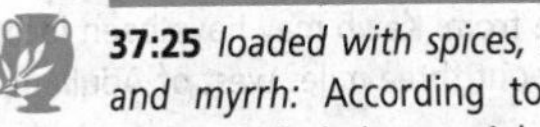

37:25 *loaded with spices, balm and myrrh:* According to the Hebrew, these included a special balm or ointment, made from trees in Gilead, known for its healing power (Jer 8:22; 46:11) and myrrh, a dark-red gum with a strong smell and a bitter taste that comes from a bush or tree grown in Arabia and Africa. Myrrh was often crushed into powder and used to make expensive perfumes and ointments. For more, see the chart called "Spices and Perfumes," p. 1278.

37:28 *Midianite merchants . . . Ishmaelites:* According to Genesis 25:1,2,12, the Midianites and Ishmaelites were descendants of Abraham, and in Judges 8:22-24 the two names describe the same people. It is possible that in this passage "Ishmaelite" has the meaning of "nomadic traders," while "Midianite" refers to the national or tribal identity of these traders.

37:28 *twenty shekels of silver:* See the note at 20:16.

37:19 Gen 37:5-10. **37:28** Acts 7:9.

[31]Then they got Joseph's robe, slaughtered a goat and dipped the robe in the blood. [32]They took the ornamented robe back to their father and said, "We found this. Examine it to see whether it is your son's robe."

[33]He recognized it and said, "It is my son's robe! Some ferocious animal has devoured him. Joseph has surely been torn to pieces."

[34]Then Jacob tore his clothes, put on sackcloth and mourned for his son many days. [35]All his sons and daughters came to comfort him, but he refused to be comforted. "No," he said, "in mourning will I go down to the grave[a] to my son." So his father wept for him.

[36]Meanwhile, the Midianites[b] sold Joseph in Egypt to Potiphar, one of Pharaoh's officials, the captain of the guard.

Judah and Tamar

38 At that time, Judah left his brothers and went down to stay with a man of Adullam named Hirah. [2]There Judah met the daughter of a Canaanite man named Shua. He married her and lay with her; [3]she became pregnant and gave birth to a son, who was named Er. [4]She conceived again and gave birth to a son and named him Onan. [5]She gave birth to still another son and named him Shelah. It was at Kezib that she gave birth to him.

[6]Judah got a wife for Er, his firstborn, and her name was Tamar. [7]But Er, Judah's firstborn, was wicked in the LORD's sight; so the LORD put him to death.

[8]Then Judah said to Onan, "Lie with your brother's wife and fulfill your duty to her as a brother-in-law to produce offspring for your brother." [9]But Onan knew that the offspring would not be his; so whenever he lay with his brother's wife, he spilled his semen on the ground to keep from producing offspring for his brother. [10]What he did was wicked in the LORD's sight; so he put him to death also.

[11]Judah then said to his daughter-in-law Tamar, "Live as a widow in your father's house until my son Shelah grows up." For he thought, "He may die too, just like his brothers." So Tamar went to live in her father's house.

[12]After a long time Judah's wife, the daughter of Shua, died. When Judah had recovered from his grief, he went up to Timnah, to the men who were shearing his sheep, and his friend Hirah the Adullamite went with him.

[13]When Tamar was told, "Your father-in-law is on his way to Timnah to shear his sheep," [14]she took off her widow's clothes, covered herself with a veil to disguise herself, and then sat down at the entrance to Enaim, which is on the road to Timnah. For she

37:34 *tore his clothes, put on sackcloth and mourned:* These are two ways ancient people showed their sadness when mourning (see also 37:29). Sackcloth was a rough, dark-colored cloth made from goat or camel hair that was usually used to make grain sacks. See also the illustration on p. 1551.

37:36 *Potiphar, one of Pharaoh's officials:* Potiphar was in charge of the personal bodyguards of the king. See also the mini-article called "King of Egypt (Pharaoh)," p. 110.

38:1-5 *Adullam . . . Kezib:* Adullam was a town southwest of Jerusalem near Bethlehem (2 Chr 11:5-7). Kezib may be the same as Aczib (Josh 15:44) and Cozeba (1 Chr 4:21,22), where Shelah's descendants were said to be from. Kezib may have been located about three miles west of Adullam.

38:2 *Judah met the daughter of a Canaanite man:* Judah was the fourth son born to Jacob and Leah (29:35). Men from the tribes of Israel were not supposed to marry Canaanite women. See the note at 28:1,2.

38:6 *Judah got a wife for Er:* In the ancient world, parents decided whom their children would marry.

38:8,9 *your duty . . . offspring would not be his:* This refers to a custom known as "levirate marriage" (from the Hebrew for brother-in-law). If a man died without having children, his brother was to marry the dead man's wife and have a child, who would be considered the child of the dead brother (Deut 25:5,6). Because Er died before he and Tamar had any children, Onan expected to receive his brother Er's share of the family inheritance when their father died. If Onan gave his brother's widow (Tamar) a son, that son would inherit Er's portion of the family inheritance, leaving Onan a smaller portion. That was why he did not want to produce offspring for his brother.

[a]**35** Hebrew *Sheol* [b]**36** Samaritan Pentateuch, Septuagint, Vulgate and Syriac (see also verse 28); Masoretic Text *Medanites*

saw that, though Shelah had now grown up, she had not been
given to him as his wife.
15 When Judah saw her, he thought she was a prostitute, for
she had covered her face. 16 Not realizing that she was his daughter-
in-law, he went over to her by the roadside and said, "Come now,
let me sleep with you."
"And what will you give me to sleep with you?" she asked.
17 "I'll send you a young goat from my flock," he said.
"Will you give me something as a pledge until you send it?"
she asked.
18 He said, "What pledge should I give you?"
"Your seal and its cord, and the staff in your hand," she
answered. So he gave them to her and slept with her, and she
became pregnant by him. 19 After she left, she took off her veil and
put on her widow's clothes again.
20 Meanwhile Judah sent the young goat by his friend the
Adullamite in order to get his pledge back from the woman, but
he did not find her. 21 He asked the men who lived there, "Where is
the shrine prostitute who was beside the road at Enaim?"
"There hasn't been any shrine prostitute here," they said.
22 So he went back to Judah and said, "I didn't find her.
Besides, the men who lived there said, 'There hasn't been any
shrine prostitute here.' "
23 Then Judah said, "Let her keep what she has, or we will
become a laughingstock. After all, I did send her this young goat,
but you didn't find her."
24 About three months later Judah was told, "Your daughter-
in-law Tamar is guilty of prostitution, and as a result she is now
pregnant."
Judah said, "Bring her out and have her burned to death!"
25 As she was being brought out, she sent a message to her
father-in-law. "I am pregnant by the man who owns these," she
said. And she added, "See if you recognize whose seal and cord and
staff these are."
26 Judah recognized them and said, "She is more righteous
than I, since I wouldn't give her to my son Shelah." And he did not
sleep with her again.
27 When the time came for her to give birth, there were twin
boys in her womb. 28 As she was giving birth, one of them put out
his hand; so the midwife took a scarlet thread and tied it on his
wrist and said, "This one came out first." 29 But when he drew back
his hand, his brother came out, and she said, "So this is how you
have broken out!" And he was named Perez.[a] 30 Then his brother,
who had the scarlet thread on his wrist, came out and he was given
the name Zerah.[b]

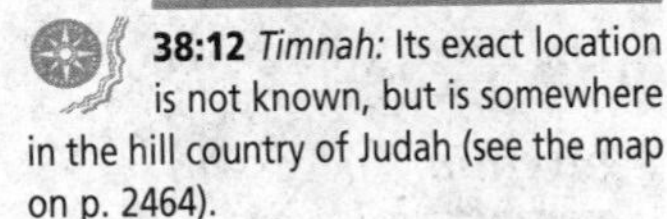

38:12 *Timnah:* Its exact location is not known, but is somewhere in the hill country of Judah (see the map on p. 2464).

38:15-21 *prostitute:* Different Hebrew words for prostitute are used in 38:15 and 21. The word in 38:15 is a less dignified term, while the one in 38:21 refers to a woman who engages in prostitution in connection with the worship of one of the Canaanite fertility gods. As Judah's friend, Hirah uses the more dignified term when speaking to the people of Enaim. See also the mini-article called "Prostitution in the Bible," p. 1688.

38:18 *Your seal . . . the staff:* The seal was actually a type of ring that could be rolled over soft clay as a way of marking a document with one's personal seal. The staff may have been just a walking stick, or it may have been a symbol of power and the sign of Judah's leadership in the tribe.

38:21 *Enaim:* This means "two springs," and was probably located between Adullam and Timnah (see the notes at 38:1-5 and 38:12).

38:24 *prostitution:* See the note at 38:15-21. The Hebrew word used for "prostitute" in this verse is the less dignified term.

38:27-30 *twin boys . . . Perez . . . Zerah:* In Hebrew "Perez" sounds like a word for "opening" and means "breaking out," and "Zerah" means "bright," probably referring to the red thread. Perez was an ancestor of King David (Ruth 4:18-22) and was named along with Zerah as two clans of the tribe of Judah (Num 26:19-22). Compare this story to the story of the birth of the twins, Jacob and Esau (25:24-26).

[a]**29** *Perez* means *breaking out.* [b]**30** *Zerah* can mean *scarlet* or *brightness.*

Joseph and Potiphar's Wife

39 Now Joseph had been taken down to Egypt. Potiphar, an Egyptian who was one of Pharaoh's officials, the captain of the guard, bought him from the Ishmaelites who had taken him there. [2]The LORD was with Joseph and he prospered, and he lived in the house of his Egyptian master. [3]When his master saw that the LORD was with him and that the LORD gave him success in everything he did, [4]Joseph found favor in his eyes and became his attendant. Potiphar put him in charge of his household, and he entrusted to his care everything he owned. [5]From the time he put him in charge of his household and of all that he owned, the LORD blessed the household of the Egyptian because of Joseph. The blessing of the LORD was on everything Potiphar had, both in the house and in the field. [6]So he left in Joseph's care everything he had; with Joseph in charge, he did not concern himself with anything except the food he ate.

Now Joseph was well-built and handsome, [7]and after a while his master's wife took notice of Joseph and said, "Come to bed with me!"

[8]But he refused. "With me in charge," he told her, "my master does not concern himself with anything in the house; everything he owns he has entrusted to my care. [9]No one is greater in this house than I am. My master has withheld nothing from me except you, because you are his wife. How then could I do such a wicked thing and sin against God?" [10]And though she spoke to Joseph day after day, he refused to go to bed with her or even be with her.

[11]One day he went into the house to attend to his duties, and none of the household servants was inside. [12]She caught him by his cloak and said, "Come to bed with me!" But he left his cloak in her hand and ran out of the house.

[13]When she saw that he had left his cloak in her hand and had run out of the house, [14]she called her household servants. "Look," she said to them, "this Hebrew has been brought to us to make sport of us! He came in here to sleep with me, but I screamed. [15]When he heard me scream for help, he left his cloak beside me and ran out of the house."

[16]She kept his cloak beside her until his master came home. [17]Then she told him this story: "That Hebrew slave you brought us came to me to make sport of me. [18]But as soon as I screamed for help, he left his cloak beside me and ran out of the house."

[19]When his master heard the story his wife told him, saying, "This is how your slave treated me," he burned with anger. [20]Joseph's master took him and put him in prison, the place where the king's prisoners were confined.

But while Joseph was there in the prison, [21]the LORD was with him; he showed him kindness and granted him favor in the eyes of the prison warden. [22]So the warden put Joseph in charge of

The LORD was with Joseph. . . . the LORD gave him success in everything he did.
Gen 39:2-3

39:1 *Potiphar . . . one of Pharaoh's officials:* See the note at 37:36.

39:2,3 *LORD:* See the note at 2:4.

39:5 *blessing:* The promise to Abraham that his descendants would be a blessing to other nations was being further fulfilled in Joseph (12:2,3).

39:9 *sin against God:* Wanting or "coveting" another person's wife or husband was prohibited in the Law of Moses (Exod 20:17). See also the mini-articles called "Sin," p. 2181 and "Ten Commandments," p. 354.

39:17 *Hebrew:* See the note at 14:13.

39:21 *the LORD was with him:* The usual punishment for rape, the crime Joseph was being accused of, was the death penalty. Imprisonment, with the hope of eventual release, was a much lighter sentence. As in other stories in GENESIS, God is being given credit for the hero's good fortune (see also the note at 31:9).

39:1-3 Gen 37:36; Acts 7:9.

all those held in the prison, and he was made responsible for all
that was done there. [23]The warden paid no attention to anything
under Joseph's care, because the LORD was with Joseph and gave
him success in whatever he did.

The Cupbearer and the Baker

40 Some time later, the cupbearer and the baker of the king of
Egypt offended their master, the king of Egypt. [2]Pharaoh was
angry with his two officials, the chief cupbearer and the chief
baker, [3]and put them in custody in the house of the captain of the
guard, in the same prison where Joseph was confined. [4]The captain of the guard assigned them to Joseph, and he attended them.
After they had been in custody for some time, [5]each of the
two men—the cupbearer and the baker of the king of Egypt, who
were being held in prison—had a dream the same night, and each
dream had a meaning of its own.
[6]When Joseph came to them the next morning, he saw that
they were dejected. [7]So he asked Pharaoh's officials who were in
custody with him in his master's house, "Why are your faces so sad
today?"
[8]"We both had dreams," they answered, "but there is no one
to interpret them."
Then Joseph said to them, "Do not interpretations belong to
God? Tell me your dreams."
[9]So the chief cupbearer told Joseph his dream. He said to
him, "In my dream I saw a vine in front of me, [10]and on the vine
were three branches. As soon as it budded, it blossomed, and its
clusters ripened into grapes. [11]Pharaoh's cup was in my hand, and
I took the grapes, squeezed them into Pharaoh's cup and put the
cup in his hand."
[12]"This is what it means," Joseph said to him. "The three
branches are three days. [13]Within three days Pharaoh will lift up
your head and restore you to your position, and you will put Pharaoh's cup in his hand, just as you used to do when you were his
cupbearer. [14]But when all goes well with you, remember me and
show me kindness; mention me to Pharaoh and get me out of this
prison. [15]For I was forcibly carried off from the land of the
Hebrews, and even here I have done nothing to deserve being put
in a dungeon."
[16]When the chief baker saw that Joseph had given a favorable
interpretation, he said to Joseph, "I too had a dream: On my head
were three baskets of bread.[a] [17]In the top basket were all kinds of
baked goods for Pharaoh, but the birds were eating them out of
the basket on my head."
[18]"This is what it means," Joseph said. "The three baskets are

[a]**16** Or *three wicker baskets*

40:1-3 *cupbearer:* The cupbearer was the king's personal servant, an important and trusted official in the royal court. Cupbearers personally served wine to the king and were sometimes asked to taste the wine before the king drank any of it to make sure it wasn't poisoned. See also the illustration on p. 874.

40:5 *each dream had a meaning of its own:* In the ancient world dreams were thought to have specific meanings and could predict the future if they were correctly interpreted. God sometimes spoke to people in dreams (Gen 20:3; 28:10-15; Matt 1:20-23).

40:15 *land of the Hebrews:* This means Canaan. See 37:1,28,36 and the note at 14:13.

40:15 *dungeon:* The Hebrew word translated "dungeon" in this verse is the same word translated as "cistern" in 37:20,24,28 earlier in the Joseph story. Through this clever word play Joseph's dungeon is compared to his being in the cistern back in Canaan.

41:1 *Pharaoh . . . Nile:* See the mini-articles called "King of Egypt (Pharaoh)," below and "Egypt," p. 135. The Nile River, the word's second longest river, floods its banks each year leaving fresh muddy soil behind that is good for growing crops. This annual flooding of the Nile was so important to maintaining the fertility of the land that the Nile itself came to be considered one of Egypt's gods. Cattle often stood in the waters of the Nile up to their necks (41:3) to stay out of the sun and keep away insects. For the location of the Nile, see the map on p. 2463; see also the illustration on p. 922.

41:6 *east wind:* A hot wind that blew from the desert area west of the Nile valley and dried up crops. This was known in the area as a "sirocco" wind.

three days. [19]Within three days Pharaoh will lift off your head and
hang you on a tree.[a] And the birds will eat away your flesh."
[20]Now the third day was Pharaoh's birthday, and he gave a
feast for all his officials. He lifted up the heads of the chief cupbearer and the chief baker in the presence of his officials: [21]He
restored the chief cupbearer to his position, so that he once again
put the cup into Pharaoh's hand, [22]but he hanged[b] the chief baker,
just as Joseph had said to them in his interpretation.
[23]The chief cupbearer, however, did not remember Joseph;
he forgot him.

Pharaoh's Dreams

41 When two full years had passed, Pharaoh had a dream: He
was standing by the Nile, [2]when out of the river there came up
seven cows, sleek and fat, and they grazed among the reeds. [3]After
them, seven other cows, ugly and gaunt, came up out of the Nile
and stood beside those on the riverbank. [4]And the cows that were
ugly and gaunt ate up the seven sleek, fat cows. Then Pharaoh
woke up.
[5]He fell asleep again and had a second dream: Seven heads of
grain, healthy and good, were growing on a single stalk. [6]After
them, seven other heads of grain sprouted—thin and scorched by
the east wind. [7]The thin heads of grain swallowed up the seven
healthy, full heads. Then Pharaoh woke up; it had been a dream.

---

[a]19 Or *and impale you on a pole* [b]22 Or *impaled*

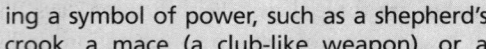

KING OF EGYPT (PHARAOH)

Pharaoh is the title for the chief ruler of Egypt and comes from two Egyptian words that mean "great house." To the pharaoh's name was added other titles of honor, such as "Son of Re" (the Egyptian sun god) or "King of Upper and Lower Egypt." About the time of Abraham, "pharaoh" meant "king," so the Bible uses both these terms to refer to the ruler of Egypt. When the Egyptian king died, he was identified with Osiris (shown here), the god who went through death and overcame it, and was thought to rule in the world of the dead. Ancient pictures of the pharaohs often show them holding a symbol of power, such as a shepherd's crook, a mace (a club-like weapon), or a curved sword. On the headpiece was a cobra snake symbol, which was supposed to protect the pharaoh from his enemies. For more on the kingdom of Egypt, see the article called "The Ancient World: Peoples, Powers, and Politics," p. 919.

A number of Egypt's pharaoh kings are mentioned in the Jewish Scriptures. For more see the chart called "Egyptian Kings (Pharaohs) in the Bible," on p. 111, and the chart called "Egyptian Dynasties" on p. 136.

EGYPTIAN KINGS (PHARAOHS) IN THE BIBLE

KING	IDENTITY OR POSSIBLE IDENTITY	SCRIPTURE PASSAGES
Unnamed	Befriended Abraham and took Sarah into his household	Gen 12:14-20
Unnamed	Put Joseph in charge of food supply in Egypt	Gen 41:37-57
Sety I (Sethos) 1291-1279 B.C.	Possibly the "new king" (Exod 1:8) who was Pharaoh during the Hebrews' time of slavery in Egypt	Exod 1–4
Rameses II 1279-1212 B.C.	Followed Sety I and may have been the Pharaoh at the time of Hebrews' exodus from Egypt	Exod 5–14
Unnamed	Father of King Solomon's Egyptian wife	1 Kgs 3:1; 7:8
Shishak 945-924 B.C.	Raided the Jerusalem temple during the reign of Rehoboam of Judah, but let King Jeroboam of Israel hide in his palace	1 Kgs 14:25,26; 2 Chr 12:2-9
So 727-720 B.C.	This may have been Pharaoh Osorkon IV, who was sent a message by King Hoshea of Israel just before the Israelites rebelled against the king of Assyria	2 Kgs 17:1-4
Tirhakah 690-664 B.C.	Called "the Cushite king of Egypt" who battled with Assyria during the reign of King Hezekiah of Judah	2 Kgs 19:9; Isa 37:9
Neco 610-595 B.C.	Killed King Josiah of Judah at Megiddo, replaced Jehoahaz with Jehoiakim as Judah's ruler, and was defeated by King Nebuchadnezzar of Babylon	2 Kgs 23:29-35; 2 Chr 35:20—36:4
Hophra 589-570 B.C.	The prophet Jeremiah said Hophra would be captured by his enemy Nebuchadnezzar of Babylonia	Jer 43:6-13; 44:30
Other unnamed kings	Little is known about these kings	1 Kgs 11:14-22; 2 Kgs 18:21; 1 Chr 4:17,18

8 In the morning his mind was troubled, so he sent for all the magicians and wise men of Egypt. Pharaoh told them his dreams, but no one could interpret them for him.

9 Then the chief cupbearer said to Pharaoh, "Today I am reminded of my shortcomings. 10 Pharaoh was once angry with his servants, and he imprisoned me and the chief baker in the house of the captain of the guard. 11 Each of us had a dream the same night, and each dream had a meaning of its own. 12 Now a young Hebrew was there with us, a servant of the captain of the guard. We told him our dreams, and he interpreted them for us, giving each man the interpretation of his dream. 13 And things turned out exactly as he interpreted them to us: I was restored to my position, and the other man was hanged.[a]"

14 So Pharaoh sent for Joseph, and he was quickly brought from the dungeon. When he had shaved and changed his clothes, he came before Pharaoh.

41:8 *magicians and wise men:* The king had advisers who practiced magic and tried to read future events by looking at how light reflected off liquids in a cup (44:5,15). The wise men may have been priests who tried to get messages (oracles) from unseen powers. See also the note at 30:27,28.

41:9 *cupbearer:* See the note at 40:1-3.

---

[a]**13** Or *impaled*

41:16 *God will give Pharaoh the answer:* The episode about the king's dreams shows that Joseph's God is more powerful than the Egyptian magic and wisdom. For other examples of how the LORD God's power is superior to that of a foreign king's court magicians, see Exodus 7:8-12; 8:16-19; 9:11; Daniel 5:8, 15-28.

41:27 *seven years of famine:* Long periods of drought and grain shortages were not common in Egypt because the Nile River overflowed nearly every year, providing water for crops.

41:38 *the spirit of God:* Pharaoh recognizes that Joseph's wisdom and ability as a manager is from God. See also the note at 39:21.

41:24 Gen 41:8.

15 Pharaoh said to Joseph, "I had a dream, and no one can
interpret it. But I have heard it said of you that when you hear a
dream you can interpret it."

16 "I cannot do it," Joseph replied to Pharaoh, "but God will
give Pharaoh the answer he desires."

17 Then Pharaoh said to Joseph, "In my dream I was standing
on the bank of the Nile, 18 when out of the river there came up
seven cows, fat and sleek, and they grazed among the reeds. 19 After
them, seven other cows came up—scrawny and very ugly and lean.
I had never seen such ugly cows in all the land of Egypt. 20 The
lean, ugly cows ate up the seven fat cows that came up first. 21 But
even after they ate them, no one could tell that they had done so;
they looked just as ugly as before. Then I woke up.

22 "In my dreams I also saw seven heads of grain, full and
good, growing on a single stalk. 23 After them, seven other heads
sprouted—withered and thin and scorched by the east wind. 24 The
thin heads of grain swallowed up the seven good heads. I told this
to the magicians, but none could explain it to me."

25 Then Joseph said to Pharaoh, "The dreams of Pharaoh are
one and the same. God has revealed to Pharaoh what he is about
to do. 26 The seven good cows are seven years, and the seven good
heads of grain are seven years; it is one and the same dream. 27 The
seven lean, ugly cows that came up afterward are seven years, and
so are the seven worthless heads of grain scorched by the east
wind: They are seven years of famine.

28 "It is just as I said to Pharaoh: God has shown Pharaoh what
he is about to do. 29 Seven years of great abundance are coming
throughout the land of Egypt, 30 but seven years of famine will follow
them. Then all the abundance in Egypt will be forgotten, and the
famine will ravage the land. 31 The abundance in the land will not be
remembered, because the famine that follows it will be so severe.
32 The reason the dream was given to Pharaoh in two forms is that
the matter has been firmly decided by God, and God will do it soon.

33 "And now let Pharaoh look for a discerning and wise man
and put him in charge of the land of Egypt. 34 Let Pharaoh appoint
commissioners over the land to take a fifth of the harvest of Egypt
during the seven years of abundance. 35 They should collect all the
food of these good years that are coming and store up the grain
under the authority of Pharaoh, to be kept in the cities for food.
36 This food should be held in reserve for the country, to be used
during the seven years of famine that will come upon Egypt, so
that the country may not be ruined by the famine."

37 The plan seemed good to Pharaoh and to all his officials.
38 So Pharaoh asked them, "Can we find anyone like this man, one
in whom is the spirit of God[a]?"

---

[a] **38** Or *of the gods*

Joseph's Granaries from a thirteenth century mosaic in the Church of San Marco, Venice, artist unknown. Joseph was a Hebrew servant of the king of Egypt (Pharaoh). He interpreted two of the Pharaoh's dreams, telling him that there would be seven years in which the people would have more than enough grain to live on, followed by seven years of famine. To save the people from starving, Joseph advised the king to store one-fifth of the crop during each of the seven years when there would be more than enough to eat. (See 41:1-36.) In this mosaic the artist made the storehouses (granaries) look like the pyramids of Egypt.

39Then Pharaoh said to Joseph, "Since God has made all this
known to you, there is no one so discerning and wise as you. 40You
shall be in charge of my palace, and all my people are to submit to
your orders. Only with respect to the throne will I be greater than
you."

Joseph in Charge of Egypt

41So Pharaoh said to Joseph, "I hereby put you in charge of
the whole land of Egypt." 42Then Pharaoh took his signet ring
from his finger and put it on Joseph's finger. He dressed him
in robes of fine linen and put a gold chain around his neck. 43He
had him ride in a chariot as his second-in-command,[a] and men
shouted before him, "Make way[b]!" Thus he put him in charge of
the whole land of Egypt.
44Then Pharaoh said to Joseph, "I am Pharaoh, but without

[a]43 Or *in the chariot of his second-in-command*; or *in his second chariot* [b]43 Or *Bow down*

41:41-43 *chariot . . . second-in-command:* The symbols of royal authority given to Joseph were a signet ring (with the king's symbol, see Esth 3:10), a special robe (see Esth 6:11), and a golden neck chain (see Dan 5:7,29). Riding in a royal chariot was a sign of great power. For more about chariots, see the article called "Trade and Travel," p. 948 and the illustration on p. 160.

41:40 Acts 7:10.

your word no one will lift hand or foot in all Egypt.” 45Pharaoh
gave Joseph the name Zaphenath-Paneah and gave him Asenath
daughter of Potiphera, priest of On,[a] to be his wife. And Joseph
went throughout the land of Egypt.
46Joseph was thirty years old when he entered the service of
Pharaoh king of Egypt. And Joseph went out from Pharaoh’s presence and traveled throughout Egypt. 47During the seven years of
abundance the land produced plentifully. 48Joseph collected all the
food produced in those seven years of abundance in Egypt and
stored it in the cities. In each city he put the food grown in the
fields surrounding it. 49Joseph stored up huge quantities of grain,
like the sand of the sea; it was so much that he stopped keeping
records because it was beyond measure.
50Before the years of famine came, two sons were born to
Joseph by Asenath daughter of Potiphera, priest of On. 51Joseph
named his firstborn Manasseh[b] and said, “It is because God has
made me forget all my trouble and all my father’s household.”
52The second son he named Ephraim[c] and said, “It is because God
has made me fruitful in the land of my suffering.”
53The seven years of abundance in Egypt came to an end,
54and the seven years of famine began, just as Joseph had said.
There was famine in all the other lands, but in the whole land of
Egypt there was food. 55When all Egypt began to feel the famine,
the people cried to Pharaoh for food. Then Pharaoh told all the
Egyptians, “Go to Joseph and do what he tells you.”
56When the famine had spread over the whole country,
Joseph opened the storehouses and sold grain to the Egyptians, for
the famine was severe throughout Egypt. 57And all the countries
came to Egypt to buy grain from Joseph, because the famine was
severe in all the world.

Joseph’s Brothers Go to Egypt

42 When Jacob learned that there was grain in Egypt, he said to
his sons, “Why do you just keep looking at each other?” 2He continued, “I have heard that there is grain in Egypt. Go down there
and buy some for us, so that we may live and not die.”
3Then ten of Joseph’s brothers went down to buy grain from
Egypt. 4But Jacob did not send Benjamin, Joseph’s brother, with
the others, because he was afraid that harm might come to him.
5So Israel’s sons were among those who went to buy grain, for the
famine was in the land of Canaan also.
6Now Joseph was the governor of the land, the one who sold
grain to all its people. So when Joseph’s brothers arrived, they
bowed down to him with their faces to the ground. 7As soon as

[a]45 That is, Heliopolis; also in verse 50 [b]51 *Manasseh* sounds like and may be derived from the Hebrew for *forget.* [c]52 *Ephraim* sounds like the Hebrew for *twice fruitful.*

41:45 *Zaphenath-Paneah . . . Asenath daughter of Potiphera:* The ceremony of making Joseph an Egyptian official ended with him receiving an Egyptian name that may mean “God speaks, he lives.” Though the king used Joseph to serve his political purposes, he did not realize that Joseph’s promotion was part of God’s greater plan (45:5-8; 50:19,20).

The name of Joseph’s new wife “Asenath,” may mean “belonging to Neith” (an Egyptian goddess). Her father Potiphera’s name may mean “given by Ra” (the Egyptian sun god).

41:45 *On:* Also translated Heliopolis. This name in Greek means “city of the sun” and was located about six miles northeast of modern Cairo.

41:51,52 *Manasseh . . . Ephraim:* In Hebrew “Manasseh” sounds like a word for “forget,” and “Ephraim” means “twice fruitful,” “fruitful,” or “pastureland.” See also the note at 49:22-26.

41:57 *all the countries:* This probably refers to all the nearby lands in the Middle East. The food shortage brings people to Egypt where one of God’s people, a descendant of Abraham, is in a position to be a blessing to them (see 12:2,3).

42:3,4 *Ten of Joseph’s brothers . . . Benjamin:* See the chart called “Jacob’s Children and Their Mothers,” p. 99. Joseph’s brothers may have thought he was dead because so much time had passed since they sold him to a caravan, or, they may have preferred to tell Joseph the same story they had told their father as a way of keeping the Egyptian official (Joseph) from learning how they had mistreated their own brother. The youngest brother was Benjamin (42:4), who was born to Rachel, making him Joseph’s only full brother. See also 29:31—30:23; 35:16-18.

41:54 Acts 7:11. **41:55** John 2:5. **42:2** Acts 7:12. **42:6,9** Gen 37:5-10.

Joseph saw his brothers, he recognized them, but he pretended to
be a stranger and spoke harshly to them. "Where do you come
from?" he asked.
"From the land of Canaan," they replied, "to buy food."
8 Although Joseph recognized his brothers, they did not recognize him. 9 Then he remembered his dreams about them and
said to them, "You are spies! You have come to see where our land
is unprotected."
10 "No, my lord," they answered. "Your servants have come to
buy food. 11 We are all the sons of one man. Your servants are honest men, not spies."
12 "No!" he said to them. "You have come to see where our
land is unprotected."
13 But they replied, "Your servants were twelve brothers, the
sons of one man, who lives in the land of Canaan. The youngest is
now with our father, and one is no more."
14 Joseph said to them, "It is just as I told you: You are spies!
15 And this is how you will be tested: As surely as Pharaoh lives, you
will not leave this place unless your youngest brother comes here.
16 Send one of your number to get your brother; the rest of you will
be kept in prison, so that your words may be tested to see if you
are telling the truth. If you are not, then as surely as Pharaoh lives,
you are spies!" 17 And he put them all in custody for three days.
18 On the third day, Joseph said to them, "Do this and you
will live, for I fear God: 19 If you are honest men, let one of your
brothers stay here in prison, while the rest of you go and take grain
back for your starving households. 20 But you must bring your
youngest brother to me, so that your words may be verified and
that you may not die." This they proceeded to do.
21 They said to one another, "Surely we are being punished
because of our brother. We saw how distressed he was when he
pleaded with us for his life, but we would not listen; that's why this
distress has come upon us."
22 Reuben replied, "Didn't I tell you not to sin against the
boy? But you wouldn't listen! Now we must give an accounting for
his blood." 23 They did not realize that Joseph could understand
them, since he was using an interpreter.
24 He turned away from them and began to weep, but then
turned back and spoke to them again. He had Simeon taken from
them and bound before their eyes.
25 Joseph gave orders to fill their bags with grain, to put each
man's silver back in his sack, and to give them provisions for their
journey. After this was done for them, 26 they loaded their grain on
their donkeys and left.
27 At the place where they stopped for the night one of them
opened his sack to get feed for his donkey, and he saw his silver in
the mouth of his sack. 28 "My silver has been returned," he said to
his brothers. "Here it is in my sack."

42:7,8 *they did not recognize him:* Joseph was a teenager when the brothers had sold him as a slave nearly twenty years earlier. He would have changed, and they would not have expected to see him as a powerful ruler in Egypt.

42:13-15 *The youngest is now with our father, and one is no more:* The youngest brother was Benjamin (42:4). The one who "is no more" was Joseph. The brothers assumed he had died, though they did not really know what had happened to him.

42:15 *As surely as Pharaoh lives:* Because pharaoh was considered to be like a god, this was a very powerful oath.

42:18 *I fear God:* Joseph's brothers might have been surprised to hear an Egyptian official declare his fear of God. See also the note at 1:1.

42:23 *interpreter:* Joseph spoke Egyptian, but Hebrew was his first language. Speaking Hebrew, however, might have given away his identity to his brothers.

42:25 *silver:* Since there were no coins or paper money at this time, people used small pieces of silver to make payments. Their value was determined by their weight. See also the note at 20:16.

42:27 *donkey:* Donkeys were commonly used to carry loads. See the article called "Trade and Travel," p. 948.

42:22 Gen 37:21,22.

Their hearts sank and they turned to each other trembling and said, "What is this that God has done to us?"

29 When they came to their father Jacob in the land of Canaan, they told him all that had happened to them. They said, 30 "The man who is lord over the land spoke harshly to us and treated us as though we were spying on the land. 31 But we said to him, 'We are honest men; we are not spies. 32 We were twelve brothers, sons of one father. One is no more, and the youngest is now with our father in Canaan.'

33 "Then the man who is lord over the land said to us, 'This is how I will know whether you are honest men: Leave one of your brothers here with me, and take food for your starving households and go. 34 But bring your youngest brother to me so I will know that you are not spies but honest men. Then I will give your brother back to you, and you can trade[a] in the land.' "

35 As they were emptying their sacks, there in each man's sack was his pouch of silver! When they and their father saw the money pouches, they were frightened. 36 Their father Jacob said to them, "You have deprived me of my children. Joseph is no more and Simeon is no more, and now you want to take Benjamin. Everything is against me!"

37 Then Reuben said to his father, "You may put both of my sons to death if I do not bring him back to you. Entrust him to my care, and I will bring him back."

38 But Jacob said, "My son will not go down there with you; his brother is dead and he is the only one left. If harm comes to him on the journey you are taking, you will bring my gray head down to the grave[b] in sorrow."

The Second Journey to Egypt

43 Now the famine was still severe in the land. 2 So when they had eaten all the grain they had brought from Egypt, their father said to them, "Go back and buy us a little more food."

3 But Judah said to him, "The man warned us solemnly, 'You will not see my face again unless your brother is with you.' 4 If you will send our brother along with us, we will go down and buy food for you. 5 But if you will not send him, we will not go down, because the man said to us, 'You will not see my face again unless your brother is with you.' "

6 Israel asked, "Why did you bring this trouble on me by telling the man you had another brother?"

7 They replied, "The man questioned us closely about ourselves and our family. 'Is your father still living?' he asked us. 'Do you have another brother?' We simply answered his questions. How were we to know he would say, 'Bring your brother down here'?"

42:28 *What is this that God has done to us?:* The brothers believed God was directing what was happening to them, and they suspected that it was punishment for their treatment of Joseph many years before (42:21,22).

42:29 *land of Canaan:* See the note at 12:4-6.

42:37,38 *both of my sons . . . the only one left:* As the oldest son, Reuben felt responsible for Benjamin's safety, as he had earlier for Joseph (37:17-22). The "only one left" to whom Jacob was referring was Benjamin, who along with Joseph, were Jacob's only sons by Rachel, his favorite wife. To lose Benjamin after already having lost Joseph would have been devastating to Jacob.

43:3-5 *Judah:* At this point in the story, Judah begins to speak for his brothers (see also 44:14-34; 46:28). The tribe of Judah eventually would become the most important among the tribes of Israel (49:8-10). David, Israel's most famous king, would be from the tribe of Judah (1 Chr 2:1-17). Compare Judah's offer in 43:9 with Reuben's offer (42:37).

42:36 Gen 37:28; 42:19,24.

[a]**34** Or *move about freely* [b]**38** Hebrew *Sheol*

8Then Judah said to Israel his father, “Send the boy along
with me and we will go at once, so that we and you and our children may live and not die. 9I myself will guarantee his safety; you
can hold me personally responsible for him. If I do not bring him
back to you and set him here before you, I will bear the blame
before you all my life. 10As it is, if we had not delayed, we could
have gone and returned twice.”
11Then their father Israel said to them, “If it must be, then
do this: Put some of the best products of the land in your bags and
take them down to the man as a gift—a little balm and a little
honey, some spices and myrrh, some pistachio nuts and almonds.
12Take double the amount of silver with you, for you must return
the silver that was put back into the mouths of your sacks. Perhaps
it was a mistake. 13Take your brother also and go back to the man
at once. 14And may God Almighty[a] grant you mercy before the
man so that he will let your other brother and Benjamin come
back with you. As for me, if I am bereaved, I am bereaved.”
15So the men took the gifts and double the amount of silver,
and Benjamin also. They hurried down to Egypt and presented
themselves to Joseph. 16When Joseph saw Benjamin with them, he
said to the steward of his house, “Take these men to my house,
slaughter an animal and prepare dinner; they are to eat with me at
noon.”
17The man did as Joseph told him and took the men to
Joseph’s house. 18Now the men were frightened when they were
taken to his house. They thought, “We were brought here because
of the silver that was put back into our sacks the first time. He
wants to attack us and overpower us and seize us as slaves and take
our donkeys.”
19So they went up to Joseph’s steward and spoke to him at
the entrance to the house. 20“Please, sir,” they said, “we came down
here the first time to buy food. 21But at the place where we stopped
for the night we opened our sacks and each of us found his silver—the exact weight—in the mouth of his sack. So we have
brought it back with us. 22We have also brought additional silver
with us to buy food. We don’t know who put our silver in our
sacks.”
23“It’s all right,” he said. “Don’t be afraid. Your God, the God
of your father, has given you treasure in your sacks; I received your
silver.” Then he brought Simeon out to them.
24The steward took the men into Joseph’s house, gave them
water to wash their feet and provided fodder for their donkeys.
25They prepared their gifts for Joseph’s arrival at noon, because
they had heard that they were to eat there.
26When Joseph came home, they presented to him the gifts
they had brought into the house, and they bowed down before

[a]14 Hebrew *El-Shaddai*

43:11 *a gift . . . spices . . . pistachio nuts and almonds:* Bringing gifts to someone who had superior power or position was an ancient custom (see 1 Kgs 10:1-13). Gifts of food during a time of famine would have been truly sacrificial. The generosity of this gift is further reflected in the fact that it includes spices and myrrh, luxury items that Israel could only have obtained by trade with caravans from distant lands. Honey may be either the sweet liquid extract from dates or wild honey made by bees. Pistachio and almond trees grew in Canaan and Syria, but not in Egypt at this time. This would have made them a specially prized gift.

43:14 *God Almighty:* The meaning of the Hebrew for this title, *El Shaddai,* is uncertain. One possible meaning is “God, the One of the Mountains” (see also Gen 35:9-11; Exod 6:2, 3). *El* was one of the most common names for god among the Canaanites, who believed that El was not the only god, but the one who ruled over all the other gods. In the Jewish Scriptures this name frequently refers to the God of Israel. See the mini-article called “Names of God,” p. 243.

43:15 *silver:* See the note at 42:25.

43:23 *God . . . has given you treasure in your sacks:* See 42:28. The steward’s words repeat the main theme of the Joseph story: God is at work directing events for the good of his chosen people.

43:24 *water to wash their feet:* See the note at 18:16.

43:29 *his brother Benjamin:* Joseph and Benjamin were the only sons of Jacob and Rachel. See also 45:22 and the note at 42:37,38.

43:32 *Egyptians could not eat with Hebrews:* The Egyptians probably sat apart from the Hebrews because of religious or ritual purity rules (see also Exod 8:26).

43:33,34 *seated . . . from the firstborn to the youngest . . . five times as much:* Joseph is both following the usual custom for treating guests and breaking the custom at the same time. He arranged the brothers at their table so that the oldest would have the place of honor, but he gave special treatment to the youngest, Benjamin, by giving him the largest portions. See also the mini-article called "Birthright," p. 80.

44:1-5 *silver . . . my cup . . . for divination:* The steward claims that Joseph's cup is important, because Joseph uses it to practice divination, or telling future events by reading objects that are put into liquid in his cup. See also the notes at 30:27,28 and 41:8.

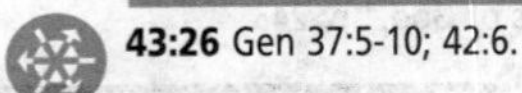
43:26 Gen 37:5-10; 42:6.

him to the ground. 27 He asked them how they were, and then he
said, "How is your aged father you told me about? Is he still
living?"
28 They replied, "Your servant our father is still alive and
well." And they bowed low to pay him honor.
29 As he looked about and saw his brother Benjamin, his own
mother's son, he asked, "Is this your youngest brother, the one you
told me about?" And he said, "God be gracious to you, my son."
30 Deeply moved at the sight of his brother, Joseph hurried out and
looked for a place to weep. He went into his private room and
wept there.
31 After he had washed his face, he came out and, controlling
himself, said, "Serve the food."
32 They served him by himself, the brothers by themselves,
and the Egyptians who ate with him by themselves, because Egyptians could not eat with Hebrews, for that is detestable to Egyptians. 33 The men had been seated before him in the order of their
ages, from the firstborn to the youngest; and they looked at each
other in astonishment. 34 When portions were served to them from
Joseph's table, Benjamin's portion was five times as much as anyone else's. So they feasted and drank freely with him.

A Silver Cup in a Sack

44 Now Joseph gave these instructions to the steward of his
house: "Fill the men's sacks with as much food as they can carry,
and put each man's silver in the mouth of his sack. 2 Then put my
cup, the silver one, in the mouth of the youngest one's sack, along
with the silver for his grain." And he did as Joseph said.
3 As morning dawned, the men were sent on their way with
their donkeys. 4 They had not gone far from the city when Joseph
said to his steward, "Go after those men at once, and when you
catch up with them, say to them, 'Why have you repaid good with
evil? 5 Isn't this the cup my master drinks from and also uses for
divination? This is a wicked thing you have done.' "
6 When he caught up with them, he repeated these words to
them. 7 But they said to him, "Why does my lord say such things?
Far be it from your servants to do anything like that! 8 We even
brought back to you from the land of Canaan the silver we found
inside the mouths of our sacks. So why would we steal silver or
gold from your master's house? 9 If any of your servants is found to
have it, he will die; and the rest of us will become my lord's slaves."
10 "Very well, then," he said, "let it be as you say. Whoever is
found to have it will become my slave; the rest of you will be free
from blame."
11 Each of them quickly lowered his sack to the ground and
opened it. 12 Then the steward proceeded to search, beginning with
the oldest and ending with the youngest. And the cup was found in

Benjamin's sack. 13 At this, they tore their clothes. Then they all
loaded their donkeys and returned to the city.
14 Joseph was still in the house when Judah and his brothers
came in, and they threw themselves to the ground before him.
15 Joseph said to them, "What is this you have done? Don't you
know that a man like me can find things out by divination?"
16 "What can we say to my lord?" Judah replied. "What can
we say? How can we prove our innocence? God has uncovered
your servants' guilt. We are now my lord's slaves—we ourselves
and the one who was found to have the cup."
17 But Joseph said, "Far be it from me to do such a thing!
Only the man who was found to have the cup will become my
slave. The rest of you, go back to your father in peace."
18 Then Judah went up to him and said: "Please, my lord, let
your servant speak a word to my lord. Do not be angry with your
servant, though you are equal to Pharaoh himself. 19 My lord asked
his servants, 'Do you have a father or a brother?' 20 And we
answered, 'We have an aged father, and there is a young son born
to him in his old age. His brother is dead, and he is the only one
of his mother's sons left, and his father loves him.'
21 "Then you said to your servants, 'Bring him down to me
so I can see him for myself.' 22 And we said to my lord, 'The boy
cannot leave his father; if he leaves him, his father will die.' 23 But
you told your servants, 'Unless your youngest brother comes down
with you, you will not see my face again.' 24 When we went back to
your servant my father, we told him what my lord had said.
25 "Then our father said, 'Go back and buy a little more food.'
26 But we said, 'We cannot go down. Only if our youngest brother
is with us will we go. We cannot see the man's face unless our
youngest brother is with us.'
27 "Your servant my father said to us, 'You know that my wife
bore me two sons. 28 One of them went away from me, and I said,
"He has surely been torn to pieces." And I have not seen him since.
29 If you take this one from me too and harm comes to him, you
will bring my gray head down to the grave[a] in misery.'
30 "So now, if the boy is not with us when I go back to your
servant my father and if my father, whose life is closely bound up
with the boy's life, 31 sees that the boy isn't there, he will die. Your
servants will bring the gray head of our father down to the grave
in sorrow. 32 Your servant guaranteed the boy's safety to my father.
I said, 'If I do not bring him back to you, I will bear the blame
before you, my father, all my life!'
33 "Now then, please let your servant remain here as my lord's
slave in place of the boy, and let the boy return with his brothers.
34 How can I go back to my father if the boy is not with me? No!
Do not let me see the misery that would come upon my father."

[a]**29** Hebrew *Sheol*; also in verse 31

44:13 *tore their clothes:* See the note at 37:34.

44:15 *find things out by divination:* See the note at 44:1-5.

44:20 *His brother is dead:* This refers to Benjamin and Joseph. Judah believes Joseph is dead.

44:27 *my wife bore me two sons:* Rachel, Jacob's favorite wife, only bore two sons Joseph, and Benjamin.

44:14 Gen 37:5-10; 42:6. **44:23** Gen 42:15,16; 43:6. **44:32** Gen 43:9.

> Joseph said, *"Do not be distressed and do not be angry with yourselves for selling me here, because it was to save lives that God sent me ahead of you."*
> Gen 45:5

45:5 *God sent me ahead of you:* God's promise to Abraham (12:1-3), the main theme of the Joseph story, is repeated again. See also Gen 50:19, 20; Acts 7:9,10.

45:8 *father to Pharaoh:* Meaning the prime minister or vizier. See the note at 41:41-43.

45:10 *Goshen:* This area of grazing land was in the eastern part of the Nile River delta of northern Egypt (see the map on p. 2463). Because Joseph's family would "be near" him in Goshen, it is assumed that the palace of the Egyptian king was in or near this region at this time.

45:18 *enjoy the fat of the land:* Ancient Egyptian writings tell how some of Egypt's kings allowed foreigners to settle in Egypt during times of famine.

45:1 Acts 7:13. **45:9-11** Acts 7:14.

Joseph Makes Himself Known

45 Then Joseph could no longer control himself before all his
attendants, and he cried out, "Have everyone leave my presence!"
So there was no one with Joseph when he made himself known to
his brothers. [2]And he wept so loudly that the Egyptians heard him,
and Pharaoh's household heard about it.

[3]Joseph said to his brothers, "I am Joseph! Is my father still
living?" But his brothers were not able to answer him, because they
were terrified at his presence.

[4]Then Joseph said to his brothers, "Come close to me." When
they had done so, he said, "I am your brother Joseph, the one you
sold into Egypt! [5]And now, do not be distressed and do not be
angry with yourselves for selling me here, because it was to save
lives that God sent me ahead of you. [6]For two years now there has
been famine in the land, and for the next five years there will not
be plowing and reaping. [7]But God sent me ahead of you to preserve for you a remnant on earth and to save your lives by a great
deliverance.[a]

[8]"So then, it was not you who sent me here, but God. He made
me father to Pharaoh, lord of his entire household and ruler of all
Egypt. [9]Now hurry back to my father and say to him, 'This is what
your son Joseph says: God has made me lord of all Egypt. Come
down to me; don't delay. [10]You shall live in the region of Goshen and
be near me—you, your children and grandchildren, your flocks and
herds, and all you have. [11]I will provide for you there, because five
years of famine are still to come. Otherwise you and your household
and all who belong to you will become destitute.'

[12]"You can see for yourselves, and so can my brother Benjamin, that it is really I who am speaking to you. [13]Tell my father
about all the honor accorded me in Egypt and about everything
you have seen. And bring my father down here quickly."

[14]Then he threw his arms around his brother Benjamin and
wept, and Benjamin embraced him, weeping. [15]And he kissed all
his brothers and wept over them. Afterward his brothers talked
with him.

[16]When the news reached Pharaoh's palace that Joseph's
brothers had come, Pharaoh and all his officials were pleased.
[17]Pharaoh said to Joseph, "Tell your brothers, 'Do this: Load your
animals and return to the land of Canaan, [18]and bring your father
and your families back to me. I will give you the best of the land of
Egypt and you can enjoy the fat of the land.'

[19]"You are also directed to tell them, 'Do this: Take some
carts from Egypt for your children and your wives, and get your
father and come. [20]Never mind about your belongings, because the
best of all Egypt will be yours.' "

---

[a]7 Or *save you as a great band of survivors*

21 So the sons of Israel did this. Joseph gave them carts, as Pharaoh had commanded, and he also gave them provisions for their journey. 22 To each of them he gave new clothing, but to Benjamin he gave three hundred shekels[a] of silver and five sets of clothes. 23 And this is what he sent to his father: ten donkeys loaded with the best things of Egypt, and ten female donkeys loaded with grain and bread and other provisions for his journey. 24 Then he sent his brothers away, and as they were leaving he said to them, "Don't quarrel on the way!"

25 So they went up out of Egypt and came to their father Jacob in the land of Canaan. 26 They told him, "Joseph is still alive! In fact, he is ruler of all Egypt." Jacob was stunned; he did not believe them. 27 But when they told him everything Joseph had said to them, and when he saw the carts Joseph had sent to carry him back, the spirit of their father Jacob revived. 28 And Israel said, "I'm convinced! My son Joseph is still alive. I will go and see him before I die."

Jacob Goes to Egypt

46 So Israel set out with all that was his, and when he reached Beersheba, he offered sacrifices to the God of his father Isaac.

2 And God spoke to Israel in a vision at night and said, "Jacob! Jacob!"

"Here I am," he replied.

3 "I am God, the God of your father," he said. "Do not be afraid to go down to Egypt, for I will make you into a great nation there. 4 I will go down to Egypt with you, and I will surely bring you back again. And Joseph's own hand will close your eyes."

5 Then Jacob left Beersheba, and Israel's sons took their father Jacob and their children and their wives in the carts that Pharaoh had sent to transport him. 6 They also took with them their livestock and the possessions they had acquired in Canaan, and Jacob and all his offspring went to Egypt. 7 He took with him to Egypt his sons and grandsons and his daughters and granddaughters—all his offspring.

8 These are the names of the sons of Israel (Jacob and his descendants) who went to Egypt:

Reuben the firstborn of Jacob.

9 The sons of Reuben:
Hanoch, Pallu, Hezron and Carmi.

10 The sons of Simeon:
Jemuel, Jamin, Ohad, Jakin, Zohar and Shaul the son of a Canaanite woman.

11 The sons of Levi:
Gershon, Kohath and Merari.

[a]**22** That is, about 7 1/2 pounds (about 3.5 kilograms)

45:21 *carts:* These may have been two-wheeled carts made of wood or woven basket material on a wooden frame, or four-wheeled wagons used mainly for hauling large items. Smaller, two-wheeled carts could be pulled by hand, but carts were usually pulled by oxen or donkeys. See also the article called, "Trade and Travel," p. 948.

45:22 *shekels of silver:* See the note at 20:16.

45:26 *ruler of all Egypt:* See the note at 41:41-43.

46:1 *Beersheba ... offered sacrifices:* See the notes at 21:14 and 21:31. Jacob's grandfather Abraham and father Isaac had also worshiped God at Beersheba (21:33; 26:23-25). For more about sacrifices, see also the note at 22:7,8.

46:5-7 *Pharaoh:* See the mini-article called "King of Egypt (Pharaoh)," p. 110.

45:22 Gen 43:34. **46:2** Gen 22:11; 26:24; Exod 3:4; 1 Sam 3:4-8. **46:3,4** Gen 12:1-3; 15:5; 17:1-6; 22:16-18; 49:33—50:1. **46:5-7** Acts 7:15. **46:8-25** Gen 29:31—30:24; 35:16-18; 41:50-52.

46:8-15 *thirty-three in all:* The list of Jacob and Leah's descendants is said to be thirty-three, but the number of names is actually thirty-four. Ohad, son of Simeon, is not listed in family lists given in Numbers 26:12-14 and 1 Chronicles 4:24.

46:19-22 *Manasseh and Ephraim . . . Asenath:* See 41:45,50-52.

46:19-22 *On:* See the note at 41:45.

46:27 *seventy in all:* This number, given in the ancient Hebrew text, includes Jacob and Joseph and the two sons born to Joseph and Asenath, who were already living in Egypt. Seventy was considered an ideal and complete number. Acts 7:14 lists the number of Jacob's descendants in Egypt as seventy-five, following the ancient Greek translation of the Hebrew Scriptures (see also Exod 1:1-5).

12 The sons of Judah:
Er, Onan, Shelah, Perez and Zerah (but Er and Onan had died in the land of Canaan).
The sons of Perez:
Hezron and Hamul.
13 The sons of Issachar:
Tola, Puah,[a] Jashub[b] and Shimron.
14 The sons of Zebulun:
Sered, Elon and Jahleel.

15 These were the sons Leah bore to Jacob in Paddan Aram,[c]
besides his daughter Dinah. These sons and daughters of his were
thirty-three in all.

16 The sons of Gad:
Zephon,[d] Haggi, Shuni, Ezbon, Eri, Arodi and Areli.
17 The sons of Asher:
Imnah, Ishvah, Ishvi and Beriah.
Their sister was Serah.
The sons of Beriah:
Heber and Malkiel.

18 These were the children born to Jacob by Zilpah, whom
Laban had given to his daughter Leah—sixteen in all.

19 The sons of Jacob's wife Rachel:
Joseph and Benjamin. 20 In Egypt, Manasseh and Ephraim were born to Joseph by Asenath daughter of Potiphera, priest of On.[e]
21 The sons of Benjamin:
Bela, Beker, Ashbel, Gera, Naaman, Ehi, Rosh, Muppim, Huppim and Ard.

22 These were the sons of Rachel who were born to Jacob—
fourteen in all.

23 The son of Dan:
Hushim.
24 The sons of Naphtali:
Jahziel, Guni, Jezer and Shillem.

25 These were the sons born to Jacob by Bilhah, whom Laban
had given to his daughter Rachel—seven in all.

26 All those who went to Egypt with Jacob—those who were
his direct descendants, not counting his sons' wives—numbered
sixty-six persons. 27 With the two sons[f] who had been born to

---

[a] **13** Samaritan Pentateuch and Syriac (see also 1 Chron. 7:1); Masoretic Text *Puvah* [b] **13** Samaritan Pentateuch and some Septuagint manuscripts (see also Num. 26:24 and 1 Chron. 7:1); Masoretic Text *Iob* [c] **15** That is, Northwest Mesopotamia [d] **16** Samaritan Pentateuch and Septuagint (see also Num. 26:15); Masoretic Text *Ziphion* [e] **20** That is, Heliopolis [f] **27** Hebrew; Septuagint *the nine children*

Joseph in Egypt, the members of Jacob's family, which went to
Egypt, were seventy[a] in all.
28Now Jacob sent Judah ahead of him to Joseph to get directions to Goshen. When they arrived in the region of Goshen,
29Joseph had his chariot made ready and went to Goshen to meet
his father Israel. As soon as Joseph appeared before him, he threw
his arms around his father[b] and wept for a long time.
30Israel said to Joseph, "Now I am ready to die, since I have
seen for myself that you are still alive."
31Then Joseph said to his brothers and to his father's household, "I will go up and speak to Pharaoh and will say to him, 'My
brothers and my father's household, who were living in the land of
Canaan, have come to me. 32The men are shepherds; they tend
livestock, and they have brought along their flocks and herds and
everything they own.' 33When Pharaoh calls you in and asks, 'What
is your occupation?' 34you should answer, 'Your servants have tended livestock from our boyhood on, just as our fathers did.' Then
you will be allowed to settle in the region of Goshen, for all shepherds are detestable to the Egyptians."
47 Joseph went and told Pharaoh, "My father and brothers, with
their flocks and herds and everything they own, have come from
the land of Canaan and are now in Goshen." 2He chose five of his
brothers and presented them before Pharaoh.
3Pharaoh asked the brothers, "What is your occupation?"
"Your servants are shepherds," they replied to Pharaoh, "just
as our fathers were." 4They also said to him, "We have come to live
here awhile, because the famine is severe in Canaan and your servants' flocks have no pasture. So now, please let your servants settle
in Goshen."
5Pharaoh said to Joseph, "Your father and your brothers have
come to you, 6and the land of Egypt is before you; settle your
father and your brothers in the best part of the land. Let them live
in Goshen. And if you know of any among them with special ability, put them in charge of my own livestock."
7Then Joseph brought his father Jacob in and presented him
before Pharaoh. After Jacob blessed[c] Pharaoh, 8Pharaoh asked him,
"How old are you?"
9And Jacob said to Pharaoh, "The years of my pilgrimage
are a hundred and thirty. My years have been few and difficult,
and they do not equal the years of the pilgrimage of my fathers."
10Then Jacob blessed[d] Pharaoh and went out from his presence.
11So Joseph settled his father and his brothers in Egypt and
gave them property in the best part of the land, the district of
Rameses, as Pharaoh directed. 12Joseph also provided his father
and his brothers and all his father's household with food, according to the number of their children.

[a]27 Hebrew (see also Exodus 1:5 and footnote); Septuagint (see also Acts 7:14) *seventy-five* [b]29 Hebrew *around him* [c]7 Or *greeted* [d]10 Or *said farewell to*

46:28 *Goshen:* See the note at 45:10.

46:34 *shepherds are detestable to the Egyptians:* Egyptians thought that the wandering sheep-herders from the east were inferior and did not like to mix with them. Joseph wanted to tell the king that his brothers were shepherds, so the king would give them their own area (Goshen), apart from Egypt's main population farther up river.

47:1,2 *Canaan . . . Goshen:* See the notes at 12:4-6 and 45:10.

47:7-10 *Jacob blessed Pharaoh:* This probably refers to a greeting that included Jacob's wishing Pharoah well-being and a long life. However, since Jacob refers to his grandparents (Abraham and Sarah), he may have used a form of the blessing found in 12:2,3.

47:11 *the district of Rameses:* The city of Rameses was located in Goshen in the northeast part of the Nile River delta. It was probably named for the Egyptian king, Rameses II, who ruled for many years after the time of Joseph (about 1279 to 1212 B.C.). The name of the city was probably added to this verse by a later editor to help readers clearly identify where Jacob's family settled. See also Exod 1:11; 12:37; Num 33:3-5; and the map on p. 2463.

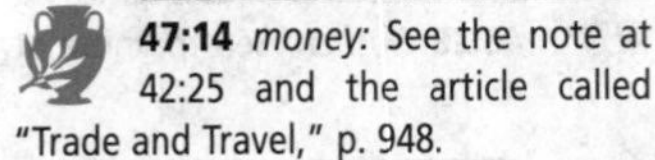

47:14 *money:* See the note at 42:25 and the article called "Trade and Travel," p. 948.

Joseph and the Famine

13There was no food, however, in the whole region because
the famine was severe; both Egypt and Canaan wasted away
because of the famine. 14Joseph collected all the money that was to
be found in Egypt and Canaan in payment for the grain they were
buying, and he brought it to Pharaoh's palace. 15When the money
of the people of Egypt and Canaan was gone, all Egypt came to
Joseph and said, "Give us food. Why should we die before your
eyes? Our money is used up."
16"Then bring your livestock," said Joseph. "I will sell you
food in exchange for your livestock, since your money is gone."
17So they brought their livestock to Joseph, and he gave them food
in exchange for their horses, their sheep and goats, their cattle and
donkeys. And he brought them through that year with food in
exchange for all their livestock.
18When that year was over, they came to him the following
year and said, "We cannot hide from our lord the fact that since
our money is gone and our livestock belongs to you, there is nothing left for our lord except our bodies and our land. 19Why should

NOMADS (WANDERING HERDERS)

The term "nomad" comes from the Greek form of a Latin word meaning "to graze." Nomads were wandering shepherds who moved their families and their flocks of sheep and goats from place to place looking for good pasture land and water. They lived in tents and took with them only what clothing and supplies they had to have. They did not often own land, but claimed the land they were using at the time, or even took it over by force. Sometimes they settled in an area after making agreements with the local people (Gen 13:5-18; 26:12-33). Wandering nomads who moved in and settled for a time in an area probably made nearby farmers or city dwellers anxious and crowded. This may be one reason that, in the ancient world, nomadic shepherds were considered to be lower class and disgusting (Gen 46:34). Nomads were known for being strong and independent. They were cautious about mixing with other peoples, but offered great hospitality to guests (Gen 18:2-8) and would protect them at great risk to themselves and their families (Gen 19:4-8).

The migration of Semitic nomads from ancient Mesopotamia west to Canaan, the Negev, and Egypt took place at regular times during ancient history. One such migration occurred around 1900 B.C. and likely included Abraham and Sarah, the ancestors of the Hebrew people. GENESIS tells how the Hebrew people moved from place to place, ranging from northern Syria (Haran) through Canaan and all the way to Egypt (Gen 42) when food supplies became scarce in Canaan.

After the Hebrews left Egypt (Exod 12–14), they continued wandering for a period of time before settling in Canaan, where they took some areas and cities by force. They were known as the nation of Israel, named for Jacob, who was also called Israel (Gen 32:22-28; 35:9-11). Some nomads had trouble adjusting to life in the city, because of their independent ways. The image of the wandering nomad or foreigner is often used in the Bible to describe God's people (1 Chr 29:15; Ps 39:12; see also Phil 3:20; Heb 11:13; 1 Pet 2:11).

Nomadic Shepherds in the Ancient World.

we perish before your eyes—we and our land as well? Buy us and
our land in exchange for food, and we with our land will be in
bondage to Pharaoh. Give us seed so that we may live and not die,
and that the land may not become desolate."
20So Joseph bought all the land in Egypt for Pharaoh. The
Egyptians, one and all, sold their fields, because the famine was too
severe for them. The land became Pharaoh's, 21and Joseph reduced
the people to servitude,[a] from one end of Egypt to the other.
22However, he did not buy the land of the priests, because they
received a regular allotment from Pharaoh and had food enough
from the allotment Pharaoh gave them. That is why they did not
sell their land.
23Joseph said to the people, "Now that I have bought you and
your land today for Pharaoh, here is seed for you so you can plant
the ground. 24But when the crop comes in, give a fifth of it to
Pharaoh. The other four-fifths you may keep as seed for the fields
and as food for yourselves and your households and your children."

47:22 *priests:* At times in ancient Egypt the priests had enough power and influence to remove one king and replace him with another, or to change a form of worship. This may be why the king of Egypt did not take the land belonging to the priests.

47:24 *a fifth:* A fifth of the crops were taken during the seven years of plenty (41:34), but now all land belonged to the king as well.

---

[a]**21** Samaritan Pentateuch and Septuagint (see also Vulgate); Masoretic Text *and he moved the people into the cities*

47:27 *Goshen:* See the note at 45:10

47:29,30 *where they are buried:* See the note at 23:9. See also 49:29-32; 50:6,13.

48:1 *Manasseh and Ephraim:* See the notes at 41:51,52 and 49:22-26.

48:3 *God Almighty:* See the note at 43:14.

48:5,6 *Ephraim and Manasseh will be mine:* By adopting Joseph's sons as his own, Jacob gave them the same status as his own oldest sons, Reuben and Simeon. Jacob named Ephraim first, even though Manasseh was older, which meant Ephraim received Jacob's main blessing (see the note at 27:4 and the mini-article called "Birthright," p. 80). Actually, because of his earlier sin (35:22), Reuben would lose his birthright to Joseph and Joseph's sons (Gen 49:3,4; 1 Chr 5:1,2). This scene explains why later in Israel's history, the Joseph tribe is divided into two tribes, Manasseh and Ephraim, each receiving land like other tribes of Israel. See also the note at 49:5-7.

48:7 *Ephrath . . . Bethlehem:* See the note at 35:15-19.

48:8-12 *bless them . . . Israel's knees:* See the notes at 27:4 and 27:33. See also 48:14-19. The two boys were placed on Jacob's knees, as a sign that he had accepted them as his sons.

48:3,4 Gen 28:13-19; 35:9-12. **48:7** Gen 35:16-20.

25"You have saved our lives," they said. "May we find favor in
the eyes of our lord; we will be in bondage to Pharaoh."
26So Joseph established it as a law concerning land in
Egypt—still in force today—that a fifth of the produce belongs to
Pharaoh. It was only the land of the priests that did not become
Pharaoh's.
27Now the Israelites settled in Egypt in the region of Goshen.
They acquired property there and were fruitful and increased
greatly in number.
28Jacob lived in Egypt seventeen years, and the years of his
life were a hundred and forty-seven. 29When the time drew near
for Israel to die, he called for his son Joseph and said to him, "If I
have found favor in your eyes, put your hand under my thigh and
promise that you will show me kindness and faithfulness. Do not
bury me in Egypt, 30but when I rest with my fathers, carry me out
of Egypt and bury me where they are buried."
"I will do as you say," he said.
31"Swear to me," he said. Then Joseph swore to him, and
Israel worshiped as he leaned on the top of his staff.[a]

Manasseh and Ephraim

48 Some time later Joseph was told, "Your father is ill." So he
took his two sons Manasseh and Ephraim along with him. 2When
Jacob was told, "Your son Joseph has come to you," Israel rallied
his strength and sat up on the bed.
3Jacob said to Joseph, "God Almighty[b] appeared to me at Luz
in the land of Canaan, and there he blessed me 4and said to me,
'I am going to make you fruitful and will increase your numbers.
I will make you a community of peoples, and I will give this land
as an everlasting possession to your descendants after you.'
5"Now then, your two sons born to you in Egypt before I
came to you here will be reckoned as mine; Ephraim and Manasseh will be mine, just as Reuben and Simeon are mine. 6Any children born to you after them will be yours; in the territory they
inherit they will be reckoned under the names of their brothers.
7As I was returning from Paddan,[c] to my sorrow Rachel died in the
land of Canaan while we were still on the way, a little distance
from Ephrath. So I buried her there beside the road to Ephrath"
(that is, Bethlehem).
8When Israel saw the sons of Joseph, he asked, "Who are these?"
9"They are the sons God has given me here," Joseph said to
his father.
Then Israel said, "Bring them to me so I may bless them."
10Now Israel's eyes were failing because of old age, and he

[a]31 Or *Israel bowed down at the head of his bed* [b]3 Hebrew *El-Shaddai*
[c]7 That is, Northwest Mesopotamia

could hardly see. So Joseph brought his sons close to him, and his
father kissed them and embraced them.
11Israel said to Joseph, "I never expected to see your face
again, and now God has allowed me to see your children too."
12Then Joseph removed them from Israel's knees and bowed
down with his face to the ground. 13And Joseph took both of them,
Ephraim on his right toward Israel's left hand and Manasseh on his
left toward Israel's right hand, and brought them close to him. 14But
Israel reached out his right hand and put it on Ephraim's head,
though he was the younger, and crossing his arms, he put his left
hand on Manasseh's head, even though Manasseh was the firstborn.
15Then he blessed Joseph and said,

"May the God before whom my fathers
Abraham and Isaac walked,
the God who has been my shepherd
all my life to this day,
16the Angel who has delivered me from all harm
—may he bless these boys.

48:13 *left . . . right:* The right side was the place of greater authority or power. Joseph placed Manasseh there because he was the oldest (see the note at 25:5,6). This is why Joseph was upset when Jacob crossed his hands and gave the blessing of the firstborn to Ephraim (48:17-19).

Jacob Blesses Manasseh and Ephraim by Rembrandt, 1656. For years Jacob (Israel) thought that his son Joseph was dead, but Joseph was alive and serving the king of Egypt. Jacob lived to see Joseph once again and to meet Joseph's two sons, Manasseh and Ephraim. Before he died, Jacob blessed these two grandsons, even before giving a blessing to his own twelve sons. (See 48:1-22.)

48:19 *his younger brother will be greater:* Later in Israel's history the tribe of Ephraim would become very powerful, and during the time when Israel was divided into two kingdoms, the whole northern kingdom was sometimes called Ephraim.

48:22 *the ridge of land I took from the Amorites:* The Hebrew word translated "ridge" is very similar to the name "Shechem," where Joseph was later buried. This phrase may refer to the events described in 34:25-29. See also the note at 10:6-20.

49:3 *Reuben:* He was Jacob's oldest son (29:32). See the note at 48:5,6 and the mini-article called "Birthright," p. 80.

49:5-7 *Simeon and Levi:* Verse 6 refers to the revenge these two brothers took against the men at Shechem because of the rape of Dinah, their sister (34:25-29). When the tribes of Israel later settled in Canaan, the tribe of Simeon was eventually absorbed into the tribe of Judah. The Levi tribe became Israel's priests (see Exod 32:26-29; Deut 10:8 and the mini-article called "Israel's Priests," p. 2344). The number of Jacob's sons was twelve and stood for the twelve tribes of Israel. But the Levi tribe could not own land (Deut 10:9). The land that would have gone to Joseph's tribe however, was divided between his two sons, Manasseh and Ephraim, making the total of land-owning tribes twelve (see the note at 48:5,6). See also the mini-article called "Israel," p. 264.

48:20-22 Heb 11:21. **49:1** Gen 32:22-28.

May they be called by my name
and the names of my fathers Abraham and Isaac,
and may they increase greatly
upon the earth."

17 When Joseph saw his father placing his right hand on
Ephraim's head he was displeased; so he took hold of his father's
hand to move it from Ephraim's head to Manasseh's head. 18 Joseph
said to him, "No, my father, this one is the firstborn; put your right
hand on his head."
19 But his father refused and said, "I know, my son, I know.
He too will become a people, and he too will become great. Nevertheless, his younger brother will be greater than he, and his
descendants will become a group of nations." 20 He blessed them
that day and said,

"In your[a] name will Israel pronounce this blessing:
'May God make you like Ephraim and Manasseh.' "

So he put Ephraim ahead of Manasseh.
21 Then Israel said to Joseph, "I am about to die, but God will
be with you[b] and take you[b] back to the land of your[b] fathers. 22 And
to you, as one who is over your brothers, I give the ridge of land[c] I
took from the Amorites with my sword and my bow."

Jacob Blesses His Sons

49 Then Jacob called for his sons and said: "Gather around so I can tell you what will happen to you in days to come.

2 "Assemble and listen, sons of Jacob;
listen to your father Israel.

3 "Reuben, you are my firstborn,
my might, the first sign of my strength,
excelling in honor, excelling in power.
4 Turbulent as the waters, you will no longer excel,
for you went up onto your father's bed,
onto my couch and defiled it.

5 "Simeon and Levi are brothers—
their swords[d] are weapons of violence.
6 Let me not enter their council,
let me not join their assembly,
for they have killed men in their anger
and hamstrung oxen as they pleased.
7 Cursed be their anger, so fierce,
and their fury, so cruel!

[a]20 The Hebrew is singular. [b]21 The Hebrew is plural. [c]22 Or *And to you I give one portion more than to your brothers—the portion* [d]5 The meaning of the Hebrew for this word is uncertain.

I will scatter them in Jacob
and disperse them in Israel.

8 "Judah,[a] your brothers will praise you;
your hand will be on the neck of your enemies;
your father's sons will bow down to you.
9 You are a lion's cub, O Judah;
you return from the prey, my son.
Like a lion he crouches and lies down,
like a lioness—who dares to rouse him?
10 The scepter will not depart from Judah,
nor the ruler's staff from between his feet,
until he comes to whom it belongs[b]
and the obedience of the nations is his.
11 He will tether his donkey to a vine,
his colt to the choicest branch;
he will wash his garments in wine,
his robes in the blood of grapes.
12 His eyes will be darker than wine,
his teeth whiter than milk.[c]

13 "Zebulun will live by the seashore
and become a haven for ships;
his border will extend toward Sidon.

14 "Issachar is a rawboned[d] donkey
lying down between two saddlebags.[e]
15 When he sees how good is his resting place
and how pleasant is his land,
he will bend his shoulder to the burden
and submit to forced labor.

16 "Dan[f] will provide justice for his people
as one of the tribes of Israel.
17 Dan will be a serpent by the roadside,
a viper along the path,
that bites the horse's heels
so that its rider tumbles backward.

18 "I look for your deliverance, O LORD.

19 "Gad[g] will be attacked by a band of raiders,
but he will attack them at their heels.

20 "Asher's food will be rich;
he will provide delicacies fit for a king.

---

[a]8 *Judah* sounds like and may be derived from the Hebrew for *praise.* [b]10 Or *until Shiloh comes;* or *until he comes to whom tribute belongs* [c]12 Or *will be dull from wine, / his teeth white from milk* [d]14 Or *strong* [e]14 Or *campfires* [f]16 *Dan* here means *he provides justice.* [g]19 *Gad* can mean *attack* and *band of raiders.*

49:8-12 *Judah:* Judah was the fourth son born to Jacob and Leah (29:35), but his older brothers (Reuben, Simeon, and Levi) had done things that made them lose their rights of leadership (see 35:22; 34:25-29). Judah would become the leading tribe in the south. King David belonged to the Judah tribe (see the note at 43:3-5).

49:13-15 *Zebulun . . . Issachar:* Zebulun was bordered on the west by Asher and Manasseh, but they were close enough to the Mediterranean Sea to make a living off it (see Deut 33:19). Issachar is compared to a donkey that is satisfied to rest in the meadows and willing to become a slave to others.

49:16-21 *Dan . . . Gad . . . Asher . . . Naphtali:* Dan would later occupy a small area of Canaan (Josh 19:40-48). Samson, one of Israel's famous judges, came from the Dan tribe (Judg 13:2-5). The reference to Dan as a serpent may be to its sneak attack on Laish (Judg 18:1-2,27-29). In Hebrew "Dan" means "justice" or "judgment," and "Gad" is like a word that means "attack." The tribe of Gad settled east of the Jordan River, where they were open to attack by the Moabites (Josh 13:24-28; 2 Kgs 3:4,5). The tribe of Asher settled on fertile farmland (Josh 19:24-31), which meant they would always have plenty of food. The Naphtali tribe settled in the hill country north of the Sea of Galilee (Josh 19:32-39) and may have been known for being independent and free, like deer that roam the woods.

49:9 Num 24:9; Rev 5:5.

49:22-26 *Joseph:* The Joseph tribe was divided according to his two sons, Ephraim and Manasseh (see the note at 48:5, 6). The "fruitful vine" probably refers to Ephraim, whose name in Hebrew sounds like the word for "fruitful." As vines tend to grow over whatever surrounds them, the Joseph tribes tended to try to expand the boundaries of their land (Josh 17:14-18). The Joseph tribes were large (49:25) and were blessed by much wealth.

49:24 *Mighty One . . . Shepherd . . . Rock:* See the note at 43:14 (God Almighty). Shepherds lead and protect their flocks, just as God leads and protects his people (Ps 23:1; Isa 40:11). The ideal leader of Israel would be like a good shepherd (Ezek 34:23; John 10:14-16). "Rock" is often used to describe God, who is Israel's defense (Deut 32:15; Ps 18:2).

49:27 *Benjamin:* See the note at 35:18. Some of the descendants of Benjamin were fierce and brutal warriors (Judg 3:12-30; 19:1—21:24).

49:28 *twelve tribes of Israel:* See the notes at 48:5,6 and 49:5-7.

49:29-31 *cave in the field of Machpelah, near Mamre:* See 23:3-20; 25:9,10. See also the notes at 23:3 (Hitites); 23:9 (cave); and 13:18 (Mamre).

49:33 Acts 7:15.

21 "Naphtali is a doe set free
that bears beautiful fawns.[a]

22 "Joseph is a fruitful vine,
a fruitful vine near a spring,
whose branches climb over a wall.[b]
23 With bitterness archers attacked him;
they shot at him with hostility.
24 But his bow remained steady,
his strong arms stayed[c] limber,
because of the hand of the Mighty One of Jacob,
because of the Shepherd, the Rock of Israel,
25 because of your father's God, who helps you,
because of the Almighty,[d] who blesses you
with blessings of the heavens above,
blessings of the deep that lies below,
blessings of the breast and womb.
26 Your father's blessings are greater
than the blessings of the ancient mountains,
than[e] the bounty of the age-old hills.
Let all these rest on the head of Joseph,
on the brow of the prince among[f] his brothers.

27 "Benjamin is a ravenous wolf;
in the morning he devours the prey,
in the evening he divides the plunder."

28 All these are the twelve tribes of Israel, and this is what
their father said to them when he blessed them, giving each the
blessing appropriate to him.

The Death of Jacob

29 Then he gave them these instructions: "I am about to be
gathered to my people. Bury me with my fathers in the cave in the
field of Ephron the Hittite, 30 the cave in the field of Machpelah,
near Mamre in Canaan, which Abraham bought as a burial place
from Ephron the Hittite, along with the field. 31 There Abraham
and his wife Sarah were buried, there Isaac and his wife Rebekah
were buried, and there I buried Leah. 32 The field and the cave in it
were bought from the Hittites.[g]"

33 When Jacob had finished giving instructions to his sons, he
drew his feet up into the bed, breathed his last and was gathered to
his people.

50 Joseph threw himself upon his father and wept over him and
kissed him. 2 Then Joseph directed the physicians in his service to

[a]21 Or *free; / he utters beautiful words* [b]22 Or *Joseph is a wild colt, / a wild colt near a spring, / a wild donkey on a terraced hill* [c]23,24 Or *archers will attack . . . will shoot . . . will remain . . . will stay* [d]25 Hebrew *Shaddai* [e]26 Or *of my progenitors, / as great as* [f]26 Or *the one separated from* [g]32 Or *the sons of Heth*

embalm his father Israel. So the physicians embalmed him, [3]taking a full forty days, for that was the time required for embalming. And the Egyptians mourned for him seventy days.

[4]When the days of mourning had passed, Joseph said to Pharaoh's court, "If I have found favor in your eyes, speak to Pharaoh for me. Tell him, [5]'My father made me swear an oath and said, "I am about to die; bury me in the tomb I dug for myself in the land of Canaan." Now let me go up and bury my father; then I will return.' "

[6]Pharaoh said, "Go up and bury your father, as he made you swear to do."

[7]So Joseph went up to bury his father. All Pharaoh's officials accompanied him—the dignitaries of his court and all the dignitaries of Egypt— [8]besides all the members of Joseph's household and his brothers and those belonging to his father's household. Only their children and their flocks and herds were left in Goshen. [9]Chariots and horsemen[a] also went up with him. It was a very large company.

[10]When they reached the threshing floor of Atad, near the Jordan, they lamented loudly and bitterly; and there Joseph observed a seven-day period of mourning for his father. [11]When the Canaanites who lived there saw the mourning at the threshing floor of Atad, they said, "The Egyptians are holding a solemn ceremony of mourning." That is why that place near the Jordan is called Abel Mizraim.[b]

[12]So Jacob's sons did as he had commanded them: [13]They carried him to the land of Canaan and buried him in the cave in the field of Machpelah, near Mamre, which Abraham had bought as a burial place from Ephron the Hittite, along with the field. [14]After burying his father, Joseph returned to Egypt, together with his brothers and all the others who had gone with him to bury his father.

Joseph Reassures His Brothers

[15]When Joseph's brothers saw that their father was dead, they said, "What if Joseph holds a grudge against us and pays us back for all the wrongs we did to him?" [16]So they sent word to Joseph, saying, "Your father left these instructions before he died: [17]'This is what you are to say to Joseph: I ask you to forgive your brothers the sins and the wrongs they committed in treating you so badly.' Now please forgive the sins of the servants of the God of your father." When their message came to him, Joseph wept.

[18]His brothers then came and threw themselves down before him. "We are your slaves," they said.

[a]9 Or *charioteers* [b]11 *Abel Mizraim* means *mourning of the Egyptians.*

50:2-4 *embalmed . . . mourning:* Embalming was an ancient Egyptian custom that was done by removing internal organs and using linen and spices to fill the body cavities. In Egypt the bodies of important kings were also wrapped in long linen bandages, becoming mummies. The process of embalming took forty days, and the time of mourning for Jacob lasted seventy days, or about the same amount of time the Egyptian people mourned the death of one of their kings. See the mini-article "Burial," p. 1998

50:7-9 *Chariots and horsemen:* See the note at 41:41-43. The horsemen were the king's horse-riding soldiers.

50:10 *threshing floor of Atad, near the Jordan:* Atad's threshing floor was likely a flat area located in a high open place exposed to the wind. During threshing, grain stalks were crushed on the floor, and then thrown into the air. The heavier grain fell to the floor, but the light chaff was blown away in the wind.

The Jordan River begins in the streams near Mount Hermon, which come together and run south into the Sea of Galilee. The river then flows south from the Sea of Galilee to the Dead Sea. It formed a natural boundary between Canaan and its neighbors to the east (see the map on p. 2464).

50:13 *cave . . . Machpelah . . . Ephron the Hittite:* See 23:3-20; 25:9,10; 49:29-31; Acts 7:16. See also the notes at 23:3 (Hittites) and 23:9 (cave).

50:5 Gen 47:29-31. **50:18** Gen 37:5-10; 42:6,9.

50:20 *God intended it for good:* Here is one final statement of this key theme in the Joseph stories: God is at work in human events, and can make good things happen even when a person's intentions are evil (see the note at 31:9). With Joseph, the people of Israel have begun to fulfill God's promise that they would be a blessing to others (12:1-3).

50:23 *children of Makir son of Manasseh . . . Joseph's knees:* Joseph likely adopted Makir as Jacob had adopted Joseph's sons (see the note at 48:5,6). The descendants of Makir are described as a warlike clan that settled in Gilead (Num 32:39, 40; Josh 17:1).

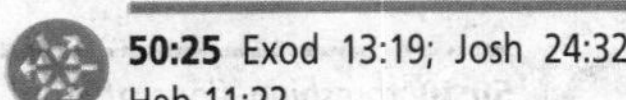

50:25 Exod 13:19; Josh 24:32; Heb 11:22.

19 But Joseph said to them, "Don't be afraid. Am I in the place of God? 20 You intended to harm me, but God intended it for good to accomplish what is now being done, the saving of many lives. 21 So then, don't be afraid. I will provide for you and your children." And he reassured them and spoke kindly to them.

The Death of Joseph

22 Joseph stayed in Egypt, along with all his father's family. He lived a hundred and ten years 23 and saw the third generation of Ephraim's children. Also the children of Makir son of Manasseh were placed at birth on Joseph's knees.[a]

24 Then Joseph said to his brothers, "I am about to die. But God will surely come to your aid and take you up out of this land to the land he promised on oath to Abraham, Isaac and Jacob." 25 And Joseph made the sons of Israel swear an oath and said, "God will surely come to your aid, and then you must carry my bones up from this place."

26 So Joseph died at the age of a hundred and ten. And after they embalmed him, he was placed in a coffin in Egypt.

[a]23 That is, were counted as his

QUESTIONS ABOUT GENESIS 37:1—50:26

1. Who was Joseph and what were his dreams? (37:5-9) How did Joseph's brothers react to his dreams? Why? What did they do to Joseph? (37:10-34)
2. What responsibilities did Potiphar give to Joseph at first? (39:1-6) Why? How did Joseph end up in jail, and how did this bad situation turn out for the best for Joseph? (39:7—41:57)
3. How was Joseph able to interpret the true meaning of dreams? (40:8; 41:15, 16,28,37-39)
4. What brought Joseph's brothers to Egypt? Describe their first meeting. What did Joseph tell them to do? (42:1-24)
5. When Joseph finally revealed who he was to his brothers, how did he explain their earlier evil action against him? (45:4-8; 50:20)
6. Compare Jacob's blessing of Joseph's sons, Manasseh and Ephraim (48:1-19) to Isaac's earlier blessing of Jacob and his brother Esau (27:1-40). How were the situations similar? Explain how Joseph's sons each became an ancestor of one of the twelve tribes of Israel, when Jacob (Israel) already had twelve sons of his own.
7. Compare Genesis 50:20 to Romans 8:28. How does God bring good results out of bad situations? What examples can you think of?
8. What is the overall message of the story of Joseph in the Bible?
9. Complete these statements.
   - My favorite part of GENESIS is . . . because. . . .
   - One new thing I learned from reading GENESIS is. . . .
   - After reading GENESIS, one question I still have is. . . .

EXODUS

Who was Moses, and how was he involved in two of the most important events in the history of the people of Israel?

WHAT MAKES EXODUS SPECIAL?

"Exodus" comes from the Greek word meaning "exit" or "the way out." Those who translated the Greek version of the Old Testament (the Septuagint) named the book EXODUS to emphasize how God chose Moses to lead the Hebrew people out of slavery in Egypt. The Hebrew title of the book means "These are the names," a phrase that appears in Genesis 46:8 and again in Exodus 1:1 and lists the names of some of Israel's ancestors. This title emphasizes how EXODUS continues the story of God's people, begun in GENESIS (see the Introduction to the Pentateuch, p. 35).

WHY WAS EXODUS WRITTEN?

EXODUS describes two key events in the history of the people of Israel. The first event is the exodus from Egypt. It begins with the birth of Moses, who becomes an Egyptian prince but later obeys God's command to free his Hebrew people from slavery in Egypt. The exodus story includes a description of the great plagues that God sent upon the Egyptian people in order to force their king (called Pharaoh) to let the people of Israel leave Egypt. The dramatic escape from Egypt includes the miraculous crossing of the Red Sea. All future generations would remember the exodus as the great example of God's saving help.

The second key event in the book occurs at Mount Sinai, where God gives Moses and the people the Ten Commandments and the laws that are to guide how they will worship and live together as God's people. Also included were instructions for making the tabernacle, its furnishings, and the priestly clothes. The covenant God made with the people at Sinai was built on the promises God had first made to Abraham (33:1-3; see also Gen 12:1-3; 15:18-21; 17:1-8). But in order to receive God's promised blessings the people had to be loyal to God alone and follow God's commands (23:20-33).

WHAT'S THE STORY BEHIND THE SCENE?

According to 1 Kings 6:1, the exodus from Egypt occurred 480 years before the fourth year of King Solomon's reign. Solomon ruled from about 970 to 931 B.C. That would mean that the exodus occurred around 1446 B.C. However, 480 may be a symbolic number for twelve generations. The small amount of historical evidence that exists (the name Rameses in 1:11) seems to point to Sety I and Rameses II as the Egyptian Pharaohs at the time of Israel's slavery and escape from Egypt (see the mini-article called "King of Egypt (Pharaoh)," p. 110. This would date the exodus shortly after 1300 B.C.

Mount Sinai: This mountain (also called Horeb) plays an important role in the story of Moses and the people of Israel as told in the last four books of the Pentateuch (EXODUS through DEUTERONOMY). It was on this holy mountain that Moses saw the burning bush and heard the voice of the God who was worshiped by Abraham, Isaac, and Jacob, the ancestors of the Israelites (3:1-6). The LORD revealed to Moses his intention to rescue the people from their life of slavery and told Moses that he had been chosen to lead the people out of Egypt (3:7-10). The LORD even revealed to Moses his personal name (3:14,15). Mount Sinai was also the place where the LORD later gave the Ten Commandments and the rest of the laws to Moses and the people of Israel (see 19–40).

Mount Sinai is located somewhere on the large Sinai Peninsula, but archaeologists and biblical scholars are uncertain about its exact location. As many as twenty different mountains have been suggested. The two shown here are the ones most frequently proposed.

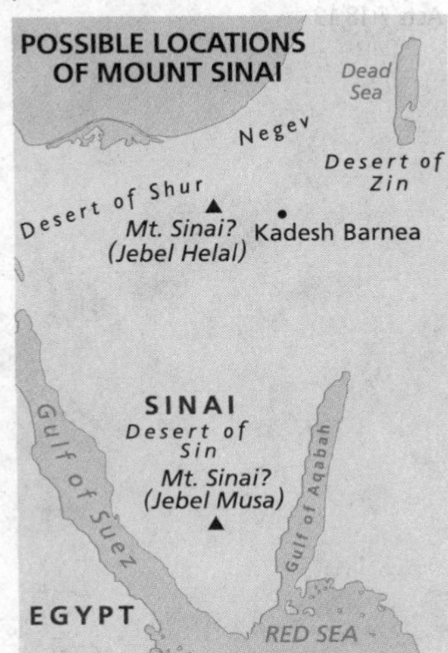

How is Exodus constructed?

The following outline divides the book into three major sections, based primarily on the location of events.

Moses leads the people out of Egypt (1:1—13:16)
Troubled times for Israel and Moses (1:1—2:25)
God chooses Moses (3:1—4:31)
The God of Israel versus Pharaoh (5:1—11:10)
Passover and the exodus (12:1—13:16)

Moses leads the people in the desert (13:17—18:27)
Escape through the sea (13:17—15:21)
God provides water and food (15:22—17:7)
Victory in battle and the appointment of judges (17:8—18:27)

Moses and the people of Israel at Mount Sinai (19:1—40:38)
God gives Moses the Law (19:1—24:18)
God gives instructions for worship (25:1—31:18)
The people rebel, but God remains faithful (32:1—33:23)
God's instructions are carried out (34:1—40:38)

1:1-7 *Jacob . . . descendants:* Jacob was the grandson of Abraham and son of Isaac (Gen 25:19-26). Jacob's son Joseph had been sold by his jealous brothers to slave traders and ended up in Egypt (Gen 37:12-36), where he eventually became second-in-command over all Egypt (Gen 41:37-57). When famine hit Canaan, Jacob's sons went to Egypt to ask for food and were reunited with Joseph. Shortly after, Jacob and his sons and their families moved to Egypt (Gen 46:8-27). They were given their own land in the region of Egypt known as Goshen (Gen 47:27), where they settled. The tribes of Israel were named for Jacob's sons (see Gen 48,49; Josh 13–21).

1:7 *the land was filled with them:* The Israelites lived in Goshen, an area of pastureland in the eastern part of the Nile River delta on the Mediterranean coast (see the map on p. 2463). The palace of the Egyptian king was in or near this region at this time. As the Hebrews filled the land, God's promise of many descendants was coming true (Gen 17:1,2; 22:17; Acts 7:17).

1:8 *new king:* The identity of this king is uncertain, but it may have been Sety I, who ruled Egypt from about 1291 to 1279 B.C. The Hebrew word for the Egyptian kings is "pharaoh." See the mini-article called "King of Egypt (Pharaoh)," p. 110. See also Acts 7:18,19.

Moses Leads the People Out of Egypt

The people of Israel are suffering in Egypt as slaves, but God hears their cries and chooses Moses to lead them out of slavery. With his brother Aaron's help, Moses shows God's power to Pharaoh, the Egyptian king, in the form of ten terrible plagues. Finally, the stubborn Pharaoh lets the Israelite people go. As they prepare to leave, Moses tells the people to prepare a special meal that will be celebrated by future generations as Passover.

TROUBLED TIMES FOR ISRAEL AND MOSES

Years after the death of Joseph (1:8) the people of Israel have become slaves in Egypt. During this time, Moses is born to a Hebrew woman but is adopted by the daughter of the Pharaoh. Moses grows up and flees Egypt after killing an Egyptian guard.

The Israelites Oppressed

1 These are the names of the sons of Israel who went to Egypt
with Jacob, each with his family: [2]Reuben, Simeon, Levi and Judah;
[3]Issachar, Zebulun and Benjamin; [4]Dan and Naphtali; Gad and
Asher. [5]The descendants of Jacob numbered seventy[a] in all; Joseph
was already in Egypt.

---

[a]5 Masoretic Text (see also Gen. 46:27); Dead Sea Scrolls and Septuagint (see also Acts 7:14 and note at Gen. 46:27) *seventy-five*

[6]Now Joseph and all his brothers and all that generation
died, [7]but the Israelites were fruitful and multiplied greatly and
became exceedingly numerous, so that the land was filled with
them.
[8]Then a new king, who did not know about Joseph, came to
power in Egypt. [9]"Look," he said to his people, "the Israelites have
become much too numerous for us. [10]Come, we must deal shrewdly with them or they will become even more numerous and, if war
breaks out, will join our enemies, fight against us and leave the
country."
[11]So they put slave masters over them to oppress them with
forced labor, and they built Pithom and Rameses as store cities for
Pharaoh. [12]But the more they were oppressed, the more they multiplied and spread; so the Egyptians came to dread the Israelites
[13]and worked them ruthlessly. [14]They made their lives bitter with
hard labor in brick and mortar and with all kinds of work in the
fields; in all their hard labor the Egyptians used them ruthlessly.
[15]The king of Egypt said to the Hebrew midwives, whose
names were Shiphrah and Puah, [16]"When you help the Hebrew
women in childbirth and observe them on the delivery stool, if it
is a boy, kill him; but if it is a girl, let her live." [17]The midwives,
however, feared God and did not do what the king of Egypt had
told them to do; they let the boys live. [18]Then the king of Egypt
summoned the midwives and asked them, "Why have you done
this? Why have you let the boys live?"

1:11 *Pithom and Rameses:* The exact location of Pithom is unknown. In Egyptian, it means "House of (the sun god) Atum." The city of Rameses was the home of Rameses II and was probably located in Goshen in the northeast part of the Nile River delta (see the map on p. 2463).

1:13,14 *hard labor in brick and mortar:* Hand-made mud bricks were made of a mixture of river-mud or clay plus a bit of straw to help them hold together better. Mortar was made of clay and sand or chalky lime or gypsum rock mixed with water. It was used to hold the bricks in place or to cover the bricks like plaster. See the illustration on p. 143, which shows ancient brick-making.

1:16 *if it is a boy, kill him:* In ancient Hebrew cultures the family line was passed on through the males, so killing the male babies was thought to be the way to wipe out that culture.

EGYPT

Egypt is located at the meeting point between northeastern Africa and southwestern Asia (see the maps on pp. 2462-2463). Egypt was one of the great centers of civilization in the world from as early as 4500 B.C. Then, as now, most Egyptians lived in two main areas of the country. The first area is the fertile strip of land along the Nile River that stretches more than 800 miles from the south to northern part of Egypt. The second main area is the far northern end of the river where it spreads out across a valley that is more than one hundred miles wide. This area is called the Nile River delta. Heavy rainfall in central Africa, where the Nile begins, causes the Nile to overflow its banks each year. Because of this, farmers in Egypt could count on plenty of water to grow rich crops of grain each year. In ancient times when Palestine and Syria got little or no rain, people would move west toward Egypt, where they could be sure of a food supply.

Many of the huge temples and tombs of Egypt have survived down to the present day. Some of these are known as the pyramids. French scholars in the time of Napoleon (late eighteenth century) discovered an ancient stone tablet called the "Rosetta Stone," which had the same passage repeated in three different languages, including Egyptian and Greek. The scholars' knowledge of Greek made it possible to decipher the Egyptian text and use what they learned to help them translate other ancient Egyptian documents and monument inscriptions that had been found. These writings showed that the history of Egypt was to be divided into a series of periods called "dynasties."

1:22 *all his people:* Since the Egyptian people participated in trying to get rid of Hebrew male babies, they suffered the consequences of God's judgment. See the mini-article "Disasters (Plagues)," p. 151.

2:1 *house of Levi:* These descendants of Jacob's son Levi (Gen 29:34) became the family line for Israel's priests (6:16-25; Deut 10:8,9).

19The midwives answered Pharaoh, "Hebrew women are not
like Egyptian women; they are vigorous and give birth before the
midwives arrive."
20So God was kind to the midwives and the people increased
and became even more numerous. 21And because the midwives
feared God, he gave them families of their own.
22Then Pharaoh gave this order to all his people: "Every boy
that is born[a] you must throw into the Nile, but let every girl live."

[a]22 Masoretic Text; Samaritan Pentateuch, Septuagint and Targums *born to the Hebrews*

EGYPTIAN DYNASTIES

DYNASTIES AND ACHIEVEMENTS	APPROX. DATES
Pre-Dynastic Period. Early Egyptian village groups began to band together.	3400-2950 B.C.
First and Second Dynasties. The Nile River valley and delta were brought under one ruler.	2950-2675 B.C.
Old Kingdom—Third to Sixth Dynasties. The great pyramids were built near Memphis.	2675-2180 B.C.
First Intermediate Period—Seventh to Tenth Dynasties. Outsiders controlled the delta—Libyans from the west and Asians from the east.	2180-1970 B.C.
Middle Kingdom—Eleventh to Twelfth Dynasties. Egypt was again unified with its capital at Thebes. This period was the high point of Egyptian art. Abraham was in Egypt during this time (Gen 12:10-20).	1970-1756 B.C.
Second Intermediate Period—Thirteenth to Seventeenth Dynasties. Egypt was ruled by the Hyksos, Asian invaders who had high technical and military skills. Based in the delta, Hyksos traded with Syria and Palestine. Possibly the period when Joseph and his family were in Egypt.	1756-1520 B.C.
New Kingdom—Eighteenth to Twentieth Dynasties. Many famous Egyptian rulers lived in this period, such as Amenhotep IV, who worshiped only Aton, god of the sun; Tutankhamen, also known as "King Tut," who restored the worship of Amon, the traditional god of the Egyptians; Rameses II, who may have been the Pharaoh when the Hebrews were led out of Egypt by Moses.	1539-1075 B.C.
Third Intermediate Period—Twenty-First to Twenty-Fifth Dynasties. A Pharaoh from one of these dynasties gave his daughter in marriage to Solomon (1 Kgs 9:16). The Egyptians could not prevent the Assyrians from invading Egypt.	1075-656 B.C.
Late Period—Twenty-Sixth to Thirty-First Dynasties. After struggles with the Assyrians, Egypt was conquered by the Persians. Then Alexander the Great of Macedonia took over Egypt in 332 B.C. Alexander built a new capital city on the Mediterranean coast where the Nile emptied into the sea and named it after himself. For 600 years Alexandria was one of the great centers of learning in the world.	664-343 B.C.
Ptolemaic Dynasty—Final Period. When Alexander the Great died, one of his generals, Ptolemy Soter, seized control of Egypt and founded the Ptolemaic Dynasty. The Ptolemies fought with the Seleucid dynasty of northern Syria for control of Palestine. Egypt became more dependent on the Roman empire. After the Ptolemaic queen Cleopatra fell from power in 30 B.C., Egypt was directly ruled by Rome.	332 B.C.-A.D. 324

The Birth of Moses

2 Now a man of the house of Levi married a Levite woman, [2]and
she became pregnant and gave birth to a son. When she saw that
he was a fine child, she hid him for three months. [3]But when she
could hide him no longer, she got a papyrus basket for him and
coated it with tar and pitch. Then she placed the child in it and put
it among the reeds along the bank of the Nile. [4]His sister stood at
a distance to see what would happen to him.

[5]Then Pharaoh's daughter went down to the Nile to bathe,
and her attendants were walking along the river bank. She saw the
basket among the reeds and sent her slave girl to get it. [6]She
opened it and saw the baby. He was crying, and she felt sorry for
him. "This is one of the Hebrew babies," she said.

[7]Then his sister asked Pharaoh's daughter, "Shall I go and get
one of the Hebrew women to nurse the baby for you?"

[8]"Yes, go," she answered. And the girl went and got the baby's
mother. [9]Pharaoh's daughter said to her, "Take this baby and nurse
him for me, and I will pay you." So the woman took the baby and
nursed him. [10]When the child grew older, she took him to Pharaoh's daughter and he became her son. She named him Moses,[a]
saying, "I drew him out of the water."

Moses Flees to Midian

[11]One day, after Moses had grown up, he went out to where
his own people were and watched them at their hard labor. He saw
an Egyptian beating a Hebrew, one of his own people. [12]Glancing
this way and that and seeing no one, he killed the Egyptian and
hid him in the sand. [13]The next day he went out and saw two
Hebrews fighting. He asked the one in the wrong, "Why are you
hitting your fellow Hebrew?"

[14]The man said, "Who made you ruler and judge over us? Are
you thinking of killing me as you killed the Egyptian?" Then Moses
was afraid and thought, "What I did must have become known."

[15]When Pharaoh heard of this, he tried to kill Moses, but
Moses fled from Pharaoh and went to live in Midian, where he sat
down by a well. [16]Now a priest of Midian had seven daughters, and
they came to draw water and fill the troughs to water their father's
flock. [17]Some shepherds came along and drove them away, but
Moses got up and came to their rescue and watered their flock.

[18]When the girls returned to Reuel their father, he asked
them, "Why have you returned so early today?"

[19]They answered, "An Egyptian rescued us from the shepherds. He even drew water for us and watered the flock."

[20]"And where is he?" he asked his daughters. "Why did you
leave him? Invite him to have something to eat."

[a]10 *Moses* sounds like the Hebrew for *draw out.*

2:3 *basket:* The word translated here as "basket" is related to an Egyptian word that is also the basis of the Hebrew word for Noah's ark (Gen 6:14). This basket was made of papyrus reeds woven together and covered with tar to make it watertight.

2:3 *the Nile:* The Nile River is the world's second longest river and an important means of travel in Egypt. Egypt's fertility depended on the flood waters of the Nile, which was considered one of Egypt's gods. See the map on p. 2462.

2:4 *sister:* This probably is Miriam, the sister of Moses and Aaron (15:20).

2:10 *Moses:* In Hebrew the word "Moses" sounds like the word for "pull out" or "the one who pulls out." Moses is an Egyptian name that means "is born" and was part of Egyptian names such as Thutmose and Rameses. For more, see the mini-article called "Moses," p. 2335. See also Acts 7:21.

2:15 *Midian:* This was a hilly region in northern Arabia along the east coast of the Gulf of Aqabah (see the map on p. 2463). The Midianites (Gen 25:2) were nomads descended from Abraham and his wife Keturah. See also Acts 7:29; Heb 11:27.

2:16 *a priest of Midian:* Though this verse in Hebrew does not give the name "Jethro," it is assumed from later verses (3:1; 4:18; 18:1,2). In the Hebrew of 2:18, he is spoken of as "Reuel," which may have been the name of the tribe Jethro belonged to. The term "priest" may simply refer to his position of leadership in the tribe, and not a religious office.

2:19 *Egyptian:* Moses was actually a Hebrew, but he was wearing Egyptian clothing and had his hair cut in an Egyptian style, having been adopted by the Egyptian royal family.

2:2 Acts 7:20; Heb 11:23. **2:11-14** Acts 7:23-28; Heb 11:24,25.

Pharaoh's Daughter Finding the Infant Moses, wall painting from a third century synagogue, Dura Europos, Syria. Many years after the death of Joseph and his brothers, a new king came to power in Egypt. He was afraid of the Hebrews. He ordered all the baby boys killed, but Moses' mother saved him by placing him in a basket and putting the basket in the Nile where he was found by Pharaoh's daughter. (See 2:1-10.)

21Moses agreed to stay with the man, who gave his daughter
Zipporah to Moses in marriage. 22Zipporah gave birth to a son,
and Moses named him Gershom,[a] saying, "I have become an alien
in a foreign land."

23During that long period, the king of Egypt died. The
Israelites groaned in their slavery and cried out, and their cry for
help because of their slavery went up to God. 24God heard their
groaning and he remembered his covenant with Abraham, with
Isaac and with Jacob. 25So God looked on the Israelites and was
concerned about them.

GOD CHOOSES MOSES

The LORD, the God of Moses' ancestors, chooses Moses to return to Egypt and lead the Israelite people out of slavery. Though Moses is not sure he can do this job, God promises to give Moses great help. Moses also finds out God's name.

Moses and the Burning Bush

3 Now Moses was tending the flock of Jethro his father-in-law,
the priest of Midian, and he led the flock to the far side of the
desert and came to Horeb, the mountain of God. 2There the angel
of the LORD appeared to him in flames of fire from within a bush.
Moses saw that though the bush was on fire it did not burn up.

[a]22 *Gershom* sounds like the Hebrew for *an alien there.*

2:22 *Gershom:* In Hebrew "Gershom" sounds like the word for "foreigner."

2:23 *king of Egypt died:* See the note at 1:8. The new king (possibly Rameses II) was as cruel as the previous king had been. See also the mini-article called "King of Egypt (Pharaoh)," p. 110 and the chart "Egyptian Kings (Pharaohs) in the Bible," on p. 111.

2:24 *covenant:* God's help was based on covenants made to the Israelites' ancestors: Abraham (Gen 15:13-18; 17:1-9), Isaac (Gen 17:19; 26:24), and Jacob (Gen 35:9-12).

3:1 *Horeb, the mountain of God:* Horeb is also called Mount Sinai. See the note and map on p. 133.

3:2 *flames . . . fire:* Fire and smoke often signal the presence of God. See Gen 15:17,18; Exod 13:21, 22; 19:16-19; Judg 13:20.

3:2-10 Acts 7:30-34.

3So Moses thought, "I will go over and see this strange sight—why
the bush does not burn up."
4When the LORD saw that he had gone over to look, God
called to him from within the bush, "Moses! Moses!"
And Moses said, "Here I am."
5"Do not come any closer," God said. "Take off your sandals,
for the place where you are standing is holy ground." 6Then he
said, "I am the God of your father, the God of Abraham, the God
of Isaac and the God of Jacob." At this, Moses hid his face, because
he was afraid to look at God.
7The LORD said, "I have indeed seen the misery of my people
in Egypt. I have heard them crying out because of their slave drivers, and I am concerned about their suffering. 8So I have come
down to rescue them from the hand of the Egyptians and to bring
them up out of that land into a good and spacious land, a land
flowing with milk and honey—the home of the Canaanites, Hittites, Amorites, Perizzites, Hivites and Jebusites. 9And now the cry
of the Israelites has reached me, and I have seen the way the Egyptians are oppressing them. 10So now, go. I am sending you to Pharaoh to bring my people the Israelites out of Egypt."
11But Moses said to God, "Who am I, that I should go to
Pharaoh and bring the Israelites out of Egypt?"
12And God said, "I will be with you. And this will be the sign
to you that it is I who have sent you: When you have brought the
people out of Egypt, you[a] will worship God on this mountain."
13Moses said to God, "Suppose I go to the Israelites and say
to them, 'The God of your fathers has sent me to you,' and they
ask me, 'What is his name?' Then what shall I tell them?"
14God said to Moses, "I AM WHO I AM.[b] This is what you are
to say to the Israelites: 'I AM has sent me to you.'"
15God also said to Moses, "Say to the Israelites, 'The LORD,[c] the
God of your fathers—the God of Abraham, the God of Isaac and the
God of Jacob—has sent me to you.' This is my name forever, the name
by which I am to be remembered from generation to generation.
16"Go, assemble the elders of Israel and say to them, 'The
LORD, the God of your fathers—the God of Abraham, Isaac and
Jacob—appeared to me and said: I have watched over you and
have seen what has been done to you in Egypt. 17And I have
promised to bring you up out of your misery in Egypt into the
land of the Canaanites, Hittites, Amorites, Perizzites, Hivites and
Jebusites—a land flowing with milk and honey.'
18"The elders of Israel will listen to you. Then you and the
elders are to go to the king of Egypt and say to him, 'The LORD, the
God of the Hebrews, has met with us. Let us take a three-day journey into the desert to offer sacrifices to the LORD our God.' 19But I

[a]**12** The Hebrew is plural. [b]**14** Or *I WILL BE WHAT I WILL BE* [c]**15** The Hebrew for *LORD* sounds like and may be derived from the Hebrew for *I AM* in verse 14.

3:4 *LORD:* See the mini-article called "LORD (YHWH)," on p. 140.

3:5 *Take off your sandals . . . holy ground:* Removing sandals may have been an ancient custom connected with holy places, though it was not required in the Law of Moses.

3:8 *Canaanites . . . Jebusites:* The Canaanites were descendants of Noah's son Ham, and the Hittites were a powerful people descended from Heth, grandson of Ham (Gen 10:6-20). The Amorites lived in the hill country at the time the Israelites invaded (Num 21:21-35; Josh 2:10). It is not clear who the Perizzites were. The Hivites may have settled in the area around Mount Seir but were later pushed out by the descendants of Esau. The Jebusites were located in and around Jerusalem until King David took over (2 Sam 5:6-9). See also Num 13:29; Deut 7:1.

3:16 *elders of Israel:* The Hebrew word here refers to "those with beards," meaning the older and experienced men who were the heads of each clan or tribe.

3:18 *king of Egypt:* See the note at 2:23.

3:18 *offer sacrifices:* Offering sacrifices to gods and goddesses was a common worship practice in the ancient world (Gen 22:13,14). These sacrifices were a way to maintain, restore, or celebrate the relationship between the giver and God. Before the Law of Moses commanded sacrifices to be done by Israel's priests, sacrifices were offered by the head of each family. See also the chart called "Sacrifices and Offerings," p. 219.

3:13 Exod 6:2,3. **3:14,15** Rev 1:4,8.

4:2,3 *A staff . . . snake:* The king of Egypt often wore a headpiece that included a metal cobra, or snake, which symbolized the king's majesty and power. Turning the staff into a snake and back again may have been meant to show that the LORD was more powerful than Egypt's king, who was considered a god by the Egyptians.

3:21,22 Exod 12:35,36. **4:5** Exod 3:6.

know that the king of Egypt will not let you go unless a mighty hand
compels him. 20So I will stretch out my hand and strike the Egyptians with all the wonders that I will perform among them. After
that, he will let you go.
21"And I will make the Egyptians favorably disposed toward this
people, so that when you leave you will not go empty-handed. 22Every
woman is to ask her neighbor and any woman living in her house for
articles of silver and gold and for clothing, which you will put on your
sons and daughters. And so you will plunder the Egyptians."

Signs for Moses

4 Moses answered, "What if they do not believe me or listen to
me and say, 'The LORD did not appear to you'?"
2Then the LORD said to him, "What is that in your hand?"
"A staff," he replied.
3The LORD said, "Throw it on the ground."
Moses threw it on the ground and it became a snake, and he
ran from it. 4Then the LORD said to him, "Reach out your hand and
take it by the tail." So Moses reached out and took hold of the
snake and it turned back into a staff in his hand. 5"This," said the
LORD, "is so that they may believe that the LORD, the God of their

LORD (YHWH)

God's personal name appears over 5,700 times in the Old Testament. This name was revealed to Moses at the burning bush (Exod 3:1-15). In Hebrew it is written as the four letters "YHWH" and probably is meant to be pronounced *Yahweh* (YAH-way). The exact pronunciation is unknown because the Jews came to consider this name so holy that they would not say it out loud, except at special times, such as the Day of Atonement. Even then, only a particular chosen priest was allowed to speak God's name.

When Jews read YHWH in their Bible they carefully substituted another word for God that emphasizes God's power. This word is *Adonai* and means "my lord." The Jewish Scriptures (which Christians call the Old Testament) were written in Hebrew with consonants but no vowels. Hundreds of years after the Scriptures were first written down, scholars who copied the Bible wrote the vowels for *Adonai* under the consonants for *Yahweh* to remind the reader not to pronounce God's holy name. If it was pronounced with this mix of vowels and consonants it sounded like *Yehovah*, or Jehovah, but this is not natural to Hebrew pronunciation.

When the Old Testament was translated into Greek in the second or third centuries B.C., the translators did not translate this holy name. Instead, they used the Greek word for *Adonai*, which is *kyrios*, and means "lord." Many modern Bible translations, including the NIV, show the Hebrew word YHWH (*Yahweh*) as LORD, written with small capital letters. See also the mini-article called "I Am," p. 2081.

fathers—the God of Abraham, the God of Isaac and the God of
Jacob—has appeared to you."
[6]Then the LORD said, "Put your hand inside your cloak." So
Moses put his hand into his cloak, and when he took it out, it was
leprous,[a] like snow.
[7]"Now put it back into your cloak," he said. So Moses put his
hand back into his cloak, and when he took it out, it was restored,
like the rest of his flesh.
[8]Then the LORD said, "If they do not believe you or pay
attention to the first miraculous sign, they may believe the second.
[9]But if they do not believe these two signs or listen to you, take
some water from the Nile and pour it on the dry ground. The
water you take from the river will become blood on the ground."
[10]Moses said to the LORD, "O Lord, I have never been eloquent, neither in the past nor since you have spoken to your servant. I am slow of speech and tongue."
[11]The LORD said to him, "Who gave man his mouth? Who
makes him deaf or mute? Who gives him sight or makes him
blind? Is it not I, the LORD? [12]Now go; I will help you speak and
will teach you what to say."
[13]But Moses said, "O Lord, please send someone else to
do it."
[14]Then the LORD's anger burned against Moses and he said,
"What about your brother, Aaron the Levite? I know he can speak
well. He is already on his way to meet you, and his heart will be
glad when he sees you. [15]You shall speak to him and put words in
his mouth; I will help both of you speak and will teach you what
to do. [16]He will speak to the people for you, and it will be as if he
were your mouth and as if you were God to him. [17]But take this
staff in your hand so you can perform miraculous signs with it."

Moses Returns to Egypt

[18]Then Moses went back to Jethro his father-in-law and said
to him, "Let me go back to my own people in Egypt to see if any
of them are still alive."
Jethro said, "Go, and I wish you well."
[19]Now the LORD had said to Moses in Midian, "Go back to
Egypt, for all the men who wanted to kill you are dead." [20]So Moses
took his wife and sons, put them on a donkey and started back to
Egypt. And he took the staff of God in his hand.
[21]The LORD said to Moses, "When you return to Egypt, see
that you perform before Pharaoh all the wonders I have given you
the power to do. But I will harden his heart so that he will not let
the people go. [22]Then say to Pharaoh, 'This is what the LORD says:
Israel is my firstborn son, [23]and I told you, "Let my son go, so he

[a]6 The Hebrew word was used for various diseases affecting the skin—not necessarily leprosy.

4:6 *leprous:* Moses' hand had turned white with leprosy. The word "leprosy" was used for many different kinds of skin diseases.

4:9 *Nile:* See the note at 2:3 and the mini-article called "Egypt," p. 135.

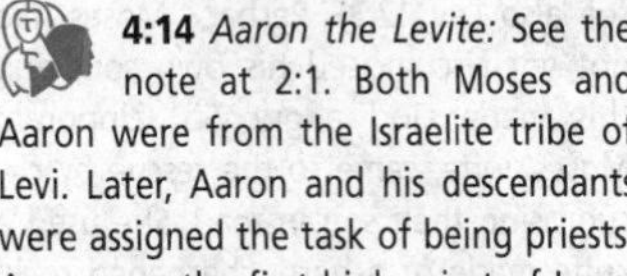

4:14 *Aaron the Levite:* See the note at 2:1. Both Moses and Aaron were from the Israelite tribe of Levi. Later, Aaron and his descendants were assigned the task of being priests. Aaron was the first high priest of Israel (27:21—28:3).

4:18 *Jethro:* See the note at 2:16.

4:19 *Midian . . . Egypt:* See the note at 2:15, 16 (Midian) and the mini-article called "Egypt," p. 135.

4:21 *perform . . . all the wonders:* See 4:2-9 and the note at 4:2,3.

4:22 *Israel is my firstborn son:* Jacob, the grandson of Abraham, was renamed "Israel" (Gen 32:28). Jacob's (Israel's) sons were the ancestors of the tribes of Israel (see the note at 1:1-7). Ancient laws allowed for a father to give a greater share of his property to his oldest son. As God's "firstborn," the people of Israel had the special privileges and inheritance reserved for the firstborn (Deut 21:15-17). See also the mini-article called "Birthright," p. 80.

4:23 Exod 12:29.

4:25,26 *circumcision:* "Circumcision" was the ceremony of cutting off the foreskin of a male's penis. According to God's covenant with Abraham, Hebrew fathers were responsible for making sure the males in their families were circumcised. This was to show that Abraham's descendants were God's chosen people (Gen 17:1-14; 34:21-23; see also Lev 12:3). Perhaps Moses had not yet circumcised his own son, and this made God angry. So, Zipporah, Moses' wife, came to the rescue by circumcising their son instead. She used a knife made of a hard, sharpened rock. As a daughter of a priest (2:15,16), she was likely familiar with religious rituals. She put some of the blood which flowed from the cut on Moses' or the boy's leg, which probably was meant to symbolize the genitals. Blood was believed to have saving or protective power (see 12:21–23). See also the mini-articles called "Blood," p. 180 and "Circumcision," p. 2251.

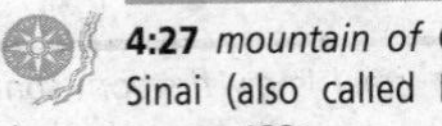

4:27 *mountain of God:* Mount Sinai (also called Horeb). See the note on p. 133.

4:29 *elders of the Israelites:* See the note at 3:16.

5:1 *Pharaoh:* See the notes at 1:8 and 2:23.

5:3 *God of the Hebrews . . . sacrifices:* "Hebrews" is another name for Israelites, the descendants of Abraham, Isaac, and Jacob. Ancient sources other than the Bible speak of a people known as *Habiru* or *Apiru*, which may be related to the name Hebrew. These people were described as poor immigrants or foreigners who wandered from place to place but did not own land or property in a specific place. For more about sacrifices, see the note at 3:18 (offer sacrifices).

4:28 Exod 4:1-9.

may worship me." But you refused to let him go; so I will kill your
firstborn son.' "
24 At a lodging place on the way, the LORD met ⌞Moses⌟[a] and was
about to kill him. 25 But Zipporah took a flint knife, cut off her son's
foreskin and touched ⌞Moses'⌟ feet with it.[b] "Surely you are a bridegroom of blood to me," she said. 26 So the LORD let him alone. (At that
time she said "bridegroom of blood," referring to circumcision.)
27 The LORD said to Aaron, "Go into the desert to meet
Moses." So he met Moses at the mountain of God and kissed him.
28 Then Moses told Aaron everything the LORD had sent him to say,
and also about all the miraculous signs he had commanded him to
perform.
29 Moses and Aaron brought together all the elders of the
Israelites, 30 and Aaron told them everything the LORD had said to
Moses. He also performed the signs before the people, 31 and they
believed. And when they heard that the LORD was concerned
about them and had seen their misery, they bowed down and
worshiped.

THE GOD OF ISRAEL VERSUS PHARAOH

Moses and Aaron go to Pharaoh and tell him what the LORD God of Israel demands: Let the Israelite people be released from slavery in Egypt. Each time Pharaoh refuses, God sends a different plague upon Egypt as an example of God's power.

Bricks Without Straw

5 Afterward Moses and Aaron went to Pharaoh and said, "This is
what the LORD, the God of Israel, says: 'Let my people go, so that
they may hold a festival to me in the desert.' "
2 Pharaoh said, "Who is the LORD, that I should obey him and
let Israel go? I do not know the LORD and I will not let Israel go."
3 Then they said, "The God of the Hebrews has met with us.
Now let us take a three-day journey into the desert to offer sacrifices to the LORD our God, or he may strike us with plagues or with
the sword."
4 But the king of Egypt said, "Moses and Aaron, why are you
taking the people away from their labor? Get back to your work!"
5 Then Pharaoh said, "Look, the people of the land are now
numerous, and you are stopping them from working."
6 That same day Pharaoh gave this order to the slave drivers
and foremen in charge of the people: 7 "You are no longer to supply the people with straw for making bricks; let them go and gather their own straw. 8 But require them to make the same number of
bricks as before; don't reduce the quota. They are lazy; that is why

[a]24 Or *⌞Moses' son⌟*; Hebrew *him* [b]25 Or *and drew near ⌞Moses'⌟ feet*

Making Bricks. In ancient times, bricks were made by adding straw or sand to a mud or clay mixture. Workers mixed the straw and mud together with a stick or by hand, sometimes standing right in the mud pit. The wet mud and straw mixture was put in wooden brick-shaped molds, and the wet bricks were laid out in rows so that they could dry in the hot sun. As the bricks dried and became hard, the straw made the mud bricks stronger and kept them from shrinking, cracking, or losing their shape. Bricks were the most widely used building material in the ancient Near East.

they are crying out, 'Let us go and sacrifice to our God.' 9Make the
work harder for the men so that they keep working and pay no
attention to lies."

10Then the slave drivers and the foremen went out and said
to the people, "This is what Pharaoh says: 'I will not give you any
more straw. 11Go and get your own straw wherever you can find
it, but your work will not be reduced at all.'" 12So the people scattered all over Egypt to gather stubble to use for straw. 13The slave
drivers kept pressing them, saying, "Complete the work required
of you for each day, just as when you had straw." 14The Israelite
foremen appointed by Pharaoh's slave drivers were beaten and
were asked, "Why didn't you meet your quota of bricks yesterday
or today, as before?"

15Then the Israelite foremen went and appealed to Pharaoh:
"Why have you treated your servants this way? 16Your servants are
given no straw, yet we are told, 'Make bricks!' Your servants are
being beaten, but the fault is with your own people."

5:7,8 *straw . . . same number of bricks:* In ancient times, bricks were often made by adding straw to a mud or clay mixture. Collecting enough straw to make large numbers of bricks would have taken a lot of time. Though this job was added to the Hebrew slaves' brick making, the number of bricks they had to make did not change. They had to work longer and harder to complete their assigned tasks. See also the note at 1:13,14.

The LORD said to Moses, *"I am the LORD, and I will bring you out from under the yoke of the Egyptians. I will free you from being slaves to them, and I will redeem you. . . . I will take you as my own people, and I will be your God."*
Exod 6:6,7

6:2,3 *I am the LORD . . . God Almighty:* For more about LORD, see the mini-article called "LORD (YHWH)," on p. 140. In Hebrew "God Almighty" is *El Shaddai*, which means "God, the One of the Mountains" (Gen 35:9-11). *El* was one of the most common names for god among the Canaanites. The Canaanites did not believe that *El* was the only god, but they believed that he ruled over all the other gods. In the Jewish Scriptures (Old Testament) this name frequently refers to the God of Israel. See also Gen 17:1; 28:3.

6:4-8 *I also established my covenant . . . bring you to the land:* See the notes at 2:24 and 3:8.

[17]Pharaoh said, "Lazy, that's what you are—lazy! That is why you keep saying, 'Let us go and sacrifice to the LORD.' [18]Now get to work. You will not be given any straw, yet you must produce your full quota of bricks."

[19]The Israelite foremen realized they were in trouble when they were told, "You are not to reduce the number of bricks required of you for each day." [20]When they left Pharaoh, they found Moses and Aaron waiting to meet them, [21]and they said, "May the LORD look upon you and judge you! You have made us a stench to Pharaoh and his officials and have put a sword in their hand to kill us."

God Promises Deliverance

[22]Moses returned to the LORD and said, "O Lord, why have you brought trouble upon this people? Is this why you sent me? [23]Ever since I went to Pharaoh to speak in your name, he has brought trouble upon this people, and you have not rescued your people at all."

6 Then the LORD said to Moses, "Now you will see what I will do to Pharaoh: Because of my mighty hand he will let them go; because of my mighty hand he will drive them out of his country."

[2]God also said to Moses, "I am the LORD. [3]I appeared to Abraham, to Isaac and to Jacob as God Almighty,[a] but by my name the LORD[b] I did not make myself known to them.[c] [4]I also established my covenant with them to give them the land of Canaan, where they lived as aliens. [5]Moreover, I have heard the groaning of the Israelites, whom the Egyptians are enslaving, and I have remembered my covenant.

[6]"Therefore, say to the Israelites: 'I am the LORD, and I will bring you out from under the yoke of the Egyptians. I will free you from being slaves to them, and I will redeem you with an outstretched arm and with mighty acts of judgment. [7]I will take you as my own people, and I will be your God. Then you will know that I am the LORD your God, who brought you out from under the yoke of the Egyptians. [8]And I will bring you to the land I swore with uplifted hand to give to Abraham, to Isaac and to Jacob. I will give it to you as a possession. I am the LORD.' "

[9]Moses reported this to the Israelites, but they did not listen to him because of their discouragement and cruel bondage.

[10]Then the LORD said to Moses, [11]"Go, tell Pharaoh king of Egypt to let the Israelites go out of his country."

[12]But Moses said to the LORD, "If the Israelites will not listen to me, why would Pharaoh listen to me, since I speak with faltering lips[d]?"

---

[a]3 Hebrew *El-Shaddai* [b]3 See note at Exodus 3:15. [c]3 Or *Almighty, and by my name the LORD did I not let myself be known to them?* [d]12 Hebrew *I am uncircumcised of lips*; also in verse 30

Family Record of Moses and Aaron

13Now the LORD spoke to Moses and Aaron about the
Israelites and Pharaoh king of Egypt, and he commanded them to
bring the Israelites out of Egypt.

14These were the heads of their families[a]:

The sons of Reuben the firstborn son of Israel were
Hanoch and Pallu, Hezron and Carmi. These were the clans
of Reuben.

15The sons of Simeon were Jemuel, Jamin, Ohad, Jakin,
Zohar and Shaul the son of a Canaanite woman. These were
the clans of Simeon.

16These were the names of the sons of Levi according to
their records: Gershon, Kohath and Merari. Levi lived 137 years.
17The sons of Gershon, by clans, were Libni and Shimei.
18The sons of Kohath were Amram, Izhar, Hebron and
Uzziel. Kohath lived 133 years.
19The sons of Merari were Mahli and Mushi.
These were the clans of Levi according to their records.
20Amram married his father's sister Jochebed, who bore
him Aaron and Moses. Amram lived 137 years.
21The sons of Izhar were Korah, Nepheg and Zicri.
22The sons of Uzziel were Mishael, Elzaphan and Sithri.
23Aaron married Elisheba, daughter of Amminadab and
sister of Nahshon, and she bore him Nadab and Abihu,
Eleazar and Ithamar.
24The sons of Korah were Assir, Elkanah and Abiasaph.
These were the Korahite clans.
25Eleazar son of Aaron married one of the daughters of
Putiel, and she bore him Phinehas.

These were the heads of the Levite families, clan by clan.

26It was this same Aaron and Moses to whom the LORD said,
"Bring the Israelites out of Egypt by their divisions." 27They were
the ones who spoke to Pharaoh king of Egypt about bringing the
Israelites out of Egypt. It was the same Moses and Aaron.

Aaron to Speak for Moses

28Now when the LORD spoke to Moses in Egypt, 29he said to
him, "I am the LORD. Tell Pharaoh king of Egypt everything I tell
you."

30But Moses said to the LORD, "Since I speak with faltering lips, why would Pharaoh listen to me?"
7 Then the LORD said to Moses, "See, I have made you like God
to Pharaoh, and your brother Aaron will be your prophet. 2You are

[a]14 The Hebrew for *families* here and in verse 25 refers to units larger than clans.

6:14-25 *heads of their families:* Ancestral clans are groups of extended families who are descended from a common male ancestor. Tribes are made up of all the clans who are descended from a single male ancestor (for Israelites, one of Jacob's sons). See also the mini-articles called "Genealogies in the Bible," p. 734 and "Israel," p. 264.

Only the three oldest of Jacob's twelve sons are mentioned in this list (genealogy), since the story is mainly concerned with describing the family history of Moses and Aaron. They were from the tribe of Levi and so were part of the family that became Israel's priests (see the note at 2:1).

6:29 *Pharaoh king of Egypt:* See the notes at 1:8 and 2:23.

7:1,2 *prophet:* A prophet is someone who speaks God's message. The message the prophet speaks is called a "prophecy." While the prophets of the Bible sometimes told what would happen in the future, they mainly observed what was happening around them and then delivered God's message for that situation. Because Aaron would be speaking for God and for Moses, God here calls him a prophet (4:13-16). See also the article called "Prophets and Prophecy," p. 935.

6:16-19 Num 3:17-20; 26:57,58; 1 Chr 6:16-30.

to say everything I command you, and your brother Aaron is to tell Pharaoh to let the Israelites go out of his country. [3]But I will harden Pharaoh's heart, and though I multiply my miraculous signs and wonders in Egypt, [4]he will not listen to you. Then I will lay my hand on Egypt and with mighty acts of judgment I will bring out my divisions, my people the Israelites. [5]And the Egyptians will know that I am the LORD when I stretch out my hand against Egypt and bring the Israelites out of it."

[6]Moses and Aaron did just as the LORD commanded them. [7]Moses was eighty years old and Aaron eighty-three when they spoke to Pharaoh.

Aaron's Staff Becomes a Snake

[8]The LORD said to Moses and Aaron, [9]"When Pharaoh says to you, 'Perform a miracle,' then say to Aaron, 'Take your staff and throw it down before Pharaoh,' and it will become a snake."

[10]So Moses and Aaron went to Pharaoh and did just as the LORD commanded. Aaron threw his staff down in front of Pharaoh and his officials, and it became a snake. [11]Pharaoh then summoned wise men and sorcerers, and the Egyptian magicians also did the same things by their secret arts: [12]Each one threw down his staff and it became a snake. But Aaron's staff swallowed up their staffs. [13]Yet Pharaoh's heart became hard and he would not listen to them, just as the LORD had said.

The Plague of Blood

[14]Then the LORD said to Moses, "Pharaoh's heart is unyielding; he refuses to let the people go. [15]Go to Pharaoh in the morning as he goes out to the water. Wait on the bank of the Nile to meet him, and take in your hand the staff that was changed into a snake. [16]Then say to him, 'The LORD, the God of the Hebrews, has sent me to say to you: Let my people go, so that they may worship me in the desert. But until now you have not listened. [17]This is what the LORD says: By this you will know that I am the LORD: With the staff that is in my hand I will strike the water of the Nile, and it will be changed into blood. [18]The fish in the Nile will die, and the river will stink; the Egyptians will not be able to drink its water.' "

[19]The LORD said to Moses, "Tell Aaron, 'Take your staff and stretch out your hand over the waters of Egypt—over the streams and canals, over the ponds and all the reservoirs'—and they will turn to blood. Blood will be everywhere in Egypt, even in the wooden buckets and stone jars."

[20]Moses and Aaron did just as the LORD had commanded. He raised his staff in the presence of Pharaoh and his officials and struck the water of the Nile, and all the water was changed into blood. [21]The fish in the Nile died, and the river smelled so bad that

7:3,4 *I will harden Pharaoh's heart:* Throughout the story, Pharaoh hardens his heart on his own (7:13,14,22; 8:15,19,32; 9:7), or the LORD acts to harden Pharaoh's heart (9:12; 10:1,20,27; 11:10; 14:8). Pharaoh's stubbornness leads to many plagues that reveal the power of Israel's God (9:16).

7:7 *eighty years old:* Compare to 2:11, where Moses is said to be "grown up." Acts 7:23 tells us that he was forty years old when he went to visit the Israelites, killed the man, and ran away. That means that he spent at least forty years in Midian before returning to Egypt.

7:9-11 *Pharaoh . . . wise men and sorcerers . . . magicians:* See the notes at 1:8 and 2:23. In ancient Egypt, many gods were worshiped, and they were believed to control the forces of nature. The king of Egypt himself was considered a god. Great temples were built to the gods, and priests were assigned to serve the gods or get messages from them. The wise men may have been such priests, who sometimes tried to predict the future by looking at how light reflected off liquids in a cup (Gen 44:5-15). Magicians may have been people who did magic tricks and claimed they were miracles of the gods. When Aaron's staff swallowed the snakes thrown down by the magicians, it showed the LORD's power over the Egyptian gods. See also the article called "Miracles, Magic, and Medicine," p. 1838.

7:15 *Nile:* See the note at 2:3 (the Nile). This disaster was especially horrible because it struck the river, which the Egyptians saw as the source of life.

7:3,4 Exod 3:19,20; 4:21. **7:17** Rev 16:4.

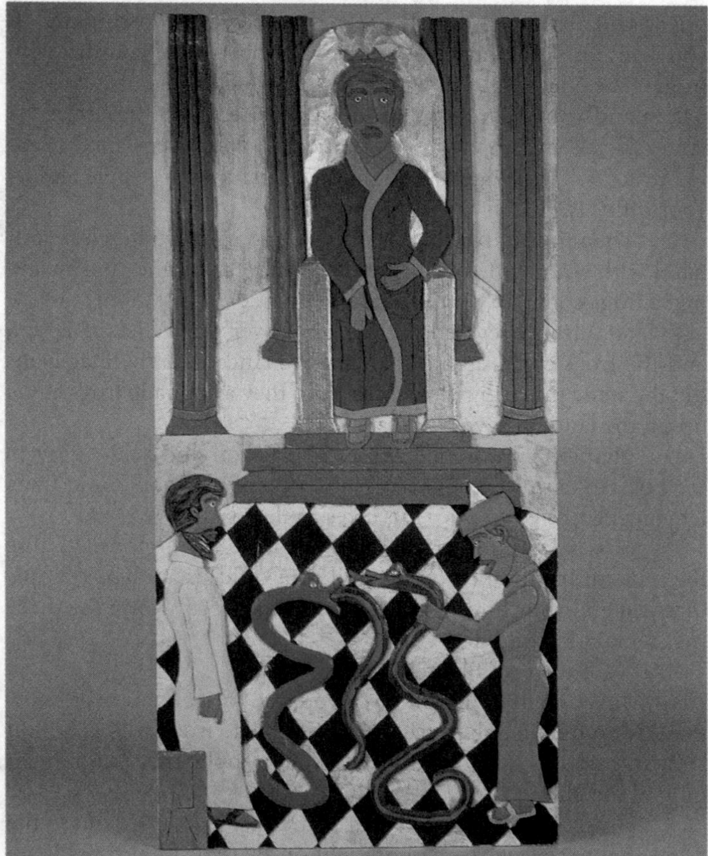

Moses and Aaron by Leroy Almon, Sr., 1988. The LORD told Moses and Aaron to go to Pharaoh and ask him to let the people of Israel leave Egypt where they had been living as slaves. The LORD told them to throw Aaron's staff (walking stick) down in front of the king. They did, and the staff turned into a snake. When the king's magicians did the same miracle, the LORD's snake swallowed up the snakes of the magicians. Even so, Pharaoh would not let the Israelites leave Egypt. (See 7:8-13.)

the Egyptians could not drink its water. Blood was everywhere in
Egypt.
22 But the Egyptian magicians did the same things by their
secret arts, and Pharaoh's heart became hard; he would not listen
to Moses and Aaron, just as the LORD had said. 23 Instead, he turned
and went into his palace, and did not take even this to heart. 24 And
all the Egyptians dug along the Nile to get drinking water, because
they could not drink the water of the river.

The Plague of Frogs

8 25 Seven days passed after the LORD struck the Nile. 1 Then the
LORD said to Moses, "Go to Pharaoh and say to him, 'This is what

7:19 *stretch out your hand:* The outstretched arm is often a symbol of God's power or protection in the Bible (15:12,16; Deut 5:15; Isa 14:27; 40:10). Here Aaron not only speaks for Moses but also performs the action that causes God's miracle to happen. Similarly, in EXODUS, the outstretched arms of Moses represent God's power and willingness to help his chosen people (14:21,27; 17:10-13).

7:19-24 *waters of Egypt:* Any water that came from streams, ponds, and irrigation canals fed by the river turned to blood, even water collected in wooden buckets or stone jars. The Bible doesn't explain where the Egyptian magicians found fresh water to turn to blood, but in doing so, they only made matters worse. The devastating effect of what Moses and Aaron had done by God's power was so great that the Egyptians had to dig wells to find underground water that didn't come from the river.

7:25 *Seven days:* The number "seven" symbolized completeness. See the chart called "Numbers in the Bible," p. 2405.

the LORD says: Let my people go, so that they may worship me. 2 If
you refuse to let them go, I will plague your whole country with
frogs. 3 The Nile will teem with frogs. They will come up into your
palace and your bedroom and onto your bed, into the houses of
your officials and on your people, and into your ovens and kneading troughs. 4 The frogs will go up on you and your people and all
your officials.' "
5 Then the LORD said to Moses, "Tell Aaron, 'Stretch out your
hand with your staff over the streams and canals and ponds, and
make frogs come up on the land of Egypt.' "
6 So Aaron stretched out his hand over the waters of Egypt,
and the frogs came up and covered the land. 7 But the magicians
did the same things by their secret arts; they also made frogs come
up on the land of Egypt.
8 Pharaoh summoned Moses and Aaron and said, "Pray to
the LORD to take the frogs away from me and my people, and I will
let your people go to offer sacrifices to the LORD."
9 Moses said to Pharaoh, "I leave to you the honor of setting
the time for me to pray for you and your officials and your people
that you and your houses may be rid of the frogs, except for those
that remain in the Nile."
10 "Tomorrow," Pharaoh said.
Moses replied, "It will be as you say, so that you may know
there is no one like the LORD our God. 11 The frogs will leave you
and your houses, your officials and your people; they will remain
only in the Nile."
12 After Moses and Aaron left Pharaoh, Moses cried out to the
LORD about the frogs he had brought on Pharaoh. 13 And the LORD
did what Moses asked. The frogs died in the houses, in the courtyards and in the fields. 14 They were piled into heaps, and the land
reeked of them. 15 But when Pharaoh saw that there was relief, he
hardened his heart and would not listen to Moses and Aaron, just
as the LORD had said.

The Plague of Gnats

16 Then the LORD said to Moses, "Tell Aaron, 'Stretch out your
staff and strike the dust of the ground,' and throughout the land of
Egypt the dust will become gnats." 17 They did this, and when
Aaron stretched out his hand with the staff and struck the dust of
the ground, gnats came upon men and animals. All the dust
throughout the land of Egypt became gnats. 18 But when the magicians tried to produce gnats by their secret arts, they could not.
And the gnats were on men and animals.
19 The magicians said to Pharaoh, "This is the finger of God."
But Pharaoh's heart was hard and he would not listen, just as the
LORD had said.

8:2 *frogs:* Frogs thrive in marshes and along rivers. They were known to be a nuisance in regions near the Nile River. A huge swarm of frogs was a disaster the people of Egypt would have been very familiar with, though the one described here was clearly bigger than usual.

8:5,6 *Aaron stretched out his hand:* See the note at 7:19.

8:7 *magicians:* See the note at 7:9-11. Again, the fact that the magicians can also produce frogs only makes matters worse.

8:8 *offer sacrifices:* See the note at 3:18 (offer sacrifices).

8:10 *LORD:* See the note at 6:2, 3.

8:16 *gnats:* These tiny biting insects typically hatch in flooded fields around the Nile in the late autumn.

8:19 Exod 7:5; 10:7; Luke 11:20.

The Plague of Flies

[20]Then the LORD said to Moses, "Get up early in the morning and confront Pharaoh as he goes to the water and say to him, 'This is what the LORD says: Let my people go, so that they may worship me. [21]If you do not let my people go, I will send swarms of flies on you and your officials, on your people and into your houses. The houses of the Egyptians will be full of flies, and even the ground where they are.

[22]" 'But on that day I will deal differently with the land of Goshen, where my people live; no swarms of flies will be there, so that you will know that I, the LORD, am in this land. [23]I will make a distinction[a] between my people and your people. This miraculous sign will occur tomorrow.' "

[24]And the LORD did this. Dense swarms of flies poured into Pharaoh's palace and into the houses of his officials, and throughout Egypt the land was ruined by the flies.

[25]Then Pharaoh summoned Moses and Aaron and said, "Go, sacrifice to your God here in the land."

[26]But Moses said, "That would not be right. The sacrifices we offer the LORD our God would be detestable to the Egyptians. And if we offer sacrifices that are detestable in their eyes, will they not stone us? [27]We must take a three-day journey into the desert to offer sacrifices to the LORD our God, as he commands us."

[28]Pharaoh said, "I will let you go to offer sacrifices to the LORD your God in the desert, but you must not go very far. Now pray for me."

[29]Moses answered, "As soon as I leave you, I will pray to the LORD, and tomorrow the flies will leave Pharaoh and his officials and his people. Only be sure that Pharaoh does not act deceitfully again by not letting the people go to offer sacrifices to the LORD."

[30]Then Moses left Pharaoh and prayed to the LORD, [31]and the LORD did what Moses asked: The flies left Pharaoh and his officials and his people; not a fly remained. [32]But this time also Pharaoh hardened his heart and would not let the people go.

The Plague on Livestock

9 Then the LORD said to Moses, "Go to Pharaoh and say to him, 'This is what the LORD, the God of the Hebrews, says: "Let my people go, so that they may worship me." [2]If you refuse to let them go and continue to hold them back, [3]the hand of the LORD will bring a terrible plague on your livestock in the field—on your horses and donkeys and camels and on your cattle and sheep and goats. [4]But the LORD will make a distinction between the livestock of Israel and that of Egypt, so that no animal belonging to the Israelites will die.' "

[a]**23** Septuagint and Vulgate; Hebrew *will put a deliverance*

8:22 *Goshen:* See the note at 1:7. The Egyptians made the Hebrew people live apart from the general Egyptian population, because Hebrew customs and habits were different from those of the Egyptians (Gen 43:32).

8:26 *sacrifices . . . detestable to the Egyptians:* See the note at 3:18 (offer sacrifices). Apparently, the Hebrews' religious practices, which included animal sacrifices, were considered disgusting by the Egyptians. Moses demanded that the Hebrew people be allowed to go far away into the desert to offer sacrifices to God, so the Egyptians wouldn't be angered or disgusted by watching the sacrifices.

8:32 *Pharaoh hardened his heart:* See the note at 7:3,4.

9:1 *Hebrews:* See the note at 5:3.

9:3 *terrible plague:* The exact disease is not known, but swarms of flies can carry disease-causing bacteria such as anthrax, which is deadly to animals that live in herds and flocks. The Egyptians worshiped certain animal-headed gods, such as Apis (bull), Mnevis (cow), and Khnum (ram). This disaster of all the livestock dying symbolized God's power over the Egyptian animal gods.

9:8 *soot from a furnace:* The furnace was probably built out of bricks that had been hand-made by the Hebrew people. The type of sores or boils that affected the people may have been caused by the same kind of bacteria that caused the animals to get sick and die (see note at 9:3). In humans, this kind of bacteria can cause sores that burn and turn black, the color of soot or ashes.

9:11 *magicians:* See the note at 7:9-11. As the plagues continue, the power of the magicians decreases.

9:12 *the LORD hardened Pharaoh's heart:* See the note at 7:3,4.

9:16 *show you my power:* The plagues God sent upon Egypt revealed God's power (Rom 9:17). See also the note at 7:3, 4 and the mini-article called "Disasters (Plagues)," p. 151.

9:18 *tomorrow:* Moses' announcement allows time for people who believed the threat to get their animals into shelter (9:20,21).

9:22 *Stretch out your hand toward the sky:* This was a common posture for prayer (see 9:29). See also the note at 7:19.

9:10 Rev 16:2. **9:23,24** Rev 8:7; 16:21.

5The LORD set a time and said, "Tomorrow the LORD will do
this in the land." 6And the next day the LORD did it: All the livestock of the Egyptians died, but not one animal belonging to the
Israelites died. 7Pharaoh sent men to investigate and found that
not even one of the animals of the Israelites had died. Yet his heart
was unyielding and he would not let the people go.

The Plague of Boils

8Then the LORD said to Moses and Aaron, "Take handfuls of
soot from a furnace and have Moses toss it into the air in the presence of Pharaoh. 9It will become fine dust over the whole land of
Egypt, and festering boils will break out on men and animals
throughout the land."
10So they took soot from a furnace and stood before Pharaoh. Moses tossed it into the air, and festering boils broke out on
men and animals. 11The magicians could not stand before Moses
because of the boils that were on them and on all the Egyptians.
12But the LORD hardened Pharaoh's heart and he would not listen
to Moses and Aaron, just as the LORD had said to Moses.

The Plague of Hail

13Then the LORD said to Moses, "Get up early in the morning, confront Pharaoh and say to him, 'This is what the LORD, the
God of the Hebrews, says: Let my people go, so that they may worship me, 14or this time I will send the full force of my plagues
against you and against your officials and your people, so you may
know that there is no one like me in all the earth. 15For by now I
could have stretched out my hand and struck you and your people
with a plague that would have wiped you off the earth. 16But I have
raised you up[a] for this very purpose, that I might show you my
power and that my name might be proclaimed in all the earth.
17You still set yourself against my people and will not let them go.
18Therefore, at this time tomorrow I will send the worst hailstorm
that has ever fallen on Egypt, from the day it was founded till now.
19Give an order now to bring your livestock and everything you
have in the field to a place of shelter, because the hail will fall on
every man and animal that has not been brought in and is still out
in the field, and they will die.'"
20Those officials of Pharaoh who feared the word of the
LORD hurried to bring their slaves and their livestock inside. 21But
those who ignored the word of the LORD left their slaves and livestock in the field.
22Then the LORD said to Moses, "Stretch out your hand
toward the sky so that hail will fall all over Egypt—on men and
animals and on everything growing in the fields of Egypt." 23When

[a]16 Or *have spared you*

Moses stretched out his staff toward the sky, the LORD sent thunder and hail, and lightning flashed down to the ground. So the
LORD rained hail on the land of Egypt; 24hail fell and lightning
flashed back and forth. It was the worst storm in all the land of
Egypt since it had become a nation. 25Throughout Egypt hail
struck everything in the fields—both men and animals; it beat
down everything growing in the fields and stripped every tree.
26The only place it did not hail was the land of Goshen, where the
Israelites were.

9:26 *Goshen:* See the note at 1:7.

DISASTERS (PLAGUES)

In the Bible, God sometimes sends plagues (disasters) to punish evildoers, to show his chosen people that he is angry because of their disobedience, or to show his power as the supreme God of nature. These plagues are so devastating that there can be no doubting that they come from God. In Genesis 12:10-20, Abraham's wife, Sarah, goes to live with the Pharaoh, telling him that she was Abraham's sister. God sent terrible diseases on the king and those in his palace, because Sarah was Abraham's wife, and no one else was to have sexual relations with her. See other examples of plagues sent as punishment at 1 Samuel 5,6 and 2 Kings 19:35.

The most famous plagues in the Bible are those described in EXODUS which occurred before the people of Israel escaped from Egypt. These ten plagues are listed below:

PLAGUE	WHAT HAPPENED	EXODUS PASSAGE
1	Nile River's water is turned into blood	7:14-24
2	Frogs swarm all over the land	7:25—8:15
3	Gnats cover all humans and animals	8:16-19
4	Flies swarm everywhere and fill the houses	8:20-24
5	Egyptian livestock are killed by a disease	9:1-7
6	Humans and animals are covered with boils	9:8-12
7	Hail knocks down the crops	9:13-35
8	Locusts eat up all the plants	10:1-20
9	Darkness covers the whole land	10:21-29
10	Death of all firstborn Egyptian males and animals	12:1-30

Although the Egyptian magicians were able to make some of these plagues happen, only God could cause the most serious ones, and only God's people were saved from them. The magicians admitted, "This is the finger of [Israel's] God" when they couldn't undo or perform one of these miracles themselves (Exod 8:19). Jesus used a similar phrase when he was showing how he could drive demons out of people (Luke 11:20). Some psalms (Ps 78:42-52; 105:26-38; 135:8,9; 136:10) and the writings of the prophets (Amos 4:10; Hab 3:5) highlight the importance of the plagues in making possible Israel's escape from Egypt. In addition, the people of Israel were reminded that God could send such plagues on them if they did not live by the laws God gave to Moses (Num 14:12; Deut 28:21-23,58-63; 32:22-24).

[27]Then Pharaoh summoned Moses and Aaron. "This time I
have sinned," he said to them. "The LORD is in the right, and I and
my people are in the wrong. [28]Pray to the LORD, for we have had
enough thunder and hail. I will let you go; you don't have to stay
any longer."
[29]Moses replied, "When I have gone out of the city, I will
spread out my hands in prayer to the LORD. The thunder will stop
and there will be no more hail, so you may know that the earth is
the LORD's. [30]But I know that you and your officials still do not fear
the LORD God."
[31](The flax and barley were destroyed, since the barley had
headed and the flax was in bloom. [32]The wheat and spelt, however, were not destroyed, because they ripen later.)
[33]Then Moses left Pharaoh and went out of the city. He
spread out his hands toward the LORD; the thunder and hail
stopped, and the rain no longer poured down on the land. [34]When
Pharaoh saw that the rain and hail and thunder had stopped, he
sinned again: He and his officials hardened their hearts. [35]So Pharaoh's heart was hard and he would not let the Israelites go, just as
the LORD had said through Moses.

The Plague of Locusts

10 Then the LORD said to Moses, "Go to Pharaoh, for I have
hardened his heart and the hearts of his officials so that I may perform these miraculous signs of mine among them [2]that you may
tell your children and grandchildren how I dealt harshly with the
Egyptians and how I performed my signs among them, and that
you may know that I am the LORD."
[3]So Moses and Aaron went to Pharaoh and said to him,
"This is what the LORD, the God of the Hebrews, says: 'How long
will you refuse to humble yourself before me? Let my people go, so
that they may worship me. [4]If you refuse to let them go, I will
bring locusts into your country tomorrow. [5]They will cover the
face of the ground so that it cannot be seen. They will devour what
little you have left after the hail, including every tree that is growing in your fields. [6]They will fill your houses and those of all your
officials and all the Egyptians—something neither your fathers nor
your forefathers have ever seen from the day they settled in this
land till now.'" Then Moses turned and left Pharaoh.
[7]Pharaoh's officials said to him, "How long will this man be
a snare to us? Let the people go, so that they may worship the LORD
their God. Do you not yet realize that Egypt is ruined?"
[8]Then Moses and Aaron were brought back to Pharaoh. "Go,
worship the LORD your God," he said. "But just who will be going?"
[9]Moses answered, "We will go with our young and old, with
our sons and daughters, and with our flocks and herds, because we
are to celebrate a festival to the LORD."

9:27 *I have sinned:* Sin is turning away from God and disobeying God's Law. See also the mini-article called "Sin," p. 2181. The Egyptian king admits he is guilty of resisting God.

9:30 *fear the LORD God:* The Hebrew word translated as "fear" also means "to respect" or "to honor." For more about LORD, see the note at 6:2,3. The Hebrew name translated as "God" here is *Elohim*, another name Israel used for the one true God. See also the mini-article called "Names of God," p. 243.

9:31,32 *flax and barley . . . wheat and spelt:* Flax plants have flowers with five bright blue petals. The oil from flax seeds was used as food and to make some paints. The stalks of the flax plant were dried on rooftops. Then its fibers were split, combed, and woven into linen cloth.

The grain known as barley was a very cheap source of food. It was used mainly to feed cattle, but it was also used for making bread in times of emergency. The wheat crops mentioned here refer to wheat and a wheat-like grain called spelt, which has been discovered in some ancient Egyptian tombs. Wheat was considered the best grain for making flour used to bake breads; spelt was not as good, but it could grow in less fertile soil.

10:4 *locusts:* This type of grasshopper often comes in swarms and causes great damage to crops. They can cause severe food shortages called famines. In the spring, hungry young locusts often migrated west toward Egypt, blown by prevailing east winds (10:13). Locusts are described in the Bible as a symbol of God's judgment (see Joel 1:4-7; Amos 7:1-3; and the mini-article called "Locusts," p. 1708).

[10]Pharaoh said, "The LORD be with you—if I let you go,
along with your women and children! Clearly you are bent on
evil.[a] [11]No! Have only the men go; and worship the LORD, since
that's what you have been asking for." Then Moses and Aaron were
driven out of Pharaoh's presence.
[12]And the LORD said to Moses, "Stretch out your hand over
Egypt so that locusts will swarm over the land and devour everything growing in the fields, everything left by the hail."
[13]So Moses stretched out his staff over Egypt, and the LORD
made an east wind blow across the land all that day and all that
night. By morning the wind had brought the locusts; [14]they invaded all Egypt and settled down in every area of the country in great
numbers. Never before had there been such a plague of locusts,
nor will there ever be again. [15]They covered all the ground until it
was black. They devoured all that was left after the hail—everything growing in the fields and the fruit on the trees. Nothing
green remained on tree or plant in all the land of Egypt.
[16]Pharaoh quickly summoned Moses and Aaron and said, "I
have sinned against the LORD your God and against you. [17]Now
forgive my sin once more and pray to the LORD your God to take
this deadly plague away from me."
[18]Moses then left Pharaoh and prayed to the LORD. [19]And the
LORD changed the wind to a very strong west wind, which caught
up the locusts and carried them into the Red Sea.[b] Not a locust was

[a]10 Or *Be careful, trouble is in store for you!* [b]19 Hebrew *Yam Suph*; that is, Sea of Reeds

The Plague of Locusts, illuminated page from a fourteenth century *Haggadah.* Haggadahs are texts read by Jews in the celebration of Passover. They commemorate the time when the people of Israel escaped from Egypt and recall many of the events told in Exodus 4–12, including the ten plagues that the LORD sent to punish the Egyptians. The eighth plague, the plague of the locusts, is described in Exodus 10:1-20.

10:12 *Stretch out your hand:* See the notes at 7:19 and 9:22.

10:13 *east wind:* During the months of March and April, the most common winds in Egypt come from the dry areas to the east (see the map on p. 2463).

10:16,17 *sinned . . . forgive my sin:* For more about sin, see the note at 9:27. To "forgive" means to remove any penalty or judgment that one deserves because of sinful actions. For more about sin and its consequences, see the mini-article called "Sin," p. 2181.

10:14,15 Rev 9:2,3.

Now the LORD had said to Moses, "I will bring one more plague on Pharaoh and on Egypt. After that, he will let you go from here, and when he does, he will drive you out completely."
Exod 11:1

10:25 *sacrifices:* See the note at 3:18 (offer sacrifices).

10:27 *hardened Pharaoh's heart:* See the note at 7:3,4.

11:5 *Every firstborn son in Egypt . . . slave girl:* See the note at 4:22 (firstborn). The "slave girl" here refers to non-Hebrew slave woman whose task was grinding grain into flour by hand. See also Isa 47:1,2.

12:2 *This month . . . first month:* Abib (also called Nisan) is the first month of the Hebrew calendar. See also the chart called "Jewish Calendar and Festivals," p. 944.

11:9,10 Exod 6:8; 7:3,4.

left anywhere in Egypt. [20]But the LORD hardened Pharaoh's heart,
and he would not let the Israelites go.

The Plague of Darkness

[21]Then the LORD said to Moses, "Stretch out your hand
toward the sky so that darkness will spread over Egypt—darkness
that can be felt." [22]So Moses stretched out his hand toward the sky,
and total darkness covered all Egypt for three days. [23]No one could
see anyone else or leave his place for three days. Yet all the Israelites
had light in the places where they lived.
[24]Then Pharaoh summoned Moses and said, "Go, worship
the LORD. Even your women and children may go with you; only
leave your flocks and herds behind."
[25]But Moses said, "You must allow us to have sacrifices and
burnt offerings to present to the LORD our God. [26]Our livestock too
must go with us; not a hoof is to be left behind. We have to use
some of them in worshiping the LORD our God, and until we get
there we will not know what we are to use to worship the LORD."
[27]But the LORD hardened Pharaoh's heart, and he was not
willing to let them go. [28]Pharaoh said to Moses, "Get out of my
sight! Make sure you do not appear before me again! The day you
see my face you will die."
[29]"Just as you say," Moses replied, "I will never appear before
you again."

The Plague on the Firstborn

11 Now the LORD had said to Moses, "I will bring one more
plague on Pharaoh and on Egypt. After that, he will let you go
from here, and when he does, he will drive you out completely.
[2]Tell the people that men and women alike are to ask their neighbors for articles of silver and gold." [3](The LORD made the Egyptians favorably disposed toward the people, and Moses himself was
highly regarded in Egypt by Pharaoh's officials and by the people.)
[4]So Moses said, "This is what the LORD says: 'About midnight
I will go throughout Egypt. [5]Every firstborn son in Egypt will die,
from the firstborn son of Pharaoh, who sits on the throne, to the
firstborn son of the slave girl, who is at her hand mill, and all the
firstborn of the cattle as well. [6]There will be loud wailing throughout Egypt—worse than there has ever been or ever will be again.
[7]But among the Israelites not a dog will bark at any man or animal.' Then you will know that the LORD makes a distinction
between Egypt and Israel. [8]All these officials of yours will come to
me, bowing down before me and saying, 'Go, you and all the people who follow you!' After that I will leave." Then Moses, hot with
anger, left Pharaoh.
[9]The LORD had said to Moses, "Pharaoh will refuse to listen
to you—so that my wonders may be multiplied in Egypt." [10]Moses

and Aaron performed all these wonders before Pharaoh, but the
LORD hardened Pharaoh's heart, and he would not let the Israelites
go out of his country.

PASSOVER AND THE EXODUS

As the Israelite people prepare to leave Egypt, they are told to prepare a special meal that will be celebrated in future years as the Feast of Passover, a time to remember how God saved them from the final plague and led them out of slavery in Egypt.

The Passover

12 The LORD said to Moses and Aaron in Egypt, 2"This month
is to be for you the first month, the first month of your year. 3Tell
the whole community of Israel that on the tenth day of this month
each man is to take a lamb[a] for his family, one for each household.
4If any household is too small for a whole lamb, they must share
one with their nearest neighbor, having taken into account the
number of people there are. You are to determine the amount of
lamb needed in accordance with what each person will eat. 5The
animals you choose must be year-old males without defect, and
you may take them from the sheep or the goats. 6Take care of them
until the fourteenth day of the month, when all the people of the
community of Israel must slaughter them at twilight. 7Then they
are to take some of the blood and put it on the sides and tops of
the doorframes of the houses where they eat the lambs. 8That same
night they are to eat the meat roasted over the fire, along with bitter herbs, and bread made without yeast. 9Do not eat the meat raw
or cooked in water, but roast it over the fire—head, legs and inner
parts. 10Do not leave any of it till morning; if some is left till morning, you must burn it. 11This is how you are to eat it: with your
cloak tucked into your belt, your sandals on your feet and your
staff in your hand. Eat it in haste; it is the LORD's Passover.

12"On that same night I will pass through Egypt and strike
down every firstborn—both men and animals—and I will bring
judgment on all the gods of Egypt. I am the LORD. 13The blood will
be a sign for you on the houses where you are; and when I see the
blood, I will pass over you. No destructive plague will touch you
when I strike Egypt.

14"This is a day you are to commemorate; for the generations to come you shall celebrate it as a festival to the LORD—a
lasting ordinance. 15For seven days you are to eat bread made without yeast. On the first day remove the yeast from your houses, for
whoever eats anything with yeast in it from the first day through
the seventh must be cut off from Israel. 16On the first day hold a

[a]**3** The Hebrew word can mean *lamb* or *kid*; also in verse 4.

12:5 *without defect:* These animals had to be healthy and have no defects (see Lev 1:3,10).

12:7 *blood . . . doorframes:* To protect themselves from God's final punishment of the Egyptians (11:4-6; 12:29,30).

12:8,9 *meat roasted over the fire:* Roasting was the way to make sure that all the blood was removed from the meat. Blood was a symbol of life (Gen 9:4; Lev 17:11-14) and was to be returned to God when meat was eaten (Lev 17:3-6; Deut 12:5-19).

12:8,9 *bitter herbs, and bread made without yeast:* The herbs probably were endive, chicory, or other edible herbs that grew in Egypt. Their bitter taste would remind the people of their bitter years as slaves in Egypt.

Yeast is a tiny yellowish fungus that causes the dough to rise, so that the bread will not be flat when baked. Bread that has no yeast is flat and is called "unleavened bread." Unleavened bread was served at Passover as a reminder of how quickly the people had to leave Egypt. There wasn't even time to let the dough rise.

12:11 *the LORD's Passover:* "Passover" is related to the Hebrew word translated as "pass over" in 12:13,27. This festival was celebrated as a remembrance of how God saved the people from the final disaster and helped them escape from slavery in Egypt. See also the mini-article called "Passover and the Feast of Unleavened Bread," p. 2030.

12:15 *yeast:* See the note at 12:8,9.

12:1-13 Lev 23:4,5; Num 9:1-5; 28:16; Deut 16:1-8. **12:14-20** Exod 23:15; 34:18; Lev 23:4-8; Num 28:16-25; Deut 16:1-8.

12:17 *Feast of Unleavened Bread:* See the note at 12:8,9. See also the mini-article called "Passover and the Feast of Unleavened Bread," p. 2030 and the article called "People of the Law: The Religion of Israel," p. 939.

12:22 *Take a bunch of hyssop:* The hyssop plant is from the mint family. Its hairy stalk and leaves hold liquids well, so its branches could be used as brushes or as sprinklers in religious rituals (Lev 14:4-7,49-52; Num 19:6,17,18; Heb 9:19).

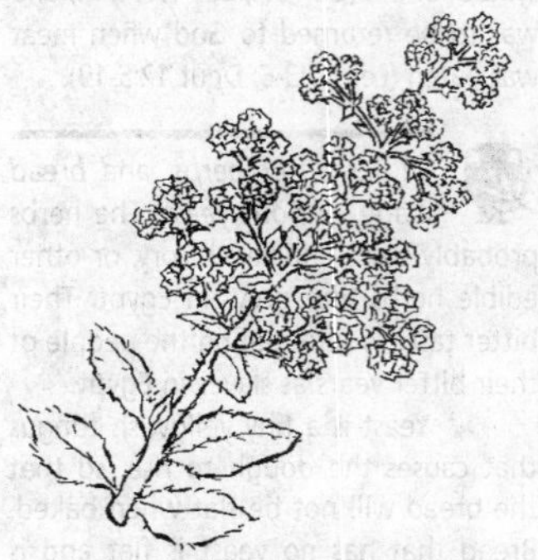

12:23 *the destroyer:* In Psalm 78:49, God is depicted as sending "a band of destroying angels" to bring judgment upon Egypt. See also 2 Sam 24:15, 16; 2 Kgs 19:35.

12:25 *enter the land:* This refers to Canaan (see the note at 3:8). About forty years passed from the time the Israelite people left Egypt until they finally entered the promised land of Canaan (Num 14:31-35).

12:34 *dough before the yeast was added:* See the note at 12:8,9.

12:21-28 Exod 12:2-20. **12:29** Exod 4:21-23; 11:4-7. **12:35,36** Exod 3:21,22.

sacred assembly, and another one on the seventh day. Do no work
at all on these days, except to prepare food for everyone to eat—
that is all you may do.
[17]"Celebrate the Feast of Unleavened Bread, because it was on
this very day that I brought your divisions out of Egypt. Celebrate
this day as a lasting ordinance for the generations to come. [18]In the
first month you are to eat bread made without yeast, from the
evening of the fourteenth day until the evening of the twenty-first
day. [19]For seven days no yeast is to be found in your houses. And
whoever eats anything with yeast in it must be cut off from the community of Israel, whether he is an alien or native-born. [20]Eat nothing
made with yeast. Wherever you live, you must eat unleavened bread."
[21]Then Moses summoned all the elders of Israel and said to
them, "Go at once and select the animals for your families and
slaughter the Passover lamb. [22]Take a bunch of hyssop, dip it into
the blood in the basin and put some of the blood on the top and on
both sides of the doorframe. Not one of you shall go out the door
of his house until morning. [23]When the LORD goes through the land
to strike down the Egyptians, he will see the blood on the top and
sides of the doorframe and will pass over that doorway, and he will
not permit the destroyer to enter your houses and strike you down.
[24]"Obey these instructions as a lasting ordinance for you and
your descendants. [25]When you enter the land that the LORD will
give you as he promised, observe this ceremony. [26]And when your
children ask you, 'What does this ceremony mean to you?' [27]then
tell them, 'It is the Passover sacrifice to the LORD, who passed over
the houses of the Israelites in Egypt and spared our homes when
he struck down the Egyptians.'" Then the people bowed down and
worshiped. [28]The Israelites did just what the LORD commanded
Moses and Aaron.
[29]At midnight the LORD struck down all the firstborn in
Egypt, from the firstborn of Pharaoh, who sat on the throne, to the
firstborn of the prisoner, who was in the dungeon, and the firstborn of all the livestock as well. [30]Pharaoh and all his officials and
all the Egyptians got up during the night, and there was loud wailing in Egypt, for there was not a house without someone dead.

The Exodus

[31]During the night Pharaoh summoned Moses and Aaron
and said, "Up! Leave my people, you and the Israelites! Go, worship the LORD as you have requested. [32]Take your flocks and herds,
as you have said, and go. And also bless me."
[33]The Egyptians urged the people to hurry and leave the
country. "For otherwise," they said, "we will all die!" [34]So the people took their dough before the yeast was added, and carried it on
their shoulders in kneading troughs wrapped in clothing. [35]The
Israelites did as Moses instructed and asked the Egyptians for
articles of silver and gold and for clothing. [36]The LORD had made

the Egyptians favorably disposed toward the people, and they gave them what they asked for; so they plundered the Egyptians.

[37]The Israelites journeyed from Rameses to Succoth. There were about six hundred thousand men on foot, besides women and children. [38]Many other people went up with them, as well as large droves of livestock, both flocks and herds. [39]With the dough they had brought from Egypt, they baked cakes of unleavened bread. The dough was without yeast because they had been driven out of Egypt and did not have time to prepare food for themselves.

[40]Now the length of time the Israelite people lived in Egypt[a] was 430 years. [41]At the end of the 430 years, to the very day, all the LORD's divisions left Egypt. [42]Because the LORD kept vigil that night to bring them out of Egypt, on this night all the Israelites are to keep vigil to honor the LORD for the generations to come.

Passover Restrictions

[43]The LORD said to Moses and Aaron, "These are the regulations for the Passover:

"No foreigner is to eat of it. [44]Any slave you have bought may eat of it after you have circumcised him, [45]but a temporary resident and a hired worker may not eat of it.

[46]"It must be eaten inside one house; take none of the meat outside the house. Do not break any of the bones. [47]The whole community of Israel must celebrate it.

[48]"An alien living among you who wants to celebrate the LORD's Passover must have all the males in his household circumcised; then he may take part like one born in the land. No uncircumcised male may eat of it. [49]The same law applies to the native-born and to the alien living among you."

[50]All the Israelites did just what the LORD had commanded Moses and Aaron. [51]And on that very day the LORD brought the Israelites out of Egypt by their divisions.

Consecration of the Firstborn

13 The LORD said to Moses, [2]"Consecrate to me every firstborn male. The first offspring of every womb among the Israelites belongs to me, whether man or animal."

[3]Then Moses said to the people, "Commemorate this day, the day you came out of Egypt, out of the land of slavery, because the LORD brought you out of it with a mighty hand. Eat nothing containing yeast. [4]Today, in the month of Abib, you are leaving. [5]When the LORD brings you into the land of the Canaanites, Hittites, Amorites, Hivites and Jebusites—the land he swore to your forefathers to give you, a land flowing with milk and honey—you are to observe

[a]40 Masoretic Text; Samaritan Pentateuch and Septuagint *Egypt and Canaan*

The LORD had made the Egyptians favorably disposed toward the people, and they gave them what they asked for; so they plundered the Egyptians.
Exod 12:36

12:37 *Rameses to Succoth:* See the note at 1:11 (Rameses). In Hebrew "Succoth" means "booths." Its location is not certain, though it may have been near the region of Pithom. See the map on p. 2463 for the possible route the Israelites traveled after leaving Egypt.

12:44,45 *Any slave . . . circumcised . . . temporary resident:* Two groups of non-Israelites are mentioned in these verses. Even though the Israelites were slaves in Egypt, they apparently also had some of their own slaves. Foreigners who lived and worked among the Israelite people were not circumcised and so could not eat the Passover meal. See 12:48 and the note at 4:25,26.

13:2 *Consecrate to me every firstborn male:* See the note at 4:22. See also Num 3:11-13; Luke 2:23.

13:4-7 *Abib . . . unleavened bread:* See the notes at 12:2 and 12:8,9 (without yeast).

13:5 *land of the Canaanites . . . Jebusites:* See the note at 3:8.

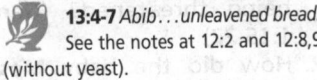

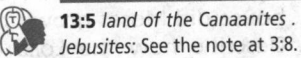

12:40,41 Gen 15:13-15; Gal 3:17. **12:46** Num 9:12; Ps 34:20; John 19:36. **13:5-8** Exod 12:17-20.

13:9 *sign on your hand . . . forehead:* Identifying seals, rings, or ornaments were tied on the hands or worn on the foreheads (see also 13:16; Deut 6:8; 11:18; Prov 3:3). This passage may have led to the later practice of writing Scripture texts on small pieces of parchment and putting them in small leather boxes called phylacteries. These were then strapped to the head and left arm before morning prayers (Deut 6:4-9; Matt 23:5).

13:13 *Redeem with a lamb every firstborn donkey:* The donkey was the only "unclean" animal that had to be redeemed; the firstborn of all the "clean" animals (sheep, goats, cattle) had to be sacrificed. Donkeys were important because they were used for transportation and for hauling or pulling loads. See also the mini-article called "Purity (Clean and Unclean)," p. 2125.

13:14 *LORD:* See the note at 6:2,3.

13:12 Exod 34:19,20; Luke 2:23.

this ceremony in this month: 6For seven days eat bread made without yeast and on the seventh day hold a festival to the LORD. 7Eat
unleavened bread during those seven days; nothing with yeast in it
is to be seen among you, nor shall any yeast be seen anywhere within your borders. 8On that day tell your son, 'I do this because of what
the LORD did for me when I came out of Egypt.' 9This observance
will be for you like a sign on your hand and a reminder on your
forehead that the law of the LORD is to be on your lips. For the LORD
brought you out of Egypt with his mighty hand. 10You must keep
this ordinance at the appointed time year after year.
11"After the LORD brings you into the land of the Canaanites
and gives it to you, as he promised on oath to you and your forefathers, 12you are to give over to the LORD the first offspring of every
womb. All the firstborn males of your livestock belong to the LORD.
13Redeem with a lamb every firstborn donkey, but if you do not
redeem it, break its neck. Redeem every firstborn among your sons.
14"In days to come, when your son asks you, 'What does this
mean?' say to him, 'With a mighty hand the LORD brought us out of
Egypt, out of the land of slavery. 15When Pharaoh stubbornly
refused to let us go, the LORD killed every firstborn in Egypt, both
man and animal. This is why I sacrifice to the LORD the first male
offspring of every womb and redeem each of my firstborn sons.'
16And it will be like a sign on your hand and a symbol on your forehead that the LORD brought us out of Egypt with his mighty hand."

QUESTIONS ABOUT EXODUS 1:1—13:16

1. In the time between Joseph's death (Gen 50:22-26) and Moses' birth (Exod 2:1,2), what had happened to the Hebrew people living in Egypt? How was God's promise to Abraham and his descendants being threatened? (Gen 17:1-8; Exod 1:15-22)
2. How did the baby Moses survive the Egyptian Pharaoh's order? In whose house did Moses grow up? (2:1-10)
3. Describe how the LORD chose Moses to lead the people of Israel out of slavery in Egypt. What was Moses worried about? How did the LORD deal with his worries? (3:1—4:23)
4. What do Moses and Aaron ask Pharaoh to do? How does Pharaoh respond to this request? (5:1-21)
5. What promise did God tell Moses to give to the people when they became discouraged? (6:2-8) Who had first received these promises? Why is it difficult to believe promises in the midst of hard times?
6. Pharaoh was stubborn, both on his own and because Israel's God made him stubborn. What happened because of Pharaoh's stubbornness? (7:14—12:30) What is your reaction to the idea that God actually made (or makes) people stubborn or unwilling to trust God?
7. What was the purpose of the ten plagues that God sent upon Egypt? (9:16) What kinds of plagues or disasters would be especially horrible in our day?
8. What people today might be especially inspired by the early chapters of EXODUS? Why?
9. Complete these sentences:
   "The most important character in Exodus 1–13 is . . . , because . . . ."
   "The character I identify with most is . . . , because . . . ."

Moses Leads the People in the Desert

After leaving the area of Goshen, Moses and the Israelites head east into the desert region of Sinai. Before they get too far, Pharaoh tries to stop them, but God clears a path through the Red Sea for them to cross and then makes the sea close on Pharaoh's army. With the Egyptian threat behind them, the people head into the desert where they face water and food shortages and hostile enemies. Even though the people complain and show a lack of trust, the LORD sends miracles to help them survive.

ESCAPE THROUGH THE SEA

God clears a path through the Red Sea, so the Israelites can escape the Egyptian army.

Crossing the Sea

17 When Pharaoh let the people go, God did not lead them
on the road through the Philistine country, though that was shorter. For God said, "If they face war, they might change their minds
and return to Egypt." 18 So God led the people around by the desert
road toward the Red Sea.[a] The Israelites went up out of Egypt
armed for battle.

19 Moses took the bones of Joseph with him because Joseph
had made the sons of Israel swear an oath. He had said, "God will
surely come to your aid, and then you must carry my bones up
with you from this place."[b]

20 After leaving Succoth they camped at Etham on the edge
of the desert. 21 By day the LORD went ahead of them in a pillar of

[a]**18** Hebrew *Yam Suph*; that is, Sea of Reeds [b]**19** See Gen. 50:25.

The Exodus with the Pillar of Fire by Shalom of Safed, 1967. The LORD was with his people day and night as he led them out of Egypt. He went ahead of them in a thick cloud during the day and in a flaming fire at night. This painting shows Moses at the front of the long procession holding a shepherd's staff. (See 13:20-22.)

13:15 *Pharaoh stubbornly refused to let us go:* See the notes at 2:23 and 7:3,4.

13:16 *sign on your hand . . . forehead:* See the note at 13:9.

13:17-20 *Philistine country . . . desert road . . . Red Sea . . . Succoth . . . Etham:* The shortest route from the Nile delta to Canaan was north along the major road that followed the Mediterranean coastline. The Philistine territory was the narrow strip of land along the sea, bordering on the southwest part of Canaan. The Israelites could easily be attacked on this main road, so God led them southeast toward Succoth, Etham, and the Red Sea.

The term "Red Sea" in Hebrew is *yam suph,* literally meaning "Sea of Reeds," one of the marshes or fresh water lakes near the eastern part of the Nile delta. This identification is based on Exodus 13:17—14:9, which lists the towns along the route the Israelites took before crossing the sea. In the Greek translation of the Scriptures made about 200 B.C., the "Sea of Reeds" was named "Red Sea." See the map on p. 2463 for the possible route taken by the Israelites.

See the note at 12:37 (Succoth). The location of Etham is uncertain.

13:19 Gen 50:25; Josh 24:32.

cloud to guide them on their way and by night in a pillar of fire to
give them light, so that they could travel by day or night. [22]Neither
the pillar of cloud by day nor the pillar of fire by night left its place
in front of the people.
14 Then the LORD said to Moses, [2]"Tell the Israelites to turn
back and encamp near Pi Hahiroth, between Migdol and the sea.
They are to encamp by the sea, directly opposite Baal Zephon.
[3]Pharaoh will think, 'The Israelites are wandering around the land
in confusion, hemmed in by the desert.' [4]And I will harden Pharaoh's heart, and he will pursue them. But I will gain glory for
myself through Pharaoh and all his army, and the Egyptians will
know that I am the LORD." So the Israelites did this.

[5]When the king of Egypt was told that the people had fled,
Pharaoh and his officials changed their minds about them and
said, "What have we done? We have let the Israelites go and have
lost their services!" [6]So he had his chariot made ready and took his
army with him. [7]He took six hundred of the best chariots, along
with all the other chariots of Egypt, with officers over all of them.
[8]The LORD hardened the heart of Pharaoh king of Egypt, so that he
pursued the Israelites, who were marching out boldly. [9]The Egyptians—all Pharaoh's horses and chariots, horsemen[a] and troops—
pursued the Israelites and overtook them as they camped by the
sea near Pi Hahiroth, opposite Baal Zephon.

[10]As Pharaoh approached, the Israelites looked up, and there
were the Egyptians, marching after them. They were terrified and
cried out to the LORD. [11]They said to Moses, "Was it because there
were no graves in Egypt that you brought us to the desert to die?
What have you done to us by bringing us out of Egypt? [12]Didn't we
say to you in Egypt, 'Leave us alone; let us serve the Egyptians'? It
would have been better for us to serve the Egyptians than to die in
the desert!"

[13]Moses answered the people, "Do not be afraid. Stand firm
and you will see the deliverance the LORD will bring you today. The
Egyptians you see today you will never see again. [14]The LORD will
fight for you; you need only to be still."

[15]Then the LORD said to Moses, "Why are you crying out to
me? Tell the Israelites to move on. [16]Raise your staff and stretch out
your hand over the sea to divide the water so that the Israelites can
go through the sea on dry ground. [17]I will harden the hearts of the
Egyptians so that they will go in after them. And I will gain glory
through Pharaoh and all his army, through his chariots and his
horsemen. [18]The Egyptians will know that I am the LORD when I
gain glory through Pharaoh, his chariots and his horsemen."

[19]Then the angel of God, who had been traveling in front of
Israel's army, withdrew and went behind them. The pillar of cloud
also moved from in front and stood behind them, [20]coming

a9 Or *charioteers*; also in verses 17, 18, 23, 26 and 28

13:21,22 *pillar of fire:* Fire and smoke often signal the presence of God in the Bible (Gen 15:17,18; Exod 3:2; 19:16-19; Judg 13:20,21).

14:2 *Pi Hahiroth . . . Migdol . . . the sea . . . Baal Zephon:* Pi Hahiroth may have been an Egyptian temple site east of Baal Zephon (Num 33:7). Baal was the Canaanite god whose home was believed to be "Zaphon," or Mount Casius on the coast of northern Syria. Baal Zephon may refer to an ancient temple site near one of the lakes in northern Sinai, either Menzaleh or Sarbonis. In Hebrew Migdol means "Tower," and may refer to a fort built along the northern Sinai coast, east of the lake area mentioned above.

The "sea" refers to the Red Sea (see the note at 13:17-20). All of the locations mentioned seem to point to a water crossing in northern Sinai and not at the location today known as the Red Sea. See the map on p. 2463.

14:6 *chariot:* A war chariot had a single axle and two wheels, and was usually drawn by one or two horses. Two or three soldiers could ride in a chariot. The speed and mobility of chariots made it easy for chariot drivers to gain on fleeing enemy armies or to quickly change positions and attack their enemies from behind.

14:9 *Pi Hahiroth . . . Baal Zephon:* See the note at 14:2.

14:11,12 Exod 15:24; 17:1-3; Num 11:1-6; 14:1-4.

between the armies of Egypt and Israel. Throughout the night the
cloud brought darkness to the one side and light to the other side;
so neither went near the other all night long.
21 Then Moses stretched out his hand over the sea, and all
that night the LORD drove the sea back with a strong east wind and
turned it into dry land. The waters were divided, 22 and the
Israelites went through the sea on dry ground, with a wall of water
on their right and on their left.
23 The Egyptians pursued them, and all Pharaoh's horses and
chariots and horsemen followed them into the sea. 24 During the
last watch of the night the LORD looked down from the pillar of
fire and cloud at the Egyptian army and threw it into confusion.
25 He made the wheels of their chariots come off[a] so that they had
difficulty driving. And the Egyptians said, "Let's get away from the
Israelites! The LORD is fighting for them against Egypt."
26 Then the LORD said to Moses, "Stretch out your hand over
the sea so that the waters may flow back over the Egyptians and
their chariots and horsemen." 27 Moses stretched out his hand over

[a]25 Or *He jammed the wheels of their chariots* (see Samaritan Pentateuch, Septuagint and Syriac)

Egyptians Drowning, an illustration by Philip Isac Levy from the *Copenhagen Haggadah,* 1739. Like the illustration on p. 153, this one from a Haggadah would have reminded Jews celebrating Passsover of God's faithfulness to his chosen people and his power to save them from Pharaoh's army. Here, the Israelites are safe on the other side of the Red Sea they had just crossed, while the Egyptian soldiers and their horses drown in the sea. (See chapter 14.)

14:14 *The LORD will fight for you:* Israel's God is often described in the Jewish Scriptures (Old Testament) as a warrior who fights for them (Exod 14:25; 15:3; Deut 1:30; Josh 10:14; 2 Sam 5:22-24; Ps 24:8). See also the mini-article called "Holy War (The LORD's Battles)," p. 306.

14:17 *chariots and his horsemen:* See the note at 14:6. Horsemen refers to warriors who ride on horseback. Because of their usefulness in warfare, horses were owned almost exclusively by kings, and the power of kings in the ancient world was often measured by the number of horses and chariots they had at their command.

14:19 *angel of God:* An angel was accompanying the people and giving them protection. In Hebrew the word for "angel" means "messenger." See also the mini-article called "Angels," p. 88. In 14:24, the LORD himself is said to be in the pillar of fire and cloud.

14:26 *Stretch out your hand over the sea:* See the notes at 7:19 and 9:22.

14:22 1 Cor 10:1,2; Heb 11:29.

the sea, and at daybreak the sea went back to its place. The Egyptians were fleeing toward[a] it, and the LORD swept them into the sea.
28 The water flowed back and covered the chariots and horsemen—
the entire army of Pharaoh that had followed the Israelites into the
sea. Not one of them survived.
29 But the Israelites went through the sea on dry ground, with
a wall of water on their right and on their left. 30 That day the LORD
saved Israel from the hands of the Egyptians, and Israel saw the
Egyptians lying dead on the shore. 31 And when the Israelites saw the
great power the LORD displayed against the Egyptians, the people
feared the LORD and put their trust in him and in Moses his servant.

The Song of Moses and Miriam

15 Then Moses and the Israelites sang this song to the LORD:

"I will sing to the LORD,
for he is highly exalted.
The horse and its rider
he has hurled into the sea.
2 The LORD is my strength and my song;
he has become my salvation.
He is my God, and I will praise him,
my father's God, and I will exalt him.
3 The LORD is a warrior;
the LORD is his name.
4 Pharaoh's chariots and his army
he has hurled into the sea.
The best of Pharaoh's officers
are drowned in the Red Sea.[b]
5 The deep waters have covered them;
they sank to the depths like a stone.

6 "Your right hand, O LORD,
was majestic in power.
Your right hand, O LORD,
shattered the enemy.
7 In the greatness of your majesty
you threw down those who opposed you.
You unleashed your burning anger;
it consumed them like stubble.
8 By the blast of your nostrils
the waters piled up.
The surging waters stood firm like a wall;
the deep waters congealed in the heart of the sea.

9 "The enemy boasted,
'I will pursue, I will overtake them.

[a]27 Or *from* [b]4 Hebrew *Yam Suph*; that is, Sea of Reeds; also in verse 22

Moses and the Israelites sang, *"The LORD is my strength and my song; he has become my salvation."* Exod 15:2

14:31 *Moses his servant:* The Hebrew word for "servant" here refers to one who serves as a high official in the court of the LORD (Num 12:8; Deut 34:5). This title was used to describe other important Israelite leaders such as, the military leader Joshua (Josh 24:29) and Israel's greatest king, David (2 Sam 3:18).

15:1-21 *this song to the LORD:* Many scholars think that portions of the songs in this chapter, especially "The Song of Miriam" (15:21), are some of the oldest writings in the entire Bible.

15:3 *LORD is a warrior:* See the note at 14:14.

15:4 *Red Sea:* See the note at 13:17-20.

15:6 *right hand:* In ancient times, the "right side" was thought to be the side of power.

14:30 Exod 14:13. **15:1,2** Ps 118:14; Isa 12:2; Rev 15:3. **15:8** Ps 66:6; 106:9-11; 136:13,14; Isa 51:10; 63:11-13.

Miriam—Prophetess and Sister of Aaron by Lucy D'Souza, contemporary painting. After the LORD rescued the people of Israel from the Egyptians who were pursuing them, Miriam, the sister of Moses and Aaron, led the Israelite women in singing praises to the LORD. (See 15:19-21.)

I will divide the spoils;
　I will gorge myself on them.
I will draw my sword
　and my hand will destroy them.'
10 But you blew with your breath,
　and the sea covered them.
They sank like lead
　in the mighty waters.
11 "Who among the gods is like you, O LORD?
　Who is like you—
　　majestic in holiness,
　　awesome in glory,
　　working wonders?
12 You stretched out your right hand
　and the earth swallowed them.
13 "In your unfailing love you will lead
　the people you have redeemed.
In your strength you will guide them
　to your holy dwelling.
14 The nations will hear and tremble;
　anguish will grip the people of Philistia.
15 The chiefs of Edom will be terrified,

15:11 *O LORD? Who is like you:* See the note at 6:2,3.

15:13 *holy dwelling:* This translates a Hebrew word that often refers to the place where shepherds live, or a field of green grass as in Psalm 23:2. Sometimes this word is used to describe the promised land of Canaan (13:5).

15:14,15 *Philistia . . . Edom . . . Moab . . . Canaan:* See the note at 13:17-20. The Philistine rulers were quite powerful and often battled with Israel in the days of the judges and later during the time of Israel's kings. The land of Edom, or Seir, was south and southeast of the Dead Sea. The Edomites descended from Esau (Gen 36:1-43). The descendants of Jacob (the Israelites) sometimes fought with the Edomites (Num 20:14-21; Obad 9,10). Moab was located to the east of the Dead Sea. The Moabites and Ammonites would later become enemies of Israel (Judg 10:11-18; 1 Sam 14:47,48; 2 Kgs 3:21-27; 2 Chr 20:10,11). See also the note at 3:8 and the maps on pp. 2463 and 2465.

15:17 *the mountain of your inheritance . . . sanctuary:* This mountain probably refers to Mount Zion in Jerusalem. King Solomon built the first temple (sanctuary) to the LORD on Mount Zion about 350 years after Moses led the Israelite people out of Egypt. See also the mini-article called "Zion," p. 1294.

15:19 *chariots and horsemen:* See the notes at 14:6 and 14:17.

15:20 *Miriam the prophetess, Aaron's sister:* Miriam is most likely the older sister who helped rescue the baby Moses by finding a Hebrew woman (Moses' own mother) to take care of him for the king's daughter who had found him in the Nile and adopted him (2:1-10).

For more about prophets, see the note at 7:1,2

15:20 *tambourine:* An instrument played by shaking or striking. See the illustration on p. 1190.

15:22 *Red Sea . . . Desert of Shur:* See the note at 13:17-20. The Desert of Shur was located east of Goshen in the northwestern part of the Sinai Peninsula (see the map on p. 2463). Moses probably found water at an oasis known as Marah (15:23), which today is often identified with a bitter spring at Hawwarah, located on the eastern shore of the Gulf of Suez.

the leaders of Moab will be seized with trembling,
the people[a] of Canaan will melt away;
16 terror and dread will fall upon them.
By the power of your arm
they will be as still as a stone—
until your people pass by, O LORD,
until the people you bought[b] pass by.
17 You will bring them in and plant them
on the mountain of your inheritance—
the place, O LORD, you made for your dwelling,
the sanctuary, O Lord, your hands established.
18 The LORD will reign
for ever and ever."

19 When Pharaoh's horses, chariots and horsemen[c] went into
the sea, the LORD brought the waters of the sea back over them, but
the Israelites walked through the sea on dry ground. 20 Then Miriam the prophetess, Aaron's sister, took a tambourine in her hand,
and all the women followed her, with tambourines and dancing.
21 Miriam sang to them:

"Sing to the LORD,
for he is highly exalted.
The horse and its rider
he has hurled into the sea."

GOD PROVIDES WATER AND FOOD

Though the people complain against Moses, God provides food and water for them in the desert.

The Waters of Marah and Elim

22 Then Moses led Israel from the Red Sea and they went into
the Desert of Shur. For three days they traveled in the desert without finding water. 23 When they came to Marah, they could not
drink its water because it was bitter. (That is why the place is called
Marah.[d]) 24 So the people grumbled against Moses, saying, "What
are we to drink?"

25 Then Moses cried out to the LORD, and the LORD showed him a piece of wood. He threw it into the water, and the water became sweet.

There the LORD made a decree and a law for them, and there
he tested them. 26 He said, "If you listen carefully to the voice of the
LORD your God and do what is right in his eyes, if you pay attention to his commands and keep all his decrees, I will not bring on
you any of the diseases I brought on the Egyptians, for I am the
LORD, who heals you."

[a]15 Or *rulers* [b]16 Or *created* [c]19 Or *charioteers* [d]23 *Marah* means *bitter.*

27 Then they came to Elim, where there were twelve springs
and seventy palm trees, and they camped there near the water.

Manna and Quail

16 The whole Israelite community set out from Elim and came
to the Desert of Sin, which is between Elim and Sinai, on the fifteenth day of the second month after they had come out of Egypt.
2 In the desert the whole community grumbled against Moses and
Aaron. 3 The Israelites said to them, "If only we had died by the
LORD's hand in Egypt! There we sat around pots of meat and ate all
the food we wanted, but you have brought us out into this desert
to starve this entire assembly to death."
4 Then the LORD said to Moses, "I will rain down bread from
heaven for you. The people are to go out each day and gather
enough for that day. In this way I will test them and see whether
they will follow my instructions. 5 On the sixth day they are to prepare what they bring in, and that is to be twice as much as they
gather on the other days."
6 So Moses and Aaron said to all the Israelites, "In the evening
you will know that it was the LORD who brought you out of Egypt,
7 and in the morning you will see the glory of the LORD, because he
has heard your grumbling against him. Who are we, that you
should grumble against us?" 8 Moses also said, "You will know that
it was the LORD when he gives you meat to eat in the evening and
all the bread you want in the morning, because he has heard your
grumbling against him. Who are we? You are not grumbling
against us, but against the LORD."
9 Then Moses told Aaron, "Say to the entire Israelite community, 'Come before the LORD, for he has heard your grumbling.' "
10 While Aaron was speaking to the whole Israelite community, they looked toward the desert, and there was the glory of the
LORD appearing in the cloud.
11 The LORD said to Moses, 12 "I have heard the grumbling of
the Israelites. Tell them, 'At twilight you will eat meat, and in the
morning you will be filled with bread. Then you will know that I
am the LORD your God.' "
13 That evening quail came and covered the camp, and in the
morning there was a layer of dew around the camp. 14 When the
dew was gone, thin flakes like frost on the ground appeared on the
desert floor. 15 When the Israelites saw it, they said to each other,
"What is it?" For they did not know what it was.
Moses said to them, "It is the bread the LORD has given you
to eat. 16 This is what the LORD has commanded: 'Each one is to
gather as much as he needs. Take an omer[a] for each person you
have in your tent.' "

a16 That is, probably about 2 quarts (about 2 liters); also in verses 18, 32, 33 and 36

The LORD said to Moses, "I will rain down bread from heaven for you."
Exod 16:4

16:1 *Elim . . . Desert of Sin . . . Sinai:* See the map on p. 2463. Elim means "large trees," and is often identified with the brook known as Gharandel, south of Hawwarah (see the note at 15:22). The Desert of Sin stretches across the Sinai Peninsula between the Gulf of Suez and the Gulf of Aqaba. See the map on p. 133.

16:4 *bread from heaven:* This was something like a thin and flaky wafer, and it was called "manna," which in Hebrew means, "What is it?" (16:15).

16:8 *meat:* Refers to the meat of quail (see 16:13), small brown or sandy-colored birds that usually migrated to the region of Palestine in large flocks during March or April.

16:10 *glory of the LORD:* See the note at 3:2.

16:13-15 *quail . . . thin flakes:* See the notes at 16:4 and 16:8.

16:4 Josh 5:12; Ps 78:24; John 6:31-35,51; Heb 9:4.

The people of Israel called the bread manna. It was white like coriander seed and tasted like wafers made with honey.
Exod 16:31

Manna from Heaven, carved wood panel from a choir stall, Cathedral of Merzeburg, Germany, fifteenth century. The Israelites were frightened and hungry in the desert. The LORD said to Moses, "I will rain down bread from heaven for you." Every morning thin flakes that looked like frost mysteriously appeared, and the people gathered enough to eat for that day. (See 16:4-36.)

17The Israelites did as they were told; some gathered much,
some little. 18And when they measured it by the omer, he who
gathered much did not have too much, and he who gathered little
did not have too little. Each one gathered as much as he needed.
19Then Moses said to them, "No one is to keep any of it until
morning."
20However, some of them paid no attention to Moses; they
kept part of it until morning, but it was full of maggots and began
to smell. So Moses was angry with them.
21Each morning everyone gathered as much as he needed,
and when the sun grew hot, it melted away. 22On the sixth day, they

gathered twice as much—two omers[a] for each person—and the
leaders of the community came and reported this to Moses. 23He
said to them, "This is what the LORD commanded: 'Tomorrow is to
be a day of rest, a holy Sabbath to the LORD. So bake what you
want to bake and boil what you want to boil. Save whatever is left
and keep it until morning.'"
24So they saved it until morning, as Moses commanded, and
it did not stink or get maggots in it. 25"Eat it today," Moses said,
"because today is a Sabbath to the LORD. You will not find any of
it on the ground today. 26Six days you are to gather it, but on the
seventh day, the Sabbath, there will not be any."
27Nevertheless, some of the people went out on the seventh
day to gather it, but they found none. 28Then the LORD said to
Moses, "How long will you[b] refuse to keep my commands and my
instructions? 29Bear in mind that the LORD has given you the Sabbath; that is why on the sixth day he gives you bread for two days.
Everyone is to stay where he is on the seventh day; no one is to go
out." 30So the people rested on the seventh day.
31The people of Israel called the bread manna.[c] It was white like
coriander seed and tasted like wafers made with honey. 32Moses said,
"This is what the LORD has commanded: 'Take an omer of manna
and keep it for the generations to come, so they can see the bread I
gave you to eat in the desert when I brought you out of Egypt.'"
33So Moses said to Aaron, "Take a jar and put an omer of
manna in it. Then place it before the LORD to be kept for the generations to come."
34As the LORD commanded Moses, Aaron put the manna in
front of the Testimony, that it might be kept. 35The Israelites ate
manna forty years, until they came to a land that was settled; they
ate manna until they reached the border of Canaan.
36(An omer is one tenth of an ephah.)

Water From the Rock

17 The whole Israelite community set out from the Desert of Sin,
traveling from place to place as the LORD commanded. They camped
at Rephidim, but there was no water for the people to drink. 2So
they quarreled with Moses and said, "Give us water to drink."
Moses replied, "Why do you quarrel with me? Why do you
put the LORD to the test?"
3But the people were thirsty for water there, and they grumbled against Moses. They said, "Why did you bring us up out of
Egypt to make us and our children and livestock die of thirst?"
4Then Moses cried out to the LORD, "What am I to do with
these people? They are almost ready to stone me."
5The LORD answered Moses, "Walk on ahead of the people.

[a]22 That is, probably about 4 quarts (about 4.5 liters) [b]28 The Hebrew is plural. [c]31 *Manna* means *What is it?* (see verse 15).

16:23 *day of rest:* The day of rest, or Sabbath, was the seventh day of the week, and commemorated the day that God rested after finishing the work of creation (Gen 2:2, 3). Sabbath means "rest" or to "stop working" and resting on the Sabbath became an important way for Jewish people to honor God (20:8-11; Deut 5:12-15). Picking up bread (manna), quail, or grain on the Sabbath would have been considered work, so it was forbidden.

For more about the Sabbath see the chart called "Jewish Calendar and Festivals," p. 944.

16:31 *manna . . . white like coriander seed . . . honey:* For more information about manna, see the note at 16:4. See also Num 11:7-9.

16:33 *jar . . . place it before the LORD:* Moses commands Aaron to do this, since he would later become the first high priest of Israel (28:1). The high priest was the only person who could place something near the ark of the covenant. This jar was said to be made of gold (Heb 9:4).

16:34 *in front of the Testimony:* The directions for building the ark of the covenant (also called the ark of the Testimony) are given in Exodus 25:10-19. See the mini-article called "The Ark of the Covenant," p. 513.

17:1 *Rephidim:* This is the last stopping place mentioned between the Red Sea and Mount Sinai. The exact location is unknown.

17:4 *stone me:* Piling or dropping stones on someone was one of the most common forms of capital punishment in Israelite society (Lev 24:23).

16:18 2 Cor 8:15. **16:35,36** Josh 5:12. **17:1-7** Num 20:1-13. **17:3** Exod 16:2,3.

17:5,6 *Nile . . . rock at Horeb:* Horeb is another name for Mount Sinai. See the note on p. 133 (Mount Sinai). When Moses struck the Nile River he made the Egyptians' water undrinkable (7:14-24), but here Moses strikes the rock to bring drinkable water to the Israelites.

17:7 *Massah . . . Meribah:* Compare this verse to Num 20:7-13 and Deut 6:16; 9:22. This location must have been near the base of Mount Sinai.

17:8-10 *Amalekites . . . Joshua . . . Hur:* The Amalekites were descendants of Amalek, grandson of Esau (Gen 36:15,16). They were a nomadic people living mostly in the area south and east of the Dead Sea. In later times, the Amalekites raided the Israelites living in Canaan (Judg 6:1-35; 1 Sam 30:1-20). See also 1 Chr 4:41-43.

Joshua, whose name means "the LORD saves," was appointed to lead Israel after the death of Moses (Deut 1:38; 31:14; 34:9).

Not much is known about Hur, but this leader from the tribe of Judah must have been important to be standing on the hilltop with Moses and Aaron. Along with Aaron, Hur would later be responsible to settle any disputes among the Israelites while Moses went up Mount Sinai to receive the Law from the LORD (24:14). Hur also is named as the grandfather of Bezalel, the craftsman chosen to make the tabernacle and its furnishings (31:2).

17:11 *held up his hands:* See the notes at 7:19 and 9:22.

18:1 *Jethro . . . priest of Midian:* See the notes at 2:15 and 2:16.

18:2-4 *Zipporah . . . Gershom . . . Eliezer:* For more about Zipporah, see the note at 4:25,26. For Gershom, see the note at 2:22. In Hebrew "Eliezer" means "God helps me," a reference to how Moses was saved from the king of Egypt (1:22—2:16). See also Acts 7:29.

17:14 Deut 25:17-19; 1 Sam 15:2-9.

Take with you some of the elders of Israel and take in your hand
the staff with which you struck the Nile, and go. 6I will stand there
before you by the rock at Horeb. Strike the rock, and water will
come out of it for the people to drink." So Moses did this in the
sight of the elders of Israel. 7And he called the place Massah[a] and
Meribah[b] because the Israelites quarreled and because they tested
the LORD saying, "Is the LORD among us or not?"

VICTORY IN BATTLE AND THE APPOINTMENT OF JUDGES

God helps the Israelites win a battle over the Amalekites, and Jethro encourages Moses to appoint judges from each tribe to help him with the work of settling disagreements.

The Amalekites Defeated

8The Amalekites came and attacked the Israelites at
Rephidim. 9Moses said to Joshua, "Choose some of our men and
go out to fight the Amalekites. Tomorrow I will stand on top of the
hill with the staff of God in my hands."
10So Joshua fought the Amalekites as Moses had ordered,
and Moses, Aaron and Hur went to the top of the hill. 11As long as
Moses held up his hands, the Israelites were winning, but whenever he lowered his hands, the Amalekites were winning. 12When
Moses' hands grew tired, they took a stone and put it under him
and he sat on it. Aaron and Hur held his hands up—one on one
side, one on the other—so that his hands remained steady till
sunset. 13So Joshua overcame the Amalekite army with the sword.
14Then the LORD said to Moses, "Write this on a scroll as
something to be remembered and make sure that Joshua hears it,
because I will completely blot out the memory of Amalek from
under heaven."
15Moses built an altar and called it The LORD is my Banner.
16He said, "For hands were lifted up to the throne of the LORD.
The[c] LORD will be at war against the Amalekites from generation to
generation."

Jethro Visits Moses

18 Now Jethro, the priest of Midian and father-in-law of Moses,
heard of everything God had done for Moses and for his people
Israel, and how the LORD had brought Israel out of Egypt.
2After Moses had sent away his wife Zipporah, his father-in-
law Jethro received her 3and her two sons. One son was named
Gershom,[d] for Moses said, "I have become an alien in a foreign

[a]7 *Massah* means *testing.* [b]7 *Meribah* means *quarreling.* [c]16 Or *"Because a hand was against the throne of the LORD, the* [d]3 *Gershom* sounds like the Hebrew for *an alien there.*

land”; 4and the other was named Eliezer,[a] for he said, “My father’s
God was my helper; he saved me from the sword of Pharaoh.”
5Jethro, Moses’ father-in-law, together with Moses’ sons and
wife, came to him in the desert, where he was camped near the
mountain of God. 6Jethro had sent word to him, “I, your father-
in-law Jethro, am coming to you with your wife and her two sons.”
7So Moses went out to meet his father-in-law and bowed down
and kissed him. They greeted each other and then went into the tent.
8Moses told his father-in-law about everything the LORD had done to
Pharaoh and the Egyptians for Israel’s sake and about all the hardships they had met along the way and how the LORD had saved them.
9Jethro was delighted to hear about all the good things the
LORD had done for Israel in rescuing them from the hand of the
Egyptians. 10He said, “Praise be to the LORD, who rescued you from
the hand of the Egyptians and of Pharaoh, and who rescued the
people from the hand of the Egyptians. 11Now I know that the
LORD is greater than all other gods, for he did this to those who
had treated Israel arrogantly.” 12Then Jethro, Moses’ father-in-law,
brought a burnt offering and other sacrifices to God, and Aaron
came with all the elders of Israel to eat bread with Moses’ father-
in-law in the presence of God.
13The next day Moses took his seat to serve as judge for the
people, and they stood around him from morning till evening.
14When his father-in-law saw all that Moses was doing for the people, he said, “What is this you are doing for the people? Why do
you alone sit as judge, while all these people stand around you
from morning till evening?”
15Moses answered him, “Because the people come to me to
seek God’s will. 16Whenever they have a dispute, it is brought to

[a]4 *Eliezer* means *my God is helper.*

Jethro shouted, *“Praise be to the LORD, who rescued you from the hand of the Egyptians and of Pharaoh, and who rescued the people from the hand of the Egyptians. Now I know that the LORD is greater than all other gods.”* Exod 18:10,11

18:5 *mountain of God:* Mount Sinai. See the note on p. 133.

18:12 *sacrifices to God:* See the note at 3:18 (offer sacrifices). A portion of the food prepared for sacrifice was used in a meal of celebration. Meals were also a common way to complete a covenant (Gen 26:30; 31:54; Exod 24:11).

QUESTIONS ABOUT EXODUS 13:17—18:27

1. Retrace the journey of the Israelites from the time they left Egypt until they reached Mount Sinai (13:17—18:27). See also the map on p. 2463. Name three key events that took place during that journey.
2. What did the Israelite people complain about? (14:10-12; 15:22-24; 16:2,3; 17:3) How did Moses, with God’s help, respond to those complaints?
3. The Red Sea (or Sea of Reeds) crossing was a great example of God’s saving power on behalf of the people of Israel. What happened to the pursuing Egyptian cavalry? What is your reaction to that? Have you ever felt as though you have been “saved”? If so, describe the situation.
4. The Israelite people sang praises and danced for joy after God delivered them from the Egyptians (15:1-21). How do you thank God for blessings?
5. Why did Moses appoint judges to help him settle disputes among the Israelites?
6. Examples of God’s miraculous help fill this section of EXODUS. In your opinion, do such miracles still happen? Explain.

18:13-20 *bring their disputes:* This refers to disputes between Israelites that had to be settled by a judge. Moses used what God had shown in order to make these kinds of judgments (see 15:25,26). See also the mini-article called "Law," p. 1160.

18:25,26 *capable men from all Israel . . . served as judges:* See the notes at 1:1-7 and 3:16. It was common in a culture of nomads for the leaders of clans to settle disputes within their clans.

19:1,2 *Rephidim . . . the mountain:* See the note at 17:1 (Rephidim). "The mountain" refers to Mount Sinai (see the note on p. 133). The Israelites left Egypt in the month of Abib (12:2). It is now two months later, or the month of Sivan (mid-May to mid-June). See the chart called "Jewish Calendar and Festivals," p. 944.

me, and I decide between the parties and inform them of God's
decrees and laws."
17 Moses' father-in-law replied, "What you are doing is not
good. 18 You and these people who come to you will only wear yourselves out. The work is too heavy for you; you cannot handle it
alone. 19 Listen now to me and I will give you some advice, and may
God be with you. You must be the people's representative before
God and bring their disputes to him. 20 Teach them the decrees and
laws, and show them the way to live and the duties they are to perform. 21 But select capable men from all the people—men who fear
God, trustworthy men who hate dishonest gain—and appoint them
as officials over thousands, hundreds, fifties and tens. 22 Have them
serve as judges for the people at all times, but have them bring every
difficult case to you; the simple cases they can decide themselves.
That will make your load lighter, because they will share it with you.
23 If you do this and God so commands, you will be able to stand the
strain, and all these people will go home satisfied."
24 Moses listened to his father-in-law and did everything he
said. 25 He chose capable men from all Israel and made them leaders
of the people, officials over thousands, hundreds, fifties and tens.
26 They served as judges for the people at all times. The difficult cases
they brought to Moses, but the simple ones they decided themselves.
27 Then Moses sent his father-in-law on his way, and Jethro
returned to his own country.

Moses and the People of Israel at Mount Sinai

While camped at Mount Sinai, Moses receives laws and instructions from God, including: the Ten Commandments; laws governing worship and daily life; instructions for the duties of the priests and their special clothing; and instructions for making the tabernacle, ark of the covenant, and other items to be kept in the tabernacle. This section also includes the story of Aaron and the people making a golden calf idol while Moses is away on the mountain.

GOD GIVES MOSES THE LAW

Moses meets the LORD on Mount Sinai and receives the Ten Commandments and many other laws that form the basis of a covenant between the LORD and the people of Israel.

At Mount Sinai

19 In the third month after the Israelites left Egypt—on the very
day—they came to the Desert of Sinai. 2 After they set out from
Rephidim, they entered the Desert of Sinai, and Israel camped
there in the desert in front of the mountain.

[3]Then Moses went up to God, and the LORD called to him
from the mountain and said, "This is what you are to say to the
house of Jacob and what you are to tell the people of Israel: [4]"You
yourselves have seen what I did to Egypt, and how I carried you
on eagles' wings and brought you to myself. [5]Now if you obey me
fully and keep my covenant, then out of all nations you will be my
treasured possession. Although the whole earth is mine, [6]you[a] will
be for me a kingdom of priests and a holy nation.' These are the
words you are to speak to the Israelites."

[7]So Moses went back and summoned the elders of the people and set before them all the words the LORD had commanded
him to speak. [8]The people all responded together, "We will do
everything the LORD has said." So Moses brought their answer back
to the LORD.

[9]The LORD said to Moses, "I am going to come to you in a
dense cloud, so that the people will hear me speaking with you and
will always put their trust in you." Then Moses told the LORD what
the people had said.

[10]And the LORD said to Moses, "Go to the people and consecrate them today and tomorrow. Have them wash their clothes
[11]and be ready by the third day, because on that day the LORD will
come down on Mount Sinai in the sight of all the people. [12]Put
limits for the people around the mountain and tell them, 'Be careful that you do not go up the mountain or touch the foot of it.
Whoever touches the mountain shall surely be put to death. [13]He
shall surely be stoned or shot with arrows; not a hand is to be laid
on him. Whether man or animal, he shall not be permitted to live.'
Only when the ram's horn sounds a long blast may they go up to
the mountain."

[14]After Moses had gone down the mountain to the people,
he consecrated them, and they washed their clothes. [15]Then he said
to the people, "Prepare yourselves for the third day. Abstain from
sexual relations."

[16]On the morning of the third day there was thunder and
lightning, with a thick cloud over the mountain, and a very loud
trumpet blast. Everyone in the camp trembled. [17]Then Moses led
the people out of the camp to meet with God, and they stood at
the foot of the mountain. [18]Mount Sinai was covered with smoke,
because the LORD descended on it in fire. The smoke billowed up
from it like smoke from a furnace, the whole mountain[b] trembled
violently, [19]and the sound of the trumpet grew louder and louder.
Then Moses spoke and the voice of God answered him.[c]

[20]The LORD descended to the top of Mount Sinai and called
Moses to the top of the mountain. So Moses went up [21]and the

19:3 *LORD:* For more about "LORD," see the note at 6:2,3. The Hebrew name translated as "God" here is *Elohim*. It is a plural form of *El*, and can refer to "gods," but here it is used with LORD (*Yahweh*) to refer to Israel's one true God. See also the mini-article called "Names of God," p. 243.

19:6 *priests:* Though the descendants of Aaron, the members of the Levi tribe, were officially appointed as Israel's priests (28:1; Num 18:20-32), all the people were God's holy people, which means that they had been chosen and dedicated to serve God. For more, see the mini-article called "Israel's Priests," p. 2344. See also 1 Pet 2:9.

19:10,11 *wash their clothes . . . be ready:* This refers to a ritual known as "consecration," which included washing clothes and the body to remove any trace of contact with something that had made them ritually unclean (19:14,15; Lev 14:8).

19:12 *Put limits . . . put to death:* God's holiness has a physical aspect. There is danger in coming into contact with God's holiness. See also Heb 12:18-20.

19:15 *Abstain from sexual relations:* Sex was not considered sinful, but was believed to make one ritually unclean for a day (Lev 15:18; Deut 23:10, 11; 1 Sam 21:4,5).

19:16-18 *thunder and lightning . . . smoke . . . fire:* Fire and smoke often signal the presence of God in the Bible (Gen 15:17,18; Exod 3:2; 13:21,22; Judg 13:20,21). See also the mini-article called "Fire," p. 2383.

19:5,6 Deut 4:20; 7:6; 14:2; 26:18,19; Isa 61:6; Rev 1:6; 5:10. **19:16-18** Deut 4:11,12; Rev 4:5. **19:21** Exod 19:12,13.

[a]**5,6** Or *possession, for the whole earth is mine. [6]You* [b]**18** Most Hebrew manuscripts; a few Hebrew manuscripts and Septuagint *all the people* [c]**19** Or *and God answered him with thunder*

19:22 *priests:* See the note at 19:6. These may be priests from the tribe of Levi and descendants of Aaron (28:1). Or, they may be the elders who served as priests before the Aaronic priesthood was established.

20:2 *I am the* LORD *your God:* The Ten Commandments (20:2-17) follow a pattern used in an ancient form of treaty between a ruler and his people. In such a treaty, the ruler identifies himself and refers to acts done on behalf of his people (20:2). Then the ruler gives the laws that the people are to live by in order to keep their part of the treaty. The ruler promises to protect and help the people, who promise in return to be loyal and obedient to the ruler alone. See also the mini-articles called "Ten Commandments," p. 354, and "Covenants (Agreements)," p. 386.

20:4,5 *idol:* Refers to objects made of wood, stone, or metal, commonly worshiped by many ancient peoples. No lifeless image could stand for Israel's God, who was a "living" God (Isa 44:9-20). See also Exod 34:17; Lev 19:4; 26:1; Deut 4:15-20; 27:15.

20:7 *misuse the name of the* LORD *your God:* This probably includes using God's name to break promises, telling lies after swearing to tell the truth, using the LORD's name as a curse word or in a magic formula, and trying to control the LORD by using the name. See also Lev 19:12; Deut 5:11.

20:8 *Sabbath:* See the note at 16:23. See also 31:12-15.

20:5,6 Exod 34:6,7; Num 14:18; Deut 7:9,10. **20:9,10** Exod 23:12; 31:12-17; 34:21; 35:2,3; Lev 23:3. **20:11** Gen 2:1-3; Exod 31:17. **20:14** Lev 20:10; Matt 5:27; 19:18; Mark 10:19; Luke 18:20; Rom 13:9; Jas 2:11. **20:15** Lev 19:11; Matt 19:18; Mark 10:19; Luke 18:20; Rom 13:9. **20:16** Exod 23:1; Matt 19:18; Mark 10:19; Luke 18:20; Rom 13:9. **20:17** Rom 7:7; 13:9.

LORD said to him, "Go down and warn the people so they do not
force their way through to see the LORD and many of them perish.
[22]Even the priests, who approach the LORD, must consecrate themselves, or the LORD will break out against them."

[23]Moses said to the LORD, "The people cannot come up
Mount Sinai, because you yourself warned us, 'Put limits around
the mountain and set it apart as holy.'"

[24]The LORD replied, "Go down and bring Aaron up with you.
But the priests and the people must not force their way through to
come up to the LORD, or he will break out against them."

[25]So Moses went down to the people and told them.

The Ten Commandments

20 And God spoke all these words:

[2]"I am the LORD your God, who brought you out of Egypt, out of the land of slavery.

[3]"You shall have no other gods before[a] me.

[4]"You shall not make for yourself an idol in the form of anything in heaven above or on the earth beneath or in the
waters below. [5]You shall not bow down to them or worship them; for I, the LORD your God, am a jealous God, punishing the children for the sin of the fathers to the
third and fourth generation of those who hate me, [6]but
showing love to a thousand ⌞generations⌟ of those who love me and keep my commandments.

[7]"You shall not misuse the name of the LORD your God, for the LORD will not hold anyone guiltless who misuses his name.

[8]"Remember the Sabbath day by keeping it holy. [9]Six days
you shall labor and do all your work, [10]but the seventh
day is a Sabbath to the LORD your God. On it you shall not do any work, neither you, nor your son or daughter, nor your manservant or maidservant, nor your animals,
nor the alien within your gates. [11]For in six days the
LORD made the heavens and the earth, the sea, and all that is in them, but he rested on the seventh day. Therefore the LORD blessed the Sabbath day and made it holy.

[12]"Honor your father and your mother, so that you may live long in the land the LORD your God is giving you.

[13]"You shall not murder.

[14]"You shall not commit adultery.

[15]"You shall not steal.

[16]"You shall not give false testimony against your neighbor.

[17]"You shall not covet your neighbor's house. You shall not covet your neighbor's wife, or his manservant or maid-

[a]3 Or *besides*

Moses Receives the Tables of the Law, illuminated page from *The Grandval Bible,* around A.D. 840. Of all the Israelites, only Moses was allowed to go up Mount Sinai to meet with the LORD. It was on Mount Sinai that the LORD gave the Law to Moses. This Law included many instructions about religious practices and how the Israelites were to live their lives. Perhaps the most famous part of this Law is the group of laws known as "The Ten Commandments." (See 20:1-17.)

And God spoke all these words: "I am the LORD your God, who brought you out of Egypt, out of the land of slavery. You shall have no other gods before me."
Exod 20:1-3

servant, his ox or donkey, or anything that belongs to
your neighbor."
[18]When the people saw the thunder and lightning and heard
the trumpet and saw the mountain in smoke, they trembled with
fear. They stayed at a distance [19]and said to Moses, "Speak to us
yourself and we will listen. But do not have God speak to us or we
will die."
[20]Moses said to the people, "Do not be afraid. God has come
to test you, so that the fear of God will be with you to keep you
from sinning."
[21]The people remained at a distance, while Moses approached
the thick darkness where God was.

Idols and Altars

[22]Then the LORD said to Moses, "Tell the Israelites this: 'You
have seen for yourselves that I have spoken to you from heaven:
[23]Do not make any gods to be alongside me; do not make for yourselves gods of silver or gods of gold.
[24]" 'Make an altar of earth for me and sacrifice on it your
burnt offerings and fellowship offerings,[a] your sheep and goats

20:12 *Honor your father and your mother:* Children were expected to care for parents and to show them the greatest respect (Lev 19:3; 20:9; Deut 27:16; Prov 23:22-25). Note that this command comes with a promise. See also Matt 15:4; 19:19; Mark 7:10; 10:19; Luke 18:20; Eph 6:2,3.

20:13 *murder:* Some modern translations substitute "kill," but this commandment does not forbid all forms of killing. Rather, it refers to taking a life without just cause. See also Gen 9:5, 6; Lev 24:17; Matt 5:21; 19:18; Mark 10:19; Luke 18:20; Rom 13:9; Jas 2:11.

20:20 *fear . . . keep you from sinning:* The visible presence of God in the thunder and smoke (19:16-19) tested the people's courage. But their fear was not to keep them from living up to their promises to trust the LORD God and to obey the LORD's commands. See also the note at 9:27.

20:24 *sacrifice:* See the note at 3:18 (offer sacrifices). The Hebrew text mentions two types of offerings: burnt offerings and fellowship offerings. See also Lev 1,3 and the chart called "Sacrifices and Offerings," p. 219.

20:18,19 Heb 12:18,19. **20:23** Exod 20:4.

[a]**24** Traditionally *peace offerings*

20:26 *nakedness be exposed:* Priests were to wear full-length clothes and special underwear (28:42). Unlike some of their ancient neighbors, the religion of Israel did not include sexual practices. This set the Israelites apart from other peoples and their religions. Requiring priests to remain fully covered in the presence of God may have been a way to make sure no such sexual practices entered Israel's religious rituals.

21:1 *These are the laws:* Moses next receives specific laws that apply to certain situations. These are sometimes known as "case" laws.

21:2 *servant:* The Israelites were not to keep other Hebrews as slaves longer than six years, unless the slave asked to continue serving his master. The slave's ear was pierced as a sign of his or her life-long commitment (21:6). See also Lev 25:39-46; Jer 34:8-20.

21:7,8 *daughter . . . redeemed:* The rights of female slaves were protected. If she did not please her owner, the owner was obligated to sell her back to her family or to another Israelite who wished to marry her. A woman who became the wife of her owner's son was to be treated as part of the family.

21:13,14 *flee to a place I will designate . . . my altar:* The "place" refers to one of several towns set aside as cities of refuge (Num 35:9-34; Deut 4:41-43; 19:1-13; Josh 20:1-9). The LORD's altar was like the cities of refuge. A person who caused accidental death could hold on to the horns of an altar and be protected from the death penalty, until proven guilty (1 Kgs 1:50-53; 2:28-34). See also the mini-article called "Cities of Refuge," p. 444.

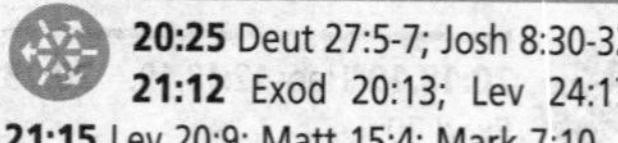

20:25 Deut 27:5-7; Josh 8:30-32. **21:12** Exod 20:13; Lev 24:17. **21:15** Lev 20:9; Matt 15:4; Mark 7:10.

and your cattle. Wherever I cause my name to be honored, I will come to you and bless you. [25]If you make an altar of stones for me, do not build it with dressed stones, for you will defile it if you use a tool on it. [26]And do not go up to my altar on steps, lest your nakedness be exposed on it.'

21 "These are the laws you are to set before them:

Hebrew Servants

[2]"If you buy a Hebrew servant, he is to serve you for six years. But in the seventh year, he shall go free, without paying anything. [3]If he comes alone, he is to go free alone; but if he has a wife when he comes, she is to go with him. [4]If his master gives him a wife and she bears him sons or daughters, the woman and her children shall belong to her master, and only the man shall go free.

[5]"But if the servant declares, 'I love my master and my wife and children and do not want to go free,' [6]then his master must take him before the judges.[a] He shall take him to the door or the doorpost and pierce his ear with an awl. Then he will be his servant for life.

[7]"If a man sells his daughter as a servant, she is not to go free as menservants do. [8]If she does not please the master who has selected her for himself,[b] he must let her be redeemed. He has no right to sell her to foreigners, because he has broken faith with her. [9]If he selects her for his son, he must grant her the rights of a daughter. [10]If he marries another woman, he must not deprive the first one of her food, clothing and marital rights. [11]If he does not provide her with these three things, she is to go free, without any payment of money.

Personal Injuries

[12]"Anyone who strikes a man and kills him shall surely be put to death. [13]However, if he does not do it intentionally, but God lets it happen, he is to flee to a place I will designate. [14]But if a man schemes and kills another man deliberately, take him away from my altar and put him to death.

[15]"Anyone who attacks[c] his father or his mother must be put to death.

[16]"Anyone who kidnaps another and either sells him or still has him when he is caught must be put to death.

[17]"Anyone who curses his father or mother must be put to death.

[18]"If men quarrel and one hits the other with a stone or with his fist[d] and he does not die but is confined to bed, [19]the one who

---

[a]6 Or *before God* [b]8 Or *master so that he does not choose her* [c]15 Or *kills*
[d]18 Or *with a tool*

struck the blow will not be held responsible if the other gets up
and walks around outside with his staff; however, he must pay the
injured man for the loss of his time and see that he is completely
healed.
20“If a man beats his male or female slave with a rod and the
slave dies as a direct result, he must be punished, 21but he is not to
be punished if the slave gets up after a day or two, since the slave
is his property.
22“If men who are fighting hit a pregnant woman and she
gives birth prematurely[a] but there is no serious injury, the offender must be fined whatever the woman's husband demands and the
court allows. 23But if there is serious injury, you are to take life for
life, 24eye for eye, tooth for tooth, hand for hand, foot for foot,
25burn for burn, wound for wound, bruise for bruise.
26“If a man hits a manservant or maidservant in the eye and
destroys it, he must let the servant go free to compensate for the
eye. 27And if he knocks out the tooth of a manservant or maidservant, he must let the servant go free to compensate for the tooth.
28“If a bull gores a man or a woman to death, the bull must
be stoned to death, and its meat must not be eaten. But the owner
of the bull will not be held responsible. 29If, however, the bull has
had the habit of goring and the owner has been warned but has
not kept it penned up and it kills a man or woman, the bull must
be stoned and the owner also must be put to death. 30However, if
payment is demanded of him, he may redeem his life by paying
whatever is demanded. 31This law also applies if the bull gores a
son or daughter. 32If the bull gores a male or female slave, the
owner must pay thirty shekels[b] of silver to the master of the slave,
and the bull must be stoned.
33“If a man uncovers a pit or digs one and fails to cover it
and an ox or a donkey falls into it, 34the owner of the pit must
pay for the loss; he must pay its owner, and the dead animal will
be his.
35“If a man's bull injures the bull of another and it dies, they
are to sell the live one and divide both the money and the dead
animal equally. 36However, if it was known that the bull had the
habit of goring, yet the owner did not keep it penned up, the
owner must pay, animal for animal, and the dead animal will
be his.

Protection of Property

22 “If a man steals an ox or a sheep and slaughters it or sells it,
he must pay back five head of cattle for the ox and four sheep for
the sheep.
2“If a thief is caught breaking in and is struck so that he dies,

[a]22 Or *she has a miscarriage* [b]32 That is, about 12 ounces (about 0.3 kilogram)

22:1-4 *ox . . . sheep . . . cattle . . . donkey:* Livestock were an important part of the Israelite economy. Donkeys and oxen were used to haul and transport things, as well as do other farming chores. Sheep were sheared for their wool, slaughtered and eaten, and used in sacrifices. Good animals were highly valued by their owners and were a sign of wealth. Their loss threatened their owners' livelihood. For more about the economic systems in the ancient world, see the article called "Trade and Travel," p. 948. In the ancient Babylonian law code of Hammurabi, a thief who could not repay what he or she had stolen would be put to death instead of being sold as a slave.

21:16 Deut 24:7. **21:24** Lev 24:19,20; Deut 19:19-21; Matt 5:38.

the defender is not guilty of bloodshed; 3but if it happens[a] after
sunrise, he is guilty of bloodshed.
"A thief must certainly make restitution, but if he has nothing, he must be sold to pay for his theft.
4"If the stolen animal is found alive in his possession—
whether ox or donkey or sheep—he must pay back double.
5"If a man grazes his livestock in a field or vineyard and lets
them stray and they graze in another man's field, he must make
restitution from the best of his own field or vineyard.
6"If a fire breaks out and spreads into thornbushes so that it
burns shocks of grain or standing grain or the whole field, the one
who started the fire must make restitution.
7"If a man gives his neighbor silver or goods for safekeeping
and they are stolen from the neighbor's house, the thief, if he is
caught, must pay back double. 8But if the thief is not found, the
owner of the house must appear before the judges[b] to determine
whether he has laid his hands on the other man's property. 9In all
cases of illegal possession of an ox, a donkey, a sheep, a garment, or
any other lost property about which somebody says, 'This is mine,'
both parties are to bring their cases before the judges. The one
whom the judges declare[c] guilty must pay back double to his
neighbor.
10"If a man gives a donkey, an ox, a sheep or any other animal to his neighbor for safekeeping and it dies or is injured or is
taken away while no one is looking, 11the issue between them will
be settled by the taking of an oath before the LORD that the neighbor did not lay hands on the other person's property. The owner is
to accept this, and no restitution is required. 12But if the animal
was stolen from the neighbor, he must make restitution to the
owner. 13If it was torn to pieces by a wild animal, he shall bring in
the remains as evidence and he will not be required to pay for the
torn animal.
14"If a man borrows an animal from his neighbor and it is
injured or dies while the owner is not present, he must make restitution. 15But if the owner is with the animal, the borrower will not
have to pay. If the animal was hired, the money paid for the hire
covers the loss.

Social Responsibility

16"If a man seduces a virgin who is not pledged to be married and sleeps with her, he must pay the bride-price, and she shall
be his wife. 17If her father absolutely refuses to give her to him, he
must still pay the bride-price for virgins.
18"Do not allow a sorceress to live.

[a]3 Or *if he strikes him* [b]8 Or *before God*; also in verse 9 [c]9 Or *whom God declares*

22:2-4 *after sunrise . . . make restitution:* Killing someone in defense of one's home during the night was allowed. During daylight, however, a person could identify a robber and later seek repayment. But killing the thief without giving the thief a chance to repay was considered murder (see the note at 20:13).

22:5 *vineyard:* This is a place where grapes are grown on vines. A vineyard was usually located on a stony hillside and was sometimes enclosed by a wall that protected it. A high watchtower was often built so someone would keep an eye out for robbers and animals.

Grape-growing and wine making would be an important part of Israel's economy once they settled in Canaan, the land God promised to them. See Num 13:23,24 and the mini-article called "Wine," p. 2047.

22:16,17 *bride-price:* It was the custom for a man to pay his wife's family a bride-price before the actual wedding ceremony took place (see also Deut 22:28,29). This payment showed that the bride now belonged to her husband's family and no longer to her father's. If the bride had already had sex, the bride price was meant to make up for the dishonor to the father whether or not he agreed to let his daughter marry the man she had slept with.

22:18 *sorceress:* One who practices magic, or witchcraft, which was forbidden by the Law of Moses (Lev 19:26; Deut 18:10,11), since relying on spirits or powers other than God showed a lack of faith in the one true God.

19“Anyone who has sexual relations with an animal must be
put to death.
20“Whoever sacrifices to any god other than the LORD must
be destroyed.[a]
21“Do not mistreat an alien or oppress him, for you were
aliens in Egypt.
22“Do not take advantage of a widow or an orphan. 23If you
do and they cry out to me, I will certainly hear their cry. 24My
anger will be aroused, and I will kill you with the sword; your
wives will become widows and your children fatherless.
25“If you lend money to one of my people among you who
is needy, do not be like a moneylender; charge him no interest.[b]
26If you take your neighbor’s cloak as a pledge, return it to him by
sunset, 27because his cloak is the only covering he has for his body.
What else will he sleep in? When he cries out to me, I will hear, for
I am compassionate.
28“Do not blaspheme God[c] or curse the ruler of your people.
29“Do not hold back offerings from your granaries or your
vats.[d]
“You must give me the firstborn of your sons. 30Do the same
with your cattle and your sheep. Let them stay with their mothers
for seven days, but give them to me on the eighth day.
31“You are to be my holy people. So do not eat the meat of
an animal torn by wild beasts; throw it to the dogs.

Laws of Justice and Mercy

23 “Do not spread false reports. Do not help a wicked man by
being a malicious witness.
2“Do not follow the crowd in doing wrong. When you give
testimony in a lawsuit, do not pervert justice by siding with the
crowd, 3and do not show favoritism to a poor man in his lawsuit.
4“If you come across your enemy’s ox or donkey wandering
off, be sure to take it back to him. 5If you see the donkey of someone who hates you fallen down under its load, do not leave it
there; be sure you help him with it.
6“Do not deny justice to your poor people in their lawsuits.
7Have nothing to do with a false charge and do not put an innocent or honest person to death, for I will not acquit the guilty.
8“Do not accept a bribe, for a bribe blinds those who see and
twists the words of the righteous.
9“Do not oppress an alien; you yourselves know how it feels
to be aliens, because you were aliens in Egypt.

[a]20 The Hebrew term refers to the irrevocable giving over of things or persons to the LORD, often by totally destroying them. [b]25 Or *excessive interest* [c]28 Or *Do not revile the judges* [d]29 The meaning of the Hebrew for this phrase is uncertain.

22:21 *alien:* The Israelites were to remember their experience as slaves in Egypt in order to act with fairness and justice toward non-Israelites and those in their society who could not easily take care of their own needs, such as widows and orphans. See also Exod 23:9; Lev 19:33,34; Deut 24:17,18; 27:19. See the mini-articles called “Foreigners (Aliens),” p. 501, and “Justice,” p. 1721.

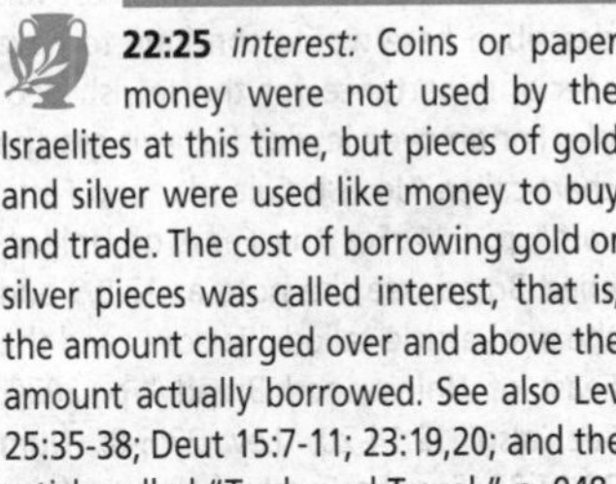

22:25 *interest:* Coins or paper money were not used by the Israelites at this time, but pieces of gold and silver were used like money to buy and trade. The cost of borrowing gold or silver pieces was called interest, that is, the amount charged over and above the amount actually borrowed. See also Lev 25:35-38; Deut 15:7-11; 23:19,20; and the article called “Trade and Travel,” p. 948.

22:29 *offerings . . . firstborn:* See the notes at 3:18 (offer sacrifices) and 4:22. See also Num 18:11,12, 25-30; Deut 26:1-15.

23:6 *justice:* God’s concern for justice toward all people, especially the poor, is clear in the Law of Moses and in the writings of Israel’s prophets (Hos 6:6; Amos 5:21-24; Isa 1:10-17). See also the mini-article called “Justice,” p. 1721.

23:9 *alien:* See the note at 22:21.

22:19 Lev 18:23; 20:15,16; Deut 27:21. **22:20** Deut 17:2-7. **22:26,27** Deut 24:10-13. **22:28** Acts 23:5. **22:31** Lev 17:15. **23:1** Exod 20:16; Lev 19:11,12; Deut 5:20. **23:2,3** Lev 19:15; Deut 16:18,19. **23:4,5** Deut 22:1-4.

23:11,12 *seventh year . . . seventh day:* Every seventh year the people were to let the land rest, just as they were to rest every seventh day. For more about this, see the note at 16:23; see also 20:9-11; 31:14,15; 34:21; 35:2; Lev 23:3; 25:1-7; Deut 5:13,14.

23:14-17 *Three times a year all the men are to appear:* Although the Israelites would come to celebrate a number of festivals, the three festivals described here would continue to have special importance for the Jewish people. For an overview of festivals see the chart called "Jewish Calendar and Festivals," p. 944. For the Feast of Unleavened Bread, see the note at 12:8,9 and the mini-article called "Passover and the Feast of Unleavened Bread," p. 2030. See also 12:14-20; Lev 23:6-8; Num 28:17-25. For the Feast of Harvest (also called the Feast of Weeks), see 34:22; Lev 23:15-21; Num 28:26-31; Deut 16:9-12. For the Feast of Ingathering (also called the Feast of Tabernacles), see 34:22; Lev 23:33-36; Deut 16:13-17; Neh 8:13-18.

23:18 *yeast:* See the note at 12:8,9 (bitter herbs . . . yeast).

23:20 *angel:* See the note at 14:19.

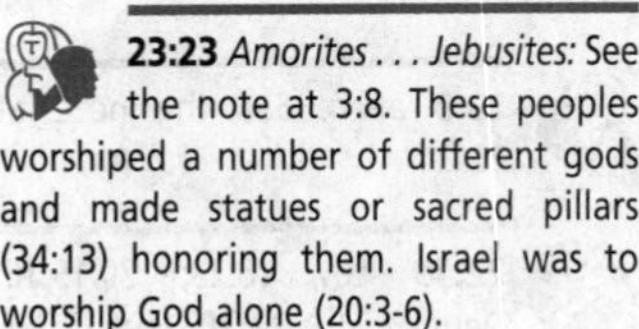

23:23 *Amorites . . . Jebusites:* See the note at 3:8. These peoples worshiped a number of different gods and made statues or sacred pillars (34:13) honoring them. Israel was to worship God alone (20:3-6).

23:31 *Red Sea . . . the desert to the River:* "Red Sea" probably refers to the northeast arm of the Red Sea. The Sea of the Philistines is the Mediterranean. The desert here probably refers to the area southeast of Canaan. The River is the great Euphrates that formed the western boundary of Mesopotamia. Only during the time of King Solomon did Israel control the amount of land mentioned in this verse (1 Kgs 4:21). See the maps on pp. 2463, 2465, and 2468.

Sabbath Laws

10“For six years you are to sow your fields and harvest the
crops, 11but during the seventh year let the land lie unplowed and
unused. Then the poor among your people may get food from it,
and the wild animals may eat what they leave. Do the same with
your vineyard and your olive grove.
12“Six days do your work, but on the seventh day do not
work, so that your ox and your donkey may rest and the slave born
in your household, and the alien as well, may be refreshed.
13“Be careful to do everything I have said to you. Do not
invoke the names of other gods; do not let them be heard on your
lips.

The Three Annual Festivals

14“Three times a year you are to celebrate a festival to me.
15“Celebrate the Feast of Unleavened Bread; for seven days
eat bread made without yeast, as I commanded you. Do this at the
appointed time in the month of Abib, for in that month you came
out of Egypt.
“No one is to appear before me empty-handed.
16“Celebrate the Feast of Harvest with the firstfruits of the
crops you sow in your field.
“Celebrate the Feast of Ingathering at the end of the year,
when you gather in your crops from the field.
17“Three times a year all the men are to appear before the
Sovereign LORD.
18“Do not offer the blood of a sacrifice to me along with
anything containing yeast.
“The fat of my festival offerings must not be kept until
morning.
19“Bring the best of the firstfruits of your soil to the house of
the LORD your God.
“Do not cook a young goat in its mother's milk.

God's Angel to Prepare the Way

20“See, I am sending an angel ahead of you to guard you
along the way and to bring you to the place I have prepared. 21Pay
attention to him and listen to what he says. Do not rebel against
him; he will not forgive your rebellion, since my Name is in him.
22If you listen carefully to what he says and do all that I say, I will
be an enemy to your enemies and will oppose those who oppose
you. 23My angel will go ahead of you and bring you into the land
of the Amorites, Hittites, Perizzites, Canaanites, Hivites and
Jebusites, and I will wipe them out. 24Do not bow down before
their gods or worship them or follow their practices. You must
demolish them and break their sacred stones to pieces. 25Worship
the LORD your God, and his blessing will be on your food and

water. I will take away sickness from among you, 26and none will
miscarry or be barren in your land. I will give you a full life span.
27"I will send my terror ahead of you and throw into confusion every nation you encounter. I will make all your enemies turn
their backs and run. 28I will send the hornet ahead of you to drive
the Hivites, Canaanites and Hittites out of your way. 29But I will
not drive them out in a single year, because the land would
become desolate and the wild animals too numerous for you. 30Lit-
tle by little I will drive them out before you, until you have
increased enough to take possession of the land.
31"I will establish your borders from the Red Sea[a] to the Sea
of the Philistines,[b] and from the desert to the River.[c] I will hand
over to you the people who live in the land and you will drive
them out before you. 32Do not make a covenant with them or with
their gods. 33Do not let them live in your land, or they will cause
you to sin against me, because the worship of their gods will certainly be a snare to you."

The Covenant Confirmed

24 Then he said to Moses, "Come up to the LORD, you and
Aaron, Nadab and Abihu, and seventy of the elders of Israel. You
are to worship at a distance, 2but Moses alone is to approach the
LORD; the others must not come near. And the people may not
come up with him."
3When Moses went and told the people all the LORD's words
and laws, they responded with one voice, "Everything the LORD has
said we will do." 4Moses then wrote down everything the LORD had
said.

He got up early the next morning and built an altar at the
foot of the mountain and set up twelve stone pillars representing
the twelve tribes of Israel. 5Then he sent young Israelite men, and
they offered burnt offerings and sacrificed young bulls as fellowship
offerings[d] to the LORD. 6Moses took half of the blood and put it in
bowls, and the other half he sprinkled on the altar. 7Then he took
the Book of the Covenant and read it to the people. They responded, "We will do everything the LORD has said; we will obey."
8Moses then took the blood, sprinkled it on the people and
said, "This is the blood of the covenant that the LORD has made
with you in accordance with all these words."
9Moses and Aaron, Nadab and Abihu, and the seventy elders
of Israel went up 10and saw the God of Israel. Under his feet was
something like a pavement made of sapphire,[e] clear as the sky
itself. 11But God did not raise his hand against these leaders of the
Israelites; they saw God, and they ate and drank.

[a]**31** Hebrew *Yam Suph*; that is, Sea of Reeds [b]**31** That is, the Mediterranean
[c]**31** That is, the Euphrates [d]**5** Traditionally *peace offerings* [e]**10** Or *lapis lazuli*

23:33 *sin:* See the notes at 9:27 and 20:4,5.

24:1-4 *Nadab and Abihu . . . seventy of the elders . . . twelve tribes:* Nadab and Abihu were Aaron's oldest sons (6:23). Eleazar, not Nadab, would become high priest after Aaron because Nadab and Abihu were killed for disobeying the LORD (Lev 10:1,2; Num 3:4; 20:25-28). For elders, see the note at 3:16. Seventy was considered a complete or full number. The leaders probably represented each of Israel's twelve tribes (see also 19:7).

24:5,6 *burnt offerings . . . fellowship offerings . . . blood:* See the notes at 3:18 (offer sacrifices) and 20:24 (sacrifice). Fellowship offerings is often translated "peace offerings," which were to make peace between God and the Israelite people.

For more about blood, see the mini-article on p. 180.

24:10 *sapphire:* A precious blue stone. See also Ezek 1:26.

24:11 *saw God:* Moses had been warned not to let the people come close enough to see God, because this could cause death (19:20-22). Only those selected to represent the people (Moses and the priests) could come into the presence of God. Here, Israel's leaders are allowed to see God up close. See also Ezek 44:3.

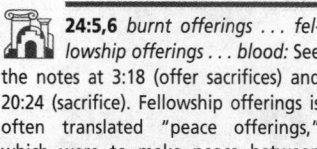

23:19 Exod 34:26; Deut 14:21; 26:2. **24:8** Matt 26:28; Mark 14:24; Luke 22:20; 1 Cor 11:25; Heb 9:19, 20; 10:29.

24:13,14 *Joshua . . . Aaron and Hur:* See the notes at 17:8-10 and 4:14.

24:15 *the mountain:* Referring to Mount Sinai (also called Horeb). See the note on p. 133.

24:16-18 *a consuming fire . . . forty days and forty nights:* The number forty stands for a long time or for a generation. See the chart called "Numbers in the Bible," p. 2405. See also Deut 9:9-11.

For more about fire and the presence of God, see the note at 13:21,22.

12 The LORD said to Moses, "Come up to me on the mountain and stay here, and I will give you the tablets of stone, with the
law and commands I have written for their instruction."
13 Then Moses set out with Joshua his aide, and Moses went
up on the mountain of God. 14 He said to the elders, "Wait here for
us until we come back to you. Aaron and Hur are with you, and
anyone involved in a dispute can go to them."
15 When Moses went up on the mountain, the cloud covered
it, 16 and the glory of the LORD settled on Mount Sinai. For six days
the cloud covered the mountain, and on the seventh day the LORD
called to Moses from within the cloud. 17 To the Israelites the glory
of the LORD looked like a consuming fire on top of the mountain.
18 Then Moses entered the cloud as he went on up the mountain.
And he stayed on the mountain forty days and forty nights.

BLOOD

In the Bible the power of life is understood to be present in blood. This is true of animals (Gen 9:4) and of humans (Gen 4:10). No one was to eat meat that still had the blood in it (Lev 17:10-12; Deut 12:23,24) or touch a bloody dead animal (Lev 17:15, 16). To kill another human being is to "shed blood," and the blood of the victim is "on the head" of the murderer (see for example, 1 Kgs 2:31-33). The shedding of innocent blood could make the land itself cursed (Gen 4:10-12) or ritually unclean (Num 35:33, 34). Because David spilled so much blood by fighting with his enemies he was said to be unfit to build the LORD's temple (1 Chr 22:8; 28:3).

Blood was considered evidence of God-given life. Because of this, Israel's priests used blood to prepare the sacrifices they offered to God for the benefit of the people. The altar was to be made ready for sacrifices by the sprinkling of blood (Lev 1:5-9; 4:3-7; 6:24-30; 8:15), and the priests had to have blood put on them so they could become fit to come into God's presence (Exod 29:19-21; Lev 8:22-30). When the people of Israel were preparing to escape from Egypt, they were told to sprinkle blood on the doorframes of their houses to protect them as the LORD passed over Egypt and took the life of the oldest son in each family (Exod 12). At Mount Sinai, blood was poured out to make firm the covenant between God and the Israelite people (Exod 24:8). In the place where they worshiped God, blood continued to cleanse them and to confirm their special relationship (Lev 1).

Because of the Old Testament beliefs about blood and sacrifice, Jesus' death had special meaning for New Testament writers like Paul. Paul describes Jesus' death on the cross as a "sacrifice," and understood that Christ offered his blood so people could be forgiven and be made acceptable to God (Rom 3:25,26; see also Col 1:20). The writer of HEBREWS says that the blood of Jesus has a more powerful purifying effect than the blood sacrifices of ancient Israel (Heb 9:20-22; 10:3-14). Christ's blood (death) makes it possible for believers to have a complete and everlasting relationship with God (John 6:53-56; Heb 10:19-22). In 1 PETER, Christ is described as the "lamb without blemish or defect," whose blood rescues people from being slaves to sin (1 Pet 1:18,19). When Christians take part in the Lord's Supper, they are sharing in the body and blood of Jesus (Luke 22:19, 20; 1 Cor 11:23-32).

GOD GIVES INSTRUCTIONS FOR WORSHIP

Moses receives instructions about how to make a portable place of worship, a large tent (tabernacle) that will house the ark of the covenant, table for the bread of the Presence, special lampstand, and altar for offering sacrifices. Instructions for how the priests are to dress and perform their duties are also given.

Offerings for the Tabernacle

25 The LORD said to Moses, 2“Tell the Israelites to bring me an
offering. You are to receive the offering for me from each man
whose heart prompts him to give. 3These are the offerings you are
to receive from them: gold, silver and bronze; 4blue, purple and
scarlet yarn and fine linen; goat hair; 5ram skins dyed red and
hides of sea cows[a]; acacia wood; 6olive oil for the light; spices for
the anointing oil and for the fragrant incense; 7and onyx stones
and other gems to be mounted on the ephod and breastpiece.
8“Then have them make a sanctuary for me, and I will dwell
among them. 9Make this tabernacle and all its furnishings exactly
like the pattern I will show you.

The Ark

10“Have them make a chest of acacia wood—two and a half
cubits long, a cubit and a half wide, and a cubit and a half high.[b]
11Overlay it with pure gold, both inside and out, and make a gold
molding around it. 12Cast four gold rings for it and fasten them to
its four feet, with two rings on one side and two rings on the other.
13Then make poles of acacia wood and overlay them with gold.
14Insert the poles into the rings on the sides of the chest to carry
it. 15The poles are to remain in the rings of this ark; they are not
to be removed. 16Then put in the ark the Testimony, which I will
give you.
17“Make an atonement cover[c] of pure gold—two and a half
cubits long and a cubit and a half wide.[d] 18And make two cherubim
out of hammered gold at the ends of the cover. 19Make one cherub
on one end and the second cherub on the other; make the cherubim of one piece with the cover, at the two ends. 20The cherubim
are to have their wings spread upward, overshadowing the cover
with them. The cherubim are to face each other, looking toward
the cover. 21Place the cover on top of the ark and put in the ark the
Testimony, which I will give you. 22There, above the cover between
the two cherubim that are over the ark of the Testimony, I will
meet with you and give you all my commands for the Israelites.

[a]**5** That is, dugongs [b]**10** That is, about 3 3/4 feet (about 1.1 meters) long and 2 1/4 feet (about 0.7 meter) wide and high [c]**17** Traditionally *a mercy seat* [d]**17** That is, about 3 3/4 feet (about 1.1 meters) long and 2 1/4 feet (about 0.7 meter) wide

25:4-6 *blue, purple and scarlet yarn and fine linen . . . anointing oil:* Linen was woven from thread made from the stalks of flax plants. The colors of wool requested were considered royal colors because these shades of dyes were expensive to make.

Oil extracted from olives had many uses in the ancient world. It was used for cooking and food preparation; as fuel for lamps, as an important ingredient in perfumes and medicinal ointments. As indicated here, it was also used for ceremonial purposes (ordaining priests and dedicating sacred objects). See also the note at 29:1.

25:10 *chest of acacia wood:* Also known as the ark of the covenant. For more about this important sacred object from early Israelite history, see the mini-article called "The Ark of the Covenant," p. 513.

Acacia wood comes from a kind of evergreen tree. Its beautiful wood is harder and darker in color than oak.

25:16 *the Testimony:* Referring to the tablets of the Ten Commandments (see 20:2-17 and the note at 20:2). When these stones were put into the ark of the covenant, they made the ark too holy to touch (2 Sam 6:6,7). Because the commandments were stored there, it is called the ark of the covenant.

25:17-20 *atonement cover . . . cherubim:* The lid of the ark of the covenant has also been called the "mercy seat," where God sat and judged the people with overwhelming kindness (mercy) and told them what they must do (25:22). The winged creatures, called cherubim, probably looked like the Sphinx of Egypt, having a human head and lion's body (Ezek 41:18-20) or like the human-headed bulls and lions that guarded ancient Mesopotamian temples. See also 2 Sam 6:2; 1 Kgs 6:22-29; 2 Kgs 19:15; Ezek 10:2.

25:17 Heb 9:5.

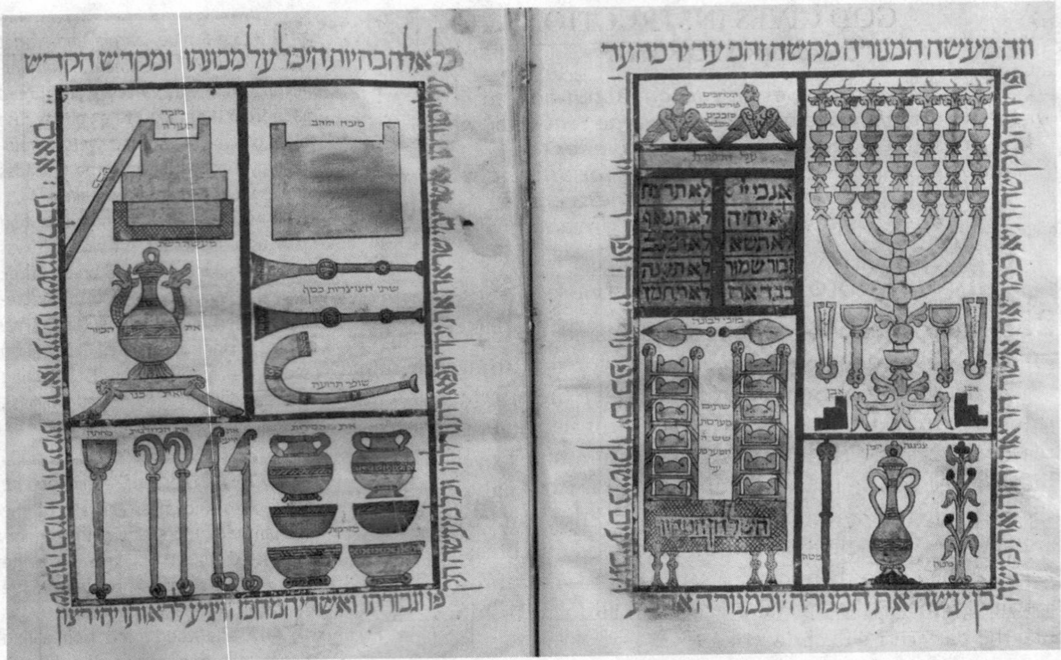

Sanctuary Furnishings, illuminated page from a late thirteenth century Hebrew Bible, possibly by the artist Solomon ben Raphael. The LORD gave Moses instructions about the kinds of items the people of Israel were to create for use in the tabernacle, the place where the people were to worship the LORD and offer sacrifices (see chapters 25–27). These included: (left-hand page, clockwise from top left) an altar for burnt offerings; an incense altar; trumpets and horns; pots for ashes and basins for catching the blood of sacrificed animals; shovels, flesh hooks, a firepan; a laver (bronze basin or urn on a stand; see 30:17-21); (right-hand page, clockwise from top left) the ark of the covenant (ark of the Testimony) containing the two stone tablets with the Law; the gold lampstand with tongs and snuffers; a jar containing manna (see 16:33) flanked by two representations of Aaron's walking staff (one budding, see Num 17); the table with the bread of the Presence. Later, when Solomon was king of Israel, these items were placed in the temple in Jerusalem. The Hebrew text around the edges of the pages includes the phrase "May it be Your will that the Temple be speedily rebuilt in our days so that our eyes may behold it and our heart rejoice."

25:23-30 *table . . . bread of the Presence:* This table probably resembled a modern coffee table with a raised rim all around its top (see the illustration above). It also had rings of gold and poles for carrying it. Twelve sacred loaves, one for each of Israel's twelve tribes, were to be placed fresh on the table every Sabbath (Lev 24:5-9). The loaves, called the bread of the Presence, were an ongoing offering to God and a reminder of God's blessings. The bread could only be eaten by Aaron's descendants, the priests of Israel.

The Table

23"Make a table of acacia wood—two cubits long, a cubit
wide and a cubit and a half high.[a] 24Overlay it with pure gold and
make a gold molding around it. 25Also make around it a rim a
handbreadth[b] wide and put a gold molding on the rim. 26Make
four gold rings for the table and fasten them to the four corners,
where the four legs are. 27The rings are to be close to the rim to
hold the poles used in carrying the table. 28Make the poles of acacia wood, overlay them with gold and carry the table with them.
29And make its plates and dishes of pure gold, as well as its pitchers and bowls for the pouring out of offerings. 30Put the bread of
the Presence on this table to be before me at all times.

[a]**23** That is, about 3 feet (about 0.9 meter) long and 1 1/2 feet (about 0.5 meter) wide and 2 1/4 feet (about 0.7 meter) high [b]**25** That is, about 3 inches (about 8 centimeters)

The Lampstand

31“Make a lampstand of pure gold and hammer it out, base
and shaft; its flowerlike cups, buds and blossoms shall be of one
piece with it. 32Six branches are to extend from the sides of the
lampstand—three on one side and three on the other. 33Three cups
shaped like almond flowers with buds and blossoms are to be on
one branch, three on the next branch, and the same for all six
branches extending from the lampstand. 34And on the lampstand
there are to be four cups shaped like almond flowers with buds
and blossoms. 35One bud shall be under the first pair of branches
extending from the lampstand, a second bud under the second
pair, and a third bud under the third pair—six branches in all.
36The buds and branches shall all be of one piece with the lampstand, hammered out of pure gold.
37“Then make its seven lamps and set them up on it so that
they light the space in front of it. 38Its wick trimmers and trays are
to be of pure gold. 39A talent[a] of pure gold is to be used for the
lampstand and all these accessories. 40See that you make them
according to the pattern shown you on the mountain.

The Tabernacle

26 “Make the tabernacle with ten curtains of finely twisted linen
and blue, purple and scarlet yarn, with cherubim worked into
them by a skilled craftsman. 2All the curtains are to be the same
size—twenty-eight cubits long and four cubits wide.[b] 3Join five of
the curtains together, and do the same with the other five. 4Make
loops of blue material along the edge of the end curtain in one set,
and do the same with the end curtain in the other set. 5Make fifty
loops on one curtain and fifty loops on the end curtain of the
other set, with the loops opposite each other. 6Then make fifty gold
clasps and use them to fasten the curtains together so that the tabernacle is a unit.
7“Make curtains of goat hair for the tent over the tabernacle—eleven altogether. 8All eleven curtains are to be the same size—
thirty cubits long and four cubits wide.[c] 9Join five of the curtains
together into one set and the other six into another set. Fold the
sixth curtain double at the front of the tent. 10Make fifty loops
along the edge of the end curtain in one set and also along the
edge of the end curtain in the other set. 11Then make fifty bronze
clasps and put them in the loops to fasten the tent together as a
unit. 12As for the additional length of the tent curtains, the half
curtain that is left over is to hang down at the rear of the tabernacle. 13The tent curtains will be a cubit[d] longer on both sides;

[a]**39** That is, about 75 pounds (about 34 kilograms) [b]**2** That is, about 42 feet (about 12.5 meters) long and 6 feet (about 1.8 meters) wide [c]**8** That is, about 45 feet (about 13.5 meters) long and 6 feet (about 1.8 meters) wide [d]**13** That is, about 1 1/2 feet (about 0.5 meter)

25:31 *lampstand of pure gold:* The lampstand had seven branches with small clay saucer-like lamps attached to the end of each branch. Seven was a number symbolizing completeness. The light from the lamps represented the glory of God. The lampstand was decorated with golden flowers, buds and petals patterned after the almond tree, one of the first trees to bloom each spring in Canaan.

26:1-7 *the tabernacle . . . linen . . . cherubim . . . goat hair:* This tabernacle was the place where the people were to meet God (29:42,43), who lived among the people (25:8). "Tabernacle" means "dwelling place." It became the place of worship, where the people brought gifts and priests offered sacrifices to God. The tabernacle's curtains were made of fine red, blue, or purple linen (see the note at 25:4–6) and were decorated with cherubim like those that were on the lid of the ark of the covenant (see the note at 25:17-20). The tabernacle itself was made of coarse goat hair woven in eleven sections, ram skins dyed red, and fine leather. See the mini-article called "The Tabernacle," p. 2346.

25:40 Acts 7:44; Heb 8:5.

what is left will hang over the sides of the tabernacle so as to cover
it. 14 Make for the tent a covering of ram skins dyed red, and over
that a covering of hides of sea cows.[a]

15 "Make upright frames of acacia wood for the tabernacle.
16 Each frame is to be ten cubits long and a cubit and a half wide,[b]
17 with two projections set parallel to each other. Make all the
frames of the tabernacle in this way. 18 Make twenty frames for the
south side of the tabernacle 19 and make forty silver bases to go
under them—two bases for each frame, one under each projection. 20 For the other side, the north side of the tabernacle, make
twenty frames 21 and forty silver bases—two under each frame.
22 Make six frames for the far end, that is, the west end of the tabernacle, 23 and make two frames for the corners at the far end. 24 At
these two corners they must be double from the bottom all the
way to the top, and fitted into a single ring; both shall be like that.
25 So there will be eight frames and sixteen silver bases—two under
each frame.

26 "Also make crossbars of acacia wood: five for the frames on
one side of the tabernacle, 27 five for those on the other side, and
five for the frames on the west, at the far end of the tabernacle.
28 The center crossbar is to extend from end to end at the middle of
the frames. 29 Overlay the frames with gold and make gold rings to
hold the crossbars. Also overlay the crossbars with gold.

30 "Set up the tabernacle according to the plan shown you on
the mountain.

31 "Make a curtain of blue, purple and scarlet yarn and finely twisted linen, with cherubim worked into it by a skilled craftsman. 32 Hang it with gold hooks on four posts of acacia wood
overlaid with gold and standing on four silver bases. 33 Hang the
curtain from the clasps and place the ark of the Testimony behind
the curtain. The curtain will separate the Holy Place from the
Most Holy Place. 34 Put the atonement cover on the ark of the Testimony in the Most Holy Place. 35 Place the table outside the curtain on the north side of the tabernacle and put the lampstand
opposite it on the south side.

36 "For the entrance to the tent make a curtain of blue, purple and scarlet yarn and finely twisted linen—the work of an
embroiderer. 37 Make gold hooks for this curtain and five posts of
acacia wood overlaid with gold. And cast five bronze bases for
them.

The Altar of Burnt Offering

27 "Build an altar of acacia wood, three cubits[c] high; it is to be
square, five cubits long and five cubits wide.[d] 2 Make a horn at each

[a]14 That is, dugongs [b]16 That is, about 15 feet (about 4.5 meters) long and 2 1/4 feet (about 0.7 meter) wide [c]1 That is, about 4 1/2 feet (about 1.3 meters) [d]1 That is, about 7 1/2 feet (about 2.3 meters) long and wide

The LORD said to Moses, *"Set up the tabernacle according to the plan shown you on the mountain."* Exod 26:30

26:15 *frames of acacia wood:* The tabernacle was supported by a framework of acacia wood slats or frames placed on heavy silver bases and connected with five crossbars. See the note at 25:10.

26:31-34 *curtain . . . Holy Place . . . Most Holy Place:* Inside the tabernacle, a linen curtain was hung to separate the Holy Place, which contained the table for the bread of the Presence, the lampstand, the altar of incense (30:1-6), and the lamp (27:20,21), from the Most Holy Place, where it was believed that God had his earthly throne on the atonement cover of the ark of the covenant (26:34; see also the note at 25:17-20).

26:36 *entrance:* The entrance was made of fine linen (see the note at 25:4-6), embroidered with wool, not woven like the curtain separating the holy spaces inside the tabernacle (see 26:31-34).

27:1-8 *altar . . . hollow:* The main altar used for offering sacrifices was made of acacia wood covered with bronze. The altar was to have a decorative bronze edge all the way around the top with corners that resembled bulls' horns. See the illustration on p. 182.

26:33 Heb 6:19; 9:3-5.

of the four corners, so that the horns and the altar are of one piece,
and overlay the altar with bronze. 3Make all its utensils of
bronze—its pots to remove the ashes, and its shovels, sprinkling
bowls, meat forks and firepans. 4Make a grating for it, a bronze
network, and make a bronze ring at each of the four corners of the
network. 5Put it under the ledge of the altar so that it is halfway up
the altar. 6Make poles of acacia wood for the altar and overlay
them with bronze. 7The poles are to be inserted into the rings so
they will be on two sides of the altar when it is carried. 8Make the
altar hollow, out of boards. It is to be made just as you were shown
on the mountain.

The Courtyard

9"Make a courtyard for the tabernacle. The south side shall
be a hundred cubits[a] long and is to have curtains of finely twisted
linen, 10with twenty posts and twenty bronze bases and with silver
hooks and bands on the posts. 11The north side shall also be a
hundred cubits long and is to have curtains, with twenty posts and
twenty bronze bases and with silver hooks and bands on the posts.
12"The west end of the courtyard shall be fifty cubits[b] wide
and have curtains, with ten posts and ten bases. 13On the east end,
toward the sunrise, the courtyard shall also be fifty cubits wide.
14Curtains fifteen cubits[c] long are to be on one side of the entrance,
with three posts and three bases, 15and curtains fifteen cubits long
are to be on the other side, with three posts and three bases.
16"For the entrance to the courtyard, provide a curtain twenty cubits[d] long, of blue, purple and scarlet yarn and finely twisted
linen—the work of an embroiderer—with four posts and four
bases. 17All the posts around the courtyard are to have silver bands
and hooks, and bronze bases. 18The courtyard shall be a hundred
cubits long and fifty cubits wide,[e] with curtains of finely twisted
linen five cubits[f] high, and with bronze bases. 19All the other articles used in the service of the tabernacle, whatever their function,
including all the tent pegs for it and those for the courtyard, are to
be of bronze.

Oil for the Lampstand

20"Command the Israelites to bring you clear oil of pressed
olives for the light so that the lamps may be kept burning. 21In the
Tent of Meeting, outside the curtain that is in front of the Testimony, Aaron and his sons are to keep the lamps burning before

[a]**9** That is, about 150 feet (about 46 meters); also in verse 11 [b]**12** That is, about 75 feet (about 23 meters); also in verse 13 [c]**14** That is, about 22 1/2 feet (about 6.9 meters); also in verse 15 [d]**16** That is, about 30 feet (about 9 meters)
[e]**18** That is, about 150 feet (about 46 meters) long and 75 feet (about 23 meters) wide [f]**18** That is, about 7 1/2 feet (about 2.3 meters)

27:9-15 *courtyard:* The enclosure, or courtyard, surrounding the tabernacle was about half the size of an American football field. The curtain surrounding the courtyard was about seven and a half feet high (27:18), or about half the height of the tabernacle itself. In the courtyard were the bronze altar (27:1-7) and the large bronze basin used by the priests to wash their hands and feet (30:18-21). The tabernacle took up the western half of the courtyard, and the bronze altar of sacrifice was in the middle of the eastern half. The entrance to the courtyard was on the east end of the courtyard, so the tabernacle opening faced east toward the rising sun. See the illustration on p. 2345.

27:20 *oil of pressed olives . . . lamps:* See the note at 25:4-6. Olive oil was collected by crushing olives in a bowl and then pouring the olive pulp into a cloth basket. Clear oil burns with very little smoke. See also the illustration on p. 1326. The lamp in the Holy Place was probably a simple oil lamp that had to be filled with enough oil at sunset so it would burn until sunrise, when it was likely put out (see 30:8; 1 Sam 3:3). This lamp symbolized God's presence in the tabernacle.

27:21 *Aaron and his sons:* See the notes at 2:1 and 4:14, and the mini-article called "Israel's Priests," p. 2344. See also the note at 24:1-4.

28:2 *sacred garments:* The clothes are described in detail in 28:4-43. Israel's high priest was in charge of the other priests and was the only one who could enter the Most Holy Place in the tabernacle (Lev 16:1-19). Aaron would later be anointed and consecrated as Israel's first high priest (see 29:5-7).

28:4 *breastpiece . . . sash:* These items are described in detail in 28:6-39. See also the illustration on p. 187 and the article called "People of the Law: The Religion of Israel," p. 939.

28:6 *ephod:* This ephod, or vest, was made of fine linen woven with royal shades of wool (see the note at 25:4-6). The sash was like a wide belt used to help hold the vest in place. On the shoulder straps two onyx stones were engraved with the names of the twelve sons of Jacob. See the mini-article called "Israel," p. 264 and the illustration on p. 187.

28:15 *breastpiece:* The breastpiece was like a flat wool and linen pouch that contained an inner pocket, formed by doubling over the material (28:16). In the pouch were kept the small objects used to receive answers from God (see the note at 28:30).

28:17 *four rows of precious stones:* The exact translation of Hebrew and Greek terms for these stones is difficult. The stones listed in this translation may be briefly defined as follows: ruby is red in color; topaz is yellow; beryl is green or bluish green; turquoise is sky blue; sapphire is blue; emerald is green; jacinth is orange; agate has swirls of brown and white; amethyst is deep purple; chrysolite is yellow; onyx is translucent; jasper is sometimes reddish-brown, but the kind mentioned in this verse is probably green or clear.

the LORD from evening till morning. This is to be a lasting ordinance among the Israelites for the generations to come.

The Priestly Garments

28 "Have Aaron your brother brought to you from among the
Israelites, along with his sons Nadab and Abihu, Eleazar and
Ithamar, so they may serve me as priests. [2]Make sacred garments
for your brother Aaron, to give him dignity and honor. [3]Tell all the
skilled men to whom I have given wisdom in such matters that
they are to make garments for Aaron, for his consecration, so he
may serve me as priest. [4]These are the garments they are to make:
a breastpiece, an ephod, a robe, a woven tunic, a turban and a sash.
They are to make these sacred garments for your brother Aaron
and his sons, so they may serve me as priests. [5]Have them use gold,
and blue, purple and scarlet yarn, and fine linen.

The Ephod

[6]"Make the ephod of gold, and of blue, purple and scarlet
yarn, and of finely twisted linen—the work of a skilled craftsman.
[7]It is to have two shoulder pieces attached to two of its corners, so
it can be fastened. [8]Its skillfully woven waistband is to be like it—
of one piece with the ephod and made with gold, and with blue,
purple and scarlet yarn, and with finely twisted linen.
[9]"Take two onyx stones and engrave on them the names of
the sons of Israel [10]in the order of their birth—six names on one
stone and the remaining six on the other. [11]Engrave the names of
the sons of Israel on the two stones the way a gem cutter engraves
a seal. Then mount the stones in gold filigree settings [12]and fasten
them on the shoulder pieces of the ephod as memorial stones for
the sons of Israel. Aaron is to bear the names on his shoulders as a
memorial before the LORD. [13]Make gold filigree settings [14]and two
braided chains of pure gold, like a rope, and attach the chains to
the settings.

The Breastpiece

[15]"Fashion a breastpiece for making decisions—the work of
a skilled craftsman. Make it like the ephod: of gold, and of blue,
purple and scarlet yarn, and of finely twisted linen. [16]It is to be
square—a span[a] long and a span wide—and folded double. [17]Then
mount four rows of precious stones on it. In the first row there
shall be a ruby, a topaz and a beryl; [18]in the second row a
turquoise, a sapphire[b] and an emerald; [19]in the third row a jacinth,
an agate and an amethyst; [20]in the fourth row a chrysolite, an onyx
and a jasper.[c] Mount them in gold filigree settings. [21]There are to

[a]**16** That is, about 9 inches (about 22 centimeters) [b]**18** Or *lapis lazuli*
[c]**20** The precise identification of some of these precious stones is uncertain.

The High Priest and His Breastpiece. The LORD told Moses to make clothes for Aaron that were beautiful and worthy of a high priest. Over a robe of blue wool the high priest was to wear a fine linen vest. And over the vest he was to wear a breastpiece, nine inches square, that would hold twelve precious stones representing the twelve tribes of Israel. Although no one but the high priest was allowed to go into the Most Holy Place, all of Israel would be remembered by the LORD because their names were engraved on the breastpiece and therefore over his heart whenever he enters the presence of the LORD. The stones on the breastpiece were (1) ruby, (2) topaz, (3) beryl, (4) turquoise, (5) sapphire, (6) emerald, (7) jacinth, (8) agate, (9) amethyst, (10) chrysolite, (11) onyx, and (12) jasper. It is not known which stones represented which tribes. (See 28:1-39.)

be twelve stones, one for each of the names of the sons of Israel,
each engraved like a seal with the name of one of the twelve tribes.
22"For the breastpiece make braided chains of pure gold, like
a rope. 23Make two gold rings for it and fasten them to two corners
of the breastpiece. 24Fasten the two gold chains to the rings at the
corners of the breastpiece, 25and the other ends of the chains to the
two settings, attaching them to the shoulder pieces of the ephod at
the front. 26Make two gold rings and attach them to the other two
corners of the breastpiece on the inside edge next to the ephod.
27Make two more gold rings and attach them to the bottom of the
shoulder pieces on the front of the ephod, close to the seam just
above the waistband of the ephod. 28The rings of the breastpiece are
to be tied to the rings of the ephod with blue cord, connecting it to
the waistband, so that the breastpiece will not swing out from the
ephod.
29"Whenever Aaron enters the Holy Place, he will bear the
names of the sons of Israel over his heart on the breastpiece of
decision as a continuing memorial before the LORD. 30Also put the
Urim and the Thummim in the breastpiece, so they may be over
Aaron's heart whenever he enters the presence of the LORD. Thus

28:29 *Holy Place:* See the note at 26:31-34.

28:30 *the Urim and the Thummim:* Two objects in the breastpiece used by the priest to determine God's will. It is not known precisely how they were used. These objects may have been made of wood, stone, or metal. See also Num 27:21; Deut 33:8; Ezra 2:63; Neh 7:65.

Aaron will always bear the means of making decisions for the
Israelites over his heart before the LORD.

Other Priestly Garments

[31]"Make the robe of the ephod entirely of blue cloth, [32]with
an opening for the head in its center. There shall be a woven edge
like a collar[a] around this opening, so that it will not tear. [33]Make
pomegranates of blue, purple and scarlet yarn around the hem of
the robe, with gold bells between them. [34]The gold bells and the
pomegranates are to alternate around the hem of the robe. [35]Aaron
must wear it when he ministers. The sound of the bells will be
heard when he enters the Holy Place before the LORD and when he
comes out, so that he will not die.

[36]"Make a plate of pure gold and engrave on it as on a seal:
HOLY TO THE LORD. [37]Fasten a blue cord to it to attach it to the tur-
ban; it is to be on the front of the turban. [38]It will be on Aaron's
forehead, and he will bear the guilt involved in the sacred gifts the
Israelites consecrate, whatever their gifts may be. It will be on
Aaron's forehead continually so that they will be acceptable to the
LORD.

[39]"Weave the tunic of fine linen and make the turban of fine
linen. The sash is to be the work of an embroiderer. [40]Make tunics,
sashes and headbands for Aaron's sons, to give them dignity and
honor. [41]After you put these clothes on your brother Aaron and his
sons, anoint and ordain them. Consecrate them so they may serve
me as priests.

[42]"Make linen undergarments as a covering for the body,
reaching from the waist to the thigh. [43]Aaron and his sons must
wear them whenever they enter the Tent of Meeting or approach
the altar to minister in the Holy Place, so that they will not incur
guilt and die.

"This is to be a lasting ordinance for Aaron and his descendants.

Consecration of the Priests

29 "This is what you are to do to consecrate them, so they may
serve me as priests: Take a young bull and two rams without
defect. [2]And from fine wheat flour, without yeast, make bread, and
cakes mixed with oil, and wafers spread with oil. [3]Put them in a
basket and present them in it—along with the bull and the two
rams. [4]Then bring Aaron and his sons to the entrance to the Tent
of Meeting and wash them with water. [5]Take the garments and
dress Aaron with the tunic, the robe of the ephod, the ephod itself
and the breastpiece. Fasten the ephod on him by its skillfully
woven waistband. [6]Put the turban on his head and attach the

[a]32 The meaning of the Hebrew for this word is uncertain.

28:31-35 *robe . . . pomegranates . . . bells:* The long robe made of blue wool was worn under the vest. At the bottom of the robe were to be woven shapes in the form of pomegranates of blue, purple, and red wool. In the ancient world one was not supposed to approach rulers without being formally announced. The sound of the bells was intended to announce to God that the high priest was coming into the Holy Place.

28:36-38 *plate of pure gold . . . on Aaron's forehead . . . bear the guilt:* If an Israelite or one of the priests mistakenly sinned, that is, did not follow proper procedures while offering a sacrifice, his error (sin) would fall on the high priest's head, at least in a symbolic way (see Lev 22:3, for example). So, the gold plate may have been thought to act as a sort of magnet, attracting these improper actions.

28:37 *turban:* This headdress included cloth rolled at its base which was thick enough to support the gold strip. See 28:28 (blue cord).

28:40 *Aaron's sons:* See the notes at 2:1 and 4:14, and the mini-article called "Israel's Priests," p. 2344.

28:40-42 *tunics . . . linen undergarments:* The robes were full-length and made of wool and linen (see the note at 25:4-6). The turbans were wound in the shape of a cone. See also the note at 20:26.

28:41 *anoint and ordain:* See the note at 29:1.

29:1 *consecrate:* To consecrate meant "to choose and to set apart for a special purpose." Olive oil was poured on the head of the person being dedicated or chosen (28:41; 29:7). This pouring of oil is also known as "anointing," and was a practice the Israelites employed when dedicating the kings God chose for them (see, for example, 1 Sam 10:1; 16:13; 2 Kgs 23:30). See also the mini-article called "Messiah (Chosen One)," p. 1124.

sacred diadem to the turban. [7]Take the anointing oil and anoint him by pouring it on his head. [8]Bring his sons and dress them in tunics [9]and put headbands on them. Then tie sashes on Aaron and his sons.[a] The priesthood is theirs by a lasting ordinance. In this way you shall ordain Aaron and his sons.

[10]"Bring the bull to the front of the Tent of Meeting, and Aaron and his sons shall lay their hands on its head. [11]Slaughter it in the LORD's presence at the entrance to the Tent of Meeting. [12]Take some of the bull's blood and put it on the horns of the altar with your finger, and pour out the rest of it at the base of the altar. [13]Then take all the fat around the inner parts, the covering of the liver, and both kidneys with the fat on them, and burn them on the altar. [14]But burn the bull's flesh and its hide and its offal outside the camp. It is a sin offering.

[15]"Take one of the rams, and Aaron and his sons shall lay their hands on its head. [16]Slaughter it and take the blood and sprinkle it against the altar on all sides. [17]Cut the ram into pieces and wash the inner parts and the legs, putting them with the head and the other pieces. [18]Then burn the entire ram on the altar. It is a burnt offering to the LORD, a pleasing aroma, an offering made to the LORD by fire.

[19]"Take the other ram, and Aaron and his sons shall lay their hands on its head. [20]Slaughter it, take some of its blood and put it on the lobes of the right ears of Aaron and his sons, on the thumbs of their right hands, and on the big toes of their right feet. Then sprinkle blood against the altar on all sides. [21]And take some of the blood on the altar and some of the anointing oil and sprinkle it on Aaron and his garments and on his sons and their garments. Then he and his sons and their garments will be consecrated.

[22]"Take from this ram the fat, the fat tail, the fat around the inner parts, the covering of the liver, both kidneys with the fat on them, and the right thigh. (This is the ram for the ordination.) [23]From the basket of bread made without yeast, which is before the LORD, take a loaf, and a cake made with oil, and a wafer. [24]Put all these in the hands of Aaron and his sons and wave them before the LORD as a wave offering. [25]Then take them from their hands and burn them on the altar along with the burnt offering for a pleasing aroma to the LORD, an offering made to the LORD by fire. [26]After you take the breast of the ram for Aaron's ordination, wave it before the LORD as a wave offering, and it will be your share.

[27]"Consecrate those parts of the ordination ram that belong to Aaron and his sons: the breast that was waved and the thigh that was presented. [28]This is always to be the regular share from the Israelites for Aaron and his sons. It is the contribution the Israelites are to make to the LORD from their fellowship offerings.[b]

[29]"Aaron's sacred garments will belong to his descendants so

---

[a]**9** Hebrew; Septuagint *on them* [b]**28** Traditionally *peace offerings*

29:4 *wash them with water:* Washing the hands and feet was a requirement before offering sacrifices (30:18-21). If a priest had touched something that was ritually unclean, he could likely make the sacrifice unclean and unfit for God (Lev 16:3,4; Heb 10:22). See also the mini-article called "Purity (Clean and Unclean)," p. 2125.

29:5-9 *garments . . . sashes:* See the notes at 28:6 and 28:40-42.

29:10-12 *bull . . . blood:* A bull was offered as a sin offering (29:14). For more about "Blood," see the mini-article on p. 180. The choicest parts of the bull were burned on the altar (Lev 4).

29:14 *sin offering:* The contents of the bull's stomach were thought of as containing the sins and were to be burned outside the camp (Heb 13:11-13). When a sin offering was made for someone other than priests, the part that was not burned on the altar could be eaten by the priests (Lev 5:13; 6:26).

29:20,21 *blood . . . right ears . . . their garments:* The blood was believed to have purifying power and to keep the priest safe from ritual uncleanness. See the mini-article called "Blood" on p. 180. See also Lev 14:14-20.

29:22 *right thigh:* This was usually given to the priest in charge of the sacrifice (Lev 7:32,33).

29:27 *Consecrate:* See the note at 29:1. For more about the wave offering, see Lev 7:28-36.

29:18 Gen 8:20, 21; Lev 1; Eph 5:2; Phil 4:18. **29:23** Exod 29:2,3. **29:29,30** Exod 29:35-37; Num 20:26.

29:33 *offerings by which atonement was made:* See the note at 29:14.

29:35-37 *seven days . . . the altar will be most holy:* The number seven was considered a sacred number signifying completeness (see also the note at 23:11,12). Olive oil was used to consecrate or "anoint" people or things in order to make them holy (see the notes at 25:4-6 and 29:1). To be holy meant "to be set apart," usually for a special purpose, or to be dedicated to God. See also 30:22-33; Lev 6:18,27; 8:10,11.

29:38 *offer on the altar regularly each day:* The priests were to offer daily sacrifices on the altar (27:1-8) in the courtyard outside the entrance to the tabernacle (see the illustration, p. 2345). The sacrifices offered in the morning and in the evening included a one-year-old lamb, two pounds of fine wheat flour and one quart of pure olive oil (see the note at 27:20).

29:43-45 *my glory . . . dwell among the Israelites:* See the notes at 3:2; 19:16-18. See also 25:8 and the note at 25:17-20.

30:1 *altar of acacia wood for burning incense:* See the note at 25:10. Incense was made of frankincense, other gums and spices, and salt, which together produced a sweet smell when burned. The smoke from the burning incense represented the prayers that went up to God (Ps 141:2; Rev 5:8). The altar for burning incense was in the Holy Place (see the illustration on p. 2345).

29:32 Exod 29:2,3. **29:46** Exod 12:31-41; 20:2.

that they can be anointed and ordained in them. 30The son who
succeeds him as priest and comes to the Tent of Meeting to minister in the Holy Place is to wear them seven days.

31"Take the ram for the ordination and cook the meat in a
sacred place. 32At the entrance to the Tent of Meeting, Aaron and
his sons are to eat the meat of the ram and the bread that is in the
basket. 33They are to eat these offerings by which atonement was
made for their ordination and consecration. But no one else may
eat them, because they are sacred. 34And if any of the meat of the
ordination ram or any bread is left over till morning, burn it up. It
must not be eaten, because it is sacred.

35"Do for Aaron and his sons everything I have commanded
you, taking seven days to ordain them. 36Sacrifice a bull each day as
a sin offering to make atonement. Purify the altar by making
atonement for it, and anoint it to consecrate it. 37For seven days
make atonement for the altar and consecrate it. Then the altar will
be most holy, and whatever touches it will be holy.

38"This is what you are to offer on the altar regularly each
day: two lambs a year old. 39Offer one in the morning and the
other at twilight. 40With the first lamb offer a tenth of an ephah[a] of
fine flour mixed with a quarter of a hin[b] of oil from pressed olives,
and a quarter of a hin of wine as a drink offering. 41Sacrifice the
other lamb at twilight with the same grain offering and its drink
offering as in the morning—a pleasing aroma, an offering made to
the LORD by fire.

42"For the generations to come this burnt offering is to be
made regularly at the entrance to the Tent of Meeting before the
LORD. There I will meet you and speak to you; 43there also I will meet
with the Israelites, and the place will be consecrated by my glory.

44"So I will consecrate the Tent of Meeting and the altar and
will consecrate Aaron and his sons to serve me as priests. 45Then I
will dwell among the Israelites and be their God. 46They will know
that I am the LORD their God, who brought them out of Egypt so
that I might dwell among them. I am the LORD their God.

The Altar of Incense

30 "Make an altar of acacia wood for burning incense. 2It is to
be square, a cubit long and a cubit wide, and two cubits high[c]—its
horns of one piece with it. 3Overlay the top and all the sides and
the horns with pure gold, and make a gold molding around it.
4Make two gold rings for the altar below the molding—two on
opposite sides—to hold the poles used to carry it. 5Make the poles
of acacia wood and overlay them with gold. 6Put the altar in front

[a]**40** That is, probably about 2 quarts (about 2 liters) [b]**40** That is, probably about 1 quart (about 1 liter) [c]**2** That is, about 1 1/2 feet (about 0.5 meter) long and wide and about 3 feet (about 0.9 meter) high

of the curtain that is before the ark of the Testimony—before the atonement cover that is over the Testimony—where I will meet with you.
7"Aaron must burn fragrant incense on the altar every morn-
ing when he tends the lamps. 8He must burn incense again when
he lights the lamps at twilight so incense will burn regularly before
the LORD for the generations to come. 9Do not offer on this altar
any other incense or any burnt offering or grain offering, and do
not pour a drink offering on it. 10Once a year Aaron shall make
atonement on its horns. This annual atonement must be made with the blood of the atoning sin offering for the generations to come. It is most holy to the LORD."

Atonement Money

11Then the LORD said to Moses, 12"When you take a census of
the Israelites to count them, each one must pay the LORD a ransom for his life at the time he is counted. Then no plague will come on
them when you number them. 13Each one who crosses over to
those already counted is to give a half shekel,[a] according to the sanctuary shekel, which weighs twenty gerahs. This half shekel is
an offering to the LORD. 14All who cross over, those twenty years
old or more, are to give an offering to the LORD. 15The rich are not
to give more than a half shekel and the poor are not to give less when you make the offering to the LORD to atone for your lives.
16Receive the atonement money from the Israelites and use it for the service of the Tent of Meeting. It will be a memorial for the Israelites before the LORD, making atonement for your lives."

Basin for Washing

17Then the LORD said to Moses, 18"Make a bronze basin, with
its bronze stand, for washing. Place it between the Tent of Meeting
and the altar, and put water in it. 19Aaron and his sons are to wash
their hands and feet with water from it. 20Whenever they enter the
Tent of Meeting, they shall wash with water so that they will not die. Also, when they approach the altar to minister by presenting
an offering made to the LORD by fire, 21they shall wash their hands
and feet so that they will not die. This is to be a lasting ordinance for Aaron and his descendants for the generations to come."

Anointing Oil

22Then the LORD said to Moses, 23"Take the following fine
spices: 500 shekels[b] of liquid myrrh, half as much (that is, 250
shekels) of fragrant cinnamon, 250 shekels of fragrant cane, 24500

[a]**13** That is, about 1/5 ounce (about 6 grams); also in verse 15 [b]**23** That is, about 12 1/2 pounds (about 6 kilograms)

30:6 *where I will meet with you:* See the notes at 25:10 and 25:17-20.

30:10 *its horns:* Four projections on the four corners of the altar.

30:13-16 *atonement money:* A count (census) of the number of Israelite men twenty years old or older was taken every so often to determine who had duty as a priest, and to keep track of offerings made to support the tabernacle, and later, the temple in Jerusalem. The amount owed by each Israelite male was half a shekel, which at this time was a piece of gold or silver that weighed about one fifth of an ounce. Coins were not yet in use. See also 38:25,26; Matt 17:24.

30:17-21 *bronze basin ... washing:* The basin was made from mirrors donated by Israelite women (see 38:8). Bronze was made by melting and mixing together copper and tin. See the notes at 19:10,11 and 29:4.

30:7,8 Exod 27:21.

shekels of cassia—all according to the sanctuary shekel—and a hin[a] of olive oil. 25Make these into a sacred anointing oil, a fragrant blend, the work of a perfumer. It will be the sacred anointing oil. 26Then use it to anoint the Tent of Meeting, the ark of the Testimony, 27the table and all its articles, the lampstand and its accessories, the altar of incense, 28the altar of burnt offering and all its utensils, and the basin with its stand. 29You shall consecrate them so they will be most holy, and whatever touches them will be holy.

30"Anoint Aaron and his sons and consecrate them so they may serve me as priests. 31Say to the Israelites, 'This is to be my sacred anointing oil for the generations to come. 32Do not pour it on men's bodies and do not make any oil with the same formula. It is sacred, and you are to consider it sacred. 33Whoever makes perfume like it and whoever puts it on anyone other than a priest must be cut off from his people.' "

Incense

34Then the LORD said to Moses, "Take fragrant spices—gum resin, onycha and galbanum—and pure frankincense, all in equal amounts, 35and make a fragrant blend of incense, the work of a perfumer. It is to be salted and pure and sacred. 36Grind some of it to powder and place it in front of the Testimony in the Tent of Meeting, where I will meet with you. It shall be most holy to you. 37Do not make any incense with this formula for yourselves; consider it holy to the LORD. 38Whoever makes any like it to enjoy its fragrance must be cut off from his people."

Bezalel and Oholiab

31 Then the LORD said to Moses, 2"See, I have chosen Bezalel son of Uri, the son of Hur, of the tribe of Judah, 3and I have filled him with the Spirit of God, with skill, ability and knowledge in all kinds of crafts— 4to make artistic designs for work in gold, silver and bronze, 5to cut and set stones, to work in wood, and to engage in all kinds of craftsmanship. 6Moreover, I have appointed Oholiab son of Ahisamach, of the tribe of Dan, to help him. Also I have given skill to all the craftsmen to make everything I have commanded you: 7the Tent of Meeting, the ark of the Testimony with the atonement cover on it, and all the other furnishings of the tent— 8the table and its articles, the pure gold lampstand and all its accessories, the altar of incense, 9the altar of burnt offering and all its utensils, the basin with its stand— 10and also the woven garments, both the sacred garments for Aaron the priest and the garments for his sons when they serve as priests, 11and the anointing oil and fragrant incense for the Holy Place. They are to make them just as I commanded you."

[a]**24** That is, probably about 4 quarts (about 4 liters)

30:22-32 *olive oil . . . anointing oil:* For more about the use of olive oil, see the notes at 25:4-6 and 29:1. Myrrh and cinnamon are described in the chart called "Spices and Perfumes," p. 1278. Cassia was derived from the dried flowers of the cinnamon plant. This oil and spice mixture described here was used to consecrate items in the tabernacle and to ordain priests.

30:34-36 *fragrant spices . . . the Testimony:* Gum resin is sweet-smelling, similar to myrrh. Onycha comes from mollusk shells, and galbanum is a resin that comes from the milky juice of the root of a carrot-like plant that was plentiful in Persia and Syria. Frankincense comes from a white gummy substance produced by certain trees in the Middle East. It was often pounded into a valuable powder that was burned to make a sweet smell. See also the chart called "Spices and Perfumes," p. 1278.

"The Testimony" is another way of referring to the ark of the covenant. See the mini-article called "The Ark of the Covenant," p. 513.

30:37 *holy:* See the note at 29:35-37.

31:2 *Bezalel . . . tribe of Judah:* In Hebrew *Bezalel* means "In the Shadow (Protection) of God." The tribe of Judah would settle in the area west of the Dead Sea after the Israelites settled in Canaan, the land God promised to them (see the map on p. 2464). King David, Israel's greatest king, and his son Solomon, who built the first temple to the LORD in Jerusalem, were from the tribe of Judah.

31:3 *I have filled him:* This refers to the presence of God, which gives special gifts or abilities.

31:6 *Oholiab . . . tribe of Dan:* His name means "My Tent Is the Father (God)." The members of the Dan tribe eventually settled just to the north of the Judah tribe.

31:7-11 Exod 25:1—30:38.

The Sabbath

[12]Then the LORD said to Moses, [13]"Say to the Israelites, 'You must observe my Sabbaths. This will be a sign between me and you for the generations to come, so you may know that I am the LORD, who makes you holy.[a]

[14]" 'Observe the Sabbath, because it is holy to you. Anyone who desecrates it must be put to death; whoever does any work on that day must be cut off from his people. [15]For six days, work is to be done, but the seventh day is a Sabbath of rest, holy to the LORD. Whoever does any work on the Sabbath day must be put to death. [16]The Israelites are to observe the Sabbath, celebrating it for the generations to come as a lasting covenant. [17]It will be a sign between me and the Israelites forever, for in six days the LORD made the heavens and the earth, and on the seventh day he abstained from work and rested.' "

[18]When the LORD finished speaking to Moses on Mount Sinai, he gave him the two tablets of the Testimony, the tablets of stone inscribed by the finger of God.

THE PEOPLE REBEL, BUT GOD REMAINS FAITHFUL

While Moses is on the mountain for forty days (24:17, 18) receiving the LORD's laws for the people (24:12), the people become anxious and ask Aaron to make a statue of a god that they can worship. Moses discovers the people worshiping the idol and breaks the stones that contain God's laws. The LORD punishes the people (32:35) but then renews his promise to be with them (33:14).

The Golden Calf

32 When the people saw that Moses was so long in coming down from the mountain, they gathered around Aaron and said, "Come, make us gods[b] who will go before us. As for this fellow Moses who brought us up out of Egypt, we don't know what has happened to him."

[2]Aaron answered them, "Take off the gold earrings that your wives, your sons and your daughters are wearing, and bring them to me." [3]So all the people took off their earrings and brought them to Aaron. [4]He took what they handed him and made it into an idol cast in the shape of a calf, fashioning it with a tool. Then they said, "These are your gods,[c] O Israel, who brought you up out of Egypt."

[5]When Aaron saw this, he built an altar in front of the calf and announced, "Tomorrow there will be a festival to the LORD." [6]So the next day the people rose early and sacrificed burnt

[a]**13** Or *who sanctifies you*; or *who sets you apart as holy* [b]**1** Or *a god*; also in verses 23 and 31 [c]**4** Or *This is your god*; also in verse 8

The LORD had said to Moses, *"The Israelites are to observe the Sabbath, celebrating it for the generations to come as a lasting covenant. It will be a sign between me and the Israelites forever, for in six days the LORD made the heavens and the earth, and on the seventh day he abstained from work and rested."*
Exod 31:16,17

31:14 *Sabbath:* See the note at 16:23 and the chart called "Jewish Calendar and Festivals," p. 944.

32:1 *make us gods:* The people wanted a statue or an idol (32:4), which was forbidden in the laws Moses received from the LORD on Mount Sinai (20:3-5). See also the note at 20:4,5.

32:4 *calf:* The statue may have looked like the Egyptian bull-god Apis or one of the gods worshiped by the Canaanites. Many centuries later, King Jeroboam of Israel (northern kingdom) used similar words to describe the golden calves he set up as objects of worship in the towns of Bethel and Dan (1 Kgs 12:26-30). See also Acts 7:41.

31:15 Exod 20:8-11; 23:12; 34:21; 35:2; Lev 23:3; Deut 5:12-15. **32:1** Acts 7:40. **32:6** 1 Cor 10:7.

The Golden Calf by Ora Lerman, 1987. While Moses was on Mount Sinai receiving the Law from the LORD, the people of Israel became restless and asked Moses' brother Aaron to make them an image of a god. Aaron collected the gold jewelry the people had taken from the Egyptians, melted it down, and made an idol in the shape of a calf. The people worshiped this idol with dancing and sacrifices, which made the LORD very angry. (See chapter 32.)

offerings and presented fellowship offerings.[a] Afterward they sat down to eat and drink and got up to indulge in revelry.
7Then the LORD said to Moses, "Go down, because your people, whom you brought up out of Egypt, have become corrupt.
8They have been quick to turn away from what I commanded them and have made themselves an idol cast in the shape of a calf. They have bowed down to it and sacrificed to it and have said, 'These are your gods, O Israel, who brought you up out of Egypt.'
9"I have seen these people," the LORD said to Moses, "and they are a stiff-necked people. 10Now leave me alone so that my anger may burn against them and that I may destroy them. Then I will make you into a great nation."
11But Moses sought the favor of the LORD his God. "O LORD," he said, "why should your anger burn against your people, whom you brought out of Egypt with great power and a mighty hand?
12Why should the Egyptians say, 'It was with evil intent that he brought them out, to kill them in the mountains and to wipe them off the face of the earth'? Turn from your fierce anger; relent and do not bring disaster on your people. 13Remember your servants Abraham, Isaac and Israel, to whom you swore by your own self: 'I will make your descendants as numerous as the stars in the sky and I will give your descendants all this land I promised them, and it will be their inheritance forever.' " 14Then the LORD relented and did not bring on his people the disaster he had threatened.

32:11 *why should your anger burn:* Moses' prayers had an effect on the LORD's actions toward the Hebrew people. The people broke their earlier promise to worship only God, and so they deserved punishment. Moses pleaded with God not to destroy the people he had chosen. See also Num 14:13-19.

32:13 *to whom you swore:* See the note at 2:24.

 **32:13** Gen 22:16,17.

---

[a]**6** Traditionally *peace offerings*

15Moses turned and went down the mountain with the two
tablets of the Testimony in his hands. They were inscribed on both
sides, front and back. 16The tablets were the work of God; the writing was the writing of God, engraved on the tablets.
17When Joshua heard the noise of the people shouting, he
said to Moses, "There is the sound of war in the camp."
18Moses replied:

"It is not the sound of victory,
 it is not the sound of defeat;
 it is the sound of singing that I hear."

19When Moses approached the camp and saw the calf and
the dancing, his anger burned and he threw the tablets out of his
hands, breaking them to pieces at the foot of the mountain. 20And
he took the calf they had made and burned it in the fire; then he
ground it to powder, scattered it on the water and made the
Israelites drink it.
21He said to Aaron, "What did these people do to you, that
you led them into such great sin?"
22"Do not be angry, my lord," Aaron answered. "You know
how prone these people are to evil. 23They said to me, 'Make us
gods who will go before us. As for this fellow Moses who brought
us up out of Egypt, we don't know what has happened to him.'
24So I told them, 'Whoever has any gold jewelry, take it off.' Then
they gave me the gold, and I threw it into the fire, and out came
this calf!"
25Moses saw that the people were running wild and that
Aaron had let them get out of control and so become a laughingstock to their enemies. 26So he stood at the entrance to the camp
and said, "Whoever is for the LORD, come to me." And all the
Levites rallied to him.
27Then he said to them, "This is what the LORD, the God of
Israel, says: 'Each man strap a sword to his side. Go back and forth
through the camp from one end to the other, each killing his
brother and friend and neighbor.' " 28The Levites did as Moses
commanded, and that day about three thousand of the people
died. 29Then Moses said, "You have been set apart to the LORD
today, for you were against your own sons and brothers, and he
has blessed you this day."
30The next day Moses said to the people, "You have committed a great sin. But now I will go up to the LORD; perhaps I can
make atonement for your sin."
31So Moses went back to the LORD and said, "Oh, what a
great sin these people have committed! They have made themselves gods of gold. 32But now, please forgive their sin—but if not,
then blot me out of the book you have written."
33The LORD replied to Moses, "Whoever has sinned against
me I will blot out of my book. 34Now go, lead the people to the

32:17 Joshua: See the note at 17:8-10. Joshua had gone up the mountain with Moses (24:13).

32:18 *sound . . . singing:* Victory over an enemy was celebrated by a special kind of high-pitched shouting. Sometimes a sort of yodel-like singing was done at weddings and funerals. What Moses heard was not a victory shout but wild, disorganized singing and yelling.

32:19 *calf . . . threw the tablets:* See the note at 32:4. The people broke their covenant to worship only the LORD, so Moses broke the tablets. See also the mini-article called "Covenants (Agreements)," p. 386.

32:21 *sin:* See the note at 9:27 and the mini-article called "Sin," p. 2181.

32:26 *all the Levites:* Not all the Levites joined Moses, since Exodus 32:29 and Deuteronomy 33:9 suggest that some were later killed. At first, all the descendants of Levi may have been considered Israel's priests. Eventually, only those members of the tribe of Levi who could prove they were descendants of Aaron were considered Israel's true priests (Num 18:20-32; Ezra 2:61-63). "Levites" then came to mean those members of the tribe of Levi who were not descended from Aaron. Their job was to take care of the Tent of Meeting (tabernacle) and to assist the priests. See also the mini-article called "Israel's Priests," p. 2344 and the illustration on p. 2345.

32:32 *the book:* The people of Israel believed that the LORD kept a record of the names of his people, and anyone whose name was removed from the book of the living no longer belonged to the LORD. See also Ps 9:5; 69:28; Isa 4:3; Mal 3:16; Rev 3:5.

32:15,16 Exod 31:18. **32:20** Deut 9:21; 2 Kgs 23:15.

place I spoke of, and my angel will go before you. However, when
the time comes for me to punish, I will punish them for their sin."
35And the LORD struck the people with a plague because of
what they did with the calf Aaron had made.
33 Then the LORD said to Moses, "Leave this place, you and the
people you brought up out of Egypt, and go up to the land I
promised on oath to Abraham, Isaac and Jacob, saying, 'I will give
it to your descendants.' 2I will send an angel before you and drive
out the Canaanites, Amorites, Hittites, Perizzites, Hivites and
Jebusites. 3Go up to the land flowing with milk and honey. But I
will not go with you, because you are a stiff-necked people and I
might destroy you on the way."
4When the people heard these distressing words, they began
to mourn and no one put on any ornaments. 5For the LORD had
said to Moses, "Tell the Israelites, 'You are a stiff-necked people. If
I were to go with you even for a moment, I might destroy you.
Now take off your ornaments and I will decide what to do with
you.' " 6So the Israelites stripped off their ornaments at Mount
Horeb.

The Tent of Meeting

7Now Moses used to take a tent and pitch it outside the
camp some distance away, calling it the "tent of meeting." Anyone
inquiring of the LORD would go to the tent of meeting outside the
camp. 8And whenever Moses went out to the tent, all the people
rose and stood at the entrances to their tents, watching Moses until
he entered the tent. 9As Moses went into the tent, the pillar of
cloud would come down and stay at the entrance, while the LORD
spoke with Moses. 10Whenever the people saw the pillar of cloud
standing at the entrance to the tent, they all stood and worshiped,
each at the entrance to his tent. 11The LORD would speak to Moses
face to face, as a man speaks with his friend. Then Moses would
return to the camp, but his young aide Joshua son of Nun did not
leave the tent.

Moses and the Glory of the LORD

12Moses said to the LORD, "You have been telling me, 'Lead
these people,' but you have not let me know whom you will send
with me. You have said, 'I know you by name and you have found
favor with me.' 13If you are pleased with me, teach me your ways so
I may know you and continue to find favor with you. Remember
that this nation is your people."
14The LORD replied, "My Presence will go with you, and I will
give you rest."
15Then Moses said to him, "If your Presence does not go
with us, do not send us up from here. 16How will anyone know
that you are pleased with me and with your people unless you go

32:35 *plague:* The people may have become ill from drinking the water that had gold powder in it (32:20), but this is not certain. The retelling of this event in DEUTERONOMY does not include this detail (see Deut 9:7-29).

33:1 *the land I promised:* See the notes at 2:24 and 3:8.

33:2 *Canaanites . . . Jebusites:* See the note at 3:8.

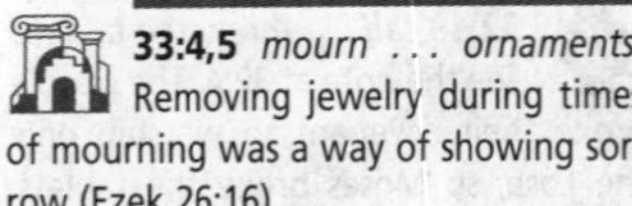

33:4,5 *mourn . . . ornaments:* Removing jewelry during times of mourning was a way of showing sorrow (Ezek 26:16).

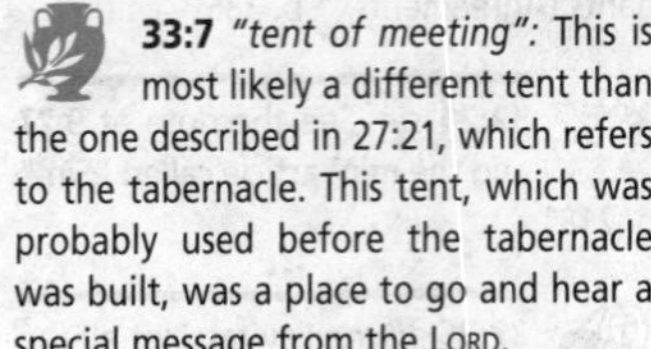

33:7 *"tent of meeting":* This is most likely a different tent than the one described in 27:21, which refers to the tabernacle. This tent, which was probably used before the tabernacle was built, was a place to go and hear a special message from the LORD.

33:11 *Joshua:* See the note at 17:8-10.

33:15 *from here:* Meaning Mount Sinai; see the note on p. 133.

33:1 Gen 12:1-7; 26:3; 28:13.
33:12 Exod 3:12.

with us? What else will distinguish me and your people from all
the other people on the face of the earth?"
17And the LORD said to Moses, "I will do the very thing you
have asked, because I am pleased with you and I know you by
name."
18Then Moses said, "Now show me your glory."
19And the LORD said, "I will cause all my goodness to pass in
front of you, and I will proclaim my name, the LORD, in your presence. I will have mercy on whom I will have mercy, and I will have
compassion on whom I will have compassion. 20But," he said, "you
cannot see my face, for no one may see me and live."
21Then the LORD said, "There is a place near me where you
may stand on a rock. 22When my glory passes by, I will put you in
a cleft in the rock and cover you with my hand until I have passed
by. 23Then I will remove my hand and you will see my back; but
my face must not be seen."

GOD'S INSTRUCTIONS ARE CARRIED OUT

After the people sin against God by worshiping an idol, God renews his earlier instructions to Moses. The people begin working to make those things mentioned in chapters 20–31 of EXODUS.

The New Stone Tablets

34 The LORD said to Moses, "Chisel out two stone tablets like
the first ones, and I will write on them the words that were on the
first tablets, which you broke. 2Be ready in the morning, and then
come up on Mount Sinai. Present yourself to me there on top of
the mountain. 3No one is to come with you or be seen anywhere
on the mountain; not even the flocks and herds may graze in front
of the mountain."
4So Moses chiseled out two stone tablets like the first ones
and went up Mount Sinai early in the morning, as the LORD had
commanded him; and he carried the two stone tablets in his
hands. 5Then the LORD came down in the cloud and stood there
with him and proclaimed his name, the LORD. 6And he passed in
front of Moses, proclaiming, "The LORD, the LORD, the compassionate and gracious God, slow to anger, abounding in love and
faithfulness, 7maintaining love to thousands, and forgiving wickedness, rebellion and sin. Yet he does not leave the guilty unpunished; he punishes the children and their children for the sin of the
fathers to the third and fourth generation."
8Moses bowed to the ground at once and worshiped.
9"O Lord, if I have found favor in your eyes," he said, "then let the
Lord go with us. Although this is a stiff-necked people, forgive our
wickedness and our sin, and take us as your inheritance."
10Then the LORD said: "I am making a covenant with you.

The LORD told Moses, *"I will cause all my goodness to pass in front of you, and I will proclaim my name, the LORD, in your presence. I will have mercy on whom I will have mercy, and I will have compassion on whom I will have compassion."* Exod 33:19

33:18 *your glory:* See the notes at 3:2 and 19:16-18.

34:5 *proclaimed his name, the LORD:* See the note at 6:2,3 and the mini-article called "LORD (YHWH)," p. 140. See also the note at 9:30.

34:6,7 *compassionate and gracious God . . . third and fourth generation:* These verses use formula-style language to describe several characteristics of God's nature. First, they speak of God's love and faithfulness (see also Neh 9:17; Ps 86:15; 103:8; 145:8; Jonah 4:2). But they also say God hates sin and punishes those who are unfaithful or disobedient. Here, God's anger is described as being so great that even the descendants of the rebellious person are punished (see also 20:5; Num 14:18; Nah 1:3). Later in Israelite history, the prophets Jeremiah and Ezekiel speak of a time when people will be responsible for their own sins and no child will be punished for the sins of the parent (see Jer 31:29, 30; Ezek 18:1-32).

33:19,20 Deut 5:26; John 1:18; Rom 9:15; 1 John 4:12. **34:1** Exod 24:12; 32:19. **34:6,7** Exod 20:5,6; Num 14:18; Deut 5:9,10; 7:9,10.

34:11 *Canaanites . . . Jebusites:* See the note at 3:8.

34:13 *Asherah poles:* This refers to sacred trees or to wooden poles and symbols cut and carved in the image of Asherah, the Canaanite goddess of fertility. See also Deut 16:21 and the mini-article called "Canaanite Gods and Goddesses," p. 469.

34:15,16 *prostitute themselves . . . sacrifice:* To eat food that had been sacrificed to a foreign god would mean being disloyal to the LORD God of Israel (1 Cor 8; 10:18-21). The sacrificial meals of the Moabites and Canaanites sometimes included ritual prostitution (Num 25:1, 2; Judg 2:17; 8:33; Hos 9:10). Marriage between Hebrew men and foreign women was also a temptation to follow other gods. At various times in Israel's history, such intermarriage was viewed as a severe problem (see, for example, Ezra 9:1-4).

34:18 *Feast of Unleavened Bread . . . Abib:* See the notes at 12:8,9 and 12:2. See also 12:14-20; Lev 23:6-8; Num 28:16-25.

34:19,20 *firstborn . . . donkey:* See the notes at 4:22 and 13:13. See also 13:2; Num 3:11-13.

34:22,23 *Three times a year:* See the note at 23:14-17. See also Lev 23:15-21; 23:39-43; Num 28:26-31.

34:25 *yeast . . . Passover:* See the notes at 12:8,9 (without yeast) and 12:11. See also 12:10.

34:28 *forty days . . . Ten Commandments:* See the notes at 24:16-18 and 20:2.

34:14,17 Exod 20:2-5; Lev 19:4; Deut 5:8,9; 27:15. **34:21** Exod 20:8-11; 23:12; 31:14-17; 35:2; Lev 23:3; Deut 5:13-15. **34:26** Exod 23:19; Deut 14:21; 26:2.

Before all your people I will do wonders never before done in any
nation in all the world. The people you live among will see how
awesome is the work that I, the LORD, will do for you. 11Obey what
I command you today. I will drive out before you the Amorites,
Canaanites, Hittites, Perizzites, Hivites and Jebusites. 12Be careful
not to make a treaty with those who live in the land where you are
going, or they will be a snare among you. 13Break down their
altars, smash their sacred stones and cut down their Asherah
poles.[a] 14Do not worship any other god, for the LORD, whose name
is Jealous, is a jealous God.

15"Be careful not to make a treaty with those who live in the
land; for when they prostitute themselves to their gods and sacrifice to them, they will invite you and you will eat their sacrifices.
16And when you choose some of their daughters as wives for your
sons and those daughters prostitute themselves to their gods, they
will lead your sons to do the same.

17"Do not make cast idols.

18"Celebrate the Feast of Unleavened Bread. For seven days
eat bread made without yeast, as I commanded you. Do this at the
appointed time in the month of Abib, for in that month you came
out of Egypt.

19"The first offspring of every womb belongs to me, including all the firstborn males of your livestock, whether from herd or
flock. 20Redeem the firstborn donkey with a lamb, but if you do
not redeem it, break its neck. Redeem all your firstborn sons.

"No one is to appear before me empty-handed.

21"Six days you shall labor, but on the seventh day you shall
rest; even during the plowing season and harvest you must rest.

22"Celebrate the Feast of Weeks with the firstfruits of the
wheat harvest, and the Feast of Ingathering at the turn of the year.[b]
23Three times a year all your men are to appear before the Sovereign LORD, the God of Israel. 24I will drive out nations before you
and enlarge your territory, and no one will covet your land when
you go up three times each year to appear before the LORD your
God.

25"Do not offer the blood of a sacrifice to me along with
anything containing yeast, and do not let any of the sacrifice from
the Passover Feast remain until morning.

26"Bring the best of the firstfruits of your soil to the house of
the LORD your God.

"Do not cook a young goat in its mother's milk."

27Then the LORD said to Moses, "Write down these words, for
in accordance with these words I have made a covenant with you
and with Israel." 28Moses was there with the LORD forty days and
forty nights without eating bread or drinking water. And he wrote
on the tablets the words of the covenant—the Ten Commandments.

---

[a]**13** That is, symbols of the goddess Asherah [b]**22** That is, in the fall

The Radiant Face of Moses

29When Moses came down from Mount Sinai with the two
tablets of the Testimony in his hands, he was not aware that his face
was radiant because he had spoken with the LORD. 30When Aaron
and all the Israelites saw Moses, his face was radiant, and they were
afraid to come near him. 31But Moses called to them; so Aaron and
all the leaders of the community came back to him, and he spoke to
them. 32Afterward all the Israelites came near him, and he gave
them all the commands the LORD had given him on Mount Sinai.
33When Moses finished speaking to them, he put a veil over
his face. 34But whenever he entered the LORD's presence to speak
with him, he removed the veil until he came out. And when he
came out and told the Israelites what he had been commanded,
35they saw that his face was radiant. Then Moses would put the veil
back over his face until he went in to speak with the LORD.

Sabbath Regulations

35 Moses assembled the whole Israelite community and said to
them, "These are the things the LORD has commanded you to do:
2For six days, work is to be done, but the seventh day shall be your
holy day, a Sabbath of rest to the LORD. Whoever does any work on
it must be put to death. 3Do not light a fire in any of your
dwellings on the Sabbath day."

Materials for the Tabernacle

4Moses said to the whole Israelite community, "This is what
the LORD has commanded: 5From what you have, take an offering
for the LORD. Everyone who is willing is to bring to the LORD an
offering of gold, silver and bronze; 6blue, purple and scarlet yarn
and fine linen; goat hair; 7ram skins dyed red and hides of sea
cows[a]; acacia wood; 8olive oil for the light; spices for the anointing
oil and for the fragrant incense; 9and onyx stones and other gems
to be mounted on the ephod and breastpiece.
10"All who are skilled among you are to come and make
everything the LORD has commanded: 11the tabernacle with its tent
and its covering, clasps, frames, crossbars, posts and bases; 12the
ark with its poles and the atonement cover and the curtain that
shields it; 13the table with its poles and all its articles and the bread
of the Presence; 14the lampstand that is for light with its accessories, lamps and oil for the light; 15the altar of incense with its
poles, the anointing oil and the fragrant incense; the curtain for
the doorway at the entrance to the tabernacle; 16the altar of burnt
offering with its bronze grating, its poles and all its utensils; the
bronze basin with its stand; 17the curtains of the courtyard with its

[a]7 That is, dugongs; also in verse 23

34:29-35 *face was radiant . . . veil:* Moses' face reflected God's glory (Exod 29:42,43; 33:18). The veil acted to hide Moses' shining face, because some were afraid of it or because he did not want the people to see the glory of God fade from his face. See also 2 Cor 3:7-16.

35:3 *Sabbath:* See the note at 16:23. See also 20:8-11; 23:12; 31:15; 34:21; Lev 23:3; Deut 5:12-14.

35:5-9 *offering . . . ephod and breastpiece:* Many of the items mentioned in these verses were described as being used to create parts of the tabernacle and its furnishings. See the notes at 25:4-6; 27:20; and 30:34-36.

35:10 *All who are skilled . . . make everything:* In addition to bringing physical gifts (35:5-9), the people were encouraged to share their skill and energy to make the tabernacle and the many objects that were to be used in worship. The notes describing these various objects can be found as follows: ark of the covenant (25:10; 25:17-20); the table for the bread of the Presence (25:23-30); the lampstand (25:31); altar for burning incense (30:1); sweet-smelling incense and anointing oil (30:22-32; 30:34-36); altar for sacrifices (27:1-8); bronze basin (30:17-21); enclosure, or courtyard, for the tabernacle (27:9-15). For a description of priestly clothes, see 28:1-43. See also the illustrations on pp. 182 and 187 and the article called "People of the Law: The Religion of Israel," p. 939.

35:23,24 *fine linen . . . goat hair . . . acacia wood:* See the notes at 25:4-6 and 25:10.

35:27 *gems . . . breastpiece:* See the notes at 28:15 and 28:17.

35:28 *spices . . . anointing oil . . . incense:* See the notes at 30:1; 30:22-32; 27:20.

35:30 *Bezalel . . . tribe of Judah:* See the note at 31:2.

35:31-33 *filled him with the Spirit of God:* See the note at 31:3 and the mini-article called "Holy Spirit," p. 2082.

35:34 *Oholiab . . . tribe of Dan:* See the note at 31:6. Like Bezalel, Oholiab was chosen by the LORD to do the important work of creating everything that was needed for the tabernacle. But it is the LORD who prepared them for this work and who gave them the skills to carry it out according to the instructions the LORD gave to Moses, including the ability to teach others.

36:3 *offerings:* See the note at 30:13-16.

posts and bases, and the curtain for the entrance to the courtyard;
18the tent pegs for the tabernacle and for the courtyard, and their
ropes; 19the woven garments worn for ministering in the sanctuary—both the sacred garments for Aaron the priest and the garments for his sons when they serve as priests."

20Then the whole Israelite community withdrew from
Moses' presence, 21and everyone who was willing and whose heart
moved him came and brought an offering to the LORD for the
work on the Tent of Meeting, for all its service, and for the sacred
garments. 22All who were willing, men and women alike, came and
brought gold jewelry of all kinds: brooches, earrings, rings and
ornaments. They all presented their gold as a wave offering to the
LORD. 23Everyone who had blue, purple or scarlet yarn or fine
linen, or goat hair, ram skins dyed red or hides of sea cows brought
them. 24Those presenting an offering of silver or bronze brought it
as an offering to the LORD, and everyone who had acacia wood for
any part of the work brought it. 25Every skilled woman spun with
her hands and brought what she had spun—blue, purple or scarlet yarn or fine linen. 26And all the women who were willing and
had the skill spun the goat hair. 27The leaders brought onyx stones
and other gems to be mounted on the ephod and breastpiece.
28They also brought spices and olive oil for the light and for the
anointing oil and for the fragrant incense. 29All the Israelite men
and women who were willing brought to the LORD freewill offerings for all the work the LORD through Moses had commanded
them to do.

Bezalel and Oholiab

30Then Moses said to the Israelites, "See, the LORD has chosen
Bezalel son of Uri, the son of Hur, of the tribe of Judah, 31and he
has filled him with the Spirit of God, with skill, ability and knowledge in all kinds of crafts— 32to make artistic designs for work in
gold, silver and bronze, 33to cut and set stones, to work in wood
and to engage in all kinds of artistic craftsmanship. 34And he has
given both him and Oholiab son of Ahisamach, of the tribe of
Dan, the ability to teach others. 35He has filled them with skill to
do all kinds of work as craftsmen, designers, embroiderers in
blue, purple and scarlet yarn and fine linen, and weavers—all of
36 them master craftsmen and designers. 1So Bezalel, Oholiab
and every skilled person to whom the LORD has given skill and
ability to know how to carry out all the work of constructing the
sanctuary are to do the work just as the LORD has commanded."

2Then Moses summoned Bezalel and Oholiab and every
skilled person to whom the LORD had given ability and who was
willing to come and do the work. 3They received from Moses all
the offerings the Israelites had brought to carry out the work of
constructing the sanctuary. And the people continued to bring
freewill offerings morning after morning. 4So all the skilled crafts-

men who were doing all the work on the sanctuary left their work
5 and said to Moses, "The people are bringing more than enough
for doing the work the LORD commanded to be done."
6 Then Moses gave an order and they sent this word
throughout the camp: "No man or woman is to make anything
else as an offering for the sanctuary." And so the people were
restrained from bringing more, 7 because what they already had
was more than enough to do all the work.

> The workers told Moses: *"The people are bringing more than enough for doing the work the LORD commanded to be done."*
> Exod 36:5

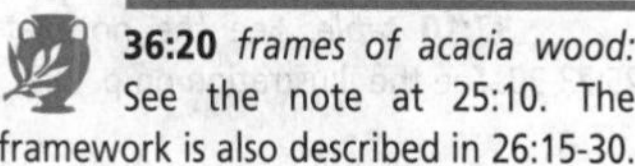

36:20 *frames of acacia wood:* See the note at 25:10. The framework is also described in 26:15-30.

36:8-19 Exod 26:1-14.

The Tabernacle

8 All the skilled men among the workmen made the tabernacle with ten curtains of finely twisted linen and blue, purple and
scarlet yarn, with cherubim worked into them by a skilled craftsman. 9 All the curtains were the same size—twenty-eight cubits
long and four cubits wide.[a] 10 They joined five of the curtains
together and did the same with the other five. 11 Then they made
loops of blue material along the edge of the end curtain in one set,
and the same was done with the end curtain in the other set.
12 They also made fifty loops on one curtain and fifty loops on the
end curtain of the other set, with the loops opposite each other.
13 Then they made fifty gold clasps and used them to fasten the two
sets of curtains together so that the tabernacle was a unit.
14 They made curtains of goat hair for the tent over the tabernacle—eleven altogether. 15 All eleven curtains were the same
size—thirty cubits long and four cubits wide.[b] 16 They joined five of
the curtains into one set and the other six into another set. 17 Then
they made fifty loops along the edge of the end curtain in one set
and also along the edge of the end curtain in the other set. 18 They
made fifty bronze clasps to fasten the tent together as a unit.
19 Then they made for the tent a covering of ram skins dyed red,
and over that a covering of hides of sea cows.[c]
20 They made upright frames of acacia wood for the tabernacle. 21 Each frame was ten cubits long and a cubit and a half
wide,[d] 22 with two projections set parallel to each other. They made
all the frames of the tabernacle in this way. 23 They made twenty
frames for the south side of the tabernacle 24 and made forty silver
bases to go under them—two bases for each frame, one under each
projection. 25 For the other side, the north side of the tabernacle,
they made twenty frames 26 and forty silver bases—two under each
frame. 27 They made six frames for the far end, that is, the west end
of the tabernacle, 28 and two frames were made for the corners of
the tabernacle at the far end. 29 At these two corners the frames
were double from the bottom all the way to the top and fitted into

[a] **9** That is, about 42 feet (about 12.5 meters) long and 6 feet (about 1.8 meters) wide [b] **15** That is, about 45 feet (about 13.5 meters) long and 6 feet (about 1.8 meters) wide [c] **19** That is, dugongs [d] **21** That is, about 15 feet (about 4.5 meters) long and 2 1/4 feet (about 0.7 meter) wide

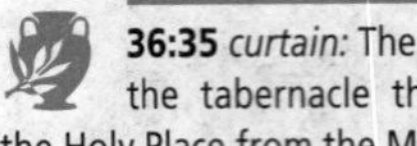

36:35 *curtain:* The curtain inside the tabernacle that separated the Holy Place from the Most Holy Place (see the note at 26:31-34). See also the notes at 25:4-6 and 25:17-20.

37:1 *Bezalel:* See the note at 31:2.

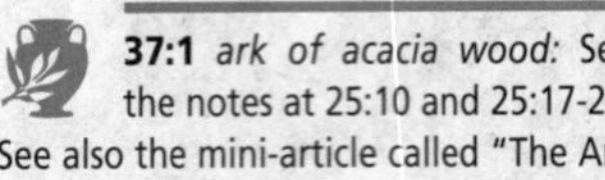

37:1 *ark of acacia wood:* See the notes at 25:10 and 25:17-20. See also the mini-article called "The Ark of the Covenant," p. 513.

37:10 *table:* See the note at 25:23-30. See the illustration on p. 182.

a single ring; both were made alike. 30 So there were eight frames
and sixteen silver bases—two under each frame.

31 They also made crossbars of acacia wood: five for the
frames on one side of the tabernacle, 32 five for those on the other
side, and five for the frames on the west, at the far end of the tabernacle. 33 They made the center crossbar so that it extended from
end to end at the middle of the frames. 34 They overlaid the frames
with gold and made gold rings to hold the crossbars. They also
overlaid the crossbars with gold.

35 They made the curtain of blue, purple and scarlet yarn and
finely twisted linen, with cherubim worked into it by a skilled
craftsman. 36 They made four posts of acacia wood for it and overlaid them with gold. They made gold hooks for them and cast their
four silver bases. 37 For the entrance to the tent they made a curtain of blue, purple and scarlet yarn and finely twisted linen—the
work of an embroiderer; 38 and they made five posts with hooks for
them. They overlaid the tops of the posts and their bands with
gold and made their five bases of bronze.

The Ark

37 Bezalel made the ark of acacia wood—two and a half cubits
long, a cubit and a half wide, and a cubit and a half high.[a] 2 He
overlaid it with pure gold, both inside and out, and made a gold
molding around it. 3 He cast four gold rings for it and fastened
them to its four feet, with two rings on one side and two rings on
the other. 4 Then he made poles of acacia wood and overlaid them
with gold. 5 And he inserted the poles into the rings on the sides of
the ark to carry it.

6 He made the atonement cover of pure gold—two and a half
cubits long and a cubit and a half wide.[b] 7 Then he made two cherubim out of hammered gold at the ends of the cover. 8 He made one
cherub on one end and the second cherub on the other; at the two
ends he made them of one piece with the cover. 9 The cherubim had
their wings spread upward, overshadowing the cover with them.
The cherubim faced each other, looking toward the cover.

The Table

10 They[c] made the table of acacia wood—two cubits long, a
cubit wide, and a cubit and a half high.[d] 11 Then they overlaid it
with pure gold and made a gold molding around it. 12 They also
made around it a rim a handbreadth[e] wide and put a gold molding

---

[a] **1** That is, about 3 3/4 feet (about 1.1 meters) long and 2 1/4 feet (about 0.7 meter) wide and high [b] **6** That is, about 3 3/4 feet (about 1.1 meters) long and 2 1/4 feet (about 0.7 meter) wide [c] **10** Or *He*; also in verses 11-29 [d] **10** That is, about 3 feet (about 0.9 meter) long, 1 1/2 feet (about 0.5 meter) wide, and 2 1/4 feet (about 0.7 meter) high [e] **12** That is, about 3 inches (about 8 centimeters)

on the rim. [13]They cast four gold rings for the table and fastened
them to the four corners, where the four legs were. [14]The rings were
put close to the rim to hold the poles used in carrying the table.
[15]The poles for carrying the table were made of acacia wood and
were overlaid with gold. [16]And they made from pure gold the articles for the table—its plates and dishes and bowls and its pitchers
for the pouring out of drink offerings.

The Lampstand

[17]They made the lampstand of pure gold and hammered it
out, base and shaft; its flowerlike cups, buds and blossoms were of
one piece with it. [18]Six branches extended from the sides of the
lampstand—three on one side and three on the other. [19]Three cups
shaped like almond flowers with buds and blossoms were on one
branch, three on the next branch and the same for all six
branches extending from the lampstand. [20]And on the lampstand
were four cups shaped like almond flowers with buds and blossoms. [21]One bud was under the first pair of branches extending
from the lampstand, a second bud under the second pair, and a
third bud under the third pair—six branches in all. [22]The buds and
the branches were all of one piece with the lampstand, hammered
out of pure gold.

[23]They made its seven lamps, as well as its wick trimmers
and trays, of pure gold. [24]They made the lampstand and all its
accessories from one talent[a] of pure gold.

The Altar of Incense

[25]They made the altar of incense out of acacia wood. It was
square, a cubit long and a cubit wide, and two cubits high[b]—its
horns of one piece with it. [26]They overlaid the top and all the sides
and the horns with pure gold, and made a gold molding around it.
[27]They made two gold rings below the molding—two on opposite
sides—to hold the poles used to carry it. [28]They made the poles of
acacia wood and overlaid them with gold.

[29]They also made the sacred anointing oil and the pure, fragrant incense—the work of a perfumer.

The Altar of Burnt Offering

38 They[c] built the altar of burnt offering of acacia wood, three
cubits[d] high; it was square, five cubits long and five cubits wide.[e]
[2]They made a horn at each of the four corners, so that the horns
and the altar were of one piece, and they overlaid the altar with

[a]24 That is, about 75 pounds (about 34 kilograms) [b]25 That is, about 1 1/2 feet (about 0.5 meter) long and wide, and about 3 feet (about 0.9 meter) high
[c]1 Or *He*; also in verses 2-9 [d]1 That is, about 4 1/2 feet (about 1.3 meters)
[e]1 That is, about 7 1/2 feet (about 2.3 meters) long and wide

37:17-24 *lampstand . . . accessories:* See the note at 25:31.

37:25 *altar of incense:* See the note at 30:1 and the illustration on p. 182.

37:29 *sacred anointing oil . . . fragrant incense:* See the notes at 29:35-37; 30:22-32; and 30:34-36.

38:1 *altar of burnt offering of acacia wood:* See the notes at 25:10 (acacia) and 27:1-8 (altar). See also the illustration on p. 182.

The curtain for the entrance to the courtyard was of blue, purple and scarlet yarn and finely twisted linen—the work of an embroiderer.
Exod 38:18

38:8 *bronze basin:* See the note at 30:17-21 and the illustration on p. 798.

38:9 *courtyard:* See the note at 27:9-15 and the illustration on p. 2345.

bronze. [3]They made all its utensils of bronze—its pots, shovels, sprinkling bowls, meat forks and firepans. [4]They made a grating for the altar, a bronze network, to be under its ledge, halfway up the altar. [5]They cast bronze rings to hold the poles for the four corners of the bronze grating. [6]They made the poles of acacia wood and overlaid them with bronze. [7]They inserted the poles into the rings so they would be on the sides of the altar for carrying it. They made it hollow, out of boards.

Basin for Washing

[8]They made the bronze basin and its bronze stand from the mirrors of the women who served at the entrance to the Tent of Meeting.

The Courtyard

[9]Next they made the courtyard. The south side was a hundred cubits[a] long and had curtains of finely twisted linen, [10]with twenty posts and twenty bronze bases, and with silver hooks and bands on the posts. [11]The north side was also a hundred cubits long and had twenty posts and twenty bronze bases, with silver hooks and bands on the posts.

[12]The west end was fifty cubits[b] wide and had curtains, with ten posts and ten bases, with silver hooks and bands on the posts. [13]The east end, toward the sunrise, was also fifty cubits wide. [14]Curtains fifteen cubits[c] long were on one side of the entrance, with three posts and three bases, [15]and curtains fifteen cubits long were on the other side of the entrance to the courtyard, with three posts and three bases. [16]All the curtains around the courtyard were of finely twisted linen. [17]The bases for the posts were bronze. The hooks and bands on the posts were silver, and their tops were overlaid with silver; so all the posts of the courtyard had silver bands.

[18]The curtain for the entrance to the courtyard was of blue, purple and scarlet yarn and finely twisted linen—the work of an embroiderer. It was twenty cubits[d] long and, like the curtains of the courtyard, five cubits[e] high, [19]with four posts and four bronze bases. Their hooks and bands were silver, and their tops were overlaid with silver. [20]All the tent pegs of the tabernacle and of the surrounding courtyard were bronze.

The Materials Used

[21]These are the amounts of the materials used for the tabernacle, the tabernacle of the Testimony, which were recorded at Moses' command by the Levites under the direction of Ithamar

---

[a]**9** That is, about 150 feet (about 46 meters) [b]**12** That is, about 75 feet (about 23 meters) [c]**14** That is, about 22 1/2 feet (about 6.9 meters) [d]**18** That is, about 30 feet (about 9 meters) [e]**18** That is, about 7 1/2 feet (about 2.3 meters)

son of Aaron, the priest. 22(Bezalel son of Uri, the son of Hur, of the tribe of Judah, made everything the LORD commanded Moses; 23with him was Oholiab son of Ahisamach, of the tribe of Dan—a craftsman and designer, and an embroiderer in blue, purple and scarlet yarn and fine linen.) 24The total amount of the gold from the wave offering used for all the work on the sanctuary was 29 talents and 730 shekels,[a] according to the sanctuary shekel.

25The silver obtained from those of the community who were counted in the census was 100 talents and 1,775 shekels,[b] according to the sanctuary shekel— 26one beka per person, that is, half a shekel,[c] according to the sanctuary shekel, from everyone who had crossed over to those counted, twenty years old or more, a total of 603,550 men. 27The 100 talents[d] of silver were used to cast the bases for the sanctuary and for the curtain—100 bases from the 100 talents, one talent for each base. 28They used the 1,775 shekels[e] to make the hooks for the posts, to overlay the tops of the posts, and to make their bands.

29The bronze from the wave offering was 70 talents and 2,400 shekels.[f] 30They used it to make the bases for the entrance to the Tent of Meeting, the bronze altar with its bronze grating and all its utensils, 31the bases for the surrounding courtyard and those for its entrance and all the tent pegs for the tabernacle and those for the surrounding courtyard.

38:22,23 *Bezalel . . . Oholiab:* See the notes at 31:2 and 31:6.

38:24-26 *sanctuary shekel:* The weights of gold, silver, and bronze are in shekels and talents. The sanctuary shekel was a type of official standard for weight. A talent was equal to about 75 pounds. So, for example, the amount of gold in 38:24, "29 talents and 730 shekels" was equal to about 2,209 pounds. The amount of silver given was over 100 talents (7,550 pounds). A shekel was about 2/5 of an ounce. So, each pound (sixteen ounces) would equal about 40 shekels. That would make a total of nearly 302,000 shekels of silver, or about a half a shekel for each of the 603,550 men mentioned in verse 26. See also the chart called "Table of Weights and Measures," p. 1644.

It is interesting to note that the total number of men mentioned here seems to be based on the census taken in Numbers 1:20-46. See also Exod 30:11-16 and Matt 17:24.

39:1 *garments:* See the notes at 28:2; 28:4; and 28:6. See the illustrations on p. 187.

The Priestly Garments

39 From the blue, purple and scarlet yarn they made woven garments for ministering in the sanctuary. They also made sacred garments for Aaron, as the LORD commanded Moses.

The Ephod

2They[g] made the ephod of gold, and of blue, purple and scarlet yarn, and of finely twisted linen. 3They hammered out thin sheets of gold and cut strands to be worked into the blue, purple and scarlet yarn and fine linen—the work of a skilled craftsman. 4They made shoulder pieces for the ephod, which were attached to two of its corners, so it could be fastened. 5Its skillfully woven waistband was like it—of one piece with the ephod and made with gold, and with blue, purple and scarlet yarn, and with finely twisted linen, as the LORD commanded Moses.

6They mounted the onyx stones in gold filigree settings and engraved them like a seal with the names of the sons of Israel.

---

[a]24 The weight of the gold was a little over one ton (about 1 metric ton).
[b]25 The weight of the silver was a little over 3 3/4 tons (about 3.4 metric tons). [c]26 That is, about 1/5 ounce (about 5.5 grams) [d]27 That is, about 3 3/4 tons (about 3.4 metric tons) [e]28 That is, about 45 pounds (about 20 kilograms) [f]29 The weight of the bronze was about 2 1/2 tons (about 2.4 metric tons). [g]2 Or *He*; also in verses 7, 8 and 22

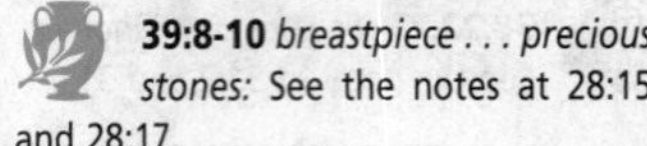

39:8-10 *breastpiece . . . precious stones:* See the notes at 28:15 and 28:17.

39:22-31 *robe . . . pomegranates . . . turban:* See the notes at 28:31-35; 28:37; and 28:40-42.

[7]Then they fastened them on the shoulder pieces of the ephod as memorial stones for the sons of Israel, as the LORD commanded Moses.

The Breastpiece

[8]They fashioned the breastpiece—the work of a skilled craftsman. They made it like the ephod: of gold, and of blue, purple and scarlet yarn, and of finely twisted linen. [9]It was square—a span[a] long and a span wide—and folded double. [10]Then they mounted four rows of precious stones on it. In the first row there was a ruby, a topaz and a beryl; [11]in the second row a turquoise, a sapphire[b] and an emerald; [12]in the third row a jacinth, an agate and an amethyst; [13]in the fourth row a chrysolite, an onyx and a jasper.[c] They were mounted in gold filigree settings. [14]There were twelve stones, one for each of the names of the sons of Israel, each engraved like a seal with the name of one of the twelve tribes.

[15]For the breastpiece they made braided chains of pure gold, like a rope. [16]They made two gold filigree settings and two gold rings, and fastened the rings to two of the corners of the breastpiece. [17]They fastened the two gold chains to the rings at the corners of the breastpiece, [18]and the other ends of the chains to the two settings, attaching them to the shoulder pieces of the ephod at the front. [19]They made two gold rings and attached them to the other two corners of the breastpiece on the inside edge next to the ephod. [20]Then they made two more gold rings and attached them to the bottom of the shoulder pieces on the front of the ephod, close to the seam just above the waistband of the ephod. [21]They tied the rings of the breastpiece to the rings of the ephod with blue cord, connecting it to the waistband so that the breastpiece would not swing out from the ephod—as the LORD commanded Moses.

Other Priestly Garments

[22]They made the robe of the ephod entirely of blue cloth—the work of a weaver— [23]with an opening in the center of the robe like the opening of a collar,[d] and a band around this opening, so that it would not tear. [24]They made pomegranates of blue, purple and scarlet yarn and finely twisted linen around the hem of the robe. [25]And they made bells of pure gold and attached them around the hem between the pomegranates. [26]The bells and pomegranates alternated around the hem of the robe to be worn for ministering, as the LORD commanded Moses.

[27]For Aaron and his sons, they made tunics of fine linen—the work of a weaver— [28]and the turban of fine linen, the linen

---

[a]**9** That is, about 9 inches (about 22 centimeters) [b]**11** Or *lapis lazuli* [c]**13** The precise identification of some of these precious stones is uncertain. [d]**23** The meaning of the Hebrew for this word is uncertain.

headbands and the undergarments of finely twisted linen. 29The
sash was of finely twisted linen and blue, purple and scarlet yarn—
the work of an embroiderer—as the LORD commanded Moses.
30They made the plate, the sacred diadem, out of pure gold
and engraved on it, like an inscription on a seal: HOLY TO THE LORD.
31Then they fastened a blue cord to it to attach it to the turban, as
the LORD commanded Moses.

Moses Inspects the Tabernacle

32So all the work on the tabernacle, the Tent of Meeting, was
completed. The Israelites did everything just as the LORD commanded Moses. 33Then they brought the tabernacle to Moses: the
tent and all its furnishings, its clasps, frames, crossbars, posts and
bases; 34the covering of ram skins dyed red, the covering of hides
of sea cows[a] and the shielding curtain; 35the ark of the Testimony
with its poles and the atonement cover; 36the table with all its articles and the bread of the Presence; 37the pure gold lampstand with
its row of lamps and all its accessories, and the oil for the light;
38the gold altar, the anointing oil, the fragrant incense, and the curtain for the entrance to the tent; 39the bronze altar with its bronze
grating, its poles and all its utensils; the basin with its stand; 40the
curtains of the courtyard with its posts and bases, and the curtain
for the entrance to the courtyard; the ropes and tent pegs for the
courtyard; all the furnishings for the tabernacle, the Tent of Meeting; 41and the woven garments worn for ministering in the sanctuary, both the sacred garments for Aaron the priest and the
garments for his sons when serving as priests.
42The Israelites had done all the work just as the LORD had
commanded Moses. 43Moses inspected the work and saw that they
had done it just as the LORD had commanded. So Moses blessed
them.

Setting Up the Tabernacle

40 Then the LORD said to Moses: 2"Set up the tabernacle, the
Tent of Meeting, on the first day of the first month. 3Place the ark
of the Testimony in it and shield the ark with the curtain. 4Bring in
the table and set out what belongs on it. Then bring in the lampstand and set up its lamps. 5Place the gold altar of incense in front
of the ark of the Testimony and put the curtain at the entrance to
the tabernacle.
6"Place the altar of burnt offering in front of the entrance to
the tabernacle, the Tent of Meeting; 7place the basin between
the Tent of Meeting and the altar and put water in it. 8Set up the
courtyard around it and put the curtain at the entrance to the
courtyard.

[a]**34** That is, dugongs

39:30 *HOLY TO THE LORD:* See the note at 29:35-37.

39:33-41 *tent . . . garments:* See chapters 25–31 and the notes in that section.

39:43 *Moses blessed:* Moses blessed them for their gifts and for the work they did in creating the tabernacle and its furnishings.

40:2 *first day of the first month:* Abib (also called Nisan) is the first month of the Hebrew calendar, from mid-March to mid-April. See also the chart called "Jewish Calendar and Festivals," p. 944.

40:3 *ark of the Testimony . . . curtain:* See the notes at 25:10 and 26:31-34.

40:4-7 *table . . . basin:* For the items named in these verses, see the notes at 25:23-30 (table); 25:31 (lampstand); altar for burning incense (30:1); ark of the covenant (25:10); curtain (26:31-34); altar for offering sacrifices (27:1-8); and bronze basin (30:17-21).

39:32 Exod 25:40.

40:9 *anointing oil . . . holy:* See the notes at 30:22-32; 29:1; 27:20; and 29:35-37.

40:12 *wash them:* See the notes at 19:10,11 and 29:4.

40:13-15 *sacred garments . . . priests:* See the notes about priestly garments in chapter 28.

40:17 *first day . . . second year:* See the note at 40:2. The tabernacle was set up exactly one year after the Israelite people began their exodus out of Egypt and celebrated the first Passover (12:2-41).

40:20 *Testimony . . . atonement cover:* "Testimony" refers to the tablets of the Ten Commandments. For atonement cover (also called the mercy seat), see the note at 25:17-20.

40:31 *wash:* See the notes at 19:10,11 and 29:4.

40:20 Exod 25:21. **40:33** Exod 27:9-15. **40:34** 1 Kgs 8:10,11; Isa 6:4; Ezek 43:4, 5; Rev 15:8.

9"Take the anointing oil and anoint the tabernacle and
everything in it; consecrate it and all its furnishings, and it will be
holy. 10Then anoint the altar of burnt offering and all its utensils;
consecrate the altar, and it will be most holy. 11Anoint the basin
and its stand and consecrate them.

12"Bring Aaron and his sons to the entrance to the Tent of
Meeting and wash them with water. 13Then dress Aaron in the
sacred garments, anoint him and consecrate him so he may serve
me as priest. 14Bring his sons and dress them in tunics. 15Anoint
them just as you anointed their father, so they may serve me as
priests. Their anointing will be to a priesthood that will continue
for all generations to come." 16Moses did everything just as the
LORD commanded him.

17So the tabernacle was set up on the first day of the first
month in the second year. 18When Moses set up the tabernacle, he
put the bases in place, erected the frames, inserted the crossbars
and set up the posts. 19Then he spread the tent over the tabernacle
and put the covering over the tent, as the LORD commanded him.

20He took the Testimony and placed it in the ark, attached
the poles to the ark and put the atonement cover over it. 21Then he
brought the ark into the tabernacle and hung the shielding curtain
and shielded the ark of the Testimony, as the LORD commanded
him.

22Moses placed the table in the Tent of Meeting on the north
side of the tabernacle outside the curtain 23and set out the bread
on it before the LORD, as the LORD commanded him.

24He placed the lampstand in the Tent of Meeting opposite
the table on the south side of the tabernacle 25and set up the lamps
before the LORD, as the LORD commanded him.

26Moses placed the gold altar in the Tent of Meeting in front
of the curtain 27and burned fragrant incense on it, as the LORD
commanded him. 28Then he put up the curtain at the entrance to
the tabernacle.

29He set the altar of burnt offering near the entrance to the
tabernacle, the Tent of Meeting, and offered on it burnt offerings
and grain offerings, as the LORD commanded him.

30He placed the basin between the Tent of Meeting and the
altar and put water in it for washing, 31and Moses and Aaron and
his sons used it to wash their hands and feet. 32They washed whenever
they entered the Tent of Meeting or approached the altar, as
the LORD commanded Moses.

33Then Moses set up the courtyard around the tabernacle
and altar and put up the curtain at the entrance to the courtyard.
And so Moses finished the work.

The Glory of the LORD

34Then the cloud covered the Tent of Meeting, and the glory
of the LORD filled the tabernacle. 35Moses could not enter the Tent
of Meeting because the cloud had settled upon it, and the glory of
the LORD filled the tabernacle.

36In all the travels of the Israelites, whenever the cloud lifted
from above the tabernacle, they would set out; 37but if the cloud
did not lift, they did not set out—until the day it lifted. 38So the
cloud of the LORD was over the tabernacle by day, and fire was in
the cloud by night, in the sight of all the house of Israel during all
their travels.

> *So the cloud of the LORD was over the tabernacle by day, and fire was in the cloud by night, in the sight of all the house of Israel during all their travels.*
> Exod 40:38

40:34-38 *glory of the LORD . . . fire:* See the notes at 3:2 and 19:16-18.

QUESTIONS ABOUT EXODUS 19:1—40:38

1. Describe the scene at Mount Sinai when the LORD God came to give the laws and instructions to Moses and the Israelite people (19:16-25).
2. How does 20:2 serve as a bridge between the events of the exodus and the giving of the laws and instructions? Which of the commandments in 20:2-17 relate to the people's relationship with God? Which relate to their relationships with one another?
3. How would you describe the purpose of the laws given in 21:1—23:9? In your opinion, what is the purpose of laws in modern society? How are our civil laws similar and different from the laws given in this section of EXODUS?
4. What three festivals are mentioned in 23:14-19? Why was each to be celebrated?
5. What was the ark of the covenant, and where was it to be kept? What was to be kept in it? What was important about the lid of the ark? (25:10-22)
6. What was the purpose for the following items: table of the bread of the Presence, golden lampstand, curtain inside the tabernacle; altar for offering sacrifices; altar for burning incense; large bronze bowl? (25:23—27:8; 30:1-10,17-21)
7. Who were chosen to serve as Israel's priests? What does consecration mean? Who was consecrated? How were olive oil and incense used in the ordination ceremony? (30:22-38)
8. How did the people rebel against God? (chapter 32) What was their punishment?
9. In the covenant between God and the Israelites at Sinai, what did God promise? What did God demand in return? (34:10-28)
10. How were the commands regarding the making of the tabernacle, its furnishings, and the priestly clothes carried out? (35:4-29; 39:32-43)
11. Complete this sentence: "After reading EXODUS, I wonder. . . ."

LEVITICUS

Blood sacrifices, grain offerings, and special holy days—read Leviticus to find out how these were an important part of the ongoing relationship between the people of Israel and the Lord.

tabernacle and altar: Exodus describes in detail the tabernacle (also called the Tent of Meeting) that God commanded Moses and the people to build (Exod 25–27; 30). It was to be the center of Israel's worship and the place where God would live among his people (Exod 25:8). In Leviticus the priests of Israel are shown offering sacrifices on the altar in front of the entrance to the tabernacle. This altar was made of acacia wood and covered with bronze (Exod 27:1-8). A smaller altar for burning incense was inside the tabernacle (Exod 30:1-5). For an artist's rendering of what the tabernacle, the altar, and other furnishings may have looked like, see the illustration on p. 2345. See also the mini-article called "The Tabernacle," p. 2346.

priests: Aaron, the brother of Moses, was the first high priest of Israel (Exod 28:1). His descendants were expected to serve as Israel's priests. For more, see the mini-article called "Israel's Priests," p. 2344.

holiness: In Leviticus, holiness usually refers to something (or someone) that has been "set apart" or "dedicated" for a special purpose. For a fuller explanation, see the mini-article called "Holiness," p. 1626.

What makes Leviticus special?

The name of this book in the Hebrew Scriptures is taken from the first word of the book, which is translated in English as "the Lord spoke." "Leviticus" is the name given to this book in the Greek version of the Old Testament (the Septuagint). It is related to "Levites," the descendants of Levi who had special assigned duties in Israel's priesthood. But this book mentions the Levites only once (25:32-34), and most of the duties described in the book were to be done by the priests from Aaron's family, who actually performed the sacrifices. The Levites did the basic work of preparing sacrifices and maintaining the tabernacle. As the people of Israel traveled, the Levites were responsible for carrying the sacred objects used in Israel's worship.

Why was Leviticus written?

Leviticus is also known by the name it is given by Jewish rabbis, "the Priest's Manual." Much of Leviticus does read like a "how-to" manual for carrying out the sacrifices and cleansing rituals that set Israel apart as God's holy people. But it also emphasizes the "why" of doing these rituals. God's overwhelming love and concern for Israel was made clear in the exodus from Egypt. The laws that were given at Sinai provided further evidence that God cared for Israel—those laws were given as a protective umbrella or foundation for the Israelite people. If the people remained true to God and observed the laws and rituals God commanded, they would have a good life. But if they turned away from God, followed idols, or refused to live within the protective bounds of the Law, they could expect suffering and even death.

It is important to keep this "why" of Leviticus in mind while reading the detailed responsibilities of the priests, which included: making sure that proper sacrifices were offered to God, teaching the people what was clean and unclean, and making arrangements for Israel's yearly religious festivals. The book also contains laws about which animals could be used for food, what materials could be used for clothing, how the people were to treat one another, and what the penalties were for sinning against God or against a neighbor.

Leviticus emphasizes the role of Israel's priests as the chosen representatives of the people before God. In their ritual acts of sacrifice the priests offer thanks to God, seek God's blessings and forgiveness, and make people clean who have become ritually unclean. The priests are the key links in the chain that holds God and God's people together.

What's the story behind the scene?

LEVITICUS is the third book in the Pentateuch, as the first five books of the Old Testament are called by Christians (see the Introduction to the Pentateuch, p. 35). It follows EXODUS, which describes the laws God gave at Mount Sinai and provides instructions for building the Tent of Meeting (tabernacle), and for all the holy objects that were to be used in worship. LEVITICUS provides a detailed look at the everyday activities of the priests and God's people as they are settled in camp. NUMBERS, the book that follows LEVITICUS, describes God's people on the move.

In the opinion of some biblical scholars, LEVITICUS as it exists today probably combines material from the time of Moses with teachings about God's Law that reflect the settled life of Israel in Canaan many years after Moses' death. By then, the people were no longer worshiping in the movable tabernacle that they had used for so many years in the Desert of Sinai and in Canaan, but were worshiping the LORD in the glorious temple built by Solomon in Jerusalem around 950 B.C. Even so, much of the religious practices described in LEVITICUS continued to be carried out by the priests in the temple.

How is Leviticus constructed?

The following outline divides the book into two main sections with a number of important divisions.

Israel: Community sacrifice and cleanness (1:1—16:34)
- Five kinds of offerings (1:1—7:38)
- The ordination and work of Israel's priests (8:1—10:20)
- Cleaning out impurity (11:1—16:34)

Israel: God's holy people (17:1—27:34)
- Laws for all God's people (17:1—20:27)
- Laws for the priests and religious festivals (21:1—25:55)
- Keeping promises: The blessings of obedience (26:1—27:34)

Israel: Community Sacrifice and Cleanness

The first sixteen chapters of LEVITICUS focus on the sacrifices the priests are to offer to God, on the rituals and sacrifices connected with the ordination of the priests, and on the laws that defined who or what was clean or unclean. Also, the Day of Atonement is described as a yearly event when the sins of the people of Israel are forgiven.

FIVE KINDS OF OFFERINGS

The five types of sacrifices that Israel's priests were to offer to God are described. These include burnt offerings, grain offerings, fellowship offerings, sin offerings, and guilt offerings.

The Burnt Offering

1 The LORD called to Moses and spoke to him from the Tent of
Meeting. He said, 2"Speak to the Israelites and say to them: 'When

1:1 *LORD:* In the NIV, "LORD" is usually the translation for the Hebrew name for God, *Yahweh.* See also the mini-article called "LORD (YHWH)," p. 140.

1:1 *Tent of Meeting:* See the note on p. 210 (tabernacle).

1:3 *burnt offering:* An offering in which the whole animal was burned on the altar. A main purpose of such an offering was to gain God's favor with the odor of the sacrifice.

In ancient times, offering burnt sacrifices was a way to worship God and to maintain, restore, or celebrate the relationship between the giver and God. Before the Law of Moses commanded sacrifices to be done by Israel's priests, sacrifices were offered by the head of each family. See also the chart called "Sacrifices and Offerings," p. 219.

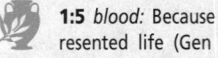

1:4 *lay his hand on:* This was done to show that the sins of the one who brought the animal to be sacrificed were transferred to the animal, and that God would accept the sacrifice and forgive these sins.

1:4 *make atonement for him:* Sin is turning away from God and disobeying God's laws. Israel's priests offered animal sacrifices for the sins of the people, making "atonement" for them (correcting their relationship with God). The animals took the punishment that the people deserved for doing wrong. See also 4:1—6:30.

1:5 *Aaron's sons the priests:* See the note on p. 210 (priests).

1:5 *blood:* Because blood represented life (Gen 4:10,11), it was sacred and not to be eaten (7:26, 27; 17:10-14; 19:26; Deut 12:16,23,24; 15:23). It also had power to protect (Exod 12:7,13) and was a sign of the bond between God and the people. Blood put on the altar or on the people had cleansing power and showed that something or someone was dedicated to God (Exod 29:10-21). See also the mini-article called "Blood," p. 180.

1:9 *aroma pleasing to the* LORD*:* See the note at 1:3.

1:11 *sprinkle its blood:* See the note at 1:5 (blood).

1:15 *altar:* See the note on p. 210 (tabernacle).

any of you brings an offering to the LORD, bring as your offering
an animal from either the herd or the flock.
3 "'If the offering is a burnt offering from the herd, he is to offer
a male without defect. He must present it at the entrance to the Tent
of Meeting so that it[a] will be acceptable to the LORD. 4 He is to lay his
hand on the head of the burnt offering, and it will be accepted on his
behalf to make atonement for him. 5 He is to slaughter the young bull
before the LORD, and then Aaron's sons the priests shall bring the
blood and sprinkle it against the altar on all sides at the entrance to
the Tent of Meeting. 6 He is to skin the burnt offering and cut it into
pieces. 7 The sons of Aaron the priest are to put fire on the altar and
arrange wood on the fire. 8 Then Aaron's sons the priests shall arrange
the pieces, including the head and the fat, on the burning wood that
is on the altar. 9 He is to wash the inner parts and the legs with water,
and the priest is to burn all of it on the altar. It is a burnt offering, an
offering made by fire, an aroma pleasing to the LORD.
10 "'If the offering is a burnt offering from the flock, from
either the sheep or the goats, he is to offer a male without defect.
11 He is to slaughter it at the north side of the altar before the LORD,
and Aaron's sons the priests shall sprinkle its blood against the
altar on all sides. 12 He is to cut it into pieces, and the priest shall
arrange them, including the head and the fat, on the burning
wood that is on the altar. 13 He is to wash the inner parts and the
legs with water, and the priest is to bring all of it and burn it on
the altar. It is a burnt offering, an offering made by fire, an aroma
pleasing to the LORD.
14 "'If the offering to the LORD is a burnt offering of birds, he
is to offer a dove or a young pigeon. 15 The priest shall bring it to
the altar, wring off the head and burn it on the altar; its blood shall
be drained out on the side of the altar. 16 He is to remove the crop
with its contents[b] and throw it to the east side of the altar, where
the ashes are. 17 He shall tear it open by the wings, not severing it
completely, and then the priest shall burn it on the wood that is
on the fire on the altar. It is a burnt offering, an offering made by
fire, an aroma pleasing to the LORD.

The Grain Offering

2 "'When someone brings a grain offering to the LORD, his offering is to be of fine flour. He is to pour oil on it, put incense on it
2 and take it to Aaron's sons the priests. The priest shall take a
handful of the fine flour and oil, together with all the incense, and
burn this as a memorial portion on the altar, an offering made by
fire, an aroma pleasing to the LORD. 3 The rest of the grain offering
belongs to Aaron and his sons; it is a most holy part of the offerings made to the LORD by fire.

---

[a]**3** Or *he* [b]**16** Or *crop and the feathers*; the meaning of the Hebrew for this word is uncertain.

Israelites Making a Sacrifice to the LORD, stone relief from Sainte Chapelle, Paris, thirteenth century. Although GENESIS tells of people like Abel, Noah, and Abraham who sacrificed animals as a way of worshiping God, it is LEVITICUS that gives the most thorough descriptions of the different kinds of offerings and sacrifices the people of Israel were expected to make. These sacrifices were to be made for the people by priests from the tribe of Levi. People were expected to offer up animals that were healthy and had nothing wrong with them. Different sacrifices were done for different reasons, but the smoke that rose from the altar was always "an offering made by fire, an aroma pleasing to the LORD."

4"'If you bring a grain offering baked in an oven, it is to consist of fine flour: cakes made without yeast and mixed with oil, or[a]
wafers made without yeast and spread with oil. 5If your grain
offering is prepared on a griddle, it is to be made of fine flour
mixed with oil, and without yeast. 6Crumble it and pour oil on it;
it is a grain offering. 7If your grain offering is cooked in a pan, it is
to be made of fine flour and oil. 8Bring the grain offering made of
these things to the LORD; present it to the priest, who shall take it
to the altar. 9He shall take out the memorial portion from the
grain offering and burn it on the altar as an offering made by fire,
an aroma pleasing to the LORD. 10The rest of the grain offering
belongs to Aaron and his sons; it is a most holy part of the offerings made to the LORD by fire.
11"'Every grain offering you bring to the LORD must be made
without yeast, for you are not to burn any yeast or honey in an
offering made to the LORD by fire. 12You may bring them to the
LORD as an offering of the firstfruits, but they are not to be offered

[a]4 Or *and*

1:16 *east side of the altar, where the ashes are:* Ashes were piled up on the east side of the altar, possibly because this side was opposite the entrance of the tabernacle. Once a day they were taken to the large ash heap outside the camp (4:11,12; 6:10,11).

2:1 *grain offering:* This sacrifice was made to thank the LORD with a gift of grain and secure God's favor. See also the note at 1:3.

2:1 *oil . . . incense:* Olive oil was mixed with incense and flour and burned to make an offering of thanks to God. Incense was made of spices and gums, including frankincense (Exod 30:7,8,34,35).

2:3 *rest of the grain offering:* Unlike the burnt offerings (1:3), which had to be completely burned up, a portion of these grain offerings was to be saved and eaten by the priests in the courtyard of the tabernacle (6:16, 17). Israel's priests came from the Levite tribe, which did not hold tribal land. So, Israel's priests and their families were supported by the tribes that did receive land. This meant that Levites could keep portions of the offerings brought by the people (Num 18:21-24).

2:4-7 *grain offering baked in an oven:* Four kinds of bread could be used for sacrifices: oven-baked cakes or wafers (2:4), bread cooked on a griddle (2:5,6) or fried in a covered pan (2:7).

2:11 *yeast or honey:* Yeast and honey ferment easily. Because the fermentation process, though beneficial, is a form of decay, these items were not to be used in offerings made to God.

2:12 *firstfruits:* The first harvested grains and the foods made from the first grains were given to honor God and to remember that the people's blessings came from God (23:9-12; Num 18:11,12,25-30; Deut 26:1-15).

2:13 *salt:* Salt was used to preserve food. It was sprinkled on offerings as a symbol of the lasting covenant between God and his people.

3:1 *fellowship offering:* Traditionally called "peace offering" or "offering of well-being." A main purpose was to give thanks to God and have fellowship with him.

3:2 *lay his hand on the head of his offering:* See the note at 1:4 (lay his hand on).

3:2 *Aaron's sons the priests shall sprinkle the blood:* See the notes on p. 210 (priests) and at 1:5 (blood).

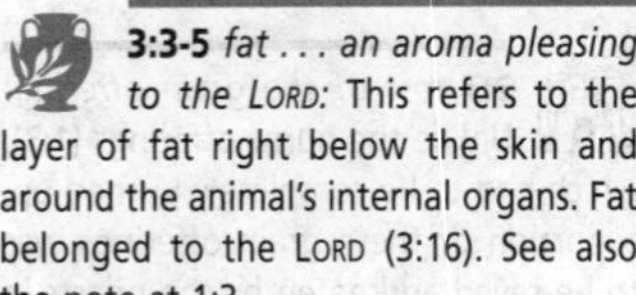

3:3-5 *fat . . . an aroma pleasing to the Lord:* This refers to the layer of fat right below the skin and around the animal's internal organs. Fat belonged to the LORD (3:16). See also the note at 1:3.

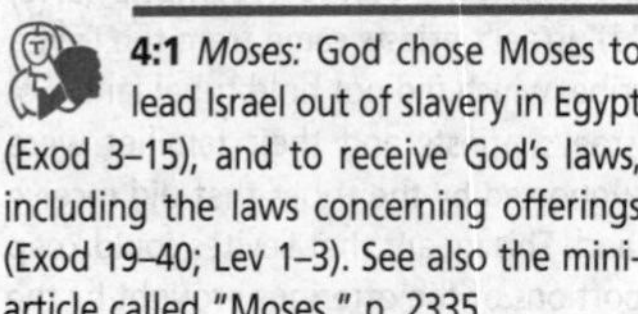

4:1 *Moses:* God chose Moses to lead Israel out of slavery in Egypt (Exod 3–15), and to receive God's laws, including the laws concerning offerings (Exod 19–40; Lev 1–3). See also the mini-article called "Moses," p. 2335.

4:3 *If the anointed priest sins . . . a young bull:* Israel's high priest was in charge of the other priests and was the only one who could enter the Most Holy Place in the tabernacle. As a religious leader, his sins would bring guilt on the entire nation. Aaron was ordained as Israel's first high priest (Exod 29:5-7). The best animals, rather than injured animals, were to be offered to God. Bulls were an especially valuable sacrifice (4:4-12).

on the altar as a pleasing aroma. 13Season all your grain offerings
with salt. Do not leave the salt of the covenant of your God out of
your grain offerings; add salt to all your offerings.
14"'If you bring a grain offering of firstfruits to the LORD,
offer crushed heads of new grain roasted in the fire. 15Put oil and
incense on it; it is a grain offering. 16The priest shall burn the
memorial portion of the crushed grain and the oil, together with
all the incense, as an offering made to the LORD by fire.

The Fellowship Offering

3 "'If someone's offering is a fellowship offering,[a] and he offers
an animal from the herd, whether male or female, he is to present
before the LORD an animal without defect. 2He is to lay his hand on
the head of his offering and slaughter it at the entrance to the Tent
of Meeting. Then Aaron's sons the priests shall sprinkle the blood
against the altar on all sides. 3From the fellowship offering he is to
bring a sacrifice made to the LORD by fire: all the fat that covers the
inner parts or is connected to them, 4both kidneys with the fat on
them near the loins, and the covering of the liver, which he will
remove with the kidneys. 5Then Aaron's sons are to burn it on the
altar on top of the burnt offering that is on the burning wood, as
an offering made by fire, an aroma pleasing to the LORD.
6"'If he offers an animal from the flock as a fellowship offering to the LORD, he is to offer a male or female without defect. 7If
he offers a lamb, he is to present it before the LORD. 8He is to lay his
hand on the head of his offering and slaughter it in front of the
Tent of Meeting. Then Aaron's sons shall sprinkle its blood against
the altar on all sides. 9From the fellowship offering he is to bring a
sacrifice made to the LORD by fire: its fat, the entire fat tail cut off
close to the backbone, all the fat that covers the inner parts or is
connected to them, 10both kidneys with the fat on them near the
loins, and the covering of the liver, which he will remove with the
kidneys. 11The priest shall burn them on the altar as food, an offering made to the LORD by fire.
12"'If his offering is a goat, he is to present it before the LORD.
13He is to lay his hand on its head and slaughter it in front of the
Tent of Meeting. Then Aaron's sons shall sprinkle its blood against
the altar on all sides. 14From what he offers he is to make this offering to the LORD by fire: all the fat that covers the inner parts or is
connected to them, 15both kidneys with the fat on them near the
loins, and the covering of the liver, which he will remove with the
kidneys. 16The priest shall burn them on the altar as food, an offering made by fire, a pleasing aroma. All the fat is the LORD's.
17"'This is a lasting ordinance for the generations to come,
wherever you live: You must not eat any fat or any blood.'"

a1 Traditionally *peace offering*; also in verses 3, 6 and 9

The Sin Offering

4 The LORD said to Moses, 2"Say to the Israelites: 'When anyone
sins unintentionally and does what is forbidden in any of the
LORD's commands—

3" 'If the anointed priest sins, bringing guilt on the people,
he must bring to the LORD a young bull without defect as a sin
offering for the sin he has committed. 4He is to present the bull at
the entrance to the Tent of Meeting before the LORD. He is to lay
his hand on its head and slaughter it before the LORD. 5Then the
anointed priest shall take some of the bull's blood and carry it into
the Tent of Meeting. 6He is to dip his finger into the blood and
sprinkle some of it seven times before the LORD, in front of the
curtain of the sanctuary. 7The priest shall then put some of the
blood on the horns of the altar of fragrant incense that is before
the LORD in the Tent of Meeting. The rest of the bull's blood he
shall pour out at the base of the altar of burnt offering at the
entrance to the Tent of Meeting. 8He shall remove all the fat from
the bull of the sin offering—the fat that covers the inner parts or
is connected to them, 9both kidneys with the fat on them near the
loins, and the covering of the liver, which he will remove with the
kidneys— 10just as the fat is removed from the ox[a] sacrificed as a
fellowship offering.[b] Then the priest shall burn them on the altar
of burnt offering. 11But the hide of the bull and all its flesh, as well
as the head and legs, the inner parts and offal— 12that is, all the
rest of the bull—he must take outside the camp to a place ceremonially clean, where the ashes are thrown, and burn it in a wood
fire on the ash heap.

13" 'If the whole Israelite community sins unintentionally
and does what is forbidden in any of the LORD's commands, even
though the community is unaware of the matter, they are guilty.
14When they become aware of the sin they committed, the assembly must bring a young bull as a sin offering and present it before
the Tent of Meeting. 15The elders of the community are to lay their
hands on the bull's head before the LORD, and the bull shall be
slaughtered before the LORD. 16Then the anointed priest is to take
some of the bull's blood into the Tent of Meeting. 17He shall dip
his finger into the blood and sprinkle it before the LORD seven
times in front of the curtain. 18He is to put some of the blood on
the horns of the altar that is before the LORD in the Tent of Meeting. The rest of the blood he shall pour out at the base of the altar
of burnt offering at the entrance to the Tent of Meeting. 19He shall
remove all the fat from it and burn it on the altar, 20and do with
this bull just as he did with the bull for the sin offering. In this way
the priest will make atonement for them, and they will be forgiven.

a10 The Hebrew word can include both male and female. **b10** Traditionally *peace offering*; also in verses 26, 31 and 35

4:3 *a sin offering for the sin he has committed:* Referred to as "sin offerings," they are intended to clean or purify one who unintentionally sinned or accidentally did something that was against God's law. Different objects of offering were used for different individuals and for the whole people.

4:5-7 *blood . . . seven times . . . altar:* See the note at 1:5 (blood). The sprinkling of blood purified the altar. This was done seven times, because seven was a sacred number symbolizing perfection or completeness. The directions for building the ark of the covenant are given in Exodus 25:10-22. See also the note on p. 210 (tabernacle). The altar for burning incense (Exod 30:1-10) was in the Holy Place of the tabernacle.

4:10 *fellowship offering:* See the note at 3:1. See also 3:3-5.

4:12 *ashes:* See the note at 1:16.

4:13 *whole Israelite community sins:* The idea that all the people of the nation are guilty because of the actions of a few was an important understanding for ancient Israel. A bull was also used as an offering for the sins of the whole nation.

4:15 *elders of the community:* They represented the whole nation (Exod 3:16; 12:21; 24:9). See also the note at 1:4 (lay his hand on).

4:26 *fellowship offering:* The sin offering followed a pattern similar to the fellowship offering (see the note at 3:1).

4:27-32 *a member of the community . . . female goat . . . lamb:* People who were not priests or leaders were to bring a female goat or a lamb as a sin offering.

4:32 *lamb . . . a female without defect:* Meaning it could have no blemish or deformity (22:21-24). See also the note at 4:3 (anointed priest).

5:2 *ceremonially unclean . . . carcasses . . . become unclean and is guilty:* The Law of Moses declared some animals ritually unclean. They could not be eaten or even touched without making the one who touched them ritually impure. See chapter 11 for a list of such animals. See also the mini-article called "Purity (Clean and Unclean)," p. 2125.

4:27-31 Num 15:27,28.

21 Then he shall take the bull outside the camp and burn it as he
burned the first bull. This is the sin offering for the community.

22 " 'When a leader sins unintentionally and does what is forbidden in any of the commands of the LORD his God, he is guilty.
23 When he is made aware of the sin he committed, he must bring
as his offering a male goat without defect. 24 He is to lay his hand
on the goat's head and slaughter it at the place where the burnt
offering is slaughtered before the LORD. It is a sin offering. 25 Then
the priest shall take some of the blood of the sin offering with his
finger and put it on the horns of the altar of burnt offering and
pour out the rest of the blood at the base of the altar. 26 He shall
burn all the fat on the altar as he burned the fat of the fellowship
offering. In this way the priest will make atonement for the man's
sin, and he will be forgiven.

27 " 'If a member of the community sins unintentionally and
does what is forbidden in any of the LORD's commands, he is
guilty. 28 When he is made aware of the sin he committed, he must
bring as his offering for the sin he committed a female goat without defect. 29 He is to lay his hand on the head of the sin offering
and slaughter it at the place of the burnt offering. 30 Then the priest
is to take some of the blood with his finger and put it on the horns
of the altar of burnt offering and pour out the rest of the blood at
the base of the altar. 31 He shall remove all the fat, just as the fat is
removed from the fellowship offering, and the priest shall burn it
on the altar as an aroma pleasing to the LORD. In this way the
priest will make atonement for him, and he will be forgiven.

32 " 'If he brings a lamb as his sin offering, he is to bring a
female without defect. 33 He is to lay his hand on its head and
slaughter it for a sin offering at the place where the burnt offering
is slaughtered. 34 Then the priest shall take some of the blood of the
sin offering with his finger and put it on the horns of the altar of
burnt offering and pour out the rest of the blood at the base of the
altar. 35 He shall remove all the fat, just as the fat is removed from
the lamb of the fellowship offering, and the priest shall burn it on
the altar on top of the offerings made to the LORD by fire. In this
way the priest will make atonement for him for the sin he has
committed, and he will be forgiven.

5 " 'If a person sins because he does not speak up when he hears
a public charge to testify regarding something he has seen or
learned about, he will be held responsible.

2 " 'Or if a person touches anything ceremonially unclean—
whether the carcasses of unclean wild animals or of unclean livestock or of unclean creatures that move along the ground—even
though he is unaware of it, he has become unclean and is guilty.

3 " 'Or if he touches human uncleanness—anything that
would make him unclean—even though he is unaware of it, when
he learns of it he will be guilty.

4“ ‘Or if a person thoughtlessly takes an oath to do anything,
whether good or evil—in any matter one might carelessly swear
about—even though he is unaware of it, in any case when he
learns of it he will be guilty.
5“ ‘When anyone is guilty in any of these ways, he must confess in what way he has sinned 6and, as a penalty for the sin he has
committed, he must bring to the LORD a female lamb or goat from
the flock as a sin offering; and the priest shall make atonement for
him for his sin.
7“ ‘If he cannot afford a lamb, he is to bring two doves or two
young pigeons to the LORD as a penalty for his sin—one for a sin
offering and the other for a burnt offering. 8He is to bring them to
the priest, who shall first offer the one for the sin offering. He is to
wring its head from its neck, not severing it completely, 9and is to
sprinkle some of the blood of the sin offering against the side of
the altar; the rest of the blood must be drained out at the base of
the altar. It is a sin offering. 10The priest shall then offer the other
as a burnt offering in the prescribed way and make atonement for
him for the sin he has committed, and he will be forgiven.
11“ ‘If, however, he cannot afford two doves or two young
pigeons, he is to bring as an offering for his sin a tenth of an
ephah[a] of fine flour for a sin offering. He must not put oil or
incense on it, because it is a sin offering. 12He is to bring it to the
priest, who shall take a handful of it as a memorial portion and
burn it on the altar on top of the offerings made to the LORD by
fire. It is a sin offering. 13In this way the priest will make atonement for him for any of these sins he has committed, and he will
be forgiven. The rest of the offering will belong to the priest, as in
the case of the grain offering.’ ”

The Guilt Offering

14The LORD said to Moses: 15“When a person commits a violation and sins unintentionally in regard to any of the LORD’s holy
things, he is to bring to the LORD as a penalty a ram from the flock,
one without defect and of the proper value in silver, according to
the sanctuary shekel.[b] It is a guilt offering. 16He must make restitution for what he has failed to do in regard to the holy things, add
a fifth of the value to that and give it all to the priest, who will
make atonement for him with the ram as a guilt offering, and he
will be forgiven.
17“If a person sins and does what is forbidden in any of the
LORD’s commands, even though he does not know it, he is guilty
and will be held responsible. 18He is to bring to the priest as a guilt
offering a ram from the flock, one without defect and of the proper value. In this way the priest will make atonement for him for

5:7-11 *cannot afford ... two doves or two young pigeons ... a tenth of an ephah of fine flour:* The objects of sacrifice were determined according to a person’s place in Israelite society. The poor were in the lowest place in society, so they could bring the least expensive animals (doves or pigeons) or even two pounds of flour. These objects were brought to the priest who first made a sin offering (5:8) followed by a burnt offering (5:10).

5:13 *rest of the offering will belong to the priest:* See the note at 2:3.

5:15 *sins unintentionally ... ram ... sanctuary shekel:* This refers to accidentally breaking or misusing the sacred objects in and around the tabernacle. When such an offense occurred, a ram or the amount of money equal to the price of a ram was to be offered. Coins or paper money were not used by the Israelites at this time, but pieces of silver called shekels (each weighing about one fifth of an ounce) were used as payment.

5:16 *restitution ... atonement ... guilt offering:* This kind of sacrifice was like a sin offering, except that the offender also paid a fine for the damages. This payment included the cost of fixing or replacing the broken object plus twenty percent (a fifth). The sin offering was used for situations when the offender was not able to pay a fine in order to replace what was broken. The repayment offering was sometimes called a “guilt” offering. A main purpose of this sacrifice was to relieve guilt and to pay for the offense, even if the sin had been unintentional.

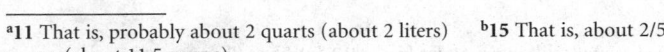

a11 That is, probably about 2 quarts (about 2 liters) **b15** That is, about 2/5 ounce (about 11.5 grams)

6:2-7 *stolen . . . cheats . . . restitution in full, add a fifth:* See the note at 5:16. A person had to return the stolen property plus twenty percent, and provide a ram for a sacrifice. See also Num 5:5-8.

6:9 *Aaron and his sons:* See the note on p. 210 (priests).

6:9 *burnt offering . . . throughout the night:* In ancient Israel a new day was said to begin at sunset, so the priests placed the animal for the daily burnt offering on the altar in the evening and let it burn all night long.

6:10,11 *priest . . . linen clothes . . . remove the ashes:* See the note at 8:7-9. See Exodus 28 and its accompanying notes for a complete description of the garments worn by the priests and high priest. Linen (6:10) was made from the fibers of the flax plant. For more about the handling of ashes, see the note at 1:16.

6:12 *fellowship offerings:* See the note at 3:1.

6:13 *fire . . . burning on the altar continuously:* The very first sacrifices offered by Aaron on the altar were consumed by a fire sent from the LORD (9:24). The fire was to be kept burning so that all later sacrifices could be consumed by fire that had its beginning with the LORD's miraculous fire.

6:14,15 *grain offering . . . incense:* See the notes at 2:1.

6:16,17 *must not be baked with yeast . . . most holy:* See the notes at 2:4-7 and 2:11. For more on holiness, see the note on p. 210 (holiness).

the wrong he has committed unintentionally, and he will be
forgiven. 19 It is a guilt offering; he has been guilty of[a] wrongdoing against the LORD."
6 The LORD said to Moses: 2 "If anyone sins and is unfaithful to
the LORD by deceiving his neighbor about something entrusted to
him or left in his care or stolen, or if he cheats him, 3 or if he finds
lost property and lies about it, or if he swears falsely, or if he commits any such sin that people may do— 4 when he thus sins and
becomes guilty, he must return what he has stolen or taken by
extortion, or what was entrusted to him, or the lost property he
found, 5 or whatever it was he swore falsely about. He must make
restitution in full, add a fifth of the value to it and give it all to the
owner on the day he presents his guilt offering. 6 And as a penalty
he must bring to the priest, that is, to the LORD, his guilt offering,
a ram from the flock, one without defect and of the proper value.
7 In this way the priest will make atonement for him before the
LORD, and he will be forgiven for any of these things he did that
made him guilty."

The Burnt Offering

8 The LORD said to Moses: 9 "Give Aaron and his sons this
command: 'These are the regulations for the burnt offering: The
burnt offering is to remain on the altar hearth throughout the
night, till morning, and the fire must be kept burning on the altar.
10 The priest shall then put on his linen clothes, with linen undergarments next to his body, and shall remove the ashes of the burnt
offering that the fire has consumed on the altar and place them
beside the altar. 11 Then he is to take off these clothes and put on
others, and carry the ashes outside the camp to a place that is ceremonially clean. 12 The fire on the altar must be kept burning; it
must not go out. Every morning the priest is to add firewood and
arrange the burnt offering on the fire and burn the fat of the fellowship offerings[b] on it. 13 The fire must be kept burning on the
altar continuously; it must not go out.

The Grain Offering

14 " 'These are the regulations for the grain offering: Aaron's
sons are to bring it before the LORD, in front of the altar. 15 The priest
is to take a handful of fine flour and oil, together with all the incense
on the grain offering, and burn the memorial portion on the altar as
an aroma pleasing to the LORD. 16 Aaron and his sons shall eat the
rest of it, but it is to be eaten without yeast in a holy place; they are
to eat it in the courtyard of the Tent of Meeting. 17 It must not be
baked with yeast; I have given it as their share of the offerings made
to me by fire. Like the sin offering and the guilt offering, it is most

[a] **19** Or *has made full expiation for his* [b] **12** Traditionally *peace offerings*

SACRIFICES AND OFFERINGS

The practice of offering objects to the gods was common in the ancient world. Offerings were made to give thanks, to ask for something like rainfall or good crops, and to keep the gods from becoming angry. The laws God gave to Moses and the people of Israel called for a number of specific kinds of sacrifices or offerings. The objects offered for sacrifice were brought by the common people and their leaders, but only the priests could perform the sacrifices, which were to be offered only to Israel's LORD (*Yahweh*). LEVITICUS describes five basic kinds of sacrifices that Israel's priests were to offer for the people.

TYPE OF SACRIFICE	OBJECT TO BE SACRIFICED	REASON FOR SACRIFICE	LEVITICUS PASSAGES
Burnt offering	Bull, male sheep or goat without blemish; or a dove or pigeon for the poor	To worship God, show devotion to God, and to ask for God's forgiveness; the entire object is burned	1:1-17 6:8-13 8:18-21 16:2
Grain offering	A mixture of fine wheat flour, olive oil and incense; bread baked without yeast (unleavened) or honey in loaves or wafers; salt added sometimes; sometimes used along with burnt offerings or fellowship offerings	To worship God by giving thanks; to recognize that God is the giver of blessings and provider of good things	2:1-16 6:14-23
Fellowship offering	Fat and certain inner organs from a bull, cow, sheep, or goat that has nothing wrong with it; various kinds of bread made without yeast (unleavened bread)	To worship God and ask for God's blessing; some of the meat is kept and eaten by the priests	3:1-17 7:11-34
Sin offering	• A young bull for the high priest and the whole nation • A male goat for a tribal leader • A female goat or lamb for ordinary people • Two doves or pigeons for the poor • Two pounds of fine flour for the very poor • Two goats and a ram on the Day of Atonement (one goat carries the sins of the whole nation into the desert)	To ask for God's forgiveness; to make up for specific unintentional sins; to become clean after becoming ritually unclean	4:1—5:13 6:24-30 8:14-17 16:3-22
Guilt offering	A ram that has nothing wrong with it, or the price of the ram; in addition, the guilty person is to pay back the value of what was stolen or destroyed plus twenty percent	To make up for cheating the LORD or for unintentionally destroying something that belonged to the LORD; to make up for robbing or cheating another person	5:14—6:7 7:1-6

holy. [18]Any male descendant of Aaron may eat it. It is his regular share of the offerings made to the LORD by fire for the generations to come. Whatever touches them will become holy.[a]"

[19]The LORD also said to Moses, [20]"This is the offering Aaron and his sons are to bring to the LORD on the day he[b] is anointed: a tenth of an ephah[c] of fine flour as a regular grain offering, half of it in the morning and half in the evening. [21]Prepare it with oil on a griddle; bring it well-mixed and present the grain offering broken[d] in pieces as an aroma pleasing to the LORD. [22]The son who is to succeed him as anointed priest shall prepare it. It is the LORD's regular share and is to be burned completely. [23]Every grain offering of a priest shall be burned completely; it must not be eaten."

The Sin Offering

[24]The LORD said to Moses, [25]"Say to Aaron and his sons: 'These are the regulations for the sin offering: The sin offering is to be slaughtered before the LORD in the place the burnt offering is slaughtered; it is most holy. [26]The priest who offers it shall eat it; it is to be eaten in a holy place, in the courtyard of the Tent of Meeting. [27]Whatever touches any of the flesh will become holy, and if any of the blood is spattered on a garment, you must wash it in a holy place. [28]The clay pot the meat is cooked in must be broken; but if it is cooked in a bronze pot, the pot is to be scoured and rinsed with water. [29]Any male in a priest's family may eat it; it is most holy. [30]But any sin offering whose blood is brought into the Tent of Meeting to make atonement in the Holy Place must not be eaten; it must be burned.

The Guilt Offering

7 "'These are the regulations for the guilt offering, which is most holy: [2]The guilt offering is to be slaughtered in the place where the burnt offering is slaughtered, and its blood is to be sprinkled against the altar on all sides. [3]All its fat shall be offered: the fat tail and the fat that covers the inner parts, [4]both kidneys with the fat on them near the loins, and the covering of the liver, which is to be removed with the kidneys. [5]The priest shall burn them on the altar as an offering made to the LORD by fire. It is a guilt offering. [6]Any male in a priest's family may eat it, but it must be eaten in a holy place; it is most holy.

[7]"'The same law applies to both the sin offering and the guilt offering: They belong to the priest who makes atonement with them. [8]The priest who offers a burnt offering for anyone may keep its hide for himself. [9]Every grain offering baked in an oven or

[a]18 Or *Whoever touches them must be holy*; similarly in verse 27 [b]20 Or *each* [c]20 That is, probably about 2 quarts (about 2 liters) [d]21 The meaning of the Hebrew for this word is uncertain.

6:18 *descendant of Aaron:* See the note on p. 210 (priests).

6:20 *the day he is anointed:* People who were anointed were chosen and set apart for a special purpose, or dedicated to the LORD. Olive oil was poured on their head as a sign that they had been chosen (Exod 28:41; 29:7). The full description of the consecration (ordination) of Israel's priests is given in Exodus 29 and Leviticus 8.

6:20 *regular grain offering . . . morning . . . evening:* Ordination offerings included a one-pound grain offering at the regular time of the morning and evening sacrifices. See the note at 2:4-7 and see Exod 29:38-43.

6:25,26 *sin offering . . . eaten in a holy place:* See the note at 4:3. Some sacrifices for sin offerings were "holy" and were to be eaten by the priest who offered the sacrifice (6:26,29). But sacrifices for sin that required blood to be brought into the tabernacle (4:1-21) were burned completely on the altar (6:30).

6:27,28 *wash it . . . clay pot . . . bronze pot:* The sacrificial meat and juices were thought to absorb the sin or impurity the sacrifice was meant to get rid of. Persons or objects that came into contact with this sacrifice could become polluted by the impurities that the sacrifice had absorbed. Clay pots that held the sacrifice had to be broken, since clay absorbed the juices and could not be fully cleansed. Metal pots did not absorb the juices, so they were to be cleaned just like the priest's clothing.

7:1 *guilt offering:* See the note at 5:16. The sacrificial animal was killed near the entrance of the tabernacle (see the note on p. 210, tabernacle). This sacrifice was very holy (see the note on p. 210, holiness) and was to be eaten by the priests in a holy place, the courtyard of the Tent of Meeting (see 6:16).

cooked in a pan or on a griddle belongs to the priest who offers it, [10]and every grain offering, whether mixed with oil or dry, belongs equally to all the sons of Aaron.

The Fellowship Offering

[11]"'These are the regulations for the fellowship offering[a] a person may present to the LORD:

[12]"'If he offers it as an expression of thankfulness, then along with this thank offering he is to offer cakes of bread made without yeast and mixed with oil, wafers made without yeast and spread with oil, and cakes of fine flour well-kneaded and mixed with oil. [13]Along with his fellowship offering of thanksgiving he is to present an offering with cakes of bread made with yeast. [14]He is to bring one of each kind as an offering, a contribution to the LORD; it belongs to the priest who sprinkles the blood of the fellowship offerings. [15]The meat of his fellowship offering of thanksgiving must be eaten on the day it is offered; he must leave none of it till morning.

[16]"'If, however, his offering is the result of a vow or is a freewill offering, the sacrifice shall be eaten on the day he offers it, but anything left over may be eaten on the next day. [17]Any meat of the sacrifice left over till the third day must be burned up. [18]If any meat of the fellowship offering is eaten on the third day, it will not be accepted. It will not be credited to the one who offered it, for it is impure; the person who eats any of it will be held responsible.

[19]"'Meat that touches anything ceremonially unclean must not be eaten; it must be burned up. As for other meat, anyone ceremonially clean may eat it. [20]But if anyone who is unclean eats any meat of the fellowship offering belonging to the LORD, that person must be cut off from his people. [21]If anyone touches something unclean—whether human uncleanness or an unclean animal or any unclean, detestable thing—and then eats any of the meat of the fellowship offering belonging to the LORD, that person must be cut off from his people.'"

Eating Fat and Blood Forbidden

[22]The LORD said to Moses, [23]"Say to the Israelites: 'Do not eat any of the fat of cattle, sheep or goats. [24]The fat of an animal found dead or torn by wild animals may be used for any other purpose, but you must not eat it. [25]Anyone who eats the fat of an animal from which an offering by fire may be[b] made to the LORD must be cut off from his people. [26]And wherever you live, you must not eat the blood of any bird or animal. [27]If anyone eats blood, that person must be cut off from his people.'"

[a]11 Traditionally *peace offering;* also in verses 13-37 [b]25 Or *fire is*

7:7-10 *They belong to the priest:* Certain parts of the sacrifices were eaten by the priest performing the sacrifice. These included the guilt offerings, the sin offerings, and the grain offerings. The priest could keep the skin of the burnt offering (see the note at 1:3, burnt offering), but everything else had to be burned. The grain offerings were to be divided among the priests.

7:11 *fellowship offering:* See the note at 3:1. Rules for three different kinds of fellowship offerings are given. This first is a grain offering using four different kinds of bread (see the note at 2:4-7). Note the addition of a loaf of bread made "with yeast" (7:13). The food (bread or meat) must be eaten the same day it is sacrificed. With fellowship offerings that involved making a vow to God or giving a gift to God, the meat could be saved and eaten the following day. But any left after the second day had to be burned (7:16,17).

7:19 *unclean:* See the note at 5:2.

7:26 *must not eat the blood:* See the note at 1:5 (blood). See also Gen 9:4; Lev 17:10-14; 19:26; Deut 12:16-24; 15:23.

7:23 Lev 3:16,17.

7:29 *fellowship offering:* See the note at 3:1. Also called "wave offering" (7:30). The choice ribs were to be kept and eaten by the priest who offered the sacrifice. These ribs were to be waved above the priest's head to show that they were presented as a special gift to the LORD.

7:35 *Aaron and his sons . . . presented to serve the LORD as priests:* See the notes on p. 210 (priests) and at 6:20 (anointed).

7:38 *Mount Sinai . . . in the Desert of Sinai:* God gave the Ten Commandments and the rest of the laws to Moses and the people at Mount Sinai, which was probably located somewhere on the dry Sinai Peninsula (Exod 19:1,18). See the note and map on p. 133.

8:2 *garments . . . bread made without yeast:* See the notes at 8:7-9; 6:20 (anointed); 4:3; 2:4-7; and 2:11.

8:6 *washed them:* To make themselves ritually clean, not just to remove dirt. See the note at 5:2.

8:7-9 *tunic . . . ephod . . . breastpiece . . . Urim and Thummin:* The tunic was a special embroidered shirt (Exod 28:4,5), and the ephod, or sacred vest, was made of fine linen and colorful wool (Exod 28:6-14). The ephod had two onyx stones, each engraved with six of the names of the twelve tribes of Israel, who were named after the sons of Jacob (Gen 35:23-26).

The breastpiece was like a flat wool and linen pouch that contained an inner pocket, formed by doubling over the material (Exod 28:15-30). In the pouch were kept the Urim and Thummin, two objects used by the priest to determine God's will. It is not known precisely how they were used. The breastpiece had four rows of three precious stones each, one for each of the twelve tribes of Israel. The turban was a kind of headdress that included cloth rolled at its base that was thick enough to support a gold strip. For more detail about the priestly clothing, see the notes in Exodus 28 and the illustration on p. 1908.

The Priests' Share

28 The LORD said to Moses, 29 "Say to the Israelites: 'Anyone
who brings a fellowship offering to the LORD is to bring part of it
as his sacrifice to the LORD. 30 With his own hands he is to bring the
offering made to the LORD by fire; he is to bring the fat, together
with the breast, and wave the breast before the LORD as a wave
offering. 31 The priest shall burn the fat on the altar, but the breast
belongs to Aaron and his sons. 32 You are to give the right thigh of
your fellowship offerings to the priest as a contribution. 33 The son
of Aaron who offers the blood and the fat of the fellowship offering shall have the right thigh as his share. 34 From the fellowship
offerings of the Israelites, I have taken the breast that is waved and
the thigh that is presented and have given them to Aaron the priest
and his sons as their regular share from the Israelites.'"

35 This is the portion of the offerings made to the LORD by
fire that were allotted to Aaron and his sons on the day they were
presented to serve the LORD as priests. 36 On the day they were
anointed, the LORD commanded that the Israelites give this to
them as their regular share for the generations to come.

37 These, then, are the regulations for the burnt offering, the
grain offering, the sin offering, the guilt offering, the ordination
offering and the fellowship offering, 38 which the LORD gave Moses
on Mount Sinai on the day he commanded the Israelites to bring
their offerings to the LORD, in the Desert of Sinai.

THE ORDINATION AND WORK OF ISRAEL'S PRIESTS

A special seven-day ceremony marks the ordination of Israel's priests, and their work of offering sacrifices for the people begins. Two of Aaron's sons die when they fail to follow the LORD's instructions about proper procedures for offering sacrifices.

The Ordination of Aaron and His Sons

8 The LORD said to Moses, 2 "Bring Aaron and his sons, their garments, the anointing oil, the bull for the sin offering, the two rams
and the basket containing bread made without yeast, 3 and gather
the entire assembly at the entrance to the Tent of Meeting." 4 Moses
did as the LORD commanded him, and the assembly gathered at
the entrance to the Tent of Meeting.

5 Moses said to the assembly, "This is what the LORD has
commanded to be done." 6 Then Moses brought Aaron and his sons
forward and washed them with water. 7 He put the tunic on Aaron,
tied the sash around him, clothed him with the robe and put the
ephod on him. He also tied the ephod to him by its skillfully
woven waistband; so it was fastened on him. 8 He placed the breastpiece on him and put the Urim and Thummim in the breastpiece.
9 Then he placed the turban on Aaron's head and set the gold plate,

the sacred diadem, on the front of it, as the LORD commanded
Moses.
10 Then Moses took the anointing oil and anointed the tabernacle and everything in it, and so consecrated them. 11 He sprinkled some of the oil on the altar seven times, anointing the altar
and all its utensils and the basin with its stand, to consecrate them.
12 He poured some of the anointing oil on Aaron's head and
anointed him to consecrate him. 13 Then he brought Aaron's sons
forward, put tunics on them, tied sashes around them and put
headbands on them, as the LORD commanded Moses.
14 He then presented the bull for the sin offering, and Aaron
and his sons laid their hands on its head. 15 Moses slaughtered the
bull and took some of the blood, and with his finger he put it on
all the horns of the altar to purify the altar. He poured out the rest
of the blood at the base of the altar. So he consecrated it to make
atonement for it. 16 Moses also took all the fat around the inner
parts, the covering of the liver, and both kidneys and their fat, and
burned it on the altar. 17 But the bull with its hide and its flesh and
its offal he burned up outside the camp, as the LORD commanded
Moses.
18 He then presented the ram for the burnt offering, and
Aaron and his sons laid their hands on its head. 19 Then Moses
slaughtered the ram and sprinkled the blood against the altar on
all sides. 20 He cut the ram into pieces and burned the head, the
pieces and the fat. 21 He washed the inner parts and the legs with
water and burned the whole ram on the altar as a burnt offering,
a pleasing aroma, an offering made to the LORD by fire, as the LORD
commanded Moses.
22 He then presented the other ram, the ram for the ordination, and Aaron and his sons laid their hands on its head. 23 Moses
slaughtered the ram and took some of its blood and put it on the
lobe of Aaron's right ear, on the thumb of his right hand and on
the big toe of his right foot. 24 Moses also brought Aaron's sons forward and put some of the blood on the lobes of their right ears, on
the thumbs of their right hands and on the big toes of their right
feet. Then he sprinkled blood against the altar on all sides. 25 He
took the fat, the fat tail, all the fat around the inner parts, the covering of the liver, both kidneys and their fat and the right thigh.
26 Then from the basket of bread made without yeast, which was
before the LORD, he took a cake of bread, and one made with oil,
and a wafer; he put these on the fat portions and on the right
thigh. 27 He put all these in the hands of Aaron and his sons and
waved them before the LORD as a wave offering. 28 Then Moses took
them from their hands and burned them on the altar on top of the
burnt offering as an ordination offering, a pleasing aroma, an
offering made to the LORD by fire. 29 He also took the breast—
Moses' share of the ordination ram—and waved it before the LORD
as a wave offering, as the LORD commanded Moses.

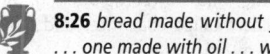

8:11,12 *sprinkled some of the oil . . . seven times:* For more about the number seven see the note at 4:5-7 and the chart called "Numbers in the Bible," p. 2405. See also the note at 6:20 (anointed).

8:15 *blood . . . poured out . . . consecrated it:* See the notes at 1:5 (blood) and 4:3. See also 4:3-7.

8:18 *burnt offering:* See the note at 1:3 (burnt offering). In the ceremony of ordination, the sin offering (8:14) was followed by a burnt offering and a grain offering (8:26).

8:23 *put it . . . Aaron's right ear . . . thumb . . . big toe:* The practice of smearing blood on persons or statues of gods was common in the ancient Near East. The words spoken during these rituals showed that the smearing was intended to protect the person or object from evil forces.

8:26 *bread made without yeast . . . one made with oil . . . wafer:* See the note at 2:4-7. This bread was made from the finest wheat flour. Olive oil was mixed into part of the dough, and some of it was made into thin wafers brushed with oil (see also Exod 29:2,3).

8:27,29 *wave offering:* See the note at 7:29.

Moses said to Aaron and his sons, *"What has been done today was commanded by the LORD to make atonement for you."* Lev 8:34

8:30 *oil . . . blood . . . sprinkled them:* See the notes at 8:7-9; 6:20 (anointed); and 1:5 (blood).

9:1 *the eighth day:* That is, after the seven-day ordination ceremony was over (Exod 29:35). The priests began their official duties by offering sacrifices for the people.

9:2 *sin offering . . . burnt offering:* See the notes at 4:3 (sin offering) and 1:3 (burnt offering), and the chart called "Sacrifices and Offerings," p. 219.

9:4 *fellowship offering . . . grain offering:* See the notes at 3:1 and 2:1 (grain offering).

9:5-7 *the Tent of Meeting . . . the altar:* Also called the tabernacle. See the note on p. 210 (tabernacle).

9:8 *sin offering for himself:* "Himself" refers to the high priest. Aaron is making this sacrifice for his own sins. Later, high priests, who were to be descendants of Aaron, would be required to make similar sacrifices. See also the notes at 4:3.

8:31-33 Exod 29:31-35. **9:7** Lev 9:2,3; Heb 7:27.

30 Then Moses took some of the anointing oil and some of the blood from the altar and sprinkled them on Aaron and his garments and on his sons and their garments. So he consecrated Aaron and his garments and his sons and their garments.

31 Moses then said to Aaron and his sons, "Cook the meat at the entrance to the Tent of Meeting and eat it there with the bread from the basket of ordination offerings, as I commanded, saying,[a] 'Aaron and his sons are to eat it.' 32 Then burn up the rest of the meat and the bread. 33 Do not leave the entrance to the Tent of Meeting for seven days, until the days of your ordination are completed, for your ordination will last seven days. 34 What has been done today was commanded by the LORD to make atonement for you. 35 You must stay at the entrance to the Tent of Meeting day and night for seven days and do what the LORD requires, so you will not die; for that is what I have been commanded." 36 So Aaron and his sons did everything the LORD commanded through Moses.

The Priests Begin Their Ministry

9 On the eighth day Moses summoned Aaron and his sons and the elders of Israel. 2 He said to Aaron, "Take a bull calf for your sin offering and a ram for your burnt offering, both without defect, and present them before the LORD. 3 Then say to the Israelites: 'Take a male goat for a sin offering, a calf and a lamb—both a year old and without defect—for a burnt offering, 4 and an ox[b] and a ram for a fellowship offering[c] to sacrifice before the LORD, together with a grain offering mixed with oil. For today the LORD will appear to you.'"

5 They took the things Moses commanded to the front of the Tent of Meeting, and the entire assembly came near and stood before the LORD. 6 Then Moses said, "This is what the LORD has commanded you to do, so that the glory of the LORD may appear to you."

7 Moses said to Aaron, "Come to the altar and sacrifice your sin offering and your burnt offering and make atonement for yourself and the people; sacrifice the offering that is for the people and make atonement for them, as the LORD has commanded."

8 So Aaron came to the altar and slaughtered the calf as a sin offering for himself. 9 His sons brought the blood to him, and he dipped his finger into the blood and put it on the horns of the altar; the rest of the blood he poured out at the base of the altar. 10 On the altar he burned the fat, the kidneys and the covering of the liver from the sin offering, as the LORD commanded Moses; 11 the flesh and the hide he burned up outside the camp.

---

[a]31 Or *I was commanded:* [b]4 The Hebrew word can include both male and female; also in verses 18 and 19. [c]4 Traditionally *peace offering;* also in verses 18 and 22

12 Then he slaughtered the burnt offering. His sons handed him the blood, and he sprinkled it against the altar on all sides. 13 They handed him the burnt offering piece by piece, including the head, and he burned them on the altar. 14 He washed the inner parts and the legs and burned them on top of the burnt offering on the altar.

15 Aaron then brought the offering that was for the people. He took the goat for the people's sin offering and slaughtered it and offered it for a sin offering as he did with the first one.

16 He brought the burnt offering and offered it in the prescribed way. 17 He also brought the grain offering, took a handful of it and burned it on the altar in addition to the morning's burnt offering.

18 He slaughtered the ox and the ram as the fellowship offering for the people. His sons handed him the blood, and he sprinkled it against the altar on all sides. 19 But the fat portions of the ox and the ram—the fat tail, the layer of fat, the kidneys and the covering of the liver— 20 these they laid on the breasts, and then Aaron burned the fat on the altar. 21 Aaron waved the breasts and the right thigh before the LORD as a wave offering, as Moses commanded.

22 Then Aaron lifted his hands toward the people and blessed them. And having sacrificed the sin offering, the burnt offering and the fellowship offering, he stepped down.

23 Moses and Aaron then went into the Tent of Meeting. When they came out, they blessed the people; and the glory of the LORD appeared to all the people. 24 Fire came out from the presence of the LORD and consumed the burnt offering and the fat portions on the altar. And when all the people saw it, they shouted for joy and fell facedown.

The Death of Nadab and Abihu

10 Aaron's sons Nadab and Abihu took their censers, put fire in them and added incense; and they offered unauthorized fire before the LORD, contrary to his command. 2 So fire came out from the presence of the LORD and consumed them, and they died before the LORD. 3 Moses then said to Aaron, "This is what the LORD spoke of when he said:

"'Among those who approach me
    I will show myself holy;
in the sight of all the people
    I will be honored.'"

Aaron remained silent.

4 Moses summoned Mishael and Elzaphan, sons of Aaron's uncle Uzziel, and said to them, "Come here; carry your cousins

9:12 *burnt offering:* See the notes at 1:3 (burnt offering) and 1:5 (blood).

9:17 *grain offering . . . morning's burnt offering:* See the note at 6:20 (morning, evening).

9:18 *fellowship offering:* See 3:1-11. See also the note at 3:1.

9:22 *blessed them:* Aaron may have used the words of blessing given at Numbers 6:22-26.

9:23,24 *the glory of the LORD . . . Fire:* Flames, fire, and smoke often signal God's presence in the Bible (Gen 15:17; Exod 3:1-6; 13:21,22; 19:16-19; Judg 13:20,21; Rev 1:12-16). The fire may have come from the Most Holy Place in the tabernacle (Exod 25:22).

10:1 *Nadab and Abihu:* They were part of a group of Israel's top leaders (Exod 6:23; 24:1-10; 28:1). NUMBERS emphasizes their deaths, which were considered even more tragic because they died without having any children (Num 3:2,4; 26:60,61; 1 Chr 6:3; 24:1,2).

10:4,5 *Mishael and Elzaphan . . . carry your cousins:* These men were Aaron's cousins, sons of his uncle Uzziel (Exod 6:22).

9:15,16 Lev 4:27-31. **10:3** Lev 21:5,6; Isa 5:16; Ezek 28:22.

outside the camp, away from the front of the sanctuary." 5 So they came and carried them, still in their tunics, outside the camp, as Moses ordered.

6 Then Moses said to Aaron and his sons Eleazar and Ithamar, "Do not let your hair become unkempt,[a] and do not tear your clothes, or you will die and the LORD will be angry with the whole community. But your relatives, all the house of Israel, may mourn for those the LORD has destroyed by fire. 7 Do not leave the entrance to the Tent of Meeting or you will die, because the LORD's anointing oil is on you." So they did as Moses said.

8 Then the LORD said to Aaron, 9 "You and your sons are not to drink wine or other fermented drink whenever you go into the Tent of Meeting, or you will die. This is a lasting ordinance for the generations to come. 10 You must distinguish between the holy and the common, between the unclean and the clean, 11 and you must teach the Israelites all the decrees the LORD has given them through Moses."

12 Moses said to Aaron and his remaining sons, Eleazar and Ithamar, "Take the grain offering left over from the offerings made to the LORD by fire and eat it prepared without yeast beside the altar, for it is most holy. 13 Eat it in a holy place, because it is your share and your sons' share of the offerings made to the LORD by fire; for so I have been commanded. 14 But you and your sons and your daughters may eat the breast that was waved and the thigh that was presented. Eat them in a ceremonially clean place; they have been given to you and your children as your share of the Israelites' fellowship offerings.[b] 15 The thigh that was presented and the breast that was waved must be brought with the fat portions of the offerings made by fire, to be waved before the LORD as a wave offering. This will be the regular share for you and your children, as the LORD has commanded."

16 When Moses inquired about the goat of the sin offering and found that it had been burned up, he was angry with Eleazar and Ithamar, Aaron's remaining sons, and asked, 17 "Why didn't you eat the sin offering in the sanctuary area? It is most holy; it was given to you to take away the guilt of the community by making atonement for them before the LORD. 18 Since its blood was not taken into the Holy Place, you should have eaten the goat in the sanctuary area, as I commanded."

19 Aaron replied to Moses, "Today they sacrificed their sin offering and their burnt offering before the LORD, but such things as this have happened to me. Would the LORD have been pleased if I had eaten the sin offering today?" 20 When Moses heard this, he was satisfied.

[a] 6 Or *Do not uncover your heads* [b] 14 Traditionally *peace offerings*

10:6,7 *Do not let your hair become unkempt, and do not tear your clothes*: These acts were done to show extreme sadness (Gen 37:29; Lev 13:45; Jonah 3:4-9), like wearing sackcloth and rubbing ashes on the body and face. But God warned Aaron and his sons not to mourn in these ways, although other relatives and the community could do so. Aaron and his other sons were not to leave the camp and join the other mourners. That would have made them ritually unclean and unfit to perform priestly duties.

10:9 *wine or other fermented drink:* The priests could not drink alcoholic beverages while on duty, because drinking too much might impair a priest's judgment, causing him to make mistakes when trying to follow the correct procedures for making a sacrifice.

10:10 *the holy and the common:* See the notes on p. 210 (holiness) and at 11:4-8.

10:12 *grain offering:* See the note at 2:1 (grain offering). See also 6:14-18.

10:14 *ceremonially clean place . . . fellowship offerings:* See the note at 7:29. The "clean place" mentioned here is the courtyard of the tabernacle (6:16).

10:17 *eat the sin offering . . . most holy:* See 6:29 and the note at 7:7-10.

10:19 *such things as this have happened to me:* Aaron was most likely referring to the death of his older sons. Aaron, Eleazar, and Ithamar burned the sin offering but did not eat any of it. Aaron explained that they were not trying to be disobedient but that they did not feel it appropriate to eat the sacrifice after the tragedy that had just occurred.

10:14,15 Lev 7:29-34. **10:18** Lev 6:26-30.

CLEANING OUT IMPURITY

These chapters give detailed instructions about how the Israelite people can be acceptable to God (ritually clean), especially after they have become unclean because of disease, bodily discharge, or by touching someone or something that is unclean.

Clean and Unclean Food

11 The LORD said to Moses and Aaron, [2]"Say to the Israelites:
'Of all the animals that live on land, these are the ones you may
eat: [3]You may eat any animal that has a split hoof completely
divided and that chews the cud.

[4]" 'There are some that only chew the cud or only have a split
hoof, but you must not eat them. The camel, though it chews the
cud, does not have a split hoof; it is ceremonially unclean for you.
[5]The coney,[a] though it chews the cud, does not have a split hoof; it
is unclean for you. [6]The rabbit, though it chews the cud, does not
have a split hoof; it is unclean for you. [7]And the pig, though it has
a split hoof completely divided, does not chew the cud; it is
unclean for you. [8]You must not eat their meat or touch their carcasses; they are unclean for you.

[9]" 'Of all the creatures living in the water of the seas and the
streams, you may eat any that have fins and scales. [10]But all creatures in the seas or streams that do not have fins and scales—
whether among all the swarming things or among all the other
living creatures in the water—you are to detest. [11]And since you
are to detest them, you must not eat their meat and you must
detest their carcasses. [12]Anything living in the water that does not
have fins and scales is to be detestable to you.

[13]" 'These are the birds you are to detest and not eat because
they are detestable: the eagle, the vulture, the black vulture, [14]the
red kite, any kind of black kite, [15]any kind of raven, [16]the horned
owl, the screech owl, the gull, any kind of hawk, [17]the little owl, the
cormorant, the great owl, [18]the white owl, the desert owl, the
osprey, [19]the stork, any kind of heron, the hoopoe and the bat.[b]

[20]" 'All flying insects that walk on all fours are to be
detestable to you. [21]There are, however, some winged creatures that
walk on all fours that you may eat: those that have jointed legs for
hopping on the ground. [22]Of these you may eat any kind of locust,
katydid, cricket or grasshopper. [23]But all other winged creatures
that have four legs you are to detest.

[24]" 'You will make yourselves unclean by these; whoever
touches their carcasses will be unclean till evening. [25]Whoever
picks up one of their carcasses must wash his clothes, and he will
be unclean till evening.

[26]" 'Every animal that has a split hoof not completely divided

---

[a]5 That is, the hyrax or rock badger [b]19 The precise identification of some of the birds, insects and animals in this chapter is uncertain.

11:3 *the cud:* Some animals that eat grass and leaves have more than one stomach and chew their food a second time after it has been partly digested in the first stomach. This partially digested food is called the "cud."

11:4-8 *unclean:* Animals that "chew the cud" are cattle, sheep, and goats. They eat mostly grass and other plants. Pigs, which do not "chew the cud," eat a wide variety of things, including carrion. This may be one reason they were considered unclean. See also Deut 14:4-21 and the mini-article called "Purity (Clean and Unclean)," p. 2125.

11:9-12 *creatures living in the water of the seas and the streams:* Fish with scales were clean, but other water creatures like eels were considered unclean.

11:24-28 *animals:* These animals include pigs (see the note at 11:4-8), cats, dogs, and other four-footed animals with paws.

"I am the LORD your God; consecrate yourselves and be holy, because I am holy."
Lev 11:44

11:32,33 *unclean . . . wood, cloth, hide or sackcloth . . . clay:* Unclean things could also transfer their impurity to other objects. Most things could be washed to remove the impurity, but clay pots had to be broken, since the porous clay soaked up the impurity. If they weren't broken, anything that was put in the pot would become unclean, as would anyone who ate something from an unclean pot. See also 6:27,28.

11:35,36 *oven or cooking pot . . . spring . . . cistern:* Many cooking ovens and pots were made from clay and would be considered unclean. Water sources that came out of the ground, however, were not made unclean by the body of a dead animal.

11:44,45 *holy . . . brought you up out of Egypt:* God chose the Israelite people, the descendants of Abraham (Gen 12:1-3), to be a great nation. Later, God led them out of slavery in Egypt (Exod 12–15) and gave the Law to Moses and the people at Mount Sinai (Exod 19–40). The Law included rules about what was clean and unclean. Because God chose the people of Israel and gave them laws, Israel was set apart from their neighbors who worshiped other gods and did not follow the same laws of purity. "Be holy" was a command, but a command based on the fact that God had chosen the people of Israel and had overwhelming love for them. See also the mini-article called "Holiness," p. 1626.

11:41,42 Lev 11:20-23,29,30.
11:44 Lev 19:2; 1 Pet 1:16.

or that does not chew the cud is unclean for you; whoever touches ⌞the carcass of⌟ any of them will be unclean. 27Of all the animals that walk on all fours, those that walk on their paws are unclean for you; whoever touches their carcasses will be unclean till evening. 28Anyone who picks up their carcasses must wash his clothes, and he will be unclean till evening. They are unclean for you.

29" 'Of the animals that move about on the ground, these are unclean for you: the weasel, the rat, any kind of great lizard, 30the gecko, the monitor lizard, the wall lizard, the skink and the chameleon. 31Of all those that move along the ground, these are unclean for you. Whoever touches them when they are dead will be unclean till evening. 32When one of them dies and falls on something, that article, whatever its use, will be unclean, whether it is made of wood, cloth, hide or sackcloth. Put it in water; it will be unclean till evening, and then it will be clean. 33If one of them falls into a clay pot, everything in it will be unclean, and you must break the pot. 34Any food that could be eaten but has water on it from such a pot is unclean, and any liquid that could be drunk from it is unclean. 35Anything that one of their carcasses falls on becomes unclean; an oven or cooking pot must be broken up. They are unclean, and you are to regard them as unclean. 36A spring, however, or a cistern for collecting water remains clean, but anyone who touches one of these carcasses is unclean. 37If a carcass falls on any seeds that are to be planted, they remain clean. 38But if water has been put on the seed and a carcass falls on it, it is unclean for you.

39" 'If an animal that you are allowed to eat dies, anyone who touches the carcass will be unclean till evening. 40Anyone who eats some of the carcass must wash his clothes, and he will be unclean till evening. Anyone who picks up the carcass must wash his clothes, and he will be unclean till evening.

41" 'Every creature that moves about on the ground is detestable; it is not to be eaten. 42You are not to eat any creature that moves about on the ground, whether it moves on its belly or walks on all fours or on many feet; it is detestable. 43Do not defile yourselves by any of these creatures. Do not make yourselves unclean by means of them or be made unclean by them. 44I am the LORD your God; consecrate yourselves and be holy, because I am holy. Do not make yourselves unclean by any creature that moves about on the ground. 45I am the LORD who brought you up out of Egypt to be your God; therefore be holy, because I am holy.

46" 'These are the regulations concerning animals, birds, every living thing that moves in the water and every creature that moves about on the ground. 47You must distinguish between the unclean and the clean, between living creatures that may be eaten and those that may not be eaten.' "

Purification After Childbirth

12 The LORD said to Moses, 2“Say to the Israelites: ‘A woman
who becomes pregnant and gives birth to a son will be ceremonially unclean for seven days, just as she is unclean during her
monthly period. 3On the eighth day the boy is to be circumcised.
4Then the woman must wait thirty-three days to be purified from
her bleeding. She must not touch anything sacred or go to the
sanctuary until the days of her purification are over. 5If she gives
birth to a daughter, for two weeks the woman will be unclean, as
during her period. Then she must wait sixty-six days to be purified
from her bleeding.

6“ ‘When the days of her purification for a son or daughter
are over, she is to bring to the priest at the entrance to the Tent of
Meeting a year-old lamb for a burnt offering and a young pigeon
or a dove for a sin offering. 7He shall offer them before the LORD to
make atonement for her, and then she will be ceremonially clean
from her flow of blood.

“ ‘These are the regulations for the woman who gives birth to
a boy or a girl. 8If she cannot afford a lamb, she is to bring two
doves or two young pigeons, one for a burnt offering and the other
for a sin offering. In this way the priest will make atonement for
her, and she will be clean.’ ”

Regulations About Infectious Skin Diseases

13 The LORD said to Moses and Aaron, 2“When anyone has a
swelling or a rash or a bright spot on his skin that may become an
infectious skin disease,[a] he must be brought to Aaron the priest or
to one of his sons[b] who is a priest. 3The priest is to examine the sore
on his skin, and if the hair in the sore has turned white and the sore
appears to be more than skin deep,[c] it is an infectious skin disease.
When the priest examines him, he shall pronounce him ceremonially unclean. 4If the spot on his skin is white but does not appear to
be more than skin deep and the hair in it has not turned white, the
priest is to put the infected person in isolation for seven days. 5On
the seventh day the priest is to examine him, and if he sees that the
sore is unchanged and has not spread in the skin, he is to keep him
in isolation another seven days. 6On the seventh day the priest is to
examine him again, and if the sore has faded and has not spread in
the skin, the priest shall pronounce him clean; it is only a rash. The
man must wash his clothes, and he will be clean. 7But if the rash
does spread in his skin after he has shown himself to the priest to
be pronounced clean, he must appear before the priest again. 8The
priest is to examine him, and if the rash has spread in the skin, he
shall pronounce him unclean; it is an infectious disease.

[a]2 Traditionally *leprosy*; the Hebrew word was used for various diseases affecting the skin—not necessarily leprosy; also elsewhere in this chapter. [b]2 Or *descendants* [c]3 Or *be lower than the rest of the skin*; also elsewhere in this chapter

12:2 *woman . . . son . . . ceremonially unclean for seven days:* A woman was considered ritually unclean for seven days because of the flow of blood connected with childbirth (see the note at 1:5, blood). On the eighth day a baby boy was to be circumcised. (See the mini-article called “Circumcision,” p. 2251.) God commanded circumcision as a physical sign that Abraham’s descendants were God’s chosen people (Gen 17:11-13). See also Luke 2:21.

12:5 *daughter . . . woman . . . sixty-six days:* The reason for the longer period of uncleanness is not clear.

12:6 *days of her purification for a son or daughter . . . burnt offering . . . sin offering:* The time periods mentioned in 12:2,5 were considered necessary to remove the ritual impurity connected to the women’s post-delivery blood flow. Then she must bring a burnt offering (see the note at 1:3, burnt offering) and a sin offering (see the note at 4:3, sin offering), which is really a purification offering that allows her to go to the place of worship once again. See also Luke 2:24.

13:3 *infectious skin disease:* Many different kinds of skin diseases, such as vitiligo, psoriasis, and scale disease, are traditionally called “leprosy.” The strict rules about what was clean and unclean helped to stop the spread of infectious skin diseases. Some kinds of skin disease were very serious and contagious, but some other skin diseases and burns were not contagious. See also Num 5:2-4; Deut 24:8,9.

13:8 *if the rash has spread . . . unclean:* Nonspreading sores were not considered unclean.

Priest Examining People for Leprosy, eighteenth century woodcut. The Hebrew word for "leprosy" can refer to any number of skin diseases, not just to the medical condition called leprosy today. The various symptoms that people experienced are catalogued in Leviticus 13 and 14. It was one of the duties of the priests to examine people to determine who had leprosy and who didn't. People who did were considered ritually unclean and had to live apart from the rest of the community. They could only live among the people again when the priest said they were healed and when the proper sacrifices had been made.

13:18,19 *boil . . . swelling:* This probably refers to boils or other skin swelling due to infections.

9"When anyone has an infectious skin disease, he must be
brought to the priest. 10The priest is to examine him, and if there
is a white swelling in the skin that has turned the hair white and if
there is raw flesh in the swelling, 11it is a chronic skin disease and
the priest shall pronounce him unclean. He is not to put him in
isolation, because he is already unclean.

12"If the disease breaks out all over his skin and, so far as the
priest can see, it covers all the skin of the infected person from
head to foot, 13the priest is to examine him, and if the disease has
covered his whole body, he shall pronounce that person clean.
Since it has all turned white, he is clean. 14But whenever raw flesh
appears on him, he will be unclean. 15When the priest sees the raw
flesh, he shall pronounce him unclean. The raw flesh is unclean;
he has an infectious disease. 16Should the raw flesh change and
turn white, he must go to the priest. 17The priest is to examine
him, and if the sores have turned white, the priest shall pronounce
the infected person clean; then he will be clean.

18"When someone has a boil on his skin and it heals, 19and in
the place where the boil was, a white swelling or reddish-white

spot appears, he must present himself to the priest. [20]The priest is
to examine it, and if it appears to be more than skin deep and the
hair in it has turned white, the priest shall pronounce him
unclean. It is an infectious skin disease that has broken out where
the boil was. [21]But if, when the priest examines it, there is no white
hair in it and it is not more than skin deep and has faded, then the
priest is to put him in isolation for seven days. [22]If it is spreading
in the skin, the priest shall pronounce him unclean; it is infectious.
[23]But if the spot is unchanged and has not spread, it is only a scar
from the boil, and the priest shall pronounce him clean.

[24]"When someone has a burn on his skin and a reddish-
white or white spot appears in the raw flesh of the burn, [25]the
priest is to examine the spot, and if the hair in it has turned white,
and it appears to be more than skin deep, it is an infectious disease that has broken out in the burn. The priest shall pronounce
him unclean; it is an infectious skin disease. [26]But if the priest
examines it and there is no white hair in the spot and if it is not
more than skin deep and has faded, then the priest is to put him in
isolation for seven days. [27]On the seventh day the priest is to examine him, and if it is spreading in the skin, the priest shall pronounce him unclean; it is an infectious skin disease. [28]If, however,
the spot is unchanged and has not spread in the skin but has
faded, it is a swelling from the burn, and the priest shall pronounce him clean; it is only a scar from the burn.

[29]"If a man or woman has a sore on the head or on the chin,
[30]the priest is to examine the sore, and if it appears to be more
than skin deep and the hair in it is yellow and thin, the priest shall
pronounce that person unclean; it is an itch, an infectious disease
of the head or chin. [31]But if, when the priest examines this kind of
sore, it does not seem to be more than skin deep and there is no
black hair in it, then the priest is to put the infected person in isolation for seven days. [32]On the seventh day the priest is to examine
the sore, and if the itch has not spread and there is no yellow hair
in it and it does not appear to be more than skin deep, [33]he must
be shaved except for the diseased area, and the priest is to keep him
in isolation another seven days. [34]On the seventh day the priest is
to examine the itch, and if it has not spread in the skin and
appears to be no more than skin deep, the priest shall pronounce
him clean. He must wash his clothes, and he will be clean. [35]But if
the itch does spread in the skin after he is pronounced clean, [36]the
priest is to examine him, and if the itch has spread in the skin, the
priest does not need to look for yellow hair; the person is unclean.
[37]If, however, in his judgment it is unchanged and black hair has
grown in it, the itch is healed. He is clean, and the priest shall pronounce him clean.

[38]"When a man or woman has white spots on the skin, [39]the
priest is to examine them, and if the spots are dull white, it is a
harmless rash that has broken out on the skin; that person is clean.

13:25 *the spot . . . broken out in the burn:* Burns don't turn to skin disease, but burns that become infected were considered leprous and unclean. See also the note at 13:3.

13:29 *sore on the head . . . chin:* Persons with diseases or sores on the head that were only skin deep and didn't spread would be declared clean after seven days (13:33). Normal baldness didn't make one unclean, but sores that broke out on the bald spot could be called unclean.

13:45 *wear torn clothes . . . hair be unkempt:* Tearing the clothes was done as a sign of mourning. See the note at 10:6,7.

13:47-52 *clothing is contaminated with mildew . . . unclean:* Mildew caused clothing or leather to be unclean. Those who wore clothes with mildew would be considered ritually unclean. If mildew spread on leather or a garment, the garment was to be destroyed. The Hebrew word for "dreaded skin disease" and "mildew" is the same.

14:2 *diseased person:* See the note at 13:3. A person who had recovered from a dreaded skin disease needed to show himself to the priest so that the priest could confirm that the person was healed. If so, the healed person could make the prescribed sacrifice and rejoin the Israelite community. Jesus was aware of this practice and insisted that the people with skin disease he healed show themselves to a priest. See Matt 8:4; Mark 1:44; Luke 5:14; 17:14.

[40]"When a man has lost his hair and is bald, he is clean. [41]If he has lost his hair from the front of his scalp and has a bald forehead, he is clean. [42]But if he has a reddish-white sore on his bald head or forehead, it is an infectious disease breaking out on his head or forehead. [43]The priest is to examine him, and if the swollen sore on his head or forehead is reddish-white like an infectious skin disease, [44]the man is diseased and is unclean. The priest shall pronounce him unclean because of the sore on his head.

[45]"The person with such an infectious disease must wear torn clothes, let his hair be unkempt,[a] cover the lower part of his face and cry out, 'Unclean! Unclean!' [46]As long as he has the infection he remains unclean. He must live alone; he must live outside the camp.

Regulations About Mildew

[47]"If any clothing is contaminated with mildew—any woolen or linen clothing, [48]any woven or knitted material of linen or wool, any leather or anything made of leather— [49]and if the contamination in the clothing, or leather, or woven or knitted material, or any leather article, is greenish or reddish, it is a spreading mildew and must be shown to the priest. [50]The priest is to examine the mildew and isolate the affected article for seven days. [51]On the seventh day he is to examine it, and if the mildew has spread in the clothing, or the woven or knitted material, or the leather, whatever its use, it is a destructive mildew; the article is unclean. [52]He must burn up the clothing, or the woven or knitted material of wool or linen, or any leather article that has the contamination in it, because the mildew is destructive; the article must be burned up.

[53]"But if, when the priest examines it, the mildew has not spread in the clothing, or the woven or knitted material, or the leather article, [54]he shall order that the contaminated article be washed. Then he is to isolate it for another seven days. [55]After the affected article has been washed, the priest is to examine it, and if the mildew has not changed its appearance, even though it has not spread, it is unclean. Burn it with fire, whether the mildew has affected one side or the other. [56]If, when the priest examines it, the mildew has faded after the article has been washed, he is to tear the contaminated part out of the clothing, or the leather, or the woven or knitted material. [57]But if it reappears in the clothing, or in the woven or knitted material, or in the leather article, it is spreading, and whatever has the mildew must be burned with fire. [58]The clothing, or the woven or knitted material, or any leather article that has been washed and is rid of the mildew, must be washed again, and it will be clean."

[a]**45** Or *clothes, uncover his head*

59These are the regulations concerning contamination by
mildew in woolen or linen clothing, woven or knitted material, or
any leather article, for pronouncing them clean or unclean.

Cleansing From Infectious Skin Diseases

14 The LORD said to Moses, 2"These are the regulations for the
diseased person at the time of his ceremonial cleansing, when he is
brought to the priest: 3The priest is to go outside the camp and
examine him. If the person has been healed of his infectious skin
disease,[a] 4the priest shall order that two live clean birds and some
cedar wood, scarlet yarn and hyssop be brought for the one to be
cleansed. 5Then the priest shall order that one of the birds be killed
over fresh water in a clay pot. 6He is then to take the live bird and
dip it, together with the cedar wood, the scarlet yarn and the hyssop, into the blood of the bird that was killed over the fresh water.
7Seven times he shall sprinkle the one to be cleansed of the infectious disease and pronounce him clean. Then he is to release the
live bird in the open fields.

8"The person to be cleansed must wash his clothes, shave off
all his hair and bathe with water; then he will be ceremonially
clean. After this he may come into the camp, but he must stay outside his tent for seven days. 9On the seventh day he must shave off
all his hair; he must shave his head, his beard, his eyebrows and the
rest of his hair. He must wash his clothes and bathe himself with
water, and he will be clean.

10"On the eighth day he must bring two male lambs and one
ewe lamb a year old, each without defect, along with three-tenths
of an ephah[b] of fine flour mixed with oil for a grain offering, and
one log[c] of oil. 11The priest who pronounces him clean shall present both the one to be cleansed and his offerings before the LORD
at the entrance to the Tent of Meeting.

12"Then the priest is to take one of the male lambs and offer
it as a guilt offering, along with the log of oil; he shall wave them
before the LORD as a wave offering. 13He is to slaughter the lamb in
the holy place where the sin offering and the burnt offering are
slaughtered. Like the sin offering, the guilt offering belongs to the
priest; it is most holy. 14The priest is to take some of the blood of
the guilt offering and put it on the lobe of the right ear of the one
to be cleansed, on the thumb of his right hand and on the big toe
of his right foot. 15The priest shall then take some of the log of oil,
pour it in the palm of his own left hand, 16dip his right forefinger
into the oil in his palm, and with his finger sprinkle some of it
before the LORD seven times. 17The priest is to put some of the oil

[a]3 Traditionally *leprosy*; the Hebrew word was used for various diseases affecting the skin—not necessarily leprosy; also elsewhere in this chapter. [b]10 That is, probably about 6 quarts (about 6.5 liters) [c]10 That is, probably about 2/3 pint (about 0.3 liter); also in verses 12, 15, 21 and 24

14:2-7 *ceremonial cleansing:* The cedar wood is probably chosen because of its reddish color. The reddish wood and the scarlet yarn are the color of life or blood. The hyssop plant's hairy stalk and leaves held liquids well, so it was often used as brush or sprinkler in religious rituals (Exod 12:22; Num 19:6,17,18; Heb 9:19). See the note at 4:5-7. These objects, as well as the live bird, were dipped into the blood of the bird the priest had killed. The objects may have been thought to transfer the person's uncleanness to the blood, which had the power to purify. The live bird then flew away carrying the impurity with it.

14:8 *wash . . . shave:* After washing and shaving twice, washing his clothes and staying out of his tent for seven days, a person was considered clean and could once again be part of his family and the whole people of God.

14:12 *guilt offering . . . wave offering:* See the notes at 5:16 and 7:1. Part of this sacrifice was to be presented as a special gift to the LORD (see the note at 7:29). This sacrifice was done in case the unclean person had touched a sacred object or entered a holy space while unclean. Like other kinds of sacrifices, this was to be done at the entrance to the tabernacle (see 1:1-3; 4:4). For more about the tabernacle (also called the Tent of Meeting), see the note on p. 210.

14:14-16 *blood . . . sprinkle . . . seven times:* See the notes at 1:5 (blood); 8:23; and 4:5-7.

14:17 *oil:* See the notes at 2:1 (oil) and 6:20 (anointed).

14:19 *sin offering ... burnt offering:* See the notes at 4:3 (sin offering) and 1:3 (burnt offering).

14:21 *poor and cannot afford these:* The Law includes a number of instructions on how the Israelites were to treat the poor. See also the note at 25:35.

14:21 *a guilt offering to be waved:* See the notes at 7:11 and 7:29.

14:34,35 *Canaan:* Canaan was the land God promised to give Abraham and his descendants (Gen 17:7,8; Exod 3:8). See the map on p. 2464 and the mini-article called "Palestine," p. 410.

14:34,35 *mildew:* See the note at 13:47-52.

14:23-31 Lev 14:10-20.

remaining in his palm on the lobe of the right ear of the one to be
cleansed, on the thumb of his right hand and on the big toe of his
right foot, on top of the blood of the guilt offering. 18The rest of
the oil in his palm the priest shall put on the head of the one to be
cleansed and make atonement for him before the LORD.

19"Then the priest is to sacrifice the sin offering and make
atonement for the one to be cleansed from his uncleanness. After
that, the priest shall slaughter the burnt offering 20and offer it on
the altar, together with the grain offering, and make atonement for
him, and he will be clean.

21"If, however, he is poor and cannot afford these, he must
take one male lamb as a guilt offering to be waved to make atonement for him, together with a tenth of an ephah[a] of fine flour
mixed with oil for a grain offering, a log of oil, 22and two doves or
two young pigeons, which he can afford, one for a sin offering and
the other for a burnt offering.

23"On the eighth day he must bring them for his cleansing to
the priest at the entrance to the Tent of Meeting, before the LORD.
24The priest is to take the lamb for the guilt offering, together with
the log of oil, and wave them before the LORD as a wave offering. 25He
shall slaughter the lamb for the guilt offering and take some of its
blood and put it on the lobe of the right ear of the one to be cleansed,
on the thumb of his right hand and on the big toe of his right foot.
26The priest is to pour some of the oil into the palm of his own left
hand, 27and with his right forefinger sprinkle some of the oil from his
palm seven times before the LORD. 28Some of the oil in his palm he is
to put on the same places he put the blood of the guilt offering—on
the lobe of the right ear of the one to be cleansed, on the thumb of
his right hand and on the big toe of his right foot. 29The rest of the
oil in his palm the priest shall put on the head of the one to be
cleansed, to make atonement for him before the LORD. 30Then he
shall sacrifice the doves or the young pigeons, which the person can
afford, 31one[b] as a sin offering and the other as a burnt offering,
together with the grain offering. In this way the priest will make
atonement before the LORD on behalf of the one to be cleansed."

32These are the regulations for anyone who has an infectious
skin disease and who cannot afford the regular offerings for his
cleansing.

Cleansing From Mildew

33The LORD said to Moses and Aaron, 34"When you enter the
land of Canaan, which I am giving you as your possession, and I
put a spreading mildew in a house in that land, 35the owner of the
house must go and tell the priest, 'I have seen something that looks
like mildew in my house.' 36The priest is to order the house to be

---

[a]**21** That is, probably about 2 quarts (about 2 liters) [b]**31** Septuagint and Syriac; Hebrew *31such as the person can afford, one*

emptied before he goes in to examine the mildew, so that nothing in the house will be pronounced unclean. After this the priest is to go in and inspect the house. 37He is to examine the mildew on the walls, and if it has greenish or reddish depressions that appear to be deeper than the surface of the wall, 38the priest shall go out the doorway of the house and close it up for seven days. 39On the seventh day the priest shall return to inspect the house. If the mildew has spread on the walls, 40he is to order that the contaminated stones be torn out and thrown into an unclean place outside the town. 41He must have all the inside walls of the house scraped and the material that is scraped off dumped into an unclean place outside the town. 42Then they are to take other stones to replace these and take new clay and plaster the house.

43"If the mildew reappears in the house after the stones have been torn out and the house scraped and plastered, 44the priest is to go and examine it and, if the mildew has spread in the house, it is a destructive mildew; the house is unclean. 45It must be torn down—its stones, timbers and all the plaster—and taken out of the town to an unclean place.

46"Anyone who goes into the house while it is closed up will be unclean till evening. 47Anyone who sleeps or eats in the house must wash his clothes.

48"But if the priest comes to examine it and the mildew has not spread after the house has been plastered, he shall pronounce the house clean, because the mildew is gone. 49To purify the house he is to take two birds and some cedar wood, scarlet yarn and hyssop. 50He shall kill one of the birds over fresh water in a clay pot. 51Then he is to take the cedar wood, the hyssop, the scarlet yarn and the live bird, dip them into the blood of the dead bird and the fresh water, and sprinkle the house seven times. 52He shall purify the house with the bird's blood, the fresh water, the live bird, the cedar wood, the hyssop and the scarlet yarn. 53Then he is to release the live bird in the open fields outside the town. In this way he will make atonement for the house, and it will be clean."

54These are the regulations for any infectious skin disease, for an itch, 55for mildew in clothing or in a house, 56and for a swelling, a rash or a bright spot, 57to determine when something is clean or unclean.

These are the regulations for infectious skin diseases and mildew.

Discharges Causing Uncleanness

15 The LORD said to Moses and Aaron, 2"Speak to the Israelites and say to them: 'When any man has a bodily discharge, the discharge is unclean. 3Whether it continues flowing from his body or is blocked, it will make him unclean. This is how his discharge will bring about uncleanness:

4"'Any bed the man with a discharge lies on will be unclean, and anything he sits on will be unclean. 5Anyone who touches his

14:40 *unclean place outside the town:* This probably refers to a dumping area for garbage and other unclean items.

14:45-47 *torn down . . . wash his clothes:* If mildew reappeared in the house, the whole building was to be destroyed and taken away from the camp or city. Anyone who entered a diseased house was considered unclean and had to wash to purify himself.

14:49-53 *purify the house:* See the note at 14:2-7.

15:2,3 *bodily discharge . . . unclean:* Fluids that came from infections or sexual diseases were unclean. Anything an infected man rested on or sat on also became unclean, as did a person who touched the man or his clothes, or who was touched by the man before he had washed his hands.

The LORD said to Moses and Aaron, *"You must keep the Israelites separate from things that make them unclean, so they will not die in their uncleanness for defiling my dwelling place, which is among them."* Lev 15:31

15:12 *clay pot:* See the note at 6:27,28.

15:13-15 *seven days . . . wash . . . sin offering . . . burnt offering:* See the note at 4:5-7. Washing clothes and bathing in fresh spring water were done and sacrifices were offered in order for the man to be declared clean. See the notes at 4:3 (sin offering) and 1:3 (burnt offering).

15:16 *emission of semen:* The natural flow of semen caused a man to be unclean for a day. Intercourse made both a man and the woman he slept with unclean for a day. Like blood, semen was considered sacred, since it carried the "seed" of life.

15:19 *woman has her regular flow of blood:* See the note at 12:2. The woman could stay at home and carry on her duties, but family members were to avoid touching anything she rested on or sat on to avoid becoming unclean as well.

bed must wash his clothes and bathe with water, and he will be
unclean till evening. 6Whoever sits on anything that the man with
a discharge sat on must wash his clothes and bathe with water, and
he will be unclean till evening.

7" 'Whoever touches the man who has a discharge must wash
his clothes and bathe with water, and he will be unclean till
evening.

8" 'If the man with the discharge spits on someone who is
clean, that person must wash his clothes and bathe with water, and
he will be unclean till evening.

9" 'Everything the man sits on when riding will be unclean,
10and whoever touches any of the things that were under him will
be unclean till evening; whoever picks up those things must wash
his clothes and bathe with water, and he will be unclean till
evening.

11" 'Anyone the man with a discharge touches without rins-
ing his hands with water must wash his clothes and bathe with
water, and he will be unclean till evening.

12" 'A clay pot that the man touches must be broken, and any
wooden article is to be rinsed with water.

13" 'When a man is cleansed from his discharge, he is to
count off seven days for his ceremonial cleansing; he must wash
his clothes and bathe himself with fresh water, and he will be
clean. 14On the eighth day he must take two doves or two young
pigeons and come before the LORD to the entrance to the Tent of
Meeting and give them to the priest. 15The priest is to sacrifice
them, the one for a sin offering and the other for a burnt offering.
In this way he will make atonement before the LORD for the man
because of his discharge.

16" 'When a man has an emission of semen, he must bathe
his whole body with water, and he will be unclean till evening.
17Any clothing or leather that has semen on it must be washed
with water, and it will be unclean till evening. 18When a man lies
with a woman and there is an emission of semen, both must bathe
with water, and they will be unclean till evening.

19" 'When a woman has her regular flow of blood, the impurity of her monthly period will last seven days, and anyone who
touches her will be unclean till evening.

20" 'Anything she lies on during her period will be unclean,
and anything she sits on will be unclean. 21Whoever touches her
bed must wash his clothes and bathe with water, and he will be
unclean till evening. 22Whoever touches anything she sits on must
wash his clothes and bathe with water, and he will be unclean till
evening. 23Whether it is the bed or anything she was sitting on,
when anyone touches it, he will be unclean till evening.

24" 'If a man lies with her and her monthly flow touches him,
he will be unclean for seven days; any bed he lies on will be
unclean.

[25]"'When a woman has a discharge of blood for many days
at a time other than her monthly period or has a discharge that
continues beyond her period, she will be unclean as long as she has
the discharge, just as in the days of her period. [26]Any bed she lies
on while her discharge continues will be unclean, as is her bed
during her monthly period, and anything she sits on will be
unclean, as during her period. [27]Whoever touches them will be
unclean; he must wash his clothes and bathe with water, and he
will be unclean till evening.
[28]"'When she is cleansed from her discharge, she must count
off seven days, and after that she will be ceremonially clean. [29]On
the eighth day she must take two doves or two young pigeons and
bring them to the priest at the entrance to the Tent of Meeting.
[30]The priest is to sacrifice one for a sin offering and the other for a
burnt offering. In this way he will make atonement for her before
the LORD for the uncleanness of her discharge.
[31]"'You must keep the Israelites separate from things that
make them unclean, so they will not die in their uncleanness for
defiling my dwelling place,[a] which is among them.'"
[32]These are the regulations for a man with a discharge, for
anyone made unclean by an emission of semen, [33]for a woman in
her monthly period, for a man or a woman with a discharge, and
for a man who lies with a woman who is ceremonially unclean.

The Day of Atonement

16 The LORD spoke to Moses after the death of the two sons of
Aaron who died when they approached the LORD. [2]The LORD said
to Moses: "Tell your brother Aaron not to come whenever he
chooses into the Most Holy Place behind the curtain in front of
the atonement cover on the ark, or else he will die, because I
appear in the cloud over the atonement cover.
[3]"This is how Aaron is to enter the sanctuary area: with a
young bull for a sin offering and a ram for a burnt offering. [4]He is to
put on the sacred linen tunic, with linen undergarments next to his
body; he is to tie the linen sash around him and put on the linen turban. These are sacred garments; so he must bathe himself with water
before he puts them on. [5]From the Israelite community he is to take
two male goats for a sin offering and a ram for a burnt offering.
[6]"Aaron is to offer the bull for his own sin offering to make
atonement for himself and his household. [7]Then he is to take the
two goats and present them before the LORD at the entrance to the
Tent of Meeting. [8]He is to cast lots for the two goats—one lot for
the LORD and the other for the scapegoat.[b] [9]Aaron shall bring the
goat whose lot falls to the LORD and sacrifice it for a sin offering.

[a]**31** Or *my tabernacle* [b]**8** That is, the goat of removal; Hebrew *azazel*; also in verses 10 and 26

15:28-30 *seven days . . . offering:* Seven days after her monthly period stopped, a woman was to bring a sin offering (see the note at 4:3) and a burnt offering (see the note at 1:3). Then she would be considered clean again.

15:31 *defiling my dwelling place:* People who were unclean were to stay away from the rest of the community and the tabernacle so that they would not defile the people or the place of worship. That meant that a woman had to spend a significant part of each month at home and not go near the place of worship.

16:2 *cloud over the atonement cover:* In the Bible, the LORD's appearance is sometimes related to fire or a cloud of smoke (see the note at 9:23,24). On the lid of the ark of the covenant (also called the ark of the Testimony) was the atonement cover or "place of mercy," where God sat and judged the people with overwhelming kindness and told them what they must do (Exod 25:22). The ark of the covenant was seen as the royal throne where God ruled (1 Sam 4:4; 2 Sam 6:2; Ps 99:1). See the mini-article called "The Ark of the Covenant," on p. 513. The ark was kept in the Most Holy Place of the tabernacle (Exod 26:31-35).

16:3 *sanctuary area . . . offering:* See the note at 16:2 and the article called "People of the Law: The Religion of Israel," p. 939. See also Heb 9:7.

16:4 *sacred garments:* See the note at 8:7-9.

16:7,8 *goats . . . scapegoat:* On the Day of Atonement two goats were to be offered for the people's sins (compare this to 4:13-15, which says a bull is to be offered for the whole community of Israel). One goat was killed and sacrificed, and the other (called the scapegoat) was sent away into the desert. See also the chart called "Jewish Calendar and Festivals," p. 944.

16:1 Lev 10:1,2. **16:2** Heb 6:19. **16:6** Lev 4:3.

The Day of Atonement by Jacob Kramer, 1919. The Day of Atonement *(Yom Kippur)* continues to be one of the holiest days in the Jewish calendar. On this day the high priest of Israel sacrificed a bull for his sins and a goat for the sins of the people. The blood from these animals was used to purify the tabernacle, the bronze altar, the people, and the Most Holy Place. On this holy day, the people were to go without eating and to show sorrow for their sins. (See chapter 16.)

10But the goat chosen by lot as the scapegoat shall be presented
alive before the LORD to be used for making atonement by sending
it into the desert as a scapegoat.
11"Aaron shall bring the bull for his own sin offering to make
atonement for himself and his household, and he is to slaughter
the bull for his own sin offering. 12He is to take a censer full of
burning coals from the altar before the LORD and two handfuls of
finely ground fragrant incense and take them behind the curtain.
13He is to put the incense on the fire before the LORD, and the
smoke of the incense will conceal the atonement cover above the
Testimony, so that he will not die. 14He is to take some of the bull's
blood and with his finger sprinkle it on the front of the atonement
cover; then he shall sprinkle some of it with his finger seven times
before the atonement cover.
15"He shall then slaughter the goat for the sin offering for the
people and take its blood behind the curtain and do with it as he
did with the bull's blood: He shall sprinkle it on the atonement
cover and in front of it. 16In this way he will make atonement for
the Most Holy Place because of the uncleanness and rebellion of
the Israelites, whatever their sins have been. He is to do the same
for the Tent of Meeting, which is among them in the midst of their
uncleanness. 17No one is to be in the Tent of Meeting from the
time Aaron goes in to make atonement in the Most Holy Place

16:12 *censer . . . altar . . . incense:* The censer (also called a firepan) was made of bronze and was used at the altar of sacrifice (Exod 27:1-3). See the note on p. 210 (tabernacle).

16:13 *atonement cover above the Testimony:* See the note at 16:2. The smoke from the burning incense was to cover God's presence on the place of mercy (atonement cover) and protect the high priest who came into God's presence.

16:14 *blood . . . sprinkle it:* The blood sprinkled seven times in front of the ark of the covenant was from the bull (16:11). Then Aaron sprinkled blood from the goat inside the Most Holy Place, in order to take away the sins of the people (16:15). See the notes at 1:5 (blood) and 4:5-7. See also Heb 9:12.

until he comes out, having made atonement for himself, his household and the whole community of Israel.

[18]"Then he shall come out to the altar that is before the LORD and make atonement for it. He shall take some of the bull's blood and some of the goat's blood and put it on all the horns of the altar. [19]He shall sprinkle some of the blood on it with his finger seven times to cleanse it and to consecrate it from the uncleanness of the Israelites.

[20]"When Aaron has finished making atonement for the Most Holy Place, the Tent of Meeting and the altar, he shall bring forward the live goat. [21]He is to lay both hands on the head of the live goat and confess over it all the wickedness and rebellion of the Israelites—all their sins—and put them on the goat's head. He shall send the goat away into the desert in the care of a man appointed for the task. [22]The goat will carry on itself all their sins to a solitary place; and the man shall release it in the desert.

[23]"Then Aaron is to go into the Tent of Meeting and take off the linen garments he put on before he entered the Most Holy Place, and he is to leave them there. [24]He shall bathe himself with water in a holy place and put on his regular garments. Then he shall come out and sacrifice the burnt offering for himself and the burnt offering for the people, to make atonement for himself and for the people. [25]He shall also burn the fat of the sin offering on the altar.

[26]"The man who releases the goat as a scapegoat must wash his clothes and bathe himself with water; afterward he may come into the camp. [27]The bull and the goat for the sin offerings, whose

16:21 *lay both hands on . . . confess:* See the note at 1:4 (lay his hand on). The confession of sins along with the laying of hands transferred the sins of the Israelites to the goat. The goat that was driven off into the desert is called the "scapegoat" (16:10)

16:23 *linen garments:* The garments the high priest had worn in the Most Holy Place were left behind, because they had been in the presence of God.

16:18 Lev 4:25. **16:23,24** Ezek 44:19.

QUESTIONS ABOUT LEVITICUS 1:1—16:34

1. The LORD gave Moses instructions for five different types of sacrifices. What was the purpose of each kind of sacrifice? Who was assigned the task of making these sacrifices? (chapters 1–5)
2. How did the laws of sacrifice help define the relationship between God and the Israelite people?
3. What was the significance and power of blood in the sacrifices? (1:5; 4:5-7) What was the meaning of the oil used in sacrifices and in the ordination of the priests? (6:20; 8:10,11)
4. Describe some of the reasons the sin offerings were to be made (4:1—5:13). For what reasons did people have to bring a guilt offering or payment to makes things right? (5:14—6:7) When you think of "making things right" in society today, what comes to mind?
5. What does it mean to be "holy"? What do the laws of sacrifice and cleanness have to do with being holy? Read Leviticus 11:44,45. How is it possible to live up to that command?
6. Why do you think there was so much emphasis put on laws and rituals concerning skin disease and mildew?
7. Describe what happened on the Day of Atonement (16:1-34). Who alone could enter the Most Holy Place in the tabernacle on that day? What was the "scapegoat"?
8. Complete this sentence: "So far, the most important thing I have discovered in reading LEVITICUS is . . ."

blood was brought into the Most Holy Place to make atonement, must be taken outside the camp; their hides, flesh and offal are to be burned up. [28]The man who burns them must wash his clothes and bathe himself with water; afterward he may come into the camp.

[29]"This is to be a lasting ordinance for you: On the tenth day of the seventh month you must deny yourselves[a] and not do any work—whether native-born or an alien living among you— [30]because on this day atonement will be made for you, to cleanse you. Then, before the LORD, you will be clean from all your sins. [31]It is a sabbath of rest, and you must deny yourselves; it is a lasting ordinance. [32]The priest who is anointed and ordained to succeed his father as high priest is to make atonement. He is to put on the sacred linen garments [33]and make atonement for the Most Holy Place, for the Tent of Meeting and the altar, and for the priests and all the people of the community.

[34]"This is to be a lasting ordinance for you: Atonement is to be made once a year for all the sins of the Israelites."

And it was done, as the LORD commanded Moses.

Israel: God's Holy People

The focus of Leviticus 17–27 is on how the people of Israel will live together as God's holy people. A number of laws and their punishments are given, as well as instructions to the priests about the special religious festivals that are to be celebrated. The LORD promises to bless those who obey but punish those who disobey.

LAWS FOR ALL GOD'S PEOPLE

God's people are to follow laws that protect them and set them apart from their neighbors. Strong penalties for disobeying these laws are also given.

Eating Blood Forbidden

17 The LORD said to Moses, [2]"Speak to Aaron and his sons and to all the Israelites and say to them: 'This is what the LORD has commanded: [3]Any Israelite who sacrifices an ox,[b] a lamb or a goat in the camp or outside of it [4]instead of bringing it to the entrance to the Tent of Meeting to present it as an offering to the LORD in front of the tabernacle of the LORD—that man shall be considered guilty of bloodshed; he has shed blood and must be cut off from his people. [5]This is so the Israelites will bring to the LORD the sacrifices they are now making in the open fields. They must bring them to the priest, that is, to the LORD, at the entrance to the Tent of Meet-

[a]**29** Or *must fast*; also in verse 31 [b]**3** The Hebrew word can include both male and female.

The LORD said to Moses, *"This is to be a lasting ordinance for you: Atonement is to be made once a year for all the sins of the Israelites."*
Lev 16:34

16:29 *seventh month:* Tishri (also called Ethanim), the seventh month of the Hebrew calendar, from about mid-September to mid-October.

16:29-31 *deny yourselves and not do any work:* The people denied themselves by fasting (going without eating). People fasted during times of mourning. Here, fasting is done to show sorrow for sins on the Day of Atonement. They did no work because it was a holy day, a Sabbath, the weekly day of rest that began at sunset on Friday and ended with a blessing (benediction) at sunset on Saturday. Observing the Sabbath, which means to "rest" or to "stop working" was a rule for all Jewish people (Exod 20:8-11; Deut 5:12-15). See also the chart called "Jewish Calendar and Festivals," p. 944. See also 23:26-32; Num 29:7-11.

17:2 *Aaron and his sons:* See the note on p. 210 (priests).

17:3,4 *Tent of Meeting . . . blood:* See the note on p. 210 (tabernacle), and the notes on blood at 1:5 and 4:5-7.

17:5 *fellowship offerings:* See the notes at 3:1 and 7:11.

ing and sacrifice them as fellowship offerings.[a] [6]The priest is to sprinkle the blood against the altar of the LORD at the entrance to the Tent of Meeting and burn the fat as an aroma pleasing to the LORD. [7]They must no longer offer any of their sacrifices to the goat idols[b] to whom they prostitute themselves. This is to be a lasting ordinance for them and for the generations to come.'

[8]"Say to them: 'Any Israelite or any alien living among them who offers a burnt offering or sacrifice [9]and does not bring it to the entrance to the Tent of Meeting to sacrifice it to the LORD—that man must be cut off from his people.

[10]" 'Any Israelite or any alien living among them who eats any blood—I will set my face against that person who eats blood and will cut him off from his people. [11]For the life of a creature is in the blood, and I have given it to you to make atonement for yourselves on the altar; it is the blood that makes atonement for one's life. [12]Therefore I say to the Israelites, "None of you may eat blood, nor may an alien living among you eat blood."

[13]" 'Any Israelite or any alien living among you who hunts any animal or bird that may be eaten must drain out the blood and cover it with earth, [14]because the life of every creature is its blood. That is why I have said to the Israelites, "You must not eat the blood of any creature, because the life of every creature is its blood; anyone who eats it must be cut off."

[15]" 'Anyone, whether native-born or alien, who eats anything found dead or torn by wild animals must wash his clothes and bathe with water, and he will be ceremonially unclean till evening; then he will be clean. [16]But if he does not wash his clothes and bathe himself, he will be held responsible.' "

Unlawful Sexual Relations

18 The LORD said to Moses, [2]"Speak to the Israelites and say to them: 'I am the LORD your God. [3]You must not do as they do in Egypt, where you used to live, and you must not do as they do in the land of Canaan, where I am bringing you. Do not follow their practices. [4]You must obey my laws and be careful to follow my decrees. I am the LORD your God. [5]Keep my decrees and laws, for the man who obeys them will live by them. I am the LORD.

[6]" 'No one is to approach any close relative to have sexual relations. I am the LORD.

[7]" 'Do not dishonor your father by having sexual relations with your mother. She is your mother; do not have relations with her.

[8]" 'Do not have sexual relations with your father's wife; that would dishonor your father.

[9]" 'Do not have sexual relations with your sister, either your

[a]5 Traditionally *peace offerings* [b]7 Or *demons*

17:7 *goat idols:* See also Exod 20:3-6; 34:15,16.

17:11 *life . . . is in the blood:* See the note at 1:5 (blood). See also Heb 9:22. Blood drained from an animal killed while hunting was to be covered with dirt, so it could not be used in an improper ceremony, such as idol worship involving blood.

18:3 *Egypt . . . Canaan:* See the notes at 11:44,45 and 14:34,35 (Canaan). See the map on p. 2463. The Israelites were told not to follow the evil customs of the people who lived in these countries.

18:5 *I am the LORD:* See the note at 1:1 (LORD). What set the people of Israel apart from their neighbors was that God had chosen them and given them laws that they were to follow with loyalty and obedience. See also Exod 20:1-17; Ezek 18:9; 20:11,12.

18:6 *close relative . . . sexual relations:* Just as the people's faith in the LORD was to set them apart from their neighbors, so was their lifestyle. Following strict rules about sexual behavior was one way to set themselves apart.

17:10 Gen 9:4; Lev 7:26,27; 19:26; Deut 12:23-25; 15:23. **17:15** Lev 11:39,40. **18:2,3** Exod 20:2,3. **18:8** Lev 20:11; Deut 22:30; 27:20. **18:9** Lev 20:17; Deut 27:22.

18:17 *sexual relations . . . close relatives . . . wickedness:* See the mini-article called "Purity (Clean and Unclean)," p. 2125. See also 20:14; Deut 27:14-26.

18:19 *monthly period:* See the note at 15:19. See also 20:18.

18:21 *Molech:* This name is related to the Hebrew name for "king" (*melech*) but it is changed slightly, so that it sounds like the word for "shame." People sacrificed their children to this Ammonite god by burning them in the Valley of Ben Hinnom near Jerusalem (20:1-5; Deut 12:31; 2 Kgs 16:3; 17:17; 23:10; Jer 7:30,31; 19:4,5; Ezek 16:20,21; 20:31).

18:24 *defile yourselves . . . the nations:* See the note at 18:3. Though Israel had not yet entered Canaan, this verse refers to the people they would drive out when they took over that land. See also the mini-article called "Canaanite Gods and Goddesses," p. 469.

18:25 *the land was defiled:* Immoral living pollutes the land itself (makes it unclean). This is part of the basis for the idea of a "holy land," which remains clean (acceptable to God) if all people who live there, including foreigners (17:8,10), obey God's laws.

19:2 *holy:* See the note on p. 210 (holiness). See also 11:44,45; 1 Pet 1:16.

18:12-14 Lev 20:19,20. **18:15,16** Lev 20:12,21. **18:20** Lev 20:10. **18:22** Lev 20:13; Rom 1:26,27. **18:23** Exod 22:19; Lev 20:15,16; Deut 27:21.

father's daughter or your mother's daughter, whether she was born
in the same home or elsewhere.
10" 'Do not have sexual relations with your son's daughter or
your daughter's daughter; that would dishonor you.
11" 'Do not have sexual relations with the daughter of your
father's wife, born to your father; she is your sister.
12" 'Do not have sexual relations with your father's sister; she
is your father's close relative.
13" 'Do not have sexual relations with your mother's sister,
because she is your mother's close relative.
14" 'Do not dishonor your father's brother by approaching
his wife to have sexual relations; she is your aunt.
15" 'Do not have sexual relations with your daughter-in-law.
She is your son's wife; do not have relations with her.
16" 'Do not have sexual relations with your brother's wife;
that would dishonor your brother.
17" 'Do not have sexual relations with both a woman and her
daughter. Do not have sexual relations with either her son's daughter or her daughter's daughter; they are her close relatives. That is
wickedness.
18" 'Do not take your wife's sister as a rival wife and have sexual relations with her while your wife is living.
19" 'Do not approach a woman to have sexual relations during the uncleanness of her monthly period.
20" 'Do not have sexual relations with your neighbor's wife
and defile yourself with her.
21" 'Do not give any of your children to be sacrificed[a] to Molech, for you must not profane the name of your God. I am the
LORD.
22" 'Do not lie with a man as one lies with a woman; that is
detestable.
23" 'Do not have sexual relations with an animal and defile
yourself with it. A woman must not present herself to an animal to
have sexual relations with it; that is a perversion.
24" 'Do not defile yourselves in any of these ways, because
this is how the nations that I am going to drive out before you
became defiled. 25Even the land was defiled; so I punished it for its
sin, and the land vomited out its inhabitants. 26But you must keep
my decrees and my laws. The native-born and the aliens living
among you must not do any of these detestable things, 27for all
these things were done by the people who lived in the land before
you, and the land became defiled. 28And if you defile the land, it
will vomit you out as it vomited out the nations that were before
you.
29" 'Everyone who does any of these detestable things—such
persons must be cut off from their people. 30Keep my requirements

[a]**21** Or *to be passed through* ⌊*the fire*⌋

and do not follow any of the detestable customs that were practiced before you came and do not defile yourselves with them. I
am the LORD your God.’”

Various Laws

19 The LORD said to Moses, 2“Speak to the entire assembly of
Israel and say to them: ‘Be holy because I, the LORD your God, am
holy.

3“ ‘Each of you must respect his mother and father, and you
must observe my Sabbaths. I am the LORD your God.

4“ ‘Do not turn to idols or make gods of cast metal for yourselves. I am the LORD your God.

5“ ‘When you sacrifice a fellowship offering[a] to the LORD, sacrifice it in such a way that it will be accepted on your behalf. 6It
shall be eaten on the day you sacrifice it or on the next day; anything left over until the third day must be burned up. 7If any of it
is eaten on the third day, it is impure and will not be accepted.
8Whoever eats it will be held responsible because he has desecrated what is holy to the LORD; that person must be cut off from his
people.

9“ ‘When you reap the harvest of your land, do not reap to
the very edges of your field or gather the gleanings of your harvest. 10Do not go over your vineyard a second time or pick up the
grapes that have fallen. Leave them for the poor and the alien. I am
the LORD your God.

[a]5 Traditionally *peace offering*

19:5 *fellowship offering:* See the note at 3:1.

19:9 *gleanings:* Being a holy people did not simply mean Israelites shall avoid doing things that would make them unclean. It also meant they should look out for the needs of others, especially the poor, who were allowed to pick up leftover grain (“gleanings”) after the harvest (23:22). See also Deut 24:19-22; Ruth 2:1-3.

19:3 ***a*** Exod 20:12; Deut 5:16; ***b*** Exod 20:8-11; Deut 5:12-15. **19:4** Exod 20:4-6,23; 34:17; Lev 26:1; Deut 5:8-10; 17:2-7. **19:5-7** Lev 7:16-18.

NAMES OF GOD

Of the many words used to name God in the Bible, the following are especially important. The most common is the general noun *Elohim*, usually translated as “God” when it refers to the God of Israel, or “gods” when it refers to other gods. This name is related to *El*, the Semitic word for god that appears in many ancient languages. *El* is frequently used with other terms, creating various names such as: *El Shaddai* (God All-Powerful), *El Elyon* (God Most High), and *El Olam* (Eternal God).

The most important word for God in the Old Testament is *Yahweh*. In English Bibles it usually appears as “the LORD.” But this is not a translation. *Yahweh* is God’s personal name that God made known to Moses from the burning bush (Exod 3:13-15). For a more complete explanation, see the mini-article called “LORD (YHWH),” p. 140.

Unlike the other names for God, “The LORD Almighty” is a title. In 1 Samuel 1:3 it is the name used in the worship of God at Shiloh. It is commonly used in the books of the prophets. Literally, the Hebrew phrase means “The LORD of Hosts,” though it is unclear whether the “hosts” are the armies of Israel, or the sun, moon, and stars, or the angels and heavenly forces that are ready to obey God.

19:13 *wages . . . overnight:* Day laborers needed their wages to buy food for their evening meal, which was the main meal of the day.

19:19 *Do not mate different kinds of animals:* This may be based on the belief that in creation God separated everything according to their own species (Gen 1). Keeping things separate was seen as following the natural order of God's created world. See Deut 22:9-11.

19:24 *fruit will be holy:* Meaning set apart or presented as holy to the LORD.

19:26 *Do not eat any meat with the blood still in it . . . divination or sorcery:* See the note at 1:5 (blood) and see Gen 9:4. Divination and sorcery included casting spells, fortune telling, and trying to talk to the spirits of the dead (19:31; Deut 18:10,11). Witchcraft was forbidden by the Law of Moses. See also 20:6,27.

19:29 *prostitute:* This may refer to the practice of women serving as prostitutes at the temple of a foreign god such as the fertility god Baal (Hos 4:11-14). It was believed that intercourse with these prostitutes assured fertile fields and herds. But such activities disgraced the land (see the note at 18:25).

19:30 *Sabbaths:* See the note at 16:29-31. See also 26:2.

19:11 ***a*** Exod 20:15; Deut 5:19; ***b*** Exod 20:16; Deut 5:20. **19:12** Exod 20:4-7; Deut 5:11; Matt 5:33. **19:13** Deut 24:14,15. **19:14** Deut 27:17,18. **19:15** Exod 23:6-8; Deut 16:18,19. **19:17** Matt 18:15. **19:18** Prov 20:22; Matt 5:39-48; 19:19; 22:39; Mark 12:31; Luke 10:27; Rom 13:9; Gal 5:14; Jas 2:8. **19:27,28** Lev 21:5; Deut 14:1. **19:29** Deut 23:17.

11"'Do not steal.
"'Do not lie.
"'Do not deceive one another.
12"'Do not swear falsely by my name and so profane the
name of your God. I am the LORD.
13"'Do not defraud your neighbor or rob him.
"'Do not hold back the wages of a hired man overnight.
14"'Do not curse the deaf or put a stumbling block in front
of the blind, but fear your God. I am the LORD.
15"'Do not pervert justice; do not show partiality to the poor
or favoritism to the great, but judge your neighbor fairly.
16"'Do not go about spreading slander among your people.
"'Do not do anything that endangers your neighbor's life. I
am the LORD.
17"'Do not hate your brother in your heart. Rebuke your
neighbor frankly so you will not share in his guilt.
18"'Do not seek revenge or bear a grudge against one of your
people, but love your neighbor as yourself. I am the LORD.
19"'Keep my decrees.
"'Do not mate different kinds of animals.
"'Do not plant your field with two kinds of seed.
"'Do not wear clothing woven of two kinds of material.
20"'If a man sleeps with a woman who is a slave girl
promised to another man but who has not been ransomed or
given her freedom, there must be due punishment. Yet they are not
to be put to death, because she had not been freed. 21The man,
however, must bring a ram to the entrance to the Tent of Meeting
for a guilt offering to the LORD. 22With the ram of the guilt offering the priest is to make atonement for him before the LORD for
the sin he has committed, and his sin will be forgiven.
23"'When you enter the land and plant any kind of fruit tree,
regard its fruit as forbidden.[a] For three years you are to consider it
forbidden[a]; it must not be eaten. 24In the fourth year all its fruit
will be holy, an offering of praise to the LORD. 25But in the fifth
year you may eat its fruit. In this way your harvest will be
increased. I am the LORD your God.
26"'Do not eat any meat with the blood still in it.
"'Do not practice divination or sorcery.
27"'Do not cut the hair at the sides of your head or clip off
the edges of your beard.
28"'Do not cut your bodies for the dead or put tattoo marks
on yourselves. I am the LORD.
29"'Do not degrade your daughter by making her a prostitute,
or the land will turn to prostitution and be filled with wickedness.
30"'Observe my Sabbaths and have reverence for my sanctuary. I am the LORD.

[a]23 Hebrew *uncircumcised*

[31]"'Do not turn to mediums or seek out spiritists, for you
will be defiled by them. I am the LORD your God.
[32]"'Rise in the presence of the aged, show respect for the
elderly and revere your God. I am the LORD.
[33]"'When an alien lives with you in your land, do not mistreat him. [34]The alien living with you must be treated as one of
your native-born. Love him as yourself, for you were aliens in
Egypt. I am the LORD your God.
[35]"'Do not use dishonest standards when measuring length,
weight or quantity. [36]Use honest scales and honest weights, an
honest ephah[a] and an honest hin.[b] I am the LORD your God, who
brought you out of Egypt.
[37]"'Keep all my decrees and all my laws and follow them.
I am the LORD.'"

Punishments for Sin

20 The LORD said to Moses, [2]"Say to the Israelites: 'Any Israelite
or any alien living in Israel who gives[c] any of his children to
Molech must be put to death. The people of the community are to
stone him. [3]I will set my face against that man and I will cut him
off from his people; for by giving his children to Molech, he has
defiled my sanctuary and profaned my holy name. [4]If the people of
the community close their eyes when that man gives one of his
children to Molech and they fail to put him to death, [5]I will set my
face against that man and his family and will cut off from their
people both him and all who follow him in prostituting themselves
to Molech.
[6]"'I will set my face against the person who turns to mediums and spiritists to prostitute himself by following them, and I
will cut him off from his people.
[7]"'Consecrate yourselves and be holy, because I am the LORD
your God. [8]Keep my decrees and follow them. I am the LORD, who
makes you holy.[d]
[9]"'If anyone curses his father or mother, he must be put to
death. He has cursed his father or his mother, and his blood will be
on his own head.
[10]"'If a man commits adultery with another man's wife—
with the wife of his neighbor—both the adulterer and the adulteress must be put to death.
[11]"'If a man sleeps with his father's wife, he has dishonored
his father. Both the man and the woman must be put to death;
their blood will be on their own heads.
[12]"'If a man sleeps with his daughter-in-law, both of them

[a]**36** An ephah was a dry measure. [b]**36** A hin was a liquid measure. [c]**2** Or *sacrifices*; also in verses 3 and 4 [d]**8** Or *who sanctifies you*; or *who sets you apart as holy*

19:31 *mediums . . . spiritists:* See the note at 19:26. See also 20:6; 1 Sam 28:3; Isa 8:19.

19:34 *you were aliens in Egypt:* See the note at 11:44,45. See also Exod 22:21; Lev 18:3; Deut 24:17, 18; 27:19.

20:2 *Molech:* See the note at 18:21.

20:2 *stone him:* Dropping or placing heavy stones on someone was one of the most common forms of execution in Israelite society.

19:35,36 Deut 25:13-16; Prov 20:10; Ezek 45:10. **20:7** Lev 11:44,45. **20:9** Exod 21:17; Matt 15:4; Mark 7:10. **20:10** Exod 20:14; Lev 18:20; Deut 5:18. **20:11** Lev 18:8; Deut 22:30; 27:20. **20:12** Lev 18:15.

must be put to death. What they have done is a perversion; their
blood will be on their own heads.

13“‘If a man lies with a man as one lies with a woman, both
of them have done what is detestable. They must be put to death;
their blood will be on their own heads.

14“‘If a man marries both a woman and her mother, it is
wicked. Both he and they must be burned in the fire, so that no
wickedness will be among you.

15“‘If a man has sexual relations with an animal, he must be
put to death, and you must kill the animal.

16“‘If a woman approaches an animal to have sexual relations with it, kill both the woman and the animal. They must be
put to death; their blood will be on their own heads.

17“‘If a man marries his sister, the daughter of either his
father or his mother, and they have sexual relations, it is a disgrace.
They must be cut off before the eyes of their people. He has dishonored his sister and will be held responsible.

18“‘If a man lies with a woman during her monthly period
and has sexual relations with her, he has exposed the source of her
flow, and she has also uncovered it. Both of them must be cut off
from their people.

19“‘Do not have sexual relations with the sister of either your
mother or your father, for that would dishonor a close relative;
both of you would be held responsible.

20“‘If a man sleeps with his aunt, he has dishonored his
uncle. They will be held responsible; they will die childless.

21“‘If a man marries his brother’s wife, it is an act of impurity; he has dishonored his brother. They will be childless.

22“‘Keep all my decrees and laws and follow them, so that the
land where I am bringing you to live may not vomit you out. 23You
must not live according to the customs of the nations I am going
to drive out before you. Because they did all these things, I
abhorred them. 24But I said to you, “You will possess their land; I
will give it to you as an inheritance, a land flowing with milk and
honey.” I am the LORD your God, who has set you apart from the
nations.

25“‘You must therefore make a distinction between clean and
unclean animals and between unclean and clean birds. Do not
defile yourselves by any animal or bird or anything that moves
along the ground—those which I have set apart as unclean for
you. 26You are to be holy to me[a] because I, the LORD, am holy, and
I have set you apart from the nations to be my own.

27“‘A man or woman who is a medium or spiritist among
you must be put to death. You are to stone them; their blood will
be on their own heads.’”

[a]**26** Or *be my holy ones*

“I am the LORD your God, who has set you apart from the nations.”
Lev 20:24

20:18 *monthly period:* See the note at 15:19. See also 18:19.

20:21 *marries his brother’s wife:* Compare with Deuteronomy 25:5,6, which says a man was supposed to marry his brother’s widow if his brother died without having children. Otherwise, such marriages were forbidden (see also 18:16; Matt 22:23-33; Mark 12:18-27; Luke 20:27-40).

20:23 *I am going to drive out before you:* See the notes at 14:34,35 (Canaan) and 18:24.

20:25 *clean . . . unclean:* See the note at 11:4-8.

20:27 *medium or spiritist:* This refers to a person who claims to have the power to get messages from dead people. See also 20:6 and the note at 19:26.

20:13 Lev 18:22; Rom 1:26-28. **20:14** Lev 18:17; Deut 27:23. **20:15,16** Exod 22:19; Lev 18:23; Deut 27:21. **20:17** Lev 18:9. **20:18** Lev 18:19. **20:19,20** Lev 18:12-14. **20:26** Lev 11:44, 45; 20:7.

LAWS FOR THE PRIESTS AND RELIGIOUS FESTIVALS

More laws define how the priests are to avoid becoming ritually impure and to make acceptable sacrifices. The whole community of Israel receives the laws concerning when and how to celebrate major religious festivals.

Rules for Priests

21 The LORD said to Moses, "Speak to the priests, the sons of Aaron, and say to them: 'A priest must not make himself ceremonially unclean for any of his people who die, 2except for a close relative, such as his mother or father, his son or daughter, his brother, 3or an unmarried sister who is dependent on him since she has no husband—for her he may make himself unclean. 4He must not make himself unclean for people related to him by marriage,[a] and so defile himself.

5" 'Priests must not shave their heads or shave off the edges of their beards or cut their bodies. 6They must be holy to their God and must not profane the name of their God. Because they present the offerings made to the LORD by fire, the food of their God, they are to be holy.

7" 'They must not marry women defiled by prostitution or divorced from their husbands, because priests are holy to their God. 8Regard them as holy, because they offer up the food of your God. Consider them holy, because I the LORD am holy—I who make you holy.[b]

9" 'If a priest's daughter defiles herself by becoming a prostitute, she disgraces her father; she must be burned in the fire.

10" 'The high priest, the one among his brothers who has had the anointing oil poured on his head and who has been ordained to wear the priestly garments, must not let his hair become unkempt[c] or tear his clothes. 11He must not enter a place where there is a dead body. He must not make himself unclean, even for his father or mother, 12nor leave the sanctuary of his God or desecrate it, because he has been dedicated by the anointing oil of his God. I am the LORD.

13" 'The woman he marries must be a virgin. 14He must not marry a widow, a divorced woman, or a woman defiled by prostitution, but only a virgin from his own people, 15so he will not defile his offspring among his people. I am the LORD, who makes him holy.[d]' "

16The LORD said to Moses, 17"Say to Aaron: 'For the generations to come none of your descendants who has a defect may come near to offer the food of his God. 18No man who has any

[a]4 Or *unclean as a leader among his people* [b]8 Or *who sanctify you*; or *who set you apart as holy* [c]10 Or *not uncover his head* [d]15 Or *who sanctifies him*; or *who sets him apart as holy*

21:1 *priests, the sons of Aaron:* See the note on p. 210 (priests). The regulations in chapter 21 were given to keep the priests from becoming ritually unclean, making them unfit to do their work on behalf of the people.

21:1,2 *make himself ceremonially unclean:* Coming into contact with a dead body made a person unclean (Num 19:11-21). The uncleanness connected with a human corpse lasted seven days. To become clean again, a person had to go through a ceremonial washing. The priests were given permission to bury blood relatives, but not relatives by marriage, including the priest's own wife and members of her family. But the rules for the high priest were even more strict (21:10,11).

21:6 *be holy:* See the notes on p. 210 (holiness) and at 11:44,45.

21:7 *defiled by prostitution:* See the note at 19:29.

21:10 *high priest:* See the note at 4:3 (priest).

21:13-15 *must be a virgin:* Since the office of high priest was passed on within a family, a young man would know he was next in line to be high priest even while his father was still the acting high priest (6:22).

21:17-23 *defect:* Just as animals given for sacrifice could not have any defects, so those who handled the sacrifices or entered the Holy Place of the tabernacle were to be without defect. By modern standards, this seems harsh, but this rule was based on the Israelite understanding of holiness, which meant that all things chosen and dedicated to God were to represent the perfection of God's creation. Although men with such defects could not serve at the altar, they were not abandoned by the community. They could eat the food the priests ate and likely helped the priests with certain tasks.

21:5 Lev 19:27,28; Deut 14:1.
21:10 Lev 10:6,7.

21:23 *curtain . . . altar:* The curtain probably refers to the one that separated the Holy Place and Most Holy Place in the tabernacle (Exod 26:33). Since those who had defects could eat food offered to God, they could be in the sacred courtyard outside the tabernacle itself (6:16). See the mini-article called "The Tabernacle," p. 2346.

22:3 *unclean:* See the note at 11:4-8.

22:8 *found dead or torn by wild animals:* The rule for ordinary people was not as strict (17:15). The priests were to rely on the food that came from portions of the sacrifices they offered. To eat food from other sources showed a lack of faith. This rule was more than a diet restriction; it had to do with the priests trusting in God to provide for their needs.

22:9 *I am the* LORD *. . . holy:* See the notes at 1:1 (LORD) and on p. 210 (holiness).

22:10,11 *hired worker . . . slave:* Paid laborers could not eat any of the sacred food, that is, portions of the sacrificial meat, bread, and grains. But slaves who lived in the households of the priestly families could eat the sacred food. Even though the Israelites had themselves been slaves in Egypt, they apparently also had some slaves. The Hebrew people were not to keep slaves longer than six years, unless the slave asked to continue serving his master. The slave's ear was then pierced as a sign of his life-long commitment (Exod 21:6). See also 25:39-46; Jer 34:8-20.

22:4,5 Lev 13:1—14:32; 15:1-17.

defect may come near: no man who is blind or lame, disfigured or
deformed; 19no man with a crippled foot or hand, 20or who is
hunchbacked or dwarfed, or who has any eye defect, or who has
festering or running sores or damaged testicles. 21No descendant
of Aaron the priest who has any defect is to come near to present
the offerings made to the LORD by fire. He has a defect; he must
not come near to offer the food of his God. 22He may eat the most
holy food of his God, as well as the holy food; 23yet because of his
defect, he must not go near the curtain or approach the altar,
and so desecrate my sanctuary. I am the LORD, who makes them
holy.[a]' "

24So Moses told this to Aaron and his sons and to all the
Israelites.

22 The LORD said to Moses, 2"Tell Aaron and his sons to treat
with respect the sacred offerings the Israelites consecrate to me, so
they will not profane my holy name. I am the LORD.

3"Say to them: 'For the generations to come, if any of your
descendants is ceremonially unclean and yet comes near the sacred
offerings that the Israelites consecrate to the LORD, that person
must be cut off from my presence. I am the LORD.

4" 'If a descendant of Aaron has an infectious skin disease[b]
or a bodily discharge, he may not eat the sacred offerings until he
is cleansed. He will also be unclean if he touches something defiled
by a corpse or by anyone who has an emission of semen, 5or if he
touches any crawling thing that makes him unclean, or any person
who makes him unclean, whatever the uncleanness may be. 6The
one who touches any such thing will be unclean till evening. He
must not eat any of the sacred offerings unless he has bathed himself with water. 7When the sun goes down, he will be clean, and
after that he may eat the sacred offerings, for they are his food. 8He
must not eat anything found dead or torn by wild animals, and so
become unclean through it. I am the LORD.

9" 'The priests are to keep my requirements so that they do
not become guilty and die for treating them with contempt. I am
the LORD, who makes them holy.[c]

10" 'No one outside a priest's family may eat the sacred offering, nor may the guest of a priest or his hired worker eat it. 11But
if a priest buys a slave with money, or if a slave is born in his
household, that slave may eat his food. 12If a priest's daughter marries anyone other than a priest, she may not eat any of the sacred
contributions. 13But if a priest's daughter becomes a widow or is
divorced, yet has no children, and she returns to live in her father's
house as in her youth, she may eat of her father's food. No unauthorized person, however, may eat any of it.

[a]**23** Or *who sanctifies them*; or *who sets them apart as holy* [b]**4** Traditionally *leprosy*; the Hebrew word was used for various diseases affecting the skin—not necessarily leprosy. [c]**9** Or *who sanctifies them*; or *who sets them apart as holy*; also in verse 16

[14]"'If anyone eats a sacred offering by mistake, he must make
restitution to the priest for the offering and add a fifth of the value
to it. [15]The priests must not desecrate the sacred offerings the
Israelites present to the LORD [16]by allowing them to eat the sacred
offerings and so bring upon them guilt requiring payment. I am
the LORD, who makes them holy.'"

Unacceptable Sacrifices

[17]The LORD said to Moses, [18]"Speak to Aaron and his sons
and to all the Israelites and say to them: 'If any of you—either an
Israelite or an alien living in Israel—presents a gift for a burnt
offering to the LORD, either to fulfill a vow or as a freewill offering,
[19]you must present a male without defect from the cattle, sheep or
goats in order that it may be accepted on your behalf. [20]Do not
bring anything with a defect, because it will not be accepted on
your behalf. [21]When anyone brings from the herd or flock a fellowship offering[a] to the LORD to fulfill a special vow or as a freewill
offering, it must be without defect or blemish to be acceptable.
[22]Do not offer to the LORD the blind, the injured or the maimed, or
anything with warts or festering or running sores. Do not place
any of these on the altar as an offering made to the LORD by fire.
[23]You may, however, present as a freewill offering an ox[b] or a sheep
that is deformed or stunted, but it will not be accepted in fulfillment of a vow. [24]You must not offer to the LORD an animal whose
testicles are bruised, crushed, torn or cut. You must not do this in
your own land, [25]and you must not accept such animals from the
hand of a foreigner and offer them as the food of your God. They
will not be accepted on your behalf, because they are deformed
and have defects.'"

[26]The LORD said to Moses, [27]"When a calf, a lamb or a goat is
born, it is to remain with its mother for seven days. From the eighth
day on, it will be acceptable as an offering made to the LORD by fire.
[28]Do not slaughter a cow or a sheep and its young on the same day.

[29]"When you sacrifice a thank offering to the LORD, sacrifice
it in such a way that it will be accepted on your behalf. [30]It must be
eaten that same day; leave none of it till morning. I am the LORD.

[31]"Keep my commands and follow them. I am the LORD.
[32]Do not profane my holy name. I must be acknowledged as holy
by the Israelites. I am the LORD, who makes[c] you holy[d] [33]and who
brought you out of Egypt to be your God. I am the LORD."

23 The LORD said to Moses, [2]"Speak to the Israelites and say to
them: 'These are my appointed feasts, the appointed feasts of the
LORD, which you are to proclaim as sacred assemblies.

[a]21 Traditionally *peace offering* [b]23 The Hebrew word can include both male and female. [c]32 Or *made* [d]32 Or *who sanctifies you*; or *who sets you apart as holy*

"Do not profane my holy name. I must be acknowledged as holy by the Israelites. I am the LORD, who makes you holy and who brought you out of Egypt to be your God. I am the LORD."
Lev 22:32,33

22:21 *fellowship offering:* See the note at 3:1.

22:25 *foreigner:* This means someone who was not born into an Israelite family. Only animals bred and raised by the Israelites could be used for sacrifices. See also the mini-article called "Foreigners (Aliens)," p. 501.

22:26,27 *seven days:* See the note at 4:5-7.

22:29 *sacrifice a thank offering:* This is not the grain offering described in chapter 2, which involved grain and bread offerings. This sacrifice of thanksgiving can include an animal sacrifice (7:12-16).

22:33 *brought you out of Egypt:* See the note at 11:44,45.

22:19-22 Lev 1:10; 3:1; Deut 17:1; Mal 1:8. **22:28** Deut 22:6,7.

23:3 *Sabbath:* See the note at 16:29-31 and the chart called "Jewish Calendar and Festivals," p. 944. See also Exod 20:8-10; 23:12; 31:14-16; 34:21; 35:2; Deut 5:12-15.

23:5 *Passover ... first month:* The "Passover" is related to the Hebrew verb translated as "pass over" in Exodus 12. This festival was celebrated as a remembrance of how God acted to save the Israelite people from slavery in Egypt. See also Deut 16:1,2. The first month of the Hebrew calendar is Abib (also called Nisan), which lasts from about mid-March to mid-April. See also the chart called "Jewish Calendar and Festivals," p. 944.

23:6 *Feast of Unleavened Bread:* This feast began the day after Passover and lasted seven days (Num 28:16-25). The unleavened bread that was to be eaten during Passover and the Feast of Unleavened Bread was a reminder of how quickly the people had to leave Egypt. They did not have time to let the dough for their bread rise. See also Exod 23:15; 34:18; Deut 16:3-8 and the mini-article called "Passover and the Feast of Unleavened Bread," p. 2030.

23:9,10 *reap its harvest ... sheaf of the first grain:* Traditionally called the offering of firstfruits. See also the note at 2:12.

23:11,12 *Sabbath ... burnt offering:* See the notes at 16:29-31 and 1:3 (burnt offering).

The Sabbath

3"'There are six days when you may work, but the seventh
day is a Sabbath of rest, a day of sacred assembly. You are not to do
any work; wherever you live, it is a Sabbath to the LORD.

The Passover and Unleavened Bread

4"'These are the LORD's appointed feasts, the sacred assemblies you are to proclaim at their appointed times: 5The LORD's
Passover begins at twilight on the fourteenth day of the first
month. 6On the fifteenth day of that month the LORD's Feast of
Unleavened Bread begins; for seven days you must eat bread made
without yeast. 7On the first day hold a sacred assembly and do no
regular work. 8For seven days present an offering made to the LORD
by fire. And on the seventh day hold a sacred assembly and do no
regular work.'"

The Kiddush at the Sabbath Meal by Dora Holzhandler, 1996. The LORD told Moses, "There are six days when you may work, but the seventh day is a Sabbath of rest, a day of sacred assembly. You are not to do any work; wherever you live, it is a Sabbath to the LORD" (23:3). While other festivals were celebrated on a monthly or yearly basis, the Sabbath, or day of rest, was to be celebrated each week. In this contemporary painting a family has gathered together on the Sabbath and the mother prepares to read the Kiddush (blessing) before the meal.

Firstfruits

9The LORD said to Moses, 10"Speak to the Israelites and say
to them: 'When you enter the land I am going to give you and you
reap its harvest, bring to the priest a sheaf of the first grain you
harvest. 11He is to wave the sheaf before the LORD so it will be
accepted on your behalf; the priest is to wave it on the day after
the Sabbath. 12On the day you wave the sheaf, you must sacrifice
as a burnt offering to the LORD a lamb a year old without defect,
13together with its grain offering of two-tenths of an ephah[a] of
fine flour mixed with oil—an offering made to the LORD by fire,
a pleasing aroma—and its drink offering of a quarter of a hin[b]
of wine. 14You must not eat any bread, or roasted or new grain,
until the very day you bring this offering to your God. This is to
be a lasting ordinance for the generations to come, wherever you
live.

Feast of Weeks

15" 'From the day after the Sabbath, the day you brought the
sheaf of the wave offering, count off seven full weeks. 16Count off
fifty days up to the day after the seventh Sabbath, and then present
an offering of new grain to the LORD. 17From wherever you live,
bring two loaves made of two-tenths of an ephah of fine flour,
baked with yeast, as a wave offering of firstfruits to the LORD. 18Pre-
sent with this bread seven male lambs, each a year old and without
defect, one young bull and two rams. They will be a burnt offering
to the LORD, together with their grain offerings and drink offerings—an offering made by fire, an aroma pleasing to the LORD.
19Then sacrifice one male goat for a sin offering and two lambs,
each a year old, for a fellowship offering.[c] 20The priest is to wave
the two lambs before the LORD as a wave offering, together with
the bread of the firstfruits. They are a sacred offering to the LORD
for the priest. 21On that same day you are to proclaim a sacred
assembly and do no regular work. This is to be a lasting ordinance
for the generations to come, wherever you live.

22" 'When you reap the harvest of your land, do not reap
to the very edges of your field or gather the gleanings of your
harvest. Leave them for the poor and the alien. I am the LORD
your God.' "

Feast of Trumpets

23The LORD said to Moses, 24"Say to the Israelites: 'On the
first day of the seventh month you are to have a day of rest, a
sacred assembly commemorated with trumpet blasts. 25Do no regular work, but present an offering made to the LORD by fire.' "

23:14 *new grain:* The newest (first-cut) grain belonged to God. Requiring this offering reminded the people that God was the source of the peoples' blessings.

23:16 *fifty days . . . day after the seventh Sabbath:* Fifty days after offering the first grain offering during the Feast of Unleavened Bread, a new offering was brought to the Feast of Harvest, also known as the Feast of Weeks and later as Pentecost (see Acts 2:1; 20:16; 1 Cor 16:8). The people presented grain to God as a sign of thanks and to show confidence that God would continue to meet their needs. See also Exod 23:16; 34:22; Deut 16:9-12.

23:18 *burnt offering . . . drink offerings:* See the note at 1:3 (burnt offering). Compare to Numbers 15:1-16, which gives specific amounts of wine to be used in certain offerings. See also Deut 32:38; 2 Kgs 16:13, 15; Ezra 7:17.

23:19 *fellowship offering:* See the note at 3:1.

23:22 *Leave them for the poor and the alien:* See the note at 19:9.

23:23,24 *seventh month . . . trumpet blasts:* See the note at 16:29. The Feast of Trumpets was observed by trumpet blasts, special sacrifices, and rest from work. Trumpets were also blown on the first day of every month ("new moon," Ps 81:3). These trumpets were probably hammered metal horns made of silver (Num 10:2) that measured about a foot long. Today, this first day of the seventh month is known as *Rosh Hashanah*, meaning "the beginning of the year."

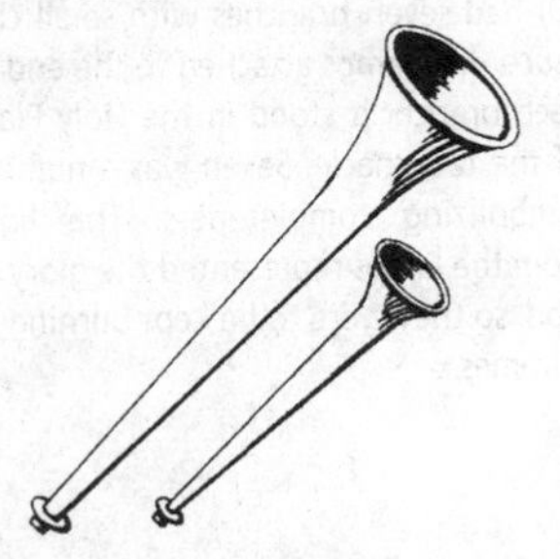

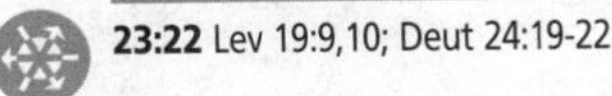

23:22 Lev 19:9,10; Deut 24:19-22.

[a]**13** That is, probably about 4 quarts (about 4.5 liters); also in verse 17 [b]**13** That is, probably about 1 quart (about 1 liter) [c]**19** Traditionally *peace offering*

23:26,27 *Day of Atonement:* See the note at 16:29. This festival is also known as *Yom Kippur.*

23:29-32 *deny himself . . . rest:* See the note at 16:29-31.

23:33,34 *Feast of Tabernacles:* This festival took place at the end of the fall harvest (Deut 16:13-17) and lasted for seven days. In addition to giving thanks to God for the fall harvest, the people were to build and live in shelters made of tree branches (23:40-42). The temporary shelters were to be a reminder of how the people lived in the wilderness after leaving Egypt. This festival is traditionally known as *Sukkoth*, the Feast of Booths, or the Feast of Shelters.

23:40-42 *fruit . . . leafy branches . . . booths:* The kind of fruit is unclear. The shelters were to be made of the branches of leafy trees, such as the olive, myrtle, and palm. See also Neh 8:13-16.

23:43 *Egypt:* See the note at 11:44,45.

24:2-4 *clear oil of pressed olives . . . lamps:* See the note at 2:1 (oil). The gold lampstand (Exod 25:31-40) had seven branches with small clay saucer-like lamps attached to the end of each branch. It stood in the Holy Place of the tabernacle. Seven was a number symbolizing completeness. The light from the lamps represented the glory of God, so they were to be kept burning at all times.

Day of Atonement

[26]The LORD said to Moses, [27]"The tenth day of this seventh month is the Day of Atonement. Hold a sacred assembly and deny yourselves,[a] and present an offering made to the LORD by fire. [28]Do no work on that day, because it is the Day of Atonement, when atonement is made for you before the LORD your God. [29]Anyone who does not deny himself on that day must be cut off from his people. [30]I will destroy from among his people anyone who does any work on that day. [31]You shall do no work at all. This is to be a lasting ordinance for the generations to come, wherever you live. [32]It is a sabbath of rest for you, and you must deny yourselves. From the evening of the ninth day of the month until the following evening you are to observe your sabbath."

Feast of Tabernacles

[33]The LORD said to Moses, [34]"Say to the Israelites: 'On the fifteenth day of the seventh month the LORD's Feast of Tabernacles begins, and it lasts for seven days. [35]The first day is a sacred assembly; do no regular work. [36]For seven days present offerings made to the LORD by fire, and on the eighth day hold a sacred assembly and present an offering made to the LORD by fire. It is the closing assembly; do no regular work.

[37](" 'These are the LORD's appointed feasts, which you are to proclaim as sacred assemblies for bringing offerings made to the LORD by fire—the burnt offerings and grain offerings, sacrifices and drink offerings required for each day. [38]These offerings are in addition to those for the LORD's Sabbaths and[b] in addition to your gifts and whatever you have vowed and all the freewill offerings you give to the LORD.)

[39]" 'So beginning with the fifteenth day of the seventh month, after you have gathered the crops of the land, celebrate the festival to the LORD for seven days; the first day is a day of rest, and the eighth day also is a day of rest. [40]On the first day you are to take choice fruit from the trees, and palm fronds, leafy branches and poplars, and rejoice before the LORD your God for seven days. [41]Celebrate this as a festival to the LORD for seven days each year. This is to be a lasting ordinance for the generations to come; celebrate it in the seventh month. [42]Live in booths for seven days: All native-born Israelites are to live in booths [43]so your descendants will know that I had the Israelites live in booths when I brought them out of Egypt. I am the LORD your God.' "

[44]So Moses announced to the Israelites the appointed feasts of the LORD.

---

[a]**27** Or *and fast;* also in verses 29 and 32 [b]**38** Or *These feasts are in addition to the LORD's Sabbaths, and these offerings are*

Oil and Bread Set Before the LORD

24 The LORD said to Moses, [2]"Command the Israelites to bring you clear oil of pressed olives for the light so that the lamps may be kept burning continually. [3]Outside the curtain of the Testimony in the Tent of Meeting, Aaron is to tend the lamps before the LORD from evening till morning, continually. This is to be a lasting ordinance for the generations to come. [4]The lamps on the pure gold lampstand before the LORD must be tended continually.

[5]"Take fine flour and bake twelve loaves of bread, using two-tenths of an ephah[a] for each loaf. [6]Set them in two rows, six in each row, on the table of pure gold before the LORD. [7]Along each row put some pure incense as a memorial portion to represent the bread and to be an offering made to the LORD by fire. [8]This bread is to be set out before the LORD regularly, Sabbath after Sabbath, on behalf of the Israelites, as a lasting covenant. [9]It belongs to Aaron and his sons, who are to eat it in a holy place, because it is a most holy part of their regular share of the offerings made to the LORD by fire."

A Blasphemer Stoned

[10]Now the son of an Israelite mother and an Egyptian father went out among the Israelites, and a fight broke out in the camp between him and an Israelite. [11]The son of the Israelite woman blasphemed the Name with a curse; so they brought him to Moses. (His mother's name was Shelomith, the daughter of Dibri the Danite.) [12]They put him in custody until the will of the LORD should be made clear to them.

[13]Then the LORD said to Moses: [14]"Take the blasphemer outside the camp. All those who heard him are to lay their hands on his head, and the entire assembly is to stone him. [15]Say to the Israelites: 'If anyone curses his God, he will be held responsible; [16]anyone who blasphemes the name of the LORD must be put to death. The entire assembly must stone him. Whether an alien or native-born, when he blasphemes the Name, he must be put to death.

[17]"'If anyone takes the life of a human being, he must be put to death. [18]Anyone who takes the life of someone's animal must make restitution—life for life. [19]If anyone injures his neighbor, whatever he has done must be done to him: [20]fracture for fracture, eye for eye, tooth for tooth. As he has injured the other, so he is to be injured. [21]Whoever kills an animal must make restitution, but whoever kills a man must be put to death. [22]You are to have the same law for the alien and the native-born. I am the LORD your God.'"

[23]Then Moses spoke to the Israelites, and they took the

[a]5 That is, probably about 4 quarts (about 4.5 liters)

24:5,6 *flour . . . twelve loaves:* The finest flour was made of wheat. Twelve fresh loaves representing the twelve tribes of Israel were to be placed in the presence of the LORD (24:8), and were called the bread of the Presence. The loaves were an ongoing offering to God and a reminder of God's blessings.

24:7 *pure incense:* See the note at 2:1 (oil). The incense was burned on an incense altar in the Holy Place of the tabernacle (Exod 30:1-10). See the illustration on p. 2345.

24:8 *Sabbath:* See the note at 16:29-31.

24:9 *eat it in a holy place:* See the notes at 6:25,26 and 24:5,6. Only the priests were to eat this bread (but see 1 Sam 21:1-6; Matt 12:4; Mark 2:26; Luke 6:4).

24:10,11 *blasphemed the Name with a curse:* This phrase can mean a number of things, such as using God's name to break promises, telling lies after swearing to tell the truth, using the LORD's name as a curse word or a magic formula, or trying to control the LORD by using the name. But the young man here may have said the sacred name of God, which was not to be spoken aloud. See also Exod 3:14,15; Lev 19:12; Deut 5:11.

24:10,11 *Danite:* This refers to the tribe named after Dan, one of the sons of Jacob (Gen 30:4-6). See also Josh 19:40-48.

24:14 *lay their hands on his head . . . stone him:* Speaking God's sacred name aloud affected not only the speaker but all those who heard it as well. The laying on of hands transferred the bad effect (guilt) from the hearers back to the one who spoke the name. See the note at 20:2.

24:5,6 Exod 25:30. **24:17** Exod 21:12; Deut 5:17. **24:18** Exod 22:14. **24:20** Exod 21:23-25; Deut 19:21; Matt 5:38-42. **24:22** Num 15:15,16.

Aaron Pouring Oil into One of the Lamps of the Menorah, thirteenth-century illuminated manuscript, France. The gold lampstand (menorah) was an important furnishing in the tabernacle. It stood in front of the curtain that separated the Holy Place from the Most Holy Place. Oil pressed from olives was needed to keep the flames of the lampstand burning. It was one of the responsibilities of Aaron and his sons to see that the lamps had enough oil each night. (See 24:1-4.)

25:4 *seventh year . . . Do not sow your fields:* The year of rest (Sabbath year) was intended to help the soil regain some of the nutrients lost in the previous growing season. The plants and grasses that grew up during the year of rest would be plowed into the soil to make it richer and more fertile. See also Exodus 23:10,11, which says the poor were to eat what grows naturally during the seventh year. Leviticus 25:6,7 says landowners and their servants can eat what grows naturally.

blasphemer outside the camp and stoned him. The Israelites did
as the LORD commanded Moses.

The Sabbath Year

25 The LORD said to Moses on Mount Sinai, 2“Speak to the
Israelites and say to them: ‘When you enter the land I am going to
give you, the land itself must observe a sabbath to the LORD. 3For
six years sow your fields, and for six years prune your vineyards
and gather their crops. 4But in the seventh year the land is to have
a sabbath of rest, a sabbath to the LORD. Do not sow your fields or
prune your vineyards. 5Do not reap what grows of itself or harvest
the grapes of your untended vines. The land is to have a year of
rest. 6Whatever the land yields during the sabbath year will be food
for you—for yourself, your manservant and maidservant, and the

hired worker and temporary resident who live among you, 7as well
as for your livestock and the wild animals in your land. Whatever
the land produces may be eaten.

The Year of Jubilee

8"'Count off seven sabbaths of years—seven times seven
years—so that the seven sabbaths of years amount to a period of
forty-nine years. 9Then have the trumpet sounded everywhere on
the tenth day of the seventh month; on the Day of Atonement
sound the trumpet throughout your land. 10Consecrate the fiftieth
year and proclaim liberty throughout the land to all its inhabitants. It shall be a jubilee for you; each one of you is to return to his
family property and each to his own clan. 11The fiftieth year shall
be a jubilee for you; do not sow and do not reap what grows of
itself or harvest the untended vines. 12For it is a jubilee and is to be
holy for you; eat only what is taken directly from the fields.
13"'In this Year of Jubilee everyone is to return to his own
property.
14"'If you sell land to one of your countrymen or buy any
from him, do not take advantage of each other. 15You are to buy
from your countryman on the basis of the number of years since
the Jubilee. And he is to sell to you on the basis of the number of
years left for harvesting crops. 16When the years are many, you are
to increase the price, and when the years are few, you are to
decrease the price, because what he is really selling you is the number of crops. 17Do not take advantage of each other, but fear your
God. I am the LORD your God.
18"'Follow my decrees and be careful to obey my laws, and
you will live safely in the land. 19Then the land will yield its fruit,
and you will eat your fill and live there in safety. 20You may ask,
"What will we eat in the seventh year if we do not plant or harvest
our crops?" 21I will send you such a blessing in the sixth year that
the land will yield enough for three years. 22While you plant during the eighth year, you will eat from the old crop and will continue to eat from it until the harvest of the ninth year comes in.
23"'The land must not be sold permanently, because the land
is mine and you are but aliens and my tenants. 24Throughout the
country that you hold as a possession, you must provide for the
redemption of the land.
25"'If one of your countrymen becomes poor and sells some
of his property, his nearest relative is to come and redeem what his
countryman has sold. 26If, however, a man has no one to redeem it
for him but he himself prospers and acquires sufficient means to
redeem it, 27he is to determine the value for the years since he sold
it and refund the balance to the man to whom he sold it; he can
then go back to his own property. 28But if he does not acquire the
means to repay him, what he sold will remain in the possession of

25:9,10 *seventh month . . . fiftieth year:* See the note at 16:29. The last year of seven seven-year cycles was the Year of Jubilee. During this year all property was to be restored to its original owner (25:11,13). This was done so that each Israelite tribe could hold on to the land they were given when they first entered the land of Canaan (Num 34:1-29; Josh 15:1-14). Deuteronomy 15:1-11 adds that during this year debts should be canceled and any crops that grew on their own were to be left for the poor.

25:15 *Jubilee:* See the note at 25:9,10. Land bought one year before the Year of Jubilee had to be restored to the family that originally owned it. The price would be low, since the land would only have one year to produce crops. The price of the land was really a rental fee paid for the right to grow crops on the land and sell its produce (see also 25:23).

25:23,24 *not be sold permanently:* If property was sold in a year other than the Year of Jubilee, the original owner was to be given first chance to buy it back. In the Year of Jubilee, the land returned to the original owners for free.

25:25 *nearest relative is to come and redeem:* If a relative could not buy the land, it could be sold, but the original owner had to buy it back along with a fair rental price when he could afford it.

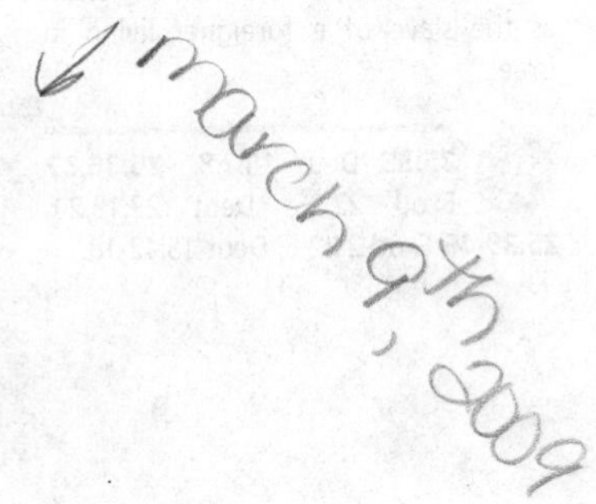

the buyer until the Year of Jubilee. It will be returned in the Jubilee, and he can then go back to his property.

29“ ‘If a man sells a house in a walled city, he retains the right of redemption a full year after its sale. During that time he may redeem it. 30If it is not redeemed before a full year has passed, the house in the walled city shall belong permanently to the buyer and his descendants. It is not to be returned in the Jubilee. 31But houses in villages without walls around them are to be considered as open country. They can be redeemed, and they are to be returned in the Jubilee.

32“ ‘The Levites always have the right to redeem their houses in the Levitical towns, which they possess. 33So the property of the Levites is redeemable—that is, a house sold in any town they hold—and is to be returned in the Jubilee, because the houses in the towns of the Levites are their property among the Israelites. 34But the pastureland belonging to their towns must not be sold; it is their permanent possession.

35“ ‘If one of your countrymen becomes poor and is unable to support himself among you, help him as you would an alien or a temporary resident, so he can continue to live among you. 36Do not take interest of any kind[a] from him, but fear your God, so that your countryman may continue to live among you. 37You must not lend him money at interest or sell him food at a profit. 38I am the LORD your God, who brought you out of Egypt to give you the land of Canaan and to be your God.

39“ ‘If one of your countrymen becomes poor among you and sells himself to you, do not make him work as a slave. 40He is to be treated as a hired worker or a temporary resident among you; he is to work for you until the Year of Jubilee. 41Then he and his children are to be released, and he will go back to his own clan and to the property of his forefathers. 42Because the Israelites are my servants, whom I brought out of Egypt, they must not be sold as slaves. 43Do not rule over them ruthlessly, but fear your God.

44“ ‘Your male and female slaves are to come from the nations around you; from them you may buy slaves. 45You may also buy some of the temporary residents living among you and members of their clans born in your country, and they will become your property. 46You can will them to your children as inherited property and can make them slaves for life, but you must not rule over your fellow Israelites ruthlessly.

47“ ‘If an alien or a temporary resident among you becomes rich and one of your countrymen becomes poor and sells himself to the alien living among you or to a member of the alien’s clan, 48he retains the right of redemption after he has sold himself. One of his relatives may redeem him: 49An uncle or a cousin or any blood relative in his clan may redeem him. Or if he prospers, he

[a]**36** Or *take excessive interest*; similarly in verse 37

25:29 *sells a house:* Houses were not like land, which always belonged to the original owner. If an owner wanted to buy back his house within a year of selling it, the new owner had to sell it back. But after a year, the new owner owned the house and could decide what to do with it.

25:32 *Levites:* The Levites were descendants of Levi, the son of Jacob and Leah (Gen 29:34). The Levi tribe did not receive a share of the land of Canaan when the Israelites settled there (Deut 10:9), but they were given towns and nearby pasturelands (Num 35:1-8; Josh 21:1-42).

25:35 *poor:* The poor were those who were forced to sell their property or land, so they were no longer able to make a living from it. A poor Israelite could rely on a relative’s help (25:25), become a servant of another Israelite (25:39), or become a slave for a foreigner living in the land of the Israelites (25:47-50). The people of God were to look after the needs of the poor (Exod 22:25; Isa 1:17; Amos 5:10-13). See the mini-articles called “Foreigners (Aliens),” p. 501, and “The Poor,” p. 2362.

25:38 *Egypt . . . Canaan:* See the notes at 11:44,45 and 14:34, 35 (Canaan). See also 18:2,3.

25:39 *as a slave:* This refers to poor Israelites who became paid servants of other Israelites (see the note at 25:35). In the Year of Jubilee they returned to their families, who once again would own the land originally given to them (see the note at 25:15).

25:44 *slaves:* This refers to people who worked without wages. A relative could buy the freedom of an Israelite who had sold himself or herself as the slave of a foreigner living in Israel.

25:35 Deut 15:7,8. **25:36,37** Exod 22:25; Deut 23:19,20. **25:39-46** Exod 21:2-6; Deut 15:12-18.

may redeem himself. 50He and his buyer are to count the time
from the year he sold himself up to the Year of Jubilee. The price
for his release is to be based on the rate paid to a hired man for
that number of years. 51If many years remain, he must pay for his
redemption a larger share of the price paid for him. 52If only a few
years remain until the Year of Jubilee, he is to compute that and
pay for his redemption accordingly. 53He is to be treated as a man
hired from year to year; you must see to it that his owner does not
rule over him ruthlessly.
54" 'Even if he is not redeemed in any of these ways, he and
his children are to be released in the Year of Jubilee, 55for the
Israelites belong to me as servants. They are my servants, whom I
brought out of Egypt. I am the LORD your God.

KEEPING PROMISES: THE BLESSINGS OF OBEDIENCE

Blessings are promised to those who obey the LORD, but punishment will happen to those who disobey by failing to follow the LORD's commands. The final chapters focus on promises made to the LORD as well as certain offerings required of God's people.

Reward for Obedience

26 " 'Do not make idols or set up an image or a sacred stone for
yourselves, and do not place a carved stone in your land to bow
down before it. I am the LORD your God.
2" 'Observe my Sabbaths and have reverence for my sanctuary.
I am the LORD.
3" 'If you follow my decrees and are careful to obey my commands, 4I will send you rain in its season, and the ground will yield
its crops and the trees of the field their fruit. 5Your threshing will
continue until grape harvest and the grape harvest will continue
until planting, and you will eat all the food you want and live in
safety in your land.
6" 'I will grant peace in the land, and you will lie down and
no one will make you afraid. I will remove savage beasts from the
land, and the sword will not pass through your country. 7You will
pursue your enemies, and they will fall by the sword before you.
8Five of you will chase a hundred, and a hundred of you will chase
ten thousand, and your enemies will fall by the sword before you.
9" 'I will look on you with favor and make you fruitful and
increase your numbers, and I will keep my covenant with you.
10You will still be eating last year's harvest when you will have to
move it out to make room for the new. 11I will put my dwelling
place[a] among you, and I will not abhor you. 12I will walk among
you and be your God, and you will be my people. 13I am the LORD

[a]11 Or *my tabernacle*

"I will walk among you and be your God, and you will be my people."
Lev 26:12

25:54 *Year of Jubilee:* See the note at 25:15. Freedom was based on God's freeing of the Israelites when they were slaves in Egypt (25:55). The Israelite people were to serve the LORD and not others.

26:1 *the LORD your God:* See the note at 1:1 (LORD).

26:2 *Sabbaths . . . sanctuary:* See the note at 16:29-31. The place of worship refers to the tabernacle and courtyard (see the note on p. 210, tabernacle). During King Solomon's reign Israel's "sanctuary" later became the temple in Jerusalem.

26:3-6 *obey my commands . . . I will grant peace:* If the people obey God's laws, God will give the blessings of rain and plentiful crops (26:4,5, 10), peace and protection from dangerous animals and human enemies (26:6-8), God's continuous presence (26:12), and freedom (26:13). See also Deut 7:12-15; 11:13-15; 28:1-14; 2 Cor 6:16.

26:1 Exod 20:4-6; Lev 19:4; Deut 5:8; 16:21,22. **26:13** Lev 11:44, 45; 18:2,3.

your God, who brought you out of Egypt so that you would no
longer be slaves to the Egyptians; I broke the bars of your yoke and
enabled you to walk with heads held high.

Punishment for Disobedience

14“‘But if you will not listen to me and carry out all these
commands, 15and if you reject my decrees and abhor my laws and
fail to carry out all my commands and so violate my covenant,
16then I will do this to you: I will bring upon you sudden terror,
wasting diseases and fever that will destroy your sight and drain
away your life. You will plant seed in vain, because your enemies
will eat it. 17I will set my face against you so that you will be defeated by your enemies; those who hate you will rule over you, and
you will flee even when no one is pursuing you.

18“‘If after all this you will not listen to me, I will punish you
for your sins seven times over. 19I will break down your stubborn
pride and make the sky above you like iron and the ground
beneath you like bronze. 20Your strength will be spent in vain,
because your soil will not yield its crops, nor will the trees of the
land yield their fruit.

21“‘If you remain hostile toward me and refuse to listen to
me, I will multiply your afflictions seven times over, as your sins
deserve. 22I will send wild animals against you, and they will rob
you of your children, destroy your cattle and make you so few in
number that your roads will be deserted.

23“‘If in spite of these things you do not accept my correction but continue to be hostile toward me, 24I myself will be hostile toward you and will afflict you for your sins seven times over.
25And I will bring the sword upon you to avenge the breaking of
the covenant. When you withdraw into your cities, I will send a
plague among you, and you will be given into enemy hands.
26When I cut off your supply of bread, ten women will be able to
bake your bread in one oven, and they will dole out the bread by
weight. You will eat, but you will not be satisfied.

27“‘If in spite of this you still do not listen to me but continue to be hostile toward me, 28then in my anger I will be hostile
toward you, and I myself will punish you for your sins seven times
over. 29You will eat the flesh of your sons and the flesh of your
daughters. 30I will destroy your high places, cut down your incense
altars and pile your dead bodies on the lifeless forms of your idols,
and I will abhor you. 31I will turn your cities into ruins and lay
waste your sanctuaries, and I will take no delight in the pleasing
aroma of your offerings. 32I will lay waste the land, so that your
enemies who live there will be appalled. 33I will scatter you among
the nations and will draw out my sword and pursue you. Your land
will be laid waste, and your cities will lie in ruins. 34Then the land
will enjoy its sabbath years all the time that it lies desolate and you
are in the country of your enemies; then the land will rest and

26:18 *seven times:* The number seven symbolized completeness or perfection. Israel's punishment would be total and complete. See also the chart called "Numbers in the Bible," p. 2405.

26:19 *the sky . . . like iron:* Ancient Hebrews understood the sky to be like a solid bowl or dome set over the earth (Gen 1:6-8), and high mountains held up the sky like pillars (Job 26:11). The sky had to be solid in order to hold back the flood of water above. Rain and snow were said to fall when God opened doors or windows in the sky (Ps 78:23). A sky dome made of "iron" would be solid, meaning no rain would come.

26:20 *soil will not yield:* Just the opposite of the plentiful harvest as a blessing for faithfulness (26:4,5,10).

26:30 *destroy your high places:* This probably refers to worship places dedicated to worshiping idols. This describes the situation that would come to pass in Israel some centuries after the time of Moses, when the people of Israel had built shrines to honor Canaanite gods and goddesses (1 Kgs 16:29-33; 22:52,53; 2 Kgs 14:3,4).

26:33-35 *scatter you among the nations:* In 722 B.C. the Assyrians defeated the northern kingdom (Israel) and carried many of its people away. About 125 years later the Babylonians defeated the southern kingdom (Judah) and took many of the Jewish people into exile in Babylon. See also the mini-article called "Exile," p. 1541.

26:14-33 Deut 28:15-68.

enjoy its sabbaths. [35]All the time that it lies desolate, the land will
have the rest it did not have during the sabbaths you lived in it.
[36]" 'As for those of you who are left, I will make their hearts
so fearful in the lands of their enemies that the sound of a windblown leaf will put them to flight. They will run as though fleeing
from the sword, and they will fall, even though no one is pursuing
them. [37]They will stumble over one another as though fleeing from
the sword, even though no one is pursuing them. So you will not
be able to stand before your enemies. [38]You will perish among the
nations; the land of your enemies will devour you. [39]Those of you
who are left will waste away in the lands of their enemies because
of their sins; also because of their fathers' sins they will waste away.
[40]" 'But if they will confess their sins and the sins of their
fathers—their treachery against me and their hostility toward me,
[41]which made me hostile toward them so that I sent them into the
land of their enemies—then when their uncircumcised hearts are
humbled and they pay for their sin, [42]I will remember my covenant
with Jacob and my covenant with Isaac and my covenant with
Abraham, and I will remember the land. [43]For the land will be
deserted by them and will enjoy its sabbaths while it lies desolate
without them. They will pay for their sins because they rejected my
laws and abhorred my decrees. [44]Yet in spite of this, when they are
in the land of their enemies, I will not reject them or abhor them
so as to destroy them completely, breaking my covenant with
them. I am the LORD their God. [45]But for their sake I will remember the covenant with their ancestors whom I brought out of
Egypt in the sight of the nations to be their God. I am the LORD.' "
[46]These are the decrees, the laws and the regulations that the
LORD established on Mount Sinai between himself and the
Israelites through Moses.

26:39 *because of their sins:* Here "sins" refers to Israel's people worshiping idols and treating their neighbors or the poor among them unfairly (Isa 48:1-11; Jer 11:9-13; Mic 2:1-3; Amos 2:4,5; 5:10-15).

26:42 *Jacob . . . Isaac . . . Abraham:* God promised Israel's earliest ancestors land and many descendants. God also promised to bless them, so that they could be a blessing to other nations (Gen 12:1-3). See also Gen 17:7,8; 26:3,4; 28:13,14.

27:2 *a special vow to dedicate persons to the LORD:* This refers to people who had been dedicated to serving the LORD by a promise or vow.

27:3-7 *shekels of silver . . . sanctuary shekel:* See the note at 5:15. The standard payments probably were based on how much work an individual would be able to do. A strong mature male would normally be able to do more work that required physical strength. See also Num 3:47; 18:16; 1 Sam 1:11.

26:45 Exod 12; Lev 11:44,45.

Redeeming What Is the LORD's

27 The LORD said to Moses, [2]"Speak to the Israelites and say to
them: 'If anyone makes a special vow to dedicate persons to the
LORD by giving equivalent values, [3]set the value of a male between
the ages of twenty and sixty at fifty shekels[a] of silver, according to
the sanctuary shekel[b]; [4]and if it is a female, set her value at thirty
shekels.[c] [5]If it is a person between the ages of five and twenty, set
the value of a male at twenty shekels[d] and of a female at ten
shekels.[e] [6]If it is a person between one month and five years, set
the value of a male at five shekels[f] of silver and that of a female at
three shekels[g] of silver. [7]If it is a person sixty years old or more, set

[a]3 That is, about 1 1/4 pounds (about 0.6 kilogram); also in verse 16 [b]3 That is, about 2/5 ounce (about 11.5 grams); also in verse 25 [c]4 That is, about 12 ounces (about 0.3 kilogram) [d]5 That is, about 8 ounces (about 0.2 kilogram) [e]5 That is, about 4 ounces (about 110 grams); also in verse 7 [f]6 That is, about 2 ounces (about 55 grams) [g]6 That is, about 1 1/4 ounces (about 35 grams)

"A tithe of everything from the land, whether grain from the soil or fruit from the trees, belongs to the LORD; it is holy to the LORD."
Lev 27:30

the value of a male at fifteen shekels[a] and of a female at ten shekels.
[8]If anyone making the vow is too poor to pay the specified
amount, he is to present the person to the priest, who will set the
value for him according to what the man making the vow can
afford.

[9]" 'If what he vowed is an animal that is acceptable as an
offering to the LORD, such an animal given to the LORD becomes
holy. [10]He must not exchange it or substitute a good one for a bad
one, or a bad one for a good one; if he should substitute one animal for another, both it and the substitute become holy. [11]If what
he vowed is a ceremonially unclean animal—one that is not
acceptable as an offering to the LORD—the animal must be presented to the priest, [12]who will judge its quality as good or bad.
Whatever value the priest then sets, that is what it will be. [13]If the
owner wishes to redeem the animal, he must add a fifth to its
value.

[14]" 'If a man dedicates his house as something holy to the
LORD, the priest will judge its quality as good or bad. Whatever
value the priest then sets, so it will remain. [15]If the man who dedicates his house redeems it, he must add a fifth to its value, and the
house will again become his.

[16]" 'If a man dedicates to the LORD part of his family land, its
value is to be set according to the amount of seed required for it—
fifty shekels of silver to a homer[b] of barley seed. [17]If he dedicates
his field during the Year of Jubilee, the value that has been set
remains. [18]But if he dedicates his field after the Jubilee, the priest
will determine the value according to the number of years that
remain until the next Year of Jubilee, and its set value will be
reduced. [19]If the man who dedicates the field wishes to redeem it,
he must add a fifth to its value, and the field will again become his.
[20]If, however, he does not redeem the field, or if he has sold it to
someone else, it can never be redeemed. [21]When the field is
released in the Jubilee, it will become holy, like a field devoted to
the LORD; it will become the property of the priests.[c]

[22]" 'If a man dedicates to the LORD a field he has bought,
which is not part of his family land, [23]the priest will determine its
value up to the Year of Jubilee, and the man must pay its value on
that day as something holy to the LORD. [24]In the Year of Jubilee the
field will revert to the person from whom he bought it, the one
whose land it was. [25]Every value is to be set according to the sanctuary shekel, twenty gerahs to the shekel.

[26]" 'No one, however, may dedicate the firstborn of an animal, since the firstborn already belongs to the LORD; whether an
ox[d] or a sheep, it is the LORD's. [27]If it is one of the unclean animals,

[a]**7** That is, about 6 ounces (about 170 grams) [b]**16** That is, probably about 6 bushels (about 220 liters) [c]**21** Or *priest* [d]**26** The Hebrew word can include both male and female.

27:9 *vowed . . . holy:* An animal promised as a sacrificial offering became holy, that is, "dedicated to the LORD," and couldn't be set free or exchanged for a different animal. Unclean animals, such as donkeys, that had been promised could be bought back for the priest's price plus an additional twenty percent.

27:16-21 *family land . . . property of the priests:* See the note at 25:9,10. Israel's land was divided among the descendants of Israel's twelve tribes. Families within each tribe were probably given their own pieces of land. The sale of lands dedicated to the LORD was complicated. Buying back dedicated family land was charged according to ten pieces of silver for every bushel of seed. This figure in 27:16 may be a yearly price, based on 27:17,18, which values the land according to the number of years till the next Year of Jubilee, when the land can be bought back by the family (27:19). However, once someone else has bought the land and dedicated it to the LORD, it becomes the property of the priests at the next Year of Jubilee.

27:25 *sanctuary shekel:* See the notes at 5:15 and 27:3-7.

27:26 *firstborn already belongs to the LORD:* The firstborn of the flocks belonged to the LORD (Exod 34:19, 20), just as the first harvested crops were to be given to the LORD (23:9,10). See also Exod 13:2; Num 3:11-13.

27:27 Lev 27:11-13.

he may buy it back at its set value, adding a fifth of the value to it.
If he does not redeem it, it is to be sold at its set value.
28“‘But nothing that a man owns and devotes[a] to the LORD—
whether man or animal or family land—may be sold or redeemed;
everything so devoted is most holy to the LORD.
29“‘No person devoted to destruction[b] may be ransomed; he
must be put to death.
30“‘A tithe of everything from the land, whether grain from
the soil or fruit from the trees, belongs to the LORD; it is holy to
the LORD. 31If a man redeems any of his tithe, he must add a fifth
of the value to it. 32The entire tithe of the herd and flock—every
tenth animal that passes under the shepherd's rod—will be holy to
the LORD. 33He must not pick out the good from the bad or make
any substitution. If he does make a substitution, both the animal
and its substitute become holy and cannot be redeemed.’”

34These are the commands the LORD gave Moses on Mount
Sinai for the Israelites.

[a]28 The Hebrew term refers to the irrevocable giving over of things or persons to the LORD. [b]29 The Hebrew term refers to the irrevocable giving over of things or persons to the LORD, often by totally destroying them.

27:28,29 *most holy to the LORD . . . put to death:* In order to show that something was dedicated completely to the LORD and could not be used by anyone else, it was destroyed. This law most often applied to towns and people captured in war (Josh 6:16, 17). See also Num 21:1-3; 1 Sam 15:3; and the mini-article called "Holy War (The LORD's Battles)," p. 306.

27:30 *tithe:* This passage says that a tenth is holy, or dedicated to the LORD's sacred place of worship. Compare this to the other tithe offerings described in Numbers 18:21-29 and Deuteronomy 14:22-29. See also 2 Chr 31:5,6.

27:34 *Mount Sinai:* See the note at 7:38.

27:28 Num 18:14.

QUESTIONS ABOUT LEVITICUS 17:1—27:34

1. Why were the laws forbidding certain kinds of sex so specific? (chapter 18) How do the rules in chapter 18 compare to written or unwritten laws concerning sexual activity today? In your opinion, what is the purpose of human sexual love?
2. Review the laws in chapter 19. Which do you think are most relevant for life today? Why? Which laws do you wish people were more careful about following? Why?
3. For what reason did the rule in 21:16-23 exist? How did you respond to that rule when you read it? Why?
4. Review the religious festivals in chapter 23. What was the purpose of each festival?
5. What was the purpose of the year of rest every seventh year, and the purpose of the Year of Jubilee? (chapter 25)
6. How were the laws of ancient Israel set up to help the poor? (25:35-55)
7. What blessings were promised to those who faithfully obeyed God's laws? (chapter 26) What were the punishments for disobeying?
8. Much of what is described in LEVITICUS is not part of our common modern-day life. But what words, phrases, or passages are especially helpful to you in understanding the meaning of LEVITICUS? How do you think people should understand the laws given in LEVITICUS today?

NUMBERS

God was leading the Israelites to the promised land, so why was their trip bumpy and filled with detours?

1:1 *LORD:* The translation for the Hebrew *Yahweh*, which is used in the Old Testament for God's personal name. It means "I Am" (see Exod 3:14, 15). See also the mini-article called "LORD (YHWH)," p. 140.

1:1 *Desert of Sinai . . . Egypt:* Just over a year before the narrative of NUMBERS begins, Moses had led the Israelite people out of slavery in Egypt (see Exod 12–15). After a time of wandering, they settled at Mount Sinai (see Exod 19–40 and Lev 1–27). There God made a covenant with Moses and the Israelites based on laws which set them apart as God's holy people. Mount Sinai was located in the Desert of Sinai on the Sinai Peninsula, but its exact location is unknown (see the map on p. 133).

WHAT MAKES NUMBERS SPECIAL?

The title NUMBERS comes from the Greek (*Arithmoi*) and Latin (*Numeri*) names for this book. The title in Hebrew is based on a word that means "in the desert." Both titles reflect what the book is about. Many lists of groups and numbers of people are included (see 1:20-46; 3:21-43; 7:12-83; 26:5-62), but more important is the description of the Israelites' desert journey toward the land God promised them. The promised land represented true freedom and escape from slavery in Egypt.

WHY WAS NUMBERS WRITTEN?

NUMBERS describes the Israelites' journey in the desert. There they learn how God wishes them to be organized, and how the Levites are to help Israel's priests. They also find out who will be chosen to lead them when they enter Canaan.

But the Israelites' journey also shows the rebellious side of the people. They complain that God has brought them out to the desert to starve or to die of thirst. They plot to get rid of their leaders, Moses and Aaron. After hearing the report of the spies who were sent to explore Canaan, they fearfully refuse to enter the land. Because of these sins, God does not allow them an easy, straight path to the land of promise. Instead, all those in the older generation who left Egypt (including Moses) must wander for forty years and eventually die in the desert. Only those in the younger generation would follow the faithful leaders, Joshua and Caleb, into Canaan. The lesson is about trust in God. Those who obey and trust God will receive God's blessings. Those who don't will not receive the blessings connected with God's promises.

The goal of entering the land of promise is what drives the Israelites' journey, but those who already live in and near the land are against the Israelites. To these people the Israelites are a threat. NUMBERS introduces the idea of a Holy War, in which God helps the Israelite people fight against and destroy their enemies.

WHAT'S THE STORY BEHIND THE SCENE?

NUMBERS is the fourth book of the five-part section of the Old Testament known as the Pentateuch (see the Introduction to the Pentateuch, p. 35). It continues the story of the wandering Israelite people begun in EXODUS and continued in LEVITICUS. While LEVITICUS describes the Israelite people learning God's laws concerning holiness as they camp at Mount Sinai, NUMBERS depicts the Israelite people on the move. Moses has traditionally been identified as the book's author, and much of the central material in the book may date to the time of Moses. Many scholars believe it is likely that scribes and editors who lived centuries later put the book in the form we know today.

How is Numbers constructed?

Numbers is made up of many different kinds of material. Those who have tried to find a structure usually point to two different ways of looking at its organization. One divides the book based on the two generations of Israelites who wandered in the desert. Chapters 1–25 focus on the older, disobedient generation, while chapters 26–36 mainly focus on the younger generation, who would enter the promised land of Canaan.

The second way of organizing Numbers divides the book according to where the action takes place. The following outline uses this geographical way of structuring the book:

Israel in camp at Sinai (1:1—10:10)
- The people are counted and organized (1:1—2:34)
- The duties of the priests and Levites (3:1—4:49)
- Instructions for God's holy people (5:1—10:10)

Israel's journey from Sinai to Moab (10:11—21:35)
- From Sinai to the Desert of Paran (10:11—12:16)
- Trouble in the camp at Kadesh (13:1—20:13)
- From Kadesh to Moab (20:14—21:35)

The Moab camp: Preparing to enter Canaan (22:1—36:13)
- The stories of Balaam and the worship of Baal (22:1—25:18)
- Counting and instructing a new generation (26:1—30:16)
- Getting ready to cross the Jordan River (31:1—36:13)

1:1 *second month:* Ziv, the second month of the Hebrew calendar, falls from about mid-April to mid-May. See also the chart called "Jewish Calendar and Festivals," p. 944.

1:1 *the Israelites:* The Israelites are traditionally understood to be the descendants of Abraham's grandson Jacob (who was also called Israel). The Israelites believed they were the inheritors of the promise God made to Abraham (Gen 12:1-7) and reaffirmed with Jacob (Gen 28:10-15). This promise includes the gift of the land of Canaan. For more about Jacob's sons, see the chart called "Jacob's Children and Their Mothers," p. 99. The blessings each son received from Jacob are described in Genesis 48:1—49:28. The blessings Moses gave to the twelve tribes before they entered Canaan are described in Deuteronomy 33. See also the mini-article called "Israel," p. 264.

1:2,3 *census . . . clans and families . . . Aaron:* Each of Israel's twelve tribes was divided into clans, and each clan included a number of families. Only males twenty years old or older were to be counted in this census, because they were the ones expected to fight in battle. Moses and his brother Aaron, Israel's first high priest (Exod 27:21—28:3), were given the task of taking the census.

1:1-46 Num 26:1-51.

Israel in Camp at Sinai

A year after leaving Egypt, Israel is still camped at Sinai. There the Lord *commands Moses to count the people and to set Israel's tribes in order around the tabernacle. The Levite tribe is counted, given special duties, and dedicated to the* Lord. *Other laws and regulations are given as the people prepare to leave Sinai and begin their journey toward the promised land of Canaan.*

THE PEOPLE ARE COUNTED AND ORGANIZED

With the help of tribal leaders, Moses and Aaron count Israel's males twenty and older, and they organize Israel's tribes in a special order around the tabernacle.

The Census

1 The Lord spoke to Moses in the Tent of Meeting in the Desert
of Sinai on the first day of the second month of the second year
after the Israelites came out of Egypt. He said: 2"Take a census of
the whole Israelite community by their clans and families, listing
every man by name, one by one. 3You and Aaron are to number by

The people indicated their ancestry by their clans and families, . . . as the LORD commanded Moses.
Num 1:18,19

their divisions all the men in Israel twenty years old or more who
are able to serve in the army. 4One man from each tribe, each the
head of his family, is to help you. 5These are the names of the men
who are to assist you:

from Reuben, Elizur son of Shedeur;
6from Simeon, Shelumiel son of Zurishaddai;
7from Judah, Nahshon son of Amminadab;
8from Issachar, Nethanel son of Zuar;

ISRAEL

The name "Israel" is used in several different, but interrelated, ways in the Bible. The following summary describes these different uses.

The Name. The Hebrew word for "Israel" means "one who wrestles with God" or "May God join in the struggle!" The second meaning implies "May God defeat the forces that oppose God and the people of God." The name "Israel" was given to Jacob, the son of Isaac and Rebekah and grandson of Abraham and Sarah, after Jacob wrestled with someone who seemed to be a human but later turned out to be God (Gen 32:22-32). Later, Israel's twelve tribes were named for the sons of Jacob (Israel) and for two of his grandsons (see Gen 48,49).

The Nation. About 1000 B.C. the people from the separate tribes began to come together under their first king, Saul (1 Sam 9,10). But it was King David who brought all the tribes together in one unified nation under one ruler (2 Sam 5:1-5). Jerusalem became the nation's capital and the central place for the people to worship God. David's son, King Solomon, built a temple in Jerusalem where all Israel could come together to worship the LORD (2 Sam 7; 1 Kgs 6). Under Solomon, the territory known as Israel stretched from the Gulf of Aqaba and the northern boundaries of Egypt in the south to Kadesh and the Euphrates River in northern Syria.

After Solomon died (924 B.C.), the ten northern tribes broke away from the two southern tribes known as Judah. These northern tribes built their own temple in the north at Samaria, and called themselves "Israel" (1 Kgs 12; 16:32). In 722 B.C. the Assyrians invaded from the north and deported the people of the northern kingdom (Israel), sending them into various regions in the Assyrian empire. The people in the southern kingdom (Judah) were not captured by the Assyrians, but in 586 B.C. Judah was defeated by the Babylonians and many of its people sent to live throughout Babylonia. This period in the history of Israel is known as "the exile." For more, see the mini-article called "Exile," p. 1541. During the time before and after the exile, "Israel" was often used by the prophets as the name for all God's people (Ezek 36; Hos 4,5).

God's Holy People. After the time of the Babylonian exile, the Israelites who returned to Judah were governed by the Persians and, later, by the Greeks. At this time the people of Israel, regardless of where they lived, came to be known as "Jews," a term derived from the Greco-Latin term "Judea," meaning Judah. Because they lived in so many different places, the Jewish people did not base their identity so much on the geographic area they controlled or on political power, but on their commitment to following God's Law. This desire to obey God is what set them apart from other nations. At the time of Jesus, the people of Israel were ruled by the Romans but continued to follow the traditions, ceremonies, and festivals that made them God's holy people.

[9] from Zebulun, Eliab son of Helon;
[10] from the sons of Joseph:
from Ephraim, Elishama son of Ammihud;
from Manasseh, Gamaliel son of Pedahzur;
[11] from Benjamin, Abidan son of Gideoni;
[12] from Dan, Ahiezer son of Ammishaddai;
[13] from Asher, Pagiel son of Ocran;
[14] from Gad, Eliasaph son of Deuel;
[15] from Naphtali, Ahira son of Enan."

[16] These were the men appointed from the community, the
leaders of their ancestral tribes. They were the heads of the clans of
Israel.
[17] Moses and Aaron took these men whose names had been
given, [18] and they called the whole community together on the first
day of the second month. The people indicated their ancestry by
their clans and families, and the men twenty years old or more
were listed by name, one by one, [19] as the LORD commanded Moses.
And so he counted them in the Desert of Sinai:

[20] From the descendants of Reuben the firstborn son of Israel:
All the men twenty years old or more who were able to
serve in the army were listed by name, one by one, according to the records of their clans and families. [21] The number from the tribe of Reuben was 46,500.

[22] From the descendants of Simeon:
All the men twenty years old or more who were able to
serve in the army were counted and listed by name, one
by one, according to the records of their clans and families. [23] The number from the tribe of Simeon was 59,300.

[24] From the descendants of Gad:
All the men twenty years old or more who were able to
serve in the army were listed by name, according to the
records of their clans and families. [25] The number from the
tribe of Gad was 45,650.

[26] From the descendants of Judah:
All the men twenty years old or more who were able to
serve in the army were listed by name, according to the
records of their clans and families. [27] The number from the
tribe of Judah was 74,600.

[28] From the descendants of Issachar:
All the men twenty years old or more who were able to
serve in the army were listed by name, according to the
records of their clans and families. [29] The number from the
tribe of Issachar was 54,400.

[30] From the descendants of Zebulun:
All the men twenty years old or more who were able to

1:5-16 *leaders of their ancestral tribes . . . heads of the clans:* These verses list the twelve tribes that would later be given land in Canaan. The tribes were named for the sons of Jacob. Ephraim and Manasseh were the sons of Jacob's son Joseph. Each received a share of land in Canaan (see Gen 48). The tribe of Levi was given special duties but did not receive a share of the land (see the note at 1:47). See similar lists in chapters 2; 7; 26; and 34. See also Gen 29:31—30:24.

1:24 *Gad:* Gad is listed third in this list, instead of eleventh as in the previous list (1:14). This is probably because the family was supposed to camp on the south side of the tabernacle next to Reuben and Simeon (2:10-16).

The LORD said to Moses, *"You must not count the tribe of Levi or include them in the census of the other Israelites. Instead, appoint the Levites to be in charge of the tabernacle of the Testimony."* Num 1:49,50

serve in the army were listed by name, according to the
records of their clans and families. [31]The number from the
tribe of Zebulun was 57,400.

[32]From the sons of Joseph:
From the descendants of Ephraim:
All the men twenty years old or more who were able to
serve in the army were listed by name, according to the
records of their clans and families. [33]The number from the
tribe of Ephraim was 40,500.
[34]From the descendants of Manasseh:

ISRAEL COUNTED TWICE

NUMBERS describes two censuses organized by Moses. The LORD asked Moses to make a list of all the men twenty years or older who would be able to fight in battle. The first census took place at Sinai a year after the Israelites came out of Egypt. It counted the generation of Israelites the LORD would not allow to enter Canaan, because of their lack of trust in God (Num 14:21-35). The second census took place in the plains of Moab about thirty-eight years later (Num 26). It counted the generation that would eventually enter Canaan. Between the censuses, some tribes lost many people as a punishment for disobeying God. The LORD also asked Moses to count all the men and boys in the tribe of Levi who were at least one month old. The Levites would not own land in Canaan; instead, they were to serve the entire nation as priests and by taking care of the tabernacle.

TRIBES ENTITLED TO LAND AND REQUESTED TO FIGHT IN BATTLE		
Israel's Tribes	**Numbers 1:20-46**	**Numbers 26:1-65**
Reuben	46,500	43,730
Simeon	59,300	22,200
Gad	45,650	40,500
Judah	74,600	76,500
Issachar	54,400	64,300
Zebulun	57,400	60,500
Ephraim	40,500	32,500
Manasseh	32,200	52,700
Benjamin	35,400	45,600
Dan	62,700	64,400
Asher	41,500	53,400
Naphtali	53,400	45,400
SUBTOTALS	**603,550**	**601,730**
PRIESTLY TRIBE IN CHARGE OF THE SACRED TENT		
Levites	22,000	23,000
TOTAL	**625,550**	**624,730**

All the men twenty years old or more who were able to
serve in the army were listed by name, according to the
records of their clans and families. [35]The number from the
tribe of Manasseh was 32,200.

[36]From the descendants of Benjamin:
All the men twenty years old or more who were able to
serve in the army were listed by name, according to the
records of their clans and families. [37]The number from the
tribe of Benjamin was 35,400.

[38]From the descendants of Dan:
All the men twenty years old or more who were able to
serve in the army were listed by name, according to the
records of their clans and families. [39]The number from the
tribe of Dan was 62,700.

[40]From the descendants of Asher:
All the men twenty years old or more who were able to
serve in the army were listed by name, according to the
records of their clans and families. [41]The number from the
tribe of Asher was 41,500.

[42]From the descendants of Naphtali:
All the men twenty years old or more who were able to
serve in the army were listed by name, according to the
records of their clans and families. [43]The number from the
tribe of Naphtali was 53,400.

[44]These were the men counted by Moses and Aaron and the
twelve leaders of Israel, each one representing his family. [45]All the
Israelites twenty years old or more who were able to serve in
Israel's army were counted according to their families. [46]The total
number was 603,550.

[47]The families of the tribe of Levi, however, were not counted along with the others. [48]The LORD had said to Moses: [49]"You
must not count the tribe of Levi or include them in the census of
the other Israelites. [50]Instead, appoint the Levites to be in charge of
the tabernacle of the Testimony—over all its furnishings and
everything belonging to it. They are to carry the tabernacle and all
its furnishings; they are to take care of it and encamp around it.
[51]Whenever the tabernacle is to move, the Levites are to take it
down, and whenever the tabernacle is to be set up, the Levites shall
do it. Anyone else who goes near it shall be put to death. [52]The
Israelites are to set up their tents by divisions, each man in his own
camp under his own standard. [53]The Levites, however, are to set up
their tents around the tabernacle of the Testimony so that wrath
will not fall on the Israelite community. The Levites are to be
responsible for the care of the tabernacle of the Testimony."

[54]The Israelites did all this just as the LORD commanded
Moses.

1:46 *The total number:* The total of 603,550 fighting men has been questioned by many Bible scholars as being too large, but an agreement has not been reached on what may be a more accurate number.

1:47 *tribe of Levi:* Descendants of Levi, the son of Jacob and Leah (Gen 29:34). The Levite tribe did not receive a share of the land of Canaan (Deut 10:9), but they were given towns and nearby pasturelands (see 35:1-8; Josh 21:1-42). The Levites helped the priests by taking care of the tabernacle and its furnishings and by carrying them from camp to camp.

1:52,53 *standard . . . tabernacle:* A standard was probably a flag used by the tribes in battle; each tribe having its own unique standard. The Levites camped close to the tabernacle to protect it (see the note at Lev 15:31). See Exodus 25–27 and 30 for a description of the tabernacle.

2:3-9 *Judah . . . Zebulun:* The first tribes mentioned are called by the names of the fourth, fifth, and sixth sons of Jacob and Leah (Gen 29:35; 30:16-20). Judah was given a place of honor among his brothers when Jacob blessed his sons (Gen 49:8-10). Judah's warriors were to lead the other tribes into battle. See the chart called "Israel on the March," p. 288, showing the order in which the tribes were to march.

2:10-16 *Reuben . . . Gad:* Reuben and Simeon were the first and second sons of Jacob and Leah (Gen 29:31-33). Reuben lost his position as Jacob's firstborn son because he slept with Bilhah, one of Jacob's wives. See Gen 35:22; 49:3,4. Gad was Jacob's seventh son and his first son by Leah's maid Zilpah (Gen 30:9-11).

2:17 *Levites:* See the note at 1:47. Levi was the third son of Jacob and Leah (Gen 29:34). Levi was also passed over for leadership because he had helped Simeon massacre the Hivite men (Gen 34; 49:5-7). Some of the Levites led the march of the Israelite tribes because they carried the ark of the covenant (10:33). See the chart called "Israel on the March," p. 288, showing the order of Israel's tribes as they marched.

2:18-24 *Ephraim . . . Benjamin:* Ephraim and Manasseh were the sons of Joseph, Jacob's first son by Rachel (Gen 30:22-24). Benjamin was Jacob's youngest son, also born to Rachel (Gen 35:16-18).

The Arrangement of the Tribal Camps

2 The LORD said to Moses and Aaron: [2]"The Israelites are to
camp around the Tent of Meeting some distance from it, each man
under his standard with the banners of his family."

[3]On the east, toward the sunrise, the divisions of the
camp of Judah are to encamp under their standard. The leader
of the people of Judah is Nahshon son of Amminadab. [4]His
division numbers 74,600.
[5]The tribe of Issachar will camp next to them. The
leader of the people of Issachar is Nethanel son of Zuar. [6]His
division numbers 54,400.
[7]The tribe of Zebulun will be next. The leader of the
people of Zebulun is Eliab son of Helon. [8]His division numbers 57,400.
[9]All the men assigned to the camp of Judah, according
to their divisions, number 186,400. They will set out first.
[10]On the south will be the divisions of the camp of
Reuben under their standard. The leader of the people of
Reuben is Elizur son of Shedeur. [11]His division numbers
46,500.
[12]The tribe of Simeon will camp next to them. The
leader of the people of Simeon is Shelumiel son of Zurishaddai. [13]His division numbers 59,300.
[14]The tribe of Gad will be next. The leader of the people
of Gad is Eliasaph son of Deuel.[a] [15]His division numbers
45,650.
[16]All the men assigned to the camp of Reuben, according to their divisions, number 151,450. They will set out second.

[17]Then the Tent of Meeting and the camp of the Levites
will set out in the middle of the camps. They will set out in
the same order as they encamp, each in his own place under
his standard.
[18]On the west will be the divisions of the camp of
Ephraim under their standard. The leader of the people of
Ephraim is Elishama son of Ammihud. [19]His division numbers 40,500.
[20]The tribe of Manasseh will be next to them. The leader
of the people of Manasseh is Gamaliel son of Pedahzur. [21]His
division numbers 32,200.
[22]The tribe of Benjamin will be next. The leader of the
people of Benjamin is Abidan son of Gideoni. [23]His division
numbers 35,400.

---

a14 Many manuscripts of the Masoretic Text, Samaritan Pentateuch and Vulgate (see also Num. 1:14); most manuscripts of the Masoretic Text *Reuel*

24 All the men assigned to the camp of Ephraim, according to their divisions, number 108,100. They will set out third.

25 On the north will be the divisions of the camp of Dan,
under their standard. The leader of the people of Dan is
Ahiezer son of Ammishaddai. 26 His division numbers 62,700.
27 The tribe of Asher will camp next to them. The leader

2:25-31 *Dan . . . Naphtali:* Dan led the northern camp as the firstborn son of Jacob and Rachel's maid Bilhah (Gen 30:4-6). Naphtali was Jacob and Bilhah's second son (Gen 30:7,8), and Asher was Jacob's second son with Leah's maid Zilpah (Gen 30:9-13).

Twelve Tents of the Tribes of Israel, page from an illuminated manuscript, seventeenth century. The tabernacle was important to the people of Israel during the forty years they wandered in the desert. Each time the people settled in a place, the tabernacle (Tent of Meeting) was set up in the center of the encampment and the tents of the twelve tribes were set up at a distance on all four sides (see 2:2). The ark of the covenant, guarded by two cherubim, was placed inside the tabernacle. The ark held the stone tablets with God's commandments written on them, a jar of manna, and Aaron's staff (see Exod 25:10-22; Num 17:10; Heb 9:4). Also shown here is a jar containing blood from an animal sacrifice, and an "eternal lamp."

of the people of Asher is Pagiel son of Ocran. [28]His division numbers 41,500.

[29]The tribe of Naphtali will be next. The leader of the people of Naphtali is Ahira son of Enan. [30]His division numbers 53,400.

[31]All the men assigned to the camp of Dan number 157,600. They will set out last, under their standards.

[32]These are the Israelites, counted according to their families. All those in the camps, by their divisions, number 603,550. [33]The Levites, however, were not counted along with the other Israelites, as the LORD commanded Moses.

[34]So the Israelites did everything the LORD commanded Moses; that is the way they encamped under their standards, and that is the way they set out, each with his clan and family.

THE DUTIES OF THE PRIESTS AND LEVITES

Moses is told to count the Levite tribe and to explain the duties of the Levite clans.

The Levites

3 This is the account of the family of Aaron and Moses at the time the LORD talked with Moses on Mount Sinai.

[2]The names of the sons of Aaron were Nadab the firstborn and Abihu, Eleazar and Ithamar. [3]Those were the names of Aaron's sons, the anointed priests, who were ordained to serve as priests. [4]Nadab and Abihu, however, fell dead before the LORD when they made an offering with unauthorized fire before him in the Desert of Sinai. They had no sons; so only Eleazar and Ithamar served as priests during the lifetime of their father Aaron.

[5]The LORD said to Moses, [6]"Bring the tribe of Levi and present them to Aaron the priest to assist him. [7]They are to perform duties for him and for the whole community at the Tent of Meeting by doing the work of the tabernacle. [8]They are to take care of all the furnishings of the Tent of Meeting, fulfilling the obligations of the Israelites by doing the work of the tabernacle. [9]Give the Levites to Aaron and his sons; they are the Israelites who are to be given wholly to him.[a] [10]Appoint Aaron and his sons to serve as priests; anyone else who approaches the sanctuary must be put to death."

[11]The LORD also said to Moses, [12]"I have taken the Levites from among the Israelites in place of the first male offspring of every Israelite woman. The Levites are mine, [13]for all the firstborn are mine. When I struck down all the firstborn in Egypt, I set apart

[a]9 Most manuscripts of the Masoretic Text; some manuscripts of the Masoretic Text, Samaritan Pentateuch and Septuagint (see also Num. 8:16) *to me*

2:33 *Levites . . . not counted:* See the note at 1:47.

2:34 *standards . . . set out:* See the chart called "Israel on the March," p. 288.

2:34 *clan:* Clans are groups of extended families who are descended from a common male ancestor. Tribes are made up of all the clans who are descended from a single male ancestor (for the Israelites, one of Jacob's sons). See also the mini-article called "Genealogies in the Bible," p. 734.

3:2,3 *sons of Aaron . . . anointed priests . . . ordained:* All of Aaron's sons were ordained by Moses at Mount Sinai (Exod 29:1-37; 30:30; 40:12-15; Lev 8). To "ordain" means to choose or to set apart to serve God. Nadab and Abihu died when they did not follow correct procedures for offering a sacrifice (Lev 10:1,2). See also Lev 10:12; Num 26:60,61.

3:6 *tribe of Levi:* See the note at 1:47.

3:11-13 *firstborn:* In ancient societies, the firstborn son often held a special place in the family structure. As Israel was preparing to leave Egypt, the LORD told Moses that Israel's firstborn sons and the firstborn of the flocks were to be dedicated, that is, set apart to honor and serve the LORD (Exod 13:1,2,11-16; see also Lev 27:26). See the note at 3:44-48. Now, the Levites are to take the place of firstborn sons.

for myself every firstborn in Israel, whether man or animal. They
are to be mine. I am the LORD."
14 The LORD said to Moses in the Desert of Sinai, 15 "Count
the Levites by their families and clans. Count every male a month
old or more." 16 So Moses counted them, as he was commanded by
the word of the LORD.
17 These were the names of the sons of Levi:
Gershon, Kohath and Merari.
18 These were the names of the Gershonite clans:
Libni and Shimei.
19 The Kohathite clans:
Amram, Izhar, Hebron and Uzziel.
20 The Merarite clans:
Mahli and Mushi.
These were the Levite clans, according to their families.

21 To Gershon belonged the clans of the Libnites and
Shimeites; these were the Gershonite clans. 22 The number of all the
males a month old or more who were counted was 7,500. 23 The
Gershonite clans were to camp on the west, behind the tabernacle.
24 The leader of the families of the Gershonites was Eliasaph son of
Lael. 25 At the Tent of Meeting the Gershonites were responsible for
the care of the tabernacle and tent, its coverings, the curtain at the
entrance to the Tent of Meeting, 26 the curtains of the courtyard,
the curtain at the entrance to the courtyard surrounding the tabernacle and altar, and the ropes—and everything related to their use.

27 To Kohath belonged the clans of the Amramites, Izharites,
Hebronites and Uzzielites; these were the Kohathite clans. 28 The
number of all the males a month old or more was 8,600.[a]
The Kohathites were responsible for the care of the sanctuary.
29 The Kohathite clans were to camp on the south side of the tabernacle. 30 The leader of the families of the Kohathite clans was Elizaphan son of Uzziel. 31 They were responsible for the care of the ark,
the table, the lampstand, the altars, the articles of the sanctuary
used in ministering, the curtain, and everything related to their
use. 32 The chief leader of the Levites was Eleazar son of Aaron, the
priest. He was appointed over those who were responsible for the
care of the sanctuary.

33 To Merari belonged the clans of the Mahlites and the
Mushites; these were the Merarite clans. 34 The number of all
the males a month old or more who were counted was 6,200. 35 The
leader of the families of the Merarite clans was Zuriel son of
Abihail; they were to camp on the north side of the tabernacle.
36 The Merarites were appointed to take care of the frames of the

[a] **28** Hebrew; some Septuagint manuscripts *8,300*

3:14 *Desert of Sinai:* See the note on 1:1 (Desert of Sinai).

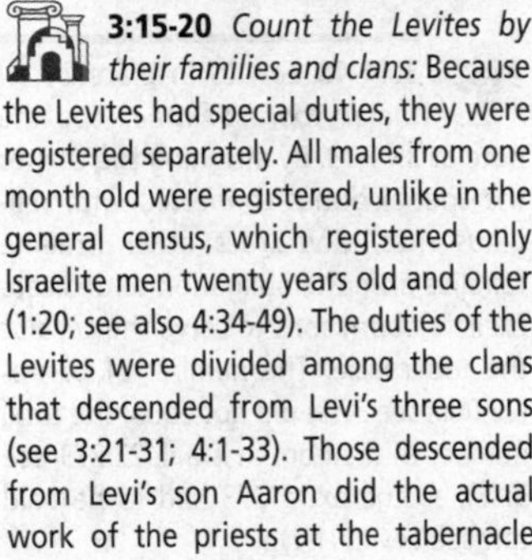

3:15-20 *Count the Levites by their families and clans:* Because the Levites had special duties, they were registered separately. All males from one month old were registered, unlike in the general census, which registered only Israelite men twenty years old and older (1:20; see also 4:34-49). The duties of the Levites were divided among the clans that descended from Levi's three sons (see 3:21-31; 4:1-33). Those descended from Levi's son Aaron did the actual work of the priests at the tabernacle (3:32).

3:21 *Gershonite clans:* This clan camped behind the tabernacle on the west side, opposite the entrance. They were in charge of putting up and taking down the covering and curtains of the tabernacle, except the curtain in front of the Most Holy Place (3:31; see also the notes at Exod 26 and the chart called "Israel on the March," p. 288).

3:27 *Kohathite clans:* This clan camped on the south side of the tabernacle, in the second most important position. The Kohathites took care of the sacred objects (see Exod 25:10-40; 30:1-10) in the tabernacle. They were not allowed to touch or look at these sacred objects, so the priests from Aaron's family covered them first (4:4-12). Then the Kohath clan could carry them from place to place.

3:32 *chief leader . . . Eleazar:* Aaron and his sons Eleazar and Ithamar were the leaders of the Levite clans. They functioned as Israel's priests and made sure the other clans did their assigned work. They camped in the most important location, near the entrance of the tabernacle on the east side.

3:33 *Merarite clans:* Camped on the north side of the tabernacle. They were responsible for carrying, setting up, and taking down the framework that held the tabernacle together (see Exod 26:15-30).

3:39 *22,000:* The total of the clans as given in 3:22, 28, and 34 is 22,300.

3:44-48 *Levites in place of all the firstborn of Israel:* See the note at 3:11-13. By assigning the Levites the special duties connected with religious rites, God frees other Israelite families from the obligation to dedicate their firstborn sons to serve the LORD at the tabernacle. The number of Levites (22,000; see 3:39) did not equal the total number of firstborn in Israel (22,273; see 3:46), so the extra 273 had to be paid for (see Lev 27:1-7).

The Israelites did not use coins and paper money at this time. Pieces of silver called "shekels" (each weighing about one-fifth of an ounce) served as the official currency. See also the chart called "Banking and Money in the Ancient World," p. 951.

4:2 *Kohathite:* See the note at 3:27.

4:6,7 *poles . . . table of the Presence:* The Kohathites carried the sacred objects by putting wood poles covered with gold through gold loops attached to corners or legs of those objects (Exod 25:12-14, 26-28). The table held the bread of the Presence that was offered to the LORD and was a symbol of the LORD's presence in the tabernacle. Twelve loaves representing the twelve tribes of Israel were placed fresh on the holy table every Sabbath (Lev 24:5-9). The table made of acacia wood and covered with gold probably looked like a modern coffee table with a raised ridge all around its top.

tabernacle, its crossbars, posts, bases, all its equipment, and everything related to their use, [37]as well as the posts of the surrounding
courtyard with their bases, tent pegs and ropes.

[38]Moses and Aaron and his sons were to camp to the east of
the tabernacle, toward the sunrise, in front of the Tent of Meeting.
They were responsible for the care of the sanctuary on behalf of
the Israelites. Anyone else who approached the sanctuary was to be
put to death.

[39]The total number of Levites counted at the LORD's command by Moses and Aaron according to their clans, including
every male a month old or more, was 22,000.

[40]The LORD said to Moses, "Count all the firstborn Israelite
males who are a month old or more and make a list of their
names. [41]Take the Levites for me in place of all the firstborn of the
Israelites, and the livestock of the Levites in place of all the firstborn of the livestock of the Israelites. I am the LORD."
[42]So Moses counted all the firstborn of the Israelites, as the
LORD commanded him. [43]The total number of firstborn males a
month old or more, listed by name, was 22,273.
[44]The LORD also said to Moses, [45]"Take the Levites in place
of all the firstborn of Israel, and the livestock of the Levites in
place of their livestock. The Levites are to be mine. I am the LORD.
[46]To redeem the 273 firstborn Israelites who exceed the number of
the Levites, [47]collect five shekels[a] for each one, according to the
sanctuary shekel, which weighs twenty gerahs. [48]Give the money
for the redemption of the additional Israelites to Aaron and his
sons."
[49]So Moses collected the redemption money from those who
exceeded the number redeemed by the Levites. [50]From the firstborn of the Israelites he collected silver weighing 1,365 shekels,[b]
according to the sanctuary shekel. [51]Moses gave the redemption
money to Aaron and his sons, as he was commanded by the word
of the LORD.

The Kohathites

4 The LORD said to Moses and Aaron: [2]"Take a census of the
Kohathite branch of the Levites by their clans and families. [3]Count
all the men from thirty to fifty years of age who come to serve in
the work in the Tent of Meeting.
[4]"This is the work of the Kohathites in the Tent of Meeting:
the care of the most holy things. [5]When the camp is to move,
Aaron and his sons are to go in and take down the shielding cur-

[a]**47** That is, about 2 ounces (about 55 grams) [b]**50** That is, about 35 pounds (about 15.5 kilograms)

tain and cover the ark of the Testimony with it. 6Then they are to
cover this with hides of sea cows,[a] spread a cloth of solid blue over
that and put the poles in place.

7“Over the table of the Presence they are to spread a blue
cloth and put on it the plates, dishes and bowls, and the jars for
drink offerings; the bread that is continually there is to remain on
it. 8Over these they are to spread a scarlet cloth, cover that with
hides of sea cows and put its poles in place.

9“They are to take a blue cloth and cover the lampstand that
is for light, together with its lamps, its wick trimmers and trays,
and all its jars for the oil used to supply it. 10Then they are to wrap
it and all its accessories in a covering of hides of sea cows and put
it on a carrying frame.

11“Over the gold altar they are to spread a blue cloth and
cover that with hides of sea cows and put its poles in place.

12“They are to take all the articles used for ministering in the
sanctuary, wrap them in a blue cloth, cover that with hides of sea
cows and put them on a carrying frame.

13“They are to remove the ashes from the bronze altar and
spread a purple cloth over it. 14Then they are to place on it all the
utensils used for ministering at the altar, including the firepans,
meat forks, shovels and sprinkling bowls. Over it they are to spread
a covering of hides of sea cows and put its poles in place.

15“After Aaron and his sons have finished covering the holy
furnishings and all the holy articles, and when the camp is ready to
move, the Kohathites are to come to do the carrying. But they
must not touch the holy things or they will die. The Kohathites are
to carry those things that are in the Tent of Meeting.

16“Eleazar son of Aaron, the priest, is to have charge of the
oil for the light, the fragrant incense, the regular grain offering and
the anointing oil. He is to be in charge of the entire tabernacle and
everything in it, including its holy furnishings and articles.”

17The LORD said to Moses and Aaron, 18“See that the
Kohathite tribal clans are not cut off from the Levites. 19So that
they may live and not die when they come near the most holy
things, do this for them: Aaron and his sons are to go into the
sanctuary and assign to each man his work and what he is to carry.
20But the Kohathites must not go in to look at the holy things, even
for a moment, or they will die.”

The Gershonites

21The LORD said to Moses, 22“Take a census also of the Gershonites by their families and clans. 23Count all the men from thirty to fifty years of age who come to serve in the work at the Tent
of Meeting.

4:9-11 *lampstand . . . oil . . . gold altar:* The lampstand (see Exod 25:31-40) was made of pure gold and had seven branches with small clay saucer-like lamps attached to the end of each branch (see the illustration on p. 2345). The light from the lamps represented the glory of God (Exod 29:43). Pure olive oil was burned in the lamps. The incense altar in the Holy Place of the tabernacle was made of acacia wood and covered with gold (see Exod 30:1-10). Incense was made from tree resins, spices and salt, which together produced a sweet-smelling smoke when burned. The smoke represented the prayers that went up to God (Ps 141:2; Rev 5:8).

4:13,14 *bronze altar:* The altar used for offering sacrifices was outside the entrance to the tabernacle. It was made of acacia wood covered with bronze, a metal alloy made by melting and mixing copper and tin (see Exod 27:1-8). All the equipment used at the altar was also made of bronze.

4:15 *must not touch . . . will die:* The sacred objects were holy and were not to be touched by anyone except the priests who represented the people before God. Touching a sacred object could be disastrous (see 2 Sam 6:1-7).

4:16 *anointing oil:* Objects or people could be consecrated, or dedicated, to the LORD, that is, set apart to honor or serve him. Consecration of a person chosen for a specific task, such as a priest or king, was usually accompanied by pouring oil on the person's head as a sign of being chosen. This pouring of oil is also known as “anointing.” See also Exod 29:1-7; Lev 8:12; 1 Sam 10:1; 16:12,13.

4:18,19 *not die when they come near the most holy things:* See the note at 4:15.

4:22-26 *Gershonites . . . curtains:* See the note at 3:21.

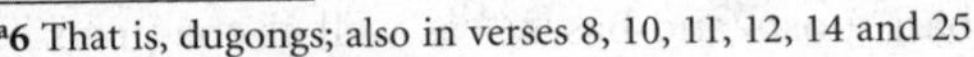

[a]**6** That is, dugongs; also in verses 8, 10, 11, 12, 14 and 25

At the LORD's command through Moses, each was assigned his work and told what to carry. Thus they were counted, as the LORD commanded Moses.
Num 4:49

4:29-32 *Merarites . . . frames of the tabernacle:* See the note at 3:33.

The Ark of the Covenant, stone carving from the synagogue in Capernaum, Galilee, around the third century A.D. The tribe of Levi was responsible for the tabernacle and its furnishings and for performing the sacrifices that the LORD commanded. Each clan within the tribe of Levi had its own set of duties. The Kohathites were responsible for moving the ark of the covenant (ark of the Testimony) whenever the Israelites changed their campsite (see 4:4-6). The ark was not large and the Kohathites carried it on poles. This carving shows the ark on an ox cart, which is not how it was to be transported (2 Sam 6:3; 1 Chr 15:15).

24"This is the service of the Gershonite clans as they work
and carry burdens: 25They are to carry the curtains of the tabernacle, the Tent of Meeting, its covering and the outer covering of
hides of sea cows, the curtains for the entrance to the Tent of
Meeting, 26the curtains of the courtyard surrounding the tabernacle and altar, the curtain for the entrance, the ropes and all the
equipment used in its service. The Gershonites are to do all that
needs to be done with these things. 27All their service, whether carrying or doing other work, is to be done under the direction of
Aaron and his sons. You shall assign to them as their responsibility all they are to carry. 28This is the service of the Gershonite clans
at the Tent of Meeting. Their duties are to be under the direction
of Ithamar son of Aaron, the priest.

The Merarites

29"Count the Merarites by their clans and families. 30Count
all the men from thirty to fifty years of age who come to serve in
the work at the Tent of Meeting. 31This is their duty as they perform service at the Tent of Meeting: to carry the frames of the
tabernacle, its crossbars, posts and bases, 32as well as the posts of

the surrounding courtyard with their bases, tent pegs, ropes, all
their equipment and everything related to their use. Assign to each
man the specific things he is to carry. [33]This is the service of the
Merarite clans as they work at the Tent of Meeting under the
direction of Ithamar son of Aaron, the priest."

The Numbering of the Levite Clans

[34]Moses, Aaron and the leaders of the community counted
the Kohathites by their clans and families. [35]All the men from
thirty to fifty years of age who came to serve in the work in the
Tent of Meeting, [36]counted by clans, were 2,750. [37]This was the
total of all those in the Kohathite clans who served in the Tent of
Meeting. Moses and Aaron counted them according to the LORD's
command through Moses.

[38]The Gershonites were counted by their clans and families.
[39]All the men from thirty to fifty years of age who came to serve in
the work at the Tent of Meeting, [40]counted by their clans and families, were 2,630. [41]This was the total of those in the Gershonite
clans who served at the Tent of Meeting. Moses and Aaron counted them according to the LORD's command.

[42]The Merarites were counted by their clans and families. [43]All
the men from thirty to fifty years of age who came to serve in the
work at the Tent of Meeting, [44]counted by their clans, were 3,200.
[45]This was the total of those in the Merarite clans. Moses and Aaron
counted them according to the LORD's command through Moses.

[46]So Moses, Aaron and the leaders of Israel counted all the
Levites by their clans and families. [47]All the men from thirty to
fifty years of age who came to do the work of serving and carrying
the Tent of Meeting [48]numbered 8,580. [49]At the LORD's command
through Moses, each was assigned his work and told what to carry.

Thus they were counted, as the LORD commanded Moses.

4:34-48 *Levites by their clans and families . . . numbered 8,580:* The first Levite census (3:14-39) counted all Levite males one month and older (22,000), whereas this second census counts males between thirty and fifty years old, those directly responsible for the tabernacle and its objects.

5:2,3 *skin disease . . . defile:* There are many kinds of skin diseases referred to in the Bible, not just the disease now known as Hansen's disease, traditionally called leprosy (Lev 13). In the Old Testament "clean" and "unclean" refer to whatever makes a person, animal, or object acceptable or unacceptable to God. See also Deut 14:3-21 and the mini-article called "Purity (Clean and Unclean)," p. 2125. Bodily discharges included blood (including blood flow from menstruation or childbirth), semen, and pus from sores or infections (see Lev 12; 15; 17:10-14). Touching a dead body or certain dead animals could also make a person ritually unclean (Lev 11:35,39,40; 21:1-12).

INSTRUCTIONS FOR GOD'S HOLY PEOPLE

The people receive various instructions, including the rules for jealous husbands, the vows one must take to be a Nazirite, and the process for ordaining Israel's priests and Levites. As they prepare to leave the Sinai region, they hear again the instructions for celebrating Passover.

The Purity of the Camp

5 The LORD said to Moses, [2]"Command the Israelites to send
away from the camp anyone who has an infectious skin disease[a] or
a discharge of any kind, or who is ceremonially unclean because of
a dead body. [3]Send away male and female alike; send them outside

[a]2 Traditionally *leprosy*; the Hebrew word was used for various diseases affecting the skin—not necessarily leprosy.

5:7,8 *sin . . . atonement:* Sin is turning away from God and disobeying God's laws. In this case the LORD is talking about cheating a neighbor in any way (see Lev 6:1-7). To remove the guilt of the sin, the neighbor was to be repaid in full plus twenty percent. In addition, a sacrifice was to be offered by the priest. For more, see the mini-article called "Sin," p. 2181.

5:9 *contributions:* Contributions for the upkeep of the tabernacle were given to the priests as God's representatives. Here, the contributions may also refer to offerings brought to the tabernacle but not put on the altar, such as grain (Lev 2:1-3), meat (Lev 7:7-10), or the first ten percent of the harvest (Lev 27:30). Some donations would be given to specific priests; others were shared by all the priests.

5:12-14 *no witness:* The Law of Moses said that two witnesses were needed to convict someone of a crime (Deut 17:6; 19:15). If a woman's unfaithfulness had been observed by witnesses, she would have been tried in the normal way and likely punished by death (Lev 20:10). Here, however, the man suspects his wife's guilt but cannot prove it, so the punishment can't be death.

5:15 *barley:* A very cheap source of food, used mainly to feed cattle and to make bread in times of emergency. Other sacrifices used the finer wheat grain and flour (Lev 2:1; 6:14,15).

5:17 *holy water in a clay jar:* The holy water was taken from the bronze bowl that stood between the altar and the entrance to the tabernacle (Exod 30:18-21). A clay jar was used and then broken so that the curses dissolved in the water it held.

the camp so they will not defile their camp, where I dwell among them." [4]The Israelites did this; they sent them outside the camp. They did just as the LORD had instructed Moses.

Restitution for Wrongs

[5]The LORD said to Moses, [6]"Say to the Israelites: 'When a man or woman wrongs another in any way[a] and so is unfaithful to the LORD, that person is guilty [7]and must confess the sin he has committed. He must make full restitution for his wrong, add one fifth to it and give it all to the person he has wronged. [8]But if that person has no close relative to whom restitution can be made for the wrong, the restitution belongs to the LORD and must be given to the priest, along with the ram with which atonement is made for him. [9]All the sacred contributions the Israelites bring to a priest will belong to him. [10]Each man's sacred gifts are his own, but what he gives to the priest will belong to the priest.' "

The Test for an Unfaithful Wife

[11]Then the LORD said to Moses, [12]"Speak to the Israelites and say to them: 'If a man's wife goes astray and is unfaithful to him [13]by sleeping with another man, and this is hidden from her husband and her impurity is undetected (since there is no witness against her and she has not been caught in the act), [14]and if feelings of jealousy come over her husband and he suspects his wife and she is impure—or if he is jealous and suspects her even though she is not impure— [15]then he is to take his wife to the priest. He must also take an offering of a tenth of an ephah[b] of barley flour on her behalf. He must not pour oil on it or put incense on it, because it is a grain offering for jealousy, a reminder offering to draw attention to guilt.

[16]" 'The priest shall bring her and have her stand before the LORD. [17]Then he shall take some holy water in a clay jar and put some dust from the tabernacle floor into the water. [18]After the priest has had the woman stand before the LORD, he shall loosen her hair and place in her hands the reminder offering, the grain offering for jealousy, while he himself holds the bitter water that brings a curse. [19]Then the priest shall put the woman under oath and say to her, "If no other man has slept with you and you have not gone astray and become impure while married to your husband, may this bitter water that brings a curse not harm you. [20]But if you have gone astray while married to your husband and you have defiled yourself by sleeping with a man other than your husband"— [21]here the priest is to put the woman under this curse of the oath—"may the LORD cause your people to curse and

---

[a]**6** Or *woman commits any wrong common to mankind* [b]**15** That is, probably about 2 quarts (about 2 liters)

denounce you when he causes your thigh to waste away and your abdomen to swell.[a] 22May this water that brings a curse enter your body so that your abdomen swells and your thigh wastes away.[b]"

" 'Then the woman is to say, "Amen. So be it."

23" 'The priest is to write these curses on a scroll and then wash them off into the bitter water. 24He shall have the woman drink the bitter water that brings a curse, and this water will enter her and cause bitter suffering. 25The priest is to take from her hands the grain offering for jealousy, wave it before the LORD and bring it to the altar. 26The priest is then to take a handful of the grain offering as a memorial offering and burn it on the altar; after that, he is to have the woman drink the water. 27If she has defiled herself and been unfaithful to her husband, then when she is made to drink the water that brings a curse, it will go into her and cause bitter suffering; her abdomen will swell and her thigh waste away,[c] and she will become accursed among her people. 28If, however, the woman has not defiled herself and is free from impurity, she will be cleared of guilt and will be able to have children.

29" 'This, then, is the law of jealousy when a woman goes astray and defiles herself while married to her husband, 30or when feelings of jealousy come over a man because he suspects his wife. The priest is to have her stand before the LORD and is to apply this entire law to her. 31The husband will be innocent of any wrongdoing, but the woman will bear the consequences of her sin.' "

The Nazirite

6 The LORD said to Moses, 2"Speak to the Israelites and say to them: 'If a man or woman wants to make a special vow, a vow of separation to the LORD as a Nazirite, 3he must abstain from wine and other fermented drink and must not drink vinegar made from wine or from other fermented drink. He must not drink grape juice or eat grapes or raisins. 4As long as he is a Nazirite, he must not eat anything that comes from the grapevine, not even the seeds or skins.

5" 'During the entire period of his vow of separation no razor may be used on his head. He must be holy until the period of his separation to the LORD is over; he must let the hair of his head grow long. 6Throughout the period of his separation to the LORD he must not go near a dead body. 7Even if his own father or mother or brother or sister dies, he must not make himself ceremonially unclean on account of them, because the symbol of his separation to God is on his head. 8Throughout the period of his separation he is consecrated to the LORD.

[a]21 Or *causes you to have a miscarrying womb and barrenness* [b]22 Or *body and cause you to be barren and have a miscarrying womb* [c]27 Or *suffering; she will have barrenness and a miscarrying womb*

5:23 *write . . . bitter water:* The priest probably wrote the curses on some kind of parchment, using a substance that would dissolve when the paper was put into the water. (5:23).

5:31 *husband will be innocent:* The husband had the right to accuse his wife, but there was no comparable law that allowed a woman to accuse her husband of being unfaithful if no witnesses were available (5:12-14).

6:2 *Nazirite:* Nazirite comes from a Hebrew word that means "to separate." Nazirites were not priests. They were people who dedicated themselves to being ritually clean and serving God. This dedication meant they did things that set them apart from others. They didn't drink alcohol, and they didn't cut their hair, because even their hair was considered holy, that is, dedicated to God. (See the story of Samson in Judg 13–16.) See also Luke 1:15.

5:25 Lev 7:28-30; 14:11,12,21.

6:9-12 *consecrate his head . . . dedicate himself:* If a Nazirite did touch a dead body, he or she also had to go through a cleansing ritual that included shaving off the hair and bringing sacrifices used as a sin offering (see the note at 8:8) and a burnt offering (see Lev 1:1-3, and the note at 7:87). Even priests who were made unclean by touching a dead body did not have to go through a purification ritual this elaborate.

6:14,15 *without defect . . . without yeast:* The animals to be offered had to be in perfect health (see Lev 22:21-24). Fellowship offerings have traditionally been called "peace offerings" or "offerings of well-being." A main purpose was to give thanks to God and have fellowship with him. See also the chart called "Sacrifices and Offerings," p. 219. Yeast is a fungus used to make dough rise when mixed with water and flour. Bread that has no yeast, or leaven, is flat and is called unleavened bread. See Lev 2:1-7.

6:23 *bless the Israelites:* One function of the priests was to bless the people of Israel (see also Lev 9:22,23; Deut 10:8; 21:5; 2 Chr 30:27). The word translated "peace" in 6:26 is from the Hebrew word *shalom,* which means total well-being, not simply an absence of war.

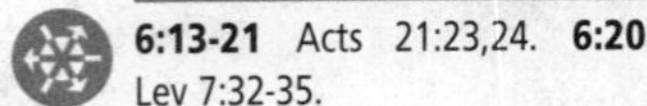

6:13-21 Acts 21:23,24. **6:20** Lev 7:32-35.

9" 'If someone dies suddenly in his presence, thus defiling
the hair he has dedicated, he must shave his head on the day of his
cleansing—the seventh day. 10Then on the eighth day he must
bring two doves or two young pigeons to the priest at the entrance
to the Tent of Meeting. 11The priest is to offer one as a sin offering
and the other as a burnt offering to make atonement for him
because he sinned by being in the presence of the dead body. That
same day he is to consecrate his head. 12He must dedicate himself
to the LORD for the period of his separation and must bring a year-
old male lamb as a guilt offering. The previous days do not count,
because he became defiled during his separation.

13" 'Now this is the law for the Nazirite when the period of
his separation is over. He is to be brought to the entrance to the
Tent of Meeting. 14There he is to present his offerings to the LORD:
a year-old male lamb without defect for a burnt offering, a year-old
ewe lamb without defect for a sin offering, a ram without defect for
a fellowship offering,[a] 15together with their grain offerings and
drink offerings, and a basket of bread made without yeast—cakes
made of fine flour mixed with oil, and wafers spread with oil.

16" 'The priest is to present them before the LORD and make
the sin offering and the burnt offering. 17He is to present the basket of unleavened bread and is to sacrifice the ram as a fellowship
offering to the LORD, together with its grain offering and drink
offering.

18" 'Then at the entrance to the Tent of Meeting, the Nazirite
must shave off the hair that he dedicated. He is to take the hair and
put it in the fire that is under the sacrifice of the fellowship offering.

19" 'After the Nazirite has shaved off the hair of his dedication, the priest is to place in his hands a boiled shoulder of the
ram, and a cake and a wafer from the basket, both made without
yeast. 20The priest shall then wave them before the LORD as a wave
offering; they are holy and belong to the priest, together with the
breast that was waved and the thigh that was presented. After that,
the Nazirite may drink wine.

21" 'This is the law of the Nazirite who vows his offering to
the LORD in accordance with his separation, in addition to whatever else he can afford. He must fulfill the vow he has made,
according to the law of the Nazirite.' "

The Priestly Blessing

22The LORD said to Moses, 23"Tell Aaron and his sons, 'This is
how you are to bless the Israelites. Say to them:

24" ' "The LORD bless you
and keep you;

[a]**14** Traditionally *peace offering*; also in verses 17 and 18

[25]the LORD make his face shine upon you
and be gracious to you;
[26]the LORD turn his face toward you
and give you peace." '

[27]"So they will put my name on the Israelites, and I will bless
them."

Offerings at the Dedication of the Tabernacle

7 When Moses finished setting up the tabernacle, he anointed it
and consecrated it and all its furnishings. He also anointed and
consecrated the altar and all its utensils. [2]Then the leaders of Israel, the heads of families who were the tribal leaders in charge of
those who were counted, made offerings. [3]They brought as their
gifts before the LORD six covered carts and twelve oxen—an ox
from each leader and a cart from every two. These they presented
before the tabernacle.
[4]The LORD said to Moses, [5]"Accept these from them, that
they may be used in the work at the Tent of Meeting. Give them to
the Levites as each man's work requires."
[6]So Moses took the carts and oxen and gave them to the
Levites. [7]He gave two carts and four oxen to the Gershonites, as
their work required, [8]and he gave four carts and eight oxen to the
Merarites, as their work required. They were all under the direction of Ithamar son of Aaron, the priest. [9]But Moses did not give
any to the Kohathites, because they were to carry on their shoulders the holy things, for which they were responsible.
[10]When the altar was anointed, the leaders brought their
offerings for its dedication and presented them before the altar.
[11]For the LORD had said to Moses, "Each day one leader is to bring
his offering for the dedication of the altar."

[12]The one who brought his offering on the first day was Nahshon
son of Amminadab of the tribe of Judah.
[13]His offering was one silver plate weighing a hundred and
thirty shekels,[a] and one silver sprinkling bowl weighing seventy shekels,[b] both according to the sanctuary shekel, each
filled with fine flour mixed with oil as a grain offering; [14]one
gold dish weighing ten shekels,[c] filled with incense; [15]one
young bull, one ram and one male lamb a year old, for a burnt
offering; [16]one male goat for a sin offering; [17]and two oxen,
five rams, five male goats and five male lambs a year old, to be
sacrificed as a fellowship offering.[d] This was the offering of
Nahshon son of Amminadab.

7:2 *heads of families . . . tribal leaders:* See 1:1-19 and the note at 1:5-16.

7:3 *carts and twelve oxen:* Probably two-wheeled wagons. Oxen were strong animals used for hauling large objects and pulling plows. For more, see the article called "Trade and Travel," p. 948.

7:5 *Accept these:* Referring to offerings from the people for use in and maintenance of the tabernacle (7:2).

7:7-9 *Gershonites . . . Kohathites:* The Gershonites (3:21-26) and Merarites (3:33-37) could use wagons to haul the tabernacle curtains and framing, but the Kohathites (3:27-31) had to carry the sacred objects from the tabernacle by hand. See also the note at 4:6,7.

7:10 *leaders:* See 1:1-19 and the note at 1:5-16.

7:12-83 *Judah . . . Naphtali:* See the note at 1:5-16.

6:25,26 Ps 4:6; 31:16; 80:3. **7:1** Exod 40:1-33.

[a]**13** That is, about 3 1/4 pounds (about 1.5 kilograms); also elsewhere in this chapter [b]**13** That is, about 1 3/4 pounds (about 0.8 kilogram); also elsewhere in this chapter [c]**14** That is, about 4 ounces (about 110 grams); also elsewhere in this chapter [d]**17** Traditionally *peace offering*; also elsewhere in this chapter

[18]On the second day Nethanel son of Zuar, the leader of Issachar,
brought his offering.
[19]The offering he brought was one silver plate weighing a hundred and thirty shekels, and one silver sprinkling bowl weighing seventy shekels, both according to the sanctuary shekel,
each filled with fine flour mixed with oil as a grain offering;
[20]one gold dish weighing ten shekels, filled with incense; [21]one
young bull, one ram and one male lamb a year old, for a burnt
offering; [22]one male goat for a sin offering; [23]and two oxen,
five rams, five male goats and five male lambs a year old, to be
sacrificed as a fellowship offering. This was the offering of
Nethanel son of Zuar.

[24]On the third day, Eliab son of Helon, the leader of the people of
Zebulun, brought his offering.
[25]His offering was one silver plate weighing a hundred and
thirty shekels, and one silver sprinkling bowl weighing seventy shekels, both according to the sanctuary shekel, each filled
with fine flour mixed with oil as a grain offering; [26]one gold
dish weighing ten shekels, filled with incense; [27]one young
bull, one ram and one male lamb a year old, for a burnt offering; [28]one male goat for a sin offering; [29]and two oxen, five
rams, five male goats and five male lambs a year old, to be sacrificed as a fellowship offering. This was the offering of Eliab
son of Helon.

[30]On the fourth day Elizur son of Shedeur, the leader of the people of Reuben, brought his offering.
[31]His offering was one silver plate weighing a hundred and
thirty shekels, and one silver sprinkling bowl weighing seventy shekels, both according to the sanctuary shekel, each filled
with fine flour mixed with oil as a grain offering; [32]one gold
dish weighing ten shekels, filled with incense; [33]one young
bull, one ram and one male lamb a year old, for a burnt offering; [34]one male goat for a sin offering; [35]and two oxen, five
rams, five male goats and five male lambs a year old, to be sacrificed as a fellowship offering. This was the offering of Elizur
son of Shedeur.

[36]On the fifth day Shelumiel son of Zurishaddai, the leader of the
people of Simeon, brought his offering.
[37]His offering was one silver plate weighing a hundred and
thirty shekels, and one silver sprinkling bowl weighing seventy
shekels, both according to the sanctuary shekel, each filled with
fine flour mixed with oil as a grain offering; [38]one gold dish
weighing ten shekels, filled with incense; [39]one young bull, one
ram and one male lamb a year old, for a burnt offering; [40]one
male goat for a sin offering; [41]and two oxen, five rams, five
male goats and five male lambs a year old, to be sacrificed as a

fellowship offering. This was the offering of Shelumiel son of
Zurishaddai.

42 On the sixth day Eliasaph son of Deuel, the leader of the people
of Gad, brought his offering.

43 His offering was one silver plate weighing a hundred and
thirty shekels, and one silver sprinkling bowl weighing seventy shekels, both according to the sanctuary shekel, each filled
with fine flour mixed with oil as a grain offering; 44 one gold
dish weighing ten shekels, filled with incense; 45 one young
bull, one ram and one male lamb a year old, for a burnt offering; 46 one male goat for a sin offering; 47 and two oxen, five
rams, five male goats and five male lambs a year old, to be sacrificed as a fellowship offering. This was the offering of Eliasaph son of Deuel.

48 On the seventh day Elishama son of Ammihud, the leader of the
people of Ephraim, brought his offering.

49 His offering was one silver plate weighing a hundred and
thirty shekels, and one silver sprinkling bowl weighing seventy shekels, both according to the sanctuary shekel, each filled
with fine flour mixed with oil as a grain offering; 50 one gold
dish weighing ten shekels, filled with incense; 51 one young
bull, one ram and one male lamb a year old, for a burnt offering; 52 one male goat for a sin offering; 53 and two oxen, five
rams, five male goats and five male lambs a year old, to be sacrificed as a fellowship offering. This was the offering of
Elishama son of Ammihud.

54 On the eighth day Gamaliel son of Pedahzur, the leader of the
people of Manasseh, brought his offering.

55 His offering was one silver plate weighing a hundred and
thirty shekels, and one silver sprinkling bowl weighing seventy shekels, both according to the sanctuary shekel, each filled
with fine flour mixed with oil as a grain offering; 56 one gold
dish weighing ten shekels, filled with incense; 57 one young
bull, one ram and one male lamb a year old, for a burnt offering; 58 one male goat for a sin offering; 59 and two oxen, five
rams, five male goats and five male lambs a year old, to be sacrificed as a fellowship offering. This was the offering of
Gamaliel son of Pedahzur.

60 On the ninth day Abidan son of Gideoni, the leader of the people of Benjamin, brought his offering.

61 His offering was one silver plate weighing a hundred and
thirty shekels, and one silver sprinkling bowl weighing seventy shekels, both according to the sanctuary shekel, each filled
with fine flour mixed with oil as a grain offering; 62 one gold
dish weighing ten shekels, filled with incense; 63 one young
bull, one ram and one male lamb a year old, for a burnt

When Moses entered the Tent of Meeting to speak with the Lord, he heard the voice speaking to him from between the two cherubim above the atonement cover on the ark of the Testimony. And he spoke with him.
Num 7:89

7:87 *burnt offering:* The offerings included two silver bowls. One was used to catch the blood from an offering so it could be sprinkled on the altar (Lev 16:18,19). Burnt offerings have traditionally been called "whole burnt offerings" because the whole animal was burned on the altar. A main purpose of such an offering was to gain God's favor with the odor of the sacrifice. See also the chart called "Sacrifices and Offerings," p. 219.

offering; 64 one male goat for a sin offering; 65 and two oxen, five rams, five male goats and five male lambs a year old, to be sacrificed as a fellowship offering. This was the offering of Abidan son of Gideoni.

66 On the tenth day Ahiezer son of Ammishaddai, the leader of the people of Dan, brought his offering.

67 His offering was one silver plate weighing a hundred and thirty shekels, and one silver sprinkling bowl weighing seventy shekels, both according to the sanctuary shekel, each filled with fine flour mixed with oil as a grain offering; 68 one gold dish weighing ten shekels, filled with incense; 69 one young bull, one ram and one male lamb a year old, for a burnt offering; 70 one male goat for a sin offering; 71 and two oxen, five rams, five male goats and five male lambs a year old, to be sacrificed as a fellowship offering. This was the offering of Ahiezer son of Ammishaddai.

72 On the eleventh day Pagiel son of Ocran, the leader of the people of Asher, brought his offering.

73 His offering was one silver plate weighing a hundred and thirty shekels, and one silver sprinkling bowl weighing seventy shekels, both according to the sanctuary shekel, each filled with fine flour mixed with oil as a grain offering; 74 one gold dish weighing ten shekels, filled with incense; 75 one young bull, one ram and one male lamb a year old, for a burnt offering; 76 one male goat for a sin offering; 77 and two oxen, five rams, five male goats and five male lambs a year old, to be sacrificed as a fellowship offering. This was the offering of Pagiel son of Ocran.

78 On the twelfth day Ahira son of Enan, the leader of the people of Naphtali, brought his offering.

79 His offering was one silver plate weighing a hundred and thirty shekels, and one silver sprinkling bowl weighing seventy shekels, both according to the sanctuary shekel, each filled with fine flour mixed with oil as a grain offering; 80 one gold dish weighing ten shekels, filled with incense; 81 one young bull, one ram and one male lamb a year old, for a burnt offering; 82 one male goat for a sin offering; 83 and two oxen, five rams, five male goats and five male lambs a year old, to be sacrificed as a fellowship offering. This was the offering of Ahira son of Enan.

84 These were the offerings of the Israelite leaders for the dedication of the altar when it was anointed: twelve silver plates, twelve silver sprinkling bowls and twelve gold dishes. 85 Each silver plate weighed a hundred and thirty shekels, and each sprinkling bowl seventy shekels. Altogether, the silver dishes weighed two

thousand four hundred shekels,[a] according to the sanctuary shekel. 86The twelve gold dishes filled with incense weighed ten shekels each, according to the sanctuary shekel. Altogether, the gold dishes weighed a hundred and twenty shekels.[b] 87The total number of animals for the burnt offering came to twelve young bulls, twelve rams and twelve male lambs a year old, together with their grain offering. Twelve male goats were used for the sin offering. 88The total number of animals for the sacrifice of the fellowship offering came to twenty-four oxen, sixty rams, sixty male goats and sixty male lambs a year old. These were the offerings for the dedication of the altar after it was anointed.

89When Moses entered the Tent of Meeting to speak with the LORD, he heard the voice speaking to him from between the two cherubim above the atonement cover on the ark of the Testimony. And he spoke with him.

Setting Up the Lamps

8 The LORD said to Moses, 2"Speak to Aaron and say to him, 'When you set up the seven lamps, they are to light the area in front of the lampstand.' "

3Aaron did so; he set up the lamps so that they faced forward on the lampstand, just as the LORD commanded Moses. 4This is how the lampstand was made: It was made of hammered gold—from its base to its blossoms. The lampstand was made exactly like the pattern the LORD had shown Moses.

The Setting Apart of the Levites

5The LORD said to Moses: 6"Take the Levites from among the other Israelites and make them ceremonially clean. 7To purify them, do this: Sprinkle the water of cleansing on them; then have them shave their whole bodies and wash their clothes, and so purify themselves. 8Have them take a young bull with its grain offering of fine flour mixed with oil; then you are to take a second young bull for a sin offering. 9Bring the Levites to the front of the Tent of Meeting and assemble the whole Israelite community. 10You are to bring the Levites before the LORD, and the Israelites are to lay their hands on them. 11Aaron is to present the Levites before the LORD as a wave offering from the Israelites, so that they may be ready to do the work of the LORD.

12"After the Levites lay their hands on the heads of the bulls, use the one for a sin offering to the LORD and the other for a burnt offering, to make atonement for the Levites. 13Have the Levites stand in front of Aaron and his sons and then present them as a wave offering to the LORD. 14In this way you are to set the Levites apart from the other Israelites, and the Levites will be mine.

[a]**85** That is, about 60 pounds (about 28 kilograms) [b]**86** That is, about 3 pounds (about 1.4 kilograms)

7:89 *atonement cover:* The atonement cover on the ark of the Testimony (or ark of the covenant) has also been called a "mercy seat," where God said he would sit and judge the people and tell them what they must do (Exod 25:22). The winged cherubim were hybrid creatures, but were always connected with the LORD. They are pictured as looking like the Sphinx of Egypt, having a human head and lion's body (Ezek 41:18,19) or like the human-headed bulls and lions that guarded ancient Mesopotamian temples. See also 1 Sam 4:4; 2 Sam 6:2; Ps 80:1.

8:2 *seven lamps . . . lampstand:* See the note at 4:9-11. See also Exod 25:31-40; 37:17-24.

8:6,7 *Take the Levites . . . ceremonially clean:* The Levites (see the note at 1:47) had to become ritually clean (see the note at 5:2,3) before they could serve at the tabernacle. This was done by sprinkling them with the water that washes away sins (19:9,17-19), which was not the same as the holy water (5:17). They also had to shave their bodies and wash their clothes (see Lev 16:23,24; 21:5).

8:8 *offering:* Grain offerings were made to thank the LORD and secure God's favor (Lev 2). The sin offering was done to purify those who had unintentionally sinned by disobeying God's laws or those who had accidentally done something God told them not to do. The Levites were to offer a bull (see Lev 4:3). See also the chart called "Sacrifices and Offerings," p. 219.

8:10 *lay their hands on them:* This connected the people with those chosen for the special work, just as the laying of hands identified the one making a sacrifice with the object sacrificed (see Lev 3:2).

8:12 *sin offering . . . burnt offering:* See the notes at 8:8 and 7:87. See also Lev 1:1-13.

8:14,15 *set the Levites apart . . . purified:* See the notes at 8:6,7 and 4:16.

8:16 *in place of the firstborn:* See the notes at 3:11-13 and 3:44-48. See also Exod 13:2.

8:21 *purified ... washed:* See the notes at 8:6,7 and 8:8.

9:1 *Desert of Sinai ... first month:* The first month of the Hebrew calendar is Abib (also called Nisan), which lasts from about mid-March to mid-April. NUMBERS begins in the second month of the second year (see 1:1), so 9:1-5 refers to a Passover celebration that had already taken place. See the note at 1:1 (Desert of Sinai).

9:2,3 *Passover ... this month:* The name "Passover" is related to the Hebrew verb translated as "pass over" in Exodus 12:13,23,27. This festival celebrated how God acted to save the Israelite people from slavery in Egypt. See also the mini-article called "Passover and the Feast of Unleavened Bread," p. 2030.

9:6 *ceremonially unclean ... dead body:* See the note at 5:2,3.

8:19 Num 3:6-10. **9:1-5** Exod 12:1-13.

15“After you have purified the Levites and presented them as
a wave offering, they are to come to do their work at the Tent of
Meeting. 16They are the Israelites who are to be given wholly to
me. I have taken them as my own in place of the firstborn, the first
male offspring from every Israelite woman. 17Every firstborn male
in Israel, whether man or animal, is mine. When I struck down all
the firstborn in Egypt, I set them apart for myself. 18And I have
taken the Levites in place of all the firstborn sons in Israel. 19Of all
the Israelites, I have given the Levites as gifts to Aaron and his sons
to do the work at the Tent of Meeting on behalf of the Israelites
and to make atonement for them so that no plague will strike the
Israelites when they go near the sanctuary.”

20Moses, Aaron and the whole Israelite community did with
the Levites just as the LORD commanded Moses. 21The Levites
purified themselves and washed their clothes. Then Aaron presented them as a wave offering before the LORD and made atonement for them to purify them. 22After that, the Levites came to do
their work at the Tent of Meeting under the supervision of Aaron
and his sons. They did with the Levites just as the LORD commanded Moses.

23The LORD said to Moses, 24“This applies to the Levites: Men
twenty-five years old or more shall come to take part in the work
at the Tent of Meeting, 25but at the age of fifty, they must retire
from their regular service and work no longer. 26They may assist
their brothers in performing their duties at the Tent of Meeting,
but they themselves must not do the work. This, then, is how you
are to assign the responsibilities of the Levites.”

The Passover

9 The LORD spoke to Moses in the Desert of Sinai in the first
month of the second year after they came out of Egypt. He said,
2“Have the Israelites celebrate the Passover at the appointed time.
3Celebrate it at the appointed time, at twilight on the fourteenth
day of this month, in accordance with all its rules and regulations.”

4So Moses told the Israelites to celebrate the Passover, 5and
they did so in the Desert of Sinai at twilight on the fourteenth day
of the first month. The Israelites did everything just as the LORD
commanded Moses.

6But some of them could not celebrate the Passover on that
day because they were ceremonially unclean on account of a dead
body. So they came to Moses and Aaron that same day 7and said to
Moses, “We have become unclean because of a dead body, but why
should we be kept from presenting the LORD’s offering with the
other Israelites at the appointed time?”

8Moses answered them, “Wait until I find out what the LORD
commands concerning you.”

9Then the LORD said to Moses, 10“Tell the Israelites: ‘When

The Pillar of Cloud, a fresco from the Vatican, school of Raphael, around 1500. During the time the Israelites wandered in the desert the LORD showed the people where they were to set up camp. When the thick cloud that covered the tabernacle moved, the Israelites knew it was time to move to the next place the LORD had chosen for them. The people followed the cloud and wherever it stopped, they set up camp and stayed there, whether it was one night, a few days or months, or even a year. (See 9:15-23.)

any of you or your descendants are unclean because of a dead
body or are away on a journey, they may still celebrate the LORD's
Passover. 11They are to celebrate it on the fourteenth day of the
second month at twilight. They are to eat the lamb, together with
unleavened bread and bitter herbs. 12They must not leave any of it
till morning or break any of its bones. When they celebrate the
Passover, they must follow all the regulations. 13But if a man who
is ceremonially clean and not on a journey fails to celebrate the
Passover, that person must be cut off from his people because he
did not present the LORD's offering at the appointed time. That
man will bear the consequences of his sin.
14" 'An alien living among you who wants to celebrate the
LORD's Passover must do so in accordance with its rules and regulations. You must have the same regulations for the alien and the
native-born.' "

The Cloud Above the Tabernacle

15On the day the tabernacle, the Tent of the Testimony, was
set up, the cloud covered it. From evening till morning the cloud
above the tabernacle looked like fire. 16That is how it continued to
be; the cloud covered it, and at night it looked like fire. 17Whenever
the cloud lifted from above the Tent, the Israelites set out; wherever

9:11 *second month:* See the note at 1:1 (second month). Those who were considered ritually unclean at the time of the actual Passover could celebrate a month later after they had become acceptable to God again. See also 2 Chr 30:1-3.

9:11 *lamb . . . unleavened bread and bitter herbs:* Lamb was served at the first Passover (Exod 12:3) along with unleavened bread (see the note at 6:14,15) and bitter herbs (Exod 12:8), which symbolized the Israelites' bitter years of slavery in Egypt.

9:14 *alien:* Refers to foreigners who had settled among the Israelite people. The non-Israelite males could celebrate Passover as long as they were circumcised (see Exod 12:48,49). They were not punished if they decided not to celebrate the Passover, but Israelites were (9:13). See also the mini-articles called "Foreigners (Aliens)," p. 501 and "Circumcision," p. 2251.

9:15,16 *Tent . . . was set up:* According to Exodus 40:17, the Tent (tabernacle) was first set up on the first day of the first month of the second year of the Israelites' period of wandering in the desert.

9:15,16 *cloud . . . fire:* Flames, fire, smoke and a cloud are often symbols of God's presence in the Bible (see also Gen 15:17,18; Exod 3:1-6; 16:10; 19:16-19; 24:15-18; Judg 13:20; Rev 1:12-16). These are connected with God's glory, a visible reminder that God was with the people and lived in the tabernacle. In Israel's time of wandering, God used the cloud to guide their journey (see also Exod 13:20-22; 14:19,20).

9:12 Exod 12:46; Ps 34:20; John 19:36.

10:2 *two trumpets:* These silver trumpets were shaped like modern bugles, measuring about one foot long. They were used to celebrate religious festivals (10:10; 29:1-6), to call the people together (10:5-8), and to sound the signal for battle (10:9). The Egyptian trumpets shown here are from the tomb of Tutankhamen, eighteenth century B.C.

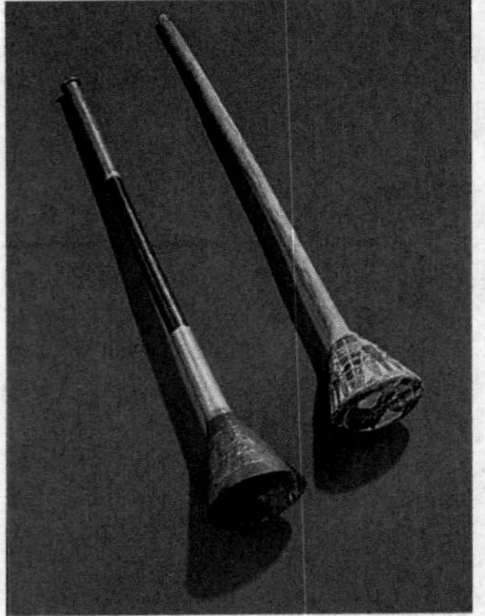

the cloud settled, the Israelites encamped. 18At the LORD's command the Israelites set out, and at his command they encamped.
As long as the cloud stayed over the tabernacle, they remained in
camp. 19When the cloud remained over the tabernacle a long time,
the Israelites obeyed the LORD's order and did not set out. 20Some-
times the cloud was over the tabernacle only a few days; at the
LORD's command they would encamp, and then at his command
they would set out. 21Sometimes the cloud stayed only from
evening till morning, and when it lifted in the morning, they set
out. Whether by day or by night, whenever the cloud lifted, they
set out. 22Whether the cloud stayed over the tabernacle for two
days or a month or a year, the Israelites would remain in camp and
not set out; but when it lifted, they would set out. 23At the LORD's
command they encamped, and at the LORD's command they set
out. They obeyed the LORD's order, in accordance with his command through Moses.

The Silver Trumpets

10 The LORD said to Moses: 2"Make two trumpets of hammered
silver, and use them for calling the community together and for
having the camps set out. 3When both are sounded, the whole
community is to assemble before you at the entrance to the Tent of
Meeting. 4If only one is sounded, the leaders—the heads of the
clans of Israel—are to assemble before you. 5When a trumpet blast
is sounded, the tribes camping on the east are to set out. 6At the
sounding of a second blast, the camps on the south are to set out.
The blast will be the signal for setting out. 7To gather the assembly,
blow the trumpets, but not with the same signal.

8"The sons of Aaron, the priests, are to blow the trumpets.
This is to be a lasting ordinance for you and the generations to
come. 9When you go into battle in your own land against an

QUESTIONS ABOUT NUMBERS 1:1—10:10

1. Who helped Moses and Aaron count the people of Israel? Why were the people counted? (chapter 1)
2. Even though the Levites were an important Israelite tribe, they were not counted as warriors and would not receive land when the people moved into Canaan. What were the special duties of the Levite clans? (2:17; 3:5—4:49)
3. Describe the ceremony that was used when a jealous husband suspected his wife of being unfaithful. (5:11-30) What is your reaction to this ceremony?
4. Who were the Nazirites? (chapter 6) How does a person today show that his or her life is dedicated to serving God?
5. Describe how the Levites were ordained and dedicated to the LORD. (8:5-26)
6. What happened during the celebration of Passover? (9:1-14) What important event was being remembered in this celebration?
7. For what reasons were the silver trumpets blown? (10:1-10)

enemy who is oppressing you, sound a blast on the trumpets. Then
you will be remembered by the LORD your God and rescued from
your enemies. [10]Also at your times of rejoicing—your appointed
feasts and New Moon festivals—you are to sound the trumpets
over your burnt offerings and fellowship offerings,[a] and they will
be a memorial for you before your God. I am the LORD your God."

10:10 *appointed feasts and New Moon festivals:* Trumpets were blown on the first day of every month, which began with the "new moon" (Ps 81:3). Special sacrifices were offered on this day (28:11-15). See also the note at 29:1 (seventh month) and the chart called "Jewish Calendar and Festivals," p. 944.

10:11 *second month . . . second year:* The Israelites broke camp nineteen days after the first counting of the people (see 1:1). They had been at Sinai for eleven months and nineteen days (see Exod 19:1).

Israel's Journey from Sinai to Moab

The Israelites break camp in the Desert of Sinai and journey toward Canaan. Along the way, God provides food and water in the desert, in spite of the people's complaints. The reports of the twelve tribal leaders chosen to explore Canaan frighten the people. Eventually some Israelites rebel against Moses and Aaron, but God punishes them and vows that no one of the older generation, except Joshua and Caleb, would live to enter the promised land. As Israel nears Moab, they battle and defeat people living in the lands east of Canaan.

FROM SINAI TO THE DESERT OF PARAN

The Israelites march in formation according to God's command. Leaders are chosen to help Moses. The people grumble about being hungry, so God sends manna and quail. Moses' sister Miriam is punished for being jealous of Moses.

The Israelites Leave Sinai

[11]On the twentieth day of the second month of the second
year, the cloud lifted from above the tabernacle of the Testimony.
[12]Then the Israelites set out from the Desert of Sinai and traveled
from place to place until the cloud came to rest in the Desert of
Paran. [13]They set out, this first time, at the LORD's command
through Moses.
[14]The divisions of the camp of Judah went first, under their
standard. Nahshon son of Amminadab was in command.
[15]Nethanel son of Zuar was over the division of the tribe of
Issachar, [16]and Eliab son of Helon was over the division of the tribe
of Zebulun. [17]Then the tabernacle was taken down, and the Gershonites and Merarites, who carried it, set out.
[18]The divisions of the camp of Reuben went next, under
their standard. Elizur son of Shedeur was in command. [19]Shelu-
miel son of Zurishaddai was over the division of the tribe of Simeon, [20]and Eliasaph son of Deuel was over the division of the tribe
of Gad. [21]Then the Kohathites set out, carrying the holy things.
The tabernacle was to be set up before they arrived.
[22]The divisions of the camp of Ephraim went next, under
their standard. Elishama son of Ammihud was in command.

10:12 *Desert of Sinai . . . Desert of Paran:* See the note at 1:1 (Desert of Sinai). The location of the Desert of Paran is unknown, but it is often assumed to be in the northern or central part of the Sinai peninsula, west of the Arabah, the riff valley that runs through Palestine from the Sea of Galilee to the Red Sea (see the map on p. 2463).

10:12 *the cloud:* See the note at 9:15,16 (cloud).

10:14-27 *Judah . . . tribe of Naphtali:* See the notes describing Israel's tribes and their camp arrangement at 2:3-9; 2:10-16; 2:18-24; 2:25-31.

10:14 *standard:* See the note at 1:52,53.

10:17 *Gershonites and Merarites:* Two of the Levite clans responsible for taking down and carrying the tabernacle (see the note at 1:52, 53). For more, see the notes at 3:21 and 3:33.

10:21 *Kohathites:* See 4:4-15 and the note at 3:27.

a10 Traditionally *peace offerings*

ISRAEL ON THE MARCH

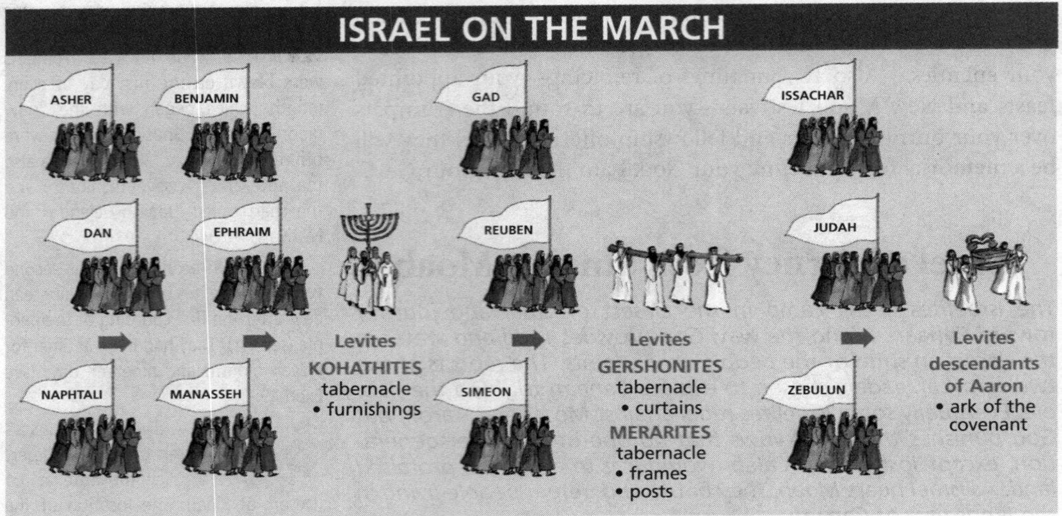

The LORD gave Moses instructions about how the Israelites were to arrange their camp during the time they wandered in the Desert of Sinai (see 2:1-34). When the Israelites moved to the next place the LORD chose for them, they were to march in the formation shown here. Levites carrying the ark of the covenant would lead the way. Judah would lead the first row of warrior tribes, and Dan would lead the tribes responsible for protecting the Israelites from behind (see 10:11-28).

10:29 *Hobab . . . Midianite:* After killing an Egyptian guard (Exod 2:11-14) Moses ran away to Midian where he married the daughter of Reuel (Exod 2:18-21), who is called Jethro in Exodus 18. Hobab was Moses' brother-in-law. The Midianites were descendants of Abraham and Keturah (Gen 25:1-4). The Israelites and Midianites were sometimes at peace (Exod 18), sometimes in conflict (22:4,7; 25:17; 31:2; Judg 6–8).

10:33 *mountain of the LORD:* See the note at 1:1 (Desert of Sinai).

10:33 *ark of the covenant:* See the note at 7:89 and the mini-article called "The Ark of the Covenant" p. 513.

10:34 *cloud:* See 10:12 and the note at 9:15,16 (cloud).

10:35 Ps 68:1.

23 Gamaliel son of Pedahzur was over the division of the tribe of
Manasseh, 24 and Abidan son of Gideoni was over the division of the
tribe of Benjamin.

25 Finally, as the rear guard for all the units, the divisions of
the camp of Dan set out, under their standard. Ahiezer son of
Ammishaddai was in command. 26 Pagiel son of Ocran was over
the division of the tribe of Asher, 27 and Ahira son of Enan was over
the division of the tribe of Naphtali. 28 This was the order of march
for the Israelite divisions as they set out.

29 Now Moses said to Hobab son of Reuel the Midianite,
Moses' father-in-law, "We are setting out for the place about which
the LORD said, 'I will give it to you.' Come with us and we will treat
you well, for the LORD has promised good things to Israel."

30 He answered, "No, I will not go; I am going back to my
own land and my own people."

31 But Moses said, "Please do not leave us. You know where
we should camp in the desert, and you can be our eyes. 32 If you
come with us, we will share with you whatever good things the
LORD gives us."

33 So they set out from the mountain of the LORD and traveled for three days. The ark of the covenant of the LORD went
before them during those three days to find them a place to rest.
34 The cloud of the LORD was over them by day when they set out
from the camp.

35 Whenever the ark set out, Moses said,

"Rise up, O LORD!
May your enemies be scattered;
may your foes flee before you."

36Whenever it came to rest, he said,

"Return, O LORD,
to the countless thousands of Israel."

Fire From the LORD

11 Now the people complained about their hardships in the
hearing of the LORD, and when he heard them his anger was
aroused. Then fire from the LORD burned among them and consumed some of the outskirts of the camp. 2When the people cried
out to Moses, he prayed to the LORD and the fire died down. 3So
that place was called Taberah,[a] because fire from the LORD had
burned among them.

Quail From the LORD

4The rabble with them began to crave other food, and again
the Israelites started wailing and said, "If only we had meat to eat!
5We remember the fish we ate in Egypt at no cost—also the
cucumbers, melons, leeks, onions and garlic. 6But now we have lost
our appetite; we never see anything but this manna!"
7The manna was like coriander seed and looked like resin.
8The people went around gathering it, and then ground it in a
handmill or crushed it in a mortar. They cooked it in a pot or
made it into cakes. And it tasted like something made with olive
oil. 9When the dew settled on the camp at night, the manna also
came down.
10Moses heard the people of every family wailing, each at the
entrance to his tent. The LORD became exceedingly angry, and
Moses was troubled. 11He asked the LORD, "Why have you brought
this trouble on your servant? What have I done to displease you
that you put the burden of all these people on me? 12Did I conceive all these people? Did I give them birth? Why do you tell me
to carry them in my arms, as a nurse carries an infant, to the land
you promised on oath to their forefathers? 13Where can I get meat
for all these people? They keep wailing to me, 'Give us meat to eat!'
14I cannot carry all these people by myself; the burden is too heavy
for me. 15If this is how you are going to treat me, put me to death
right now—if I have found favor in your eyes—and do not let me
face my own ruin."
16The LORD said to Moses: "Bring me seventy of Israel's
elders who are known to you as leaders and officials among the
people. Have them come to the Tent of Meeting, that they may

[a]3 *Taberah* means *burning.*

11:1 *fire:* See the note at 9:15, 16 (cloud . . . fire). Fire is often a sign of God's judgment in the Bible (see the mini-article "Fire," p. 2383). Here the fire may have been lightning or wild fire caused by lightning.

11:4 *rabble with them:* The "rabble" refers to foreigners who had joined Israel. Food was scarce on the journey, and some of those who had come with the Israelites when they left Egypt missed the food available there. Their complaining caused the Israelites to complain too.

11:6 *manna:* God provided this food (described as white, sweet, thin cakes) every day except the Sabbath (see Exod 16:1-31). In Hebrew, "manna" means "What is it?" after the reaction of the Israelites upon finding it on the ground for the first time.

11:12 *land you promised on oath:* Canaan, the land God promised to give Abraham and his descendants (Gen 17:7,8; Exod 3:8). See the map on p. 2464.

11:16 *seventy . . . leaders:* The number seven symbolized completeness and perfection. Because it is a multiple of seven, "seventy" was also considered an important number. The leaders led the clans in each tribe. See also Exod 18:13-25, and the chart called "Numbers in the Bible," p. 2405.

11:1 Exod 15:22-24; 16:1-3.
11:15 Exod 32:31,32.

The LORD answered Moses, "Is the LORD's arm too short? You will now see whether or not what I say will come true for you."
Num 11:23

11:18 *Consecrate yourselves:* The people were to prepare for this gift from God by bathing themselves and washing their clothes to make themselves ritually clean and by abstaining from sex (see Exod 19:10-15).

11:21 *six hundred thousand men:* Refers to the men who were eligible to be Israel's soldiers (see Exod 12:37; Num 1:20-46).

11:25 *LORD . . . Spirit . . . prophesied:* The Spirit refers to God's power, which gives special gifts or abilities. In ancient Israel, prophets were sometimes described as having ecstatic experiences after the LORD's spirit took control of them (see, for example, 1 Sam 10:5,6; 19:20-24). In these verses, the elders had similar experiences that showed God had chosen them for a special task. For more, see the article called "Prophets and Prophecy," p. 935.

11:28 *Joshua:* Joshua was later appointed to lead Israel after Moses died (Deut 1:38; 31:14; 34:9). See also Exod 17:9-14.

11:31 *quail:* A small brown or sandy-colored bird that usually migrated to the region of Palestine in large flocks during March or April. See also Exod 16:13 and the illustration on p. 165. The people were only to eat what they needed, to show that they trusted God would continue to provide food for them, but many took baskets full of quail in order to dry the meat for eating later.

stand there with you. 17I will come down and speak with you there,
and I will take of the Spirit that is on you and put the Spirit on
them. They will help you carry the burden of the people so that
you will not have to carry it alone.
18"Tell the people: 'Consecrate yourselves in preparation for
tomorrow, when you will eat meat. The LORD heard you when you
wailed, "If only we had meat to eat! We were better off in Egypt!"
Now the LORD will give you meat, and you will eat it. 19You will not
eat it for just one day, or two days, or five, ten or twenty days, 20but
for a whole month—until it comes out of your nostrils and you
loathe it—because you have rejected the LORD, who is among you,
and have wailed before him, saying, "Why did we ever leave
Egypt?" ' "
21But Moses said, "Here I am among six hundred thousand
men on foot, and you say, 'I will give them meat to eat for a whole
month!' 22Would they have enough if flocks and herds were
slaughtered for them? Would they have enough if all the fish in the
sea were caught for them?"
23The LORD answered Moses, "Is the LORD's arm too short?
You will now see whether or not what I say will come true for you."
24So Moses went out and told the people what the LORD had
said. He brought together seventy of their elders and had them
stand around the Tent. 25Then the LORD came down in the cloud
and spoke with him, and he took of the Spirit that was on him and
put the Spirit on the seventy elders. When the Spirit rested on
them, they prophesied, but they did not do so again.[a]
26However, two men, whose names were Eldad and Medad,
had remained in the camp. They were listed among the elders, but
did not go out to the Tent. Yet the Spirit also rested on them, and
they prophesied in the camp. 27A young man ran and told Moses,
"Eldad and Medad are prophesying in the camp."
28Joshua son of Nun, who had been Moses' aide since youth,
spoke up and said, "Moses, my lord, stop them!"
29But Moses replied, "Are you jealous for my sake? I wish that
all the LORD's people were prophets and that the LORD would put
his Spirit on them!" 30Then Moses and the elders of Israel returned
to the camp.
31Now a wind went out from the LORD and drove quail in
from the sea. It brought them[b] down all around the camp to about
three feet[c] above the ground, as far as a day's walk in any direction.
32All that day and night and all the next day the people went out
and gathered quail. No one gathered less than ten homers.[d] Then
they spread them out all around the camp. 33But while the meat was
still between their teeth and before it could be consumed, the anger
of the LORD burned against the people, and he struck them with a

[a]25 Or *prophesied and continued to do so* [b]31 Or *They flew* [c]31 Hebrew *two cubits* (about 1 meter) [d]32 That is, probably about 60 bushels (about 2.2 kiloliters)

severe plague. [34]Therefore the place was named Kibroth Hattaavah,[a] because there they buried the people who had craved other food.

[35]From Kibroth Hattaavah the people traveled to Hazeroth and stayed there.

Miriam and Aaron Oppose Moses

12 Miriam and Aaron began to talk against Moses because of his Cushite wife, for he had married a Cushite. [2]"Has the LORD spoken only through Moses?" they asked. "Hasn't he also spoken through us?" And the LORD heard this.

[3](Now Moses was a very humble man, more humble than anyone else on the face of the earth.)

[4]At once the LORD said to Moses, Aaron and Miriam, "Come out to the Tent of Meeting, all three of you." So the three of them came out. [5]Then the LORD came down in a pillar of cloud; he stood at the entrance to the Tent and summoned Aaron and Miriam. When both of them stepped forward, [6]he said, "Listen to my words:

"When a prophet of the LORD is among you,
I reveal myself to him in visions,
I speak to him in dreams.
[7]But this is not true of my servant Moses;
he is faithful in all my house.
[8]With him I speak face to face,
clearly and not in riddles;
he sees the form of the LORD.
Why then were you not afraid
to speak against my servant Moses?"

[9]The anger of the LORD burned against them, and he left them.

[10]When the cloud lifted from above the Tent, there stood Miriam—leprous,[b] like snow. Aaron turned toward her and saw that she had leprosy; [11]and he said to Moses, "Please, my lord, do not hold against us the sin we have so foolishly committed. [12]Do not let her be like a stillborn infant coming from its mother's womb with its flesh half eaten away."

[13]So Moses cried out to the LORD, "O God, please heal her!"

[14]The LORD replied to Moses, "If her father had spit in her face, would she not have been in disgrace for seven days? Confine her outside the camp for seven days; after that she can be brought back." [15]So Miriam was confined outside the camp for seven days, and the people did not move on till she was brought back.

[16]After that, the people left Hazeroth and encamped in the Desert of Paran.

[a]34 *Kibroth Hattaavah* means *graves of craving*. [b]10 The Hebrew word was used for various diseases affecting the skin—not necessarily leprosy.

11:35 *Hazeroth:* The exact location is unknown (see also 33:16-36; Deut 1:1).

12:1 *Miriam and Aaron . . . Cushite wife:* Moses' sister and brother (see Exod 4:14; 15:20; Num 26:59). Cush, or Ethiopia, is a region to the south of Egypt. The "Cushite wife" is not identified by name anywhere in the Bible. Some scholars think she may have been a woman Moses married some time after marrying Zipporah the Midianite (Exod 18:2-4). Others have suggested that the word translated as "Cush" can also refer to a place in northern Arabia and could include areas where Midianites lived. If so, Aaron and Miriam could actually be objecting to Moses' marriage to Zipporah.

12:6 *visions . . . dreams:* In the Bible God is frequently shown using visions and dreams to speak to people (see Gen 15:1; 40:1—41:57; Joel 2:28; Matt 1:20-24; 2:13-15) and to special religious leaders called prophets (Isa 6; Dan 7–12; Zech 1–6).

12:10 *leprosy:* See the note at 5:2,3.

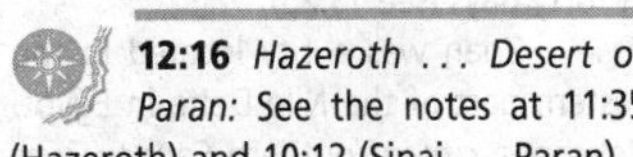

12:16 *Hazeroth . . . Desert of Paran:* See the notes at 11:35 (Hazeroth) and 10:12 (Sinai . . . Paran).

12:7 Heb 3:2. **12:14** Num 5:2,3.

13:3 *Desert of Paran:* See the note at 10:12 (Sinai . . . Paran).

13:3-15 *leaders:* See the note at 1:5-16. These leaders were not necessarily the same leaders who helped count the people.

13:3-15 *Israelites:* See the notes at 1:2,3 and 1:5-16.

13:17-22 *explore Canaan:* The twelve men traveled from the Desert of Paran (13:3) north to the Desert of Zin (13:21; Josh 15:1-4). The hill country may refer to the hilly area of the southern wilderness or to the hills of southern Canaan itself (see 14:40). The twelve spies were to go as far north as Rehob near Lebo Hamath. The location of Rehob itself is unknown. Lebo Hamath (sometimes called Hamath Pass) may refer to the pass near Mount Hermon at the entrance to southern Lebanon, or it may refer to the city north of Damascus on the Orontes River, which would correspond to Israel's northern boundary at the time of King David (2 Sam 10:6-19). Assuming the more southern location of Israel's northern border, the men would have had to cover the five hundred-mile round-trip in forty days (see 13:25).

Zoan was a city located in the eastern part of the Nile Delta in Egypt. Hebron, a city in southern Canaan, was where the spies saw the descendants of Anak.

13:22 *the descendants of Anak:* Canaanite clans mentioned in the Bible and often described as being tall, strong, and fierce warriors (see Deut 1:28; 2:10-21; 9:2; Josh 11:21,22; 15:14; Judg 1:10).

TROUBLE IN THE CAMP AT KADESH

Ten of the twelve leaders sent to Canaan return with reports that frighten the Israelites and lead them to rebel against Moses. The other two, Joshua and Caleb, try to calm the people's fear. God punishes the people for rebelling and for lacking faith. The Israelites' wandering will continue for forty years, and the older generation who came out of Egypt, including Moses, will not be allowed to enter the promised land of Canaan.

Exploring Canaan

13 The LORD said to Moses, [2]"Send some men to explore the
land of Canaan, which I am giving to the Israelites. From each
ancestral tribe send one of its leaders."

[3]So at the LORD's command Moses sent them out from the
Desert of Paran. All of them were leaders of the Israelites. [4]These
are their names:

from the tribe of Reuben, Shammua son of Zaccur;
[5]from the tribe of Simeon, Shaphat son of Hori;
[6]from the tribe of Judah, Caleb son of Jephunneh;
[7]from the tribe of Issachar, Igal son of Joseph;
[8]from the tribe of Ephraim, Hoshea son of Nun;
[9]from the tribe of Benjamin, Palti son of Raphu;
[10]from the tribe of Zebulun, Gaddiel son of Sodi;
[11]from the tribe of Manasseh (a tribe of Joseph), Gaddi son of Susi;
[12]from the tribe of Dan, Ammiel son of Gemalli;
[13]from the tribe of Asher, Sethur son of Michael;
[14]from the tribe of Naphtali, Nahbi son of Vophsi;
[15]from the tribe of Gad, Geuel son of Maki.

[16]These are the names of the men Moses sent to explore the land.
(Moses gave Hoshea son of Nun the name Joshua.)

[17]When Moses sent them to explore Canaan, he said, "Go up
through the Negev and on into the hill country. [18]See what the
land is like and whether the people who live there are strong or
weak, few or many. [19]What kind of land do they live in? Is it good
or bad? What kind of towns do they live in? Are they unwalled or
fortified? [20]How is the soil? Is it fertile or poor? Are there trees on
it or not? Do your best to bring back some of the fruit of the land."
(It was the season for the first ripe grapes.)

[21]So they went up and explored the land from the Desert of
Zin as far as Rehob, toward Lebo[a] Hamath. [22]They went up
through the Negev and came to Hebron, where Ahiman, Sheshai
and Talmai, the descendants of Anak, lived. (Hebron had been
built seven years before Zoan in Egypt.) [23]When they reached the
Valley of Eshcol,[b] they cut off a branch bearing a single cluster of

[a]**21** Or *toward the entrance to* [b]**23** *Eshcol* means *cluster*; also in verse 24.

Grapes of Canaan by Sadao Watanabe, 1983. Moses sent twelve tribal leaders into Canaan to explore the land the LORD was going to give them. They were to report back concerning how strong the people were who lived in Canaan and whether the land was good for growing crops. When they got to the Valley of Eshcol, they cut some grapes, figs, and pomegranates to take back to Moses. The bunch of grapes they cut was so huge it took two men to carry it on a pole. (See 13:1-25.)

grapes. Two of them carried it on a pole between them, along with
some pomegranates and figs. 24That place was called the Valley of
Eshcol because of the cluster of grapes the Israelites cut off there.
25At the end of forty days they returned from exploring the land.

Report on the Exploration

26They came back to Moses and Aaron and the whole
Israelite community at Kadesh in the Desert of Paran. There they
reported to them and to the whole assembly and showed them the
fruit of the land. 27They gave Moses this account: "We went into
the land to which you sent us, and it does flow with milk and
honey! Here is its fruit. 28But the people who live there are powerful, and the cities are fortified and very large. We even saw descendants of Anak there. 29The Amalekites live in the Negev; the
Hittites, Jebusites and Amorites live in the hill country; and the
Canaanites live near the sea and along the Jordan."

30Then Caleb silenced the people before Moses and said, "We
should go up and take possession of the land, for we can certainly
do it."

13:23 *Valley of Eshcol:* Eshcol in Hebrew means "bunch of grapes." The location of this valley is unknown. See also 32:9 and Deut 1:24.

13:23 *pomegranates and figs:* The pomegranate is a bright red fruit about the size of a large apple that has a lot of seeds surrounded by a sweet-tasting pulp. See the illustration on p. 1277. Figs are sweet fruits from bushy trees that grow as high as thirty feet.

13:26 *Kadesh . . . Desert of Paran:* Kadesh probably refers to an oasis located about fifty miles south of Beersheba in the Desert of Zin (see 20:1) Also known as Kadesh Barnea (see 32:8; 34:4).

13:28,29 *people who live there are powerful:* See the note at 13:22. The Amalekites were nomadic tribes who lived mostly in the Negev (an area south and east of the Dead Sea). They were enemies of Israel (Exod 17:8-14). The Hittites were a powerful people who were descended from Heth, grandson of Ham (Gen 10:6-20). They established an empire in Asia Minor and were a dominant force in Canaan from the time of Abraham until the twelfth century B.C. The Jebusites ruled Jerusalem until King David drove them out (2 Sam 5:6-9). The Amorites lived in the hill country of Canaan at the time the Israelites invaded (21:21-35; Josh 2:10). The Canaanites were descendants of Noah's son, Ham (Gen 10:6-20), and lived in cities or villages near the Jordan River and the Mediterranean Sea northwest of Jerusalem.

13:29 *near the sea and along the Jordan:* The Mediterranean Sea formed Canaan's western boundary, and the Jordan River was Canaan's main river. See the map on p. 2464.

13:27 Exod 3:8.

13:33 *descendants of Anak:* Also called Nephilim, meaning "fallen ones." This is a legendary race of giant people with human mothers and heavenly beings as fathers (see Gen 6:4). The reports from Canaan compared the Anakim to these legendary giants. Only Caleb and Joshua (14:5-9) argued that the Israelites, with God on their side, could conquer them easily.

14:6 *tore their clothes:* Tearing one's clothing was a way ancient people showed sorrow or sadness. See also Gen 37:29,34; Judg 11:35.

14:10 *glory of the Lord . . . Tent of Meeting:* See the notes at 9:15,16 (cloud . . . fire) and 1:52,53.

14:2,3 Exod 16:2,3; Num 11:1,4,5; Deut 1:26-28. **14:9** Heb 3:16. **14:13-16** Exod 12:29-41; 13:20-22; 14:19-22.

[31]But the men who had gone up with him said, "We can't attack those people; they are stronger than we are." [32]And they spread among the Israelites a bad report about the land they had explored. They said, "The land we explored devours those living in it. All the people we saw there are of great size. [33]We saw the Nephilim there (the descendants of Anak come from the Nephilim). We seemed like grasshoppers in our own eyes, and we looked the same to them."

The People Rebel

14 That night all the people of the community raised their voices and wept aloud. [2]All the Israelites grumbled against Moses and Aaron, and the whole assembly said to them, "If only we had died in Egypt! Or in this desert! [3]Why is the Lord bringing us to this land only to let us fall by the sword? Our wives and children will be taken as plunder. Wouldn't it be better for us to go back to Egypt?" [4]And they said to each other, "We should choose a leader and go back to Egypt."

[5]Then Moses and Aaron fell facedown in front of the whole Israelite assembly gathered there. [6]Joshua son of Nun and Caleb son of Jephunneh, who were among those who had explored the land, tore their clothes [7]and said to the entire Israelite assembly, "The land we passed through and explored is exceedingly good. [8]If the Lord is pleased with us, he will lead us into that land, a land flowing with milk and honey, and will give it to us. [9]Only do not rebel against the Lord. And do not be afraid of the people of the land, because we will swallow them up. Their protection is gone, but the Lord is with us. Do not be afraid of them."

[10]But the whole assembly talked about stoning them. Then the glory of the Lord appeared at the Tent of Meeting to all the Israelites. [11]The Lord said to Moses, "How long will these people treat me with contempt? How long will they refuse to believe in me, in spite of all the miraculous signs I have performed among them? [12]I will strike them down with a plague and destroy them, but I will make you into a nation greater and stronger than they."

[13]Moses said to the Lord, "Then the Egyptians will hear about it! By your power you brought these people up from among them. [14]And they will tell the inhabitants of this land about it. They have already heard that you, O Lord, are with these people and that you, O Lord, have been seen face to face, that your cloud stays over them, and that you go before them in a pillar of cloud by day and a pillar of fire by night. [15]If you put these people to death all at one time, the nations who have heard this report about you will say, [16]'The Lord was not able to bring these people into the land he promised them on oath; so he slaughtered them in the desert.'

[17]"Now may the Lord's strength be displayed, just as you have declared: [18]'The Lord is slow to anger, abounding in love and

forgiving sin and rebellion. Yet he does not leave the guilty unpunished; he punishes the children for the sin of the fathers to the
third and fourth generation.' [19]In accordance with your great love,
forgive the sin of these people, just as you have pardoned them
from the time they left Egypt until now."
[20]The LORD replied, "I have forgiven them, as you asked.
[21]Nevertheless, as surely as I live and as surely as the glory of the
LORD fills the whole earth, [22]not one of the men who saw my glory
and the miraculous signs I performed in Egypt and in the desert
but who disobeyed me and tested me ten times— [23]not one of
them will ever see the land I promised on oath to their forefathers.
No one who has treated me with contempt will ever see it. [24]But
because my servant Caleb has a different spirit and follows me
wholeheartedly, I will bring him into the land he went to, and his
descendants will inherit it. [25]Since the Amalekites and Canaanites
are living in the valleys, turn back tomorrow and set out toward
the desert along the route to the Red Sea.[a]"
[26]The LORD said to Moses and Aaron: [27]"How long will this
wicked community grumble against me? I have heard the complaints
of these grumbling Israelites. [28]So tell them, 'As surely as I live,
declares the LORD, I will do to you the very things I heard you say:
[29]In this desert your bodies will fall—every one of you twenty years
old or more who was counted in the census and who has grumbled
against me. [30]Not one of you will enter the land I swore with uplifted hand to make your home, except Caleb son of Jephunneh and
Joshua son of Nun. [31]As for your children that you said would be
taken as plunder, I will bring them in to enjoy the land you have
rejected. [32]But you—your bodies will fall in this desert. [33]Your children will be shepherds here for forty years, suffering for your unfaithfulness, until the last of your bodies lies in the desert. [34]For forty
years—one year for each of the forty days you explored the land—
you will suffer for your sins and know what it is like to have me
against you.' [35]I, the LORD, have spoken, and I will surely do these
things to this whole wicked community, which has banded together
against me. They will meet their end in this desert; here they will die."
[36]So the men Moses had sent to explore the land, who
returned and made the whole community grumble against him by
spreading a bad report about it— [37]these men responsible for
spreading the bad report about the land were struck down and
died of a plague before the LORD. [38]Of the men who went to
explore the land, only Joshua son of Nun and Caleb son of
Jephunneh survived.
[39]When Moses reported this to all the Israelites, they
mourned bitterly. [40]Early the next morning they went up toward
the high hill country. "We have sinned," they said. "We will go up
to the place the LORD promised."

[a]25 Hebrew *Yam Suph*; that is, Sea of Reeds

14:22 *not one:* These are the older generation of Israelites who escaped from Egypt. They will die in the desert during the forty-year period of wandering because they complained and tested God too often (14:29,34). See also Heb 3:18.

14:24 *Caleb:* Caleb was from the tribe of Judah. For his trust in God, he and his descendants were later given choice land in Canaan (see Josh 14:6-14).

14:25 *valleys . . . route to the Red Sea:* The valley routes to Canaan from the south were blocked by the Amalekites and Canaanites (see the note at 13:28,29), so the Israelites had to go southeast toward the northeastern arm of the Red Sea. The Hebrew term can be translated "Sea of Reeds" (see Exod 13:17—14:9).

14:27,28 *wicked community . . . I will do to you the very things I heard you say:* Their sin is lack of trust. God promises to give them what they asked for in 14:2, to die in the desert.

14:33 *children will be shepherds here for forty years:* Though the older generation will die, God hears Moses' prayer for mercy and will allow their children to enter Canaan, after first suffering hardship in the desert for forty years. The number forty is an important number in the Bible. It is used to stand for a long period of time. The flood during the time of Noah (Gen 7:12) lasted forty days and nights. Jesus was tempted in the wilderness for forty days (Mark 1:13). For other examples, see the chart called "Numbers in the Bible," p. 2405. See also Acts 7:36.

14:17-19 Exod 32:11-14. **14:18** Exod 20:5,6; 34:6,7; Deut 5:9, 10; 7:9,10. **14:29** Heb 3:17.

14:43 *Amalekites . . . Canaanites:* See the note at 13:28,29.

14:44,45 *hill country . . . Hormah:* The hill country here refers to southern Canaan. The exact location of Hormah is uncertain, but it probably was somewhere just south of Beersheba. See Deut 1:44 and Judg 1:17.

14:44 *ark of the LORD's covenant:* See the note at 7:89. God was present with the Israelites as long as they carried the ark of the covenant. When they tried to enter Canaan without it, they were doing so without God's blessing.

15:3 *burnt offerings . . . vows:* See the note at 7:87. Some sacrifices were also connected to making a vow to God (see Lev 27:9-11).

15:6 *flour mixed with . . . oil:* The flour was probably wheat flour. Olive oil was collected by crushing olives in a bowl and then pouring the olive pulp into a cloth basket. The oil that dripped through the cloth was used in cooking and burned in lamps. See the illustration on p. 1326.

15:7 *aroma pleasing to the LORD:* See the note at 7:87.

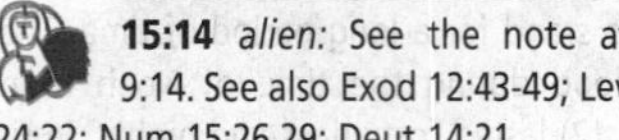

15:14 *alien:* See the note at 9:14. See also Exod 12:43-49; Lev 24:22; Num 15:26,29; Deut 14:21.

41 But Moses said, "Why are you disobeying the LORD's command? This will not succeed! 42 Do not go up, because the LORD is
not with you. You will be defeated by your enemies, 43 for the
Amalekites and Canaanites will face you there. Because you have
turned away from the LORD, he will not be with you and you will
fall by the sword."
44 Nevertheless, in their presumption they went up toward
the high hill country, though neither Moses nor the ark of the
LORD's covenant moved from the camp. 45 Then the Amalekites and
Canaanites who lived in that hill country came down and attacked
them and beat them down all the way to Hormah.

Supplementary Offerings

15 The LORD said to Moses, 2 "Speak to the Israelites and say to
them: 'After you enter the land I am giving you as a home 3 and you
present to the LORD offerings made by fire, from the herd or the
flock, as an aroma pleasing to the LORD—whether burnt offerings or
sacrifices, for special vows or freewill offerings or festival offerings—
4 then the one who brings his offering shall present to the LORD a
grain offering of a tenth of an ephah[a] of fine flour mixed with a
quarter of a hin[b] of oil. 5 With each lamb for the burnt offering or the
sacrifice, prepare a quarter of a hin of wine as a drink offering.
6 " 'With a ram prepare a grain offering of two-tenths of an
ephah[c] of fine flour mixed with a third of a hin[d] of oil, 7 and a third
of a hin of wine as a drink offering. Offer it as an aroma pleasing
to the LORD.
8 " 'When you prepare a young bull as a burnt offering or sacrifice, for a special vow or a fellowship offering[e] to the LORD, 9 bring
with the bull a grain offering of three-tenths of an ephah[f] of fine
flour mixed with half a hin[g] of oil. 10 Also bring half a hin of wine
as a drink offering. It will be an offering made by fire, an aroma
pleasing to the LORD. 11 Each bull or ram, each lamb or young goat,
is to be prepared in this manner. 12 Do this for each one, for as
many as you prepare.
13 " 'Everyone who is native-born must do these things in this
way when he brings an offering made by fire as an aroma pleasing
to the LORD. 14 For the generations to come, whenever an alien or
anyone else living among you presents an offering made by fire as
an aroma pleasing to the LORD, he must do exactly as you do. 15 The
community is to have the same rules for you and for the alien
living among you; this is a lasting ordinance for the generations to

[a]**4** That is, probably about 2 quarts (about 2 liters) [b]**4** That is, probably about 1 quart (about 1 liter); also in verse 5 [c]**6** That is, probably about 4 quarts (about 4.5 liters) [d]**6** That is, probably about 1 1/4 quarts (about 1.2 liters); also in verse 7 [e]**8** Traditionally *peace offering* [f]**9** That is, probably about 6 quarts (about 6.5 liters) [g]**9** That is, probably about 2 quarts (about 2 liters); also in verse 10

come. You and the alien shall be the same before the LORD: [16]The
same laws and regulations will apply both to you and to the alien
living among you.' "
[17]The LORD said to Moses, [18]"Speak to the Israelites and say
to them: 'When you enter the land to which I am taking you [19]and
you eat the food of the land, present a portion as an offering to the
LORD. [20]Present a cake from the first of your ground meal and present it as an offering from the threshing floor. [21]Throughout the
generations to come you are to give this offering to the LORD from
the first of your ground meal.

Offerings for Unintentional Sins

[22]" 'Now if you unintentionally fail to keep any of these commands the LORD gave Moses— [23]any of the LORD's commands to
you through him, from the day the LORD gave them and continuing through the generations to come— [24]and if this is done unintentionally without the community being aware of it, then the
whole community is to offer a young bull for a burnt offering as
an aroma pleasing to the LORD, along with its prescribed grain
offering and drink offering, and a male goat for a sin offering.
[25]The priest is to make atonement for the whole Israelite community, and they will be forgiven, for it was not intentional and they
have brought to the LORD for their wrong an offering made by fire
and a sin offering. [26]The whole Israelite community and the aliens
living among them will be forgiven, because all the people were
involved in the unintentional wrong.
[27]" 'But if just one person sins unintentionally, he must bring
a year-old female goat for a sin offering. [28]The priest is to make
atonement before the LORD for the one who erred by sinning unintentionally, and when atonement has been made for him, he will
be forgiven. [29]One and the same law applies to everyone who sins
unintentionally, whether he is a native-born Israelite or an alien.
[30]" 'But anyone who sins defiantly, whether native-born or
alien, blasphemes the LORD, and that person must be cut off from
his people. [31]Because he has despised the LORD's word and broken
his commands, that person must surely be cut off; his guilt
remains on him.' "

The Sabbath-Breaker Put to Death

[32]While the Israelites were in the desert, a man was found
gathering wood on the Sabbath day. [33]Those who found him gathering wood brought him to Moses and Aaron and the whole
assembly, [34]and they kept him in custody, because it was not clear
what should be done to him. [35]Then the LORD said to Moses, "The
man must die. The whole assembly must stone him outside the

15:24 *unintentionally:* Breaking God's laws, even without meaning to, still called for offering sacrifices (see the note at 8:8). Unintentional sins, such as touching sacred objects or going near the tabernacle when ritually unclean, affected the whole people of God, and so everyone needed forgiveness. See also Lev 4:27-31.

15:32 *Sabbath:* The Sabbath was the weekly day of rest that began at sunset on Friday and ended at sunset on Saturday. For more, see the chart called "Jewish Calendar and Festivals," p. 944.

15:35 *stone him:* Stoning was a common form of capital punishment in Israelite society. It was inflicted for crimes against God, such as working on the Sabbath. Stoning was done outside the camp to keep from disturbing the holiness of the camp. See also Lev 24:14,23.

camp.” 36So the assembly took him outside the camp and stoned
him to death, as the LORD commanded Moses.

Tassels on Garments

37The LORD said to Moses, 38“Speak to the Israelites and say
to them: ‘Throughout the generations to come you are to make
tassels on the corners of your garments, with a blue cord on each
tassel. 39You will have these tassels to look at and so you will
remember all the commands of the LORD, that you may obey them
and not prostitute yourselves by going after the lusts of your own
hearts and eyes. 40Then you will remember to obey all my commands and will be consecrated to your God. 41I am the LORD your
God, who brought you out of Egypt to be your God. I am the
LORD your God.’ ”

Korah, Dathan and Abiram

16 Korah son of Izhar, the son of Kohath, the son of Levi, and
certain Reubenites—Dathan and Abiram, sons of Eliab, and On
son of Peleth—became insolent[a] 2and rose up against Moses. With
them were 250 Israelite men, well-known community leaders who
had been appointed members of the council. 3They came as a
group to oppose Moses and Aaron and said to them, “You have
gone too far! The whole community is holy, every one of them,
and the LORD is with them. Why then do you set yourselves above
the LORD’s assembly?”

4When Moses heard this, he fell facedown. 5Then he said to
Korah and all his followers: “In the morning the LORD will show
who belongs to him and who is holy, and he will have that person
come near him. The man he chooses he will cause to come near
him. 6You, Korah, and all your followers are to do this: Take
censers 7and tomorrow put fire and incense in them before the
LORD. The man the LORD chooses will be the one who is holy. You
Levites have gone too far!”

8Moses also said to Korah, “Now listen, you Levites! 9Isn’t it
enough for you that the God of Israel has separated you from the
rest of the Israelite community and brought you near himself to
do the work at the LORD’s tabernacle and to stand before the community and minister to them? 10He has brought you and all your
fellow Levites near himself, but now you are trying to get the
priesthood too. 11It is against the LORD that you and all your followers have banded together. Who is Aaron that you should grumble against him?”

12Then Moses summoned Dathan and Abiram, the sons of
Eliab. But they said, “We will not come! 13Isn’t it enough that you
have brought us up out of a land flowing with milk and honey to

a1 Or *Peleth—took ⌞men⌟*

15:38 *tassels:* The tassels would wave about when people walked reminding them to obey God’s laws and teachings. Today Jewish prayer shawls still include such tassels. See also Deut 22:12.

16:1,2 *Korah . . . On son of Peleth:* Korah was a Levite from the Kohathite clan (3:27-31; 4:1-20). See Exod 6:16-24 for Korah’s family history, and see 1 Chr 6:22-24,33-38, which mentions Korah as an ancestor of Israel’s temple musicians. Korah and other Levites who did not belong to Aaron’s family were not allowed to perform the duties of the priests (3:1-10). They rebelled because they wanted to have the same priestly privileges as Aaron’s sons. Dathan, Abiram, and On from the Reuben tribe believed that all the members of the community belong to the LORD (16:3) and deserved the same privileges as the priests from Aaron’s family. The rest of chapter 16 relates Moses’ answers to these separate challenges to priestly privilege. See also Jude 11.

16:6,7 *censers . . . the LORD chooses:* The censers (firepans) were special implements used to hold burning coals in the ceremony to offer sacrifices (see Lev 16:12; Exod 27:3). Only priests could offer incense at the sacred altar; anyone else who tried would be killed (3:10; see also Lev 10:1, 2). In this case, the man who lived would be the one the LORD had chosen.

15:41 Exod 6:6-8; 20:2; Lev 26:13; Deut 5:6. **16:8,9** Num 3:5—4:49.

kill us in the desert? And now you also want to lord it over us?
14Moreover, you haven't brought us into a land flowing with milk
and honey or given us an inheritance of fields and vineyards. Will
you gouge out the eyes of[a] these men? No, we will not come!"
15Then Moses became very angry and said to the LORD, "Do
not accept their offering. I have not taken so much as a donkey
from them, nor have I wronged any of them."
16Moses said to Korah, "You and all your followers are to
appear before the LORD tomorrow—you and they and Aaron.
17Each man is to take his censer and put incense in it—250 censers
in all—and present it before the LORD. You and Aaron are to present your censers also." 18So each man took his censer, put fire and
incense in it, and stood with Moses and Aaron at the entrance to
the Tent of Meeting. 19When Korah had gathered all his followers
in opposition to them at the entrance to the Tent of Meeting, the
glory of the LORD appeared to the entire assembly. 20The LORD said
to Moses and Aaron, 21"Separate yourselves from this assembly so
I can put an end to them at once."
22But Moses and Aaron fell facedown and cried out, "O God,
God of the spirits of all mankind, will you be angry with the entire
assembly when only one man sins?"
23Then the LORD said to Moses, 24"Say to the assembly, 'Move
away from the tents of Korah, Dathan and Abiram.' "
25Moses got up and went to Dathan and Abiram, and the
elders of Israel followed him. 26He warned the assembly, "Move
back from the tents of these wicked men! Do not touch anything
belonging to them, or you will be swept away because of all their
sins." 27So they moved away from the tents of Korah, Dathan and
Abiram. Dathan and Abiram had come out and were standing
with their wives, children and little ones at the entrances to their
tents.
28Then Moses said, "This is how you will know that the LORD
has sent me to do all these things and that it was not my idea: 29If
these men die a natural death and experience only what usually
happens to men, then the LORD has not sent me. 30But if the LORD
brings about something totally new, and the earth opens its mouth
and swallows them, with everything that belongs to them, and they
go down alive into the grave,[b] then you will know that these men
have treated the LORD with contempt."
31As soon as he finished saying all this, the ground under
them split apart 32and the earth opened its mouth and swallowed
them, with their households and all Korah's men and all their possessions. 33They went down alive into the grave, with everything
they owned; the earth closed over them, and they perished and
were gone from the community. 34At their cries, all the Israelites
around them fled, shouting, "The earth is going to swallow us too!"

---

[a]**14** Or *you make slaves of*; or *you deceive*   [b]**30** Hebrew *Sheol*; also in verse 33

16:14 *you haven't brought us into a land:* Dathan and Abiram's complaint seems to focus on the fact that Moses' promise to lead the people to the rich land of Canaan is taking too long. They claim that they would be better off going back to Egypt where they had rich farmland. They have already begun to forget that they were also slaves in Egypt.

16:17 *put incense in it:* The story returns to the priestly test brought on by Korah's rebellion. See the note at 16:6,7.

16:19 *the glory of the LORD appeared:* See the note at 9:15,16 (cloud).

16:37-39 *censers are holy:* Eleazar, Aaron's son, took the censers from the fire, probably because the high priest (Aaron) was not allowed to touch anything that was dead (see Lev 21:10,11). The censers were considered holy, or sacred, because they had been used to offer incense to the LORD.

16:40 *no one except a descendant of Aaron:* See the notes at 16:1,2 (Korah); 3:2,3 (sons of Aaron).

16:42 *glory of the LORD:* See the note at 9:15,16 (cloud).

16:46,47 *incense . . . made atonement for them:* Offering incense was not the usual way for priests to make offerings and sacrifices to forgive the sins of the people, but in this case speed was important because the people had already started dying.

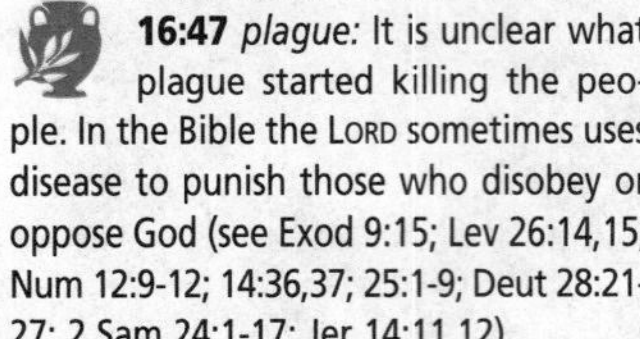

16:47 *plague:* It is unclear what plague started killing the people. In the Bible the LORD sometimes uses disease to punish those who disobey or oppose God (see Exod 9:15; Lev 26:14,15; Num 12:9-12; 14:36,37; 25:1-9; Deut 28:21-27; 2 Sam 24:1-17; Jer 14:11,12).

17:2 *twelve ...leader of each of their ancestral tribes:* See the note at 1:5-16.

17:2-4 *twelve staffs . . . in front of the Testimony:* A staff symbolized a leader's power and authority (see Exod 7:8-12; 14:15-17). The "Testimony" refers to the ark of the covenant which was in the most holy part of the tabernacle, where only Moses and the high priest were allowed to go.

16:35 Num 16:1,2.

35 And fire came out from the LORD and consumed the 250 men who were offering the incense.

36 The LORD said to Moses, 37 "Tell Eleazar son of Aaron, the priest, to take the censers out of the smoldering remains and scatter the coals some distance away, for the censers are holy— 38 the censers of the men who sinned at the cost of their lives. Hammer the censers into sheets to overlay the altar, for they were presented before the LORD and have become holy. Let them be a sign to the Israelites."

39 So Eleazar the priest collected the bronze censers brought by those who had been burned up, and he had them hammered out to overlay the altar, 40 as the LORD directed him through Moses. This was to remind the Israelites that no one except a descendant of Aaron should come to burn incense before the LORD, or he would become like Korah and his followers.

41 The next day the whole Israelite community grumbled against Moses and Aaron. "You have killed the LORD's people," they said.

42 But when the assembly gathered in opposition to Moses and Aaron and turned toward the Tent of Meeting, suddenly the cloud covered it and the glory of the LORD appeared. 43 Then Moses and Aaron went to the front of the Tent of Meeting, 44 and the LORD said to Moses, 45 "Get away from this assembly so I can put an end to them at once." And they fell facedown.

46 Then Moses said to Aaron, "Take your censer and put incense in it, along with fire from the altar, and hurry to the assembly to make atonement for them. Wrath has come out from the LORD; the plague has started." 47 So Aaron did as Moses said, and ran into the midst of the assembly. The plague had already started among the people, but Aaron offered the incense and made atonement for them. 48 He stood between the living and the dead, and the plague stopped. 49 But 14,700 people died from the plague, in addition to those who had died because of Korah. 50 Then Aaron returned to Moses at the entrance to the Tent of Meeting, for the plague had stopped.

The Budding of Aaron's Staff

17 The LORD said to Moses, 2 "Speak to the Israelites and get twelve staffs from them, one from the leader of each of their ancestral tribes. Write the name of each man on his staff. 3 On the staff of Levi write Aaron's name, for there must be one staff for the head of each ancestral tribe. 4 Place them in the Tent of Meeting in front of the Testimony, where I meet with you. 5 The staff belonging to the man I choose will sprout, and I will rid myself of this constant grumbling against you by the Israelites."

6 So Moses spoke to the Israelites, and their leaders gave him twelve staffs, one for the leader of each of their ancestral tribes,

and Aaron's staff was among them. [7]Moses placed the staffs before the LORD in the Tent of the Testimony.

[8]The next day Moses entered the Tent of the Testimony and saw that Aaron's staff, which represented the house of Levi, had not only sprouted but had budded, blossomed and produced almonds. [9]Then Moses brought out all the staffs from the LORD's presence to all the Israelites. They looked at them, and each man took his own staff.

[10]The LORD said to Moses, "Put back Aaron's staff in front of the Testimony, to be kept as a sign to the rebellious. This will put an end to their grumbling against me, so that they will not die." [11]Moses did just as the LORD commanded him.

[12]The Israelites said to Moses, "We will die! We are lost, we are all lost! [13]Anyone who even comes near the tabernacle of the LORD will die. Are we all going to die?"

Duties of Priests and Levites

18 The LORD said to Aaron, "You, your sons and your father's family are to bear the responsibility for offenses against the sanctuary, and you and your sons alone are to bear the responsibility for offenses against the priesthood. [2]Bring your fellow Levites from your ancestral tribe to join you and assist you when you and your sons minister before the Tent of the Testimony. [3]They are to be responsible to you and are to perform all the duties of the Tent, but they must not go near the furnishings of the sanctuary or the altar, or both they and you will die. [4]They are to join you and be responsible for the care of the Tent of Meeting—all the work at the Tent—and no one else may come near where you are.

[5]"You are to be responsible for the care of the sanctuary and the altar, so that wrath will not fall on the Israelites again. [6]I myself have selected your fellow Levites from among the Israelites as a gift to you, dedicated to the LORD to do the work at the Tent of Meeting. [7]But only you and your sons may serve as priests in connection with everything at the altar and inside the curtain. I am giving you the service of the priesthood as a gift. Anyone else who comes near the sanctuary must be put to death."

Offerings for Priests and Levites

[8]Then the LORD said to Aaron, "I myself have put you in charge of the offerings presented to me; all the holy offerings the Israelites give me I give to you and your sons as your portion and regular share. [9]You are to have the part of the most holy offerings that is kept from the fire. From all the gifts they bring me as most holy offerings, whether grain or sin or guilt offerings, that part belongs to you and your sons. [10]Eat it as something most holy; every male shall eat it. You must regard it as holy.

[11]"This also is yours: whatever is set aside from the gifts of all

> The LORD said to Aaron, *"I myself have selected your fellow Levites from among the Israelites as a gift to you, dedicated to the LORD to do the work at the Tent of Meeting."*
> Num 18:6

17:8 *blossomed . . . almonds:* Almond trees grow wild in Palestine and Syria and reach a height of fourteen to eighteen feet. They blossom as early as January and produce a pulpy fruit with a hard stone surrounding the almond seed or nut.

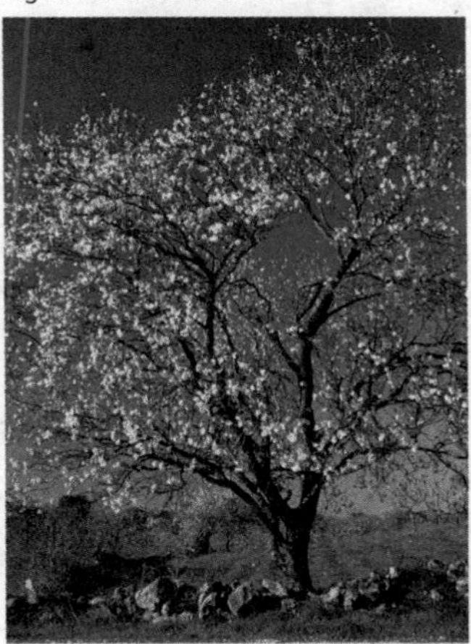

18:1-7 *Aaron . . . your sons . . . Levites:* See the note at 3:2,3. The Levites helped the priests (1:47-53), but they could not go near the sacred objects or altar to offer sacrifices.

18:8 *holy offerings . . . I give to you:* See the note at 5:9. When the Israelites entered the land of Canaan, the Levite tribe could not farm the land because they were needed to take care of the tabernacle. Therefore God tells Aaron that they deserve a part of the people's offerings to support themselves and their families.

17:8-10 Heb 9:4.

18:14 *devoted to the* LORD: Those things unconditionally dedicated to the LORD are taken away from humans and given to God forever. Sometimes they were even destroyed (see Josh 6:15-19). See also Lev 27:28; Num 21:1-3; 1 Sam 15:3. But here God says that these things can be used by the priests.

18:15,16 *redeem them:* This refers to the price of a child who had been dedicated to the LORD (see Lev 27:1-7). The parents would pay that price to "buy back" the child. See the notes at 3:11-13; 3:44-48.

18:17 *Sprinkle their blood:* Blood thrown or smeared on the altar or on the people had cleansing power and showed that something or someone was dedicated to God (see also Exod 29:10-21). See the mini-article called "Blood," p. 180.

18:20 *no inheritance:* See the notes at 1:5-16 and 1:47.

18:21 *tithes:* This tithe, ten percent, was given to the Levites in return for their care of the tabernacle and because they did not receive a share of land. See also Lev 27:30-33; Deut 14:22-29; 2 Chr 31:5,6.

18:26 *present a tenth of that tithe:* The Levites had to offer a tenth of the gifts given to them (18:21) to the LORD. These gifts went to the priests from Aaron's family.

19:2 *red heifer without defect:* The cow was to be burned as a sacrifice and its ashes used in a ceremony to remove ritual uncleanness (19:9) and to cleanse someone who had touched a corpse (19:11,12). It had to be an animal that had no defects (see Lev 4:28; 14:10; 22:19) and one that had not been used for work (see Deut 15:19; 21:3). The cow's red color probably was meant to connect it with the color of blood, which had the power to purify (see the note at 18:17).

18:18,19 Lev 6:18; 7:28-36; 22:10-16.

the wave offerings of the Israelites. I give this to you and your sons
and daughters as your regular share. Everyone in your household
who is ceremonially clean may eat it.
12"I give you all the finest olive oil and all the finest new wine
and grain they give the LORD as the firstfruits of their harvest. 13All
the land's firstfruits that they bring to the LORD will be yours.
Everyone in your household who is ceremonially clean may eat it.
14"Everything in Israel that is devoted[a] to the LORD is yours.
15The first offspring of every womb, both man and animal, that is
offered to the LORD is yours. But you must redeem every firstborn
son and every firstborn male of unclean animals. 16When they are
a month old, you must redeem them at the redemption price set at
five shekels[b] of silver, according to the sanctuary shekel, which
weighs twenty gerahs.
17"But you must not redeem the firstborn of an ox, a sheep or
a goat; they are holy. Sprinkle their blood on the altar and burn
their fat as an offering made by fire, an aroma pleasing to the LORD.
18Their meat is to be yours, just as the breast of the wave offering
and the right thigh are yours. 19Whatever is set aside from the holy
offerings the Israelites present to the LORD I give to you and your
sons and daughters as your regular share. It is an everlasting
covenant of salt before the LORD for both you and your offspring."
20The LORD said to Aaron, "You will have no inheritance in
their land, nor will you have any share among them; I am your
share and your inheritance among the Israelites.
21"I give to the Levites all the tithes in Israel as their inheritance in return for the work they do while serving at the Tent of
Meeting. 22From now on the Israelites must not go near the Tent of
Meeting, or they will bear the consequences of their sin and will
die. 23It is the Levites who are to do the work at the Tent of Meeting and bear the responsibility for offenses against it. This is a lasting ordinance for the generations to come. They will receive no
inheritance among the Israelites. 24Instead, I give to the Levites as
their inheritance the tithes that the Israelites present as an offering
to the LORD. That is why I said concerning them: 'They will have
no inheritance among the Israelites.' "
25The LORD said to Moses, 26"Speak to the Levites and say to
them: 'When you receive from the Israelites the tithe I give you as
your inheritance, you must present a tenth of that tithe as the
LORD's offering. 27Your offering will be reckoned to you as grain
from the threshing floor or juice from the winepress. 28In this way
you also will present an offering to the LORD from all the tithes you
receive from the Israelites. From these tithes you must give the
LORD's portion to Aaron the priest. 29You must present as the LORD's
portion the best and holiest part of everything given to you.'

---

[a]**14** The Hebrew term refers to the irrevocable giving over of things or persons to the LORD. [b]**16** That is, about 2 ounces (about 55 grams)

30“Say to the Levites: ‘When you present the best part, it will
be reckoned to you as the product of the threshing floor or the
winepress. 31You and your households may eat the rest of it anywhere, for it is your wages for your work at the Tent of Meeting.
32By presenting the best part of it you will not be guilty in this
matter; then you will not defile the holy offerings of the Israelites,
and you will not die.’ ”

The Water of Cleansing

19 The LORD said to Moses and Aaron: 2“This is a requirement
of the law that the LORD has commanded: Tell the Israelites to
bring you a red heifer without defect or blemish and that has never
been under a yoke. 3Give it to Eleazar the priest; it is to be taken
outside the camp and slaughtered in his presence. 4Then Eleazar
the priest is to take some of its blood on his finger and sprinkle it
seven times toward the front of the Tent of Meeting. 5While he
watches, the heifer is to be burned—its hide, flesh, blood and offal.
6The priest is to take some cedar wood, hyssop and scarlet wool
and throw them onto the burning heifer. 7After that, the priest
must wash his clothes and bathe himself with water. He may then
come into the camp, but he will be ceremonially unclean till
evening. 8The man who burns it must also wash his clothes and
bathe with water, and he too will be unclean till evening.
9“A man who is clean shall gather up the ashes of the heifer
and put them in a ceremonially clean place outside the camp. They
shall be kept by the Israelite community for use in the water of
cleansing; it is for purification from sin. 10The man who gathers
up the ashes of the heifer must also wash his clothes, and he too
will be unclean till evening. This will be a lasting ordinance both
for the Israelites and for the aliens living among them.
11“Whoever touches the dead body of anyone will be
unclean for seven days. 12He must purify himself with the water on
the third day and on the seventh day; then he will be clean. But if
he does not purify himself on the third and seventh days, he will
not be clean. 13Whoever touches the dead body of anyone and fails
to purify himself defiles the LORD’s tabernacle. That person must
be cut off from Israel. Because the water of cleansing has not been
sprinkled on him, he is unclean; his uncleanness remains on him.
14“This is the law that applies when a person dies in a tent:
Anyone who enters the tent and anyone who is in it will be
unclean for seven days, 15and every open container without a lid
fastened on it will be unclean.
16“Anyone out in the open who touches someone who has
been killed with a sword or someone who has died a natural death,
or anyone who touches a human bone or a grave, will be unclean
for seven days.
17“For the unclean person, put some ashes from the burned
purification offering into a jar and pour fresh water over them.

19:3 *Eleazar . . . outside the camp:* The high priest (Aaron) was not allowed to leave the tabernacle area (Lev 21:11,12), so Eleazar (Aaron’s son) took the cow outside the camp.

19:4,5 *blood . . . seven times:* See the note at 18:17. Seven is a sacred number symbolizing a complete cycle in the Bible (see Gen 2:3; Lev 4:6; 23:3). Eleazar sprinkled the blood in the direction of the tabernacle where the LORD was present. In this sacrifice the whole cow was burned.

19:6 *cedar wood, hyssop and scarlet wool:* Sweet-smelling wood such as cedar was used in water purifying ceremonies in Mesopotamia, but here the cedar wood is probably chosen because of its red color. Along with the scarlet wool, it symbolized the color of life or blood. The hyssop plant has white flowers and sweet-smelling leaves. Liquid clings to its furry stalk and leaves, so it was often used as a brush or sprinkler in religious rituals (see Exod 12:22; Lev 14:6,7; Heb 9:19).

19:10 *unclean:* Because the cow had been sacrificed to God, it was considered holy. Touching holy things could make a person ritually unclean and could even be dangerous (see Exod 19:10-15; Heb 9:13).

19:11 *touches the dead body . . . unclean for seven days:* Coming into contact with a corpse made a person ritually unclean (see also Lev 11:24,25; 21:1; Num 31:19-24). To become clean again, a person had to go through a ceremonial washing using the ashes of a red heifer (see the note at 19:2). “Seven” was a number symbolizing a complete cycle. See also Lev 12:2; 14:8; 15.

19:13 *defiles the LORD’s tabernacle:* See the note at 5:2,3. A person who was unclean had to stay away from both the rest of the community and the tabernacle to avoid defiling them (see Lev 15:31).

19:7,8 Lev 11:24-28,40; 16:26-28; 22:6,7.

19:18,19 *ceremonially clean . . . wash:* These are more specific instructions than those given in 19:11-13. See also the note at 19:4,5.

19:21 *anyone who touches the water:* Even the person who sprinkled the unclean person with the water (19:17,18) is made unclean. But this uncleanness is temporary, lasting only until evening.

20:1 *Desert of Zin . . . Kadesh:* See the notes at 13:17-22 and 13:26. It is unclear how many years have passed, but it may be near the end of the forty-year period in the desert.

20:1 *Miriam:* See the note at 12:1.

20:5 *Why . . . out of Egypt:* See the notes at 1:1 (Egypt) and 16:14.

20:5 *figs . . . pomegranates:* See the note at 13:23.

20:12 *did not trust in me:* Though not clear in this story, other Bible passages describe the sin of Moses and Aaron as rebellion (20:24; 27:14), unfaithfulness to God in the presence of the people of Israel (Deut 32:50,51), or speaking in anger (Ps 106:32,33).

20:2-13 Exod 17:1-7. **20:3** Num 14:2,27-29; 16:41-49.

[18]Then a man who is ceremonially clean is to take some hyssop, dip it in the water and sprinkle the tent and all the furnishings and the people who were there. He must also sprinkle anyone who has touched a human bone or a grave or someone who has been killed or someone who has died a natural death. [19]The man who is clean is to sprinkle the unclean person on the third and seventh days, and on the seventh day he is to purify him. The person being cleansed must wash his clothes and bathe with water, and that evening he will be clean. [20]But if a person who is unclean does not purify himself, he must be cut off from the community, because he has defiled the sanctuary of the LORD. The water of cleansing has not been sprinkled on him, and he is unclean. [21]This is a lasting ordinance for them.

"The man who sprinkles the water of cleansing must also wash his clothes, and anyone who touches the water of cleansing will be unclean till evening. [22]Anything that an unclean person touches becomes unclean, and anyone who touches it becomes unclean till evening."

Water From the Rock

20 In the first month the whole Israelite community arrived at the Desert of Zin, and they stayed at Kadesh. There Miriam died and was buried.

[2]Now there was no water for the community, and the people gathered in opposition to Moses and Aaron. [3]They quarreled with Moses and said, "If only we had died when our brothers fell dead before the LORD! [4]Why did you bring the LORD's community into this desert, that we and our livestock should die here? [5]Why did you bring us up out of Egypt to this terrible place? It has no grain or figs, grapevines or pomegranates. And there is no water to drink!"

[6]Moses and Aaron went from the assembly to the entrance to the Tent of Meeting and fell facedown, and the glory of the LORD appeared to them. [7]The LORD said to Moses, [8]"Take the staff, and you and your brother Aaron gather the assembly together. Speak to that rock before their eyes and it will pour out its water. You will bring water out of the rock for the community so they and their livestock can drink."

[9]So Moses took the staff from the LORD's presence, just as he commanded him. [10]He and Aaron gathered the assembly together in front of the rock and Moses said to them, "Listen, you rebels, must we bring you water out of this rock?" [11]Then Moses raised his arm and struck the rock twice with his staff. Water gushed out, and the community and their livestock drank.

[12]But the LORD said to Moses and Aaron, "Because you did not trust in me enough to honor me as holy in the sight of the Israelites, you will not bring this community into the land I give them."

[13]These were the waters of Meribah,[a] where the Israelites quarreled with the LORD and where he showed himself holy among them.

FROM KADESH TO MOAB

The Israelites leave Kadesh but are not allowed to pass through Edom, so they have to go a different way. During this journey Aaron dies, venomous snakes kill many, and the Israelites defeat the Amorite king and King Og of Bashan before reaching the plains of Moab.

Edom Denies Israel Passage

[14]Moses sent messengers from Kadesh to the king of Edom, saying:

"This is what your brother Israel says: You know about all the hardships that have come upon us. [15]Our forefathers went down into Egypt, and we lived there many years. The Egyptians mistreated us and our fathers, [16]but when we cried out to the LORD, he heard our cry and sent an angel and brought us out of Egypt.

"Now we are here at Kadesh, a town on the edge of your territory. [17]Please let us pass through your country. We will not go through any field or vineyard, or drink water from any well. We will travel along the king's highway and not turn to the right or to the left until we have passed through your territory."

[18]But Edom answered:

"You may not pass through here; if you try, we will march out and attack you with the sword."

[19]The Israelites replied:

"We will go along the main road, and if we or our livestock drink any of your water, we will pay for it. We only want to pass through on foot—nothing else."

[20]Again they answered:

"You may not pass through."

Then Edom came out against them with a large and powerful army. [21]Since Edom refused to let them go through their territory, Israel turned away from them.

The Death of Aaron

[22]The whole Israelite community set out from Kadesh and came to Mount Hor. [23]At Mount Hor, near the border of Edom,

[a]13 *Meribah* means *quarreling.*

20:13 *Meribah:* The rock must have been near Kadesh (see the note at 13:26). See 20:3, which gives the people's complaint. The carving shown here depicts this miracle. It is from a third century Christian gravestone (called a sarcophagus).

20:14 *Kadesh . . . Edom:* See the note at 13:26. The people of Edom were descendants of Jacob's brother Esau (Gen 25:24-26; 36:1) and usually described as enemies of Israel (Num 24:18; 1 Sam 14:47; 2 Sam 8:13, 14). Edom was directly south of the Dead Sea between Desert of Zin and Moab (see the map on p. 2463).

20:17 *king's highway:* An important trade route through what is today the country of Jordan. It connected the city of Damascus in Syria with the Red Sea. See also the article called "Trade and Travel," p. 948.

20:21,22 *turned away . . . Mount Hor:* They went south of Edom toward the Red Sea (see 21:4). The location of Mount Hor is not known.

20:29 *mourned . . . thirty days:* The normal time of mourning was seven days (see Gen 50:10; 1 Sam 31:13), but the people mourned Aaron's death for thirty days.

21:1 *Arad . . . Atharim:* Arad was about fifty miles north of Kadesh in the southern part of Canaan (see the note at 13:17-22). The location of Atharim is unknown. See also 33:40.

21:2 *totally destroy:* Sometimes the spoils of war were destroyed to prove they belonged only to God.

20:24 Num 20:12; 27:14; Deut 32:50,51. **20:28** Exod 29:29; Num 33:38; Deut 10:6.

the LORD said to Moses and Aaron, 24"Aaron will be gathered to
his people. He will not enter the land I give the Israelites, because
both of you rebelled against my command at the waters of
Meribah. 25Get Aaron and his son Eleazar and take them up
Mount Hor. 26Remove Aaron's garments and put them on his son
Eleazar, for Aaron will be gathered to his people; he will die
there."

27Moses did as the LORD commanded: They went up Mount
Hor in the sight of the whole community. 28Moses removed
Aaron's garments and put them on his son Eleazar. And Aaron
died there on top of the mountain. Then Moses and Eleazar came
down from the mountain, 29and when the whole community
learned that Aaron had died, the entire house of Israel mourned
for him thirty days.

Arad Destroyed

21 When the Canaanite king of Arad, who lived in the Negev,
heard that Israel was coming along the road to Atharim, he attacked
the Israelites and captured some of them. 2Then Israel made this
vow to the LORD: "If you will deliver these people into our hands,

HOLY WAR (THE LORD'S BATTLES)

Early Israel's understanding of warfare is closely connected with their conception of God as a mighty warrior (Exod 15:3; Ps 24:8; Deut 7; 20). The LORD was a warrior who had made Israel his people by defeating the Egyptians (Deut 4:32-34) and who protects and defends them (2 Sam 22:35-37; Ps 144:1). Because the LORD was the God of Israel's army (1 Sam 17:45), the Israelites understood that God would lead them into battle (Judg 4:14). They would pray for God's approval and involvement before engaging in war (2 Sam 5:17-19).

Though they might be outnumbered, with the Divine Warrior on their side, the size of the army was unimportant (Judg 7:1-9; 1 Sam 14:6). But even with God's help, preparation was necessary. Often information was gathered from behind enemy lines (Num 13; Josh 2:1), sacrifices were offered (1 Sam 7:9,10), and stirring speeches were given to inspire the warriors to have no fear. God would be with them to deliver their enemies into their hands (Deut 20:2-4; 2 Chr 20:20). The battle began with priests sounding the trumpet (Num 10:9) and bringing out the ark of the covenant, a symbol of God's presence in the field (Josh 6:2-13). The battle ended when God sent terror into the hearts of the enemy. (Sometimes in their fear and panic they destroyed themselves.) This is the miraculous victory that God provides. The Israelites' responsibility was to trust completely in the power of God and to face the enemy unafraid (Exod 14:14).

Following the battle, the Israelites would often destroy part or all of the city or country along with its people, animals, and possessions. This practice, known as "the ban," meant devoting or setting aside the spoils of war for God. No Israelite was permitted to take anything as a souvenir of war or to capture enemies and make them slaves once a town had been put under a ban. And anyone who did so was severely punished (Josh 7).

Moses Gives Water to the Tribes, wall painting from the synagogue at Dura Europos, Syria, third century A.D. Water was especially important to the people of Israel during their time of wandering in the desert. But the LORD always gave the people what they needed. First, the LORD gave them water from a rock near Kadesh (see 20:1-13). Then, when the people encamped near the town of Beer in Moab, the LORD told Moses, "Gather the people together and I will give them water." The people rejoiced and sang a song about the well the LORD had provided. (See 21:10-20.)

we will totally destroy[a] their cities." 3The LORD listened to Israel's
plea and gave the Canaanites over to them. They completely
destroyed them and their towns; so the place was named Hormah.[b]

The Bronze Snake

4They traveled from Mount Hor along the route to the Red
Sea,[c] to go around Edom. But the people grew impatient on the
way; 5they spoke against God and against Moses, and said, "Why
have you brought us up out of Egypt to die in the desert? There is
no bread! There is no water! And we detest this miserable food!"
6Then the LORD sent venomous snakes among them; they bit
the people and many Israelites died. 7The people came to Moses
and said, "We sinned when we spoke against the LORD and against
you. Pray that the LORD will take the snakes away from us." So
Moses prayed for the people.
8The LORD said to Moses, "Make a snake and put it up on a
pole; anyone who is bitten can look at it and live." 9So Moses made
a bronze snake and put it up on a pole. Then when anyone was
bitten by a snake and looked at the bronze snake, he lived.

[a]2 The Hebrew term refers to the irrevocable giving over of things or persons to the LORD, often by totally destroying them; also in verse 3. [b]3 *Hormah* means *destruction.* [c]4 Hebrew *Yam Suph*; that is, Sea of Reeds

21:3 *Hormah:* See the note at 14:44,45. Hormah is many miles northwest of the Edom location mentioned in 20:21 and opposite the direction the Israelites had to travel to "go around Edom" in 21:4.

21:4 *Red Sea . . . go around Edom:* See the notes at 20:14 and 14:25. See also Deut 2:1 and the map on p. 2463.

21:6 *venomous snakes:* Because the Hebrew word translated as "venomous snakes" comes from a word for fire, the bite of these creatures probably caused a burning pain.

21:9 *bronze snake:* Bronze is made by mixing copper and tin. Many centuries later, King Hezekiah destroyed this bronze snake, which some people had begun to worship (2 Kgs 18:4). See also John 3:14.

21:5-9 Exod 17:1-7; Num 11:1-6; 14:1-3; 20:2-5; 1 Cor 10:9.

21:10-16 *Oboth . . . well:* The Israelites traveled to the east of Moab (see the map on p. 2465). The Zered River gorge lay between northern Edom and southern Moab. From the Zered they traveled north to the Arnon River which flows into the Dead Sea and formed the boundary between Moab and Ammon. The location of this well is uncertain.

21:14 *Book of the Wars:* This may be a collection of ancient war songs. See also Josh 10:12,13.

21:17,18 *song . . . scepters:* The song may be from the "Book of the Wars" (21:14). A scepter is a ceremonial staff that was a symbol of a ruler's power.

21:18-20 *Mattanah . . . Pisgah:* The location of Mattanah and Nahaliel are unknown. Bamoth, which means "high places," could refer to a number of sites, such as Bamoth Baal (see 22:41; Josh 13:17) or Beth Bamoth. Pisgah probably refers to the highest peak in the Abarim Mountains in Moab. From this spot, the Israelites could likely see the land of Canaan beyond the southern Jordan River valley.

21:21 *Sihon king of the Amorites:* Also called "Sihon king of Heshbon" (Deut 2:26; 3:6; Josh 12:5), because Heshbon was where the king ruled (21:25; Deut 1:4; Josh 12:2; 13:10). The Amorites who were related to the Canaanites, lived in Canaan in the area that would later be claimed by the tribe of Judah (Exod 3:8; 1 Chr 1:14; Deut 1:19-27) and in the hill country east of the Jordan River. They were Israel's enemies until King Solomon defeated them (1 Kgs 9:20,21).

21:22 *king's highway:* See the note at 20:17.

21:24 *Arnon to the Jabbok . . . Ammonites:* See the note at 21:10-16. The Jabbok River formed the southern boundary of Ammon, a land east of the Jordan River valley and north of Moab (see the map on p. 2464). The Ammonites and Moabites had a common ancestor, and both were enemies of Israel.

The Journey to Moab

10 The Israelites moved on and camped at Oboth. 11 Then they
set out from Oboth and camped in Iye Abarim, in the desert that
faces Moab toward the sunrise. 12 From there they moved on and
camped in the Zered Valley. 13 They set out from there and camped
alongside the Arnon, which is in the desert extending into
Amorite territory. The Arnon is the border of Moab, between
Moab and the Amorites. 14 That is why the Book of the Wars of the
LORD says:

". . . Waheb in Suphah[a] and the ravines,
  the Arnon 15 and[b] the slopes of the ravines
that lead to the site of Ar
  and lie along the border of Moab."

16 From there they continued on to Beer, the well where the LORD
said to Moses, "Gather the people together and I will give them
water."

17 Then Israel sang this song:

"Spring up, O well!
  Sing about it,
18 about the well that the princes dug,
  that the nobles of the people sank—
  the nobles with scepters and staffs."

Then they went from the desert to Mattanah, 19 from Mattanah to
Nahaliel, from Nahaliel to Bamoth, 20 and from Bamoth to the valley
in Moab where the top of Pisgah overlooks the wasteland.

Defeat of Sihon and Og

21 Israel sent messengers to say to Sihon king of the
Amorites:

22 "Let us pass through your country. We will not turn
aside into any field or vineyard, or drink water from any well.
We will travel along the king's highway until we have passed
through your territory."

23 But Sihon would not let Israel pass through his territory.
He mustered his entire army and marched out into the desert
against Israel. When he reached Jahaz, he fought with Israel.
24 Israel, however, put him to the sword and took over his land
from the Arnon to the Jabbok, but only as far as the Ammonites,
because their border was fortified. 25 Israel captured all the cities of
the Amorites and occupied them, including Heshbon and all its
surrounding settlements. 26 Heshbon was the city of Sihon king of

---

[a] **14** The meaning of the Hebrew for this phrase is uncertain. [b] **14,15** Or *"I have been given from Suphah and the ravines / of the Arnon 15 to*

the Amorites, who had fought against the former king of Moab
and had taken from him all his land as far as the Arnon.
27 That is why the poets say:

"Come to Heshbon and let it be rebuilt;
let Sihon's city be restored.
28 "Fire went out from Heshbon,
a blaze from the city of Sihon.
It consumed Ar of Moab,
the citizens of Arnon's heights.
29 Woe to you, O Moab!
You are destroyed, O people of Chemosh!
He has given up his sons as fugitives
and his daughters as captives
to Sihon king of the Amorites.

30 "But we have overthrown them;
Heshbon is destroyed all the way to Dibon.
We have demolished them as far as Nophah,
which extends to Medeba."

31 So Israel settled in the land of the Amorites.
32 After Moses had sent spies to Jazer, the Israelites captured

21:25 *Heshbon:* The capital city of the Amorite territory that King Sihon had taken from the Moabites (21:29,30).

21:29 *Moab . . . Chemosh:* Moab was located east of the Dead Sea. See also the note at 21:24. Chemosh, the god of the Moabites, is mentioned in the Moabite Stone and in various Old Testament passages (1 Kgs 11:7,33; 2 Kgs 23:13; Jer 48:4-7,13,45, 46). See also the mini-article called "Canaanite Gods and Goddesses," p. 469.

21:30 *Heshbon . . . Medeba:* See the note at 21:25. Dibon and Medeba represent sites about twenty to thirty miles southwest of modern Amman in Jordan. See also Josh 13:8-10.

21:31,32 *Amorites . . . Jazer:* See the note at 21:21. The exact location of Jazer is unknown. See also 32:1-5; Josh 13:24,25.

QUESTIONS ABOUT NUMBERS 10:11—21:35

1. How did the Israelites know when to break camp in the Desert of Sinai? In what order did they march? (10:11-28) Where did the Levite clans (Gershonites, Merarites, and Kohathites) march, and what did they carry?
2. What did the people complain to Moses about as they traveled? (11:1-15) How did God respond? (11:31-34) Why did Miriam and Aaron complain? What happened to them? (chapter 12)
3. Who was sent to Canaan and what was the task they were given? (13:1-25) What did these men report and how did the people respond? (13:26—14:4) What did Josha and Caleb say? (14:5-9) Have you ever been asked to do something that seemed impossible? If so, how did you react? What do you rely upon to help you overcome your fears?
4. Describe the rebellion of Korah, Dathan, and Abiram. (chapter 16) What happened to them and their families?
5. Why did the priests and Levites receive a portion of the people's offerings? (chapter 18) What were the Levites supposed to offer to God? What kinds of offerings do people make to God today? What can you "offer" to God?
6. Why was the cleansing ceremony important to the people of Israel? (chapter 19) Notice that the reference to defiling the LORD's sanctuary (tabernacle) occurs twice. (19:13,20) What does this mean? What is the relationship between "being clean" and belonging to God's people?
7. In chapter 20, what did the people complain about? How did Moses and Aaron respond to the complaint? Why did God decide to punish Aaron and Moses? (20:1-13)
8. What did the people complain about after leaving Mount Hor? (21:4-9) What did the LORD do to them? What did the LORD tell Moses to do when Moses asked the LORD for help?

its surrounding settlements and drove out the Amorites who were
there. 33 Then they turned and went up along the road toward
Bashan, and Og king of Bashan and his whole army marched out
to meet them in battle at Edrei.
34 The LORD said to Moses, "Do not be afraid of him, for I
have handed him over to you, with his whole army and his land.
Do to him what you did to Sihon king of the Amorites, who
reigned in Heshbon."
35 So they struck him down, together with his sons and his
whole army, leaving them no survivors. And they took possession
of his land.

The Moab Camp: Preparing to Enter Canaan

King Balak of Moab tries to hire Balaam to curse the Israelites, but his plan backfires. Some of the Israelites do turn from God and worship the Canaanite god Baal. The Israelites are counted a second time, and the new generation prepares to enter Canaan under Joshua's leadership. Laws about sacrifices for special festival days are given, as are laws about the Levite towns. The Israelites fight and defeat the Midianites, and God gives the order to conquer Canaan.

THE STORIES OF BALAAM AND THE WORSHIP OF BAAL

King Balak of Moab fears the Israelites and hires Balaam to curse them so they will leave his land, but God tells Balaam to bless the people instead. At the Shittim camp some Israelites turn to worshiping the god Baal, and God punishes them.

Balak Summons Balaam

22 Then the Israelites traveled to the plains of Moab and
camped along the Jordan across from Jericho.[a]
2 Now Balak son of Zippor saw all that Israel had done to the
Amorites, 3 and Moab was terrified because there were so many
people. Indeed, Moab was filled with dread because of the
Israelites.
4 The Moabites said to the elders of Midian, "This horde is
going to lick up everything around us, as an ox licks up the grass
of the field."
So Balak son of Zippor, who was king of Moab at that time,
5 sent messengers to summon Balaam son of Beor, who was at
Pethor, near the River,[b] in his native land. Balak said:

[a]1 Hebrew *Jordan of Jericho*; possibly an ancient name for the Jordan River
[b]5 That is, the Euphrates

21:33 *Bashan . . . Edrei:* Bashan was a wide area of fertile land on the eastern side of the Jordan River, known for its rich pastures, forests, and herds of cattle (see Ps 22:12; Isa 2:13; Ezek 27:6; Zech 11:2). Edrei was located about thirty miles east of the Sea of Galilee and about sixty miles south of Damascus in Syria.

22:1 *plains of Moab . . . Jordan . . . Jericho:* These plains bordered Canaan, the land God promised the Israelites. It was west of the Jordan River, the main waterway in the area running south from the Sea of Galilee to the Dead Sea. Jericho was a very ancient city controlled at this time by the Canaanites. See the map on p. 2463.

22:2-4 *Balak . . . king of Moab:* All that is known about Balak is found in chapters 22–24, but he is mentioned in Josh 24:9; Judg 11:25; Mic 6:5. See the note at 21:29. For more on the Midianites, see the note at 10:29.

22:5 *Balaam son of Beor . . . River:* Balaam had a reputation as a fortuneteller and diviner (see the note at 22:7,8). In the Bible he is remembered in both negative and positive ways (see 31:8,16; Deut 23:3-6; Josh 13:22; 24:9, 10; 2 Pet 2:15,16; Jude 11). The exact location of Pethor is unclear. If it is the ancient city of Pitru in northern Syria, as some scholars suggest, it was nearly four hundred miles from Moab. Other scholars think Pethor is somewhere in Ammon. If this is true, Balaam's journey would have been a reasonable distance. The exact name of the River is also unknown.

"A people has come out of Egypt; they cover the face of the land and have settled next to me. 6Now come and put a curse on these people, because they are too powerful for me. Perhaps then I will be able to defeat them and drive them out of the country. For I know that those you bless are blessed, and those you curse are cursed."

7The elders of Moab and Midian left, taking with them the fee for divination. When they came to Balaam, they told him what Balak had said.

8"Spend the night here," Balaam said to them, "and I will bring you back the answer the LORD gives me." So the Moabite princes stayed with him.

9God came to Balaam and asked, "Who are these men with you?"

10Balaam said to God, "Balak son of Zippor, king of Moab, sent me this message: 11'A people that has come out of Egypt covers the face of the land. Now come and put a curse on them for me. Perhaps then I will be able to fight them and drive them away.' "

12But God said to Balaam, "Do not go with them. You must not put a curse on those people, because they are blessed."

13The next morning Balaam got up and said to Balak's princes, "Go back to your own country, for the LORD has refused to let me go with you."

14So the Moabite princes returned to Balak and said, "Balaam refused to come with us."

15Then Balak sent other princes, more numerous and more distinguished than the first. 16They came to Balaam and said:

> "This is what Balak son of Zippor says: Do not let anything keep you from coming to me, 17because I will reward you handsomely and do whatever you say. Come and put a curse on these people for me."

18But Balaam answered them, "Even if Balak gave me his palace filled with silver and gold, I could not do anything great or small to go beyond the command of the LORD my God. 19Now stay here tonight as the others did, and I will find out what else the LORD will tell me."

20That night God came to Balaam and said, "Since these men have come to summon you, go with them, but do only what I tell you."

Balaam's Donkey

21Balaam got up in the morning, saddled his donkey and went with the princes of Moab. 22But God was very angry when he went, and the angel of the LORD stood in the road to oppose him. Balaam was riding on his donkey, and his two servants were with him. 23When the donkey saw the angel of the LORD standing in the

22:7,8 *fee for divination . . . the answer the LORD gives:* Balaam worked as a prophet of the gods and a diviner. Divination was the practice of trying to discover information about the future by looking at the inner organs of a sacrificed animal or by reading the pattern of oil droplets in a cup of water. Balaam was not an Israelite and did not follow Israel's LORD (Yahweh), so it is surprising when he tells Balak's officials that he will report what the LORD tells him. For more, see the articles called "Prophets and Prophecy," p. 935 and "Miracles, Magic, and Medicine," p. 1838.

22:9 *God:* The Hebrew name translated as "God" in these verses is *Elohim*. See also the mini-article called "Names of God," p. 243.

22:22-26 *God was very angry . . . angel of the LORD:* The story does not tell exactly why God was angry, since God had already given Balaam permission to go (22:20,35). In Hebrew the word for "angel" also means "messenger." In the Bible, angels act both as messengers and servants of God. In this case, this was the "angel of the LORD" which may have been a preincarnate visit by Christ. See also the mini-article called "Angels," p. 88.

Balaam and His Donkey, Ukrainian folk picture, nineteenth century. King Balak of Moab hired the prophet Balaam to curse the Israelites who were living in his land and becoming powerful. But Balaam promised the king to say only what the LORD told him to. On his way to see the king, Balaam's donkey was stopped three times by an angel holding a sword. Each time the donkey stopped, the prophet struck it with his staff. The donkey spoke, complaining about its treatment. Finally, the angel of the LORD appeared to the prophet himself and told him he could continue on his journey. (See 22:21-35.)

22:24 *vineyards:* Vineyards in the ancient world were often enclosed by stone walls to protect them from thieves and from destruction by livestock and wild animals. For more about grape farming, see the mini-article called "Wine," p. 2047. Balaam and his donkey were standing between two vineyards. The space was too narrow for the donkey to turn around (22:26).

road with a drawn sword in his hand, she turned off the road into
a field. Balaam beat her to get her back on the road.
24 Then the angel of the LORD stood in a narrow path
between two vineyards, with walls on both sides. 25 When the donkey saw the angel of the LORD, she pressed close to the wall, crushing Balaam's foot against it. So he beat her again.
26 Then the angel of the LORD moved on ahead and stood in
a narrow place where there was no room to turn, either to the
right or to the left. 27 When the donkey saw the angel of the LORD,
she lay down under Balaam, and he was angry and beat her with
his staff. 28 Then the LORD opened the donkey's mouth, and she
said to Balaam, "What have I done to you to make you beat me
these three times?"
29 Balaam answered the donkey, "You have made a fool of
me! If I had a sword in my hand, I would kill you right now."
30 The donkey said to Balaam, "Am I not your own donkey,
which you have always ridden, to this day? Have I been in the habit
of doing this to you?"
"No," he said.
31 Then the LORD opened Balaam's eyes, and he saw the angel
of the LORD standing in the road with his sword drawn. So he
bowed low and fell facedown.
32 The angel of the LORD asked him, "Why have you beaten

your donkey these three times? I have come here to oppose you
because your path is a reckless one before me.[a] 33 The donkey saw
me and turned away from me these three times. If she had not
turned away, I would certainly have killed you by now, but I would
have spared her."
34 Balaam said to the angel of the LORD, "I have sinned. I did
not realize you were standing in the road to oppose me. Now if
you are displeased, I will go back."
35 The angel of the LORD said to Balaam, "Go with the men, but
speak only what I tell you." So Balaam went with the princes of Balak.
36 When Balak heard that Balaam was coming, he went out
to meet him at the Moabite town on the Arnon border, at the edge
of his territory. 37 Balak said to Balaam, "Did I not send you an
urgent summons? Why didn't you come to me? Am I really not
able to reward you?"
38 "Well, I have come to you now," Balaam replied. "But can I
say just anything? I must speak only what God puts in my mouth."
39 Then Balaam went with Balak to Kiriath Huzoth. 40 Balak
sacrificed cattle and sheep, and gave some to Balaam and the
princes who were with him. 41 The next morning Balak took Balaam up to Bamoth Baal, and from there he saw part of the people.

Balaam's First Oracle

23 Balaam said, "Build me seven altars here, and prepare seven
bulls and seven rams for me." 2 Balak did as Balaam said, and the
two of them offered a bull and a ram on each altar.
3 Then Balaam said to Balak, "Stay here beside your offering
while I go aside. Perhaps the LORD will come to meet with me.
Whatever he reveals to me I will tell you." Then he went off to a
barren height.
4 God met with him, and Balaam said, "I have prepared seven
altars, and on each altar I have offered a bull and a ram."
5 The LORD put a message in Balaam's mouth and said, "Go
back to Balak and give him this message."
6 So he went back to him and found him standing beside his
offering, with all the princes of Moab. 7 Then Balaam uttered his
oracle:

"Balak brought me from Aram,
    the king of Moab from the eastern mountains.
'Come,' he said, 'curse Jacob for me;
    come, denounce Israel.'
8 How can I curse
    those whom God has not cursed?
How can I denounce
    those whom the LORD has not denounced?

[a]32 The meaning of the Hebrew for this clause is uncertain.

22:39-41 *Kirath Huzoth . . . Bamoth Baal:* The location of Kiriath Huzoth, which means "city of streets," is unknown. Bamoth Baal means "the high places of Baal," and may refer to the hills dedicated to the worship of Baal. It also may be the same as the place mentioned in 21:19. From this high place, Balaam could see the Israelites below.

22:41 *he saw part of the people:* For a curse to be effective, the people or thing being cursed had to be within the field of vision of the person uttering the curse.

23:1 *seven altars . . . rams:* Seven was a sacred number in ancient times. See also Gen 21:28; Job 42:8; and the note at 11:16. The altars may have been made of wood, but more likely they were made from stones found in the area. Balaam asked Balak to provide the offerings for God as the correct ceremony for receiving God's message. Bulls and rams were the most valuable of Israel's animal sacrifices (see Lev 4; 5:14—6:7).

23:7 *Aram . . . mountains:* Aram is another name for Syria. The mountains were most likely the high mountains of the northeastern Syrian desert. See also the note at 22:5.

22:38 Num 22:20,35.

Balaam said, *"Let me die the death of the righteous, and may my end be like theirs!"* Num 23:10

23:11 *Balak . . . Balaam:* See the notes at 22:2-4 and 22:5.

23:14 *Pisgah . . . seven altars:* See the notes at 21:18-20 and 23:1.

23:16 *message:* Messages spoken by prophets are sometimes called "oracles."

23:20 *he has blessed:* God's blessing could not be taken away once it was promised (see 22:12; see also Gen 27:1-40).

23:21 *The LORD their God . . . the King:* Though the books of the Bible are not necessarily arranged as they were written, this is the first place in the Old Testament that Israel's God is described as a king (see also Ps 145:1; Isa 41:21-24). See the notes at 1:1 (LORD) and 22:9 (God). It is noteworthy that this affirmation of Israel's God is made by Balaam, a foreigner (see the note at 22:7,8).

23:23 *no sorcery . . . no divination:* As a diviner, Balaam may also have practiced magic, but his words here point out that magic charms could not work against the Israelites because they were protected by God.

23:22 Exod 12–15; Lev 26:13.

9 From the rocky peaks I see them,
from the heights I view them.
I see a people who live apart
and do not consider themselves one of the nations.
10 Who can count the dust of Jacob
or number the fourth part of Israel?
Let me die the death of the righteous,
and may my end be like theirs!"

11 Balak said to Balaam, "What have you done to me? I
brought you to curse my enemies, but you have done nothing but
bless them!"
12 He answered, "Must I not speak what the LORD puts in my
mouth?"

Balaam's Second Oracle

13 Then Balak said to him, "Come with me to another place
where you can see them; you will see only a part but not all of
them. And from there, curse them for me." 14 So he took him to the
field of Zophim on the top of Pisgah, and there he built seven
altars and offered a bull and a ram on each altar.
15 Balaam said to Balak, "Stay here beside your offering while
I meet with him over there."
16 The LORD met with Balaam and put a message in his
mouth and said, "Go back to Balak and give him this message."
17 So he went to him and found him standing beside his
offering, with the princes of Moab. Balak asked him, "What did the
LORD say?"
18 Then he uttered his oracle:

"Arise, Balak, and listen;
hear me, son of Zippor.
19 God is not a man, that he should lie,
nor a son of man, that he should change his mind.
Does he speak and then not act?
Does he promise and not fulfill?
20 I have received a command to bless;
he has blessed, and I cannot change it.

21 "No misfortune is seen in Jacob,
no misery observed in Israel.[a]
The LORD their God is with them;
the shout of the King is among them.
22 God brought them out of Egypt;
they have the strength of a wild ox.
23 There is no sorcery against Jacob,
no divination against Israel.

---

[a]**21** Or *He has not looked on Jacob's offenses / or on the wrongs found in Israel.*

It will now be said of Jacob
    and of Israel, 'See what God has done!'
[24]The people rise like a lioness;
    they rouse themselves like a lion
that does not rest till he devours his prey
    and drinks the blood of his victims."

[25]Then Balak said to Balaam, "Neither curse them at all nor
bless them at all!"
[26]Balaam answered, "Did I not tell you I must do whatever
the LORD says?"

Balaam's Third Oracle

[27]Then Balak said to Balaam, "Come, let me take you to
another place. Perhaps it will please God to let you curse them for
me from there." [28]And Balak took Balaam to the top of Peor, overlooking the wasteland.
[29]Balaam said, "Build me seven altars here, and prepare seven
bulls and seven rams for me." [30]Balak did as Balaam had said, and
offered a bull and a ram on each altar.
24 Now when Balaam saw that it pleased the LORD to bless
Israel, he did not resort to sorcery as at other times, but turned his
face toward the desert. [2]When Balaam looked out and saw Israel
encamped tribe by tribe, the Spirit of God came upon him [3]and
he uttered his oracle:

"The oracle of Balaam son of Beor,
    the oracle of one whose eye sees clearly,
[4]the oracle of one who hears the words of God,
    who sees a vision from the Almighty,[a]
    who falls prostrate, and whose eyes are opened:

[5]"How beautiful are your tents, O Jacob,
    your dwelling places, O Israel!

[6]"Like valleys they spread out,
    like gardens beside a river,
like aloes planted by the LORD,
    like cedars beside the waters.
[7]Water will flow from their buckets;
    their seed will have abundant water.

"Their king will be greater than Agag;
    their kingdom will be exalted.

[8]"God brought them out of Egypt;
    they have the strength of a wild ox.
They devour hostile nations
    and break their bones in pieces;

[a]4 Hebrew *Shaddai*; also in verse 16

23:28 *top of Peor:* Not mentioned anywhere else in the Bible, Mount Peor may have been near Beth Peor (see Deut 3:29; 34:6; Josh 13:20).

24:1 *did not resort to sorcery:* See the notes at 22:7,8 and 23:23. Balaam may have examined the inner organs of the sacrificed animals (see 22:40), but there is no evidence that he had relied on magic when he received the first two messages from God.

24:1 *desert:* North of the Dead Sea on the east side of the Jordan River (see 23:28).

24:2 *Spirit of God:* See the note at 11:25.

24:4 *a vision from the Almighty:* For more about the "Almighty" see the mini-article called "Names of God," p. 243. The prophets were sometimes in a kind of trance when they received visions from God (see 11:24-29; 1 Sam 10:5-13; 19:20-24).

24:6 *aloes:* The aloe tree should not be confused with the aloe plant. It is valued for its bark's sweet-smelling resin.

24:7 *Agag:* Agag was one of the most powerful kings of the Amalekites (see the note at 13:28,29), long-time enemies of the Israelites.

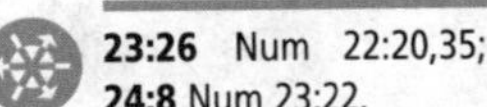

23:26 Num 22:20,35; 23:12.
24:8 Num 23:22.

24:16 *Most High . . . Almighty:* "Most High" is a translation of the Hebrew *El Elyon,* here identified with the Almighty God (see also Deut 32:8 and the note at 24:4).

24:17 *A star will come out of Jacob . . . crush the foreheads of Moab:* King David of Israel (the "star" out of Jacob) defeated the Moabites and Edomites (2 Sam 8:2,13,14) at least two hundred years after Balaam's message. For Moabites, see the notes at 21:24; 21:29.

24:18 *Edom:* See the note at 20:14.

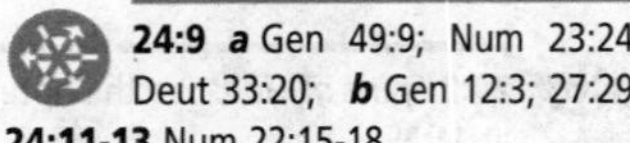

24:9 ***a*** Gen 49:9; Num 23:24; Deut 33:20; ***b*** Gen 12:3; 27:29.
24:11-13 Num 22:15-18.

with their arrows they pierce them.
9 Like a lion they crouch and lie down,
like a lioness—who dares to rouse them?

"May those who bless you be blessed
and those who curse you be cursed!"

10 Then Balak's anger burned against Balaam. He struck his
hands together and said to him, "I summoned you to curse my
enemies, but you have blessed them these three times. 11 Now leave
at once and go home! I said I would reward you handsomely, but
the LORD has kept you from being rewarded."
12 Balaam answered Balak, "Did I not tell the messengers you
sent me, 13 'Even if Balak gave me his palace filled with silver and gold,
I could not do anything of my own accord, good or bad, to go
beyond the command of the LORD—and I must say only what the
LORD says'? 14 Now I am going back to my people, but come, let me
warn you of what this people will do to your people in days to come."

Balaam's Fourth Oracle

15 Then he uttered his oracle:

"The oracle of Balaam son of Beor,
the oracle of one whose eye sees clearly,
16 the oracle of one who hears the words of God,
who has knowledge from the Most High,
who sees a vision from the Almighty,
who falls prostrate, and whose eyes are opened:

17 "I see him, but not now;
I behold him, but not near.
A star will come out of Jacob;
a scepter will rise out of Israel.
He will crush the foreheads of Moab,
the skulls[a] of[b] all the sons of Sheth.[c]
18 Edom will be conquered;
Seir, his enemy, will be conquered,
but Israel will grow strong.
19 A ruler will come out of Jacob
and destroy the survivors of the city."

Balaam's Final Oracles

20 Then Balaam saw Amalek and uttered his oracle:

"Amalek was first among the nations,
but he will come to ruin at last."

---

[a]**17** Samaritan Pentateuch (see also Jer. 48:45); the meaning of the word in the Masoretic Text is uncertain. [b]**17** Or possibly *Moab, / batter* [c]**17** Or *all the noisy boasters*

21 Then he saw the Kenites and uttered his oracle:

"Your dwelling place is secure,
your nest is set in a rock;
22 yet you Kenites will be destroyed
when Asshur takes you captive."

23 Then he uttered his oracle:

"Ah, who can live when God does this?[a]
24 Ships will come from the shores of Kittim;
they will subdue Asshur and Eber,
but they too will come to ruin."

25 Then Balaam got up and returned home and Balak went
his own way.

Moab Seduces Israel

25 While Israel was staying in Shittim, the men began to
indulge in sexual immorality with Moabite women, 2 who invited
them to the sacrifices to their gods. The people ate and bowed
down before these gods. 3 So Israel joined in worshiping the Baal
of Peor. And the LORD's anger burned against them.
4 The LORD said to Moses, "Take all the leaders of these people, kill them and expose them in broad daylight before the LORD,
so that the LORD's fierce anger may turn away from Israel."
5 So Moses said to Israel's judges, "Each of you must put to
death those of your men who have joined in worshiping the Baal
of Peor."
6 Then an Israelite man brought to his family a Midianite
woman right before the eyes of Moses and the whole assembly of
Israel while they were weeping at the entrance to the Tent of Meeting. 7 When Phinehas son of Eleazar, the son of Aaron, the priest,
saw this, he left the assembly, took a spear in his hand 8 and followed the Israelite into the tent. He drove the spear through both
of them—through the Israelite and into the woman's body. Then
the plague against the Israelites was stopped; 9 but those who died
in the plague numbered 24,000.
10 The LORD said to Moses, 11 "Phinehas son of Eleazar, the son
of Aaron, the priest, has turned my anger away from the Israelites;
for he was as zealous as I am for my honor among them, so that in
my zeal I did not put an end to them. 12 Therefore tell him I am
making my covenant of peace with him. 13 He and his descendants
will have a covenant of a lasting priesthood, because he was zealous
for the honor of his God and made atonement for the Israelites."
14 The name of the Israelite who was killed with the Midianite woman was Zimri son of Salu, the leader of a Simeonite family.

a23 Masoretic Text; with a different word division of the Hebrew *A people will gather from the north.*

24:21,22 *Kenites ... Asshur:* The Kenites were a Canaanite tribe that lived in the desert south of Israel (see Gen 15:19). They were descendants of Hobab, the brother-in-law of Moses (Judg 4:11). "Asshur" is Assyria, a very powerful country in Biblical times.

24:24 *Kittim ... Asshur and Eber:* Kittim is Cyprus, which may stand for the island of Cyprus or may refer to a number of peoples who sailed from the west to invade the Middle East (see Jer 2:10; Dan 11:30). Asshur is Assyria (see the note on 24:21,22). Eber may refer to a land to the east of the Euphrates River, such as Babylonia. In Genesis 10:21-31 Eber is listed as one of Israel's ancestors.

25:1 *Shittim:* Also called Acacia, Shittim is the area of Moab across the Jordan River from Jericho, where the Israelites were camped (see 22:1; 33:41-49; Josh 2:1; 3:1).

25:2,3 *sacrifices to their gods ... Baal of Peor:* After having sex, the Moabite women convinced the Israelite men to join in a sacrifice feast to the Moabite gods, which included Baal of Peor. Baal was the name of a number of fertility gods worshiped in different parts of the region. Peor refers to the place this particular Baal was worshiped. (See also 31:16; Deut 4:3; Hos 9:10.)

25:5 *judges:* Special leaders who were probably responsible for an entire tribe or part of a tribe (see also Exod 18:25,26 and the notes at Num 1:5-16 and 11:16).

25:6 *Midianite:* See the note at 10:29. Here used as a general term for various peoples who lived east of the Jordan River. Some of these people were probably ruled by the Moabite king (see Gen 36:35).

25:8 *plague:* The text does not say what this plague was, but verse 6 seems to show the people's reaction to it.

25:14 *Simeonite family:* See the note at 2:10-16.

26:1 *Eleazar:* After Aaron died, his son Eleazar became Israel's high priest (20:27,28).

26:2 *Take a census:* Forty years had passed since the first census (see 1:1-46). This second census counted the Israelite men in the next generation, those who would be allowed to enter the promised land of Canaan (14:20-23, 29-32).

26:3,4 *plains of Moab . . . Jericho:* See the note at 22:1.

26:5-18 *Reuben . . . Simeon . . . Gad:* See the note at 2:10-16 and the chart called "Israel Counted Twice," on p. 266.

26:2 Num 1:1-46. **26:9,10** Num 16:1-35.

15 And the name of the Midianite woman who was put to death
was Cozbi daughter of Zur, a tribal chief of a Midianite family.
16 The LORD said to Moses, 17 "Treat the Midianites as enemies
and kill them, 18 because they treated you as enemies when they
deceived you in the affair of Peor and their sister Cozbi, the daughter of a Midianite leader, the woman who was killed when the
plague came as a result of Peor."

COUNTING AND INSTRUCTING A NEW GENERATION

The LORD tells Moses to count the Israelite men a second time, and Joshua is chosen to lead this new generation into Canaan. As the people prepare to enter Canaan, they receive laws concerning festival celebrations and making promises to the LORD.

The Second Census

26 After the plague the LORD said to Moses and Eleazar son of
Aaron, the priest, 2 "Take a census of the whole Israelite community by families—all those twenty years old or more who are able to
serve in the army of Israel." 3 So on the plains of Moab by the Jordan across from Jericho,[a] Moses and Eleazar the priest spoke with
them and said, 4 "Take a census of the men twenty years old or
more, as the LORD commanded Moses."

These were the Israelites who came out of Egypt:

5 The descendants of Reuben, the firstborn son of Israel, were:
through Hanoch, the Hanochite clan;
through Pallu, the Palluite clan;
6 through Hezron, the Hezronite clan;
through Carmi, the Carmite clan.
7 These were the clans of Reuben; those numbered were 43,730.
8 The son of Pallu was Eliab, 9 and the sons of Eliab were
Nemuel, Dathan and Abiram. The same Dathan and Abiram were
the community officials who rebelled against Moses and Aaron
and were among Korah's followers when they rebelled against the
LORD. 10 The earth opened its mouth and swallowed them along
with Korah, whose followers died when the fire devoured the 250
men. And they served as a warning sign. 11 The line of Korah, however, did not die out.

12 The descendants of Simeon by their clans were:
through Nemuel, the Nemuelite clan;
through Jamin, the Jaminite clan;
through Jakin, the Jakinite clan;
13 through Zerah, the Zerahite clan;

[a] **3** Hebrew *Jordan of Jericho*; possibly an ancient name for the Jordan River; also in verse 63

through Shaul, the Shaulite clan.
14These were the clans of Simeon; there were 22,200 men.

15The descendants of Gad by their clans were:
through Zephon, the Zephonite clan;
through Haggi, the Haggite clan;
through Shuni, the Shunite clan;
16through Ozni, the Oznite clan;
through Eri, the Erite clan;
17through Arodi,[a] the Arodite clan;
through Areli, the Arelite clan.
18These were the clans of Gad; those numbered were 40,500.

19Er and Onan were sons of Judah, but they died in Canaan.
20The descendants of Judah by their clans were:
through Shelah, the Shelanite clan;
through Perez, the Perezite clan;
through Zerah, the Zerahite clan.
21The descendants of Perez were:
through Hezron, the Hezronite clan;
through Hamul, the Hamulite clan.
22These were the clans of Judah; those numbered were 76,500.

23The descendants of Issachar by their clans were:
through Tola, the Tolaite clan;
through Puah, the Puite[b] clan;
24through Jashub, the Jashubite clan;
through Shimron, the Shimronite clan.
25These were the clans of Issachar; those numbered were 64,300.

26The descendants of Zebulun by their clans were:
through Sered, the Seredite clan;
through Elon, the Elonite clan;
through Jahleel, the Jahleelite clan.
27These were the clans of Zebulun; those numbered were 60,500.

28The descendants of Joseph by their clans through Manasseh and Ephraim were:

29The descendants of Manasseh:
through Makir, the Makirite clan (Makir was the father of Gilead);
through Gilead, the Gileadite clan.
30These were the descendants of Gilead:
through Iezer, the Iezerite clan;
through Helek, the Helekite clan;
31through Asriel, the Asrielite clan;
through Shechem, the Shechemite clan;

26:19-27 *Judah . . . Issachar . . . Zebulun:* See the note at 2:3-9. For Judah's sons, see Gen 38:1-10.

26:28-38 *Manasseh . . . Ephraim . . . Benjamin:* See the note at 2:18-24. Notice that Ephraim and Manasseh have changed places in this second counting. For Zelophehad and his five daughters, see 27:1-11; 36:1-12.

---

[a]**17** Samaritan Pentateuch and Syriac (see also Gen. 46:16); Masoretic Text *Arod* [b]**23** Samaritan Pentateuch, Septuagint, Vulgate and Syriac (see also 1 Chron. 7:1); Masoretic Text *through Puvah, the Punite*

26:42-50 *Dan . . . Naphtali:* See the note at 2:25-31.

[32]through Shemida, the Shemidaite clan;
through Hepher, the Hepherite clan.
[33](Zelophehad son of Hepher had no sons; he had only daughters, whose names were Mahlah, Noah, Hoglah, Milcah and Tirzah.)
[34]These were the clans of Manasseh; those numbered were 52,700.

[35]These were the descendants of Ephraim by their clans:
through Shuthelah, the Shuthelahite clan;
through Beker, the Bekerite clan;
through Tahan, the Tahanite clan.
[36]These were the descendants of Shuthelah:
through Eran, the Eranite clan.
[37]These were the clans of Ephraim; those numbered were 32,500.

These were the descendants of Joseph by their clans.

[38]The descendants of Benjamin by their clans were:
through Bela, the Belaite clan;
through Ashbel, the Ashbelite clan;
through Ahiram, the Ahiramite clan;
[39]through Shupham,[a] the Shuphamite clan;
through Hupham, the Huphamite clan.
[40]The descendants of Bela through Ard and Naaman were:
through Ard,[b] the Ardite clan;
through Naaman, the Naamite clan.
[41]These were the clans of Benjamin; those numbered were 45,600.

[42]These were the descendants of Dan by their clans:
through Shuham, the Shuhamite clan.
These were the clans of Dan: [43]All of them were Shuhamite clans;
and those numbered were 64,400.

[44]The descendants of Asher by their clans were:
through Imnah, the Imnite clan;
through Ishvi, the Ishvite clan;
through Beriah, the Beriite clan;
[45]and through the descendants of Beriah:
through Heber, the Heberite clan;
through Malkiel, the Malkielite clan.
[46](Asher had a daughter named Serah.)
[47]These were the clans of Asher; those numbered were 53,400.

[48]The descendants of Naphtali by their clans were:
through Jahzeel, the Jahzeelite clan;
through Guni, the Gunite clan;

[a]**39** A few manuscripts of the Masoretic Text, Samaritan Pentateuch, Vulgate and Syriac (see also Septuagint); most manuscripts of the Masoretic Text *Shephupham*
[b]**40** Samaritan Pentateuch and Vulgate (see also Septuagint); Masoretic Text does not have *through Ard.*

[49]through Jezer, the Jezerite clan;
through Shillem, the Shillemite clan.
[50]These were the clans of Naphtali; those numbered were 45,400.

[51]The total number of the men of Israel was 601,730.

[52]The LORD said to Moses, [53]"The land is to be allotted to
them as an inheritance based on the number of names. [54]To a
larger group give a larger inheritance, and to a smaller group a
smaller one; each is to receive its inheritance according to the
number of those listed. [55]Be sure that the land is distributed by lot.
What each group inherits will be according to the names for its
ancestral tribe. [56]Each inheritance is to be distributed by lot among
the larger and smaller groups."

[57]These were the Levites who were counted by their clans:
through Gershon, the Gershonite clan;
through Kohath, the Kohathite clan;
through Merari, the Merarite clan.
[58]These also were Levite clans:
the Libnite clan,
the Hebronite clan,
the Mahlite clan,
the Mushite clan,
the Korahite clan.
(Kohath was the forefather of Amram; [59]the name of Amram's
wife was Jochebed, a descendant of Levi, who was born to the
Levites[a] in Egypt. To Amram she bore Aaron, Moses and their
sister Miriam. [60]Aaron was the father of Nadab and Abihu,
Eleazar and Ithamar. [61]But Nadab and Abihu died when they
made an offering before the LORD with unauthorized fire.)

[62]All the male Levites a month old or more numbered 23,000.
They were not counted along with the other Israelites because they
received no inheritance among them.

[63]These are the ones counted by Moses and Eleazar the priest
when they counted the Israelites on the plains of Moab by the Jordan across from Jericho. [64]Not one of them was among those
counted by Moses and Aaron the priest when they counted the
Israelites in the Desert of Sinai. [65]For the LORD had told those
Israelites they would surely die in the desert, and not one of them
was left except Caleb son of Jephunneh and Joshua son of Nun.

Zelophehad's Daughters

27 The daughters of Zelophehad son of Hepher, the son of Gilead,
the son of Makir, the son of Manasseh, belonged to the clans of

[a]59 Or *Jochebed, a daughter of Levi, who was born to Levi*

26:51 *total number:* Compare this total to the total in 1:46. In the second counting, the clans of each tribe are also listed.

26:53 *land is to be allotted:* The tribe of Levi was not given a share of the land (26:62; see also the note at 1:47). The results of the second counting were also used to determine how much land would be given to each tribe. See also Joshua 13:8—19:48 for another account of how the land was divided among Israel's tribes. The author of JOSHUA says that Moses gave land east of the Jordan River to Reuben, Gad, and half of the tribe of Manasseh (Josh 13:8; 14:1,2). It was Joshua who later divided the land among those in Canaan, to the west of the Jordan River. See also 34:13.

26:57 *Levites . . . clans:* See the notes at 1:47 and 2:17 (Levites); 3:21 (Gershon); 3:27 (Kohath); and 3:33 (Merari).

26:63 *plains of Moab . . . Jericho:* See the note at 22:1.

26:60,61 Lev 10:1,2; Num 3:2-4. **26:65** Num 14:26-35. **27:1** Num 36:1-12.

The Daughters of Zelophehad by Gloria Ortiz Hernandez, 1999. In the ancient Near East, a man's property usually was passed on to his sons or other male relatives when he died. NUMBERS, however, tells of a case in which a man's lands were passed on to his daughters. When their father died without a son, Zelophehad's five daughters went to Moses and asked for some land so that their father's name would not die out. Moses asked the LORD and the LORD said Zelophehad's daughters were right. (See 27:1-11; 36:1-12.)

Manasseh son of Joseph. The names of the daughters were Mahlah,
Noah, Hoglah, Milcah and Tirzah. They approached 2the entrance to
the Tent of Meeting and stood before Moses, Eleazar the priest, the
leaders and the whole assembly, and said, 3"Our father died in the
desert. He was not among Korah's followers, who banded together
against the LORD, but he died for his own sin and left no sons. 4Why
should our father's name disappear from his clan because he had no
son? Give us property among our father's relatives."
5So Moses brought their case before the LORD 6and the LORD
said to him, 7"What Zelophehad's daughters are saying is right. You
must certainly give them property as an inheritance among their
father's relatives and turn their father's inheritance over to them.
8"Say to the Israelites, 'If a man dies and leaves no son, turn
his inheritance over to his daughter. 9If he has no daughter, give
his inheritance to his brothers. 10If he has no brothers, give his
inheritance to his father's brothers. 11If his father had no brothers,
give his inheritance to the nearest relative in his clan, that he may

27:2 *Eleazar:* See the note at 26:1.

27:3 *Our father died . . . no sons:* Zelophehad died along with the others who were punished for rebelling against God (13:1—14:45). In Israel, property was usually passed from father to son. In this case, a law was made to allow the daughters to inherit the land (27:8-11).

possess it. This is to be a legal requirement for the Israelites, as the
LORD commanded Moses.' "

Joshua to Succeed Moses

12 Then the LORD said to Moses, "Go up this mountain in the
Abarim range and see the land I have given the Israelites. 13 After
you have seen it, you too will be gathered to your people, as your
brother Aaron was, 14 for when the community rebelled at the
waters in the Desert of Zin, both of you disobeyed my command
to honor me as holy before their eyes." (These were the waters of
Meribah Kadesh, in the Desert of Zin.)
15 Moses said to the LORD, 16 "May the LORD, the God of the spirits of all mankind, appoint a man over this community 17 to go out
and come in before them, one who will lead them out and bring them
in, so the LORD's people will not be like sheep without a shepherd."
18 So the LORD said to Moses, "Take Joshua son of Nun, a
man in whom is the spirit,[a] and lay your hand on him. 19 Have him
stand before Eleazar the priest and the entire assembly and commission him in their presence. 20 Give him some of your authority
so the whole Israelite community will obey him. 21 He is to stand
before Eleazar the priest, who will obtain decisions for him by
inquiring of the Urim before the LORD. At his command he and
the entire community of the Israelites will go out, and at his command they will come in."
22 Moses did as the LORD commanded him. He took Joshua
and had him stand before Eleazar the priest and the whole assembly. 23 Then he laid his hands on him and commissioned him, as
the LORD instructed through Moses.

Daily Offerings

28 The LORD said to Moses, 2 "Give this command to the
Israelites and say to them: 'See that you present to me at the
appointed time the food for my offerings made by fire, as an
aroma pleasing to me.' 3 Say to them: 'This is the offering made by
fire that you are to present to the LORD: two lambs a year old without defect, as a regular burnt offering each day. 4 Prepare one lamb
in the morning and the other at twilight, 5 together with a grain
offering of a tenth of an ephah[b] of fine flour mixed with a quarter
of a hin[c] of oil from pressed olives. 6 This is the regular burnt offering instituted at Mount Sinai as a pleasing aroma, an offering
made to the LORD by fire. 7 The accompanying drink offering is to
be a quarter of a hin of fermented drink with each lamb. Pour out
the drink offering to the LORD at the sanctuary. 8 Prepare the

[a]**18** Or *Spirit* [b]**5** That is, probably about 2 quarts (about 2 liters); also in verses 13, 21 and 29 [c]**5** That is, probably about 1 quart (about 1 liter); also in verses 7 and 14

27:12-14 *Abarim range . . . waters of Meribah Kadesh, in the Desert of Zin:* The Abarim Mountains stretched around the northern end of the Dead Sea on the east side of the Jordan River. See 20:1-12 and the notes at 20:13 (Meribah) and 13:26 (Kadesh).

27:13,14 *gathered to your people . . . you disobeyed:* "Gathered to your people" means death. Moses' disobedience is recorded in 20:1-12. Aaron's death is described in 20:22-29, and the story of Moses' death is in Deuteronomy 34:1-8. See also Deut 3:23-27; 32:48-52.

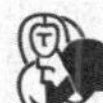

27:18 *Joshua . . . lay your hand on him:* See the note at 11:28. Moses laid his hands on Joshua to show that his power would be passed on to Joshua. Laying hands on a person was also a way to show that the person was chosen for a special task. See also 27:23; Exod 24:13.

27:21 *stand before Eleazar the priest:* Joshua was Israel's military leader, but he had to get advice from the high priest Eleazar who used pieces of wood or stone called Urim and Thummim to find out what the LORD wanted. See also Exod 28:30; 1 Sam 28:6.

28:2,3 *offerings made by fire:* See the notes at 7:87 and 6:14, 15. This kind of sacrifice was offered for various reasons, including the daily sacrifices offered in the morning and evening by the priests (see Exod 29:38-42; Lev 6:8-13; Num 28:9,10).

27:17 1 Kgs 22:17; Ezek 34:5; Matt 9:36; Mark 6:34. **27:23** Deut 31:23; 32:44-47; 34:9.

second lamb at twilight, along with the same kind of grain offering and drink offering that you prepare in the morning. This is an offering made by fire, an aroma pleasing to the LORD.

Sabbath Offerings

[9]“ ‘On the Sabbath day, make an offering of two lambs a year old without defect, together with its drink offering and a grain offering of two-tenths of an ephah[a] of fine flour mixed with oil. [10]This is the burnt offering for every Sabbath, in addition to the regular burnt offering and its drink offering.

Monthly Offerings

[11]“ ‘On the first of every month, present to the LORD a burnt offering of two young bulls, one ram and seven male lambs a year old, all without defect. [12]With each bull there is to be a grain offering of three-tenths of an ephah[b] of fine flour mixed with oil; with the ram, a grain offering of two-tenths of an ephah of fine flour mixed with oil; [13]and with each lamb, a grain offering of a tenth of an ephah of fine flour mixed with oil. This is for a burnt offering, a pleasing aroma, an offering made to the LORD by fire. [14]With each bull there is to be a drink offering of half a hin[c] of wine; with the ram, a third of a hin[d]; and with each lamb, a quarter of a hin. This is the monthly burnt offering to be made at each new moon during the year. [15]Besides the regular burnt offering with its drink offering, one male goat is to be presented to the LORD as a sin offering.

The Passover

[16]“ ‘On the fourteenth day of the first month the LORD’s Passover is to be held. [17]On the fifteenth day of this month there is to be a festival; for seven days eat bread made without yeast. [18]On the first day hold a sacred assembly and do no regular work. [19]Present to the LORD an offering made by fire, a burnt offering of two young bulls, one ram and seven male lambs a year old, all without defect. [20]With each bull prepare a grain offering of three-tenths of an ephah of fine flour mixed with oil; with the ram, two-tenths; [21]and with each of the seven lambs, one-tenth. [22]Include one male goat as a sin offering to make atonement for you. [23]Prepare these in addition to the regular morning burnt offering. [24]In this way prepare the food for the offering made by fire every day for seven days as an aroma pleasing to the LORD; it is to be prepared in addition to the regular burnt offering and its drink offering. [25]On the seventh day hold a sacred assembly and do no regular work.

[a]**9** That is, probably about 4 quarts (about 4.5 liters); also in verses 12, 20 and 28
[b]**12** That is, probably about 6 quarts (about 6.5 liters); also in verses 20 and 28
[c]**14** That is, probably about 2 quarts (about 2 liters) [d]**14** That is, probably about 1 1/4 quarts (about 1.2 liters)

28:9,10 *burnt offering for every Sabbath:* See the notes at 15:32 and 28:2,3.

28:11-13 *first of every month . . . a pleasing aroma:* See the notes at 10:10 (New Moon) and 7:87.

28:12 *flour . . . oil:* See the note at 15:6.

28:15 *regular burnt offering:* See 28:1-8 and the note at 28:2,3.

28:16,17 *Passover . . . seven days:* See the note at 9:2,3 (Passover). The Feast of Unleavened Bread began the day after Passover and lasted seven days. Unleavened bread (bread made without yeast) was to be eaten during the festival as a reminder of how quickly the people had to leave Egypt. See also Exod 12:1-20; 23:15; 34:18; Deut 16:1-8, and the chart called “Jewish Calendar and Festivals,” p. 944.

28:19-24 *offering made by fire:* See the notes at 28:2,3 and 7:87.

Feast of Weeks

26“ ‘On the day of firstfruits, when you present to the LORD
an offering of new grain during the Feast of Weeks, hold a sacred
assembly and do no regular work. 27Present a burnt offering of two
young bulls, one ram and seven male lambs a year old as an aroma
pleasing to the LORD. 28With each bull there is to be a grain offering of three-tenths of an ephah of fine flour mixed with oil; with
the ram, two-tenths; 29and with each of the seven lambs, one-
tenth. 30Include one male goat to make atonement for you. 31Pre-
pare these together with their drink offerings, in addition to the
regular burnt offering and its grain offering. Be sure the animals
are without defect.

Feast of Trumpets

29 “ ‘On the first day of the seventh month hold a sacred assembly and do no regular work. It is a day for you to sound the trumpets. 2As an aroma pleasing to the LORD, prepare a burnt offering
of one young bull, one ram and seven male lambs a year old, all
without defect. 3With the bull prepare a grain offering of three-
tenths of an ephah[a] of fine flour mixed with oil; with the ram, two-
tenths[b]; 4and with each of the seven lambs, one-tenth.[c] 5Include
one male goat as a sin offering to make atonement for you. 6These
are in addition to the monthly and daily burnt offerings with their
grain offerings and drink offerings as specified. They are offerings
made to the LORD by fire—a pleasing aroma.

Day of Atonement

7“ ‘On the tenth day of this seventh month hold a sacred
assembly. You must deny yourselves[d] and do no work. 8Present as
an aroma pleasing to the LORD a burnt offering of one young bull,
one ram and seven male lambs a year old, all without defect. 9With
the bull prepare a grain offering of three-tenths of an ephah of fine
flour mixed with oil; with the ram, two-tenths; 10and with each of
the seven lambs, one-tenth. 11Include one male goat as a sin offering, in addition to the sin offering for atonement and the regular
burnt offering with its grain offering, and their drink offerings.

Feast of Tabernacles

12“ ‘On the fifteenth day of the seventh month, hold a sacred
assembly and do no regular work. Celebrate a festival to the LORD
for seven days. 13Present an offering made by fire as an aroma
pleasing to the LORD, a burnt offering of thirteen young bulls, two
rams and fourteen male lambs a year old, all without defect.

[a]**3** That is, probably about 6 quarts (about 6.5 liters); also in verses 9 and 14
[b]**3** That is, probably about 4 quarts (about 4.5 liters); also in verses 9 and 14
[c]**4** That is, probably about 2 quarts (about 2 liters); also in verses 10 and 15
[d]**7** Or *must fast*

28:26 *Feast of Weeks:* This feast, also known as the Feast of Harvest, took place fifty days after the Feast of Unleavened Bread (Lev 23:15,16). The people presented grain to God as a sign of thanks and to show confidence that God would continue to meet their needs. See also Exod 23:16; 34:22; Deut 16:9-12; and the chart called "Jewish Calendar and Festivals," p. 944.

28:27-31 *burnt offering . . . grain offering:* See the notes at 7:87 and 8:8.

28:31 *regular burnt offering and its grain offering:* See the note at 28:2,3.

29:1 *seventh month . . . sacred assembly:* The seventh month of the Hebrew calendar, Tishri (also known as Ethanim), runs from about mid-September to mid-October. The first day of this month was the start of the New Year Festival, which was observed by horn blasts, special sacrifices, and rest from work. Today, this first day of the seventh month is known as *Rosh Hashanah,* meaning "the beginning of the year." It is not clear why the seventh month marks the beginning of a new year. For more, see the chart called "Jewish Calendar and Festivals," p. 944. See also Lev 23:23-25; Amos 8:5.

29:1 *trumpets:* See the note at 10:2.

29:2 *burnt offering:* See the notes at 7:87; 8:8; and 28:2,3. Numbers 28:11-15 describes the sacrifices offered on the first day of each month. For more, see the chart called "Sacrifices and Offerings," p. 219.

29:7 *seventh month . . . sacred assembly:* See the note at 29:1 (seventh month). See Leviticus 16 for a detailed description of the Day of Atonement. See also Lev 23:26-34.

29:12 *a festival to the LORD for seven days:* This was the Feast of Tabernacles. It took place at the end of the fall harvest (Deut 16:13-17). The people were to build shelters made of tree branches. They were to live in them for seven days (Lev 23:42) to recall the temporary shelters their ancestors lived in as they wandered in the desert. See the chart called "Jewish Calendar and Festivals," p. 944.

The LORD said to Moses, *"Present an offering made by fire as an aroma pleasing to the* LORD, *a burnt offering of one bull, one ram and seven male lambs a year old, all without defect."*
Num 29:36

14 With each of the thirteen bulls prepare a grain offering of three-tenths of an ephah of fine flour mixed with oil; with each of the two rams, two-tenths; 15 and with each of the fourteen lambs, one-tenth. 16 Include one male goat as a sin offering, in addition to the regular burnt offering with its grain offering and drink offering.

17 " 'On the second day prepare twelve young bulls, two rams and fourteen male lambs a year old, all without defect. 18 With the bulls, rams and lambs, prepare their grain offerings and drink offerings according to the number specified. 19 Include one male goat as a sin offering, in addition to the regular burnt offering with its grain offering, and their drink offerings.

20 " 'On the third day prepare eleven bulls, two rams and fourteen male lambs a year old, all without defect. 21 With the bulls, rams and lambs, prepare their grain offerings and drink offerings according to the number specified. 22 Include one male goat as a sin offering, in addition to the regular burnt offering with its grain offering and drink offering.

23 " 'On the fourth day prepare ten bulls, two rams and fourteen male lambs a year old, all without defect. 24 With the bulls, rams and lambs, prepare their grain offerings and drink offerings according to the number specified. 25 Include one male goat as a sin offering, in addition to the regular burnt offering with its grain offering and drink offering.

26 " 'On the fifth day prepare nine bulls, two rams and fourteen male lambs a year old, all without defect. 27 With the bulls, rams and lambs, prepare their grain offerings and drink offerings according to the number specified. 28 Include one male goat as a sin offering, in addition to the regular burnt offering with its grain offering and drink offering.

29 " 'On the sixth day prepare eight bulls, two rams and fourteen male lambs a year old, all without defect. 30 With the bulls, rams and lambs, prepare their grain offerings and drink offerings according to the number specified. 31 Include one male goat as a sin offering, in addition to the regular burnt offering with its grain offering and drink offering.

32 " 'On the seventh day prepare seven bulls, two rams and fourteen male lambs a year old, all without defect. 33 With the bulls, rams and lambs, prepare their grain offerings and drink offerings according to the number specified. 34 Include one male goat as a sin offering, in addition to the regular burnt offering with its grain offering and drink offering.

35 " 'On the eighth day hold an assembly and do no regular work. 36 Present an offering made by fire as an aroma pleasing to the LORD, a burnt offering of one bull, one ram and seven male lambs a year old, all without defect. 37 With the bull, the ram and the lambs, prepare their grain offerings and drink offerings according to the number specified. 38 Include one male goat as a sin

offering, in addition to the regular burnt offering with its grain offering and drink offering.

39“ ‘In addition to what you vow and your freewill offerings, prepare these for the LORD at your appointed feasts: your burnt offerings, grain offerings, drink offerings and fellowship offerings.[a] ’ ”

40Moses told the Israelites all that the LORD commanded him.

Vows

30 Moses said to the heads of the tribes of Israel: “This is what the LORD commands: 2When a man makes a vow to the LORD or takes an oath to obligate himself by a pledge, he must not break his word but must do everything he said.

3“When a young woman still living in her father’s house makes a vow to the LORD or obligates herself by a pledge 4and her father hears about her vow or pledge but says nothing to her, then all her vows and every pledge by which she obligated herself will stand. 5But if her father forbids her when he hears about it, none of her vows or the pledges by which she obligated herself will stand; the LORD will release her because her father has forbidden her.

6“If she marries after she makes a vow or after her lips utter a rash promise by which she obligates herself 7and her husband hears about it but says nothing to her, then her vows or the pledges by which she obligated herself will stand. 8But if her husband forbids her when he hears about it, he nullifies the vow that obligates her or the rash promise by which she obligates herself, and the LORD will release her.

9“Any vow or obligation taken by a widow or divorced woman will be binding on her.

10“If a woman living with her husband makes a vow or obligates herself by a pledge under oath 11and her husband hears about it but says nothing to her and does not forbid her, then all her vows or the pledges by which she obligated herself will stand. 12But if her husband nullifies them when he hears about them, then none of the vows or pledges that came from her lips will stand. Her husband has nullified them, and the LORD will release her. 13Her husband may confirm or nullify any vow she makes or any sworn pledge to deny herself. 14But if her husband says nothing to her about it from day to day, then he confirms all her vows or the pledges binding on her. He confirms them by saying nothing to her when he hears about them. 15If, however, he nullifies them some time after he hears about them, then he is responsible for her guilt.”

16These are the regulations the LORD gave Moses concerning relationships between a man and his wife, and between a father and his young daughter still living in his house.

[a]39 Traditionally *peace offerings*

30:2 *vow to the LORD:* Either a promise of a gift or the promise to do something. Vows were taken very seriously. Once a person made a vow, it could not be taken back. See also Deut 23:21-23; Matt 5:33; and the mini-article called “Making Vows,” on p. 328.

30:3-16 *young woman . . . vow:* The laws concerning vows made by women show that men were in charge of ancient Israelite society. Fathers could overrule a vow made by an unmarried daughter living at home, and husbands could overrule promises made by their wives. But the husband had only one day to object to his wife’s vow. Widows and divorced women who made vows were expected to keep any promises they made to the LORD.

MAKING VOWS

Vows are spoken promises made to God, and are often made in response to help received from God. A person making a vow can offer a thing, an action, or the promise of a future action. It is an act of trust between people and God. A person making a vow is expected to fulfill it by doing what is promised. Vows were used in various ways in the Bible.

A vow is not the same as an oath. In general, an oath reassures others that the speaker of the oath is being truthful, whereas a vow involves a promise to God. The New Testament states that oaths should be avoided (Matt 5:34-37; Jas 5:12).

Sometimes vows were made to get something from God. In return for God's help or blessing, the person making the vow promised to do something or give something. For example, Jacob promised to worship God and give God a tenth of everything he owned if God would protect him (Gen 28:20-22). The brave warrior Jephthah promised God he would sacrifice whatever greeted him after battling the Ammonites if God let him win the battle (Judg 11). Hannah prayed for God to give her a son, and in return she vowed to dedicate him to serve the LORD at Shiloh (1 Sam 1).

Other vows were simply made to thank God. Nothing was expected in return. King David promised that he would not rest until he had found a home for the LORD and the ark of the covenant (Ps 132:2-5). The sailors with Jonah made vows to God after the LORD calmed a violent storm at sea (Jonah 1:13-16).

God also made promises. See the mini-article called "Covenants (Agreements)," on p. 386. God's promises are always kept (see Num 23:19). Though David didn't ask for it, God promised that someone in David's family would always be king (2 Sam 7; Ps 132:11, 12). Some other examples of God's promises or vows can be found in GENESIS. In Genesis 8:21, the LORD promised never again to destroy "all living creatures" or to punish the earth for the sinful things its people do. In Genesis 12:2,3, the LORD promised to bless Abram and make his descendants into a great nation, and in Genesis 15:5 the LORD promised Abram as many descendants as there are stars in the sky.

The Law of Moses had rules for making promises or vows. There were laws about offerings given when making a vow (Lev 7:16-18) and about what kind of offering was acceptable when making a sacrifice for a vow (Lev 22:17-25; Num 15:1-12). Laws also set the price to buy back people or property promised to God (Lev 27). There were special rules for those who dedicated themselves to God by vowing to become Nazirites (Num 6:1-21). It is possible that the apostle Paul cut his hair at Cenchrea because of a kind of Nazirite vow he had made to God (Acts 18:18; see also Acts 21:23).

Numbers 30 deals mostly with vows made by women. A young woman living at home could make a vow, but her father had the power to cancel it. If he did, she no longer had to keep the promise and would not be blamed. The same was true of a husband who disapproved of his wife's vow. Widows and divorced women could make vows and were expected to keep them, because no one had the power to cancel their vows. Making a vow to the LORD was not required, but when a vow was made, the LORD expected it to be kept (Deut 23:21-23; Eccl 5:4,5).

Jephthah's daughter was the first to greet Jephthah after he returned from defeating the Ammonites. This caused him great sadness because he had made a solemn vow to God to sacrifice whatever came out to meet him on his return from battle.

GETTING READY TO CROSS THE JORDAN RIVER

The Israelites battle the Midianites and settle in the land east of the Jordan. Their journey from Egypt to Moab is summarized, and the LORD gives the command to conquer Canaan. Various rules are set down, including those for establishing towns, punishing criminals, and distributing land.

Vengeance on the Midianites

31 The LORD said to Moses, [2]"Take vengeance on the Midianites
for the Israelites. After that, you will be gathered to your people."
[3]So Moses said to the people, "Arm some of your men to go
to war against the Midianites and to carry out the LORD's
vengeance on them. [4]Send into battle a thousand men from each
of the tribes of Israel." [5]So twelve thousand men armed for battle,
a thousand from each tribe, were supplied from the clans of Israel.
[6]Moses sent them into battle, a thousand from each tribe, along
with Phinehas son of Eleazar, the priest, who took with him articles from the sanctuary and the trumpets for signaling.
[7]They fought against Midian, as the LORD commanded
Moses, and killed every man. [8]Among their victims were Evi,
Rekem, Zur, Hur and Reba—the five kings of Midian. They also
killed Balaam son of Beor with the sword. [9]The Israelites captured
the Midianite women and children and took all the Midianite
herds, flocks and goods as plunder. [10]They burned all the towns
where the Midianites had settled, as well as all their camps. [11]They
took all the plunder and spoils, including the people and animals,
[12]and brought the captives, spoils and plunder to Moses and
Eleazar the priest and the Israelite assembly at their camp on the
plains of Moab, by the Jordan across from Jericho.[a]
[13]Moses, Eleazar the priest and all the leaders of the community went to meet them outside the camp. [14]Moses was angry
with the officers of the army—the commanders of thousands and
commanders of hundreds—who returned from the battle.
[15]"Have you allowed all the women to live?" he asked them.
[16]"They were the ones who followed Balaam's advice and were the
means of turning the Israelites away from the LORD in what happened at Peor, so that a plague struck the LORD's people. [17]Now kill
all the boys. And kill every woman who has slept with a man, [18]but
save for yourselves every girl who has never slept with a man.
[19]"All of you who have killed anyone or touched anyone who
was killed must stay outside the camp seven days. On the third
and seventh days you must purify yourselves and your captives.
[20]Purify every garment as well as everything made of leather, goat
hair or wood."
[21]Then Eleazar the priest said to the soldiers who had gone
into battle, "This is the requirement of the law that the LORD gave

[a]12 Hebrew *Jordan of Jericho*; possibly an ancient name for the Jordan River

31:2 *Midianites:* See the note at 10:29. See also 22:4; 25:6-18.

31:6 *Phinehas . . . articles from the sanctuary:* Eleazar, the high priest, was not allowed to leave the tabernacle area or touch corpses, so Phinehas was sent out with the army as Israel's priest. The battle with the Midianites was considered a Holy War because the priest and holy objects were present (see also Deut 20; Josh 6:1-21). It is not clear which articles were taken into battle. It could have been the trumpets, the Urim and Thummin, or "lots," used to ask God what he wanted done (see 27:21), or even the ark of the covenant itself. See also the mini-article called "Holy War (The LORD'S Battles)," p. 306.

31:8 *Balaam son of Beor:* See the note at 22:5.

31:9-18 *captured the Midianite women:* Because the war against Midian was a Holy War, the people and property captured were to be consecrated to the LORD. This meant killing the men and destroying the towns. According to Deuteronomy 20:16 and Leviticus 27:28,29 all people and animals consecrated to God and captured in a Holy War were to be destroyed. But Deuteronomy 20:10-15 says women and children were to be kept as slaves. In this case, Moses wanted all the women who were not virgins killed, because some of them had persuaded the Israelites to worship Baal of Peor and had had sex with some Israelite men (see 25:1-18). Virgins were to be kept as slaves.

31:19 *purify yourselves:* See the note at 19:11 and the mini-article called "Purity (Clean and Unclean)," p. 2125.

Moses and Eleazar the priest accepted the gold from the commanders of thousands and commanders of hundreds and brought it into the Tent of Meeting as a memorial for the Israelites before the LORD.
Num 31:54

31:28-30 *Give them to the Levites:* A portion of everything captured in battle, as well as a portion of anything grown, went to the priest and Levites. See the notes at 5:9 and 18:21.

Moses: [22]Gold, silver, bronze, iron, tin, lead [23]and anything else that can withstand fire must be put through the fire, and then it will be clean. But it must also be purified with the water of cleansing. And whatever cannot withstand fire must be put through that water. [24]On the seventh day wash your clothes and you will be clean. Then you may come into the camp."

Dividing the Spoils

[25]The LORD said to Moses, [26]"You and Eleazar the priest and the family heads of the community are to count all the people and animals that were captured. [27]Divide the spoils between the soldiers who took part in the battle and the rest of the community. [28]From the soldiers who fought in the battle, set apart as tribute for the LORD one out of every five hundred, whether persons, cattle, donkeys, sheep or goats. [29]Take this tribute from their half share and give it to Eleazar the priest as the LORD's part. [30]From the Israelites' half, select one out of every fifty, whether persons, cattle, donkeys, sheep, goats or other animals. Give them to the Levites, who are responsible for the care of the LORD's tabernacle." [31]So Moses and Eleazar the priest did as the LORD commanded Moses.

[32]The plunder remaining from the spoils that the soldiers took was 675,000 sheep, [33]72,000 cattle, [34]61,000 donkeys [35]and 32,000 women who had never slept with a man.

[36]The half share of those who fought in the battle was:

337,500 sheep, [37]of which the tribute for the LORD was 675;
[38]36,000 cattle, of which the tribute for the LORD was 72;
[39]30,500 donkeys, of which the tribute for the LORD was 61;
[40]16,000 people, of which the tribute for the LORD was 32.

[41]Moses gave the tribute to Eleazar the priest as the LORD's part, as the LORD commanded Moses.

[42]The half belonging to the Israelites, which Moses set apart from that of the fighting men— [43]the community's half—was 337,500 sheep, [44]36,000 cattle, [45]30,500 donkeys [46]and 16,000 people. [47]From the Israelites' half, Moses selected one out of every fifty persons and animals, as the LORD commanded him, and gave them to the Levites, who were responsible for the care of the LORD's tabernacle.

[48]Then the officers who were over the units of the army—the commanders of thousands and commanders of hundreds—went to Moses [49]and said to him, "Your servants have counted the soldiers under our command, and not one is missing. [50]So we have brought as an offering to the LORD the gold articles each of us acquired—armlets, bracelets, signet rings, earrings and necklaces—to make atonement for ourselves before the LORD."

[51]Moses and Eleazar the priest accepted from them the gold—all the crafted articles. [52]All the gold from the commanders

of thousands and commanders of hundreds that Moses and
Eleazar presented as a gift to the LORD weighed 16,750 shekels.[a]
53 Each soldier had taken plunder for himself. 54 Moses and Eleazar
the priest accepted the gold from the commanders of thousands
and commanders of hundreds and brought it into the Tent of
Meeting as a memorial for the Israelites before the LORD.

The Transjordan Tribes

32 The Reubenites and Gadites, who had very large herds and
flocks, saw that the lands of Jazer and Gilead were suitable for livestock. 2 So they came to Moses and Eleazar the priest and to the
leaders of the community, and said, 3 "Ataroth, Dibon, Jazer, Nimrah, Heshbon, Elealeh, Sebam, Nebo and Beon— 4 the land the
LORD subdued before the people of Israel—are suitable for livestock, and your servants have livestock. 5 If we have found favor in
your eyes," they said, "let this land be given to your servants as our
possession. Do not make us cross the Jordan."
6 Moses said to the Gadites and Reubenites, "Shall your countrymen go to war while you sit here? 7 Why do you discourage the
Israelites from going over into the land the LORD has given them?
8 This is what your fathers did when I sent them from Kadesh
Barnea to look over the land. 9 After they went up to the Valley of
Eshcol and viewed the land, they discouraged the Israelites from
entering the land the LORD had given them. 10 The LORD's anger was
aroused that day and he swore this oath: 11 'Because they have not
followed me wholeheartedly, not one of the men twenty years old
or more who came up out of Egypt will see the land I promised on
oath to Abraham, Isaac and Jacob— 12 not one except Caleb son of
Jephunneh the Kenizzite and Joshua son of Nun, for they followed
the LORD wholeheartedly.' 13 The LORD's anger burned against Israel
and he made them wander in the desert forty years, until the
whole generation of those who had done evil in his sight was gone.
14 "And here you are, a brood of sinners, standing in the place
of your fathers and making the LORD even more angry with Israel.
15 If you turn away from following him, he will again leave all this
people in the desert, and you will be the cause of their destruction."
16 Then they came up to him and said, "We would like to
build pens here for our livestock and cities for our women and children. 17 But we are ready to arm ourselves and go ahead of the
Israelites until we have brought them to their place. Meanwhile our
women and children will live in fortified cities, for protection from
the inhabitants of the land. 18 We will not return to our homes until
every Israelite has received his inheritance. 19 We will not receive any
inheritance with them on the other side of the Jordan, because our
inheritance has come to us on the east side of the Jordan."

a52 That is, about 420 pounds (about 190 kilograms)

32:1 *Reubenites and Gadites:* See the note at 2:10-16.

32:1 *lands of Jazer and Gilead:* Jazer's exact location is unknown (21:32), but it probably was in the same general area as Gilead, a high area of fertile grasslands east of the Jordan River (see Gen 31:21,47,48). See the map on p. 2464.

32:3,4 *Ataroth . . . Beon:* The location of many of these towns is not certain. For Heshbon, see the note at 21:25. For Dibon, see the note at 21:30. The town of Nebo is not the same as Mount Nebo, where Moses died (see Deut 34:1).

32:16,17 *build pens . . . ready to arm ourselves:* Moses and the tribes of Reuben and Gad reached a compromise. The Reuben and Gad tribes would fight in Canaan to the west of the Jordan River, but once the other tribes were settled in the land, they could come back and own the land east of the Jordan (32:20-22). See the map showing how the Israelite tribes settled the land, p. 2464.

32:8,9 Num 13:17-33. **32:10-13** Num 14:20-35.

Moses said, *"Build cities for your women and children, and pens for your flocks, but do what you have promised."*
Num 32:24

32:29 *Gilead:* See the note at 32:1.

32:33 *Manasseh . . . Sihon king of the Amorites . . . Bashan:* For Manasseh, see 1:10 and the note at 2:18-24. For more about King Sihon, see the notes at 21:21 and 21:25. For Bashan, see the note at 21:33.

32:34-37 *Gadites . . . Reubenites:* See Joshua 13:8-33 for another account of the lands given to the tribes of Reuben, Gad, and the half-tribe of Manasseh.

32:39-42 *Makir . . . Nobah:* Makir was one of Manasseh's sons (see Josh 13:30,31). This tribe (Manasseh) also owned land west of the Jordan River after the Israelites took over Canaan (Josh 17:1-13). For Amorites, see the note at 21:21. Jair was probably in the Bashan region (see Josh 13:30,31). Nobah is usually identified with the Nobah mentioned in Judges 8:11, which would place it in the region west or northwest of modern-day Amman, Jordan.

32:28-32 Josh 1:12-15. **32:31,32** Num 32:16-19.

20Then Moses said to them, "If you will do this—if you will
arm yourselves before the LORD for battle, 21and if all of you will go
armed over the Jordan before the LORD until he has driven his enemies out before him— 22then when the land is subdued before the
LORD, you may return and be free from your obligation to the
LORD and to Israel. And this land will be your possession before
the LORD.

23"But if you fail to do this, you will be sinning against the
LORD; and you may be sure that your sin will find you out. 24Build
cities for your women and children, and pens for your flocks, but
do what you have promised."

25The Gadites and Reubenites said to Moses, "We your servants will do as our lord commands. 26Our children and wives, our
flocks and herds will remain here in the cities of Gilead. 27But your
servants, every man armed for battle, will cross over to fight before
the LORD, just as our lord says."

28Then Moses gave orders about them to Eleazar the priest
and Joshua son of Nun and to the family heads of the Israelite
tribes. 29He said to them, "If the Gadites and Reubenites, every
man armed for battle, cross over the Jordan with you before the
LORD, then when the land is subdued before you, give them the
land of Gilead as their possession. 30But if they do not cross over
with you armed, they must accept their possession with you in
Canaan."

31The Gadites and Reubenites answered, "Your servants will
do what the LORD has said. 32We will cross over before the LORD
into Canaan armed, but the property we inherit will be on this side
of the Jordan."

33Then Moses gave to the Gadites, the Reubenites and the
half-tribe of Manasseh son of Joseph the kingdom of Sihon king of
the Amorites and the kingdom of Og king of Bashan—the whole
land with its cities and the territory around them.

34The Gadites built up Dibon, Ataroth, Aroer, 35Atroth Sho-
phan, Jazer, Jogbehah, 36Beth Nimrah and Beth Haran as fortified
cities, and built pens for their flocks. 37And the Reubenites rebuilt
Heshbon, Elealeh and Kiriathaim, 38as well as Nebo and Baal Meon
(these names were changed) and Sibmah. They gave names to the
cities they rebuilt.

39The descendants of Makir son of Manasseh went to Gilead,
captured it and drove out the Amorites who were there. 40So
Moses gave Gilead to the Makirites, the descendants of Manasseh,
and they settled there. 41Jair, a descendant of Manasseh, captured
their settlements and called them Havvoth Jair.[a] 42And Nobah captured Kenath and its surrounding settlements and called it Nobah
after himself.

---

[a]**41** Or *them the settlements of Jair*

Stages in Israel's Journey

33 Here are the stages in the journey of the Israelites when they
came out of Egypt by divisions under the leadership of Moses and
Aaron. 2 At the LORD's command Moses recorded the stages in their
journey. This is their journey by stages:

3 The Israelites set out from Rameses on the fifteenth day
of the first month, the day after the Passover. They marched
out boldly in full view of all the Egyptians, 4 who were burying
all their firstborn, whom the LORD had struck down among
them; for the LORD had brought judgment on their gods.
5 The Israelites left Rameses and camped at Succoth.
6 They left Succoth and camped at Etham, on the edge of
the desert.
7 They left Etham, turned back to Pi Hahiroth, to the
east of Baal Zephon, and camped near Migdol.
8 They left Pi Hahiroth[a] and passed through the sea into
the desert, and when they had traveled for three days in the
Desert of Etham, they camped at Marah.
9 They left Marah and went to Elim, where there were
twelve springs and seventy palm trees, and they camped there.
10 They left Elim and camped by the Red Sea.[b]
11 They left the Red Sea and camped in the Desert of Sin.
12 They left the Desert of Sin and camped at Dophkah.
13 They left Dophkah and camped at Alush.
14 They left Alush and camped at Rephidim, where there
was no water for the people to drink.
15 They left Rephidim and camped in the Desert of Sinai.
16 They left the Desert of Sinai and camped at Kibroth
Hattaavah.
17 They left Kibroth Hattaavah and camped at Hazeroth.
18 They left Hazeroth and camped at Rithmah.
19 They left Rithmah and camped at Rimmon Perez.
20 They left Rimmon Perez and camped at Libnah.
21 They left Libnah and camped at Rissah.
22 They left Rissah and camped at Kehelathah.
23 They left Kehelathah and camped at Mount Shepher.
24 They left Mount Shepher and camped at Haradah.
25 They left Haradah and camped at Makheloth.
26 They left Makheloth and camped at Tahath.
27 They left Tahath and camped at Terah.
28 They left Terah and camped at Mithcah.
29 They left Mithcah and camped at Hashmonah.
30 They left Hashmonah and camped at Moseroth.

33:2 *Moses recorded:* See 33:1-47 for a summary of the Israelites' forty-year journey from Egypt to the lowlands of Moab.

33:3 *Rameses . . . first month:* The city of Rameses was probably located in Goshen in the northeast part of the Nile River Delta. See the note at 9:1 (first month). See also Exod 12:1-3.

33:5-15 *Succoth . . . Desert of Sinai:* Succoth may have been near Pithom, and Pi Hahiroth may have been near Baal Zephon, an ancient temple site close to one of the lakes in northern Sinai. In Hebrew *Migdol* means "Tower," and may refer to a fort built along the northern Sinai coast, Baal Zephon. Here the Red Sea refers to the northwestern arm of the Red Sea known as the Gulf of Suez. The location of the Desert of Etham is unknown. Elim means "large trees," and is often said to be near the brook known as Gharandel. The Desert of Sinai stretches across the Sinai Peninsula between the Gulf of Suez and the Gulf of Aqaba. Rephidim was the last stopping place between the Red Sea and Mount Sinai (see Exod 17:1-7). For more, see Exod 13:17—19:1 and the map on p. 133.

33:16-37 *Desert of Sinai . . . Edom:* For a full description of these travels, see 10:11—22:1. For the Desert of Zin, see the note at 13:17-22. For a further discussion of other places mentioned here, see the notes at 13:26 and 20:14. The location of Mount Hor is not known.

---

a8 Many manuscripts of the Masoretic Text, Samaritan Pentateuch and Vulgate; most manuscripts of the Masoretic Text *left from before Hahiroth* **b10** Hebrew *Yam Suph*; that is, Sea of Reeds; also in verse 11

The LORD said to Moses, *"Take possession of the land and settle in it, for I have given you the land to possess."* Num 33:53

33:38,39 *fifth month:* Ab, the fifth month of the Hebrew calendar, falls from about mid-July to mid-August. See also the chart called "Jewish Calendar and Festivals," p. 944.

33:40 *the Negev of Canaan:* Referring to southern Canaan. See the note at 13:17-22. See also 21:1.

33:41-49 *Moab . . . Abel Shittim:* See the note at 21:29. For other locations mentioned here, see the notes at 27:12-14; 22:1; and 25:1.

33:51 *Canaan:* See the notes at 11:12 and 13:28,29, and the mini-article called "Palestine," p. 410. See also Exod 23:23-33; Deut 7:1-6; 12:2-4; and the mini-article called "Canaanite Gods and Goddesses," p. 469.

33:38,39 Num 20:22-29; Deut 10:6; 32:50. **33:54** Num 26:53-56; Josh 13:8—19:51.

31 They left Moseroth and camped at Bene Jaakan.
32 They left Bene Jaakan and camped at Hor Haggidgad.
33 They left Hor Haggidgad and camped at Jotbathah.
34 They left Jotbathah and camped at Abronah.
35 They left Abronah and camped at Ezion Geber.
36 They left Ezion Geber and camped at Kadesh, in the
Desert of Zin.
37 They left Kadesh and camped at Mount Hor, on the
border of Edom. 38 At the LORD's command Aaron the priest
went up Mount Hor, where he died on the first day of the fifth
month of the fortieth year after the Israelites came out of
Egypt. 39 Aaron was a hundred and twenty-three years old
when he died on Mount Hor.
40 The Canaanite king of Arad, who lived in the Negev of
Canaan, heard that the Israelites were coming.
41 They left Mount Hor and camped at Zalmonah.
42 They left Zalmonah and camped at Punon.
43 They left Punon and camped at Oboth.
44 They left Oboth and camped at Iye Abarim, on the
border of Moab.
45 They left Iyim[a] and camped at Dibon Gad.
46 They left Dibon Gad and camped at Almon Diblathaim.
47 They left Almon Diblathaim and camped in the
mountains of Abarim, near Nebo.
48 They left the mountains of Abarim and camped on
the plains of Moab by the Jordan across from Jericho.[b] 49 There
on the plains of Moab they camped along the Jordan from
Beth Jeshimoth to Abel Shittim.

50 On the plains of Moab by the Jordan across from Jericho
the LORD said to Moses, 51 "Speak to the Israelites and say to them:
'When you cross the Jordan into Canaan, 52 drive out all the inhabitants of the land before you. Destroy all their carved images and
their cast idols, and demolish all their high places. 53 Take possession of the land and settle in it, for I have given you the land to
possess. 54 Distribute the land by lot, according to your clans. To a
larger group give a larger inheritance, and to a smaller group a
smaller one. Whatever falls to them by lot will be theirs. Distribute
it according to your ancestral tribes.

55 " 'But if you do not drive out the inhabitants of the land,
those you allow to remain will become barbs in your eyes and
thorns in your sides. They will give you trouble in the land where
you will live. 56 And then I will do to you what I plan to do to
them.' "

[a]**45** That is, Iye Abarim [b]**48** Hebrew *Jordan of Jericho*; possibly an ancient name for the Jordan River; also in verse 50

Boundaries of Canaan

34 The LORD said to Moses, 2"Command the Israelites and say
to them: 'When you enter Canaan, the land that will be allotted to
you as an inheritance will have these boundaries:

3" 'Your southern side will include some of the Desert of Zin
along the border of Edom. On the east, your southern boundary
will start from the end of the Salt Sea,[a] 4cross south of Scorpion[b]
Pass, continue on to Zin and go south of Kadesh Barnea. Then it
will go to Hazar Addar and over to Azmon, 5where it will turn, join
the Wadi of Egypt and end at the Sea.[c]

6" 'Your western boundary will be the coast of the Great Sea.
This will be your boundary on the west.

7" 'For your northern boundary, run a line from the Great
Sea to Mount Hor 8and from Mount Hor to Lebo[d] Hamath. Then
the boundary will go to Zedad, 9continue to Ziphron and end at
Hazar Enan. This will be your boundary on the north.

10" 'For your eastern boundary, run a line from Hazar Enan
to Shepham. 11The boundary will go down from Shepham to
Riblah on the east side of Ain and continue along the slopes east of
the Sea of Kinnereth.[e] 12Then the boundary will go down along the
Jordan and end at the Salt Sea.

" 'This will be your land, with its boundaries on every side.' "

13Moses commanded the Israelites: "Assign this land by lot
as an inheritance. The LORD has ordered that it be given to the nine
and a half tribes, 14because the families of the tribe of Reuben, the
tribe of Gad and the half-tribe of Manasseh have received their
inheritance. 15These two and a half tribes have received their
inheritance on the east side of the Jordan of Jericho,[f] toward the
sunrise."

16The LORD said to Moses, 17"These are the names of the
men who are to assign the land for you as an inheritance: Eleazar
the priest and Joshua son of Nun. 18And appoint one leader from
each tribe to help assign the land. 19These are their names:

Caleb son of Jephunneh,
from the tribe of Judah;
20Shemuel son of Ammihud,
from the tribe of Simeon;
21Elidad son of Kislon,
from the tribe of Benjamin;
22Bukki son of Jogli,
the leader from the tribe of Dan;
23Hanniel son of Ephod,
the leader from the tribe of Manasseh son of Joseph;

34:2-12 *boundaries:* The borders described in these verses do not accurately describe Israel's borders at any one time in its history. Also, the land in Canaan is limited here to lands west of the Jordan River and does not include the lands promised to Reuben, Gad, and the half-tribe of Manasseh (see Num 32). The southern boundary ran from the south end of the Dead Sea southwest through the Desert of Zin (see the note at 13:17-22) through the Scorpion Pass (location unknown) to Kadesh Barnea (see the note at 13:26). Then it turned northwest following the Egyptian Gorge, probably modern Wadi el-Arish (Kadesh Barnea), ending at the Mediterranean Sea, which formed the western boundary. The northern boundary began at a point on the Mediterranean parallel to Mount Hor (not the Mount Hor where Aaron died, see 20:22) and ran east to Lebo Hamath (see the note at 13:17-22). The exact location of Zedad is unknown, but may have been northeast of Damascus. The eastern boundary went south from Hazar Enan (unknown) to the Sea of Galilee. From there it followed the Jordan River into the Salt Sea (Dead Sea). The map on p. 2464 gives one possible view of the boundaries described in these verses.

34:17,18 *Eleazar . . . Joshua . . . one leader from each tribe:* Eleazar was Aaron's son (see 20:26). For Joshua, see the note at 11:28. Other than Caleb, the leaders listed in 34:19-28 are new names who represent the new generation of Israelites who will enter Canaan. Eleazar and Joshua will lead this new generation (see 14:20-35; 27:12-23). The tribes are listed from south to north (see the map on p. 2464), except for Manasseh, which is listed before Ephraim because Manasseh was the firstborn of Joseph's two sons (Gen 41:50-52).

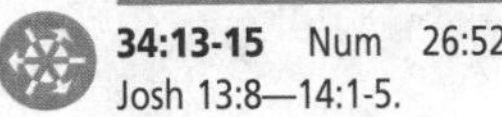
34:13-15 Num 26:52-56; 32; Josh 13:8—14:1-5.

a3 That is, the Dead Sea; also in verse 12 **b4** Hebrew *Akrabbim* **c5** That is, the Mediterranean; also in verses 6 and 7 **d8** Or *to the entrance to* **e11** That is, Galilee **f15** *Jordan of Jericho* was possibly an ancient name for the Jordan River.

35:1 *plains of Moab:* See the note at 21:29.

35:2 *give the Levites towns . . . pasturelands:* See the note at 1:47. See also Josh 21:1-42.

35:6 *cities of refuge:* These cities of refuge were set aside to protect those who accidentally killed someone. At this time in Israel's history, the male relative closest to the victim had the right to avenge the death (35:16-19). A person found guilty of murder at a trial would be taken from the city of refuge and put to death. If found innocent, the person could stay in the city of refuge, protected from the relative's revenge (35:25). For more, see the mini-article called "Cities of Refuge," p. 444. "Anyone" in 35:15 is understood as including non-Israelite strangers and those traveling through the land. See also Exod 21:12-14; Deut 4:41-43; 19:2-4; Josh 20:1-9.

24 Kemuel son of Shiphtan,
the leader from the tribe of Ephraim son of Joseph;
25 Elizaphan son of Parnach,
the leader from the tribe of Zebulun;
26 Paltiel son of Azzan,
the leader from the tribe of Issachar;
27 Ahihud son of Shelomi,
the leader from the tribe of Asher;
28 Pedahel son of Ammihud,
the leader from the tribe of Naphtali."

29 These are the men the LORD commanded to assign the inheritance to the Israelites in the land of Canaan.

Towns for the Levites

35 On the plains of Moab by the Jordan across from Jericho,[a] the LORD said to Moses, 2 "Command the Israelites to give the Levites towns to live in from the inheritance the Israelites will possess. And give them pasturelands around the towns. 3 Then they will have towns to live in and pasturelands for their cattle, flocks and all their other livestock.

4 "The pasturelands around the towns that you give the Levites will extend out fifteen hundred feet[b] from the town wall. 5 Outside the town, measure three thousand feet[c] on the east side, three thousand on the south side, three thousand on the west and three thousand on the north, with the town in the center. They will have this area as pastureland for the towns.

Cities of Refuge

6 "Six of the towns you give the Levites will be cities of refuge, to which a person who has killed someone may flee. In addition, give them forty-two other towns. 7 In all you must give the Levites forty-eight towns, together with their pasturelands. 8 The towns you give the Levites from the land the Israelites possess are to be given in proportion to the inheritance of each tribe: Take many towns from a tribe that has many, but few from one that has few."

9 Then the LORD said to Moses: 10 "Speak to the Israelites and say to them: 'When you cross the Jordan into Canaan, 11 select some towns to be your cities of refuge, to which a person who has killed someone accidentally may flee. 12 They will be places of refuge from the avenger, so that a person accused of murder may not die before he stands trial before the assembly. 13 These six towns you give will be your cities of refuge. 14 Give three on this side of the Jordan and three in Canaan as cities of refuge. 15 These

---

[a]**1** Hebrew *Jordan of Jericho*; possibly an ancient name for the Jordan River
[b]**4** Hebrew *a thousand cubits* (about 450 meters) [c]**5** Hebrew *two thousand cubits* (about 900 meters)

six towns will be a place of refuge for Israelites, aliens and any
other people living among them, so that anyone who has killed
another accidentally can flee there.
16“ ‘If a man strikes someone with an iron object so that he
dies, he is a murderer; the murderer shall be put to death. 17Or if
anyone has a stone in his hand that could kill, and he strikes someone so that he dies, he is a murderer; the murderer shall be put to
death. 18Or if anyone has a wooden object in his hand that could
kill, and he hits someone so that he dies, he is a murderer; the
murderer shall be put to death. 19The avenger of blood shall put
the murderer to death; when he meets him, he shall put him to
death. 20If anyone with malice aforethought shoves another or
throws something at him intentionally so that he dies 21or if in
hostility he hits him with his fist so that he dies, that person shall
be put to death; he is a murderer. The avenger of blood shall put
the murderer to death when he meets him.
22“ ‘But if without hostility someone suddenly shoves another or throws something at him unintentionally 23or, without seeing
him, drops a stone on him that could kill him, and he dies, then
since he was not his enemy and he did not intend to harm him,
24the assembly must judge between him and the avenger of blood
according to these regulations. 25The assembly must protect the
one accused of murder from the avenger of blood and send him
back to the city of refuge to which he fled. He must stay there until
the death of the high priest, who was anointed with the holy oil.
26“ ‘But if the accused ever goes outside the limits of the city
of refuge to which he has fled 27and the avenger of blood finds him
outside the city, the avenger of blood may kill the accused without
being guilty of murder. 28The accused must stay in his city of
refuge until the death of the high priest; only after the death of the
high priest may he return to his own property.
29“ ‘These are to be legal requirements for you throughout
the generations to come, wherever you live.
30“ ‘Anyone who kills a person is to be put to death as a murderer only on the testimony of witnesses. But no one is to be put
to death on the testimony of only one witness.
31“ ‘Do not accept a ransom for the life of a murderer, who
deserves to die. He must surely be put to death.
32“ ‘Do not accept a ransom for anyone who has fled to a city
of refuge and so allow him to go back and live on his own land
before the death of the high priest.
33“ ‘Do not pollute the land where you are. Bloodshed pollutes the land, and atonement cannot be made for the land on
which blood has been shed, except by the blood of the one who
shed it. 34Do not defile the land where you live and where I dwell,
for I, the LORD, dwell among the Israelites.’ ”

35:28 *death of the high priest:* The shedding of blood, whether accidental or intentional, was against God's Law (Exod 20:13) and polluted the land (Gen 4:10,11; Num 35:33). Penalties had to be paid and sacrifices offered to make the person and the land clean again (see Exod 21:12-36; Lev 4:1—5:19). The high priest's death was considered sufficient payment for the blood of victims who were killed while he was high priest. See also Deut 17:5-7; 19:15.

36:1-4 *Gilead . . . property will be taken:* Gilead was a grandson of Joseph's son Manasseh. The Gilead clan leaders spoke with Moses about his ruling concerning the daughters of Zelophehad (27:1-11). They were worried that daughters who married outside their clan would transfer land to the husbands' clans.

36:4-9 *Year of Jubilee . . . inheritance:* This sacred year for Israel occurred every fiftieth year, after seven cycles of seven years each (see Lev 25:8-55). During this year, all property had to go back to its original owner. But here, if a daughter married outside the tribe, the property belonged to her husband's tribe and so could not be returned. To protect the Manasseh tribe from losing the land given to Zelophehad's daughters, Moses made the daughters marry men from one of the Manasseh clans. Then the rule was made to apply to all daughters who inherited land (36:8, 9).

Inheritance of Zelophehad's Daughters

36 The family heads of the clan of Gilead son of Makir, the son
of Manasseh, who were from the clans of the descendants of
Joseph, came and spoke before Moses and the leaders, the heads of
the Israelite families. 2They said, "When the LORD commanded my
lord to give the land as an inheritance to the Israelites by lot, he
ordered you to give the inheritance of our brother Zelophehad to
his daughters. 3Now suppose they marry men from other Israelite
tribes; then their inheritance will be taken from our ancestral
inheritance and added to that of the tribe they marry into. And so
part of the inheritance allotted to us will be taken away. 4When the
Year of Jubilee for the Israelites comes, their inheritance will be
added to that of the tribe into which they marry, and their property
will be taken from the tribal inheritance of our forefathers."

5Then at the LORD's command Moses gave this order to the
Israelites: "What the tribe of the descendants of Joseph is saying is
right. 6This is what the LORD commands for Zelophehad's daughters:
They may marry anyone they please as long as they marry
within the tribal clan of their father. 7No inheritance in Israel is to
pass from tribe to tribe, for every Israelite shall keep the tribal land
inherited from his forefathers. 8Every daughter who inherits land

QUESTIONS ABOUT NUMBERS 22:1—36:13

1. Why did King Balak and the Midianite leaders hire the prophet Balaam? (22:1—24:25) Did Balak get what he expected from Balaam? Summarize the key points of Balaam's four messages.
2. What happened at the camp at Shittim that made the LORD angry with the Israelites? (chapter 25) Which of the Ten Commandments (see Exod 20:1-17) was being broken here? How was the problem resolved and what was the lasting effect of the sin committed by the Israelite men?
3. Forty years passed between the first census of the Israelite people (chapter 1) and the second census. (chapter 26) What had happened to the older generation of Israelites that had come out of Egypt?
4. Who were the daughters of Zelophehad, and what did they want? (27:1-11) What was God's response to their request? How was this ruling adjusted later? (chapter 36)
5. How important was the offering of sacrifices to God to the Israelites in daily life, worship, and special feasts? (chapters 28, 29) How important in daily life are offerings, worship, and religious ceremonies today?
6. Describe the Israelites' battle with the Midianites. (chapter 31) What happened to the Midianites' lands? Read the note at 31:9-18. What is your reaction to the concept of a "Holy War"? Explain.
7. What did the men from the tribes of Reuben and Gad want, and how did Moses respond to their request? (chapter 32) What other tribe was included in Moses' decision?
8. Why were towns given to the Levites? (35:1-8) What were the cities of refuge, and what did they have to do with the laws about accidental killing or murder? (35:9-15)
9. Think of NUMBERS as a family travel album or diary with pictures. What pictures from this album stand out in your mind? Are there any pictures you would not want to show other people? Why or why not?

in any Israelite tribe must marry someone in her father's tribal
clan, so that every Israelite will possess the inheritance of his
fathers. 9No inheritance may pass from tribe to tribe, for each
Israelite tribe is to keep the land it inherits."
10So Zelophehad's daughters did as the LORD commanded
Moses. 11Zelophehad's daughters—Mahlah, Tirzah, Hoglah, Milcah and Noah—married their cousins on their father's side. 12They
married within the clans of the descendants of Manasseh son of
Joseph, and their inheritance remained in their father's clan and
tribe.
13These are the commands and regulations the LORD gave
through Moses to the Israelites on the plains of Moab by the Jordan across from Jericho.[a]

36:10,11 Num 27:1. **36:13** Num 22:1; 26:3; 33:48-50; Deut 34:1,8.

[a]**13** Hebrew *Jordan of Jericho*; possibly an ancient name for the Jordan River

DEUTERONOMY

Was Deuteronomy the ancient Book of the Law discovered in the temple during the reign of King Josiah? If so, it may have been the first book of the Bible to be recognized as Holy Scripture. Listen as Moses speaks powerful words about God's Law to the people of Israel.

Moses: Moses led the Hebrew people, the Israelites, out of slavery in Egypt, received the Law of the LORD at Mount Sinai, and led the people in battle during their time of wandering in the desert. As DEUTERONOMY begins, Moses is nearing the end of his life, and he knows he will not be able to enter the promised land of Canaan (1:37). For more, see the mini-article called "Moses," p. 2335.

Throughout DEUTERONOMY Moses speaks the words of God in much the same way that Israel's prophets would speak God's messages to the people. His speeches contain words of warning and judgment, as well as words of promise and blessing.

Israel: In Hebrew, one meaning of "Israel" is "one who wrestles with God" as when the name of Jacob, the grandson of Abraham, was changed to Israel (Gen 32:28; 35:9-12). The descendants of Abraham then became known as the people of Israel or Israelites. God promised to give the land of Canaan to Abraham and his descendants (Gen 17:7, 8). When Moses delivers the speeches in DEUTERONOMY, the Israelites are preparing to cross into the promised land. For more, see the mini-article called "Israel," p. 264.

WHAT MAKES DEUTERONOMY SPECIAL?

DEUTERONOMY comes from a Greek word meaning *second law.* Those who prepared the Greek version of the Old Testament (the Septuagint) thought the copy of God's law mentioned in Deuteronomy 17:18 was a *second law.* But DEUTERONOMY is not to be understood as a *second law.* Rather, it is a retelling or renewal of the Law God gave Moses on Mount Sinai. The Hebrew title of the book, *"These are the words (that Moses spoke),"* more correctly sums up what DEUTERONOMY is all about. The "words" are a series of speeches that Moses made to the people of Israel before his death.

DEUTERONOMY is located at an important place in the Old Testament. It is the fifth and concluding book in the section of the Bible known as "The Law," or *Torah*, which means *"teaching"* (see also the Introduction to the Pentateuch, p. 35). It continues the story of God's people that began in EXODUS. The LORD chose the people of Israel, brought them out of slavery in Egypt, and at Sinai gave to them and their leader Moses the laws and commandments that they were to live by. In this way, DEUTERONOMY looks backward, emphasizing what the LORD has already done. But the words of Moses also look forward and are meant to be teaching for future generations as well. God's covenant with the people of Israel, as presented in DEUTERONOMY, forms the basis of and provides an introduction to the history of Israel found in the books of JOSHUA, JUDGES, 1 and 2 SAMUEL, and 1 and 2 KINGS.

WHY WAS DEUTERONOMY WRITTEN?

DEUTERONOMY is presented as Moses' last words to the generation of Israelites who are ready to enter the promised land. Though Moses has traditionally been seen as the book's author, some scholars believe the final form of the book also applies the traditions of Moses and the Law to the religious and political situations of a later time. This is done in two ways. First, Israel can use the message of DEUTERONOMY to judge its national successes and failures: Obeying the terms of God's covenant with Israel will result in good fortune; disobedience will bring death and destruction. Second, DEUTERONOMY repeats this key point throughout the book: God has chosen Israel out of love, so Israel should respond to this love by loving God in return and by remaining faithful to the terms of God's covenant with them.

What's the story behind the scene?

Second Kings tells the story of a great reform in Israel in 621 B.C. (2 Kgs 22,23). While workers were repairing the temple in Jerusalem, they found the Book of the Law. When King Josiah of Judah heard what it had to say, he tore his clothes in sorrow and called together the older leaders of the people. Josiah realized that the people had not been following the Law, so he ordered reforms suggested by the Book. These reforms included breaking down and burning all the altars, shrines, and high places honoring gods other than the Lord God of Israel. Most biblical scholars believe that Josiah's Book of the Law was the book we know as Deuteronomy, or at least its middle section (Deut 12–26).

Where did the Book of the Law come from, and how did it end up in storage in the temple? This is not clear. Some scholars think that the ancient writings were brought to Jerusalem by Levite priests who were running away from Assyrian persecution in the north sometime during the reign of Manasseh (687-642 B.C.). What does this have to say about when Deuteronomy was written? Though much of the material in Deuteronomy may date back to the time of Moses, it was likely put in its present form by later scribes and editors.

How is Deuteronomy constructed?

The following outline divides the book into five sections, based primarily on the speeches of Moses:

Setting the scene (1:1-8)

The first speech: Moses reviews the past (1:9—4:43)
- God's faithfulness in the desert (1:9—3:29)
- Challenge to hear the word of the Lord (4:1-43)

The second speech: Moses tells what the Lord demands (4:44—28:68)
- Love God and obey God's laws (4:44—11:32)
- How to live as God's people (12:1—26:15)
- Renewing the covenant (26:16—28:68)

The third speech: Israel must keep its covenant with the Lord (29:1—30:20)

Final speeches and the death of Moses (31:1—34:12)
- A leader for the people and a place for the Law (31:1-29)
- The song and the blessing of Moses (31:30—33:29)
- Moses dies (34:1-12)

Mezuzah: The word means doorpost. Many Jews today continue the practice of memorizing the Law (Scripture), placing verses in containers and attaching them to the doorposts of their houses. See the note at 6:6-8. The importance of the Law is a key theme in Deuteronomy.

Jordan, Heshbon, Paran, Horeb, and Moab: See the maps on pp. 2463-2465 for the location of the many places mentioned in 1:1-5. The Jordan River flows south from Mount Hermon into the Dead Sea. It separates the eastern and western sides of Canaan. Paran is a desert area west of Edom, north of Sinai, and south of Judah. But the location of the towns of Paran, Suph, Tophel, Laban, Hazeroth, and Dizahab are not known.

Heshbon was the capital city of the land of the Amorites. The region of Bashan was an area known for its rich pastures, forests, and herds of cattle (Ps 22:12; Isa 2:13; Ezek 27:6; Amos 4:1; Zech 11:2). Ashtaroth and Edrei were located in Bashan, east of the Sea of Galilee and north of Ramoth. Moab was a strip of fertile land between the east side of the Dead Sea and the desert.

Horeb is another name for Mount Sinai, sometimes called the "holy mountain" because this is where God gave the Ten Commandments and the rest of the laws to Moses and the people (Exod 19–40). The mountain is located somewhere on the large, dry Sinai Peninsula, but the exact location is uncertain (see the map on p. 2463 for possible locations).

Kadesh Barnea, also known as Kadesh, probably refers to an oasis located about fifty miles south of Beersheba in the Desert of Zin (Num 20:1), which borders the Desert of Paran on the north. Edom was the area directly south of the Dead Sea, and stood between the Desert of Zin and the land of Moab. Within the hills of Edom was a road that ran its entire length, called the Mount Seir road. The people of Edom were descendants of Jacob's brother Esau (Gen 25:24-26; 36:1). The nation of Edom is usually described in the Bible as an enemy of Israel (Num 24:18; 2 Sam 8:13,14; Isa 34:5-17).

1:1 *Moses spoke to all Israel:* See the note on p. 340 (Moses).

1:1-5 *Jordan . . . Paran . . . Horeb . . . Heshbon . . . Moab:* See the note on p. 341 (Jordan . . . Moab).

1:3 *fortieth year . . . eleventh month:* The number "forty" is an important number in the Bible. It stands for a long period of time or for a generation. See the chart called "Numbers in the Bible" p. 2405. Here it refers to the fortieth year after Israel had left Egypt. The story of Moses leading the Hebrew people out of Egypt and through the desert is told in detail in Exodus 13–40 and Numbers 1–36. The Israelites were about to enter Canaan, but they would have entered the land from Kadesh Barnea forty years earlier if they had not rebelled against God (Num 14:1-45; Deut 1:26-45). For more, see the article called "The Ancient World: Peoples, Powers, and Politics," p. 919.

The eleventh month of the Hebrew calendar is the Shebat, which runs from about mid-January to mid-February. See also the chart called "Jewish Calendar and Festivals," p. 944.

1:3-5 *Lord . . . this law:* See the mini-article called "Lord (YHWH)," p. 140.

The "law" here refers to the Law of Moses, which includes the Ten Commandments and other laws that God gave Moses on Mount Sinai (see Exod 19–40). See also the mini-articles called "Covenants (Agreements)," p. 386, and "Law," p. 1160.

1:4 *Sihon king of the Amorites . . . Og king of Bashan:* King Sihon did not want the Israelites to pass through the land of the Amorites on their way to Canaan. He joined with King Og to try to stop the Israelites, but the Israelites defeated their combined armies (Num 21:21-35). The territories of King Sihon and King Og were divided among several of the tribes of Israel (Num 32:33,34; Josh 13). For more about Heshbon and Bashan, see the note on p. 341 (Jordan . . . Moab).

Mount Sinai. Jebel Musa, a tall mountain in the Jebel Safsafa range in the southern part of the Sinai Peninsula, is the mountain most often considered to be the Mount Sinai of the Bible. It was at Mount Sinai that Moses received the Law from the Lord after he had led the people out of slavery in Egypt. Deuteronomy is made up of a number of sermons Moses gave to explain the Law while the people were still living in the desert.

Setting the Scene

This brief introduction sets the scene for the rest of Deuteronomy. As the book begins, the people of Israel are camped in the territory of Moab east of the Jordan River, forty years after having left a life of slavery in Egypt.

The Command to Leave Horeb

1 These are the words Moses spoke to all Israel in the desert east
of the Jordan—that is, in the Arabah—opposite Suph, between
Paran and Tophel, Laban, Hazeroth and Dizahab. 2(It takes eleven
days to go from Horeb to Kadesh Barnea by the Mount Seir road.)
3In the fortieth year, on the first day of the eleventh month,
Moses proclaimed to the Israelites all that the Lord had commanded him concerning them. 4This was after he had defeated
Sihon king of the Amorites, who reigned in Heshbon, and at Edrei
had defeated Og king of Bashan, who reigned in Ashtaroth.

5East of the Jordan in the territory of Moab, Moses began to
expound this law, saying:

6The Lord our God said to us at Horeb, "You have stayed
long enough at this mountain. 7Break camp and advance into the
hill country of the Amorites; go to all the neighboring peoples in
the Arabah, in the mountains, in the western foothills, in the
Negev and along the coast, to the land of the Canaanites and to
Lebanon, as far as the great river, the Euphrates. 8See, I have given

you this land. Go in and take possession of the land that the LORD
swore he would give to your fathers—to Abraham, Isaac and
Jacob—and to their descendants after them."

The First Speech: Moses Reviews the Past

Moses' first speech reviews Israel's desert journey from Mount Sinai to where they are now camping in the plains of Moab. As they are preparing to cross the Jordan River into the promised land of Canaan, Moses tells the people that they must obey the LORD and not worship idols.

GOD'S FAITHFULNESS IN THE DESERT

Moses describes how the first generation of Israelites that came out of Egypt were unfaithful during the forty years they wandered in the desert. That generation had died in the desert as a result of all their grumbling and rebellion (1:34-36). Even so, God remained faithful to the people of Israel, giving them what they needed to survive and helping them to defeat their enemies.

The Appointment of Leaders

9 At that time I said to you, "You are too heavy a burden for
me to carry alone. 10 The LORD your God has increased your numbers so that today you are as many as the stars in the sky. 11 May
the LORD, the God of your fathers, increase you a thousand times
and bless you as he has promised! 12 But how can I bear your problems and your burdens and your disputes all by myself? 13 Choose
some wise, understanding and respected men from each of your
tribes, and I will set them over you."

14 You answered me, "What you propose to do is good."

15 So I took the leading men of your tribes, wise and respected men, and appointed them to have authority over you—as commanders of thousands, of hundreds, of fifties and of tens and as
tribal officials. 16 And I charged your judges at that time: Hear the
disputes between your brothers and judge fairly, whether the case
is between brother Israelites or between one of them and an alien.
17 Do not show partiality in judging; hear both small and great
alike. Do not be afraid of any man, for judgment belongs to God.
Bring me any case too hard for you, and I will hear it. 18 And at that
time I told you everything you were to do.

Spies Sent Out

19 Then, as the LORD our God commanded us, we set out
from Horeb and went toward the hill country of the Amorites
through all that vast and dreadful desert that you have seen, and so
we reached Kadesh Barnea. 20 Then I said to you, "You have reached

1:6 *The LORD our God:* This phrase occurs almost three hundred times in DEUTERONOMY. See also the note at 1:3-5.

1:6,7 *mountain . . . camp:* Forty years earlier, the Israelites had camped by Horeb (Mount Sinai, see Num 11:11-13). See also the note on p. 341 (Jordan . . . Moab).

1:7,8 *Amorites . . . Canaanites . . . Abraham, Isaac and Jacob:* The Amorites lived in the hill country of Canaan at the time the Israelites came into the land (Num 21:21-35; Josh 2:10). The Canaanites lived in the land God promised to give Abraham and his descendants (Gen 15:18-21; 17:7,8). See the map on p. 2464.

In Hebrew "Abraham" sounds like "ancestor of many" (Gen 17:4,5). God promised Abraham that his descendants would form a great nation (Gen 12:1-3; 15:4-6). This promise was repeated to Isaac, Abraham and Sarah's son (Gen 26:2-4), and again to Jacob, Abraham's grandson (Gen 28:13; 35:9-12).

1:10 *increased your numbers:* God's promised blessing (Gen 15:5) resulted in a growing Israelite population that was becoming too big for Moses to lead alone.

1:15-17 *leading men:* The leaders were older men who were in charge of the clans in each tribe (Exod 18:13-25). "Officials" (1:15) have a variety of civil and military duties. Judges (1:16) have the duty of deciding disputes. Even aliens, those who were not part of the Israelite people, are to be treated fairly. Only the most difficult cases are to be brought to Moses (1:17).

1:19-21 *the LORD our God:* See the note at 1:6.

1:19 *Horeb . . . Kadesh Barnea:* Horeb is another name for Mount Sinai. See the note on p. 341 (Jordan . . . Moab).

1:19-21 *Amorites:* See the note at 1:7,8.

the hill country of the Amorites, which the LORD our God is giving us. 21 See, the LORD your God has given you the land. Go up and
take possession of it as the LORD, the God of your fathers, told you.
Do not be afraid; do not be discouraged."

22 Then all of you came to me and said, "Let us send men
ahead to spy out the land for us and bring back a report about the
route we are to take and the towns we will come to."

23 The idea seemed good to me; so I selected twelve of you,
one man from each tribe. 24 They left and went up into the hill
country, and came to the Valley of Eshcol and explored it. 25 Taking
with them some of the fruit of the land, they brought it down to us
and reported, "It is a good land that the LORD our God is giving us."

Rebellion Against the LORD

26 But you were unwilling to go up; you rebelled against the
command of the LORD your God. 27 You grumbled in your tents
and said, "The LORD hates us; so he brought us out of Egypt to
deliver us into the hands of the Amorites to destroy us. 28 Where
can we go? Our brothers have made us lose heart. They say, 'The
people are stronger and taller than we are; the cities are large, with
walls up to the sky. We even saw the Anakites there.' "

29 Then I said to you, "Do not be terrified; do not be afraid of
them. 30 The LORD your God, who is going before you, will fight for
you, as he did for you in Egypt, before your very eyes, 31 and in the
desert. There you saw how the LORD your God carried you, as a father
carries his son, all the way you went until you reached this place."

32 In spite of this, you did not trust in the LORD your God,
33 who went ahead of you on your journey, in fire by night and in
a cloud by day, to search out places for you to camp and to show
you the way you should go.

34 When the LORD heard what you said, he was angry and
solemnly swore: 35 "Not a man of this evil generation shall see the
good land I swore to give your forefathers, 36 except Caleb son of
Jephunneh. He will see it, and I will give him and his descendants
the land he set his feet on, because he followed the LORD wholeheartedly."

37 Because of you the LORD became angry with me also and
said, "You shall not enter it, either. 38 But your assistant, Joshua son
of Nun, will enter it. Encourage him, because he will lead Israel to
inherit it. 39 And the little ones that you said would be taken captive, your children who do not yet know good from bad—they will
enter the land. I will give it to them and they will take possession
of it. 40 But as for you, turn around and set out toward the desert
along the route to the Red Sea.[a]"

41 Then you replied, "We have sinned against the LORD. We

[a]**40** Hebrew *Yam Suph*; that is, Sea of Reeds

1:23 *twelve . . . one man from each tribe:* The twelve men are named in Numbers 13:3-15. Israel was made up of twelve tribes descended from the twelve sons of Jacob. The promised land was eventually divided up among these twelve tribes. The tribe of Joseph was divided into two tribes representing his sons, Ephraim and Manasseh. That would make thirteen, but the Bible always counts only twelve. The tribe of Levi is not counted, because it was not given land in Canaan (Num 35:1-8; Deut 10:9; Josh 21:1-42).

1:26-28 *you rebelled:* The Israelites refused to take possession of the land the LORD gave them (1:20,21). Their fear was stronger than their memory of God's power. The tragic story is told in Numbers 14. See also 9:23; Heb 3:16.

1:28 *Anakites:* See the note at 2:10,11.

1:30-32 *LORD your God . . . will fight for you:* God brought disasters and death upon the Egyptians to force them to release the Israelites from slavery (Exod 7:14—15:21). As the people made their way through the desert, God continued to care for them (Exod 15:22—18:27). When it came to entering this new land, however, they failed to trust that God would do as he promised.

1:33 *fire . . . cloud:* Clouds, fire, and smoke often signal the presence of God in the Bible (Gen 15:17, 18; Exod 3:1-6; 19:16-19; 24:15-18; Judg 13:20). They are connected with God's glory, a visible reminder that God was with the people. See also Exod 13:20-22; 14:19,20; 40:34-38; Num 9:15-23.

1:35 *this evil generation:* The first generation of Israelites who left Egypt but rebelled against the LORD in the desert (Num 14:26-30).

1:31 Acts 13:18. **1:32** Heb 3:16-19.

will go up and fight, as the LORD our God commanded us." So
every one of you put on his weapons, thinking it easy to go up into
the hill country.
42But the LORD said to me, "Tell them, 'Do not go up and
fight, because I will not be with you. You will be defeated by your
enemies.' "
43So I told you, but you would not listen. You rebelled
against the LORD's command and in your arrogance you marched
up into the hill country. 44The Amorites who lived in those hills
came out against you; they chased you like a swarm of bees and
beat you down from Seir all the way to Hormah. 45You came back
and wept before the LORD, but he paid no attention to your weeping and turned a deaf ear to you. 46And so you stayed in Kadesh
many days—all the time you spent there.

Wanderings in the Desert

2 Then we turned back and set out toward the desert along the
route to the Red Sea,[a] as the LORD had directed me. For a long time
we made our way around the hill country of Seir.
2Then the LORD said to me, 3"You have made your way around
this hill country long enough; now turn north. 4Give the people these
orders: 'You are about to pass through the territory of your brothers
the descendants of Esau, who live in Seir. They will be afraid of you,
but be very careful. 5Do not provoke them to war, for I will not give
you any of their land, not even enough to put your foot on. I have
given Esau the hill country of Seir as his own. 6You are to pay them
in silver for the food you eat and the water you drink.' "
7The LORD your God has blessed you in all the work of your
hands. He has watched over your journey through this vast desert.
These forty years the LORD your God has been with you, and you
have not lacked anything.
8So we went on past our brothers the descendants of Esau,
who live in Seir. We turned from the Arabah road, which comes up
from Elath and Ezion Geber, and traveled along the desert road of
Moab.
9Then the LORD said to me, "Do not harass the Moabites or
provoke them to war, for I will not give you any part of their land.
I have given Ar to the descendants of Lot as a possession."
10(The Emites used to live there—a people strong and
numerous, and as tall as the Anakites. 11Like the Anakites, they too
were considered Rephaites, but the Moabites called them Emites.
12Horites used to live in Seir, but the descendants of Esau drove
them out. They destroyed the Horites from before them and settled in their place, just as Israel did in the land the LORD gave them
as their possession.)

[a]1 Hebrew *Yam Suph*; that is, Sea of Reeds

1:35 *good land:* See the note at 1:7,8.

1:36-38 *Caleb . . . Joshua:* Caleb and Joshua encouraged the people to trust God and enter Canaan (Num 13:25—14:10). Caleb and his descendants were later given some of the best land in Canaan (Josh 14:6-14). Joshua was chosen to lead the people of Israel (31:3). See also the note at 3:28 (Joshua). Moses cannot enter the promised land because he had sinned (Num 20:1-12). See also 32:48-52.

1:40 *Red Sea:* Here "Red Sea" probably refers to the Gulf of Aqabah, since the term is extended to include the northeastern arm of the Red Sea (see the map on p. 2463).

1:44 *Amorites:* See the note at 1:7,8.

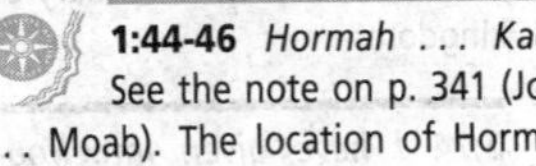
1:44-46 *Hormah . . . Kadesh:* See the note on p. 341 (Jordan . . . Moab). The location of Hormah is uncertain.

2:3-19 *turn north . . . Do not provoke them:* The LORD had warned the Israelites not to create a conflict with the Edomites (2:4-7), the Moabites (2:8,9), or the Ammonites (2:18,19).

2:7 *These forty years:* See the note at 1:3.

2:8,9 *Elath . . . Ar:* Archaeologists think that Elath was another name for Ezion Geber, a port city in Edom. For Moab, see the note at 1:1-5. Ar was one of the main cities of Moab (Num 21:28; Isa 15:1), but here it refers to all of Moab.

2:10,11 *Emites . . . Anakites . . . Rephaites:* May refer to a group or groups of very tall people that lived in or near Canaan before the Israelites. See 1:28; Deut 2:20; see also Num 13:33.

2:12 *Horites . . . Seir:* The Hebrew word *hor* means "cave," so the Horites may have been cave-dwelling people in Seir (another name for Edom).

2:13-19 *Zered Valley . . . Kadesh Barnea . . . Moab . . . Ammonites:* See the map on p. 2463. See also Gen 19:38 and the note on p. 341 (Jordan . . . Moab).

2:14 *Thirty-eight years passed:* God made the Israelites wander for forty years as punishment for their rebellion (2:7; Num 14:27-35). See also the note at 1:3.

2:20-22 *Rephaites . . . Ammonites . . . Zamzummites:* See the notes at 2:3-19; 2:10,11; and 2:13-19. The exact meaning of "Zamzummites" is uncertain.

2:23 *Avvites:* Little is known about the Avvite peoples who lived in Gaza (see the map on p. 2462).

2:24 *Arnon Gorge:* This formed the northern boundary of Moab's territory and the southern boundary of Sihon's kingdom.

2:24 *I have given into your hand:* See the note at 3:6.

2:26-29 *desert of Kedemoth:* The desert of Kedemoth was east of the Dead Sea and Jordan River, and south of Heshbon (see the map on p. 2465).

2:29 *the LORD our God:* See the note at 1:6.

2:30 *The LORD . . . made his spirit stubborn:* Just as the LORD had made Egypt's king stubborn (Exod 4:21), the LORD causes Sihon to be stubborn and eager to fight the Israelites. See also Num 21:21-35.

2:32–37 *Jahaz . . . Gilead:* The location of Jahaz is unknown. Gilead was a high area of fertile grasslands east of the Jordan River (Gen 31:21,47,48). See also the map on p. 2467.

2:19 Gen 19:38.

13 And the LORD said, "Now get up and cross the Zered Valley." So we crossed the valley.
14 Thirty-eight years passed from the time we left Kadesh
Barnea until we crossed the Zered Valley. By then, that entire generation of fighting men had perished from the camp, as the LORD
had sworn to them. 15 The LORD's hand was against them until he
had completely eliminated them from the camp.
16 Now when the last of these fighting men among the people
had died, 17 the LORD said to me, 18 "Today you are to pass by the
region of Moab at Ar. 19 When you come to the Ammonites, do not
harass them or provoke them to war, for I will not give you possession of any land belonging to the Ammonites. I have given it as
a possession to the descendants of Lot."
20 (That too was considered a land of the Rephaites, who
used to live there; but the Ammonites called them Zamzummites.
21 They were a people strong and numerous, and as tall as the
Anakites. The LORD destroyed them from before the Ammonites,
who drove them out and settled in their place. 22 The LORD had
done the same for the descendants of Esau, who lived in Seir, when
he destroyed the Horites from before them. They drove them out
and have lived in their place to this day. 23 And as for the Avvites
who lived in villages as far as Gaza, the Caphtorites coming out
from Caphtor[a] destroyed them and settled in their place.)

Defeat of Sihon King of Heshbon

24 "Set out now and cross the Arnon Gorge. See, I have given
into your hand Sihon the Amorite, king of Heshbon, and his country. Begin to take possession of it and engage him in battle. 25 This
very day I will begin to put the terror and fear of you on all the
nations under heaven. They will hear reports of you and will tremble and be in anguish because of you."
26 From the desert of Kedemoth I sent messengers to Sihon
king of Heshbon offering peace and saying, 27 "Let us pass through
your country. We will stay on the main road; we will not turn aside
to the right or to the left. 28 Sell us food to eat and water to drink
for their price in silver. Only let us pass through on foot— 29 as the
descendants of Esau, who live in Seir, and the Moabites, who live
in Ar, did for us—until we cross the Jordan into the land the LORD
our God is giving us." 30 But Sihon king of Heshbon refused to let
us pass through. For the LORD your God had made his spirit stubborn and his heart obstinate in order to give him into your hands,
as he has now done.
31 The LORD said to me, "See, I have begun to deliver Sihon
and his country over to you. Now begin to conquer and possess
his land."

[a]**23** That is, Crete

32When Sihon and all his army came out to meet us in battle
at Jahaz, 33the LORD our God delivered him over to us and we struck
him down, together with his sons and his whole army. 34At that time
we took all his towns and completely destroyed[a] them—men,
women and children. We left no survivors. 35But the livestock and
the plunder from the towns we had captured we carried off for ourselves. 36From Aroer on the rim of the Arnon Gorge, and from the
town in the gorge, even as far as Gilead, not one town was too strong
for us. The LORD our God gave us all of them. 37But in accordance
with the command of the LORD our God, you did not encroach on
any of the land of the Ammonites, neither the land along the course
of the Jabbok nor that around the towns in the hills.

Defeat of Og King of Bashan

3 Next we turned and went up along the road toward Bashan,
and Og king of Bashan with his whole army marched out to meet
us in battle at Edrei. 2The LORD said to me, "Do not be afraid of
him, for I have handed him over to you with his whole army and
his land. Do to him what you did to Sihon king of the Amorites,
who reigned in Heshbon."
3So the LORD our God also gave into our hands Og king of
Bashan and all his army. We struck them down, leaving no survivors. 4At that time we took all his cities. There was not one of the
sixty cities that we did not take from them—the whole region of
Argob, Og's kingdom in Bashan. 5All these cities were fortified
with high walls and with gates and bars, and there were also a great
many unwalled villages. 6We completely destroyed[a] them, as we
had done with Sihon king of Heshbon, destroying[a] every city—
men, women and children. 7But all the livestock and the plunder
from their cities we carried off for ourselves.
8So at that time we took from these two kings of the Amorites the territory east of the Jordan, from the Arnon Gorge as far
as Mount Hermon. 9(Hermon is called Sirion by the Sidonians; the
Amorites call it Senir.) 10We took all the towns on the plateau, and
all Gilead, and all Bashan as far as Salecah and Edrei, towns of Og's
kingdom in Bashan. 11(Only Og king of Bashan was left of the
remnant of the Rephaites. His bed[b] was made of iron and was
more than thirteen feet long and six feet wide.[c] It is still in Rabbah
of the Ammonites.)

Division of the Land

12Of the land that we took over at that time, I gave the
Reubenites and the Gadites the territory north of Aroer by the

[a]**34,6** The Hebrew term refers to the irrevocable giving over of things or persons to the LORD, often by totally destroying them. [b]**11** Or *sarcophagus* [c]**11** Hebrew *nine cubits long and four cubits wide* (about 4 meters long and 1.8 meters wide)

2:34 *completely destroyed them . . . no survivors:* According to 20:16 and Leviticus 27:28,29 all people and animals captured in a holy war were to be destroyed (see also the notes at 3:6 and 7:2).

3:1,2 *Og . . . Sihon:* See the note at 1:4.

3:3-10 *Argob . . . Edrei:* The Argob region east of the Jordan River formed part of the kingdom of Og. Mount Hermon is over 9,200 feet high. Salecah marked the eastern boundary of Bashan. See the notes on p. 341 (Jordan . . . Moab) and at 1:7,8. See also the maps on pp. 2464-2465.

3:6 *destroyed:* The complete destruction of a city and its people provided stunning evidence of the LORD's power. It also served another practical purpose. Any person or object that might turn the Israelites away from worshiping the LORD God was to be destroyed. See also the mini-article called "Holy War (The LORD's Battles)," p. 306.

3:11 *bed . . . thirteen feet long:* The size of the king's bed supports the idea that the Rephaites were large people (see the note at 2:10,11). Rabbah bordered the Ammonite territory.

3:12 *Reubenites . . . Gadites:* These tribes were descendants of Abraham's grandson Jacob (Israel). Reuben was Jacob and Leah's first son (Gen 29:31). Gad was the first son of Jacob and Leah's maid Zilpah (Gen 30:9-11). See also the notes on p. 340 (Moses, Israel) and at 1:23.

3:12-17 *Arnon Gorge . . . slopes of Pisgah:* See the note at 2:24 (Arnon Gorge). These are the areas given to the Reuben and Gad tribes (see the map on p. 2464). Kinnereth is another name for the Sea of Galilee. The Sea of the Arabah and the Salt Sea are other names for the Dead Sea. Mount Pisgah is probably one of the mountains north of Mount Nebo.

3:13-15 *Manasseh . . . Jair . . . Makir:* Manasseh received a blessing from his grandfather Jacob (Gen 48:12-22). Jair and Makir were the sons of Manasseh. The Makir clan was part of the Manasseh tribe. Here, they represent one-half of the tribe of Manasseh. See also Num 32:39-42 and the notes on p. 340 (Moses, Israel) and at 1:23.

3:18-20 *at that time . . . until the* LORD *gives rest to your brothers:* The tribes of Reuben, Gad, and the half tribe of Manasseh were to help the armies of the other tribes to conquer Canaan. See also Josh 1:12-15.

3:21,22 *the* LORD *your God . . . will fight for you:* See the notes at 1:6; 2:34; and 3:6.

3:23-26 *I pleaded:* Moses was not allowed to enter the promised land of Canaan (Num 20:1-13; see also Deut 1:37; 32:49-52).

3:25-29 *beyond the Jordan . . . Beth Peor:* Canaan lay west of the Jordan River. Moses was allowed to see Canaan from the top of Mount Nebo (32:48-52; Num 27:12-14; 33:47). Beth Peor was located about twenty miles east of the north end of the Dead Sea. See the map on p. 2464.

3:28 *Joshua:* Joshua was on Mount Sinai (Horeb) when Moses received the Law (Exod 32:17). He was a military general (Exod 17:8-13) and one of the spies Moses sent into Canaan (see Num 13:8, where he is called Hoshea). See also 34:9.

Arnon Gorge, including half the hill country of Gilead, together with its towns. 13 The rest of Gilead and also all of Bashan, the kingdom of Og, I gave to the half tribe of Manasseh. (The whole region of Argob in Bashan used to be known as a land of the Rephaites. 14 Jair, a descendant of Manasseh, took the whole region of Argob as far as the border of the Geshurites and the Maacathites; it was named after him, so that to this day Bashan is called Havvoth Jair.[a]) 15 And I gave Gilead to Makir. 16 But to the Reubenites and the Gadites I gave the territory extending from Gilead down to the Arnon Gorge (the middle of the gorge being the border) and out to the Jabbok River, which is the border of the Ammonites. 17 Its western border was the Jordan in the Arabah, from Kinnereth to the Sea of the Arabah (the Salt Sea[b]), below the slopes of Pisgah.

18 I commanded you at that time: "The LORD your God has given you this land to take possession of it. But all your able-bodied men, armed for battle, must cross over ahead of your brother Israelites. 19 However, your wives, your children and your livestock (I know you have much livestock) may stay in the towns I have given you, 20 until the LORD gives rest to your brothers as he has to you, and they too have taken over the land that the LORD your God is giving them, across the Jordan. After that, each of you may go back to the possession I have given you."

Moses Forbidden to Cross the Jordan

21 At that time I commanded Joshua: "You have seen with your own eyes all that the LORD your God has done to these two kings. The LORD will do the same to all the kingdoms over there where you are going. 22 Do not be afraid of them; the LORD your God himself will fight for you."

23 At that time I pleaded with the LORD: 24 "O Sovereign LORD, you have begun to show to your servant your greatness and your strong hand. For what god is there in heaven or on earth who can do the deeds and mighty works you do? 25 Let me go over and see the good land beyond the Jordan—that fine hill country and Lebanon."

26 But because of you the LORD was angry with me and would not listen to me. "That is enough," the LORD said. "Do not speak to me anymore about this matter. 27 Go up to the top of Pisgah and look west and north and south and east. Look at the land with your own eyes, since you are not going to cross this Jordan. 28 But commission Joshua, and encourage and strengthen him, for he will lead this people across and will cause them to inherit the land that you will see." 29 So we stayed in the valley near Beth Peor.

---

[a] **14** Or *called the settlements of Jair* [b] **17** That is, the Dead Sea

CHALLENGE TO HEAR THE WORD OF THE LORD

Moses challenges the new generation of Israelites to obey the LORD, so they can go in and take the land the LORD promised to give them. They are to be especially careful not to worship idols.

Obedience Commanded

4 Hear now, O Israel, the decrees and laws I am about to teach
you. Follow them so that you may live and may go in and take possession of the land that the LORD, the God of your fathers, is giving you. [2]Do not add to what I command you and do not subtract
from it, but keep the commands of the LORD your God that I give
you.
[3]You saw with your own eyes what the LORD did at Baal Peor.
The LORD your God destroyed from among you everyone who followed the Baal of Peor, [4]but all of you who held fast to the LORD
your God are still alive today.
[5]See, I have taught you decrees and laws as the LORD my God
commanded me, so that you may follow them in the land you are
entering to take possession of it. [6]Observe them carefully, for this
will show your wisdom and understanding to the nations, who
will hear about all these decrees and say, "Surely this great nation
is a wise and understanding people." [7]What other nation is so great
as to have their gods near them the way the LORD our God is near
us whenever we pray to him? [8]And what other nation is so great as
to have such righteous decrees and laws as this body of laws I am
setting before you today?
[9]Only be careful, and watch yourselves closely so that you do
not forget the things your eyes have seen or let them slip from
your heart as long as you live. Teach them to your children and to
their children after them. [10]Remember the day you stood before
the LORD your God at Horeb, when he said to me, "Assemble the
people before me to hear my words so that they may learn to
revere me as long as they live in the land and may teach them to
their children." [11]You came near and stood at the foot of the
mountain while it blazed with fire to the very heavens, with black
clouds and deep darkness. [12]Then the LORD spoke to you out of the
fire. You heard the sound of words but saw no form; there was
only a voice. [13]He declared to you his covenant, the Ten Commandments, which he commanded you to follow and then wrote
them on two stone tablets. [14]And the LORD directed me at that time
to teach you the decrees and laws you are to follow in the land that
you are crossing the Jordan to possess.

Idolatry Forbidden

[15]You saw no form of any kind the day the LORD spoke
to you at Horeb out of the fire. Therefore watch yourselves very

4:1 *the land:* See the note at 1:7,8.

4:1-4 *Follow them so that you may live:* Moses recalls how God destroyed the Israelites who worshiped the god Baal of Peor (Num 25). He reminds the people that if they obey and honor God, they will live; but if they turn away from God, they will die.

4:3 *Baal Peor:* Worshiping the Baal of Peor, a Moabite fertility god, may have included Israelite men having sex with Moabite women (Num 25:1-9).

4:7,8 *righteous decrees and laws:* The laws God gave Israel were a sign of God's special relationship with that nation. See also the note at 1:3-5.

4:9 *do not forget . . . Teach them to your children:* Remembering God's saving acts is a frequent theme in DEUTERONOMY (5:15; 7:18; 8:2; 11:2-4; 16:1-4; 24:18,22; 32:7).

4:10 *Horeb:* Another name for Mount Sinai. In the incident recalled here (Exod 19,20), God spoke the words of the Ten Commandments. See also the note on p. 341 (Jordan . . . Moab).

4:14 *the land . . . possess:* See the note at 1:7,8.

4:11,12 Exod 19:16-18; 20:18-21; Heb 12:18,19. **4:13** Exod 20:1-17; 31:18; 34:28; Deut 9:9-11. **4:14** Exod 21:1. **4:15** Exod 19:18,19; Deut 4:11,12.

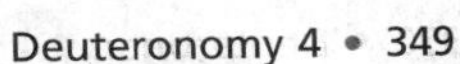

4:16-18 *idol:* Israel's LORD God was a living God, and no image or idol could be made that could represent God. See also Exod 20:4,5; 34:17; Lev 26:1; Deut 5:8,9; 27:15; Isa 44:6-20.

4:19 *the sun, the moon and the stars:* Some ancient religions made gods of the stars and constellations, as well as the sun and moon. But Israel was chosen for a special relationship with the one true God, who led them out of slavery in Egypt (Exod 12–14). No other god was to be the object of Israel's worship. See also Exod 20:4; Lev 26:1; Deut 5:8; 17:3.

4:20 *the people of his inheritance:* Moses reminds the people that they were chosen by the LORD (Exod 19:5; Deut 7:6; 14:2; 26:18; see also Titus 2:14; 1 Pet 2:9). And the LORD helped them through overwhelming hardships such as escaping slavery in Egypt.

4:21 *The LORD was angry with me:* See the notes at 1:36-38 and 3:23-26.

4:25-31 *have lived in the land a long time:* Moses warns the people not to forget the law and not to worship idols. If they do, the nation will be destroyed, and the few remaining people will be forced to leave the promised land. But if the people turn back to God and worship only God, God will keep the promises made with the people and show them mercy. See also Jer 29:13; and the article called, "From Joshua to the Exile: The People of Israel in the Promised Land," p. 924.

4:17,18 Rom 1:23. **4:21** Num 20:12. **4:24** Heb 12:29. **4:27,28** Deut 28:36.

carefully, [16]so that you do not become corrupt and make for yourselves an idol, an image of any shape, whether formed like a man or a woman, [17]or like any animal on earth or any bird that flies in the air, [18]or like any creature that moves along the ground or any fish in the waters below. [19]And when you look up to the sky and see the sun, the moon and the stars—all the heavenly array—do not be enticed into bowing down to them and worshiping things the LORD your God has apportioned to all the nations under heaven. [20]But as for you, the LORD took you and brought you out of the iron-smelting furnace, out of Egypt, to be the people of his inheritance, as you now are.

[21]The LORD was angry with me because of you, and he solemnly swore that I would not cross the Jordan and enter the good land the LORD your God is giving you as your inheritance. [22]I will die in this land; I will not cross the Jordan; but you are about to cross over and take possession of that good land. [23]Be careful not to forget the covenant of the LORD your God that he made with you; do not make for yourselves an idol in the form of anything the LORD your God has forbidden. [24]For the LORD your God is a consuming fire, a jealous God.

[25]After you have had children and grandchildren and have lived in the land a long time—if you then become corrupt and make any kind of idol, doing evil in the eyes of the LORD your God and provoking him to anger, [26]I call heaven and earth as witnesses against you this day that you will quickly perish from the land that you are crossing the Jordan to possess. You will not live there long but will certainly be destroyed. [27]The LORD will scatter you among the peoples, and only a few of you will survive among the nations to which the LORD will drive you. [28]There you will worship man-made gods of wood and stone, which cannot see or hear or eat or smell. [29]But if from there you seek the LORD your God, you will find him if you look for him with all your heart and with all your soul. [30]When you are in distress and all these things have happened to you, then in later days you will return to the LORD your God and obey him. [31]For the LORD your God is a merciful God; he will not abandon or destroy you or forget the covenant with your forefathers, which he confirmed to them by oath.

The LORD Is God

[32]Ask now about the former days, long before your time, from the day God created man on the earth; ask from one end of the heavens to the other. Has anything so great as this ever happened, or has anything like it ever been heard of? [33]Has any other people heard the voice of God[a] speaking out of fire, as you have,

[a]**33** Or *of a god*

and lived? [34]Has any god ever tried to take for himself one nation
out of another nation, by testings, by miraculous signs and wonders, by war, by a mighty hand and an outstretched arm, or by
great and awesome deeds, like all the things the LORD your God
did for you in Egypt before your very eyes?
[35]You were shown these things so that you might know that
the LORD is God; besides him there is no other. [36]From heaven he
made you hear his voice to discipline you. On earth he showed you
his great fire, and you heard his words from out of the fire.
[37]Because he loved your forefathers and chose their descendants
after them, he brought you out of Egypt by his Presence and his
great strength, [38]to drive out before you nations greater and
stronger than you and to bring you into their land to give it to you
for your inheritance, as it is today.
[39]Acknowledge and take to heart this day that the LORD is
God in heaven above and on the earth below. There is no other.
[40]Keep his decrees and commands, which I am giving you today, so
that it may go well with you and your children after you and that
you may live long in the land the LORD your God gives you for all
time.

Cities of Refuge

[41]Then Moses set aside three cities east of the Jordan, [42]to
which anyone who had killed a person could flee if he had unintentionally killed his neighbor without malice aforethought. He
could flee into one of these cities and save his life. [43]The cities
were these: Bezer in the desert plateau, for the Reubenites;
Ramoth in Gilead, for the Gadites; and Golan in Bashan, for the
Manassites.

4:34 *miraculous signs and wonders:* This likely refers to the way God acted to save the people in Egypt (see the note at 1:30-32).

4:41 *three cities:* These "cities of refuge" were set aside to protect those who accidentally killed someone. At this time in Israel's history, "revenge killing" was an accepted form of execution. A victim's clan could appoint a close male relative to track down and kill a person who had killed a member of their clan. If the person who killed someone was found guilty of intentional murder at a trial, he or she could be taken from the city of refuge and put to death. If found innocent, the person could remain in the city of refuge to be protected from the revenge of the victim's relatives (Num 35:25-27). See also Exod 21:12-14; Num 35:6-18; Deut 19:1-13; Josh 20:2-9.

For the general location of the cities mentioned in this passage, see the maps on pp. 2464-2465. See also the notes at 3:12 (Reuben and Gad) and 3:13-15 (Manasseh).

4:35 Mark 12:32.

QUESTIONS ABOUT DEUTERONOMY 1:1—4:43

1. At the beginning of DEUTERONOMY, where are the Israelite people, and what are they preparing to do? (1:1-8) What is so important about the land of the Canaanites?
2. Why did God cause the Israelites to wander in the desert for forty years? (1:26—2:7)
3. What events does Moses recall to prove to the people that the LORD is the only true God? (4:1-14,32-40)
4. What must the people of Israel do in order to take the land God promised to give them? (4:1,2)
5. Do you agree or disagree with this statement: "Those who don't study the past are doomed to repeat the mistakes of the past"? Explain your opinion. How would such a statement apply to the beginning chapters of DEUTERONOMY?

The Second Speech: Moses Tells What the LORD Demands

Moses' second speech contains the heart of Israel's religion—the Law that God gave to Moses and the people. The speech begins with the Ten Commandments and continues with a sermon on the importance of the first commandment and Israel's duty to worship God alone (chapters 5–11). Chapters 12–26 present the religious, social, civil, and criminal laws that Israel is to follow in the land. In a special ceremony described in chapters 27 and 28, the people agree to live by God's rules.

LOVE GOD AND OBEY GOD'S LAWS

DEUTERONOMY contains two sets of rules. Those appearing in chapters 5–11 are more general and provide the basic laws that will be made more specific in the second set of rules (12–26). These basic rules of the LORD are clearly set forth in the Ten Commandments, repeated almost exactly from Exodus 20. Chapters 5–11 are probably part of the book that was found in the temple in 621 B.C. (see also the Introduction to DEUTERONOMY).

4:44-49 *Egypt . . . Beth Peor . . . slopes of Pisgah:* These verses are a second introduction to DEUTERONOMY. It took forty years of wandering for the Israelites to reach this camp at Beth Peor (see the notes at 2:14 and 3:25-29). After defeating kings and peoples on the east side of the Jordan River, they are getting ready to cross over to the lands west of the river. See also the notes on p. 341 (Jordan . . . Moab) and at 1:7,8. See the note at 3:3-10 for more information about Mount Siyon (Hermon).

5:1 *the decrees and laws I declare in your hearing:* These words serve as a title to the chapter. Similar titles are found at 6:1 and 12:1. The theme of obedience is repeated. See also the note at 4:9.

5:2 *covenant . . . Horeb:* The covenant God made with Israel at Horeb (Mount Sinai) was for all generations. See also the notes at 1:3-5; 4:7, 8; and 4:9.

Introduction to the Law

[44]This is the law Moses set before the Israelites. [45]These are
the stipulations, decrees and laws Moses gave them when they
came out of Egypt [46]and were in the valley near Beth Peor east of
the Jordan, in the land of Sihon king of the Amorites, who reigned
in Heshbon and was defeated by Moses and the Israelites as they
came out of Egypt. [47]They took possession of his land and the land
of Og king of Bashan, the two Amorite kings east of the Jordan.
[48]This land extended from Aroer on the rim of the Arnon Gorge to
Mount Siyon[a] (that is, Hermon), [49]and included all the Arabah east
of the Jordan, as far as the Sea of the Arabah,[b] below the slopes of
Pisgah.

The Ten Commandments

5 Moses summoned all Israel and said:
Hear, O Israel, the decrees and laws I declare in your hearing
today. Learn them and be sure to follow them. [2]The LORD our God
made a covenant with us at Horeb. [3]It was not with our fathers
that the LORD made this covenant, but with us, with all of us who
are alive here today. [4]The LORD spoke to you face to face out of the
fire on the mountain. [5](At that time I stood between the LORD and
you to declare to you the word of the LORD, because you were
afraid of the fire and did not go up the mountain.) And he said:

[a]**48** Hebrew; Syriac (see also Deut. 3:9) *Sirion* [b]**49** That is, the Dead Sea

"And He led us before Mount Sinai and gave us the Torah," manuscript illumination by Philip Isac Levy, 1739. This illustration from the *Copenhagen Haggadah* shows the people of Israel gathered on the lower slopes of Mount Sinai. Moses stands on top of the mountain holding the two stone tablets containing the Ten Commandments; his brother Aaron stands apart, a little further up the mountain from the other people, a sign of his special status as the first in a long line of priests. (See 5:1-22.)

6 "I am the LORD your God, who brought you out of
Egypt, out of the land of slavery.
7 "You shall have no other gods before[a] me.
8 "You shall not make for yourself an idol in the form of anything in heaven above or on the earth beneath or in the
waters below. 9 You shall not bow down to them or worship them; for I, the LORD your God, am a jealous God,
punishing the children for the sin of the fathers to the
third and fourth generation of those who hate me, 10 but
showing love to a thousand ⌞generations⌟ of those who
love me and keep my commandments.
11 "You shall not misuse the name of the LORD your God, for
the LORD will not hold anyone guiltless who misuses his
name.
12 "Observe the Sabbath day by keeping it holy, as the LORD
your God has commanded you. 13 Six days you shall
labor and do all your work, 14 but the seventh day is a
Sabbath to the LORD your God. On it you shall not do
any work, neither you, nor your son or daughter, nor

[a]7 Or *besides*

5:6 *I am the LORD your God:* The Commandments are introduced by establishing the relationship between the LORD and the people being addressed (Israel). See the notes at 1:6 and 4:7,8.

5:7-9 *no other gods before me:* See the note at 4:16-18. See also Lev 26:1; Deut 4:15-18; 27:14-26.

5:11 *misuse the name:* Probably includes using God's name to make promises, telling lies after swearing to tell the truth, using the LORD's name as a curse word or in a magic formula, and trying to control the LORD by using the LORD's name. See also Exod 20:7 and Lev 19:12.

5:12 *Sabbath:* Sabbath means "rest" and resting on the seventh day of the week became a rule for all Jewish people. The emphasis here is that servants and animals get a day of rest. See also Exod 16:23-30; 20:8-11; 23:12; 31:12-15; 34:21; 35:2; and Lev 23:3.

5:9,10 Exod 34:6,7; Num 14:18; Deut 7:9,10.

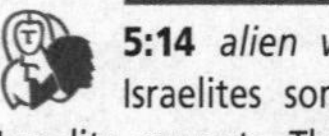

5:14 *alien within your gates:* Israelites sometimes had non-Israelite servants. Their need for a day of rest was also respected. See also the mini-article called "Foreigners (Aliens)," p. 501.

your manservant or maidservant, nor your ox, your
donkey or any of your animals, nor the alien within your
gates, so that your manservant and maidservant may
rest, as you do. 15 Remember that you were slaves in
Egypt and that the LORD your God brought you out of
there with a mighty hand and an outstretched arm.
Therefore the LORD your God has commanded you to
observe the Sabbath day.

TEN COMMANDMENTS

The list of commands known as the "Ten Commandments" is the most familiar of all the laws that the LORD gave to the people of Israel. They are recorded in two slightly different versions in Exodus 20:1-17 and Deuteronomy 5:6-21. Scholars have observed that the form of the Ten Commandments is similar to ancient Near Eastern treaties or agreements between a ruler and the people he rules. In such treaties, the ruler promised to protect the people, and the people, in turn, promised to be loyal to the ruler. The Ten Commandments is more than just a list of "do's" and "don'ts." More importantly, they define a relationship. Notice how the commands are introduced with God's statement: "I am the LORD your God, who brought you out of Egypt, out of the land of slavery" (Exod 20:2). When the LORD chose the people of Israel and saved them from slavery, a sacred relationship was formed.

The commands were given to strengthen the relationship that God had already established. Because God chose Israel, they were to be loyal to God alone. They were to worship only God and not make or worship idols that represented other gods. And because God's name is holy, the people weren't to misuse it in any way (see Exod 20:7 and the note). The relationship with God also included setting aside a day for rest, as God did at creation (Gen 2:2, 3; Exod 20:8-11). The day of rest is "a Sabbath to the LORD" (Exod 20:10), meaning it was to be a day to worship God and to remember what God had done for the people (Deut 5:12-15). Observing this special day each week was to set the people of Israel apart from their neighbors. By resting, worshiping, and giving servants (and even animals) time off, the people would remind the world of their unique relationship with God.

The rest of the commands help define the relationship that the people were to have with one another. These commands are like important foundation stones or pillars helping to support Israel's life as a community and to protect it from danger. If these "foundation" commands were not obeyed, lives would be affected in negative ways. Individuals and whole families would be hurt. Marriages would be broken up, and the peace and blessing intended for those who live under God's care would be replaced with pain and chaos.

Notice that neither list of commandments (Exod 20:1-17; Deut 5:6-21) includes a "one through ten" numbering. Different religious traditions number the Ten Commandments in slightly different ways. Some combine the command to worship only God (Exod 20:3) with the command which bans the making and worshiping of idols (Exod 20:4-6). The final command about "not coveting" what belongs to someone else is then divided into two commands, so the list will equal "ten." What's most important about the Ten Commandments is not how they are numbered, but rather that they show God's people how to live with one another and how to honor God.

16 "Honor your father and your mother, as the LORD your God
has commanded you, so that you may live long and that
it may go well with you in the land the LORD your God
is giving you.
17 "You shall not murder.
18 "You shall not commit adultery.
19 "You shall not steal.
20 "You shall not give false testimony against your neighbor.
21 "You shall not covet your neighbor's wife. You shall not set
your desire on your neighbor's house or land, his manservant or maidservant, his ox or donkey, or anything
that belongs to your neighbor."

22 These are the commandments the LORD proclaimed in a
loud voice to your whole assembly there on the mountain from
out of the fire, the cloud and the deep darkness; and he added
nothing more. Then he wrote them on two stone tablets and gave
them to me.
23 When you heard the voice out of the darkness, while the
mountain was ablaze with fire, all the leading men of your tribes
and your elders came to me. 24 And you said, "The LORD our God
has shown us his glory and his majesty, and we have heard his voice
from the fire. Today we have seen that a man can live even if God
speaks with him. 25 But now, why should we die? This great fire will
consume us, and we will die if we hear the voice of the LORD our
God any longer. 26 For what mortal man has ever heard the voice of
the living God speaking out of fire, as we have, and survived? 27 Go
near and listen to all that the LORD our God says. Then tell us whatever the LORD our God tells you. We will listen and obey."
28 The LORD heard you when you spoke to me and the LORD
said to me, "I have heard what this people said to you. Everything
they said was good. 29 Oh, that their hearts would be inclined to
fear me and keep all my commands always, so that it might go well
with them and their children forever!
30 "Go, tell them to return to their tents. 31 But you stay here
with me so that I may give you all the commands, decrees and laws
you are to teach them to follow in the land I am giving them to
possess."
32 So be careful to do what the LORD your God has commanded you; do not turn aside to the right or to the left. 33 Walk in
all the way that the LORD your God has commanded you, so that
you may live and prosper and prolong your days in the land that
you will possess.

Love the LORD Your God

6 These are the commands, decrees and laws the LORD your God
directed me to teach you to observe in the land that you are crossing the Jordan to possess, 2 so that you, your children and their

5:16 *Honor:* Children were to care for parents and to show them the greatest respect (Exod 20:12; Lev 19:3,4; 20:9). This command comes with a promise.

5:17 *murder:* Some modern translations substitute "kill." This commandment does not forbid all forms of killing, but rather refers to taking a life without just cause.

5:18 *adultery:* Forbids sex between a married and an unmarried person or between married persons not married to each other.

5:19 *steal:* Also refers to kidnapping and selling someone into slavery (24:7).

5:20 *false testimony:* Includes spreading rumors and giving false testimony that would cause an innocent person to be condemned or help a criminal escape the consequences of his crimes (Exod 23:1).

5:21 *You shall not covet:* This refers both to greedy attitudes (jealousy) and actions. Compare this list to the list in Exodus 20:17. See also Rom 7:7; 13:9.

5:22 *assembly there on the mountain:* Refers to the people of Israel gathered at Mount Sinai (Exod 19). See the note at 1:1-5. See also the notes at 1:33 and Heb 12:18,19.

5:28-31 *commands, decrees and laws:* The LORD gives Moses the laws and teachings that he will pass on to the people.

6:1 *LORD your God directed me to teach you:* See the note at 4:7,8.

5:16 Deut 27:16; Matt 15:4; 19:19; Mark 7:10; 10:19; Luke 18:20; Eph 6:2,3. **5:17** Gen 9:5,6; Lev 24:17; Matt 5:21; 19:18; Mark 10:19; Luke 18:20; Rom 13:9; Jas 2:11. **5:18** Lev 20:10; Matt 5:27; 19:18; Mark 10:19; Luke 18:20; Rom 13:9; Jas 2:11. **5:19** Exod 22:1; Lev 19:11; Matt 19:18; Mark 10:19; Luke 18:20; Rom 13:9. **5:20** Matt 19:18; Mark 10:19; Luke 18:20.

children after them may fear the LORD your God as long as you live
by keeping all his decrees and commands that I give you, and so
that you may enjoy long life. 3 Hear, O Israel, and be careful to obey
so that it may go well with you and that you may increase greatly
in a land flowing with milk and honey, just as the LORD, the God
of your fathers, promised you.

4 Hear, O Israel: The LORD our God, the LORD is one.[a] 5 Love
the LORD your God with all your heart and with all your soul and
with all your strength. 6 These commandments that I give you
today are to be upon your hearts. 7 Impress them on your children.
Talk about them when you sit at home and when you walk along
the road, when you lie down and when you get up. 8 Tie them as
symbols on your hands and bind them on your foreheads. 9 Write
them on the doorframes of your houses and on your gates.

10 When the LORD your God brings you into the land he
swore to your fathers, to Abraham, Isaac and Jacob, to give you—
a land with large, flourishing cities you did not build, 11 houses
filled with all kinds of good things you did not provide, wells you
did not dig, and vineyards and olive groves you did not plant—
then when you eat and are satisfied, 12 be careful that you do not
forget the LORD, who brought you out of Egypt, out of the land of
slavery.

13 Fear the LORD your God, serve him only and take your
oaths in his name. 14 Do not follow other gods, the gods of the peoples around you; 15 for the LORD your God, who is among you, is a
jealous God and his anger will burn against you, and he will
destroy you from the face of the land. 16 Do not test the LORD your
God as you did at Massah. 17 Be sure to keep the commands of the
LORD your God and the stipulations and decrees he has given you.
18 Do what is right and good in the LORD's sight, so that it may go
well with you and you may go in and take over the good land that
the LORD promised on oath to your forefathers, 19 thrusting out all
your enemies before you, as the LORD said.

20 In the future, when your son asks you, "What is the meaning of the stipulations, decrees and laws the LORD our God has
commanded you?" 21 tell him: "We were slaves of Pharaoh in Egypt,
but the LORD brought us out of Egypt with a mighty hand. 22 Before
our eyes the LORD sent miraculous signs and wonders—great and
terrible—upon Egypt and Pharaoh and his whole household. 23 But
he brought us out from there to bring us in and give us the land
that he promised on oath to our forefathers. 24 The LORD commanded us to obey all these decrees and to fear the LORD our God,
so that we might always prosper and be kept alive, as is the case
today. 25 And if we are careful to obey all this law before the LORD
our God, as he has commanded us, that will be our righteousness."

[a]4 Or *The LORD our God is one LORD*; or *The LORD is our God, the LORD is one*; or *The LORD is our God, the LORD alone*

6:4,5 *Hear, O Israel:* Jewish tradition calls these verses the "Shema," which means "listen" or "hear." This confession of faith in the LORD is to be recited twice a day. To love with one's heart, soul, and strength was to love with one's entire being. See also 10:12,13; 11:13-15; 13:3-5; 26:16; 30:2,6, 8-10; Mark 12:29,30.

6:6-8 *These commandments . . . Tie them as symbols on your hands . . . foreheads:* Some Jewish people put Scripture passages in small leather pouches (phylacteries) and tie them to their arms and foreheads. See also the note on p. 341 (Mezuzah).

6:10 *the land:* See the note at 1:7, 8.

6:10,11 *cities . . . wells:* Canaan was already a settled area. The people of Israel would not have to build houses, dig wells, or plant vineyards.

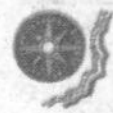

6:16 *Massah:* Where the people tested God's patience with their complaining (Exod 17:1-7).

6:20 *What is the meaning of the stipulations, decrees and laws:* See also the notes at 1:3-5 and 6:4,5.

6:10 Gen 12:7; 26:3; 28:13. **6:13** Matt 4:10; Luke 4:8.

Driving Out the Nations

7 When the LORD your God brings you into the land you are
entering to possess and drives out before you many nations—the
Hittites, Girgashites, Amorites, Canaanites, Perizzites, Hivites and
Jebusites, seven nations larger and stronger than you— 2 and when
the LORD your God has delivered them over to you and you have
defeated them, then you must destroy them totally.[a] Make no
treaty with them, and show them no mercy. 3 Do not intermarry
with them. Do not give your daughters to their sons or take their
daughters for your sons, 4 for they will turn your sons away from
following me to serve other gods, and the LORD's anger will burn
against you and will quickly destroy you. 5 This is what you are to
do to them: Break down their altars, smash their sacred stones, cut
down their Asherah poles[b] and burn their idols in the fire. 6 For you
are a people holy to the LORD your God. The LORD your God has
chosen you out of all the peoples on the face of the earth to be his
people, his treasured possession.

7 The LORD did not set his affection on you and choose you
because you were more numerous than other peoples, for you
were the fewest of all peoples. 8 But it was because the LORD loved
you and kept the oath he swore to your forefathers that he brought
you out with a mighty hand and redeemed you from the land of
slavery, from the power of Pharaoh king of Egypt. 9 Know therefore that the LORD your God is God; he is the faithful God, keeping his covenant of love to a thousand generations of those who
love him and keep his commands. 10 But

> those who hate him he will repay to their face by
> destruction;
> he will not be slow to repay to their face those who
> hate him.

11 Therefore, take care to follow the commands, decrees and laws I
give you today.

12 If you pay attention to these laws and are careful to follow
them, then the LORD your God will keep his covenant of love with
you, as he swore to your forefathers. 13 He will love you and bless
you and increase your numbers. He will bless the fruit of your
womb, the crops of your land—your grain, new wine and oil—the
calves of your herds and the lambs of your flocks in the land that
he swore to your forefathers to give you. 14 You will be blessed more
than any other people; none of your men or women will be childless, nor any of your livestock without young. 15 The LORD will keep
you free from every disease. He will not inflict on you the horrible
diseases you knew in Egypt, but he will inflict them on all who

[a] 2 The Hebrew term refers to the irrevocable giving over of things or persons to the LORD, often by totally destroying them; also in verse 26. [b] 5 That is, symbols of the goddess Asherah; here and elsewhere in Deuteronomy

7:1 *Hittites . . . Jebusites:* The Hittites were a strong force in Canaan from the time of Abraham to around 1300 B.C. (see also Gen 10:6-20). The Girgashites came from Canaan, the son of Ham and grandson of Noah (Gen 10:16). The Perizzites may have lived in the open country as opposed to the Canaanites who lived in walled cities. The Hivites may also be the people known as the Horites, and may have settled in the mountainous area around Edom. The Jebusites lived in and around Jerusalem until King David took over that city (2 Sam 5:6-9). See also Acts 13:19 and the note at 1:7, 8.

7:2 *destroy them totally:* This translates the Hebrew word *herem*, a term used in holy war settings. Total destruction of the enemy was intended to remove temptations that would cause Israel to turn their backs on the LORD. See also Exod 20:1-20 and the notes at 2:34 and 3:6.

7:5 *altars . . . sacred stones . . . Asherah poles:* The people of Israel were to tear down these sacred objects and destroy these altar stones. Carved wooden poles were set up in honor of Asherah, the Canaanite goddess of fertility. See also 12:3.

7:8 *mighty hand . . . Egypt:* The term "mighty hand" is often used to describe the LORD's protection or power, especially in battle (Exod 15:12, 16; Deut 5:15; Isa 40:10). See also the note at 1:3.

7:12-15 *bless you:* If the people obey God's laws, they will be blessed. See also 11:13-17; 28:1-14; Lev 26:3-13.

7:15 *diseases:* This probably refers to the kind of diseases that the Egyptians suffered (Exod 9:8-11; 15:26).

7:6 Exod 19:5; Deut 4:20; 14:2; 26:18; Titus 2:14; 1 Pet 2:9. **7:9,10** Exod 20:5, 6; 34:6, 7; Num 14:18; Deut 5:9, 10.

Moses told the people, *"Do not be terrified by them, for the LORD your God, who is among you, is a great and awesome God."* Deut 7:21

7:16-25 *do not serve their gods:* See the notes at 7:2 and 7:5.

7:26 *Utterly abhor and detest it:* Regarding idols, the Hebrew text uses the word *toebhah*, which is the strongest word used in the Old Testament for something that is totally displeasing to God. It shows how terrible the worship of idols was considered to be. To worship another god was to reject the LORD.

8:1 *follow every command:* See also 6:1-3; 10:12,13; 11:22, 23.

8:2 *these forty years:* See the notes at 1:3 and 2:14.

8:3 *manna:* God provided this unusual food in the desert (Exod 16:13-31). In Hebrew, "manna" means "What is it?" At night, insects feeding on tamarisk trees in the southern desert secrete a sticky white substance that Arabs call *man*. It has a sweet taste like the manna that tasted like honey wafers. Though God gave food to keep their bodies alive, Moses makes the point that the LORD's word (commands, 8:6) is the true source of life. See also Matt 4:4; Luke 4:4.

8:7 *good land:* See the note at 1:7,8.

8:8,9 *fig trees, pomegranates . . . iron:* Figs were an important source of food, producing two crops each year. A pomegranate is a bright red fruit that has red seeds surrounded by sweet-tasting pulp. Copper and iron ore are found in the mountains of Lebanon and in regions east of the Sea of Galilee. Ancient copper mines dating back to Israel's King Solomon have also been discovered south of the Dead Sea.

hate you. 16You must destroy all the peoples the LORD your God
gives over to you. Do not look on them with pity and do not serve
their gods, for that will be a snare to you.

17You may say to yourselves, "These nations are stronger
than we are. How can we drive them out?" 18But do not be afraid
of them; remember well what the LORD your God did to Pharaoh
and to all Egypt. 19You saw with your own eyes the great trials, the
miraculous signs and wonders, the mighty hand and outstretched
arm, with which the LORD your God brought you out. The LORD
your God will do the same to all the peoples you now fear. 20More-
over, the LORD your God will send the hornet among them until
even the survivors who hide from you have perished. 21Do not be
terrified by them, for the LORD your God, who is among you, is a
great and awesome God. 22The LORD your God will drive out those
nations before you, little by little. You will not be allowed to eliminate them all at once, or the wild animals will multiply around
you. 23But the LORD your God will deliver them over to you, throwing them into great confusion until they are destroyed. 24He will
give their kings into your hand, and you will wipe out their names
from under heaven. No one will be able to stand up against you;
you will destroy them. 25The images of their gods you are to burn
in the fire. Do not covet the silver and gold on them, and do not
take it for yourselves, or you will be ensnared by it, for it is
detestable to the LORD your God. 26Do not bring a detestable thing
into your house or you, like it, will be set apart for destruction.
Utterly abhor and detest it, for it is set apart for destruction.

Do Not Forget the LORD

8 Be careful to follow every command I am giving you today, so
that you may live and increase and may enter and possess the land
that the LORD promised on oath to your forefathers. 2Remember
how the LORD your God led you all the way in the desert these
forty years, to humble you and to test you in order to know what
was in your heart, whether or not you would keep his commands.
3He humbled you, causing you to hunger and then feeding you
with manna, which neither you nor your fathers had known, to
teach you that man does not live on bread alone but on every word
that comes from the mouth of the LORD. 4Your clothes did not
wear out and your feet did not swell during these forty years.
5Know then in your heart that as a man disciplines his son, so the
LORD your God disciplines you.

6Observe the commands of the LORD your God, walking in
his ways and revering him. 7For the LORD your God is bringing you
into a good land—a land with streams and pools of water, with
springs flowing in the valleys and hills; 8a land with wheat and barley, vines and fig trees, pomegranates, olive oil and honey; 9a land
where bread will not be scarce and you will lack nothing; a land

where the rocks are iron and you can dig copper out of the hills.
[10]When you have eaten and are satisfied, praise the LORD
your God for the good land he has given you. [11]Be careful that you
do not forget the LORD your God, failing to observe his commands, his laws and his decrees that I am giving you this day.
[12]Otherwise, when you eat and are satisfied, when you build fine
houses and settle down, [13]and when your herds and flocks grow
large and your silver and gold increase and all you have is multiplied, [14]then your heart will become proud and you will forget the
LORD your God, who brought you out of Egypt, out of the land of
slavery. [15]He led you through the vast and dreadful desert, that
thirsty and waterless land, with its venomous snakes and scorpions. He brought you water out of hard rock. [16]He gave you
manna to eat in the desert, something your fathers had never
known, to humble and to test you so that in the end it might go
well with you. [17]You may say to yourself, "My power and the
strength of my hands have produced this wealth for me." [18]But
remember the LORD your God, for it is he who gives you the ability to produce wealth, and so confirms his covenant, which he
swore to your forefathers, as it is today.
[19]If you ever forget the LORD your God and follow other
gods and worship and bow down to them, I testify against you
today that you will surely be destroyed. [20]Like the nations the LORD
destroyed before you, so you will be destroyed for not obeying the
LORD your God.

Not Because of Israel's Righteousness

9 Hear, O Israel. You are now about to cross the Jordan to go in
and dispossess nations greater and stronger than you, with large
cities that have walls up to the sky. [2]The people are strong and
tall—Anakites! You know about them and have heard it said:
"Who can stand up against the Anakites?" [3]But be assured today
that the LORD your God is the one who goes across ahead of you
like a devouring fire. He will destroy them; he will subdue them
before you. And you will drive them out and annihilate them
quickly, as the LORD has promised you.
[4]After the LORD your God has driven them out before you,
do not say to yourself, "The LORD has brought me here to take possession of this land because of my righteousness." No, it is on
account of the wickedness of these nations that the LORD is going
to drive them out before you. [5]It is not because of your righteousness or your integrity that you are going in to take possession of
their land; but on account of the wickedness of these nations, the
LORD your God will drive them out before you, to accomplish what
he swore to your fathers, to Abraham, Isaac and Jacob. [6]Under-
stand, then, that it is not because of your righteousness that the
LORD your God is giving you this good land to possess, for you are
a stiff-necked people.

8:10-20 *praise the LORD your God . . . you will be destroyed:* Moses reminds the people to guard against pride when they begin to enjoy the rich blessings waiting for them in Canaan. They should not forget how the LORD has saved them in the past—by freeing them from slavery in Egypt (Exod 12–14) and by providing them with water (Num 20:2-13) and manna in the desert (see the note at 8:3). They are to remember that what they have was not something they earned by their own efforts, but was a gift from God (8:17, 18). If they forget the LORD or fail to thank the LORD for these blessings, they may be punished.

9:1-5 *devouring fire. He will destroy them:* This passage presents the reasons for the holy war soon to take place when Israel enters Canaan. See the notes at 2:34; 3:6; and 7:2. The Israelites are not stronger, and they are not to think of themselves as "righteous" people. But the LORD will help the Israelites gain victory because the other nations are evil and because God made a promise to give the land to the descendants of Abraham, Isaac, and Jacob (see the note at 1:7,8). For Anakites, see the note at 2:10, 11.

8:11-16 Hos 13:5, 6.

9:8 *Horeb:* For more about Horeb (Mount Sinai), see the notes on p. 341 and at 5:2.

9:8-21 *aroused the LORD's wrath . . . idol cast in the shape of a calf:* While Moses was away on the mountain for forty days and nights (Exod 24:17,18), the Hebrew people made a metal calf idol (Exod 32:1-6) that may have looked like the Egyptian bull-god Apis. The LORD was angry with the people but decided not to destroy them when Moses prayed on their behalf (Exod 32:11-14; Deut 9:18-20). Moses melted the idol, ground it into powder, and mixed it with the people's drinking water (Exod 32:20; Deut 9:21). The small gold and bronze bull shown here is from Byblos, 1800 to 1500 B.C.

9:22,23 *Taberah . . . Kadesh Barnea:* The exact location of Taberah is unknown. For Massah, see Exod 17:1-7 and the note at 6:16. The first place the Israelites stopped after leaving Mount Sinai was Kibroth Hattaavah (Num 11:34). Kadesh Barnea was the oasis where the Israelites stayed after leaving Mount Sinai. See Num 13–14. See the map on p. 2463.

9:25 *before the LORD:* In front of the tabernacle. A detailed description of the tabernacle can be found in Exodus 26. See the mini-article called "The Tabernacle," p. 2346.

9:7 Exod 15:22-24; 16:1-3; 32:1-35; Num 11:1-15; 14:1-35; 16:1-50; 25:1-16. **9:18-20** Heb 12:21. **9:23** Deut 1:20,21,26. **10:10** Exod 34:28.

The Golden Calf

7 Remember this and never forget how you provoked the
LORD your God to anger in the desert. From the day you left Egypt
until you arrived here, you have been rebellious against the LORD.
8 At Horeb you aroused the LORD's wrath so that he was angry
enough to destroy you. 9 When I went up on the mountain to
receive the tablets of stone, the tablets of the covenant that the
LORD had made with you, I stayed on the mountain forty days and
forty nights; I ate no bread and drank no water. 10 The LORD gave
me two stone tablets inscribed by the finger of God. On them were
all the commandments the LORD proclaimed to you on the mountain out of the fire, on the day of the assembly.

11 At the end of the forty days and forty nights, the LORD gave
me the two stone tablets, the tablets of the covenant. 12 Then the
LORD told me, "Go down from here at once, because your people
whom you brought out of Egypt have become corrupt. They have
turned away quickly from what I commanded them and have
made a cast idol for themselves."

13 And the LORD said to me, "I have seen this people, and they
are a stiff-necked people indeed! 14 Let me alone, so that I may
destroy them and blot out their name from under heaven. And I
will make you into a nation stronger and more numerous than
they."

15 So I turned and went down from the mountain while it
was ablaze with fire. And the two tablets of the covenant were in
my hands.[a] 16 When I looked, I saw that you had sinned against the
LORD your God; you had made for yourselves an idol cast in the
shape of a calf. You had turned aside quickly from the way that the
LORD had commanded you. 17 So I took the two tablets and threw
them out of my hands, breaking them to pieces before your eyes.

18 Then once again I fell prostrate before the LORD for forty
days and forty nights; I ate no bread and drank no water, because
of all the sin you had committed, doing what was evil in the LORD's
sight and so provoking him to anger. 19 I feared the anger and
wrath of the LORD, for he was angry enough with you to destroy
you. But again the LORD listened to me. 20 And the LORD was angry
enough with Aaron to destroy him, but at that time I prayed for
Aaron too. 21 Also I took that sinful thing of yours, the calf you had
made, and burned it in the fire. Then I crushed it and ground it to
powder as fine as dust and threw the dust into a stream that flowed
down the mountain.

22 You also made the LORD angry at Taberah, at Massah and
at Kibroth Hattaavah.

23 And when the LORD sent you out from Kadesh Barnea, he
said, "Go up and take possession of the land I have given you." But

[a] **15** Or *And I had the two tablets of the covenant with me, one in each hand*

you rebelled against the command of the LORD your God. You did
not trust him or obey him. 24 You have been rebellious against the
LORD ever since I have known you.

25 I lay prostrate before the LORD those forty days and forty
nights because the LORD had said he would destroy you. 26 I prayed
to the LORD and said, "O Sovereign LORD, do not destroy your people, your own inheritance that you redeemed by your great power
and brought out of Egypt with a mighty hand. 27 Remember your
servants Abraham, Isaac and Jacob. Overlook the stubbornness of
this people, their wickedness and their sin. 28 Otherwise, the country from which you brought us will say, 'Because the LORD was not
able to take them into the land he had promised them, and
because he hated them, he brought them out to put them to death
in the desert.' 29 But they are your people, your inheritance that you
brought out by your great power and your outstretched arm."

Tablets Like the First Ones

10 At that time the LORD said to me, "Chisel out two stone
tablets like the first ones and come up to me on the mountain.
Also make a wooden chest.[a] 2 I will write on the tablets the words
that were on the first tablets, which you broke. Then you are to put
them in the chest."

3 So I made the ark out of acacia wood and chiseled out two
stone tablets like the first ones, and I went up on the mountain
with the two tablets in my hands. 4 The LORD wrote on these tablets
what he had written before, the Ten Commandments he had proclaimed to you on the mountain, out of the fire, on the day of the
assembly. And the LORD gave them to me. 5 Then I came back down
the mountain and put the tablets in the ark I had made, as the
LORD commanded me, and they are there now.

6 (The Israelites traveled from the wells of the Jaakanites to
Moserah. There Aaron died and was buried, and Eleazar his son
succeeded him as priest. 7 From there they traveled to Gudgodah
and on to Jotbathah, a land with streams of water. 8 At that time
the LORD set apart the tribe of Levi to carry the ark of the
covenant of the LORD, to stand before the LORD to minister and to
pronounce blessings in his name, as they still do today. 9 That is
why the Levites have no share or inheritance among their brothers; the LORD is their inheritance, as the LORD your God told
them.)

10 Now I had stayed on the mountain forty days and nights,
as I did the first time, and the LORD listened to me at this time also.
It was not his will to destroy you. 11 "Go," the LORD said to me, "and
lead the people on their way, so that they may enter and possess
the land that I swore to their fathers to give them."

[a] 1 That is, an ark

10:1-3 *stone tablets . . . ark . . . acacia wood:* These stone tablets may have been like other ancient "steles" (upright stones) that were carved with words and illustrations. The LORD's commandments were placed in the ark of the covenant (Exod 25:10-22), which was kept in the Most Holy Place in the tabernacle. See also the mini-article called "The Ark of the Covenant," p. 513. The wood of an acacia, a short evergreen tree, is harder and darker in color than oak.

10:4 *Ten Commandments:* See the notes at 1:3-5 and 4:7, 8. See also 5:1-22 and the mini-article called "Ten Commandments," p. 354.

10:6,7 *wells of the Jaakanites . . . Jotbathah:* The location of Moserah is uncertain. Other passages say that Aaron was buried on Mount Hor, not Moserah (Num 33:38,39; Deut 32:50). Gudgodah's location is unknown. Jotbathah was possibly located at et-Taba, twenty miles north of Aqaba.

10:6 *Aaron:* Aaron was the brother of Moses and Miriam. He served as Israel's first high priest (Exod 28:1-3; Lev 8, 9; Num 18:1-20). Aaron was not allowed to enter the promised land (Num 20:7-13). Moses took Aaron up Mount Hor and gave Aaron's high priest's clothing to Aaron's son Eleazar. Aaron died there at the age of 123 (Num 20:23-28).

10:8 *tribe of Levi:* Levi was the son of Jacob and Leah (Gen 29:34). His descendants became Israel's priests (Exod 6:16-25; Num 3:5-8). In later periods, only Levites who could prove they were descendants of Aaron were considered Israel's priests (Num 18:20-32; Neh 11:10-18). Levite men not descended from Aaron were assigned to take care of the tabernacle and assist the priests. See the mini-article called "Israel's Priests," p. 2344.

10:11 *lead the people:* Moses would disobey the LORD and be unable to lead the people into the land (Num 20:10-12; Deut 1:37; 3:23-28).

10:12,13 *the* LORD *your God . . . walk in all his ways:* See the notes at 1:6; 6:3-5, and 7:12-15.

10:18,19 *the fatherless and the widow . . . the alien:* The Israelites were to treat such people fairly, just as God does (10:17), and just as God treated the Israelites when they were defenseless slaves in Egypt (10:19). See also Exod 22:21-24; Lev 19:33; and the mini-article called "Justice," p. 1721.

10:22 *numerous as the stars in the sky:* The number of Jacob's descendants fulfilled the LORD's promise to Abraham (Gen 15:5; 22:17).

11:4 *Red Sea:* Refers to one of the marshes or freshwater lakes near the eastern Nile Delta. This identification is based on Exodus 13:17—14:9.

11:6 *Dathan and Abiram:* These two men rebelled against Moses, but the LORD punished them and their families (Num 16:1-33).

11:8 *so that you may . . . take over the land:* Moses repeats the promise as the people are camped in Moab east of the Jordan River (1:1-5). See the notes on p. 341 and at 1:7, 8. Conquering the land will happen only if the people obey the laws they received at Sinai.

11:10,11 *irrigated:* Egypt had very little rain, so most water for crops had to come from the Nile River.

10:17 Acts 10:34; Rom 2:11; Gal 2:6; Eph 6:9; 1 Tim 6:15; Rev 17:14; 19:16. **11:1** Deut 6:4, 5. **11:3** Exod 7:8—12:13. **11:4** Exod 14:28.

Fear the LORD

12 And now, O Israel, what does the LORD your God ask of
you but to fear the LORD your God, to walk in all his ways, to love
him, to serve the LORD your God with all your heart and with all
your soul, 13 and to observe the LORD's commands and decrees that
I am giving you today for your own good?
14 To the LORD your God belong the heavens, even the highest heavens, the earth and everything in it. 15 Yet the LORD set his
affection on your forefathers and loved them, and he chose you,
their descendants, above all the nations, as it is today. 16 Circumcise
your hearts, therefore, and do not be stiff-necked any longer. 17 For
the LORD your God is God of gods and Lord of lords, the great
God, mighty and awesome, who shows no partiality and accepts
no bribes. 18 He defends the cause of the fatherless and the widow,
and loves the alien, giving him food and clothing. 19 And you are to
love those who are aliens, for you yourselves were aliens in Egypt.
20 Fear the LORD your God and serve him. Hold fast to him and
take your oaths in his name. 21 He is your praise; he is your God,
who performed for you those great and awesome wonders you saw
with your own eyes. 22 Your forefathers who went down into Egypt
were seventy in all, and now the LORD your God has made you as
numerous as the stars in the sky.

Love and Obey the LORD

11 Love the LORD your God and keep his requirements, his
decrees, his laws and his commands always. 2 Remember today that
your children were not the ones who saw and experienced the discipline of the LORD your God: his majesty, his mighty hand, his
outstretched arm; 3 the signs he performed and the things he did
in the heart of Egypt, both to Pharaoh king of Egypt and to his
whole country; 4 what he did to the Egyptian army, to its horses
and chariots, how he overwhelmed them with the waters of the
Red Sea[a] as they were pursuing you, and how the LORD brought
lasting ruin on them. 5 It was not your children who saw what he
did for you in the desert until you arrived at this place, 6 and what
he did to Dathan and Abiram, sons of Eliab the Reubenite, when
the earth opened its mouth right in the middle of all Israel and
swallowed them up with their households, their tents and every
living thing that belonged to them. 7 But it was your own eyes that
saw all these great things the LORD has done.
8 Observe therefore all the commands I am giving you today,
so that you may have the strength to go in and take over the land
that you are crossing the Jordan to possess, 9 and so that you may
live long in the land that the LORD swore to your forefathers to give
to them and their descendants, a land flowing with milk and

[a] **4** Hebrew *Yam Suph*; that is, Sea of Reeds

honey. [10]The land you are entering to take over is not like the land
of Egypt, from which you have come, where you planted your seed
and irrigated it by foot as in a vegetable garden. [11]But the land you
are crossing the Jordan to take possession of is a land of mountains and valleys that drinks rain from heaven. [12]It is a land the
LORD your God cares for; the eyes of the LORD your God are continually on it from the beginning of the year to its end.
[13]So if you faithfully obey the commands I am giving you
today—to love the LORD your God and to serve him with all your
heart and with all your soul— [14]then I will send rain on your land
in its season, both autumn and spring rains, so that you may gather in your grain, new wine and oil. [15]I will provide grass in the
fields for your cattle, and you will eat and be satisfied.
[16]Be careful, or you will be enticed to turn away and worship
other gods and bow down to them. [17]Then the LORD's anger will
burn against you, and he will shut the heavens so that it will not
rain and the ground will yield no produce, and you will soon perish from the good land the LORD is giving you. [18]Fix these words of
mine in your hearts and minds; tie them as symbols on your hands
and bind them on your foreheads. [19]Teach them to your children,
talking about them when you sit at home and when you walk
along the road, when you lie down and when you get up. [20]Write
them on the doorframes of your houses and on your gates, [21]so
that your days and the days of your children may be many in the
land that the LORD swore to give your forefathers, as many as the
days that the heavens are above the earth.
[22]If you carefully observe all these commands I am giving you
to follow—to love the LORD your God, to walk in all his ways and
to hold fast to him— [23]then the LORD will drive out all these
nations before you, and you will dispossess nations larger and
stronger than you. [24]Every place where you set your foot will be
yours: Your territory will extend from the desert to Lebanon, and
from the Euphrates River to the western sea.[a] [25]No man will be able
to stand against you. The LORD your God, as he promised you, will
put the terror and fear of you on the whole land, wherever you go.
[26]See, I am setting before you today a blessing and a curse—
[27]the blessing if you obey the commands of the LORD your God
that I am giving you today; [28]the curse if you disobey the commands of the LORD your God and turn from the way that I command you today by following other gods, which you have not
known. [29]When the LORD your God has brought you into the land
you are entering to possess, you are to proclaim on Mount Gerizim the blessings, and on Mount Ebal the curses. [30]As you know,
these mountains are across the Jordan, west of the road,[b] toward
the setting sun, near the great trees of Moreh, in the territory of
those Canaanites living in the Arabah in the vicinity of Gilgal.

[a]24 That is, the Mediterranean [b]30 Or *Jordan, westward*

11:13-15 *obey the commands ... I will send rain:* See the notes at 4:1-4; 4:25-31; and 7:12-15. See also 28:1-14 and Lev 26:3-13.

11:14 *autumn and spring rains:* In Palestine, almost all the rain for the year comes during the months from October through April.

11:18 *tie them ... hands ... foreheads:* See 6:6-8 and the note on p. 341 (Mezuzah). Many Jews today continue the practice of attaching mezuzahs, like the one shown here, to their doorposts.

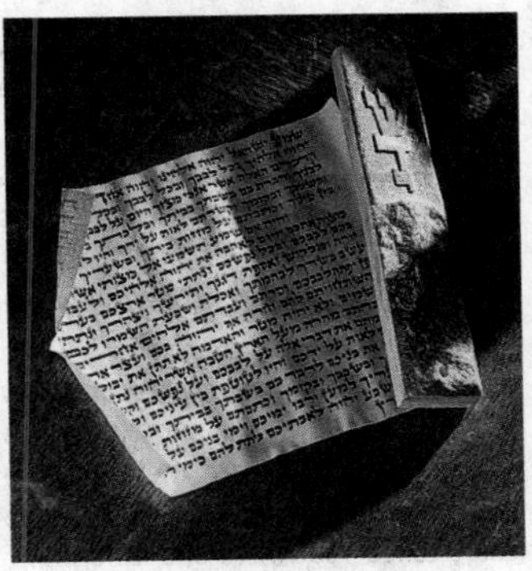

11:24 *desert to Lebanon ... Euphrates River to the western sea:* The places mentioned formed the approximate south-north and east-west boundaries of Israel's kingdom as it existed during the reigns of David (2 Sam 8:1-12) and Solomon (1 Kgs 4:20-25). See also Josh 1:3-5 and the maps on pp. 2464-2465.

11:26-28 *blessing ... curse:* See 11:13-17 and 27:9—28:68.

11:29,30 *Mount Gerizim ... Gilgal:* See the map on p. 2464. The ceremony mentioned is explained in 27:11-26. The great trees of Moreh were near Shechem. See Gen 12:6-18; 35:4. Gilgal means "circle," and probably refers to a circle of stones.

11:21 Jer 33:25,26.

> Moses told the people, *"Be careful to obey all these regulations I am giving you, so that it may always go well with you and your children after you, because you will be doing what is good and right in the eyes of the LORD your God."*
> Deut 12:28

31 You are about to cross the Jordan to enter and take possession of
the land the LORD your God is giving you. When you have taken it
over and are living there, 32 be sure that you obey all the decrees
and laws I am setting before you today.

HOW TO LIVE AS GOD'S PEOPLE

After presenting the Ten Commandments, the main focus of chapters 5–11 is on the first commandment—to love and worship only the LORD God. Chapters 12–26 present more laws that provide more detail for the Ten Commandments. These laws focus on six main areas: proper worship, the role of leaders, civil laws, holiness (purity) laws, proper relationships, and celebrating God's covenant and promises.

The One Place of Worship

12 These are the decrees and laws you must be careful to follow
in the land that the LORD, the God of your fathers, has given you
to possess—as long as you live in the land. 2 Destroy completely all
the places on the high mountains and on the hills and under every
spreading tree where the nations you are dispossessing worship
their gods. 3 Break down their altars, smash their sacred stones and
burn their Asherah poles in the fire; cut down the idols of their
gods and wipe out their names from those places.
4 You must not worship the LORD your God in their way. 5 But
you are to seek the place the LORD your God will choose from
among all your tribes to put his Name there for his dwelling. To
that place you must go; 6 there bring your burnt offerings and sacrifices, your tithes and special gifts, what you have vowed to give
and your freewill offerings, and the firstborn of your herds and
flocks. 7 There, in the presence of the LORD your God, you and your
families shall eat and shall rejoice in everything you have put your
hand to, because the LORD your God has blessed you.
8 You are not to do as we do here today, everyone as he sees
fit, 9 since you have not yet reached the resting place and the inheritance the LORD your God is giving you. 10 But you will cross the
Jordan and settle in the land the LORD your God is giving you as an
inheritance, and he will give you rest from all your enemies around
you so that you will live in safety. 11 Then to the place the LORD
your God will choose as a dwelling for his Name—there you are to
bring everything I command you: your burnt offerings and sacrifices, your tithes and special gifts, and all the choice possessions
you have vowed to the LORD. 12 And there rejoice before the LORD
your God, you, your sons and daughters, your menservants and
maidservants, and the Levites from your towns, who have no allotment or inheritance of their own. 13 Be careful not to sacrifice your
burnt offerings anywhere you please. 14 Offer them only at the place
the LORD will choose in one of your tribes, and there observe
everything I command you.

12:1 *laws . . . the LORD:* See the notes at 1:3-5 and 4:7, 8.

12:2-4 *their gods:* See the notes at 4:19 and 7:5; and the mini-article called "Canaanite Gods and Goddesses," p. 469.

12:6 *bring your burnt offerings and sacrifices:* The main purpose of such sacrifices was to please the LORD with the aroma of the sacrifice. See the chart called "Sacrifices and Offerings," p. 219.

12:6 *tithes and special gifts . . . firstborn:* The Israelites had to give one-tenth (a tithe) of their harvest to the LORD each year (Lev 27:30-33; Deut 14:22-29; 26:12,13). Israel's firstborn sons and the firstborn of the flocks were to be dedicated to the LORD (Exod 13:2). See also Lev 27:26; Deut 15:19-22.

12:7 *in the presence of the LORD . . . eat . . . rejoice:* Some sacrifices were completely burned on the altar. In other sacrifices, part of the animal was burned and part was given to the priests, but most of the meat was eaten by the worshipers as a sacred meal (Lev 7:11-15).

12:10 *cross the Jordan:* See the note at 11:8.

12:12 *Levites:* See the note at 10:8.

[15]Nevertheless, you may slaughter your animals in any of
your towns and eat as much of the meat as you want, as if it were
gazelle or deer, according to the blessing the LORD your God gives
you. Both the ceremonially unclean and the clean may eat it. [16]But
you must not eat the blood; pour it out on the ground like water.
[17]You must not eat in your own towns the tithe of your grain and
new wine and oil, or the firstborn of your herds and flocks, or
whatever you have vowed to give, or your freewill offerings or special gifts. [18]Instead, you are to eat them in the presence of the LORD
your God at the place the LORD your God will choose—you, your
sons and daughters, your menservants and maidservants, and the
Levites from your towns—and you are to rejoice before the LORD
your God in everything you put your hand to. [19]Be careful not to
neglect the Levites as long as you live in your land.
[20]When the LORD your God has enlarged your territory as he
promised you, and you crave meat and say, "I would like some
meat," then you may eat as much of it as you want. [21]If the place
where the LORD your God chooses to put his Name is too far away
from you, you may slaughter animals from the herds and flocks
the LORD has given you, as I have commanded you, and in your
own towns you may eat as much of them as you want. [22]Eat them
as you would gazelle or deer. Both the ceremonially unclean and
the clean may eat. [23]But be sure you do not eat the blood, because
the blood is the life, and you must not eat the life with the meat.
[24]You must not eat the blood; pour it out on the ground like water.
[25]Do not eat it, so that it may go well with you and your children
after you, because you will be doing what is right in the eyes of the
LORD.
[26]But take your consecrated things and whatever you have
vowed to give, and go to the place the LORD will choose. [27]Present
your burnt offerings on the altar of the LORD your God, both the
meat and the blood. The blood of your sacrifices must be poured
beside the altar of the LORD your God, but you may eat the meat.
[28]Be careful to obey all these regulations I am giving you, so that it
may always go well with you and your children after you, because
you will be doing what is good and right in the eyes of the LORD
your God.
[29]The LORD your God will cut off before you the nations you
are about to invade and dispossess. But when you have driven
them out and settled in their land, [30]and after they have been
destroyed before you, be careful not to be ensnared by inquiring
about their gods, saying, "How do these nations serve their gods?
We will do the same." [31]You must not worship the LORD your God
in their way, because in worshiping their gods, they do all kinds of
detestable things the LORD hates. They even burn their sons and
daughters in the fire as sacrifices to their gods.
[32]See that you do all I command you; do not add to it or take
away from it.

12:15 *slaughter your animals . . . eat:* Butchering animals for food was permitted at home, as long as the blood was not eaten. Since this meat is not eaten as part of a sacrifice, those eating it do not have to be "clean" (12:22).

12:15 *unclean:* See the mini-article called "Purity (Clean and Unclean)," p. 2125.

12:16 *must not eat the blood:* See also the mini-article called "Blood," p. 180.

12:20 *meat:* Meat was usually eaten only on special occasions, such as during a sacred meal when sacrifices were offered to the LORD.

12:21-26 *the place where the LORD your God chooses to put his Name . . . the place the LORD will choose:* The law in Exodus 20:24 allowed the worship of the LORD at several different locations. But Moses' words suggest that in the land of Canaan, one place of worship will be established. This likely refers to King David setting up the tabernacle in Jerusalem (2 Sam 6:16-18) and to King Solomon building Israel's first temple there (1 Kgs 8:1-21).

12:22 *unclean and the clean:* Only those who were properly prepared for worship, or "clean," could eat a sacred meal, but anyone could eat this kind of meat.

12:28 *obey . . . it may always go well:* See the note at 7:12-15.

12:31 *worshiping their gods . . . burn their sons and daughters:* See the note at 7:5. The practice of sacrificing children by fire was especially true of the cult of the god Molech (Lev 18:21; 20:2-5; Deut 18:10, 11; 2 Kgs 21:4-7; 23:10; Jer 7:31).

12:23,24 Lev 17:10-14. **12:32** Deut 4:2; Rev 22:18, 19.

13:1,2 *prophet . . . sign or wonder:* A prophet is God's messenger. The message the prophet speaks is called a "prophecy." The prophets of the Bible sometimes foretold what would happen in the future, but they mainly observed what was happening around them and then delivered God's message for that situation. Some Israelites assumed that anyone who performed miracles was a prophet who received that power from God. But any person who tries to lead the people to worship other gods is not a prophet of God and should not be followed. God used such a person as a test of the people's faithfulness. See also the article called "Prophets and Prophecy," p. 935.

13:9,10 *put him to death . . . Stone him:* Stoning someone was one of the most common forms of capital punishment among the Israelites. The accused persons were forced to stand in a small pit, and people would throw large rocks down on them in order to crush and kill them.

13:14 *detestable thing:* This refers to the worship of an idol. See also the note at 7:26.

13:15,16 *Destroy it completely . . . burnt offering:* A city that worships other gods is to be destroyed, just like cities that are captured in holy war, so it can be purified and dedicated to God. See the notes at 2:34; 3:6; and 7:2.

14:1 *Do not cut yourselves or shave:* Shaving the head (Job 1:20; Isa 3:24; 15:2; 22:12; Ezek 7:18; Amos 8:10; Mic 1:16) or gashing the skin (Jer 16:6; 41:5) were done as signs of mourning. But here and in Leviticus 19:27,28 and 21:5 such shaving and gashing is forbidden, probably because it was connected with the worship of other gods.

Worshiping Other Gods

13 If a prophet, or one who foretells by dreams, appears among
you and announces to you a miraculous sign or wonder, 2and if
the sign or wonder of which he has spoken takes place, and he
says, "Let us follow other gods" (gods you have not known) "and
let us worship them," 3you must not listen to the words of that
prophet or dreamer. The LORD your God is testing you to find out
whether you love him with all your heart and with all your soul. 4It
is the LORD your God you must follow, and him you must revere.
Keep his commands and obey him; serve him and hold fast to
him. 5That prophet or dreamer must be put to death, because he
preached rebellion against the LORD your God, who brought you
out of Egypt and redeemed you from the land of slavery; he has
tried to turn you from the way the LORD your God commanded
you to follow. You must purge the evil from among you.

6If your very own brother, or your son or daughter, or the
wife you love, or your closest friend secretly entices you, saying,
"Let us go and worship other gods" (gods that neither you nor
your fathers have known, 7gods of the peoples around you,
whether near or far, from one end of the land to the other), 8do
not yield to him or listen to him. Show him no pity. Do not spare
him or shield him. 9You must certainly put him to death. Your
hand must be the first in putting him to death, and then the hands
of all the people. 10Stone him to death, because he tried to turn
you away from the LORD your God, who brought you out of Egypt,
out of the land of slavery. 11Then all Israel will hear and be afraid,
and no one among you will do such an evil thing again.

12If you hear it said about one of the towns the LORD your
God is giving you to live in 13that wicked men have arisen among
you and have led the people of their town astray, saying, "Let us go
and worship other gods" (gods you have not known), 14then you
must inquire, probe and investigate it thoroughly. And if it is true
and it has been proved that this detestable thing has been done
among you, 15you must certainly put to the sword all who live in
that town. Destroy it completely,[a] both its people and its livestock.
16Gather all the plunder of the town into the middle of the public
square and completely burn the town and all its plunder as a
whole burnt offering to the LORD your God. It is to remain a ruin
forever, never to be rebuilt. 17None of those condemned things[a]
shall be found in your hands, so that the LORD will turn from his
fierce anger; he will show you mercy, have compassion on you, and
increase your numbers, as he promised on oath to your forefathers, 18because you obey the LORD your God, keeping all his
commands that I am giving you today and doing what is right in
his eyes.

[a]15,17 The Hebrew term refers to the irrevocable giving over of things or persons to the LORD, often by totally destroying them.

Clean and Unclean Food

14 You are the children of the LORD your God. Do not cut yourselves or shave the front of your heads for the dead, 2 for you are a
people holy to the LORD your God. Out of all the peoples on the face
of the earth, the LORD has chosen you to be his treasured possession.
3 Do not eat any detestable thing. 4 These are the animals you
may eat: the ox, the sheep, the goat, 5 the deer, the gazelle, the roe
deer, the wild goat, the ibex, the antelope and the mountain sheep.[a]
6 You may eat any animal that has a split hoof divided in two and
that chews the cud. 7 However, of those that chew the cud or that
have a split hoof completely divided you may not eat the camel,
the rabbit or the coney.[b] Although they chew the cud, they do not
have a split hoof; they are ceremonially unclean for you. 8 The pig
is also unclean; although it has a split hoof, it does not chew the
cud. You are not to eat their meat or touch their carcasses.
9 Of all the creatures living in the water, you may eat any that
has fins and scales. 10 But anything that does not have fins and
scales you may not eat; for you it is unclean.
11 You may eat any clean bird. 12 But these you may not eat:
the eagle, the vulture, the black vulture, 13 the red kite, the black
kite, any kind of falcon, 14 any kind of raven, 15 the horned owl, the
screech owl, the gull, any kind of hawk, 16 the little owl, the great
owl, the white owl, 17 the desert owl, the osprey, the cormorant,
18 the stork, any kind of heron, the hoopoe and the bat.
19 All flying insects that swarm are unclean to you; do not eat
them. 20 But any winged creature that is clean you may eat.
21 Do not eat anything you find already dead. You may give it
to an alien living in any of your towns, and he may eat it, or you
may sell it to a foreigner. But you are a people holy to the LORD
your God.

Do not cook a young goat in its mother's milk.

Tithes

22 Be sure to set aside a tenth of all that your fields produce
each year. 23 Eat the tithe of your grain, new wine and oil, and the
firstborn of your herds and flocks in the presence of the LORD your
God at the place he will choose as a dwelling for his Name, so that
you may learn to revere the LORD your God always. 24 But if that
place is too distant and you have been blessed by the LORD your
God and cannot carry your tithe (because the place where the
LORD will choose to put his Name is so far away), 25 then exchange
your tithe for silver, and take the silver with you and go to
the place the LORD your God will choose. 26 Use the silver to buy
whatever you like: cattle, sheep, wine or other fermented drink, or

14:2 *the LORD your God . . . has chosen you:* The Israelites were chosen by God and so were to set themselves apart from those who worshiped other gods. See also Exod 19:5; Deut 4:20; 7:6; 26:18; Isa 41:8, 9; Titus 2:14; 1 Pet 2:9.

14:3-20 *Do not eat . . . unclean:* Part of being God's holy people meant eating only proper ("clean") foods. Some animals were considered clean, and others were unclean. The exact reason for this is unclear.

Some of the birds in this list, such as hoopoes, are difficult to identify. "Any winged creature that is clean you may eat" (14:20) refers to locusts, crickets, and grasshoppers (Lev 11:20-23). See also the mini-article called "Purity (Clean and Unclean)," p. 2125.

14:21 *already dead:* An animal that had died naturally would contain blood, which could not be eaten. See the mini-article called "Blood," p. 180.

14:21 *goat in its mother's milk:* Some religions prepared a sacrifice by cooking it in milk. The Israelites may have been forbidden to do so to avoid imitating such pagan customs. This law forms the basis for the dietary practice of not mixing meat and dairy foods in later Judaism. See also Exod 23:19; 34:26.

14:22-29 *bring all the tithes:* People were to give a tenth of their vegetables, fruits, and grains, and the firstborn of their livestock as an offering to God. These offerings were to be taken to the place of worship and used for a holy meal eaten by the one making the offering and the Levites. Those unable to transport the items to the place of worship could use money to buy food for the holy meal. Every third year, the tithe was to remain in the local town. The tithe was also to be used by the Levites and given to groups in need (14:28, 29). Compare to Lev 27:30-33; Num 18:21-29; and 2 Chr 31:5, 6.

---

[a]**5** The precise identification of some of the birds and animals in this chapter is uncertain. [b]**7** That is, the hyrax or rock badger

15:1-10 *every seven years you must cancel debts:* Every seven years, all debts owed by Israelites to each other are to be canceled. The law does not apply to non-Jews (foreigners). Only DEUTERONOMY says that debts should be canceled every seven years. In the other books of the Pentateuch the emphasis is placed on allowing the land to rest every seven years so that the poor can what grows naturally during that year (Exod 23:10, 11; Lev 25:1-5).

15:11 *poor and needy:* The law (15:4-6) was supposed to eliminate poverty in Israel, but this verse suggests that people will not always properly care for the poor and needy who live in the land. See also Matt 26:11; Mark 14:7; John 12:8.

15:12-15 *sells himself:* Slavery was extremely common in the ancient Near East. The Israelites had slaves, including some of their own people. Israelites also bought slaves from slave traders, such as the Midianites (Gen 37:28, 36). The Israelites were not to keep slaves longer than six years, and when the slaves were freed, the owners were to provide them with enough so that they could remain independent. If a male slave wanted to continue serving his master, the slave's ear was pierced as a sign of lifelong commitment (Exod 21:6). Compare this to the rules concerning female slaves (21:10-14). See also Lev 25:39-46; Jer 34:8-20; and the mini-article called "Slaves and Servants in the Time of Jesus," p. 2006.

anything you wish. Then you and your household shall eat there in the presence of the LORD your God and rejoice. 27And do not neglect the Levites living in your towns, for they have no allotment or inheritance of their own.

28At the end of every three years, bring all the tithes of that year's produce and store it in your towns, 29so that the Levites (who have no allotment or inheritance of their own) and the aliens, the fatherless and the widows who live in your towns may come and eat and be satisfied, and so that the LORD your God may bless you in all the work of your hands.

The Year for Canceling Debts

15 At the end of every seven years you must cancel debts. 2This is how it is to be done: Every creditor shall cancel the loan he has made to his fellow Israelite. He shall not require payment from his fellow Israelite or brother, because the LORD's time for canceling debts has been proclaimed. 3You may require payment from a foreigner, but you must cancel any debt your brother owes you. 4However, there should be no poor among you, for in the land the LORD your God is giving you to possess as your inheritance, he will richly bless you, 5if only you fully obey the LORD your God and are careful to follow all these commands I am giving you today. 6For the LORD your God will bless you as he has promised, and you will lend to many nations but will borrow from none. You will rule over many nations but none will rule over you.

7If there is a poor man among your brothers in any of the towns of the land that the LORD your God is giving you, do not be hardhearted or tightfisted toward your poor brother. 8Rather be openhanded and freely lend him whatever he needs. 9Be careful not to harbor this wicked thought: "The seventh year, the year for canceling debts, is near," so that you do not show ill will toward your needy brother and give him nothing. He may then appeal to the LORD against you, and you will be found guilty of sin. 10Give generously to him and do so without a grudging heart; then because of this the LORD your God will bless you in all your work and in everything you put your hand to. 11There will always be poor people in the land. Therefore I command you to be openhanded toward your brothers and toward the poor and needy in your land.

Freeing Servants

12If a fellow Hebrew, a man or a woman, sells himself to you and serves you six years, in the seventh year you must let him go free. 13And when you release him, do not send him away empty-handed. 14Supply him liberally from your flock, your threshing floor and your winepress. Give to him as the LORD your God has blessed you. 15Remember that you were slaves in Egypt and the

LORD your God redeemed you. That is why I give you this command today.
[16]But if your servant says to you, "I do not want to leave
you," because he loves you and your family and is well off with
you, [17]then take an awl and push it through his ear lobe into the
door, and he will become your servant for life. Do the same for
your maidservant.
[18]Do not consider it a hardship to set your servant free,
because his service to you these six years has been worth twice as
much as that of a hired hand. And the LORD your God will bless
you in everything you do.

The Firstborn Animals

[19]Set apart for the LORD your God every firstborn male of
your herds and flocks. Do not put the firstborn of your oxen to
work, and do not shear the firstborn of your sheep. [20]Each year
you and your family are to eat them in the presence of the LORD
your God at the place he will choose. [21]If an animal has a defect, is
lame or blind, or has any serious flaw, you must not sacrifice it to
the LORD your God. [22]You are to eat it in your own towns. Both the
ceremonially unclean and the clean may eat it, as if it were gazelle
or deer. [23]But you must not eat the blood; pour it out on the
ground like water.

Passover

16 Observe the month of Abib and celebrate the Passover of the
LORD your God, because in the month of Abib he brought you out
of Egypt by night. [2]Sacrifice as the Passover to the LORD your God
an animal from your flock or herd at the place the LORD will
choose as a dwelling for his Name. [3]Do not eat it with bread made
with yeast, but for seven days eat unleavened bread, the bread of
affliction, because you left Egypt in haste—so that all the days of
your life you may remember the time of your departure from
Egypt. [4]Let no yeast be found in your possession in all your land
for seven days. Do not let any of the meat you sacrifice on the
evening of the first day remain until morning.
[5]You must not sacrifice the Passover in any town the LORD
your God gives you [6]except in the place he will choose as a
dwelling for his Name. There you must sacrifice the Passover in the
evening, when the sun goes down, on the anniversary[a] of your
departure from Egypt. [7]Roast it and eat it at the place the LORD
your God will choose. Then in the morning return to your tents.
[8]For six days eat unleavened bread and on the seventh day hold an
assembly to the LORD your God and do no work.

[a]**6** Or *down, at the time of day*

Moses said, *"Remember that you were slaves in Egypt and the LORD your God redeemed you."* Deut 15:15

15:19 *firstborn:* Firstborn male animals were to be offered as a sacrifice to God at God's chosen place of worship. If the animal was unfit for sacrifice (15:21), it could be eaten at home like any other meat. See also the notes at 12:6 and 12:15.

15:23 *blood:* See the mini-article called "Blood," on p. 180. See also Gen 9:4; Lev 7:26, 27; 17:10-14; 19:26; Deut 12:5-19, 23, 24.

16:1 *the LORD your God:* See the notes at 1:3-5 and 1:6.

16:1 *in the month of Abib:* Abib (also called Nisan), is the first month of the Hebrew calendar, from about mid-March to mid-April.

16:3 *for seven days:* This period was called the Feast of Unleavened Bread. "Passover" is related to the Hebrew word translated as "pass over" in Exodus 12:1-20 and 13:3-8. Passover was celebrated as a remembrance of how God saved the people and acted to help them escape from slavery in Egypt. It was to be celebrated on the fourteenth day of the first month starting at twilight. The Feast of Unleavened Bread was to begin the next day and to last for seven days (Lev 23:4-8; Num 28:16-25). See also the mini-article called "Passover and the Feast of Unleavened Bread," p. 2030.

16:8 *unleavened bread:* The unleavened bread was made without using yeast and was eaten as a reminder that the Hebrew people had to leave Egypt so quickly that they didn't have time to let their dough rise before baking it.

15:19 Exod 13:12.

16:10 *Feast of Weeks:* During the Feast of Weeks (also called the Feast of Ingathering), the people thanked God by bringing gifts of grain (Exod 23:16; 34:22; Lev 23:15-21; Num 28:26-31). This festival was known in New Testament times as "Pentecost." See also the chart called "Jewish Calendar and Festivals," p. 944.

16:13 *Feast of Tabernacles:* During the seven-day celebration of the Feast of Tabernacles, the people were to give thanks to God for the fall harvest and to build and live in shelters (or booths) made of tree branches (Lev 23:39-43). These shelters recalled the temporary shelters their ancestors lived in after they left Egypt. See also Num 29:12-38; Neh 8; and the chart called "Jewish Calendar and Festivals," p. 944.

16:16 *Feast of Unleavened Bread . . . Feast of Weeks . . . Feast of Tabernacles:* For a fuller explanation of these feasts, see Numbers 28:16-31 and 29:12-40.

16:18,19 *Appoint judges and officials:* It is not clear if this system of selecting judges differed from the system described earlier (Exod 18:13-27; Deut 1:9-17). It is clear that judges must be fair and honest (Exod 23:6-8; Lev 19:15). Israel's system of local government and courts was unique, because it was based on God's laws and the command to treat all people equally, whether they were rich or poor, powerful or weak.

16:20 *Follow justice:* See the note at 10:18,19.

16:21,22 *the altar you build to the Lord your God:* No altars or symbols honoring other gods were to be put up beside Israel's altar of sacrifice. See the notes at 7:5 and 12:21-26. See also Exod 34:13.

17:1 *defect:* Any animal offered as a sacrifice was to be in perfect condition (Exod 12:4, 5; Lev 22:20-25).

16:22 Lev 26:1.

Feast of Weeks

[9]Count off seven weeks from the time you begin to put the sickle to the standing grain. [10]Then celebrate the Feast of Weeks to the LORD your God by giving a freewill offering in proportion to the blessings the LORD your God has given you. [11]And rejoice before the LORD your God at the place he will choose as a dwelling for his Name—you, your sons and daughters, your menservants and maidservants, the Levites in your towns, and the aliens, the fatherless and the widows living among you. [12]Remember that you were slaves in Egypt, and follow carefully these decrees.

Feast of Tabernacles

[13]Celebrate the Feast of Tabernacles for seven days after you have gathered the produce of your threshing floor and your winepress. [14]Be joyful at your Feast—you, your sons and daughters, your menservants and maidservants, and the Levites, the aliens, the fatherless and the widows who live in your towns. [15]For seven days celebrate the Feast to the LORD your God at the place the LORD will choose. For the LORD your God will bless you in all your harvest and in all the work of your hands, and your joy will be complete.

[16]Three times a year all your men must appear before the LORD your God at the place he will choose: at the Feast of Unleavened Bread, the Feast of Weeks and the Feast of Tabernacles. No man should appear before the LORD empty-handed: [17]Each of you must bring a gift in proportion to the way the LORD your God has blessed you.

Judges

[18]Appoint judges and officials for each of your tribes in every town the LORD your God is giving you, and they shall judge the people fairly. [19]Do not pervert justice or show partiality. Do not accept a bribe, for a bribe blinds the eyes of the wise and twists the words of the righteous. [20]Follow justice and justice alone, so that you may live and possess the land the LORD your God is giving you.

Worshiping Other Gods

[21]Do not set up any wooden Asherah pole[a] beside the altar you build to the LORD your God, [22]and do not erect a sacred stone, for these the LORD your God hates.

17 Do not sacrifice to the LORD your God an ox or a sheep that has any defect or flaw in it, for that would be detestable to him.

[2]If a man or woman living among you in one of the towns

[a]**21** Or *Do not plant any tree dedicated to Asherah*

the LORD gives you is found doing evil in the eyes of the LORD your God in violation of his covenant, [3]and contrary to my command has worshiped other gods, bowing down to them or to the sun or the moon or the stars of the sky, [4]and this has been brought to your attention, then you must investigate it thoroughly. If it is true and it has been proved that this detestable thing has been done in Israel, [5]take the man or woman who has done this evil deed to your city gate and stone that person to death. [6]On the testimony of two or three witnesses a man shall be put to death, but no one shall be put to death on the testimony of only one witness. [7]The hands of the witnesses must be the first in putting him to death, and then the hands of all the people. You must purge the evil from among you.

Law Courts

[8]If cases come before your courts that are too difficult for you to judge—whether bloodshed, lawsuits or assaults—take them to the place the LORD your God will choose. [9]Go to the priests, who are Levites, and to the judge who is in office at that time. Inquire of them and they will give you the verdict. [10]You must act according to the decisions they give you at the place the LORD will choose. Be careful to do everything they direct you to do. [11]Act according to the law they teach you and the decisions they give you. Do not turn aside from what they tell you, to the right or to the left. [12]The man who shows contempt for the judge or for the priest who stands ministering there to the LORD your God must be put to death. You must purge the evil from Israel. [13]All the people will hear and be afraid, and will not be contemptuous again.

The King

[14]When you enter the land the LORD your God is giving you and have taken possession of it and settled in it, and you say, "Let us set a king over us like all the nations around us," [15]be sure to appoint over you the king the LORD your God chooses. He must be from among your own brothers. Do not place a foreigner over you, one who is not a brother Israelite. [16]The king, moreover, must not acquire great numbers of horses for himself or make the people return to Egypt to get more of them, for the LORD has told you, "You are not to go back that way again." [17]He must not take many wives, or his heart will be led astray. He must not accumulate large amounts of silver and gold.

[18]When he takes the throne of his kingdom, he is to write for himself on a scroll a copy of this law, taken from that of the priests, who are Levites. [19]It is to be with him, and he is to read it all the days of his life so that he may learn to revere the LORD his God and follow carefully all the words of this law and these decrees [20]and not consider himself better than his brothers and turn from the

17:3 *sun . . . moon . . . stars:* Some people worshiped these as gods. See the note at 4:19.

17:6 *two or three witnesses:* This requirement was meant to keep people from falsely accusing someone. Two witnesses were needed (Num 35:30; Deut 19:15), so one person alone could not charge someone falsely. These requirements show God's concern for justice. See also Matt 18:16; 2 Cor 13:1; 1 Tim 5:19; Heb 10:28.

17:8,9 *too difficult . . . to judge . . . Go to the priests:* Cases that are too difficult for the local judges to decide (16:18-20) are to be taken to a court at the place of worship. God chose the place, the judge, and the priests who interpret the law, so the decision is to be taken as the LORD's. For more about priests, see the note at 10:8.

17:14 *a king:* Each tribe had leaders, and in times of national danger, God chose a special leader to help the people fight off their enemies (see JUDGES). Eventually, the people begged for a king (1 Sam 8:4-22). Unlike other nations, Israel's king was to be chosen by God and was to rule according to God's laws (17:19, 20). The LORD God alone was to be the supreme ruler of Israel, and the king's future was in God's hands.

17:17 *many wives . . . led astray:* When making treaties, kings might marry each other's daughters. These foreign women would naturally want to worship their own gods, and would want their husband the king to do so as well. This happened to Solomon (1 Kgs 11:1-13) and to other kings of Israel.

17:16 1 Kgs 10:28; 2 Chr 1:16; 9:28. **17:17** 1 Kgs 10:14-22, 27; 11:1-8; 2 Chr 1:15; 9:27.

law to the right or to the left. Then he and his descendants will
reign a long time over his kingdom in Israel.

Offerings for Priests and Levites

18 The priests, who are Levites—indeed the whole tribe of
Levi—are to have no allotment or inheritance with Israel. They
shall live on the offerings made to the LORD by fire, for that is their
inheritance. 2They shall have no inheritance among their brothers;
the LORD is their inheritance, as he promised them.

3This is the share due the priests from the people who sacrifice a bull or a sheep: the shoulder, the jowls and the inner parts.
4You are to give them the firstfruits of your grain, new wine and
oil, and the first wool from the shearing of your sheep, 5for the
LORD your God has chosen them and their descendants out of all
your tribes to stand and minister in the LORD's name always.

6If a Levite moves from one of your towns anywhere in Israel
where he is living, and comes in all earnestness to the place the
LORD will choose, 7he may minister in the name of the LORD his
God like all his fellow Levites who serve there in the presence of
the LORD. 8He is to share equally in their benefits, even though he
has received money from the sale of family possessions.

Detestable Practices

9When you enter the land the LORD your God is giving you,
do not learn to imitate the detestable ways of the nations there.
10Let no one be found among you who sacrifices his son or daughter in[a] the fire, who practices divination or sorcery, interprets
omens, engages in witchcraft, 11or casts spells, or who is a medium
or spiritist or who consults the dead. 12Anyone who does these
things is detestable to the LORD, and because of these detestable
practices the LORD your God will drive out those nations before
you. 13You must be blameless before the LORD your God.

The Prophet

14The nations you will dispossess listen to those who practice
sorcery or divination. But as for you, the LORD your God has not
permitted you to do so. 15The LORD your God will raise up for you
a prophet like me from among your own brothers. You must listen
to him. 16For this is what you asked of the LORD your God at Horeb
on the day of the assembly when you said, "Let us not hear the voice
of the LORD our God nor see this great fire anymore, or we will die."

17The LORD said to me: "What they say is good. 18I will raise
up for them a prophet like you from among their brothers; I will
put my words in his mouth, and he will tell them everything I

[a]10 Or *who makes his son or daughter pass through*

18:1 *tribe of Levi . . . live on the offerings:* See the notes at 10:8 and 14:22-29. See also Lev 6:16,17; 22:10-16; Num 18:8-24; Deut 18:5.

18:3 *inner parts:* Certain portions of the sacrificed animal were considered a delicacy.

18:4 *grain . . . oil:* The first part of the harvest was offered as a gift to the LORD (Lev 23:10,11). See also the note at 12:6 (tithes).

18:6 *If a Levite moves:* The priests and other Levites would later be assigned to work at the temple in Jerusalem for a time each year. While serving at the temple, they would receive portions of the food offerings brought by the people (see the note at 18:1). See also the note at 12:21-26 and the mini-article called "Israel's Priests," p. 2344.

18:9 *the land:* See the note at 1:7, 8.

18:9 *the LORD your God:* See the notes at 1:3-5 and 1:6.

18:10,11 *sacrifices his son or daughter . . . medium or spiritist:* See the note at 12:31. Telling fortunes or practicing witchcraft were forbidden by God's Law (Exod 22:18; Lev 19:26, 31; Deut 18:14).

18:12 *detestable practices:* See the notes at 7:26 and 13:14.

18:15 *prophet like me:* Moses is described as a prophet (Deut 34:10; Acts 3:22; 7:37). He did not receive the visions and dreams God gave to other "prophets," but God spoke directly to Moses (Num 12:6-8). See also the note at 13:1, 2.

18:16 *Horeb:* Another name for Mount Sinai. See the note on p. 341 (Jordan . . . Moab).

18:10,11 Exod 22:18; Lev 19:26, 31; Deut 18:14. **18:13** Matt 5:48.

command him. 19If anyone does not listen to my words that the prophet speaks in my name, I myself will call him to account. 20But a prophet who presumes to speak in my name anything I have not commanded him to say, or a prophet who speaks in the name of other gods, must be put to death."

21You may say to yourselves, "How can we know when a message has not been spoken by the LORD?" 22If what a prophet proclaims in the name of the LORD does not take place or come true, that is a message the LORD has not spoken. That prophet has spoken presumptuously. Do not be afraid of him.

Cities of Refuge

19 When the LORD your God has destroyed the nations whose land he is giving you, and when you have driven them out and settled in their towns and houses, 2then set aside for yourselves three cities centrally located in the land the LORD your God is giving you to possess. 3Build roads to them and divide into three parts the land the LORD your God is giving you as an inheritance, so that anyone who kills a man may flee there.

4This is the rule concerning the man who kills another and flees there to save his life—one who kills his neighbor unintentionally, without malice aforethought. 5For instance, a man may go into the forest with his neighbor to cut wood, and as he swings his ax to fell a tree, the head may fly off and hit his neighbor and kill him. That man may flee to one of these cities and save his life. 6Otherwise, the avenger of blood might pursue him in a rage, overtake him if the distance is too great, and kill him even though he is not deserving of death, since he did it to his neighbor without malice aforethought. 7This is why I command you to set aside for yourselves three cities.

8If the LORD your God enlarges your territory, as he promised on oath to your forefathers, and gives you the whole land he promised them, 9because you carefully follow all these laws I command you today—to love the LORD your God and to walk always in his ways—then you are to set aside three more cities. 10Do this so that innocent blood will not be shed in your land, which the LORD your God is giving you as your inheritance, and so that you will not be guilty of bloodshed.

11But if a man hates his neighbor and lies in wait for him, assaults and kills him, and then flees to one of these cities, 12the elders of his town shall send for him, bring him back from the city, and hand him over to the avenger of blood to die. 13Show him no pity. You must purge from Israel the guilt of shedding innocent blood, so that it may go well with you.

14Do not move your neighbor's boundary stone set up by your predecessors in the inheritance you receive in the land the LORD your God is giving you to possess.

18:16 *LORD your God . . . great fire:* See the notes at 1:33 and 5:22.

18:18-22 *what a prophet proclaims . . . does not take place or come true:* This is the way to test whether a prophet was truly speaking God's words.

19:1 *the LORD your God has destroyed:* See the notes at 1:6; 2:34; 3:6; and 7:2.

19:1 *land . . . giving you:* See the note at 1:7, 8.

19:4-13 *set aside for yourselves three cities:* See the note at 4:41. If an innocent person is killed because a city of refuge is too far away, the whole nation is guilty of murder (19:10), and anyone guilty of murder is to die without mercy (19:13). See also Josh 20:1-9.

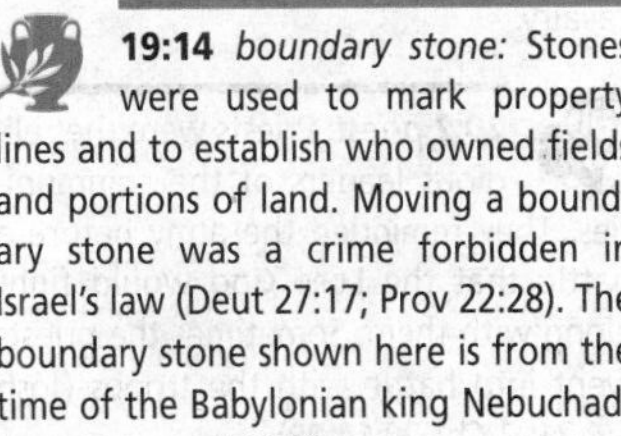

19:14 *boundary stone:* Stones were used to mark property lines and to establish who owned fields and portions of land. Moving a boundary stone was a crime forbidden in Israel's law (Deut 27:17; Prov 22:28). The boundary stone shown here is from the time of the Babylonian king Nebuchadnezzar, around 1140 B.C.

18:19 Acts 3:23.

Witnesses

15 One witness is not enough to convict a man accused of any crime or offense he may have committed. A matter must be established by the testimony of two or three witnesses.

16 If a malicious witness takes the stand to accuse a man of a crime, 17 the two men involved in the dispute must stand in the presence of the LORD before the priests and the judges who are in office at the time. 18 The judges must make a thorough investigation, and if the witness proves to be a liar, giving false testimony against his brother, 19 then do to him as he intended to do to his brother. You must purge the evil from among you. 20 The rest of the people will hear of this and be afraid, and never again will such an evil thing be done among you. 21 Show no pity: life for life, eye for eye, tooth for tooth, hand for hand, foot for foot.

Going to War

20 When you go to war against your enemies and see horses and chariots and an army greater than yours, do not be afraid of them, because the LORD your God, who brought you up out of Egypt, will be with you. 2 When you are about to go into battle, the priest shall come forward and address the army. 3 He shall say: "Hear, O Israel, today you are going into battle against your enemies. Do not be fainthearted or afraid; do not be terrified or give way to panic before them. 4 For the LORD your God is the one who goes with you to fight for you against your enemies to give you victory."

5 The officers shall say to the army: "Has anyone built a new house and not dedicated it? Let him go home, or he may die in battle and someone else may dedicate it. 6 Has anyone planted a vineyard and not begun to enjoy it? Let him go home, or he may die in battle and someone else enjoy it. 7 Has anyone become pledged to a woman and not married her? Let him go home, or he may die in battle and someone else marry her." 8 Then the officers shall add, "Is any man afraid or fainthearted? Let him go home so that his brothers will not become disheartened too." 9 When the officers have finished speaking to the army, they shall appoint commanders over it.

10 When you march up to attack a city, make its people an offer of peace. 11 If they accept and open their gates, all the people in it shall be subject to forced labor and shall work for you. 12 If they refuse to make peace and they engage you in battle, lay siege to that city. 13 When the LORD your God delivers it into your hand, put to the sword all the men in it. 14 As for the women, the children, the livestock and everything else in the city, you may take these as plunder for yourselves. And you may use the plunder the LORD your God gives you from your enemies. 15 This is how you are to treat all the cities that are at a distance from you and do not belong to the nations nearby.

19:15 *witness:* See the note at 17:6. Israel's justice system depended heavily on witnesses. Any witness who was discovered lying was severely punished (19:18-21).

20:1 *chariots:* A chariot had a single axle and two wheels, and was usually drawn by horses. Two or three soldiers rode in each chariot. The riders would often use the chariots to rush behind their enemies and attack them from the rear. See also the article called "Trade and Travel," p. 948.

20:1 *the LORD your God . . . will be with you:* In a holy war, the side having the most soldiers, horses, and chariots will not necessarily win the battle, because victory comes from God. Israel is reminded how the LORD helped them cross the Red Sea, where the LORD destroyed the Egyptians' chariots and cavalry.

20:2 *priest:* Priests were the religious leaders of the communities. They reminded the army before a battle that the LORD God would fight along with them. Sometimes the priests went into battle with the troops (Josh 6:4-21; 2 Chr 20:14-23).

20:5-9 *Let him go home:* Certain groups could be excused from fighting. One reason was fairness: new home builders, those who have not experienced the joy of their first grape harvest, and anyone engaged to be married did not have to serve. A second reason was army spirit and confidence: those who are afraid to fight might discourage the rest of the soldiers.

20:15 *cities that are at a distance:* A city outside the boundaries of Canaan was allowed to surrender. If it did, the people would become slaves; if not, all the men were to be killed and the women, children, and property were to be divided among the soldiers. See also the note at 15:12-15.

19:19-21 Exod 21:23-25; Lev 24:19, 20; Matt 5:38.

[16]However, in the cities of the nations the LORD your God is giving you as an inheritance, do not leave alive anything that breathes. [17]Completely destroy[a] them—the Hittites, Amorites, Canaanites, Perizzites, Hivites and Jebusites—as the LORD your God has commanded you. [18]Otherwise, they will teach you to follow all the detestable things they do in worshiping their gods, and you will sin against the LORD your God.

[19]When you lay siege to a city for a long time, fighting against it to capture it, do not destroy its trees by putting an ax to them, because you can eat their fruit. Do not cut them down. Are the trees of the field people, that you should besiege them?[b] [20]However, you may cut down trees that you know are not fruit trees and use them to build siege works until the city at war with you falls.

Atonement for an Unsolved Murder

21 If a man is found slain, lying in a field in the land the LORD your God is giving you to possess, and it is not known who killed him, [2]your elders and judges shall go out and measure the distance from the body to the neighboring towns. [3]Then the elders of the town nearest the body shall take a heifer that has never been worked and has never worn a yoke [4]and lead her down to a valley that has not been plowed or planted and where there is a flowing stream. There in the valley they are to break the heifer's neck. [5]The priests, the sons of Levi, shall step forward, for the LORD your God has chosen them to minister and to pronounce blessings in the name of the LORD and to decide all cases of dispute and assault. [6]Then all the elders of the town nearest the body shall wash their hands over the heifer whose neck was broken in the valley, [7]and they shall declare: "Our hands did not shed this blood, nor did our eyes see it done. [8]Accept this atonement for your people Israel, whom you have redeemed, O LORD, and do not hold your people guilty of the blood of an innocent man." And the bloodshed will be atoned for. [9]So you will purge from yourselves the guilt of shedding innocent blood, since you have done what is right in the eyes of the LORD.

Marrying a Captive Woman

[10]When you go to war against your enemies and the LORD your God delivers them into your hands and you take captives, [11]if you notice among the captives a beautiful woman and are attracted to her, you may take her as your wife. [12]Bring her into your home and have her shave her head, trim her nails [13]and put aside the clothes she was wearing when captured. After she has lived in

---

[a]17 The Hebrew term refers to the irrevocable giving over of things or persons to the LORD, often by totally destroying them. [b]19 Or *down to use in the siege, for the fruit trees are for the benefit of man.*

20:16 *cities of the nations:* Captured towns in the land of Canaan were to be completely destroyed in order to purify them and to prevent the people living in them from trying to persuade the Israelites to worship other gods (see the note at 7:26). See also the notes at 2:34; 3:6; and 7:2.

20:19 *do not destroy its trees:* This area had many apple, fig, apricot, and olive trees. Because these could provide food for Israel, they were not to be destroyed unnecessarily.

21:1-9 *If a man is found slain:* Murder was against God's Law (Exod 20:13; Deut 5:17), and the spilled blood of a murder victim made the land "unclean" and useless until the murderer was found and executed (Gen 4:10, 11; Num 35:33, 34). If the murderer was not found, the town nearest to the murder had to conduct a ceremony of purification to remove that guilt and make the land clean again. After breaking the neck of a young cow, the town leaders were to wash their hands over the dead body as the blood of the cow washed down the stream. This symbolized the washing away of guilt. By performing this ceremony and asking God's forgiveness, the community took responsibility for the crime. See also the mini-article called "Purity (Clean and Unclean)," p. 2125.

21:3 *heifer:* The heifer is executed in place of the murderer.

21:11 *beautiful woman:* The laws of holy war allowed soldiers to keep and marry women they captured (20:10-15).

21:15-17 *two wives . . . firstborn:* This law protects the rights of a man's firstborn son, even if he is not the son of the most-favored wife. Ancient laws allowed for a man to give a greater share of his property to his oldest son. Because a widow depended on her son for support, this law also protected the less-favored wife. See also the mini-article called "Birthright," p. 80.

21:18-21 *stubborn and rebellious . . . stone him:* Stoning a rebellious son to death was meant to serve as a lesson to others and to protect the family. See also 5:16 and the note at 13:9, 10.

21:19 *elders at the gate:* Walls were built around cities for protection. A town wall usually had a central gate, where people could enter the city. The town gate was also a gathering place where the town leaders heard and decided disputes. See the note at 16:18, 19.

21:22 *body is hung on a tree:* Because the hanged body was considered cursed by God, it had to be buried by evening so that the land would not become "unclean." See also the note at 21:1-9.

22:1 *take it back:* Lost property was to be cared for and returned. See also Exod 23:4, 5.

22:8 *the roof:* In the ancient Near East, roofs were sometimes used for sleeping and entertaining guests.

22:9-11 *two kinds:* Breeding, planting, and even the making of cloth were to follow the natural order of God's created world. See Lev 19:19.

22:11 *linen:* Stalks of flax plants were soaked in water, and dried. Then fibers were separated and spun into thread, which was woven into linen cloth. See illustration on p. 1829.

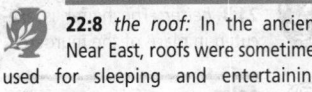

21:22,23 Gal 3:13.

your house and mourned her father and mother for a full month,
then you may go to her and be her husband and she shall be your
wife. 14 If you are not pleased with her, let her go wherever she
wishes. You must not sell her or treat her as a slave, since you have
dishonored her.

The Right of the Firstborn

15 If a man has two wives, and he loves one but not the other,
and both bear him sons but the firstborn is the son of the wife he
does not love, 16 when he wills his property to his sons, he must not
give the rights of the firstborn to the son of the wife he loves in
preference to his actual firstborn, the son of the wife he does not
love. 17 He must acknowledge the son of his unloved wife as the
firstborn by giving him a double share of all he has. That son is
the first sign of his father's strength. The right of the firstborn
belongs to him.

A Rebellious Son

18 If a man has a stubborn and rebellious son who does not
obey his father and mother and will not listen to them when they
discipline him, 19 his father and mother shall take hold of him and
bring him to the elders at the gate of his town. 20 They shall say to
the elders, "This son of ours is stubborn and rebellious. He will not
obey us. He is a profligate and a drunkard." 21 Then all the men of
his town shall stone him to death. You must purge the evil from
among you. All Israel will hear of it and be afraid.

Various Laws

22 If a man guilty of a capital offense is put to death and his
body is hung on a tree, 23 you must not leave his body on the tree
overnight. Be sure to bury him that same day, because anyone who
is hung on a tree is under God's curse. You must not desecrate the
land the LORD your God is giving you as an inheritance.
22 If you see your brother's ox or sheep straying, do not ignore
it but be sure to take it back to him. 2 If the brother does not live
near you or if you do not know who he is, take it home with you
and keep it until he comes looking for it. Then give it back to him.
3 Do the same if you find your brother's donkey or his cloak or
anything he loses. Do not ignore it.
4 If you see your brother's donkey or his ox fallen on the
road, do not ignore it. Help him get it to its feet.
5 A woman must not wear men's clothing, nor a man wear
women's clothing, for the LORD your God detests anyone who does
this.

6 If you come across a bird's nest beside the road, either in a
tree or on the ground, and the mother is sitting on the young or
on the eggs, do not take the mother with the young. 7 You may take

the young, but be sure to let the mother go, so that it may go well
with you and you may have a long life.
[8]When you build a new house, make a parapet around your
roof so that you may not bring the guilt of bloodshed on your
house if someone falls from the roof.
[9]Do not plant two kinds of seed in your vineyard; if you do,
not only the crops you plant but also the fruit of the vineyard will
be defiled.[a]
[10]Do not plow with an ox and a donkey yoked together.
[11]Do not wear clothes of wool and linen woven together.
[12]Make tassels on the four corners of the cloak you wear.

Marriage Violations

[13]If a man takes a wife and, after lying with her, dislikes her
[14]and slanders her and gives her a bad name, saying, "I married
this woman, but when I approached her, I did not find proof of
her virginity," [15]then the girl's father and mother shall bring proof
that she was a virgin to the town elders at the gate. [16]The girl's
father will say to the elders, "I gave my daughter in marriage to this
man, but he dislikes her. [17]Now he has slandered her and said, 'I
did not find your daughter to be a virgin.' But here is the proof of
my daughter's virginity." Then her parents shall display the cloth
before the elders of the town, [18]and the elders shall take the man
and punish him. [19]They shall fine him a hundred shekels of silver[b]
and give them to the girl's father, because this man has given an
Israelite virgin a bad name. She shall continue to be his wife; he
must not divorce her as long as he lives.
[20]If, however, the charge is true and no proof of the girl's virginity can be found, [21]she shall be brought to the door of her
father's house and there the men of her town shall stone her to
death. She has done a disgraceful thing in Israel by being promiscuous while still in her father's house. You must purge the evil
from among you.
[22]If a man is found sleeping with another man's wife, both
the man who slept with her and the woman must die. You must
purge the evil from Israel.
[23]If a man happens to meet in a town a virgin pledged to be
married and he sleeps with her, [24]you shall take both of them to
the gate of that town and stone them to death—the girl because
she was in a town and did not scream for help, and the man
because he violated another man's wife. You must purge the evil
from among you.
[25]But if out in the country a man happens to meet a girl
pledged to be married and rapes her, only the man who has done
this shall die. [26]Do nothing to the girl; she has committed no sin

[a]9 Or *be forfeited to the sanctuary* [b]19 That is, about 2 1/2 pounds (about 1 kilogram)

22:12 *tassels on the four corners:* Jewish prayer shawls today still include such tassels. See also Num 15:37-41.

22:13-21 *man . . . stone her to death:* Women were expected to be virgins at the time of the wedding. If a man proved that a woman was not a virgin when she married, she was executed outside her father's door as a public show of the shame she had brought upon her family. A man could be beaten and heavily fined for falsely claiming his bride was not a virgin. The fine was paid to her father, not to her (22:19, 28, 29).

22:19 *a hundred shekels of silver:* Twice what a man paid the father to marry his daughter (22:28, 29).

22:22 *sleeping with another man's wife:* This law forbidding sex with another man's wife (adultery) was intended to protect a husband's rights over his wife. An engaged woman was considered legally married. If a man had sex with a woman, not his wife, whether married or engaged, both were to die. But an engaged woman could avoid death if she was heard screaming for help (22:23, 24). If the act took place where no one could hear her (22:27), the man was guilty of rape and was put to death. If a man had sex with a woman who was not married or engaged, he was to pay her father, marry her, and support her for life. See also Exod 22:16, 17.

22:30 *his father's wife:* This may refer to a widow or divorced stepmother.

23:1,2 *emasculated . . . born of a forbidden marriage:* A man who has been castrated is called a "eunuch." Eunuchs usually served as court officials, often in charge of the women's living areas. Excluding eunuchs from membership in God's community reflects the belief that all things dedicated to God were to represent the perfection of God's creation. Those born outside of marriage were considered unfit, too, as they were born outside of God's Law.

23:3-7 *Ammonite or Moabite . . . Edomite . . . Egyptian:* The king of Moab hired Balaam to curse Israel (Num 22:1-6). The Edomites had refused to let Israel pass through their land, but they will be included in the assembly of the LORD because they are relatives. The Egyptians, who had held the Israelites as slaves (Exod 1:1-22), will be included because they helped Joseph and his father Jacob's family (Gen 41:37-57; 46:1—47:26).

23:17 *shrine prostitute:* Refers to young unmarried women who were expected to have sex with the worshipers of Baal, the Canaanite god of rain and fertility. The men who had sex with these prostitutes believed ritual sex would cause the gods to make the land fertile. See Lev 19:29; Hos 4:10-15; and the mini-article called "Prostitution in the Bible," p. 1688.

23:18 *earnings:* Part of the money temple prostitutes earned was given as a gift to a god. No such offering was acceptable to the LORD God.

23:19 *interest:* Israelites gave loans to those suffering hardship, but those who loaned money were not supposed to earn a profit because of the other person's need. Loans to foreigners usually were business loans and benefited both parties.

deserving death. This case is like that of someone who attacks and
murders his neighbor, 27 for the man found the girl out in the
country, and though the betrothed girl screamed, there was no one
to rescue her.

28 If a man happens to meet a virgin who is not pledged to be
married and rapes her and they are discovered, 29 he shall pay the
girl's father fifty shekels of silver.[a] He must marry the girl, for he
has violated her. He can never divorce her as long as he lives.

30 A man is not to marry his father's wife; he must not dishonor his father's bed.

Exclusion From the Assembly

23 No one who has been emasculated by crushing or cutting
may enter the assembly of the LORD.

2 No one born of a forbidden marriage[b] nor any of his
descendants may enter the assembly of the LORD, even down to the
tenth generation.

3 No Ammonite or Moabite or any of his descendants may
enter the assembly of the LORD, even down to the tenth generation.
4 For they did not come to meet you with bread and water on your
way when you came out of Egypt, and they hired Balaam son of
Beor from Pethor in Aram Naharaim[c] to pronounce a curse on
you. 5 However, the LORD your God would not listen to Balaam but
turned the curse into a blessing for you, because the LORD your
God loves you. 6 Do not seek a treaty of friendship with them as
long as you live.

7 Do not abhor an Edomite, for he is your brother. Do not
abhor an Egyptian, because you lived as an alien in his country.
8 The third generation of children born to them may enter the
assembly of the LORD.

Uncleanness in the Camp

9 When you are encamped against your enemies, keep away
from everything impure. 10 If one of your men is unclean because
of a nocturnal emission, he is to go outside the camp and stay
there. 11 But as evening approaches he is to wash himself, and at
sunset he may return to the camp.

12 Designate a place outside the camp where you can go to
relieve yourself. 13 As part of your equipment have something to
dig with, and when you relieve yourself, dig a hole and cover up
your excrement. 14 For the LORD your God moves about in your
camp to protect you and to deliver your enemies to you. Your
camp must be holy, so that he will not see among you anything
indecent and turn away from you.

---

[a] **29** That is, about 1 1/4 pounds (about 0.6 kilogram) [b] **2** Or *one of illegitimate birth* [c] **4** That is, Northwest Mesopotamia

Miscellaneous Laws

[15]If a slave has taken refuge with you, do not hand him over
to his master. [16]Let him live among you wherever he likes and in
whatever town he chooses. Do not oppress him.

[17]No Israelite man or woman is to become a shrine prostitute. [18]You must not bring the earnings of a female prostitute or of
a male prostitute[a] into the house of the LORD your God to pay any
vow, because the LORD your God detests them both.

[19]Do not charge your brother interest, whether on money or
food or anything else that may earn interest. [20]You may charge a
foreigner interest, but not a brother Israelite, so that the LORD your
God may bless you in everything you put your hand to in the land
you are entering to possess.

[21]If you make a vow to the LORD your God, do not be slow to
pay it, for the LORD your God will certainly demand it of you and
you will be guilty of sin. [22]But if you refrain from making a vow,
you will not be guilty. [23]Whatever your lips utter you must be sure
to do, because you made your vow freely to the LORD your God
with your own mouth.

[24]If you enter your neighbor's vineyard, you may eat all the
grapes you want, but do not put any in your basket. [25]If you enter
your neighbor's grainfield, you may pick kernels with your hands,
but you must not put a sickle to his standing grain.

24 If a man marries a woman who becomes displeasing to
him because he finds something indecent about her, and he
writes her a certificate of divorce, gives it to her and sends her
from his house, [2]and if after she leaves his house she becomes the
wife of another man, [3]and her second husband dislikes her and
writes her a certificate of divorce, gives it to her and sends her
from his house, or if he dies, [4]then her first husband, who
divorced her, is not allowed to marry her again after she has been
defiled. That would be detestable in the eyes of the LORD. Do not
bring sin upon the land the LORD your God is giving you as an
inheritance.

[5]If a man has recently married, he must not be sent to war or
have any other duty laid on him. For one year he is to be free to
stay at home and bring happiness to the wife he has married.

[6]Do not take a pair of millstones—not even the upper one—
as security for a debt, because that would be taking a man's livelihood as security.

[7]If a man is caught kidnapping one of his brother Israelites
and treats him as a slave or sells him, the kidnapper must die. You
must purge the evil from among you.

[8]In cases of leprous[b] diseases be very careful to do exactly as
the priests, who are Levites, instruct you. You must follow carefully

[a]**18** Hebrew *of a dog* [b]**8** The Hebrew word was used for various diseases affecting the skin—not necessarily leprosy.

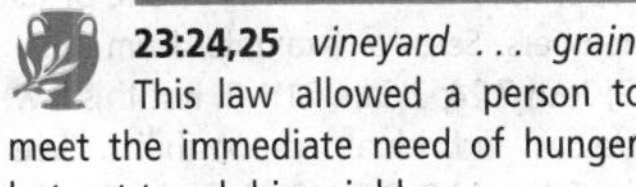

23:21 *do not be slow to pay for it:* Vows were taken very seriously. Once a person made a vow, it could not be taken back. See also Num 30:1-16; Matt 5:33; and the mini-article called "Making Vows," p. 328.

23:24,25 *vineyard . . . grain:* This law allowed a person to meet the immediate need of hunger, but not to rob his neighbor.

24:1,2 *certificate of divorce:* In ancient Israel, a husband could easily divorce his wife. If the woman remarried, the husband who divorced her could not marry her again, even if the second husband died. This law probably was intended to discourage men from deciding too quickly to write out a certificate of divorce. See Matt 5:31; 19:7; Mark 10:4.

24:6 *millstones:* Grain was placed on a flat stone, and then another stone was used to crush the grain into flour. Millstones ranged in size from small hand-held ones to very large ones powered by water, animals, or humans. Every household had to have a millstone in order to grind grain into flour for making bread and other basic foods. Someone who lends money could not take a millstone as guarantee of repayment of the loan.

24:8 *leprous diseases:* Some skin diseases were contagious, but skin diseases and burns that were not contagious were also treated as if they made a person unclean. See also Num 5:2-4; Lev 13:1—14:32.

24:8 *priests:* See the note at 10:8. The priests were responsible for making sure the people and the land remained acceptable to God (ritually clean).

23:5 Num 23, 24. **24:7** Exod 21:16.

what I have commanded them. [9]Remember what the LORD your God did to Miriam along the way after you came out of Egypt.

[10]When you make a loan of any kind to your neighbor, do not go into his house to get what he is offering as a pledge. [11]Stay outside and let the man to whom you are making the loan bring the pledge out to you. [12]If the man is poor, do not go to sleep with his pledge in your possession. [13]Return his cloak to him by sunset so that he may sleep in it. Then he will thank you, and it will be regarded as a righteous act in the sight of the LORD your God.

[14]Do not take advantage of a hired man who is poor and needy, whether he is a brother Israelite or an alien living in one of your towns. [15]Pay him his wages each day before sunset, because he is poor and is counting on it. Otherwise he may cry to the LORD against you, and you will be guilty of sin.

[16]Fathers shall not be put to death for their children, nor children put to death for their fathers; each is to die for his own sin.

[17]Do not deprive the alien or the fatherless of justice, or take the cloak of the widow as a pledge. [18]Remember that you were slaves in Egypt and the LORD your God redeemed you from there. That is why I command you to do this.

[19]When you are harvesting in your field and you overlook a sheaf, do not go back to get it. Leave it for the alien, the fatherless and the widow, so that the LORD your God may bless you in all the work of your hands. [20]When you beat the olives from your trees, do not go over the branches a second time. Leave what remains for the alien, the fatherless and the widow. [21]When you harvest the grapes in your vineyard, do not go over the vines again. Leave what remains for the alien, the fatherless and the widow. [22]Remember that you were slaves in Egypt. That is why I command you to do this.

25 When men have a dispute, they are to take it to court and the judges will decide the case, acquitting the innocent and condemning the guilty. [2]If the guilty man deserves to be beaten, the judge shall make him lie down and have him flogged in his presence with the number of lashes his crime deserves, [3]but he must not give him more than forty lashes. If he is flogged more than that, your brother will be degraded in your eyes.

[4]Do not muzzle an ox while it is treading out the grain.

[5]If brothers are living together and one of them dies without a son, his widow must not marry outside the family. Her husband's brother shall take her and marry her and fulfill the duty of a brother-in-law to her. [6]The first son she bears shall carry on the name of the dead brother so that his name will not be blotted out from Israel.

[7]However, if a man does not want to marry his brother's wife, she shall go to the elders at the town gate and say, "My husband's brother refuses to carry on his brother's name in Israel. He

24:15 *Pay him his wages each day:* Poor workers probably used most of the money they earned for food. See also Lev 19:13.

24:16 *put to death:* The entire family or community was often held responsible for the actions of one of its members. See, for example, Num 16:1-33; Josh 7:24; 2 Sam 21:1-9. But this law stresses individual responsibility. See also 2 Kgs 14:6; 2 Chr 25:4; Ezek 18:4-20.

24:17 *alien . . . fatherless:* See the note at 10:18, 19. See also Exod 23:9; Lev 19:33, 34; Deut 27:19; and the mini-article called "Foreigners (Aliens)," p. 501.

24:19-21 *overlook . . . Leave what remains:* Some grain or fruit was to be left behind in fields, orchards, and vineyards, so the poor could pick it and eat. See Lev 19:9,10; 23:22; Ruth 2:2-7.

25:1-3 *not give him more than forty lashes:* Beating as a punishment was allowed, but only after a trial and in view of a judge. The limit of forty lashes was later changed to thirty-nine to allow for a miscount (2 Cor 11:24).

25:4 *muzzle . . . treading out the grain:* Not muzzling an ox allowed the ox to eat as he worked, which was an act of kindness. See the note at 24:6 and the illustration on p. 730.

24:9 Num 12. **24:10-13** Exod 22:25-27 **25:4** 1 Cor 9:9; 1 Tim 5:18.

will not fulfill the duty of a brother-in-law to me." 8Then the elders
of his town shall summon him and talk to him. If he persists in
saying, "I do not want to marry her," 9his brother's widow shall go
up to him in the presence of the elders, take off one of his sandals,
spit in his face and say, "This is what is done to the man who will
not build up his brother's family line." 10That man's line shall be
known in Israel as The Family of the Unsandaled.
11If two men are fighting and the wife of one of them comes
to rescue her husband from his assailant, and she reaches out and
seizes him by his private parts, 12you shall cut off her hand. Show
her no pity.
13Do not have two differing weights in your bag—one heavy,
one light. 14Do not have two differing measures in your house—
one large, one small. 15You must have accurate and honest weights
and measures, so that you may live long in the land the LORD your
God is giving you. 16For the LORD your God detests anyone who
does these things, anyone who deals dishonestly.
17Remember what the Amalekites did to you along the way
when you came out of Egypt. 18When you were weary and worn
out, they met you on your journey and cut off all who were lag-
ging behind; they had no fear of God. 19When the LORD your God
gives you rest from all the enemies around you in the land he is
giving you to possess as an inheritance, you shall blot out the
memory of Amalek from under heaven. Do not forget!

Firstfruits and Tithes

26 When you have entered the land the LORD your God is giving you as an inheritance and have taken possession of it and settled in it, 2take some of the firstfruits of all that you produce from
the soil of the land the LORD your God is giving you and put them
in a basket. Then go to the place the LORD your God will choose as
a dwelling for his Name 3and say to the priest in office at the time,
"I declare today to the LORD your God that I have come to the land
the LORD swore to our forefathers to give us." 4The priest shall take
the basket from your hands and set it down in front of the altar of
the LORD your God. 5Then you shall declare before the LORD your
God: "My father was a wandering Aramean, and he went down
into Egypt with a few people and lived there and became a great
nation, powerful and numerous. 6But the Egyptians mistreated us
and made us suffer, putting us to hard labor. 7Then we cried out to
the LORD, the God of our fathers, and the LORD heard our voice
and saw our misery, toil and oppression. 8So the LORD brought us
out of Egypt with a mighty hand and an outstretched arm, with
great terror and with miraculous signs and wonders. 9He brought
us to this place and gave us this land, a land flowing with milk and
honey; 10and now I bring the firstfruits of the soil that you,
O LORD, have given me." Place the basket before the LORD your

25:5-9 *dies without a son:* The law assured that a man who died without a son could have his name carried on and his property kept in the family (Gen 38:6-26; Ruth 4:10; Matt 22:24; Mark 12:19). To make a deal legal, one person took off a sandal and gave it to the other (Ruth 4:7, 8).

25:13,14 *two differing weights:* Dishonest business practices were forbidden (Exod 20:15; Lev 19:35, 36; Prov 20:10; Amos 8:5).

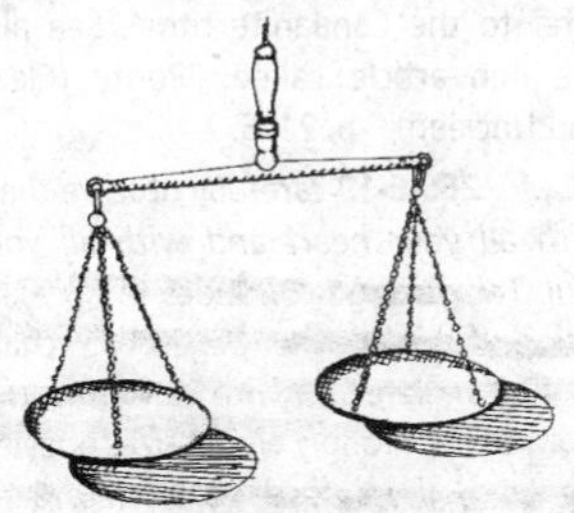

25:17 *Amalekites:* Descendants of Amalek (Gen 36:15, 16), they attacked the Israelites on their way out of Egypt (Exod 17:8-14).

26:2-11 *firstfruits:* When the first part of the harvest is presented to God at the place of worship, the people are to remember that God rescued them from Egypt and give thanks for the gift of a new land.

26:2 *the LORD your God:* See the note at 1:6.

26:3-11 *priest . . . Levites:* Israel's priests offered sacrifices to God, taught the people what was ritually clean and unclean, and made arrangements for Israel's yearly religious festivals. Part of thanksgiving offerings were eaten by the priests and their families (see Lev 6:18; 7:11-21; and the note at 14:22-29).

26:5 *wandering Aramean:* Refers to Jacob, who wandered from southern Canaan to Haran and back (Gen 27–35), later went to Egypt (Gen 46:3-7), and was married to two Aramean women (Gen 28:5; 29:16-28). During Jacob's time in Egypt, his family grew to great numbers (Exod 1:1-7).

26:11 *aliens:* See the note at 10:18, 19.

26:12 *third year, the year of the tithe:* Probably the third and sixth years of the seven-year cycle described in 15:1-11. See 14:28, 29 and the note at 14:22-29.

26:14 *mourning . . . offered any of it to the dead:* Touching the dead made a person unclean and unfit to worship God (Lev 11:24-38; Num 19:11-22). Offering to spirits of the dead may refer to the Canaanite ritual. See also the mini-article called "Purity (Clean and Unclean)," p. 2125.

26:16-19 *carefully observe them with all your heart and with all your soul:* This passage concludes the presentation of the law that began with chapter 12 (compare 12:1 with 26:16). Though 12:1—26:15 strongly emphasizes obeying the LORD, these final verses (26:16-19) emphasize that obeying God is not simply a duty, but a loving response to the care and blessing they have first received from the LORD God.

27:2-4 *crossed the Jordan . . . Mount Ebal:* While the Israelites camped in Moab, east of the Jordan River, Moses gave instructions for a ceremony at Mount Ebal near Shechem. The ceremony presented here calls for announcing both blessings and curses, but only the curses appear in 27:14–26.

27:2-5 *large stones . . . altar:* A mixture of clay and lime "plaster" was added to give the stones a smooth, light surface for the writing. It is not known why the altar stones were not to be cut with iron tools. See also Exod 20:25, and the notes at 7:5 and 10:1-3.

26:15 1 Kgs 8:30; 2 Chr 30:27; Ps 68:4. **27:2-8** Josh 8:30-32.

God and bow down before him. 11 And you and the Levites and the
aliens among you shall rejoice in all the good things the LORD your
God has given to you and your household.
12 When you have finished setting aside a tenth of all your
produce in the third year, the year of the tithe, you shall give it to
the Levite, the alien, the fatherless and the widow, so that they may
eat in your towns and be satisfied. 13 Then say to the LORD your
God: "I have removed from my house the sacred portion and have
given it to the Levite, the alien, the fatherless and the widow,
according to all you commanded. I have not turned aside from
your commands nor have I forgotten any of them. 14 I have not
eaten any of the sacred portion while I was in mourning, nor have
I removed any of it while I was unclean, nor have I offered any of
it to the dead. I have obeyed the LORD my God; I have done everything you commanded me. 15 Look down from heaven, your holy
dwelling place, and bless your people Israel and the land you have
given us as you promised on oath to our forefathers, a land flowing with milk and honey."

RENEWING THE COVENANT

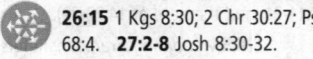

Moses describes a ceremony for renewing the covenant that the LORD made with Israel at Mount Sinai. The ceremony is to take place at Mount Ebal near Shechem after the people cross the Jordan River (27:1-26). Moses presents a list of blessings (material rewards) if Israel keeps the covenant (28:1-14), and a much longer list of curses (punishments) if they do not (28:15-68).

Follow the LORD's Commands

16 The LORD your God commands you this day to follow
these decrees and laws; carefully observe them with all your heart
and with all your soul. 17 You have declared this day that the LORD
is your God and that you will walk in his ways, that you will keep
his decrees, commands and laws, and that you will obey him.
18 And the LORD has declared this day that you are his people, his
treasured possession as he promised, and that you are to keep all
his commands. 19 He has declared that he will set you in praise,
fame and honor high above all the nations he has made and that
you will be a people holy to the LORD your God, as he promised.

The Altar on Mount Ebal

27 Moses and the elders of Israel commanded the people: "Keep
all these commands that I give you today. 2 When you have crossed
the Jordan into the land the LORD your God is giving you, set up
some large stones and coat them with plaster. 3 Write on them all
the words of this law when you have crossed over to enter the land
the LORD your God is giving you, a land flowing with milk and

honey, just as the LORD, the God of your fathers, promised you.
[4]And when you have crossed the Jordan, set up these stones on
Mount Ebal, as I command you today, and coat them with plaster.
[5]Build there an altar to the LORD your God, an altar of stones. Do
not use any iron tool upon them. [6]Build the altar of the LORD your
God with fieldstones and offer burnt offerings on it to the LORD
your God. [7]Sacrifice fellowship offerings[a] there, eating them and
rejoicing in the presence of the LORD your God. [8]And you shall
write very clearly all the words of this law on these stones you have
set up."

Curses From Mount Ebal

[9]Then Moses and the priests, who are Levites, said to all
Israel, "Be silent, O Israel, and listen! You have now become the
people of the LORD your God. [10]Obey the LORD your God and follow his commands and decrees that I give you today."

[11]On the same day Moses commanded the people:
[12]When you have crossed the Jordan, these tribes shall stand
on Mount Gerizim to bless the people: Simeon, Levi, Judah,
Issachar, Joseph and Benjamin. [13]And these tribes shall stand on
Mount Ebal to pronounce curses: Reuben, Gad, Asher, Zebulun,
Dan and Naphtali.
[14]The Levites shall recite to all the people of Israel in a loud
voice:

[15]"Cursed is the man who carves an image or casts an idol—a thing detestable to the LORD, the work of the craftsman's hands—and sets it up in secret."

Then all the people shall say, "Amen!"

[16]"Cursed is the man who dishonors his father or his mother."

Then all the people shall say, "Amen!"

[17]"Cursed is the man who moves his neighbor's boundary stone."

Then all the people shall say, "Amen!"

[18]"Cursed is the man who leads the blind astray on the road."

Then all the people shall say, "Amen!"

[19]"Cursed is the man who withholds justice from the alien, the fatherless or the widow."

Then all the people shall say, "Amen!"

[20]"Cursed is the man who sleeps with his father's wife, for he dishonors his father's bed."

Then all the people shall say, "Amen!"

[21]"Cursed is the man who has sexual relations with any animal."

Then all the people shall say, "Amen!"

[a]7 Traditionally *peace offerings*

27:6 *burnt offerings:* See the note at 12:6 (burnt offerings).

27:7 *fellowship offerings:* Traditionally called "peace offerings" or "offerings of well-being." The main purpose was to give thanks to God and have fellowship with him.

27:9 *priests:* See the notes at 20:2 and 24:8 (priests).

27:9 *You have now become the people of the LORD your God:* This statement is based on the covenant recorded in 26:16-19. This new covenant does not replace the first covenant made at Mount Sinai, but renews it.

27:12,13 *Mount Gerizim ... Mount Ebal:* See the note at 11:29, 30; see also Josh 8:33-35.

27:14 *The Levites:* See the note at 10:8.

27:15-26 *Cursed:* In Israelite thought, the spoken word was powerful. This was especially true of curses and blessings. Some of the curses were for those who disobeyed various commandments: idol worship (Exod 20:4, 5; Lev 19:4); disrespecting parents (Exod 20:12; Lev 19:3); murder (Exod 20:13). Other curses were for various other laws: moving property lines (see 19:14); causing a blind person to stumble (Lev 19:14); treating the poor unfairly (Lev 19:33, 34; Deut 24:17, 18); improper sexual relations (Lev 18:8, 9, 23; Deut 22:22-30); and taking bribes (see 16:18, 19). Following each curse, the people would say "Amen," to show that they understand and agree with what is being said.

27:14-26 Jer 11:1-4; Gal 3:10.

[22]"Cursed is the man who sleeps with his sister, the
daughter of his father or the daughter of his mother."
Then all the people shall say, "Amen!"
[23]"Cursed is the man who sleeps with his mother-
in-law."
Then all the people shall say, "Amen!"
[24]"Cursed is the man who kills his neighbor secretly."
Then all the people shall say, "Amen!"
[25]"Cursed is the man who accepts a bribe to kill an
innocent person."
Then all the people shall say, "Amen!"
[26]"Cursed is the man who does not uphold the words of
this law by carrying them out."
Then all the people shall say, "Amen!"

Blessings for Obedience

28 If you fully obey the LORD your God and carefully follow all
his commands I give you today, the LORD your God will set you
high above all the nations on earth. [2]All these blessings will come
upon you and accompany you if you obey the LORD your God:

[3]You will be blessed in the city and blessed in the country.
[4]The fruit of your womb will be blessed, and the crops
of your land and the young of your livestock—the calves of
your herds and the lambs of your flocks.
[5]Your basket and your kneading trough will be blessed.
[6]You will be blessed when you come in and blessed
when you go out.

[7]The LORD will grant that the enemies who rise up against
you will be defeated before you. They will come at you from one
direction but flee from you in seven.
[8]The LORD will send a blessing on your barns and on everything you put your hand to. The LORD your God will bless you in
the land he is giving you.
[9]The LORD will establish you as his holy people, as he
promised you on oath, if you keep the commands of the LORD
your God and walk in his ways. [10]Then all the peoples on earth will
see that you are called by the name of the LORD, and they will fear
you. [11]The LORD will grant you abundant prosperity—in the fruit
of your womb, the young of your livestock and the crops of your
ground—in the land he swore to your forefathers to give you.
[12]The LORD will open the heavens, the storehouse of his
bounty, to send rain on your land in season and to bless all the
work of your hands. You will lend to many nations but will borrow
from none. [13]The LORD will make you the head, not the tail. If you
pay attention to the commands of the LORD your God that I give

28:1-14 *obey . . . blessings:* The blessings in 28:1-14 correspond to the curses given in 28:15-44. A list of blessings and curses was often included in ancient treaties. They were meant to assure that both sides would act according to the terms of the treaty. In DEUTERONOMY, blessings and curses are used in the same way. Israel will receive blessings if they obey the LORD's laws and teachings and do not worship other gods, but curses will follow disobedience.

28:4 *fruit of your womb . . . crops . . . livestock:* Children were considered proof of God's love and blessing, as were good crops and large herds and flocks. A large family was a special blessing (Ps 127:3-5).

28:5 *kneading trough:* Bread made from grain and kneaded in a kneading trough was the main food of the Israelites. For more, see the mini-article called "Bread," p. 2058.

28:12 *open the heavens:* In ancient times, God was said to keep the rain, snow, hail, and wind in storehouses above the sky dome that covered the earth. When God opened a window in the sky, rain or snow would fall through and water the earth. See Gen 1:6-8; 8:2; Job 38:22-30; Ps 135:7; Jer 10:13; 51:16.

you this day and carefully follow them, you will always be at the top, never at the bottom. [14]Do not turn aside from any of the commands I give you today, to the right or to the left, following other gods and serving them.

Curses for Disobedience

[15]However, if you do not obey the LORD your God and do not carefully follow all his commands and decrees I am giving you today, all these curses will come upon you and overtake you:

> [16]You will be cursed in the city and cursed in the country.
> [17]Your basket and your kneading trough will be cursed.
> [18]The fruit of your womb will be cursed, and the crops of your land, and the calves of your herds and the lambs of your flocks.
> [19]You will be cursed when you come in and cursed when you go out.

[20]The LORD will send on you curses, confusion and rebuke in everything you put your hand to, until you are destroyed and come to sudden ruin because of the evil you have done in forsaking him.[a] [21]The LORD will plague you with diseases until he has destroyed you from the land you are entering to possess. [22]The LORD will strike you with wasting disease, with fever and inflammation, with scorching heat and drought, with blight and mildew, which will plague you until you perish. [23]The sky over your head will be bronze, the ground beneath you iron. [24]The LORD will turn the rain of your country into dust and powder; it will come down from the skies until you are destroyed.

[25]The LORD will cause you to be defeated before your enemies. You will come at them from one direction but flee from them in seven, and you will become a thing of horror to all the kingdoms on earth. [26]Your carcasses will be food for all the birds of the air and the beasts of the earth, and there will be no one to frighten them away. [27]The LORD will afflict you with the boils of Egypt and with tumors, festering sores and the itch, from which you cannot be cured. [28]The LORD will afflict you with madness, blindness and confusion of mind. [29]At midday you will grope about like a blind man in the dark. You will be unsuccessful in everything you do; day after day you will be oppressed and robbed, with no one to rescue you.

[30]You will be pledged to be married to a woman, but another will take her and ravish her. You will build a house, but you will not live in it. You will plant a vineyard, but you will not even begin to enjoy its fruit. [31]Your ox will be slaughtered before your eyes, but you will eat none of it. Your donkey will be forcibly taken from

---

[a]**20** Hebrew *me*

Moses said, *"Do not turn aside from any of the commands I give you today, to the right or to the left, following other gods and serving them."* Deut 28:14

28:18 *fruit of your womb will be cursed:* See the note at 28:4.

28:22 *wasting disease:* The exact diseases are not known. Diseases often were connected to the LORD's punishment (Lev 26:16; 1 Kgs 8:37; Jer 14:12). One of the plagues that God sent upon Egypt was an epidemic of sores on people and animals (Exod 9:9).

28:23,24 *sky over your head will be bronze:* This passage gives a picture of drought conditions when crops dry up and animals die of thirst. Dry times also produced severe dust and sandstorms that blew over the land from the desert areas to the east and south of Canaan.

28:30 Deut 20:5-7.

you and will not be returned. Your sheep will be given to your enemies, and no one will rescue them. 32Your sons and daughters will be given to another nation, and you will wear out your eyes watching for them day after day, powerless to lift a hand. 33A people that you do not know will eat what your land and labor produce, and you will have nothing but cruel oppression all your days. 34The sights you see will drive you mad. 35The LORD will afflict your knees and legs with painful boils that cannot be cured, spreading from the soles of your feet to the top of your head.

COVENANTS (AGREEMENTS)

The Bible often speaks of covenants, agreements, pacts, alliances, or treaties between individuals or groups of equal or unequal standing. Often these agreements were designed to make clear the relationship that existed between them. In Hebrew, people were said to "cut a covenant" with each other. This may refer to the practice of cutting a sacrificial animal in half and then walking between the two parts as a way to pledge loyalty to the covenant (Gen 15:7-21; Jer 34:18, 19). In Genesis 21:22-34 Abraham and Abimelech agreed that the well at Beersheba belonged to Abraham; Solomon and Hiram made a peace treaty that included trade agreements (1 Kgs 5:1-12); marriage was a covenant made between husband and wife that included obligations with God serving as a witness (Mal 2:14).

Covenants were usually completed with some act, such as eating a meal together (Gen 26:26-31), giving gifts (1 Sam 18:3, 4), setting up a stone or a pile of rocks as a reminder (Gen 31:43-55), giving someone a sandal (Ruth 4:7, 8), or even a simple handshake (2 Kgs 10:15). Covenants were designed to establish loyalty and faithfulness, and breaking a covenant was thought to be a very serious matter.

This way of thinking about relationships guided Israel's faith from the beginning. The most important covenants were those that God made with his people. Some of these include God's covenants with Noah (Gen 6:18), Abraham (Gen 12:1-7; 15:4-21; 17:1-16), Phineas (Num 25:10-15), and the tribes of Israel under Joshua (Josh 24:25). God promised to establish David's family as kings forever (2 Sam 7:12-16; 2 Chr 13:5; see also 1 Kgs 8:22-26; 2 Chr 6:12-15). This promise became the basis of Israel's hope for the Messiah that Christians see fulfilled in Jesus.

The most significant covenant in the Old Testament took place on Mount Sinai. There God reminded the people of Israel that he had chosen them and was giving them commandments and laws that would guide their worship and life together. For their part, Israel promised to obey the LORD's laws and worship only the LORD. This covenant was sealed when Moses sprinked blood on the people and on an altar he had set up for that purpose (Exod 24). The history of Israel was closely connected with this covenant. If the people obeyed this covenant and continued to be faithful to God, they would receive the blessings God had promised. But if they disobeyed God's Law and worshiped other gods, they would be punished (Deut 4:1, 2, 39, 40; 7:12-16; 8:19, 20).

The prophet Jeremiah spoke of a "new covenant," one the LORD would write on the hearts and minds of the people (Jer 31:31-37). Christians see Jesus' words at the Last Supper (Matt 26:28) as the fulfillment of this prophecy. See also Heb 10:16 and the mini-article called "Salvation," p. 2021.

36The LORD will drive you and the king you set over you to a
nation unknown to you or your fathers. There you will worship
other gods, gods of wood and stone. 37You will become a thing of
horror and an object of scorn and ridicule to all the nations where
the LORD will drive you.
38You will sow much seed in the field but you will harvest little, because locusts will devour it. 39You will plant vineyards and
cultivate them but you will not drink the wine or gather the
grapes, because worms will eat them. 40You will have olive trees
throughout your country but you will not use the oil, because the
olives will drop off. 41You will have sons and daughters but you will
not keep them, because they will go into captivity. 42Swarms of
locusts will take over all your trees and the crops of your land.
43The alien who lives among you will rise above you higher
and higher, but you will sink lower and lower. 44He will lend to
you, but you will not lend to him. He will be the head, but you will
be the tail.
45All these curses will come upon you. They will pursue you
and overtake you until you are destroyed, because you did not
obey the LORD your God and observe the commands and decrees
he gave you. 46They will be a sign and a wonder to you and your
descendants forever. 47Because you did not serve the LORD your
God joyfully and gladly in the time of prosperity, 48therefore in
hunger and thirst, in nakedness and dire poverty, you will serve the
enemies the LORD sends against you. He will put an iron yoke on
your neck until he has destroyed you.
49The LORD will bring a nation against you from far away,
from the ends of the earth, like an eagle swooping down, a nation
whose language you will not understand, 50a fierce-looking nation
without respect for the old or pity for the young. 51They will
devour the young of your livestock and the crops of your land
until you are destroyed. They will leave you no grain, new wine or
oil, nor any calves of your herds or lambs of your flocks until you
are ruined. 52They will lay siege to all the cities throughout your
land until the high fortified walls in which you trust fall down.
They will besiege all the cities throughout the land the LORD your
God is giving you.
53Because of the suffering that your enemy will inflict on you
during the siege, you will eat the fruit of the womb, the flesh of the
sons and daughters the LORD your God has given you. 54Even the
most gentle and sensitive man among you will have no compassion on his own brother or the wife he loves or his surviving children, 55and he will not give to one of them any of the flesh of his
children that he is eating. It will be all he has left because of the
suffering your enemy will inflict on you during the siege of all
your cities. 56The most gentle and sensitive woman among you—
so sensitive and gentle that she would not venture to touch the
ground with the sole of her foot—will begrudge the husband she

28:36 *to a nation unknown to you:* This curse is the opposite of the promise of national greatness for Israel (28:7, 10, 13). This curse did come true in Israel's later history. The Assyrians defeated the northern kingdom of Israel in 722 B.C. and took many of its people into exile (2 Kgs 17:5-23). In 587 or 586 B.C. Babylonia defeated the southern kingdom of Judah and many of its leaders, including the king, were captured and taken to live in exile in Babylonia (2 Kgs 24:8—25:21). The people would have been introduced to the gods worshiped in those countries. It was sometimes thought that only the gods of a country could be worshiped within the borders of that country. See also the article called "From Joshua to the Exile: The People of Israel in the Promised Land," p. 924.

28:38 *locusts:* This is a type of grasshopper that comes in swarms and causes great damage to plant life. See Joel 1:4-10 and the mini-article called "Locusts," p. 1708.

28:40 *olive trees . . . oil:* Olive oil was used for cooking and for making ointments for the skin and hair. It was also burned in clay lamps to provide light.

28:45 *curses will come upon you:* See the note at 27:15-26.

28:48-57 *in hunger and thirst . . . you will serve the enemies:* These verses reflect what the Israelite people experienced when the Babylonians attacked the walled cities of Judah (28:52) and captured Jerusalem (see the note at 28:36). People inside the surrounded cities ran out of food and began to starve. These horrible conditions are seen as just punishment for Israel's refusal to honor the LORD and worship him alone (28:47).

28:56,57 2 Kgs 6:28, 29; Lam 4:10.

loves and her own son or daughter [57]the afterbirth from her womb and the children she bears. For she intends to eat them secretly during the siege and in the distress that your enemy will inflict on you in your cities.

[58]If you do not carefully follow all the words of this law, which are written in this book, and do not revere this glorious and awesome name—the LORD your God— [59]the LORD will send fearful plagues on you and your descendants, harsh and prolonged disasters, and severe and lingering illnesses. [60]He will bring upon you all the diseases of Egypt that you dreaded, and they will cling to you. [61]The LORD will also bring on you every kind of sickness and disaster not recorded in this Book of the Law, until you are destroyed. [62]You who were as numerous as the stars in the sky will be left but few in number, because you did not obey the LORD your God. [63]Just as it pleased the LORD to make you prosper and increase in number, so it will please him to ruin and destroy you. You will be uprooted from the land you are entering to possess.

[64]Then the LORD will scatter you among all nations, from one end of the earth to the other. There you will worship other gods—gods of wood and stone, which neither you nor your fathers have known. [65]Among those nations you will find no repose, no resting place for the sole of your foot. There the LORD will give you an anxious mind, eyes weary with longing, and a despairing heart. [66]You will live in constant suspense, filled with dread both night and day, never sure of your life. [67]In the morning you will say, "If only it were evening!" and in the evening, "If only it were morning!"—because of the terror that will fill your hearts and the sights that your eyes will see. [68]The LORD will send you back in ships to Egypt on a journey I said you should never make again. There you will offer yourselves for sale to your enemies as male and female slaves, but no one will buy you.

Moses said:
"You are standing here in order to enter into a covenant with the LORD your God, a covenant the LORD is making with you this day and sealing with an oath, to confirm you this day as his people, that he may be your God as he promised you and as he swore to your fathers, Abraham, Isaac and Jacob."
Deut 29:12, 13

28:58 *words of this law ... written in this book:* This probably refers to 12:1—26:15 (see the Introduction to DEUTERONOMY on p. 340).

28:59,60 *diseases of Egypt:* See the note at 28:22.

28:64 *scatter you among all nations:* See the note at 28:36.

28:62 Gen 22:15-18.

QUESTIONS ABOUT DEUTERONOMY 4:44—28:68

1. Moses' "Second Speech" (4:44—29:68) is long, but it repeats several key themes. What are this speech's key themes?
2. Name three laws from 4:44—28:68 that no longer seem to be in effect today. Why do you think this is so?
3. What, if anything, surprises you about the laws or the culture reflected in this section of DEUTERONOMY?
4. What does the LORD God want from his people? (6:4-9; 10:12, 13)
5. Why was it important in chapter 12 to claim that there was only one place (Jerusalem) to worship the LORD? Why do you think this has changed?
6. Chapter 20 describes warfare that is often called "holy war." Have you heard this term used today? If so, what does it refer to? How does the "holy war" idea in DEUTERONOMY fit with your idea of war today?
7. One message of DEUTERONOMY is that God blesses the faithful and curses the unfaithful. What reaction do you have to this message?

The Third Speech: Israel Must Keep Its Covenant with the LORD

In this summary of his earlier speeches, Moses reminds the people how God delivered them from the Egyptians and led them through the desert. The LORD God has promised to be their God (29:13-15), so they should show that they are the LORD's people by keeping the covenant he made with them. Moses reminds the people that their decision will have consequences (30:15). If they are unfaithful, they will be scattered to the countries of their enemies. If they are faithful, they will live a long time in the land the LORD promised to give their ancestors (30:20).

Renewal of the Covenant

29 These are the terms of the covenant the LORD commanded
Moses to make with the Israelites in Moab, in addition to the
covenant he had made with them at Horeb.
2 Moses summoned all the Israelites and said to them:

Your eyes have seen all that the LORD did in Egypt to
Pharaoh, to all his officials and to all his land. 3 With your own eyes
you saw those great trials, those miraculous signs and great wonders. 4 But to this day the LORD has not given you a mind that
understands or eyes that see or ears that hear. 5 During the forty
years that I led you through the desert, your clothes did not wear
out, nor did the sandals on your feet. 6 You ate no bread and drank
no wine or other fermented drink. I did this so that you might
know that I am the LORD your God.
7 When you reached this place, Sihon king of Heshbon and
Og king of Bashan came out to fight against us, but we defeated
them. 8 We took their land and gave it as an inheritance to the
Reubenites, the Gadites and the half-tribe of Manasseh.
9 Carefully follow the terms of this covenant, so that you may
prosper in everything you do. 10 All of you are standing today in the
presence of the LORD your God—your leaders and chief men, your
elders and officials, and all the other men of Israel, 11 together with
your children and your wives, and the aliens living in your camps
who chop your wood and carry your water. 12 You are standing here
in order to enter into a covenant with the LORD your God, a
covenant the LORD is making with you this day and sealing with
an oath, 13 to confirm you this day as his people, that he may be
your God as he promised you and as he swore to your fathers,
Abraham, Isaac and Jacob. 14 I am making this covenant, with its
oath, not only with you 15 who are standing here with us today in
the presence of the LORD our God but also with those who are not
here today.
16 You yourselves know how we lived in Egypt and how we
passed through the countries on the way here. 17 You saw among

29:1 *covenant . . . Moab . . . Horeb:* The covenant at Moab contains much of what is found in DEUTERONOMY, beginning with Moses' speech at 4:1. This covenant is similar to the first covenant that the LORD made with Moses and the people at Horeb, also called Mount Sinai (Exod 19–40). Both covenants include the Ten Commandments, but each has much material that is different from the other. See also the note at 1:3-5.

29:2,3 *Egypt . . . great wonders:* See Exod 1–12, and the note at 1:3. This review of God's saving acts is a typical Israelite way to confess faith in God.

29:5,6 *forty years . . . so that you might know:* See 1:32—2:19 and the notes. Even God's miracles and saving help did not convince the people to be faithful. This would take a change of heart (see the note at 6:3-5). See also Jer 31:31-34.

29:7,8 *Sihon . . . Og . . . Reubenites, the Gadites and the half-tribe of Manasseh:* See Num 21:21-35; Deut 2:26—3:11; and the note at 1:4.

See also Num 32:33 and the notes at 3:12 and 3:13-15.

29:10,11 *leaders:* See the note at 1:15-17.

29:13 *Abraham, Isaac and Jacob:* See the note at 1:7, 8.

29:16,17 *Egypt . . . detestable images and idols:* The ancient Egyptians worshiped many gods, including animal-headed gods such as Apis (bull), Mnevis (cow), and Khnum (ram). The Nile River was worshiped like a god, because its floods made the land fertile. The king of Egypt (pharaoh) was also considered a god. See also the notes at 4:16-18; 7:26 and the mini-article called "King of Egypt (Pharaoh)," p. 110.

29:18 *no root among you that produces such bitter poison:* One person worshiping idols could influence the rest of the Israelite people and lead to punishment for all (29:19). See also Heb 12:15.

29:20,21 *All the curses:* See 27:9-26; 28:15-68; and the note at 27:15-26.

29:21 *Book of the Law:* See the note at 28:58.

29:23 *Sodom ... Zeboiim:* The LORD destroyed Sodom and Gomorrah because of the evil people who lived there (Gen 18:16-28; 19:24, 25). Admah and Zeboiim were located near Sodom and Gomorrah (Gen 10:19) and were likely destroyed at the same time (Hos 11:8).

29:25 *people abandoned the covenant:* The nations wonder why God's chosen people have been defeated and sent into exile (see the note at 28:36). The answer: Israel worshiped other gods. This act of disobedience caused the LORD to punish them with curses (see the note at 27:15-26).

30:1 *take them to heart:* The LORD hopes that when these events happen, the people will remember and return to their God. See 28:1-14 and the note. See also 27:9-26; 28:15-68; the note at 27:15-26; and the note at 6:3-5.

30:3,4 *gather you again from ... where he scattered you:* In this passage, it sounds as if Israel is already in exile (see the note at 28:36). But they are reminded that if they turn back to God and obey God's laws, God will return them to the land and bless them. This promise would be told to the people of Israel again by a number of Israel's prophets many centuries after the time of Moses (see Isa 48; 49; Jer 3:12-19; Ezek 11:15-21; Hos 14:1-9).

29:22 Deut 28:21-23, 27.

them their detestable images and idols of wood and stone, of silver and gold. [18]Make sure there is no man or woman, clan or tribe among you today whose heart turns away from the LORD our God to go and worship the gods of those nations; make sure there is no root among you that produces such bitter poison.

[19]When such a person hears the words of this oath, he invokes a blessing on himself and therefore thinks, "I will be safe, even though I persist in going my own way." This will bring disaster on the watered land as well as the dry.[a] [20]The LORD will never be willing to forgive him; his wrath and zeal will burn against that man. All the curses written in this book will fall upon him, and the LORD will blot out his name from under heaven. [21]The LORD will single him out from all the tribes of Israel for disaster, according to all the curses of the covenant written in this Book of the Law.

[22]Your children who follow you in later generations and foreigners who come from distant lands will see the calamities that have fallen on the land and the diseases with which the LORD has afflicted it. [23]The whole land will be a burning waste of salt and sulfur—nothing planted, nothing sprouting, no vegetation growing on it. It will be like the destruction of Sodom and Gomorrah, Admah and Zeboiim, which the LORD overthrew in fierce anger. [24]All the nations will ask: "Why has the LORD done this to this land? Why this fierce, burning anger?"

[25]And the answer will be: "It is because this people abandoned the covenant of the LORD, the God of their fathers, the covenant he made with them when he brought them out of Egypt. [26]They went off and worshiped other gods and bowed down to them, gods they did not know, gods he had not given them. [27]Therefore the LORD's anger burned against this land, so that he brought on it all the curses written in this book. [28]In furious anger and in great wrath the LORD uprooted them from their land and thrust them into another land, as it is now."

[29]The secret things belong to the LORD our God, but the things revealed belong to us and to our children forever, that we may follow all the words of this law.

Prosperity After Turning to the LORD

30 When all these blessings and curses I have set before you come upon you and you take them to heart wherever the LORD your God disperses you among the nations, [2]and when you and your children return to the LORD your God and obey him with all your heart and with all your soul according to everything I command you today, [3]then the LORD your God will restore your

[a]19 Or *way, in order to add drunkenness to thirst.*"

fortunes[a] and have compassion on you and gather you again from
all the nations where he scattered you. 4 Even if you have been banished to the most distant land under the heavens, from there the
LORD your God will gather you and bring you back. 5 He will bring
you to the land that belonged to your fathers, and you will take
possession of it. He will make you more prosperous and numerous
than your fathers. 6 The LORD your God will circumcise your hearts
and the hearts of your descendants, so that you may love him with
all your heart and with all your soul, and live. 7 The LORD your God
will put all these curses on your enemies who hate and persecute
you. 8 You will again obey the LORD and follow all his commands I
am giving you today. 9 Then the LORD your God will make you
most prosperous in all the work of your hands and in the fruit of
your womb, the young of your livestock and the crops of your
land. The LORD will again delight in you and make you prosperous, just as he delighted in your fathers, 10 if you obey the LORD
your God and keep his commands and decrees that are written in
this Book of the Law and turn to the LORD your God with all your
heart and with all your soul.

The Offer of Life or Death

11 Now what I am commanding you today is not too difficult
for you or beyond your reach. 12 It is not up in heaven, so that you
have to ask, "Who will ascend into heaven to get it and proclaim it
to us so we may obey it?" 13 Nor is it beyond the sea, so that you
have to ask, "Who will cross the sea to get it and proclaim it to us
so we may obey it?" 14 No, the word is very near you; it is in your
mouth and in your heart so you may obey it.

15 See, I set before you today life and prosperity, death and
destruction. 16 For I command you today to love the LORD your
God, to walk in his ways, and to keep his commands, decrees and
laws; then you will live and increase, and the LORD your God will
bless you in the land you are entering to possess.

---

[a]3 Or *will bring you back from captivity*

> Moses told the people: *"The word is very near you; it is in your mouth and in your heart so you may obey it."*
> Deut 30:14

30:15 *set before you today:* Here, choosing life means obeying the laws and commands God gave the people. Those who obey are promised a life full of blessings. See also John 11:25,26; 14:6.

QUESTIONS ABOUT DEUTERONOMY 29:1—30:20

1. Idol worship is described as being like a poison in the community. (29:18) Explain what this means. What "idols" are worshiped in modern culture? How does worship of idols "poison" our communities?
2. Compare Deuteronomy 30:11-14 and Romans 10:1-13. According to Paul (the writer of ROMANS), what has become even more important than obeying the Law?
3. What was the historical situation that Israel understood to be its punishment for disobedience? What is the reward for changing? (30:1-10)
4. The challenge to choose life or disaster is described clearly in the words of Moses. Why did the Israelites have difficulty choosing life? How can you "choose life"? (30:15-20)

> *"Love the LORD your God, listen to his voice, and hold fast to him. For the LORD is your life, and he will give you many years in the land he swore to give to your fathers, Abraham, Isaac and Jacob."*
> Deut 30:20

30:18 *the land:* See the notes on p. 340 (Moses, Israel) and at 1:7, 8.

31:2 *hundred and twenty years old:* This is three times forty years. Since the Hebrews considered a generation to be about forty years, this may simply mean that Moses was a man old enough to have seen his grandchildren become adults. See also the note at 1:3.

31:2,3 *shall not cross the Jordan . . . Joshua also will cross over ahead of you:* Moses was not allowed to cross into the promised land because of disobedience (Num 20:1-12). See the notes at 1:36-38 and 3:28.

31:4 *Sihon and Og:* See Num 21:21-35; Deut 2:26—3:11; and the note at 1:4.

31:7 *go with this people into the land:* See the note at 1:7, 8.

31:2 Num 20:12.

17But if your heart turns away and you are not obedient, and if you are drawn away to bow down to other gods and worship them, 18I declare to you this day that you will certainly be destroyed. You will not live long in the land you are crossing the Jordan to enter and possess.

19This day I call heaven and earth as witnesses against you that I have set before you life and death, blessings and curses. Now choose life, so that you and your children may live 20and that you may love the LORD your God, listen to his voice, and hold fast to him. For the LORD is your life, and he will give you many years in the land he swore to give to your fathers, Abraham, Isaac and Jacob.

Final Speeches and the Death of Moses

Just before he dies, Moses makes a number of arrangements for Israel's future. These include transferring leadership to Joshua (31:1-8, 14-23), providing for the care and reading of the Law (31:9-13, 24-29), singing of God's deliverance of Israel (31:30—32:43), and blessing the tribes of Israel in the same way that Jacob had blessed his sons on his deathbed (Gen 49). Before Moses dies, God allows him to see the promised land.

A LEADER FOR THE PEOPLE AND A PLACE FOR THE LAW

God promises to continue to be with Israel after Moses dies. With Joshua, their new leader, the people of Israel will begin to conquer the promised land (31:1-8,14-23). The newly delivered Law will be kept safe in the ark of the covenant and read at a special gathering every seven years (31:9-13, 24-29).

Joshua to Succeed Moses

31 Then Moses went out and spoke these words to all Israel: 2"I am now a hundred and twenty years old and I am no longer able to lead you. The LORD has said to me, 'You shall not cross the Jordan.' 3The LORD your God himself will cross over ahead of you. He will destroy these nations before you, and you will take possession of their land. Joshua also will cross over ahead of you, as the LORD said. 4And the LORD will do to them what he did to Sihon and Og, the kings of the Amorites, whom he destroyed along with their land. 5The LORD will deliver them to you, and you must do to them all that I have commanded you. 6Be strong and courageous. Do not be afraid or terrified because of them, for the LORD your God goes with you; he will never leave you nor forsake you."

7Then Moses summoned Joshua and said to him in the presence of all Israel, "Be strong and courageous, for you must go with

Reading the Law, a detail from a wall-painting in the synagogue at Dura-Europos, Syria, third century A.D. Many scholars identify this figure as Moses, the great prophet and leader of the people of Israel who received the Law from the LORD at Mount Sinai. DEUTERONOMY tells how Moses wrote down all the laws and teachings and commanded the priests to read them to the people during the festivals (see 31:9-13). Other scholars believe this is an image of Ezra, teacher of the Law who helped to re-establish obedience to the Law after the people returned from exile in Babylonia. Both interpretations show the importance of the Law for the people of Israel.

this people into the land that the LORD swore to their forefathers to
give them, and you must divide it among them as their inheritance. 8 The LORD himself goes before you and will be with you; he
will never leave you nor forsake you. Do not be afraid; do not be
discouraged."

The Reading of the Law

9 So Moses wrote down this law and gave it to the priests,
the sons of Levi, who carried the ark of the covenant of the LORD,
and to all the elders of Israel. 10 Then Moses commanded them:
"At the end of every seven years, in the year for canceling debts,
during the Feast of Tabernacles, 11 when all Israel comes to appear
before the LORD your God at the place he will choose, you shall
read this law before them in their hearing. 12 Assemble the

31:9 *wrote down this law:* This is the covenant the people made with God at Mount Sinai and the explanations and teachings about it (chapters 4–28). In ancient times, copies of agreements between nations were often placed before the gods at the worship centers of the nations involved. Israel was commanded to keep its covenant with God in the ark of the covenant at God's chosen place of worship. See also the note at 1:3-5.

31:9 *priests, the sons of Levi:* See the note at 10:8.

31:9 *ark of the covenant:* See the note at 10:1-3.

31:10 *every seven years . . . Feast of Tabernacles:* See the note at 16:13. Reading the law and teaching it to the people of Israel was one of the main jobs of a priest (33:10; Mal 2:4-9). Every seven years the laws were to be read at one of the required festivals, so that each generation would hear and learn them. See also the note at 15:1-10.

31:8 Josh 1:5; Heb 13:5. **31:10, 11** Deut 5:1, 2; 16:13-17.

people—men, women and children, and the aliens living in your
towns—so they can listen and learn to fear the LORD your God and
follow carefully all the words of this law. 13 Their children, who do
not know this law, must hear it and learn to fear the LORD your
God as long as you live in the land you are crossing the Jordan to
possess."

Israel's Rebellion Predicted

14 The LORD said to Moses, "Now the day of your death is
near. Call Joshua and present yourselves at the Tent of Meeting,
where I will commission him." So Moses and Joshua came and
presented themselves at the Tent of Meeting.
15 Then the LORD appeared at the Tent in a pillar of cloud,
and the cloud stood over the entrance to the Tent. 16 And the LORD
said to Moses: "You are going to rest with your fathers, and these
people will soon prostitute themselves to the foreign gods of the
land they are entering. They will forsake me and break the
covenant I made with them. 17 On that day I will become angry
with them and forsake them; I will hide my face from them, and
they will be destroyed. Many disasters and difficulties will come
upon them, and on that day they will ask, 'Have not these disasters
come upon us because our God is not with us?' 18 And I will certainly hide my face on that day because of all their wickedness in
turning to other gods.
19 "Now write down for yourselves this song and teach it to the
Israelites and have them sing it, so that it may be a witness for me
against them. 20 When I have brought them into the land flowing
with milk and honey, the land I promised on oath to their forefathers, and when they eat their fill and thrive, they will turn to other
gods and worship them, rejecting me and breaking my covenant.
21 And when many disasters and difficulties come upon them, this
song will testify against them, because it will not be forgotten by
their descendants. I know what they are disposed to do, even before
I bring them into the land I promised them on oath." 22 So Moses
wrote down this song that day and taught it to the Israelites.
23 The LORD gave this command to Joshua son of Nun: "Be
strong and courageous, for you will bring the Israelites into the
land I promised them on oath, and I myself will be with you."
24 After Moses finished writing in a book the words of this
law from beginning to end, 25 he gave this command to the Levites
who carried the ark of the covenant of the LORD: 26 "Take this Book
of the Law and place it beside the ark of the covenant of the LORD
your God. There it will remain as a witness against you. 27 For I
know how rebellious and stiff-necked you are. If you have been
rebellious against the LORD while I am still alive and with you, how
much more will you rebel after I die! 28 Assemble before me all the
elders of your tribes and all your officials, so that I can speak these
words in their hearing and call heaven and earth to testify against

31:14 *Moses and Joshua:* See the notes on p. 340 (Moses, Israel) and at 3:28.

31:14 *Tent of Meeting:* Also called the tabernacle. See the mini-article called "The Tabernacle," p. 2346.

31:15 *pillar of cloud:* See the note at 1:33.

31:16 *break the covenant:* See 29:9—30:9 and the notes at 1:3-5; 4:7, 8; 4:25-31; and 7:26.

31:16 *land they are entering:* This refers to Canaan. See the notes at 1:3; 1:7, 8; and 7:5.

31:19 *write down . . . this song:* The words of the song are given in 32:1-43. The song will not be forgotten and will stand as proof that the Israelites know God's laws and have no excuse for breaking them (31:21).

31:21 *I know what they are disposed to do:* This refers to Israel worshiping other gods after they have settled in the promised land. See also the notes at 28:36 and 29:25.

31:23 *the LORD gave this command:* This verse continues the thought begun in 31:14. See also Num 27:23; Josh 1:6-8.

31:24-26 *Book of the Law . . . beside the ark of the covenant:* These verses continue the thought begun in 31:9-13. The Book of the Law (see the note at 28:58) is to be used along with the laws (commandments) written on stone tablets and kept with the ark of the covenant. See the notes at 5:2 and 10:1-3.

31:25 *Levites:* See the note at 10:8.

31:28 *call heaven and earth to testify:* See 30:19.

them. 29 For I know that after my death you are sure to become
utterly corrupt and to turn from the way I have commanded you.
In days to come, disaster will fall upon you because you will do evil
in the sight of the LORD and provoke him to anger by what your
hands have made."

> Moses said, *"He is the Rock, his works are perfect, and all his ways are just. A faithful God who does no wrong, upright and just is he."*
> Deut 32:4

THE SONG AND THE BLESSING OF MOSES

Moses' "song" (32:1-43) is presented in the form of a lawsuit. God charges Israel with being unfaithful to their covenant (32:5, 6). Despite God's past blessings (32:7-14), Israel rebelled (32:15-18), and God was forced to punish them (32:19-27). But God promises to overthrow the nations that oppose Israel (32:28-42). In this way, Israel will be cleansed of its sin and restored to a faithful relationship with God (32:43). Moses' blessing poem (33:2-29) is placed within a victory song celebrating God's deliverance (33:2-5, 26-29). Moses asks God to continue to bless each tribe of Israel.

The Song of Moses

30 And Moses recited the words of this song from beginning
to end in the hearing of the whole assembly of Israel:

32 Listen, O heavens, and I will speak;
hear, O earth, the words of my mouth.
2 Let my teaching fall like rain
and my words descend like dew,
like showers on new grass,
like abundant rain on tender plants.

3 I will proclaim the name of the LORD.
Oh, praise the greatness of our God!
4 He is the Rock, his works are perfect,
and all his ways are just.
A faithful God who does no wrong,
upright and just is he.

5 They have acted corruptly toward him;
to their shame they are no longer his children,
but a warped and crooked generation.[a]
6 Is this the way you repay the LORD,
O foolish and unwise people?
Is he not your Father, your Creator,[b]
who made you and formed you?

7 Remember the days of old;
consider the generations long past.
Ask your father and he will tell you,
your elders, and they will explain to you.

---

[a] **5** Or *Corrupt are they and not his children, / a generation warped and twisted to their shame* [b] **6** Or *Father, who bought you*

32:1 *heavens . . . earth:* See 30:19 and 31:28.

32:3 *name . . . LORD:* See the notes at 1:3-5 and 1:6.

32:4 *He is the Rock:* In Hebrew poetry the LORD's protection is sometimes compared to a mountain where his people can run for safety (Ps 18:2, 46; Isa 17:10; Hab 1:12).

32:8 *Most High:* The name "Most High" emphasizes God's control over all of creation (Gen 14:19). See also the mini-article called "Names of God," p. 243.

32:13 *He made him ride on the heights of the land:* Moses' song is written in a way that sounds as if the people have already taken over Canaan and have been living in the land.

32:13 *honey . . . oil:* Most oil came from olive trees that often grew on rocky hillsides, and bees sometimes built their hives between rocks. See also the note at 28:40.

32:15,18 *Rock his Savior:* See the note at 32:4.

32:16,17 *detestable idols:* The gods of other nations were not like Israel's living LORD God, so they were useless to help. See also the notes at 4:16-18; 7:5; and 7:26.

32:20,21 *perverse generation . . . unfaithful:* Though the LORD saved the people of Israel from slavery in Egypt and helped them take over the land of Canaan, they turned their backs on the LORD by worshiping other gods (see the notes at 28:36 and 29:25).

32:8 Acts 17:26. **32:17** 1 Cor 10:20.

8 When the Most High gave the nations their inheritance,
when he divided all mankind,
he set up boundaries for the peoples
according to the number of the sons of Israel.[a]
9 For the LORD's portion is his people,
Jacob his allotted inheritance.

10 In a desert land he found him,
in a barren and howling waste.
He shielded him and cared for him;
he guarded him as the apple of his eye,
11 like an eagle that stirs up its nest
and hovers over its young,
that spreads its wings to catch them
and carries them on its pinions.
12 The LORD alone led him;
no foreign god was with him.

13 He made him ride on the heights of the land
and fed him with the fruit of the fields.
He nourished him with honey from the rock,
and with oil from the flinty crag,
14 with curds and milk from herd and flock
and with fattened lambs and goats,
with choice rams of Bashan
and the finest kernels of wheat.
You drank the foaming blood of the grape.

15 Jeshurun[b] grew fat and kicked;
filled with food, he became heavy and sleek.
He abandoned the God who made him
and rejected the Rock his Savior.
16 They made him jealous with their foreign gods
and angered him with their detestable idols.
17 They sacrificed to demons, which are not God—
gods they had not known,
gods that recently appeared,
gods your fathers did not fear.
18 You deserted the Rock, who fathered you;
you forgot the God who gave you birth.

19 The LORD saw this and rejected them
because he was angered by his sons and daughters.
20 "I will hide my face from them," he said,
"and see what their end will be;
for they are a perverse generation,
children who are unfaithful.

[a]**8** Masoretic Text; Dead Sea Scrolls (see also Septuagint) *sons of God*
[b]**15** *Jeshurun* means *the upright one*, that is, Israel.

21 They made me jealous by what is no god
and angered me with their worthless idols.
I will make them envious by those who are not a people;
I will make them angry by a nation that has no
understanding.
22 For a fire has been kindled by my wrath,
one that burns to the realm of death[a] below.
It will devour the earth and its harvests
and set afire the foundations of the mountains.
23 "I will heap calamities upon them
and spend my arrows against them.
24 I will send wasting famine against them,
consuming pestilence and deadly plague;
I will send against them the fangs of wild beasts,
the venom of vipers that glide in the dust.
25 In the street the sword will make them childless;
in their homes terror will reign.
Young men and young women will perish,
infants and gray-haired men.
26 I said I would scatter them
and blot out their memory from mankind,
27 but I dreaded the taunt of the enemy,
lest the adversary misunderstand
and say, 'Our hand has triumphed;
the LORD has not done all this.' "
28 They are a nation without sense,
there is no discernment in them.
29 If only they were wise and would understand this
and discern what their end will be!
30 How could one man chase a thousand,
or two put ten thousand to flight,
unless their Rock had sold them,
unless the LORD had given them up?
31 For their rock is not like our Rock,
as even our enemies concede.
32 Their vine comes from the vine of Sodom
and from the fields of Gomorrah.
Their grapes are filled with poison,
and their clusters with bitterness.
33 Their wine is the venom of serpents,
the deadly poison of cobras.
34 "Have I not kept this in reserve
and sealed it in my vaults?
35 It is mine to avenge; I will repay.
In due time their foot will slip;

[a]22 Hebrew *to Sheol*

32:22 *a fire has been kindled by my wrath . . . realm of death:* Fire is often connected with the LORD's judgment against those who are evil or disobedient (Gen 19:23-29; Lev 10:1, 2; Isa 4:4; Joel 2:1-3; Matt 13:36-42). See also the note at 1:33.

In ancient Hebrew thought, the "realm of death" was a deep underground pit that lay beneath a great underground sea. The Hebrew name for the underground world of the dead was *Sheol*, described in the Bible as a totally silent place where no one knows or feels anything (Job 10:21, 22; Ps 88:12; 94:17).

32:26 *I would scatter them:* It is important that other nations not misunderstand Israel's punishment as a lack of God's authority. If Israel is spared, it will be to prove God's power to others, not because the people deserve it. See also 28:64 and the note at 28:36.

32:32 *Sodom . . . Gomorrah:* See the note at 29:23.

32:21 Rom 10:19; 1 Cor 10:22.

their day of disaster is near
and their doom rushes upon them."

36 The LORD will judge his people
and have compassion on his servants
when he sees their strength is gone
and no one is left, slave or free.
37 He will say: "Now where are their gods,
the rock they took refuge in,
38 the gods who ate the fat of their sacrifices
and drank the wine of their drink offerings?
Let them rise up to help you!
Let them give you shelter!

39 "See now that I myself am He!
There is no god besides me.
I put to death and I bring to life,
I have wounded and I will heal,
and no one can deliver out of my hand.
40 I lift my hand to heaven and declare:
As surely as I live forever,
41 when I sharpen my flashing sword
and my hand grasps it in judgment,
I will take vengeance on my adversaries
and repay those who hate me.
42 I will make my arrows drunk with blood,
while my sword devours flesh:
the blood of the slain and the captives,
the heads of the enemy leaders."
43 Rejoice, O nations, with his people,[a,b]
for he will avenge the blood of his servants;
he will take vengeance on his enemies
and make atonement for his land and people.

44 Moses came with Joshua[c] son of Nun and spoke all the words of this song in the hearing of the people. 45 When Moses finished reciting all these words to all Israel, 46 he said to them, "Take to heart all the words I have solemnly declared to you this day, so that you may command your children to obey carefully all the words of this law. 47 They are not just idle words for you—they are your life. By them you will live long in the land you are crossing the Jordan to possess."

Moses to Die on Mount Nebo

48 On that same day the LORD told Moses, 49 "Go up into the Abarim Range to Mount Nebo in Moab, across from Jericho, and

---

[a] 43 Or *Make his people rejoice, O nations* [b] 43 Masoretic Text; Dead Sea Scrolls (see also Septuagint) *people, / and let all the angels worship him /* [c] 44 Hebrew *Hoshea*, a variant of *Joshua*

The LORD said, *"See now that I myself am He! There is no god besides me. I put to death and I bring to life, I have wounded and I will heal, and no one can deliver out of my hand."*
Deut 32:39

32:36 *and have compassion on his servants:* God will allow Israel to rebuild. See also Ps 135:14; Isa 40:1, 2; 49:13-18.

32:38 *Let them rise up to help you:* The first part of Israel's wine, grain, and livestock were to be sacrificed as a gift of thanks to the LORD (see the note at 18:4). But some Israelites offered these things to other gods, especially the Canaanite gods that were believed to be responsible for giving rain and making the land fertile for growing good crops. See also Hos 2:8 and the notes at 6:3-5 and 7:5.

32:46,47 *all the words I have solemnly declared:* God's teachings refer to the commandments and laws given to Moses and the people, and is included in parts of the first five books of the Old Testament. Those who obey God's teachings are often described as choosing the path of life and blessing (Ps 1:2, 3; Prov 4:10-13). See also the note at 30:15 and the mini-article called "Law," p. 1160.

32:49 *Abarim Range . . . Mount Nebo . . . Canaan:* See the note at 3:25-29.

32:39 Deut 5:7; Isa 46:9. **32:43** Rom 15:10; Rev 19:2.

view Canaan, the land I am giving the Israelites as their own possession. 50There on the mountain that you have climbed you will die and be gathered to your people, just as your brother Aaron died on Mount Hor and was gathered to his people. 51This is because both of you broke faith with me in the presence of the Israelites at the waters of Meribah Kadesh in the Desert of Zin and because you did not uphold my holiness among the Israelites. 52Therefore, you will see the land only from a distance; you will not enter the land I am giving to the people of Israel."

Moses Blesses the Tribes

33 This is the blessing that Moses the man of God pronounced on the Israelites before his death. 2He said:

"The LORD came from Sinai
and dawned over them from Seir;
he shone forth from Mount Paran.
He came with[a] myriads of holy ones
from the south, from his mountain slopes.[b]
3Surely it is you who love the people;
all the holy ones are in your hand.
At your feet they all bow down,
and from you receive instruction,
4the law that Moses gave us,
the possession of the assembly of Jacob.
5He was king over Jeshurun[c]
when the leaders of the people assembled,
along with the tribes of Israel.

6"Let Reuben live and not die,
nor[d] his men be few."

7And this he said about Judah:

"Hear, O LORD, the cry of Judah;
bring him to his people.
With his own hands he defends his cause.
Oh, be his help against his foes!"

8About Levi he said:

"Your Thummim and Urim belong
to the man you favored.
You tested him at Massah;
you contended with him at the waters of Meribah.
9He said of his father and mother,
'I have no regard for them.'

[a]2 Or *from* [b]2 The meaning of the Hebrew for this phrase is uncertain.
[c]5 *Jeshurun* means *the upright one,* that is, Israel; also in verse 26. [d]6 Or *but let*

32:50 *Aaron died on Mount Hor:* See the note at 10:6.

33:1 *Moses the man of God:* See the notes on p. 340 (Moses, Israel) and at 13:1, 2.

33:2 *Sinai . . . Seir . . . Mount Paran:* See the note on p. 341 (Jordan . . . Moab). Seir is another name for Edom. Mount Paran may be the same as Mount Sinai. If not, its location is not known. The Desert of Paran (Num 10:12) is often assumed to be on the Sinai peninsula, south of the Negev and west of the Arabah (see the map on p. 2463). See also Judg 5:4, 5; Hab 3:3.

33:2 *shone forth:* See the note at 1:33.

33:4 *the law:* See the notes at 1:3-5 and 32:46, 47.

33:6 *Reuben:* See the note at 3:12 (Reubenites). Reuben lost his right as firstborn son to inherit leadership of the family because he had an affair with one of his father's wives (Gen 35:22; 49:4). The tribe is described here as being very small. It disappeared by the tenth century B.C.

33:7 *Judah:* Judah was Jacob and Leah's fourth son. He was a leader among his brothers and was given a special blessing by Jacob (Gen 49:8-12). Moses speaks of the tribe as having trouble with an enemy. Judah did suffer at the hands of the Philistines in the eleventh century B.C.

33:8 *Massah . . . waters of Meribah:* See the note at 6:16 (Massah). See also Exod 17:1-7.

33:8 *Levi:* Levi was Jacob and Leah's third son. See the notes at 1:23; 10:8.

32:51 Num 20:1-13; 27:12-14; Deut 3:23-27.

He did not recognize his brothers
or acknowledge his own children,
but he watched over your word
and guarded your covenant.
10 He teaches your precepts to Jacob
and your law to Israel.
He offers incense before you
and whole burnt offerings on your altar.
11 Bless all his skills, O LORD,
and be pleased with the work of his hands.
Smite the loins of those who rise up against him;
strike his foes till they rise no more."

12 About Benjamin he said:

"Let the beloved of the LORD rest secure in him,
for he shields him all day long,
and the one the LORD loves rests between his shoulders."

13 About Joseph he said:

"May the LORD bless his land
with the precious dew from heaven above
and with the deep waters that lie below;
14 with the best the sun brings forth
and the finest the moon can yield;
15 with the choicest gifts of the ancient mountains
and the fruitfulness of the everlasting hills;
16 with the best gifts of the earth and its fullness
and the favor of him who dwelt in the burning bush.
Let all these rest on the head of Joseph,
on the brow of the prince among[a] his brothers.
17 In majesty he is like a firstborn bull;
his horns are the horns of a wild ox.
With them he will gore the nations,
even those at the ends of the earth.
Such are the ten thousands of Ephraim;
such are the thousands of Manasseh."

18 About Zebulun he said:

"Rejoice, Zebulun, in your going out,
and you, Issachar, in your tents.
19 They will summon peoples to the mountain
and there offer sacrifices of righteousness;
they will feast on the abundance of the seas,
on the treasures hidden in the sand."

33:9 *guarded your covenant:* The Levites were in charge of the ark of the covenant that contained the laws God gave to the people (4:1-6), and they were to camp near the tabernacle to make sure the Israelites worshiped in the proper way (Num 3:38).

33:12 *Benjamin:* Benjamin was Jacob's youngest son. His mother was Rachel. The tribe of Benjamin became known as warriors, living up to the name of "ravenous wolf" (Gen 49:27). Israel's first king, Saul, came from this tribe (1 Sam 9:21).

33:13-17 *Joseph . . . Ephraim . . . Manasseh:* Joseph was Jacob and Rachel's first son. Joseph's two sons, Ephraim and Manasseh, were adopted by Jacob. See also the notes at 1:23 and 3:13-15. Several important leaders in Israel's history came from the tribe of Ephraim, including Joshua (Num 13:8 where he is called Hoshea, also Josh 1:1-11), Samuel (1 Sam 1:1; 3:19, 20), and Jeroboam (1 Kgs 11:26-40).

33:18 *Zebulun:* Zebulun was Jacob's tenth son and Leah's sixth and final son. See also Gen 49:13.

33:18 *Issachar:* Issachar was Jacob's ninth son and Leah's first. See also Gen 49:14, 15.

33:19 *treasures hidden in the sand:* This may refer to glass made from sand; glass was rare and very valuable.

a16 Or *of the one separated from*

Testament and Death of Moses, a detail from a fresco by Luca Signorelli, around 1483. The author of DEUTERONOMY reports that Moses died in Moab when he was one hundred twenty years old. Moses was allowed to see the land that the LORD promised the people of Israel, but the LORD did not allow Moses to cross the Jordan River and settle there with them. (See 32:48-52; 34:1-8.)

20 About Gad he said:

"Blessed is he who enlarges Gad's domain!
Gad lives there like a lion,
tearing at arm or head.
21 He chose the best land for himself;
the leader's portion was kept for him.
When the heads of the people assembled,
he carried out the LORD's righteous will,
and his judgments concerning Israel."

22 About Dan he said:

"Dan is a lion's cub,
springing out of Bashan."

23 About Naphtali he said:

"Naphtali is abounding with the favor of the LORD
and is full of his blessing;
he will inherit southward to the lake."

24 About Asher he said:

"Most blessed of sons is Asher;
let him be favored by his brothers,

33:20,21 *Gad:* Gad was Jacob's seventh son. His mother was Zilpah, Leah's maid. When Leah could no longer have children, she saw Gad's birth as a sign of good fortune and so named him Gad, which means "luck" (Gen 30:11). Gad was the strongest of the tribes and was known for its fine warriors (1 Chr 12:8). The Gad tribe asked for some of the land east of the Jordan River, but promised that their warriors would cross the Jordan and help the other tribes take over the land west of the Jordan (Num 32:1-33; Josh 4:10-13). See also Gen 49:19.

33:22 *Dan:* Dan was Jacob's fifth son. His mother was Rachel's maid, Bilhah (Gen 30:6), who was also the mother of Naphtali. See also Gen 49:16, 17.

33:23 *Naphtali:* Naphtali was Jacob's sixth son. His mother was Bilhah, Rachel's maid. His name means "fight," and reflects the struggles between Rachel and Leah (Gen 30:1-8). See also Gen 49:21.

33:24 *Asher:* Asher was Jacob's eighth son. His mother was Leah's maid, Zilpah, who was also the mother of Gad. See also Gen 49:20.

33:29 *shield:* A piece of equipment made of wood, leather, or metal that soldiers used for protection in battle. See also 2 Sam 22:3; Ps 7:10.

34:1-3 *Moab . . . City of Palms . . . Zoar:* Moses is following God's command (32:48-52). See the notes on p. 341 (Jordan . . . Moab) and at 3:12-17. Mount Nebo was probably one peak of the ridge known as Mount Pisgah. The City of Palms was Jericho, a Canaanite city just west of the Jordan River and north of the Dead Sea (Josh 5:13—6:27). See the note at 2:32-37 for Gilead. Zoar was probably located near the southern shore of the Dead Sea. See the maps on pp. 2464-2465.

34:6 *Beth Peor:* See the note at 3:25-29.

34:7 *hundred and twenty years old:* See the note at 31:2.

34:4 Gen 12:7; 26:3; 28:13.

and let him bathe his feet in oil.
25 The bolts of your gates will be iron and bronze,
and your strength will equal your days.

26 "There is no one like the God of Jeshurun,
who rides on the heavens to help you
and on the clouds in his majesty.
27 The eternal God is your refuge,
and underneath are the everlasting arms.
He will drive out your enemy before you,
saying, 'Destroy him!'
28 So Israel will live in safety alone;
Jacob's spring is secure
in a land of grain and new wine,
where the heavens drop dew.
29 Blessed are you, O Israel!
Who is like you,
a people saved by the LORD?
He is your shield and helper
and your glorious sword.
Your enemies will cower before you,
and you will trample down their high places.[a]"

MOSES DIES

Moses, Israel's great leader and lawgiver dies as he gazes at the promised land he is not allowed to enter. This scene and the words written in his honor (34:10-12) bring the Pentateuch, traditionally called the "Books of Moses," to a close. But they also look ahead to the historical books, sometimes called the Deuteronomistic History.

The Death of Moses

34 Then Moses climbed Mount Nebo from the plains of Moab
to the top of Pisgah, across from Jericho. There the LORD showed

[a] **29** Or *will tread upon their bodies*

QUESTIONS ABOUT DEUTERONOMY 31:1—34:12

1. The Israelites celebrated God's place in their history and in their lives several times a year. (31:9-13; see also 16:1-17) How do you celebrate your relationship with God?
2. Why did God not allow Moses to enter Canaan, the promised land? (32:49-52; see also 3:21-29; Num 20:1-13)
3. What familiar images of God were reinforced by your reading of DEUTERONOMY? What new images of God did you discover?
4. How does your new understanding of DEUTERONOMY affect the way you understand other parts of the Bible?
5. What did DEUTERONOMY have to say about the past, present, and future of the people of Israel? What does it say about these for people today?

him the whole land—from Gilead to Dan, [2]all of Naphtali, the territory of Ephraim and Manasseh, all the land of Judah as far as the western sea,[a] [3]the Negev and the whole region from the Valley of Jericho, the City of Palms, as far as Zoar. [4]Then the LORD said to him, "This is the land I promised on oath to Abraham, Isaac and Jacob when I said, 'I will give it to your descendants.' I have let you see it with your eyes, but you will not cross over into it."

[5]And Moses the servant of the LORD died there in Moab, as the LORD had said. [6]He buried him[b] in Moab, in the valley opposite Beth Peor, but to this day no one knows where his grave is. [7]Moses was a hundred and twenty years old when he died, yet his eyes were not weak nor his strength gone. [8]The Israelites grieved for Moses in the plains of Moab thirty days, until the time of weeping and mourning was over.

[9]Now Joshua son of Nun was filled with the spirit[c] of wisdom because Moses had laid his hands on him. So the Israelites listened to him and did what the LORD had commanded Moses.

[10]Since then, no prophet has risen in Israel like Moses, whom the LORD knew face to face, [11]who did all those miraculous signs and wonders the LORD sent him to do in Egypt—to Pharaoh and to all his officials and to his whole land. [12]For no one has ever shown the mighty power or performed the awesome deeds that Moses did in the sight of all Israel.

34:9 *Joshua:* See Num 27:15-23 and the notes at 1:36-38 and 3:28.

34:9 *wisdom:* See the mini-article called "Wisdom," p. 2206.

34:9 *what the LORD had commanded Moses:* See the note at 1:3-5.

34:10-12 *no prophet . . . like Moses:* See the note at 13:1,2 and the mini-article called "Moses," p. 2335.

34:10 Exod 33:9-11; Num 12:6-8; Deut 18:15-22; Hos 12:13.

[a]**2** That is, the Mediterranean [b]**6** Or *He was buried* [c]**9** Or *Spirit*

Historical Books

THE FINAL BOOK of the Pentateuch, DEUTERONOMY, ends with the tribes of Israel camped in Moab, east of the Jordan River. The Israelites are prepared to enter Canaan, the land God had promised to them (Deut 1:1-8; 34:1-8). The final words of DEUTERONOMY tell about the death of Moses and the choice of Joshua as the next leader of Israel.

Christians call the Old Testament books that follow the Pentateuch, beginning with JOSHUA and ending with ESTHER, the Historical Books. These books describe Israel's history as a people in the land of Canaan. Although these books are called "historical," they are different from history books of today. The descriptions of events in these books are concerned with important religious teachings about God and God's relationship with Israel rather than about simply recording the historical facts of the events themselves. So the Historical Books read much more like exciting stories than like straightforward historical accounts. In fact, two of the books in this section, RUTH and ESTHER, are more like short stories than history books.

These books can be thought of as telling one long story that took place from around 1250 B.C. to 400 B.C. Within this story are several key events and main characters.

KEY EVENTS OF THE HISTORICAL BOOKS. The first key event of the Historical Books is Israel's **settlement** in the land of Canaan. JOSHUA and JUDGES describe how the people of Israel entered Canaan and settled in various regions and cities. Sometimes this settlement was peaceful, but at other times it was more difficult for the Israelites. These two books also describe how the twelve tribes were allotted specific territories and functioned with tribal leaders. The Israelites' system of government has been called a "theocracy," meaning that God was, in a real sense, their King. The book of JUDGES demonstrates Israel's repeated rejection of that relationship, leading to recurring cycles of spiritual unfaithfulness, foreign oppression, cries to God for help, and deliverance. The LORD brought that deliverance through a number of Spirit-empowered leaders known as "judges" (Judg 2:10-19).

The second key event describes the establishment of a **monarchy** ruled by a human king. The books of 1 and 2 SAMUEL tell how Saul was chosen to be the first king of Israel and describe the events that led to David becoming the second king of Israel. An important part of this event was David's choosing of Jerusalem to be the capital of Israel.

David's son Solomon became king after David died. Solomon built the first temple in Jerusalem and increased the influence and wealth of Israel. But his policies of heavy taxation and conscription of labor and military forces, together with his sin of allowing the worship of foreign idols, led to a revolt shortly after his death. The result was a **divided monarchy**, the third key event of the Historical Books. The books of 1 and 2 KINGS and 1 and 2 CHRONICLES describe the reigns of the kings who ruled the northern and southern kingdoms from about 931 B.C. to 586 B.C.

The fourth key event was the time of **defeat and exile** of these two kingdoms. Though warned by prophets like Amos and Hosea, the northern kingdom (Israel) continued to worship idols and to disobey God's Law. This led to their defeat by the Assyrians in 722 B.C. The southern kingdom (Judah) was ruled by kings descended from David, but it, too, did not listen to the warnings of prophets like Isaiah, Jeremiah, and Ezekiel. When the people and some of their leaders were unfaithful to the LORD, the LORD allowed the Babylonians to defeat them in 586 B.C. and force many of Judah's leading citizens to live as exiles in Babylonia.

In 539 B.C. King Cyrus of Persia defeated Babylonia and allowed the Jewish people living in exile to return home and reclaim their land. This **return from exile** is the fifth key event in the Historical Books. EZRA and NEHEMIAH describe how the people were able to return to Judah, rebuild the walls and temple of Jerusalem, and rededicate themselves to being God's people.

IMPORTANT CHARACTERS IN THE HISTORICAL BOOKS. Four characters are particularly important in the Historical Books. **Joshua** was the leader of the Israelites after Moses died who led the people into Canaan and helped them settle into the land by tribes. **Samuel** was the last of Israel's "judges." The people begged Samuel to choose a king for them, but he warned them that their request for a king showed a lack of faith in God's leadership. **David** was Israel's most important and best-loved king. Many of the events described in the Historical Books tell of David's faithfulness to God, who promised that one of David's descendants would always be king. But these books do not hide David's sins and the grave consequences that they brought as a result. **Ezra** was a leader who helped the people of Israel who returned from exile to commit themselves to worshiping and obeying the LORD once again.

JOSHUA

God keeps promises. Read JOSHUA to learn how the courage and faith of the people of Israel were tested by the LORD's holy war.

WHAT MAKES JOSHUA SPECIAL?

JOSHUA describes how the tribes of Israel conquered and divided the promised land of Canaan. The title of the book comes from its leading character, Joshua, who was chosen to lead Israel after Moses died (1:1-3). But the real hero is the LORD, who helped the people conquer the land. By doing so, the LORD kept the promise that was part of the covenants made with Israel's ancestors. In the first covenant, the LORD promised Abraham that his descendants would one day have a land they could call their own (Gen 12:1-3; 15:13-21; 17:8). This promise was repeated to Moses (Exod 3:7,8), who later received God's second covenant based on the Law. The people had experienced God's help in the past, and so they were challenged to trust God and obey God's Law before they entered the land of Canaan (1:6-9) and again after they had conquered the land (24:15).

The name "Joshua" means "The LORD saves," and this is the book's lesson. Those who trust in the LORD will receive the LORD's help. God's plan to give the land of Canaan to the people of Israel unfolds through individuals (Joshua, Eleazar, Rahab, Caleb), and God's power is demonstrated through miraculous acts (crossing the Jordan River, the destruction of Jericho, large hailstones in a battle).

WHY WAS JOSHUA WRITTEN?

JOSHUA is part of the great story, DEUTERONOMY through 2 KINGS, which tells of Israel's life as God's special people in the promised land. A key theme in this entire work is that the land is a gift from the LORD, and remaining loyal to the LORD and the LORD's Law are the conditions for keeping the land. Israel could only win the land with the LORD's help. And, they could only keep it by obeying the LORD's Law. This theme is emphasized in two speeches given by Joshua at the end of the book (23:1—24:27)

The events described in JOSHUA also answer two important questions: How did the people of Israel enter the land of Canaan? and How was the land divided among the tribes? Many scholars believe JOSHUA records events that took place around 1250 to 1225 B.C. JOSHUA records a series of "holy wars" against the people of Canaan, and reports the swift and sometimes miraculous capture of many Canaanite cities and towns. For example, in the battle at Jericho, the LORD made the walls collapse (6:20). Later, in the battle at Gibeon the LORD made huge hailstones fall from the sky and crush the enemy soldiers (10:11). With Joshua in command, the united tribes of Israel crossed the Jordan River and cut through the center of the land, eventually taking over the lands to the

Jordan River and the Palestinian rift valley: A basic understanding of the geography of Palestine can be helpful to understanding the history of Israel. The land where the Hebrew people would settle was divided in two by a deep rift valley that ran from the Sea of Galilee in the north to the Red Sea in the south. The Jordan River, which begins in the Lebanon Mountains, runs through this rift valley into the Sea of Galilee, and then, from the Sea of Galilee into the Dead Sea sixty-five miles further south. It is the world's lowest river, the length from the Sea of Galilee to the Dead Sea being well below sea level. Most of the tribes of Israel settled in the hill country west of the Jordan and east of the coastal plain which was usually controlled by the Philistines and Phoenicians. The area east of the Jordan is usually referred to as Transjordan. About fifteen miles south of the Sea of Galilee and to the west of the Jordan River is the Valley of Jezreel, a fertile area and an important pass connecting the coastal plain to the west with the Jordan Valley. See the map on p. 2464.

The Jordan River, therefore, is an important boundary in the stories related in JOSHUA. When the people cross the Jordan and enter the promised land for the first time, its waters are stopped to allow the people to safely cross. (3:1-17), a miracle similar to the one the LORD performed at the Red Sea. After the people began to settle into their tribal lands, the tribes of Reuben and Gad and the half-tribe of Manasseh crossed back into Transjordan to settle in the lands which Moses said would be theirs. The story of how this crossing created tension for the people of Israel is told in chapter 22.

> The LORD said, *"Have I not commanded you? Be strong and courageous. Do not be terrified; do not be discouraged, for the LORD your God will be with you wherever you go."*
> Josh 1:9

1:1 *Moses . . . Joshua:* Moses, the great leader who had brought the Hebrews out of Egypt and through the desert wanderings of forty years, was dead. Joshua had been appointed by God to take his place (Deut 34:1-10). For more, see the mini-article called "Moses," p. 2335.

Since his youth, Joshua had been Moses' helper (Exod 24:13; 33:9-11; Num 11:28). Before Moses died, he placed his hands on Joshua to show that he would take Moses' place as the leader of the twelve tribes of Israel (Num 27:12-23; Deut 31:1-8). Here in Joshua 1:2-9 the LORD orders Joshua to lead Israel into Canaan and promises to be with Joshua and the people wherever they go.

south and to the north. But at certain points in the story, individual clans are described as trying on their own to take over land with only partial success.

The second part of the book (13:1—24:33) describes how each tribe received its land. This included land in Canaan to the west of the Jordan River and some territory east of the Jordan River that had already been promised to the tribes of Gad, Reuben, and half of Manasseh (Num 32). The book also explains why the special servants of the LORD, the Levite tribe, did not receive a large share of land like the other tribes. Instead, they were given towns scattered throughout the whole country.

WHAT'S THE STORY BEHIND THE SCENE?

Archaeologists have discovered evidence that parts of Canaan were attacked in the period between 1300 and 1200 B.C. The towns of Bethel, Lachish, and Debir were completely destroyed. While some key places were destroyed or captured under Joshua, not all the places where Canaanites lived were taken over by the people of Israel (Judg 1). It was not until the time of King David (around 1000 B.C.) that the tribes of Israel were united in one kingdom and were solidly in place in the land of Canaan. Even then, Canaanite culture and religion continued to influence the people of Israel for many more centuries. According to the biblical authors, it was the worship of Canaanite idols that led, in part, to the fall of the northern kingdom (Israel) in 722 B.C. and to the fall of the southern kingdom (Judah) in 586 B.C. See also the article called "From Joshua to the Exile: The People of Israel in the Promised Land," p. 924.

HOW IS JOSHUA CONSTRUCTED?

The book of JOSHUA has two main parts. The first half (1–12) is a series of stories about the capture of key cities and towns in Canaan. It includes many stories that explain the origin of a landmark in Israel. The second half (13–22) consists of tribal boundaries and city lists. The twelve tribes each got a share of the land, while the Levites were given special cities scattered throughout Israel. The concluding chapters of the book (23,24) report Joshua's farewell and death as well as the important gathering at Shechem where the people of Israel promised to obey the LORD God, now that they had settled in the promised land. The book may be outlined in the following way:

Conquest of major Canaanite cities (1:1—12:24)
- Entering the promised land (1:1—5:12)
- The LORD leads Israel in battle (5:13—12:24)

Division of the promised land (13:1—22:34)

The last days of Joshua (23:1—24:33)
- Joshua's farewell address (23:1-16)
- The ceremony at Shechem and three burials (24:1-33)

Conquest of Major Canaanite Cities

Moses is dead and the Israelites are ready to end their forty years of wandering in the desert. Their new leader, Joshua, leads the people across the Jordan River westward into hostile Canaanite territory. Beginning with Jericho, the people attack key cities in western Canaan. Their attacks are made successful by the LORD *God, who provides miraculous help.*

ENTERING THE PROMISED LAND

The LORD *assures Joshua and the people of success based on the promises made to Moses. Spies are sent into Jericho, and the Israelites cross the Jordan River in a manner similar to their earlier crossing of the Red Sea.*

The LORD Commands Joshua

1 After the death of Moses the servant of the LORD, the LORD said
to Joshua son of Nun, Moses' aide: 2"Moses my servant is dead.
Now then, you and all these people, get ready to cross the Jordan
River into the land I am about to give to them—to the Israelites. 3I
will give you every place where you set your foot, as I promised
Moses. 4Your territory will extend from the desert to Lebanon, and
from the great river, the Euphrates—all the Hittite country—to the
Great Sea[a] on the west. 5No one will be able to stand up against
you all the days of your life. As I was with Moses, so I will be with
you; I will never leave you nor forsake you.

6"Be strong and courageous, because you will lead these people to inherit the land I swore to their forefathers to give them. 7Be
strong and very courageous. Be careful to obey all the law my servant Moses gave you; do not turn from it to the right or to the left,
that you may be successful wherever you go. 8Do not let this Book
of the Law depart from your mouth; meditate on it day and night,
so that you may be careful to do everything written in it. Then you
will be prosperous and successful. 9Have I not commanded you?
Be strong and courageous. Do not be terrified; do not be discouraged, for the LORD your God will be with you wherever you go."

10So Joshua ordered the officers of the people: 11"Go through
the camp and tell the people, 'Get your supplies ready. Three days
from now you will cross the Jordan here to go in and take possession of the land the LORD your God is giving you for your own.' "

12But to the Reubenites, the Gadites and the half-tribe of
Manasseh, Joshua said, 13"Remember the command that Moses the
servant of the LORD gave you: 'The LORD your God is giving you
rest and has granted you this land.' 14Your wives, your children and
your livestock may stay in the land that Moses gave you east of the
Jordan, but all your fighting men, fully armed, must cross over

[a]4 That is, the Mediterranean

1:2-4 *Jordan River ... Great Sea:* The land promised to Moses (Exod 3:8) and described here covered more than the land of Canaan. It included the entire area between the Jordan River to the Mediterranean Sea (here called the Great Sea). Its southern boundary was a desert known as the Negev. It stretched north to the Lebanon Mountains and included parts of Syria. The Hittite country refers to the northern part of Syria, which had been the southernmost part of the Hittite empire which stretches across much of Asia Minor. See the map on p. 2464.

1:6-8 *the land I swore to their forefathers . . . Book of the Law:* The promise of a land the people could call their own was first given to Abraham (Gen 17:7,8). But obeying God's Law became a condition both for taking the land and remaining in the land. The Book of the Law, here probably refers to the core of what is now DEUTERONOMY (most likely Deut 12–26). See 2 Kgs 22:8 and the Introduction to DEUTERONOMY. See also Deut 7:1-15.

1:12 *Reubenites, the Gadites and the half-tribe of Manasseh:* The Israelites were divided into tribes. Each tribe descended from a common ancestor, one of Jacob's twelve sons. (Jacob's name was changed to "Israel," Gen 32:28.) The tribes are named after each son (Gen 35:23-26; 48; 49).

The tribes of Reuben, Gad, and half the tribe of Manasseh will eventually settle east of the Jordan River. This plan dates from the time of Moses, when this promise was made to them (Num 32:28-32; Deut 3:18-20; Josh 22:1-9).

1:3-5 Deut 11:24,25; Heb 13:5.
1:9 Deut 31:6,7,23.

1:14,15 *help your brothers:* The men of the two-and-a-half eastern tribes (1:12) were ordered to lead the attack on Canaan.

ahead of your brothers. You are to help your brothers 15 until the
LORD gives them rest, as he has done for you, and until they too
have taken possession of the land that the LORD your God is giving
them. After that, you may go back and occupy your own land,
which Moses the servant of the LORD gave you east of the Jordan
toward the sunrise."

16 Then they answered Joshua, "Whatever you have commanded us we will do, and wherever you send us we will go. 17 Just
as we fully obeyed Moses, so we will obey you. Only may the LORD
your God be with you as he was with Moses. 18 Whoever rebels
against your word and does not obey your words, whatever you
may command them, will be put to death. Only be strong and
courageous!"

PALESTINE

Palestine refers to the area of land along the east coast of the Mediterranean Sea from Gaza in the south to southern Lebanon, then east to the areas bordering the Jordan River. It was also known as the land of Canaan or the Holy Land. In the Bible it is known as the "land flowing with milk and honey" (Deut 6:3; 26:15), or as the promised land, because God promised to give the land to Abraham and his descendants (Gen 17:7, 8; Num 34:1-12). Abraham's descendants, the tribes of Israel, made this land their geographical and spiritual homeland after years of slavery in Egypt and after wandering in the desert for forty years.

The region of Palestine was originally called Canaan and the people who lived there before the Israelites were called Canaanites. It came to be known as Israel after the twelve tribes conquered the land. The region came to be known as Palestine in the time when the Greeks ruled the region beginning in about 333 B.C. The name "Palestine" comes from "Philistines," the name of the people who settled in the narrow strip of land along the southwestern part of the Mediterranean coastline some time after 1200 B.C. (see the map on p. 2464). Today, "Palestine" refers to the area covered by Israel, Gaza, and Jordan.

The distance from Dan to Beersheba, the traditional northern and southern limits of Palestine, is around 150 miles. Two long valleys run north and south, one along the Mediterranean coast and the other along the Jordan River. Between these fertile farmlands are many small mountain ranges suitable for raising sheep. Deserts lie to the east of the Jordan and to the south and west of the Dead Sea.

There are only two seasons: a cold, wet winter and a hot, dry summer. The rains begin in the month of Tishri (starting in mid-September) and end in the month of Nisan (from mid-March to mid-April). For more about Palestine's climate see the chart called "Jewish Calendar and Festivals," p. 944.

This tiny region was an important land bridge between Africa and Asia. Traders had to pass through Palestine to carry their goods overland or to reach shipping harbors on the Mediterranean. Rival armies often battled for control of the region. Because Palestine served as a coastal passage for many hostile peoples, the foreign influences on the Israelites were a constant source of trouble. In spite of their dangerous position in the region, the Israelites never wavered in their belief that this land was God's gift to them.

Palestine, the land promised to the Israelites. God promised Abraham that his descendants would live in a land flowing with milk and honey. When Joshua led the people across the Jordan River, they entered a fertile valley that produced many crops: grains (such as wheat and barley), grapes, and olives. Bordering the valley were small mountain ranges ideal for sheep herding.

Rahab and the Spies

2 Then Joshua son of Nun secretly sent two spies from Shittim.
"Go, look over the land," he said, "especially Jericho." So they went
and entered the house of a prostitute[a] named Rahab and stayed there.
2 The king of Jericho was told, "Look! Some of the Israelites
have come here tonight to spy out the land." 3 So the king of Jericho sent this message to Rahab: "Bring out the men who came to
you and entered your house, because they have come to spy out
the whole land."
4 But the woman had taken the two men and hidden them.
She said, "Yes, the men came to me, but I did not know where they
had come from. 5 At dusk, when it was time to close the city gate,
the men left. I don't know which way they went. Go after them
quickly. You may catch up with them." 6 (But she had taken them
up to the roof and hidden them under the stalks of flax she had
laid out on the roof.) 7 So the men set out in pursuit of the spies on
the road that leads to the fords of the Jordan, and as soon as the
pursuers had gone out, the gate was shut.

2:1 *Shittim . . . Jericho:* The exact location of the Israelite camp at Shittim is unknown, but it was in Moab east of the Jordan River and northeast of the Dead Sea (see the map on p. 2464). See also Num 22:1; 33:41-49.

2:1 *Rahab:* Possibly an innkeeper, Rahab is identified here as a prostitute. She and her family would later become part of the Hebrew people (Josh 6:21-25). She is described in Hebrews 11:31 as a hero of faith. See also Jas 2:24,25.

2:2 *king of Jericho:* The king knew Rahab's house (or inn) would be a likely place to find the spies.

---

[a]1 Or possibly *an innkeeper*

[8]Before the spies lay down for the night, she went up on the roof [9]and said to them, "I know that the LORD has given this land to you and that a great fear of you has fallen on us, so that all who live in this country are melting in fear because of you. [10]We have heard how the LORD dried up the water of the Red Sea[a] for you when you came out of Egypt, and what you did to Sihon and Og, the two kings of the Amorites east of the Jordan, whom you completely destroyed.[b] [11]When we heard of it, our hearts melted and everyone's courage failed because of you, for the LORD your God is God in heaven above and on the earth below. [12]Now then, please swear to me by the LORD that you will show kindness to my family, because I have shown kindness to you. Give me a sure sign [13]that you will spare the lives of my father and mother, my brothers and sisters, and all who belong to them, and that you will save us from death."

[14]"Our lives for your lives!" the men assured her. "If you don't tell what we are doing, we will treat you kindly and faithfully when the LORD gives us the land."

[15]So she let them down by a rope through the window, for the house she lived in was part of the city wall. [16]Now she had said to them, "Go to the hills so the pursuers will not find you. Hide yourselves there three days until they return, and then go on your way."

[17]The men said to her, "This oath you made us swear will not be binding on us [18]unless, when we enter the land, you have tied this scarlet cord in the window through which you let us down, and unless you have brought your father and mother, your brothers and all your family into your house. [19]If anyone goes outside your house into the street, his blood will be on his own head; we will not be responsible. As for anyone who is in the house with you, his blood will be on our head if a hand is laid on him. [20]But if you tell what we are doing, we will be released from the oath you made us swear."

[21]"Agreed," she replied. "Let it be as you say." So she sent them away and they departed. And she tied the scarlet cord in the window.

[22]When they left, they went into the hills and stayed there three days, until the pursuers had searched all along the road and returned without finding them. [23]Then the two men started back. They went down out of the hills, forded the river and came to Joshua son of Nun and told him everything that had happened to them. [24]They said to Joshua, "The LORD has surely given the whole land into our hands; all the people are melting in fear because of us."

2:10 *dried up the water of the Red Sea:* Refers to one of the marshes or freshwater lakes near the eastern part of the Nile River delta (see the map on p. 2463). This identification is based on Exodus 13:17—14:9. In the Greek translation of the Hebrew Scriptures made about 200 B.C., the "Sea of Reeds" was named "Red Sea." For the report Rahab heard, see Exodus 14:21,22.

2:10 *Sihon and Og:* While Moses was still alive, King Sihon refused to let the Israelites pass through Amorite land. But the Israelites defeated King Sihon's army near Jahaz and King Og's army at Edrei (Num 21:21-35).

2:15 *part of the city wall:* In ancient times, cities and larger towns had high walls around them to protect them against attack. Sometimes houses were built against the wall so that the city wall formed one wall of the house. This added strength to the city wall.

2:24 *The LORD has surely given the whole land into our hands:* The Israelite spies express their confidence and show that they accept what God wants to do for the Israelite people (1:9). Their confidence, most likely, was reinforced by Rahab's words. Although she was a Canaanite, she knew the LORD was going to give the land to the Israelites (2:9).

a10 Hebrew *Yam Suph*; that is, Sea of Reeds **b10** The Hebrew term refers to the irrevocable giving over of things or persons to the LORD, often by totally destroying them.

Rahab and the Israelite spies, fourteenth-century illuminated manuscript, National Library, Florence. Rahab was a prostitute in Jericho who hid Joshua's spies from the king of Jericho, and then later helped them to escape. She lowered them from a window with a rope. Because of this, she and her family were spared when the Israelites invaded the city. (See 2:1-24; 6:25.)

Crossing the Jordan

3 Early in the morning Joshua and all the Israelites set out from
Shittim and went to the Jordan, where they camped before crossing over. [2]After three days the officers went throughout the camp,
[3]giving orders to the people: "When you see the ark of the
covenant of the LORD your God, and the priests, who are Levites,
carrying it, you are to move out from your positions and follow it.
[4]Then you will know which way to go, since you have never been
this way before. But keep a distance of about a thousand yards[a]
between you and the ark; do not go near it."
[5]Joshua told the people, "Consecrate yourselves, for tomorrow the LORD will do amazing things among you."
[6]Joshua said to the priests, "Take up the ark of the covenant
and pass on ahead of the people." So they took it up and went
ahead of them.
[7]And the LORD said to Joshua, "Today I will begin to exalt you
in the eyes of all Israel, so they may know that I am with you as I was
with Moses. [8]Tell the priests who carry the ark of the covenant: 'When
you reach the edge of the Jordan's waters, go and stand in the river.'"

[a]4 Hebrew *about two thousand cubits* (about 900 meters)

3:1 *Shittim . . . Jordan:* See the note at 2:1 (Shittim). The Israelites camped on the east side of the Jordan for three days (3:2) before trying to cross.

3:3 *ark of the covenant . . . the priests, who are Levites, carrying it:* The ark of the covenant was considered the place where God was present with the people of Israel (Exod 25:18-22). The priests who came from the Levite clan of Kohath had earlier been assigned the task of carrying the ark (Num 4:1-6). See also the mini-article called "The Ark of the Covenant," p. 513. When the tribes of Israel moved from one place to another, the priests of the Levi tribe carried the ark of the covenant ahead of the people, who were supposed to keep their distance from it because of its power.

3:5 *Consecrate yourselves:* People had to perform specific rituals to purify themselves in order to worship the LORD (Lev 7:20,21; 15:2,33; 22:4-8; Deut 23:10,11) or to prepare for battle (Deut 20:1-9; 23:9-14; 1 Sam 21:2-5). The people's crossing of the Jordan River into the promised land of Canaan includes the parts of a religious ceremony—a rite of purification (3:5), a procession (3:6), a sermon (3:9-13), and setting up a memorial (4:9).

3:7 *I will begin to exalt you . . . as I was with Moses:* The LORD sets in motion the promise made to Joshua in 1:5. The parting of the waters in 3:16, 17 is compared to Moses' parting of the Red Sea (Exod 14:21,22).

[9]Joshua said to the Israelites, "Come here and listen to the words of the LORD your God. [10]This is how you will know that the living God is among you and that he will certainly drive out before you the Canaanites, Hittites, Hivites, Perizzites, Girgashites, Amorites and Jebusites. [11]See, the ark of the covenant of the Lord of all the earth will go into the Jordan ahead of you. [12]Now then, choose twelve men from the tribes of Israel, one from each tribe. [13]And as soon as the priests who carry the ark of the LORD—the Lord of all the earth—set foot in the Jordan, its waters flowing downstream will be cut off and stand up in a heap."

[14]So when the people broke camp to cross the Jordan, the priests carrying the ark of the covenant went ahead of them. [15]Now the Jordan is at flood stage all during harvest. Yet as soon as the priests who carried the ark reached the Jordan and their feet touched the water's edge, [16]the water from upstream stopped flowing. It piled up in a heap a great distance away, at a town called Adam in the vicinity of Zarethan, while the water flowing down to the Sea of the Arabah (the Salt Sea[a]) was completely cut off. So the people crossed over opposite Jericho. [17]The priests who carried the ark of the covenant of the LORD stood firm on dry ground in the middle of the Jordan, while all Israel passed by until the whole nation had completed the crossing on dry ground.

4 When the whole nation had finished crossing the Jordan, the LORD said to Joshua, [2]"Choose twelve men from among the people, one from each tribe, [3]and tell them to take up twelve stones from the middle of the Jordan from right where the priests stood and to carry them over with you and put them down at the place where you stay tonight."

[4]So Joshua called together the twelve men he had appointed from the Israelites, one from each tribe, [5]and said to them, "Go over before the ark of the LORD your God into the middle of the Jordan. Each of you is to take up a stone on his shoulder, according to the number of the tribes of the Israelites, [6]to serve as a sign among you. In the future, when your children ask you, 'What do these stones mean?' [7]tell them that the flow of the Jordan was cut off before the ark of the covenant of the LORD. When it crossed the Jordan, the waters of the Jordan were cut off. These stones are to be a memorial to the people of Israel forever."

[8]So the Israelites did as Joshua commanded them. They took twelve stones from the middle of the Jordan, according to the number of the tribes of the Israelites, as the LORD had told Joshua; and they carried them over with them to their camp, where they put them down. [9]Joshua set up the twelve stones that had been[b] in the middle of the Jordan at the spot where the priests who carried the ark of the covenant had stood. And they are there to this day.

[10]Now the priests who carried the ark remained standing in

[a]**16** That is, the Dead Sea [b]**9** Or *Joshua also set up twelve stones*

3:10 *Canaanites . . . Jebusites:* This was a common list of the peoples living in Palestine at the time of the conquest (see also Exod 3:8; Num 13:29; Deut 7:1). The Canaanites were said to be descendants of Noah's son Ham (Gen 10:6-20). "Canaan" probably first meant "land of the purple." The Canaanites used purple dye from a shellfish found along the coast of the Mediterranean Sea. The Greeks later called the coastal area "Phoenicia" from a Greek word also meaning "purple." The Hittites were a dominant force in Canaan from the time of Abraham to around 1300 B.C. (see also Gen 10:6-20). The exact identity of the Hivites, Perizzites, and Girgashites is not certain (but see also the note at Deut 7:1). The Amorites lived in the hill country of Canaan at the time the Israelites invaded (Num 21:21-35). According to Joshua 10:3-5, they also occupied cities to the south of Jerusalem. The Jebusites controlled the area around Jerusalem until Israel's King David took over that city (2 Sam 5:6-9).

3:12 *twelve . . . one from each tribe:* The number of the tribes comes from the twelve sons of Jacob, who was later named "Israel" (Gen 32:22-29)

3:14,15 *flood stage all during harvest:* The Jordan River often flooded in late spring at the end of the rainy season. This made the crossing even more dramatic. There were no bridges the people could use to cross over the swollen river.

3:14–16 *priests . . . water . . . completely cut off:* See the notes at 3:3 and 3:7. This miracle recalls the earlier miracle when the LORD helped the Hebrews cross the Red Sea (Exod 14).

3:16 *Adam . . . Sea of the Arabah (the Salt Sea):* Adam was eighteen miles north of Jericho. The Jordan flows south into the Dead Sea (also called Sea of the Arabah and Salt Sea), which has a salt content so high (one part salt to two parts water) that no animals or plants can live in it. Its bottom is 2,600 feet below sea level.

The Ark Passes over the Jordan, James Tissot, about 1880. Joshua told the Israelites that when the priests stepped into the Jordan River carrying the ark of the covenant containing the stones with the Ten Commandments written on them, the water would stop flowing. They could then cross over on dry land. As soon as the priests' feet touched the water, the river stopped. (See 3:1-17.)

the middle of the Jordan until everything the LORD had commanded Joshua was done by the people, just as Moses had directed Joshua. The people hurried over, 11and as soon as all of them
had crossed, the ark of the LORD and the priests came to the other
side while the people watched. 12The men of Reuben, Gad and the
half-tribe of Manasseh crossed over, armed, in front of the
Israelites, as Moses had directed them. 13About forty thousand
armed for battle crossed over before the LORD to the plains of Jericho for war.

14That day the LORD exalted Joshua in the sight of all Israel;
and they revered him all the days of his life, just as they had
revered Moses.

15Then the LORD said to Joshua, 16"Command the priests
carrying the ark of the Testimony to come up out of the Jordan."

17So Joshua commanded the priests, "Come up out of the
Jordan."

18And the priests came up out of the river carrying the ark of
the covenant of the LORD. No sooner had they set their feet on the
dry ground than the waters of the Jordan returned to their place
and ran at flood stage as before.

19On the tenth day of the first month the people went up
from the Jordan and camped at Gilgal on the eastern border of
Jericho. 20And Joshua set up at Gilgal the twelve stones they had
taken out of the Jordan. 21He said to the Israelites, "In the future

4:3 *take up twelve stones:* Two descriptions of the monument stones are given here, perhaps indicating two different sets of stones. One monument was set up at the Gilgal camp (4:1-3,19,20), while the other was placed in the bed of the Jordan River (4:9).

4:6 *when your children ask:* As in Exodus 13:14 and Deuteronomy 6:20, the concern is for future generations to know and remember the ways that the LORD has acted on behalf of the people.

4:11 *ark of the LORD:* Referring to the ark of the covenant (see the note at 3:3). The army was marching past the ark, the symbol of God's throne on earth (Exod 25:10-22; 37:1-9; 1 Sam 4:4).

4:12 *men of Reuben, Gad and the half-tribe of Manasseh:* See the notes at 1:12 and 1:14,15. The men from these two-and-a-half tribes now take over the advance from the priests (1:12-16).

4:14 *That day the LORD exalted Joshua:* Joshua's role as leader is demonstrated by this crossing, as promised by the LORD in 1:5,17,18; 3:7. When Moses died his leadership was honored, but many stories in EXODUS and NUMBERS show how the Israelites had questioned Moses' leadership. See also the mini-article called "Moses," p. 2335.

4:19 *first month:* The first month of the Hebrew calendar is Abib (also called Nisan), which is from about mid-March to mid-April. See also the chart called "Jewish Calendar and Festivals," p. 944.

4:19 *Gilgal:* Located near Jericho, Gilgal was an important worship site before Jerusalem was established as the only proper place for Israelites to make sacrifices (see 1 Sam 11:15; 2 Sam 19:15).

4:23 *Red Sea:* See the note at 2:10 (dried up).

5:1 *Amorite . . . Canaanite:* These terms are used loosely to describe the groups of people who lived in Palestine. See the notes at 2:10 (Sihon and Og) and 3:10. Compare also Josh 9:1,2. Each Canaanite city had its own king (ruler).

5:2 *flint knives . . . circumcise:* Flint is a stone that can be chipped until it forms a very sharp edge. Bronze tools had replaced stone by this time, but the ancient stone tools were required for this circumcision ritual (Exod 4:25,26). God commanded circumcision as a permanent physical sign that Abraham's descendants were God's chosen people (Gen 17:9-14). See the mini-article called "Circumcision," p. 2251.

5:5 *all the people born in the desert . . . had not:* See Num 14:27-35. The new generation, those not born in Egypt, were to be circumcised in preparation for the Passover celebration (5:10).

5:10 *Passover:* Passover was celebrated as a remembrance of how God acted to save the Israelite people from slavery in Egypt. See also Exod 12:1-13 and the mini-article called "Passover and the Feast of Unleavened Bread," p. 2030.

when your descendants ask their fathers, 'What do these stones
mean?' 22 tell them, 'Israel crossed the Jordan on dry ground.' 23 For
the LORD your God dried up the Jordan before you until you had
crossed over. The LORD your God did to the Jordan just what he
had done to the Red Sea[a] when he dried it up before us until we
had crossed over. 24 He did this so that all the peoples of the earth
might know that the hand of the LORD is powerful and so that you
might always fear the LORD your God."

Circumcision at Gilgal

5 Now when all the Amorite kings west of the Jordan and all the
Canaanite kings along the coast heard how the LORD had dried up
the Jordan before the Israelites until we had crossed over, their hearts
melted and they no longer had the courage to face the Israelites.
2 At that time the LORD said to Joshua, "Make flint knives and
circumcise the Israelites again." 3 So Joshua made flint knives and
circumcised the Israelites at Gibeath Haaraloth.[b]
4 Now this is why he did so: All those who came out of
Egypt—all the men of military age—died in the desert on the way
after leaving Egypt. 5 All the people that came out had been circumcised, but all the people born in the desert during the journey
from Egypt had not. 6 The Israelites had moved about in the desert
forty years until all the men who were of military age when they
left Egypt had died, since they had not obeyed the LORD. For the
LORD had sworn to them that they would not see the land that he
had solemnly promised their fathers to give us, a land flowing with
milk and honey. 7 So he raised up their sons in their place, and
these were the ones Joshua circumcised. They were still uncircumcised because they had not been circumcised on the way. 8 And
after the whole nation had been circumcised, they remained where
they were in camp until they were healed.
9 Then the LORD said to Joshua, "Today I have rolled away the
reproach of Egypt from you." So the place has been called Gilgal[c]
to this day.

[a]23 Hebrew *Yam Suph*; that is, Sea of Reeds [b]3 *Gibeath Haaraloth* means *hill of foreskins.* [c]9 *Gilgal* sounds like the Hebrew for *roll.*

QUESTIONS ABOUT JOSHUA 1:1—5:12

1. Who was Joshua, and what does the LORD promise him? (1:1-9)
2. How does the foreigner Rahab show her faith in the LORD? (2:1-11) How is she to be "rewarded" for her actions? (2:12-14)
3. Compare the crossing of the Jordan River (3:1-17) with the crossing of the Red Sea under Moses. (Exod 14:15-22) How are the situations similar? How are they different? What purpose was this miraculous crossing meant to serve? (3:10; 4:5-7, 22-24)
4. In what ways does the material in chapter 5 mark the end of an old era and the beginning of the new?
5. What person or event in Joshua 1–5 do you find most inspiring? Why?

10 On the evening of the fourteenth day of the month, while camped at Gilgal on the plains of Jericho, the Israelites celebrated the Passover. 11 The day after the Passover, that very day, they ate some of the produce of the land: unleavened bread and roasted grain. 12 The manna stopped the day after[a] they ate this food from the land; there was no longer any manna for the Israelites, but that year they ate of the produce of Canaan.

THE LORD LEADS ISRAEL IN BATTLE

The next section tells how the LORD leads the people of Israel in their conquest of Canaan. Some of the victories are a result of the LORD's mighty miracles. Three major attacks are described: in central Canaan (5:13—10:28), southern Canaan (10:29-43), and northern Canaan (11:1-15).

The Fall of Jericho

13 Now when Joshua was near Jericho, he looked up and saw a man standing in front of him with a drawn sword in his hand. Joshua went up to him and asked, "Are you for us or for our enemies?"

14 "Neither," he replied, "but as commander of the army of the LORD I have now come." Then Joshua fell facedown to the ground in reverence, and asked him, "What message does my Lord[b] have for his servant?"

15 The commander of the LORD's army replied, "Take off your sandals, for the place where you are standing is holy." And Joshua did so.

6 Now Jericho was tightly shut up because of the Israelites. No one went out and no one came in.

2 Then the LORD said to Joshua, "See, I have delivered Jericho into your hands, along with its king and its fighting men. 3 March around the city once with all the armed men. Do this for six days. 4 Have seven priests carry trumpets of rams' horns in front of the ark. On the seventh day, march around the city seven times, with the priests blowing the trumpets. 5 When you hear them sound a long blast on the trumpets, have all the people give a loud shout; then the wall of the city will collapse and the people will go up, every man straight in."

6 So Joshua son of Nun called the priests and said to them, "Take up the ark of the covenant of the LORD and have seven priests carry trumpets in front of it." 7 And he ordered the people, "Advance! March around the city, with the armed guard going ahead of the ark of the LORD."

8 When Joshua had spoken to the people, the seven priests

[a]12 Or *the day* [b]14 Or *lord*

5:11,12 *unleavened bread and roasted grain . . . manna:* These verses mark the end of one era and the beginning of another. Now that they were beginning a settled life in Canaan, they could grow the grains that would be an important part of their diet. Israelites were supposed to eat bread made without yeast (unleavened) for the week following Passover during the Feast of Unleavened Bread (Exod 12:14-20; Num 28:16,17). Manna was the special food that God provided for the Israelites while they were in the desert (Exod 16:13-36; Num 11:4-9).

5:15 *Take off your sandals:* This was done to show respect for God, just as Moses had done when he encountered God on Mount Sinai (Exod 3:5).

6:1 *Jericho was tightly shut up:* See the note at 2:15. The entrances to walled cities were huge gates. By shutting down its gates, the city protected itself.

6:4 *ark . . . trumpets:* See the note at 3:3. The trumpets were hollowed-out ram's horns (see the photograph on p. 2223). Note that the trumpets were blown by seven priests, who represented Israel. The number "seven" was understood to symbolize perfection. For more, see the chart called "Numbers in the Bible," p. 2405. Although the priests and soldiers had their tasks to perform, the victory would be led by God.

6:4 *march around the city:* Jericho was located at the crossroads of several important trade routes in the Jordan River valley. Though it was a center for trade and business, Jericho was small by modern standards, only six acres in size. So, the Israelites are able to march around it slowly seven times in one day.

Joshua had commanded the people, "Do not give a war cry, do not raise your voices, do not say a word until the day I tell you to shout. Then shout!"
Josh 6:10

6:15 *marched around the city seven times:* This strategy made the enemy afraid while giving the troops exercise and keeping their morale high. The way Israel marched around Jericho is more like a religious ritual than a true battle plan.

6:17 *devoted to the LORD:* That everything was to be "devoted to the LORD" meant complete destruction. Destroying a city and everything in it showed that it belonged to the LORD. These actions signaled a complete break with the condemned culture. See also Lev 27:28,29; Deut 20:16-18; and the mini-article called "Holy War (The LORD's Battles)," p. 306.

The Fall of Jericho, Edmund Dulac (1882-1953). For six days the Israelite army marched around the walled city of Jericho. On the seventh day, while the priests blew their trumpets, the people marched around the city seven times. When Joshua gave the signal, the priests blew their trumpets again and all the people shouted as loud as they could. The walls of Jericho fell flat. (See 6:1-20.)

carrying the seven trumpets before the LORD went forward, blowing their trumpets, and the ark of the LORD's covenant followed
them. 9The armed guard marched ahead of the priests who blew
the trumpets, and the rear guard followed the ark. All this time the
trumpets were sounding. 10But Joshua had commanded the people, "Do not give a war cry, do not raise your voices, do not say a
word until the day I tell you to shout. Then shout!" 11So he had the
ark of the LORD carried around the city, circling it once. Then the
people returned to camp and spent the night there.
12Joshua got up early the next morning and the priests
took up the ark of the LORD. 13The seven priests carrying the
seven trumpets went forward, marching before the ark of the
LORD and blowing the trumpets. The armed men went ahead of
them and the rear guard followed the ark of the LORD, while the
trumpets kept sounding. 14So on the second day they marched

around the city once and returned to the camp. They did this
for six days.
[15]On the seventh day, they got up at daybreak and marched
around the city seven times in the same manner, except that on
that day they circled the city seven times. [16]The seventh time
around, when the priests sounded the trumpet blast, Joshua commanded the people, "Shout! For the LORD has given you the city!
[17]The city and all that is in it are to be devoted[a] to the LORD. Only
Rahab the prostitute[b] and all who are with her in her house shall
be spared, because she hid the spies we sent. [18]But keep away from
the devoted things, so that you will not bring about your own
destruction by taking any of them. Otherwise you will make the
camp of Israel liable to destruction and bring trouble on it. [19]All
the silver and gold and the articles of bronze and iron are sacred to
the LORD and must go into his treasury."
[20]When the trumpets sounded, the people shouted, and at
the sound of the trumpet, when the people gave a loud shout, the
wall collapsed; so every man charged straight in, and they took the
city. [21]They devoted the city to the LORD and destroyed with the
sword every living thing in it—men and women, young and old,
cattle, sheep and donkeys.
[22]Joshua said to the two men who had spied out the land,
"Go into the prostitute's house and bring her out and all who
belong to her, in accordance with your oath to her." [23]So the young
men who had done the spying went in and brought out Rahab, her
father and mother and brothers and all who belonged to her. They
brought out her entire family and put them in a place outside the
camp of Israel.
[24]Then they burned the whole city and everything in it, but
they put the silver and gold and the articles of bronze and iron
into the treasury of the LORD's house. [25]But Joshua spared Rahab
the prostitute, with her family and all who belonged to her,
because she hid the men Joshua had sent as spies to Jericho—and
she lives among the Israelites to this day.
[26]At that time Joshua pronounced this solemn oath: "Cursed
before the LORD is the man who undertakes to rebuild this city,
Jericho:

"At the cost of his firstborn son
will he lay its foundations;
at the cost of his youngest
will he set up its gates."

[27]So the LORD was with Joshua, and his fame spread
throughout the land.

---

[a]17 The Hebrew term refers to the irrevocable giving over of things or persons to the LORD, often by totally destroying them; also in verses 18 and 21. [b]17 Or possibly *innkeeper*; also in verses 22 and 25

6:17 *Rahab . . . spies:* See 2:1-24 and the note at 2:1 (Rahab).

6:18 *keep away from the devoted things . . . destruction:* Despite the warning, this is exactly what happens in 7:1.

6:19 *bronze:* This metal was made by melting and mixing copper and tin. Because it was harder than copper, bronze could be used to make stronger weapons.

6:21,22 *destroyed with the sword every living thing . . . bring her out . . . oath to her:* For the total destruction, see the note at 6:17 (devoted). Rahab and her family were brought to safety as promised earlier (2:17-20)

6:23 *outside the camp of Israel:* Rahab and her family were Canaanites and were considered ritually unclean. Only those people and things that were acceptable to the LORD could be in the Israelite camp. If Rahab and her family stayed in the Israelite army camp, the LORD would not help the Israelite army in battle (see Deut 23:9-14). See also the mini-article called "Purity (Clean and Unclean)," p. 2125. In Matthew 1:2-6, Rahab is listed as one of Jesus' ancestors. See also Heb 11:31; Jas 2:25.

6:24 *the LORD's house:* Israel's place of worship, which at the time was the tabernacle. See the mini-article called "The Tabernacle," p. 2346.

6:26 *Cursed before the LORD . . . rebuild this city, Jericho:* This is exactly what happened to Hiel of Bethel many years later (see 1 Kgs 16:34).

6:20 Heb 11:30.

Achan's Sin

7 But the Israelites acted unfaithfully in regard to the devoted things[a]; Achan son of Carmi, the son of Zimri,[b] the son of Zerah, of the tribe of Judah, took some of them. So the LORD's anger burned against Israel.

[2]Now Joshua sent men from Jericho to Ai, which is near Beth Aven to the east of Bethel, and told them, "Go up and spy out the region." So the men went up and spied out Ai.

[3]When they returned to Joshua, they said, "Not all the people will have to go up against Ai. Send two or three thousand men to take it and do not weary all the people, for only a few men are there." [4]So about three thousand men went up; but they were routed by the men of Ai, [5]who killed about thirty-six of them. They chased the Israelites from the city gate as far as the stone quarries[c] and struck them down on the slopes. At this the hearts of the people melted and became like water.

[6]Then Joshua tore his clothes and fell facedown to the ground before the ark of the LORD, remaining there till evening. The elders of Israel did the same, and sprinkled dust on their heads. [7]And Joshua said, "Ah, Sovereign LORD, why did you ever bring this people across the Jordan to deliver us into the hands of the Amorites to destroy us? If only we had been content to stay on the other side of the Jordan! [8]O Lord, what can I say, now that Israel has been routed by its enemies? [9]The Canaanites and the other people of the country will hear about this and they will surround us and wipe out our name from the earth. What then will you do for your own great name?"

[10]The LORD said to Joshua, "Stand up! What are you doing down on your face? [11]Israel has sinned; they have violated my covenant, which I commanded them to keep. They have taken some of the devoted things; they have stolen, they have lied, they have put them with their own possessions. [12]That is why the Israelites cannot stand against their enemies; they turn their backs and run because they have been made liable to destruction. I will not be with you anymore unless you destroy whatever among you is devoted to destruction.

[13]"Go, consecrate the people. Tell them, 'Consecrate yourselves in preparation for tomorrow; for this is what the LORD, the God of Israel, says: That which is devoted is among you, O Israel. You cannot stand against your enemies until you remove it.

[14]" 'In the morning, present yourselves tribe by tribe. The tribe that the LORD takes shall come forward clan by clan; the clan that the LORD takes shall come forward family by family; and the family that the LORD takes shall come forward man by man.

a1 The Hebrew term refers to the irrevocable giving over of things or persons to the LORD, often by totally destroying them; also in verses 11, 12, 13 and 15. **b1** See Septuagint and 1 Chron. 2:6; Hebrew *Zabdi*; also in verses 17 and 18. **c5** Or *as far as Shebarim*

7:1 *Israelites acted unfaithfully . . . Achan:* The Israelites were commanded to destroy Jericho as a way of showing that the city belonged to the LORD (6:17). Achan violated this command. Even though Achan was the only person who disobeyed, it meant that the LORD's instructions to the people of Israel had not been followed, and the whole nation was held responsible.

7:2 *Ai:* The site was eleven miles north of Jerusalem and two miles east of Bethel. Ai was an unwalled village at that time. See the map on p. 2464.

7:6 *tore his clothes . . . dust on their heads:* The men did these things to show their grief (see also Gen 37:34; 44:13; Job 1:20; 2:12). In spite of the small size of Ai, Israel is defeated. Joshua does not yet know the reason for the defeat (given in 7:11).

7:7 *why did you ever bring this people:* The first readers of JOSHUA would have recognized the complaint the Israelites made to Moses when they were being pursued by the Egyptian army after leaving Egypt (see Exod 14:11,12).

7:9 *will hear about this:* These words echo Moses' prayer in Numbers 14:13-16 on behalf of the Israelites. See also Jer 14:21.

7:12 *unless you destroy:* See the note at 6:17 (devoted).

7:14 *tribe that the LORD takes . . . family . . . man:* The guilty tribe, family, and individual would be picked out by using the Urim and Thummin, also known as choosing lots. These consisted of different sized stones or pieces of wood (see the note at Exod 28:30). Though this method appears to be based on chance, the Israelites understood God to be guiding the outcome.

15 He who is caught with the devoted things shall be destroyed by fire, along with all that belongs to him. He has violated the covenant of the LORD and has done a disgraceful thing in Israel!' "

16 Early the next morning Joshua had Israel come forward by tribes, and Judah was taken. 17 The clans of Judah came forward, and he took the Zerahites. He had the clan of the Zerahites come forward by families, and Zimri was taken. 18 Joshua had his family come forward man by man, and Achan son of Carmi, the son of Zimri, the son of Zerah, of the tribe of Judah, was taken.

19 Then Joshua said to Achan, "My son, give glory to the LORD,[a] the God of Israel, and give him the praise.[b] Tell me what you have done; do not hide it from me."

20 Achan replied, "It is true! I have sinned against the LORD, the God of Israel. This is what I have done: 21 When I saw in the plunder a beautiful robe from Babylonia,[c] two hundred shekels[d] of silver and a wedge of gold weighing fifty shekels,[e] I coveted them and took them. They are hidden in the ground inside my tent, with the silver underneath."

22 So Joshua sent messengers, and they ran to the tent, and there it was, hidden in his tent, with the silver underneath. 23 They took the things from the tent, brought them to Joshua and all the Israelites and spread them out before the LORD.

24 Then Joshua, together with all Israel, took Achan son of Zerah, the silver, the robe, the gold wedge, his sons and daughters, his cattle, donkeys and sheep, his tent and all that he had, to the Valley of Achor. 25 Joshua said, "Why have you brought this trouble on us? The LORD will bring trouble on you today."

Then all Israel stoned him, and after they had stoned the rest, they burned them. 26 Over Achan they heaped up a large pile of rocks, which remains to this day. Then the LORD turned from his fierce anger. Therefore that place has been called the Valley of Achor[f] ever since.

Ai Destroyed

8 Then the LORD said to Joshua, "Do not be afraid; do not be discouraged. Take the whole army with you, and go up and attack Ai. For I have delivered into your hands the king of Ai, his people, his city and his land. 2 You shall do to Ai and its king as you did to Jericho and its king, except that you may carry off their plunder and livestock for yourselves. Set an ambush behind the city."

3 So Joshua and the whole army moved out to attack Ai. He chose thirty thousand of his best fighting men and sent them out at night 4 with these orders: "Listen carefully. You are to set an ambush behind the city. Don't go very far from it. All of you be on

---

[a]19 A solemn charge to tell the truth [b]19 Or *and confess to him* [c]21 Hebrew *Shinar* [d]21 That is, about 5 pounds (about 2.3 kilograms) [e]21 That is, about 1 1/4 pounds (about 0.6 kilogram) [f]26 *Achor* means *trouble.*

7:15 *violated the covenant:* Obedience to God's Law was necessary to maintain ritual purity. Stolen items might include idols representing other gods.

7:20 *It is true! I have sinned:* The suspense has mounted as the circle draws closer and closer, finally centering on Achan. When asked, he confesses his guilt.

7:24 *took Achan . . . all that he had:* In ancient Israel, guilt was not limited to an individual. It often extended to the individual's family, livestock, and possessions. This is why Achan's whole family was crushed to death with stones and then burned along with their possessions. See also Num 16:1-33, but compare Deut 24:16; Ezek 18:1-32.

7:26 *Valley of Achor:* Achor means "trouble." The location is uncertain, but in 15:7 the Valley of Achor is the border between the tribal territories of Judah and Benjamin.

8:1 *Do not be afraid . . . I have delivered:* The LORD tells Joshua to forget about the Israelites' earlier defeat at Ai (7:4,5). The LORD will direct a new plan that will be successful. See the note at 6:17 (devoted).

8:3 *thirty thousand of his best fighting men:* Compare to 8:12. This number includes an ambush party, made up of his best soldiers who were sent out at night to wait.

LOVING GOD
IS THIS GOD SHOWING HIS COMPASSION FOR THE FIRST DEFEAT EVEN THOUGH IT WAS BROUGHT ON BY DISOBEDIENCE?

Ancient city of Ai. Although the location of the city of Ai is not certain, most scholars locate it at the site of the modern city of et-Tell. "Ai" means "ruin" in Hebrew. The author of JOSHUA describes how the Israelites ambushed and destroyed this city when they entered the land that God promised them. (See 8:1-29.)

8:5 *we will flee from them:* The plan calls for a force under Joshua to act as decoys, drawing the enemy army out of the city. This force is positioned to the north of Ai, while the ambush force is west of the town.

8:9 *Bethel:* Bethel was located eleven miles north of Jerusalem and two miles west of Ai (see the map on p. 2464). It was an important town in Israel's history. Jacob had a dream there and set up a monument to honor God (Gen 28:10-22). Later, King Jeroboam of the northern kingdom established Bethel as a place to worship the Canaanite gods (1 Kgs 12:26-33).

the alert. 5I and all those with me will advance on the city, and
when the men come out against us, as they did before, we will flee
from them. 6They will pursue us until we have lured them away
from the city, for they will say, 'They are running away from us as
they did before.' So when we flee from them, 7you are to rise up
from ambush and take the city. The LORD your God will give it
into your hand. 8When you have taken the city, set it on fire. Do
what the LORD has commanded. See to it; you have my orders."

9Then Joshua sent them off, and they went to the place of
ambush and lay in wait between Bethel and Ai, to the west of Ai—
but Joshua spent that night with the people.

10Early the next morning Joshua mustered his men, and he
and the leaders of Israel marched before them to Ai. 11The entire
force that was with him marched up and approached the city and
arrived in front of it. They set up camp north of Ai, with the valley between them and the city. 12Joshua had taken about five thousand men and set them in ambush between Bethel and Ai, to the
west of the city. 13They had the soldiers take up their positions—
all those in the camp to the north of the city and the ambush to
the west of it. That night Joshua went into the valley.

14 When the king of Ai saw this, he and all the men of the city
hurried out early in the morning to meet Israel in battle at a certain place overlooking the Arabah. But he did not know that an
ambush had been set against him behind the city. 15 Joshua and all
Israel let themselves be driven back before them, and they fled
toward the desert. 16 All the men of Ai were called to pursue them,
and they pursued Joshua and were lured away from the city. 17 Not
a man remained in Ai or Bethel who did not go after Israel. They
left the city open and went in pursuit of Israel.
18 Then the LORD said to Joshua, "Hold out toward Ai the
javelin that is in your hand, for into your hand I will deliver the
city." So Joshua held out his javelin toward Ai. 19 As soon as he did
this, the men in the ambush rose quickly from their position and
rushed forward. They entered the city and captured it and quickly
set it on fire.
20 The men of Ai looked back and saw the smoke of the city
rising against the sky, but they had no chance to escape in any direction, for the Israelites who had been fleeing toward the desert had
turned back against their pursuers. 21 For when Joshua and all Israel
saw that the ambush had taken the city and that smoke was going
up from the city, they turned around and attacked the men of Ai.
22 The men of the ambush also came out of the city against them, so
that they were caught in the middle, with Israelites on both sides.
Israel cut them down, leaving them neither survivors nor fugitives.
23 But they took the king of Ai alive and brought him to Joshua.
24 When Israel had finished killing all the men of Ai in the
fields and in the desert where they had chased them, and when
every one of them had been put to the sword, all the Israelites
returned to Ai and killed those who were in it. 25 Twelve thousand
men and women fell that day—all the people of Ai. 26 For Joshua
did not draw back the hand that held out his javelin until he had
destroyed[a] all who lived in Ai. 27 But Israel did carry off for themselves the livestock and plunder of this city, as the LORD had
instructed Joshua.
28 So Joshua burned Ai and made it a permanent heap of
ruins, a desolate place to this day. 29 He hung the king of Ai on a
tree and left him there until evening. At sunset, Joshua ordered
them to take his body from the tree and throw it down at the
entrance of the city gate. And they raised a large pile of rocks over
it, which remains to this day.

The Covenant Renewed at Mount Ebal

30 Then Joshua built on Mount Ebal an altar to the LORD, the
God of Israel, 31 as Moses the servant of the LORD had commanded

[a]26 The Hebrew term refers to the irrevocable giving over of things or persons to the LORD, often by totally destroying them.

8:17 *left the city open:* The decoy attack works. The northern war party draws the troops out of the city, the western ambush easily captures the city (8:19), and the men of Ai are caught between the two forces (see 8:22-24).

8:18 *javelin:* A javelin was a kind of spear. Joshua acts as Moses did in Exodus 17:8-13.

8:24 *every one of them:* See the note at 6:17 (devoted).

8:28,29 *permanent heap of ruins:* As with Jericho (6:17), nothing is to remain of Canaanite, pagan influences. The dead king's body is to be taken down as commanded in Deuteronomy 21:22,23. The Israelites set up memorial stones here as they had previously next to the Jordan River (4:9) and in the Valley of Achor (7:26). They could still be seen at the time JOSHUA was written.

8:30 *Mount Ebal:* Located about twenty miles from Ai in central Canaan. The ceremony in 8:30-35 is similar to the one in 24:1-28. See also Deut 11:29,30; 27:2-8.

8:31 *uncut stones . . . no iron tool:* Following the command of God in Exodus 20:25.

8:31 *burnt offerings:* These sacrifices have been traditionally called "whole burnt offerings" because the whole animal was burned on the altar. See also Lev 1.

8:31 *fellowship offerings:* A main purpose of these offerings was to give thanks to God and have fellowship with him. See also Lev 3 and the chart called "Sacrifices and Offerings," p. 219.

8:27 Josh 8:1,2.

8:33 *Mount Gerizim . . . Mount Ebal . . . the aliens:* Between Mounts Gerizim and Ebal is a valley and the city of Shechem. By gaining control of the high ground above this mountain pass, the Israelites could control a large area in central Palestine. It is unclear exactly who the "aliens" (foreigners) are, but they are allowed to participate in the blessing (see Deut 10:19).

8:34 *Book of the Law:* See the note at 1:6-8.

9:1 *kings west of the Jordan . . . Hittites . . . Jebusites:* Kings or rulers in Canaan ruled cities or tribal groups. See the note at 3:10.

9:3 *people of Gibeon:* Gibeon was six miles northwest of Jerusalem. Having heard of Israel's victories, the Gibeonites decided to try and trick the Israelites into signing a peace treaty.

9:4 *wineskins:* Wine was carried in leather pouches (see the illustration on p. 1985). Old wineskins often cracked and had to be patched.

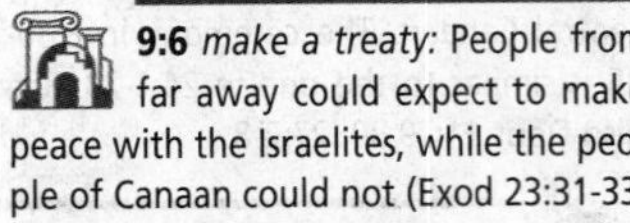

9:6 *make a treaty:* People from far away could expect to make peace with the Israelites, while the people of Canaan could not (Exod 23:31-33; 34:11-16; Deut 7:1-4; 20:10-18).

9:9,10 *Egypt . . . Sihon . . . Og:* The Gibeonites say that they know about the Israelites' escape from Egypt and how they defeated the Amorite kings, Sihon and Og (Num 21:21-35), but they make no mention of what happened at the nearby cities of Jericho or Ai, even though they are aware of it (9:3).

8:33-35 Deut 11:29; 27:11-14.

the Israelites. He built it according to what is written in the Book
of the Law of Moses—an altar of uncut stones, on which no iron
tool had been used. On it they offered to the LORD burnt offerings
and sacrificed fellowship offerings.[a] 32There, in the presence of the
Israelites, Joshua copied on stones the law of Moses, which he had
written. 33All Israel, aliens and citizens alike, with their elders, officials and judges, were standing on both sides of the ark of the
covenant of the LORD, facing those who carried it—the priests,
who were Levites. Half of the people stood in front of Mount Gerizim and half of them in front of Mount Ebal, as Moses the servant of the LORD had formerly commanded when he gave
instructions to bless the people of Israel.
34Afterward, Joshua read all the words of the law—the blessings and the curses—just as it is written in the Book of the Law.
35There was not a word of all that Moses had commanded that
Joshua did not read to the whole assembly of Israel, including the
women and children, and the aliens who lived among them.

The Gibeonite Deception

9 Now when all the kings west of the Jordan heard about these
things—those in the hill country, in the western foothills, and
along the entire coast of the Great Sea[b] as far as Lebanon (the
kings of the Hittites, Amorites, Canaanites, Perizzites, Hivites and
Jebusites)— 2they came together to make war against Joshua and
Israel.
3However, when the people of Gibeon heard what Joshua
had done to Jericho and Ai, 4they resorted to a ruse: They went as
a delegation whose donkeys were loaded[c] with worn-out sacks and
old wineskins, cracked and mended. 5The men put worn and
patched sandals on their feet and wore old clothes. All the bread of
their food supply was dry and moldy. 6Then they went to Joshua in
the camp at Gilgal and said to him and the men of Israel, "We have
come from a distant country; make a treaty with us."
7The men of Israel said to the Hivites, "But perhaps you live
near us. How then can we make a treaty with you?"
8"We are your servants," they said to Joshua.
But Joshua asked, "Who are you and where do you come
from?"
9They answered: "Your servants have come from a very distant country because of the fame of the LORD your God. For we
have heard reports of him: all that he did in Egypt, 10and all that he
did to the two kings of the Amorites east of the Jordan—Sihon
king of Heshbon, and Og king of Bashan, who reigned in
Ashtaroth. 11And our elders and all those living in our country said

[a]31 Traditionally *peace offerings* [b]1 That is, the Mediterranean [c]4 Most Hebrew manuscripts; some Hebrew manuscripts, Vulgate and Syriac (see also Septuagint) *They prepared provisions and loaded their donkeys*

to us, 'Take provisions for your journey; go and meet them and say
to them, "We are your servants; make a treaty with us." ' 12This
bread of ours was warm when we packed it at home on the day we
left to come to you. But now see how dry and moldy it is. 13And
these wineskins that we filled were new, but see how cracked they
are. And our clothes and sandals are worn out by the very long
journey."

14The men of Israel sampled their provisions but did not
inquire of the LORD. 15Then Joshua made a treaty of peace with
them to let them live, and the leaders of the assembly ratified it by
oath.

16Three days after they made the treaty with the Gibeonites,
the Israelites heard that they were neighbors, living near them. 17So
the Israelites set out and on the third day came to their cities:
Gibeon, Kephirah, Beeroth and Kiriath Jearim. 18But the Israelites
did not attack them, because the leaders of the assembly had
sworn an oath to them by the LORD, the God of Israel.

The whole assembly grumbled against the leaders, 19but all
the leaders answered, "We have given them our oath by the LORD,
the God of Israel, and we cannot touch them now. 20This is what
we will do to them: We will let them live, so that wrath will not fall
on us for breaking the oath we swore to them." 21They continued,
"Let them live, but let them be woodcutters and water carriers for
the entire community." So the leaders' promise to them was kept.

22Then Joshua summoned the Gibeonites and said, "Why did
you deceive us by saying, 'We live a long way from you,' while actually you live near us? 23You are now under a curse: You will never
cease to serve as woodcutters and water carriers for the house of
my God."

24They answered Joshua, "Your servants were clearly told
how the LORD your God had commanded his servant Moses to
give you the whole land and to wipe out all its inhabitants from
before you. So we feared for our lives because of you, and that is
why we did this. 25We are now in your hands. Do to us whatever
seems good and right to you."

26So Joshua saved them from the Israelites, and they did not
kill them. 27That day he made the Gibeonites woodcutters and water
carriers for the community and for the altar of the LORD at the place
the LORD would choose. And that is what they are to this day.

The Sun Stands Still

10 Now Adoni-Zedek king of Jerusalem heard that Joshua had
taken Ai and totally destroyed[a] it, doing to Ai and its king as he
had done to Jericho and its king, and that the people of Gibeon

[a]1 The Hebrew term refers to the irrevocable giving over of things or persons to the LORD, often by totally destroying them; also in verses 28, 35, 37, 39 and 40.

9:14,15 *sampled their provisions . . . ratified it by oath:* The Israelites may have tried the Gibeonites' food to see if it really was old or to simply show that they wanted peace. Ancient treaties often included the sharing of gifts or a meal (Gen 21:22-31). By making an oath, the leaders were committed to the peace treaty (see the note at 9:19).

9:17 *Gibeon . . . Kiriath Jearim:* These towns were twenty to thirty miles west of the Israelite camp at Gilgal. Kephirah, Beeroth, and Kiriath Jearim are towns within a five mile radius of Gibeon (Gibeah). See the map on p. 2464.

9:19 *given them our oath:* The Gibeonites were not harmed, because once a treaty is made it cannot be broken. See also Gen 27 (especially 27:33), and the mini-article called "Making Vows," p. 328.

9:23 *the house of my God:* See the note at 6:24.

9:27 *the altar of the LORD:* This probably refers to the altar in front of the tabernacle (see Exod 27:1-8; Deut 12:5-19). Eventually, the only proper place for offering sacrifices would be at the temple in Jerusalem.

9:27 *to this day:* The Gibeonites admit their trickery and then agree to be servants of the Israelites (9:24). Joshua stops the angry Israelites from killing the Gibeonites, who are made to serve Israel's priests. Years later, King David also protected the Gibeonites (2 Sam 21:2).

10:1 *Jerusalem:* Jerusalem was not an Israelite city at this time. It was first settled by the Jebusites. The Israelites burned the city (Judg 1:8), but it was evidently resettled (Judg 1:21). Eventually David captured it (2 Sam 5:6-10), made it the capital of Israel, and renamed it the City of David. See the mini-article called "Jerusalem," p. 574.

10:3,4 *Adoni-Zedek . . . help me attack Gibeon:* This alliance is made up of five kings, or chiefs, of five cities to the south of Gibeon (see the map on p. 2464). This is their first attempt at an offensive action. However, the action is aimed at Gibeon, not Israel. The peace treaty of 9:15 meant that Israel would let Gibeon live; it also meant that Israel would defend the Gibeonites against their enemies.

10:5 *Amorites:* The Amorites are described in Genesis 10:6-20 as descendants of Noah's grandson Canaan. See also the note at 3:10.

10:6 *Gilgal:* See the note at 4:19 (Gilgal).

10:9 *all-night march from Gilgal:* Joshua leads the troops on a march at night in preparation for a surprise attack as he did at Ai (8:3,4). The march from Gilgal to the area near Gibeon would have been a difficult, mostly uphill march of nearly twenty miles.

10:10-12 *Beth Horon . . . Makkedah . . . Valley of Aijalon:* The distance from Gibeon to Makkedah is about twenty-five miles. The Valley of Aijalon was located southwest of Beth Horon Pass.

10:13 *the sun stood still, and the moon stopped:* Compare to Judges 5:20 where the poet speaks of the stars fighting against Sisera. This passage is a powerful image of God's "long day" of victories.

10:13 *Book of Jashar:* This book, now lost, may have been a collection of ancient war songs praising national heroes. See also 2 Sam 1:18.

10:14 *the LORD was fighting:* The LORD fulfills the promise made to Joshua (1:5). See also Josh 23:9; Deut 7:23,24; and the mini-article called "Holy War (The LORD's Battles)," p. 306.

had made a treaty of peace with Israel and were living near them. [2]He and his people were very much alarmed at this, because Gibeon was an important city, like one of the royal cities; it was larger than Ai, and all its men were good fighters. [3]So Adoni-Zedek king of Jerusalem appealed to Hoham king of Hebron, Piram king of Jarmuth, Japhia king of Lachish and Debir king of Eglon. [4]"Come up and help me attack Gibeon," he said, "because it has made peace with Joshua and the Israelites."

[5]Then the five kings of the Amorites—the kings of Jerusalem, Hebron, Jarmuth, Lachish and Eglon—joined forces. They moved up with all their troops and took up positions against Gibeon and attacked it.

[6]The Gibeonites then sent word to Joshua in the camp at Gilgal: "Do not abandon your servants. Come up to us quickly and save us! Help us, because all the Amorite kings from the hill country have joined forces against us."

[7]So Joshua marched up from Gilgal with his entire army, including all the best fighting men. [8]The LORD said to Joshua, "Do not be afraid of them; I have given them into your hand. Not one of them will be able to withstand you."

[9]After an all-night march from Gilgal, Joshua took them by surprise. [10]The LORD threw them into confusion before Israel, who defeated them in a great victory at Gibeon. Israel pursued them along the road going up to Beth Horon and cut them down all the way to Azekah and Makkedah. [11]As they fled before Israel on the road down from Beth Horon to Azekah, the LORD hurled large hailstones down on them from the sky, and more of them died from the hailstones than were killed by the swords of the Israelites.

[12]On the day the LORD gave the Amorites over to Israel, Joshua said to the LORD in the presence of Israel:

"O sun, stand still over Gibeon,
O moon, over the Valley of Aijalon."
[13]So the sun stood still,
and the moon stopped,
till the nation avenged itself on[a] its enemies,

as it is written in the Book of Jashar.

The sun stopped in the middle of the sky and delayed going down about a full day. [14]There has never been a day like it before or since, a day when the LORD listened to a man. Surely the LORD was fighting for Israel!

[15]Then Joshua returned with all Israel to the camp at Gilgal.

Five Amorite Kings Killed

[16]Now the five kings had fled and hidden in the cave at Makkedah. [17]When Joshua was told that the five kings had been

[a]**13** Or *nation triumphed over*

found hiding in the cave at Makkedah, [18]he said, "Roll large rocks up to the mouth of the cave, and post some men there to guard it. [19]But don't stop! Pursue your enemies, attack them from the rear and don't let them reach their cities, for the LORD your God has given them into your hand."

[20]So Joshua and the Israelites destroyed them completely—almost to a man—but the few who were left reached their fortified cities. [21]The whole army then returned safely to Joshua in the camp at Makkedah, and no one uttered a word against the Israelites.

[22]Joshua said, "Open the mouth of the cave and bring those five kings out to me." [23]So they brought the five kings out of the cave—the kings of Jerusalem, Hebron, Jarmuth, Lachish and Eglon. [24]When they had brought these kings to Joshua, he summoned all the men of Israel and said to the army commanders who had come with him, "Come here and put your feet on the necks of these kings." So they came forward and placed their feet on their necks.

[25]Joshua said to them, "Do not be afraid; do not be discouraged. Be strong and courageous. This is what the LORD will do to all the enemies you are going to fight." [26]Then Joshua struck and killed the kings and hung them on five trees, and they were left hanging on the trees until evening.

[27]At sunset Joshua gave the order and they took them down from the trees and threw them into the cave where they had been hiding. At the mouth of the cave they placed large rocks, which are there to this day.

[28]That day Joshua took Makkedah. He put the city and its king to the sword and totally destroyed everyone in it. He left no survivors. And he did to the king of Makkedah as he had done to the king of Jericho.

Southern Cities Conquered

[29]Then Joshua and all Israel with him moved on from Makkedah to Libnah and attacked it. [30]The LORD also gave that city and its king into Israel's hand. The city and everyone in it Joshua put to the sword. He left no survivors there. And he did to its king as he had done to the king of Jericho.

[31]Then Joshua and all Israel with him moved on from Libnah to Lachish; he took up positions against it and attacked it. [32]The LORD handed Lachish over to Israel, and Joshua took it on the second day. The city and everyone in it he put to the sword, just as he had done to Libnah. [33]Meanwhile, Horam king of Gezer had come up to help Lachish, but Joshua defeated him and his army—until no survivors were left.

[34]Then Joshua and all Israel with him moved on from Lachish to Eglon; they took up positions against it and attacked it. [35]They captured it that same day and put it to the sword and totally destroyed everyone in it, just as they had done to Lachish.

Joshua said, *"The LORD your God has given them into your hand."* Josh 10:19

10:16 *five kings had fled and hidden in the cave at Makkedah:* The defeated chiefs hide in a cave as David would later do when running from Saul (1 Sam 22:1), but with a different result.

10:20 *few who were left:* While the conquest of southern Palestine is successful, it is not total or complete. Wiping out all the inhabitants would only make a wasteland (Deut 7:22). The presence of Canaanites in their walled cities would continue to be an issue after the death of Joshua (see Judg 1).

10:24 *put your feet on the necks:* This custom was done as a gesture of total domination and defeat (Ps 110:1).

10:26,27 *hung them . . . until evening . . . large rocks:* See the note at 8:28,29. Another large pile of rocks still existed at Makkedah (exact location unknown) at the time this section of JOSHUA was written.

10:28-34 *Makkedah . . . Libnah . . . Lachish . . . Eglon:* See the notes at 10:3,4 and 10:10-12. Joshua takes the chief towns that guarded the approach to the southern highlands. No details are given.

Joshua and the Amorites, seventeenth century, stained glass in Wragny Church, Switzerland. The LORD promised Joshua victory over the Amorites, one of the tribes which lived in Canaan. At noon on the day of battle, Joshua prayed to the LORD. The sun and the moon stood still until Israel defeated its enemy and won the land God promised to its ancestors. (See 10:12, 13.)

[36]Then Joshua and all Israel with him went up from Eglon to
Hebron and attacked it. [37]They took the city and put it to the
sword, together with its king, its villages and everyone in it. They
left no survivors. Just as at Eglon, they totally destroyed it and
everyone in it.
[38]Then Joshua and all Israel with him turned around and
attacked Debir. [39]They took the city, its king and its villages, and
put them to the sword. Everyone in it they totally destroyed. They
left no survivors. They did to Debir and its king as they had done
to Libnah and its king and to Hebron.
[40]So Joshua subdued the whole region, including the hill
country, the Negev, the western foothills and the mountain slopes,
together with all their kings. He left no survivors. He totally
destroyed all who breathed, just as the LORD, the God of Israel, had
commanded. [41]Joshua subdued them from Kadesh Barnea to Gaza
and from the whole region of Goshen to Gibeon. [42]All these kings
and their lands Joshua conquered in one campaign, because the
LORD, the God of Israel, fought for Israel.
[43]Then Joshua returned with all Israel to the camp at Gilgal.

All these kings and their lands Joshua conquered in one campaign, because the LORD, the God of Israel, fought for Israel.
Josh 10:42

10:36-39 *Hebron . . . Debir:* Hebron was nineteen miles south of Jerusalem; Debir was twelve miles southwest of Hebron. The king of Hebron had already been killed (10:23-26). The capture (perhaps recapture) of Hebron and Debir by the tribe of Judah is also described in Judges 1:9-11.

10:40 *Joshua subdued the whole region:* This is a summary of the conquest of the south. The Negev is an arid region south of Beersheba. Joshua does as the LORD commanded, offering up the enemy as a sacrifice to God. See the note at 6:17 (devoted).

10:41 *from Kadesh Barnea to Gaza . . . Goshen:* See the map on p. 2464. Gaza was a Philistine city. Goshen was a region between the hill country of Judah and the desert further south. This is not the same Goshen as the one in Egypt where the Hebrew slaves settled at the time of Joseph (Gen 47:4-6).

11:1 *Jabin king of Hazor:* This powerful king organized an army of troops from surrounding cities in the far north country of Palestine. Jabin was a noted enemy of Israel (see Judg 4:1-24). Hazor, nine miles north of the Sea of Galilee, was noted in Egyptian and Mesopotamian records as a chief Canaanite city.

Northern Kings Defeated

11 When Jabin king of Hazor heard of this, he sent word to
Jobab king of Madon, to the kings of Shimron and Acshaph, [2]and
to the northern kings who were in the mountains, in the Arabah
south of Kinnereth, in the western foothills and in Naphoth Dor[a]
on the west; [3]to the Canaanites in the east and west; to the Amorites, Hittites, Perizzites and Jebusites in the hill country; and to
the Hivites below Hermon in the region of Mizpah. [4]They came
out with all their troops and a large number of horses and chariots—a huge army, as numerous as the sand on the seashore. [5]All
these kings joined forces and made camp together at the Waters of
Merom, to fight against Israel.

[6]The LORD said to Joshua, "Do not be afraid of them,
because by this time tomorrow I will hand all of them over
to Israel, slain. You are to hamstring their horses and burn their
chariots."

[7]So Joshua and his whole army came against them suddenly
at the Waters of Merom and attacked them, [8]and the LORD gave
them into the hand of Israel. They defeated them and pursued
them all the way to Greater Sidon, to Misrephoth Maim, and to the
Valley of Mizpah on the east, until no survivors were left. [9]Joshua
did to them as the LORD had directed: He hamstrung their horses
and burned their chariots.

[10]At that time Joshua turned back and captured Hazor and
put its king to the sword. (Hazor had been the head of all these
kingdoms.) [11]Everyone in it they put to the sword. They totally destroyed[b] them, not sparing anything that breathed, and he burned
up Hazor itself.

[12]Joshua took all these royal cities and their kings and put
them to the sword. He totally destroyed them, as Moses the servant of the LORD had commanded. [13]Yet Israel did not burn any of
the cities built on their mounds—except Hazor, which Joshua
burned. [14]The Israelites carried off for themselves all the plunder
and livestock of these cities, but all the people they put to the
sword until they completely destroyed them, not sparing anyone
that breathed. [15]As the LORD commanded his servant Moses, so
Moses commanded Joshua, and Joshua did it; he left nothing
undone of all that the LORD commanded Moses.

[16]So Joshua took this entire land: the hill country, all the
Negev, the whole region of Goshen, the western foothills, the
Arabah and the mountains of Israel with their foothills, [17]from
Mount Halak, which rises toward Seir, to Baal Gad in the Valley of
Lebanon below Mount Hermon. He captured all their kings and
struck them down, putting them to death. [18]Joshua waged war

---

[a]2 Or *in the heights of Dor* [b]11 The Hebrew term refers to the irrevocable giving over of things or persons to the LORD, often by totally destroying them; also in verses 12, 20 and 21.

11:3 *region of Mizpah:* This is probably the same region as the Valley of Mizpah in 11:8, but different from other places named Mizpah: of Judah in 15:38; of Benjamin in 18:26 and 1 Samuel 7:16,17; of Gilead in Genesis 31:49 and Judges 10:17.

11:4 *troops . . . numerous as the sand on the seashore:* The terrifying odds against Israel in the north of Palestine were made more threatening by the enemies' horses and chariots. Israel did not have horses or chariots at this time. See also Josh 17:16.

11:5 *Waters of Merom:* This pond probably contained waters that flowed from the high mountains of upper Galilee southward into the northwest part of the Sea of Galilee.

11:8 *Greater Sidon:* Joshua pursued the enemy alliance all the way to the northern border of Palestine at Sidon. See the map on p. 2464.

11:9 *hamstrung their horses and burned their chariots:* Horses and chariots were a great military advantage at this time. Since the Israelites would not have horses to use in battle until the time of Solomon (970-931 B.C.), crippling the enemies' horses helped to undermine their enemies' advantage (1 Kgs 10:26-29). Depending on chariots and a cavalry indicates trust in material resources and not in God (Isa 31:1).

11:13 *Israel did not burn:* The old walled cities of the lowlands were not destroyed. The Israelites had their greatest success in the hills where the Canaanite chariots could not be used. See also the note at 6:17 (devoted).

11:16-18 *Mount Halak . . . Mount Hermon:* This is a summary of Israel's conquests as in 10:40-43, with the addition of northern Palestine. For Goshen, see the note at 10:41. But battles against the kings in the north continued for a long time.

11:20 *the LORD himself who hardened their hearts:* The LORD causes the Canaanites' determination to fight, just as it is God who made the king of Egypt stubborn (Exod 4:21).

11:21 *the Anakites:* This group of very tall people who lived in Palestine before the Israelites. Sons of Anak, they are described as descendants of the legendary giants called Nephilim (Gen 6:4). See also Num 13:33 and Deut 2:10,11,20,21.

11:22 *Gaza, Gath and Ashdod:* These were cities in Philistia on the coastal plain. These three cities, plus Ashkelon and Ekron, made up the five cities of the Philistine alliance. The giant Goliath came from Gath (1 Sam 17:4). King David finally defeated the Philistines and brought them under control (2 Sam 5:25). Gaza and Ashdod had temples dedicated to Dagon, a fertility god.

12:1 *Arnon Gorge to Mount Hermon:* The Arnon Gorge formed the boundary between Moab and Ammon. Mount Hermon was located near the southern border of Lebanon.

12:1-4 *kings . . . Sihon . . . Og:* See Num 21:21-35 and the note at 2:10 (Sihon and Og). The summary here in chapter 12 draws from Deuteronomy 2:24—3:11.

12:3-5 *Sea of Kinnereth . . . Sea of the Arabah:* The Sea of Kinnereth is the Sea of Galilee. The Sea of the Arabah (Salt Sea) is also the Dead Sea. See the map on p. 2467.

12:4 *Rephaites:* Like the Anakites (11:21), this may have been a group of tall people who lived in Palestine before the Israelites (Deut 2:10,11).

12:6 *Moses . . . gave their land:* Joshua promises to carry out Moses' gift to these tribes (see the note at 1:12). See also 22:1-34; Num 32:33; Deut 3:12-17.

against all these kings for a long time. 19 Except for the Hivites living in Gibeon, not one city made a treaty of peace with the
Israelites, who took them all in battle. 20 For it was the LORD himself who hardened their hearts to wage war against Israel, so that
he might destroy them totally, exterminating them without mercy,
as the LORD had commanded Moses.

21 At that time Joshua went and destroyed the Anakites from
the hill country: from Hebron, Debir and Anab, from all the hill
country of Judah, and from all the hill country of Israel. Joshua
totally destroyed them and their towns. 22 No Anakites were left in
Israelite territory; only in Gaza, Gath and Ashdod did any survive.
23 So Joshua took the entire land, just as the LORD had directed
Moses, and he gave it as an inheritance to Israel according to their
tribal divisions.

Then the land had rest from war.

List of Defeated Kings

12 These are the kings of the land whom the Israelites had
defeated and whose territory they took over east of the Jordan,
from the Arnon Gorge to Mount Hermon, including all the eastern side of the Arabah:

2 Sihon king of the Amorites,
who reigned in Heshbon. He ruled from Aroer on the rim of
the Arnon Gorge—from the middle of the gorge—to the Jabbok River, which is the border of the Ammonites. This included half of Gilead. 3 He also ruled over the eastern Arabah from
the Sea of Kinnereth[a] to the Sea of the Arabah (the Salt Sea[b]),
to Beth Jeshimoth, and then southward below the slopes of
Pisgah.

4 And the territory of Og king of Bashan,
one of the last of the Rephaites, who reigned in Ashtaroth and
Edrei. 5 He ruled over Mount Hermon, Salecah, all of Bashan
to the border of the people of Geshur and Maacah, and half of
Gilead to the border of Sihon king of Heshbon.

6 Moses, the servant of the LORD, and the Israelites conquered
them. And Moses the servant of the LORD gave their land to the
Reubenites, the Gadites and the half-tribe of Manasseh to be their
possession.

7 These are the kings of the land that Joshua and the Israelites
conquered on the west side of the Jordan, from Baal Gad in the
Valley of Lebanon to Mount Halak, which rises toward Seir (their
lands Joshua gave as an inheritance to the tribes of Israel according to their tribal divisions— 8 the hill country, the western

[a]3 That is, Galilee [b]3 That is, the Dead Sea

foothills, the Arabah, the mountain slopes, the desert and the Negev—the lands of the Hittites, Amorites, Canaanites, Perizzites, Hivites and Jebusites):

9 the king of Jericho	one
the king of Ai (near Bethel)	one
10 the king of Jerusalem	one
the king of Hebron	one
11 the king of Jarmuth	one
the king of Lachish	one
12 the king of Eglon	one
the king of Gezer	one
13 the king of Debir	one
the king of Geder	one
14 the king of Hormah	one
the king of Arad	one
15 the king of Libnah	one
the king of Adullam	one
16 the king of Makkedah	one
the king of Bethel	one
17 the king of Tappuah	one
the king of Hepher	one
18 the king of Aphek	one
the king of Lasharon	one
19 the king of Madon	one
the king of Hazor	one
20 the king of Shimron Meron	one
the king of Acshaph	one
21 the king of Taanach	one
the king of Megiddo	one
22 the king of Kedesh	one
the king of Jokneam in Carmel	one
23 the king of Dor (in Naphoth Dor[a])	one
the king of Goyim in Gilgal	one
24 the king of Tirzah	one

thirty-one kings in all.

[a]23 Or *in the heights of Dor*

So Joshua took the entire land, just as the LORD *had directed Moses.*
Josh 11:23

12:7-24 *west side of the Jordan . . . thirty-one kings in all:* Thirty-one Canaanite towns are listed. These lists of towns and kings concludes the JOSHUA account of the conquest of Canaan.

12:7 *Baal Gad . . . Seir:* This wide expanse of territory was the homeland of the many peoples mentioned (see the note at 3:10 and the map on p. 2464). Seir is also called Edom.

QUESTIONS ABOUT JOSHUA 5:13—12:24

1. What were the "rules" of holy war? (chapter 6) Why were these rules so important at that time in Israel's history?
2. What things did Achan keep? (7:20,21) When you read, "remove it" (7:13), what might that command mean for you today?
3. What did the Gibeonites hope for? What did they actually get? (chapter 9)
4. How does the account of the war against the five kings (10:1-15) make it clear that the LORD was fighting for Israel? Who does God "fight for" today?

Division of the Promised Land

Though not all the land of Canaan is under Israel's control, the LORD tells Joshua to divide the land west of the Jordan River. Careful records are made of the portions of land to be given to each of the twelve tribes. In addition, special towns are set aside for the Levites, who do not receive their own territory because of the special priestly duties they are expected to perform on behalf of the people of Israel.

13:1 *Joshua was old:* This verse seems to pick up where 11:23 ends. Joshua, now an old man (as in 23:1,2), is commanded to divide western Canaan among the nine-and-a-half tribes (Num 33:54).

13:2-7 *the land that remains . . . divide it:* The Geshurites may have been from Gezer, a town north of Ekron that the Israelites did not capture (Judg 1:29). The Geshurites are not the same Geshur as in 12:5 and 13:11. See the note at 11:22 for Philistine cities. The location of the Avvites is uncertain. The Sidonians lived in Sidon and in Phoenecian strongholds between the Mediterranean coast and the Lebanon Mountains (including Tyre, Arvad, and Byblos). See the mini-article called "Phoenicia," p. 1604. See also the note at 3:10. The border town Aphek mentioned in these verses is not the same Aphek as in 12:18. These are the lands that have yet to be conquered by Israel. This roughly describes the regions captured by King David some two hundred years after the time of Joshua (see the map on p. 2465). Although Israel never held all these lands, they were regarded as Canaanite lands promised to Israel by God.

13:8 *Moses had given:* See the note at 1:12.

13:9 *It extended:* Referring to the territory of the two-and-a-half tribes that settled on the east side of the Jordan River. See the notes at 1:12 and 12:1.

13:13 *did not drive out the people:* Evidence here and in 15:63; 16:10; 17:12,13 shows that the conquest was not completed under Joshua. The continued presence of non-Israelite peoples in Canaan is a dominant theme in JUDGES. Geshur and Maacah were states northeast and east of the Sea of Galilee.

13:6 Num 33:54.

Land Still to Be Taken

13 When Joshua was old and well advanced in years, the LORD
said to him, "You are very old, and there are still very large areas of
land to be taken over.

2 "This is the land that remains: all the regions of the
Philistines and Geshurites: 3 from the Shihor River on the east
of Egypt to the territory of Ekron on the north, all of it count-
ed as Canaanite (the territory of the five Philistine rulers in
Gaza, Ashdod, Ashkelon, Gath and Ekron—that of the
Avvites); 4 from the south, all the land of the Canaanites, from
Arah of the Sidonians as far as Aphek, the region of the
Amorites, 5 the area of the Gebalites[a]; and all Lebanon to the
east, from Baal Gad below Mount Hermon to Lebo[b] Hamath.

6 "As for all the inhabitants of the mountain regions from
Lebanon to Misrephoth Maim, that is, all the Sidonians, I myself
will drive them out before the Israelites. Be sure to allocate this
land to Israel for an inheritance, as I have instructed you, 7 and
divide it as an inheritance among the nine tribes and half of the
tribe of Manasseh."

Division of the Land East of the Jordan

8 The other half of Manasseh,[c] the Reubenites and the Gadites had
received the inheritance that Moses had given them east of the Jordan, as he, the servant of the LORD, had assigned it to them.

9 It extended from Aroer on the rim of the Arnon Gorge, and
from the town in the middle of the gorge, and included the
whole plateau of Medeba as far as Dibon, 10 and all the towns
of Sihon king of the Amorites, who ruled in Heshbon, out to
the border of the Ammonites. 11 It also included Gilead, the
territory of the people of Geshur and Maacah, all of Mount
Hermon and all Bashan as far as Salecah— 12 that is, the whole
kingdom of Og in Bashan, who had reigned in Ashtaroth and
Edrei and had survived as one of the last of the Rephaites.
Moses had defeated them and taken over their land. 13 But the

[a] 5 That is, the area of Byblos [b] 5 Or *to the entrance to* [c] 8 Hebrew *With it* (that is, with the other half of Manasseh)

Israelites did not drive out the people of Geshur and Maacah, so they continue to live among the Israelites to this day.

[14]But to the tribe of Levi he gave no inheritance, since the offerings made by fire to the LORD, the God of Israel, are their inheritance, as he promised them.

[15]This is what Moses had given to the tribe of Reuben, clan by clan:

[16]The territory from Aroer on the rim of the Arnon Gorge,
and from the town in the middle of the gorge, and the whole
plateau past Medeba [17]to Heshbon and all its towns on the
plateau, including Dibon, Bamoth Baal, Beth Baal Meon,
[18]Jahaz, Kedemoth, Mephaath, [19]Kiriathaim, Sibmah, Zereth
Shahar on the hill in the valley, [20]Beth Peor, the slopes of Pisgah, and Beth Jeshimoth [21]—all the towns on the plateau and
the entire realm of Sihon king of the Amorites, who ruled at
Heshbon. Moses had defeated him and the Midianite chiefs,
Evi, Rekem, Zur, Hur and Reba—princes allied with Sihon—
who lived in that country. [22]In addition to those slain in battle, the Israelites had put to the sword Balaam son of Beor,
who practiced divination. [23]The boundary of the Reubenites
was the bank of the Jordan. These towns and their villages
were the inheritance of the Reubenites, clan by clan.

[24]This is what Moses had given to the tribe of Gad, clan by clan:

[25]The territory of Jazer, all the towns of Gilead and half the
Ammonite country as far as Aroer, near Rabbah; [26]and from
Heshbon to Ramath Mizpah and Betonim, and from
Mahanaim to the territory of Debir; [27]and in the valley, Beth
Haram, Beth Nimrah, Succoth and Zaphon with the rest of
the realm of Sihon king of Heshbon (the east side of the Jor-
dan, the territory up to the end of the Sea of Kinnereth[a]).
[28]These towns and their villages were the inheritance of the
Gadites, clan by clan.

[29]This is what Moses had given to the half-tribe of Manasseh, that is, to half the family of the descendants of Manasseh, clan by clan:

[30]The territory extending from Mahanaim and including all of
Bashan, the entire realm of Og king of Bashan—all the settlements of Jair in Bashan, sixty towns, [31]half of Gilead, and
Ashtaroth and Edrei (the royal cities of Og in Bashan). This
was for the descendants of Makir son of Manasseh—for half
of the sons of Makir, clan by clan.

[32]This is the inheritance Moses had given when he was in the
plains of Moab across the Jordan east of Jericho. [33]But to the tribe

[a]**27** That is, Galilee

13:14 *the tribe of Levi:* Israel's priests came from the tribe of Levi (see Num 3:5-10 and the mini-article called "Israel's Priests," p. 2344). The Levites were not given territory of their own but were instead supported by the other tribes of Israel. The Levites and priests were to receive a portion of the meat, grain, and wine offerings the people brought to be used in making sacrifices (Num 18:8-24; Deut 18:1,2).

13:15 *tribe of Reuben:* Reuben and Simeon, Jacob's first and second sons (Gen 29:31-33), lost their normal position of leadership among the tribes because of their evil actions (Gen 49:3-7). The tribe of Reuben was given territory to the east of the Dead Sea.

13:15-23 *Heshbon . . . Pisgah:* On the northern border of the tribe of Reuben, the city of Heshbon had belonged to King Sihon, who was defeated by Moses (see the note at 2:10, Sihon and Og). The slopes of Pisgah refers to Mount Pisgah, the highest peak in the Abiram Mountains in Moab. From this spot, the Israelites could likely see the land of Canaan (see Num 23:14; Deut 3:27; 34:1-4).

13:22 *Balaam:* Balaam was a fortune-teller hired by the Moabite King Balak to curse the Israelites. Balaam had invited the people to worship the Canaanite god Baal (Num 22–24; 31:7-16).

13:24 *tribe of Gad:* Gad was the firstborn son of Jacob and Leah's maid Zilpah (Gen 30:9-11).

13:25 *Aroer . . . Rabbah:* This "Aroer" is not the same town as the Aroer in 13:16. Rabbah was the capital city of the Ammonites.

13:28 *inheritance of the Gadites:* Included the highlands north and south of the Jabbok River.

13:29-31 *Manasseh . . . Makir:* Manasseh and Ephraim were the sons of Jacob's son Joseph. Each received a share of land in Canaan (see Gen 48:5,6). "Makir" stands for western Manasseh.

14:2 *inheritances were assigned by lot to the nine-and-a-half tribes:* The nine-and-a-half tribes that settled on the west side of the Jordan River. This division of the land west of the Jordan was first reported in Numbers 26:52-56; 34:13,14. The tribes of Reuben, Gad, and East Manasseh had already received their portion under Moses, (Num 32:1-27; Deut 3:12-17; Josh 1:12-15). Joseph's sons Ephraim and Manasseh were blessed by Jacob and counted as his own (Gen 48:5). The tribe of Levi was set apart for the service of the LORD and didn't receive a share of land.

14:1 *Eleazar:* Eleazar, the high priest, was the son of Aaron, Israel's first high priest (Exod 28:1-3; Deut 10:6).

14:6 *Caleb:* Only Caleb and Joshua encouraged the people to enter the land (see Num 13,14). Because they were faithful, Joshua and Caleb were the only two of that generation allowed to enter the promised land (Num 14:30).

14:11 *just as vigorous:* Caleb is still ready for battle at age eighty-five.

14:12 *hill country . . . Anakites:* Though the land is occupied by the Anakites (see the note at 11:21), Caleb is not afraid to ask for it, trusting in God's promise.

15:1 *tribe of Judah:* Judah was the son of Jacob and Leah (Gen 29:35). Israel's King David was from the tribe of Judah.

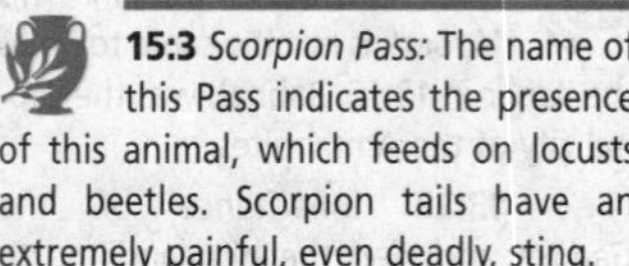

15:3 *Scorpion Pass:* The name of this Pass indicates the presence of this animal, which feeds on locusts and beetles. Scorpion tails have an extremely painful, even deadly, sting.

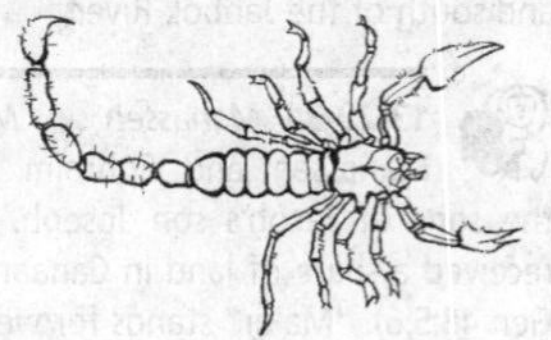

of Levi, Moses had given no inheritance; the LORD, the God of Israel, is their inheritance, as he promised them.

Division of the Land West of the Jordan

14 Now these are the areas the Israelites received as an inheritance in the land of Canaan, which Eleazar the priest, Joshua son of
Nun and the heads of the tribal clans of Israel allotted to them.
2 Their inheritances were assigned by lot to the nine-and-a-half
tribes, as the LORD had commanded through Moses. 3 Moses had
granted the two-and-a-half tribes their inheritance east of the Jordan but had not granted the Levites an inheritance among the rest,
4 for the sons of Joseph had become two tribes—Manasseh and
Ephraim. The Levites received no share of the land but only towns
to live in, with pasturelands for their flocks and herds. 5 So the
Israelites divided the land, just as the LORD had commanded Moses.

Hebron Given to Caleb

6 Now the men of Judah approached Joshua at Gilgal, and
Caleb son of Jephunneh the Kenizzite said to him, "You know what
the LORD said to Moses the man of God at Kadesh Barnea about
you and me. 7 I was forty years old when Moses the servant of the
LORD sent me from Kadesh Barnea to explore the land. And I
brought him back a report according to my convictions, 8 but my
brothers who went up with me made the hearts of the people melt
with fear. I, however, followed the LORD my God wholeheartedly.
9 So on that day Moses swore to me, 'The land on which your feet
have walked will be your inheritance and that of your children
forever, because you have followed the LORD my God wholeheartedly.'[a]
10 "Now then, just as the LORD promised, he has kept me alive
for forty-five years since the time he said this to Moses, while Israel
moved about in the desert. So here I am today, eighty-five years
old! 11 I am still as strong today as the day Moses sent me out; I'm
just as vigorous to go out to battle now as I was then. 12 Now give
me this hill country that the LORD promised me that day. You
yourself heard then that the Anakites were there and their cities
were large and fortified, but, the LORD helping me, I will drive
them out just as he said."
13 Then Joshua blessed Caleb son of Jephunneh and gave him
Hebron as his inheritance. 14 So Hebron has belonged to Caleb son
of Jephunneh the Kenizzite ever since, because he followed the
LORD, the God of Israel, wholeheartedly. 15 (Hebron used to be
called Kiriath Arba after Arba, who was the greatest man among
the Anakites.)

Then the land had rest from war.

---

[a] **9** Deut. 1:36

Allotment for Judah

15 The allotment for the tribe of Judah, clan by clan, extended
down to the territory of Edom, to the Desert of Zin in the extreme
south.
2Their southern boundary started from the bay at the
southern end of the Salt Sea,[a] 3crossed south of Scorpion[b]
Pass, continued on to Zin and went over to the south of
Kadesh Barnea. Then it ran past Hezron up to Addar and
curved around to Karka. 4It then passed along to Azmon and
joined the Wadi of Egypt, ending at the sea. This is their[c]
southern boundary.
5The eastern boundary is the Salt Sea as far as the mouth of
the Jordan.
The northern boundary started from the bay of the sea at
the mouth of the Jordan, 6went up to Beth Hoglah and continued north of Beth Arabah to the Stone of Bohan son of
Reuben. 7The boundary then went up to Debir from the Valley of Achor and turned north to Gilgal, which faces the Pass
of Adummim south of the gorge. It continued along to the
waters of En Shemesh and came out at En Rogel. 8Then it ran
up the Valley of Ben Hinnom along the southern slope of the
Jebusite city (that is, Jerusalem). From there it climbed to the
top of the hill west of the Hinnom Valley at the northern end
of the Valley of Rephaim. 9From the hilltop the boundary
headed toward the spring of the waters of Nephtoah, came
out at the towns of Mount Ephron and went down toward
Baalah (that is, Kiriath Jearim). 10Then it curved westward
from Baalah to Mount Seir, ran along the northern slope of
Mount Jearim (that is, Kesalon), continued down to Beth
Shemesh and crossed to Timnah. 11It went to the northern
slope of Ekron, turned toward Shikkeron, passed along to
Mount Baalah and reached Jabneel. The boundary ended at
the sea.
12The western boundary is the coastline of the Great Sea.[d]
These are the boundaries around the people of Judah by their clans.
13In accordance with the LORD's command to him, Joshua
gave to Caleb son of Jephunneh a portion in Judah—Kiriath Arba,
that is, Hebron. (Arba was the forefather of Anak.) 14From Hebron
Caleb drove out the three Anakites—Sheshai, Ahiman and Talmai—
descendants of Anak. 15From there he marched against the people
living in Debir (formerly called Kiriath Sepher). 16And Caleb said, "I
will give my daughter Acsah in marriage to the man who attacks and
captures Kiriath Sepher." 17Othniel son of Kenaz, Caleb's brother,
took it; so Caleb gave his daughter Acsah to him in marriage.

[a]**2** That is, the Dead Sea; also in verse 5 [b]**3** Hebrew *Akrabbim* [c]**4** Hebrew *your* [d]**12** That is, the Mediterranean; also in verse 47

15:3 *Kadesh Barnea:* This town in the Desert of Paran was southwest of the Dead Sea. See the map on p. 2465.

15:6 *Stone of Bohan:* This may refer to a natural rock formation.

15:7 *Debir . . . Valley of Achor . . . Gilgal:* This Debir is not the same town as in 10:38,39. The Valley of Achor is where Achan was stoned to death after the capture of Jericho (7:25,26). This Gilgal is not the same as in 4:19.

15:8 *Jebusite city:* The Canaanite clan known as the Jebusites lived in Jerusalem and in the surrounding hills (Judg 19:10,11). Israel's King David would later take over Jerusalem from the Jebusites (2 Sam 5:6-9). See the note at 10:1.

15:10 *Beth Shemesh:* Probably the same town as the Ir Shemesh of 19:41. Two other towns were also named Beth Shemesh (see 19:22 and 19:38).

15:12 *western boundary is the coastline of the Great Sea:* The cities along the Mediterranean Sea coastal plain were never under Israelite control until King David's time.

15:13,14 *Caleb . . . Anak:* See 14:6 and the note (Caleb). For more about Anak and his descendants the Anakites, see the note at 11:21. While given the land by Joshua in 14:13, Caleb must still take his territory by force. See also Judg 1:20.

15:16 *give my daughter:* Compare Caleb's promise with the promise made by King Saul (1 Sam 17:25).

15:17 *Othniel:* He later was chosen to be a leader (judge) of Israel for forty years (Judg 3:7-11).

15:16-19 Judg 1:12-15.

15:19 *springs of water:* These springs were vital for life to survive in this dry desert land.

15:20-63 *inheritance . . . towns:* The towns of Judah are divided into territories drawn up for administrative purposes sometime after the reign of David and emphasize the importance of the tribe of Judah.

15:21-32 *Kabzeel . . . Rimmon:* This large region was in the south with Beersheba as its center.

15:33-36 *Eshtaol . . . Gederah:* This region was in the lowlands or plains west of Judah's central mountains, with Adullam being the southernmost city and Gederah the northernmost.

15:37-41 *Zenan . . . Makkedah:* Most of the towns named are unknown. For Lachish and Eglon see the note at 10:28-34.

15:42-44 *Libnah . . . Mareshah:* This region is centered around Mareshah, fourteen miles northwest of Hebron.

15:45-47 *Ekron . . . Gaza:* This region includes the major Philistine cities above and Ashdod. See the note at 11:22.

15:48-51 *Shamir . . . Giloh:* This region was north of the first region. Debir is one of its important cities (see 15:15).

15:52-54 *Arab . . . Zior:* This region was in the heart of the southern highlands. Its center is Hebron, where many years later, the people of Judah crowned David king (2 Sam 2:4).

15:55-57 *Maon . . . Timnah:* This region was on the eastern edge of the highlands south of Hebron. Jezreel is not the same city as in 19:18; Gibeah is not the same as in 18:28.

15:58,59 *Halhul . . . Eltekon:* These cities were scattered throughout the small region that extended from Hebron in the south to the area just north of Bethlehem.

18 One day when she came to Othniel, she urged him[a] to ask
her father for a field. When she got off her donkey, Caleb asked
her, "What can I do for you?"
19 She replied, "Do me a special favor. Since you have given
me land in the Negev, give me also springs of water." So Caleb gave
her the upper and lower springs.

20 This is the inheritance of the tribe of Judah, clan by clan:
21 The southernmost towns of the tribe of Judah in the Negev
toward the boundary of Edom were:
Kabzeel, Eder, Jagur, 22 Kinah, Dimonah, Adadah, 23 Kedesh,
Hazor, Ithnan, 24 Ziph, Telem, Bealoth, 25 Hazor Hadattah, Kerioth Hezron (that is, Hazor), 26 Amam, Shema, Moladah, 27 Hazar
Gaddah, Heshmon, Beth Pelet, 28 Hazar Shual, Beersheba, Bizio-
thiah, 29 Baalah, Iim, Ezem, 30 Eltolad, Kesil, Hormah, 31 Ziklag,
Madmannah, Sansannah, 32 Lebaoth, Shilhim, Ain and Rimmon—a total of twenty-nine towns and their villages.

33 In the western foothills:
Eshtaol, Zorah, Ashnah, 34 Zanoah, En Gannim, Tappuah,
Enam, 35 Jarmuth, Adullam, Socoh, Azekah, 36 Shaaraim,
Adithaim and Gederah (or Gederothaim)[b]—fourteen towns
and their villages.
37 Zenan, Hadashah, Migdal Gad, 38 Dilean, Mizpah, Joktheel,
39 Lachish, Bozkath, Eglon, 40 Cabbon, Lahmas, Kitlish,
41 Gederoth, Beth Dagon, Naamah and Makkedah—sixteen
towns and their villages.
42 Libnah, Ether, Ashan, 43 Iphtah, Ashnah, Nezib, 44 Keilah,
Aczib and Mareshah—nine towns and their villages.
45 Ekron, with its surrounding settlements and villages;
46 west of Ekron, all that were in the vicinity of Ashdod,
together with their villages; 47 Ashdod, its surrounding settlements and villages; and Gaza, its settlements and villages, as
far as the Wadi of Egypt and the coastline of the Great Sea.

48 In the hill country:
Shamir, Jattir, Socoh, 49 Dannah, Kiriath Sannah (that is,
Debir), 50 Anab, Eshtemoh, Anim, 51 Goshen, Holon and
Giloh—eleven towns and their villages.
52 Arab, Dumah, Eshan, 53 Janim, Beth Tappuah, Aphekah,
54 Humtah, Kiriath Arba (that is, Hebron) and Zior—nine
towns and their villages.
55 Maon, Carmel, Ziph, Juttah, 56 Jezreel, Jokdeam, Zanoah,
57 Kain, Gibeah and Timnah—ten towns and their villages.
58 Halhul, Beth Zur, Gedor, 59 Maarath, Beth Anoth and
Eltekon—six towns and their villages.

---

[a]**18** Hebrew and some Septuagint manuscripts; other Septuagint manuscripts (see also note at Judges 1:14) *Othniel, he urged her* [b]**36** Or *Gederah and Gederothaim*

60 Kiriath Baal (that is, Kiriath Jearim) and Rabbah—two
towns and their villages.

61 In the desert:
Beth Arabah, Middin, Secacah, 62 Nibshan, the City of Salt
and En Gedi—six towns and their villages.

63 Judah could not dislodge the Jebusites, who were living in
Jerusalem; to this day the Jebusites live there with the people of
Judah.

Allotment for Ephraim and Manasseh

16 The allotment for Joseph began at the Jordan of Jericho,[a] east of the waters of Jericho, and went up from there
through the desert into the hill country of Bethel. 2 It went on
from Bethel (that is, Luz),[b] crossed over to the territory of the
Arkites in Ataroth, 3 descended westward to the territory of the
Japhletites as far as the region of Lower Beth Horon and on to
Gezer, ending at the sea.

4 So Manasseh and Ephraim, the descendants of Joseph, received
their inheritance.

5 This was the territory of Ephraim, clan by clan:
The boundary of their inheritance went from Ataroth Addar
in the east to Upper Beth Horon 6 and continued to the sea.
From Micmethath on the north it curved eastward to Taanath
Shiloh, passing by it to Janoah on the east. 7 Then it went down
from Janoah to Ataroth and Naarah, touched Jericho and came
out at the Jordan. 8 From Tappuah the border went west to the
Kanah Ravine and ended at the sea. This was the inheritance of
the tribe of the Ephraimites, clan by clan. 9 It also included all
the towns and their villages that were set aside for the
Ephraimites within the inheritance of the Manassites.

10 They did not dislodge the Canaanites living in Gezer; to this day
the Canaanites live among the people of Ephraim but are required
to do forced labor.

17 This was the allotment for the tribe of Manasseh as Joseph's
firstborn, that is, for Makir, Manasseh's firstborn. Makir was the
ancestor of the Gileadites, who had received Gilead and Bashan
because the Makirites were great soldiers. 2 So this allotment was
for the rest of the people of Manasseh—the clans of Abiezer,
Helek, Asriel, Shechem, Hepher and Shemida. These are the other
male descendants of Manasseh son of Joseph by their clans.

3 Now Zelophehad son of Hepher, the son of Gilead, the son
of Makir, the son of Manasseh, had no sons but only daughters,
whose names were Mahlah, Noah, Hoglah, Milcah and Tirzah.

[a]1 *Jordan of Jericho* was possibly an ancient name for the Jordan River.
[b]2 Septuagint; Hebrew *Bethel to Luz*

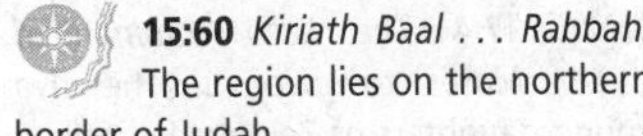

15:60 *Kiriath Baal . . . Rabbah:* The region lies on the northern border of Judah.

15:61,62 *Beth Arabah . . . En Gedi:* En Gedi is about midway along the western shore of the Dead Sea.

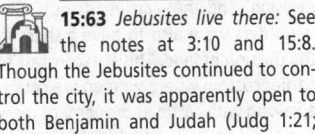

15:63 *Jebusites live there:* See the notes at 3:10 and 15:8. Though the Jebusites continued to control the city, it was apparently open to both Benjamin and Judah (Judg 1:21; see also 1 Chr 11:4).

16:2,3 *Ataroth . . . Gezer:* This is the same Ataroth as Ataroth Addar in 16:5, but a different Ataroth from the one in 16:6-8. Gezer was later given to Solomon as a wedding gift by the Egyptian king (1 Kgs 9:16).

16:4 *Manasseh and Ephraim:* See the notes at 13:29-31 and 14:1-5. Ephraim was the larger of the two, and one of the most powerful tribes.

16:10 *They did not dislodge the Canaanites living in Gezer:* See also Judg 1:29. Because their horses and chariots helped them defend the plains region of Palestine, some Canaanites remained in Ephraim tribal lands. Their status as "slaves" reflects different conditions from that of the conquest. Over two hundred years later, Israel's King Solomon also used the Canaanite population for forced labor (1 Kgs 9:20,21). Intermarriage between Israelites and Canaanites and the worship of Canaanite gods caused ongoing problems for Israel's tribes. See the notes at 16:2,3 (Gezer) and 13:2-7.

17:1 *Manasseh as Joseph's firstborn:* See the notes at 13:29-31 and 14:1-5. For more on Gezer, see the note at 16:2,3. In Numbers 26:28-34, six clans of Manasseh are listed as descendants of Makir's son Gilead. The names of three of his sons are also the names of Canaanite cities (Shechem, Hepher, and Tirzah).

4They went to Eleazar the priest, Joshua son of Nun, and the leaders and said, "The LORD commanded Moses to give us an inheritance among our brothers." So Joshua gave them an inheritance
along with the brothers of their father, according to the LORD's
command. 5Manasseh's share consisted of ten tracts of land
besides Gilead and Bashan east of the Jordan, 6because the daughters of the tribe of Manasseh received an inheritance among the
sons. The land of Gilead belonged to the rest of the descendants of
Manasseh.

7The territory of Manasseh extended from Asher to
Micmethath east of Shechem. The boundary ran southward
from there to include the people living at En Tappuah. 8(Manasseh had the land of Tappuah, but Tappuah itself, on the
boundary of Manasseh, belonged to the Ephraimites.) 9Then
the boundary continued south to the Kanah Ravine. There
were towns belonging to Ephraim lying among the towns of
Manasseh, but the boundary of Manasseh was the northern
side of the ravine and ended at the sea. 10On the south the
land belonged to Ephraim, on the north to Manasseh. The
territory of Manasseh reached the sea and bordered Asher on
the north and Issachar on the east.

11Within Issachar and Asher, Manasseh also had Beth Shan,
Ibleam and the people of Dor, Endor, Taanach and Megiddo,
together with their surrounding settlements (the third in the
list is Naphoth[a]).
12Yet the Manassites were not able to occupy these towns, for the
Canaanites were determined to live in that region. 13However,
when the Israelites grew stronger, they subjected the Canaanites to
forced labor but did not drive them out completely.

14The people of Joseph said to Joshua, "Why have you given
us only one allotment and one portion for an inheritance? We are
a numerous people and the LORD has blessed us abundantly."

15"If you are so numerous," Joshua answered, "and if the hill
country of Ephraim is too small for you, go up into the forest and
clear land for yourselves there in the land of the Perizzites and
Rephaites."

16The people of Joseph replied, "The hill country is not
enough for us, and all the Canaanites who live in the plain have
iron chariots, both those in Beth Shan and its settlements and
those in the Valley of Jezreel."

17But Joshua said to the house of Joseph—to Ephraim and
Manasseh—"You are numerous and very powerful. You will have
not only one allotment 18but the forested hill country as well. Clear
it, and its farthest limits will be yours; though the Canaanites have
iron chariots and though they are strong, you can drive them out."

17:4 *The LORD commanded Moses to give us:* The five young daughters of Zelophehad talked with Moses about getting their fair share, and the LORD declared that they were right (Num 27:1-11; 36:1-12). Now their descendants remind Joshua of this decision and he carries it out. The daughters were also to have a share in the division of land. This is in contrast to earlier custom where women are counted along with cattle as property of men. The five daughters asked for justice, and they received it from the LORD.

17:7 *territory of Manasseh:* The land described in 17:7-11 is the land given to the part of the Manasseh tribe that settled west of the Jordan River. Combined with the east Manasseh lands, this tribe held the most territory of all the tribes.

17:12 *Canaanites were determined to live in that region:* See Judg 1:27,28 and the note at 16:10. Mention of Canaanite slaves reflects a much later time.

17:14 *people of Joseph:* This refers to the tribes of Ephraim and Manasseh (see the notes at 13:29-31 and 14:1-5). The tribes of Ephraim and Manasseh that lived west of the Jordan act here as one tribe, as they were treated in 16:1-4. Their request for more land is based on two arguments: God has continually shown mercy to them, and they have too many people for the land area they were given. Their dissatisfaction is evidence of quarreling among the tribes.

17:15 *hill country . . . forest:* The rugged hill country that covered a good portion of the Joseph tribal territories was difficult to farm. The dissatisfied descendants of Joseph were invited to clear the forests of the Perizzites (see the note at 3:10) and the Rephaites (see the note at 12:4).

a11 That is, Naphoth Dor

Division of the Rest of the Land

18 The whole assembly of the Israelites gathered at Shiloh and set up the Tent of Meeting there. The country was brought under their control, 2but there were still seven Israelite tribes who had not yet received their inheritance.

3So Joshua said to the Israelites: "How long will you wait before you begin to take possession of the land that the LORD, the God of your fathers, has given you? 4Appoint three men from each tribe. I will send them out to make a survey of the land and to write a description of it, according to the inheritance of each. Then they will return to me. 5You are to divide the land into seven parts. Judah is to remain in its territory on the south and the house of Joseph in its territory on the north. 6After you have written descriptions of the seven parts of the land, bring them here to me and I will cast lots for you in the presence of the LORD our God. 7The Levites, however, do not get a portion among you, because the priestly service of the LORD is their inheritance. And Gad, Reuben and the half-tribe of Manasseh have already received their inheritance on the east side of the Jordan. Moses the servant of the LORD gave it to them."

8As the men started on their way to map out the land, Joshua instructed them, "Go and make a survey of the land and write a description of it. Then return to me, and I will cast lots for you here at Shiloh in the presence of the LORD." 9So the men left and went through the land. They wrote its description on a scroll, town by town, in seven parts, and returned to Joshua in the camp at Shiloh. 10Joshua then cast lots for them in Shiloh in the presence of the LORD, and there he distributed the land to the Israelites according to their tribal divisions.

Allotment for Benjamin

11The lot came up for the tribe of Benjamin, clan by clan. Their allotted territory lay between the tribes of Judah and Joseph:

12On the north side their boundary began at the Jordan, passed the northern slope of Jericho and headed west into the hill country, coming out at the desert of Beth Aven. 13From there it crossed to the south slope of Luz (that is, Bethel) and went down to Ataroth Addar on the hill south of Lower Beth Horon.

14From the hill facing Beth Horon on the south the boundary turned south along the western side and came out at Kiriath Baal (that is, Kiriath Jearim), a town of the people of Judah. This was the western side.

15The southern side began at the outskirts of Kiriath Jearim on the west, and the boundary came out at the spring of the waters of Nephtoah. 16The boundary went down to the foot of the hill facing the Valley of Ben Hinnom, north of the

18:1 *gathered at Shiloh:* For this religious ceremony the scene has shifted from Gilgal (4:19) to Shiloh, an important religious site for Israel in the time before David (Judg 18:30,31). It was where the ark of the covenant was kept in the tabernacle until the ark was taken by the Philistines around 1050 B.C. (1 Sam 4:3-11). See the mini-article called "The Tabernacle," p. 2346.

18:5-7 *Judah . . . Joseph . . . Levites:* For the lands already given to Judah, see 15:1-63. For the Joseph tribes (Ephraim and Manasseh), see chapters 16 and 17, and the note at 17:14. For the Levites, see the note at 13:14. There were still seven tribes without land because Gad and Reuben had already settled east of the Jordan River, and Levi could not own land outright.

18:6 *written descriptions . . . cast lots:* Lots were cast to determine who got what land (see the notes at 7:14; 14:1-5).

18:11 *Benjamin . . . Joseph:* Benjamin was the youngest son of Jacob and Rachel (Gen 35:16-18). Years after settling in the land, Israel's first king, Saul, would come from the tribe of Benjamin. When Samuel told Saul that he was to be king, Saul objected, saying he was from the smallest tribe in Israel (1 Sam 9:21). The Benjamin lands were very small and were located between the Judah and Ephraim lands (see the map on p. 2464). See also the note at 17:14.

18:13 *Bethel:* This important site was a holy place in central Canaan, eleven miles north of Jerusalem on the way to Shechem. "Bethel," meaning "house of God," was the name given to it by Jacob after having a vision in a dream there (see Gen 28:18,19). The town is given to Ephraim in 16:1. Border towns like Bethel probably housed people from two different tribes and were claimed by both. See also the note at 8:9.

18:17 *Stone of Bohan:* Or "Bohan Rock," possibly a natural rock formation. See also 15:6.

18:28 *the Jebusite city (that is, Jerusalem):* See the notes at 10:1 and 15:8. Jerusalem seems to have been partly on Judah's land and partly on Benjamin's (15:63; Judg 1:21).

19:1-9 *Simeon . . . within the territory of Judah:* The second son born to Jacob and Leah (Gen 29:31-33; 49:3-7). The tribal boundaries for Simeon are not given because Simeon became absorbed into the larger tribe of Judah. Territorial boundaries were adjusted because Judah's portion was more than they needed for their population. The towns listed for Simeon are in the southern part of Judah (see the map on p. 2464).

19:10 *Zebulun:* The sixth son born to Jacob and Leah (Gen 30:20). Zebulun's region is roughly the western half of the southern Galilean hills (see the map on p. 2464).

19:1-9 1 Chr 4:24-43.

Valley of Rephaim. It continued down the Hinnom Valley
along the southern slope of the Jebusite city and so to En
Rogel. 17It then curved north, went to En Shemesh, continued
to Geliloth, which faces the Pass of Adummim, and ran down
to the Stone of Bohan son of Reuben. 18It continued to the
northern slope of Beth Arabah[a] and on down into the Arabah.
19It then went to the northern slope of Beth Hoglah and came
out at the northern bay of the Salt Sea,[b] at the mouth of the
Jordan in the south. This was the southern boundary.
20The Jordan formed the boundary on the eastern side.
These were the boundaries that marked out the inheritance of the
clans of Benjamin on all sides.

21The tribe of Benjamin, clan by clan, had the following cities:
Jericho, Beth Hoglah, Emek Keziz, 22Beth Arabah, Zemaraim, Bethel, 23Avvim, Parah, Ophrah, 24Kephar Ammoni,
Ophni and Geba—twelve towns and their villages.
25Gibeon, Ramah, Beeroth, 26Mizpah, Kephirah, Mozah,
27Rekem, Irpeel, Taralah, 28Zelah, Haeleph, the Jebusite city
(that is, Jerusalem), Gibeah and Kiriath—fourteen towns and
their villages.
This was the inheritance of Benjamin for its clans.

Allotment for Simeon

19 The second lot came out for the tribe of Simeon, clan by
clan. Their inheritance lay within the territory of Judah. 2It included:
Beersheba (or Sheba),[c] Moladah, 3Hazar Shual, Balah,
Ezem, 4Eltolad, Bethul, Hormah, 5Ziklag, Beth Marcaboth,
Hazar Susah, 6Beth Lebaoth and Sharuhen—thirteen towns
and their villages;
7Ain, Rimmon, Ether and Ashan—four towns and their villages— 8and all the villages around these towns as far as
Baalath Beer (Ramah in the Negev).
This was the inheritance of the tribe of the Simeonites, clan by
clan. 9The inheritance of the Simeonites was taken from the share
of Judah, because Judah's portion was more than they needed. So
the Simeonites received their inheritance within the territory of
Judah.

Allotment for Zebulun

10The third lot came up for Zebulun, clan by clan:
The boundary of their inheritance went as far as Sarid.
11Going west it ran to Maralah, touched Dabbesheth, and
extended to the ravine near Jokneam. 12It turned east from

[a]**18** Septuagint; Hebrew *slope facing the Arabah* [b]**19** That is, the Dead Sea
[c]**2** Or *Beersheba, Sheba*; 1 Chron. 4:28 does not have *Sheba.*

Sarid toward the sunrise to the territory of Kisloth Tabor and
went on to Daberath and up to Japhia. 13 Then it continued
eastward to Gath Hepher and Eth Kazin; it came out at Rimmon and turned toward Neah. 14 There the boundary went
around on the north to Hannathon and ended at the Valley of
Iphtah El. 15 Included were Kattath, Nahalal, Shimron, Idalah
and Bethlehem. There were twelve towns and their villages.
16 These towns and their villages were the inheritance of Zebulun,
clan by clan.

Allotment for Issachar

17 The fourth lot came out for Issachar, clan by clan. 18 Their territory included:
Jezreel, Kesulloth, Shunem, 19 Hapharaim, Shion, Anaharath,
20 Rabbith, Kishion, Ebez, 21 Remeth, En Gannim, En Haddah
and Beth Pazzez. 22 The boundary touched Tabor, Shahazumah
and Beth Shemesh, and ended at the Jordan. There were sixteen towns and their villages.
23 These towns and their villages were the inheritance of the tribe of
Issachar, clan by clan.

Allotment for Asher

24 The fifth lot came out for the tribe of Asher, clan by clan. 25 Their
territory included:
Helkath, Hali, Beten, Acshaph, 26 Allammelech, Amad and
Mishal. On the west the boundary touched Carmel and Shihor Libnath. 27 It then turned east toward Beth Dagon,
touched Zebulun and the Valley of Iphtah El, and went north
to Beth Emek and Neiel, passing Cabul on the left. 28 It went to
Abdon,[a] Rehob, Hammon and Kanah, as far as Greater Sidon.
29 The boundary then turned back toward Ramah and went to
the fortified city of Tyre, turned toward Hosah and came out
at the sea in the region of Aczib, 30 Ummah, Aphek and Rehob.
There were twenty-two towns and their villages.
31 These towns and their villages were the inheritance of the tribe of
Asher, clan by clan.

Allotment for Naphtali

32 The sixth lot came out for Naphtali, clan by clan:
33 Their boundary went from Heleph and the large tree in
Zaanannim, passing Adami Nekeb and Jabneel to Lakkum
and ending at the Jordan. 34 The boundary ran west through
Aznoth Tabor and came out at Hukkok. It touched Zebulun
on the south, Asher on the west and the Jordan[b] on the east.

---

[a]**28** Some Hebrew manuscripts (see also Joshua 21:30); most Hebrew manuscripts *Ebron* [b]**34** Septuagint; Hebrew *west, and Judah, the Jordan,*

19:15 *Bethlehem:* Northern town different from the Bethlehem in north central Judah's hill country.

19:17 *Issachar:* The fifth son of Jacob and Leah (Gen 30:16-18). In Genesis 49:14,15 Issachar is compared to a donkey. That may refer to the tribe's later service of King Solomon or to serving its Canaanite neighbors. This tribe's territory forms a rough square (see the map on p. 2464).

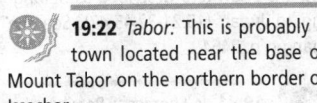

19:22 *Tabor:* This is probably a town located near the base of Mount Tabor on the northern border of Issachar.

19:22 *Beth Shemesh:* This is not the same Beth Shemesh as in 15:10 or 19:38.

19:24 *Asher:* Jacob's second son with Leah's servant Zilpah (Gen 30:12,13). The Asher tribe's northern border ran along the Galilean mountains to the territory of Tyre (see the map on p. 2464).

19:29 *Ramah . . . Tyre:* This is not the same Ramah as in 18:25 or 19:36. Tyre, a Phoenician walled city, was built on an island in the Mediterranean Sea about half a mile from shore. Years later, its king, Hiram, would be an important ally of Israel (see 1 Kgs 5:1-12). See also the mini-article called "Phoenicia," p. 1604.

19:32 *Naphtali:* Naphtali was the second son of Jacob and Rachel's servant Bilhah (Gen 30:7,8). This tribe held land in the Galilean highlands. See the map on p. 2464.

19:33 *Jabneel:* This town is not the same Jabneel as in 15:11.

19:36-38 *Ramah . . . Edrei . . . Beth Shemesh:* This is not the same Ramah listed in 18:25 or 19:36. This Edrei is not the same as the town in Bashan where King Og lived (see 12:4; 13:12,31). This Beth Shemesh is not the same town as mentioned in 15:10 or 19:22.

19:40 *Dan:* The firstborn son of Jacob and Rachel's servant Bilhah (Gen 30:4-6). No border list is given for this tribe. The towns listed fall in regions elsewhere described as belonging to Judah (15:21-32,45-47). See the map on p. 2464.

19:41 *Ir Shemesh:* Possibly the Beth Shemesh of 15:10.

19:47 *had difficulty:* Ancient tradition locates Dan in the south along the Mediterranean coastal plain (see the note at 19:40). Sometime before David became king of Israel, the tribe migrated north. The had difficulty conquering their allotted territory, so they went where it would be easier. For an account of the migration see Judges 17,18. The town renamed Dan later became a center for idol worship (Judg 18:27-31).

19:49,50 *Joshua . . . Timnath Serah:* Located seventeen miles southwest of Shechem and ten miles northwest of Bethel. Joshua is from the tribe of Ephraim (Num 13:8, where he is called Hoshea).

19:51 *assigned by lot at Shiloh:* This is where the land distribution took place (see the note at 18:1).

35 The fortified cities were Ziddim, Zer, Hammath, Rakkath,
Kinnereth, 36 Adamah, Ramah, Hazor, 37 Kedesh, Edrei, En
Hazor, 38 Iron, Migdal El, Horem, Beth Anath and Beth Shemesh. There were nineteen towns and their villages.
39 These towns and their villages were the inheritance of the tribe of Naphtali, clan by clan.

Allotment for Dan

40 The seventh lot came out for the tribe of Dan, clan by clan. 41 The
territory of their inheritance included:
Zorah, Eshtaol, Ir Shemesh, 42 Shaalabbin, Aijalon, Ithlah,
43 Elon, Timnah, Ekron, 44 Eltekeh, Gibbethon, Baalath, 45 Jehud,
Bene Berak, Gath Rimmon, 46 Me Jarkon and Rakkon, with the area facing Joppa.
47 (But the Danites had difficulty taking possession of their territory, so they went up and attacked Leshem, took it, put it to the sword and occupied it. They settled in Leshem and named it Dan after their forefather.)
48 These towns and their villages were the inheritance of the tribe of Dan, clan by clan.

Allotment for Joshua

49 When they had finished dividing the land into its allotted portions, the Israelites gave Joshua son of Nun an inheritance
among them, 50 as the LORD had commanded. They gave him the town he asked for—Timnath Serah[a] in the hill country of Ephraim. And he built up the town and settled there.
51 These are the territories that Eleazar the priest, Joshua son of Nun and the heads of the tribal clans of Israel assigned by lot at Shiloh in the presence of the LORD at the entrance to the Tent of Meeting. And so they finished dividing the land.

Cities of Refuge

20 Then the LORD said to Joshua: 2 "Tell the Israelites to designate the cities of refuge, as I instructed you through Moses, 3 so
that anyone who kills a person accidentally and unintentionally may flee there and find protection from the avenger of blood.
4 "When he flees to one of these cities, he is to stand in the entrance of the city gate and state his case before the elders of that city. Then they are to admit him into their city and give him
a place to live with them. 5 If the avenger of blood pursues him, they must not surrender the one accused, because he killed his
neighbor unintentionally and without malice aforethought. 6 He
is to stay in that city until he has stood trial before the assembly

[a]**50** Also known as *Timnath Heres* (see Judges 2:9)

and until the death of the high priest who is serving at that time. Then he may go back to his own home in the town from which he fled."

[7]So they set apart Kedesh in Galilee in the hill country of Naphtali, Shechem in the hill country of Ephraim, and Kiriath Arba (that is, Hebron) in the hill country of Judah. [8]On the east side of the Jordan of Jericho[a] they designated Bezer in the desert on the plateau in the tribe of Reuben, Ramoth in Gilead in the tribe of Gad, and Golan in Bashan in the tribe of Manasseh. [9]Any of the Israelites or any alien living among them who killed someone accidentally could flee to these designated cities and not be killed by the avenger of blood prior to standing trial before the assembly.

Towns for the Levites

21 Now the family heads of the Levites approached Eleazar the priest, Joshua son of Nun, and the heads of the other tribal families of Israel [2]at Shiloh in Canaan and said to them, "The LORD commanded through Moses that you give us towns to live in, with pasturelands for our livestock." [3]So, as the LORD had commanded, the Israelites gave the Levites the following towns and pasturelands out of their own inheritance:

[4]The first lot came out for the Kohathites, clan by clan. The Levites who were descendants of Aaron the priest were allotted thirteen towns from the tribes of Judah, Simeon and Benjamin. [5]The rest of Kohath's descendants were allotted ten towns from the clans of the tribes of Ephraim, Dan and half of Manasseh.

[6]The descendants of Gershon were allotted thirteen towns from the clans of the tribes of Issachar, Asher, Naphtali and the half-tribe of Manasseh in Bashan.

[7]The descendants of Merari, clan by clan, received twelve towns from the tribes of Reuben, Gad and Zebulun.

[8]So the Israelites allotted to the Levites these towns and their pasturelands, as the LORD had commanded through Moses.

[9]From the tribes of Judah and Simeon they allotted the following towns by name [10](these towns were assigned to the descendants of Aaron who were from the Kohathite clans of the Levites, because the first lot fell to them):

> [11]They gave them Kiriath Arba (that is, Hebron), with its surrounding pastureland, in the hill country of Judah. (Arba was the forefather of Anak.) [12]But the fields and villages around the city they had given to Caleb son of Jephunneh as his possession.
>
> [13]So to the descendants of Aaron the priest they gave Hebron (a city of refuge for one accused of murder), Libnah, [14]Jattir, Eshtemoa, [15]Holon, Debir, [16]Ain, Juttah and Beth

---

[a]**8** *Jordan of Jericho* was possibly an ancient name for the Jordan River.

20:2 *cities of refuge:* God tells Moses about the cities of refuge in Numbers 35:6-15; Moses tells Israel about the cities of refuge in Deuteronomy 4:41-43; 19:1-13. See the mini-article called "Cities of Refuge," p. 444. All six of these cities belong to the Levites.

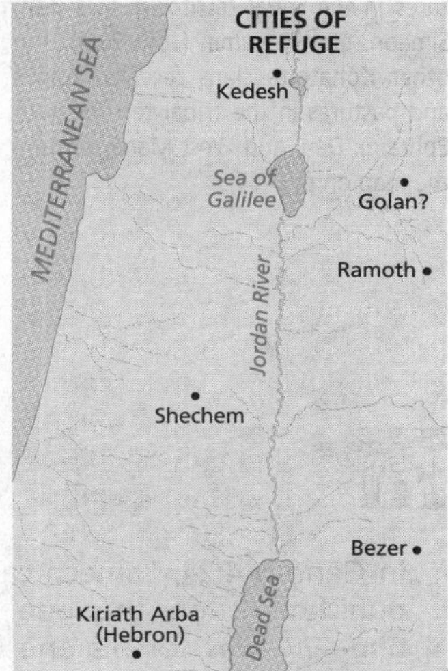

20:9 *alien:* The cities provided protection for foreigners as well.

21:1,2 *Levites . . . give us towns:* See the note at 13:14. The Levites were given forty-eight towns (21:41,42) with pasturelands by the other tribes. This division of the land ensured that the priests were scattered among the tribes. The actual selection of the Levite towns was determined by casting lots (18:6). See the note at 14:1 for Eleazar. See also Num 35:1-8.

21:4-7 *Kohathites . . . Gershon . . . Merari:* Names of the three major clans of the tribe of Levi. See Num 4:1-33. Although Gershon was Levi's oldest son, the Kohath clan gets the most towns, most likely because Israel's first high priest, Aaron, was a member of this clan (see Exod 6:16-20).

21:11 *Hebron:* Hebron was given to Caleb (14:13-15). For more about Anak, see the note at 11:21.

21:20 *Kohathite clans of the Levites:* The Kohathites took care of the sacred objects in the tabernacle (see Exod 25:10-40; 30:1-10). See also Num 4:1-20. The Kohathite clans that descended from Aaron, Israel's first high priest, were given towns and pastures in the tribal territories of Judah, Simeon, and Benjamin (Josh 21:4). The other Kohathite clans received towns and pastures in the tribal territories of Ephraim, Dan, and West Manasseh (see the map on p. 2464).

Shemesh, together with their pasturelands—nine towns from
these two tribes.
17 And from the tribe of Benjamin they gave them Gibeon,
Geba, 18 Anathoth and Almon, together with their pasturelands—four towns.
19 All the towns for the priests, the descendants of Aaron, were thirteen, together with their pasturelands.
20 The rest of the Kohathite clans of the Levites were allotted towns
from the tribe of Ephraim:
21 In the hill country of Ephraim they were given Shechem
(a city of refuge for one accused of murder) and Gezer,
22 Kibzaim and Beth Horon, together with their pasturelands—four towns.

CITIES OF REFUGE

In Genesis 4:24, Lamech called for a severe punishment on the one who might kill him—77 lives for his one life. However, in cases of serious injury, the Law of Moses called for "eye for eye, tooth for tooth"—even "life for life" (Exod 21:23-25; Lev 24:18). The earliest Hebrew tradition says the punishment must fit the crime, putting an end to the age-old practice of blood feuds. The clan could appoint a close male relative to find and kill a person who had killed a member of their clan (Num 35:16-19).

Early laws also provided places of safety, which were off limits to any avenging family members. The accused could expect to be protected by holding on to the Lord's altar (Exod 21:13, 14), provided the killing was not committed in anger or planned in advance.

With the conquest of Canaan, the Israelites were able to set aside cities of refuge, which provided more protection than one altar could. The cities of refuge sheltered a person who had accidentally caused a death. Accused people were given refuge until their cases could be tried. In the city of refuge, they were safe from angry family members seeking "eye for eye, life for life."

First, the accused would approach the city gate (Josh 20:3, 4), the place for a preliminary hearing by the elders. The gates, standing more than one story tall, had enclosed rooms where the town leaders would hear the case. If the elders approved, the person would then be allowed to stay in the city until a public hearing could be held, with the citizens of the town acting as a sort of jury (Josh 20:6).

Careful attention was paid to the intentions of the accused. If the cause of death was an accident (Deut 19:4-6), the accused could not be convicted of murder. However, if hatred was involved, the accused was guilty of murder and the citizens of the city of refuge were to let the victim's relatives kill the murderer (Num 35:16-21; Deut 19:11-13). The message is this: Show no mercy to a murderer, but do all you can to protect the accused until means and motive can be established.

The accused person, if found innocent of hatred or intention to kill, stayed in the city of refuge throughout the lifetime of the high priest (Josh 20:6). This gave time for tempers to cool. When the present high priest died, the accused could eventually go back home without fear of revenge from the victim's family.

23 Also from the tribe of Dan they received Eltekeh, Gibbethon,
24 Aijalon and Gath Rimmon, together with their pasturelands—
four towns.
25 From half the tribe of Manasseh they received Taanach
and Gath Rimmon, together with their pasturelands—two
towns.
26 All these ten towns and their pasturelands were given to the rest
of the Kohathite clans.

27 The Levite clans of the Gershonites were given:
from the half-tribe of Manasseh,
Golan in Bashan (a city of refuge for one accused of murder)
and Be Eshtarah, together with their pasturelands—two
towns;
28 from the tribe of Issachar,
Kishion, Daberath, 29 Jarmuth and En Gannim, together with
their pasturelands—four towns;
30 from the tribe of Asher,
Mishal, Abdon, 31 Helkath and Rehob, together with their pasturelands—four towns;
32 from the tribe of Naphtali,
Kedesh in Galilee (a city of refuge for one accused of murder),
Hammoth Dor and Kartan, together with their pasturelands—three towns.
33 All the towns of the Gershonite clans were thirteen, together with
their pasturelands.

34 The Merarite clans (the rest of the Levites) were given:
from the tribe of Zebulun,
Jokneam, Kartah, 35 Dimnah and Nahalal, together with their
pasturelands—four towns;
36 from the tribe of Reuben,
Bezer, Jahaz, 37 Kedemoth and Mephaath, together with their
pasturelands—four towns;
38 from the tribe of Gad,
Ramoth in Gilead (a city of refuge for one accused of murder), Mahanaim, 39 Heshbon and Jazer, together with their pasturelands—four towns in all.
40 All the towns allotted to the Merarite clans, who were the rest of
the Levites, were twelve.
41 The towns of the Levites in the territory held by the
Israelites were forty-eight in all, together with their pasturelands.
42 Each of these towns had pasturelands surrounding it; this was
true for all these towns.

43 So the LORD gave Israel all the land he had sworn to give
their forefathers, and they took possession of it and settled there.
44 The LORD gave them rest on every side, just as he had sworn to
their forefathers. Not one of their enemies withstood them; the

So the LORD gave Israel all the land he had sworn to give their forefathers, and they took possession of it and settled there.
Josh 21:43

21:27 *clans of the Gershonites:* This clan was in charge of setting up and taking down the tabernacle's covering and curtains, except the curtain in front of the Most Holy Place (Num 4:21-28). The Gershonite towns and pastures were in the tribal territories of East Manasseh, Issachar, Asher, and Naphtali (see the map on p. 2464).

21:34 *Merarite clans:* The Merarites were responsible for setting up and taking down the framework that held the tabernacle together (Num 4:29-33). They also carried these objects when the Israelite tribes moved to a new location. The Merarite towns and pastures were in the tribal territories of Zebulun, Reuben, and Gad (see the map on p. 2464).

21:41,42 *forty-eight in all:* This is an ideal number, consisting of four cities in each of the twelve tribes.

21:43-45 *the LORD gave . . . every one was fulfilled:* This summary of the conquest emphasizes the LORD's role in helping Israel capture and settle Canaan. This fulfilled the ancient promises made to Israel (see the note at 1:6-8). Though Israel had settled in the land, the enemies around them were not yet completely under Israel's control. Battles continue off and on for many years.

LORD handed all their enemies over to them. [45]Not one of all the
LORD's good promises to the house of Israel failed; every one was
fulfilled.

Eastern Tribes Return Home

22 Then Joshua summoned the Reubenites, the Gadites and the
half-tribe of Manasseh [2]and said to them, "You have done all that
Moses the servant of the LORD commanded, and you have obeyed
me in everything I commanded. [3]For a long time now—to this
very day—you have not deserted your brothers but have carried
out the mission the LORD your God gave you. [4]Now that the LORD
your God has given your brothers rest as he promised, return to
your homes in the land that Moses the servant of the LORD gave
you on the other side of the Jordan. [5]But be very careful to keep
the commandment and the law that Moses the servant of the LORD
gave you: to love the LORD your God, to walk in all his ways, to
obey his commands, to hold fast to him and to serve him with all
your heart and all your soul."

[6]Then Joshua blessed them and sent them away, and they
went to their homes. [7](To the half-tribe of Manasseh Moses had
given land in Bashan, and to the other half of the tribe Joshua gave
land on the west side of the Jordan with their brothers.) When
Joshua sent them home, he blessed them, [8]saying, "Return to your
homes with your great wealth—with large herds of livestock, with
silver, gold, bronze and iron, and a great quantity of clothing—and
divide with your brothers the plunder from your enemies."

[9]So the Reubenites, the Gadites and the half-tribe of Manasseh left the Israelites at Shiloh in Canaan to return to Gilead,
their own land, which they had acquired in accordance with the
command of the LORD through Moses.

[10]When they came to Geliloth near the Jordan in the land of
Canaan, the Reubenites, the Gadites and the half-tribe of Manasseh
built an imposing altar there by the Jordan. [11]And when the
Israelites heard that they had built the altar on the border of
Canaan at Geliloth near the Jordan on the Israelite side, [12]the whole
assembly of Israel gathered at Shiloh to go to war against them.

[13]So the Israelites sent Phinehas son of Eleazar, the priest, to
the land of Gilead—to Reuben, Gad and the half-tribe of Manasseh. [14]With him they sent ten of the chief men, one for each of
the tribes of Israel, each the head of a family division among the
Israelite clans.

[15]When they went to Gilead—to Reuben, Gad and the half-
tribe of Manasseh—they said to them: [16]"The whole assembly of
the LORD says: 'How could you break faith with the God of Israel
like this? How could you turn away from the LORD and build yourselves an altar in rebellion against him now? [17]Was not the sin of
Peor enough for us? Up to this very day we have not cleansed our-

Joshua said, *"Be very careful to keep the commandment and the law that Moses the servant of the LORD gave you: to love the LORD your God, to walk in all his ways, to obey his commands, to hold fast to him and to serve him with all your heart and all your soul."*
Josh 22:5

22:1 *Reubenites, the Gadites and the half-tribe of Manasseh:* See the notes at 1:12 and 14:1-5. Joshua is addressing the specially trained army of these two-and-a-half tribes. Their homes and families on the east side of the Jordan River await their return.

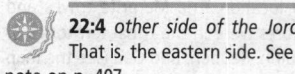

22:4 *other side of the Jordan:* That is, the eastern side. See the note on p. 407.

22:6-8 *great wealth . . . divide with your brothers:* Reuben, Gad, and the half-tribe of Manasseh have fulfilled their obligations to help; now they can return home. They go back with a share of the things taken from those they had conquered. See also Num 31:25-27; 1 Sam 30:22-25.

22:9 *Shiloh:* See the note at 18:1.

22:10-12 *imposing altar . . . go to war:* According to Deuteronomy 12:5, the LORD wanted the Israelites to have only one altar for offering sacrifices. To build another altar would have been to disobey the LORD. When the other tribes heard that the eastern tribes had built their own altar, they prepared to go to war.

22:2,3 Num 32:20-32; Josh 1:12-15. **22:16** Deut 12:5-19.

selves from that sin, even though a plague fell on the community
of the LORD! [18]And are you now turning away from the LORD?
" 'If you rebel against the LORD today, tomorrow he will be
angry with the whole community of Israel. [19]If the land you possess is defiled, come over to the LORD's land, where the LORD's
tabernacle stands, and share the land with us. But do not rebel
against the LORD or against us by building an altar for yourselves,
other than the altar of the LORD our God. [20]When Achan son of
Zerah acted unfaithfully regarding the devoted things,[a] did not
wrath come upon the whole community of Israel? He was not the
only one who died for his sin.' "
[21]Then Reuben, Gad and the half-tribe of Manasseh replied to
the heads of the clans of Israel: [22]"The Mighty One, God, the LORD!
The Mighty One, God, the LORD! He knows! And let Israel know! If
this has been in rebellion or disobedience to the LORD, do not spare
us this day. [23]If we have built our own altar to turn away from the
LORD and to offer burnt offerings and grain offerings, or to sacrifice
fellowship offerings[b] on it, may the LORD himself call us to account.
[24]"No! We did it for fear that some day your descendants might
say to ours, 'What do you have to do with the LORD, the God of
Israel? [25]The LORD has made the Jordan a boundary between us and
you—you Reubenites and Gadites! You have no share in the LORD.' So
your descendants might cause ours to stop fearing the LORD.
[26]"That is why we said, 'Let us get ready and build an altar—
but not for burnt offerings or sacrifices.' [27]On the contrary, it is to
be a witness between us and you and the generations that follow,
that we will worship the LORD at his sanctuary with our burnt
offerings, sacrifices and fellowship offerings. Then in the future
your descendants will not be able to say to ours, 'You have no share
in the LORD.'
[28]"And we said, 'If they ever say this to us, or to our descendants, we will answer: Look at the replica of the LORD's altar, which
our fathers built, not for burnt offerings and sacrifices, but as a
witness between us and you.'
[29]"Far be it from us to rebel against the LORD and turn away
from him today by building an altar for burnt offerings, grain
offerings and sacrifices, other than the altar of the LORD our God
that stands before his tabernacle."
[30]When Phinehas the priest and the leaders of the community—the heads of the clans of the Israelites—heard what Reuben,
Gad and Manasseh had to say, they were pleased. [31]And Phinehas
son of Eleazar, the priest, said to Reuben, Gad and Manasseh,
"Today we know that the LORD is with us, because you have not

[a]**20** The Hebrew term refers to the irrevocable giving over of things or persons to the LORD, often by totally destroying them. [b]**23** Traditionally *peace offerings*; also in verse 27

22:13 *Phinehas:* The eagerness of Phinehas is first seen in Numbers 25:6-13. He is grandson of Aaron and son of Eleazar, the high priest during the conquest. This is the first time he is mentioned in JOSHUA.

22:17 *the sin of Peor:* At the time of the wanderings in the desert, the Israelites worshiped the Moabite gods and the Canaanite god Baal of Peor at Shittim. Phinehas's fierce, swift action stopped the deadly disease sent by the LORD as a punishment (Num 25).

22:20 *Achan:* The leaders accuse the two-and-a-half tribes of rebelling against the LORD (22:16), just as Achan had disobeyed his command (7:1-26). The sin of an individual reflects on the entire people. The leaders' argument is this: If one individual (Achan) could bring tragedy on the whole nation, how much more suffering will the sin of these tribes cause?

22:24 *We did it for fear:* The east Jordan tribes explain their action. They fear that at some future time, the tribes in western Palestine might disown them. So, they set up the altar, not for sacrifices (22:23), but as a sign of their unity with the rest of Israel.

22:26 *not for burnt offerings or sacrifices:* See the note at 8:31 (burnt offerings).

22:27 *his sanctuary:* At this time, the tabernacle was portable, and so was the altar used for sacrifices (see Exod 25:1—27:8; Num 4:1-33). The tabernacle was set up at Shiloh, west of the Jordan River. The issue here is that only one place for sacrifices is commanded by Moses (Deuteronomy 12:5-19). The eastern tribes insist they have not built an altar for sacrifices, but as a memorial. These verses provide evidence of conflict and a potential feud between the tribes east of the Jordan and the tribes west of the Jordan.

Joshua told the people, *"It was the* LORD *your God who fought for you."* Josh 23:3

22:33 *talked no more . . . war:* The explosive situation is calmed and the crisis passes.

23:1,2 *Joshua . . . summoned all Israel:* The place is not known. This is not the same assembly as in chapter 24. Joshua's speech here is a fitting conclusion to the book, balancing the material in 1:1-9 and drawing together the themes first raised at the beginning of the book. For other farewell speeches, see Moses' speech in Deuteronomy 29–31, Samuel's in 1 Samuel 12, and David's in 1 Kings 2:1-9.

23:4 *I have allotted as an inheritance:* While the land is not entirely theirs (13:1-7), it has been given out to the tribes (chapters 13–21). It is up to the tribes to settle the land, which will entirely become theirs, if they are obedient to the LORD.

23:6 *Book of the Law of Moses:* See the note at 1:6-8.

23:10 *the* LORD *your God fights for you:* See the note at 10:14.

23:3 Josh 2:9-11; 4:22-24; 10:14, 42,43. **23:7** Exod 23:13. **23:10** Deut 3:22; 32:30.

acted unfaithfully toward the LORD in this matter. Now you have
rescued the Israelites from the LORD's hand."
32Then Phinehas son of Eleazar, the priest, and the leaders
returned to Canaan from their meeting with the Reubenites and
Gadites in Gilead and reported to the Israelites. 33They were glad
to hear the report and praised God. And they talked no more
about going to war against them to devastate the country where
the Reubenites and the Gadites lived.
34And the Reubenites and the Gadites gave the altar this
name: A Witness Between Us that the LORD is God.

The Last Days of Joshua

The story of the conquest concludes. Joshua has successfully led the tribes through this crucial period in their history. It is time for him to say farewell and for the people to declare their loyalty to their covenant with the LORD. *Joshua urges the people to remain faithful to the* LORD. *The final scene in the book tells of the burial of Joshua.*

JOSHUA'S FAREWELL ADDRESS

Now at a ripe old age, Joshua reviews the terms of the covenant God made with the people of Israel.

Joshua's Farewell to the Leaders

23 After a long time had passed and the LORD had given Israel
rest from all their enemies around them, Joshua, by then old and
well advanced in years, 2summoned all Israel—their elders, leaders,
judges and officials—and said to them: "I am old and well
advanced in years. 3You yourselves have seen everything the LORD
your God has done to all these nations for your sake; it was the
LORD your God who fought for you. 4Remember how I have allotted as an inheritance for your tribes all the land of the nations that
remain—the nations I conquered—between the Jordan and the
Great Sea[a] in the west. 5The LORD your God himself will drive them
out of your way. He will push them out before you, and you will
take possession of their land, as the LORD your God promised you.
6"Be very strong; be careful to obey all that is written in the
Book of the Law of Moses, without turning aside to the right or to
the left. 7Do not associate with these nations that remain among
you; do not invoke the names of their gods or swear by them. You
must not serve them or bow down to them. 8But you are to hold
fast to the LORD your God, as you have until now.
9"The LORD has driven out before you great and powerful
nations; to this day no one has been able to withstand you. 10One of

[a]**4** That is, the Mediterranean

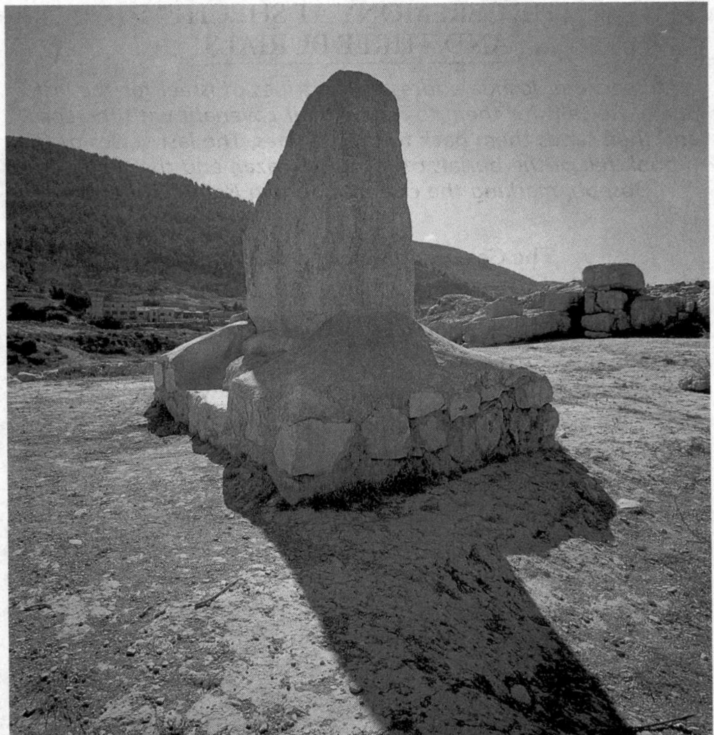

Altar at Shechem, Israel. The LORD first appeared to Abraham at Shechem and told him this was the land he and his descendants would inherit. Abraham built an altar there. Later, Jacob, Abraham's grandson, dug a well at the same site. (See 24:25-27.)

you routs a thousand, because the LORD your God fights for you,
just as he promised. [11]So be very careful to love the LORD your God.
[12]"But if you turn away and ally yourselves with the survivors of these nations that remain among you and if you intermarry with them and associate with them, [13]then you may be sure
that the LORD your God will no longer drive out these nations
before you. Instead, they will become snares and traps for you,
whips on your backs and thorns in your eyes, until you perish
from this good land, which the LORD your God has given you.
[14]"Now I am about to go the way of all the earth. You know
with all your heart and soul that not one of all the good promises
the LORD your God gave you has failed. Every promise has been fulfilled; not one has failed. [15]But just as every good promise of the
LORD your God has come true, so the LORD will bring on you all the
evil he has threatened, until he has destroyed you from this good
land he has given you. [16]If you violate the covenant of the LORD
your God, which he commanded you, and go and serve other gods
and bow down to them, the LORD's anger will burn against you, and
you will quickly perish from the good land he has given you."

23:11,12 *love the LORD . . . if you turn away:* This teaching, indeed the entire farewell address, closely follows Moses' speech in Deuteronomy 6,7. For verse 11, see Deut 6:5. On marriage with foreigners, see Deut 7:1-4. This is a significant warning which recognizes that intermarriage can cause divided loyalties. See the mini-article called "Foreigners (Aliens)," p. 501.

23:13 *snares and traps . . . thorns:* Foreign nations are described here as a source of constant trouble, as in Judges 2:3. The biggest danger is that the people of Israel will lose the land that they have begun to settle. This view of foreigners contrasts sharply with the message of RUTH and with God's plan for Israel as reported in Isaiah 49:6; 51:4,5; 55:5; 56:6-8. God is warning the people that they are to be influences for him, and not be influenced by the foreigners and their gods.

23:16 *violate the covenant:* The covenant is based on the Book of the Law of Moses and calls for being faithful to the LORD and not worshiping other gods (Josh 23:6). See also Deut 11:26-32; 28:1-68; and the mini-article called "Covenants (Agreements)," p. 386.

24:1 *Shechem:* This town in central Canaan was the site of a sacred tree during the time of Abraham (Gen 12:6) and an altar built by Jacob (Gen 33:18-20). See also the note at 8:33-35 (Mount Gerizim).

24:2 *the River:* Referring to the Euphrates River. Israel's ancestor Abraham lived in Mesopotamia by the Euphrates River before the LORD told him to go to Canaan (Gen 11:26-28). See also the map on p. 2462.

24:4 *hill country of Seir to Esau:* Esau and his descendants lived in Seir (also called Edom), the highlands southwest of the Dead Sea (Gen 32:3). See the map on p. 2463.

24:5 *I afflicted the Egyptians:* This refers to the plagues God sent upon Egypt when Pharaoh would not release the Hebrew people from slavery. See the mini-article called "Disasters (Plagues)," p. 151.

24:7 *you lived in the desert:* This summary of the history of God's saving acts follows the biblical record and Deuteronomy 26:5-11, but does not mention the events at Mount Sinai or the desert wanderings (Exod 15:22—40:38; Num 1–20).

24:9 *Balak . . . Balaam:* See the note at 13:22.

24:11,12 *crossed the Jordan . . . drove them out before you:* This is a summary of Joshua 1–12. For crossing the Jordan, see 3:14-17.

24:11 *Amorites . . . Jebusites:* See the note at 3:10.

24:12 *the two Amorite kings:* This refers to Sihon and Og (see the note at 2:10, Sihon and Og).

24:3 Gen 12:1-9; 21:1-3. **24:4** Gen 25:24-26; 36:8; 46:1-7; Deut 2:5. **24:5-7** Exod 3:1—12:42; 14:1-31. **24:8** Num 21:21-35. **24:12** Exod 23:28; Deut 7:20. **24:13** Deut 6:10,11.

THE CEREMONY AT SHECHEM AND THREE BURIALS

At Shechem, Joshua addresses the tribes of Israel for the last time. He calls for them to renew their covenant with the LORD and then sends them back to their homes. The last verses of the book tell of the burials of Joshua, Eleazar, and the bones of Joseph, marking the end of an era in Israelite history.

The Covenant Renewed at Shechem

24 Then Joshua assembled all the tribes of Israel at Shechem.
He summoned the elders, leaders, judges and officials of Israel, and
they presented themselves before God.
2 Joshua said to all the people, "This is what the LORD, the
God of Israel, says: 'Long ago your forefathers, including Terah the
father of Abraham and Nahor, lived beyond the River[a] and worshiped other gods. 3 But I took your father Abraham from the land
beyond the River and led him throughout Canaan and gave him
many descendants. I gave him Isaac, 4 and to Isaac I gave Jacob and
Esau. I assigned the hill country of Seir to Esau, but Jacob and his
sons went down to Egypt.
5 " 'Then I sent Moses and Aaron, and I afflicted the Egyptians by what I did there, and I brought you out. 6 When I brought
your fathers out of Egypt, you came to the sea, and the Egyptians
pursued them with chariots and horsemen[b] as far as the Red Sea.[c]
7 But they cried to the LORD for help, and he put darkness between
you and the Egyptians; he brought the sea over them and covered
them. You saw with your own eyes what I did to the Egyptians.
Then you lived in the desert for a long time.
8 " 'I brought you to the land of the Amorites who lived east
of the Jordan. They fought against you, but I gave them into your
hands. I destroyed them from before you, and you took possession
of their land. 9 When Balak son of Zippor, the king of Moab, prepared to fight against Israel, he sent for Balaam son of Beor to put
a curse on you. 10 But I would not listen to Balaam, so he blessed
you again and again, and I delivered you out of his hand.
11 " 'Then you crossed the Jordan and came to Jericho. The
citizens of Jericho fought against you, as did also the Amorites,
Perizzites, Canaanites, Hittites, Girgashites, Hivites and Jebusites,
but I gave them into your hands. 12 I sent the hornet ahead of you,
which drove them out before you—also the two Amorite kings.
You did not do it with your own sword and bow. 13 So I gave you a
land on which you did not toil and cities you did not build; and
you live in them and eat from vineyards and olive groves that you
did not plant.'

[a]**2** That is, the Euphrates; also in verses 3, 14 and 15 [b]**6** Or *charioteers*
[c]**6** Hebrew *Yam Suph*; that is, Sea of Reeds

14“Now fear the LORD and serve him with all faithfulness.
Throw away the gods your forefathers worshiped beyond the River
and in Egypt, and serve the LORD. 15But if serving the LORD seems
undesirable to you, then choose for yourselves this day whom you
will serve, whether the gods your forefathers served beyond the
River, or the gods of the Amorites, in whose land you are living.
But as for me and my household, we will serve the LORD.”
16Then the people answered, “Far be it from us to forsake the
LORD to serve other gods! 17It was the LORD our God himself who
brought us and our fathers up out of Egypt, from that land of slavery, and performed those great signs before our eyes. He protected
us on our entire journey and among all the nations through which
we traveled. 18And the LORD drove out before us all the nations,
including the Amorites, who lived in the land. We too will serve
the LORD, because he is our God.”
19Joshua said to the people, “You are not able to serve the
LORD. He is a holy God; he is a jealous God. He will not forgive
your rebellion and your sins. 20If you forsake the LORD and serve
foreign gods, he will turn and bring disaster on you and make an
end of you, after he has been good to you.”
21But the people said to Joshua, “No! We will serve the
LORD.”
22Then Joshua said, “You are witnesses against yourselves
that you have chosen to serve the LORD.”
“Yes, we are witnesses,” they replied.
23“Now then,” said Joshua, “throw away the foreign gods that
are among you and yield your hearts to the LORD, the God of Israel.”
24And the people said to Joshua, “We will serve the LORD our
God and obey him.”

24:14 *Throw away the gods:* Joshua's speech provided an opportunity for the Israelites who had been living according to the Law of Moses (see the note at 1:6-8) to rededicate themselves to worshiping the LORD. Others who had been taken into the people of Israel during the time of settlement were also challenged to "choose for yourselves this day" whether to worship the LORD or keep worshiping their other gods. In Egypt the people had worshiped the gold bull-calf representing the fertility god Apis. The gods of Mesopotamia beyond the Euphrates River included Marduk, the chief god of Babylon, and Bel, who was similar to the Canaanite fertility god Baal.

24:17,18 *from that land of slavery . . . drove out before us:* The events described in 24:17 are retold in EXODUS and NUMBERS. For the defeat of the Amorites, see Numbers 21:21-32.

24:18 *serve the LORD:* Joshua challenges the people and warns them that breaking their covenant with the LORD will lead to terrible things, including their destruction as a nation. The covenant calls for their discipline and devotion.

24:23 *throw away the foreign gods:* The Israelites did not destroy all the sacred places where Canaanite gods were worshiped. Some Israelites even joined in the rituals honoring these gods (Hos 4:12-19).

QUESTIONS ABOUT JOSHUA 13:1—24:33

1. Why were the Levites singled out as special among the twelve tribes? (13:14,33) How did their special duties affect where they lived when Canaan was settled by Israel? (21:1-42)
2. What was the purpose of the cities of refuge? (20:1-6) What does their existence reveal about the relationship of punishment and justice in Israelite society?
3. Re-read Joshua's farewell speech (23:1-16). What were his key points? What were his instructions concerning how the Israelites were to live in relationship to the other people in the land? Would Joshua's advice work in today's world? Why or why not?
4. Why did Joshua call the Israelites together at Shechem? (24:1-27) What did he ask them to do? What does Joshua's speech reveal about what God is like?
5. Name two things you learned from studying JOSHUA.

24:25 *made a covenant:* For an earlier ceremony, see Exodus 24:3-8. The covenant in Joshua 24 is patterned on treaties made in ancient times.

24:26 *the Book of the Law of God:* See the note at 1:6-8.

24:27 *stone:* Witnesses were required to make a treaty official. Here, the witness is a sacred stone at the worship site.

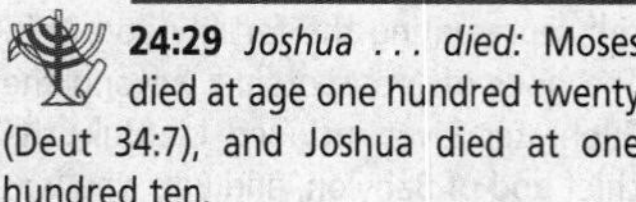

24:29 *Joshua . . . died:* Moses died at age one hundred twenty (Deut 34:7), and Joshua died at one hundred ten.

24:32 *Joseph's bones . . . Jacob:* It was Joseph's last wish to be buried in the field his father had bought (Gen 33:19; 50:24,25; Exod 13:19).

24:33 *Eleazar:* See the note at 14:1. The death of these leaders marks the end of an era of faithfulness (24:31; see also Judg 2:10-15).

24:32 John 4:5; Acts 7:16.

25 On that day Joshua made a covenant for the people, and
there at Shechem he drew up for them decrees and laws. 26 And
Joshua recorded these things in the Book of the Law of God. Then
he took a large stone and set it up there under the oak near the
holy place of the LORD.
27 "See!" he said to all the people. "This stone will be a witness against us. It has heard all the words the LORD has said to us.
It will be a witness against you if you are untrue to your God."

Buried in the Promised Land

28 Then Joshua sent the people away, each to his own
inheritance.
29 After these things, Joshua son of Nun, the servant of the
LORD, died at the age of a hundred and ten. 30 And they buried him
in the land of his inheritance, at Timnath Serah[a] in the hill country of Ephraim, north of Mount Gaash.
31 Israel served the LORD throughout the lifetime of Joshua
and of the elders who outlived him and who had experienced
everything the LORD had done for Israel.
32 And Joseph's bones, which the Israelites had brought up
from Egypt, were buried at Shechem in the tract of land that Jacob
bought for a hundred pieces of silver[b] from the sons of Hamor, the
father of Shechem. This became the inheritance of Joseph's descendants.
33 And Eleazar son of Aaron died and was buried at Gibeah,
which had been allotted to his son Phinehas in the hill country of
Ephraim.

---

[a]**30** Also known as *Timnath Heres* (see Judges 2:9) [b]**32** Hebrew *hundred kesitahs*; a kesitah was a unit of money of unknown weight and value.

JUDGES

Who were the "judges" of Israel, and how did God use them? Read JUDGES to find out.

WHAT MAKES JUDGES SPECIAL?

JUDGES is part of the great story, from DEUTERONOMY through 2 KINGS, that tells of God's special people, the Israelites, in the promised land of Canaan. JUDGES describes the time after the tribes of Israel began to settle in Canaan but before they were united as one nation under a king. It was during this time that the LORD chose special leaders known as "judges" to help the tribes defeat their enemies. Some judges may have led all the tribes together, but usually a judge led a few tribes at the most. The stories about these heroes of Israel make up the largest part of JUDGES.

WHY WAS JUDGES WRITTEN?

In order for the people of Israel to survive as a nation, they had to obey God's Law and worship the LORD God only. If they did this, they would remain in the land of Canaan and receive the LORD's blessings (Deut 7:1-16). But if the people worshiped other gods, the LORD would allow their enemies to defeat them (2:1-3).

The Israelites did not show a strong and lasting commitment to the covenant they had made with the LORD. JUDGES describes how the behavior of the people of Israel followed a pattern:

1. The people disobeyed the LORD and worshiped other gods;
2. the LORD allowed Israel's enemies to oppress them;
3. the people cried out in distress to the LORD;
4. the LORD chose a deliverer, or "judge," to lead the people in battle against their enemies; and
5. when a judge would die, the cycle would begin again.

So, the conquest of Canaan was a power struggle told on two levels: The Israelite tribes and the native peoples battled for control of the land, while the faith of Israel was severely tested by the religions of its neighbors. The people had to learn that they were to worship only the LORD, and that when they were unfaithful, the LORD would punish them. But the book also shows that the LORD was ready and willing to offer the Israelite people the opportunity for a fresh start. Even though they often abandoned the LORD, the LORD did not give up on them.

WHAT'S THE STORY BEHIND THE SCENE?

The period of the judges starts with the death of Joshua around 1200 B.C. and continues at least until Samuel, the last of the judges, anoints Saul as the first king of Israel in about 1030 B.C. (1 Sam 12). Israel at this time was a loosely bound group of

Israelites, Canaanites, and Perizzites: The Israelites were the chosen people of God (Deut 7:6-8). They had been led out of slavery in Egypt by Moses, who received the LORD's commandments and laws. After Moses died, Joshua led the people into Canaan, the land God promised to give the people. As JUDGES begins, Joshua has died and the tribes of Israel have not yet captured all of Canaan. See also the mini-article called "Israel," p. 264.

Judah was an important tribe of Israel that settled in southern Canaan. The tribe of Simeon was southwest of Judah and partially surrounded by it (see the map on p. 2464). The opening battle in JUDGES shows that the people of Israel did not have one united army. Tribes or groups of tribes battled the non-Israelite people living in the areas that Joshua had assigned to each of the tribes of Israel (see Josh 13–19).

The Canaanites and other peoples (Deut 7:1) lived in Canaan before the Israelites. The Israelites were to drive the Canaanite people out of the land so that the people of Israel would not be influenced by Canaanite customs or begin to worship Canaanite gods. For the land of Canaan, see the map on p. 2462.

The Perizzites may be named for a word that means "rustic," which may indicate that they lived in the open country, as opposed to the Canaanites who lived in walled cities.

Whenever the LORD raised up a judge for them, he was with the judge and saved them out of the hands of their enemies as long as the judge lived; for the LORD had compassion on them as they groaned under those who oppressed and afflicted them.
Judg 2:18

tribes rather than a single, united country. The judges would unite some or all of the people for a time, but the writer summarizes this time in Israel's history in this way: "everyone did as he saw fit" (21:25). Canaanite culture and religion remained a heavy influence that tempted the Israelites to disobey and forget God. But individuals and tribes of Israel also treated other individuals and tribes badly.

The judges who led Israel during this violent and unsettled time were not judges in a legal sense, although Deborah and Samuel did sometimes play a legal role. For more information, see the article called "From Joshua to the Exile: The People of Israel in the Promised Land," p. 924.

HOW IS JUDGES CONSTRUCTED?

JUDGES mainly consists of a series of independent stories that focus on the leaders (judges) that God raised up to rescue Israel's tribes (3:7—16:31). The actions of some of the judges are described in detail, while a few more "minor" judges are only briefly mentioned.

The opening two chapters set the stage for the stories of the judges, while the final chapters of the book (17–21) do not mention the judges at all. In the final chapters, the threat to Israel is not from outside enemies but from those inside Israel who continued to turn away from the LORD. The final chapters make it clear that Israel was suffering from a lack of leadership and from a lack of loyalty to the LORD. These chapters hint that Israel's problems might begin to be solved if a king could be chosen to rule over all the tribes.

The following summary is one way the book can be outlined:

Israel invades Canaan but turns away from the LORD (1:1—3:6)

The stories of Israel's chosen leaders, the judges (3:7—16:31)
- Othniel, Ehud, and Shamgar (3:7-31)
- Deborah (4:1—5:31)
- Gideon (6:1—8:35)
- Abimelech, Tola, and Jair (9:1—10:5)
- Jephthah, Ibzan, Elon, and Abdon (10:6—12:15)
- Samson (13:1—16:31)

Israel's troubled times continue (17:1—21:25)
- The tribe of Dan and their place of worship (17:1—18:31)
- The crime at Gibeah and civil war against the tribe of Benjamin (19:1—21:25)

Israel Invades Canaan but Turns Away from the LORD

Joshua has died, and the capture of the promised land is not complete. Israel's tribes try to drive out the Canaanites and Amorites with mixed success. Time passes and the Israelite people have no leader like Joshua who is faithful to the LORD. They begin to worship the gods of the Canaanites and other nearby nations (2:10-13). The LORD gets angry and allows neighboring nations to oppress the Israelites. But the LORD also promises to choose leaders (judges) to help Israel overcome its enemies.

Israel Fights the Remaining Canaanites

1 After the death of Joshua, the Israelites asked the LORD, "Who will be the first to go up and fight for us against the Canaanites?"

[2]The LORD answered, "Judah is to go; I have given the land into their hands."

[3]Then the men of Judah said to the Simeonites their brothers, "Come up with us into the territory allotted to us, to fight against the Canaanites. We in turn will go with you into yours." So the Simeonites went with them.

[4]When Judah attacked, the LORD gave the Canaanites and Perizzites into their hands and they struck down ten thousand men at Bezek. [5]It was there that they found Adoni-Bezek and fought against him, putting to rout the Canaanites and Perizzites. [6]Adoni-Bezek fled, but they chased him and caught him, and cut off his thumbs and big toes.

[7]Then Adoni-Bezek said, "Seventy kings with their thumbs and big toes cut off have picked up scraps under my table. Now God has paid me back for what I did to them." They brought him to Jerusalem, and he died there.

[8]The men of Judah attacked Jerusalem also and took it. They put the city to the sword and set it on fire.

[9]After that, the men of Judah went down to fight against the Canaanites living in the hill country, the Negev and the western foothills. [10]They advanced against the Canaanites living in Hebron (formerly called Kiriath Arba) and defeated Sheshai, Ahiman and Talmai.

[11]From there they advanced against the people living in Debir (formerly called Kiriath Sepher). [12]And Caleb said, "I will give my daughter Acsah in marriage to the man who attacks and captures Kiriath Sepher." [13]Othniel son of Kenaz, Caleb's younger brother, took it; so Caleb gave his daughter Acsah to him in marriage.

[14]One day when she came to Othniel, she urged him[a] to ask her father for a field. When she got off her donkey, Caleb asked her, "What can I do for you?"

---

[a]**14** Hebrew; Septuagint and Vulgate *Othniel, he urged her*

1:1 *Joshua:* As a youth, Joshua had been Moses' helper (Exod 24:13; 33:9-11; Num 11:28). Before Moses died, he laid his hands on Joshua and passed on to him the leadership of the twelve tribes of Israel (Num 27:12-23). Unlike Moses, Joshua did not appoint a leader to take his place when he died (Josh 24:29-31).

1:1-4 *Israelites . . . Canaanites . . . Judah . . . Simeonites . . . Perizzites:* See the note on p. 953.

1:4 *Bezek:* The location of Bezek is uncertain.

1:7 *Seventy . . . thumbs . . . big toes cut off:* Cutting off the thumbs and toes of a king made him an unfit military leader, because he could not hold a sword and no longer had good balance needed for hand-to-hand fighting. Seventy here is meant to symbolize a very large number. See the chart called "Numbers in the Bible," p. 2405.

1:8-11 *Jerusalem . . . Hebron . . . Debir:* Verse 8 probably refers to towns and villages in Judah's territory south of the Jerusalem city wall. Jerusalem itself was just inside Benjamin's territory and was not captured by Israel at this time (see 2:21; Josh 15:5-9; 18:15-18).

Hebron was south of Jerusalem in the southern highlands. It is listed as a Levite town in Joshua 21:13. The Negev was a desert area southwest of Hebron. The exact location of Debir is uncertain. See the map on p. 2464 for these locations.

1:12 *Caleb:* Caleb was one of the leaders of Judah. See Num 13:3-15, 30; 14:6, 24; Josh 14:6-14; 15:13-19.

15 She replied, "Do me a special favor. Since you have given
me land in the Negev, give me also springs of water." Then Caleb
gave her the upper and lower springs.
16 The descendants of Moses' father-in-law, the Kenite, went
up from the City of Palms[a] with the men of Judah to live among
the people of the Desert of Judah in the Negev near Arad.
17 Then the men of Judah went with the Simeonites their
brothers and attacked the Canaanites living in Zephath, and they
totally destroyed[b] the city. Therefore it was called Hormah.[c] 18 The
men of Judah also took[d] Gaza, Ashkelon and Ekron—each city
with its territory.

19 The LORD was with the men of Judah. They took possession of the hill country, but they were unable to drive the people
from the plains, because they had iron chariots. 20 As Moses had
promised, Hebron was given to Caleb, who drove from it the three
sons of Anak. 21 The Benjamites, however, failed to dislodge the
Jebusites, who were living in Jerusalem; to this day the Jebusites
live there with the Benjamites.
22 Now the house of Joseph attacked Bethel, and the LORD
was with them. 23 When they sent men to spy out Bethel (formerly
called Luz), 24 the spies saw a man coming out of the city and they
said to him, "Show us how to get into the city and we will see that
you are treated well." 25 So he showed them, and they put the city to
the sword but spared the man and his whole family. 26 He then
went to the land of the Hittites, where he built a city and called it
Luz, which is its name to this day.
27 But Manasseh did not drive out the people of Beth Shan or
Taanach or Dor or Ibleam or Megiddo and their surrounding settlements, for the Canaanites were determined to live in that land.
28 When Israel became strong, they pressed the Canaanites into
forced labor but never drove them out completely. 29 Nor did
Ephraim drive out the Canaanites living in Gezer, but the Canaanites continued to live there among them. 30 Neither did Zebulun
drive out the Canaanites living in Kitron or Nahalol, who remained
among them; but they did subject them to forced labor. 31 Nor did
Asher drive out those living in Acco or Sidon or Ahlab or Aczib or
Helbah or Aphek or Rehob, 32 and because of this the people of
Asher lived among the Canaanite inhabitants of the land. 33 Neither
did Naphtali drive out those living in Beth Shemesh or Beth Anath;
but the Naphtalites too lived among the Canaanite inhabitants of
the land, and those living in Beth Shemesh and Beth Anath became
forced laborers for them. 34 The Amorites confined the Danites to the
hill country, not allowing them to come down into the plain. 35 And
the Amorites were determined also to hold out in Mount Heres,

[a]16 That is, Jericho [b]17 The Hebrew term refers to the irrevocable giving over of things or persons to the LORD, often by totally destroying them. [c]17 *Hormah* means *destruction.* [d]18 Hebrew; Septuagint *Judah did not take*

1:16 *Kenite:* The Kenites lived in the northern part of the Sinai Peninsula, an area rich in copper mines. See also 1 Sam 15:6.

1:16 *City of Palms . . . Arad:* See the map on p. 2464. The City of Palms was another name for Jericho, an important city on the trade routes from the east. It was the first city the Israelites captured after crossing into Canaan (Josh 6). Arad was fifteen miles south of Hebron (see the note at 1:8-11).

1:17 *destroyed:* This word translates a term that means that the town was to be dedicated completely to the LORD and so no trace of any foreign gods would remain. See also the mini-article called "Holy War (The LORD's Battles),"p. 306.

1:18 *Gaza, Ashkelon and Ekron:* Three of the five main Philistine cities. The Philistines controlled the land along the Mediterranean coast and were often at war with Israel. Israel never controlled these cities. See the map on p. 2464.

1:20 *sons of Anak:* The descendants of Anak were very large people that lived in Canaan before the Israelites (Num 13:33; Deut 2:21).

1:22,23 *house of Joseph . . . Bethel:* The "house of Joseph" refers to the tribes of Ephraim and Manasseh, named for Joseph's two sons (Gen 48:1-19). Ephraim was one of Israel's most powerful tribes. Bethel was a holy place in central Canaan, about twelve miles north of Jerusalem. See the map on p. 2464.

1:24 *Show us . . . city:* The men were looking for some way to get past the wall that surrounded the city. Sometimes there were small doors in the wall that could be opened from the inside even when the main town gates were shut and locked. In some walled towns, small houses were built against the inside wall and one of its windows might face outside the wall (Josh 2:14-16). See also the note at 9:35.

Aijalon and Shaalbim, but when the power of the house of Joseph
increased, they too were pressed into forced labor. [36]The boundary
of the Amorites was from Scorpion[a] Pass to Sela and beyond.

The Angel of the LORD at Bokim

2 The angel of the LORD went up from Gilgal to Bokim and said,
"I brought you up out of Egypt and led you into the land that I
swore to give to your forefathers. I said, 'I will never break my
covenant with you, [2]and you shall not make a covenant with the
people of this land, but you shall break down their altars.' Yet you
have disobeyed me. Why have you done this? [3]Now therefore I tell
you that I will not drive them out before you; they will be ⌞thorns⌟
in your sides and their gods will be a snare to you."
[4]When the angel of the LORD had spoken these things to all
the Israelites, the people wept aloud, [5]and they called that place
Bokim.[b] There they offered sacrifices to the LORD.

Disobedience and Defeat

[6]After Joshua had dismissed the Israelites, they went to take
possession of the land, each to his own inheritance. [7]The people
served the LORD throughout the lifetime of Joshua and of the
elders who outlived him and who had seen all the great things the
LORD had done for Israel.
[8]Joshua son of Nun, the servant of the LORD, died at the age
of a hundred and ten. [9]And they buried him in the land of his
inheritance, at Timnath Heres[c] in the hill country of Ephraim,
north of Mount Gaash.
[10]After that whole generation had been gathered to their
fathers, another generation grew up, who knew neither the LORD
nor what he had done for Israel. [11]Then the Israelites did evil in
the eyes of the LORD and served the Baals. [12]They forsook the LORD,
the God of their fathers, who had brought them out of Egypt.
They followed and worshiped various gods of the peoples around
them. They provoked the LORD to anger [13]because they forsook
him and served Baal and the Ashtoreths. [14]In his anger against
Israel the LORD handed them over to raiders who plundered them.
He sold them to their enemies all around, whom they were no
longer able to resist. [15]Whenever Israel went out to fight, the hand
of the LORD was against them to defeat them, just as he had sworn
to them. They were in great distress.
[16]Then the LORD raised up judges,[d] who saved them out of
the hands of these raiders. [17]Yet they would not listen to their
judges but prostituted themselves to other gods and worshiped
them. Unlike their fathers, they quickly turned from the way in

[a]36 Hebrew *Akrabbim* [b]5 *Bokim* means *weepers.* [c]9 Also known as *Timnath Serah* (see Joshua 19:50 and 24:30) [d]16 Or *leaders*; similarly in verses 17-19

2:1 *angel of the LORD:* A supernatural being who tells God's messages to people. See also the mini-article called "Angels," p. 88.

2:1,2 *I will never break my covenant ... you have disobeyed:* See Exod 3:7, 8; 23:31-33; 34:12, 13; Deut 7:2-5. The Israelites broke their covenant with God and worshiped other gods (Num 25; Judg 2:11-13). See also the mini-article called "Covenants (Agreements)," p. 386.

2:5 *offered sacrifices:* Grain and animal sacrifices were offered to God in order to give thanks or to ask for God's help or forgiveness. See also the chart called "Sacrifices and Offerings," p. 219.

2:8 *Joshua:* See the note at 1:1. For more about the land Joshua chose for himself, see also Joshua 19: 49-51.

2:13 *served Baal and the Ashtoreths:* The Canaanites believed that Baal was the most powerful god. Ashtoreth (also called Asherah) was the Canaanite goddess of fertility. Those who worshiped her believed she could give them many children, abundant crops, and their animals lots of young. See also the mini-article called "Canaanite Gods and Goddesses," p. 469.

2:16 *LORD raised up judges:* These special leaders, called judges, became military leaders of their own tribe or several tribes. After defeating enemies, the judges governed until they died. In addition to leading Israelites in battle, many of these judges also decided legal cases and performed religious duties. See also the Introduction to JUDGES, p. 453.

2:17-19 *judge died, the people returned to ways even more corrupt:* The pattern described here repeats several times. The Israelites worship other gods; an enemy oppresses them; they pray to God for help; and God sends a judge to help deliver them from an enemy. See also 3:7-16; 4:1-3; 10:6-16.

> *Yet they would not listen to their judges but prostituted themselves to other gods and worshiped them. Unlike their fathers, they quickly turned from the way in which their fathers had walked, the way of obedience to the LORD's commands.*
> Judg 2:17

which their fathers had walked, the way of obedience to the LORD's
commands. [18]Whenever the LORD raised up a judge for them, he
was with the judge and saved them out of the hands of their enemies as long as the judge lived; for the LORD had compassion on
them as they groaned under those who oppressed and afflicted
them. [19]But when the judge died, the people returned to ways even
more corrupt than those of their fathers, following other gods and
serving and worshiping them. They refused to give up their evil
practices and stubborn ways.

[20]Therefore the LORD was very angry with Israel and said,
"Because this nation has violated the covenant that I laid down for
their forefathers and has not listened to me, [21]I will no longer drive
out before them any of the nations Joshua left when he died. [22]I
will use them to test Israel and see whether they will keep the way
of the LORD and walk in it as their forefathers did." [23]The LORD
had allowed those nations to remain; he did not drive them out at
once by giving them into the hands of Joshua.

3 These are the nations the LORD left to test all those Israelites
who had not experienced any of the wars in Canaan [2](he did this
only to teach warfare to the descendants of the Israelites who had
not had previous battle experience): [3]the five rulers of the
Philistines, all the Canaanites, the Sidonians, and the Hivites living in the Lebanon mountains from Mount Baal Hermon to Lebo[a]
Hamath. [4]They were left to test the Israelites to see whether they
would obey the LORD's commands, which he had given their forefathers through Moses.

[5]The Israelites lived among the Canaanites, Hittites, Amorites, Perizzites, Hivites and Jebusites. [6]They took their daughters
in marriage and gave their own daughters to their sons, and served
their gods. TOTAL DISOBEDIENCE

[a]3 Or *to the entrance to*

2:20—3:6 *violated the covenant . . . test Israel . . . served their gods:* Israel broke their covenant with the LORD by worshiping other gods (see 2:1,2 and 2:13 and the notes). These verses give three reasons why the Canaanites were still present in the promised land. Foreign peoples were left in Canaan as a test to see if the Israelites would hold to the terms of their covenant with the LORD (2:22). The second reason why enemies were still present is that each generation must learn how to defend itself against its enemies (3:1,2). The third reason is that Israelites had married them (3:6). Marrying these people caused divided loyalties, and in Israel's case, it led to the worship of foreign gods. See Deut 7:1-4.

QUESTIONS ABOUT JUDGES 1:1—3:6

1. In the first chapter of JUDGES, what is the situation for Israel's tribes in Canaan?
2. What promise had God made to Israel's ancestors regarding the land of Canaan? What did the Israelites promise to do in return? Why did the LORD stop helping Israel defeat its enemies? (2:1-3)
3. Why had Joshua been such an important leader for an earlier generation? What happened to Israel after Joshua died? (2:6-15)
4. What was the main role of Israel's judges? (2:16-19) How is this role different from or similar to what you might expect?
5. Why were many of Israel's enemies still in Canaan, even after the Israelites had invaded the land? (2:20—3:6)

The Stories of Israel's Chosen Leaders, the Judges

Israel's tribes sin against the LORD by worshiping idols. So, the LORD gets angry and lets neighboring nations oppress Israel. When the people cry for help, the LORD sends special leaders (judges) to help them defeat their enemies. The next fourteen chapters include the stories of these judges.

OTHNIEL, EHUD, AND SHAMGAR

Three brief stories are told of heroes who fight successfully against Israel's enemies.

Othniel

[7]The Israelites did evil in the eyes of the LORD; they forgot
the LORD their God and served the Baals and the Asherahs. [8]The
anger of the LORD burned against Israel so that he sold them into
the hands of Cushan-Rishathaim king of Aram Naharaim,[a] to
whom the Israelites were subject for eight years. [9]But when they
cried out to the LORD, he raised up for them a deliverer, Othniel
son of Kenaz, Caleb's younger brother, who saved them. [10]The
Spirit of the LORD came upon him, so that he became Israel's
judge[b] and went to war. The LORD gave Cushan-Rishathaim king
of Aram into the hands of Othniel, who overpowered him. [11]So the
land had peace for forty years, until Othniel son of Kenaz died.

Ehud

[12]Once again the Israelites did evil in the eyes of the LORD,
and because they did this evil the LORD gave Eglon king of Moab
power over Israel. [13]Getting the Ammonites and Amalekites to join
him, Eglon came and attacked Israel, and they took possession of
the City of Palms.[c] [14]The Israelites were subject to Eglon king of
Moab for eighteen years.
[15]Again the Israelites cried out to the LORD, and he gave them
a deliverer—Ehud, a left-handed man, the son of Gera the Benjamite. The Israelites sent him with tribute to Eglon king of Moab.
[16]Now Ehud had made a double-edged sword about a foot and a
half[d] long, which he strapped to his right thigh under his clothing.
[17]He presented the tribute to Eglon king of Moab, who was a very
fat man. [18]After Ehud had presented the tribute, he sent on their
way the men who had carried it. [19]At the idols[e] near Gilgal he himself turned back and said, "I have a secret message for you, O king."
The king said, "Quiet!" And all his attendants left him.
[20]Ehud then approached him while he was sitting alone in

[a]8 That is, Northwest Mesopotamia [b]10 Or *leader* [c]13 That is, Jericho
[d]16 Hebrew *a cubit* (about 0.5 meter) [e]19 Or *the stone quarries*; also in verse 26

3:7 *Baals . . . Asherahs:* See the note at 2:13.

3:8-10 *Cushan-Rishathaim . . . Othniel . . . Spirit of the LORD:* Cushan ruled in Northern Syria, also known as the land of the Arameans (see the map on p. 2465). Nothing else is known about this king.

Othniel is the hero of 1:13 and Joshua 15:17. The "Spirit" is the power of the LORD at work in the world. It is when the Spirit of the LORD takes control of him that Othniel becomes victorious. See also the mini-article called "Holy Spirit," p. 2082.

3:11 *peace for forty years:* Peace lasts for forty years here, in 5:31 and in 8:28. It lasts eighty (forty times two) years in 3:30. Forty is used symbolically here, representing a long period of time or about two generations. See the chart called "Numbers in the Bible," p. 2405.

3:12,13 *Moab . . . Ammonites . . . Amalekites . . . City of Palms:* For the location of Moab and Ammon, see the map on p. 2464. The Moabites and Ammonites were said to be the descendants of Lot's sons (Gen 19:30-38). Historically, both nations were enemies of Israel (Num 22:2-11; Judg 10:11-18; 1 Sam 14:47, 48; 2 Sam 8:2; 2 Kgs 3:21-27; Jer 48:1—49:6). The Amalekites were nomadic tribes who lived mostly in the area southeast of the Dead Sea. They were early enemies of Israel (Exod 17:8–14). The City of Palms is another name for Jericho (see the note at 1:16).

3:15 *Ehud . . . Benjamite:* Benjamites were descendants of Jacob's youngest son (Gen 35:16-18). For the land assigned to this tribe, see the map on p. 2464. An unusually high number of men from the Benjamin tribe, including Ehud, were left-handed (20:15, 16). Ehud could more easily grab the dagger from its hiding place on his right thigh because he was left-handed.

the upper room of his summer palace[a] and said, "I have a message
from God for you." As the king rose from his seat, 21 Ehud reached
with his left hand, drew the sword from his right thigh and
plunged it into the king's belly. 22 Even the handle sank in after the
blade, which came out his back. Ehud did not pull the sword out,
and the fat closed in over it. 23 Then Ehud went out to the porch[b];
he shut the doors of the upper room behind him and locked them.
24 After he had gone, the servants came and found the doors
of the upper room locked. They said, "He must be relieving himself in the inner room of the house." 25 They waited to the point of
embarrassment, but when he did not open the doors of the room,
they took a key and unlocked them. There they saw their lord fall-
en to the floor, dead.
26 While they waited, Ehud got away. He passed by the idols
and escaped to Seirah. 27 When he arrived there, he blew a trumpet
in the hill country of Ephraim, and the Israelites went down with
him from the hills, with him leading them.
28 "Follow me," he ordered, "for the LORD has given Moab,
your enemy, into your hands." So they followed him down and,
taking possession of the fords of the Jordan that led to Moab, they
allowed no one to cross over. 29 At that time they struck down
about ten thousand Moabites, all vigorous and strong; not a man
escaped. 30 That day Moab was made subject to Israel, and the land
had peace for eighty years.

Shamgar

31 After Ehud came Shamgar son of Anath, who struck down
six hundred Philistines with an oxgoad. He too saved Israel.

DEBORAH

Once again, the Israelites disobey God and are punished by a Canaanite attack. God chooses a female prophet, Deborah, to lead the people in battle against Jabin of Hazor. She praises God with a victory song after defeating Jabin's army (5:1-31).

Deborah

4 After Ehud died, the Israelites once again did evil in the eyes of
the LORD. 2 So the LORD sold them into the hands of Jabin, a king
of Canaan, who reigned in Hazor. The commander of his army
was Sisera, who lived in Harosheth Haggoyim. 3 Because he had
nine hundred iron chariots and had cruelly oppressed the Israelites
for twenty years, they cried to the LORD for help.
4 Deborah, a prophetess, the wife of Lappidoth, was leading[c]
Israel at that time. 5 She held court under the Palm of Deborah

[a]20 The meaning of the Hebrew for this phrase is uncertain. [b]23 The meaning of the Hebrew for this word is uncertain. [c]4 Traditionally *judging*

3:20 *upper room:* The upper room probably refers to a room built on the roof of the house. Houses usually had flat roofs, and in this hot climate a room sometimes was built on one corner of the roof where it could best catch the breeze.

3:27 *trumpet:* This was probably a hollowed out ram's horn. Ehud signals the troops and blocks the Moabite forces from retreating across the Jordan River.

3:31 *Shamgar . . . Philistines:* Mentioned only here and in 5:6, Shamgar uses an unusual method to gain victory over the enemy. Philistia was on the coastal plain along the Mediterranean Sea (see the map on p. 2464). The Philistines were a persistent problem during the era of the judges (13:1).

4:2 *Jabin:* This king organized nearby Canaanite kings to fight against Joshua and the Israelites (see Josh 11:1-11).

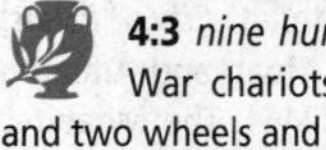

4:3 *nine hundred iron chariots:* War chariots had a single axle and two wheels and were usually drawn by one or two horses. Military leaders who had chariots had a distinct advantage over enemies who did not. Nine hundred chariots would have been a large and intimidating number of chariots to the Israelites who did not have chariots at this time.

4:4-6 *Deborah . . . disputes decided . . . Barak:* As a prophetess, Deborah would have spoken God's message. See also the article called "Prophets and Prophecy," p. 935. She also made legal decisions, as modern judges do. But she is best remembered for her role in leading two of Israel's tribes (4:6) in battle against the forces of Jabin. The "Palm of Deborah" in 4:5 is sometimes confused with the oak tree near Bethel where a different Deborah had been buried (Gen 35:8).

Deborah and Barak Attack Sisera and His Chariot Drivers, from an illuminated manuscript around 1250, France. Deborah was a leader and prophet in Israel in the time before Israel had a king. Because the Israelites began to disobey the LORD, the LORD let King Jabin of Hazor rule over them. Finally, the LORD told Deborah to call on Barak, a commander in the Israelite army, to lead its forces into battle against the Hazorites. In battle, the LORD confused Sisera, the leader of the Hazorite army, and all the Hazorite chariot drivers. The Israelites won the battle. Sisera escaped death on the battlefield, but was slain later by a woman, just as Deborah had prophesied. (See chapters 4, 5.)

between Ramah and Bethel in the hill country of Ephraim, and the
Israelites came to her to have their disputes decided. 6She sent for
Barak son of Abinoam from Kedesh in Naphtali and said to him,
"The LORD, the God of Israel, commands you: 'Go, take with you
ten thousand men of Naphtali and Zebulun and lead the way to
Mount Tabor. 7I will lure Sisera, the commander of Jabin's army,
with his chariots and his troops to the Kishon River and give him
into your hands.' "

8Barak said to her, "If you go with me, I will go; but if you
don't go with me, I won't go."

9"Very well," Deborah said, "I will go with you. But because
of the way you are going about this,[a] the honor will not be yours,
for the LORD will hand Sisera over to a woman." So Deborah went
with Barak to Kedesh, 10where he summoned Zebulun and Naphtali. Ten thousand men followed him, and Deborah also went
with him.

11Now Heber the Kenite had left the other Kenites, the
descendants of Hobab, Moses' brother-in-law,[b] and pitched his
tent by the great tree in Zaanannim near Kedesh.

12When they told Sisera that Barak son of Abinoam had
gone up to Mount Tabor, 13Sisera gathered together his nine hundred iron chariots and all the men with him, from Harosheth Haggoyim to the Kishon River.

4:6,7 *Mount Tabor . . . Kishon River:* Mount Tabor stands alone in the northeast corner of the Valley of Jezreel, southeast of the Sea of Galilee. See the map on p. 2464. The Kishon River is actually a stream that flows west through the Esdraelon Plain.

4:11 *Heber the Kenite:* See the note at 1:16 (Kenite).

4:13 Judg 4:3.

---

[a]9 Or *But on the expedition you are undertaking* [b]11 Or *father-in-law*

4:14 *Has not the LORD gone ahead of you:* Deborah declares that the battle is actually the LORD's, and the victory will be God's as well. See also Deut 20:4 and the mini-article called "Holy War (The LORD's Battles)," p. 306.

4:17 *Jael, the wife of Heber the Kenite:* The tent of Heber the Kenite was at Kedesh (4:11), about forty miles northeast of the battle site at the foot of Mount Tabor (see the note at 4:6, 7). Sisera thought he would be protected by Heber's family because they had a peace treaty with the king of Hazor. But Heber's wife Jael is more loyal to the Kenites' friends, the Israelites. She kills Sisera, fulfilling Deborah's prediction that a woman would defeat Sisera (4:9).

5:1 *this song:* This song is similar in style to ancient victory songs sung in Egypt and Assyria at this time. So, it is likely that this song is very close to the way Deborah originally wrote it around 1200 B.C. Most likely it was written for a worship celebration. The poem is a wonderful example of ancient poetry.

5:3 *the LORD, the God of Israel:* In the *NIV* "LORD" is used for the Hebrew, *Yahweh*. The LORD is Israel's personal God, who chose them and lives among them (Exod 19:3-6; 25:18-22; Isa 41:8,9). See also the mini-article called "LORD (YHWH)," p. 140.

5:4 *Seir:* This is another name for Edom, southeast of the Dead Sea (see the map on p. 2465). The LORD is pictured coming from a desert area, bringing a heavy rain that causes the Kishon River to flood and the enemy chariots to be stuck in the mud (5:21,22). All nature responds as God comes to Israel's aid.

5:5 Exod 19:18.

14Then Deborah said to Barak, "Go! This is the day the LORD has given Sisera into your hands. Has not the LORD gone ahead of you?" So Barak went down Mount Tabor, followed by ten thousand men. 15At Barak's advance, the LORD routed Sisera and all his chariots and army by the sword, and Sisera abandoned his chariot and fled on foot. 16But Barak pursued the chariots and army as far as Harosheth Haggoyim. All the troops of Sisera fell by the sword; not a man was left.

17Sisera, however, fled on foot to the tent of Jael, the wife of Heber the Kenite, because there were friendly relations between Jabin king of Hazor and the clan of Heber the Kenite.

18Jael went out to meet Sisera and said to him, "Come, my lord, come right in. Don't be afraid." So he entered her tent, and she put a covering over him.

19"I'm thirsty," he said. "Please give me some water." She opened a skin of milk, gave him a drink, and covered him up.

20"Stand in the doorway of the tent," he told her. "If someone comes by and asks you, 'Is anyone here?' say 'No.' "

21But Jael, Heber's wife, picked up a tent peg and a hammer and went quietly to him while he lay fast asleep, exhausted. She drove the peg through his temple into the ground, and he died.

22Barak came by in pursuit of Sisera, and Jael went out to meet him. "Come," she said, "I will show you the man you're looking for." So he went in with her, and there lay Sisera with the tent peg through his temple—dead.

23On that day God subdued Jabin, the Canaanite king, before the Israelites. 24And the hand of the Israelites grew stronger and stronger against Jabin, the Canaanite king, until they destroyed him.

The Song of Deborah

5 On that day Deborah and Barak son of Abinoam sang this song:

2"When the princes in Israel take the lead,
when the people willingly offer themselves—
praise the LORD!

3"Hear this, you kings! Listen, you rulers!
I will sing to[a] the LORD, I will sing;
I will make music to[b] the LORD, the God of Israel.

4"O LORD, when you went out from Seir,
when you marched from the land of Edom,
the earth shook, the heavens poured,
the clouds poured down water.
5The mountains quaked before the LORD, the One of Sinai,
before the LORD, the God of Israel.

[a]3 Or *of* [b]3 Or / *with song I will praise*

6 "In the days of Shamgar son of Anath,
in the days of Jael, the roads were abandoned;
travelers took to winding paths.
7 Village life[a] in Israel ceased,
ceased until I,[b] Deborah, arose,
arose a mother in Israel.
8 When they chose new gods,
war came to the city gates,
and not a shield or spear was seen
among forty thousand in Israel.
9 My heart is with Israel's princes,
with the willing volunteers among the people.
Praise the LORD!

10 "You who ride on white donkeys,
sitting on your saddle blankets,
and you who walk along the road,
consider 11 the voice of the singers[c] at the watering places.
They recite the righteous acts of the LORD,
the righteous acts of his warriors[d] in Israel.

"Then the people of the LORD
went down to the city gates.
12 'Wake up, wake up, Deborah!
Wake up, wake up, break out in song!
Arise, O Barak!
Take captive your captives, O son of Abinoam.'

13 "Then the men who were left
came down to the nobles;
the people of the LORD
came to me with the mighty.
14 Some came from Ephraim, whose roots were in Amalek;
Benjamin was with the people who followed you.
From Makir captains came down,
from Zebulun those who bear a commander's staff.
15 The princes of Issachar were with Deborah;
yes, Issachar was with Barak,
rushing after him into the valley.
In the districts of Reuben
there was much searching of heart.
16 Why did you stay among the campfires[e]
to hear the whistling for the flocks?
In the districts of Reuben
there was much searching of heart.

a7 Or *Warriors* b7 Or *you* c11 Or *archers*; the meaning of the Hebrew for this word is uncertain. d11 Or *villagers* e16 Or *saddlebags*

5:6 *Shamgar:* See the note at 3:31.

5:7 *a mother in Israel:* In Isaiah 66:10-13, this image is used for God's care of Jerusalem. See also Matt 23:37.

5:8 *chose new gods:* See the notes at 2:1,2 and 2:13.

5:10-18 *people of the LORD:* This great procession echoes Psalm 68:24-27, including the roll call of Israel's tribes. "Makir" in 5:14 is the Manasseh tribe (see 1:22-28). For more about the tribes mentioned, see 1:29 (Ephraim); 3:15,16 (Benjamin); 1:30-33 (Zebulun, Asher, Naphtali); and 1:34,35 (Dan). Reuben, the tribe descended from Jacob's oldest son (Gen 29:32), settled in the land east of the Dead Sea. Reuben, Gad, Dan, and Asher do not join the battle, possibly because their territories were not immediately threatened. For 5:16, compare Ps 68:11-13. See the map on p. 2464 and the mini-article called "Israel," p. 264.

5:19 *Taanach . . . Megiddo:* These two cities were in the northern hill country. The "waters" probably refers to one of the streams that flows into the Kishon River. It was common practice for the army that won a battle to take everything of value ("silver") from the dead enemy soldiers.

5:20,21 *the stars fought:* In ancient times, the stars were sometimes regarded as supernatural beings. The poetry here has the heavens above and the waters below fighting on God's side for Israel (see also Josh 10:12-14).

5:22 *horses':* Israelite armies marched on foot rather than horseback. It was not until the time of Solomon that horses were used by Israel for military purposes (1 Kgs 10:26-29). Depending on chariots and a cavalry indicated trust in material resources and not in God (Ps 20:7; 33:17; Isa 31:1).

5:23 *Meroz:* Its exact location is unknown.

5:24 *Jael:* See 4:17-22 and the note at 4:17. Jael is not an Israelite, but God used her to put an end to the enemy commander Sisera.

5:28-30 *Sisera's mother:* Sisera's mother and other Canaanite women wait for their husbands and sons to return from battle. They are worried about how long the battle is taking, but are hopeful that the delay is for good reasons. The reader, on the other hand, knows that all the Canaanite soldiers are dead.

6:1 *Again:* After another forty years of peace (see also 3:11), Israel resumes the cycle of disobedience first outlined in 2:18,19.

17 Gilead stayed beyond the Jordan.
And Dan, why did he linger by the ships?
Asher remained on the coast
and stayed in his coves.
18 The people of Zebulun risked their very lives;
so did Naphtali on the heights of the field.

19 "Kings came, they fought;
the kings of Canaan fought
at Taanach by the waters of Megiddo,
but they carried off no silver, no plunder.
20 From the heavens the stars fought,
from their courses they fought against Sisera.
21 The river Kishon swept them away,
the age-old river, the river Kishon.
March on, my soul; be strong!
22 Then thundered the horses' hoofs—
galloping, galloping go his mighty steeds.
23 'Curse Meroz,' said the angel of the LORD.
'Curse its people bitterly,
because they did not come to help the LORD,
to help the LORD against the mighty.'

24 "Most blessed of women be Jael,
the wife of Heber the Kenite,
most blessed of tent-dwelling women.
25 He asked for water, and she gave him milk;
in a bowl fit for nobles she brought him curdled milk.
26 Her hand reached for the tent peg,
her right hand for the workman's hammer.
She struck Sisera, she crushed his head,
she shattered and pierced his temple.
27 At her feet he sank,
he fell; there he lay.
At her feet he sank, he fell;
where he sank, there he fell—dead.

28 "Through the window peered Sisera's mother;
behind the lattice she cried out,
'Why is his chariot so long in coming?
Why is the clatter of his chariots delayed?'
29 The wisest of her ladies answer her;
indeed, she keeps saying to herself,
30 'Are they not finding and dividing the spoils:
a girl or two for each man,
colorful garments as plunder for Sisera,
colorful garments embroidered,
highly embroidered garments for my neck—
all this as plunder?'

31 “So may all your enemies perish, O LORD!
But may they who love you be like the sun
when it rises in its strength.”

Then the land had peace forty years.

GIDEON

Gideon, a mighty warrior, is not easily convinced that God truly is choosing him to be a leader for Israel.

Gideon

6 Again the Israelites did evil in the eyes of the LORD, and for
seven years he gave them into the hands of the Midianites.
2 Because the power of Midian was so oppressive, the Israelites prepared shelters for themselves in mountain clefts, caves and strongholds. 3 Whenever the Israelites planted their crops, the Midianites,
Amalekites and other eastern peoples invaded the country. 4 They
camped on the land and ruined the crops all the way to Gaza and
did not spare a living thing for Israel, neither sheep nor cattle nor
donkeys. 5 They came up with their livestock and their tents like
swarms of locusts. It was impossible to count the men and their
camels; they invaded the land to ravage it. 6 Midian so impover-
ished the Israelites that they cried out to the LORD for help.
7 When the Israelites cried to the LORD because of Midian,
8 he sent them a prophet, who said, “This is what the LORD, the God
of Israel, says: I brought you up out of Egypt, out of the land of
slavery. 9 I snatched you from the power of Egypt and from the
hand of all your oppressors. I drove them from before you and
gave you their land. 10 I said to you, ‘I am the LORD your God; do
not worship the gods of the Amorites, in whose land you live.’ But
you have not listened to me.”
11 The angel of the LORD came and sat down under the oak in
Ophrah that belonged to Joash the Abiezrite, where his son Gideon
was threshing wheat in a winepress to keep it from the Midianites.
12 When the angel of the LORD appeared to Gideon, he said, “The
LORD is with you, mighty warrior.”
13 “But sir,” Gideon replied, “if the LORD is with us, why has
all this happened to us? Where are all his wonders that our fathers
told us about when they said, ‘Did not the LORD bring us up out of
Egypt?’ But now the LORD has abandoned us and put us into the
hand of Midian.”
14 The LORD turned to him and said, “Go in the strength you
have and save Israel out of Midian’s hand. Am I not sending you?”
15 “But Lord,[a]” Gideon asked, “how can I save Israel? My clan
is the weakest in Manasseh, and I am the least in my family.”

[a]15 Or *sir*

6:3 *Midianites, Amalekites:* The Midianites mainly lived in the eastern part of the Arabian Desert (see the map on p. 2463), but as nomads they lived in tents and moved from place to place looking for good pasturelands and water for their herds. Perhaps food and water shortages led the Midianites and other peoples who lived in the eastern part of the Arabian Desert to move into Israel’s tribal lands in Canaan. See the mini-article called “Nomads (Wandering Herders),” p. 124, and the notes at 1:16 (Kenite) and 3:12,13.

6:4 *Gaza:* This Philistine city was near Israel’s western borders (see the map on p. 2464).

6:5 *locusts . . . camels:* Locusts are insects similar to grasshoppers. They travel in swarms and cause great damage to crops. See the mini-article called “Locusts,” p. 1708.

Camels are well adapted for life in dry regions. They can carry heavy loads, they have large cushioned feet that help them walk on sand, a hump with a reserve store of fat, and stomach cells that hold enough water to last for several days.

6:8 *prophet:* Prophets spoke God’s messages and, at times, told what would happen in the future. See also the note at 4:4-6.

6:11 *angel of the LORD:* See the note at 2:1.

6:11 *Abiezrite:* This was a clan of the Manasseh tribe (Josh 17:1-6). See the note at 1:22,23.

6:11 *threshing wheat:* In threshing, stalks of wheat were beaten by hand or walked on by oxen in order to separate the kernels from the chaff. Threshing was done outdoors on a hard floor made of packed clay soil or rock. Usually the chaff was thrown in the air so the wind would blow it away while the heavier grain kernels fell back down to the threshing floor. Joash was threshing in a pit, so a cloud of dust and chaff would not attract a Midianite raid (6:3-6).

6:15-17 *how can I save Israel . . . give me a sign:* Gideon argues that he is not a good choice for the job. Other important Israelites made this same argument to God (Exod 3:1—4:17; 1 Sam 9:21; Jer 1:6). Also, like Gideon in 6:17, others asked for (or received in advance) a sign that would prove it was really God speaking (Exod 3:1-4; 4:7-30; 1 Sam 10:1-7; 2 Kgs 19:29).

6:19 *bread without yeast:* Unleavened does not rise, and is flat as a result.

6:22 *I have seen the angel of the* LORD*:* It was not until the angel vanished that Gideon realized who his visitor was. Some people believed that if they saw one of the LORD's angels, they would die (13:22).

6:25 *altar to Baal . . . Asherah pole:* Baal, the Canaanite god of fertility, was being worshiped at this time by Gideon's family and by the other people of the town. A bull was often used as a symbol for Baal. Asherah was the Canaanite goddess of fertility. See the mini-article called "Canaanite Gods and Goddesses," p. 469.

6:26 *altar to the* LORD*:* An altar was a raised structure where sacrifices and offerings were presented to God or to foreign gods. Gideon was to replace the pagan worship site with an altar to God.

6:33 *Midianites, Amalekites:* See the note at 6:3.

6:33 *Valley of Jezreel:* See the map on p. 2464. See also the note at 6:11 (threshing).

6:34 *the Spirit of the* LORD *came upon:* This phrase is used frequently in JUDGES to indicate the moment when a person becomes one of God's chosen leaders. See also 3:10; 11:29; 13:25.

16 The LORD answered, "I will be with you, and you will strike
down all the Midianites together."
17 Gideon replied, "If now I have found favor in your eyes, give
me a sign that it is really you talking to me. 18 Please do not go away
until I come back and bring my offering and set it before you."
And the LORD said, "I will wait until you return."
19 Gideon went in, prepared a young goat, and from an
ephah[a] of flour he made bread without yeast. Putting the meat in
a basket and its broth in a pot, he brought them out and offered
them to him under the oak.
20 The angel of God said to him, "Take the meat and the
unleavened bread, place them on this rock, and pour out the
broth." And Gideon did so. 21 With the tip of the staff that was in
his hand, the angel of the LORD touched the meat and the unleavened bread. Fire flared from the rock, consuming the meat and the
bread. And the angel of the LORD disappeared. 22 When Gideon
realized that it was the angel of the LORD, he exclaimed, "Ah, Sovereign LORD! I have seen the angel of the LORD face to face!"
23 But the LORD said to him, "Peace! Do not be afraid. You are
not going to die."
24 So Gideon built an altar to the LORD there and called it The
LORD is Peace. To this day it stands in Ophrah of the Abiezrites.
25 That same night the LORD said to him, "Take the second
bull from your father's herd, the one seven years old.[b] Tear down
your father's altar to Baal and cut down the Asherah pole[c] beside
it. 26 Then build a proper kind of[d] altar to the LORD your God on
the top of this height. Using the wood of the Asherah pole that you
cut down, offer the second[e] bull as a burnt offering."
27 So Gideon took ten of his servants and did as the LORD
told him. But because he was afraid of his family and the men of
the town, he did it at night rather than in the daytime.
28 In the morning when the men of the town got up, there
was Baal's altar, demolished, with the Asherah pole beside it cut
down and the second bull sacrificed on the newly built altar!
29 They asked each other, "Who did this?"
When they carefully investigated, they were told, "Gideon
son of Joash did it."
30 The men of the town demanded of Joash, "Bring out your
son. He must die, because he has broken down Baal's altar and cut
down the Asherah pole beside it."
31 But Joash replied to the hostile crowd around him, "Are
you going to plead Baal's cause? Are you trying to save him? Whoever fights for him shall be put to death by morning! If Baal really

[a]**19** That is, probably about 3/5 bushel (about 22 liters) [b]**25** Or *Take a full-grown, mature bull from your father's herd* [c]**25** That is, a symbol of the goddess Asherah; here and elsewhere in Judges [d]**26** Or *build with layers of stone an* [e]**26** Or *full-grown*; also in verse 28

is a god, he can defend himself when someone breaks down his
altar." 32 So that day they called Gideon "Jerub-Baal,[a]" saying, "Let
Baal contend with him," because he broke down Baal's altar.
33 Now all the Midianites, Amalekites and other eastern peoples joined forces and crossed over the Jordan and camped in the
Valley of Jezreel. 34 Then the Spirit of the LORD came upon Gideon,
and he blew a trumpet, summoning the Abiezrites to follow him.
35 He sent messengers throughout Manasseh, calling them to arms,
and also into Asher, Zebulun and Naphtali, so that they too went
up to meet them.
36 Gideon said to God, "If you will save Israel by my hand as
you have promised— 37 look, I will place a wool fleece on the
threshing floor. If there is dew only on the fleece and all the ground
is dry, then I will know that you will save Israel by my hand, as you
said." 38 And that is what happened. Gideon rose early the next day;
he squeezed the fleece and wrung out the dew—a bowlful of water.
39 Then Gideon said to God, "Do not be angry with me. Let
me make just one more request. Allow me one more test with the
fleece. This time make the fleece dry and the ground covered with
dew." 40 That night God did so. Only the fleece was dry; all the
ground was covered with dew.

Gideon Defeats the Midianites

7 Early in the morning, Jerub-Baal (that is, Gideon) and all his
men camped at the spring of Harod. The camp of Midian was
north of them in the valley near the hill of Moreh. 2 The LORD said
to Gideon, "You have too many men for me to deliver Midian into
their hands. In order that Israel may not boast against me that her
own strength has saved her, 3 announce now to the people, 'Anyone
who trembles with fear may turn back and leave Mount Gilead.' "
So twenty-two thousand men left, while ten thousand remained.
4 But the LORD said to Gideon, "There are still too many men.
Take them down to the water, and I will sift them for you there. If
I say, 'This one shall go with you,' he shall go; but if I say, 'This one
shall not go with you,' he shall not go."
5 So Gideon took the men down to the water. There the LORD
told him, "Separate those who lap the water with their tongues like
a dog from those who kneel down to drink." 6 Three hundred men
lapped with their hands to their mouths. All the rest got down on
their knees to drink.
7 The LORD said to Gideon, "With the three hundred men
that lapped I will save you and give the Midianites into your
hands. Let all the other men go, each to his own place." 8 So Gideon
sent the rest of the Israelites to their tents but kept the three hundred, who took over the provisions and trumpets of the others.

[a]32 *Jerub-Baal* means *let Baal contend.*

6:34 *trumpet:* See the note at 3:27. Gideon is from the Abiezer clan, part of the Manasseh tribe (6:11).

6:36-39 *one more request:* As in 6:17, Gideon asks for a sign that it is really God leading him. God honors his request, but then Gideon again asks God for proof. Even persons of faith, such as Gideon, may sometimes have doubts. See also Heb 11:32-34.

7:1 *spring of Harod. . . . hill of Moreh:* The spring of Harod is at the base of Mount Gilboa in the Valley of Jezreel. The hill of Moreh is about five miles north of the spring of Harod.

7:2 *too many men:* God will fight on behalf of Israel. This is God's battle and God's victory. Israel will be so outnumbered that it cannot win by its power alone. See also the notes at 1:17 and 4:14.

7:3 *Mount Gilead:* Usually "Gilead" refers to an area east of the Jordan River, but in this verse it refers to a place near the Valley of Jezreel west of the Jordan.

7:5 *lap the water . . . kneel down to drink:* The soldiers who knelt most likely put their faces directly into the water. This would have made it impossible for them to see an enemy approach and suggests that they might not be alert fighters in the battlefield. Additionally, the soldiers who lapped water from their hands were probably better prepared to grab their weapons at a moment's notice. If so, then God seems to have chosen the more astute warriors. Even so, the emphasis in this passage, as in other parts of JUDGES, is that God is the one who brings victory and he does not need a large army to do so.

7:3 Deut 20:1-8.

7:10 *If you are afraid:* The LORD is prepared to give yet another sign if Gideon needs it (see 6:17, 36, 37, 39). Note that the sign requires Gideon to be daring; he must overcome fear in order to enter the huge enemy camp.

7:12 *locusts . . . camels:* The situation is serious; the enemy camp is huge. See the note at 6:5.

7:13 *a dream . . . barley:* In the Bible, God often gives messages to people in dreams (Gen 28:10-15; 40:1-23; Zech 1:7, 8; Matt 1:20, 21; 2:13-15). Barley is a cheap grain used mainly for feeding cattle. But this modest object became for Gideon a symbol for the victory that the LORD would give his troops.

Now the camp of Midian lay below him in the valley. 9 During that night the LORD said to Gideon, "Get up, go down against
the camp, because I am going to give it into your hands. 10 If you
are afraid to attack, go down to the camp with your servant Purah
11 and listen to what they are saying. Afterward, you will be encouraged to attack the camp." So he and Purah his servant went down
to the outposts of the camp. 12 The Midianites, the Amalekites and
all the other eastern peoples had settled in the valley, thick as
locusts. Their camels could no more be counted than the sand on
the seashore.

13 Gideon arrived just as a man was telling a friend his dream.
"I had a dream," he was saying. "A round loaf of barley bread came

Gideon Selects Three Hundred Soldiers, by Ryohei Koiso, around 1971. The LORD promised to help Gideon rescue the Israelites from the Midianites, but he did not want the Israelites to think they defeated them on their own. He ordered Gideon to reduce the size of his army—first by sending away anyone who was too afraid to fight, and then by rejecting any soldiers who did not drink water from the spring by lapping it with their hands. When Gideon had done what the LORD told him to, he had an army of three hundred men. (See 7:1-8.)

tumbling into the Midianite camp. It struck the tent with such
force that the tent overturned and collapsed."
14 His friend responded, "This can be nothing other than the
sword of Gideon son of Joash, the Israelite. God has given the
Midianites and the whole camp into his hands."
15 When Gideon heard the dream and its interpretation, he
worshiped God. He returned to the camp of Israel and called out,
"Get up! The LORD has given the Midianite camp into your hands."
16 Dividing the three hundred men into three companies, he placed
trumpets and empty jars in the hands of all of them, with torches
inside.
17 "Watch me," he told them. "Follow my lead. When I get to
the edge of the camp, do exactly as I do. 18 When I and all who are
with me blow our trumpets, then from all around the camp blow
yours and shout, 'For the LORD and for Gideon.'"
19 Gideon and the hundred men with him reached the edge
of the camp at the beginning of the middle watch, just after they
had changed the guard. They blew their trumpets and broke the

7:19-22 *the middle watch . . . turn on each other:* The night was divided into three periods called "watches," each about four hours long. A different set of guards would come on duty at the beginning of each watch. The first watch began at sunset, so the beginning of the middle watch would have been shortly after ten o'clock.

The effect of all the smashed jars and loud trumpets (7:19) was to shock the enemy soldiers, who began to kill each other off in panic. No mention is made of the Israelites actually using their own swords at the campsite (see 7:20).

CANAANITE GODS AND GODDESSES

The Canaanites worshiped many gods and goddesses who, together, formed a council. *El* ("god"), the father of the other gods and humanity, was head of the council. He lived in a cosmic paradise where the other gods came to see him.

Baal ("master, lord") also was known as *Hadad.* As the most popular god among the people, Baal gradually took over many of the roles and characteristics of El. He was worshiped by the Canaanites as the storm god who brought rain and made the land and flocks fertile. Once the Israelites settled in Canaan and became farmers, some of them started worshiping Baal instead of the LORD because they hoped he would give them abundant crops and fertile flocks. Statues of Baal show him wearing a cone-shaped hat with bull horns that represent his fertility. The club he holds in his right hand points to his strength, while the lightning bolt he holds in his left hand emphasizes his role as storm god.

The enemies of the fertility god were known as *Mot* ("death") and *Yam* ("sea"). Canaanite stories describe the struggles of Baal, the god of fertility, with these representatives of the forces of chaos, death, and sterility. The story speaks of Baal dying in the summer heat only to be reborn with the fall rains.

Other Canaanite gods, very similar to Baal and probably local versions of Baal, included *Melkart,* the god of Tyre; *Chemosh,* the god of Moab; *Milcom, Molek*, or *Moloch,* the Ammonite god; *Tammuz,* a type of dying and rising nature god worshiped in Syria; and *Dagon,* a vegetation god similar to Tammuz but worshiped by the Philistines.

The Canaanite goddesses were primarily fertility goddesses who were believed to provide healthy crops and large harvests, as well as increases in the flocks. *Asherah* (also known as *Ashtoreth*) was the mother of seventy of the gods, and the wife of El in the early myths. In later stories, however, she supported Baal when he asked El for power. The term "Asherah" was also used for sacred poles or trees that were put up as fertility symbols (1 Kgs 14:23; Deut 16:21).

Anath was Baal's sister as well as his wife. As a war goddess, she is best known for gory acts of violence done to those who opposed her.

7:22 *Beth Shittah . . . Zererah . . . Abel Meholah . . . Tabbath:* These were places east of the Jordan River. The Midianites scrambled off toward the desert, their home.

7:23 *all Manasseh:* Referring to both parts of the tribe. Half of Manasseh lived east of the Jordan River, and the other half lived west of the river (see the map on p. 2464). Gideon first asked men from these tribes to join his army shortly after becoming a leader (6:35). At this point, Gideon needed more than the little army of three hundred to chase away the Midianites.

8:1 *Why have you treated us like this:* Ephraim was the last tribe that Gideon called to this battle with the Midianites (7:24), and so they felt slighted. This conflict probably reflects the long rivalry between the tribes of Manasseh (Gideon's tribe) and Ephraim. Ephraim was always the more powerful of the two tribes. See also Gen 48:1-20.

8:2 *compared to you:* In his speech, Gideon shows great diplomatic skill. He shrewdly constrasts the little his clan has done with what the Ephraimites did to capture the Midianite chiefs. His humble words have a calming effect (8:3).

8:5 *Succoth:* This town was on the east side of the Jordan River in the territory of Gad.

8:5 *kings of Midian:* The two named here are unknown. They are more likely clan chieftains rather than kings.

8:8-11 *Peniel . . . Karkor . . . route of the nomads:* Peniel was several miles east of Succoth on the Jabbok River. Karkor was about one hundred miles east of the Dead Sea, in the Arabian Desert. The road at the edge of the desert was known as "route of the nomads." See the mini-article called "Nomads (Wandering Herders)," p. 124.

jars that were in their hands. [20]The three companies blew the
trumpets and smashed the jars. Grasping the torches in their left
hands and holding in their right hands the trumpets they were to
blow, they shouted, "A sword for the LORD and for Gideon!"
[21]While each man held his position around the camp, all the Midianites ran, crying out as they fled.

[22]When the three hundred trumpets sounded, the LORD
caused the men throughout the camp to turn on each other with
their swords. The army fled to Beth Shittah toward Zererah as far
as the border of Abel Meholah near Tabbath. [23]Israelites from
Naphtali, Asher and all Manasseh were called out, and they pursued the Midianites. [24]Gideon sent messengers throughout the hill
country of Ephraim, saying, "Come down against the Midianites
and seize the waters of the Jordan ahead of them as far as Beth
Barah."

So all the men of Ephraim were called out and they took the
waters of the Jordan as far as Beth Barah. [25]They also captured two
of the Midianite leaders, Oreb and Zeeb. They killed Oreb at the
rock of Oreb, and Zeeb at the winepress of Zeeb. They pursued the
Midianites and brought the heads of Oreb and Zeeb to Gideon,
who was by the Jordan.

Zebah and Zalmunna

8 Now the Ephraimites asked Gideon, "Why have you treated us
like this? Why didn't you call us when you went to fight Midian?"
And they criticized him sharply.

[2]But he answered them, "What have I accomplished compared to you? Aren't the gleanings of Ephraim's grapes better than
the full grape harvest of Abiezer? [3]God gave Oreb and Zeeb, the
Midianite leaders, into your hands. What was I able to do compared to you?" At this, their resentment against him subsided.

[4]Gideon and his three hundred men, exhausted yet keeping
up the pursuit, came to the Jordan and crossed it. [5]He said to the
men of Succoth, "Give my troops some bread; they are worn out,
and I am still pursuing Zebah and Zalmunna, the kings of Midian."

[6]But the officials of Succoth said, "Do you already have the
hands of Zebah and Zalmunna in your possession? Why should we
give bread to your troops?"

[7]Then Gideon replied, "Just for that, when the LORD has
given Zebah and Zalmunna into my hand, I will tear your flesh
with desert thorns and briers."

[8]From there he went up to Peniel[a] and made the same
request of them, but they answered as the men of Succoth had. [9]So
he said to the men of Peniel, "When I return in triumph, I will tear
down this tower."

---

[a]**8** Hebrew *Penuel,* a variant of *Peniel;* also in verses 9 and 17

10 Now Zebah and Zalmunna were in Karkor with a force of
about fifteen thousand men, all that were left of the armies of the
eastern peoples; a hundred and twenty thousand swordsmen had
fallen. 11 Gideon went up by the route of the nomads east of Nobah
and Jogbehah and fell upon the unsuspecting army. 12 Zebah and
Zalmunna, the two kings of Midian, fled, but he pursued them and
captured them, routing their entire army.
13 Gideon son of Joash then returned from the battle by the
Pass of Heres. 14 He caught a young man of Succoth and questioned him, and the young man wrote down for him the names of
the seventy-seven officials of Succoth, the elders of the town.
15 Then Gideon came and said to the men of Succoth, "Here are
Zebah and Zalmunna, about whom you taunted me by saying, 'Do
you already have the hands of Zebah and Zalmunna in your possession? Why should we give bread to your exhausted men?' " 16 He
took the elders of the town and taught the men of Succoth a lesson by punishing them with desert thorns and briers. 17 He also
pulled down the tower of Peniel and killed the men of the town.
18 Then he asked Zebah and Zalmunna, "What kind of men
did you kill at Tabor?"

"Men like you," they answered, "each one with the bearing
of a prince."
19 Gideon replied, "Those were my brothers, the sons of my
own mother. As surely as the LORD lives, if you had spared their
lives, I would not kill you." 20 Turning to Jether, his oldest son, he
said, "Kill them!" But Jether did not draw his sword, because he
was only a boy and was afraid.
21 Zebah and Zalmunna said, "Come, do it yourself. 'As is the
man, so is his strength.' " So Gideon stepped forward and killed
them, and took the ornaments off their camels' necks.

Gideon's Ephod

22 The Israelites said to Gideon, "Rule over us—you, your son
and your grandson—because you have saved us out of the hand of
Midian."
23 But Gideon told them, "I will not rule over you, nor will
my son rule over you. The LORD will rule over you." 24 And he said,
"I do have one request, that each of you give me an earring from
your share of the plunder." (It was the custom of the Ishmaelites to
wear gold earrings.)
25 They answered, "We'll be glad to give them." So they spread
out a garment, and each man threw a ring from his plunder onto
it. 26 The weight of the gold rings he asked for came to seventeen
hundred shekels,[a] not counting the ornaments, the pendants and
the purple garments worn by the kings of Midian or the chains

[a]**26** That is, about 43 pounds (about 19.5 kilograms)

8:14 *young man wrote down . . . seventy-seven officials:* Not everyone knew how to write, so writing was a valuable skill, particularly in areas of trade and government where written records were very important. Since seven is a symbolic number meaning completeness, "seventy-seven officials" probably represents a complete list.

8:18 *Tabor:* See the note at 4:6, 7. The passage reveals why Gideon has chased the Midianite kings so far out into the desert.

8:20 *Jether . . . only a boy:* Gideon wanted to insult the kings by having a young boy kill them. But his son doesn't have the heart to kill them.

8:22,23 *Rule over us . . . The LORD will rule over you:* The Israelites will later make a similar request for a king in 1 Samuel 8:4, 5. As God's special people, the only ruler they were to have was God. To ask for an earthly king showed a lack of faith or even rejection of God (1 Sam 10:19). See also the mini-article called "Kingship in Israel," p. 650.

8:24 *Ishmaelites:* The Ishmaelites are also called Midianites (Gen 37:25-28). They were descended from Abraham by Keturah, as recorded in Genesis 25:1, 2. See the note at 6:3.

8:26 *the gold rings:* The Ishmaelites (Midianites) were nomadic traders and so they carried their wealth with them. The treasure taken from the Midianites was a huge amount.

8:3-5 Ps 83:11.

8:30,31 *many wives . . . concubine:* At this time Israelite men had as many wives as they could support. Concubines were legally bound to the man, but did not have the full privileges of a primary wife. Apparently, Gideon's concubine lived with her parents, and Gideon visited her from time to time.

8:31 *Shechem:* This was the site of a sacred tree during the time of Abraham (Gen 12:6) and of an altar later built by Jacob (Gen 33:18-20).

8:33 *prostituted themselves to the Baals:* The Israelites again began worshiping idols, images or statues that represented foreign gods. See the mini-article called "Canaanite Gods and Goddesses," p. 469.

9:1 *Abimelech:* His father, Gideon, rejected the offer of kingship (8:23). His mother was a concubine from Shechem (8:31), a city where Baal was worshiped (9:4), and the home of earlier Canaanite kings or chieftains (9:28). Abimelech was influenced by his background and Caananite relatives to seek to become king of the lands controlled by the Shechemites. It is clear that God was not behind this plan, because the author does not call Abimelech a "judge" or say that the LORD's Spirit took control of him. See the note at 6:34 (Spirit of the LORD). God is only mentioned in 9:23 and 9:56,57 in this story, and then only as one who punishes Abimelech.

9:5 *murdered his seventy brothers:* See 8:30. Abimelech's wickedness is confirmed. Seventy is used in a symbolic way here, perhaps to refer to Gideon's entire family. See the note at 1:7.

9:6 *great tree at the pillar in Shechem:* Abimelech takes office at this site, sacred since early Canaanite times. See the note at 8:31. See also Josh 24:26.

9:7 *Mount Gerizim:* This mountain was located south of Shechem in the territory of Ephraim (see the map on p. 2464).

that were on their camels' necks. [27]Gideon made the gold into an ephod, which he placed in Ophrah, his town. All Israel prostituted themselves by worshiping it there, and it became a snare to Gideon and his family.

Gideon's Death

[28]Thus Midian was subdued before the Israelites and did not raise its head again. During Gideon's lifetime, the land enjoyed peace forty years.

[29]Jerub-Baal son of Joash went back home to live. [30]He had seventy sons of his own, for he had many wives. [31]His concubine, who lived in Shechem, also bore him a son, whom he named Abimelech. [32]Gideon son of Joash died at a good old age and was buried in the tomb of his father Joash in Ophrah of the Abiezrites.

[33]No sooner had Gideon died than the Israelites again prostituted themselves to the Baals. They set up Baal-Berith as their god and [34]did not remember the LORD their God, who had rescued them from the hands of all their enemies on every side. [35]They also failed to show kindness to the family of Jerub-Baal (that is, Gideon) for all the good things he had done for them.

ABIMELECH, TOLA, AND JAIR

Even though God does not choose Abimelech to be a special leader, Abimelech sets himself up as king of Shechem.

Abimelech

9 Abimelech son of Jerub-Baal went to his mother's brothers in Shechem and said to them and to all his mother's clan, [2]"Ask all the citizens of Shechem, 'Which is better for you: to have all seventy of Jerub-Baal's sons rule over you, or just one man?' Remember, I am your flesh and blood."

[3]When the brothers repeated all this to the citizens of Shechem, they were inclined to follow Abimelech, for they said, "He is our brother." [4]They gave him seventy shekels[a] of silver from the temple of Baal-Berith, and Abimelech used it to hire reckless adventurers, who became his followers. [5]He went to his father's home in Ophrah and on one stone murdered his seventy brothers, the sons of Jerub-Baal. But Jotham, the youngest son of Jerub-Baal, escaped by hiding. [6]Then all the citizens of Shechem and Beth Millo gathered beside the great tree at the pillar in Shechem to crown Abimelech king.

[7]When Jotham was told about this, he climbed up on the top of Mount Gerizim and shouted to them, "Listen to me, citizens of Shechem, so that God may listen to you. [8]One day the trees went

---

a4 That is, about 1 3/4 pounds (about 0.8 kilogram)

out to anoint a king for themselves. They said to the olive tree, ‘Be
our king.’
9“But the olive tree answered, ‘Should I give up my oil, by
which both gods and men are honored, to hold sway over the
trees?’
10“Next, the trees said to the fig tree, ‘Come and be our king.’
11“But the fig tree replied, ‘Should I give up my fruit, so good
and sweet, to hold sway over the trees?’
12“Then the trees said to the vine, ‘Come and be our king.’
13“But the vine answered, ‘Should I give up my wine, which
cheers both gods and men, to hold sway over the trees?’
14“Finally all the trees said to the thornbush, ‘Come and be
our king.’
15“The thornbush said to the trees, ‘If you really want to
anoint me king over you, come and take refuge in my shade; but if
not, then let fire come out of the thornbush and consume the
cedars of Lebanon!’
16“Now if you have acted honorably and in good faith when
you made Abimelech king, and if you have been fair to Jerub-Baal
and his family, and if you have treated him as he deserves— 17and
to think that my father fought for you, risked his life to rescue you
from the hand of Midian 18(but today you have revolted against
my father’s family, murdered his seventy sons on a single stone,
and made Abimelech, the son of his slave girl, king over the citizens of Shechem because he is your brother)— 19if then you have
acted honorably and in good faith toward Jerub-Baal and his family today, may Abimelech be your joy, and may you be his, too!
20But if you have not, let fire come out from Abimelech and consume you, citizens of Shechem and Beth Millo, and let fire come
out from you, citizens of Shechem and Beth Millo, and consume
Abimelech!”
21Then Jotham fled, escaping to Beer, and he lived there
because he was afraid of his brother Abimelech.
22After Abimelech had governed Israel three years, 23God
sent an evil spirit between Abimelech and the citizens of Shechem,
who acted treacherously against Abimelech. 24God did this in order
that the crime against Jerub-Baal’s seventy sons, the shedding of
their blood, might be avenged on their brother Abimelech and on
the citizens of Shechem, who had helped him murder his brothers.
25In opposition to him these citizens of Shechem set men on the
hilltops to ambush and rob everyone who passed by, and this was
reported to Abimelech.
26Now Gaal son of Ebed moved with his brothers into
Shechem, and its citizens put their confidence in him. 27After they
had gone out into the fields and gathered the grapes and trodden
them, they held a festival in the temple of their god. While they
were eating and drinking, they cursed Abimelech. 28Then Gaal son
of Ebed said, “Who is Abimelech, and who is Shechem, that we

9:7 *Listen to me:* Jotham tells a story which is a fable. This fable has talking trees and a moral—that the monarchy can bring trouble. Also note that the king is not chosen by God, but is picked as a last resort.

9:8-15 *olive tree . . . cedars of Lebanon:* The trees and vines mentioned in these verses were common but provided much needed products. Olive trees produced fruit that was eaten and crushed to collect oil used in cooking, grooming, and oil lamps. The fig tree gave two harvests of nourishing sweet fruit each year. Grape vines produced fruit that was eaten or crushed to make wine. The thornbush provided some shade in a sunny, dry climate, but often they were burned for fuel. The tall cedar trees that grew in the Lebanon mountains were some of the largest trees in that part of the world. They were used for all sorts of big building projects.

The fact that the thornbush agrees to be king instead of all the other more useful trees or vines is meant to ridicule the whole idea of having a king rule over Israel. Compare to 1 Sam 8 and 2 Sam 12.

9:17,18 *Midian . . . slave girl:* See the notes at 6:3 and 8:30, 31.

9:21 *Beer:* The exact location of this place is unknown, but most likely it was somewhere north of Shechem and south of the Sea of Galilee. "Beer" means "well" and frequently appears as part of place names throughout Palestine.

9:22 *governed Israel three years:* As a result of his military campaigns, Abimelech ruled Shechem and some other Canaanite and Israelite cities (9:41), but he did not rule over all of Israel. It must be noted, too, that he was made king of Shechem by the elders there, not by the LORD.

9:27 *gathered the grapes and trodden them:* This was a festival time. Note that the celebration takes place in Shechem in a temple of one of the Canaanite gods.

9:28 *Hamor:* He was the first Canaanite ruler of Shechem (Gen 33:18, 19; Josh 24:32). Gaal calls on the people of Shechem to remember the old days and the old Canaanite kings (here, chiefs of the city of Shechem). The point of Gaal's speech is that Abimelech is not a Shechemite, and that he should be overthrown. Zebul, Abimelech's deputy, sends this news to Abimelech (9:31).

9:34 *concealed positions:* They were camped at Arumah, about five miles from Shechem (9:41).

9:35 *the city gate:* Many towns and cities were surrounded by high walls with heavy gates that were closed at night for protection. See the note at 1:24.

9:37 *down from the center of the land:* Shechem was located between the mountains of Gerizim and Ebal (see the maps on pp. 2464 and 2473). The "soothsayers' tree" may have been near a road that probably led to Gerizim, which was thought to link heaven and earth.

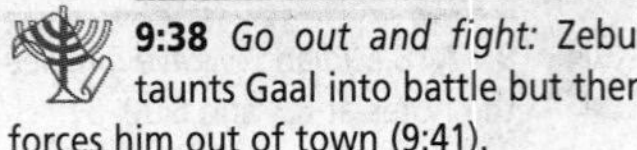

9:38 *Go out and fight:* Zebul taunts Gaal into battle but then forces him out of town (9:41).

9:41 *Arumah:* This town was about five miles southeast of Shechem.

9:45 *scattered salt over it:* This may have been part of a ceremony to place a curse on the land. Excavations have shown that the city was destroyed in the twelfth century B.C.

9:46-49 *stronghold of the temple . . . set it on fire:* Some leaders hid out in the temple of the Canaanite god they served, perhaps thinking their god would protect them from Abimelech's soldiers. Instead, they die by fire, which fulfills Jotham's curse upon them (9:15-20).

should be subject to him? Isn't he Jerub-Baal's son, and isn't Zebul
his deputy? Serve the men of Hamor, Shechem's father! Why
should we serve Abimelech? [29]If only this people were under my
command! Then I would get rid of him. I would say to Abimelech,
'Call out your whole army!' "[a]

[30]When Zebul the governor of the city heard what Gaal son
of Ebed said, he was very angry. [31]Under cover he sent messengers
to Abimelech, saying, "Gaal son of Ebed and his brothers have
come to Shechem and are stirring up the city against you. [32]Now
then, during the night you and your men should come and lie in
wait in the fields. [33]In the morning at sunrise, advance against the
city. When Gaal and his men come out against you, do whatever
your hand finds to do."

[34]So Abimelech and all his troops set out by night and took
up concealed positions near Shechem in four companies. [35]Now
Gaal son of Ebed had gone out and was standing at the entrance to
the city gate just as Abimelech and his soldiers came out from their
hiding place.

[36]When Gaal saw them, he said to Zebul, "Look, people are
coming down from the tops of the mountains!"

Zebul replied, "You mistake the shadows of the mountains
for men."

[37]But Gaal spoke up again: "Look, people are coming down
from the center of the land, and a company is coming from the
direction of the soothsayers' tree."

[38]Then Zebul said to him, "Where is your big talk now, you
who said, 'Who is Abimelech that we should be subject to him?'
Aren't these the men you ridiculed? Go out and fight them!"

[39]So Gaal led out[b] the citizens of Shechem and fought Abimelech. [40]Abimelech chased him, and many fell wounded in the
flight—all the way to the entrance to the gate. [41]Abimelech stayed
in Arumah, and Zebul drove Gaal and his brothers out of
Shechem.

[42]The next day the people of Shechem went out to the fields,
and this was reported to Abimelech. [43]So he took his men, divided
them into three companies and set an ambush in the fields. When
he saw the people coming out of the city, he rose to attack them.
[44]Abimelech and the companies with him rushed forward to a position at the entrance to the city gate. Then two companies rushed
upon those in the fields and struck them down. [45]All that day Abimelech pressed his attack against the city until he had captured it and
killed its people. Then he destroyed the city and scattered salt over it.

[46]On hearing this, the citizens in the tower of Shechem went
into the stronghold of the temple of El-Berith. [47]When Abimelech
heard that they had assembled there, [48]he and all his men went up

[a]**29** Septuagint; Hebrew *him." Then he said to Abimelech, "Call out your whole army!"* [b]**39** Or *Gaal went out in the sight of*

Mount Zalmon. He took an ax and cut off some branches, which
he lifted to his shoulders. He ordered the men with him, "Quick!
Do what you have seen me do!" 49So all the men cut branches and
followed Abimelech. They piled them against the stronghold and
set it on fire over the people inside. So all the people in the tower
of Shechem, about a thousand men and women, also died.
50Next Abimelech went to Thebez and besieged it and captured it. 51Inside the city, however, was a strong tower, to which all
the men and women—all the people of the city—fled. They locked
themselves in and climbed up on the tower roof. 52Abimelech went
to the tower and stormed it. But as he approached the entrance to
the tower to set it on fire, 53a woman dropped an upper millstone
on his head and cracked his skull.
54Hurriedly he called to his armor-bearer, "Draw your sword
and kill me, so that they can't say, 'A woman killed him.' " So his
servant ran him through, and he died. 55When the Israelites saw
that Abimelech was dead, they went home.
56Thus God repaid the wickedness that Abimelech had done
to his father by murdering his seventy brothers. 57God also made
the men of Shechem pay for all their wickedness. The curse of
Jotham son of Jerub-Baal came on them.

Tola

10 After the time of Abimelech a man of Issachar, Tola son of
Puah, the son of Dodo, rose to save Israel. He lived in Shamir, in
the hill country of Ephraim. 2He led[a] Israel twenty-three years;
then he died, and was buried in Shamir.

Jair

3He was followed by Jair of Gilead, who led Israel twenty-
two years. 4He had thirty sons, who rode thirty donkeys. They controlled thirty towns in Gilead, which to this day are called Havvoth
Jair.[b] 5When Jair died, he was buried in Kamon.

JEPHTHAH, IBZAN, ELON, AND ABDON

Israel has sinned again, and so the Ammonites are making life difficult for them. The Israelites ask Jephthah to be their leader. He is a military success, but his personal life is filled with tragedy. Brief summaries are given for the minor judges, Ibzan, Elon, and Abdon.

Jephthah

6Again the Israelites did evil in the eyes of the LORD. They
served the Baals and the Ashtoreths, and the gods of Aram, the
gods of Sidon, the gods of Moab, the gods of the Ammonites and

[a]2 Traditionally *judged*; also in verse 3 [b]4 Or *called the settlements of Jair*

9:50 *Thebez:* This town was about twelve miles northeast of Shechem.

9:53 *millstone:* This was a stone used to grind grain. Grinding grain was not usually done on the roof, so the woman must have taken the stone with her to defend herself. See also 2 Sam 11:21.

9:54-57 *kill me . . . curse of Jotham:* It was considered a disgrace for a man to be killed by a woman. See also 1 Sam 31:3,4.

Shechem already has been punished (9:3-6,42-49) for supporting Abimelech as king because he wasn't worthy. Now, with Abimelech's death, Jotham's curse is fulfilled (9:15,19-21).

10:1,2 *Tola:* Of the total of twelve special leaders named in JUDGES, some are only mentioned briefly, including Tola and Jair in 10:3-5. Tola is from the Issachar tribe (Num 26:23-25). It is unclear which nation was oppressing Israel at this time or how Tola helped Israel. See also the note at 2:16.

10:3,4 *Jair . . . thirty donkeys:* Jair was a special leader who had many sons and many donkeys, a sign that the family was wealthy.

10:3-5 *Gilead . . . towns . . . Kamon:* Gilead was the territory east of the Jordan River in the highlands north and south of the Jabbok River (see the map on p. 2467). Each of the thirty towns was governed by one of Jair's sons. See also Josh 13:30,31. The exact location of Kamon is unknown.

10:6 *served the Baals and the Ashtoreths, and the gods:* See the notes at 2:1,2 and 2:13. Baal and Ashtoreth were the chief Caananite gods, while the other nations surrounding Israel's tribes turned to similar gods for protection and blessings. See also the mini-article called "Canaanite Gods and Goddesses," p. 469.

the gods of the Philistines. And because the Israelites forsook the
LORD and no longer served him, [7]he became angry with them. He
sold them into the hands of the Philistines and the Ammonites,
[8]who that year shattered and crushed them. For eighteen years
they oppressed all the Israelites on the east side of the Jordan in
Gilead, the land of the Amorites. [9]The Ammonites also crossed the
Jordan to fight against Judah, Benjamin and the house of Ephraim;
and Israel was in great distress. [10]Then the Israelites cried out to
the LORD, "We have sinned against you, forsaking our God and
serving the Baals."

[11]The LORD replied, "When the Egyptians, the Amorites, the
Ammonites, the Philistines, [12]the Sidonians, the Amalekites and
the Maonites[a] oppressed you and you cried to me for help, did
I not save you from their hands? [13]But you have forsaken me and
served other gods, so I will no longer save you. [14]Go and cry out
to the gods you have chosen. Let them save you when you are in
trouble!"

[15]But the Israelites said to the LORD, "We have sinned. Do
with us whatever you think best, but please rescue us now." [16]Then
they got rid of the foreign gods among them and served the LORD.
And he could bear Israel's misery no longer.

[17]When the Ammonites were called to arms and camped in
Gilead, the Israelites assembled and camped at Mizpah. [18]The leaders of the people of Gilead said to each other, "Whoever will
launch the attack against the Ammonites will be the head of all
those living in Gilead."

11 Jephthah the Gileadite was a mighty warrior. His father was
Gilead; his mother was a prostitute. [2]Gilead's wife also bore him
sons, and when they were grown up, they drove Jephthah away.
"You are not going to get any inheritance in our family," they said,
"because you are the son of another woman." [3]So Jephthah fled
from his brothers and settled in the land of Tob, where a group of
adventurers gathered around him and followed him.

[4]Some time later, when the Ammonites made war on Israel,
[5]the elders of Gilead went to get Jephthah from the land of Tob.
[6]"Come," they said, "be our commander, so we can fight the
Ammonites."

[7]Jephthah said to them, "Didn't you hate me and drive me
from my father's house? Why do you come to me now, when
you're in trouble?"

[8]The elders of Gilead said to him, "Nevertheless, we are turning to you now; come with us to fight the Ammonites, and you
will be our head over all who live in Gilead."

[9]Jephthah answered, "Suppose you take me back to fight the
Ammonites and the LORD gives them to me—will I really be your
head?"

---

[a]**12** Hebrew; some Septuagint manuscripts *Midianites*

10:7 *Philistines . . . Ammonites:* See the notes at 3:31 and 3:12, 13. The Ammonites, who lived east of the Jordan River, began crossing the Jordan River to attack the tribes west of the southern part of the Jordan (see the map on p. 2464).

10:8 *Gilead:* See the note at 10:3-5.

10:10 *cried out . . . sinned against you:* The Israelites say that they are sorry for worshiping other gods, but God is not swayed at first (10:13,14). Eventually, the people get rid of the Canaanite idols, so the LORD helps them (10:16).

10:16 *he could bear Israel's misery no longer:* See the note at 2:17-19.

10:17 *Mizpah:* In chapters 10–12, Mizpah is the name of a town in Gilead east of the Jordan River (see 11:29). It is not the same town as the Mizpah of chapters 20–21, which is in the Benjamin territory.

11:1 *Jephthah . . . mother was a prostitute:* As the son of a prostitute, Jephthah was not a likely candidate for leadership. Nevertheless he is a military hero, and a special leader appointed by God (11:29). See also the mini-article called "Prostitution in the Bible," p. 1688.

11:3 *the land of Tob:* This area, fifteen miles east of Jephthah's home, was where he led the life of an adventurer.

11:6 *Ammonites:* See the note at 10:7.

11:10 *The LORD is our witness:* See Genesis 31:45-49, where a covenant is made between Jacob and Laban at this same site. See also the mini-article called "Making Vows," p. 328.

[10]The elders of Gilead replied, "The LORD is our witness; we
will certainly do as you say." [11]So Jephthah went with the elders of
Gilead, and the people made him head and commander over
them. And he repeated all his words before the LORD in Mizpah.
[12]Then Jephthah sent messengers to the Ammonite king
with the question: "What do you have against us that you have
attacked our country?"
[13]The king of the Ammonites answered Jephthah's messengers, "When Israel came up out of Egypt, they took away my land
from the Arnon to the Jabbok, all the way to the Jordan. Now give
it back peaceably."
[14]Jephthah sent back messengers to the Ammonite king,
[15]saying:

"This is what Jephthah says: Israel did not take the land of
Moab or the land of the Ammonites. [16]But when they came up
out of Egypt, Israel went through the desert to the Red Sea[a]
and on to Kadesh. [17]Then Israel sent messengers to the king of
Edom, saying, 'Give us permission to go through your country,' but the king of Edom would not listen. They sent also to
the king of Moab, and he refused. So Israel stayed at Kadesh.
[18]"Next they traveled through the desert, skirted the
lands of Edom and Moab, passed along the eastern side of the
country of Moab, and camped on the other side of the Arnon.
They did not enter the territory of Moab, for the Arnon was
its border.
[19]"Then Israel sent messengers to Sihon king of the
Amorites, who ruled in Heshbon, and said to him, 'Let us pass
through your country to our own place.' [20]Sihon, however, did
not trust Israel[b] to pass through his territory. He mustered all
his men and encamped at Jahaz and fought with Israel.
[21]"Then the LORD, the God of Israel, gave Sihon and all
his men into Israel's hands, and they defeated them. Israel
took over all the land of the Amorites who lived in that country, [22]capturing all of it from the Arnon to the Jabbok and
from the desert to the Jordan.
[23]"Now since the LORD, the God of Israel, has driven the
Amorites out before his people Israel, what right have you to
take it over? [24]Will you not take what your god Chemosh gives
you? Likewise, whatever the LORD our God has given us, we
will possess. [25]Are you better than Balak son of Zippor, king of
Moab? Did he ever quarrel with Israel or fight with them?
[26]For three hundred years Israel occupied Heshbon, Aroer, the
surrounding settlements and all the towns along the Arnon.
Why didn't you retake them during that time? [27]I have not

[a]16 Hebrew *Yam Suph*; that is, Sea of Reeds [b]20 Or *however, would not make an agreement for Israel*

11:11 *Mizpah:* See the note at 10:17. Jephthah returns to his home and is made a leader of the people.

11:13,14 *they took away my land . . . Jephthah sent back messengers to the Ammonite king:* The king of Ammon declares that he deserves to have the land back because it was stolen from him (11:13). Jephthah argues that the Israelites moved into the land after conquering it at the time of Moses (11:14-27). At that time it did not belong to either Ammon or Moab, but to the Amorites (under King Sihon). However, the argument does not convince the king of Ammon (11:28). According to Joshua 13:15-32, two-and-a-half tribes (Reuben, Gad, and the half-tribe of Manasseh) settled east of the Jordan River. This land was promised to them from the time of Moses (Num 32:28-32; Deut 3:18-20; Josh 22:1-9). See the map on p. 2464.

11:24 *your god Chemosh:* Chemosh was actually the national god of Moab, not Ammon. The land that Ammon was trying to take over had belonged to the Moabites before belonging to the Amorites (see Num 21:26). So the Ammonites may have thought that Chemosh controlled it.

11:25 *Balak:* A Moabite king at the time the people of Israel were on their way to settle in the promised land of Canaan (Num 22:1-6).

11:26 *Heshbon:* This city on the northern border of the Reuben tribe had belonged to the Amorite King Sihon before its capture by the Israelites. The "three hundred years" of Israelite settlement may refer to the number of years the judges mentioned in the book had served so far plus the eighteen years that Ammon oppressed the Israelites in Gilead (see 10:8). But it is unlikely that the Israelite people had been settled near Heshbon this long. (For more, see the Introduction to JUDGES, p. 453).

11:17 Num 20:14-21. **11:18** Num 21:13. **11:19-22** Num 21:21-24.

wronged you, but you are doing me wrong by waging war against me. Let the LORD, the Judge,[a] decide the dispute this day between the Israelites and the Ammonites."

28 The king of Ammon, however, paid no attention to the message Jephthah sent him.

29 Then the Spirit of the LORD came upon Jephthah. He crossed Gilead and Manasseh, passed through Mizpah of Gilead, and from there he advanced against the Ammonites. 30 And Jephthah made a vow to the LORD: "If you give the Ammonites into my hands, 31 whatever comes out of the door of my house to meet me when I return in triumph from the Ammonites will be the LORD's, and I will sacrifice it as a burnt offering."

32 Then Jephthah went over to fight the Ammonites, and the LORD gave them into his hands. 33 He devastated twenty towns from Aroer to the vicinity of Minnith, as far as Abel Keramim. Thus Israel subdued Ammon.

34 When Jephthah returned to his home in Mizpah, who should come out to meet him but his daughter, dancing to the sound of tambourines! She was an only child. Except for her he had neither son nor daughter. 35 When he saw her, he tore his clothes and cried, "Oh! My daughter! You have made me miserable and wretched, because I have made a vow to the LORD that I cannot break."

36 "My father," she replied, "you have given your word to the LORD. Do to me just as you promised, now that the LORD has avenged you of your enemies, the Ammonites. 37 But grant me this one request," she said. "Give me two months to roam the hills and weep with my friends, because I will never marry."

38 "You may go," he said. And he let her go for two months. She and the girls went into the hills and wept because she would never marry. 39 After the two months, she returned to her father and he did to her as he had vowed. And she was a virgin.

From this comes the Israelite custom 40 that each year the young women of Israel go out for four days to commemorate the daughter of Jephthah the Gileadite.

Jephthah and Ephraim

12 The men of Ephraim called out their forces, crossed over to Zaphon and said to Jephthah, "Why did you go to fight the Ammonites without calling us to go with you? We're going to burn down your house over your head."

2 Jephthah answered, "I and my people were engaged in a great struggle with the Ammonites, and although I called, you didn't save me out of their hands. 3 When I saw that you wouldn't help, I took my life in my hands and crossed over to fight the Ammonites, and the LORD gave me the victory over them. Now why have you come up today to fight me?"

---

[a]27 Or *Ruler*

11:30,31 *vow . . . I will sacrifice it as a burnt offering:* The tragedy of this bargain with God is that it is not necessary. Jephthah is already possessed by the Spirit (11:29), so his victory is assured. See also the mini-article called "Making Vows," p. 328.

11:34 *daughter:* The unnamed girl, unaware of the vow, greets her father. The results of Jephthah's senseless vow is heartbreaking for him and fatal for his only child.

11:35,36 *I have made a vow . . . Do to me just as you promised:* In Hebrew thought and practice, once a promise was made it could not be taken back. Ironically, the girl herself makes sure that her father does not take back his vow.

11:40 *each year . . . four days:* This religious rite was probably performed at some point in Israel's history, but it is not mentioned anywhere else in the Bible.

12:1-5 *men of Ephraim . . . Gilead:* See the notes at 1:22, 23 and 10:3-5. The tribe of Ephraim complained that they were not involved in the war against the Ammonites, perhaps because they wanted a share of the money and goods that had been captured. The men of Ephraim then claim that the people of Gilead are living on land that actually belongs to Ephraim (12:4). So Jephthah squashes the Ephraim threat and orders tight security placed on the east bank of the Jordan River so no one from Ephraim can get into Gilead (the tribal land belonging to Gad). See also the note at 8:1.

12:6 *Shibboleth:* This is Hebrew for "ear of corn." The Ephraimites apparently had their own pronunciation for this word, and so their dialect gave them away.

11:35 Num 30:2.

[4]Jephthah then called together the men of Gilead and fought against Ephraim. The Gileadites struck them down because the Ephraimites had said, "You Gileadites are renegades from Ephraim and Manasseh." [5]The Gileadites captured the fords of the Jordan leading to Ephraim, and whenever a survivor of Ephraim said, "Let me cross over," the men of Gilead asked him, "Are you an Ephraimite?" If he replied, "No," [6]they said, "All right, say 'Shibboleth.' " If he said, "Sibboleth," because he could not pronounce the word correctly, they seized him and killed him at the fords of the Jordan. Forty-two thousand Ephraimites were killed at that time.

[7]Jephthah led[a] Israel six years. Then Jephthah the Gileadite died, and was buried in a town in Gilead.

Ibzan, Elon and Abdon

[8]After him, Ibzan of Bethlehem led Israel. [9]He had thirty sons and thirty daughters. He gave his daughters away in marriage to those outside his clan, and for his sons he brought in thirty young women as wives from outside his clan. Ibzan led Israel seven years. [10]Then Ibzan died, and was buried in Bethlehem.

[11]After him, Elon the Zebulunite led Israel ten years. [12]Then Elon died, and was buried in Aijalon in the land of Zebulun.

[13]After him, Abdon son of Hillel, from Pirathon, led Israel. [14]He had forty sons and thirty grandsons, who rode on seventy donkeys. He led Israel eight years. [15]Then Abdon son of Hillel died, and was buried at Pirathon in Ephraim, in the hill country of the Amalekites.

[a]7 Traditionally *judged*; also in verses 8-14

12:7 *led Israel:* See the note at 2:16.

12:8 *Ibzan of Bethlehem:* Ibzan was from the town of Bethlehem in the territory of Zebulun, not Bethlehem in Judah. See the map on p. 2464.

12:9 *thirty sons and thirty daughters:* Ibzan's many children were a sign of his wealth and importance. Compare to 10:4.

12:12 *Aijalon:* This is not the Aijalon in the Manasseh or Ephraim territory (1:35), but another Aijalon farther north in the Zebulun territory.

12:13,14 *Abdon . . . forty sons . . . seventy donkeys:* See the note at 10:3, 4. Donkeys at this time were commonly used as pack animals and for transportation, though not everyone could afford to keep one. The fact that each son owned a donkey was a sign that the family was wealthy. It was not until the time of King Solomon (around 970 B.C.) that the horse came to be used in Palestine.

QUESTIONS ABOUT JUDGES 3:7—12:15

1. Compare the story of Ehud in 3:12-30 with the story of Jael in 4:17-22. How are these stories similar? What is your reaction to the stories?
2. Who was Deborah? In what ways does she show special leadership? (4:1-14)
3. When Gideon was chosen to be a judge, how did he respond? (6:11-24) How many times did Gideon ask for proof from the LORD? (6:17-40) Why do you think he needed this proof?
4. After Gideon was successful in defeating the Midianites, the people asked him to be their king. How did Gideon respond? (8:22, 23) If his response was a high point, what "low point" quickly followed? (8:24-31)
5. How did Abimelech come to leadership? (9:1-6) What differences do you see between Abimelech and his father Gideon?
6. What point does Jotham's fable make about kingship? (9:7-15)
7. According to Jephthah's message to the king of Ammon, why can the Israelites claim the land as their own? (11:16-27)
8. What horror resulted from Jephthah's vow? (11:29-40) What does the behavior of the father and the daughter tell you about this era in history? What do you think of the fact that neither Jephthah nor his daughter asked God to release Jephthah from his vow?
9. What qualities do you want in your political and religious leaders?

13:1 *did evil in the eyes of the Lord:* See the notes at 2:1, 2 and 2:13. See also 2:17; 3:7, 12; 4:1; 6:1; 10:6.

13:1 *Philistines:* See the note at 3:31.

13:2 *Zorah:* Located on the border between Judah and Dan fifteen miles west of Jerusalem (see the map on p. 2464).

13:3 *angel of the Lord:* See the note at 2:1. Manoah's wife refers to the angel as a "man of God" in 13:6,8.

13:5 *a Nazirite, set apart to God:* Nazirites had to follow special rules to show their commitment. Their strict lifestyle is outlined in Numbers 6:1-21. Among other things, they were not to cut their hair, drink wine or beer, or have any contact with a dead body. They were also supposed to follow the laws concerning clean and unclean food (Lev 11). See also the mini-article called "Purity (Clean and Unclean)," p. 2125.

13:15,16 *prepare a young goat:* Offering food was an act of hospitality. See also Gen 18:1-8 and Judg 6:19-22.

13:19 *sacrificed it on a rock to the Lord:* Sacrifices were gifts to God that included certain animals, grains, fruits, and sweet-smelling spices. See also the chart called "Sacrifices and Offerings," p. 219.

13:22 *doomed to die . . . We have seen God:* See the note at 6:22.

SAMSON

Samson, a local hero, has a series of adventures and takes revenge against the Philistines. He is known for his superhuman strength, but note his other personality traits in the stories in chapters 13–16.

The Birth of Samson

13 Again the Israelites did evil in the eyes of the LORD, so the
LORD delivered them into the hands of the Philistines for forty
years.
2 A certain man of Zorah, named Manoah, from the clan of
the Danites, had a wife who was sterile and remained childless.
3 The angel of the LORD appeared to her and said, "You are sterile
and childless, but you are going to conceive and have a son. 4 Now
see to it that you drink no wine or other fermented drink and that
you do not eat anything unclean, 5 because you will conceive and
give birth to a son. No razor may be used on his head, because the
boy is to be a Nazirite, set apart to God from birth, and he will
begin the deliverance of Israel from the hands of the Philistines."
6 Then the woman went to her husband and told him, "A
man of God came to me. He looked like an angel of God, very
awesome. I didn't ask him where he came from, and he didn't tell
me his name. 7 But he said to me, 'You will conceive and give birth
to a son. Now then, drink no wine or other fermented drink and
do not eat anything unclean, because the boy will be a Nazirite of
God from birth until the day of his death.' "
8 Then Manoah prayed to the LORD: "O Lord, I beg you, let
the man of God you sent to us come again to teach us how to
bring up the boy who is to be born."
9 God heard Manoah, and the angel of God came again to the
woman while she was out in the field; but her husband Manoah
was not with her. 10 The woman hurried to tell her husband, "He's
here! The man who appeared to me the other day!"
11 Manoah got up and followed his wife. When he came to
the man, he said, "Are you the one who talked to my wife?"
"I am," he said.
12 So Manoah asked him, "When your words are fulfilled,
what is to be the rule for the boy's life and work?"
13 The angel of the LORD answered, "Your wife must do all that
I have told her. 14 She must not eat anything that comes from the
grapevine, nor drink any wine or other fermented drink nor eat
anything unclean. She must do everything I have commanded her."
15 Manoah said to the angel of the LORD, "We would like you
to stay until we prepare a young goat for you."
16 The angel of the LORD replied, "Even though you detain
me, I will not eat any of your food. But if you prepare a burnt

offering, offer it to the LORD." (Manoah did not realize that it was
the angel of the LORD.)
17Then Manoah inquired of the angel of the LORD, "What
is your name, so that we may honor you when your word
comes true?"
18He replied, "Why do you ask my name? It is beyond understanding.[a]" 19Then Manoah took a young goat, together with the
grain offering, and sacrificed it on a rock to the LORD. And the
LORD did an amazing thing while Manoah and his wife watched:
20As the flame blazed up from the altar toward heaven, the angel of
the LORD ascended in the flame. Seeing this, Manoah and his wife
fell with their faces to the ground. 21When the angel of the LORD
did not show himself again to Manoah and his wife, Manoah realized that it was the angel of the LORD.
22"We are doomed to die!" he said to his wife. "We have
seen God!"
23But his wife answered, "If the LORD had meant to kill us,
he would not have accepted a burnt offering and grain offering
from our hands, nor shown us all these things or now told us
this."
24The woman gave birth to a boy and named him Samson.
He grew and the LORD blessed him, 25and the Spirit of the LORD
began to stir him while he was in Mahaneh Dan, between Zorah
and Eshtaol.

Samson's Marriage

14 Samson went down to Timnah and saw there a young Philistine woman. 2When he returned, he said to his father and mother,
"I have seen a Philistine woman in Timnah; now get her for me as
my wife."
3His father and mother replied, "Isn't there an acceptable
woman among your relatives or among all our people? Must you
go to the uncircumcised Philistines to get a wife?"
But Samson said to his father, "Get her for me. She's the
right one for me." 4(His parents did not know that this was from
the LORD, who was seeking an occasion to confront the Philistines;
for at that time they were ruling over Israel.) 5Samson went down
to Timnah together with his father and mother. As they
approached the vineyards of Timnah, suddenly a young lion came
roaring toward him. 6The Spirit of the LORD came upon him in
power so that he tore the lion apart with his bare hands as he
might have torn a young goat. But he told neither his father nor
his mother what he had done. 7Then he went down and talked
with the woman, and he liked her.
8Some time later, when he went back to marry her, he turned

[a]**18** Or *is wonderful*

The woman gave birth to a boy and named him Samson. He grew and the LORD blessed him.
Judg 13:24

13:24 *Samson:* This name is related to the Hebrew word for sun. A miracle birth (13:2), concerned parents (13:8), and God's blessing are typical ways for biblical authors to call attention to special individuals.

13:25 *the Spirit of the LORD:* See the note at 3:8-10.

14:1 *Timnah:* This town was located about four miles southwest of Dan's camp. For the presence of Philistines, see 13:1 and the note at 3:31.

14:2 *get her for me as my wife:* Samson was strong physically, but seemed to be weak in other ways. He was stubborn and had to have his own way, and he was attracted to non-Israelite women. Marriage with foreigners was forbidden throughout much of Israel's history because such marriages could lead to worshiping foreign gods (3:5, 6).

At this time, marriage was not a matter of personal choice. Rather, parents (or the father alone) chose whom their children would marry (Gen 24:1-4; 38:6).

14:5 *young lion:* This large strong animal was dangerous not only to domestic animals but also to humans. Lions often hide in small hallows in the ground and wait for their prey to pass by. They can kill smaller animals with a blow of the paw and kill larger ones by biting them on the throat.

14:9,10 *did not tell them . . . lion's carcass . . . feast:* Samson didn't tell his parents because eating anything that had touched a skeleton was against God's laws (Lev 11:24-40). Further, as a Nazirite, Samson was not permitted to go close to a dead body. See Num 6:6, 7 and the note at 13:5.

The Hebrew term for "feast" here means a social gathering that involves a lot of drinking. Again, as a Nazirite, Samson was not allowed to drink wine, beer, or even grape juice (see Num 6:2-4).

14:12,13 *riddle:* A riddle was a saying with a hidden meaning. Riddles were often used in the ancient world to test a person's intelligence and wisdom. People who could answer difficult riddles were usually considered more worthy of rewards and positions of authority. See, for example, 1 Kgs 10:1-3; Dan 5:12. See also the Introduction to the Books of Wisdom and Poetry, p. 959.

14:18 *on the seventh day:* At this time, marriage was official after the seventh day of the wedding festivities. However, Samson leaves the woman's home before sunset of the last day, meaning the marriage rite has not been completed or made official.

Samson and the Lion, bronze vessel, thirteenth century. JUDGES includes many stories about Samson, a heroic leader from the tribe of Dan. His parents dedicated him to God from the day he was born, and as he grew the LORD blessed him. The first time the LORD's Spirit took control of Samson was when he was attacked by a lion and he was given the strength to tear it apart with his bare hands. (See 14:5,6.)

aside to look at the lion's carcass. In it was a swarm of bees and
some honey, 9 which he scooped out with his hands and ate as he
went along. When he rejoined his parents, he gave them some, and
they too ate it. But he did not tell them that he had taken the
honey from the lion's carcass.

10 Now his father went down to see the woman. And Samson
made a feast there, as was customary for bridegrooms. 11 When he
appeared, he was given thirty companions.

12 "Let me tell you a riddle," Samson said to them. "If you can
give me the answer within the seven days of the feast, I will give
you thirty linen garments and thirty sets of clothes. 13 If you can't
tell me the answer, you must give me thirty linen garments and
thirty sets of clothes."

"Tell us your riddle," they said. "Let's hear it."

14 He replied,

"Out of the eater, something to eat;
out of the strong, something sweet."

For three days they could not give the answer.

15 On the fourth[a] day, they said to Samson's wife, "Coax your
husband into explaining the riddle for us, or we will burn you and
your father's household to death. Did you invite us here to rob us?"
16 Then Samson's wife threw herself on him, sobbing, "You
hate me! You don't really love me. You've given my people a riddle,
but you haven't told me the answer."
"I haven't even explained it to my father or mother," he
replied, "so why should I explain it to you?" 17 She cried the whole
seven days of the feast. So on the seventh day he finally told her,
because she continued to press him. She in turn explained the riddle to her people.
18 Before sunset on the seventh day the men of the town said
to him,

"What is sweeter than honey?
What is stronger than a lion?"

Samson said to them,

"If you had not plowed with my heifer,
you would not have solved my riddle."

19 Then the Spirit of the LORD came upon him in power. He
went down to Ashkelon, struck down thirty of their men, stripped
them of their belongings and gave their clothes to those who had
explained the riddle. Burning with anger, he went up to his father's
house. 20 And Samson's wife was given to the friend who had
attended him at his wedding.

Samson's Vengeance on the Philistines

15 Later on, at the time of wheat harvest, Samson took a young
goat and went to visit his wife. He said, "I'm going to my wife's
room." But her father would not let him go in.
2 "I was so sure you thoroughly hated her," he said, "that I
gave her to your friend. Isn't her younger sister more attractive?
Take her instead."
3 Samson said to them, "This time I have a right to get even
with the Philistines; I will really harm them." 4 So he went out and
caught three hundred foxes and tied them tail to tail in pairs. He
then fastened a torch to every pair of tails, 5 lit the torches and let
the foxes loose in the standing grain of the Philistines. He burned
up the shocks and standing grain, together with the vineyards and
olive groves.
6 When the Philistines asked, "Who did this?" they were told,
"Samson, the Timnite's son-in-law, because his wife was given to
his friend."
So the Philistines went up and burned her and her father to

14:19 *the Spirit of the LORD:* See the note at 3:8-10. In contrast to other leaders, Samson never leads an army, and his feuds are motivated by personal revenge not by a desire to rescue the Israelite tribes from hostile neighbors. When the LORD's power takes control of him, Samson gains superhuman strength (see also 14:6; 15:13,14; 16:28-30).

14:19 *Ashkelon:* This was a major Philistine town on the southern Mediterranean coast, about twenty miles from Timnah (see the map on p. 2464). Samson robs Ashkelon in order to pay his personal debt to Timnah.

15:1 *took a young goat and went to visit his wife:* The gift was in exchange for sexual relations (Gen 38:15-17).

15:1,2 *his wife . . . I gave her to your friend:* Deuteronomy 24:1 suggests that in Israelite law a husband could end his marriage if he thought his wife had done something disgraceful or if she displeased him in some way. Apparently, the father of the woman Samson was to marry thought Samson intended to divorce his daughter when Samson left before the seven-day wedding feast was over (see the note at 14:18).

15:4 *foxes:* The Hebrew word is also used for jackals, animals very much like foxes. Jackals stay together in packs during the day and sometimes hide in caves where hunters try to trap and kill them.

[a]15 Some Septuagint manuscripts and Syriac; Hebrew *seventh*

death. [7]Samson said to them, "Since you've acted like this, I won't stop until I get my revenge on you." [8]He attacked them viciously and slaughtered many of them. Then he went down and stayed in a cave in the rock of Etam.

[9]The Philistines went up and camped in Judah, spreading out near Lehi. [10]The men of Judah asked, "Why have you come to fight us?"

"We have come to take Samson prisoner," they answered, "to do to him as he did to us."

[11]Then three thousand men from Judah went down to the cave in the rock of Etam and said to Samson, "Don't you realize that the Philistines are rulers over us? What have you done to us?"

He answered, "I merely did to them what they did to me."

[12]They said to him, "We've come to tie you up and hand you over to the Philistines."

Samson said, "Swear to me that you won't kill me yourselves."

[13]"Agreed," they answered. "We will only tie you up and hand you over to them. We will not kill you." So they bound him with two new ropes and led him up from the rock. [14]As he approached Lehi, the Philistines came toward him shouting. The Spirit of the LORD came upon him in power. The ropes on his arms became like charred flax, and the bindings dropped from his hands. [15]Finding a fresh jawbone of a donkey, he grabbed it and struck down a thousand men.

[16]Then Samson said,

"With a donkey's jawbone
    I have made donkeys of them.[a]
With a donkey's jawbone
    I have killed a thousand men."

[17]When he finished speaking, he threw away the jawbone; and the place was called Ramath Lehi.[b]

[18]Because he was very thirsty, he cried out to the LORD, "You have given your servant this great victory. Must I now die of thirst and fall into the hands of the uncircumcised?" [19]Then God opened up the hollow place in Lehi, and water came out of it. When Samson drank, his strength returned and he revived. So the spring was called En Hakkore,[c] and it is still there in Lehi.

[20]Samson led[d] Israel for twenty years in the days of the Philistines.

Samson and Delilah

16 One day Samson went to Gaza, where he saw a prostitute. He went in to spend the night with her. [2]The people of Gaza were told,

[a]16 Or *made a heap or two*; the Hebrew for *donkey* sounds like the Hebrew for *heap.* [b]17 *Ramath Lehi* means *jawbone hill.* [c]19 *En Hakkore* means *caller's spring.* [d]20 Traditionally *judged*

15:8,9 *cave in the rock of Etam . . . Judah:* Samson belonged to the Dan tribe, but the rock of Etam was a few miles southwest of Bethlehem in the territory of the tribe of Judah (see the map on p. 2464). The people of Judah do not want a confrontation with the Philistines (15:10), and they have no reason to support this wild man from Dan.

15:14 *Spirit of the LORD:* See the note at 14:19.

15:15 *jawbone of a donkey:* After snapping the ropes tied around him, Samson uses a jawbone as a curved, sickle-like weapon. As a Nazirite, he is to have no contact with corpses or skeletons (see the note at 14:9,10). The story, however, would have delighted Israelites who were tired of foreign oppressors.

15:19 *God opened up the hollow place . . . water came out of it:* In Hebrew *Hakkore* means "caller." The story explains how Hakkore received its name. See Exod 17:1-7; Num 20:7, 8; Deut 8:15.

15:20 *led Israel for twenty years:* See the note at 2:16. Nothing is known about Samson's leadership of all of Israel, or even any one individual tribe.

16:1 *Gaza:* See the notes at 1:18 and 6:4. Gaza is the most southern of the major Philistine cities. See also the note at 16:3.

16:2 *lay in wait for him all night at the city gate:* The gate was often in a part of the town wall that was thicker and taller than the rest of the wall. The people would have waited for Samson in small rooms inside the city wall adjacent to the gate. See also the notes at 1:24 and 9:35.

Samson Carrying away the City Gates of Gaza, illuminated page from a Bible, mid-fifteenth century. The people of Gaza wanted to kill Samson. In the night, they hid in the guardrooms on each side of the city gate so that they could ambush him as he walked through the gate in the morning. But Samson escaped by pulling the gate doors and doorposts out of the wall and carrying them forty miles away where he set them down on a hill overlooking Hebron. (See 16:1-3.)

"Samson is here!" So they surrounded the place and lay in wait for
him all night at the city gate. They made no move during the
night, saying, "At dawn we'll kill him."
3But Samson lay there only until the middle of the night.
Then he got up and took hold of the doors of the city gate, together with the two posts, and tore them loose, bar and all. He lifted
them to his shoulders and carried them to the top of the hill that
faces Hebron.
4Some time later, he fell in love with a woman in the Valley
of Sorek whose name was Delilah. 5The rulers of the Philistines

16:3 *Hebron:* Hebron was in the southern highlands of Judah, about a forty-mile uphill walk from Gaza (see the map on p. 2464). This story of Samson's superhuman strength no doubt thrilled early listeners. Many would have wondered what could defeat him.

16:4 *Delilah:* She is the only woman given a name in the Samson stories. Delilah lived in a valley that begins thirteen miles southwest of Jerusalem. Although the Philistine rulers hired her, it is not clear whether she herself was a Philistine.

16:5 *rulers of the Philistines:* The cities of Gaza, Gath, Ashdod, Ashkelon, and Ekron made up the five cities of the Philistine alliance. A king or chieftain ruled each. See the map on p. 2465.

16:5 *silver:* Each of the five kings offered eleven hundred pieces of silver, which all together equaled about one hundred forty pounds, an enormous reward.

16:6 *the secret of your great strength:* Though told to trick Samson, Delilah instead asks him directly what she wants to know. Samson approaches the question as a game, similar to his actions in 14:12.

16:7 *seven fresh thongs that have not been dried:* The string for a bow was often made from sinews or internal organs of animals. These strings (here called thongs) were made while the animal tissues were still moist. He snaps them (16:8,9) as he did the ropes in 15:13,14.

16:13 *loom:* This is a large wooden frame used to weave together strands of wool or flax into cloth. For more, see the illustration on p. 1829.

16:15 *How can you say, 'I love you':* Compare to 14:16.

16:17-21 *set apart to God . . . gouged out his eyes:* "Set apart to God" is a reference to the Nazirite vow. See the note at 13:5. Putting out someone's eyes was a humiliating form of punishment also used by Israel's enemies in 1 Samuel 11:2; 2 Kings 25:7.

went to her and said, "See if you can lure him into showing you the secret of his great strength and how we can overpower him so we may tie him up and subdue him. Each one of us will give you eleven hundred shekels[a] of silver."

6 So Delilah said to Samson, "Tell me the secret of your great strength and how you can be tied up and subdued."

7 Samson answered her, "If anyone ties me with seven fresh thongs[b] that have not been dried, I'll become as weak as any other man."

8 Then the rulers of the Philistines brought her seven fresh thongs that had not been dried, and she tied him with them. 9 With men hidden in the room, she called to him, "Samson, the Philistines are upon you!" But he snapped the thongs as easily as a piece of string snaps when it comes close to a flame. So the secret of his strength was not discovered.

10 Then Delilah said to Samson, "You have made a fool of me; you lied to me. Come now, tell me how you can be tied."

11 He said, "If anyone ties me securely with new ropes that have never been used, I'll become as weak as any other man."

12 So Delilah took new ropes and tied him with them. Then, with men hidden in the room, she called to him, "Samson, the Philistines are upon you!" But he snapped the ropes off his arms as if they were threads.

13 Delilah then said to Samson, "Until now, you have been making a fool of me and lying to me. Tell me how you can be tied."

He replied, "If you weave the seven braids of my head into the fabric ⌞on the loom⌟ and tighten it with the pin, I'll become as weak as any other man." So while he was sleeping, Delilah took the seven braids of his head, wove them into the fabric 14 and[c] tightened it with the pin.

Again she called to him, "Samson, the Philistines are upon you!" He awoke from his sleep and pulled up the pin and the loom, with the fabric.

15 Then she said to him, "How can you say, 'I love you,' when you won't confide in me? This is the third time you have made a fool of me and haven't told me the secret of your great strength." 16 With such nagging she prodded him day after day until he was tired to death.

17 So he told her everything. "No razor has ever been used on my head," he said, "because I have been a Nazirite set apart to God since birth. If my head were shaved, my strength would leave me, and I would become as weak as any other man."

18 When Delilah saw that he had told her everything, she sent word to the rulers of the Philistines, "Come back once more; he

---

[a]5 That is, about 28 pounds (about 13 kilograms) [b]7 Or *bowstrings*; also in verses 8 and 9 [c]13,14 Some Septuagint manuscripts; Hebrew "⌞*I can*⌟ *if you weave the seven braids of my head into the fabric* ⌞*on the loom*⌟." 14 *So she*

has told me everything." So the rulers of the Philistines returned
with the silver in their hands. 19Having put him to sleep on her lap,
she called a man to shave off the seven braids of his hair, and so
began to subdue him.[a] And his strength left him.
20Then she called, "Samson, the Philistines are upon you!"
He awoke from his sleep and thought, "I'll go out as before and
shake myself free." But he did not know that the LORD had left him.
21Then the Philistines seized him, gouged out his eyes and
took him down to Gaza. Binding him with bronze shackles, they
set him to grinding in the prison. 22But the hair on his head began
to grow again after it had been shaved.

The Death of Samson

23Now the rulers of the Philistines assembled to offer a great
sacrifice to Dagon their god and to celebrate, saying, "Our god has
delivered Samson, our enemy, into our hands."
24When the people saw him, they praised their god, saying,

"Our god has delivered our enemy
    into our hands,
the one who laid waste our land
    and multiplied our slain."

25While they were in high spirits, they shouted, "Bring out
Samson to entertain us." So they called Samson out of the prison,
and he performed for them.
When they stood him among the pillars, 26Samson said to
the servant who held his hand, "Put me where I can feel the pillars
that support the temple, so that I may lean against them." 27Now
the temple was crowded with men and women; all the rulers of the
Philistines were there, and on the roof were about three thousand
men and women watching Samson perform. 28Then Samson
prayed to the LORD, "O Sovereign LORD, remember me. O God,
please strengthen me just once more, and let me with one blow get
revenge on the Philistines for my two eyes." 29Then Samson
reached toward the two central pillars on which the temple stood.
Bracing himself against them, his right hand on the one and his
left hand on the other, 30Samson said, "Let me die with the
Philistines!" Then he pushed with all his might, and down came
the temple on the rulers and all the people in it. Thus he killed
many more when he died than while he lived.
31Then his brothers and his father's whole family went down
to get him. They brought him back and buried him between Zorah
and Eshtaol in the tomb of Manoah his father. He had led[b] Israel
twenty years.

[a]**19** Hebrew; some Septuagint manuscripts *and he began to weaken*
[b]**31** Traditionally *judged*

Samson prayed, *"O Sovereign LORD, remember me. O God, please strengthen me just once more, and let me with one blow get revenge on the Philistines for my two eyes."* Judg 16:28

16:21 *Gaza:* See the notes at 1:18; 6:4; and 16:1.

16:23 *Dagon their god:* This Philistine god was the father of Baal and the god of grain, with temples in Ashdod and Gaza. See the note at 2:13 and the mini-article called "Canaanite Gods and Goddesses," p. 469. The temple had a large flat roof where the celebration took place.

16:24,25 *among the pillars:* The large middle pillars of the building.

16:27,28 *watching Samson . . . prayed:* Samson may have been in a courtyard visible from the roof. In his prayer, Samson claims that his power comes from God (see also 15:18).

16:31 *buried him:* Several family members were often buried in one tomb, which was often a cave cut into bedrock. See the mini-article called "Burial," p. 1998. See also 15:20.

16:31 *Zorah and Eshtaol:* These towns were listed as part of the Dan tribal territory in Joshua 19:40-46, but in Joshua 15:33 they are listed as part of Judah.

17:1 *Micah . . . Ephraim:* A number of people in the Bible are called Micah, a name that means "who is like the LORD?" This Micah should not be confused with the prophet who lived at the same time as the prophet Isaiah. See the note at 1:22,23.

17:2 *utter a curse . . . bless you:* Like a vow (see the note at 11:35,36), a curse could not be taken back once uttered. But a curse could be made powerless by a blessing.

17:2-4 *shekels of silver . . . cast idol:* The large amount (eleven hundred pieces) was equal to about twenty-eight pounds. Two hundred pieces weighed about five pounds. See also the notes at 2:13 and 8:33.

17:6 *Israel had no king:* These words are used four times in the final chapters of JUDGES (see also 18:1; 19:1; 21:25) to emphasize the lawless and chaotic situation that existed in Israel before the kingship was established. A more negative attitude toward this monarchy is reflected in such passages as Deuteronomy 17:14-20; 1 Samuel 8:1-22.

17:7 *A young Levite:* God chose the men of one Levite family, the descendants of Moses' brother Aaron, to be Israel's priests. The other men from this tribe helped with work in the tabernacle and later in the Temple (see Num 3:5-10 and the mini-article called "Israel's Priests," p. 2344). The Levites were not given territory like the other tribes. Instead, they were to be supported by the rest of the tribes by receiving a portion of the offerings given to the LORD (Num 18:21-24; Deut 18:1,2).

17:7 *Bethlehem:* This town six miles south of Jerusalem was where Rachel was buried (Gen 35:19) and where Israel's greatest king, David, was born (1 Sam 17:12).

17:6 Judg 21:25.

Israel's Troubled Times Continue

The final chapters of JUDGES do not tell of more judges, but continue to describe a period of lawlessness, evil, and civil war among the people of Israel. The writer of the book suggests that life for Israel's tribes was filled with turmoil because they did not have one leader, a king, to rule over them.

THE TRIBE OF DAN AND THEIR PLACE OF WORSHIP

Taking Micah's idols and a Levite priest with them, the tribe of Dan searches for a new home in the north and settles there.

Micah's Idols

17 Now a man named Micah from the hill country of Ephraim
2 said to his mother, "The eleven hundred shekels[a] of silver that
were taken from you and about which I heard you utter a curse—
I have that silver with me; I took it."
Then his mother said, "The LORD bless you, my son!"
3 When he returned the eleven hundred shekels of silver to
his mother, she said, "I solemnly consecrate my silver to the LORD
for my son to make a carved image and a cast idol. I will give it
back to you."
4 So he returned the silver to his mother, and she took two
hundred shekels[b] of silver and gave them to a silversmith, who made
them into the image and the idol. And they were put in Micah's
house.
5 Now this man Micah had a shrine, and he made an ephod
and some idols and installed one of his sons as his priest. 6 In those
days Israel had no king; everyone did as he saw fit.
7 A young Levite from Bethlehem in Judah, who had been
living within the clan of Judah, 8 left that town in search of some
other place to stay. On his way[c] he came to Micah's house in the
hill country of Ephraim.
9 Micah asked him, "Where are you from?"
"I'm a Levite from Bethlehem in Judah," he said, "and I'm
looking for a place to stay."
10 Then Micah said to him, "Live with me and be my father
and priest, and I'll give you ten shekels[d] of silver a year, your
clothes and your food." 11 So the Levite agreed to live with him, and
the young man was to him like one of his sons. 12 Then Micah
installed the Levite, and the young man became his priest and
lived in his house. 13 And Micah said, "Now I know that the LORD
will be good to me, since this Levite has become my priest."

[a] **2** That is, about 28 pounds (about 13 kilograms) [b] **4** That is, about 5 pounds (about 2.3 kilograms) [c] **8** Or *To carry on his profession* [d] **10** That is, about 4 ounces (about 110 grams)

Danites Settle in Laish

18 In those days Israel had no king.
And in those days the tribe of the Danites was seeking a
place of their own where they might settle, because they had not
yet come into an inheritance among the tribes of Israel. 2 So the
Danites sent five warriors from Zorah and Eshtaol to spy out the
land and explore it. These men represented all their clans. They
told them, "Go, explore the land."
The men entered the hill country of Ephraim and came to
the house of Micah, where they spent the night. 3 When they were
near Micah's house, they recognized the voice of the young Levite;
so they turned in there and asked him, "Who brought you here?
What are you doing in this place? Why are you here?"
4 He told them what Micah had done for him, and said, "He
has hired me and I am his priest."
5 Then they said to him, "Please inquire of God to learn
whether our journey will be successful."
6 The priest answered them, "Go in peace. Your journey has
the LORD's approval."
7 So the five men left and came to Laish, where they saw that
the people were living in safety, like the Sidonians, unsuspecting
and secure. And since their land lacked nothing, they were prosperous.[a] Also, they lived a long way from the Sidonians and had no
relationship with anyone else.[b]
8 When they returned to Zorah and Eshtaol, their brothers
asked them, "How did you find things?"
9 They answered, "Come on, let's attack them! We have seen
that the land is very good. Aren't you going to do something?
Don't hesitate to go there and take it over. 10 When you get there,
you will find an unsuspecting people and a spacious land that God
has put into your hands, a land that lacks nothing whatever."
11 Then six hundred men from the clan of the Danites, armed
for battle, set out from Zorah and Eshtaol. 12 On their way they set
up camp near Kiriath Jearim in Judah. This is why the place west of
Kiriath Jearim is called Mahaneh Dan[c] to this day. 13 From there they
went on to the hill country of Ephraim and came to Micah's house.
14 Then the five men who had spied out the land of Laish said
to their brothers, "Do you know that one of these houses has an
ephod, other household gods, a carved image and a cast idol? Now
you know what to do." 15 So they turned in there and went to
the house of the young Levite at Micah's place and greeted him.
16 The six hundred Danites, armed for battle, stood at the entrance
to the gate. 17 The five men who had spied out the land went inside
and took the carved image, the ephod, the other household gods
and the cast idol while the priest and the six hundred armed men
stood at the entrance to the gate.

---

[a]7 The meaning of the Hebrew for this clause is uncertain. [b]7 Hebrew; some Septuagint manuscripts *with the Arameans* [c]12 *Mahaneh Dan* means *Dan's camp.*

17:10 *be my father and priest:* Micah had already made his son the household priest (17:5). Now he seizes the opportunity to get a genuine Levite for the job. Micah is convinced that he then will have God's favor, or perhaps simply have better luck.

18:1 *Israel had no king:* This negative comment on the situation is repeated several times in JUDGES (see 17:6; 19:1; and 21:25). The stories in these last chapters of the book show the chaos in Israel's society and the disintegration of true worship. The writer suggests that a good king would not have allowed these practices. Whenever a leader died, Israel forgot its promises to God. See also the note at 8:22,23.

18:1 *tribe of the Danites:* Ancient tradition locates the tribe of Dan in the south along the Mediterranean coastal plain (Josh 19:40-48). They were hemmed in by the tribe of Ephraim to the north, the tribes of Benjamin and Judah to the east, and the Philistines to the south. See the map on p. 2464.

18:2 *Zorah and Eshtaol . . . Ephraim:* See the note at 16:31 (Zorah and Eshtaol). The warriors left the area heading to the north. Zorah was fifteen miles west of Jerusalem.

18:7 *Laish . . . Sidonians:* Laish was southwest of Mount Hermon in the north, at the headwaters of the Jordan River. Sidon was in Phoenician territory on the Mediterranean coast twenty miles north of Tyre (see the map on p. 2464). Laish was peaceful but defenseless, and had no allies.

18:24 *the gods I made:* See 17:2-4 and the note. Compare to Isa 44:9-20.

18:27,28 *Laish:* See the note at 18:7. The defenseless people of the town are wiped out. For another account of the migration of the tribe of Dan to the lands near the Lebanon Mountains, see Joshua 19:47,48.

18:30,31 *Danites set up for themselves the idols . . . Shiloh:* Dan later became a center for idol worship (1 Kgs 12:28-30). Located twenty miles north of Jerusalem, Shiloh was an important religious site for Israel and many other ancient peoples. Israel kept the ark of the covenant—containing the stone tablets with the Ten Commandments written on them—at Shiloh, until the Philistines stole it around 1050 B.C. (1 Sam 4:3-11). Eventually, Israel's King David defeated the Philistines and got the ark back. See also the mini-article called "The Ark of the Covenant," p. 513.

The "captivity" anticipated here occurred in 722 B.C. when Assyria conquered the northern kingdom of Israel and forced many of Israel's citizens to live in other lands. See the article called "From Joshua to the Exile: The People of Israel in the Promised Land," p. 924, and the mini-article called "Exile," p. 1541.

19:1 *Israel had no king:* See the note at 18:1 (no king). While the exact time is not specified in Israel's history, this comment shows that the stories come from a period of chaos.

19:1 *a Levite . . . concubine:* See the note at 17:7 (A young Levite). The Levites did not have tribal land, but were scattered throughout all the tribes to serve as priests. For "concubine," see the note at 8:30,31.

[18]When these men went into Micah's house and took the
carved image, the ephod, the other household gods and the cast
idol, the priest said to them, "What are you doing?"
[19]They answered him, "Be quiet! Don't say a word. Come
with us, and be our father and priest. Isn't it better that you serve
a tribe and clan in Israel as priest rather than just one man's
household?" [20]Then the priest was glad. He took the ephod, the
other household gods and the carved image and went along with
the people. [21]Putting their little children, their livestock and their
possessions in front of them, they turned away and left.
[22]When they had gone some distance from Micah's house, the
men who lived near Micah were called together and overtook the
Danites. [23]As they shouted after them, the Danites turned and said
to Micah, "What's the matter with you that you called out your
men to fight?"
[24]He replied, "You took the gods I made, and my priest, and
went away. What else do I have? How can you ask, 'What's the matter with you?' "
[25]The Danites answered, "Don't argue with us, or some hot-tempered men will attack you, and you and your family will lose
your lives." [26]So the Danites went their way, and Micah, seeing that
they were too strong for him, turned around and went back home.
[27]Then they took what Micah had made, and his priest, and went
on to Laish, against a peaceful and unsuspecting people. They attacked
them with the sword and burned down their city. [28]There was no one
to rescue them because they lived a long way from Sidon and had no
relationship with anyone else. The city was in a valley near Beth Rehob.
The Danites rebuilt the city and settled there. [29]They named
it Dan after their forefather Dan, who was born to Israel—though
the city used to be called Laish. [30]There the Danites set up for
themselves the idols, and Jonathan son of Gershom, the son of
Moses,[a] and his sons were priests for the tribe of Dan until the
time of the captivity of the land. [31]They continued to use the idols
Micah had made, all the time the house of God was in Shiloh.

THE CRIME AT GIBEAH AND CIVIL WAR AGAINST THE TRIBE OF BENJAMIN

The last chapters give gruesome stories explaining why the tribes of Israel went to war against the Benjamin tribe, and how that tribe survived after nearly being wiped out.

A Levite and His Concubine

19 In those days Israel had no king.
Now a Levite who lived in a remote area in the hill country of Ephraim took a concubine from Bethlehem in Judah. [2]But

[a]**30** An ancient Hebrew scribal tradition, some Septuagint manuscripts and Vulgate; Masoretic Text *Manasseh*

she was unfaithful to him. She left him and went back to her
father's house in Bethlehem, Judah. After she had been there four
months, 3her husband went to her to persuade her to return. He
had with him his servant and two donkeys. She took him into her
father's house, and when her father saw him, he gladly welcomed
him. 4His father-in-law, the girl's father, prevailed upon him to
stay; so he remained with him three days, eating and drinking, and
sleeping there.

5On the fourth day they got up early and he prepared to
leave, but the girl's father said to his son-in-law, "Refresh yourself
with something to eat; then you can go." 6So the two of them sat
down to eat and drink together. Afterward the girl's father said,
"Please stay tonight and enjoy yourself." 7And when the man got
up to go, his father-in-law persuaded him, so he stayed there that
night. 8On the morning of the fifth day, when he rose to go, the
girl's father said, "Refresh yourself. Wait till afternoon!" So the two
of them ate together.

9Then when the man, with his concubine and his servant,
got up to leave, his father-in-law, the girl's father, said, "Now look,
it's almost evening. Spend the night here; the day is nearly over.
Stay and enjoy yourself. Early tomorrow morning you can get up
and be on your way home." 10But, unwilling to stay another night,
the man left and went toward Jebus (that is, Jerusalem), with his
two saddled donkeys and his concubine.

11When they were near Jebus and the day was almost gone,
the servant said to his master, "Come, let's stop at this city of the
Jebusites and spend the night."

12His master replied, "No. We won't go into an alien city,
whose people are not Israelites. We will go on to Gibeah." 13He
added, "Come, let's try to reach Gibeah or Ramah and spend the
night in one of those places." 14So they went on, and the sun set as
they neared Gibeah in Benjamin. 15There they stopped to spend
the night. They went and sat in the city square, but no one took
them into his home for the night.

16That evening an old man from the hill country of
Ephraim, who was living in Gibeah (the men of the place were
Benjamites), came in from his work in the fields. 17When he
looked and saw the traveler in the city square, the old man asked,
"Where are you going? Where did you come from?"

18He answered, "We are on our way from Bethlehem in
Judah to a remote area in the hill country of Ephraim where I live.
I have been to Bethlehem in Judah and now I am going to the
house of the LORD. No one has taken me into his house. 19We have
both straw and fodder for our donkeys and bread and wine for
ourselves your servants—me, your maidservant, and the young
man with us. We don't need anything."

20"You are welcome at my house," the old man said. "Let me
supply whatever you need. Only don't spend the night in the

19:10-14 *Jebus . . . Ramah . . . Gibeah . . . Benjamin:* Not yet under Israelite control, Jebus was a Canaanite town, named for the Jebusite clan who settled there first. Israel captured Jebus (Jerusalem) in King David's time (2 Sam 5:6, 7; 1 Chr 11:4), but even then the Jebusites were not forced to leave. See also the mini-article called "Jerusalem" on p. 574.

The Levite refuses to stop in Jebus, deciding to travel on another three miles north to Gibeah in the territory of Benjamin, and hoping to make it to Ramah, another three miles north. See the map on p. 2464. For more about "Benjamin," see the note at 20:3.

19:15 *spend the night:* People usually considered it a duty to ask travelers to spend the night in their homes, since there were often no other places to stay. This lack of hospitality proved to be the least of their troubles in Gibeah.

19:16 *old man from . . . Ephraim:* While the Benjamites failed to do the proper thing, the old man from Ephraim extends an invitation to the weary travelers.

square." [21]So he took him into his house and fed his donkeys. After they had washed their feet, they had something to eat and drink.

[22]While they were enjoying themselves, some of the wicked men of the city surrounded the house. Pounding on the door, they shouted to the old man who owned the house, "Bring out the man who came to your house so we can have sex with him."

[23]The owner of the house went outside and said to them, "No, my friends, don't be so vile. Since this man is my guest, don't do this disgraceful thing. [24]Look, here is my virgin daughter, and his concubine. I will bring them out to you now, and you can use them and do to them whatever you wish. But to this man, don't do such a disgraceful thing."

[25]But the men would not listen to him. So the man took his concubine and sent her outside to them, and they raped her and abused her throughout the night, and at dawn they let her go. [26]At daybreak the woman went back to the house where her master was staying, fell down at the door and lay there until daylight.

[27]When her master got up in the morning and opened the door of the house and stepped out to continue on his way, there lay his concubine, fallen in the doorway of the house, with her hands on the threshold. [28]He said to her, "Get up; let's go." But there was no answer. Then the man put her on his donkey and set out for home.

[29]When he reached home, he took a knife and cut up his concubine, limb by limb, into twelve parts and sent them into all the areas of Israel. [30]Everyone who saw it said, "Such a thing has never been seen or done, not since the day the Israelites came up out of Egypt. Think about it! Consider it! Tell us what to do!"

Israelites Fight the Benjamites

20 Then all the Israelites from Dan to Beersheba and from the land of Gilead came out as one man and assembled before the LORD in Mizpah. [2]The leaders of all the people of the tribes of Israel took their places in the assembly of the people of God, four hundred thousand soldiers armed with swords. [3](The Benjamites heard that the Israelites had gone up to Mizpah.) Then the Israelites said, "Tell us how this awful thing happened."

[4]So the Levite, the husband of the murdered woman, said, "I and my concubine came to Gibeah in Benjamin to spend the night. [5]During the night the men of Gibeah came after me and surrounded the house, intending to kill me. They raped my concubine, and she died. [6]I took my concubine, cut her into pieces and sent one piece to each region of Israel's inheritance, because they committed this lewd and disgraceful act in Israel. [7]Now, all you Israelites, speak up and give your verdict."

[8]All the people rose as one man, saying, "None of us will go home. No, not one of us will return to his house. [9]But now this is

19:21 *washed their feet:* Seeing that one's guests' feet were washed was an important part of hospitality, since people wore open sandals and their feet got dirty after walking on the dusty roads or working in the fields.

19:22-24 *Bring out the man . . . here is my virgin daughter . . . concubine:* For a similar situation, see Gen 19:4-8. According to customs of hospitality, the old man was expected to protect his male guest. Offering the Benjamite men his daughter and the Levite's concubine shows how strongly he felt about his duty to his guest. It also shows that men often controlled what happened to women and that women had few legal rights. Though the Law of Moses did have strong rules against illegal sex, including rape (Deut 22:22-27), the story is another example of the lawlessness of the time.

19:29 *cut up his concubine . . . sent them into all the areas of Israel:* The Levite seems to be unfeeling and indifferent toward his concubine, who had such a horrifying night while he slept. The gruesome act of cutting up the dead woman's body and distributing the pieces to Israel's twelve tribes is a dramatic call to action. Her murder is seen as not just a personal tragedy, but an insult to all the people of Israel. Ironically, her dismemberment brings the people together and makes them act as one to avenge this insult. For other symbolic divisions, see 1 Sam 11:7; 1 Kgs 11:29-31.

20:1,2 *Dan . . . Beersheba . . . Mizpah:* People from every tribe gathered in Mizpah in the Benjamin district, a worship site eight miles north of Jerusalem. "From Dan to Beersheba" indicates the whole of Canaan from north to south (see the map on p. 2464).

20:3 *Benjamites:* Benjamin was the smallest of the tribes (1 Sam 9:21). This tribe ignores the summons, supports the town of Gibeah, and prepares for war. The men of Gibeah who raped the Levite's concubine should have been judged according to the Law of Moses, but because this was a lawless time, their evil act leads to a civil war.

what we'll do to Gibeah: We'll go up against it as the lot directs.
10We'll take ten men out of every hundred from all the tribes of
Israel, and a hundred from a thousand, and a thousand from ten
thousand, to get provisions for the army. Then, when the army
arrives at Gibeah[a] in Benjamin, it can give them what they deserve
for all this vileness done in Israel." 11So all the men of Israel got
together and united as one man against the city.

12The tribes of Israel sent men throughout the tribe of Benjamin, saying, "What about this awful crime that was committed
among you? 13Now surrender those wicked men of Gibeah so that
we may put them to death and purge the evil from Israel."

But the Benjamites would not listen to their fellow Israelites.
14From their towns they came together at Gibeah to fight against
the Israelites. 15At once the Benjamites mobilized twenty-six thousand swordsmen from their towns, in addition to seven hundred
chosen men from those living in Gibeah. 16Among all these soldiers there were seven hundred chosen men who were left-handed,
each of whom could sling a stone at a hair and not miss.

17Israel, apart from Benjamin, mustered four hundred thousand swordsmen, all of them fighting men.

18The Israelites went up to Bethel[b] and inquired of God. They
said, "Who of us shall go first to fight against the Benjamites?"

The LORD replied, "Judah shall go first."

19The next morning the Israelites got up and pitched camp
near Gibeah. 20The men of Israel went out to fight the Benjamites
and took up battle positions against them at Gibeah. 21The Benjamites came out of Gibeah and cut down twenty-two thousand
Israelites on the battlefield that day. 22But the men of Israel
encouraged one another and again took up their positions where
they had stationed themselves the first day. 23The Israelites went up
and wept before the LORD until evening, and they inquired of the
LORD. They said, "Shall we go up again to battle against the Benjamites, our brothers?"

The LORD answered, "Go up against them."

24Then the Israelites drew near to Benjamin the second day.
25This time, when the Benjamites came out from Gibeah to oppose
them, they cut down another eighteen thousand Israelites, all of
them armed with swords.

26Then the Israelites, all the people, went up to Bethel, and
there they sat weeping before the LORD. They fasted that day until
evening and presented burnt offerings and fellowship offerings[c]
to the LORD. 27And the Israelites inquired of the LORD. (In those
days the ark of the covenant of God was there, 28with Phinehas son
of Eleazar, the son of Aaron, ministering before it.) They asked,

[a]**10** One Hebrew manuscript; most Hebrew manuscripts *Geba,* a variant of *Gibeah* [b]**18** Or *to the house of God*; also in verse 26 [c]**26** Traditionally *peace offerings*

20:9 *as the lot directs:* Answers to questions put to the LORD were often determined by a method known as drawing lots. Small pieces of wood or stone called "lots" were used to find out what God wanted the people to do. It was similar to flipping a coin or drawing straws, but it was believed that God controlled the outcome.

20:15 *Benjamites:* See the note at 20:3.

20:15,16 *sling a stone:* Benjamin's warriors were known as sharpshooters, using slings made from leather straps to hurl stones with precision (1 Chr 12:2).

20:18 *inquired of God . . . Judah:* They asked God by casting "lots" (see the note at 20:9). The men of the Judah tribe chose the lot that sent them to war first. See also Judg 1:1,2.

20:26 *weeping . . . fasted:* After being defeated by the tribe of Benjamin, the Israelites mourned their losses by crying out to God and by fasting (not eating). Mourning was also done by tearing one's clothes and rubbing dirt on one's body (see Josh 7:6). The slaughter of the Israelites was immense.

20:26 *burnt offerings and fellowship offerings:* See Lev 1–3 and the relevant notes. See also the note at 2:5.

20:27,28 *ark of the covenant:* See the note at 18:30,31 and the mini-article called "The Ark of the Covenant," p. 513.

20:27,28 *Phinehas:* Phinehas is the grandson of Aaron and son of Eleazar, the high priest during the conquest of Canaan. See Exod 6:25; Num 25:6-13; Josh 22:13.

20:29 *set an ambush:* The battle plan used here is similar to that used by Joshua in the campaign against the town of Ai (Josh 8).

20:40 *column of smoke:* The smoke signals the destruction of Gibeah and the ambush. Just when the Benjamites thought all was going well, the rest of Israel defeats them. Twenty-five thousand men of Benjamin were killed and only six hundred survived (20:47).

20:45 *rock of Rimmon:* This was located about three miles east of Bethel (see the map on p. 2464).

20:48 *put all the towns to the sword:* The civil war ends with the tribe of Benjamin almost completely wiped out (21:15, 16). See the note at 1:17. The "Holy War" tactics that had guided the Israelites in their defeat of foreign enemies in Canaan were now used against one of their own tribes (Benjamin). Only six hundred male survivors were left at the rock of Rimmon (20:47).

"Shall we go up again to battle with Benjamin our brother, or not?"

The LORD responded, "Go, for tomorrow I will give them into your hands."

[29]Then Israel set an ambush around Gibeah. [30]They went up against the Benjamites on the third day and took up positions against Gibeah as they had done before. [31]The Benjamites came out to meet them and were drawn away from the city. They began to inflict casualties on the Israelites as before, so that about thirty men fell in the open field and on the roads—the one leading to Bethel and the other to Gibeah.

[32]While the Benjamites were saying, "We are defeating them as before," the Israelites were saying, "Let's retreat and draw them away from the city to the roads."

[33]All the men of Israel moved from their places and took up positions at Baal Tamar, and the Israelite ambush charged out of its place on the west[a] of Gibeah.[b] [34]Then ten thousand of Israel's finest men made a frontal attack on Gibeah. The fighting was so heavy that the Benjamites did not realize how near disaster was. [35]The LORD defeated Benjamin before Israel, and on that day the Israelites struck down 25,100 Benjamites, all armed with swords. [36]Then the Benjamites saw that they were beaten.

Now the men of Israel had given way before Benjamin, because they relied on the ambush they had set near Gibeah. [37]The men who had been in ambush made a sudden dash into Gibeah, spread out and put the whole city to the sword. [38]The men of Israel had arranged with the ambush that they should send up a great cloud of smoke from the city, [39]and then the men of Israel would turn in the battle.

The Benjamites had begun to inflict casualties on the men of Israel (about thirty), and they said, "We are defeating them as in the first battle." [40]But when the column of smoke began to rise from the city, the Benjamites turned and saw the smoke of the whole city going up into the sky. [41]Then the men of Israel turned on them, and the men of Benjamin were terrified, because they realized that disaster had come upon them. [42]So they fled before the Israelites in the direction of the desert, but they could not escape the battle. And the men of Israel who came out of the towns cut them down there. [43]They surrounded the Benjamites, chased them and easily[c] overran them in the vicinity of Gibeah on the east. [44]Eighteen thousand Benjamites fell, all of them valiant fighters. [45]As they turned and fled toward the desert to the rock of Rimmon, the Israelites cut down five thousand men along the roads. They kept pressing after the Benjamites as far as Gidom and struck down two thousand more.

---

[a]**33** Some Septuagint manuscripts and Vulgate; the meaning of the Hebrew for this word is uncertain. [b]**33** Hebrew *Geba,* a variant of *Gibeah* [c]**43** The meaning of the Hebrew for this word is uncertain.

46 On that day twenty-five thousand Benjamite swordsmen
fell, all of them valiant fighters. 47 But six hundred men turned and
fled into the desert to the rock of Rimmon, where they stayed four
months. 48 The men of Israel went back to Benjamin and put all the
towns to the sword, including the animals and everything else they
found. All the towns they came across they set on fire.

Wives for the Benjamites

21 The men of Israel had taken an oath at Mizpah: "Not one of
us will give his daughter in marriage to a Benjamite."
2 The people went to Bethel,[a] where they sat before God until
evening, raising their voices and weeping bitterly. 3 "O LORD, the
God of Israel," they cried, "why has this happened to Israel? Why
should one tribe be missing from Israel today?"
4 Early the next day the people built an altar and presented
burnt offerings and fellowship offerings.[b]
5 Then the Israelites asked, "Who from all the tribes of Israel
has failed to assemble before the LORD?" For they had taken a
solemn oath that anyone who failed to assemble before the LORD at
Mizpah should certainly be put to death.
6 Now the Israelites grieved for their brothers, the Benjamites. "Today one tribe is cut off from Israel," they said. 7 "How
can we provide wives for those who are left, since we have taken
an oath by the LORD not to give them any of our daughters in marriage?" 8 Then they asked, "Which one of the tribes of Israel failed
to assemble before the LORD at Mizpah?" They discovered that no
one from Jabesh Gilead had come to the camp for the assembly.
9 For when they counted the people, they found that none of the
people of Jabesh Gilead were there.
10 So the assembly sent twelve thousand fighting men with
instructions to go to Jabesh Gilead and put to the sword those living there, including the women and children. 11 "This is what you
are to do," they said. "Kill every male and every woman who is not
a virgin." 12 They found among the people living in Jabesh Gilead
four hundred young women who had never slept with a man, and
they took them to the camp at Shiloh in Canaan.
13 Then the whole assembly sent an offer of peace to the Benjamites at the rock of Rimmon. 14 So the Benjamites returned at
that time and were given the women of Jabesh Gilead who had
been spared. But there were not enough for all of them.
15 The people grieved for Benjamin, because the LORD had
made a gap in the tribes of Israel. 16 And the elders of the assembly
said, "With the women of Benjamin destroyed, how shall we provide wives for the men who are left? 17 The Benjamite survivors
must have heirs," they said, "so that a tribe of Israel will not be

[a]2 Or *to the house of God* [b]4 Traditionally *peace offerings*

21:1 *taken an oath:* They make a vow that cannot be taken back (see the note at 11:35,36). See also the mini-article called "Making Vows," p. 328.

21:2,3 *Bethel . . . weeping bitterly:* Bethel was a holy place in central Canaan, situated between Jerusalem and Shechem. Jacob named this place "Bethel," which means "house of God" (Gen 28:10-19). The town is given to Ephraim in Joshua 16:1-4. See the note at 20:26 (weeping).

21:4 *burnt offerings and fellowship offerings:* See the chart called "Sacrifices and Offerings," p. 219.

21:5 *solemn oath . . . put to death:* See the first oath at 21:1. Here we find out that a second oath was made at the meeting of the tribes at Mizpah (20:1-3). This oath to kill anyone who didn't come to the meeting at Mizpah would cause more bloodshed and death, but it also allowed the Israelite tribes to make things up to the men of the Benjamin tribe that had been nearly wiped out. See also the notes at 21:12 and 21:22.

21:10 *Jabesh Gilead:* It was determined that no one from Jabesh Gilead had attended the meeting. Gilead was east of the Jordan River in the territory of Gad (see the map on p. 2464). The town of Jabesh is also tied with Benjamin later, through the Benjamite King Saul (1 Sam 11:1-11; 31:11-13).

21:12 *four hundred young women who had never slept with a man:* These virgins are given as wives to the surviving men of the Benjamin tribe, since all the women of the Benjamin tribe had been killed. Sparing young virgins' lives and then claiming them as war prizes is also seen in Numbers 31:17,18 and Judges 5:30. But the four hundred women mentioned here are not enough for the six hundred warriors (20:47).

wiped out. 18 We can't give them our daughters as wives, since we
Israelites have taken this oath: 'Cursed be anyone who gives a wife
to a Benjamite.' 19 But look, there is the annual festival of the LORD
in Shiloh, to the north of Bethel, and east of the road that goes
from Bethel to Shechem, and to the south of Lebonah."
20 So they instructed the Benjamites, saying, "Go and hide in
the vineyards 21 and watch. When the girls of Shiloh come out to
join in the dancing, then rush from the vineyards and each of you
seize a wife from the girls of Shiloh and go to the land of Benjamin. 22 When their fathers or brothers complain to us, we will say
to them, 'Do us a kindness by helping them, because we did not
get wives for them during the war, and you are innocent, since you
did not give your daughters to them.' "
23 So that is what the Benjamites did. While the girls were
dancing, each man caught one and carried her off to be his wife.
Then they returned to their inheritance and rebuilt the towns and
settled in them.
24 At that time the Israelites left that place and went home to
their tribes and clans, each to his own inheritance.
25 In those days Israel had no king; everyone did as he saw fit.

21:19 *annual festival . . . Shiloh:* For Shiloh, see the note at 18:30, 31. This annual festival in Shiloh might have been a common practice during the period of the judges (see also 1 Sam 1:3, 21).

21:22 *innocent:* The promise of 21:1 was not technically violated, as the women were kidnapped, and their parents did not actually give them to the Benjamites.

21:24,25 *Israel had no king:* The book seems to end with the tribes of Israel at peace, but the writer repeats a phrase (17:6; 18:1; 19:1), which leaves the impression that Israel will continue to have a difficult time until a king rules all the tribes. Until then, every person and every tribe will do as they please, meaning that civil war, needless violence, and acts of cruelty and injustice will continue.

QUESTIONS ABOUT JUDGES 13:1—21:25

1. What were the miraculous events that accompanied Samson's birth? (13:2-25)
2. Samson was to be given to God as a Nazirite. According to Numbers 6:1-8, what strict vows were Nazirites supposed to keep? Which of these vows did Samson keep? Which did he violate?
3. In what ways does Samson fit the role of a judge? How is he different from other judges in the book? What are your thoughts or questions about God's choice of Samson as a leader?
4. Do you believe that Micah's mother or the Levite thought they were worshiping God properly? (Judg 17; 18:15-26) If so, what does it say about the state of worship in Israel at this time? What might it say about the need for leadership in the teaching of faith, both then and now?
5. Why did the tribe of Dan wish to move from the south? Why did they choose to invade Laish? (18:1-7) What do you think of what the men of Dan say in 18:9,10?
6. Which, if any, of the events in chapters 19–21 would not be tolerated in our society today? Why? What seems to have been the attitude toward women in the ancient times? What was women's status?
7. What point does the writer of JUDGES seem to be making in 21:25? (also 17:6; 18:1; 19:1) How does this fit with Gideon's response in 8:22, 23?
8. How is the idea of everyone doing as they see fit encouraged in our society today? How does this idea fit with honoring God and living a life of faith?
9. What other questions do you still have regarding what you have read and studied in JUDGES?

RUTH

Trying to survive when the odds are against you can be difficult. Read the story of Ruth and her mother-in-law Naomi to find out how a brave and loyal woman survived under difficult circumstances to become the great-grandmother of King David.

WHAT MAKES RUTH SPECIAL?

RUTH is a beautiful story that teaches many things, among them:

- God's purposes may be fulfilled in unexpected ways;
- God works in the lives of people who are faithful;
- Helping others and being loyal to family and friends can change lives and bring happiness;
- God's goodness is for everyone, not just for people who are born Jews;
- God cares about all people and is at work in their everyday lives.

WHY WAS RUTH WRITTEN?

The story of Ruth showed the people it was written for, the people of Israel, how God can use not only the Jews but people of other nations to work out God's plans in the world. Ruth was not from any of the tribes of Israel but from Moab. She left the security of her own family to live in Israel with her mother-in-law Naomi and to take care of this childless widow. The last verses of the story (4:13-22) tell how Ruth and her descendants became ancestors of Israel's greatest king, David.

WHAT'S THE STORY BEHIND THE SCENE?

The story of Ruth tells about events that happened during the time of the judges, a period of around two hundred years which ended shortly before David became king of Israel in about 1000 B.C. (See the Introduction to JUDGES p. 453). Many of the Hebrew terms and customs that are mentioned in the story come from this time, but some biblical scholars believe that some of the language and laws at work in the book come from as late as 250 B.C. This may mean that the final version of the story was written down centuries after the time when the events in the story took place.

HOW IS RUTH CONSTRUCTED?

RUTH is like a short story with interesting characters and a plot that leads to a happy conclusion. But, it is a story with an important message about God and God's people. It can be divided into two main sections:

Ruth decides to leave Moab (1:1-22)

Ruth in Israel (2:1—4:22)

Moab: Moab was a land east of the Dead Sea. The people of Moab were not part of Israel, but were considered to be descendants of Lot, the nephew of Abraham (Gen 11:31; 19:30-38). The tribes of Israel stayed in Moab (Num 22–24) on their way from Egypt to Canaan, the land God had promised to give them. The people of Moab worshiped idols and were enemies of the people of Israel (Deut 23:3-6).

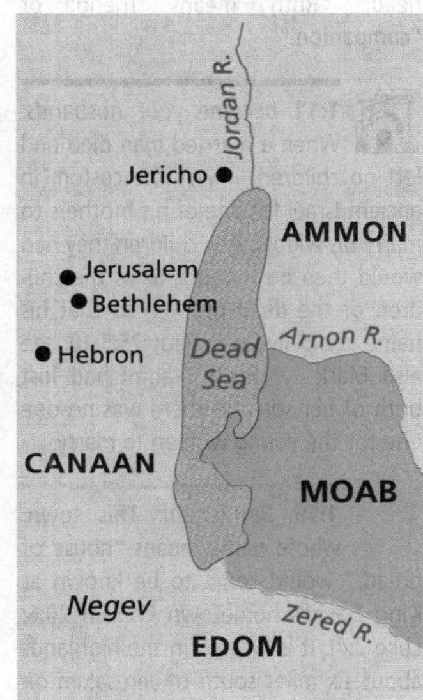

1:1 *when the judges ruled:* After Joshua led the Israelite people into the land of Canaan, the land was divided among Israel's twelve tribes. See the map on p. 2464. During this time, God chose leaders known as "judges" to help the people protect their land and to remind them to remain faithful to God. See also the Introduction to JUDGES, p. 453.

1:1 *Moab:* See the note on p. 497.

1:2 *Elimelech . . . Naomi . . . Mahlon and Kilion . . . Ephrathites:* In Hebrew, "Elimelech" means "My God is king" and "Naomi" means "pleasant" or "beloved," "Mahlon" means "sickness," and "Kilion" means "weakness." Elimelech and Naomi were from the tribe of Judah. They are called Ephrathites because they were from Ephrathah, a name for the area around Bethlehem.

1:4 *Orpah . . . Ruth:* In Hebrew "Orpah" means "neck" or "back of the head." "Ruth" means "friend" or "companion."

1:11 *become your husbands:* When a married man died and left no children, it was the custom in ancient Israel for one of his brothers to marry his widow. Any children they had would then be thought of as the children of the dead brother, so that his name could live on (Deut 25:5-10; see also Mark 12:18-27). Naomi had lost both of her sons, so there was no one else for the young women to marry.

1:19 *Bethlehem:* This town, whose name means "house of bread," would come to be known as King David's hometown (1 Sam 20:6; Luke 2:4). It is located in the highlands about six miles south of Jerusalem on the main north-south ridge that runs through Palestine. See the map on p. 497.

Ruth Decides to Leave Moab

An Israelite woman named Naomi moves to Moab but later decides to return to Israel after her husband and sons die. Naomi's daughter-in-law Ruth, who is from Moab, decides to leave her own family and friends and move to Israel to help Naomi.

Naomi and Ruth

1 In the days when the judges ruled,[a] there was a famine in the
land, and a man from Bethlehem in Judah, together with his wife
and two sons, went to live for a while in the country of Moab. 2 The
man's name was Elimelech, his wife's name Naomi, and the names
of his two sons were Mahlon and Kilion. They were Ephrathites
from Bethlehem, Judah. And they went to Moab and lived there.
3 Now Elimelech, Naomi's husband, died, and she was left
with her two sons. 4 They married Moabite women, one named
Orpah and the other Ruth. After they had lived there about ten
years, 5 both Mahlon and Kilion also died, and Naomi was left
without her two sons and her husband.
6 When she heard in Moab that the LORD had come to the aid
of his people by providing food for them, Naomi and her
daughters-in-law prepared to return home from there. 7 With her
two daughters-in-law she left the place where she had been living
and set out on the road that would take them back to the land of
Judah.
8 Then Naomi said to her two daughters-in-law, "Go back, each
of you, to your mother's home. May the LORD show kindness to you,
as you have shown to your dead and to me. 9 May the LORD grant that
each of you will find rest in the home of another husband."
Then she kissed them and they wept aloud 10 and said to her,
"We will go back with you to your people."
11 But Naomi said, "Return home, my daughters. Why would
you come with me? Am I going to have any more sons, who could
become your husbands? 12 Return home, my daughters; I am too
old to have another husband. Even if I thought there was still hope
for me—even if I had a husband tonight and then gave birth to
sons— 13 would you wait until they grew up? Would you remain
unmarried for them? No, my daughters. It is more bitter for me
than for you, because the LORD's hand has gone out against me!"
14 At this they wept again. Then Orpah kissed her mother-in-
law good-by, but Ruth clung to her.
15 "Look," said Naomi, "your sister-in-law is going back to her
people and her gods. Go back with her."
16 But Ruth replied, "Don't urge me to leave you or to turn
back from you. Where you go I will go, and where you stay I will
stay. Your people will be my people and your God my God.

[a]1 Traditionally *judged*

Story of Ruth by John August Swanson, twentieth century. This brightly colored serigraph depicts many of the key scenes in this short and lively book about Ruth, the loyal daughter-in-law of the Israelite widow Naomi. The last panel shows Naomi holding her new grandson, Obed, who would one day become the grandfather to Israel's greatest king, David.

17 Where you die I will die, and there I will be buried. May the LORD
deal with me, be it ever so severely, if anything but death separates
you and me." 18 When Naomi realized that Ruth was determined to
go with her, she stopped urging her.
19 So the two women went on until they came to Bethlehem.
When they arrived in Bethlehem, the whole town was stirred
because of them, and the women exclaimed, "Can this be Naomi?"
20 "Don't call me Naomi,[a]" she told them. "Call me Mara,[b]
because the Almighty[c] has made my life very bitter. 21 I went away
full, but the LORD has brought me back empty. Why call me
Naomi? The LORD has afflicted[d] me; the Almighty has brought
misfortune upon me."
22 So Naomi returned from Moab accompanied by Ruth the
Moabitess, her daughter-in-law, arriving in Bethlehem as the barley harvest was beginning.

1:20 *Call me Mara:* In Hebrew "Mara" means "bitter," and "Naomi" means "pleasant." In her misfortune, Naomi clearly feels the irony of her given name. See also Exod 15:23.

1:22 *barley harvest:* Barley and wheat were the two most important grains in the ancient Near East. Barley was the cheaper of the two and was used mainly to feed cattle, but it was also used by poor people for making bread. In times of emergency even wealthier people would use it in place of wheat. The barley harvest comes in March or April in the area around Bethlehem.

[a]**20** *Naomi* means *pleasant*; also in verse 21. [b]**20** *Mara* means *bitter.*
[c]**20** Hebrew *Shaddai*; also in verse 21 [d]**21** Or *has testified against*

Ruth in Israel

While picking leftover stalks of grain in a nearby field, Ruth meets Boaz, a relative of Naomi's dead husband. Naomi makes plans for Ruth to marry Boaz, but first he must bargain with another relative who also has the right to marry Ruth. After Boaz and Ruth marry, they have a child who later becomes the grandfather of King David.

Ruth Meets Boaz

2 Now Naomi had a relative on her husband's side, from the clan
of Elimelech, a man of standing, whose name was Boaz.
[2]And Ruth the Moabitess said to Naomi, "Let me go to the
fields and pick up the leftover grain behind anyone in whose eyes
I find favor."
Naomi said to her, "Go ahead, my daughter." [3]So she went
out and began to glean in the fields behind the harvesters. As it
turned out, she found herself working in a field belonging to Boaz,
who was from the clan of Elimelech.
[4]Just then Boaz arrived from Bethlehem and greeted the harvesters, "The LORD be with you!"
"The LORD bless you!" they called back.
[5]Boaz asked the foreman of his harvesters, "Whose young
woman is that?"
[6]The foreman replied, "She is the Moabitess who came back
from Moab with Naomi. [7]She said, 'Please let me glean and gather
among the sheaves behind the harvesters.' She went into the field
and has worked steadily from morning till now, except for a short
rest in the shelter."
[8]So Boaz said to Ruth, "My daughter, listen to me. Don't go
and glean in another field and don't go away from here. Stay here
with my servant girls. [9]Watch the field where the men are harvesting, and follow along after the girls. I have told the men not to
touch you. And whenever you are thirsty, go and get a drink from
the water jars the men have filled."
[10]At this, she bowed down with her face to the ground. She
exclaimed, "Why have I found such favor in your eyes that you
notice me—a foreigner?"
[11]Boaz replied, "I've been told all about what you have done
for your mother-in-law since the death of your husband—how you
left your father and mother and your homeland and came to live
with a people you did not know before. [12]May the LORD repay you
for what you have done. May you be richly rewarded by the LORD,
the God of Israel, under whose wings you have come to take refuge."
[13]"May I continue to find favor in your eyes, my lord," she
said. "You have given me comfort and have spoken kindly to your
servant—though I do not have the standing of one of your servant
girls."

2:1 *Boaz:* Boaz was a wealthy relative of Elimelech. His name means "strength" or "sharp mind."

2:2 *pick up the leftover grain:* It was the custom at harvest time to leave some stalks of grain in the field for poor people, widows, orphans, and foreigners to pick up (Lev 19:9,10; 23:22; Deut 24:19-22). Naomi and Ruth had little money or food after coming back to Bethlehem from Moab. As widows, it would not have been unusual for them to take advantage of the law allowing them to pick unharvested grain. This was called "gleaning."

2:10 *a foreigner:* Because the people of Moab were sometimes enemies of Israel (Deut 23:3-6), the Jewish people who first heard this story might have been surprised that Boaz was so kind toward Ruth, who was from Moab. For more about what the Bible has to say about how foreigners should be treated, see the mini-article called "Foreigners (Aliens)," p. 501.

2:15,16 *pull out some stalks for her . . . leave them for her:* See the note at 2:2. Boaz was being more generous than the Law or custom required him to be.

14 At mealtime Boaz said to her, "Come over here. Have some
bread and dip it in the wine vinegar."
When she sat down with the harvesters, he offered her some
roasted grain. She ate all she wanted and had some left over. 15 As
she got up to glean, Boaz gave orders to his men, "Even if she gathers among the sheaves, don't embarrass her. 16 Rather, pull out
some stalks for her from the bundles and leave them for her to
pick up, and don't rebuke her."
17 So Ruth gleaned in the field until evening. Then she
threshed the barley she had gathered, and it amounted to about an
ephah.[a] 18 She carried it back to town, and her mother-in-law saw

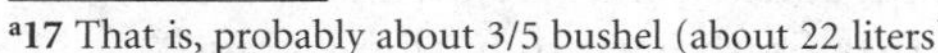

[a]17 That is, probably about 3/5 bushel (about 22 liters)

2:17 *gleaned . . . threshed:* See the note at 2:2. Threshing was done with wooden sticks, used to beat the grain stalks until all the grain and husks fell to the ground. The empty stalks were either thrown away, used for weaving things, burned as kindling, or fed to animals in the dry season.

FOREIGNERS (ALIENS)

GENESIS tells the story of Abraham and Sarah who left their country in the East to live in Canaan as foreigners (Gen 12–23). Their grandson Jacob moved his family to Egypt during a time of famine after his own son Joseph rose to a position of power there (Gen 43–50). Later, Jacob's descendants, the people of Israel, became slaves in Egypt. It was then that God chose Moses to lead them out of Egypt into Canaan, the land God had promised to give them as their own.

They settled there under the leadership of Joshua. The laws they had received from God taught them to treat the foreigners living among them with the same fairness and freedom that they had finally come to enjoy (Exod 12:49; Lev 24:22). The Israelites were commanded to respect foreigners and to give them full legal rights, remembering that they themselves had once lived as foreigners in Egypt (Lev 19:33,34; Deut 10:18,19; 23:7).

However, the Jewish Scriptures also warned the Israelites to be careful about becoming too friendly with the people who lived in the land of Canaan. The Canaanites and their false gods were to be driven out (Exod 23:31-33). If the Canaanites remained in the land, they were not to participate in the religion of Israel, unless the males allowed themselves to be circumcised (Exod 12:48,49).

Years later, the people of Israel became foreigners once again, when they were taken as captives into exile in Babylon. The Israelites were allowed to return to their own land in 539 B.C. Their leaders at this time were Ezra and Nehemiah, who taught the people to be very strict about separating themselves from foreigners when they prayed or worshiped God. And they told the Israelite men who had married foreign women to divorce these wives and send them and their children away (Ezra 9,10).

Some of Israel's prophets, however, taught that God had a plan that included foreigners and the enemies of Israel. For example, the prophets Isaiah and Ezekiel declared that in the future, foreigners would join Israel in worshiping Israel's God and even share in possession of the promised land (Isa 56:1-8; Ezek 47:21-23).

In the New Testament, Jesus' actions showed that God's love and care are for all people. The story he told his followers about the Good Samaritan (Luke 10:25-37) showed how a man who was not a Jew (the Samaritan) acted in a very neighborly way toward a Jewish man who had been robbed and beaten. Jesus also reached out to Gentiles (non-Jews) when he healed the servant of an officer in the Roman army (Matt 8:5-13) and the daughter of a Canaanite woman (Matt 15:21-28).

2:23 *wheat:* Wheat is a highly valued grain that is usually harvested in late May or early June, several weeks after the harvesting of barley. People ground wheat into flour and used it for making bread and other baked foods.

3:1 *try to find a home for you:* In ancient Israel, unmarried women and widows had a difficult time supporting themselves. Since property was owned by men who passed it on to their sons, it was very important for a woman to have a husband or sons to protect her and take care of her.

3:4 *uncover his feet and lie down:* By telling Ruth to lie under the cover next to Boaz, Naomi was hoping that Boaz would want to marry Ruth. Although the Law of Moses required Boaz to take care of the needs of the widow of his dead relative (see Num 36:1-9; Deut 25:5-10), the Law did not require him to marry Ruth.

3:7 *in good spirits:* Boaz was likely feeling very relaxed from the food and from the wine he had been drinking. It was customary to sleep in the fields during harvest time in order to protect the newly-cut grain from robbers.

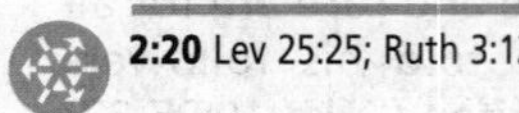

2:20 Lev 25:25; Ruth 3:12.

how much she had gathered. Ruth also brought out and gave her
what she had left over after she had eaten enough.
[19]Her mother-in-law asked her, "Where did you glean today?
Where did you work? Blessed be the man who took notice of you!"
Then Ruth told her mother-in-law about the one at whose
place she had been working. "The name of the man I worked with
today is Boaz," she said.
[20]"The LORD bless him!" Naomi said to her daughter-in-law.
"He has not stopped showing his kindness to the living and the
dead." She added, "That man is our close relative; he is one of our
kinsman-redeemers."
[21]Then Ruth the Moabitess said, "He even said to me, 'Stay
with my workers until they finish harvesting all my grain.'"
[22]Naomi said to Ruth her daughter-in-law, "It will be good
for you, my daughter, to go with his girls, because in someone
else's field you might be harmed."
[23]So Ruth stayed close to the servant girls of Boaz to glean
until the barley and wheat harvests were finished. And she lived
with her mother-in-law.

Ruth and Boaz at the Threshing Floor

3 One day Naomi her mother-in-law said to her, "My daughter,
should I not try to find a home[a] for you, where you will be well
provided for? [2]Is not Boaz, with whose servant girls you have been,
a kinsman of ours? Tonight he will be winnowing barley on the
threshing floor. [3]Wash and perfume yourself, and put on your best
clothes. Then go down to the threshing floor, but don't let him
know you are there until he has finished eating and drinking.
[4]When he lies down, note the place where he is lying. Then go and
uncover his feet and lie down. He will tell you what to do."
[5]"I will do whatever you say," Ruth answered. [6]So she went
down to the threshing floor and did everything her mother-in-law
told her to do.
[7]When Boaz had finished eating and drinking and was in
good spirits, he went over to lie down at the far end of the grain
pile. Ruth approached quietly, uncovered his feet and lay down. [8]In
the middle of the night something startled the man, and he turned
and discovered a woman lying at his feet.
[9]"Who are you?" he asked.
"I am your servant Ruth," she said. "Spread the corner of
your garment over me, since you are a kinsman-redeemer."
[10]"The LORD bless you, my daughter," he replied. "This kindness is greater than that which you showed earlier: You have not run
after the younger men, whether rich or poor. [11]And now, my daughter, don't be afraid. I will do for you all you ask. All my fellow towns-

[a]1 Hebrew *find rest* (see Ruth 1:9)

men know that you are a woman of noble character. [12]Although it is
true that I am near of kin, there is a kinsman-redeemer nearer than
I. [13]Stay here for the night, and in the morning if he wants to
redeem, good; let him redeem. But if he is not willing, as surely as
the LORD lives I will do it. Lie here until morning."

[14]So she lay at his feet until morning, but got up before anyone could be recognized; and he said, "Don't let it be known that a woman came to the threshing floor."

[15]He also said, "Bring me the shawl you are wearing and hold it out." When she did so, he poured into it six measures of barley and put it on her. Then he[a] went back to town.

[16]When Ruth came to her mother-in-law, Naomi asked, "How did it go, my daughter?"

Then she told her everything Boaz had done for her [17]and
added, "He gave me these six measures of barley, saying, 'Don't go back to your mother-in-law empty-handed.' "

[18]Then Naomi said, "Wait, my daughter, until you find out what happens. For the man will not rest until the matter is settled today."

Boaz Marries Ruth

4 Meanwhile Boaz went up to the town gate and sat there. When the kinsman-redeemer he had mentioned came along, Boaz said, "Come over here, my friend, and sit down." So he went over and sat down.

[2]Boaz took ten of the elders of the town and said, "Sit here,"
and they did so. [3]Then he said to the kinsman-redeemer, "Naomi,
who has come back from Moab, is selling the piece of land that
belonged to our brother Elimelech. [4]I thought I should bring the
matter to your attention and suggest that you buy it in the presence of these seated here and in the presence of the elders of my people. If you will redeem it, do so. But if you[b] will not, tell me, so I will know. For no one has the right to do it except you, and I am next in line."

"I will redeem it," he said.

[5]Then Boaz said, "On the day you buy the land from Naomi and from Ruth the Moabitess, you acquire[c] the dead man's widow, in order to maintain the name of the dead with his property."

[6]At this, the kinsman-redeemer said, "Then I cannot redeem it because I might endanger my own estate. You redeem it yourself. I cannot do it."

[7](Now in earlier times in Israel, for the redemption and transfer of property to become final, one party took off his sandal

[a]15 Most Hebrew manuscripts; many Hebrew manuscripts, Vulgate and Syriac *she*
[b]4 Many Hebrew manuscripts, Septuagint, Vulgate and Syriac; most Hebrew manuscripts *he* [c]5 Hebrew; Vulgate and Syriac *Naomi, you acquire Ruth the Moabitess,*

3:12 *a kinsman-redeemer nearer than I:* A kinsman-redeemer was a relative who would help take care of his extended family, especially widows who had no one else on whom to depend. Boaz knew that the Law of Moses gave Ruth's closest male relative the first chance to marry her. If that relative refused, then Boaz would be free to marry Ruth. See also 2:20.

3:14 *Don't let it be known:* Ruth left before daylight, so people would not know she had slept beside Boaz the night before. If people had seen Ruth, they could have said that Boaz had already made a commitment to marry her.

4:1 *town gate:* The town gate was a place where business was carried out and where leaders of the city gathered to make decisions about the life of their people.

4:6 *I might endanger my own estate:* Boaz invited Ruth's other close relative to buy the land that had belonged to Naomi's husband Elimelech. If he bought the land, it would mean that he agreed to support Elimelech's whole family and that he agreed to marry Ruth. If he married Ruth, part of his property would have to be passed on to Ruth and any children she would have.

4:8 *removed his sandal:* This custom was a public sign in ancient Israel that a purchase involving land or property was complete. See also Deut 25:9.

4:12 *Perez, whom Tamar bore to Judah:* Perez was one of the sons of Judah (Gen 38:27-30) and Tamar, a Canaanite woman who had been married to another of Judah's sons. Perez was an ancestor of Boaz and of many others who lived in Bethlehem. See also verses 18-22.

4:10 Deut 25:5, 6. **4:11** Gen 29:31—30:24.

and gave it to the other. This was the method of legalizing transactions in Israel.)

8So the kinsman-redeemer said to Boaz, "Buy it yourself."
And he removed his sandal.

9Then Boaz announced to the elders and all the people,
"Today you are witnesses that I have bought from Naomi all the
property of Elimelech, Kilion and Mahlon. 10I have also acquired
Ruth the Moabitess, Mahlon's widow, as my wife, in order to maintain the name of the dead with his property, so that his name will not disappear from among his family or from the town records. Today you are witnesses!"

11Then the elders and all those at the gate said, "We are witnesses. May the LORD make the woman who is coming into your home like Rachel and Leah, who together built up the house of Israel. May you have standing in Ephrathah and be famous in
Bethlehem. 12Through the offspring the LORD gives you by this
young woman, may your family be like that of Perez, whom Tamar bore to Judah."

QUESTIONS ABOUT RUTH

1. When Naomi's sons died, Naomi believed that God had turned against her and Ruth. (1:1–21) Why did she feel so desperate? Have you ever felt this desperate or have you known anyone who felt bitter like Naomi? If so, what caused these feelings and how did you or your friend get through this difficult period?
2. Naomi's daughters-in-law both loved Naomi but made very different decisions about how to go on with their lives. (1:6-18) What did Orpah do? What did Ruth do? Why do you think Ruth chose to do what she did?
3. What did Ruth do to help Naomi when they got to Bethlehem in Judah? (2:1-18) What seemed to have been the risks for women who did this kind of work? How could the fact that Ruth was a foreigner (from Moab) have made the situation even more difficult? Are there people with different cultural or religious backgrounds living in your community? If so, how are they treated? What can you do to make them feel more accepted?
4. The field Ruth chooses to work in belongs to a rich and important man named Boaz. (2:3-23) What kind of person does he seem to be? How does he treat Ruth? The Law of Moses required faithful Jews to allow foreigners and widows to pick up stalks of grain after a field was harvested. In what way did Boaz do more than what the law required? What can you learn from Boaz's actions?
5. In chapter 3, Naomi helps Ruth to find a husband. Why do you think she felt this was an important thing to do?
6. Read the notes about the Jewish customs relating to marriage. (See the notes at 1:11; 3:4; 3:12; 4:6.) What impressed Boaz about Ruth? (3:10) What prevented Boaz from offering to marry Ruth right away? (3:12,13) What did Boaz do to solve this problem? (4:1-8) How did this help Naomi as well as Ruth? (4:9,10)
7. How would you describe the mood at the end of the story? How are Naomi's feelings after the birth of her grandson (4:14-17) different from her feelings at the end of chapter 1? How does she show her gratitude? How did Naomi's grandson Obed become a blessing for all the people of Israel?

The Genealogy of David

[13]So Boaz took Ruth and she became his wife. Then he went
to her, and the LORD enabled her to conceive, and she gave birth to
a son. [14]The women said to Naomi: "Praise be to the LORD, who
this day has not left you without a kinsman-redeemer. May he
become famous throughout Israel! [15]He will renew your life and
sustain you in your old age. For your daughter-in-law, who loves
you and who is better to you than seven sons, has given him birth."

[16]Then Naomi took the child, laid him in her lap and cared
for him. [17]The women living there said, "Naomi has a son." And
they named him Obed. He was the father of Jesse, the father of
David.

[18]This, then, is the family line of Perez:

Perez was the father of Hezron,
19 Hezron the father of Ram,
Ram the father of Amminadab,
20 Amminadab the father of Nahshon,
Nahshon the father of Salmon,[a]
21 Salmon the father of Boaz,
Boaz the father of Obed,
22 Obed the father of Jesse,
and Jesse the father of David.

---

[a]**20** A few Hebrew manuscripts, some Septuagint manuscripts and Vulgate (see also verse 21 and Septuagint of 1 Chron. 2:11); most Hebrew manuscripts *Salma*

4:14,15 *Praise be to the LORD:* These words, like other blessings in the Bible (Gen 12:1-3; 27:27-29), are a declaration of the many good things God has done and will do in the future. See also the mini-article called "Blessed (Happy)," p. 1026.

4:17 *Naomi has a son:* Even though Obed was not technically the son or grandson of Naomi, the women of Bethlehem knew that because of Ruth's son Naomi's family would continue and Naomi's place in the community was once again secure. See the note at 1:11.

4:17 *Obed . . . Jesse . . . David:* In Hebrew, "Obed" means "worshiper." Obed's grandson was David, Israel's greatest king. David was the son of Jesse, a wealthy sheep farmer. See also the mini-article called "David," p. 1028.

4:18-22 *the family line:* Knowing one's ancestors was important in ancient Israel. See also the mini-article called "Genealogies in the Bible," p. 734.

1 SAMUEL

Exciting stories of Samuel, Saul, and David fill the pages of 1 SAMUEL. Read how they struggled with themselves, with each other, and with God, and how they transformed Israel from a group of tribes governed by judges to a nation ruled by a king.

The nation Israel: Before Saul became king, the Israelites did not think of themselves as a unified nation, but as a loose collection of tribes living close to each other. Surrounded by non-Israelite peoples like the Philistines and Ammonites, several Israelite tribes would sometimes join together to defend themselves. The Israelites' religious center described in 1 SAMUEL was at Shiloh, where the ark of the covenant was kept for a time. See the mini-article called "The Ark of the Covenant" on p. 513. See also the mini-article called "Israel," p. 264 and the map on p. 2465.

WHAT MAKES 1 SAMUEL SPECIAL?

FIRST SAMUEL is the first half of one long book that was split in two because it was too long to fit on one scroll. (SECOND SAMUEL is the second half.) Together they tell of the lives of Samuel, Saul, and David—three people who were chosen by the LORD. But the real story in these books is how all three, in spite of their human flaws, helped to make Israel a strong nation.

WHY WAS 1 SAMUEL WRITTEN?

The book of 1 SAMUEL tells how God chose the earliest kings in ancient Israel. For two centuries the Israelites had been loosely organized as a group of twelve tribes ruled by temporary leaders, called judges, chosen by God in times of need. (See the Introduction to JUDGES on p. 453.) Samuel, the last of these leaders, had to deal with God because of Israel's request for a new kind of leader—a king like the ones that ruled other nations (8:5,19,20). Chapters 8–12 of 1 SAMUEL present a tension. On the one hand, the LORD directs Samuel to give the people a king. But on the other hand, the request for a human king goes against Israel's ancient belief in God as king (Exod 15:18; Deut 33:5), particularly because the people wanted a king like the nations around them had—one to lead them in battle and provide national unity.

God reluctantly agreed to let Israel have a king. God knew it would bring big changes to the people of Israel, and that not all of the changes would be good ones. After choosing a king, God reminded Israel and its king that they must still keep their solemn promise to obey the LORD (Gen 17:7-9; Exod 24). But Saul did not obey and did not want to be replaced by David, the new king chosen by God. As David himself would later learn, even kings must obey the LORD.

WHAT'S THE STORY BEHIND THE SCENE?

The two books of SAMUEL cover just over a century of Israel's history from 1080 to 970 B.C., from Samuel's birth to David's death. JUDGES tells how Israel slid into lawless confusion after conquering the promised land. JUDGES ends by saying "In those days Israel had no king; everyone did as he saw fit" (Judg 21:25). Besides internal turmoil, Israel also faced a constant outside military threat from the aggressive Philistines, who lived on the Mediterranean coast just west of Israel.

But this would soon change. As 1 SAMUEL opens, Israel is a

loosely organized group of twelve tribes trembling before their Philistine enemies. By the end of 2 SAMUEL, however, David is described as the king of a unified and powerful nation. The story of Israel's religious growth during the same time is also impressive. In 1 SAMUEL, the Israelites gathered several times a year to worship and offer sacrifices to the LORD. As 2 SAMUEL closes, Jerusalem has become the center of worship, and David has built an altar at the place where his son Solomon would later build a magnificent temple. For more about this period in Israel's history, see the article called "From Joshua to the Exile: The People of Israel in the Promised Land," p. 924.

HOW IS 1 SAMUEL CONSTRUCTED?

The book can be divided into three major sections, one for each of its main characters—Samuel, Saul, and David:

Samuel (1:1—7:17)
- Samuel's childhood (1:1—2:11)
- Samuel at the house of the LORD (2:12—4:1a)
- War with the Philistines (4:1b—7:2)
- Samuel leads Israel (7:3-17)

Saul (8:1—15:35)
- Israel pleads with Samuel (8:1-22)
- Saul becomes king (9:1—11:15)
- Samuel's reminds the people to worship and obey the LORD (12:1-25)
- Saul disobeys the LORD and is rejected (13:1—15:35)

David (16:1—31:13)
- The LORD chooses David (16:1—17:58)
- Saul turns against David (18:1—19:17)
- David runs away (19:18—27:12)
- Saul and his sons die (28:1—31:13)

Samuel

This part of 1 SAMUEL begins and ends in Ramah, Samuel's home town. It describes Samuel's life and service to God. As the last of the judges and as a priest who becomes a prophet, Samuel carries out God's will in choosing and rejecting kings as Israel struggles with becoming a monarchy.

SAMUEL'S CHILDHOOD

Born in answer to the prayers of his childless mother Hannah, Samuel's early life points to his later service to God as a priest, leader, and prophet.

The Birth of Samuel

1 There was a certain man from Ramathaim, a Zuphite[a] from the hill country of Ephraim, whose name was Elkanah son of

[a]1 Or *from Ramathaim Zuphim*

1:1 *Ramathaim . . . hill country of Ephraim . . . Ephraimite:* "Ramathaim" is a longer form of "Ramah," which is used in 1:19. The hill country of Ephraim was the area of Canaan given to the tribe of Ephraim when the people of Israel moved into the land and divided it among the twelve tribes of Israel. (See the map on p. 2464.) Each tribe was descended from one of Jacob's twelve sons. The tribe of Joseph was divided between Ephraim and Manasseh, tribes that were named after the two sons of Joseph. That would make thirteen tribes, but the Bible normally lists only twelve. That may be because Ephraim and Manasseh are sometimes counted as one tribe. Also, the Levi tribe was sometimes not counted at all, since they did not have their own tribal lands but instead served as priests for all the tribes and were scattered throughout Canaan. See also the mini-article called "Israel," on p. 264.

1:2 *two wives:* Having more than one wife was considered acceptable in many cultures in the ancient Near East.

1:3 *Year after year . . . worship and sacrifice:* Israelite males were required to go to the central place of worship three times each year (Exod 23:14-19; 34:23; Deut 16:16). Elkanah probably went during the Feast of Weeks, when the people thanked God for their harvests. Sacrifices were gifts to God that included certain animals, grains, fruits, and sweet-smelling spices. See also Lev 3:7-17; 7:11-18 and the chart called "Sacrifices and Offerings," p. 219.

1:3 *LORD Almighty:* See the mini-articles called "LORD (YHWH)," p. 140 and "Names of God," p. 243.

1:5 *closed her womb:* Many Israelites believed that children were gifts that God would give or withhold (Gen 16:2; 30:1,2,22,23). Children were also considered a sign of God's blessing (Ps 127:3-5). Seeing others celebrate God's blessings, it is natural that Hannah would be upset that she did not have a child.

1:7 *house of the LORD:* Another name for the place of worship at Shiloh. This may have been a temple that was later destroyed by the Philistines. More likely, it refers to the tabernacle that the LORD told Moses to set up and where the people made sacrifices and worshiped the LORD. For more see the mini-article called "The Tabernacle," p. 2346.

1:11 *I will give him to the LORD . . . no razor:* Hannah's promise is like what God had required of Samson's mother (Judg 13:3-5). Each of their sons would serve God. Leaving the child's hair uncut showed that he would belong to the LORD forever. See also Num 6:1-21.

1:13 *drunk:* In those times, people usually prayed aloud. Hannah prayed silently. When Eli saw her lips moving, he thought she had had too much to drink and was mumbling to herself.

Jeroham, the son of Elihu, the son of Tohu, the son of Zuph, an Ephraimite. [2]He had two wives; one was called Hannah and the other Peninnah. Peninnah had children, but Hannah had none.

[3]Year after year this man went up from his town to worship and sacrifice to the LORD Almighty at Shiloh, where Hophni and Phinehas, the two sons of Eli, were priests of the LORD. [4]Whenever the day came for Elkanah to sacrifice, he would give portions of the meat to his wife Peninnah and to all her sons and daughters. [5]But to Hannah he gave a double portion because he loved her, and the LORD had closed her womb. [6]And because the LORD had closed her womb, her rival kept provoking her in order to irritate her. [7]This went on year after year. Whenever Hannah went up to the house of the LORD, her rival provoked her till she wept and would not eat. [8]Elkanah her husband would say to her, "Hannah, why are you weeping? Why don't you eat? Why are you downhearted? Don't I mean more to you than ten sons?"

[9]Once when they had finished eating and drinking in Shiloh, Hannah stood up. Now Eli the priest was sitting on a chair by the doorpost of the LORD's temple.[a] [10]In bitterness of soul Hannah wept much and prayed to the LORD. [11]And she made a vow, saying, "O LORD Almighty, if you will only look upon your servant's misery and remember me, and not forget your servant but give her a son, then I will give him to the LORD for all the days of his life, and no razor will ever be used on his head."

[12]As she kept on praying to the LORD, Eli observed her mouth. [13]Hannah was praying in her heart, and her lips were moving but her voice was not heard. Eli thought she was drunk [14]and said to her, "How long will you keep on getting drunk? Get rid of your wine."

[15]"Not so, my lord," Hannah replied, "I am a woman who is deeply troubled. I have not been drinking wine or beer; I was pouring out my soul to the LORD. [16]Do not take your servant for a wicked woman; I have been praying here out of my great anguish and grief."

[17]Eli answered, "Go in peace, and may the God of Israel grant you what you have asked of him."

[18]She said, "May your servant find favor in your eyes." Then she went her way and ate something, and her face was no longer downcast.

[19]Early the next morning they arose and worshiped before the LORD and then went back to their home at Ramah. Elkanah lay with Hannah his wife, and the LORD remembered her. [20]So in the course of time Hannah conceived and gave birth to a son. She named him Samuel,[b] saying, "Because I asked the LORD for him."

---

[a]**9** That is, tabernacle [b]**20** *Samuel* sounds like the Hebrew for *heard of God.*

Hannah Presents Samuel to the LORD, stained glass window from Canterbury Cathedral, late twelfth century. The story of Hannah, the mother of the prophet Samuel, is a beautiful illustration of God's mercy. Hannah wanted a son so much that she offered to give her first son to the LORD if only God would help her to conceive. After Samuel was born, Hannah kept her promise. When he was old enough to be separated from her, Hannah and her husband Elkanah took Samuel to Shiloh and presented him to the priest Eli. (See 1:1—2:11, 18-21.) Hannah is one of several childless women in the Bible who, by God's mercy, eventually gave birth to an important son. See, for example, the stories of Sarah (Gen 18:1-15; 21:1-8) and Elizabeth (Luke 1:5-25, 57-80).

Hannah Dedicates Samuel

21 When the man Elkanah went up with all his family to offer
the annual sacrifice to the LORD and to fulfill his vow, 22 Hannah did
not go. She said to her husband, "After the boy is weaned, I will take
him and present him before the LORD, and he will live there always."
23 "Do what seems best to you," Elkanah her husband told
her. "Stay here until you have weaned him; only may the LORD
make good his[a] word." So the woman stayed at home and nursed
her son until she had weaned him.
24 After he was weaned, she took the boy with her, young as
he was, along with a three-year-old bull,[b] an ephah[c] of flour and a

[a]**23** Masoretic Text; Dead Sea Scrolls, Septuagint and Syriac *your* [b]**24** Dead Sea Scrolls, Septuagint and Syriac; Masoretic Text *with three bulls* [c]**24** That is, probably about 3/5 bushel (about 22 liters)

1:20 *Samuel:* In Hebrew "Samuel" means "name of God," and is here related to the Hebrew verb for "ask."

1:22 *weaned:* Babies were breast-fed up to three years.

Hannah prayed, "My heart rejoices in the LORD . . . There is no one holy like the LORD; there is no one besides you; there is no Rock like our God."
1 Sam 2:1,2

2:1-10 *Hannah prayed:* Beginning and ending books with similar expressions was common in Hebrew literature. Several phrases in Hannah's prayer are repeated in David's prayer at the end of these books (2 Sam 22). Scholars believe that parts of this prayer are taken from older prayers that were used to give thanks after receiving God's help. The prayer celebrates God's power to change human situations from bad to good so that those in need are helped. For example, the hungry are given food, and a woman without a child is given seven children.

2:6 *the grave:* The dead were thought to live as shadows far beneath the earth in a place called Sheol. This is different from hell, but see the mini-article called "Hell," p. 1944, for more about ancient beliefs about what happens to people when they die.

2:10 *his king:* Although, Israelites did not have a king at this point in their history, this phrase in Hannah's prayer is a hint that one day God would choose a king to rule over them.

2:1-10 Luke 1:46-55.

skin of wine, and brought him to the house of the LORD at Shiloh.
25 When they had slaughtered the bull, they brought the boy to Eli,
26 and she said to him, "As surely as you live, my lord, I am the
woman who stood here beside you praying to the LORD. 27 I prayed
for this child, and the LORD has granted me what I asked of him.
28 So now I give him to the LORD. For his whole life he will be given
over to the LORD." And he worshiped the LORD there.

Hannah's Prayer

2 Then Hannah prayed and said:

"My heart rejoices in the LORD;
in the LORD my horn[a] is lifted high.
My mouth boasts over my enemies,
for I delight in your deliverance.

2 "There is no one holy[b] like the LORD;
there is no one besides you;
there is no Rock like our God.

3 "Do not keep talking so proudly
or let your mouth speak such arrogance,
for the LORD is a God who knows,
and by him deeds are weighed.

4 "The bows of the warriors are broken,
but those who stumbled are armed with strength.
5 Those who were full hire themselves out for food,
but those who were hungry hunger no more.
She who was barren has borne seven children,
but she who has had many sons pines away.

6 "The LORD brings death and makes alive;
he brings down to the grave[c] and raises up.
7 The LORD sends poverty and wealth;
he humbles and he exalts.
8 He raises the poor from the dust
and lifts the needy from the ash heap;
he seats them with princes
and has them inherit a throne of honor.

"For the foundations of the earth are the LORD's;
upon them he has set the world.
9 He will guard the feet of his saints,
but the wicked will be silenced in darkness.

"It is not by strength that one prevails;
10 those who oppose the LORD will be shattered.

a1 *Horn* here symbolizes strength; also in verse 10. **b2** Or *no Holy One*
c6 Hebrew *Sheol*

He will thunder against them from heaven;
the LORD will judge the ends of the earth.

"He will give strength to his king
and exalt the horn of his anointed."

[11]Then Elkanah went home to Ramah, but the boy ministered before the LORD under Eli the priest.

SAMUEL AT THE HOUSE OF THE LORD

Eli's Wicked Sons

[12]Eli's sons were wicked men; they had no regard for the LORD.
[13]Now it was the practice of the priests with the people that whenever anyone offered a sacrifice and while the meat was being boiled,
the servant of the priest would come with a three-pronged fork in
his hand. [14]He would plunge it into the pan or kettle or caldron or
pot, and the priest would take for himself whatever the fork brought
up. This is how they treated all the Israelites who came to Shiloh.
[15]But even before the fat was burned, the servant of the priest would
come and say to the man who was sacrificing, "Give the priest some
meat to roast; he won't accept boiled meat from you, but only raw."
[16]If the man said to him, "Let the fat be burned up first, and
then take whatever you want," the servant would then answer, "No,
hand it over now; if you don't, I'll take it by force."
[17]This sin of the young men was very great in the LORD's
sight, for they[a] were treating the LORD's offering with contempt.
[18]But Samuel was ministering before the LORD—a boy wearing a linen ephod. [19]Each year his mother made him a little robe
and took it to him when she went up with her husband to offer
the annual sacrifice. [20]Eli would bless Elkanah and his wife, saying,
"May the LORD give you children by this woman to take the place
of the one she prayed for and gave to the LORD." Then they would
go home. [21]And the LORD was gracious to Hannah; she conceived
and gave birth to three sons and two daughters. Meanwhile, the
boy Samuel grew up in the presence of the LORD.
[22]Now Eli, who was very old, heard about everything his
sons were doing to all Israel and how they slept with the women
who served at the entrance to the Tent of Meeting. [23]So he said to
them, "Why do you do such things? I hear from all the people
about these wicked deeds of yours. [24]No, my sons; it is not a good
report that I hear spreading among the LORD's people. [25]If a man
sins against another man, God[b] may mediate for him; but if a man
sins against the LORD, who will intercede for him?" His sons, however, did not listen to their father's rebuke, for it was the LORD's
will to put them to death.

[a]17 Or *men* [b]25 Or *the judges*

2:15 *fat was burned:* The fat of the animal belonged to the LORD and was supposed to be burned as a sacrifice before the rest of the animal was cooked and eaten (Lev 3:3,4,9,10, 14,15). See also the chart called "Sacrifices and Offerings" on p. 219.

2:18,19 *a linen ephod . . . a little robe:* Fine linen was a luxury and a symbol of purity. Priests wore sacred linen garments nobody else could wear: a robe with a sash, an embroidered shirt, and other things (see Exod 28). Samuel was a small child, but his mother made him clothes just like the ones Eli wore. The Hebrew word translated here as "little robe" means a long, sleeveless vest.

2:20 *Eli would bless:* Eli probably blessed Elkanah and Hannah because he knew that they would be blessed by the LORD for carrying out their promise. But only the LORD could decide what form the blessing would take.

2:30 *be disdained:* To be disdained by the LORD means to be cut off from God's blessings.

3:3 *lamp of God had not yet gone out:* The Hebrew text has "The lamp was still burning." An olive oil lamp would go out after a few hours if the wick was not adjusted, so they could not have slept very long. For more about the lamp that was to be lighted each evening in the tabernacle, see Exodus 27:20,21. See also the illustration on p. 2345.

3:3 *lying down in the temple . . . ark of God:* Samuel may have slept on a mat, a cloth sack with wool, feathers, or straw inside, or a pad of animal skins in the tabernacle. The ark of God refers to the ark of the covenant where God's presence was with his people (Exod 25:22). See the mini-articles called "The Tabernacle," p. 2346, and "The Ark of the Covenant," p. 513.

2:26 Luke 2:52. **2:28,29** Exod 28:1-4; Lev 7:34,35; 1 Sam 2:15. **2:34** 1 Sam 4:11.

26 And the boy Samuel continued to grow in stature and in
favor with the LORD and with men.

Prophecy Against the House of Eli

27 Now a man of God came to Eli and said to him, "This is
what the LORD says: 'Did I not clearly reveal myself to your father's
house when they were in Egypt under Pharaoh? 28 I chose your
father out of all the tribes of Israel to be my priest, to go up to my
altar, to burn incense, and to wear an ephod in my presence. I also
gave your father's house all the offerings made with fire by the
Israelites. 29 Why do you[a] scorn my sacrifice and offering that I prescribed for my dwelling? Why do you honor your sons more than
me by fattening yourselves on the choice parts of every offering
made by my people Israel?'
30 "Therefore the LORD, the God of Israel, declares: 'I
promised that your house and your father's house would minister
before me forever.' But now the LORD declares: 'Far be it from me!
Those who honor me I will honor, but those who despise me will
be disdained. 31 The time is coming when I will cut short your
strength and the strength of your father's house, so that there will
not be an old man in your family line 32 and you will see distress in
my dwelling. Although good will be done to Israel, in your family
line there will never be an old man. 33 Every one of you that I do
not cut off from my altar will be spared only to blind your eyes
with tears and to grieve your heart, and all your descendants will
die in the prime of life.
34 " 'And what happens to your two sons, Hophni and Phinehas, will be a sign to you—they will both die on the same day. 35 I
will raise up for myself a faithful priest, who will do according to
what is in my heart and mind. I will firmly establish his house, and
he will minister before my anointed one always. 36 Then everyone
left in your family line will come and bow down before him for a
piece of silver and a crust of bread and plead, "Appoint me to some
priestly office so I can have food to eat." ' "

The LORD Calls Samuel

3 The boy Samuel ministered before the LORD under Eli. In those
days the word of the LORD was rare; there were not many visions.
2 One night Eli, whose eyes were becoming so weak that he
could barely see, was lying down in his usual place. 3 The lamp of
God had not yet gone out, and Samuel was lying down in the
temple[b] of the LORD, where the ark of God was. 4 Then the LORD
called Samuel.
Samuel answered, "Here I am." 5 And he ran to Eli and said,
"Here I am; you called me."

---

[a]29 The Hebrew is plural. [b]3 That is, tabernacle

But Eli said, "I did not call; go back and lie down." So he
went and lay down.
6 Again the LORD called, "Samuel!" And Samuel got up and
went to Eli and said, "Here I am; you called me."
"My son," Eli said, "I did not call; go back and lie down."
7 Now Samuel did not yet know the LORD: The word of the
LORD had not yet been revealed to him.
8 The LORD called Samuel a third time, and Samuel got up
and went to Eli and said, "Here I am; you called me."
Then Eli realized that the LORD was calling the boy. 9 So Eli
told Samuel, "Go and lie down, and if he calls you, say, 'Speak,
LORD, for your servant is listening.' " So Samuel went and lay down
in his place.

> *"Speak, LORD, for your servant is listening."*
> 1 Sam 3:9

THE ARK OF THE COVENANT

The ark of the covenant (also called the ark of the Testimony) was the acacia wood box or chest that accompanied the Hebrews on their desert wanderings in the time of Moses, and housed the two stone tablets with the Ten Commandments written on them.

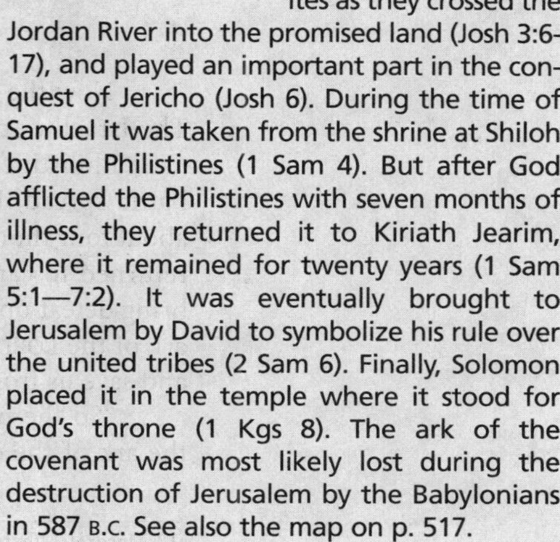

Biblical descriptions of ancient Israel's most important religious symbol vary. EXODUS presents an elaborate picture of a chest forty-five inches long, twenty-seven inches wide, and twenty-seven inches high made of acacia wood and covered inside and out with gold, constructed by the skilled craftsman, Bezalel. A lid of pure gold with two winged creatures (cherubim), also of pure gold, covered the chest. It was carried about on gold poles which passed through gold rings attached to the sides (Exod 25:10-22; 31:2,7; 35:30-35; 37:1-9). A much simpler description is found in Deuteronomy 10:1-5. Here Moses is said to have constructed a plain wooden box of acacia wood to hold the new stone tablets with the Ten Commandments written on them that replaced the ones he had broken when he saw the people worshiping a gold statue of a calf.

In addition to holding the Ten Commandments, the ark of the covenant symbolized the presence of the living God among his people (Num 10:33-36). Normally kept in the Most Holy Place of the tabernacle (Exod 26:34), the poles allowed the Levitical priests to carry the chest on their shoulders (Deut 10:8); anyone else who touched it would die (2 Sam 6:6,7). During the desert wanderings, the ark of the covenant led the way (Num 10:33). It led the Israelites as they crossed the Jordan River into the promised land (Josh 3:6-17), and played an important part in the conquest of Jericho (Josh 6). During the time of Samuel it was taken from the shrine at Shiloh by the Philistines (1 Sam 4). But after God afflicted the Philistines with seven months of illness, they returned it to Kiriath Jearim, where it remained for twenty years (1 Sam 5:1—7:2). It was eventually brought to Jerusalem by David to symbolize his rule over the united tribes (2 Sam 6). Finally, Solomon placed it in the temple where it stood for God's throne (1 Kgs 8). The ark of the covenant was most likely lost during the destruction of Jerusalem by the Babylonians in 587 B.C. See also the map on p. 517.

10 The LORD came and stood there, calling as at the other
times, "Samuel! Samuel!"
Then Samuel said, "Speak, for your servant is listening."
11 And the LORD said to Samuel: "See, I am about to do something in Israel that will make the ears of everyone who hears of it
tingle. 12 At that time I will carry out against Eli everything I spoke
against his family—from beginning to end. 13 For I told him that I
would judge his family forever because of the sin he knew about;
his sons made themselves contemptible,[a] and he failed to restrain
them. 14 Therefore, I swore to the house of Eli, 'The guilt of Eli's
house will never be atoned for by sacrifice or offering.' "
15 Samuel lay down until morning and then opened the
doors of the house of the LORD. He was afraid to tell Eli the vision,
16 but Eli called him and said, "Samuel, my son."
Samuel answered, "Here I am."
17 "What was it he said to you?" Eli asked. "Do not hide it
from me. May God deal with you, be it ever so severely, if you hide
from me anything he told you." 18 So Samuel told him everything,
hiding nothing from him. Then Eli said, "He is the LORD; let him
do what is good in his eyes."
19 The LORD was with Samuel as he grew up, and he let none
of his words fall to the ground. 20 And all Israel from Dan to Beersheba recognized that Samuel was attested as a prophet of the
LORD. 21 The LORD continued to appear at Shiloh, and there he
revealed himself to Samuel through his word.
4 And Samuel's word came to all Israel.

WAR WITH THE PHILISTINES

The Philistines capture the ark of the covenant during a war with the Israelites. As the leader of the Israelites, Samuel inspires hope among the people.

The Philistines Capture the Ark

Now the Israelites went out to fight against the Philistines.
The Israelites camped at Ebenezer, and the Philistines at Aphek.
2 The Philistines deployed their forces to meet Israel, and as the
battle spread, Israel was defeated by the Philistines, who killed
about four thousand of them on the battlefield. 3 When the soldiers
returned to camp, the elders of Israel asked, "Why did the LORD
bring defeat upon us today before the Philistines? Let us bring the
ark of the LORD's covenant from Shiloh, so that it[b] may go with us
and save us from the hand of our enemies."
4 So the people sent men to Shiloh, and they brought back
the ark of the covenant of the LORD Almighty, who is enthroned

[a]13 Masoretic Text; an ancient Hebrew scribal tradition and Septuagint *sons blasphemed God* [b]3 Or *he*

3:18 *let him do what is good in his eyes:* Eli realized that Samuel's message indeed came from God, since God had already told Eli these things (2:27-36).

3:20 *prophet:* Prophets received messages from God to pass on to other people. Prophets were important Israelite leaders and advisers through much of Israel's history. See the article called "Prophets and Prophecies," p. 935.

4:1 *Philistines:* The Philistines lived in an area along the Mediterranean Sea about fifty miles long and twenty miles wide. They had five main cities in that small area: Ekron, Gath, Ashdod, Ashkelon, and Gaza. (See the map on p. 2464.) Although each city had its own ruler, the rulers worked together to make the Philistines stronger. They were often at war with Israel.

4:3 *ark of the LORD's covenant:* The LORD's covenant with Israel was written on two stone tablets with the Ten Commandments that were kept in the ark of the covenant. See the mini-articles called "Ten Commandments," p. 354 and "Covenants (Agreements)," p. 386.

4:4 Exod 25:17-22.

between the cherubim. And Eli's two sons, Hophni and Phinehas, were there with the ark of the covenant of God.

5 When the ark of the LORD's covenant came into the camp, all Israel raised such a great shout that the ground shook. 6 Hearing the uproar, the Philistines asked, "What's all this shouting in the Hebrew camp?"

When they learned that the ark of the LORD had come into the camp, 7 the Philistines were afraid. "A god has come into the camp," they said. "We're in trouble! Nothing like this has happened before. 8 Woe to us! Who will deliver us from the hand of these mighty gods? They are the gods who struck the Egyptians with all kinds of plagues in the desert. 9 Be strong, Philistines! Be men, or you will be subject to the Hebrews, as they have been to you. Be men, and fight!"

10 So the Philistines fought, and the Israelites were defeated and every man fled to his tent. The slaughter was very great; Israel lost thirty thousand foot soldiers. 11 The ark of God was captured, and Eli's two sons, Hophni and Phinehas, died.

Death of Eli

12 That same day a Benjamite ran from the battle line and went to Shiloh, his clothes torn and dust on his head. 13 When he arrived, there was Eli sitting on his chair by the side of the road, watching, because his heart feared for the ark of God. When the man entered the town and told what had happened, the whole town sent up a cry.

14 Eli heard the outcry and asked, "What is the meaning of this uproar?"

The man hurried over to Eli, 15 who was ninety-eight years old and whose eyes were set so that he could not see. 16 He told Eli, "I have just come from the battle line; I fled from it this very day."

Eli asked, "What happened, my son?"

17 The man who brought the news replied, "Israel fled before the Philistines, and the army has suffered heavy losses. Also your two sons, Hophni and Phinehas, are dead, and the ark of God has been captured."

18 When he mentioned the ark of God, Eli fell backward off his chair by the side of the gate. His neck was broken and he died, for he was an old man and heavy. He had led[a] Israel forty years.

19 His daughter-in-law, the wife of Phinehas, was pregnant and near the time of delivery. When she heard the news that the ark of God had been captured and that her father-in-law and her husband were dead, she went into labor and gave birth, but was overcome by her labor pains. 20 As she was dying, the women attending her said, "Don't despair; you have given birth to a son." But she did not respond or pay any attention.

a18 Traditionally *judged*

4:4 *cherubim:* Symbols of God's majesty and associated with his presence. Also referred to as "living creatures" or "winged creatures." See Exod 25:18-20.

4:6 *the Hebrew camp:* In the Jewish Scriptures, the use of the word "Hebrew" (instead of "Israelite") usually shows that the person who is speaking is not an Israelite. See also Gen 39:17; Exod 1:16,19; 2:6.

4:7 *A god:* The Philistines worshiped several gods and might have assumed the Israelites did, too. But the Israelites were God's special people since they had agreed to worship only the LORD.

4:8 *struck the Egyptians with all kinds of plagues:* God brought disasters and death upon the Egyptians to force them to let the Israelites leave for the promised land (Exod 7:14–15:21). The Philistines had heard the story of Israel's God.

4:12 *a Benjamite:* From the tribe of Benjamin, named after Jacob's youngest son. Jacob called Benjamin a "ravenous wolf" when he blessed him (Gen 49:27), and men of the tribe of Benjamin were known as warriors.

4:21 *Ichabod:* Ichabod means "where is the glory?" or "there is no glory." Phinehas's wife saw the loss of the ark of the covenant as losing the LORD, because a cloud with a dazzling light marked the LORD's presence at the ark (Exod 40:34).

5:2 *Dagon's temple:* Dagon was a god of rain and fertility and the Philistines' most important god. Dagon was originally worshiped in Mesopotamia but by 2000 B.C. was more widely worshiped throughout the ancient Near East. As the Canaanites began to trade with Mesopotamia they learned about their god Dagon, and adopted him as their own. When the Philistines conquered Canaan, Dagon also became their god. The bronze statue shown here is from the Mediterranean city Byblos, from around the fourteenth century B.C. See also Judg 16:23; 1 Chr 10:10.

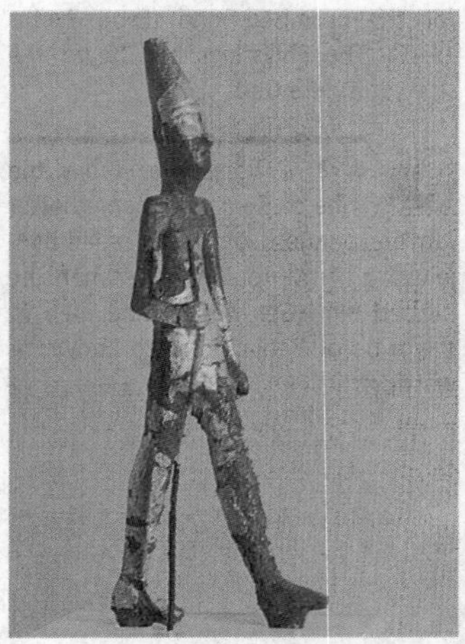

5:5 *neither the priests . . . nor any others . . . step on the threshold:* The author might have been trying to explain a strange ritual that had continued for many years.

5:6 *tumors:* Probably bubonic plague, a disease spread by fleas carried by rats or mice. See the note at 6:4.

21She named the boy Ichabod,[a] saying, "The glory has departed from Israel"—because of the capture of the ark of God and the
deaths of her father-in-law and her husband. 22She said, "The glory
has departed from Israel, for the ark of God has been captured."

The Ark in Ashdod and Ekron

5 After the Philistines had captured the ark of God, they took it
from Ebenezer to Ashdod. 2Then they carried the ark into Dagon's
temple and set it beside Dagon. 3When the people of Ashdod rose
early the next day, there was Dagon, fallen on his face on the
ground before the ark of the LORD! They took Dagon and put him
back in his place. 4But the following morning when they rose,
there was Dagon, fallen on his face on the ground before the ark of
the LORD! His head and hands had been broken off and were lying
on the threshold; only his body remained. 5That is why to this day
neither the priests of Dagon nor any others who enter Dagon's
temple at Ashdod step on the threshold.

6The LORD's hand was heavy upon the people of Ashdod and
its vicinity; he brought devastation upon them and afflicted them
with tumors.[b] 7When the men of Ashdod saw what was happening, they said, "The ark of the god of Israel must not stay here with
us, because his hand is heavy upon us and upon Dagon our god."
8So they called together all the rulers of the Philistines and asked
them, "What shall we do with the ark of the god of Israel?"

They answered, "Have the ark of the god of Israel moved to
Gath." So they moved the ark of the God of Israel.

9But after they had moved it, the LORD's hand was against
that city, throwing it into a great panic. He afflicted the people of
the city, both young and old, with an outbreak of tumors.[c] 10So
they sent the ark of God to Ekron.

As the ark of God was entering Ekron, the people of Ekron
cried out, "They have brought the ark of the god of Israel around
to us to kill us and our people." 11So they called together all the
rulers of the Philistines and said, "Send the ark of the god of Israel
away; let it go back to its own place, or it[d] will kill us and our people." For death had filled the city with panic; God's hand was very
heavy upon it. 12Those who did not die were afflicted with tumors,
and the outcry of the city went up to heaven.

The Ark Returned to Israel

6 When the ark of the LORD had been in Philistine territory
seven months, 2the Philistines called for the priests and the diviners and said, "What shall we do with the ark of the LORD? Tell us
how we should send it back to its place."

[a]21 *Ichabod* means *no glory.* [b]6 Hebrew; Septuagint and Vulgate *tumors. And rats appeared in their land, and death and destruction were throughout the city* [c]9 Or *with tumors in the groin* (see Septuagint) [d]11 Or *he*

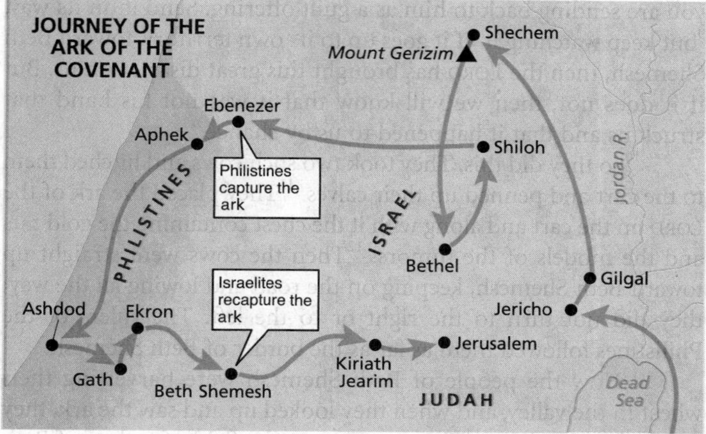

Journey of the Ark of the Covenant. The LORD told Moses to have the Israelites make a sacred chest, called the ark of the covenant, for holding the two stone tablets with the Ten Commandments written on them. The people brought the ark with them out of the desert and into the land God promised to them. They carried it into battle when they conquered Jericho (Josh 6). They brought the ark with them when they settled for a time in the valley between Mount Ebal and Mount Gerizim (Josh 8:33-35), and later in Bethel (Judg 20:26-28). The ark was in Shiloh when Eli was the LORD's priest but was captured by the Philistines in a battle near Ebenezer (4:1-11). As it was passed from town to town in the land of the Philistines it made them break out in sores (chapter 5). Finally, the Philistines sent the ark back to the Israelites (5:11—6:18) and it stayed for a while in Kiriath Jearim (6:19—7:2). After David became king, he had the ark of the covenant brought to his new capital, Jerusalem (2 Sam 6:1-19).

3They answered, "If you return the ark of the god of Israel,
do not send it away empty, but by all means send a guilt offering
to him. Then you will be healed, and you will know why his hand
has not been lifted from you."
4The Philistines asked, "What guilt offering should we send
to him?"
They replied, "Five gold tumors and five gold rats, according
to the number of the Philistine rulers, because the same plague has
struck both you and your rulers. 5Make models of the tumors and
of the rats that are destroying the country, and pay honor to
Israel's god. Perhaps he will lift his hand from you and your gods
and your land. 6Why do you harden your hearts as the Egyptians
and Pharaoh did? When he[a] treated them harshly, did they not
send the Israelites out so they could go on their way?
7"Now then, get a new cart ready, with two cows that have
calved and have never been yoked. Hitch the cows to the cart, but
take their calves away and pen them up. 8Take the ark of the LORD
and put it on the cart, and in a chest beside it put the gold objects

[a]**6** That is, God

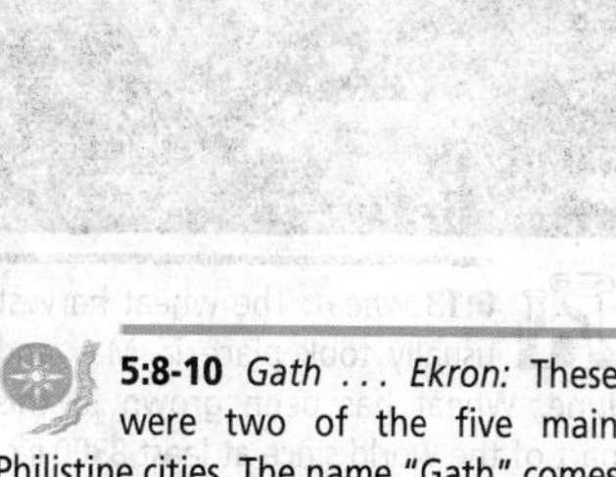

5:8-10 *Gath . . . Ekron:* These were two of the five main Philistine cities. The name "Gath" comes from a word meaning "winepress," something that was very common throughout the region because there were so many vineyards. As a result, many cities were called Gath, but most had a second name to help tell them apart (Gath Rimmon and Moresheth Gath, for example). The Philistines' Gath might have been about twelve miles east of Ashdod. See the map above.

6:4 *Five gold tumors and five gold rats:* The Philistines used gold to try to impress God. When they sent the models of the tumors and the rats, they were admitting that Israel's God had sent the plague and rats. The Philistines also might have hoped that by sending away the symbols of the plague, they could send away the plague itself.

6:7 *two cows that have calved and have never been yoked:* Cows have to be trained to pull a cart (yoked), and usually cows will not leave a nursing calf. The Philistines believed that if untrained cows left their calves and pulled the cart away, that would be a clear sign that God had caused the disease and was taking the ark of the covenant back to the Israelites.

6:9 *Beth Shemesh:* Four cities with this name appear in the Jewish Scriptures. This one was near the Philistine border, about sixteen miles southwest of Jerusalem. Archaeologists have excavated Beth Shemesh three times in this century and have concluded that people lived here as early as 2000 B.C.

6:13 *wheat:* The wheat harvest usually took place in May and June. Wheat has been grown in this part of the world since at least 8300 B.C. and was a regular part of the ancient Near Eastern diet.

6:15 *The Levites:* Only priests could touch the ark of the covenant. The Levites descended from Levi, one of Jacob's sons (Gen 29:34), and were the tribe God chose to be his priests (Exod 6:16-25; 32:26-29; Num 3:5-8). The Levites did not get land in Canaan when the other tribes did, because they served all of the tribes and were scattered throughout the land belonging to the other tribes. See also the mini-article called "Israel's Priests," p. 2344, and the Introduction to LEVITICUS, p. 210.

you are sending back to him as a guilt offering. Send it on its way,
9 but keep watching it. If it goes up to its own territory, toward Beth
Shemesh, then the LORD has brought this great disaster on us. But
if it does not, then we will know that it was not his hand that
struck us and that it happened to us by chance."
10 So they did this. They took two such cows and hitched them
to the cart and penned up their calves. 11 They placed the ark of the
LORD on the cart and along with it the chest containing the gold rats
and the models of the tumors. 12 Then the cows went straight up
toward Beth Shemesh, keeping on the road and lowing all the way;
they did not turn to the right or to the left. The rulers of the
Philistines followed them as far as the border of Beth Shemesh.
13 Now the people of Beth Shemesh were harvesting their
wheat in the valley, and when they looked up and saw the ark, they
rejoiced at the sight. 14 The cart came to the field of Joshua of Beth
Shemesh, and there it stopped beside a large rock. The people
chopped up the wood of the cart and sacrificed the cows as a burnt
offering to the LORD. 15 The Levites took down the ark of the LORD,
together with the chest containing the gold objects, and placed
them on the large rock. On that day the people of Beth Shemesh
offered burnt offerings and made sacrifices to the LORD. 16 The five
rulers of the Philistines saw all this and then returned that same
day to Ekron.
17 These are the gold tumors the Philistines sent as a guilt
offering to the LORD—one each for Ashdod, Gaza, Ashkelon, Gath
and Ekron. 18 And the number of the gold rats was according to the
number of Philistine towns belonging to the five rulers—the fortified towns with their country villages. The large rock, on which[a]
they set the ark of the LORD, is a witness to this day in the field of
Joshua of Beth Shemesh.

[a] **18** A few Hebrew manuscripts (see also Septuagint); most Hebrew manuscripts *villages as far as Greater Abel, where*

QUESTIONS ABOUT 1 SAMUEL 1:1—7:17

1. Samuel was an important figure in Israel's history, but most of the first two chapters tell his mother Hannah's story. Why do you think that is?
2. Hannah gave her very young son Samuel to be raised by the priest Eli. How difficult would it have been for her to make that decision? Why? (See 2:21-26.)
3. The twelve tribes of Israel were living in the land promised to them by God (Gen 17:8). Why did they continue to face threats from their neighbors?
4. What were Eli's strengths and weaknesses as a priest and as a father? How did these affect the Israelites? (1:9-17; 2:12-36)
5. The Philistines became afraid when they heard that the ark of the covenant was in the Israelites' camp. If they were afraid, why do you think they captured it? (4:6-11) Why did they return it? (5:1—6:21) What was the the importance of the ark of the covenant to the Israelites?
6. What examples of the power of prayer do you find in 1 Samuel 1–7?

19But God struck down some of the men of Beth Shemesh,
putting seventy[a] of them to death because they had looked into the
ark of the LORD. The people mourned because of the heavy blow
the LORD had dealt them, 20and the men of Beth Shemesh asked,
"Who can stand in the presence of the LORD, this holy God? To
whom will the ark go up from here?"
21Then they sent messengers to the people of Kiriath Jearim,
saying, "The Philistines have returned the ark of the LORD.
7 Come down and take it up to your place." 1So the men of Kiriath
Jearim came and took up the ark of the LORD. They took it to Abinadab's house on the hill and consecrated Eleazar his son to guard
the ark of the LORD.

SAMUEL LEADS ISRAEL

Samuel Subdues the Philistines at Mizpah

2It was a long time, twenty years in all, that the ark remained
at Kiriath Jearim, and all the people of Israel mourned and sought
after the LORD. 3And Samuel said to the whole house of Israel, "If
you are returning to the LORD with all your hearts, then rid yourselves of the foreign gods and the Ashtoreths and commit yourselves to the LORD and serve him only, and he will deliver you out
of the hand of the Philistines." 4So the Israelites put away their
Baals and Ashtoreths, and served the LORD only.
5Then Samuel said, "Assemble all Israel at Mizpah and I will
intercede with the LORD for you." 6When they had assembled at
Mizpah, they drew water and poured it out before the LORD. On
that day they fasted and there they confessed, "We have sinned
against the LORD." And Samuel was leader[b] of Israel at Mizpah.
7When the Philistines heard that Israel had assembled at
Mizpah, the rulers of the Philistines came up to attack them. And
when the Israelites heard of it, they were afraid because of the
Philistines. 8They said to Samuel, "Do not stop crying out to the
LORD our God for us, that he may rescue us from the hand of
the Philistines." 9Then Samuel took a suckling lamb and offered it
up as a whole burnt offering to the LORD. He cried out to the LORD
on Israel's behalf, and the LORD answered him.
10While Samuel was sacrificing the burnt offering, the
Philistines drew near to engage Israel in battle. But that day the LORD
thundered with loud thunder against the Philistines and threw them
into such a panic that they were routed before the Israelites. 11The
men of Israel rushed out of Mizpah and pursued the Philistines,
slaughtering them along the way to a point below Beth Car.

[a]**19** A few Hebrew manuscripts; most Hebrew manuscripts and Septuagint *50,070*
[b]**6** Traditionally *judge*

6:19 *putting seventy of them to death . . . looked into the ark of the LORD:* In the Bible, seventy often stands for a large number rather than an exact amount. See the chart called "Numbers in the Bible," p. 2405. Looking inside the ark of the covenant to see God was so disrespectful that those who did it were struck dead (see also 2 Sam 6:6,7).

6:21 *Kiriath Jearim:* The "city of forests" was a border town of the tribes of Judah, Benjamin, and Dan and was about eight miles north of Jerusalem. Once it was called Kiriath Baal, "city of the god Baal" (Josh 15:60).

7:3,4 *rid yourselves of the foreign gods . . . Baals and Ashtoreths:* Foreign gods were represented by idols, objects made of wood, stone, metal, or baked clay. Many places in the Jewish Scriptures claim that the God of Israel could not be contained in such a hand-made image. See also Exod 34:17; Lev 19:4; 26:1; Deut 27:15.

"Baal" means "owner" or "lord" and is used in the Bible as both a common and proper noun. Here it is used as the name of a weather god, who was worshiped from a number of locations in Canaan. Baal's worshipers believed he brought thunderstorms and fertility to the land. Ashtoreth is also known as "Asherah," the goddess of fertility. Her worshipers believed that she made the land produce crops and gave them many children. See also the mini-article called "Canaanite Gods and Goddesses," p. 469.

7:5-11 *Mizpah . . . Beth Car:* At least five places were called "Mizpah," a word that means watchtower. The Mizpah in this verse was probably near Kiriath Jearim (6:21). Beth Car's location is not known.

7:6 *they fasted:* Fasting, or going without eating, was a common way of showing sorrow or regret.

7:1 2 Sam 6:2-11; 1 Chr 13:5-7.

7:15-17 *judge over Israel:* The Hebrew word translated as "judge" here could mean an army commander, a judge, or a religious leader. Samuel was all three. Judges in ancient Israel did more than just settle disputes. An Israelite judge guided people toward making the right decisions.

7:16 *Bethel to Gilgal to Mizpah:* The places Samuel visited as ruler and judge were a small part of Israelite lands, but they were very important and were at the center of what would one day be the united Israelite Kingdom.

Mizpah, Shiloh, and Gilgal formed a triangle, and Bethel was near Mizpah. See the map on p. 2464 and the note at 7:5-11. Bethel, once named Luz (Gen 28:19), was important in Israel's religious history. Abraham built an altar near Bethel (Gen 12:8); Jacob also built an altar there (Gen 35:1-16); and the ark of the covenant was kept there for a while (Judg 20:26-28).

Many places were called Gilgal. This Gilgal was probably near Jericho.

8:1 *Samuel grew old:* About twenty years have gone by since the victory at Mizpah (7:12, 13). Samuel would be about sixty-five years old.

8:2 *Beersheba:* Beersheba was an important city in the semi-desert area at the southern end of the Israelites' lands (see the map on p. 2464).

8:1-5 *judges . . . appoint a king:* See the note at 7:15-17. Kings ruled most of Israel's neighbors. The Israelites hoped that a king would unite their tribes as a nation and protect them from the Philistines and Ammonites. They used Samuel's age and the behavior of his sons as an excuse to ask for a different kind of leader (8:19,20; 10:19; 12:12). See also Deut 17:14-20.

8:7 *they have rejected me as their king:* When the Israelites asked for a king, the LORD knew that they were breaking their promise to rely only on God to save and protect them (Num 23:21; 1 Sam 12:12). Years earlier, Moses had said they would reject God and ask for a king (Deut 17:14).

12 Then Samuel took a stone and set it up between Mizpah
and Shen. He named it Ebenezer,[a] saying, "Thus far has the LORD
helped us." 13 So the Philistines were subdued and did not invade
Israelite territory again.

Throughout Samuel's lifetime, the hand of the LORD was
against the Philistines. 14 The towns from Ekron to Gath that the
Philistines had captured from Israel were restored to her, and Israel
delivered the neighboring territory from the power of the
Philistines. And there was peace between Israel and the Amorites.

15 Samuel continued as judge over Israel all the days of his
life. 16 From year to year he went on a circuit from Bethel to Gilgal
to Mizpah, judging Israel in all those places. 17 But he always went
back to Ramah, where his home was, and there he also judged
Israel. And he built an altar there to the LORD.

Saul

This part of SAMUEL also begins and ends in Ramah, Samuel's home. Israel asks for a king like the ones that ruled other nations. Saul is chosen, but fails in the end.

ISRAEL PLEADS WITH SAMUEL

When the Israelites ask for a king, Samuel reminds them that God is king in Israel.

Israel Asks for a King

8 When Samuel grew old, he appointed his sons as judges for
Israel. 2 The name of his firstborn was Joel and the name of his second was Abijah, and they served at Beersheba. 3 But his sons did
not walk in his ways. They turned aside after dishonest gain and
accepted bribes and perverted justice.

4 So all the elders of Israel gathered together and came to
Samuel at Ramah. 5 They said to him, "You are old, and your sons
do not walk in your ways; now appoint a king to lead[b] us, such as
all the other nations have."

6 But when they said, "Give us a king to lead us," this displeased Samuel; so he prayed to the LORD. 7 And the LORD told him:
"Listen to all that the people are saying to you; it is not you they
have rejected, but they have rejected me as their king. 8 As they have
done from the day I brought them up out of Egypt until this day,
forsaking me and serving other gods, so they are doing to you.
9 Now listen to them; but warn them solemnly and let them know
what the king who will reign over them will do."

10 Samuel told all the words of the LORD to the people who

[a]**12** *Ebenezer* means *stone of help.* [b]**5** Traditionally *judge*; also in verses 6 and 20

were asking him for a king. 11He said, “This is what the king who
will reign over you will do: He will take your sons and make them
serve with his chariots and horses, and they will run in front of his
chariots. 12Some he will assign to be commanders of thousands
and commanders of fifties, and others to plow his ground and reap
his harvest, and still others to make weapons of war and equipment for his chariots. 13He will take your daughters to be per-
fumers and cooks and bakers. 14He will take the best of your fields
and vineyards and olive groves and give them to his attendants.
15He will take a tenth of your grain and of your vintage and give it
to his officials and attendants. 16Your menservants and maidservants and the best of your cattle[a] and donkeys he will take for
his own use. 17He will take a tenth of your flocks, and you yourselves will become his slaves. 18When that day comes, you will cry
out for relief from the king you have chosen, and the LORD will not
answer you in that day.”

19But the people refused to listen to Samuel. “No!” they said.
“We want a king over us. 20Then we will be like all the other
nations, with a king to lead us and to go out before us and fight
our battles.”

21When Samuel heard all that the people said, he repeated it
before the LORD. 22The LORD answered, “Listen to them and give
them a king.”

Then Samuel said to the men of Israel, “Everyone go back to
his town.”

SAUL BECOMES KING

Samuel Anoints Saul

9 There was a Benjamite, a man of standing, whose name was
Kish son of Abiel, the son of Zeror, the son of Becorath, the son of
Aphiah of Benjamin. 2He had a son named Saul, an impressive
young man without equal among the Israelites—a head taller than
any of the others.

3Now the donkeys belonging to Saul’s father Kish were lost,
and Kish said to his son Saul, “Take one of the servants with you
and go and look for the donkeys.” 4So he passed through the hill
country of Ephraim and through the area around Shalisha, but
they did not find them. They went on into the district of Shaalim,
but the donkeys were not there. Then he passed through the territory of Benjamin, but they did not find them.

5When they reached the district of Zuph, Saul said to the
servant who was with him, “Come, let’s go back, or my father will
stop thinking about the donkeys and start worrying about us.”

6But the servant replied, “Look, in this town there is a man

[a]16 Septuagint; Hebrew *young men*

“We want a king over us. Then we will be like all the other nations, with a king to lead us and to go out before us and fight our battles.”
1 Sam 8:19, 20

8:10 *asking:* In this story, the Hebrew word translated here as “asking” is also translated “inquiring,” “finding out,” or “praying.” In each case, it is a pun on Saul’s name, which in Hebrew is another form of the same word. The pun on Saul’s name becomes more obvious when Saul, “the one asked for” (10:22; 12:13,17,19), is the one doing the asking (14:37; 17:58; 28:6).

8:11 *This is what the king . . . will do:* Samuel reminded the Israelites that it could cost them dearly to have a king. When he told them they would have to give up their sons and daughters, part of their property, and some of the food that they raise, Samuel hoped to make them think again about wanting a king.

9:2 *Saul:* Saul became the first king of Israel, and reigned from about 1030 to 1000 B.C.

9:4 *Ephraim . . . Shalisha . . . Shaalim . . . Benjamin:* For Ephraim and Benjamin, see the notes at 1:1 and 4:12. Shalisha (also known as Baal Shalisha) is thought to be in the territory of Ephraim. Shaalim’s exact location is not known.

9:5 *district of Zuph:* The Zuph clan lived in this region. It was Samuel’s father’s clan and part of the tribe of Ephraim. A clan was a group of families who were related to each other and often lived close to each other. A group of clans made up a tribe. See the note at 1:1.

9:9-11 *some girls coming out to draw water:* Towns were often built on a hill with a source of water in a valley outside of the town. Women usually had the job of drawing water for their families.

9:12,13 *He's ahead of you . . . bless the sacrifice:* As the priest, Samuel had to bless the meat from the sacrifice before it could be eaten. See also the note at 1:3 (sacrifice).

9:16 *Anoint him leader:* Olive oil was poured on the head of someone who was chosen to perform the special duties as a priest, a prophet, or a king. This practice was called "anointing."

9:22 *at the head:* People were seated at the table according to their importance. Samuel treated Saul as if Saul were already the king.

of God; he is highly respected, and everything he says comes true.
Let's go there now. Perhaps he will tell us what way to take."
7Saul said to his servant, "If we go, what can we give the
man? The food in our sacks is gone. We have no gift to take to the
man of God. What do we have?"
8The servant answered him again. "Look," he said, "I have a
quarter of a shekel[a] of silver. I will give it to the man of God so that
he will tell us what way to take." 9(Formerly in Israel, if a man went
to inquire of God, he would say, "Come, let us go to the seer,"
because the prophet of today used to be called a seer.)
10"Good," Saul said to his servant. "Come, let's go." So they
set out for the town where the man of God was.
11As they were going up the hill to the town, they met some
girls coming out to draw water, and they asked them, "Is the seer
here?"
12"He is," they answered. "He's ahead of you. Hurry now; he
has just come to our town today, for the people have a sacrifice at
the high place. 13As soon as you enter the town, you will find him
before he goes up to the high place to eat. The people will not
begin eating until he comes, because he must bless the sacrifice;
afterward, those who are invited will eat. Go up now; you should
find him about this time."
14They went up to the town, and as they were entering it, there
was Samuel, coming toward them on his way up to the high place.
15Now the day before Saul came, the LORD had revealed this
to Samuel: 16"About this time tomorrow I will send you a man
from the land of Benjamin. Anoint him leader over my people
Israel; he will deliver my people from the hand of the Philistines. I
have looked upon my people, for their cry has reached me."
17When Samuel caught sight of Saul, the LORD said to him,
"This is the man I spoke to you about; he will govern my people."
18Saul approached Samuel in the gateway and asked, "Would
you please tell me where the seer's house is?"
19"I am the seer," Samuel replied. "Go up ahead of me to the
high place, for today you are to eat with me, and in the morning I
will let you go and will tell you all that is in your heart. 20As for the
donkeys you lost three days ago, do not worry about them; they
have been found. And to whom is all the desire of Israel turned, if
not to you and all your father's family?"
21Saul answered, "But am I not a Benjamite, from the smallest tribe of Israel, and is not my clan the least of all the clans of the
tribe of Benjamin? Why do you say such a thing to me?"
22Then Samuel brought Saul and his servant into the hall
and seated them at the head of those who were invited—about
thirty in number. 23Samuel said to the cook, "Bring the piece of
meat I gave you, the one I told you to lay aside."

[a]**8** That is, about 1/10 ounce (about 3 grams)

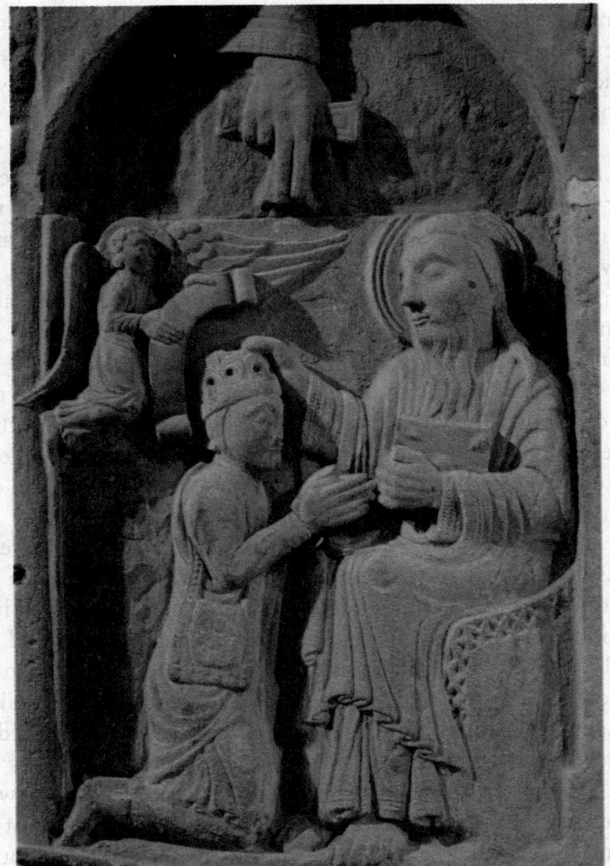

Samuel and Saul, bas relief carving from the Freiburg Cathedral, Freiburg, Germany, around 1300. The people of Israel wanted to be like the nations around them and to have a king who would rule them and lead them into battle. At first the LORD gave the prophet Samuel a message to warn the people about what a king would do to them, but when the people continued to ask for a king, the LORD agreed and led Saul, from the tribe of Benjamin, to Samuel. Although this Gothic carving doesn't show the prophet pouring oil on the kneeling Saul's head, the "hand of God" reaching down from heaven is the artist's way of showing that the LORD chose Saul to be Israel's leader. (See chapters 8–10.)

24 So the cook took up the leg with what was on it and set it
in front of Saul. Samuel said, "Here is what has been kept for you.
Eat, because it was set aside for you for this occasion, from the
time I said, 'I have invited guests.' " And Saul dined with Samuel
that day.
25 After they came down from the high place to the town,
Samuel talked with Saul on the roof of his house. 26 They rose
about daybreak and Samuel called to Saul on the roof, "Get ready,
and I will send you on your way." When Saul got ready, he and

9:25 *on the roof of his house:* Houses in ancient times usually had flat roofs. Guests often slept on the roof of their host's house so they could enjoy the cool breeze.

10:1 *oil . . . poured it . . . kissed him:* See the note at 9:16. Relatives or close friends often greeted one another with a kiss. But this may have been a ceremonial kiss after Samuel poured oil on Saul's head to indicate that he would be the king.

10:2 *Rachel's tomb, at Zelzah . . . border of Benjamin:* Rachel was one of the wives of Jacob (whose sons were the ancestors of the twelve tribes Israel) and the mother of Joseph and Benjamin. In this verse, Rachel's tomb is said to be in the territory of Benjamin, north of Jerusalem. Elsewhere in the Bible, it is said to be south of Jerusalem near Bethlehem (Gen 35:16-19; 48:7).

10:3-5 *Tabor . . . Bethel . . . Gibeah:* Tabor was probably in the territory of Benjamin. For Bethel, see the note at 7:16. Gibeah was a few miles north of Jerusalem. Archaeologists have suggested that Saul took over the Philistine's "camp" at Gibeah and made it his palace.

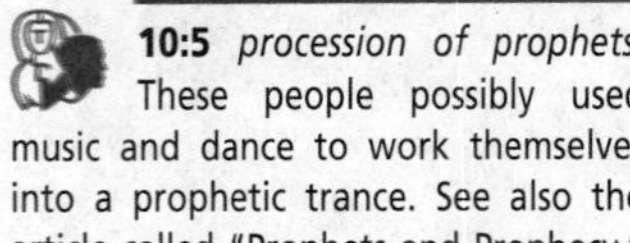

10:5 *procession of prophets:* These people possibly used music and dance to work themselves into a prophetic trance. See also the article called "Prophets and Prophecy," p. 935.

10:8 *Gilgal:* See the note at 7:16.

10:12 1 Sam 19:23, 24.

Samuel went outside together. 27 As they were going down to the
edge of the town, Samuel said to Saul, "Tell the servant to go on
ahead of us"—and the servant did so—"but you stay here awhile,
so that I may give you a message from God."

10 Then Samuel took a flask of oil and poured it on Saul's head
and kissed him, saying, "Has not the LORD anointed you leader
over his inheritance?[a] 2 When you leave me today, you will meet
two men near Rachel's tomb, at Zelzah on the border of Benjamin.
They will say to you, 'The donkeys you set out to look for have
been found. And now your father has stopped thinking about
them and is worried about you. He is asking, "What shall I do
about my son?"'

3 "Then you will go on from there until you reach the great
tree of Tabor. Three men going up to God at Bethel will meet you
there. One will be carrying three young goats, another three loaves
of bread, and another a skin of wine. 4 They will greet you and offer
you two loaves of bread, which you will accept from them.

5 "After that you will go to Gibeah of God, where there is a
Philistine outpost. As you approach the town, you will meet a procession of prophets coming down from the high place with lyres,
tambourines, flutes and harps being played before them, and they
will be prophesying. 6 The Spirit of the LORD will come upon you
in power, and you will prophesy with them; and you will be
changed into a different person. 7 Once these signs are fulfilled, do
whatever your hand finds to do, for God is with you.

8 "Go down ahead of me to Gilgal. I will surely come down to
you to sacrifice burnt offerings and fellowship offerings,[b] but you
must wait seven days until I come to you and tell you what you are
to do."

Saul Made King

9 As Saul turned to leave Samuel, God changed Saul's heart,
and all these signs were fulfilled that day. 10 When they arrived at
Gibeah, a procession of prophets met him; the Spirit of God came
upon him in power, and he joined in their prophesying. 11 When
all those who had formerly known him saw him prophesying with
the prophets, they asked each other, "What is this that has happened to the son of Kish? Is Saul also among the prophets?"

12 A man who lived there answered, "And who is their
father?" So it became a saying: "Is Saul also among the prophets?"
13 After Saul stopped prophesying, he went to the high place.

14 Now Saul's uncle asked him and his servant, "Where have
you been?"

---

[a]**1** Hebrew; Septuagint and Vulgate *over his people Israel? You will reign over the LORD's people and save them from the power of their enemies round about. And this will be a sign to you that the LORD has anointed you leader over his inheritance:*
[b]**8** Traditionally *peace offerings*

"Looking for the donkeys," he said. "But when we saw they
were not to be found, we went to Samuel."
15 Saul's uncle said, "Tell me what Samuel said to you."
16 Saul replied, "He assured us that the donkeys had been
found." But he did not tell his uncle what Samuel had said about
the kingship.
17 Samuel summoned the people of Israel to the LORD at Mizpah 18 and said to them, "This is what the LORD, the God of Israel,
says: 'I brought Israel up out of Egypt, and I delivered you from
the power of Egypt and all the kingdoms that oppressed you.' 19 But
you have now rejected your God, who saves you out of all your
calamities and distresses. And you have said, 'No, set a king over
us.' So now present yourselves before the LORD by your tribes and
clans."
20 When Samuel brought all the tribes of Israel near, the tribe
of Benjamin was chosen. 21 Then he brought forward the tribe of
Benjamin, clan by clan, and Matri's clan was chosen. Finally Saul
son of Kish was chosen. But when they looked for him, he was not
to be found. 22 So they inquired further of the LORD, "Has the man
come here yet?"
And the LORD said, "Yes, he has hidden himself among the
baggage."
23 They ran and brought him out, and as he stood among the
people he was a head taller than any of the others. 24 Samuel said to
all the people, "Do you see the man the LORD has chosen? There is
no one like him among all the people."
Then the people shouted, "Long live the king!"
25 Samuel explained to the people the regulations of the kingship. He wrote them down on a scroll and deposited it before the
LORD. Then Samuel dismissed the people, each to his own home.
26 Saul also went to his home in Gibeah, accompanied by
valiant men whose hearts God had touched. 27 But some troublemakers said, "How can this fellow save us?" They despised him and
brought him no gifts. But Saul kept silent.

Saul Rescues the City of Jabesh

11 Nahash the Ammonite went up and besieged Jabesh Gilead.
And all the men of Jabesh said to him, "Make a treaty with us, and
we will be subject to you."
2 But Nahash the Ammonite replied, "I will make a treaty
with you only on the condition that I gouge out the right eye of
every one of you and so bring disgrace on all Israel."
3 The elders of Jabesh said to him, "Give us seven days so we
can send messengers throughout Israel; if no one comes to rescue
us, we will surrender to you."
4 When the messengers came to Gibeah of Saul and reported
these terms to the people, they all wept aloud. 5 Just then Saul was
returning from the fields, behind his oxen, and he asked, "What is

Samuel said, *"You have now rejected your God, who saves you out of all your calamities and distresses. And you have said, 'No, set a king over us.'"*
1 Sam 10:19

10:17 *Mizpah:* See the notes at 7:5-11 and 7:16.

10:19 *by your tribes and clans:* See the notes at 1:1 and 9:5.

10:20,21 *chosen:* The Hebrew verb refers to the special way priests would get answers from God to simple yes or no questions. Priests kept objects of wood, stone, or metal in a pouch (breastpiece) attached to the front of their vest. These objects were marked Urim ("curses") for no, and Thummim ("perfections") for yes. God would guide the priest in determining the answer (Exod 28).

11:1 *Nahash the Ammonite:* The Ammonites were related to the Israelites (Gen 19:30-38) and lived east of Israel and north of Moab (Deut 2:17-19). When the Israelites came out of Egypt they asked the Ammonites for help, but the Ammonites refused to help them. Later, the Ammonites became a constant threat to the Israelites (Judg 11:1-5). See also the map on p. 2464.

11:1 *Jabesh Gilead:* A city east of the Jordan River about forty miles north of the Dead Sea. See the map on p. 2464.

11:2 *gouge out the right eye:* Since the shield was held in the left hand and covered the left eye, the loss of the right eye would make warriors useless, giving Nahash a military advantage.

> *Samuel said to all Israel, "I have listened to everything you said to me and have set a king over you. Now you have a king as your leader."*
> 1 Sam 12:1,2

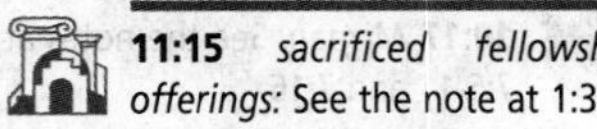
11:15 *sacrificed fellowship offerings:* See the note at 1:3.

wrong with the people? Why are they weeping?" Then they repeated to him what the men of Jabesh had said.
[6]When Saul heard their words, the Spirit of God came upon
him in power, and he burned with anger. [7]He took a pair of oxen,
cut them into pieces, and sent the pieces by messengers throughout Israel, proclaiming, "This is what will be done to the oxen of anyone who does not follow Saul and Samuel." Then the terror of the LORD fell on the people, and they turned out as one man.
[8]When Saul mustered them at Bezek, the men of Israel numbered
three hundred thousand and the men of Judah thirty thousand.
[9]They told the messengers who had come, "Say to the men of
Jabesh Gilead, 'By the time the sun is hot tomorrow, you will be delivered.' " When the messengers went and reported this to the
men of Jabesh, they were elated. [10]They said to the Ammonites,
"Tomorrow we will surrender to you, and you can do to us whatever seems good to you."
[11]The next day Saul separated his men into three divisions;
during the last watch of the night they broke into the camp of the Ammonites and slaughtered them until the heat of the day. Those who survived were scattered, so that no two of them were left together.

Saul Confirmed as King

[12]The people then said to Samuel, "Who was it that asked,
'Shall Saul reign over us?' Bring these men to us and we will put them to death."
[13]But Saul said, "No one shall be put to death today, for this
day the LORD has rescued Israel."
[14]Then Samuel said to the people, "Come, let us go to Gilgal
and there reaffirm the kingship." [15]So all the people went to Gilgal
and confirmed Saul as king in the presence of the LORD. There they sacrificed fellowship offerings[a] before the LORD, and Saul and all the Israelites held a great celebration.

SAMUEL REMINDS THE PEOPLE TO WORSHIP AND OBEY THE LORD

Samuel's Farewell Speech

12 Samuel said to all Israel, "I have listened to everything you
said to me and have set a king over you. [2]Now you have a king as
your leader. As for me, I am old and gray, and my sons are here with you. I have been your leader from my youth until this day.
[3]Here I stand. Testify against me in the presence of the LORD and
his anointed. Whose ox have I taken? Whose donkey have I taken?

[a]15 Traditionally *peace offerings*

Whom have I cheated? Whom have I oppressed? From whose hand
have I accepted a bribe to make me shut my eyes? If I have done
any of these, I will make it right."
4"You have not cheated or oppressed us," they replied. "You
have not taken anything from anyone's hand."
5Samuel said to them, "The LORD is witness against you, and
also his anointed is witness this day, that you have not found anything in my hand."
"He is witness," they said.
6Then Samuel said to the people, "It is the LORD who
appointed Moses and Aaron and brought your forefathers up out
of Egypt. 7Now then, stand here, because I am going to confront
you with evidence before the LORD as to all the righteous acts performed by the LORD for you and your fathers.
8"After Jacob entered Egypt, they cried to the LORD for help,
and the LORD sent Moses and Aaron, who brought your forefathers
out of Egypt and settled them in this place.
9"But they forgot the LORD their God; so he sold them into
the hand of Sisera, the commander of the army of Hazor, and into
the hands of the Philistines and the king of Moab, who fought
against them. 10They cried out to the LORD and said, 'We have
sinned; we have forsaken the LORD and served the Baals and the
Ashtoreths. But now deliver us from the hands of our enemies, and
we will serve you.' 11Then the LORD sent Jerub-Baal,[a] Barak,[b] Jephthah and Samuel,[c] and he delivered you from the hands of your
enemies on every side, so that you lived securely.
12"But when you saw that Nahash king of the Ammonites was
moving against you, you said to me, 'No, we want a king to rule over
us'—even though the LORD your God was your king. 13Now here is
the king you have chosen, the one you asked for; see, the LORD has
set a king over you. 14If you fear the LORD and serve and obey him
and do not rebel against his commands, and if both you and the
king who reigns over you follow the LORD your God—good! 15But
if you do not obey the LORD, and if you rebel against his commands, his hand will be against you, as it was against your fathers.
16"Now then, stand still and see this great thing the LORD is
about to do before your eyes! 17Is it not wheat harvest now? I will call
upon the LORD to send thunder and rain. And you will realize what an
evil thing you did in the eyes of the LORD when you asked for a king."
18Then Samuel called upon the LORD, and that same day the
LORD sent thunder and rain. So all the people stood in awe of the
LORD and of Samuel.
19The people all said to Samuel, "Pray to the LORD your God
for your servants so that we will not die, for we have added to all
our other sins the evil of asking for a king."

[a]11 Also called *Gideon* [b]11 Some Septuagint manuscripts and Syriac; Hebrew *Bedan* [c]11 Hebrew; some Septuagint manuscripts and Syriac *Samson*

12:5 *witness against you:* The law required at least two witnesses for proof (Deut 19:15). Samuel asked the Israelites if what he said about his service to God was true, and in front of witnesses, they said it was. This reminded the people that the rest of what he would say was also true.

12:6 *forefathers up out of Egypt:* The people of Israel had been slaves in Egypt (see Exod 6:26 and the Introduction to EXODUS). For more about Moses, see the mini-article called "Moses," p. 2335. Moses' brother Aaron was Israel's first high priest (Exod 28:1-3).

12:11 *Jerub-Baal, Barak, Jephthah and Samuel:* Samuel was reminding the Israelites that God had taken care of them, and that so far they had not needed a king. The people would have known these Israelite judges from the past. Gideon (also called Jerub-Baal, see Judg 7:1) rescued Israel from the Midianites (Judg 6:11—8:21). Jephthah delivered Israel from the Ammonites (Judg 10:6—12:7). Samuel led the people against the Philistines (1 Sam 7). Unless this Barak is the same one who helped the judge Deborah defeat Sisera's army (Judg 4), his contribution is not clear. Some scholars think that "Barak" (Hebrew "Bedan") might be another name for "Jephthah."

12:17 *wheat harvest . . . thunder and rain:* The wheat harvest was usually in late spring, the beginning of the dry season. The Hebrew word for thunder is literally "voices" (Exod 9:33). It suggests that the thunder in storms is God's loud voice (7:9,10; Ps 29:3-9). Samuel asked God to create thunder and rain during a dry season to show the people they were wrong to ask for a king.

12:8 Exod 2:23-25; 3:9. **12:9** ***a*** Judg 4:2; ***b*** Judg 13:1; ***c*** Judg 3:12. **12:10** Judg 10:10-15. **12:11** ***a*** Judg 7:1; ***b*** Judg 11:29; ***c*** 1 Sam 3:20. **12:12** 1 Sam 8:19, 20.

12:21 *useless idols:* See the note at 7:3, 4.

12:22 *the LORD will not reject his people:* God promised Abraham that his descendants, the Israelites, would form a great nation (Gen 12:2). See also the mini-article called "Israel," p. 264.

13:2,3 *three thousand . . . Jonathan . . . Philistine:* The three thousand men were full-time soldiers, those sent home would fight alongside the army only when the nation was in danger. Jonathan was Saul's son (see also 13:16). For the Philistines, see the note at 4:1.

13:3 *trumpet:* Here, probably a shofar. Made from the horn of a ram or other animal, it could make several different sounds. These were used to signal events, danger, or the death of important people (Judg 3:27, 28; Neh 4:18-20). The shofar is still used as part of Jewish religious celebrations. The photograph below is of an Orthodox Jew sounding the shofar at the New Year (Rosh Hashanah) celebration at the Western Wall in Jerusalem.

13:5 *as numerous as the sand on the seashore:* This exaggeration is a way of saying the Philistines would be hard to defeat.

13:5 *Beth Aven:* May be another name for Bethel (see Hos 4:15; 5:8; 10:5), or may be a town located about a mile southwest of Micmash.

20 "Do not be afraid," Samuel replied. "You have done all this
evil; yet do not turn away from the LORD, but serve the LORD with
all your heart. 21 Do not turn away after useless idols. They can do
you no good, nor can they rescue you, because they are useless.
22 For the sake of his great name the LORD will not reject his people,
because the LORD was pleased to make you his own. 23 As for me, far
be it from me that I should sin against the LORD by failing to pray
for you. And I will teach you the way that is good and right. 24 But
be sure to fear the LORD and serve him faithfully with all your heart;
consider what great things he has done for you. 25 Yet if you persist
in doing evil, both you and your king will be swept away."

SAUL DISOBEYS THE LORD AND IS REJECTED

Samuel Rebukes Saul

13 Saul was ⌞thirty⌟[a] years old when he became king, and he
reigned over Israel ⌞forty-⌟[b] two years.
2 Saul[c] chose three thousand men from Israel; two thousand
were with him at Micmash and in the hill country of Bethel, and a
thousand were with Jonathan at Gibeah in Benjamin. The rest of
the men he sent back to their homes.
3 Jonathan attacked the Philistine outpost at Geba, and the
Philistines heard about it. Then Saul had the trumpet blown
throughout the land and said, "Let the Hebrews hear!" 4 So all Israel
heard the news: "Saul has attacked the Philistine outpost, and now
Israel has become a stench to the Philistines." And the people were
summoned to join Saul at Gilgal.
5 The Philistines assembled to fight Israel, with three thousand[d] chariots, six thousand charioteers, and soldiers as numerous
as the sand on the seashore. They went up and camped at Micmash, east of Beth Aven. 6 When the men of Israel saw that their situation was critical and that their army was hard pressed, they hid in
caves and thickets, among the rocks, and in pits and cisterns. 7 Some
Hebrews even crossed the Jordan to the land of Gad and Gilead.
Saul remained at Gilgal, and all the troops with him were
quaking with fear. 8 He waited seven days, the time set by Samuel;
but Samuel did not come to Gilgal, and Saul's men began to scatter.
9 So he said, "Bring me the burnt offering and the fellowship offerings.[e]" And Saul offered up the burnt offering. 10 Just as he finished
making the offering, Samuel arrived, and Saul went out to greet him.
11 "What have you done?" asked Samuel.
Saul replied, "When I saw that the men were scattering, and

[a]1 A few late manuscripts of the Septuagint; Hebrew does not have *thirty.*
[b]1 See the round number in Acts 13:21; Hebrew does not have *forty-.* [c]1,2 Or *and when he had reigned over Israel two years, 2he* [d]5 Some Septuagint manuscripts and Syriac; Hebrew *thirty thousand* [e]9 Traditionally *peace offerings*

that you did not come at the set time, and that the Philistines were
assembling at Micmash, [12]I thought, 'Now the Philistines will come
down against me at Gilgal, and I have not sought the LORD's favor.'
So I felt compelled to offer the burnt offering."
[13]"You acted foolishly," Samuel said. "You have not kept the
command the LORD your God gave you; if you had, he would have
established your kingdom over Israel for all time. [14]But now your
kingdom will not endure; the LORD has sought out a man after his
own heart and appointed him leader of his people, because you
have not kept the LORD's command."
[15]Then Samuel left Gilgal[a] and went up to Gibeah in Benjamin, and Saul counted the men who were with him. They numbered about six hundred.

Israel Without Weapons

[16]Saul and his son Jonathan and the men with them were
staying in Gibeah[b] in Benjamin, while the Philistines camped at
Micmash. [17]Raiding parties went out from the Philistine camp in
three detachments. One turned toward Ophrah in the vicinity of
Shual, [18]another toward Beth Horon, and the third toward the bor-
derland overlooking the Valley of Zeboim facing the desert.
[19]Not a blacksmith could be found in the whole land of
Israel, because the Philistines had said, "Otherwise the Hebrews
will make swords or spears!" [20]So all Israel went down to the
Philistines to have their plowshares, mattocks, axes and sickles[c]
sharpened. [21]The price was two thirds of a shekel[d] for sharpening
plowshares and mattocks, and a third of a shekel[e] for sharpening
forks and axes and for repointing goads.
[22]So on the day of the battle not a soldier with Saul and
Jonathan had a sword or spear in his hand; only Saul and his son
Jonathan had them.

Jonathan Attacks the Philistines

[23]Now a detachment of Philistines had gone out to the pass
14 at Micmash. [1]One day Jonathan son of Saul said to the young
man bearing his armor, "Come, let's go over to the Philistine outpost on the other side." But he did not tell his father.
[2]Saul was staying on the outskirts of Gibeah under a pomegranate tree in Migron. With him were about six hundred men,
[3]among whom was Ahijah, who was wearing an ephod. He was a
son of Ichabod's brother Ahitub son of Phinehas, the son of Eli, the
LORD's priest in Shiloh. No one was aware that Jonathan had left.

---

[a]15 Hebrew; Septuagint *Gilgal and went his way; the rest of the people went after Saul to meet the army, and they went out of Gilgal* [b]16 Two Hebrew manuscripts; most Hebrew manuscripts *Geba*, a variant of *Gibeah* [c]20 Septuagint; Hebrew *plowshares* [d]21 Hebrew *pim*; that is, about 1/4 ounce (about 8 grams) [e]21 That is, about 1/8 ounce (about 4 grams)

13:7 *Some Hebrews:* See the note at 14:21.

13:8-12 *I felt compelled to offer the burnt offering:* As a king chosen by God, Saul was supposed to follow God's Law and know that the prophet Samuel's word was God's word. Samuel had advised Saul to wait—that he would tell Saul what to do after he came and offered sacrifices (10:8). Saul panicked, ignored Samuel's instructions, and went ahead on his own.

13:13 *he would have established your kingdom over Israel for all time:* Because Saul broke his promise to obey God, his son Jonathan and all of Saul's other descendants lost the right to become kings of Israel. See 2 Sam 7:15, 16.

13:14 *a man after his own heart:* Referring to David. See also Acts 13:22.

13:19-21 *blacksmith . . . sickles . . . goads:* Forged iron was preferred for tools and weapons because of its strength. Blacksmiths made the tools, farming implements, and weapons. Plows and hoes were used to work the ground. Axes were used for cutting trees and thick plants or for hewing (cutting and shaping) stone. Sickles were used for cutting grain. Goads were used to poke cattle and make them move.

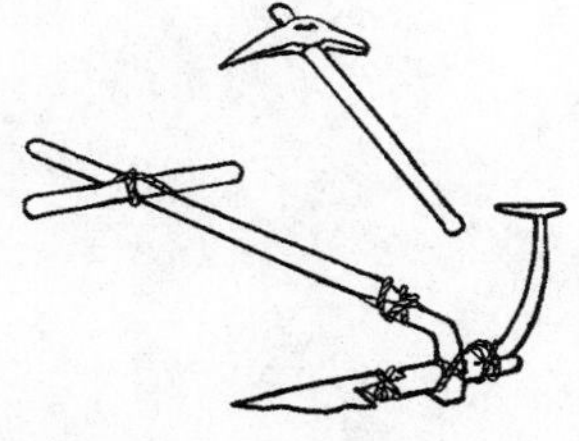

14:2 *pomegranate tree:* A pomegranate is a bright red fruit that looks like an apple. It had special meaning for the Israelites. See Deut 8:8,9.

14:4,5 *Micmash . . . Geba:* Micmash and Geba guarded an important travel route between Jericho and the Mediterranean coast. That route went through the pass that Jonathan and the soldier crossed to surprise the Philistines.

14:9,10 *if they say . . . that will be our sign:* Jonathan was looking for a sign that they were fighting on God's side.

14:18 *Bring the ark of God:* Referring to the ark of the covenant, symbolizing God's presence with the people.

14:21 *Those Hebrews:* This translates a Hebrew word which may be used to refer to wandering groups of people who sometimes became outlaws or hired soldiers. See also 13:7 and the note at 4:6.

4 On each side of the pass that Jonathan intended to cross to
reach the Philistine outpost was a cliff; one was called Bozez, and
the other Seneh. 5 One cliff stood to the north toward Micmash,
the other to the south toward Geba.

6 Jonathan said to his young armor-bearer, "Come, let's go
over to the outpost of those uncircumcised fellows. Perhaps the
LORD will act in our behalf. Nothing can hinder the LORD from
saving, whether by many or by few."

7 "Do all that you have in mind," his armor-bearer said. "Go
ahead; I am with you heart and soul."

8 Jonathan said, "Come, then; we will cross over toward the
men and let them see us. 9 If they say to us, 'Wait there until we
come to you,' we will stay where we are and not go up to them.
10 But if they say, 'Come up to us,' we will climb up, because that
will be our sign that the LORD has given them into our hands."

11 So both of them showed themselves to the Philistine outpost. "Look!" said the Philistines. "The Hebrews are crawling out of
the holes they were hiding in." 12 The men of the outpost shouted to
Jonathan and his armor-bearer, "Come up to us and we'll teach you
a lesson."

So Jonathan said to his armor-bearer, "Climb up after me;
the LORD has given them into the hand of Israel."

13 Jonathan climbed up, using his hands and feet, with his
armor-bearer right behind him. The Philistines fell before
Jonathan, and his armor-bearer followed and killed behind him.
14 In that first attack Jonathan and his armor-bearer killed some
twenty men in an area of about half an acre.[a]

Israel Routs the Philistines

15 Then panic struck the whole army—those in the camp and
field, and those in the outposts and raiding parties—and the
ground shook. It was a panic sent by God.[b]

16 Saul's lookouts at Gibeah in Benjamin saw the army melting away in all directions. 17 Then Saul said to the men who were
with him, "Muster the forces and see who has left us." When they
did, it was Jonathan and his armor-bearer who were not there.

18 Saul said to Ahijah, "Bring the ark of God." (At that time it
was with the Israelites.)[c] 19 While Saul was talking to the priest, the
tumult in the Philistine camp increased more and more. So Saul
said to the priest, "Withdraw your hand."

20 Then Saul and all his men assembled and went to the battle. They found the Philistines in total confusion, striking each
other with their swords. 21 Those Hebrews who had previously
been with the Philistines and had gone up with them to their camp

[a]14 Hebrew *half a yoke*; a "yoke" was the land plowed by a yoke of oxen in one day. [b]15 Or *a terrible panic* [c]18 Hebrew; Septuagint *"Bring the ephod." (At that time he wore the ephod before the Israelites.)*

went over to the Israelites who were with Saul and Jonathan.
22When all the Israelites who had hidden in the hill country of
Ephraim heard that the Philistines were on the run, they joined the
battle in hot pursuit. 23So the LORD rescued Israel that day, and the
battle moved on beyond Beth Aven.

Jonathan Eats Honey

24Now the men of Israel were in distress that day, because
Saul had bound the people under an oath, saying, "Cursed be any
man who eats food before evening comes, before I have avenged
myself on my enemies!" So none of the troops tasted food.
25The entire army[a] entered the woods, and there was honey
on the ground. 26When they went into the woods, they saw the
honey oozing out, yet no one put his hand to his mouth, because
they feared the oath. 27But Jonathan had not heard that his father
had bound the people with the oath, so he reached out the end of
the staff that was in his hand and dipped it into the honeycomb.
He raised his hand to his mouth, and his eyes brightened.[b] 28Then
one of the soldiers told him, "Your father bound the army under a
strict oath, saying, 'Cursed be any man who eats food today!' That
is why the men are faint."
29Jonathan said, "My father has made trouble for the country. See how my eyes brightened[c] when I tasted a little of this
honey. 30How much better it would have been if the men had eaten
today some of the plunder they took from their enemies. Would
not the slaughter of the Philistines have been even greater?"
31That day, after the Israelites had struck down the Philistines
from Micmash to Aijalon, they were exhausted. 32They pounced on
the plunder and, taking sheep, cattle and calves, they butchered
them on the ground and ate them, together with the blood. 33Then
someone said to Saul, "Look, the men are sinning against the LORD
by eating meat that has blood in it."

"You have broken faith," he said. "Roll a large stone over here
at once." 34Then he said, "Go out among the men and tell them,
'Each of you bring me your cattle and sheep, and slaughter them
here and eat them. Do not sin against the LORD by eating meat
with blood still in it.' "

So everyone brought his ox that night and slaughtered it
there. 35Then Saul built an altar to the LORD; it was the first time he
had done this.
36Saul said, "Let us go down after the Philistines by night and
plunder them till dawn, and let us not leave one of them alive."

"Do whatever seems best to you," they replied.

But the priest said, "Let us inquire of God here."

37So Saul asked God, "Shall I go down after the Philistines?

[a]25 Or *Now all the people of the land* [b]27 Or *his strength was renewed* [c]29 Or *my strength was renewed*

14:23 *Beth Aven:* See the note at 13:5 (Beth Aven).

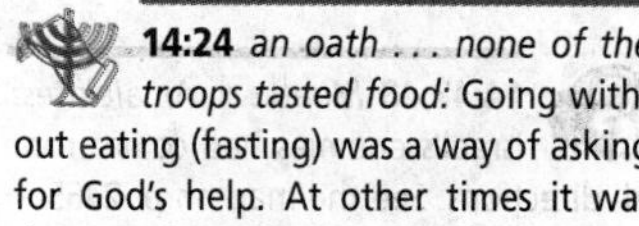

14:24 *an oath . . . none of the troops tasted food:* Going without eating (fasting) was a way of asking for God's help. At other times it was done to show sorrow.

14:31 *Aijalon:* About twenty miles west of Micmash.

14:32 *sheep, cattle and calves . . . butchered them . . . blood:* In spite of what Jonathan said, the Israelite army waited until they had won the fight before they began to eat. After all, they had fasted to get God's help in winning. But the Israelites were so hungry, they forgot they were supposed to drain the blood from a butchered animal before the meat was cooked and eaten (Gen 9:4; Lev 17:10-14; Deut 12:23,24).

14:33,34 *large stone . . . slaughter:* Saul meant for the people to slaughter their animals on a big stone, that is, up off the ground so the blood could drain out.

14:36-41 *Let us inquire of God:* See the note at 10:20,21. See also Num 27:21; 1 Sam 28:6.

14:33 Gen 9:4; Lev 7:26, 27; 17:10-14; 19:26; Deut 12:5-19, 23,24; 15:23.

14:41 *taken by lot:* Probably with the Urim and Thummim. See the note at 10:20, 21.

14:47,48 *Moab . . . Amalekites:* Israel's enemies had come from all directions. See the map on p. 2465.

14:49 *Ishvi . . . Michal:* Ishvi was also known as Esh-Baal (1 Chr 8:33; 9:39) and Ish-Bosheth (2 Sam 2:8-13; 3:8-15; 4:5-12). Michal, Saul's younger daughter would later be given in marriage to one of Saul's best warriors, David, who would become Israel's king after Saul's death. See 1 Sam 18:27.

Will you give them into Israel's hand?" But God did not answer him that day.

38 Saul therefore said, "Come here, all you who are leaders of the army, and let us find out what sin has been committed today. 39 As surely as the LORD who rescues Israel lives, even if it lies with my son Jonathan, he must die." But not one of the men said a word.

40 Saul then said to all the Israelites, "You stand over there; I and Jonathan my son will stand over here."

"Do what seems best to you," the men replied.

41 Then Saul prayed to the LORD, the God of Israel, "Give me the right answer."[a] And Jonathan and Saul were taken by lot, and the men were cleared. 42 Saul said, "Cast the lot between me and Jonathan my son." And Jonathan was taken.

43 Then Saul said to Jonathan, "Tell me what you have done."

So Jonathan told him, "I merely tasted a little honey with the end of my staff. And now must I die?"

44 Saul said, "May God deal with me, be it ever so severely, if you do not die, Jonathan."

45 But the men said to Saul, "Should Jonathan die—he who has brought about this great deliverance in Israel? Never! As surely as the LORD lives, not a hair of his head will fall to the ground, for he did this today with God's help." So the men rescued Jonathan, and he was not put to death.

46 Then Saul stopped pursuing the Philistines, and they withdrew to their own land.

47 After Saul had assumed rule over Israel, he fought against their enemies on every side: Moab, the Ammonites, Edom, the kings[b] of Zobah, and the Philistines. Wherever he turned, he inflicted punishment on them.[c] 48 He fought valiantly and defeated the Amalekites, delivering Israel from the hands of those who had plundered them.

Saul's Family

49 Saul's sons were Jonathan, Ishvi and Malki-Shua. The name of his older daughter was Merab, and that of the younger was Michal. 50 His wife's name was Ahinoam daughter of Ahimaaz. The name of the commander of Saul's army was Abner son of Ner, and Ner was Saul's uncle. 51 Saul's father Kish and Abner's father Ner were sons of Abiel.

52 All the days of Saul there was bitter war with the Philistines, and whenever Saul saw a mighty or brave man, he took him into his service.

---

[a]**41** Hebrew; Septuagint *"Why have you not answered your servant today? If the fault is in me or my son Jonathan, respond with Urim, but if the men of Israel are at fault, respond with Thummim."* [b]**47** Masoretic Text; Dead Sea Scrolls and Septuagint *king* [c]**47** Hebrew; Septuagint *he was victorious*

The LORD Rejects Saul as King

15 Samuel said to Saul, "I am the one the LORD sent to anoint
you king over his people Israel; so listen now to the message from
the LORD. 2This is what the LORD Almighty says: 'I will punish the
Amalekites for what they did to Israel when they waylaid them as
they came up from Egypt. 3Now go, attack the Amalekites and
totally destroy[a] everything that belongs to them. Do not spare
them; put to death men and women, children and infants, cattle
and sheep, camels and donkeys.' "

4So Saul summoned the men and mustered them at
Telaim—two hundred thousand foot soldiers and ten thousand
men from Judah. 5Saul went to the city of Amalek and set an
ambush in the ravine. 6Then he said to the Kenites, "Go away, leave
the Amalekites so that I do not destroy you along with them; for
you showed kindness to all the Israelites when they came up out of
Egypt." So the Kenites moved away from the Amalekites.

7Then Saul attacked the Amalekites all the way from Havilah to Shur, to the east of Egypt. 8He took Agag king of the
Amalekites alive, and all his people he totally destroyed with the
sword. 9But Saul and the army spared Agag and the best of the
sheep and cattle, the fat calves[b] and lambs—everything that was
good. These they were unwilling to destroy completely, but everything that was despised and weak they totally destroyed.

10Then the word of the LORD came to Samuel: 11"I am
grieved that I have made Saul king, because he has turned away
from me and has not carried out my instructions." Samuel was
troubled, and he cried out to the LORD all that night.

12Early in the morning Samuel got up and went to meet
Saul, but he was told, "Saul has gone to Carmel. There he has set
up a monument in his own honor and has turned and gone on
down to Gilgal."

13When Samuel reached him, Saul said, "The LORD bless you!
I have carried out the LORD's instructions."

14But Samuel said, "What then is this bleating of sheep in my
ears? What is this lowing of cattle that I hear?"

15Saul answered, "The soldiers brought them from the
Amalekites; they spared the best of the sheep and cattle to sacrifice
to the LORD your God, but we totally destroyed the rest."

16"Stop!" Samuel said to Saul. "Let me tell you what the LORD
said to me last night."

"Tell me," Saul replied.

17Samuel said, "Although you were once small in your own
eyes, did you not become the head of the tribes of Israel? The LORD
anointed you king over Israel. 18And he sent you on a mission,

---

[a]3 The Hebrew term refers to the irrevocable giving over of things or persons to the LORD, often by totally destroying them; also in verses 8, 9, 15, 18, 20 and 21.

[b]9 Or *the grown bulls*; the meaning of the Hebrew for this phrase is uncertain.

15:3 *go, attack . . . destroy everything:* This is what God required of the Israelites when they captured towns in the land God gave them. See also Deut 20:10-18 and the mini-article called "Holy War (The LORD's Battles)," p. 306.

15:6 *Kenites:* The Kenites were a group of nomads in the southern part of the Israelites' land. They would later become part of the tribe of Judah (30:27-31). See also Judg 1:16.

15:9 *spared . . . everything that was good:* God had forbidden the Israelites from keeping things of value. See the note at 15:3.

15:12 *Carmel:* A city about seven miles south of Hebron near the Amalekite territory. See 25:2,3.

15:15 *totally destroyed:* These animals had been unconditionally dedicated to the LORD and had to be destroyed (see Lev 27:28).

15:1 1 Sam 10:1. **15:2** Exod 17:8-14; Deut 25:17-19.

Saul said, *"I have sinned. I violated the LORD's command and your instructions. I was afraid of the people and so I gave in to them."*
1 Sam 15:24

15:26-28 *You have rejected . . . The LORD has torn:* Saul still didn't understand. He seemed to think that he could do what he wanted, as long as he gave sacrifices and offerings (15:22). Samuel's torn cloak was symbolic of the removal of Saul's kingship. See also 1 Kgs 11:29-31. Saul no longer measured up to God's rule that kings must obey God's law. See also 1 Sam 28:17.

saying, 'Go and completely destroy those wicked people, the
Amalekites; make war on them until you have wiped them out.'
19Why did you not obey the LORD? Why did you pounce on the
plunder and do evil in the eyes of the LORD?"
20"But I did obey the LORD," Saul said. "I went on the mission the LORD assigned me. I completely destroyed the Amalekites
and brought back Agag their king. 21The soldiers took sheep and
cattle from the plunder, the best of what was devoted to God, in
order to sacrifice them to the LORD your God at Gilgal."
22But Samuel replied:

"Does the LORD delight in burnt offerings and sacrifices
as much as in obeying the voice of the LORD?
To obey is better than sacrifice,
and to heed is better than the fat of rams.
23For rebellion is like the sin of divination,
and arrogance like the evil of idolatry.
Because you have rejected the word of the LORD,
he has rejected you as king."

24Then Saul said to Samuel, "I have sinned. I violated the
LORD's command and your instructions. I was afraid of the people
and so I gave in to them. 25Now I beg you, forgive my sin and come
back with me, so that I may worship the LORD."
26But Samuel said to him, "I will not go back with you. You
have rejected the word of the LORD, and the LORD has rejected you
as king over Israel!"
27As Samuel turned to leave, Saul caught hold of the hem of
his robe, and it tore. 28Samuel said to him, "The LORD has torn the
kingdom of Israel from you today and has given it to one of your

QUESTIONS ABOUT 1 SAMUEL 8:1—15:35

1. The behavior of Eli's sons led to his replacement as a leader (2:12-17, 22-25; 3:11-18). By contrast, how did the behavior of Samuel's sons affect Samuel's leadership? (8:1-5)
2. The Israelites wanted to be like other nations and be led by a king (8:5, 19, 20). What reasons did they give? Why was it hard for them to trust in God alone? (12:19, 20)
3. Samuel indicated that Saul was to be Israel's king by pouring oil on his head, but then almost immediately reminded the people not to put all their trust in a king. Why do you think he did so? (11:14, 15; 12:1-17)
4. Saul offered a sacrifice to the LORD instead of waiting for Samuel (13:7-15). What did that say about Saul's character? How did Saul react to Samuel's angry response?
5. Read 15:1-23 and the mini-article called "Holy War (The LORD's Battles)," p. 306. How did the Israelites' understanding of holy war relate to their being God's chosen people?
6. Samuel was a priest, a prophet, and a judge. Pick an incident that shows his strengths in each role. How are these roles similar? How are they different?
7. Read 15:22. Rewrite this verse in your own words to make it more meaningful in today's culture.

neighbors—to one better than you. [29]He who is the Glory of Israel
does not lie or change his mind; for he is not a man, that he should
change his mind."

[30]Saul replied, "I have sinned. But please honor me before
the elders of my people and before Israel; come back with me, so
that I may worship the LORD your God." [31]So Samuel went back
with Saul, and Saul worshiped the LORD.

[32]Then Samuel said, "Bring me Agag king of the Amalekites."

Agag came to him confidently,[a] thinking, "Surely the bitterness of death is past."

[33]But Samuel said,

"As your sword has made women childless,
so will your mother be childless among women."

And Samuel put Agag to death before the LORD at Gilgal.

[34]Then Samuel left for Ramah, but Saul went up to his home
in Gibeah of Saul. [35]Until the day Samuel died, he did not go to
see Saul again, though Samuel mourned for him. And the LORD
was grieved that he had made Saul king over Israel.

David

This third and last part of 1 Samuel moves the story away from Ramah as Saul continues to falter and David is being prepared to be king.

THE LORD CHOOSES DAVID

Samuel pours oil on David's head to show that God has chosen David to be king. David has courage and faith in God, while Saul's fear and anxiety continue to grow.

Samuel Anoints David

16 The LORD said to Samuel, "How long will you mourn for
Saul, since I have rejected him as king over Israel? Fill your horn
with oil and be on your way; I am sending you to Jesse of Bethlehem. I have chosen one of his sons to be king."

[2]But Samuel said, "How can I go? Saul will hear about it and
kill me."

The LORD said, "Take a heifer with you and say, 'I have come
to sacrifice to the LORD.' [3]Invite Jesse to the sacrifice, and I will
show you what to do. You are to anoint for me the one I indicate."

[4]Samuel did what the LORD said. When he arrived at Bethlehem, the elders of the town trembled when they met him. They
asked, "Do you come in peace?"

[5]Samuel replied, "Yes, in peace; I have come to sacrifice to the

[a]32 Or *him trembling, yet*

15:33 *put Agag to death:* Samuel wanted to make sure that God was obeyed, so he did what Saul was supposed to have done.

16:1 *Fill your horn with oil:* See the note at 9:16. Olive oil was often stored in the hollowed out horns of animals.

16:1 *Jesse:* The son of Obed and grandson of Boaz and Ruth (Ruth 4:17-22). Bethlehem is only a few miles south of Jerusalem. See the map on p. 2464.

16:3-5 *to the sacrifice . . . Consecrate yourselves:* After a sacrifice, part of the animal might be eaten in a sacred meal, but only by people who were properly prepared. A number of things could make a person unfit to eat the meal (see Lev 7:20,21; 15:2,31; 22:4-8; Deut 23:10,11). See also the mini-article called "Purity (Clean and Unclean)," p. 2125.

The LORD said, *"The LORD does not look at the things man looks at. Man looks at the outward appearance, but the LORD looks at the heart."*
1 Sam 16:7

16:6 *Surely the LORD's anointed stands here:* Samuel thought he knew who God's choice would be. But even Samuel had to be shown what God was looking for.

16:11 *the youngest . . . tending the sheep:* David's humble beginnings as a shepherd would later be understood as a symbol for his role as a kind of shepherd (leader) of God's chosen people (17:34,35; 2 Sam 7:7,8; Ps 78:71,72). See the mini-article called "David," p. 1028.

16:12 *anoint him:* See the note at 9:16. Although David's brothers watched, they might not have known exactly what was happening. See, for example, Eliab's angry outburst at 17:28.

16:14 *an evil spirit from the LORD:* Saul probably was suffering from depression or a similar illness. People believed evil spirits caused such conditions, and that God sent both evil spirits and good spirits. See also 16:13; 18:10-12; 19:9, 10; 1 Kgs 22:19-23; Luke 11:24-26.

Samuel Anoints David, wall painting from the synagogue at Dura Europos, thirteenth century. The LORD was sorry he had made Saul king of Israel. He told Samuel to go to the town of Bethlehem because a man named Jesse lived there, and he had a son that the LORD had chosen to be Israel's new king. When David, the youngest of Jesse's sons, came before Samuel the LORD said, "Rise and anoint him; he is the one." (See 16:1-13.)

LORD. Consecrate yourselves and come to the sacrifice with me." Then
he consecrated Jesse and his sons and invited them to the sacrifice.
[6]When they arrived, Samuel saw Eliab and thought, "Surely
the LORD's anointed stands here before the LORD."
[7]But the LORD said to Samuel, "Do not consider his appearance or his height, for I have rejected him. The LORD does not look
at the things man looks at. Man looks at the outward appearance,
but the LORD looks at the heart."
[8]Then Jesse called Abinadab and had him pass in front of
Samuel. But Samuel said, "The LORD has not chosen this one
either." [9]Jesse then had Shammah pass by, but Samuel said, "Nor
has the LORD chosen this one." [10]Jesse had seven of his sons pass
before Samuel, but Samuel said to him, "The LORD has not chosen
these." [11]So he asked Jesse, "Are these all the sons you have?"
"There is still the youngest," Jesse answered, "but he is tending the sheep."
Samuel said, "Send for him; we will not sit down[a] until he
arrives."
[12]So he sent and had him brought in. He was ruddy, with a
fine appearance and handsome features.
Then the LORD said, "Rise and anoint him; he is the one."
[13]So Samuel took the horn of oil and anointed him in the

[a]**11** Some Septuagint manuscripts; Hebrew *not gather around*

presence of his brothers, and from that day on the Spirit of the
LORD came upon David in power. Samuel then went to Ramah.

David in Saul's Service

[14]Now the Spirit of the LORD had departed from Saul, and an
evil[a] spirit from the LORD tormented him.
[15]Saul's attendants said to him, "See, an evil spirit from God
is tormenting you. [16]Let our lord command his servants here to
search for someone who can play the harp. He will play when the
evil spirit from God comes upon you, and you will feel better."
[17]So Saul said to his attendants, "Find someone who plays
well and bring him to me."
[18]One of the servants answered, "I have seen a son of Jesse of
Bethlehem who knows how to play the harp. He is a brave man
and a warrior. He speaks well and is a fine-looking man. And the
LORD is with him."
[19]Then Saul sent messengers to Jesse and said, "Send me
your son David, who is with the sheep." [20]So Jesse took a donkey
loaded with bread, a skin of wine and a young goat and sent them
with his son David to Saul.
[21]David came to Saul and entered his service. Saul liked him
very much, and David became one of his armor-bearers. [22]Then
Saul sent word to Jesse, saying, "Allow David to remain in my service, for I am pleased with him."
[23]Whenever the spirit from God came upon Saul, David
would take his harp and play. Then relief would come to Saul; he
would feel better, and the evil spirit would leave him.

David and Goliath

17 Now the Philistines gathered their forces for war and assembled at Socoh in Judah. They pitched camp at Ephes Dammim,
between Socoh and Azekah. [2]Saul and the Israelites assembled and
camped in the Valley of Elah and drew up their battle line to meet
the Philistines. [3]The Philistines occupied one hill and the Israelites
another, with the valley between them.
[4]A champion named Goliath, who was from Gath, came out
of the Philistine camp. He was over nine feet[b] tall. [5]He had a
bronze helmet on his head and wore a coat of scale armor of
bronze weighing five thousand shekels[c]; [6]on his legs he wore bronze
greaves, and a bronze javelin was slung on his back. [7]His spear shaft
was like a weaver's rod, and its iron point weighed six hundred
shekels.[d] His shield bearer went ahead of him.
[8]Goliath stood and shouted to the ranks of Israel, "Why do
you come out and line up for battle? Am I not a Philistine, and are

---

a14 Or *injurious*; also in verses 15, 16 and 23 b4 Hebrew *was six cubits and a span* (about 3 meters) c5 That is, about 125 pounds (about 57 kilograms) d7 That is, about 15 pounds (about 7 kilograms)

16:16 *harp:* Here, probably a lyre, a small stringed musical instrument. See the illustration on p. 897.

16:19 *Send me your son:* Saul did not yet know that David had been chosen by God to replace him as king.

16:20 *a skin of wine:* Wine was sometimes kept in leather containers often made of goatskin sewn up with the fur on the outside. See also the mini-article called "Wine," on p. 2047.

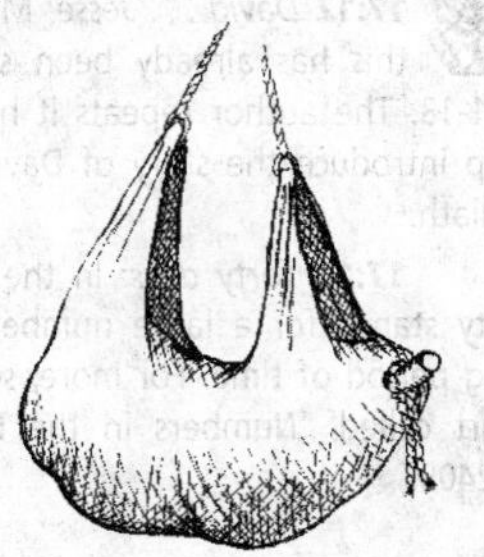

17:1,2 *Socoh and Azekah . . . Valley of Elah:* This area was about fifteen miles west of the hills of southern Judah. At the time, Socoh was controlled by the Israelites, and Azekah was controlled by the Philistines.

17:4-10 *Goliath . . . Choose a man . . . fight each other:* Goliath came out between the two armies and challenged the Israelites to choose a man to fight with him in one-on-one combat. The result of that fight would decide which army won the battle. This way of fighting kept the loss of life to a minimum.

17:5-7 *a bronze helmet . . . spear shaft:* Even though Goliath wore a heavy armor and carried a huge sword, David would be able to defeat him with a few stones because he had the LORD Almighty on his side. See the illustrations on pp. 1149, 881, and 1088.

David asked, *"Who is this uncircumcised Philistine that he should defy the armies of the living God?"*
1 Sam 17:26

17:12 *David . . . Jesse:* Much of this has already been said in 16:1-13. The author repeats it here to help introduce the story of David and Goliath.

17:16 *forty days:* In the Bible, forty stands for a large number or a long period of time. For more, see the chart called "Numbers in the Bible," p. 2405.

you not the servants of Saul? Choose a man and have him come down to me. 9 If he is able to fight and kill me, we will become your subjects; but if I overcome him and kill him, you will become our subjects and serve us." 10 Then the Philistine said, "This day I defy the ranks of Israel! Give me a man and let us fight each other." 11 On hearing the Philistine's words, Saul and all the Israelites were dismayed and terrified.

12 Now David was the son of an Ephrathite named Jesse, who was from Bethlehem in Judah. Jesse had eight sons, and in Saul's time he was old and well advanced in years. 13 Jesse's three oldest sons had followed Saul to the war: The firstborn was Eliab; the second, Abinadab; and the third, Shammah. 14 David was the youngest. The three oldest followed Saul, 15 but David went back and forth from Saul to tend his father's sheep at Bethlehem.

16 For forty days the Philistine came forward every morning and evening and took his stand.

17 Now Jesse said to his son David, "Take this ephah[a] of roasted grain and these ten loaves of bread for your brothers and hurry to their camp. 18 Take along these ten cheeses to the commander of their unit.[b] See how your brothers are and bring back some assurance[c] from them. 19 They are with Saul and all the men of Israel in the Valley of Elah, fighting against the Philistines."

20 Early in the morning David left the flock with a shepherd, loaded up and set out, as Jesse had directed. He reached the camp as the army was going out to its battle positions, shouting the war cry. 21 Israel and the Philistines were drawing up their lines facing each other. 22 David left his things with the keeper of supplies, ran to the battle lines and greeted his brothers. 23 As he was talking with them, Goliath, the Philistine champion from Gath, stepped out from his lines and shouted his usual defiance, and David heard it. 24 When the Israelites saw the man, they all ran from him in great fear.

25 Now the Israelites had been saying, "Do you see how this man keeps coming out? He comes out to defy Israel. The king will give great wealth to the man who kills him. He will also give him his daughter in marriage and will exempt his father's family from taxes in Israel."

26 David asked the men standing near him, "What will be done for the man who kills this Philistine and removes this disgrace from Israel? Who is this uncircumcised Philistine that he should defy the armies of the living God?"

27 They repeated to him what they had been saying and told him, "This is what will be done for the man who kills him."

28 When Eliab, David's oldest brother, heard him speaking with the men, he burned with anger at him and asked, "Why have you come down here? And with whom did you leave those few

---

[a]**17** That is, probably about 3/5 bushel (about 22 liters) [b]**18** Hebrew *thousand*
[c]**18** Or *some token*; or *some pledge of spoils*

sheep in the desert? I know how conceited you are and how wicked
your heart is; you came down only to watch the battle.”

29“Now what have I done?” said David. “Can’t I even speak?”
30He then turned away to someone else and brought up the same
matter, and the men answered him as before. 31What David said
was overheard and reported to Saul, and Saul sent for him.

32David said to Saul, “Let no one lose heart on account of
this Philistine; your servant will go and fight him.”

33Saul replied, “You are not able to go out against this Philistine and fight him; you are only a boy, and he has been a fighting
man from his youth.”

34But David said to Saul, “Your servant has been keeping his
father’s sheep. When a lion or a bear came and carried off a sheep
from the flock, 35I went after it, struck it and rescued the sheep
from its mouth. When it turned on me, I seized it by its hair,
struck it and killed it. 36Your servant has killed both the lion and
the bear; this uncircumcised Philistine will be like one of them,
because he has defied the armies of the living God. 37The LORD
who delivered me from the paw of the lion and the paw of the bear
will deliver me from the hand of this Philistine.”

Saul said to David, “Go, and the LORD be with you.”

38Then Saul dressed David in his own tunic. He put a coat
of armor on him and a bronze helmet on his head. 39David fastened on his sword over the tunic and tried walking around,
because he was not used to them.

“I cannot go in these,” he said to Saul, “because I am not
used to them.” So he took them off. 40Then he took his staff in his
hand, chose five smooth stones from the stream, put them in the
pouch of his shepherd’s bag and, with his sling in his hand,
approached the Philistine.

41Meanwhile, the Philistine, with his shield bearer in front of
him, kept coming closer to David. 42He looked David over and saw
that he was only a boy, ruddy and handsome, and he despised him.
43He said to David, “Am I a dog, that you come at me with sticks?”
And the Philistine cursed David by his gods. 44“Come here,” he
said, “and I’ll give your flesh to the birds of the air and the beasts
of the field!”

45David said to the Philistine, “You come against me with
sword and spear and javelin, but I come against you in the name of
the LORD Almighty, the God of the armies of Israel, whom you
have defied. 46This day the LORD will hand you over to me, and I’ll
strike you down and cut off your head. Today I will give the carcasses of the Philistine army to the birds of the air and the beasts
of the earth, and the whole world will know that there is a God in
Israel. 47All those gathered here will know that it is not by sword or
spear that the LORD saves; for the battle is the LORD’s, and he will
give all of you into our hands.”

48As the Philistine moved closer to attack him, David ran

17:34,35 *keeping his father’s sheep . . . lion or a bear:* Shepherds and shepherding are mentioned over two hundred times in the Bible. Shepherds fed, watered, and protected their sheep day and night. The term “shepherd” is used to describe Israel’s leaders and kings, as well as for describing God (Ps 23; Isa 40:11; Ezek 34; John 10:7-17; Heb 13:20, 21). For more, see the mini-article called “Shepherds,” p. 1972.

17:40 *staff . . . stones . . . bag . . . sling:* The shepherd used the wooden staff for support when walking in the hills and carried a few day’s supply of food in the bag, which was worn over the shoulder.

The sling was a hand-held weapon used to throw stones. Leather strings or straps were attached to both sides of a wider leather band or pocket. A stone was put in the leather pocket, and the thrower held on to both straps while swinging it above his head. When the thrower let go of one strap, the stone would fly out of the sling at speeds of up to 100 miles per hour.

17:43 *dog:* To call someone a dog was an insult. Most dogs were considered unclean, but some were kept as pets or used by shepherds (Job 30:1). When dogs are mentioned in the Bible, it is usually in a negative way (Exod 22:31; 1 Kgs 14:11; Prov 26:11,17; Matt 7:6; 15:26,27; Luke 16:21).

17:45-47 *LORD Almighty . . . the LORD saves:* David knew that when he was fighting on God’s side, God would help him win. See also Deut 7:16-24; Ps 33:16-19.

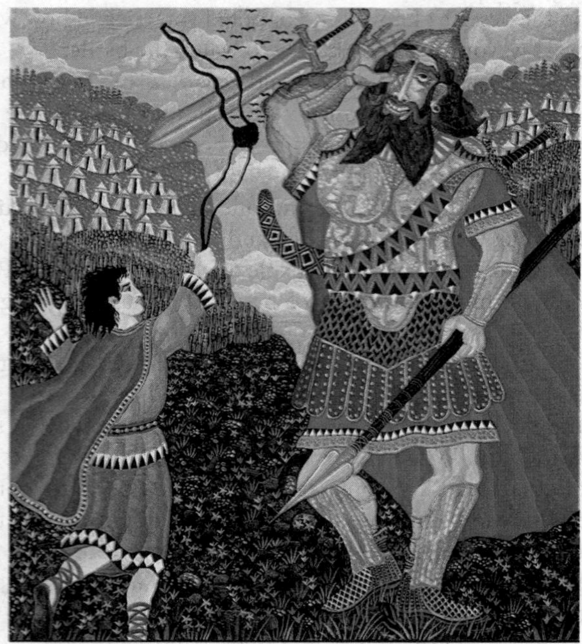

David Slays Goliath by Esben Hanefelt Kristensen, 1993. Goliath dared the Israelites to send out someone to fight him. Israel's warriors were afraid. But David accepted the giant's challenge, saying, "This day the LORD will hand you over to me . . . the whole world will know that there is a God in Israel." (See 17:41-54.)

quickly toward the battle line to meet him. 49Reaching into his bag
and taking out a stone, he slung it and struck the Philistine on the
forehead. The stone sank into his forehead, and he fell facedown
on the ground.
50So David triumphed over the Philistine with a sling and a
stone; without a sword in his hand he struck down the Philistine
and killed him.
51David ran and stood over him. He took hold of the Philistine's sword and drew it from the scabbard. After he killed him, he
cut off his head with the sword.
When the Philistines saw that their hero was dead, they
turned and ran. 52Then the men of Israel and Judah surged forward with a shout and pursued the Philistines to the entrance of
Gath[a] and to the gates of Ekron. Their dead were strewn along the
Shaaraim road to Gath and Ekron. 53When the Israelites returned
from chasing the Philistines, they plundered their camp. 54David
took the Philistine's head and brought it to Jerusalem, and he put
the Philistine's weapons in his own tent.

17:52–54 *Gath . . . Ekron . . . Shaaraim . . . Jerusalem:* For Gath and Ekron, see the note at 5:8-10. Shaaraim was a town in Judah. Since the Jebusites still held Jerusalem, it is not likely that David would not have gone there at this time. Perhaps he took Goliath's head to Jerusalem later, after he conquered and made it the capital of Israel (2 Sam 5:1-9).

17:50,51 2 Sam 21:19.

[a]52 Some Septuagint manuscripts; Hebrew *a valley*

55As Saul watched David going out to meet the Philistine, he said to Abner, commander of the army, "Abner, whose son is that young man?"

Abner replied, "As surely as you live, O king, I don't know."

56The king said, "Find out whose son this young man is."

57As soon as David returned from killing the Philistine, Abner took him and brought him before Saul, with David still holding the Philistine's head.

58"Whose son are you, young man?" Saul asked him.

David said, "I am the son of your servant Jesse of Bethlehem."

SAUL TURNS AGAINST DAVID

Jealous of David's success, Saul plots against him and tries to have him killed.

Saul's Jealousy of David

18 After David had finished talking with Saul, Jonathan became
one in spirit with David, and he loved him as himself. 2From that
day Saul kept David with him and did not let him return to his
father's house. 3And Jonathan made a covenant with David
because he loved him as himself. 4Jonathan took off the robe he
was wearing and gave it to David, along with his tunic, and even
his sword, his bow and his belt.

5Whatever Saul sent him to do, David did it so successfully[a]
that Saul gave him a high rank in the army. This pleased all the
people, and Saul's officers as well.

6When the men were returning home after David had killed
the Philistine, the women came out from all the towns of Israel to
meet King Saul with singing and dancing, with joyful songs and
with tambourines and lutes. 7As they danced, they sang:

"Saul has slain his thousands,
and David his tens of thousands."

8Saul was very angry; this refrain galled him. "They have
credited David with tens of thousands," he thought, "but me with
only thousands. What more can he get but the kingdom?" 9And
from that time on Saul kept a jealous eye on David.

10The next day an evil[b] spirit from God came forcefully upon
Saul. He was prophesying in his house, while David was playing
the harp, as he usually did. Saul had a spear in his hand 11and he
hurled it, saying to himself, "I'll pin David to the wall." But David
eluded him twice.

12Saul was afraid of David, because the LORD was with David
but had left Saul. 13So he sent David away from him and gave him

[a]5 Or *wisely* [b]10 Or *injurious*

17:55 *whose son:* It seems strange that Saul did not recognize David as Jesse's son who had played the harp for him (16:14-23). The following verses may be part of another story of how Saul comes to know David. They also reflect (like 16:14-23) Saul's positive feelings about David when they first met. See also 18:5.

18:1 *Jonathan:* Saul's oldest son and an officer in the king's army. See 13:16—14:15.

18:4 *took off the robe he was wearing and gave it to David:* It was probably too soon for Jonathan to have recognized David as the future king. But David's taking the robe from Jonathan can be seen as a symbol of the transfer of royal power from Saul to David, rather than to his own son. The transfer of military gear indicates that David would soon surpass Saul and Jonathan in military skill and success.

18:9,10 *a jealous eye on David . . . evil spirit from God:* This marks an important turning point in the relationship between Saul and David. Saul's jealousy and crazy behavior are clear signs that he is no longer in God's favor. Similarly, David's military successes, the affection and loyalty shown to him by Saul's own children, and the honorable way David continues to respect Saul as God's chosen king, show that David is increasing in God's favor. For more about the evil spirit, see 19:9 and the note at 16:14.

18:7 1 Sam 21:11; 29:5.

David and King Saul by Leslie Xuereb, contemporary painting. After the Spirit of the LORD had departed from King Saul, he was troubled by evil spirits. Saul's officials persuaded him to let them find someone who could play music for him to make him feel better. They found the shepherd boy David, who was good at playing the harp, and brought him to the king. Even though Saul was pleased by David's music, the king was still seized by evil spirits and even threw his spear at David when David was playing his harp. (See 16:14-23; 18:10, 11.)

command over a thousand men, and David led the troops in their
campaigns. 14In everything he did he had great success,[a] because
the LORD was with him. 15When Saul saw how successful[b] he was,
he was afraid of him. 16But all Israel and Judah loved David,
because he led them in their campaigns.

17Saul said to David, "Here is my older daughter Merab. I
will give her to you in marriage; only serve me bravely and fight
the battles of the LORD." For Saul said to himself, "I will not raise a
hand against him. Let the Philistines do that!"

18But David said to Saul, "Who am I, and what is my family
or my father's clan in Israel, that I should become the king's son-
in-law?" 19So[c] when the time came for Merab, Saul's daughter, to
be given to David, she was given in marriage to Adriel of Meholah.

20Now Saul's daughter Michal was in love with David, and
when they told Saul about it, he was pleased. 21"I will give her to
him," he thought, "so that she may be a snare to him and so that the
hand of the Philistines may be against him." So Saul said to David,
"Now you have a second opportunity to become my son-in-law."

22Then Saul ordered his attendants: "Speak to David privately and say, 'Look, the king is pleased with you, and his attendants
all like you; now become his son-in-law.' "

18:17-21 *give her to you in marriage:* Kings in the ancient world often relied on political marriages as a way of cementing alliances and preventing rebellions. Even though Saul was suspicious of David (18:9), allowing this popular warrior to marry one of his daughters made it look like he trusted him. If Saul's subjects believed this they would be less likely to suspect the king of having arranged David's death, should David die in battle.

18:18 *Who am I, and what is my family:* Family ties and status were very important among the scattered Israelite tribes. It was common courtly practice to speak humbly to the king as David is doing here. Compare his statement to what Saul said to Samuel (9:21). Unlike Saul, however, David is in reality the son of a wealthy man who was respected by the community (see 16:20; 17:12-15).

[a]**14** Or *he was very wise* [b]**15** Or *wise* [c]**19** Or *However,*

[23]They repeated these words to David. But David said, "Do you think it is a small matter to become the king's son-in-law? I'm only a poor man and little known."

[24]When Saul's servants told him what David had said, [25]Saul replied, "Say to David, 'The king wants no other price for the bride than a hundred Philistine foreskins, to take revenge on his enemies.'" Saul's plan was to have David fall by the hands of the Philistines.

[26]When the attendants told David these things, he was pleased to become the king's son-in-law. So before the allotted time elapsed, [27]David and his men went out and killed two hundred Philistines. He brought their foreskins and presented the full number to the king so that he might become the king's son-in-law. Then Saul gave him his daughter Michal in marriage.

[28]When Saul realized that the LORD was with David and that his daughter Michal loved David, [29]Saul became still more afraid of him, and he remained his enemy the rest of his days.

[30]The Philistine commanders continued to go out to battle, and as often as they did, David met with more success[a] than the rest of Saul's officers, and his name became well known.

Saul Tries to Kill David

19 Saul told his son Jonathan and all the attendants to kill David. But Jonathan was very fond of David [2]and warned him, "My father Saul is looking for a chance to kill you. Be on your guard tomorrow morning; go into hiding and stay there. [3]I will go out and stand with my father in the field where you are. I'll speak to him about you and will tell you what I find out."

[4]Jonathan spoke well of David to Saul his father and said to him, "Let not the king do wrong to his servant David; he has not wronged you, and what he has done has benefited you greatly. [5]He took his life in his hands when he killed the Philistine. The LORD won a great victory for all Israel, and you saw it and were glad. Why then would you do wrong to an innocent man like David by killing him for no reason?"

[6]Saul listened to Jonathan and took this oath: "As surely as the LORD lives, David will not be put to death."

[7]So Jonathan called David and told him the whole conversation. He brought him to Saul, and David was with Saul as before.

[8]Once more war broke out, and David went out and fought the Philistines. He struck them with such force that they fled before him.

[9]But an evil[b] spirit from the LORD came upon Saul as he was sitting in his house with his spear in his hand. While David was playing the harp, [10]Saul tried to pin him to the wall with his spear, but David eluded him as Saul drove the spear into the wall. That night David made good his escape.

[a]30 Or *David acted more wisely* [b]9 Or *injurious*

18:23 *a poor man:* The bride's father had to approve of the marriage, so a prospective groom usually offered something valuable in order to marry his daughter. It would take a large amount of silver or gold to marry the daughter of a king.

18:25 *Philistine foreskins:* In ancient times, soldiers would sometimes cut off body parts of dead enemies to prove how many they had killed. Here the foreskins would prove that the dead were not Israelites, who would have been circumcised (Lev 12:3).

19:9 *an evil spirit from the LORD:* Saul had promised in 19:6 not to have David killed. Saul's inability to keep the promises he made is further evidence that he had lost control of his faculties and was no longer fit to be king. See also the note at 16:14.

19:12 *down through a window:* The house was probably built into the town wall, allowing David to come down outside the wall, where the guards could not see him.

19:18 *Ramah:* Samuel was born here. See also the note at 1:1.

19:19,20 *Naioth ... group of prophets:* Prophets in the ancient Near East may have lived together in large groups to help support one another's work and show their legitimacy as prophets.

19:22 *great cistern:* A large hole dug down into the rock and used for storing rainwater.

19:24 *stripped off his robes:* Prophets were understood to be under God's control while they were prophesying, and so could no longer control their own actions. See also the article called "Prophets and Prophecy," p. 935.

20:1-42 *David fled ... went back to the town:* In this chapter Jonathan cannot believe Saul would want to kill David (20:2). The previous chapter, however, tells that Jonathan knew of Saul's plans to kill David once (19:1-3). Saul had already attacked David (19:9,10), causing David to run away. Now in 20:5, Saul has invited David to a special dinner. These verses probably reflect different stories of Saul's relationship with David. Also, the author may be using these different stories to show Saul's unstable attitude toward David. See also the note at 17:55.

19:11 Ps 59 Title. **19:24** 1 Sam 10:10, 11.

11 Saul sent men to David's house to watch it and to kill him
in the morning. But Michal, David's wife, warned him, "If you
don't run for your life tonight, tomorrow you'll be killed." 12 So
Michal let David down through a window, and he fled and
escaped. 13 Then Michal took an idol[a] and laid it on the bed, covering it with a garment and putting some goats' hair at the head.
14 When Saul sent the men to capture David, Michal said,
"He is ill."
15 Then Saul sent the men back to see David and told them,
"Bring him up to me in his bed so that I may kill him." 16 But when
the men entered, there was the idol in the bed, and at the head was
some goats' hair.
17 Saul said to Michal, "Why did you deceive me like this and
send my enemy away so that he escaped?"
Michal told him, "He said to me, 'Let me get away. Why
should I kill you?' "

DAVID RUNS AWAY

Saul pursues David in a jealous rage, and David escapes time and again. Finally, David escapes by joining the Philistines and agreeing to help them fight against Israel.

18 When David had fled and made his escape, he went to
Samuel at Ramah and told him all that Saul had done to him. Then
he and Samuel went to Naioth and stayed there. 19 Word came to Saul:
"David is in Naioth at Ramah"; 20 so he sent men to capture him. But
when they saw a group of prophets prophesying, with Samuel standing there as their leader, the Spirit of God came upon Saul's men and
they also prophesied. 21 Saul was told about it, and he sent more men,
and they prophesied too. Saul sent men a third time, and they also
prophesied. 22 Finally, he himself left for Ramah and went to the great
cistern at Secu. And he asked, "Where are Samuel and David?"
"Over in Naioth at Ramah," they said.
23 So Saul went to Naioth at Ramah. But the Spirit of God
came even upon him, and he walked along prophesying until he
came to Naioth. 24 He stripped off his robes and also prophesied in
Samuel's presence. He lay that way all that day and night. This is
why people say, "Is Saul also among the prophets?"

David and Jonathan

20 Then David fled from Naioth at Ramah and went to
Jonathan and asked, "What have I done? What is my crime? How
have I wronged your father, that he is trying to take my life?"
2 "Never!" Jonathan replied. "You are not going to die! Look,
my father doesn't do anything, great or small, without confiding
in me. Why would he hide this from me? It's not so!"

---

[a]**13** Hebrew *teraphim*; also in verse 16

3But David took an oath and said, "Your father knows very
well that I have found favor in your eyes, and he has said to himself, 'Jonathan must not know this or he will be grieved.' Yet as surely as the LORD lives and as you live, there is only a step between me and death."

4Jonathan said to David, "Whatever you want me to do, I'll do for you."

5So David said, "Look, tomorrow is the New Moon festival,
and I am supposed to dine with the king; but let me go and hide
in the field until the evening of the day after tomorrow. 6If your
father misses me at all, tell him, 'David earnestly asked my permission to hurry to Bethlehem, his hometown, because an annual
sacrifice is being made there for his whole clan.' 7If he says, 'Very
well,' then your servant is safe. But if he loses his temper, you can
be sure that he is determined to harm me. 8As for you, show kindness to your servant, for you have brought him into a covenant with you before the LORD. If I am guilty, then kill me yourself! Why hand me over to your father?"

9"Never!" Jonathan said. "If I had the least inkling that my father was determined to harm you, wouldn't I tell you?"

10David asked, "Who will tell me if your father answers you harshly?"

11"Come," Jonathan said, "let's go out into the field." So they went there together.

12Then Jonathan said to David: "By the LORD, the God of
Israel, I will surely sound out my father by this time the day after
tomorrow! If he is favorably disposed toward you, will I not send
you word and let you know? 13But if my father is inclined to harm
you, may the LORD deal with me, be it ever so severely, if I do not
let you know and send you away safely. May the LORD be with you
as he has been with my father. 14But show me unfailing kindness
like that of the LORD as long as I live, so that I may not be killed,
15and do not ever cut off your kindness from my family—not even when the LORD has cut off every one of David's enemies from the face of the earth."

16So Jonathan made a covenant with the house of David,
saying, "May the LORD call David's enemies to account." 17And
Jonathan had David reaffirm his oath out of love for him, because he loved him as he loved himself.

18Then Jonathan said to David: "Tomorrow is the New
Moon festival. You will be missed, because your seat will be empty.
19The day after tomorrow, toward evening, go to the place where
you hid when this trouble began, and wait by the stone Ezel. 20I
will shoot three arrows to the side of it, as though I were shooting
at a target. 21Then I will send a boy and say, 'Go, find the arrows.'
If I say to him, 'Look, the arrows are on this side of you; bring them here,' then come, because, as surely as the LORD lives, you are
safe; there is no danger. 22But if I say to the boy, 'Look, the arrows

> Jonathan said to David, *"May the LORD be with you as he has been with my father. But show me unfailing kindness like that of the LORD . . . and do not ever cut off your kindness from my family."*
> 1 Sam 20:13-15

20:5 *New Moon festival:* The first day of the month, when Israelites offered special sacrifices to the LORD and had special sacred meals. See also Num 28:11.

20:13 *May the LORD be with you . . . my father:* This seems to show that Jonathan believes David would be king after Saul, not himself.

20:14,15 *show me unfailing kindness . . . my family:* Saul was Israel's first king, and Jonathan was his son. Often in the ancient world when a new ruler came to power, members of the old royal household were killed. Jonathan asked David not to do that in Israel. Even after Jonathan died in battle, David honored Jonathan's request by letting Jonathan's son live (2 Sam 9).

"Why should he be put to death? What has he done?" Jonathan asked his father.
1 Sam 20:32

20:26 *he is unclean:* See the note at 16:3-5. Since many things could make a person impure (unclean), it is impossible to know what Saul had in mind.

20:41 *kissed:* Although kissing was a common way of greeting or saying good-bye in ancient times, the kiss between David and Jonathan is a symbol of their deep friendship.

are beyond you,' then you must go, because the LORD has sent you away. 23 And about the matter you and I discussed—remember, the LORD is witness between you and me forever."

24 So David hid in the field, and when the New Moon festival came, the king sat down to eat. 25 He sat in his customary place by the wall, opposite Jonathan,[a] and Abner sat next to Saul, but David's place was empty. 26 Saul said nothing that day, for he thought, "Something must have happened to David to make him ceremonially unclean—surely he is unclean." 27 But the next day, the second day of the month, David's place was empty again. Then Saul said to his son Jonathan, "Why hasn't the son of Jesse come to the meal, either yesterday or today?"

28 Jonathan answered, "David earnestly asked me for permission to go to Bethlehem. 29 He said, 'Let me go, because our family is observing a sacrifice in the town and my brother has ordered me to be there. If I have found favor in your eyes, let me get away to see my brothers.' That is why he has not come to the king's table."

30 Saul's anger flared up at Jonathan and he said to him, "You son of a perverse and rebellious woman! Don't I know that you have sided with the son of Jesse to your own shame and to the shame of the mother who bore you? 31 As long as the son of Jesse lives on this earth, neither you nor your kingdom will be established. Now send and bring him to me, for he must die!"

32 "Why should he be put to death? What has he done?" Jonathan asked his father. 33 But Saul hurled his spear at him to kill him. Then Jonathan knew that his father intended to kill David.

34 Jonathan got up from the table in fierce anger; on that second day of the month he did not eat, because he was grieved at his father's shameful treatment of David.

35 In the morning Jonathan went out to the field for his meeting with David. He had a small boy with him, 36 and he said to the boy, "Run and find the arrows I shoot." As the boy ran, he shot an arrow beyond him. 37 When the boy came to the place where Jonathan's arrow had fallen, Jonathan called out after him, "Isn't the arrow beyond you?" 38 Then he shouted, "Hurry! Go quickly! Don't stop!" The boy picked up the arrow and returned to his master. 39 (The boy knew nothing of all this; only Jonathan and David knew.) 40 Then Jonathan gave his weapons to the boy and said, "Go, carry them back to town."

41 After the boy had gone, David got up from the south side ⌞of the stone⌟ and bowed down before Jonathan three times, with his face to the ground. Then they kissed each other and wept together—but David wept the most.

42 Jonathan said to David, "Go in peace, for we have sworn friendship with each other in the name of the LORD, saying, 'The LORD is witness between you and me, and between your

---

[a]25 Septuagint; Hebrew *wall. Jonathan arose*

descendants and my descendants forever.' " Then David left, and
Jonathan went back to the town.

David at Nob

21 David went to Nob, to Ahimelech the priest. Ahimelech
trembled when he met him, and asked, "Why are you alone? Why
is no one with you?"
2David answered Ahimelech the priest, "The king charged me
with a certain matter and said to me, 'No one is to know anything
about your mission and your instructions.' As for my men, I have told
them to meet me at a certain place. 3Now then, what do you have on
hand? Give me five loaves of bread, or whatever you can find."
4But the priest answered David, "I don't have any ordinary
bread on hand; however, there is some consecrated bread here—
provided the men have kept themselves from women."
5David replied, "Indeed women have been kept from us, as
usual whenever[a] I set out. The men's things[b] are holy even on missions that are not holy. How much more so today!" 6So the priest
gave him the consecrated bread, since there was no bread there
except the bread of the Presence that had been removed from before
the LORD and replaced by hot bread on the day it was taken away.
7Now one of Saul's servants was there that day, detained
before the LORD; he was Doeg the Edomite, Saul's head shepherd.
8David asked Ahimelech, "Don't you have a spear or a sword
here? I haven't brought my sword or any other weapon, because
the king's business was urgent."
9The priest replied, "The sword of Goliath the Philistine,
whom you killed in the Valley of Elah, is here; it is wrapped in a
cloth behind the ephod. If you want it, take it; there is no sword
here but that one."
David said, "There is none like it; give it to me."

David at Gath

10That day David fled from Saul and went to Achish king of
Gath. 11But the servants of Achish said to him, "Isn't this David,
the king of the land? Isn't he the one they sing about in their
dances:

" 'Saul has slain his thousands,
and David his tens of thousands'?"

12David took these words to heart and was very much afraid
of Achish king of Gath. 13So he pretended to be insane in their
presence; and while he was in their hands he acted like a madman,
making marks on the doors of the gate and letting saliva run down
his beard.

---

[a]5 Or *from us in the past few days since* [b]5 Or *bodies*

21:1 *Nob:* Nob was in Benjamin, not too far from Jerusalem (Isa 10:32).

21:4-6 *consecrated bread:* In Israel, objects were considered to be either "common," "sacred," or "banned." Common objects could be used by anyone. Sacred (or consecrated) objects were put aside for God, and people other than priests usually could not use them. Banned objects were totally dedicated to God and had to be destroyed.

The consecrated bread (called bread of the Presence) was set out in the place of worship every week as a way of thanking God for providing the bread people needed each day. At the end of the week, the priests ate the bread; no one else was allowed to eat it (Lev 24:5-9). But Ahimelech made an exception and gave some of the consecrated bread to David.

21:4 *kept themselves from women:* Having sex was one of the things that would make someone temporarily unfit to take part in worship or a sacred meal (Exod 19:15; Lev 15:18). See the note at 16:3-5.

21:7 *the Edomite:* Doeg was from a country south of Israel. See the map on p. 2465.

21:10 *Gath:* One of the five main Philistine towns. See also the note at 5:8-10.

21:1-6 Matt 12:3, 4; Mark 2:25, 26; Luke 6:3, 4. **21:6** Lev 24:5-9. **21:9** 1 Sam 17:51. **21:11** 1 Sam 18:7; 29:5. **21:12** Ps 56 Title. **21:13** Ps 34 Title.

22:1 *cave of Adullam:* Adullam was about eighteen miles southwest of Gibeah and nine miles southeast of Gath.

22:3 *Mizpah in Moab:* The exact location of this Mizpah is unknown. Moab was located east of the Dead Sea. The Moabites were enemies of Israel (Judg 3:12-30; 1 Sam 14:47,48; 2 Kgs 3:21-27). David probably thought Moab's king would help him because both of them were now enemies of Saul, and also because David's great-grandmother was a Moabite (Ruth 4:13-17).

22:5 *forest of Hereth:* The exact location of this forest is not known, but it is thought to have been a few miles south of Adullam.

22:5 *the prophet Gad:* God would use this prophet to guide David at other times (2 Sam 24:11-13; 2 Chr 29:25). The author of 1 CHRONICLES reports that Gad, along with Samuel and Nathan, wrote a history of David's reign (1 Chr 29:29).

22:6 *Saul . . . under the tamarisk tree:* Ancient rulers are sometimes described as sitting under a well-known tree to hold court and make important decisions. Saul is at the highest point of his hometown of Gibeah. See also Judg 4:5.

22:7 *men of Benjamin:* Saul warned that David would give the tribe of Judah special privileges if he became king. This echoed Samuel's warning about what a king would do (8:11-15). But Saul's words show that he has done the same thing by giving special favors to his own tribe, the tribe of Benjamin.

22:1 Ps 57 Title; Ps 142 Title. **22:9,10** 1 Sam 21:7-9; Ps 52 Title.

[14]Achish said to his servants, "Look at the man! He is insane! Why bring him to me? [15]Am I so short of madmen that you have to bring this fellow here to carry on like this in front of me? Must this man come into my house?"

David at Adullam and Mizpah

22 David left Gath and escaped to the cave of Adullam. When his brothers and his father's household heard about it, they went down to him there. [2]All those who were in distress or in debt or discontented gathered around him, and he became their leader. About four hundred men were with him.

[3]From there David went to Mizpah in Moab and said to the king of Moab, "Would you let my father and mother come and stay with you until I learn what God will do for me?" [4]So he left them with the king of Moab, and they stayed with him as long as David was in the stronghold.

[5]But the prophet Gad said to David, "Do not stay in the stronghold. Go into the land of Judah." So David left and went to the forest of Hereth.

Saul Kills the Priests of Nob

[6]Now Saul heard that David and his men had been discovered. And Saul, spear in hand, was seated under the tamarisk tree on the hill at Gibeah, with all his officials standing around him. [7]Saul said to them, "Listen, men of Benjamin! Will the son of Jesse give all of you fields and vineyards? Will he make all of you commanders of thousands and commanders of hundreds? [8]Is that why you have all conspired against me? No one tells me when my son makes a covenant with the son of Jesse. None of you is concerned about me or tells me that my son has incited my servant to lie in wait for me, as he does today."

[9]But Doeg the Edomite, who was standing with Saul's officials, said, "I saw the son of Jesse come to Ahimelech son of Ahitub at Nob. [10]Ahimelech inquired of the LORD for him; he also gave him provisions and the sword of Goliath the Philistine."

[11]Then the king sent for the priest Ahimelech son of Ahitub and his father's whole family, who were the priests at Nob, and they all came to the king. [12]Saul said, "Listen now, son of Ahitub."

"Yes, my lord," he answered.

[13]Saul said to him, "Why have you conspired against me, you and the son of Jesse, giving him bread and a sword and inquiring of God for him, so that he has rebelled against me and lies in wait for me, as he does today?"

[14]Ahimelech answered the king, "Who of all your servants is as loyal as David, the king's son-in-law, captain of your bodyguard and highly respected in your household? [15]Was that day the first time I inquired of God for him? Of course not! Let not the king

accuse your servant or any of his father's family, for your servant
knows nothing at all about this whole affair."
16 But the king said, "You will surely die, Ahimelech, you and
your father's whole family."
17 Then the king ordered the guards at his side: "Turn and kill
the priests of the LORD, because they too have sided with David.
They knew he was fleeing, yet they did not tell me."
But the king's officials were not willing to raise a hand to
strike the priests of the LORD.
18 The king then ordered Doeg, "You turn and strike down
the priests." So Doeg the Edomite turned and struck them down.
That day he killed eighty-five men who wore the linen ephod. 19 He
also put to the sword Nob, the town of the priests, with its men
and women, its children and infants, and its cattle, donkeys and
sheep.
20 But Abiathar, a son of Ahimelech son of Ahitub, escaped
and fled to join David. 21 He told David that Saul had killed the
priests of the LORD. 22 Then David said to Abiathar: "That day,
when Doeg the Edomite was there, I knew he would be sure to tell
Saul. I am responsible for the death of your father's whole family.
23 Stay with me; don't be afraid; the man who is seeking your life is
seeking mine also. You will be safe with me."

David Saves Keilah

23 When David was told, "Look, the Philistines are fighting
against Keilah and are looting the threshing floors," 2 he inquired
of the LORD, saying, "Shall I go and attack these Philistines?"
The LORD answered him, "Go, attack the Philistines and save
Keilah."
3 But David's men said to him, "Here in Judah we are afraid.
How much more, then, if we go to Keilah against the Philistine
forces!"
4 Once again David inquired of the LORD, and the LORD
answered him, "Go down to Keilah, for I am going to give the
Philistines into your hand." 5 So David and his men went to Keilah,
fought the Philistines and carried off their livestock. He inflicted
heavy losses on the Philistines and saved the people of Keilah.
6 (Now Abiathar son of Ahimelech had brought the ephod down
with him when he fled to David at Keilah.)

Saul Pursues David

7 Saul was told that David had gone to Keilah, and he said,
"God has handed him over to me, for David has imprisoned himself by entering a town with gates and bars." 8 And Saul called up
all his forces for battle, to go down to Keilah to besiege David and
his men.
9 When David learned that Saul was plotting against him, he

22:18 *Doeg . . . killed eighty-five men who wore the linen ephod:* Saul's men were still loyal to God and knew better than to strike his priests. Doeg was not an Israelite and was loyal only to Saul, so he was not afraid to kill the priests.

22:19 *put to the sword Nob:* God had warned Eli that there would be such a punishment (2:31).

22:20 *Abiathar:* Abiathar would stay in David's life (23:6-9; 30:7). He served as a high priest in Israel until David's son Solomon removed him from that position (1 Kgs 2:26, 27).

23:1 *Keilah:* Keilah was just south of Adullam, where David was staying. It probably was not controlled by Israelites at this time. See the note at 22:1.

23:1 *looting the threshing floors:* The Philistines might have wanted the grain for their people, or they may have stolen the grain simply to starve the Israelites and weaken their ability to fight.

23:6-11 *ephod . . . tell your servant:* See the note at 10:20, 21.

said to Abiathar the priest, "Bring the ephod." [10]David said, "O LORD, God of Israel, your servant has heard definitely that Saul plans to come to Keilah and destroy the town on account of me. [11]Will the citizens of Keilah surrender me to him? Will Saul come down, as your servant has heard? O LORD, God of Israel, tell your servant."

And the LORD said, "He will."

[12]Again David asked, "Will the citizens of Keilah surrender me and my men to Saul?"

And the LORD said, "They will."

[13]So David and his men, about six hundred in number, left Keilah and kept moving from place to place. When Saul was told that David had escaped from Keilah, he did not go there.

[14]David stayed in the desert strongholds and in the hills of the Desert of Ziph. Day after day Saul searched for him, but God did not give David into his hands.

[15]While David was at Horesh in the Desert of Ziph, he learned that Saul had come out to take his life. [16]And Saul's son Jonathan went to David at Horesh and helped him find strength in God. [17]"Don't be afraid," he said. "My father Saul will not lay a hand on you. You will be king over Israel, and I will be second to you. Even my father Saul knows this." [18]The two of them made a covenant before the LORD. Then Jonathan went home, but David remained at Horesh.

[19]The Ziphites went up to Saul at Gibeah and said, "Is not David hiding among us in the strongholds at Horesh, on the hill of Hakilah, south of Jeshimon? [20]Now, O king, come down whenever it pleases you to do so, and we will be responsible for handing him over to the king."

[21]Saul replied, "The LORD bless you for your concern for me. [22]Go and make further preparation. Find out where David usually goes and who has seen him there. They tell me he is very crafty. [23]Find out about all the hiding places he uses and come back to me with definite information.[a] Then I will go with you; if he is in the area, I will track him down among all the clans of Judah."

[24]So they set out and went to Ziph ahead of Saul. Now David and his men were in the Desert of Maon, in the Arabah south of Jeshimon. [25]Saul and his men began the search, and when David was told about it, he went down to the rock and stayed in the Desert of Maon. When Saul heard this, he went into the Desert of Maon in pursuit of David.

[26]Saul was going along one side of the mountain, and David and his men were on the other side, hurrying to get away from Saul. As Saul and his forces were closing in on David and his men to capture them, [27]a messenger came to Saul, saying, "Come quickly! The Philistines are raiding the land." [28]Then Saul broke off his

23:14 *Desert of Ziph:* A rocky area south of Hebron near the Negev.

23:16,17 *Jonathan . . . I will be second to you:* See the note at 18:4. Jonathan is not jealous of the favor God is showing David, and he wishes to continue to show his loyalty by serving David as a trusted official.

23:23 *among all the clans of Judah:* That is, the family groups that occupied the land of Judah. Because David was from the tribe of Judah, Saul had good reason to suspect that the people from related clans would help hide David from him. It is not clear why the people of Ziph were willing to help Saul. See also the notes at 1:1 and 9:5.

23:18 1 Sam 18:3. **23:19** Ps 54 Title.

[a]**23** Or *me at Nacon*

David Shears Off a Piece of Saul's Mantle in the Cave at En Gedi, illuminated page from *Old Testament Miniatures,* around 1250. Saul was jealous and afraid of David because David was such a successful warrior, and because Saul could see that the LORD was helping his young rival. He tried several times to kill David, but David always managed to escape. Saul even took three thousand soldiers and went looking for David at the Crags of the Wild Goats in the Desert of En Gedi, where David hid in a cave. When the king came into the cave, he did not see David. David cut off a piece of Saul's robe but did not harm Saul, because Saul was God's chosen king. (See 24:1-22.)

pursuit of David and went to meet the Philistines. That is why they
call this place Sela Hammahlekoth.[a] 29 And David went up from
there and lived in the strongholds of En Gedi.

David Spares Saul's Life

24 After Saul returned from pursuing the Philistines, he was
told, "David is in the Desert of En Gedi." 2 So Saul took three thousand chosen men from all Israel and set out to look for David and
his men near the Crags of the Wild Goats.

3 He came to the sheep pens along the way; a cave was there,
and Saul went in to relieve himself. David and his men were far
back in the cave. 4 The men said, "This is the day the LORD spoke of
when he said[b] to you, 'I will give your enemy into your hands for
you to deal with as you wish.' " Then David crept up unnoticed
and cut off a corner of Saul's robe.

5 Afterward, David was conscience-stricken for having cut off
a corner of his robe. 6 He said to his men, "The LORD forbid that I

23:29 *En Gedi:* A spring on the western shore of the Dead Sea. It was an important source of fresh water.

24:4 *a corner of Saul's robe:* In the Bible, a person's robe or cloak can represent that person's authority. See, for example, 18:4; 1 Kgs 19:19; 2 Kgs 2:13, 14.

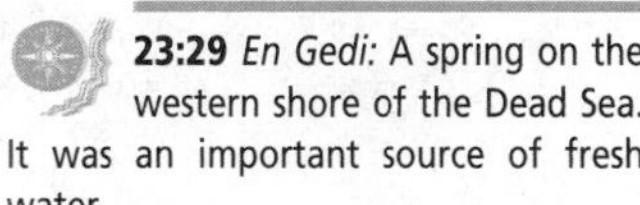

Later in this story, David will use this piece of Saul's robe as evidence that he could have killed the king but refused out of his respect for Saul. See also the note at 18:9,10.

24:3 Ps 57 Title; Ps 142 Title.

[a]**28** *Sela Hammahlekoth* means *rock of parting.* [b]**4** Or *"Today the LORD is saying*

should do such a thing to my master, the LORD's anointed, or lift
my hand against him; for he is the anointed of the LORD." [7]With
these words David rebuked his men and did not allow them to
attack Saul. And Saul left the cave and went his way.

[8]Then David went out of the cave and called out to Saul, "My
lord the king!" When Saul looked behind him, David bowed down
and prostrated himself with his face to the ground. [9]He said to Saul,
"Why do you listen when men say, 'David is bent on harming you'?
[10]This day you have seen with your own eyes how the LORD delivered
you into my hands in the cave. Some urged me to kill you, but I
spared you; I said, 'I will not lift my hand against my master, because
he is the LORD's anointed.' [11]See, my father, look at this piece of your
robe in my hand! I cut off the corner of your robe but did not kill
you. Now understand and recognize that I am not guilty of wrongdoing or rebellion. I have not wronged you, but you are hunting me
down to take my life. [12]May the LORD judge between you and me.
And may the LORD avenge the wrongs you have done to me, but my
hand will not touch you. [13]As the old saying goes, 'From evildoers
come evil deeds,' so my hand will not touch you.

[14]"Against whom has the king of Israel come out? Whom are
you pursuing? A dead dog? A flea? [15]May the LORD be our judge
and decide between us. May he consider my cause and uphold it;
may he vindicate me by delivering me from your hand."

[16]When David finished saying this, Saul asked, "Is that your
voice, David my son?" And he wept aloud. [17]"You are more righteous than I," he said. "You have treated me well, but I have treated
you badly. [18]You have just now told me of the good you did to me;
the LORD delivered me into your hands, but you did not kill me.
[19]When a man finds his enemy, does he let him get away
unharmed? May the LORD reward you well for the way you treated
me today. [20]I know that you will surely be king and that the kingdom of Israel will be established in your hands. [21]Now swear to me
by the LORD that you will not cut off my descendants or wipe out
my name from my father's family."

[22]So David gave his oath to Saul. Then Saul returned home,
but David and his men went up to the stronghold.

David, Nabal and Abigail

25 Now Samuel died, and all Israel assembled and mourned for
him; and they buried him at his home in Ramah.

Then David moved down into the Desert of Maon.[a] [2]A certain man in Maon, who had property there at Carmel, was very
wealthy. He had a thousand goats and three thousand sheep, which
he was shearing in Carmel. [3]His name was Nabal and his wife's
name was Abigail. She was an intelligent and beautiful woman, but
her husband, a Calebite, was surly and mean in his dealings.

---

[a]1 Some Septuagint manuscripts; Hebrew *Paran*

24:6 *my master, the LORD's anointed:* David did not forget that Saul was chosen by God. See also 26:11.

24:16-20 *David my son . . . wept aloud . . . you will surely be king:* Saul was David's father-in-law. Moved by David's mercy, Saul finally admitted that David would be the next king (23:17). In spite of this realization, Saul's jealousy would again overtake him (see 26:1-25).

24:21 *not cut off my descendants or wipe out my name:* Jonathan had earlier asked David for the same favor (see the note at 20:14, 15). Saul might have been worried that if his family died out, there would be no one left to remember him.

25:1 *at his home:* Hebrew "in the house." Family tombs were sometimes underneath the house or in the courtyard of the home.

25:2,3 *Carmel:* See the note at 15:12.

24:14 1 Sam 26:20.

4While David was in the desert, he heard that Nabal was
shearing sheep. 5So he sent ten young men and said to them, "Go
up to Nabal at Carmel and greet him in my name. 6Say to him:
'Long life to you! Good health to you and your household! And
good health to all that is yours!

7" 'Now I hear that it is sheep-shearing time. When your
shepherds were with us, we did not mistreat them, and the whole
time they were at Carmel nothing of theirs was missing. 8Ask your
own servants and they will tell you. Therefore be favorable toward
my young men, since we come at a festive time. Please give your
servants and your son David whatever you can find for them.' "

9When David's men arrived, they gave Nabal this message in
David's name. Then they waited.

10Nabal answered David's servants, "Who is this David? Who
is this son of Jesse? Many servants are breaking away from their
masters these days. 11Why should I take my bread and water, and
the meat I have slaughtered for my shearers, and give it to men
coming from who knows where?"

12David's men turned around and went back. When they
arrived, they reported every word. 13David said to his men, "Put on
your swords!" So they put on their swords, and David put on his.
About four hundred men went up with David, while two hundred
stayed with the supplies.

14One of the servants told Nabal's wife Abigail: "David sent
messengers from the desert to give our master his greetings, but he
hurled insults at them. 15Yet these men were very good to us. They
did not mistreat us, and the whole time we were out in the fields
near them nothing was missing. 16Night and day they were a wall
around us all the time we were herding our sheep near them.
17Now think it over and see what you can do, because disaster is
hanging over our master and his whole household. He is such a
wicked man that no one can talk to him."

18Abigail lost no time. She took two hundred loaves of bread,
two skins of wine, five dressed sheep, five seahs[a] of roasted grain,
a hundred cakes of raisins and two hundred cakes of pressed figs,
and loaded them on donkeys. 19Then she told her servants, "Go on
ahead; I'll follow you." But she did not tell her husband Nabal.

20As she came riding her donkey into a mountain ravine,
there were David and his men descending toward her, and she met
them. 21David had just said, "It's been useless—all my watching
over this fellow's property in the desert so that nothing of his was
missing. He has paid me back evil for good. 22May God deal with
David,[b] be it ever so severely, if by morning I leave alive one male
of all who belong to him!"

23When Abigail saw David, she quickly got off her donkey

---

[a]**18** That is, probably about a bushel (about 37 liters) [b]**22** Some Septuagint manuscripts; Hebrew *with David's enemies*

25:7 *nothing of theirs was missing:* When the Philistines and Amalekites attacked walled towns (23:1; 30:1, 2), the shepherds out in the fields had nowhere to go for protection and were in danger. David reminded Nabal that he and his men had protected Nabal's shepherds and sheep. See also 25:14-16.

25:8 *a festive time:* Sheep owners like Nabal were expected to remember that God had blessed them by giving them healthy sheep that produced good wool. During sheep-shearing time, they were to be especially kind and generous to others. This would have been a very good time for David to ask a favor.

25:13 *Put on your swords:* This might seem like a surprising reaction by David, since he had invited himself to Nabal's celebration (25:8). But the rules for hosts and guests were very rigid in the ancient Near East, where many people wandered from place to place. If strangers were not a threat, the host was expected to welcome them as guests. David proved he and his men were not threats to Nabal by reminding him how they protected the shepherds (25:7). Nabal's response (25:10, 11) was an insult, and refusing to let David's group eat with him was like calling them enemies.

25:25 *Nabal . . . his name is Fool:* This word play is a good example of how the Bible sometimes uses a person's name to reveal something about that person's character. The name Nabal in Hebrew means "a fool." When Abigail said Nabal was a fool, she meant he did not have any common sense.

25:30,31 *appointed him leader over Israel:* Abigail is aware that David is to be the next king. God uses her to save David from wrongly shedding blood.

25:41 *wash the feet of my master's servants:* At that time, people walked almost everywhere and usually wore sandals. A traveler's feet became extremely tired and dirty after a day of walking on dirt roads and paths. Washing the feet both cleaned and comforted them, and seeing that a guest's feet were washed was an expected part of being a host. Since it was thought to be a lowly task, it was usually done by servants. Servants normally would not be treated to such hospitality, so Abigail was really telling David how deeply she appreciated his decision not to punish Nabal. See also Gen 18:4; Luke 7:38; John 13:1-20.

25:43 *Ahinoam of Jezreel:* Ahinoam was David's second wife (27:2, 3). The Jezreel mentioned here was probably southwest of Hebron in the hill country of southern Judah. Hebron is on the map on p. 2464.

25:43 *they both were his wives:* Referring to Ahinoam and Abigail. See the note at 1:2. See also 2 Sam 3:2-5.

and bowed down before David with her face to the ground. [24]She fell at his feet and said: "My lord, let the blame be on me alone. Please let your servant speak to you; hear what your servant has to say. [25]May my lord pay no attention to that wicked man Nabal. He is just like his name—his name is Fool, and folly goes with him. But as for me, your servant, I did not see the men my master sent.

[26]"Now since the LORD has kept you, my master, from bloodshed and from avenging yourself with your own hands, as surely as the LORD lives and as you live, may your enemies and all who intend to harm my master be like Nabal. [27]And let this gift, which your servant has brought to my master, be given to the men who follow you. [28]Please forgive your servant's offense, for the LORD will certainly make a lasting dynasty for my master, because he fights the LORD's battles. Let no wrongdoing be found in you as long as you live. [29]Even though someone is pursuing you to take your life, the life of my master will be bound securely in the bundle of the living by the LORD your God. But the lives of your enemies he will hurl away as from the pocket of a sling. [30]When the LORD has done for my master every good thing he promised concerning him and has appointed him leader over Israel, [31]my master will not have on his conscience the staggering burden of needless bloodshed or of having avenged himself. And when the LORD has brought my master success, remember your servant."

[32]David said to Abigail, "Praise be to the LORD, the God of Israel, who has sent you today to meet me. [33]May you be blessed for your good judgment and for keeping me from bloodshed this day and from avenging myself with my own hands. [34]Otherwise, as surely as the LORD, the God of Israel, lives, who has kept me from harming you, if you had not come quickly to meet me, not one male belonging to Nabal would have been left alive by daybreak."

[35]Then David accepted from her hand what she had brought him and said, "Go home in peace. I have heard your words and granted your request."

[36]When Abigail went to Nabal, he was in the house holding a banquet like that of a king. He was in high spirits and very drunk. So she told him nothing until daybreak. [37]Then in the morning, when Nabal was sober, his wife told him all these things, and his heart failed him and he became like a stone. [38]About ten days later, the LORD struck Nabal and he died.

[39]When David heard that Nabal was dead, he said, "Praise be to the LORD, who has upheld my cause against Nabal for treating me with contempt. He has kept his servant from doing wrong and has brought Nabal's wrongdoing down on his own head."

Then David sent word to Abigail, asking her to become his wife. [40]His servants went to Carmel and said to Abigail, "David has sent us to you to take you to become his wife."

[41]She bowed down with her face to the ground and said,

"Here is your maidservant, ready to serve you and wash the feet of
my master's servants." 42 Abigail quickly got on a donkey and,
attended by her five maids, went with David's messengers and
became his wife. 43 David had also married Ahinoam of Jezreel, and
they both were his wives. 44 But Saul had given his daughter Michal,
David's wife, to Paltiel[a] son of Laish, who was from Gallim.

David Again Spares Saul's Life

26 The Ziphites went to Saul at Gibeah and said, "Is not David
hiding on the hill of Hakilah, which faces Jeshimon?"
2 So Saul went down to the Desert of Ziph, with his three
thousand chosen men of Israel, to search there for David. 3 Saul
made his camp beside the road on the hill of Hakilah facing Jeshimon, but David stayed in the desert. When he saw that Saul had
followed him there, 4 he sent out scouts and learned that Saul had
definitely arrived.[b]
5 Then David set out and went to the place where Saul had
camped. He saw where Saul and Abner son of Ner, the commander of the army, had lain down. Saul was lying inside the camp, with
the army encamped around him.
6 David then asked Ahimelech the Hittite and Abishai son of
Zeruiah, Joab's brother, "Who will go down into the camp with me
to Saul?"

"I'll go with you," said Abishai.
7 So David and Abishai went to the army by night, and there
was Saul, lying asleep inside the camp with his spear stuck in the
ground near his head. Abner and the soldiers were lying around him.
8 Abishai said to David, "Today God has delivered your
enemy into your hands. Now let me pin him to the ground with
one thrust of my spear; I won't strike him twice."
9 But David said to Abishai, "Don't destroy him! Who can lay
a hand on the LORD's anointed and be guiltless? 10 As surely as the
LORD lives," he said, "the LORD himself will strike him; either his
time will come and he will die, or he will go into battle and perish.
11 But the LORD forbid that I should lay a hand on the LORD's
anointed. Now get the spear and water jug that are near his head,
and let's go."
12 So David took the spear and water jug near Saul's head,
and they left. No one saw or knew about it, nor did anyone wake
up. They were all sleeping, because the LORD had put them into a
deep sleep.
13 Then David crossed over to the other side and stood on
top of the hill some distance away; there was a wide space between
them. 14 He called out to the army and to Abner son of Ner, "Aren't
you going to answer me, Abner?"

[a] **44** Hebrew *Palti*, a variant of *Paltiel* [b] **4** Or *had come to Nacon*

25:44 *Michal:* David's first wife. Taking Michal away from David and marrying her to someone else shows how much Saul distrusted and feared David. If Michal had a son by David, that child would have a legitimate claim to the throne (see 18:20—19:17). Later, David would demand her return (2 Sam 3:14-16).

26:1 *Ziphites:* David had been betrayed by the people of Ziph before (23:19). See also Ps 54 Title.

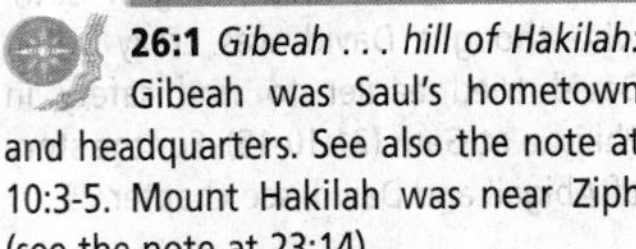

26:1 *Gibeah . . . hill of Hakilah:* Gibeah was Saul's hometown and headquarters. See also the note at 10:3-5. Mount Hakilah was near Ziph (see the note at 23:14).

26:6 *Ahimelech the Hittite:* This is not Ahimelech the priest (21:1). The Hittites came from what is now Turkey. They conquered much of the ancient Near East between 1600 and 1200 B.C. (see the map on p. 2462). Some Hittites settled in areas that later belonged to the Israelites (Gen 23:3; Num 13:29; Josh 1:4). The few who remained by David's time had joined the Israelite community and taken Hebrew names, with "the Hittite" added to the end.

26:6 *Abishai:* Hebrew "Abishai the son of Zeruiah." Zeruiah was David's older sister, so Abishai and Joab were David's nephews (see 1 Chr 2:12-17 and 2 Sam 17:25).

26:11 *spear and water jug:* Many kinds of clay jugs were used for carrying and dispensing water. This one might have been a clay jug with a handle and a spout for drinking, or it could have been a flat bottle that had two handles and was used like a modern canteen. Some water jars also had several spouts to drink from.

David will use these two personal items of Saul's to show that he could have killed the king to make himself king (26:16), just as he used a piece of Saul's robe before (24:11).

26:11 1 Sam 24:6, 7.

26:17 *my son:* See 24:16 and the note at 24:16-20.

27:1 *land of the Philistines:* See the note at 4:1. Saul probably did not have the military strength to risk going after David in Philistia. The Philistines were one of Israel's traditional enemies. It is ironic that David, who would one day be Israel's greatest king, should turn to them for protection.

27:2,3 *Achish . . . Abigail:* This is the same Achish, king of Gath, who thought David was crazy when David tried earlier to find safety in Philistia at Gath (21:10-15). For the story of Abigail and David, see chapter 25.

Abner replied, "Who are you who calls to the king?"
[15]David said, "You're a man, aren't you? And who is like you
in Israel? Why didn't you guard your lord the king? Someone came
to destroy your lord the king. [16]What you have done is not good.
As surely as the LORD lives, you and your men deserve to die,
because you did not guard your master, the LORD's anointed. Look
around you. Where are the king's spear and water jug that were
near his head?"
[17]Saul recognized David's voice and said, "Is that your voice,
David my son?"
David replied, "Yes it is, my lord the king." [18]And he added,
"Why is my lord pursuing his servant? What have I done, and what
wrong am I guilty of? [19]Now let my lord the king listen to his servant's words. If the LORD has incited you against me, then may he
accept an offering. If, however, men have done it, may they be
cursed before the LORD! They have now driven me from my share
in the LORD's inheritance and have said, 'Go, serve other gods.'
[20]Now do not let my blood fall to the ground far from the presence of the LORD. The king of Israel has come out to look for a
flea—as one hunts a partridge in the mountains."
[21]Then Saul said, "I have sinned. Come back, David my son.
Because you considered my life precious today, I will not try to harm
you again. Surely I have acted like a fool and have erred greatly."
[22]"Here is the king's spear," David answered. "Let one of your
young men come over and get it. [23]The LORD rewards every man
for his righteousness and faithfulness. The LORD delivered you into
my hands today, but I would not lay a hand on the LORD's anointed. [24]As surely as I valued your life today, so may the LORD value
my life and deliver me from all trouble."
[25]Then Saul said to David, "May you be blessed, my son
David; you will do great things and surely triumph."
So David went on his way, and Saul returned home.

David Among the Philistines

27 But David thought to himself, "One of these days I will be
destroyed by the hand of Saul. The best thing I can do is to escape
to the land of the Philistines. Then Saul will give up searching for
me anywhere in Israel, and I will slip out of his hand."
[2]So David and the six hundred men with him left and went
over to Achish son of Maoch king of Gath. [3]David and his men
settled in Gath with Achish. Each man had his family with him,
and David had his two wives: Ahinoam of Jezreel and Abigail of
Carmel, the widow of Nabal. [4]When Saul was told that David had
fled to Gath, he no longer searched for him.
[5]Then David said to Achish, "If I have found favor in your
eyes, let a place be assigned to me in one of the country towns,
that I may live there. Why should your servant live in the royal city
with you?"

6 So on that day Achish gave him Ziklag, and it has belonged
to the kings of Judah ever since. 7 David lived in Philistine territory
a year and four months.
8 Now David and his men went up and raided the Geshurites,
the Girzites and the Amalekites. (From ancient times these peoples
had lived in the land extending to Shur and Egypt.) 9 Whenever
David attacked an area, he did not leave a man or woman alive,
but took sheep and cattle, donkeys and camels, and clothes. Then
he returned to Achish.
10 When Achish asked, "Where did you go raiding today?"
David would say, "Against the Negev of Judah" or "Against the
Negev of Jerahmeel" or "Against the Negev of the Kenites." 11 He
did not leave a man or woman alive to be brought to Gath, for he
thought, "They might inform on us and say, 'This is what David
did.'" And such was his practice as long as he lived in Philistine
territory. 12 Achish trusted David and said to himself, "He has
become so odious to his people, the Israelites, that he will be my
servant forever."

SAUL AND HIS SONS DIE

Samuel's ghost predicts Saul's death in a battle with the Philistines.

Saul and the Witch of Endor

28 In those days the Philistines gathered their forces to fight
against Israel. Achish said to David, "You must understand that
you and your men will accompany me in the army."
2 David said, "Then you will see for yourself what your servant can do."
Achish replied, "Very well, I will make you my bodyguard for
life."
3 Now Samuel was dead, and all Israel had mourned for him
and buried him in his own town of Ramah. Saul had expelled the
mediums and spiritists from the land.
4 The Philistines assembled and came and set up camp at
Shunem, while Saul gathered all the Israelites and set up camp at
Gilboa. 5 When Saul saw the Philistine army, he was afraid; terror
filled his heart. 6 He inquired of the LORD, but the LORD did not
answer him by dreams or Urim or prophets. 7 Saul then said to his
attendants, "Find me a woman who is a medium, so I may go and
inquire of her."
"There is one in Endor," they said.
8 So Saul disguised himself, putting on other clothes, and at
night he and two men went to the woman. "Consult a spirit for
me," he said, "and bring up for me the one I name."
9 But the woman said to him, "Surely you know what Saul
has done. He has cut off the mediums and spiritists from the land.
Why have you set a trap for my life to bring about my death?"

27:6 *Ziklag:* The exact location is unknown. Many scholars believe it was near the Philistine border, about ten miles northeast of Beersheba in southern Judah. There is some question whether the Philistines ever controlled Ziklag. See the map on p. 2465.

27:8,9 *attacked an area, he did not leave a man or woman alive:* David wanted Achish to think he was raiding Israelite towns when he was really attacking towns belonging to Israel's enemies. David completely destroyed the towns he attacked, leaving no witnesses to let Achish know what he was really doing (27:11). See also the note at 15:3.

27:10 *Jerahmeel . . . Kenites:* These were clans of the Judah tribe. See the notes at 1:1; 9:5; and 15:6. See also the mini-article called "Israel," p. 264.

28:3 *Samuel was dead:* For Samuel's death, see 25:1.

28:3 *expelled the mediums and spiritists:* Many people in the ancient Near East believed that it was possible to communicate with the spirits of the dead through mediums or fortune-tellers and that these spirits could tell the future. But it was against God's Law to consult such people (Lev 20:27; Deut 18:10,11).

28:4 *Shunem . . . Gilboa:* Shunem was about ten miles north of Mount Gilboa. The armies faced each other across the Valley of Jezreel. See the map on p. 2464.

28:6,7 *dreams or Urim or prophets . . . a medium:* Dreams or visions, priests, and prophets were ways in which God spoke to people and kings (see Num 12:6; 27:19-21; see the note at 10:20,21). None of these worked for Saul, so he decided to break God's Law and ask someone to talk to the dead to learn what God wanted him to do (Lev 20:27; Deut 18:10,11). See also 15:10,11 and 16:14.

28:17 *he predicted through me:* The deceased Samuel is reminding Saul of the conversation they had after Saul disobeyed the LORD by not following the LORD's battle instruction (see 15:10-35).

28:19 *tomorrow . . . be with me:* Samuel meant Saul and his sons would die the next day.

28:24 *bread without yeast:* That is, unleavened, since there was no time to let the bread rise.

28:17 1 Sam 15:28. **28:18** 1 Sam 15:3-9.

10 Saul swore to her by the LORD, "As surely as the LORD lives, you will not be punished for this."

11 Then the woman asked, "Whom shall I bring up for you?"

"Bring up Samuel," he said.

12 When the woman saw Samuel, she cried out at the top of her voice and said to Saul, "Why have you deceived me? You are Saul!"

13 The king said to her, "Don't be afraid. What do you see?"

The woman said, "I see a spirit[a] coming up out of the ground."

14 "What does he look like?" he asked.

"An old man wearing a robe is coming up," she said.

Then Saul knew it was Samuel, and he bowed down and prostrated himself with his face to the ground.

15 Samuel said to Saul, "Why have you disturbed me by bringing me up?"

"I am in great distress," Saul said. "The Philistines are fighting against me, and God has turned away from me. He no longer answers me, either by prophets or by dreams. So I have called on you to tell me what to do."

16 Samuel said, "Why do you consult me, now that the LORD has turned away from you and become your enemy? 17 The LORD has done what he predicted through me. The LORD has torn the kingdom out of your hands and given it to one of your neighbors—to David. 18 Because you did not obey the LORD or carry out his fierce wrath against the Amalekites, the LORD has done this to you today. 19 The LORD will hand over both Israel and you to the Philistines, and tomorrow you and your sons will be with me. The LORD will also hand over the army of Israel to the Philistines."

20 Immediately Saul fell full length on the ground, filled with fear because of Samuel's words. His strength was gone, for he had eaten nothing all that day and night.

21 When the woman came to Saul and saw that he was greatly shaken, she said, "Look, your maidservant has obeyed you. I took my life in my hands and did what you told me to do. 22 Now please listen to your servant and let me give you some food so you may eat and have the strength to go on your way."

23 He refused and said, "I will not eat."

But his men joined the woman in urging him, and he listened to them. He got up from the ground and sat on the couch.

24 The woman had a fattened calf at the house, which she butchered at once. She took some flour, kneaded it and baked bread without yeast. 25 Then she set it before Saul and his men, and they ate. That same night they got up and left.

[a]13 Or *see spirits*; or *see gods*

Achish Sends David Back to Ziklag

29 The Philistines gathered all their forces at Aphek, and Israel
camped by the spring in Jezreel. 2As the Philistine rulers marched
with their units of hundreds and thousands, David and his men
were marching at the rear with Achish. 3The commanders of the
Philistines asked, "What about these Hebrews?"
Achish replied, "Is this not David, who was an officer of Saul
king of Israel? He has already been with me for over a year, and
from the day he left Saul until now, I have found no fault in him."
4But the Philistine commanders were angry with him and
said, "Send the man back, that he may return to the place you
assigned him. He must not go with us into battle, or he will turn
against us during the fighting. How better could he regain his master's favor than by taking the heads of our own men? 5Isn't this the
David they sang about in their dances:

" 'Saul has slain his thousands,
and David his tens of thousands'?"

6So Achish called David and said to him, "As surely as the
LORD lives, you have been reliable, and I would be pleased to have
you serve with me in the army. From the day you came to me until
now, I have found no fault in you, but the rulers don't approve of
you. 7Turn back and go in peace; do nothing to displease the
Philistine rulers."
8"But what have I done?" asked David. "What have you
found against your servant from the day I came to you until now?
Why can't I go and fight against the enemies of my lord the king?"
9Achish answered, "I know that you have been as pleasing in
my eyes as an angel of God; nevertheless, the Philistine commanders have said, 'He must not go up with us into battle.' 10Now get up
early, along with your master's servants who have come with you,
and leave in the morning as soon as it is light."
11So David and his men got up early in the morning to go
back to the land of the Philistines, and the Philistines went up to
Jezreel.

David Destroys the Amalekites

30 David and his men reached Ziklag on the third day. Now the
Amalekites had raided the Negev and Ziklag. They had attacked
Ziklag and burned it, 2and had taken captive the women and all
who were in it, both young and old. They killed none of them, but
carried them off as they went on their way.
3When David and his men came to Ziklag, they found it
destroyed by fire and their wives and sons and daughters taken
captive. 4So David and his men wept aloud until they had no
strength left to weep. 5David's two wives had been captured—
Ahinoam of Jezreel and Abigail, the widow of Nabal of Carmel.

29:1 *Aphek:* The events of chapter 29 probably happened before the Philistines reached Shunem (28:4).

30:1 *Ziklag:* See the note at 27:6. This would have been an eighty-mile march over rough land.

30:2-4 *taken captive the women . . . wept aloud:* The women and children most likely were to be sold into slavery. Loud, long crying was a normal way to express grief in this part of the world. Grieving this way can be emotionally and physically tiring, and the men were already exhausted from their difficult trip home.

29:5 1 Sam 18:7; 21:11. **30:5** 1 Sam 25:42,43.

David said, *"No, my brothers, you must not do that with what the* LORD *has given us. He has protected us and handed over to us the forces that came against us."*
1 Sam 30:23

30:6 *talking of stoning him:* Dropping or piling heavy stones on a person until they died was a common form of capital punishment. Adultery, blasphemy, infant sacrifice, worshiping idols, failure to observe the Sabbath, witchcraft, and treason were among the crimes that were sometimes punished by stoning (see, for example, Lev 24:14-16; Num 15:32-36; Deut 17:2-7; 22:22-24). David's men may have felt he had betrayed them by leaving the women and children without protection.

30:7 *Abiathar the priest:* See the note at 22:20.

30:7 *Bring me the ephod:* See the note at 10:20,21.

30:23 *what the* LORD *has given us:* David reminded his men that the victory was the LORD's. Since even those who guarded the camp were serving the LORD, everyone should have a share in what had been taken from the Amalekites. See also the note at 17:45-47. See also Deut 1:42,43; 3:1-6; 7:16-24; 20:1-4; and Ps 33:16-19.

30:27-31 *He sent it:* David probably hoped to win their favor and support by sharing the loot that was taken back from the Amalekites. But since some of it had been stolen from Judah, David could also have been returning things to their owners.

Hebron was the most important of the towns mentioned here (see the map on p. 2464). David made Hebron his capital when he became king of Judah (2 Sam 2:1-7).

6 David was greatly distressed because the men were talking of
stoning him; each one was bitter in spirit because of his sons and
daughters. But David found strength in the LORD his God.
7 Then David said to Abiathar the priest, the son of Ahimelech, "Bring me the ephod." Abiathar brought it to him, 8 and
David inquired of the LORD, "Shall I pursue this raiding party? Will
I overtake them?"
"Pursue them," he answered. "You will certainly overtake
them and succeed in the rescue."
9 David and the six hundred men with him came to the Besor
Ravine, where some stayed behind, 10 for two hundred men were
too exhausted to cross the ravine. But David and four hundred
men continued the pursuit.
11 They found an Egyptian in a field and brought him to
David. They gave him water to drink and food to eat— 12 part of a
cake of pressed figs and two cakes of raisins. He ate and was
revived, for he had not eaten any food or drunk any water for three
days and three nights.
13 David asked him, "To whom do you belong, and where do
you come from?"
He said, "I am an Egyptian, the slave of an Amalekite. My
master abandoned me when I became ill three days ago. 14 We
raided the Negev of the Kerethites and the territory belonging to
Judah and the Negev of Caleb. And we burned Ziklag."
15 David asked him, "Can you lead me down to this raiding
party?"
He answered, "Swear to me before God that you will not kill
me or hand me over to my master, and I will take you down to
them."
16 He led David down, and there they were, scattered over the
countryside, eating, drinking and reveling because of the great
amount of plunder they had taken from the land of the Philistines
and from Judah. 17 David fought them from dusk until the evening
of the next day, and none of them got away, except four hundred
young men who rode off on camels and fled. 18 David recovered
everything the Amalekites had taken, including his two wives.
19 Nothing was missing: young or old, boy or girl, plunder or anything else they had taken. David brought everything back. 20 He
took all the flocks and herds, and his men drove them ahead of the
other livestock, saying, "This is David's plunder."
21 Then David came to the two hundred men who had been
too exhausted to follow him and who were left behind at the Besor
Ravine. They came out to meet David and the people with him. As
David and his men approached, he greeted them. 22 But all the evil
men and troublemakers among David's followers said, "Because
they did not go out with us, we will not share with them the plunder we recovered. However, each man may take his wife and children and go."

23David replied, “No, my brothers, you must not do that with
what the LORD has given us. He has protected us and handed over
to us the forces that came against us. 24Who will listen to what you
say? The share of the man who stayed with the supplies is to be the
same as that of him who went down to the battle. All will share
alike.” 25David made this a statute and ordinance for Israel from
that day to this.
26When David arrived in Ziklag, he sent some of the plunder
to the elders of Judah, who were his friends, saying, “Here is a present for you from the plunder of the LORD’s enemies.”
27He sent it to those who were in Bethel, Ramoth Negev and
Jattir; 28to those in Aroer, Siphmoth, Eshtemoa 29and Racal; to
those in the towns of the Jerahmeelites and the Kenites; 30to those
in Hormah, Bor Ashan, Athach 31and Hebron; and to those in all
the other places where David and his men had roamed.

Saul Takes His Life

31 Now the Philistines fought against Israel; the Israelites fled
before them, and many fell slain on Mount Gilboa. 2The Philistines
pressed hard after Saul and his sons, and they killed his sons
Jonathan, Abinadab and Malki-Shua. 3The fighting grew fierce
around Saul, and when the archers overtook him, they wounded
him critically.
4Saul said to his armor-bearer, “Draw your sword and run
me through, or these uncircumcised fellows will come and run me
through and abuse me.”

31:1 *Mount Gilboa:* See the note at 28:4.

31:3-5 *wounded him critically . . . took his own sword and fell on it:* Saul was supposed to be the one who would rescue Israel from the Philistines (9:16). But in the final example of his failure, he died fighting them. Saul killed himself to avoid being humiliated and abused like Samson had been (Judg 16:23-25). The servant refused to kill Saul, perhaps because he knew that God would punish anyone who killed God’s chosen king (26:9). It was common in the ancient world for a military leader’s servant to kill himself when his master died in battle.

David’s reaction in similar situations was to gather strength from God (23:16; 30:6), but this was something Saul could no longer do.

Suicide is extremely rare in the Bible. It is mentioned only three other times, and only in connection with the most serious betrayal or blatant disobedience to the LORD (2 Sam 17:23; 1 Kgs 16:18; Matt 27:5).

QUESTIONS ABOUT 1 SAMUEL 16:1—31:13

1. God told Samuel, “Man looks at the outward appearance, but the LORD looks at the heart” (16:7). According to 1 SAMUEL what was in David’s heart that prepared him to be the future king? (16:18)
2. In chapters 17, 24, and 25 David fought against various enemies. What do the different ways he treated these enemies show about his character?
3. Describe in your own words the role David and Jonathan’s friendship played in the up-and-down relationship of King Saul and David (18:1-4; 19:1-8; 20:1-42; and 23:14-18).
4. David has several chances to kill Saul, but each time he spares the king’s life. What differences do you see between the incidents in chapters 24 and 26?
5. Jonathan put loyalty to David, the future king, above loyalty to his own father, the ruling king. Why do you think Jonathan acted in this way? What does loyalty mean to you? When is it justified? When is it misplaced?
6. Even after David knew he would one day be king of Israel, he did not always seem to act in the best interest of Israel (see, for example, chapter 21). How do you think he would have explained his actions to others? How might he have explained them to God?
7. What do you think were David’s best qualities as a leader? What were his worst qualities? Describe the qualities you look for in a leader.

31:7 *the valley:* Referring to the Valley of Jezreel. Shunem and Mount Gilboa (see 28:4) were across the Valley of Jezreel from each other.

31:9 *cut off his head and stripped off his armor:* Bringing back the head and the armor of a slain enemy was common practice in the ancient Near East. They were displayed to announce victory and to warn other enemies. David had done this after killing Goliath (17:51,54).

31:10 *Beth Shan:* Located where the Valley of Jezreel and Jordan Valley meet, near Jabesh (see the map on p. 2464).

31:11-13 *the people of Jabesh Gilead . . . fasted seven days:* One of the first things Saul had done as king was to rescue the people of Jabesh (11:1-11). They had not forgotten, and they showed their gratitude by bringing the bodies of Saul and his sons to Jabesh, in spite of the danger. David later moved the bones to Saul's family burial place in Benjamin (2 Sam 21:11-14).

But his armor-bearer was terrified and would not do it; so
Saul took his own sword and fell on it. 5When the armor-bearer
saw that Saul was dead, he too fell on his sword and died with him.
6So Saul and his three sons and his armor-bearer and all his men
died together that same day.

7When the Israelites along the valley and those across the
Jordan saw that the Israelite army had fled and that Saul and his
sons had died, they abandoned their towns and fled. And the
Philistines came and occupied them.

8The next day, when the Philistines came to strip the dead,
they found Saul and his three sons fallen on Mount Gilboa. 9They
cut off his head and stripped off his armor, and they sent messengers throughout the land of the Philistines to proclaim the news in
the temple of their idols and among their people. 10They put his
armor in the temple of the Ashtoreths and fastened his body to the
wall of Beth Shan.

11When the people of Jabesh Gilead heard of what the
Philistines had done to Saul, 12all their valiant men journeyed
through the night to Beth Shan. They took down the bodies of
Saul and his sons from the wall of Beth Shan and went to Jabesh,
where they burned them. 13Then they took their bones and buried
them under a tamarisk tree at Jabesh, and they fasted seven days.

2 SAMUEL

David is remembered as Israel's most powerful king and as a human being who made some terrible mistakes. Read about his struggles and see how one man's relationship with God affects the fate of the nation he rules.

What makes 2 Samuel special?

Some of the best stories about people in the Jewish Scriptures (Old Testament) are in 1 and 2 SAMUEL. In 2 SAMUEL the story of David, begun in the second half of 1 SAMUEL, is continued. It tells of David's triumphs and failures and shows how important one person's relationship with God can be in shaping the course of his life and the life of the nation he rules.

Why was 2 Samuel written?

The second half of one book that was split into two, 2 SAMUEL continues the story of Israel's first kings. What is now called 1 SAMUEL ended with the death of King Saul, and 2 SAMUEL picks up with David's reign, from about 1010 to 970 B.C. The first dramatic section tells how David became king of Judah, then king of all Israel, in a series of military victories and with an extraordinary promise from God. But troubles followed his triumphs, and David's life unraveled when he sinned with Bathsheba, arranged a murder, and watched his family come apart.

What's the story behind the scene?

Instead of writing only about David's strengths, the author also showed David's weaknesses. Some biblical scholars believe that JOSHUA, JUDGES, 1 and 2 SAMUEL, and 1 and 2 KINGS, which contain common lesson themes for Israel, were brought together some time in the sixth century B.C. They repeatedly describe what happens when individuals or groups of people don't live up to their covenant with God. Israel had agreed to be faithful to the LORD (see Deut 7:12). Their peace and prosperity depended on it, but Israel failed again and again. The authors of these books struggled to understand who was to blame for the division of Israel, its defeat by two powerful kingdoms in the east, and its eventual exile into Babylonia.

Key to understanding 2 SAMUEL is the covenant God made with David (7:16). God promised David that one of his descendants would always be king. This promise led the people of Israel to expect a *messiah,* or "chosen one." See the mini-article called "Messiah (Chosen One)," p. 1124. Later, when the line of kings descended from David came to an end with the capture of Jerusalem (2 Kgs 25:7, 8), people wondered how God would continue to keep the promise he made to David. In later generations, several of Israel's prophets would speak of a new king descended

crown: Crowns were worn by people with special honors or positions, such as priests and kings. The practice of making crowns from metal probably began when tribal leaders began to decorate their cloth headpieces (turbans) with metal ornaments and jewels. See, for example, Exod 29:4-6. God chose David to be the next king (1 Sam 16), so it was fitting that Saul's crown should be brought to David after Saul's death (1:10). When David conquered the city of Rabbah he took the crown from the statue of the Ammonite god Milcom which was made of gold, weighed 75 pounds, and had a precious jewel in it (2 Sam 12:29, 30).

The copper crown shown here was found in the "Cave of the Treasure" in the southern Judean desert along with numerous other copper items that seem to have had ritual significance. In the fifth millennium B.C., humans began to mine, smelt (refine), and work copper, the first metal to be used for ornaments and utensils. The objects from the "Cave of the Treasure" probably date from the fourth millennium B.C.

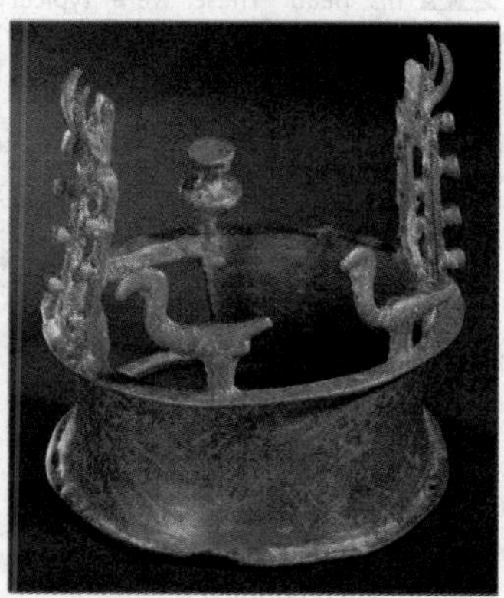

from David (Jer 33:15; Dan 9:25). In New Testament times Jesus' early apostles understood Jesus to be this new king (Matt 1:1; Acts 2:29,30; Rom 1:3, 4).

How is 2 Samuel constructed?

The book of 2 Samuel can be divided into two major sections—one for David's triumphs and one for his troubles. Added to these is a third section of other stories about David.

David's triumphs (1:1—10:19)
- David mourns for Saul and Jonathan (1:1-27)
- Israel's two kings (2:1—4:12)
- David unites all of Israel (5:1—6:23)
- God's promise and David's response (7:1-29)
- David defeats Israel's enemies (8:1—10:19)

David's troubles (11:1—20:26)
- David sins and suffers because of it (11:1—12:31)
- Violence tears David's family apart (13:1—14:33)
- Absalom challenges his father (15:1—19:43)
- Sheba's rebellion (20:1-26)

Other stories about David (21:1—24:25)
- A famine in Israel (21:1-14)
- Other victories (21:15-22)
- David's songs (22:1—23:7)
- David's warriors (23:8-39)
- David's sin brings an angel of destruction (24:1-25)

David's Triumphs

David rises to power by first becoming king of his own tribe of Judah, then of all Israel. He makes Jerusalem the capital of the united kingdom, defeats Israel's enemies, and fulfills the promise he made to Jonathan.

DAVID MOURNS FOR SAUL AND JONATHAN

David Hears of Saul's Death

1 After the death of Saul, David returned from defeating the
Amalekites and stayed in Ziklag two days. 2On the third day a man
arrived from Saul's camp, with his clothes torn and with dust on
his head. When he came to David, he fell to the ground to pay him
honor.
3"Where have you come from?" David asked him.
He answered, "I have escaped from the Israelite camp."
4"What happened?" David asked. "Tell me."
He said, "The men fled from the battle. Many of them fell
and died. And Saul and his son Jonathan are dead."
5Then David said to the young man who brought him the
report, "How do you know that Saul and his son Jonathan are
dead?"
6"I happened to be on Mount Gilboa," the young man said,

1:1 *Saul, David . . . Amalekites:* Saul was Israel's first king and ruled from about 1030 to 1010 B.C. (1 Sam 9:15-17; 10:1).

David was king from about 1010 to 970 B.C. After Saul disobeyed God, God chose David to replace Saul (1 Sam 16:1-13). David had to wait over seven years to become king of all Israel, because Saul's family challenged David's right to rule. But in the end, David prevailed and God promised him that one of his descendants would always be king (2 Sam 7:16). See also the mini-article called "David," p. 1028.

The Amalekites were nomads who lived mostly south and west of the Dead Sea. They were enemies of Israel that both Saul and David had fought (see 1 Sam 15:1-9; 30:1-20). Even before the Israelites had settled in Canaan they had conflicts with the Amalekites (Exod 17:8-16).

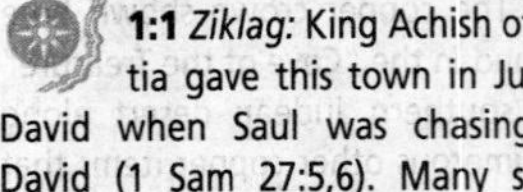

1:1 *Ziklag:* King Achish of Philistia gave this town in Judah to David when Saul was chasing after David (1 Sam 27:5,6). Many scholars believe it was located close to the border of the Philistine territory, about ten miles northeast of Beersheba. See the map on p. 2465.

1:2 *his clothes torn . . . dust on his head:* These were typical ways of showing grief and sorrow. See also 13:19,31; 15:30; 1 Kgs 21:27 and the note at 3:31.

1:4 *Jonathan:* Jonathan, the son of Israel's first king (Saul), was the best friend of David who was chosen by God to be king after Saul. The dramatic story of their loyal friendship is told in 1 Samuel 18–20.

1:6 *Mount Gilboa:* Saul had gathered his army here to fight the attacking Philistines. See 1 Sam 31 and the map on p. 2464.

1:8 *Amalekite:* This man probably was not actually in Saul's army (1:4), since Saul and the Israelites considered the Amalekites to be enemies. See 1 Sam 15.

"and there was Saul, leaning on his spear, with the chariots and
riders almost upon him. [7]When he turned around and saw me, he
called out to me, and I said, 'What can I do?'
[8]"He asked me, 'Who are you?'
" 'An Amalekite,' I answered.
[9]"Then he said to me, 'Stand over me and kill me! I am in
the throes of death, but I'm still alive.'
[10]"So I stood over him and killed him, because I knew that
after he had fallen he could not survive. And I took the crown that
was on his head and the band on his arm and have brought them
here to my lord."
[11]Then David and all the men with him took hold of their
clothes and tore them. [12]They mourned and wept and fasted till
evening for Saul and his son Jonathan, and for the army of the
LORD and the house of Israel, because they had fallen by the sword.
[13]David said to the young man who brought him the report,
"Where are you from?"
"I am the son of an alien, an Amalekite," he answered.
[14]David asked him, "Why were you not afraid to lift your
hand to destroy the LORD's anointed?"
[15]Then David called one of his men and said, "Go, strike him
down!" So he struck him down, and he died. [16]For David had said
to him, "Your blood be on your own head. Your own mouth testified against you when you said, 'I killed the LORD's anointed.' "

David's Lament for Saul and Jonathan

[17]David took up this lament concerning Saul and his son
Jonathan, [18]and ordered that the men of Judah be taught this
lament of the bow (it is written in the Book of Jashar):

[19]"Your glory, O Israel, lies slain on your heights.
How the mighty have fallen!

[20]"Tell it not in Gath,
proclaim it not in the streets of Ashkelon,
lest the daughters of the Philistines be glad,
lest the daughters of the uncircumcised rejoice.

[21]"O mountains of Gilboa,
may you have neither dew nor rain,
nor fields that yield offerings ⌞of grain⌟.
For there the shield of the mighty was defiled,
the shield of Saul—no longer rubbed with oil.
[22]From the blood of the slain,
from the flesh of the mighty,
the bow of Jonathan did not turn back,
the sword of Saul did not return unsatisfied.
[23]"Saul and Jonathan—
in life they were loved and gracious,

1:9-15 *strike him down:* The end of 1 SAMUEL reports that Saul killed himself (1 Sam 31). Since Saul was David's enemy, the Amalekite may have hoped David would reward him if he said he killed Saul. But David was outraged that anyone would dare to kill God's chosen king (1 Sam 24:6,7; 26:9,23).

1:10 *crown . . . band on his arm:* See the note on p. 563.

1:11,12 *tore them . . . fasted:* See the note at 1:2.

1:17-27 *took up this lament:* David created many songs, which are included in PSALMS. This song is one of the earliest known pieces of Hebrew literature. David showed his own sadness as well as Israel's when he sang in memory of Saul and Jonathan.

1:18 *the Book of Jashar:* May have been a collection of ancient war songs. See also Josh 10:12,13.

1:20 *Gath . . . Ashkelon:* These two Philistine cities stand for all of Philistia in this song. The Philistines lived in Philistia, an area along the Mediterranean Sea. They were often at war with Israel. See the map on p. 2464.

1:20 *daughters . . . rejoice:* Women would sing and dance to greet victorious soldiers returning from battle. Moses' sister Miriam celebrated in this way after the LORD defeated the Egyptian army (Exod 15:20,21).

1:21 *mountains of Gilboa . . . neither dew nor rain:* David cursed the place where Saul and Jonathan died. The Israelites believed the spoken word had a life and power of its own. Once spoken, a curse could not be taken back.

1:21 *shield . . . no longer rubbed with oil:* Rubbing a shield with oil was a way of polishing it. This might mean that the Philistines would leave Saul's shield as it was, rather than risk honoring him by polishing it.

1:6-10 1 Sam 31:1-6; 1 Chr 10:1-6.

and in death they were not parted.
They were swifter than eagles,
they were stronger than lions.

24 "O daughters of Israel,
weep for Saul,
who clothed you in scarlet and finery,
who adorned your garments with ornaments
of gold.

25 "How the mighty have fallen in battle!
Jonathan lies slain on your heights.

26 I grieve for you, Jonathan my brother;
you were very dear to me.
Your love for me was wonderful,
more wonderful than that of women.

27 "How the mighty have fallen!
The weapons of war have perished!"

ISRAEL'S TWO KINGS

The people of Judah pour oil on David's head to show they have chosen him as their king, but Saul's son Ish-Bosheth claims his father's throne. Abner, the commander of Saul's army, offers to help unite all of Israel under David, but is killed by David's army commander Joab before he can this bring this about. Some time after Abner's death, King Ish-Bosheth is also assassinated.

David Anointed King Over Judah

2 In the course of time, David inquired of the LORD. "Shall I go
up to one of the towns of Judah?" he asked.

The LORD said, "Go up."

David asked, "Where shall I go?"

"To Hebron," the LORD answered.

2 So David went up there with his two wives, Ahinoam of
Jezreel and Abigail, the widow of Nabal of Carmel. 3 David also
took the men who were with him, each with his family, and they
settled in Hebron and its towns. 4 Then the men of Judah came to
Hebron and there they anointed David king over the house of
Judah.

When David was told that it was the men of Jabesh Gilead
who had buried Saul, 5 he sent messengers to the men of Jabesh
Gilead to say to them, "The LORD bless you for showing this kindness to Saul your master by burying him. 6 May the LORD now
show you kindness and faithfulness, and I too will show you the
same favor because you have done this. 7 Now then, be strong and
brave, for Saul your master is dead, and the house of Judah has
anointed me king over them."

1:24 *daughters of Israel, weep:* Women were often the ones who began the formal mourning in a community, just as they were usually the first to celebrate victories (1:20).

1:24 *clothed you in scarlet and finery . . . ornaments of gold:* These precious objects were some of the things taken in war that Saul had generously shared with the people.

1:27 *weapons:* This may refer to Saul and Jonathan.

2:1 *LORD:* See the mini-article called "LORD (YHWH)," p. 140.

2:1,2 *Judah . . . Hebron . . . Jezreel . . . Carmel:* Before Saul became king, the Israelites were a loose confederation of tribes. Each tribe had its own area. (See also the mini-article called "Israel," p. 264, and the maps on p. 2464 and p. 2465).

Hebron was the most important city in the area claimed by Judah and would be David's capital while he was king of Judah. It has been continuously occupied since 3300 B.C., making it one of the oldest cities in the world.

The Jezreel mentioned here is a fertile region in southern Judah. Carmel was about seven miles south of Hebron.

2:2 *Ahinoam . . . Abigail . . . widow of Nabal:* At this time, men often had more than one wife, although this was against God's Law (Gen 2:24). Ahinoam was David's second wife and Abigail was his third (1 Sam 25:42,43; 27:2,3). Abigail was the mother of his second son, Kileab (2 Sam 3:3). David's first wife was Michal (1 Sam 18:27).

Nabal was a rich sheep owner from Maon in southern Judah. For the story of Abigail, Nabal, and David, see 1 Samuel 25.

2:4 *anointed:* Olive oil was poured on the head of someone chosen to be a priest, a prophet, or a king.

2:4 *Jabesh Gilead:* A city east of the Jordan River. See also 1 Sam 31:11,12 and the map on p. 2464.

The Coronation of David, illuminated page from the *Psalter of Paris,* fourteenth century. David was Israel's second king. Even while Saul was still king, Samuel poured oil on David's head to show that God had chosen David to be the next king, rather than one of Saul's sons (1 Sam 16:12,13). But David didn't become king of Judah until after Saul died (2 Sam 2:4), and then king of all of Israel seven and a half years after that (2 Sam 5:3-5). Although the kings of Israel wore crowns on special occasions, the ceremony for making someone king was called an "anointing" (meaning to pour oil on his head) not a "coronation" (placing a crown on him).

War Between the Houses of David and Saul

[8]Meanwhile, Abner son of Ner, the commander of Saul's
army, had taken Ish-Bosheth son of Saul and brought him over to
Mahanaim. [9]He made him king over Gilead, Ashuri[a] and Jezreel,
and also over Ephraim, Benjamin and all Israel.
[10]Ish-Bosheth son of Saul was forty years old when he became
king over Israel, and he reigned two years. The house of Judah, however, followed David. [11]The length of time David was king in Hebron
over the house of Judah was seven years and six months.

[a]**9** Or *Asher*

2:8 *Abner son of Ner:* Saul's cousin and faithful general (1 Sam 14:50). Abner was the real power behind the throne, since he proclaimed Ish-Bosheth as king.

2:8 *Ish-Bosheth:* Ish-Bosheth was probably called Ishvi in 1 Samuel 14:49 and Esh-Baal in 1 Chronicles 8:33. In Hebrew "baal" means "lord" and was the name of a Canaanite god. Later, the Israelites would change "baal" to "bosheth" in people's names to avoid mentioning Baal (Hos 2:17). "Bosheth" means "shame."

2:8 *Mahanaim:* This was in the territory of Gad near where the Jabbok River flows into the Jordan (see the general area on the map on p. 2464).

2:9 *Israel:* Sometimes "Israel" meant only the northern tribes and did not include the southern tribes. That is how it is used in this verse and in chapters 3,4, and 5.

2:10,11 *forty years old . . . seven years and six months:* The numbers for Ish-Bosheth's age and how long he ruled are puzzling. He apparently did not fight at the battle at Mount Gilboa (1 Sam 31:1-3, 8), which could mean he was too young to fight. But if he was too young, he could not have been forty when he became king. David and Ish-Bosheth both became kings after Saul died. That means that Ish-Bosheth and David would have ruled separately for about the same length of time, around seven and a half years. David ruled in Hebron for seven and a half years, but some of that time might have been as king of all Israel.

2:13 *Joab son of Zeruiah:* Joab was David's nephew, since Zeruiah was David's older sister. Joab became an important military leader for David, but Joab's brutality stood out against David's gentleness (10:7-14; 11:1; 18:9-15; 1 Kgs 11:15,16).

2:13 *pool:* This large pool was just inside Gibeon's city wall and was used for storing water. It was in the shape of a circle and was thirty-six feet wide and thirty-six feet deep.

2:28 *trumpet:* Probably a shofar, or ram's horn. (See the illustration on p. 528.) Shofars can make several different sounds and were used to signal events, danger, or the death of important people (Judg 3:27, 28; Neh 4:18-20). The shofar is still used today in synagogues for celebrating important holidays.

12 Abner son of Ner, together with the men of Ish-Bosheth
son of Saul, left Mahanaim and went to Gibeon. 13 Joab son of
Zeruiah and David's men went out and met them at the pool of
Gibeon. One group sat down on one side of the pool and one
group on the other side.
14 Then Abner said to Joab, "Let's have some of the young
men get up and fight hand to hand in front of us."
"All right, let them do it," Joab said.
15 So they stood up and were counted off—twelve men for
Benjamin and Ish-Bosheth son of Saul, and twelve for David.
16 Then each man grabbed his opponent by the head and thrust his
dagger into his opponent's side, and they fell down together. So
that place in Gibeon was called Helkath Hazzurim.[a]
17 The battle that day was very fierce, and Abner and the men
of Israel were defeated by David's men.
18 The three sons of Zeruiah were there: Joab, Abishai and Asahel. Now Asahel was as fleet-footed as a wild gazelle. 19 He chased
Abner, turning neither to the right nor to the left as he pursued him.
20 Abner looked behind him and asked, "Is that you, Asahel?"
"It is," he answered.
21 Then Abner said to him, "Turn aside to the right or to the
left; take on one of the young men and strip him of his weapons."
But Asahel would not stop chasing him.
22 Again Abner warned Asahel, "Stop chasing me! Why
should I strike you down? How could I look your brother Joab in
the face?"
23 But Asahel refused to give up the pursuit; so Abner thrust
the butt of his spear into Asahel's stomach, and the spear came out
through his back. He fell there and died on the spot. And every
man stopped when he came to the place where Asahel had fallen
and died.
24 But Joab and Abishai pursued Abner, and as the sun was
setting, they came to the hill of Ammah, near Giah on the way to
the wasteland of Gibeon. 25 Then the men of Benjamin rallied
behind Abner. They formed themselves into a group and took
their stand on top of a hill.
26 Abner called out to Joab, "Must the sword devour forever?
Don't you realize that this will end in bitterness? How long before
you order your men to stop pursuing their brothers?"
27 Joab answered, "As surely as God lives, if you had not spoken, the men would have continued the pursuit of their brothers
until morning.[b]"
28 So Joab blew the trumpet, and all the men came to a halt;
they no longer pursued Israel, nor did they fight anymore.

---

a16 *Helkath Hazzurim* means *field of daggers* or *field of hostilities.* **b27** Or *spoken this morning, the men would not have taken up the pursuit of their brothers*; or *spoken, the men would have given up the pursuit of their brothers by morning*

29 All that night Abner and his men marched through the
Arabah. They crossed the Jordan, continued through the whole
Bithron[a] and came to Mahanaim.
30 Then Joab returned from pursuing Abner and assembled
all his men. Besides Asahel, nineteen of David's men were found
missing. 31 But David's men had killed three hundred and sixty
Benjamites who were with Abner. 32 They took Asahel and buried
him in his father's tomb at Bethlehem. Then Joab and his men
marched all night and arrived at Hebron by daybreak.
3 The war between the house of Saul and the house of David
lasted a long time. David grew stronger and stronger, while the
house of Saul grew weaker and weaker.
2 Sons were born to David in Hebron:

His firstborn was Amnon the son of Ahinoam of Jezreel;
3 his second, Kileab the son of Abigail the widow of Nabal of
Carmel;
the third, Absalom the son of Maacah daughter of Talmai
king of Geshur;
4 the fourth, Adonijah the son of Haggith;
the fifth, Shephatiah the son of Abital;
5 and the sixth, Ithream the son of David's wife Eglah.
These were born to David in Hebron.

Abner Goes Over to David

6 During the war between the house of Saul and the house of
David, Abner had been strengthening his own position in the
house of Saul. 7 Now Saul had had a concubine named Rizpah
daughter of Aiah. And Ish-Bosheth said to Abner, "Why did you
sleep with my father's concubine?"
8 Abner was very angry because of what Ish-Bosheth said and
he answered, "Am I a dog's head—on Judah's side? This very day I
am loyal to the house of your father Saul and to his family and
friends. I haven't handed you over to David. Yet now you accuse
me of an offense involving this woman! 9 May God deal with
Abner, be it ever so severely, if I do not do for David what the LORD
promised him on oath 10 and transfer the kingdom from the house
of Saul and establish David's throne over Israel and Judah from
Dan to Beersheba." 11 Ish-Bosheth did not dare to say another word
to Abner, because he was afraid of him.
12 Then Abner sent messengers on his behalf to say to David,
"Whose land is it? Make an agreement with me, and I will help you
bring all Israel over to you."
13 "Good," said David. "I will make an agreement with you.
But I demand one thing of you: Do not come into my presence
unless you bring Michal daughter of Saul when you come to see

[a]29 Or *morning*; or *ravine*; the meaning of the Hebrew for this word is uncertain.

3:7 *concubine:* This translates a Hebrew word for a woman who was legally bound to a man, but without the full privileges of a wife. As a kind of slave, these wives would pass to the next ruler because they were considered part of the property of the royal household. Ish-Bosheth accused Abner of trying to take the king's place by sleeping with Rizpah, a royal concubine. Such an act was considered as making a claim to the king's property—his throne.

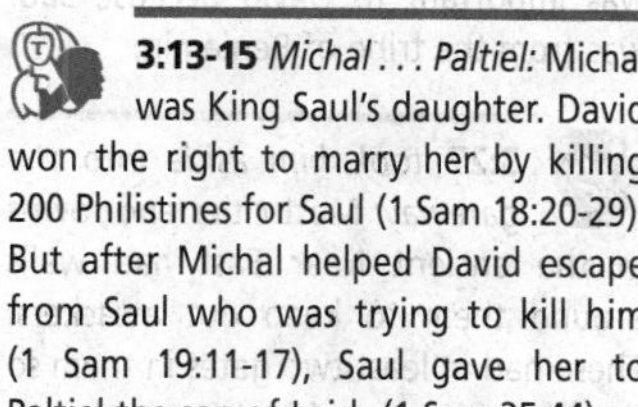

3:13-15 *Michal . . . Paltiel:* Michal was King Saul's daughter. David won the right to marry her by killing 200 Philistines for Saul (1 Sam 18:20-29). But after Michal helped David escape from Saul who was trying to kill him (1 Sam 19:11-17), Saul gave her to Paltiel the son of Laish (1 Sam 25:44).

David probably had more than one reason for asking Michal to be brought back to him. He may have truly loved her and missed her; he may have wanted to test Abner's sincerity and loyalty; and he may have understood how being married to someone from the household of the previous king would strengthen his own claim to be king of all Israel.

3:10 1 Sam 15:28.

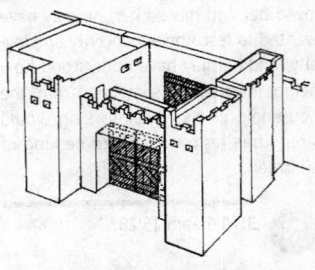

3:17-19 *elders of Israel . . . Benjamites:* In the Bible, Israel is made up of twelve tribes descended from Jacob. The tribe of Judah was mentioned in 2:1. Benjamin was Jacob's youngest son, and his descendants became the Benjamites. Jacob called Benjamin a "ravenous wolf" when he blessed him (Gen 49:27), and the tribe of Benjamin became known as warriors. See also the mini-article called "Israel," p. 264. The approval of the Benjamites was important to David because Saul was from the tribe of Benjamin.

3:27 *took him aside into the gateway:* Most cities and towns in the ancient Near East had walls around them to keep out attackers. These had at least two gates in them so that the citizens could let in merchants, farmers, and friendly visitors. See also the note at 18:24.

3:29 *his blood fall upon the head of Joab:* David put a curse on Joab and his family. See the note at 1:21 (mountains). It would not be until shortly before his own death that David would command that Joab be punished for murdering Abner (1 Kgs 2:5, 6, 28-35).

Joab was guilty of murdering Abner. Killing during war was not seen as unlawful in ancient Israel, but Joab's killing of Abner was not an act of war, because David had just sent Abner away in peace (3:21). Also, Joab's act was not considered a kind of lawful blood revenge (Deut 19:11-13). Although Abner had killed Joab's brother Asahel, it was during battle and Abner had tried to avoid it (2 Sam 2:18-23). David's cursing of Joab would have shown the Israelites that he had not arranged to have Abner murdered for his own political gain.

me." [14]Then David sent messengers to Ish-Bosheth son of Saul, demanding, "Give me my wife Michal, whom I betrothed to myself for the price of a hundred Philistine foreskins."

[15]So Ish-Bosheth gave orders and had her taken away from her husband Paltiel son of Laish. [16]Her husband, however, went with her, weeping behind her all the way to Bahurim. Then Abner said to him, "Go back home!" So he went back.

[17]Abner conferred with the elders of Israel and said, "For some time you have wanted to make David your king. [18]Now do it! For the LORD promised David, 'By my servant David I will rescue my people Israel from the hand of the Philistines and from the hand of all their enemies.' "

[19]Abner also spoke to the Benjamites in person. Then he went to Hebron to tell David everything that Israel and the whole house of Benjamin wanted to do. [20]When Abner, who had twenty men with him, came to David at Hebron, David prepared a feast for him and his men. [21]Then Abner said to David, "Let me go at once and assemble all Israel for my lord the king, so that they may make a compact with you, and that you may rule over all that your heart desires." So David sent Abner away, and he went in peace.

Joab Murders Abner

[22]Just then David's men and Joab returned from a raid and brought with them a great deal of plunder. But Abner was no longer with David in Hebron, because David had sent him away, and he had gone in peace. [23]When Joab and all the soldiers with him arrived, he was told that Abner son of Ner had come to the king and that the king had sent him away and that he had gone in peace.

[24]So Joab went to the king and said, "What have you done? Look, Abner came to you. Why did you let him go? Now he is gone! [25]You know Abner son of Ner; he came to deceive you and observe your movements and find out everything you are doing."

[26]Joab then left David and sent messengers after Abner, and they brought him back from the well of Sirah. But David did not know it. [27]Now when Abner returned to Hebron, Joab took him aside into the gateway, as though to speak with him privately. And there, to avenge the blood of his brother Asahel, Joab stabbed him in the stomach, and he died.

[28]Later, when David heard about this, he said, "I and my kingdom are forever innocent before the LORD concerning the blood of Abner son of Ner. [29]May his blood fall upon the head of Joab and upon all his father's house! May Joab's house never be without someone who has a running sore or leprosy[a] or who leans on a crutch or who falls by the sword or who lacks food."

[a]**29** The Hebrew word was used for various diseases affecting the skin—not necessarily leprosy.

30(Joab and his brother Abishai murdered Abner because he had killed their brother Asahel in the battle at Gibeon.)

31Then David said to Joab and all the people with him, "Tear your clothes and put on sackcloth and walk in mourning in front of Abner." King David himself walked behind the bier. 32They buried Abner in Hebron, and the king wept aloud at Abner's tomb. All the people wept also.

33The king sang this lament for Abner:

"Should Abner have died as the lawless die?
34 Your hands were not bound,
your feet were not fettered.
You fell as one falls before wicked men."

And all the people wept over him again.

35Then they all came and urged David to eat something while it was still day; but David took an oath, saying, "May God deal with me, be it ever so severely, if I taste bread or anything else before the sun sets!"

36All the people took note and were pleased; indeed, everything the king did pleased them. 37So on that day all the people and all Israel knew that the king had no part in the murder of Abner son of Ner.

38Then the king said to his men, "Do you not realize that a prince and a great man has fallen in Israel this day? 39And today, though I am the anointed king, I am weak, and these sons of Zeruiah are too strong for me. May the LORD repay the evildoer according to his evil deeds!"

Ish-Bosheth Murdered

4 When Ish-Bosheth son of Saul heard that Abner had died in Hebron, he lost courage, and all Israel became alarmed. 2Now Saul's son had two men who were leaders of raiding bands. One was named Baanah and the other Recab; they were sons of Rimmon the Beerothite from the tribe of Benjamin—Beeroth is considered part of Benjamin, 3because the people of Beeroth fled to Gittaim and have lived there as aliens to this day.

4(Jonathan son of Saul had a son who was lame in both feet. He was five years old when the news about Saul and Jonathan came from Jezreel. His nurse picked him up and fled, but as she hurried to leave, he fell and became crippled. His name was Mephibosheth.)

5Now Recab and Baanah, the sons of Rimmon the Beerothite, set out for the house of Ish-Bosheth, and they arrived there in the heat of the day while he was taking his noonday rest. 6They went into the inner part of the house as if to get some wheat, and they stabbed him in the stomach. Then Recab and his brother Baanah slipped away.

3:31 *sackcloth:* Sackcloth was a rough, dark-colored cloth made from goat or camel hair and was used to make grain sacks. Because of its rough texture and unrefined appearance, people wore sackcloth in times of trouble or sorrow. See the illustration on p. 1551. Tearing one's clothes was another way of showing sorrow (see also the note at 1:2).

4:3 *lived there as aliens:* They did not have the full legal rights of citizens.

4:4 *news about Saul and Jonathan:* See 1 Sam 31:1-6.

4:6-12 *cut off his head . . . cut off their hands and feet and hung the bodies:* Taking the head of a slain enemy was a common practice in the ancient Near East. Displaying the head was a way to announce the victory and to warn other enemies. David had done this after killing Goliath (1 Sam 17:51, 54). David ordered that the criminals' bodies be displayed for similar reasons (4:12). Executing the killers also demonstrated that David did not approve of how they had eliminated his rival for the throne. (See also Deut 21:22.)

4:4 2 Sam 9:3.

5:1 *your own flesh and blood:* Members of all the tribes of Israel were related. See the note at 3:17-19.

5:4 *forty years:* Forty stands for a large number or a long period of time. See the chart called "Numbers in the Bible," p. 2405.

5:6 *Jerusalem . . . Jebusites:* Jebusites lived in Canaan long before the Israelites. Jerusalem, one of the towns of the Jebusites, was on the border between the tribes of Judah and Benjamin. See also the mini-article called "Jerusalem," p. 574.

5:7 *fortress of Zion, the City of David:* The fortress of Zion was the name for one of the hills on which Jerusalem was built. Jerusalem came to be called "the City of David" (1 Kgs 8:1; Neh 12:37; Isa 22:9). See also the mini-article called "Zion," p. 1294.

4:10 2 Sam 1:1-16. **5:4,5** 1 Kgs 2:10, 11; 1 Chr 3:1-4; 29:26, 27. **5:6** Josh 15:63; Judg 1:21.

7They had gone into the house while he was lying on the bed
in his bedroom. After they stabbed and killed him, they cut off his
head. Taking it with them, they traveled all night by way of the
Arabah. 8They brought the head of Ish-Bosheth to David at
Hebron and said to the king, "Here is the head of Ish-Bosheth son
of Saul, your enemy, who tried to take your life. This day the LORD
has avenged my lord the king against Saul and his offspring."

9David answered Recab and his brother Baanah, the sons of
Rimmon the Beerothite, "As surely as the LORD lives, who has
delivered me out of all trouble, 10when a man told me, 'Saul is
dead,' and thought he was bringing good news, I seized him and
put him to death in Ziklag. That was the reward I gave him for
his news! 11How much more—when wicked men have killed an
innocent man in his own house and on his own bed—should I
not now demand his blood from your hand and rid the earth of
you!"

12So David gave an order to his men, and they killed them.
They cut off their hands and feet and hung the bodies by the pool
in Hebron. But they took the head of Ish-Bosheth and buried it in
Abner's tomb at Hebron.

DAVID UNITES ALL OF ISRAEL

The leaders of the northern tribes accept David as king. David leads a united Israel in capturing Jerusalem from the Jebusites and in fighting the Philistines. With Jerusalem secure, David and his soldiers go to Kiriath Jearim to get the ark of the covenant and bring it to his new capital.

David Becomes King Over Israel

5 All the tribes of Israel came to David at Hebron and said, "We
are your own flesh and blood. 2In the past, while Saul was king
over us, you were the one who led Israel on their military campaigns. And the LORD said to you, 'You will shepherd my people
Israel, and you will become their ruler.'"

3When all the elders of Israel had come to King David at
Hebron, the king made a compact with them at Hebron before the
LORD, and they anointed David king over Israel.

4David was thirty years old when he became king, and he
reigned forty years. 5In Hebron he reigned over Judah seven years
and six months, and in Jerusalem he reigned over all Israel and
Judah thirty-three years.

David Conquers Jerusalem

6The king and his men marched to Jerusalem to attack the
Jebusites, who lived there. The Jebusites said to David, "You will
not get in here; even the blind and the lame can ward you off."

They thought, "David cannot get in here." 7Nevertheless, David
captured the fortress of Zion, the City of David.

8On that day, David said, "Anyone who conquers the
Jebusites will have to use the water shaft[a] to reach those 'lame and
blind' who are David's enemies.[b]" That is why they say, "The 'blind
and lame' will not enter the palace."

9David then took up residence in the fortress and called it
the City of David. He built up the area around it, from the supporting terraces[c] inward. 10And he became more and more powerful, because the LORD God Almighty was with him.

11Now Hiram king of Tyre sent messengers to David, along
with cedar logs and carpenters and stonemasons, and they built a
palace for David. 12And David knew that the LORD had established
him as king over Israel and had exalted his kingdom for the sake of
his people Israel.

13After he left Hebron, David took more concubines and
wives in Jerusalem, and more sons and daughters were born to
him. 14These are the names of the children born to him there:
Shammua, Shobab, Nathan, Solomon, 15Ibhar, Elishua, Nepheg,
Japhia, 16Elishama, Eliada and Eliphelet.

David Defeats the Philistines

17When the Philistines heard that David had been anointed
king over Israel, they went up in full force to search for him, but
David heard about it and went down to the stronghold. 18Now the
Philistines had come and spread out in the Valley of Rephaim; 19so
David inquired of the LORD, "Shall I go and attack the Philistines?
Will you hand them over to me?"

The LORD answered him, "Go, for I will surely hand the Philistines over to you."

20So David went to Baal Perazim, and there he defeated
them. He said, "As waters break out, the LORD has broken out
against my enemies before me." So that place was called Baal Perazim.[d] 21The Philistines abandoned their idols there, and David
and his men carried them off.

22Once more the Philistines came up and spread out in the
Valley of Rephaim; 23so David inquired of the LORD, and he
answered, "Do not go straight up, but circle around behind them
and attack them in front of the balsam trees. 24As soon as you hear
the sound of marching in the tops of the balsam trees, move
quickly, because that will mean the LORD has gone out in front of
you to strike the Philistine army." 25So David did as the LORD commanded him, and he struck down the Philistines all the way from
Gibeon[e] to Gezer.

[a]8 Or *use scaling hooks* [b]8 Or *are hated by David* [c]9 Or *the Millo* [d]20 *Baal Perazim* means *the lord who breaks out.* [e]25 Septuagint (see also 1 Chron. 14:16); Hebrew *Geba*

5:8 *water shaft:* Archaeologists have discovered a tunnel running under the city wall from the Gihon Spring to a storage pool inside the city wall. People could get water without going outside the walls for water. This was a true advantage when the city was under attack.

5:8 *'lame and blind':* David used the Jebusites' own words to ridicule their boasting (5:6).

5:9 *supporting terraces:* Probably a section on the steep eastern ridge of the city.

5:10 *LORD God Almighty:* See the mini-article called "LORD (YHWH)," p. 140.

5:11 *Tyre:* Tyre was an important Phoenician seaport on the Mediterranean coast. See also the mini-article called "Phoenicia," p. 1604.

5:13 *concubines and wives:* See the notes at 2:2 and 3:7.

5:16 *Eliada:* Eliada is listed in 1 Chronicles 3:8, but 1 Chronicles 14:7 has "Beeliada."

5:17 *Philistines:* See the note at 1:20.

5:17 *stronghold:* This could be Adullam, David's former hideout (1 Sam 22:1; 24:22), or it could refer to Jerusalem, called the "fortress of Zion" in 5:7.

5:18 *Valley of Rephaim:* A few miles southwest of Jerusalem.

5:20 *Baal Perazim:* This name in Hebrew means "LORD of the Breakthrough."

5:21 *idols . . . carried them off:* The Philistines worshiped many gods. Idols were objects that represented these gods. See also the note at 1 Sam 7:3,4.

JERUSALEM

Jerusalem, in the hill country eighteen miles west of the north end of the Dead Sea, began as a small settlement around 3500 B.C. It grew around the Gihon Spring, one of only two sources of water in the area around what would later be called the "temple mount." The city is mentioned in ancient Egyptian writings and at one time was known as Salem (Gen 14:18).

When David became king of Israel, he captured the walled city of Jerusalem around 1000 B.C. from the Jebusites (2 Sam 5, 6) and made it Israel's new capital. This decision helped to unify the country, since this neutral city was located between the feuding northern and southern tribes of Israel. The city grew under David's son, King Solomon, who extended the city to the north and built his palace and a temple to the LORD on the eastern hill. King Hezekiah (ruled 716-687 B.C.) further enlarged the city to include the western hill. In 586 B.C., when Judah's most important citizens were taken off to Babylonia as prisoners, much of Jerusalem was left in ruins. Under the Jewish Maccabean kings (140-63 B.C.) it became prominent once again. By the time of Herod's rule (40-4 B.C.), Jerusalem covered more than 200 acres and had a population of forty thousand.

Solomon's temple, which the Babylonians destroyed in 586 B.C., was rebuilt on a smaller scale (516 B.C.) by returned exiles led by Zerubbabel after the Persians allowed the Jews to return to their land, then known as Judea (445 B.C.). When Alexander the Great (356-323 B.C.) conquered the Near East, the influence of Greek culture began to spread throughout the world. The Syrian (Seleucid) rulers who took over control of Palestine after Alexander's death had been influenced by the Greeks, and so began to turn Jerusalem into a typical Greek-style city. In 168 B.C., Antiochus IV of Syria made the temple a shrine to the Greek god Zeus. He also built a fortress just north of the temple so that his troops could keep an eye on the city and surrounding area. When the Jewish family known as the Maccabees came to power around 140 B.C., they made the western hill their seat of government. See the map on p. 2466.

The Romans took over Judea in 63 B.C., but it wasn't until 37 B.C. that Herod was able to capture Jerusalem. He expanded the city by enlarging the temple area on the eastern hill. He built a huge stone platform for the temple and its courtyards that covered more than one and a half million square feet. He lived in a palace on the western hill, surrounded by his wealthy supporters. Massive towers protected the palace, and a bridge crossed the valley between two hills. Another huge tower was built north of the temple area. A grand staircase led south from the temple mount to the older, poorer part of the city below. The northern city wall connected the tower overlooking the temple with Herod's palace. All of these structures would still have been in place in Jesus' day. See the map on p. 2474.

During the first Jewish revolt against the Romans (A.D. 66-70), the temple and much of the city were destroyed. After the second revolt (A.D. 130-135), the Romans built a new temple to their god Jupiter on the temple mount. They renamed the city Aelia Capitolina, and would not allow the Jews into the city in an effort to prevent any new uprisings. Since then, many different groups have controlled Jerusalem, including Byzantine Christians, Islamic rulers, Latin Christians, and Ottoman Turks. Today it is the capital of the Jewish state of Israel, as well as a holy city for Jews, Christians, and Muslims around the world.

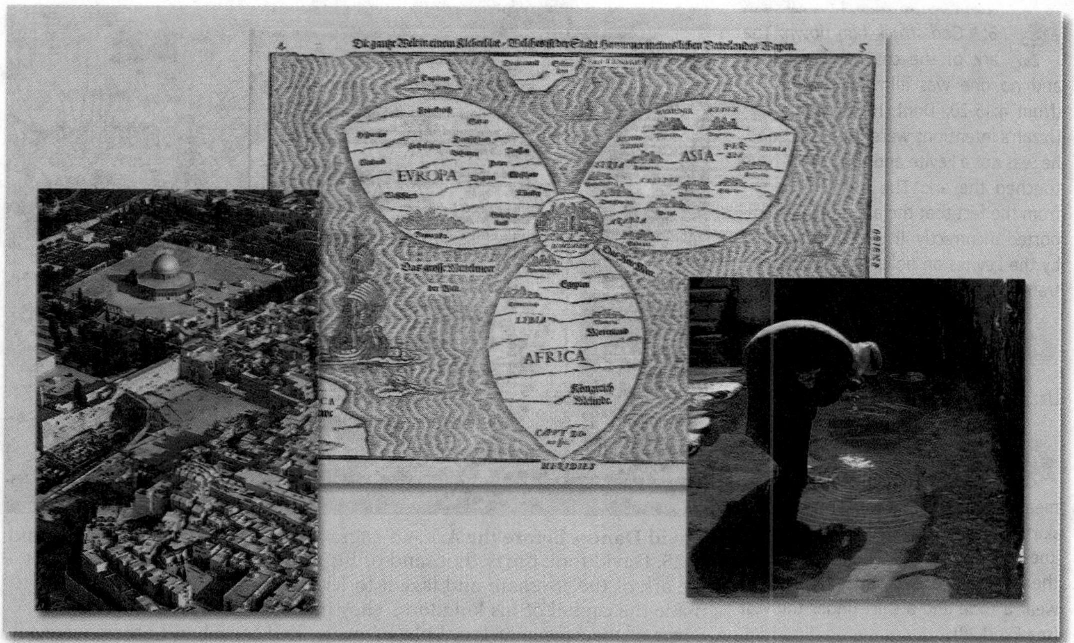

Jerusalem. Jerusalem began as a small settlement near the Gihon Spring over four thousand years ago. It has been an important site of Western religious history since David captured the city from the Jebusites around 1000 B.C. The sixteenth century map above illustrates this continuing importance: Jerusalem is at the center of a three-leafed clover representing all the known continents—Asia, Africa, and Europe. The Dome of the Rock, now a Muslim mosque, is located on the Temple Mount where Solomon's temple once stood. In biblical times, waters from the Pool of Siloam, fed by the Gihon Spring, were used for ritual cleansing.

The Ark Brought to Jerusalem

6 David again brought together out of Israel chosen men, thirty
thousand in all. [2]He and all his men set out from Baalah of Judah[a]
to bring up from there the ark of God, which is called by the
Name,[b] the name of the LORD Almighty, who is enthroned between
the cherubim that are on the ark. [3]They set the ark of God on a
new cart and brought it from the house of Abinadab, which was
on the hill. Uzzah and Ahio, sons of Abinadab, were guiding the
new cart [4]with the ark of God on it,[c] and Ahio was walking in
front of it. [5]David and the whole house of Israel were celebrating
with all their might before the LORD, with songs[d] and with harps,
lyres, tambourines, sistrums and cymbals.
[6]When they came to the threshing floor of Nacon, Uzzah
reached out and took hold of the ark of God, because the oxen

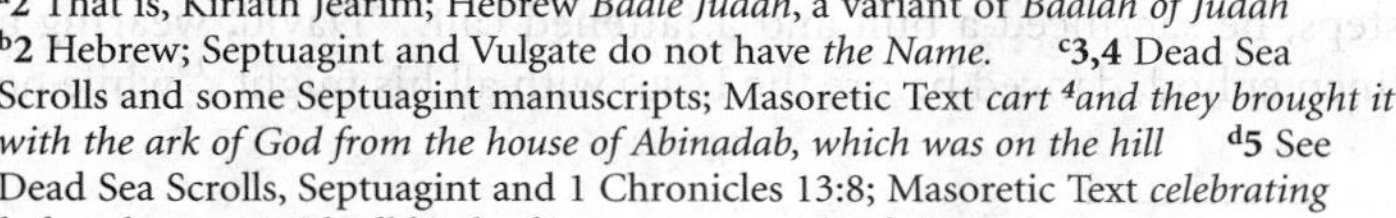

[a]2 That is, Kiriath Jearim; Hebrew *Baale Judah*, a variant of *Baalah of Judah* [b]2 Hebrew; Septuagint and Vulgate do not have *the Name.* [c]3,4 Dead Sea Scrolls and some Septuagint manuscripts; Masoretic Text *cart [4]and they brought it with the ark of God from the house of Abinadab, which was on the hill* [d]5 See Dead Sea Scrolls, Septuagint and 1 Chronicles 13:8; Masoretic Text *celebrating before the LORD with all kinds of instruments made of pine.*

6:2,3 *ark of God:* This refers to the ark of the covenant, which held the two stone tablets that had the Ten Commandments written on them. See the mini-article called "The Ark of the Covenant," p. 513. Bringing the ark of the covenant to Jerusalem would make the city the religious as well as political center of Israel. See also the map on p. 517.

6:6 *threshing floor:* Where harvested stalks of grain were beaten with hand tools or walked over by oxen to separate the seeds (kernels) from the stalks and husks (chaff). It would be done outdoors on a hard floor of packed clay, soil, or rock. Threshing areas were often on hills so that the wind could more easily blow away the chaff.

6:2 Exod 25:22. **6:3** 1 Sam 7:1,2.

6:7 *God struck him down:* The ark of the covenant was holy and no one was allowed to touch it (Num 4:15-20; Deut 10:8,9). Although Uzzah's intentions were probably good, he was not a Levite and should not have touched the ark. The problem begins from the fact that the ark is being transported incorrectly. It was to be carried by the Levites on poles (Exod 37:5), not transported on a cart.

6:8 *Perez Uzzah:* This name in Hebrew means "Punishment of Uzzah."

6:14 *linen ephod:* The Hebrew word translated "ephod" can mean either a piece of clothing like a skirt that went from the waist to the knee or a long vest or a jacket that only the priests wore. Priests would also wear a robe and a shirt under the vest (see Exod 28).

6:16 *despised him:* Michal seemed to be concerned that David was not behaving like a king. But David thought of himself as God's servant celebrating God's victories (7:18-20).

6:17-19 *sacrificed burnt offerings and fellowship offerings:* The Hebrew text mentions two kinds of sacrifices. In one kind of sacrifice, the whole animal was burned on the altar. In the other, only part of it was burned, and the worshipers ate the rest. See also Lev 1:1-17; 3:1-17 and the chart called "Sacrifices and Offerings," p. 219.

6:23 *Michal . . . had no children:* This could be because David stopped having sexual relations with her, or because God was punishing her for despising David's joy (6:16,20). Whatever the reason, the fact that Michal and David never had children means that none of David's children would also be a descendant of Saul (see 1 Sam 15:28).

6:11,12 1 Chr 26:4,5.

David Dances before the Ark, an engraving by Matthäus Merian, around 1625. David took thirty thousand of his soldiers to Kiriath Jearim to get the ark of the covenant and take it to Jerusalem, the city David had made the capital of his kingdom. They put the ark on a new ox cart. Some of the people of Israel played music and David and others were so happy that they began "celebrating with all their might before the LORD." When the ox cart started to tip, Uzzah reached out and took hold of the ark. Since Uzzah was not a priest, the LORD got angry and killed him immediately. This frightened David, who temporarily had the ark of the covenant moved to Gath. (See 6:1-19.)

stumbled. [7]The LORD's anger burned against Uzzah because of his irreverent act; therefore God struck him down and he died there beside the ark of God.

[8]Then David was angry because the LORD's wrath had broken out against Uzzah, and to this day that place is called Perez Uzzah.[a]

[9]David was afraid of the LORD that day and said, "How can the ark of the LORD ever come to me?" [10]He was not willing to take the ark of the LORD to be with him in the City of David. Instead, he took it aside to the house of Obed-Edom the Gittite. [11]The ark of the LORD remained in the house of Obed-Edom the Gittite for three months, and the LORD blessed him and his entire household.

[12]Now King David was told, "The LORD has blessed the household of Obed-Edom and everything he has, because of the ark of God." So David went down and brought up the ark of God from the house of Obed-Edom to the City of David with rejoicing. [13]When those who were carrying the ark of the LORD had taken six steps, he sacrificed a bull and a fattened calf. [14]David, wearing a linen ephod, danced before the LORD with all his might, [15]while he

---

[a]**8** *Perez Uzzah* means *outbreak against Uzzah.*

and the entire house of Israel brought up the ark of the LORD with
shouts and the sound of trumpets.
[16]As the ark of the LORD was entering the City of David,
Michal daughter of Saul watched from a window. And when she saw
King David leaping and dancing before the LORD, she despised him
in her heart.
[17]They brought the ark of the LORD and set it in its place
inside the tent that David had pitched for it, and David sacrificed
burnt offerings and fellowship offerings[a] before the LORD. [18]After
he had finished sacrificing the burnt offerings and fellowship
offerings, he blessed the people in the name of the LORD Almighty.
[19]Then he gave a loaf of bread, a cake of dates and a cake of raisins
to each person in the whole crowd of Israelites, both men and
women. And all the people went to their homes.
[20]When David returned home to bless his household, Michal
daughter of Saul came out to meet him and said, "How the king of
Israel has distinguished himself today, disrobing in the sight of the
slave girls of his servants as any vulgar fellow would!"
[21]David said to Michal, "It was before the LORD, who chose
me rather than your father or anyone from his house when he
appointed me ruler over the LORD's people Israel—I will celebrate
before the LORD. [22]I will become even more undignified than this,
and I will be humiliated in my own eyes. But by these slave girls
you spoke of, I will be held in honor."
[23]And Michal daughter of Saul had no children to the day of
her death.

GOD'S PROMISE AND DAVID'S RESPONSE

With Israel at peace, God makes a promise to David. The LORD tells David that one of his descendants will always be king and that David's son, not David, will be the one to build a temple for the LORD.

God's Promise to David

7 After the king was settled in his palace and the LORD had given
him rest from all his enemies around him, [2]he said to Nathan the
prophet, "Here I am, living in a palace of cedar, while the ark of
God remains in a tent."
[3]Nathan replied to the king, "Whatever you have in mind, go
ahead and do it, for the LORD is with you."
[4]That night the word of the LORD came to Nathan, saying:
[5]"Go and tell my servant David, 'This is what the LORD
says: Are you the one to build me a house to dwell in? [6]I have
not dwelt in a house from the day I brought the Israelites up
out of Egypt to this day. I have been moving from place to

[a]17 Traditionally *peace offerings*; also in verse 18

7:1 *the LORD had given him rest:* It is not certain whether David had defeated all of his enemies at this time. The next chapter lists more of David's victories.

7:2,3 *Nathan the prophet . . . go ahead and do it:* This is the first time Nathan is mentioned. Prophets received messages from God to pass on to other people. But here Nathan spoke before hearing God's word, and was wrong to tell David to go ahead with his building plans. He corrected that error after God appeared to him in a vision (7:4-16). For more about the role of prophets in the history of the people of Israel, see the article called "Prophets and Prophecy," p. 935.

7:5-16 *my servant David . . . throne will be established forever:* In the Hebrew text, God's promise to David plays on different meanings of the word "temple." In effect, God is saying, "Do not build a temple for me (7:5-7), but I will build a house (provide descendants) for you (7:10, 11), and one of your sons will build a temple for me" (7:12, 13).

In a political sense, the "House of David" did not last, falling to the Babylonians in 587 B.C. But God's promise to David has been the basis of the hope for a new "chosen one" (*Messiah*). See Ps 89:3,4,36,37; 132:11; Isa 11:1,2,10. Jesus' apostles understood that Jesus' claim to be bringing about the "kingdom of God" rested partly on the fact that Jesus was descended from David. See John 7:42; Acts 2:30.

7:6 *brought the Israelites up out of Egypt . . . with a tent as my dwelling:* For the story of the Israelites leaving Egypt, see Exodus 6–12. EXODUS goes on to describe the building and furnishing of the tabernacle and the ark of the covenant (Exod 25–27). See also the mini-article called "The Tabernacle," p. 2346.

6:19,20 1 Chr 16:2,3,43.

The LORD told David, *"I will also give you rest from all your enemies. 'The LORD declares to you that the LORD himself will establish a house for you.'"* 2 Sam 7:11

7:18 *sat before the LORD:* At that time, people normally stood or kneeled for prayer. David's sitting might have reflected his special relationship to God (see Ps 16:11; 110:1).

7:12 Ps 89:3,4; 132:11; John 7:42; Acts 2:30. **7:14** Ps 89:26,27; 2 Cor 6:18; Heb 1:5. **7:16** Ps 89:36,37.

place with a tent as my dwelling. [7]Wherever I have moved
with all the Israelites, did I ever say to any of their rulers
whom I commanded to shepherd my people Israel, "Why have
you not built me a house of cedar?" '

[8]"Now then, tell my servant David, 'This is what the
LORD Almighty says: I took you from the pasture and from
following the flock to be ruler over my people Israel. [9]I have
been with you wherever you have gone, and I have cut off all
your enemies from before you. Now I will make your name
great, like the names of the greatest men of the earth. [10]And I
will provide a place for my people Israel and will plant them
so that they can have a home of their own and no longer be
disturbed. Wicked people will not oppress them anymore, as
they did at the beginning [11]and have done ever since the time
I appointed leaders[a] over my people Israel. I will also give you
rest from all your enemies.

" 'The LORD declares to you that the LORD himself will
establish a house for you: [12]When your days are over and you
rest with your fathers, I will raise up your offspring to succeed
you, who will come from your own body, and I will establish
his kingdom. [13]He is the one who will build a house for my
Name, and I will establish the throne of his kingdom forever.
[14]I will be his father, and he will be my son. When he does
wrong, I will punish him with the rod of men, with floggings
inflicted by men. [15]But my love will never be taken away from
him, as I took it away from Saul, whom I removed from
before you. [16]Your house and your kingdom will endure forever before me[b]; your throne will be established forever.' "

[17]Nathan reported to David all the words of this entire
revelation.

David's Prayer

[18]Then King David went in and sat before the LORD, and he
said:

"Who am I, O Sovereign LORD, and what is my family,
that you have brought me this far? [19]And as if this were not
enough in your sight, O Sovereign LORD, you have also spoken about the future of the house of your servant. Is this your
usual way of dealing with man, O Sovereign LORD?

[20]"What more can David say to you? For you know your
servant, O Sovereign LORD. [21]For the sake of your word and
according to your will, you have done this great thing and
made it known to your servant.

[a]**11** Traditionally *judges* [b]**16** Some Hebrew manuscripts and Septuagint; most Hebrew manuscripts *you*

22“How great you are, O Sovereign LORD! There is no
one like you, and there is no God but you, as we have heard
with our own ears. 23And who is like your people Israel—the
one nation on earth that God went out to redeem as a people
for himself, and to make a name for himself, and to perform
great and awesome wonders by driving out nations and their
gods from before your people, whom you redeemed from
Egypt?[a] 24You have established your people Israel as your very
own forever, and you, O LORD, have become their God.
25“And now, LORD God, keep forever the promise you
have made concerning your servant and his house. Do as you
promised, 26so that your name will be great forever. Then men
will say, ‘The LORD Almighty is God over Israel!’ And the
house of your servant David will be established before you.
27“O LORD Almighty, God of Israel, you have revealed this
to your servant, saying, ‘I will build a house for you.’ So your
servant has found courage to offer you this prayer. 28O Sovereign
LORD, you are God! Your words are trustworthy, and you have
promised these good things to your servant. 29Now be pleased to
bless the house of your servant, that it may continue forever in
your sight; for you, O Sovereign LORD, have spoken, and with
your blessing the house of your servant will be blessed forever.”

DAVID DEFEATS ISRAEL’S ENEMIES

David defeats the Philistines and conquers many of the neighboring nations, including Moab, the Aramean kingdom, and Edom. But David is kind to Mephibosheth, Saul’s grandson, because of a promise David made to Jonathan.

David’s Victories

8 In the course of time, David defeated the Philistines and subdued them, and he took Metheg Ammah from the control of the Philistines.
2David also defeated the Moabites. He made them lie down on
the ground and measured them off with a length of cord. Every two
lengths of them were put to death, and the third length was allowed
to live. So the Moabites became subject to David and brought tribute.
3Moreover, David fought Hadadezer son of Rehob, king of
Zobah, when he went to restore his control along the Euphrates
River. 4David captured a thousand of his chariots, seven thousand
charioteers[b] and twenty thousand foot soldiers. He hamstrung all
but a hundred of the chariot horses.

[a]**23** See Septuagint and 1 Chron. 17:21; Hebrew *wonders for your land and before your people, whom you redeemed from Egypt, from the nations and their gods.*
[b]**4** Septuagint (see also Dead Sea Scrolls and 1 Chron. 18:4); Masoretic Text *captured seventeen hundred of his charioteers*

7:22-29 *Sovereign LORD . . . blessed forever:* David’s prayer of thanks recalled other promises that the LORD had made and kept with Israel. He asked the LORD to keep this promise, too. But David recognized that he and his descendants would have to continue to serve the LORD if they were to be the chosen kings. For the earlier promises, see Deut 5:1-3; 7:6-9; Exod 20:1-17, and the mini-articles called “Ten Commandments,” p. 354, and “Covenants (Agreements),” p. 386. For what the LORD expected of kings, see Deut 17:14-20.

7:23 *great and awesome wonders by driving out nations:* See Deut 4:32-38; Josh 3:1-17; 24:5,6,16-18.

8:1-14 *David defeated . . . became subject:* The lack of detail in the descriptions of David’s victories helps to emphasize that these were the LORD’s victories, especially with the repetition in verses 6 and 14. Saul had also fought the same enemies, but only to stop their raiding of Israelite lands (1 Sam 14:47, 48). The area David secured was that promised in Genesis 15:18-21 and Joshua 1:2-5. Zobah was northeast of Damascus and controlled the land to the Euphrates River. See also the map on p. 2465.

8:2 *Moabites:* David had taken his parents to Moab to protect them when he fled Israel (1 Sam 22:3,4).

8:3 *Euphrates River:* God promised to give Abraham’s descendants the land between Egypt and the Euphrates River. The part of the river referred to here is the upper Euphrates, which rises in modern Turkey and flows through Syria. See the map on p. 2462.

8:4 *chariots:* David might not have considered chariots to be of much use in the hills of the Israelite kingdom. But he also could have had Moses’ warning in mind that “The king, moreover, must not acquire great numbers of horses for himself” (Deut 17:16).

5 When the Arameans of Damascus came to help Hadadezer
king of Zobah, David struck down twenty-two thousand of them.
6 He put garrisons in the Aramean kingdom of Damascus, and the
Arameans became subject to him and brought tribute. The LORD
gave David victory wherever he went.
7 David took the gold shields that belonged to the officers of
Hadadezer and brought them to Jerusalem. 8 From Tebah[a] and
Berothai, towns that belonged to Hadadezer, King David took a
great quantity of bronze.
9 When Tou[b] king of Hamath heard that David had defeated
the entire army of Hadadezer, 10 he sent his son Joram[c] to King
David to greet him and congratulate him on his victory in battle
over Hadadezer, who had been at war with Tou. Joram brought
with him articles of silver and gold and bronze.
11 King David dedicated these articles to the LORD, as he had
done with the silver and gold from all the nations he had subdued:
12 Edom[d] and Moab, the Ammonites and the Philistines, and Amalek.
He also dedicated the plunder taken from Hadadezer son of Rehob,
king of Zobah.
13 And David became famous after he returned from striking
down eighteen thousand Edomites[e] in the Valley of Salt.
14 He put garrisons throughout Edom, and all the Edomites
became subject to David. The LORD gave David victory wherever
he went.

David's Officials

15 David reigned over all Israel, doing what was just and right
for all his people. 16 Joab son of Zeruiah was over the army;
Jehoshaphat son of Ahilud was recorder; 17 Zadok son of Ahitub
and Ahimelech son of Abiathar were priests; Seraiah was secretary;
18 Benaiah son of Jehoiada was over the Kerethites and Pelethites;
and David's sons were royal advisers.[f]

David and Mephibosheth

9 David asked, "Is there anyone still left of the house of Saul to
whom I can show kindness for Jonathan's sake?"
2 Now there was a servant of Saul's household named Ziba.
They called him to appear before David, and the king said to him,
"Are you Ziba?"
"Your servant," he replied.
3 The king asked, "Is there no one still left of the house of
Saul to whom I can show God's kindness?"

---

a8 See some Septuagint manuscripts (see also 1 Chron. 18:8); Hebrew *Betah*.
b9 Hebrew *Toi*, a variant of *Tou*; also in verse 10 c10 A variant of *Hadoram*
d12 Some Hebrew manuscripts, Septuagint and Syriac (see also 1 Chron. 18:11); most Hebrew manuscripts *Aram* e13 A few Hebrew manuscripts, Septuagint and Syriac (see also 1 Chron. 18:12); most Hebrew manuscripts *Aram* (that is, Arameans) f18 Or *were priests*

The LORD gave David victory wherever he went.
2 Sam 8:14

8:5 *Arameans of Damascus:* Damascus was the largest independent Aramean (Syrian) city-state. It is perhaps the world's oldest continuously occupied city and a major trading and transportation center. By defeating Damascus, David gained control over much of Syria.

8:11 *dedicated these articles to the LORD:* Later, Solomon used part of these precious metals to build the temple (1 Chr 18:8).

8:13 *Valley of Salt:* Probably located south and east of the Dead Sea in Edom. In one place Joab gets credit for the victory at the Valley of Salt (Ps 60 Title) and in another Abishai does (1 Chr 18:12).

Many years later, one of David's descendants, Amaziah, the ninth king of Judah, would also defeat the Edomites at the Valley of Salt (2 Kgs 14:1-7).

8:18 *Kerethites and Pelethites:* Some of David's officials were hired fighters (mercenaries) who were not Israelites. There were Kerethites, who were probably originally from Crete, and Pelethites, who were probably originally from somewhere around the Aegean Sea or Asia Minor. Since the Kerethites and Pelethites had settled in Philistia, David may have won their loyalty during the time he had offered his services to King Achish of Gath (1 Sam 27). They may have served the king as his bodyguards.

8:18 *David's sons were royal advisers:* See 1 Chr 18:14-17.

9:1 *for Jonathan's sake:* See 1 Sam 20:14-17.

9:3 2 Sam 4:4.

Ziba answered the king, "There is still a son of Jonathan; he
is crippled in both feet."
4"Where is he?" the king asked.
Ziba answered, "He is at the house of Makir son of Ammiel
in Lo Debar."
5So King David had him brought from Lo Debar, from the
house of Makir son of Ammiel.
6When Mephibosheth son of Jonathan, the son of Saul, came
to David, he bowed down to pay him honor.
David said, "Mephibosheth!"
"Your servant," he replied.
7"Don't be afraid," David said to him, "for I will surely show
you kindness for the sake of your father Jonathan. I will restore to
you all the land that belonged to your grandfather Saul, and you
will always eat at my table."
8Mephibosheth bowed down and said, "What is your servant, that you should notice a dead dog like me?"
9Then the king summoned Ziba, Saul's servant, and said to
him, "I have given your master's grandson everything that
belonged to Saul and his family. 10You and your sons and your
servants are to farm the land for him and bring in the crops, so
that your master's grandson may be provided for. And Mephibosheth, grandson of your master, will always eat at my table." (Now
Ziba had fifteen sons and twenty servants.)
11Then Ziba said to the king, "Your servant will do whatever
my lord the king commands his servant to do." So Mephibosheth
ate at David's[a] table like one of the king's sons.
12Mephibosheth had a young son named Mica, and all the
members of Ziba's household were servants of Mephibosheth.
13And Mephibosheth lived in Jerusalem, because he always ate at
the king's table, and he was crippled in both feet.

David Defeats the Ammonites

10 In the course of time, the king of the Ammonites died, and
his son Hanun succeeded him as king. 2David thought, "I will
show kindness to Hanun son of Nahash, just as his father showed
kindness to me." So David sent a delegation to express his sympathy to Hanun concerning his father.
When David's men came to the land of the Ammonites, 3the
Ammonite nobles said to Hanun their lord, "Do you think David
is honoring your father by sending men to you to express sympathy? Hasn't David sent them to you to explore the city and spy
it out and overthrow it?" 4So Hanun seized David's men, shaved
off half of each man's beard, cut off their garments in the middle
at the buttocks, and sent them away.

[a]**11** Septuagint; Hebrew *my*

9:4 *Lo Debar:* A town in Gilead, east of the Jordan.

9:7 *land that belonged to your grandfather Saul:* This land became David's when he succeeded Saul as king of Israel.

9:7 *always eat at my table:* David was honoring Mephibosheth with a place at his table, not offering charity. David might also have hoped to secure Mephibosheth's loyalty.

9:8 *a dead dog:* Mephibosheth might have been humbling himself out of fear that David wanted to destroy all of Saul's family. See also 1 Sam 17:43; 24:14.

10:1 *his son Hanun:* Nahash was most likely the same person who threatened the town of Jabesh Gilead and whose army was defeated by Saul (1 Sam 11:1-14). It is not known what kindness Nahash had done for David, though it is possible that Nahash helped David in some way when David was fleeing from Saul.

10:4 *shaved off half of each man's beard, cut off their garments:* Shaving a man's beard this way was extremely humiliating. Beards were a symbol of a man's honor and masculinity, and were shaved only in times of mourning (Isa 15:2; Jer 41:5).

Exposing the body also was considered shameful. Cutting the robes so short that the men's buttocks showed was so humiliating that normally it would only be done to prisoners of war.

5When David was told about this, he sent messengers to
meet the men, for they were greatly humiliated. The king said,
"Stay at Jericho till your beards have grown, and then come back."
6When the Ammonites realized that they had become a stench
in David's nostrils, they hired twenty thousand Aramean foot soldiers from Beth Rehob and Zobah, as well as the king of Maacah
with a thousand men, and also twelve thousand men from Tob.
7On hearing this, David sent Joab out with the entire army
of fighting men. 8The Ammonites came out and drew up in battle
formation at the entrance to their city gate, while the Arameans of
Zobah and Rehob and the men of Tob and Maacah were by themselves in the open country.
9Joab saw that there were battle lines in front of him and
behind him; so he selected some of the best troops in Israel and
deployed them against the Arameans. 10He put the rest of the men
under the command of Abishai his brother and deployed them
against the Ammonites. 11Joab said, "If the Arameans are too
strong for me, then you are to come to my rescue; but if the
Ammonites are too strong for you, then I will come to rescue you.
12Be strong and let us fight bravely for our people and the cities of
our God. The LORD will do what is good in his sight."
13Then Joab and the troops with him advanced to fight the
Arameans, and they fled before him. 14When the Ammonites saw

Joab told Abishai and his fighting men, *"Be strong and let us fight bravely for our people and the cities of our God. The LORD will do what is good in his sight."* 2 Sam 10:12

10:5 *Jericho:* Located about five miles west of the Jordan River and seven miles north of the Dead Sea, Jericho was an important city on the trade routes from the east to Palestine. Joshua had a major victory here after the Israelites crossed the Jordan (Josh 6). It is one of the oldest cities in the world with evidence of building on the site as early as 9250 B.C. See the map on p. 2465.

QUESTIONS ABOUT 2 SAMUEL 1:1—10:19

1. What did David do when he heard about Saul and Jonathan's deaths? (chapter 1) Do you think he was sincere? Why or why not? What kinds of loss have you experienced? How did you express your sorrow?
2. In 1 SAMUEL we learn how God rejected Saul as king and chose David, rather than one of Saul's sons, to be the next king (1 Sam 16:1-13). After Saul died, what kept David from immediately taking his place as God's chosen king? (2 Sam 1–4)
3. Three of David's rivals died violently: Saul (1 Sam 31:4), Abner (2 Sam 3:22-39), and Ish-Bosheth (4:5-12). What was different about David's reactions to each of their deaths?
4. In chapters 5 and 6, David becomes king of Israel, captures Jerusalem, and brings the ark of the covenant to Jerusalem. How are these events related and what do they signify? How do the people react when the ark is brought to Jerusalem? What important events do you celebrate? How do you celebrate them?
5. What is the important message the LORD's prophet Nathan brings to David in chapter 7? How is the covenant the LORD is making with David different from the one the LORD made with Saul? What will the relationship be between the LORD and one of David's sons? What will this son do for the LORD?
6. Read David's prayer of thanks to the LORD (7:18-29). What key points does he make about what God is like and what he has done for his chosen people Israel? Notice how many times the word "forever" occurs in this passage. What does this word mean to you?
7. Who were Mephibosheth and Ziba? (9:1-13) What did David do for them? What was David's motive?
8. How did King Hanun of Ammon insult David? (chapter 10) How did David respond?

that the Arameans were fleeing, they fled before Abishai and went inside the city. So Joab returned from fighting the Ammonites and came to Jerusalem.

[15]After the Arameans saw that they had been routed by Israel, they regrouped. [16]Hadadezer had Arameans brought from beyond the River[a]; they went to Helam, with Shobach the commander of Hadadezer's army leading them.

[17]When David was told of this, he gathered all Israel, crossed the Jordan and went to Helam. The Arameans formed their battle lines to meet David and fought against him. [18]But they fled before Israel, and David killed seven hundred of their charioteers and forty thousand of their foot soldiers.[b] He also struck down Shobach the commander of their army, and he died there. [19]When all the kings who were vassals of Hadadezer saw that they had been defeated by Israel, they made peace with the Israelites and became subject to them.

So the Arameans were afraid to help the Ammonites anymore.

10:19 *made peace with the Israelites . . . Arameans:* This would be David's last major military campaign against two enemies working together. Though some Arameans accepted David as their ruler, other Arameans beyond the Euphrates River remained loyal to Hadadezer.

11:1 *spring . . . kings go off to war:* This was probably about ten years after David took over Jerusalem. More men and food would be available for warfare after the spring rains and the grain harvest in April or May. See also 1 Kgs 20:22,26; 1 Chr 20:1.

11:2 *roof:* Houses usually had flat roofs. In hot weather it was cooler on the roof than in the house, and so roofs would be used for relaxing, entertaining, and sleeping.

David's Troubles

David has been successful in uniting the tribes of Israel and in defeating its many enemies. But when David commits sin by sleeping with Bathsheba, the beautiful wife of Uriah, and then arranges for Uriah's death in battle, his fortunes change. From this point on, David begins to have problems within his own family, especially from his son Absalom.

DAVID SINS AND SUFFERS BECAUSE OF IT

While David's soldiers are off fighting the Ammonites, David sins by sleeping with Uriah's wife, Bathsheba. When she becomes pregnant, David tries to hide his sin by sending Uriah off to battle where he will be killed. But the LORD knows what David has done, and sends the prophet Nathan to the king to tell him what his punishment will be.

David and Bathsheba

11 In the spring, at the time when kings go off to war, David sent Joab out with the king's men and the whole Israelite army. They destroyed the Ammonites and besieged Rabbah. But David remained in Jerusalem.

[2]One evening David got up from his bed and walked around on the roof of the palace. From the roof he saw a woman bathing. The woman was very beautiful, [3]and David sent someone to find out about her. The man said, "Isn't this Bathsheba, the daughter of

---

[a]**16** That is, the Euphrates [b]**18** Some Septuagint manuscripts (see also 1 Chron. 19:18); Hebrew *horsemen*

Eliam and the wife of Uriah the Hittite?" 4 Then David sent messengers to get her. She came to him, and he slept with her. (She had purified herself from her uncleanness.) Then[a] she went back home. 5 The woman conceived and sent word to David, saying, "I am pregnant."

6 So David sent this word to Joab: "Send me Uriah the Hittite." And Joab sent him to David. 7 When Uriah came to him, David asked him how Joab was, how the soldiers were and how the war was going. 8 Then David said to Uriah, "Go down to your house and wash your feet." So Uriah left the palace, and a gift from the king was sent after him. 9 But Uriah slept at the entrance to the palace with all his master's servants and did not go down to his house.

10 When David was told, "Uriah did not go home," he asked him, "Haven't you just come from a distance? Why didn't you go home?"

11 Uriah said to David, "The ark and Israel and Judah are staying in tents, and my master Joab and my lord's men are camped in the open fields. How could I go to my house to eat and drink and lie with my wife? As surely as you live, I will not do such a thing!"

12 Then David said to him, "Stay here one more day, and tomorrow I will send you back." So Uriah remained in Jerusalem that day and the next. 13 At David's invitation, he ate and drank with him, and David made him drunk. But in the evening Uriah went out to sleep on his mat among his master's servants; he did not go home.

14 In the morning David wrote a letter to Joab and sent it with Uriah. 15 In it he wrote, "Put Uriah in the front line where the fighting is fiercest. Then withdraw from him so he will be struck down and die."

16 So while Joab had the city under siege, he put Uriah at a place where he knew the strongest defenders were. 17 When the men of the city came out and fought against Joab, some of the men in David's army fell; moreover, Uriah the Hittite died.

18 Joab sent David a full account of the battle. 19 He instructed the messenger: "When you have finished giving the king this account of the battle, 20 the king's anger may flare up, and he may ask you, 'Why did you get so close to the city to fight? Didn't you know they would shoot arrows from the wall? 21 Who killed Abimelech son of Jerub-Besheth[b]? Didn't a woman throw an upper millstone on him from the wall, so that he died in Thebez? Why did you get so close to the wall?' If he asks you this, then say to him, 'Also, your servant Uriah the Hittite is dead.' "

22 The messenger set out, and when he arrived he told David

[a]4 Or *with her. When she purified herself from her uncleanness,* [b]21 Also known as *Jerub-Baal* (that is, Gideon)

11:3 *Uriah the Hittite:* The Hittites came from what is now modern Turkey, and once controlled much of the ancient Near East (see the map on p. 2462). Some Hittites settled in areas that later belonged to the Israelites (Gen 23:3; Num 13:29; Josh 1:4). The few who remained by David's time had joined the Israelite community and taken Hebrew names, with "the Hittite" added to the end.

11:4 *purified herself from her uncleanness:* Most likely Bathsheba had just completed the purification rites following menstruation (Lev 15:19-30). This statement makes it clear that she was not already pregnant by her husband when she slept with David.

11:11 *The ark . . . staying in tents:* The ark of the covenant held the two stone tablets with the Ten Commandments written on them. See the note at 6:2,3 and the mini-article called "The Ark of the Covenant," p. 513. Even though David had brought the ark of the covenant to Jerusalem (6:2-19), it was apparently still taken by the Israelites into battle so that the LORD would be with the people and help them defeat their enemies.

11:11 *lie with my wife . . . not do such a thing:* Soldiers were not allowed to have sexual intercourse before battle. That would make them unclean and not fit to fight for the LORD. See 1 Sam 21:4,5. Uriah showed far more integrity and self-control than David did.

11:14,15 *David wrote a letter to Joab . . . so he will be struck down and die:* Many readers have wondered why David would allow Uriah to deliver a letter that contained his own death sentence. Perhaps Uriah could not read or perhaps David counted on Uriah being too honest to unseal and read the letter. In any case, this action is an indication of the extent of David's spiritual blindness and sinful lust.

11:21 Judg 9:53.

David and Bathsheba by Gui-jie Zhang, around 1990. When David's army was at war with the Ammonites, David stayed behind in Jerusalem. One afternoon he saw Bathsheba bathing in her courtyard and had her brought to his palace so that he could sleep with her. When she became pregnant, David arranged to have her husband sent to the front line of the battle so that he would be killed. After Uriah died, David married Bathsheba, and they had a son. But the LORD was unhappy with what David had done. The prophet Nathan brought David the LORD's message: "The sword will never depart from your house, because you despised me." (See 11:1—12:15.)

everything Joab had sent him to say. 23The messenger said to
David, "The men overpowered us and came out against us in the
open, but we drove them back to the entrance to the city gate.
24Then the archers shot arrows at your servants from the wall, and
some of the king's men died. Moreover, your servant Uriah the
Hittite is dead."

25David told the messenger, "Say this to Joab: 'Don't let this
upset you; the sword devours one as well as another. Press the
attack against the city and destroy it.' Say this to encourage Joab."

26When Uriah's wife heard that her husband was dead, she
mourned for him. 27After the time of mourning was over, David
had her brought to his house, and she became his wife and bore
him a son. But the thing David had done displeased the LORD.

11:20 *shoot arrows from the wall:* Many cities were surrounded by walls thick enough to be walked on and with narrow windows through which soldiers could shoot at an enemy. See also the note at 3:27.

11:27 *time of mourning:* The usual amount of time allowed for mourning is seven days (Gen 50:10).

Nathan Rebukes David

12 The LORD sent Nathan to David. When he came to him, he
said, "There were two men in a certain town, one rich and the
other poor. 2The rich man had a very large number of sheep and
cattle, 3but the poor man had nothing except one little ewe lamb
he had bought. He raised it, and it grew up with him and his children. It shared his food, drank from his cup and even slept in his
arms. It was like a daughter to him.

12:1 *Nathan:* See the note at 7:2,3. See also Psalm 51 for David's prayer for forgiveness for disobeying the LORD.

12:6 *four times over:* God's Law required this payment (Exod 22:1).

12:10,11 *bring calamity . . . lie with your wives:* Three of David's sons would die violently: Amnon (13:28,29), Absalom (18:14), and Adonijah (1 Kgs 2:25); and one of these sons, Absalom, would steal David's throne (15:1-15) and sleep openly with David's wives (16:22).

12:16 *fasted:* Going without food was a way of showing grief and sorrow.

4"Now a traveler came to the rich man, but the rich man
refrained from taking one of his own sheep or cattle to prepare a
meal for the traveler who had come to him. Instead, he took the
ewe lamb that belonged to the poor man and prepared it for the
one who had come to him."

5David burned with anger against the man and said to
Nathan, "As surely as the LORD lives, the man who did this deserves
to die! 6He must pay for that lamb four times over, because he did
such a thing and had no pity."

7Then Nathan said to David, "You are the man! This is what
the LORD, the God of Israel, says: 'I anointed you king over Israel,
and I delivered you from the hand of Saul. 8I gave your master's
house to you, and your master's wives into your arms. I gave you
the house of Israel and Judah. And if all this had been too little, I
would have given you even more. 9Why did you despise the word
of the LORD by doing what is evil in his eyes? You struck down
Uriah the Hittite with the sword and took his wife to be your own.
You killed him with the sword of the Ammonites. 10Now, therefore,
the sword will never depart from your house, because you despised
me and took the wife of Uriah the Hittite to be your own.'

11"This is what the LORD says: 'Out of your own household I
am going to bring calamity upon you. Before your very eyes I will
take your wives and give them to one who is close to you, and he
will lie with your wives in broad daylight. 12You did it in secret, but
I will do this thing in broad daylight before all Israel.' "

13Then David said to Nathan, "I have sinned against the LORD."

Nathan replied, "The LORD has taken away your sin. You are
not going to die. 14But because by doing this you have made the
enemies of the LORD show utter contempt,[a] the son born to you
will die."

15After Nathan had gone home, the LORD struck the child
that Uriah's wife had borne to David, and he became ill. 16David
pleaded with God for the child. He fasted and went into his house
and spent the nights lying on the ground. 17The elders of his
household stood beside him to get him up from the ground, but
he refused, and he would not eat any food with them.

18On the seventh day the child died. David's servants were
afraid to tell him that the child was dead, for they thought, "While
the child was still living, we spoke to David but he would not listen to us. How can we tell him the child is dead? He may do something desperate."

19David noticed that his servants were whispering among
themselves and he realized the child was dead. "Is the child dead?"
he asked.

"Yes," they replied, "he is dead."

---

[a]**14** Masoretic Text; an ancient Hebrew scribal tradition *this you have shown utter contempt for the LORD*

20 Then David got up from the ground. After he had washed,
put on lotions and changed his clothes, he went into the house of
the LORD and worshiped. Then he went to his own house, and at
his request they served him food, and he ate.
21 His servants asked him, "Why are you acting this way?
While the child was alive, you fasted and wept, but now that the
child is dead, you get up and eat!"
22 He answered, "While the child was still alive, I fasted and
wept. I thought, 'Who knows? The LORD may be gracious to me
and let the child live.' 23 But now that he is dead, why should I fast?
Can I bring him back again? I will go to him, but he will not
return to me."
24 Then David comforted his wife Bathsheba, and he went to
her and lay with her. She gave birth to a son, and they named him
Solomon. The LORD loved him; 25 and because the LORD loved him,
he sent word through Nathan the prophet to name him Jedidiah.[a]
26 Meanwhile Joab fought against Rabbah of the Ammonites
and captured the royal citadel. 27 Joab then sent messengers to David,
saying, "I have fought against Rabbah and taken its water supply.
28 Now muster the rest of the troops and besiege the city and capture
it. Otherwise I will take the city, and it will be named after me."
29 So David mustered the entire army and went to Rabbah,
and attacked and captured it. 30 He took the crown from the head
of their king[b]—its weight was a talent[c] of gold, and it was set with
precious stones—and it was placed on David's head. He took a
great quantity of plunder from the city 31 and brought out the people who were there, consigning them to labor with saws and with
iron picks and axes, and he made them work at brickmaking.[d] He
did this to all the Ammonite towns. Then David and his entire
army returned to Jerusalem.

VIOLENCE TEARS DAVID'S FAMILY APART

Amnon and Tamar

13 In the course of time, Amnon son of David fell in love with
Tamar, the beautiful sister of Absalom son of David.
2 Amnon became frustrated to the point of illness on account
of his sister Tamar, for she was a virgin, and it seemed impossible
for him to do anything to her.
3 Now Amnon had a friend named Jonadab son of Shimeah,
David's brother. Jonadab was a very shrewd man. 4 He asked
Amnon, "Why do you, the king's son, look so haggard morning
after morning? Won't you tell me?"

---

[a]25 *Jedidiah* means *loved by the LORD.* [b]30 Or *of Milcom* (that is, Molech)
[c]30 That is, about 75 pounds (about 34 kilograms) [d]31 The meaning of the
Hebrew for this clause is uncertain.

Bathsheba . . . gave birth to a son, and they named him Solomon.
2 Sam 12:24

12:23 *I will go to him:* David was speaking of the world of the dead, or *Sheol,* described as a place under the earth where people went after they died, never to return (Job 7:9, 10). See also the mini-article called "Hell," p. 1944.

12:25 *Jedidiah:* In Hebrew this name means "Beloved of the LORD."

12:27 *taken its water supply:* Water was necessary to a city's survival and so its supply source was carefully guarded. See 5:8.

12:31 *consigning them to labor:* When towns were captured, often the people who lived there were made slaves.

13:1 *Amnon . . . Tamar . . . Absalom:* See 3:2-5 for a list of David's sons who were born in Hebron. Absalom and Tamar's mother was Maacah and Amnon's mother was Ahinoam. Amnon was David's oldest son and heir to the throne. Absalom was next in line to the throne. David's second son, Kileab, probably died young as he is only mentioned once in the Bible.

Amnon said to him, "I'm in love with Tamar, my brother Absalom's sister."

5"Go to bed and pretend to be ill," Jonadab said. "When your father comes to see you, say to him, 'I would like my sister Tamar to come and give me something to eat. Let her prepare the food in my sight so I may watch her and then eat it from her hand.' "

6So Amnon lay down and pretended to be ill. When the king came to see him, Amnon said to him, "I would like my sister Tamar to come and make some special bread in my sight, so I may eat from her hand."

7David sent word to Tamar at the palace: "Go to the house of your brother Amnon and prepare some food for him." 8So Tamar went to the house of her brother Amnon, who was lying down. She took some dough, kneaded it, made the bread in his sight and baked it. 9Then she took the pan and served him the bread, but he refused to eat.

"Send everyone out of here," Amnon said. So everyone left him. 10Then Amnon said to Tamar, "Bring the food here into my bedroom so I may eat from your hand." And Tamar took the bread she had prepared and brought it to her brother Amnon in his bedroom. 11But when she took it to him to eat, he grabbed her and said, "Come to bed with me, my sister."

12"Don't, my brother!" she said to him. "Don't force me. Such a thing should not be done in Israel! Don't do this wicked thing. 13What about me? Where could I get rid of my disgrace? And what about you? You would be like one of the wicked fools in Israel. Please speak to the king; he will not keep me from being married to you." 14But he refused to listen to her, and since he was stronger than she, he raped her.

15Then Amnon hated her with intense hatred. In fact, he hated her more than he had loved her. Amnon said to her, "Get up and get out!"

16"No!" she said to him. "Sending me away would be a greater wrong than what you have already done to me."

But he refused to listen to her. 17He called his personal servant and said, "Get this woman out of here and bolt the door after her." 18So his servant put her out and bolted the door after her. She was wearing a richly ornamented[a] robe, for this was the kind of garment the virgin daughters of the king wore. 19Tamar put ashes on her head and tore the ornamented[b] robe she was wearing. She put her hand on her head and went away, weeping aloud as she went.

20Her brother Absalom said to her, "Has that Amnon, your brother, been with you? Be quiet now, my sister; he is your brother. Don't take this thing to heart." And Tamar lived in her brother Absalom's house, a desolate woman.

13:12,13 *wicked thing:* Tamar was not just talking about rape. Men were not permitted to have sex with a half-sister (Lev 18:9; Deut 27:22). Also, women were expected to stay virgins until their wedding night (Deut 22:13-21). This would have been especially important for a king's daughter (princess) who would not have been able to find a suitable husband from another royal family if she were not a virgin.

13:18,19 *kind of garment the virgin daughters of the king wore . . . weeping aloud:* Tamar's robe identified her both as royalty and as a virgin. Tamar tore her robe, wore ashes, covered her face, and cried because she was twice shamed—raped by her half-brother, and no longer a virgin. See also the note at 1:2.

a18 The meaning of the Hebrew for this phrase is uncertain. **b19** The meaning of the Hebrew for this word is uncertain.

21When King David heard all this, he was furious. 22Absalom
never said a word to Amnon, either good or bad; he hated Amnon
because he had disgraced his sister Tamar.

Absalom Kills Amnon

23Two years later, when Absalom's sheepshearers were at Baal
Hazor near the border of Ephraim, he invited all the king's sons to
come there. 24Absalom went to the king and said, "Your servant has
had shearers come. Will the king and his officials please join me?"
25"No, my son," the king replied. "All of us should not go; we
would only be a burden to you." Although Absalom urged him, he
still refused to go, but gave him his blessing.
26Then Absalom said, "If not, please let my brother Amnon
come with us."
The king asked him, "Why should he go with you?" 27But
Absalom urged him, so he sent with him Amnon and the rest of
the king's sons.
28Absalom ordered his men, "Listen! When Amnon is in high
spirits from drinking wine and I say to you, 'Strike Amnon down,'
then kill him. Don't be afraid. Have not I given you this order? Be
strong and brave." 29So Absalom's men did to Amnon what Absalom had ordered. Then all the king's sons got up, mounted their
mules and fled.
30While they were on their way, the report came to David:
"Absalom has struck down all the king's sons; not one of them is
left." 31The king stood up, tore his clothes and lay down on the
ground; and all his servants stood by with their clothes torn.
32But Jonadab son of Shimeah, David's brother, said, "My
lord should not think that they killed all the princes; only Amnon
is dead. This has been Absalom's expressed intention ever since the
day Amnon raped his sister Tamar. 33My lord the king should not
be concerned about the report that all the king's sons are dead.
Only Amnon is dead."
34Meanwhile, Absalom had fled.
Now the man standing watch looked up and saw many people on the road west of him, coming down the side of the hill. The
watchman went and told the king, "I see men in the direction of
Horonaim, on the side of the hill."[a]
35Jonadab said to the king, "See, the king's sons are here; it
has happened just as your servant said."
36As he finished speaking, the king's sons came in, wailing
loudly. The king, too, and all his servants wept very bitterly.
37Absalom fled and went to Talmai son of Ammihud, the
king of Geshur. But King David mourned for his son every day.
38After Absalom fled and went to Geshur, he stayed there

[a]**34** Septuagint; Hebrew does not have this sentence.

13:23 *invited all the king's sons:* Shearing the sheep was a time for celebrating as well as working (1 Sam 25:2-8). See also the mini-article called "Shepherds," p. 1972.

13:29 *mules:* Mules are a cross between a mare (female horse) and a male donkey. Since cross-breeding was forbidden by the Law (Lev 19:19), the king's sons' mules were probably acquired from some other nation. At this time, mules seem to have been used mainly by royalty (1 Kgs 1:33), and horses mostly in warfare.

13:31 *tore his clothes:* See the note at 1:2.

13:37,38 *Geshur:* A region east of the Sea of Galilee. See the map on p. 2465.

13:37,38 *Talmai:* Absalom's grandfather (see 3:2-5).

13:37,38 2 Sam 3:2-5.

14:1 *Joab:* See the note at 2:13 (Joab).

14:2 *wise woman:* A woman who is skilled at making an argument. See 20:16-22 for the story about what a wise woman did to save her city.

14:2 *Tekoa:* Tekoa was a few miles south of Bethlehem. Two centuries later this town would be the home of the prophet Amos (Amos 1:1).

14:3 *Joab put the words in her mouth:* Joab used the woman and a made-up story to help David see his own situation more clearly. Nathan had also used a story to confront David about Bathsheba (12:1-15).

14:7 *Hand over the one who struck his brother down . . . leaving . . . neither name nor descendant:* God's Law allowed a murder victim's closest relatives to put the murderer to death (Deut 19:12). But the Law also recognized the importance of continuing a family line (Deut 25:5-10). David was being asked to decide between these two competing concepts.

three years. 39 And the spirit of the king[a] longed to go to Absalom, for he was consoled concerning Amnon's death.

Absalom Returns to Jerusalem

14 Joab son of Zeruiah knew that the king's heart longed for Absalom. 2 So Joab sent someone to Tekoa and had a wise woman brought from there. He said to her, "Pretend you are in mourning. Dress in mourning clothes, and don't use any cosmetic lotions. Act like a woman who has spent many days grieving for the dead. 3 Then go to the king and speak these words to him." And Joab put the words in her mouth.

4 When the woman from Tekoa went[b] to the king, she fell with her face to the ground to pay him honor, and she said, "Help me, O king!"

5 The king asked her, "What is troubling you?"

She said, "I am indeed a widow; my husband is dead. 6 I your servant had two sons. They got into a fight with each other in the field, and no one was there to separate them. One struck the other and killed him. 7 Now the whole clan has risen up against your servant; they say, 'Hand over the one who struck his brother down, so that we may put him to death for the life of his brother whom he killed; then we will get rid of the heir as well.' They would put out the only burning coal I have left, leaving my husband neither name nor descendant on the face of the earth."

8 The king said to the woman, "Go home, and I will issue an order in your behalf."

9 But the woman from Tekoa said to him, "My lord the king, let the blame rest on me and on my father's family, and let the king and his throne be without guilt."

10 The king replied, "If anyone says anything to you, bring him to me, and he will not bother you again."

11 She said, "Then let the king invoke the LORD his God to prevent the avenger of blood from adding to the destruction, so that my son will not be destroyed."

"As surely as the LORD lives," he said, "not one hair of your son's head will fall to the ground."

12 Then the woman said, "Let your servant speak a word to my lord the king."

"Speak," he replied.

13 The woman said, "Why then have you devised a thing like this against the people of God? When the king says this, does he not convict himself, for the king has not brought back his banished son? 14 Like water spilled on the ground, which cannot be recovered, so we must die. But God does not take away life;

---

[a]**39** Dead Sea Scrolls and some Septuagint manuscripts; Masoretic Text *But* ⌞*the spirit of*⌟ *David the king* [b]**4** Many Hebrew manuscripts, Septuagint, Vulgate and Syriac; most Hebrew manuscripts *spoke*

instead, he devises ways so that a banished person may not remain
estranged from him.
15“And now I have come to say this to my lord the king
because the people have made me afraid. Your servant thought, ‘I
will speak to the king; perhaps he will do what his servant asks.
16Perhaps the king will agree to deliver his servant from the hand
of the man who is trying to cut off both me and my son from the
inheritance God gave us.’
17“And now your servant says, ‘May the word of my lord the
king bring me rest, for my lord the king is like an angel of God in
discerning good and evil. May the LORD your God be with you.’ ”
18Then the king said to the woman, “Do not keep from me
the answer to what I am going to ask you.”
“Let my lord the king speak,” the woman said.
19The king asked, “Isn’t the hand of Joab with you in all this?”
The woman answered, “As surely as you live, my lord the
king, no one can turn to the right or to the left from anything my
lord the king says. Yes, it was your servant Joab who instructed me
to do this and who put all these words into the mouth of your
servant. 20Your servant Joab did this to change the present situation. My lord has wisdom like that of an angel of God—he knows
everything that happens in the land.”
21The king said to Joab, “Very well, I will do it. Go, bring
back the young man Absalom.”
22Joab fell with his face to the ground to pay him honor, and
he blessed the king. Joab said, “Today your servant knows that he
has found favor in your eyes, my lord the king, because the king
has granted his servant’s request.”
23Then Joab went to Geshur and brought Absalom back to
Jerusalem. 24But the king said, “He must go to his own house; he
must not see my face.” So Absalom went to his own house and did
not see the face of the king.
25In all Israel there was not a man so highly praised for his
handsome appearance as Absalom. From the top of his head to the
sole of his foot there was no blemish in him. 26Whenever he cut
the hair of his head—he used to cut his hair from time to time
when it became too heavy for him—he would weigh it, and its
weight was two hundred shekels[a] by the royal standard.
27Three sons and a daughter were born to Absalom. The
daughter’s name was Tamar, and she became a beautiful woman.
28Absalom lived two years in Jerusalem without seeing the
king’s face. 29Then Absalom sent for Joab in order to send him to
the king, but Joab refused to come to him. So he sent a second
time, but he refused to come. 30Then he said to his servants, “Look,
Joab’s field is next to mine, and he has barley there. Go and set it
on fire.” So Absalom’s servants set the field on fire.

In all Israel there was not a man so highly praised for his handsome appearance as Absalom. From the top of his head to the sole of his foot there was no blemish in him.
2 Sam 14:25

14:26 *hair . . . weight was two hundred shekels:* Or about five pounds. Thick, heavy hair was considered beautiful.

14:17 2 Sam 19:27.

[a]**26** That is, about 5 pounds (about 2.3 kilograms)

15:1 *chariot and horses . . . fifty men:* See the notes at 8:4 and 13:29. The fifty men may have been bodyguards (see the note at 8:18). Absalom is surrounding himself with the trappings of royalty.

15:4 *judge in the land . . . justice:* Absalom seems to be exploiting a weakness in David's rule. A king was expected to resolve disputes that lesser officials could not (see 1 Kgs 4:16-28). The Law of Moses set a very high standard of justice. See also the mini-article called "Justice," p. 1721.

15:7 *fulfill a vow:* Spoken vows were taken very seriously in most ancient cultures. See, for instance, 1 Sam 14:24-45 and the mini-article called "Making Vows," p. 328.

15:8 *Geshur in Aram . . . Hebron:* See the notes at 13:37,38 (Geshur) and 2:1,2.

15:10-12 2 Sam 12:11.

31 Then Joab did go to Absalom's house and he said to him,
"Why have your servants set my field on fire?"
32 Absalom said to Joab, "Look, I sent word to you and said,
'Come here so I can send you to the king to ask, "Why have I come
from Geshur? It would be better for me if I were still there!"' Now
then, I want to see the king's face, and if I am guilty of anything,
let him put me to death."
33 So Joab went to the king and told him this. Then the king
summoned Absalom, and he came in and bowed down with his
face to the ground before the king. And the king kissed Absalom.

ABSALOM CHALLENGES HIS FATHER

David's son Absalom tries to undermine David by winning the favor of the northern tribes, and David is soon forced to flee from Jerusalem. When war breaks out between the soldiers of Absalom and David in the forest of Ephraim, Absalom is killed against the king's wishes by David's commander, Joab. David mourns the death of his son, but eventually returns to Jerusalem and tries to reunite Israel and Judah.

Absalom's Conspiracy

15 In the course of time, Absalom provided himself with a chariot and horses and with fifty men to run ahead of him. 2 He would
get up early and stand by the side of the road leading to the city
gate. Whenever anyone came with a complaint to be placed before
the king for a decision, Absalom would call out to him, "What
town are you from?" He would answer, "Your servant is from one
of the tribes of Israel." 3 Then Absalom would say to him, "Look,
your claims are valid and proper, but there is no representative of
the king to hear you." 4 And Absalom would add, "If only I were
appointed judge in the land! Then everyone who has a complaint
or case could come to me and I would see that he gets justice."
5 Also, whenever anyone approached him to bow down before
him, Absalom would reach out his hand, take hold of him and kiss
him. 6 Absalom behaved in this way toward all the Israelites who
came to the king asking for justice, and so he stole the hearts of the
men of Israel.
7 At the end of four[a] years, Absalom said to the king, "Let me
go to Hebron and fulfill a vow I made to the LORD. 8 While your
servant was living at Geshur in Aram, I made this vow: 'If the LORD
takes me back to Jerusalem, I will worship the LORD in Hebron.[b]'"
9 The king said to him, "Go in peace." So he went to Hebron.
10 Then Absalom sent secret messengers throughout the
tribes of Israel to say, "As soon as you hear the sound of the trumpets, then say, 'Absalom is king in Hebron.'" 11 Two hundred men

---

[a]7 Some Septuagint manuscripts, Syriac and Josephus; Hebrew *forty* [b]8 Some Septuagint manuscripts; Hebrew does not have *in Hebron.*

from Jerusalem had accompanied Absalom. They had been invited
as guests and went quite innocently, knowing nothing about the
matter. 12While Absalom was offering sacrifices, he also sent for
Ahithophel the Gilonite, David's counselor, to come from Giloh,
his hometown. And so the conspiracy gained strength, and Absalom's following kept on increasing.

David Flees

13A messenger came and told David, "The hearts of the men
of Israel are with Absalom."
14Then David said to all his officials who were with him in
Jerusalem, "Come! We must flee, or none of us will escape from
Absalom. We must leave immediately, or he will move quickly to
overtake us and bring ruin upon us and put the city to the sword."
15The king's officials answered him, "Your servants are ready
to do whatever our lord the king chooses."
16The king set out, with his entire household following him;
but he left ten concubines to take care of the palace. 17So the king
set out, with all the people following him, and they halted at a place
some distance away. 18All his men marched past him, along with all
the Kerethites and Pelethites; and all the six hundred Gittites who
had accompanied him from Gath marched before the king.
19The king said to Ittai the Gittite, "Why should you come
along with us? Go back and stay with King Absalom. You are a foreigner, an exile from your homeland. 20You came only yesterday.
And today shall I make you wander about with us, when I do not
know where I am going? Go back, and take your countrymen. May
kindness and faithfulness be with you."
21But Ittai replied to the king, "As surely as the LORD lives,
and as my lord the king lives, wherever my lord the king may be,
whether it means life or death, there will your servant be."
22David said to Ittai, "Go ahead, march on." So Ittai the Gittite
marched on with all his men and the families that were with him.
23The whole countryside wept aloud as all the people passed
by. The king also crossed the Kidron Valley, and all the people
moved on toward the desert.
24Zadok was there, too, and all the Levites who were with
him were carrying the ark of the covenant of God. They set down
the ark of God, and Abiathar offered sacrifices[a] until all the people
had finished leaving the city.
25Then the king said to Zadok, "Take the ark of God back
into the city. If I find favor in the LORD's eyes, he will bring me
back and let me see it and his dwelling place again. 26But if he says,
'I am not pleased with you,' then I am ready; let him do to me
whatever seems good to him."

15:12 *Ahithophel:* It is not clear why one of David's advisers would join with Absalom, especially when Ahithophel's son Eliam was one of David's top warriors (23:34). But Bathsheba's husband, Uriah the Hittite, was also one of David's top warriors, and her father was named Eliam. If Ahithopel was Bathsheba's grandfather, that would explain why he wanted revenge against David (chapter 11).

15:16. *concubines:* See the note at 3:7.

15:18 *Kerethites and Pelethites; and all the six hundred Gittites . . . from Gath:* See the note at 8:18 (Kerethites and Pelethites). The six hundred soldiers were the Philistine soldiers who were loyal to David.

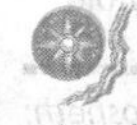

15:23 *Kidron Valley:* This was the eastern boundary of Jerusalem (John 18:1).

15:24 *Zadok . . . Abiathar:* Zadok, previously mentioned in 8:17, would continue to be loyal to David. Abiathar was David's priest and close friend (1 Sam 22:18-22; 23:9). Later, David would choose Zadok over Abiathar to assist Nathan in making Solomon the next king (1 Kgs 1:32-35, 44,45).

15:24 *ark of the covenant:* See the note at 11:11 (the ark).

15:25 *Take the ark of God back into the city:* The ark of the covenant was God's throne on earth, but as the Philistines found out, possessing it did not guarantee victory (see 1 Sam 4:3-11; 5:11—6:3). David knew that the ark of the covenant belonged with God's people in Jerusalem.

[a]**24** Or *Abiathar went up*

[27]The king also said to Zadok the priest, "Aren't you a seer?
Go back to the city in peace, with your son Ahimaaz and Jonathan
son of Abiathar. You and Abiathar take your two sons with you. [28]I
will wait at the fords in the desert until word comes from you to
inform me." [29]So Zadok and Abiathar took the ark of God back to
Jerusalem and stayed there.

[30]But David continued up the Mount of Olives, weeping as
he went; his head was covered and he was barefoot. All the people
with him covered their heads too and were weeping as they went
up. [31]Now David had been told, "Ahithophel is among the con-
spirators with Absalom." So David prayed, "O LORD, turn
Ahithophel's counsel into foolishness."

[32]When David arrived at the summit, where people used to
worship God, Hushai the Arkite was there to meet him, his robe
torn and dust on his head. [33]David said to him, "If you go with me,
you will be a burden to me. [34]But if you return to the city and say
to Absalom, 'I will be your servant, O king; I was your father's
servant in the past, but now I will be your servant,' then you can
help me by frustrating Ahithophel's advice. [35]Won't the priests
Zadok and Abiathar be there with you? Tell them anything you
hear in the king's palace. [36]Their two sons, Ahimaaz son of Zadok
and Jonathan son of Abiathar, are there with them. Send them to
me with anything you hear."

[37]So David's friend Hushai arrived at Jerusalem as Absalom
was entering the city.

David and Ziba

16 When David had gone a short distance beyond the summit,
there was Ziba, the steward of Mephibosheth, waiting to meet him.
He had a string of donkeys saddled and loaded with two hundred
loaves of bread, a hundred cakes of raisins, a hundred cakes of figs
and a skin of wine.

[2]The king asked Ziba, "Why have you brought these?"

Ziba answered, "The donkeys are for the king's household to
ride on, the bread and fruit are for the men to eat, and the wine is
to refresh those who become exhausted in the desert."

[3]The king then asked, "Where is your master's grandson?"

Ziba said to him, "He is staying in Jerusalem, because he
thinks, 'Today the house of Israel will give me back my grandfather's kingdom.'"

[4]Then the king said to Ziba, "All that belonged to Mephibosheth is now yours."

"I humbly bow," Ziba said. "May I find favor in your eyes,
my lord the king."

Shimei Curses David

[5]As King David approached Bahurim, a man from the same
clan as Saul's family came out from there. His name was Shimei

15:30 *Mount of Olives:* A high hill just east of Jerusalem, across the Kidron Valley. Its peak is taller than the highest part of Jerusalem and so this Mount sometimes served as Jerusalem's "watchtower." See also Matt 24:3; Mark 14:26; Luke 19:29; John 8:1.

15:30 *head was covered . . . barefoot:* See the note at 1:2.

15:32 *Hushai the Arkite:* Hushai was one of David's advisers. The Arkites were part of the tribe of Benjamin (Josh 16:1-4). See also the note at 3:17-19.

15:32 *robe torn and dust on his head:* See the note at 1:2.

15:33 *you will be a burden:* Hushai was probably very old.

16:1-4 *Ziba . . . Mephibosheth:* Ziba had been a servant of Saul's family (9:9). Mephibosheth was Saul's grandson and Jonathan's son. David returned Saul's property to Mephibosheth and treated him like a son (9:10-13) because of a promise he had made to Jonathan (1 Sam 20:14, 15). To hear Mephibosheth's side of the story, see 19:24-30.

16:5 *Bahurim:* Located on the road from Jerusalem to Jericho, not far from the Mount of Olives.

16:5-14 *Saul's family . . . Shimei:* For more about how David and his son Solomon ultimately responded to Shimei, see 2 Samuel 19:16-23 and 1 Kings 2:8,9,36-46.

16:1 2 Sam 9:9, 10. **16:3** 2 Sam 19:25-27.

son of Gera, and he cursed as he came out. [6]He pelted David and all the king's officials with stones, though all the troops and the special guard were on David's right and left. [7]As he cursed, Shimei said, "Get out, get out, you man of blood, you scoundrel! [8]The LORD has repaid you for all the blood you shed in the household of Saul, in whose place you have reigned. The LORD has handed the kingdom over to your son Absalom. You have come to ruin because you are a man of blood!"

[9]Then Abishai son of Zeruiah said to the king, "Why should this dead dog curse my lord the king? Let me go over and cut off his head."

[10]But the king said, "What do you and I have in common, you sons of Zeruiah? If he is cursing because the LORD said to him, 'Curse David,' who can ask, 'Why do you do this?' "

[11]David then said to Abishai and all his officials, "My son, who is of my own flesh, is trying to take my life. How much more, then, this Benjamite! Leave him alone; let him curse, for the LORD has told him to. [12]It may be that the LORD will see my distress and repay me with good for the cursing I am receiving today."

[13]So David and his men continued along the road while Shimei was going along the hillside opposite him, cursing as he went and throwing stones at him and showering him with dirt. [14]The king and all the people with him arrived at their destination exhausted. And there he refreshed himself.

The Advice of Hushai and Ahithophel

[15]Meanwhile, Absalom and all the men of Israel came to Jerusalem, and Ahithophel was with him. [16]Then Hushai the Arkite, David's friend, went to Absalom and said to him, "Long live the king! Long live the king!"

[17]Absalom asked Hushai, "Is this the love you show your friend? Why didn't you go with your friend?"

[18]Hushai said to Absalom, "No, the one chosen by the LORD, by these people, and by all the men of Israel—his I will be, and I will remain with him. [19]Furthermore, whom should I serve? Should I not serve the son? Just as I served your father, so I will serve you."

[20]Absalom said to Ahithophel, "Give us your advice. What should we do?"

[21]Ahithophel answered, "Lie with your father's concubines whom he left to take care of the palace. Then all Israel will hear that you have made yourself a stench in your father's nostrils, and the hands of everyone with you will be strengthened." [22]So they pitched a tent for Absalom on the roof, and he lay with his father's concubines in the sight of all Israel.

[23]Now in those days the advice Ahithophel gave was like that of one who inquires of God. That was how both David and Absalom regarded all of Ahithophel's advice.

16:21,22 *father's concubines:* For "concubines," see the note at 3:7. Nathan had told David that another man would openly have sex with David's wives (12:11, 12). This prophecy was now being fulfilled.

16:22 *tent:* This was a wedding tent in which a bride and groom would spend their first night together.

17:3 *death of the man you seek:* Ahithophel's advice that Absalom kill only David seemed good, because Ahithophel knew that the nation was divided in its loyalties between David and Absalom. If, however, a civil war broke out it would be difficult for either side to win, and the victor would still not have the loyalty of all the people.

17:14 *the LORD had determined:* As good as Ahithophel's advice was perceived to be, it still did not come from God (16:23). David was still God's chosen king and it would be wrong for anyone to kill him. For earlier examples of how God helped David and approved of him as a leader, see 7:1; 8:6,14.

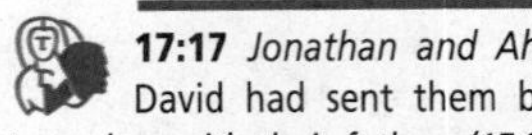

17:17 *Jonathan and Ahimaaz:* David had sent them back to Jerusalem with their fathers (15:27).

17:17 *En Rogel:* En Rogel was a spring south of Jerusalem in the Kidron Valley on the border between lands belonging to the tribe of Judah and the tribe of Benjamin. See the map on p. 2466.

17:17 *servant girl:* Using a servant girl as a messenger would arouse little suspicion, because they were the ones who usually went for water.

17 Ahithophel said to Absalom, "I would[a] choose twelve thousand
men and set out tonight in pursuit of David. 2 I would[b] attack him
while he is weary and weak. I would[b] strike him with terror, and then
all the people with him will flee. I would[b] strike down only the king
3 and bring all the people back to you. The death of the man you seek
will mean the return of all; all the people will be unharmed." 4 This
plan seemed good to Absalom and to all the elders of Israel.

5 But Absalom said, "Summon also Hushai the Arkite, so we
can hear what he has to say." 6 When Hushai came to him, Absalom said, "Ahithophel has given this advice. Should we do what he
says? If not, give us your opinion."

7 Hushai replied to Absalom, "The advice Ahithophel has
given is not good this time. 8 You know your father and his men;
they are fighters, and as fierce as a wild bear robbed of her cubs.
Besides, your father is an experienced fighter; he will not spend the
night with the troops. 9 Even now, he is hidden in a cave or some
other place. If he should attack your troops first,[c] whoever hears
about it will say, 'There has been a slaughter among the troops
who follow Absalom.' 10 Then even the bravest soldier, whose heart
is like the heart of a lion, will melt with fear, for all Israel knows
that your father is a fighter and that those with him are brave.

11 "So I advise you: Let all Israel, from Dan to Beersheba—as
numerous as the sand on the seashore—be gathered to you, with
you yourself leading them into battle. 12 Then we will attack him
wherever he may be found, and we will fall on him as dew settles
on the ground. Neither he nor any of his men will be left alive. 13 If
he withdraws into a city, then all Israel will bring ropes to that city,
and we will drag it down to the valley until not even a piece of it
can be found."

14 Absalom and all the men of Israel said, "The advice of
Hushai the Arkite is better than that of Ahithophel." For the LORD
had determined to frustrate the good advice of Ahithophel in
order to bring disaster on Absalom.

15 Hushai told Zadok and Abiathar, the priests, "Ahithophel
has advised Absalom and the elders of Israel to do such and such,
but I have advised them to do so and so. 16 Now send a message
immediately and tell David, 'Do not spend the night at the fords in
the desert; cross over without fail, or the king and all the people
with him will be swallowed up.' "

17 Jonathan and Ahimaaz were staying at En Rogel. A servant
girl was to go and inform them, and they were to go and tell King
David, for they could not risk being seen entering the city. 18 But a
young man saw them and told Absalom. So the two of them left
quickly and went to the house of a man in Bahurim. He had a well
in his courtyard, and they climbed down into it. 19 His wife took a

[a]1 Or *Let me* [b]2 Or *will* [c]9 Or *When some of the men fall at the first attack*

covering and spread it out over the opening of the well and scattered grain over it. No one knew anything about it.

[20]When Absalom's men came to the woman at the house, they asked, "Where are Ahimaaz and Jonathan?"

The woman answered them, "They crossed over the brook."[a] The men searched but found no one, so they returned to Jerusalem.

[21]After the men had gone, the two climbed out of the well and went to inform King David. They said to him, "Set out and cross the river at once; Ahithophel has advised such and such against you."
[22]So David and all the people with him set out and crossed the Jordan. By daybreak, no one was left who had not crossed the Jordan.

[23]When Ahithophel saw that his advice had not been followed, he saddled his donkey and set out for his house in his hometown. He put his house in order and then hanged himself. So he died and was buried in his father's tomb.

[24]David went to Mahanaim, and Absalom crossed the Jordan
with all the men of Israel. [25]Absalom had appointed Amasa over the army in place of Joab. Amasa was the son of a man named Jether,[b] an Israelite[c] who had married Abigail,[d] the daughter of Nahash and sister of Zeruiah the mother of Joab. [26]The Israelites and Absalom camped in the land of Gilead.

[27]When David came to Mahanaim, Shobi son of Nahash from Rabbah of the Ammonites, and Makir son of Ammiel from Lo Debar, and Barzillai the Gileadite from Rogelim [28]brought bedding and bowls and articles of pottery. They also brought wheat and barley, flour and roasted grain, beans and lentils,[e] [29]honey and curds, sheep, and cheese from cows' milk for David and his people to eat. For they said, "The people have become hungry and tired and thirsty in the desert."

Absalom's Death

18 David mustered the men who were with him and appointed over them commanders of thousands and commanders of hundreds. [2]David sent the troops out—a third under the command of Joab, a third under Joab's brother Abishai son of Zeruiah, and a third under Ittai the Gittite. The king told the troops, "I myself will surely march out with you."

[3]But the men said, "You must not go out; if we are forced to flee, they won't care about us. Even if half of us die, they won't care; but you are worth ten thousand of us.[f] It would be better now for you to give us support from the city."

17:19 *spread it out over the opening of the well and scattered grain over it:* The cover for the well would have been at ground level. It would look like the woman was drying grain on a mat that she had spread on the ground.

17:23 *hanged himself:* Ahithophel probably realized that Absalom would fail and that he could face death for betraying David. Suicide is extremely rare in the Bible. It is mentioned only three other times (1 Sam 31:4,5; 1 Kgs 16:18; Matt 27:5).

17:23 *in his father's tomb:* Many families showed respect for the dead by burying them in family tombs. These burial places could be natural caves or cut out of the side of a hill or dug into the ground. Some of the most famous examples are at Genesis 49:29-31; 50:5-14; and Joshua 24:32,33. See also the mini-article called "Burial," p. 1998.

17:25-27 *Amasa . . . Abigail . . . Shobi:* Abigail and Zeruiah (Joab's mother) were full sisters, and David was evidently their half-brother with the same mother, but a different father. This made Amasa one of David's nephews (see 1 Chr 2:12-17).

Shobi, one of the sons of Nahash, had probably been appointed the new king of the Ammonites after David captured Rabbah (see 10:1-3; 12:26-31).

---

[a]**20** Or *"They passed by the sheep pen toward the water."* [b]**25** Hebrew *Ithra,* a variant of *Jether* [c]**25** Hebrew and some Septuagint manuscripts; other Septuagint manuscripts (see also 1 Chron. 2:17) *Ishmaelite* or *Jezreelite* [d]**25** Hebrew *Abigal,* a variant of *Abigail* [e]**28** Most Septuagint manuscripts and Syriac; Hebrew *lentils, and roasted grain* [f]**3** Two Hebrew manuscripts, some Septuagint manuscripts and Vulgate; most Hebrew manuscripts *care; for now there are ten thousand like us*

The Hanging of Absalom, by Faith Robinson Trumbull, needlework, around 1770. David's son Absalom rebelled against his father and united all the leaders in the north who had a complaint against the king. Nathan's prophecy that David would not have peace in his family was coming true. Absalom even took the advice of one of David's disloyal advisers, and slept with his father's concubines. Eventually, father and son went to war against each other. As Absalom was riding his mule through the forest of Ephraim his head got caught in a tree. His mule ran away, leaving the young prince behind. When David's military leader Joab heard about this, he went to where Absalom was hanging and stabbed him through the chest with his spears. (See 18:6-18.)

18:6 *forest of Ephraim:* The exact location is not known, but it was probably east of the Jordan River, close enough to Mahanaim so that David could send additional soldiers. It may have gotten its name from the fact that people from the tribe of Ephraim (whose territory was west of the Jordan) settled there. Or, it may be because the word "Ephraim" means "fruitful place." See also the note at 2:8 (Mahanaim).

18:9 *Absalom's head got caught in the tree:* The word "head" could also be translated "hair." Absalom had very thick, heavy hair (14:26). The writer seems to want to call attention to the fact that Absalom's most renowned feature is the one that brings about his death.

4The king answered, "I will do whatever seems best to you."
So the king stood beside the gate while all the men marched
out in units of hundreds and of thousands. 5The king commanded Joab, Abishai and Ittai, "Be gentle with the young man Absalom
for my sake." And all the troops heard the king giving orders concerning Absalom to each of the commanders.

6The army marched into the field to fight Israel, and the battle took place in the forest of Ephraim. 7There the army of Israel
was defeated by David's men, and the casualties that day were
great—twenty thousand men. 8The battle spread out over the
whole countryside, and the forest claimed more lives that day than
the sword.

9Now Absalom happened to meet David's men. He was riding his mule, and as the mule went under the thick branches of a
large oak, Absalom's head got caught in the tree. He was left hanging in midair, while the mule he was riding kept on going.

10When one of the men saw this, he told Joab, "I just saw
Absalom hanging in an oak tree."

11Joab said to the man who had told him this, "What! You
saw him? Why didn't you strike him to the ground right there?
Then I would have had to give you ten shekels[a] of silver and a warrior's belt."
12But the man replied, "Even if a thousand shekels[b] were
weighed out into my hands, I would not lift my hand against the
king's son. In our hearing the king commanded you and Abishai
and Ittai, 'Protect the young man Absalom for my sake.'[c] 13And if I
had put my life in jeopardy[d]—and nothing is hidden from the
king—you would have kept your distance from me."
14Joab said, "I'm not going to wait like this for you." So he took
three javelins in his hand and plunged them into Absalom's heart
while Absalom was still alive in the oak tree. 15And ten of Joab's
armor-bearers surrounded Absalom, struck him and killed him.
16Then Joab sounded the trumpet, and the troops stopped
pursuing Israel, for Joab halted them. 17They took Absalom, threw
him into a big pit in the forest and piled up a large heap of rocks
over him. Meanwhile, all the Israelites fled to their homes.
18During his lifetime Absalom had taken a pillar and erected
it in the King's Valley as a monument to himself, for he thought, "I
have no son to carry on the memory of my name." He named the
pillar after himself, and it is called Absalom's Monument to this
day.

David Mourns

19Now Ahimaaz son of Zadok said, "Let me run and take the
news to the king that the LORD has delivered him from the hand of
his enemies."
20"You are not the one to take the news today," Joab told
him. "You may take the news another time, but you must not do so
today, because the king's son is dead."
21Then Joab said to a Cushite, "Go, tell the king what you
have seen." The Cushite bowed down before Joab and ran off.
22Ahimaaz son of Zadok again said to Joab, "Come what
may, please let me run behind the Cushite."
But Joab replied, "My son, why do you want to go? You don't
have any news that will bring you a reward."
23He said, "Come what may, I want to run."
So Joab said, "Run!" Then Ahimaaz ran by way of the plain[e]
and outran the Cushite.
24While David was sitting between the inner and outer gates,
the watchman went up to the roof of the gateway by the wall. As

[a]**11** That is, about 4 ounces (about 115 grams) [b]**12** That is, about 25 pounds (about 11 kilograms) [c]**12** A few Hebrew manuscripts, Septuagint, Vulgate and Syriac; most Hebrew manuscripts may be translated *Absalom, whoever you may be.* [d]**13** Or *Otherwise, if I had acted treacherously toward him* [e]**23** That is, the plain of the Jordan

18:11 *ten shekels of silver and a warrior's belt:* A very large reward. In Judges 17:10, ten shekels of silver was a year's wages for a priest.

18:17 *piled up a large heap of rocks:* This burial does not show the respect usually given to the dead, much less the respect deserved by a king's son. The pile of rocks might have been put there to keep the body from being moved easily, or to mock the monument Absalom had erected to himself (18:18). See also the note at 17:23 (father's tomb).

18:18 *King's Valley:* The exact location of this valley is unknown, but it may be the same as the Kidron Valley just east of Jerusalem.

18:18 *I have no son . . . to this day:* According to 14:27, Absalom had three sons. But they may have died young or been put to death for Absalom's murder of Amnon.

"To this day" means at the time of writing. This monument is not the same structure now known as "Absalom's Tomb," which was built at least 600 years later.

18:20 *You are not the one to take the news today:* Who was chosen to carry a message was a sign of whether the message contained good or bad news (18:24-27).

18:24 *between . . . gates:* The city gate was often like a tower in the city wall, with one gate on the outside of the wall and another gate on the inside of the wall. See also the note and illustration at 3:27.

David kept saying, *"O my son Absalom! My son, my son Absalom! If only I had died instead of you— O Absalom, my son, my son!"*
2 Sam 18:33

18:33—19:4 *The king was shaken ... day was turned into mourning:* The story of King David as told in 2 SAMUEL is punctuated with episodes of profound loss and grief. See, for instance 1:1-27 (death of Saul and Jonathan); 3:28-39 (death of Abner); 12:15-23 (death of David and Bathsheba's first son); and 13:29-38 (death of Amnon). PSALMS, a book of songs and prayers, includes a number of laments that may have been written by David (see Ps 10; 22; 35).

he looked out, he saw a man running alone. 25The watchman
called out to the king and reported it.

The king said, "If he is alone, he must have good news." And
the man came closer and closer.

26Then the watchman saw another man running, and he
called down to the gatekeeper, "Look, another man running
alone!"

The king said, "He must be bringing good news, too."

27The watchman said, "It seems to me that the first one runs
like Ahimaaz son of Zadok."

"He's a good man," the king said. "He comes with good
news."

28Then Ahimaaz called out to the king, "All is well!" He
bowed down before the king with his face to the ground and said,
"Praise be to the LORD your God! He has delivered up the men
who lifted their hands against my lord the king."

29The king asked, "Is the young man Absalom safe?"

Ahimaaz answered, "I saw great confusion just as Joab was
about to send the king's servant and me, your servant, but I don't
know what it was."

30The king said, "Stand aside and wait here." So he stepped
aside and stood there.

31Then the Cushite arrived and said, "My lord the king, hear
the good news! The LORD has delivered you today from all who
rose up against you."

32The king asked the Cushite, "Is the young man Absalom
safe?"

The Cushite replied, "May the enemies of my lord the king
and all who rise up to harm you be like that young man."

33The king was shaken. He went up to the room over the
gateway and wept. As he went, he said: "O my son Absalom! My
son, my son Absalom! If only I had died instead of you—O Absalom, my son, my son!"

19 Joab was told, "The king is weeping and mourning for Absalom." 2And for the whole army the victory that day was turned into
mourning, because on that day the troops heard it said, "The king
is grieving for his son." 3The men stole into the city that day as
men steal in who are ashamed when they flee from battle. 4The
king covered his face and cried aloud, "O my son Absalom!
O Absalom, my son, my son!"

5Then Joab went into the house to the king and said, "Today
you have humiliated all your men, who have just saved your life
and the lives of your sons and daughters and the lives of your
wives and concubines. 6You love those who hate you and hate
those who love you. You have made it clear today that the commanders and their men mean nothing to you. I see that you would
be pleased if Absalom were alive today and all of us were dead.
7Now go out and encourage your men. I swear by the LORD that if

you don't go out, not a man will be left with you by nightfall. This will be worse for you than all the calamities that have come upon you from your youth till now."

[8]So the king got up and took his seat in the gateway. When the men were told, "The king is sitting in the gateway," they all came before him.

David Returns to Jerusalem

Meanwhile, the Israelites had fled to their homes. [9]Throughout the tribes of Israel, the people were all arguing with each other, saying, "The king delivered us from the hand of our enemies; he is the one who rescued us from the hand of the Philistines. But now he has fled the country because of Absalom; [10]and Absalom, whom we anointed to rule over us, has died in battle. So why do you say nothing about bringing the king back?"

[11]King David sent this message to Zadok and Abiathar, the priests: "Ask the elders of Judah, 'Why should you be the last to bring the king back to his palace, since what is being said throughout Israel has reached the king at his quarters? [12]You are my brothers, my own flesh and blood. So why should you be the last to bring back the king?' [13]And say to Amasa, 'Are you not my own flesh and blood? May God deal with me, be it ever so severely, if from now on you are not the commander of my army in place of Joab.' "

[14]He won over the hearts of all the men of Judah as though they were one man. They sent word to the king, "Return, you and all your men." [15]Then the king returned and went as far as the Jordan.

Now the men of Judah had come to Gilgal to go out and meet the king and bring him across the Jordan. [16]Shimei son of Gera, the Benjamite from Bahurim, hurried down with the men of Judah to meet King David. [17]With him were a thousand Benjamites, along with Ziba, the steward of Saul's household, and his fifteen sons and twenty servants. They rushed to the Jordan, where the king was. [18]They crossed at the ford to take the king's household over and to do whatever he wished.

When Shimei son of Gera crossed the Jordan, he fell prostrate before the king [19]and said to him, "May my lord not hold me guilty. Do not remember how your servant did wrong on the day my lord the king left Jerusalem. May the king put it out of his mind. [20]For I your servant know that I have sinned, but today I have come here as the first of the whole house of Joseph to come down and meet my lord the king."

[21]Then Abishai son of Zeruiah said, "Shouldn't Shimei be put to death for this? He cursed the LORD's anointed."

[22]David replied, "What do you and I have in common, you sons of Zeruiah? This day you have become my adversaries! Should anyone be put to death in Israel today? Do I not know that

19:12 *my own flesh and blood . . . bring back the king:* David was from the tribe of Judah, and was king of Judah (2:1-4) before becoming king of all Israel (5:1-3).

19:13 *Amasa . . . commander . . . place of Joab:* Joab had finally gone too far by murdering Absalom (18:4-6,12-14). Considering the severity of the crime, it is surprising that all David did was replace him as army commander with someone else. Although Amasa was David's nephew, he had commanded Absalom's army.

19:16 *Shimei . . . the Benjamite:* See the note at 16:5-14.

19:24-29 *Mephibosheth . . . Ziba:* David had returned Saul's property to Mephibosheth and treated him like a son (9:1-13). But after the servant Ziba said Mephibosheth had stayed in Jerusalem so he could rule the kingdom that was once his grandfather's, David took the property away from Mephibosheth and gave it to Ziba (16:1-4).

19:31 2 Sam 17:27-29.

today I am king over Israel?" 23So the king said to Shimei, "You
shall not die." And the king promised him on oath.
24Mephibosheth, Saul's grandson, also went down to meet
the king. He had not taken care of his feet or trimmed his mustache or washed his clothes from the day the king left until the day
he returned safely. 25When he came from Jerusalem to meet the
king, the king asked him, "Why didn't you go with me, Mephibosheth?"
26He said, "My lord the king, since I your servant am lame, I
said, 'I will have my donkey saddled and will ride on it, so I can go
with the king.' But Ziba my servant betrayed me. 27And he has
slandered your servant to my lord the king. My lord the king is like
an angel of God; so do whatever pleases you. 28All my grandfather's descendants deserved nothing but death from my lord the king, but you gave your servant a place among those who eat at your table. So what right do I have to make any more appeals to the king?"
29The king said to him, "Why say more? I order you and Ziba
to divide the fields."
30Mephibosheth said to the king, "Let him take everything,
now that my lord the king has arrived home safely."
31Barzillai the Gileadite also came down from Rogelim to
cross the Jordan with the king and to send him on his way from
there. 32Now Barzillai was a very old man, eighty years of age. He
had provided for the king during his stay in Mahanaim, for he was
a very wealthy man. 33The king said to Barzillai, "Cross over with
me and stay with me in Jerusalem, and I will provide for you."
34But Barzillai answered the king, "How many more years will
I live, that I should go up to Jerusalem with the king? 35I am now
eighty years old. Can I tell the difference between what is good and what is not? Can your servant taste what he eats and drinks? Can I still hear the voices of men and women singers? Why should your
servant be an added burden to my lord the king? 36Your servant will
cross over the Jordan with the king for a short distance, but why
should the king reward me in this way? 37Let your servant return,
that I may die in my own town near the tomb of my father and mother. But here is your servant Kimham. Let him cross over with my lord the king. Do for him whatever pleases you."
38The king said, "Kimham shall cross over with me, and I
will do for him whatever pleases you. And anything you desire from me I will do for you."
39So all the people crossed the Jordan, and then the king
crossed over. The king kissed Barzillai and gave him his blessing, and Barzillai returned to his home.
40When the king crossed over to Gilgal, Kimham crossed
with him. All the troops of Judah and half the troops of Israel had taken the king over.
41Soon all the men of Israel were coming to the king and say-

ing to him, "Why did our brothers, the men of Judah, steal the
king away and bring him and his household across the Jordan,
together with all his men?"
42All the men of Judah answered the men of Israel, "We did
this because the king is closely related to us. Why are you angry
about it? Have we eaten any of the king's provisions? Have we
taken anything for ourselves?"
43Then the men of Israel answered the men of Judah, "We
have ten shares in the king; and besides, we have a greater claim
on David than you have. So why do you treat us with contempt?
Were we not the first to speak of bringing back our king?"
But the men of Judah responded even more harshly than the
men of Israel.

SHEBA'S REBELLION

A Benjamite named Sheba leads a group of Israelites in a new rebellion against David. Joab and his best soldiers pursue Sheba to the town of Abel Beth Maacah where a wise woman saves her city from destruction by having the rebel beheaded.

Sheba Rebels Against David

20 Now a troublemaker named Sheba son of Bicri, a Benjamite,
happened to be there. He sounded the trumpet and shouted,

"We have no share in David,
no part in Jesse's son!
Every man to his tent, O Israel!"

2So all the men of Israel deserted David to follow Sheba son
of Bicri. But the men of Judah stayed by their king all the way from
the Jordan to Jerusalem.
3When David returned to his palace in Jerusalem, he took
the ten concubines he had left to take care of the palace and put
them in a house under guard. He provided for them, but did not
lie with them. They were kept in confinement till the day of their
death, living as widows.
4Then the king said to Amasa, "Summon the men of Judah
to come to me within three days, and be here yourself." 5But when
Amasa went to summon Judah, he took longer than the time the
king had set for him.
6David said to Abishai, "Now Sheba son of Bicri will do us
more harm than Absalom did. Take your master's men and pursue
him, or he will find fortified cities and escape from us." 7So Joab's
men and the Kerethites and Pelethites and all the mighty warriors
went out under the command of Abishai. They marched out from
Jerusalem to pursue Sheba son of Bicri.
8While they were at the great rock in Gibeon, Amasa came to
meet them. Joab was wearing his military tunic, and strapped over

19:43 *men of Israel . . . men of Judah:* In this verse "men of Israel" stands for the northern tribes, "men of Judah" for the tribe of Judah in the south. See also the note at 2:1,2 and the mini-article called "Israel," p. 264.

20:3 *ten concubines . . . widows:* Absalom had slept with these concubines (see 16:21,22). Perhaps David did not trust them and wanted to be sure they did not have any sons who would betray him as Absalom had done.

20:7 *Kerethites and Pelethites:* See the note at 8:18 (Kerethites and Pelethites).

20:1 1 Kgs 12:15-19; 2 Chr 10:15-19.

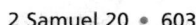

20:15 *seige ramp . . . fortifications . . . battering the wall:* Most cities in the ancient Near East were surrounded by thick walls made of bricks, stones, or earth. When a city was under attack the citizens closed their gates and mounted archers on top of the walls. The attacking forces used large seige engines, enclosed structures equipped with battering rams, to break through the city's walls. See the illustration, p. 772.

it at his waist was a belt with a dagger in its sheath. As he stepped
forward, it dropped out of its sheath.
[9]Joab said to Amasa, "How are you, my brother?" Then Joab
took Amasa by the beard with his right hand to kiss him. [10]Amasa
was not on his guard against the dagger in Joab's hand, and Joab
plunged it into his belly, and his intestines spilled out on the
ground. Without being stabbed again, Amasa died. Then Joab and
his brother Abishai pursued Sheba son of Bicri.
[11]One of Joab's men stood beside Amasa and said, "Whoever
favors Joab, and whoever is for David, let him follow Joab!"
[12]Amasa lay wallowing in his blood in the middle of the road, and
the man saw that all the troops came to a halt there. When he realized that everyone who came up to Amasa stopped, he dragged
him from the road into a field and threw a garment over him.
[13]After Amasa had been removed from the road, all the men went
on with Joab to pursue Sheba son of Bicri.
[14]Sheba passed through all the tribes of Israel to Abel Beth
Maacah[a] and through the entire region of the Berites, who gathered
together and followed him. [15]All the troops with Joab came and
besieged Sheba in Abel Beth Maacah. They built a siege ramp up to
the city, and it stood against the outer fortifications. While they

[a]**14** Or *Abel, even Beth Maacah*; also in verse 15

QUESTIONS ABOUT 2 SAMUEL 11:1—20:26

1. Read the story of David and Bathsheba (chapter 11). What did David do wrong? How did he make things worse? How did the prophet get David to confess his guilt? (12:1-15) What happened as a result of David's sin?
2. Both Saul and David disobeyed God at points in their lives. Compare 1 Sam 13:11-14 and 2 Sam 12:13,14. How were the punishments similar and different? Why do you think that was?
3. Part of the LORD's message that Nathan delivered to David was, "The sword will never depart from your house, because you despised me" (12:10). What are David's "family problems" as described in chapters 13–16? How did David react to each of these problems? Do you agree with the choices he made in each case? Why or why not?
4. Why do you think Joab had so much influence over David? (Some passages you may want to look at before answering are 3:19-31; 11:6-25; 12:26-31; 14:1-3, 19-24, 28-33; 18:4-17; 19:4-8; 20:7-23.) To whom do you turn for advice and support when you have difficult decisions to make? How do you know that person is trustworthy?
5. In 1 and 2 Samuel there are many examples of covenants and promises that people made with one another, and that God made with people. How did David treat the covenant he made with Jonathan in 1 Samuel 20:11-17 when dealing with Jonathan's son Mephibosheth? Read chapter 9 for background, then read 16:1-4 and 19:24-30. What kinds of promises or agreements have you made with other people? When, if ever, do you feel it is okay to break an agreement you've made with someone? Why? What keeps you from breaking an agreement you've made? What do you do when someone breaks a promise he or she made to you?

were battering the wall to bring it down, [16]a wise woman called from the city, "Listen! Listen! Tell Joab to come here so I can speak to him." [17]He went toward her, and she asked, "Are you Joab?"

"I am," he answered.

She said, "Listen to what your servant has to say."

"I'm listening," he said.

[18]She continued, "Long ago they used to say, 'Get your answer at Abel,' and that settled it. [19]We are the peaceful and faithful in Israel. You are trying to destroy a city that is a mother in Israel. Why do you want to swallow up the LORD's inheritance?"

[20]"Far be it from me!" Joab replied, "Far be it from me to swallow up or destroy! [21]That is not the case. A man named Sheba son of Bicri, from the hill country of Ephraim, has lifted up his hand against the king, against David. Hand over this one man, and I'll withdraw from the city."

The woman said to Joab, "His head will be thrown to you from the wall."

[22]Then the woman went to all the people with her wise advice, and they cut off the head of Sheba son of Bicri and threw it to Joab. So he sounded the trumpet, and his men dispersed from the city, each returning to his home. And Joab went back to the king in Jerusalem.

[23]Joab was over Israel's entire army; Benaiah son of Jehoiada was over the Kerethites and Pelethites; [24]Adoniram[a] was in charge of forced labor; Jehoshaphat son of Ahilud was recorder; [25]Sheva was secretary; Zadok and Abiathar were priests; [26]and Ira the Jairite was David's priest.

20:16 *wise woman:* See the note at 14:2 (wise woman).

20:23-26 *Joab . . . Ira:* Most of these names were also on the list at 8:16-18, so they probably served David during most of the time he was king.

20:23 *Kerethites and Pelethites:* See the note at 8:18 (Kerethites and Pelethites).

Other Stories About David

The last four chapters of 2 SAMUEL are a loose collection of stories and songs drawn from different periods of David's life.

A FAMINE IN ISRAEL

Saul's guilt had become a curse on Israel that resulted in famine. For this curse to be removed, the Gibeonites would have to ask the LORD to be kind to Israel.

The Gibeonites Avenged

21 During the reign of David, there was a famine for three successive years; so David sought the face of the LORD. The LORD said, "It is on account of Saul and his blood-stained house; it is because he put the Gibeonites to death."

---

[a]**24** Some Septuagint manuscripts (see also 1 Kings 4:6 and 5:14); Hebrew *Adoram*

21:2 *Gibeonites:* The people who lived in and around Gibeon, a town about five miles northwest of Jerusalem. Though Israel's promise to the Gibeonites is recorded in Joshua 9:3-27, Saul's attempt to kill them is not recorded in the Bible.

21:8 *Rizpah . . . Merab . . . Barzillai:* Rizpah was the wife of Saul that Abner, Saul's army commander, had slept with after Saul's death (3:7-11). Merab was Saul's daughter who married Adriel from Meholah, even though Saul had promised her to David (1 Sam 18:19). Saul then allowed David to marry his other daughter, Michal, instead. Michal didn't have any children (6:23). It is not certain if Barzillai is the same person mentioned in 19:31-39.

21:9 *as the barley harvest was beginning:* This would have been late in April.

21:10 *sackcloth:* See the note at 3:31.

21:10 *till the rain poured down:* Normally bodies were buried within 24 hours of death. These were left unburied as a mark of dishonor. She protected the bodies from the additional dishonor of being picked at by buzzards, jackals, and crows. Unless the rains came early she would have done this for about six months, until the start of the rainy season in September or October.

21:12 *where the Philistines had hung them:* It was common practice in the ancient Near East to bring back at least the head and the armor of the slain enemy, perhaps as proof of victory. The head and other body parts were displayed to announce the victory and to serve as a warning to other enemies. David followed this custom after killing Goliath (1 Sam 17:51,54). See also 1 Sam 31:8-13.

21:7 1 Sam 20:14-17; 2 Sam 9:1-7.

2 The king summoned the Gibeonites and spoke to them.
(Now the Gibeonites were not a part of Israel but were survivors of
the Amorites; the Israelites had sworn to ⌞spare⌟ them, but Saul in
his zeal for Israel and Judah had tried to annihilate them.) 3 David
asked the Gibeonites, "What shall I do for you? How shall I make
amends so that you will bless the LORD's inheritance?"
4 The Gibeonites answered him, "We have no right to
demand silver or gold from Saul or his family, nor do we have the
right to put anyone in Israel to death."
"What do you want me to do for you?" David asked.
5 They answered the king, "As for the man who destroyed us
and plotted against us so that we have been decimated and have
no place anywhere in Israel, 6 let seven of his male descendants be
given to us to be killed and exposed before the LORD at Gibeah of
Saul—the LORD's chosen one."
So the king said, "I will give them to you."
7 The king spared Mephibosheth son of Jonathan, the son of
Saul, because of the oath before the LORD between David and
Jonathan son of Saul. 8 But the king took Armoni and Mephibosheth, the two sons of Aiah's daughter Rizpah, whom she had
borne to Saul, together with the five sons of Saul's daughter
Merab,[a] whom she had borne to Adriel son of Barzillai the Meho-
lathite. 9 He handed them over to the Gibeonites, who killed and
exposed them on a hill before the LORD. All seven of them fell
together; they were put to death during the first days of the harvest, just as the barley harvest was beginning.
10 Rizpah daughter of Aiah took sackcloth and spread it out
for herself on a rock. From the beginning of the harvest till the
rain poured down from the heavens on the bodies, she did not let
the birds of the air touch them by day or the wild animals by
night. 11 When David was told what Aiah's daughter Rizpah, Saul's
concubine, had done, 12 he went and took the bones of Saul and his
son Jonathan from the citizens of Jabesh Gilead. (They had taken
them secretly from the public square at Beth Shan, where the
Philistines had hung them after they struck Saul down on Gilboa.)
13 David brought the bones of Saul and his son Jonathan from
there, and the bones of those who had been killed and exposed
were gathered up.
14 They buried the bones of Saul and his son Jonathan in the
tomb of Saul's father Kish, at Zela in Benjamin, and did everything
the king commanded. After that, God answered prayer in behalf of
the land.

[a]**8** Two Hebrew manuscripts, some Septuagint manuscripts and Syriac (see also 1 Samuel 18:19); most Hebrew and Septuagint manuscripts *Michal*

OTHER VICTORIES

Wars Against the Philistines

15 Once again there was a battle between the Philistines and
Israel. David went down with his men to fight against the
Philistines, and he became exhausted. 16 And Ishbi-Benob, one of
the descendants of Rapha, whose bronze spearhead weighed three
hundred shekels[a] and who was armed with a new ⸤sword⸥, said he
would kill David. 17 But Abishai son of Zeruiah came to David's
rescue; he struck the Philistine down and killed him. Then David's
men swore to him, saying, "Never again will you go out with us to
battle, so that the lamp of Israel will not be extinguished."

18 In the course of time, there was another battle with the
Philistines, at Gob. At that time Sibbecai the Hushathite killed
Saph, one of the descendants of Rapha.

19 In another battle with the Philistines at Gob, Elhanan son
of Jaare-Oregim[b] the Bethlehemite killed Goliath[c] the Gittite, who
had a spear with a shaft like a weaver's rod.

20 In still another battle, which took place at Gath, there was
a huge man with six fingers on each hand and six toes on each
foot—twenty-four in all. He also was descended from Rapha.
21 When he taunted Israel, Jonathan son of Shimeah, David's
brother, killed him.

22 These four were descendants of Rapha in Gath, and they
fell at the hands of David and his men.

DAVID'S SONGS

Two poems celebrate God's promise to be faithful.

David's Song of Praise

22 David sang to the LORD the words of this song when the
LORD delivered him from the hand of all his enemies and from the
hand of Saul. 2 He said:

"The LORD is my rock, my fortress and my deliverer;
3 my God is my rock, in whom I take refuge,
my shield and the horn[d] of my salvation.
He is my stronghold, my refuge and my savior—
from violent men you save me.

[a]16 That is, about 7 1/2 pounds (about 3.5 kilograms) [b]19 Or *son of Jair the weaver* [c]19 Hebrew and Septuagint; 1 Chron. 20:5 *son of Jair killed Lahmi the brother of Goliath* [d]3 *Horn* here symbolizes strength.

21:13,14 *David brought the bones . . . God answered prayer:* David was moved by the way Rizpah protected the bodies of Saul's sons and grandsons. He restored some of the honor to the fallen king and his descendants by having them all buried in the grave of Saul's father Kish. See the note at 17:23 (father's tomb). "God answered prayer" indicates that justice has been done and the famine that had begun three years before (21:1) is now over.

21:16 *descendants of Rapha:* A group of people (also called Rephaites), famous for their large size, who lived in the area before the Israelites did.

21:17 *Abishai:* David's nephew, the brother of Joab.

21:19 *Goliath:* According to 1 Samuel 17, David killed a giant named Goliath who made fun of Israel. The Goliath mentioned here may be a different warrior, perhaps "the brother of Goliath" as indicated in 1 Chronicles 20:5.

21:19 *spear with a shaft like a weaver's rod:* Looms were large wooden structures with sturdy cross beams that supported many rows of yarn. This giant's spear was very large indeed.

22:1-51 *David sang . . . forever:* David's victory song, one of the oldest major poems in the Jewish Scriptures was also collected, in a slightly different form, in PSALMS (Ps 18). In verses 21 to 25, David makes it clear that he thought the LORD supported him because he was innocent by God's standards and because he obeyed the LORD.

22:2,3 *my rock, my fortress:* In Hebrew, "rock" and "fortress" are sometimes used in poetry to compare the LORD to a mountain where his people can run for protection from their enemies.

21:17 1 Kgs 11:36; Ps 132:17.

King David Kneeling in Prayer, by Philip Isac Levy, an illuminated page from the *Copenhagen Haggadah,* 1739. King David was known for two important things: his prayerful trust in the LORD and for the songs (psalms) he composed to celebrate what the LORD did for him and for the people of Israel. The song David sings in chapter 22 recalls how the LORD repeatedly rescued him from his enemies and concludes with a powerful affirmation: "He gives his king great victories; he shows unfailing kindness to his anointed, to David and his descendants forever."

22:4 *my enemies:* See the mini-article called "Enemies (The Wicked)," p. 1084.

22:7 *From his temple:* God's temple is heaven (Ps 11:4). The temple David's son Solomon would later build in Jerusalem would be considered God's throne on earth.

22:8 *foundations of the heavens shook:* The sky was sometimes described as a dome held up by a foundation or pillars (Gen 1:6-8).

4 I call to the LORD, who is worthy of praise,
and I am saved from my enemies.

5 "The waves of death swirled about me;
the torrents of destruction overwhelmed me.
6 The cords of the grave[a] coiled around me;
the snares of death confronted me.
7 In my distress I called to the LORD;
I called out to my God.
From his temple he heard my voice;
my cry came to his ears.

8 "The earth trembled and quaked,
the foundations of the heavens[b] shook;
they trembled because he was angry.

[a]**6** Hebrew *Sheol* [b]**8** Hebrew; Vulgate and Syriac (see also Psalm 18:7) *mountains*

9 Smoke rose from his nostrils;
consuming fire came from his mouth,
burning coals blazed out of it.
10 He parted the heavens and came down;
dark clouds were under his feet.
11 He mounted the cherubim and flew;
he soared[a] on the wings of the wind.
12 He made darkness his canopy around him—
the dark[b] rain clouds of the sky.
13 Out of the brightness of his presence
bolts of lightning blazed forth.
14 The LORD thundered from heaven;
the voice of the Most High resounded.
15 He shot arrows and scattered ⌞the enemies⌟,
bolts of lightning and routed them.
16 The valleys of the sea were exposed
and the foundations of the earth laid bare
at the rebuke of the LORD,
at the blast of breath from his nostrils.

17 "He reached down from on high and took hold of me;
he drew me out of deep waters.
18 He rescued me from my powerful enemy,
from my foes, who were too strong for me.
19 They confronted me in the day of my disaster,
but the LORD was my support.
20 He brought me out into a spacious place;
he rescued me because he delighted in me.

21 "The LORD has dealt with me according to my righteousness;
according to the cleanness of my hands he has
rewarded me.
22 For I have kept the ways of the LORD;
I have not done evil by turning from my God.
23 All his laws are before me;
I have not turned away from his decrees.
24 I have been blameless before him
and have kept myself from sin.
25 The LORD has rewarded me according to my righteousness,
according to my cleanness[c] in his sight.

26 "To the faithful you show yourself faithful,
to the blameless you show yourself blameless,

22:11 *cherubim:* Most likely some kind of supernatural beings, like the ones represented on the top of the ark of the covenant. See the mini-article called "The Ark of the Covenant," p. 513.

22:14 *The* LORD *thundered . . . Most High:* See the note at 1 Sam 12:17 (thunder and rain). See also the mini-article called "Names of God," p. 243.

[a]11 Many Hebrew manuscripts (see also Psalm 18:10); most Hebrew manuscripts *appeared* [b]12 Septuagint and Vulgate (see also Psalm 18:11); Hebrew *massed* [c]25 Hebrew; Septuagint and Vulgate (see also Psalm 18:24) *to the cleanness of my hands*

22:29 *You are my lamp . . . light:* These are symbols of life (see Prov 13:9). Light also stands for the wisdom and truth that come from God, as opposed to darkness, which symbolizes evil. Previously, the author of 2 SAMUEL related how David's soldiers called him "the lamp of Israel" (2 Sam 21:17), meaning he was their source of hope.

22:30 *I can scale a wall:* See the note at 20:15.

22:34 Hab 3:19.

27 to the pure you show yourself pure,
but to the crooked you show yourself shrewd.
28 You save the humble,
but your eyes are on the haughty to bring them low.
29 You are my lamp, O LORD;
the LORD turns my darkness into light.
30 With your help I can advance against a troop[a];
with my God I can scale a wall.

31 "As for God, his way is perfect;
the word of the LORD is flawless.
He is a shield
for all who take refuge in him.
32 For who is God besides the LORD?
And who is the Rock except our God?
33 It is God who arms me with strength[b]
and makes my way perfect.
34 He makes my feet like the feet of a deer;
he enables me to stand on the heights.
35 He trains my hands for battle;
my arms can bend a bow of bronze.
36 You give me your shield of victory;
you stoop down to make me great.
37 You broaden the path beneath me,
so that my ankles do not turn.

38 "I pursued my enemies and crushed them;
I did not turn back till they were destroyed.
39 I crushed them completely, and they could not rise;
they fell beneath my feet.
40 You armed me with strength for battle;
you made my adversaries bow at my feet.
41 You made my enemies turn their backs in flight,
and I destroyed my foes.
42 They cried for help, but there was no one to save them—
to the LORD, but he did not answer.
43 I beat them as fine as the dust of the earth;
I pounded and trampled them like mud in the streets.

44 "You have delivered me from the attacks of my people;
you have preserved me as the head of nations.
People I did not know are subject to me,
45 and foreigners come cringing to me;
as soon as they hear me, they obey me.

---

[a]**30** Or *can run through a barricade* [b]**33** Dead Sea Scrolls, some Septuagint manuscripts, Vulgate and Syriac (see also Psalm 18:32); Masoretic Text *who is my strong refuge*

46 They all lose heart;
they come trembling[a] from their strongholds.

47 "The LORD lives! Praise be to my Rock!
Exalted be God, the Rock, my Savior!
48 He is the God who avenges me,
who puts the nations under me,
49 who sets me free from my enemies.
You exalted me above my foes;
from violent men you rescued me.
50 Therefore I will praise you, O LORD, among the nations;
I will sing praises to your name.
51 He gives his king great victories;
he shows unfailing kindness to his anointed,
to David and his descendants forever."

The Last Words of David

23 These are the last words of David:

"The oracle of David son of Jesse,
the oracle of the man exalted by the
Most High,
the man anointed by the God of Jacob,
Israel's singer of songs[b]:

2 "The Spirit of the LORD spoke through me;
his word was on my tongue.
3 The God of Israel spoke,
the Rock of Israel said to me:
'When one rules over men in righteousness,
when he rules in the fear of God,
4 he is like the light of morning at sunrise
on a cloudless morning,
like the brightness after rain
that brings the grass from the earth.'

5 "Is not my house right with God?
Has he not made with me an everlasting covenant,
arranged and secured in every part?
Will he not bring to fruition my salvation
and grant me my every desire?
6 But evil men are all to be cast aside like thorns,
which are not gathered with the hand.
7 Whoever touches thorns
uses a tool of iron or the shaft of a spear;
they are burned up where they lie."

---

[a]**46** Some Septuagint manuscripts and Vulgate (see also Psalm 18:45); Masoretic Text *they arm themselves.* [b]**1** Or *Israel's beloved singer*

> The protector of Israel said to me:
> *"When one rules over men in righteousness, when he rules in the fear of God, he is like the light of morning at sunrise on a cloudless morning, like the brightness after rain that brings the grass from the earth."*
> 2 Sam 23:3,4

22:47 *Rock . . . my Savior:* See the note at 22:2,3.

22:51 *his anointed . . . David and his descendants forever:* God promised David that one of David's descendants always would be on the throne (7:12-16). See also the mini-article called "David," p. 1028 and "Messiah (Chosen One)," p. 1124.

23:1-7 *last words of David:* Verse 1 calls David a great king. David summarized his own life as one of serving God—as a prophet (23:2) and as a fair and just ruler (23:3,4)—so that God's promise to him would never be broken.

23:5 *an everlasting covenant:* See the note at 22:51 and the mini-article called "Covenants (Agreements)," p. 386.

22:50 Rom 15:9. **23:5** 2 Sam 7:12-16; 22:51.

23:8 *the Three:* The most honored group of soldiers. They might have been part of the Thirty. See 23:13,18,23.

23:13 *cave of Adullam:* This might have happened during the time that David was an outlaw (1 Sam 22:1-6).

23:20 *Benaiah:* Benaiah was the commander of the Kerethites and Pelethites (8:18; 20:23) and one of David's army commanders (1 Chr 27:1-15). Later he would support Solomon, David's son, when Solomon inherited the throne (1 Kgs 1,2), and was made the commander of Solomon's army (1 Kgs 2:35).

23:8-17 1 Chr 11:10-19. **23:18-39** 1 Chr 11:20-47.

DAVID'S WARRIORS

David inspires brave deeds and unquestioning loyalty among his soldiers.

David's Mighty Men

8 These are the names of David's mighty men:
Josheb-Basshebeth,[a] a Tahkemonite,[b] was chief of the Three;
he raised his spear against eight hundred men, whom he killed[c] in
one encounter.
9 Next to him was Eleazar son of Dodai the Ahohite. As one
of the three mighty men, he was with David when they taunted the
Philistines gathered at Pas Dammim[d] for battle. Then the men of
Israel retreated, 10 but he stood his ground and struck down the
Philistines till his hand grew tired and froze to the sword. The
LORD brought about a great victory that day. The troops returned
to Eleazar, but only to strip the dead.
11 Next to him was Shammah son of Agee the Hararite. When
the Philistines banded together at a place where there was a field
full of lentils, Israel's troops fled from them. 12 But Shammah took
his stand in the middle of the field. He defended it and struck the
Philistines down, and the LORD brought about a great victory.
13 During harvest time, three of the thirty chief men came down
to David at the cave of Adullam, while a band of Philistines was
encamped in the Valley of Rephaim. 14 At that time David was in the
stronghold, and the Philistine garrison was at Bethlehem. 15 David
longed for water and said, "Oh, that someone would get me a drink
of water from the well near the gate of Bethlehem!" 16 So the three
mighty men broke through the Philistine lines, drew water from the
well near the gate of Bethlehem and carried it back to David. But he
refused to drink it; instead, he poured it out before the LORD. 17 "Far be
it from me, O LORD, to do this!" he said. "Is it not the blood of men
who went at the risk of their lives?" And David would not drink it.
Such were the exploits of the three mighty men.
18 Abishai the brother of Joab son of Zeruiah was chief of the
Three.[e] He raised his spear against three hundred men, whom he
killed, and so he became as famous as the Three. 19 Was he not held
in greater honor than the Three? He became their commander,
even though he was not included among them.
20 Benaiah son of Jehoiada was a valiant fighter from Kabzeel,
who performed great exploits. He struck down two of Moab's best
men. He also went down into a pit on a snowy day and killed a lion.

---

[a]**8** Hebrew; some Septuagint manuscripts suggest *Ish-Bosheth,* that is, *Esh-Baal* (see also 1 Chron. 11:11 *Jashobeam*). [b]**8** Probably a variant of *Hacmonite* (see 1 Chron. 11:11) [c]**8** Some Septuagint manuscripts (see also 1 Chron. 11:11); Hebrew and other Septuagint manuscripts *Three; it was Adino the Eznite who killed eight hundred men* [d]**9** See 1 Chron. 11:13; Hebrew *gathered there.* [e]**18** Most Hebrew manuscripts (see also 1 Chron. 11:20); two Hebrew manuscripts and Syriac *Thirty*

[21]And he struck down a huge Egyptian. Although the Egyptian had
a spear in his hand, Benaiah went against him with a club. He
snatched the spear from the Egyptian's hand and killed him with
his own spear. [22]Such were the exploits of Benaiah son of Jehoiada;
he too was as famous as the three mighty men. [23]He was held in
greater honor than any of the Thirty, but he was not included
among the Three. And David put him in charge of his bodyguard.

[24]Among the Thirty were:
Asahel the brother of Joab,
Elhanan son of Dodo from Bethlehem,
[25]Shammah the Harodite,
Elika the Harodite,
[26]Helez the Paltite,
Ira son of Ikkesh from Tekoa,
[27]Abiezer from Anathoth,
Mebunnai[a] the Hushathite,
[28]Zalmon the Ahohite,
Maharai the Netophathite,
[29]Heled[b] son of Baanah the Netophathite,
Ithai son of Ribai from Gibeah in Benjamin,
[30]Benaiah the Pirathonite,
Hiddai[c] from the ravines of Gaash,
[31]Abi-Albon the Arbathite,
Azmaveth the Barhumite,
[32]Eliahba the Shaalbonite,
the sons of Jashen,
Jonathan [33]son of[d] Shammah the Hararite,
Ahiam son of Sharar[e] the Hararite,
[34]Eliphelet son of Ahasbai the Maacathite,
Eliam son of Ahithophel the Gilonite,
[35]Hezro the Carmelite,
Paarai the Arbite,
[36]Igal son of Nathan from Zobah,
the son of Hagri,[f]
[37]Zelek the Ammonite,
Naharai the Beerothite, the armor-bearer of Joab son of Zeruiah,
[38]Ira the Ithrite,
Gareb the Ithrite
[39]and Uriah the Hittite.
There were thirty-seven in all.

23:23 *the Thirty:* The second most honored group of soldiers. They also may have been officers in the army (see the note at 23:8).

[a]**27** Hebrew; some Septuagint manuscripts (see also 1 Chron. 11:29) *Sibbecai* [b]**29** Some Hebrew manuscripts and Vulgate (see also 1 Chron. 11:30); most Hebrew manuscripts *Heleb* [c]**30** Hebrew; some Septuagint manuscripts (see also 1 Chron. 11:32) *Hurai* [d]**33** Some Septuagint manuscripts (see also 1 Chron. 11:34); Hebrew does not have *son of.* [e]**33** Hebrew; some Septuagint manuscripts (see also 1 Chron. 11:35) *Sacar* [f]**36** Some Septuagint manuscripts (see also 1 Chron. 11:38); Hebrew *Haggadi*

> Joab said, *"May the* LORD *your God multiply the troops a hundred times over, and may the eyes of my lord the king see it. But why does my lord the king want to do such a thing?"*
> 2 Sam 24:3

24:1-3 *anger of the* LORD *burned . . . take a census:* Wanting to count the people might have been a sign that David's trust in the LORD was weakening. Leaders had counted the Israelites in the past, but only when the LORD told them to do so. Joab tried to remind David that God would provide any soldiers that would be needed, no matter how many that was. After all, the LORD had repeatedly promised to help Israel fight and win (see, for example, Deut 20:1-4).

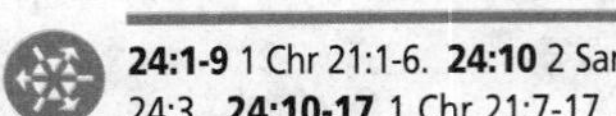
24:1-9 1 Chr 21:1-6. **24:10** 2 Sam 24:3. **24:10-17** 1 Chr 21:7-17.

DAVID'S SIN BRINGS AN ANGEL OF DESTRUCTION

God sends a horrible disease against Israel because David counted his troops. The plague does not stop until David buys Araunah's threshing floor, builds an altar, and makes a sacrifice there.

David Counts the Fighting Men

24 Again the anger of the LORD burned against Israel, and he incited David against them, saying, "Go and take a census of Israel and Judah."

2 So the king said to Joab and the army commanders[a] with him, "Go throughout the tribes of Israel from Dan to Beersheba and enroll the fighting men, so that I may know how many there are."

3 But Joab replied to the king, "May the LORD your God multiply the troops a hundred times over, and may the eyes of my lord the king see it. But why does my lord the king want to do such a thing?"

4 The king's word, however, overruled Joab and the army commanders; so they left the presence of the king to enroll the fighting men of Israel.

5 After crossing the Jordan, they camped near Aroer, south of the town in the gorge, and then went through Gad and on to Jazer. 6 They went to Gilead and the region of Tahtim Hodshi, and on to Dan Jaan and around toward Sidon. 7 Then they went toward the fortress of Tyre and all the towns of the Hivites and Canaanites. Finally, they went on to Beersheba in the Negev of Judah.

8 After they had gone through the entire land, they came back to Jerusalem at the end of nine months and twenty days.

9 Joab reported the number of the fighting men to the king: In Israel there were eight hundred thousand able-bodied men who could handle a sword, and in Judah five hundred thousand.

10 David was conscience-stricken after he had counted the fighting men, and he said to the LORD, "I have sinned greatly in what I have done. Now, O LORD, I beg you, take away the guilt of your servant. I have done a very foolish thing."

11 Before David got up the next morning, the word of the LORD had come to Gad the prophet, David's seer: 12 "Go and tell David, 'This is what the LORD says: I am giving you three options. Choose one of them for me to carry out against you.' "

13 So Gad went to David and said to him, "Shall there come upon you three[b] years of famine in your land? Or three months of fleeing from your enemies while they pursue you? Or three days of plague in your land? Now then, think it over and decide how I should answer the one who sent me."

---

[a] **2** Septuagint (see also verse 4 and 1 Chron. 21:2); Hebrew *Joab the army commander* [b] **13** Septuagint (see also 1 Chron. 21:12); Hebrew *seven*

[14]David said to Gad, "I am in deep distress. Let us fall into
the hands of the LORD, for his mercy is great; but do not let me fall
into the hands of men."
[15]So the LORD sent a plague on Israel from that morning
until the end of the time designated, and seventy thousand of the
people from Dan to Beersheba died. [16]When the angel stretched
out his hand to destroy Jerusalem, the LORD was grieved because of
the calamity and said to the angel who was afflicting the people,
"Enough! Withdraw your hand." The angel of the LORD was then at
the threshing floor of Araunah the Jebusite.
[17]When David saw the angel who was striking down the people, he said to the LORD, "I am the one who has sinned and done
wrong. These are but sheep. What have they done? Let your hand
fall upon me and my family."

24:18 *altar:* A raised structure where sacrifices and offerings could be presented to the LORD. See the illustration on p. 1811.

24:17 2 Sam 5:2; 7:7. **24:18-25** 1 Chr 21:18—22:1.

David Builds an Altar

[18]On that day Gad went to David and said to him, "Go up
and build an altar to the LORD on the threshing floor of Araunah

QUESTIONS ABOUT 2 SAMUEL 21:1—24:25

1. What happened because Saul broke a promise the Israelites had made to the Gibeonites? (21:1-9) What did David do to make things right? How do you feel about this? When someone does something that harms another person today, what kind of punishment do you think is appropriate? What can a society do to see that justice is done and all people are treated fairly?
2. Read the key passages in 2 SAMUEL that deal with mourning for the dead: (a) David mourns for Saul and Jonathan, 1:17-27, (b) David mourns for Abner, 3:28-39, (c) David mourns for his infant son, 12:15-23, (d) David mourns for Amnon, 13:30—14:24, (e) David mourns for Absalom, 18:33—19:8, (f) Rizpah mourns for her relatives who were executed, 21:10. How are these stories similar? How are they different? Have you experienced the loss of a loved one? If so, how did you mourn? Where did you find your comfort?
3. Read 21:17. Make a list of David's qualities that you think led to the devotion and honor his soldiers give him. What do these qualities have to do with David's relationship with God? Read what David has to say about himself in 22:21-25. Does this sound like boasting? Why or why not? What qualities do you have that might inspire respect from other people? How can improving your relationship with God improve your relationships with friends, family, and co-workers?
4. Why did David want to count the people of Israel and Judah? (24:1-17) What did Joab say when David told him that he wanted to do this? (24:3) How did David feel afterwards? (24:10) What message did the prophet Gad bring to David and how did David respond? (24:11-14) Look back through 2 SAMUEL for an example of David asking for, trusting, and following God's direction. How was this different from the time David counted the people?
5. David was a great leader of the people of Israel and a man who put his trust in God, yet he was guilty of many sins. Why do you think God continued to forgive David? What does this tell you about God?

24:22 *offer it up:* These gifts to God included certain animals, grains, fruits, and sweet-smelling spices. See also the note at 6:17-19 and the chart called "Sacrifices and Offerings," p. 219.

24:22 *threshing sledges:* See the note at 6:6. Threshing sledges were heavy boards with bits of rock or metal on the bottom. They were dragged across the grain to separate the husks from the kernels. See also the illustration on p. 730.

the Jebusite." [19]So David went up, as the LORD had commanded
through Gad. [20]When Araunah looked and saw the king and his
men coming toward him, he went out and bowed down before the
king with his face to the ground.
[21]Araunah said, "Why has my lord the king come to his
servant?"

"To buy your threshing floor," David answered, "so I can build an altar to the LORD, that the plague on the people may be stopped."

[22]Araunah said to David, "Let my lord the king take whatever pleases him and offer it up. Here are oxen for the burnt offering, and here are threshing sledges and ox yokes for the wood.
[23]O king, Araunah gives all this to the king." Araunah also said to
him, "May the LORD your God accept you."
[24]But the king replied to Araunah, "No, I insist on paying
you for it. I will not sacrifice to the LORD my God burnt offerings
that cost me nothing."

So David bought the threshing floor and the oxen and paid
fifty shekels[a] of silver for them. [25]David built an altar to the LORD
there and sacrificed burnt offerings and fellowship offerings.[b]
Then the LORD answered prayer in behalf of the land, and the
plague on Israel was stopped.

[a]**24** That is, about 1 1/4 pounds (about 0.6 kilogram) [b]**25** Traditionally *peace offerings*

1 KINGS

Israel experienced its "golden age" of peace and prosperity under King Solomon. But even Israel's wisest king wasn't perfect. Read 1 Kings to see what happened to the peace Israel enjoyed because of Solomon's disobedience to the Lord.

What makes 1 Kings special?

The book called 1 Kings is actually the first half of a single book that was divided into two parts, 1 and 2 Kings, because they were too long to fit on one scroll. Together the books continue the history of Israel that began in the books of Samuel, but 1 and 2 Kings tell the history in a special way. The story moves back and forth between reports of the kings of Judah and reports of the kings of Israel so that we can always compare what was going on in the north (Israel) with what was going on in the south (Judah).

In addition, the kings of the separate kingdoms are introduced in different ways. The reports of kings of Judah begin with the following standard outline:

1. the date the king began to rule in terms of how long the current king in Israel had been ruling,
2. his age,
3. the name of his mother, and
4. an evaluation of his conduct measured against the conduct of Israel's greatest king, David.

The kings of Israel, however, are introduced with the following standard outline:

1. the date he began to rule Israel in terms of how long the current king of Judah had been ruling,
2. the location of his capital,
3. the period of time he ruled, and
4. a negative judgment of the king.

Why was 1 Kings written?

The books of 1 and 2 Kings were written to complete the history of Israel begun in 1 and 2 Samuel, but they also serve another purpose. The history of the nation is told through the lives of the kings and several prophets to explain the tragic history of Israel as a failure of the nation to keep the covenant its people made with God as it is presented in Deuteronomy. The northern kingdom (Israel) had been destroyed by the Assyrians in 722 B.C. In 586 B.C., the southern kingdom (Judah) had fallen to Nebuchadnezzar and the Babylonians. The temple was burned to the ground, Jerusalem was destroyed, and Judah's high-ranking citizens, including its king, were deported to Babylon. To those Israelites living in exile in Babylon when the books of Kings were being written, it must have seemed as if God had abandoned them.

But 1 and 2 Kings present a different view: God has not been unfaithful to his chosen people; rather, the kings have been

King David: David was king of Israel from about 1010 to 970 B.C., and is the most famous king Israel ever had. Because of a promise the Lord made to David (2 Sam 7:16), many of the people of Israel expected that one of his descendants would always be their king. See also the mini-article called "David," p. 1028.

The Aramaic inscription on this stele (stone marker) from the ninth century B.C. found in the ruins of the ancient city of Dan in northern Israel tells of a battle between the king of Aram and the "House of David" (meaning one of the kings descended from David).

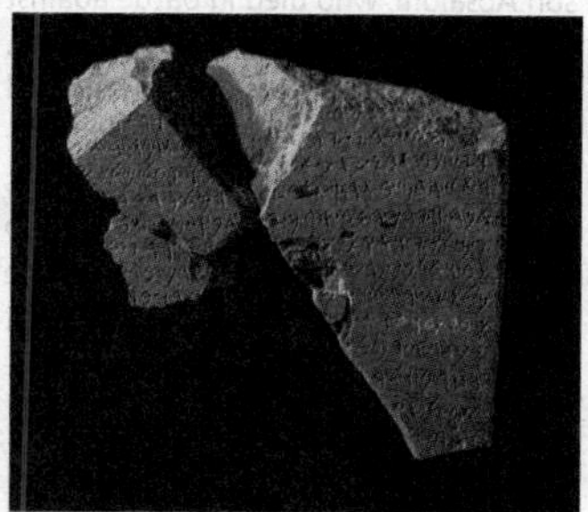

1:1-3 *King David . . . Abishag:* For David, see the note on p. 617. Having more than one wife was allowed at this time. Abishag's status may have been that of a "concubine," a woman legally bound to a man, but without the full privileges of a wife. The fact that David does not have sexual relations with this wife is probably the author's way of indicating that David was no longer a powerful ruler.

1:3 *Shunammite:* Shunem was a town in northern Israel, just north of the Valley of Jezreel.

1:5 *chariots and horses:* A chariot was a two-wheeled cart that was open at the back and pulled by horses. Chariots were especially useful during war because they could carry an archer into battle, they could move quickly, and they were easy to steer. The fact that Adonijah was acquiring chariots and horses shows that he intended to be king and knew he might have to go into battle to win the throne.

1:5,6 *Adonijah . . . Absalom:* The tragic story of David and his son Absalom, who died in battle against his father, is told in 2 Samuel 13–18. Absalom's mother was Maacah and Adonijah's mother was Haggith. With Absalom dead, Adonijah was now David's oldest surviving son (2 Sam 3:2-5) and so may have expected to inherit the throne. Adonijah also may have thought his father was no longer capable of ruling (see the note at 1:1-3).

unfaithful through their failure to obey God's law. These books, therefore, retell the history of Israel by looking at each king and judging him according to his faithfulness. If a king of Judah was faithful and obeyed God's Law, especially by worshiping in the place the LORD chose, that is, in Jerusalem (Deut 12:5-19), he was praised as being good. If he disobeyed by tolerating the worship of other gods or by allowing the people to worship from places other than Jerusalem, he was condemned as being evil. Some of the kings of Judah were judged to be good, especially Hezekiah and Josiah, because they enforced worship at the temple in Jerusalem. All the kings of Israel were judged to be evil, because they worshiped at the rival shrines of Bethel and Dan.

For more about this important period of Israelite history, see the article called "From Joshua to the Exile: The People of Israel in the Promised Land," p. 924.

WHAT'S THE STORY BEHIND THE SCENE?

The books of 1 and 2 KINGS were perhaps finally put together in Babylon from a number of sources sometime during the exile (586-539 B.C.). The original compilation of the material may have been written during the reign of Josiah who died in 609 B.C. This version saw Josiah as the fulfillment of God's promises to David. By showing the evil of the preceding kings the authors hoped to support the reforms begun by Josiah (2 Kgs 22, 23). During the disillusionment of the exile, however, a revision most likely was undertaken to expand the earlier version to show that God's judgment on Israel was fair. This "second edition" makes clear that Israel needed to accept God's punishment for the people's disobedience and to turn back to God if they are ever to be allowed to return to the land God promised to their ancestors.

HOW IS 1 KINGS CONSTRUCTED?

The following outline divides the book into three major sections. The first (1 Kgs 1,2) tells about the last years of David's life and how Solomon, his son, became king of Israel. The second (1 Kgs 3–11) reports what Solomon did as king, especially the building and dedication of the temple in Jerusalem. The last section (1 Kgs 12–22) begins with the story of the northern tribes' rejection of Solomon's son Rehoboam as king after Solomon's death, and the splitting of the nation into two separate kingdoms—Israel in the north and Judah in the south. This section then reports the activities of the various kings of both kingdoms through the middle of the ninth century B.C. These sections can be further subdivided as follows:

Solomon becomes king (1:1—2:46)

Israel under King Solomon (3:1—11:43)
- Solomon's wisdom and administration (3:1—4:34)
- Solomon builds and dedicates the temple (5:1—8:66)
- Solomon's wealth and wisdom (9:1—10:29)
- Solomon's failings (11:1-43)

The kingdom divides (12:1—22:53)
- The northern tribes rebel (12:1—14:31)
- Early kings of Judah and Israel (15:1—16:34)
- Elijah the prophet (17:1—19:21)
- King Ahab and Queen Jezebel (20:1—22:40)
- King Jehoshaphat of Judah and King Ahaziah of Israel (22:41-53)

Solomon Becomes King

***First Kings** opens with the conclusion of the court history of David that began in 2 Samuel 9 and then proceeds to relate the story of who would follow David as king: David's eldest living son, Adonijah, or his son by Bathsheba, Solomon.*

Adonijah Sets Himself Up as King

1 When King David was old and well advanced in years, he
could not keep warm even when they put covers over him. 2So his
servants said to him, "Let us look for a young virgin to attend the
king and take care of him. She can lie beside him so that our lord
the king may keep warm."
3Then they searched throughout Israel for a beautiful girl
and found Abishag, a Shunammite, and brought her to the king.
4The girl was very beautiful; she took care of the king and waited
on him, but the king had no intimate relations with her.
5Now Adonijah, whose mother was Haggith, put himself forward and said, "I will be king." So he got chariots and horses[a]
ready, with fifty men to run ahead of him. 6(His father had never
interfered with him by asking, "Why do you behave as you do?" He
was also very handsome and was born next after Absalom.)
7Adonijah conferred with Joab son of Zeruiah and with Abiathar the priest, and they gave him their support. 8But Zadok the
priest, Benaiah son of Jehoiada, Nathan the prophet, Shimei and
Rei[b] and David's special guard did not join Adonijah.
9Adonijah then sacrificed sheep, cattle and fattened calves at
the Stone of Zoheleth near En Rogel. He invited all his brothers,
the king's sons, and all the men of Judah who were royal officials,
10but he did not invite Nathan the prophet or Benaiah or the special guard or his brother Solomon.
11Then Nathan asked Bathsheba, Solomon's mother, "Have
you not heard that Adonijah, the son of Haggith, has become king
without our lord David's knowing it? 12Now then, let me advise
you how you can save your own life and the life of your son
Solomon. 13Go in to King David and say to him, 'My lord the king,
did you not swear to me your servant: "Surely Solomon your son
shall be king after me, and he will sit on my throne"? Why then
has Adonijah become king?' 14While you are still there talking to
the king, I will come in and confirm what you have said."
15So Bathsheba went to see the aged king in his room, where
Abishag the Shunammite was attending him. 16Bathsheba bowed
low and knelt before the king.
"What is it you want?" the king asked.
17She said to him, "My lord, you yourself swore to me your
servant by the LORD your God: 'Solomon your son shall be king
after me, and he will sit on my throne.' 18But now Adonijah has

[a]5 Or *charioteers* [b]8 Or *and his friends*

1:7,8 *Joab son of Zeruiah . . . Abiathar . . . Zadok . . . Benaiah . . . Nathan:* Zeruiah was David's older sister, so Joab was David's nephew. Joab was an important military leader who had served King David (2 Sam 10:7-14; 11:1; 1 Kgs 11:15,16). He commanded the troops in the field during battle, but would not have had men at his immediate command to support Adonijah in his claim as the new king.

Abiathar was the son of Ahimelech, a priest whom Saul had killed for helping David (1 Sam 22:11-23). Abiathar became David's close friend and was now David's priest (1 Sam 22:20-22; 23:9).

Zadok, a priest, is first mentioned in 2 Samuel 8:17, and was continually loyal to David.

Benaiah was the commander of the standing army, a group of paid foreign soldiers who acted as David's bodyguards (see the note at 1:38 and 2 Sam 23:20). The man Benaiah supports would have troops at his immediate command.

Nathan was a prophet who advised David (2 Sam 7:2,3; 12:1,25). For more about the role of prophets, see the article called "Prophets and Prophecy," p. 935.

1:9 *sacrificed:* This sacrificing of animals was part of a ceremony where Adonijah was made the new king.

1:11 *Bathsheba:* David slept with Bathsheba while she was still the wife of one of his soldiers, Uriah. When she became pregnant, David arranged for Uriah to be killed in battle and then married Bathsheba (2 Sam 11:2-27). The baby from their union died as punishment for David's sin. Solomon was their second son (2 Sam 12:24). See the mini-article called "Solomon," p. 776.

1:17 *you yourself swore:* This promise is not recorded anywhere in the Bible, but may be suggested in 2 Samuel 12:24,25. David either remembers making this promise or is convinced that if Nathan and Bathsheba believe he made this promise, then he surely must have (1:29,30).

1:33 *mule:* Mules are strong animals that are a cross between a mare (female horse) and a male donkey. Since Jewish law did not allow cross-breeding, mules were either imported or captured during war. They were mostly used by royalty (see also 2 Sam 13:29).

1:33 *Gihon:* This spring was Jerusalem's primary source of water. Archaeologists have discovered a tunnel running from the Gihon spring outside Jerusalem's walls to a pool under the city. Water jugs were lowered down a vertical shaft to the pool, giving the city access to water without going outside its walls. This was a real advantage during times when the city was under attack.

1:34 *anoint him:* This was a ceremonial act in which olive oil was poured on the head of the newly chosen king. See 1 Sam 10:1; 2 Sam 2:4.

1:34 *trumpet:* Here, probably a straight metal pipe-like instrument with a flared end. Among other things, these were used by priests to announce a temple sacrifice or ceremony (Num 10:1-10; 2 Chr 5:11-14). See the illustration on p. 251.

Another type of trumpet was a shofar, or ram's horn. It had a limit of two to three notes and was used to signal events, danger, or the death of important people (Judg 3:27; Neh 4:18-20). This ancient instrument is still used in synagogues today to announce the new year on Rosh Hashanah.

become king, and you, my lord the king, do not know about it.
[19]He has sacrificed great numbers of cattle, fattened calves, and
sheep, and has invited all the king's sons, Abiathar the priest and
Joab the commander of the army, but he has not invited Solomon
your servant. [20]My lord the king, the eyes of all Israel are on you,
to learn from you who will sit on the throne of my lord the king
after him. [21]Otherwise, as soon as my lord the king is laid to rest
with his fathers, I and my son Solomon will be treated as
criminals."

[22]While she was still speaking with the king, Nathan the prophet
arrived. [23]And they told the king, "Nathan the prophet is here." So
he went before the king and bowed with his face to the ground.

[24]Nathan said, "Have you, my lord the king, declared that
Adonijah shall be king after you, and that he will sit on your
throne? [25]Today he has gone down and sacrificed great numbers of
cattle, fattened calves, and sheep. He has invited all the king's sons,
the commanders of the army and Abiathar the priest. Right now
they are eating and drinking with him and saying, 'Long live King
Adonijah!' [26]But me your servant, and Zadok the priest, and Benaiah son of Jehoiada, and your servant Solomon he did not invite.
[27]Is this something my lord the king has done without letting his
servants know who should sit on the throne of my lord the king
after him?"

David Makes Solomon King

[28]Then King David said, "Call in Bathsheba." So she came
into the king's presence and stood before him.

[29]The king then took an oath: "As surely as the LORD lives,
who has delivered me out of every trouble, [30]I will surely carry out
today what I swore to you by the LORD, the God of Israel: Solomon
your son shall be king after me, and he will sit on my throne in my
place."

[31]Then Bathsheba bowed low with her face to the ground
and, kneeling before the king, said, "May my lord King David live
forever!"

[32]King David said, "Call in Zadok the priest, Nathan the
prophet and Benaiah son of Jehoiada." When they came before the
king, [33]he said to them: "Take your lord's servants with you and set
Solomon my son on my own mule and take him down to Gihon.
[34]There have Zadok the priest and Nathan the prophet anoint him
king over Israel. Blow the trumpet and shout, 'Long live King
Solomon!' [35]Then you are to go up with him, and he is to come
and sit on my throne and reign in my place. I have appointed him
ruler over Israel and Judah."

[36]Benaiah son of Jehoiada answered the king, "Amen! May
the LORD, the God of my lord the king, so declare it. [37]As the LORD
was with my lord the king, so may he be with Solomon to make
his throne even greater than the throne of my lord King David!"

38 So Zadok the priest, Nathan the prophet, Benaiah son of
Jehoiada, the Kerethites and the Pelethites went down and put
Solomon on King David's mule and escorted him to Gihon.
39 Zadok the priest took the horn of oil from the sacred tent and
anointed Solomon. Then they sounded the trumpet and all the
people shouted, "Long live King Solomon!" 40 And all the people
went up after him, playing flutes and rejoicing greatly, so that the
ground shook with the sound.
41 Adonijah and all the guests who were with him heard it as
they were finishing their feast. On hearing the sound of the trumpet, Joab asked, "What's the meaning of all the noise in the city?"
42 Even as he was speaking, Jonathan son of Abiathar the
priest arrived. Adonijah said, "Come in. A worthy man like you
must be bringing good news."
43 "Not at all!" Jonathan answered. "Our lord King David has
made Solomon king. 44 The king has sent with him Zadok the
priest, Nathan the prophet, Benaiah son of Jehoiada, the Kerethites
and the Pelethites, and they have put him on the king's mule, 45 and
Zadok the priest and Nathan the prophet have anointed him king
at Gihon. From there they have gone up cheering, and the city
resounds with it. That's the noise you hear. 46 Moreover, Solomon
has taken his seat on the royal throne. 47 Also, the royal officials
have come to congratulate our lord King David, saying, 'May your
God make Solomon's name more famous than yours and his
throne greater than yours!' And the king bowed in worship on his
bed 48 and said, 'Praise be to the LORD, the God of Israel, who has
allowed my eyes to see a successor on my throne today.' "
49 At this, all Adonijah's guests rose in alarm and dispersed.
50 But Adonijah, in fear of Solomon, went and took hold of the
horns of the altar. 51 Then Solomon was told, "Adonijah is afraid of
King Solomon and is clinging to the horns of the altar. He says,
'Let King Solomon swear to me today that he will not put his servant to death with the sword.' "
52 Solomon replied, "If he shows himself to be a worthy man,
not a hair of his head will fall to the ground; but if evil is found in
him, he will die." 53 Then King Solomon sent men, and they
brought him down from the altar. And Adonijah came and bowed
down to King Solomon, and Solomon said, "Go to your home."

David's Charge to Solomon

2 When the time drew near for David to die, he gave a charge to
Solomon his son.
2 "I am about to go the way of all the earth," he said. "So be
strong, show yourself a man, 3 and observe what the LORD your
God requires: Walk in his ways, and keep his decrees and commands, his laws and requirements, as written in the Law of Moses,
so that you may prosper in all you do and wherever you go, 4 and
that the LORD may keep his promise to me: 'If your descendants

1:38 *Zadok . . . Kerethites and the Pelethites:* By sending his officials (1:33), a priest (Zadok), a prophet (Nathan), his military commander (Benaiah), and the Kerethites and Pelethites to participate in the ceremony to make Solomon king, David shows that he supports Solomon, not Adonijah.

The Kerethites were probably originally from Crete, and the Pelethites were probably originally from somewhere around the Aegean Sea or Asia Minor. Since the Kerethites and Pelethites had settled in Philistia, David may have won their loyalty during the time he had offered his services to King Achish of Gath (1 Sam 27). They may have become David's bodyguards and hired fighters (mercenaries) See also 2 Sam 8:18.

1:39 *the sacred tent:* The sacred tent is usually called the "tabernacle," which means "dwelling place." When the people of Israel were wandering in the desert after leaving Egypt, the LORD told Moses to set up the tabernacle as the place where the people could worship the LORD and bring gifts, and where the priests could offer sacrifices according to the Law God gave Moses (Exod 26). When the people settled in the land God promised to them, they brought the tabernacle with them. Eventually, King David had it put up in Jerusalem. See also the mini-article called "The Tabernacle," p. 2346.

1:42 *A worthy man . . . good news:* Who carried the message was a sign of whether the message was good or bad news (see 2 Sam 18:27).

1:50 *in fear . . . took hold of the horns of the altar:* The four corners of some ancient altars looked like animal horns. Since the entire altar was sacred, anyone holding on to its corners was supposed to be safe from being killed. This protection, however, was not for people who intentionally committed murder (Exod 21:14).

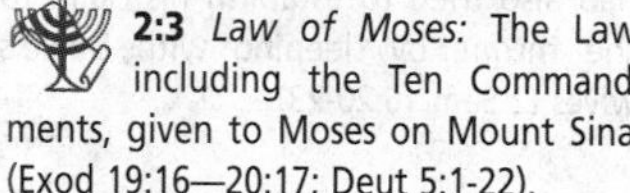

2:3 *Law of Moses:* The Law, including the Ten Commandments, given to Moses on Mount Sinai (Exod 19:16—20:17; Deut 5:1-22).

watch how they live, and if they walk faithfully before me with all
their heart and soul, you will never fail to have a man on the
throne of Israel.'
5"Now you yourself know what Joab son of Zeruiah did to
me—what he did to the two commanders of Israel's armies, Abner
son of Ner and Amasa son of Jether. He killed them, shedding their
blood in peacetime as if in battle, and with that blood stained the
belt around his waist and the sandals on his feet. 6Deal with him
according to your wisdom, but do not let his gray head go down to
the grave[a] in peace.
7"But show kindness to the sons of Barzillai of Gilead and
let them be among those who eat at your table. They stood by me
when I fled from your brother Absalom.
8"And remember, you have with you Shimei son of Gera, the
Benjamite from Bahurim, who called down bitter curses on me the
day I went to Mahanaim. When he came down to meet me at
the Jordan, I swore to him by the LORD: 'I will not put you to death
by the sword.' 9But now, do not consider him innocent. You are a
man of wisdom; you will know what to do to him. Bring his gray
head down to the grave in blood."
10Then David rested with his fathers and was buried in the
City of David. 11He had reigned forty years over Israel—seven
years in Hebron and thirty-three in Jerusalem. 12So Solomon sat
on the throne of his father David, and his rule was firmly established.

Solomon's Throne Established

13Now Adonijah, the son of Haggith, went to Bathsheba,
Solomon's mother. Bathsheba asked him, "Do you come peacefully?"
He answered, "Yes, peacefully." 14Then he added, "I have
something to say to you."
"You may say it," she replied.
15"As you know," he said, "the kingdom was mine. All Israel
looked to me as their king. But things changed, and the kingdom
has gone to my brother; for it has come to him from the LORD.
16Now I have one request to make of you. Do not refuse me."
"You may make it," she said.
17So he continued, "Please ask King Solomon—he will not
refuse you—to give me Abishag the Shunammite as my wife."
18"Very well," Bathsheba replied, "I will speak to the king
for you."
19When Bathsheba went to King Solomon to speak to him
for Adonijah, the king stood up to meet her, bowed down to her
and sat down on his throne. He had a throne brought for the
king's mother, and she sat down at his right hand.

[a]6 Hebrew *Sheol*; also in verse 9

2:5,6 *He killed them . . . Deal with him:* See 2 Sam 3:22-27 and 20:7-10.

2:7,8 *sons of Barzillai . . . Absalom . . . Shimei:* Barzillai from Gilead, the region east of the Jordan River, was among those who helped David when David's son Absalom tried to take the throne from David (2 Sam 17:27-29).

Shimei son of Gera was a distant relative of King Saul who blamed David for Saul's death and cursed David (2 Sam 16:5-13; 19:16-23).

2:8 *called down bitter curses on me:* A curse is the opposite of a blessing. A person who curses another asks for harm or destruction to happen to that person. Once spoken, a curse (like a blessing) could not be taken back, because it was believed that the spoken word had a life and power of its own, with the ability to make happen what was spoken. Only a blessing or other special action is able to control the evil intent of a curse.

2:10 *City of David:* From this time, "City of David" becomes another term for Jerusalem. See also the mini-article called "Jerusalem," p. 574.

2:11 *reigned forty years:* David and Solomon are both said to have ruled for forty years (see 11:42; 2 Sam 5:4, 5; 1 Chr 3:1-4). Forty often is used to mean a long period of time or a generation. See the chart called "Numbers in the Bible," p. 2405.

2:13 *Adonijah . . . Bathsheba:* See the notes at 1:5, 6 and 1:11.

2:17 *Abishag:* Whoever inherited the king's wives was considered to have inherited the throne. Abishag was one of David's wives (1 Kgs 1:3, 4). Solomon considers Adonijah's request to marry one of their father's wives as another attempt to establish himself as king. Solomon's older brother Absalom had also tried to establish his claim to the throne by sleeping with David's wives (2 Sam 16:20-23).

20“I have one small request to make of you,” she said. “Do
not refuse me.”
The king replied, “Make it, my mother; I will not refuse you.”
21So she said, “Let Abishag the Shunammite be given in marriage to your brother Adonijah.”
22King Solomon answered his mother, “Why do you request
Abishag the Shunammite for Adonijah? You might as well request
the kingdom for him—after all, he is my older brother—yes, for
him and for Abiathar the priest and Joab son of Zeruiah!”
23Then King Solomon swore by the LORD: “May God deal
with me, be it ever so severely, if Adonijah does not pay with his
life for this request! 24And now, as surely as the LORD lives—he
who has established me securely on the throne of my father David
and has founded a dynasty for me as he promised—Adonijah shall
be put to death today!” 25So King Solomon gave orders to Benaiah
son of Jehoiada, and he struck down Adonijah and he died.
26To Abiathar the priest the king said, “Go back to your fields
in Anathoth. You deserve to die, but I will not put you to death
now, because you carried the ark of the Sovereign LORD before my
father David and shared all my father’s hardships.” 27So Solomon
removed Abiathar from the priesthood of the LORD, fulfilling the
word the LORD had spoken at Shiloh about the house of Eli.
28When the news reached Joab, who had conspired with
Adonijah though not with Absalom, he fled to the tent of the LORD
and took hold of the horns of the altar. 29King Solomon was told that
Joab had fled to the tent of the LORD and was beside the altar. Then
Solomon ordered Benaiah son of Jehoiada, “Go, strike him down!”
30So Benaiah entered the tent of the LORD and said to Joab,
“The king says, ‘Come out!’ ”
But he answered, “No, I will die here.”
Benaiah reported to the king, “This is how Joab answered me.”
31Then the king commanded Benaiah, “Do as he says. Strike
him down and bury him, and so clear me and my father’s house of
the guilt of the innocent blood that Joab shed. 32The LORD will
repay him for the blood he shed, because without the knowledge
of my father David he attacked two men and killed them with the
sword. Both of them—Abner son of Ner, commander of Israel’s
army, and Amasa son of Jether, commander of Judah’s army—
were better men and more upright than he. 33May the guilt of their
blood rest on the head of Joab and his descendants forever. But on
David and his descendants, his house and his throne, may there be
the LORD’s peace forever.”
34So Benaiah son of Jehoiada went up and struck down Joab
and killed him, and he was buried on his own land[a] in the desert.

[a]**34** Or *buried in his tomb*

2:19 *she sat down at his right hand:* The place of honor.

2:26 *Abiathar:* See the note at 1:7,8 and the notes at 1 Sam 22:20; and 2 Sam 15:24 (Zadok . . . Abiathar).

2:26 *you carried the ark of the Sovereign LORD:* The ark of the covenant was the acacia wood box that accompanied the Hebrews on their desert wanderings in the time of Moses and housed the two stone tablets that had the Ten Commandments written on them. It was understood to be the throne of the LORD Almighty from which God ruled his people. See also the mini-article called "The Ark of the Covenant," p. 513.

2:26,27 *Go back to your fields . . . fulfilling the word the LORD had spoken:* Priests were protected from execution, so the only way Solomon could punish Abiathar was by sending him away.

Eli, Abiathar's great-grandfather, was told by a prophet that his family would lose its position as Israel's priests (1 Sam 2:27-36).

2:28 *took hold of the horns of the altar:* See the note at 1:50.

2:34,35 *struck down Joab . . . replaced Abiathar with Zadok the priest:* Perhaps Joab is not given the protection of the altar (see the note at 1:50) because his killings were murder, not accidental (2:31,32). Joab was buried near his home in Bethlehem (2 Sam 2:18,32).

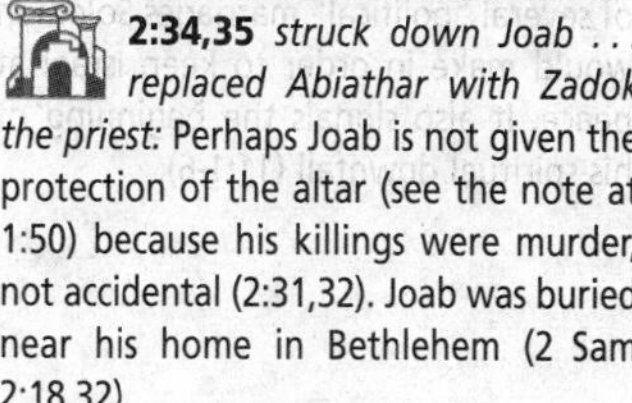

Priests led the worship in the tabernacle or in the temple and offered sacrifices to the LORD for the sake of the people. From this time on, only Zadok and his descendants are considered legitimate priests. See also the mini-article called "Israel's Priests," p. 2344.

2:12 1 Chr 29:23.

> Solomon said to God, *"Give your servant a discerning heart to govern your people and to distinguish between right and wrong. For who is able to govern this great people of yours?"*
> 1 Kgs 3:9

2:36,37 *Jerusalem . . . Kidron Valley:* Jerusalem was Israel's political capital and the place where people were to worship God. See also the note at 2:10. The Kidron Valley was considered the eastern boundary of Jerusalem. See the map on p. 2465 and the mini-article called "Jerusalem," p. 574.

2:46 *struck Shimei down:* Killing Shimei ends the curse Shimei made on David, because Shimei had first broken the promise he had made to Solomon never to leave Jerusalem (2:36-38). See also the notes at 2:7,8 and 2:8.

3:1 *made an alliance . . . married his daughter:* This marriage protected Israel against Egypt. It is the first of several "political" marriages Solomon would make in order to keep Israel at peace. It also signals the beginning of his spiritual downfall (11:1-6).

35 The king put Benaiah son of Jehoiada over the army in Joab's
position and replaced Abiathar with Zadok the priest.
36 Then the king sent for Shimei and said to him, "Build
yourself a house in Jerusalem and live there, but do not go anywhere else. 37 The day you leave and cross the Kidron Valley, you
can be sure you will die; your blood will be on your own head."
38 Shimei answered the king, "What you say is good. Your
servant will do as my lord the king has said." And Shimei stayed in
Jerusalem for a long time.
39 But three years later, two of Shimei's slaves ran off to
Achish son of Maacah, king of Gath, and Shimei was told, "Your
slaves are in Gath." 40 At this, he saddled his donkey and went to
Achish at Gath in search of his slaves. So Shimei went away and
brought the slaves back from Gath.
41 When Solomon was told that Shimei had gone from
Jerusalem to Gath and had returned, 42 the king summoned Shimei
and said to him, "Did I not make you swear by the LORD and warn
you, 'On the day you leave to go anywhere else, you can be sure
you will die'? At that time you said to me, 'What you say is good. I
will obey.' 43 Why then did you not keep your oath to the LORD and
obey the command I gave you?"
44 The king also said to Shimei, "You know in your heart all
the wrong you did to my father David. Now the LORD will repay
you for your wrongdoing. 45 But King Solomon will be blessed, and
David's throne will remain secure before the LORD forever."
46 Then the king gave the order to Benaiah son of Jehoiada,
and he went out and struck Shimei down and killed him.
The kingdom was now firmly established in Solomon's hands.

Israel Under King Solomon

Israel under Solomon is seen as experiencing a "golden age." Given the gift of wisdom by God, Solomon organizes the nation to be more efficient, brings them peace and prosperity, and builds a temple for the LORD in Jerusalem, majestic palaces, and strong forts. But Solomon is not always wise. He uses forced labor to complete his building projects and taxes the people too heavily. His big sin, however, is that he builds shrines to the gods his foreign wives worship.

SOLOMON'S WISDOM AND ADMINISTRATION

When the LORD appears to Solomon in a dream, the young king asks God for the wisdom to rule his people. God is so pleased that Solomon has asked for wisdom that God promises to make him rich and respected as well.

Solomon Asks for Wisdom

3 Solomon made an alliance with Pharaoh king of Egypt and
married his daughter. He brought her to the City of David until he
finished building his palace and the temple of the LORD, and the

wall around Jerusalem. [2]The people, however, were still sacrificing at the high places, because a temple had not yet been built for the Name of the LORD. [3]Solomon showed his love for the LORD by walking according to the statutes of his father David, except that he offered sacrifices and burned incense on the high places.

[4]The king went to Gibeon to offer sacrifices, for that was the most important high place, and Solomon offered a thousand burnt offerings on that altar. [5]At Gibeon the LORD appeared to Solomon during the night in a dream, and God said, "Ask for whatever you want me to give you."

[6]Solomon answered, "You have shown great kindness to your servant, my father David, because he was faithful to you and righteous and upright in heart. You have continued this great kindness to him and have given him a son to sit on his throne this very day.

[7]"Now, O LORD my God, you have made your servant king in place of my father David. But I am only a little child and do not know how to carry out my duties. [8]Your servant is here among the people you have chosen, a great people, too numerous to count or number. [9]So give your servant a discerning heart to govern your people and to distinguish between right and wrong. For who is able to govern this great people of yours?"

[10]The Lord was pleased that Solomon had asked for this. [11]So God said to him, "Since you have asked for this and not for long life or wealth for yourself, nor have asked for the death of your enemies but for discernment in administering justice, [12]I will do what you have asked. I will give you a wise and discerning heart, so that there will never have been anyone like you, nor will there ever be. [13]Moreover, I will give you what you have not asked for—both riches and honor—so that in your lifetime you will have no equal among kings. [14]And if you walk in my ways and obey my statutes and commands as David your father did, I will give you a long life." [15]Then Solomon awoke—and he realized it had been a dream.

He returned to Jerusalem, stood before the ark of the Lord's covenant and sacrificed burnt offerings and fellowship offerings.[a] Then he gave a feast for all his court.

A Wise Ruling

[16]Now two prostitutes came to the king and stood before him. [17]One of them said, "My lord, this woman and I live in the same house. I had a baby while she was there with me. [18]The third day after my child was born, this woman also had a baby. We were alone; there was no one in the house but the two of us.

[19]"During the night this woman's son died because she lay on him. [20]So she got up in the middle of the night and took my son from my side while I your servant was asleep. She put him by her breast

[a]**15** Traditionally *peace offerings*

3:2 *high places:* Many of the Israelites' altars were on hills, at places where foreign gods once had been worshiped. God's Law required that these altars be destroyed (Num 33:52; Deut 7:5; 12:3), and that worship take place only at the one place chosen by the LORD, Jerusalem (Deut 12:5).

3:4 *Gibeon:* Located in the area of Benjamin about six miles northwest of Jerusalem. See the map on p. 2464.

3:6 *David:* See the note on p. 617.

3:7 *you have made your servant king:* These words show that Solomon understands his place as king of Israel. The LORD God is the true king. Israel's earthly kings were chosen by God and were expected to carry out God's will. For more, see the mini-article called "Kingship in Israel," p. 650.

3:15 *ark of the Lord's covenant:* See the note at 2:26 (ark).

3:15 *burnt offerings and fellowship offerings:* For burnt offerings, the whole animal was burned on the altar. A main purpose of such an offering was to gain God's favor with the odor of the sacrifice. See Lev 1:1-17.

A main purpose of fellowship offerings was to give thanks to God and have fellowship with him. See Lev 3:1-17. See also the chart called "Sacrifices and Offerings," p. 219.

3:16 *prostitutes:* These women were not sacred prostitutes (see the note at 14:24). Most likely they worked at an inn, a profession that was not considered very honorable. See also the mini-article called "Prostitution in the Bible," p. 1688.

When all Israel heard the verdict the king had given, they held the king in awe, because they saw that he had wisdom from God to administer justice.
1 Kgs 3:28

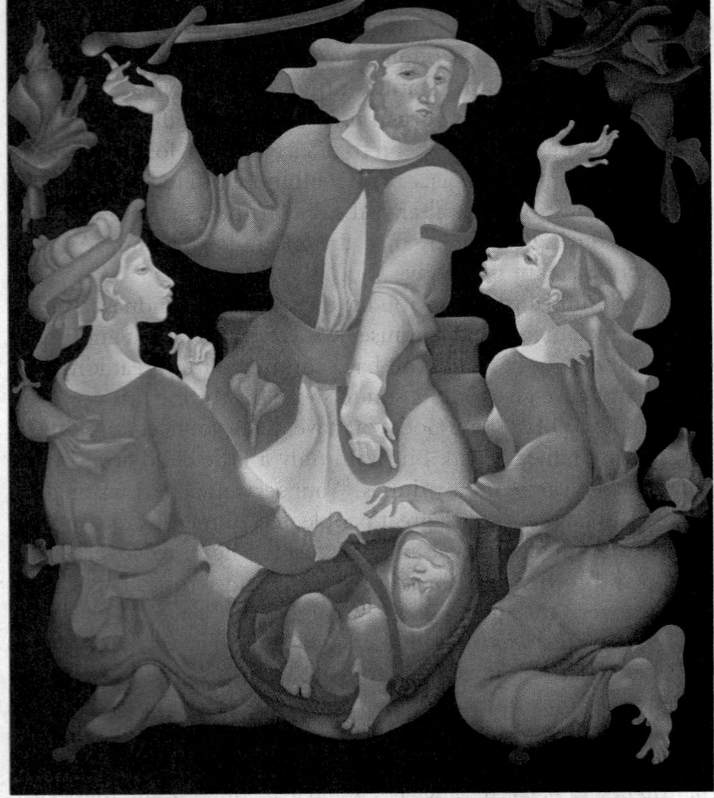

Solomon's Decision by Emmanuil and Janet Snitkovsky, 1989. Solomon prayed for wisdom, and the LORD promised to make him wiser than anyone who ever lived (3:12). One day, two women came to Solomon, both claiming to be the rightful mother of the same baby boy. Solomon listened to their stories and then decided the baby should be cut in two so that each mother could have half. Solomon knew the real mother would rather lose her child than see it destroyed in this way. When the real mother cried out in horror, Solomon gave the baby to her. All Israel was amazed at the wisdom of Solomon's decision. (See 3:16-28.)

and put her dead son by my breast. 21The next morning, I got up to
nurse my son—and he was dead! But when I looked at him closely in
the morning light, I saw that it wasn't the son I had borne."
22The other woman said, "No! The living one is my son; the
dead one is yours."
But the first one insisted, "No! The dead one is yours; the living one is mine." And so they argued before the king.
23The king said, "This one says, 'My son is alive and your son is
dead,' while that one says, 'No! Your son is dead and mine is alive.'"
24Then the king said, "Bring me a sword." So they brought a
sword for the king. 25He then gave an order: "Cut the living child
in two and give half to one and half to the other."

[26]The woman whose son was alive was filled with compassion for her son and said to the king, "Please, my lord, give her the
living baby! Don't kill him!"

But the other said, "Neither I nor you shall have him. Cut
him in two!"

[27]Then the king gave his ruling: "Give the living baby to the
first woman. Do not kill him; she is his mother."

[28]When all Israel heard the verdict the king had given, they
held the king in awe, because they saw that he had wisdom from
God to administer justice.

Solomon's Officials and Governors

4 So King Solomon ruled over all Israel. [2]And these were his
chief officials:

Azariah son of Zadok—the priest;
[3]Elihoreph and Ahijah, sons of Shisha—secretaries;
Jehoshaphat son of Ahilud—recorder;
[4]Benaiah son of Jehoiada—commander in chief;
Zadok and Abiathar—priests;
[5]Azariah son of Nathan—in charge of the district officers;
Zabud son of Nathan—a priest and personal adviser to the king;
[6]Ahishar—in charge of the palace;
Adoniram son of Abda—in charge of forced labor.

[7]Solomon also had twelve district governors over all Israel,
who supplied provisions for the king and the royal household.
Each one had to provide supplies for one month in the year.
[8]These are their names:

Ben-Hur—in the hill country of Ephraim;
[9]Ben-Deker—in Makaz, Shaalbim, Beth Shemesh and Elon Bethhanan;
[10]Ben-Hesed—in Arubboth (Socoh and all the land of Hepher were his);
[11]Ben-Abinadab—in Naphoth Dor[a] (he was married to Taphath daughter of Solomon);
[12]Baana son of Ahilud—in Taanach and Megiddo, and in all of Beth Shan next to Zarethan below Jezreel, from Beth Shan to Abel Meholah across to Jokmeam;
[13]Ben-Geber—in Ramoth Gilead (the settlements of Jair son of Manasseh in Gilead were his, as well as the district of Argob in Bashan and its sixty large walled cities with bronze gate bars);
[14]Ahinadab son of Iddo—in Mahanaim;

[a]**11** Or *in the heights of Dor*

3:28 *wisdom:* The story in 3:16-28 reflects the Israelites' understanding that "wisdom" is the ability to understand the human mind and intentions in order to see that God's justice is carried out. Other understandings of "wisdom" are revealed in the spoken and written literature of the people of Israel, particularly in their proverbs, songs, and riddles (see 4:32). See also the mini-article called "Wisdom," p. 2206 and the Introduction to the Books of Wisdom and Poetry, p. 959.

4:2-4 *Azariah . . . Zadok and Abiathar:* This list has puzzled scholars because it names Zadok's son Azariah as a priest as well as Zadok himself and Abiathar, David's priest that Solomon had sent away (2:26, 27). Parts of the list may be from early in Solomon's reign and other parts from later. See also the note at 1:7,8.

Running the nation required the appointment of high-ranking officials (an administrative cabinet) and giving them authority over the various aspects of government. Unlike the twelve district governors (4:7-19), these officials governed with Solomon in Jerusalem.

4:7-19 *twelve district governors over all Israel:* Solomon divided the kingdom into twelve districts, each with its own governor. The district boundaries are somewhat different from the boundaries that separated the twelve tribes. Solomon may have hoped that this would break old tribal loyalties and work toward creating a more united nation. In the end, it may have contributed to the revolt after his death (see 12:1-20), especially since Judah (Solomon's own tribal territory) appears to have been a thirteenth territory that was not required to support the king in the same way as the others.

During Solomon's lifetime Judah and Israel, from Dan to Beersheba, lived in safety, each man under his own vine and fig tree.
1 Kgs 4:25

4:20 *Judah and Israel:* Before David united the kingdom as a whole under the name of Israel (and then again after the revolt under Rehoboam), "Israel" refers to the ten northern tribes (led by the tribe of Ephraim) and "Judah" to the two southern tribes (Simeon and Judah, with the tribe of Judah leading). See the map on p. 2464 and the mini-article called "Israel," p. 264.

4:21 *the River:* Referring to the Euphrates River, the longest, largest river in Western Asia, originating in the Armenian Mountains and flowing to the Persian Gulf. See the map on p. 2462.

4:21 *land of the Philistines:* Philistia, homeland of the Philistines, was a strip of land along the eastern coast of the Mediterranean Sea. It included five main cities, each with its own ruler: Ekron, Ashdod, Ashkelon, Gath, and Gaza. Israel fought many wars against the Philistines.

4:21 *the border of Egypt:* See the mini-article called "Egypt," p. 135.

4:23 *gazelles:* A small, swift antelope that lived in the wild and hilly areas of Israel.

4:24 *Tiphsah . . . Gaza:* Tiphsah was a city on the Euphrates River on the northern border of Solomon's kingdom. Gaza was one of the southernmost cities of the kingdom.

4:21 Gen 15:18-21; 2 Chr 9:26. **4:26** 1 Kgs 10:26; 2 Chr 1:14; 9:25. **4:27** 1 Sam 8:11-18. **4:32** Prov 1:1; 10:1; 25:1; Song 1:1.

[15] Ahimaaz—in Naphtali (he had married Basemath daughter of Solomon);
[16] Baana son of Hushai—in Asher and in Aloth;
[17] Jehoshaphat son of Paruah—in Issachar;
[18] Shimei son of Ela—in Benjamin;
[19] Geber son of Uri—in Gilead (the country of Sihon king of the Amorites and the country of Og king of Bashan). He was the only governor over the district.

Solomon's Daily Provisions

[20] The people of Judah and Israel were as numerous as the
sand on the seashore; they ate, they drank and they were happy.
[21] And Solomon ruled over all the kingdoms from the River[a] to the
land of the Philistines, as far as the border of Egypt. These countries brought tribute and were Solomon's subjects all his life.
[22] Solomon's daily provisions were thirty cors[b] of fine flour
and sixty cors[c] of meal, [23] ten head of stall-fed cattle, twenty of
pasture-fed cattle and a hundred sheep and goats, as well as deer,
gazelles, roebucks and choice fowl. [24] For he ruled over all the
kingdoms west of the River, from Tiphsah to Gaza, and had peace
on all sides. [25] During Solomon's lifetime Judah and Israel, from
Dan to Beersheba, lived in safety, each man under his own vine
and fig tree.
[26] Solomon had four[d] thousand stalls for chariot horses, and
twelve thousand horses.[e]
[27] The district officers, each in his month, supplied provisions
for King Solomon and all who came to the king's table. They saw
to it that nothing was lacking. [28] They also brought to the proper
place their quotas of barley and straw for the chariot horses and
the other horses.

Solomon's Wisdom

[29] God gave Solomon wisdom and very great insight, and a
breadth of understanding as measureless as the sand on the
seashore. [30] Solomon's wisdom was greater than the wisdom of all
the men of the East, and greater than all the wisdom of Egypt. [31] He
was wiser than any other man, including Ethan the Ezrahite—
wiser than Heman, Calcol and Darda, the sons of Mahol. And his
fame spread to all the surrounding nations. [32] He spoke three thousand proverbs and his songs numbered a thousand and five. [33] He
described plant life, from the cedar of Lebanon to the hyssop that
grows out of walls. He also taught about animals and birds, reptiles

[a] **21** That is, the Euphrates; also in verse 24 [b] **22** That is, probably about 185 bushels (about 6.6 kiloliters) [c] **22** That is, probably about 375 bushels (about 13.2 kiloliters) [d] **26** Some Septuagint manuscripts (see also 2 Chron. 9:25); Hebrew *forty* [e] **26** Or *charioteers*

and fish. 34 Men of all nations came to listen to Solomon's wisdom,
sent by all the kings of the world, who had heard of his wisdom.

SOLOMON BUILDS AND DEDICATES THE TEMPLE

With the help of King Hiram of Tyre, Solomon builds a temple for the LORD to replace the tabernacle in Jerusalem and dedicates it during the Feast of Tabernacles. But Solomon is warned in a dream that the LORD will desert the temple and the land if the people disobey God's commands and start worshiping foreign gods.

Preparations for Building the Temple

5 When Hiram king of Tyre heard that Solomon had been
anointed king to succeed his father David, he sent his envoys to
Solomon, because he had always been on friendly terms with
David. 2 Solomon sent back this message to Hiram:

> 3 "You know that because of the wars waged against my
> father David from all sides, he could not build a temple for the
> Name of the LORD his God until the LORD put his enemies under
> his feet. 4 But now the LORD my God has given me rest on every
> side, and there is no adversary or disaster. 5 I intend, therefore, to
> build a temple for the Name of the LORD my God, as the LORD
> told my father David, when he said, 'Your son whom I will put
> on the throne in your place will build the temple for my Name.'
> 6 "So give orders that cedars of Lebanon be cut for me.
> My men will work with yours, and I will pay you for your men
> whatever wages you set. You know that we have no one so
> skilled in felling timber as the Sidonians."

7 When Hiram heard Solomon's message, he was greatly
pleased and said, "Praise be to the LORD today, for he has given
David a wise son to rule over this great nation."
8 So Hiram sent word to Solomon:

> "I have received the message you sent me and will do all
> you want in providing the cedar and pine logs. 9 My men will
> haul them down from Lebanon to the sea, and I will float
> them in rafts by sea to the place you specify. There I will sep-
> arate them and you can take them away. And you are to grant
> my wish by providing food for my royal household."

10 In this way Hiram kept Solomon supplied with all the
cedar and pine logs he wanted, 11 and Solomon gave Hiram
twenty thousand cors[a] of wheat as food for his household, in addition to twenty thousand baths[b,c] of pressed olive oil. Solomon

---

[a]**11** That is, probably about 125,000 bushels (about 4,400 kiloliters)
[b]**11** Septuagint (see also 2 Chron. 2:10); Hebrew *twenty cors* [c]**11** That is, about 115,000 gallons (about 440 kiloliters)

> Solomon said,
> *"I intend, therefore, to build a temple for the Name of the LORD my God."*
> 1 Kgs 5:5

5:1 *Hiram king of Tyre:* King Hiram, who ruled the city state of Tyre from around 970 to 935 B.C., had sent lumber and workmen to help David build his palace (2 Sam 5:11). His strong trade and military relations with David and Solomon was an important reason why the Philistines ceased to be a major threat to Israel during Solomon's reign.

5:1 *Tyre:* The most important city in Phoenicia. It was located on the coast of the Mediterranean Sea north of Israel, in what is today southern Lebanon. See the mini-article called "Phoenicia," p. 1604.

5:6 *cedars of Lebanon:* Cedar is an extremely hard wood that resists rotting and insects, is suitable for carving, and is valued for its distinctive smell. See the photograph on p. 858. At one time cedar forests covered most of the Lebanon mountain range that stretches for around one hundred miles along the Syrian coast between Tyre and Arvad.

5:6 *your men:* The Phoenicians were well-known in the ancient world for their skills in many crafts.

5:9 *the sea:* The Mediterranean is the large body of water separating Africa and Europe. It formed the western boundary of Solomon's kingdom. See the maps on pp. 2465 and 2471. The huge cedar logs would be shipped from Phoenicia south to Israel.

5:5 2 Sam 7:12,13; 1 Chr 17:11, 12.

5:18 *Gebal:* Also called Byblos. This was a seaport famous for its skilled stonemasons and shipbuilders. See the map on p. 2465.

6:1 *Israelites . . . Egypt . . . Ziv:* Some historians have used this verse to establish a probable date for the exodus, that is, 1446 B.C., the time when the Hebrew people were freed from their captivity in Egypt. Other historians, however, take "four hundred eighty" to be a figurative way of saying twelve generations of forty years and do not use it to calculate the date of the exodus. Based on Genesis 47:11 and other considerations, they place the exodus at 1290 B.C. The Bible Timeline on p. 2458 and other notes in the Learning Bible use the later date.

Ziv is the second month of the Hebrew calendar, from about mid-April to mid-May. See also the chart called "Jewish Calendar and Festivals," p. 944.

6:7 *at the quarry:* Besides the reason given here, another reason for cutting and shaping the stones at the quarry may have been tied to an earlier belief that once stones were brought onto an altar site they became sacred. See also the illustration on p. 862.

6:16 *Most Holy Place:* The Most Holy Place in the temple is its inner sanctuary. This, the Holy Place, and the outer courtyard were the three major areas of the temple. Only the high priest could enter the Most Holy Place, and even he could enter it only once a year on the Day of Atonement. The Most Holy Place traditionally has been called "the Holy of Holies."

continued to do this for Hiram year after year. [12]The LORD gave
Solomon wisdom, just as he had promised him. There were peaceful relations between Hiram and Solomon, and the two of them made a treaty.

[13]King Solomon conscripted laborers from all Israel—thirty thousand men. [14]He sent them off to Lebanon in shifts of ten thousand a month, so that they spent one month in Lebanon and two months at home. Adoniram was in charge of the forced labor.
[15]Solomon had seventy thousand carriers and eighty thousand stonecutters in the hills, [16]as well as thirty-three hundred[a] foremen who supervised the project and directed the workmen. [17]At the king's command they removed from the quarry large blocks of quality stone to provide a foundation of dressed stone for the temple. [18]The craftsmen of Solomon and Hiram and the men of Gebal[b] cut and prepared the timber and stone for the building of the temple.

Solomon Builds the Temple

6 In the four hundred and eightieth[c] year after the Israelites had come out of Egypt, in the fourth year of Solomon's reign over Israel, in the month of Ziv, the second month, he began to build the temple of the LORD.

[2]The temple that King Solomon built for the LORD was sixty cubits long, twenty wide and thirty high.[d] [3]The portico at the front of the main hall of the temple extended the width of the temple, that is twenty cubits,[e] and projected ten cubits[f] from the front of the temple. [4]He made narrow clerestory windows in the temple.
[5]Against the walls of the main hall and inner sanctuary he built a structure around the building, in which there were side rooms.
[6]The lowest floor was five cubits[g] wide, the middle floor six cubits[h] and the third floor seven.[i] He made offset ledges around the outside of the temple so that nothing would be inserted into the temple walls.

[7]In building the temple, only blocks dressed at the quarry were used, and no hammer, chisel or any other iron tool was heard at the temple site while it was being built.

[8]The entrance to the lowest[j] floor was on the south side of the temple; a stairway led up to the middle level and from there to the third. [9]So he built the temple and completed it, roofing it with beams and cedar planks. [10]And he built the side rooms all along

---

[a]16 Hebrew; some Septuagint manuscripts (see also 2 Chron. 2:2, 18) *thirty-six hundred* [b]18 That is, Byblos [c]1 Hebrew; Septuagint *four hundred and fortieth* [d]2 That is, about 90 feet (about 27 meters) long and 30 feet (about 9 meters) wide and 45 feet (about 13.5 meters) high [e]3 That is, about 30 feet (about 9 meters) [f]3 That is, about 15 feet (about 4.5 meters) [g]6 That is, about 7 1/2 feet (about 2.3 meters); also in verses 10 and 24 [h]6 That is, about 9 feet (about 2.7 meters) [i]6 That is, about 10 1/2 feet (about 3.1 meters) [j]8 Septuagint; Hebrew *middle*

the temple. The height of each was five cubits, and they were
attached to the temple by beams of cedar.
11The word of the LORD came to Solomon: 12"As for this temple you are building, if you follow my decrees, carry out my regulations and keep all my commands and obey them, I will fulfill
through you the promise I gave to David your father. 13And I will
live among the Israelites and will not abandon my people Israel."
14So Solomon built the temple and completed it. 15He lined
its interior walls with cedar boards, paneling them from the floor
of the temple to the ceiling, and covered the floor of the temple
with planks of pine. 16He partitioned off twenty cubits[a] at the rear
of the temple with cedar boards from floor to ceiling to form within the temple an inner sanctuary, the Most Holy Place. 17The main
hall in front of this room was forty cubits[b] long. 18The inside of
the temple was cedar, carved with gourds and open flowers. Everything was cedar; no stone was to be seen.
19He prepared the inner sanctuary within the temple to set
the ark of the covenant of the LORD there. 20The inner sanctuary
was twenty cubits long, twenty wide and twenty high.[c] He overlaid
the inside with pure gold, and he also overlaid the altar of cedar.
21Solomon covered the inside of the temple with pure gold, and he
extended gold chains across the front of the inner sanctuary, which
was overlaid with gold. 22So he overlaid the whole interior with
gold. He also overlaid with gold the altar that belonged to the
inner sanctuary.
23In the inner sanctuary he made a pair of cherubim of olive
wood, each ten cubits[d] high. 24One wing of the first cherub was five
cubits long, and the other wing five cubits—ten cubits from wing
tip to wing tip. 25The second cherub also measured ten cubits, for
the two cherubim were identical in size and shape. 26The height of
each cherub was ten cubits. 27He placed the cherubim inside the
innermost room of the temple, with their wings spread out. The
wing of one cherub touched one wall, while the wing of the other
touched the other wall, and their wings touched each other in the
middle of the room. 28He overlaid the cherubim with gold.
29On the walls all around the temple, in both the inner and
outer rooms, he carved cherubim, palm trees and open flowers.
30He also covered the floors of both the inner and outer rooms of
the temple with gold.
31For the entrance of the inner sanctuary he made doors of
olive wood with five-sided jambs. 32And on the two olive wood
doors he carved cherubim, palm trees and open flowers, and overlaid the cherubim and palm trees with beaten gold. 33In the same
way he made four-sided jambs of olive wood for the entrance to

[a]**16** That is, about 30 feet (about 9 meters) [b]**17** That is, about 60 feet (about 18 meters) [c]**20** That is, about 30 feet (about 9 meters) long, wide and high [d]**23** That is, about 15 feet (about 4.5 meters)

The LORD said to Solomon, *"As for this temple you are building, if you follow my decrees, carry out my regulations and keep all my commands and obey them, I will fulfill through you the promise I gave to David your father. And I will live among the Israelites and will not abandon my people Israel."*
1 Kgs 6:12, 13

6:19-23 *ark of the covenant . . . gold . . . cherubim:* For ark of the covenant, see the note at 2:26 (ark).

Large forests were not common in this part of the world, and so wood, especially cedar, was precious. In addition to using precious woods, a layer of gold apparently covered almost everything in the Most Holy Place. See also Exod 25:18-20; 26:31-34; 30:1-3.

The cherubim were statues of winged creatures symbolizing the LORD's throne on earth (see Exod 25:18-22). Similar statues are described as having human, lion, eagle, or ox heads (Gen 3:24; Ezek 1:10; 10:12-14; 41:18-20), sometimes with more than one of these on the same winged body. They may have been similar to the human-headed bull and lions that guarded Mesopotamian temples. Such winged creatures guarding sacred objects or places are commonly seen in Egyptian and Phoenician art as well.

Temple of Solomon, illustration from a Moravian *Haggadah,* 1729. When Solomon was king, Israel was at peace with its neighbors. He decided to build a temple for the LORD to replace the tabernacle where the people worshiped and offered sacrifices to God. To do this, he made a pact with King Hiram of Tyre for materials and workmen. The temple took seven years to build. After the workers finished the outside of the temple, the LORD told Solomon, "I will live among the Israelites and will not abandon my people Israel." (See 5:1—6:38.)

6:37,38 *Ziv . . . Bul:* For Ziv, see the note at 6:1. Bul is the eighth month of the Hebrew calendar, from about mid-October to mid-November. See also the chart called "Jewish Calendar and Festivals," p. 944.

7:2,3 *Palace of the Forest of Lebanon:* A large ceremonial hall in the palace, probably so called because it was paneled in cedar.

the main hall. [34]He also made two pine doors, each having two
leaves that turned in sockets. [35]He carved cherubim, palm trees
and open flowers on them and overlaid them with gold hammered
evenly over the carvings.

[36]And he built the inner courtyard of three courses of
dressed stone and one course of trimmed cedar beams.

[37]The foundation of the temple of the LORD was laid in the
fourth year, in the month of Ziv. [38]In the eleventh year in the month
of Bul, the eighth month, the temple was finished in all its details
according to its specifications. He had spent seven years building it.

Solomon Builds His Palace

7 It took Solomon thirteen years, however, to complete the construction of his palace. [2]He built the Palace of the Forest of Lebanon
a hundred cubits long, fifty wide and thirty high,[a] with four rows of
cedar columns supporting trimmed cedar beams. [3]It was roofed
with cedar above the beams that rested on the columns—forty-five
beams, fifteen to a row. [4]Its windows were placed high in sets of

[a]2 That is, about 150 feet (about 46 meters) long, 75 feet (about 23 meters) wide and 45 feet (about 13.5 meters) high

three, facing each other. 5All the doorways had rectangular frames;
they were in the front part in sets of three, facing each other.[a]
6He made a colonnade fifty cubits long and thirty wide.[b] In
front of it was a portico, and in front of that were pillars and an
overhanging roof.
7He built the throne hall, the Hall of Justice, where he was to
judge, and he covered it with cedar from floor to ceiling.[c] 8And the
palace in which he was to live, set farther back, was similar in
design. Solomon also made a palace like this hall for Pharaoh's
daughter, whom he had married.
9All these structures, from the outside to the great courtyard
and from foundation to eaves, were made of blocks of high-grade
stone cut to size and trimmed with a saw on their inner and outer
faces. 10The foundations were laid with large stones of good quality, some measuring ten cubits[d] and some eight.[e] 11Above were
high-grade stones, cut to size, and cedar beams. 12The great courtyard was surrounded by a wall of three courses of dressed stone
and one course of trimmed cedar beams, as was the inner courtyard of the temple of the LORD with its portico.

The Temple's Furnishings

13King Solomon sent to Tyre and brought Huram,[f] 14whose
mother was a widow from the tribe of Naphtali and whose father
was a man of Tyre and a craftsman in bronze. Huram was highly
skilled and experienced in all kinds of bronze work. He came to
King Solomon and did all the work assigned to him.
15He cast two bronze pillars, each eighteen cubits high and
twelve cubits around,[g] by line. 16He also made two capitals of cast
bronze to set on the tops of the pillars; each capital was five cubits[h]
high. 17A network of interwoven chains festooned the capitals on
top of the pillars, seven for each capital. 18He made pomegranates
in two rows[i] encircling each network to decorate the capitals on
top of the pillars.[j] He did the same for each capital. 19The capitals
on top of the pillars in the portico were in the shape of lilies, four
cubits[k] high. 20On the capitals of both pillars, above the bowl-
shaped part next to the network, were the two hundred pomegranates in rows all around. 21He erected the pillars at the portico
of the temple. The pillar to the south he named Jakin[l] and the one

[a]5 The meaning of the Hebrew for this verse is uncertain. [b]6 That is, about 75 feet (about 23 meters) long and 45 feet (about 13.5 meters) wide [c]7 Vulgate and Syriac; Hebrew *floor* [d]10 That is, about 15 feet (about 4.5 meters) [e]10 That is, about 12 feet (about 3.6 meters) [f]13 Hebrew *Hiram*, a variant of *Huram*; also in verses 40 and 45 [g]15 That is, about 27 feet (about 8.1 meters) high and 18 feet (about 5.4 meters) around [h]16 That is, about 7 1/2 feet (about 2.3 meters); also in verse 23 [i]18 Two Hebrew manuscripts and Septuagint; most Hebrew manuscripts *made the pillars, and there were two rows* [j]18 Many Hebrew manuscripts and Syriac; most Hebrew manuscripts *pomegranates* [k]19 That is, about 6 feet (about 1.8 meters); also in verse 38 [l]21 *Jakin* probably means *he establishes.*

7:14 *bronze work:* The bronze furnishings were made near the Jordan River between Sukkoth and Zarethan, because the clay soil was needed to make the molds for the objects. Bronze is a strong metal that is yellowish-brown in color and can be easily burnished and fashioned into attractive and useful objects. It is an alloy made of copper and a second metal, usually tin, both of which were available in this area.

7:15 *pillars:* These were not building supports, but freestanding columns. It was common at the time to have such pillars at the entrance to a temple, although the ones described here seem to have been particularly large. See 7:21.

7:18 *pomegranates:* A pomegranate is a bright red fruit. In ancient times, it was a symbol of life. See the photograph on p. 1025.

7:21 *Jakin ... Boaz:* Jakin sounds like the Hebrew for "he (God) establishes." Boaz sounds like the Hebrew for "by his (God's) strength."

7:8 1 Kgs 3:1.

7:23 *Sea of cast metal:* The priests used the water in this huge basin (thus called a "Sea") for ritual cleansing (see 2 Chr 4:6). This bronze tank may have symbolized God's separation of the waters that covered the earth to make the sky, land, and ocean in the creation story (Gen 1:6-10).

7:48-50 *altar . . . bread of the Presence . . . lampstands . . . bowls, dishes and censers:* The golden altar was used for burning incense (Exod 25:23-30; 30:1-10,27,34,35).

The bread of the Presence was offered to the LORD and was a symbol of the LORD's presence in the temple. It was put on a special table, and was replaced with fresh bread each week (Lev 24:5-9).

The ten lampstands had a center piece with three branches on either side, each with a small saucer-like lamp attached to its end (Exod 25:31-40). The light from the lamps symbolized the glory of God. The small lamps probably were simple oil lamps that were filled with enough oil to burn from sunset to sunrise (Exod 27:20). Tongs and lamp snuffers were used to cover a flame to extinguish it or to trim the wicks. See Exod 25:31-40.

Bowls and other dishes were used in the preparation for an animal sacrifice. Censers were metal pans used to burn incense, carry hot coals, and clean up the ashes after sacrifices. See the illustrations on p. 182.

7:38 Exod 30:17-21.

to the north Boaz.[a] 22The capitals on top were in the shape of lilies.
And so the work on the pillars was completed.
23He made the Sea of cast metal, circular in shape, measuring ten cubits[b] from rim to rim and five cubits high. It took a line
of thirty cubits[c] to measure around it. 24Below the rim, gourds
encircled it—ten to a cubit. The gourds were cast in two rows in
one piece with the Sea.
25The Sea stood on twelve bulls, three facing north, three facing west, three facing south and three facing east. The Sea rested
on top of them, and their hindquarters were toward the center. 26It
was a handbreadth[d] in thickness, and its rim was like the rim of a
cup, like a lily blossom. It held two thousand baths.[e]
27He also made ten movable stands of bronze; each was four
cubits long, four wide and three high.[f] 28This is how the stands
were made: They had side panels attached to uprights. 29On the
panels between the uprights were lions, bulls and cherubim—and
on the uprights as well. Above and below the lions and bulls were
wreaths of hammered work. 30Each stand had four bronze wheels
with bronze axles, and each had a basin resting on four supports,
cast with wreaths on each side. 31On the inside of the stand there
was an opening that had a circular frame one cubit[g] deep. This
opening was round, and with its basework it measured a cubit and
a half.[h] Around its opening there was engraving. The panels of the
stands were square, not round. 32The four wheels were under
the panels, and the axles of the wheels were attached to the stand.
The diameter of each wheel was a cubit and a half. 33The wheels
were made like chariot wheels; the axles, rims, spokes and hubs
were all of cast metal.
34Each stand had four handles, one on each corner, projecting from the stand. 35At the top of the stand there was a circular
band half a cubit[i] deep. The supports and panels were attached to
the top of the stand. 36He engraved cherubim, lions and palm trees
on the surfaces of the supports and on the panels, in every available space, with wreaths all around. 37This is the way he made the
ten stands. They were all cast in the same molds and were identical in size and shape.
38He then made ten bronze basins, each holding forty baths[j]
and measuring four cubits across, one basin to go on each of the
ten stands. 39He placed five of the stands on the south side of the
temple and five on the north. He placed the Sea on the south side,

---

[a]21 *Boaz* probably means *in him is strength.* [b]**23** That is, about 15 feet (about 4.5 meters) [c]**23** That is, about 45 feet (about 13.5 meters) [d]**26** That is, about 3 inches (about 8 centimeters) [e]**26** That is, probably about 11,500 gallons (about 44 kiloliters); the Septuagint does not have this sentence. [f]**27** That is, about 6 feet (about 1.8 meters) long and wide and about 4 1/2 feet (about 1.3 meters) high [g]**31** That is, about 1 1/2 feet (about 0.5 meter) [h]**31** That is, about 2 1/4 feet (about 0.7 meter); also in verse 32 [i]**35** That is, about 3/4 foot (about 0.2 meter) [j]**38** That is, about 230 gallons (about 880 liters)

at the southeast corner of the temple. 40He also made the basins
and shovels and sprinkling bowls.

So Huram finished all the work he had undertaken for King
Solomon in the temple of the LORD:

41 the two pillars;
the two bowl-shaped capitals on top of the pillars;
the two sets of network decorating the two bowl-shaped capitals on top of the pillars;
42 the four hundred pomegranates for the two sets of network
(two rows of pomegranates for each network, decorating the bowl-shaped capitals on top of the pillars);
43 the ten stands with their ten basins;
44 the Sea and the twelve bulls under it;
45 the pots, shovels and sprinkling bowls.

All these objects that Huram made for King Solomon for the
temple of the LORD were of burnished bronze. 46The king had
them cast in clay molds in the plain of the Jordan between Succoth and Zarethan. 47Solomon left all these things unweighed,
because there were so many; the weight of the bronze was not
determined.
48Solomon also made all the furnishings that were in the
LORD's temple:

the golden altar;
the golden table on which was the bread of the Presence;
49 the lampstands of pure gold (five on the right and five on the left, in front of the inner sanctuary);
the gold floral work and lamps and tongs;
50 the pure gold basins, wick trimmers, sprinkling bowls, dishes and censers;
and the gold sockets for the doors of the innermost room, the Most Holy Place, and also for the doors of the main hall of the temple.

51When all the work King Solomon had done for the temple
of the LORD was finished, he brought in the things his father David
had dedicated—the silver and gold and the furnishings—and he
placed them in the treasuries of the LORD's temple.

The Ark Brought to the Temple

8 Then King Solomon summoned into his presence at Jerusalem
the elders of Israel, all the heads of the tribes and the chiefs of the
Israelite families, to bring up the ark of the LORD's covenant from
Zion, the City of David. 2All the men of Israel came together to
King Solomon at the time of the festival in the month of Ethanim,
the seventh month.

3When all the elders of Israel had arrived, the priests took up
the ark, 4and they brought up the ark of the LORD and the Tent of

7:51 *brought in the things his father David had dedicated:* These were objects that were given to David in tribute by foreign kings, or that David took as booty in war. See 2 Sam 8:9-12; 1 Chr 18:11.

8:1 *Zion, the City of David:* Zion was a hill in the southernmost part of Jerusalem. The Jebusite fortress that David conquered there was called the "City of David." Later, both "Zion" and "City of David" are used to mean all of Jerusalem. See the mini-article called "Zion," p. 1294 and the map on p. 2466. See also 2 Sam 6:11-16; 1 Chr 15:25-29.

8:2 *the festival in the month of Ethanim:* This festival would be the Feast of Tabernacles, one of three yearly pilgrimage celebrations. It took place at the end of the fall harvest (Lev 23:33–36) and lasted for seven days. In addition to giving thanks to God for the harvest, the people built and lived in shelters (or booths) made of tree branches (Lev 23:39-42) as a way of commemorating the temporary shelters the Hebrews lived in after they left Egypt and wandered in the desert. A description of this festival is given in Nehemiah 8:13-17. The amount of animals, grain, and oil used for sacrifice was to be the same as that used during Passover (Ezek 45:25). See also Num 29:12-38; Lev 23:33, 34.

Ethanim, also called Tishri, is the seventh month of the Hebrew calendar, from about mid-September to mid-October. See also the chart, "Jewish Calendar and Festivals," p. 944.

8:3,4 *ark of the LORD and the Tent of Meeting:* See the notes at 2:26 (ark) and 1:39.

8:4 *Levites:* Priests were Levites descended from Aaron (Num 3:1-13). Later in the Israelites' history, during the period known as the exile, the Levites would lose the position of priesthood and would become only special temple servants (Num 18:1-6; Ezek 44:10-14). See also the mini-articles called "Israel's Priests," p. 2344 and "Exile," p. 1541.

8:8,9 *poles . . . stone tablets:* Poles were put through rings on the sides of the ark so that the ark itself would not be touched when carried. These poles always were to remain in the rings (Exod 25:13-15).

The Ten Commandments were written on two stone tablets. See also Deut 10:1-5 and the mini-article called "Ten Commandments," p. 354.

8:11-13 *the glory of the* LORD *. . . dwell forever:* Here as elsewhere, a cloud surrounds and covers God's presence before the people (Exod 14:19,20; 33:9-11; 40:34-37; Ps 18:11; 97:2; Isa 6:4; Mark 9:7). At other times, God appears in fire (Exod 3:2-4; Ezek 1:27). Verse 12 notes that God lives in clouds and darkness. It is for this reason that in this glorious temple, the Most Holy Place is completely dark, and it is there that the ark of the covenant is placed (see the note at 2:26, ark).

Though God's earthly home will be within the Most Holy Place, heaven also is still God's home (see 8:27-30).

8:15,16 2 Sam 7:4-11; 1 Chr 17:3-10. **8:17,18** 2 Sam 7:1,2; 1 Chr 17:1. **8:19** 2 Sam 7:12, 13; 1 Chr 17:11,12.

Meeting and all the sacred furnishings in it. The priests and Levites
carried them up, [5]and King Solomon and the entire assembly of
Israel that had gathered about him were before the ark, sacrificing so
many sheep and cattle that they could not be recorded or counted.
[6]The priests then brought the ark of the LORD's covenant to
its place in the inner sanctuary of the temple, the Most Holy Place,
and put it beneath the wings of the cherubim. [7]The cherubim
spread their wings over the place of the ark and overshadowed the
ark and its carrying poles. [8]These poles were so long that their
ends could be seen from the Holy Place in front of the inner sanctuary,
but not from outside the Holy Place; and they are still there
today. [9]There was nothing in the ark except the two stone tablets
that Moses had placed in it at Horeb, where the LORD made a
covenant with the Israelites after they came out of Egypt.
[10]When the priests withdrew from the Holy Place, the cloud
filled the temple of the LORD. [11]And the priests could not perform
their service because of the cloud, for the glory of the LORD filled
his temple.
[12]Then Solomon said, "The LORD has said that he would
dwell in a dark cloud; [13]I have indeed built a magnificent temple
for you, a place for you to dwell forever."
[14]While the whole assembly of Israel was standing there, the
king turned around and blessed them. [15]Then he said:

> "Praise be to the LORD, the God of Israel, who with his
> own hand has fulfilled what he promised with his own mouth
> to my father David. For he said, [16]'Since the day I brought my
> people Israel out of Egypt, I have not chosen a city in any
> tribe of Israel to have a temple built for my Name to be there,
> but I have chosen David to rule my people Israel.'
> [17]"My father David had it in his heart to build a temple
> for the Name of the LORD, the God of Israel. [18]But the LORD
> said to my father David, 'Because it was in your heart to build
> a temple for my Name, you did well to have this in your heart.
> [19]Nevertheless, you are not the one to build the temple, but
> your son, who is your own flesh and blood—he is the one
> who will build the temple for my Name.'
> [20]"The LORD has kept the promise he made: I have succeeded
> David my father and now I sit on the throne of Israel,
> just as the LORD promised, and I have built the temple for the
> Name of the LORD, the God of Israel. [21]I have provided a place
> there for the ark, in which is the covenant of the LORD that he
> made with our fathers when he brought them out of Egypt."

Solomon's Prayer of Dedication

[22]Then Solomon stood before the altar of the LORD in front
of the whole assembly of Israel, spread out his hands toward
heaven [23]and said:

"O LORD, God of Israel, there is no God like you in
heaven above or on earth below—you who keep your
covenant of love with your servants who continue wholeheartedly in your way. 24 You have kept your promise to your
servant David my father; with your mouth you have promised
and with your hand you have fulfilled it—as it is today.

25 "Now LORD, God of Israel, keep for your servant
David my father the promises you made to him when you
said, 'You shall never fail to have a man to sit before me on the
throne of Israel, if only your sons are careful in all they do to
walk before me as you have done.' 26 And now, O God of Israel,
let your word that you promised your servant David my father
come true.

27 "But will God really dwell on earth? The heavens, even
the highest heaven, cannot contain you. How much less this
temple I have built! 28 Yet give attention to your servant's
prayer and his plea for mercy, O LORD my God. Hear the cry
and the prayer that your servant is praying in your presence
this day. 29 May your eyes be open toward this temple night
and day, this place of which you said, 'My Name shall be
there,' so that you will hear the prayer your servant prays
toward this place. 30 Hear the supplication of your servant and
of your people Israel when they pray toward this place. Hear
from heaven, your dwelling place, and when you hear, forgive.

31 "When a man wrongs his neighbor and is required to
take an oath and he comes and swears the oath before your
altar in this temple, 32 then hear from heaven and act. Judge
between your servants, condemning the guilty and bringing
down on his own head what he has done. Declare the innocent not guilty, and so establish his innocence.

33 "When your people Israel have been defeated by an
enemy because they have sinned against you, and when they
turn back to you and confess your name, praying and making
supplication to you in this temple, 34 then hear from heaven
and forgive the sin of your people Israel and bring them back
to the land you gave to their fathers.

35 "When the heavens are shut up and there is no rain
because your people have sinned against you, and when they
pray toward this place and confess your name and turn from
their sin because you have afflicted them, 36 then hear from
heaven and forgive the sin of your servants, your people Israel.
Teach them the right way to live, and send rain on the land
you gave your people for an inheritance.

37 "When famine or plague comes to the land, or blight
or mildew, locusts or grasshoppers, or when an enemy
besieges them in any of their cities, whatever disaster or disease may come, 38 and when a prayer or plea is made by any of
your people Israel—each one aware of the afflictions of his

Solomon prayed,
"O LORD, God of Israel, there is no God like you in heaven above or on earth below—you who keep your covenant of love with your servants who continue wholeheartedly in your way."
1 Kgs 8:23

8:37 *locusts:* A type of grasshopper that comes in swarms and causes great damage to plant life. See also the mini-article called "Locusts," p. 1708.

8:25 1 Kgs 2:4. **8:27** 2 Chr 2:6. **8:29** Deut 12:5-19.

8:39,40 *you know his heart . . . they will fear you:* Solomon understands that God looks at people's motives as well as at their actions (outward behavior). This is similar to the message the prophet Jeremiah would later give the people of Israel and Judah about a new covenant, one in which the LORD would write his laws on people's hearts and minds (Jer 31:31-34). See also 1 Sam 16:7; Mark 7:20-23.

Fearing the LORD in the Bible means to completely honor and deeply revere God. People who fear the LORD happily obey his commands.

8:41 *the foreigner who does not belong:* See also the mini-article called "Foreigners (Aliens)," p. 501.

8:43 *so that all people of the earth may know your name:* Solomon is aware that God's blessings were not for the Israelites alone, but as God had promised Abraham, all the peoples of the world would be blessed by what God would do for the Israelites (see Gen 12:1-3).

8:44 *their enemies:* See the mini-article called "Enemies (The Wicked)," p. 1084.

8:46 *sin against you:* See the mini-article called "Sin," p. 2181.

8:48,49 *pray to you . . . hear their prayer:* In the middle of Solomon's prayer of dedication he speaks of a time in the future known as the exile when prayer would be especially important to the Jewish people. For more, see the mini-articles called "Exile," p. 1541 and "Prayer," p. 2287.

own heart, and spreading out his hands toward this temple—
39 then hear from heaven, your dwelling place. Forgive and act;
deal with each man according to all he does, since you know
his heart (for you alone know the hearts of all men), 40 so that
they will fear you all the time they live in the land you gave
our fathers.

41 "As for the foreigner who does not belong to your
people Israel but has come from a distant land because of
your name— 42 for men will hear of your great name and your
mighty hand and your outstretched arm—when he comes
and prays toward this temple, 43 then hear from heaven, your
dwelling place, and do whatever the foreigner asks of you, so
that all the peoples of the earth may know your name and fear
you, as do your own people Israel, and may know that this
house I have built bears your Name.

44 "When your people go to war against their enemies,
wherever you send them, and when they pray to the LORD
toward the city you have chosen and the temple I have built
for your Name, 45 then hear from heaven their prayer and their
plea, and uphold their cause.

46 "When they sin against you—for there is no one who
does not sin—and you become angry with them and give them
over to the enemy, who takes them captive to his own land, far
away or near; 47 and if they have a change of heart in the land
where they are held captive, and repent and plead with you in
the land of their conquerors and say, 'We have sinned, we have
done wrong, we have acted wickedly'; 48 and if they turn back
to you with all their heart and soul in the land of their enemies
who took them captive, and pray to you toward the land you
gave their fathers, toward the city you have chosen and the
temple I have built for your Name; 49 then from heaven, your
dwelling place, hear their prayer and their plea, and uphold
their cause. 50 And forgive your people, who have sinned against
you; forgive all the offenses they have committed against you,
and cause their conquerors to show them mercy; 51 for they are
your people and your inheritance, whom you brought out of
Egypt, out of that iron-smelting furnace.

52 "May your eyes be open to your servant's plea and to
the plea of your people Israel, and may you listen to them
whenever they cry out to you. 53 For you singled them out
from all the nations of the world to be your own inheritance,
just as you declared through your servant Moses when you,
O Sovereign LORD, brought our fathers out of Egypt."

54 When Solomon had finished all these prayers and supplications to the LORD, he rose from before the altar of the LORD,
where he had been kneeling with his hands spread out toward
heaven. 55 He stood and blessed the whole assembly of Israel in a
loud voice, saying:

56"Praise be to the LORD, who has given rest to his people
Israel just as he promised. Not one word has failed of all the
good promises he gave through his servant Moses. 57May the
LORD our God be with us as he was with our fathers; may he
never leave us nor forsake us. 58May he turn our hearts to him,
to walk in all his ways and to keep the commands, decrees and
regulations he gave our fathers. 59And may these words of
mine, which I have prayed before the LORD, be near to the
LORD our God day and night, that he may uphold the cause of
his servant and the cause of his people Israel according to each
day's need, 60so that all the peoples of the earth may know that
the LORD is God and that there is no other. 61But your hearts
must be fully committed to the LORD our God, to live by his
decrees and obey his commands, as at this time."

The Dedication of the Temple

62Then the king and all Israel with him offered sacrifices
before the LORD. 63Solomon offered a sacrifice of fellowship offerings[a] to the LORD: twenty-two thousand cattle and a hundred and
twenty thousand sheep and goats. So the king and all the Israelites
dedicated the temple of the LORD.

64On that same day the king consecrated the middle part of
the courtyard in front of the temple of the LORD, and there he
offered burnt offerings, grain offerings and the fat of the fellowship offerings, because the bronze altar before the LORD was too
small to hold the burnt offerings, the grain offerings and the fat of
the fellowship offerings.

65So Solomon observed the festival at that time, and all Israel
with him—a vast assembly, people from Lebo[b] Hamath to the
Wadi of Egypt. They celebrated it before the LORD our God for
seven days and seven days more, fourteen days in all. 66On the following day he sent the people away. They blessed the king and
then went home, joyful and glad in heart for all the good things
the LORD had done for his servant David and his people Israel.

SOLOMON'S WEALTH AND WISDOM

Originally, Solomon had asked God to make him wise so that he would know difference between right and wrong and so he would be able to rule God's people. Now he uses his wisdom to make himself wealthy and famous. This turns out to be the beginning of his decline as king.

The LORD Appears to Solomon

9 When Solomon had finished building the temple of the LORD
and the royal palace, and had achieved all he had desired to do,

[a]63 Traditionally *peace offerings*; also in verse 64 [b]65 Or *from the entrance to*

Solomon said to the people, *"Praise be to the LORD, who has given rest to his people Israel just as he promised. Not one word has failed of all the good promises he gave through his servant Moses."*
1 Kgs 8:56

8:56 *Praise be to the LORD . . . all the good promises:* The completion of the temple fulfills two important promises that God made to the nation of Israel. The first is the promise to David that his son would follow him as king and be the one to build the temple (2 Sam 7). The second is that Israel would have a time of peace after conquering the promised land (Canaan) and establishing a central place of worship at the one place God would choose. See also Deut 12:5-19; Josh 21:44,45.

8:56 *LORD:* See the mini-article called "LORD (YHWH)," on p. 140.

8:62-65 *fellowship offerings . . . burnt offerings:* See the note at 3:15 (burnt offerings).

8:65 *the festival:* Referring to the Feast of Tabernacles. See the note at 8:2.

8:65 *Lebo Hamath to the Wadi of Egypt:* Because Hamath was on the northern border and the Wadi (brook) of Egypt on the southern border, this expression means all of Israel. The temple was to unite the people religiously the way the success of the king was to unite them politically. See the map on p. 2463.

9:2 *Gibeon:* See the note at 3:4. See also 1 Kgs 3:4, 5; 2 Chr 1:5-7.

9:6 *other gods:* See the note at 11:2.

9:11-13 *twenty towns in Galilee . . . Land of Cabul:* See the map on p. 2465. The name Hiram gives to this region, Cabul, sounds like *kebal,* the Hebrew word for "worthless." See 5:9, 10 for the original terms of payment agreed upon by Hiram and Solomon. It is not clear whether Solomon had trouble making his agreed-upon payments or whether his building projects were more ambitious than he had anticipated. Either way, Solomon's debt and the hint of tension he is having with his close ally are signs that things are beginning to go badly for Israel's king.

9:15-17 *supporting terraces . . . Lower Beth Horon:* Solomon increased the size of Jerusalem by filling in land on the east side and extending the wall around it. See the map on p. 2466; for the extent of Solomon's expansion.

Other cities important to Israel's defense and economy also were fortified with strong walls and gates. Hazor, in northern Galilee, controlled the trade route that ran north and south between the Euphrates River and Egypt. Megiddo was an important business and military center located at the intersection of the north-south trade route, and controlled the pass through the Carmel mountain range between the Plains of Jezreel and Sharon. Gezer was at the crossroads of the north-south trade route and the east-west route between Jerusalem and the port at Joppa. Lower Beth Horon also protected the route between Jerusalem and the sea. See the map on p. 2465.

9:5 1 Kgs 2:4. **9:8** 2 Kgs 25:9-21; 2 Chr 36:19.

2the LORD appeared to him a second time, as he had appeared to
him at Gibeon. 3The LORD said to him:

"I have heard the prayer and plea you have made before
me; I have consecrated this temple, which you have built, by
putting my Name there forever. My eyes and my heart will
always be there.

4"As for you, if you walk before me in integrity of heart
and uprightness, as David your father did, and do all I command
and observe my decrees and laws, 5I will establish your
royal throne over Israel forever, as I promised David your
father when I said, 'You shall never fail to have a man on the
throne of Israel.'

6"But if you[a] or your sons turn away from me and do
not observe the commands and decrees I have given you[a] and
go off to serve other gods and worship them, 7then I will cut
off Israel from the land I have given them and will reject this
temple I have consecrated for my Name. Israel will then
become a byword and an object of ridicule among all peoples.
8And though this temple is now imposing, all who pass by will
be appalled and will scoff and say, 'Why has the LORD done
such a thing to this land and to this temple?' 9People will
answer, 'Because they have forsaken the LORD their God, who
brought their fathers out of Egypt, and have embraced other
gods, worshiping and serving them—that is why the LORD
brought all this disaster on them.' "

Solomon's Other Activities

10At the end of twenty years, during which Solomon built
these two buildings—the temple of the LORD and the royal palace—
11King Solomon gave twenty towns in Galilee to Hiram king of
Tyre, because Hiram had supplied him with all the cedar and pine
and gold he wanted. 12But when Hiram went from Tyre to see the
towns that Solomon had given him, he was not pleased with them.
13"What kind of towns are these you have given me, my brother?"
he asked. And he called them the Land of Cabul,[b] a name they have
to this day. 14Now Hiram had sent to the king 120 talents[c] of gold.

15Here is the account of the forced labor King Solomon conscripted
to build the LORD's temple, his own palace, the supporting
terraces,[d] the wall of Jerusalem, and Hazor, Megiddo and Gezer.
16(Pharaoh king of Egypt had attacked and captured Gezer. He had
set it on fire. He killed its Canaanite inhabitants and then gave it as
a wedding gift to his daughter, Solomon's wife. 17And Solomon
rebuilt Gezer.) He built up Lower Beth Horon, 18Baalath, and

[a]**6** The Hebrew is plural. [b]**13** *Cabul* sounds like the Hebrew for *good-for-nothing.* [c]**14** That is, about 4 1/2 tons (about 4 metric tons) [d]**15** Or *the Millo*; also in verse 24

Tadmor[a] in the desert, within his land, [19]as well as all his store cities and the towns for his chariots and for his horses[b]—whatever he desired to build in Jerusalem, in Lebanon and throughout all the territory he ruled.

[20]All the people left from the Amorites, Hittites, Perizzites, Hivites and Jebusites (these peoples were not Israelites), [21]that is, their descendants remaining in the land, whom the Israelites could not exterminate[c]—these Solomon conscripted for his slave labor force, as it is to this day. [22]But Solomon did not make slaves of any of the Israelites; they were his fighting men, his government officials, his officers, his captains, and the commanders of his chariots and charioteers. [23]They were also the chief officials in charge of Solomon's projects—550 officials supervising the men who did the work.

[24]After Pharaoh's daughter had come up from the City of David to the palace Solomon had built for her, he constructed the supporting terraces.

[25]Three times a year Solomon sacrificed burnt offerings and fellowship offerings[d] on the altar he had built for the LORD, burning incense before the LORD along with them, and so fulfilled the temple obligations.

[26]King Solomon also built ships at Ezion Geber, which is near Elath in Edom, on the shore of the Red Sea.[e] [27]And Hiram sent his men—sailors who knew the sea—to serve in the fleet with Solomon's men. [28]They sailed to Ophir and brought back 420 talents[f] of gold, which they delivered to King Solomon.

The Queen of Sheba Visits Solomon

10 When the queen of Sheba heard about the fame of Solomon and his relation to the name of the LORD, she came to test him with hard questions. [2]Arriving at Jerusalem with a very great caravan—with camels carrying spices, large quantities of gold, and precious stones—she came to Solomon and talked with him about all that she had on her mind. [3]Solomon answered all her questions; nothing was too hard for the king to explain to her. [4]When the queen of Sheba saw all the wisdom of Solomon and the palace he had built, [5]the food on his table, the seating of his officials, the attending servants in their robes, his cupbearers, and the burnt offerings he made at[g] the temple of the LORD, she was overwhelmed.

[6]She said to the king, "The report I heard in my own country about your achievements and your wisdom is true. [7]But I did not believe these things until I came and saw with my own eyes.

---

[a]18 The Hebrew may also be read *Tamar.* [b]19 Or *charioteers* [c]21 The Hebrew term refers to the irrevocable giving over of things or persons to the LORD, often by totally destroying them. [d]25 Traditionally *peace offerings* [e]26 Hebrew *Yam Suph*; that is, Sea of Reeds [f]28 That is, about 16 tons (about 14.5 metric tons) [g]5 Or *the ascent by which he went up to*

The queen of Sheba said to Solomon, *"The report I heard in my own country about your achievements and your wisdom is true."* 1 Kgs 10:6

9:22 *Solomon did not make slaves of any of the Israelites:* This seems to contradict 5:13-18 and the complaint the people from the northern tribes would later make to Solomon's son (12:4).

9:25 *Three times a year:* Israelite men were required to worship at the temple three times a year: at Passover and the Feast of Unleavened Bread, the Feast of Weeks, and the Feast of Tabernacles (see the note at 8:2). Because this required travel to Jerusalem, these are sometimes called "pilgrimage festivals." See Exod 23:17; 34:23; Deut 16:16. See also the chart called "Jewish Calendar and Festivals," p. 944.

9:26-28 *Ezion Geber . . . Ophir:* The city of Ezion Geber is on the northeastern arm of the Red Sea. The location of Ophir is not known, though southern Africa and India have been suggested as possibilities.

10:1 *queen of Sheba:* The exact location of Sheba is not certain, though many believe it may be the same place as Seba, a wealthy kingdom in southwest Arabia that traded luxury items from India and east Africa. The queen's interest in visiting Solomon may have been partially a concern that Israel's control of major land and sea trade routes posed a threat to the trade relationships she had already established. See also the article called "Trade and Travel," p. 948.

10:1-10 Matt 12:42; Luke 11:31.

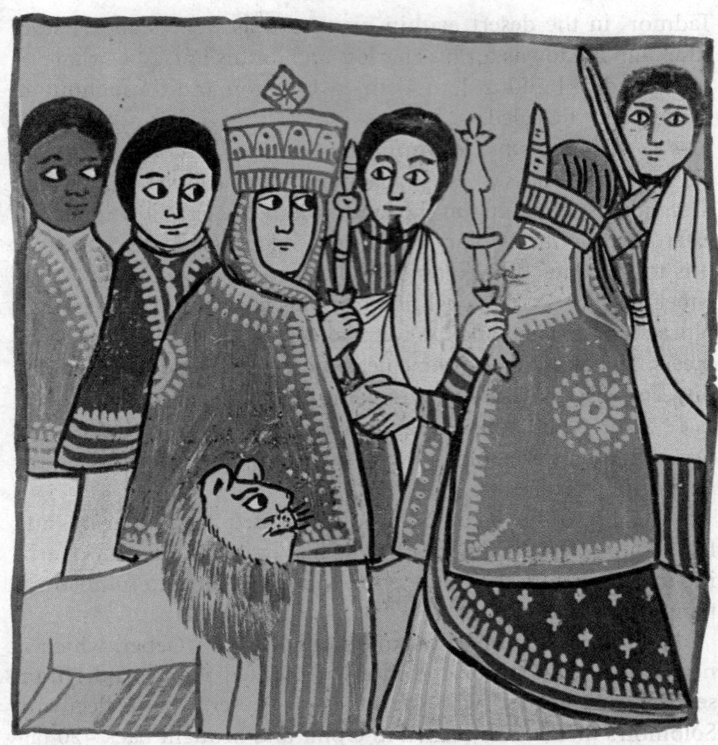

Solomon and the Queen of Sheba, a contemporary manuscript painting in the traditional Ethiopian style of the sixteenth century, artist unknown. Solomon's fame had reached all parts of the ancient world. Even the Queen of Sheba had heard of Solomon's wisdom and the splendor of his palace. She came to Jerusalem to test his wisdom and to see for herself how wealthy he was. Before leaving him she said, "Praise be to the LORD your God . . . Because of the LORD's eternal love for Israel, he has made you king." (See 10:1-13.)

10:11,12 *Almugwood . . . lyres:* Almugwood is also called juniper wood. It is a very hard wood that can be smoothly polished.

A lyre is a hand-held stringed musical instrument. See the illustration on p. 1190.

Indeed, not even half was told me; in wisdom and wealth you have
far exceeded the report I heard. [8]How happy your men must be!
How happy your officials, who continually stand before you and
hear your wisdom! [9]Praise be to the LORD your God, who has
delighted in you and placed you on the throne of Israel. Because of
the LORD's eternal love for Israel, he has made you king, to maintain justice and righteousness."

[10]And she gave the king 120 talents[a] of gold, large quantities
of spices, and precious stones. Never again were so many spices
brought in as those the queen of Sheba gave to King Solomon.

[11](Hiram's ships brought gold from Ophir; and from there
they brought great cargoes of almugwood[b] and precious stones.
[12]The king used the almugwood to make supports for the temple

---

[a]**10** That is, about 4 1/2 tons (about 4 metric tons) [b]**11** Probably a variant of *algumwood*; also in verse 12

of the LORD and for the royal palace, and to make harps and lyres
for the musicians. So much almugwood has never been imported
or seen since that day.)
13 King Solomon gave the queen of Sheba all she desired and
asked for, besides what he had given her out of his royal bounty.
Then she left and returned with her retinue to her own country.

Solomon's Splendor

14 The weight of the gold that Solomon received yearly was 666
talents,[a] 15 not including the revenues from merchants and traders
and from all the Arabian kings and the governors of the land.
16 King Solomon made two hundred large shields of hammered gold; six hundred bekas[b] of gold went into each shield. 17 He
also made three hundred small shields of hammered gold, with
three minas[c] of gold in each shield. The king put them in the
Palace of the Forest of Lebanon.
18 Then the king made a great throne inlaid with ivory and
overlaid with fine gold. 19 The throne had six steps, and its back had
a rounded top. On both sides of the seat were armrests, with a lion
standing beside each of them. 20 Twelve lions stood on the six steps,
one at either end of each step. Nothing like it had ever been made
for any other kingdom. 21 All King Solomon's goblets were gold,
and all the household articles in the Palace of the Forest of
Lebanon were pure gold. Nothing was made of silver, because silver was considered of little value in Solomon's days. 22 The king had
a fleet of trading ships[d] at sea along with the ships of Hiram. Once
every three years it returned, carrying gold, silver and ivory, and
apes and baboons.
23 King Solomon was greater in riches and wisdom than all
the other kings of the earth. 24 The whole world sought audience
with Solomon to hear the wisdom God had put in his heart. 25 Year
after year, everyone who came brought a gift—articles of silver and
gold, robes, weapons and spices, and horses and mules.
26 Solomon accumulated chariots and horses; he had fourteen
hundred chariots and twelve thousand horses,[e] which he kept in the
chariot cities and also with him in Jerusalem. 27 The king made silver
as common in Jerusalem as stones, and cedar as plentiful as
sycamore-fig trees in the foothills. 28 Solomon's horses were imported from Egypt[f] and from Kue[g]—the royal merchants purchased
them from Kue. 29 They imported a chariot from Egypt for six hundred shekels[h] of silver, and a horse for a hundred and fifty.[i] They also
exported them to all the kings of the Hittites and of the Arameans.

10:16 *shields:* Large oblong shields that covered the whole body were the type normally used in battle. These probably were used more for ceremonies, as were the smaller round shields. See the illustration on p. 1088.

10:17 *Palace of the Forest of Lebanon:* See 7:2,3 and the note.

10:28,29 *Egypt and from Kue . . . Hittites . . . Arameans:* Solomon is acting in direct contradiction of the instructions recorded in DEUTERONOMY where the king is advised not to have horses from Egypt (Deut 17:16). The author of 1 KINGS is showing that Solomon is no longer acting wisely and in obedience to the LORD.

The Hittites would have been descendants of the people who controlled much of Asia Minor from 1600 to 1200 B.C. but who now controlled the smaller state of Hamath and northern Syria. The Arameans (Syrians) controlled the area around Damascus.

10:26 Deut 17:16; 1 Sam 8:11; 1 Kgs 4:26. **10:27** Deut 17:17. **10:28,29** Deut 17:16.

a14 That is, about 25 tons (about 23 metric tons) **b16** That is, about 7 1/2 pounds (about 3.5 kilograms) **c17** That is, about 3 3/4 pounds (about 1.7 kilograms) **d22** Hebrew *of ships of Tarshish* **e26** Or *charioteers* **f28** Or possibly *Muzur*, a region in Cilicia; also in verse 29 **g28** Probably *Cilicia* **h29** That is, about 15 pounds (about 7 kilograms) **i29** That is, about 3 3/4 pounds (about 1.7 kilograms)

SOLOMON'S FAILINGS

Because Solomon disobeys the LORD by worshiping the gods of his foreign wives, Solomon's kingdom begins to face troubles from enemies inside and outside of Israel.

Solomon's Wives

11 King Solomon, however, loved many foreign women besides
Pharaoh's daughter—Moabites, Ammonites, Edomites, Sidonians
and Hittites. [2]They were from nations about which the LORD had
told the Israelites, "You must not intermarry with them, because
they will surely turn your hearts after their gods." Nevertheless,
Solomon held fast to them in love. [3]He had seven hundred wives of
royal birth and three hundred concubines, and his wives led him
astray. [4]As Solomon grew old, his wives turned his heart after other
gods, and his heart was not fully devoted to the LORD his God, as
the heart of David his father had been. [5]He followed Ashtoreth the
goddess of the Sidonians, and Molech[a] the detestable god of the
Ammonites. [6]So Solomon did evil in the eyes of the LORD; he did
not follow the LORD completely, as David his father had done.
[7]On a hill east of Jerusalem, Solomon built a high place for
Chemosh the detestable god of Moab, and for Molech the
detestable god of the Ammonites. [8]He did the same for all his foreign wives, who burned incense and offered sacrifices to their gods.
[9]The LORD became angry with Solomon because his heart
had turned away from the LORD, the God of Israel, who had
appeared to him twice. [10]Although he had forbidden Solomon to
follow other gods, Solomon did not keep the LORD's command.
[11]So the LORD said to Solomon, "Since this is your attitude and you
have not kept my covenant and my decrees, which I commanded
you, I will most certainly tear the kingdom away from you and give
it to one of your subordinates. [12]Nevertheless, for the sake of David
your father, I will not do it during your lifetime. I will tear it out
of the hand of your son. [13]Yet I will not tear the whole kingdom
from him, but will give him one tribe for the sake of David my
servant and for the sake of Jerusalem, which I have chosen."

Solomon's Adversaries

[14]Then the LORD raised up against Solomon an adversary,
Hadad the Edomite, from the royal line of Edom. [15]Earlier when
David was fighting with Edom, Joab the commander of the army,
who had gone up to bury the dead, had struck down all the men
in Edom. [16]Joab and all the Israelites stayed there for six months,
until they had destroyed all the men in Edom. [17]But Hadad, still
only a boy, fled to Egypt with some Edomite officials who had
served his father. [18]They set out from Midian and went to Paran.

[a]5 Hebrew *Milcom*; also in verse 33

11:2 *their gods:* Foreign gods worshiped by Israel's neighbors or by the Canaanites living in Israel. God chose Israel to be his special people and gave them laws, including the Ten Commandments to show them how to live (see Deut 5:6-21).

11:3 *seven hundred wives . . . three hundred concubines:* Israelite men were instructed not to marry women from other nations (11:2) because the men might be tempted to worship gods from their wives' homelands. Many of Solomon's marriages were for political reasons or to seal agreements with other kings. See also Deut 17:17. "Concubines" translates a Hebrew word for a woman who was legally bound to a man, but without the full privileges of a wife.

11:5-7 *Ashtoreth . . . Molech . . . Chemosh:* Ashtoreth was a Canaanite fertility goddess. Molech, also known as Milcom, was the national god of the Ammonites and was worshiped with human sacrifice. Chemosh was a god of the Moabites and most likely the god to whom Moab's king would sacrifice his son when facing defeat in battle (2 Kgs 3:26, 27). See also the mini-article called "Canaanite Gods and Goddesses," p. 469.

11:6 *Solomon did evil in the eyes of the LORD:* In other words, he worshiped idols. Often in the Bible the word "detestable" is used to identify something that is unclean and totally displeasing to God. Worshiping foreign gods, known as idolatry, was especially detestable. See also Deut 7:26.

11:14 *the LORD raised up:* The Israelites understood that God controlled everything in creation, including the actions of foreign rulers.

Then taking men from Paran with them, they went to Egypt, to
Pharaoh king of Egypt, who gave Hadad a house and land and
provided him with food.
19 Pharaoh was so pleased with Hadad that he gave him a sister of his own wife, Queen Tahpenes, in marriage. 20 The sister of
Tahpenes bore him a son named Genubath, whom Tahpenes
brought up in the royal palace. There Genubath lived with Pharaoh's
own children.
21 While he was in Egypt, Hadad heard that David rested with
his fathers and that Joab the commander of the army was also
dead. Then Hadad said to Pharaoh, "Let me go, that I may return
to my own country."
22 "What have you lacked here that you want to go back to
your own country?" Pharaoh asked.
"Nothing," Hadad replied, "but do let me go!"
23 And God raised up against Solomon another adversary,
Rezon son of Eliada, who had fled from his master, Hadadezer
king of Zobah. 24 He gathered men around him and became the
leader of a band of rebels when David destroyed the forces[a] ⌞of
Zobah⌟; the rebels went to Damascus, where they settled and took
control. 25 Rezon was Israel's adversary as long as Solomon lived,
adding to the trouble caused by Hadad. So Rezon ruled in Aram
and was hostile toward Israel.

Jeroboam Rebels Against Solomon

26 Also, Jeroboam son of Nebat rebelled against the king. He
was one of Solomon's officials, an Ephraimite from Zeredah, and
his mother was a widow named Zeruah.
27 Here is the account of how he rebelled against the king:
Solomon had built the supporting terraces[b] and had filled in the
gap in the wall of the city of David his father. 28 Now Jeroboam was
a man of standing, and when Solomon saw how well the young
man did his work, he put him in charge of the whole labor force of
the house of Joseph.
29 About that time Jeroboam was going out of Jerusalem, and
Ahijah the prophet of Shiloh met him on the way, wearing a new
cloak. The two of them were alone out in the country, 30 and Ahijah took hold of the new cloak he was wearing and tore it into
twelve pieces. 31 Then he said to Jeroboam, "Take ten pieces for
yourself, for this is what the LORD, the God of Israel, says: 'See, I
am going to tear the kingdom out of Solomon's hand and give you
ten tribes. 32 But for the sake of my servant David and the city of
Jerusalem, which I have chosen out of all the tribes of Israel, he
will have one tribe. 33 I will do this because they have[c] forsaken me

[a]**24** Hebrew *destroyed them* [b]**27** Or *the Millo* [c]**33** Hebrew; Septuagint, Vulgate and Syriac *because he has*

11:15-18 *Edom ... Midian ... Paran:* Edom was the area directly south of the Dead Sea and stood between the Desert of Zin and the land of Moab. The people of Edom were descendants of Jacob's brother, Esau (see Gen 25:24-26; 36:1). The nation of Edom is usually described in the Bible as an enemy of Israel (see Num 24:18; 2 Sam 8:13,14; Isa 34:5-17).

Midian was an area to the east of Egypt including the Sinai Peninsula and extending into northern Arabia. The Midianites, also known as the Kenites (Judg 1:16), were descendants of Abraham and Keturah (Gen 25:1-4) and lived as nomads and traders (Gen 37:28). The relationship between the Israelites and Midianites was at times good and peaceful (Exod 2:11-22; 18; Judg 4:11; 1 Sam 15:6), but at other times the Midianites were Israel's enemies (Num 22:4, 7; 25:6-8; Judg 6–8). Paran is a desert area west of Edom and south of Judah. See the map on p. 2463.

11:23,24 *Hadadezer ... rebels went to Damascus:* David's defeat of Hadadezer was one of several victories that freed Israel from the control of its enemies (2 Sam 8:3-6). Having Damascus fall into enemy hands was a serious problem, because many of Israel's trade routes passed through that city. See the map on p. 2465.

11:29,30 *Ahijah ... tore it into twelve pieces:* Sometimes prophets used dramatic or symbolic actions to illustrate their messages from God. Later Ahijah will prophesy to Jeroboam's wife (14:1-6).

11:31,32 *ten tribes ... one tribe:* By this time the tribe of Simeon had become part of the tribe of Judah. "One tribe" refers to Judah. God tears Israel apart but keeps his promises to David and to Solomon, even though Solomon has rejected God to worship foreign gods (see 11:33-39).

and worshiped Ashtoreth the goddess of the Sidonians, Chemosh
the god of the Moabites, and Molech the god of the Ammonites,
and have not walked in my ways, nor done what is right in my
eyes, nor kept my statutes and laws as David, Solomon's father, did.
34“ ‘But I will not take the whole kingdom out of Solomon's
hand; I have made him ruler all the days of his life for the sake of
David my servant, whom I chose and who observed my commands and statutes. 35I will take the kingdom from his son's hands
and give you ten tribes. 36I will give one tribe to his son so that
David my servant may always have a lamp before me in Jerusalem,
the city where I chose to put my Name. 37However, as for you, I
will take you, and you will rule over all that your heart desires; you
will be king over Israel. 38If you do whatever I command you and
walk in my ways and do what is right in my eyes by keeping my

11:37,38 *I will take you, and you will rule . . . I will build you a dynasty:* God gives Jeroboam a promise that is very similar to the one David and Solomon had been given (2 Sam 7:8-16; 1 Kgs 3:14).

QUESTIONS ABOUT 1 KINGS 1:1—11:43

1. Quickly review chapters 1 and 2. Which two of David's many sons thought they should be the next king? How did each of them go about making his claim? Who did each one of them turn to for support? What were David's final instructions to Solomon? (2:1-9)
2. In 2:13-46 King Solomon arranges for the execution of three men: (1) Adonijah, his brother, (2) Joab, a military leader who had served his father, and (3) Shimei, a relative of Saul who had cursed David. Why were these men killed? Do you think Solomon was being fair and reasonable? Why or why not? How do you expect leaders today to treat their political rivals and enemies?
3. Read 3:5-15. In this dream, what did Solomon ask the LORD for? What was the LORD's response? What would you have asked for if you were chosen to be a ruler of a great country?
4. How would you define "wisdom"? Does the example of the difficult decision Solomon made in 3:16-28 fit your definition? Why or why not? Read the note at 3:28. How does this information change your understanding of what wisdom is? How can this kind of wisdom change your relationship with God? With others?
5. Skim over chapters 5–8. What, if anything, impresses you about the description of the temple given in these chapters? What puzzles you? What don't you understand about the purpose of the temple and its place in the life of the Israelites? Make a list of things you'd like to know, and then read the article called "People of the Law: The Religion of Israel," p. 939.
6. Read Solomon's prayer at the temple (8:22-53). What does this prayer have to say about human nature? About what God is like? About forgiveness? About prayer?
7. Read 10:14—11:6. How is Solomon's behavior in these passages different from what it was like when he first became king? What seems to have brought about this change? Can you think of examples in your own life where a "gift" has been misused? What gifts have you been given? What can you do to see that these gifts are used in good, rather than selfish, ways?
8. Go back and read David's statement about obedience and success in 2:3. List some of the events or situations in these first chapters of 1 KINGS that point to the truth of this statement. Do you think this applies just to leaders? Do you think this instruction can also apply to you? If so, how does your answer depend on how you define success?

statutes and commands, as David my servant did, I will be with you. I will build you a dynasty as enduring as the one I built for David and will give Israel to you. [39]I will humble David's descendants because of this, but not forever.' "

[40]Solomon tried to kill Jeroboam, but Jeroboam fled to Egypt, to Shishak the king, and stayed there until Solomon's death.

Solomon's Death

[41]As for the other events of Solomon's reign—all he did and the wisdom he displayed—are they not written in the book of the annals of Solomon? [42]Solomon reigned in Jerusalem over all Israel forty years. [43]Then he rested with his fathers and was buried in the city of David his father. And Rehoboam his son succeeded him as king.

The Kingdom Divides

After Solomon dies, Jeroboam, one of Solomon's former officials, leads the northern tribes in a rebellion against Rehoboam, Solomon's heir. The remainder of 1 Kings focuses on the religious loyalties of the kings of Israel in the north and the kings of Judah in the south. The kings of Israel are strongly condemned because they choose to worship at Bethel and Dan, the holy places set up by Jeroboam (chapter 12), rather than to worship God in Jerusalem. The story of the divided kingdom continues in 2 Kings.

THE NORTHERN TRIBES REBEL

The people from the northern tribes promise to obey and serve Rehoboam on the condition that he lighten their work load. Rehoboam refuses and the people from the north break away, uniting under Jeroboam, who makes Shechem his capital. He also sets up gold statues of calves in Dan and Bethel. Rehoboam also sins by allowing the people of Judah to build shrines and worship foreign gods.

Israel Rebels Against Rehoboam

12 Rehoboam went to Shechem, for all the Israelites had gone there to make him king. [2]When Jeroboam son of Nebat heard this (he was still in Egypt, where he had fled from King Solomon), he returned from[a] Egypt. [3]So they sent for Jeroboam, and he and the whole assembly of Israel went to Rehoboam and said to him: [4]"Your father put a heavy yoke on us, but now lighten the harsh labor and the heavy yoke he put on us, and we will serve you."

[5]Rehoboam answered, "Go away for three days and then come back to me." So the people went away.

[6]Then King Rehoboam consulted the elders who had served

[a]2 Or *he remained in*

11:42,43 *forty years . . . Rehoboam his son succeeded him as king:* While "forty" is sometimes used in a symbolic way to express a long and complete period of time, here it is also probably the actual number of years Solomon ruled, from approximately 970 to 931 B.C. See also the note at 2:11.

12:1 *Shechem:* Shechem was on an important trade route and figured repeatedly in the religious and political history of Israel, making it a good place to crown a new king. A sacred tree at Shechem is where Abram (Abraham) first worshiped God in the promised land (Gen 12:6, 7) and where Abraham's grandson Jacob built an altar (Gen 33:18-20). It is also where Joseph, one of Jacob's sons, was buried (Josh 24:32). In addition, Joshua called a meeting of the tribes of Israel at Shechem in order to renew the covenant made with the LORD in the desert before entering Canaan (Josh 24).

12:11 *scourge you with scorpions:* An animal with a painful stinger (see the illustration on p. 434).

12:15-18 *Ahijah . . . Adoniram:* Adoniram also had been in control of David's and Solomon's labor forces (2 Sam 20:24; 1 Kgs 4:6). For Ahijah, see the note at 11:29, 30.

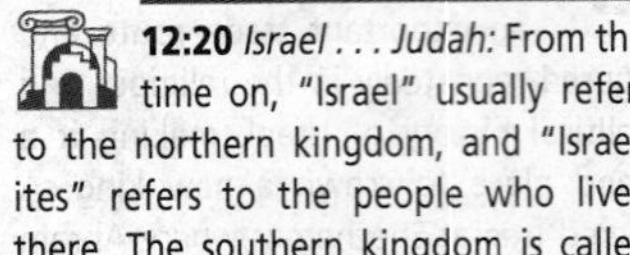

12:20 *Israel . . . Judah:* From this time on, "Israel" usually refers to the northern kingdom, and "Israelites" refers to the people who lived there. The southern kingdom is called "Judah." See also the note at 4:20.

12:23,24 *Judah and Benjamin . . . your brothers:* Judah and Benjamin, like all the twelve tribes, were descended from Jacob whose name was changed to Israel (Gen 32:22-32). See also the mini-article called "Israel," p. 264.

12:15-19 2 Sam 20:1. **12:28** Exod 32:4.

his father Solomon during his lifetime. "How would you advise me
to answer these people?" he asked.
7They replied, "If today you will be a servant to these people
and serve them and give them a favorable answer, they will always
be your servants."
8But Rehoboam rejected the advice the elders gave him and
consulted the young men who had grown up with him and were
serving him. 9He asked them, "What is your advice? How should
we answer these people who say to me, 'Lighten the yoke your
father put on us'?"
10The young men who had grown up with him replied, "Tell
these people who have said to you, 'Your father put a heavy yoke
on us, but make our yoke lighter'—tell them, 'My little finger is
thicker than my father's waist. 11My father laid on you a heavy
yoke; I will make it even heavier. My father scourged you with
whips; I will scourge you with scorpions.' "
12Three days later Jeroboam and all the people returned to
Rehoboam, as the king had said, "Come back to me in three days."
13The king answered the people harshly. Rejecting the advice given
him by the elders, 14he followed the advice of the young men and
said, "My father made your yoke heavy; I will make it even heavier. My father scourged you with whips; I will scourge you with
scorpions." 15So the king did not listen to the people, for this turn
of events was from the LORD, to fulfill the word the LORD had spoken to Jeroboam son of Nebat through Ahijah the Shilonite.
16When all Israel saw that the king refused to listen to them,
they answered the king:

COURT RECORDS AND SOURCES FOR 1 AND 2 KINGS

The author of 1 and 2 KINGS drew upon existing material to tell the stories of the kings of Israel and Judah. Some of the sources were probably court records kept by officials who served these kings. Today, the source documents no longer exist. Many people, however, find evidence of these texts in the Scripture passages listed below.

SOURCE DOCUMENTS	SCRIPTURE PASSAGES
The book of the annals of Solomon	1 Kings 11:41
The book of the annals of the kings of Judah	1 Kings 14:29; 15:7, 23; 22:43-46; 2 Kings 8:23; 12:19; 14:18-20; 15:6, 36; 16:19; 20:20; 21:17, 24-26; 23:28; 24:5
The book of the annals of the kings of Israel	1 Kings 14:19; 15:31; 16:5, 14, 20, 27; 22:39; 2 Kings 1:18; 10:34; 13:8, 12; 14:15, 28; 15:11, 15, 21, 26, 31
The Book of the Law (or Book of the Covenant)	2 Kings 22:8-11; 23:2, 21

"What share do we have in David,
what part in Jesse's son?
To your tents, O Israel!
Look after your own house, O David!"

So the Israelites went home. 17 But as for the Israelites who were living in the towns of Judah, Rehoboam still ruled over them.
18 King Rehoboam sent out Adoniram,[a] who was in charge of
forced labor, but all Israel stoned him to death. King Rehoboam,
however, managed to get into his chariot and escape to Jerusalem.
19 So Israel has been in rebellion against the house of David to this
day.
20 When all the Israelites heard that Jeroboam had returned,
they sent and called him to the assembly and made him king over all
Israel. Only the tribe of Judah remained loyal to the house of David.
21 When Rehoboam arrived in Jerusalem, he mustered the
whole house of Judah and the tribe of Benjamin—a hundred and
eighty thousand fighting men—to make war against the house of
Israel and to regain the kingdom for Rehoboam son of Solomon.
22 But this word of God came to Shemaiah the man of God:
23 "Say to Rehoboam son of Solomon king of Judah, to the whole
house of Judah and Benjamin, and to the rest of the people, 24 'This
is what the LORD says: Do not go up to fight against your brothers,
the Israelites. Go home, every one of you, for this is my doing.' " So
they obeyed the word of the LORD and went home again, as the
LORD had ordered.

Golden Calves at Bethel and Dan

25 Then Jeroboam fortified Shechem in the hill country of
Ephraim and lived there. From there he went out and built up
Peniel.[b]
26 Jeroboam thought to himself, "The kingdom will now
likely revert to the house of David. 27 If these people go up to offer
sacrifices at the temple of the LORD in Jerusalem, they will again
give their allegiance to their lord, Rehoboam king of Judah. They
will kill me and return to King Rehoboam."
28 After seeking advice, the king made two golden calves. He
said to the people, "It is too much for you to go up to Jerusalem. Here
are your gods, O Israel, who brought you up out of Egypt." 29 One he
set up in Bethel, and the other in Dan. 30 And this thing became a sin;
the people went even as far as Dan to worship the one there.
31 Jeroboam built shrines on high places and appointed
priests from all sorts of people, even though they were not Levites.
32 He instituted a festival on the fifteenth day of the eighth month,
like the festival held in Judah, and offered sacrifices on the altar.

[a] **18** Some Septuagint manuscripts and Syriac (see also 1 Kings 4:6 and 5:14); Hebrew *Adoram* [b] **25** Hebrew *Penuel,* a variant of *Peniel*

12:25 *Shechem . . . Ephraim . . . Peniel:* Although Shechem was originally part of the territory of Manasseh (see the map on p. 2464), apparently the boundary between Manasseh and Ephraim changed at some point in Israelite history. Ephraim was one of the largest and most important tribes of Israel. Two early religious sites, Bethel and Shiloh, were located here. Joshua, who led the people of Israel into the promised land, was an Ephraimite (Num 13:3-16, where he is called Hoshea); as was the prophet and judge Samuel (1 Sam 1:1,19,20). Peniel was located east of the Jordan River near the Jabbok River.

12:28-31 *two golden calves . . . built shrines on high places:* It is not clear what Jeroboam's intentions were. Either he meant for these statues to represent the LORD or to represent the Canaanite god Baal. Either way, this kind of statue was clearly forbidden by the Law (see Deut 4:15-20; 5:7-10). Jeroboam sinned by making idols to represent God and by encouraging the people to worship in places other than the temple in Jerusalem. See the note at 3:2.

12:29 *Bethel . . . Dan:* Bethel was in the area of Benjamin, close to the border of Ephraim. This placed it in the southernmost part of Israel, about twelve miles north of Jerusalem in Judah. It had been a special place of worship at several times in Israel's history (Gen 12:8; 28:11-19; 35:6, 7). Dan was near Mount Hermon located in the far north of Israel. In the period when judges ruled the tribes of Israel some Danites worshiped foreign gods there (Judg 18:28-31).

12:32 *like the festival held in Judah:* This probably refers to the Feast of Tabernacles. See the note at 8:2. Jeroboam appears to be reestablishing former customs of the northern tribes, perhaps in an attempt to build a national identity for the northern kingdom that would set it apart from the southern kingdom.

13:1 *Judah . . . Bethel:* The prophet from the southern kingdom brings a message to Jeroboam at Bethel in the northern kingdom to warn him about what will result because of his improper worship at Bethel's altar. See the notes at 12:20 and 12:29.

13:1,2 2 Kgs 23:15,16.

This he did in Bethel, sacrificing to the calves he had made. And at
Bethel he also installed priests at the high places he had made.
33 On the fifteenth day of the eighth month, a month of his own
choosing, he offered sacrifices on the altar he had built at Bethel.
So he instituted the festival for the Israelites and went up to the
altar to make offerings.

The Man of God From Judah

13 By the word of the LORD a man of God came from Judah to
Bethel, as Jeroboam was standing by the altar to make an offering.

KINGSHIP IN ISRAEL

Although surrounded by nations that had been governed by kings for many years—Assyria, Babylonia, Egypt, and the nations of Canaan—kingship and a centralized form of government did not appear in Israel until about 1000 B.C. Before that time, the Jewish Scriptures say that "In those days Israel had no king; everyone did as he saw fit" (Judg 21:25). During this period the various tribes of Israel enjoyed a more or less independent existence. When attacked by a mutual enemy, however, they would join forces under the direction of special leaders chosen by God and called "judges." As these attacks became more frequent many people in Israel felt the need for a more permanent form of leadership. Finally, the people said, "Appoint a king to lead us, such as all the other nations have" (1 Sam 8:5).

This demand caused serious problems for Israel. The people clearly needed a strong military leader to deal with the political situation. But when Israel wanted to be like "all the other nations," they denied their special relationship with God. From the time of Moses, the people of Israel saw themselves as God's chosen people with God, rather than a human being, as their king. Samuel, a prophet and the last judge of Israel, warned the people about the dangers of having a human king (1 Sam 8:11-18). In the end, however, he agreed to take the matter to the LORD who allowed the Israelites to have a king. But this king would have to be chosen by God and would be expected to make God's invisible rule over the people visible. In this way, the people had their "king," but God would continue to rule over them.

The Jewish Scriptures reflect both positive and negative evaluations of how well kingship worked for Israel. For example, the first king, Saul, forgot his role as God's appointed leader soon after he was anointed king. Saul's kingship ended very sadly and tragically (1 Sam 15; 31). On the other hand, David is clearly the best example of a faithful king. God rewarded David for his obedience by promising that someone from David's family would always rule Israel (2 Sam 7). Some kings after David refused to obey God's Law and did not rule according to God's instructions. Very often these kings, like Ahaziah (2 Kgs 8:25-29; 9:29) and Amon (2 Kgs 21:19-26), were killed and quickly forgotten. Others, like Hezekiah and Josiah, did their best to serve God and were rewarded for their faithfulness with many years as king.

Israel's four-hundred-year experiment with kingship began to come to an end in 722 B.C. when the northern kingdom (Israel) was destroyed by Assyria. When the Babylonians defeated the southern kingdom (Judah) and took King Zedekiah and its leading citizens into captivity (586 B.C.), kingship in Israel ended for good.

See the article called "From Joshua to the Exile: The People of Israel in the Promised Land," p. 924.

2 He cried out against the altar by the word of the LORD: "O altar,
altar! This is what the LORD says: 'A son named Josiah will be born
to the house of David. On you he will sacrifice the priests of the
high places who now make offerings here, and human bones will
be burned on you.' " 3 That same day the man of God gave a sign:
"This is the sign the LORD has declared: The altar will be split apart
and the ashes on it will be poured out."
4 When King Jeroboam heard what the man of God cried out
against the altar at Bethel, he stretched out his hand from the altar
and said, "Seize him!" But the hand he stretched out toward the
man shriveled up, so that he could not pull it back. 5 Also, the altar
was split apart and its ashes poured out according to the sign given
by the man of God by the word of the LORD.
6 Then the king said to the man of God, "Intercede with the
LORD your God and pray for me that my hand may be restored." So
the man of God interceded with the LORD, and the king's hand was
restored and became as it was before.
7 The king said to the man of God, "Come home with me
and have something to eat, and I will give you a gift."
8 But the man of God answered the king, "Even if you were to
give me half your possessions, I would not go with you, nor would
I eat bread or drink water here. 9 For I was commanded by the
word of the LORD: 'You must not eat bread or drink water or
return by the way you came.' " 10 So he took another road and did
not return by the way he had come to Bethel.
11 Now there was a certain old prophet living in Bethel,
whose sons came and told him all that the man of God had done
there that day. They also told their father what he had said to the
king. 12 Their father asked them, "Which way did he go?" And his
sons showed him which road the man of God from Judah had
taken. 13 So he said to his sons, "Saddle the donkey for me." And
when they had saddled the donkey for him, he mounted it 14 and
rode after the man of God. He found him sitting under an oak tree
and asked, "Are you the man of God who came from Judah?"

"I am," he replied.

15 So the prophet said to him, "Come home with me and eat."
16 The man of God said, "I cannot turn back and go with
you, nor can I eat bread or drink water with you in this place. 17 I
have been told by the word of the LORD: 'You must not eat bread
or drink water there or return by the way you came.' "
18 The old prophet answered, "I too am a prophet, as you are.
And an angel said to me by the word of the LORD: 'Bring him back
with you to your house so that he may eat bread and drink
water.' " (But he was lying to him.) 19 So the man of God returned
with him and ate and drank in his house.
20 While they were sitting at the table, the word of the LORD
came to the old prophet who had brought him back. 21 He cried
out to the man of God who had come from Judah, "This is what

13:1 *altar:* A raised structure where sacrifices and offerings were presented to God or to pagan gods. Altars could be made of rocks, packed earth, metal, or pottery. See the illustration on p. 1811.

13:2 *Josiah . . . house of David:* Josiah would not become king of Judah until almost three hundred years later. He ruled from 640 to 609 B.C. His dramatic reform is described in 2 Kings 22,23. See also the mini-article called "Josiah," p. 843.

13:2 *human bones will be burned on you:* Burning a dead person's bones on an altar made the altar unfit for any sacred purpose.

13:11 *old prophet:* One test for a true prophet is whether what the prophet says comes true (Deut 18:21,22). The "old prophet" is at first a false prophet, but he is later used by God as a true prophet (13:16-24). See also the article called "Prophets and Prophecy," p. 935.

13:22 *not to eat . . . body will not be buried:* Refusing to eat or drink at a place was a sign of disapproval (13:7-9).

In the ancient world it was very important to people to be buried near their ancestors and other family members, because they believed that the only comfort a person had following death was to sleep alongside one's relatives. See also the mini-article called "Burial," p. 1998.

13:24 *lion:* Lions are predatory cats. The lion mentioned here is probably the smaller Asian lion. Asian lions were found in many parts of the Middle East until the nineteenth century. In 1 and 2 KINGS, lions are shown as bringing punishment to people who make fun of the LORD or the LORD's prophets. See also 20:36 and 2 Kgs 17:25.

13:33 *priests:* See the note at 2:34, 35.

14:3 *ten loaves of bread . . . cakes . . . honey:* The gifts are part of the disguise as they are typical of what a common person would bring, not a queen.

the LORD says: 'You have defied the word of the LORD and have not
kept the command the LORD your God gave you. [22]You came back
and ate bread and drank water in the place where he told you not
to eat or drink. Therefore your body will not be buried in the
tomb of your fathers.' "
[23]When the man of God had finished eating and drinking,
the prophet who had brought him back saddled his donkey for
him. [24]As he went on his way, a lion met him on the road and
killed him, and his body was thrown down on the road, with both
the donkey and the lion standing beside it. [25]Some people who
passed by saw the body thrown down there, with the lion standing
beside the body, and they went and reported it in the city where
the old prophet lived.
[26]When the prophet who had brought him back from his
journey heard of it, he said, "It is the man of God who defied the
word of the LORD. The LORD has given him over to the lion, which
has mauled him and killed him, as the word of the LORD had
warned him."
[27]The prophet said to his sons, "Saddle the donkey for me,"
and they did so. [28]Then he went out and found the body thrown
down on the road, with the donkey and the lion standing beside it.
The lion had neither eaten the body nor mauled the donkey. [29]So
the prophet picked up the body of the man of God, laid it on the
donkey, and brought it back to his own city to mourn for him and
bury him. [30]Then he laid the body in his own tomb, and they
mourned over him and said, "Oh, my brother!"
[31]After burying him, he said to his sons, "When I die, bury
me in the grave where the man of God is buried; lay my bones
beside his bones. [32]For the message he declared by the word of the
LORD against the altar in Bethel and against all the shrines on the
high places in the towns of Samaria will certainly come true."
[33]Even after this, Jeroboam did not change his evil ways, but
once more appointed priests for the high places from all sorts of
people. Anyone who wanted to become a priest he consecrated for
the high places. [34]This was the sin of the house of Jeroboam that
led to its downfall and to its destruction from the face of the earth.

Ahijah's Prophecy Against Jeroboam

14 At that time Abijah son of Jeroboam became ill, [2]and Jeroboam said to his wife, "Go, disguise yourself, so you won't be recognized as the wife of Jeroboam. Then go to Shiloh. Ahijah the
prophet is there—the one who told me I would be king over this
people. [3]Take ten loaves of bread with you, some cakes and a jar of
honey, and go to him. He will tell you what will happen to the
boy." [4]So Jeroboam's wife did what he said and went to Ahijah's
house in Shiloh.

Now Ahijah could not see; his sight was gone because of his
age. [5]But the LORD had told Ahijah, "Jeroboam's wife is coming to ask

you about her son, for he is ill, and you are to give her such and such
an answer. When she arrives, she will pretend to be someone else."
6 So when Ahijah heard the sound of her footsteps at the
door, he said, "Come in, wife of Jeroboam. Why this pretense? I
have been sent to you with bad news. 7 Go, tell Jeroboam that this is
what the LORD, the God of Israel, says: 'I raised you up from among
the people and made you a leader over my people Israel. 8 I tore the
kingdom away from the house of David and gave it to you, but you
have not been like my servant David, who kept my commands and
followed me with all his heart, doing only what was right in my
eyes. 9 You have done more evil than all who lived before you. You
have made for yourself other gods, idols made of metal; you have
provoked me to anger and thrust me behind your back.
10 "'Because of this, I am going to bring disaster on the house
of Jeroboam. I will cut off from Jeroboam every last male in
Israel—slave or free. I will burn up the house of Jeroboam as one
burns dung, until it is all gone. 11 Dogs will eat those belonging to
Jeroboam who die in the city, and the birds of the air will feed on
those who die in the country. The LORD has spoken!'
12 "As for you, go back home. When you set foot in your city,
the boy will die. 13 All Israel will mourn for him and bury him. He
is the only one belonging to Jeroboam who will be buried, because
he is the only one in the house of Jeroboam in whom the LORD,
the God of Israel, has found anything good.
14 "The LORD will raise up for himself a king over Israel who
will cut off the family of Jeroboam. This is the day! What? Yes, even
now.[a] 15 And the LORD will strike Israel, so that it will be like a reed
swaying in the water. He will uproot Israel from this good land
that he gave to their forefathers and scatter them beyond the
River,[b] because they provoked the LORD to anger by making Asherah poles.[c] 16 And he will give Israel up because of the sins Jeroboam has committed and has caused Israel to commit."
17 Then Jeroboam's wife got up and left and went to Tirzah.
As soon as she stepped over the threshold of the house, the boy
died. 18 They buried him, and all Israel mourned for him, as the
LORD had said through his servant the prophet Ahijah.
19 The other events of Jeroboam's reign, his wars and how he
ruled, are written in the book of the annals of the kings of Israel.
20 He reigned for twenty-two years and then rested with his fathers.
And Nadab his son succeeded him as king.

Rehoboam King of Judah

21 Rehoboam son of Solomon was king in Judah. He was
forty-one years old when he became king, and he reigned

[a]**14** The meaning of the Hebrew for this sentence is uncertain. [b]**15** That is, the Euphrates [c]**15** That is, symbols of the goddess Asherah; here and elsewhere in 1 Kings

14:11 *Dogs will eat:* This accurate description of what happened to bodies left in the open was thought to be a horrible ending to one's life. First, Jeroboam and his descendants' last contact will be with dogs, animals that were considered unclean because they fed on dead animals. Second, they will not be buried. See Deut 28:26 and the note at 13:22. See also the mini-article called "Purity (Clean and Unclean)," p. 2125.

14:15 *Asherah:* Also known as Astarte, the Canaanite goddess of fertility. See the mini-article "Canaanite Gods and Godesses," p. 469.

14:17 *Tirzah:* Jeroboam appears to have established this city as the capital of the northern kingdom, although some scholars believe it was actually King Baasha (1 Kgs 15:33). Tirzah was known for its beauty (Song 6:4), and is thought to have been about seven miles northeast of Shechem. See the map on p. 2467.

14:10 1 Kgs 15:29.

14:24 *prostitutes:* Men and women sometimes served at the local shrines as prostitutes in the worship of Canaanite gods, but the LORD had forbidden the people of Israel to worship in this way (Deut 23:17,18). See also the mini-article called "Prostitution in the Bible," p. 1688.

14:25 *Shishak king of Egypt:* Not the father of Solomon's wife (3:1). Shishak is the first Egyptian ruler actually named in the Old Testament. See 2 Chr 12:2-8. See also the mini-article called " Egypt," p. 135 and the chart called "Egyptian Kings (Pharaohs) in the Bible," p. 111.

14:26 *gold shields:* See the note at 10:16. See also 1 Kgs 10:16, 17; 2 Chr 9:15,16.

14:31 *City of David:* See the note at 2:10.

15:5 *Uriah:* A man who served in David's army. David's sin against him is described in 2 Samuel 11:1-27. Even though David sinned against Uriah, he is held up as a standard of obedience because he did not worship other gods.

15:12,13 *prostitutes . . . queen mother:* For prostitutes, see the note at 14:24. The "queen mother" was the mother of the king, an important position in royal courts of the ancient world. See 2:19 for an example of the kind of respect a king in power was expected to show the queen mother.

14:23 2 Kgs 17:9,10. **15:4,5** 1 Kgs 11:36. **15:6,7** 2 Chr 13:3-21. **15:12** 2 Chr 15:8-15.

seventeen years in Jerusalem, the city the LORD had chosen out of
all the tribes of Israel in which to put his Name. His mother's
name was Naamah; she was an Ammonite.
[22]Judah did evil in the eyes of the LORD. By the sins they
committed they stirred up his jealous anger more than their
fathers had done. [23]They also set up for themselves high places,
sacred stones and Asherah poles on every high hill and under
every spreading tree. [24]There were even male shrine prostitutes in
the land; the people engaged in all the detestable practices of the
nations the LORD had driven out before the Israelites.
[25]In the fifth year of King Rehoboam, Shishak king of Egypt
attacked Jerusalem. [26]He carried off the treasures of the temple of
the LORD and the treasures of the royal palace. He took everything,
including all the gold shields Solomon had made. [27]So King
Rehoboam made bronze shields to replace them and assigned
these to the commanders of the guard on duty at the entrance to
the royal palace. [28]Whenever the king went to the LORD's temple,
the guards bore the shields, and afterward they returned them to
the guardroom.
[29]As for the other events of Rehoboam's reign, and all he did,
are they not written in the book of the annals of the kings of
Judah? [30]There was continual warfare between Rehoboam and Jeroboam. [31]And Rehoboam rested with his fathers and was buried
with them in the City of David. His mother's name was Naamah;
she was an Ammonite. And Abijah[a] his son succeeded him as king.

EARLY KINGS OF JUDAH AND ISRAEL

Abijah and Asa continue the line of David on the throne of Judah for a total of forty-four years. Leadership in Israel is less stable due to shifting loyalties among military and political leaders. Under Omri, however, a new capital is set up for Israel in the city of Samaria. This section ends with Omri's son, Ahab, coming to power.

Abijah King of Judah

15 In the eighteenth year of the reign of Jeroboam son of Nebat,
Abijah[b] became king of Judah, [2]and he reigned in Jerusalem three
years. His mother's name was Maacah daughter of Abishalom.[c]
[3]He committed all the sins his father had done before him;
his heart was not fully devoted to the LORD his God, as the heart of
David his forefather had been. [4]Nevertheless, for David's sake the
LORD his God gave him a lamp in Jerusalem by raising up a son to
succeed him and by making Jerusalem strong. [5]For David had
done what was right in the eyes of the LORD and had not failed to

[a]31 Some Hebrew manuscripts and Septuagint (see also 2 Chron. 12:16); most Hebrew manuscripts *Abijam* [b]1 Some Hebrew manuscripts and Septuagint (see also 2 Chron. 12:16); most Hebrew manuscripts *Abijam*; also in verses 7 and 8 [c]2 A variant of *Absalom*; also in verse 10

keep any of the LORD's commands all the days of his life—except
in the case of Uriah the Hittite.
[6]There was war between Rehoboam[a] and Jeroboam throughout ⌊Abijah's⌋ lifetime. [7]As for the other events of Abijah's reign,
and all he did, are they not written in the book of the annals of the
kings of Judah? There was war between Abijah and Jeroboam.
[8]And Abijah rested with his fathers and was buried in the City of
David. And Asa his son succeeded him as king.

Asa King of Judah

[9]In the twentieth year of Jeroboam king of Israel, Asa became
king of Judah, [10]and he reigned in Jerusalem forty-one years. His
grandmother's name was Maacah daughter of Abishalom.
[11]Asa did what was right in the eyes of the LORD, as his father
David had done. [12]He expelled the male shrine prostitutes from the
land and got rid of all the idols his fathers had made. [13]He even
deposed his grandmother Maacah from her position as queen
mother, because she had made a repulsive Asherah pole. Asa cut the
pole down and burned it in the Kidron Valley. [14]Although he did
not remove the high places, Asa's heart was fully committed to the
LORD all his life. [15]He brought into the temple of the LORD the silver and gold and the articles that he and his father had dedicated.
[16]There was war between Asa and Baasha king of Israel
throughout their reigns. [17]Baasha king of Israel went up against
Judah and fortified Ramah to prevent anyone from leaving or
entering the territory of Asa king of Judah.
[18]Asa then took all the silver and gold that was left in the
treasuries of the LORD's temple and of his own palace. He entrusted it to his officials and sent them to Ben-Hadad son of Tabrim-
mon, the son of Hezion, the king of Aram, who was ruling in
Damascus. [19]"Let there be a treaty between me and you," he said,
"as there was between my father and your father. See, I am sending you a gift of silver and gold. Now break your treaty with
Baasha king of Israel so he will withdraw from me."
[20]Ben-Hadad agreed with King Asa and sent the commanders of his forces against the towns of Israel. He conquered Ijon,
Dan, Abel Beth Maacah and all Kinnereth in addition to Naphtali.
[21]When Baasha heard this, he stopped building Ramah and withdrew to Tirzah. [22]Then King Asa issued an order to all Judah—no
one was exempt—and they carried away from Ramah the stones
and timber Baasha had been using there. With them King Asa built
up Geba in Benjamin, and also Mizpah.
[23]As for all the other events of Asa's reign, all his achievements, all he did and the cities he built, are they not written in the

[a]**6** Most Hebrew manuscripts; some Hebrew manuscripts and Syriac *Abijam* (that is, Abijah)

15:12,13 *idols ... repulsive Asherah pole:* God's Law did not allow the worship of idols. See Exod 20:4; 34:17; Lev 19:4; and the notes at 11:6 and 14:15.

15:13 *Kidron Valley:* A deep valley on the eastern side of Jerusalem. See the map on p. 2466. Beginning with Asa, the Kidron Valley was used as a place where kings who were obedient to God's laws destroyed idols (2 Kgs 23:4-6; 2 Chr 29:16).

15:17 *Baasha:* Baasha was king of Israel from around 909 to 886 B.C. His rule is described in 15:33—16:7.

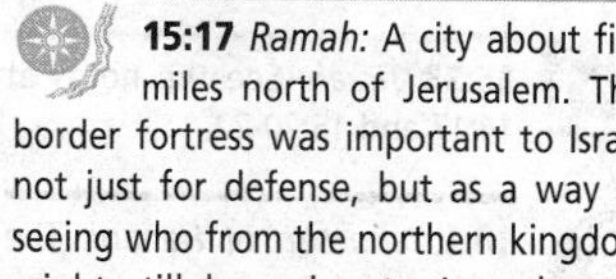

15:17 *Ramah:* A city about five miles north of Jerusalem. This border fortress was important to Israel not just for defense, but as a way of seeing who from the northern kingdom might still be going to Jerusalem to make sacrifices at the temple.

15:18 *Ben-Hadad ... king of Aram:* This is the first of three kings with this name who are mentioned in the Bible. The other two are this man's son and the son of Hazael who seized the second Ben-Hadad's crown (2 Kgs 13:24). Aram took over several cities and areas in the north of Israel, forcing Baasha to leave Ramah to defend the northern area of his kingdom.

15:20-22 *Dan ... Tirzah ... Geba ... Mizpah:* The places named in verse 20 are all at the northern end of Israel, in the territories of Dan and Naphtali. In earlier times Dan was known as Laish (Josh 19:47; Judg 18:7). See also the note at 12:29. The listing of these places indicates that Ben-Hadad had taken all of Israel's northwest territory. Tirzah (15:21) was the capital of the northern kingdom at this time (see the note at 14:17). The exact locations of Geba and Mizpah are not certain, but both are believed to have been close to the border of Judah and Israel.

15:25,26 *Nadab . . . walking in the ways of his father:* Nadab ruled Israel from about 910 to 909 B.C. Jeroboam, Nadab's father, made religious changes that led to idol worship. For doing this, God promised to destroy Jeroboam's entire family (1 Kgs 14:6-16).

15:29 *destroyed them all:* Baasha carries out God's judgment against Jeroboam (1 Kgs 14:10), but not knowingly. Baasha is simply following the common practice of killing all members of a ruler's family after seizing that ruler's throne. This was done so that no one would be left to take revenge or lay claim to the throne. See 1 Sam 24:20,21; 2 Kgs 10:17.

15:33 *Tirzah:* See the notes at 14:17 and 15:20-22.

16:1 *Jehu son of Hanani:* The author of 2 CHRONICLES mentions Jehu as one of the authors of the book of the kings of Israel (2 Chr 20:34).

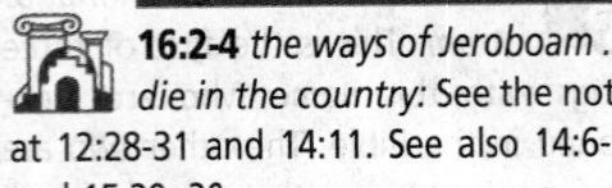

16:2-4 *the ways of Jeroboam . . . die in the country:* See the notes at 12:28-31 and 14:11. See also 14:6-16 and 15:29, 30.

16:7 *Baasha . . . evil he had done:* Even though Baasha's actions fulfilled God's judgment against Jeroboam, Baasha did them for personal gain and with evil intentions.

book of the annals of the kings of Judah? In his old age, however,
his feet became diseased. [24]Then Asa rested with his fathers and
was buried with them in the city of his father David. And
Jehoshaphat his son succeeded him as king.

Nadab King of Israel

[25]Nadab son of Jeroboam became king of Israel in the second year of Asa king of Judah, and he reigned over Israel two
years. [26]He did evil in the eyes of the LORD, walking in the ways of
his father and in his sin, which he had caused Israel to commit.
[27]Baasha son of Ahijah of the house of Issachar plotted
against him, and he struck him down at Gibbethon, a Philistine
town, while Nadab and all Israel were besieging it. [28]Baasha killed
Nadab in the third year of Asa king of Judah and succeeded him as
king.
[29]As soon as he began to reign, he killed Jeroboam's whole
family. He did not leave Jeroboam anyone that breathed, but
destroyed them all, according to the word of the LORD given
through his servant Ahijah the Shilonite— [30]because of the sins
Jeroboam had committed and had caused Israel to commit, and
because he provoked the LORD, the God of Israel, to anger.
[31]As for the other events of Nadab's reign, and all he did, are
they not written in the book of the annals of the kings of Israel?
[32]There was war between Asa and Baasha king of Israel throughout
their reigns.

Baasha King of Israel

[33]In the third year of Asa king of Judah, Baasha son of Ahijah became king of all Israel in Tirzah, and he reigned twenty-four
years. [34]He did evil in the eyes of the LORD, walking in the ways of
Jeroboam and in his sin, which he had caused Israel to commit.
16 Then the word of the LORD came to Jehu son of Hanani
against Baasha: [2]"I lifted you up from the dust and made you
leader of my people Israel, but you walked in the ways of Jeroboam
and caused my people Israel to sin and to provoke me to anger by
their sins. [3]So I am about to consume Baasha and his house, and I
will make your house like that of Jeroboam son of Nebat. [4]Dogs
will eat those belonging to Baasha who die in the city, and the
birds of the air will feed on those who die in the country."
[5]As for the other events of Baasha's reign, what he did and
his achievements, are they not written in the book of the annals of
the kings of Israel? [6]Baasha rested with his fathers and was buried
in Tirzah. And Elah his son succeeded him as king.
[7]Moreover, the word of the LORD came through the prophet
Jehu son of Hanani to Baasha and his house, because of all the evil
he had done in the eyes of the LORD, provoking him to anger by
the things he did, and becoming like the house of Jeroboam—and
also because he destroyed it.

Elah King of Israel

[8]In the twenty-sixth year of Asa king of Judah, Elah son of
Baasha became king of Israel, and he reigned in Tirzah two years.
[9]Zimri, one of his officials, who had command of half his
chariots, plotted against him. Elah was in Tirzah at the time, getting drunk in the home of Arza, the man in charge of the palace at
Tirzah. [10]Zimri came in, struck him down and killed him in the
twenty-seventh year of Asa king of Judah. Then he succeeded him
as king.
[11]As soon as he began to reign and was seated on the throne,
he killed off Baasha's whole family. He did not spare a single male,
whether relative or friend. [12]So Zimri destroyed the whole family
of Baasha, in accordance with the word of the LORD spoken against
Baasha through the prophet Jehu— [13]because of all the sins Baasha
and his son Elah had committed and had caused Israel to commit,
so that they provoked the LORD, the God of Israel, to anger by their
worthless idols.
[14]As for the other events of Elah's reign, and all he did, are
they not written in the book of the annals of the kings of Israel?

Zimri King of Israel

[15]In the twenty-seventh year of Asa king of Judah, Zimri
reigned in Tirzah seven days. The army was encamped near Gibbethon, a Philistine town. [16]When the Israelites in the camp heard
that Zimri had plotted against the king and murdered him, they
proclaimed Omri, the commander of the army, king over Israel
that very day there in the camp. [17]Then Omri and all the Israelites
with him withdrew from Gibbethon and laid siege to Tirzah.
[18]When Zimri saw that the city was taken, he went into the citadel
of the royal palace and set the palace on fire around him. So he
died, [19]because of the sins he had committed, doing evil in the eyes
of the LORD and walking in the ways of Jeroboam and in the sin he
had committed and had caused Israel to commit.
[20]As for the other events of Zimri's reign, and the rebellion
he carried out, are they not written in the book of the annals of
the kings of Israel?

Omri King of Israel

[21]Then the people of Israel were split into two factions; half
supported Tibni son of Ginath for king, and the other half supported Omri. [22]But Omri's followers proved stronger than those of
Tibni son of Ginath. So Tibni died and Omri became king.
[23]In the thirty-first year of Asa king of Judah, Omri became
king of Israel, and he reigned twelve years, six of them in Tirzah.
[24]He bought the hill of Samaria from Shemer for two talents[a] of

[a]**24** That is, about 150 pounds (about 70 kilograms)

16:11-13 *killed off Baasha's whole family . . . worthless idols:* Baasha's family suffers the same judgment as did Jeroboam's (see 16:2-4).

16:21-23 *split . . . Tibni . . . Omri:* While Judah was enjoying stability under Asa, Israel was going through a civil war that would last four years (16:15,16).

16:21 *Omri:* Omri was a much more successful leader than is indicated here (16:21-28). He conquered Moab, formed an alliance with Sidon (16:31), and built up Samaria as his capital. However, this brilliant administrator was a failure as a religious leader (see 16:25, 26; Mic 6:16).

16:24 *Samaria:* See the note at 22:37.

16:29-31 *Ahab . . . Jezebel:* Ahab's wife encouraged him to promote the worship of other gods. See the notes at 11:2; 11:3; and 18:1,2.

16:31 *Sidonians:* Sidon was one of the most important cities in Phoenicia.

16:31-33 *serve Baal and worship him . . . made an Asherah pole:* Baal, a weather god, was believed by the Canaanites to be the most powerful god. In artwork, he was often depicted holding a lightning bolt, as in this relief from the first or second century B.C. For Asherah, see the notes at 14:15 and 15:13, and the mini-article called "Canaanite Gods and Goddesses," p. 469.

16:32 *altar for Baal in the temple of Baal:* For more about altars, see the note at 13:1 (altar). By building a temple for Baal, Ahab gives official approval for the people of Israel to worship Baal along with or in place of the LORD God.

16:34 *Hiel of Bethel rebuilt Jericho:* This event fulfills a statement Joshua made after the Israelites destroyed Jericho when they first entered Canaan (Josh 6:26).

silver and built a city on the hill, calling it Samaria, after Shemer, the name of the former owner of the hill.

[25]But Omri did evil in the eyes of the LORD and sinned more than all those before him. [26]He walked in all the ways of Jeroboam son of Nebat and in his sin, which he had caused Israel to commit, so that they provoked the LORD, the God of Israel, to anger by their worthless idols.

[27]As for the other events of Omri's reign, what he did and the things he achieved, are they not written in the book of the annals of the kings of Israel? [28]Omri rested with his fathers and was buried in Samaria. And Ahab his son succeeded him as king.

Ahab Becomes King of Israel

[29]In the thirty-eighth year of Asa king of Judah, Ahab son of Omri became king of Israel, and he reigned in Samaria over Israel twenty-two years. [30]Ahab son of Omri did more evil in the eyes of the LORD than any of those before him. [31]He not only considered it trivial to commit the sins of Jeroboam son of Nebat, but he also married Jezebel daughter of Ethbaal king of the Sidonians, and began to serve Baal and worship him. [32]He set up an altar for Baal in the temple of Baal that he built in Samaria. [33]Ahab also made an Asherah pole and did more to provoke the LORD, the God of Israel, to anger than did all the kings of Israel before him.

[34]In Ahab's time, Hiel of Bethel rebuilt Jericho. He laid its foundations at the cost of his firstborn son Abiram, and he set up its gates at the cost of his youngest son Segub, in accordance with the word of the LORD spoken by Joshua son of Nun.

ELIJAH THE PROPHET

The unfolding story of the kings of Israel and Judah is put aside momentarily so that the author of 1 KINGS can describe the work of the prophet Elijah, whose name means "the LORD is my God." Elijah challenges King Ahab and Queen Jezebel of Israel who followed the Canaanite god Baal.

Elijah Fed by Ravens

17 Now Elijah the Tishbite, from Tishbe[a] in Gilead, said to Ahab, "As the LORD, the God of Israel, lives, whom I serve, there will be neither dew nor rain in the next few years except at my word."

[2]Then the word of the LORD came to Elijah: [3]"Leave here, turn eastward and hide in the Kerith Ravine, east of the Jordan. [4]You will drink from the brook, and I have ordered the ravens to feed you there."

---

[a]1 Or *Tishbite, of the settlers*

5So he did what the LORD had told him. He went to the Kerith Ravine, east of the Jordan, and stayed there. 6The ravens brought him bread and meat in the morning and bread and meat in the evening, and he drank from the brook.

The Widow at Zarephath

7Some time later the brook dried up because there had been no rain in the land. 8Then the word of the LORD came to him: 9"Go at once to Zarephath of Sidon and stay there. I have commanded a widow in that place to supply you with food." 10So he went to Zarephath. When he came to the town gate, a widow was there gathering sticks. He called to her and asked, "Would you bring me a little water in a jar so I may have a drink?" 11As she was going to get it, he called, "And bring me, please, a piece of bread."

12"As surely as the LORD your God lives," she replied, "I don't have any bread—only a handful of flour in a jar and a little oil in a jug. I am gathering a few sticks to take home and make a meal for myself and my son, that we may eat it—and die."

13Elijah said to her, "Don't be afraid. Go home and do as you have said. But first make a small cake of bread for me from what you have and bring it to me, and then make something for yourself and your son. 14For this is what the LORD, the God of Israel, says: 'The jar of flour will not be used up and the jug of oil will not run dry until the day the LORD gives rain on the land.' "

15She went away and did as Elijah had told her. So there was food every day for Elijah and for the woman and her family. 16For the jar of flour was not used up and the jug of oil did not run dry, in keeping with the word of the LORD spoken by Elijah.

17Some time later the son of the woman who owned the house became ill. He grew worse and worse, and finally stopped breathing. 18She said to Elijah, "What do you have against me, man of God? Did you come to remind me of my sin and kill my son?"

19"Give me your son," Elijah replied. He took him from her arms, carried him to the upper room where he was staying, and laid him on his bed. 20Then he cried out to the LORD, "O LORD my God, have you brought tragedy also upon this widow I am staying with, by causing her son to die?" 21Then he stretched himself out on the boy three times and cried to the LORD, "O LORD my God, let this boy's life return to him!"

22The LORD heard Elijah's cry, and the boy's life returned to him, and he lived. 23Elijah picked up the child and carried him down from the room into the house. He gave him to his mother and said, "Look, your son is alive!"

24Then the woman said to Elijah, "Now I know that you are a man of God and that the word of the LORD from your mouth is the truth."

17:1 *Elijah:* A prophet was someone who spoke God's message to the people or to their rulers. Some of the prophets in 1 KINGS are not named; others are named, but not mentioned in any other part of the Bible. Elijah, however, would continue to have significance for Jews many centuries after the events reported in these few chapters (1 Kgs 17–21; 2 Kgs 1, 2). Many Jews in later centuries thought that Elijah would return to prepare the people for the day of judgment or for the coming of the Messiah (Mal 4:1-6; Matt 17:10,11; Mark 9:11,12). See also the mini-article called "Elijah," p. 1816.

17:1-3 *Tishbe in Gilead . . . Kerith Ravine:* Tishbe's exact location is unknown except that it was in Gilead, an area east of the Jordan River. See the map on p. 2467. The location of Kerith Ravine is unknown, but may have been a gorge through which the heavy waters of the rainy season ran into the Jordan River.

17:1 *neither dew nor rain:* The drought will punish the people for their wickedness and demonstrate that the LORD God, not Baal, is in control of the rains. See the note at 16:31-33. See also Jas 5:17.

17:9 *Zarephath of Sidon:* Zarephath was on the Mediterranean coast about eight miles south of the city of Sidon, Queen Jezebel's hometown. The worship of Baal would have been strong in this area (see 16:31).

17:19-23 *Give me your son . . . three times . . . your son is alive:* Elijah's bringing the dead boy back to life not only proves that he is a true prophet (17:24), but shows that the LORD, not Baal, has power over life and death. Doing something "three times" was considered the "right number" in ancient rituals.

17:9 Luke 4:25, 26. **17:21** 2 Kgs 4:34, 35.

18:1 *Ahab:* See the note at 16:29-31. Ahab's marriage to the Phoenician princess Jezebel most likely brought economic and political benefits to Israel: it would have opened new trade routes and brought assurance that the Phoenician king would not invade Israel. But it was more important that a king of Israel lead the people in faithfulness to God.

18:2 *Samaria:* See the note at 22:37.

18:3,4 *Obadiah . . . Jezebel . . . the LORD's prophets:* Many men named Obadiah appear in the Jewish Scriptures. The name means "Servant of the LORD." The official mentioned here is not the author of OBADIAH. Jezebel, a Phoenician princess by birth (16:31) was Ahab's wife and the one who encouraged the king to allow the worship of Baal in Israel. The LORD's prophets were attached to particular shrines or roamed the countryside. These prophets were most likely part of groups or schools of prophets (1 Sam 10:5; 19:20; 2 Kgs 4:38). See also the article called "Prophets and Prophecy," on p. 935.

18:12 *where the Spirit of the LORD may carry you:* It is not clear why Obadiah says this. Later, Elijah would be taken up into heaven in a miraculous way (2 Kgs 2:11,12).

18:15 *the LORD Almighty . . . whom I serve:* When Elijah declares that he serves the LORD, he is using language customarily applied to the kings of Israel, who were expected to rule as servants of God and to lead God's people and keep them faithful to God's laws. Israel's kings were not being faithful to God, however, and many of God's people were worshiping foreign gods while those who remained faithful were being persecuted. Elijah's task as a prophet and servant of the LORD was to lead people back to God.

Elijah and Obadiah

18 After a long time, in the third year, the word of the LORD
came to Elijah: "Go and present yourself to Ahab, and I will send
rain on the land." 2So Elijah went to present himself to Ahab.
Now the famine was severe in Samaria, 3and Ahab had summoned Obadiah, who was in charge of his palace. (Obadiah was a
devout believer in the LORD. 4While Jezebel was killing off the
LORD's prophets, Obadiah had taken a hundred prophets and hidden them in two caves, fifty in each, and had supplied them with
food and water.) 5Ahab had said to Obadiah, "Go through the land
to all the springs and valleys. Maybe we can find some grass to
keep the horses and mules alive so we will not have to kill any of
our animals." 6So they divided the land they were to cover, Ahab
going in one direction and Obadiah in another.
7As Obadiah was walking along, Elijah met him. Obadiah
recognized him, bowed down to the ground, and said, "Is it really
you, my lord Elijah?"
8"Yes," he replied. "Go tell your master, 'Elijah is here.' "
9"What have I done wrong," asked Obadiah, "that you are
handing your servant over to Ahab to be put to death? 10As surely
as the LORD your God lives, there is not a nation or kingdom where
my master has not sent someone to look for you. And whenever a
nation or kingdom claimed you were not there, he made them
swear they could not find you. 11But now you tell me to go to my
master and say, 'Elijah is here.' 12I don't know where the Spirit of
the LORD may carry you when I leave you. If I go and tell Ahab and
he doesn't find you, he will kill me. Yet I your servant have worshiped the LORD since my youth. 13Haven't you heard, my lord,
what I did while Jezebel was killing the prophets of the LORD? I hid
a hundred of the LORD's prophets in two caves, fifty in each, and
supplied them with food and water. 14And now you tell me to go
to my master and say, 'Elijah is here.' He will kill me!"
15Elijah said, "As the LORD Almighty lives, whom I serve, I
will surely present myself to Ahab today."

Elijah on Mount Carmel

16So Obadiah went to meet Ahab and told him, and Ahab
went to meet Elijah. 17When he saw Elijah, he said to him, "Is that
you, you troubler of Israel?"
18"I have not made trouble for Israel," Elijah replied. "But
you and your father's family have. You have abandoned the LORD's
commands and have followed the Baals. 19Now summon the people from all over Israel to meet me on Mount Carmel. And bring
the four hundred and fifty prophets of Baal and the four hundred
prophets of Asherah, who eat at Jezebel's table."
20So Ahab sent word throughout all Israel and assembled the
prophets on Mount Carmel. 21Elijah went before the people and

said, "How long will you waver between two opinions? If the LORD
is God, follow him; but if Baal is God, follow him."
But the people said nothing.
22 Then Elijah said to them, "I am the only one of the LORD's
prophets left, but Baal has four hundred and fifty prophets. 23 Get
two bulls for us. Let them choose one for themselves, and let them
cut it into pieces and put it on the wood but not set fire to it. I will
prepare the other bull and put it on the wood but not set fire to it.
24 Then you call on the name of your god, and I will call on the
name of the LORD. The god who answers by fire—he is God."
Then all the people said, "What you say is good."
25 Elijah said to the prophets of Baal, "Choose one of the
bulls and prepare it first, since there are so many of you. Call on
the name of your god, but do not light the fire." 26 So they took the
bull given them and prepared it.
Then they called on the name of Baal from morning till
noon. "O Baal, answer us!" they shouted. But there was no
response; no one answered. And they danced around the altar they
had made.
27 At noon Elijah began to taunt them. "Shout louder!" he
said. "Surely he is a god! Perhaps he is deep in thought, or busy, or
traveling. Maybe he is sleeping and must be awakened." 28 So they
shouted louder and slashed themselves with swords and spears, as
was their custom, until their blood flowed. 29 Midday passed, and
they continued their frantic prophesying until the time for the
evening sacrifice. But there was no response, no one answered, no
one paid attention.
30 Then Elijah said to all the people, "Come here to me." They
came to him, and he repaired the altar of the LORD, which was in
ruins. 31 Elijah took twelve stones, one for each of the tribes descended from Jacob, to whom the word of the LORD had come, saying,
"Your name shall be Israel." 32 With the stones he built an altar in the
name of the LORD, and he dug a trench around it large enough to
hold two seahs[a] of seed. 33 He arranged the wood, cut the bull into
pieces and laid it on the wood. Then he said to them, "Fill four large
jars with water and pour it on the offering and on the wood."
34 "Do it again," he said, and they did it again.
"Do it a third time," he ordered, and they did it the third time.
35 The water ran down around the altar and even filled the trench.
36 At the time of sacrifice, the prophet Elijah stepped forward
and prayed: "O LORD, God of Abraham, Isaac and Israel, let it be
known today that you are God in Israel and that I am your servant and have done all these things at your command. 37 Answer me,
O LORD, answer me, so these people will know that you, O LORD,
are God, and that you are turning their hearts back again."
38 Then the fire of the LORD fell and burned up the sacrifice,

[a]32 That is, probably about 13 quarts (about 15 liters)

18:19 *Mount Carmel:* A tall mountain on the Mediterranean coast near the western entrance to the Jezreel Valley. See the map on p. 2467.

18:19 *prophets . . . who eat at Jezebel's table:* Though Jezebel attempted to kill all the LORD's prophets (18:3, 4), she continues to support hundreds of prophets of Baal and Asherah, even in the midst of drought and famine.

18:21 *How long will you waver between two opinions:* Elijah means all of God's people, Israel. Elijah will challenge the people three times during this contest between the powers of Baal and God: he will accuse them of worshiping Baal rather than God (18:21); he will engage them in a demonstration of who is greater, God or Baal (18:22-24); and he will call them to destroy the prophets of Baal (18:39,40).

18:28 *slashed themselves:* Cutting oneself as part of rituals like mourning or idol worship was common (Lev 19:28; 21:5). Ecstatic prophets often cut themselves to bring on a loss of consciousness due to lack of blood. See also the article called "Prophets and Prophecy," p. 935.

18:33 *Fill four large jars with water:* Due to the drought this water was as precious as the blood shed by Baal's prophets (18:28). Pouring water on the altar was symbolic of the pouring rains the people desired. It also made the igniting of the fire more difficult, and the resulting miracle more amazing, proving the superiority of the LORD over Baal.

18:31,32 Gen 32:28; 35:9-11.

18:41 *Go, eat and drink:* People were fasting as a way of asking God to end the famine. Telling Ahab to eat again was Elijah's way of saying it was time to celebrate because the famine was about to end.

18:46 *ran ahead of Ahab . . . to Jezreel:* Ahab had a second royal home in Jezreel, a city about seventeen miles northwest of Mount Gilboa. See the map on p. 2467. In yet another miraculous event, Elijah runs so fast that Ahab's chariots and horses only can follow behind. By placing Elijah ahead of Ahab, the author is showing that the true leader is the prophet of the LORD, not the king.

19:3 *Beersheba in Judah:* Beersheba was on the southern border of Judah, in the Negev (or Southern Desert) and served as an important commercial center between Israel and Egypt. See the map on p. 2467. It also was an important city in Israel's history because Abraham had made a treaty there (Gen 21:30-33), and because Isaac and Jacob had made sacrifices to the LORD there (Gen 26:23-25; 46:1-5).

19:4 *broom tree:* A tree which grows up to ten feet tall but providing only a small amount of shade.

19:5 *angel:* A supernatural being who brings God's messages to people or protects those who belong to God. See also the mini-article called "Angels," p. 88.

19:8 *forty days and forty nights:* Moses spent forty days on Mount Sinai (Exod 24:15-18; 34:28). Forty often is used as a symbolic number, meaning a long period of time. In the New Testament, Jesus is said to have spent forty days in the desert before beginning his ministry of preaching and healing (Matt 4:2). See the chart called "Numbers in the Bible," p. 2405.

18:42-46 Jas 5:17,18.

the wood, the stones and the soil, and also licked up the water in
the trench.
[39]When all the people saw this, they fell prostrate and cried,
"The LORD—he is God! The LORD—he is God!"
[40]Then Elijah commanded them, "Seize the prophets of Baal.
Don't let anyone get away!" They seized them, and Elijah had them
brought down to the Kishon Valley and slaughtered there.
[41]And Elijah said to Ahab, "Go, eat and drink, for there is the
sound of a heavy rain." [42]So Ahab went off to eat and drink, but
Elijah climbed to the top of Carmel, bent down to the ground and
put his face between his knees.
[43]"Go and look toward the sea," he told his servant. And he
went up and looked.
"There is nothing there," he said.
Seven times Elijah said, "Go back."
[44]The seventh time the servant reported, "A cloud as small as
a man's hand is rising from the sea."
So Elijah said, "Go and tell Ahab, 'Hitch up your chariot and
go down before the rain stops you.' "
[45]Meanwhile, the sky grew black with clouds, the wind rose,
a heavy rain came on and Ahab rode off to Jezreel. [46]The power of
the LORD came upon Elijah and, tucking his cloak into his belt, he
ran ahead of Ahab all the way to Jezreel.

Elijah Flees to Horeb

19 Now Ahab told Jezebel everything Elijah had done and how
he had killed all the prophets with the sword. [2]So Jezebel sent a
messenger to Elijah to say, "May the gods deal with me, be it ever
so severely, if by this time tomorrow I do not make your life like
that of one of them."
[3]Elijah was afraid[a] and ran for his life. When he came to
Beersheba in Judah, he left his servant there, [4]while he himself
went a day's journey into the desert. He came to a broom tree, sat
down under it and prayed that he might die. "I have had enough,
LORD," he said. "Take my life; I am no better than my ancestors."
[5]Then he lay down under the tree and fell asleep.
All at once an angel touched him and said, "Get up and eat."
[6]He looked around, and there by his head was a cake of bread
baked over hot coals, and a jar of water. He ate and drank and then
lay down again.
[7]The angel of the LORD came back a second time and touched
him and said, "Get up and eat, for the journey is too much for you."
[8]So he got up and ate and drank. Strengthened by that food, he
traveled forty days and forty nights until he reached Horeb, the
mountain of God. [9]There he went into a cave and spent the night.

[a]3 Or *Elijah saw*

A Still, Small Voice by Sister Genevieve, twentieth century. King Ahab's wife Jezebel wanted to kill Elijah because Elijah had killed one hundred fifty prophets of Baal. Elijah ran and hid in the desert. He walked for forty days until he reached Mount Sinai. While he was hiding in a cave the LORD spoke to Elijah and told the prophet he wanted Elijah to see him. A powerful wind tore the mountain apart. This was followed by an earthquake and a fire. The LORD was not in any of these. Instead, the LORD was in the gentle whisper that followed these frightening events. The LORD then told Elijah what he should do next and reminded him that there were seven thousand Israelites who were still faithful to the LORD. (See 19:9-13.)

The LORD Appears to Elijah

And the word of the LORD came to him: "What are you
doing here, Elijah?"
10He replied, "I have been very zealous for the LORD God
Almighty. The Israelites have rejected your covenant, broken down
your altars, and put your prophets to death with the sword. I am
the only one left, and now they are trying to kill me too."
11The LORD said, "Go out and stand on the mountain in the
presence of the LORD, for the LORD is about to pass by."

Then a great and powerful wind tore the mountains apart

19:8 *Horeb, the mountain of God:* Also called Mount Sinai. This was considered holy because this is where God gave the Law, including the Ten Commandments, to Moses and the people (see Exod 19–40; Deut 5:1-22). For the possible location of this mountain, see the map on p. 133. See also the photograph on p. 342.

19:10-12 *LORD God Almighty . . . wind . . . earthquake . . . fire:* For more about the "LORD God Almighty," see the mini-article called "Names of God," p. 243. Wind, earthquakes, and fire often are associated with God's presence (Exod 19:16,18; Ps 18:7-15).

19:10 *The Israelites have rejected your covenant:* The covenant God made with the people on Mount Sinai (Exod 19:1-7; 20:1-17). See also the mini-articles called "Ten Commandments," p. 354 and "Covenants (Agreements)," p. 386.

19:10,18 Rom 11:2-4.

Elijah went from there and found Elisha son of Shaphat. He was plowing with twelve yoke of oxen . . . Elijah went up to him and threw his cloak around him.
1 Kgs 19:19

19:15,16 *Damascus . . . Aram . . . Israel:* Aram (Syria) was a nation directly north of Israel and southwest of Assyria. Its capital Damascus, located northeast of Mount Hermon, was a major trading and transportation center. Damascus is thought to be the world's oldest continually inhabited city. See the note at 15:18 and the map on p. 2467.

"Israel" here refers to the ten tribes that made up the northern kingdom. See also the notes at 4:20 and 12:20.

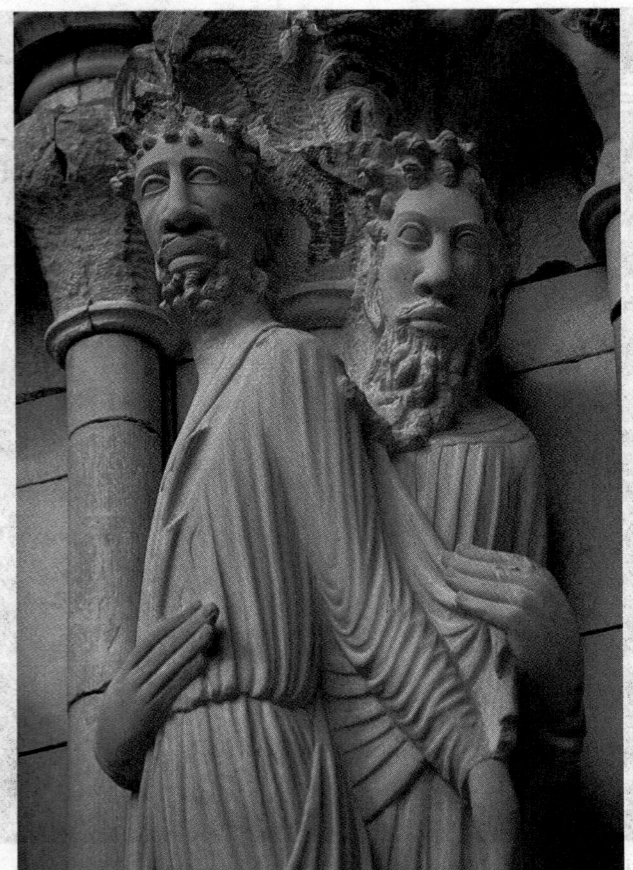

Elijah and Elisha, stone carvings by master stonecarver Simon Verity from the Portal of Paradise, Cathedral of St. John the Divine, New York City. The LORD ordered Elijah to pick Elisha to take his place as the LORD's prophet. Elijah found Elisha plowing a field, went over to him, and put his cloak on Elisha to show that he had been selected to take his place (19:19-21). See also 2 Kgs 2:1-18.

and shattered the rocks before the LORD, but the LORD was not in
the wind. After the wind there was an earthquake, but the LORD
was not in the earthquake. 12 After the earthquake came a fire, but
the LORD was not in the fire. And after the fire came a gentle whisper. 13 When Elijah heard it, he pulled his cloak over his face and
went out and stood at the mouth of the cave.

Then a voice said to him, "What are you doing here, Elijah?"
14 He replied, "I have been very zealous for the LORD God
Almighty. The Israelites have rejected your covenant, broken down
your altars, and put your prophets to death with the sword. I am
the only one left, and now they are trying to kill me too."
15 The LORD said to him, "Go back the way you came, and go

to the Desert of Damascus. When you get there, anoint Hazael king
over Aram. 16Also, anoint Jehu son of Nimshi king over Israel, and
anoint Elisha son of Shaphat from Abel Meholah to succeed you as
prophet. 17Jehu will put to death any who escape the sword of Hazael, and Elisha will put to death any who escape the sword of Jehu.
18Yet I reserve seven thousand in Israel—all whose knees have not
bowed down to Baal and all whose mouths have not kissed him."

The Call of Elisha

19So Elijah went from there and found Elisha son of
Shaphat. He was plowing with twelve yoke of oxen, and he himself
was driving the twelfth pair. Elijah went up to him and threw his
cloak around him. 20Elisha then left his oxen and ran after Elijah.
"Let me kiss my father and mother good-by," he said, "and then I
will come with you."

"Go back," Elijah replied. "What have I done to you?"

21So Elisha left him and went back. He took his yoke of oxen
and slaughtered them. He burned the plowing equipment to cook
the meat and gave it to the people, and they ate. Then he set out to
follow Elijah and became his attendant.

KING AHAB AND QUEEN JEZEBEL

This section is a collection of stories about King Ahab and Queen Jezebel. First, it tells of Ahab's battle with King Ben-Hadad of Syria and the message of condemnation an unnamed prophet of the LORD brings to Ahab (chapter 20). This is followed by the story of how Jezebel plots to get Naboth's vineyard for her husband, and Elijah's words of condemnation to the king and queen (chapter 21). The prophet Micaiah warns Ahab that he will die in battle against the Syrians.

Ben-Hadad Attacks Samaria

20 Now Ben-Hadad king of Aram mustered his entire army.
Accompanied by thirty-two kings with their horses and chariots,
he went up and besieged Samaria and attacked it. 2He sent messengers into the city to Ahab king of Israel, saying, "This is what
Ben-Hadad says: 3'Your silver and gold are mine, and the best of
your wives and children are mine.' "
4The king of Israel answered, "Just as you say, my lord the
king. I and all I have are yours."
5The messengers came again and said, "This is what Ben-
Hadad says: 'I sent to demand your silver and gold, your wives and
your children. 6But about this time tomorrow I am going to send
my officials to search your palace and the houses of your officials.
They will seize everything you value and carry it away.' "
7The king of Israel summoned all the elders of the land and
said to them, "See how this man is looking for trouble! When he
sent for my wives and my children, my silver and my gold, I did
not refuse him."

19:15,16 *anoint Hazael . . . Jehu . . . Elisha:* Anointing included a ceremony in which olive oil was poured on the head of a person to show that he was the chosen king. The prophet Samuel had been given a similar instruction by the LORD when he was told to make Saul, and later, David king (1 Sam 10:1; 16:1-13). Unlike Samuel, however, Elijah is called to anoint a leader for a non-Israelite nation (Aram). This shows that the LORD is not just a local deity, but the God of all nations. Elijah then anointed Elisha to show that he was the one God chose to be Elijah's successor.

19:18 *seven thousand:* Seven often symbolizes completeness in the Bible. Although seven thousand may not seem like a large number, it was enough to assure Elijah that he is not alone in his faithfulness to God. See Rom 11:2-6. See also the chart called "Numbers in the Bible," p. 2405.

19:19 *threw his cloak around him:* This was a sign that Elijah wanted Elisha to follow him and become a prophet. See also 2 Kgs 2:13-15.

20:1 *Ben-Hadad king of Aram . . . thirty-two kings:* This king of Aram is probably not the same Ben-Hadad mentioned in 15:18-21. The thirty-two kings are probably from towns or states under Ben-Hadad's control.

20:1 *Samaria:* King Ahab's capital. See the note at 22:37.

20:3 *your wives:* Apparently Ahab had other wives and concubines in addition to his queen Jezebel. Having more than one wife was allowed in these times and was common for kings. See also the note at 1:1-3.

19:15 2 Kgs 8:7-13. **19:16** 2 Kgs 9:1-6.

20:21 *horses and chariots:* See the note at 1:5. Besides being used to pull chariots, horses were also ridden into battle. See the illustrations on pp. 160 and 772.

20:22 *the prophet:* This is the same unnamed prophet who had told Ahab that he would defeat Ben-Hadad in 20:13.

20:22 *next spring:* In this part of the ancient world kings would wait until after the spring rains and grain harvest before going to war so that they would have enough food and soldiers to fight. See also 2 Sam 11:1; 1 Chr 20:1.

20:26 *Aphek:* Several cities had this name. Many scholars believe this Aphek was located east of the Jordan River near the Sea of Galilee; others believe it was a city somewhere in the hill country between Joppa and Shechem.

8 The elders and the people all answered, "Don't listen to him
or agree to his demands."
9 So he replied to Ben-Hadad's messengers, "Tell my lord the
king, 'Your servant will do all you demanded the first time, but this
demand I cannot meet.' " They left and took the answer back to
Ben-Hadad.
10 Then Ben-Hadad sent another message to Ahab: "May the
gods deal with me, be it ever so severely, if enough dust remains in
Samaria to give each of my men a handful."
11 The king of Israel answered, "Tell him: 'One who puts on
his armor should not boast like one who takes it off.' "
12 Ben-Hadad heard this message while he and the kings were
drinking in their tents,[a] and he ordered his men: "Prepare to
attack." So they prepared to attack the city.

Ahab Defeats Ben-Hadad

13 Meanwhile a prophet came to Ahab king of Israel and
announced, "This is what the LORD says: 'Do you see this vast
army? I will give it into your hand today, and then you will know
that I am the LORD.' "
14 "But who will do this?" asked Ahab.
The prophet replied, "This is what the LORD says: 'The young
officers of the provincial commanders will do it.' "
"And who will start the battle?" he asked.
The prophet answered, "You will."
15 So Ahab summoned the young officers of the provincial
commanders, 232 men. Then he assembled the rest of the
Israelites, 7,000 in all. 16 They set out at noon while Ben-Hadad and
the 32 kings allied with him were in their tents getting drunk.
17 The young officers of the provincial commanders went out first.
Now Ben-Hadad had dispatched scouts, who reported, "Men
are advancing from Samaria."
18 He said, "If they have come out for peace, take them alive;
if they have come out for war, take them alive."
19 The young officers of the provincial commanders marched
out of the city with the army behind them 20 and each one struck
down his opponent. At that, the Arameans fled, with the Israelites
in pursuit. But Ben-Hadad king of Aram escaped on horseback
with some of his horsemen. 21 The king of Israel advanced and
overpowered the horses and chariots and inflicted heavy losses on
the Arameans.
22 Afterward, the prophet came to the king of Israel and said,
"Strengthen your position and see what must be done, because
next spring the king of Aram will attack you again."
23 Meanwhile, the officials of the king of Aram advised him,

[a]**12** Or *in Succoth*; also in verse 16

"Their gods are gods of the hills. That is why they were too strong
for us. But if we fight them on the plains, surely we will be stronger
than they. 24 Do this: Remove all the kings from their commands
and replace them with other officers. 25 You must also raise an army
like the one you lost—horse for horse and chariot for chariot—so
we can fight Israel on the plains. Then surely we will be stronger
than they." He agreed with them and acted accordingly.
26 The next spring Ben-Hadad mustered the Arameans and
went up to Aphek to fight against Israel. 27 When the Israelites were
also mustered and given provisions, they marched out to meet
them. The Israelites camped opposite them like two small flocks of
goats, while the Arameans covered the countryside.
28 The man of God came up and told the king of Israel, "This
is what the LORD says: 'Because the Arameans think the LORD is a
god of the hills and not a god of the valleys, I will deliver this vast
army into your hands, and you will know that I am the LORD.' "
29 For seven days they camped opposite each other, and on
the seventh day the battle was joined. The Israelites inflicted a
hundred thousand casualties on the Aramean foot soldiers in one
day. 30 The rest of them escaped to the city of Aphek, where the wall
collapsed on twenty-seven thousand of them. And Ben-Hadad fled
to the city and hid in an inner room.
31 His officials said to him, "Look, we have heard that the
kings of the house of Israel are merciful. Let us go to the king of
Israel with sackcloth around our waists and ropes around our
heads. Perhaps he will spare your life."
32 Wearing sackcloth around their waists and ropes around
their heads, they went to the king of Israel and said, "Your servant
Ben-Hadad says: 'Please let me live.' "
The king answered, "Is he still alive? He is my brother."
33 The men took this as a good sign and were quick to pick
up his word. "Yes, your brother Ben-Hadad!" they said.
"Go and get him," the king said. When Ben-Hadad came
out, Ahab had him come up into his chariot.
34 "I will return the cities my father took from your father,"
Ben-Hadad offered. "You may set up your own market areas in
Damascus, as my father did in Samaria."
⌞Ahab said,⌟ "On the basis of a treaty I will set you free." So
he made a treaty with him, and let him go.

A Prophet Condemns Ahab

35 By the word of the LORD one of the sons of the prophets
said to his companion, "Strike me with your weapon," but the man
refused.
36 So the prophet said, "Because you have not obeyed the
LORD, as soon as you leave me a lion will kill you." And after the
man went away, a lion found him and killed him.
37 The prophet found another man and said, "Strike me,

20:30 *the wall collapsed:* Many ancient cities had tall walls built around them for protection. These were usually made of clay and bricks. Stone walls were more durable, but stones were not always plentiful. (The stone wall shown here is from Arad in the Negev and dates from around 2700 B.C.) Walled cities like Nineveh and Babylon had walls that were wide enough to support a roadway that allowed up to six rows of chariots to travel side by side. Guardrooms, towers, and gates were built into city walls so that the citizens could control who entered the city.

Many scholars believe the walls at Aphek actually fell as described. However, to say a city's walls "collapsed" also was a way of saying the city was captured, so other scholars believe this verse simply describes the number of lives lost when the city was taken.

20:31 *sackcloth . . . ropes:* During their time as slaves in Egypt, the Israelites wore loincloths made of dark, coarse goat or camel hair called *"saq."* This garment, known as sackcloth, became a symbol of slavery, humiliation, and great sadness and was worn at times of trouble or sorrow. It is not certain why the ropes are worn here, but they also may symbolize the ropes used to tie and lead the slaves in Egypt. See also the illustration on p. 1551.

20:34 *cities my father took:* These were taken by the earlier Ben-Hadad in a deal made with King Asa of Judah (15:16-21).

20:34 *Damascus:* See the note at 19:15, 16 (Damascus).

20:36 1 Kgs 13:24.

21:1 *vineyard:* A vineyard is a place where grapes are grown. Vineyards were usually located on a stony hillside and were sometimes enclosed by a wall that protected it. See the illustration on p. 1892 and the mini-article called "Wine," p. 2047.

21:1 *Jezreel:* The Jezreel mentioned here was about twenty miles southeast of Mount Carmel at the foot of Mount Gilboa. See the map on p. 2467.

21:2 *Let me have your vineyard:* As an Israelite, Naboth had the right to own this piece of the promised land that he inherited from his father. It belonged to Naboth's past, present, and future family and so it was not his alone to sell or trade (Lev 25:25-31), and not even a king could take it. Ahab accepts this, but Jezebel, who comes from another culture, does not (16:30, 31).

21:7 *Is this how you act as king:* The Law God gave to Moses listed certain limitations on the power of a king (Deut 17:14-20). Before Israel had its first king and the people were asking their leader Samuel to give them a king like the other nations had, Samuel warned them that a king would take their best fields, vineyards, and orchards (1 Sam 8:14). Samuel's statement was coming true in the actions of Ahab, Israel's most disobedient king.

please." So the man struck him and wounded him. [38]Then the
prophet went and stood by the road waiting for the king. He disguised himself with his headband down over his eyes. [39]As the king
passed by, the prophet called out to him, "Your servant went into
the thick of the battle, and someone came to me with a captive and
said, 'Guard this man. If he is missing, it will be your life for his
life, or you must pay a talent[a] of silver.' [40]While your servant was
busy here and there, the man disappeared."

"That is your sentence," the king of Israel said. "You have
pronounced it yourself."

[41]Then the prophet quickly removed the headband from his
eyes, and the king of Israel recognized him as one of the prophets.
[42]He said to the king, "This is what the LORD says: 'You have set free
a man I had determined should die.[b] Therefore it is your life for
his life, your people for his people.' " [43]Sullen and angry, the king
of Israel went to his palace in Samaria.

Naboth's Vineyard

21 Some time later there was an incident involving a vineyard
belonging to Naboth the Jezreelite. The vineyard was in Jezreel,
close to the palace of Ahab king of Samaria. [2]Ahab said to Naboth,
"Let me have your vineyard to use for a vegetable garden, since it
is close to my palace. In exchange I will give you a better vineyard
or, if you prefer, I will pay you whatever it is worth."

[3]But Naboth replied, "The LORD forbid that I should give
you the inheritance of my fathers."

[4]So Ahab went home, sullen and angry because Naboth the
Jezreelite had said, "I will not give you the inheritance of my
fathers." He lay on his bed sulking and refused to eat.

[5]His wife Jezebel came in and asked him, "Why are you so
sullen? Why won't you eat?"

[6]He answered her, "Because I said to Naboth the Jezreelite,
'Sell me your vineyard; or if you prefer, I will give you another
vineyard in its place.' But he said, 'I will not give you my vineyard.' "

[7]Jezebel his wife said, "Is this how you act as king over Israel?
Get up and eat! Cheer up. I'll get you the vineyard of Naboth the
Jezreelite."

[8]So she wrote letters in Ahab's name, placed his seal on
them, and sent them to the elders and nobles who lived in
Naboth's city with him. [9]In those letters she wrote:

> "Proclaim a day of fasting and seat Naboth in a promi-
> nent place among the people. [10]But seat two scoundrels oppo-

[a]**39** That is, about 75 pounds (about 34 kilograms) [b]**42** The Hebrew term refers to the irrevocable giving over of things or persons to the LORD, often by totally destroying them.

King Ahab's Coveting: Ahab and Jezebel by Thomas Matthews Rooke, 1879. King Ahab wanted to buy Naboth's vineyard and turn it into a vegetable garden. When Naboth refused to sell it to the king, Queen Jezebel devised a plan that would make it possible for her husband to take the vineyard. She arranged to have two men falsely accuse Naboth of cursing God and the king so that the people of his town would stone him to death. This unjust act did not go unnoticed. The LORD sent Elijah to King Ahab with strong words about what God was going to do to Ahab and his queen. (See 21:1-29.)

site him and have them testify that he has cursed both God and the king. Then take him out and stone him to death."

11So the elders and nobles who lived in Naboth's city did as
Jezebel directed in the letters she had written to them. 12They proclaimed a fast and seated Naboth in a prominent place among the
people. 13Then two scoundrels came and sat opposite him and brought charges against Naboth before the people, saying, "Naboth has cursed both God and the king." So they took him outside the
city and stoned him to death. 14Then they sent word to Jezebel:
"Naboth has been stoned and is dead."
15As soon as Jezebel heard that Naboth had been stoned to death, she said to Ahab, "Get up and take possession of the vineyard of Naboth the Jezreelite that he refused to sell you. He is no
longer alive, but dead." 16When Ahab heard that Naboth was
dead, he got up and went down to take possession of Naboth's vineyard.
17Then the word of the LORD came to Elijah the Tishbite:
18"Go down to meet Ahab king of Israel, who rules in Samaria. He

21:9,10 *day of fasting . . . cursed both God and the king . . . stone him:* People sometimes came together to worship and to fast as a way of showing that they were sorry for their sin and as a way of asking God for help during a time of crisis.

For more about what "cursing God and the king" means, see the note at 2:8. The accusation that Naboth had cursed God and the king was serious. If the accusation had been true, it would have been impossible to stop the curse except by taking some special action like killing the one who had spoken the curse. According to 2 KINGS, Naboth's sons also were stoned to death, probably so that they could not carry out the curse Naboth was supposed to have made (2 Kgs 9:25, 26).

21:20 *my enemy:* This harsh term recalls what Ahab had previously called Elijah, a "troubler of Israel" (18:17). Elijah is Ahab's enemy, because Elijah serves the LORD while Ahab serves false gods.

21:22 *Jeroboam . . . Baasha:* Jeroboam was the first king of the northern kingdom (see 12:20). See 14:7-11 for the message the prophet Ahijah brought him concerning how the LORD would punish him. Baasha was the third king of Israel (see the note at 15:17, Baasha). See 16:1-7 for the prophet Jehu's message to him.

21:26,27 *going after idols . . . sackcloth:* See the notes at 11:6 and 20:31.

21:26 *Amorites:* A name sometimes used for the people who lived in Canaan before the Israelites.

21:29 *I will not bring this disaster . . . days of his son:* The body of Ahab's son, Joram, was thrown on Naboth's land (2 Kgs 9:25, 26). Ahab was killed in battle and dogs licked the blood from the chariot that carried his body to Samaria (1 Kgs 22:29-38). See also 2 Kgs 9:36 and the note at 14:11.

22:2 *Jehoshaphat king of Judah . . . king of Israel:* Jehoshaphat, the son of King Asa of Judah, ruled the southern kingdom from 870 to 848 B.C. and maintained friendly relationships with Israel. King Ahab of Israel was the son of King Omri of Israel and ruled Israel from 874 to 853 B.C. See also the note at 16:29-31.

22:3 *Ramoth Gilead:* Ramoth Gilead was east of the Jordan River and south of the Yarmuk River, and had been an Israelite city since the time of Moses (Deut 4:41-43; 1 Kgs 4:13). Though not mentioned by name, it was one of the towns Ben-Hadad had taken from Israel (15:16-21) and that was later returned (1 Kgs 20:34).

21:23 2 Kgs 9:30-37.

is now in Naboth's vineyard, where he has gone to take possession
of it. [19]Say to him, 'This is what the LORD says: Have you not murdered a man and seized his property?' Then say to him, 'This is
what the LORD says: In the place where dogs licked up Naboth's
blood, dogs will lick up your blood—yes, yours!' "
[20]Ahab said to Elijah, "So you have found me, my enemy!"
"I have found you," he answered, "because you have sold
yourself to do evil in the eyes of the LORD. [21]"I am going to bring
disaster on you. I will consume your descendants and cut off from
Ahab every last male in Israel—slave or free. [22]I will make your
house like that of Jeroboam son of Nebat and that of Baasha son
of Ahijah, because you have provoked me to anger and have
caused Israel to sin.'
[23]"And also concerning Jezebel the LORD says: 'Dogs will
devour Jezebel by the wall of[a] Jezreel.'
[24]"Dogs will eat those belonging to Ahab who die in the city,
and the birds of the air will feed on those who die in the country."
[25](There was never a man like Ahab, who sold himself to do
evil in the eyes of the LORD, urged on by Jezebel his wife. [26]He
behaved in the vilest manner by going after idols, like the Amorites
the LORD drove out before Israel.)
[27]When Ahab heard these words, he tore his clothes, put on
sackcloth and fasted. He lay in sackcloth and went around meekly.
[28]Then the word of the LORD came to Elijah the Tishbite:
[29]"Have you noticed how Ahab has humbled himself before me?
Because he has humbled himself, I will not bring this disaster in
his day, but I will bring it on his house in the days of his son."

Micaiah Prophesies Against Ahab

22 For three years there was no war between Aram and Israel.
[2]But in the third year Jehoshaphat king of Judah went down to see
the king of Israel. [3]The king of Israel had said to his officials,
"Don't you know that Ramoth Gilead belongs to us and yet we are
doing nothing to retake it from the king of Aram?"
[4]So he asked Jehoshaphat, "Will you go with me to fight
against Ramoth Gilead?"
Jehoshaphat replied to the king of Israel, "I am as you are,
my people as your people, my horses as your horses." [5]But
Jehoshaphat also said to the king of Israel, "First seek the counsel
of the LORD."
[6]So the king of Israel brought together the prophets—about
four hundred men—and asked them, "Shall I go to war against
Ramoth Gilead, or shall I refrain?"

[a]23 Most Hebrew manuscripts; a few Hebrew manuscripts, Vulgate and Syriac (see also 2 Kings 9:26) *the plot of ground at*

"Go," they answered, "for the Lord will give it into the king's
hand."
7 But Jehoshaphat asked, "Is there not a prophet of the LORD
here whom we can inquire of?"
8 The king of Israel answered Jehoshaphat, "There is still one
man through whom we can inquire of the LORD, but I hate him
because he never prophesies anything good about me, but always
bad. He is Micaiah son of Imlah."
"The king should not say that," Jehoshaphat replied.
9 So the king of Israel called one of his officials and said,
"Bring Micaiah son of Imlah at once."
10 Dressed in their royal robes, the king of Israel and
Jehoshaphat king of Judah were sitting on their thrones at the threshing floor by the entrance of the gate of Samaria, with all the prophets
prophesying before them. 11 Now Zedekiah son of Kenaanah had
made iron horns and he declared, "This is what the LORD says:
'With these you will gore the Arameans until they are destroyed.'"
12 All the other prophets were prophesying the same thing.
"Attack Ramoth Gilead and be victorious," they said, "for the LORD
will give it into the king's hand."
13 The messenger who had gone to summon Micaiah said to
him, "Look, as one man the other prophets are predicting success
for the king. Let your word agree with theirs, and speak favorably."
14 But Micaiah said, "As surely as the LORD lives, I can tell him
only what the LORD tells me."
15 When he arrived, the king asked him, "Micaiah, shall we go
to war against Ramoth Gilead, or shall I refrain?"
"Attack and be victorious," he answered, "for the LORD will
give it into the king's hand."
16 The king said to him, "How many times must I make you
swear to tell me nothing but the truth in the name of the LORD?"
17 Then Micaiah answered, "I saw all Israel scattered on the
hills like sheep without a shepherd, and the LORD said, 'These people have no master. Let each one go home in peace.'"
18 The king of Israel said to Jehoshaphat, "Didn't I tell you
that he never prophesies anything good about me, but only bad?"
19 Micaiah continued, "Therefore hear the word of the LORD:
I saw the LORD sitting on his throne with all the host of heaven
standing around him on his right and on his left. 20 And the LORD
said, 'Who will entice Ahab into attacking Ramoth Gilead and
going to his death there?'
"One suggested this, and another that. 21 Finally, a spirit came
forward, stood before the LORD and said, 'I will entice him.'
22 " 'By what means?' the LORD asked.
" 'I will go out and be a lying spirit in the mouths of all his
prophets,' he said.
" 'You will succeed in enticing him,' said the LORD. 'Go and
do it.'

22:10 *threshing floor . . . gate:* A threshing floor is where harvested stalks of grain are beaten with hand tools or walked over by oxen to separate the seeds (kernels) from the stalks and husks (chaff). Threshing was done outdoors on a hard floor of packed clay, soil, or rock. Threshing floors were often on hills so that the wind could more easily blow away the chaff. See also the illustration on p. 730.

Many cities, particularly those important to a nation's defense, were walled and had a central gate through which people could enter and leave the city. This gate often had a room where guards kept watch. The area just inside the town gate was a very active place where people gathered to make agreements and settle disputes.

22:17 *I saw:* In ancient times, prophets often told about future events from what they had seen in visions or dreams.

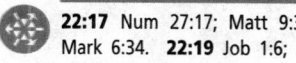

22:17 Num 27:17; Matt 9:36; Mark 6:34. **22:19** Job 1:6; Isa 6:1.

22:37 *Samaria:* Built on the hill of the same name, the city of Samaria stood three hundred feet above the surrounding plain, giving it great defensive strength. It was approximately forty miles north of Jerusalem and midway between the Jordan River and the Mediterranean Sea. Eventually it became known as the burial place for the kings of Israel (1 Kgs 16:28; 2 Kgs 10:35; 13:13). See the map on p. 2467.

23“So now the LORD has put a lying spirit in the mouths of all
these prophets of yours. The LORD has decreed disaster for you.”
24Then Zedekiah son of Kenaanah went up and slapped
Micaiah in the face. “Which way did the spirit from[a] the LORD go
when he went from me to speak to you?” he asked.
25Micaiah replied, “You will find out on the day you go to
hide in an inner room.”
26The king of Israel then ordered, “Take Micaiah and send
him back to Amon the ruler of the city and to Joash the king’s son
27and say, ‘This is what the king says: Put this fellow in prison and
give him nothing but bread and water until I return safely.’ ”
28Micaiah declared, “If you ever return safely, the LORD has
not spoken through me.” Then he added, “Mark my words, all you
people!”

Ahab Killed at Ramoth Gilead

29So the king of Israel and Jehoshaphat king of Judah went
up to Ramoth Gilead. 30The king of Israel said to Jehoshaphat, “I
will enter the battle in disguise, but you wear your royal robes.” So
the king of Israel disguised himself and went into battle.
31Now the king of Aram had ordered his thirty-two chariot
commanders, “Do not fight with anyone, small or great, except the
king of Israel.” 32When the chariot commanders saw Jehoshaphat,
they thought, “Surely this is the king of Israel.” So they turned to
attack him, but when Jehoshaphat cried out, 33the chariot commanders saw that he was not the king of Israel and stopped pursuing him.
34But someone drew his bow at random and hit the king of
Israel between the sections of his armor. The king told his chariot
driver, “Wheel around and get me out of the fighting. I’ve been
wounded.” 35All day long the battle raged, and the king was
propped up in his chariot facing the Arameans. The blood from
his wound ran onto the floor of the chariot, and that evening he
died. 36As the sun was setting, a cry spread through the army:
“Every man to his town; everyone to his land!”
37So the king died and was brought to Samaria, and they
buried him there. 38They washed the chariot at a pool in Samaria
(where the prostitutes bathed),[b] and the dogs licked up his blood,
as the word of the LORD had declared.
39As for the other events of Ahab’s reign, including all he did,
the palace he built and inlaid with ivory, and the cities he fortified,
are they not written in the book of the annals of the kings of
Israel? 40Ahab rested with his fathers. And Ahaziah his son succeeded him as king.

---

[a]**24** Or *Spirit of* [b]**38** Or *Samaria and cleaned the weapons*

KING JEHOSHAPHAT OF JUDAH AND KING AHAZIAH OF ISRAEL

For a brief period there is cooperation and peace between the kings of Judah and Israel.

22:41 *Jehoshaphat:* See the note at 22:2.

22:46 *prostitutes:* See the note at 14:24.

Jehoshaphat King of Judah

41 Jehoshaphat son of Asa became king of Judah in the fourth
year of Ahab king of Israel. 42 Jehoshaphat was thirty-five years old
when he became king, and he reigned in Jerusalem twenty-five
years. His mother's name was Azubah daughter of Shilhi. 43 In
everything he walked in the ways of his father Asa and did not
stray from them; he did what was right in the eyes of the LORD.
The high places, however, were not removed, and the people continued to offer sacrifices and burn incense there. 44 Jehoshaphat was
also at peace with the king of Israel.

45 As for the other events of Jehoshaphat's reign, the things
he achieved and his military exploits, are they not written in the
book of the annals of the kings of Judah? 46 He rid the land of the
rest of the male shrine prostitutes who remained there even after
the reign of his father Asa. 47 There was then no king in Edom; a
deputy ruled.

QUESTIONS ABOUT 1 KINGS 12:1—22:53

1. Why did the Israelites from the northern tribes decide to break away and choose their own king rather than follow Solomon's heir, Rehoboam? (12) Who did they choose to be their leader instead? What did this leader do that upset the LORD?
2. List some of the temptations that drew the people and their kings into disobedience. What temptations draw people and their leaders away from God today?
3. Which of the rulers in 1 KINGS is most memorable? Why? Does the author of 1 KINGS describe this ruler as faithful or evil? What are the reasons the author gives?
4. The book of 1 KINGS includes stories about a number of prophets. Some them are named (like Nathan, Elijah, and Micaiah), but others are unnamed. How would you describe their relationships with people in power? Which is your favorite story concerning a prophet? Why? Take time to read the article called "Prophets and Prophecy," p. 935. How does the information in this article change your understanding of what the prophets in 1 KINGS were trying to do in the situations they found themselves?
5. Prophets don't just "preach" against injustice. Often they dramatize what they have to say (see, for example, 20:38-42). Is there an injustice in your community that you're concerned about? What would you like to say to the people who have the power to change this injustice? How could you dramatize your statement?
6. Suppose a friend said, "Jezebel wasn't so wicked. She acted as a faithful follower of her own god to encourage his worship." How would you respond?
7. A major theme in 1 KINGS is that God rewards those who obey God's Law and punishes those who disobey it. Compare this with what Jesus says in Luke 13:1-5.

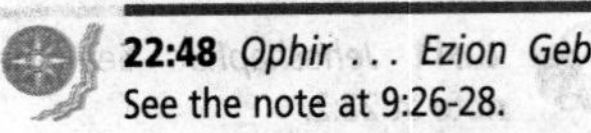
22:48 *Ophir . . . Ezion Geber:* See the note at 9:26-28.

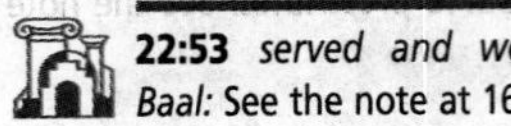
22:53 *served and worshiped Baal:* See the note at 16:31-33.

48Now Jehoshaphat built a fleet of trading ships[a] to go to
Ophir for gold, but they never set sail—they were wrecked at
Ezion Geber. 49At that time Ahaziah son of Ahab said to
Jehoshaphat, "Let my men sail with your men," but Jehoshaphat
refused.

50Then Jehoshaphat rested with his fathers and was buried
with them in the city of David his father. And Jehoram his son succeeded him.

Ahaziah King of Israel

51Ahaziah son of Ahab became king of Israel in Samaria in
the seventeenth year of Jehoshaphat king of Judah, and he reigned
over Israel two years. 52He did evil in the eyes of the LORD, because
he walked in the ways of his father and mother and in the ways of
Jeroboam son of Nebat, who caused Israel to sin. 53He served and
worshiped Baal and provoked the LORD, the God of Israel, to
anger, just as his father had done.

[a]48 Hebrew *of ships of Tarshish*

2 KINGS

This book continues the story of those who ruled Israel and Judah. Read 2 Kings to find out which rulers were faithful to God and which were not. And read about a real hero, Elisha the prophet.

What makes 2 Kings special?

Second Kings is actually the second half of a single book (1 and 2 Kings) that was divided into two parts because they were too long to fit on one scroll. Together the books continue the history of the nation that was begun in 1 and 2 Samuel. As in 1 Kings, the history is told in a special way. The story moves back and forth between reports of the kings in Judah (the southern kingdom) and reports of the kings in Israel (the northern kingdom). That allows the reader to compare what was going on in the south with what was going on in the north.

Why was 2 Kings written?

The destruction of Jerusalem in 586 B.C. was the major event that prompted the writing of 2 Kings. The smashing of the city walls, the burning of the temple, and the humiliation of the people resulted in a religious crisis among the survivors. God had promised to allow a descendant of King David to rule forever. But when Jerusalem was destroyed and the temple was burned, the line of rulers from David's family line also came to an end. Together, these events threatened to destroy the people's trust in God, who seemed to have abandoned them.

The history as recorded in 1 and 2 Kings was completed after the destruction of Jerusalem, so the books are a response to this event. Second Kings shows the people that their kings, and not God, had been unfaithful. God had been very patient with Israel and Judah, even after the people and their leaders disobeyed God and worshiped idols. Prophets were sent repeatedly to warn the people and their kings to stop worshiping other gods and turn back to him. Finally, the people were punished. The two kingdoms were destroyed, and the people were forced to live in foreign nations.

The Lord's promise through the prophet Nathan that one of David's descendants would always rule Israel (2 Sam 7) is repeated often in 1 and 2 Kings. This repeated promise was intended to encourage the people to have hope that one day in the future, Israel's punishment would end, and they would once again be ruled by a king descended from David's family.

Elijah the prophet from Tishbe: Elijah's name means "the Lord is my God." He represented the loyal followers of God against Israel's King Ahab and Queen Jezebel, who encouraged their followers to worship the Canaanite god Baal (1 Kgs 17–22; 2 Kgs 1,2).

Prophets spoke God's message, which at times included telling what would happen in the future. Elijah spoke God's message in the early ninth century B.C. In later centuries many Jewish people expected Elijah to return to get everything ready for the day of judgment or for the coming of a Messiah (Mal 4:1-6; Matt 17:10,11; Mark 9:11, 12). See also the mini-article called "Elijah," p. 1816 and the article called "Prophets and Prophecy," p. 935.

Tishbe's exact location is unknown. It was in Gilead, an area east of the Jordan River between the Jabbok River in the south and the Yarmuk River in the north. See the map on p. 2467.

1:1,2 *Ahab . . . Ahaziah:* Ahab, Israel's seventh king, ruled from 874 to 853 B.C. He died in battle against the Arameans at Ramoth Gilead (1 Kgs 22:29-40). His son Ahaziah became Israel's eighth king, but he ruled only a brief time (853-852 B.C.).

1:1,2 *Moab . . . Samaria . . . Ekron:* For these locations, see the map on p. 2467. The Moabites were enemies of Israel (Judg 10:11-18; 1 Sam 14:47,48). Omri, Israel's sixth king, conquered Moab, and it remained under Israel's control for forty years until its rebellion during the reign of Israel's King Ahaziah.

The city of Samaria stood three hundred feet above the surrounding plain, giving it great defensive strength. Omri made Samaria the capital of the northern kingdom of Israel (1 Kgs 16:21-24). Eventually it became known as the burial place for the kings of Israel (1 Kgs 16:28; 22:37; 2 Kgs 10:35; 13:13).

Ekron was an important Philistine town.

WHAT'S THE STORY BEHIND THE SCENE?

SECOND KINGS is presented as an historical account of three hundred years of the monarchies of Israel and Judah. But it is important to realize that the author was also writing this history as an interpretation of the events that led to the destruction of the nation. As a result, these pages are also filled with an emphasis on traditional values, with frequent warnings against unfaithfulness, and with calls for obedience to God's commandments.

On several occasions the author explains why certain events have taken place (2 Kgs 17:7-23) or whether or not a particular king was good or bad. Sometimes these explanations appear in the speeches or statements made by God, a king, or a prophet (2 Kgs 20:16-18; 22:15-20).

HOW IS 2 KINGS CONSTRUCTED?

The following outline divides the book into three major sections. The first section (1:1—8:15) relates many stories about the prophet Elisha. The second section (8:16—17:41) reports the history of the two kingdoms until 722 B.C. when the Assyrians defeated the northern kingdom of Israel, destroyed Samaria, its capital city, and led the people away as captives. That left Judah, the southern kingdom, alone as an independent nation. The final section (chapters 18–25) reports the history of Judah until 586 B.C., when it was defeated by King Nebuchadnezzar of Babylon. The capital city of Jerusalem was destroyed along with the temple that Solomon had built, and many of the people were taken to Babylonia as prisoners. The book ends on a somewhat hopeful note with the release of King Jehoiachin from prison.

The prophet Elisha (1:1—8:15)
- Elisha follows Elijah as prophet (1:1—2:25)
- Elisha and Joram (3:1-27)
- Elisha's miracles (4:1—8:15)

Kings of Judah and Israel (8:16—17:41)
- Jehu and his house (9:1—14:29)
- The last days of Israel (15:1—17:41)

Judah alone (18:1—25:30)
- King Hezekiah and the Assyrian invasion (18:1—20:21)
- Two evil kings: Manasseh and Amon (21:1-26)
- King Josiah and his reform (22:1—23:30)
- The fall of Jerusalem (23:31—25:30)

The Prophet Elisha

SECOND KINGS begins with the last of the stories about Elijah the prophet. He condemns King Ahaziah (chapter 1) and then he goes up into heaven, leaving Elisha to carry on the work of being the LORD's prophet (2:1-18). The section that follows in 2:19—8:15 tells of Elisha's meeting with Joram and of the many miracles he does for people. The miracles, rather than messages condemning the religious practices of the kings, are the main focus of the Elisha stories.

ELISHA FOLLOWS ELIJAH AS PROPHET

The life and work of the prophet Elijah are nearly at an end. Three stories about Elisha's faithfulness as a disciple of Elijah (2:1-8) are followed by three stories demonstrating the transfer of prophetic power (2:13-25) from Elijah to Elisha.

The LORD's Judgment on Ahaziah

1 After Ahab's death, Moab rebelled against Israel. 2 Now Ahaziah
had fallen through the lattice of his upper room in Samaria and
injured himself. So he sent messengers, saying to them, "Go and
consult Baal-Zebub, the god of Ekron, to see if I will recover from
this injury."
3 But the angel of the LORD said to Elijah the Tishbite, "Go up
and meet the messengers of the king of Samaria and ask them, 'Is
it because there is no God in Israel that you are going off to consult Baal-Zebub, the god of Ekron?' 4 Therefore this is what the
LORD says: 'You will not leave the bed you are lying on. You will
certainly die!' " So Elijah went.
5 When the messengers returned to the king, he asked them,
"Why have you come back?"
6 "A man came to meet us," they replied. "And he said to us,
'Go back to the king who sent you and tell him, "This is what the
LORD says: Is it because there is no God in Israel that you are sending men to consult Baal-Zebub, the god of Ekron? Therefore you
will not leave the bed you are lying on. You will certainly die!" ' "
7 The king asked them, "What kind of man was it who came
to meet you and told you this?"
8 They replied, "He was a man with a garment of hair and
with a leather belt around his waist."
The king said, "That was Elijah the Tishbite."
9 Then he sent to Elijah a captain with his company of fifty
men. The captain went up to Elijah, who was sitting on the top of
a hill, and said to him, "Man of God, the king says, 'Come down!' "
10 Elijah answered the captain, "If I am a man of God, may
fire come down from heaven and consume you and your fifty
men!" Then fire fell from heaven and consumed the captain and
his men.
11 At this the king sent to Elijah another captain with his fifty

1:1,2 *the lattice of his upper room:* In the ancient Near East, many buildings had flat roofs. Roofs would be used for relaxing, entertaining, and for sleeping during hot evenings. Ahaziah's upper room probably had trellis-like walls with windows cut out. The trellis created shade and privacy while the windows let the air flow through. See also the article called "Archaeology and the Bible," p. 27.

1:1,2 *Baal-Zebub:* Meaning "lord of flies," this name may have been used by local Baal worshipers to refer to a storm god who was thought to control diseases brought by flies. Or, it may have been an insulting nickname for "Baal-Zebul," which means "Baal the Prince," and refers to Baal, a Canaanite fertility god. The New Testament uses the similar name "Beelzebub" as a name for Satan (Matt 12:24; Mark 3:22; Luke 11:15). See also the mini-article called "Canaanite Gods and Goddesses," p. 469.

1:3 *angel of the LORD:* See the mini-article called "Angels," p. 88.

1:3 *Elijah the Tishbite:* See the note on p. 675.

1:8 *garment of hair . . . leather belt:* Elijah may have worn a coat made of camel hair or sheepskin and tied with a strip of leather. According to Zechariah 13:4 and Matthew 7:15, prophets wore unusual clothing. In Matthew 3:4 and Mark 1:6, John the Baptist wears similar clothing.

1:9 *a hill:* This probably refers to Mount Carmel (see the map on p. 2467).

1:9 *Man of God:* Another name for a prophet of the LORD.

1:10 *fire fell from heaven:* Fire was often associated with God's presence and judgment (Exod 19:16, 18; Ps 18:7-15; Luke 9:54). See also 1 Kgs 18:38 and the mini-article called "Fire," p. 2383.

men. The captain said to him, “Man of God, this is what the king
says, ‘Come down at once!’ ”
12“If I am a man of God,” Elijah replied, “may fire come
down from heaven and consume you and your fifty men!” Then
the fire of God fell from heaven and consumed him and his
fifty men.
13So the king sent a third captain with his fifty men. This
third captain went up and fell on his knees before Elijah. “Man of
God,” he begged, “please have respect for my life and the lives of
these fifty men, your servants! 14See, fire has fallen from heaven
and consumed the first two captains and all their men. But now
have respect for my life!”
15The angel of the LORD said to Elijah, “Go down with him;
do not be afraid of him.” So Elijah got up and went down with
him to the king.
16He told the king, “This is what the LORD says: Is it because
there is no God in Israel for you to consult that you have sent messengers to consult Baal-Zebub, the god of Ekron? Because you have
done this, you will never leave the bed you are lying on. You will
certainly die!” 17So he died, according to the word of the LORD that
Elijah had spoken.

Because Ahaziah had no son, Joram[a] succeeded him as king
in the second year of Jehoram son of Jehoshaphat king of Judah.
18As for all the other events of Ahaziah’s reign, and what he did, are
they not written in the book of the annals of the kings of Israel?

Elijah Taken Up to Heaven

2 When the LORD was about to take Elijah up to heaven in a
whirlwind, Elijah and Elisha were on their way from Gilgal. 2Elijah
said to Elisha, “Stay here; the LORD has sent me to Bethel.”
But Elisha said, “As surely as the LORD lives and as you live, I
will not leave you.” So they went down to Bethel.
3The company of the prophets at Bethel came out to Elisha
and asked, “Do you know that the LORD is going to take your master from you today?”
“Yes, I know,” Elisha replied, “but do not speak of it.”
4Then Elijah said to him, “Stay here, Elisha; the LORD has
sent me to Jericho.”
And he replied, “As surely as the LORD lives and as you live, I
will not leave you.” So they went to Jericho.
5The company of the prophets at Jericho went up to Elisha
and asked him, “Do you know that the LORD is going to take your
master from you today?”
“Yes, I know,” he replied, “but do not speak of it.”
6Then Elijah said to him, “Stay here; the LORD has sent me
to the Jordan.”

[a]17 Hebrew *Jehoram,* a variant of *Joram*

1:17 *he died . . . second year of Jehoram:* According to 3:1, this was also the eighteenth year of Jehoshaphat’s rule in Judah. In biblical times, a father and son would sometimes rule as kings at the same time. This way, when the father died, the son already had control of the kingdom (see also 8:16).

2:1 *Elisha:* Elijah already had chosen Elisha to follow him as a prophet (1 Kgs 19:19). Elisha’s story will continue through 2 Kings 13:20. See also the note on p. 675 and the article called “Prophets and Prophecy,” p. 935.

2:1-4 *Gilgal . . . Bethel . . . Jericho:* It appears that the LORD leads Elijah to pay a last visit to the prophets who were at each of these locations (see the map on p. 2467).

This Gilgal was several miles north of Bethel, and is not the Gilgal just north and east of Jericho. Bethel was about twelve miles north of Jerusalem in Judah. It had been a special place of worship at several times in Israel’s history (Gen 12:8; 28:11-19; 35:6,7).

Jericho was an important city on the trade routes from the east to Palestine. It is one of the oldest cities in the world with evidence of building on the site as early as 9000 B.C.

2:6 *the Jordan:* The Jordan River is the longest and most important river in Palestine. See the map on p. 2467.

And he replied, "As surely as the LORD lives and as you live, I
will not leave you." So the two of them walked on.
[7]Fifty men of the company of the prophets went and stood
at a distance, facing the place where Elijah and Elisha had stopped
at the Jordan. [8]Elijah took his cloak, rolled it up and struck the
water with it. The water divided to the right and to the left, and
the two of them crossed over on dry ground.
[9]When they had crossed, Elijah said to Elisha, "Tell me, what
can I do for you before I am taken from you?"

2:8 ***struck the water . . . on dry ground:*** Elijah uses his rolled-up coat to part the water of the Jordan River much as Moses had used his walking stick to part the waters of the Red Sea (Exod 14:15-22). After crossing to the east bank of the Jordan, Elijah comes to the area where Moses died and where his own life also will end (2:11).

The Fiery Ascension of the Prophet Elijah, Greek icon, late seventeenth century. When Elisha knew that the LORD was going to take away his master, Elijah, he asked the prophet to give him twice as much power as he would give to any other prophet. Elijah said this would happen only if Elisha saw him being taken away. As the two prophets were walking and talking, a chariot of fire passed between them. Elijah was taken away, but his cloak fell off. When Elisha struck the Jordan River with Elijah's cloak, a dry path opened up for him, and he knew the request he had made of Elijah had been answered. (See 2:1-18.)

2:9 *double portion:* In Israel at this time, sons received a share of their father's possessions, but the firstborn son was entitled to a double share. Much like a firstborn son, Elisha asks for a double share of Elijah's power. See also Deut 21:15-17.

2:11 *chariot . . . whirlwind:* Chariots drawn by horses were used in warfare and were the fastest means of transportation at this time. See also 2 Kgs 13:14 and the note at 1:10.

2:13 *cloak:* The cloak marked Elisha as now having Elijah's powers (2:14,15). See also the note at 1:8.

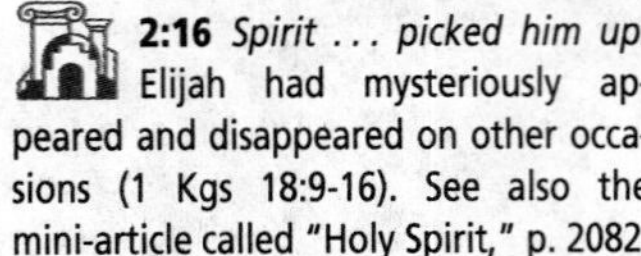

2:16 *Spirit . . . picked him up:* Elijah had mysteriously appeared and disappeared on other occasions (1 Kgs 18:9-16). See also the mini-article called "Holy Spirit," p. 2082.

2:20 *salt:* This is the first of several events that show the miraculous power God gives Elisha.

2:23,24 *baldhead . . . curse:* Baldness was unusual in this culture. Criminals and captured soldiers sometimes had their heads shaved as a sign of humiliation. By using the term "baldhead" to ridicule the shaven or apparently bald Elisha, they insulted and ridiculed God.

A curse is the opposite of blessing. It calls for harm or destruction to someone or something. Once spoken, a curse or blessing could not be taken back, because it was believed that the spoken word had a life and causative power of its own.

2:24 *two bears:* Bears mentioned in the Bible are most likely Syrian bears that eat mostly vegetables, roots, berries, nuts, and ants, but are known to also feed on livestock and other animals. They will attack humans when provoked (2 Sam 17:8). Like lions, they were feared and admired for their strength. Syrian bears can grow to about six and a half feet long.

"Let me inherit a double portion of your spirit," Elisha
replied.
10"You have asked a difficult thing," Elijah said, "yet if
you see me when I am taken from you, it will be yours—otherwise not."
11As they were walking along and talking together, suddenly
a chariot of fire and horses of fire appeared and separated the two
of them, and Elijah went up to heaven in a whirlwind. 12Elisha saw
this and cried out, "My father! My father! The chariots and horsemen of Israel!" And Elisha saw him no more. Then he took hold of
his own clothes and tore them apart.

13He picked up the cloak that had fallen from Elijah and
went back and stood on the bank of the Jordan. 14Then he took the
cloak that had fallen from him and struck the water with it.
"Where now is the LORD, the God of Elijah?" he asked. When he
struck the water, it divided to the right and to the left, and he
crossed over.

15The company of the prophets from Jericho, who were
watching, said, "The spirit of Elijah is resting on Elisha." And they
went to meet him and bowed to the ground before him. 16"Look,"
they said, "we your servants have fifty able men. Let them go and
look for your master. Perhaps the Spirit of the LORD has picked
him up and set him down on some mountain or in some valley."

"No," Elisha replied, "do not send them."

17But they persisted until he was too ashamed to refuse. So
he said, "Send them." And they sent fifty men, who searched for
three days but did not find him. 18When they returned to Elisha,
who was staying in Jericho, he said to them, "Didn't I tell you not
to go?"

Healing of the Water

19The men of the city said to Elisha, "Look, our lord, this
town is well situated, as you can see, but the water is bad and the
land is unproductive."

20"Bring me a new bowl," he said, "and put salt in it." So they
brought it to him.

21Then he went out to the spring and threw the salt into it,
saying, "This is what the LORD says: 'I have healed this water. Never
again will it cause death or make the land unproductive.' " 22And
the water has remained wholesome to this day, according to the
word Elisha had spoken.

Elisha Is Jeered

23From there Elisha went up to Bethel. As he was walking
along the road, some youths came out of the town and jeered at
him. "Go on up, you baldhead!" they said. "Go on up, you baldhead!" 24He turned around, looked at them and called down a
curse on them in the name of the LORD. Then two bears came out

of the woods and mauled forty-two of the youths. [25]And he went
on to Mount Carmel and from there returned to Samaria.

ELISHA AND JORAM

The war with Moab shows how the relationship between the godly prophets and Israel's disobedient kings was often tense.

Moab Revolts

3 Joram[a] son of Ahab became king of Israel in Samaria in the
eighteenth year of Jehoshaphat king of Judah, and he reigned
twelve years. [2]He did evil in the eyes of the LORD, but not as his
father and mother had done. He got rid of the sacred stone of Baal
that his father had made. [3]Nevertheless he clung to the sins of Jeroboam son of Nebat, which he had caused Israel to commit; he did
not turn away from them.

[4]Now Mesha king of Moab raised sheep, and he had to supply the king of Israel with a hundred thousand lambs and with the
wool of a hundred thousand rams. [5]But after Ahab died, the king
of Moab rebelled against the king of Israel. [6]So at that time King
Joram set out from Samaria and mobilized all Israel. [7]He also sent
this message to Jehoshaphat king of Judah: "The king of Moab has
rebelled against me. Will you go with me to fight against Moab?"

"I will go with you," he replied. "I am as you are, my people
as your people, my horses as your horses."

[8]"By what route shall we attack?" he asked.

"Through the Desert of Edom," he answered.

[9]So the king of Israel set out with the king of Judah and the
king of Edom. After a roundabout march of seven days, the army
had no more water for themselves or for the animals with them.

[10]"What!" exclaimed the king of Israel. "Has the LORD called
us three kings together only to hand us over to Moab?"

[11]But Jehoshaphat asked, "Is there no prophet of the LORD
here, that we may inquire of the LORD through him?"

An officer of the king of Israel answered, "Elisha son of
Shaphat is here. He used to pour water on the hands of Elijah.[b]"

[12]Jehoshaphat said, "The word of the LORD is with him." So
the king of Israel and Jehoshaphat and the king of Edom went
down to him.

[13]Elisha said to the king of Israel, "What do we have to do
with each other? Go to the prophets of your father and the
prophets of your mother."

"No," the king of Israel answered, "because it was the LORD
who called us three kings together to hand us over to Moab."

[14]Elisha said, "As surely as the LORD Almighty lives, whom I

---

[a]**1** Hebrew *Jehoram,* a variant of *Joram*; also in verse 6 [b]**11** That is, he was Elijah's personal servant.

2:25 *Mount Carmel . . . Samaria:* See the notes at 1:9 (a hill) and 1:1,2 (Samaria).

3:1-3 *Joram son of Ahab . . . Jehoshaphat . . . Jeroboam:* Joram, Israel's ninth king, ruled from 852 to 841 B.C. He continued the evil policies of Jeroboam, who sinned against the LORD by making two gold statues of calves and putting them in Bethel and Dan (1 Kgs 12:26-30). The statues were meant to represent God, but this was against God's commandments (Exod 20:3,4). He also encouraged the people to worship in places other than the temple in Jerusalem.

3:1 *Samaria:* See the note at 1:1,2 (Samaria).

3:2 *sacred stone of Baal:* This sacred stone was an idol. Idols were objects made of wood, metal, or stone to represent gods. They were worshiped by many ancient peoples.

Baal, a Canaanite god, was believed to bring rain to make crops grow. See also the mini-article called "Canaanite Gods and Goddesses," p. 469.

3:4 *Moab:* See the note at 1:1,2 (Moab).

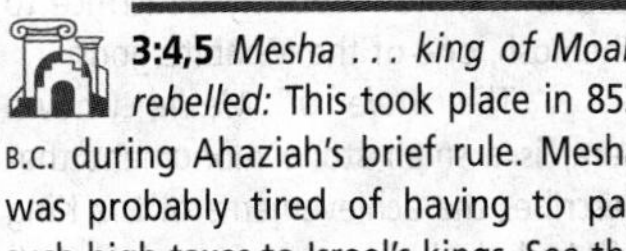

3:4,5 *Mesha . . . king of Moab rebelled:* This took place in 853 B.C. during Ahaziah's brief rule. Mesha was probably tired of having to pay such high taxes to Israel's kings. See the note at 1:1,2 (Ahaziah).

3:8 *Desert of Edom:* Mesha's forces had a firm hold in the north, so the combined forces of Israel and Judah could more easily attack Moab from the south (see the map on p. 2467).

3:13 *the prophets of your father . . . mother:* These were prophets of the Canaanite god Baal and the goddess Asherah. See 1 Kgs 16:30-33; 18:19.

3:15 *harpist:* This probably refers to someone who played a small stringed musical instrument known as a lyre. See the illustration on p. 1190.

3:19 *fortified city:* Many cities, particularly those important to a nation's defense, were walled and had a central gate that could be closed. The area near the gate was also where city leaders heard and decided disputes.

3:20 *the sacrifice:* This was a required daily sacrifice (Exod 29:38-43; Num 28:3,4). See also the chart called "Sacrifices and Offerings," p. 219.

3:25 *Kir Hareseth:* Moab's capital city. See the map on p. 2467.

3:25 *slings:* A sling is a hand-held weapon used to throw rocks. Leather strings or straps were attached to both sides of a wider leather band or pocket. A rock was put in the leather pocket, and the thrower held on to both straps while swinging it above his head. When the thrower let go of one strap, the rock would fly out of the sling at speeds of up to 100 miles per hour (see 1 Sam 17:40).

3:27 *offered him as a sacrifice:* This was probably a sacrifice to Chemosh, one of the Moabite gods.

The *Stele of Mesha* (shown here) is a small stone monument that describes the achievements of the King of Moab, including the successful rebellion of the Moabites in 852 B.C. against the Israelites.

serve, if I did not have respect for the presence of Jehoshaphat king of Judah, I would not look at you or even notice you. 15 But now bring me a harpist."

While the harpist was playing, the hand of the LORD came upon Elisha 16 and he said, "This is what the LORD says: Make this valley full of ditches. 17 For this is what the LORD says: You will see neither wind nor rain, yet this valley will be filled with water, and you, your cattle and your other animals will drink. 18 This is an easy thing in the eyes of the LORD; he will also hand Moab over to you. 19 You will overthrow every fortified city and every major town. You will cut down every good tree, stop up all the springs, and ruin every good field with stones."

20 The next morning, about the time for offering the sacrifice, there it was—water flowing from the direction of Edom! And the land was filled with water.

21 Now all the Moabites had heard that the kings had come to fight against them; so every man, young and old, who could bear arms was called up and stationed on the border. 22 When they got up early in the morning, the sun was shining on the water. To the Moabites across the way, the water looked red—like blood. 23 "That's blood!" they said. "Those kings must have fought and slaughtered each other. Now to the plunder, Moab!"

24 But when the Moabites came to the camp of Israel, the Israelites rose up and fought them until they fled. And the Israelites invaded the land and slaughtered the Moabites. 25 They destroyed the towns, and each man threw a stone on every good field until it was covered. They stopped up all the springs and cut down every good tree. Only Kir Hareseth was left with its stones in place, but men armed with slings surrounded it and attacked it as well.

26 When the king of Moab saw that the battle had gone against him, he took with him seven hundred swordsmen to break through to the king of Edom, but they failed. 27 Then he took his firstborn son, who was to succeed him as king, and offered him as a sacrifice on the city wall. The fury against Israel was great; they withdrew and returned to their own land.

ELISHA'S MIRACLES

The stories about Elisha demonstrate the power of the prophetic word in all areas of life. The contrast between the power of the prophet and the ineffective power of the kings is deliberate.

The Widow's Oil

4 The wife of a man from the company of the prophets cried out to Elisha, "Your servant my husband is dead, and you know that he revered the LORD. But now his creditor is coming to take my two boys as his slaves."

2 Elisha replied to her, "How can I help you? Tell me, what do you have in your house?"

"Your servant has nothing there at all," she said, "except a
little oil."

3Elisha said, "Go around and ask all your neighbors for
empty jars. Don't ask for just a few. 4Then go inside and shut the
door behind you and your sons. Pour oil into all the jars, and as
each is filled, put it to one side."

5She left him and afterward shut the door behind her and
her sons. They brought the jars to her and she kept pouring.
6When all the jars were full, she said to her son, "Bring me another one."

But he replied, "There is not a jar left." Then the oil stopped
flowing.

7She went and told the man of God, and he said, "Go,
sell the oil and pay your debts. You and your sons can live on what
is left."

The Shunammite's Son Restored to Life

8One day Elisha went to Shunem. And a well-to-do woman
was there, who urged him to stay for a meal. So whenever he came
by, he stopped there to eat. 9She said to her husband, "I know that
this man who often comes our way is a holy man of God. 10Let's
make a small room on the roof and put in it a bed and a table, a
chair and a lamp for him. Then he can stay there whenever he
comes to us."

11One day when Elisha came, he went up to his room and lay
down there. 12He said to his servant Gehazi, "Call the Shunammite." So he called her, and she stood before him. 13Elisha said to
him, "Tell her, 'You have gone to all this trouble for us. Now what
can be done for you? Can we speak on your behalf to the king or
the commander of the army?' "

She replied, "I have a home among my own people."

14"What can be done for her?" Elisha asked.

Gehazi said, "Well, she has no son and her husband is old."

15Then Elisha said, "Call her." So he called her, and she stood
in the doorway. 16"About this time next year," Elisha said, "you will
hold a son in your arms."

"No, my lord," she objected. "Don't mislead your servant,
O man of God!"

17But the woman became pregnant, and the next year about
that same time she gave birth to a son, just as Elisha had told her.

18The child grew, and one day he went out to his father, who
was with the reapers. 19"My head! My head!" he said to his father.

His father told a servant, "Carry him to his mother." 20After
the servant had lifted him up and carried him to his mother, the
boy sat on her lap until noon, and then he died. 21She went up and
laid him on the bed of the man of God, then shut the door and
went out.

22She called her husband and said, "Please send me one of

4:1 *his slaves:* If a loan could not be repaid, the law allowed the lender to take the borrower's children as payment. Such slaves were to be treated as servants, and the length of their slavery was limited (Lev 25:39-43).

4:2 *oil:* The oil that came from crushed olives was very valuable. It was used in cooking, medicine, grooming, and special anointing ceremonies (see 1 Chr 11:3). It was also burned in lamps for light and was one of the ingredients in certain offerings to God.

4:8 *Shunem:* A town in Israel, about twenty-five miles north of Samaria. See the map on p. 2467.

4:13 *speak on your behalf:* Elisha may have meant that he could ask these leaders to lower her taxes.

4:14 *no son and her husband is old:* Without a son, the family name would not continue, and the family line would be destroyed. Also, a woman depended on her son to protect her and provide for her if her husband died.

4:16 Gen 18:14.

the servants and a donkey so I can go to the man of God quickly
and return."
[23]"Why go to him today?" he asked. "It's not the New Moon
or the Sabbath."
"It's all right," she said.
[24]She saddled the donkey and said to her servant, "Lead on;
don't slow down for me unless I tell you." [25]So she set out and
came to the man of God at Mount Carmel.
When he saw her in the distance, the man of God said to his
servant Gehazi, "Look! There's the Shunammite! [26]Run to meet her
and ask her, 'Are you all right? Is your husband all right? Is your
child all right?' "
"Everything is all right," she said.
[27]When she reached the man of God at the mountain, she
took hold of his feet. Gehazi came over to push her away, but the
man of God said, "Leave her alone! She is in bitter distress, but the
LORD has hidden it from me and has not told me why."
[28]"Did I ask you for a son, my lord?" she said. "Didn't I tell
you, 'Don't raise my hopes'?"
[29]Elisha said to Gehazi, "Tuck your cloak into your belt, take
my staff in your hand and run. If you meet anyone, do not greet
him, and if anyone greets you, do not answer. Lay my staff on the
boy's face."
[30]But the child's mother said, "As surely as the LORD lives and
as you live, I will not leave you." So he got up and followed her.
[31]Gehazi went on ahead and laid the staff on the boy's face,
but there was no sound or response. So Gehazi went back to meet
Elisha and told him, "The boy has not awakened."
[32]When Elisha reached the house, there was the boy lying
dead on his couch. [33]He went in, shut the door on the two of them
and prayed to the LORD. [34]Then he got on the bed and lay upon
the boy, mouth to mouth, eyes to eyes, hands to hands. As he
stretched himself out upon him, the boy's body grew warm.
[35]Elisha turned away and walked back and forth in the room and
then got on the bed and stretched out upon him once more. The
boy sneezed seven times and opened his eyes.
[36]Elisha summoned Gehazi and said, "Call the Shunammite."
And he did. When she came, he said, "Take your son." [37]She came
in, fell at his feet and bowed to the ground. Then she took her son
and went out.

Death in the Pot

[38]Elisha returned to Gilgal and there was a famine in that
region. While the company of the prophets was meeting with him,
he said to his servant, "Put on the large pot and cook some stew
for these men."
[39]One of them went out into the fields to gather herbs and
found a wild vine. He gathered some of its gourds and filled the

4:23 *New Moon . . . Sabbath:* The Sabbath and the New Moon Festival were holy days, and probably were considered more appropriate times to visit a prophet. The New Moon Festival was held on the day of the new moon. This day was always the first day of the month for the Hebrew calendar. This festival was a time for worship, sacrifices, celebration, eating, and rest from work. See also Num 28:1—29:39. The Sabbath was the weekly day of rest that began at sunset on Friday and ended at sunset on Saturday. No work was to be done on the Sabbath, which means "rest" or to "stop working" (Exod 20:8-11; 31:12-17; Num 28:9,10; Deut 5:12-15).

4:25 *Mount Carmel:* See the note at 1:9 (a hill).

4:27 *took hold of his feet:* This was a sign of humility and respect.

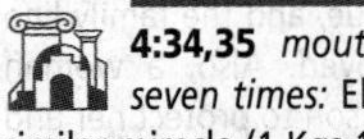

4:34,35 *mouth to mouth . . . seven times:* Elijah performed a similar miracle (1 Kgs 17:21).

The number seven symbolized perfection. The book's original readers would have seen the seven sneezes as indicating the boy was restored to full life and breath. See also the chart called "Numbers in the Bible," p. 2405.

4:38 *Gilgal:* See the note at 2:1-4. The failure of crops in Gilgal is God's judgment upon the people for their disobedience (see also Lev 26:26-29; Deut 28:15-24.) God's power was also apparent in Elisha's sprinkling of flour to make the bitter stew edible. Normally, a sprinkling of flour would not have such an effect.

4:39 *wild vine:* This may refer to a colocynthis, a bitter orange-shaped fruit that can cause vomiting and is poisonous in large amounts.

The Shunammite's Son, wood engraving, nineteenth century. After the LORD took the prophet Elijah away, Elisha put on Elijah's cloak and began to perform miracles as great as the ones his master performed. Just as Elijah had raised to life the son of a widow from Zarephath (1 Kgs 17:17-24), Elisha brought back to life the son of the rich woman from Shunem. (See 4:8-37.)

fold of his cloak. When he returned, he cut them up into the pot
of stew, though no one knew what they were. 40The stew was
poured out for the men, but as they began to eat it, they cried out,
"O man of God, there is death in the pot!" And they could not
eat it.

41Elisha said, "Get some flour." He put it into the pot and
said, "Serve it to the people to eat." And there was nothing harmful in the pot.

Feeding of a Hundred

42A man came from Baal Shalishah, bringing the man of
God twenty loaves of barley bread baked from the first ripe grain,
along with some heads of new grain. "Give it to the people to eat,"
Elisha said.

4:42 *Baal Shalishah:* The exact location of this town is not known, but it was probably somewhere near Shechem.

4:42 *first ripe grain, along with some heads of new grain:* The first part of a harvest was to be brought to the place of worship and offered to God (Lev 2:14; Deut 18:3-5). It appears that prophets as well as priests could receive the offering at this time. The offering recognized that everything comes from and belongs to God. Once a portion of the first harvest was offered to God, the rest could be used by the people. It is not clear whether the offering here is a one-time event or part of the Feast of Harvest (Exod 23:16; Lev 23:15-21; Num 28:26–31) or the Feast of Tabernacles (Lev 23:33-43; Num 29:12-39).

4:42-44 Matt 14:13-21; 15:32-38.

5:1 *Aram:* Aram (Syria) was located to the north and west of Israel (see the map on p. 2467). The Arameans traditionally had been enemies of Israel.

5:1 *leprosy:* The word translated "leprosy" was used for many different kinds of skin diseases.

5:3 *prophet:* See the note on p. 675.

5:3 *Samaria:* Elisha kept a home in Samaria. See also the note at 1:1,2 (Samaria).

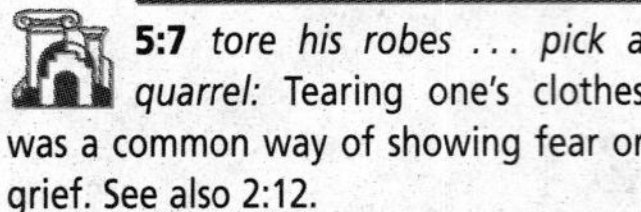

5:7 *tore his robes . . . pick a quarrel:* Tearing one's clothes was a common way of showing fear or grief. See also 2:12.

The king's concern over the Aramean king trying to pick a fight, and the raids mentioned in 5:2 both indicate that Aram had power over Israel at this time.

5:9 *horses and chariots:* A chariot was a two-wheeled cart that was open at the back and was pulled by horses. Horses were also ridden into battle and were a sign of wealth. See also the illustration on p. 160.

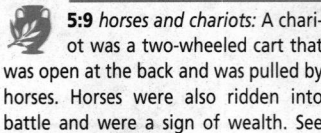

5:12 *Abana and Pharpar, the rivers of Damascus:* The Abana River's clean waters flowed from the Lebanon mountains to Damascus, while the Pharpar River flowed from east of Mount Hermon to south of Damascus. Both rivers were much cleaner than the muddy waters of the Jordan River (see the note at 2:6).

Damascus was Aram's capital and a major trading and transportation center. The two rivers flowing into it and feeding its orchards and gardens made it a beautiful oasis in the middle of the desert. See the map on p. 2467.

5:1-14 Luke 4:27.

43 "How can I set this before a hundred men?" his servant asked.

But Elisha answered, "Give it to the people to eat. For this is what the LORD says: 'They will eat and have some left over.' " 44 Then he set it before them, and they ate and had some left over, according to the word of the LORD.

Naaman Healed of Leprosy

5 Now Naaman was commander of the army of the king of Aram. He was a great man in the sight of his master and highly regarded, because through him the LORD had given victory to Aram. He was a valiant soldier, but he had leprosy.[a]

2 Now bands from Aram had gone out and had taken captive a young girl from Israel, and she served Naaman's wife. 3 She said to her mistress, "If only my master would see the prophet who is in Samaria! He would cure him of his leprosy."

4 Naaman went to his master and told him what the girl from Israel had said. 5 "By all means, go," the king of Aram replied. "I will send a letter to the king of Israel." So Naaman left, taking with him ten talents[b] of silver, six thousand shekels[c] of gold and ten sets of clothing. 6 The letter that he took to the king of Israel read: "With this letter I am sending my servant Naaman to you so that you may cure him of his leprosy."

7 As soon as the king of Israel read the letter, he tore his robes and said, "Am I God? Can I kill and bring back to life? Why does this fellow send someone to me to be cured of his leprosy? See how he is trying to pick a quarrel with me!"

8 When Elisha the man of God heard that the king of Israel had torn his robes, he sent him this message: "Why have you torn your robes? Have the man come to me and he will know that there is a prophet in Israel." 9 So Naaman went with his horses and chariots and stopped at the door of Elisha's house. 10 Elisha sent a messenger to say to him, "Go, wash yourself seven times in the Jordan, and your flesh will be restored and you will be cleansed."

11 But Naaman went away angry and said, "I thought that he would surely come out to me and stand and call on the name of the LORD his God, wave his hand over the spot and cure me of my leprosy. 12 Are not Abana and Pharpar, the rivers of Damascus, better than any of the waters of Israel? Couldn't I wash in them and be cleansed?" So he turned and went off in a rage.

13 Naaman's servants went to him and said, "My father, if the prophet had told you to do some great thing, would you not have done it? How much more, then, when he tells you, 'Wash and be cleansed'!" 14 So he went down and dipped himself in the Jordan

---

a1 The Hebrew word was used for various diseases affecting the skin—not necessarily leprosy; also in verses 3, 6, 7, 11 and 27. **b5** That is, about 750 pounds (about 340 kilograms) **c5** That is, about 150 pounds (about 70 kilograms)

seven times, as the man of God had told him, and his flesh was
restored and became clean like that of a young boy.
[15]Then Naaman and all his attendants went back to the man
of God. He stood before him and said, "Now I know that there is
no God in all the world except in Israel. Please accept now a gift
from your servant."
[16]The prophet answered, "As surely as the LORD lives, whom
I serve, I will not accept a thing." And even though Naaman urged
him, he refused.
[17]"If you will not," said Naaman, "please let me, your servant, be given as much earth as a pair of mules can carry, for your
servant will never again make burnt offerings and sacrifices to any
other god but the LORD. [18]But may the LORD forgive your servant
for this one thing: When my master enters the temple of Rimmon
to bow down and he is leaning on my arm and I bow there also—
when I bow down in the temple of Rimmon, may the LORD forgive your servant for this."
[19]"Go in peace," Elisha said.
After Naaman had traveled some distance, [20]Gehazi, the
servant of Elisha the man of God, said to himself, "My master was
too easy on Naaman, this Aramean, by not accepting from him
what he brought. As surely as the LORD lives, I will run after him
and get something from him."
[21]So Gehazi hurried after Naaman. When Naaman saw him
running toward him, he got down from the chariot to meet him.
"Is everything all right?" he asked.
[22]"Everything is all right," Gehazi answered. "My master sent
me to say, 'Two young men from the company of the prophets
have just come to me from the hill country of Ephraim. Please give
them a talent[a] of silver and two sets of clothing.' "
[23]"By all means, take two talents," said Naaman. He urged
Gehazi to accept them, and then tied up the two talents of silver in
two bags, with two sets of clothing. He gave them to two of his
servants, and they carried them ahead of Gehazi. [24]When Gehazi
came to the hill, he took the things from the servants and put
them away in the house. He sent the men away and they left.
[25]Then he went in and stood before his master Elisha.
"Where have you been, Gehazi?" Elisha asked.
"Your servant didn't go anywhere," Gehazi answered.
[26]But Elisha said to him, "Was not my spirit with you when
the man got down from his chariot to meet you? Is this the time to
take money, or to accept clothes, olive groves, vineyards, flocks,
herds, or menservants and maidservants? [27]Naaman's leprosy will
cling to you and to your descendants forever." Then Gehazi went
from Elisha's presence and he was leprous, as white as snow.

[a]**22** That is, about 75 pounds (about 34 kilograms)

Naaman said, *"Now I know that there is no God in all the world except in Israel."*
2 Kgs 5:15

5:17 *as much earth as a pair of mules can carry:* It was believed that the LORD had to be worshiped in Israel or on soil taken from Israel.

5:18 *Rimmon:* Another name for Hadad, a chief god of the Arameans. As the Aramean king's servant, Naaman was required to go with the king to worship at the temple of Rimmon.

5:27 *leprosy:* See the note at 5:1 (leprosy).

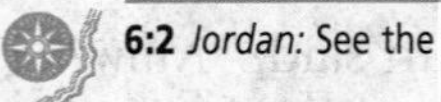

6:2 *Jordan:* See the note at 2:6.

6:4 *trees:* The trees common to this area (willow, tamarisk, and acacia) produced lightweight lumber that was used to build smaller buildings but not great palaces or temples.

6:8 *king of Aram:* This probably refers to Ben-Hadad II. By leaving him unnamed, the author may be emphasizing how unimportant the kings are compared to God or God's prophets. See also 1 Kgs 15:18.

6:13 *Dothan:* This town was located north of Samaria and twelve miles south of Jezreel. It controlled a main mountain pass along the road that connected Damascus and Egypt. See the map on p. 2467.

6:17 *horses and chariots of fire:* Those with Elisha were God's heavenly army (Josh 5:14; 2 Chr 32:7,8). See also the notes at 2:11 and 1:10.

An Axhead Floats

6 The company of the prophets said to Elisha, "Look, the place
where we meet with you is too small for us. 2Let us go to the Jordan, where each of us can get a pole; and let us build a place there
for us to live."
And he said, "Go."
3Then one of them said, "Won't you please come with your
servants?"
"I will," Elisha replied. 4And he went with them.
They went to the Jordan and began to cut down trees. 5As
one of them was cutting down a tree, the iron axhead fell into the
water. "Oh, my lord," he cried out, "it was borrowed!"
6The man of God asked, "Where did it fall?" When he
showed him the place, Elisha cut a stick and threw it there, and
made the iron float. 7"Lift it out," he said. Then the man reached
out his hand and took it.

Elisha Traps Blinded Arameans

8Now the king of Aram was at war with Israel. After confer-
ring with his officers, he said, "I will set up my camp in such and
such a place."
9The man of God sent word to the king of Israel: "Beware of
passing that place, because the Arameans are going down there."
10So the king of Israel checked on the place indicated by the man
of God. Time and again Elisha warned the king, so that he was on
his guard in such places.
11This enraged the king of Aram. He summoned his officers
and demanded of them, "Will you not tell me which of us is on
the side of the king of Israel?"
12"None of us, my lord the king," said one of his officers,
"but Elisha, the prophet who is in Israel, tells the king of Israel the
very words you speak in your bedroom."
13"Go, find out where he is," the king ordered, "so I can send
men and capture him." The report came back: "He is in Dothan."
14Then he sent horses and chariots and a strong force there. They
went by night and surrounded the city.
15When the servant of the man of God got up and went out
early the next morning, an army with horses and chariots had surrounded the city. "Oh, my lord, what shall we do?" the servant
asked.
16"Don't be afraid," the prophet answered. "Those who are
with us are more than those who are with them."
17And Elisha prayed, "O LORD, open his eyes so he may see."
Then the LORD opened the servant's eyes, and he looked and saw
the hills full of horses and chariots of fire all around Elisha.
18As the enemy came down toward him, Elisha prayed to the
LORD, "Strike these people with blindness." So he struck them with
blindness, as Elisha had asked.

19 Elisha told them, "This is not the road and this is not the city. Follow me, and I will lead you to the man you are looking for." And he led them to Samaria.

20 After they entered the city, Elisha said, "LORD, open the eyes of these men so they can see." Then the LORD opened their eyes and they looked, and there they were, inside Samaria.

21 When the king of Israel saw them, he asked Elisha, "Shall I kill them, my father? Shall I kill them?"

22 "Do not kill them," he answered. "Would you kill men you have captured with your own sword or bow? Set food and water before them so that they may eat and drink and then go back to their master."
23 So he prepared a great feast for them, and after they had finished eating and drinking, he sent them away, and they returned to their master. So the bands from Aram stopped raiding Israel's territory.

Famine in Besieged Samaria

24 Some time later, Ben-Hadad king of Aram mobilized his entire army and marched up and laid siege to Samaria. 25 There was a great famine in the city; the siege lasted so long that a donkey's head sold for eighty shekels[a] of silver, and a quarter of a cab[b] of seed pods[c] for five shekels.[d]

26 As the king of Israel was passing by on the wall, a woman cried to him, "Help me, my lord the king!"

27 The king replied, "If the LORD does not help you, where can I get help for you? From the threshing floor? From the winepress?"
28 Then he asked her, "What's the matter?"

She answered, "This woman said to me, 'Give up your son so we may eat him today, and tomorrow we'll eat my son.' 29 So we cooked my son and ate him. The next day I said to her, 'Give up your son so we may eat him,' but she had hidden him."

30 When the king heard the woman's words, he tore his robes. As he went along the wall, the people looked, and there, underneath, he had sackcloth on his body. 31 He said, "May God deal with me, be it ever so severely, if the head of Elisha son of Shaphat remains on his shoulders today!"

32 Now Elisha was sitting in his house, and the elders were sitting with him. The king sent a messenger ahead, but before he arrived, Elisha said to the elders, "Don't you see how this murderer is sending someone to cut off my head? Look, when the messenger comes, shut the door and hold it shut against him. Is not the sound of his master's footsteps behind him?"

33 While he was still talking to them, the messenger came down to him. And ⌞the king⌟ said, "This disaster is from the LORD. Why should I wait for the LORD any longer?"

---

[a]25 That is, about 2 pounds (about 1 kilogram) [b]25 That is, probably about 1/2 pint (about 0.3 liter) [c]25 Or *of doves' dung* [d]25 That is, about 2 ounces (about 55 grams)

6:23 *great feast:* In the ancient Near East, such a meal often was part of sealing an agreement or settlement.

6:24 *Ben-Hadad king of Aram:* This may or may not be the same Ben-Hadad mentioned in 1 Kings 20:1. Several of the Aramean kings were named Ben-Hadad.

6:25 *donkey's head . . . cab of seed pods:* There was so little food that even undesirable parts of "unclean" animals, such as donkeys, were sold for high prices. See also the mini-article called "Purity (Clean and Unclean)," p. 2125.

The seed pods may have been roasted beans or for the shells of certain seeds.

6:26 *the king of Israel:* This refers to either Jehoahaz or Jehoash, but possibly even Joram. Once again, the writer emphasizes how insignificant the kings are by omitting the actual ruler's name.

6:26 *the wall:* Many cities were surrounded by walls that were wide enough to walk on. Narrow windows in the walls were used by archers to shoot arrows at an enemy.

6:28 *eat my son:* The Israelites' situation is so desperate that the woman is not ashamed to admit she has eaten her own child. Instead, she is concerned only with getting her fair share of the meat from another woman's child. See also Deut 28:56,57; Lam 4:10.

6:30 *tore his robes . . . sackcloth:* In times of trouble and sadness people tore their clothes and wore sackcloth. See also 2:12 and the note at 5:7.

During their time as slaves in Egypt, the Israelites wore clothing made of dark, coarse goat or camel hair called *"saq."* This garment, known as sackcloth, became a symbol of slavery, humiliation, and great sadness. As a result, it was worn at times of trouble or sorrow.

7:3 *men with leprosy:* See the note at 5:1 (leprosy).

7:6 *Hittite and Egyptian kings:* The Hittites once had a vast empire in Asia Minor and threatened Aram from the north. Hittites are mentioned as being settled in Canaan before the people of Israel took over the land (Gen 23:3; Num 13:29; Josh 1:4). At various times in history, Egypt was a great military power and attacked areas of the ancient Near East as far north as Aram.

7:7 *tents and their horses and donkeys:* These soldiers were part of the cavalry, who rode horses into battle. Donkeys were used for carrying supplies.

7 Elisha said, "Hear the word of the LORD. This is what the LORD
says: About this time tomorrow, a seah[a] of flour will sell for
a shekel[b] and two seahs[c] of barley for a shekel at the gate of
Samaria."
2 The officer on whose arm the king was leaning said to the
man of God, "Look, even if the LORD should open the floodgates of
the heavens, could this happen?"
"You will see it with your own eyes," answered Elisha, "but
you will not eat any of it!"

The Siege Lifted

3 Now there were four men with leprosy[d] at the entrance of
the city gate. They said to each other, "Why stay here until we die?
4 If we say, 'We'll go into the city'—the famine is there, and we will
die. And if we stay here, we will die. So let's go over to the camp of
the Arameans and surrender. If they spare us, we live; if they kill
us, then we die."
5 At dusk they got up and went to the camp of the Arameans.
When they reached the edge of the camp, not a man was there, 6 for
the Lord had caused the Arameans to hear the sound of chariots
and horses and a great army, so that they said to one another,
"Look, the king of Israel has hired the Hittite and Egyptian kings
to attack us!" 7 So they got up and fled in the dusk and abandoned
their tents and their horses and donkeys. They left the camp as it
was and ran for their lives.
8 The men who had leprosy reached the edge of the camp
and entered one of the tents. They ate and drank, and carried away
silver, gold and clothes, and went off and hid them. They returned
and entered another tent and took some things from it and hid
them also.
9 Then they said to each other, "We're not doing right. This is
a day of good news and we are keeping it to ourselves. If we wait
until daylight, punishment will overtake us. Let's go at once and
report this to the royal palace."
10 So they went and called out to the city gatekeepers and told
them, "We went into the Aramean camp and not a man was
there—not a sound of anyone—only tethered horses and donkeys,
and the tents left just as they were." 11 The gatekeepers shouted the
news, and it was reported within the palace.
12 The king got up in the night and said to his officers, "I will
tell you what the Arameans have done to us. They know we are
starving; so they have left the camp to hide in the countryside,

---

[a] **1** That is, probably about 7 quarts (about 7.3 liters); also in verses 16 and 18
[b] **1** That is, about 2/5 ounce (about 11 grams); also in verses 16 and 18 [c] **1** That is, probably about 13 quarts (about 15 liters); also in verses 16 and 18 [d] **3** The Hebrew word is used for various diseases affecting the skin—not necessarily leprosy; also in verse 8.

thinking, 'They will surely come out, and then we will take them
alive and get into the city.' "
13 One of his officers answered, "Have some men take five of
the horses that are left in the city. Their plight will be like that of
all the Israelites left here—yes, they will only be like all these
Israelites who are doomed. So let us send them to find out what
happened."
14 So they selected two chariots with their horses, and the
king sent them after the Aramean army. He commanded the drivers, "Go and find out what has happened." 15 They followed them as
far as the Jordan, and they found the whole road strewn with the
clothing and equipment the Arameans had thrown away in their
headlong flight. So the messengers returned and reported to the
king. 16 Then the people went out and plundered the camp of the
Arameans. So a seah of flour sold for a shekel, and two seahs of
barley sold for a shekel, as the LORD had said.
17 Now the king had put the officer on whose arm he leaned
in charge of the gate, and the people trampled him in the gateway,
and he died, just as the man of God had foretold when the king
came down to his house. 18 It happened as the man of God had said
to the king: "About this time tomorrow, a seah of flour will sell for
a shekel and two seahs of barley for a shekel at the gate of
Samaria."
19 The officer had said to the man of God, "Look, even if the
LORD should open the floodgates of the heavens, could this happen?" The man of God had replied, "You will see it with your own
eyes, but you will not eat any of it!" 20 And that is exactly what happened to him, for the people trampled him in the gateway, and he
died.

The Shunammite's Land Restored

8 Now Elisha had said to the woman whose son he had restored
to life, "Go away with your family and stay for a while wherever
you can, because the LORD has decreed a famine in the land that
will last seven years." 2 The woman proceeded to do as the man of
God said. She and her family went away and stayed in the land of
the Philistines seven years.
3 At the end of the seven years she came back from the land
of the Philistines and went to the king to beg for her house and
land. 4 The king was talking to Gehazi, the servant of the man of
God, and had said, "Tell me about all the great things Elisha has
done." 5 Just as Gehazi was telling the king how Elisha had restored
the dead to life, the woman whose son Elisha had brought back to
life came to beg the king for her house and land.
Gehazi said, "This is the woman, my lord the king, and this
is her son whom Elisha restored to life." 6 The king asked the
woman about it, and she told him.
Then he assigned an official to her case and said to him,

7:14 *chariots:* See the notes at 2:11 (chariot) and 5:9.

8:1 *Elisha . . . son he had restored to life:* This miracle is described in 4:8-37.

8:2 *land of the Philistines:* This area was west of Judah along the Mediterranean Sea. It included five main cities, each with its own ruler: Ashdod, Ashkelon, Ekron, Gath, and Gaza (see the map on p. 2467). The Philistines often had been at war with Israel.

8:3 *went to the king to beg for her house and land:* The king was the highest judge in the land.

8:7 *Damascus:* See the note at 5:12.

8:7,8 *Ben-Hadad king of Aram . . . Hazael:* See the notes at 6:8 and 6:24. Hazael probably was one of Ben-Hadad's officials.

8:9 *finest wares of Damascus:* The finest merchandise from all over the ancient Near East could be found in Damascus, because it was a major trade center. See also the note at 5:12.

It was the custom to bring a gift to a prophet when asking about God's will (1 Sam 9:7; 1 Kgs 14:2,3).

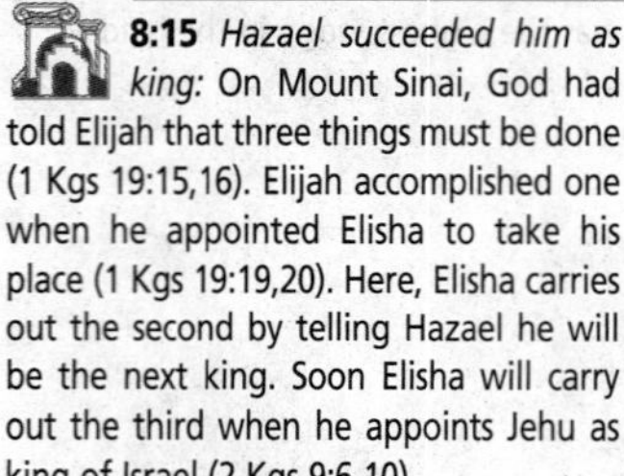

8:15 *Hazael succeeded him as king:* On Mount Sinai, God had told Elijah that three things must be done (1 Kgs 19:15,16). Elijah accomplished one when he appointed Elisha to take his place (1 Kgs 19:19,20). Here, Elisha carries out the second by telling Hazael he will be the next king. Soon Elisha will carry out the third when he appoints Jehu as king of Israel (2 Kgs 9:6-10).

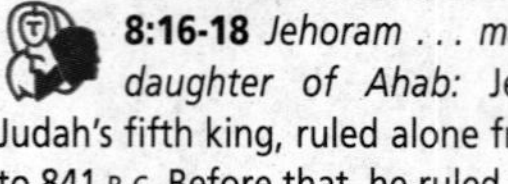

8:16-18 *Jehoram . . . married a daughter of Ahab:* Jehoram, Judah's fifth king, ruled alone from 848 to 841 B.C. Before that, he ruled for four years with his father, Jehoshaphat (see the note at 1:17). See also the note at 3:1-3 (Joram).

Athaliah may have been the daughter of Israel's King Ahab and Queen Jezebel. But, some believe she was the daughter of Omri, Ahab's father, but that Ahab raised her.

"Give back everything that belonged to her, including all the income from her land from the day she left the country until now."

Hazael Murders Ben-Hadad

7 Elisha went to Damascus, and Ben-Hadad king of Aram
was ill. When the king was told, "The man of God has come all the
way up here," 8 he said to Hazael, "Take a gift with you and go to
meet the man of God. Consult the LORD through him; ask him,
'Will I recover from this illness?' "
9 Hazael went to meet Elisha, taking with him as a gift forty
camel-loads of all the finest wares of Damascus. He went in and
stood before him, and said, "Your son Ben-Hadad king of Aram
has sent me to ask, 'Will I recover from this illness?' "
10 Elisha answered, "Go and say to him, 'You will certainly
recover'; but[a] the LORD has revealed to me that he will in fact die."
11 He stared at him with a fixed gaze until Hazael felt ashamed.
Then the man of God began to weep.
12 "Why is my lord weeping?" asked Hazael.
"Because I know the harm you will do to the Israelites," he
answered. "You will set fire to their fortified places, kill their young
men with the sword, dash their little children to the ground, and
rip open their pregnant women."
13 Hazael said, "How could your servant, a mere dog, accomplish such a feat?"
"The LORD has shown me that you will become king of
Aram," answered Elisha.
14 Then Hazael left Elisha and returned to his master. When
Ben-Hadad asked, "What did Elisha say to you?" Hazael replied,
"He told me that you would certainly recover." 15 But the next day
he took a thick cloth, soaked it in water and spread it over the
king's face, so that he died. Then Hazael succeeded him as king.

[a] **10** The Hebrew may also be read *Go and say, 'You will certainly not recover,' for.*

QUESTIONS ABOUT 2 KINGS 1:1—8:15

1. How are Elijah and Elisha alike? How are they different? What words or phrases would you say best describe Elisha? Who functions like an Elisha in our world today?
2. Elisha performed about twice as many miracles as Elijah. Do you think that is what he meant when he asked for "a double portion" of Elijah's power? (2:9) See also Deut 21:15-17. Explain your answer.
3. What happened to the chief officer who doubted God's power? (7:1,2,17-20) Do you believe God finds all doubt unacceptable? Why or why not?
4. Why does the author often not mention the specific names of Israelite or foreign kings in the stories about Elisha?

Kings of Judah and Israel

The stories about the kings of Judah and Israel are interrupted by the Elijah and Elisha stories (1 Kgs 17:1—2 Kgs 8:15). But now the writers of 1 and 2 KINGS resume their descriptions of the reigns of these kings. The stories alternate between the two kingdoms and focus mainly on the way the kings sinned against God by allowing idol worship. The disobedience of Israel's rulers eventually leads to Israel being defeated by Assyria.

Jehoram King of Judah

[16]In the fifth year of Joram son of Ahab king of Israel, when Jehoshaphat was king of Judah, Jehoram son of Jehoshaphat began his reign as king of Judah. [17]He was thirty-two years old when he became king, and he reigned in Jerusalem eight years. [18]He walked in the ways of the kings of Israel, as the house of Ahab had done, for he married a daughter of Ahab. He did evil in the eyes of the LORD. [19]Nevertheless, for the sake of his servant David, the LORD was not willing to destroy Judah. He had promised to maintain a lamp for David and his descendants forever.

[20]In the time of Jehoram, Edom rebelled against Judah and set up its own king. [21]So Jehoram[a] went to Zair with all his chariots. The Edomites surrounded him and his chariot commanders, but he rose up and broke through by night; his army, however, fled back home. [22]To this day Edom has been in rebellion against Judah. Libnah revolted at the same time.

[23]As for the other events of Jehoram's reign, and all he did, are they not written in the book of the annals of the kings of Judah? [24]Jehoram rested with his fathers and was buried with them in the City of David. And Ahaziah his son succeeded him as king.

Ahaziah King of Judah

[25]In the twelfth year of Joram son of Ahab king of Israel, Ahaziah son of Jehoram king of Judah began to reign. [26]Ahaziah was twenty-two years old when he became king, and he reigned in Jerusalem one year. His mother's name was Athaliah, a granddaughter of Omri king of Israel. [27]He walked in the ways of the house of Ahab and did evil in the eyes of the LORD, as the house of Ahab had done, for he was related by marriage to Ahab's family.

[28]Ahaziah went with Joram son of Ahab to war against Hazael king of Aram at Ramoth Gilead. The Arameans wounded Joram; [29]so King Joram returned to Jezreel to recover from the wounds the Arameans had inflicted on him at Ramoth[b] in his battle with Hazael king of Aram.

Then Ahaziah son of Jehoram king of Judah went down to Jezreel to see Joram son of Ahab, because he had been wounded.

[a]**21** Hebrew *Joram,* a variant of *Jehoram*; also in verses 23 and 24 [b]**29** Hebrew *Ramah,* a variant of *Ramoth*

8:18 *as the house of Ahab . . . did evil in the eyes of the LORD:* Jehoram allowed Baal worship in Judah, just as Ahab had during his rule as king of Israel (see 1 Kgs 16:29-33).

8:20-22,24 *Edom . . . Zair . . . Libnah . . . City of David:* In the Bible, Edom is usually described as Israel's enemy (Num 24:18; 2 Sam 8:13,14; Isa 34:5-17). Zair's location is not known. Libnah was a town on the border between Philistia and Judah. With uprisings both from Libnah and Edom, Jehoram faced rebellion on two sides of his kingdom. The City of David is another name for Jerusalem.

8:20 *Edom rebelled:* The Edomites were descendants of Esau, brother of Jacob who was the ancestor of Israel (see Gen 25:24-26; 36:1; 27:40). About 250 years prior to the time of Jehoram, Israel's King David, a descendant of Jacob, had conquered Edom (2 Sam 8:13,14).

8:25-27 *Ahaziah . . . was related by marriage to Ahab's family:* Ahaziah, Judah's sixth king, ruled for one year in 841 B.C. His mother was Athaliah, the daughter of Israel's former king Ahab (see the note at 8:16-18).

The reference to Omri in 8:26 is a tribute to his greatness. Omri conquered Moab, formed an alliance with Sidon, and wisely built up Samaria as Israel's capital. A hundred years after his reign, Assyrian kings still called Israel "the land of Omri." However, this brilliant civilian and military leader was a failure as a religious leader for God's people (1 Kgs 16:25,26; Mic 6:16).

8:28,29 *Ramoth Gilead . . . Jezreel:* Ramoth Gilead had been an Israelite city since the time of Moses (Deut 4:41-43; 1 Kgs 4:13). It fell to Aram in 922 B.C., about seventy years before this time. Ahab lost his life trying to reclaim it (1 Kgs 22:29-40).

During his reign, Ahab had a second royal home in Jezreel. For these locations, see the map on p. 2467.

8:19 1 Kgs 11:36.

JEHU AND HIS HOUSE

Jehu, an army officer who becomes king of Israel, fulfills Elijah's prophecy (1 Kgs 19:16, 17) by overthrowing Omri's ruling family. Under the leadership of the next king, Jeroboam II, the northern kingdom of Israel enjoys its most prosperous period.

Jehu Anointed King of Israel

9 The prophet Elisha summoned a man from the company of
the prophets and said to him, "Tuck your cloak into your belt, take
this flask of oil with you and go to Ramoth Gilead. 2 When you get
there, look for Jehu son of Jehoshaphat, the son of Nimshi. Go to
him, get him away from his companions and take him into an
inner room. 3 Then take the flask and pour the oil on his head and
declare, 'This is what the LORD says: I anoint you king over Israel.'
Then open the door and run; don't delay!"

4 So the young man, the prophet, went to Ramoth Gilead.
5 When he arrived, he found the army officers sitting together. "I
have a message for you, commander," he said.

"For which of us?" asked Jehu.

"For you, commander," he replied.

6 Jehu got up and went into the house. Then the prophet
poured the oil on Jehu's head and declared, "This is what the LORD,
the God of Israel, says: 'I anoint you king over the LORD's people
Israel. 7 You are to destroy the house of Ahab your master, and I
will avenge the blood of my servants the prophets and the blood of
all the LORD's servants shed by Jezebel. 8 The whole house of Ahab
will perish. I will cut off from Ahab every last male in Israel—slave
or free. 9 I will make the house of Ahab like the house of Jeroboam
son of Nebat and like the house of Baasha son of Ahijah. 10 As for
Jezebel, dogs will devour her on the plot of ground at Jezreel, and
no one will bury her.'" Then he opened the door and ran.

11 When Jehu went out to his fellow officers, one of them asked
him, "Is everything all right? Why did this madman come to you?"

"You know the man and the sort of things he says," Jehu replied.

12 "That's not true!" they said. "Tell us."

Jehu said, "Here is what he told me: 'This is what the LORD
says: I anoint you king over Israel.'"

13 They hurried and took their cloaks and spread them under
him on the bare steps. Then they blew the trumpet and shouted,
"Jehu is king!"

Jehu Kills Joram and Ahaziah

14 So Jehu son of Jehoshaphat, the son of Nimshi, conspired
against Joram. (Now Joram and all Israel had been defending
Ramoth Gilead against Hazael king of Aram, 15 but King Joram[a]

9:1 *Elisha . . . prophets:* Elisha was the prophet who was chosen to follow Elijah (1 Kgs 19:19-21; 2 Kgs 2:1-15). See also the note at 2:1.

9:2 *Jehu:* Jehu, Israel's tenth king, ruled from 841 to 814 B.C. God told Elijah that Jehu would become king and kill anyone who worshiped Baal (1 Kgs 19:16,17).

9:6 *the prophet poured the oil on Jehu's head:* Olive oil was often poured on the head of someone who was chosen to be a priest, a prophet, or a king. This process also was called "anointing." Elijah had been told that Jehu was to become king (1 Kgs 19:16). See also the note at 4:2.

9:7 *Jezebel:* This woman, King Ahab's wife, encouraged Ahab to allow the people of Israel to worship Baal and Asherah, the Canaanite god and goddess of fertility (see 1 Kgs 16:31-33). She also tried to destroy God's prophets (1 Kgs 18:3,4).

9:13 *trumpet:* This straight metal pipe-like instrument with a flared end probably was made of silver. Trumpets were used by priests to announce a temple sacrifice, ceremony, religious festival, or to draw attention to a public announcement (Num 10:1-10; 2 Chr 5:11-13). See the illustration on p. 251.

9:13 *cloaks . . . spread them . . . Jehu is king:* The officers hold a ceremony, making a type of throne with their coats spread on the steps. They complete the ceremony with a trumpet call and the customary shouting of "Jehu is king!"

9:10 1 Kgs 21:23.

[a] **15** Hebrew *Jehoram,* a variant of *Joram;* also in verses 17 and 21-24

had returned to Jezreel to recover from the wounds the Arameans
had inflicted on him in the battle with Hazael king of Aram.) Jehu
said, "If this is the way you feel, don't let anyone slip out of the city
to go and tell the news in Jezreel." 16 Then he got into his chariot
and rode to Jezreel, because Joram was resting there and Ahaziah
king of Judah had gone down to see him.

17 When the lookout standing on the tower in Jezreel saw
Jehu's troops approaching, he called out, "I see some troops
coming."

"Get a horseman," Joram ordered. "Send him to meet them
and ask, 'Do you come in peace?' "

18 The horseman rode off to meet Jehu and said, "This is
what the king says: 'Do you come in peace?' "

"What do you have to do with peace?" Jehu replied. "Fall in
behind me."

The lookout reported, "The messenger has reached them,
but he isn't coming back."

19 So the king sent out a second horseman. When he came to
them he said, "This is what the king says: 'Do you come in
peace?' "

Jehu replied, "What do you have to do with peace? Fall in
behind me."

20 The lookout reported, "He has reached them, but he isn't
coming back either. The driving is like that of Jehu son of
Nimshi—he drives like a madman."

21 "Hitch up my chariot," Joram ordered. And when it was
hitched up, Joram king of Israel and Ahaziah king of Judah rode
out, each in his own chariot, to meet Jehu. They met him at the
plot of ground that had belonged to Naboth the Jezreelite. 22 When
Joram saw Jehu he asked, "Have you come in peace, Jehu?"

"How can there be peace," Jehu replied, "as long as all the
idolatry and witchcraft of your mother Jezebel abound?"

23 Joram turned about and fled, calling out to Ahaziah,
"Treachery, Ahaziah!"

24 Then Jehu drew his bow and shot Joram between the
shoulders. The arrow pierced his heart and he slumped down in
his chariot. 25 Jehu said to Bidkar, his chariot officer, "Pick him up
and throw him on the field that belonged to Naboth the Jezreelite.
Remember how you and I were riding together in chariots behind
Ahab his father when the LORD made this prophecy about him:
26 'Yesterday I saw the blood of Naboth and the blood of his sons,
declares the LORD, and I will surely make you pay for it on this plot
of ground, declares the LORD.'[a] Now then, pick him up and throw
him on that plot, in accordance with the word of the LORD."

27 When Ahaziah king of Judah saw what had happened, he
fled up the road to Beth Haggan.[b] Jehu chased him, shouting, "Kill

[a]**26** See 1 Kings 21:19. [b]**27** Or *fled by way of the garden house*

9:21 *Naboth:* Ahab and Jezebel had earlier plotted to kill Naboth so they could steal his land (1 Kgs 21:1-16). The prophet Elijah warned Ahab that his body would end up in Naboth's field, and his family would be wiped out (1 Kgs 21:17-22). Jehu's killing of Ahab's sons, Joram and Ahaziah, fulfill Elijah's prophecy in part. But see also 2 Kgs 10:6-17.

9:27 *Beth Haggan:* About seven miles southwest of Jezreel.

9:29 *Ahaziah . . . king of Judah:* He ruled Judah briefly in 841 B.C. before being killed by Jehu. He was the son of Athaliah, the daughter of Ahab. He ruled in Judah, because his mother had earlier married King Jehoram of Judah.

9:30-32 *painted her eyes:* She probably put on eye shadow that was a black powder mixed with oil and applied with a brush. The queen probably wore it on occasions when she appeared in public. She is defiant toward Jehu, but no one volunteers to help her. Her last public appearance is a humiliating death.

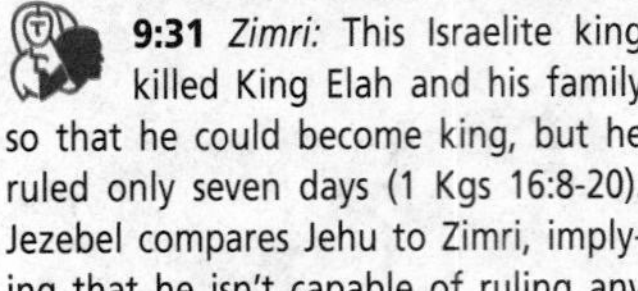

9:31 *Zimri:* This Israelite king killed King Elah and his family so that he could become king, but he ruled only seven days (1 Kgs 16:8-20). Jezebel compares Jehu to Zimri, implying that he isn't capable of ruling any longer than Zimri had.

9:34 *king's daughter:* Jezebel's father was King Ethbaal of Sidon (1 Kgs 16:31).

10:1 *Samaria:* See the note at 1:1,2 (Samaria).

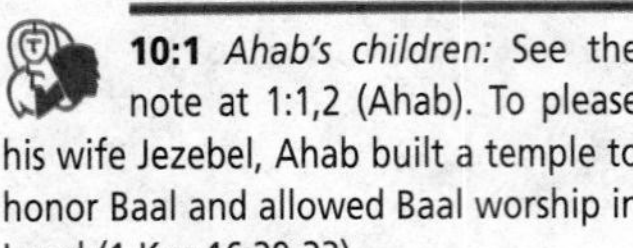

10:1 *Ahab's children:* See the note at 1:1,2 (Ahab). To please his wife Jezebel, Ahab built a temple to honor Baal and allowed Baal worship in Israel (1 Kgs 16:29-33).

Ahab had many wives (1 Kgs 20:5), and so would have had many children. Here, seventy may be a symbolic number for all of Ahab's male children (his sons and grandsons). A new ruler often killed all the male descendants of a former ruler so that none of them would lay claim to the throne (Num 35:12, 16-19).

10:2 *chariots and horses:* See the notes at 2:11 and 7:5-8 (horses).

9:36 1 Kgs 21:23.

him too!" They wounded him in his chariot on the way up to Gur
near Ibleam, but he escaped to Megiddo and died there. 28 His servants took him by chariot to Jerusalem and buried him with his
fathers in his tomb in the City of David. 29 (In the eleventh year of
Joram son of Ahab, Ahaziah had become king of Judah.)

Jezebel Killed

30 Then Jehu went to Jezreel. When Jezebel heard about it, she
painted her eyes, arranged her hair and looked out of a window.
31 As Jehu entered the gate, she asked, "Have you come in peace,
Zimri, you murderer of your master?"[a]
32 He looked up at the window and called out, "Who is on my
side? Who?" Two or three eunuchs looked down at him. 33 "Throw
her down!" Jehu said. So they threw her down, and some of her
blood spattered the wall and the horses as they trampled her
underfoot.
34 Jehu went in and ate and drank. "Take care of that cursed
woman," he said, "and bury her, for she was a king's daughter."
35 But when they went out to bury her, they found nothing except
her skull, her feet and her hands. 36 They went back and told Jehu,
who said, "This is the word of the LORD that he spoke through his
servant Elijah the Tishbite: On the plot of ground at Jezreel dogs
will devour Jezebel's flesh.[b] 37 Jezebel's body will be like refuse on
the ground in the plot at Jezreel, so that no one will be able to say,
'This is Jezebel.' "

Ahab's Family Killed

10 Now there were in Samaria seventy sons of the house of
Ahab. So Jehu wrote letters and sent them to Samaria: to the officials of Jezreel,[c] to the elders and to the guardians of Ahab's children. He said, 2 "As soon as this letter reaches you, since your
master's sons are with you and you have chariots and horses, a fortified city and weapons, 3 choose the best and most worthy of your
master's sons and set him on his father's throne. Then fight for
your master's house."
4 But they were terrified and said, "If two kings could not
resist him, how can we?"
5 So the palace administrator, the city governor, the elders
and the guardians sent this message to Jehu: "We are your servants
and we will do anything you say. We will not appoint anyone as
king; you do whatever you think best."
6 Then Jehu wrote them a second letter, saying, "If you are on
my side and will obey me, take the heads of your master's sons and
come to me in Jezreel by this time tomorrow."

---

[a]**31** Or *"Did Zimri have peace, who murdered his master?"* [b]**36** See 1 Kings 21:23. [c]**1** Hebrew; some Septuagint manuscripts and Vulgate *of the city*

Now the royal princes, seventy of them, were with the leading men of the city, who were rearing them. [7]When the letter
arrived, these men took the princes and slaughtered all seventy of
them. They put their heads in baskets and sent them to Jehu in
Jezreel. [8]When the messenger arrived, he told Jehu, "They have
brought the heads of the princes."

Then Jehu ordered, "Put them in two piles at the entrance of
the city gate until morning."

[9]The next morning Jehu went out. He stood before all the
people and said, "You are innocent. It was I who conspired against
my master and killed him, but who killed all these? [10]Know then,
that not a word the LORD has spoken against the house of Ahab
will fail. The LORD has done what he promised through his servant
Elijah." [11]So Jehu killed everyone in Jezreel who remained of the
house of Ahab, as well as all his chief men, his close friends and
his priests, leaving him no survivor.

[12]Jehu then set out and went toward Samaria. At Beth Eked
of the Shepherds, [13]he met some relatives of Ahaziah king of Judah
and asked, "Who are you?"

They said, "We are relatives of Ahaziah, and we have come
down to greet the families of the king and of the queen mother."

[14]"Take them alive!" he ordered. So they took them alive and
slaughtered them by the well of Beth Eked—forty-two men. He
left no survivor.

[15]After he left there, he came upon Jehonadab son of Recab,
who was on his way to meet him. Jehu greeted him and said, "Are
you in accord with me, as I am with you?"

"I am," Jehonadab answered.

"If so," said Jehu, "give me your hand." So he did, and Jehu
helped him up into the chariot. [16]Jehu said, "Come with me
and see my zeal for the LORD." Then he had him ride along in his
chariot.

[17]When Jehu came to Samaria, he killed all who were left
there of Ahab's family; he destroyed them, according to the word
of the LORD spoken to Elijah.

Ministers of Baal Killed

[18]Then Jehu brought all the people together and said to
them, "Ahab served Baal a little; Jehu will serve him much. [19]Now
summon all the prophets of Baal, all his ministers and all his
priests. See that no one is missing, because I am going to hold a
great sacrifice for Baal. Anyone who fails to come will no longer
live." But Jehu was acting deceptively in order to destroy the ministers of Baal.

[20]Jehu said, "Call an assembly in honor of Baal." So they proclaimed it. [21]Then he sent word throughout Israel, and all the ministers of Baal came; not one stayed away. They crowded into the
temple of Baal until it was full from one end to the other. [22]And

10:3-5 *fight for your master's house:* Jehu seems to want to force a confrontation with the leaders of Samaria. Because he had already killed Joram and Ahaziah, the leaders and officials believe they can't resist Jehu's power. See also the notes at 9:2 (Jehu); 3:1-3 (Joram); and 8:25-27 (Ahaziah).

10:6 *take the heads:* It was a common practice in the ancient Near East to bring back the head of a slain enemy, perhaps as proof of victory. The head and other body parts often were displayed to announce the victory and to serve as a warning to other enemies (see 10:8). King David followed this custom after the deaths of Goliath (1 Sam 17:51,54), and Recab and Baanah (2 Sam 4:5-7,12).

10:8 *city gate:* See the note at 3:19.

10:10 *not a word . . . will fail:* The destruction of Ahab's family was predicted by Elijah many years earlier (see 1 Kgs 21:17-24 and the note at 9:21).

10:15 *Jehonadab son of Recab:* Ancient texts indicate that Jehu and Jehonadab were long-time friends. Jehonadab's father, Recab, was one of the two men who murdered Saul's son Ish-Bosheth (2 Sam 4:1-12). Jehonadab was a faithful servant who obeyed God's laws. His descendants, the Recabites, followed his example of faithfulness. Well over two hundred years later, the prophet Jeremiah mentioned Jehonadab and the Recabites as examples of faithfulness and loyalty in contrast to the unfaithful people of Judah (Jer 35).

10:18 *Baal:* See the note at 3:2.

10:21 *temple of Baal:* This refers to the temple Ahab built in Samaria (1 Kgs 16:31,32).

10:11 Hos 1:4.

Jehu said to the keeper of the wardrobe, "Bring robes for all the ministers of Baal." So he brought out robes for them.

23 Then Jehu and Jehonadab son of Recab went into the temple of Baal. Jehu said to the ministers of Baal, "Look around and see that no servants of the LORD are here with you—only ministers of Baal." 24 So they went in to make sacrifices and burnt offerings. Now Jehu had posted eighty men outside with this warning: "If one of you lets any of the men I am placing in your hands escape, it will be your life for his life."

25 As soon as Jehu had finished making the burnt offering, he ordered the guards and officers: "Go in and kill them; let no one escape." So they cut them down with the sword. The guards and officers threw the bodies out and then entered the inner shrine of the temple of Baal. 26 They brought the sacred stone out of the temple of Baal and burned it. 27 They demolished the sacred stone of Baal and tore down the temple of Baal, and people have used it for a latrine to this day.

28 So Jehu destroyed Baal worship in Israel. 29 However, he did not turn away from the sins of Jeroboam son of Nebat, which he had caused Israel to commit—the worship of the golden calves at Bethel and Dan.

30 The LORD said to Jehu, "Because you have done well in accomplishing what is right in my eyes and have done to the house of Ahab all I had in mind to do, your descendants will sit on the throne of Israel to the fourth generation." 31 Yet Jehu was not careful to keep the law of the LORD, the God of Israel, with all his heart. He did not turn away from the sins of Jeroboam, which he had caused Israel to commit.

32 In those days the LORD began to reduce the size of Israel. Hazael overpowered the Israelites throughout their territory 33 east of the Jordan in all the land of Gilead (the region of Gad, Reuben and Manasseh), from Aroer by the Arnon Gorge through Gilead to Bashan.

34 As for the other events of Jehu's reign, all he did, and all his achievements, are they not written in the book of the annals of the kings of Israel?

35 Jehu rested with his fathers and was buried in Samaria. And Jehoahaz his son succeeded him as king. 36 The time that Jehu reigned over Israel in Samaria was twenty-eight years.

Athaliah and Joash

11 When Athaliah the mother of Ahaziah saw that her son was dead, she proceeded to destroy the whole royal family. 2 But Jehosheba, the daughter of King Jehoram[a] and sister of Ahaziah, took Joash son of Ahaziah and stole him away from among the royal princes, who were about to be murdered. She put him and

[a]2 Hebrew *Joram,* a variant of *Jehoram*

10:29 *golden calves at Bethel and Dan:* See 1 Kgs 12:26-30 and the note at 3:1-3.

11:1 *Athaliah:* Athaliah, Judah's only queen and seventh "ruler," ruled from 841 to 835 B.C. When her son was killed she tried to kill her own nephews and others who might claim to be king. See also the note at 8:16-18.

11:2-4 *Jehosheba . . . Jehoiada:* Jehosheba was the wife of Jehoiada the faithful high priest (2 Chr 22:11). That is why she could hide Joash in one of the private bedrooms used only by the priests. See also 2 Chr 24:14-16.

his nurse in a bedroom to hide him from Athaliah; so he was not
killed. 3He remained hidden with his nurse at the temple of the
LORD for six years while Athaliah ruled the land.

4In the seventh year Jehoiada sent for the commanders of
units of a hundred, the Carites and the guards and had them
brought to him at the temple of the LORD. He made a covenant
with them and put them under oath at the temple of the LORD.
Then he showed them the king's son. 5He commanded them, saying, "This is what you are to do: You who are in the three companies that are going on duty on the Sabbath—a third of you
guarding the royal palace, 6a third at the Sur Gate, and a third at
the gate behind the guard, who take turns guarding the temple—
7and you who are in the other two companies that normally go off
Sabbath duty are all to guard the temple for the king. 8Station
yourselves around the king, each man with his weapon in his
hand. Anyone who approaches your ranks[a] must be put to death.
Stay close to the king wherever he goes."

9The commanders of units of a hundred did just as Jehoiada the priest ordered. Each one took his men—those who were
going on duty on the Sabbath and those who were going off
duty—and came to Jehoiada the priest. 10Then he gave the commanders the spears and shields that had belonged to King David
and that were in the temple of the LORD. 11The guards, each with
his weapon in his hand, stationed themselves around the king—
near the altar and the temple, from the south side to the north side
of the temple.

12Jehoiada brought out the king's son and put the crown on
him; he presented him with a copy of the covenant and proclaimed him king. They anointed him, and the people clapped
their hands and shouted, "Long live the king!"

13When Athaliah heard the noise made by the guards and the
people, she went to the people at the temple of the LORD. 14She
looked and there was the king, standing by the pillar, as the custom
was. The officers and the trumpeters were beside the king, and all
the people of the land were rejoicing and blowing trumpets. Then
Athaliah tore her robes and called out, "Treason! Treason!"

15Jehoiada the priest ordered the commanders of units of a
hundred, who were in charge of the troops: "Bring her out
between the ranks[b] and put to the sword anyone who follows her."
For the priest had said, "She must not be put to death in the temple of the LORD." 16So they seized her as she reached the place
where the horses enter the palace grounds, and there she was put
to death.

17Jehoiada then made a covenant between the LORD and the
king and people that they would be the LORD's people. He also
made a covenant between the king and the people. 18All the people

a8 Or *approaches the precincts* **b15** Or *out from the precincts*

11:3 *the temple of the LORD:* The temple in Jerusalem that had been built by Solomon (1 Kgs 7). See also the mini-article called "Solomon," p. 776, and the article called "People of the Law: The Religion of Israel," p. 939, which includes an illustration showing what Solomon's temple might have looked like.

11:6 *Sur Gate:* This may have been the gate that connected the temple with the palace.

11:10 *spears and shields . . . King David:* After defeating King Hadadezer of Zobah, David brought the things he took from Hadadezer and his soldiers to Jerusalem and dedicated them to God (2 Sam 8:3-12).

11:12 *crown . . . copy of the covenant . . . anointed him:* A crown was a headpiece worn by royalty and sometimes by other people in special positions, such as a high priest (Exod 29:4-6). Because a crown was a symbol of authority, a ruler wore it on the throne and when leading an army into battle. Metal crowns probably had their beginnings in the cloth headpieces or headbands that tribal leaders wore. The "copy of the covenant" may have been official papers that dealt with the king's position and duties. Some scholars feel it included a copy of the Ten Commandments or the entire Law of Moses. For anointing, see the note at 9:6.

11:14 *standing by the pillar:* These may have been the two large columns on each side of the front door of the temple (1 Kgs 7:15-21), or one of the pillars by the platform that Solomon built in the center of the outer courtyard (2 Chr 6:12,13). See also 2 Kgs 23:3.

11:15 *She must not be put to death in the temple of the LORD:* Perhaps Jehoiada did not want to make the temple area "unclean" by shedding the blood of the queen and her followers there. See also 2 Chr 24:21,22.

of the land went to the temple of Baal and tore it down. They smashed the altars and idols to pieces and killed Mattan the priest of Baal in front of the altars.

Then Jehoiada the priest posted guards at the temple of the LORD. [19]He took with him the commanders of hundreds, the Carites, the guards and all the people of the land, and together they brought the king down from the temple of the LORD and went into the palace, entering by way of the gate of the guards. The king then took his place on the royal throne, [20]and all the people of the land rejoiced. And the city was quiet, because Athaliah had been slain with the sword at the palace.

[21]Joash[a] was seven years old when he began to reign.

Joash Repairs the Temple

12 In the seventh year of Jehu, Joash[b] became king, and he reigned in Jerusalem forty years. His mother's name was Zibiah; she was from Beersheba. [2]Joash did what was right in the eyes of the LORD all the years Jehoiada the priest instructed him. [3]The high places, however, were not removed; the people continued to offer sacrifices and burn incense there.

[4]Joash said to the priests, "Collect all the money that is brought as sacred offerings to the temple of the LORD—the money collected in the census, the money received from personal vows and the money brought voluntarily to the temple. [5]Let every priest receive the money from one of the treasurers, and let it be used to repair whatever damage is found in the temple."

[6]But by the twenty-third year of King Joash the priests still had not repaired the temple. [7]Therefore King Joash summoned Jehoiada the priest and the other priests and asked them, "Why aren't you repairing the damage done to the temple? Take no more money from your treasurers, but hand it over for repairing the temple." [8]The priests agreed that they would not collect any more money from the people and that they would not repair the temple themselves.

[9]Jehoiada the priest took a chest and bored a hole in its lid. He placed it beside the altar, on the right side as one enters the temple of the LORD. The priests who guarded the entrance put into the chest all the money that was brought to the temple of the LORD. [10]Whenever they saw that there was a large amount of money in the chest, the royal secretary and the high priest came, counted the money that had been brought into the temple of the LORD and put it into bags. [11]When the amount had been determined, they gave the money to the men appointed to supervise the work on the temple. With it they paid those who worked on the temple of the LORD—the carpenters and builders, [12]the masons

11:18 *temple of Baal:* Athaliah encouraged Baal worship in Judah, just as her mother Jezebel had encouraged it in Israel.

12:1 *Joash:* Joash was Judah's seventh king but eighth ruler (see the note at 11:2-4). He ruled from 835 to 796 B.C.

12:4 *money:* Each male over twenty years of age was required to pay taxes for the work of the priests at the place of worship. See Exod 30:11-16; Lev 22:17-23; 27:1-7; Deut 16:10,11.

---

[a]**21** Hebrew *Jehoash,* a variant of *Joash* [b]**1** Hebrew *Jehoash,* a variant of *Joash*; also in verses 2, 4, 6, 7 and 18

and stonecutters. They purchased timber and dressed stone for the
repair of the temple of the LORD, and met all the other expenses of
restoring the temple.
13 The money brought into the temple was not spent for
making silver basins, wick trimmers, sprinkling bowls, trumpets or
any other articles of gold or silver for the temple of the LORD; 14 it
was paid to the workmen, who used it to repair the temple. 15 They
did not require an accounting from those to whom they gave the
money to pay the workers, because they acted with complete honesty. 16 The money from the guilt offerings and sin offerings was
not brought into the temple of the LORD; it belonged to the priests.
17 About this time Hazael king of Aram went up and attacked
Gath and captured it. Then he turned to attack Jerusalem. 18 But
Joash king of Judah took all the sacred objects dedicated by his
fathers—Jehoshaphat, Jehoram and Ahaziah, the kings of Judah—
and the gifts he himself had dedicated and all the gold found in
the treasuries of the temple of the LORD and of the royal palace,
and he sent them to Hazael king of Aram, who then withdrew
from Jerusalem.
19 As for the other events of the reign of Joash, and all he did,
are they not written in the book of the annals of the kings of
Judah? 20 His officials conspired against him and assassinated him
at Beth Millo, on the road down to Silla. 21 The officials who murdered him were Jozabad son of Shimeath and Jehozabad son of
Shomer. He died and was buried with his fathers in the City of
David. And Amaziah his son succeeded him as king.

Jehoahaz King of Israel

13 In the twenty-third year of Joash son of Ahaziah king of
Judah, Jehoahaz son of Jehu became king of Israel in Samaria, and
he reigned seventeen years. 2 He did evil in the eyes of the LORD by
following the sins of Jeroboam son of Nebat, which he had caused
Israel to commit, and he did not turn away from them. 3 So the
LORD's anger burned against Israel, and for a long time he kept them
under the power of Hazael king of Aram and Ben-Hadad his son.
4 Then Jehoahaz sought the LORD's favor, and the LORD listened to him, for he saw how severely the king of Aram was
oppressing Israel. 5 The LORD provided a deliverer for Israel, and
they escaped from the power of Aram. So the Israelites lived in
their own homes as they had before. 6 But they did not turn away
from the sins of the house of Jeroboam, which he had caused
Israel to commit; they continued in them. Also, the Asherah pole[a]
remained standing in Samaria.
7 Nothing had been left of the army of Jehoahaz except fifty
horsemen, ten chariots and ten thousand foot soldiers, for the king

12:13 *wick trimmers, sprinkling bowls:* Wick trimmers were used to cover a flame to extinguish it or to trim wicks. See Exod 25:31-40.

Sprinkling bowls were used in the preparation for an animal sacrifice. See also the illustrations on p. 182.

12:16 *money . . . belonged to the priests:* This money provided an income for the priests and so it was not used to repair the temple. See also Lev 7:6,7.

12:17 *Gath . . . Jerusalem:* Gath was one of the five major cities of Philistia. Its exact location is not known, but is thought to have been about twenty-five miles southwest of Jerusalem. At one time, Gath belonged to Judah (2 Chr 11:5-8).

For Jerusalem, see the mini-article called "Jerusalem," p. 574.

Hazael appears to have gained the control of much of Judah. See also 8:13-15.

13:1,2 *Jehoahaz . . . Jeroboam:* Jehoahaz, Israel's eleventh king, ruled from 814 to 798 B.C. Jeroboam was Israel's first king and ruled from 931 to 910 B.C. The sin of idol worship that began with his rule continued through the reigns of all of Israel's kings. See 1 Kgs 12:25-33 and the note at 3:1-3.

13:5 *a deliverer:* The name of this leader is not given, but it may refer to Elisha the prophet, King Jehoash of Israel, or his son King Jeroboam II.

13:6 *Asherah pole:* Carved wooden poles were set up to honor Asherah, the Canaanite goddess of fertility. See also the notes at 3:2 and 3:13.

13:6 *Samaria:* See the note at 1:1,2 (Samaria).

12:15 2 Kgs 22:7.

---

a6 That is, a symbol of the goddess Asherah; here and elsewhere in 2 Kings

They did not turn away from the sins of the house of Jeroboam, which he had caused Israel to commit.
2 Kgs 13:6

13:10-13 *Jehoash . . . Jeroboam:* Jehoash, Israel's twelfth king, ruled from 798 to 783 B.C. He is not to be confused with Joash (sometimes spelled Jehoash), Judah's king from 835 to 796 B.C.

"Jeroboam" in 13:11 refers to the first king of Israel (see the note at 3:1-3), whereas "Jeroboam" in 13:13 is Joash's son, Jeroboam II.

13:14 *Elisha:* Elisha was the prophet who was chosen to follow Elijah (1 Kgs 19:19-21; 2 Kgs 2:1-15). See also the note at 2:1.

13:17 *Aphek:* Aphek was located near the source of the Yarkon River in the Plain of Sharon (see the map on p. 2464). In the New Testament, this city is known as Antipatris.

13:19,20 *Aram . . . Moabite:* Following the death of Solomon and the division of the united Israel into the northern and southern kingdoms (1 Kgs 11:41—12:20), Aram occupied a large area north of Israel.

See the note at 1:1,2 (Moab).

13:21 *tomb:* A burial room cut into solid rock.

13:23 *covenant . . . Abraham, Isaac and Jacob:* God promised Abraham that his descendants would form a great nation (Gen 12:1-3). The covenant was repeated to Isaac, Abraham's son (Gen 26:2-4), and still again to Jacob, Abraham's grandson (Gen 35:9-12). See also the mini-article called "Covenants (Agreements)," p. 386.

13:14 2 Kgs 2:12.

of Aram had destroyed the rest and made them like the dust at
threshing time.
8 As for the other events of the reign of Jehoahaz, all he did and
his achievements, are they not written in the book of the annals of
the kings of Israel? 9 Jehoahaz rested with his fathers and was buried
in Samaria. And Jehoash[a] his son succeeded him as king.

Jehoash King of Israel

10 In the thirty-seventh year of Joash king of Judah, Jehoash
son of Jehoahaz became king of Israel in Samaria, and he reigned
sixteen years. 11 He did evil in the eyes of the LORD and did not turn
away from any of the sins of Jeroboam son of Nebat, which he had
caused Israel to commit; he continued in them.
12 As for the other events of the reign of Jehoash, all he did
and his achievements, including his war against Amaziah king of
Judah, are they not written in the book of the annals of the kings
of Israel? 13 Jehoash rested with his fathers, and Jeroboam succeeded him on the throne. Jehoash was buried in Samaria with the
kings of Israel.
14 Now Elisha was suffering from the illness from which he
died. Jehoash king of Israel went down to see him and wept over
him. "My father! My father!" he cried. "The chariots and horsemen
of Israel!"
15 Elisha said, "Get a bow and some arrows," and he did so.
16 "Take the bow in your hands," he said to the king of Israel. When
he had taken it, Elisha put his hands on the king's hands.
17 "Open the east window," he said, and he opened it.
"Shoot!" Elisha said, and he shot. "The LORD's arrow of victory, the
arrow of victory over Aram!" Elisha declared. "You will completely destroy the Arameans at Aphek."
18 Then he said, "Take the arrows," and the king took them.
Elisha told him, "Strike the ground." He struck it three times and
stopped. 19 The man of God was angry with him and said, "You
should have struck the ground five or six times; then you would
have defeated Aram and completely destroyed it. But now you will
defeat it only three times."
20 Elisha died and was buried.
Now Moabite raiders used to enter the country every spring.
21 Once while some Israelites were burying a man, suddenly they
saw a band of raiders; so they threw the man's body into Elisha's
tomb. When the body touched Elisha's bones, the man came to life
and stood up on his feet.
22 Hazael king of Aram oppressed Israel throughout the reign
of Jehoahaz. 23 But the LORD was gracious to them and had compassion and showed concern for them because of his covenant

[a]9 Hebrew *Joash,* a variant of *Jehoash;* also in verses 12-14 and 25

with Abraham, Isaac and Jacob. To this day he has been unwilling
to destroy them or banish them from his presence.
24Hazael king of Aram died, and Ben-Hadad his son succeeded him as king. 25Then Jehoash son of Jehoahaz recaptured
from Ben-Hadad son of Hazael the towns he had taken in battle
from his father Jehoahaz. Three times Jehoash defeated him, and
so he recovered the Israelite towns.

Amaziah King of Judah

14 In the second year of Jehoash[a] son of Jehoahaz king of Israel,
Amaziah son of Joash king of Judah began to reign. 2He was
twenty-five years old when he became king, and he reigned in
Jerusalem twenty-nine years. His mother's name was Jehoaddin;
she was from Jerusalem. 3He did what was right in the eyes of the
LORD, but not as his father David had done. In everything he followed the example of his father Joash. 4The high places, however,
were not removed; the people continued to offer sacrifices and
burn incense there.
5After the kingdom was firmly in his grasp, he executed the
officials who had murdered his father the king. 6Yet he did not put
the sons of the assassins to death, in accordance with what is written in the Book of the Law of Moses where the LORD commanded:
"Fathers shall not be put to death for their children, nor children
put to death for their fathers; each is to die for his own sins."[b]
7He was the one who defeated ten thousand Edomites in the
Valley of Salt and captured Sela in battle, calling it Joktheel, the
name it has to this day.
8Then Amaziah sent messengers to Jehoash son of Jehoahaz,
the son of Jehu, king of Israel, with the challenge: "Come, meet me
face to face."
9But Jehoash king of Israel replied to Amaziah king of Judah:
"A thistle in Lebanon sent a message to a cedar in Lebanon, 'Give
your daughter to my son in marriage.' Then a wild beast in
Lebanon came along and trampled the thistle underfoot. 10You
have indeed defeated Edom and now you are arrogant. Glory in
your victory, but stay at home! Why ask for trouble and cause your
own downfall and that of Judah also?"
11Amaziah, however, would not listen, so Jehoash king of
Israel attacked. He and Amaziah king of Judah faced each other at
Beth Shemesh in Judah. 12Judah was routed by Israel, and every
man fled to his home. 13Jehoash king of Israel captured Amaziah
king of Judah, the son of Joash, the son of Ahaziah, at Beth
Shemesh. Then Jehoash went to Jerusalem and broke down the
wall of Jerusalem from the Ephraim Gate to the Corner Gate—a
section about six hundred feet long.[c] 14He took all the gold and

14:1 *Amaziah:* Amaziah was Judah's eighth king. The actual length of rule is uncertain. During many of these twenty-nine years (796-766 B.C.), his son, Azariah, ruled with him (see the note at 1:17).

14:3 *his father David:* The term "father" is sometimes used for "ancestor." See the mini-article "David," p. 1028. David was not sinless, but he did continue to worship God. Amaziah, one of the more faithful kings, worshiped the Edomite gods (2 Chr 25:14-16).

14:4 *high places:* God's law required that foreign altars be destroyed (Num 33:52; Deut 7:5; 12:3).

14:5 *executed the officials:* Amaziah took revenge on these who rebelled against his father Joash (2 Kgs 12:20,21).

14:7 *Edomites:* See the note at 8:20.

14:7 *Valley of Salt . . . Sela . . . Joktheel:* The Valley of Salt was a passage south and east of the Dead Sea. Many scholars identify Sela (Joktheel) as Petra, Edom's capital city. Petra was carved out of the side of a mountain. See the map on p. 2465.

14:9 *thistle . . . cedar:* The thistle is a worthless plant, while the cedar is a majestic tree prized for its beauty and aromatic wood.

14:11 *Beth Shemesh:* A town west of Jerusalem.

14:13,14 *Ephraim Gate to the Corner Gate . . . took all the gold and silver:* See the map of Jerusalem on p. 2466.

There probably was not much of value in the treasury at this time, because Joash of Judah had sent it to King Hazael of Aram (12:17,18).

[a]1 Hebrew *Joash,* a variant of *Jehoash;* also in verses 13, 23 and 27 [b]6 Deut. 24:16 [c]13 Hebrew *four hundred cubits* (about 180 meters)

14:14 *Samaria:* See the note at 1:1, 2 (Samaria).

14:19 *Lachish:* Lachish was the second largest city in Judah. See the map on p. 2467.

14:19 *sent men after him . . . killed him:* Amaziah is killed by his own people, perhaps because they had suffered due to his pride (14:13,14).

14:23 *Jeroboam:* This is Jeroboam II, Israel's thirteenth king. He ruled from 783 to 743 B.C., eleven years alongside his father, Jehoash. See the note at 3:1-3.

14:25 *Lebo Hamath . . . Sea of the Arabah:* Lebo Hamath was north of Damascus, on the Orontes River. The Sea of the Arabah is another name for the Dead Sea or Salt Sea because it is four times saltier than ocean water and so cannot support fish and many water plants. It is located 1300 feet below sea level (see the map on p. 2467).

Jeroboam II regained much of the land that had been lost to Hazael and Ben-Hadad of Aram (10:32; 12:17; 13:3,22,25), and brought Israel's boundaries close to what they had been under Solomon's glorious rule (1 Kgs 8:65; 2 Chr 8:4).

14:25 *the word of the LORD . . . Jonah:* This was Jonah, the prophet (see Jonah 1:1).

silver and all the articles found in the temple of the LORD and in
the treasuries of the royal palace. He also took hostages and
returned to Samaria.
15 As for the other events of the reign of Jehoash, what he did
and his achievements, including his war against Amaziah king of
Judah, are they not written in the book of the annals of the kings
of Israel? 16 Jehoash rested with his fathers and was buried in
Samaria with the kings of Israel. And Jeroboam his son succeeded
him as king.

17 Amaziah son of Joash king of Judah lived for fifteen years
after the death of Jehoash son of Jehoahaz king of Israel. 18 As for
the other events of Amaziah's reign, are they not written in the
book of the annals of the kings of Judah?

19 They conspired against him in Jerusalem, and he fled to
Lachish, but they sent men after him to Lachish and killed him
there. 20 He was brought back by horse and was buried in Jerusalem
with his fathers, in the City of David.

21 Then all the people of Judah took Azariah,[a] who was sixteen years old, and made him king in place of his father Amaziah.
22 He was the one who rebuilt Elath and restored it to Judah after
Amaziah rested with his fathers.

Jeroboam II King of Israel

23 In the fifteenth year of Amaziah son of Joash king of
Judah, Jeroboam son of Jehoash king of Israel became king in
Samaria, and he reigned forty-one years. 24 He did evil in the eyes
of the LORD and did not turn away from any of the sins of Jeroboam son of Nebat, which he had caused Israel to commit. 25 He
was the one who restored the boundaries of Israel from Lebo[b]
Hamath to the Sea of the Arabah,[c] in accordance with the word of
the LORD, the God of Israel, spoken through his servant Jonah son
of Amittai, the prophet from Gath Hepher.

26 The LORD had seen how bitterly everyone in Israel, whether
slave or free, was suffering; there was no one to help them. 27 And
since the LORD had not said he would blot out the name of Israel
from under heaven, he saved them by the hand of Jeroboam son of
Jehoash.

28 As for the other events of Jeroboam's reign, all he did, and
his military achievements, including how he recovered for Israel
both Damascus and Hamath, which had belonged to Yaudi,[d] are
they not written in the book of the annals of the kings of Israel?
29 Jeroboam rested with his fathers, the kings of Israel. And
Zechariah his son succeeded him as king.

---

[a]21 Also called *Uzziah* [b]25 Or *from the entrance to* [c]25 That is, the Dead Sea [d]28 Or *Judah*

THE LAST DAYS OF ISRAEL

After Jeroboam II, the fall of the northern kingdom became inevitable. The destruction of Israel is blamed upon the failure of the people and the kings to obey God's commands.

Azariah King of Judah

15 In the twenty-seventh year of Jeroboam king of Israel, Azariah son of Amaziah king of Judah began to reign. 2He was sixteen
years old when he became king, and he reigned in Jerusalem fifty-
two years. His mother's name was Jecoliah; she was from
Jerusalem. 3He did what was right in the eyes of the LORD, just as
his father Amaziah had done. 4The high places, however, were not
removed; the people continued to offer sacrifices and burn incense
there.
5The LORD afflicted the king with leprosy[a] until the day he
died, and he lived in a separate house.[b] Jotham the king's son had
charge of the palace and governed the people of the land.
6As for the other events of Azariah's reign, and all he did, are
they not written in the book of the annals of the kings of Judah?
7Azariah rested with his fathers and was buried near them in the
City of David. And Jotham his son succeeded him as king.

Zechariah King of Israel

8In the thirty-eighth year of Azariah king of Judah, Zechariah son of Jeroboam became king of Israel in Samaria, and he
reigned six months. 9He did evil in the eyes of the LORD, as his
fathers had done. He did not turn away from the sins of Jeroboam
son of Nebat, which he had caused Israel to commit.
10Shallum son of Jabesh conspired against Zechariah. He
attacked him in front of the people,[c] assassinated him and succeeded him as king. 11The other events of Zechariah's reign are
written in the book of the annals of the kings of Israel. 12So the
word of the LORD spoken to Jehu was fulfilled: "Your descendants
will sit on the throne of Israel to the fourth generation."[d]

Shallum King of Israel

13Shallum son of Jabesh became king in the thirty-ninth year
of Uzziah king of Judah, and he reigned in Samaria one month.
14Then Menahem son of Gadi went from Tirzah up to Samaria. He
attacked Shallum son of Jabesh in Samaria, assassinated him and
succeeded him as king.
15The other events of Shallum's reign, and the conspiracy he
led, are written in the book of the annals of the kings of Israel.

[a]5 The Hebrew word was used for various diseases affecting the skin—not necessarily leprosy. [b]5 Or *in a house where he was relieved of responsibility* [c]10 Hebrew; some Septuagint manuscripts *in Ibleam* [d]12 2 Kings 10:30

15:1-4 *Azariah . . . high places . . . not removed:* Azariah (also known as Uzziah) was Judah's ninth king. He ruled from 781 to 740 B.C. Isaiah the prophet began his ministry during Azariah's (Uzziah's) reign (Isa 1:1).

Azariah's reign was a time of increased growth and wealth for Judah. He successfully battled the Philistines to expand Judah's territory, built new cities, secured trade routes, and created new and successful agricultural methods. But he did not destroy the local shrines where idol worship took place.

15:5 *leprosy:* See the note at 5:1 (leprosy).

15:8 *Zechariah:* Zechariah was Israel's fourteenth king and ruled for six months in 743 B.C.

15:8 *Samaria:* See the note at 1:1,2 (Samaria).

15:9 *Jeroboam son of Nebat:* See the notes at 3:1-3 and 13:1,2.

15:12 *the word of the LORD:* See 10:28-31 for the LORD's promise to Jehu.

15:13 *Shallum:* Shallum, Israel's fifteenth king, ruled for one month in 743 B.C.

15:7 Isa 6:1; 2 Chr 26:23.

15:16 *Tirzah . . . Tiphsah:* Tirzah had been the capital of the northern kingdom at one time (1 Kgs 14:17; 15:21,33).

Tiphsah was on the Euphrates River about 325 miles northeast of Samaria, leading scholars to believe that town meant here is actually Tappuah, a town about fifteen miles southwest of Tirzah.

15:19 *Pul king of Assyria:* Pul is also called Tiglath-Pileser. He ruled Assyria from 745 to 727 B.C. When he invaded Israel, Israel's King Menahem paid Pul (Tiglath-Pileser) a high tax in order to keep Pul from capturing all of Israel. Later, Pul put down a rebellion by the combined forces of Tyre, Israel, and Aram (see 2 Kgs 16:5-9).

15:19 *Assyria:* Around 911 B.C. Assyria began to expand its power and continued to do so throughout the period of the Israelite kings (931-722 B.C.). Its expansion into Palestine had begun around 855 B.C. At this time, Tiglath-Pileser III (Pul) ruled Assyria. In expanding his empire, he gained control of conquered areas in part by exiling native people to other lands owned by Assyria. See the map on p. 2468 and the mini-article called "Assyria," p. 711.

15:23,25 *Pekahiah:* Pekahiah, Israel's sixteenth king, ruled from 738 to 737 B.C. Pekah was probably a military commander in Gilead, as it was men from Gilead who help him kill Pekahiah.

15:29 *Gilead and Galilee . . . Naphtali:* The listing of the cities in this verse indicates that Assyria had taken all of Israel's northwest territory. See the maps on pp. 2467 and 2464.

These same areas were taken by Ben-Hadad I one hundred fifty years earlier in an agreement with Judah (1 Kgs 15:16-20) and later returned (1 Kgs 20:34). Being taken as prisoners to other Assyrian lands was Israel's punishment for disobeying God (Deut 28:32-36).

16 At that time Menahem, starting out from Tirzah, attacked Tiphsah and everyone in the city and its vicinity, because they refused to open their gates. He sacked Tiphsah and ripped open all the pregnant women.

Menahem King of Israel

17 In the thirty-ninth year of Azariah king of Judah, Menahem son of Gadi became king of Israel, and he reigned in Samaria ten years. 18 He did evil in the eyes of the LORD. During his entire reign he did not turn away from the sins of Jeroboam son of Nebat, which he had caused Israel to commit.

19 Then Pul[a] king of Assyria invaded the land, and Menahem gave him a thousand talents[b] of silver to gain his support and strengthen his own hold on the kingdom. 20 Menahem exacted this money from Israel. Every wealthy man had to contribute fifty shekels[c] of silver to be given to the king of Assyria. So the king of Assyria withdrew and stayed in the land no longer.

21 As for the other events of Menahem's reign, and all he did, are they not written in the book of the annals of the kings of Israel? 22 Menahem rested with his fathers. And Pekahiah his son succeeded him as king.

Pekahiah King of Israel

23 In the fiftieth year of Azariah king of Judah, Pekahiah son of Menahem became king of Israel in Samaria, and he reigned two years. 24 Pekahiah did evil in the eyes of the LORD. He did not turn away from the sins of Jeroboam son of Nebat, which he had caused Israel to commit. 25 One of his chief officers, Pekah son of Remaliah, conspired against him. Taking fifty men of Gilead with him, he assassinated Pekahiah, along with Argob and Arieh, in the citadel of the royal palace at Samaria. So Pekah killed Pekahiah and succeeded him as king.

26 The other events of Pekahiah's reign, and all he did, are written in the book of the annals of the kings of Israel.

Pekah King of Israel

27 In the fifty-second year of Azariah king of Judah, Pekah son of Remaliah became king of Israel in Samaria, and he reigned twenty years. 28 He did evil in the eyes of the LORD. He did not turn away from the sins of Jeroboam son of Nebat, which he had caused Israel to commit.

29 In the time of Pekah king of Israel, Tiglath-Pileser king of Assyria came and took Ijon, Abel Beth Maacah, Janoah, Kedesh and Hazor. He took Gilead and Galilee, including all the land of

---

[a] **19** Also called *Tiglath-Pileser* [b] **19** That is, about 37 tons (about 34 metric tons) [c] **20** That is, about 1 1/4 pounds (about 0.6 kilogram)

Naphtali, and deported the people to Assyria. [30]Then Hoshea son
of Elah conspired against Pekah son of Remaliah. He attacked and
assassinated him, and then succeeded him as king in the twentieth
year of Jotham son of Uzziah.
[31]As for the other events of Pekah's reign, and all he did, are
they not written in the book of the annals of the kings of Israel?

Jotham King of Judah

[32]In the second year of Pekah son of Remaliah king of
Israel, Jotham son of Uzziah king of Judah began to reign. [33]He
was twenty-five years old when he became king, and he reigned
in Jerusalem sixteen years. His mother's name was Jerusha daughter of Zadok. [34]He did what was right in the eyes of the LORD, just
as his father Uzziah had done. [35]The high places, however, were
not removed; the people continued to offer sacrifices and burn
incense there. Jotham rebuilt the Upper Gate of the temple of the
LORD.
[36]As for the other events of Jotham's reign, and what he did,
are they not written in the book of the annals of the kings of
Judah? [37](In those days the LORD began to send Rezin king of Aram
and Pekah son of Remaliah against Judah.) [38]Jotham rested with
his fathers and was buried with them in the City of David, the city
of his father. And Ahaz his son succeeded him as king.

Ahaz King of Judah

16 In the seventeenth year of Pekah son of Remaliah, Ahaz son
of Jotham king of Judah began to reign. [2]Ahaz was twenty years
old when he became king, and he reigned in Jerusalem sixteen
years. Unlike David his father, he did not do what was right in the
eyes of the LORD his God. [3]He walked in the ways of the kings of
Israel and even sacrificed his son in[a] the fire, following the
detestable ways of the nations the LORD had driven out before the
Israelites. [4]He offered sacrifices and burned incense at the high
places, on the hilltops and under every spreading tree.
[5]Then Rezin king of Aram and Pekah son of Remaliah king
of Israel marched up to fight against Jerusalem and besieged Ahaz,
but they could not overpower him. [6]At that time, Rezin king of
Aram recovered Elath for Aram by driving out the men of Judah.
Edomites then moved into Elath and have lived there to this day.
[7]Ahaz sent messengers to say to Tiglath-Pileser king of
Assyria, "I am your servant and vassal. Come up and save me out
of the hand of the king of Aram and of the king of Israel, who are
attacking me." [8]And Ahaz took the silver and gold found in the
temple of the LORD and in the treasuries of the royal palace and
sent it as a gift to the king of Assyria. [9]The king of Assyria

[a]3 Or *even made his son pass through*

15:32-38 *Jotham . . . Uzziah . . . Jerusha . . . Zadok:* Jotham, Judah's tenth king, ruled from 740 to 736 B.C. Though he is said to have ruled sixteen years (15:33), a number of these years were probably as a powerless ruler under Assyrian control. The Zadok here is not the loyal priest and friend of King David and who made Solomon king (1 Kgs 1:28-46). Aram and Israel attacked Judah during Jotham's reign (15:37), because Judah would not join them in their rebellion against Assyria.

15:35 *Upper Gate:* This probably refers to the gate in the wall along the north side of the temple. It may have been knocked down at the time Jehoash of Israel invaded Judah after King Amaziah foolishly challenged Israel to fight (14:8-13). See the illustration on p. 2466.

16:1 *Ahaz:* Judah's eleventh king, he ruled from 736 to 716 B.C. Though said to have ruled only sixteen years (16:2), there were additional years during which he ruled along with Azariah, Jotham, and Hezekiah.

16:3 *sacrificed his son:* Human sacrifice was part of the worship of certain foreign gods, such as Molech or Chemosh (see 3:27 and note). All worship of foreign gods was forbidden and disgusting to God. See Lev 18:21; 20:1-5; Deut 12:31; 13:1-5.

16:5-9 *Rezin . . . Pekah . . . Tiglath-Pileser:* The events in these verses probably took place around 734 B.C., before the events described in 15:29. Rezin of Aram and Pekah of Israel tried to force Ahaz out of Judah, so they could install a ruler of their choice in Jerusalem and force Judah's armies to join them against Assyria. See also Isa 7:1-16. But Ahaz saved Judah by taking money from the temple treasury and giving it to Assyria's leader, Tiglath-Pileser. By taking over Damascus, Aram's capital, Tiglath-Pileser began to put down the rebellion.

All this took place because the Israelites had sinned against the LORD *their God.*
2 Kgs 17:7

16:10 *Ahaz went to Damascus:* After receiving Tiglath-Pileser's help, Ahaz went to Damascus to thank the Assyrian king and to honor him.

16:13 *offered up his burnt offering . . . fellowship offerings:* These are described in Leviticus 1–3. See also the chart called "Sacrifices and Offerings," p. 219.

16:17,18 *the Sea . . . royal entryway:* The Sea was a huge basin that the priests may have used for ritual cleansing. See also 1 Kgs 7:23-39; 2 Chr 4:2-6. The royal entryway may have been a canopy where the king stood during worship on the Sabbath.

16:20 *City of David:* See the note at 8:20-22, 24.

17:1 *Hoshea:* Hoshea was Israel's nineteenth and last king. He ruled from 732 to 723 B.C.

17:1 *Samaria:* See the note at 1:1,2 (Samaria).

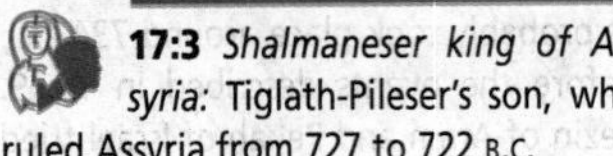
17:3 *Shalmaneser king of Assyria:* Tiglath-Pileser's son, who ruled Assyria from 727 to 722 B.C.

16:14 Exod 27:1, 2; 2 Chr 4:1.
16:20 Isa 14:28-32.

complied by attacking Damascus and capturing it. He deported its
inhabitants to Kir and put Rezin to death.
[10]Then King Ahaz went to Damascus to meet Tiglath-Pileser
king of Assyria. He saw an altar in Damascus and sent to Uriah the
priest a sketch of the altar, with detailed plans for its construction.
[11]So Uriah the priest built an altar in accordance with all the plans
that King Ahaz had sent from Damascus and finished it before
King Ahaz returned. [12]When the king came back from Damascus
and saw the altar, he approached it and presented offerings[a] on it.
[13]He offered up his burnt offering and grain offering, poured out
his drink offering, and sprinkled the blood of his fellowship offerings[b] on the altar. [14]The bronze altar that stood before the LORD he
brought from the front of the temple—from between the new altar
and the temple of the LORD—and put it on the north side of the
new altar.
[15]King Ahaz then gave these orders to Uriah the priest: "On
the large new altar, offer the morning burnt offering and the
evening grain offering, the king's burnt offering and his grain
offering, and the burnt offering of all the people of the land, and
their grain offering and their drink offering. Sprinkle on the altar
all the blood of the burnt offerings and sacrifices. But I will use the
bronze altar for seeking guidance." [16]And Uriah the priest did just
as King Ahaz had ordered.
[17]King Ahaz took away the side panels and removed the
basins from the movable stands. He removed the Sea from the
bronze bulls that supported it and set it on a stone base. [18]He took
away the Sabbath canopy[c] that had been built at the temple and
removed the royal entryway outside the temple of the LORD, in def-
erence to the king of Assyria.
[19]As for the other events of the reign of Ahaz, and what he
did, are they not written in the book of the annals of the kings of
Judah? [20]Ahaz rested with his fathers and was buried with them in
the City of David. And Hezekiah his son succeeded him as king.

Hoshea Last King of Israel

17 In the twelfth year of Ahaz king of Judah, Hoshea son of
Elah became king of Israel in Samaria, and he reigned nine years.
[2]He did evil in the eyes of the LORD, but not like the kings of Israel
who preceded him.
[3]Shalmaneser king of Assyria came up to attack Hoshea, who
had been Shalmaneser's vassal and had paid him tribute. [4]But the
king of Assyria discovered that Hoshea was a traitor, for he had
sent envoys to So[d] king of Egypt, and he no longer paid tribute to
the king of Assyria, as he had done year by year. Therefore Shalmaneser seized him and put him in prison. [5]The king of Assyria

[a]**12** Or *and went up* (see Septuagint) [b]**13** Traditionally *peace offerings* [c]**18** Or *the dais of his throne* [d]**4** Or *to Sais, to the*; *So* is possibly an abbreviation for *Osorkon.*

invaded the entire land, marched against Samaria and laid siege to
it for three years. [6]In the ninth year of Hoshea, the king of Assyria
captured Samaria and deported the Israelites to Assyria. He settled
them in Halah, in Gozan on the Habor River and in the towns of
the Medes.

Israel Exiled Because of Sin

[7]All this took place because the Israelites had sinned against
the LORD their God, who had brought them up out of Egypt from
under the power of Pharaoh king of Egypt. They worshiped other
gods [8]and followed the practices of the nations the LORD had driv-
en out before them, as well as the practices that the kings of Israel
had introduced. [9]The Israelites secretly did things against the LORD
their God that were not right. From watchtower to fortified city
they built themselves high places in all their towns. [10]They set up
sacred stones and Asherah poles on every high hill and under
every spreading tree. [11]At every high place they burned incense, as
the nations whom the LORD had driven out before them had done.
They did wicked things that provoked the LORD to anger. [12]They
worshiped idols, though the LORD had said, "You shall not do
this."[a] [13]The LORD warned Israel and Judah through all his
prophets and seers: "Turn from your evil ways. Observe my commands and decrees, in accordance with the entire Law that I commanded your fathers to obey and that I delivered to you through
my servants the prophets."

[14]But they would not listen and were as stiff-necked as their
fathers, who did not trust in the LORD their God. [15]They rejected
his decrees and the covenant he had made with their fathers and
the warnings he had given them. They followed worthless idols
and themselves became worthless. They imitated the nations
around them although the LORD had ordered them, "Do not do as
they do," and they did the things the LORD had forbidden them
to do.

[16]They forsook all the commands of the LORD their God and
made for themselves two idols cast in the shape of calves, and an
Asherah pole. They bowed down to all the starry hosts, and they
worshiped Baal. [17]They sacrificed their sons and daughters in[b] the
fire. They practiced divination and sorcery and sold themselves to
do evil in the eyes of the LORD, provoking him to anger.

[18]So the LORD was very angry with Israel and removed them
from his presence. Only the tribe of Judah was left, [19]and even Judah
did not keep the commands of the LORD their God. They followed
the practices Israel had introduced. [20]Therefore the LORD rejected all
the people of Israel; he afflicted them and gave them into the hands
of plunderers, until he thrust them from his presence.

[a]**12** Exodus 20:4, 5 [b]**17** Or *They made their sons and daughters pass through*

17:6 *king of Assyria captured Samaria:* This probably refers to Sargon II, who followed Shalmaneser as king of Assyria. Shalmaneser died after the city of Samaria was captured (722 B.C.), but before the people of Israel were taken away as prisoners (720 B.C.). Sargon ruled Assyria from 722 to 705 B.C.

17:6 *Halah, in Gozan on the Habor River and in the towns of the Medes:* Halah's exact location is unknown. The Habor River in Gozan was a northern branch of the Euphrates River. The Medes lived in an area east of the Tigris River. See the map on p. 2468.

17:7 *brought them up out of Egypt:* See Exod 2–20.

17:9,10 *high places . . . Asherah poles:* See the notes at 14:4 and 15:1-4, and the note at 13:6 (Asherah pole). See also 1 Kgs 14:23.

17:12 *idols:* See the note at 3:2. See also Exod 20:4,5; Lev 19:3,4.

17:13 *prophets:* See the note on p. 675. See also Jer 4:1; 35:15; Hos 4:17-19; Mic 5:10-15.

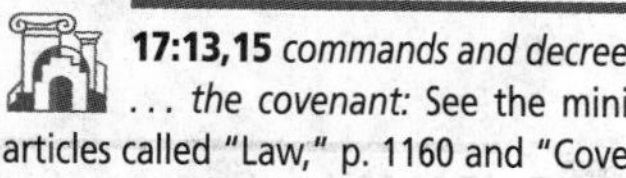

17:13,15 *commands and decrees . . . the covenant:* See the mini-articles called "Law," p. 1160 and "Covenants (Agreements)," p. 386.

17:16 *idols cast in the shape of calves . . . Asherah pole . . . Baal:* Jeroboam, Israel's first king, made two gold statues of calves and encouraged the people to worship them (1 Kgs 12:28).

See also the notes at 3:2 (Baal) and 13:6 (Asherah pole).

17:17 Deut 18:10,11.

Assyria. The Assyrians conquered almost the entire Near East. At its greatest extent (around 700 B.C.) the empire stretched from Egypt and the Mediterranean coast to Asia Minor in the west, and the Mesopotamian valley to the Persian Gulf in the east. The Assyrian army, highly trained and feared for its cruelty, was equipped with chariots, siege-engines, spear throwers, slingers and archers. During the rule of King Tiglath-Pileser III (745-727 B.C.) and his successor Shalmaneser V (727-722 B.C.) Israel was brought under Assyrian control. The next Assyrian king, Sargon II (721-705 B.C.), deported 27,000 Israelites to Assyria, bringing a final end to the northern kingdom. Sargon II decorated his palace at Khorsobad with human-headed, winged bulls.

17:21-23 *tore Israel away from the house of David . . . taken from their homeland into exile in Assyria:* David's son, Solomon, was the final king to rule over the united tribes of Israel. But he did not remain faithful and obey God, and so God split the tribes into the northern and southern kingdoms. David's family continued to rule in the southern kingdom of Judah where Jerusalem was located. See 1 Kgs 11:29-39 and the note at 3:1-3.

After the fall of Samaria, the northern kingdom of Israel came to an end, and the people were scattered to other lands.

21 When he tore Israel away from the house of David, they
made Jeroboam son of Nebat their king. Jeroboam enticed Israel
away from following the LORD and caused them to commit a great
sin. 22 The Israelites persisted in all the sins of Jeroboam and did
not turn away from them 23 until the LORD removed them from his
presence, as he had warned through all his servants the prophets.
So the people of Israel were taken from their homeland into exile
in Assyria, and they are still there.

Samaria Resettled

24 The king of Assyria brought people from Babylon, Cuthah,
Avva, Hamath and Sepharvaim and settled them in the towns of
Samaria to replace the Israelites. They took over Samaria and lived
in its towns. 25 When they first lived there, they did not worship the
LORD; so he sent lions among them and they killed some of the
people. 26 It was reported to the king of Assyria: "The people you
deported and resettled in the towns of Samaria do not know what

the god of that country requires. He has sent lions among them,
which are killing them off, because the people do not know what
he requires."
27 Then the king of Assyria gave this order: "Have one of the
priests you took captive from Samaria go back to live there and
teach the people what the god of the land requires." 28 So one of the
priests who had been exiled from Samaria came to live in Bethel
and taught them how to worship the LORD.
29 Nevertheless, each national group made its own gods in the
several towns where they settled, and set them up in the shrines
the people of Samaria had made at the high places. 30 The men
from Babylon made Succoth Benoth, the men from Cuthah made
Nergal, and the men from Hamath made Ashima; 31 the Avvites
made Nibhaz and Tartak, and the Sepharvites burned their children in the fire as sacrifices to Adrammelech and Anammelech, the
gods of Sepharvaim. 32 They worshiped the LORD, but they also

17:24 *Babylon, Cuthah, Avva, Hamath, and Sepharvaim . . . Samaria:* Babylon and Cuthah were in southern Mesopotamia. The locations of Avva and Sepharvaim are unknown. Hamath, also known as Lebo-Hamath, was about one hundred twenty miles north of Damascus, on the Orontes River. See also the note at 1:1,2 (Samaria) and the map on p. 2468.

17:30,31 *Succoth Benoth . . . Nergal . . . Ashima . . . Nibhaz . . . Tartak . . . Adrammelech and Anammelech:* Little is known about these gods except for Nergal, who was the Mesopotamian god of plagues and the land of the dead.

ASSYRIA

Ancient Assyria was located north of Babylonia in the valley between the Tigris and Euphrates rivers (see the map on p. 2468). Various peoples have ruled the area down through the ages, among the most important being the Sumerians and the Babylonians. As far back as the thirteenth century B.C., the Assyrians began to have an influence on world history. The Assyrians were known for their organizational skill and military tactics. A series of brilliant Assyrian kings eventually created an army powerful enough to take over Mesopotamia. Around 900 B.C., Assyria turned its attention to the south and west, and made its power and influence felt in Syria and Israel.

All the peoples of the ancient world feared the cruelty of the Assyrians. They were known for piercing the jawbones of their captives in order to chain them together as they led them off to other parts of the empire. Often, the Assyrians repopulated a captured territory by bringing captives from other conquered lands.

Israel faced a severe threat from Assyria for many years. The words of the prophets Amos, Hosea, Micah, and Isaiah are filled with warnings that God sent Assyria in order to punish the people of Israel for their lack of faithfulness (Isa 10:5). Some of the Assyrian invasions of Israel are described in 2 KINGS (15:29; 17:3, 6, 24; 18:9, 13-25; 19:35-37). One important battle, the one fought at Qarqar in north Syria in 853 B.C., is not mentioned in the Bible. This is surprising, since King Ahab of Israel was part of a coalition of kings who fought against Shalmaneser III and temporarily halted Assyrian expansion.

Ultimately, the northern kingdom of Israel fell to the Assyrians in 722 B.C. Its capital, Samaria, was destroyed and many of its people were led away as prisoners to live in other lands controlled by Assyria. Jerusalem, in the south, narrowly escaped destruction by Sennacherib in 701 B.C., though they paid heavy taxes to Assyria for years to avoid being overrun (2 Kgs 18:13—19:36).

With Asshurbanipal's capture of Egypt in 651 B.C., the Assyrian empire reached its greatest extent. But soon after, Assyria's empire began to crumble. In 612 B.C. the Babylonians destroyed Assyria's capital city, Nineveh. The prophet Nahum spoke about the day when Assyria would be no more.

The LORD *said, "Do not forget the covenant I have made with you, and do not worship other gods."*
2 Kgs 17:38

17:34 *descendants of Jacob:* Another name for the people of Israel. Jacob, the grandson of Abraham, became known as "Israel" after he wrestled with God (Gen 32:28). His descendants were the people of Israel. In the Bible, Israel is the nation made up of the twelve tribes descended from Jacob, but in 2 KINGS it most often refers to just the northern kingdom. See also the mini-article called "Israel," p. 264.

17:35-39 *Do not worship any other gods . . . worship the* LORD *your God:* The basis of the covenant God made with the Israelites. The Israelites' failure to keep this covenant caused the punishment they continued to suffer. See Exod 20:2-5; Deut 5:9; 6:13.

appointed all sorts of their own people to officiate for them as
priests in the shrines at the high places. 33 They worshiped the
LORD, but they also served their own gods in accordance with the
customs of the nations from which they had been brought.
34 To this day they persist in their former practices. They neither worship the LORD nor adhere to the decrees and ordinances,
the laws and commands that the LORD gave the descendants of
Jacob, whom he named Israel. 35 When the LORD made a covenant
with the Israelites, he commanded them: "Do not worship any
other gods or bow down to them, serve them or sacrifice to them.
36 But the LORD, who brought you up out of Egypt with mighty
power and outstretched arm, is the one you must worship. To him
you shall bow down and to him offer sacrifices. 37 You must always
be careful to keep the decrees and ordinances, the laws and commands he wrote for you. Do not worship other gods. 38 Do not forget the covenant I have made with you, and do not worship other
gods. 39 Rather, worship the LORD your God; it is he who will deliver you from the hand of all your enemies."
40 They would not listen, however, but persisted in their former practices. 41 Even while these people were worshiping the
LORD, they were serving their idols. To this day their children and
grandchildren continue to do as their fathers did.

QUESTIONS ABOUT 2 KINGS 8:16—17:41

1. Review the story of King Jehu's reign as king of the northern kingdom (9:1—10:36). What means did he use to come to power? What is your reaction to the killing of Ahab and the other acts of violence in these chapters? Compare the description of how the prophet Elisha commissioned Jehu to rescue Israel from the King Ahab (9:4-10) with the words of the prophet Hosea (Hos 1:4,5). What do you make of these passages?
2. The author of 2 KINGS consistently condemns the kings of Israel for allowing the people to worship idols. Why do you think the people of Israel and their leaders were attracted to worshiping the Canaanite fertility gods?
3. Idols in 2 KINGS are statues made of wood or stone. But idols can also be understood as anything other than God that people turn to for comfort and protection. What are some idols that people worship today? How does this affect people's relationship with God?
4. Some historians have identified King Jeroboam II as one of Israel's most important political and military leaders. Israel (the northern kingdom) experienced prosperity and a certain amount of political stability during his rule. The Bible, however, has little to say about this king's accomplishments (14:23-29). Why do you think that is so? What does the author of 2 KINGS want the reader to understand about Jeroboam as a ruler of the Israelites? For further insight into the problems Israel faced during Jeroboam's reign, read the words of the prophet Amos (Amos 2:6-8; 5:10-13; 6:4-14; 8:4-6).

Judah Alone

This final major section relates the history of Judah, the surviving southern kingdom, from 722 B.C. until its own destruction and captivity in 586 B.C. Most of these chapters are concerned with two of Judah's greatest kings, Hezekiah (18:1—20:21) and Josiah (22:1—23:30). Even these godly kings, however, could not undo the evil of Judah's worst king, Manasseh (21:1-18), or prevent the coming disaster.

KING HEZEKIAH AND THE ASSYRIAN INVASION

Hezekiah, one of Judah's greatest kings, struggled to free his people from Assyrian domination and was the first king to eliminate the local shrines (high places) honoring other gods.

Hezekiah King of Judah

18 In the third year of Hoshea son of Elah king of Israel, Hezekiah son of Ahaz king of Judah began to reign. 2He was twenty-five
years old when he became king, and he reigned in Jerusalem
twenty-nine years. His mother's name was Abijah[a] daughter of
Zechariah. 3He did what was right in the eyes of the LORD, just as his
father David had done. 4He removed the high places, smashed the
sacred stones and cut down the Asherah poles. He broke into pieces
the bronze snake Moses had made, for up to that time the Israelites
had been burning incense to it. (It was called[b] Nehushtan.[c])
5Hezekiah trusted in the LORD, the God of Israel. There was
no one like him among all the kings of Judah, either before him or
after him. 6He held fast to the LORD and did not cease to follow
him; he kept the commands the LORD had given Moses. 7And the
LORD was with him; he was successful in whatever he undertook.
He rebelled against the king of Assyria and did not serve him.
8From watchtower to fortified city, he defeated the Philistines, as
far as Gaza and its territory.
9In King Hezekiah's fourth year, which was the seventh year
of Hoshea son of Elah king of Israel, Shalmaneser king of Assyria
marched against Samaria and laid siege to it. 10At the end of three
years the Assyrians took it. So Samaria was captured in Hezekiah's
sixth year, which was the ninth year of Hoshea king of Israel. 11The
king of Assyria deported Israel to Assyria and settled them in
Halah, in Gozan on the Habor River and in towns of the Medes.
12This happened because they had not obeyed the LORD their God,
but had violated his covenant—all that Moses the servant of the
LORD commanded. They neither listened to the commands nor
carried them out.

[a]2 Hebrew *Abi*, a variant of *Abijah* [b]4 Or *He called it* [c]4 *Nehushtan* sounds like the Hebrew for *bronze* and *snake* and *unclean thing*.

18:1,2 *Hezekiah . . . Zechariah:* Hezekiah, Judah's twelfth king, ruled from 716 to 687 B.C. See also the mini-article called "Hezekiah," p. 1293. Hezekiah's grandfather was Zechariah, a former king of Israel.

18:4 *removed the high places . . . Asherah poles . . . the bronze snake . . . Nehushtan:* See notes at 14:4 and 15:1-4, and the note at 13:6 (Asherah pole). See also Numbers 21:8,9, which describes the bronze snake Moses made. "Nehushtan" is a nickname that sounds like the Hebrew words for "snake" and "bronze."

18:7,8 *Assyria . . . Gaza:* Judah came under Assyrian control when Hezekiah's father, Ahaz, was king (see the notes at 16:5-9 and 16:10). Because Assyria had such a powerful army, Hezekiah's rebellion demanded that he have great faith and trust that the LORD would protect him and the people of Judah.

Gaza was one of five main cities in Philistia, a nation along the Mediterranean Sea. The Philistines were often at war with Israel. See the map on p. 2467.

18:9 *King Hezekiah's fourth year . . . Shalmaneser . . . Samaria:* Though the beginning of Hezekiah's rule is given as 716 B.C., he probably had begun to rule beside his father Ahaz when Shalmaneser invaded Israel and finally captured Samaria in 722 B.C.

18:11 *The king of Assyria:* This probably refers to Sargon. See the note at 17:6 (king of Assyria).

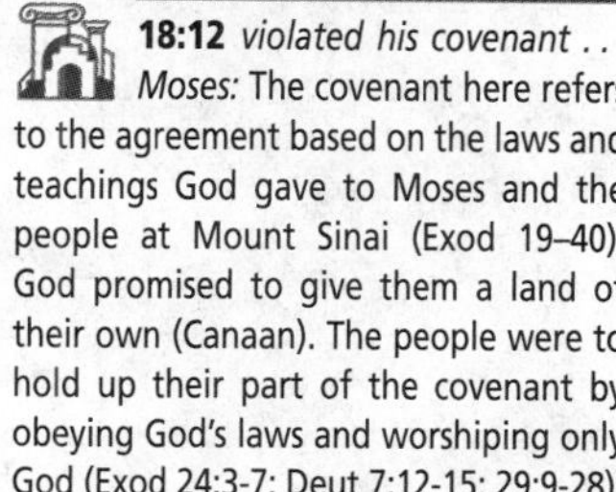

18:12 *violated his covenant . . . Moses:* The covenant here refers to the agreement based on the laws and teachings God gave to Moses and the people at Mount Sinai (Exod 19–40). God promised to give them a land of their own (Canaan). The people were to hold up their part of the covenant by obeying God's laws and worshiping only God (Exod 24:3-7; Deut 7:12-15; 29:9-28).

18:13 *Sennacherib king of Assyria . . . fortified cities:* Sennacherib ruled Assyria from 705 to 681 B.C. This event probably took place in 701 B.C. See also the note at 3:19.

18:15,16 *all the silver . . . the gold:* This was not the first time a king removed gold and silver from the temple treasury. See 1 Kgs 7:51; 14:26; 15:18; 2 Kgs 12:18; 14:13,14; 16:8.

18:22 *worship:* The Assyrian leader is confused, thinking that the many altars Hezekiah had torn down were to be used to worship the LORD God of Israel. Actually, Hezekiah had torn down the places where idols were worshiped, and he told the people to worship the LORD at one place of worship in Jerusalem.

18:24-26 *chariots and horsemen:* See the notes at 2:11 and 7:5-8 (horses). An army with horses and chariots was assumed to be stronger than an army that had only foot soldiers.

18:26 *Aramaic . . . Hebrew . . . people on the wall:* Many ancient cities had tall walls built around them as protection. The leaders from Jerusalem who spoke to the Assyrian army commander wanted him to speak in Aramaic, a language used by representatives from various countries in the region. The common people of Israel spoke Hebrew and so may not have understood the commander's threats if he spoke in Aramaic.

13 In the fourteenth year of King Hezekiah's reign, Sennacherib king of Assyria attacked all the fortified cities of Judah and captured them. 14 So Hezekiah king of Judah sent this message to the king of Assyria at Lachish: "I have done wrong. Withdraw from me, and I will pay whatever you demand of me." The king of Assyria exacted from Hezekiah king of Judah three hundred talents[a] of silver and thirty talents[b] of gold. 15 So Hezekiah gave him all the silver that was found in the temple of the LORD and in the treasuries of the royal palace.

16 At this time Hezekiah king of Judah stripped off the gold with which he had covered the doors and doorposts of the temple of the LORD, and gave it to the king of Assyria.

Sennacherib Threatens Jerusalem

17 The king of Assyria sent his supreme commander, his chief officer and his field commander with a large army, from Lachish to King Hezekiah at Jerusalem. They came up to Jerusalem and stopped at the aqueduct of the Upper Pool, on the road to the Washerman's Field. 18 They called for the king; and Eliakim son of Hilkiah the palace administrator, Shebna the secretary, and Joah son of Asaph the recorder went out to them.

19 The field commander said to them, "Tell Hezekiah:

" 'This is what the great king, the king of Assyria, says: On what are you basing this confidence of yours? 20 You say you have strategy and military strength—but you speak only empty words. On whom are you depending, that you rebel against me? 21 Look now, you are depending on Egypt, that splintered reed of a staff, which pierces a man's hand and wounds him if he leans on it! Such is Pharaoh king of Egypt to all who depend on him. 22 And if you say to me, "We are depending on the LORD our God"—isn't he the one whose high places and altars Hezekiah removed, saying to Judah and Jerusalem, "You must worship before this altar in Jerusalem"?

23 " 'Come now, make a bargain with my master, the king of Assyria: I will give you two thousand horses—if you can put riders on them! 24 How can you repulse one officer of the least of my master's officials, even though you are depending on Egypt for chariots and horsemen[c]? 25 Furthermore, have I come to attack and destroy this place without word from the LORD? The LORD himself told me to march against this country and destroy it.' "

26 Then Eliakim son of Hilkiah, and Shebna and Joah said to the field commander, "Please speak to your servants in Aramaic,

---

[a]14 That is, about 11 tons (about 10 metric tons) [b]14 That is, about 1 ton (about 1 metric ton) [c]24 Or *charioteers*

since we understand it. Don't speak to us in Hebrew in the hearing
of the people on the wall."
27But the commander replied, "Was it only to your master
and you that my master sent me to say these things, and not to the
men sitting on the wall—who, like you, will have to eat their own
filth and drink their own urine?"
28Then the commander stood and called out in Hebrew:
"Hear the word of the great king, the king of Assyria! 29This is
what the king says: Do not let Hezekiah deceive you. He cannot
deliver you from my hand. 30Do not let Hezekiah persuade you to
trust in the LORD when he says, 'The LORD will surely deliver us;
this city will not be given into the hand of the king of Assyria.'
31"Do not listen to Hezekiah. This is what the king of Assyria
says: Make peace with me and come out to me. Then every one of
you will eat from his own vine and fig tree and drink water from
his own cistern, 32until I come and take you to a land like your
own, a land of grain and new wine, a land of bread and vineyards,
a land of olive trees and honey. Choose life and not death!
"Do not listen to Hezekiah, for he is misleading you when
he says, 'The LORD will deliver us.' 33Has the god of any nation ever
delivered his land from the hand of the king of Assyria? 34Where
are the gods of Hamath and Arpad? Where are the gods of Sepharvaim, Hena and Ivvah? Have they rescued Samaria from my hand?
35Who of all the gods of these countries has been able to save his
land from me? How then can the LORD deliver Jerusalem from my
hand?"
36But the people remained silent and said nothing in reply,
because the king had commanded, "Do not answer him."
37Then Eliakim son of Hilkiah the palace administrator,
Shebna the secretary and Joah son of Asaph the recorder went to
Hezekiah, with their clothes torn, and told him what the field
commander had said.

Jerusalem's Deliverance Foretold

19 When King Hezekiah heard this, he tore his clothes and put
on sackcloth and went into the temple of the LORD. 2He sent Eliakim the palace administrator, Shebna the secretary and the leading priests, all wearing sackcloth, to the prophet Isaiah son of
Amoz. 3They told him, "This is what Hezekiah says: This day is a
day of distress and rebuke and disgrace, as when children come to
the point of birth and there is no strength to deliver them. 4It may
be that the LORD your God will hear all the words of the field commander, whom his master, the king of Assyria, has sent to ridicule
the living God, and that he will rebuke him for the words the LORD
your God has heard. Therefore pray for the remnant that still
survives."
5When King Hezekiah's officials came to Isaiah, 6Isaiah said
to them, "Tell your master, 'This is what the LORD says: Do not be

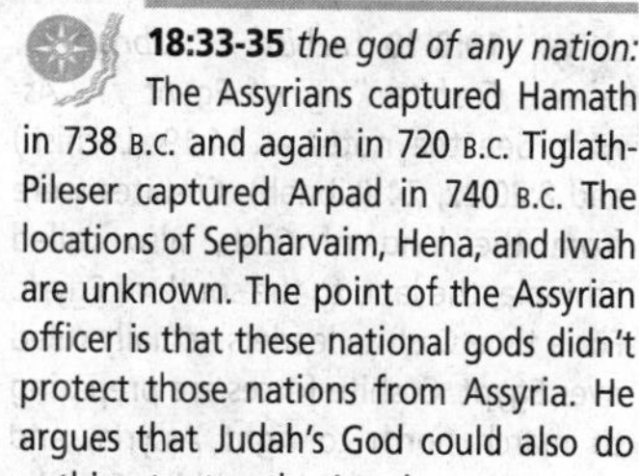

18:33-35 *the god of any nation:* The Assyrians captured Hamath in 738 B.C. and again in 720 B.C. Tiglath-Pileser captured Arpad in 740 B.C. The locations of Sepharvaim, Hena, and Ivvah are unknown. The point of the Assyrian officer is that these national gods didn't protect those nations from Assyria. He argues that Judah's God could also do nothing to stop the Assyrians.

18:37 *clothes torn:* See the note at 5:7.

19:1 *Hezekiah:* See the note at 18:1,2.

19:1 *tore his clothes . . . sack-cloth:* See the note at 6:30.

19:2 *Isaiah:* The prophet Isaiah had been bringing God's messages of judgment and hope to Judah since the last year of Azariah's reign, forty years before this time. However, this is the first time he is mentioned in 1 and 2 KINGS. ISAIAH includes parallel accounts of the Hezekiah stories given here in 2 KINGS. Isaiah is mentioned in 2 Chronicles 26:22 as the writer of a history of King Azariah (also called Uzziah). See also the Introduction to ISAIAH, p. 1289, and the article called "Prophets and Prophecy," p. 935.

19:8-10 *Lachish . . . Libnah . . . Cushite king of Egypt . . . Assyria:* See the notes at 14:19 (Lachish) and 8:20-22, 24 (Libnah). Cushites were from the land of Cush, also called Ethiopia, the land to the south of Egypt. For a time Cushite leaders actually ruled over Egypt. Cushite forces are preparing to march north to fight Assyria, and Judah is caught in the middle. See the notes at 15:19.

19:12,13 *the gods of the nations that were destroyed:* The cities listed here are meant to impress Hezekiah with the power Assyria has already shown in Mesopotamia (19:12) and Aram (19:13). See also the note at 18:33-35 and the maps on pp. 2468 and 2469.

19:14,15 *temple . . . cherubim:* See the note at 11:3. The cherubim were the two winged creatures made of gold that sat on the top of the ark of the covenant and were symbols of the LORD's throne on earth (Exod 25:18-22; 2 Sam 6:2). Other cherubim are described as having human, lion, eagle, or ox heads (Gen 3:24; Ezek 1:10; 10:12-14; 41:18-20). Cherubim may have been similar to the human-headed bull and lion statues that guarded Mesopotamian temples. Winged creatures guarding sacred objects or places are commonly seen in Egyptian and Phoenician art. See also the mini-article called "The Ark of the Covenant" and the illustration on p. 513.

19:18 *gods . . . wood and stone:* See the note at 3:2.

19:20 *Sennacherib king of Assyria:* See the note at 18:13.

19:21-28 *despises you and mocks you . . . I will make you return:* These verses were written in a song style that was used in songs of sadness (laments) or satire. Here the song is used to make fun of King Sennacherib.

19:15 Exod 25:22.

afraid of what you have heard—those words with which the
underlings of the king of Assyria have blasphemed me. 7Listen!
I am going to put such a spirit in him that when he hears a certain
report, he will return to his own country, and there I will have him
cut down with the sword.' "

8When the field commander heard that the king of Assyria
had left Lachish, he withdrew and found the king fighting against
Libnah.

9Now Sennacherib received a report that Tirhakah, the
Cushite[a] king ⌞of Egypt⌟, was marching out to fight against him.
So he again sent messengers to Hezekiah with this word: 10"Say to
Hezekiah king of Judah: Do not let the god you depend on deceive
you when he says, 'Jerusalem will not be handed over to the king
of Assyria.' 11Surely you have heard what the kings of Assyria have
done to all the countries, destroying them completely. And will
you be delivered? 12Did the gods of the nations that were destroyed
by my forefathers deliver them: the gods of Gozan, Haran, Rezeph
and the people of Eden who were in Tel Assar? 13Where is the king
of Hamath, the king of Arpad, the king of the city of Sepharvaim,
or of Hena or Ivvah?"

Hezekiah's Prayer

14Hezekiah received the letter from the messengers and read it.
Then he went up to the temple of the LORD and spread it out before
the LORD. 15And Hezekiah prayed to the LORD: "O LORD, God of
Israel, enthroned between the cherubim, you alone are God over all
the kingdoms of the earth. You have made heaven and earth. 16Give
ear, O LORD, and hear; open your eyes, O LORD, and see; listen to the
words Sennacherib has sent to insult the living God.

17"It is true, O LORD, that the Assyrian kings have laid waste
these nations and their lands. 18They have thrown their gods into
the fire and destroyed them, for they were not gods but only wood
and stone, fashioned by men's hands. 19Now, O LORD our God,
deliver us from his hand, so that all kingdoms on earth may know
that you alone, O LORD, are God."

Isaiah Prophesies Sennacherib's Fall

20Then Isaiah son of Amoz sent a message to Hezekiah: "This
is what the LORD, the God of Israel, says: I have heard your prayer
concerning Sennacherib king of Assyria. 21This is the word that the
LORD has spoken against him:

" 'The Virgin Daughter of Zion
despises you and mocks you.
The Daughter of Jerusalem
tosses her head as you flee.

[a]9 That is, from the upper Nile region

22 Who is it you have insulted and blasphemed?
Against whom have you raised your voice
and lifted your eyes in pride?
Against the Holy One of Israel!
23 By your messengers
you have heaped insults on the Lord.
And you have said,
"With my many chariots
I have ascended the heights of the mountains,
the utmost heights of Lebanon.
I have cut down its tallest cedars,
the choicest of its pines.
I have reached its remotest parts,
the finest of its forests.
24 I have dug wells in foreign lands
and drunk the water there.
With the soles of my feet
I have dried up all the streams of Egypt."

25 " 'Have you not heard?
Long ago I ordained it.
In days of old I planned it;
now I have brought it to pass,
that you have turned fortified cities
into piles of stone.
26 Their people, drained of power,
are dismayed and put to shame.
They are like plants in the field,
like tender green shoots,
like grass sprouting on the roof,
scorched before it grows up.

27 " 'But I know where you stay
and when you come and go
and how you rage against me.
28 Because you rage against me
and your insolence has reached my ears,
I will put my hook in your nose
and my bit in your mouth,
and I will make you return
by the way you came.'

29 "This will be the sign for you, O Hezekiah:

"This year you will eat what grows by itself,
and the second year what springs from that.
But in the third year sow and reap,
plant vineyards and eat their fruit.
30 Once more a remnant of the house of Judah
will take root below and bear fruit above.

19:22 *Holy One of Israel:* This phrase is common in ISAIAH (Isa 1:4; 43:14). It refers to God as special and different from other nations' gods. It emphasizes that Israel's LORD God controls what happens (19:25,26,28) and saves those who are faithful.

19:26 *tender green shoots . . . scorched:* Many of the houses had roofs made of packed earth. Grass would sometimes grow out of a roof, but would die quickly because of the sun and hot winds.

19:28 *bit in your mouth:* A piece of metal or wood (bit) was attached to leather straps and put inside the mouth of a horse or donkey in order to control it and make it turn or stop. The Assyrians sometimes used metal hooks, rings, and bits to control their human prisoners. But now the LORD will treat Sennacherib the same way. The Assyrians will be steered to destruction.

19:29 *sow and reap:* Farmers in this part of the world commonly planted grains like wheat, barley, and millet. During harvest, some seeds would drop to the ground and produce new plants the following year. But a crop produced this way would not be very large. God is preparing the people for hunger during Assyria's two-year battle to overtake Judah. God also assures the people that in the third year they will again be able to plant, harvest, and eat plenty of food.

19:30,31 *Judah:* The tribe of Judah occupied the hill country west of the Dead Sea. Following the death of Solomon, the ten northern tribes of Israel broke away. The tribes of Judah and Benjamin were left to form the southern kingdom, which they also called "Judah." Here, God assures Hezekiah that Judah will not experience total destruction and that he will keep his promise to David (2 Sam 7).

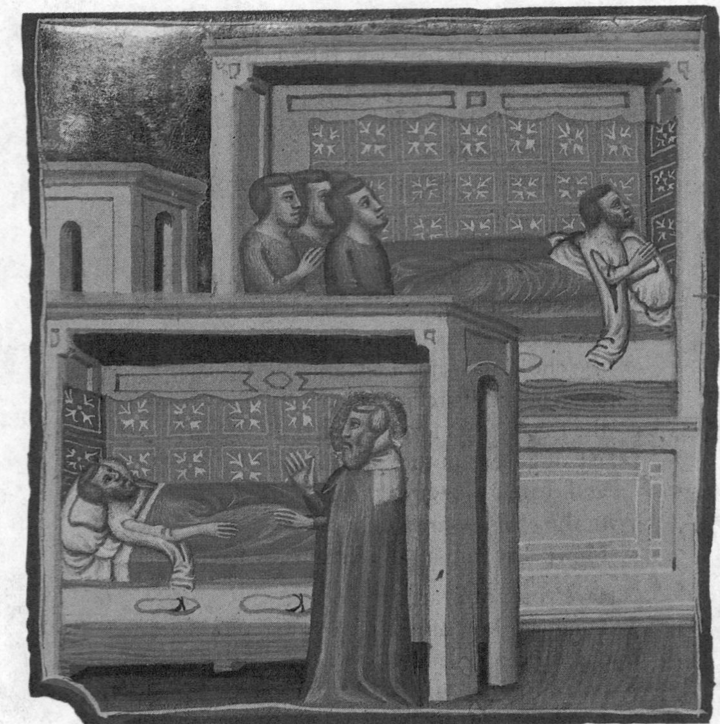

King Hezekiah, illuminated page from the *Naples Bible*, fourteenth century. Once, when King Hezekiah was sick, the prophet Isaiah came to him and told him that the LORD said he would never recover. Hezekiah turned to the wall and prayed, asking God to remember that he had always obeyed the LORD with his whole heart. The LORD heard Hezekiah's prayer and decided to heal him. Even before Isaiah had a chance to leave the king's palace, the LORD sent him back to Hezekiah to tell him that he would be healed and would live for fifteen more years. (See 20:1-11.)

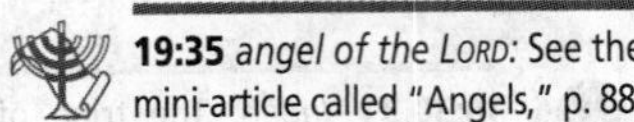

19:35 *angel of the LORD:* See the mini-article called "Angels," p. 88.

31 For out of Jerusalem will come a remnant,
and out of Mount Zion a band of survivors.

The zeal of the LORD Almighty will accomplish this.

32 "Therefore this is what the LORD says concerning the
king of Assyria:

"He will not enter this city
or shoot an arrow here.
He will not come before it with shield
or build a siege ramp against it.
33 By the way that he came he will return;
he will not enter this city,
declares the LORD.
34 I will defend this city and save it,
for my sake and for the sake of David my servant."

35 That night the angel of the LORD went out and put to death
a hundred and eighty-five thousand men in the Assyrian camp.
When the people got up the next morning—there were all the
dead bodies! 36 So Sennacherib king of Assyria broke camp and
withdrew. He returned to Nineveh and stayed there.
37 One day, while he was worshiping in the temple of his god
Nisroch, his sons Adrammelech and Sharezer cut him down with
the sword, and they escaped to the land of Ararat. And Esarhaddon his son succeeded him as king.

Hezekiah's Illness

20 In those days Hezekiah became ill and was at the point of
death. The prophet Isaiah son of Amoz went to him and said,
"This is what the LORD says: Put your house in order, because you
are going to die; you will not recover."
2 Hezekiah turned his face to the wall and prayed to the
LORD, 3 "Remember, O LORD, how I have walked before you faithfully and with wholehearted devotion and have done what is good
in your eyes." And Hezekiah wept bitterly.
4 Before Isaiah had left the middle court, the word of the
LORD came to him: 5 "Go back and tell Hezekiah, the leader of my
people, 'This is what the LORD, the God of your father David, says:
I have heard your prayer and seen your tears; I will heal you. On
the third day from now you will go up to the temple of the LORD.
6 I will add fifteen years to your life. And I will deliver you and this
city from the hand of the king of Assyria. I will defend this city for
my sake and for the sake of my servant David.' "
7 Then Isaiah said, "Prepare a poultice of figs." They did so
and applied it to the boil, and he recovered.
8 Hezekiah had asked Isaiah, "What will be the sign that the
LORD will heal me and that I will go up to the temple of the LORD
on the third day from now?"
9 Isaiah answered, "This is the LORD's sign to you that the
LORD will do what he has promised: Shall the shadow go forward
ten steps, or shall it go back ten steps?"
10 "It is a simple matter for the shadow to go forward ten
steps," said Hezekiah. "Rather, have it go back ten steps."
11 Then the prophet Isaiah called upon the LORD, and the
LORD made the shadow go back the ten steps it had gone down on
the stairway of Ahaz.

Envoys From Babylon

12 At that time Merodach-Baladan son of Baladan king of
Babylon sent Hezekiah letters and a gift, because he had heard of
Hezekiah's illness. 13 Hezekiah received the messengers and showed
them all that was in his storehouses—the silver, the gold, the spices
and the fine oil—his armory and everything found among his

19:36,37 *Nineveh . . . land of Ararat:* Nineveh was the capital city of Assyria. It was in northeastern Mesopotamia (now modern-day Iraq) on the Tigris River. The land of Ararat is a mountainous region about two hundred miles north of Nineveh, in what is now eastern Turkey. Noah's ark is said to have settled on the mountains of Ararat (Gen 8:4). The traditional site is shown here. See also the maps on pp. 2462 and 2468. Nineveh's wickedness is described in Nahum 2:8—3:19.

19:37 *Esarhaddon:* He ruled Assyria from 681 to 669 B.C.

20:1 *Hezekiah became ill:* See the mini-article called "Hezekiah," p. 1293.

20:1 *Put your house in order:* Tell his family his final wishes.

20:7 *poultice of figs:* Figs are the sweet fruit of fig trees. A mixture made of figs was also placed on infected skin boils or ulcers to help drain the infection out of them.

20:11 *stairway of Ahaz:* See the note at 16:1 (Ahaz). It's possible that the steps were designed to measure time with shadows, much as a sundial does. See also Isa 38:8.

20:12 *Merodach-Baladan . . . Babylon:* Merodach-Baladan ruled Babylonia during 722 to 710 B.C. and again, briefly, from 704 to 703 B.C. Assyria was a constant threat during his reign. Here the king of Babylonia appears to be building an alliance with Hezekiah, since there would be little reason otherwise for Hezekiah to show where all his wealth and weapons were stored (20:13).

See the map on p. 2468 and the mini-article called "Babylon," p. 1363.

20:20 *pool . . . tunnel:* In A.D. 1838, archaeologists discovered a tunnel seventeen hundred feet long running from the Gihon Spring outside Jerusalem's walls to the pool of Siloam within the city. The tunnel was filled with rocks and other debris left by Jerusalem's destruction in 586 B.C. But the tunnel was cleared out in 1909. This tunnel was probably not the first to bring water into the city, since David had entered the city through a water tunnel three hundred years earlier (2 Sam 5:6-9).

21:1-3 *Manasseh . . . high places . . . starry hosts:* Manasseh, Judah's thirteenth king, ruled from 687 to 642 B.C. His "fifty-five"-year reign includes ten years ruling with his father Hezekiah.

Manasseh undid his father's reforms (see 18:4 and note). He rebuilt high places (see the note at 14:4), and he set up altars to honor Baal and sacred poles to honor Asherah (see the notes at 3:2 and 13:6), and worshiped the stars, sun, and moon as gods. (See Jer 15:4.)

21:4,5 *in the temple:* See the note at 11:3 and also 2 Sam 7:13. Manasseh went so far as to set up altars and sacred poles honoring foreign gods right in the temple area, making that holy and sacred place ritually unclean.

21:6 *sacrificed his own son in the fire . . . sorcery and divination:* These actions further showed Manasseh's disregard for God's Law. See Lev 19:31; Deut 18:9-12.

21:7 *David . . . Solomon:* See the notes at 14:3 (David), and 17:21-23. See also 2 Sam 7:8-16; 1 Kgs 9:3-9.

21:7 *Jerusalem:* See the note at 8:20-22, 24.

20:17 2 Kgs 24:13; 2 Chr 36:10.
20:18 2 Kgs 24:14,15; Dan 1:1-7.
21:7,8 1 Kgs 9:3-9; 2 Chr 7:12-18.

treasures. There was nothing in his palace or in all his kingdom
that Hezekiah did not show them.

[14]Then Isaiah the prophet went to King Hezekiah and asked,
"What did those men say, and where did they come from?"

"From a distant land," Hezekiah replied. "They came from
Babylon."

[15]The prophet asked, "What did they see in your palace?"

"They saw everything in my palace," Hezekiah said. "There is
nothing among my treasures that I did not show them."

[16]Then Isaiah said to Hezekiah, "Hear the word of the LORD:
[17]The time will surely come when everything in your palace, and
all that your fathers have stored up until this day, will be carried
off to Babylon. Nothing will be left, says the LORD. [18]And some of
your descendants, your own flesh and blood, that will be born to
you, will be taken away, and they will become eunuchs in the
palace of the king of Babylon."

[19]"The word of the LORD you have spoken is good," Hezekiah replied. For he thought, "Will there not be peace and security in
my lifetime?"

[20]As for the other events of Hezekiah's reign, all his achievements and how he made the pool and the tunnel by which he
brought water into the city, are they not written in the book of the
annals of the kings of Judah? [21]Hezekiah rested with his fathers.
And Manasseh his son succeeded him as king.

TWO EVIL KINGS: MANASSEH AND AMON

Manasseh ruled Judah for fifty-five years, longer than any other king of Israel or Judah. He is remembered as an evil and sinful king.

Manasseh King of Judah

21 Manasseh was twelve years old when he became king, and he
reigned in Jerusalem fifty-five years. His mother's name was Hephzibah. [2]He did evil in the eyes of the LORD, following the detestable
practices of the nations the LORD had driven out before the
Israelites. [3]He rebuilt the high places his father Hezekiah had
destroyed; he also erected altars to Baal and made an Asherah pole,
as Ahab king of Israel had done. He bowed down to all the starry
hosts and worshiped them. [4]He built altars in the temple of the
LORD, of which the LORD had said, "In Jerusalem I will put my
Name." [5]In both courts of the temple of the LORD, he built altars to
all the starry hosts. [6]He sacrificed his own son in[a] the fire, practiced
sorcery and divination, and consulted mediums and spiritists. He
did much evil in the eyes of the LORD, provoking him to anger.

[7]He took the carved Asherah pole he had made and put it in
the temple, of which the LORD had said to David and to his son

a6 Or *He made his own son pass through*

Solomon, "In this temple and in Jerusalem, which I have chosen
out of all the tribes of Israel, I will put my Name forever. 8I will
not again make the feet of the Israelites wander from the land I
gave their forefathers, if only they will be careful to do everything
I commanded them and will keep the whole Law that my servant
Moses gave them." 9But the people did not listen. Manasseh led
them astray, so that they did more evil than the nations the LORD
had destroyed before the Israelites.
10The LORD said through his servants the prophets: 11"Manasseh king of Judah has committed these detestable sins. He has
done more evil than the Amorites who preceded him and has led
Judah into sin with his idols. 12Therefore this is what the LORD, the
God of Israel, says: I am going to bring such disaster on Jerusalem
and Judah that the ears of everyone who hears of it will tingle. 13I
will stretch out over Jerusalem the measuring line used against
Samaria and the plumb line used against the house of Ahab. I will
wipe out Jerusalem as one wipes a dish, wiping it and turning it
upside down. 14I will forsake the remnant of my inheritance and
hand them over to their enemies. They will be looted and plundered by all their foes, 15because they have done evil in my eyes
and have provoked me to anger from the day their forefathers
came out of Egypt until this day."
16Moreover, Manasseh also shed so much innocent blood
that he filled Jerusalem from end to end—besides the sin that he
had caused Judah to commit, so that they did evil in the eyes of
the LORD.
17As for the other events of Manasseh's reign, and all he did,
including the sin he committed, are they not written in the book
of the annals of the kings of Judah? 18Manasseh rested with his
fathers and was buried in his palace garden, the garden of Uzza.
And Amon his son succeeded him as king.

Amon King of Judah

19Amon was twenty-two years old when he became king, and
he reigned in Jerusalem two years. His mother's name was
Meshullemeth daughter of Haruz; she was from Jotbah. 20He did evil
in the eyes of the LORD, as his father Manasseh had done. 21He
walked in all the ways of his father; he worshiped the idols his father
had worshiped, and bowed down to them. 22He forsook the LORD,
the God of his fathers, and did not walk in the way of the LORD.
23Amon's officials conspired against him and assassinated the
king in his palace. 24Then the people of the land killed all who had
plotted against King Amon, and they made Josiah his son king in
his place.
25As for the other events of Amon's reign, and what he did,
are they not written in the book of the annals of the kings of
Judah? 26He was buried in his grave in the garden of Uzza. And
Josiah his son succeeded him as king.

21:8 *the whole Law:* See the mini-articles called "Law," p. 1160 and "Covenants (Agreements)," p. 386.

21:11 *Amorites:* Here used in the general sense of nations that lived in Canaan before the Israelites.

21:11 *idols:* See the note at 21:1-3.

21:13 *stretch out over Jerusalem the measuring line used against Samaria:* During his rule of Israel, Ahab not only promoted the worship of other gods, but allowed his wife Jezebel to murder those who were faithful to God (1 Kgs 18:13). Manasseh also killed the innocent (2 Kgs 21:16) and openly encouraged the worship of other gods. This made Judah and its capital Jerusalem as guilty as Israel and its capital Samaria had been earlier. See also the note at 1:1,2 (Samaria).

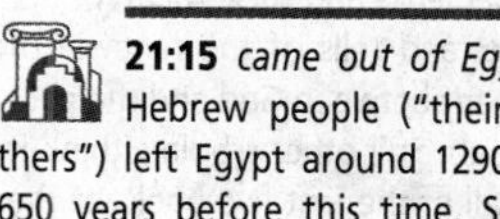

21:15 *came out of Egypt:* The Hebrew people ("their forefathers") left Egypt around 1290 B.C., or 650 years before this time. See Exod 2–20.

21:18 *garden of Uzza:* Manasseh's private burial place was along the temple wall in the palace garden.

21:19 *Amon:* Amon, Judah's fourteenth king, ruled from 642 to 640 B.C. He followed his father's evil example. He was murdered by his own officials, who were then murdered by the people so that Amon's son, Josiah, could become king. Murder plots and assassinations had been common in the northern kingdom, and now they were happening in Judah as well.

22:1 *Josiah:* Josiah, Judah's fifteenth king, ruled from 640 to 609 B.C. See also Jer 3:6, and the mini-article called "Josiah," p. 843.

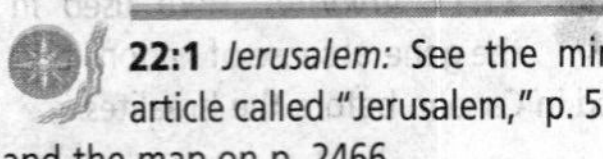

22:1 *Jerusalem:* See the mini-article called "Jerusalem," p. 574 and the map on p. 2466.

22:4-7 *money ... collected from the people:* King Joash (12:9-15) used a similar method to collect money for repairing the temple during his rule as king about two hundred years earlier.

22:8 *Book of the Law:* Many scholars feel this may have been a portion of DEUTERONOMY that includes the law God gave to Moses. Some think it was Deuteronomy 5, which includes the Ten Commandments. Others believe it was Deuteronomy 28–30, which explains how God would bless the people for obedience and curse them for disobedience, and tells of the renewal of the covenant between God and the people at Moab. Still other scholars think it refers to all of the first five books of the Bible, but this is less likely, since Shaphan read it twice in one day (22:8,10).

22:11 *tore his robes:* See the note at 5:7.

22:14 *the prophetess Huldah:* Huldah is one of the woman prophets named in the Bible. Two other famous female prophets are Miriam (Exod 15:20,21) and Deborah (Judg 4:4). See also the article called "Prophets and Prophecy," p. 935.

22:17 *idols:* See the note at 3:2.

22:20 *buried in peace:* Since Josiah died before Jerusalem was destroyed, it could be said that he died at peace with God. Josiah actually was killed by the Egyptians in 609 B.C., who attacked at Megiddo when he was trying to make plans for Judah to become independent from Assyria. His death in battle (see 2 Chr 35:23-25) put an end to reforms in Judah.

KING JOSIAH AND HIS REFORM

Josiah begins religious reforms in Judah after Hilkiah discovers the Book of the Law in the temple.

The Book of the Law Found

22 Josiah was eight years old when he became king, and he
reigned in Jerusalem thirty-one years. His mother's name was Jedi-
dah daughter of Adaiah; she was from Bozkath. 2 He did what was
right in the eyes of the LORD and walked in all the ways of his
father David, not turning aside to the right or to the left.
3 In the eighteenth year of his reign, King Josiah sent the secretary, Shaphan son of Azaliah, the son of Meshullam, to the temple of the LORD. He said: 4 "Go up to Hilkiah the high priest and
have him get ready the money that has been brought into the temple of the LORD, which the doorkeepers have collected from the
people. 5 Have them entrust it to the men appointed to supervise
the work on the temple. And have these men pay the workers who
repair the temple of the LORD— 6 the carpenters, the builders and
the masons. Also have them purchase timber and dressed stone to
repair the temple. 7 But they need not account for the money
entrusted to them, because they are acting faithfully."
8 Hilkiah the high priest said to Shaphan the secretary, "I
have found the Book of the Law in the temple of the LORD." He
gave it to Shaphan, who read it. 9 Then Shaphan the secretary went
to the king and reported to him: "Your officials have paid out the
money that was in the temple of the LORD and have entrusted it to
the workers and supervisors at the temple." 10 Then Shaphan the
secretary informed the king, "Hilkiah the priest has given me a
book." And Shaphan read from it in the presence of the king.
11 When the king heard the words of the Book of the Law, he
tore his robes. 12 He gave these orders to Hilkiah the priest, Ahikam
son of Shaphan, Acbor son of Micaiah, Shaphan the secretary and
Asaiah the king's attendant: 13 "Go and inquire of the LORD for me
and for the people and for all Judah about what is written in this
book that has been found. Great is the LORD's anger that burns
against us because our fathers have not obeyed the words of this
book; they have not acted in accordance with all that is written
there concerning us."
14 Hilkiah the priest, Ahikam, Acbor, Shaphan and Asaiah
went to speak to the prophetess Huldah, who was the wife of Shallum son of Tikvah, the son of Harhas, keeper of the wardrobe. She
lived in Jerusalem, in the Second District.
15 She said to them, "This is what the LORD, the God of Israel,
says: Tell the man who sent you to me, 16 'This is what the LORD
says: I am going to bring disaster on this place and its people,
according to everything written in the book the king of Judah has
read. 17 Because they have forsaken me and burned incense to other

gods and provoked me to anger by all the idols their hands have
made,[a] my anger will burn against this place and will not be
quenched.' 18Tell the king of Judah, who sent you to inquire of the
LORD, 'This is what the LORD, the God of Israel, says concerning
the words you heard: 19Because your heart was responsive and you
humbled yourself before the LORD when you heard what I have
spoken against this place and its people, that they would become
accursed and laid waste, and because you tore your robes and wept
in my presence, I have heard you, declares the LORD. 20Therefore I
will gather you to your fathers, and you will be buried in peace.
Your eyes will not see all the disaster I am going to bring on this
place.'"

So they took her answer back to the king.

Josiah Renews the Covenant

23 Then the king called together all the elders of Judah and
Jerusalem. 2He went up to the temple of the LORD with the men of
Judah, the people of Jerusalem, the priests and the prophets—all
the people from the least to the greatest. He read in their hearing
all the words of the Book of the Covenant, which had been found
in the temple of the LORD. 3The king stood by the pillar and
renewed the covenant in the presence of the LORD—to follow the
LORD and keep his commands, regulations and decrees with all his
heart and all his soul, thus confirming the words of the covenant
written in this book. Then all the people pledged themselves to the
covenant.

4The king ordered Hilkiah the high priest, the priests next in
rank and the doorkeepers to remove from the temple of the LORD
all the articles made for Baal and Asherah and all the starry hosts.
He burned them outside Jerusalem in the fields of the Kidron
Valley and took the ashes to Bethel. 5He did away with the pagan
priests appointed by the kings of Judah to burn incense on the
high places of the towns of Judah and on those around Jerusalem—those who burned incense to Baal, to the sun and moon,
to the constellations and to all the starry hosts. 6He took the Asherah pole from the temple of the LORD to the Kidron Valley outside
Jerusalem and burned it there. He ground it to powder and scattered the dust over the graves of the common people. 7He also
tore down the quarters of the male shrine prostitutes, which were
in the temple of the LORD and where women did weaving for
Asherah.

8Josiah brought all the priests from the towns of Judah and
desecrated the high places, from Geba to Beersheba, where the
priests had burned incense. He broke down the shrines[b] at the
gates—at the entrance to the Gate of Joshua, the city governor,

[a]17 Or *by everything they have done* [b]8 Or *high places*

23:2 *Book of the Covenant:* Also called the Book of the Law. See the note at 22:8.

23:4 *remove from the temple . . . burned them:* The temple was to be a holy place of worship, and only things and people who were ritually "clean" were supposed to enter the temple area. But the leaders of Judah had filled the temple with altars and sacred poles honoring Baal and Asherah (see 21:1-3 and the note).

23:4 *Kidron Valley:* See the map on p. 2466.

23:4-6 *The king ordered . . . scattered the dust over the graves of the common people:* Josiah undoes what his father Manasseh had done, just as Manasseh undid what his own father Hezekiah had done. See 2 Kgs 21:3; 2 Chr 33:3.

Wealthy people were buried in private tombs cut out of rock walls on a hillside or in caves. Common people were buried in a large pit called a public cemetery. According to the Law of Moses, contact with the dead made things or people unclean and unfit for holy use. (At this time, even things used in idol worship could be considered holy or sacred.) By scattering the ashes of the idols on the graves, Josiah makes certain the idols are completely and forever polluted and unholy.

23:6 *Asherah pole:* See the note at 13:6.

23:7 *male shrine prostitutes:* Young men or boys sometimes served as prostitutes in the worship of Canaanite gods, but the LORD had forbidden the people of Israel and Judah to worship in this way (Deut 23:17,18). See also Hos 4:12, 14.

23:8 *Geba . . . Beersheba:* Geba is believed to have been north of Jerusalem close to the border between Judah and Israel. Beersheba was on the southern border of Judah. See the map on p. 2467.

which is on the left of the city gate. 9 Although the priests of the high places did not serve at the altar of the LORD in Jerusalem, they ate unleavened bread with their fellow priests.

10 He desecrated Topheth, which was in the Valley of Ben Hinnom, so no one could use it to sacrifice his son or daughter in[a] the fire to Molech. 11 He removed from the entrance to the temple of the LORD the horses that the kings of Judah had dedicated to the sun. They were in the court near the room of an official named Nathan-Melech. Josiah then burned the chariots dedicated to the sun.

12 He pulled down the altars the kings of Judah had erected on the roof near the upper room of Ahaz, and the altars Manasseh had built in the two courts of the temple of the LORD. He removed them from there, smashed them to pieces and threw the rubble into the Kidron Valley. 13 The king also desecrated the high places that were east of Jerusalem on the south of the Hill of Corruption—the ones Solomon king of Israel had built for Ashtoreth the vile goddess of the Sidonians, for Chemosh the vile god of Moab, and for Molech[b] the detestable god of the people of Ammon. 14 Josiah smashed the sacred stones and cut down the Asherah poles and covered the sites with human bones.

15 Even the altar at Bethel, the high place made by Jeroboam son of Nebat, who had caused Israel to sin—even that altar and high place he demolished. He burned the high place and ground it to powder, and burned the Asherah pole also. 16 Then Josiah looked around, and when he saw the tombs that were there on the hillside, he had the bones removed from them and burned on the altar to defile it, in accordance with the word of the LORD proclaimed by the man of God who foretold these things.

17 The king asked, "What is that tombstone I see?"

The men of the city said, "It marks the tomb of the man of God who came from Judah and pronounced against the altar of Bethel the very things you have done to it."

18 "Leave it alone," he said. "Don't let anyone disturb his bones." So they spared his bones and those of the prophet who had come from Samaria.

19 Just as he had done at Bethel, Josiah removed and defiled all the shrines at the high places that the kings of Israel had built in the towns of Samaria that had provoked the LORD to anger. 20 Josiah slaughtered all the priests of those high places on the altars and burned human bones on them. Then he went back to Jerusalem.

21 The king gave this order to all the people: "Celebrate the Passover to the LORD your God, as it is written in this Book of the Covenant." 22 Not since the days of the judges who led Israel, nor throughout the days of the kings of Israel and the kings of Judah,

23:9 *unleavened bread:* This may be either the pieces of thin bread made without yeast to be eaten during the Passover Festival (23:21-23) or the baked flour used in the grain offering (Lev 2:4,5).

23:11 *horses . . . chariots:* The horses and chariots were probably used in some type of parade to honor the sun god who was often pictured as riding in a winged chariot.

23:13 *the ones Solomon king of Israel had built for Ashtoreth:* See 1 Kgs 11:5-7. Ashtoreth was a Canaanite fertility goddess. Chemosh was a god of the Moabites and most likely the god to whom Moab's king sacrificed his son when facing defeat in battle (2 Kgs 3:26,27). Molech, also known as Milcom, was the national god of the Ammonites and was worshiped with human sacrifice. See 2 Chr 33:6,7. Molech, Milcom, and Chemosh may all be names for Nergal, the Mesopotamian god of death and the underworld. See the mini-article called "Canaanite Gods and Goddesses," p. 469.

23:14 *human bones:* This made the whole area unfit for the worship of any god (see the note at 23:4-6).

23:15 *Bethel:* See the note at 2:1-4. See also 1 Kgs 12:32,33.

23:21 *Passover . . . Book of the Covenant:* The "Passover" is related to the Hebrew word translated as "pass over" in Exodus 12:12,13,23,27. Passover was celebrated as a remembrance of how God saved the people from the final plague and acted to help them escape from slavery in Egypt. The kings of Israel and Judah were not faithful, and so Passover probably had not been celebrated properly since the time of the judges almost four hundred years earlier. See also the mini-article called "Passover and the Feast of Unleavened Bread," p. 2030, and the note at 22:9.

23:12 2 Kgs 21:5; 2 Chr 33:5.
23:16,17 1 Kgs 13:1,2,30-32.

[a] **10** Or *to make his son or daughter pass through* [b] **13** Hebrew *Milcom*

King Josiah Hears the Book of God's Law, an engraving by Schnorr von Carolsfeld, nineteenth century. After Josiah had been king of Judah for eighteen years, the high priest Hilkiah found the Book of the Law in the temple. He gave it to Shaphan, one of the king's highest officials, who read it to the king. When Josiah heard the Law, he realized that everyone in Judah had disobeyed it, and he tore his clothes in sorrow. He then had all the people of Judah gather at the temple so that they, too, could hear the Law. When he finished reading it to them, he asked everyone to promise to obey the LORD and follow his commands. (See 22:1—23:3.)

had any such Passover been observed. 23But in the eighteenth year
of King Josiah, this Passover was celebrated to the LORD in
Jerusalem.

24Furthermore, Josiah got rid of the mediums and spiritists,
the household gods, the idols and all the other detestable things
seen in Judah and Jerusalem. This he did to fulfill the requirements
of the law written in the book that Hilkiah the priest had discovered in the temple of the LORD. 25Neither before nor after Josiah
was there a king like him who turned to the LORD as he did—with
all his heart and with all his soul and with all his strength, in accordance with all the Law of Moses.

26Nevertheless, the LORD did not turn away from the heat of
his fierce anger, which burned against Judah because of all that
Manasseh had done to provoke him to anger. 27So the LORD said, "I
will remove Judah also from my presence as I removed Israel, and
I will reject Jerusalem, the city I chose, and this temple, about
which I said, 'There shall my Name be.'[a]"

[a]**27** 1 Kings 8:29

23:24 *detestable:* Often in the Bible the word "detestable" is used in connection with foreign gods and the worship of these gods. Its use is an indication that the worship of idols or other gods is the worst of sins. See also Deut 7:26.

23:24 *the law . . . the book:* See 22:3-13 and the note at 22:8.

23:27 2 Sam 7:13; 2 Kgs 21:10-15.

[28]As for the other events of Josiah's reign, and all he did, are
they not written in the book of the annals of the kings of Judah?
[29]While Josiah was king, Pharaoh Neco king of Egypt went
up to the Euphrates River to help the king of Assyria. King Josiah
marched out to meet him in battle, but Neco faced him and killed
him at Megiddo. [30]Josiah's servants brought his body in a chariot
from Megiddo to Jerusalem and buried him in his own tomb. And
the people of the land took Jehoahaz son of Josiah and anointed
him and made him king in place of his father.

THE FALL OF JERUSALEM

Following the death of Josiah, the fall of Jerusalem became inevitable.

Jehoahaz King of Judah

[31]Jehoahaz was twenty-three years old when he became king,
and he reigned in Jerusalem three months. His mother's name was
Hamutal daughter of Jeremiah; she was from Libnah. [32]He did evil
in the eyes of the LORD, just as his fathers had done. [33]Pharaoh
Neco put him in chains at Riblah in the land of Hamath[a] so that he
might not reign in Jerusalem, and he imposed on Judah a levy of
a hundred talents[b] of silver and a talent[c] of gold. [34]Pharaoh Neco
made Eliakim son of Josiah king in place of his father Josiah and
changed Eliakim's name to Jehoiakim. But he took Jehoahaz and
carried him off to Egypt, and there he died. [35]Jehoiakim paid
Pharaoh Neco the silver and gold he demanded. In order to do so,
he taxed the land and exacted the silver and gold from the people
of the land according to their assessments.

Jehoiakim King of Judah

[36]Jehoiakim was twenty-five years old when he became king,
and he reigned in Jerusalem eleven years. His mother's name was
Zebidah daughter of Pedaiah; she was from Rumah. [37]And he did
evil in the eyes of the LORD, just as his fathers had done.
24 During Jehoiakim's reign, Nebuchadnezzar king of Babylon
invaded the land, and Jehoiakim became his vassal for three years.
But then he changed his mind and rebelled against Nebuchadnezzar. [2]The LORD sent Babylonian,[d] Aramean, Moabite and Ammonite raiders against him. He sent them to destroy Judah, in
accordance with the word of the LORD proclaimed by his servants
the prophets. [3]Surely these things happened to Judah according to
the LORD's command, in order to remove them from his presence
because of the sins of Manasseh and all he had done, [4]including

---

[a]33 Hebrew; Septuagint (see also 2 Chron. 36:3) *Neco at Riblah in Hamath removed him* [b]33 That is, about 3 3/4 tons (about 3.4 metric tons) [c]33 That is, about 75 pounds (about 34 kilograms) [d]2 Or *Chaldean*

23:29 *killed:* At this time, King Neco of Egypt (609-595 B.C.) was fighting on the side of the Assyrians. He marched north to fight the Babylonian army and help Assyria keep control of its land. Since Josiah considered Assyria an enemy, he set out to stop Neco and the Egyptian troops. See also 2 Chr 35:20-27.

23:29 *Megiddo:* Megiddo was an important business and military center located on an important north-south trade route. Whoever controlled Megiddo also controlled the pass through the Carmel mountain range between the Valley of Jezreel and the Plain of Sharon.

23:31 *Jehoahaz:* Jehoahaz, Judah's sixteenth king, ruled for only three months in 609 B.C.

23:33 *Riblah:* Neco of Egypt set up his military headquarters at this important town in Aram on the Orontes River.

23:34-36 *Jehoiakim:* Neco of Egypt removed Jehoahaz from Judah's throne and took him prisoner (23:34). Then he set up Jehoiakim (609-598 B.C.) as Judah's seventeenth king. Now that Judah was controlled by Egypt, it faced a great threat of being attacked by Babylon, Egypt's enemy.

24:1 *Nebuchadnezzar king of Babylon . . . Jehoiakim . . . rebelled:* Nebuchadnezzar ruled Babylon from 605 to 562 B.C. He defeated the Egyptian army in 605 B.C. at the town of Carchemish on the Euphrates River in northern Aram. After that Babylon was in control of the territory of Judah. Against the prophet Jeremiah's advice, Jehoiakim rebelled against Babylon. This led to Nebuchadnezzar's first major invasion of Judah in 598 B.C. After Jehoiakim died, Nebuchadnezzar took Jehoiakim's son Jehoiachin into captivity along with many leaders of the land. He then put Zedekiah (24:15-18) on the throne as a puppet king and forced Judah to pay heavy taxes.

the shedding of innocent blood. For he had filled Jerusalem with
innocent blood, and the LORD was not willing to forgive.
[5]As for the other events of Jehoiakim's reign, and all he did,
are they not written in the book of the annals of the kings of
Judah? [6]Jehoiakim rested with his fathers. And Jehoiachin his son
succeeded him as king.
[7]The king of Egypt did not march out from his own country
again, because the king of Babylon had taken all his territory, from
the Wadi of Egypt to the Euphrates River.

Jehoiachin King of Judah

[8]Jehoiachin was eighteen years old when he became king,
and he reigned in Jerusalem three months. His mother's name was
Nehushta daughter of Elnathan; she was from Jerusalem. [9]He did
evil in the eyes of the LORD, just as his father had done.
[10]At that time the officers of Nebuchadnezzar king of Babylon advanced on Jerusalem and laid siege to it, [11]and Nebuchadnezzar himself came up to the city while his officers were besieging
it. [12]Jehoiachin king of Judah, his mother, his attendants, his nobles
and his officials all surrendered to him.
In the eighth year of the reign of the king of Babylon, he
took Jehoiachin prisoner. [13]As the LORD had declared, Nebuchadnezzar removed all the treasures from the temple of the LORD and
from the royal palace, and took away all the gold articles that
Solomon king of Israel had made for the temple of the LORD. [14]He
carried into exile all Jerusalem: all the officers and fighting men,
and all the craftsmen and artisans—a total of ten thousand. Only
the poorest people of the land were left.
[15]Nebuchadnezzar took Jehoiachin captive to Babylon. He
also took from Jerusalem to Babylon the king's mother, his wives,
his officials and the leading men of the land. [16]The king of Babylon also deported to Babylon the entire force of seven thousand
fighting men, strong and fit for war, and a thousand craftsmen and
artisans. [17]He made Mattaniah, Jehoiachin's uncle, king in his place
and changed his name to Zedekiah.

Zedekiah King of Judah

[18]Zedekiah was twenty-one years old when he became king,
and he reigned in Jerusalem eleven years. His mother's name was
Hamutal daughter of Jeremiah; she was from Libnah. [19]He did evil
in the eyes of the LORD, just as Jehoiakim had done. [20]It was
because of the LORD's anger that all this happened to Jerusalem
and Judah, and in the end he thrust them from his presence.

The Fall of Jerusalem

Now Zedekiah rebelled against the king of Babylon.
25 So in the ninth year of Zedekiah's reign, on the tenth day of
the tenth month, Nebuchadnezzar king of Babylon marched

24:7 *king of Babylon had taken all his territory:* See the note at 24:1.

24:8,9 *Jehoiachin . . . did evil:* Jehoiachin, Judah's eighteenth king, ruled for only three months in 598 B.C. He also disobeyed God by worshiping other gods.

24:12 *eighth year . . . took Jehoiachin prisoner:* These events took place in 597 B.C. Soon the nation and land of the Israelites would be ruled by non-Israelites. See also the note at 24:1 and Jer 22:24-30; 24:1-10; 29:1,2.

24:13 *As the LORD had declared:* The prophet Isaiah warned Judah's King Hezekiah that this would happen (20:16-18).

24:14-16 *carried into exile . . . officers and fighting men . . . craftsmen and artisans:* The Assyrians took most of the people they had conquered away as prisoners and replaced them with foreigners. The Babylonian strategy was different. They took the important leaders, skilled workers, and best soldiers, but allowed many others to stay in their homeland (see also the note at 25:12).

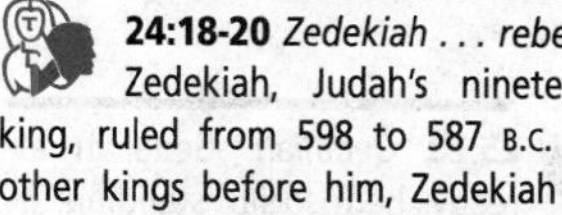

24:18-20 *Zedekiah . . . rebelled:* Zedekiah, Judah's nineteenth king, ruled from 598 to 587 B.C. Like other kings before him, Zedekiah also disobeyed the LORD, meaning he allowed the worship of idols in Judah. See also Jer 27:1-22; 28:1-17 and the note at 24:1.

Apries, King Neco's grandson, reclaimed the Egyptian crown from Babylonia in 588 B.C. He may have encouraged Zedekiah's rebellion. See also Ezek 17:15-18.

25:1 *tenth month . . . marched:* Zedekiah's treaty with Egypt caused Nebuchadnezzar to launch a second major attack against Judah (see also the note at 24:1). This happened in Tebeth, the tenth month of the Hebrew calendar, from about mid-December to mid-January, in 588 B.C. The Babylonians surrounded Jerusalem, causing starvation in the city (25:2,3). See also Jer 21:1-10; 34:1-5; Ezek 24:2.

25:3 *fourth month:* Tammuz, the fourth month of the Hebrew calendar, from about mid-June to mid-July.

25:4 *city wall was broken through:* Jerusalem was destroyed in 586 B.C. See also the note at 3:19 and the map on p. 2466.

25:5,6 *Jericho . . . Riblah:* See the notes at 2:1-4 and 23:33. See the map on p. 2467.

25:7 *put out his eyes:* The prophet Ezekiel had prophesied that Zedekiah would be taken to Babylon, but would not see it (Ezek 12:13).

25:12 *poorest people:* The Babylonians took only the important leaders and the strong citizens of a conquered nation (see the note at 24:14-16). The poor who were left behind were given property and leadership, which usually made them loyal to the Babylonian rulers.

25:17 *pomegranates:* The pomegranate fruit has red seeds surrounded by sweet-tasting pulp. See also Exod 28:33,34 and the illustration on p. 1277.

25:22 *Gedaliah:* Gedaliah already had social standing in Judah. His father (Ahikam) and grandfather (Shaphan) were trusted servants in Josiah's court (22:3-13). An identification seal found at Lachish indicates that Gedaliah was also an official in Zedekiah's court. His kind, peaceful nature won him support, but also may have led to his death. See 25:24-26 and Jer 40:5—41:11.

24:15 Ezek 17:12. **24:17** Jer 37:1; Ezek 17:13. **25:4** Ezek 33:21. **25:9** 1 Kgs 9:8. **25:13,14** 1 Kgs 7:15-26, 45; 2 Chr 3:15-17; 4:2-5,16.

against Jerusalem with his whole army. He encamped outside the
city and built siege works all around it. 2The city was kept under
siege until the eleventh year of King Zedekiah. 3By the ninth day of
the ⌞fourth⌟[a] month the famine in the city had become so severe
that there was no food for the people to eat. 4Then the city wall was
broken through, and the whole army fled at night through
the gate between the two walls near the king's garden, though the
Babylonians[b] were surrounding the city. They fled toward the
Arabah,[c] 5but the Babylonian[d] army pursued the king and overtook
him in the plains of Jericho. All his soldiers were separated from
him and scattered, 6and he was captured. He was taken to the king
of Babylon at Riblah, where sentence was pronounced on him.
7They killed the sons of Zedekiah before his eyes. Then they put out
his eyes, bound him with bronze shackles and took him to Babylon.

8On the seventh day of the fifth month, in the nineteenth year
of Nebuchadnezzar king of Babylon, Nebuzaradan commander of the
imperial guard, an official of the king of Babylon, came to Jerusalem.
9He set fire to the temple of the LORD, the royal palace and all the
houses of Jerusalem. Every important building he burned down. 10The
whole Babylonian army, under the commander of the imperial guard,
broke down the walls around Jerusalem. 11Nebuzaradan the commander
of the guard carried into exile the people who remained in
the city, along with the rest of the populace and those who had gone
over to the king of Babylon. 12But the commander left behind some of
the poorest people of the land to work the vineyards and fields.

13The Babylonians broke up the bronze pillars, the movable
stands and the bronze Sea that were at the temple of the LORD and
they carried the bronze to Babylon. 14They also took away the pots,
shovels, wick trimmers, dishes and all the bronze articles used
in the temple service. 15The commander of the imperial guard
took away the censers and sprinkling bowls—all that were made
of pure gold or silver.

16The bronze from the two pillars, the Sea and the movable
stands, which Solomon had made for the temple of the LORD, was
more than could be weighed. 17Each pillar was twenty-seven feet[e]
high. The bronze capital on top of one pillar was four and a half
feet[f] high and was decorated with a network and pomegranates of
bronze all around. The other pillar, with its network, was similar.

18The commander of the guard took as prisoners Seraiah the
chief priest, Zephaniah the priest next in rank and the three doorkeepers.
19Of those still in the city, he took the officer in charge of
the fighting men and five royal advisers. He also took the secretary
who was chief officer in charge of conscripting the people of the
land and sixty of his men who were found in the city. 20Neb-

[a]3 See Jer. 52:6. [b]4 Or *Chaldeans*; also in verses 13, 25 and 26 [c]4 Or *the Jordan Valley* [d]5 Or *Chaldean*; also in verses 10 and 24 [e]17 Hebrew *eighteen cubits* (about 8.1 meters) [f]17 Hebrew *three cubits* (about 1.3 meters)

uzaradan the commander took them all and brought them to the
king of Babylon at Riblah. [21]There at Riblah, in the land of
Hamath, the king had them executed.

So Judah went into captivity, away from her land.

[22]Nebuchadnezzar king of Babylon appointed Gedaliah son
of Ahikam, the son of Shaphan, to be over the people he had left
behind in Judah. [23]When all the army officers and their men heard
that the king of Babylon had appointed Gedaliah as governor, they
came to Gedaliah at Mizpah—Ishmael son of Nethaniah, Johanan
son of Kareah, Seraiah son of Tanhumeth the Netophathite, Jaazaniah the son of the Maacathite, and their men. [24]Gedaliah took an
oath to reassure them and their men. "Do not be afraid of the
Babylonian officials," he said. "Settle down in the land and serve
the king of Babylon, and it will go well with you."

[25]In the seventh month, however, Ishmael son of Nethaniah,
the son of Elishama, who was of royal blood, came with ten men
and assassinated Gedaliah and also the men of Judah and the
Babylonians who were with him at Mizpah. [26]At this, all the people from the least to the greatest, together with the army officers,
fled to Egypt for fear of the Babylonians.

Jehoiachin Released

[27]In the thirty-seventh year of the exile of Jehoiachin king of
Judah, in the year Evil-Merodach[a] became king of Babylon, he
released Jehoiachin from prison on the twenty-seventh day of the
twelfth month. [28]He spoke kindly to him and gave him a seat of
honor higher than those of the other kings who were with him in
Babylon. [29]So Jehoiachin put aside his prison clothes and for the
rest of his life ate regularly at the king's table. [30]Day by day the king
gave Jehoiachin a regular allowance as long as he lived.

[a]27 Also called *Amel-Marduk*

25:23 *Mizpah:* Gedaliah probably set up headquarters in a new city because Jerusalem was destroyed and because keeping Jerusalem as the capital may have been unacceptable to the ruler of Babylon. See also 1 Kgs 15:22.

25:27 *Jehoiachin . . . Evil-Merodach . . . Babylon:* Jehoiachin had been captured and taken to Babylon during Nebuchadnezzar's first invasion of Judah in 597 B.C. (see 24:10-12 and the note). Evil-Merodach was the son of Nebuchadnezzar and ruled Babylonia from 562 to 560 B.C. "Evil" was his actual name and is not a description of his personality.

25:27 *twelfth month:* Adar, the twelfth month of the Hebrew calendar, from about mid-February to mid-March.

25:29 *ate regularly at the king's table:* This was a high honor. The freeing of Jehoiachin provided the people of Judah with some hope for the future during the dark days of the exile in Babylon. See also the mini-article called "Exile," p. 1541.

25:22-24 Jer 40:7-9 **25:25** Jer 41:1-3. **25:26** Jer 43:5-7.

QUESTIONS ABOUT 2 KINGS 18:1—25:30

1. Why were the reforms of the good kings Hezekiah and Josiah not enough to turn away God's anger and prevent the destruction of Jerusalem by Babylon? (23:26,27)
2. Why do 1 and 2 KINGS generally criticize the kings of the northern kingdom (Israel) more severely than those of the southern kingdom (Judah)?
3. What did Hilkiah the priest find in the temple, and how did King Josiah respond to what he found? (22:3—23:23)
4. How much do you think national and world leaders are guided by their personal faith? How does your own faith affect your opinions about political leaders?
5. Why might Evil-Merodach's unexpected kindness toward Jehoiachin have raised the hopes of the first readers of 2 KINGS? (25:27-30)
6. Name two important things you learned while reading and studying 2 KINGS. What questions do you still have about the people, events, or key themes in the book?

1 CHRONICLES

Important stories are worth repeating. Although the story of David is told in 1 and 2 Samuel, the author of 1 Chronicles offers another viewpoint on the life of Israel's greatest king.

threshing floor: 1 CHRONICLES tells how David purchased a threshing floor from a Jebusite named Araunah. There, David wanted to make a sacrifice to the LORD and ask him to put an end to a plague the LORD had sent upon the Israelites for a sin David had committed (see 1 Chr 21:1—22:1). The LORD heard David's prayer and sent fire down to the altar, a sign that the LORD accepted David's sacrifice and agreed not to let any more people die. The author of CHRONICLES goes on to say that David decided this threshing floor was where a temple to the LORD should be built. And before he died, David gave his son Solomon instructions to do just that.

Threshing floors were important to farmers who raised grains like wheat and barley. At a threshing floor bundles of grain stalks were beaten, trampled, or crushed in order to separate the kernels from the outer husks (chaff). Often, threshing boards, like the one shown here, were dragged across the grain by oxen or donkeys. These heavy boards had bits of rock or metal on the bottom which helped them separate the husks and kernels. Sometimes workers would ride the threshing board in order to add weight and improve its efficiency. Threshing was done outdoors on a hard floor made of packed earth or rock. Often threshing floors were on hills so that the wind could more easily blow away the chaff.

WHAT MAKES 1 CHRONICLES SPECIAL?

The long family lists that begin 1 CHRONICLES make this book special. For the writer of 1 CHRONICLES and his audience, who had recently returned from exile in Babylon, these long family lists were very good news. The people were worried about their relationship with God, and they wondered if the promises God made to their ancestors still applied to them. The writer uses these lists to connect his own generation to ancestors going all the way back to Adam (1 Chr 1:1). For those who were worried that God had lost interest in them, the lists showed that Israel was still special to, and loved by, God.

WHY WAS 1 CHRONICLES WRITTEN?

FIRST CHRONICLES retells the story of King David, already familiar from 2 SAMUEL, from a more uplifting point of view. This is done by linking David to the ark of the covenant, worship in Jerusalem, and above all, to the careful preparations for the building of the temple. Some stories from 2 SAMUEL that might present David in an unfavorable light are left out. His adultery with Bathsheba, David's arranging of the death of her husband Uriah, and Nathan's criticism of David (2 Sam 11,12) are not included in the record of 1 CHRONICLES.

The purpose of presenting David's story in this way is to show his strengths rather than his human weaknesses, and to present his faith and devotion to God as a model for Israel's leaders. After God chose David and his family to lead Israel and build the temple, David is shown making the land safe, getting the temple site, organizing for worship there, and planning for the temple's construction. Later, David's son, Solomon, continues what his father began by actually building the temple (see 2 CHRONICLES).

WHAT'S THE STORY BEHIND THE SCENE?

For many years there were reasons to think that 1 and 2 CHRONICLES formed a single work with the books of EZRA and NEHEMIAH, with Ezra as the possible author. For example, the same decree of Cyrus appears at the ending of 2 CHRONICLES and at the beginning of EZRA (2 Chr 36:23; Ezra 1:1-4). Also, *1 Esdras,* an early Greek language version of the story, quotes from 2 Chronicles 35 and much of EZRA, indicating that these two books were once joined. In addition, 1 and 2 CHRONICLES are written in a style similar to that of

Ezra and Nehemiah, and they share many examples of similar vocabulary. Finally, 1 and 2 Chronicles, Ezra, and Nehemiah all share a strong interest in worship and lists.

Today, many scholars think that 1 and 2 Chronicles should be separated from Ezra and Nehemiah. While the overlap between the end of 2 Chronicles and the beginning of Ezra may show an original joining of these works, it could also represent an attempt to join two previously separate works. Similarly, it is not clear that *1 Esdras* represents an early stage in the relationship between 1 and 2 Chronicles and Ezra. It may instead indicate a stage after these books were connected for other reasons. Also, that these books are written in similar Hebrew is true. But that does not prove that the same person wrote them. Of greater importance, however, is the fact that these books are very different in significant ways. Differences include their handling of the identity of "Israel," the Sabbath, mixed marriages, God's promise that David's ancestors would always rule, the role of prophecy, the function of the Levites, and the importance of the exodus from Egypt.

How is 1 Chronicles constructed?

First Chronicles falls into two major sections. The first section, 1 Chronicles 1–9, makes use of long family lists to trace the history of God's people from Adam to the end of the Babylonian exile. The second section, 1 Chronicles 10–29, is devoted to retelling the story of David in terms of his contributions to the worship life of Israel.

From Adam to the exile (1:1—9:34)
- From Adam to Esau and Israel (1:1—2:1)
- Judah, David, and his family (2:2—4:23)
- The rest of the tribes of Israel (4:24—8:40)
- Lists of the families returning to Jerusalem (9:1-34)

David, founder of the temple (9:35—29:30)
- Introduction: The death of Saul (9:35—10:14)
- David rules in Jerusalem (11:1—17:27)
- David's wars (18:1—20:8)
- David plans the temple (21:1—29:30)

From Adam to the Exile

First Chronicles opens with nine chapters of genealogies that trace Israel's ancestors back to Adam. This shows that from the beginning of humanity Israel was chosen to be unique among the nations of the world. The lists emphasize the importance of David and the significance of the tribe of Levi and the role it plays in worship. The genealogies connect historical Israel (chapters 1–8) with the community at the time of the writer of 1 Chronicles (chapter 9).

FROM ADAM TO ESAU AND ISRAEL

This first genealogy charts the history of the Israelites from Adam, the father of humanity, to Abraham, the father of the faithful. The lists of Abraham's sons are arranged according to who their mothers were: Hagar (1:29-31); Keturah (1:32, 33); and Sarah (1:34). Abraham and Sarah's son Isaac is the father of Esau and Israel. Esau's family list includes the Edomite people (1:35-54), while Jacob's sons are the ancestors of the tribes of Israel (2:1, 2).

Historical Records From Adam to Abraham

To Noah's Sons

1 Adam, Seth, Enosh, 2 Kenan, Mahalalel, Jared, 3 Enoch, Methuselah, Lamech, Noah.

4 The sons of Noah:[a]
Shem, Ham and Japheth.

The Japhethites

5 The sons[b] of Japheth:
Gomer, Magog, Madai, Javan, Tubal, Meshech and Tiras.
6 The sons of Gomer:
Ashkenaz, Riphath[c] and Togarmah.
7 The sons of Javan:
Elishah, Tarshish, the Kittim and the Rodanim.

The Hamites

8 The sons of Ham:
Cush, Mizraim,[d] Put and Canaan.
9 The sons of Cush:
Seba, Havilah, Sabta, Raamah and Sabteca.
The sons of Raamah:
Sheba and Dedan.

[a]**4** Septuagint; Hebrew does not have *The sons of Noah:* [b]**5** *Sons* may mean *descendants* or *successors* or *nations*; also in verses 6-10, 17 and 20. [c]**6** Many Hebrew manuscripts and Vulgate (see also Septuagint and Gen. 10:3); most Hebrew manuscripts *Diphath* [d]**8** That is, Egypt; also in verse 11

1:1-4 *Adam . . . Noah:* Adam was the name of the first human God created. In Hebrew "Adam" and "man" are the same word. See also Gen 1:26; 5:1, 2; Ps 8:5-8.

Noah and his family were saved from the great flood that God sent to destroy the earth's living creatures as punishment for man's sinfulness (Gen 6–9). See also the mini-article called "Covenants (Agreements)," p. 386.

1:5-7 *Japheth . . . Rodanim:* The kingdoms of Japheth's descendants were located mostly in Asia Minor and the upper Euphrates River region. Elishah could refer to the island of Cyprus, whose ancient name was Alashia. Tarshish may refer to southern Spain, and the Rodanim may be the people of the island of Rhodes. See also Gen 10 and the map on p. 2462.

1:8-16 *sons of Ham . . . Hamathites:* The descendants of Ham, one of Noah's sons, ruled kingdoms located mainly in northeastern Africa and Canaan. The warrior Nimrod ruled city-states in Babylonia (another name for southern Mesopotamia) and Nineveh in Assyria, which was in the northern part of the Tigris and Euphrates River valleys. The Jebusites were located in and around Jerusalem, until King David drove them out and took over Jerusalem (2 Sam 5:6-9). The Amorites lived in the hill country of Canaan at the time the Israelites invaded (Num 21:21-35; Josh 2:10). The other Canaanite groups listed were located in city-states in Canaan. See the map on p. 2462 and the article called "The Ancient World: Peoples, Powers, and Politics," p. 919.

1:13 *Canaan:* In a curse, Noah declared that Canaan, Ham's son, would be his brothers' slave (Gen 9:18-27). This curse was fulfilled when Canaan (the land of Canaan's descendants) was taken over by the Israelites (descendants of Canaan's brother, Shem). It is the land that God promised to give to Abraham and his descendants (Gen 15:7; 17:7, 8; Exod 3:8).

[10] Cush was the father[a] of
Nimrod, who grew to be a mighty warrior on earth.
[11] Mizraim was the father of
the Ludites, Anamites, Lehabites, Naphtuhites, [12] Pathru-
sites, Casluhites (from whom the Philistines came) and
Caphtorites.
[13] Canaan was the father of
Sidon his firstborn,[b] and of the Hittites, [14] Jebusites, Amorites, Girgashites, [15] Hivites, Arkites, Sinites, [16] Arvadites,
Zemarites and Hamathites.

The Semites

[17] The sons of Shem:
Elam, Asshur, Arphaxad, Lud and Aram.
The sons of Aram[c]:
Uz, Hul, Gether and Meshech.
[18] Arphaxad was the father of Shelah,
and Shelah the father of Eber.
[19] Two sons were born to Eber:
One was named Peleg,[d] because in his time the earth was
divided; his brother was named Joktan.
[20] Joktan was the father of
Almodad, Sheleph, Hazarmaveth, Jerah, [21] Hadoram, Uzal,
Diklah, [22] Obal,[e] Abimael, Sheba, [23] Ophir, Havilah and
Jobab. All these were sons of Joktan.
[24] Shem, Arphaxad,[f] Shelah,
[25] Eber, Peleg, Reu,
[26] Serug, Nahor, Terah
[27] and Abram (that is, Abraham).

The Family of Abraham

[28] The sons of Abraham:
Isaac and Ishmael.

Descendants of Hagar

[29] These were their descendants:
Nebaioth the firstborn of Ishmael, Kedar, Adbeel, Mibsam,
[30] Mishma, Dumah, Massa, Hadad, Tema, [31] Jetur, Naphish
and Kedemah. These were the sons of Ishmael.

1:17-27 *sons of Shem . . . Abram (that is, Abraham):* Shem's descendants were called "Shemites," which became the modern word "Semites." The people known as Israel descended from the Hebrews (children of "Eber"), one group of ancient Semitic peoples. Elam was located just east of the mouth of the Tigris River, and Aram was an early name for Syria. Sheba was probably located in southwest Arabia. The queen of Sheba made a famous visit to King Solomon of Israel (1 Kgs 10:1-13; 2 Chr 9:1-12). Ophir, in southern Arabia or in Africa, was an important source of gold for Solomon's elaborate building projects (1 Kgs 9:27, 28; 10:11-13). See the map on p. 2462.

1:19 *Peleg:* In Hebrew, "Peleg" means "division." This division of the earth refers to Noah's sons being assigned tribal territories following the flood (Gen 10) and to how God scattered those tribes over all the earth by confusing their common language (Gen 11:1-9).

1:28-33 *Abraham . . . Eldaah:* God promised Abraham and his wife Sarah that they would have more descendants than could be counted (Gen 12:1-7; 17:1—18:15). See also the mini-article called "Abraham," p. 2254.

Isaac was the son God promised Abraham and Sarah (see also the note at 1:34-37).

Ishmael, the son of Abraham and Sarah's servant Hagar, was actually Abraham's oldest son. Ancient laws allowed for a man to give a greater share of his property to his oldest son (see also Deut 21:15-17). Abraham gave most of his property to Isaac, his son with Sarah, even though he wasn't the oldest. God blessed Ishmael, however, by making him the ancestor of twelve tribes (Gen 17:20; 25:12-16), just as Israel was later organized into twelve tribes (Gen 49:1-28; Josh 13:14—19:51).

Abraham and Keturah's descendants were the first ancestors of certain Arabic tribes, including the Midianite desert wanderers who were the tribe of Moses' wife and her father Jethro (Exod 2:15-22; 18:1; Num 31).

[a] **10** *Father* may mean *ancestor* or *predecessor* or *founder*; also in verses 11, 13, 18 and 20. [b] **13** Or *of the Sidonians, the foremost* [c] **17** One Hebrew manuscript and some Septuagint manuscripts (see also Gen. 10:23); most Hebrew manuscripts do not have this line. [d] **19** *Peleg* means *division.* [e] **22** Some Hebrew manuscripts and Syriac (see also Gen. 10:28); most Hebrew manuscripts *Ebal* [f] **24** Hebrew; some Septuagint manuscripts *Arphaxad, Cainan* (see also note at Gen. 11:10)

1:34 *Isaac . . . Israel:* Isaac married Rebekah, and together they had twin sons, Esau and Jacob. God later gave Jacob the new name "Israel" (Gen 32:22-28), which the author of 1 CHRONICLES prefers to use. Jacob tricked his older brother Esau out of his birthright and, with his mother's help, also tricked his father into giving him the special blessing that was meant for Esau. See also the mini-article called "Birthright," p. 80.

Descendants of Keturah

32 The sons born to Keturah, Abraham's concubine:
Zimran, Jokshan, Medan, Midian, Ishbak and Shuah.
The sons of Jokshan:
Sheba and Dedan.
33 The sons of Midian:
Ephah, Epher, Hanoch, Abida and Eldaah.
All these were descendants of Keturah.

Descendants of Sarah

34 Abraham was the father of Isaac.
The sons of Isaac:
Esau and Israel.

GENEALOGIES IN THE BIBLE

People in ancient Israel placed great importance on who their family's ancestors were. The Bible includes genealogies (family lists) in order to show where certain families came from and why they were important. GENESIS lists the male head of each family from Adam to Noah (Gen 5:1-32), from Noah through the descendants of his three sons, Japheth, Ham, and Shem, and from Shem to Abraham (Gen 11:10-26). Isaac was the son God promised to give Abraham and Sarah. GENESIS tells the story of Isaac's descendants, but the genealogy in 25:12-18 is a reminder that Abraham also had a son named Ishmael with Hagar, Sarah's slave. The names listed in this passage are based on village names in areas surrounding Canaan, but are not really part of the land promised to Abraham and his descendants. Many of the names included in the lists from GENESIS are of tribes or places rather than individuals (for example, see Gen 10). Even so, they show how God's purpose works through the historical experiences of groups as well as of individuals.

The only proper family line for Israel's priests was from Levi (Exod 6:16-25). The long list of worthy ancestors of Israel's first king, Saul, is given in 1 Chronicles 1:1—9:44. Those who wanted to be priests or kings had to show they were descended from these families. After the Jews returned from exile in Babylon, beginning in about 538 B.C., family lists were emphasized for purity reasons. Lists from EZRA show which families could serve as priests and temple workers and which were questionable (Ezra 2). Ezra 10 lists those who wanted to remain priests but first had to agree to divorce their foreign wives (10:18-44).

Israel's future kings were to be descendants of King David (2 Sam 7:16; Isa 11:1-5; Ps 89:3, 4). Both of the genealogies of Jesus (Matt 1:1-17; Luke 3:23-38) link him with David, although they differ in details in their lists. MATTHEW emphasizes Jesus as the fulfillment of God's promises to Israel, so his list begins with Abraham, the father of God's people (Gen 12:1-3). Then his list moves through David, Israel's model king, and through leaders of the Jewish people when they returned from exile (Matt 1:17). The list in LUKE goes backwards beginning with Joseph, Jesus' legal father, through David the king, Jacob, Abraham, and all the way back to Adam, the first human. This line shows that Jesus was important, not only for Israel, but for the whole human race.

Esau's Sons

[35]The sons of Esau:
Eliphaz, Reuel, Jeush, Jalam and Korah.
[36]The sons of Eliphaz:
Teman, Omar, Zepho,[a] Gatam and Kenaz;
by Timna: Amalek.[b]
[37]The sons of Reuel:
Nahath, Zerah, Shammah and Mizzah.

The People of Seir in Edom

[38]The sons of Seir:
Lotan, Shobal, Zibeon, Anah, Dishon, Ezer and Dishan.
[39]The sons of Lotan:
Hori and Homam. Timna was Lotan's sister.
[40]The sons of Shobal:
Alvan,[c] Manahath, Ebal, Shepho and Onam.
The sons of Zibeon:
Aiah and Anah.
[41]The son of Anah:
Dishon.
The sons of Dishon:
Hemdan,[d] Eshban, Ithran and Keran.
[42]The sons of Ezer:
Bilhan, Zaavan and Akan.[e]
The sons of Dishan[f]:
Uz and Aran.

The Rulers of Edom

[43]These were the kings who reigned in Edom before any
Israelite king reigned[g]:
Bela son of Beor, whose city was named Dinhabah.
[44]When Bela died, Jobab son of Zerah from Bozrah succeeded
him as king.
[45]When Jobab died, Husham from the land of the Temanites
succeeded him as king.
[46]When Husham died, Hadad son of Bedad, who defeated
Midian in the country of Moab, succeeded him as king.
His city was named Avith.
[47]When Hadad died, Samlah from Masrekah succeeded him as
king.

1:38-54 *Seir . . . Edom:* The land of Edom, or Seir, was south and southeast of the Dead Sea (see the map on p. 2465). The Edomites were descended from Esau (Gen 36:1-43). The descendants of Jacob (the Israelites) often battled with the Edomites (Num 20:14-21; Obad 9,10).

---

[a]**36** Many Hebrew manuscripts, some Septuagint manuscripts and Syriac (see also Gen. 36:11); most Hebrew manuscripts *Zephi* [b]**36** Some Septuagint manuscripts (see also Gen. 36:12); Hebrew *Gatam, Kenaz, Timna and Amalek* [c]**40** Many Hebrew manuscripts and some Septuagint manuscripts (see also Gen. 36:23); most Hebrew manuscripts *Alian* [d]**41** Many Hebrew manuscripts and some Septuagint manuscripts (see also Gen. 36:26); most Hebrew manuscripts *Hamran* [e]**42** Many Hebrew and Septuagint manuscripts (see also Gen. 36:27); most Hebrew manuscripts *Zaavan, Jaakan* [f]**42** Hebrew *Dishon,* a variant of *Dishan* [g]**43** Or *before an Israelite king reigned over them*

Judah, stained glass window by Marc Chagall, 1960. Judah, the fourth son of Jacob, was called a lion when Jacob blessed him (Gen 49:9). This stained glass window depicts the "Lion of Judah" against the walls of Jerusalem. The hands holding a crown are a traditional gesture of blessing and a sign of the kingship of Judah and his descendants, David and Solomon.

48 When Samlah died, Shaul from Rehoboth on the river[a] succeeded him as king.
49 When Shaul died, Baal-Hanan son of Acbor succeeded him as king.
50 When Baal-Hanan died, Hadad succeeded him as king. His city was named Pau,[b] and his wife's name was Mehetabel daughter of Matred, the daughter of Me-Zahab.
51 Hadad also died.

[a]**48** Possibly the Euphrates [b]**50** Many Hebrew manuscripts, some Septuagint manuscripts, Vulgate and Syriac (see also Gen. 36:39); most Hebrew manuscripts *Pai*

The chiefs of Edom were:
Timna, Alvah, Jetheth, 52 Oholibamah, Elah, Pinon,
53 Kenaz, Teman, Mibzar, 54 Magdiel and Iram. These were
the chiefs of Edom.

Israel's Sons

2 These were the sons of Israel:
Reuben, Simeon, Levi, Judah, Issachar, Zebulun, 2 Dan,
Joseph, Benjamin, Naphtali, Gad and Asher.

JUDAH, DAVID, AND HIS FAMILY

All of the sons of Israel are listed (2:1, 2), but Judah's genealogy list comes first and is longer than that of the other tribes, because both King David and most of the audience of 1 CHRONICLES were descendants of Judah.

Judah

To Hezron's Sons

3 The sons of Judah:
Er, Onan and Shelah. These three were born to him by a
Canaanite woman, the daughter of Shua. Er, Judah's firstborn, was wicked in the LORD's sight; so the LORD put him
to death. 4 Tamar, Judah's daughter-in-law, bore him Perez
and Zerah. Judah had five sons in all.

5 The sons of Perez:
Hezron and Hamul.
6 The sons of Zerah:
Zimri, Ethan, Heman, Calcol and Darda[a]—five in all.
7 The son of Carmi:
Achar,[b] who brought trouble on Israel by violating the ban
on taking devoted things.[c]
8 The son of Ethan:
Azariah.
9 The sons born to Hezron were:
Jerahmeel, Ram and Caleb.[d]

From Ram Son of Hezron

10 Ram was the father of
Amminadab, and Amminadab the father of Nahshon, the
leader of the people of Judah. 11 Nahshon was the father of

[a]6 Many Hebrew manuscripts, some Septuagint manuscripts and Syriac (see also 1 Kings 4:31); most Hebrew manuscripts *Dara* [b]7 *Achar* means *trouble*; *Achar* is called *Achan* in Joshua. [c]7 The Hebrew term refers to the irrevocable giving over of things or persons to the LORD, often by totally destroying them.
[d]9 Hebrew *Kelubai,* a variant of *Caleb*

2:1,2 *Israel . . . Asher:* Jacob, the son of Isaac and grandson of Abraham, was the Israelites' third great ancestor. His name was changed to Israel when he struggled with God at Peniel near the Jabbok River (Gen 32:22-32). In Hebrew, one meaning of "Israel" is "he struggles" or "a man who wrestles with God." See also the note at 1:34–37.

Each of the twelve tribes of Israel traces its beginning to one of Jacob's twelve sons. See also the mini-article called "Israel," p. 264, and the chart "Jacob's Children and their Mothers" on p. 99.

2:3 *Judah:* The fourth son born to Jacob and Leah (Gen 29:35). The tribe of Judah eventually became the most important among the tribes of Israel (Gen 49:8-10). Judah's descendants included King David and Jesus (Matt 1:1-17; Luke 3:23-33).

2:3 *wicked in the LORD's sight:* This may refer to Er worshiping other gods.

2:9-15 *Hezron . . . David:* The writer of 1 CHRONICLES considers Hezron to be the most important of Judah's clans because David's ancestry is traced to Hezron's son, Ram.

2:7 Josh 7:1-26.

2:2 *Gilead:* This area was east of the Jordan River between the Jabbok River in the south and the Yarmuk River in the north. See the map on p. 2467.

Salmon,[a] Salmon the father of Boaz, 12 Boaz the father of
Obed and Obed the father of Jesse.

13 Jesse was the father of
Eliab his firstborn; the second son was Abinadab, the third
Shimea, 14 the fourth Nethanel, the fifth Raddai, 15 the sixth
Ozem and the seventh David. 16 Their sisters were Zeruiah
and Abigail. Zeruiah's three sons were Abishai, Joab and
Asahel. 17 Abigail was the mother of Amasa, whose father
was Jether the Ishmaelite.

Caleb Son of Hezron

18 Caleb son of Hezron had children by his wife Azubah (and
by Jerioth). These were her sons: Jesher, Shobab and
Ardon. 19 When Azubah died, Caleb married Ephrath, who
bore him Hur. 20 Hur was the father of Uri, and Uri the
father of Bezalel.

21 Later, Hezron lay with the daughter of Makir the father of
Gilead (he had married her when he was sixty years old),
and she bore him Segub. 22 Segub was the father of Jair,
who controlled twenty-three towns in Gilead. 23 (But Geshur and Aram captured Havvoth Jair,[b] as well as Kenath
with its surrounding settlements—sixty towns.) All these
were descendants of Makir the father of Gilead.

24 After Hezron died in Caleb Ephrathah, Abijah the wife of
Hezron bore him Ashhur the father[c] of Tekoa.

Jerahmeel Son of Hezron

25 The sons of Jerahmeel the firstborn of Hezron:
Ram his firstborn, Bunah, Oren, Ozem and[d] Ahijah. 26 Jerahmeel had another wife, whose name was Atarah; she
was the mother of Onam.

27 The sons of Ram the firstborn of Jerahmeel:
Maaz, Jamin and Eker.

28 The sons of Onam:
Shammai and Jada.

The sons of Shammai:
Nadab and Abishur.

29 Abishur's wife was named Abihail, who bore him Ahban and
Molid.

30 The sons of Nadab:
Seled and Appaim. Seled died without children.

31 The son of Appaim:
Ishi, who was the father of Sheshan.

---

[a] **11** Septuagint (see also Ruth 4:21); Hebrew *Salma* [b] **23** Or *captured the settlements of Jair* [c] **24** *Father* may mean *civic leader* or *military leader*; also in verses 42, 45, 49-52 and possibly elsewhere. [d] **25** Or *Oren and Ozem, by*

Sheshan was the father of Ahlai.
[32]The sons of Jada, Shammai's brother:
Jether and Jonathan. Jether died without children.
[33]The sons of Jonathan:
Peleth and Zaza.
These were the descendants of Jerahmeel.
[34]Sheshan had no sons—only daughters.
He had an Egyptian servant named Jarha. [35]Sheshan gave
his daughter in marriage to his servant Jarha, and she bore
him Attai.
[36]Attai was the father of Nathan,
Nathan the father of Zabad,
[37]Zabad the father of Ephlal,
Ephlal the father of Obed,
[38]Obed the father of Jehu,
Jehu the father of Azariah,
[39]Azariah the father of Helez,
Helez the father of Eleasah,
[40]Eleasah the father of Sismai,
Sismai the father of Shallum,
[41]Shallum the father of Jekamiah,
and Jekamiah the father of Elishama.

The Clans of Caleb

[42]The sons of Caleb the brother of Jerahmeel:
Mesha his firstborn, who was the father of Ziph, and his
son Mareshah,[a] who was the father of Hebron.
[43]The sons of Hebron:
Korah, Tappuah, Rekem and Shema. [44]Shema was the
father of Raham, and Raham the father of Jorkeam.
Rekem was the father of Shammai. [45]The son of Shammai
was Maon, and Maon was the father of Beth Zur.
[46]Caleb's concubine Ephah was the mother of Haran, Moza
and Gazez. Haran was the father of Gazez.
[47]The sons of Jahdai:
Regem, Jotham, Geshan, Pelet, Ephah and Shaaph.
[48]Caleb's concubine Maacah was the mother of Sheber and
Tirhanah. [49]She also gave birth to Shaaph the father of
Madmannah and to Sheva the father of Macbenah and
Gibea. Caleb's daughter was Acsah. [50]These were the
descendants of Caleb.

The sons of Hur the firstborn of Ephrathah:
Shobal the father of Kiriath Jearim, [51]Salma the father of
Bethlehem, and Hareph the father of Beth Gader.
[52]The descendants of Shobal the father of Kiriath Jearim were:

[a]**42** The meaning of the Hebrew for this phrase is uncertain.

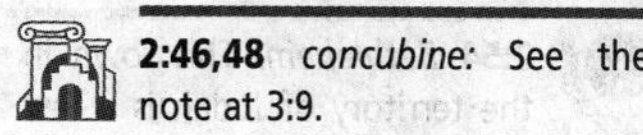

2:46,48 *concubine:* See the note at 3:9.

Haroeh, half the Manahathites, 53 and the clans of Kiriath
Jearim: the Ithrites, Puthites, Shumathites and Mishraites.
From these descended the Zorathites and Eshtaolites.

54 The descendants of Salma:
Bethlehem, the Netophathites, Atroth Beth Joab, half the
Manahathites, the Zorites, 55 and the clans of scribes[a] who
lived at Jabez: the Tirathites, Shimeathites and Sucathites.
These are the Kenites who came from Hammath, the
father of the house of Recab.[b]

The Sons of David

3 These were the sons of David born to him in Hebron:
The firstborn was Amnon the son of Ahinoam of Jezreel;
the second, Daniel the son of Abigail of Carmel;
2 the third, Absalom the son of Maacah daughter of Talmai
king of Geshur;
the fourth, Adonijah the son of Haggith;
3 the fifth, Shephatiah the son of Abital;
and the sixth, Ithream, by his wife Eglah.
4 These six were born to David in Hebron, where he reigned
seven years and six months.
David reigned in Jerusalem thirty-three years, 5 and these were the
children born to him there:
Shammua,[c] Shobab, Nathan and Solomon. These four
were by Bathsheba[d] daughter of Ammiel. 6 There were also
Ibhar, Elishua,[e] Eliphelet, 7 Nogah, Nepheg, Japhia, 8 Elishama, Eliada and Eliphelet—nine in all. 9 All these were the
sons of David, besides his sons by his concubines. And
Tamar was their sister.

The Kings of Judah

10 Solomon's son was Rehoboam,
Abijah his son,
Asa his son,
Jehoshaphat his son,
11 Jehoram[f] his son,
Ahaziah his son,
Joash his son,
12 Amaziah his son,
Azariah his son,
Jotham his son,
13 Ahaz his son,

[a]55 Or *of the Sopherites* [b]55 Or *father of Beth Recab* [c]5 Hebrew *Shimea*, a variant of *Shammua* [d]5 One Hebrew manuscript and Vulgate (see also Septuagint and 2 Samuel 11:3); most Hebrew manuscripts *Bathshua* [e]6 Two Hebrew manuscripts (see also 2 Samuel 5:15 and 1 Chron. 14:5); most Hebrew manuscripts *Elishama* [f]11 Hebrew *Joram*, a variant of *Jehoram*

2:54 *Bethlehem:* This town in the territory of Judah is a few miles south of Jerusalem (see the map on p. 2464). Bethlehem is where Jesus would be born (Luke 2:4-7).

2:55 *Kenites:* The Kenites originally were not part of the Israelite people, but later many became part of Judah (Judg 1:16).

3:1,2 *David ... Absalom ... Adonijah:* David, the most famous king Israel ever had, was king from about 1010 to 970 B.C. Many of the people of Israel hoped that one of his descendants would always be their king. See also the mini-article called "David," p. 1028.

The tragic story of David and his son Absalom, who died in battle fighting against his father, is found in 2 Samuel 13–18. Adonijah attempted to take over David's kingship just prior to David's death but lost it to Solomon, his younger brother, who later had him killed (1 Kgs 1; 2:13-25).

3:1-4 *Hebron ... Jerusalem:* Hebron was David's capital during the seven-and-a-half years he was king of Judah but not yet king of all Israel. Hebron is located about twenty miles southwest of Jerusalem (see the map on p. 2465). Archaeological evidence shows that the city has been continuously occupied since about 1600 B.C. (see also Num 13:22). Hebron was also where Abram settled after he and Lot separated (Gen 13:14-18), and where Absalom began his revolt against his father, David (2 Sam 15:7-12). See also 2 Sam 5:4, 5; 1 Kgs 2:10, 11; 1 Chr 29:27.

Jerusalem is also known as "the City of David." When David conquered Jerusalem and brought the ark of the covenant to that city, he made it the political and religious center of the Israelite nation. See the mini-article called "Jerusalem," p. 574.

3:5 *Solomon ... Bathsheba:* Solomon, David and Bathsheba's second son (2 Sam 12:24), followed his father as king of Israel. Solomon built the temple at Jerusalem, majestic palaces, and strong forts.

Hezekiah his son,
Manasseh his son,
14 Amon his son,
Josiah his son.
15 The sons of Josiah:
Johanan the firstborn,
Jehoiakim the second son,
Zedekiah the third,
Shallum the fourth.
16 The successors of Jehoiakim:
Jehoiachin[a] his son,
and Zedekiah.

The Royal Line After the Exile

17 The descendants of Jehoiachin the captive:
Shealtiel his son, 18 Malkiram, Pedaiah, Shenazzar, Jekamiah, Hoshama and Nedabiah.
19 The sons of Pedaiah:
Zerubbabel and Shimei.
The sons of Zerubbabel:
Meshullam and Hananiah.
Shelomith was their sister.
20 There were also five others:
Hashubah, Ohel, Berekiah, Hasadiah and Jushab-Hesed.
21 The descendants of Hananiah:
Pelatiah and Jeshaiah, and the sons of Rephaiah, of Arnan, of Obadiah and of Shecaniah.
22 The descendants of Shecaniah:
Shemaiah and his sons:
Hattush, Igal, Bariah, Neariah and Shaphat—six in all.
23 The sons of Neariah:
Elioenai, Hizkiah and Azrikam—three in all.
24 The sons of Elioenai:
Hodaviah, Eliashib, Pelaiah, Akkub, Johanan, Delaiah and Anani—seven in all.

Other Clans of Judah

4 The descendants of Judah:
Perez, Hezron, Carmi, Hur and Shobal.
2 Reaiah son of Shobal was the father of Jahath, and Jahath the father of Ahumai and Lahad. These were the clans of the Zorathites.
3 These were the sons[b] of Etam:
Jezreel, Ishma and Idbash. Their sister was named

[a]16 Hebrew *Jeconiah,* a variant of *Jehoiachin*; also in verse 17 [b]3 Some Septuagint manuscripts (see also Vulgate); Hebrew *father*

3:9 *besides his sons by his concubines:* In the ancient world, an important man, such as a king, might have many wives. Some wives were considered true wives, meaning they and their children had special privileges and their children were entitled to inherit a portion of the husband's wealth. Other "wives" were known as concubines. They were legally bound to their "husband," but they and their children did not have the same privileges. They were more like servants who could be bought and sold or easily sent away.

3:10-16 *Rehoboam . . . Zedekiah:* Rehoboam was the first and Zedekiah the last of Judah's kings after the division of Israel into the northern kingdom of Israel and the southern kingdom of Judah. They and the other kings named in these verses ruled Judah from 931 to 587 B.C. See also the article called "From Joshua to the Exile: The People of Israel in the Promised Land," p. 924.

3:17-19 *Shealtiel . . . Zerubbabel:* Elsewhere, Zerubbabel is called the son of Shealtiel (Ezra 3:2). The list here is of David's descendants following Israel's exile in Babylonia. After the people returned to Judah beginning in 538 B.C., Zerubbabel served as governor in Jerusalem and led the people in beginning the work of rebuilding the temple (Hag 1, 2).

4:1 *Judah:* See the note at 2:3 (Judah).

Jabez cried out to the God of Israel, "Oh, that you would bless me and enlarge my territory! Let your hand be with me, and keep me from harm so that I will be free from pain."
1 Chr 4:10

4:4,5 *Bethlehem . . . Tekoa:* See the note at 2:54. "Father" may refer to a leader of a town rather than to the biological father of a person. The prophet Amos came from Tekoa (Amos 1:1), a village in the hill country near Bethlehem.

4:9 *Jabez . . . pain:* In Hebrew "Jabez" sounds like "pain."

4:17,18 *Mered:* Mered must have been a person of some importance to marry the daughter of an Egyptian king.

Hazzelelponi. 4 Penuel was the father of Gedor, and Ezer
the father of Hushah.

These were the descendants of Hur, the firstborn of
Ephrathah and father[a] of Bethlehem.

5 Ashhur the father of Tekoa had two wives, Helah and Naarah.
6 Naarah bore him Ahuzzam, Hepher, Temeni and Haa-
hashtari. These were the descendants of Naarah.
7 The sons of Helah:
Zereth, Zohar, Ethnan, 8 and Koz, who was the father of
Anub and Hazzobebah and of the clans of Aharhel son of
Harum.

9 Jabez was more honorable than his brothers. His mother
had named him Jabez,[b] saying, "I gave birth to him in pain."
10 Jabez cried out to the God of Israel, "Oh, that you would bless
me and enlarge my territory! Let your hand be with me, and keep
me from harm so that I will be free from pain." And God granted
his request.

11 Kelub, Shuhah's brother, was the father of Mehir, who was the
father of Eshton. 12 Eshton was the father of Beth Rapha,
Paseah and Tehinnah the father of Ir Nahash.[c] These were
the men of Recah.

13 The sons of Kenaz:
Othniel and Seraiah.
The sons of Othniel:
Hathath and Meonothai.[d] 14 Meonothai was the father of
Ophrah.
Seraiah was the father of Joab,
the father of Ge Harashim.[e] It was called this because its
people were craftsmen.
15 The sons of Caleb son of Jephunneh:
Iru, Elah and Naam.
The son of Elah:
Kenaz.
16 The sons of Jehallelel:
Ziph, Ziphah, Tiria and Asarel.
17 The sons of Ezrah:
Jether, Mered, Epher and Jalon. One of Mered's wives gave
birth to Miriam, Shammai and Ishbah the father of Eshte-
moa. 18 (His Judean wife gave birth to Jered the father of
Gedor, Heber the father of Soco, and Jekuthiel the father
of Zanoah.) These were the children of Pharaoh's daughter Bithiah, whom Mered had married.

[a]**4** *Father* may mean *civic leader* or *military leader*; also in verses 12, 14, 17, 18 and possibly elsewhere. [b]**9** *Jabez* sounds like the Hebrew for *pain.* [c]**12** Or *of the city of Nahash* [d]**13** Some Septuagint manuscripts and Vulgate; Hebrew does not have *and Meonothai.* [e]**14** *Ge Harashim* means *valley of craftsmen.*

19 The sons of Hodiah's wife, the sister of Naham:
the father of Keilah the Garmite, and Eshtemoa the Maacathite.
20 The sons of Shimon:
Amnon, Rinnah, Ben-Hanan and Tilon.
The descendants of Ishi:
Zoheth and Ben-Zoheth.
21 The sons of Shelah son of Judah:
Er the father of Lecah, Laadah the father of Mareshah and the clans of the linen workers at Beth Ashbea, [22]Jokim, the men of Cozeba, and Joash and Saraph, who ruled in Moab and Jashubi Lehem. (These records are from ancient times.) [23]They were the potters who lived at Netaim and Gederah; they stayed there and worked for the king.

THE REST OF THE TRIBES OF ISRAEL

Because the other tribes are less important to the writer of 1 Chronicles than Judah, their genealogies are shorter. Levi (chapter 6), however, receives special attention because those who served in the "house of God" came from his tribe (6:48), and the priests came from Aaron's line within the tribe (6:49).

Simeon

24 The descendants of Simeon:
Nemuel, Jamin, Jarib, Zerah and Shaul;
25 Shallum was Shaul's son, Mibsam his son and Mishma his son.
26 The descendants of Mishma:
Hammuel his son, Zaccur his son and Shimei his son.
27 Shimei had sixteen sons and six daughters, but his brothers
did not have many children; so their entire clan did not become as
numerous as the people of Judah. [28]They lived in Beersheba,
Moladah, Hazar Shual, [29]Bilhah, Ezem, Tolad, [30]Bethuel, Hormah,
Ziklag, [31]Beth Marcaboth, Hazar Susim, Beth Biri and Shaaraim.
These were their towns until the reign of David. [32]Their surrounding villages were Etam, Ain, Rimmon, Token and Ashan—five
towns— [33]and all the villages around these towns as far as
Baalath.[a] These were their settlements. And they kept a genealogical record.

34 Meshobab, Jamlech, Joshah son of Amaziah, [35]Joel, Jehu son
of Joshibiah, the son of Seraiah, the son of Asiel, [36]also Elioenai, Jaakobah, Jeshohaiah, Asaiah, Adiel, Jesimiel, Benaiah,
[37]and Ziza son of Shiphi, the son of Allon, the son of Jedaiah,
the son of Shimri, the son of Shemaiah.

[a]**33** Some Septuagint manuscripts (see also Joshua 19:8); Hebrew *Baal*

4:21 *linen workers:* Cloth was woven on a loom in a manner still used today. Linen from the flax plant, wool from sheep and goats, and camel hair were the most common fibers used (Exod 35:25, 26; Prov 31:13, 19,24).

4:22 *Moab:* Moab was located to the east of the Dead Sea. The Moabites were enemies of Israel (Judg 3:12-30; 1 Sam 14:47, 48). Omri, Israel's sixth king, conquered Moab. Moab remained under Israel's control for forty years, until it rebelled during the reign of Ahaziah, Israel's eighth king, in 853 B.C. See the map on p. 2465.

4:28-33 *They lived in . . . These were their settlements:* The Simeon tribe, descended from Jacob's second son (Gen 29:31-33), lost its normal position of leadership among the tribes because of the evil actions of Simeon and his brother Levi (Gen 34:25-30; 49:5-7). The area described here is immediately southwest of Judah. Eventually the Simeon tribe was, for all practical purposes, absorbed into Judah. See Josh 19:2-8 and the map on p. 2464.

4:39-42 *Gedor . . . Seir:* Gedor is possibly Gerar on the Philistine border and was known for its rich pasturelands.

Seir is another name for Edom, a land directly south of the Dead Sea. See the note at 1:38-54 (Seir) and the map on p. 2465.

4:40 *Hamites:* See the note at 1:8-16.

5:1 *firstborn of Israel:* See the note at 2:1,2.

5:1 *rights as firstborn:* The firstborn son inherited the largest amount of property and leadership of the family. See Deut 21:15-17 and the mini-article called "Birthright," p. 80. Because Reuben sinned (Gen 35:22), he lost his birthright to Joseph and his descendants (Gen 49:3,4; Gen 48:19,20).

5:2 *a ruler came from him:* This is a reference to David. See also Gen 49:8-10.

5:6 *Tiglath-Pileser king of Assyria:* From 745 to 727 B.C., Assyria threatened and invaded the northern kingdom of Israel. The event in this verse probably took place around 733 B.C. See also the map on p. 2468 and the mini-article called "Assyria," p. 711.

5:9 *Euphrates River . . . Gilead:* The Euphrates River was one of the four rivers flowing out of Eden (Gen 2:14). See the map on p. 2462. For Gilead, see the note at 2:22 and the map on p. 2467.

5:10 *Hagrites:* The Hagrites were nomads from northern Arabia. See the map on p. 2464 and the mini-article called "Nomads (Wandering Herders)," p. 124.

5:6 2 Kgs 15:29.

[38]The men listed above by name were leaders of their clans.
Their families increased greatly, [39]and they went to the outskirts of
Gedor to the east of the valley in search of pasture for their flocks.
[40]They found rich, good pasture, and the land was spacious, peaceful and quiet. Some Hamites had lived there formerly.
[41]The men whose names were listed came in the days of
Hezekiah king of Judah. They attacked the Hamites in their
dwellings and also the Meunites who were there and completely
destroyed[a] them, as is evident to this day. Then they settled in their
place, because there was pasture for their flocks. [42]And five hundred of these Simeonites, led by Pelatiah, Neariah, Rephaiah and
Uzziel, the sons of Ishi, invaded the hill country of Seir. [43]They
killed the remaining Amalekites who had escaped, and they have
lived there to this day.

Reuben

5 The sons of Reuben the firstborn of Israel (he was the firstborn, but when he defiled his father's marriage bed, his rights as
firstborn were given to the sons of Joseph son of Israel; so he could
not be listed in the genealogical record in accordance with his
birthright, [2]and though Judah was the strongest of his brothers
and a ruler came from him, the rights of the firstborn belonged to
Joseph)— [3]the sons of Reuben the firstborn of Israel:
Hanoch, Pallu, Hezron and Carmi.
[4]The descendants of Joel:
Shemaiah his son, Gog his son,
Shimei his son, [5]Micah his son,
Reaiah his son, Baal his son,
[6]and Beerah his son, whom Tiglath-Pileser[b] king of
Assyria took into exile. Beerah was a leader of the Reubenites.
[7]Their relatives by clans, listed according to their genealogical
records:
Jeiel the chief, Zechariah, [8]and Bela son of Azaz, the son of
Shema, the son of Joel. They settled in the area from Aroer
to Nebo and Baal Meon. [9]To the east they occupied the
land up to the edge of the desert that extends to the
Euphrates River, because their livestock had increased in
Gilead.
[10]During Saul's reign they waged war against the
Hagrites, who were defeated at their hands; they occupied
the dwellings of the Hagrites throughout the entire region
east of Gilead.

[a]**41** The Hebrew term refers to the irrevocable giving over of things or persons to the LORD, often by totally destroying them. [b]**6** Hebrew *Tilgath-Pilneser,* a variant of *Tiglath-Pileser*; also in verse 26

Gad

[11]The Gadites lived next to them in Bashan, as far as Salecah:
[12]Joel was the chief, Shapham the second, then Janai and Shaphat, in Bashan.
[13]Their relatives, by families, were:
Michael, Meshullam, Sheba, Jorai, Jacan, Zia and Eber—seven in all.
[14]These were the sons of Abihail son of Huri, the son of Jaroah, the son of Gilead, the son of Michael, the son of Jeshishai, the son of Jahdo, the son of Buz.
[15]Ahi son of Abdiel, the son of Guni, was head of their family.
[16]The Gadites lived in Gilead, in Bashan and its outlying villages, and on all the pasturelands of Sharon as far as they extended.
[17]All these were entered in the genealogical records during the reigns of Jotham king of Judah and Jeroboam king of Israel.

[18]The Reubenites, the Gadites and the half-tribe of Manasseh
had 44,760 men ready for military service—able-bodied men who
could handle shield and sword, who could use a bow, and who
were trained for battle. [19]They waged war against the Hagrites,
Jetur, Naphish and Nodab. [20]They were helped in fighting them,
and God handed the Hagrites and all their allies over to them,
because they cried out to him during the battle. He answered their
prayers, because they trusted in him. [21]They seized the livestock of
the Hagrites—fifty thousand camels, two hundred fifty thousand
sheep and two thousand donkeys. They also took one hundred
thousand people captive, [22]and many others fell slain, because the
battle was God's. And they occupied the land until the exile.

The Half-Tribe of Manasseh

[23]The people of the half-tribe of Manasseh were numerous;
they settled in the land from Bashan to Baal Hermon, that is, to
Senir (Mount Hermon).
[24]These were the heads of their families: Epher, Ishi, Eliel,
Azriel, Jeremiah, Hodaviah and Jahdiel. They were brave warriors,
famous men, and heads of their families. [25]But they were unfaithful to the God of their fathers and prostituted themselves to the
gods of the peoples of the land, whom God had destroyed before
them. [26]So the God of Israel stirred up the spirit of Pul king of
Assyria (that is, Tiglath-Pileser king of Assyria), who took the
Reubenites, the Gadites and the half-tribe of Manasseh into exile.
He took them to Halah, Habor, Hara and the river of Gozan,
where they are to this day.

5:16 *Gilead . . . Bashan . . . Sharon:* The tribe of Gad (Gen 30:9, 10) was larger and more important than Reuben (Deut 33:6, 20, 21). See the map on p. 2464. For Gilead, see the note at 2:22. Bashan was known for its rich pastures, forests, and herds of cattle (Ps 22:12; Isa 2:13; Ezek 27:6; Zech 11:2). "Sharon" here probably means pasture-lands east of the Jordan. See the map on p. 2465.

5:18 *shield and sword . . . bow:* See 1 Sam 13:19-22; 17:5-40; 20:35-40; 2 Chr 25:5.

5:20-22 *the battle was God's:* A favorite theme of the writer of 1 CHRONICLES: Those who trust God in battle will be victorious over their enemies. See the mini-article called "Holy War (The LORD's Battles)," p. 306.

5:22 *the exile:* See 5:26 and the note at 5:6; also 2 Kgs 15:29; 17:5-23. See also the mini-article called "Exile," p. 1541.

5:23 *half-tribe of Manasseh:* Ephraim and Manasseh were the sons of Jacob's son Joseph. Each received a share of land in Canaan (see Gen 48:5, 6 and the note). But half the tribe of Manasseh chose to settle on the east side of the Jordan River, along with the tribes of Reuben and Gad, while the other half of Manasseh joined the rest of the Israelites on the west side of the Jordan. See the map on p. 2464. See also Josh 13:29-33.

5:23 *Baal Hermon:* The location of this place is unknown.

5:26 2 Kgs 15:19,29; 17:6.

6:1-30 *Levi . . . descendants of Merari:* Verses 1-15 trace the ancestry of Israel's high priesthood from Levi to Aaron, from Aaron to Eleazar, and from Eleazar to Phinehas. God had promised that Phinehas's descendants would always be priests (Num 25:11-13). Verses 16-30 record the clans of the tribe of Levi.

See Numbers 4:1-33, which describes the specific duties of the Levite clans of Kohath, Gershon, and Merari. For more about the Levites, see Num 3:5-10; 18:1-6, 20-32; 35:1-8; and the mini-article called "Israel's Priests," p. 2344.

6:8-14 *Zadok . . . Hilkiah:* It is not clear why Zadok is listed twice. Solomon appointed him high priest in Jerusalem because Zadok had favored Solomon over Adonijah as David's successor (1 Kgs 1:5-8, 39; 2:35). Hilkiah was the priest who found the Book of the Law (2 Kgs 22:8-13; 2 Chr 34:14-21).

6:15 *deported . . . Nebuchadnezzar:* See the mini-articles called "Nebuchadnezzar," p. 1469, and "Exile," p. 1541. See also 2 Kgs 24:8-17; 25:1-21.

6:16-19 Exod 6:16-19.

Levi

6 The sons of Levi:
Gershon, Kohath and Merari.
2 The sons of Kohath:
Amram, Izhar, Hebron and Uzziel.
3 The children of Amram:
Aaron, Moses and Miriam.
The sons of Aaron:
Nadab, Abihu, Eleazar and Ithamar.
4 Eleazar was the father of Phinehas,
Phinehas the father of Abishua,
5 Abishua the father of Bukki,
Bukki the father of Uzzi,
6 Uzzi the father of Zerahiah,
Zerahiah the father of Meraioth,
7 Meraioth the father of Amariah,
Amariah the father of Ahitub,
8 Ahitub the father of Zadok,
Zadok the father of Ahimaaz,
9 Ahimaaz the father of Azariah,
Azariah the father of Johanan,
10 Johanan the father of Azariah (it was he who served as
priest in the temple Solomon built in Jerusalem),
11 Azariah the father of Amariah,
Amariah the father of Ahitub,
12 Ahitub the father of Zadok,
Zadok the father of Shallum,
13 Shallum the father of Hilkiah,
Hilkiah the father of Azariah,
14 Azariah the father of Seraiah,
and Seraiah the father of Jehozadak.
15 Jehozadak was deported when the LORD sent Judah and
Jerusalem into exile by the hand of Nebuchadnezzar.

16 The sons of Levi:
Gershon,[a] Kohath and Merari.
17 These are the names of the sons of Gershon:
Libni and Shimei.
18 The sons of Kohath:
Amram, Izhar, Hebron and Uzziel.
19 The sons of Merari:
Mahli and Mushi.
These are the clans of the Levites listed according to their
fathers:
20 Of Gershon:
Libni his son, Jehath his son,
Zimmah his son, 21 Joah his son,

[a]**16** Hebrew *Gershom,* a variant of *Gershon;* also in verses 17, 20, 43, 62 and 71

Iddo his son, Zerah his son
and Jeatherai his son.
22 The descendants of Kohath:
Amminadab his son, Korah his son,
Assir his son, 23 Elkanah his son,
Ebiasaph his son, Assir his son,
24 Tahath his son, Uriel his son,
Uzziah his son and Shaul his son.
25 The descendants of Elkanah:
Amasai, Ahimoth,
26 Elkanah his son,[a] Zophai his son,
Nahath his son, 27 Eliab his son,
Jeroham his son, Elkanah his son
and Samuel his son.[b]
28 The sons of Samuel:
Joel[c] the firstborn
and Abijah the second son.
29 The descendants of Merari:
Mahli, Libni his son,
Shimei his son, Uzzah his son,
30 Shimea his son, Haggiah his son
and Asaiah his son.

The Temple Musicians

31 These are the men David put in charge of the music in the
house of the LORD after the ark came to rest there. 32 They ministered
with music before the tabernacle, the Tent of Meeting, until
Solomon built the temple of the LORD in Jerusalem. They performed
their duties according to the regulations laid down for them.
33 Here are the men who served, together with their sons:
From the Kohathites:
Heman, the musician,
the son of Joel, the son of Samuel,
34 the son of Elkanah, the son of Jeroham,
the son of Eliel, the son of Toah,
35 the son of Zuph, the son of Elkanah,
the son of Mahath, the son of Amasai,
36 the son of Elkanah, the son of Joel,
the son of Azariah, the son of Zephaniah,
37 the son of Tahath, the son of Assir,
the son of Ebiasaph, the son of Korah,
38 the son of Izhar, the son of Kohath,
the son of Levi, the son of Israel;

[a]**26** Some Hebrew manuscripts, Septuagint and Syriac; most Hebrew manuscripts *Ahimoth* [26]*and Elkanah. The sons of Elkanah:* [b]**27** Some Septuagint manuscripts (see also 1 Samuel 1:19,20 and 1 Chron. 6:33,34); Hebrew does not have *and Samuel his son.* [c]**28** Some Septuagint manuscripts and Syriac (see also 1 Samuel 8:2 and 1 Chron. 6:33); Hebrew does not have *Joel.*

6:28 *Samuel:* Elsewhere, Samuel is said to be of the tribe of Ephraim (1 Sam 1:1-19). Perhaps his role as priest and prophet led to the assumption that he had family ties to the Levites. Samuel also is listed as an ancestor of the temple musicians (6:33).

6:31 *men David put in charge of the music:* David is given credit for establishing the tradition of musicians for the temple. The Levites from the families listed here were given the duty of singing God's praises. Those families are listed in order of importance or rank in 6:33-47. In later times, the Levite musicians began the tradition of choosing and singing psalms that were suitable to particular occasions, sacrifices, or festivals, much as this is done today.

6:31,32 *the ark . . . Jerusalem:* The ark of the covenant contained Israel's covenant with God (the tablets of the Ten Commandments) and functioned as the throne of the LORD (Exod 25:10-22). See also the note at 3:5 and the mini-article called "The Ark of the Covenant," p. 513.

For the story of how David conquered Jerusalem, see 11:4-9. See also the note at 3:1-4.

6:48 *tabernacle:* The word "tabernacle" means "dwelling place." It is described in Exodus 26. See the mini-article called "The Tabernacle," p. 2346.

6:49 *offerings:* These gifts to God included certain animals, grains, fruits, and sweet-smelling spices. Israelites offered sacrifices to give thanks to God, to ask for God's forgiveness and blessing, and to make a payment for doing wrong. See the chart called "Sacrifices and Offerings," p. 219.

6:49 *Moses:* He is the prophet who led the people of Israel when God rescued them from slavery in Egypt. It was on their journey from Egypt to the promised land that God gave Moses the laws and teachings that revealed how the Israelites should live. Along with the Law came a promise that the people of Israel were God's special people. See Exod 2–12; 20:2; Deut 5:15; 1 Sam 12:6-25 and the mini-article called "Moses," p. 2335.

6:54-81 *settlements ... pasturelands:* The Levites were not given complete ownership of the cities. Rather, they were given certain privileges and property rights within those cities (Lev 25:32-34; Num 35:1-8). See also the note at 6:1-30 and the map on p. 2464.

6:57 *city of refuge:* Special towns called cities of refuge were set aside as places where a person who had accidentally killed someone could run for protection from the victim's relatives (Num 35:9-15; Deut 19:1-13; Josh 20:1-9). See also the mini-article called "Cities of Refuge," p. 444.

39 and Heman's associate Asaph, who served at his right hand:
Asaph son of Berekiah, the son of Shimea,
40 the son of Michael, the son of Baaseiah,[a]
the son of Malkijah, 41 the son of Ethni,
the son of Zerah, the son of Adaiah,
42 the son of Ethan, the son of Zimmah,
the son of Shimei, 43 the son of Jahath,
the son of Gershon, the son of Levi;
44 and from their associates, the Merarites, at his left hand:
Ethan son of Kishi, the son of Abdi,
the son of Malluch, 45 the son of Hashabiah,
the son of Amaziah, the son of Hilkiah,
46 the son of Amzi, the son of Bani,
the son of Shemer, 47 the son of Mahli,
the son of Mushi, the son of Merari,
the son of Levi.

48 Their fellow Levites were assigned to all the other duties of
the tabernacle, the house of God. 49 But Aaron and his descendants
were the ones who presented offerings on the altar of burnt offering and on the altar of incense in connection with all that was done in the Most Holy Place, making atonement for Israel, in accordance with all that Moses the servant of God had commanded.

50 These were the descendants of Aaron:
Eleazar his son, Phinehas his son,
Abishua his son, 51 Bukki his son,
Uzzi his son, Zerahiah his son,
52 Meraioth his son, Amariah his son,
Ahitub his son, 53 Zadok his son
and Ahimaaz his son.

54 These were the locations of their settlements allotted as their territory (they were assigned to the descendants of Aaron who were from the Kohathite clan, because the first lot was for them):
55 They were given Hebron in Judah with its surrounding pasturelands. 56 But the fields and villages around the city were given to Caleb son of Jephunneh.
57 So the descendants of Aaron were given Hebron (a
city of refuge), and Libnah,[b] Jattir, Eshtemoa, 58 Hilen, Debir,
59 Ashan, Juttah[c] and Beth Shemesh, together with their pasturelands. 60 And from the tribe of Benjamin they were given Gibeon,[d] Geba, Alemeth and Anathoth, together with their pasturelands.

[a]**40** Most Hebrew manuscripts; some Hebrew manuscripts, one Septuagint manuscript and Syriac *Maaseiah* [b]**57** See Joshua 21:13; Hebrew *given the cities of refuge: Hebron, Libnah.* [c]**59** Syriac (see also Septuagint and Joshua 21:16); Hebrew does not have *Juttah.* [d]**60** See Joshua 21:17; Hebrew does not have *Gibeon.*

These towns, which were distributed among the
Kohathite clans, were thirteen in all.
61The rest of Kohath's descendants were allotted ten towns
from the clans of half the tribe of Manasseh.
62The descendants of Gershon, clan by clan, were allotted
thirteen towns from the tribes of Issachar, Asher and Naphtali, and
from the part of the tribe of Manasseh that is in Bashan.
63The descendants of Merari, clan by clan, were allotted
twelve towns from the tribes of Reuben, Gad and Zebulun.
64So the Israelites gave the Levites these towns and their pasturelands. 65From the tribes of Judah, Simeon and Benjamin they
allotted the previously named towns.
66Some of the Kohathite clans were given as their territory
towns from the tribe of Ephraim.

67In the hill country of Ephraim they were given
Shechem (a city of refuge), and Gezer,[a] 68Jokmeam, Beth Horon, 69Aijalon and Gath Rimmon, together with their pasturelands.

70And from half the tribe of Manasseh the Israelites gave
Aner and Bileam, together with their pasturelands, to the rest
of the Kohathite clans.

71The Gershonites received the following:
From the clan of the half-tribe of Manasseh
they received Golan in Bashan and also Ashtaroth, together with their pasturelands;
72from the tribe of Issachar
they received Kedesh, Daberath, 73Ramoth and Anem,
together with their pasturelands;
74from the tribe of Asher
they received Mashal, Abdon, 75Hukok and Rehob, together with their pasturelands;
76and from the tribe of Naphtali
they received Kedesh in Galilee, Hammon and Kiriathaim, together with their pasturelands.

77The Merarites (the rest of the Levites) received the following:
From the tribe of Zebulun
they received Jokneam, Kartah,[b] Rimmono and Tabor, together with their pasturelands;
78from the tribe of Reuben across the Jordan east of Jericho
they received Bezer in the desert, Jahzah, 79Kedemoth and
Mephaath, together with their pasturelands;
80and from the tribe of Gad
they received Ramoth in Gilead, Mahanaim, 81Heshbon
and Jazer, together with their pasturelands.

6:65 *allotted:* The LORD chose the locations for the tribes. Pieces of wood or stone called "lots" were used to find out what God wanted his people to do (Josh 18:3-6). This is similar to drawing straws or flipping a coin today. But "casting lots" was not considered mere chance, since it was believed that God guided which lots were chosen and who chose them.

[a]**67** See Joshua 21:21; Hebrew *given the cities of refuge: Shechem, Gezer.* [b]**77** See Septuagint and Joshua 21:34; Hebrew does not have *Jokneam, Kartah.*

7:1-5 *Issachar:* Issachar was the fifth son of Jacob and Leah (Gen 30:16-18). The genealogies of Israel's northern tribes begin with the descendants of Issachar. As the listing includes only four generations, the writer of 1 CHRONICLES probably had only limited family records and military census figures available. See the map on p. 2464.

7:6-12 *Benjamin:* Benjamin was Jacob and Rachel's youngest son (Gen 35:16-18). It would be more logical for the genealogy of Zebulun rather than Benjamin to follow the genealogy of Issachar (see 2:1; 12:23-37; 27:16-22). The small Benjamin tribe was in the south next to Judah (see the map on p. 2464). Benjamin's genealogy appears again in chapter 8, while there is no genealogy for Zebulun in chapters 2–9. The list here does not match other lists of either Zebulun or Benjamin (Gen 46:8-22; Num 26:26, 27; 38-41).

7:13,14 *Naphtali: . . . descendants of Bilhah:* Naphtali was the son of Jacob and Rachel's servant Bilhah (Gen 30:1-8; see also Gen 46:23-25). The Naphtali tribe settled the region north and west of the Sea of Galilee. See also Matt 4:13-16.

Issachar

7 The sons of Issachar:
Tola, Puah, Jashub and Shimron—four in all.
2 The sons of Tola:
Uzzi, Rephaiah, Jeriel, Jahmai, Ibsam and Samuel—heads of their families. During the reign of David, the descendants of Tola listed as fighting men in their genealogy numbered 22,600.
3 The son of Uzzi:
Izrahiah.
The sons of Izrahiah:
Michael, Obadiah, Joel and Isshiah. All five of them were chiefs.
4 According to their family genealogy, they had 36,000 men ready for battle, for they had many wives and children.
5 The relatives who were fighting men belonging to all the clans of Issachar, as listed in their genealogy, were 87,000 in all.

Benjamin

6 Three sons of Benjamin:
Bela, Beker and Jediael.
7 The sons of Bela:
Ezbon, Uzzi, Uzziel, Jerimoth and Iri, heads of families—five in all. Their genealogical record listed 22,034 fighting men.
8 The sons of Beker:
Zemirah, Joash, Eliezer, Elioenai, Omri, Jeremoth, Abijah, Anathoth and Alemeth. All these were the sons of Beker.
9 Their genealogical record listed the heads of families and 20,200 fighting men.
10 The son of Jediael:
Bilhan.
The sons of Bilhan:
Jeush, Benjamin, Ehud, Kenaanah, Zethan, Tarshish and Ahishahar.
11 All these sons of Jediael were heads of families. There were 17,200 fighting men ready to go out to war.
12 The Shuppites and Huppites were the descendants of Ir, and the Hushites the descendants of Aher.

Naphtali

13 The sons of Naphtali:
Jahziel, Guni, Jezer and Shillem[a]—the descendants of Bilhah.

---

[a] **13** Some Hebrew and Septuagint manuscripts (see also Gen. 46:24 and Num. 26:49); most Hebrew manuscripts *Shallum*

Manasseh

[14]The descendants of Manasseh:
Asriel was his descendant through his Aramean concubine. She gave birth to Makir the father of Gilead. [15]Makir
took a wife from among the Huppites and Shuppites. His
sister's name was Maacah.
Another descendant was named Zelophehad, who had
only daughters.
[16]Makir's wife Maacah gave birth to a son and named
him Peresh. His brother was named Sheresh, and his sons
were Ulam and Rakem.
[17]The son of Ulam:
Bedan.
These were the sons of Gilead son of Makir, the son of Manasseh. [18]His sister Hammoleketh gave birth to Ishhod,
Abiezer and Mahlah.
[19]The sons of Shemida were:
Ahian, Shechem, Likhi and Aniam.

Ephraim

[20]The descendants of Ephraim:
Shuthelah, Bered his son,
Tahath his son, Eleadah his son,
Tahath his son, [21]Zabad his son
and Shuthelah his son.
Ezer and Elead were killed by the native-born men of
Gath, when they went down to seize their livestock. [22]Their
father Ephraim mourned for them many days, and his relatives came to comfort him. [23]Then he lay with his wife again,
and she became pregnant and gave birth to a son. He named
him Beriah,[a] because there had been misfortune in his family. [24]His daughter was Sheerah, who built Lower and Upper
Beth Horon as well as Uzzen Sheerah.
[25]Rephah was his son, Resheph his son,[b]
Telah his son, Tahan his son,
[26]Ladan his son, Ammihud his son,
Elishama his son, [27]Nun his son
and Joshua his son.
[28]Their lands and settlements included Bethel and its surrounding villages, Naaran to the east, Gezer and its villages to the
west, and Shechem and its villages all the way to Ayyah and its villages. [29]Along the borders of Manasseh were Beth Shan, Taanach,
Megiddo and Dor, together with their villages. The descendants of
Joseph son of Israel lived in these towns.

7:14 *concubine:* See the note at 3:9.

7:20-29 *Ephraim ... descendants of Joseph:* See the note at 5:23.

7:23 *Beriah ... misfortune in his family:* In Hebrew "Beriah" sounds like "in misery" or "misfortune."

[a]**23** *Beriah* sounds like the Hebrew for *misfortune.* [b]**25** Some Septuagint manuscripts; Hebrew does not have *his son.*

7:30-40 *Asher:* Asher was the second son of Jacob and his wife Leah's servant Zilpah (Gen 30:9-13). The Asher tribe settled in the north along the Mediterranean coast (see Josh 19:24-31 and the map on p. 2464).

8:1-40 *Benjamin . . . Saul:* See the note at 7:6-12. The family line of Benjamin is given extra attention, probably because it was the tribe of Saul, Israel's first king (8:33), and because Benjamites were among those who helped in the rebuilding of Jerusalem under Nehemiah after the exile (Neh 11:7-9). Jerusalem is located in what was the original territory of the Benjamin tribe (see the map on p. 2464).

Note that though Saul was Israel's first king, his genealogy is given in chapter 8 while David's genealogy is given first in chapter 3. See also the article called "From Joshua to the Exile: The People of Israel in the Promised Land," p. 924.

8:6 *Geba:* Geba is believed to have been north of Jerusalem close to the border between Judah and Israel.

8:8 *Moab:* See the note at 4:22. Aijalon was north and east of Gibeah.

8:13 *Gath:* Gath was probably the most important of the five major cities of Philistia. Its exact location is not known, but it is thought to have been to the southwest of Jerusalem. At one time, Gath belonged to Judah (2 Chr 11:5-8). Goliath, the Philistine giant who fought David, was from Gath (1 Sam 17:4-54).

8:28 *Jerusalem:* See the note at 3:1-4. For all locations, see the map on p. 2464.

8:29 *Gibeon:* This city was within the tribal lands of Benjamin about five-and-a-half miles north of Jerusalem. For key events in this city's history, see Josh 9:1—10:14; 1 Kgs 3:4,5; 1 Chr 16:39; 2 Chr 1:3,13.

Asher

30 The sons of Asher:
Imnah, Ishvah, Ishvi and Beriah. Their sister was Serah.
31 The sons of Beriah:
Heber and Malkiel, who was the father of Birzaith.
32 Heber was the father of Japhlet, Shomer and Hotham and of
their sister Shua.
33 The sons of Japhlet:
Pasach, Bimhal and Ashvath.
These were Japhlet's sons.
34 The sons of Shomer:
Ahi, Rohgah,[a] Hubbah and Aram.
35 The sons of his brother Helem:
Zophah, Imna, Shelesh and Amal.
36 The sons of Zophah:
Suah, Harnepher, Shual, Beri, Imrah, 37 Bezer, Hod, Shamma,
Shilshah, Ithran[b] and Beera.
38 The sons of Jether:
Jephunneh, Pispah and Ara.
39 The sons of Ulla:
Arah, Hanniel and Rizia.
40 All these were descendants of Asher—heads of families,
choice men, brave warriors and outstanding leaders. The number
of men ready for battle, as listed in their genealogy, was 26,000.

The Genealogy of Saul the Benjamite

8 Benjamin was the father of Bela his firstborn,
Ashbel the second son, Aharah the third,
2 Nohah the fourth and Rapha the fifth.
3 The sons of Bela were:
Addar, Gera, Abihud,[c] 4 Abishua, Naaman, Ahoah, 5 Gera,
Shephuphan and Huram.
6 These were the descendants of Ehud, who were heads of families of those living in Geba and were deported to Manahath:
7 Naaman, Ahijah, and Gera, who deported them and who
was the father of Uzza and Ahihud.
8 Sons were born to Shaharaim in Moab after he had divorced
his wives Hushim and Baara. 9 By his wife Hodesh he had
Jobab, Zibia, Mesha, Malcam, 10 Jeuz, Sakia and Mirmah.
These were his sons, heads of families. 11 By Hushim he
had Abitub and Elpaal.
12 The sons of Elpaal:
Eber, Misham, Shemed (who built Ono and Lod with its

[a]34 Or *of his brother Shomer: Rohgah* [b]37 Possibly a variant of *Jether* [c]3 Or *Gera the father of Ehud*

surrounding villages), [13]and Beriah and Shema, who were
heads of families of those living in Aijalon and who drove
out the inhabitants of Gath.
[14]Ahio, Shashak, Jeremoth, [15]Zebadiah, Arad, Eder, [16]Michael,
Ishpah and Joha were the sons of Beriah.
[17]Zebadiah, Meshullam, Hizki, Heber, [18]Ishmerai, Izliah and
Jobab were the sons of Elpaal.
[19]Jakim, Zicri, Zabdi, [20]Elienai, Zillethai, Eliel, [21]Adaiah, Bera-
iah and Shimrath were the sons of Shimei.
[22]Ishpan, Eber, Eliel, [23]Abdon, Zicri, Hanan, [24]Hananiah, Elam,
Anthothijah, [25]Iphdeiah and Penuel were the sons of
Shashak.
[26]Shamsherai, Shehariah, Athaliah, [27]Jaareshiah, Elijah and
Zicri were the sons of Jeroham.
[28]All these were heads of families, chiefs as listed in their
genealogy, and they lived in Jerusalem.

[29]Jeiel[a] the father[b] of Gibeon lived in Gibeon.
His wife's name was Maacah, [30]and his firstborn son
was Abdon, followed by Zur, Kish, Baal, Ner,[c] Nadab,
[31]Gedor, Ahio, Zeker [32]and Mikloth, who was the father
of Shimeah. They too lived near their relatives in Jerusalem.
[33]Ner was the father of Kish, Kish the father of Saul, and Saul
the father of Jonathan, Malki-Shua, Abinadab and Esh-
Baal.[d]
[34]The son of Jonathan:
Merib-Baal,[e] who was the father of Micah.
[35]The sons of Micah:
Pithon, Melech, Tarea and Ahaz.
[36]Ahaz was the father of Jehoaddah, Jehoaddah was the
father of Alemeth, Azmaveth and Zimri, and Zimri was
the father of Moza. [37]Moza was the father of Binea;
Raphah was his son, Eleasah his son and Azel his son.
[38]Azel had six sons, and these were their names:
Azrikam, Bokeru, Ishmael, Sheariah, Obadiah and Hanan.
All these were the sons of Azel.
[39]The sons of his brother Eshek:
Ulam his firstborn, Jeush the second son and Eliphelet the
third. [40]The sons of Ulam were brave warriors who could
handle the bow. They had many sons and grandsons—150
in all.
All these were the descendants of Benjamin.

8:28 *lived in Jerusalem:* Many Benjamites were probably living in Jerusalem at the time of the writing of 1 CHRONICLES.

8:33 *Saul . . . Jonathan:* Saul, Israel's first king, ruled from about 1030 to 1010 B.C. See 1 Sam 9:15-17; 10:1.

Jonathan, Saul's son, was the best friend of David, the second king of Israel. The dramatic story of the loyal friendship between Jonathan and David is told in 1 Samuel 18–20 (see also 2 Sam 1:26).

8:29-38 1 Chr 9:35-44.

---

[a]**29** Some Septuagint manuscripts (see also 1 Chron. 9:35); Hebrew does not have *Jeiel.* [b]**29** *Father* may mean *civic leader* or *military leader.* [c]**30** Some Septuagint manuscripts (see also 1 Chron. 9:36); Hebrew does not have *Ner.* [d]**33** Also known as *Ish-Bosheth* [e]**34** Also known as *Mephibosheth*

9:1 *the book of the kings of Israel:* This may refer to a census or to some other historical documents.

9:1 *taken captive to Babylon:* See the mini-articles called "Babylon," p. 1363 and "Exile," p. 1541.

9:2 *some Israelites:* Before Saul, and then David, united the whole kingdom under the name "Israel," the name sometimes referred to the ten northern tribes led by the tribe of Ephraim. "Judah" referred to the two southern tribes led by the tribe of Judah. Following the death of King Solomon, the nation of Israel was divided (1 Kgs 12:1-20). From that time on, "Israel" usually referred to the northern kingdom, and the people who lived there were called "Israelites," as is the case in this verse. The southern kingdom was called "Judah." Some of the people left the northern kingdom and became citizens of Jerusalem so that they could worship God in that city as God's Law required. As a result, Judah had citizens from the northern tribes such as Ephraim and Manasseh (9:3) as well as from the southern tribes of Judah and Benjamin.

9:2-34 *first to resettle . . . lived in Jerusalem:* These lists show the concern the writer of 1 Chronicles had for rank within the community that returned to Jerusalem. The common citizens among the Israelites are listed (9:4-9), followed by the priests (9:10-13), then the Levites (9:14-16), and finally, the gatekeepers (9:17-21).

The gatekeepers are of special interest to the writer, who carefully lists their duties in 9:22-32. As members of the priestly family of Levi through the line of Korah (6:22-24), their position began in the time of Moses (9:18-20). But the writer credits David and Samuel for choosing those families that now served in the temple. See also the note at 26:1.

9:2,3 Ezra 2:21-42; Neh 7:73.

LISTS OF THE FAMILIES RETURNING TO JERUSALEM

The writer of 1 Chronicles uses these lists, modified from Nehemiah 11:3-24, to help his people see themselves as part of the people of God described in chapters 1–8.

9 All Israel was listed in the genealogies recorded in the book of the kings of Israel.

The People in Jerusalem

The people of Judah were taken captive to Babylon because of their unfaithfulness.
2 Now the first to resettle on their own property in their own towns were some Israelites, priests, Levites and temple servants.

3 Those from Judah, from Benjamin, and from Ephraim and Manasseh who lived in Jerusalem were:

4 Uthai son of Ammihud, the son of Omri, the son of Imri, the son of Bani, a descendant of Perez son of Judah.

5 Of the Shilonites:
Asaiah the firstborn and his sons.

6 Of the Zerahites:
Jeuel.
The people from Judah numbered 690.

7 Of the Benjamites:
Sallu son of Meshullam, the son of Hodaviah, the son of Hassenuah;

8 Ibneiah son of Jeroham; Elah son of Uzzi, the son of Micri; and Meshullam son of Shephatiah, the son of Reuel, the son of Ibnijah.

9 The people from Benjamin, as listed in their genealogy, numbered 956. All these men were heads of their families.

10 Of the priests:
Jedaiah; Jehoiarib; Jakin;

11 Azariah son of Hilkiah, the son of Meshullam, the son of Zadok, the son of Meraioth, the son of Ahitub, the official in charge of the house of God;

12 Adaiah son of Jeroham, the son of Pashhur, the son of Malkijah; and Maasai son of Adiel, the son of Jahzerah, the son of Meshullam, the son of Meshillemith, the son of Immer.

13 The priests, who were heads of families, numbered 1,760. They were able men, responsible for ministering in the house of God.

14 Of the Levites:
Shemaiah son of Hasshub, the son of Azrikam, the son of Hashabiah, a Merarite;
15 Bakbakkar, Heresh, Galal and Mattaniah son of Mica, the son of Zicri, the son of Asaph;
16 Obadiah son of Shemaiah, the son of Galal, the son of

Jeduthun; and Berekiah son of Asa, the son of Elkanah,
who lived in the villages of the Netophathites.
17 The gatekeepers:
Shallum, Akkub, Talmon, Ahiman and their brothers,
Shallum their chief 18 being stationed at the King's Gate
on the east, up to the present time. These were the gatekeepers belonging to the camp of the Levites. 19 Shallum
son of Kore, the son of Ebiasaph, the son of Korah, and
his fellow gatekeepers from his family (the Korahites)
were responsible for guarding the thresholds of the Tent[a]
just as their fathers had been responsible for guarding the
entrance to the dwelling of the LORD. 20 In earlier times
Phinehas son of Eleazar was in charge of the gatekeepers,
and the LORD was with him. 21 Zechariah son of Meshelemiah was the gatekeeper at the entrance to the Tent of
Meeting.
22 Altogether, those chosen to be gatekeepers at the thresholds numbered 212. They were registered by genealogy in their
villages. The gatekeepers had been assigned to their positions of
trust by David and Samuel the seer. 23 They and their descendants were in charge of guarding the gates of the house of the
LORD—the house called the Tent. 24 The gatekeepers were on the
four sides: east, west, north and south. 25 Their brothers in their
villages had to come from time to time and share their duties
for seven-day periods. 26 But the four principal gatekeepers, who
were Levites, were entrusted with the responsibility for the
rooms and treasuries in the house of God. 27 They would spend
the night stationed around the house of God, because they had
to guard it; and they had charge of the key for opening it each
morning.
28 Some of them were in charge of the articles used in the
temple service; they counted them when they were brought in and

[a]19 That is, the temple; also in verses 21 and 23

9:18,19 *King's Gate ... the dwelling of the LORD:* Many cities, particularly those important to a nation's defense, were walled and had one or more gates. These gates were often topped with a roofed room where guards kept a watch out for enemies. The exact location of the King's Gate is unclear. It may have been the one that the king used to enter and leave the city. See the map on p. 2466.

The "Tent" here refers to the temple and the "dwelling of the LORD" refers to the tabernacle. See the note at 6:48, 49.

9:22-27 *gatekeepers ... numbered 212:* Three shifts every day at each of the twenty-four guard stations (see 26:16-18) meant that seventy-two men were on duty each week. With 212 men, each group of seventy-two would be on duty about once every three weeks. When they weren't on duty, the guards returned home to be with their families. Four full-time guards supervised all the others.

QUESTIONS ABOUT 1 CHRONICLES 1:1—9:34

1. The author of 1 CHRONICLES wrote this history for those Israelites who had returned from exile in Babylon. Why would the long genealogies be important to them?
2. Why had the Israelites been in exile in Babylon? (9:1, 2) Why do you think the writer reminds the readers of this?
3. Why do you think the writer gave additional attention to the tribes of Judah and Levi? In the end, what do you think will be of greater importance to the Israelites, the continuation of the kingly line of David or the continuation of proper worship?
4. What do you know about your family's history? How can our knowledge or understanding of the past affect how we live in the present and future?

9:29-32 *incense . . . offering bread . . . every Sabbath:* Incense was made of frankincense, other gums and spices, and a seasoning of salt, which together produced a sweet smell when burned (Exod 30:34-38). The smoke from the burning incense represented the prayers that went up to God (Ps 141:2; Rev 5:8). The altar for burning incense (1 Chr 6:49) was in the Holy Place in the temple.

Bread offerings could be prepared in several ways: oven-baked loaves, oven-baked wafers, bread made over the fire in a shallow pan, or bread fried in a covered pan. The dough for each was made of fine wheat and olive oil. But no recipe was to include yeast, a tiny yellowish fungus that causes dough to rise when mixed with water and flour. Yeast also is called leaven. Bread that has no yeast, or leaven, is flat and is called unleavened bread. See also Lev 2:2-7 and the mini-article called "Temple Offerings," p. 2027.

On each Sabbath, twelve loaves of fresh bread, representing the twelve tribes of Israel, were to be placed on the table in the Holy Place. The loaves were an ongoing offering to God and a reminder of God's blessings. See Lev 24:5-9 and the mini-article called "Bread," p. 2058.

10:1 *Philistines:* Philistia had five main cities, each with its own ruler: Ashdod, Ashkelon, Ekron, Gath, and Gaza. The Philistines were often at war with Israel. See the map on p. 2465.

10:1 *Mount Gilboa:* This mountain was just south and east of Jezreel (see the map on p. 2464).

10:4,6 *abuse me . . . all his house died:* Saul killed himself (1 Sam 31:1-13) rather than be humiliated as Samson had been (Judg 16:23-25). Not all of Saul's male relatives died. His son Ish-Bosheth took over his father's rule following Saul's death (2 Sam 2:8-11).

when they were taken out. 29Others were assigned to take care of
the furnishings and all the other articles of the sanctuary, as well as
the flour and wine, and the oil, incense and spices. 30But some of
the priests took care of mixing the spices. 31A Levite named Mattithiah, the firstborn son of Shallum the Korahite, was entrusted
with the responsibility for baking the offering bread. 32Some of
their Kohathite brothers were in charge of preparing for every Sabbath the bread set out on the table.

33Those who were musicians, heads of Levite families, stayed
in the rooms of the temple and were exempt from other duties
because they were responsible for the work day and night.

34All these were heads of Levite families, chiefs as listed in
their genealogy, and they lived in Jerusalem.

David, Founder of the Temple

David is not pictured as a brave shepherd boy, a military hero, or an expert in administration in 1 Chronicles. Rather, David is a faithful follower of the Lord who creates and finances an elaborate system of temple worship and assigns gifted musicians to lead its worship services. The primary goal of David's kingship is to prepare for the construction and furnishing of the temple, and to create a structure for proper worship.

INTRODUCTION: THE DEATH OF SAUL

This repetition of Saul's genealogy from 1 Chronicles 8:29-40 and the story of his death is the background for the story of David that will occupy the rest of the book.

The Genealogy of Saul

35Jeiel the father[a] of Gibeon lived in Gibeon.
His wife's name was Maacah, 36and his firstborn son was
Abdon, followed by Zur, Kish, Baal, Ner, Nadab, 37Gedor,
Ahio, Zechariah and Mikloth. 38Mikloth was the father of
Shimeam. They too lived near their relatives in Jerusalem.
39Ner was the father of Kish, Kish the father of Saul, and Saul the
father of Jonathan, Malki-Shua, Abinadab and Esh-Baal.[b]
40The son of Jonathan:
Merib-Baal,[c] who was the father of Micah.
41The sons of Micah:
Pithon, Melech, Tahrea and Ahaz.[d]
42Ahaz was the father of Jadah, Jadah[e] was the father of

[a]35 *Father* may mean *civic leader* or *military leader.* [b]39 Also known as *Ish-Bosheth* [c]40 Also known as *Mephibosheth* [d]41 Vulgate and Syriac (see also Septuagint and 1 Chron. 8:35); Hebrew does not have *and Ahaz.* [e]42 Some Hebrew manuscripts and Septuagint (see also 1 Chron. 8:36); most Hebrew manuscripts *Jarah, Jarah*

Alemeth, Azmaveth and Zimri, and Zimri was the father
of Moza. 43Moza was the father of Binea; Rephaiah was his
son, Eleasah his son and Azel his son.
44 Azel had six sons, and these were their names:
Azrikam, Bokeru, Ishmael, Sheariah, Obadiah and Hanan.
These were the sons of Azel.

Saul Takes His Life

10 Now the Philistines fought against Israel; the Israelites fled
before them, and many fell slain on Mount Gilboa. 2The Philistines
pressed hard after Saul and his sons, and they killed his sons Jonathan, Abinadab and Malki-Shua. 3The fighting grew fierce around
Saul, and when the archers overtook him, they wounded him.
4Saul said to his armor-bearer, "Draw your sword and run
me through, or these uncircumcised fellows will come and
abuse me."
But his armor-bearer was terrified and would not do it; so
Saul took his own sword and fell on it. 5When the armor-bearer
saw that Saul was dead, he too fell on his sword and died. 6So Saul
and his three sons died, and all his house died together.
7When all the Israelites in the valley saw that the army had
fled and that Saul and his sons had died, they abandoned their
towns and fled. And the Philistines came and occupied them.
8The next day, when the Philistines came to strip the dead,
they found Saul and his sons fallen on Mount Gilboa. 9They
stripped him and took his head and his armor, and sent messengers throughout the land of the Philistines to proclaim the news
among their idols and their people. 10They put his armor in the
temple of their gods and hung up his head in the temple of Dagon.
11When all the inhabitants of Jabesh Gilead heard of everything the Philistines had done to Saul, 12all their valiant men went
and took the bodies of Saul and his sons and brought them to
Jabesh. Then they buried their bones under the great tree in
Jabesh, and they fasted seven days.
13Saul died because he was unfaithful to the LORD; he did not
keep the word of the LORD and even consulted a medium for guidance, 14and did not inquire of the LORD. So the LORD put him to
death and turned the kingdom over to David son of Jesse.

DAVID RULES IN JERUSALEM

David's rule is marked by the importance of worship, the movement of the ark of the covenant to Jerusalem (chapters 13–16), and God's choice of Solomon as temple builder (chapter 17).

David Becomes King Over Israel

11 All Israel came together to David at Hebron and said, "We
are your own flesh and blood. 2In the past, even while Saul was

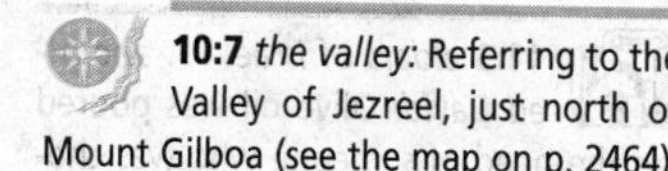

10:7 *the valley:* Referring to the Valley of Jezreel, just north of Mount Gilboa (see the map on p. 2464).

10:9,10 *took his head . . . Dagon:* It was common practice in the ancient Near East to display the head and other body parts to announce the victory and to serve as a warning to other enemies.

Dagon was the Philistines' most important god. As early as 2000 B.C., a large temple was built in Dagon's honor in the seaside city of Ugarit. Ugaritic documents say that Dagon was the father of the important god, Baal. See also Judg 16:23.

10:12 *Jabesh:* A city east of the Jordan River (see the map on p. 2464). One of the first things Saul did as king was to rescue the people of Jabesh (1 Sam 11:1-13). So, when Saul died, they brought the body of Saul and his sons to Jabesh for a proper burial. See also 2 Sam 21:11-14 and the mini-article called "Burial," p. 1998.

10:12 *fasted:* In ancient times people went without eating in times of grief or to show that they were sorry for their sins.

10:13 *consulted a medium for guidance:* Saul became impatient and broke God's Law by seeking advice from the dead in an attempt to know God's will (Lev 19:31; 20:6,27; Deut 18:10,11; 1 Sam 28:7,8).

11:1 *All Israel:* Here, it seems that all of Israel's tribal leaders immediately supported David as their king following Saul's death. But 2 Samuel 1–4 tells how the ten northern tribes first supported Saul's son Ish-Bosheth, while the two southern tribes supported David.

11:1 *Hebron:* See the note at 3:1-4.

10:13 1 Sam 13:8-14; 15:1-24; 28:7,8.

11:3 *elders of Israel . . . anointed David:* Olive oil was poured on the head of someone who was chosen to be a priest, a prophet, or a king (Exod 28:41; 29:7; 2 Sam 2:4; 5:3).

11:5 *fortress of Zion, the City of David:* Both "Zion" and "City of David" became alternative names for Jerusalem. See the map on p. 2466 and the mini-articles called "Jerusalem," p. 574 and "Zion," p. 1294.

11:6 *Joab:* David's nephew who became an important, but violent, military leader of David's army (2 Sam 10:7-14; 11:1; 1 Kgs 11:15,16).

11:9 *Lord Almighty:* Sometimes translated as "Lord of hosts." See also the mini-article called "Names of God," p. 243.

11:10—12:40 *as the Lord had promised . . . there was joy in Israel:* In this section, the writer of 1 Chronicles puts forth the idea that all of Israel united to make David their king, with God at David's side (11:9, 10). The writer does so by listing the warriors of each tribe who fought with David in the conquest of Jerusalem and by pointing out that even while Saul was alive men from Saul's own tribe of Benjamin and from the northern tribes of Gad and Manasseh supported David (12:1-23). See also the note at 11:1 (All Israel).

11:4 Josh 15:63; Judg 1:21.

king, you were the one who led Israel on their military campaigns.
And the Lord your God said to you, 'You will shepherd my people
Israel, and you will become their ruler.' "
[3]When all the elders of Israel had come to King David at
Hebron, he made a compact with them at Hebron before the Lord,
and they anointed David king over Israel, as the Lord had
promised through Samuel.

David Conquers Jerusalem

[4]David and all the Israelites marched to Jerusalem (that is,
Jebus). The Jebusites who lived there [5]said to David, "You will not
get in here." Nevertheless, David captured the fortress of Zion, the
City of David.
[6]David had said, "Whoever leads the attack on the Jebusites
will become commander-in-chief." Joab son of Zeruiah went up
first, and so he received the command.
[7]David then took up residence in the fortress, and so it was
called the City of David. [8]He built up the city around it, from the
supporting terraces[a] to the surrounding wall, while Joab restored
the rest of the city. [9]And David became more and more powerful,
because the Lord Almighty was with him.

David's Mighty Men

[10]These were the chiefs of David's mighty men—they,
together with all Israel, gave his kingship strong support to extend
it over the whole land, as the Lord had promised— [11]this is the list
of David's mighty men:
Jashobeam,[b] a Hacmonite, was chief of the officers[c]; he
raised his spear against three hundred men, whom he killed in one
encounter.
[12]Next to him was Eleazar son of Dodai the Ahohite, one of the
three mighty men. [13]He was with David at Pas Dammim when the
Philistines gathered there for battle. At a place where there was a field
full of barley, the troops fled from the Philistines. [14]But they took
their stand in the middle of the field. They defended it and struck the
Philistines down, and the Lord brought about a great victory.
[15]Three of the thirty chiefs came down to David to the rock
at the cave of Adullam, while a band of Philistines was encamped
in the Valley of Rephaim. [16]At that time David was in the stronghold, and the Philistine garrison was at Bethlehem. [17]David longed
for water and said, "Oh, that someone would get me a drink of
water from the well near the gate of Bethlehem!" [18]So the Three
broke through the Philistine lines, drew water from the well near
the gate of Bethlehem and carried it back to David. But he refused

---

[a]**8** Or *the Millo* [b]**11** Possibly a variant of *Jashob-Baal* [c]**11** Or *Thirty*; some Septuagint manuscripts *Three* (see also 2 Samuel 23:8)

to drink it; instead, he poured it out before the LORD. [19]"God forbid that I should do this!" he said. "Should I drink the blood of
these men who went at the risk of their lives?" Because they risked
their lives to bring it back, David would not drink it.

Such were the exploits of the three mighty men.

[20]Abishai the brother of Joab was chief of the Three. He
raised his spear against three hundred men, whom he killed, and
so he became as famous as the Three. [21]He was doubly honored
above the Three and became their commander, even though he
was not included among them.

[22]Benaiah son of Jehoiada was a valiant fighter from Kabzeel,
who performed great exploits. He struck down two of Moab's best
men. He also went down into a pit on a snowy day and killed a
lion. [23]And he struck down an Egyptian who was seven and a half
feet[a] tall. Although the Egyptian had a spear like a weaver's rod in
his hand, Benaiah went against him with a club. He snatched the
spear from the Egyptian's hand and killed him with his own spear.
[24]Such were the exploits of Benaiah son of Jehoiada; he too was as
famous as the three mighty men. [25]He was held in greater honor
than any of the Thirty, but he was not included among the Three.
And David put him in charge of his bodyguard.

[26]The mighty men were:
Asahel the brother of Joab,
Elhanan son of Dodo from Bethlehem,
[27]Shammoth the Harorite,
Helez the Pelonite,
[28]Ira son of Ikkesh from Tekoa,
Abiezer from Anathoth,
[29]Sibbecai the Hushathite,
Ilai the Ahohite,
[30]Maharai the Netophathite,
Heled son of Baanah the Netophathite,
[31]Ithai son of Ribai from Gibeah in Benjamin,
Benaiah the Pirathonite,
[32]Hurai from the ravines of Gaash,
Abiel the Arbathite,
[33]Azmaveth the Baharumite,
Eliahba the Shaalbonite,
[34]the sons of Hashem the Gizonite,
Jonathan son of Shagee the Hararite,
[35]Ahiam son of Sacar the Hararite,
Eliphal son of Ur,
[36]Hepher the Mekerathite,
Ahijah the Pelonite,
[37]Hezro the Carmelite,

David became more and more powerful, because the LORD Almighty was with him.
1 Chr 11:9

11:19 *drink the blood . . . risk of their lives:* The men risked their own lives, or blood, to get the water for David. As a result, David may have poured out the water to make a drink offering of this precious gift back to God. Or he may have seen the water as being like blood, which God's laws would not allow him to touch. Blood was considered sacred and not to be eaten or drunk (Lev 17:10-16; Deut 12:5-27; 2 Kgs 16:13-15; Hos 9:4). See also the mini-articles called "Purity (Clean and Unclean)," p. 2125 and "Blood," p. 180.

[a]23 Hebrew *five cubits* (about 2.3 meters)

Amasai said, *"We are yours, O David! We are with you, O son of Jesse! Success, success to you, and success to those who help you, for your God will help you."*
1 Chr 12:18

Naarai son of Ezbai,
38 Joel the brother of Nathan,
Mibhar son of Hagri,
39 Zelek the Ammonite,
Naharai the Berothite, the armor-bearer of Joab son of Zeruiah,
40 Ira the Ithrite,
Gareb the Ithrite,
41 Uriah the Hittite,
Zabad son of Ahlai,
42 Adina son of Shiza the Reubenite, who was chief of the Reubenites, and the thirty with him,
43 Hanan son of Maacah,
Joshaphat the Mithnite,
44 Uzzia the Ashterathite,
Shama and Jeiel the sons of Hotham the Aroerite,
45 Jediael son of Shimri,
his brother Joha the Tizite,
46 Eliel the Mahavite,
Jeribai and Joshaviah the sons of Elnaam,
Ithmah the Moabite,
47 Eliel, Obed and Jaasiel the Mezobaite.

Warriors Join David

12 These were the men who came to David at Ziklag, while he
was banished from the presence of Saul son of Kish (they were
among the warriors who helped him in battle; 2 they were armed
with bows and were able to shoot arrows or to sling stones right-handed or left-handed; they were kinsmen of Saul from the tribe of Benjamin):

3 Ahiezer their chief and Joash the sons of Shemaah the
Gibeathite; Jeziel and Pelet the sons of Azmaveth; Beracah,
Jehu the Anathothite, 4 and Ishmaiah the Gibeonite, a mighty
man among the Thirty, who was a leader of the Thirty; Jeremiah, Jahaziel, Johanan, Jozabad the Gederathite, 5 Eluzai, Jerimoth, Bealiah, Shemariah and Shephatiah the Haruphite;
6 Elkanah, Isshiah, Azarel, Joezer and Jashobeam the Korahites;
7 and Joelah and Zebadiah the sons of Jeroham from Gedor.

8 Some Gadites defected to David at his stronghold in the
desert. They were brave warriors, ready for battle and able to handle the shield and spear. Their faces were the faces of lions, and they were as swift as gazelles in the mountains.
9 Ezer was the chief,
Obadiah the second in command, Eliab the third,
10 Mishmannah the fourth, Jeremiah the fifth,
11 Attai the sixth, Eliel the seventh,

12:1 *David at Ziklag . . . in battle:* Ziklag was the Philistine town that King Achish of Gath gave David in return for his loyalty (1 Sam 27:6). Since this happened when David was living as an outlaw, the events in this chapter actually took place before David became king.

12:2 *kinsmen of Saul from the tribe of Benjamin:* The story emphasizes that warriors from King Saul's own Benjamin tribe abandoned Saul and joined David's army. See also the note at 11:10—12:40.

[12]Johanan the eighth, Elzabad the ninth,
[13]Jeremiah the tenth and Macbannai the eleventh.

[14]These Gadites were army commanders; the least was a
match for a hundred, and the greatest for a thousand. [15]It was they
who crossed the Jordan in the first month when it was overflowing
all its banks, and they put to flight everyone living in the valleys, to
the east and to the west.

[16]Other Benjamites and some men from Judah also came to
David in his stronghold. [17]David went out to meet them and said
to them, "If you have come to me in peace, to help me, I am ready
to have you unite with me. But if you have come to betray me to
my enemies when my hands are free from violence, may the God
of our fathers see it and judge you."

[18]Then the Spirit came upon Amasai, chief of the Thirty, and
he said:

"We are yours, O David!
We are with you, O son of Jesse!
Success, success to you,
and success to those who help you,
for your God will help you."

So David received them and made them leaders of his raiding bands.

[19]Some of the men of Manasseh defected to David when he
went with the Philistines to fight against Saul. (He and his men did
not help the Philistines because, after consultation, their rulers sent
him away. They said, "It will cost us our heads if he deserts to his master Saul.") [20]When David went to Ziklag, these were the men of Manasseh who defected to him: Adnah, Jozabad, Jediael, Michael, Jozabad,
Elihu and Zillethai, leaders of units of a thousand in Manasseh. [21]They
helped David against raiding bands, for all of them were brave warriors, and they were commanders in his army. [22]Day after day men
came to help David, until he had a great army, like the army of God.[a]

Others Join David at Hebron

[23]These are the numbers of the men armed for battle who
came to David at Hebron to turn Saul's kingdom over to him, as
the LORD had said:

[24]men of Judah, carrying shield and spear—6,800 armed for battle;
[25]men of Simeon, warriors ready for battle—7,100;
[26]men of Levi—4,600, [27]including Jehoiada, leader of the family of Aaron, with 3,700 men, [28]and Zadok, a brave young
warrior, with 22 officers from his family;
[29]men of Benjamin, Saul's kinsmen—3,000, most of whom had remained loyal to Saul's house until then;

[a]22 Or *a great and mighty army*

Day after day men came to help David, until he had a great army, like the army of God.
1 Chr 12:22

12:15 *Jordan . . . overflowing all its banks:* This may refer to March or April when the melting snow from the north can fill the Jordan River to overflowing. Or it may simply refer to a flood caused by heavy rains.

12:23-40 *to turn Saul's kingdom over . . . there was joy in Israel:* David ruled from Hebron for seven and a half years before he was made king of all Israel and moved to Jerusalem (2 Sam 5:1-5). But here Israelites from the northern tribes come to Hebron to convince David to be king over all Israel (12:38). The celebration in 12:38-40 is in honor of David being made king.

12:19,20 1 Sam 29. **12:21,22** 1 Sam 30.

13:3 *the ark of our God:* Referring to the ark of the covenant. See the note at 6:31, 32.

13:5,6 *Shihor River in Egypt to Lebo Hamath ... Baalah of Judah:* The Shihor River and Lebo Hamath represent the southern and northern boundaries of Israel. The Shihor may be the river that runs through the Egyptian Gorge in the northern Sinai Peninsula. Lebo Hamath was somewhere to the north of Lebanon near the Orontes River. See the map on p. 2465. Baalah (Kiriath Jearim) is where the ark was sent after the Philistines returned it to the Israelites (1 Sam 7:1, 2).

13:6 *ark of God ... cherubim:* See the note at 6:31, 32. Two cherubim, golden statues of winged creatures, were on top of the ark of the covenant. The LORD's throne on earth was said to be above these creatures (Exod 25:18-22; 1 Kgs 8:1-13; Ps 80:1).

30 men of Ephraim, brave warriors, famous in their own clans—20,800;
31 men of half the tribe of Manasseh, designated by name to come and make David king—18,000;
32 men of Issachar, who understood the times and knew what Israel should do—200 chiefs, with all their relatives under their command;
33 men of Zebulun, experienced soldiers prepared for battle with every type of weapon, to help David with undivided loyalty—50,000;
34 men of Naphtali—1,000 officers, together with 37,000 men carrying shields and spears;
35 men of Dan, ready for battle—28,600;
36 men of Asher, experienced soldiers prepared for battle—40,000;
37 and from east of the Jordan, men of Reuben, Gad and the half-tribe of Manasseh, armed with every type of weapon—120,000.

38 All these were fighting men who volunteered to serve in
the ranks. They came to Hebron fully determined to make David
king over all Israel. All the rest of the Israelites were also of one
mind to make David king. 39 The men spent three days there with
David, eating and drinking, for their families had supplied provisions for them. 40 Also, their neighbors from as far away as Issachar,
Zebulun and Naphtali came bringing food on donkeys, camels,
mules and oxen. There were plentiful supplies of flour, fig cakes,
raisin cakes, wine, oil, cattle and sheep, for there was joy in Israel.

Bringing Back the Ark

13 David conferred with each of his officers, the commanders
of thousands and commanders of hundreds. 2 He then said to the
whole assembly of Israel, "If it seems good to you and if it is the
will of the LORD our God, let us send word far and wide to the rest
of our brothers throughout the territories of Israel, and also to the
priests and Levites who are with them in their towns and pasturelands, to come and join us. 3 Let us bring the ark of our God back
to us, for we did not inquire of[a] it[b] during the reign of Saul." 4 The
whole assembly agreed to do this, because it seemed right to all the
people.

5 So David assembled all the Israelites, from the Shihor River
in Egypt to Lebo[c] Hamath, to bring the ark of God from Kiriath
Jearim. 6 David and all the Israelites with him went to Baalah of
Judah (Kiriath Jearim) to bring up from there the ark of God the
LORD, who is enthroned between the cherubim—the ark that is
called by the Name.

[a] **3** Or *we neglected* [b] **3** Or *him* [c] **5** Or *to the entrance to*

City of Jerusalem during the First Temple Period. Jerusalem was a small Jebusite city on top of a hill just west of the Kidron Valley when David chose it to be his capital. He expanded it, building a palace and other royal buildings. A Jebusite water shaft and wall fragment are almost all that remain of the city from the time of David. This model shows what Jerusalem may have looked like in the time of David's son Solomon, after he built the first temple (middle right) to the LORD there. (See 14:1, 2.)

7They moved the ark of God from Abinadab's house on a
new cart, with Uzzah and Ahio guiding it. 8David and all the
Israelites were celebrating with all their might before God, with
songs and with harps, lyres, tambourines, cymbals and trumpets.
9When they came to the threshing floor of Kidon, Uzzah
reached out his hand to steady the ark, because the oxen stumbled.
10The LORD's anger burned against Uzzah, and he struck him down
because he had put his hand on the ark. So he died there before
God.
11Then David was angry because the LORD's wrath had broken out against Uzzah, and to this day that place is called Perez
Uzzah.[a]
12David was afraid of God that day and asked, "How can I
ever bring the ark of God to me?" 13He did not take the ark to be
with him in the City of David. Instead, he took it aside to the
house of Obed-Edom the Gittite. 14The ark of God remained with
the family of Obed-Edom in his house for three months, and the
LORD blessed his household and everything he had.

David's House and Family

14 Now Hiram king of Tyre sent messengers to David, along
with cedar logs, stonemasons and carpenters to build a palace for
him. 2And David knew that the LORD had established him as king

[a]11 *Perez Uzzah* means *outbreak against Uzzah.*

13:7 *ark of God . . . Abinadab's house:* For more details, see 1 Sam 6:19—7:2.

13:8 *harps . . . trumpets:* The harps were either small ten-stringed harps (see Ps 33:2) or lyres. See also Ps 150 and the illustration on p. 897.

13:10 *The LORD's anger burned:* No one was to touch the ark of the covenant. Only the Levites were allowed to move the ark, and even they had to carry it with poles that were inserted in rings along the sides of the chest. See also Num 3:30,31; 4:14,15; 2 Sam 6:1-12; and the chart called "Israel on the March" on p. 288.

13:13,14 *Obed-Edom:* According to 26:1-5, Obed-Edom was a member of the Levite tribe, making him an acceptable person to care for the ark of the covenant. These verses in 1 Chronicles 26 also demonstrate that the gift of many sons was one way God had blessed Obed-Edom.

14:1 *Hiram king of Tyre:* According to 1 Kings 5:1-18, Hiram provided David's son Solomon with cedar and pine logs for building the temple. Tyre was an important Phoenician seaport on the Mediterranean coast. Good relationships with Israel were important to Tyre, because most of the inland trade routes Tyre used for transporting goods passed through territory controlled by Israel. Israel also supplied much of Tyre's food. See also the article called "Trade and Travel," p. 948.

14:2 *David knew that the LORD had established him:* David sees God's many blessings as signs that God was the power that had made him king of all Israel.

over Israel and that his kingdom had been highly exalted for the
sake of his people Israel.
3 In Jerusalem David took more wives and became the father
of more sons and daughters. 4 These are the names of the children
born to him there: Shammua, Shobab, Nathan, Solomon, 5 Ibhar,
Elishua, Elpelet, 6 Nogah, Nepheg, Japhia, 7 Elishama, Beeliada[a] and
Eliphelet.

David Defeats the Philistines

8 When the Philistines heard that David had been anointed
king over all Israel, they went up in full force to search for him, but
David heard about it and went out to meet them. 9 Now the
Philistines had come and raided the Valley of Rephaim; 10 so David
inquired of God: "Shall I go and attack the Philistines? Will you
hand them over to me?"
The LORD answered him, "Go, I will hand them over to you."
11 So David and his men went up to Baal Perazim, and there
he defeated them. He said, "As waters break out, God has broken
out against my enemies by my hand." So that place was called Baal
Perazim.[b] 12 The Philistines had abandoned their gods there, and
David gave orders to burn them in the fire.
13 Once more the Philistines raided the valley; 14 so David
inquired of God again, and God answered him, "Do not go
straight up, but circle around them and attack them in front of the
balsam trees. 15 As soon as you hear the sound of marching in the
tops of the balsam trees, move out to battle, because that will mean
God has gone out in front of you to strike the Philistine army."
16 So David did as God commanded him, and they struck down the
Philistine army, all the way from Gibeon to Gezer.
17 So David's fame spread throughout every land, and the
LORD made all the nations fear him.

The Ark Brought to Jerusalem

15 After David had constructed buildings for himself in the City
of David, he prepared a place for the ark of God and pitched a tent
for it. 2 Then David said, "No one but the Levites may carry the ark
of God, because the LORD chose them to carry the ark of the LORD
and to minister before him forever."
3 David assembled all Israel in Jerusalem to bring up the ark
of the LORD to the place he had prepared for it. 4 He called together the descendants of Aaron and the Levites:

5 From the descendants of Kohath,
Uriel the leader and 120 relatives;
6 from the descendants of Merari,
Asaiah the leader and 220 relatives;

[a] 7 A variant of *Eliada* [b] 11 *Baal Perazim* means *the lord who breaks out.*

The LORD answered him, "Go, I will hand them over to you."
1 Chr 14:10

14:3 *took more wives:* Some of these women were concubines (see the note at 3:9). Since a man was supposed to be able to support his wives, having many wives and children was a sign of wealth and importance.

14:4 *Solomon:* See the note at 3:5.

14:8-17 *Philistines . . . the LORD made all the nations fear him:* The Philistines may have hoped to destroy David before he had a chance to build Israel. In relating David's victory against the Philistines, the writer of 1 CHRONICLES clearly gives the credit for that victory to God. The victory also shows that David is indeed the one God supported as king of all Israel, especially since Saul's defense of Israel against the Philistines ended in defeat (1 Sam 28:16-25; 31:1-13). See also the note at 5:20-22 and the mini-article called "Holy War (The LORD's Battles)," p. 306.

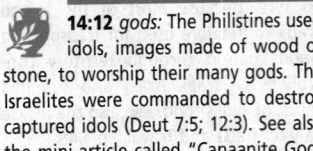

14:12 *gods:* The Philistines used idols, images made of wood or stone, to worship their many gods. The Israelites were commanded to destroy captured idols (Deut 7:5; 12:3). See also the mini-article called "Canaanite Gods and Goddesses," p. 469.

15:1 *ark of God . . . tent:* Proper respect for the ark of the covenant demanded that a special place be provided for it. See also the note at 6:31, 32.

15:2 *No one but the Levites:* Levites had not carried the ark of the covenant in David's disastrous earlier attempt to bring the ark to Jerusalem (13:5-14; 15:13). See also Num 4:4-8; Deut 10:8; and the note at 13:10.

7 from the descendants of Gershon,[a]
Joel the leader and 130 relatives;
8 from the descendants of Elizaphan,
Shemaiah the leader and 200 relatives;
9 from the descendants of Hebron,
Eliel the leader and 80 relatives;
10 from the descendants of Uzziel,
Amminadab the leader and 112 relatives.

11 Then David summoned Zadok and Abiathar the priests,
and Uriel, Asaiah, Joel, Shemaiah, Eliel and Amminadab the
Levites. 12 He said to them, "You are the heads of the Levitical families; you and your fellow Levites are to consecrate yourselves and
bring up the ark of the LORD, the God of Israel, to the place I have
prepared for it. 13 It was because you, the Levites, did not bring it
up the first time that the LORD our God broke out in anger against
us. We did not inquire of him about how to do it in the prescribed
way." 14 So the priests and Levites consecrated themselves in order
to bring up the ark of the LORD, the God of Israel. 15 And the
Levites carried the ark of God with the poles on their shoulders, as
Moses had commanded in accordance with the word of the LORD.

16 David told the leaders of the Levites to appoint their brothers as singers to sing joyful songs, accompanied by musical instruments: lyres, harps and cymbals.

17 So the Levites appointed Heman son of Joel; from his
brothers, Asaph son of Berekiah; and from their brothers the Merarites, Ethan son of Kushaiah; 18 and with them their brothers next
in rank: Zechariah,[b] Jaaziel, Shemiramoth, Jehiel, Unni, Eliab,
Benaiah, Maaseiah, Mattithiah, Eliphelehu, Mikneiah, Obed-Edom
and Jeiel,[c] the gatekeepers.

19 The musicians Heman, Asaph and Ethan were to sound the
bronze cymbals; 20 Zechariah, Aziel, Shemiramoth, Jehiel, Unni,
Eliab, Maaseiah and Benaiah were to play the lyres according to
alamoth,[d] 21 and Mattithiah, Eliphelehu, Mikneiah, Obed-Edom,
Jeiel and Azaziah were to play the harps, directing according to
sheminith.[d] 22 Kenaniah the head Levite was in charge of the
singing; that was his responsibility because he was skillful at it.

23 Berekiah and Elkanah were to be doorkeepers for the ark.
24 Shebaniah, Joshaphat, Nethanel, Amasai, Zechariah, Benaiah and
Eliezer the priests were to blow trumpets before the ark of God.
Obed-Edom and Jehiah were also to be doorkeepers for the ark.

25 So David and the elders of Israel and the commanders of
units of a thousand went to bring up the ark of the covenant of
the LORD from the house of Obed-Edom, with rejoicing. 26 Because
God had helped the Levites who were carrying the ark of the

---

[a]7 Hebrew *Gershom*, a variant of *Gershon* [b]18 Three Hebrew manuscripts and most Septuagint manuscripts (see also verse 20 and 1 Chron. 16:5); most Hebrew manuscripts *Zechariah son and* or *Zechariah, Ben and* [c]18 Hebrew; Septuagint (see also verse 21) *Jeiel and Azaziah* [d]20,21 Probably a musical term

15:12 *consecrate yourselves:* In Old Testament times, a person who was acceptable to worship God was called "clean." A person who had certain kinds of diseases, who had touched a dead body, or who had broken certain laws became "unclean," and was unacceptable to worship God. If a person was unclean because of disease, the disease would have to be cured before the person could be clean again. Becoming clean involved performing certain ceremonies that sometimes included sacrifices, special baths, and not having sex. Priests went through particular rituals to assure that they were "clean" and fit to perform their duties. See Exod 30:18-21; 40:31,32 and the mini-article called "Purity (Clean and Unclean)," p. 2125.

15:15 *poles:* See Exod 25:13-15 and the note at 13:10.

15:26 *seven bulls and seven rams were sacrificed:* This was an offering of thanks. "Seven" was considered a perfect or complete number. See the note at 6:49 (offerings).

15:25 1 Chr 13:12-14.

15:27 *ephod:* The Hebrew word can mean either a piece of clothing like a skirt that went from the waist to the knee or a garment like a vest or jacket that the priests wore. Linen cloth was made from the dried fibers of the flax plant. See also Exod 28:31-43.

15:29 *Michal:* She was one of David's wives. Michal, King Saul's daughter (1 Sam 18:27), felt David's dancing and leaping (2 Sam 6:16) were improper for one chosen to be king.

16:1-3 *burnt offerings and fellowship offerings ... blessed the people ... gave a loaf of bread:* David supervises the sacrifices and performs the priestly tasks of blessing the people and giving them food (Lev 7:11-19; Num 6:22-27). A main purpose of the burnt offerings was to please the LORD with the smell of the sacrifice. The main purpose of the fellowship offerings was to ask for the LORD's blessing.

16:4,5 *He appointed some of the Levites:* David is given credit for selecting people to lead worship, including Asaph (see also Ps 50 title).

16:7-36 *Give thanks to the LORD ... Praise be to the LORD:* The writer of 1 CHRONICLES includes portions of three psalms (Ps 105:1-15; 96:1-13; 106:1,47,48) as part of the worshiping community's celebration.

16:8-12 *what he has done ... wonderful acts ... wonders:* God's miracles in the past, including saving them from slavery in Egypt (Exod 2–15; also Ps 77:11-16; 105:26-29), providing food and water for them in the desert (Exod 15:22—17:7), giving them the Law at Sinai (Exod 19–24), helping them cross the Jordan River into Canaan (Josh 3), and helping them to take over the land (Canaan).

16:7 1 Chr 15:16-21.

covenant of the LORD, seven bulls and seven rams were sacrificed.
[27]Now David was clothed in a robe of fine linen, as were all the
Levites who were carrying the ark, and as were the singers, and
Kenaniah, who was in charge of the singing of the choirs. David
also wore a linen ephod. [28]So all Israel brought up the ark of the
covenant of the LORD with shouts, with the sounding of rams'
horns and trumpets, and of cymbals, and the playing of lyres and
harps.
[29]As the ark of the covenant of the LORD was entering
the City of David, Michal daughter of Saul watched from a window. And when she saw King David dancing and celebrating,
she despised him in her heart.

16 They brought the ark of God and set it inside the tent that
David had pitched for it, and they presented burnt offerings and
fellowship offerings[a] before God. [2]After David had finished sacrificing the burnt offerings and fellowship offerings, he blessed the
people in the name of the LORD. [3]Then he gave a loaf of bread, a
cake of dates and a cake of raisins to each Israelite man and
woman.
[4]He appointed some of the Levites to minister before the ark
of the LORD, to make petition, to give thanks, and to praise the
LORD, the God of Israel: [5]Asaph was the chief, Zechariah second,
then Jeiel, Shemiramoth, Jehiel, Mattithiah, Eliab, Benaiah, Obed-
Edom and Jeiel. They were to play the lyres and harps, Asaph was to
sound the cymbals, [6]and Benaiah and Jahaziel the priests were to
blow the trumpets regularly before the ark of the covenant of God.

David's Psalm of Thanks

[7]That day David first committed to Asaph and his associates
this psalm of thanks to the LORD:

[8]Give thanks to the LORD, call on his name;
make known among the nations what he has done.
[9]Sing to him, sing praise to him;
tell of all his wonderful acts.
[10]Glory in his holy name;
let the hearts of those who seek the LORD rejoice.
[11]Look to the LORD and his strength;
seek his face always.
[12]Remember the wonders he has done,
his miracles, and the judgments he pronounced,
[13]O descendants of Israel his servant,
O sons of Jacob, his chosen ones.

[14]He is the LORD our God;
his judgments are in all the earth.

[a]1 Traditionally *peace offerings*; also in verse 2

15 He remembers[a] his covenant forever,
the word he commanded, for a thousand generations,
16 the covenant he made with Abraham,
the oath he swore to Isaac.
17 He confirmed it to Jacob as a decree,
to Israel as an everlasting covenant:
18 "To you I will give the land of Canaan
as the portion you will inherit."

19 When they were but few in number,
few indeed, and strangers in it,
20 they[b] wandered from nation to nation,
from one kingdom to another.
21 He allowed no man to oppress them;
for their sake he rebuked kings:
22 "Do not touch my anointed ones;
do my prophets no harm."
23 Sing to the LORD, all the earth;
proclaim his salvation day after day.
24 Declare his glory among the nations,
his marvelous deeds among all peoples.
25 For great is the LORD and most worthy of praise;
he is to be feared above all gods.
26 For all the gods of the nations are idols,
but the LORD made the heavens.
27 Splendor and majesty are before him;
strength and joy in his dwelling place.
28 Ascribe to the LORD, O families of nations,
ascribe to the LORD glory and strength,
29 ascribe to the LORD the glory due his name.
Bring an offering and come before him;
worship the LORD in the splendor of his[c] holiness.
30 Tremble before him, all the earth!
The world is firmly established; it cannot be moved.
31 Let the heavens rejoice, let the earth be glad;
let them say among the nations, "The LORD reigns!"
32 Let the sea resound, and all that is in it;
let the fields be jubilant, and everything in them!
33 Then the trees of the forest will sing,
they will sing for joy before the LORD,
for he comes to judge the earth.

34 Give thanks to the LORD, for he is good;
his love endures forever.

---

[a]**15** Some Septuagint manuscripts (see also Psalm 105:8); Hebrew *Remember*
[b]**18-20** One Hebrew manuscript, Septuagint and Vulgate (see also Psalm 105:12); most Hebrew manuscripts *inherit,* / [19]*though you are but few in number,* / *few indeed, and strangers in it."* / [20]*They* [c]**29** Or *LORD with the splendor of*

Sing to the LORD, all the earth; proclaim his salvation day after day. Declare his glory among the nations, his marvelous deeds among all peoples.
1 Chr 16:23,24

16:13 *Israel his servant . . . chosen ones:* Beginning with their ancestor Abraham, the people of Israel were chosen to receive God's blessings, so they would be able to bless others (Gen 12:1-3; Exod 19:3-6; Deut 7:6-9; Isa 41:8, 9). See the note at 2:1, 2.

16:14-18 *covenant:* The covenant was made with Abraham, Isaac, and Jacob (Gen 12:7; 26:3; 28:13). Israel could keep the land God promised to give them if they worshiped God alone and obeyed God's Law (Josh 23:15,16).

16:31-33 *The LORD reigns . . . comes to judge the earth:* In addition to choosing Israel and saving it in times of trouble, the LORD God also rules the whole universe, which he created, and all the nations on earth (Ps 5:2). God is also often referred to as the one who will judge Israel and the nations (see the mini-article called "Day of the LORD," p. 1727).

16:21,22 Gen 20:3-7. **16:34** 2 Chr 5:13; 7:3; Ezra 3:11; Ps 100:5; 106:1; 107:1; 118:1; 136:1-26; Jer 33:11.

35 Cry out, "Save us, O God our Savior;
gather us and deliver us from the nations,
that we may give thanks to your holy name,
that we may glory in your praise."
36 Praise be to the LORD, the God of Israel,
from everlasting to everlasting.

Then all the people said "Amen" and "Praise the LORD."

37 David left Asaph and his associates before the ark of the
covenant of the LORD to minister there regularly, according to each
day's requirements. 38 He also left Obed-Edom and his sixty-eight
associates to minister with them. Obed-Edom son of Jeduthun,
and also Hosah, were gatekeepers.

39 David left Zadok the priest and his fellow priests before the
tabernacle of the LORD at the high place in Gibeon 40 to present
burnt offerings to the LORD on the altar of burnt offering regularly, morning and evening, in accordance with everything written in
the Law of the LORD, which he had given Israel. 41 With them were
Heman and Jeduthun and the rest of those chosen and designated
by name to give thanks to the LORD, "for his love endures forever."
42 Heman and Jeduthun were responsible for the sounding of the
trumpets and cymbals and for the playing of the other instruments for sacred song. The sons of Jeduthun were stationed at the
gate.

43 Then all the people left, each for his own home, and David
returned home to bless his family.

God's Promise to David

17 After David was settled in his palace, he said to Nathan the
prophet, "Here I am, living in a palace of cedar, while the ark of
the covenant of the LORD is under a tent."

2 Nathan replied to David, "Whatever you have in mind, do
it, for God is with you."

3 That night the word of God came to Nathan, saying:

4 "Go and tell my servant David, 'This is what the LORD
says: You are not the one to build me a house to dwell in. 5 I
have not dwelt in a house from the day I brought Israel up
out of Egypt to this day. I have moved from one tent site to
another, from one dwelling place to another. 6 Wherever I have
moved with all the Israelites, did I ever say to any of their
leaders[a] whom I commanded to shepherd my people, "Why
have you not built me a house of cedar?" '

7 "Now then, tell my servant David, 'This is what the
LORD Almighty says: I took you from the pasture and from
following the flock, to be ruler over my people Israel. 8 I have

[a]6 Traditionally *judges*; also in verse 10

16:37-42 *David left Asaph . . . David left Zadok:* David's intention to worship at both Jerusalem and Gibeon and his emphasis on the use of music in worship are signs of his respect for God and his concern that worship be done in a proper manner. See the note at 16:4,5.

16:37,39 *ark of the covenant . . . tabernacle:* The ark of the covenant was in a tent in Jerusalem that David had set up for it (15:1; 16:1). The tabernacle stayed in Gibeon until Solomon finished building the temple in Jerusalem (2 Chr 1:2-5,13; 5:4,5). See also the mini-articles called "The Ark of the Covenant," p. 513 and "The Tabernacle," p. 2346.

16:39 *Gibeon:* See the note at 8:29. It was at the shrine in Gibeon that God spoke to Solomon and gave him the gift of wisdom (1 Kgs 3:4-15).

17:1-27 *David . . . blessed forever:* This section relates God's promise to David that someone from David's family always would rule Israel. See also 2 Sam 7:1-29.

17:1 *Nathan the prophet:* A prophet was someone who spoke God's message. At first, Nathan speaks before hearing God's word and incorrectly advises David. He corrects that error after God appears to him in a vision (17:2-15).

17:5 *I have not dwelt in a house . . . I brought Israel up out of Egypt . . . tent:* For the story of the Israelites leaving Egypt, see Exod 6–14. The tabernacle with its furnishings (see Exod 25–27) was considered the LORD's home as the people moved from place to place. But now with the people settled in the land and being ruled by a strong king, it may have seemed like the right time to create a more permanent place for worshiping God.

been with you wherever you have gone, and I have cut off all
your enemies from before you. Now I will make your name
like the names of the greatest men of the earth. 9And I will
provide a place for my people Israel and will plant them so
that they can have a home of their own and no longer be disturbed. Wicked people will not oppress them anymore, as they
did at the beginning 10and have done ever since the time I
appointed leaders over my people Israel. I will also subdue all
your enemies.
" 'I declare to you that the LORD will build a house for
you: 11When your days are over and you go to be with your
fathers, I will raise up your offspring to succeed you, one of
your own sons, and I will establish his kingdom. 12He is the
one who will build a house for me, and I will establish his
throne forever. 13I will be his father, and he will be my son. I
will never take my love away from him, as I took it away from
your predecessor. 14I will set him over my house and my kingdom forever; his throne will be established forever.' "

15Nathan reported to David all the words of this entire revelation.

David's Prayer

16Then King David went in and sat before the LORD, and he
said:

"Who am I, O LORD God, and what is my family, that
you have brought me this far? 17And as if this were not
enough in your sight, O God, you have spoken about the
future of the house of your servant. You have looked on me as
though I were the most exalted of men, O LORD God.
18"What more can David say to you for honoring your
servant? For you know your servant, 19O LORD. For the sake of
your servant and according to your will, you have done this
great thing and made known all these great promises.
20"There is no one like you, O LORD, and there is no
God but you, as we have heard with our own ears. 21And who
is like your people Israel—the one nation on earth whose God
went out to redeem a people for himself, and to make a name
for yourself, and to perform great and awesome wonders by
driving out nations from before your people, whom you
redeemed from Egypt? 22You made your people Israel your
very own forever, and you, O LORD, have become their God.
23"And now, LORD, let the promise you have made concerning your servant and his house be established forever. Do
as you promised, 24so that it will be established and that your
name will be great forever. Then men will say, 'The LORD
Almighty, the God over Israel, is Israel's God!' And the house
of your servant David will be established before you.

"There is no one like you, O LORD, and there is no God but you . . . And who is like your people Israel—the one nation on earth whose God went out to redeem a people for himself?"
1 Chr 17:20,21

17:10-14 *I declare to you . . . throne will be established forever:* God promises that there always will be a descendant of David on the throne. This promise did remain true for about four hundred years until 587 B.C. when the Babylonians conquered Jerusalem and took many of its people into exile. David's descendants no longer ruled over Israel. Christians believe that Jesus, who is of the line of David, restores David's kingdom. See Isa 11:1,2,10; Ps 89:3,4,36,37; 132:11; John 7:42; Acts 2:30. See also the mini-article called "Messiah (Chosen One)," p. 1124.

17:16 *sat before the LORD:* Sitting, as we define it, is not a prayer posture of David's time and culture. The reference here is probably to a position of kneeling and sitting back on one's heels.

17:17-22 *There is no one like you, O LORD:* God's promise is for David and for all of Israel. David knows that there is only one true God, the God of Israel (17:20). David then repeats the covenant God made with Israel that they would be God's special people (17:22). See also the mini-article called "Covenants (Agreements)," p. 386.

16:43 2 Sam 6:19,20. **17:13** 2 Sam 7:14; 2 Cor 6:18; Heb 1:5.

18:1-6 *The LORD gave David victory everywhere he went:* David fights a series of battles that defeat Israel's enemies on all sides. Earlier, David had defeated the Amalekites to the south (1 Sam 30:16-20). Now he defeats the Philistines to the west (18:1), the Moabites to the east (18:2), and Hadadezer of Zobah and the Aramean kingdom of Damascus to the north (18:3,5). Zobah was an Aramean kingdom north of Damascus. The Arameans (Syrians), including Zobah, were controlled by Damascus, perhaps the world's oldest continually occupied city and a major trading and transportation center. Later, David's troops will further secure Israel's southern borders by defeating the Edomites (18:12,13). See the notes at 10:1 (Philistines); 4:22; and 1:38-54. See also the map on p. 2465.

18:4 *chariot horses:* A chariot was a two-wheeled cart that was open at the back and that was pulled by horses. Horses were also ridden into battle. See 1 Sam 8:11,12; 2 Sam 8:4 and the illustration on p. 160.

18:7,8 *gold shields . . . the bronze Sea:* The gold shields were probably used for ceremonies rather than for battle. The "bronze Sea" was a huge basin that held water that possibly was used by the priests for ritual cleansing. It may have symbolized God's separation of the waters that covered the earth to make the sky, land, and seas in the creation story (Gen 1:6-10; 1 Kgs 7:23-26). See also 1 Kgs 7:40-47; 2 Chr 4:11-18.

18:12,13 *Valley of Salt . . . Edom:* The Valley of Salt probably refers to the area at the southern end of the Dead Sea, near where Edom's northern border meets Judah's southern border (see the map on p. 2467). See also Ps 60 Title.

[25]"You, my God, have revealed to your servant that you
will build a house for him. So your servant has found courage
to pray to you. [26]O LORD, you are God! You have promised
these good things to your servant. [27]Now you have been
pleased to bless the house of your servant, that it may continue forever in your sight; for you, O LORD, have blessed it, and
it will be blessed forever."

DAVID'S WARS

David is unbeatable in war when he trusts God's rule. His victories also provide the wealth used for building the temple.

David's Victories

18 In the course of time, David defeated the Philistines and subdued them, and he took Gath and its surrounding villages from
the control of the Philistines.

[2]David also defeated the Moabites, and they became subject
to him and brought tribute.

[3]Moreover, David fought Hadadezer king of Zobah, as far as
Hamath, when he went to establish his control along the Euphrates
River. [4]David captured a thousand of his chariots, seven thousand
charioteers and twenty thousand foot soldiers. He hamstrung all
but a hundred of the chariot horses.

[5]When the Arameans of Damascus came to help Hadadezer
king of Zobah, David struck down twenty-two thousand of them.
[6]He put garrisons in the Aramean kingdom of Damascus, and the
Arameans became subject to him and brought tribute. The LORD
gave David victory everywhere he went.

[7]David took the gold shields carried by the officers of
Hadadezer and brought them to Jerusalem. [8]From Tebah[a] and
Cun, towns that belonged to Hadadezer, David took a great quantity of bronze, which Solomon used to make the bronze Sea, the
pillars and various bronze articles.

[9]When Tou king of Hamath heard that David had defeated
the entire army of Hadadezer king of Zobah, [10]he sent his son Hadoram to King David to greet him and congratulate him on his victory in battle over Hadadezer, who had been at war with Tou.
Hadoram brought all kinds of articles of gold and silver and bronze.

[11]King David dedicated these articles to the LORD, as he had
done with the silver and gold he had taken from all these nations:
Edom and Moab, the Ammonites and the Philistines, and Amalek.

[12]Abishai son of Zeruiah struck down eighteen thousand
Edomites in the Valley of Salt. [13]He put garrisons in Edom, and all
the Edomites became subject to David. The LORD gave David victory everywhere he went.

---

[a]8 Hebrew *Tibhath,* a variant of *Tebah*

David's Officials

[14]David reigned over all Israel, doing what was just and right for all his people. [15]Joab son of Zeruiah was over the army; Jehoshaphat son of Ahilud was recorder; [16]Zadok son of Ahitub and Ahimelech[a] son of Abiathar were priests; Shavsha was secretary; [17]Benaiah son of Jehoiada was over the Kerethites and Pelethites; and David's sons were chief officials at the king's side.

The Battle Against the Ammonites

19 In the course of time, Nahash king of the Ammonites died, and his son succeeded him as king. [2]David thought, "I will show kindness to Hanun son of Nahash, because his father showed kindness to me." So David sent a delegation to express his sympathy to Hanun concerning his father.

When David's men came to Hanun in the land of the Ammonites to express sympathy to him, [3]the Ammonite nobles said to Hanun, "Do you think David is honoring your father by sending men to you to express sympathy? Haven't his men come to you to explore and spy out the country and overthrow it?" [4]So Hanun seized David's men, shaved them, cut off their garments in the middle at the buttocks, and sent them away.

[5]When someone came and told David about the men, he sent messengers to meet them, for they were greatly humiliated. The king said, "Stay at Jericho till your beards have grown, and then come back."

[6]When the Ammonites realized that they had become a stench in David's nostrils, Hanun and the Ammonites sent a thousand talents[b] of silver to hire chariots and charioteers from Aram Naharaim,[c] Aram Maacah and Zobah. [7]They hired thirty-two thousand chariots and charioteers, as well as the king of Maacah with his troops, who came and camped near Medeba, while the Ammonites were mustered from their towns and moved out for battle.

[8]On hearing this, David sent Joab out with the entire army of fighting men. [9]The Ammonites came out and drew up in battle formation at the entrance to their city, while the kings who had come were by themselves in the open country.

[10]Joab saw that there were battle lines in front of him and behind him; so he selected some of the best troops in Israel and deployed them against the Arameans. [11]He put the rest of the men under the command of Abishai his brother, and they were deployed against the Ammonites. [12]Joab said, "If the Arameans are too strong for me, then you are to rescue me; but if the Ammonites are too strong for you, then I will rescue you.

---

[a]16 Some Hebrew manuscripts, Vulgate and Syriac (see also 2 Samuel 8:17); most Hebrew manuscripts *Abimelech* [b]6 That is, about 37 tons (about 34 metric tons) [c]6 That is, Northwest Mesopotamia

18:15,16 *Joab . . . Zadok:* For Jacob, see 11:4-6 and the note at 11:6. For Zadok, see 2 Sam 8:17; 1 Chr 16:39; and the note at 6:8-14.

19:4 *shaved them, cut off their garments:* In this culture, beards were a symbol of honor and manliness and were shaved only in times of mourning (Isa 15:2; Jer 41:5). Even plucking the beard was an insult; so to shave a man's beard in this way was extremely humiliating. Exposing the body was also considered shameful. Cutting the garments so short that the lower body showed caused such great humiliation that it was normally done only to prisoners of war.

19:5 *Jericho:* Jericho was an important city on the trade routes from the east to Palestine (see the map on p. 2464). It is one of the oldest cities in the world with evidence of building on the site before 5000 B.C. It was the first city the people of Israel captured when they crossed into Canaan (Josh 5:13—6:26).

19:6-15 *Ammonites:* The Ammonites were said to be the descendants of Lot's sons (Gen 19:30-38). The Ammonites lived east of the Jordan River and often battled with Israel (Judg 10:11-18; 1 Sam 14:47,48; 2 Chr 20:10,11; Jer 49:1-6).

19:9 *their city:* This probably refers to Rabbah, the capital city of Ammon.

Ancient Warfare. The methods of warfare in the ancient Near East were constantly changing. The development of walled cities for protection resulted in weapons that could penetrate or overcome them, like battering rams and siege towers with scaling ladders. Sometimes a moat was dug around a city and filled with water. Soldiers swam across on air-inflated bladders made from animal skins. These methods of warfare, along with others, are shown in these wall reliefs commemorating Assyrian military victories, most dating from the seventh and eighth centuries B.C.

19:13 *Be strong . . . The LORD will do what is good:* As military commander, Joab plans the battle (19:10-12), but he puts its outcome in God's hands and is rewarded with an easy victory (19:14,15). See also 14:8-17 and the note at 5:20-22.

19:17-19 *David . . . advanced against them:* This is the last time David leads a major military campaign against combined foreign powers. Though Hadadezer's subjects accept David as their ruler, we have no evidence that Hadadezer himself did so.

13 Be strong and let us fight bravely for our people and the cities of
our God. The LORD will do what is good in his sight."
14 Then Joab and the troops with him advanced to fight the
Arameans, and they fled before him. 15 When the Ammonites saw
that the Arameans were fleeing, they too fled before his brother
Abishai and went inside the city. So Joab went back to Jerusalem.
16 After the Arameans saw that they had been routed by
Israel, they sent messengers and had Arameans brought from
beyond the River,[a] with Shophach the commander of Hadadezer's
army leading them.
17 When David was told of this, he gathered all Israel and
crossed the Jordan; he advanced against them and formed his battle lines opposite them. David formed his lines to meet the
Arameans in battle, and they fought against him. 18 But they fled
before Israel, and David killed seven thousand of their charioteers
and forty thousand of their foot soldiers. He also killed Shophach
the commander of their army.

[a]16 That is, the Euphrates

[19]When the vassals of Hadadezer saw that they had been
defeated by Israel, they made peace with David and became subject to him.

So the Arameans were not willing to help the Ammonites
anymore.

The Capture of Rabbah

20 In the spring, at the time when kings go off to war, Joab led
out the armed forces. He laid waste the land of the Ammonites and
went to Rabbah and besieged it, but David remained in Jerusalem.
Joab attacked Rabbah and left it in ruins. [2]David took the crown
from the head of their king[a]—its weight was found to be a talent[b]
of gold, and it was set with precious stones—and it was placed on
David's head. He took a great quantity of plunder from the city
[3]and brought out the people who were there, consigning them to
labor with saws and with iron picks and axes. David did this to all
the Ammonite towns. Then David and his entire army returned to
Jerusalem.

War With the Philistines

[4]In the course of time, war broke out with the Philistines, at
Gezer. At that time Sibbecai the Hushathite killed Sippai, one of the
descendants of the Rephaites, and the Philistines were subjugated.
[5]In another battle with the Philistines, Elhanan son of Jair
killed Lahmi the brother of Goliath the Gittite, who had a spear
with a shaft like a weaver's rod.
[6]In still another battle, which took place at Gath, there was a
huge man with six fingers on each hand and six toes on each
foot—twenty-four in all. He also was descended from Rapha.
[7]When he taunted Israel, Jonathan son of Shimea, David's brother, killed him.
[8]These were descendants of Rapha in Gath, and they fell at
the hands of David and his men.

DAVID PLANS THE TEMPLE

Chapters 21, 22, 28, and 29 relate David's final preparations for the construction of the temple. Chapters 23–27 describe his organization of the people who will run the temple.

David Numbers the Fighting Men

21 Satan rose up against Israel and incited David to take a census of Israel. [2]So David said to Joab and the commanders of the
troops, "Go and count the Israelites from Beersheba to Dan. Then
report back to me so that I may know how many there are."

[a]2 Or *of Milcom,* that is, Molech [b]2 That is, about 75 pounds (about 34 kilograms)

20:4 *Gezer:* Gezer was at the crossroads of the north-south trade route and the east-west route between Jerusalem and the port at Joppa. Lower Beth Horon also protected the route between Jerusalem and the sea. See the map on p. 2465.

20:4 *the Rephaites:* This may refer to a group of people who lived in Palestine before the Israelites and who were famous for their large size (see also Josh 12:4; Deut 2:10,11,20,21).

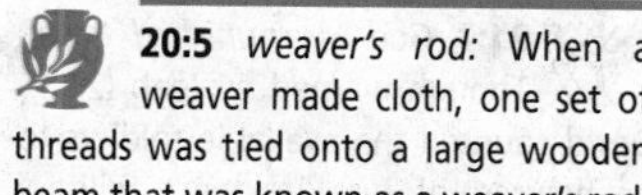

20:5 *weaver's rod:* When a weaver made cloth, one set of threads was tied onto a large wooden beam that was known as a weaver's rod.

21:1 *Satan:* Here, Satan makes David count the people (compare to 2 Sam 24:1). But God allows Satan to do so, and David must bear the responsibility of his own actions (21:7-13). See also the mini-article called "Satan," p. 963.

20:1 2 Sam 11:1—12:25. **20:5** 1 Sam 17:4-7.

21:5,6 *one million one hundred thousand . . . did not include Levi and Benjamin:* These numbers differ from those in 2 Samuel 24:9. Levites did not have to serve in the military, because they were responsible for Israel's religious life (Num 1:47-51). Because both the tabernacle in Gibeon (21:29,30) and the ark of the covenant in Jerusalem (15:1; 16:1) were in Benjamin territory (Josh 18:25-28), the tribe of Benjamin may also have been excused from military service.

21:7 *God . . . punished Israel:* Though warned by Joab (21:3), David counted the available soldiers to be assured of his kingdom's military strength, rather than trusting in God's complete leadership and control.

21:9 *Gad, David's seer:* The friendship of Gad and David goes back to the time when David was hiding from Saul, who wanted to kill him (1 Sam 22:5).

21:15 *angel:* See also the mini-article called "Angels," p. 88.

21:16 *sackcloth:* This rough cloth made from goat or camel hair was worn in times of trouble or sorrow.

21:18,23 *threshing floor of Araunah . . . threshing sledges:* This is believed to be the flat rock under the Dome of the Rock in present-day Jerusalem. At a threshing floor, bundles of grain stalks were beaten or crushed in order to separate the kernels from the outer husk. Often threshing floors were on hills so that the wind could more easily blow away the chaff. Threshing sledges were heavy boards with bits of rock or metal on the bottom. They were dragged across the grain by oxen or donkeys to separate the husks from the kernels. See also the note on p. 730.

3But Joab replied, "May the LORD multiply his troops a hundred times over. My lord the king, are they not all my lord's subjects? Why does my lord want to do this? Why should he bring
guilt on Israel?"

4The king's word, however, overruled Joab; so Joab left and
went throughout Israel and then came back to Jerusalem. 5Joab
reported the number of the fighting men to David: In all Israel
there were one million one hundred thousand men who could
handle a sword, including four hundred and seventy thousand in
Judah.

6But Joab did not include Levi and Benjamin in the numbering, because the king's command was repulsive to him. 7This
command was also evil in the sight of God; so he punished Israel.
8Then David said to God, "I have sinned greatly by doing
this. Now, I beg you, take away the guilt of your servant. I have
done a very foolish thing."

9The LORD said to Gad, David's seer, 10"Go and tell David,
'This is what the LORD says: I am giving you three options. Choose
one of them for me to carry out against you.'"

11So Gad went to David and said to him, "This is what the
LORD says: 'Take your choice: 12three years of famine, three months
of being swept away[a] before your enemies, with their swords over-
taking you, or three days of the sword of the LORD—days of plague
in the land, with the angel of the LORD ravaging every part of Israel.'
Now then, decide how I should answer the one who sent me."

13David said to Gad, "I am in deep distress. Let me fall into
the hands of the LORD, for his mercy is very great; but do not let
me fall into the hands of men."

14So the LORD sent a plague on Israel, and seventy thousand
men of Israel fell dead. 15And God sent an angel to destroy
Jerusalem. But as the angel was doing so, the LORD saw it and was
grieved because of the calamity and said to the angel who was
destroying the people, "Enough! Withdraw your hand." The angel
of the LORD was then standing at the threshing floor of Araunah[b]
the Jebusite.

16David looked up and saw the angel of the LORD standing
between heaven and earth, with a drawn sword in his hand
extended over Jerusalem. Then David and the elders, clothed in
sackcloth, fell facedown.

17David said to God, "Was it not I who ordered the fighting
men to be counted? I am the one who has sinned and done wrong.
These are but sheep. What have they done? O LORD my God, let
your hand fall upon me and my family, but do not let this plague
remain on your people."

18Then the angel of the LORD ordered Gad to tell David to go

[a]12 Hebrew; Septuagint and Vulgate (see also 2 Samuel 24:13) *of fleeing*
[b]15 Hebrew *Ornan,* a variant of *Araunah;* also in verses 18-28

up and build an altar to the LORD on the threshing floor of Araunah the Jebusite. [19]So David went up in obedience to the word that Gad had spoken in the name of the LORD.

[20]While Araunah was threshing wheat, he turned and saw the angel; his four sons who were with him hid themselves. [21]Then David approached, and when Araunah looked and saw him, he left the threshing floor and bowed down before David with his face to the ground.

[22]David said to him, "Let me have the site of your threshing floor so I can build an altar to the LORD, that the plague on the people may be stopped. Sell it to me at the full price."

[23]Araunah said to David, "Take it! Let my lord the king do whatever pleases him. Look, I will give the oxen for the burnt offerings, the threshing sledges for the wood, and the wheat for the grain offering. I will give all this."

[24]But King David replied to Araunah, "No, I insist on paying the full price. I will not take for the LORD what is yours, or sacrifice a burnt offering that costs me nothing."

[25]So David paid Araunah six hundred shekels[a] of gold for the site. [26]David built an altar to the LORD there and sacrificed burnt offerings and fellowship offerings.[b] He called on the LORD, and the LORD answered him with fire from heaven on the altar of burnt offering.

[27]Then the LORD spoke to the angel, and he put his sword back into its sheath. [28]At that time, when David saw that the LORD had answered him on the threshing floor of Araunah the Jebusite, he offered sacrifices there. [29]The tabernacle of the LORD, which Moses had made in the desert, and the altar of burnt offering were at that time on the high place at Gibeon. [30]But David could not go before it to inquire of God, because he was afraid of the sword of the angel of the LORD.

22 Then David said, "The house of the LORD God is to be here, and also the altar of burnt offering for Israel."

Preparations for the Temple

[2]So David gave orders to assemble the aliens living in Israel, and from among them he appointed stonecutters to prepare dressed stone for building the house of God. [3]He provided a large amount of iron to make nails for the doors of the gateways and for the fittings, and more bronze than could be weighed. [4]He also provided more cedar logs than could be counted, for the Sidonians and Tyrians had brought large numbers of them to David.

[5]David said, "My son Solomon is young and inexperienced, and the house to be built for the LORD should be of great magnificence and fame and splendor in the sight of all the nations.

[a]**25** That is, about 15 pounds (about 7 kilograms) [b]**26** Traditionally *peace offerings*

21:26 *burnt offerings and fellowship offerings:* See the note at 16:1-3.

21:26 *fire from heaven on the altar:* In the Bible, fire is often associated with God's presence (Exod 19:18; 1 Kgs 18:38; Ps 18:7, 8). Here, it also signals God's acceptance of David's prayer and approval of the future site of the temple. See also Lev 9:24; 2 Chr 7:1-3 and the mini-article called "Fire," p. 2383.

21:27 *angel:* See 21:15,16 and the mini-article called "Angels," p. 88.

21:28 *threshing floor ... offered sacrifices:* With the Levites prepared for their work (chapter 15) and the ark of the covenant already in Jerusalem (chapter 16), this approval by God of a new site for the offering of sacrifices indicates that all is now ready for the building of the temple.

22:2 *aliens:* Non-Israelites who were descendants of the Canaanites, or slaves taken in war. See the mini-article called "Foreigners (Aliens)," p. 501.

22:3,4 *bronze ... cedar logs:* Bronze is made by melting and mixing copper and tin. Ancient copper mines dating back at least to the time of Solomon have been discovered in the Arabah south of the Dead Sea.

Cedar is an extremely hard wood that has a beautiful tight grain for carving, and is valued for its distinctive smell. At one time cedar forests covered most of the Lebanon mountain range. See the map on p. 2465.

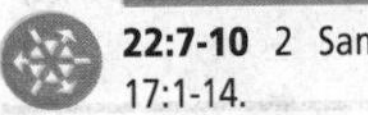

22:9 *son . . . man of peace and rest . . . Solomon:* The Hebrew word for "Solomon" sounds like the word for "peace" (*shalom*). Solomon will rule in a time of peace, while David spent much of his time at war. The writer of 1 CHRONICLES suggests that it was not only the time spent in war that kept David from building the temple (1 Kgs 5:3, 4), but that the blood shed by David made him unfit for the task.

22:7-10 2 Sam 7:1-16; 1 Chr 17:1-14.

Therefore I will make preparations for it." So David made extensive preparations before his death.

[6]Then he called for his son Solomon and charged him to build a house for the LORD, the God of Israel. [7]David said to Solomon: "My son, I had it in my heart to build a house for the Name of the LORD my God. [8]But this word of the LORD came to me: 'You have shed much blood and have fought many wars. You are not to build a house for my Name, because you have shed much blood on the earth in my sight. [9]But you will have a son who will be a man of peace and rest, and I will give him rest from all his enemies on every side. His name will be Solomon,[a] and I will grant Israel peace and quiet during his reign. [10]He is the one who will build a house for my Name. He will be my son, and I will be his father. And I will establish the throne of his kingdom over Israel forever.'

[a]9 *Solomon* sounds like and may be derived from the Hebrew for *peace.*

SOLOMON

Solomon, the tenth son of David and the second son of Bathsheba, became the third king of Israel in 970 B.C. and reigned for forty years. Though his path to the throne was marked by the murder of his political rivals (1 Kgs 2:25, 34, 46), Solomon's kingship was regarded as Israel's "Golden Age." It was a time of peace, prosperity, and great cultural achievements. The name "Solomon" in Hebrew means "peaceful." Only one military campaign is recorded during his time (2 Chr 8:3). The long period of peace during Solomon's reign caused great unity in Israel and loyalty to the throne. It also provided the time and wealth needed for Solomon's most important project, the construction of the Jerusalem temple. It was built from the materials generously provided by David (1 Chr 22) and, like the tabernacle before it, the temple symbolized God's continuing presence with his people.

Solomon earned large amounts of tax money by controlling major trade routes that went through Israel (1 Kgs 9:26-28; 10:14, 15). Even so, he was always in debt because of his many other building projects (1 Kgs 7:1-12). His financial problems forced him to give up territory (1 Kgs 9:10-12), to charge the people heavy taxes, and to make many people work in his projects without pay (1 Kgs 5:13-16). Unrest grew throughout the empire. While the taxes continued to be paid during his lifetime (1 Kgs 4:21), many places, such as the countries of Edom and Damascus, became increasingly independent (1 Kgs 11:14, 23-25).

More serious was Solomon's spiritual failure, which was due, in part, to the influence of his many non-Israelite wives, who worshiped foreign gods (1 Kgs 11:1-9). God was prompted to say, "Since this is your attitude and you have not kept my covenant and my decrees, which I commanded you, I will most certainly tear the kingdom away from you and give it to one of your subordinates" (1 Kgs 11:11). When Solomon died, his son Rehoboam became king. He could not keep the northern tribes from breaking away and forming their own nation. The descendants of David and Solomon continued to rule over the two southernmost tribes, which became known as the nation of Judah. That way, David would always have a descendant ruling in Jerusalem (1 Kgs 11:12, 13, 34-36).

11“Now, my son, the LORD be with you, and may you have success and build the house of the LORD your God, as he said you
would. 12May the LORD give you discretion and understanding when
he puts you in command over Israel, so that you may keep the law
of the LORD your God. 13Then you will have success if you are careful to observe the decrees and laws that the LORD gave Moses for
Israel. Be strong and courageous. Do not be afraid or discouraged.
14“I have taken great pains to provide for the temple of the
LORD a hundred thousand talents[a] of gold, a million talents[b] of
silver, quantities of bronze and iron too great to be weighed, and
wood and stone. And you may add to them. 15You have many
workmen: stonecutters, masons and carpenters, as well as men
skilled in every kind of work 16in gold and silver, bronze and
iron—craftsmen beyond number. Now begin the work, and the
LORD be with you.”
17Then David ordered all the leaders of Israel to help his son
Solomon. 18He said to them, “Is not the LORD your God with you?
And has he not granted you rest on every side? For he has handed
the inhabitants of the land over to me, and the land is subject to
the LORD and to his people. 19Now devote your heart and soul to
seeking the LORD your God. Begin to build the sanctuary of the
LORD God, so that you may bring the ark of the covenant of the
LORD and the sacred articles belonging to God into the temple that
will be built for the Name of the LORD.”

The Levites

23 When David was old and full of years, he made his son
Solomon king over Israel.
2He also gathered together all the leaders of Israel, as well as
the priests and Levites. 3The Levites thirty years old or more were
counted, and the total number of men was thirty-eight thousand.
4David said, “Of these, twenty-four thousand are to supervise the
work of the temple of the LORD and six thousand are to be officials
and judges. 5Four thousand are to be gatekeepers and four thousand are to praise the LORD with the musical instruments I have
provided for that purpose.”
6David divided the Levites into groups corresponding to the
sons of Levi: Gershon, Kohath and Merari.

Gershonites

7Belonging to the Gershonites:
Ladan and Shimei.
8The sons of Ladan:
Jehiel the first, Zetham and Joel—three in all.

---

[a]**14** That is, about 3,750 tons (about 3,450 metric tons) [b]**14** That is, about 37,500 tons (about 34,500 metric tons)

David said to Israel's leaders, *"Now devote your heart and soul to seeking the LORD your God."* 1 Chr 22:19

22:12,13 *discretion and understanding . . . decrees and laws:* Solomon is given this wisdom by God (1 Kgs 3:5-14; 2 Chr 1:7-12). The wisdom that God gives is often closely related to God's Law or to obeying the Law (see Prov 1:7; 2:4-7). See also the mini-article called "Wisdom," p. 2206. David tells Solomon that he will be successful as long as he obeys God's Law, which includes the Ten Commandments and the rest of the laws God gave to Moses and the people at Mount Sinai (see Exod 19–40; Deut 5:1-22; and the mini-article called "Law," p. 1160).

22:14 *gold . . . silver . . . bronze and iron . . . wood and stone:* David's preparations included enormous amounts of precious resources from those kingdoms he had conquered (18:1-13).

23:3 *thirty years old:* The age of the Levites who were considered able to serve in the temple varied from time to time even in Moses' day (Num 4:1-3; 8:24, 25). David changes the age again (1 Chr 23:24).

23:6 *divided the Levites into groups . . . Gershon, Kohath and Merari:* See the note at 6:1-30. The Levites are divided just as they were in Moses' time (Num 3:14-17).

22:13 Josh 1:6-9. **23:1** 1 Kgs 1:1-40.

Aaron was set apart, he and his descendants forever, to consecrate the most holy things, to offer sacrifices before the LORD, to minister before him and to pronounce blessings in his name forever.
1 Chr 23:13

23:13-15 *Aaron was set apart:* Aaron's descendants were considered to be Israel's true priests (Exod 28:1; Num 3:5-8; 18:1), while Moses' descendants, along with the rest of the Levites, were to be assistants to the priests (23:28). For more about the priests, see chapter 24.

[9]The sons of Shimei:
Shelomoth, Haziel and Haran—three in all.
These were the heads of the families of Ladan.
[10]And the sons of Shimei:
Jahath, Ziza,[a] Jeush and Beriah.
These were the sons of Shimei—four in all.
[11]Jahath was the first and Ziza the second, but Jeush and
Beriah did not have many sons; so they were counted as
one family with one assignment.

Kohathites

[12]The sons of Kohath:
Amram, Izhar, Hebron and Uzziel—four in all.
[13]The sons of Amram:
Aaron and Moses.
Aaron was set apart, he and his descendants forever, to
consecrate the most holy things, to offer sacrifices before
the LORD, to minister before him and to pronounce blessings in his name forever. [14]The sons of Moses the man of
God were counted as part of the tribe of Levi.
[15]The sons of Moses:
Gershom and Eliezer.
[16]The descendants of Gershom:
Shubael was the first.
[17]The descendants of Eliezer:
Rehabiah was the first.
Eliezer had no other sons, but the sons of Rehabiah were
very numerous.
[18]The sons of Izhar:
Shelomith was the first.
[19]The sons of Hebron:
Jeriah the first, Amariah the second, Jahaziel the third and
Jekameam the fourth.
[20]The sons of Uzziel:
Micah the first and Isshiah the second.

Merarites

[21]The sons of Merari:
Mahli and Mushi.
The sons of Mahli:
Eleazar and Kish.
[22]Eleazar died without having sons: he had only daughters.
Their cousins, the sons of Kish, married them.

---

[a]**10** One Hebrew manuscript, Septuagint and Vulgate (see also verse 11); most Hebrew manuscripts *Zina*

23 The sons of Mushi:
Mahli, Eder and Jerimoth—three in all.

24 These were the descendants of Levi by their families—the
heads of families as they were registered under their names and
counted individually, that is, the workers twenty years old or more
who served in the temple of the LORD. 25 For David had said, "Since
the LORD, the God of Israel, has granted rest to his people and has
come to dwell in Jerusalem forever, 26 the Levites no longer need to
carry the tabernacle or any of the articles used in its service."
27 According to the last instructions of David, the Levites were
counted from those twenty years old or more.

28 The duty of the Levites was to help Aaron's descendants in
the service of the temple of the LORD: to be in charge of the courtyards, the side rooms, the purification of all sacred things and the
performance of other duties at the house of God. 29 They were in
charge of the bread set out on the table, the flour for the grain
offerings, the unleavened wafers, the baking and the mixing, and
all measurements of quantity and size. 30 They were also to stand
every morning to thank and praise the LORD. They were to do the
same in the evening 31 and whenever burnt offerings were presented to the LORD on Sabbaths and at New Moon festivals and at
appointed feasts. They were to serve before the LORD regularly in
the proper number and in the way prescribed for them.

32 And so the Levites carried out their responsibilities for
the Tent of Meeting, for the Holy Place and, under their brothers
the descendants of Aaron, for the service of the temple of the
LORD.

The Divisions of Priests

24 These were the divisions of the sons of Aaron:
The sons of Aaron were Nadab, Abihu, Eleazar and Ithamar.
2 But Nadab and Abihu died before their father did, and they had
no sons; so Eleazar and Ithamar served as the priests. 3 With the
help of Zadok a descendant of Eleazar and Ahimelech a descendant of Ithamar, David separated them into divisions for their
appointed order of ministering. 4 A larger number of leaders were
found among Eleazar's descendants than among Ithamar's, and
they were divided accordingly: sixteen heads of families from
Eleazar's descendants and eight heads of families from Ithamar's
descendants. 5 They divided them impartially by drawing lots, for
there were officials of the sanctuary and officials of God among
the descendants of both Eleazar and Ithamar.

6 The scribe Shemaiah son of Nethanel, a Levite, recorded
their names in the presence of the king and of the officials: Zadok
the priest, Ahimelech son of Abiathar and the heads of families of
the priests and of the Levites—one family being taken from
Eleazar and then one from Ithamar.

23:25,26 *dwell in Jerusalem . . . no longer need to carry the tabernacle:* God's earthly home, or dwelling place, now will be within the temple in Jerusalem, not in the portable tabernacle. See also the notes at 6:48 and 13:6.

23:29 *all measurements of quantity and size:* In the morning and at twilight before sunset the priests were to offer sacrifices that included a young lamb, two pounds of flour mixed with a quart of pure olive oil, and a quart of wine. See also Exod 29:38-41.

23:31 *New Moon festivals:* These religious festivals were held on the day of the new moon, the day when only a thin edge of the moon can be seen. This day was always the first day of the month for the Hebrew calendar. The New Moon festival was a time of worship, sacrifices, celebration, feasting, and rest from work. See also the article called "People of the Law: The Religion of Israel," which gives a full summary of all the Jewish religious festivals, p. 939.

24:3 *Zadok:* Zadok served as priest at the tabernacle in Gibeon (1 Chr 16:39). See also 2 Sam 8:17 and the note at 1 Chr 6:8-14.

24:4 *sixteen . . . eight:* In addition to organizing the Levites (chapter 23), David organizes the priests by creating twenty-four divisions of duties. This allowed the priests to work in monthly shifts or for two-week shifts once a year as will be done in New Testament times (Luke 1:5–9). See also the mini-article called "Israel's Priests," p. 2344.

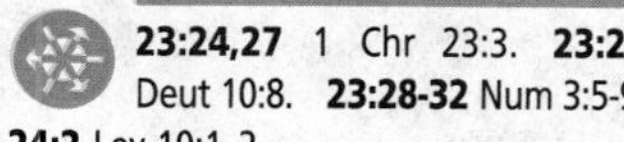

23:24,27 1 Chr 23:3. **23:26** Deut 10:8. **23:28-32** Num 3:5-9. **24:2** Lev 10:1, 2.

David, together with the commanders of the army, set apart some of the sons of Asaph, Heman and Jeduthun for the ministry of prophesying, accompanied by harps, lyres and cymbals.
1 Chr 25:1

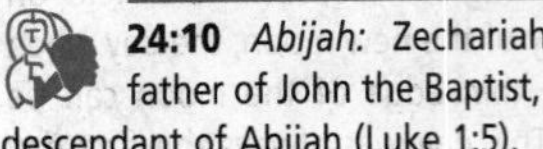
24:10 *Abijah:* Zechariah, the father of John the Baptist, was a descendant of Abijah (Luke 1:5).

[7]The first lot fell to Jehoiarib,
the second to Jedaiah,
[8]the third to Harim,
the fourth to Seorim,
[9]the fifth to Malkijah,
the sixth to Mijamin,
[10]the seventh to Hakkoz,
the eighth to Abijah,
[11]the ninth to Jeshua,
the tenth to Shecaniah,
[12]the eleventh to Eliashib,
the twelfth to Jakim,
[13]the thirteenth to Huppah,
the fourteenth to Jeshebeab,
[14]the fifteenth to Bilgah,
the sixteenth to Immer,
[15]the seventeenth to Hezir,
the eighteenth to Happizzez,
[16]the nineteenth to Pethahiah,
the twentieth to Jehezkel,
[17]the twenty-first to Jakin,
the twenty-second to Gamul,
[18]the twenty-third to Delaiah
and the twenty-fourth to Maaziah.

[19]This was their appointed order of ministering when they entered the temple of the LORD, according to the regulations prescribed for them by their forefather Aaron, as the LORD, the God of Israel, had commanded him.

The Rest of the Levites

[20]As for the rest of the descendants of Levi:
from the sons of Amram: Shubael;
from the sons of Shubael: Jehdeiah.
[21]As for Rehabiah, from his sons:
Isshiah was the first.
[22]From the Izharites: Shelomoth;
from the sons of Shelomoth: Jahath.
[23]The sons of Hebron: Jeriah the first,[a] Amariah the second,
Jahaziel the third and Jekameam the fourth.
[24]The son of Uzziel: Micah;
from the sons of Micah: Shamir.
[25]The brother of Micah: Isshiah;
from the sons of Isshiah: Zechariah.
[26]The sons of Merari: Mahli and Mushi.
The son of Jaaziah: Beno.

[a]**23** Two Hebrew manuscripts and some Septuagint manuscripts (see also 1 Chron. 23:19); most Hebrew manuscripts *The sons of Jeriah:*

27 The sons of Merari:
from Jaaziah: Beno, Shoham, Zaccur and Ibri.
28 From Mahli: Eleazar, who had no sons.
29 From Kish: the son of Kish:
Jerahmeel.
30 And the sons of Mushi: Mahli, Eder and Jerimoth.

These were the Levites, according to their families. 31 They
also cast lots, just as their brothers the descendants of Aaron did,
in the presence of King David and of Zadok, Ahimelech, and the
heads of families of the priests and of the Levites. The families of
the oldest brother were treated the same as those of the youngest.

The Singers

25 David, together with the commanders of the army, set apart
some of the sons of Asaph, Heman and Jeduthun for the ministry
of prophesying, accompanied by harps, lyres and cymbals. Here is
the list of the men who performed this service:

2 From the sons of Asaph:
Zaccur, Joseph, Nethaniah and Asarelah. The sons of Asaph were under the supervision of Asaph, who prophesied under the king's supervision.
3 As for Jeduthun, from his sons:
Gedaliah, Zeri, Jeshaiah, Shimei,[a] Hashabiah and Mattithiah, six in all, under the supervision of their father Jeduthun, who prophesied, using the harp in thanking and praising the LORD.
4 As for Heman, from his sons:
Bukkiah, Mattaniah, Uzziel, Shubael and Jerimoth; Hananiah,
Hanani, Eliathah, Giddalti and Romamti-Ezer; Joshbekashah,
Mallothi, Hothir and Mahazioth. 5 All these were sons of
Heman the king's seer. They were given him through the
promises of God to exalt him.[b] God gave Heman fourteen
sons and three daughters.

6 All these men were under the supervision of their fathers
for the music of the temple of the LORD, with cymbals, lyres and
harps, for the ministry at the house of God. Asaph, Jeduthun and
Heman were under the supervision of the king. 7 Along with their
relatives—all of them trained and skilled in music for the LORD—
they numbered 288. 8 Young and old alike, teacher as well as student, cast lots for their duties.

9 The first lot, which was for Asaph, fell to Joseph,
his sons and relatives,[c] 12[d]

[a]3 One Hebrew manuscript and some Septuagint manuscripts (see also verse 17); most Hebrew manuscripts do not have *Shimei.* [b]5 Hebrew *exalt the horn* [c]9 See Septuagint; Hebrew does not have *his sons and relatives.* [d]9 See the total in verse 7; Hebrew does not have *twelve.*

25:1 *sons of Asaph, Heman and Jeduthun:* In other lists of David's chief musicians, Ethan is named rather than Jeduthun (compare 6:31-48; 15:16-24; 16:37-42).

25:1 *harps, lyres and cymbals:* Cymbals were either two round plates, raised in the center and held by straps, or cone-shaped bronze cylinders with handles. Sound was created by striking the two plates or cylinders together.

See also the note at 13:8. Music was part of the offering of praise to God and helped people experience worship and hear God's word more easily (2 Chr 29:25-31).

25:5 *the king's seer . . . fourteen sons and three daughters:* In both 1 and 2 CHRONICLES musicians and music are commonly associated with prophecy (see 2 Chr 29:25; 35:15). See the note at 17:1.

Heman's large family was a sign of God's special blessing (Ps 127:3-5).

25:7-31 *they numbered 288 . . . The first lot:* As he had with the priests, David divides the musicians into twenty-four groups. Each group has twelve members for a total of 288 leaders of the four thousand musicians who were to play at the temple (23:5).

24:31 1 Chr 24:3-5.

the second to Gedaliah,
he and his relatives and sons, 12
10 the third to Zaccur,
his sons and relatives, 12
11 the fourth to Izri,[a]
his sons and relatives, 12
12 the fifth to Nethaniah,
his sons and relatives, 12
13 the sixth to Bukkiah,
his sons and relatives, 12
14 the seventh to Jesarelah,[b]
his sons and relatives, 12
15 the eighth to Jeshaiah,
his sons and relatives, 12
16 the ninth to Mattaniah,
his sons and relatives, 12
17 the tenth to Shimei,
his sons and relatives, 12
18 the eleventh to Azarel,[c]
his sons and relatives, 12
19 the twelfth to Hashabiah,
his sons and relatives, 12
20 the thirteenth to Shubael,
his sons and relatives, 12
21 the fourteenth to Mattithiah,
his sons and relatives, 12
22 the fifteenth to Jerimoth,
his sons and relatives, 12
23 the sixteenth to Hananiah,
his sons and relatives, 12
24 the seventeenth to Joshbekashah,
his sons and relatives, 12
25 the eighteenth to Hanani,
his sons and relatives, 12
26 the nineteenth to Mallothi,
his sons and relatives, 12
27 the twentieth to Eliathah,
his sons and relatives, 12
28 the twenty-first to Hothir,
his sons and relatives, 12
29 the twenty-second to Giddalti,
his sons and relatives, 12
30 the twenty-third to Mahazioth,
his sons and relatives, 12
31 the twenty-fourth to Romamti-Ezer,
his sons and relatives, 12

a11 A variant of *Zeri* **b14** A variant of *Asarelah* **c18** A variant of *Uzziel*

The Gatekeepers

26 The divisions of the gatekeepers:

From the Korahites: Meshelemiah son of Kore, one of the
sons of Asaph.
2 Meshelemiah had sons:
Zechariah the firstborn,
Jediael the second,
Zebadiah the third,
Jathniel the fourth,
3 Elam the fifth,
Jehohanan the sixth
and Eliehoenai the seventh.
4 Obed-Edom also had sons:
Shemaiah the firstborn,
Jehozabad the second,
Joah the third,
Sacar the fourth,
Nethanel the fifth,
5 Ammiel the sixth,
Issachar the seventh
and Peullethai the eighth.
(For God had blessed Obed-Edom.)

6 His son Shemaiah also had sons, who were leaders in their
father's family because they were very capable men. 7 The
sons of Shemaiah: Othni, Rephael, Obed and Elzabad; his
relatives Elihu and Semakiah were also able men. 8 All these
were descendants of Obed-Edom; they and their sons and
their relatives were capable men with the strength to do the
work—descendants of Obed-Edom, 62 in all.
9 Meshelemiah had sons and relatives, who were able men—18
in all.
10 Hosah the Merarite had sons: Shimri the first (although he
was not the firstborn, his father had appointed him the
first), 11 Hilkiah the second, Tabaliah the third and
Zechariah the fourth. The sons and relatives of Hosah
were 13 in all.

12 These divisions of the gatekeepers, through their chief
men, had duties for ministering in the temple of the LORD, just as
their relatives had. 13 Lots were cast for each gate, according to their
families, young and old alike.

14 The lot for the East Gate fell to Shelemiah.[a] Then lots were
cast for his son Zechariah, a wise counselor, and the lot for the
North Gate fell to him. 15 The lot for the South Gate fell to Obed-
Edom, and the lot for the storehouse fell to his sons. 16 The lots for

26:1 *gatekeepers . . . the sons of:* In addition to guarding the temple and opening and closing its doors, the gatekeepers kept records of the gifts brought to the temple, ordered supplies and food for the priests and sacrifices, kept all equipment and utensils in order, and mixed spices for incense. See also 9:17-32.

The "sons of" someone were part of a clan, a group of families who were related to each other and who often lived close to each other. A group of clans made up a tribe. Israel was organized into twelve tribes (Gen 49:1-28; Josh 13:14—19:51). See the note at 2:1, 2.

26:4,5 *God had blessed Obed-Edom:* Having many children was a sign of God's blessing. See 2 Sam 6:11,12; 1 Chr 13:14; and the note at 13:13,14.

26:14-16 *East Gate . . . West Gate:* The four main gates to the temple each faced a different direction. The East Gate was the main entrance and had six guard posts. The others had four. The South Gate was closest to the palaces of David and Solomon. The honor of guarding it was probably given to Obed-Edom because he had taken care of the ark of the covenant (13:13,14). Particular laws governed how the people were to enter and leave by the gates (Ezek 46:1-10). See also the map on p. 2466.

[a]**14** A variant of *Meshelemiah*

the West Gate and the Shalleketh Gate on the upper road fell to
Shuppim and Hosah.
Guard was alongside of guard: [17]There were six Levites a day
on the east, four a day on the north, four a day on the south and
two at a time at the storehouse. [18]As for the court to the west, there
were four at the road and two at the court itself.
[19]These were the divisions of the gatekeepers who were
descendants of Korah and Merari.

The Treasurers and Other Officials

[20]Their fellow Levites were[a] in charge of the treasuries of the
house of God and the treasuries for the dedicated things.
[21]The descendants of Ladan, who were Gershonites through
Ladan and who were heads of families belonging to Ladan the Gershonite, were Jehieli, [22]the sons of Jehieli, Zetham and his brother
Joel. They were in charge of the treasuries of the temple of the LORD.
[23]From the Amramites, the Izharites, the Hebronites and the
Uzzielites:

[24]Shubael, a descendant of Gershom son of Moses, was the
officer in charge of the treasuries. [25]His relatives through
Eliezer: Rehabiah his son, Jeshaiah his son, Joram his son,
Zicri his son and Shelomith his son. [26]Shelomith and his
relatives were in charge of all the treasuries for the things
dedicated by King David, by the heads of families who
were the commanders of thousands and commanders of
hundreds, and by the other army commanders. [27]Some of
the plunder taken in battle they dedicated for the repair
of the temple of the LORD. [28]And everything dedicated by
Samuel the seer and by Saul son of Kish, Abner son of Ner
and Joab son of Zeruiah, and all the other dedicated
things were in the care of Shelomith and his relatives.
[29]From the Izharites: Kenaniah and his sons were assigned duties
away from the temple, as officials and judges over Israel.
[30]From the Hebronites: Hashabiah and his relatives—seventeen
hundred able men—were responsible in Israel west of the
Jordan for all the work of the LORD and for the king's service. [31]As for the Hebronites, Jeriah was their chief according to the genealogical records of their families. In the
fortieth year of David's reign a search was made in the
records, and capable men among the Hebronites were
found at Jazer in Gilead. [32]Jeriah had twenty-seven hundred relatives, who were able men and heads of families,
and King David put them in charge of the Reubenites, the
Gadites and the half-tribe of Manasseh for every matter
pertaining to God and for the affairs of the king.

[a]**20** Septuagint; Hebrew *As for the Levites, Ahijah was*

26:20 *treasuries:* These included the gifts the people brought, the precious furnishings and equipment, and those things taken in warfare (26:26, 27; 2 Chr 5:1).

26:28 *Samuel . . . Saul . . . Abner . . . Joab:* Samuel served Israel as a priest, prophet, and judge, and named Saul as its first king (1 Sam 10:1, 18–21). See the note at 8:33.

Abner was King Saul's cousin and faithful general (see 1 Sam 14:49-51). For Joab, see the note at 11:6.

26:29-32 *assigned duties away from the temple:* These verses tell which of the six thousand Levites (23:4) served outside of the temple. They were in charge of all religious and government business (26:30,32), which shows that in Israel there was no difference between religious and civil law. Because God was the true king of Israel, God's law was Israel's law.

The fortieth year of David's rule (26:31) was also his last.

Army Divisions

27 This is the list of the Israelites—heads of families, commanders of thousands and commanders of hundreds, and their officers, who served the king in all that concerned the army divisions that were on duty month by month throughout the year. Each division consisted of 24,000 men.

2 In charge of the first division, for the first month, was Jashobeam son of Zabdiel. There were 24,000 men in his
division. 3 He was a descendant of Perez and chief of all the army officers for the first month.

4 In charge of the division for the second month was Dodai the Ahohite; Mikloth was the leader of his division. There were 24,000 men in his division.

5 The third army commander, for the third month, was Benaiah son of Jehoiada the priest. He was chief and there were
24,000 men in his division. 6 This was the Benaiah who was a mighty man among the Thirty and was over the Thirty. His son Ammizabad was in charge of his division.

7 The fourth, for the fourth month, was Asahel the brother of Joab; his son Zebadiah was his successor. There were 24,000 men in his division.

8 The fifth, for the fifth month, was the commander Shamhuth the Izrahite. There were 24,000 men in his division.

9 The sixth, for the sixth month, was Ira the son of Ikkesh the Tekoite. There were 24,000 men in his division.

10 The seventh, for the seventh month, was Helez the Pelonite, an Ephraimite. There were 24,000 men in his division.

11 The eighth, for the eighth month, was Sibbecai the Hushathite, a Zerahite. There were 24,000 men in his division.

12 The ninth, for the ninth month, was Abiezer the Anathothite, a Benjamite. There were 24,000 men in his division.

13 The tenth, for the tenth month, was Maharai the Netophathite, a Zerahite. There were 24,000 men in his division.

14 The eleventh, for the eleventh month, was Benaiah the Pirathonite, an Ephraimite. There were 24,000 men in his division.

15 The twelfth, for the twelfth month, was Heldai the Netophathite, from the family of Othniel. There were 24,000 men in his division.

Officers of the Tribes

16 The officers over the tribes of Israel:

over the Reubenites: Eliezer son of Zicri;
over the Simeonites: Shephatiah son of Maacah;
17 over Levi: Hashabiah son of Kemuel;

27:1-15 *list of the . . . commanders:* The regular army of Israel was made up of twelve divisions of 24,000 men each. The commanders of these divisions are listed here, and they are also are named in the list of David's warriors (11:11-14,20-47). This may indicate that David rewarded those who were faithful to him when he ran away from Saul (1 Sam 21–24). Besides the regular monthly army, many other warriors were available if a full-scale war broke out (21:5).

27:16-22 *officers over the tribes of Israel:* The officers of ten of the tribes are named along with the officers of the Levites and the descendants of Aaron, but the tribes of Asher and Gad are not mentioned. See also the mini-article called "Israel," p. 264, and the chart "Jacob's Children and Their Mothers" on p. 99.

David said, *"Acknowledge the God of your father, and serve him with wholehearted devotion and with a willing mind, for the LORD searches every heart and understands every motive behind the thoughts."*
1 Chr 28:9

27:17-21 *Zadok . . . Elihu . . . Abner:* For more on Zadok, see the note at 6:8-14. Elihu is not named as a brother of David elsewhere in the Bible, though the number of Jesse's sons is given as both seven (2:13-15) and eight (1 Sam 17:12). He may be the eighth son who is not named in 2:13-15. Elihu might also be another name for Eliab (1 Sam 16:6; 17:13,14), Jesse's oldest son (as in the Greek translation, see 1 Sam 16:6; 17:13, 14; 1 Chr 2:3–15). Or "brother" may be used here as "relative."

For more on Abner, see the note at 26:28.

27:25-31 *royal storehouses . . . King David's property:* This list is evidence of David's great wealth. As there is no evidence that David ever taxed the people of Israel, it appears he was able to finance the nation by way of trade, earnings from his land, valuables captured in wars, and taxes (tribute) paid by conquered nations.

27:27,28 *vineyards . . . olive and sycamore-fig trees . . . olive oil:* A vineyard is a place where grapes are grown on vines. Often a vineyard was located on a rocky hillside and had a protective wall around it (see the illustration on p. 1892). Sycamore trees were wide trees with branches that spread out close to the ground, making them easy to climb (Luke 19:3, 4). Egyptians used sycamore wood for their coffins because of its durability. Its fig-like fruit is bitter and was eaten primarily by the poor. Olive oil comes from the fruit of olive trees that were common in the area.

over Aaron: Zadok;
18 over Judah: Elihu, a brother of David;
over Issachar: Omri son of Michael;
19 over Zebulun: Ishmaiah son of Obadiah;
over Naphtali: Jerimoth son of Azriel;
20 over the Ephraimites: Hoshea son of Azaziah;
over half the tribe of Manasseh: Joel son of Pedaiah;
21 over the half-tribe of Manasseh in Gilead: Iddo son of Zechariah;
over Benjamin: Jaasiel son of Abner;
22 over Dan: Azarel son of Jeroham.
These were the officers over the tribes of Israel.

23 David did not take the number of the men twenty years
old or less, because the LORD had promised to make Israel as
numerous as the stars in the sky. 24 Joab son of Zeruiah began to
count the men but did not finish. Wrath came on Israel on
account of this numbering, and the number was not entered in the
book[a] of the annals of King David.

The King's Overseers

25 Azmaveth son of Adiel was in charge of the royal storehouses.

Jonathan son of Uzziah was in charge of the storehouses in the outlying districts, in the towns, the villages and the watchtowers.

26 Ezri son of Kelub was in charge of the field workers who farmed the land.

27 Shimei the Ramathite was in charge of the vineyards.

Zabdi the Shiphmite was in charge of the produce of the vineyards for the wine vats.

28 Baal-Hanan the Gederite was in charge of the olive and sycamore-fig trees in the western foothills.

Joash was in charge of the supplies of olive oil.

29 Shitrai the Sharonite was in charge of the herds grazing in Sharon.

Shaphat son of Adlai was in charge of the herds in the valleys.

30 Obil the Ishmaelite was in charge of the camels.

Jehdeiah the Meronothite was in charge of the donkeys.

31 Jaziz the Hagrite was in charge of the flocks.

All these were the officials in charge of King David's property.

32 Jonathan, David's uncle, was a counselor, a man of insight
and a scribe. Jehiel son of Hacmoni took care of the king's sons.
33 Ahithophel was the king's counselor.

[a]**24** Septuagint; Hebrew *number*

Hushai the Arkite was the king's friend. 34 Ahithophel was
succeeded by Jehoiada son of Benaiah and by Abiathar.
Joab was the commander of the royal army.

David's Plans for the Temple

28 David summoned all the officials of Israel to assemble at
Jerusalem: the officers over the tribes, the commanders of the divisions in the service of the king, the commanders of thousands and
commanders of hundreds, and the officials in charge of all the
property and livestock belonging to the king and his sons, together
with the palace officials, the mighty men and all the brave
warriors.
2 King David rose to his feet and said: "Listen to me, my
brothers and my people. I had it in my heart to build a house as a
place of rest for the ark of the covenant of the LORD, for the footstool of our God, and I made plans to build it. 3 But God said to
me, 'You are not to build a house for my Name, because you are a
warrior and have shed blood.'
4 "Yet the LORD, the God of Israel, chose me from my whole
family to be king over Israel forever. He chose Judah as leader, and
from the house of Judah he chose my family, and from my father's
sons he was pleased to make me king over all Israel. 5 Of all my
sons—and the LORD has given me many—he has chosen my son
Solomon to sit on the throne of the kingdom of the LORD over
Israel. 6 He said to me: 'Solomon your son is the one who will build
my house and my courts, for I have chosen him to be my son, and
I will be his father. 7 I will establish his kingdom forever if he is
unswerving in carrying out my commands and laws, as is being
done at this time.'
8 "So now I charge you in the sight of all Israel and of the
assembly of the LORD, and in the hearing of our God: Be careful to
follow all the commands of the LORD your God, that you may possess this good land and pass it on as an inheritance to your descendants forever.
9 "And you, my son Solomon, acknowledge the God of your
father, and serve him with wholehearted devotion and with a willing mind, for the LORD searches every heart and understands every
motive behind the thoughts. If you seek him, he will be found by
you; but if you forsake him, he will reject you forever. 10 Consider
now, for the LORD has chosen you to build a temple as a sanctuary.
Be strong and do the work."
11 Then David gave his son Solomon the plans for the portico of the temple, its buildings, its storerooms, its upper parts, its
inner rooms and the place of atonement. 12 He gave him the plans
of all that the Spirit had put in his mind for the courts of the temple of the LORD and all the surrounding rooms, for the treasuries
of the temple of God and for the treasuries for the dedicated

28:1 *Jerusalem:* See the note at 3:1-4.

28:3 *You are not to build a house for my Name:* See the note at 22:9.

28:8,9 *Be careful to follow all the commands:* Just as the temple was to be God's permanent home on earth (28:2), Canaan was to be Israel's permanent home on earth. David reminds the people and Solomon that this promise and the promise of God's great blessing depend on their obedience to God's laws. See also Deut 5:29, 33; 6:1-8; and the note at 1 Chr 22:12, 13.

28:11,14-18 *inner rooms . . . lampstands . . . altar of incense . . . cherubim . . . ark of the covenant:* The "inner rooms" would refer to the Holy Place and Most Holy Place in the temple. The ark of the covenant was kept in the Most Holy Place. The cherubim on the ark of the covenant were symbols of the LORD's throne on earth (Exod 25:18-22; 1 Kgs 8:1-13; Ps 80:1). These may have been similar to the human-headed bulls and lions that guarded Mesopotamian temples. Such winged creatures guarding sacred objects or places are common in Egyptian and Phoenician art. The chariot mentioned here may be a reference to the description of the LORD's glory (see Ezek 1).

The lampstands were to line the north and south walls of the Holy Place. Elsewhere, these are described as having a center piece with three branches on either side, each with a small saucer-like lamp attached to its end (Exod 25:31-40). The lamps probably were simple oil lamps that were filled with enough oil to burn through the night from sunset to sunrise (Exod 27:20).

A description of the altar of incense can be found at Exod 30:1-5. For these and other furnishings of the temple, see the illustration on p. 182.

27:23 Gen 15:5; 22:17; 26:4. **27:24** 2 Sam 24:1-17; 1 Chr 21:1-14. **27:33** 2 Sam 15:31-37; 17:1-23. **28:2-7** 2 Sam 7:1-16; 1 Chr 17:1-14.

28:19 *from the hand of the Lord:* Just as Moses was given God's Law, which showed the people how to live (Exod 20), David was given the plans for the temple where the people would worship God in the proper way.

29:1 *Solomon, the one whom God has chosen:* The Hebrew word for "chosen" used here and in 28:5,6,10 is only used in reference to Solomon and to no other king after David.

29:2-8 *gold . . . marble . . . iron . . . precious stones:* Compare the gifts David requested be brought for the temple to the gifts Moses asked the people to give to the original tent of meeting (Exod 35:4-9,20-29).

29:1,2 1 Chr 22:5.

things. [13]He gave him instructions for the divisions of the priests
and Levites, and for all the work of serving in the temple of the
Lord, as well as for all the articles to be used in its service. [14]He
designated the weight of gold for all the gold articles to be used in
various kinds of service, and the weight of silver for all the silver
articles to be used in various kinds of service: [15]the weight of gold
for the gold lampstands and their lamps, with the weight for each
lampstand and its lamps; and the weight of silver for each silver
lampstand and its lamps, according to the use of each lampstand;
[16]the weight of gold for each table for consecrated bread; the
weight of silver for the silver tables; [17]the weight of pure gold for
the forks, sprinkling bowls and pitchers; the weight of gold for
each gold dish; the weight of silver for each silver dish; [18]and the
weight of the refined gold for the altar of incense. He also gave him
the plan for the chariot, that is, the cherubim of gold that spread
their wings and shelter the ark of the covenant of the Lord.

[19]"All this," David said, "I have in writing from the hand of
the Lord upon me, and he gave me understanding in all the details
of the plan."

[20]David also said to Solomon his son, "Be strong and courageous, and do the work. Do not be afraid or discouraged, for the
Lord God, my God, is with you. He will not fail you or forsake you
until all the work for the service of the temple of the Lord is finished. [21]The divisions of the priests and Levites are ready for all the
work on the temple of God, and every willing man skilled in any
craft will help you in all the work. The officials and all the people
will obey your every command."

Gifts for Building the Temple

29 Then King David said to the whole assembly: "My son Solomon,
the one whom God has chosen, is young and inexperienced. The task
is great, because this palatial structure is not for man but for the Lord
God. [2]With all my resources I have provided for the temple of my
God—gold for the gold work, silver for the silver, bronze for the
bronze, iron for the iron and wood for the wood, as well as onyx for
the settings, turquoise,[a] stones of various colors, and all kinds of fine
stone and marble—all of these in large quantities. [3]Besides, in my
devotion to the temple of my God I now give my personal treasures of
gold and silver for the temple of my God, over and above everything
I have provided for this holy temple: [4]three thousand talents[b] of gold
(gold of Ophir) and seven thousand talents[c] of refined silver, for the
overlaying of the walls of the buildings, [5]for the gold work and the silver work, and for all the work to be done by the craftsmen. Now, who
is willing to consecrate himself today to the Lord?"

[a]2 The meaning of the Hebrew for this word is uncertain. [b]4 That is, about 110 tons (about 100 metric tons) [c]4 That is, about 260 tons (about 240 metric tons)

[6]Then the leaders of families, the officers of the tribes of
Israel, the commanders of thousands and commanders of hundreds, and the officials in charge of the king's work gave willingly.
[7]They gave toward the work on the temple of God five thousand
talents[a] and ten thousand darics[b] of gold, ten thousand talents[c] of
silver, eighteen thousand talents[d] of bronze and a hundred thousand talents[e] of iron. [8]Any who had precious stones gave them to
the treasury of the temple of the LORD in the custody of Jehiel the
Gershonite. [9]The people rejoiced at the willing response of their
leaders, for they had given freely and wholeheartedly to the LORD.
David the king also rejoiced greatly.

David praised the LORD . . . saying, "Yours, O LORD, is the kingdom; you are exalted as head over all. Wealth and honor come from you; you are the ruler of all things."
1 Chr 29:10-12

David's Prayer

[10]David praised the LORD in the presence of the whole
assembly, saying,

"Praise be to you, O LORD,
God of our father Israel,
from everlasting to everlasting.
[11]Yours, O LORD, is the greatness and the power
and the glory and the majesty and the splendor,
for everything in heaven and earth is yours.
Yours, O LORD, is the kingdom;
you are exalted as head over all.
[12]Wealth and honor come from you;
you are the ruler of all things.
In your hands are strength and power
to exalt and give strength to all.
[13]Now, our God, we give you thanks,
and praise your glorious name.

[14]"But who am I, and who are my people, that we should be
able to give as generously as this? Everything comes from you, and
we have given you only what comes from your hand. [15]We are
aliens and strangers in your sight, as were all our forefathers. Our
days on earth are like a shadow, without hope. [16]O LORD our God,
as for all this abundance that we have provided for building you a
temple for your Holy Name, it comes from your hand, and all of it
belongs to you. [17]I know, my God, that you test the heart and are
pleased with integrity. All these things have I given willingly and
with honest intent. And now I have seen with joy how willingly
your people who are here have given to you. [18]O LORD, God of our
fathers Abraham, Isaac and Israel, keep this desire in the hearts of
your people forever, and keep their hearts loyal to you. [19]And give

29:10 *our father Israel:* Referring to Jacob. See the note at 2:1,2.

29:18 *our fathers Abraham, Isaac and Israel:* Abraham's son was Isaac; Isaac's son was Jacob (also called Israel). See the notes at 1:28-33 and 2:1,2.

[a]7 That is, about 190 tons (about 170 metric tons) [b]7 That is, about 185 pounds (about 84 kilograms) [c]7 That is, about 375 tons (about 345 metric tons) [d]7 That is, about 675 tons (about 610 metric tons) [e]7 That is, about 3,750 tons (about 3,450 metric tons)

The LORD highly exalted Solomon in the sight of all Israel and bestowed on him royal splendor such as no king over Israel ever had before.
1 Chr 29:25

29:21 *sacrifices to the LORD:* See the note at 16:1-3.

Solomon Crowned King, illustration by Jean Fouquet from a printed edition of Josephus's *Antiquities of the Jews,* around 1474. FIRST CHRONICLES names nineteen of David's many sons (3:1-9). Solomon was one of the four sons David had by Bathsheba, and he was the one the LORD wanted to be king after David. The LORD told David, "You will have a son . . . I will give him rest from all his enemies on every side" (22:9). The day Solomon was finally crowned king, the Israelites celebrated by slaughtering a thousand bulls, a thousand rams, and a thousand lambs (29:21-25).

my son Solomon the wholehearted devotion to keep your commands, requirements and decrees and to do everything to build the palatial structure for which I have provided."
[20]Then David said to the whole assembly, "Praise the LORD your God." So they all praised the LORD, the God of their fathers; they bowed low and fell prostrate before the LORD and the king.

Solomon Acknowledged as King

[21]The next day they made sacrifices to the LORD and presented burnt offerings to him: a thousand bulls, a thousand rams

and a thousand male lambs, together with their drink offerings,
and other sacrifices in abundance for all Israel. 22They ate and
drank with great joy in the presence of the LORD that day.
Then they acknowledged Solomon son of David as king a
second time, anointing him before the LORD to be ruler and Zadok
to be priest. 23So Solomon sat on the throne of the LORD as king in
place of his father David. He prospered and all Israel obeyed him.
24All the officers and mighty men, as well as all of King David's
sons, pledged their submission to King Solomon.
25The LORD highly exalted Solomon in the sight of all Israel
and bestowed on him royal splendor such as no king over Israel
ever had before.

The Death of David

26David son of Jesse was king over all Israel. 27He ruled over
Israel forty years—seven in Hebron and thirty-three in Jerusalem.
28He died at a good old age, having enjoyed long life, wealth and
honor. His son Solomon succeeded him as king.
29As for the events of King David's reign, from beginning to
end, they are written in the records of Samuel the seer, the records
of Nathan the prophet and the records of Gad the seer, 30together
with the details of his reign and power, and the circumstances that
surrounded him and Israel and the kingdoms of all the other
lands.

29:22 *anointing . . . Zadok to be priest:* See the note at 11:3. Zadok's loyalty to David, Solomon, and God made him the likely choice for high priest. For more about Zadok's loyalty and for another account of Solomon's becoming king, see 1 Kings 1:1—2:27.

29:24 *pledged their submission to King Solomon:* This ignores the events recorded in 1 Kings 1, which describes Adonijah and others attempting to take the throne from David.

29:29,30 *written in the records of Samuel the seer . . . Nathan . . . Gad:* These three are given credit for writing the books of SAMUEL and KINGS, or some other separate unknown history of David.

29:23 1 Kgs 2:12. **29:27** 2 Sam 5:4,5; 1 Chr 3:1-4.

QUESTIONS ABOUT 1 CHRONICLES 9:35—29:30

1. David was promised that when he became king, everyone in Israel would support him (11:10). When David is at Hebron, what evidence is given that he will receive unified support from Israel's tribes? (12:1-40)
2. Why was it so important for David to bring the ark of the covenant to Jerusalem? (13:1—16:43)
3. What is your reaction to God's severe punishment of Uzzah? (13:9-11) Why was God so angry? What is the positive lesson this story seeks to teach?
4. Read 5:20-22; 14:8-17; and the mini-article called "Holy War (The LORD's Battles)," p. 306. What does the Holy War concept have to do with David's kingship? Where have you heard of the concept of "Holy War" in today's society? In your opinion, are any wars being fought today true "holy wars"? Why or why not?
5. What was God's promise to David? (17:3-15) How is this promise significant to David? To the people of Israel? To Christians?
6. List at least five things David contributed toward the building and functioning of the temple (22:1—29:30).
7. "Solomon" is related to the Hebrew word for "peace." How does this help us to understand why God chose Solomon rather than David to build the temple? (22:6-9)
8. After reading 1 CHRONICLES, what questions, if any, do you have?

2 CHRONICLES

Remembering a golden age from the past can give people strength and hope even when they are living in exile. Read 2 Chronicles and see how God's chosen people were encouraged by recalling their faithful leaders from the past.

What makes 2 Chronicles special?

The book of 2 Chronicles continues the story told in 1 Chronicles, and before that, in the books of Samuel and Kings. But 2 Chronicles introduces a new point of view. The writer of 2 Chronicles is more concerned with the ways of proper worship than with political matters.

In telling the story of Solomon, the writer concentrates on Solomon's building of the temple, leaving out the less appealing details of how Solomon came to the throne (1 Kgs 1, 2) and his later fall from faith (1 Kgs 11). In dealing with the kings who came after Solomon, the writer pays particular attention to Asa, Jehoshaphat, Hezekiah, and Josiah, four kings who were especially faithful and dedicated to bringing the people back to God.

Why was 2 Chronicles written?

Like 1 Chronicles, 2 Chronicles was written to give encouragement to the people who had returned from exile in Babylon. The writer of 2 Chronicles makes the point that God's plan for them was not affected by the fall of Judah or by their long stay in a foreign land. Though they might feel that their hopes as God's people had perished with the destruction of Jerusalem and the temple, the writer intends to show them that this was just another stage in the accomplishment of God's purpose. The writer wants to encourage them to reestablish their religious practices and institutions in the tradition of those who had gone before them.

What's the story behind the scene?

The book of 2 Chronicles repeats many stories that are found in 1 and 2 Kings, but from the point of view of devotion to faith. The stories needed to be retold, because the situation of their audience was quite different from that of the people who had first read 1 and 2 Kings. The original readers of those earlier books had lived during the exile and had experienced the destruction of Jerusalem and the end of the rule by David's ancestors. Their lives were filled with questions, such as "Why did this happen to us?" and "Did God's plan fail?" The books of 1 and 2 Kings answer these questions by showing that God did not fail. God fulfilled his warning that the people would be punished for their failure to live up to their agreement to obey God's word.

But the books of Chronicles are addressed to people who have returned from exile in Babylon. Their questions are different and require a different telling of the story. Instead of asking "Why

Solomon and David: Solomon was the second son of David and Bathsheba (2 Sam 12:24). He followed his father as king and was chosen by God to build the temple in Jerusalem (1 Chr 28:1—29:2). The writer of 2 Chronicles is primarily concerned with Solomon's greatness as king and builder of the temple, and so ignores the violence that was part of his path to the throne (1 Kgs 1,2). See also the mini-article called "Solomon," p. 776.

David was king of Israel from about 1010 to 970 B.C., and was the most famous king Israel ever had. Many of the people of Israel hoped that one of his descendants would always be their king. See also the mini-article called "David," p. 1028.

did this happen to us?" the people want to ask about their relationship to the past: "Are we still the people of God?" and "What do God's promises to David mean for us?" The books of CHRONICLES retell the story of Israel's past in ways that speak to these questions.

HOW IS 2 CHRONICLES CONSTRUCTED?

The book of 2 CHRONICLES is told in three major sections. The first section (2 Chr 1–9) tells the story of Solomon, the builder of the temple. The second section (2 Chr 10–28) retells the story of the divided monarchy following the rebellion of the northern tribes, but it records only the history of the southern kingdom, Judah. The third section (2 Chr 29–36) presents the story of the monarchy from the conquest of the northern kingdom by the Assyrians until the exile of the people of Judah to Babylon. At the close of 2 CHRONICLES, King Cyrus of Persia declares the end of the exile, and the people are allowed to return to Judah.

1:1 *Solomon . . . David:* See the note on p. 792.

1:3-5 *Tent of Meeting . . . ark of God . . . bronze altar . . . tabernacle:* The ark of God refers to the ark of the covenant that contained the tablets of the Ten Commandments and functioned as the throne of the LORD Almighty. See also the mini-article called "The Ark of the Covenant," p. 513.

The bronze altar was a raised structure where sacrifices and offerings were presented to God. The Tent of Meeting was another name for the tabernacle—the portable tent which functioned as a place of worship where the people brought gifts and the priests offered sacrifices to God during the wandering in the desert. It is described in Exodus 26. At this time, the tabernacle was located in Gideon. See also the mini-article called "The Tabernacle," p. 2346.

David had also pitched a tent in Jerusalem when he moved the ark of the covenant there (2 Sam 6:17). This tent housed the ark until Solomon built the temple.

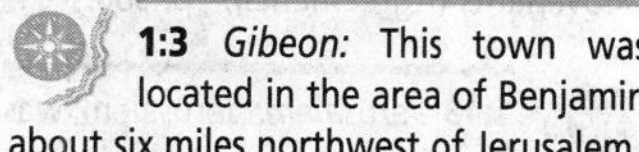

1:3 *Gibeon:* This town was located in the area of Benjamin about six miles northwest of Jerusalem.

Solomon, Builder of the Temple

The story of Solomon, as told by the writer of 2 CHRONICLES, is concerned primarily with the building of the temple. This construction project is seen to be the result of the combined efforts of David, who planned and provided for its construction, and Solomon, the one chosen by God to do the actual building.

SOLOMON'S WISDOM AND WEALTH

Solomon Asks for Wisdom

1 Solomon son of David established himself firmly over his kingdom, for the LORD his God was with him and made him exceedingly great.

2 Then Solomon spoke to all Israel—to the commanders of thousands and commanders of hundreds, to the judges and to all the leaders in Israel, the heads of families— 3 and Solomon and the whole assembly went to the high place at Gibeon, for God's Tent of Meeting was there, which Moses the LORD's servant had made in the

desert. [4]Now David had brought up the ark of God from Kiriath Jearim to the place he had prepared for it, because he had pitched a tent for it in Jerusalem. [5]But the bronze altar that Bezalel son of Uri, the son of Hur, had made was in Gibeon in front of the tabernacle of the LORD; so Solomon and the assembly inquired of him there. [6]Solomon went up to the bronze altar before the LORD in the Tent of Meeting and offered a thousand burnt offerings on it.

[7]That night God appeared to Solomon and said to him, "Ask for whatever you want me to give you."

[8]Solomon answered God, "You have shown great kindness to David my father and have made me king in his place. [9]Now, LORD God, let your promise to my father David be confirmed, for you have made me king over a people who are as numerous as the dust of the earth. [10]Give me wisdom and knowledge, that I may lead this people, for who is able to govern this great people of yours?"

[11]God said to Solomon, "Since this is your heart's desire and you have not asked for wealth, riches or honor, nor for the death of your enemies, and since you have not asked for a long life but for wisdom and knowledge to govern my people over whom I have made you king, [12]therefore wisdom and knowledge will be given you. And I will also give you wealth, riches and honor, such as no king who was before you ever had and none after you will have."

[13]Then Solomon went to Jerusalem from the high place at Gibeon, from before the Tent of Meeting. And he reigned over Israel.

[14]Solomon accumulated chariots and horses; he had fourteen hundred chariots and twelve thousand horses,[a] which he kept in the chariot cities and also with him in Jerusalem. [15]The king made silver and gold as common in Jerusalem as stones, and cedar as plentiful as sycamore-fig trees in the foothills. [16]Solomon's horses were imported from Egypt[b] and from Kue[c]—the royal merchants purchased them from Kue. [17]They imported a chariot from Egypt for six hundred shekels[d] of silver, and a horse for a hundred and fifty.[e] They also exported them to all the kings of the Hittites and of the Arameans.

SOLOMON BUILDS THE TEMPLE

Besides emphasizing Solomon's role as its builder, this section describes the temple's location, interior, and furnishings.

Preparations for Building the Temple

2 Solomon gave orders to build a temple for the Name of the LORD and a royal palace for himself. [2]He conscripted seventy thou-

[a]14 Or *charioteers* [b]16 Or possibly *Muzur,* a region in Cilicia; also in verse 17 [c]16 Probably Cilicia [d]17 That is, about 15 pounds (about 7 kilograms) [e]17 That is, about 3 3/4 pounds (about 1.7 kilograms)

1:5 *Bezalel:* Bezalel was the skilled craftsman chosen by God to make the tabernacle and its furnishings, including the bronze altar mentioned here (Exod 31:1-11; 38:1-20).

1:6 *burnt offerings:* These offerings traditionally have been called "whole burnt offerings" because the whole animal was burned on the altar. A main purpose of such sacrifices was to please the LORD with the smell of the sacrifice. See also the chart called "Sacrifices and Offerings," p. 219.

1:7,8 *God appeared to Solomon . . . have made me king:* God spoke to people in dreams and visions. Solomon's statement that God made him king shows his proper understanding of kingship in Israel. God chooses Israel's earthly kings, who then carry out God's will.

1:9 *your promise to my father David:* God promised that a descendant of David would always rule God's people. See 2 Sam 7:10-16; 1 Chr 17:7-14; and the mini-article called "Covenants (Agreements)," p. 386.

1:13 *Jerusalem:* Jerusalem was Israel's political and religious capital. See the map on p. 2465 and the mini-article called "Jerusalem," p. 574.

1:14 *chariots . . . horses:* A chariot was a two-wheeled cart that was open at the back and was pulled by horses. Horses were also ridden into battle and were a sign of wealth. See 1 Sam 8:11,12; 2 Sam 8:4; 1 Kgs 4:26; and the illustration on p. 160.

1:4 2 Sam 6:1-17; 1 Chr 13:5-14; 15:1—16:1. **1:5** Exod 38:1-7. **1:9** Gen 13:16; 28:14. **1:16,17** Deut 17:16.

Cutting Down Cedars for the Construction of the Temple, engraving by Gustave Doré, around 1866. Solomon was famous for his many building projects. He built a palace for himself and a temple for the LORD in Jerusalem. This required the finest lumber. The cedars that grew in the Lebanon mountains were famous throughout the ancient Near East for their strength and for the beauty of their wood. These trees were cut down in Lebanon by King Hiram's workmen, shipped in rafts along the coast of the Mediterranean Sea to Joppa, and then carried overland to Jerusalem. See 2:1-16.

sand men as carriers and eighty thousand as stonecutters in the
hills and thirty-six hundred as foremen over them.
3 Solomon sent this message to Hiram[a] king of Tyre:

"Send me cedar logs as you did for my father David
when you sent him cedar to build a palace to live in. 4 Now I
am about to build a temple for the Name of the LORD my God
and to dedicate it to him for burning fragrant incense before
him, for setting out the consecrated bread regularly, and for
making burnt offerings every morning and evening and on

[a]3 Hebrew *Huram,* a variant of *Hiram;* also in verses 11 and 12

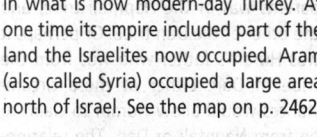

1:16,17 *Hittites . . . Arameans:* The Hittite nation had its capital in what is now modern-day Turkey. At one time its empire included part of the land the Israelites now occupied. Aram (also called Syria) occupied a large area north of Israel. See the map on p. 2462.

2:1 *royal palace:* Solomon's palace and its construction are described in 1 Kings 7:1-12.

2:3 *Hiram king of Tyre:* Tyre was the most important city in Phoenicia. It was located north of Israel on the coast of the Mediterranean Sea, in modern south Lebanon. See also 2 Sam 5:11 and the map on p. 2467.

Sabbaths and New Moons and at the appointed feasts of the LORD our God. This is a lasting ordinance for Israel.

5“The temple I am going to build will be great, because our God is greater than all other gods. 6But who is able to build a temple for him, since the heavens, even the highest heavens, cannot contain him? Who then am I to build a temple for him, except as a place to burn sacrifices before him?

7“Send me, therefore, a man skilled to work in gold and silver, bronze and iron, and in purple, crimson and blue yarn, and experienced in the art of engraving, to work in Judah and Jerusalem with my skilled craftsmen, whom my father David provided.

8“Send me also cedar, pine and algum[a] logs from Lebanon, for I know that your men are skilled in cutting timber there. My men will work with yours 9to provide me with plenty of lumber, because the temple I build must be large and magnificent. 10I will give your servants, the woodsmen who cut the timber, twenty thousand cors[b] of ground wheat, twenty thousand cors of barley, twenty thousand baths[c] of wine and twenty thousand baths of olive oil.”

11Hiram king of Tyre replied by letter to Solomon:

“Because the LORD loves his people, he has made you their king.”

12And Hiram added:

“Praise be to the LORD, the God of Israel, who made heaven and earth! He has given King David a wise son, endowed with intelligence and discernment, who will build a temple for the LORD and a palace for himself.

13“I am sending you Huram-Abi, a man of great skill, 14whose mother was from Dan and whose father was from Tyre. He is trained to work in gold and silver, bronze and iron, stone and wood, and with purple and blue and crimson yarn and fine linen. He is experienced in all kinds of engraving and can execute any design given to him. He will work with your craftsmen and with those of my lord, David your father.

15“Now let my lord send his servants the wheat and barley and the olive oil and wine he promised, 16and we will cut all the logs from Lebanon that you need and will float them in rafts by sea down to Joppa. You can then take them up to Jerusalem.”

17Solomon took a census of all the aliens who were in Israel, after the census his father David had taken; and they were found to be 153,600. 18He assigned 70,000 of them to be carriers and 80,000

---

[a]**8** Probably a variant of *almug*; possibly juniper [b]**10** That is, probably about 125,000 bushels (about 4,400 kiloliters) [c]**10** That is, probably about 115,000 gallons (about 440 kiloliters)

2:6 *who is able to build a temple for him:* Though the tabernacle, and now the temple, have been seen as both places of worship and as God's home on earth, Solomon here recognizes that no place can contain God. This verse emphasizes the temple as a place of worship. See also the note at 1:3-5 (ark of God).

2:7 *a man skilled . . . experienced:* The Phoenicians were well-known in the ancient world for their skills in many crafts. See also 1 Chr 22:15,16 and the mini-article called "Phoenicia," p. 1604.

2:8 *cedar, pine and algum logs:* Cedar is an extremely hard wood that resists dry rot and insects, has a beautiful tight grain for carving, and is valued for its distinctive smell. At one time, cedar forests covered most of the Lebanon mountain range that runs north of Tyre for about 100 miles along the coast. See the map on p. 2465. In general, however, large forests were not common in this part of the world, and so all wood was precious. Algum may be another name for juniper.

2:13,14 *Huram-Abi . . . from Dan:* FIRST KINGS says that Huram's mother was from the tribe of Naphtali (1 Kgs 7:14). Perhaps one of his mother's parents was of the Naphtali tribe, and the other of the Dan tribe. Or perhaps it was Huram's father who was from the tribe of Dan. Either of these circumstances would allow Huram to claim to be from Naphtali or Dan. The relationship to the Israelite community is what is important.

2:16 *Joppa:* This major port city is on the coast of the Mediterranean Sea. See the map on p. 2465, and the article called "Trade and Travel," p. 948.

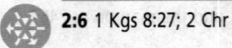

2:6 1 Kgs 8:27; 2 Chr 6:18.

to be stonecutters in the hills, with 3,600 foremen over them to keep the people working.

Solomon Builds the Temple

3 Then Solomon began to build the temple of the LORD in Jerusalem on Mount Moriah, where the LORD had appeared to his father David. It was on the threshing floor of Araunah[a] the Jebusite, the place provided by David. [2]He began building on the second day of the second month in the fourth year of his reign.

[3]The foundation Solomon laid for building the temple of God was sixty cubits long and twenty cubits wide[b] (using the cubit of the old standard). [4]The portico at the front of the temple was twenty cubits[c] long across the width of the building and twenty cubits[d] high.

He overlaid the inside with pure gold. [5]He paneled the main hall with pine and covered it with fine gold and decorated it with palm tree and chain designs. [6]He adorned the temple with precious stones. And the gold he used was gold of Parvaim. [7]He overlaid the ceiling beams, doorframes, walls and doors of the temple with gold, and he carved cherubim on the walls.

[8]He built the Most Holy Place, its length corresponding to the width of the temple—twenty cubits long and twenty cubits wide. He overlaid the inside with six hundred talents[e] of fine gold. [9]The gold nails weighed fifty shekels.[f] He also overlaid the upper parts with gold.

[10]In the Most Holy Place he made a pair of sculptured cherubim and overlaid them with gold. [11]The total wingspan of the cherubim was twenty cubits. One wing of the first cherub was five cubits[g] long and touched the temple wall, while its other wing, also five cubits long, touched the wing of the other cherub. [12]Similarly one wing of the second cherub was five cubits long and touched the other temple wall, and its other wing, also five cubits long, touched the wing of the first cherub. [13]The wings of these cherubim extended twenty cubits. They stood on their feet, facing the main hall.[h]

[14]He made the curtain of blue, purple and crimson yarn and fine linen, with cherubim worked into it.

[15]In the front of the temple he made two pillars, which ⌊together⌋ were thirty-five cubits[i] long, each with a capital on top measuring five cubits. [16]He made interwoven chains[j] and put them

---

a1 Hebrew *Ornan*, a variant of *Araunah* **b3** That is, about 90 feet (about 27 meters) long and 30 feet (about 9 meters) wide **c4** That is, about 30 feet (about 9 meters); also in verses 8, 11 and 13 **d4** Some Septuagint and Syriac manuscripts; Hebrew *and a hundred and twenty* **e8** That is, about 23 tons (about 21 metric tons) **f9** That is, about 1 1/4 pounds (about 0.6 kilogram) **g11** That is, about 7 1/2 feet (about 2.3 meters); also in verse 15 **h13** Or *facing inward* **i15** That is, about 52 feet (about 16 meters) **j16** Or possibly *made chains in the inner sanctuary*; the meaning of the Hebrew for this phrase is uncertain.

3:2 *second month:* Ziv, the second month of the Hebrew calendar, from about mid-April to mid-May. See 1 Kgs 6:1. See also the chart "Jewish Calendar and Festivals," p. 944.

3:3 *using the cubit of the old standard:* There may have been two different standards of measurement during Israel's history.

3:6 *Parvaim:* The location of this place is unknown. Perhaps its gold was of extremely fine quality.

3:8,10,14 *Most Holy Place . . . sculptured cherubim . . . curtain:* The Most Holy Place is the inner sanctuary of the temple. It, along with the Holy Place and the outer courtyard, were the major parts of the temple. Only the high priest could enter the Most Holy Place on the Day of Atonement (Lev 16:1-28). The Most Holy Place traditionally has been called "the Holy of Holies." It was separated from view by the curtain (Exod 26:31-34).

Two cherubim (golden statues of winged creatures) were on top of the ark of the covenant. The LORD's throne on earth was said to be above these creatures (Exod 25:18-22; 1 Kgs 8:1-13; Ps 80:1). See also the note at 1 Chr 28:11,14–18.

The curtain separated the Most Holy Place from the main room of the temple (Exod 26:31-34). For more about these and other temple areas and furnishings see the article called "People of the Law: The Religion of Israel," p. 939.

3:15,16 *two pillars . . . pomegranates:* The pillars appear to be freestanding. It was common at the time to have such columns at the entrance to a temple, although these are particularly large.

A pomegranate is a small red fruit. In ancient times it was a symbol of life. See the illustration on p. 1277.

3:1,2 Gen 22:2; 1 Chr 21:15,18.

on top of the pillars. He also made a hundred pomegranates and
attached them to the chains. [17]He erected the pillars in the front of
the temple, one to the south and one to the north. The one to the
south he named Jakin[a] and the one to the north Boaz.[b]

The Temple's Furnishings

4 He made a bronze altar twenty cubits long, twenty cubits wide
and ten cubits high.[c] [2]He made the Sea of cast metal, circular in
shape, measuring ten cubits from rim to rim and five cubits[d] high.
It took a line of thirty cubits[e] to measure around it. [3]Below the
rim, figures of bulls encircled it—ten to a cubit.[f] The bulls were
cast in two rows in one piece with the Sea.

[4]The Sea stood on twelve bulls, three facing north, three facing west, three facing south and three facing east. The Sea rested
on top of them, and their hindquarters were toward the center. [5]It
was a handbreadth[g] in thickness, and its rim was like the rim of a
cup, like a lily blossom. It held three thousand baths.[h]

[6]He then made ten basins for washing and placed five on the
south side and five on the north. In them the things to be used for
the burnt offerings were rinsed, but the Sea was to be used by the
priests for washing.

[7]He made ten gold lampstands according to the specifications for them and placed them in the temple, five on the south
side and five on the north.

[8]He made ten tables and placed them in the temple, five on
the south side and five on the north. He also made a hundred gold
sprinkling bowls.

[9]He made the courtyard of the priests, and the large court
and the doors for the court, and overlaid the doors with bronze.
[10]He placed the Sea on the south side, at the southeast corner.

[11]He also made the pots and shovels and sprinkling bowls.
So Huram finished the work he had undertaken for King
Solomon in the temple of God:

[12]the two pillars;
the two bowl-shaped capitals on top of the pillars;
the two sets of network decorating the two bowl-shaped capitals on top of the pillars;
[13]the four hundred pomegranates for the two sets of network (two rows of pomegranates for each network, decorating the bowl-shaped capitals on top of the pillars);
[14]the stands with their basins;

[a]17 *Jakin* probably means *he establishes.* [b]17 *Boaz* probably means *in him is strength.* [c]1 That is, about 30 feet (about 9 meters) long and wide, and about 15 feet (about 4.5 meters) high [d]2 That is, about 7 1/2 feet (about 2.3 meters) [e]2 That is, about 45 feet (about 13.5 meters) [f]3 That is, about 1 1/2 feet (about 0.5 meter) [g]5 That is, about 3 inches (about 8 centimeters) [h]5 That is, about 17,500 gallons (about 66 kiloliters)

4:1,2 *bronze altar . . . the Sea:* The bronze altar was the main altar where sacrifices were offered. This bronze altar outside the entrance to the temple was solid bronze while the one inside the tabernacle and the earlier altar were bronze over wood (Exod 27:1-8; 38:1,2). See also the note at 1:3-5.

The Sea was possibly used by the priests for ritual cleansing (2 Chr 4:6; Exod 30:17-21). It may have symbolized God's separation of the waters that covered the earth to make the sky, land, and seas in the creation story (Gen 1:6-10; 1 Kgs 7:23-26; 1 Chr 18:8).

4:7,8 *lampstands . . . sprinkling bowls:* The ten lampstands are described elsewhere as having a center piece with three branches on either side, each with a small saucer-like lamp attached to its end (Exod 25:31-40).

Sprinkling bowls were used in the preparations for an animal sacrifice. For more about the temple and its furnishings see the illustration on p. 182 and the article called "People of the Law: The Religion of Israel," p. 939.

4:13 *pomegranates:* See the note at 3:15,16.

4:8 Exod 25:23-30.

[15]the Sea and the twelve bulls under it;
[16]the pots, shovels, meat forks and all related articles.

All the objects that Huram-Abi made for King Solomon for
the temple of the LORD were of polished bronze. [17]The king had
them cast in clay molds in the plain of the Jordan between Succoth and Zarethan.[a] [18]All these things that Solomon made
amounted to so much that the weight of the bronze was not determined.

[19]Solomon also made all the furnishings that were in God's
temple:

the golden altar;
the tables on which was the bread of the Presence;
[20]the lampstands of pure gold with their lamps, to burn in
front of the inner sanctuary as prescribed;
[21]the gold floral work and lamps and tongs (they were solid
gold);
[22]the pure gold wick trimmers, sprinkling bowls, dishes and
censers; and the gold doors of the temple: the inner doors
to the Most Holy Place and the doors of the main hall.

5 When all the work Solomon had done for the temple of the
LORD was finished, he brought in the things his father David had
dedicated—the silver and gold and all the furnishings—and he
placed them in the treasuries of God's temple.

SOLOMON DEDICATES THE TEMPLE

After Solomon moves the ark of the covenant to the completed temple, God promises to forgive Israel whenever the people humbly pray, turn back to God, and stop sinning.

The Ark Brought to the Temple

[2]Then Solomon summoned to Jerusalem the elders of Israel,
all the heads of the tribes and the chiefs of the Israelite families, to
bring up the ark of the LORD's covenant from Zion, the City of
David. [3]And all the men of Israel came together to the king at the
time of the festival in the seventh month.

[4]When all the elders of Israel had arrived, the Levites took up
the ark, [5]and they brought up the ark and the Tent of Meeting and
all the sacred furnishings in it. The priests, who were Levites, carried them up; [6]and King Solomon and the entire assembly of Israel
that had gathered about him were before the ark, sacrificing so
many sheep and cattle that they could not be recorded or counted.
[7]The priests then brought the ark of the LORD's covenant to
its place in the inner sanctuary of the temple, the Most Holy Place,

[a]17 Hebrew *Zeredatha,* a variant of *Zarethan*

4:17 *the plain of the Jordan between Succoth and Zarethan:* The bronze furnishings were made here because the clay soil was needed to make the molds for the objects. Bronze itself is made by mixing copper and tin.

4:19 *bread of the Presence:* This bread was a symbol of the LORD's presence in the temple. It was put out on special tables and was replaced with fresh bread every week (Lev 24:5-9).

5:1 *temple . . . finished:* The temple took seven and a half years to build and was completed in Solomon's eleventh year as king, or about 959 B.C. See also 1 Kgs 6:37, 38.

5:1 *the things his father David had dedicated:* Foreign kings offered gifts to David, and David collected valuable things from enemies he defeated (2 Sam 8:9-12; 1 Chr 18:11). These things were dedicated to the LORD (1 Chr 29:1-8).

5.2 *Zion, the City of David:* Mount Zion was a hill in Jerusalem. The City of David was the Jebusite fortress on Mount Zion that David conquered. See the map on p. 2466. See also 2 Sam 5:6-12; 6:11-16; 1 Chr 15:25-29 and the mini-article called "Zion," p. 1294.

5:3 *the festival in the seventh month:* This would be the Feast of Tabernacles that took place at the end of the fall harvest (Lev 23:33-36) and lasted for seven days. In addition to giving thanks to God for the fall harvest, the people were to build and live in shelters made of tree branches during the celebration to remember the temporary shelters their ancestors lived in after they left Egypt and wandered in the desert (Lev 23:33-42). See also Num 29:12-38; Neh 8:13-17; Ezek 45:25.

5:9,10 *poles . . . tablets:* Poles were put through rings on the sides of the ark of the covenant so that the chest itself would not be touched when carried (Exod 25:13-15).

The stone tablets recorded the Ten Commandments. See also Deut 10:1-5. Earlier, the ark of the covenant also contained a jar of manna (Exod 16:32-34) and Aaron's staff (Num 17:10; Heb 9:4).

5:11,12 *consecrated themselves . . . Levites:* This ceremony may have involved washing themselves with water taken from the large bronze bowl known as the Sea (see 4:1,2 and the note).

Levi was the son of Jacob and Leah (Gen 29:34). The "Levites" were members of the tribe of Levi who were not descended from Aaron (Num 18:1-6; 20-32). David is given credit for establishing the tradition of musicians for the temple (1 Chr 6:31-47). In later times, the Levite musicians began the tradition of choosing and singing psalms that were suitable to particular occasions, sacrifices, or festivals, much as this is done today. See also the note at 11:13.

5:14 *the glory of the* LORD*:* Here as elsewhere, a cloud surrounds and covers God's appearance before the people (Exod 14:19, 20; 33:9-11; 40:34-37; Ps 18:11; Isa 6:4; Mark 9:7). At other times, God appears under the cover of fire (Exod 3:2-4; 2 Chr 7:3; Ezek 1:27).

6:5 *out of Egypt:* See Exod 6–14.

5:11-14 Exod 40:34, 35; 1 Chr 16:34, 41; 2 Chr 7:3; Ezra 3:11; Ps 100:5; 106:1; 107:1; 118:1; 136:1; Jer 33:11. **6:6-9** 2 Sam 7:1-13; 1 Chr 17:1-12; 22:6-10.

and put it beneath the wings of the cherubim. 8The cherubim
spread their wings over the place of the ark and covered the ark
and its carrying poles. 9These poles were so long that their ends,
extending from the ark, could be seen from in front of the inner
sanctuary, but not from outside the Holy Place; and they are still
there today. 10There was nothing in the ark except the two tablets
that Moses had placed in it at Horeb, where the LORD made a
covenant with the Israelites after they came out of Egypt.

11The priests then withdrew from the Holy Place. All the
priests who were there had consecrated themselves, regardless of
their divisions. 12All the Levites who were musicians—Asaph,
Heman, Jeduthun and their sons and relatives—stood on the east
side of the altar, dressed in fine linen and playing cymbals, harps
and lyres. They were accompanied by 120 priests sounding trumpets. 13The trumpeters and singers joined in unison, as with one
voice, to give praise and thanks to the LORD. Accompanied by
trumpets, cymbals and other instruments, they raised their voices
in praise to the LORD and sang:

"He is good;
his love endures forever."

Then the temple of the LORD was filled with a cloud, 14and
the priests could not perform their service because of the cloud,
for the glory of the LORD filled the temple of God.

6 Then Solomon said, "The LORD has said that he would dwell in
a dark cloud; 2I have built a magnificent temple for you, a place for
you to dwell forever."

3While the whole assembly of Israel was standing there, the
king turned around and blessed them. 4Then he said:

"Praise be to the LORD, the God of Israel, who with his
hands has fulfilled what he promised with his mouth to my
father David. For he said, 5'Since the day I brought my people
out of Egypt, I have not chosen a city in any tribe of Israel to
have a temple built for my Name to be there, nor have I chosen anyone to be the leader over my people Israel. 6But now I
have chosen Jerusalem for my Name to be there, and I have
chosen David to rule my people Israel.'

7"My father David had it in his heart to build a temple
for the Name of the LORD, the God of Israel. 8But the LORD
said to my father David, 'Because it was in your heart to build
a temple for my Name, you did well to have this in your heart.
9Nevertheless, you are not the one to build the temple, but
your son, who is your own flesh and blood—he is the one
who will build the temple for my Name.'

10"The LORD has kept the promise he made. I have succeeded David my father and now I sit on the throne of Israel,
just as the LORD promised, and I have built the temple for the

Name of the LORD, the God of Israel. 11 There I have placed the
ark, in which is the covenant of the LORD that he made with
the people of Israel."

Solomon's Prayer of Dedication

12 Then Solomon stood before the altar of the LORD in front
of the whole assembly of Israel and spread out his hands. 13 Now he
had made a bronze platform, five cubits[a] long, five cubits wide and
three cubits[b] high, and had placed it in the center of the outer
court. He stood on the platform and then knelt down before the
whole assembly of Israel and spread out his hands toward heaven.
14 He said:

"O LORD, God of Israel, there is no God like you in
heaven or on earth—you who keep your covenant of love
with your servants who continue wholeheartedly in your way.
15 You have kept your promise to your servant David my
father; with your mouth you have promised and with your
hand you have fulfilled it—as it is today.

16 "Now LORD, God of Israel, keep for your servant
David my father the promises you made to him when you
said, 'You shall never fail to have a man to sit before me on the
throne of Israel, if only your sons are careful in all they do to
walk before me according to my law, as you have done.' 17 And
now, O LORD, God of Israel, let your word that you promised
your servant David come true.

18 "But will God really dwell on earth with men? The
heavens, even the highest heavens, cannot contain you. How
much less this temple I have built! 19 Yet give attention to your
servant's prayer and his plea for mercy, O LORD my God. Hear
the cry and the prayer that your servant is praying in your
presence. 20 May your eyes be open toward this temple day and
night, this place of which you said you would put your Name
there. May you hear the prayer your servant prays toward this
place. 21 Hear the supplications of your servant and of your
people Israel when they pray toward this place. Hear from
heaven, your dwelling place; and when you hear, forgive.

22 "When a man wrongs his neighbor and is required to
take an oath and he comes and swears the oath before your
altar in this temple, 23 then hear from heaven and act. Judge
between your servants, repaying the guilty by bringing down
on his own head what he has done. Declare the innocent not
guilty and so establish his innocence.

24 "When your people Israel have been defeated by an
enemy because they have sinned against you and when they

---

[a]**13** That is, about 7 1/2 feet (about 2.3 meters) [b]**13** That is, about 4 1/2 feet (about 1.3 meters)

Solomon prayed, *"O LORD, God of Israel, there is no God like you in heaven or on earth—you who keep your covenant of love with your servants who continue wholeheartedly in your way."* 2 Chr 6:14

6:11 *ark:* See the notes at 1:3-5 and 5:9,10. The "covenant" here is a reference to the stone tablets containing the Ten Commandments.

5:10 *covenant:* This refers to the covenant God made with the people of Israel at Horeb, or Mount Sinai (Exod 19:1-7; 20:1-17), and more specifically to the Ten Commandments. See 5:10 and the mini-article called "Ten Commandments," p. 354.

6:13 *bronze platform:* It was common for kings or priests to offer prayers from a special raised platform they had made. The platform was in the courtyard near the altar used for sacrifice, not inside the temple itself.

6:16 *the promises you made to him:* Solomon's prayer refers to the promise God made to David that someone from his family would always be king of Israel (2 Sam 7:11-16). See also 1 Kgs 2:4.

6:18 2 Chr 2:6. **6:20** Deut 12:5-19.

Solomon prayed, *"When they pray toward this place and confess your name and turn from their sin because you have afflicted them, then hear from heaven and forgive the sin of your servants."*
2 Chr 6:26,27

6:28 *locusts:* This is a type of grasshopper that comes in swarms and causes great damage to crops. See the mini-article called "Locusts," p. 1708.

6:36-39 *When they sin against you . . . takes them captive . . . forgive your people:* Solomon's prayer includes prophetic words about Israel's future. The people did sin by turning their backs on God, disobeying God's Law, and worshiping idols. Many people in Israel were taken captive by the Assyrians around 721 B.C. and later by the Babylonians in 587 B.C. after they destroyed Jerusalem and Solomon's temple. The exile was seen as God's punishment for the sins of the people of Israel. See also the article called "From Joshua to the Exile: The People of Israel in the Promised Land," p. 924.

turn back and confess your name, praying and making supplication before you in this temple, 25then hear from heaven
and forgive the sin of your people Israel and bring them back
to the land you gave to them and their fathers.

26"When the heavens are shut up and there is no rain
because your people have sinned against you, and when they
pray toward this place and confess your name and turn from
their sin because you have afflicted them, 27then hear from
heaven and forgive the sin of your servants, your people Israel.
Teach them the right way to live, and send rain on the land
you gave your people for an inheritance.

28"When famine or plague comes to the land, or blight
or mildew, locusts or grasshoppers, or when enemies besiege
them in any of their cities, whatever disaster or disease may
come, 29and when a prayer or plea is made by any of your
people Israel—each one aware of his afflictions and pains, and
spreading out his hands toward this temple— 30then hear
from heaven, your dwelling place. Forgive, and deal with each
man according to all he does, since you know his heart (for
you alone know the hearts of men), 31so that they will fear you
and walk in your ways all the time they live in the land you
gave our fathers.

32"As for the foreigner who does not belong to your
people Israel but has come from a distant land because of
your great name and your mighty hand and your outstretched
arm—when he comes and prays toward this temple, 33then
hear from heaven, your dwelling place, and do whatever the
foreigner asks of you, so that all the peoples of the earth may
know your name and fear you, as do your own people Israel,
and may know that this house I have built bears your Name.

34"When your people go to war against their enemies,
wherever you send them, and when they pray to you toward
this city you have chosen and the temple I have built for your
Name, 35then hear from heaven their prayer and their plea,
and uphold their cause.

36"When they sin against you—for there is no one who
does not sin—and you become angry with them and give them
over to the enemy, who takes them captive to a land far away or
near; 37and if they have a change of heart in the land where
they are held captive, and repent and plead with you in the
land of their captivity and say, 'We have sinned, we have done
wrong and acted wickedly'; 38and if they turn back to you with
all their heart and soul in the land of their captivity where they
were taken, and pray toward the land you gave their fathers,
toward the city you have chosen and toward the temple I have
built for your Name; 39then from heaven, your dwelling place,
hear their prayer and their pleas, and uphold their cause. And
forgive your people, who have sinned against you.

40"Now, my God, may your eyes be open and your ears
attentive to the prayers offered in this place.

41"Now arise, O LORD God, and come to your resting place,
you and the ark of your might.
May your priests, O LORD God, be clothed with salvation,
may your saints rejoice in your goodness.
42O LORD God, do not reject your anointed one.
Remember the great love promised to David your
servant."

The Dedication of the Temple

7 When Solomon finished praying, fire came down from heav-
en and consumed the burnt offering and the sacrifices, and the
glory of the LORD filled the temple. 2The priests could not enter
the temple of the LORD because the glory of the LORD filled it.
3When all the Israelites saw the fire coming down and the glory of
the LORD above the temple, they knelt on the pavement with their
faces to the ground, and they worshiped and gave thanks to the
LORD, saying,

"He is good;
his love endures forever."

4Then the king and all the people offered sacrifices before the
LORD. 5And King Solomon offered a sacrifice of twenty-two thousand head of cattle and a hundred and twenty thousand sheep and
goats. So the king and all the people dedicated the temple of God.
6The priests took their positions, as did the Levites with the LORD's
musical instruments, which King David had made for praising the
LORD and which were used when he gave thanks, saying, "His love
endures forever." Opposite the Levites, the priests blew their trumpets, and all the Israelites were standing.

7Solomon consecrated the middle part of the courtyard in
front of the temple of the LORD, and there he offered burnt offerings and the fat of the fellowship offerings,[a] because the bronze
altar he had made could not hold the burnt offerings, the grain
offerings and the fat portions.

8So Solomon observed the festival at that time for seven
days, and all Israel with him—a vast assembly, people from Lebo[b]
Hamath to the Wadi of Egypt. 9On the eighth day they held an
assembly, for they had celebrated the dedication of the altar for
seven days and the festival for seven days more. 10On the twenty-
third day of the seventh month he sent the people to their homes,
joyful and glad in heart for the good things the LORD had done for
David and Solomon and for his people Israel.

[a]7 Traditionally *peace offerings* [b]8 Or *from the entrance to*

7:1 *fire came down . . . consumed the burnt offering and the sacrifices:* Fire coming down and burning up the offerings is a sign of God's presence and approval. See also Lev 9:23,24; 1 Kgs 18:38. Fire can also be a sign of God's disapproval for an improper offering (see Lev 10:2).

7:7 *burnt offerings:* See the note at 1:6.

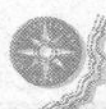

7:8 *from Lebo Hamath to the Wadi of Egypt:* See the map on p. 2465.

7:8-10 *festival . . . seven days . . . seventh month:* It appears that the temple dedication was celebrated on the eighth to fourteenth days of the month and the Feast of Tabernacles on the fifteenth to twenty-second days of the month. See the note at 5:3. The Day of Atonement fell on the tenth day of the month. On the Day of Atonement, the sins of the priests and the people were forgiven. Today this festival is known as *Yom Kippur*.

6:41,42 Ps 132:8-10. **7:3** 1 Chr 16:34; 2 Chr 5:13; Ezra 3:11; Ps 100:5; 106:1; 107:1; 118:1; 136:1; Jer 33:11.

7:13 *locusts:* See the note at 6:28.

7:14-22 *if my people . . . seek my face . . . But if you turn away . . . I will uproot:* The people will be blessed if they remain obedient to God. If they do not, great suffering will result (1 Chr 22:12,13; 28:8-10; 2 Chr 12:1,2; 14:7,12-15; 15:2-7; 16:7-9; 24:21-22,24). This truth becomes more and more apparent as the story told in this book unfolds (2 Chr 36:17-21).

8:1,2 *twenty years . . . villages that Hiram had given him:* The completion of both the temple and palace would have been about 946 B.C. (1 Kgs 6:38; 7:1).

In 1 Kings 9:10-14, Solomon gave these towns to Hiram, who rejected them because of their poor condition.

8:3-6 *Hamath Zobah . . . Baalath:* Hamath Zobah and Tadmor were located over one hundred miles north of Damascus. See the map on p. 2468.

Beth Horon was on an important road that connected Jerusalem to the Mediterranean seaport of Joppa. See the map on p. 2465. Baalath was about thirty miles west of Jerusalem.

8:5 *fortified cities, with walls and with gates and bars:* Many cities were walled and had one or more gates used for entering and leaving the city. The area near the gate to a city was the place where disputes were heard and decided. See also the note at 32:18.

8:7-9 *Hittites, Amorites, Perizzites, Hivites and Jebusites:* All of these groups lived in Canaan at the time the Israelites invaded. See also Exod 3:8 and note; 1 Kgs 9:20-22.

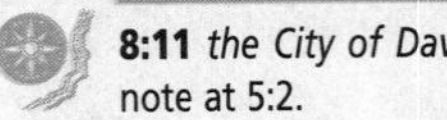

8:11 *the City of David:* See the note at 5:2.

7:12 2 Chr 1:7. **7:15** 2 Chr 6:40. **7:18** 1 Kgs 2:4.

The LORD Appears to Solomon

[11]When Solomon had finished the temple of the LORD and
the royal palace, and had succeeded in carrying out all he had in
mind to do in the temple of the LORD and in his own palace, [12]the
LORD appeared to him at night and said:

"I have heard your prayer and have chosen this place for
myself as a temple for sacrifices.
[13]"When I shut up the heavens so that there is no rain,
or command locusts to devour the land or send a plague
among my people, [14]if my people, who are called by my name,
will humble themselves and pray and seek my face and turn
from their wicked ways, then will I hear from heaven and will
forgive their sin and will heal their land. [15]Now my eyes will
be open and my ears attentive to the prayers offered in this
place. [16]I have chosen and consecrated this temple so that my
Name may be there forever. My eyes and my heart will always
be there.
[17]"As for you, if you walk before me as David your
father did, and do all I command, and observe my decrees and
laws, [18]I will establish your royal throne, as I covenanted with
David your father when I said, 'You shall never fail to have a
man to rule over Israel.'
[19]"But if you[a] turn away and forsake the decrees and
commands I have given you[a] and go off to serve other gods
and worship them, [20]then I will uproot Israel from my land,
which I have given them, and will reject this temple I have
consecrated for my Name. I will make it a byword and an
object of ridicule among all peoples. [21]And though this temple
is now so imposing, all who pass by will be appalled and say,
'Why has the LORD done such a thing to this land and to this
temple?' [22]People will answer, 'Because they have forsaken the
LORD, the God of their fathers, who brought them out of
Egypt, and have embraced other gods, worshiping and serving
them—that is why he brought all this disaster on them.' "

SOLOMON'S LONG RULE

Solomon's successes in politics (8:1-11), religion (8:12-16), and trade (8:17, 18) increase his wealth and fame.

Solomon's Other Activities

8 At the end of twenty years, during which Solomon built the
temple of the LORD and his own palace, [2]Solomon rebuilt the
villages that Hiram[b] had given him, and settled Israelites in them.
[3]Solomon then went to Hamath Zobah and captured it. [4]He also

[a]19 The Hebrew is plural. [b]2 Hebrew *Huram,* a variant of *Hiram*; also in verse 18

built up Tadmor in the desert and all the store cities he had built
in Hamath. 5He rebuilt Upper Beth Horon and Lower Beth Horon
as fortified cities, with walls and with gates and bars, 6as well as
Baalath and all his store cities, and all the cities for his chariots and
for his horses[a]—whatever he desired to build in Jerusalem, in
Lebanon and throughout all the territory he ruled.

7All the people left from the Hittites, Amorites, Perizzites,
Hivites and Jebusites (these peoples were not Israelites), 8that is,
their descendants remaining in the land, whom the Israelites had
not destroyed—these Solomon conscripted for his slave labor
force, as it is to this day. 9But Solomon did not make slaves of the
Israelites for his work; they were his fighting men, commanders of
his captains, and commanders of his chariots and charioteers.
10They were also King Solomon's chief officials—two hundred and
fifty officials supervising the men.

11Solomon brought Pharaoh's daughter up from the City of
David to the palace he had built for her, for he said, "My wife must
not live in the palace of David king of Israel, because the places the
ark of the LORD has entered are holy."

12On the altar of the LORD that he had built in front of the
portico, Solomon sacrificed burnt offerings to the LORD, 13according
to the daily requirement for offerings commanded by Moses for
Sabbaths, New Moons and the three annual feasts—the Feast of
Unleavened Bread, the Feast of Weeks and the Feast of Tabernacles.
14In keeping with the ordinance of his father David, he appointed
the divisions of the priests for their duties, and the Levites to lead
the praise and to assist the priests according to each day's requirement. He also appointed the gatekeepers by divisions for the various gates, because this was what David the man of God had ordered.
15They did not deviate from the king's commands to the priests or to
the Levites in any matter, including that of the treasuries.

16All Solomon's work was carried out, from the day the
foundation of the temple of the LORD was laid until its completion. So the temple of the LORD was finished.

17Then Solomon went to Ezion Geber and Elath on the coast
of Edom. 18And Hiram sent him ships commanded by his own
officers, men who knew the sea. These, with Solomon's men, sailed
to Ophir and brought back four hundred and fifty talents[b] of gold,
which they delivered to King Solomon.

The Queen of Sheba Visits Solomon

9 When the queen of Sheba heard of Solomon's fame, she came
to Jerusalem to test him with hard questions. Arriving with a very
great caravan—with camels carrying spices, large quantities of
gold, and precious stones—she came to Solomon and talked with

---

[a]**6** Or *charioteers* [b]**18** That is, about 17 tons (about 16 metric tons)

8:12,13 *Solomon sacrificed burnt offerings . . . Sabbaths . . . the Feast of Unleavened Bread . . . Weeks . . . Tabernacles:* Solomon performs the work usually done only by priests. For sacrifices, see the chart called "Sacrifices and Offerings," p. 219.

The Sabbath was the weekly day of rest that began at sunset on Friday and ended with a blessing (benediction) at sunset on Saturday. No work was to be done on the Sabbath, which means "rest" or to "stop working" (see also Exod 20:8-11; 31:12-17; Num 28:9, 10; Deut 5:12-15).

For the Feast of Unleavened Bread, see Deut 16:3, 4 and the mini-article called "Passover and the Feast of Unleavened Bread," p. 2030.

The Feast of Weeks (also called Feast of Harvest and Pentecost) took place fifty days after the Feast of Unleavened Bread (Lev 23:6-8). See also Exod 23:16; 34:22; Lev 23:15-22; Deut 16:9-12.

See also the note at 5:3; and Exod 23:14-17; 34:22, 23; Num 28:11—29:39; Deut 16:16.

8:17,18 *coast of Edom . . . Ophir:* This was probably the Gulf of Aqaba, the northeastern arm of the Red Sea. See also the note at Exod 13:17-20 and the map on p. 2463. Evidently Hiram (see the note at 2:3) began the ship-building process in Phoenicia and transported the parts over land, where they were assembled at the port of Ezion Geber.

Ophir may have been located in India, southern Arabia, or Africa.

9:1 *queen of Sheba:* Archaeological evidence points to the queen having come from Saba (or Seba), a wealthy kingdom in southwest Arabia that traded luxury items from India and east Africa. The queen's interest in Solomon may have partially been a concern that Israel's control of major land and sea trade routes posed a threat to that trade. See also the article called "Trade and Travel," p. 948.

8:14,15 1 Chr 23–26. **9:1-9** Matt 12:42; Luke 11:31.

9:3-5 *wisdom of Solomon:* In Scripture, Solomon is described as a wise man, and he is given credit for writing many wise sayings (1 Kgs 3:10-12; 5:12; Prov 1:1; 10:1).

9:15,16 *large shields of hammered gold:* These were probably used for ceremonies, as were the smaller round shields. See also 1 Chr 18:7, 8 and the note.

9:25 *stalls for horses and chariots:* See the note at 1:14. Horses and chariots were an important part of a king's wealth in the ancient Near East. Archaeologists believe that the stables at Megiddo (shown here) could have housed 450 horses. Though called "Solomon's Stables," they were probably built by King Ahab seventy years after the time of Solomon upon the site of Solomon's stables.

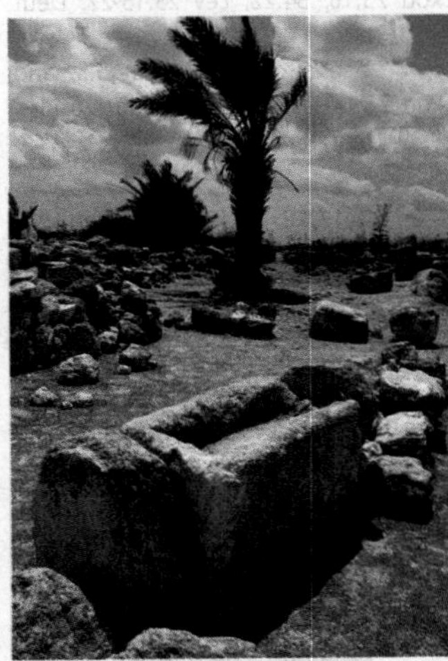

him about all she had on her mind. [2]Solomon answered all her
questions; nothing was too hard for him to explain to her. [3]When
the queen of Sheba saw the wisdom of Solomon, as well as the
palace he had built, [4]the food on his table, the seating of his officials, the attending servants in their robes, the cupbearers in their
robes and the burnt offerings he made at[a] the temple of the LORD,
she was overwhelmed.

[5]She said to the king, "The report I heard in my own country about your achievements and your wisdom is true. [6]But I did
not believe what they said until I came and saw with my own eyes.
Indeed, not even half the greatness of your wisdom was told me;
you have far exceeded the report I heard. [7]How happy your men
must be! How happy your officials, who continually stand before
you and hear your wisdom! [8]Praise be to the LORD your God, who
has delighted in you and placed you on his throne as king to rule
for the LORD your God. Because of the love of your God for Israel
and his desire to uphold them forever, he has made you king over
them, to maintain justice and righteousness."

[9]Then she gave the king 120 talents[b] of gold, large quantities
of spices, and precious stones. There had never been such spices as
those the queen of Sheba gave to King Solomon.

[10](The men of Hiram and the men of Solomon brought gold
from Ophir; they also brought algumwood[c] and precious stones.
[11]The king used the algumwood to make steps for the temple of
the LORD and for the royal palace, and to make harps and lyres for
the musicians. Nothing like them had ever been seen in Judah.)

[12]King Solomon gave the queen of Sheba all she desired and
asked for; he gave her more than she had brought to him. Then
she left and returned with her retinue to her own country.

Solomon's Splendor

[13]The weight of the gold that Solomon received yearly was
666 talents,[d] [14]not including the revenues brought in by merchants
and traders. Also all the kings of Arabia and the governors of the
land brought gold and silver to Solomon.

[15]King Solomon made two hundred large shields of hammered gold; six hundred bekas[e] of hammered gold went into each
shield. [16]He also made three hundred small shields of hammered
gold, with three hundred bekas[f] of gold in each shield. The king
put them in the Palace of the Forest of Lebanon.

[17]Then the king made a great throne inlaid with ivory and
overlaid with pure gold. [18]The throne had six steps, and a footstool
of gold was attached to it. On both sides of the seat were armrests,

[a]**4** Or *the ascent by which he went up to* [b]**9** That is, about 4 1/2 tons (about 4 metric tons) [c]**10** Probably a variant of *almugwood* [d]**13** That is, about 25 tons (about 23 metric tons) [e]**15** That is, about 7 1/2 pounds (about 3.5 kilograms) [f]**16** That is, about 3 3/4 pounds (about 1.7 kilograms)

with a lion standing beside each of them. 19 Twelve lions stood on
the six steps, one at either end of each step. Nothing like it had ever
been made for any other kingdom. 20 All King Solomon's goblets
were gold, and all the household articles in the Palace of the Forest of Lebanon were pure gold. Nothing was made of silver,
because silver was considered of little value in Solomon's day.
21 The king had a fleet of trading ships[a] manned by Hiram's[b] men.
Once every three years it returned, carrying gold, silver and ivory,
and apes and baboons.
22 King Solomon was greater in riches and wisdom than all
the other kings of the earth. 23 All the kings of the earth sought
audience with Solomon to hear the wisdom God had put in his
heart. 24 Year after year, everyone who came brought a gift—articles of silver and gold, and robes, weapons and spices, and horses
and mules.
25 Solomon had four thousand stalls for horses and chariots,
and twelve thousand horses,[c] which he kept in the chariot cities and
also with him in Jerusalem. 26 He ruled over all the kings from the
River[d] to the land of the Philistines, as far as the border of Egypt.
27 The king made silver as common in Jerusalem as stones, and
cedar as plentiful as sycamore-fig trees in the foothills. 28 Solomon's
horses were imported from Egypt[e] and from all other countries.

Solomon's Death

29 As for the other events of Solomon's reign, from beginning
to end, are they not written in the records of Nathan the prophet,

[a]21 Hebrew *of ships that could go to Tarshish* [b]21 Hebrew *Huram,* a variant of *Hiram* [c]25 Or *charioteers* [d]26 That is, the Euphrates [e]28 Or possibly *Muzur,* a region in Cilicia

The queen of Sheba said to Solomon, *"Praise be to the LORD your God, who has delighted in you and placed you on his throne as king to rule for the LORD your God."* 2 Chr 9:8

9:26 *the River ... Egypt:* Solomon's dominion extended all the way from the Euphrates to the border of Egypt. See the map on p. 2462.

9:29 *the other events of Solomon's reign:* In keeping with his desire to emphasize the greatness of Solomon, the writer of 2 CHRONICLES chooses not to include Solomon's failings (1 Kgs 11:1-13).

9:25 1 Kgs 4:26. **9:26** Gen 15:18; 1 Kgs 4:21. **9:28** Deut 17:16.

QUESTIONS ABOUT 2 CHRONICLES 1:1—9:31

1. Solomon is best known for his wisdom, wealth, and worship. Find two examples of each.
2. David's bringing of the ark of the covenant to Jerusalem made the city the central place for both the political and religious lives of the people. How did Solomon's building of the temple complete this process and make it permanent? (6:1—7:22)
3. Compare the Israelites' understanding of the connection between the temple and God to your own understanding of the connection that exists between places of worship and God.
4. Read 7:1-3. (See also Lev 9:1-24; and 1 Kgs 18:20-40.) What characteristics of fire make it an effective symbol of God's presence and acceptance?
5. How did the people celebrate the dedication of the temple? (7:4-10) Why was the completion of the temple such an important event in the lives of the people of Israel?
6. Name two or three big events that you have been a part of celebrating. Why do we mark important life events with celebrations?

in the prophecy of Ahijah the Shilonite and in the visions of Iddo
the seer concerning Jeroboam son of Nebat? [30]Solomon reigned in
Jerusalem over all Israel forty years. [31]Then he rested with his
fathers and was buried in the city of David his father. And
Rehoboam his son succeeded him as king.

9:30,31 *forty years . . . Rehoboam his son succeeded him:* While the number forty is often used in a symbolic sense, here it can be taken literally. Solomon is believed to have reigned from approximately 970 to 931 B.C. See also the chart called "Numbers in the Bible," p. 2405.

Rehoboam ruled from 931 to 913 B.C. Almost as soon as he came to power, the people of the northern tribes revolted and formed the northern kingdom (Israel) under the rule of Jeroboam. Rehoboam was left as ruler only of the tribes of Judah and Benjamin in what became known as the southern kingdom (Judah). See 1 Kgs 12:1-24.

The Divided Monarchy

After Solomon's death, the people who had been united under a Davidic king in Jerusalem split into two kingdoms, shattering the ideal vision of Israel held by the writer of 2 Chronicles. The chapters that follow are almost entirely devoted to the kings of Judah and their acts of faith. Unlike 1 and 2 Kings, the kings of the north are mentioned only when they have some relationship to the south.

INTRODUCTION: THE NORTH REVOLTS

Rehoboam continues the harsher policies of his father, Solomon. The northern tribes rebel and set up a rival kingdom.

Israel Rebels Against Rehoboam

10 Rehoboam went to Shechem, for all the Israelites had gone
there to make him king. [2]When Jeroboam son of Nebat heard this
(he was in Egypt, where he had fled from King Solomon), he
returned from Egypt. [3]So they sent for Jeroboam, and he and all
Israel went to Rehoboam and said to him: [4]"Your father put a
heavy yoke on us, but now lighten the harsh labor and the heavy
yoke he put on us, and we will serve you."

[5]Rehoboam answered, "Come back to me in three days." So
the people went away.

[6]Then King Rehoboam consulted the elders who had served
his father Solomon during his lifetime. "How would you advise me
to answer these people?" he asked.

[7]They replied, "If you will be kind to these people and please
them and give them a favorable answer, they will always be your
servants."

[8]But Rehoboam rejected the advice the elders gave him and
consulted the young men who had grown up with him and were
serving him. [9]He asked them, "What is your advice? How should
we answer these people who say to me, 'Lighten the yoke your
father put on us'?"

[10]The young men who had grown up with him replied, "Tell
the people who have said to you, 'Your father put a heavy yoke on
us, but make our yoke lighter'—tell them, 'My little finger is
thicker than my father's waist. [11]My father laid on you a heavy
yoke; I will make it even heavier. My father scourged you with
whips; I will scourge you with scorpions.'"

10:1 *Shechem:* Significant in Israel's history and central for the northern tribes, Shechem was a logical place for the installation of a king. A sacred tree at Shechem is where Abram (later renamed Abraham) first worshiped God in the promised land (Gen 12:6,7). In addition, Jacob built an altar in Shechem (Gen 33:18,20), and Joseph was buried there (Josh 24:32). Joshua led the people in renewing their covenant with the Lord at Shechem (Josh 24:1-27). See the map on p. 2467.

10:2 *Jeroboam:* See the notes at 13:1,2 and 13:4-12.

10:11 *scorpions:* May be figurative for long leather bags tightly packed with sand and studded with metal spikes.

[12]Three days later Jeroboam and all the people returned to
Rehoboam, as the king had said, "Come back to me in three days."
[13]The king answered them harshly. Rejecting the advice of the
elders, [14]he followed the advice of the young men and said, "My
father made your yoke heavy; I will make it even heavier. My father
scourged you with whips; I will scourge you with scorpions." [15]So
the king did not listen to the people, for this turn of events was
from God, to fulfill the word the LORD had spoken to Jeroboam
son of Nebat through Ahijah the Shilonite.
[16]When all Israel saw that the king refused to listen to them,
they answered the king:

"What share do we have in David,
what part in Jesse's son?
To your tents, O Israel!
Look after your own house, O David!"

So all the Israelites went home. [17]But as for the Israelites who were
living in the towns of Judah, Rehoboam still ruled over them.
[18]King Rehoboam sent out Adoniram,[a] who was in charge of
forced labor, but the Israelites stoned him to death. King Rehoboam, however, managed to get into his chariot and escape to
Jerusalem. [19]So Israel has been in rebellion against the house of
David to this day.
11 When Rehoboam arrived in Jerusalem, he mustered the
house of Judah and Benjamin—a hundred and eighty thousand
fighting men—to make war against Israel and to regain the kingdom for Rehoboam.
[2]But this word of the LORD came to Shemaiah the man of
God: [3]"Say to Rehoboam son of Solomon king of Judah and to all
the Israelites in Judah and Benjamin, [4]'This is what the LORD says:
Do not go up to fight against your brothers. Go home, every one
of you, for this is my doing.' " So they obeyed the words of the
LORD and turned back from marching against Jeroboam.

KINGS OF JUDAH

"Good" kings are rewarded with wealth, wisdom, peace, building projects, and large families. "Bad" kings suffer illness or defeat in war.

Rehoboam Fortifies Judah

[5]Rehoboam lived in Jerusalem and built up towns for
defense in Judah: [6]Bethlehem, Etam, Tekoa, [7]Beth Zur, Soco, Adullam, [8]Gath, Mareshah, Ziph, [9]Adoraim, Lachish, Azekah, [10]Zorah,
Aijalon and Hebron. These were fortified cities in Judah and

[a]**18** Hebrew *Hadoram,* a variant of *Adoniram*

10:15-18 *Ahijah . . . Adoniram:* The writer of 2 CHRONICLES assumes the reader is familiar with the prophet Ahijah's message for Jeroboam prior to Solomon's death. Ahijah predicted that Jeroboam would become king of the north because of Solomon's disobedience to God (1 Kgs 11:29-40). The writer claims this revolt fulfilled these prophetic words from God. See also the article called "Prophets and Prophecy," p. 935.

Adoniram was in charge of the forced labor used by David and Solomon. See also 2 Sam 20:24; 1 Kgs 4:1-6; 5:14.

10:19 *Israel has been in rebellion:* Though the writer of 2 CHRONICLES previously included the people of the south in his concept of Israel, from this time on, the term "Israel" primarily refers to the northern kingdom. The southern kingdom is called "Judah."

11:4 *your brothers:* Judah and Benjamin, like all the other tribes, were descended from Jacob, whose name was changed to Israel (Gen 32:22-32).

11:5-12 *fortified cities in Judah and Benjamin:* At this time, thick walls with gates and guard towers were built around cities to fortify, or strengthen, them against attack. This list is intended to show Judah's strength. See also 14:6,7 and the map on p. 2467.

10:16 2 Sam 20:1.

Benjamin. [11]He strengthened their defenses and put commanders
in them, with supplies of food, olive oil and wine. [12]He put shields
and spears in all the cities, and made them very strong. So Judah
and Benjamin were his.

[13]The priests and Levites from all their districts throughout
Israel sided with him. [14]The Levites even abandoned their pasturelands and property, and came to Judah and Jerusalem because Jeroboam and his sons had rejected them as priests of the LORD.
[15]And he appointed his own priests for the high places and for the
goat and calf idols he had made. [16]Those from every tribe of Israel
who set their hearts on seeking the LORD, the God of Israel, followed the Levites to Jerusalem to offer sacrifices to the LORD, the
God of their fathers. [17]They strengthened the kingdom of Judah
and supported Rehoboam son of Solomon three years, walking in
the ways of David and Solomon during this time.

11:13 *priests and Levites:* Priests led worship and offered sacrifices. The Levites who were descended from Moses' brother, Aaron, could serve as priests (Num 3:1-13). Other Levites were assigned positions as temple servants. They took care of the temple and assisted the priests. See also the note at 5:11,12 and the mini-article called "Israel's Priests," p. 2344.

11:15 *high places . . . goat and calf idols:* These idols represented false gods. The people worshiped them in places other than the temple in Jerusalem. Also, calves (bulls) were a symbol for the Canaanite god, Baal (1 Kgs 18:19-40). See Exod 20:4; 32:4; 34:17; Lev 19:4; 1 Kgs 12:28-31. See also the illustration on p. 194 and the mini-article called "Canaanite Gods and Goddesses," p. 469.

12:6,7 2 Chr 7:14; 12:12.

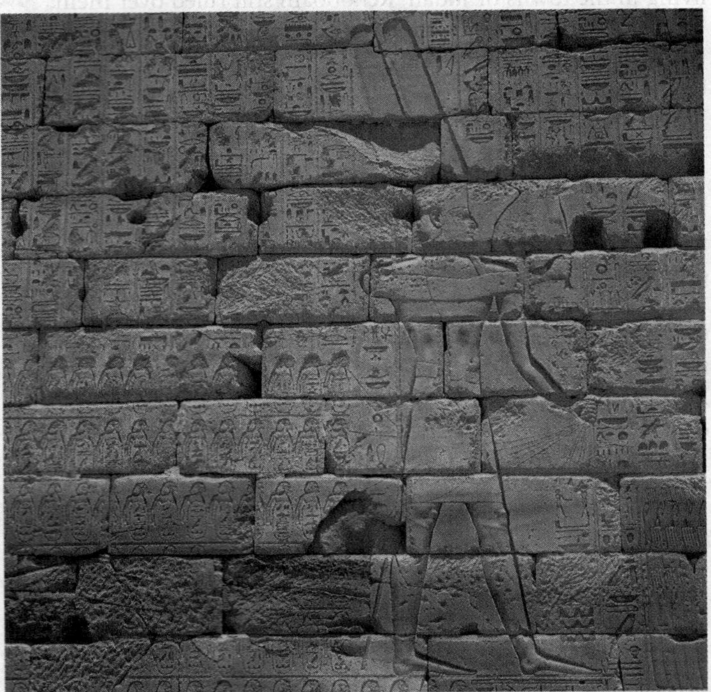

King Shishak before the God Amun, unfinished relief from the temple of Amun at Karnak. In Luxor (formerly Thebes), there are many temples to the Egyptian gods. This relief shows the king (lower right with arms raised in prayer) honoring the god Amun. When Rehoboam became the king of the southern kingdom (Judah), the prophet Shemaiah told Rehoboam that the LORD had abandoned him and would not help him when King Shishak of Egypt attacked him (see 2 Chr 12:2-5). The inscription on this relief lists 154 towns the Egyptians claimed to have destroyed around 925 B.C. Not only did Shishak attack Judah, but towns in the northern kingdom (Israel) as well.

Rehoboam's Family

[18]Rehoboam married Mahalath, who was the daughter of David's son Jerimoth and of Abihail, the daughter of Jesse's son Eliab. [19]She bore him sons: Jeush, Shemariah and Zaham. [20]Then he married Maacah daughter of Absalom, who bore him Abijah, Attai, Ziza and Shelomith. [21]Rehoboam loved Maacah daughter of Absalom more than any of his other wives and concubines. In all, he had eighteen wives and sixty concubines, twenty-eight sons and sixty daughters.

[22]Rehoboam appointed Abijah son of Maacah to be the chief prince among his brothers, in order to make him king. [23]He acted wisely, dispersing some of his sons throughout the districts of Judah and Benjamin, and to all the fortified cities. He gave them abundant provisions and took many wives for them.

Shishak Attacks Jerusalem

12 After Rehoboam's position as king was established and he had become strong, he and all Israel[a] with him abandoned the law of the LORD. [2]Because they had been unfaithful to the LORD, Shishak king of Egypt attacked Jerusalem in the fifth year of King Rehoboam. [3]With twelve hundred chariots and sixty thousand horsemen and the innumerable troops of Libyans, Sukkites and Cushites[b] that came with him from Egypt, [4]he captured the fortified cities of Judah and came as far as Jerusalem.

[5]Then the prophet Shemaiah came to Rehoboam and to the leaders of Judah who had assembled in Jerusalem for fear of Shishak, and he said to them, "This is what the LORD says, 'You have abandoned me; therefore, I now abandon you to Shishak.' "

[6]The leaders of Israel and the king humbled themselves and said, "The LORD is just."

[7]When the LORD saw that they humbled themselves, this word of the LORD came to Shemaiah: "Since they have humbled themselves, I will not destroy them but will soon give them deliverance. My wrath will not be poured out on Jerusalem through Shishak. [8]They will, however, become subject to him, so that they may learn the difference between serving me and serving the kings of other lands."

[9]When Shishak king of Egypt attacked Jerusalem, he carried off the treasures of the temple of the LORD and the treasures of the royal palace. He took everything, including the gold shields Solomon had made. [10]So King Rehoboam made bronze shields to replace them and assigned these to the commanders of the guard on duty at the entrance to the royal palace. [11]Whenever the king went to the LORD's temple, the guards went with him, bearing the shields, and afterward they returned them to the guardroom.

[a]1 That is, Judah, as frequently in 2 Chronicles [b]3 That is, people from the upper Nile region

11:18-21 *Rehoboam married Mahalath . . . Maacah . . . concubines:* Two of Rehoboam's wives, Mahalath and Maacah, were related to David. Though never encouraged by God in the biblical record, to have more than one wife was culturally acceptable at this time, since many marriages were arranged as part of a political or financial alliance. It was also necessary that a man be able to support these wives and the children that resulted. Rehoboam's many children are a sign that God chose to bless him.

Concubines were women who were legally bound to a man, but without the full privileges of a wife.

11:21,22 *appointed Abijah son of Maacah:* It was common, but not required, that the eldest son follow his father as king. Rehoboam chose Abijah, who was not his oldest son but the son of his favorite wife Maacah.

12:1,2 *Because they had been unfaithful to the LORD . . . attacked:* This same attack is reported in 1 Kings 14:25-28, but the writer of 2 CHRONICLES stresses the idea that it was God's punishment for disobedience, just as chapter 11 stressed that obedience brought God's blessings. See also the note at 7:14-22.

12:2 *Shishak:* Shishak ruled Egypt from about 945 to 924 B.C. According to Shishak's own inscription on the wall of the temple of Amun at Karnak (Thebes), this attack went as far north as Megiddo (see the map on p. 2467), putting Judah and several important trade routes in both Judah and Israel under Egypt's control.

12:5 *the prophet Shemaiah:* A prophet is someone who delivers God's messages. See the article called "Prophets and Prophecy," p. 935.

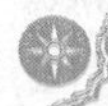

12:9 *Jerusalem:* See the note at 1:13.

12:9 *gold shields:* See the note at 9:15,16. See also 1 Kgs 10:16,17.

12 Because Rehoboam humbled himself, the LORD's anger
turned from him, and he was not totally destroyed. Indeed, there
was some good in Judah.
13 King Rehoboam established himself firmly in Jerusalem
and continued as king. He was forty-one years old when he
became king, and he reigned seventeen years in Jerusalem, the city
the LORD had chosen out of all the tribes of Israel in which to put
his Name. His mother's name was Naamah; she was an Ammonite.
14 He did evil because he had not set his heart on seeking the LORD.
15 As for the events of Rehoboam's reign, from beginning to
end, are they not written in the records of Shemaiah the prophet
and of Iddo the seer that deal with genealogies? There was continual warfare between Rehoboam and Jeroboam. 16 Rehoboam rested
with his fathers and was buried in the City of David. And Abijah
his son succeeded him as king.

Abijah King of Judah

13 In the eighteenth year of the reign of Jeroboam, Abijah
became king of Judah, 2 and he reigned in Jerusalem three years.
His mother's name was Maacah,[a] a daughter[b] of Uriel of Gibeah.
There was war between Abijah and Jeroboam. 3 Abijah went
into battle with a force of four hundred thousand able fighting
men, and Jeroboam drew up a battle line against him with eight
hundred thousand able troops.
4 Abijah stood on Mount Zemaraim, in the hill country of
Ephraim, and said, "Jeroboam and all Israel, listen to me! 5 Don't
you know that the LORD, the God of Israel, has given the kingship
of Israel to David and his descendants forever by a covenant of salt?
6 Yet Jeroboam son of Nebat, an official of Solomon son of David,
rebelled against his master. 7 Some worthless scoundrels gathered
around him and opposed Rehoboam son of Solomon when he was
young and indecisive and not strong enough to resist them.
8 "And now you plan to resist the kingdom of the LORD,
which is in the hands of David's descendants. You are indeed a vast
army and have with you the golden calves that Jeroboam made to
be your gods. 9 But didn't you drive out the priests of the LORD, the
sons of Aaron, and the Levites, and make priests of your own as
the peoples of other lands do? Whoever comes to consecrate himself with a young bull and seven rams may become a priest of what
are not gods.
10 "As for us, the LORD is our God, and we have not forsaken
him. The priests who serve the LORD are sons of Aaron, and the
Levites assist them. 11 Every morning and evening they present
burnt offerings and fragrant incense to the LORD. They set out the

[a]2 Most Septuagint manuscripts and Syriac (see also 2 Chron. 11:20 and 1 Kings 15:2); Hebrew *Micaiah* [b]2 Or *granddaughter*

13:1,2 *Abijah . . . Jeroboam:* Abijah ruled Judah from 913 to 911 B.C. See 11:21,22 and the note there, and 1 Kgs 15:1-8. Jeroboam was the first king of the northern kingdom (Israel) and ruled from 931 to 910 B.C. (1 Kgs 11:26—14:20).

13:3 *four hundred thousand . . . eight hundred thousand:* These high numbers fit with David's census (1 Chr 21:5). Each nation was prepared for a major effort. Since Judah was outnumbered by two to one, the writer of 2 CHRONICLES stresses God's ability to give victory against all odds.

13:4 *Mount Zemaraim:* Probably located on the northern border of the territory of Benjamin.

13:4-12 *Jeroboam and all Israel . . . God is with us:* In this passage and elsewhere, the message is repeated that the southern kingdom will keep God's favor by obeying God's laws and keeping itself separate from the sinful northern kingdom (16:7-9; 19:2-11; 25:7-9). The northern kingdom will not be able to defeat the southern kingdom, because one of David's ancestors remains on Judah's throne (1 Chr 17:13,14; 2 Chr 7:17,18).

Further, Jeroboam set up altars in honor of the Canaanite god Baal and appointed non-Levites as priests (see also 1 Kgs 12:25-33). See also the notes at 11:13 and 11:15.

13:7 *young:* Rehoboam was forty-one at the time (12:13).

13:11 *burnt offerings . . . bread . . . gold lampstand:* See the notes at 1:6 and 4:7,8. The sacred loaves of bread were a symbol of the LORD's presence in the temple. They were called the bread of the Presence and were offered to the LORD on a special table. The loaves were replaced with fresh bread each week (Lev 24:5-9).

13:14 *trumpets:* Probably a ram's horn, used to signal danger, solemn events, or the deaths of important people (Exod 19:16-19; Judg 3:27,28; Neh 4:18-20).

bread on the ceremonially clean table and light the lamps on the
gold lampstand every evening. We are observing the requirements
of the LORD our God. But you have forsaken him. 12God is with us;
he is our leader. His priests with their trumpets will sound the battle cry against you. Men of Israel, do not fight against the LORD,
the God of your fathers, for you will not succeed."
13Now Jeroboam had sent troops around to the rear, so that
while he was in front of Judah the ambush was behind them.
14Judah turned and saw that they were being attacked at both front
and rear. Then they cried out to the LORD. The priests blew their
trumpets 15and the men of Judah raised the battle cry. At the
sound of their battle cry, God routed Jeroboam and all Israel
before Abijah and Judah. 16The Israelites fled before Judah, and
God delivered them into their hands. 17Abijah and his men inflicted heavy losses on them, so that there were five hundred thousand
casualties among Israel's able men. 18The men of Israel were subdued on that occasion, and the men of Judah were victorious
because they relied on the LORD, the God of their fathers.
19Abijah pursued Jeroboam and took from him the towns of
Bethel, Jeshanah and Ephron, with their surrounding villages.
20Jeroboam did not regain power during the time of Abijah. And
the LORD struck him down and he died.
21But Abijah grew in strength. He married fourteen wives
and had twenty-two sons and sixteen daughters.
22The other events of Abijah's reign, what he did and what
he said, are written in the annotations of the prophet Iddo.
14 And Abijah rested with his fathers and was buried in the City
of David. Asa his son succeeded him as king, and in his days the
country was at peace for ten years.

Asa King of Judah

2Asa did what was good and right in the eyes of the LORD his
God. 3He removed the foreign altars and the high places, smashed
the sacred stones and cut down the Asherah poles.[a] 4He commanded Judah to seek the LORD, the God of their fathers, and to
obey his laws and commands. 5He removed the high places and
incense altars in every town in Judah, and the kingdom was at
peace under him. 6He built up the fortified cities of Judah, since
the land was at peace. No one was at war with him during those
years, for the LORD gave him rest.
7"Let us build up these towns," he said to Judah, "and put
walls around them, with towers, gates and bars. The land is still
ours, because we have sought the LORD our God; we sought him
and he has given us rest on every side." So they built and prospered.
8Asa had an army of three hundred thousand men from
Judah, equipped with large shields and with spears, and two

[a]3 That is, symbols of the goddess Asherah; here and elsewhere in 2 Chronicles

13:18 *men of Judah were victorious:* Victory came to those who trusted in God, not from personal strength or military power. See also Deut 7:16-24; 2 Chr 13:12-16; 14:11-13; Ps 33:16-19; and the mini-article called "Holy War (The LORD's Battles)," p. 306.

13:19 *Bethel, Jeshanah and Ephron:* Bethel was in the area of Benjamin, about twelve miles north of Jerusalem. It had been a special place of worship at several times in Israel's history (Gen 12:8; 28:11-19; 35:6-15). The exact locations of Jeshanah and Ephron are unknown.

13:21 *Abijah grew in strength . . . sons . . . daughters:* SECOND CHRONICLES stresses the good rather than the negative aspects (1 Kgs 15:3) of Abijah's rule. Abijah was blessed by God with many children.

14:1 *Asa:* Asa, Judah's third king, ruled from 911 to 870 B.C. The book of 2 CHRONICLES gives a much more detailed account of Asa's reign than that in 1 Kings 15:9-24. Three examples in this account (14:1-15; 15:1-19; 16:1-13) again point out the idea that obedience brings blessing and disobedience brings punishment.

14:3 *foreign altars . . . high places . . . sacred stones . . . Asherah poles:* All worship of foreign gods was forbidden and disgusting to God. The high places were local places to worship foreign gods.

The Asherah poles were used as symbols for Asherah, a Canaanite fertility goddess. See also 1 Kgs 14:23. Asherah was linked with Baal, a Canaanite god who was believed by many to be the most powerful of all the gods. Those who worshiped Asherah believed that she gave them fertile land and many children, and that she helped their animals give birth to many young.

14:6 *the LORD gave him rest:* Asa's obedience is rewarded.

hundred and eighty thousand from Benjamin, armed with small shields and with bows. All these were brave fighting men.

[9]Zerah the Cushite marched out against them with a vast army[a] and three hundred chariots, and came as far as Mareshah. [10]Asa went out to meet him, and they took up battle positions in the Valley of Zephathah near Mareshah.

[11]Then Asa called to the LORD his God and said, "LORD, there is no one like you to help the powerless against the mighty. Help us, O LORD our God, for we rely on you, and in your name we have come against this vast army. O LORD, you are our God; do not let man prevail against you."

[12]The LORD struck down the Cushites before Asa and Judah. The Cushites fled, [13]and Asa and his army pursued them as far as Gerar. Such a great number of Cushites fell that they could not recover; they were crushed before the LORD and his forces. The men of Judah carried off a large amount of plunder. [14]They destroyed all the villages around Gerar, for the terror of the LORD had fallen upon them. They plundered all these villages, since there was much booty there. [15]They also attacked the camps of the herdsmen and carried off droves of sheep and goats and camels. Then they returned to Jerusalem.

Asa's Reform

15 The Spirit of God came upon Azariah son of Oded. [2]He went out to meet Asa and said to him, "Listen to me, Asa and all Judah and Benjamin. The LORD is with you when you are with him. If you seek him, he will be found by you, but if you forsake him, he will forsake you. [3]For a long time Israel was without the true God, without a priest to teach and without the law. [4]But in their distress they turned to the LORD, the God of Israel, and sought him, and he was found by them. [5]In those days it was not safe to travel about, for all the inhabitants of the lands were in great turmoil. [6]One nation was being crushed by another and one city by another, because God was troubling them with every kind of distress. [7]But as for you, be strong and do not give up, for your work will be rewarded."

[8]When Asa heard these words and the prophecy of Azariah son of[b] Oded the prophet, he took courage. He removed the detestable idols from the whole land of Judah and Benjamin and from the towns he had captured in the hills of Ephraim. He repaired the altar of the LORD that was in front of the portico of the LORD's temple.

[9]Then he assembled all Judah and Benjamin and the people

a9 Hebrew *with an army of a thousand thousands* or *with an army of thousands upon thousands* **b8** Vulgate and Syriac (see also Septuagint and verse 1); Hebrew does not have *Azariah son of.*

14:9-13 *Zerah the Cushite . . . Gerar:* Zerah was from Cush, a region south of Egypt.

Mareshah was about twenty-five miles southwest of Jerusalem. The Valley of Zephathah led to the hills of Jerusalem. Gerar was located south of Gaza near the Mediterranean coast. See the maps on pp. 2465 and 2469.

14:12-15 *The LORD struck down the Cushites:* Judah's foot soldiers were able to defeat a huge army which included chariots.

15:1,2 *Azariah . . . Asa:* Azariah means "The LORD has helped." Although a number of men in 1 and 2 CHRONICLES have this name, this is the only mention of the prophet Azariah. For more about Asa, see the note at 14:1.

15:2-7 *The LORD is with you when you are with him:* See the notes at 7:14-22 and 14:1. See also Deut 20:1; 1 Chr 28:9; Jer 29:12-14.

15:9 *Ephraim, Manasseh and Simeon . . . come over to him from Israel:* These tribes were among those that formed the northern kingdom, but some of their people moved to Jerusalem so that they could worship God properly.

15:10 *in the third month:* Sivan, which ran from about mid-May to mid-June. During Sivan the Feast of Weeks was celebrated. See the note at 8:12,13.

15:12-14 *entered into a covenant:* For other such promises of faithfulness to God, see Exod 24:1-18; Deut 17:2-7; Deut 29:1; Josh 8:30-35; Josh 24:24,25.

14:11,12 2 Chr 13:18.

from Ephraim, Manasseh and Simeon who had settled among
them, for large numbers had come over to him from Israel when
they saw that the LORD his God was with him.
[10]They assembled at Jerusalem in the third month of the fifteenth year of Asa's reign. [11]At that time they sacrificed to the LORD
seven hundred head of cattle and seven thousand sheep and goats
from the plunder they had brought back. [12]They entered into a
covenant to seek the LORD, the God of their fathers, with all their
heart and soul. [13]All who would not seek the LORD, the God of
Israel, were to be put to death, whether small or great, man or
woman. [14]They took an oath to the LORD with loud acclamation,
with shouting and with trumpets and horns. [15]All Judah rejoiced
about the oath because they had sworn it wholeheartedly. They
sought God eagerly, and he was found by them. So the LORD gave
them rest on every side.
[16]King Asa also deposed his grandmother Maacah from her
position as queen mother, because she had made a repulsive
Asherah pole. Asa cut the pole down, broke it up and burned it in
the Kidron Valley. [17]Although he did not remove the high places
from Israel, Asa's heart was fully committed ⌞to the LORD⌟ all his
life. [18]He brought into the temple of God the silver and gold and
the articles that he and his father had dedicated.
[19]There was no more war until the thirty-fifth year of Asa's
reign.

Asa's Last Years

16 In the thirty-sixth year of Asa's reign Baasha king of Israel
went up against Judah and fortified Ramah to prevent anyone
from leaving or entering the territory of Asa king of Judah.
[2]Asa then took the silver and gold out of the treasuries of the
LORD's temple and of his own palace and sent it to Ben-Hadad
king of Aram, who was ruling in Damascus. [3]"Let there be a treaty
between me and you," he said, "as there was between my father and
your father. See, I am sending you silver and gold. Now break your
treaty with Baasha king of Israel so he will withdraw from me."
[4]Ben-Hadad agreed with King Asa and sent the commanders
of his forces against the towns of Israel. They conquered Ijon, Dan,
Abel Maim[a] and all the store cities of Naphtali. [5]When Baasha
heard this, he stopped building Ramah and abandoned his work.
[6]Then King Asa brought all the men of Judah, and they carried
away from Ramah the stones and timber Baasha had been using.
With them he built up Geba and Mizpah.
[7]At that time Hanani the seer came to Asa king of Judah and
said to him: "Because you relied on the king of Aram and not on
the LORD your God, the army of the king of Aram has escaped

[a]**4** Also known as *Abel Beth Maacah*

15:16,17 *Asherah pole . . . high places:* See the notes at 11:15 and 14:3.

15:16 *Kidron Valley:* Beginning with Asa, kings obedient to God's laws used this valley east of Jerusalem as a place to destroy idols. See also 2 Kgs 23:4, 6, 12 and the map on p. 2466.

16:1 *Baasha king of Israel:* Baasha was king of Israel from 909 to 886 B.C. (1 Kgs 15:33—16:7).

16:1 *Ramah:* A city in the area of Benjamin about five miles north of Jerusalem.

16:2 *Ben-Hadad king of Aram:* This is the first of at least three Aramean kings with this name. Another attacked Israel during King Ahab's rule (1 Kgs 20:1). A third was the son of Hazael who seized the second Ben-Hadad's crown (2 Kgs 8:7-15; 13:24).

Aram was north of Israel. Ben-Hadad begins by capturing several cities in northern Israel (16:4), forcing Baasha to leave Ramah in the south in order to defend the northern area of his kingdom. See the map on p. 2465.

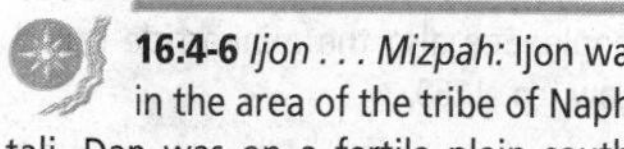

16:4-6 *Ijon . . . Mizpah:* Ijon was in the area of the tribe of Naphtali. Dan was on a fertile plain southwest of Mount Hermon. In earlier times it was known as Leshem (Josh 19:47, 48) or Laish (Judg 18:7). Abel Maim (known in 1 Kgs 15:20 as Abel Beth Maacah) was near Dan, but in the territory of the tribe of Naphtali. The listing of these cities and areas indicates that Ben-Hadad had taken all of Israel's northwest territory. See the maps on pp. 2464 and 2465.

Geba and Mizpah are believed to have been north of Jerusalem.

16:7-9 *You have done a foolish thing:* See the note at 13:4-12. See also 14:9-14.

15:16 2 Chr 11:20-22; 12:16; 14:1.

from your hand. 8Were not the Cushites[a] and Libyans a mighty
army with great numbers of chariots and horsemen[b]? Yet when
you relied on the LORD, he delivered them into your hand. 9For the
eyes of the LORD range throughout the earth to strengthen those
whose hearts are fully committed to him. You have done a foolish
thing, and from now on you will be at war."
10Asa was angry with the seer because of this; he was so
enraged that he put him in prison. At the same time Asa brutally
oppressed some of the people.
11The events of Asa's reign, from beginning to end, are written in the book of the kings of Judah and Israel. 12In the thirty-
ninth year of his reign Asa was afflicted with a disease in his feet.
Though his disease was severe, even in his illness he did not seek
help from the LORD, but only from the physicians. 13Then in the
forty-first year of his reign Asa died and rested with his fathers.
14They buried him in the tomb that he had cut out for himself in
the City of David. They laid him on a bier covered with spices and
various blended perfumes, and they made a huge fire in his honor.

Jehoshaphat King of Judah

17 Jehoshaphat his son succeeded him as king and strengthened
himself against Israel. 2He stationed troops in all the fortified cities
of Judah and put garrisons in Judah and in the towns of Ephraim
that his father Asa had captured.
3The LORD was with Jehoshaphat because in his early years
he walked in the ways his father David had followed. He did not
consult the Baals 4but sought the God of his father and followed
his commands rather than the practices of Israel. 5The LORD established the kingdom under his control; and all Judah brought gifts
to Jehoshaphat, so that he had great wealth and honor. 6His heart
was devoted to the ways of the LORD; furthermore, he removed the
high places and the Asherah poles from Judah.
7In the third year of his reign he sent his officials Ben-Hail,
Obadiah, Zechariah, Nethanel and Micaiah to teach in the towns of
Judah. 8With them were certain Levites—Shemaiah, Nethaniah, Zebadiah, Asahel, Shemiramoth, Jehonathan, Adonijah, Tobijah and Tob-
Adonijah—and the priests Elishama and Jehoram. 9They taught
throughout Judah, taking with them the Book of the Law of the LORD;
they went around to all the towns of Judah and taught the people.
10The fear of the LORD fell on all the kingdoms of the lands
surrounding Judah, so that they did not make war with Jehoshaphat. 11Some Philistines brought Jehoshaphat gifts and silver as
tribute, and the Arabs brought him flocks: seven thousand seven
hundred rams and seven thousand seven hundred goats.
12Jehoshaphat became more and more powerful; he built

[a]8 That is, people from the upper Nile region [b]8 Or *charioteers*

16:12 *disease in his feet:* The kind of disease is not clear. It apparently played some role in Asa's death about two years later. This is one of several biblical examples of disease occurring in connection with sin (2 Kgs 15:5; 2 Chr 21:18, 19; 26:16-23). The way Asa relies on doctors rather than God is related to his not trusting God for help in battle (16:7-9).

16:14 *tomb . . . huge fire:* Tombs cut into rock or hillsides were common burial places. Asa's long reign and many accomplishments earned him the honor of a bonfire despite his sinful later years (in contrast to Jehoram's burial at 21:19). See also the mini-article called "Burial," p. 1998.

17:1 *Jehoshaphat:* Jehoshaphat, the son of King Asa of Judah, ruled Judah from 870 to 848 B.C.

17:3-6 *Baals . . . Asherah poles:* See the notes at 11:15 and 14:3.

17:6 *high places:* See the notes at 11:15; 14:3; and 20:33.

17:9 *They taught . . . the Book of the Law:* Religious and state law were one and the same for God's people. See also the mini-article called "Law," p. 1160.

17:11 *Philistines:* The Philistines were people from Philistia, an area on the eastern coast of the Mediterranean Sea. Israel fought many wars against the Philistines. See 1 Chr 14:8-17 and the map on p. 2467.

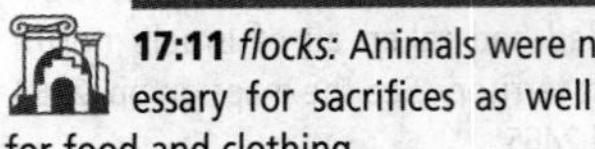

17:11 *flocks:* Animals were necessary for sacrifices as well as for food and clothing.

17:12-19 *Jehoshaphat became more and more powerful:* God rewarded Jehoshaphat for being obedient (17:3-7). See also the notes at 7:14-22; 12:1, 2; and 14:1.

17:10 1 Chr 14:17; 2 Chr 14:14; 20:29.

forts and store cities in Judah 13and had large supplies in the towns
of Judah. He also kept experienced fighting men in Jerusalem.
14Their enrollment by families was as follows:

From Judah, commanders of units of 1,000:
Adnah the commander, with 300,000 fighting men;
15next, Jehohanan the commander, with 280,000;
16next, Amasiah son of Zicri, who volunteered himself for the
service of the LORD, with 200,000.
17From Benjamin:
Eliada, a valiant soldier, with 200,000 men armed with bows
and shields;
18next, Jehozabad, with 180,000 men armed for battle.

19These were the men who served the king, besides those he stationed in the fortified cities throughout Judah.

Micaiah Prophesies Against Ahab

18 Now Jehoshaphat had great wealth and honor, and he allied
himself with Ahab by marriage. 2Some years later he went down
to visit Ahab in Samaria. Ahab slaughtered many sheep and cattle
for him and the people with him and urged him to attack Ramoth
Gilead. 3Ahab king of Israel asked Jehoshaphat king of Judah, "Will
you go with me against Ramoth Gilead?"

Jehoshaphat replied, "I am as you are, and my people as your
people; we will join you in the war." 4But Jehoshaphat also said to
the king of Israel, "First seek the counsel of the LORD."

5So the king of Israel brought together the prophets—four
hundred men—and asked them, "Shall we go to war against
Ramoth Gilead, or shall I refrain?"

"Go," they answered, "for God will give it into the king's
hand."

6But Jehoshaphat asked, "Is there not a prophet of the LORD
here whom we can inquire of?"

7The king of Israel answered Jehoshaphat, "There is still one
man through whom we can inquire of the LORD, but I hate him
because he never prophesies anything good about me, but always
bad. He is Micaiah son of Imlah."

"The king should not say that," Jehoshaphat replied.

8So the king of Israel called one of his officials and said,
"Bring Micaiah son of Imlah at once."

9Dressed in their royal robes, the king of Israel and
Jehoshaphat king of Judah were sitting on their thrones at the
threshing floor by the entrance to the gate of Samaria, with all
the prophets prophesying before them. 10Now Zedekiah son of
Kenaanah had made iron horns, and he declared, "This is what the
LORD says: 'With these you will gore the Arameans until they are
destroyed.' "

17:14 *families:* Referring to a "clan" or group of families who were related to each other. A group of clans made up a tribe. Ten of the twelve tribes of Israel formed the northern kingdom (Israel), while the other two formed the southern kingdom (Judah).

18:1 *allied himself with Ahab by marriage:* King Ahab ruled the northern kingdom (Israel) from 874 to 853 B.C. The marriage between Jehoshaphat's son Jehoram and Ahab's daughter Athaliah was a military alliance and therefore a sin (2 Kgs 8:16-18), because it showed a lack of trust in God's ability to protect Judah. Athaliah later became Judah's seventh ruler and only queen. During her rule (841-835 B.C.), she killed almost all of David's descendants (22:10) and helped bring the worship of foreign gods back to Judah. This eventually led to the destruction of the nation (36:17-21).

18:2 *Samaria . . . Ramoth Gilead:* Samaria was Israel's capital. Built on the hill of the same name, the city stood three hundred feet above the surrounding plain, giving it great defensive strength. It was approximately forty miles north of Jerusalem and midway between the Jordan River and the Mediterranean Sea. Ramoth Gilead was east of the Jordan River. It had been an Israelite city since the time of Moses (Deut 4:41-43; 1 Kgs 4:13). The Arameans had taken control of it (1 Kgs 22:3, 4).

18:5 *prophets—four hundred men:* Ahab's false prophets told the kings what they wanted to hear, unlike the true prophet who spoke God's message (18:14-34).

18:9 *threshing floor . . . gate:* Regarding the gate, see the note at 8:5. At a threshing floor, bundles of grain were beaten or trampled in order to separate the kernels from their outer husks. It was done outdoors on hilltops so that the wind could more easily blow away the light husks as the heavier grains fell back down to the threshing floor. See the illustration on p. 730.

11All the other prophets were prophesying the same thing.
"Attack Ramoth Gilead and be victorious," they said, "for the LORD
will give it into the king's hand."
12The messenger who had gone to summon Micaiah said to
him, "Look, as one man the other prophets are predicting success
for the king. Let your word agree with theirs, and speak favorably."
13But Micaiah said, "As surely as the LORD lives, I can tell him
only what my God says."
14When he arrived, the king asked him, "Micaiah, shall we go
to war against Ramoth Gilead, or shall I refrain?"
"Attack and be victorious," he answered, "for they will be
given into your hand."
15The king said to him, "How many times must I make you
swear to tell me nothing but the truth in the name of the LORD?"
16Then Micaiah answered, "I saw all Israel scattered on the
hills like sheep without a shepherd, and the LORD said, 'These people have no master. Let each one go home in peace.' "
17The king of Israel said to Jehoshaphat, "Didn't I tell you
that he never prophesies anything good about me, but only bad?"
18Micaiah continued, "Therefore hear the word of the LORD:
I saw the LORD sitting on his throne with all the host of heaven
standing on his right and on his left. 19And the LORD said, 'Who
will entice Ahab king of Israel into attacking Ramoth Gilead and
going to his death there?'
"One suggested this, and another that. 20Finally, a spirit came
forward, stood before the LORD and said, 'I will entice him.'
" 'By what means?' the LORD asked.
21" 'I will go and be a lying spirit in the mouths of all his
prophets,' he said.
" 'You will succeed in enticing him,' said the LORD. 'Go and
do it.'
22"So now the LORD has put a lying spirit in the mouths of
these prophets of yours. The LORD has decreed disaster for you."
23Then Zedekiah son of Kenaanah went up and slapped
Micaiah in the face. "Which way did the spirit from[a] the LORD go
when he went from me to speak to you?" he asked.
24Micaiah replied, "You will find out on the day you go to
hide in an inner room."
25The king of Israel then ordered, "Take Micaiah and send
him back to Amon the ruler of the city and to Joash the king's son,
26and say, 'This is what the king says: Put this fellow in prison and
give him nothing but bread and water until I return safely.' "
27Micaiah declared, "If you ever return safely, the LORD has
not spoken through me." Then he added, "Mark my words, all you
people!"

[a]23 Or *Spirit of*

Jehoshaphat told the judges, *"Let the fear of the LORD be upon you. Judge carefully, for with the LORD our God there is no injustice or partiality or bribery."*
2 Chr 19:7

18:16 *I saw all Israel scattered . . . shepherd:* In ancient times, prophets were able to tell about future events because of what they had seen in visions or dreams (Num 12:6; Ezek 1:1—3:15; Amos 7:1-3; 8:1-3).

In the Bible kings are often referred to as shepherds because it is their responsibility to protect their "flock," the people of their nation (Ps 78:70-72). By telling both kings that Israel is without a shepherd, Micaiah is telling Ahab and Jehoshaphat that they are both failures as kings. The true king of Israel is the LORD, who rules from his throne in heaven (18:18). See also Ezek 34.

18:16 Num 27:17; Ezek 34:5; Matt 9:36; Mark 6:34.

Ahab Killed at Ramoth Gilead

28 So the king of Israel and Jehoshaphat king of Judah went up to Ramoth Gilead. 29 The king of Israel said to Jehoshaphat, "I will enter the battle in disguise, but you wear your royal robes." So the king of Israel disguised himself and went into battle.

30 Now the king of Aram had ordered his chariot commanders, "Do not fight with anyone, small or great, except the king of Israel." 31 When the chariot commanders saw Jehoshaphat, they thought, "This is the king of Israel." So they turned to attack him, but Jehoshaphat cried out, and the LORD helped him. God drew them away from him, 32 for when the chariot commanders saw that he was not the king of Israel, they stopped pursuing him.

33 But someone drew his bow at random and hit the king of Israel between the sections of his armor. The king told the chariot driver, "Wheel around and get me out of the fighting. I've been wounded." 34 All day long the battle raged, and the king of Israel propped himself up in his chariot facing the Arameans until evening. Then at sunset he died.

19 When Jehoshaphat king of Judah returned safely to his palace in Jerusalem, 2 Jehu the seer, the son of Hanani, went out to meet him and said to the king, "Should you help the wicked and love[a] those who hate the LORD? Because of this, the wrath of the LORD is upon you. 3 There is, however, some good in you, for you have rid the land of the Asherah poles and have set your heart on seeking God."

Jehoshaphat Appoints Judges

4 Jehoshaphat lived in Jerusalem, and he went out again among the people from Beersheba to the hill country of Ephraim and turned them back to the LORD, the God of their fathers. 5 He appointed judges in the land, in each of the fortified cities of Judah. 6 He told them, "Consider carefully what you do, because you are not judging for man but for the LORD, who is with you whenever you give a verdict. 7 Now let the fear of the LORD be upon you. Judge carefully, for with the LORD our God there is no injustice or partiality or bribery."

8 In Jerusalem also, Jehoshaphat appointed some of the Levites, priests and heads of Israelite families to administer the law of the LORD and to settle disputes. And they lived in Jerusalem. 9 He gave them these orders: "You must serve faithfully and wholeheartedly in the fear of the LORD. 10 In every case that comes before you from your fellow countrymen who live in the cities—whether bloodshed or other concerns of the law, commands, decrees or ordinances—you are to warn them not to sin against the LORD; otherwise his wrath will come on you and your brothers. Do this, and you will not sin.

---

[a]2 Or *and make alliances with*

18:33 *drew his bow at random and hit the king of Israel:* Ahab's death by an unaimed arrow reveals it as God's doing (18:19).

19:2,3 *Should you help the wicked:* See the note at 18:1. Jehoshaphat's treaty with Ahab was considered sinful, but most of what Jehoshaphat did was considered good.

19:3 *Asherah poles:* See the note at 14:3.

19:5 *judges:* Jehoshaphat, whose name means "the LORD judges," reformed the justice system by placing godly judges throughout the country and by establishing a "court of appeals," or higher court, in Jerusalem (19:8-11). See also Deut 17:8-13.

19:7 *bribery:* Payments given to influence someone else's acts or decisions. See also Exod 23:6-8; Lev 19:15; Deut 16:18, 19. The practice of giving and taking bribes was often criticized by Israel's prophets. Bribing officials kept God's true justice from being carried out (see Isa 1:21-23; Amos 5:12; Mic 2:9-11).

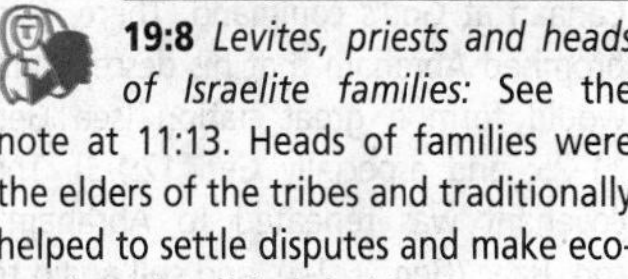

19:8 *Levites, priests and heads of Israelite families:* See the note at 11:13. Heads of families were the elders of the tribes and traditionally helped to settle disputes and make economic and political decisions.

A judicial system was not new to Israel or to other nations. Israel's system was based on God's command to treat all people equally, without regard to their standing in society (Lev 19:15; Deut 16:18-20). See also the mini-article called "Justice," p. 1721.

18:31 1 Kgs 22:32, 33.

20:1 *Moabites and Ammonites . . . Meunites:* Moab was located to the east of the Dead Sea. The Moabites were longtime enemies of Israel (Num 22:1-6; 1 Sam 14:47, 48; 2 Chr 20:10).

Ammon was a nation east of the northern kingdom (Israel). Like the Moabites, the Ammonites were related to the Israelites through Lot (Gen 19:36-38), but refused to help Israel and often warred against them (Deut 23:3-6; 1 Sam 11:1, 2; Ezek 25:1-11).

The Meunites lived in Edom near Mount Seir. See the map on p. 2467.

20:3 *proclaimed a fast:* People sometimes went without eating in times of crisis and sadness, or to show they were sorry for their sins.

20:5 *the temple of the* LORD*:* The temple in Jerusalem, built by Solomon (1 Kgs 6,7; 2 Chr 2–5), was considered God's home on earth and the place of worship for Israel's people.

20:7 *Abraham:* In Hebrew, "Abraham" sounds like "father of many nations" (Gen 17:4,5). Abraham was the ancestor of the Israelite (Hebrew) nation. He left his home in Ur to go to Canaan at God's command. There, God promised Abraham that his descendants would form a great nation (see Gen 11–25; and especially Gen 12:1-3). The covenant was repeated to Abraham's son, Isaac (Gen 26:2-4), and still again to Abraham's grandson, Jacob (Gen 35:9-12). See also the mini-article called "Covenants (Agreements)," p. 386.

20:10 *men from Ammon, Moab and Mount Seir:* See the note at 20:1 and Deut 2:4-19.

20:7 Isa 41:8; Jas 2:23. **20:9** 2 Chr 6:14-42; 7:12-22.

11 "Amariah the chief priest will be over you in any matter
concerning the LORD, and Zebadiah son of Ishmael, the leader of
the tribe of Judah, will be over you in any matter concerning the
king, and the Levites will serve as officials before you. Act with
courage, and may the LORD be with those who do well."

Jehoshaphat Defeats Moab and Ammon

20 After this, the Moabites and Ammonites with some of the
Meunites[a] came to make war on Jehoshaphat.
2 Some men came and told Jehoshaphat, "A vast army is coming against you from Edom,[b] from the other side of the Sea.[c] It is
already in Hazazon Tamar" (that is, En Gedi). 3 Alarmed, Jehoshaphat resolved to inquire of the LORD, and he proclaimed a fast for
all Judah. 4 The people of Judah came together to seek help from the
LORD; indeed, they came from every town in Judah to seek him.
5 Then Jehoshaphat stood up in the assembly of Judah and
Jerusalem at the temple of the LORD in the front of the new courtyard 6 and said:

"O LORD, God of our fathers, are you not the God who
is in heaven? You rule over all the kingdoms of the nations.
Power and might are in your hand, and no one can withstand
you. 7 O our God, did you not drive out the inhabitants of this
land before your people Israel and give it forever to the
descendants of Abraham your friend? 8 They have lived in it
and have built in it a sanctuary for your Name, saying, 9 'If
calamity comes upon us, whether the sword of judgment, or
plague or famine, we will stand in your presence before this
temple that bears your Name and will cry out to you in our
distress, and you will hear us and save us.'
10 "But now here are men from Ammon, Moab and
Mount Seir, whose territory you would not allow Israel to
invade when they came from Egypt; so they turned away from
them and did not destroy them. 11 See how they are repaying
us by coming to drive us out of the possession you gave us as
an inheritance. 12 O our God, will you not judge them? For we
have no power to face this vast army that is attacking us. We
do not know what to do, but our eyes are upon you."

13 All the men of Judah, with their wives and children and little ones, stood there before the LORD.
14 Then the Spirit of the LORD came upon Jahaziel son of
Zechariah, the son of Benaiah, the son of Jeiel, the son of Mattaniah, a Levite and descendant of Asaph, as he stood in the
assembly.

---

[a]1 Some Septuagint manuscripts; Hebrew *Ammonites* [b]2 One Hebrew manuscript; most Hebrew manuscripts, Septuagint and Vulgate *Aram* [c]2 That is, the Dead Sea

15He said: "Listen, King Jehoshaphat and all who live in
Judah and Jerusalem! This is what the LORD says to you: 'Do not be
afraid or discouraged because of this vast army. For the battle is
not yours, but God's. 16Tomorrow march down against them. They
will be climbing up by the Pass of Ziz, and you will find them at
the end of the gorge in the Desert of Jeruel. 17You will not have to
fight this battle. Take up your positions; stand firm and see the
deliverance the LORD will give you, O Judah and Jerusalem. Do not
be afraid; do not be discouraged. Go out to face them tomorrow,
and the LORD will be with you.' "
18Jehoshaphat bowed with his face to the ground, and all
the people of Judah and Jerusalem fell down in worship before
the LORD. 19Then some Levites from the Kohathites and Korahites
stood up and praised the LORD, the God of Israel, with very loud
voice.
20Early in the morning they left for the Desert of Tekoa. As
they set out, Jehoshaphat stood and said, "Listen to me, Judah and
people of Jerusalem! Have faith in the LORD your God and you will
be upheld; have faith in his prophets and you will be successful."
21After consulting the people, Jehoshaphat appointed men to sing
to the LORD and to praise him for the splendor of his[a] holiness as
they went out at the head of the army, saying:

"Give thanks to the LORD,
for his love endures forever."

22As they began to sing and praise, the LORD set ambushes
against the men of Ammon and Moab and Mount Seir who were
invading Judah, and they were defeated. 23The men of Ammon and
Moab rose up against the men from Mount Seir to destroy and
annihilate them. After they finished slaughtering the men from
Seir, they helped to destroy one another.
24When the men of Judah came to the place that overlooks
the desert and looked toward the vast army, they saw only dead
bodies lying on the ground; no one had escaped. 25So Jehoshaphat
and his men went to carry off their plunder, and they found
among them a great amount of equipment and clothing[b] and also
articles of value—more than they could take away. There was so
much plunder that it took three days to collect it. 26On the fourth
day they assembled in the Valley of Beracah, where they praised
the LORD. This is why it is called the Valley of Beracah[c] to this day.
27Then, led by Jehoshaphat, all the men of Judah and
Jerusalem returned joyfully to Jerusalem, for the LORD had given
them cause to rejoice over their enemies. 28They entered Jerusalem
and went to the temple of the LORD with harps and lutes and
trumpets.

[a]21 Or *him with the splendor of* [b]25 Some Hebrew manuscripts and Vulgate; most Hebrew manuscripts *corpses* [c]26 *Beracah* means *praise.*

Jehoshaphat said,
"Power and might are in your hand, and no one can withstand you . . . . we have no power to face this vast army that is attacking us. We do not know what to do, but our eyes are upon you."
2 Chr 20:6,12

20:16 *gorge in the Desert of Jeruel:* This is an area between En Gedi on the Dead Sea and Tekoa (20:20), fewer than twenty miles northwest of En Gedi and about ten miles south of Jerusalem. It includes the pass that leads from En Gedi to Jerusalem. See the map on p. 2464.

20:21-24 *sing to the LORD . . . saw only dead bodies:* The people's trust in God's power was so great that they were given victory by God without even having to fight. See also Judg 7:15-22 and the mini-article called "Holy War (The LORD's Battles)," p. 306.

20:26 *Valley of Beracah:* In Hebrew the name "Beracah" means "praise."

20:15-17 Exod 14:13, 14; Deut 20:1-4.

20:33 *high places . . . were not removed:* This verse appears to contradict 17:6. Perhaps Jehoshaphat destroyed the shrines initially, but could not keep the people from rebuilding them. See the note at 14:3.

21:1 *buried with them:* Burial in one's family burial place was very important. It was believed that the only comfort one had following death was to be buried near one's relatives. See also the mini-article called "Burial," p. 1998.

21:1 *Jehoram:* Jehoram was Judah's fifth king and ruled alone from 848 to 841 B.C. Before that, he ruled for four years with his father, Jehoshaphat. In biblical times, a father and son would sometimes rule as kings at the same time. That way, when the father died, his son would already have control of the kingdom.

21:2-4 *All these were sons of Jehoshaphat king of Israel . . . put all his brothers to the sword:* Having many children was a sign of God's blessing (Ps 127:3). By contrast, only one of Jehoram's children would be left after Judah was invaded (21:17).

It was not unusual for a new king to remove or kill anyone who might try to take the throne from him, but Jehoram's murder of his own brothers is particularly evil (21:13). Later, Athaliah acts in a similar way (22:10).

21:6 *walked in the ways of the kings of Israel:* Jehoram allows the worship of foreign gods in Judah, just as his father-in-law Ahab and other kings had done in Israel (1 Kgs 15:26,34; 16:13,19,25,29-33).

21:8 *Edom:* Edom is usually described in the Bible as Israel's enemy (Num 24:18; 1 Sam 14:47; Isa 34:5-17). See the map on p. 2467.

20:29 Exod 23:27; Josh 2:9-11; 2 Chr 17:10. **21:7** 1 Kgs 11:36.

[29]The fear of God came upon all the kingdoms of the countries when they heard how the LORD had fought against the enemies of Israel. [30]And the kingdom of Jehoshaphat was at peace, for
his God had given him rest on every side.

The End of Jehoshaphat's Reign

[31]So Jehoshaphat reigned over Judah. He was thirty-five
years old when he became king of Judah, and he reigned in
Jerusalem twenty-five years. His mother's name was Azubah
daughter of Shilhi. [32]He walked in the ways of his father Asa and
did not stray from them; he did what was right in the eyes of the
LORD. [33]The high places, however, were not removed, and the people still had not set their hearts on the God of their fathers.
[34]The other events of Jehoshaphat's reign, from beginning to
end, are written in the annals of Jehu son of Hanani, which are
recorded in the book of the kings of Israel.
[35]Later, Jehoshaphat king of Judah made an alliance with
Ahaziah king of Israel, who was guilty of wickedness. [36]He agreed
with him to construct a fleet of trading ships.[a] After these were built
at Ezion Geber, [37]Eliezer son of Dodavahu of Mareshah prophesied
against Jehoshaphat, saying, "Because you have made an alliance
with Ahaziah, the LORD will destroy what you have made." The ships
were wrecked and were not able to set sail to trade.[b]
21 Then Jehoshaphat rested with his fathers and was buried
with them in the City of David. And Jehoram his son succeeded
him as king. [2]Jehoram's brothers, the sons of Jehoshaphat, were
Azariah, Jehiel, Zechariah, Azariahu, Michael and Shephatiah. All
these were sons of Jehoshaphat king of Israel.[c] [3]Their father had
given them many gifts of silver and gold and articles of value, as
well as fortified cities in Judah, but he had given the kingdom to
Jehoram because he was his firstborn son.

Jehoram King of Judah

[4]When Jehoram established himself firmly over his father's
kingdom, he put all his brothers to the sword along with some of
the princes of Israel. [5]Jehoram was thirty-two years old when he
became king, and he reigned in Jerusalem eight years. [6]He walked
in the ways of the kings of Israel, as the house of Ahab had done,
for he married a daughter of Ahab. He did evil in the eyes of the
LORD. [7]Nevertheless, because of the covenant the LORD had made
with David, the LORD was not willing to destroy the house of
David. He had promised to maintain a lamp for him and his
descendants forever.
[8]In the time of Jehoram, Edom rebelled against Judah and

[a]36 Hebrew *of ships that could go to Tarshish* [b]37 Hebrew *sail for Tarshish*
[c]2 That is, Judah, as frequently in 2 Chronicles

set up its own king. 9So Jehoram went there with his officers and
all his chariots. The Edomites surrounded him and his chariot
commanders, but he rose up and broke through by night. 10To this
day Edom has been in rebellion against Judah.

Libnah revolted at the same time, because Jehoram had forsaken the LORD, the God of his fathers. 11He had also built high
places on the hills of Judah and had caused the people of
Jerusalem to prostitute themselves and had led Judah astray.

12Jehoram received a letter from Elijah the prophet, which said:

"This is what the LORD, the God of your father David, says:
'You have not walked in the ways of your father Jehoshaphat
or of Asa king of Judah. 13But you have walked in the ways of
the kings of Israel, and you have led Judah and the people of
Jerusalem to prostitute themselves, just as the house of Ahab
did. You have also murdered your own brothers, members of
your father's house, men who were better than you. 14So now
the LORD is about to strike your people, your sons, your wives
and everything that is yours, with a heavy blow. 15You yourself
will be very ill with a lingering disease of the bowels, until the
disease causes your bowels to come out.' "

16The LORD aroused against Jehoram the hostility of the
Philistines and of the Arabs who lived near the Cushites. 17They
attacked Judah, invaded it and carried off all the goods found in
the king's palace, together with his sons and wives. Not a son was
left to him except Ahaziah,[a] the youngest.

18After all this, the LORD afflicted Jehoram with an incurable
disease of the bowels. 19In the course of time, at the end of the second year, his bowels came out because of the disease, and he died
in great pain. His people made no fire in his honor, as they had for
his fathers.

20Jehoram was thirty-two years old when he became king,
and he reigned in Jerusalem eight years. He passed away, to no
one's regret, and was buried in the City of David, but not in the
tombs of the kings.

Ahaziah King of Judah

22 The people of Jerusalem made Ahaziah, Jehoram's youngest
son, king in his place, since the raiders, who came with the Arabs
into the camp, had killed all the older sons. So Ahaziah son of
Jehoram king of Judah began to reign.

2Ahaziah was twenty-two[b] years old when he became king,
and he reigned in Jerusalem one year. His mother's name was
Athaliah, a granddaughter of Omri.

[a]17 Hebrew *Jehoahaz,* a variant of *Ahaziah* [b]2 Some Septuagint manuscripts and Syriac (see also 2 Kings 8:26); Hebrew *forty-two*

21:8 *Edom rebelled:* The Edomites were descendants of Esau (Gen 25:24-26; 36:1). David had conquered Edom about two hundred and fifty years prior to this time (2 Sam 8:13,14). Isaac, Esau's father, had said that Esau's descendants would be ruled by his brother Jacob's descendants, but that one day they would rebel and be free (Gen 27:40).

21:10 *Libnah:* This was a town on the border between Philistia and Judah, which means that Jehoram was facing rebellion on both sides of his kingdom. See the map on p. 2467.

21:11 *high places:* See the note at 14:3.

21:12 *Elijah the prophet:* The name Elijah means "the LORD is my God." During the reigns of King Ahab, Queen Jezebel, and King Ahaziah (1 Kgs 17—2 Kgs 2:11), Elijah brought God's messages to Israel and fought against the worship of Baal. See also the mini-article called "Elijah," p. 1816.

21:15 *disease of the bowels:* Compare Jehoram's disease with Asa's (see 16:12 and the note).

21:16 *Cushites:* See the note at 14:9-13.

21:17 *Ahaziah:* This is not the same Ahaziah who was Israel's king. That Ahaziah was Ahab's son and Athaliah's brother. See the notes at 22:1 and 22:5.

22:1 *Ahaziah:* Ahaziah was Judah's sixth king and ruled for one year in 841 B.C. His mother was Athaliah, whose father (Ahab) and brothers (Ahaziah and Joram) were kings of Israel (1 Kgs 16:29; 22:51; 2 Kgs 1:17). See also the note at 18:1.

21:19,20 2 Chr 16:14; 24:25, 26.
22:1 2 Chr 21:16,17.

3He too walked in the ways of the house of Ahab, for his
mother encouraged him in doing wrong. 4He did evil in the eyes of
the LORD, as the house of Ahab had done, for after his father's
death they became his advisers, to his undoing. 5He also followed
their counsel when he went with Joram[a] son of Ahab king of Israel
to war against Hazael king of Aram at Ramoth Gilead. The
Arameans wounded Joram; 6so he returned to Jezreel to recover
from the wounds they had inflicted on him at Ramoth[b] in his battle with Hazael king of Aram.

Then Ahaziah[c] son of Jehoram king of Judah went down to
Jezreel to see Joram son of Ahab because he had been wounded.
7Through Ahaziah's visit to Joram, God brought about
Ahaziah's downfall. When Ahaziah arrived, he went out with
Joram to meet Jehu son of Nimshi, whom the LORD had anointed
to destroy the house of Ahab. 8While Jehu was executing judgment
on the house of Ahab, he found the princes of Judah and the sons
of Ahaziah's relatives, who had been attending Ahaziah, and he
killed them. 9He then went in search of Ahaziah, and his men captured him while he was hiding in Samaria. He was brought to Jehu
and put to death. They buried him, for they said, "He was a son of
Jehoshaphat, who sought the LORD with all his heart." So there was
no one in the house of Ahaziah powerful enough to retain the
kingdom.

Athaliah and Joash

10When Athaliah the mother of Ahaziah saw that her son
was dead, she proceeded to destroy the whole royal family of the
house of Judah. 11But Jehosheba,[d] the daughter of King Jehoram,
took Joash son of Ahaziah and stole him away from among the
royal princes who were about to be murdered and put him and his
nurse in a bedroom. Because Jehosheba,[d] the daughter of King
Jehoram and wife of the priest Jehoiada, was Ahaziah's sister, she
hid the child from Athaliah so she could not kill him. 12He
remained hidden with them at the temple of God for six years
while Athaliah ruled the land.

23 In the seventh year Jehoiada showed his strength. He made a
covenant with the commanders of units of a hundred: Azariah son
of Jeroham, Ishmael son of Jehohanan, Azariah son of Obed, Maaseiah son of Adaiah, and Elishaphat son of Zicri. 2They went
throughout Judah and gathered the Levites and the heads of
Israelite families from all the towns. When they came to Jerusalem,
3the whole assembly made a covenant with the king at the temple
of God.

---

[a]5 Hebrew *Jehoram,* a variant of *Joram*; also in verses 6 and 7 [b]6 Hebrew *Ramah,* a variant of *Ramoth* [c]6 Some Hebrew manuscripts, Septuagint, Vulgate and Syriac (see also 2 Kings 8:29); most Hebrew manuscripts *Azariah* [d]11 Hebrew *Jehoshabeath,* a variant of *Jehosheba*

22:5 *Joram . . . Hazael:* Joram was ninth king of Israel's northern kingdom and ruled from 852 to 841 B.C. He was the brother of Ahaziah, Israel's eighth king (2 Kgs 1:17), and Athaliah, making him the uncle of Ahaziah, Judah's sixth king. See also the note at 22:1.

Hazael became Aram's king by killing King Ben-Hadad (2 Kgs 8:7-15). He went on to fulfill the words of Elisha the prophet by bringing oppression and pain to Israel (2 Kgs 10:32; 12:17, 18).

22:5,6 *Ramoth Gilead . . . Jezreel:* See the note at 18:2. Jezreel was about seventeen miles northwest of Mount Gilboa. Ahab had a royal home there. See the map on p. 2467.

22:7 *Jehu:* Jehu was Israel's tenth king and ruled from 841 to 814 B.C. God told Elijah that Jehu would become king and kill the worshipers of Baal (1 Kgs 19:16,17).

22:10-12 *Athaliah . . . Joash:* See the note at 18:1. Joash became Judah's seventh king. He ruled from 835 to 796 B.C. See 2 Chr 23, 24.

23:1,2 *Jehoiada . . . Levites . . . heads of Israelite families:* Jehoiada, the high priest (22:11; 24:6), provides religious leadership by leading the revolt against Athaliah and establishing Joash as the rightful ruler.

See the notes at 11:13 and 17:14.

23:3 *as the LORD promised concerning the descendants of David:* Joash is the last of David's descendants and so must become king for the promise to be kept (see also 2 Sam 7:12-16).

23:5 *Foundation Gate:* This may have been the gate that connected the temple with the palace.

22:7 2 Kgs 8:28—9:28. **22:10** 2 Chr 21:4.

Jehoiada said to them, "The king's son shall reign, as the LORD promised concerning the descendants of David. [4]Now this is what you are to do: A third of you priests and Levites who are going on duty on the Sabbath are to keep watch at the doors, [5]a third of you at the royal palace and a third at the Foundation Gate, and all the other men are to be in the courtyards of the temple of the LORD. [6]No one is to enter the temple of the LORD except the priests and Levites on duty; they may enter because they are consecrated, but all the other men are to guard what the LORD has assigned to them.[a] [7]The Levites are to station themselves around the king, each man with his weapons in his hand. Anyone who enters the temple must be put to death. Stay close to the king wherever he goes."

[8]The Levites and all the men of Judah did just as Jehoiada the priest ordered. Each one took his men—those who were going on duty on the Sabbath and those who were going off duty—for Jehoiada the priest had not released any of the divisions. [9]Then he gave the commanders of units of a hundred the spears and the large and small shields that had belonged to King David and that were in the temple of God. [10]He stationed all the men, each with his weapon in his hand, around the king—near the altar and the temple, from the south side to the north side of the temple.

[11]Jehoiada and his sons brought out the king's son and put the crown on him; they presented him with a copy of the covenant and proclaimed him king. They anointed him and shouted, "Long live the king!"

[12]When Athaliah heard the noise of the people running and cheering the king, she went to them at the temple of the LORD. [13]She looked, and there was the king, standing by his pillar at the entrance. The officers and the trumpeters were beside the king, and all the people of the land were rejoicing and blowing trumpets, and singers with musical instruments were leading the praises. Then Athaliah tore her robes and shouted, "Treason! Treason!"

[14]Jehoiada the priest sent out the commanders of units of a hundred, who were in charge of the troops, and said to them: "Bring her out between the ranks[b] and put to the sword anyone who follows her." For the priest had said, "Do not put her to death at the temple of the LORD." [15]So they seized her as she reached the entrance of the Horse Gate on the palace grounds, and there they put her to death.

[16]Jehoiada then made a covenant that he and the people and the king[c] would be the LORD's people. [17]All the people went to the temple of Baal and tore it down. They smashed the altars and idols and killed Mattan the priest of Baal in front of the altars.

---

[a]**6** Or *to observe the LORD's command* ⌞*not to enter*⌟ [b]**14** Or *out from the precincts* [c]**16** Or *covenant between* ⌞*the LORD*⌟ *and the people and the king that they* (see 2 Kings 11:17)

23:6 *consecrated:* To be "consecrated" means to be cleansed. In Old Testament times, a person who was acceptable to worship God was called "clean." A person who had certain kinds of diseases, who had touched a dead body, or who had broken certain laws became "unclean," and was unacceptable to worship God. If a person was unclean because of disease, the disease would have to be cured before the person could be clean again. Becoming clean (being consecrated) involved performing certain ceremonies that sometimes included sacrifices, special baths, and not having sex. Priests went through particular rituals to assure that they were "clean" and fit to perform their duties. See Exod 30:18-21; 40:31, 32; and the mini-article called "Purity (Clean and Unclean)," p. 2125.

23:11 *crown . . . copy of the covenant . . . anointed:* The crown was a headpiece or headband worn by royalty, or sometimes by others with special honors or position, such as a high priest (Exod 29:4-6).

The "copy of the covenant" may have been official papers that dealt with the king's position and duties.

Olive oil was poured on the head of someone who was chosen to be a priest, a prophet, or a king (Exod 28:41; 29:7; 2 Sam 2:4; 5:3).

23:14 *Do not put her to death at the temple of the LORD:* Killing was not allowed at the LORD's temple (Ezek 21:14; 1 Kgs 1:50,51). Interestingly, Athaliah was killed near the Horse Gate, while years earlier her mother Jezebel's body was trampled by horses (2 Kgs 9:33).

23:16 *Jehoiada then made a covenant:* Here, Jehoiada joins with the king and the people in a covenant to be faithful to the LORD.

23:17 *temple of Baal . . . altars and idols:* Athaliah's parents, Ahab and Jezebel, built a temple to Baal (1 Kgs 16:30-33) and allowed Baal worship in Israel (1 Kgs 16–22).

23:18,19 *priests . . . Levites . . . doorkeepers:* The writer describes the priests, Levites, and doorkeepers assuming their duties just as David had intended (1 Chr 23–27). See also 2 Kgs 11:18, 19; and the note at 11:13.

23:20 *Upper Gate:* Probably the Upper Benjamin Gate in the wall along the north side of the temple. See the map on p. 2466.

24:1 *Joash:* See the notes at 22:10-12 and 23:3.

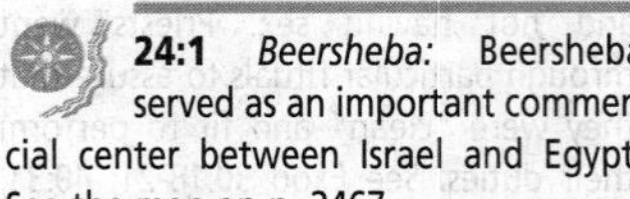

24:1 *Beersheba:* Beersheba served as an important commercial center between Israel and Egypt. See the map on p. 2467.

24:2,3 *did what was right . . . two wives for him:* Doing "right" meant obeying God's laws and worshiping only God. The writers of both KINGS and CHRONICLES state that Joash did what was right all the years Jehoiada the priest instructed him (2 Kgs 12:2). But 2 Chronicles 24:17-25 adds that Joash became unfaithful to the LORD after Jehoiada died (see the note at 24:15,16).

For "two wives," see the note at 11:18-21.

24:8 *a chest was made:* Such collection boxes were common in ancient Near Eastern temples. Temple practices at that time did not allow the people to enter the inner court where the altar was placed. In the earlier account, the box is put by the altar (2 Kgs 12:9).

24:4 2 Chr 24:7. **24:6** Exod 30:11-16.

18 Then Jehoiada placed the oversight of the temple of the
LORD in the hands of the priests, who were Levites, to whom David
had made assignments in the temple, to present the burnt offerings of the LORD as written in the Law of Moses, with rejoicing and
singing, as David had ordered. 19 He also stationed doorkeepers at
the gates of the LORD's temple so that no one who was in any way
unclean might enter.
20 He took with him the commanders of hundreds, the
nobles, the rulers of the people and all the people of the land and brought the king down from the temple of the LORD. They went into the palace through the Upper Gate and seated the king on the
royal throne, 21 and all the people of the land rejoiced. And the city
was quiet, because Athaliah had been slain with the sword.

Joash Repairs the Temple

24 Joash was seven years old when he became king, and he reigned in Jerusalem forty years. His mother's name was Zibiah;
she was from Beersheba. 2 Joash did what was right in the eyes of
the LORD all the years of Jehoiada the priest. 3 Jehoiada chose two
wives for him, and he had sons and daughters.
4 Some time later Joash decided to restore the temple of the
LORD. 5 He called together the priests and Levites and said to them, "Go to the towns of Judah and collect the money due annually from all Israel, to repair the temple of your God. Do it now." But the Levites did not act at once.
6 Therefore the king summoned Jehoiada the chief priest and said to him, "Why haven't you required the Levites to bring in from Judah and Jerusalem the tax imposed by Moses the servant of the LORD and by the assembly of Israel for the Tent of the Testimony?"
7 Now the sons of that wicked woman Athaliah had broken into the temple of God and had used even its sacred objects for the Baals.
8 At the king's command, a chest was made and placed out-
side, at the gate of the temple of the LORD. 9 A proclamation was
then issued in Judah and Jerusalem that they should bring to the LORD the tax that Moses the servant of God had required of Israel
in the desert. 10 All the officials and all the people brought their contributions gladly, dropping them into the chest until it was full.
11 Whenever the chest was brought in by the Levites to the king's officials and they saw that there was a large amount of money, the royal secretary and the officer of the chief priest would come and empty the chest and carry it back to its place. They did this regularly and collected a great amount of money. 12 The king and
Jehoiada gave it to the men who carried out the work required for the temple of the LORD. They hired masons and carpenters to restore the LORD's temple, and also workers in iron and bronze to repair the temple.
13 The men in charge of the work were diligent, and the

repairs progressed under them. They rebuilt the temple of God
according to its original design and reinforced it. 14When they had
finished, they brought the rest of the money to the king and Jehoiada, and with it were made articles for the LORD's temple: articles for
the service and for the burnt offerings, and also dishes and other
objects of gold and silver. As long as Jehoiada lived, burnt offerings
were presented continually in the temple of the LORD.
15Now Jehoiada was old and full of years, and he died at the
age of a hundred and thirty. 16He was buried with the kings in the
City of David, because of the good he had done in Israel for God
and his temple.

The Wickedness of Joash

17After the death of Jehoiada, the officials of Judah came and
paid homage to the king, and he listened to them. 18They abandoned the temple of the LORD, the God of their fathers, and worshiped Asherah poles and idols. Because of their guilt, God's anger
came upon Judah and Jerusalem. 19Although the LORD sent
prophets to the people to bring them back to him, and though
they testified against them, they would not listen.
20Then the Spirit of God came upon Zechariah son of
Jehoiada the priest. He stood before the people and said, "This is
what God says: 'Why do you disobey the LORD's commands? You
will not prosper. Because you have forsaken the LORD, he has forsaken you.' "
21But they plotted against him, and by order of the king they
stoned him to death in the courtyard of the LORD's temple. 22King
Joash did not remember the kindness Zechariah's father Jehoiada
had shown him but killed his son, who said as he lay dying, "May
the LORD see this and call you to account."
23At the turn of the year,[a] the army of Aram marched against
Joash; it invaded Judah and Jerusalem and killed all the leaders of
the people. They sent all the plunder to their king in Damascus.
24Although the Aramean army had come with only a few men, the
LORD delivered into their hands a much larger army. Because Judah
had forsaken the LORD, the God of their fathers, judgment was executed on Joash. 25When the Arameans withdrew, they left Joash
severely wounded. His officials conspired against him for murdering the son of Jehoiada the priest, and they killed him in his bed.
So he died and was buried in the City of David, but not in the
tombs of the kings.
26Those who conspired against him were Zabad,[b] son of
Shimeath an Ammonite woman, and Jehozabad, son of Shimrith[c]
a Moabite woman. 27The account of his sons, the many prophecies
about him, and the record of the restoration of the temple of God

[a]23 Probably in the spring [b]26 A variant of *Jozabad* [c]26 A variant of *Shomer*

24:14 *burnt offerings:* See the note at 1:6.

24:15,16 *at the age of a hundred and thirty . . . buried with the kings:* A long life was seen as God's reward for a godly life. Jehoiada's burial reflects his faithful leadership of God's people and is used by the writer of 2 CHRONICLES to divide Joash's reign into two periods. While Jehoiada was alive Joash was faithful. After the death of the priest, Joash turned away from God.

24:18 *Asherah poles:* See the note at 14:3.

24:21,22 *May the LORD see this and call you to account:* Zechariah's words reflect the belief that God blesses those who are faithful and punishes those who are not. See also the note at 7:14-22.

24:23 *army of Aram . . . king in Damascus:* For Aram, see the note at 1:16, 17.

Damascus, a major trading and transportation center, was Aram's political headquarters (see the map on p. 2467). It is located northeast of Mount Hermon, and is one of the world's oldest continuously occupied cities.

24:25 *he died . . . not in the tombs of the kings:* Joash was assassinated at age 47 (see 24:1), and then deprived of the burial given to highly honored kings. Compare this to Joash's godly mentor Jehoiada, as seen in the note at 24:15,16.

24:14 2 Kgs 12:13, 14. **24:20-22** Matt 23:35; Luke 11:51.

25:1 *Amaziah:* Amaziah was Judah's eighth king. Though he is said to have ruled twenty-nine years (from about 796 to 766 B.C.), the actual length of his rule is uncertain. During many of the years his son Uzziah ruled with him; Amaziah's active rule is thought to have been from 796 to 781 B.C. See also 2 Kgs 14:1-22.

25:5,6 *three hundred thousand . . . a hundred thousand:* Jehoshaphat's army (17:14-19) numbered over one million soldiers. Amaziah's much smaller army shows how much power Judah had lost in eighty years.

25:7 *a man of God . . . the LORD is not with Israel:* "A man of God" is another way of referring to a prophet. For more on this unnamed prophet's message, see the note at 13:4-12.

25:11 *men of Seir:* A reference to the Edomites. See the note at 21:8.

25:11,13 *Valley of Salt . . . Samaria to Beth Horon:* The Valley of Salt was a passage south of the Dead Sea between Jerusalem and Edom.

For Samaria and Beth Horon, see the notes at 18:2 and 8:3-6. However, it isn't logical to connect "Judean towns" with the capital of the northern kingdom. Since there was no known town by that name in the southern kingdom (Judah), this reference may be a copyist's error. Or perhaps the men from Israel gathered in Samaria and launched their raids into Judah from there.

25:14 *brought back the gods:* Amaziah may have been acting on a common belief of this time that the gods of a defeated nation sometimes added their loyalties to the victorious nation.

25:4 Deut 24:16.

are written in the annotations on the book of the kings. And Amaziah his son succeeded him as king.

Amaziah King of Judah

25 Amaziah was twenty-five years old when he became king, and he reigned in Jerusalem twenty-nine years. His mother's name was Jehoaddin[a]; she was from Jerusalem. [2]He did what was right in the eyes of the LORD, but not wholeheartedly. [3]After the kingdom was firmly in his control, he executed the officials who had murdered his father the king. [4]Yet he did not put their sons to death, but acted in accordance with what is written in the Law, in the Book of Moses, where the LORD commanded: "Fathers shall not be put to death for their children, nor children put to death for their fathers; each is to die for his own sins."[b]

[5]Amaziah called the people of Judah together and assigned them according to their families to commanders of thousands and commanders of hundreds for all Judah and Benjamin. He then mustered those twenty years old or more and found that there were three hundred thousand men ready for military service, able to handle the spear and shield. [6]He also hired a hundred thousand fighting men from Israel for a hundred talents[c] of silver.

[7]But a man of God came to him and said, "O king, these troops from Israel must not march with you, for the LORD is not with Israel—not with any of the people of Ephraim. [8]Even if you go and fight courageously in battle, God will overthrow you before the enemy, for God has the power to help or to overthrow."

[9]Amaziah asked the man of God, "But what about the hundred talents I paid for these Israelite troops?"

The man of God replied, "The LORD can give you much more than that."

[10]So Amaziah dismissed the troops who had come to him from Ephraim and sent them home. They were furious with Judah and left for home in a great rage.

[11]Amaziah then marshaled his strength and led his army to the Valley of Salt, where he killed ten thousand men of Seir. [12]The army of Judah also captured ten thousand men alive, took them to the top of a cliff and threw them down so that all were dashed to pieces.

[13]Meanwhile the troops that Amaziah had sent back and had not allowed to take part in the war raided Judean towns from Samaria to Beth Horon. They killed three thousand people and carried off great quantities of plunder.

[14]When Amaziah returned from slaughtering the Edomites, he brought back the gods of the people of Seir. He set them up as his own gods, bowed down to them and burned sacrifices to them.

---

a1 Hebrew *Jehoaddan,* a variant of *Jehoaddin* **b4** Deut. 24:16 **c6** That is, about 3 3/4 tons (about 3.4 metric tons); also in verse 9

15 The anger of the LORD burned against Amaziah, and he sent a prophet to him, who said, "Why do you consult this people's gods, which could not save their own people from your hand?"

16 While he was still speaking, the king said to him, "Have we appointed you an adviser to the king? Stop! Why be struck down?"

So the prophet stopped but said, "I know that God has determined to destroy you, because you have done this and have not listened to my counsel."

17 After Amaziah king of Judah consulted his advisers, he sent this challenge to Jehoash[a] son of Jehoahaz, the son of Jehu, king of Israel: "Come, meet me face to face."

18 But Jehoash king of Israel replied to Amaziah king of Judah: "A thistle in Lebanon sent a message to a cedar in Lebanon, 'Give your daughter to my son in marriage.' Then a wild beast in Lebanon came along and trampled the thistle underfoot. 19 You say to yourself that you have defeated Edom, and now you are arrogant and proud. But stay at home! Why ask for trouble and cause your own downfall and that of Judah also?"

20 Amaziah, however, would not listen, for God so worked that he might hand them over to ⌞Jehoash⌟, because they sought the gods of Edom. 21 So Jehoash king of Israel attacked. He and Amaziah king of Judah faced each other at Beth Shemesh in Judah. 22 Judah was routed by Israel, and every man fled to his home. 23 Jehoash king of Israel captured Amaziah king of Judah, the son of Joash, the son of Ahaziah,[b] at Beth Shemesh. Then Jehoash brought him to Jerusalem and broke down the wall of Jerusalem from the Ephraim Gate to the Corner Gate—a section about six hundred feet[c] long. 24 He took all the gold and silver and all the articles found in the temple of God that had been in the care of Obed-Edom, together with the palace treasures and the hostages, and returned to Samaria.

25 Amaziah son of Joash king of Judah lived for fifteen years after the death of Jehoash son of Jehoahaz king of Israel. 26 As for the other events of Amaziah's reign, from beginning to end, are they not written in the book of the kings of Judah and Israel? 27 From the time that Amaziah turned away from following the LORD, they conspired against him in Jerusalem and he fled to Lachish, but they sent men after him to Lachish and killed him there. 28 He was brought back by horse and was buried with his fathers in the City of Judah.

Uzziah King of Judah

26 Then all the people of Judah took Uzziah,[d] who was sixteen years old, and made him king in place of his father Amaziah. 2 He

---

[a] 17 Hebrew *Joash,* a variant of *Jehoash*; also in verses 18, 21, 23 and 25

[b] 23 Hebrew *Jehoahaz,* a variant of *Ahaziah*

[c] 23 Hebrew *four hundred cubits* (about 180 meters)

[d] 1 Also called *Azariah*

25:16 *God has determined to destroy you:* See the notes at 7:14-22 and 24:21, 22.

25:17 *Jehoash:* Jehoash was the twelfth king of the northern kingdom of Israel. He ruled from 798 to 783 B.C. He should not be confused with Joash (sometimes spelled Jehoash), Judah's prior king and Amaziah's father.

25:18 *thistle ... cedar in Lebanon:* King Jehoash of Israel is comparing Judah to an annoying thistle that can be easily crushed. Thistles and thornbushes are common in dry areas of Palestine, often choking out desirable plants if left to grow unchecked. In the Bible they often are used as symbols of God's punishment or judgment, or of false prophecy or stumbling blocks to belief (Gen 3:18; 2 Sam 23:6; Isa 32:13; Jer 4:3; Matt 7:16; 13:7, 22). The cedar tree, by comparison, is highly valued for both its beauty and its fragrant wood. See also the note at 2:8.

25:21 *Beth Shemesh:* One of the cities given to the Levites (Josh 21:9-19; 1 Chr 6:57-59).

25:23 *wall . . . Ephraim Gate . . . Corner Gate:* See the note at 8:5. These gates were most likely on the northern wall of the city.

25:24 *Obed-Edom:* He cared for the ark of the covenant (2 Sam 6:10-12). See also 1 Chr 13:13, 14; 26:15.

25:24 *Samaria:* See the note at 18:2.

25:27 *conspired against him . . . killed him:* Amaziah was killed by his own people, perhaps because of the losses they had suffered due to his foolish disobedience to God (25:18-20).

was the one who rebuilt Elath and restored it to Judah after Amaziah rested with his fathers.

[3]Uzziah was sixteen years old when he became king, and he reigned in Jerusalem fifty-two years. His mother's name was Jecoliah; she was from Jerusalem. [4]He did what was right in the eyes of the LORD, just as his father Amaziah had done. [5]He sought God during the days of Zechariah, who instructed him in the fear[a] of God. As long as he sought the LORD, God gave him success.

[6]He went to war against the Philistines and broke down the walls of Gath, Jabneh and Ashdod. He then rebuilt towns near Ashdod and elsewhere among the Philistines. [7]God helped him against the Philistines and against the Arabs who lived in Gur Baal and against the Meunites. [8]The Ammonites brought tribute to Uzziah, and his fame spread as far as the border of Egypt, because he had become very powerful.

[9]Uzziah built towers in Jerusalem at the Corner Gate, at the Valley Gate and at the angle of the wall, and he fortified them. [10]He also built towers in the desert and dug many cisterns, because he had much livestock in the foothills and in the plain. He had people working his fields and vineyards in the hills and in the fertile lands, for he loved the soil.

[11]Uzziah had a well-trained army, ready to go out by divisions according to their numbers as mustered by Jeiel the secretary and Maaseiah the officer under the direction of Hananiah, one of the royal officials. [12]The total number of family leaders over the fighting men was 2,600. [13]Under their command was an army of 307,500 men trained for war, a powerful force to support the king against his enemies. [14]Uzziah provided shields, spears, helmets, coats of armor, bows and slingstones for the entire army. [15]In Jerusalem he made machines designed by skillful men for use on the towers and on the corner defenses to shoot arrows and hurl large stones. His fame spread far and wide, for he was greatly helped until he became powerful.

[16]But after Uzziah became powerful, his pride led to his downfall. He was unfaithful to the LORD his God, and entered the temple of the LORD to burn incense on the altar of incense. [17]Azariah the priest with eighty other courageous priests of the LORD followed him in. [18]They confronted him and said, "It is not right for you, Uzziah, to burn incense to the LORD. That is for the priests, the descendants of Aaron, who have been consecrated to burn incense. Leave the sanctuary, for you have been unfaithful; and you will not be honored by the LORD God."

[19]Uzziah, who had a censer in his hand ready to burn incense, became angry. While he was raging at the priests in their presence before the incense altar in the LORD's temple, leprosy[b]

---

[a]5 Many Hebrew manuscripts, Septuagint and Syriac; other Hebrew manuscripts *vision* [b]19 The Hebrew word was used for various diseases affecting the skin—not necessarily leprosy; also in verses 20, 21 and 23.

26:2 *Elath:* A city on the northeastern arm of the Red Sea. See the map on p. 2463.

26:6 *Philistines:* See the note at 17:11 (Philistines).

26:6 *Gath, Jabneh and Ashdod:* Gath and Ashdod were Philistine cities. Jabneh was also known as Jabneel (Josh 15:11) and later as Jamnia.

26:7,8 *Meunites . . . Ammonites:* See the note at 20:1.

26:10 *cisterns:* Cisterns are deep holes cut into rock or earth and used to store rainwater or spring water. The remains of hundreds of small private cisterns and large public ones have been found in this part of the world. See also the mini-article called "Water," p. 1647.

26:14,15 *shields . . . slingstones . . . machines:* The weapons mentioned were used by Uzziah's large army of infantry. For more examples of ancient weapons, see 1 Sam 17:38-40; 2 Kgs 3:25,26.

26:16 *entered the temple of the LORD to burn incense:* The smoke from the burning incense represented the prayers that went up to God (Ps 141:2; Rev 5:8). The altar for burning incense was in the Holy Place. See also Exod 30:34-38. Only the priests were to enter the Holy Place to burn incense as an offering to the LORD (Exod 30:1-10; Num 16:39,40). Uzziah disobeyed God's Law by making such an offering. See also the mini-article called "Israel's Priests," p. 2344.

26:19,20 *leprosy . . . hurried him out:* The word translated as "leprosy" was used for many different kinds of skin diseases. Skin diseases made a person unclean and therefore unable to be in the temple. See the note at 23:6. See also Lev 13:1—14:57; Num 5:2-4; and the mini-article called "Purity (Clean and Unclean)," p. 2125.

26:18 Exod 30:7,8; Num 3:10.

broke out on his forehead. [20]When Azariah the chief priest and all
the other priests looked at him, they saw that he had leprosy on
his forehead, so they hurried him out. Indeed, he himself was
eager to leave, because the LORD had afflicted him.
[21]King Uzziah had leprosy until the day he died. He lived in
a separate house[a]—leprous, and excluded from the temple of the
LORD. Jotham his son had charge of the palace and governed the
people of the land.
[22]The other events of Uzziah's reign, from beginning to end,
are recorded by the prophet Isaiah son of Amoz. [23]Uzziah rested
with his fathers and was buried near them in a field for burial that
belonged to the kings, for people said, "He had leprosy." And
Jotham his son succeeded him as king.

Jotham King of Judah

27 Jotham was twenty-five years old when he became king, and he
reigned in Jerusalem sixteen years. His mother's name was Jerusha
daughter of Zadok. [2]He did what was right in the eyes of the LORD,
just as his father Uzziah had done, but unlike him he did not enter the
temple of the LORD. The people, however, continued their corrupt
practices. [3]Jotham rebuilt the Upper Gate of the temple of the LORD
and did extensive work on the wall at the hill of Ophel. [4]He built
towns in the Judean hills and forts and towers in the wooded areas.
[5]Jotham made war on the king of the Ammonites and conquered them. That year the Ammonites paid him a hundred talents[b] of silver, ten thousand cors[c] of wheat and ten thousand cors
of barley. The Ammonites brought him the same amount also in
the second and third years.
[6]Jotham grew powerful because he walked steadfastly before
the LORD his God.
[7]The other events in Jotham's reign, including all his wars
and the other things he did, are written in the book of the kings of
Israel and Judah. [8]He was twenty-five years old when he became
king, and he reigned in Jerusalem sixteen years. [9]Jotham rested
with his fathers and was buried in the City of David. And Ahaz his
son succeeded him as king.

Ahaz King of Judah

28 Ahaz was twenty years old when he became king, and he
reigned in Jerusalem sixteen years. Unlike David his father, he did
not do what was right in the eyes of the LORD. [2]He walked in the
ways of the kings of Israel and also made cast idols for worshiping
the Baals. [3]He burned sacrifices in the Valley of Ben Hinnom and

[a]**21** Or *in a house where he was relieved of responsibilities* [b]**5** That is, about 3 3/4 tons (about 3.4 metric tons) [c]**5** That is, probably about 62,000 bushels (about 2,200 kiloliters)

26:23 *buried near them:* Uzziah's leprosy may have been why he was buried close to, but not in, the royal tombs. See the note at 24:25. His remains are believed to be marked by a gravestone from eight hundred years later. The inscription on the stone reads, "Hither were brought the bones of Uzziah, king of Judah; do not open."

27:1 *Jotham:* Jotham was Judah's tenth king. He ruled from 740 to 736 B.C. Though he is said to have ruled sixteen years, a number of these years overlapped with the reign of Uzziah.

28:1 *Ahaz:* Ahaz was Judah's eleventh king. He ruled from 736 to 716 B.C. Though he is said to have ruled only sixteen years, there were additional years when he ruled along with Jotham.

Ahaz restored Baal worship to Judah, participated in child sacrifice (28:3), and bought Assyria's help against Israel and Aram with treasures taken from the temple in Jerusalem (28:20, 21).

28:2,3 *Baals . . . sacrificed his sons:* For Baal, see the note at 14:3. Human sacrifice was part of the worship of certain foreign gods such as Molech or Chemosh. The Law of Moses strictly forbids child sacrifice (Lev 20:1-5). See also (Lev 18:21; 20:1-5; Deut 12:31; 13:1-5).

28:3 *Valley of Ben Hinnom:* This burning and dumping ground southwest of Jerusalem had been used to offer human sacrifice to the god Molech (2 Kgs 23:10). This earned it the name "Valley of Slaughter" (Jer 19:6).

28:4 *high places:* See the note at 14:3.

28:5 *took many of his people as prisoners ... inflicted heavy casualties:* This probably took place around 734 B.C. See also 2 Kgs 16:5, 6; Isa 7:1-16.

28:5,8 *Damascus ... Samaria:* See the notes at 24:23 and 18:2.

28:9 *a prophet of the LORD named Oded:* This Oded should not be confused with the father of Azariah the prophet (15:1). For "prophet," see the article called "Prophets and Prophecy," p. 935.

28:15 *Jericho:* Jericho was an important city on the trade routes from the east (see the map on p. 2467).

28:16,17 *king of Assyria ... Edomites:* Assyria began to expand its power and continued to do so throughout the period of the Israelite kings (931-722 B.C.). Its expansion into Israel had begun around 855 B.C. During the rule of Tiglath-Pileser III (745-727 B.C.), the Assyrian expansion continued, gaining control of conquered areas in part by forcing native peoples to leave their homelands and move to other lands owned by Assyria. See the map on p. 2468 and the mini-article called "Assyria," p. 711.

For "Edomites," see the two notes at 21:8.

28:9 Isa 10:5-19. **28:10,11** Lev 25:39-55.

sacrificed his sons in the fire, following the detestable ways of the
nations the LORD had driven out before the Israelites. 4He offered
sacrifices and burned incense at the high places, on the hilltops
and under every spreading tree.

5Therefore the LORD his God handed him over to the king of
Aram. The Arameans defeated him and took many of his people as
prisoners and brought them to Damascus.

He was also given into the hands of the king of Israel, who
inflicted heavy casualties on him. 6In one day Pekah son of Remaliah killed a hundred and twenty thousand soldiers in Judah—
because Judah had forsaken the LORD, the God of their fathers.
7Zicri, an Ephraimite warrior, killed Maaseiah the king's son,
Azrikam the officer in charge of the palace, and Elkanah, second to
the king. 8The Israelites took captive from their kinsmen two hundred thousand wives, sons and daughters. They also took a great
deal of plunder, which they carried back to Samaria.

9But a prophet of the LORD named Oded was there, and he
went out to meet the army when it returned to Samaria. He said to
them, "Because the LORD, the God of your fathers, was angry with
Judah, he gave them into your hand. But you have slaughtered
them in a rage that reaches to heaven. 10And now you intend to
make the men and women of Judah and Jerusalem your slaves. But
aren't you also guilty of sins against the LORD your God? 11Now listen to me! Send back your fellow countrymen you have taken as
prisoners, for the LORD's fierce anger rests on you."

12Then some of the leaders in Ephraim—Azariah son of
Jehohanan, Berekiah son of Meshillemoth, Jehizkiah son of Shallum, and Amasa son of Hadlai—confronted those who were arriving from the war. 13"You must not bring those prisoners here," they
said, "or we will be guilty before the LORD. Do you intend to add to
our sin and guilt? For our guilt is already great, and his fierce anger
rests on Israel."

14So the soldiers gave up the prisoners and plunder in the
presence of the officials and all the assembly. 15The men designated by name took the prisoners, and from the plunder they clothed
all who were naked. They provided them with clothes and sandals,
food and drink, and healing balm. All those who were weak they
put on donkeys. So they took them back to their fellow countrymen at Jericho, the City of Palms, and returned to Samaria.

16At that time King Ahaz sent to the king[a] of Assyria for
help. 17The Edomites had again come and attacked Judah and carried away prisoners, 18while the Philistines had raided towns in
the foothills and in the Negev of Judah. They captured and occupied Beth Shemesh, Aijalon and Gederoth, as well as Soco, Timnah and Gimzo, with their surrounding villages. 19The LORD had

[a]**16** One Hebrew manuscript, Septuagint and Vulgate (see also 2 Kings 16:7); most Hebrew manuscripts *kings*

humbled Judah because of Ahaz king of Israel,[a] for he had promoted wickedness in Judah and had been most unfaithful to the
LORD. 20Tiglath-Pileser[b] king of Assyria came to him, but he gave
him trouble instead of help. 21Ahaz took some of the things from
the temple of the LORD and from the royal palace and from the
princes and presented them to the king of Assyria, but that did
not help him.
22In his time of trouble King Ahaz became even more
unfaithful to the LORD. 23He offered sacrifices to the gods of Damascus, who had defeated him; for he thought, "Since the gods of
the kings of Aram have helped them, I will sacrifice to them so
they will help me." But they were his downfall and the downfall of
all Israel.
24Ahaz gathered together the furnishings from the temple of
God and took them away.[c] He shut the doors of the LORD's temple
and set up altars at every street corner in Jerusalem. 25In every
town in Judah he built high places to burn sacrifices to other gods
and provoked the LORD, the God of his fathers, to anger.
26The other events of his reign and all his ways, from beginning to end, are written in the book of the kings of Judah and
Israel. 27Ahaz rested with his fathers and was buried in the city of
Jerusalem, but he was not placed in the tombs of the kings of
Israel. And Hezekiah his son succeeded him as king.

[a]19 That is, Judah, as frequently in 2 Chronicles **[b]20** Hebrew *Tilgath-Pilneser,* a variant of *Tiglath-Pileser* **[c]24** Or *and cut them up*

28:20,21 *Tiglath-Pileser king of Assyria came to him . . . trouble instead of help:* This is somewhat different from the account in 2 KINGS (2 Kgs 15:29; 16:5-9). The writer of 2 CHRONICLES stresses the end result: because they put trust in the Assyrian king instead of in God, Ahaz and the people of Judah are severely punished.

28:24 *Jerusalem:* See the note at 1:13.

28:25 *high places:* See the note at 14:3.

28:22-27 2 Kgs 16:10-20. **28:27** Isa 14:28.

QUESTIONS ABOUT 2 CHRONICLES 10:1—28:27

1. Why did the northern tribes rebel (10:1—11:17)? Name something Judah gained and something Judah lost as a result of this.
2. Why do you think the writer of 2 CHRONICLES seems to judge the kings only on the basis of their religious faithfulness and not on their political achievements? In your opinion, what would the writer say about our leaders today?
3. Jehoshaphat's prayer (20:6-12) has been described as a "model" prayer. Why do you think this is? Compare this prayer to your own prayers and those you hear offered in worship.
4. Read the introduction to the section at 11:5. Which kings provide examples of how God rewards faithful kings and punishes the unfaithful? Is this concept of reward and punishment true in your experience? Why or why not?
5. What might the words of 20:20 have meant to those living at the time this history was written? What do these words mean to you?

The End of the Divided Monarchy

The period of the divided monarchy comes to a close with the fall of the north to Assyria in 722 B.C. Hezekiah, as a king in the tradition of his ancestors David and Solomon, restores Judah and unites the people around the temple in Jerusalem. Josiah will also contribute to this restoration.

HEZEKIAH'S REFORM

The book of 2 KINGS stressed Hezekiah's revolt against Assyria. The writer of 2 CHRONICLES stresses his religious reforms.

Hezekiah Purifies the Temple

29 Hezekiah was twenty-five years old when he became king,
and he reigned in Jerusalem twenty-nine years. His mother's name
was Abijah daughter of Zechariah. [2]He did what was right in the
eyes of the LORD, just as his father David had done.
[3]In the first month of the first year of his reign, he opened
the doors of the temple of the LORD and repaired them. [4]He
brought in the priests and the Levites, assembled them in the
square on the east side [5]and said: "Listen to me, Levites! Consecrate yourselves now and consecrate the temple of the LORD, the
God of your fathers. Remove all defilement from the sanctuary.
[6]Our fathers were unfaithful; they did evil in the eyes of the LORD
our God and forsook him. They turned their faces away from the
LORD's dwelling place and turned their backs on him. [7]They also
shut the doors of the portico and put out the lamps. They did not
burn incense or present any burnt offerings at the sanctuary to the
God of Israel. [8]Therefore, the anger of the LORD has fallen on
Judah and Jerusalem; he has made them an object of dread and
horror and scorn, as you can see with your own eyes. [9]This is why
our fathers have fallen by the sword and why our sons and daughters and our wives are in captivity. [10]Now I intend to make a
covenant with the LORD, the God of Israel, so that his fierce anger
will turn away from us. [11]My sons, do not be negligent now, for the
LORD has chosen you to stand before him and serve him, to minister before him and to burn incense."
[12]Then these Levites set to work:
from the Kohathites,
Mahath son of Amasai and Joel son of Azariah;
from the Merarites,
Kish son of Abdi and Azariah son of Jehallelel;
from the Gershonites,
Joah son of Zimmah and Eden son of Joah;
[13]from the descendants of Elizaphan,
Shimri and Jeiel;

29:1 *Hezekiah:* Hezekiah was Judah's twelfth king, ruling from 716 to 687 B.C. One of Judah's greatest kings, he struggled to free his people from Assyrian domination and was the first king to eliminate the high places completely. See the mini-article called "Hezekiah," p. 1293.

In 2 CHRONICLES, Hezekiah shares many similarities with Solomon: his attention to the temple as a place of worship (2:4; 29:5,10,20-36), his celebration of Passover (7:8,9; 30:1-5, 23-26), and his wealth (9:13,14; 32:27-29).

29:3 *first month:* This is Abib (also called Nisan), the first month of the Hebrew calendar, from about mid-March to mid-April.

29:3 *opened the doors of the temple:* King Ahaz had locked the doors and stopped everyone from worshiping the LORD (28:24,25).

29:4 *priests . . . Levites:* See the note at 11:13.

29:5 *Consecrate yourselves:* See the notes at 5:11,12 and 23:6.

29:8,9 *the anger of the LORD . . . captivity:* Because he was writing after the exile, the writer of 2 CHRONICLES can borrow language here from Jeremiah's later description of the horror of the exile (Jer 29:16-19). The writer lets Hezekiah use the words to depict the earlier defeats Ahaz and the people of Judah suffered because of their sinfulness.

29:8 Jer 19:8; 25:9,18; 29:16-19.

from the descendants of Asaph,
Zechariah and Mattaniah;
[14]from the descendants of Heman,
Jehiel and Shimei;
from the descendants of Jeduthun,
Shemaiah and Uzziel.
[15]When they had assembled their brothers and consecrated
themselves, they went in to purify the temple of the LORD, as the
king had ordered, following the word of the LORD. [16]The priests
went into the sanctuary of the LORD to purify it. They brought out
to the courtyard of the LORD's temple everything unclean that they
found in the temple of the LORD. The Levites took it and carried it
out to the Kidron Valley. [17]They began the consecration on the first
day of the first month, and by the eighth day of the month they
reached the portico of the LORD. For eight more days they consecrated the temple of the LORD itself, finishing on the sixteenth day
of the first month.
[18]Then they went in to King Hezekiah and reported: "We
have purified the entire temple of the LORD, the altar of burnt
offering with all its utensils, and the table for setting out the consecrated bread, with all its articles. [19]We have prepared and consecrated all the articles that King Ahaz removed in his unfaithfulness
while he was king. They are now in front of the LORD's altar."
[20]Early the next morning King Hezekiah gathered the city
officials together and went up to the temple of the LORD. [21]They
brought seven bulls, seven rams, seven male lambs and seven male
goats as a sin offering for the kingdom, for the sanctuary and for
Judah. The king commanded the priests, the descendants of Aaron,
to offer these on the altar of the LORD. [22]So they slaughtered the
bulls, and the priests took the blood and sprinkled it on the altar;
next they slaughtered the rams and sprinkled their blood on the
altar; then they slaughtered the lambs and sprinkled their blood on
the altar. [23]The goats for the sin offering were brought before the
king and the assembly, and they laid their hands on them. [24]The
priests then slaughtered the goats and presented their blood on the
altar for a sin offering to atone for all Israel, because the king had
ordered the burnt offering and the sin offering for all Israel.
[25]He stationed the Levites in the temple of the LORD with
cymbals, harps and lyres in the way prescribed by David and Gad
the king's seer and Nathan the prophet; this was commanded by
the LORD through his prophets. [26]So the Levites stood ready with
David's instruments, and the priests with their trumpets.
[27]Hezekiah gave the order to sacrifice the burnt offering on
the altar. As the offering began, singing to the LORD began also,
accompanied by trumpets and the instruments of David king of
Israel. [28]The whole assembly bowed in worship, while the singers

29:16 *Kidron Valley:* See the note at 15:16.

29:17 *first month:* See the note at 29:3 (first month).

29:18 *altar of burnt offering . . . consecrated bread:* See the notes at 4:1,2 and 13:11.

29:21,22 *seven bulls . . . sprinkled their blood:* Seven is a number that symbolized perfection and is often not meant literally, though here it probably is. See the chart called "Numbers in the Bible," p. 2405.

Because blood carried the life force, it was considered sacred (Gen 4:10, 11; Lev 17:14). It was not to be eaten (Lev 7:26, 27; 17:10-14; 19:26; Deut 12:23, 24; 15:23). It also had power to protect (Exod 12:7). Blood sprinkled on the altar, on other objects, or on the people had cleansing power and showed that the object or person was dedicated to God (Exod 29:10-21). See also the mini-article called "Blood," p. 180.

29:23,24 *laid their hands on them . . . sin offering for all Israel:* The laying on of hands was to connect the offerer to the animal in order to get rid of the person's sins through the animal (Lev 4:15; 16:21; Num 8:12). Here the sacrificial animals represented the entire nation.

29:27-35 *Hezekiah gave the order . . . burnt offerings in abundance:* This is similar to Solomon's dedication of the temple (7:4-7).

29:18 2 Chr 2:4. **29:26** 1 Chr 23:5.

29:32-34 *burnt offerings ... consecrating themselves:* See the notes at 1:6; 5:11,12; and 23:6.

30:1,2 *Passover ... second month:* Passover was celebrated as a remembrance of how God saved the people from disaster in Egypt. It was to be celebrated beginning at twilight on the fourteenth day of Nisan/Abib, the first month of the Hebrew calendar (from about mid-March to mid-April), not in the second month. But in these extraordinary circumstances (30:3-5; see also 30:26 and the note) the decision was made to celebrate the Passover a month later. See also Num 9:9-14 and the mini-article called "Passover and the Feast of Unleavened Bread," p. 2030.

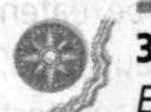

30:1,5 *all Israel and Judah ... Ephraim and Manasseh ... from Beersheba to Dan:* These widespread locations indicate Hezekiah's desire to bring all of Israel back to proper worship in Jerusalem. Unfortunately, the only Israelites still in the northern kingdom at this time were those who had been left behind or escaped after Assyria invaded and took the people away as prisoners in 722 B.C. (Num 9:9-11; 2 Kgs 17:1-23; 18:9-12).

For "Israel and Judah," see the notes at 9:30, 31 and 10:15-18. Ephraim and Manasseh were the leading tribes of the northern kingdom. Beersheba and Dan are expressions for all of Israel from south to north, respectively.

30:6 *Abraham, Isaac and Israel:* Jacob was also called Israel (Gen 32:28). See the note at 20:7 (Abraham). Hezekiah is warning here that the people of both kingdoms should learn from what has happened to Israel.

sang and the trumpeters played. All this continued until the sacrifice of the burnt offering was completed.

[29]When the offerings were finished, the king and everyone present with him knelt down and worshiped. [30]King Hezekiah and his officials ordered the Levites to praise the LORD with the words of David and of Asaph the seer. So they sang praises with gladness and bowed their heads and worshiped.

[31]Then Hezekiah said, "You have now dedicated yourselves to the LORD. Come and bring sacrifices and thank offerings to the temple of the LORD." So the assembly brought sacrifices and thank offerings, and all whose hearts were willing brought burnt offerings.

[32]The number of burnt offerings the assembly brought was seventy bulls, a hundred rams and two hundred male lambs—all of them for burnt offerings to the LORD. [33]The animals consecrated as sacrifices amounted to six hundred bulls and three thousand sheep and goats. [34]The priests, however, were too few to skin all the burnt offerings; so their kinsmen the Levites helped them until the task was finished and until other priests had been consecrated, for the Levites had been more conscientious in consecrating themselves than the priests had been. [35]There were burnt offerings in abundance, together with the fat of the fellowship offerings[a] and the drink offerings that accompanied the burnt offerings.

So the service of the temple of the LORD was reestablished. [36]Hezekiah and all the people rejoiced at what God had brought about for his people, because it was done so quickly.

Hezekiah Celebrates the Passover

30 Hezekiah sent word to all Israel and Judah and also wrote letters to Ephraim and Manasseh, inviting them to come to the temple of the LORD in Jerusalem and celebrate the Passover to the LORD, the God of Israel. [2]The king and his officials and the whole assembly in Jerusalem decided to celebrate the Passover in the second month. [3]They had not been able to celebrate it at the regular time because not enough priests had consecrated themselves and the people had not assembled in Jerusalem. [4]The plan seemed right both to the king and to the whole assembly. [5]They decided to send a proclamation throughout Israel, from Beersheba to Dan, calling the people to come to Jerusalem and celebrate the Passover to the LORD, the God of Israel. It had not been celebrated in large numbers according to what was written.

[6]At the king's command, couriers went throughout Israel and Judah with letters from the king and from his officials, which read:

[a]35 Traditionally *peace offerings*

"People of Israel, return to the LORD, the God of Abraham, Isaac and Israel, that he may return to you who are left,
who have escaped from the hand of the kings of Assyria. [7]Do
not be like your fathers and brothers, who were unfaithful to
the LORD, the God of their fathers, so that he made them an
object of horror, as you see. [8]Do not be stiff-necked, as your
fathers were; submit to the LORD. Come to the sanctuary,
which he has consecrated forever. Serve the LORD your God,
so that his fierce anger will turn away from you. [9]If you return
to the LORD, then your brothers and your children will be
shown compassion by their captors and will come back to this
land, for the LORD your God is gracious and compassionate.
He will not turn his face from you if you return to him."

[10]The couriers went from town to town in Ephraim and
Manasseh, as far as Zebulun, but the people scorned and ridiculed
them. [11]Nevertheless, some men of Asher, Manasseh and Zebulun
humbled themselves and went to Jerusalem. [12]Also in Judah the
hand of God was on the people to give them unity of mind to
carry out what the king and his officials had ordered, following the
word of the LORD.

[13]A very large crowd of people assembled in Jerusalem to
celebrate the Feast of Unleavened Bread in the second month.
[14]They removed the altars in Jerusalem and cleared away the
incense altars and threw them into the Kidron Valley.

[15]They slaughtered the Passover lamb on the fourteenth day
of the second month. The priests and the Levites were ashamed
and consecrated themselves and brought burnt offerings to the
temple of the LORD. [16]Then they took up their regular positions as
prescribed in the Law of Moses the man of God. The priests sprinkled the blood handed to them by the Levites. [17]Since many in the
crowd had not consecrated themselves, the Levites had to kill the
Passover lambs for all those who were not ceremonially clean and
could not consecrate ⌊their lambs⌋ to the LORD. [18]Although most of
the many people who came from Ephraim, Manasseh, Issachar and
Zebulun had not purified themselves, yet they ate the Passover,
contrary to what was written. But Hezekiah prayed for them, saying, "May the LORD, who is good, pardon everyone [19]who sets his
heart on seeking God—the LORD, the God of his fathers—even if
he is not clean according to the rules of the sanctuary." [20]And the
LORD heard Hezekiah and healed the people.

[21]The Israelites who were present in Jerusalem celebrated the
Feast of Unleavened Bread for seven days with great rejoicing,
while the Levites and priests sang to the LORD every day, accompanied by the LORD's instruments of praise.[a]

[a]**21** Or *priests praised the LORD every day with resounding instruments belonging to the LORD*

King Hezekiah wrote, *"People of Israel, return to the LORD, the God of Abraham, Isaac and Israel, that he may return to you who are left, who have escaped from the hand of the kings of Assyria."*
2 Chr 30:6

30:13 *Feast of Unleavened Bread:* The celebration of this feast began one day after Passover, and so these two festivals were often referred to as one. See the notes at 8:12,13 and 30:1,2.

30:13 *second month:* See the note at 3:2.

30:15 *consecrated themselves and brought burnt offerings:* See the notes at 5:11,12 and 23:6. See also the note at 1:6.

30:16 *Moses the man of God:* Moses was the one God chose to lead Israel out of slavery in Egypt and to give God's laws and covenant to the people (Exod 2–25). See also the mini-article called "Moses," p. 2335.

30:14 2 Chr 28:25. **30:18,19** 2 Chr 6:21, 29-31; 7:14,15.

30:26 *since the days of Solomon:* Like Solomon more than two hundred and fifteen years earlier, Hezekiah brings the people together in proper worship.

31:1 *sacred stones . . . Asherah poles . . . high places . . . altars:* Objects related to gods which were commonly worshiped by many ancient peoples.

See the notes at 11:15 and 14:3.

31:3 *Sabbaths, New Moons and appointed feasts:* See the note at 8:12,13.

The New Moon festivals were held each month on the day of the new moon, the day when only a thin edge of the moon can be seen. This day was always the first day of the month for the Hebrew calendar. This festival was a time for worship, sacrifices, celebration, eating, and rest from work.

See also Num 28:1—29:39 and the article called "People of the Law: The Religion of Israel," which gives a full summary of all the Jewish religious festivals, p. 939.

31:7 *third month:* This is Sivan, the third month of the Hebrew calendar, from about mid-May to mid-June.

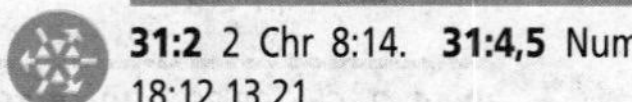

31:2 2 Chr 8:14. **31:4,5** Num 18:12,13,21.

[22]Hezekiah spoke encouragingly to all the Levites, who showed good understanding of the service of the LORD. For the seven days they ate their assigned portion and offered fellowship offerings[a] and praised the LORD, the God of their fathers.

[23]The whole assembly then agreed to celebrate the festival seven more days; so for another seven days they celebrated joyfully. [24]Hezekiah king of Judah provided a thousand bulls and seven thousand sheep and goats for the assembly, and the officials provided them with a thousand bulls and ten thousand sheep and goats. A great number of priests consecrated themselves. [25]The entire assembly of Judah rejoiced, along with the priests and Levites and all who had assembled from Israel, including the aliens who had come from Israel and those who lived in Judah. [26]There was great joy in Jerusalem, for since the days of Solomon son of David king of Israel there had been nothing like this in Jerusalem. [27]The priests and the Levites stood to bless the people, and God heard them, for their prayer reached heaven, his holy dwelling place.

31 When all this had ended, the Israelites who were there went out to the towns of Judah, smashed the sacred stones and cut down the Asherah poles. They destroyed the high places and the altars throughout Judah and Benjamin and in Ephraim and Manasseh. After they had destroyed all of them, the Israelites returned to their own towns and to their own property.

Contributions for Worship

[2]Hezekiah assigned the priests and Levites to divisions—each of them according to their duties as priests or Levites—to offer burnt offerings and fellowship offerings,[a] to minister, to give thanks and to sing praises at the gates of the LORD's dwelling. [3]The king contributed from his own possessions for the morning and evening burnt offerings and for the burnt offerings on the Sabbaths, New Moons and appointed feasts as written in the Law of the LORD. [4]He ordered the people living in Jerusalem to give the portion due the priests and Levites so they could devote themselves to the Law of the LORD. [5]As soon as the order went out, the Israelites generously gave the firstfruits of their grain, new wine, oil and honey and all that the fields produced. They brought a great amount, a tithe of everything. [6]The men of Israel and Judah who lived in the towns of Judah also brought a tithe of their herds and flocks and a tithe of the holy things dedicated to the LORD their God, and they piled them in heaps. [7]They began doing this in the third month and finished in the seventh month. [8]When Hezekiah and his officials came and saw the heaps, they praised the LORD and blessed his people Israel.

[9]Hezekiah asked the priests and Levites about the heaps;

---

[a]**22,2** Traditionally *peace offerings*

10 and Azariah the chief priest, from the family of Zadok, answered, "Since the people began to bring their contributions to the temple of the LORD, we have had enough to eat and plenty to spare, because the LORD has blessed his people, and this great amount is left over."

11 Hezekiah gave orders to prepare storerooms in the temple of the LORD, and this was done. 12 Then they faithfully brought in the contributions, tithes and dedicated gifts. Conaniah, a Levite, was in charge of these things, and his brother Shimei was next in rank. 13 Jehiel, Azaziah, Nahath, Asahel, Jerimoth, Jozabad, Eliel, Ismakiah, Mahath and Benaiah were supervisors under Conaniah and Shimei his brother, by appointment of King Hezekiah and Azariah the official in charge of the temple of God.

14 Kore son of Imnah the Levite, keeper of the East Gate, was in charge of the freewill offerings given to God, distributing the contributions made to the LORD and also the consecrated gifts. 15 Eden, Miniamin, Jeshua, Shemaiah, Amariah and Shecaniah assisted him faithfully in the towns of the priests, distributing to their fellow priests according to their divisions, old and young alike.

16 In addition, they distributed to the males three years old or more whose names were in the genealogical records—all who would enter the temple of the LORD to perform the daily duties of their various tasks, according to their responsibilities and their divisions. 17 And they distributed to the priests enrolled by their families in the genealogical records and likewise to the Levites twenty years old or more, according to their responsibilities and their divisions. 18 They included all the little ones, the wives, and the sons and daughters of the whole community listed in these genealogical records. For they were faithful in consecrating themselves.

19 As for the priests, the descendants of Aaron, who lived on the farm lands around their towns or in any other towns, men were designated by name to distribute portions to every male among them and to all who were recorded in the genealogies of the Levites.

20 This is what Hezekiah did throughout Judah, doing what was good and right and faithful before the LORD his God. 21 In everything that he undertook in the service of God's temple and in obedience to the law and the commands, he sought his God and worked wholeheartedly. And so he prospered.

Sennacherib Threatens Jerusalem

32 After all that Hezekiah had so faithfully done, Sennacherib king of Assyria came and invaded Judah. He laid siege to the fortified cities, thinking to conquer them for himself. 2 When Hezekiah saw that Sennacherib had come and that he intended to make war on Jerusalem, 3 he consulted with his officials and military staff about blocking off the water from the springs outside the city, and they helped him. 4 A large force of men assembled, and they

> Azariah said, *"Since the people began to bring their contributions to the temple of the LORD, we have had enough to eat and plenty to spare, because the LORD has blessed his people, and this great amount is left over."*
> 2 Chr 31:10

31:14 *East Gate:* There were four main gates to the temple, each facing a different geographical direction. The East Gate was the main entrance and had six guard posts.

31:14-19 *freewill offerings . . . distributed to the priests . . . and likewise to the Levites:* Because the tribe of Levi was set apart for priestly service to all the tribes, they were not given their own land in Canaan. Instead, they were scattered throughout the land belonging to the other tribes and were supported with a portion of the offerings brought by the people (Num 18:8-14; 2 Chr 31:19). See also the note at 11:13 (priests and Levites) and the mini-article called "Israel's Priests," p. 2344.

32:1 *Sennacherib king of Assyria . . . fortified cities:* Sennacherib ruled Assyria from 705 to 681 B.C. This event probably took place in 701 B.C.

For fortified cities, see the notes at 8:5 and 32:18.

31:19 Josh 21:1-42.

blocked all the springs and the stream that flowed through the land. "Why should the kings[a] of Assyria come and find plenty of water?" they said. 5 Then he worked hard repairing all the broken sections of the wall and building towers on it. He built another wall outside that one and reinforced the supporting terraces[b] of the City of David. He also made large numbers of weapons and shields.

6 He appointed military officers over the people and assembled them before him in the square at the city gate and encouraged them with these words: 7 "Be strong and courageous. Do not be afraid or discouraged because of the king of Assyria and the vast army with him, for there is a greater power with us than with him. 8 With him is only the arm of flesh, but with us is the LORD our God to help us and to fight our battles." And the people gained confidence from what Hezekiah the king of Judah said.

9 Later, when Sennacherib king of Assyria and all his forces were laying siege to Lachish, he sent his officers to Jerusalem with this message for Hezekiah king of Judah and for all the people of Judah who were there:

10 "This is what Sennacherib king of Assyria says: On what are you basing your confidence, that you remain in Jerusalem under siege? 11 When Hezekiah says, 'The LORD our God will save us from the hand of the king of Assyria,' he is misleading you, to let you die of hunger and thirst. 12 Did not Hezekiah himself remove this god's high places and altars, saying to Judah and Jerusalem, 'You must worship before one altar and burn sacrifices on it'?

13 "Do you not know what I and my fathers have done to all the peoples of the other lands? Were the gods of those nations ever able to deliver their land from my hand? 14 Who of all the gods of these nations that my fathers destroyed has been able to save his people from me? How then can your god deliver you from my hand? 15 Now do not let Hezekiah deceive you and mislead you like this. Do not believe him, for no god of any nation or kingdom has been able to deliver his people from my hand or the hand of my fathers. How much less will your god deliver you from my hand!"

16 Sennacherib's officers spoke further against the LORD God and against his servant Hezekiah. 17 The king also wrote letters insulting the LORD, the God of Israel, and saying this against him: "Just as the gods of the peoples of the other lands did not rescue their people from my hand, so the god of Hezekiah will not rescue his people from my hand." 18 Then they called out in Hebrew to the people of Jerusalem who were on the wall, to terrify them and make them afraid in order to capture the city. 19 They spoke about

[a]4 Hebrew; Septuagint and Syriac *king* [b]5 Or *the Millo*

King Hezekiah said, *"Be strong and courageous. Do not be afraid or discouraged because of the king of Assyria and the vast army with him, for there is a greater power with us than with him."*
2 Chr 32:7

32:12 *Did not Hezekiah himself remove this god's high places and altars:* Hezekiah actually had torn down the places where idols were worshiped, and he had told the people to worship the LORD at one place of worship in Jerusalem. But the Assyrian leader was confused and thought that all of these were places to worship the LORD.

32:18 *people . . . on the wall:* People may have gathered on the walls to listen, as many ancient cities had tall walls built around them for protection. These were usually made of clay and reed bricks. Some walls were extremely thick. Those at Nineveh are believed to have been wide enough on top to drive three chariots side by side, and those at Babylon wide enough to drive six chariots side by side. Rooms built into city walls were used to keep watch for approaching enemies and to defend the city when it was attacked.

the God of Jerusalem as they did about the gods of the other peoples of the world—the work of men's hands.
[20]King Hezekiah and the prophet Isaiah son of Amoz cried
out in prayer to heaven about this. [21]And the LORD sent an angel,
who annihilated all the fighting men and the leaders and officers in the camp of the Assyrian king. So he withdrew to his own land in disgrace. And when he went into the temple of his god, some of his sons cut him down with the sword.
[22]So the LORD saved Hezekiah and the people of Jerusalem
from the hand of Sennacherib king of Assyria and from the hand
of all others. He took care of them[a] on every side. [23]Many brought
offerings to Jerusalem for the LORD and valuable gifts for Hezekiah king of Judah. From then on he was highly regarded by all the nations.

Hezekiah's Pride, Success and Death

[24]In those days Hezekiah became ill and was at the point of death. He prayed to the LORD, who answered him and gave him a
miraculous sign. [25]But Hezekiah's heart was proud and he did not respond to the kindness shown him; therefore the LORD's wrath
was on him and on Judah and Jerusalem. [26]Then Hezekiah repent-
ed of the pride of his heart, as did the people of Jerusalem; therefore the LORD's wrath did not come upon them during the days of Hezekiah.
[27]Hezekiah had very great riches and honor, and he made treasuries for his silver and gold and for his precious stones, spices,
shields and all kinds of valuables. [28]He also made buildings to store the harvest of grain, new wine and oil; and he made stalls for various kinds of cattle, and pens for the flocks. [29]He built villages and
acquired great numbers of flocks and herds, for God had given him very great riches.
[30]It was Hezekiah who blocked the upper outlet of the Gihon spring and channeled the water down to the west side of the City
of David. He succeeded in everything he undertook. [31]But when
envoys were sent by the rulers of Babylon to ask him about the miraculous sign that had occurred in the land, God left him to test him and to know everything that was in his heart.
[32]The other events of Hezekiah's reign and his acts of devo-
tion are written in the vision of the prophet Isaiah son of Amoz
in the book of the kings of Judah and Israel. [33]Hezekiah rested
with his fathers and was buried on the hill where the tombs of David's descendants are. All Judah and the people of Jerusalem honored him when he died. And Manasseh his son succeeded him as king.

[a]22 Hebrew; Septuagint and Vulgate *He gave them rest*

32:20 *the prophet Isaiah:* See the Introduction to ISAIAH, p. 1289.

32:21 *angel:* A supernatural being who brings God's messages to people or protects those who are faithful to God. See also the mini-article called "Angels," p. 88.

32:27-29 *Hezekiah had very great riches:* See the note at 29:1.

32:30 *Gihon spring . . . channeled the water:* In A.D. 1838, archaeologists discovered a tunnel seventeen hundred feet long running from the Gihon spring outside Jerusalem's walls to the Pool of Siloam within the city (see the map on p. 2466). In places the tunnel is sixty feet deep and tall enough to walk through. The debris in the tunnel left by Jerusalem's destruction in 586 B.C. was cleared out in A.D. 1909. This tunnel was probably not the first that brought water into the city. David had entered the city through a water tunnel three hundred years prior to this (2 Sam 5:6-8).

32:31 *Babylon:* Babylonia, like Assyria, was a large empire of Old Testament times. Its capital, Babylon, was located in south-central Mesopotamia. This is the empire that would conquer Judah. See the map on p. 2468 and the mini-article called "Babylon," p. 1363.

32:24 2 Kgs 20:8-11.

33:1 *Manasseh:* Manasseh was Judah's thirteenth king, ruling from 687 to 642 B.C. The "fifty-five years" mentioned in this verse is the longest reign in the Bible, though it includes an extra ten years during which Manasseh ruled alongside his father.

33:2-6 *He did evil in the eyes of the LORD . . . provoking him to anger:* Manasseh brought the worship of the Canaanite gods back to Judah. He built altars honoring these gods right in the temple area and rebuilt local shrines that his father had torn down (see 31:1 and the note). See also the notes at 11:15 and 14:3.

Manasseh also built altars honoring the stars, sun, and moon. He encouraged the practice of magic and witchcraft, as well as the practice of trying to talk to the spirits of the dead. Both were forbidden by the Law of Moses (Exod 22:18; Lev 19:31). He even sacrificed his own son to the god Molech in the Valley of Ben Hinnom, a practice that was also forbidden (Lev 18:21). See the note at 28:3.

33:7 *David . . . Solomon:* See the note on p. 792.

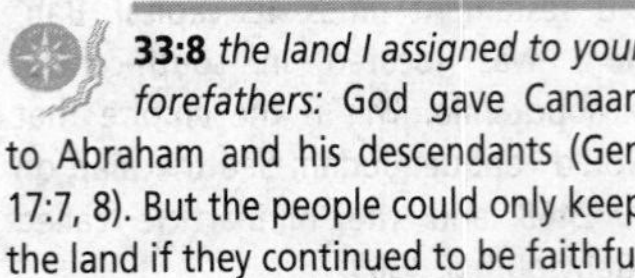

33:8 *the land I assigned to your forefathers:* God gave Canaan to Abraham and his descendants (Gen 17:7, 8). But the people could only keep the land if they continued to be faithful to the LORD alone (Deut 11:1-15).

33:8 *laws, decrees and ordinances given through Moses:* See the notes at 17:9 and 30:16 (Moses). See also Deut 10:1-5.

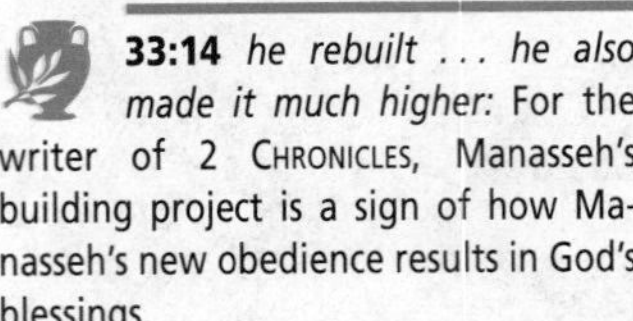

33:14 *he rebuilt . . . he also made it much higher:* For the writer of 2 CHRONICLES, Manasseh's building project is a sign of how Manasseh's new obedience results in God's blessings.

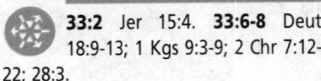

33:2 Jer 15:4. **33:6-8** Deut 18:9-13; 1 Kgs 9:3-9; 2 Chr 7:12-22; 28:3.

MANASSEH AND AMON

Manasseh and Amon do much evil, despite Manasseh's late return to God. Much of Hezekiah's work is undone, and Josiah is left with a nation desperately in need of reform.

Manasseh King of Judah

33 Manasseh was twelve years old when he became king, and he reigned in Jerusalem fifty-five years. 2He did evil in the eyes of the LORD, following the detestable practices of the nations the LORD had driven out before the Israelites. 3He rebuilt the high places his father Hezekiah had demolished; he also erected altars to the Baals and made Asherah poles. He bowed down to all the starry hosts and worshiped them. 4He built altars in the temple of the LORD, of which the LORD had said, "My Name will remain in Jerusalem forever." 5In both courts of the temple of the LORD, he built altars to all the starry hosts. 6He sacrificed his sons in[a] the fire in the Valley of Ben Hinnom, practiced sorcery, divination and witchcraft, and consulted mediums and spiritists. He did much evil in the eyes of the LORD, provoking him to anger.

7He took the carved image he had made and put it in God's temple, of which God had said to David and to his son Solomon, "In this temple and in Jerusalem, which I have chosen out of all the tribes of Israel, I will put my Name forever. 8I will not again make the feet of the Israelites leave the land I assigned to your forefathers, if only they will be careful to do everything I commanded them concerning all the laws, decrees and ordinances given through Moses." 9But Manasseh led Judah and the people of Jerusalem astray, so that they did more evil than the nations the LORD had destroyed before the Israelites.

10The LORD spoke to Manasseh and his people, but they paid no attention. 11So the LORD brought against them the army commanders of the king of Assyria, who took Manasseh prisoner, put a hook in his nose, bound him with bronze shackles and took him to Babylon. 12In his distress he sought the favor of the LORD his God and humbled himself greatly before the God of his fathers. 13And when he prayed to him, the LORD was moved by his entreaty and listened to his plea; so he brought him back to Jerusalem and to his kingdom. Then Manasseh knew that the LORD is God.

14Afterward he rebuilt the outer wall of the City of David, west of the Gihon spring in the valley, as far as the entrance of the Fish Gate and encircling the hill of Ophel; he also made it much higher. He stationed military commanders in all the fortified cities in Judah.

15He got rid of the foreign gods and removed the image from the temple of the LORD, as well as all the altars he had built on the temple hill and in Jerusalem; and he threw them out of the city.

[a]6 Or *He made his sons pass through*

[16]Then he restored the altar of the LORD and sacrificed fellowship
offerings[a] and thank offerings on it, and told Judah to serve the
LORD, the God of Israel. [17]The people, however, continued to sacrifice at the high places, but only to the LORD their God.
[18]The other events of Manasseh's reign, including his prayer
to his God and the words the seers spoke to him in the name of
the LORD, the God of Israel, are written in the annals of the kings
of Israel.[b] [19]His prayer and how God was moved by his entreaty, as
well as all his sins and unfaithfulness, and the sites where he built
high places and set up Asherah poles and idols before he humbled
himself—all are written in the records of the seers.[c] [20]Manasseh
rested with his fathers and was buried in his palace. And Amon his
son succeeded him as king.

Amon King of Judah

[21]Amon was twenty-two years old when he became king, and
he reigned in Jerusalem two years. [22]He did evil in the eyes of the
LORD, as his father Manasseh had done. Amon worshiped and
offered sacrifices to all the idols Manasseh had made. [23]But unlike

a16 Traditionally *peace offerings* **b18** That is, Judah, as frequently in 2 Chronicles **c19** One Hebrew manuscript and Septuagint; most Hebrew manuscripts *of Hozai*

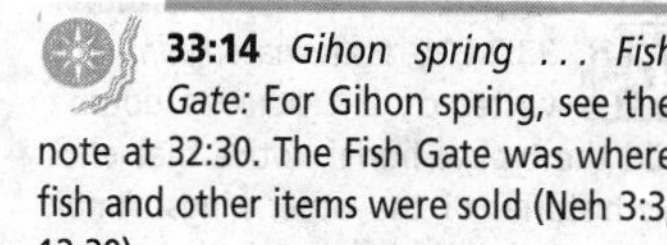

33:14 *Gihon spring . . . Fish Gate:* For Gihon spring, see the note at 32:30. The Fish Gate was where fish and other items were sold (Neh 3:3; 12:39).

33:16 *fellowship offerings and thank offerings:* See the chart called "Sacrifices and Offerings," p. 219.

33:20 *buried in his palace:* In 2 Kings 21:18, Manasseh is said to be buried in the garden of Uzza near the palace. Since the reference to Uzza may have been to a foreign god, the writer of 2 CHRONICLES may not have given the name of the garden because of a feeling that this was not a proper place to bury a king who had returned to a proper faith in God.

33:21 *Amon:* Amon was Judah's fourteenth king, ruling from 642 to 640 B.C.

JOSIAH

Josiah was one of Judah's best kings, even though he was the son of one of Judah's worst kings. He took the throne in Jerusalem at the age of eight, after his father Amon was killed by his own officials, and ruled Judah for thirty-one years, from 640 to 609 B.C. The decline of the Assyrian empire before the fall of Nineveh in 612 B.C. allowed Josiah to restore Judah's political independence and expand its borders.

Josiah is best known, however, for his religious reforms. As the author of 2 KINGS says, "Neither before nor after Josiah was there a king like him who turned to the LORD as he did" (2 Kgs 23:25). While repairs were being made to the temple in 621 B.C., Hilkiah the high priest found the "Book of the Law," which was probably some version of DEUTERONOMY. Shaphan the scribe read it aloud to Josiah. The young king was deeply troubled when he heard that God would severely punish Israel for worshiping other gods (Deut 29:25-28). So, Josiah immediately began to reform the worship practices of the people. He asked the people to promise to obey the LORD, removed priests who worshiped other gods, broke down altars dedicated to those gods, got rid of the high places, and celebrated the feast of Passover (2 Kgs 23; 2 Chr 34, 35). As a reward for Josiah's faithfulness, God promised him through Huldah the prophet that Judah would not be destroyed in Josiah's lifetime (2 Kgs 22:14-20; 2 Chr 34:22-28).

Judah received a serious setback when this faithful king and follower of the LORD was killed at the battle of Megiddo against Pharaoh Neco king of Egypt (2 Kgs 23:28-30; 2 Chr 35:20-24). The prophet Jeremiah was prompted to write a funeral song in Josiah's honor (2 Chr 35:25).

his father Manasseh, he did not humble himself before the LORD;
Amon increased his guilt.
24 Amon's officials conspired against him and assassinated
him in his palace. 25 Then the people of the land killed all who had
plotted against King Amon, and they made Josiah his son king in
his place.

JOSIAH'S REFORM

Josiah is a hero in 2 Kings because of his path of reform. Here, he serves to restore the good that Hezekiah had done before.

Josiah's Reforms

34 Josiah was eight years old when he became king, and he
reigned in Jerusalem thirty-one years. 2 He did what was right in
the eyes of the LORD and walked in the ways of his father David,
not turning aside to the right or to the left.
3 In the eighth year of his reign, while he was still young, he
began to seek the God of his father David. In his twelfth year he
began to purge Judah and Jerusalem of high places, Asherah poles,
carved idols and cast images. 4 Under his direction the altars of the
Baals were torn down; he cut to pieces the incense altars that were
above them, and smashed the Asherah poles, the idols and the
images. These he broke to pieces and scattered over the graves of
those who had sacrificed to them. 5 He burned the bones of the
priests on their altars, and so he purged Judah and Jerusalem. 6 In
the towns of Manasseh, Ephraim and Simeon, as far as Naphtali,
and in the ruins around them, 7 he tore down the altars and the
Asherah poles and crushed the idols to powder and cut to pieces
all the incense altars throughout Israel. Then he went back to Jerusalem.
8 In the eighteenth year of Josiah's reign, to purify the land
and the temple, he sent Shaphan son of Azaliah and Maaseiah the
ruler of the city, with Joah son of Joahaz, the recorder, to repair the
temple of the LORD his God.
9 They went to Hilkiah the high priest and gave him
the money that had been brought into the temple of God, which
the Levites who were the doorkeepers had collected from the people of Manasseh, Ephraim and the entire remnant of Israel and
from all the people of Judah and Benjamin and the inhabitants of
Jerusalem. 10 Then they entrusted it to the men appointed to supervise the work on the LORD's temple. These men paid the workers
who repaired and restored the temple. 11 They also gave money to
the carpenters and builders to purchase dressed stone, and timber
for joists and beams for the buildings that the kings of Judah had
allowed to fall into ruin.
12 The men did the work faithfully. Over them to direct them
were Jahath and Obadiah, Levites descended from Merari, and

33:24,25 *assassinated him:* The writer of 2 CHRONICLES doesn't add the typical burial notice that ends his histories of the other kings. Amon was buried near his father in the garden of Uzza by the palace (2 Kgs 21:17,18, 23-26). See also the note at 33:20.

34:1 *Josiah:* Josiah was Judah's fifteenth king, ruling from 640 to 609 B.C. See also Jer 3:6 and the mini-article called "Josiah," p. 843.

34:1 *Jerusalem:* See the note at 1:13.

34:3 *high places, Asherah poles, carved idols and cast images:* These were all used to worship other gods and had been promoted by Manasseh (2 Kgs 21:3; 2 Chr 33:3). See the notes at 14:3 and 11:15.

34:4,5 *scattered over the graves . . . burned the bones:* Contact with the dead made things unclean and unfit for holy use. (At this time, some in Israel felt that even objects used in idol worship could be considered holy or sacred.) By scattering the pieces of the broken idols on the graves, Josiah made sure that the idols were completely and forever destroyed. By burning the bones of the pagan priests on the altars, Josiah made the altars unclean so that they could not be used in worshiping any god. See also 1 Kgs 13:1,2.

34:6 *Manasseh, Ephraim and Simeon . . . Naphtali:* Josiah's reforms reach into the northern kingdom of Israel and cover a territory similar to that ruled by David and Solomon (see the map on p. 2464). The writer of 2 CHRONICLES compares Josiah and Hezekiah to kings David and Solomon, who had ruled when Judah and Israel were united as one kingdom of Israel. The people of both nations shared common ancestors who had made a special covenant with God.

Zechariah and Meshullam, descended from Kohath. The Levites—all who were skilled in playing musical instruments— [13]had charge of the laborers and supervised all the workers from job to job. Some of the Levites were secretaries, scribes and doorkeepers.

The Book of the Law Found

[14]While they were bringing out the money that had been taken into the temple of the LORD, Hilkiah the priest found the Book of the Law of the LORD that had been given through Moses.
[15]Hilkiah said to Shaphan the secretary, "I have found the Book of the Law in the temple of the LORD." He gave it to Shaphan.
[16]Then Shaphan took the book to the king and reported to him: "Your officials are doing everything that has been committed to them. [17]They have paid out the money that was in the temple of the LORD and have entrusted it to the supervisors and workers."
[18]Then Shaphan the secretary informed the king, "Hilkiah the priest has given me a book." And Shaphan read from it in the presence of the king.
[19]When the king heard the words of the Law, he tore his robes. [20]He gave these orders to Hilkiah, Ahikam son of Shaphan, Abdon son of Micah,[a] Shaphan the secretary and Asaiah the king's attendant: [21]"Go and inquire of the LORD for me and for the remnant in Israel and Judah about what is written in this book that has been found. Great is the LORD's anger that is poured out on us because our fathers have not kept the word of the LORD; they have not acted in accordance with all that is written in this book."
[22]Hilkiah and those the king had sent with him[b] went to speak to the prophetess Huldah, who was the wife of Shallum son of Tokhath,[c] the son of Hasrah,[d] keeper of the wardrobe. She lived in Jerusalem, in the Second District.
[23]She said to them, "This is what the LORD, the God of Israel, says: Tell the man who sent you to me, [24]'This is what the LORD says: I am going to bring disaster on this place and its people—all the curses written in the book that has been read in the presence of the king of Judah. [25]Because they have forsaken me and burned incense to other gods and provoked me to anger by all that their hands have made,[e] my anger will be poured out on this place and will not be quenched.' [26]Tell the king of Judah, who sent you to inquire of the LORD, 'This is what the LORD, the God of Israel, says concerning the words you heard: [27]Because your heart was responsive and you humbled yourself before God when you heard what he spoke against this place and its people, and because you humbled yourself before me and tore your robes and wept in my presence, I have heard you, declares the LORD. [28]Now I will gather you

[a]20 Also called *Acbor son of Micaiah* [b]22 One Hebrew manuscript, Vulgate and Syriac; most Hebrew manuscripts do not have *had sent with him.* [c]22 Also called *Tikvah* [d]22 Also called *Harhas* [e]25 Or *by everything they have done*

34:8 *repair the temple:* The temple restoration begun by Hezekiah had not been continued during the many years that Manasseh and Amon ruled.

34:9 *Hilkiah . . . the money:* King Joash also had collected money for repairing the temple during his rule approximately two hundred years earlier (24:8-14; 2 Kgs 12:9-15).

34:15 *Book of the Law:* Many scholars feel this may have been a portion of DEUTERONOMY, which includes the laws given to Moses. Some point to Deuteronomy 5, which gives the Ten Commandments, or to Deuteronomy 28–30, which tells how God would bless the people for obedience and curse them for disobedience, and also includes the renewal of the covenant between God and the people at Moab. Others think this "Book" may have been the text of all of the first five books of the Bible.

34:19 *tore his robes:* Tearing one's clothes was a common way of showing fear or grief. See Josh 7:6; 2 Sam 13:31; Job 1:20.

34:20 *Abdon son of Micah:* Also called "Acbor son of Micaiah" (see 2 Kgs 22:12).

34:22 *prophetess Huldah:* Huldah is one of several female prophets named in the Bible. Miriam (Exod 15:20), Deborah (Judg 4:4), Noadiah (Neh 6:14), and Anna (Luke 2:36) are other women who served as prophetesses. See also the article called "Prophets and Prophecy," p. 935.

Josiah removed all the detestable idols from all the territory belonging to the Israelites, and he had all who were present in Israel serve the LORD their God.
2 Chr 34:33

34:30 *temple of the LORD:* See the note at 20:5.

35:1 *Passover . . . first month:* See the notes at 30:1,2 and 29:3 (first month).

35:3 *Levites:* See the note at 11:13.

35:3 *sacred ark:* Referring to the ark of the covenant. See the note at 1:3-5.

35:4 2 Chr 8:14.

to your fathers, and you will be buried in peace. Your eyes will not
see all the disaster I am going to bring on this place and on those
who live here.' "

So they took her answer back to the king.
29Then the king called together all the elders of Judah and
Jerusalem. 30He went up to the temple of the LORD with the men of
Judah, the people of Jerusalem, the priests and the Levites—all the
people from the least to the greatest. He read in their hearing all
the words of the Book of the Covenant, which had been found
in the temple of the LORD. 31The king stood by his pillar and
renewed the covenant in the presence of the LORD—to follow the
LORD and keep his commands, regulations and decrees with all his
heart and all his soul, and to obey the words of the covenant written in this book.
32Then he had everyone in Jerusalem and Benjamin pledge
themselves to it; the people of Jerusalem did this in accordance
with the covenant of God, the God of their fathers.
33Josiah removed all the detestable idols from all the territory belonging to the Israelites, and he had all who were present in
Israel serve the LORD their God. As long as he lived, they did not
fail to follow the LORD, the God of their fathers.

Josiah Celebrates the Passover

35 Josiah celebrated the Passover to the LORD in Jerusalem, and
the Passover lamb was slaughtered on the fourteenth day of the
first month. 2He appointed the priests to their duties and encouraged them in the service of the LORD's temple. 3He said to the
Levites, who instructed all Israel and who had been consecrated to
the LORD: "Put the sacred ark in the temple that Solomon son of
David king of Israel built. It is not to be carried about on your
shoulders. Now serve the LORD your God and his people Israel.
4Prepare yourselves by families in your divisions, according to the
directions written by David king of Israel and by his son Solomon.
5"Stand in the holy place with a group of Levites for each
subdivision of the families of your fellow countrymen, the lay people. 6Slaughter the Passover lambs, consecrate yourselves and prepare ⌊the lambs⌋ for your fellow countrymen, doing what the LORD
commanded through Moses."
7Josiah provided for all the lay people who were there a total
of thirty thousand sheep and goats for the Passover offerings, and
also three thousand cattle—all from the king's own possessions.
8His officials also contributed voluntarily to the people and
the priests and Levites. Hilkiah, Zechariah and Jehiel, the administrators of God's temple, gave the priests twenty-six hundred
Passover offerings and three hundred cattle. 9Also Conaniah along
with Shemaiah and Nethanel, his brothers, and Hashabiah, Jeiel
and Jozabad, the leaders of the Levites, provided five thousand
Passover offerings and five hundred head of cattle for the Levites.

10 The service was arranged and the priests stood in their places with the Levites in their divisions as the king had ordered. 11 The Passover lambs were slaughtered, and the priests sprinkled the blood handed to them, while the Levites skinned the animals. 12 They set aside the burnt offerings to give them to the subdivisions of the families of the people to offer to the LORD, as is written in the Book of Moses. They did the same with the cattle. 13 They roasted the Passover animals over the fire as prescribed, and boiled the holy offerings in pots, caldrons and pans and served them quickly to all the people. 14 After this, they made preparations for themselves and for the priests, because the priests, the descendants of Aaron, were sacrificing the burnt offerings and the fat portions until nightfall. So the Levites made preparations for themselves and for the Aaronic priests.

15 The musicians, the descendants of Asaph, were in the places prescribed by David, Asaph, Heman and Jeduthun the king's seer. The gatekeepers at each gate did not need to leave their posts, because their fellow Levites made the preparations for them.

16 So at that time the entire service of the LORD was carried out for the celebration of the Passover and the offering of burnt offerings on the altar of the LORD, as King Josiah had ordered. 17 The Israelites who were present celebrated the Passover at that time and observed the Feast of Unleavened Bread for seven days. 18 The Passover had not been observed like this in Israel since the days of the prophet Samuel; and none of the kings of Israel had ever celebrated such a Passover as did Josiah, with the priests, the Levites and all Judah and Israel who were there with the people of Jerusalem. 19 This Passover was celebrated in the eighteenth year of Josiah's reign.

The Death of Josiah

20 After all this, when Josiah had set the temple in order, Neco king of Egypt went up to fight at Carchemish on the Euphrates, and Josiah marched out to meet him in battle. 21 But Neco sent messengers to him, saying, "What quarrel is there between you and me, O king of Judah? It is not you I am attacking at this time, but the house with which I am at war. God has told me to hurry; so stop opposing God, who is with me, or he will destroy you."

22 Josiah, however, would not turn away from him, but disguised himself to engage him in battle. He would not listen to what Neco had said at God's command but went to fight him on the plain of Megiddo.

23 Archers shot King Josiah, and he told his officers, "Take me away; I am badly wounded." 24 So they took him out of his chariot, put him in the other chariot he had and brought him to Jerusalem, where he died. He was buried in the tombs of his fathers, and all Judah and Jerusalem mourned for him.

35:18 *Passover had not been observed like this in Israel since . . . Samuel:* The Passover celebration under Hezekiah had been held a month late, and many of the people had not made themselves clean (30:1-4,18,19). See also the note at 23:6.

In Hebrew "Samuel" sounds like "Someone from God" or "Heard of God" or "His name is God." Samuel served Israel as a priest, prophet, and judge, and anointed its first king, Saul (1 Sam 10:17-25).

35:20-22 *Neco king of Egypt:* At this time, King Neco of Egypt (609-595 B.C.) was fighting on the side of the Assyrians. He marched north to fight the Babylonian army and to help Assyria keep control of its land. Neco is also doing God's work here.

35:22 *Megiddo:* Megiddo was an important business and military center located at the intersection of the north-south trade route. Whoever controlled Megiddo also controlled the pass through the Carmel mountain range between the Valley of Jezreel and the Plain of Sharon. This is also the place called Armageddon (Rev 16:16). See the map on p. 2467.

35:13 Exod 12:8,9. **35:15** 1 Chr 25:1. **35:17** Exod 12:1-20.

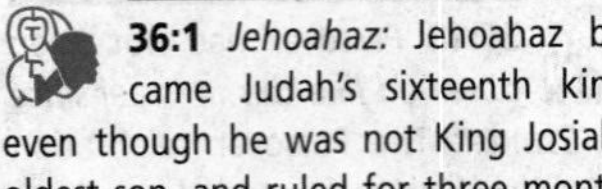

36:1 *Jehoahaz:* Jehoahaz became Judah's sixteenth king, even though he was not King Josiah's oldest son, and ruled for three months in 609 B.C.

36:4,6 *changed Eliakim's name to Jehoiakim . . . Nebuchadnezzar . . . Jeremiah:* Jehoiakim was Judah's seventeenth king, and ruled from 609 to 598 B.C.

The meaning of a name was very important during this period. By changing Jehoahaz's older brother's name from Eliakim ("God has established") to Jehoiakim ("the LORD has established"), perhaps Neco was claiming to be the lord of Judah, displacing God. Now that Judah was controlled politically by Egypt, it faced the threat of being attacked by Babylon, Egypt's enemy.

Nebuchadnezzar ruled Babylon from 605 to 562 B.C. and ordered the attacks on Jerusalem in 597 and 587 B.C. See also the mini-article called "Nebuchadnezzar," p. 1469.

36:9 *Jehoiachin . . . did evil:* Jehoiachin was Judah's eighteenth king, and ruled for three months in 598 B.C. He disobeyed God by worshiping other gods.

36:10 *In the spring, King Nebuchadnezzar sent for him:* These events took place in 597 B.C. See also Jer 22:24-30; 24:1-10; 29:1,2; 37:1; Ezek 17:12,13.

25 Jeremiah composed laments for Josiah, and to this day all
the men and women singers commemorate Josiah in the laments.
These became a tradition in Israel and are written in the Laments.
26 The other events of Josiah's reign and his acts of devotion,
according to what is written in the Law of the LORD— 27 all the
events, from beginning to end, are written in the book of the kings
36 of Israel and Judah. 1 And the people of the land took
Jehoahaz son of Josiah and made him king in Jerusalem in place of
his father.

JUDAH'S DEFEAT, EXILE, AND RETURN

The story of Judah's last four kings, who are all led away by conquerors, provides an explanation for the Babylonian exile that finally came to Judah. But King Cyrus's words of hope, also found at the beginning of EZRA, remind the people that their story does not end in exile in Babylon.

Jehoahaz King of Judah

2 Jehoahaz[a] was twenty-three years old when he became
king, and he reigned in Jerusalem three months. 3 The king of
Egypt dethroned him in Jerusalem and imposed on Judah a levy
of a hundred talents[b] of silver and a talent[c] of gold. 4 The king of
Egypt made Eliakim, a brother of Jehoahaz, king over Judah and
Jerusalem and changed Eliakim's name to Jehoiakim. But Neco
took Eliakim's brother Jehoahaz and carried him off to Egypt.

Jehoiakim King of Judah

5 Jehoiakim was twenty-five years old when he became king,
and he reigned in Jerusalem eleven years. He did evil in the eyes of
the LORD his God. 6 Nebuchadnezzar king of Babylon attacked him
and bound him with bronze shackles to take him to Babylon.
7 Nebuchadnezzar also took to Babylon articles from the temple of
the LORD and put them in his temple[d] there.
8 The other events of Jehoiakim's reign, the detestable things
he did and all that was found against him, are written in the book
of the kings of Israel and Judah. And Jehoiachin his son succeeded him as king.

Jehoiachin King of Judah

9 Jehoiachin was eighteen[e] years old when he became king,
and he reigned in Jerusalem three months and ten days. He did
evil in the eyes of the LORD. 10 In the spring, King Nebuchadnezzar

---

a2 Hebrew *Joahaz,* a variant of *Jehoahaz;* also in verse 4 b3 That is, about 3 3/4 tons (about 3.4 metric tons) c3 That is, about 75 pounds (about 34 kilograms) d7 Or *palace* e9 One Hebrew manuscript, some Septuagint manuscripts and Syriac (see also 2 Kings 24:8); most Hebrew manuscripts *eight*

King Cyrus Orders the Rebuilding of the Temple, an illuminated page from *Antiquities of the Jews* by Josephus, France, fifteenth century. Cyrus II (known as Cyrus the Great) was the king of Persia from around 549 until 530 B.C. He is one of the few non-Israelite monarchs that the biblical authors speak of with admiration and praise. After conquering the Babylonians, he issued a decree allowing captured peoples to return to their homelands. This allowed the Jews the chance to rebuild Jerusalem and its temple.

sent for him and brought him to Babylon, together with articles of value from the temple of the LORD, and he made Jehoiachin's uncle,[a] Zedekiah, king over Judah and Jerusalem.

Zedekiah King of Judah

[11]Zedekiah was twenty-one years old when he became king,
and he reigned in Jerusalem eleven years. [12]He did evil in the eyes
of the LORD his God and did not humble himself before Jeremiah
the prophet, who spoke the word of the LORD. [13]He also rebelled

[a]**10** Hebrew *brother,* that is, relative (see 2 Kings 24:17)

36:11,12 *Zedekiah . . . Jeremiah:* Zedekiah was Judah's nineteenth king, ruling from 598 to 587 B.C. Nebuchadnezzar changed Zedekiah's name from Mattaniah ("gift of the LORD") to Zedekiah ("righteousness of the LORD"). Perhaps Nebuchadnezzar was showing that he was lord over Zedekiah. See also 2 Kgs 24:17; Jer 27:1-22; 28:1-17.

The prophet Jeremiah began bringing God's message to the people about 627 B.C., during Josiah's rule (see Jer 1:2,3).

36:13 *rebelled against King Nebuchadnezzar:* Hophra (also known as Apries), the king of Egypt from 589 to 570 B.C., may have encouraged Zedekiah's rebellion. See also Jer 44:30; Ezek 17:15-18.

36:15 *his messengers:* Referring to the prophets. Ezekiel and probably Habakkuk were also prophets at this time, in addition to Jeremiah. See the note at 36:11,12. See also Ezek 1:1-3; Hab 1:6.

36:17-20 *He brought up against them the king of the Babylonians . . . carried into exile:* The writer says that the LORD sent Nebuchadnezzar to show that the defeat of Jerusalem was punishment for the sins of the leaders and people of Judah. The city and temple were destroyed in 586 B.C. See also 1 Kgs 9:8; Jer 21:1-10; 34:1-5.

36:21 *seventy years . . . spoken by Jeremiah:* Jeremiah the prophet warned the people of Judah that they would spend seventy years in captivity in Babylon (Jer 25:11). He also said that later they would be set free (Jer 29:10).

The actual length of the exile was about fifty years. See also the mini-article called "Exile," p. 1541.

against King Nebuchadnezzar, who had made him take an oath in
God's name. He became stiff-necked and hardened his heart and
would not turn to the LORD, the God of Israel. [14]Furthermore, all
the leaders of the priests and the people became more and more
unfaithful, following all the detestable practices of the nations and
defiling the temple of the LORD, which he had consecrated in
Jerusalem.

The Fall of Jerusalem

[15]The LORD, the God of their fathers, sent word to them
through his messengers again and again, because he had pity on
his people and on his dwelling place. [16]But they mocked God's
messengers, despised his words and scoffed at his prophets until
the wrath of the LORD was aroused against his people and there
was no remedy. [17]He brought up against them the king of the Babylonians,[a] who killed their young men with the sword in the sanctuary, and spared neither young man nor young woman, old man
or aged. God handed all of them over to Nebuchadnezzar. [18]He
carried to Babylon all the articles from the temple of God, both
large and small, and the treasures of the LORD's temple and the
treasures of the king and his officials. [19]They set fire to God's temple and broke down the wall of Jerusalem; they burned all the
palaces and destroyed everything of value there.

[20]He carried into exile to Babylon the remnant, who escaped
from the sword, and they became servants to him and his sons
until the kingdom of Persia came to power. [21]The land enjoyed its
sabbath rests; all the time of its desolation it rested, until the seventy years were completed in fulfillment of the word of the LORD
spoken by Jeremiah.

[a]17 Or *Chaldeans*

QUESTIONS ABOUT 2 CHRONICLES 29:1—36:23

1. Compare Hezekiah and Josiah (see chapters 29–32 and 34,35). Which one do you think was more important and why?
2. A number of prayers are found in 1 and 2 CHRONICLES. They tend to be group prayers for worship, rather than private or devotional prayers. What is the place of private prayer in the life of faith?
3. What aspect of a king's life is most important for the writer of 2 CHRONICLES?
4. Manasseh was one of Israel's most wicked kings, yet unlike the author of the books of KINGS, the writer of 2 CHRONICLES takes the trouble to stress Manasseh's repentance late in life. What reasons might there be for this? (2 Kgs 21; 2 Chr 33)
5. The Israelites had lost a great deal. What did they still have to help them rebuild?
6. What new thing(s) did you learn by reading 2 CHRONICLES?

22 In the first year of Cyrus king of Persia, in order to fulfill
the word of the LORD spoken by Jeremiah, the LORD moved the
heart of Cyrus king of Persia to make a proclamation throughout
his realm and to put it in writing:

23 "This is what Cyrus king of Persia says:
" 'The LORD, the God of heaven, has given me all the
kingdoms of the earth and he has appointed me to build a
temple for him at Jerusalem in Judah. Anyone of his people
among you—may the LORD his God be with him, and let him
go up.' "

36:22 *the first year of Cyrus king of Persia:* This probably refers to 538 B.C., after Cyrus captured Babylonia.

36:22 *Cyrus:* Cyrus II, "the Great," ruled the Persian empire from 549 to 530 B.C. The capture of Babylon in 539 B.C. was his greatest military victory. The prophet Isaiah praises Cyrus as God's chosen one, since he was the one God used to allow the people of Judah to go back to its own land and worship God there (Isa 45:1-4).

36:22 *Persia:* See the mini-article called "Persia," p. 859, and the map on p. 2469.

36:23 *appointed me to build a temple for him at Jerusalem:* The Assyrians and Babylonians reorganized their empires by forcing conquered peoples to move to other areas. After defeating the Babylonians, the Persians tried to win the loyalty of those conquered peoples by encouraging them to return to their own lands. Cyrus's actions, then, may have been politically motivated. See Isa 44:28 and the article called "After the Exile: God's People Return to Judea," p. 931.

EZRA

Going home can be an exciting time. As you read Ezra, look for the different experiences God's people had when they returned with Zerubbabel and Ezra.

What makes Ezra special?

Ezra and the next book in the Bible, Nehemiah, were originally one book. Together they make up the most important source for the history of 538 to 430 B.C. This period saw the restoration of the Jewish religious community in Judah following the Babylonian exile. Ezra the priest, as the main religious leader of this time, and Nehemiah, as appointed governor, were largely responsible for the shape this community was to take.

Why was Ezra written?

Ezra was written to help the Jewish community in Jerusalem understand who they were as God's people. It does this by remembering how the community began and by describing how some of them returned home to Judah and struggled to obey the Law of Moses, rebuild the city and the temple, and keep themselves pure in the midst of foreign peoples.

What's the story behind the scene?

A number of historical and literary questions surround Ezra and Nehemiah. The traditional view sees Ezra beginning his mission in the seventh year of the reign of Artaxerxes I (458 B.C.; Ezra 7:8) and Nehemiah arriving thirteen years later in the twentieth year of Artaxerxes' reign (445 B.C.; Neh 2:1). Others suggest the opposite order is more accurate, because it better explains certain difficulties in the text. In this view, Nehemiah still arrives at Jerusalem in 445 B.C., but Ezra comes much later, in the seventh year of Artaxerxes II (398 B.C.). Still others place Ezra's arrival after Nehemiah's but insist that their ministries overlapped. This view must change the text of Ezra 7:8,9 from "seventh" to either "twenty-seventh" or "thirty-seventh." There is no agreement as to which order is most accurate.

The author of Ezra and Nehemiah probably used several different sources in writing these books. The most important ones are the first-person accounts called the "Memoirs of Ezra" that form the basis of Ezra 8–10 and Nehemiah 8, 9, and the "Memoirs of Nehemiah" which lie behind Nehemiah 1–7; 11:1,2; 12:31-43; and 13:4-31. The author also draws upon a number of Persian documents written in Aramaic (Ezra 1:2-4; 4:8—6:18; 7:12-28), and many lists of people.

How is Ezra constructed?

Originally, Ezra and Nehemiah were one book that told the story of God restoring the Jewish people to their homeland in Israel.

Babylonia and Persia: Jerusalem was conquered by the Babylonians in 586 B.C. The temple was destroyed and its treasures taken by the conquerors. Many of the leading citizens of Judah and Jerusalem were forced to move to other parts of the Babylonian empire. See the mini-article called "Exile," p. 1541. The Israelites' time and experiences in Babylonia strongly influenced later Jewish thought, business, and worship. See the map on p. 2468 and the mini-article called "Babylon," p. 1363.

Persia was one of the greatest empires in biblical times and dominated the Middle East for nearly 200 years. Today the western part of what was once Persia is called Iran, and the eastern part is Afghanistan and Pakistan. See the map on p. 2469 and the mini-article called "Persia," p. 859.

1:1-3 *In the first year . . . in Jerusalem:* These verses are nearly the same as the final verses of 2 Chronicles. This may indicate that the same person wrote 1 and 2 Chronicles, Ezra, and Nehemiah. Since Ezra and Nehemiah come before 1 and 2 Chronicles in the Hebrew Bible, the repetition of the verses is probably a way to connect these works.

It is structured around the decrees of two Persian kings, Cyrus and Artaxerxes. Cyrus's decree that allowed the Jews to return home and rebuild the temple (Ezra 1:2-4) is followed by the story of their homecoming and the rebuilding of the temple (Ezra 1–6). In Ezra 7:12-26, Artaxerxes calls for all Jews to obey the Law of Moses. This is followed by Ezra's mission. His reading of the Law to the people becomes the basis for several changes he makes in response to various problems he finds in the community (Ezra 7–10; Neh 8–10; 13). Artaxerxes also authorizes Nehemiah to return to Jerusalem (Neh 2) to rebuild and dedicate the city's walls (Neh 2–7; 12).

EZRA can be outlined in the following way:

God's people return from exile and begin rebuilding the temple (1:1—6:22)
- God's people come home (1:1—4:24)
- Work on the temple continues (5:1—6:22)

Ezra returns and restores the people (7:1—10:44)
- Ezra and his mission (7:1—8:36)
- Ezra deals with problems in the community (9:1—10:44)

God's People Return from Exile and Begin Rebuilding the Temple

The first six chapters of this book tell about the many Israelites who returned from exile in Babylonia (1:1—2:70) and struggled to rebuild the temple (3:1—6:22). These events happened between 538 and 516 B.C., long before the appearance of Ezra.

GOD'S PEOPLE COME HOME

After defeating the Babylonians, King Cyrus of Persia issues an order that allows the Israelites, who had been held captive in Babylonia for seventy years, to return to their home area near Jerusalem and rebuild their temple.

Cyrus Helps the Exiles to Return

1 In the first year of Cyrus king of Persia, in order to fulfill the
word of the LORD spoken by Jeremiah, the LORD moved the heart
of Cyrus king of Persia to make a proclamation throughout his
realm and to put it in writing:

2 "This is what Cyrus king of Persia says:

" 'The LORD, the God of heaven, has given me all the
kingdoms of the earth and he has appointed me to build a
temple for him at Jerusalem in Judah. 3 Anyone of his people
among you—may his God be with him, and let him go up to
Jerusalem in Judah and build the temple of the LORD, the God
of Israel, the God who is in Jerusalem. 4 And the people of any

1:1 *Cyrus king of Persia:* Cyrus II ("Cyrus the Great") founded the Achaemenid dynasty and the Kingdom of Persia, and ruled it from 549 to 530 B.C. The capture of Babylonia in 539 B.C. was his greatest military victory. The prophet Isaiah praised Cyrus as God's "anointed" (Isa 45:1-4), since he was the one God used to allow the Israelites to go back to their own land in Judea and to worship God there. Isaiah also said Cyrus would lead Israel in the rebuilding of the temple (Isa 44:28).

1:1 *fulfill the word of the LORD spoken by Jeremiah:* Through the prophet Jeremiah, God told the people of Israel they would spend seventy years in captivity in Babylonia (Jer 25:11). God also promised that after that time, they would be set free (Jer 29:10). According to Daniel 1:1, it was in 605 B.C., or about seventy years earlier, that the first group of Jews had been forced to move to Babylonia.

1:1 *a proclamation:* Cyrus originally spoke the message. The version in 1:2-4 was written in Hebrew, the ancient language of the Israelites. Another version of this message appears in 6:3-5 and is written in Aramaic, which is similar to Hebrew and became the official language of the Persian empire.

1:2 *he has appointed me to build a temple:* The Assyrians and Babylonians moved those they conquered out of their homelands and into other lands of their empires. After defeating the Babylonians, the Persians tried to win the loyalty of these displaced people by encouraging them to return to their own lands. Though Cyrus's actions may have been politically motivated, Ezra says that God caused Cyrus to be kind toward the people of Israel. See also Isa 44:28.

1:2 *Jerusalem:* This was the Israelites' religious and political capital. See the mini-article called "Jerusalem," p. 574.

1:5 *family heads of Judah and Benjamin, and the priests and Levites:* The family heads were political leaders of the two tribes that made up the southern kingdom, Judah and Benjamin. The priests were all members of the tribe of Levi who could prove they were descendants of Aaron, a descendant of Levi and Israel's first high priest (Num 18:21-32). The Levites who had been in exile in Babylonia were thought to have worshiped the Canaanite gods and so were considered unfit to do anything except work as janitors in the temple (Ezek 44:10-14). However, some were given other special duties in the temple, (1 Chr 15:11-15; 16:4-37).

1:7,8 *Nebuchadnezzar . . . Sheshbazzar:* Nebuchadnezzar II, ruled Babylonia from 605 to 562 B.C. In 586 B.C. he captured Jerusalem, destroyed the temple, and took many of the people to Babylonia. See also the mini-article called "Nebuchadnezzar," p. 1469. Sheshbazzar had been appointed governor of Judah by Cyrus. Little more is known about him. He may have been the same person as Shenazzar (1 Chr 3:18), the fourth son of Jehoiachin (Jeconiah).

1:7 *his god:* The most important of these gods was Marduk, the main god of Babylonia.

1:11 *Babylon:* See the note on p. 852 (Babylonia and Persia).

Cyrus Cylinder, around 538 B.C. In the ancient world, the victories and achievements of kings were often commemorated on stone tablets, monuments, and objects like this clay cylinder. This text, written in Akkadian using cuneiform, tells how the Persian king, Cyrus the Great, captured the great Babylonian empire without a battle. Cyrus allowed the people that the Babylonians had taken prisoner to return to their homelands. The Cylinder describes Cyrus as a tolerant ruler who also allowed the different peoples of his empire to worship their own gods. It was during his rule that the Jews would begin returning to Jerusalem to rebuild the temple.

place where survivors may now be living are to provide him with silver and gold, with goods and livestock, and with freewill offerings for the temple of God in Jerusalem.' "

5Then the family heads of Judah and Benjamin, and the
priests and Levites—everyone whose heart God had moved—prepared to go up and build the house of the LORD in Jerusalem. 6All
their neighbors assisted them with articles of silver and gold, with
goods and livestock, and with valuable gifts, in addition to all the
freewill offerings. 7Moreover, King Cyrus brought out the articles
belonging to the temple of the LORD, which Nebuchadnezzar had
carried away from Jerusalem and had placed in the temple of his
god.[a] 8Cyrus king of Persia had them brought by Mithredath the
treasurer, who counted them out to Sheshbazzar the prince of
Judah.

9This was the inventory:

gold dishes	30
silver dishes	1,000
silver pans[b]	29
10 gold bowls	30
matching silver bowls	410
other articles	1,000

11In all, there were 5,400 articles of gold and of silver. Sheshbazzar brought all these along when the exiles came up from Babylon to Jerusalem.

[a]7 Or *gods* [b]9 The meaning of the Hebrew for this word is uncertain.

The List of the Exiles Who Returned

2 Now these are the people of the province who came up from
the captivity of the exiles, whom Nebuchadnezzar king of Babylon
had taken captive to Babylon (they returned to Jerusalem and
Judah, each to his own town, 2 in company with Zerubbabel,
Jeshua, Nehemiah, Seraiah, Reelaiah, Mordecai, Bilshan, Mispar,
Bigvai, Rehum and Baanah):

The list of the men of the people of Israel:

3 the descendants of Parosh	2,172
4 of Shephatiah	372
5 of Arah	775
6 of Pahath-Moab (through the line of Jeshua and Joab)	2,812
7 of Elam	1,254
8 of Zattu	945
9 of Zaccai	760
10 of Bani	642
11 of Bebai	623
12 of Azgad	1,222
13 of Adonikam	666
14 of Bigvai	2,056
15 of Adin	454
16 of Ater (through Hezekiah)	98
17 of Bezai	323
18 of Jorah	112
19 of Hashum	223
20 of Gibbar	95

21 the men of Bethlehem	123
22 of Netophah	56
23 of Anathoth	128
24 of Azmaveth	42
25 of Kiriath Jearim,[a] Kephirah and Beeroth	743
26 of Ramah and Geba	621
27 of Micmash	122
28 of Bethel and Ai	223
29 of Nebo	52
30 of Magbish	156
31 of the other Elam	1,254
32 of Harim	320
33 of Lod, Hadid and Ono	725
34 of Jericho	345
35 of Senaah	3,630

[a]**25** See Septuagint (see also Neh. 7:29); Hebrew *Kiriath Arim.*

2:1-70 *Now these are the people:* This list is almost the same as that found in Nehemiah 7:4-73. It lists the Israelites who returned to Judah in terms of families (2:3-20), towns (2:21-35), families of priests (2:36-39), families of Levites (2:40-42), and various temple servants (2:43-58).

2:2 *Zerubbabel . . . Baanah:* If the first eleven names in this verse are a listing of those who, at various times, had led groups back to Jerusalem, then Zerubbabel and Jeshua may be the governor and priest mentioned in Ezra 3:2. Nehemiah is perhaps the governor named in Nehemiah 1:1, but may be simply a leader of the people who returned with Sheshbazzar. Seraiah is Ezra's father (Ezra 7:1-6), and Bigvai was a later governor of Judah.

2:40 *Levites:* See the note at 1:5.

2:61 *a man who married a daughter of Barzillai:* Barzillai is the only man in the Old Testament to take his wife's family name.

2:63 *governor:* In Nehemiah 8:9 and 10:1 this same title is used for Nehemiah, but here it more likely refers to another Persian official.

2:63 *Urim and Thummim:* The priests used these sacred objects in some way to receive answers from God (Exod 28:30).

2:66,67 *horses . . . donkeys:* People rode on horses and mules when they traveled, but belongings and food were carried by camels and donkeys. See also the article called "Trade and Travel," p. 948.

2:68 *heads of the families:* See the note at 1:5.

36 The priests:

the descendants of Jedaiah
(through the family of Jeshua) 973
37 of Immer 1,052
38 of Pashhur 1,247
39 of Harim 1,017

40 The Levites:

the descendants of Jeshua and Kadmiel
(through the line of Hodaviah) 74

41 The singers:

the descendants of Asaph 128

42 The gatekeepers of the temple:

the descendants of
Shallum, Ater, Talmon, Akkub,
Hatita and Shobai 139

43 The temple servants:

the descendants of
Ziha, Hasupha, Tabbaoth,
44 Keros, Siaha, Padon,
45 Lebanah, Hagabah, Akkub,
46 Hagab, Shalmai, Hanan,
47 Giddel, Gahar, Reaiah,
48 Rezin, Nekoda, Gazzam,
49 Uzza, Paseah, Besai,
50 Asnah, Meunim, Nephussim,
51 Bakbuk, Hakupha, Harhur,
52 Bazluth, Mehida, Harsha,
53 Barkos, Sisera, Temah,
54 Neziah and Hatipha

55 The descendants of the servants of Solomon:

the descendants of
Sotai, Hassophereth, Peruda,
56 Jaala, Darkon, Giddel,
57 Shephatiah, Hattil,
Pokereth-Hazzebaim and Ami

58 The temple servants and the descendants
of the servants of Solomon 392

59 The following came up from the towns of Tel Melah, Tel Harsha, Kerub, Addon and Immer, but they could not show that their families were descended from Israel:

60 The descendants of
Delaiah, Tobiah and Nekoda 652

61 And from among the priests:
The descendants of
Hobaiah, Hakkoz and Barzillai (a man who had married a daughter of Barzillai the Gileadite and was called by that name).
62 These searched for their family records, but they could not find them and so were excluded from the priesthood as unclean.
63 The governor ordered them not to eat any of the most sacred food until there was a priest ministering with the Urim and Thummim.

64 The whole company numbered 42,360, 65 besides their 7,337 menservants and maidservants; and they also had 200 men and women singers.
66 They had 736 horses, 245 mules,
67 435 camels and 6,720 donkeys.

68 When they arrived at the house of the LORD in Jerusalem, some of the heads of the families gave freewill offerings toward the rebuilding of the house of God on its site.
69 According to their ability they gave to the treasury for this work 61,000 drachmas[a] of gold, 5,000 minas[b] of silver and 100 priestly garments.

70 The priests, the Levites, the singers, the gatekeepers and the temple servants settled in their own towns, along with some of the other people, and the rest of the Israelites settled in their towns.

Rebuilding the Altar

3 When the seventh month came and the Israelites had settled in their towns, the people assembled as one man in Jerusalem.
2 Then Jeshua son of Jozadak and his fellow priests and Zerubbabel son of Shealtiel and his associates began to build the altar of the God of Israel to sacrifice burnt offerings on it, in accordance with what is written in the Law of Moses the man of God.
3 Despite their fear of the peoples around them, they built the altar on its foundation and sacrificed burnt offerings on it to the LORD, both the morning and evening sacrifices.
4 Then in accordance with what is written, they celebrated the Feast of Tabernacles with the required number of burnt offerings prescribed for each day.
5 After that, they presented the regular burnt offerings, the New Moon sacrifices and the sacrifices for all the appointed sacred feasts of the LORD, as well as those brought as freewill offerings to the LORD.
6 On the first day of the seventh month they began to offer burnt offerings to the LORD, though the foundation of the LORD's temple had not yet been laid.

[a]69 That is, about 1,100 pounds (about 500 kilograms) [b]69 That is, about 3 tons (about 2.9 metric tons)

3:1 *seventh month:* This could mean the seventh month after the people left Babylonia, but probably means the seventh month of the Hebrew calendar, Tishri. It lasts from mid-September to mid-October and includes many important religious festivals. See the chart called "Jewish Calendar and Festivals," p. 944.

The year may be either 538 B.C., the first year of Cyrus's reign, or 520 B.C. during the second year of Darius's reign.

3:2 *Jeshua son of Jozadak . . . Moses the man of God:* It is possible that Jeshua is listed first here because this is a religious occasion. Jozadak was the high priest at the time of the exile, 587 B.C. (1 Chr 6:15). For Moses, see the mini-article called "Moses," p. 2335.

3:3 *peoples around them:* Foreigners or other non-Israelites who had been forced by the Assyrians to move to the area around Jerusalem.

3:4,5 *Feast of Tabernacles . . . New Moon sacrifices:* The Feast of Tabernacles was celebrated as a reminder of how God protected the people of Israel in the desert (see Lev 23:33-36). The new moon marked the beginning of the month and was a holy day (Num 28:11-15). See also the chart called "Jewish Calendar and Festivals," p. 944.

3:5 *sacrifices:* These sacrifices are sometimes called "burnt offerings" (Lev 1:1-16). See the chart called "Sacrifices and Offerings," p. 219.

2:63 Num 27:21. **2:70** 1 Chr 9:2; Neh 11:3. **3:2** Exod 27:1. **3:3** Num 28:1-8. **3:5** Num 28:11—29:39.

3:7 *Sidon and Tyre . . . Joppa:* Sidon and Tyre were the leading cities of Phoenicia. Joppa was a small city on the coast. The lumber used to construct Solomon's temple was shipped here (2 Chr 2:16), and then transported overland to Jerusalem.

3:7 *cedar logs:* Cedars are evergreen trees that can grow to 100 feet tall. Their wood is excellent for building because it resists rotting. See also 2 Chr 2:8, 16; 1 Kgs 5:6-12.

3:8 *second month:* Ziv is the second month of the Hebrew calendar.

3:10 *David:* See the mini- article called "David," p. 1028.

3:11,12 *praise and thanksgiving . . . wept . . . shouted for joy:* The song of thanksgiving recalls the song of praise sung at the dedication of Solomon's temple (2 Chr 5:11-13; 7:3; Ps 136:1). See also 1 Chr 16:34; Ps 100:5; 106:1; 107:1; 118:1; Jer 33:11. The people were reminded of the destruction of Solomon's temple in 586 B.C., and cried because they knew the new smaller temple never could compare with the glory of the one Solomon had built (Hag 2:3).

4:1,2 *enemies . . . Esarhaddon:* The enemies were the people who had been captured by Assyrian and Babylonian kings and forced to settle in Palestine when the northern kingdom (Israel) fell in 722 B.C. Esarhaddon, the son of Sennacherib, ruled Assyria from 681 to 669 B.C. He continued the policy of relocating conquered people to other lands.

Rebuilding the Temple

[7]Then they gave money to the masons and carpenters, and gave food and drink and oil to the people of Sidon and Tyre, so that they would bring cedar logs by sea from Lebanon to Joppa, as authorized by Cyrus king of Persia.

[8]In the second month of the second year after their arrival at the house of God in Jerusalem, Zerubbabel son of Shealtiel, Jeshua son of Jozadak and the rest of their brothers (the priests and the Levites and all who had returned from the captivity to Jerusalem) began the work, appointing Levites twenty years of age and older to supervise the building of the house of the LORD. [9]Jeshua and his sons and brothers and Kadmiel and his sons (descendants of Hodaviah[a]) and the sons of Henadad and their sons and brothers—all Levites—joined together in supervising those working on the house of God.

[10]When the builders laid the foundation of the temple of the LORD, the priests in their vestments and with trumpets, and the Levites (the sons of Asaph) with cymbals, took their places to praise the LORD, as prescribed by David king of Israel. [11]With praise and thanksgiving they sang to the LORD:

"He is good;
his love to Israel endures forever."

And all the people gave a great shout of praise to the LORD, because the foundation of the house of the LORD was laid. [12]But many of the older priests and Levites and family heads, who had seen the former temple, wept aloud when they saw the foundation of this temple being laid, while many others shouted for joy. [13]No one could distinguish the sound of the shouts of joy from the sound of weeping, because the people made so much noise. And the sound was heard far away.

Opposition to the Rebuilding

4 When the enemies of Judah and Benjamin heard that the exiles were building a temple for the LORD, the God of Israel, [2]they came to Zerubbabel and to the heads of the families and said, "Let us help you build because, like you, we seek your God and have been sacrificing to him since the time of Esarhaddon king of Assyria, who brought us here."

[3]But Zerubbabel, Jeshua and the rest of the heads of the families of Israel answered, "You have no part with us in building a temple to our God. We alone will build it for the LORD, the God of Israel, as King Cyrus, the king of Persia, commanded us."

[4]Then the peoples around them set out to discourage the people of Judah and make them afraid to go on building.[b] [5]They

---

[a]9 Hebrew *Yehudah,* probably a variant of *Hodaviah*   [b]4 Or *and troubled them as they built*

hired counselors to work against them and frustrate their plans
during the entire reign of Cyrus king of Persia and down to the
reign of Darius king of Persia.

Later Opposition Under Xerxes and Artaxerxes

6At the beginning of the reign of Xerxes,[a] they lodged an
accusation against the people of Judah and Jerusalem.
7And in the days of Artaxerxes king of Persia, Bishlam,
Mithredath, Tabeel and the rest of his associates wrote a letter to
Artaxerxes. The letter was written in Aramaic script and in the
Aramaic language.[b,c]
8Rehum the commanding officer and Shimshai the secretary
wrote a letter against Jerusalem to Artaxerxes the king as follows:

9Rehum the commanding officer and Shimshai the secretary,
together with the rest of their associates—the judges and officials over the men from Tripolis, Persia,[d] Erech and Babylon,

4:2 *we seek your God and have been sacrificing to him:* This was only half true. They also continued to worship their own gods (2 Kgs 17:24-41).

4:4,5 *people of Judah . . . Darius king of Persia:* The "people of Judah" refers to the one of the tribes of Israel. Darius I ruled from 522 to 486 B.C.

4:5 *frustrate their plans:* Constant problems caused by neighboring people halted the rebuilding of the temple, from 536 to 520 B.C.

4:6 *the beginning of the reign of Xerxes:* This was either the end of 486 B.C. or early in 485 B.C. The Hebrew text has the king's Persian name "Ahasuerus."

3:10 1 Chr 16:4-6; 25:1. **4:6** Esth 1:1,2.

[a]6 Hebrew *Ahasuerus,* a variant of Xerxes' Persian name [b]7 Or *written in Aramaic and translated* [c]7 The text of Ezra 4:8—6:18 is in Aramaic. [d]9 Or *officials, magistrates and governors over the men from*

PERSIA

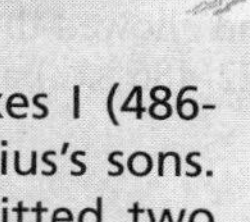

Ancient Persia was similar in size and location to modern-day Iran. From 550 to 330 B.C., however, the Persians ruled over a vast empire stretching from the Aegean Sea in the west to the Indus Valley in the east and from Asia Minor in the north to Egypt in the south.

Persia became a world power under Cyrus the Great who united the Medes and the Persians in 549 B.C. In 546 B.C. he conquered Lydia and added the former Babylonian empire in 539 B.C. Cyrus was also the king who permitted the exiled Jews in Babylonia to return to their homeland (2 Chr 36:20-22; Ezra 1). His son and successor, Cambyses II, added Egypt to the Persian empire in 525 B.C. But it was Darius I (the Great) who expanded the empire to its greatest size and who efficiently organized it into states (*satrapies*), each with its own governor.

It was during the rule of Darius I (522-486 B.C.) that the temple in Jerusalem was rebuilt (Ezra 3–6). The legendary story of ESTHER is set in the time of Xerxes I (486-465 B.C.). Xerxes was one of Darius's sons. Artaxerxes I (465-423 B.C.) permitted two other groups of Jewish exiles to return to Palestine during the time of Ezra and Nehemiah.

Unlike the Assyrians and the Babylonians before them, who uprooted and deported the people they conquered, the Persians were very tolerant of local religious beliefs. This policy resulted in several occasions where the exiles from Judah were encouraged to return to their homeland and rebuild their temple.

Persia's own religion developed out of the principles of Zoroaster, one of their prophets. Their belief in angels, Satan, paradise, and the struggle between good (represented by Ahura Mazda) and evil (represented by Ahriman) had an effect on both Judaism and Christianity.

In 330 B.C. the Persian empire was captured by Alexander the Great (356-323 B.C.).

The Persian Empire. For 200 years the Persian empire was the largest the world had seen. It stretched from India in the east to Greece in the west, and included Egypt in the south. The king's court was located at the magnificent palace at Persepolis and was famous for the luxury of its furnishings and the skill of its craftsmen. The first Persian king, Cyrus II (the Great) conquered the Babylonians in 539 B.C. and allowed the Jewish people to return to their homeland. The third Persian king, Darius I (the Great, 522-486 B.C.) authorized the rebuilding of the temple in Jerusalem (see chapters 4–6).

the Elamites of Susa,
10 and the other people whom the great
and honorable Ashurbanipal[a] deported and settled in the city
of Samaria and elsewhere in Trans-Euphrates.

11 (This is a copy of the letter they sent him.)

To King Artaxerxes,

From your servants, the men of Trans-Euphrates:

12 The king should know that the Jews who came up to
us from you have gone to Jerusalem and are rebuilding that
rebellious and wicked city. They are restoring the walls and
repairing the foundations.
13 Furthermore, the king should know that if this city is
built and its walls are restored, no more taxes, tribute or duty
will be paid, and the royal revenues will suffer.
14 Now since we
are under obligation to the palace and it is not proper for us to
see the king dishonored, we are sending this message to inform

4:8-10 *Ashurbanipal:* King of Assyria, ruled from 669 to 633 (or possibly until 627) B.C. and continued the policies of his father, Esarhaddon (see the note at 4:1,2).

4:10 *Samaria . . . Trans-Euphrates:* See the map on p. 2469. Omri, the sixth king of Israel (885-874 B.C.), made Samaria the capital of the northern kingdom (Israel). Eventually, Samaria became the name used for the entire northern kingdom. The Trans-Euphrates was the land from the Euphrates River west to the Mediterranean Sea.

4:14 *we are under obligation to the palace:* May indicate that there had been a treaty or special agreement between the Samaritan officials and the Persian authorities.

a10 Aramaic *Osnappar,* a variant of *Ashurbanipal*

the king, 15so that a search may be made in the archives of your predecessors. In these records you will find that this city is a rebellious city, troublesome to kings and provinces, a place of rebellion from ancient times. That is why this city was destroyed. 16We inform the king that if this city is built and its walls are restored, you will be left with nothing in Trans-Euphrates.

17The king sent this reply:

To Rehum the commanding officer, Shimshai the secretary and the rest of their associates living in Samaria and elsewhere in Trans-Euphrates:

Greetings.

18The letter you sent us has been read and translated in my presence. 19I issued an order and a search was made, and it was found that this city has a long history of revolt against kings and has been a place of rebellion and sedition. 20Jerusalem has had powerful kings ruling over the whole of Trans-Euphrates, and taxes, tribute and duty were paid to them. 21Now issue an order to these men to stop work, so that this city will not be rebuilt until I so order. 22Be careful not to neglect this matter. Why let this threat grow, to the detriment of the royal interests?

23As soon as the copy of the letter of King Artaxerxes was read to Rehum and Shimshai the secretary and their associates, they went immediately to the Jews in Jerusalem and compelled them by force to stop.

24Thus the work on the house of God in Jerusalem came to a standstill until the second year of the reign of Darius king of Persia.

WORK ON THE TEMPLE CONTINUES

Work on the temple had stopped from 535 to 520 B.C., but the prophets Haggai and Zechariah persuade the people to start again.

Tattenai's Letter to Darius

5 Now Haggai the prophet and Zechariah the prophet, a descendant of Iddo, prophesied to the Jews in Judah and Jerusalem in the name of the God of Israel, who was over them. 2Then Zerubbabel son of Shealtiel and Jeshua son of Jozadak set to work to rebuild the house of God in Jerusalem. And the prophets of God were with them, helping them.

3At that time Tattenai, governor of Trans-Euphrates, and Shethar-Bozenai and their associates went to them and asked, "Who authorized you to rebuild this temple and restore this structure?" 4They also asked, "What are the names of the men constructing this

4:21 *so that this city will not be rebuilt:* See Neh 2:1-9. In 444 B.C. this same king will give Nehemiah permission to resume the rebuilding of Jerusalem.

4:24 *came to a standstill until the second year of the reign of Darius:* That is 520 B.C.; see the note at 4:4, 5. This verse resumes the story of the rebuilding of the temple that was interrupted at 4:5. That interruption (verses 6-23) told of the later rebuilding of the city. See also Hag 1:1 and Zech 1:1.

5:1,3 *Haggai the prophet and Zechariah ... Tattenai ... Shethar-Bozenai:* See Hag 1:1 and Zech 1:1. The story of Haggai and Zechariah urging the people to complete the rebuilding of the temple is found throughout the book of HAGGAI and the first eight chapters of ZECHARIAH.

A Babylonian record dated 502 B.C. mentions Tattenai as governor of the Trans-Euphrates. Shethar-Bozenai probably held a lower office.

5:3 *Trans-Euphrates:* See the note at 4:10 (Trans-Euphrates).

5:1 Hag 1:1; Zech 1:1. **5:2** Hag 1:12; Zech 4:6-9.

building?"[a] 5But the eye of their God was watching over the elders of the Jews, and they were not stopped until a report could go to Darius and his written reply be received.

6This is a copy of the letter that Tattenai, governor of Trans-Euphrates, and Shethar-Bozenai and their associates, the officials of Trans-Euphrates, sent to King Darius. 7The report they sent him read as follows:

To King Darius:

Cordial greetings.

8The king should know that we went to the district of Judah, to the temple of the great God. The people are building it with large stones and placing the timbers in the walls. The work is being carried on with diligence and is making rapid progress under their direction.

9We questioned the elders and asked them, "Who authorized you to rebuild this temple and restore this structure?" 10We also asked them their names, so that we could write down the names of their leaders for your information.

11This is the answer they gave us:

"We are the servants of the God of heaven and earth, and we are rebuilding the temple that was built many years ago, one that a great king of Israel built and finished. 12But because our fathers angered the God of heaven, he handed them over to Nebuchadnezzar the Chaldean, king of Babylon, who destroyed this temple and deported the people to Babylon.

13"However, in the first year of Cyrus king of Babylon, King Cyrus issued a decree to rebuild this house of God. 14He even removed from the temple[b] of Babylon the gold and silver articles of the house of God, which Nebuchadnezzar had taken from the temple in Jerusalem and brought to the temple[b] in Babylon.

"Then King Cyrus gave them to a man named Sheshbazzar, whom he had appointed governor, 15and he told him, 'Take these articles and go and deposit them in the temple in Jerusalem. And rebuild the house of God on its site.' 16So this Sheshbazzar came and laid the foundations of the house of God in Jerusalem. From that day to the present it has been under construction but is not yet finished."

17Now if it pleases the king, let a search be made in the royal archives of Babylon to see if King Cyrus did in fact issue a decree to rebuild this house of God in Jerusalem. Then let the king send us his decision in this matter.

---

[a]4 See Septuagint; Aramaic *4We told them the names of the men constructing this building.* [b]14 Or *palace*

5:6 *copy of the letter:* The first two years of Darius's rule witnessed many revolts within the empire. This forced even minor Persian officials to be on the alert for any suspicious activity.

5:8 *building it with large stones:* In the ancient world, only special buildings like temples and palaces were made from blocks of cut stone. To cut blocks to the right size, stonecutters would make a row of holes with a chisel. Then they would put wooden pegs in the holes, and then soak the wood with water. When the wood swelled the pressure caused the stone to split exactly where the stonecutters wanted it to.

5:11 *a great king of Israel:* Refers to Solomon, King David's son, who ruled from about 970 to 931 B.C. It took Solomon seven years to build Israel's first temple (1 Kgs 6:37, 38).

5:14 *Sheshbazzar . . . appointed governor:* See the notes at 1:7, 8 (Sheshbazzar). The exact meaning of the title "governor" here is unclear, because this same title is applied to Tattenai, another Persian official in 5:6.

5:12 2 Kgs 25:8-12; 2 Chr 36:17-20; Jer 52:12-15. **5:13-15** Ezra 1:2-11.

The Decree of Darius

6 King Darius then issued an order, and they searched in the
archives stored in the treasury at Babylon. 2 A scroll was found in
the citadel of Ecbatana in the province of Media, and this was
written on it:

Memorandum:

3 In the first year of King Cyrus, the king issued a decree
concerning the temple of God in Jerusalem:

Let the temple be rebuilt as a place to present sacrifices,
and let its foundations be laid. It is to be ninety feet[a] high and
ninety feet wide, 4 with three courses of large stones and one of
timbers. The costs are to be paid by the royal treasury. 5 Also,
the gold and silver articles of the house of God, which Nebuchadnezzar took from the temple in Jerusalem and brought
to Babylon, are to be returned to their places in the temple in
Jerusalem; they are to be deposited in the house of God.

6 Now then, Tattenai, governor of Trans-Euphrates, and
Shethar-Bozenai and you, their fellow officials of that province,
stay away from there. 7 Do not interfere with the work on this
temple of God. Let the governor of the Jews and the Jewish
elders rebuild this house of God on its site.

8 Moreover, I hereby decree what you are to do for these
elders of the Jews in the construction of this house of God:

The expenses of these men are to be fully paid out of
the royal treasury, from the revenues of Trans-Euphrates, so
that the work will not stop. 9 Whatever is needed—young
bulls, rams, male lambs for burnt offerings to the God of
heaven, and wheat, salt, wine and oil, as requested by the
priests in Jerusalem—must be given them daily without fail,
10 so that they may offer sacrifices pleasing to the God of heav-
en and pray for the well-being of the king and his sons.
11 Furthermore, I decree that if anyone changes this edict,
a beam is to be pulled from his house and he is to be lifted up
and impaled on it. And for this crime his house is to be made
a pile of rubble. 12 May God, who has caused his Name to dwell
there, overthrow any king or people who lifts a hand to change
this decree or to destroy this temple in Jerusalem.

I Darius have decreed it. Let it be carried out with diligence.

Completion and Dedication of the Temple

13 Then, because of the decree King Darius had sent, Tattenai, governor of Trans-Euphrates, and Shethar-Bozenai and their
associates carried it out with diligence. 14 So the elders of the Jews

---

[a]3 Aramaic *sixty cubits* (about 27 meters)

6:2 *scroll:* Long rolls made of smaller pieces of papyrus or leather that were glued or sewn together into long strips (Isa 34:4; Jer 36:20-25; Ezek 2:9, 10). See also the mini-article called "Scrolls," p. 1491.

6:2 *Ecbatana:* The Persian kings spent their summers in this city.

6:3 *ninety feet high and ninety feet wide:* See 1 Kings 6:2 for the dimensions of Solomon's temple. It is unclear why Cyrus orders different dimensions for the new temple, especially if it was to be built on the same foundation. See also Hag 2:3.

6:10 *sacrifices pleasing:* Literally, this means "sweet smelling sacrifices." Pagan religions often regarded sacrifices as food for the gods. For the Israelites, the important thing was that the smell of the sacrifices pleased God (Lev 1:1-17; 6:21; Num 15:3-10).

6:14 *decrees of Cyrus, Darius and Artaxerxes, kings of Persia:* Credit for the building of the temple is given both to God and the Persian kings. God works through worldly authorities to carry out his purposes.

6:14 *Artaxerxes:* This possibly refers to Artaxerxes II (405-358 B.C.), who ruled in the next century. Establishing dates and sequence of events has been especially difficult with the books of EZRA and NEHEMIAH (see the Introduction to EZRA).

6:15 *Adar . . . sixth year . . . Darius:* Adar is the twelfth month of the Hebrew calendar, from about mid-February to about mid-March. The "sixth year" would be 515 B.C.

6:17 *each of the tribes of Israel:* A sacrificial goat was offered for each of the original twelve tribes of Israel, even the ten northern tribes that had largely disappeared after most of them were taken into exile by the Assyrians in 722 B.C.

6:18 *priests . . . groups for the service of God:* Although Moses gave the original instructions from the LORD about the duties of the priests (see Exod 29, for example), it was King David who actually first established a schedule for them (1 Chr 24:1-19).

6:19-22 *Passover . . . Feast of Unleavened Bread:* See the mini-article called "Passover and The Feast of Unleavened Bread," p. 2030, and the chart called "Jewish Calendar and Festivals," p. 944.

6:22 *king of Assyria:* This would mean the king of Persia, because Assyria was now taken over by the Persian empire.

7:1 *After these things . . . Artaxerxes:* If Artaxerxes I is the king intended here (see the Introduction to EZRA), this story jumps from the completion of the temple toward the end of the sixth century (516 B.C.) to the middle of the fifth century (458 B.C.). The opposition to the rebuilding of Jerusalem (4:6) occurred during the 57-year gap between the events of chapters 6 and 7.

6:17 2 Chr 7:4-7. **6:19** Exod 12:1-20.

continued to build and prosper under the preaching of Haggai the
prophet and Zechariah, a descendant of Iddo. They finished building the temple according to the command of the God of Israel and
the decrees of Cyrus, Darius and Artaxerxes, kings of Persia. [15]The
temple was completed on the third day of the month Adar, in the
sixth year of the reign of King Darius.

[16]Then the people of Israel—the priests, the Levites and the
rest of the exiles—celebrated the dedication of the house of God
with joy. [17]For the dedication of this house of God they offered a
hundred bulls, two hundred rams, four hundred male lambs and,
as a sin offering for all Israel, twelve male goats, one for each of the
tribes of Israel. [18]And they installed the priests in their divisions
and the Levites in their groups for the service of God at Jerusalem,
according to what is written in the Book of Moses.

The Passover

[19]On the fourteenth day of the first month, the exiles celebrated the Passover. [20]The priests and Levites had purified themselves and were all ceremonially clean. The Levites slaughtered the
Passover lamb for all the exiles, for their brothers the priests and
for themselves. [21]So the Israelites who had returned from the exile
ate it, together with all who had separated themselves from the
unclean practices of their Gentile neighbors in order to seek the
LORD, the God of Israel. [22]For seven days they celebrated with joy
the Feast of Unleavened Bread, because the LORD had filled them
with joy by changing the attitude of the king of Assyria, so that he
assisted them in the work on the house of God, the God of Israel.

Ezra Returns and Restores the People

The last four chapters of EZRA deal with Ezra's own activities. Chapters 7 and 8 introduce Ezra and describe his leading a group out of Babylonia and into Jerusalem. Chapters 9 and 10 record his dealing with the problem of mixed marriages, meaning marriages between Jews and non-Jews.

EZRA AND HIS MISSION

Artaxerxes gives Ezra support and permission to return to Jerusalem along with many Jewish leaders and their families.

Ezra Comes to Jerusalem

7 After these things, during the reign of Artaxerxes king of Persia, Ezra son of Seraiah, the son of Azariah, the son of Hilkiah, [2]the
son of Shallum, the son of Zadok, the son of Ahitub, [3]the son of
Amariah, the son of Azariah, the son of Meraioth, [4]the son of Zerahiah, the son of Uzzi, the son of Bukki, [5]the son of Abishua, the

The Scribe Ezra Rewriting the Sacred Records, an illuminated page from an early eighth century manuscript. Ezra was a priest and an expert in the Law of Moses. King Artaxerxes of Persia allowed him and other Jews who were living in Persia to return to Jerusalem and encouraged them to worship the LORD there again. Ezra spent his whole life studying and obeying the Law of the LORD (7:10). Chapters 8 and 9 of EZRA are sometimes called the "Memoirs of Ezra" because they are written in the first person (using "I" instead of "he" as in the rest of the book).

son of Phinehas, the son of Eleazar, the son of Aaron the chief
priest— 6this Ezra came up from Babylon. He was a teacher well
versed in the Law of Moses, which the LORD, the God of Israel, had
given. The king had granted him everything he asked, for the hand
of the LORD his God was on him. 7Some of the Israelites, including
priests, Levites, singers, gatekeepers and temple servants, also came
up to Jerusalem in the seventh year of King Artaxerxes.

8Ezra arrived in Jerusalem in the fifth month of the seventh
year of the king. 9He had begun his journey from Babylon on the
first day of the first month, and he arrived in Jerusalem on the first
day of the fifth month, for the gracious hand of his God was on

7:1-6 *Ezra:* Ezra had three different jobs. One of his jobs was as a priest. Ezra's long family history proves he is a descendant of priests and so is qualified to be a priest himself. Ezra's ancestors include Aaron, the first high priest of Israel, and Zadok, the man Solomon made high priest instead of Abiathar (1 Kgs 1:28-53; 4:2). Following the exile the high priest had to be a descendant of Zadok.

Ezra also was an expert in the Law. In the Hebrew those words literally mean "ready scribe" or "capable writer." Scribes were experts in reading and writing. Before the exile, they functioned as royal secretaries responsible for letter writing and accounting (2 Kgs 12:10-12). During and after the exile, their duties became copying, studying, and teaching the Scriptures. Eventually they became the official interpreters of the Law.

Lastly, Ezra was in a position of high favor at the court of Artaxerxes (7:11-26), during the time following the Babylonian captivity when Jerusalem was rebuilt. With Artaxerxes' blessing, he led 1,500 Jewish settlers and 258 Levites (8:1-20) back to Jerusalem. After restoring the proper worship of God (Ezra 8:31-35) and ending the marriages between Jewish men and foreign women (Ezra 9:1—10:44), he helped to reestablish Israel's special relationship with God by reading and teaching the Law of Moses to the people (Neh 8:1-18).

7:1-6 *Law of Moses:* This refers to the *Torah* (first five books of the Old Testament). See the Introduction to the Pentatuch p. 35.

7:8,9 *fifth month . . . first month:* Ezra's journey took four months and began in the same month (sometime in March) as the exodus from Egypt under Moses (Exod 12:2).

7:9 *the gracious hand of his God was on him:* Different forms of this phrase appear several times in the next chapters (7:28; 8:18,22,31) and in NEHEMIAH (Neh 2:8,18). These phrases emphasize that God was guiding Ezra's work and giving him a sense of support.

Ezra had devoted himself to the study and observance of the Law of the Lord, and to teaching its decrees and laws in Israel.
Ezra 7:10

7:10 *devoted himself to the study and observance of the Law:* Ezra would become a model for those in later centuries who spent their lives studying and explaining the Law of Moses.

7:11 *letter:* Like the earlier correspondence (4:11-21; 5:6-17; 6:2-12), this letter (7:12-26) is in Aramaic, the language used in the Persian empire for official communications. See the note at 1:1 (proclamation).

7:21 *Trans-Euphrates:* See the note at 4:8-10 (Trans-Euphrates).

7:22 *wheat . . . wine . . . olive oil . . . salt:* Wheat, oil, and salt were needed for the sacrifices to give thanks to the Lord, also called "grain offerings" (Lev 2:1-16; Num 15:1-6). Wine was needed for the drink offerings (Lev 23:13). See also 6:9.

7:23 *Why should there be wrath:* Artaxerxes, like Cyrus and Darius before him, was motivated by more than generosity. He wanted to please the gods of the people he now controlled and keep his subjects happy.

him. [10]For Ezra had devoted himself to the study and observance of the Law of the Lord, and to teaching its decrees and laws in Israel.

King Artaxerxes' Letter to Ezra

[11]This is a copy of the letter King Artaxerxes had given to Ezra the priest and teacher, a man learned in matters concerning the commands and decrees of the Lord for Israel:

[12][a]Artaxerxes, king of kings,

To Ezra the priest, a teacher of the Law of the God of heaven:

Greetings.

[13]Now I decree that any of the Israelites in my kingdom, including priests and Levites, who wish to go to Jerusalem with you, may go. [14]You are sent by the king and his seven advisers to inquire about Judah and Jerusalem with regard to the Law of your God, which is in your hand. [15]Moreover, you are to take with you the silver and gold that the king and his advisers have freely given to the God of Israel, whose dwelling is in Jerusalem, [16]together with all the silver and gold you may obtain from the province of Babylon, as well as the freewill offerings of the people and priests for the temple of their God in Jerusalem. [17]With this money be sure to buy bulls, rams and male lambs, together with their grain offerings and drink offerings, and sacrifice them on the altar of the temple of your God in Jerusalem.

[18]You and your brother Jews may then do whatever seems best with the rest of the silver and gold, in accordance with the will of your God. [19]Deliver to the God of Jerusalem all the articles entrusted to you for worship in the temple of your God. [20]And anything else needed for the temple of your God that you may have occasion to supply, you may provide from the royal treasury.

[21]Now I, King Artaxerxes, order all the treasurers of Trans-Euphrates to provide with diligence whatever Ezra the priest, a teacher of the Law of the God of heaven, may ask of you— [22]up to a hundred talents[b] of silver, a hundred cors[c] of wheat, a hundred baths[d] of wine, a hundred baths[d] of olive oil, and salt without limit. [23]Whatever the God of heaven has prescribed, let it be done with diligence for the temple of the God of heaven. Why should there be wrath against the realm of the king and of his sons? [24]You are also to know that you have no authority to impose taxes, tribute or duty on any of the

[a]**12** The text of Ezra 7:12-26 is in Aramaic. [b]**22** That is, about 3 3/4 tons (about 3.4 metric tons) [c]**22** That is, probably about 600 bushels (about 22 kiloliters) [d]**22** That is, probably about 600 gallons (about 2.2 kiloliters)

priests, Levites, singers, gatekeepers, temple servants or other
workers at this house of God.
[25]And you, Ezra, in accordance with the wisdom of your
God, which you possess, appoint magistrates and judges to
administer justice to all the people of Trans-Euphrates—all
who know the laws of your God. And you are to teach any
who do not know them. [26]Whoever does not obey the law of
your God and the law of the king must surely be punished by
death, banishment, confiscation of property, or imprisonment.

[27]Praise be to the LORD, the God of our fathers, who has put
it into the king's heart to bring honor to the house of the LORD in
Jerusalem in this way [28]and who has extended his good favor to me
before the king and his advisers and all the king's powerful officials. Because the hand of the LORD my God was on me, I took
courage and gathered leading men from Israel to go up with me.

List of the Family Heads Returning With Ezra

8 These are the family heads and those registered with them who
came up with me from Babylon during the reign of King Artaxerxes:
[2]of the descendants of Phinehas, Gershom;
of the descendants of Ithamar, Daniel;
of the descendants of David, Hattush [3]of the descendants
of Shecaniah;

of the descendants of Parosh, Zechariah, and with him were
registered 150 men;
[4]of the descendants of Pahath-Moab, Eliehoenai son of Zerahiah, and with him 200 men;
[5]of the descendants of Zattu,[a] Shecaniah son of Jahaziel, and
with him 300 men;
[6]of the descendants of Adin, Ebed son of Jonathan, and with
him 50 men;
[7]of the descendants of Elam, Jeshaiah son of Athaliah, and
with him 70 men;
[8]of the descendants of Shephatiah, Zebadiah son of Michael,
and with him 80 men;
[9]of the descendants of Joab, Obadiah son of Jehiel, and with
him 218 men;
[10]of the descendants of Bani,[b] Shelomith son of Josiphiah,
and with him 160 men;
[11]of the descendants of Bebai, Zechariah son of Bebai, and with
him 28 men;

[a]**5** Some Septuagint manuscripts (also 1 Esdras 8:32); Hebrew does not have *Zattu.* [b]**10** Some Septuagint manuscripts (also 1 Esdras 8:36); Hebrew does not have *Bani.*

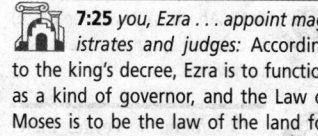

7:25 *you, Ezra . . . appoint magistrates and judges:* According to the king's decree, Ezra is to function as a kind of governor, and the Law of Moses is to be the law of the land for the Jews. The Persian king offered Ezra and the Jewish people remarkable privileges and religious protection.

7:28 *good favor:* The Hebrew word translated here as "favor" refers to the special love God promised his people. This love was based on God's loyalty, commitment, and faithfulness to the covenants that he had made with the people (see Gen 15:1-21; Exod 24:1-7; 2 Sam 7:1-17). As a result, God's people were to respond in the same way. See also the mini-article called "Covenants (Agreements)," p. 386.

7:28 *leading men from Israel:* Civil leaders in the community. See the note at 1:5.

8:1 *came up with me:* Meaning with Ezra. Beginning here and continuing through chapter 9 is a passage that scholars have called the "Memoirs of Ezra." Its beginning is marked by a switch to first person speech ("me").

8:15 *Ahava:* A town (or place) in Babylonia, but the exact location is unknown.

8:15 *I found no Levites there:* This may be because they preferred to stay in Babylonia where they had greater position and importance than they expected to have in Jerusalem and Judah. See note at 1:5. The Levites listed in 2:40-42 are also very few, less than two percent of the total.

8:17 *Casiphia:* The location might be the same as Ctesiphon, on the Tigris River, near Baghdad.

8:20 *David:* See the note at 3:10 (David).

8:21 *I proclaimed:* See the note at 8:1.

8:21 *a fast:* On special occasions the Jewish people went without eating (called fasting) to show that they were sorry for disobeying God or to ask for God's help in a difficult situation.

8:22 *ashamed . . . soldiers:* Ezra does not mean he felt sorry or guilty. Rather, he means he did not want to show a lack of faith in God by asking for human help. However, the mention of the soldiers and cavalry shows that Ezra was aware of the dangerous nature of the journey he was asking the people to take with him.

8:24 *I set apart twelve:* Ezra chose twelve because there were twelve tribes of Israel. See the chart called "Numbers in the Bible," p. 2405.

8:28 *consecrated:* The Hebrew is "are holy to," which means set aside for God's own use. Both the gifts and those in charge of them were set aside for God's own use.

8:31 *first month:* Nisan. See the chart called "Jewish Calendar and Festivals," p. 944.

12 of the descendants of Azgad, Johanan son of Hakkatan, and
with him 110 men;
13 of the descendants of Adonikam, the last ones, whose names
were Eliphelet, Jeuel and Shemaiah, and with them 60 men;
14 of the descendants of Bigvai, Uthai and Zaccur, and with
them 70 men.

The Return to Jerusalem

15 I assembled them at the canal that flows toward Ahava, and
we camped there three days. When I checked among the people and
the priests, I found no Levites there. 16 So I summoned Eliezer, Ariel,
Shemaiah, Elnathan, Jarib, Elnathan, Nathan, Zechariah and Meshullam, who were leaders, and Joiarib and Elnathan, who were men of
learning, 17 and I sent them to Iddo, the leader in Casiphia. I told them
what to say to Iddo and his kinsmen, the temple servants in Casiphia,
so that they might bring attendants to us for the house of our God.
18 Because the gracious hand of our God was on us, they brought us
Sherebiah, a capable man, from the descendants of Mahli son of Levi,
the son of Israel, and Sherebiah's sons and brothers, 18 men; 19 and
Hashabiah, together with Jeshaiah from the descendants of Merari,
and his brothers and nephews, 20 men. 20 They also brought 220 of
the temple servants—a body that David and the officials had established to assist the Levites. All were registered by name.

21 There, by the Ahava Canal, I proclaimed a fast, so that we
might humble ourselves before our God and ask him for a safe
journey for us and our children, with all our possessions. 22 I was
ashamed to ask the king for soldiers and horsemen to protect us
from enemies on the road, because we had told the king, "The gracious hand of our God is on everyone who looks to him, but his
great anger is against all who forsake him." 23 So we fasted and peti-
tioned our God about this, and he answered our prayer.

24 Then I set apart twelve of the leading priests, together with
Sherebiah, Hashabiah and ten of their brothers, 25 and I weighed
out to them the offering of silver and gold and the articles that the
king, his advisers, his officials and all Israel present there had
donated for the house of our God. 26 I weighed out to them 650 talents[a] of silver, silver articles weighing 100 talents,[b] 100 talents[b] of
gold, 27 20 bowls of gold valued at 1,000 darics,[c] and two fine articles of polished bronze, as precious as gold.

28 I said to them, "You as well as these articles are consecrated to the LORD. The silver and gold are a freewill offering to the
LORD, the God of your fathers. 29 Guard them carefully until you
weigh them out in the chambers of the house of the LORD in

[a]26 That is, about 25 tons (about 22 metric tons) [b]26 That is, about 3 3/4 tons (about 3.4 metric tons) [c]27 That is, about 19 pounds (about 8.5 kilograms)

Jerusalem before the leading priests and the Levites and the family heads of Israel." [30]Then the priests and Levites received the silver and gold and sacred articles that had been weighed out to be taken to the house of our God in Jerusalem.

[31]On the twelfth day of the first month we set out from the Ahava Canal to go to Jerusalem. The hand of our God was on us, and he protected us from enemies and bandits along the way. [32]So we arrived in Jerusalem, where we rested three days.

[33]On the fourth day, in the house of our God, we weighed out the silver and gold and the sacred articles into the hands of Meremoth son of Uriah, the priest. Eleazar son of Phinehas was with him, and so were the Levites Jozabad son of Jeshua and Noadiah son of Binnui. [34]Everything was accounted for by number and weight, and the entire weight was recorded at that time.

[35]Then the exiles who had returned from captivity sacrificed burnt offerings to the God of Israel: twelve bulls for all Israel, ninety-six rams, seventy-seven male lambs and, as a sin offering, twelve male goats. All this was a burnt offering to the LORD. [36]They also delivered the king's orders to the royal satraps and to the governors of Trans-Euphrates, who then gave assistance to the people and to the house of God.

EZRA DEALS WITH PROBLEMS IN THE COMMUNITY

God returned the people to the land so that they could worship according to the Law of Moses. But the people too often ignored the Law, for instance by marrying non-Israelites. In these last two chapters, Ezra deals with that and other problems (see Neh 10:28-30; 13:23-30).

Ezra's Prayer About Intermarriage

9 After these things had been done, the leaders came to me and said, "The people of Israel, including the priests and the Levites, have not kept themselves separate from the neighboring peoples with their detestable practices, like those of the Canaanites, Hittites, Perizzites, Jebusites, Ammonites, Moabites, Egyptians and Amorites. [2]They have taken some of their daughters as wives for themselves and their sons, and have mingled the holy race with the peoples around them. And the leaders and officials have led the way in this unfaithfulness."

[3]When I heard this, I tore my tunic and cloak, pulled hair from my head and beard and sat down appalled. [4]Then everyone who trembled at the words of the God of Israel gathered around me because of this unfaithfulness of the exiles. And I sat there appalled until the evening sacrifice.

[5]Then, at the evening sacrifice, I rose from my self-abasement, with my tunic and cloak torn, and fell on my knees with my hands spread out to the LORD my God [6]and prayed:

8:31 *Ahava Canal:* See the note at 8:15 (Ahava).

8:36 *Trans-Euphrates:* See the note at 4:10 (Trans-Euphrates).

9:1 *me:* Ezra. See the note at 8:1.

9:1 *neighboring peoples:* Includes the foreign people the Assyrians had relocated in Samaria, but also other Semitic people who had been living in the region (see the note at 9:1, Canaanites).

9:1 *detestable practices:* Refers to the worship of other gods.

9:1 *Canaanites . . . Amorites:* These eight groups were among the original inhabitants of Canaan before the Israelites conquered the land. They were included on a list of groups the Israelites were forbidden to marry (Deut 7:1-4). The Ammonites, Moabites, and Egyptians were still present in Ezra's time. The Phoenicians, who were linked to the ancient Canaanites by a common religion and culture, continued to live in the north coastal areas of Palestine.

9:2 *mingled the holy race with the peoples around them:* This phrase means that God's special people had mixed with foreigners by marrying them. The sin was not that Jewish men married women of a different race or culture, but that by doing so they married women who did not follow the God of Israel. Such marriages could lead to the adoption of sinful religious practices and the worship of foreign gods.

9:3 *pulled hair from my head and beard:* Ezra's response to the people's sin is typical of how people at that time showed mourning or grief (Num 14:6; Josh 7:6; Job 1:20; Isa 22:12).

9:4,5 *until the evening sacrifice . . . knees . . . hands:* The time here is 3:00 p.m., the customary time for prayer and confession (Exod 29:38-46). Ezra's posture is that of a beggar before God, asking for mercy.

9:6-8 *our sins . . . a remnant:* After beginning his prayer with "I" (9:6), Ezra immediately shifts to "our" and "we" to show that he includes himself as one of the people, although he was innocent. Since the nation as a whole was bound together in the covenant made with God, all the people were threatened by this sin.

"Remnant" refers to the prophecy that a faithful portion of the Israelites would survive God's judgment and continue God's work in the world (see Isa 1:9; 10:20-23; 11:11,12).

9:9 *we are slaves:* The Persians did not treat the Israelites as actual slaves, but because they were subjects of the Persian empire they lacked national independence.

9:11 *detestable practices:* This probably refers to worshiping idols.

10:1 *Ezra:* The "Memoirs of Ezra" that began at 8:1 ends at the conclusion of his prayer (9:15). From 10:1 on, EZRA continues in the third person.

10:5 *leading priests and Levites:* "Leading priests" probably refers to those who were in charge of the temple worship and daily sacrifices. See also the note at 1:5.

10:5 *under oath:* To take an oath was like saying, "If I don't keep my promise, I accept a curse upon myself." To make a person take an oath to do something was a way to be certain that the person kept his or her promise. The first five verses of this chapter emphasize that the most important thing the people can do in their situation is to renew their covenant with God. See also the mini-article called "Making Vows," p. 328.

9:12 Exod 34:11-16; Deut 7:1-5.

"O my God, I am too ashamed and disgraced to lift up
my face to you, my God, because our sins are higher than our
heads and our guilt has reached to the heavens. 7From the
days of our forefathers until now, our guilt has been great.
Because of our sins, we and our kings and our priests have
been subjected to the sword and captivity, to pillage and
humiliation at the hand of foreign kings, as it is today.
8"But now, for a brief moment, the LORD our God has
been gracious in leaving us a remnant and giving us a firm
place in his sanctuary, and so our God gives light to our eyes
and a little relief in our bondage. 9Though we are slaves, our
God has not deserted us in our bondage. He has shown us
kindness in the sight of the kings of Persia: He has granted us
new life to rebuild the house of our God and repair its ruins,
and he has given us a wall of protection in Judah and
Jerusalem.
10"But now, O our God, what can we say after this? For
we have disregarded the commands 11you gave through your
servants the prophets when you said: 'The land you are entering to possess is a land polluted by the corruption of its peoples. By their detestable practices they have filled it with their
impurity from one end to the other. 12Therefore, do not give
your daughters in marriage to their sons or take their daughters for your sons. Do not seek a treaty of friendship with
them at any time, that you may be strong and eat the good
things of the land and leave it to your children as an everlasting inheritance.'
13"What has happened to us is a result of our evil deeds
and our great guilt, and yet, our God, you have punished us
less than our sins have deserved and have given us a remnant
like this. 14Shall we again break your commands and intermarry with the peoples who commit such detestable practices? Would you not be angry enough with us to destroy us,
leaving us no remnant or survivor? 15O LORD, God of Israel,
you are righteous! We are left this day as a remnant. Here we
are before you in our guilt, though because of it not one of us
can stand in your presence."

The People's Confession of Sin

10 While Ezra was praying and confessing, weeping and throwing himself down before the house of God, a large crowd of
Israelites—men, women and children—gathered around him.
They too wept bitterly. 2Then Shecaniah son of Jehiel, one of the
descendants of Elam, said to Ezra, "We have been unfaithful to our
God by marrying foreign women from the peoples around us. But
in spite of this, there is still hope for Israel. 3Now let us make a
covenant before our God to send away all these women and their
children, in accordance with the counsel of my lord and of those

who fear the commands of our God. Let it be done according to
the Law. 4Rise up; this matter is in your hands. We will support
you, so take courage and do it."
5So Ezra rose up and put the leading priests and Levites and
all Israel under oath to do what had been suggested. And they took
the oath. 6Then Ezra withdrew from before the house of God and
went to the room of Jehohanan son of Eliashib. While he was
there, he ate no food and drank no water, because he continued to
mourn over the unfaithfulness of the exiles.
7A proclamation was then issued throughout Judah and
Jerusalem for all the exiles to assemble in Jerusalem. 8Anyone who
failed to appear within three days would forfeit all his property, in
accordance with the decision of the officials and elders, and would
himself be expelled from the assembly of the exiles.

9Within the three days, all the men of Judah and Benjamin
had gathered in Jerusalem. And on the twentieth day of the ninth
month, all the people were sitting in the square before the house of
God, greatly distressed by the occasion and because of the rain.
10Then Ezra the priest stood up and said to them, "You have been
unfaithful; you have married foreign women, adding to Israel's
guilt. 11Now make confession to the LORD, the God of your fathers,
and do his will. Separate yourselves from the peoples around you
and from your foreign wives."
12The whole assembly responded with a loud voice: "You are
right! We must do as you say. 13But there are many people here and
it is the rainy season; so we cannot stand outside. Besides, this
matter cannot be taken care of in a day or two, because we have
sinned greatly in this thing. 14Let our officials act for the whole
assembly. Then let everyone in our towns who has married a foreign woman come at a set time, along with the elders and judges of
each town, until the fierce anger of our God in this matter is
turned away from us." 15Only Jonathan son of Asahel and Jahzeiah
son of Tikvah, supported by Meshullam and Shabbethai the
Levite, opposed this.
16So the exiles did as was proposed. Ezra the priest selected
men who were family heads, one from each family division, and
all of them designated by name. On the first day of the tenth
month they sat down to investigate the cases, 17and by the first day
of the first month they finished dealing with all the men who had
married foreign women.

Those Guilty of Intermarriage

18Among the descendants of the priests, the following had
married foreign women:

From the descendants of Jeshua son of Jozadak, and his
brothers: Maaseiah, Eliezer, Jarib and Gedaliah. 19(They all
gave their hands in pledge to put away their wives, and for

10:6 *ate no food and drank no water:* Here, going without food (fasting) is not a sign of worshiping God, but is a sign of sorrow. David fasted after hearing about the death of Saul and Jonathan (2 Sam 1:12), and Nehemiah fasted upon hearing that Jerusalem remained in ruins (Neh 1:4).

10:9 *Judah and Benjamin:* See the note at 1:5.

10:9 *ninth month:* Chislev, the ninth month of the Hebrew calendar, from about mid-November to mid-December. See the chart called "Jewish Calendar and Festivals," p. 944.

10:9 *the square before the house of God:* Literally, the text says "in a wide place." It was probably the courtyard before the Water Gate (Neh 3:26; 8:1).

10:13 *sinned:* The Hebrew word translated "sinned" means "rebelled" here. The same word is used to describe the revolt of the northern tribes against Rehoboam, Solomon's son (1 Kgs 12:19).

10:14 *officials:* The elders or older men of the various villages usually formed a council that made decisions for governing the community. They were gathered from all the towns to represent God's people as a whole.

10:16 *family heads:* Civil leaders in the community. See the note at 1:5.

10:16,17 *tenth month . . . first month:* Meaning Tebeth and Nisan. See the chart called "Jewish Calendar and Festivals," p. 944.

10:19 *gave their hands in pledge:* To seal an agreement with a handshake was quite common. For another instance, see 2 Kings 10:15.

their guilt they each presented a ram from the flock as a guilt offering.)
20 From the descendants of Immer:
Hanani and Zebadiah.
21 From the descendants of Harim:
Maaseiah, Elijah, Shemaiah, Jehiel and Uzziah.
22 From the descendants of Pashhur:
Elioenai, Maaseiah, Ishmael, Nethanel, Jozabad and Elasah.

23 Among the Levites:

Jozabad, Shimei, Kelaiah (that is, Kelita), Pethahiah, Judah and Eliezer.
24 From the singers:
Eliashib.
From the gatekeepers:
Shallum, Telem and Uri.

25 And among the other Israelites:

From the descendants of Parosh:
Ramiah, Izziah, Malkijah, Mijamin, Eleazar, Malkijah and Benaiah.
26 From the descendants of Elam:
Mattaniah, Zechariah, Jehiel, Abdi, Jeremoth and Elijah.
27 From the descendants of Zattu:
Elioenai, Eliashib, Mattaniah, Jeremoth, Zabad and Aziza.
28 From the descendants of Bebai:
Jehohanan, Hananiah, Zabbai and Athlai.
29 From the descendants of Bani:
Meshullam, Malluch, Adaiah, Jashub, Sheal and Jeremoth.

QUESTIONS ABOUT EZRA

1. Why did Cyrus allow the Jews to return to Jerusalem? (1:1-3)
2. Why were foreigners not allowed to help rebuild the temple? What problems did these people cause for the returning Jews? (4:1-24)
3. What does this book reveal about Ezra and his personality? How does God help Ezra to use the gifts he has been given? What does this tell you about how God can use you?
4. How did Artaxerxes assist Ezra and the Jewish people? (7:11-26) According to Ezra, why did Artaxerxes do these things? (7:27,28)
5. The rebuilding of the temple in Jerusalem was important because it was the center of worship for the Jews and because it symbolized God's special relationship with them. What is at the center of your worship? What special symbol do you have of God's relationship with you?
6. The book of EZRA is about how the Jews tried to start over in their relationship with God. Many forces from both within and outside the community tested the Jews' faith in God and tempted them to abandon God's Law. What things in your life threaten your relationship with God?

[30]From the descendants of Pahath-Moab:
Adna, Kelal, Benaiah, Maaseiah, Mattaniah, Bezalel, Binnui and Manasseh.
[31]From the descendants of Harim:
Eliezer, Ishijah, Malkijah, Shemaiah, Shimeon, [32]Benjamin, Malluch and Shemariah.
[33]From the descendants of Hashum:
Mattenai, Mattattah, Zabad, Eliphelet, Jeremai, Manasseh and Shimei.
[34]From the descendants of Bani:
Maadai, Amram, Uel, [35]Benaiah, Bedeiah, Keluhi, [36]Vaniah,
Meremoth, Eliashib, [37]Mattaniah, Mattenai and Jaasu.
[38]From the descendants of Binnui:[a]
Shimei, [39]Shelemiah, Nathan, Adaiah, [40]Macnadebai, Shashai,
Sharai, [41]Azarel, Shelemiah, Shemariah, [42]Shallum, Amariah and Joseph.
[43]From the descendants of Nebo:
Jeiel, Mattithiah, Zabad, Zebina, Jaddai, Joel and Benaiah.

[44]All these had married foreign women, and some of them had children by these wives.[b]

10:44 *married foreign women:* The extreme action of divorce was taken in order to preserve the purity of the small group of Jewish people who had returned to Judah to rebuild the peoples' cities and renew their commitment to living as God's people. This meant being loyal to the LORD God alone.

[a]**37,38** See Septuagint (also 1 Esdras 9:34); Hebrew *Jaasu* [38]*and Bani and Binnui,* [b]**44** Or *and they sent them away with their children*

NEHEMIAH

Nehemiah faced great opposition to the task God gave him. Yet, with God's help he succeeded. Read his book to find out how.

1:1 *Nehemiah:* Nehemiah, a Jew, was a personal servant of King Artaxerxes of Persia. Later, Nehemiah was appointed governor of Judah, and carried out two missions to Jerusalem. In his first mission, he led a group of Jewish settlers back to Jerusalem, supervised the reconstruction of Jerusalem's walls, and decided which families should live in the city. He did all this, even though the governor of nearby Samaria and his allies opposed his efforts (4:1-9; 6:1-14). The Samaritans opposed the Jews' return, because the Samaritans claimed to be descendants of the Joseph tribes and true observers of the Law of Moses. They did not want Jerusalem and its temple to be rebuilt. In his second mission, Nehemiah was in charge of many social and political reforms among the people, including a return to the proper worship of God (13:4-31).

1:1 *Kislev . . . twentieth year:* Kislev is the ninth month of the Hebrew calendar, from about mid-November to mid-December. The "twentieth year" was 446 B.C.

1:1 *Susa:* This was the capital of Elam Province and the winter home of Persian kings. (see the map on p. 2462).

What makes Nehemiah special?

NEHEMIAH and EZRA were originally one book. These writings are special because we have few other biblical sources for this period of Israelite history. In addition, Nehemiah himself is a wonderful example of leadership and of how to live one's faith in the face of difficulties.

Why was Nehemiah written?

NEHEMIAH was written to continue the history of the Israelites after their return to Jerusalem from Babylonia that began in EZRA. In particular, it provides a written history of the rebuilding of the walls of Jerusalem, lists of those who returned to Jerusalem, and a report of the people's commitment to worship and remain faithful to the God of Israel.

What's the story behind the scene?

Just as EZRA is not complete without NEHEMIAH, NEHEMIAH is not complete without EZRA (see the Introduction to EZRA, page 852). Indeed, Ezra the scribe not only appears in the book of NEHEMIAH, but his reading of the Law to the Jews in Jerusalem (Neh 8, 9) is vital to the story and action of NEHEMIAH. As with the book of EZRA, the author was less concerned with exact historical dates than with simply presenting the Jews' activity following their return to Jerusalem.

Who was this Nehemiah? Nehemiah was a trusted personal servant to King Artaxerxes and had attained high rank in the Persian court. He was also a man of great ability and persuasion. Most importantly, he was a Jew who loved and sought to obey the God of Israel. It is no wonder then that he was very sad when he heard that the walls and gates of the holy city, Jerusalem, were in ruins. With Artaxerxes's support, Nehemiah returns to Jerusalem, and in the face of much opposition, supervises the rebuilding of the city's walls and gates.

How is Nehemiah constructed?

A discussion of the overall structure of EZRA and NEHEMIAH can be found in the Introduction to EZRA, p. 852. NEHEMIAH can be outlined in the following way:

Nehemiah returns and rebuilds the walls (1:1—7:73)
Nehemiah and his mission (1:1—2:10)
Nehemiah supervises the rebuilding (2:11—7:73)

A new community based on old covenants (8:1—10:39)
- Ezra teaches the people (8:1-18)
- The people respond (9:1—10:39)

Nehemiah's work continues (11:1—13:31)
- Jerusalem is repopulated (11:1—12:26)
- Joyful dedication (12:27-47)
- Nehemiah recalls his final reforms (13:1-31)

Nehemiah Returns and Rebuilds the Walls

The first part of N*EHEMIAH (the third section of* E*ZRA*-N*EHEMIAH as a whole) deals with Nehemiah's mission to return to Jerusalem and rebuild its walls. Like the missions of Sheshbazzar (Ezra 1–6) and Ezra (Ezra 7–10), this mission was authorized by the Persian king. Nehemiah's capable leadership, trusting faith, and great courage were tested as he worked to overcome the tricks and schemes of his enemies.*

NEHEMIAH AND HIS MISSION

Nehemiah's Prayer

1 The words of Nehemiah son of Hacaliah:

In the month of Kislev in the twentieth year, while I was in the citadel of Susa, [2]Hanani, one of my brothers, came from Judah with some other men, and I questioned them about the Jewish remnant that survived the exile, and also about Jerusalem.

[3]They said to me, "Those who survived the exile and are back in the province are in great trouble and disgrace. The wall of Jerusalem is broken down, and its gates have been burned with fire."

[4]When I heard these things, I sat down and wept. For some days I mourned and fasted and prayed before the God of heaven. [5]Then I said:

"O LORD, God of heaven, the great and awesome God, who keeps his covenant of love with those who love him and obey his commands, [6]let your ear be attentive and your eyes open to hear the prayer your servant is praying before you day and night for your servants, the people of Israel. I confess the sins we Israelites, including myself and my father's house, have committed against you. [7]We have acted very wickedly toward you. We have not obeyed the commands, decrees and laws you gave your servant Moses.

1:2 *Hanani . . . Jewish remnant:* Hanani was later put in charge of Jerusalem (see 7:2).

"Jewish remnant" refers to both those who had returned from exile in Babylon and those who had not been forced to go to Babylonia and remained in Judah during the exile. See also the mini-article called "Exile," p. 1541.

1:3,4 *wall of Jerusalem . . . mourned and fasted:* Like many cities, Jerusalem had tall, thick walls built around it for protection. The destruction of Jerusalem's walls and gates left the city defenseless. Most likely Nehemiah is referring to the fact that local leaders had convinced the Persian King Artaxerxes (465-424 B.C.) to command the Jews to stop rebuilding the city's walls. (see Ezra 4:7-23).

People often showed deep sadness by sitting down to cry (Ezra 9:3; Job 2:8,13; Ps 137:1) and by going without eating (1 Kgs 21:25-29; Ezra 8:23).

1:5,6 *keeps his covenant . . . confess the sins:* If the people of Israel obeyed God's commands (Deut 5:1-21,28-33; 6:1-9), then God promised to give them their own land, make them a great nation (Gen 12:1-3), and give them blessings (Deut 7:12-15). God's love for Israel is demonstrated throughout the Old Testament even though Israel sinned and rebelled. Like Ezra before him (Ezra 9:6-15), Nehemiah admits that he and his family share in the sins of the people of Israel.

1:7 *Moses:* God gave laws and commandments to Moses on Mount Sinai that explained how the Israelites should live once they entered the land God promised to them (Exod 19–40). See also the mini-article called "Moses," p. 2335.

1:4 Neh 2:4; 4:4,5; 5:19; 6:9,14; 13:14,22,29,31.

8"Remember the instruction you gave your servant Moses, saying, 'If you are unfaithful, I will scatter you among the nations, 9but if you return to me and obey my commands, then even if your exiled people are at the farthest horizon, I will gather them from there and bring them to the place I have chosen as a dwelling for my Name.'

10"They are your servants and your people, whom you redeemed by your great strength and your mighty hand. 11O Lord, let your ear be attentive to the prayer of this your servant and to the prayer of your servants who delight in revering your name. Give your servant success today by granting him favor in the presence of this man."

I was cupbearer to the king.

Artaxerxes Sends Nehemiah to Jerusalem

2 In the month of Nisan in the twentieth year of King Artaxerxes, when wine was brought for him, I took the wine and gave it to the king. I had not been sad in his presence before; 2so the king asked me, "Why does your face look so sad when you are not ill? This can be nothing but sadness of heart."

I was very much afraid, 3but I said to the king, "May the king live forever! Why should my face not look sad when the city where my fathers are buried lies in ruins, and its gates have been destroyed by fire?"

4The king said to me, "What is it you want?"

Then I prayed to the God of heaven, 5and I answered the king, "If it pleases the king and if your servant has found favor in his sight, let him send me to the city in Judah where my fathers are buried so that I can rebuild it."

6Then the king, with the queen sitting beside him, asked me, "How long will your journey take, and when will you get back?" It pleased the king to send me; so I set a time.

7I also said to him, "If it pleases the king, may I have letters to the governors of Trans-Euphrates, so that they will provide me safe-conduct until I arrive in Judah? 8And may I have a letter to Asaph, keeper of the king's forest, so he will give me timber to make beams for the gates of the citadel by the temple and for the city wall and for the residence I will occupy?" And because the gracious hand of my God was upon me, the king granted my requests. 9So I went to the governors of Trans-Euphrates and gave them the king's letters. The king had also sent army officers and cavalry with me.

10When Sanballat the Horonite and Tobiah the Ammonite official heard about this, they were very much disturbed that someone had come to promote the welfare of the Israelites.

1:11 *cupbearer to the king:* As cupbearer of King Artaxerxes (1:11; 2:1), Nehemiah not only served the king his wine, but tasted it first to be sure it was not poisoned. This earned Nehemiah the king's trust.

2:1 *Nisan:* Or Abib, the first month of the Hebrew calendar, from about mid-March to mid-April.

2:1 *Artaxerxes:* This is probably Artaxerxes I, who ruled Persia from 465 to 424 B.C.

2:3 *the city:* Nehemiah doesn't mention Jerusalem by name because of the city's reputation for rebellion (see Ezra 4:12,15).

2:6 *queen:* According to Greek sources, Damaspia was queen.

2:7 *Trans-Euphrates:* The Euphrates River is the longest (1,700 miles) and most important river in western Asia. See the map on p. 2462. Trans-Euphrates was the land from the Euphrates River west to the Mediterranean Sea.

2:8 *king's forest:* This probably refers to the cedar forests of Lebanon (see Ezra 3:7).

2:8 *the king granted my requests:* In doing so, the king reverses his earlier decision to stop the rebuilding of the city (Ezra 4:21).

2:10 *Sanballat . . . Tobiah:* Sanballat was the governor of Samaria, Judah's neighbor to the north. He probably was a native of Beth Horon (see the map on p. 2467).

Tobiah is called "the Ammonite" because he was a leader from Ammon (see the map on p. 2467). Tobiah was probably an Israelite but worked with Sanballat and Geshem to try to stop Nehemiah's attempts to rebuild Jerusalem's walls (2:19,20; 4:1-23; 6:1-19).

Nehemiah Viewing Secretly the Ruins of the Walls of Jerusalem, an engraving by Gustave Doré, around 1866. King Artaxerxes of Persia gave his homesick cupbearer, Nehemiah, permission to return to Jerusalem. After Nehemiah had been in Jerusalem for three days, he went out during the night and traveled around the city to examine the walls and gates. The next day he told the people, "Jerusalem lies in ruins . . . Come, let us rebuild the wall of Jerusalem, and we will no longer be in disgrace" (see 2:11-20).

NEHEMIAH SUPERVISES THE REBUILDING

Nehemiah's work begins with an inspection of the walls. It appears the eastern walls were mostly destroyed and were in need of rebuilding, while the other walls needed various amounts of repair. The opposition to Nehemiah's plans that began in 2:10 continues to grow throughout the story.

Nehemiah Inspects Jerusalem's Walls

11 I went to Jerusalem, and after staying there three days 12 I
set out during the night with a few men. I had not told anyone
what my God had put in my heart to do for Jerusalem. There were
no mounts with me except the one I was riding on.

2:11 *Jerusalem:* Around 1010 B.C., King David captured the walled city of Jerusalem from a Canaanite tribe called the Jebusites. He rebuilt the city and made it the capital of Israel (2 Sam 5:6-9). Jerusalem is sometimes called "the City of David." It is located in southern Palestine just north of where the Kidron and Tyropoeon Valleys come together. David's son, King Solomon, later expanded the city across the Tyropoeon Valley to the west and built the temple in the oldest part (the northern section) of the city. See the map on p. 2466 and the mini-article called "Jerusalem," p. 574.

1:8 Lev 26:33. **1:9** Deut 4:27-31; 30:1-5. **2:3** 2 Kgs 25:8-10; 2 Chr 36:19; Jer 52:12-14.

2:13-15 *Valley Gate . . . Jackal Well . . . Dung Gate . . . Fountain Gate . . . King's Pool:* The Valley Gate was probably the main gate in the western wall. Nehemiah's inspection of the walls probably began at the Valley Gate. From there he moved in a counterclockwise direction around to the southern portion of the walls where the oldest remains of the city were. Then he turned around and retraced his steps.

Jackal's Well was a well that supplied part of the city's water. It was located between the Valley Gate and the Dung Gate in Nehemiah's time. The Dung Gate probably led to the garbage dump in the Valley of Hinnom. The Fountain Gate was on the east, but near the southern end of the city where the city water supply pools were located. The King's Pool was most likely a place where water was collected from the Gihon Spring for use by the city.

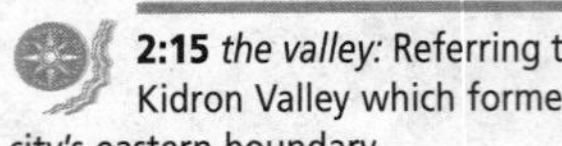

2:15 *the valley:* Referring to the Kidron Valley which formed the city's eastern boundary.

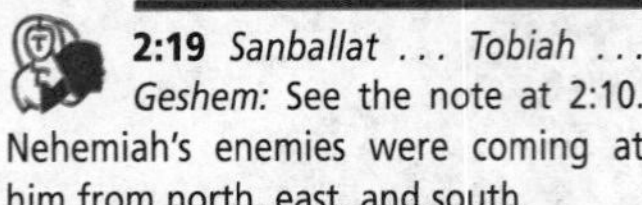

2:19 *Sanballat . . . Tobiah . . . Geshem:* See the note at 2:10. Nehemiah's enemies were coming at him from north, east, and south.

3:1-3 *Sheep Gate . . . Tower . . . Fish Gate:* The Sheep Gate was located in the northeastern part of the wall. John 5:2 locates it beside the pool Bethesda. To this day, this gate is the place where sheep are bought and sold. The name of the Tower of the Hundred may refer to the tower's height or may indicate that it housed a military unit of 100 men. Jeremiah 31:38 and Zechariah 14:10,11 suggest that the Tower of Hananel was the northernmost point in the city. Fish Gate was the site of the city's fish markets and was located near the northwest corner of the city.

3:6,8 *Jeshanah Gate . . . Broad Wall:* The Jeshanah Gate (known later as the Ancient Gate) was located in the western section of the wall. The Broad Wall may have been the western wall built by Hezekiah to enclose the city and its water supply (2 Chr 32:3-5).

13 By night I went out through the Valley Gate toward the
Jackal[a] Well and the Dung Gate, examining the walls of Jerusalem,
which had been broken down, and its gates, which had been
destroyed by fire. 14 Then I moved on toward the Fountain Gate
and the King's Pool, but there was not enough room for my mount
to get through; 15 so I went up the valley by night, examining the
wall. Finally, I turned back and reentered through the Valley Gate.
16 The officials did not know where I had gone or what I was doing,
because as yet I had said nothing to the Jews or the priests or
nobles or officials or any others who would be doing the work.

17 Then I said to them, "You see the trouble we are in:
Jerusalem lies in ruins, and its gates have been burned with fire.
Come, let us rebuild the wall of Jerusalem, and we will no longer
be in disgrace." 18 I also told them about the gracious hand of my
God upon me and what the king had said to me.

They replied, "Let us start rebuilding." So they began this
good work.

19 But when Sanballat the Horonite, Tobiah the Ammonite
official and Geshem the Arab heard about it, they mocked and
ridiculed us. "What is this you are doing?" they asked. "Are you
rebelling against the king?"

20 I answered them by saying, "The God of heaven will give us
success. We his servants will start rebuilding, but as for you, you
have no share in Jerusalem or any claim or historic right to it."

Builders of the Wall

3 Eliashib the high priest and his fellow priests went to work and
rebuilt the Sheep Gate. They dedicated it and set its doors in place,
building as far as the Tower of the Hundred, which they dedicated, and as far as the Tower of Hananel. 2 The men of Jericho built
the adjoining section, and Zaccur son of Imri built next to them.

3 The Fish Gate was rebuilt by the sons of Hassenaah. They
laid its beams and put its doors and bolts and bars in place. 4 Meremoth son of Uriah, the son of Hakkoz, repaired the next section.
Next to him Meshullam son of Berekiah, the son of Meshezabel,
made repairs, and next to him Zadok son of Baana also made
repairs. 5 The next section was repaired by the men of Tekoa, but
their nobles would not put their shoulders to the work under their
supervisors.[b]

6 The Jeshanah[c] Gate was repaired by Joiada son of Paseah
and Meshullam son of Besodeiah. They laid its beams and put its
doors and bolts and bars in place. 7 Next to them, repairs were made
by men from Gibeon and Mizpah—Melatiah of Gibeon and Jadon
of Meronoth—places under the authority of the governor of Trans-

---

[a] **13** Or *Serpent* or *Fig* [b] **5** Or *their Lord* or *the governor* [c] **6** Or *Old*

Euphrates. [8]Uzziel son of Harhaiah, one of the goldsmiths, repaired the next section; and Hananiah, one of the perfume-makers, made repairs next to that. They restored[a] Jerusalem as far as the Broad Wall. [9]Rephaiah son of Hur, ruler of a half-district of Jerusalem, repaired the next section. [10]Adjoining this, Jedaiah son of Harumaph made repairs opposite his house, and Hattush son of Hashabneiah made repairs next to him. [11]Malkijah son of Harim and Hasshub son of Pahath-Moab repaired another section and the Tower of the Ovens. [12]Shallum son of Hallohesh, ruler of a half-district of Jerusalem, repaired the next section with the help of his daughters.

[13]The Valley Gate was repaired by Hanun and the residents of Zanoah. They rebuilt it and put its doors and bolts and bars in place. They also repaired five hundred yards[b] of the wall as far as the Dung Gate.

[14]The Dung Gate was repaired by Malkijah son of Recab, ruler of the district of Beth Hakkerem. He rebuilt it and put its doors and bolts and bars in place.

[15]The Fountain Gate was repaired by Shallun son of Col-Hozeh, ruler of the district of Mizpah. He rebuilt it, roofing it over and putting its doors and bolts and bars in place. He also repaired the wall of the Pool of Siloam,[c] by the King's Garden, as far as the steps going down from the City of David. [16]Beyond him, Nehemiah son of Azbuk, ruler of a half-district of Beth Zur, made repairs up to a point opposite the tombs[d] of David, as far as the artificial pool and the House of the Heroes.

[17]Next to him, the repairs were made by the Levites under Rehum son of Bani. Beside him, Hashabiah, ruler of half the district of Keilah, carried out repairs for his district. [18]Next to him, the repairs were made by their countrymen under Binnui[e] son of Henadad, ruler of the other half-district of Keilah. [19]Next to him, Ezer son of Jeshua, ruler of Mizpah, repaired another section, from a point facing the ascent to the armory as far as the angle. [20]Next to him, Baruch son of Zabbai zealously repaired another section, from the angle to the entrance of the house of Eliashib the high priest. [21]Next to him, Meremoth son of Uriah, the son of Hakkoz, repaired another section, from the entrance of Eliashib's house to the end of it.

[22]The repairs next to him were made by the priests from the surrounding region. [23]Beyond them, Benjamin and Hasshub made repairs in front of their house; and next to them, Azariah son of Maaseiah, the son of Ananiah, made repairs beside his house.

a8 Or *They left out part of* **b13** Hebrew *a thousand cubits* (about 450 meters) **c15** Hebrew *Shelah,* a variant of *Shiloah,* that is, Siloam **d16** Hebrew; Septuagint, some Vulgate manuscripts and Syriac *tomb* **e18** Two Hebrew manuscripts and Syriac (see also Septuagint and verse 24); most Hebrew manuscripts *Bavvai*

3:9 *half-district of Jerusalem:* Judah was divided into six districts: Jerusalem (3:9,12), Beth Hakkerem (3:14), Mizpah (3:15), Beth Zur (3:16), Keilah (3:17, 18), and Jericho. Each had its own local government. At least three (Jerusalem, Beth Zur, and Keilah) were divided into two subdistricts. See the note at 3:13-15.

3:11 *Tower of the Ovens:* Perhaps one of the towers built by Uzziah (2 Chr 26:9). The ovens were used for metal work, making pottery, and baking bread.

3:12 *daughters:* This is the only reference to women helping with the rebuilding of Jerusalem's walls, although others were most likely involved.

3:13-15 *Zanoah . . . Beth Hakkerem . . . Mizpah:* Zanoah was about twenty-five miles southwest of Jerusalem. Beth Hakkerem was a district capital three miles south of Jerusalem.

Several cities are named Mizpah, which means "watch tower." Most likely this was the one located about eight miles north of Jerusalem near the border with Samaria.

3:15 *Pool of Siloam . . . City of David:* This pool was fed from the Gihon brook farther up the Kidron Valley. See the note at 2:11.

3:16,17 *Beth Zur . . . Keilah:* Beth Zur was an important district capital that marked the southern boundary of the province of Judah. Keilah was also a district capital, located about 18 miles southwest of Jerusalem.

3:17,22 *Levites . . . priests:* While both Levites and priests were members of the tribe of Levi, the Levites were not descended from Aaron and so could not serve as priests. The Levites who had been in exile in Babylonia were thought to have worshiped the foreign gods and so were considered unfit to do anything except work as janitors in the temple (Ezek 44:10–14). The priests worked on the parts of the wall near where they and the high priest had lived before the city was destroyed. See the mini-article called "Israel's Priests," p. 2344.

[24]Next to him, Binnui son of Henadad repaired another section,
from Azariah's house to the angle and the corner, [25]and Palal son
of Uzai worked opposite the angle and the tower projecting from
the upper palace near the court of the guard. Next to him, Pedaiah
son of Parosh [26]and the temple servants living on the hill of Ophel
made repairs up to a point opposite the Water Gate toward the east
and the projecting tower. [27]Next to them, the men of Tekoa
repaired another section, from the great projecting tower to the
wall of Ophel.

[28]Above the Horse Gate, the priests made repairs, each in
front of his own house. [29]Next to them, Zadok son of Immer made
repairs opposite his house. Next to him, Shemaiah son of Shecaniah, the guard at the East Gate, made repairs. [30]Next to him, Hananiah son of Shelemiah, and Hanun, the sixth son of Zalaph,
repaired another section. Next to them, Meshullam son of Berekiah made repairs opposite his living quarters. [31]Next to him, Malkijah, one of the goldsmiths, made repairs as far as the house of
the temple servants and the merchants, opposite the Inspection
Gate, and as far as the room above the corner; [32]and between the
room above the corner and the Sheep Gate the goldsmiths and
merchants made repairs.

Opposition to the Rebuilding

4 When Sanballat heard that we were rebuilding the wall, he
became angry and was greatly incensed. He ridiculed the Jews,
[2]and in the presence of his associates and the army of Samaria, he
said, "What are those feeble Jews doing? Will they restore their
wall? Will they offer sacrifices? Will they finish in a day? Can they
bring the stones back to life from those heaps of rubble—burned
as they are?"

[3]Tobiah the Ammonite, who was at his side, said, "What they
are building—if even a fox climbed up on it, he would break down
their wall of stones!"

[4]Hear us, O our God, for we are despised. Turn their insults
back on their own heads. Give them over as plunder in a land of
captivity. [5]Do not cover up their guilt or blot out their sins from
your sight, for they have thrown insults in the face of[a] the
builders.

[6]So we rebuilt the wall till all of it reached half its height, for
the people worked with all their heart.

[7]But when Sanballat, Tobiah, the Arabs, the Ammonites and
the men of Ashdod heard that the repairs to Jerusalem's walls had
gone ahead and that the gaps were being closed, they were very
angry. [8]They all plotted together to come and fight against

[a]5 Or *have provoked you to anger before*

3:26 *Ophel:* The southern part of the hill between the Kidron and Tyropoeon Valleys. Solomon built the temple and the royal palace there.

3:26 *Water Gate:* This gate led into the area of the royal palace from the Kidron Valley on the east. The large area in front of the Water Gate was where Ezra read the Law of Moses to the Jewish people (8:1,2).

3:27 *men of Tekoa:* The town leaders of Tekoa refused to work, but the citizens made up for their leaders' refusal by working on two sections of the wall. See also 3:5.

3:28,29 *Horse Gate . . . East Gate:* Since the Horse Gate was near where the priests lived, it was possibly on the east wall between the temple and the royal palace. The East Gate was most likely a gate in the eastern wall.

3:31 *Inspection Gate:* Near the northern part of the eastern temple area. Probably the place where Solomon's palace and center of government had been. Also, this may have been the designated area where a sin offering should be made (Ezek 43:21).

4:1 *Sanballat:* Nehemiah never uses the title "governor" for Sanballat, though he is identified as the governor of Samaria in other ancient sources.

4:2 *Samaria:* Samaria, meaning "mountain of watching," was the name of a prominent hill, a city, and a region in ancient Israel. Omri, the sixth king of Israel (885-874 B.C.), bought the hill of Samaria as the site for his palace and the new capital of Israel (1 Kgs 16:24).

4:2 *heaps of rubble—burned:* The stones were probably made of limestone. When the city walls were burned, many of the stones were scorched and had already begun to disintegrate.

3:30 Neh 3:8, 13.

Jerusalem and stir up trouble against it. 9But we prayed to our God
and posted a guard day and night to meet this threat.
10Meanwhile, the people in Judah said, "The strength of the
laborers is giving out, and there is so much rubble that we cannot
rebuild the wall."
11Also our enemies said, "Before they know it or see us, we
will be right there among them and will kill them and put an end
to the work."
12Then the Jews who lived near them came and told us ten
times over, "Wherever you turn, they will attack us."
13Therefore I stationed some of the people behind the lowest
points of the wall at the exposed places, posting them by families,
with their swords, spears and bows. 14After I looked things over, I
stood up and said to the nobles, the officials and the rest of the
people, "Don't be afraid of them. Remember the Lord, who is great
and awesome, and fight for your brothers, your sons and your
daughters, your wives and your homes."
15When our enemies heard that we were aware of their plot
and that God had frustrated it, we all returned to the wall, each to
his own work.
16From that day on, half of my men did the work, while the
other half were equipped with spears, shields, bows and armor.
The officers posted themselves behind all the people of Judah
17who were building the wall. Those who carried materials did
their work with one hand and held a weapon in the other, 18and
each of the builders wore his sword at his side as he worked. But
the man who sounded the trumpet stayed with me.
19Then I said to the nobles, the officials and the rest of the
people, "The work is extensive and spread out, and we are widely separated from each other along the wall. 20Wherever you hear
the sound of the trumpet, join us there. Our God will fight
for us!"
21So we continued the work with half the men holding
spears, from the first light of dawn till the stars came out. 22At that
time I also said to the people, "Have every man and his helper stay
inside Jerusalem at night, so they can serve us as guards by night
and workmen by day." 23Neither I nor my brothers nor my men
nor the guards with me took off our clothes; each had his weapon,
even when he went for water.[a]

Nehemiah Helps the Poor

5 Now the men and their wives raised a great outcry against
their Jewish brothers. 2Some were saying, "We and our sons and
daughters are numerous; in order for us to eat and stay alive, we
must get grain."

[a]23 The meaning of the Hebrew for this clause is uncertain.

4:4,5 *Turn their insults . . . Give them over:* Nehemiah's prayer is known as a "curse." The Bible has many examples of such prayers (see, for example, Ps 10; 35; 58; 109; and 137).

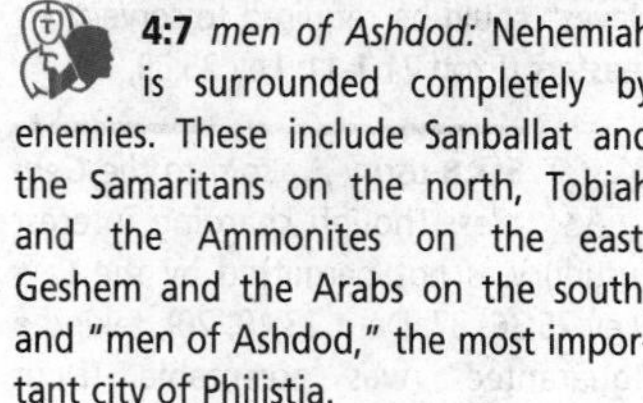

4:7 *men of Ashdod:* Nehemiah is surrounded completely by enemies. These include Sanballat and the Samaritans on the north, Tobiah and the Ammonites on the east, Geshem and the Arabs on the south, and "men of Ashdod," the most important city of Philistia.

4:13-16 *swords, spears:* Swords, the weapons most often mentioned in the Old Testament, referred to daggers and knives as well as long swords. Spears were thrown at the enemy like a javelin (1 Sam 19:9,10) or used to jab at the enemy in close combat (Num 25:7, 8).

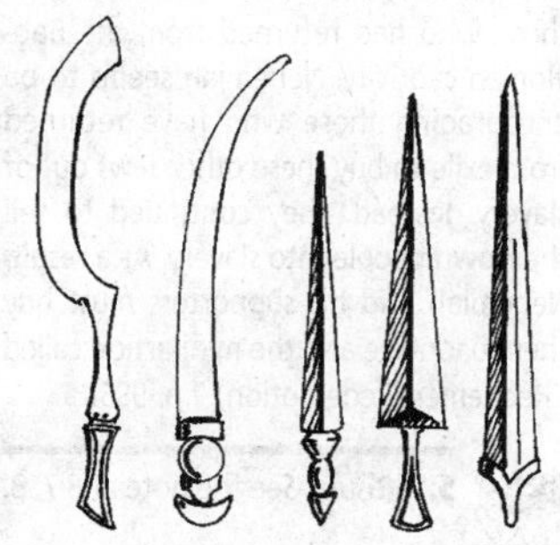

4:18 *sounded the trumpet:* This trumpet was a ram's horn.

5:1 *Jewish brothers:* These made up a privileged minority that was working with the Persian government. The shortage of food and the burden of the heavy Persian taxes had led to hunger for most people (5:2) and debts for the poor (5:3,4). The Jews in power had taken advantage of the situation by loaning money to their fellow Jews at very high rates of interest.

4:20 Exod 14:14; Deut 3:21,22; 20:4; Josh 10:14,42; 23:10.

5:5 *slavery:* Often, when a family could not pay its debts, the children were forced to become slaves until the debt was paid (see 2 Kgs 4:1). Though the Law allowed the practice, it also limited how long these "debt slaves" could be required to serve their masters (Exod 21:1-11; Lev 25:39, 40).

5:7,8 *usury . . . sold to the Gentiles:* Though charging interest (usury) was not permitted by the Law (Lev 25:36, 37; Deut 23:19, 20), taking a "guarantee" was acceptable (Deut 24:10–13). Nehemiah also had lent money in this way (5:10). Nehemiah warns that this practice, while not illegal, is "wrong" (5:9).

The Hebrew for the word translated as "sold to the Gentiles" here can mean more than one thing. It is uncertain whether Nehemiah means those sold into "debt slavery" (see the note at 5:5), or those who had returned from the Babylonian captivity. Nehemiah seems to be encouraging those who have returned from exile to buy these other Jews out of slavery. Instead, they continued to sell their own people into slavery. As a result, Nehemiah and his supporters must buy them back. See also the mini-article called "Redeemer (Redemption)," p. 995.

5:11 *usury:* See the note at 5:7, 8.

5:13 *the people:* This does not refer to the community as a whole, but to those who had been lending money.

5:14 *twentieth year . . . thirty-second year:* In the modern calendar, 445 B.C. and 433 B.C. respectively.

5:14 *Artaxerxes:* See the note at 2:1.

5:14 *ate the food allotted:* As governor, Nehemiah was allowed to require the local people to supply him with food, and to make them pay heavy taxes. But unlike his predecessors (5:15), he did not do so.

5:7 Exod 22:25; Lev 25:35, 37; Deut 23:19, 20.

3 Others were saying, "We are mortgaging our fields, our
vineyards and our homes to get grain during the famine."
4 Still others were saying, "We have had to borrow money to
pay the king's tax on our fields and vineyards. 5 Although we are of
the same flesh and blood as our countrymen and though our sons
are as good as theirs, yet we have to subject our sons and daughters to slavery. Some of our daughters have already been enslaved,
but we are powerless, because our fields and our vineyards belong
to others."

6 When I heard their outcry and these charges, I was very
angry. 7 I pondered them in my mind and then accused the nobles
and officials. I told them, "You are exacting usury from your own
countrymen!" So I called together a large meeting to deal with
them 8 and said: "As far as possible, we have bought back our Jewish brothers who were sold to the Gentiles. Now you are selling
your brothers, only for them to be sold back to us!" They kept
quiet, because they could find nothing to say.

9 So I continued, "What you are doing is not right. Shouldn't
you walk in the fear of our God to avoid the reproach of our Gentile enemies? 10 I and my brothers and my men are also lending the
people money and grain. But let the exacting of usury stop! 11 Give
back to them immediately their fields, vineyards, olive groves and
houses, and also the usury you are charging them—the hundredth
part of the money, grain, new wine and oil."

12 "We will give it back," they said. "And we will not demand
anything more from them. We will do as you say."

Then I summoned the priests and made the nobles and officials take an oath to do what they had promised. 13 I also shook out
the folds of my robe and said, "In this way may God shake out of
his house and possessions every man who does not keep this
promise. So may such a man be shaken out and emptied!"

At this the whole assembly said, "Amen," and praised the
LORD. And the people did as they had promised.

14 Moreover, from the twentieth year of King Artaxerxes,
when I was appointed to be their governor in the land of Judah,
until his thirty-second year—twelve years—neither I nor my
brothers ate the food allotted to the governor. 15 But the earlier governors—those preceding me—placed a heavy burden on the people and took forty shekels[a] of silver from them in addition to food
and wine. Their assistants also lorded it over the people. But out of
reverence for God I did not act like that. 16 Instead, I devoted myself
to the work on this wall. All my men were assembled there for the
work; we[b] did not acquire any land.

17 Furthermore, a hundred and fifty Jews and officials ate at
my table, as well as those who came to us from the surrounding

---

[a] **15** That is, about 1 pound (about 0.5 kilogram) [b] **16** Most Hebrew manuscripts; some Hebrew manuscripts, Septuagint, Vulgate and Syriac *I*

nations. 18 Each day one ox, six choice sheep and some poultry were
prepared for me, and every ten days an abundant supply of wine of
all kinds. In spite of all this, I never demanded the food allotted to
the governor, because the demands were heavy on these people.
19 Remember me with favor, O my God, for all I have done
for these people.

Further Opposition to the Rebuilding

6 When word came to Sanballat, Tobiah, Geshem the Arab and
the rest of our enemies that I had rebuilt the wall and not a gap
was left in it—though up to that time I had not set the doors in
the gates— 2 Sanballat and Geshem sent me this message: "Come,
let us meet together in one of the villages[a] on the plain of Ono."
But they were scheming to harm me; 3 so I sent messengers
to them with this reply: "I am carrying on a great project and cannot go down. Why should the work stop while I leave it and go
down to you?" 4 Four times they sent me the same message, and
each time I gave them the same answer.
5 Then, the fifth time, Sanballat sent his aide to me with the
same message, and in his hand was an unsealed letter 6 in which
was written:

> "It is reported among the nations—and Geshem[b] says it is true—that you and the Jews are plotting to revolt, and therefore you are building the wall. Moreover, according to these reports you are about to become their king 7 and have even appointed prophets to make this proclamation about you in Jerusalem: 'There is a king in Judah!' Now this report will get back to the king; so come, let us confer together."

8 I sent him this reply: "Nothing like what you are saying is
happening; you are just making it up out of your head."
9 They were all trying to frighten us, thinking, "Their hands
will get too weak for the work, and it will not be completed."
⌞But I prayed,⌟ "Now strengthen my hands."
10 One day I went to the house of Shemaiah son of Delaiah,
the son of Mehetabel, who was shut in at his home. He said, "Let
us meet in the house of God, inside the temple, and let us close the
temple doors, because men are coming to kill you—by night they
are coming to kill you."
11 But I said, "Should a man like me run away? Or should one
like me go into the temple to save his life? I will not go!" 12 I realized that God had not sent him, but that he had prophesied
against me because Tobiah and Sanballat had hired him. 13 He had
been hired to intimidate me so that I would commit a sin by doing
this, and then they would give me a bad name to discredit me.

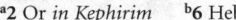

[a]**2** Or *in Kephirim* [b]**6** Hebrew *Gashmu,* a variant of *Geshem*

6:1 *Sanballat, Tobiah, Geshem:* See the notes at 2:10 and 2:19.

6:2 *plain of Ono:* This broad valley was on the coastal plain a few miles southeast of the city of Joppa. See the map on p. 2467.

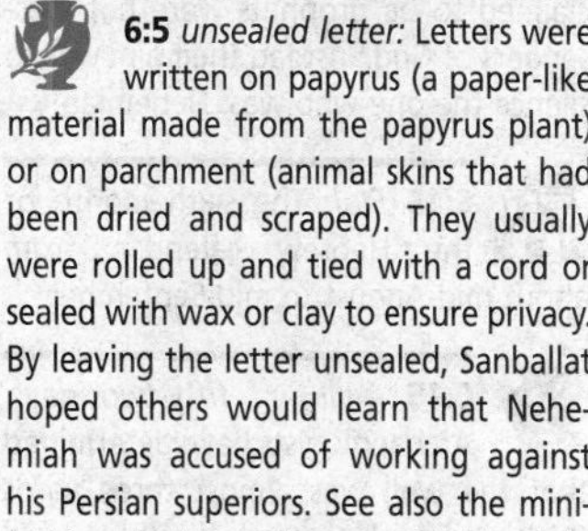

6:5 *unsealed letter:* Letters were written on papyrus (a paper-like material made from the papyrus plant) or on parchment (animal skins that had been dried and scraped). They usually were rolled up and tied with a cord or sealed with wax or clay to ensure privacy. By leaving the letter unsealed, Sanballat hoped others would learn that Nehemiah was accused of working against his Persian superiors. See also the mini-article called "Scrolls," p. 1491.

6:10 *inside the temple:* There were two curtains in the temple: one at the entrance to the Holy Place, and the other at the entrance to the Most Holy Place. Only priests were allowed to enter the Holy Place (Lev 9:1-22; Heb 9:6, 7), and only the high priest could go into the Most Holy Place. See the illustration of the temple, p. 942.

6:13 *commit a sin:* Since Nehemiah was not a priest, it would have been wrong for him to enter the temple (see the note at 6:10).

14 Remember Tobiah and Sanballat, O my God, because of what they have done; remember also the prophetess Noadiah and the rest of the prophets who have been trying to intimidate me.

The Completion of the Wall

15 So the wall was completed on the twenty-fifth of Elul, in fifty-two days. 16 When all our enemies heard about this, all the surrounding nations were afraid and lost their self-confidence, because they realized that this work had been done with the help of our God.

17 Also, in those days the nobles of Judah were sending many letters to Tobiah, and replies from Tobiah kept coming to them. 18 For many in Judah were under oath to him, since he was son-in-law to Shecaniah son of Arah, and his son Jehohanan had married the daughter of Meshullam son of Berekiah. 19 Moreover, they kept reporting to me his good deeds and then telling him what I said. And Tobiah sent letters to intimidate me.

7 After the wall had been rebuilt and I had set the doors in place, the gatekeepers and the singers and the Levites were appointed. 2 I put in charge of Jerusalem my brother Hanani, along with[a] Hananiah the commander of the citadel, because he was a man of integrity and feared God more than most men do. 3 I said to them, "The gates of Jerusalem are not to be opened until the sun is hot. While the gatekeepers are still on duty, have them shut the doors and bar them. Also appoint residents of Jerusalem as guards, some at their posts and some near their own houses."

The List of the Exiles Who Returned

4 Now the city was large and spacious, but there were few people in it, and the houses had not yet been rebuilt. 5 So my God put it into my heart to assemble the nobles, the officials and the common people for registration by families. I found the genealogical record of those who had been the first to return. This is what I found written there:

> 6 These are the people of the province who came up from the captivity of the exiles whom Nebuchadnezzar king of Babylon had taken captive (they returned to Jerusalem and Judah, each to his own town, 7 in company with Zerubbabel, Jeshua, Nehemiah, Azariah, Raamiah, Nahamani, Mordecai, Bilshan, Mispereth, Bigvai, Nehum and Baanah):
>
> The list of the men of Israel:

8 the descendants of Parosh	2,172
9 of Shephatiah	372
10 of Arah	652

[a]2 Or *Hanani, that is,*

6:14 *Remember Tobiah and Sanballat . . . prophetess Noadiah . . . intimidate me:* Rather than getting his own revenge, Nehemiah left vengeance to God and did not strike back at those who had tried to hurt him (see Deut 32:35; Rom 12:19; and the note at 4:4,5). Noadiah and others who claimed to be prophets were not messengers of God. Instead their aim was to silence the one who was: Nehemiah.

6:15 *Elul:* The sixth month of the Hebrew calendar, from about mid-August to mid-September.

6:15 *wall . . . . fifty-two days:* Archaeologists have determined that the wall was almost three yards thick and had a rough finish outside that shows it was built in a hurry. Fifty-two days is a very short time for so big a project.

6:18 *Shecaniah . . . Berekiah:* These Jews had helped rebuild the Jerusalem wall (see 3:4,29,30).

6:19 *Tobiah:* See the note at 2:10.

7:1 *gatekeepers:* The gatekeepers usually patrolled the entrance to the temple. Nehemiah stationed them at the city gates because of the danger.

7:3 *not to be opened . . . near their own houses:* These were safety measures. Usually, the gates were opened at sunrise. Keeping them shut until later in the day would make certain that everyone was awake. Having people guard the portions of the wall that were near their own homes encouraged them to do their jobs well.

7:4-73 *genealogical record of those who had been the first to return:* This list is like the one in Ezra 2, though there are many differences, partly in the names but especially in the numbers, which seem to be rounded off in Ezra. Here, the list is used to make sure that those who live within the city are of Jewish descent.

11 of Pahath-Moab (through the line of Jeshua and Joab)	2,818
12 of Elam	1,254
13 of Zattu	845
14 of Zaccai	760
15 of Binnui	648
16 of Bebai	628
17 of Azgad	2,322
18 of Adonikam	667
19 of Bigvai	2,067
20 of Adin	655
21 of Ater (through Hezekiah)	98
22 of Hashum	328
23 of Bezai	324
24 of Hariph	112
25 of Gibeon	95
26 the men of Bethlehem and Netophah	188
27 of Anathoth	128
28 of Beth Azmaveth	42
29 of Kiriath Jearim, Kephirah and Beeroth	743
30 of Ramah and Geba	621
31 of Micmash	122
32 of Bethel and Ai	123
33 of the other Nebo	52
34 of the other Elam	1,254
35 of Harim	320
36 of Jericho	345
37 of Lod, Hadid and Ono	721
38 of Senaah	3,930
39 The priests:	
the descendants of Jedaiah (through the family of Jeshua)	973
40 of Immer	1,052
41 of Pashhur	1,247
42 of Harim	1,017
43 The Levites:	
the descendants of Jeshua (through Kadmiel through the line of Hodaviah)	74
44 The singers:	
the descendants of Asaph	148
45 The gatekeepers:	
the descendants of Shallum, Ater, Talmon, Akkub, Hatita and Shobai	138

7:5 *first to return:* This was most likely 538 B.C., right after Cyrus, the ruler of Persia, had captured the city of Babylon. After this victory, Cyrus arranged for people who had been brought there by the Babylonians to return to their own lands.

7:6 *Nebuchadnezzar:* Known as Nebuchadnezzar II, he ruled Babylonia from 605 to 562 B.C. In 586 B.C., he destroyed Jerusalem and took many of its people to Babylonia. See also the mini-article called "Nebuchadnezzar," p. 1469.

7:7 *Nehemiah:* This may be another Nehemiah (see Ezra 2:2-20).

7:39-45 *priests . . . Levites:* See the note at 3:17, 22.

7:57-59 *servants of Solomon:* Refers to those descended from Israel's King Solomon, the king who built the first temple in Jerusalem about 500 years earlier. See also the mini-article called "Solomon," p. 776.

7:65 Exod 28:30; Deut 33:8.

46 The temple servants:

the descendants of
Ziha, Hasupha, Tabbaoth,
47 Keros, Sia, Padon,
48 Lebana, Hagaba, Shalmai,
49 Hanan, Giddel, Gahar,
50 Reaiah, Rezin, Nekoda,
51 Gazzam, Uzza, Paseah,
52 Besai, Meunim, Nephussim,
53 Bakbuk, Hakupha, Harhur,
54 Bazluth, Mehida, Harsha,
55 Barkos, Sisera, Temah,
56 Neziah and Hatipha

57 The descendants of the servants of Solomon:

the descendants of
Sotai, Sophereth, Perida,
58 Jaala, Darkon, Giddel,
59 Shephatiah, Hattil,
Pokereth-Hazzebaim and Amon

60 The temple servants and the descendants
of the servants of Solomon 392

61 The following came up from the towns of Tel Melah, Tel
Harsha, Kerub, Addon and Immer, but they could not show
that their families were descended from Israel:

62 the descendants of
Delaiah, Tobiah and Nekoda 642

63 And from among the priests:

the descendants of
Hobaiah, Hakkoz and Barzillai (a man who had married a daughter of Barzillai the Gileadite and was called by that name).

64 These searched for their family records, but they could
not find them and so were excluded from the priesthood as
unclean. 65 The governor, therefore, ordered them not to eat
any of the most sacred food until there should be a priest
ministering with the Urim and Thummim.

66 The whole company numbered 42,360, 67 besides their
7,337 menservants and maidservants; and they also had 245
men and women singers. 68 There were 736 horses, 245
mules,[a] 69 435 camels and 6,720 donkeys.

---

[a] **68** Some Hebrew manuscripts (see also Ezra 2:66); most Hebrew manuscripts do not have this verse.

[70]Some of the heads of the families contributed to the work. The governor gave to the treasury 1,000 drachmas[a] of gold, 50 bowls and 530 garments for priests. [71]Some of the heads of the families gave to the treasury for the work 20,000 drachmas[b] of gold and 2,200 minas[c] of silver. [72]The total given by the rest of the people was 20,000 drachmas of gold, 2,000 minas[d] of silver and 67 garments for priests.

[73]The priests, the Levites, the gatekeepers, the singers and the temple servants, along with certain of the people and the rest of the Israelites, settled in their own towns.

A New Community Based on Old Covenants

In this section, the new community of God's people is being formed. Following Ezra's public reading of the Law (8:1-18), the community confesses its sin (9:1-37) and agrees to live according to the Law of Moses (9:38—10:39). After Jerusalem's population is restored (11:1—12:26), the walls are dedicated with a joyous celebration (12:27-47). Finally, Nehemiah begins several further reforms designed to maintain the community's faithfulness (13:1-31).

EZRA TEACHES THE PEOPLE

Ezra Reads the Law

When the seventh month came and the Israelites had settled
8 in their towns, [1]all the people assembled as one man in the square before the Water Gate. They told Ezra the scribe to bring out the Book of the Law of Moses, which the LORD had commanded for Israel.

[2]So on the first day of the seventh month Ezra the priest brought the Law before the assembly, which was made up of men and women and all who were able to understand. [3]He read it aloud from daybreak till noon as he faced the square before the Water Gate in the presence of the men, women and others who could understand. And all the people listened attentively to the Book of the Law.

[4]Ezra the scribe stood on a high wooden platform built for the occasion. Beside him on his right stood Mattithiah, Shema, Anaiah, Uriah, Hilkiah and Maaseiah; and on his left were Pedaiah, Mishael, Malkijah, Hashum, Hashbaddanah, Zechariah and Meshullam.

[a]**70** That is, about 19 pounds (about 8.5 kilograms) [b]**71** That is, about 375 pounds (about 170 kilograms); also in verse 72 [c]**71** That is, about 1 1/3 tons (about 1.2 metric tons) [d]**72** That is, about 1 1/4 tons (about 1.1 metric tons)

7:73 *seventh month:* Tishri (also called Ethanim), the seventh month of the Hebrew calendar, from about mid-September to mid-October. See Ezra 3:1. See also the chart called "Jewish Calendar and Festivals," p. 944.

8:1,2 *the square . . . Water Gate . . . Law of Moses:* The open area was a square outside the temple area that was large enough so everyone could be present, even those who would have been banned from the temple. See the note at 3:26 (Water Gate).

For more about the Law of Moses, see the mini-article called "Law," p. 1160, and the "Introduction to the Pentateuch," p. 35.

8:4 *Mattithiah . . . Meshullam:* These are probably not priests, but important leaders in the community who helped the people understand the Law of Moses.

7:73 1 Chr 9:2; Neh 11:3.

8:5 *opened the book:* The "book" here is not like a modern bound book. In Ezra's day, people wrote on long strips of papyrus or parchment that were then rolled up and tied with a string. Such a document was called a scroll. See also the note at 6:5.

8:5 *stood up:* As a sign of respect for this holy book.

8:6-9 *Amen! . . . making it clear . . . mourn or weep:* The Hebrew word translated "Amen" means "it is firm, established" (Deut 27:14-26) or "Yes, it is true" (Rev 5:14). It was spoken to confirm a statement or an oath. The Law was written in Hebrew. At this time, however, the people no longer understood this language. For this reason, the Levites may have been translating (making clear) what Ezra read in Hebrew into Aramaic. The people were crying because they realized they had not kept the teachings of the Law.

8:10 *choice food:* Literally, "the fat pieces." In a sacrifice the fat pieces were considered the best parts.

8:12 *send portions of food:* Because they now understood about loving one's neighbor (Lev 19:18), the people began to share their food with those less fortunate (Deut 14:28, 29).

8:13 *heads of all the families:* The family heads were political leaders of the two major tribes of Judah, Judah and Benjamin.

8:15 *wild olive trees . . . myrtles, palms:* Olive trees symbolize beauty (Hos 14:6), blessing (Deut 7:13), and peace (Gen 8:11).

Myrtle bushes have a sweet smell. Their leaves are dark and glossy, and their pink or white flowers are used to make perfumes. They, too, were a symbol of peace (Zech 1:7-11).

A kind of palm tree that is common in Israel is the date palm, a tree that can live up to two hundred years and can grow as tall as seventy feet high.

Interior of a Succoth Shelter, from southern Germany, painted wood, around 1836. The Feast of Tabernacles, which commemorates the forty years the Israelites wandered in the desert before entering the land God promised them, is still celebrated by Jews today. Although this nineteenth century Succoth shelter is nicely decorated and made of more permanent materials, the branches that hang from the ceiling give a sense of what these temporary shelters would have been like in earlier times. The reading of the Law and commandments continues to be an important part of this autumn festival. (See 8:17, 18.)

5 Ezra opened the book. All the people could see him because
he was standing above them; and as he opened it, the people all
stood up. 6 Ezra praised the LORD, the great God; and all the people
lifted their hands and responded, "Amen! Amen!" Then they bowed
down and worshiped the LORD with their faces to the ground.
7 The Levites—Jeshua, Bani, Sherebiah, Jamin, Akkub, Shabbethai, Hodiah, Maaseiah, Kelita, Azariah, Jozabad, Hanan and
Pelaiah—instructed the people in the Law while the people were
standing there. 8 They read from the Book of the Law of God, making it clear[a] and giving the meaning so that the people could
understand what was being read.
9 Then Nehemiah the governor, Ezra the priest and scribe,
and the Levites who were instructing the people said to them all,
"This day is sacred to the LORD your God. Do not mourn or weep."
For all the people had been weeping as they listened to the words
of the Law.

[a]**8** Or *God, translating it*

10 Nehemiah said, "Go and enjoy choice food and sweet
drinks, and send some to those who have nothing prepared. This
day is sacred to our Lord. Do not grieve, for the joy of the LORD is
your strength."
11 The Levites calmed all the people, saying, "Be still, for this
is a sacred day. Do not grieve."
12 Then all the people went away to eat and drink, to send
portions of food and to celebrate with great joy, because they now
understood the words that had been made known to them.
13 On the second day of the month, the heads of all the families,
along with the priests and the Levites, gathered around Ezra the
scribe to give attention to the words of the Law. 14 They found written in the Law, which the LORD had commanded through Moses, that
the Israelites were to live in booths during the feast of the seventh
month 15 and that they should proclaim this word and spread it
throughout their towns and in Jerusalem: "Go out into the hill country and bring back branches from olive and wild olive trees, and from
myrtles, palms and shade trees, to make booths"—as it is written.[a]
16 So the people went out and brought back branches and
built themselves booths on their own roofs, in their courtyards, in
the courts of the house of God and in the square by the Water
Gate and the one by the Gate of Ephraim. 17 The whole company
that had returned from exile built booths and lived in them. From
the days of Joshua son of Nun until that day, the Israelites had not
celebrated it like this. And their joy was very great.
18 Day after day, from the first day to the last, Ezra read from
the Book of the Law of God. They celebrated the feast for seven
days, and on the eighth day, in accordance with the regulation,
there was an assembly.

THE PEOPLE RESPOND

After hearing the Law read aloud, the people respond with worship, prayer, and confession. The beautiful prayer in 9:5-37 is a summary of God's dealings with Israel. These dealings include creation (verse 6), the promise to Abraham (verses 7, 8), the exodus from Egypt (verses 9-11), their experiences in the desert and Mount Sinai (verses 12-21), the conquest of Canaan (verses 22-25), provision of judges to deliver them (verses 26-28), the time of the prophets (verses 29-31), and their present situation (verses 32-37).

The Israelites Confess Their Sins

9 On the twenty-fourth day of the same month, the Israelites
gathered together, fasting and wearing sackcloth and having dust
on their heads. 2 Those of Israelite descent had separated themselves
from all foreigners. They stood in their places and confessed their

[a]15 See Lev. 23:37-40.

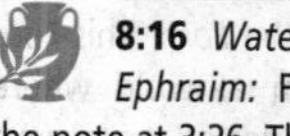

8:16 *Water Gate . . . Gate of Ephraim:* For Water Gate, see the note at 3:26. The Ephraim Gate also was known as the Jeshanah Gate (see the note at 3:6,8).

8:17 *built booths and lived in them . . . celebrated:* They celebrated the Feast of Tabernacles, a yearly festival celebrated by the Jewish people beginning on the fifteenth day of the seventh month (Tishri) and lasting eight days. Participants would construct huts or shelters of myrtle, olive, and palm branches as symbols of God's protection. The people then lived in these shelters for seven days to remember the wandering of their ancestors in the desert and God's care of them at that time. The festival included holy gatherings on the first and eighth days and animal sacrifices. See Lev 23:33-43 and Num 29:12-38. See also 2 Chr 8:13; 30:1-4; 35:18, 19; Ezra 3:4.

9:1 *twenty-fourth day . . . fasting and wearing sackcloth:* The Feast of Tabernacles ended on the twenty-second day of the month, so there was only one day between the joyous celebration of festival and this serious and sorrowful time of confession.

On special occasions the Jewish people went without eating (fasting) to show that they were sorry for disobeying God. Sackcloth was a rough, coarse cloth that often was worn in times of trouble or sorrow. People who wore sackcloth also showed how sorry they were by throwing dirt or ashes on their heads. See the illustration on p. 1551.

9:2 *foreigners:* Non-Israelites who were not permitted to take part.

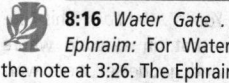

8:14,15 Lev 23:33-36, 39-43; Deut 16:13-15. **8:18** Deut 31:12,13.

9:6 *You . . . the LORD:* This confirms that, in a world where many gods and goddesses were worshiped, Israel trusted in only the one true God (Deut 5:6,7; 6:4).

9:7 *Abram:* Also known as Abraham. He was the son of Terah (Gen 11:26-28) and the ancestor of the Israelites and other related peoples of the Middle East, including the Ismaelites (Gen 25:12-18) and the Edomites (Gen 36).

God told Abram, his wife Sarah, and his nephew Lot to leave their home in Ur and go to Canaan (Gen 11:31). There, God made a covenant with Abram that he would become the ancestor of many nations (Gen 17:4,5). See the mini-article called "Abraham," p. 2254.

9:8 *promise:* God's promise to Abraham as given in Genesis 15:18-21. See the mini-article called "Covenants (Agreements)," p. 386.

9:9 *Red Sea:* The Hebrew text reads *yam suph*, "Sea of Reeds." It is one of the marshes and fresh water lakes near the eastern part of the Nile River delta. This identification is based on Exodus 13:17—14:9, which lists the towns on the route of the Israelites before crossing the sea. In the Septuagint, a Greek translation of the Scriptures that was made about 200 B.C., the "Sea of Reeds" was called "Red Sea." See the map on p. 2464.

9:9 Exod 3:7; 14:10-12. **9:10** Exod 7:8—12:32. **9:11** Exod 14:21-29; 15:4, 5. **9:12** Exod 13:21,22. **9:13,14** Exod 19:18—23:33. **9:15** Exod 16:4-15; 17:1-7; Num 20:7-13; Deut 1:20, 21. **9:16,17a** Num 14:1-4; Deut 1:26-33. **9:17b** Exod 34:6; Num 14:18.

sins and the wickedness of their fathers. 3 They stood where they
were and read from the Book of the Law of the LORD their God for
a quarter of the day, and spent another quarter in confession and in
worshiping the LORD their God. 4 Standing on the stairs were the
Levites—Jeshua, Bani, Kadmiel, Shebaniah, Bunni, Sherebiah, Bani
and Kenani—who called with loud voices to the LORD their God.
5 And the Levites—Jeshua, Kadmiel, Bani, Hashabneiah, Sherebiah,
Hodiah, Shebaniah and Pethahiah—said: "Stand up and praise the
LORD your God, who is from everlasting to everlasting.[a]"

"Blessed be your glorious name, and may it be exalted
above all blessing and praise. 6 You alone are the LORD. You made
the heavens, even the highest heavens, and all their starry host,
the earth and all that is on it, the seas and all that is in them. You
give life to everything, and the multitudes of heaven worship you.
7 "You are the LORD God, who chose Abram and brought
him out of Ur of the Chaldeans and named him Abraham.
8 You found his heart faithful to you, and you made a covenant
with him to give to his descendants the land of the Canaanites, Hittites, Amorites, Perizzites, Jebusites and Girgashites.
You have kept your promise because you are righteous.
9 "You saw the suffering of our forefathers in Egypt; you
heard their cry at the Red Sea.[b] 10 You sent miraculous signs
and wonders against Pharaoh, against all his officials and all
the people of his land, for you knew how arrogantly the Egyptians treated them. You made a name for yourself, which
remains to this day. 11 You divided the sea before them, so that
they passed through it on dry ground, but you hurled their
pursuers into the depths, like a stone into mighty waters. 12 By
day you led them with a pillar of cloud, and by night with a
pillar of fire to give them light on the way they were to take.
13 "You came down on Mount Sinai; you spoke to them
from heaven. You gave them regulations and laws that are just
and right, and decrees and commands that are good. 14 You
made known to them your holy Sabbath and gave them commands, decrees and laws through your servant Moses. 15 In
their hunger you gave them bread from heaven and in their
thirst you brought them water from the rock; you told them
to go in and take possession of the land you had sworn with
uplifted hand to give them.
16 "But they, our forefathers, became arrogant and stiff-
necked, and did not obey your commands. 17 They refused to
listen and failed to remember the miracles you performed
among them. They became stiff-necked and in their rebellion
appointed a leader in order to return to their slavery. But you
are a forgiving God, gracious and compassionate, slow to

[a] 5 Or *God for ever and ever* [b] 9 Hebrew *Yam Suph*; that is, Sea of Reeds

anger and abounding in love. Therefore you did not desert
them, [18]even when they cast for themselves an image of a calf
and said, 'This is your god, who brought you up out of Egypt,'
or when they committed awful blasphemies.
[19]"Because of your great compassion you did not abandon
them in the desert. By day the pillar of cloud did not cease to
guide them on their path, nor the pillar of fire by night to shine
on the way they were to take. [20]You gave your good Spirit to
instruct them. You did not withhold your manna from their
mouths, and you gave them water for their thirst. [21]For forty
years you sustained them in the desert; they lacked nothing,
their clothes did not wear out nor did their feet become swollen.
[22]"You gave them kingdoms and nations, allotting to
them even the remotest frontiers. They took over the country
of Sihon[a] king of Heshbon and the country of Og king of
Bashan. [23]You made their sons as numerous as the stars in the
sky, and you brought them into the land that you told their
fathers to enter and possess. [24]Their sons went in and took
possession of the land. You subdued before them the Canaanites, who lived in the land; you handed the Canaanites over to
them, along with their kings and the peoples of the land, to
deal with them as they pleased. [25]They captured fortified cities
and fertile land; they took possession of houses filled with all
kinds of good things, wells already dug, vineyards, olive groves
and fruit trees in abundance. They ate to the full and were
well-nourished; they reveled in your great goodness.
[26]"But they were disobedient and rebelled against you;
they put your law behind their backs. They killed your
prophets, who had admonished them in order to turn them
back to you; they committed awful blasphemies. [27]So you
handed them over to their enemies, who oppressed them. But
when they were oppressed they cried out to you. From heaven
you heard them, and in your great compassion you gave them
deliverers, who rescued them from the hand of their enemies.
[28]"But as soon as they were at rest, they again did what
was evil in your sight. Then you abandoned them to the hand
of their enemies so that they ruled over them. And when they
cried out to you again, you heard from heaven, and in your
compassion you delivered them time after time.
[29]"You warned them to return to your law, but they
became arrogant and disobeyed your commands. They sinned
against your ordinances, by which a man will live if he obeys
them. Stubbornly they turned their backs on you, became
stiff-necked and refused to listen. [30]For many years you were
patient with them. By your Spirit you admonished them

---

[a]22 One Hebrew manuscript and Septuagint; most Hebrew manuscripts *Sihon, that is, the country of the*

The Levites prayed, *"You are a forgiving God, gracious and compassionate, slow to anger and abounding in love."* Neh 9:17

9:14 *Sabbath:* This Jewish day of rest began at sunset on Friday when a ram's horn (shofar) was blown. It ended with a blessing at sunset on Saturday. The Sabbath was the seventh day of the week, the day that God rested after the work of creation (Gen 2:2,3). Observing the Sabbath, which means "rest" or "stop working," was required of all Jewish people (Exod 20:8-11; Deut 5:12-15). It was based on the need for everyone to have a regular time of rest. In the period following the exile, keeping the Sabbath became a major symbol of faithfulness to the Law of Moses. See also the chart called "Jewish Calendar and Festivals," p. 944.

9:20 *manna:* When the people of Israel were wandering through the desert, the LORD gave them a special kind of food to eat called "manna." In Hebrew this means, "What is it?" (Exod 16:1-36; Num 11:7-9).

9:25 *wells:* These may have been wells that led to underground sources of fresh water or cisterns, pits dug into the rock to collect and hold rainwater. See the note at 2 Chr 26:10.

9:18 Exod 32:1-4; Deut 5:7, 8; 9:15-17. **9:19-21** Deut 8:2-4. **9:22** Num 21:21-35. **9:23** Gen 15:5; 22:17; Josh 3:14-17. **9:24** Josh 11:23; 21:43. **9:25** Deut 3:8-17; 6:10, 11. **9:26-28** Judg 2:11-16; 1 Kgs 14:7-9; 2 Chr 36:15, 16. **9:29** Lev 18:5. **9:30** 2 Kgs 17:13-18; 2 Chr 36:15-20.

> The Levites prayed, *"O our God, the great, mighty and awesome God, who keeps his covenant of love . . ."*
> Neh 9:32

9:32 *from the days of the kings of Assyria until today:* The Assyrians defeated the northern kingdom (Israel) in 722 B.C. and took most of the people into exile in Assyria. "Until today" means the time of Nehemiah. See the mini-article called "Assyria," p. 711.

9:33 *you have been just:* The people viewed the victory of the Assyrians and the Babylonians as a punishment from God. Here, they are admitting that they deserved this punishment.

10:9,14 *Levites . . . leaders:* See the note at 3:17,22. For "leaders," see the note at 8:13.

9:32 2 Kgs 15:19,29; 17:3-6; Ezra 4:2,8-10.

through your prophets. Yet they paid no attention, so you
handed them over to the neighboring peoples. 31 But in your
great mercy you did not put an end to them or abandon
them, for you are a gracious and merciful God.

32 "Now therefore, O our God, the great, mighty and
awesome God, who keeps his covenant of love, do not let all
this hardship seem trifling in your eyes—the hardship that
has come upon us, upon our kings and leaders, upon our
priests and prophets, upon our fathers and all your people,
from the days of the kings of Assyria until today. 33 In all that
has happened to us, you have been just; you have acted faithfully, while we did wrong. 34 Our kings, our leaders, our priests
and our fathers did not follow your law; they did not pay
attention to your commands or the warnings you gave them.
35 Even while they were in their kingdom, enjoying your great
goodness to them in the spacious and fertile land you gave
them, they did not serve you or turn from their evil ways.

36 "But see, we are slaves today, slaves in the land you gave
our forefathers so they could eat its fruit and the other good
things it produces. 37 Because of our sins, its abundant harvest
goes to the kings you have placed over us. They rule over our
bodies and our cattle as they please. We are in great distress.

The Agreement of the People

38 "In view of all this, we are making a binding agreement,
putting it in writing, and our leaders, our Levites and our priests
are affixing their seals to it."

10 Those who sealed it were:

Nehemiah the governor, the son of Hacaliah.

Zedekiah, 2 Seraiah, Azariah, Jeremiah,
3 Pashhur, Amariah, Malkijah,
4 Hattush, Shebaniah, Malluch,
5 Harim, Meremoth, Obadiah,
6 Daniel, Ginnethon, Baruch,
7 Meshullam, Abijah, Mijamin,
8 Maaziah, Bilgai and Shemaiah.
These were the priests.

9 The Levites:

Jeshua son of Azaniah, Binnui of the sons of Henadad, Kadmiel,
10 and their associates: Shebaniah,
Hodiah, Kelita, Pelaiah, Hanan,
11 Mica, Rehob, Hashabiah,
12 Zaccur, Sherebiah, Shebaniah,
13 Hodiah, Bani and Beninu.

14 The leaders of the people:

Parosh, Pahath-Moab, Elam, Zattu, Bani,
15 Bunni, Azgad, Bebai,
16 Adonijah, Bigvai, Adin,
17 Ater, Hezekiah, Azzur,
18 Hodiah, Hashum, Bezai,
19 Hariph, Anathoth, Nebai,
20 Magpiash, Meshullam, Hezir,
21 Meshezabel, Zadok, Jaddua,
22 Pelatiah, Hanan, Anaiah,
23 Hoshea, Hananiah, Hasshub,
24 Hallohesh, Pilha, Shobek,
25 Rehum, Hashabnah, Maaseiah,
26 Ahiah, Hanan, Anan,
27 Malluch, Harim and Baanah.

28 "The rest of the people—priests, Levites, gatekeepers,
singers, temple servants and all who separated themselves
from the neighboring peoples for the sake of the Law of God,
together with their wives and all their sons and daughters who
are able to understand— 29 all these now join their brothers
the nobles, and bind themselves with a curse and an oath to
follow the Law of God given through Moses the servant of
God and to obey carefully all the commands, regulations and
decrees of the LORD our Lord.

30 "We promise not to give our daughters in marriage to
the peoples around us or take their daughters for our sons.

31 "When the neighboring peoples bring merchandise or
grain to sell on the Sabbath, we will not buy from them on the
Sabbath or on any holy day. Every seventh year we will forgo
working the land and will cancel all debts.

32 "We assume the responsibility for carrying out the
commands to give a third of a shekel[a] each year for the service
of the house of our God: 33 for the bread set out on the table;
for the regular grain offerings and burnt offerings; for the
offerings on the Sabbaths, New Moon festivals and appointed
feasts; for the holy offerings; for sin offerings to make atonement for Israel; and for all the duties of the house of our God.

34 "We—the priests, the Levites and the people—have
cast lots to determine when each of our families is to bring to
the house of our God at set times each year a contribution of
wood to burn on the altar of the LORD our God, as it is written in the Law.

35 "We also assume responsibility for bringing to the
house of the LORD each year the firstfruits of our crops and of
every fruit tree.

[a]**32** That is, about 1/8 ounce (about 4 grams)

10:29 *follow the Law of God:* The people are willing to receive God's curse if they should fail to keep their promises to God. To swear their faithfulness to God in this way was a way of showing that they took their promises seriously. See also the mini-article called "Making Vows," p. 328.

10:31-33 *Sabbath:* See the note at 9:14.

10:34 *cast lots:* See the note at 11:1.

10:35-37 *firstfruits . . . firstborn . . . tithes:* The first crops harvested (the "firstfruits") were brought to the temple. They were used to provide for the needs of the priests and the Levites (Num 18:12, 13). This offering acknowledged that the crops were God's gift and showed thankfulness for them. See also 12:44; Exod 23:19; 34:26; Deut 26:2.

The dedication of firstborn sons recalled how God killed the firstborn sons of the Egyptians when they refused to release the Israelites from slavery. See Exod 13:2, 12-15; 34:19,20; and Num 18:15,16.

The custom of giving God ten percent of one's possessions recognized that God was the ruler of the land and showed that the people were grateful for God's blessings. This ten percent (a tithe) was used to support the Levites (Num 18:21-32). See also 13:10-14.

10:30 Exod 34:16; Deut 7:3,4; Neh 13:23-27. **10:31** Exod 20:8-11; 23:10,11; Lev 25:1-7; Deut 15:1,2; Neh 13:15-22; Amos 8:5. **10:32** Exod 30:11-16.

10:38 *storerooms of the treasury:* This was where the sacred objects used for worship in the temple were kept (10:39), but it was also where the Levites kept the gifts the people had given to God (see note at 10:35-37).

11:1 *cast lots:* Lots were made of wood or stone and were thrown on the ground by a priest or official to find out how and when to do something. Though similar to flipping a coin today, the outcome was not considered to be due to luck or simple chance, since the people believed that God guided which lot was chosen.

10:38 Num 18:26. **10:39** Neh 13:11. **11:3-6** Neh 7:73.

36"As it is also written in the Law, we will bring the first-born of our sons and of our cattle, of our herds and of our flocks to the house of our God, to the priests ministering there.

37"Moreover, we will bring to the storerooms of the house of our God, to the priests, the first of our ground meal, of our grain offerings, of the fruit of all our trees and of our new wine and oil. And we will bring a tithe of our crops to the Levites, for it is the Levites who collect the tithes in all the towns where we work. 38A priest descended from Aaron is to accompany the Levites when they receive the tithes, and the Levites are to bring a tenth of the tithes up to the house of our God, to the storerooms of the treasury. 39The people of Israel, including the Levites, are to bring their contributions of grain, new wine and oil to the storerooms where the articles for the sanctuary are kept and where the ministering priests, the gatekeepers and the singers stay.

"We will not neglect the house of our God."

Nehemiah's Work Continues

These final chapters show again that Nehemiah is a dedicated, energetic, and faithful leader who does not let either success or difficulty keep him from continuing his mission.

JERUSALEM IS REPOPULATED

Chapter 11 continues the thought of 7:73. After returning from Babylonia, evidently the great majority of people preferred to live in the surrounding countryside rather than in Jerusalem. Nehemiah has the people cast lots to decide which families should live in the city. The list in 12:1-26 is made up of a series of religious servants from a variety of periods: Priests and Levites from Zerubbabel's time (520 B.C., verses 1-9), the high priests from 538 to 323 B.C. (verses 10,11), and priests and Levites from the time of Joiakim (about 520-445 B.C., verses 12-21, 24-26).

The New Residents of Jerusalem

11 Now the leaders of the people settled in Jerusalem, and the rest of the people cast lots to bring one out of every ten to live in Jerusalem, the holy city, while the remaining nine were to stay in their own towns. 2The people commended all the men who volunteered to live in Jerusalem.

3These are the provincial leaders who settled in Jerusalem (now some Israelites, priests, Levites, temple servants and descendants of Solomon's servants lived in the towns of Judah, each on his own property in the various towns, 4while other people from both Judah and Benjamin lived in Jerusalem):

From the descendants of Judah:

Athaiah son of Uzziah, the son of Zechariah, the son of Amariah, the son of Shephatiah, the son of Mahalalel, a descendant of Perez; 5 and Maaseiah son of Baruch, the son of Col-Hozeh, the son of Hazaiah, the son of Adaiah, the son of Joiarib, the son of Zechariah, a descendant of Shelah. 6 The descendants of Perez who lived in Jerusalem totaled 468 able men.

7 From the descendants of Benjamin:

Sallu son of Meshullam, the son of Joed, the son of Pedaiah, the son of Kolaiah, the son of Maaseiah, the son of Ithiel, the son of Jeshaiah, 8 and his followers, Gabbai and Sallai—928 men. 9 Joel son of Zicri was their chief officer, and Judah son of Hassenuah was over the Second District of the city.

10 From the priests:

Jedaiah; the son of Joiarib; Jakin; 11 Seraiah son of Hilkiah, the son of Meshullam, the son of Zadok, the son of Meraioth, the son of Ahitub, supervisor in the house of God, 12 and their associates, who carried on work for the temple—822 men; Adaiah son of Jeroham, the son of Pelaliah, the son of Amzi, the son of Zechariah, the son of Pashhur, the son of Malkijah, 13 and his associates, who were heads of families—242 men; Amashsai son of Azarel, the son of Ahzai, the son of Meshillemoth, the son of Immer, 14 and his[a] associates, who were able men—128. Their chief officer was Zabdiel son of Haggedolim.

15 From the Levites:

Shemaiah son of Hasshub, the son of Azrikam, the son of Hashabiah, the son of Bunni; 16 Shabbethai and Jozabad, two of the heads of the Levites, who had charge of the outside work of the house of God; 17 Mattaniah son of Mica, the son of Zabdi, the son of Asaph, the director who led in thanksgiving and prayer; Bakbukiah, second among his associates; and Abda son of Shammua, the son of Galal, the son of Jeduthun. 18 The Levites in the holy city totaled 284.

19 The gatekeepers:

Akkub, Talmon and their associates, who kept watch at the gates—172 men.

20 The rest of the Israelites, with the priests and Levites, were in all the towns of Judah, each on his ancestral property.

21 The temple servants lived on the hill of Ophel, and Ziha and Gishpa were in charge of them.

a14 Most Septuagint manuscripts; Hebrew *their*

11:10,15 *priests . . . Levites:* See the note at 3:17, 22.

11:18,21 *holy city . . . hill of Ophel:* The temple mount in Jerusalem was known as the holy hill, mountain, or city after the exile (Ps 2:6; 43:3; Isa 11:9; 27:13; 52:1; Dan 9:24). All of Ezra's and Nehemiah's work had been directed toward establishing Jerusalem as a city set apart for God. See also the note at 2:11. For "Ophel," see the note at 3:26 (Ophel).

11:19 *gatekeepers:* See the note at 7:1.

11:23 *under the king's orders:* A reminder that the Jews were not politically free, but were ruled by the Persians, who had allowed them to return from exile in Babylonia.

12:1 *Ezra:* This is not the Ezra who read the Law (8:1-5), but rather a priest who returned to Jerusalem with Zerubbabel. He is called Azariah in Nehemiah 10:2-8.

12:7 *Jeshua:* Also called Joshua, who was the high priest and a friend of Zerubbabel (see 12:1 and Hag 1:1; 2:1,2).

22 The chief officer of the Levites in Jerusalem was Uzzi son
of Bani, the son of Hashabiah, the son of Mattaniah, the son of
Mica. Uzzi was one of Asaph's descendants, who were the singers
responsible for the service of the house of God. 23 The singers were
under the king's orders, which regulated their daily activity.
24 Pethahiah son of Meshezabel, one of the descendants of
Zerah son of Judah, was the king's agent in all affairs relating to
the people.
25 As for the villages with their fields, some of the people of
Judah lived in Kiriath Arba and its surrounding settlements, in
Dibon and its settlements, in Jekabzeel and its villages, 26 in Jeshua, in
Moladah, in Beth Pelet, 27 in Hazar Shual, in Beersheba and its settlements, 28 in Ziklag, in Meconah and its settlements, 29 in En Rimmon, in Zorah, in Jarmuth, 30 Zanoah, Adullam and their villages, in
Lachish and its fields, and in Azekah and its settlements. So they
were living all the way from Beersheba to the Valley of Hinnom.
31 The descendants of the Benjamites from Geba lived in
Micmash, Aija, Bethel and its settlements, 32 in Anathoth, Nob and
Ananiah, 33 in Hazor, Ramah and Gittaim, 34 in Hadid, Zeboim and
Neballat, 35 in Lod and Ono, and in the Valley of the Craftsmen.
36 Some of the divisions of the Levites of Judah settled in
Benjamin.

Priests and Levites

12 These were the priests and Levites who returned with Zerubbabel son of Shealtiel and with Jeshua:

Seraiah, Jeremiah, Ezra,
2 Amariah, Malluch, Hattush,
3 Shecaniah, Rehum, Meremoth,
4 Iddo, Ginnethon,[a] Abijah,
5 Mijamin,[b] Moadiah, Bilgah,
6 Shemaiah, Joiarib, Jedaiah,
7 Sallu, Amok, Hilkiah and Jedaiah.

These were the leaders of the priests and their associates in the
days of Jeshua.
8 The Levites were Jeshua, Binnui, Kadmiel, Sherebiah, Judah,
and also Mattaniah, who, together with his associates, was in
charge of the songs of thanksgiving. 9 Bakbukiah and Unni, their
associates, stood opposite them in the services.
10 Jeshua was the father of Joiakim, Joiakim the father of
Eliashib, Eliashib the father of Joiada, 11 Joiada the father of
Jonathan, and Jonathan the father of Jaddua.
12 In the days of Joiakim, these were the heads of the priestly
families:

---

[a] **4** Many Hebrew manuscripts and Vulgate (see also Neh. 12:16); most Hebrew manuscripts *Ginnethoi* [b] **5** A variant of *Miniamin*

of Seraiah's family, Meraiah;
of Jeremiah's, Hananiah;
13 of Ezra's, Meshullam;
of Amariah's, Jehohanan;
14 of Malluch's, Jonathan;
of Shecaniah's,[a] Joseph;
15 of Harim's, Adna;
of Meremoth's,[b] Helkai;
16 of Iddo's, Zechariah;
of Ginnethon's, Meshullam;
17 of Abijah's, Zicri;
of Miniamin's and of Moadiah's, Piltai;
18 of Bilgah's, Shammua;
of Shemaiah's, Jehonathan;
19 of Joiarib's, Mattenai;
of Jedaiah's, Uzzi;
20 of Sallu's, Kallai;
of Amok's, Eber;
21 of Hilkiah's, Hashabiah;
of Jedaiah's, Nethanel.

22 The family heads of the Levites in the days of Eliashib,
Joiada, Johanan and Jaddua, as well as those of the priests, were
recorded in the reign of Darius the Persian. 23 The family heads
among the descendants of Levi up to the time of Johanan son of
Eliashib were recorded in the book of the annals. 24 And the leaders of the Levites were Hashabiah, Sherebiah, Jeshua son of Kadmiel, and their associates, who stood opposite them to give praise
and thanksgiving, one section responding to the other, as prescribed by David the man of God.

25 Mattaniah, Bakbukiah, Obadiah, Meshullam, Talmon and
Akkub were gatekeepers who guarded the storerooms at the gates.
26 They served in the days of Joiakim son of Jeshua, the son of
Jozadak, and in the days of Nehemiah the governor and of Ezra
the priest and scribe.

JOYFUL DEDICATION

Dedication of the Wall of Jerusalem

27 At the dedication of the wall of Jerusalem, the Levites were
sought out from where they lived and were brought to Jerusalem
to celebrate joyfully the dedication with songs of thanksgiving and
with the music of cymbals, harps and lyres. 28 The singers also were
brought together from the region around Jerusalem—from the

[a]14 Very many Hebrew manuscripts, some Septuagint manuscripts and Syriac (see also Neh. 12:3); most Hebrew manuscripts *Shebaniah's* [b]15 Some Septuagint manuscripts (see also Neh. 12:3); Hebrew *Meraioth's*

At the dedication of the wall of Jerusalem, the Levites were sought out from where they lived and were brought to Jerusalem to celebrate joyfully.
Neh 12:27

12:23 *the time of Johanan:* Probably between 408 and 405 B.C., when Darius II died.

12:27 *At the dedication of the wall:* It is not clear how long after the completion of the walls that this joyful dedication took place.

12:27 *cymbals, harps and lyres:* Cymbals were bronze or brass musical instruments often used at festivals. Some were plates raised in the center and held by straps. Others were cone-shaped with handles. Striking the cymbals together produced a clanging sound. The harp, the most frequently mentioned musical instrument in the Bible, was much smaller than our modern version and had fewer strings. It could be carried easily and held in one's lap. The other stringed instruments were similar to zithers. See also the illustration on p. 1190.

villages of the Netophathites, 29from Beth Gilgal, and from the area
of Geba and Azmaveth, for the singers had built villages for themselves around Jerusalem. 30When the priests and Levites had purified themselves ceremonially, they purified the people, the gates
and the wall.

31I had the leaders of Judah go up on top[a] of the wall. I also
assigned two large choirs to give thanks. One was to proceed on
top[b] of the wall to the right, toward the Dung Gate. 32Hoshaiah
and half the leaders of Judah followed them, 33along with Azariah,
Ezra, Meshullam, 34Judah, Benjamin, Shemaiah, Jeremiah, 35as well
as some priests with trumpets, and also Zechariah son of
Jonathan, the son of Shemaiah, the son of Mattaniah, the son of
Micaiah, the son of Zaccur, the son of Asaph, 36and his associates—Shemaiah, Azarel, Milalai, Gilalai, Maai, Nethanel, Judah
and Hanani—with musical instruments ⌞prescribed by⌟ David the
man of God. Ezra the scribe led the procession. 37At the Fountain
Gate they continued directly up the steps of the City of David on
the ascent to the wall and passed above the house of David to the
Water Gate on the east.

38The second choir proceeded in the opposite direction. I
followed them on top[c] of the wall, together with half the people—
past the Tower of the Ovens to the Broad Wall, 39over the Gate of
Ephraim, the Jeshanah[d] Gate, the Fish Gate, the Tower of Hananel
and the Tower of the Hundred, as far as the Sheep Gate. At the
Gate of the Guard they stopped.

40The two choirs that gave thanks then took their places in
the house of God; so did I, together with half the officials, 41as well
as the priests—Eliakim, Maaseiah, Miniamin, Micaiah, Elioenai,
Zechariah and Hananiah with their trumpets— 42and also Maaseiah, Shemaiah, Eleazar, Uzzi, Jehohanan, Malkijah, Elam and
Ezer. The choirs sang under the direction of Jezrahiah. 43And on
that day they offered great sacrifices, rejoicing because God had
given them great joy. The women and children also rejoiced. The
sound of rejoicing in Jerusalem could be heard far away.

44At that time men were appointed to be in charge of the
storerooms for the contributions, firstfruits and tithes. From the
fields around the towns they were to bring into the storerooms
the portions required by the Law for the priests and the Levites,
for Judah was pleased with the ministering priests and Levites.
45They performed the service of their God and the service of
purification, as did also the singers and gatekeepers, according to
the commands of David and his son Solomon. 46For long ago, in
the days of David and Asaph, there had been directors for the
singers and for the songs of praise and thanksgiving to God. 47So
in the days of Zerubbabel and of Nehemiah, all Israel contributed

[a]31 Or *go alongside* [b]31 Or *proceed alongside* [c]38 Or *them alongside*
[d]39 Or *Old*

And on that day they offered great sacrifices, rejoicing because God had given them great joy. The women and children also rejoiced. The sound of rejoicing in Jerusalem could be heard far away.
Neh 12:43

12:30 *purified themselves ceremonially:* These would have included going without food (fasting), making sacrifices, bathing and then wearing freshly washed clothes, giving up sexual intercourse for a period of time, and sprinkling the gates and walls with the blood of sacrificed animals.

12:31 *on top of the wall:* The wall that Tobiah said would not support a fox (4:3) now supports the joyful procession of two groups. One group marched counterclockwise on the southern and eastern wall. A second group marched clockwise. The two groups joined at the Gate of the Guard (12:39).

12:36 *Ezra:* The mention of Ezra in this verse may suggest that Nehemiah and Ezra were at work in the same period of time, but some scholars believe it is more likely that Ezra came several years later and finished the work Nehemiah had begun.

12:37-39 *Fountain Gate . . . Gate of the Guard:* See the notes at 2:13-15; 3:15; and 3:26 (Water Gate); 3:11; 3:6, 8; 3:1, 3. The Gate of the Guard is otherwise unknown, but may be the same as the Inspection Gate of 3:31.

12:45 *commands . . . Solomon:* Reported as given by David in 1 Chr 23–26 and carried out by Solomon in 2 Chr 8:14. See 1 Chr 25:1-8; 26:12.

12:43 Ezra 3:3-5; 6:17.

the daily portions for the singers and gatekeepers. They also set
aside the portion for the other Levites, and the Levites set aside the
portion for the descendants of Aaron.

NEHEMIAH RECALLS HIS FINAL REFORMS

The story of Nehemiah closes with a series of problems that Nehemiah faces in his second term of office.

Nehemiah's Final Reforms

13 On that day the Book of Moses was read aloud in the hearing of the people and there it was found written that no Ammonite
or Moabite should ever be admitted into the assembly of God,
2because they had not met the Israelites with food and water but
had hired Balaam to call a curse down on them. (Our God, however, turned the curse into a blessing.) 3When the people heard this
law, they excluded from Israel all who were of foreign descent.
4Before this, Eliashib the priest had been put in charge of the
storerooms of the house of our God. He was closely associated
with Tobiah, 5and he had provided him with a large room formerly used to store the grain offerings and incense and temple articles,
and also the tithes of grain, new wine and oil prescribed for the
Levites, singers and gatekeepers, as well as the contributions for the
priests.
6But while all this was going on, I was not in Jerusalem, for
in the thirty-second year of Artaxerxes king of Babylon I had
returned to the king. Some time later I asked his permission 7and
came back to Jerusalem. Here I learned about the evil thing
Eliashib had done in providing Tobiah a room in the courts of the
house of God. 8I was greatly displeased and threw all Tobiah's
household goods out of the room. 9I gave orders to purify the
rooms, and then I put back into them the equipment of the house
of God, with the grain offerings and the incense.
10I also learned that the portions assigned to the Levites had
not been given to them, and that all the Levites and singers
responsible for the service had gone back to their own fields. 11So
I rebuked the officials and asked them, "Why is the house of God
neglected?" Then I called them together and stationed them at
their posts.
12All Judah brought the tithes of grain, new wine and oil into
the storerooms. 13I put Shelemiah the priest, Zadok the scribe, and
a Levite named Pedaiah in charge of the storerooms and made
Hanan son of Zaccur, the son of Mattaniah, their assistant, because
these men were considered trustworthy. They were made responsible for distributing the supplies to their brothers.
14Remember me for this, O my God, and do not blot
out what I have so faithfully done for the house of my God and its
services.

13:1 *Ammonite . . . Moabite:* The Ammonites and Moabites were descendants of Lot, Abraham's nephew, and were frequent enemies of Israel (Num 22:2-11; 2 Sam 8:2,11,12; 12:26-31; 2 Kgs 3:4-27; 13:20; 1 Chr 20:1-3). Both nations were located east of Israel. See Deut 23:3 and the map on p. 2464.

13:2 *Balaam . . . curse:* See Num 22:1-6. King Balak of Moab hired Balaam to bring curses on the people of Israel. God, however, did not allow Balaam to deliver the curses (Num 22:12; 23:11; 24:10).

13:4 *Eliashib . . . Tobiah:* This is probably not Eliashib the high priest who was named in 3:1,2,20,21; 12:10,22; 13:28.

Tobiah was an Ammonite. Because it was against the temple laws for Ammonites to live in the temple (Deut 23:3; Neh 13:1), special cleaning was required (13:9). See the note at 2:9, 10.

13:6 *thirty-second year:* Therefore, Nehemiah's term as governor lasted twelve years, from 445 to 433 B.C. See also 1:1.

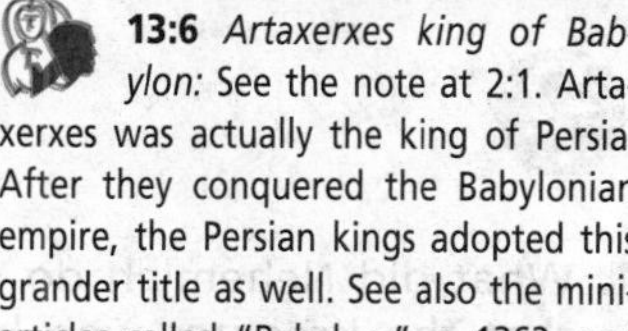

13:6 *Artaxerxes king of Babylon:* See the note at 2:1. Artaxerxes was actually the king of Persia. After they conquered the Babylonian empire, the Persian kings adopted this grander title as well. See also the mini-articles called "Babylon," p. 1363, and "Persia," p. 859.

13:11 *Why . . . neglected:* The people had not kept the promise they made in 10:39.

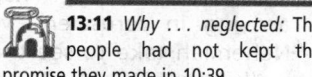

13:1,2 Deut 23:3-5 **13:10** Deut 12:4-19. **13:12** Mal 3:10.

13:15 *Sabbath:* Again, the people had not kept their promises (10:31, 37). See the note at 9:14.

13:19 *When evening shadows fell . . . Sabbath:* In the Jewish calendar, days begin at sunset, not at midnight or at sunrise as in other cultures.

13:15 Exod 20:8-10; Deut 5:12-14; Jer 17:21-24.

15 In those days I saw men in Judah treading winepresses on
the Sabbath and bringing in grain and loading it on donkeys,
together with wine, grapes, figs and all other kinds of loads. And
they were bringing all this into Jerusalem on the Sabbath. Therefore I warned them against selling food on that day. 16 Men from
Tyre who lived in Jerusalem were bringing in fish and all kinds of
merchandise and selling them in Jerusalem on the Sabbath to the
people of Judah. 17 I rebuked the nobles of Judah and said to them,
"What is this wicked thing you are doing—desecrating the Sabbath day? 18 Didn't your forefathers do the same things, so that our
God brought all this calamity upon us and upon this city? Now
you are stirring up more wrath against Israel by desecrating the
Sabbath."

19 When evening shadows fell on the gates of Jerusalem
before the Sabbath, I ordered the doors to be shut and not opened
until the Sabbath was over. I stationed some of my own men at the
gates so that no load could be brought in on the Sabbath day.
20 Once or twice the merchants and sellers of all kinds of goods
spent the night outside Jerusalem. 21 But I warned them and said,
"Why do you spend the night by the wall? If you do this again, I
will lay hands on you." From that time on they no longer came on
the Sabbath. 22 Then I commanded the Levites to purify themselves
and go and guard the gates in order to keep the Sabbath day holy.

Remember me for this also, O my God, and show mercy to
me according to your great love.

QUESTIONS ABOUT NEHEMIAH

1. What did Nehemiah do when he heard that the Israelites who had returned to Jerusalem had not begun to fix the walls and gates of the city? (1:3, 4; 2:4, 5) After arriving in Jerusalem, what steps did Nehemiah take to see that work on the walls began? (2:11-18) How did he handle the trouble nearby enemies tried to stir up in order to stop the work on the walls? (2:19, 20; 4:1-23)
2. What were some of the problems, with the community itself in Jerusalem, and how did Nehemiah work to solve them? (1:5-9; 5:1-19)
3. What part did Ezra play in helping the community return to faithful worship and obedience to God? (8:1-18) How did the people show that they were truly sorry for their sins and meant to keep their promises to God? (9:1-5, 38; 10:28-39)
4. What other problems did Nehemiah address in the community? (chapter 13:1-31)
5. What leadership qualities do you see in Nehemiah? When choosing or evaluating leaders in your own life, are these the qualities you look for? Why or why not?
6. In what ways do you identify with the Jewish community in Nehemiah? How are you like Nehemiah? What qualities did he have that you would like to develop in yourself?
7. Nehemiah had to face serious opposition at each stage of his mission. How might Nehemiah's example help you face the forces of opposition in your life?

23 Moreover, in those days I saw men of Judah who had married women from Ashdod, Ammon and Moab. 24 Half of their children spoke the language of Ashdod or the language of one of the
other peoples, and did not know how to speak the language of
Judah. 25 I rebuked them and called curses down on them. I beat
some of the men and pulled out their hair. I made them take an
oath in God's name and said: "You are not to give your daughters
in marriage to their sons, nor are you to take their daughters in
marriage for your sons or for yourselves. 26 Was it not because of
marriages like these that Solomon king of Israel sinned? Among
the many nations there was no king like him. He was loved by his
God, and God made him king over all Israel, but even he was led
into sin by foreign women. 27 Must we hear now that you too are
doing all this terrible wickedness and are being unfaithful to our
God by marrying foreign women?"

28 One of the sons of Joiada son of Eliashib the high priest
was son-in-law to Sanballat the Horonite. And I drove him away
from me.

29 Remember them, O my God, because they defiled the
priestly office and the covenant of the priesthood and of the
Levites.

30 So I purified the priests and the Levites of everything foreign, and assigned them duties, each to his own task. 31 I also made
provision for contributions of wood at designated times, and for
the firstfruits.

Remember me with favor, O my God.

13:23 *men of Judah who had married women from Ashdod:* Here, too, promises made earlier (10:28-30) had not been kept.

13:26 *Solomon king of Israel:* Solomon, King David's son, who ruled from about 960 to 931 B.C. See also the mini-article called "Solomon," p. 776.

13:28 *Sanballat:* See the note at 2:10.

13:23-25 Exod 34:11-16; Deut 7:1-5. **13:26** 2 Sam 12:24, 25; 1 Kgs 11:1-8. **13:28** Neh 4:1.

ESTHER

Elaborate feasts both begin and end this story, and no less than eight other banquets play a role in the middle. Read this story of one woman's courage and learn about the origins of the Jewish Feast of Purim.

What makes Esther special?

Esther is one of the most dramatic stories in the Bible. It has a plot full of twists and a cast of interesting characters. It is also a fully developed example of a type of story that figures elsewhere in the Jewish Scriptures (Old Testament). These stories all center around Israelites or Jews who rise to prominence in the government of a foreign king and who are able to use their positions to help their people. The first readers of Esther would have seen elements in Esther's and Mordecai's situation that would have reminded them of their ancestor Joseph, who became an important official in Egypt and was able to use his position to provide for his family when they were forced to leave their home because of a famine (see Gen 37; 39–50). Esther also has similarities to the stories told about Daniel, a Jewish exile who became an important adviser to several Babylonian kings (see Dan 1–6).

Esther, however, is unlike these other two biblical stories in that one of the key characters is a woman, Queen Esther herself. Unlike Joseph, who achieved his position without the help of other Israelites, Esther's rise was the result, in part, of the foresight and planning of her cousin Mordecai.

Another curious thing about Esther is that it is the only book of the Bible that does not mention God directly. While many Jewish and Christian readers have been bothered by this, others see God's presence clearly at work as the guiding force that makes Esther queen and allows Esther and Mordecai to use their official positions to rescue the Jewish people from certain destruction by a wicked enemy, Haman.

Why was Esther written?

One of the key reasons Esther was written was to explain the Jewish Feast of Purim which is celebrated in the month of Adar (late February/early March) and to keep alive for future generations the memory of the deliverance of the Jewish people during Xerxes' reign. Of all the major holidays still celebrated by Jews around the world, Purim and Hanukkah are the only two that do not have their basis in the exodus and desert experiences of the Israelites as described in the *Torah* (Pentateuch), and more specifically Exodus, Leviticus, Numbers, and Deuteronomy. For more, including an explanation of the origins of Hanukkah, see the chart called "Jewish Calendar and Festivals," p. 944. Purim is a

---

King Xerxes of Persia . . . governors . . . princes . . . nobles: King Xerxes was the son of King Darius, who ruled Persia from 522 to 486 B.C. (See Ezra 4:5, 6.) The nation of Persia was roughly the same area as modern-day Iran and was part of the Persian empire. This empire made major contributions to Western civilization in the areas of law, religion, and economics. It stretched from India to Ethiopia and was divided into twenty administrative areas called satrapies. Those twenty satrapies were further divided into 127 smaller provinces, each ruled by a governor (or satrap). King Xerxes' "banquet" (1:3) included these governors and countless other government leaders and army commanders. Greek writings describe Persian kings holding elaborate feasts for as many as fifteen thousand people. See also the note at 1:3,4.

1:1-3 *India . . . Cush . . . citadel of Susa . . . Persia and Media:* Susa was a city east of Babylon and a winter home for Persian kings. King Xerxes, like his father, Darius, had his main royal residence in Persepolis.

Cush (Ethiopia) was part of King Xerxes' empire. See also the note at 1:1-3. Cush was a region south of Egypt that included parts of the present countries of Ethiopia and Sudan.

The territory that is present-day India used to be part of the eastern region of the Persian empire.

The Medes lived in what is today northwest Iran. In about 550 B.C. King Cyrus conquered the Median kingdom and made it part of the Persian empire. Darius, King Xerxes' father, was a Mede (Dan 9:1,2). The kings of Persia are sometimes called the kings of Media and Persia (Dan 8:20), even though the Persian empire included other territories as well.

lively holiday in which celebrants are encouraged to let themselves go in carefree enjoyment of the moment. For example, when the book of ESTHER is read aloud in synagogues on Purim, children are given noisemakers so they can drown out Haman's name each time the reader says it.

WHAT'S THE STORY BEHIND THE SCENE?

King Cyrus the Great of Persia overcame the Babylonian empire in 539 B.C. He gave Jews who had been forced to live in Babylonia for seventy years a chance to go home. But many of the Jews liked their new home better than the ruins of Jerusalem and decided to stay where they were. In this story, Mordecai and Esther represent those who chose to stay in Babylonia.

HOW IS ESTHER CONSTRUCTED?

The queen disobeys the king (1:1-22)
Mordecai and Esther (2:1-23)
The Jews are in danger (3:1—4:17)
Esther uses her influence (5:1—7:10)
The Jews destroy their enemies (8:1—9:17)
The Feast of Purim (9:18—10:3)

The Queen Disobeys the King

In this part of the story the king and queen of Persia hold three big banquets. Huge numbers of people are invited, and one banquet lasts for one hundred and eighty days. At each of the banquets, the guests are entertained royally. When Queen Vashti refuses to leave her party and appear at King Xerxes' party, the king becomes furious.

Queen Vashti Deposed

1 This is what happened during the time of Xerxes,[a] the Xerxes
who ruled over 127 provinces stretching from India to Cush[b]: 2 At
that time King Xerxes reigned from his royal throne in the citadel
of Susa, 3 and in the third year of his reign he gave a banquet for all
his nobles and officials. The military leaders of Persia and Media,
the princes, and the nobles of the provinces were present.
4 For a full 180 days he displayed the vast wealth of his kingdom and the splendor and glory of his majesty. 5 When these days
were over, the king gave a banquet, lasting seven days, in the enclosed
garden of the king's palace, for all the people from the least to the
greatest, who were in the citadel of Susa. 6 The garden had hangings
of white and blue linen, fastened with cords of white linen and

[a]1 Hebrew *Ahasuerus*, a variant of Xerxes' Persian name; here and throughout Esther [b]1 That is, the upper Nile region

1:3-5 *banquet:* During the 180-day affair, King Xerxes generously shares the wealth of his kingdom with his Persian officials. This is very different from how he later treats the Jews in his kingdom.

King Xerxes' dinner for the men of Susa (1:5-8) is primarily a long drinking party in rich surroundings. Queen Vashti's dinner for the women of Susa (1:9) may have been a smaller celebration.

Large banquets are very important in ESTHER. Ten are mentioned throughout the book. Three pairs of these banquets mark the beginning, middle, and end of the story. There are two banquets given by King Xerxes (1:3, 4; 1:5-8), two banquets prepared by Esther (5:1-8; 7:1-10), and two celebration feasts that become the Festival of Purim (9:16, 17; 9:18). Other banquets are mentioned at 1:9; 2:18; 3:14, 15.

1:5 *all the people:* Actually, men only (see 1:9). While men could dine with women in Persia, it is likely that when King Xerxes gave his banquets, he intended them for male guests, leaving the women, mostly the wives of the male nobles and officials, in the care of his queen.

1:5-7 *enclosed garden . . . mosaic pavement . . . costly stones:* Excavations at Susa have discovered a court and objects that match this level of luxury.

purple material to silver rings on marble pillars. There were couches
of gold and silver on a mosaic pavement of porphyry, marble, mo-
ther-of-pearl and other costly stones. 7 Wine was served in goblets of
gold, each one different from the other, and the royal wine was abundant, in keeping with the king's liberality. 8 By the king's command
each guest was allowed to drink in his own way, for the king instructed all the wine stewards to serve each man what he wished.

9 Queen Vashti also gave a banquet for the women in the
royal palace of King Xerxes.

10 On the seventh day, when King Xerxes was in high spirits
from wine, he commanded the seven eunuchs who served him—
Mehuman, Biztha, Harbona, Bigtha, Abagtha, Zethar and Carcas—
11 to bring before him Queen Vashti, wearing her royal crown, in
order to display her beauty to the people and nobles, for she was
lovely to look at. 12 But when the attendants delivered the king's
command, Queen Vashti refused to come. Then the king became
furious and burned with anger.

13 Since it was customary for the king to consult experts in
matters of law and justice, he spoke with the wise men who understood the times 14 and were closest to the king—Carshena, Shethar,
Admatha, Tarshish, Meres, Marsena and Memucan, the seven
nobles of Persia and Media who had special access to the king and
were highest in the kingdom.

15 "According to law, what must be done to Queen Vashti?"
he asked. "She has not obeyed the command of King Xerxes that
the eunuchs have taken to her."

16 Then Memucan replied in the presence of the king and the
nobles, "Queen Vashti has done wrong, not only against the king
but also against all the nobles and the peoples of all the provinces
of King Xerxes. 17 For the queen's conduct will become known to
all the women, and so they will despise their husbands and say,
'King Xerxes commanded Queen Vashti to be brought before him,
but she would not come.' 18 This very day the Persian and Median
women of the nobility who have heard about the queen's conduct
will respond to all the king's nobles in the same way. There will be
no end of disrespect and discord.

19 "Therefore, if it pleases the king, let him issue a royal decree
and let it be written in the laws of Persia and Media, which cannot
be repealed, that Vashti is never again to enter the presence of King
Xerxes. Also let the king give her royal position to someone else
who is better than she. 20 Then when the king's edict is proclaimed
throughout all his vast realm, all the women will respect their husbands, from the least to the greatest."

21 The king and his nobles were pleased with this advice, so
the king did as Memucan proposed. 22 He sent dispatches to all
parts of the kingdom, to each province in its own script and to
each people in its own language, proclaiming in each people's
tongue that every man should be ruler over his own household.

1:9-12 *Queen Vashti . . . refused to come . . . furious:* Greek historians say that King Xerxes' queen was Amestris, the daughter of a Persian general. Amestris may be a Greek version of the name Vashti, or it may be a Persian name. She may have refused to come, thinking that the king was drunk and that she should wait until he came to his senses. However, this made the king furious and had disastrous results.

1:10-15 *eunuchs . . . wise men . . . nobles:* The seven eunuchs in verse 10 and the seven nobles in verse 14 all have Persian names. Memucan will speak for the group of nobles (1:16). See also Ezra 7:14.

1:17-19 *the queen's conduct will become known . . . cannot be repealed:* In biblical times, life was very difficult for women and children who did not have the support of a husband or father. At this time, the custom was that wives, even queens, had to obey their husbands without question. Most likely Queen Vashti's punishment for refusing to appear before the king would not have seemed unusual to the first readers of ESTHER.

It is not clear whether Persian laws could never be repealed (1:19), but this is not the only book of the Bible where the idea is mentioned (Dan 6:8).

1:19 *laws of Persia and Media:* Meaning the Persian empire. See the note at 1:1-3 (*India . . . Media*).

1:22 *in its own script:* Aramaic was the language used for official correspondence in the Persian empire. By claiming that the letters were written in many languages, the writer emphasizes that Xerxes' kingdom was so large that many languages were used. The governors of the provinces were responsible for translating the message from Aramaic into the languages spoken locally.

Mordecai and Esther

King Xerxes searches all over the kingdom for a new queen. Mordecai, a Jew, has a beautiful younger cousin, Esther, whom he has raised as his daughter. When she is brought to the king, he falls in love with her right away. He makes Esther queen, but he does not know she is a Jew. Mordecai becomes a palace official and overhears a plot to kill the king. He tells Esther, who then warns the king, saving his life.

Esther Made Queen

2 Later when the anger of King Xerxes had subsided, he remembered Vashti and what she had done and what he had decreed
about her. 2 Then the king's personal attendants proposed, "Let a
search be made for beautiful young virgins for the king. 3 Let the
king appoint commissioners in every province of his realm to
bring all these beautiful girls into the harem at the citadel of Susa.
Let them be placed under the care of Hegai, the king's eunuch,
who is in charge of the women; and let beauty treatments be given
to them. 4 Then let the girl who pleases the king be queen instead
of Vashti." This advice appealed to the king, and he followed it.

5 Now there was in the citadel of Susa a Jew of the tribe of
Benjamin, named Mordecai son of Jair, the son of Shimei, the son
of Kish, 6 who had been carried into exile from Jerusalem by Nebuchadnezzar king of Babylon, among those taken captive with
Jehoiachin[a] king of Judah. 7 Mordecai had a cousin named Hadassah, whom he had brought up because she had neither father nor
mother. This girl, who was also known as Esther, was lovely in
form and features, and Mordecai had taken her as his own daughter when her father and mother died.

8 When the king's order and edict had been proclaimed,
many girls were brought to the citadel of Susa and put under the
care of Hegai. Esther also was taken to the king's palace and
entrusted to Hegai, who had charge of the harem. 9 The girl pleased
him and won his favor. Immediately he provided her with her
beauty treatments and special food. He assigned to her seven
maids selected from the king's palace and moved her and her
maids into the best place in the harem.

10 Esther had not revealed her nationality and family background, because Mordecai had forbidden her to do so. 11 Every day
he walked back and forth near the courtyard of the harem to find
out how Esther was and what was happening to her.

12 Before a girl's turn came to go in to King Xerxes, she had to
complete twelve months of beauty treatments prescribed for the
women, six months with oil of myrrh and six with perfumes and
cosmetics. 13 And this is how she would go to the king: Anything
she wanted was given her to take with her from the harem to the

[a]**6** Hebrew *Jeconiah*, a variant of *Jehoiachin*

2:1 *Vashti:* See the note at 1:9-12. Note that Vashti is no longer called Queen Vashti.

2:3 *citadel of Susa:* See the note at 1:1-3.

2:5 *Mordecai . . . Jair . . . Shimei:* Mordecai's father, Jair, and his grandfather, Shimei, are named so that readers will know that Mordecai was connected to the tribe of Benjamin, one of the twelve tribes of Israel. See the mini-article called "Israel," p. 264.

2:6 *Nebuchadnezzar:* King Nebuchadnezzar ruled Babylonia from 605 to 562 B.C. In 597 B.C. Nebuchadnezzar attacked and defeated King Jehoiachin of Judah in the city of Jerusalem (see 2 Kgs 24:10-16 and 2 Chr 36:10).

2:7 *Esther:* Although Jewish, Esther is called by her Persian name which is close to the Persian word for star. Her Hebrew name, Hadassah, means "myrtle." The myrtle tree is an evergreen shrub with fragrant leaves and beautiful white flowers. In ancient times, evergreens were symbols of fertility and renewal.

2:8 *Hegai:* Hegai was King Xerxes' servant. He was in charge of the young women brought to the palace to meet King Xerxes.

2:10 *had not revealed her nationality and family background:* Esther does not tell anyone she is Jewish, probably for fear of being persecuted. The Jewish faith had many laws about how to worship and what to eat that would have made it difficult for Esther to hide her faith. It is likely she may not have openly practiced these customs. See the mini-article called "Purity (Clean and Unclean)," p. 2125.

2:1 Esth 1:10-21.

Beauty Treatments in the Ancient World. The size of a king's harem and the beauty of his concubines was a measure of a king's importance in the ancient world. The beauty treatments described in Esther 2:12-14 are quite elaborate and suggest that Xerxes was a powerful ruler. Olive oil had several uses in a woman's beauty treatment: unscented oil was rubbed on the skin to remove dirt, and then oil mixed with spices and perfumes was applied to keep her skin soft and smooth and to enhance her coloring while protecting her from sunburn. Eye makeup and face paints were made from many different natural substances, such as seeds and plant leaves. The cosmetic implements shown here are from Masada and date from around the first century B.C. For more about the substances used in beauty treatments, see the chart called "Spices and Perfumes," p. 1278.

2:14 *the concubines:* These were women who were legally bound to a man, but without the full privileges of a wife.

2:15-18 *Esther won the favor . . . he set a royal crown:* This story began in the third year of Xerxes' reign (1:3). Xerxes had now spent over three years searching for a new queen. Xerxes celebrates Esther's crowning by holding another banquet and giving expensive gifts. See also the note at 1:3-5.

2:16 *Tebeth:* The tenth month of the Hebrew calendar, from about mid-December to mid-January.

king's palace. 14In the evening she would go there and in the morning return to another part of the harem to the care of Shaashgaz,
the king's eunuch who was in charge of the concubines. She would
not return to the king unless he was pleased with her and summoned her by name.

15When the turn came for Esther (the girl Mordecai had
adopted, the daughter of his uncle Abihail) to go to the king, she
asked for nothing other than what Hegai, the king's eunuch who
was in charge of the harem, suggested. And Esther won the favor of
everyone who saw her. 16She was taken to King Xerxes in the royal
residence in the tenth month, the month of Tebeth, in the seventh
year of his reign.

17Now the king was attracted to Esther more than to any of
the other women, and she won his favor and approval more than
any of the other virgins. So he set a royal crown on her head and

made her queen instead of Vashti. [18]And the king gave a great banquet, Esther's banquet, for all his nobles and officials. He proclaimed a holiday throughout the provinces and distributed gifts
with royal liberality.

Mordecai Uncovers a Conspiracy

[19]When the virgins were assembled a second time, Mordecai
was sitting at the king's gate. [20]But Esther had kept secret her family background and nationality just as Mordecai had told her to
do, for she continued to follow Mordecai's instructions as she had
done when he was bringing her up.

[21]During the time Mordecai was sitting at the king's gate,
Bigthana[a] and Teresh, two of the king's officers who guarded the
doorway, became angry and conspired to assassinate King Xerxes.
[22]But Mordecai found out about the plot and told Queen Esther,
who in turn reported it to the king, giving credit to Mordecai.
[23]And when the report was investigated and found to be true, the
two officials were hanged on a gallows.[b] All this was recorded in
the book of the annals in the presence of the king.

The Jews Are in Danger

Haman is so angry with Mordecai for refusing to honor him that he convinces the king to kill all the Jews in the kingdom. Mordecai convinces Esther to risk her life to save her people.

Haman's Plot to Destroy the Jews

3 After these events, King Xerxes honored Haman son of
Hammedatha, the Agagite, elevating him and giving him a seat of
honor higher than that of all the other nobles. [2]All the royal officials at the king's gate knelt down and paid honor to Haman, for
the king had commanded this concerning him. But Mordecai
would not kneel down or pay him honor.

[3]Then the royal officials at the king's gate asked Mordecai,
"Why do you disobey the king's command?" [4]Day after day they
spoke to him but he refused to comply. Therefore they told Haman
about it to see whether Mordecai's behavior would be tolerated,
for he had told them he was a Jew.

[5]When Haman saw that Mordecai would not kneel down or
pay him honor, he was enraged. [6]Yet having learned who Mordecai's people were, he scorned the idea of killing only Mordecai.
Instead Haman looked for a way to destroy all Mordecai's people,
the Jews, throughout the whole kingdom of Xerxes.

[7]In the twelfth year of King Xerxes, in the first month, the

---

[a]21 Hebrew *Bigthan*, a variant of *Bigthana*; similarly elsewhere in Esther [b]23 Or *were hung* (or *impaled*) *on poles*

2:21 *officers who guarded the doorway . . . assassinate King Xerxes:* These would be the doorways to the king's private rooms, including his bedroom. That meant that the guards, Bigthana and Teresh, could easily get to the king. This plan failed but years later a similar plan was actually used to kill Xerxes.

2:23 *hanged:* Hanging was a common form of execution in ancient Persia. In some ways it resembled a crucifixion because when hanged, a person was impaled on a stake or nailed to a tree and left hanging from it. This was a slow and painful way to die. Often the person starved to death.

3:1-5 *Haman . . . the Agagite . . . seat of honor . . . Mordecai:* Haman's ancestors were from the Amalekite nation who were enemies of the Jews (see Exod 17:14-16; Deut 25:17-19). Agag was an Amalekite king who had fought against the Jews long before the time of Esther. Mordecai was a descendant of the same tribe as Saul, Israel's first king, who had defeated the Amalekites. See 1 Sam 15:1-33 and the note at 2:5. Haman's new position at court allows him to be one of the few people who can go to the king without being called by him.

3:7 *twelfth year . . . Nisan . . . Adar:* Esther was crowned queen in the seventh year of King Xerxes' reign (see 2:15-17), so at this point she has been queen for more than four years. Nisan is the first month of the Hebrew calendar, from about mid-March to mid-April. Adar is the twelfth month of the Hebrew calendar, from about mid-February to mid-March.

2:20 Esth 2:10.

3:8 *a certain people:* Haman means the Jews, but it is not clear that the king knows that. (See the note at 6:10.) Haman is bending the truth about the Jews, who did indeed have customs that were different from those of other groups in Xerxes' kingdom. The Jewish religion required that the Jews follow the law that God gave to Moses above all other laws. (See the mini-article called "Law," p. 1160). This did not necessarily mean that the Jews refused to obey all of Xerxes' laws.

3:10 *signet ring:* When a king gave his official ring to someone it was the same thing as giving his official signature and authority. Melted wax was used to seal a letter. While the wax was still soft, the king's ring was pressed in the wax and left a distinct symbol that showed that the letter had the king's approval.

3:12,13 *the language of each people . . . sent by couriers:* Xerxes' empire was so big that many languages were spoken in it. However, Aramaic was the language used for official correspondence. See the note at 1:22. The couriers who carried the letters were part of an early postal system that Cyrus established about 535 B.C.

4:1-3 *put on sackcloth and ashes . . . fasting:* Sackcloth was a rough, dark-colored cloth made from goat or camel hair and used to make grain sacks. Sometimes people wore sackcloth or sat in dust or ashes to show how sorry they were for their sins or to show their grief. A person wearing sackcloth could only go as far as the city gate (outside the palace gate) because they were considered unclean. See also the mini-article called "Purity (Clean and Unclean)," p. 2125. The Israelites would sometimes go without eating (fasting), accompanied by prayer, in times of great sorrow or danger.

month of Nisan, they cast the *pur* (that is, the lot) in the presence of Haman to select a day and month. And the lot fell on[a] the twelfth month, the month of Adar.

8 Then Haman said to King Xerxes, "There is a certain people dispersed and scattered among the peoples in all the provinces of your kingdom whose customs are different from those of all other people and who do not obey the king's laws; it is not in the king's best interest to tolerate them. 9 If it pleases the king, let a decree be issued to destroy them, and I will put ten thousand talents[b] of silver into the royal treasury for the men who carry out this business."

10 So the king took his signet ring from his finger and gave it to Haman son of Hammedatha, the Agagite, the enemy of the Jews. 11 "Keep the money," the king said to Haman, "and do with the people as you please."

12 Then on the thirteenth day of the first month the royal secretaries were summoned. They wrote out in the script of each province and in the language of each people all Haman's orders to the king's satraps, the governors of the various provinces and the nobles of the various peoples. These were written in the name of King Xerxes himself and sealed with his own ring. 13 Dispatches were sent by couriers to all the king's provinces with the order to destroy, kill and annihilate all the Jews—young and old, women and little children—on a single day, the thirteenth day of the twelfth month, the month of Adar, and to plunder their goods. 14 A copy of the text of the edict was to be issued as law in every province and made known to the people of every nationality so they would be ready for that day.

15 Spurred on by the king's command, the couriers went out, and the edict was issued in the citadel of Susa. The king and Haman sat down to drink, but the city of Susa was bewildered.

Mordecai Persuades Esther to Help

4 When Mordecai learned of all that had been done, he tore his clothes, put on sackcloth and ashes, and went out into the city, wailing loudly and bitterly. 2 But he went only as far as the king's gate, because no one clothed in sackcloth was allowed to enter it. 3 In every province to which the edict and order of the king came, there was great mourning among the Jews, with fasting, weeping and wailing. Many lay in sackcloth and ashes.

4 When Esther's maids and eunuchs came and told her about Mordecai, she was in great distress. She sent clothes for him to put on instead of his sackcloth, but he would not accept them. 5 Then Esther summoned Hathach, one of the king's eunuchs assigned to attend her, and ordered him to find out what was troubling Mordecai and why.

---

[a]7 Septuagint; Hebrew does not have *And the lot fell on.* [b]9 That is, about 375 tons (about 345 metric tons)

den dy da warten vasten solte
vnd Got für sy pitten vnd na-

Esther Sends a Letter to Mordecai, illustration from a fifteenth century manuscript, Austria. Much of what happens in ESTHER is the result of spoken or written communications that are delivered by couriers. These include the royal decrees (laws) which were translated into the many languages spoken in the Persian empire (see 1:21, 22; 3:12-15; 8:9-15) and the letters sent by Mordecai and Esther to Jews everywhere telling them to celebrate Purim (9:20-23, 29-32). But couriers also delivered personal messages like the ones exchanged by Esther and her cousin Mordecai (4:1-17).

6So Hathach went out to Mordecai in the open square of the
city in front of the king's gate. 7Mordecai told him everything that
had happened to him, including the exact amount of money
Haman had promised to pay into the royal treasury for the
destruction of the Jews. 8He also gave him a copy of the text of the
edict for their annihilation, which had been published in Susa, to
show to Esther and explain it to her, and he told him to urge her
to go into the king's presence to beg for mercy and plead with him
for her people.

9Hathach went back and reported to Esther what Mordecai
had said. 10Then she instructed him to say to Mordecai, 11"All the
king's officials and the people of the royal provinces know that for any
man or woman who approaches the king in the inner court without
being summoned the king has but one law: that he be put to death.
The only exception to this is for the king to extend the gold scepter to

4:4-6 *She sent clothes . . . Hathach went out:* Esther sent Mordecai clothes so that he could enter the palace and talk to her. Since he refused her gift she had to use a messenger, Hathach, to communicate with him.

4:8 *Susa:* See the note at 1:1-3.

4:11 *one law:* Such laws as this were usually made to protect the king from people who might want to kill him. It is not known for sure if such a law was part of Persian custom at the time.

4:11 *gold scepter:* A scepter is the official staff of a king or queen and symbolizes his or her authority. The top of a scepter is usually decorated with gold and jewels. Often a king held out his staff to welcome a person or as a signal to come forward. Such a gesture often served as a security measure, keeping possible assassins at a distance. Esther is afraid that if she tries to see the king without being invited, she might be suspected of putting him in danger and might be killed as a punishment.

4:7,8 Esth 3:9-13.

Queen Esther sent a message saying, *"I will go to the king, even though it is against the law. And if I perish, I perish."* Esth 4:16

4:14-16 *if you remain silent . . . fast for me:* Mordecai warns Esther that she cannot avoid danger by avoiding the king. He implies that they will manage to somehow survive, with God's help, if she decides not to help them, but suggests that she may have been made queen so that she could help her people, the Jews. For fasting, see the note at 4:1-3. Usually prayer was part of fasting. Esther asks the people to join her in three days of fasting to help her prepare to see the king.

5:1,2 *inner court . . . gold scepter:* The inner court is an area in front of the throne. Esther is bold in approaching the king, but keeps a respectful distance and lets him notice her. He holds out the gold scepter to welcome her. See also the notes at 4:11.

5:4-8 *a banquet . . . tomorrow . . . banquet:* See the note at 1:3-5. A private banquet with the king and queen would have been a true honor. It is not clear why Esther did not use the first banquet as an opportunity to make her request on behalf of the Jewish people. Perhaps she was waiting for Haman to get overly proud and show his true colors. In any case, the delay helps to build up suspense in the story.

him and spare his life. But thirty days have passed since I was called to go to the king."

[12]When Esther's words were reported to Mordecai, [13]he sent back this answer: "Do not think that because you are in the king's house you alone of all the Jews will escape. [14]For if you remain silent at this time, relief and deliverance for the Jews will arise from another place, but you and your father's family will perish. And who knows but that you have come to royal position for such a time as this?"

[15]Then Esther sent this reply to Mordecai: [16]"Go, gather together all the Jews who are in Susa, and fast for me. Do not eat or drink for three days, night or day. I and my maids will fast as you do. When this is done, I will go to the king, even though it is against the law. And if I perish, I perish."

[17]So Mordecai went away and carried out all of Esther's instructions.

Esther Uses Her Influence

Esther begins her clever plan to save the Jews by inviting the king and Haman to dinner. After the dinner, Haman begins his plan to kill Mordecai by building a huge gallows from which he intends to hang Mordecai. But, instead of killing Mordecai, Haman has to help honor him. Then Esther gives a second dinner for the king and Haman. At this dinner there are many surprises.

Esther's Request to the King

5 On the third day Esther put on her royal robes and stood in the inner court of the palace, in front of the king's hall. The king was sitting on his royal throne in the hall, facing the entrance. [2]When he saw Queen Esther standing in the court, he was pleased with her and held out to her the gold scepter that was in his hand. So Esther approached and touched the tip of the scepter.

[3]Then the king asked, "What is it, Queen Esther? What is your request? Even up to half the kingdom, it will be given you."

[4]"If it pleases the king," replied Esther, "let the king, together with Haman, come today to a banquet I have prepared for him."

[5]"Bring Haman at once," the king said, "so that we may do what Esther asks."

So the king and Haman went to the banquet Esther had prepared. [6]As they were drinking wine, the king again asked Esther, "Now what is your petition? It will be given you. And what is your request? Even up to half the kingdom, it will be granted."

[7]Esther replied, "My petition and my request is this: [8]If the king regards me with favor and if it pleases the king to grant my petition and fulfill my request, let the king and Haman come tomorrow to the banquet I will prepare for them. Then I will answer the king's question."

Esther Touches the King's Scepter by Barbara Garrison, 1994. Even though King Xerxes had chosen Esther to be his queen, she was not allowed to speak to him without being invited to do so. In this children's book illustration, the king is shown extending his gold scepter (a symbol of his royal authority) to Esther. This indicates that he is happy to see her and willing to hear what she has to say.

Haman's Rage Against Mordecai

9Haman went out that day happy and in high spirits. But
when he saw Mordecai at the king's gate and observed that he neither rose nor showed fear in his presence, he was filled with rage
against Mordecai. 10Nevertheless, Haman restrained himself and
went home.

Calling together his friends and Zeresh, his wife, 11Haman
boasted to them about his vast wealth, his many sons, and all the
ways the king had honored him and how he had elevated him
above the other nobles and officials. 12"And that's not all," Haman
added. "I'm the only person Queen Esther invited to accompany
the king to the banquet she gave. And she has invited me along
with the king tomorrow. 13But all this gives me no satisfaction as
long as I see that Jew Mordecai sitting at the king's gate."

14His wife Zeresh and all his friends said to him, "Have a
gallows built, seventy-five feet[a] high, and ask the king in the

[a]**14** Hebrew *fifty cubits* (about 23 meters)

5:11-13 *boasted . . . many sons . . . no satisfaction:* Haman brags about all that he has, including his many sons. It was considered a great honor to have many sons. However, the story makes it clear that even with all his wealth and honor, Haman will only be happy if no one disobeys him.

5:14 *His wife Zeresh:* The meaning of Haman's wife's name is uncertain, though some scholars have related it to ancient words for "gold" and "desirous." Zeresh is the third female character in this story. If she is the mother of Haman's many sons, then she would seem to be a good wife by ancient standards and one of the reasons Haman rose so high in the king's court. The first readers of ESTHER most likely would have seen a similarity between her advice to Haman and Jezebel's advice to her ambitious husband Ahab (see 1 Kgs 21:1-29).

5:14 *gallows:* Usually a person would be hung from a tree or stake (see the note at 2:23). If a seventy-five-foot-high gallows is used to hang Mordecai, many people will see it from a distance, and everyone will know that Haman has had his revenge.

Some scholars understand the height of the gallows to be an exaggeration intended to heighten the drama of the events being related, a common story-telling practice in ancient literature. Other examples of such exaggeration in ESTHER would be the length of Esther's beauty treatment (2:12) and the number and length of banquets (see, for instance, 1:5).

5:9 Esth 3:3-6.

morning to have Mordecai hanged on it. Then go with the king to
the dinner and be happy." This suggestion delighted Haman, and
he had the gallows built.

Mordecai Honored

6 That night the king could not sleep; so he ordered the book of
the chronicles, the record of his reign, to be brought in and read to
him. 2 It was found recorded there that Mordecai had exposed
Bigthana and Teresh, two of the king's officers who guarded the
doorway, who had conspired to assassinate King Xerxes.
3 "What honor and recognition has Mordecai received for
this?" the king asked.
"Nothing has been done for him," his attendants answered.
4 The king said, "Who is in the court?" Now Haman had just
entered the outer court of the palace to speak to the king about
hanging Mordecai on the gallows he had erected for him.
5 His attendants answered, "Haman is standing in the court."
"Bring him in," the king ordered.
6 When Haman entered, the king asked him, "What should
be done for the man the king delights to honor?"
Now Haman thought to himself, "Who is there that the
king would rather honor than me?" 7 So he answered the king,
"For the man the king delights to honor, 8 have them bring a
royal robe the king has worn and a horse the king has ridden,
one with a royal crest placed on its head. 9 Then let the robe
and horse be entrusted to one of the king's most noble princes.
Let them robe the man the king delights to honor, and lead
him on the horse through the city streets, proclaiming before
him, 'This is what is done for the man the king delights to
honor!' "
10 "Go at once," the king commanded Haman. "Get the robe
and the horse and do just as you have suggested for Mordecai the
Jew, who sits at the king's gate. Do not neglect anything you have
recommended."
11 So Haman got the robe and the horse. He robed Mordecai,
and led him on horseback through the city streets, proclaiming
before him, "This is what is done for the man the king delights to
honor!"
12 Afterward Mordecai returned to the king's gate. But
Haman rushed home, with his head covered in grief, 13 and told
Zeresh his wife and all his friends everything that had happened
to him.
His advisers and his wife Zeresh said to him, "Since Mordecai, before whom your downfall has started, is of Jewish origin,
you cannot stand against him—you will surely come to ruin!"
14 While they were still talking with him, the king's eunuchs
arrived and hurried Haman away to the banquet Esther had prepared.

6:8 *royal robe . . . royal crest:* To put one's own robe or fine clothes on a person was a sign of honor in ancient times (Gen 41:42; 1 Sam 18:4). In the ancient Near East, the horse was a highly valued symbol of royal authority. A fancy headdress made an impression on crowds when the king and his officials paraded through the city streets. The detail of a relief shown here is from the king's palace in Nineveh, seventh century B.C.

6:10 *Mordecai the Jew:* See the note at 2:5. The fact that King Xerxes would choose to honor a Jew in this way suggests that he may not have realized that it was the Jews he had ordered killed. See the note at 3:8.

6:12-14 *Mordecai returned . . . Haman . . . head covered in grief:* Even though Mordecai has been honored, his position at court has not yet changed. Haman's despair is a big change from his earlier boasting. Haman's wife and friends, who had earlier encouraged him to kill Mordecai, begin to warn him about the troubles he could expect once his plan fails. See 5:11-14.

6:1,2 Esth 2:21-23.

Haman Hanged

7 So the king and Haman went to dine with Queen Esther, 2and as
they were drinking wine on that second day, the king again asked,
"Queen Esther, what is your petition? It will be given you. What is
your request? Even up to half the kingdom, it will be granted."
3Then Queen Esther answered, "If I have found favor with
you, O king, and if it pleases your majesty, grant me my life—this
is my petition. And spare my people—this is my request. 4For I
and my people have been sold for destruction and slaughter and
annihilation. If we had merely been sold as male and female slaves,
I would have kept quiet, because no such distress would justify disturbing the king.[a]"
5King Xerxes asked Queen Esther, "Who is he? Where is the
man who has dared to do such a thing?"
6Esther said, "The adversary and enemy is this vile Haman."
Then Haman was terrified before the king and queen. 7The
king got up in a rage, left his wine and went out into the palace
garden. But Haman, realizing that the king had already decided his
fate, stayed behind to beg Queen Esther for his life.
8Just as the king returned from the palace garden to the banquet hall, Haman was falling on the couch where Esther was
reclining.
The king exclaimed, "Will he even molest the queen while
she is with me in the house?"
As soon as the word left the king's mouth, they covered
Haman's face. 9Then Harbona, one of the eunuchs attending the
king, said, "A gallows seventy-five feet[b] high stands by Haman's
house. He had it made for Mordecai, who spoke up to help the king."
The king said, "Hang him on it!" 10So they hanged Haman
on the gallows he had prepared for Mordecai. Then the king's fury
subsided.

The Jews Destroy Their Enemies

Esther tells King Xerxes that Mordecai is her cousin. The king makes Mordecai a high official in his court. Then Esther asks the king to make a new law that will save the Jews. King Xerxes agrees and says that the Jews may destroy anyone who is their enemy. After the fighting is over, the Jews celebrate having defeated their enemies.

The King's Edict in Behalf of the Jews

8 That same day King Xerxes gave Queen Esther the estate of
Haman, the enemy of the Jews. And Mordecai came into the

---

a4 Or *quiet, but the compensation our adversary offers cannot be compared with the loss the king would suffer* **b9** Hebrew *fifty cubits* (about 23 meters)

7:4 *sold for destruction and slaughter and annihilation:* Esther's comments refer to Haman's promise in 3:9.

7:8 *falling on the couch . . . covered Haman's face:* It was a common custom in the ancient world to bow down at someone's feet when asking for mercy. Since people in ancient Persia ate reclining on couches it is easy to see why the king interpreted Haman's falling down by Esther's couch the way he did.

The Greeks and Romans covered a person's head or face before killing them or as a sign that the person was to be killed. It is possible that the Persians also did this.

7:9 *gallows:* See 5:14. Haman's plan to destroy Mordecai is now used to destroy Haman instead. ESTHER contains many such "ironies" and changes in fortune. See also 6:4,5,14; 7:7,8.

8:1 *King Xerxes gave Queen Esther the estate of Haman:* The king had the power to take all the property of any criminal who, like Haman (7:1-10), was sentenced to death.

8:1 *Mordecai came into the presence of the king:* Mordecai's new position allows him to see and talk to the king without being called on first. Mordecai now has the privileges and the ring that the king had given Haman (3:1,10).

8:2-4 *signet ring . . . gold scepter:* See the notes at 3:10, 12 and 4:11.

8:5-8 *overruling the dispatches that Haman . . . devised:* Out of respect for the king, Esther suggests that Haman was the only one responsible for the letters ordering the killing of all the Jews and appeals to him to do the right thing for her and her people. Xerxes then allows Esther and Mordecai to write a new law to save the Jews. This new law will be as harsh as Haman's (8:11-13) since the first law is still in effect. With this second law, however, the Jews will be able to fight back against their enemies.

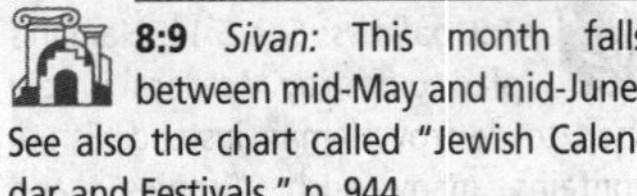

8:9 *Sivan:* This month falls between mid-May and mid-June. See also the chart called "Jewish Calendar and Festivals," p. 944.

8:9 *India to Cush:* See the note at 1:1-3.

8:9,10 *written in the script of each province . . . rode fast horses:* See the notes at 1:22 and 3:12,13.

8:15 *royal garments . . . crown . . . purple robe:* At this time, a person's clothes were a sign of that person's place in society. Some colors, like purple, were rare and expensive to produce, and were only worn by the privileged. The "crown" Mordecai is wearing is probably a special type of head wrap. Mordecai had worn kingly robes before (6:11). But this time the clothes he wears, though fine enough for a king, are his own.

presence of the king, for Esther had told how he was related to her.
2 The king took off his signet ring, which he had reclaimed from
Haman, and presented it to Mordecai. And Esther appointed him
over Haman's estate.
3 Esther again pleaded with the king, falling at his feet and
weeping. She begged him to put an end to the evil plan of Haman
the Agagite, which he had devised against the Jews. 4 Then the king
extended the gold scepter to Esther and she arose and stood before
him.
5 "If it pleases the king," she said, "and if he regards me with
favor and thinks it the right thing to do, and if he is pleased with
me, let an order be written overruling the dispatches that Haman
son of Hammedatha, the Agagite, devised and wrote to destroy the
Jews in all the king's provinces. 6 For how can I bear to see disaster
fall on my people? How can I bear to see the destruction of my
family?"
7 King Xerxes replied to Queen Esther and to Mordecai the
Jew, "Because Haman attacked the Jews, I have given his estate to
Esther, and they have hanged him on the gallows. 8 Now write
another decree in the king's name in behalf of the Jews as seems
best to you, and seal it with the king's signet ring—for no document
written in the king's name and sealed with his ring can be
revoked."
9 At once the royal secretaries were summoned—on the
twenty-third day of the third month, the month of Sivan. They
wrote out all Mordecai's orders to the Jews, and to the satraps, governors
and nobles of the 127 provinces stretching from India to
Cush.[a] These orders were written in the script of each province and
the language of each people and also to the Jews in their own script
and language. 10 Mordecai wrote in the name of King Xerxes, sealed
the dispatches with the king's signet ring, and sent them by mounted
couriers, who rode fast horses especially bred for the king.
11 The king's edict granted the Jews in every city the right to
assemble and protect themselves; to destroy, kill and annihilate any
armed force of any nationality or province that might attack them
and their women and children; and to plunder the property of
their enemies. 12 The day appointed for the Jews to do this in all the
provinces of King Xerxes was the thirteenth day of the twelfth
month, the month of Adar. 13 A copy of the text of the edict was to
be issued as law in every province and made known to the people
of every nationality so that the Jews would be ready on that day to
avenge themselves on their enemies.
14 The couriers, riding the royal horses, raced out, spurred on
by the king's command. And the edict was also issued in the citadel
of Susa.

a9 That is, the upper Nile region

15 Mordecai left the king's presence wearing royal garments
of blue and white, a large crown of gold and a purple robe of fine
linen. And the city of Susa held a joyous celebration. 16 For the Jews
it was a time of happiness and joy, gladness and honor. 17 In every
province and in every city, wherever the edict of the king went,
there was joy and gladness among the Jews, with feasting and celebrating. And many people of other nationalities became Jews
because fear of the Jews had seized them.

Triumph of the Jews

9 On the thirteenth day of the twelfth month, the month of
Adar, the edict commanded by the king was to be carried out. On
this day the enemies of the Jews had hoped to overpower them,
but now the tables were turned and the Jews got the upper hand
over those who hated them. 2 The Jews assembled in their cities in
all the provinces of King Xerxes to attack those seeking their
destruction. No one could stand against them, because the people
of all the other nationalities were afraid of them. 3 And all the
nobles of the provinces, the satraps, the governors and the king's
administrators helped the Jews, because fear of Mordecai had
seized them. 4 Mordecai was prominent in the palace; his reputation spread throughout the provinces, and he became more and
more powerful.

5 The Jews struck down all their enemies with the sword,
killing and destroying them, and they did what they pleased to
those who hated them. 6 In the citadel of Susa, the Jews killed and
destroyed five hundred men. 7 They also killed Parshandatha,
Dalphon, Aspatha, 8 Poratha, Adalia, Aridatha, 9 Parmashta, Arisai,
Aridai and Vaizatha, 10 the ten sons of Haman son of Hammedatha,
the enemy of the Jews. But they did not lay their hands on the
plunder.

11 The number of those slain in the citadel of Susa was
reported to the king that same day. 12 The king said to Queen
Esther, "The Jews have killed and destroyed five hundred men and
the ten sons of Haman in the citadel of Susa. What have they done
in the rest of the king's provinces? Now what is your petition? It
will be given you. What is your request? It will also be granted."

13 "If it pleases the king," Esther answered, "give the Jews in
Susa permission to carry out this day's edict tomorrow also, and
let Haman's ten sons be hanged on gallows."

14 So the king commanded that this be done. An edict was
issued in Susa, and they hanged the ten sons of Haman. 15 The Jews
in Susa came together on the fourteenth day of the month of Adar,
and they put to death in Susa three hundred men, but they did not
lay their hands on the plunder.

16 Meanwhile, the remainder of the Jews who were in the
king's provinces also assembled to protect themselves and get relief

8:17 *feasting and celebrating . . . fear of the Jews:* The happiness of the Jews here is a big change from their earlier fears (4:3). Now it is non-Jews who are depicted as being afraid of what may happen if they are thought to be enemies of the Jews (8:11-17).

9:1 *Adar:* See the note at 3:7. The thirteenth day of Adar is noted because it will be important to the dating of the Feast of Purim.

9:2-10 *struck down all their enemies:* Up to this point in the story, Haman (3:1-6) was the only one named as an enemy of the Jews. Here, the story says that the Jews have enemies throughout the empire. We do not know who these enemies were, but they would certainly have included all those who were willing to carry out the decree Haman wrote.

9:6-10 *killed . . . the ten sons of Haman:* Haman's losses continue. See the notes at 7:8; 7:9; 8:1; and 8:1,2.

9:10 *did not lay their hands on the plunder:* This suggests that they were fighting for survival and not riches. See also 9:15.

9:13-19 *give the Jews in Susa permission to carry out this day's edict tomorrow also:* It seems odd that there would be so many enemies for the Jews to destroy in Susa. Earlier, the story says that the citizens of Susa "held a joyous celebration" when they heard the law that saved the Jews (8:11-17). Perhaps those who had rejoiced were only the Jewish citizens of Susa.

The writer may have been trying to find a way to explain why during his time the Jews in the villages were celebrating Purim on one day (the fourteenth day of Adar, 9:16, 17) and the Jews in Susa were celebrating it on another day (the fifteenth day of Adar, 9:18). See also the note at 1:3, 4.

9:1 Esth 3:13.

from their enemies. They killed seventy-five thousand of them but did not lay their hands on the plunder. [17]This happened on the thirteenth day of the month of Adar, and on the fourteenth they rested and made it a day of feasting and joy.

The Feast of Purim

Mordecai writes a letter to all the Jews. He tells them that every year they should hold a celebration to remember and to give thanks for having defeated their enemies. This celebration is called the Feast of Purim, and Jews still celebrate it today.

Purim Celebrated

[18]The Jews in Susa, however, had assembled on the thirteenth and fourteenth, and then on the fifteenth they rested and made it a day of feasting and joy.

[19]That is why rural Jews—those living in villages—observe the fourteenth of the month of Adar as a day of joy and feasting, a day for giving presents to each other.

[20]Mordecai recorded these events, and he sent letters to all the Jews throughout the provinces of King Xerxes, near and far, [21]to have them celebrate annually the fourteenth and fifteenth days of the month of Adar [22]as the time when the Jews got relief from their enemies, and as the month when their sorrow was turned into joy and their mourning into a day of celebration. He wrote them to observe the days as days of feasting and joy and giving presents of food to one another and gifts to the poor.

[23]So the Jews agreed to continue the celebration they had begun, doing what Mordecai had written to them. [24]For Haman son of Hammedatha, the Agagite, the enemy of all the Jews, had plotted against the Jews to destroy them and had cast the *pur* (that is, the lot) for their ruin and destruction. [25]But when the plot came to the king's attention,[a] he issued written orders that the evil scheme Haman had devised against the Jews should come back onto his own head, and that he and his sons should be hanged on the gallows. [26](Therefore these days were called Purim, from the word *pur*.) Because of everything written in this letter and because of what they had seen and what had happened to them, [27]the Jews took it upon themselves to establish the custom that they and their descendants and all who join them should without fail observe these two days every year, in the way prescribed and at the time appointed. [28]These days should be remembered and observed in every generation by every family, and in every province and in every city. And these days of Purim should never cease to be

[a]**25** Or *when Esther came before the king*

Their sorrow was turned into joy and their mourning into a day of celebration. He wrote them to observe the days as days of feasting and joy and giving presents of food to one another and gifts to the poor.
Esth 9:22

9:21,22 *celebrate annually the fourteenth and fifteenth days of the month of Adar:* Rather than deciding between two dates (see the note at 9:13-19), Mordecai orders the Jews to hold a yearly celebration that includes both dates.

9:24-26 *cast the pur . . . Purim:* See also 3:7. The Jewish Feast of Purim got its name from "purim," which is the Babylonian term for the lots that Haman used to determine on which day he should have the Jews killed (3:7). Instead, fortunes changed in favor of the Jews, so the Jews survived and their enemies were destroyed. Purim is celebrated each year on the fourteenth and fifteenth of Adar, which usually falls around the first of March.

Purim is a lively festival that is still celebrated by Jews around the world today. It is preceded by a day of fasting. On Purim, ESTHER is read in synagogues. Whenever the dreaded Haman's name is read out, children are encouraged to drown out the sound of it with noisemakers. The elaborate noisemaker shown here is from Western Europe (nineteenth century).

The Hanging of Haman and His Sons, page from a Jewish prayer book (Rhenish, fourteenth century). Elaborate, hand-illustrated festival prayer books (called *Machzor*) became popular with Jewish people in the Middle Ages. The *Leipzig Machzor,* from which this illustration was reproduced, was a prayer book prepared for celebrating the Feast of Purim. Although ESTHER tells about the hanging of Haman and his sons (7:9,10; 9:5-10), this illustration includes other details (such as the suicide of Haman's daughter) not found in the biblical story.

celebrated by the Jews, nor should the memory of them die out
among their descendants.
29So Queen Esther, daughter of Abihail, along with Mordecai
the Jew, wrote with full authority to confirm this second letter
concerning Purim. 30And Mordecai sent letters to all the Jews in
the 127 provinces of the kingdom of Xerxes—words of goodwill
and assurance— 31to establish these days of Purim at their designated times, as Mordecai the Jew and Queen Esther had decreed
for them, and as they had established for themselves and their
descendants in regard to their times of fasting and lamentation.
32Esther's decree confirmed these regulations about Purim, and it
was written down in the records.

9:31 *fasting and lamentation:* The time of fasting described here was meant to recall Esther's own fasting in 4:15,16. Though ESTHER does not specify when Jews were to observe this fast, Jewish practice is to observe the Fast of Esther on the thirteenth of Adar before the celebration of the Feast of Purim. For more on fasting, see the note at 4:1-3.

> *Mordecai the Jew was second in rank to King Xerxes . . . and held in high esteem by his many fellow Jews, because he worked for the good of his people and spoke up for the welfare of all the Jews.*
> Esth 10:3

The Greatness of Mordecai

10 King Xerxes imposed tribute throughout the empire, to its
distant shores. 2 And all his acts of power and might, together with
a full account of the greatness of Mordecai to which the king had
raised him, are they not written in the book of the annals of the
kings of Media and Persia? 3 Mordecai the Jew was second in rank
to King Xerxes, preeminent among the Jews, and held in high
esteem by his many fellow Jews, because he worked for the good of
his people and spoke up for the welfare of all the Jews.

10:2 *Media and Persia:* See the note at 1:1-3.

QUESTIONS ABOUT ESTHER

1. What role do dinners, banquets, and luxury play in the story? What role do their opposites have: Mordecai's dressing in sackcloth, and Esther's fasting?
2. In this story two women, Esther and Vashti, are queens. One is originally an orphan who ends up queen. The other starts out as queen, but returns to the harem to finish out her days as a mere concubine. How does each use her position to get what she wants? Where in the book do you see women thinking for themselves, influencing and even disobeying their husbands?
3. Similarly, this story sets up a contrast between two of the king's officials, Haman and Mordecai. Review their key actions. How are their actions similar and different? How would you characterize each man's motivation? How would you account for the reversal of fortune each one experiences?
4. Who are the people you most admire in this story? Why?
5. What events in modern history or situations in today's society did you think of when you read the story of Esther? What groups of people in our times do you think have had to fight off prejudices to keep their identity?
6. ESTHER tells about the origins of the Jewish holiday of Purim (9:18-32). Do you know anyone who celebrates this holiday? If so, ask them what this festival means to them. How does understanding the holiday help to understand the book that inspired it?
7. There is no reference to God in the entire book of ESTHER. Why do you think, then, that it is included in the Bible?

THE ANCIENT WORLD: PEOPLES, POWERS, AND POLITICS

Hundreds of years before the people of Israel took over the land known as Canaan, their ancestors came from Mesopotamia, a land between the Tigris and Euphrates rivers far to the east. In fact, the word Mesopotamia means, "land between two rivers." Israelites trace their history back to Abraham, whose father Terah came from Ur (Gen 11:26-28). Abraham and his wife Sarah traveled north with Terah along the Euphrates River Valley to a place called Haran, which was located in the far northwestern part of Mesopotamia. Terah wanted to settle in the land of Canaan, to the southwest and near the Mediterranean Sea, but he died in Haran (Gen 11:31,32). God had spoken to Abraham and told him to go to Canaan, the land promised to Abraham's descendants. Abraham followed God's commands and went to Canaan around 1900 B.C.

Chapters 12–50 of GENESIS tell about Abraham and Sarah's journeys and how their children and grandchildren lived as wandering herders (nomads). One of Abraham's grandsons, Jacob, was also known by the name Israel, which means "he struggles with God" (Gen 32:27,28). Jacob had twelve sons, including Joseph, who became an important leader in Egypt (Gen 41:37-57). At the end of GENESIS, Jacob and his family, who were the ancestors of the people of Israel, travel to Egypt and are about to become the slaves of the Egyptian people. How would God's people become the nation of Israel and live in the land God promised to give them if they were slaves in another land? More will be said about this later. First, it will be helpful to take a look back to the centuries before Abraham was born and find out more about the peoples and nations that existed in the ancient Near East.

A Time before Abraham and Sarah

The most important civilizations of the ancient Near East developed in great river valleys. In the east was Mesopotamia, located in the river valleys and plains between the Tigris and Euphrates rivers. In the west was Egypt, which grew to be a strong nation beside the Nile River, the longest river in the world. In between lay the land of Canaan, west of the Jordan River. The Jordan River, fed by mountain streams, flowed past fertile land that could be used for growing crops. Perhaps even more important, Canaan was a kind of land bridge that connected Egypt and other peoples of the Mediterranean kingdoms to the people of Mesopotamia, Babylonia, and Assyria.

Discoveries at Jericho show that people lived in villages in Canaan, Egypt, and Mesopotamia even before 5000 B.C. (For more on Jericho, see the article "Archaeology and the Bible," p. 27). However, the first true civilization arose around 4000 B.C. in southern Mesopotamia near the Persian Gulf. At that time, the Sumerian people moved into the

Genesis 11:26—25:11 tells about the life of Abraham and how he traveled from his home, Ur, on the Euphrates River in the east, and eventually settled in Canaan. When Abraham was living in Mesopotamia, the LORD told him to go to the land which would be shown to him. The LORD said he would bless Abraham and make his descendants a great nation (Gen 12:1-3). Abraham is an important ancestor of the people of Israel, who would later conquer the Canaanites and settle in the land originally promised to him.

Writing in the Ancient World. *It is difficult to say exactly when human beings first began to record their thoughts in writing, but sometime before 3000 B.C. a pictorial method of recording language was being used in Mesopotamia. Hieroglyphics were a form of pictorial writing used by the ancient Egyptians. A scribe in the pharaoh's court would have needed to know seven hundred different hieroglyphics to keep the court records. At Sumer, however, the pictorial symbols developed into what is called cuneiform, a combination of pictorial and phonetic (sound-based) symbols to represent sounds and words. Alphabetic writing is a system of recording language that uses purely phonetic symbols (letters). Most cultures can represent all the words in their language using fewer than thirty letters. The Phoenicians, who lived on the eastern coast of the Mediterranean Sea, are credited with having invented the alphabet around 1500 B.C. The Greeks and the Hebrews quickly adopted alphabetic writing.*

area, possibly from south central Asia. The Sumerians built cities, made canals to bring water to their fields, and created hand-painted pottery. Around 3500 B.C., they invented a system of writing called cuneiform. From about 2860 to 2360 B.C., the Sumerian culture was made up of a number of powerful city-states. Each city-state had its own ruler and another leader who was in charge of the city's temple, which was built to honor the god of that city. Sumerians worshiped many different gods. These gods formed a kind of heavenly council led by Enlil, god of the storm. When conflicts arose between city-states, they were thought to be a result of conflicts among the gods. The Sumerians were one of the first people to develop a legal code, laws that reflected their sense of right and wrong. They believed that earthly (human) laws should reflect the laws of the gods.

The Akkadian people also lived in Mesopotamia, just north of the Sumerians. Around 2360 B.C., the Akkadian rulers gained power and created a true empire in Mesopotamia. They built palaces, which replaced the temples as the centers of power. Gradually, their language began to replace the Sumerian language.

Egyptian culture was developing in Africa. Before 3000 B.C., Egypt was divided into two main kingdoms, one in Upper Egypt (south of Cairo) and the other in Lower Egypt. (Though called "lower" because it is downsteam in the Nile Delta, Lower Egypt is actually in northern Egypt.) The kind of writing known as hieroglyphics had already been invented. Around 2900 B.C., Egypt began to unite into one kingdom. Also the first founding of dynasties, known as the Old Kingdom, occurred about 2675 to 2180 B.C.

Egyptian religion centered on the nation's leader, the pharaoh, who was not simply appointed by a god (as in Mesopotamia) but was considered to be a god. All of Egypt and its resources belonged to the pharaoh. No law code was developed in Egypt because the word of the pharaoh was the law. Egyptians believed that the world existed in a changeless order from the time of creation, and had a repeating rhythm like the floods of the Nile River. In this period, the Egyptians believed in many gods, but the main one was the pharaoh, the god-king, who was thought to live in the world of the gods after he died.

During this period, many cities sprang up in Canaan as well, but no single city-state dominated the others. The language of the Canaanites was likely the ancestor of the Hebrew language, the language spoken by the Israelite people. The Canaanite peoples also believed in a number of gods, such as Baal, the most powerful of all gods, and Astarte, the goddess of fertility.

Two centuries or so before the time of Abraham, the great kingdoms in both Mesopotamia and Egypt suffered confusing and difficult times. The Guti and other peoples from the north invaded Mesopotamia and defeated the Akkadians. Eventually, in Egypt, rival pharaohs each claimed to be the true leader of Egypt. Without one leader, local towns formed their own governments. Then, nomadic peoples (wandering herders) entered Egypt, causing more confusion. Irrigation of fields was not kept up, which led to food shortages and starvation (famines). In Canaan, nomadic peoples invaded and destroyed many cities. The area became dotted with small, poorly constructed villages.

In the century before Abraham, the Sumerian people, led by the kings of Ur, defeated the Guti people and once again ruled in Mesopotamia. But soon after, the Sumerian language began to disappear as the Sumerian and Akkadian peoples became more mixed. The Akkadian language became an important international language used throughout much of the ancient Near East. In Egypt, a powerful family in the city of Thebes (Upper Nile) was able to reunite the land and finally put an end to confusion. Egypt then entered a stable and prosperous period known as the Middle Kingdom.

From Abraham to the Time of Moses

During the nearly six hundred years between the time of Abraham and the time of Moses, Amorite people who were centered in Babylon ruled the land of Mesopotamia. Later, the Assyrians from the north took over the area. Cities such as Mari and Babylon became powerful and had many beautiful temples and palaces. The Babylonian ruler named Hammurabi (1792-1750 B.C.) is known for his famous law code, which has similarities to laws in the Old Testament. For example, the "eye for eye, tooth for tooth" law in Exodus 21:23-25 is similar to some of the laws in Hammurabi's Code. When Hittite invaders from the north defeated the Babylonians and ended their rule, much of the Near East entered a period of confusion.

Also around this time, Egypt had moved into a period known as the Middle Kingdom (around 2181 B.C.), which followed the Old Kingdom. The Middle Kingdom lasted until the Hyksos people invaded around 1800 B.C. The Hyksos were probably from northwest of Mesopotamia,

Egypt. *The life-giving waters and fertile banks of the Nile gave birth to one of the great civilizations of the ancient world, thousands of years before the time of Christ. Some of its oldest monuments, the Great Pyramids (tombs of kings called "pharaohs") and the mysterious Sphinx, were as ancient to the people of Jesus' day as the Coliseum in Rome is to us today. The Egyptians built the Temple of Karnak, with its great columns, as a model of the universe, and the Temple of Luxor as a model of the human body. Rameses II, famous for his building projects, erected a huge statue of himself at Abu Simbel. Some believe he may have been the pharaoh ruling Egypt when the Israelites set out for the promised land.*

north of the Mediterranean Sea, and they may have worshiped the gods of the Canaanites (see above). They ruled in Egypt for nearly two hundred years, until Egyptian rulers, who created what is known as the New Kingdom around 1600 B.C., drove the Hyksos out. Some time around the beginning of the New Kingdom, the descendants of Jacob (Israel) traveled to Egypt seeking food, because of a famine in Canaan (Gen 41:56—42:2; 46:1-4). They apparently stayed on in Egypt for many generations. Eventually, these descendants of Abraham, who were known as Hebrews, became slaves in Egypt (Exod 1:8-14). A child called Moses was born to Hebrew parents in Egypt at a time when the pharaoh of Egypt was trying to cut down the Hebrew population by having Hebrew male babies killed (Exod 1:1-22). Moses' mother and sister were able to save Moses from this fate and eventually he was adopted by pharaoh's daughter and raised in the royal household (Exod 2:1-10). When he was a young man, Moses killed an Egyptian guard and had to escape from

Egypt (Exod 2:11-15). He later returned (Exod 4:18-20), probably during the reign of the Egyptian pharaoh Sety I (1291-1279 B.C.). Finally, with God's help, Moses led the Hebrew people out of Egypt and toward the land God had promised to give Abraham and his descendants—Canaan.

One God, One People

God not only miraculously brought the Israelites out of bondage in Egypt, but also forged a new relationship with them. God was now to be intimately known by the covenant name "I AM," or *Yahweh* in Hebrew. When God called Moses at the burning bush to go back to Egypt, God said to him, "This is what you are to say to the Israelites: 'I AM has sent me to you'" (Exod 3:14). *Yahweh* later gave the Law to Moses as the people camped in the Sinai desert. The very first commandment in the Law said that the people were not to worship any other gods except *Yahweh* (Exod 20:1-3). While the peoples of the ancient Near East worshiped many gods, the people of Israel were to worship and follow the one true God.

The people of Israel lived in a world that had seen many struggles and wars between peoples. The lands of Egypt, Mesopotamia, and Canaan had changed hands many times. Wars would be part of Israel's history as well. But the Israelite people also lived in a world that had already made great progress in terms of building, writing, and art. Just as God had acted in history to open the way for them, they now were about to take their place in world history and make contributions that continue to affect us today.

FROM JOSHUA TO THE EXILE: THE PEOPLE OF ISRAEL IN THE PROMISED LAND

Moses led the people of Israel in the desert for forty years after they escaped from slavery in Egypt. But when the people were camped in the lowlands of Moab on the east side of the Jordan River, Moses died, and Joshua became their new leader. The promise God made more than five hundred years earlier to Abraham (Gen 12:1,2; 15:7-21) and repeated to Joshua (Josh 1:1-8) was about to be fulfilled. Abraham's descendants, the people of Israel, were ready to take over the land of Canaan. But this would not be easy. Other people had lived in Canaan for thousands of years. They had built walled cities and farmed the land, and they were not simply going to give their land to the people of Israel.

The People of Israel Enter the Promised Land

The story of how the people of Israel conquered the people of Canaan is told in JOSHUA. Like the biblical books that tell about how Moses led the people (Exodus, Numbers, Deuteronomy), JOSHUA is full of miracles. Before the people of Israel could enter Canaan, they had to cross the Jordan River. Once again, God was with them and helped them in a miraculous way. Just as God had helped Moses by opening up the waters of the Red Sea (Exod 14), so God made the waters of the Jordan River stop flowing when the priests of Israel stepped into the river (Josh 3:15-17). After they crossed the river and came to Gilgal, the people made a monument using twelve rocks, one rock for each tribe of Israel. Then they set up camp there.

Here the people of Israel prepared to capture Jericho, a nearby walled city that stood on a mound along an important east-west trade route in the fertile Jordan River Valley. The conquest of Jericho is another miraculous story. After the Israelite priests and army marched around the city for

ABOVE: The land promised to the people of Israel as it looks today. The Valley of Jezreel at the foot of Mount Gilboa is rich and productive farmland. RIGHT: Jericho, sometimes called "the oldest walled settlement in the world," dates back to around 9000 B.C. Shown here are the remains of a fortification wall.

seven days as the LORD had instructed, the priests blew their trumpets and the people shouted. The walls of the city fell flat and the Israelites captured the city (Josh 6). From Jericho, Joshua and the people moved into other parts of Canaan, capturing other cities in battle or making agreements with the people who already lived in the land.

The Tribes of Israel and Their Lands

Eventually Joshua gave different parts of the land of Canaan to each of Israel's twelve tribes (Josh 13–21; see also the map on p. 2464). These tribes were like big extended families, with the oldest male (father) serving as the center of authority. As the tribes took ownership of their pieces of land, they settled down to build towns, grow crops, and raise herds of sheep and goats. The land allotted to each tribe and each family within that tribe was a gift, or "inheritance," from God. The land was to remain perpetually in the family of the first settlers. Every fiftieth year, the Year of Jubilee, the land was to revert to its original owners (See Lev 25:8-17,23-28; and the chart called "Jewish Calendar and Festivals," p. 944). An Israelite family could not permanently sell their land, though they could sell the *use* of the land—the value of the property being calculated by projecting the value of the crops between the time of sale and the Year of Jubilee. This system, in a sense, redistributed wealth, and gave the poor the means for making a fresh start.

The tribe of Levi did not get their own land, because they were given a special task and would not be farmers or herders. The Law of Moses said they would be in charge of offering sacrifices to God (Deut 18:1). The other tribes were to provide these sacrifices, and the Levites were allowed to keep some of the food sacrifices for themselves. Thus, the Levites (priests from the tribe of Levi) had an important place as the religious leaders of the other tribes: they would be the priests for all Israel.

Even though the twelve tribes were scattered in different areas around Canaan, they shared a common history and followed the Law of Moses. Just before Joshua died, he called all the tribes together for a meeting at Shechem. He challenged them to remain faithful to God and never to worship other gods (Josh 24:4-24). The people promised to remain faithful, and Joshua set up a stone as a witness to their promises (Josh 24:25-27).

Judges Are Chosen To Rule the People of Israel

After Joshua died, the tribes of Israel continued to fight against the Canaanites (Judg 1), but they did not drive out all the people who had lived in the land. In addition, the tribes of Israel were surrounded by other peoples who were not friendly.

At this time, the Israelites began to forget the promises they had made to the LORD while Joshua was still alive. Some of them worshiped the Canaanite gods, Baal and Ashtoreth, as well as idols of other gods from nearby lands (see the article called "The Ancient World: Peoples, Powers, and Politics," p. 919). The LORD was so angry that he let the surrounding nations raid Israel's lands and steal their crops and possessions (Judg 2:6-15).

When the people cried out for help, God felt sorry for them. Help came from special leaders known as judges. The "judges" sometimes settled legal cases (see Judg 4:4,5), but most of them were more well known as military leaders chosen by God to lead the Israelites in battle against their enemies. The lives of these judges are described in Rom 3–16 (see also the Introduction to JUDGES, p. 453).

THE JUDGES OF ISRAEL

JUDGE	YEARS OF SERVICE	CHIEF ENEMY	ACCOMPLISHMENTS	SCRIPTURE PASSAGE
Othniel	40	Northern Aram	Helped Israel defeat King Cushan-Rishathaim of Aram Naharaim and brought Israel forty years of peace.	Judg 3:7-11
Ehud	80	Moabites and Amalekites	Killed King Eglon of Moab and defeated the Moabites, who had joined with the Amalekites to attack Israel.	Judg 3:12-30
Shamgar	10	Philistines	Rescued Israel by killing 600 Philistines.	Judg 3:31
Deborah and Barak	40	Canaanites	Defeated the army of Canaanite King Jabin of Hazor and his commander Sisera.	Judg 4:1—5:31
Gideon	40	Midianites and Amalekites	Built an altar for worshiping the LORD and pulled down the altar where his father had worshiped the Canaanite god Baal. Defeated the Midianites who had joined with the Amalekites to steal Israel's livestock and crops. Honored the LORD by refusing to be made king.	Judg 6:1—8:35
Tola	23	Not stated in the Bible	The Bible says he rescued Israel but gives very little information about this judge.	Judg 10:1,2
Jair	22	Not stated in the Bible	The Bible says little about this judge's accomplishments, but it does say he had thirty sons, each one in charge of a town in Gilead.	Judg 10:3-5
Jephthah	6	Ammonites and Ephraimites	Defeated the Ammonites who had invaded Gilead. Battled the army of the Israelite tribe of Ephraim.	Judg 11:1—12:7
Ibzan	7	Not stated in the Bible	The Bible says little about this judge's accomplishments, but it does say he had thirty daughters and thirty sons.	Judg 12:8-10
Elon	10	Not stated in the Bible	The Bible gives no specific information about this judge's accomplishments.	Judg 12:11,12
Abdon	8	Not stated in the Bible	The Bible says little about this judge's accomplishments, but it does say he had forty sons and thirty grandsons.	Judg 12:13-15
Samson	20	Philistines	Took revenge on the Philistine leaders and people who burned his wife and family.	Judg 13:1—16:31

Samuel: Prophet, Priest, and Judge

Near the end of the period of the judges, a boy named Samuel was born to Hannah and Elkanah (1 Sam 1). They took him to Shiloh, where he was dedicated to the LORD by the priest Eli. Samuel stayed with Eli in Shiloh and helped Eli serve the LORD. While Samuel was still very young (1 Sam 3), the LORD chose him to be his special servant and he grew up to be the LORD's prophet (1 Sam 3:19—4:1; 7:3-5). Samuel also served as a priest (1 Sam 7:9,10) and was considered a judge, or leader, all his life (1 Sam 7:15).

Kings and Kingdoms

When Samuel was getting old, the leaders of Israel's tribes asked him to choose a king to rule over them, because all the lands around them were ruled by kings. Samuel did not really like this idea. He believed that a king would not treat the people well (1 Sam 8:9-18), and he thought that the people's request for a king showed their lack of trust in the LORD as their leader (1 Sam 10:17-19). But when Samuel prayed about the situation, the LORD told him to go ahead and give the people a king (1 Sam 8:1-22). This was a major change in the history of the Israelite people. For a long time they had been a loosely connected group of tribes with one God but separate leaders. Now, they were about to become a single nation made up of tribes united not only by one God, but also under a king.

The people of ancient Israel were ruled by kings from the time of Saul (about 1030 to 1010 B.C.) and David (1010 to 970 B.C.) to the reign of Zedekiah (597 to 587 B.C.). Some of the kings were strong rulers who remained faithful to God. But other kings actually led the people away from worshiping God, made bad agreements with Israel's enemies, and treated the people cruelly and unfairly. The history of the kings is told in 1 and 2 SAMUEL, 1 and 2 KINGS, and is retold in 1 and 2 CHRONICLES. See the chart called, "The Kings of Israel," p. 929, for the names of all of the kings of Israel mentioned in the Bible.

Ashurnasirpal, the king of Assyria from 883 to 859 B.C., shown in a royal procession. After settling in the land God had promised to them, the people of Israel wanted to have a king like the ones that ruled Israel's neighbors.

Saul: Israel's First King

The period of the kings is divided into two main parts. The first part is known as the time of the United Israelite Kingdom, when there was just one king for all of the Israelite people and tribes. Samuel chose Saul to be the first king of Israel (1 Sam 9; 10) and he was accepted by the tribal leaders because of his courage and military abilities (1 Sam 11). He ruled for about twenty years and did much to bring the tribes together and to defeat some of Israel's enemies. But Saul was also a troubled man who was unfaithful to God at times (1 Sam 13; 15).

David Becomes Israel's King

While Saul was still king the LORD told Samuel to go to Bethlehem to find the next king. This turned out to be David, the youngest son of Jesse (1 Sam 16:1-13). David soon entered Saul's court as a special servant who played the harp to console the troubled king (1 Sam 16:14-23). Another account of David's life shows him to be an amazingly brave soldier who trusted in the LORD. David killed the giant Philistine Goliath (1 Sam 17:1-54) and impressed the king so much that Saul made him a high officer in the army (1 Sam 18:5). Eventually, the king became suspicious of David and jealous of his military successes. Saul tried several times to have David killed, but was never successful. Eventually, Saul committed suicide after being injured in battle against the Philistines (1 Sam 31:1-13).

After Saul's death, there was a short period when the people of Israel were divided between loyalty to Saul's only living son, Ish-bosheth, and to David, the powerful military leader. David became king of the people of Judah at Hebron (2 Sam 2:4), and then king of all of Israel after the murder of Saul's son (2 Sam 5:1-3). He then conquered the Jebusite city Jerusalem and made it the capital of the United Israelite Kingdom (2 Sam 5:6-12). He put the ark of the covenant (see the mini-articles called "The Ark of the Covenant," p. 513, and "The Tabernacle," p. 2346) on the hilltop where the temple would later be built (2 Sam 6:1-19). The prophet Nathan told David that God would dwell in the great temple in Jerusalem some day. But he said that David's son would build it, not David (2 Sam 7:1-17).

One of greatest things David did was to defeat the Philistines in battle and take control of all the land east of the Jordan River and north of Damascus in Syria as far as the Euphrates River (2 Sam 8). PSALMS and books of the prophets describe David as a model king who had a close relationship with God. In many ways, he became a symbol of new life for God's people and of God's rule in the world (2 Sam 23:5; Ps 89:3, 4; Isa 9:1-7; Jer 33:14-26; Mic 5:2-5). However, David also had his faults; he was not always perfect (2 Sam 11; 12). See also the mini-article called "David," p. 1028.

Solomon: Israel's Wisest King

David's son, Solomon, became king after David died and ruled from about 970 to 931 B.C. Solomon was known as a wise man (1 Kgs 2:9; 3:12,28; 4:29-34), and he was in charge of building Israel's first temple in Jerusalem (1 Kgs 5–8). He expanded his father David's kingdom, built an enormous palace (1 Kgs 7:1-12) and many fortresses, established store cities, and made Israel a very rich country (1 Kgs 4:20-28). But in doing this he married foreign wives and allowed them to set up shrines and monuments to other gods (1 Kgs 11:1-13), things which were certainly not pleasing to the LORD.

The Kingdom Is Divided

When Solomon died around 922 B.C., his son Rehoboam became king. Shortly after that, the ten northern tribes rebelled against the king and formed their own kingdom. This period of Israel's history became known as the Divided Kingdom.

The tribes of Judah and Benjamin in the south became known as the kingdom of Judah (or the southern kingdom). The rest of the tribes to the north formed the

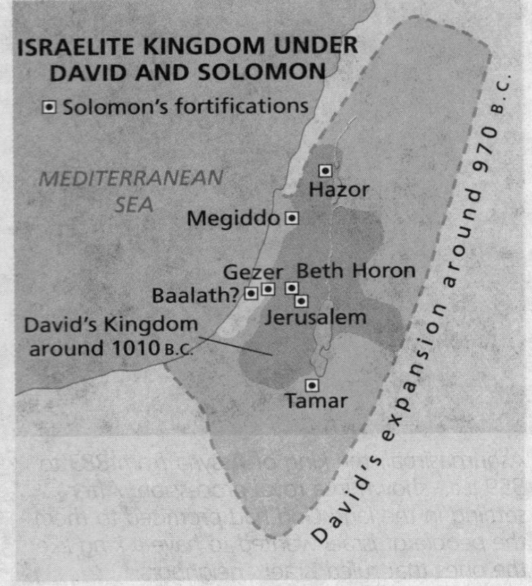

THE KINGS OF ISRAEL

This chart lists all of the kings of Israel starting with the three who ruled the United Israelite Kingdom. After Solomon's death the northern tribes broke away from the southern tribes and continued to call themselves Israel. From that time on the southern tribes came to be known as Judah. The prophets, shown in *italic*, sometimes spoke to the people of the northern or southern kingdoms, and sometimes to both.

DATE	THE UNITED ISRAELITE KINGDOM	
1050 B.C.	Saul (1030–1010)	*Eli* *Samuel*
1000 B.C.	David (1010–970)	
	Nathan	
950 B.C.	Solomon (970–931)	

DATE	JUDAH (SOUTHERN KINGDOM)	THE KINGDOM DIVIDES *Prophets*	ISRAEL (NORTHERN KINGDOM)
950 B.C.	Rehoboam (931–913) Abijah (913–911) Asa (911–870)		Jeroboam (931–910) Nadab (910–909) Baasha (909–886)
900 B.C.			Elah (886–885) Zimri (7 days in 885) Omri (885–874)
	Jehoshaphat (870–848)	*Elijah*	Ahab (874–853) Ahaziah (853–852)
850 B.C.	Jehoram (848–841) Ahaziah (of Judah, 841) Queen Athaliah (841–835) Joash (835–796)	*Elisha*	Joram (852–841) Jehu (841–814) Jehoahaz (814–798)
800 B.C.	Amaziah (796–781) Azariah (Uzziah) (781–740)	*Jonah* *Amos*	Jehoash (798–783) Jeroboam II (783–743)
750 B.C.	Jotham (740–736) Ahaz (736–716)	*Isaiah* *Micah* *Hosea*	Zechariah (6 mos. in 743) Shallum (1 mo. in 743) Menahem (743–738) Pekah (737–732)
	Hezekiah (716 – 687)		Hoshea (732–723)
700 B.C.	Manasseh (687 – 642)		**Assyrians defeat Israel and capture its capital, Samaria, 722.** **Kingdom of Israel ends.**
650 B.C.	Amon (642 – 640) Josiah (640 – 609)	*Zephaniah (640-609)* *Nahum (663-612)* *Jeremiah*	
	Jehoahaz (3 mos. in 609) Jehoiakim (609 – 598) Jehoiachin (3 mos. in 598)	*Habakkuk* *Ezekiel* (620-597)	
600 B.C.	Zedekiah (598 – 587)		

Babylonians defeat Judah and destroy Jerusalem, 587 or 586.
The exile in Babylon, 586-538.

All dates are approximate.

Kings who ruled for one year or less are in smaller type.

kingdom of Israel (or the northern kingdom). See the map called "The Kingdoms of Israel and Judah," p. 2467. Each kingdom had its own king. In Judah, the kings continued to be descendants of King David, but in Israel the tribal and military leaders had to fight to become king. Sometimes a family would reign for a period of years, only to be defeated by an opponent who then ruled for a time.

The capital of Judah was still Jerusalem where the people of Judah continued to worship the LORD in the temple. But in Israel, King Jeroboam I made a shrine in Bethel so that people could offer sacrifices there instead of going to the temple in Jerusalem (1 Kgs 12:25-33). Later, Samaria became the capital city of Israel (1 Kgs 16:24-29).

Israel: The Northern Kingdom

In the northern kingdom of Israel, some rulers allowed the people to worship idols such as the Canaanite god Baal. This practice was condemned by a number of the prophets who preached in Israel during this time. For example, the prophet Elijah spoke out against King Ahab and his wife Queen Jezebel, who openly encouraged the worship of Baal and supported Baal's prophets (see 1 Kgs 18:1—19:18).

The practice of allowing the people to worship other gods led to Israel's downfall. They fought civil wars with Judah and battled with neighbors like Aram and Moab. Eventually, the Assyrians invaded Israel and attacked the capital city of Samaria. In 722 B.C. the city was conquered and many of the Israelites were captured and taken away to Assyria as prisoners. Others stayed in the area, lived with, and sometimes married the people the Assyrians brought in to settle the land. The northern kingdom of Israel never regained its power as a nation.

Judah: The Southern Kingdom

Meanwhile, Judah in the south had its own problems. Though many of its kings, such as Hezekiah and especially Josiah, were faithful to God and followed the teachings of the Law of Moses (2 Kgs 18:1-8; 2 Kgs 22:1—23:25), other kings, like Manasseh, did things to make the LORD angry (2 Kgs 21:1-18). Eventually Judah could no longer hold out against the attacks of its powerful neighbors. The kingdom of Babylon finally invaded and destroyed Jerusalem and its temple in 587 B.C. Many of the people of Judah were taken to Babylon as prisoners. During the next fifty years this group of Israelites remained in Babylon and could not return to their own land. This period of time is known as "the exile." (See the mini-article called "Exile," p. 1541.) To learn about how the people of Israel were allowed to return to their homeland, read the next article, "After the Exile: God's People Return to Judea."

The Hanging Gardens of Babylon, *one of the "Seven Wonders of the Ancient World." The Gardens were built during the time of King Nebuchadnezzar, who ruled Babylonia from around 605 to 562 B.C. It was during this period that the Babylonians conquered Jerusalem and took the people of Judah into captivity.*

AFTER THE EXILE: GOD'S PEOPLE RETURN TO JUDEA

In Babylon

The Bible provides little information about the years in the sixth century B.C. when many of the Israelite people lived in exile in Babylon. Though the people could no longer worship God in the temple in Jerusalem, the Babylonians allowed them to gather and practice their religion. The Israelites told the stories of their ancestors, heard the words of prophets, and studied the Law of Moses. Some believe that it was during the time of the exile that some of Israel's priests added to the old Scriptures and wrote new ones, so the people would not forget who they were and where they came from.

Back Home in Judea

Many of the Jewish people had been sent into exile between the years 597 to 582 B.C. In 539 B.C., Cyrus of Persia conquered Babylonia. About one year later he gave the Jewish people permission to return to their homeland of Judea. The books of EZRA and

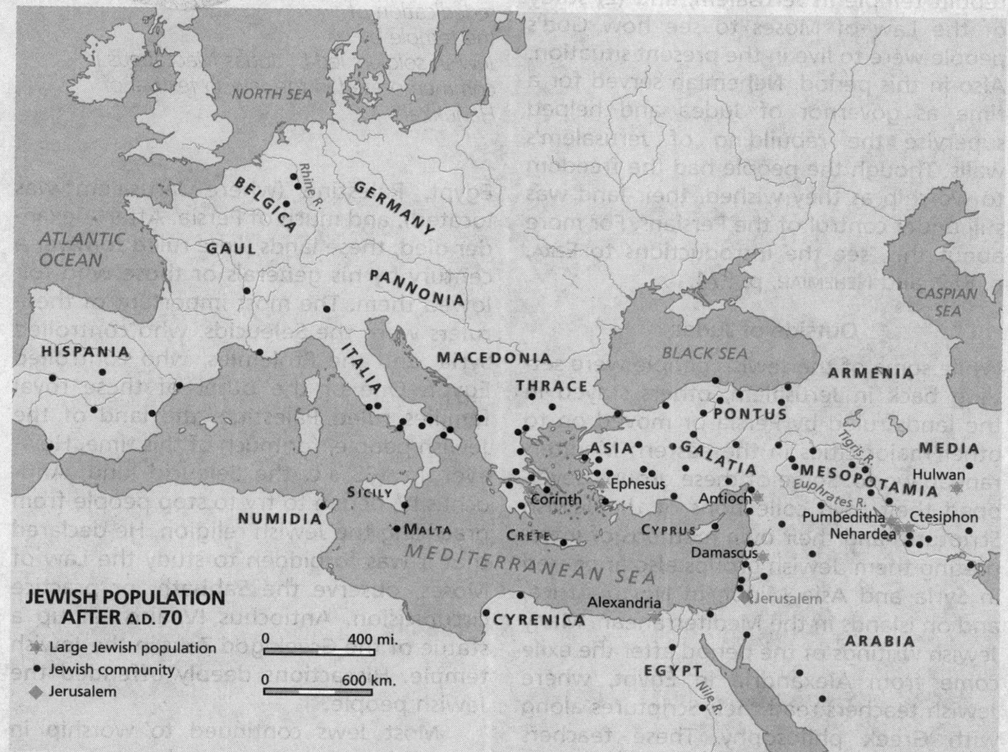

Jewish Communities in the Mediterranean World. *By the time of Jesus there were far more Jews living outside Palestine than in Palestine. This was due to both negative causes (war and exile) and to positive ones (commerce, improved travel, and Roman tolerance of the Jewish religion). After the destruction of the temple in Jerusalem in A.D. 70, the Jewish communities outside Palestine, called the "Diaspora" (meaning "scattered abroad"), would become increasingly important. When the first followers of Jesus left Judea to take the gospel to other parts of the Roman Empire, they usually went first to cities with large Jewish populations. This map shows how far from Jerusalem many Jews lived in the first century.*

Nehemiah in the Old Testament tell about the hundred-year period that followed the time of the exile. The books of the prophets Haggai and Zechariah also come from this time. Sometime between 500 and 425 B.C. the priest named Ezra encouraged the people to return to their Jewish traditions and to obey the Law of Moses. He went so far as to force Jewish men to give up their foreign wives (Ezra 9; 10).

Two religious issues were most important to the people who had returned from exile: (1) worship of the God of Israel in the rebuilt temple in Jerusalem, and (2) study of the Law of Moses to see how God's people were to live in the present situation. Also in this period, Nehemiah served for a time as governor of Judea and helped supervise the rebuilding of Jerusalem's walls. Though the people had the freedom to worship as they wished, their land was still under control of the Persians. For more about this, see the Introductions to Ezra, p. 852, and Nehemiah, p. 874.

Antiochus IV, called "Epiphanes" ("the manifested one"), *ruled Judea from 175 to 164 B.C. His cruelty toward his Jewish subjects and his enactment of laws that prohibited many customs that were required by the Law of Moses led to Jewish rebellion. The military capture, purification, and the rededication of the temple by Jewish soldiers led by Judas Maccabeus is commemorated in the Jewish festival of Hanukkah.*

Outside of Judea

While some of the Jewish people were settling back in Jerusalem, others stayed in the lands ruled by Persia or moved on to other major cities in the eastern Mediterranean world. Some of these groups developed their own collections of the Jewish Scriptures and their own methods of interpreting them. Jewish groups also appeared in Syria and Asia Minor, in North Africa, and on islands in the Mediterranean. Many Jewish writings of the period after the exile come from Alexandria in Egypt, where Jewish teachers read their Scriptures along with Greek philosophy. These teachers believed that this approach would help people to understand the basic truths of the Bible.

The Influence of Alexander the Great

Between 336 B.C. and 323 B.C., Alexander the Great of Macedonia conquered much of the eastern Mediterranean world, including Egypt, Palestine (where Jerusalem was located), and much of Persia. After Alexander died, these lands were ruled for over a century by his generals or those who followed them. The most important of these rulers were the Seleucids, who controlled Syria, and the Ptolemies, who controlled Egypt. One or the other of these royal families ruled Palestine, the land of the Jewish people, for much of this time. However, in 168 B.C. the Seleucid king, Antiochus IV, began to try to stop people from practicing the Jewish religion. He declared that it was forbidden to study the Law of Moses, observe the Sabbath, or practice circumcision. Antiochus IV also set up a statue of the Greek god Zeus in the Jewish temple. His actions deeply offended the Jewish people.

Most Jews continued to worship in Jerusalem and to pay yearly fees to support the temple and its priests. From the time of their captivity in Babylon, Jews had met informally in homes or in public halls to study the Scriptures. The moral teachings and the understanding of God contained in the Jewish Scriptures attracted many non-Jews (Gentiles) to these meetings. Some

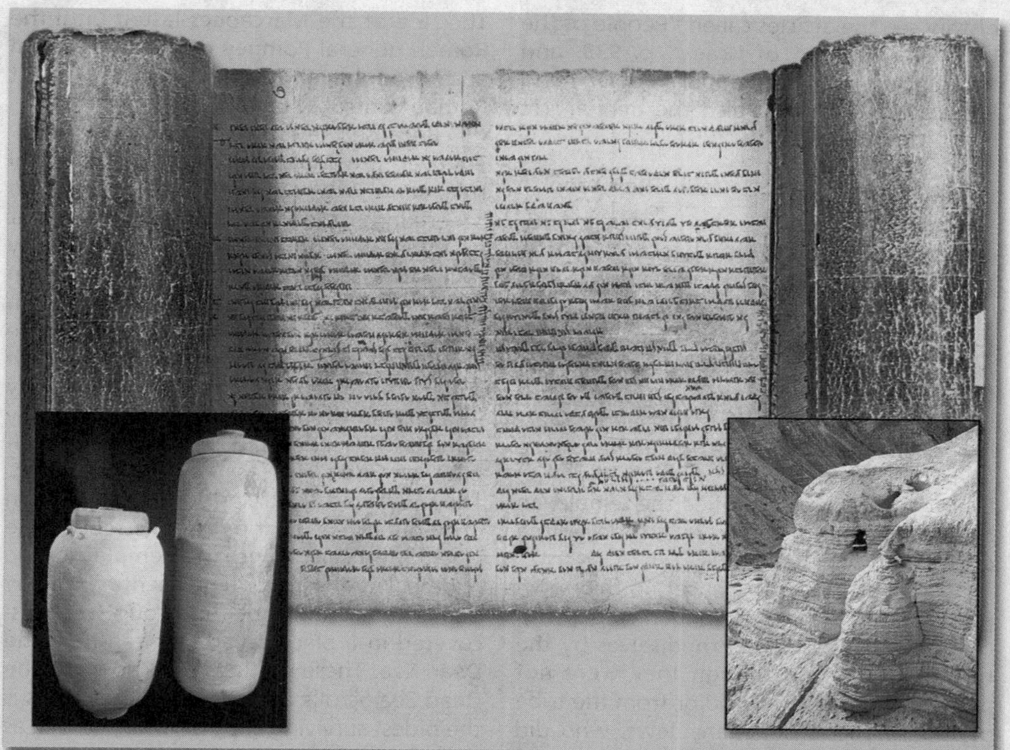

Dead Sea Scrolls. *The most important archaeological find of the twentieth century was the discovery beginning in 1947 of over eight hundred documents from a Jewish group (most likely Essenes) who lived near the Dead Sea from the middle of the second century B.C. until their defeat by the Romans around A.D. 68. Many of these leather or papyrus scrolls were stored in clay jars and hidden away in caves to keep them safe. Although most of the documents are mere scraps, a nearly complete version of ISAIAH was found. This important manuscript is older than any other copy of ISAIAH that exists.*

non-Jewish men were circumcised in order to become full members of the Jewish community (see Acts 2:11; 16:1-3; see also the note on circumcision at Gen 17:10,11).

Greek, Roman, and Persian philosophies and ideas influenced Jewish writings of the time. This influence is apparent in many of the books that are included in some editions of the Bible and known as "deuterocanonical" or "apocryphal." (See the article called "What Books Belong in the Bible?," p. 13). Jewish writers also copied the style and form of a kind of popular Roman literature called "sibylline oracles," which told of prophecies concerning Caesar and the Roman people. The Jewish Sibylline Oracles told about God's plan for the future of his people.

The religion of the Jewish people after the exile in Babylon did not move toward one single pattern or style. People were practicing Judaism and living as Jews in a variety of ways. This was the situation when Jesus came to teach the people many new things about God and God's kingdom. For a description of this next phase in Jewish history see the articles called "People of the Law: The Religion of Israel," p. 939, and "The World of Jesus: Peoples, Powers, and Politics," p. 1821. See also the mini-article called "Synagogues," p. 1857.

The Jewish People Reclaim Their Land

The Jewish people revolted against Antiochus. The rebellion broke out suddenly. Soon the rebellion had a leader named Judas Maccabeus. (One of the possible meanings for his last name is "the hammer.") Led by Judas Maccabeus, the small bands of Jewish fighters defeated the mighty army of Antiochus. This revolt is described *1* and *2 Maccabees* in the Apocrypha. (See the article "What Books Belong in the Bible?" p. 13.) Eventually the rebels purified the temple, an event still remembered by Jews today in the celebration of Hanukkah.

Finally, the Maccabees set up their own government. Those Maccabean rulers who came after Judas called themselves by the title of king, even though they were not descendants of King David or from the tribe of Judah. This upset many Jews, who did not like the Maccabeans' cruel style of control and the agreements they made with Rome in order to remain in power. The rule of the Maccabees lasted until the Roman general Pompey invaded Jerusalem and brought all the land under direct Roman control in 63 B.C.

Because they were bitterly disappointed over the Maccabean style of political rule, some of the Jewish people turned to other kinds of religions or philosophies. For example, one group of Jews became very disappointed with the temple priests in Jerusalem who seemed to love the wealth and power connected with running the temple. This group withdrew from Jewish society and lived as a separate community in a barren area near the Dead Sea. They remained there, living in complete obedience to God's Law as they understood it. They believed that God would help them drive out the present priests and rebuild the city of Jerusalem and the temple. In the middle of the twentieth century, many books and writings of this group were discovered in a place called Qumran near the Dead Sea. These writings are known as the Dead Sea Scrolls. Included in these scrolls is the oldest surviving copy of ISAIAH, as well as the rule books for this community. For more about this, see the article called "Archaeology and the Bible," p. 27.

PROPHETS AND PROPHECY

A prophet is someone who speaks God's message. The message the prophet speaks is called a "prophecy." And to speak as a prophet is to "prophesy." In general culture, prophets are sometimes compared with fortunetellers or those who predict future events. The prophets of the Old Testament, however, were somewhat different. Their task was to deliver God's message for their time and place. But those prophecies weren't simply reactions to the events and situations of the day. God's message did not depend on the needs of the audience and did not have to agree with the popular human wisdom of the times, even from the perspective of the prophet himself. As 2 Peter 1:20,21 states, "No prophecy of Scripture came about by the prophet's own interpretation. For prophecy never had its origin in the will of man, but men spoke from God as they were carried along by the Holy Spirit." The messages of the prophets were given both to God's people and to those who did not trust in Israel's God. Sometimes the message was a reminder to the people or their leaders that they were not obeying God, and that they should change their ways. This kind of message sometimes included strong warnings about God's judgment. At other times, the prophets brought words of hope in tough times, or said that even though things were bad in the present, God would cause things to change for the better in the future.

Prophets in the Old Testament

The Old Testament includes sixteen books written by or called by the names of different prophets, but these sixteen are not the only prophets who had an impact on the people of Israel. At least one prophet mentioned in the Old Testament was not part of God's chosen people, the Israelites: Balaam of Pethor was hired by the king of Moab to put a curse on Israel (Num 22:1—24:25). Using the very broad definition of prophet as one who speaks God's message, certain people from Israel's earliest history were called prophets: Abraham (Gen 20:7), Aaron (Exod 7:1), Miriam (Exod 15:20), Moses (Deut 18:18; 34:10), and Deborah (Judg 4:4). Moses certainly passed God's message to the people of Israel, but he also spoke to God for them. This was also the task of prophets. (See the mini-article called, "Moses," on p. 2335.) Samuel, a judge of Israel, was also known as a prophet (1 Sam 3:20). He heard and followed God's command to anoint Saul as Israel's first king (1 Sam 10:1).

The Old Testament often mentions the existence of false prophets who exerted influence in Israel. In contrast to the LORD's true prophets, they typically gained the favor of Israel's wicked kings. At one point some of these prophets had a contest with Israel's prophet, Elijah (875-845 B.C.), to try to prove who was stronger, Israel's God *Yahweh*, or the Canaanite god, Baal. The prophets of Baal acted like they were caught up in a trance. As they cried out to Baal they had what looked like a seizure and began to dance around. They even used their swords to cut themselves until blood poured out (1 Kgs 18:24-29). Elijah also opposed King Ahab of the northern kingdom of Israel and his wife Jezebel, who encouraged the people to worship the Canaanite god Baal (1 Kgs 17–21).

A few other examples of Old Testament prophets include the prophet Nathan, who gave King David the good news that his descendants would always rule the people of Israel (2 Sam 7:4-17), but Nathan also delivered God's angry message after David had arranged the death of a man named Uriah so that he could have Uriah's wife Bathsheba. Because of this evil action, Nathan told David that David and Bathsheba's son would die (2 Sam 12:1-14). Another prophet named Micaiah warned King Ahab that he would die in battle against the Aramean (Syrian) army (1 Kgs 22:5-38). Elisha became Elijah's assistant and eventually took his place (1 Kgs 19:19-21; 2 Kgs 2:1-18). God used Elisha to bring healing to Naaman, the commander of the army

King David and the Prophet Nathan *from a Byzantine Psalter (around A.D. 950). The Bible tells of many prophets who brought difficult news to powerful rulers. Nathan told King David that David's son would die because of his sin.*

of Aram (2 Kgs 5:1-14). Another prophet, Huldah, gave advice to King Josiah (640-609 B.C.) when Josiah asked what he should do with *The Book of the Law* that had been found in the temple (2 Kgs 22:14-20).

The Writings of the Prophets

The kingdom of Israel split into two sections (northern and southern) around 931 B.C., after the death of King Solomon. Each of these kingdoms had its own temple and king, and prophets in both parts of Israel gave warnings and encouragement to the rulers and the people. The first books of the prophets probably date back to just after 800 B.C. The prophecies of Amos and Hosea were written for the rulers and the people of the northern kingdom (Israel). They warned the leaders and the people who had grown rich to care for the poor and stop worshiping idols. About the same time or a little later, the prophets Micah and Isaiah delivered their prophecies in the southern kingdom (Judah). Isaiah warned that a king would come from the east to take over the land and force the people to leave. He called the people to obey God in order to avoid the punishment that he predicted, but he also gave them the promise that God would help them triumph in the end. The suffering they would undergo was to be seen as punishment from God. Though Isaiah's message began in the 700s B.C., many scholars believe that followers of Isaiah continued writing prophecy in his name even after the Babylonian exile in 586 B.C. Jeremiah, Zephaniah, Nahum, and Habakkuk were prophets in Judah during the time just before it was defeated by Babylon and many of its people were taken off as captives in 586 B.C. About the time Jeremiah was finishing his work as a prophet, Ezekiel began to bring God's message to the people. His prophecies were given to the people of Judah before they were taken away from their homes and forced to live in exile, and continued into the period of the exile in Babylon, where Ezekiel was also taken as captive. The last part of his prophecy includes a great vision of the future when God would rebuild the temple in Jerusalem and bring a new day for God's people (Ezek 40–46).

After the people of Judah were allowed to leave Babylon and return home, the prophets Haggai and Zechariah delivered God's message. Speaking around 520 B.C., Haggai told the people that God wanted them to rebuild the temple. About the same time Zechariah told the people the LORD's chosen king would again rule in Jerusalem and that all people on earth would someday worship Israel's God. Still later came the prophecies of Malachi, who told the priests to be faithful to the covenant the LORD had made with Israel. The time of the prophet Obadiah is unclear, though he probably wrote some time after 587 B.C. when the country of Edom helped Babylon defeat Judah. It is not clear when the prophet Joel delivered his message of both judgment and hope, though it was most likely some time after the people returned from captivity in Babylon.

JONAH is different from the other prophetic books because it gives only one sentence of what Jonah preached (3:4). The rest of the book tells about how Jonah tried to run away when God told him to preach to the people of Nineveh, the capital of Assyria, who were enemies of Israel. The first half of DANIEL tells about Daniel and what happened to him as he lived in exile in Babylon. The second half of DANIEL tells of Daniel's vision of the future when God would help bring victory to his people. Daniel's vision belongs to a kind of writing known as "apocalyptic." (See the article called "Different Kinds of Literature in the Bible," p. 19, and the mini-article called "Apocalyptic Writing," p. 1656.)

Prophecy and the New Testament

The New Testament focuses on the life and work of Jesus Christ. The New Testament writers used the Jewish Scriptures, especially the writings of the prophets, to show that Jesus was God's promised Messiah. For example, MATTHEW often uses the phrase, "to fulfill what was said by the prophet" which is followed by a quote from one of the Old Testament prophets (Matt 1:22; 2:5, 17; 4:14-16). Each quote is meant to show that Jesus' life fulfills what was said by one of the prophets hundreds of years earlier. In his letters, the apostle Paul quoted the Old Testament prophets to show that Jesus was God's chosen one who had come to save all people, Jews and Gentiles alike (Rom 9:25, 26,33; 15:11,12).

The New Testament writers also used the words of the prophet Isaiah to show that John the Baptist was the one who had been sent to prepare the way for Jesus (Matt 3:1-3; Luke 3:3-6). And John preached like a prophet, telling the people to turn to God and get ready for the one (Jesus) who was coming to baptize them with the Holy Spirit (Mark 1:7,8; Luke 3:15-17).

Jesus quoted the Old Testament prophets to show that he was the Son of Man who would come from heaven with power and great glory (Matt 24:29,30 quotes Isa 13:10 and 34:4; Matt 26:64 quotes Dan 7:13,14). Jesus also said that he was the shepherd who would be rejected and struck down (Matt 26:31 quotes Zech 13:7). He applied the writing of the prophet Isaiah to himself, explaining why he had come to earth (Luke 4:16-21 quotes

St. John the Baptist *by Sally Barton Elliott. John, like many of the prophets of the Old Testament, gave the people of his time strong warnings and told them to turn to God and get ready for the one God was sending to save them.*

Isa 61:1). Paul said it was because God's purpose for people and all creation was fulfilled in Jesus (1 Cor 15:20-28), who overcame the powers of evil.

Prophecy and the Church

Some of the followers of Jesus received the special gift of prophecy from God's Spirit (Rom 12:6; 1 Cor 12:27-31). These New Testament prophets were to use this gift to speak God's messages of truth (1 Cor 14:29-32). God's followers are also warned in the New Testament to watch out for false prophets who would try to lead them away from the truth about God (1 Tim 6:3-5; 2 Pet 2:1-3). REVELATION warns of a false prophet who would perform fake miracles and make false predictions in an effort to trick God's people (Rev 13:11-15), and the faithful are told to be careful to listen only to the message of God's true prophets (Rev 22:18,19).

For more about prophets and prophecy see the Introduction to Prophetic Books, p. 1287, and the introduction to each of the books in that section of *The Learning Bible.*

PEOPLE OF THE LAW: THE RELIGION OF ISRAEL

The faith of Israel, now more commonly known as the Jewish faith, did not begin as a set of religious practices or system of beliefs. Rather, it began when God commanded Abraham to leave his home and take his wife Sarah and family to a new land called Canaan. Along with this command, God promised Abraham three things: (1) he would have many descendants who would become a great nation; (2) his descendants would be famous and have a land they could call their own; and (3) God would bless Abraham's descendants, and everyone on earth would be blessed because of them (Gen 12:1-3; 15:1-6; 17:1-8).

In return for these promises, Abraham and his descendants were to trust in God alone and obey what God told them to do. A special agreement (also known as a "covenant") had been formed. Abraham confirmed this covenant with God by having his son and all his male descendants circumcised (Gen 17:9-27). Having male children circumcised became an important sign of belonging to God's special people. See also the mini-article called "Covenants (Agreements)," p. 386, and the note on circumcision at Genesis 17:10,11.

The following things made the faith of Israel unique among the religions of the ancient world:

1. They believed that God (*Yahweh*) had selected them to be God's special (chosen) people.
2. They believed God acted in history and was involved in the life of the whole community. God's relationship was with all the people, not just with a few individuals or the community's leaders.
3. They believed only in *Yahweh* and did not worship any other gods.

The LORD Gives His Chosen People the Law

The Bible describes how God was at work in the history of the Hebrew people, the Israelites. When they went to Egypt to escape a famine (Gen 42), God took care of them. Later, God helped them escape, led by Moses, from slavery in Egypt (Exod 12–14). The festival called Passover commemorates this important event, and is observed by Jewish people today. Remembering God's blessings and guidance has been an important part of their worship life as God's people.

God made an important covenant with the Israelite people at Mount Sinai, a place in the desert where Moses and the Israelites arrived after escaping from Egypt (Exod 19:1,2). This happened before they entered Canaan, the land God promised to give them. At Sinai, God gave the Law to Moses and the people. This Law includes the Ten Commandments (Exod 20:2-17; Deut 5:6-21) and other instructions about how the Israelite people should live together and worship God (see also the mini-article called "Ten Commandments," p. 354). Other sections of this Law of Moses are given in Exodus 19–34, LEVITICUS, and DEUTERONOMY. The Law includes rules about making sacrifices to God, about how to treat others, and about who would be in charge of Israel's worship. It also included instructions about observing special festivals and holy days and explained what should happen if someone broke a law. At this point in their history, the people of Israel did not need a system of government or a constitution because they were supposed to live according to the Law of Moses. God promised that if the people followed the Law they would be rewarded. But if they were unfaithful to God and did not live according to the Law, they could expect to be punished (Exod 20:5,6; Lev 25:14-46).

The People Enter the Land God Promised Them

In addition to the Law, God also gave Moses instructions for making the tabernacle (also known as the Tent of Meeting). The people would gather to worship God and offer sacrifices (Exod 25–30). This tent had three sections:

1. **The outer area.** This is where animals were sacrificed and burned on an altar. There was also a bronze basin in this area for the priests to wash their hands (Exod 27:9-19; 30:17-21).
2. **The Holy Place.** This area had a table, a golden candlestick, and an altar where incense was burned. The altar and table were made of acacia wood and covered with gold. A special kind of bread called the bread of the Presence was kept on the table. Twelve loaves of bread, one for each of Israel's tribes, were to be set out on the table every Sabbath (the day of rest), and only the priests were permitted to eat them (Lev 24:5-9). The lampstand was made of gold and had seven branches that curved upward. An oil-burning lamp was placed on each of the seven branches (Exod 25:31-40). The lampstand had seven branches probably because seven was a holy number that symbolized the Sabbath, the seventh day of the week (the day God rested after creating the world; see Gen 2:1,2).
3. **The Most Holy Place.** This is where God was said to be present and where the ark of the covenant containing the stone tablets of the Law was kept. The ark of the covenant was covered with gold and measured about 4 feet long and was just over 2 feet wide and high. Gold rings were put on each side, so the people could carry the chest with them when they moved from place to place (Exod 25:10-22). The lid of the chest was called the atonement cover (traditionally "mercy seat" because this is where God "sat" to be among the people, to receive their sacrifices, and to meet a representative of the people; see Exod 26:34). Only Moses, and later the high priest, were allowed to enter the Most Holy Place. It was separated from the rest of the tent by a curtain, and inside the Most Holy Place was a lamp that was to be kept burning (Exod 27:20,21).

Each of the areas of the tabernacle was separated from the others by curtains. A frame made of 48 acacia wood planks supported the whole tent, and it measured about 150 feet by 75 feet. The people carried the tabernacle and the ark of the covenant with them as they journeyed. When they finally entered the land of Canaan, the tabernacle was set up at Shiloh (Josh 18:1). Later it was moved to Nob (1 Sam 21:1-6), then Gibeon (1 Chr 16:39), and finally to Jerusalem (2 Chr 5:4-6).

The covenant God had made with Abraham and Sarah was beginning to take shape. *Yahweh* had led the people of Israel out of slavery in Egypt and had helped them get their own land. With each new generation, the people of Israel grew in number and began to enjoy the blessings of living in the promised land. But the people had a difficult time being completely loyal to God, so problems arose.

JUDGES describes how God raised up special leaders, called judges, to help the people in times of crisis. (For more about these leaders see the Introduction to JUDGES, p. 453.) The Israelites lived in this way for many years, until the people begged the judge and prophet named Samuel to give them a king like the ones who ruled neighboring countries. Samuel thought the people's request showed a lack of faith, but God eventually told Samuel to choose Saul as Israel's first king (1 Sam 8–10). Later, a shepherd named David was anointed king (1 Sam 16; 2 Sam 2:4). David captured Jerusalem and made it the capital of Israel and the single place of worship for all the tribes (2 Sam 5; 6). He even set up the tabernacle in Jerusalem on a hill that was known as Zion.

David's son Solomon built the first temple to take the place of the tabernacle. Solomon asked King Hiram of Tyre to supply some materials and skilled builders to help the Israelites construct the temple. In exchange for grain and olive oil from Israel, King Hiram gave Solomon lumber for the temple. People from both kingdoms worked together and the two nations were at peace with one another (1 Kgs 5). The temple was built using cedar, olive wood, and brick, with beautiful decorations made of gold and ivory. Like the tabernacle, the temple had three areas, but in the temple a large olive wood door, instead of a curtain, separated the Holy Place from the Most Holy Place (1 Kgs 6:16; 7:13—8:13). It took seven years to build Solomon's temple, which was dedicated sometime between 960 and 950 B.C. during the Feast of Tabernacles (1 Kgs 8:62-66).

After King Solomon died, the ten northern tribes of Israel broke away and made Shechem and then Tirzah their capital. They created several places of worship (1 Kgs 12:25-33), and some of the northern leaders, such as Ahab and Jezebel, encouraged the people to worship the Canaanite god Baal (1 Kgs 18). They also built idols (such as "Asherah poles") to worship the local gods (1 Kgs 14:15). (See also the mini-article called "Canaanite Gods and Goddesses," p. 469.) This was one of the things God and God's prophets had warned the people not to do. Because the people did not remain loyal to *Yahweh* alone, they were punished. In 722 B.C. the Assyrians invaded the northern kingdom (Israel) and took most of the people from their homeland to live in Assyria (2 Kgs 17). The people of the southern kingdom (Judah) saw this as God's punishment for the northern tribes' disobedience to their covenant with God. (See also the mini-article called "Assyria," p. 711.)

Later the people of Judah also disobeyed God and were invaded by the Babylonians, who destroyed Jerusalem and the temple in 586 B.C. Solomon's temple had stood for nearly 400 years, but the Babylonian invasion put a temporary end to worship at the temple. Israel's priests and prophets were forced to discover how Israel's faith could survive in exile, far away from Jerusalem in captivity in Babylon. (See also the mini-article called "Babylon," p. 1363.)

Israel Returns and Rebuilds the Temple

The people of Israel lived in exile in Babylon for about 50 years, but the priests and teachers of Israel did not let their faith die. Although the temple was destroyed, and they were far from home, they still had God's Word in the Scriptures and in their hearts. Some scholars believe that the time of exile marked a renewed commitment to God and to studying Scripture. The Jewish people probably continued to meet for worship, but they had to do so in private homes.

In 540 B.C. the Persians defeated the Babylonians. The Persian ruler, Cyrus, followed the Persian custom of allowing captured people to return to their homelands and to worship freely, as long as they promised not to start a revolt against the Persians. Many, but not all Israelites, did return to Judah beginning in 539 B.C. They completed work on a new, smaller temple ("the second temple") in 515 B.C. (Ezra 3–6). The physical splendor of this temple could not compare with Solomon's temple, but it was used for nearly 500 years, somewhat longer than Solomon's temple was used.

Two men, Ezra and Nehemiah, were especially important leaders during the first hundred years after the people returned to Judah from exile. Ezra, a Jewish priest and scribe, studied the Law of Moses and taught it to the people (Neh 8). Copies of the Law of Moses and the historical records were recovered and again became the basic guidelines for the relationship between God and the people of Israel. Nehemiah, who was appointed by the Persian king to be governor of Judah, supervised the reconstruction of the walls of Jerusalem (Neh 2–6).

During the centuries after the second temple was built and before Jesus was born, the people of Israel were often under

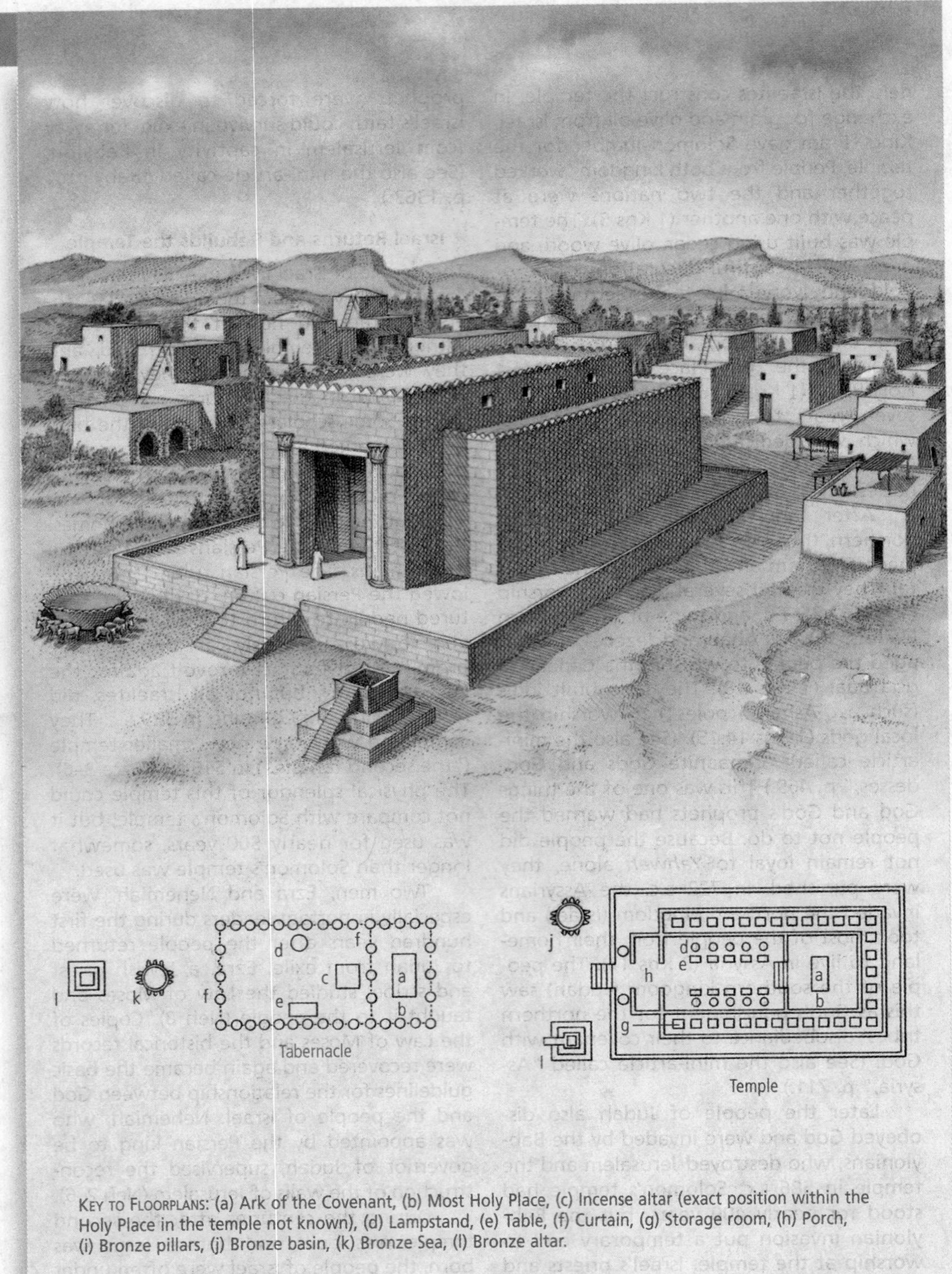

KEY TO FLOORPLANS: (a) Ark of the Covenant, (b) Most Holy Place, (c) Incense altar (exact position within the Holy Place in the temple not known), (d) Lampstand, (e) Table, (f) Curtain, (g) Storage room, (h) Porch, (i) Bronze pillars, (j) Bronze basin, (k) Bronze Sea, (l) Bronze altar.

the rule of foreign powers. This caused them to start thinking of themselves more as a religious group than as a nation with physical boundaries and a political leadership of its own. At this time, the most important feature of Israel's religion, which had come to be known as Judaism, was its stress on keeping the Law of Moses. To be a Jew meant following the Law of Moses. This included observing all the religious festivals as well as the special rules for priests and worship in the temple.

The second temple was at the center of an important event in Israel's history in the second century B.C. The Syrian king Antiochus IV Epiphanes set up an altar to the Greek god Zeus in the temple in 167 B.C. This was a horrible offense against God and the Jewish people, so the Jewish people revolted against Antiochus and restored the temple in 164 B.C. The Maccabean priests who led the revolt to free the Jews from Syrian rule set up a Jewish state with themselves as kings. It lasted until the Romans invaded in 63 B.C. For more about this period in Israel's history, see the article called "After the Exile: God's People Return to Judea," p. 931.

Herod Rebuilds and Enlarges the Temple

In 37 B.C., the Romans named a local leader ruler of Judah. In 20 B.C., Herod received permission to rebuild and expand the temple. Most of the building was completed in a year and a half, but work continued on the temple for another forty to fifty years, into the time when Jesus began his teaching (John 2:20). This expanded second temple, sometimes called "Herod's temple," was built on a huge four-sided platform that was almost a mile around its base. Its largest stones were as big as 40 feet long and 6 feet high. Some of these stones are still in place today on the temple site in Jerusalem. What is left of this "temple mount" can be seen clearly at the site called the "Western Wall" (or "Wailing Wall"), where many Jews still go to pray. The temple itself was surrounded by a large wall that had many different entrances. The outer area of the temple grounds included a court of the Gentiles, where anyone was allowed to visit. In this outer area, birds and animals suitable for sacrifice were sold to pilgrims, and foreign money was exchanged so pilgrims could pay their temple tax. In addition to the traditional sections discussed earlier—an altar area where burnt offerings were sacrificed by the priests, a holy area, where only priests were allowed, and the Most Holy Place where only the high priest was allowed to go—the second temple also included a woman's court.

The religious life of the temple went on in clear view of the Romans, who occupied the Antonia Fortress (also called the Praetorium) built right outside the northwest corner of the wall surrounding the temple area. This fortress was the living quarters for a large number of Roman soldiers, whose job was to keep peace in Jerusalem (Acts 21:34-37). The Roman governor's official residence was in Caesarea, but he usually stayed at this fortress while in Jerusalem.

During the time of Herod's temple, the Romans were in charge of Jerusalem and Judea. They did, however, allow a council of local Jewish leaders, including the high priest and other important religious and business leaders, to have some control over settling local matters, especially those having to do with the temple and religious issues. For example, no Gentile (non-Jew) was allowed in the inner parts of the temple. If someone broke this law, the Jewish leaders could call upon the Roman authorities to put the offender to death.

In Jesus' day, the temple continued to be the center of the Jewish faith. Jewish men and many of their family members traveled to Jerusalem to celebrate yearly festivals such as Passover and Pentecost. The temple priests and the rituals surrounding the temple were important to the Jewish people. Some Jews, such as the Pharisees,

JEWISH CALENDAR AND FESTIVALS

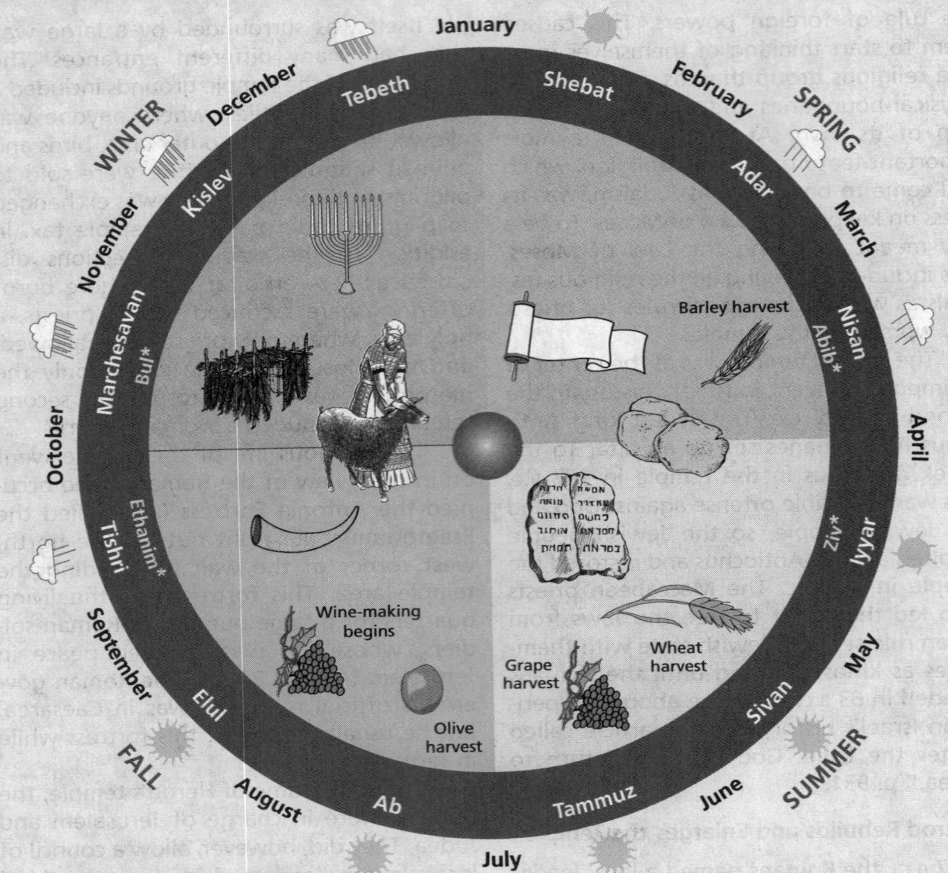

*Names of the months before the exile.

THE CALENDAR IN THE ANCIENT WORLD

As in other parts of the ancient Near East, the people of Israel developed a calendar that was based on the yearly movement of the sun and on the phases of the moon. The year was divided into twelve months, based on the observation that the moon's phases changed about twelve times in the period of days that made up a year. The number of days in the lunar (moon-based) year was about eleven days shorter than the solar (sun-based) year, so the Israelites periodically added an extra month to the calendar to make sure that the festivals they celebrated would continue to fall at their expected times in relation to the weather patterns (seasons) and agricultural cycles (planting and harvesting).

Early in Israelite history the year was considered to begin in the seventh month (around the fall fruit harvest). Later, it began in the spring on the first new moon after the vernal equinox (one of two times in the year when day and night are equal in length).

Time was measured, however, more often by season than by names of months. The year was divided into the dry season (April to September) and the rainy season (October to March). These, in turn, were divided into times for planting grain (November to December) and times for harvesting (April to June). Time was also measured by the agricultural activities that were undertaken in specific months. For example, wheat was harvested in March and April, grapes matured in June and July, and summer fruit was picked in August and September.

The months themselves had religious significance for the people of Israel. The beginning of each month (when the moon is "new") was considered a holy time and a time when the New Moon Festivals were celebrated (Num 28:11-15). Most of the yearly religious festivals had traditional associations with agricultural events, as well as to the events in Jewish history they commemorated.

FALL FESTIVALS

Feast of Trumpets (Rosh Hashanah, first day of Tishri, the seventh month)

A day to celebrate the New Year and to remember the covenant God made with the people at Mount Sinai. This holiday marks the beginning of the festival year.

Lev 23:23-25; Num 29:2-6.

Day of Atonement (Yom Kippur, tenth day of Tishri)

The day of the year when the people expressed their sorrow for their sins by going without eating (fasting) and the priest purified the Most Holy Place by sacrificing a bull for his own sins and a goat for the sins of the people. A second goat (called a scapegoat) was released into the desert to show that the people's sins were being taken away.

Lev 16:1-34; Num 29:7-11.

Feast of Tabernacles (Succoth, fifteenth day of Tishri)

A week-long celebration to remember how the people wandered for forty years in the desert before entering into the land God promised to them.

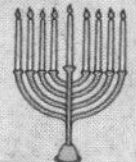

Lev 23:33-43.

Feast of Dedication (Hanukkah, twenty-fifth day of Kislev)

A week-long celebration to remember the rededication of the temple by Judas Maccabeus in 164 B.C. The story of Judas and his brothers is told in a book called *1 Maccabees*, which describes events in Jewish history from 175 to 134 B.C.

1 Maccabees 4:36-59; John 10:22.

SPRING FESTIVALS

Passover and Feast of Unleavened Bread (fifteenth Day of Nisan)

A week-long festival to recall how God delivered the people from slavery in Egypt and to give thanks for the yearly production of food crops and flocks.

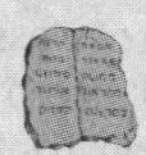

Exod 12:23-25.

Feast of Weeks (Pentecost) (Shavuoth, sixth day of Sivan)

A day to celebrate the grain harvest and the beginning of the season when the first fruits were offered. It was also a day to recall how God delivered the nation from Egypt and provided a land that could supply the needs of the people.

Lev 23:15-21; Deut 16:9-12.

Purim (thirteenth day of Adar)

A day to celebrate how Queen Esther helped stop Haman's plot against the Jews in the time of King Xerxes of Persia.

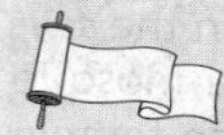

Esth 9:20-32.

PILGRIMAGE FESTIVALS

Three times a year, Jewish men were required to go to Jerusalem to celebrate these special festivals:

Feast of Tabernacles

Feast of Unleavened Bread

Feast of Weeks (Pentecost)

SABBATH: A WEEKLY FESTIVAL

The word Sabbath comes from the Hebrew verb *shabbat*, to "stop" or to "rest," and refers to the seventh day of the week, from sunset on Friday to sunset on Saturday. The ancient Israelites, like modern Jews, worshiped on the Sabbath and rested from their work.

The Bible's description of the Sabbath's origin is found in Genesis 2:1-3. These verses at the end of the creation story tell how God rested from the work of creation on the seventh day and made it a special, holy day. In EXODUS a connection is made between God's resting from creation and commanding Israel to rest from work on the Sabbath and worship the LORD (Exod 20:8-11; 31:17). This resting was not only for Israelites, but for their animals, servants (including slaves), and any foreigners living in Israel as well (Exod 23:12; Deut 5:14,15).

Related to the weekly Sabbath observance is the biblical command that every seven years the land must be allowed to rest for a full year. During this Seventh Year (or "sabbatical year") the land was not to be plowed or planted. This was done to honor the LORD, the one to whom the land truly belonged (Exod 23:10,11; Lev 25:1-7). Any crops that grew on their own were to be left in the fields for the poor and for work animals. The Seventh Year was also a time when debts were cancelled (Deut 15:1-3).

In addition, the Bible speaks of a Year of Jubilee. Each seventh Sabbatical Year (that is, every forty-nine years), land that had been sold was to be returned to its original owner, and all slaves were to be freed to their families (Lev 25:8-34). This year began on the Day of Atonement with the blowing of the ram's horn.

The Sabbath observance was one of the most important elements in Israelite religion. It reminded people of their special status as God's chosen people and that God was the Creator of the world. The three Sabbath observances of rest and freedom point to God's desire to free all of creation. Celebrating them reminds people of their own need for continual re-creation.

also emphasized the importance of studying and interpreting the Jewish Scriptures. This means that there were a number of different and important ways that Jewish people expressed their faith. If this had not been true, the Jewish faith might have died out when the temple was destroyed in A.D. 70.

Jesus' prediction that the temple would be destroyed (Mark 13:1,2) came to pass when the Romans destroyed Herod's temple while putting down a Jewish revolt that lasted between A.D. 64-70. The Roman emperor Hadrian (A.D. 117-138) crushed a second Jewish revolt about A.D. 131. In 132, Hadrian built a temple to honor the Roman god Jupiter on the same site, and in the seventh century A.D., Muslims built a mosque called the Dome of the Rock on the temple site. The shrine and mosque are still standing today, as are a few parts of Herod's original temple area.

The Role of Israel's Priests

According to the covenant God made with Moses, all the people of Israel were to serve God as priests (Exod 19:5,6). They would be God's holy nation. The Law of Moses also set aside special priests to represent the whole people in their relationship with God. The priests of Israel were to be from the tribe of Levi. Those who were not born into this tribe could not serve as priests.

The priesthood of Israel appears to fall into three levels. In the lowest level were those Levites who were not direct descendants of Moses' brother Aaron (see Num 3:5-13). They were to help the priests and take care of the furnishings in the tabernacle (and later, in the temple). At the next level were the priests who were responsible for offering sacrifices and leading the worship. These priests were also from the Levite tribe, but had to be direct descendants of Aaron. The Levites and the priests were divided into twenty-four groups or shifts. Each group served in the temple for one week on a rotating basis. With twenty-four groups, a particular priest might serve for a total of two or, very occasionally, three weeks each year. At the head of the priesthood was the

The Arch of Titus *Rome, built in A.D. 81, celebrates how this Roman general put down the First Jewish Rebellion in Palestine eleven years earlier. This relief from the Arch shows how Titus brought the temple treasures, including the gold lampstand (menorah), to the emperor and paraded them through the streets of Rome.*

high priest. He was in charge of the other priests, and was the only priest who could enter the Most Holy Place to offer sacrifices on the Day of Atonement (Lev 16:1-25). For more about the role of priests in the religious life of Israel, see the mini-article called "Israel's Priests," p. 2344.

The priests wore special clothes made of linen and other fine materials. For a description of these, see Exod 28:1—29:30. The high priest wore a special vest (ephod) and a breastpiece. The breastpiece was made partly of metal (gold) and partly of cloth (fine linen) and was to have four rows of precious stones with three in each row, representing the twelve tribes of Israel. In the early days of the priesthood, the breastpiece had a pouch in it that contained the "Urim and Thummim," objects the high priest could use to get a "yes" or "no" answer from God (Exod 28:30). Most likely, by the time the Jewish people returned from their exile in Babylonia the use of the Urim and Thummim had been discontinued. Another distinctive part of the high priest's attire was a turban. It had a gold rosette with the words "HOLY TO THE LORD" engraved on it (Exod 28:36; 39:30).

When the Jewish people returned to Jerusalem after exile in Babylonia, the Persian king would not allow them to have their own king. Because they could not have a king, the high priest became an even more significant person in the life of the people. In the centuries before Jesus and during Jesus' lifetime, the high priest was the head of the temple and of the Jewish people.

Worship and Festivals

The worship practices of Israel included the offering of sacrifices (see the chart called "Sacrifices and Offerings," p. 219), prayers, and Scripture reading. Selected texts were read for certain occasions, and sometimes songs were sung. PSALMS includes prayers and songs that were sung or said in worship by the whole people or used by individuals in private prayer. The text of Deuteronomy 6:4 ("Hear, O Israel," called the *Shema*) was to be said in prayer every morning and evening.

One of the most important aspects of the religious life of the Jewish people, both before and after the exile, was the keeping of the Sabbath (Exod 20:8-11; Exod 31:12-17). On the Sabbath, the seventh day of the week, Jews are commanded not to do any work and to rest, just as God rested after creating the world in six days (Gen 1:1—2:4). The Sabbath is also devoted to prayer and to remembering how God brought the Israelite people out of slavery in Egypt. On this day, they and their children, their servants, their visitors, and even their livestock should rest and not work (Deut 5:12-15).

The festival celebrations that were commanded in the Law of Moses and established by Jewish tradition greatly influenced Israel's life of faith. These celebrations can be grouped according to the time they were to take place as well as by purpose. See the chart on page 944-945 for an explanation of the major festivals in the Jewish calendar.

TRADE AND TRAVEL

The story of trade and travel in the ancient Near East tells how those civilizations developed. The Bible, other documents of the times, and archaeological discoveries give a general picture of how ancient peoples traded with one another, where the most important trade centers were, and how they traveled and transported their goods to these marketplaces. But the complete story has yet to be pieced together from the information available to us.

No clear evidence has been found to show how the earliest human beings traveled. Archaeologists date the earliest evidence of any kind of travel from the end of the "Ice Age," about 40,000 years ago. Evidence suggests that some kind of trading occurred in prehistoric times, since many raw materials, including "luxury" items like amber, have been found far from their likely sources. After the last glaciers of the Ice Age melted (around 12,000 years ago), people began to grow crops and raise livestock. The steady supply of food produced by farming created the conditions for people to live in towns and cities. From these early times to today, trade and travel encouraged each other to grow and expand.

Early Israelites

Before they settled in Canaan, the earliest ancestors of the Israelites were nomads, which means that they lived by moving herds of sheep and goats from place to place to find good pastures. For example, the Bible tells us how Abraham moved with Sarah and their family from Ur of the Chaldeans (at the head of the Persian Gulf) to Canaan in Palestine (Gen 11:26—12:9). Like other nomadic peoples, Abraham and his descendants lived in tents, temporary dwellings that were easy to set up and take down. Abraham's grandson Jacob moved his whole family to Egypt because there was a famine in Canaan where they lived (Gen 46:5-28). His sons and their families remained in Egypt for many years until Moses led them out of Egypt and across the Sinai peninsula. They lived there in tents for forty years as they made their way back to the land of Canaan. Besides the sheep and oxen they took with them, they may have had donkeys and camels to carry them and their belongings (Gen 12:16; 22:3; 24:10; 42:26).

The earliest Israelites traded in animals, milk, cheese, and wool. Even after they settled in Canaan, the Israelites were farmers and herders, but few were professional merchants. However, unlike more isolated areas of the world, the geography of the ancient Near East encouraged rapid change. Canaan (later known as Palestine), was a land bridge that connected northern Africa and Asia Minor with the rest of the Near East. (See the map on p. 2463.) Wandering peoples, merchants, skilled workers and artisans, and armies used this land bridge to pass from one part of the ancient world to another. They brought special skills, ideas, and products over this land bridge. Egyptians, Babylonians, Assyrians, Hittites, Greeks, Persians, and desert nomads influenced the Israelites. From about 1000 B.C. on, the Israelites became increasingly involved in trading beyond their local marketplaces.

As trading between regions and countries became more important, so did travel. In fact, trade and travel link so completely that discussing one involves discussing the other.

Improvements in transportation made it easier for merchants to trade in distant markets. In early Bible times, trade between countries probably took the form of diplomatic exchanges between kings and had little impact on the economic life of the ordinary people. Most peoples created enough goods and services in their local economies to satisfy their daily needs. However, in later times, trade would increase as transportation improved, making possible the spread of ideas, culture, and material wealth. Unfortunately, this would also give rise to wars and the struggles to maintain empires.

Local Trading and Local Economies

Ancient Palestine was largely an agricultural society. People traded farm products and animals from their flocks in the marketplaces. Farmers brought wheat and barley, grapes and wine, olives and olive oil, figs, dates, and nuts to markets in nearby towns and cities. Herders brought milk, cheese, and butter to city markets all year round. The busiest time of the year for trading was in the late spring when herders also brought young lambs and goats to market. Before the Roman period, fish was not an important food item, even though dried fish could sometimes be found in the marketplace. The development of the fishing business increased by New Testament times.

Throughout the biblical period, trading was usually conducted at the town gate or near the entrance to towns. As trading became more complex, market stalls were set up in central parts of cities. Traveling merchants from other nations also traded their goods in these marketplaces. Traders used a variety of methods to get their goods to the market. Pack animals such as donkeys and oxen carried goods overland. Small boats brought products on rivers and canals, which was often cheaper and easier than overland transport.

In the towns and cities, people made

TRADE IN OLD TESTAMENT TIMES

International trade increased during the reign of Solomon. First Kings 5–10 and Ezekiel 27 list many of the products traded in ancient times and identify which countries were involved in the international trading of these goods.

COUNTRY OR REGION	PRODUCT
Spain	Silver, iron, tin, lead
Greece, Tubal (Asia Minor), Meshech	Slaves, bronze
Beth Togarmah (Armenia)	Various breeds of horses, mules
Edom	Purple cloth, linen, embroidery; emeralds, rubies, coral
Judah, Israel	High-quality wheat, figs, olives and olive oil, honey, spices
Damascus	Wine, wool
Uzal and Javan (Mesopotamia)	Iron, spices
Dedan	Saddle blankets
Arabia	Lambs, sheep, goats, gold
Kedar	Lambs, sheep, goats
Sheba, Raamah	Gems, gold, rare spices
Haran, Canneh, Eden, Sheba, Asshur, Kilmad (Mesopotamia and Assyria)	Expensive clothing, purple and embroidered cloth, colored rugs, rope
Ophir (location uncertain)	Gems, gold, juniper wood
Egypt, Kue (Turkey)	Horses, chariots

pottery, cloth, metal tools, kettles, and weapons. They usually traded these useful items for food products. In ancient Palestine, items changed hands by a kind of trading called bartering since gold and silver were not plentiful enough to be used to buy things. The use of money in the form of minted coins was not used in Palestine until after the exile (beginning around 538 B.C.). The Persians who controlled Palestine during this time introduced the use of coins in buying and selling.

Trading with the Outside World

After the tribes of Israel were united under King David (around 1000 B.C.), international trade began to increase. Israelite rulers built storage cellars and warehouses to store wine, grain, and olive oil taken from local farmers as a form of taxation. The kings used these items in their courts or traded them with neighboring countries. Although this practice probably was a source of competition for local farmers and merchants, it also created the need for professional traders (merchants) who specialized in the business of buying and selling.

The Bible reports that trade with other nations increased during King Solomon's reign (961-922 B.C.). Solomon needed wood, gold, and precious stones to build and furnish his palace and the temple he built for the LORD in Jerusalem. He traded with King Hiram of Tyre and a trade agreement between them gave Hiram the right to use Israel's port at Ezion Geber on the Red Sea. In return, Hiram sent Solomon experienced sailors to help the Israelites' journey to Ophir (believed to be in either India or Africa) to obtain gold (1 Kgs 9:26-28). Solomon also traded with the Queen of Sheba (1 Kgs 10:1-10). He bought horses from Egypt and Kue (in today's southeast Turkey) for his many chariots (1 Kgs 10:28, 29). In addition, Solomon probably charged foreign traders tolls or taxes to pass through Israel's territory.

Israel's Imports and Exports

Because Israel was at the crossroads between Mesopotamia, Aram (Syria), Asia Minor, and Egypt, it was only a matter of time before the people became involved in trading with other nations.

Israel's main exports continued to be farm products, such as olive oil, wine, and grains (1 Kgs 5:11; Ezek 27:17). They also produced and exported dried nuts (such as pistachios and almonds), perfume, and spices (Gen 43:11). Other important products were dates, figs, wool, and clothing made from wool.

Israel imported raw materials such as tin, lead, silver, copper, iron, gold (1 Kgs 10:10-12), and timber (1 Kgs 5:6-9). White linen cloth (a fine fabric made from the flax plant) probably came regularly from Egypt and Aram, while purple-dyed wool and cloth came from Phoenicia. (See the mini-article called "Phoenicia," p. 1604.) Though Israelites made pottery, they imported special pottery from the island of Cyprus and from Greece. Gems, ivory, spices, and other things came to Israel by camel caravans across the desert and by sea from southern Arabia, Ethiopia, and India (1 Kgs 10:2,10,22).

Paying for Merchandise

As trade increased in Israel during the time of Solomon, so did the use of gold and silver to pay for goods. Around this time, merchants and a special group of money changers began to weigh and test gold and silver pieces to judge their value and purity. Even so, exchanging one kind of merchandise for another continued to be the main way of doing business.

As noted earlier, the use of money (minted coins) began in Palestine when the Persians ruled the land (530-330 B.C.). Gold darics, silver shekels, and minas were used to buy and sell things (Neh 5:15). Coins circulated from many different places. Even the Persian province of Judea was given permission to make its own silver coins. After the Jewish people won their independence under the Maccabees (164 B.C.), they again made their own coins.

In Jesus' day, Roman coins were the only form of money that could be used to pay taxes to the Roman government (see Luke 20:20-26), though coins of other countries were used in buying and selling. Although the Bible does not give a complete picture of the way local economies functioned, it does mention workers being paid for a day's wage (Matt 20:1,2), and describes the requirement to pay annual temple taxes (Matt 17:24-27). Each of these

BANKING AND MONEY IN THE ANCIENT WORLD

Ancient economies developed from a barter system in which one kind of merchandise was exchanged for another. International trade, at first, involved only exchanges between rulers and did not affect the lives of ordinary people. Silver, gold, and precious stones were used as money. Refining techniques increased the purity of precious metals and made accurate coinages possible. Yet even as the economy in cities became ever more sophisticated and complex, many rural areas continued to function using a barter system.

DATE	HISTORICAL EVENT	BANKING MILESTONE
10,000-6000 B.C.	Ancient people develop agriculture and tend livestock	Barter system: livestock and grain are used as money
3000-2000 B.C.	Banking begins in Mesopotamia	Writing is used to keep trade accounts
2250-2150 B.C.	Rulers of Cappodocia (Turkey) guarantee quality of silver ingots	The official guarantee of the purity and weight of silver increases its acceptance as money
About 1750 B.C.	The Code of Hammurabi is written	Code includes laws governing banking operations
About 640 B.C.	The first true coins are minted in Lydia (Asia Minor)	The coins are minted of *electrum*, a natural mixture of gold and silver
About 600 B.C.	The first surviving record of a merchant banker (Pythius) in the ancient world is written	Pythius trades throughout Asia Minor
After 538 B.C.	Minted coins begin to be used in Palestine	The Persians introduce coinage to Palestine after the Israelite people return from exile
336-323 B.C.	Alexander the Great helps pay his troops with captured Persian gold	Trade is stimulated throughout the ancient world
323-30 B.C.	Ptolemy Dynasty in Egypt creates first unified banking system	A central bank is created in Alexandria

passages probably refers to a denarius, a coin from Cappadocia. This was also probably the coin Jesus mentioned in Matthew 22:19. The thirty silver coins that Judas was paid to help the authorities arrest Jesus (Matt 26:15) probably amounted to the wage of a typical laborer for approximately four months of work.

Travel

Travel in biblical times, besides difficult and slow, could also be very dangerous. Robbers were a hazard to travelers and merchants as they walked along foot paths. The story of the Good Samaritan (Luke 10:25-27) is an example of the constant danger. Travelers sometimes faced unfriendly or even hostile people in certain areas or towns. Wild animals, such as lions and bears, could also be a serious threat for travelers (Judg 14:5,6; 1 Sam 17:34-36; 2 Kgs 2:23-25). There were very few places to stop for food and fresh water. Roadside inns were sometimes available, but they were also dangerous.

Throughout the biblical period, governments did not maintain most roads, and methods of constructing safe roads were not introduced until the Roman occupation of Palestine. Overgrown and mountainous routes posed hazards for travelers. Strong rains could easily wash out sections of roads or make them slippery. Sometimes rocks would fall and block roads or stick up above the surface of a road and smash the wheels of vehicles. Also there were few bridges in Palestine. Crossing a stream often meant travelers had to wait for a raft to ferry across, or had to walk to find a shallow place they could wade across.

Sea travel was also dangerous (2 Cor 11:25,26). Wind and waves could easily sink a small boat or push it off course. Weather around the Mediterranean Sea was even more stormy in winter, so very few ships tried to sail during winter (Acts 27:27; 28:11). Pirates sometimes raided merchant ships as they moved their cargo on the open sea. For most of their history, the people of Israel did not have good seaports, and unfriendly neighbors often controlled the ones they needed to use. Consequently, the Israelite people did not rely on the sea very much for travel, trading or fishing.

Travel over Land

Most travel in Bible times was done on foot. People walked along paths or roads known as "ways." Many places in the Bible describe individuals or groups of people traveling by foot. Depending on the condition of the road, people could walk up to twenty miles in a day. If the road was not in good shape, or if people were loaded down with goods and supplies, the distance they could cover in a day would be much less.

Roads. Ancient roads were well-worn paths for travel and carrying goods from place to place. As wheeled transportation became more common, roads were widened, elevated so they didn't flood over as much, and sometimes paved. A few paved roads existed in parts of the major cities of Israel, but most roads were simple pathways. Cities and fortresses were often placed near well-traveled roads, but the main roads did not usually pass directly through a city. A separate road connected the main road with the town, and a town gate allowed the people of the town to control which travelers and merchants could enter the town. The number of markets and merchants grew as new roads were built.

Roads led through major religious centers, such as Jerusalem, Samaria, and Damascus in the Near East; Ephesus in Asia Minor; and Athens on the Greek peninsula. Merchants often set up markets in these places. Some sold religious objects or gifts for presenting to the various gods. In Jerusalem, pilgrims could buy small animals and grains from merchants to make

The vast network of roads built by the Romans helped them to quickly dispatch military troops to the places they were needed most. The Appian Way (photo inset), begun in the late fourth century B.C., *connected Rome with the southern part of Italy on the Adriatic Sea.*

sacrificial offerings at the temple during special festivals.

The Persians began to build major highways throughout the Near East around 600 B.C. One famous road had inns and way stations every ten to fifteen miles to shelter royalty and wealthy people. Greek rulers who succeeded Alexander the Great extended and improved roads in Egypt and Syria.

The Romans built the best highways of ancient times. Roman roads were built to make it easier for the Roman army to move freely through the territories it conquered. As the Roman Empire grew, roads were built from the southern Jordan Valley across Asia Minor, throughout Europe, and even in remote places like northern Britain. Some Roman roads were made of large flat stones. The roads were wide enough for chariots and wagons going in different directions to pass each other. Some of these roads, which date from before the time of Christ, can still be seen today.

Main travel routes. The most important road that passed through ancient Israel was the Great Coastal Highway, or the Way of the Sea. This road connected Egypt in the south with Mesopotamia, Syria, Phoenicia, and the Land of the Hittites in the north. It followed the coastal valley along the eastern shore of the Mediterranean Sea to Mount Carmel where it split into two branches—one continuing on the eastern side of the Lebanon Mountains, and the other continuing northward along the coast through the cities of Tyre and Sidon.

The King's Highway was another very important road. It went from Egypt to Israel across the southern desert (Negev), and then turned north along the eastern side of the Great Rift Valley (the long, north-south valley that contains the Dead Sea, Jordan River, and Sea of Galilee), and on to Damascus. For these and other important roads in Palestine, see the map on p. 2470.

By the time the apostle Paul and other early Christians began to take the good news about Jesus Christ to the far corners of the Roman Empire, the value of the Roman road system was clear. Paul traveled on the Egnatian Way through Macedonia. On his final journey to Rome he traveled from Puteoli, a major port for the nearby cities of Napoli and Pompeii, to the capital city on one of the most famous highways in Italy, the Appian Way. The highways and the transportation system developed by the Romans made it easier for Christian preachers to spread the good news about Jesus, and for groups of Christians to keep in touch with and support one another.

Pack animals. Donkeys are mentioned in the Bible as an early means of transportation (Exod 4:20; Josh 15:18; 1 Sam 25:20,23; 2 Sam 16:1,2; 2 Kgs 4:22; 2 Chr 28:15). Balaam, the prophet, rode a donkey (Num 22:22-35). And the "gentle king" mentioned in Zechariah's prophecy is described

COMMON FORMS OF TRANSPORTATION IN THE ANCIENT WORLD

MEANS OF TRAVEL	DISTANCES COVERED	EXAMPLES
Walking	About 20 miles per day.	Peter walks 40 miles from Joppa to Caesarea in two days (Acts 10:23-25).
Camels	As a pack animal, a camel can carry as much as 1,000 pounds and travel almost 30 miles per day. As a saddle animal, a camel can take its rider as far as 100 miles a day.	An Ishmaelite camel caravan takes spices from Gilead to Egypt (Gen 37:25). Rebekah and her traveling companions get on camels and leave with Abraham's servant (Gen 24:61).
Donkeys	About 20 miles per day. Donkeys were used for transporting goods, and were usually not used for riding except by women, children, or those too weak to walk.	The "Good Samaritan" uses his donkey to transport the man wounded by thieves (Luke 10:34).
Horses	From 25 to 35 miles per day. If people changed horses throughout the day, they could travel greater distances.	With a change of horses at Antipatris, Paul is taken by military escort from Jerusalem to Caesarea, approximately 60 miles, in two days (Acts 23:23-31)
Chariots	Horse-drawn chariots covered distances comparable to horses alone, and were used by royalty and wealthy people.	An important Ethiopian official rides from Jerusalem to Gaza (Acts 8:28).
Sailing boats	Seagoing boats were probably not built until around 3000 B.C. when the river peoples of Egypt and southern Iraq built reed boats. Under the right conditions, sailing vessels could average from 5 to 6 knots (5 to 7 miles) per hour.	Jonah runs from the LORD by boarding a ship traveling to Tarshish, perhaps in Spain (Jonah 1:3).

as riding a donkey (Zech 9:9). Similarly, Jesus rode a young donkey into Jerusalem the week before he was to die on a cross (Matt 21:1-9). Donkeys were also used to carry supplies from place to place (Gen 44:13; Josh 9:4; 1 Sam 16:20).

Horses were more expensive than donkeys. As a means of transportation, horses were originally used only by kings and armies. Eventually, all powerful armies in the Near East used horses to transport soldiers and pull battle chariots (1 Kgs 20:21; Isa 30:16; Jer 6:23; Amos 2:15). Messengers may also have used horses to bring news quickly from place to place (2 Kgs 9:18,19; Esth 8:10). The powerful but slow-moving oxen, on the other hand, were widely used as work animals to pull carts, wagons, and plows (Num 7:3; 2 Sam 6:3-6; Job 1:14).

Caravans. Groups of merchants, pilgrims, or travelers joined together for protection as they traveled with their pack animals (either donkeys or camels, depending on the terrain). Trade and travel by caravans go back as far as recorded history (see, for example, Gen 37:25). Caravans were probably in use long before the rise of sea trade and travel.

As civilizations developed, caravans became very important to the economies of cities and empires. Cities could rise or fall depending on their closeness to important caravan routes; and empires had important interests in protecting trade routes. (See Judg 5:6,7.) Caravans were usually large and their valuable cargo required the protection of soldiers or armed guards. Wealthy travelers, like Abraham, bought slaves to use as armed guards (see Gen 14:14).

Before the time of Alexander the Great (356-323 B.C.), land caravans contributed to trade in Palestine as they moved from Asia Minor following the western edge of the Syrian Desert. They supplied the markets of Aleppo, Hamath, and Damascus before heading south into Palestine. From there, they would travel to Egypt or to places near the Red Sea.

Other caravans came from central and southern Mesopotamia. Although this land was directly east of Palestine, most of these caravans had to travel north along the Tigris and Euphrates River valleys rather than directly west through the Syrian Desert. These routes, though long, were relatively safe, and caravans could make stops along the way to refresh their animals before traveling south into Palestine. Some routes went directly west from Babylon and Akkad to Damascus, but these routes were dangerous because they crossed many miles of desert.

A north African camel caravan transporting salt. More than any other pack animal, camels are well-suited to the hardships of desert travel.

In the deserts of the ancient Near East, Egypt and northern Africa, the animal most often used in caravans was the camel. Some nomads who invaded the Israelite people rode on camels (Judg 6:3-5; 7:12; 1 Sam 30:17). Camels are the best pack animals for desert travel because they are strong, have natural protection from the environment, and can travel long distances without needing to stop for water.

In hot weather, on a long journey, a camel usually carried no more than three hundred fifty pounds. But on short journeys, in cooler weather, or to evade customs duties, a camel's load might be increased to a thousand pounds. Loads were usually divided into two parts and tied on either side of the camel's back. Passengers were often carried in large baskets tied on each side of the camel.

Camels are easier to tend during long travels through barren land. They can bite off and digest the thorny plants that grow there. Camels also have calluses on their bodies that insulate them from the heat of the desert sand. While a sandstorm might blind or injure horses or donkeys, camels have very long eyelashes to shield their eyes, and can close their nostrils to protect themselves from flying dust and sand. Because they store water in their humps, camels have the capacity to go without water for many days. They also have an acute sense of smell that makes them useful in finding sources of water.

Caravans traveled when there was enough water and pasture land. In progress, a caravan averaged two to three miles per hour for eight to fifteen hours each day or, in hot weather, each night. If possible, it was arranged to stop at a "caravansary," (an inn for caravan travelers) which was usually built on a hill or elevation, and consisted of a courtyard, surrounded on all sides by many small rooms, with stables or storerooms underneath.

Vehicles. Archaeologists guess that the invention of the wheel occurred sometime between 10,000 and 8000 B.C. From existing evidence, it appears that wheels were attached to carts no later than 4000 B.C. when the inhabitants of the ancient Mesopotamian city of Sumer placed sledges on wheels to transport goods. At first, wheels were solid disks of wood. Wheels with spokes were first introduced around 2700 B.C.

In ancient times, three types of vehicles were used: the two-wheeled cart, the four-wheeled wagon, and the chariot. Two-wheeled carts were made of wood or woven basket material. Oxen, donkeys or even people pulled them. Carts were used to transport goods, baggage, and supplies. Four-wheeled wagons hauled large items such as building supplies. Wheeled vehicles were efficient on good roads and on the level plains of Palestine. They were not as reliable on rocky and dangerous mountain roads and so were not initially used for long-distance transportation of goods. Later, Roman engineers introduced wagons with undercarriages and a pivoting front axle for easier maneuvering.

Many ancient peoples used chariots as early as 3000 B.C. Battle scenes portrayed on pottery or carved in stone depict chariots in combat. Chariots were two-wheeled vehicles that one or more horses pulled. They were large enough to hold one or two soldiers with their weapons. Chariots were used for hunting by kings or wealthy people who could afford to buy and keep their own horses. The speed and mobility of chariots made a decisive factor in military campaigns. The dominance of the Egyptians, Assyrians, and Babylonians at different periods in Bible times is partly due to their well-equipped armies and use of chariots in battle. During the time of Solomon and the divided kingdom, Israel also made extensive use of chariots (1 Kgs 4:26; 2 Chr 1:14; 9:25). A horse and chariot could easily travel thirty miles in a day; and up to forty-five miles a day when necessary.

Water Travel

Rafts, boats, and ships. Small rafts made from logs and dugout canoes were the first boats used for traveling and fishing along the Mediterranean coast. Few trees existed along the Nile River in Egypt, so ancient people made rafts and small boats from bundles of reeds. These were tied together and shaped to form boats. Reed boats were used as early as 3500 B.C. Eventually, larger wooden boats were made. Pictures painted on vases and temple walls show that these boats existed well before 2000 B.C.

Throughout the history of Egypt, boat transportation on the Nile River was very important for trade and culture. Boats traveled the four hundred miles from Syene (near modern-day Aswan) to where the river empties into the Mediterranean Sea.

Ships were used to transport people or goods on the Mediterranean and Aegean Seas. Some boats were powered by ten or more rowers, and some had both rowers and sails. Usually, these early boats were steered by large oars. Early sea travel was limited to daytime journeys along the coast with stops each night. Even so, trade and travel developed on the Mediterranean, along the Arabian Gulf, the Persian Gulf and the Indian Ocean as far as India. Sea trade was greatly advanced by the Phoenicians, who were the first to learn how to navigate by the stars. The Phoenicians (based in Tyre) traveled across the Mediterranean as far as Gibraltar and the Atlantic coasts of Spain and North Africa. Between 2000 and 1000 B.C., ship travel became more common on the Mediterranean Sea. The Minoan people of Crete, the Greeks, Syrians, and Phoenicians all built fleets of merchant ships, along with warships that could be used to defend their lands or attack their enemies. The invasion of Egypt by these "Sea Peoples" took place some years after the Hebrew people had left Egypt and settled in Canaan.

Relief showing a Roman warship from the first century A.D. Roman ships were powered by sails and by one or more banks of oars.

During the time that the Israelite people ruled all or part of Canaan (1030-586 B.C.), the Phoenicians, Greeks, and Assyrians built merchant ships and warships with two or three decks. One or two decks of rowers powered the boat. A standard-sized ship might have eight rowers per side, but a very large ship could have up to sixty rowers, thirty on each side often arranged in double rows. Israel's King Solomon built a fleet of ships at Ezion Geber (1 Kgs 9:26-28; 2 Chr 8:17,18). These ships were used to carry goods back and forth to Ophir. But since Israel did not have ports on the Mediterranean Sea, Israelites never built a strong navy and had to rely on merchants from other countries for trading and sea travel.

Small boats and fishing craft. Within Israel, however, smaller boats were important to the economy of the area around the Sea of Galilee, especially during the Roman period. Archaeologists have discovered the remains of a small boat in this freshwater lake that dates from the time of Jesus (see the photograph on p. 1981). Such small boats were used for both fishing and transportation. They are often mentioned in the Gospels (Matt 14:22; Mark 1:19; Luke 5:2; John 6:19).

Little mention is made of sea-going ships in the New Testament, except those that the apostle Paul sailed on during his trip to Rome (Acts 20:38; 21:6; 27:2; 28:11). At this time, passengers like Paul had to travel on merchant ships that carried grain or other cargo (Acts 21:1-3; 27:10). The Romans had a very active "grain fleet," which brought Egyptian grain from Alexandria to the capital city of Rome in Italy. When space allowed, these cargo ships also took passengers.

Special Reasons for Travel

Holy travel. The people of Israel traveled to special holy places such as Shiloh, Dan,

Bethel, and Jerusalem to worship and celebrate religious festivals (1 Sam 1; 1 Kgs 12:26-33; 2 Kgs 10:18-24; Amos 5:4,5). Joshua called the people of Israel together at Shechem (Josh 24). And King Solomon gathered the people in Jerusalem to celebrate the Feast of Tabernacles and to dedicate the temple they had built there for the LORD (1 Kgs 8:1-13, 62-65).

At the time of Jesus, it was the custom for the people of Israel to travel to Jerusalem three times each year to celebrate the major pilgrimage festivals—Passover and the Feast of Unleavened Bread, Pentecost, and the Feast of Tabernacles. In ACTS, Luke describes how the early apostles of Jesus traveled around preaching and teaching the gospel. More than half of the book tells about Paul's many travels by land and sea. In addition to the travel undertaken by Jews and Christians, the followers of pagan gods also made pilgrimages to holy places, shrines, and temples.

Wars. A major reason for travel concerned the movement of military forces. Israel's armies often traveled outside their boundaries to battle with unfriendly neighbors (see 2 Sam 8:1-12). Israel itself was attacked by invaders from other lands including Egypt, Assyria, and Babylonia. In 331 B.C. Alexander the Great passed through Palestine on his way to invade Egypt. His army was said to have traveled as far as forty-five miles in one day. Later, when the Roman army became the most powerful army in the world, they could conquer large areas partly because they had built good roads that made it possible for their troops and supplies to move quickly and easily.

Communication. Land or sea travel was the means of sending messages to different places. The Old Testament mentions

messengers who carried news, orders, and other messages from the king to his own military commanders or to rulers in neighboring countries (2 Sam 2:5; 3:14; 11:19).

The Roman imperial post carried messages important to the Roman Empire. A messenger would journey by carriage, changing horses at staging posts along the way. In the New Testament, Paul and other church leaders communicated with groups of Christians living in various parts of the Mediterranean world by sending letters that messengers delivered by hand. As civilization became more connected by trading, the Christian message of hope traveled throughout the ancient world.

Books of Wisdom and Poetry

THE BOOKS OF WISDOM AND POETRY, JOB through SONG OF SONGS, make up the section of the Christian Bible that follows the Pentateuch and the Historical Books. The exciting narratives of the Pentateuch and the Historical Books tell the story of the people of Israel from the creation of the world to their settlement in the land of Canaan, their defeat by foreign nations, and their return from exile in Babylonia. The Books of Wisdom and Poetry are a completely different type of literature from these narratives (see the article called "Different Kinds of Literature in the Bible" on p. 19). The books in this section include excellent examples of Hebrew poetry, with repetition of words and phrases (parallelism) and patterns of rhythm. While some of these books fall into the category of "wisdom" writings (like JOB, ECCLESIASTES, and PROVERBS), the others are collections of love poems (SONG OF SONGS) or worship prayers and songs (PSALMS).

BOOKS OF WISDOM. The Wisdom writings explore important questions about life and give advice for practical living, especially in community with others. The principle themes of these writings summarize two important understandings of wisdom found in the Hebrew Scriptures. First, true wisdom comes from God (Prov 2:6, 7). Second, God's Law offers wisdom and guidance for daily life (Prov 6:23). The writer of Psalm 1 puts it this way:

> Blessed is the man
>   who does not walk in the counsel of the wicked
> or stand in the way of sinners
>   or sit in the seat of mockers.
> But his delight is in the law of the LORD,
>   and on his law he meditates day and night.
>
> (Ps 1:1, 2)

The story of JOB focuses on the question, "Why do innocent people suffer?" Job is a faithful man who must struggle with the loss of his family, his wealth, and his health. In his sadness and despair he cries out for answers. ECCLESIASTES focuses on the question of finding meaning in life. The writer asks why human beings must work and wonders about the real source of happiness. The final verses of the book return to a common theme of the Wisdom writings: "Fear God and keep his commandments, for this is the whole duty of man" (Eccl 12:13).

PROVERBS celebrates the wisdom that comes from God's Law as the way to a happy and prosperous life. The book is filled with wise sayings and common-sense advice on issues of everyday life like honesty (11:1-3), hard work (12:24), humility (15:33; 16:18, 19), and generosity (3:27, 28). Some of these sayings are said to come from King Solomon (1:1; 10:1), but others are words of people from other nations (30:1; 31:1). While some proverbs may come from the time of Solomon, the collection called PROVERBS likely includes wisdom sayings from as many as five centuries later.

BOOKS OF POETRY. Although many of the books in the Old Testament include sections of poetry, two books in this section are written entirely in poetic form. SONG OF SONGS is a beautiful example of Hebrew poetry. It was originally written as a love poem to describe the joy and extreme happiness of two people in love. But it has also been understood in some Jewish traditions as a description of God's love for Israel, and in some Christian traditions as a description of Christ's love for the Church.

PSALMS is named after the Greek word *psalmos*, which means "song." The songs and prayers found in this book were used by the Hebrew people to express their relationship with God. They cover a whole range of human emotions from joy to anger, and from hope to despair. Some were written by David, but others were written by different poets over a period of centuries. Many of the psalms were written for use in group (communal) worship, while others were likely written as private prayers but also were used in worship. PSALMS includes songs of praise to God the Creator; songs of sorrow and anger; prayers of confession; prayers of thanksgiving; hymns to celebrate the crowning of kings; and prayers celebrating God's Law and Wisdom.

JOB

Where does suffering come from? Why do good people suffer? Read how Job and his friends try to answer these big questions.

What makes Job special?

Job tells the story of one man's troubles. But his situation prompts a series of conversations written in the form of poetry. These conversations between Job and his friends and the Lord focus on difficult life questions. In the story section of Job and when the Lord speaks (chapters 38–41), the Hebrew name for the Lord (*Yahweh*) is used. In the poetry sections, various names for God are used. Job is from the section of the Jewish Scriptures known as "The Writings" or "Wisdom" literature (see the Introduction to the Books of Wisdom and Poetry, p. 959). The Hebrew text of Job is somewhat difficult to translate, and the translators have indicated in the footnotes when the Hebrew meaning of some terms is uncertain.

Why was Job written?

Job deals with the causes of human suffering and the roles God and Satan may play in this suffering. The beginning of the story describes the main character, Job: "This man was blameless and upright; he feared God and shunned evil" (1:1). He trusted God and was blessed with many children, good health, and much wealth. But when Job loses everything and suffers terribly, the book seems to focus directly on the question of why a good and faithful person like Job has to suffer. The different characters in the story try to answer this and other questions. Is all suffering caused by human sin? Does God cause people to suffer, and if so, why? Job invites readers to struggle with these age-old questions along with the characters and, in the end, discover that the mysterious power and ways of God are sometimes beyond human understanding. But God's presence with us in times of suffering can give us the strength to go on and face the future.

What's the story behind the scene?

The story of Job is set in a time before the nation of Israel existed. Job is mentioned in Ezekiel (14:14,20), along with Noah, as a faithful man of ancient times. In Job's day, wealth was based on the number of cattle and servants a person owned, rather than on money, which was not commonly used in ancient times. The enemies of Job, the Sabeans and Chaldeans (1:15,17), are peoples that come from the time of Israel's earliest ancestors. The kind of sacrifice mentioned in the story (42:8) seems to be an ancient form of sacrifice rather than the required sacrifices that were later offered by Israel's priests. The story of Job itself appears to be very old and is similar to old stories from Babylon and Egypt.

Job: Job was blameless and upright. He feared (respected) God and refused to do evil. Other books of the Bible call this the most important kind of wisdom (Ps 119:99-101; Prov 1:7; Eccl 12:13). In ancient times, people often believed that riches, a large family, and good health were signs of God's favor. Job certainly had all these. He was the richest man for miles around.

1:1-3 *Job:* See the note on p. 961.

1:1-3 *Uz . . . the East:* The exact location of Uz, Job's homeland, is unknown, but it may be Edom in northwest Arabia, since Uz is listed among the descendants of Edom (Gen 36:28). See the map on p. 2463.

1:2 *seven . . . three:* In ancient times, the numbers seven and three were considered perfect or complete numbers. Using these numbers to describe Job's children and animals is meant to show Job had a complete and full life. See also the chart called "Numbers in the Bible," p. 2405.

1:5 *sacrifice a burnt offering . . . regular custom:* In ancient times, the head of each family offered burnt sacrifices as a way to worship God and to maintain, restore, or celebrate the relationship between the giver and God (Gen 22:13,14; Exod 3:18). Later, the laws that the LORD gave to Moses and the Israelite people included instructions for offering sacrifices to ask for forgiveness (Lev 4–7).

It is impossible to give a clear date for the writing of JOB. Scholars have argued for dating the book anywhere from the time of Moses (about 1300 B.C.) all the way to the time when the Greeks replaced the Persians as rulers of Palestine (333 B.C.).

HOW IS JOB CONSTRUCTED?

JOB is made up of a series of poems contained inside a prose story. The introduction (chapters 1 and 2) and the conclusion (42:7-17) are written in narrative or prose, while the chapters in-between (3:1—42:6) are in poetic form. The prose section tells a story of a man named Job who lost his children and everything he owned but later recovered his riches and started a new family. The poetic section is made up of speeches by Job, his three friends, another observer named Elihu, and the LORD. The following outline is one way JOB can be divided. Note that in the major section (3:1—31:40), Job and his three friends argue back and forth a number of times.

The story of Job begins (1:1—2:13)

Job speaks with his friends about his suffering (3:1—31:40)

- The first round of the debate (3:1—14:22)
- The second round of the debate (15:1—21:34)
- The third round of the debate (22:1—31:40)

Elihu speaks to Job and Job's friends (32:1—37:24)

The LORD speaks to Job, and Job replies (38:1—42:6)

The story of Job ends (42:7-17)

The Story of Job Begins

A good man named Job who respects God is blessed with many children, good health, and much wealth. But Satan challenges the LORD to take away all that Job has and make Job suffer to see if he will continue to trust in God. God agrees to this challenge, and Job's suffering begins.

Prologue

1 In the land of Uz there lived a man whose name was Job. This
man was blameless and upright; he feared God and shunned evil.
2 He had seven sons and three daughters, 3 and he owned seven
thousand sheep, three thousand camels, five hundred yoke of oxen
and five hundred donkeys, and had a large number of servants. He
was the greatest man among all the people of the East.
4 His sons used to take turns holding feasts in their homes,
and they would invite their three sisters to eat and drink with
them. 5 When a period of feasting had run its course, Job would
send and have them purified. Early in the morning he would sacrifice a burnt offering for each of them, thinking, "Perhaps my

children have sinned and cursed God in their hearts." This was
Job's regular custom.

Job's First Test

6 One day the angels[a] came to present themselves before the
LORD, and Satan[b] also came with them. 7 The LORD said to Satan,
"Where have you come from?"
Satan answered the LORD, "From roaming through the earth
and going back and forth in it."
8 Then the LORD said to Satan, "Have you considered my
servant Job? There is no one on earth like him; he is blameless and
upright, a man who fears God and shuns evil."
9 "Does Job fear God for nothing?" Satan replied. 10 "Have
you not put a hedge around him and his household and everything he has? You have blessed the work of his hands, so that his

1:6,7 *angels . . . Satan:* In Hebrew the word for "angel" means "messenger." Here, angels make up part of God's heavenly court (see the note at 15:7,8.) See the mini-article called "Angels," p. 88. In Hebrew "Satan" means the "accuser." For more about Satan, see the mini-article below.

1:10 *blessed the work of his hands:* In ancient times it was believed that God provided health and wealth for good people, and punished those who did evil by bringing sickness and poverty (4:7-9). These beliefs are evident in many of the conversations in JOB.

1:9-11 Rev 12:10.

[a]**6** Hebrew *the sons of God* [b]**6** *Satan* means *accuser.*

SATAN

In the Old Testament, Satan (the "Accuser") is described as: (1) a troublemaker who causes King David to take a census of the fighting men of Israel, demonstrating a prideful dependence on military might rather than on God (1 Chr 21); (2) the one who is allowed to cause suffering for Job (Job 1:6—2:7); and (3) the one who accuses God's chosen servant, Joshua the high priest (Zech 3:1,2). The serpent who convinces Adam and Eve to eat the fruit that God warned them not to eat (Gen 3) is understood to be Satan, though this name is not used in that story.

In the Greek translation of the Jewish Bible, this enemy of God was called the Devil, from the word *diabolos*, which also means "accuser." During the two hundred years before Jesus was born, Satan became known more and more as the force of evil that opposed God. In the Bible, the battle between God and Satan is fought in human history and will end when God defeats the powers of evil.

In Jesus' time, the powers of evil were known as the kingdom of Satan. The New Testament describes Jesus as the one who came to turn people "from darkness to light, and from the power of Satan to God" (Acts 26:18). The Gospels describe how Jesus struggled against Satan's temptations (Mark 1:12, 13; Luke 4:1-13) and drove out Satan's demons who harmed human beings (Mark 1:21-28, 32-39; 5:1-13; 7:24-30). Some people accused Jesus of working for Beelzebub, another name for Satan (Mark 3:22-26). But Jesus said that his power to defeat Satan came from God and that his victory over Satan was an example of God's kingdom at work (Luke 11:18-20).

The apostle Paul believed that Satan tried to keep him from preaching the good news about Jesus (2 Cor 12:7; 1 Thes 2:18). He also said that Satan sometimes makes himself look like an "angel of light" in order to trick God's followers (2 Cor 11:14,15). But Paul was sure that God would crush Satan (Rom 16:20). Revelation 20 describes the final battle between God and Satan, which will end with the devil being thrown into a lake of burning sulfur (Rev 20:10).

Job on the Ash-Heap, illustration from *The Nuremberg Bible,* 1483, artist unknown. God allowed Satan to take away Job's fortune and then his health, but Job did not curse God. Job sat on the ash-heap mourning his loss and told his wife, "Shall we accept good from God, and not trouble?" (See 2:8-10.)

1:15-17 *Sabeans . . . Chaldeans:* "Sabeans" may refer to caravan traders from Sheba in southwest Arabia (see also Isa 60:6; Joel 3:8). The Chaldeans were from the region of Babylonia (see the map on p. 2462).

1:16-19 *fire . . . mighty wind:* In the Bible, God's presence often is revealed by fire (Exod 3:2; 19:16-18; Acts 2:1-4). God also uses fire to punish evil people (Gen 19:24,25; Josh 7:15). See also the mini-article called "Fire," p. 2383. Wind or windstorms also signal God's presence (1 Kgs 19:11-13; Job 38:1; Jonah 1:4).

2:2 1 Pet 5:8.

flocks and herds are spread throughout the land. 11But stretch out
your hand and strike everything he has, and he will surely curse
you to your face."
12The LORD said to Satan, "Very well, then, everything he has
is in your hands, but on the man himself do not lay a finger."
Then Satan went out from the presence of the LORD.
13One day when Job's sons and daughters were feasting and
drinking wine at the oldest brother's house, 14a messenger came to
Job and said, "The oxen were plowing and the donkeys were grazing nearby, 15and the Sabeans attacked and carried them off. They
put the servants to the sword, and I am the only one who has
escaped to tell you!"
16While he was still speaking, another messenger came
and said, "The fire of God fell from the sky and burned up the
sheep and the servants, and I am the only one who has escaped to
tell you!"
17While he was still speaking, another messenger came and
said, "The Chaldeans formed three raiding parties and swept down
on your camels and carried them off. They put the servants to the
sword, and I am the only one who has escaped to tell you!"
18While he was still speaking, yet another messenger came
and said, "Your sons and daughters were feasting and drinking
wine at the oldest brother's house, 19when suddenly a mighty wind

swept in from the desert and struck the four corners of the house.
It collapsed on them and they are dead, and I am the only one who
has escaped to tell you!"
20At this, Job got up and tore his robe and shaved his head.
Then he fell to the ground in worship 21and said:

"Naked I came from my mother's womb,
and naked I will depart.[a]
The LORD gave and the LORD has taken away;
may the name of the LORD be praised."

22In all this, Job did not sin by charging God with wrongdoing.

Job's Second Test

2 On another day the angels[b] came to present themselves before
the LORD, and Satan also came with them to present himself before
him. 2And the LORD said to Satan, "Where have you come from?"
Satan answered the LORD, "From roaming through the earth
and going back and forth in it."
3Then the LORD said to Satan, "Have you considered my
servant Job? There is no one on earth like him; he is blameless and
upright, a man who fears God and shuns evil. And he still maintains his integrity, though you incited me against him to ruin him
without any reason."
4"Skin for skin!" Satan replied. "A man will give all he has for
his own life. 5But stretch out your hand and strike his flesh and
bones, and he will surely curse you to your face."
6The LORD said to Satan, "Very well, then, he is in your
hands; but you must spare his life."
7So Satan went out from the presence of the LORD and
afflicted Job with painful sores from the soles of his feet to the top

[a]21 Or *will return there* [b]1 Hebrew *the sons of God*

> Then the LORD asked, *"Have you considered my servant Job? There is no one on earth like him; he is blameless and upright, a man who fears God and shuns evil."*
> Job 2:3

1:20 *tore his robe and shaved his head:* In ancient times, people did these things to show their sadness or to show that they were sorry for their sins. Here, Job is showing his sadness about what he has lost.

1:22 *Job did not sin:* Sin is turning away from God and refusing to obey God's laws. See also the mini-article called "Sin," p. 2181. Job did not turn away from God when he lost everything. He kept on praising God (1:21) instead of cursing him, as Satan said he would do (1:11).

2:1 *angels came to present themselves before the LORD:* See the note at 1:6,7. "LORD" is used in the NIV for the Hebrew word *Yahweh,* the name of the Israel's one true God. See also the mini-article called "LORD (YHWH)," p. 140.

QUESTIONS ABOUT JOB 1:1—2:13

1. What kind of a man was Job?
2. What ceremonies did he do on behalf of his children? Why?
3. What picture do chapters 1 and 2 give of Satan? Of God?
4. List the four ways that Job lost everything (1:13-19). What did Job do after he lost these things? (1:20-22) Who was especially surprised at Job's reaction? Why?
5. What did Satan ask for next? (2:4-7) Again, what was Job's reaction? (2:10)
6. What is the first thing Job's friends did when they saw him? (2:12,13) In your opinion, was their action helpful to Job or not? Why?
7. What are some ways we can respond to people who are in great sorrow or suffering a great loss? If you were hurting like Job, what help would you want? Where would you mostly likely turn for help or comfort?

2:8 *among the ashes:* People sat in ashes or rubbed ashes on their bodies to show their sorrow (see also the note at 1:20).

2:10 *accept good from God, and not trouble:* Job expresses the belief that all things, whether good or bad, come from God.

2:11 *Temanite . . . Shuhite . . . Naamathite:* The three friends who come to give Job comfort are from Teman (a place in northern Edom), Shuah (possibly a town on the Euphrates River or else further south near the towns of Dedan and Sheba), and Naamah (possibly located on the road between modern Beirut in Lebanon, and Damascus in Syria). See the map on p. 2462.

2:12,13 *tore their robes . . . seven days:* See the notes at 1:20 and 2:8. Seven days was a common time for someone to mourn (Gen 50:10). Note that Job's friends did not say anything to Job during this seven-day period.

3:1-19 Jer 20:14-18.

of his head. 8Then Job took a piece of broken pottery and scraped
himself with it as he sat among the ashes.

9His wife said to him, "Are you still holding on to your
integrity? Curse God and die!"

10He replied, "You are talking like a foolish[a] woman. Shall we
accept good from God, and not trouble?"

In all this, Job did not sin in what he said.

Job's Three Friends

11When Job's three friends, Eliphaz the Temanite, Bildad the
Shuhite and Zophar the Naamathite, heard about all the troubles
that had come upon him, they set out from their homes and met
together by agreement to go and sympathize with him and comfort him. 12When they saw him from a distance, they could hardly
recognize him; they began to weep aloud, and they tore their robes
and sprinkled dust on their heads. 13Then they sat on the ground
with him for seven days and seven nights. No one said a word to
him, because they saw how great his suffering was.

Job Speaks with His Friends about His Suffering

The longest section of the book (chapters 3–31) contains Job's conversations with his three friends, who try to tell Job why they think he is suffering. They think he must have done something evil to deserve such punishment, but Job continues to argue that he has done nothing wrong. Job speaks with each of his three friends three times.

THE FIRST ROUND OF THE DEBATE

Chapters 3–14 contain Job's first debate with his three friends.

Job Speaks

3 After this, Job opened his mouth and cursed the day of his
birth. 2He said:

3"May the day of my birth perish,
and the night it was said, 'A boy is born!'
4That day—may it turn to darkness;
may God above not care about it;
may no light shine upon it.
5May darkness and deep shadow[b] claim it once more;
may a cloud settle over it;

[a]10 The Hebrew word rendered *foolish* denotes moral deficiency. [b]5 Or *and the shadow of death*

may blackness overwhelm its light.
6 That night—may thick darkness seize it;
may it not be included among the days of the year
nor be entered in any of the months.
7 May that night be barren;
may no shout of joy be heard in it.
8 May those who curse days[a] curse that day,
those who are ready to rouse Leviathan.
9 May its morning stars become dark;
may it wait for daylight in vain
and not see the first rays of dawn,
10 for it did not shut the doors of the womb on me
to hide trouble from my eyes.

11 "Why did I not perish at birth,
and die as I came from the womb?
12 Why were there knees to receive me
and breasts that I might be nursed?
13 For now I would be lying down in peace;
I would be asleep and at rest
14 with kings and counselors of the earth,
who built for themselves places now lying in ruins,
15 with rulers who had gold,
who filled their houses with silver.
16 Or why was I not hidden in the ground like
a stillborn child,
like an infant who never saw the light of day?
17 There the wicked cease from turmoil,
and there the weary are at rest.
18 Captives also enjoy their ease;
they no longer hear the slave driver's shout.
19 The small and the great are there,
and the slave is freed from his master.

20 "Why is light given to those in misery,
and life to the bitter of soul,
21 to those who long for death that does not come,
who search for it more than for hidden treasure,
22 who are filled with gladness
and rejoice when they reach the grave?
23 Why is life given to a man
whose way is hidden,
whom God has hedged in?
24 For sighing comes to me instead of food;
my groans pour out like water.
25 What I feared has come upon me;
what I dreaded has happened to me.

---

[a]**8** Or *the sea*

3:12 *knees to receive me:* This probably refers to placing a child on the knees of its mother or father to show that the baby was accepted as his or her child.

3:13-17 *lying down in peace . . . asleep:* This refers to the underground world of the dead, known as Sheol (see also 30:23; Ps 139:7,8; Ezek 31:16-18; Acts 2:27). Sheol is usually described as being totally silent, where no one knows or feels anything (Job 10:21,22; Ps 88:12; 94:17). Punishment and torture are not connected with Sheol. Job wants to go to this place where he can rest peacefully with kings and heroes (Isa 14:9-11), and be free from his pain, as a slave becomes free from his master when he dies (3:19).

3:21 Rev 9:6.

4:1 *Temanite:* See the note at 2:11.

4:3,4 *instructed . . . supported:* Eliphaz reminds Job of how he had been known as a counselor and a leader whose kind words and actions had helped many in the past (see 29:7-17).

4:8,9 *those who sow trouble reap it . . . destroyed:* Eliphaz uses the Israelite teaching that God punishes those who do evil. He is probably referring to Job's children doing evil and being swept away (killed) by the wind sent from God (1:19). See also the note at 1:10.

4:12-15 *secretly brought to me:* Eliphaz says that God revealed a message to him in his dreams. The breeze that blew past Eliphaz's face is like the gentle breeze that brought God's voice to Elijah (1 Kgs 19:12,13; see also Gen 15:12-16; 28:10-17; Matt 1:20-23). His message is that all humans are sinful when compared to God (4:18). Though he is a good and faithful man, Job cannot be perfect, because no human being is. So, according to Eliphaz, Job's suffering and punishment come from some wrong Job has done, even though it is not clear exactly what that wrong is.

4:12 Job 26:14. **4:19** Gen 2:7; 3:19; Job 33:6; Isa 64:8.

26 I have no peace, no quietness;
I have no rest, but only turmoil."

Eliphaz

4 Then Eliphaz the Temanite replied:

2 "If someone ventures a word with you, will you be impatient?
But who can keep from speaking?
3 Think how you have instructed many,
how you have strengthened feeble hands.
4 Your words have supported those who stumbled;
you have strengthened faltering knees.
5 But now trouble comes to you, and you are discouraged;
it strikes you, and you are dismayed.
6 Should not your piety be your confidence
and your blameless ways your hope?

7 "Consider now: Who, being innocent, has ever perished?
Where were the upright ever destroyed?
8 As I have observed, those who plow evil
and those who sow trouble reap it.
9 At the breath of God they are destroyed;
at the blast of his anger they perish.
10 The lions may roar and growl,
yet the teeth of the great lions are broken.
11 The lion perishes for lack of prey,
and the cubs of the lioness are scattered.

12 "A word was secretly brought to me,
my ears caught a whisper of it.
13 Amid disquieting dreams in the night,
when deep sleep falls on men,
14 fear and trembling seized me
and made all my bones shake.
15 A spirit glided past my face,
and the hair on my body stood on end.
16 It stopped,
but I could not tell what it was.
A form stood before my eyes,
and I heard a hushed voice:
17 'Can a mortal be more righteous than God?
Can a man be more pure than his Maker?
18 If God places no trust in his servants,
if he charges his angels with error,
19 how much more those who live in houses of clay,
whose foundations are in the dust,
who are crushed more readily than a moth!
20 Between dawn and dusk they are broken to pieces;

unnoticed, they perish forever.
21 Are not the cords of their tent pulled up,
so that they die without wisdom?"[a]

5 "Call if you will, but who will answer you?
To which of the holy ones will you turn?
2 Resentment kills a fool,
and envy slays the simple.
3 I myself have seen a fool taking root,
but suddenly his house was cursed.
4 His children are far from safety,
crushed in court without a defender.
5 The hungry consume his harvest,
taking it even from among thorns,
and the thirsty pant after his wealth.
6 For hardship does not spring from the soil,
nor does trouble sprout from the ground.
7 Yet man is born to trouble
as surely as sparks fly upward.

8 "But if it were I, I would appeal to God;
I would lay my cause before him.
9 He performs wonders that cannot be fathomed,
miracles that cannot be counted.
10 He bestows rain on the earth;
he sends water upon the countryside.
11 The lowly he sets on high,
and those who mourn are lifted to safety.
12 He thwarts the plans of the crafty,
so that their hands achieve no success.
13 He catches the wise in their craftiness,
and the schemes of the wily are swept away.
14 Darkness comes upon them in the daytime;
at noon they grope as in the night.
15 He saves the needy from the sword in their mouth;
he saves them from the clutches of the powerful.
16 So the poor have hope,
and injustice shuts its mouth.

17 "Blessed is the man whom God corrects;
so do not despise the discipline of the Almighty.[b]
18 For he wounds, but he also binds up;
he injures, but his hands also heal.
19 From six calamities he will rescue you;
in seven no harm will befall you.
20 In famine he will ransom you from death,
and in battle from the stroke of the sword.

[a]**21** Some interpreters end the quotation after verse 17. [b]**17** Hebrew *Shaddai*; here and throughout Job

5:1 *holy ones:* See the note at 1:6,7.

5:6,7 *trouble sprout from the ground . . . sparks fly upward:* In Hebrew, the word for "ground," where crops grow, is similar to the word for human being. Eliphaz's words may be a kind of pun, meaning that troubles don't just pop up from the ground by chance. Rather, they fly up like sparks from human beings, which would agree with his message in 4:17. The word translated here as "sparks" is similar to the name of the Canaanite god Resheph who was believed to bring sickness and crop failure.

5:17,18 *the Almighty:* "Almighty" here is used for the Hebrew *Shaddai.* This name for God is used thirty-one times in Job, or over half the total number of times it appears in the Old Testament. Its meaning is not certain, but it may be connected to the word for "mountain," and so mean something like "God, the one of the Mountains." Eliphaz tells Job that he should feel fortunate that God cares enough about Job to discipline ("correct") him. God punishes but will also heal those who ask for help (5:8). See also Deut 32:39; Prov 3:11,12; Hos 6:1; Heb 12:5, 6.

5:11 Ps 113:7. **5:12,13** 1 Cor 3:19. **5:15,16** 1 Sam 2:8; Ps 35:10; Luke 1:52,53; 4:18.

Job said, *"If only my anguish could be weighed and all my misery be placed on the scales!"* Job 6:2

5:25,26 *your children will be many . . . full vigor:* Many children and a long, healthy life were two important signs of God's blessing in the ancient world. See also Gen 15:5, 13-15; Ps 112:1, 2; Prov 9:10,11.

6:4 *arrows of the Almighty:* Job describes God as the one who attacks him with suffering like an archer shooting arrows (see also Lam 3:12,13; Ps 38:2). See the note at 5:17,18.

6:10 *I had not denied the words of the Holy One:* Job insists that he has never turned his back on God, even though God has made him suffer greatly.

6:12 *bronze:* This metal is made by melting and mixing copper and tin. Its strength was superior to copper alone. Many useful utensils and weapons were fashioned from bronze.

6:8 Job 3:11-17.

[21] You will be protected from the lash of the tongue,
and need not fear when destruction comes.
[22] You will laugh at destruction and famine,
and need not fear the beasts of the earth.
[23] For you will have a covenant with the stones of the field,
and the wild animals will be at peace with you.
[24] You will know that your tent is secure;
you will take stock of your property and find
nothing missing.
[25] You will know that your children will be many,
and your descendants like the grass of the earth.
[26] You will come to the grave in full vigor,
like sheaves gathered in season.
[27] "We have examined this, and it is true.
So hear it and apply it to yourself."

Job

6 Then Job replied:

[2] "If only my anguish could be weighed
and all my misery be placed on the scales!
[3] It would surely outweigh the sand of the seas—
no wonder my words have been impetuous.
[4] The arrows of the Almighty are in me,
my spirit drinks in their poison;
God's terrors are marshaled against me.
[5] Does a wild donkey bray when it has grass,
or an ox bellow when it has fodder?
[6] Is tasteless food eaten without salt,
or is there flavor in the white of an egg[a]?
[7] I refuse to touch it;
such food makes me ill.
[8] "Oh, that I might have my request,
that God would grant what I hope for,
[9] that God would be willing to crush me,
to let loose his hand and cut me off!
[10] Then I would still have this consolation—
my joy in unrelenting pain—
that I had not denied the words of the Holy One.
[11] "What strength do I have, that I should still hope?
What prospects, that I should be patient?
[12] Do I have the strength of stone?
Is my flesh bronze?
[13] Do I have any power to help myself,
now that success has been driven from me?

[a]**6** The meaning of the Hebrew for this phrase is uncertain.

14 "A despairing man should have the devotion of his friends,
even though he forsakes the fear of the Almighty.
15 But my brothers are as undependable as intermittent streams,
as the streams that overflow
16 when darkened by thawing ice
and swollen with melting snow,
17 but that cease to flow in the dry season,
and in the heat vanish from their channels.
18 Caravans turn aside from their routes;
they go up into the wasteland and perish.
19 The caravans of Tema look for water,
the traveling merchants of Sheba look in hope.
20 They are distressed, because they had been confident;
they arrive there, only to be disappointed.
21 Now you too have proved to be of no help;
you see something dreadful and are afraid.
22 Have I ever said, 'Give something on my behalf,
pay a ransom for me from your wealth,
23 deliver me from the hand of the enemy,
ransom me from the clutches of the ruthless'?

24 "Teach me, and I will be quiet;
show me where I have been wrong.
25 How painful are honest words!
But what do your arguments prove?
26 Do you mean to correct what I say,
and treat the words of a despairing man as wind?
27 You would even cast lots for the fatherless
and barter away your friend.

28 "But now be so kind as to look at me.
Would I lie to your face?
29 Relent, do not be unjust;
reconsider, for my integrity is at stake.[a]
30 Is there any wickedness on my lips?
Can my mouth not discern malice?

7 "Does not man have hard service on earth?
Are not his days like those of a hired man?
2 Like a slave longing for the evening shadows,
or a hired man waiting eagerly for his wages,
3 so I have been allotted months of futility,
and nights of misery have been assigned to me.

[a]**29** Or *my righteousness still stands*

6:14 *the Almighty:* See the note at 5:17,18.

6:18 *caravans . . . wasteland . . . perish:* In the Middle East, traveling caravans of traders and animal herders had to use travel routes that took them right through deserts. Because desert land has few landmarks, it was easy to lose one's way or to miss a watering spot. Job's disappointment with God is like the frustration of those looking for water in the desert.

6:19 *Tema . . . Sheba:* Tema was a region in northwest Arabia. For Sheba, see the note at 1:15-17.

6:22,23 *Give something . . . pay a ransom for me:* It is suggested in Jeremiah 15:10 that loaning money to or borrowing from friends can cause problems for the relationship. Job has not asked for money from his friends nor asked them to risk their lives for him, so he wonders how he has offended them enough to make them offer such hard advice.

6:29 *do not be unjust:* Job continues to argue that he hasn't done anything wrong. If his friends can't say exactly how he has offended God, their charges against him are false.

4 When I lie down I think, 'How long before
I get up?'
The night drags on, and I toss till dawn.
5 My body is clothed with worms and scabs,
my skin is broken and festering.

6 "My days are swifter than a weaver's shuttle,
and they come to an end without hope.
7 Remember, O God, that my life is but a breath;
my eyes will never see happiness again.
8 The eye that now sees me will see me no longer;
you will look for me, but I will be no more.
9 As a cloud vanishes and is gone,
so he who goes down to the grave[a] does
not return.
10 He will never come to his house again;
his place will know him no more.

11 "Therefore I will not keep silent;
I will speak out in the anguish of my spirit,
I will complain in the bitterness of my soul.
12 Am I the sea, or the monster of the deep,
that you put me under guard?
13 When I think my bed will comfort me
and my couch will ease my complaint,
14 even then you frighten me with dreams
and terrify me with visions,
15 so that I prefer strangling and death,
rather than this body of mine.
16 I despise my life; I would not live forever.
Let me alone; my days have no meaning.

17 "What is man that you make so much of him,
that you give him so much attention,
18 that you examine him every morning
and test him every moment?
19 Will you never look away from me,
or let me alone even for an instant?
20 If I have sinned, what have I done to you,
O watcher of men?
Why have you made me your target?
Have I become a burden to you?[b]
21 Why do you not pardon my offenses
and forgive my sins?
For I will soon lie down in the dust;
you will search for me, but I will be no more."

---

a9 Hebrew *Sheol* **b20** A few manuscripts of the Masoretic Text, an ancient Hebrew scribal tradition and Septuagint; most manuscripts of the Masoretic Text *I have become a burden to myself.*

7:12 *the sea, or the monster of the deep:* In the Canaanite religion, the sea was a force of chaos and disorder. According to 38:8-11, God makes the sea his prisoner by setting its boundaries.

7:20,21 *If I have sinned . . . pardon my offenses:* See the note at 1:22. God forgives, that is, "takes away" the guilt and punishment brought on by the sin. Job asks for God to forgive him, so he isn't claiming to have never sinned against God. He may have sinned without knowing it.

8:1 *the Shuhite:* See the note at 2:11.

8:3 *justice . . . the Almighty:* Justice in the Bible is not simply obeying the law, but also includes living out God's love and caring, especially for those who are poor or in need. See also the mini-article called "Justice," p. 1721. For "Almighty," see the note at 5:17,18.

8:4 *gave them over to the penalty of their sin:* See 1:18,19 and the note at 4:8,9. Bildad argues that Job's children got what they deserved.

8:5,6 *look to God . . . pure and upright:* Bildad, like Eliphaz (5:8), tells Job to turn to God for help, to live right, and to obey God. If Job does this, he will gain even more than he lost, which would be a great deal, since Job was called "the greatest man among all the people of the East" (1:3).

7:4 Job 7:13,14. **7:5,6** Job 2:7,8; 9:25. **7:17** Ps 8:4; 144:3.

Bildad

8 Then Bildad the Shuhite replied:

2 "How long will you say such things?
Your words are a blustering wind.
3 Does God pervert justice?
Does the Almighty pervert what is right?
4 When your children sinned against him,
he gave them over to the penalty of their sin.
5 But if you will look to God
and plead with the Almighty,
6 if you are pure and upright,
even now he will rouse himself on your behalf
and restore you to your rightful place.
7 Your beginnings will seem humble,
so prosperous will your future be.

8 "Ask the former generations
and find out what their fathers learned,
9 for we were born only yesterday and know nothing,
and our days on earth are but a shadow.
10 Will they not instruct you and tell you?
Will they not bring forth words from their
understanding?
11 Can papyrus grow tall where there is no marsh?
Can reeds thrive without water?
12 While still growing and uncut,
they wither more quickly than grass.
13 Such is the destiny of all who forget God;
so perishes the hope of the godless.
14 What he trusts in is fragile[a];
what he relies on is a spider's web.
15 He leans on his web, but it gives way;
he clings to it, but it does not hold.
16 He is like a well-watered plant in the sunshine,
spreading its shoots over the garden;
17 it entwines its roots around a pile of rocks
and looks for a place among the stones.
18 But when it is torn from its spot,
that place disowns it and says, 'I never saw you.'
19 Surely its life withers away,
and[b] from the soil other plants grow.

20 "Surely God does not reject a blameless man
or strengthen the hands of evildoers.
21 He will yet fill your mouth with laughter

a14 The meaning of the Hebrew for this word is uncertain. **b19** Or *Surely all the joy it has / is that*

8:8 *find out what their fathers learned:* Bildad is probably referring to the ancient ones who first taught the meaning of true wisdom (see also 15:7). While Eliphaz said that he received his wisdom and insights from a vision (4:12-19), Bildad's insights come from ancient wisdom passed on through generations.

8:11 *papyrus . . . reeds:* Papyrus reeds grow in wet areas and were especially numerous in the delta region of the Nile River in Egypt. The long flat reeds were used to make rugs, boats, baskets, and other containers. Papyrus was also used to make paper-like writing material. For more about this, see the mini-article called "Scrolls," p. 1491.

8:11-19 *papyrus . . . all who forget God . . . other plants grow:* Bildad's words can be interpreted in a number of ways. He may be comparing the papyrus reed to the person who turns away from God (8:13). Sinful people who do not recognize their sins and do not turn to God for help are like weeds that grow in a garden. Even though they scatter everywhere and attach even to rocks, they are soon pulled up and destroyed. Compare this to Eliphaz's description of evil springing up from the ground (see the note at 5:6,7).

8:20 *God does not reject a blameless man:* Bildad returns to the same argument: God doesn't brush aside the innocent or help sinners who turn away from him. Bildad does not believe Job is innocent, but he thinks Job can have hope if he turns back to God.

9:3,4 *could not answer him:* Job argues that taking God to court would be useless, since human beings can neither win an argument against God nor answer all God's questions. The truth of Job's comments will be evident when he finally faces God in Job 38–41.

9:6-9 *He shakes the earth … constellations:* These verses may be part of an ancient hymn praising God as the creator of the universe. The heavens and the earth were covered by dark waters of chaos (Gen 1:1-19). In ancient times, the sea was seen as a monster that God had to step on and tame in order to create land (see the note at 7:12). The ancient Israelites believed that the earth was flat and was built on solid pillars (2 Sam 22:8; Ps 75:3). God could upset this natural order of creation by shaking the pillars. Even in ancient times, people studied and named the constellations (stars). See also Amos 5:8.

9:2 Job 4:17; Ps 14:2,3; Rom 3:10-12. **9:6** Job 26:11; Hag 2:6,7; Heb 12:26.

and your lips with shouts of joy.
22 Your enemies will be clothed in shame,
and the tents of the wicked will be no more."

Job

9 Then Job replied:

2 "Indeed, I know that this is true.
But how can a mortal be righteous before God?
3 Though one wished to dispute with him,
he could not answer him one time out of a thousand.
4 His wisdom is profound, his power is vast.
Who has resisted him and come out unscathed?
5 He moves mountains without their knowing it
and overturns them in his anger.
6 He shakes the earth from its place
and makes its pillars tremble.
7 He speaks to the sun and it does not shine;
he seals off the light of the stars.
8 He alone stretches out the heavens
and treads on the waves of the sea.
9 He is the Maker of the Bear and Orion,
the Pleiades and the constellations of the south.
10 He performs wonders that cannot be fathomed,
miracles that cannot be counted.
11 When he passes me, I cannot see him;
when he goes by, I cannot perceive him.
12 If he snatches away, who can stop him?
Who can say to him, 'What are you doing?'
13 God does not restrain his anger;
even the cohorts of Rahab cowered at his feet.

14 "How then can I dispute with him?
How can I find words to argue with him?
15 Though I were innocent, I could not answer him;
I could only plead with my Judge for mercy.
16 Even if I summoned him and he responded,
I do not believe he would give me a hearing.
17 He would crush me with a storm
and multiply my wounds for no reason.
18 He would not let me regain my breath
but would overwhelm me with misery.
19 If it is a matter of strength, he is mighty!
And if it is a matter of justice, who will summon him[a]?
20 Even if I were innocent, my mouth would condemn me;
if I were blameless, it would pronounce me guilty.

[a]**19** See Septuagint; Hebrew *me.*

Scene from the Life of Job, Henry Ossawa Tanner, 1904, oil on canvas. Job's friends, Eliphaz, Bildad, and Zophar, came to comfort Job in his troubles. For seven days and nights they sat silently beside him. When Job began to curse the day he was born, his friends, one by one, tried to explain the reasons for his suffering and told him that misfortune is always a punishment for sin.

21 "Although I am blameless,
I have no concern for myself;
I despise my own life.
22 It is all the same; that is why I say,
'He destroys both the blameless and the wicked.'
23 When a scourge brings sudden death,
he mocks the despair of the innocent.
24 When a land falls into the hands of the wicked,
he blindfolds its judges.
If it is not he, then who is it?

25 "My days are swifter than a runner;
they fly away without a glimpse of joy.
26 They skim past like boats of papyrus,
like eagles swooping down on their prey.
27 If I say, 'I will forget my complaint,
I will change my expression, and smile,'
28 I still dread all my sufferings,
for I know you will not hold me innocent.
29 Since I am already found guilty,
why should I struggle in vain?

9:21,22 *I am blameless:* Job continues to say that he has done nothing to deserve his great suffering, but he feels defeated and no longer cares about what happens to him. He challenges his friends' arguments that God punishes evildoers and helps the innocent (see the notes at 1:10 and 4:8,9).

9:25 Job 7:6. **9:28-31** Job 9:16–20.

9:30 *soap . . . washing soda:* This refers to soap made from lye, a strong cleaner. Compare this verse to Psalm 51:7, where the writer asks God to wash him clean.

9:33 *arbitrate between us:* Job wonders if a third person could listen to Job's arguments and God's arguments and decide between them, but Job quickly realizes that no one can judge God.

10:1 *complaint:* Job's words here and in many other places are directed toward God in the form of a "lament," a cry of sadness or distress. Other examples of laments in the Bible include Psalms 22; 42; Lamentations 1:11-16.

10:13-16 *this is what you concealed in your heart:* Job realizes he cannot understand all of God's mysteries or escape from God's watchful eye. God sees everything Job does. Compare Job's words to those of the writer of Psalm 139:1-19.

10:7 Job 9:33. **10:9,11** Gen 2:7; 3:19,20; Ps 139:13-16; Isa 64:8.

30 Even if I washed myself with soap[a]
and my hands with washing soda,
31 you would plunge me into a slime pit
so that even my clothes would detest me.

32 "He is not a man like me that I might
answer him,
that we might confront each other in court.
33 If only there were someone to arbitrate between us,
to lay his hand upon us both,
34 someone to remove God's rod from me,
so that his terror would frighten me no more.
35 Then I would speak up without fear of him,
but as it now stands with me, I cannot.

10 "I loathe my very life;
therefore I will give free rein to my complaint
and speak out in the bitterness of my soul.
2 I will say to God: Do not condemn me,
but tell me what charges you have against me.
3 Does it please you to oppress me,
to spurn the work of your hands,
while you smile on the schemes of the wicked?
4 Do you have eyes of flesh?
Do you see as a mortal sees?
5 Are your days like those of a mortal
or your years like those of a man,
6 that you must search out my faults
and probe after my sin—
7 though you know that I am not guilty
and that no one can rescue me from
your hand?

8 "Your hands shaped me and made me.
Will you now turn and destroy me?
9 Remember that you molded me like clay.
Will you now turn me to dust again?
10 Did you not pour me out like milk
and curdle me like cheese,
11 clothe me with skin and flesh
and knit me together with bones and sinews?
12 You gave me life and showed me kindness,
and in your providence watched over my spirit.

13 "But this is what you concealed in your heart,
and I know that this was in your mind:
14 If I sinned, you would be watching me
and would not let my offense go unpunished.

---

[a]30 Or *snow*

15 If I am guilty—woe to me!
Even if I am innocent, I cannot lift my head,
for I am full of shame
and drowned in[a] my affliction.
16 If I hold my head high, you stalk me like a lion
and again display your awesome power against me.
17 You bring new witnesses against me
and increase your anger toward me;
your forces come against me wave upon wave.

18 "Why then did you bring me out of the womb?
I wish I had died before any eye saw me.
19 If only I had never come into being,
or had been carried straight from the womb
to the grave!
20 Are not my few days almost over?
Turn away from me so I can have a moment's joy
21 before I go to the place of no return,
to the land of gloom and deep shadow,[b]
22 to the land of deepest night,
of deep shadow and disorder,
where even the light is like darkness."

Zophar

11 Then Zophar the Naamathite replied:

2 "Are all these words to go unanswered?
Is this talker to be vindicated?
3 Will your idle talk reduce men to silence?
Will no one rebuke you when you mock?
4 You say to God, 'My beliefs are flawless
and I am pure in your sight.'
5 Oh, how I wish that God would speak,
that he would open his lips against you
6 and disclose to you the secrets of wisdom,
for true wisdom has two sides.
Know this: God has even forgotten some of your sin.

7 "Can you fathom the mysteries of God?
Can you probe the limits of the Almighty?
8 They are higher than the heavens—what can you do?
They are deeper than the depths of the grave[c]—what
can you know?
9 Their measure is longer than the earth
and wider than the sea.

10 "If he comes along and confines you in prison
and convenes a court, who can oppose him?

[a]**15** Or *and aware of* [b]**21** Or *and the shadow of death*; also in verse 22
[c]**8** Hebrew *than Sheol*

10:21,22 *land of gloom and deep shadow:* See the note at 3:13-17.

11:1 *Zophar the Naamathite:* See the note at 2:11. Zophar is the third friend to speak.

11:4-6 *pure in your sight:* Zophar claims that Job has argued that he is pure and without sin. Job did claim to be innocent of doing something that deserved God's strict punishment, but he never claimed to be pure, that is, acceptable to God because he was free of all sin (see the note at 7:20,21). Having heard Job reply to his other friends, Zophar criticizes him even more and says he deserves to be punished.

11:7-11 *mysteries:* It is a mystery why God both saves and judges people. God hands out punishment, but also shows mercy (Exod 34:6, 7; Ps 86:15; Joel 2:13; Jonah 4:2). Only God has the wisdom to know who should receive punishment or mercy.

10:18,19 Job 3:11-17.

11:13 *devote your heart to him:* Zophar repeats the advice of Eliphaz (5:8) and Bildad (8:5,6) that Job should return to God and confess his sins. Then he can sleep without fear. In ancient times the heart was considered the source of a person's intentions and behavior. But if Job doesn't follow Zophar's advice, he will be like other evil people (11:20) and get exactly what he had asked for—death (10:18-22).

12:4 *friends:* Eliphaz, Bildad, and Zophar (2:11).

12:9 *LORD:* See the note at 2:1. This is the only time this name for Israel's God is used in the poetry sections of JOB. See also the Introduction to JOB, p. 961.

11:20 Job 4:8, 9; 5:12-14. **12:4** Job 6:10.

11 Surely he recognizes deceitful men;
and when he sees evil, does he not take note?
12 But a witless man can no more become wise
than a wild donkey's colt can be born a man.[a]

13 "Yet if you devote your heart to him
and stretch out your hands to him,
14 if you put away the sin that is in your hand
and allow no evil to dwell in your tent,
15 then you will lift up your face without shame;
you will stand firm and without fear.
16 You will surely forget your trouble,
recalling it only as waters gone by.
17 Life will be brighter than noonday,
and darkness will become like morning.
18 You will be secure, because there is hope;
you will look about you and take your rest in safety.
19 You will lie down, with no one to make you afraid,
and many will court your favor.
20 But the eyes of the wicked will fail,
and escape will elude them;
their hope will become a dying gasp."

Job

12 Then Job replied:

2 "Doubtless you are the people,
and wisdom will die with you!
3 But I have a mind as well as you;
I am not inferior to you.
Who does not know all these things?

4 "I have become a laughingstock to my friends,
though I called upon God and he answered—
a mere laughingstock, though righteous and blameless!
5 Men at ease have contempt for misfortune
as the fate of those whose feet are slipping.
6 The tents of marauders are undisturbed,
and those who provoke God are secure—
those who carry their god in their hands.[b]

7 "But ask the animals, and they will teach you,
or the birds of the air, and they will tell you;
8 or speak to the earth, and it will teach you,
or let the fish of the sea inform you.
9 Which of all these does not know
that the hand of the LORD has done this?

---

[a]**12** Or *wild donkey can be born tame* [b]**6** Or *secure / in what God's hand brings them*

10 In his hand is the life of every creature
and the breath of all mankind.
11 Does not the ear test words
as the tongue tastes food?
12 Is not wisdom found among the aged?
Does not long life bring understanding?

13 "To God belong wisdom and power;
counsel and understanding are his.
14 What he tears down cannot be rebuilt;
the man he imprisons cannot be released.
15 If he holds back the waters, there is drought;
if he lets them loose, they devastate the land.
16 To him belong strength and victory;
both deceived and deceiver are his.
17 He leads counselors away stripped
and makes fools of judges.
18 He takes off the shackles put on by kings
and ties a loincloth[a] around their waist.
19 He leads priests away stripped
and overthrows men long established.
20 He silences the lips of trusted advisers
and takes away the discernment of elders.
21 He pours contempt on nobles
and disarms the mighty.
22 He reveals the deep things of darkness
and brings deep shadows into the light.
23 He makes nations great, and destroys them;
he enlarges nations, and disperses them.
24 He deprives the leaders of the earth of their reason;
he sends them wandering through a trackless waste.
25 They grope in darkness with no light;
he makes them stagger like drunkards.

13 "My eyes have seen all this,
my ears have heard and understood it.
2 What you know, I also know;
I am not inferior to you.
3 But I desire to speak to the Almighty
and to argue my case with God.
4 You, however, smear me with lies;
you are worthless physicians, all of you!
5 If only you would be altogether silent!
For you, that would be wisdom.
6 Hear now my argument;
listen to the plea of my lips.

12:13 *wisdom:* Job says that wisdom can be discovered by looking at God's creation (12:7-10) and can be passed on by earlier generations and those with experience (12:12; see also the note at 8:8). But true wisdom comes from God (see also 9:4). See also the mini-article called "Wisdom," p. 2206.

12:17-24 *leads counselors away stripped . . . makes fools of judges:* Job claims that God has power to make and destroy earthly rulers and other powerful people, just as God can shake up the earth and the stars that he created (9:5-10). Job is not confessing how great God is so much as he is pointing out how he believes God controls everything. Because he believes this, Job thinks his suffering must be caused by God. This brings him back again to his original question of what he may have done to cause God to make him suffer so much.

13:3 *the Almighty:* See the note at 5:17,18.

13:4,5 *worthless physicians . . . be altogether silent:* "Worthless physicians" refers to Job's friends. Since their advice is bad, Job says it would be better if they just keep quiet. See also Prov 17:28.

12:15 Gen 7:11,12; 8:2; Deut 11:13-15; 1 Kgs 8:35; Matt 5:45.

[a]**18** Or *shackles of kings / and ties a belt*

13:16 *my deliverance:* Since no guilty person could come into God's court without being punished, Job believes he may be able to face God and be saved from punishment, because he is not guilty.

13:18 *vindicated:* Job said earlier that he could not win an argument with God in court, since God would just find him guilty anyway (9:2-4,15-23). It looks like Job has changed his mind here, but 13:21 shows that Job still is uncertain and somewhat fearful of facing God in court. If he goes to trial with God, Job wants to be sure God will not continue punishing him.

13:23-26 *sins of my youth:* Job begs God to tell him what sin he has done to earn God's punishment, even if it is a sin he did way back when he was young.

13:27 Job 33:11.

7 Will you speak wickedly on God's behalf?
Will you speak deceitfully for him?
8 Will you show him partiality?
Will you argue the case for God?
9 Would it turn out well if he examined you?
Could you deceive him as you might deceive men?
10 He would surely rebuke you
if you secretly showed partiality.
11 Would not his splendor terrify you?
Would not the dread of him fall on you?
12 Your maxims are proverbs of ashes;
your defenses are defenses of clay.

13 "Keep silent and let me speak;
then let come to me what may.
14 Why do I put myself in jeopardy
and take my life in my hands?
15 Though he slay me, yet will I hope in him;
I will surely[a] defend my ways to his face.
16 Indeed, this will turn out for my deliverance,
for no godless man would dare come before him!
17 Listen carefully to my words;
let your ears take in what I say.
18 Now that I have prepared my case,
I know I will be vindicated.
19 Can anyone bring charges against me?
If so, I will be silent and die.

20 "Only grant me these two things, O God,
and then I will not hide from you:
21 Withdraw your hand far from me,
and stop frightening me with your terrors.
22 Then summon me and I will answer,
or let me speak, and you reply.
23 How many wrongs and sins have I committed?
Show me my offense and my sin.
24 Why do you hide your face
and consider me your enemy?
25 Will you torment a windblown leaf?
Will you chase after dry chaff?
26 For you write down bitter things against me
and make me inherit the sins of my youth.
27 You fasten my feet in shackles;
you keep close watch on all my paths
by putting marks on the soles of my feet.

28 "So man wastes away like something rotten,
like a garment eaten by moths.

---

[a]15 Or *He will surely slay me; I have no hope — / yet I will*

14 "Man born of woman
is of few days and full of trouble.
2 He springs up like a flower and withers away;
like a fleeting shadow, he does not endure.
3 Do you fix your eye on such a one?
Will you bring him[a] before you for judgment?
4 Who can bring what is pure from the impure?
No one!
5 Man's days are determined;
you have decreed the number of his months
and have set limits he cannot exceed.
6 So look away from him and let him alone,
till he has put in his time like a hired man.

7 "At least there is hope for a tree:
If it is cut down, it will sprout again,
and its new shoots will not fail.
8 Its roots may grow old in the ground
and its stump die in the soil,
9 yet at the scent of water it will bud
and put forth shoots like a plant.
10 But man dies and is laid low;
he breathes his last and is no more.
11 As water disappears from the sea
or a riverbed becomes parched and dry,
12 so man lies down and does not rise;
till the heavens are no more, men will not awake
or be roused from their sleep.

13 "If only you would hide me in the grave[b]
and conceal me till your anger has passed!
If only you would set me a time
and then remember me!
14 If a man dies, will he live again?
All the days of my hard service
I will wait for my renewal[c] to come.
15 You will call and I will answer you;
you will long for the creature your hands have made.
16 Surely then you will count my steps
but not keep track of my sin.
17 My offenses will be sealed up in a bag;
you will cover over my sin.

18 "But as a mountain erodes and crumbles
and as a rock is moved from its place,
19 as water wears away stones
and torrents wash away the soil,

Job said, "At least there is hope for a tree: If it is cut down, it will sprout again, and its new shoots will not fail. Its roots may grow old in the ground and its stump die in the soil, yet at the scent of water it will bud and put forth shoots like a plant."
Job 14:7-9

14:4 *pure . . . No one:* This appears to agree with earlier statements by Eliphaz (4:17) and Job himself (9:2), but it can also have the meaning that nothing pure can come from what is impure. If Job is speaking about being pure in a legal sense, he could mean that if he is truly guilty, he won't be found innocent. But he seems to leave the door open for the unspoken question: "If I am not guilty, then will God stop making me suffer?"

14:10-12 *he breathes his last and is no more:* A common understanding of death in ancient Israel was that it was simply the end of life. After death, there was nothing more. See also the mini-article called "Eternal Life," p. 2072.

14:13 *hide me in the grave:* See the note at 3:13-17.

14:14-22 *will he live again:* Job seems to be wondering if people can live again after they have died. This idea is suggested in a few Old Testament passages (Isa 26:19; Dan 12:2). But Job's hope for life after death is balanced by his knowledge that God has the power to destroy hopes (14:19).

14:1,2 Job 9:25,26; Ps 90:5,6; Isa 40:6,7. **14:5** Job 7:6; Ps 90:10.

[a] 3 Septuagint, Vulgate and Syriac; Hebrew *me* [b] 13 Hebrew *Sheol* [c] 14 Or *release*

so you destroy man's hope.
20 You overpower him once for all, and he is gone;
you change his countenance and send him away.
21 If his sons are honored, he does not know it;
if they are brought low, he does not see it.
22 He feels but the pain of his own body
and mourns only for himself."

THE SECOND ROUND OF THE DEBATE

Once again, Job's three friends give him advice. Job replies to them and complains to God.

Eliphaz

15 Then Eliphaz the Temanite replied:
2 "Would a wise man answer with empty notions
or fill his belly with the hot east wind?
3 Would he argue with useless words,
with speeches that have no value?
4 But you even undermine piety
and hinder devotion to God.
5 Your sin prompts your mouth;
you adopt the tongue of the crafty.
6 Your own mouth condemns you, not mine;
your own lips testify against you.

7 "Are you the first man ever born?
Were you brought forth before the hills?
8 Do you listen in on God's council?
Do you limit wisdom to yourself?
9 What do you know that we do not know?
What insights do you have that we do
not have?
10 The gray-haired and the aged are on our side,
men even older than your father.
11 Are God's consolations not enough for you,
words spoken gently to you?
12 Why has your heart carried you away,
and why do your eyes flash,
13 so that you vent your rage against God
and pour out such words from your mouth?

14 "What is man, that he could be pure,
or one born of woman, that he could be
righteous?
15 If God places no trust in his holy ones,
if even the heavens are not pure in his eyes,

15:1 *Eliphaz the Temanite:* See the note at 2:11. See Job 4, 5 for Eliphaz's first speech to Job.

15:7,8 *first man . . . listen in on God's council:* Eliphaz sarcastically asks Job if he was present when God created the world. This may be a reference to Adam (Gen 2:7; 3:20). Eliphaz also asks if Job sits in on God's council, which is a gathering of angels and others who meet to discuss matters with God (1:6; 2:1). See also 1 Kgs 22:19; Isa 6:1-4.

15:10 *gray-haired and the aged:* In ancient times, wisdom was connected to experience. Those who were old and ideas that had been tested by time were important sources of wisdom (see also the note at 8:8).

15:14-16 *pure . . . holy ones . . . evil:* See the notes at 4:12-15; 1:6,7; and 1:22. See also 4:17,18; 9:2; 25:4-6; Ps 14:2,3; Rom 3:10-12.

16 how much less man, who is vile and corrupt,
who drinks up evil like water!

17 "Listen to me and I will explain to you;
let me tell you what I have seen,
18 what wise men have declared,
hiding nothing received from their fathers
19 (to whom alone the land was given
when no alien passed among them):
20 All his days the wicked man suffers torment,
the ruthless through all the years stored up
for him.
21 Terrifying sounds fill his ears;
when all seems well, marauders attack him.
22 He despairs of escaping the darkness;
he is marked for the sword.
23 He wanders about—food for vultures[a];
he knows the day of darkness is at hand.
24 Distress and anguish fill him with terror;
they overwhelm him, like a king poised to attack,
25 because he shakes his fist at God
and vaunts himself against the Almighty,
26 defiantly charging against him
with a thick, strong shield.

27 "Though his face is covered with fat
and his waist bulges with flesh,
28 he will inhabit ruined towns
and houses where no one lives,
houses crumbling to rubble.
29 He will no longer be rich and his wealth will not endure,
nor will his possessions spread over the land.
30 He will not escape the darkness;
a flame will wither his shoots,
and the breath of God's mouth will carry him away.
31 Let him not deceive himself by trusting what is worthless,
for he will get nothing in return.
32 Before his time he will be paid in full,
and his branches will not flourish.
33 He will be like a vine stripped of its unripe grapes,
like an olive tree shedding its blossoms.
34 For the company of the godless will be barren,
and fire will consume the tents of those who
love bribes.
35 They conceive trouble and give birth to evil;
their womb fashions deceit."

[a]23 Or *about, looking for food*

Eliphaz counsels Job, saying, *"For the company of the godless will be barren, and fire will consume the tents of those who love bribes. They conceive trouble and give birth to evil."*
Job 15:34,35

15:19 *to whom alone the land was given when no alien passed among them:* It is not clear what people or which land is being described in this verse. It may refer to very ancient and wise ancestors who had not yet been influenced by foreign people and their teachings. These wise ancient ones are contrasted with those who sin (15:20-34).

15:30 *breath of God's mouth:* See the note at 1:16-19.

15:27-29 Job 27:16-18; Isa 5:8, 9; Amos 3:13-15; 5:11,12; 6:4-7.

Job said, *"Even now my witness is in heaven; my advocate is on high."*
Job 16:19

16:12,13 *target:* See the note at 6:4.

16:15 *sackcloth . . . dust:* Sackcloth is a rough dark-colored cloth made from goat hair and used to make grain sacks. It was worn in times of trouble or sorrow. People sometimes rubbed dust or dirt on themselves to show their sorrow, too. See also the note at 2:8.

16:18 *O earth, do not cover my blood:* Job wants the blood he shed in his suffering to cry out for justice, just as Abel's blood called out for justice when Cain murdered him (Gen 4:1-10). The Israelites believed that the blood of an innocent victim cried out for justice until someone took revenge against the victim's murderer (Exod 20:13; 21:12-14; Num 35:16-21; Deut 4:41-43).

16:7,8 Job 1:13—2:10. **16:9** Job 10:16, 17; Hos 6:1. **16:10** Job 12:4; 17:2; 19:13-19; Ps 22:6-8,13; 69:4.

16 Then Job replied:

2 "I have heard many things like these;
miserable comforters are you all!
3 Will your long-winded speeches never end?
What ails you that you keep on arguing?
4 I also could speak like you,
if you were in my place;
I could make fine speeches against you
and shake my head at you.
5 But my mouth would encourage you;
comfort from my lips would bring you relief.

6 "Yet if I speak, my pain is not relieved;
and if I refrain, it does not go away.
7 Surely, O God, you have worn me out;
you have devastated my entire household.
8 You have bound me—and it has become
a witness;
my gauntness rises up and testifies against me.
9 God assails me and tears me in his anger
and gnashes his teeth at me;
my opponent fastens on me his piercing eyes.
10 Men open their mouths to jeer at me;
they strike my cheek in scorn
and unite together against me.
11 God has turned me over to evil men
and thrown me into the clutches of
the wicked.
12 All was well with me, but he shattered me;
he seized me by the neck and crushed me.
He has made me his target;
13 his archers surround me.
Without pity, he pierces my kidneys
and spills my gall on the ground.
14 Again and again he bursts upon me;
he rushes at me like a warrior.

15 "I have sewed sackcloth over my skin
and buried my brow in the dust.
16 My face is red with weeping,
deep shadows ring my eyes;
17 yet my hands have been free of violence
and my prayer is pure.

18 "O earth, do not cover my blood;
may my cry never be laid to rest!
19 Even now my witness is in heaven;
my advocate is on high.

20 My intercessor is my friend[a]
as my eyes pour out tears to God;
21 on behalf of a man he pleads with God
as a man pleads for his friend.

22 "Only a few years will pass
before I go on the journey of no return.
17 1 My spirit is broken,
my days are cut short,
the grave awaits me.
2 Surely mockers surround me;
my eyes must dwell on their hostility.

3 "Give me, O God, the pledge you demand.
Who else will put up security for me?
4 You have closed their minds to understanding;
therefore you will not let them triumph.
5 If a man denounces his friends for reward,
the eyes of his children will fail.

6 "God has made me a byword to everyone,
a man in whose face people spit.
7 My eyes have grown dim with grief;
my whole frame is but a shadow.
8 Upright men are appalled at this;
the innocent are aroused against the ungodly.
9 Nevertheless, the righteous will hold to their ways,
and those with clean hands will grow stronger.

10 "But come on, all of you, try again!
I will not find a wise man among you.
11 My days have passed, my plans are shattered,
and so are the desires of my heart.
12 These men turn night into day;
in the face of darkness they say, 'Light is near.'
13 If the only home I hope for is the grave,[b]
if I spread out my bed in darkness,
14 if I say to corruption, 'You are my father,'
and to the worm, 'My mother' or 'My sister,'
15 where then is my hope?
Who can see any hope for me?
16 Will it go down to the gates of death[b]?
Will we descend together into the dust?"

Bildad

18 Then Bildad the Shuhite replied:

2 "When will you end these speeches?
Be sensible, and then we can talk.

17:3 *put up security:* Job asks God to pay a down payment as a guarantee that he is innocent. This kind of a pledge was often sealed with a handshake and an exchange of money or property. Job offers his life as the pledge of his innocence.

17:13,16 *grave . . . gates of death . . . dust:* See the note at 3:13-17.

18:1 *Bildad the Shuhite:* See the note at 2:11. See Job 8 for Bildad's first speech to Job.

17:1 Job 3:11-17; 7:6-10; Ps 88:3-5. **17:2** Job 16:10; Ps 22:7; Jer 20:7. **17:11** Job 17:1.

---

[a]**20** Or *My friends treat me with scorn* [b]**13,16** Hebrew *Sheol*

18:5,6 *lamp of the wicked:* The light of lamps is often used as a symbol for life and goodness in the Bible, while darkness is often an image for evil and death (18:18; Prov 13:9; 20:20; John 8:12). See also Job 21:17.

18:21 *the dwelling of an evil man:* Bildad repeats his earlier argument that God punishes those who sin (see the note at 1:22). The "dwelling" (life experience) of sinners includes losing their possessions (18:15), dying as forgotten people (18:17), being thrown into the darkness (18:18), and having no children to carry on the family name (18:19). The ancient Israelites did not believe in life after death, but they did believe that their lives continued on after death in the lives of their children and later generations. Having no children to carry on the family name was considered a great tragedy. Note that the bad things Bildad lists here had happened to Job already (1:13—2:10), so Bildad intends to include Job as one of the sinners he describes. See also the mini-article called "Resurrection," p. 2210.

3 Why are we regarded as cattle
and considered stupid in your sight?
4 You who tear yourself to pieces in your anger,
is the earth to be abandoned for your sake?
Or must the rocks be moved from their place?

5 "The lamp of the wicked is snuffed out;
the flame of his fire stops burning.
6 The light in his tent becomes dark;
the lamp beside him goes out.
7 The vigor of his step is weakened;
his own schemes throw him down.
8 His feet thrust him into a net
and he wanders into its mesh.
9 A trap seizes him by the heel;
a snare holds him fast.
10 A noose is hidden for him on the ground;
a trap lies in his path.
11 Terrors startle him on every side
and dog his every step.
12 Calamity is hungry for him;
disaster is ready for him when he falls.
13 It eats away parts of his skin;
death's firstborn devours his limbs.
14 He is torn from the security of his tent
and marched off to the king of terrors.
15 Fire resides[a] in his tent;
burning sulfur is scattered over his dwelling.
16 His roots dry up below
and his branches wither above.
17 The memory of him perishes from the earth;
he has no name in the land.
18 He is driven from light into darkness
and is banished from the world.
19 He has no offspring or descendants among his people,
no survivor where once he lived.
20 Men of the west are appalled at his fate;
men of the east are seized with horror.
21 Surely such is the dwelling of an evil man;
such is the place of one who knows not God."

Job

19 Then Job replied:

2 "How long will you torment me
and crush me with words?

[a]**15** Or *Nothing he had remains*

[3]Ten times now you have reproached me;
shamelessly you attack me.
[4]If it is true that I have gone astray,
my error remains my concern alone.
[5]If indeed you would exalt yourselves above me
and use my humiliation against me,
[6]then know that God has wronged me
and drawn his net around me.

[7]"Though I cry, 'I've been wronged!' I get no response;
though I call for help, there is no justice.
[8]He has blocked my way so I cannot pass;
he has shrouded my paths in darkness.
[9]He has stripped me of my honor
and removed the crown from my head.
[10]He tears me down on every side till I am gone;
he uproots my hope like a tree.
[11]His anger burns against me;
he counts me among his enemies.
[12]His troops advance in force;
they build a siege ramp against me
and encamp around my tent.

[13]"He has alienated my brothers from me;
my acquaintances are completely estranged from me.
[14]My kinsmen have gone away;
my friends have forgotten me.
[15]My guests and my maidservants count me a stranger;
they look upon me as an alien.
[16]I summon my servant, but he does not answer,
though I beg him with my own mouth.
[17]My breath is offensive to my wife;
I am loathsome to my own brothers.
[18]Even the little boys scorn me;
when I appear, they ridicule me.
[19]All my intimate friends detest me;
those I love have turned against me.
[20]I am nothing but skin and bones;
I have escaped with only the skin of my teeth.[a]

[21]"Have pity on me, my friends, have pity,
for the hand of God has struck me.
[22]Why do you pursue me as God does?
Will you never get enough of my flesh?

[23]"Oh, that my words were recorded,
that they were written on a scroll,

Job complains, *"Though I cry, 'I've been wronged!' I get no response; though I call for help, there is no justice."* Job 19:7

19:3 *Ten times:* Ten is a round number meaning "many times."

19:5 *use my humiliation against me:* See the notes at 1:10 and 4:8, 9.

19:6,7 *there is no justice:* Bildad had argued that Job is responsible for his own torment and that God would never "pervert justice" (8:3), but Job complains that God is being unjust toward him. It's as if he is already behind prison walls (19:8), even before he gets a fair trial. See also Lam 3:5-8.

19:12 Job 16:12-14; 30:12. **19:13-19** Job 12:4; 16:10; 17:2; Ps 22:6-8, 13; 69:4. **19:21** Job 16:12,13.

[a]**20** Or *only my gums*

> Job said, *"I know that my Redeemer lives, and that in the end he will stand upon the earth."* Job 19:25

19:25 *my Redeemer:* The Hebrew word (*goel*) translated here as "Redeemer" is often translated as "Savior" or "Defender." Just who Job is referring to as his Savior has been widely debated. Some believe Job is referring to God, though up to this point, Job has described God as his enemy and accuser (6:4; 7:16-19; 16:12-14; 19:7-12). Others believe Job is referring to a "redeemer" or "defender" who will argue Job's case in court against God. Or it is one who will try to buy justice for Job (see the note at 16:18), perhaps even after Job himself has died. For more, see the mini-article called "Redeemer (Redemption)," p. 995.

19:26 *see God:* It is unclear whether Job was referring to being raised to eternal life (see the notes at 14:10-12 and 14:14-22). Job hoped that even if his earthly body ("flesh") died and rotted away in the ground, he would somehow see God face to face.

19:29 *there is judgment:* This refers to a time when God would punish evildoers (Job 27:13-23; Ps 1:5; Eccl 3:17; Matt 25:31-46). See also the mini-article called "Day of the LORD," p. 1727.

20:1 *Zophar the Naamathite:* See the note at 2:11. See Job 11 for Zophar's first speech to Job.

20:3 *a rebuke that dishonors me:* By reminding Job that God punishes the wicked, Zophar and his friends think they are doing Job a favor. When Job says that his friends will also be judged by God, Zophar is insulted.

20:6 Gen 11:1-9.

24 that they were inscribed with an iron tool on[a] lead,
or engraved in rock forever!
25 I know that my Redeemer[b] lives,
and that in the end he will stand upon the earth.[c]
26 And after my skin has been destroyed,
yet[d] in[e] my flesh I will see God;
27 I myself will see him
with my own eyes—I, and not another.
How my heart yearns within me!

28 "If you say, 'How we will hound him,
since the root of the trouble lies in him,[f]'
29 you should fear the sword yourselves;
for wrath will bring punishment by the sword,
and then you will know that there is judgment.[g]"

Zophar

20 Then Zophar the Naamathite replied:

2 "My troubled thoughts prompt me to answer
because I am greatly disturbed.
3 I hear a rebuke that dishonors me,
and my understanding inspires me to reply.

4 "Surely you know how it has been from of old,
ever since man[h] was placed on the earth,
5 that the mirth of the wicked is brief,
the joy of the godless lasts but a moment.
6 Though his pride reaches to the heavens
and his head touches the clouds,
7 he will perish forever, like his own dung;
those who have seen him will say, 'Where is he?'
8 Like a dream he flies away, no more to be found,
banished like a vision of the night.
9 The eye that saw him will not see him again;
his place will look on him no more.
10 His children must make amends to the poor;
his own hands must give back his wealth.
11 The youthful vigor that fills his bones
will lie with him in the dust.

12 "Though evil is sweet in his mouth
and he hides it under his tongue,
13 though he cannot bear to let it go
and keeps it in his mouth,

[a]24 Or *and* [b]25 Or *defender* [c]25 Or *upon my grave* [d]26 Or *And after I awake, / though this ⌞body⌟ has been destroyed, / then* [e]26 Or */ apart from* [f]28 Many Hebrew manuscripts, Septuagint and Vulgate; most Hebrew manuscripts *me* [g]29 Or */ that you may come to know the Almighty* [h]4 Or *Adam*

14 yet his food will turn sour in his stomach;
  it will become the venom of serpents within him.
15 He will spit out the riches he swallowed;
  God will make his stomach vomit them up.
16 He will suck the poison of serpents;
  the fangs of an adder will kill him.
17 He will not enjoy the streams,
  the rivers flowing with honey and cream.
18 What he toiled for he must give back uneaten;
  he will not enjoy the profit from his trading.
19 For he has oppressed the poor and left them destitute;
  he has seized houses he did not build.

20 "Surely he will have no respite from his craving;
  he cannot save himself by his treasure.
21 Nothing is left for him to devour;
  his prosperity will not endure.
22 In the midst of his plenty, distress will overtake him;
  the full force of misery will come upon him.
23 When he has filled his belly,
  God will vent his burning anger against him
  and rain down his blows upon him.
24 Though he flees from an iron weapon,
  a bronze-tipped arrow pierces him.
25 He pulls it out of his back,
  the gleaming point out of his liver.
Terrors will come over him;
26   total darkness lies in wait for his treasures.
A fire unfanned will consume him
  and devour what is left in his tent.
27 The heavens will expose his guilt;
  the earth will rise up against him.
28 A flood will carry off his house,
  rushing waters[a] on the day of God's wrath.
29 Such is the fate God allots the wicked,
  the heritage appointed for them by God."

Job

21 Then Job replied:

2 "Listen carefully to my words;
  let this be the consolation you give me.
3 Bear with me while I speak,
  and after I have spoken, mock on.

4 "Is my complaint directed to man?
  Why should I not be impatient?

[a]**28** Or *The possessions in his house will be carried off, / washed away*

20:10 *make amends to the poor:* Those who were truly evil cheated the poor and did not act with justice toward others. Those who did this would also be punishing their children, since the children would also have to pay for the sins of their parents. See also Job 5:3-5; 31:16-23; Amos 2:6-8; 8:4-8.

20:12-15 *evil is sweet in his mouth . . . vomit them up:* Zophar says that sin tastes good but soon turns sour and poisonous in the sinner's stomach, making one vomit it out again.

20:17 *rivers flowing with honey and cream:* This is a description of the land that God promised to give to the people of Israel (Exod 3:16,17). The punishment described here would have been an especially painful reminder of Israel's own sins, which led to them being defeated and taken into exile away from their land.

20:23 *burning anger:* See the note at 1:16-19.

20:24 *iron weapon, a bronze-tipped arrow:* Iron was not used to make things in the ancient Near East until around 1200 B.C. See also Job 28:2; 40:18; 41:27. Bronze is a metal made by mixing copper and tin. Around the year 2000 B.C., it began to be used in place of copper alone.

20:18 Eccl 2:18-23. **20:26** Job 1:16; Ps 21:9. **20:29** Job 27:13.

21:7-12 *Why do the wicked live on:* Even though his friends all say that the wicked are punished by God and lose their wealth, Job knows that life is not so simple. Sometimes evil people get more wealth, live long enough to see their children grow up and celebrate. But Job, who has been a good man, has lost everything.

21:15 *the Almighty:* See the note at 5:17,18.

21:17 *how often is the lamp of the wicked snuffed out:* See the notes at 18:5,6 and 19:29.

21:20 *drink of the wrath:* Drinking the cup of God's wrath means to receive God's punishment (Ps 60:3; Isa 51:22; Jer 25:15-29; Rev 14:10; 16:19).

21:22 Job 36:22,23; Isa 40:12, 13; Rom 11:33,34.

5 Look at me and be astonished;
clap your hand over your mouth.
6 When I think about this, I am terrified;
trembling seizes my body.
7 Why do the wicked live on,
growing old and increasing in power?
8 They see their children established around them,
their offspring before their eyes.
9 Their homes are safe and free from fear;
the rod of God is not upon them.
10 Their bulls never fail to breed;
their cows calve and do not miscarry.
11 They send forth their children as a flock;
their little ones dance about.
12 They sing to the music of tambourine and harp;
they make merry to the sound of the flute.
13 They spend their years in prosperity
and go down to the grave[a] in peace.[b]
14 Yet they say to God, 'Leave us alone!
We have no desire to know your ways.
15 Who is the Almighty, that we should serve him?
What would we gain by praying to him?'
16 But their prosperity is not in their own hands,
so I stand aloof from the counsel of the wicked.

17 "Yet how often is the lamp of the wicked snuffed out?
How often does calamity come upon them,
the fate God allots in his anger?
18 How often are they like straw before the wind,
like chaff swept away by a gale?
19 ⌊It is said,⌋ 'God stores up a man's punishment for his sons.'
Let him repay the man himself, so that he will know it!
20 Let his own eyes see his destruction;
let him drink of the wrath of the Almighty.[c]
21 For what does he care about the family he leaves behind
when his allotted months come to an end?

22 "Can anyone teach knowledge to God,
since he judges even the highest?
23 One man dies in full vigor,
completely secure and at ease,
24 his body[d] well nourished,
his bones rich with marrow.
25 Another man dies in bitterness of soul,
never having enjoyed anything good.

[a]**13** Hebrew *Sheol* [b]**13** Or *in an instant* [c]**17-20** Verses 17 and 18 may be taken as exclamations and 19 and 20 as declarations. [d]**24** The meaning of the Hebrew for this word is uncertain.

26 Side by side they lie in the dust,
and worms cover them both.
27 "I know full well what you are thinking,
the schemes by which you would wrong me.
28 You say, 'Where now is the great man's house,
the tents where wicked men lived?'
29 Have you never questioned those who travel?
Have you paid no regard to their accounts—
30 that the evil man is spared from the day of calamity,
that he is delivered from[a] the day of wrath?
31 Who denounces his conduct to his face?
Who repays him for what he has done?
32 He is carried to the grave,
and watch is kept over his tomb.
33 The soil in the valley is sweet to him;
all men follow after him,
and a countless throng goes[b] before him.

34 "So how can you console me with your nonsense?
Nothing is left of your answers but falsehood!"

THE THIRD ROUND OF THE DEBATE

Eliphaz begins a third round of debate and Job responds. In this section, Bildad's speech is very short, and Zophar is not mentioned at all. Job does most of the talking, and sometimes his words sound like the advice of his friends, which has led to different ideas about how the text of Job reached its final form.

Eliphaz

22 Then Eliphaz the Temanite replied:
2 "Can a man be of benefit to God?
Can even a wise man benefit him?
3 What pleasure would it give the Almighty if you were righteous?
What would he gain if your ways were blameless?

4 "Is it for your piety that he rebukes you
and brings charges against you?
5 Is not your wickedness great?
Are not your sins endless?
6 You demanded security from your brothers for no reason;
you stripped men of their clothing, leaving them naked.

[a]30 Or *man is reserved for the day of calamity, / that he is brought forth to*
[b]33 Or / *as a countless throng went*

21:26 *worms cover them both:* Job continues to argue against his friends' belief that the wicked are always punished. Some who are wicked and wealthy live a long life. Some who are wealthy and good may have troubles and die at a young age. Death is the only thing all people have in common. And, since Job seems to believe that there is no life beyond this earthly one, he says some of the wicked will never be punished.

21:34 *nonsense:* Because the arguments of Job's friends aren't supported by what happens in real life, Job considers their advice meaningless.

22:1 *Eliphaz the Temanite:* See the note at 2:11. For Eliphaz's first two speeches, see Job 4, 5 and 15. Eliphaz doesn't change his advice, but his words are even more harsh and to the point.

22:3 *the Almighty:* See the note at 5:17,18.

22:5 *sins:* See the note at 1:22. Here Eliphaz presents a specific list of Job's sins, which center around his failure to act according to God's justice (see the mini-article called "Justice," p. 1721). A number of Israel's prophets accused the Israelite people of similar sins (Isa 1:11-17; Amos 2:6-8; 4:1; 5:10-12; Mic 2:1-11).

22:2,3 Job 7:17; 35:7; Ps 8:4; 143:2.

Eliphaz said to Job, "The Almighty will be your gold, the choicest silver for you. Surely then you will find delight in the Almighty and will lift up your face to God."
Job 22:25,26

22:12-14 *heights of heaven . . . vaulted heavens:* Eliphaz describes God as being distant, living at the highest point of the heavens (above "the highest stars"), where he can watch what everyone on earth is doing. Ancient people understood the sky to be like a solid bowl set over the flat earth, and they believed that high mountains held up the sky like columns (Job 9:5-10). This bowl or dome held back the flood of water above. Rain and snow were said to come through the dome when God opened windows or doors in the sky (Gen 7:11,12; Ps 78:23).

22:18-20 *fire devours their wealth:* Eliphaz is referring to Job again (see 1:4,5,16). He says Job is a disgusting sinner who won't admit that he has sinned.

22:21-23 *Submit to God . . . remove wickedness far from your tent:* Eliphaz repeats his earlier advice (5:8; see also Bildad's advice, 8:5-7). The advice to return to the LORD is good advice, but it assumes that Job is a wicked man and guilty of sins that led to God's punishment. Eliphaz also makes the point that if Job returns to God, he will get his riches back (the "prosperity" of 22:21). Then Job will once again be a hero of the faith, a good man who is able to influence God to forgive others (22:29, 30).

22:27,28 Job 33:27, 28; Ps 86:7; 97:11; Isa 30:19; Matt 7:7-11.

7 You gave no water to the weary
and you withheld food from the hungry,
8 though you were a powerful man, owning land—
an honored man, living on it.
9 And you sent widows away empty-handed
and broke the strength of the fatherless.
10 That is why snares are all around you,
why sudden peril terrifies you,
11 why it is so dark you cannot see,
and why a flood of water covers you.

12 "Is not God in the heights of heaven?
And see how lofty are the highest stars!
13 Yet you say, 'What does God know?
Does he judge through such darkness?
14 Thick clouds veil him, so he does not see us
as he goes about in the vaulted heavens.'
15 Will you keep to the old path
that evil men have trod?
16 They were carried off before their time,
their foundations washed away by a flood.
17 They said to God, 'Leave us alone!
What can the Almighty do to us?'
18 Yet it was he who filled their houses with good things,
so I stand aloof from the counsel of the wicked.

19 "The righteous see their ruin and rejoice;
the innocent mock them, saying,
20 'Surely our foes are destroyed,
and fire devours their wealth.'

21 "Submit to God and be at peace with him;
in this way prosperity will come to you.
22 Accept instruction from his mouth
and lay up his words in your heart.
23 If you return to the Almighty, you will be restored:
If you remove wickedness far from your tent
24 and assign your nuggets to the dust,
your gold of Ophir to the rocks in the ravines,
25 then the Almighty will be your gold,
the choicest silver for you.
26 Surely then you will find delight in the Almighty
and will lift up your face to God.
27 You will pray to him, and he will hear you,
and you will fulfill your vows.
28 What you decide on will be done,
and light will shine on your ways.
29 When men are brought low and you say, 'Lift them up!'
then he will save the downcast.

[30]He will deliver even one who is not innocent,
who will be delivered through the cleanness of your hands."

Job

23 Then Job replied:

[2]"Even today my complaint is bitter;
his hand[a] is heavy in spite of[b] my groaning.
[3]If only I knew where to find him;
if only I could go to his dwelling!
[4]I would state my case before him
and fill my mouth with arguments.
[5]I would find out what he would answer me,
and consider what he would say.
[6]Would he oppose me with great power?
No, he would not press charges against me.
[7]There an upright man could present his case before him,
and I would be delivered forever from my judge.

[8]"But if I go to the east, he is not there;
if I go to the west, I do not find him.
[9]When he is at work in the north, I do not see him;
when he turns to the south, I catch no glimpse of him.
[10]But he knows the way that I take;
when he has tested me, I will come forth as gold.
[11]My feet have closely followed his steps;
I have kept to his way without turning aside.
[12]I have not departed from the commands of his lips;
I have treasured the words of his mouth more than my daily bread.

[13]"But he stands alone, and who can oppose him?
He does whatever he pleases.
[14]He carries out his decree against me,
and many such plans he still has in store.
[15]That is why I am terrified before him;
when I think of all this, I fear him.
[16]God has made my heart faint;
the Almighty has terrified me.
[17]Yet I am not silenced by the darkness,
by the thick darkness that covers my face.

24 "Why does the Almighty not set times for judgment?
Why must those who know him look in vain for such days?
[2]Men move boundary stones;

23:8,9 *if I go east . . . west . . . north . . . south:* Job is expressing his frustration at being unable to find God to have his case heard and resolved. See also the note at 10:13-16.

23:11,12 *commands . . . words of his mouth:* Job responds to Eliphaz's advice (22:22) by saying that he has been following God's laws and teachings. See also 12:4.

23:16 *the Almighty:* See the note at 5:17,18.

24:2-7 *move boundary stones . . . glean in the vineyards:* Job mentions a number of ways sinners disobey God's laws and reject God's concern for justice. Moving boundary stones was an act forbidden in Israel's law (Deut 27:17; Prov 22:28), because it was the same as stealing. Widows and children had few rights and were powerless to defend themselves against those who wanted to steal their property. It was the custom at harvest time to leave some stalks of grain in the field for poor people, widows, orphans, and foreigners to pick up and eat. This was called "gleaning" (see Lev 19:9,10; 23:22; Deut 24:19-22; Ruth 2:1-3). Compare Job 24:7 to Amos 2:7,8; see also Deut 24:12,13,17.

23:2 Job 1:13—2:10. **23:13,14** Deut 6:4; Job 9:22, 23; Ps 115:3; 135:5, 6. **24:1** Mark 13:32.

[a]2 Septuagint and Syriac; Hebrew / *the hand on me* [b]2 Or *heavy on me in*

24:9 *snatched . . . seized:* One Israelite who kidnapped another could be punished by death (Deut 24:7). Taking a child as guarantee to make sure a loan was paid back was an especially terrible crime, because a poor woman's child represented her hope for future security. Children taken as guarantees against loans were sometimes forced to work as slaves (crushing olives and grapes), but were not allowed to eat or drink their masters' food and wine.

they pasture flocks they have stolen.
3 They drive away the orphan's donkey
and take the widow's ox in pledge.
4 They thrust the needy from the path
and force all the poor of the land into hiding.
5 Like wild donkeys in the desert,
the poor go about their labor of foraging food;
the wasteland provides food for their children.
6 They gather fodder in the fields
and glean in the vineyards of the wicked.
7 Lacking clothes, they spend the night naked;
they have nothing to cover themselves in the cold.
8 They are drenched by mountain rains
and hug the rocks for lack of shelter.
9 The fatherless child is snatched from the breast;
the infant of the poor is seized for a debt.
10 Lacking clothes, they go about naked;
they carry the sheaves, but still go hungry.
11 They crush olives among the terraces[a];
they tread the winepresses, yet suffer thirst.

[a]11 Or *olives between the millstones*; the meaning of the Hebrew for this word is uncertain.

Israelite redeeming (buying back) a relative from slavery.

[12]The groans of the dying rise from the city,
and the souls of the wounded cry out for help.
But God charges no one with wrongdoing.

[13]"There are those who rebel against the light,
who do not know its ways
or stay in its paths.
[14]When daylight is gone, the murderer rises up
and kills the poor and needy;
in the night he steals forth like a thief.
[15]The eye of the adulterer watches for dusk;
he thinks, 'No eye will see me,'
and he keeps his face concealed.
[16]In the dark, men break into houses,
but by day they shut themselves in;

24:13 *light:* See the note at 18:5,6.

24:15 Deut 22:22.

REDEEMER (REDEMPTION)

In the Old Testament, a redeemer (*goel*) was a person who bought back property or a house that had been sold in order to keep it in the family inheritance (Lev 25:25-34; Jer 32:6-12). Also, one family member could buy back a family member who had become a slave (Lev 25:47-55). A redeemer might also be a man who married a widow, if the woman's dead husband had no children to carry on the family name and take over the dead man's property (Deut 25:5, 6; Ruth 4:3-6). A relative chosen to take revenge for a murdered family member (called "the avenger of blood") was also regarded as a "redeemer," defending the family honor (Num 35:16-28; Deut 19:6-12; 2 Sam 14:7, 11). The Israelites believed that a murdered person's blood cried out to be avenged, until the blood of the murderer was spilled.

God is referred to as a redeemer in the Old Testament, especially as the one who saves or delivers people from slavery, exile, or disaster (Exod 6:6-8; Isa 41:14; 43:1,14; 60:16; 63:16; Jer 50:34). God also defends those who cannot defend themselves—widows, the fatherless, and the poor (Exod 22:22-24; 1 Sam 2:7,8; Isa 1:17,23; Amos 5:10-12,15).

In the New Testament, Jesus is never called "Redeemer," but the idea of redemption is used to describe his work of saving people. Redemption means "to buy back" or "to exchange one thing for another." This is closely related to the idea of paying a price or a ransom (Exod 21:30; Ps 49:7-9; 130:8). These ideas are the basis of comparing Jesus to the sacrifice Israel's high priest made to ask God's forgiveness for the people of Israel (Lev 4:1-21; 16:1-34; see also Heb 7:27; 9:27,28). And Jesus is called the Lamb of God who was sacrificed to forgive sins and to rescue sinners from death (John 1:29; Rom 3:25,26; 1 Cor 6:20; 1 Pet 1:18,19). Jesus paid his life as a ransom, so God would forgive human beings (Mark 10:45).

Why would Jesus Christ need to die in order to pay for God's forgiveness and redeem (save) the earth and its people? The answer is found in the belief that human beings cannot escape sin's hold on them (Job 4:17; 9:2; Ps 14:2,3; Rom 3:10-12,23). This fact of human existence goes all the way back to the sins of the first human beings (Gen 3). Human sin also has an effect on the rest of God's creation (Amos 4:7-9; Rom 8:19-22), so part of God's saving and redeeming work is to renew creation (2 Pet 3:12,13; Rev 21:1—22:5).

they want nothing to do with the light.
17 For all of them, deep darkness is their morning[a];
they make friends with the terrors of darkness.[b]

18 "Yet they are foam on the surface of the water;
their portion of the land is cursed,
so that no one goes to the vineyards.
19 As heat and drought snatch away the melted snow,
so the grave[c] snatches away those who have sinned.
20 The womb forgets them,
the worm feasts on them;
evil men are no longer remembered
but are broken like a tree.
21 They prey on the barren and childless woman,
and to the widow show no kindness.
22 But God drags away the mighty by his power;
though they become established, they have no
assurance of life.
23 He may let them rest in a feeling of security,
but his eyes are on their ways.
24 For a little while they are exalted, and then they are gone;
they are brought low and gathered up like all others;
they are cut off like heads of grain.

25 "If this is not so, who can prove me false
and reduce my words to nothing?"

Bildad

25 Then Bildad the Shuhite replied:

2 "Dominion and awe belong to God;
he establishes order in the heights of heaven.
3 Can his forces be numbered?
Upon whom does his light not rise?
4 How then can a man be righteous before God?
How can one born of woman be pure?
5 If even the moon is not bright
and the stars are not pure in his eyes,
6 how much less man, who is but a maggot—
a son of man, who is only a worm!"

Job

26 Then Job replied:

2 "How you have helped the powerless!
How you have saved the arm that is feeble!

[a]17 Or *them, their morning is like the shadow of death* [b]17 Or *of the shadow of death* [c]19 Hebrew *Sheol*

24:19 *the grave:* See the note at 3:13-17. See also Job 6:15-17.

25:1 *Bildad the Shuhite:* See the note at 2:11. For Bildad's first two speeches, see Job 8 and 18. Some have suggested that Bildad's short speech continues on in 26:5-14 (see the note).

26:2-4 *How you have helped the powerless . . . whose spirit spoke from your mouth:* Bildad has just described how great God is compared to human beings. Job already knows that God is great, that God acts as he wishes, and that human beings cannot be pure in God's eyes (9:1-24; 21:22-26). Job also has complained that God is making him suffer and refusing to hear his case, even though Job has obeyed God (23:1-17). So Job's reply to Bildad is probably intended to be sarcastic. Bildad has told Job nothing he doesn't already know, so his words do not comfort Job.

24:18 Job 15:27-33. **24:21** Job 22:9; 24:3,9. **24:22** Job 12:17-19; Luke 1:51-53. **25:3** Ps 147:4; 148:3, 4; Matt 5:45; Jas 1:17. **25:4** Job 4:17; 9:2.

[3]What advice you have offered to one without wisdom!
And what great insight you have displayed!
[4]Who has helped you utter these words?
And whose spirit spoke from your mouth?

[5]"The dead are in deep anguish,
those beneath the waters and all that live in them.
[6]Death[a] is naked before God;
Destruction[b] lies uncovered.
[7]He spreads out the northern ⌞skies⌟ over empty space;
he suspends the earth over nothing.
[8]He wraps up the waters in his clouds,
yet the clouds do not burst under their weight.
[9]He covers the face of the full moon,
spreading his clouds over it.
[10]He marks out the horizon on the face of the waters
for a boundary between light and darkness.
[11]The pillars of the heavens quake,
aghast at his rebuke.
[12]By his power he churned up the sea;
by his wisdom he cut Rahab to pieces.
[13]By his breath the skies became fair;
his hand pierced the gliding serpent.
[14]And these are but the outer fringe of his works;
how faint the whisper we hear of him!
Who then can understand the thunder of his power?"

27 And Job continued his discourse:

[2]"As surely as God lives, who has denied me justice,
the Almighty, who has made me taste bitterness
of soul,
[3]as long as I have life within me,
the breath of God in my nostrils,
[4]my lips will not speak wickedness,
and my tongue will utter no deceit.
[5]I will never admit you are in the right;
till I die, I will not deny my integrity.
[6]I will maintain my righteousness and never let go of it;
my conscience will not reproach me as long as I live.

[7]"May my enemies be like the wicked,
my adversaries like the unjust!
[8]For what hope has the godless when he is cut off,
when God takes away his life?
[9]Does God listen to his cry
when distress comes upon him?

a6 Hebrew *Sheol* **b6** Hebrew *Abaddon*

26:5-14 *By his breath the skies became fair:* This section is often identified as a hymn praising the power of God. Many believe it fits better with 25:6 and should be considered part of Bildad's speech (25:1-6). Job, too, knows how powerful God is and could have spoken these words (compare 9:1-13), but this hymn praising God seems out of place coming from Job at this point.

26:5,6 *those beneath the waters:* See the note at 3:13-17. Compare these verses to Ps 18:3-17.

26:10,11 *boundary . . . pillars:* Ancient Israelites believed that the horizon was the boundary where light and darkness meet. Human beings couldn't travel beyond this point to find God, since God lives beyond the horizon. The pillars probably refer to high mountains in the north (26:7; see also the note at 9:6-9).

26:12,13 *churned up the sea . . . Rahab:* In these verses, the sea monster Rahab stands for the fearsome power of the ocean. By conquering these powerful forces of chaos, God brought all heaven and earth under his control (25:2).

27:2 *the Almighty:* See the note at 5:17,18.

27:6 *I will maintain my righteousness:* Job continues to argue that he has done nothing to deserve God's harsh punishment (see 2:3; 6:8-10; 9:15, 20-22; 19:5,6).

27:7-23 *the wicked:* This passage about how God will punish the wicked sounds more like words that have been spoken earlier by Job's friends rather than by Job, who doesn't trust God to act in this way (9:22-24; 12:6; 21:7-13). That is why some scholars think that these verses might have originally been a speech by Zophar, who doesn't speak a third time as Eliphaz and Bildad do. If Job is speaking, his words are filled with sarcasm and bitterness.

28:1-6 *silver . . . gold . . . refined . . . sapphires:* Silver and gold were usually imported to Israel from countries such as Sheba (1 Kgs 10:10-13). These metals were made more pure by a process called refining, or smelting. The metal was heated until it melted into a liquid; then the hot metal was poured through a sieve to strain out particles that were not silver or gold. Jewels and gold were discovered by mining and examining rocks. The point of this section is to show how the things that humankind considers worth having can be obtained if people make the effort to bring them out of the depths of the earth. In the verses that follow (28:12-28), wisdom is known, by contrast, to be more difficult to find than these precious metals and stones. See the note at 28:12.

27:21 Job 1:18, 19; Jer 13:24.

10 Will he find delight in the Almighty?
Will he call upon God at all times?

11 "I will teach you about the power of God;
the ways of the Almighty I will not conceal.
12 You have all seen this yourselves.
Why then this meaningless talk?

13 "Here is the fate God allots to the wicked,
the heritage a ruthless man receives from the Almighty:
14 However many his children, their fate is the sword;
his offspring will never have enough to eat.
15 The plague will bury those who survive him,
and their widows will not weep for them.
16 Though he heaps up silver like dust
and clothes like piles of clay,
17 what he lays up the righteous will wear,
and the innocent will divide his silver.
18 The house he builds is like a moth's cocoon,
like a hut made by a watchman.
19 He lies down wealthy, but will do so no more;
when he opens his eyes, all is gone.
20 Terrors overtake him like a flood;
a tempest snatches him away in the night.
21 The east wind carries him off, and he is gone;
it sweeps him out of his place.
22 It hurls itself against him without mercy
as he flees headlong from its power.
23 It claps its hands in derision
and hisses him out of his place.

28 "There is a mine for silver
and a place where gold is refined.
2 Iron is taken from the earth,
and copper is smelted from ore.
3 Man puts an end to the darkness;
he searches the farthest recesses
for ore in the blackest darkness.
4 Far from where people dwell he cuts a shaft,
in places forgotten by the foot of man;
far from men he dangles and sways.
5 The earth, from which food comes,
is transformed below as by fire;
6 sapphires[a] come from its rocks,
and its dust contains nuggets of gold.
7 No bird of prey knows that hidden path,

[a] **6** Or *lapis lazuli*; also in verse 16

no falcon's eye has seen it.
8 Proud beasts do not set foot on it,
and no lion prowls there.
9 Man's hand assaults the flinty rock
and lays bare the roots of the mountains.
10 He tunnels through the rock;
his eyes see all its treasures.
11 He searches[a] the sources of the rivers
and brings hidden things to light.

12 "But where can wisdom be found?
Where does understanding dwell?
13 Man does not comprehend its worth;
it cannot be found in the land of the living.
14 The deep says, 'It is not in me';
the sea says, 'It is not with me.'
15 It cannot be bought with the finest gold,
nor can its price be weighed in silver.
16 It cannot be bought with the gold of Ophir,
with precious onyx or sapphires.
17 Neither gold nor crystal can compare with it,
nor can it be had for jewels of gold.
18 Coral and jasper are not worthy of mention;
the price of wisdom is beyond rubies.
19 The topaz of Cush cannot compare with it;
it cannot be bought with pure gold.

20 "Where then does wisdom come from?
Where does understanding dwell?
21 It is hidden from the eyes of every living thing,
concealed even from the birds of the air.
22 Destruction[b] and Death say,
'Only a rumor of it has reached our ears.'
23 God understands the way to it
and he alone knows where it dwells,
24 for he views the ends of the earth
and sees everything under the heavens.
25 When he established the force of the wind
and measured out the waters,
26 when he made a decree for the rain
and a path for the thunderstorm,
27 then he looked at wisdom and appraised it;
he confirmed it and tested it.
28 And he said to man,
'The fear of the Lord—that is wisdom,
and to shun evil is understanding.' "

a11 Septuagint, Aquila and Vulgate; Hebrew *He dams up* **b22** Hebrew *Abaddon*

And God said to man, *"The fear of the Lord—that is wisdom, and to shun evil is understanding."* Job 28:28

28:12 *wisdom:* Precious metals and gems can be found by searching, but wisdom is harder to discover. The kind of wisdom Job is referring to is wisdom that comes from God. For the people of Israel, wisdom was based on the Law that God gave to Moses and the people at Mount Sinai (Exod 19–34). This wisdom was what parents were to teach their children (Deut 6:4-9). The apostle Paul contrasted human wisdom, which is often foolishness, with the wisdom of God (1 Cor 1:18—2:16). Here Job says that only God knows the way to wisdom, and that wisdom means respecting the LORD and turning away from sin (28:28). See also the mini-article called "Wisdom," p. 2206.

28:17-19 *crystal . . . jasper . . . topaz:* In the ancient world, objects made of glass were costly. Jasper is a valuable stone, usually green or clear, and topaz is a valuable yellow or light orange crystal stone.

28:23-27 Eccl 3:11; Prov 8:22-31. **28:28** Job 37:24; Ps 111:10; Prov 1:7; 9:10.

29:3 *lamp shone upon my head:* See the note at 18:5,6.

29:7,8 *gate of the city . . . took my seat:* In ancient times, trials and important business took place near the city gate. Job apparently was a highly respected member of the city council.

29:11 *spoke well of me:* Job tells about how he helped the poor, orphans, widows, and the needy. This is a direct response to Eliphaz's earlier charges against Job (22:3-11). As part of their covenant with the LORD, the people of Israel were to show mercy and justice to the poor and powerless (see the notes at 8:3 and 22:5). See also 31:16-23.

29:20 *the bow ever new in my hand:* Bows for shooting arrows are one of the oldest weapons used for hunting and warfare. A strong archer using a good bow could shoot arrows up to a distance of 400 yards. Biblical authors often use bows as a symbol of power and strength (Gen 49:23,24; Jer 49:34,35).

29:4-6 Job 1:1-5. **29:23** Job 29:7-11.

29 Job continued his discourse:

2 “How I long for the months gone by,
for the days when God watched over me,
3 when his lamp shone upon my head
and by his light I walked through darkness!
4 Oh, for the days when I was in my prime,
when God's intimate friendship blessed my house,
5 when the Almighty was still with me
and my children were around me,
6 when my path was drenched with cream
and the rock poured out for me streams of olive oil.

7 “When I went to the gate of the city
and took my seat in the public square,
8 the young men saw me and stepped aside
and the old men rose to their feet;
9 the chief men refrained from speaking
and covered their mouths with their hands;
10 the voices of the nobles were hushed,
and their tongues stuck to the roof of their mouths.
11 Whoever heard me spoke well of me,
and those who saw me commended me,
12 because I rescued the poor who cried for help,
and the fatherless who had none to assist him.
13 The man who was dying blessed me;
I made the widow's heart sing.
14 I put on righteousness as my clothing;
justice was my robe and my turban.
15 I was eyes to the blind
and feet to the lame.
16 I was a father to the needy;
I took up the case of the stranger.
17 I broke the fangs of the wicked
and snatched the victims from their teeth.

18 “I thought, ‘I will die in my own house,
my days as numerous as the grains of sand.
19 My roots will reach to the water,
and the dew will lie all night on my branches.
20 My glory will remain fresh in me,
the bow ever new in my hand.’

21 “Men listened to me expectantly,
waiting in silence for my counsel.
22 After I had spoken, they spoke no more;
my words fell gently on their ears.
23 They waited for me as for showers
and drank in my words as the spring rain.
24 When I smiled at them, they scarcely believed it;

the light of my face was precious to them.[a]
25 I chose the way for them and sat as their chief;
I dwelt as a king among his troops;
I was like one who comforts mourners.

30 "But now they mock me,
men younger than I,
whose fathers I would have disdained
to put with my sheep dogs.
2 Of what use was the strength of their hands to me,
since their vigor had gone from them?
3 Haggard from want and hunger,
they roamed[b] the parched land
in desolate wastelands at night.
4 In the brush they gathered salt herbs,
and their food[c] was the root of the broom tree.
5 They were banished from their fellow men,
shouted at as if they were thieves.
6 They were forced to live in the dry stream beds,
among the rocks and in holes in the ground.
7 They brayed among the bushes
and huddled in the undergrowth.
8 A base and nameless brood,
they were driven out of the land.

9 "And now their sons mock me in song;
I have become a byword among them.
10 They detest me and keep their distance;
they do not hesitate to spit in my face.
11 Now that God has unstrung my bow and afflicted me,
they throw off restraint in my presence.
12 On my right the tribe[d] attacks;
they lay snares for my feet,
they build their siege ramps against me.
13 They break up my road;
they succeed in destroying me—
without anyone's helping them.[e]
14 They advance as through a gaping breach;
amid the ruins they come rolling in.
15 Terrors overwhelm me;
my dignity is driven away as by the wind,
my safety vanishes like a cloud.

16 "And now my life ebbs away;
days of suffering grip me.

[a]24 The meaning of the Hebrew for this clause is uncertain. [b]3 Or *gnawed*
[c]4 Or *fuel* [d]12 The meaning of the Hebrew for this word is uncertain.
[e]13 Or *me.* / *'No one can help him,' ⌞they say⌟.*

30:1 *now they mock me:* Job had been a wealthy and respected man (1:2,3; 29:7-11), but now people—including the poor and helpless people Job had defended and helped (29:12-17)—are making fun of him. It seems as if Job is especially hurt by being ridiculed by people who have so little (30:3-9).

30:4 *the brush:* This may refer to the roots of the large bush known as the broom tree that grows in the desert areas of Palestine and Arabia (1 Kgs 19:4).

30:1 Job 12:4; 16:10; 17:2; 19:13-19; Ps 22:6-8,13; 69:4.

Job said, *"My harp is tuned to mourning, and my flute to the sound of wailing."*
Job 30:31

30:23 *the place appointed for all the living:* See the note at 3:13-17.

30:28 *the assembly:* See the note at 29:7, 8.

30:29 *jackals:* These desert animals are related to foxes and have a very sad-sounding howl. See also Mic 1:8.

30:17-19 Job 2:8; 7:3-5. **30:21-23** Job 3:13; 6:4; 9:17; 10:20–22; 19:7–12. **31:1,2** Exod 20:14,17; Matt 5:28; 2 Pet 2:14. **31:5,6** Job 23:11-13; 27:1-6.

17 Night pierces my bones;
my gnawing pains never rest.
18 In his great power ⌞God⌟ becomes like clothing to me[a];
he binds me like the neck of my garment.
19 He throws me into the mud,
and I am reduced to dust and ashes.

20 "I cry out to you, O God, but you do not answer;
I stand up, but you merely look at me.
21 You turn on me ruthlessly;
with the might of your hand you attack me.
22 You snatch me up and drive me before the wind;
you toss me about in the storm.
23 I know you will bring me down to death,
to the place appointed for all the living.

24 "Surely no one lays a hand on a broken man
when he cries for help in his distress.
25 Have I not wept for those in trouble?
Has not my soul grieved for the poor?
26 Yet when I hoped for good, evil came;
when I looked for light, then came darkness.
27 The churning inside me never stops;
days of suffering confront me.
28 I go about blackened, but not by the sun;
I stand up in the assembly and cry for help.
29 I have become a brother of jackals,
a companion of owls.
30 My skin grows black and peels;
my body burns with fever.
31 My harp is tuned to mourning,
and my flute to the sound of wailing.

31 "I made a covenant with my eyes
not to look lustfully at a girl.
2 For what is man's lot from God above,
his heritage from the Almighty on high?
3 Is it not ruin for the wicked,
disaster for those who do wrong?
4 Does he not see my ways
and count my every step?

5 "If I have walked in falsehood
or my foot has hurried after deceit—
6 let God weigh me in honest scales
and he will know that I am blameless—
7 if my steps have turned from the path,
if my heart has been led by my eyes,

[a] **18** Hebrew; Septuagint *⌞God⌟ grasps my clothing*

or if my hands have been defiled,
8 then may others eat what I have sown,
and may my crops be uprooted.

9 "If my heart has been enticed by a woman,
or if I have lurked at my neighbor's door,
10 then may my wife grind another man's grain,
and may other men sleep with her.
11 For that would have been shameful,
a sin to be judged.
12 It is a fire that burns to Destruction[a];
it would have uprooted my harvest.

13 "If I have denied justice to my menservants and maidservants
when they had a grievance against me,
14 what will I do when God confronts me?
What will I answer when called to account?
15 Did not he who made me in the womb make them?
Did not the same one form us both within our mothers?

16 "If I have denied the desires of the poor
or let the eyes of the widow grow weary,
17 if I have kept my bread to myself,
not sharing it with the fatherless—
18 but from my youth I reared him as would a father,
and from my birth I guided the widow—
19 if I have seen anyone perishing for lack of clothing,
or a needy man without a garment,
20 and his heart did not bless me
for warming him with the fleece from my sheep,
21 if I have raised my hand against the fatherless,
knowing that I had influence in court,
22 then let my arm fall from the shoulder,
let it be broken off at the joint.
23 For I dreaded destruction from God,
and for fear of his splendor I could not do such things.

24 "If I have put my trust in gold
or said to pure gold, 'You are my security,'
25 if I have rejoiced over my great wealth,
the fortune my hands had gained,
26 if I have regarded the sun in its radiance
or the moon moving in splendor,
27 so that my heart was secretly enticed
and my hand offered them a kiss of homage,
28 then these also would be sins to be judged,
for I would have been unfaithful to God on high.

a12 Hebrew *Abaddon*

31:13-15 *Did not he who made me in the womb make them:* Though some are servants and some are masters, Job recognizes that God creates all people equal (Ps 139:13,14; Prov 22:2; Eph 6:9).

31:16-21 *widow . . . fatherless:* Job argues that he understands God's concern for widows and orphans and the poor and needy (see also 29:11 and the note).

31:26,27 *regarded the sun . . . moon . . . enticed:* The people of Israel were to worship God alone and not worship the sun and moon as gods, as some of their neighbors did (Deut 4:19; 17:2,3; 2 Kgs 21:2-7; Jer 8:1,2; Ezek 8:16-18). Job worshiped Israel's one true God, though according to the story, he lived at a time long before Moses and the people received God's laws concerning worship and daily living (see the Introduction to Job, p. 961).

31:9-11 Deut 22:22; Job 24:15.

31:31,32 *my door was always open:* It was the custom in many Near Eastern countries to welcome strangers into one's home for a meal and to rest (Gen 18:2-8). In ancient Israel, the lives of one's guests were sacred and had to be protected at any cost.

31:35 *the Almighty:* See the note at 5:17,18.

31:38 *land cries out against me:* Israel had laws that protected the land from being overused (Exod 23:10-12; Lev 25). If the land was not used properly and was abused, it was said to mourn and become no longer productive. Stealing land from its owner was considered a terrible crime that would result in severe punishment (1 Kgs 21:1-24). The land, or ground, also was affected by the way people lived. If they did not obey God, the land itself may suffer (Gen 3:18; 4:10-12; Lev 26:14-20; Isa 33:9; Jer 12:4; Hos 4:3; Joel 1:10).

31:36 Exod 28:9-12.

29 "If I have rejoiced at my enemy's misfortune
or gloated over the trouble that came to him—
30 I have not allowed my mouth to sin
by invoking a curse against his life—
31 if the men of my household have never said,
'Who has not had his fill of Job's meat?'—
32 but no stranger had to spend the night in the street,
for my door was always open to the traveler—
33 if I have concealed my sin as men do,[a]
by hiding my guilt in my heart
34 because I so feared the crowd
and so dreaded the contempt of the clans
that I kept silent and would not go outside

35 ("Oh, that I had someone to hear me!
I sign now my defense—let the Almighty answer me;
let my accuser put his indictment in writing.
36 Surely I would wear it on my shoulder,
I would put it on like a crown.
37 I would give him an account of my every step;
like a prince I would approach him.)—

38 "if my land cries out against me
and all its furrows are wet with tears,
39 if I have devoured its yield without payment
or broken the spirit of its tenants,

[a]33 Or *as Adam did*

QUESTIONS ABOUT JOB 3:1—31:40

1. When Job's three friends arrive to comfort him, how is Job feeling? How does he let his feelings be known? (3:1-26)
2. Have you ever faced suffering or sadness that is similar to Job's? If you wish, describe how this suffering felt. When you were facing this pain and suffering, what message did you want or need to hear?
3. Summarize the advice given to Job by each of his friends—Eliphaz (4; 5; 15; 22), Bildad (8; 18; 25), and Zophar (11; 20). How did Job respond to each friend?
4. Why does Job want to face God in court? Is Job's defense strong enough to stand up in court? Why or why not?
5. This large section says many things about who God is and how God acts. Name at least three. What new or surprising things have you discovered about God as you have read Job?
6. According to Job, what is true wisdom and where does it come from? (28:12-28) Does modern society define wisdom the same way as it is defined in Job? If not, what are the differences?
7. In what specific ways does Eliphaz say that Job has sinned? (22:2-11) What does Job say to defend himself against these charges? (29:4-17; 31:1-34)
8. Today, grief is often described as a process with different stages. Each of the "stages" is connected with different emotions. What "stages" of grief has Job been going through?

[40]then let briers come up instead of wheat
and weeds instead of barley."

The words of Job are ended.

Elihu Speaks to Job and Job's Friends

When Job's debate with his three friends is done, another counselor steps forward to give advice. He has been waiting patiently on the sidelines, listening to Job and his counselors, because he is younger than they are. But now he is ready to show how both Job and his friends are wrong in their thinking. Elihu is introduced in 32:1-5, and his four speeches make up Job 32:6—37:24.

Elihu

32 So these three men stopped answering Job, because he was
righteous in his own eyes. [2]But Elihu son of Barakel the Buzite, of
the family of Ram, became very angry with Job for justifying himself rather than God. [3]He was also angry with the three friends,
because they had found no way to refute Job, and yet had condemned him.[a] [4]Now Elihu had waited before speaking to Job
because they were older than he. [5]But when he saw that the three
men had nothing more to say, his anger was aroused.

[6]So Elihu son of Barakel the Buzite said:

"I am young in years,
and you are old;
that is why I was fearful,
not daring to tell you what I know.
[7]I thought, 'Age should speak;
advanced years should teach wisdom.'
[8]But it is the spirit[b] in a man,
the breath of the Almighty, that gives him
understanding.
[9]It is not only the old[c] who are wise,
not only the aged who understand what is right.

[10]"Therefore I say: Listen to me;
I too will tell you what I know.
[11]I waited while you spoke,
I listened to your reasoning;
while you were searching for words,
[12]I gave you my full attention.
But not one of you has proved Job wrong;
none of you has answered his arguments.
[13]Do not say, 'We have found wisdom;
let God refute him, not man.'

---

[a]**3** Masoretic Text; an ancient Hebrew scribal tradition *Job, and so had condemned God* [b]**8** Or *Spirit*; also in verse 18 [c]**9** Or *many*; or *great*

Elihu said, *"I thought, 'Age should speak; advanced years should teach wisdom.' But it is the spirit in a man, the breath of the Almighty, that gives him understanding."* Job 32:7,8

31:40 *let briers come up:* Job's words in 31:38-40 are an oath (compare also 31:21, 22). He is so certain that he is innocent of the charges against him (22:5) that he is willing to ask for more physical pain and for God to curse his land if he is found guilty. For more, see the mini-article called "Making Vows," p. 328.

32:2 *Elihu . . . the Buzite:* The name of Elihu's father (*Barakel*) in Hebrew means "El (God) has blessed," and Elihu's own name means "He is my God." Elihu is a descendant of Buz, nephew of Abraham (Gen 22:20-23) and brother of Uz (Job 1:1). Buz may have been an area in the territory of Edom. In Jeremiah 25:23, 24 Buz is mentioned along with Tema (see the note at 6:19). Elihu is upset at Job for blaming God and at Job's friends for being unable to give Job a good reason for his suffering.

32:6 Jer 1:6-8; 1 Tim 4:12. **32:8,9** Job 12:11-13; Prov 2:6; Jas 1:5.

Elihu said, *"I must speak and find relief; I must open my lips and reply. I will show partiality to no one, nor will I flatter any man; for if I were skilled in flattery, my Maker would soon take me away."*
Job 32:20-22

The Young Man Elihu Speaks Out by Troy Yulfo, pen and ink drawing, 1999. Elihu from Buz was much younger than Job's three friends and kept silent out of respect while they argued with Job. Finally, when he could keep silent no longer, he said, "I too will have my say . . . I am like bottled-up wine, like new wineskins ready to burst." (See 32:17-19.)

14 But Job has not marshaled his words against me,
and I will not answer him with your arguments.

15 "They are dismayed and have no more to say;
words have failed them.
16 Must I wait, now that they are silent,
now that they stand there with no reply?
17 I too will have my say;
I too will tell what I know.
18 For I am full of words,
and the spirit within me compels me;

[19]inside I am like bottled-up wine,
like new wineskins ready to burst.
[20]I must speak and find relief;
I must open my lips and reply.
[21]I will show partiality to no one,
nor will I flatter any man;
[22]for if I were skilled in flattery,
my Maker would soon take me away.

33 "But now, Job, listen to my words;
pay attention to everything I say.
[2]I am about to open my mouth;
my words are on the tip of my tongue.
[3]My words come from an upright heart;
my lips sincerely speak what I know.
[4]The Spirit of God has made me;
the breath of the Almighty gives me life.
[5]Answer me then, if you can;
prepare yourself and confront me.
[6]I am just like you before God;
I too have been taken from clay.
[7]No fear of me should alarm you,
nor should my hand be heavy upon you.

[8]"But you have said in my hearing—
I heard the very words—
[9]'I am pure and without sin;
I am clean and free from guilt.
[10]Yet God has found fault with me;
he considers me his enemy.
[11]He fastens my feet in shackles;
he keeps close watch on all my paths.'

[12]"But I tell you, in this you are not right,
for God is greater than man.
[13]Why do you complain to him
that he answers none of man's words[a]?
[14]For God does speak—now one way, now another—
though man may not perceive it.
[15]In a dream, in a vision of the night,
when deep sleep falls on men
as they slumber in their beds,
[16]he may speak in their ears
and terrify them with warnings,
[17]to turn man from wrongdoing
and keep him from pride,
[18]to preserve his soul from the pit,[b]

[a]13 Or *that he does not answer for any of his actions* [b]18 Or *preserve him from the grave*

32:19 *new wineskins ready to burst:* While the juice from grapes is becoming wine, it produces gas. The gas caused by this process of fermentation swells and stretches the skins as the juice turns to wine. Sometimes the swelling would burst the wineskins.

32:21,22 *show partiality . . . flatter:* Elihu claims that he is so completely fair that he is not able to give special honor to anyone. His attitude seems overly boastful, especially since he has not experienced the kind of suffering that Job has. Compare his vow (32:21,22) to Job's vows (31:21,22, 38-40).

33:4 *Spirit:* The Hebrew word *ruah* translated here as "Spirit" is the same word used to describe God's creating power (Gen 1:2). Elihu may also be comparing this Spirit to the source of wisdom that comes from God (32:8). See also the mini-article called, "Holy Spirit," p. 2082.

33:15,16 *dream . . . terrify them:* See the note at 4:12-15.

33:18 *the pit:* See the note at 3:13-17.

33:6 Gen 2:7; 3:19; Job 4:19; Isa 64:8. **33:11** Job 13:27.

Elihu said, *"God does all these things to a man—twice, even three times—to turn back his soul from the pit, that the light of life may shine on him."*
Job 33:29,30

33:23,24 *an angel on his side as a mediator:* See the notes at 1:6, 7 and 15:7,8. Elihu is describing an angel who defends a person in God's court (see the note at 19:25). Elihu may be referring to Job's earlier prayers for a defender (9:32-35; 16:18-22; 19:21-27).

33:27 *I sinned . . . but I did not get what I deserved:* Elihu says that God may use dreams and suffering to teach people and to get them to change their behavior (33:15-22). But here he continues the argument of Job's other friends, indicating he believes that Job has sinned and needs to turn to God for forgiveness.

33:30 *turn back his soul from the pit . . . light of life:* The word translated as "pit" here can also be translated as "death" or "grave." The pit stands for the dark world of the dead (see the note at 3:13-17). Light is a symbol of life (see the note at 18:5, 6). Elihu is saying that the suffering God has given to Job is an act of love, since Job and all other human beings actually deserve worse (compare to 11:6). See also Ps 56:12,13; Isa 53:11,12; Phil 2:13.

his life from perishing by the sword.[a]
19 Or a man may be chastened on a bed of pain
with constant distress in his bones,
20 so that his very being finds food repulsive
and his soul loathes the choicest meal.
21 His flesh wastes away to nothing,
and his bones, once hidden, now stick out.
22 His soul draws near to the pit,[b]
and his life to the messengers of death.[c]

23 "Yet if there is an angel on his side
as a mediator, one out of a thousand,
to tell a man what is right for him,
24 to be gracious to him and say,
'Spare him from going down to the pit[d];
I have found a ransom for him'—
25 then his flesh is renewed like a child's;
it is restored as in the days of his youth.
26 He prays to God and finds favor with him,
he sees God's face and shouts for joy;
he is restored by God to his righteous state.
27 Then he comes to men and says,
'I sinned, and perverted what was right,
but I did not get what I deserved.
28 He redeemed my soul from going down to the pit,[e]
and I will live to enjoy the light.'

29 "God does all these things to a man—
twice, even three times—
30 to turn back his soul from the pit,[f]
that the light of life may shine on him.

31 "Pay attention, Job, and listen to me;
be silent, and I will speak.
32 If you have anything to say, answer me;
speak up, for I want you to be cleared.
33 But if not, then listen to me;
be silent, and I will teach you wisdom."

34 Then Elihu said:

2 "Hear my words, you wise men;
listen to me, you men of learning.
3 For the ear tests words
as the tongue tastes food.
4 Let us discern for ourselves what is right;
let us learn together what is good.

---

[a]**18** Or *from crossing the River* [b]**22** Or *He draws near to the grave* [c]**22** Or *to the dead* [d]**24** Or *grave* [e]**28** Or *redeemed me from going down to the grave* [f]**30** Or *turn him back from the grave*

[5]“Job says, ‘I am innocent,
but God denies me justice.
[6]Although I am right,
I am considered a liar;
although I am guiltless,
his arrow inflicts an incurable wound.’
[7]What man is like Job,
who drinks scorn like water?
[8]He keeps company with evildoers;
he associates with wicked men.
[9]For he says, ‘It profits a man nothing
when he tries to please God.’

[10]“So listen to me, you men of understanding.
Far be it from God to do evil,
from the Almighty to do wrong.
[11]He repays a man for what he has done;
he brings upon him what his conduct deserves.
[12]It is unthinkable that God would do wrong,
that the Almighty would pervert justice.
[13]Who appointed him over the earth?
Who put him in charge of the whole world?
[14]If it were his intention
and he withdrew his spirit[a] and breath,
[15]all mankind would perish together
and man would return to the dust.

[16]“If you have understanding, hear this;
listen to what I say.
[17]Can he who hates justice govern?
Will you condemn the just and mighty One?
[18]Is he not the One who says to kings, ‘You are worthless,’
and to nobles, ‘You are wicked,’
[19]who shows no partiality to princes
and does not favor the rich over the poor,
for they are all the work of his hands?
[20]They die in an instant, in the middle of the night;
the people are shaken and they pass away;
the mighty are removed without human hand.

[21]“His eyes are on the ways of men;
he sees their every step.
[22]There is no dark place, no deep shadow,
where evildoers can hide.
[23]God has no need to examine men further,
that they should come before him for judgment.
[24]Without inquiry he shatters the mighty
and sets up others in their place.

[a]**14** Or *Spirit*

34:9 *profits a man nothing when he tries to please God:* Elihu says that Job's sin is giving up on trying to do what God wants (9:20-24). Like Job's other friends, Elihu pays little attention to how much Job's suffering may be affecting his thinking (6:11-13; 7:11-19; 10:1).

34:11 *what his conduct deserves:* Elihu repeats a key argument of Job's other friends: that God treats each person as he or she deserves to be treated (see the notes at 1:10 and 4:8,9).

34:17 *justice:* Elihu argues that God is the source of justice, so God could not act in an unjust way toward Job, as Job has claimed (27:2-6). See also the note at 8:3.

34:23 *judgment:* Elihu argues that God can judge a person at any time and in any place, so Job's request for a formal trial in God's court is unnecessary and disrespectful.

34:5,6 Job 6:29; 10:7; 23:2,11, 12. **34:11** Ps 62:12. **34:13-15** Gen 1:1—2:4, 7; 3:19; Eccl 12:7. **34:21** Job 31:4.

Elihu said, *"Suppose a man says to God, 'I am guilty but will offend no more. . . . Should God then reward you on your terms, when you refuse to repent?"* Job 34:31,33

34:31 *I am guilty:* Elihu's advice is similar to that of Bildad (8:5, 6), Zophar (11:13,14), and Eliphaz (22:23).

35:3 *what do I gain by not sinning:* See the note at 1:10.

34:36 Job 33:8-13. **35:6-8** Job 22:2,3.

25 Because he takes note of their deeds,
he overthrows them in the night and they are crushed.
26 He punishes them for their wickedness
where everyone can see them,
27 because they turned from following him
and had no regard for any of his ways.
28 They caused the cry of the poor to come before him,
so that he heard the cry of the needy.
29 But if he remains silent, who can condemn him?
If he hides his face, who can see him?
Yet he is over man and nation alike,
30 to keep a godless man from ruling,
from laying snares for the people.

31 "Suppose a man says to God,
'I am guilty but will offend no more.
32 Teach me what I cannot see;
if I have done wrong, I will not do so again.'
33 Should God then reward you on your terms,
when you refuse to repent?
You must decide, not I;
so tell me what you know.

34 "Men of understanding declare,
wise men who hear me say to me,
35 'Job speaks without knowledge;
his words lack insight.'
36 Oh, that Job might be tested to the utmost
for answering like a wicked man!
37 To his sin he adds rebellion;
scornfully he claps his hands among us
and multiplies his words against God."

35

Then Elihu said:
2 "Do you think this is just?
You say, 'I will be cleared by God.[a]'
3 Yet you ask him, 'What profit is it to me,[b]
and what do I gain by not sinning?'

4 "I would like to reply to you
and to your friends with you.
5 Look up at the heavens and see;
gaze at the clouds so high above you.
6 If you sin, how does that affect him?
If your sins are many, what does that do to him?
7 If you are righteous, what do you give to him,
or what does he receive from your hand?

[a]2 Or *My righteousness is more than God's* [b]3 Or *you*

[8]Your wickedness affects only a man like yourself,
and your righteousness only the sons of men.

[9]"Men cry out under a load of oppression;
they plead for relief from the arm of the powerful.
[10]But no one says, 'Where is God my Maker,
who gives songs in the night,
[11]who teaches more to us than to[a] the beasts of the earth
and makes us wiser than[b] the birds of the air?'
[12]He does not answer when men cry out
because of the arrogance of the wicked.
[13]Indeed, God does not listen to their empty plea;
the Almighty pays no attention to it.
[14]How much less, then, will he listen
when you say that you do not see him,
that your case is before him
and you must wait for him,
[15]and further, that his anger never punishes
and he does not take the least notice of wickedness.[c]
[16]So Job opens his mouth with empty talk;
without knowledge he multiplies words."

36 Elihu continued:

[2]"Bear with me a little longer and I will show you
that there is more to be said in God's behalf.
[3]I get my knowledge from afar;
I will ascribe justice to my Maker.
[4]Be assured that my words are not false;
one perfect in knowledge is with you.

[5]"God is mighty, but does not despise men;
he is mighty, and firm in his purpose.
[6]He does not keep the wicked alive
but gives the afflicted their rights.
[7]He does not take his eyes off the righteous;
he enthrones them with kings
and exalts them forever.
[8]But if men are bound in chains,
held fast by cords of affliction,
[9]he tells them what they have done—
that they have sinned arrogantly.
[10]He makes them listen to correction
and commands them to repent of their evil.
[11]If they obey and serve him,
they will spend the rest of their days in prosperity
and their years in contentment.

[a]11 Or *teaches us by* [b]11 Or *us wise by* [c]15 Symmachus, Theodotion and Vulgate; the meaning of the Hebrew for this word is uncertain.

35:9-14 *Men cry out under a load of oppression:* Elihu is arguing that when people in trouble cry out to God for help, their prayers are usually selfish. And when help comes, they soon forget about God. Elihu says that Job's prayers and his request to face God in court are selfish and impatient, and that Job is unwilling to trust and understand God or God's wisdom (33:10-14; Prov 8:12-36).

36:8-12 *commands them to repent of their evil:* Elihu repeats his earlier argument (see the note at 35:9-14). The earlier message that suffering is caused by sin is also repeated (see 4:8, 9; 8:20; 19:5; 22:4,5). Those who turn to God and admit their sins will be blessed. Those who don't admit their sin will face a violent death (20:4-11).

36:3 Job 34:10,11; 37:23. **36:5** Job 34:11.

Elihu said, *"Those who suffer he delivers in their suffering; he speaks to them in their affliction."* Job 36:15

36:15 *affliction:* Once again Elihu argues that God has made Job suffer in order to get Job's attention, and to make him admit his sin (36:17).

36:26 *beyond our understanding:* Elihu emphasizes how hard it is for human beings to understand God's ways, an important theme in the LORD's speeches to follow (chapters 38–41). See also 11:7-9; Isa 55:8, 9.

36:19 Deut 8:17, 18; Ps 49:5-9; Jer 9:23; 1 Tim 6:6-10, 17-19. **36:27-31** Job 5:9; 37:11; 38:28; Ps 18:9-15; 65:9-11; Isa 30:23; Acts 14:15-17.

12 But if they do not listen,
they will perish by the sword[a]
and die without knowledge.

13 "The godless in heart harbor resentment;
even when he fetters them, they do not cry for help.
14 They die in their youth,
among male prostitutes of the shrines.
15 But those who suffer he delivers in their suffering;
he speaks to them in their affliction.

16 "He is wooing you from the jaws of distress
to a spacious place free from restriction,
to the comfort of your table laden with choice food.
17 But now you are laden with the judgment due the wicked;
judgment and justice have taken hold of you.
18 Be careful that no one entices you by riches;
do not let a large bribe turn you aside.
19 Would your wealth
or even all your mighty efforts
sustain you so you would not be in distress?
20 Do not long for the night,
to drag people away from their homes.[b]
21 Beware of turning to evil,
which you seem to prefer to affliction.

22 "God is exalted in his power.
Who is a teacher like him?
23 Who has prescribed his ways for him,
or said to him, 'You have done wrong'?
24 Remember to extol his work,
which men have praised in song.
25 All mankind has seen it;
men gaze on it from afar.
26 How great is God—beyond our understanding!
The number of his years is past finding out.

27 "He draws up the drops of water,
which distill as rain to the streams[c];
28 the clouds pour down their moisture
and abundant showers fall on mankind.
29 Who can understand how he spreads out the clouds,
how he thunders from his pavilion?
30 See how he scatters his lightning about him,
bathing the depths of the sea.
31 This is the way he governs[d] the nations
and provides food in abundance.

[a]12 Or *will cross the River* [b]20 The meaning of the Hebrew for verses 18-20 is uncertain. [c]27 Or *distill from the mist as rain* [d]31 Or *nourishes*

[32]He fills his hands with lightning
and commands it to strike its mark.
[33]His thunder announces the coming storm;
even the cattle make known its approach.[a]

37 "At this my heart pounds
and leaps from its place.
[2]Listen! Listen to the roar of his voice,
to the rumbling that comes from his mouth.
[3]He unleashes his lightning beneath the whole heaven
and sends it to the ends of the earth.
[4]After that comes the sound of his roar;
he thunders with his majestic voice.
When his voice resounds,
he holds nothing back.
[5]God's voice thunders in marvelous ways;
he does great things beyond our understanding.
[6]He says to the snow, 'Fall on the earth,'
and to the rain shower, 'Be a mighty downpour.'
[7]So that all men he has made may know his work,
he stops every man from his labor.[b]
[8]The animals take cover;
they remain in their dens.
[9]The tempest comes out from its chamber,
the cold from the driving winds.
[10]The breath of God produces ice,
and the broad waters become frozen.
[11]He loads the clouds with moisture;
he scatters his lightning through them.
[12]At his direction they swirl around
over the face of the whole earth
to do whatever he commands them.
[13]He brings the clouds to punish men,
or to water his earth[c] and show his love.

[14]"Listen to this, Job;
stop and consider God's wonders.
[15]Do you know how God controls the clouds
and makes his lightning flash?
[16]Do you know how the clouds hang poised,
those wonders of him who is perfect in knowledge?
[17]You who swelter in your clothes
when the land lies hushed under the south wind,
[18]can you join him in spreading out the skies,
hard as a mirror of cast bronze?

[19]"Tell us what we should say to him;

---

[a]33 Or *announces his coming— / the One zealous against evil* [b]7 Or / *he fills all men with fear by his power* [c]13 Or *to favor them*

37:2,3 *roar of his voice . . . lightning:* Fire and smoke and thunder and lightning often signal the presence of God in the Bible (Gen 15:17,18; Exod 3:2; 13:21,22; 19:16-19; Judg 13:20; Matt 24:27). When God is revealed in this way, it is sometimes called a "theophany." See also the note at 1:16-19.

37:17,18 *south wind . . . bronze:* The south wind was a hot wind from the desert that would blow sand and dust into the air, giving the sky a gold hue, like the color of bronze, when the sun is shining (see also Deut 28:21-23). For bronze, see the notes at 6:12 and 20:24.

37:5 Job 5:9; 36:26. **37:6-8** Judg 5:4,5; 1 Kgs 18:41-45; Ps 68:7-9. **37:16** Job 36:29.

37:20 *ask to be swallowed up:* Elihu is referring to Job's wish to speak directly to God in court to prove that he is innocent. Elihu's question implies that it is wrong for Job to question God in this way.

37:23 *beyond our reach . . . justice:* Elihu summarizes some of his key arguments. God cannot be seen by humans, so it is foolish for Job to expect to face God in court. God makes himself known in dreams and is present in human suffering (33:14-22). God doesn't need to set trial dates to judge human beings, because he is watching and judging peoples' actions all the time (34:21-27). Since God's actions are always just, Job's suffering must be a punishment for something he did wrong (33:8-13; 34:5-12, 31; 36:17, 18).

37:24 *revere him:* The word translated "revere" refers to respecting, obeying, and honoring God. Sometimes it is translated as "fear." To revere or fear God in this way is truly wise (Prov 1:7).

38:1 *LORD:* See the note at 2:1.

38:1 *storm:* Storms often signal the appearance of God in the Bible (Ps 18:7-15; 50:3; Ezek 1:4; Zech 9:14). The power and effects of a windstorm can be felt and seen, but the wind itself is invisible.

we cannot draw up our case because of our darkness.
20 Should he be told that I want to speak?
Would any man ask to be swallowed up?
21 Now no one can look at the sun,
bright as it is in the skies
after the wind has swept them clean.
22 Out of the north he comes in golden splendor;
God comes in awesome majesty.
23 The Almighty is beyond our reach and exalted in power;
in his justice and great righteousness, he does not oppress.
24 Therefore, men revere him,
for does he not have regard for all the wise in heart?[a]"

The LORD Speaks to Job, and Job Replies

Finally, Job gets to hear the LORD speak directly to him out of a storm. The LORD's speeches (38:1—40:2; 40:6—41:34) are each followed by Job's replies (40:3-5; 42:1-6). The LORD does not answer Job's questions directly but rather answers Job by asking questions of his own. Job still is not sure why he suffered, since he doesn't know the role Satan played in causing his suffering (1:6-12; 2:1-7). But Job experiences God's presence in a new way, which helps him to live with his troubles and unanswered questions.

The LORD Speaks

38 Then the LORD answered Job out of the storm. He said:
2 "Who is this that darkens my counsel
with words without knowledge?

[a]24 Or *for he does not have regard for any who think they are wise.*

QUESTIONS ABOUT JOB 32:1—37:24

1. Who is Elihu, and what words would you use to describe his attitude? Why?
2. Why does Elihu criticize the arguments of Job's other friends? (32:11-14) How are Elihu's arguments similar to those of Job's other friends? What new arguments does Elihu introduce?
3. What does Elihu tell Job to do? (34:31; 36:17-23; 37:14) Do you think Elihu's advice is any better or any worse than that of Job's other friends? Why or why not?
4. What is your reaction to these statements of Elihu?
   a. "the Almighty . . . gives him understanding." (32:8)
   b. "I too have been taken from clay." (33:6)
   c. "God does all these things to a man . . . to turn back his soul from the pit." (33:29,30)
   d. "He does not answer when men cry out because of the arrogance of the wicked." (35:12)
   e. "The Almighty is beyond our reach and exalted in power." (37:23)
5. If Job were your friend, what advice would you give him?

[3] Brace yourself like a man;
I will question you,
and you shall answer me.
[4] "Where were you when I laid the earth's foundation?
Tell me, if you understand.
[5] Who marked off its dimensions? Surely you know!
Who stretched a measuring line across it?
[6] On what were its footings set,
or who laid its cornerstone—
[7] while the morning stars sang together
and all the angels[a] shouted for joy?
[8] "Who shut up the sea behind doors
when it burst forth from the womb,
[9] when I made the clouds its garment
and wrapped it in thick darkness,
[10] when I fixed limits for it
and set its doors and bars in place,

[a]7 Hebrew *the sons of God*

Then the Lord Answered Job Out of the Whirlwind, an engraving by William Blake, around 1824. After arguing with his friends and struggling to understand why God has allowed him to suffer so much, Job at last hears God's answer. The LORD spoke to Job from out of a storm. He asked Job, "Who is this that darkens my counsel with words without knowledge? Brace yourself like a man; I will question you." (See 38:2, 3.)

38:4 *when I laid the earth's foundation:* The LORD's questions in this passage focus on how the LORD created and still controls the world and the universe.

38:5 *Surely you know:* Job's earlier comments provide an answer to the LORD's questions (see 9:6-10). See also Prov 30:4.

38:8-10 *shut up the sea:* See the note at 7:12. See also Gen 1:9, 10; Jer 5:22.

38:7 Ps 148:2,3.

38:16-21 *recesses of the deep . . . gates of death . . . vast expanses:* Of course, Job cannot answer "yes" to these questions. See the note at 3:13-17. Light and darkness are described as two distinct parts of God's created universe (Gen 1:3, 4). The LORD's comment in 38:21 is meant to be sarcastic. Job can't lead the darkness and light home, and he certainly wasn't alive when God created the universe.

38:15 Job 18:5; 24:13-17; 33:29, 30. **38:24-30** Judg 5:4,5; 1 Kgs 18:41-46; Job 36:27-33; 37:6-8; Ps 68:7-9.

11 when I said, 'This far you may come and no farther;
here is where your proud waves halt'?

12 "Have you ever given orders to the morning,
or shown the dawn its place,
13 that it might take the earth by the edges
and shake the wicked out of it?
14 The earth takes shape like clay under a seal;
its features stand out like those of a garment.
15 The wicked are denied their light,
and their upraised arm is broken.

16 "Have you journeyed to the springs of the sea
or walked in the recesses of the deep?
17 Have the gates of death been shown to you?
Have you seen the gates of the shadow of death[a]?
18 Have you comprehended the vast expanses of the earth?
Tell me, if you know all this.

19 "What is the way to the abode of light?
And where does darkness reside?
20 Can you take them to their places?
Do you know the paths to their dwellings?
21 Surely you know, for you were already born!
You have lived so many years!

22 "Have you entered the storehouses of the snow
or seen the storehouses of the hail,
23 which I reserve for times of trouble,
for days of war and battle?
24 What is the way to the place where the lightning is dispersed,
or the place where the east winds are scattered over the earth?
25 Who cuts a channel for the torrents of rain,
and a path for the thunderstorm,
26 to water a land where no man lives,
a desert with no one in it,
27 to satisfy a desolate wasteland
and make it sprout with grass?
28 Does the rain have a father?
Who fathers the drops of dew?
29 From whose womb comes the ice?
Who gives birth to the frost from the heavens
30 when the waters become hard as stone,
when the surface of the deep is frozen?

[a]17 Or *gates of deep shadows*

31 "Can you bind the beautiful[a] Pleiades?
Can you loose the cords of Orion?
32 Can you bring forth the constellations in their seasons[b]
or lead out the Bear[c] with its cubs?
33 Do you know the laws of the heavens?
Can you set up ⌞God's[d]⌟ dominion over the earth?

34 "Can you raise your voice to the clouds
and cover yourself with a flood of water?
35 Do you send the lightning bolts on their way?
Do they report to you, 'Here we are'?
36 Who endowed the heart[e] with wisdom
or gave understanding to the mind[e]?
37 Who has the wisdom to count the clouds?
Who can tip over the water jars of the heavens
38 when the dust becomes hard
and the clods of earth stick together?

39 "Do you hunt the prey for the lioness
and satisfy the hunger of the lions
40 when they crouch in their dens
or lie in wait in a thicket?
41 Who provides food for the raven
when its young cry out to God
and wander about for lack of food?

39 "Do you know when the mountain goats give birth?
Do you watch when the doe bears her fawn?
2 Do you count the months till they bear?
Do you know the time they give birth?
3 They crouch down and bring forth their young;
their labor pains are ended.
4 Their young thrive and grow strong in the wilds;
they leave and do not return.

5 "Who let the wild donkey go free?
Who untied his ropes?
6 I gave him the wasteland as his home,
the salt flats as his habitat.
7 He laughs at the commotion in the town;
he does not hear a driver's shout.
8 He ranges the hills for his pasture
and searches for any green thing.

9 "Will the wild ox consent to serve you?
Will he stay by your manger at night?

---

[a]**31** Or *the twinkling*; or *the chains of the season* [b]**32** Or *the morning star in its season* [c]**32** Or *out Leo* [d]**33** Or *his*; or *their* [e]**36** The meaning of the Hebrew for this word is uncertain.

The LORD asked Job, *"Do you know the laws of the heavens? Can you set up ⌞God's⌟ dominion over the earth?"*
Job 38:33

38:31,32 *Pleiades . . . Orion . . . the Bear:* Only God has the power to rearrange the stars, so once again the questions remind Job that he is merely a human being. He is nothing compared to the LORD, the powerful creator of the whole universe. Job did earlier recognize the LORD's power (see 9:6-9 and the note).

38:39—39:30 *hunger of the lions . . . young ones feast:* These verses focus on the LORD's care for the earth's living creatures.

39:1 *mountain goats . . . doe:* The Hebrew word translated as "mountain goat" may refer to an ibex, a kind of wild goat that has shorter hair than a common goat and has horns that are slender and curve back. These animals live in the rugged hills and mountains and usually avoid people. The LORD controls the time when they will give birth to their young.

39:5-9 *wild donkey . . . wild ox:* Wild donkeys in the Middle East are larger and more lively than European donkeys. Many donkeys roamed about free, but others were captured, tamed, and used for transportation or to do work, such as pulling a millstone over grain to crush it into flour. Oxen were often used to pull loads and do work, but some oxen remained wild (Num 23:22; Deut 33:17; Ps 22:21).

38:41 Matt 6:26; Luke 12:24.

39:13-16 *ostrich:* The picture of the ostrich as a bird that does not care about its young does not fit entirely with real ostrich behavior. The male and female take turns caring for their eggs, though they do not try to hide the eggs from other animals that may try to steal and eat the eggs. Perhaps the LORD is comparing the ostrich's lack of common sense to Job's lack of wisdom.

39:19-25 *horse:* In ancient times, horses were an important part of the armies of a number of countries. They pulled chariots and were ridden by soldiers.

39:20 *locust:* Winged insects that move by jumping or flying. See also the mini-article called "Locusts," p. 1708.

39:26,27 *hawk . . . eagle:* Hawks and eagles are praised for protecting their eggs in nests built high where predators would be unable to reach them. They also provide food for their young. Job had earlier described God as watching him closely (7:20) and hunting him (16:9; 19:22), just as the eagle and hawk fly high above the earth looking for prey.

39:30 Matt 24:28; Luke 17:37.

10 Can you hold him to the furrow with a harness?
Will he till the valleys behind you?
11 Will you rely on him for his great strength?
Will you leave your heavy work to him?
12 Can you trust him to bring in your grain
and gather it to your threshing floor?

13 "The wings of the ostrich flap joyfully,
but they cannot compare with the pinions and feathers of the stork.
14 She lays her eggs on the ground
and lets them warm in the sand,
15 unmindful that a foot may crush them,
that some wild animal may trample them.
16 She treats her young harshly, as if they were not hers;
she cares not that her labor was in vain,
17 for God did not endow her with wisdom
or give her a share of good sense.
18 Yet when she spreads her feathers to run,
she laughs at horse and rider.

19 "Do you give the horse his strength
or clothe his neck with a flowing mane?
20 Do you make him leap like a locust,
striking terror with his proud snorting?
21 He paws fiercely, rejoicing in his strength,
and charges into the fray.
22 He laughs at fear, afraid of nothing;
he does not shy away from the sword.
23 The quiver rattles against his side,
along with the flashing spear and lance.
24 In frenzied excitement he eats up the ground;
he cannot stand still when the trumpet sounds.
25 At the blast of the trumpet he snorts, 'Aha!'
He catches the scent of battle from afar,
the shout of commanders and the battle cry.

26 "Does the hawk take flight by your wisdom
and spread his wings toward the south?
27 Does the eagle soar at your command
and build his nest on high?
28 He dwells on a cliff and stays there at night;
a rocky crag is his stronghold.
29 From there he seeks out his food;
his eyes detect it from afar.
30 His young ones feast on blood,
and where the slain are, there is he."

40 The LORD said to Job:

2 "Will the one who contends with the Almighty
correct him?
Let him who accuses God answer him!"

3 Then Job answered the LORD:

4 "I am unworthy—how can I reply to you?
I put my hand over my mouth.
5 I spoke once, but I have no answer—
twice, but I will say no more."

6 Then the LORD spoke to Job out of the storm:

7 "Brace yourself like a man;
I will question you,
and you shall answer me.

8 "Would you discredit my justice?
Would you condemn me to justify yourself?
9 Do you have an arm like God's,
and can your voice thunder like his?
10 Then adorn yourself with glory and splendor,
and clothe yourself in honor and majesty.
11 Unleash the fury of your wrath,
look at every proud man and bring him low,
12 look at every proud man and humble him,
crush the wicked where they stand.
13 Bury them all in the dust together;
shroud their faces in the grave.
14 Then I myself will admit to you
that your own right hand can save you.

15 "Look at the behemoth,[a]
which I made along with you
and which feeds on grass like an ox.
16 What strength he has in his loins,
what power in the muscles of his belly!
17 His tail[b] sways like a cedar;
the sinews of his thighs are close-knit.
18 His bones are tubes of bronze,
his limbs like rods of iron.
19 He ranks first among the works of God,
yet his Maker can approach him with his sword.
20 The hills bring him their produce,
and all the wild animals play nearby.
21 Under the lotus plants he lies,
hidden among the reeds in the marsh.

[a]15 Possibly the hippopotamus or the elephant [b]17 Possibly trunk

40:1,2 *LORD . . . the Almighty . . . God:* Three names for Israel's God appear in these verses. "LORD" is a translation of the name *Yahweh* (see the note at 2:1). "Almighty" is a translation of the name *Shaddai* (see the note at 5:17,18). "God" is a translation of *El*. See also the Introduction to JOB, p. 961.

40:5 *say no more:* Job recognizes how hopeless it is to argue with the LORD, so he vows to stop questioning the LORD's actions.

40:6 *storm:* See the note at 38:1.

40:8-14 *Do you have an arm like God's:* The LORD asks Job to prove his statements accusing the LORD of being unfair (9:20-23; 19:5,6; 24:1; 27:2-6). The LORD does not deal directly with Job's complaint; rather, he challenges Job to try ruling the world with true justice. If Job has the power and a voice like God, he should use it (40:9) to become like the LORD (40:10) and crush the proud and evil people of the world (40:11-13). If Job can do this, the LORD will agree that Job is innocent and has power over evil (40:14).

40:13 *shroud their faces in the grave:* In ancient times, the dead were wrapped in grave clothes made of strips of linen cloth. Sometimes spices and ointments were also put on the body. See also the mini-article called "Burial," p. 1998.

40:15-24 *behemoth . . . the Jordan:* The animal described here may be the hippopotamus. The hippopotamus and the crocodile (called leviathan, see the note at 41:1-34) can be found in Egypt, but not in the Jordan River (see the map on p. 2463). The Jordan River may have been used as an example of fast-moving water, which doesn't frighten or panic the hippopotamus.

40:18 *bronze . . . iron:* See the note at 20:24.

40:24 *can anyone capture him:* Only God can capture and control the hippopotamus, but it would be foolish for one human being (such as Job) to try to capture such a powerful and dangerous animal.

41:1-34 *leviathan:* In the Old Testament, the term translated here as "leviathan" is a symbol for powerful forces that only God can control. Such a monster can also be a symbol of evil and stand for God's enemies (Job 3:8; Ps 74:14; 104:26; Isa 27:1). In this chapter, leviathan appears at first to be the fierce crocodile, which is hard to capture (41:1, 2), difficult to tame (41:5), and has fearsome teeth (41:14) and skin made of shields (41:15). But the monster also has supernatural powers, such as breathing fire (41:18-21), and its body is as hard as iron (41:23) that cannot be hurt by weapons made by humans—the sword, spear, or arrow (41:27-29). The point is, no human could attack and defeat the monster, which God defeated (26:13), so how could a human like Job hope to attack God?

22 The lotuses conceal him in their shadow;
the poplars by the stream surround him.
23 When the river rages, he is not alarmed;
he is secure, though the Jordan should surge
against his mouth.
24 Can anyone capture him by the eyes,[a]
or trap him and pierce his nose?

41 "Can you pull in the leviathan[b] with a fishhook
or tie down his tongue with a rope?
2 Can you put a cord through his nose
or pierce his jaw with a hook?
3 Will he keep begging you for mercy?
Will he speak to you with gentle words?
4 Will he make an agreement with you
for you to take him as your slave for life?
5 Can you make a pet of him like a bird
or put him on a leash for your girls?
6 Will traders barter for him?
Will they divide him up among the merchants?
7 Can you fill his hide with harpoons
or his head with fishing spears?
8 If you lay a hand on him,
you will remember the struggle and never do it again!
9 Any hope of subduing him is false;
the mere sight of him is overpowering.
10 No one is fierce enough to rouse him.
Who then is able to stand against me?
11 Who has a claim against me that I must pay?
Everything under heaven belongs to me.
12 "I will not fail to speak of his limbs,
his strength and his graceful form.
13 Who can strip off his outer coat?
Who would approach him with a bridle?
14 Who dares open the doors of his mouth,
ringed about with his fearsome teeth?
15 His back has[c] rows of shields
tightly sealed together;
16 each is so close to the next
that no air can pass between.
17 They are joined fast to one another;
they cling together and cannot be parted.
18 His snorting throws out flashes of light;
his eyes are like the rays of dawn.
19 Firebrands stream from his mouth;
sparks of fire shoot out.

[a]24 Or *by a water hole* [b]1 Possibly the crocodile [c]15 Or *His pride is his*

Behemoth and Leviathan, engraving by William Blake, around 1824. The LORD said to Job, "Look at the behemoth, which I made . . . yet his Maker can approach him with his sword" (40:15-19). And then he asks Job, "Can you pull in the leviathan with a fishhook? . . . Firebrands stream from his mouth; sparks of fire shoot out" (41:1, 19).

The LORD said to Job, *"Who then is able to stand against me? Who has a claim against me that I must pay? Everything under heaven belongs to me."* Job 41:10,11

20 Smoke pours from his nostrils
as from a boiling pot over a fire of reeds.
21 His breath sets coals ablaze,
and flames dart from his mouth.
22 Strength resides in his neck;
dismay goes before him.
23 The folds of his flesh are tightly joined;
they are firm and immovable.
24 His chest is hard as rock,
hard as a lower millstone.
25 When he rises up, the mighty are terrified;
they retreat before his thrashing.
26 The sword that reaches him has no effect,
nor does the spear or the dart or the javelin.
27 Iron he treats like straw
and bronze like rotten wood.

41:28 *slingstones:* This weapon was made of a long narrow strip of leather with a wider holder or pocket in the middle. A thrower put a stone or piece of metal in the sling pocket and then whirled the sling above his head. After picking up speed, the thrower released one strap, hurling the stone toward the target (1 Sam 17:48-50).

42:2-6 *I know that you can do all things . . . I despise myself:* The experience of facing the LORD and the LORD's questions has made Job realize just how powerful the LORD is. The LORD is beyond Job's human understanding. Job had heard about the LORD (42:5) and knew these things in his head (9:4-14; 28:20-24), but seeing the LORD face to face appears to have turned the questioning Job into a more trusting person. Job shows his sorrow again by sitting in dust and ashes (see the notes at 1:20; 2:8), but now he seems to be showing sorrow for his sin rather than mourning about his pain and loss.

42:8 *seven bulls and seven rams:* See the note at 1:2.

42:8 *burnt offering:* These sacrifices have traditionally been called "whole burnt offerings" because the whole animal was burned on the altar. A main purpose of such a sacrifice was to please the LORD with the smell of the sacrifice. See also the chart called "Sacrifices and Offerings," p. 219.

42:3 Job 38:2. **42:4** Job 38:3.

28 Arrows do not make him flee;
slingstones are like chaff to him.
29 A club seems to him but a piece of straw;
he laughs at the rattling of the lance.
30 His undersides are jagged potsherds,
leaving a trail in the mud like a threshing sledge.
31 He makes the depths churn like a boiling caldron
and stirs up the sea like a pot of ointment.
32 Behind him he leaves a glistening wake;
one would think the deep had white hair.
33 Nothing on earth is his equal—
a creature without fear.
34 He looks down on all that are haughty;
he is king over all that are proud."

The Story of Job Ends

The LORD accuses Job's friends of not telling the whole truth and tells them to make special offerings to avoid being punished. Job prays for his friends, as the LORD tells him to do, and then Job receives the LORD's blessings. He regains his riches and has many more children

Job

42 Then Job replied to the LORD:

2 "I know that you can do all things;
no plan of yours can be thwarted.
3 ⌞You asked,⌟ 'Who is this that obscures my counsel
without knowledge?'
Surely I spoke of things I did not understand,
things too wonderful for me to know.

4 ⌞"You said,⌟ 'Listen now, and I will speak;
I will question you,
and you shall answer me.'
5 My ears had heard of you
but now my eyes have seen you.
6 Therefore I despise myself
and repent in dust and ashes."

Epilogue

7 After the LORD had said these things to Job, he said to
Eliphaz the Temanite, "I am angry with you and your two friends,
because you have not spoken of me what is right, as my servant
Job has. 8 So now take seven bulls and seven rams and go to
my servant Job and sacrifice a burnt offering for yourselves. My

servant Job will pray for you, and I will accept his prayer and not
deal with you according to your folly. You have not spoken of me
what is right, as my servant Job has." 9So Eliphaz the Temanite, Bildad the Shuhite and Zophar the Naamathite did what the LORD
told them; and the LORD accepted Job's prayer.

10After Job had prayed for his friends, the LORD made him
prosperous again and gave him twice as much as he had before.
11All his brothers and sisters and everyone who had known him
before came and ate with him in his house. They comforted and
consoled him over all the trouble the LORD had brought upon him,
and each one gave him a piece of silver[a] and a gold ring.

12The LORD blessed the latter part of Job's life more than the
first. He had fourteen thousand sheep, six thousand camels, a
thousand yoke of oxen and a thousand donkeys. 13And he also had
seven sons and three daughters. 14The first daughter he named
Jemimah, the second Keziah and the third Keren-Happuch.
15Nowhere in all the land were there found women as beautiful as
Job's daughters, and their father granted them an inheritance
along with their brothers.

16After this, Job lived a hundred and forty years; he saw his
children and their children to the fourth generation. 17And so he
died, old and full of years.

[a]11 Hebrew *him a kesitah*; a kesitah was a unit of money of unknown weight and value.

42:13-15 *three daughters ... granted them an inheritance:* In ancient times, it was unusual for daughters to inherit a share of their father's possessions and property, unless the man had no sons (Num 27:1-11).

42:10 Job 1:1-3. **42:17** Gen 25:7,8; 35:28,29.

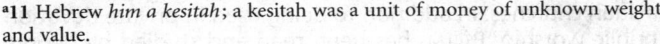

QUESTIONS ABOUT JOB 38:1—42:17

1. How did the LORD speak to Job? (38:1) Job had been hoping to argue his case in the LORD's court. Did the LORD's court appear as Job expected? Why or why not?
2. How does the LORD respond to Job's complaints and criticisms?
3. Based on the LORD's conversations with Job in chapters 38–41, how would you describe who the LORD is and what the LORD does?
4. What effect does the LORD's response have on Job? (40:3-5; 42:1-6)
5. What happens to Job and to his three friends at the end of the story?
6. The book of JOB forces the reader to consider difficult questions, such as:
   a. Where does suffering comes from?
   b. Why do good people suffer and evil people prosper?
   c. Where does evil come from?

   In your opinion, does the book give clear answers to these questions? Explain.
7. Name one new thing you have learned by studying JOB. What, if any, new questions have been raised? Which would you like to study or discuss further?

PSALMS

Read this ancient book of songs and prayers to discover what it has to say about life, about God, and about living as a person of faith.

King: This title is often used for God in PSALMS. As "King," Israel's LORD rules the whole universe, which he created (74:12-17; 95:3-5). On earth, the LORD God rules the nations (66:7; 96:10) and has chosen Israel to be his servant people (97:10-12). They are to carry out the LORD's concern for justice (99:1-5) and to reflect the glory of the LORD that shines on them (Isa 60:1-3). Israel's kings were chosen to be God's royal representatives on earth. They were to obey God and rule with justice, to encourage the priests to maintain proper worship, and to seek God's help in protecting the land and the people from their enemies (122). For other examples of psalms that celebrate the kingship of God, see 5; 47; 93; 97; and 145.

WHAT MAKES PSALMS SPECIAL?

PSALMS is the longest book in the Bible. It contains songs of praise, prayers for God's help, and poems that express trust in God. The psalms express every possible human feeling, including sorrow and joy, doubt and trust, pain and comfort, despair and hope, anger and contentment, the desire for revenge and the willingness to forgive. As models of prayer and praise, the psalms invite people to share every part of their lives with God.

WHY WAS PSALMS WRITTEN?

Many of the Bible's main ideas are echoed in PSALMS: praise, thankfulness, faith, hope, sorrow for sin, and God's loyalty and help. The individual psalms in the book were written and collected for use in worship. PSALMS became the hymnbook or prayer book that was used first in the temple in Jerusalem, then in synagogues, and later in Christian churches. In addition to being used in private devotion and public worship, PSALMS has been read and studied by people who wanted to learn more about living as faithful believers in the one true God who created and cares for the whole world and who is interested in every part of human life. For a quick overview, see the chart called "Kinds of Psalms," p. 1055.

WHAT'S THE STORY BEHIND THE SCENE?

PSALMS took shape over hundreds of years. Some psalms were probably written early in Israel's history, while others were written after the time of the exile in Babylon. The titles of seventy-three psalms mention Israel's King David, who ruled Israel from about 1010 to 970 B.C. There is little doubt that David wrote some of these psalms, but others were undoubtedly written after David's time. The persons who collected the psalms put David's name in the titles of many psalms as a way of honoring Israel's great king. The titles of thirteen psalms mention situations in David's life (for example, see Ps 3). David is presented as a model of how a person can depend upon God in difficult times. This was meant to help worshipers imagine similar situations in their own lives and how they can trust in God.

PSALMS is traditionally divided into five sections, or books (see below). Psalm 89, the final psalm in Book III, tells of God's covenant with David that one of his descendants would always rule Israel (89:1-37). But the second part of the psalm describes how God is angry and renounces this covenant (89:38-51). This has led some scholars to suggest that Books I–III may have been formed in response to the destruction of Jerusalem and the temple in 586 B.C., the exile of the Israelites from their land, and the disappearance of the line of Davidic kings. Book IV seems to respond to this crisis by announcing that God is Israel's true King and is indeed God of the whole world and all its people (see Ps 93–99). It is fitting that Psalm 90, the first psalm in Book IV, is given the title, "A prayer of Moses the man of God." It was Moses who led the people before they had a king, a land, or a temple.

Other psalms were said to have been written by various authors, such as Asaph (see the note at 50 Title) or the Sons of Korah (see the note at 42 Title). Still others have music notations (12; 22; 67; 76) or tell how and when the psalm is to be used (38; 92; 120–134).

Jesus used the psalms when he preached and taught, and they were often quoted by the writers of the New Testament. A verse from Psalm 118, for example, is directly referred to six times in the New Testament.

How is Psalms constructed?

Because Psalms is a collection of one hundred fifty separate songs, prayers, and poems, it may appear that the book has no meaningful structure. But there are smaller collections within the larger whole (see the note at 72:20). In addition, a similar concluding "amen" verse appears to divide Psalms into five smaller books (see 41:13; 72:19; 89:52; and 106:48). This five-book structure may have been meant to remind the people that the five "books" of psalms had the same purpose as the five books of Moses (Genesis—Deuteronomy), namely to teach them about God and what it means to follow God.

The five "books" that provide the outline of Psalms are:

Book I (1:1—41:13)
Book II (42:1—72:20)
Book III (73:1—89:52)
Book IV (90:1—106:48)
Book V (107:1—150:6)

1:1,2 *Blessed is the man . . . law of the Lord:* To be blessed means more than just feeling good. It means doing what God wants. The Hebrew word for "law" means "teaching." Blessings come from being constantly open to God's "teaching." See the mini-articles called "Blessed (Happy)," p. 1026 and "Law," p. 1160.

1:3 *a tree planted by streams of water:* Trees that grow beside a stream are healthy and bear fruit even in times of little rain (Jer 17:8).

One such fruit tree is the pomegranate tree, which produces fruit that has a sweet juice that is especially refreshing in warm climates. Pomegranates were frequently depicted in artwork in the ancient Near East and represented eternal life and fertility (because each pomegranate contains many seeds. See also 1 Kgs 7:18-20,40; 2 Kgs 25:17; 2 Chr 4:11; Song 4:3,13).

Book I (Psalms 1:1—41:13)

Psalms 1 and 2 serve as an introduction to Psalms. Most of the psalms in this first "book" name David as author. There are prayers that thank and praise the Lord and prayers asking for the Lord's help, protection, and forgiveness.

Psalm 1

1 Blessed is the man
who does not walk in the counsel of the wicked
or stand in the way of sinners
or sit in the seat of mockers.
2 But his delight is in the law of the Lord,
and on his law he meditates day and night.

1:3 *a tree planted by streams of water:* See the note at 1:3.

1:4,5 *the wicked will not stand in the judgment:* Those who are evil, sinful, or wicked turn away from God and disobey God's Law. Such self-centered persons are like "chaff." They have no roots. They won't survive the day of judgment, which is often described in the Bible as a day of darkness and destruction when the LORD punishes evildoers (Joel 2:1-11; Amos 5:18-20). See also the mini-articles called "Day of the LORD," p. 1727, and "Enemies (The Wicked)," p. 1084.

3 He is like a tree planted by streams of water,
which yields its fruit in season
and whose leaf does not wither.
Whatever he does prospers.

4 Not so the wicked!
They are like chaff
that the wind blows away.
5 Therefore the wicked will not stand in the judgment,
nor sinners in the assembly of the righteous.

6 For the LORD watches over the way of the righteous,
but the way of the wicked will perish.

Psalm 2

1 Why do the nations conspire[a]
and the peoples plot in vain?
2 The kings of the earth take their stand

[a]1 Hebrew; Septuagint *rage*

BLESSED (HAPPY)

Many people today think of being blessed as having possessions or money, and being happy as simply feeling good. In PSALMS and elsewhere in the Bible, to be blessed or happy means receiving God's gifts and doing what God wants done.

Sometimes blessing or happiness does involve possessions. For example, having food to eat, a place to live, and a family are signs of God's blessing (Ps 127:3; 128:4, 5; 144:12-15). All these things are gifts from God that make life and a future possible. But, there is more to life than that. True life means to be connected to God, and true blessing or happiness involves being open to God's teaching and living as God wants (Ps 1:1,2; 119:1,14,174).

This is why the psalm writers can feel blessed even when things seem to be all wrong with their lives. Many psalms are prayers for help. In these prayers, the psalmists complain bitterly of being oppressed, of being opposed by enemies, and of being surrounded by troubles of all kinds. But they still are happy because they trust that God blesses "all who take refuge in him" (Ps 2:12). Such trust is what it means to be connected to God. This kind of blessing leads people to obey God joyfully and to become like God in what they do (see Ps 41:1,2; 112:1-4). Their blessing also will result in blessings for others, as God promised Abraham (Gen 12:1-3).

Jesus described what it means to be blessed in this way. He invited people not to do what they wanted, but instead to "Repent, for the kingdom of heaven is near" (Matt 4:17). For Jesus and for his followers, this means suffering (Matt 16:21-24). But living as God wants means true blessing or happiness. According to Jesus, "Blessed are you when people insult you, persecute you and falsely say all kinds of evil against you because of me" (Matt 5:11). The prayers for help in PSALMS are prayed by people who are being insulted, mistreated, and lied about (for example, see Ps 9:13; 13:4; 17:9; 109:2-5). But because God is on their side, they know what true blessing is all about (Ps 119:92).

and the rulers gather together
against the LORD
and against his Anointed One.[a]
3 "Let us break their chains," they say,
"and throw off their fetters."

4 The One enthroned in heaven laughs;
the Lord scoffs at them.
5 Then he rebukes them in his anger
and terrifies them in his wrath, saying,
6 "I have installed my King[b]
on Zion, my holy hill."

7 I will proclaim the decree of the LORD:

He said to me, "You are my Son[c];
today I have become your Father.[d]
8 Ask of me,
and I will make the nations your inheritance,
the ends of the earth your possession.
9 You will rule them with an iron scepter[e];
you will dash them to pieces like pottery."

10 Therefore, you kings, be wise;
be warned, you rulers of the earth.
11 Serve the LORD with fear
and rejoice with trembling.
12 Kiss the Son, lest he be angry
and you be destroyed in your way,
for his wrath can flare up in a moment.
Blessed are all who take refuge in him.

Psalm 3

A psalm of David. When he fled from his son Absalom.

1 O LORD, how many are my foes!
How many rise up against me!
2 Many are saying of me,
"God will not deliver him." *Selah*[f]

3 But you are a shield around me, O LORD;
you bestow glory on me and lift[g] up my head.
4 To the LORD I cry aloud,
and he answers me from his holy hill. *Selah*

5 I lie down and sleep;
I wake again, because the LORD sustains me.

[a]2 Or *anointed one* [b]6 Or *king* [c]7 Or *son*; also in verse 12 [d]7 Or *have begotten you* [e]9 Or *will break them with a rod of iron* [f]2 A word of uncertain meaning, occurring frequently in the Psalms; possibly a musical term [g]3 Or *LORD, / my Glorious One, who lifts*

2:2 *his Anointed One:* This refers to the king chosen by God (2:6) to lead Israel. This psalm was used when new kings took office.

2:4 *The One enthroned in heaven laughs . . . the Lord:* The concept of God as king and ruler of the whole world is frequent in PSALMS.

2:6 *Zion:* The mountain in Jerusalem where the temple was built. See the mini-article called "Zion," p. 1294.

2:7-9 *You are my Son . . . your Father . . . scepter:* Each king was known as God's "son" (2 Sam 7:14). See also the mini-article called "Son of God," p. 2044. The Hebrew word for "scepter" also can mean a shepherd's walking stick. See also Ezek 34:1,2.

3 Title *David . . . Absalom:* See the mini-article called "David" p. 1028. David's son, Absalom, led a rebellion against David while David was king of Israel. Absalom was killed in battle by David's troops (2 Sam 13:37—18:17).

3:1,2 *foes . . . God will not deliver him:* Enemies appear often in PSALMS. Also called "evil" and "the wicked," they are people who try to hurt or kill God's people. Their words contradict God's promises of protection for those who trust in the LORD (see 1:6; 2:12; and 3:8). See also the mini-article called "Enemies (The Wicked)," p. 1084.

3:4 *his holy hill:* This refers to the temple on Mount Zion in Jerusalem (see the note at 2:6).

3:5-8 *sleep . . . Strike all my enemies . . . blessing be on your people:* Even though threatened by enemies, the psalmist is able to sleep, knowing that the LORD will protect him. He does not simply ask the LORD to take revenge on his enemies. He asks the LORD to exert justice on his behalf. For God's people to be protected, evil must be opposed. The psalmist asks that God act in a way that will silence people who think God won't rescue his people (3:1,2).

Answer me when I call to you, O my righteous God. Give me relief from my distress; be merciful to me and hear my prayer.
Ps 4:1

4:1,2 *prayer . . . delusions . . . false gods:* Verse 1 begins as a prayer asking for God's help, but in 4:2-5 the psalmist is addressing his enemies rather than God. In verse 2, "delusions" and "false gods" may refer to damaging lies that the enemies tell about the psalmist (see 5:6,9; 62:4), as well as to the enemies' worship of idols and false gods (see 40:4).

6 I will not fear the tens of thousands
drawn up against me on every side.

7 Arise, O LORD!
Deliver me, O my God!
Strike all my enemies on the jaw;
break the teeth of the wicked.

8 From the LORD comes deliverance.
May your blessing be on your people. *Selah*

Psalm 4

For the director of music. With stringed instruments.
A psalm of David.

1 Answer me when I call to you,
O my righteous God.
Give me relief from my distress;
be merciful to me and hear my prayer.

2 How long, O men, will you turn my glory into shame[a]?

[a]2 Or *you dishonor my Glorious One*

DAVID

David ruled from about 1010 to 970 B.C. David was a military hero (1 Sam 17:41-54; 18:6, 7), but he also was remembered as a musician and poet (1 Sam 16:14-23; 2 Sam 22:1-51; 2 Chr 29:30). The temple was not built until the reign of David's son, Solomon, but David is given credit for making the preparations for music to be played and psalms to be sung as part of worship in the temple (1 Chr 6:31, 32; 16:4-36; 25:1, 2).

David undoubtedly wrote some of the psalms, but many were written after David's time. Some of the psalms that contain David's name in their title probably were written in memory of David or in honor of later Davidic kings. The titles of Psalm 3 and twelve other psalms mention events in David's life. These titles were added by the collectors of the psalms. The intent was to invite readers to see in David and his life an example of how a psalm might apply to their own lives. For instance, the title of Psalm 3 refers to the rebellion of David's son, Absalom (see the note at Ps 3 Title).

God promised David that his family would rule forever (2 Sam 7). A long line of his family members did rule until 586 B.C., when Jerusalem was destroyed and the people of Judah were taken into exile. At that time it seemed to the Israelites that God's promise to David had been broken. Even so, the hope for a good ruler like David did not disappear. Many years later, Jesus' followers would view him as a king in David's family line (Matt 1:1; Luke 1:27, 32). Jesus was given the same titles used for King David and the kings that followed him. One of those titles was "Anointed One" (see the note at Ps 2:2). Another title was "Son of God" (Ps 2:2, 7; Mark 1:1). As God's representatives on earth, David and all of Israel's kings were to use their authority to work for justice by defending the poor (Ps 72:1-4). Compare this to the work Jesus said he had come to do (Luke 4:16-18).

How long will you love delusions and seek
false gods[a]? *Selah*
3 Know that the LORD has set apart the godly for himself;
the LORD will hear when I call to him.

4 In your anger do not sin;
when you are on your beds,
search your hearts and be silent. *Selah*
5 Offer right sacrifices
and trust in the LORD.

4:5 *right sacrifices:* Offering "right sacrifices" was done to honor and thank God, or to ask for forgiveness. For more, see the chart called "Sacrifices and Offerings," p. 219. Sacrifices were to be offered along with an attitude of "trust" and thankfulness (50:23).

4:4 Eph 4:26.

---

[a]**2** Or *seek lies*

KEY EVENTS IN DAVID'S LIFE

EVENTS	SCRIPTURE PASSAGES	RELATED PSALM
The LORD chooses David to be king	1 Sam 16:1-13	Ps 78
David plays the harp for King Saul	1 Sam 16:14-23	
David kills Goliath	1 Sam 17:1-54	
Saul becomes jealous of David	1 Sam 18:6-30	
David's marriage to Michal	1 Sam 18:20-28; 19:9-17; 2 Sam 6:20-23	Ps 59
David's friendship with Jonathan	1 Sam 18:1-4; 20:1-42; 23:14-18; 2 Sam 1:1-27	Ps 54; 63
David meets and marries Abigail	1 Sam 25:1-44	
David becomes king of Judah	2 Sam 2:1-7	
David becomes king of all Israel	2 Sam 5:1-5; 1 Chr 11:1-3; 14:1,2	
David captures Jerusalem	2 Sam 5:6-12; 1 Chr 11:4-9	
David brings the ark of the covenant to Jerusalem	2 Sam 6:1-19; 1 Chr 13:1-14; 15:1—16:43	
David and Bathsheba	2 Sam 11:1—12:23	Ps 51
Solomon is born	2 Sam 12:24,25	
Absalom rebels against his father, David	2 Sam 15:1-12	Ps 3
Absalom dies and David mourns	2 Sam 18:7—19:8	
David takes a census of Israel	2 Sam 24:1-25	
David gives instruction to his son Solomon	1 Kgs 2:1-9	
David dies	1 Kgs 2:10-12	

4:6 *Many are asking:* The question is asked by the enemies (4:2) who desire material gain. The psalmist is content to depend upon God (4:3, 7, 8).

5:2 *King:* This title is often used for God in PSALMS. For more, see the note on p. 1024.

5:3 *In the morning:* It was common for faithful followers of God to pray each morning and at other set times during the day (55:17; 88:13; 92:2).

5:7 *mercy:* The psalmist counts on the fact that God will have the same mercy on the needy that God's chosen kings were expected to have. See the note at 9:8, 9.

5:7 *your house . . . holy temple:* The Hebrew word for "temple" also can mean "palace." Because it was the "house" of God "my King" (5:2), it is fitting that the psalmist "bow down" to show his loyalty.

5:10-12 *Declare them guilty . . . Spread your protection:* The psalmist asks for God's justice. Those who lie and destroy (5:9) are to be punished because of their own evil plans and crimes (5:10). But those who love God, obey his commands and turn to him for protection will be blessed. That the enemies have rebelled against God means that God's power does not take the form of immediate enforcement. This is why the psalmist has to "wait" (5:3). God does not only use his power to destroy liars and people who do evil, he also uses it to extend his mercy to people who suffer and need his protection (5:7). God's "mercy" offers true security (see the note at 37:39, 40).

5:9 Rom 3:13. **6:8** Matt 7:23; Luke 13:27.

6 Many are asking, "Who can show us any good?"
Let the light of your face shine upon us, O LORD.
7 You have filled my heart with greater joy
than when their grain and new wine abound.
8 I will lie down and sleep in peace,
for you alone, O LORD,
make me dwell in safety.

Psalm 5

For the director of music. For flutes. A psalm of David.

1 Give ear to my words, O LORD,
consider my sighing.
2 Listen to my cry for help,
my King and my God,
for to you I pray.
3 In the morning, O LORD, you hear my voice;
in the morning I lay my requests before you
and wait in expectation.

4 You are not a God who takes pleasure in evil;
with you the wicked cannot dwell.
5 The arrogant cannot stand in your presence;
you hate all who do wrong.
6 You destroy those who tell lies;
bloodthirsty and deceitful men
the LORD abhors.

7 But I, by your great mercy,
will come into your house;
in reverence will I bow down
toward your holy temple.
8 Lead me, O LORD, in your righteousness
because of my enemies—
make straight your way before me.

9 Not a word from their mouth can be trusted;
their heart is filled with destruction.
Their throat is an open grave;
with their tongue they speak deceit.
10 Declare them guilty, O God!
Let their intrigues be their downfall.
Banish them for their many sins,
for they have rebelled against you.

11 But let all who take refuge in you be glad;
let them ever sing for joy.
Spread your protection over them,
that those who love your name may rejoice
in you.

12 For surely, O LORD, you bless the righteous;
you surround them with your favor as with a shield.

Psalm 6

For the director of music. With stringed instruments. According to *sheminith*.[a] A psalm of David.

1 O LORD, do not rebuke me in your anger
or discipline me in your wrath.
2 Be merciful to me, LORD, for I am faint;
O LORD, heal me, for my bones are in agony.
3 My soul is in anguish.
How long, O LORD, how long?

4 Turn, O LORD, and deliver me;
save me because of your unfailing love.
5 No one remembers you when he is dead.
Who praises you from the grave[b]?

6 I am worn out from groaning;
all night long I flood my bed with weeping
and drench my couch with tears.
7 My eyes grow weak with sorrow;
they fail because of all my foes.

8 Away from me, all you who do evil,
for the LORD has heard my weeping.
9 The LORD has heard my cry for mercy;
the LORD accepts my prayer.
10 All my enemies will be ashamed and dismayed;
they will turn back in sudden disgrace.

Psalm 7

A *shiggaion*[c] of David, which he sang to the LORD concerning Cush, a Benjamite.

1 O LORD my God, I take refuge in you;
save and deliver me from all who pursue me,
2 or they will tear me like a lion
and rip me to pieces with no one to rescue me.

3 O LORD my God, if I have done this
and there is guilt on my hands—
4 if I have done evil to him who is at peace with me
or without cause have robbed my foe—
5 then let my enemy pursue and overtake me;
let him trample my life to the ground
and make me sleep in the dust. *Selah*

[a]Title: Probably a musical term [b]5 Hebrew *Sheol* [c]Title: Probably a literary or musical term

6:1-4 *do not rebuke . . . Be merciful to me:* These verses suggest that this is a prayer for healing. Even if the psalmist views his sickness as punishment that comes from the LORD (6:1), the psalmist trusts that the LORD will save him, and that God's "unfailing love" will be stronger than God's anger. See also 38:1.

6:5 *dead . . . grave:* For most of the Old Testament period, people believed that death cut a person off from God. See also the notes at 9:13 and 16:10, and the mini-article called "Eternal Life," p. 2072.

6:7 *foes:* While the "enemies" did not cause the sickness (see 6:1,2), they probably made fun of the psalmist and made his suffering worse (6:10). See also the mini-article called "Enemies (The Wicked)," p. 1084.

6:8,9 *the LORD has heard . . . accepts my prayer:* The psalm ends with confidence and trust even though there is no evidence that the sickness has been cured. The psalmist is confident that his suffering is not able to separate him from God.

7 Title *Cush, a Benjamite:* It is not clear who Cush is, since no one by this name appears in the stories about David in 1 and 2 SAMUEL. The tribe of Benjamin was named for Jacob and Rachel's youngest son (Gen 35:16-18). This tribe settled in the area just north of the lands settled by the tribe of Judah. See also the map on p. 2464.

7:3-5 *if I have done this . . . then let my enemy:* The psalmist seems to have been falsely accused of something by his "enemy." In response to the false charges, he offers his innocence in the form of an oath, a very serious promise made to God. See the mini-article called "Making Vows," p. 328. This prayer and promise may have originally been spoken in the temple where the psalmist had gone to find protection.

6 Arise, O LORD, in your anger;
rise up against the rage of my enemies.
Awake, my God; decree justice.
7 Let the assembled peoples gather around you.
Rule over them from on high;
8 let the LORD judge the peoples.
Judge me, O LORD, according to my righteousness,
according to my integrity, O Most High.
9 O righteous God,
who searches minds and hearts,
bring to an end the violence of the wicked
and make the righteous secure.

10 My shield[a] is God Most High,
who saves the upright in heart.
11 God is a righteous judge,
a God who expresses his wrath every day.
12 If he does not relent,
he[b] will sharpen his sword;
he will bend and string his bow.
13 He has prepared his deadly weapons;
he makes ready his flaming arrows.

14 He who is pregnant with evil
and conceives trouble gives birth to disillusionment.
15 He who digs a hole and scoops it out
falls into the pit he has made.
16 The trouble he causes recoils on himself;
his violence comes down on his own head.

17 I will give thanks to the LORD because of his
righteousness
and will sing praise to the name of the LORD
Most High.

Psalm 8

For the director of music. According to *gittith.*[c] A psalm of David.

1 O LORD, our Lord,
how majestic is your name in all the earth!

You have set your glory
above the heavens.
2 From the lips of children and infants
you have ordained praise[d]
because of your enemies,
to silence the foe and the avenger.

---

[a]**10** Or *sovereign* [b]**12** Or *If a man does not repent, / God* [c]Title: Probably a musical term [d]**2** Or *strength*

7:6 *decree justice:* The motive for the psalmist's prayer is not only revenge. Because he is a victim (7:2), he is asking for "justice" (see 7:11 and the note at 3:5-8). Revenge belongs to God (7:11-13).

7:7 *assembled peoples . . . Rule over them from on high:* This verse suggests that God is king over all (see the note on p. 1024). One of the major responsibilities of a king was to judge (settle disputes) and to see that justice was done. See also the mini-article called "Justice," p. 1721.

7:14-16 *He who is . . . evil . . . violence comes down on his own head:* A common belief in ancient times was that evildoers would eventually be punished while those who turned to God and lived right would be blessed (for example, see Prov 1:32,33; 4:10,11,18,19). This concept—that a person always gets what he or she deserves—is referred to as "just retribution." However, a more complicated view is found in other examples of Hebrew wisdom literature (see JOB; Eccl 7:15; 8:14-17; Ps 73:2-12). See also the note at 10:5.

8:1 *LORD:* The Hebrew word *Yahweh* is translated "LORD." This is the name for God most often used in Book 1 (Psalms 1–41). See also the mini-article called "LORD (YHWH)," p. 140. The rest of the psalm tells how God rules by sharing power with human beings (8:5-8).

7:9 Rev 2:23. **8:2** Matt 21:16.

Creation of the Earth, illuminated page from a French Psalter, late thirteenth century. Many of the psalms celebrate the LORD as Creator and Ruler of all things. Here, God is shown creating the earth, dividing the waters, creating the heavens, and creating the plants. For examples of psalms that glorify God as Creator, see Psalms 8; 104; and 148.

3 When I consider your heavens,
the work of your fingers,
the moon and the stars,
which you have set in place,
4 what is man that you are mindful of him,
the son of man that you care for him?
5 You made him a little lower than the heavenly beings[a]
and crowned him with glory and honor.

6 You made him ruler over the works of your hands;
you put everything under his feet:
7 all flocks and herds,
and the beasts of the field,

When I consider your heavens, the work of your fingers, the moon and the stars, which you have set in place, what is man that you are mindful of him, the son of man that you care for him?
Ps 8:3,4

8:5-8 *You made him . . . crowned him . . . ruler:* God gave humans kingly "glory and honor" and power to rule. The language of these verses recalls Genesis 1:26-28, which says that humans will rule over the rest of creation because "God created man in his own image" (Gen 1:27). Many years after Psalm 8 was written, Christians saw in Jesus the full likeness of God, and the language of 8:6 was used to describe Jesus (1 Cor 15:27; Eph 1:22; Heb 2:8).

8:4 Job 7:17, 18; Ps 144:3; Heb 2:6-8.

[a]5 Or *than God*

9:1 *wonders:* God's "wonders" included delivering the people out of their slavery in Egypt (Exod 12:36) and sending bread ("manna") to the Israelites starving in the desert (Exod 16:1-36; Ps 78:24, 25). These and God's many other wonders always meant help for people in need or danger.

9:3 *enemies:* These are people who oppose God and who selfishly make victims of others. They are mentioned often in Psalms 9 and 10, which may have originally been one psalm. In Hebrew, every other verse of the two psalms begins with a successive letter of the Hebrew alphabet, making an acrostic (see also the note at 119:1). The evil ones or enemies are mentioned in 9:6,13,17; 10:3,4,13. See also the mini-article called "Enemies (The Wicked)," p. 1084.

9:7 *his throne:* God's throne can mean God's place in heaven, but the ark of the covenant in the tabernacle (and later the temple) was also viewed as God's throne on earth (Exod 25:17-22; 1 Kgs 8:1-13). See also the notes at 11:4 and 17:8, and the mini-article called "The Ark of the Covenant," p. 513.

9:8,9 *judge ... justice ... oppressed:* A king's main responsibility was to judge (9:4) in order to establish justice (9:16), especially for victims of injustice. See also the mini-article called "Justice," p. 1721.

Because God rules justly, the oppressed can run to God for help (9:9). The "oppressed" are the poor, the needy, the afflicted, the helpless (9:18; 10:2,9,10). See the mini-article called "The Poor," p. 2362.

9:11 *Zion:* See the note at 2:6 and the mini-article called "Zion," p. 1294.

8 the birds of the air,
and the fish of the sea,
all that swim the paths of the seas.

9 O LORD, our Lord,
how majestic is your name in all the earth!

Psalm 9[a]

For the director of music. To ⌞the tune of⌟ "The Death of the Son."
A psalm of David.

1 I will praise you, O LORD, with all my heart;
I will tell of all your wonders.
2 I will be glad and rejoice in you;
I will sing praise to your name, O Most High.

3 My enemies turn back;
they stumble and perish before you.
4 For you have upheld my right and my cause;
you have sat on your throne, judging righteously.
5 You have rebuked the nations and destroyed the wicked;
you have blotted out their name for ever and ever.
6 Endless ruin has overtaken the enemy,
you have uprooted their cities;
even the memory of them has perished.

7 The LORD reigns forever;
he has established his throne for judgment.
8 He will judge the world in righteousness;
he will govern the peoples with justice.
9 The LORD is a refuge for the oppressed,
a stronghold in times of trouble.
10 Those who know your name will trust in you,
for you, LORD, have never forsaken those who seek you.

11 Sing praises to the LORD, enthroned in Zion;
proclaim among the nations what he has done.
12 For he who avenges blood remembers;
he does not ignore the cry of the afflicted.

13 O LORD, see how my enemies persecute me!
Have mercy and lift me up from the gates of death,
14 that I may declare your praises
in the gates of the Daughter of Zion
and there rejoice in your salvation.
15 The nations have fallen into the pit they have dug;
their feet are caught in the net they have hidden.

[a]Psalms 9 and 10 may have been originally a single acrostic poem, the stanzas of which begin with the successive letters of the Hebrew alphabet. In the Septuagint they constitute one psalm.

16 The LORD is known by his justice;
the wicked are ensnared by the work
of their hands. *Higgaion.*[a] *Selah*
17 The wicked return to the grave,[b]
all the nations that forget God.
18 But the needy will not always be forgotten,
nor the hope of the afflicted ever perish.

19 Arise, O LORD, let not man triumph;
let the nations be judged in your presence.
20 Strike them with terror, O LORD;
let the nations know they are but men. *Selah*

Psalm 10[c]

1 Why, O LORD, do you stand far off?
Why do you hide yourself in times of trouble?

2 In his arrogance the wicked man hunts down the weak,
who are caught in the schemes he devises.
3 He boasts of the cravings of his heart;
he blesses the greedy and reviles the LORD.
4 In his pride the wicked does not seek him;
in all his thoughts there is no room for God.
5 His ways are always prosperous;
he is haughty and your laws are far from him;
he sneers at all his enemies.
6 He says to himself, "Nothing will shake me;
I'll always be happy and never have trouble."
7 His mouth is full of curses and lies and threats;
trouble and evil are under his tongue.
8 He lies in wait near the villages;
from ambush he murders the innocent,
watching in secret for his victims.
9 He lies in wait like a lion in cover;
he lies in wait to catch the helpless;
he catches the helpless and drags them off in
his net.
10 His victims are crushed, they collapse;
they fall under his strength.
11 He says to himself, "God has forgotten;
he covers his face and never sees."

12 Arise, LORD! Lift up your hand, O God.
Do not forget the helpless.

a16 Or *Meditation*; possibly a musical notation **b17** Hebrew *Sheol* **c**Psalms 9 and 10 may have been originally a single acrostic poem, the stanzas of which begin with the successive letters of the Hebrew alphabet. In the Septuagint they constitute one psalm.

9:13 *the gates of death:* For most of the Old Testament period, people believed that everyone who died went to the dark underground place known as "the grave" (9:17) or the "depths" (see 139:7, 8). The Hebrew word *Sheol* describes a place of total silence where no one knows or feels anything (88:12; 94:17). For more about the biblical perspectives on death and life after death, see the mini-articles called "Resurrection," p. 2210; "Hell," p. 1944; and "Eternal Life," p. 2072.

9:14 *gates of the Daughter of Zion:* This probably refers to the gate of the city of Jerusalem (9:11). In either case, it is a symbol for the life that God has given to the psalmist when the psalmist was threatened with death. See the note at 2:6.

10:1 *stand far off . . . hide yourself:* These kinds of questions appear often in the prayers for help. They are almost always balanced by the confidence that God is or will be present (compare 10:1 and 10:14).

10:2,3 *wicked man . . . the weak:* God's Law demanded that the poor be treated fairly (Deut 24:14,15,19-22). See the note at 9:8,9.

Verses 3-13 give a long description of what "the wicked" are like. See also 73:3-12 for more about what "the wicked" say and do.

10:5 *His ways are always prosperous:* A common belief was that those who were evil would suffer and those who lived right and trusted in God would prosper (see also the note at 7:14-16). But here the "wicked" are said to be prosperous (73:3). Though it may not seem as if the evildoers are being punished, they really are because they have cut themselves off from God. See also the note at 1:4,5.

10:7 Rom 3:14.

10:14 *victim . . . fatherless:* Because they had no family to provide for them, orphans were always in need (10:12,18) and of special concern to God (Exod 22:22,23; Deut 24:17-20; Ps 68:5). See also the mini-article called "The Poor," p. 2362.

11:1 *In the* LORD *I take refuge:* By "refuge," the psalmist means a place where he will be safe from attack (11:2). See also 2:12 and 5:11. He may have been thinking of God as a fortress (see 18:2; 28:8; 46:7). Fortresses were often built on the tops of mountains and had strong walls built around them. The one at Arad shown here dates back to the time of King David or Solomon.

11:4 *holy temple:* David longed to build a temple in Jerusalem, and eventually his son Solomon would do so. The temple in Jerusalem would contain the ark of the covenant that was viewed as God's throne on earth (see the note at 9:7). It was also considered to be the place where earth and heaven meet, so it was a symbol of God's "heavenly throne."

11:6 *fiery coals and burning sulfur:* Fire and burning sulfur are symbols of judgment (Gen 19:24; Joel 2:1-3; Matt 13:36-42). See also the mini-article called "Fire," p. 2383.

11:7 LORD *is righteous . . . justice . . . see his face:* See the note at 9:8,9 (justice). In some parts of the Bible, to see God's "face" is such a powerful experience that it can bring about a person's death (Exod 33:20). But this psalm says that God invites people to his house (5:7), where they "see" or experience God's presence and protection (17:15).

13 Why does the wicked man revile God?
Why does he say to himself,
"He won't call me to account"?
14 But you, O God, do see trouble and grief;
you consider it to take it in hand.
The victim commits himself to you;
you are the helper of the fatherless.
15 Break the arm of the wicked and evil man;
call him to account for his wickedness
that would not be found out.

16 The LORD is King for ever and ever;
the nations will perish from his land.
17 You hear, O LORD, the desire of the afflicted;
you encourage them, and you listen to their cry,
18 defending the fatherless and the oppressed,
in order that man, who is of the earth, may terrify
no more.

Psalm 11

For the director of music. Of David.

1 In the LORD I take refuge.
How then can you say to me:
"Flee like a bird to your mountain.
2 For look, the wicked bend their bows;
they set their arrows against the strings
to shoot from the shadows
at the upright in heart.
3 When the foundations are being destroyed,
what can the righteous do[a]?"

4 The LORD is in his holy temple;
the LORD is on his heavenly throne.
He observes the sons of men;
his eyes examine them.
5 The LORD examines the righteous,
but the wicked[b] and those who love violence
his soul hates.
6 On the wicked he will rain
fiery coals and burning sulfur;
a scorching wind will be their lot.

7 For the LORD is righteous,
he loves justice;
upright men will see his face.

[a]3 Or *what is the Righteous One doing* [b]5 Or *The LORD, the Righteous One, examines the wicked, /*

Psalm 12

For the director of music. According to *sheminith*.[a]
A psalm of David.

1 Help, LORD, for the godly are no more;
the faithful have vanished from among men.
2 Everyone lies to his neighbor;
their flattering lips speak with deception.

3 May the LORD cut off all flattering lips
and every boastful tongue
4 that says, "We will triumph with our tongues;
we own our lips[b]—who is our master?"

5 "Because of the oppression of the weak
and the groaning of the needy,
I will now arise," says the LORD.
"I will protect them from those who malign them."
6 And the words of the LORD are flawless,
like silver refined in a furnace of clay,
purified seven times.

7 O LORD, you will keep us safe
and protect us from such people forever.
8 The wicked freely strut about
when what is vile is honored among men.

Psalm 13

For the director of music. A psalm of David.

1 How long, O LORD? Will you forget me forever?
How long will you hide your face from me?
2 How long must I wrestle with my thoughts
and every day have sorrow in my heart?
How long will my enemy triumph over me?

3 Look on me and answer, O LORD my God.
Give light to my eyes, or I will sleep in death;
4 my enemy will say, "I have overcome him,"
and my foes will rejoice when I fall.

5 But I trust in your unfailing love;
my heart rejoices in your salvation.
6 I will sing to the LORD,
for he has been good to me.

[a]Title: Probably a musical term [b]4 Or / *our lips are our plowshares*

12:3,4 *flattering lips . . . boastful tongue:* See the note at 3:5-8. The wicked speak and act (12:8) in a boastful way.

12:5 *I will now arise:* The words quoted here originally may have been spoken by a prophet in the temple. They declare God's concern for justice and the poor. See the note at 10:14.

13:1,2 *How long . . . How long:* Questions like these appear often in the prayers for help (10:1; 22:1). They often are balanced by confidence and trust in God's help (13:5,6).

13:2 *my enemy:* Even when the enemy (13:4) is not the direct cause of the distress; he is present to take advantage of the situation. See the mini-article called "Enemies (The Wicked)," p. 1084.

13:5,6 *I trust in your unfailing love:* The sudden move to trust and celebration is not unusual in the prayers for help (see 6:8-10). It is possible that these verses were written later than 13:1-4, after a cure or rescue took place. But they also may be a response to a promise delivered by a priest. In this case, the psalmist looks forward with certain "trust" in God's goodness and "love." In either case, trust in God means both suffering and celebration at the same time.

Psalm 14

For the director of music. Of David.

1 The fool[a] says in his heart,
"There is no God."
They are corrupt, their deeds are vile;
there is no one who does good.

2 The LORD looks down from heaven
on the sons of men
to see if there are any who understand,
any who seek God.
3 All have turned aside,
they have together become corrupt;
there is no one who does good,
not even one.

4 Will evildoers never learn—
those who devour my people as men eat bread
and who do not call on the LORD?
5 There they are, overwhelmed with dread,
for God is present in the company of the righteous.
6 You evildoers frustrate the plans of the poor,
but the LORD is their refuge.

7 Oh, that salvation for Israel would come out of Zion!
When the LORD restores the fortunes of his people,
let Jacob rejoice and Israel be glad!

Psalm 15

A psalm of David.

1 LORD, who may dwell in your sanctuary?
Who may live on your holy hill?

2 He whose walk is blameless
and who does what is righteous,
who speaks the truth from his heart
3 and has no slander on his tongue,
who does his neighbor no wrong
and casts no slur on his fellowman,
4 who despises a vile man
but honors those who fear the LORD,
who keeps his oath
even when it hurts,
5 who lends his money without usury
and does not accept a bribe against the innocent.

He who does these things
will never be shaken.

[a]1 The Hebrew words rendered *fool* in Psalms denote one who is morally deficient.

14:1 *fool:* This is another name for the wicked. A "fool" does not lack intelligence, though he may lack wisdom. Most importantly, a fool lacks trust in God and love for others. The "fool" is a frequent subject of PROVERBS (see Prov 12:15,16; 17:12,16,21; 26:4-12).

14:6 *the poor . . . LORD is their refuge:* See the notes at 9:8,9 and 10:14.

14:7 *Israel . . . Zion . . . Jacob:* See the note at 2:6. "Jacob" is another name for the people of Israel, who were descended from Jacob's twelve sons (Gen 32:28). See also the note at 22:23.

15:1 *holy hill:* The holy hill is Mount Zion in Jerusalem where the temple, God's earthly house, would be built (see the note at 2:6). This psalm was probably used in a ceremony as worshipers entered the temple. Worshipers asked the question in 15:1 as they approached the temple, and the priest answered with 15:2-5.

15:2-5 *He whose walk is blameless:* This psalm lists a number of ways people obey God. These actions are based on God's Law. Verse 5 describes some of the ways that God's people were commanded to work for justice and prevent poverty (Exod 22:25; 23:8; Lev 25:36, 37; Deut 16:18-20).

14:1-3 Rom 3:10-12.

Shivviti, a decorative plaque from Poland, nineteenth century. "Shivviti," the first Hebrew word of Psalm 16:8, means "I have set." Plaques containing the full verse ("I have set the LORD always before me. Because he is at my right hand, I will not be shaken") were often displayed in front of people praying in synagogues.

LORD, you have assigned me my portion and my cup; you have made my lot secure.
Ps 16:5

Psalm 16

A *miktam*[a] of David.

[1] Keep me safe, O God,
for in you I take refuge.

[2] I said to the LORD, "You are my Lord;
apart from you I have no good thing."
[3] As for the saints who are in the land,
they are the glorious ones in whom is all my delight.[b]
[4] The sorrows of those will increase
who run after other gods.
I will not pour out their libations of blood
or take up their names on my lips.

[5] LORD, you have assigned me my portion and my cup;
you have made my lot secure.
[6] The boundary lines have fallen for me in pleasant places;
surely I have a delightful inheritance.

[7] I will praise the LORD, who counsels me;
even at night my heart instructs me.
[8] I have set the LORD always before me.
Because he is at my right hand,
I will not be shaken.

[a]Title: Probably a literary or musical term [b]**3** Or *As for the pagan priests who are in the land / and the nobles in whom all delight, I said:*

16:1,2 *Keep me safe . . . You are my Lord:* Although it begins as a prayer, the psalm continues as an expression of trust in God alone (16:4, 5, 7). This is in keeping with the first two commandments (Exod 20:3-6). Trusting God also sets God's people apart from the wicked (10:11; 14:1).

16:4 *libations of blood:* Throughout the ancient Near East, blood was used in ceremonies honoring various gods, either by pouring it over the altar or drinking it as an offering. Unlike other nations, Israel was forbidden to eat or drink blood (Lev 7:26, 27; 17:10-14; 19:26; Deut 12:23,24; 15:23). The blood of sacrificed animals was used by Israel's priests to ask God's forgiveness (Lev 1:5; 3:2). See also the mini-article called "Blood," p. 180. For more about Israel's sacrifices, see the chart called "Sacrifices and Offerings," p. 219.

16:10 *the grave . . . decay:* For most of the Old Testament period, people believed that death meant permanent separation from God. See the note at 9:13. Here the psalmist trusts that God will protect him from unexpected death and even expects God's presence to reach "the grave" (see the note at 139:8). New Testament writers claim that God's raising of Jesus from death to life fulfills 16:8-11 (Acts 2:25-28; 13:35).

16:11 *at your right hand:* This is the place of power and honor.

17:1,2 *vindication:* The psalmist probably was falsely accused of a crime by his enemies (7:3-5). His prayer for help originally may have been made in the tabernacle where he fled for protection (see the note at 17:8). According to ancient tradition, altars were places of worship and sacrifice but also places of protection (see Exod 21:14; 1 Kgs 1:50, 51).

17:8 *wings:* The mention of God's "wings" suggests that the prayer was offered originally in the tabernacle near the ark of the covenant. The ark, God's earthly throne, was kept in the tabernacle and later in the temple. On its lid were carved two winged creatures called cherubim (Exod 25:18-22). They were symbols of protection for the ark. This may explain why God sometimes is pictured with "wings" that protect people (36:7; 57:1; 63:7). See the note at 11:4 and the mini-article called "The Ark of the Covenant," p. 513.

17:13 *confront . . . wicked:* For innocent people to go free, oppressors must be opposed (see the notes at 3:5-8 and 7:6).

9 Therefore my heart is glad and my tongue rejoices;
my body also will rest secure,
10 because you will not abandon me to the grave,[a]
nor will you let your Holy One[b] see decay.
11 You have made[c] known to me the path of life;
you will fill me with joy in your presence,
with eternal pleasures at your right hand.

Psalm 17

A prayer of David.

1 Hear, O LORD, my righteous plea;
listen to my cry.
Give ear to my prayer—
it does not rise from deceitful lips.
2 May my vindication come from you;
may your eyes see what is right.

3 Though you probe my heart and examine me
at night,
though you test me, you will find nothing;
I have resolved that my mouth will not sin.
4 As for the deeds of men—
by the word of your lips
I have kept myself
from the ways of the violent.
5 My steps have held to your paths;
my feet have not slipped.

6 I call on you, O God, for you will answer me;
give ear to me and hear my prayer.
7 Show the wonder of your great love,
you who save by your right hand
those who take refuge in you from their foes.
8 Keep me as the apple of your eye;
hide me in the shadow of your wings
9 from the wicked who assail me,
from my mortal enemies who surround me.

10 They close up their callous hearts,
and their mouths speak with arrogance.
11 They have tracked me down, they now surround me,
with eyes alert, to throw me to the ground.
12 They are like a lion hungry for prey,
like a great lion crouching in cover.

13 Rise up, O LORD, confront them, bring them down;
rescue me from the wicked by your sword.

[a]**10** Hebrew *Sheol* [b]**10** Or *your faithful one* [c]**11** Or *You will make*

[14]O LORD, by your hand save me from such men,
from men of this world whose reward is in this life.
You still the hunger of those you cherish;
their sons have plenty,
and they store up wealth for their children.
[15]And I—in righteousness I will see your face;
when I awake, I will be satisfied with seeing your likeness.

Psalm 18

For the director of music. Of David the servant of the LORD. He sang to the LORD the words of this song when the LORD delivered him from the hand of all his enemies and from the hand of Saul. He said:

[1]I love you, O LORD, my strength.
[2]The LORD is my rock, my fortress and my deliverer;
my God is my rock, in whom I take refuge.
He is my shield and the horn[a] of my salvation,
my stronghold.
[3]I call to the LORD, who is worthy of praise,
and I am saved from my enemies.
[4]The cords of death entangled me;
the torrents of destruction overwhelmed me.
[5]The cords of the grave[b] coiled around me;
the snares of death confronted me.
[6]In my distress I called to the LORD;
I cried to my God for help.
From his temple he heard my voice;
my cry came before him, into his ears.
[7]The earth trembled and quaked,
and the foundations of the mountains shook;
they trembled because he was angry.
[8]Smoke rose from his nostrils;
consuming fire came from his mouth,
burning coals blazed out of it.
[9]He parted the heavens and came down;
dark clouds were under his feet.
[10]He mounted the cherubim and flew;
he soared on the wings of the wind.
[11]He made darkness his covering, his canopy around him—
the dark rain clouds of the sky.
[12]Out of the brightness of his presence clouds advanced,
with hailstones and bolts of lightning.

[a]2 *Horn* here symbolizes strength. [b]5 Hebrew *Sheol*

17:15 *I will see your face:* Seeing God's "face" is a way for the psalmist to say that he experienced God's presence and protection. See the note at 11:7. It is possible that the psalmist spent the night near the altar because he sought protection there (see the note at 17:1,2) or to show his dependence upon God's help. See also 3:5; 63:6; 139:18.

18 Title *David . . . Saul:* Psalm 18 is almost exactly the same as 2 Samuel 22. Centuries after the time of David, this psalm was used to express the hope that God would rescue the people of Israel from their enemies.

18:2 *my rock . . . horn of my salvation:* For "rock," see the note at 18:46. "Horn" probably refers to the horn of a powerful bull.

18:3 *enemies:* The enemies are other nations that threaten David and God's people. See also the mini-article called "Enemies (The Wicked)," p. 1084.

18:4,5 *cords of death . . . torrents . . . snares:* Death is treated like a person who attacks with "cords" and "snares." Violent water is often a symbol of death (see also 18:16).

18:6 *From his temple:* Here meaning God's heavenly temple (see the note at 11:4).

18:7-15 *The earth trembled and quaked . . . foundations:* See the note at 97:2-5. In the Canaanite religion, the god Baal was considered to control rain and wind. But here that power is recognized as belonging to God (18:31; see also the note at 29:3-9).

18:10 *cherubim:* Most likely this is a reference to the cherubim that served at the throne of God on the ark of the covenant. See 80:1; 99:1; and the mini-article called "The Ark of the Covenant," p. 513.

> *You save the humble but bring low those whose eyes are haughty.*
> Ps 18:27

18:13 *LORD . . . Most High:* "Most High" was a term used for the main Canaanite god in ancient times. But here the psalmist uses this title of honor along with "LORD," the name of Israel's one true God (see the note at 8:1). See the mini-article called "Names of God," p. 243.

18:16 *deep waters:* Water, especially deep or uncontrolled water, is a symbol of death and chaos (18:4).

18:20,24 *my righteousness:* "Righteousness" suggests that the king has obeyed God (18:23), but it also means that the king admits that his life depends completely upon God's guidance (18:22) and God's protection (18:16-19).

18:28 *lamp . . . light:* These are symbols of life (see also Prov 13:9). "Light" also stands for the wisdom and truth that come from God, as opposed to the "darkness," which symbolizes evil. David was remembered for giving "light" to his people (2 Sam 21:17). Here David shows humility (18:27) by saying that his light and life come from God.

13 The LORD thundered from heaven;
the voice of the Most High resounded.[a]
14 He shot his arrows and scattered ⌊the enemies⌋,
great bolts of lightning and routed them.
15 The valleys of the sea were exposed
and the foundations of the earth laid bare
at your rebuke, O LORD,
at the blast of breath from your nostrils.

16 He reached down from on high and took hold of me;
he drew me out of deep waters.
17 He rescued me from my powerful enemy,
from my foes, who were too strong for me.
18 They confronted me in the day of my disaster,
but the LORD was my support.
19 He brought me out into a spacious place;
he rescued me because he delighted in me.

20 The LORD has dealt with me according to my
righteousness;
according to the cleanness of my hands he has
rewarded me.
21 For I have kept the ways of the LORD;
I have not done evil by turning from my God.
22 All his laws are before me;
I have not turned away from his decrees.
23 I have been blameless before him
and have kept myself from sin.
24 The LORD has rewarded me according to my
righteousness,
according to the cleanness of my hands in his sight.

25 To the faithful you show yourself faithful,
to the blameless you show yourself blameless,
26 to the pure you show yourself pure,
but to the crooked you show yourself shrewd.
27 You save the humble
but bring low those whose eyes are haughty.
28 You, O LORD, keep my lamp burning;
my God turns my darkness into light.
29 With your help I can advance against a troop[b];
with my God I can scale a wall.

30 As for God, his way is perfect;
the word of the LORD is flawless.
He is a shield

[a]**13** Some Hebrew manuscripts and Septuagint (see also 2 Samuel 22:14); most Hebrew manuscripts *resounded, / amid hailstones and bolts of lightning* [b]**29** Or *can run through a barricade*

for all who take refuge in him.
31 For who is God besides the LORD?
And who is the Rock except our God?
32 It is God who arms me with strength
and makes my way perfect.
33 He makes my feet like the feet of a deer;
he enables me to stand on the heights.
34 He trains my hands for battle;
my arms can bend a bow of bronze.
35 You give me your shield of victory,
and your right hand sustains me;
you stoop down to make me great.
36 You broaden the path beneath me,
so that my ankles do not turn.

37 I pursued my enemies and overtook them;
I did not turn back till they were destroyed.
38 I crushed them so that they could not rise;
they fell beneath my feet.
39 You armed me with strength for battle;
you made my adversaries bow at my feet.
40 You made my enemies turn their backs in flight,
and I destroyed my foes.
41 They cried for help, but there was no one to save them—
to the LORD, but he did not answer.
42 I beat them as fine as dust borne on the wind;
I poured them out like mud in the streets.

43 You have delivered me from the attacks of the people;
you have made me the head of nations;
people I did not know are subject to me.
44 As soon as they hear me, they obey me;
foreigners cringe before me.
45 They all lose heart;
they come trembling from their strongholds.

46 The LORD lives! Praise be to my Rock!
Exalted be God my Savior!
47 He is the God who avenges me,
who subdues nations under me,
48 who saves me from my enemies.
You exalted me above my foes;
from violent men you rescued me.
49 Therefore I will praise you among the nations, O LORD;
I will sing praises to your name.
50 He gives his king great victories;
he shows unfailing kindness to his anointed,
to David and his descendants forever.

18:31 *the Rock:* See the note at 18:46.

18:33 *stand on the heights:* This is another way that the king humbly says his strength and security come from God. See also Hab 3:19.

18:34-48 *trains my hands for battle . . . from violent men you rescued me:* These verses are a victory celebration. The king thanks God for preparing him for battle (18:34) and giving him victory (18:35-48). David won many victories over Israel's opponents (see 2 Sam 2–8). God trains the king to fight so he can defend Israel against "violent men" (18:48). Nations are put under the king's power (18:47; see also 2:8) not for his personal benefit, but so that the nations will honor Israel's God and so that God's justice and peace can be established in all the earth (72:3-7). See also the mini-article called "Holy War (The LORD's Battles)," p. 306.

18:46 *my Rock:* The "Rock" is a symbol of God's strength and ability to protect people. Caves in the rocky hills and cliffs of Palestine (like these near Arbela) were good places to hide from enemies.

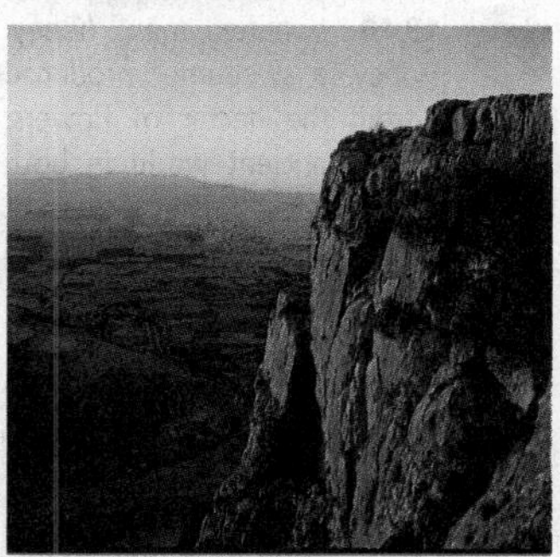

18:50 *David and his descendants:* God promised David that one of David's descendants always would be on the throne (see 2 Sam 7:10-16 and the note at 2:2). See also the mini-articles called "David," p. 1028, and "Messiah (Chosen One)," p. 1124.

18:49 Rom 15:9. **18:50** Ps 2:6-9; 72:1-17; 89:13-36.

Psalm 19

For the director of music. A psalm of David.

1 The heavens declare the glory of God;
the skies proclaim the work of his hands.
2 Day after day they pour forth speech;
night after night they display knowledge.
3 There is no speech or language
where their voice is not heard.[a]
4 Their voice[b] goes out into all the earth,
their words to the ends of the world.

In the heavens he has pitched a tent for the sun,
5 which is like a bridegroom coming forth from his pavilion,
like a champion rejoicing to run his course.
6 It rises at one end of the heavens
and makes its circuit to the other;
nothing is hidden from its heat.

7 The law of the LORD is perfect,
reviving the soul.
The statutes of the LORD are trustworthy,
making wise the simple.
8 The precepts of the LORD are right,
giving joy to the heart.
The commands of the LORD are radiant,
giving light to the eyes.
9 The fear of the LORD is pure,
enduring forever.
The ordinances of the LORD are sure
and altogether righteous.
10 They are more precious than gold,
than much pure gold;
they are sweeter than honey,
than honey from the comb.
11 By them is your servant warned;
in keeping them there is great reward.

12 Who can discern his errors?
Forgive my hidden faults.
13 Keep your servant also from willful sins;
may they not rule over me.
Then will I be blameless,
innocent of great transgression.

14 May the words of my mouth and the meditation of my heart

[a]3 Or *They have no speech, there are no words; / no sound is heard from them*
[b]4 Septuagint, Jerome and Syriac; Hebrew *line*

19:1 *The heavens declare . . . the skies proclaim:* In PSALMS, songs of praise often invite the whole creation to praise God (96:10-13; 103:22; 148:13).

19:4 *the sun:* The sun was worshiped as a god in the ancient world, sometimes even by the people of Israel (Jer 8:1, 2; Ezek 8:16-18). It is possible that Psalm 19 had its origin as a song of praise to the sun. If so, it was changed to become a song of praise to God.

19:7,8 *law of the LORD . . . reviving the soul:* The Hebrew word for "law" means "teaching." God's "teaching" included written commandments given in the *Torah* (Pentateuch), but prophets and priests were constantly reinterpreting this material. Obeying the LORD's teaching brings protection and wisdom (Prov 1:7; 2:1-9). See also the mini-articles called "Law," p. 1160, and "Wisdom," p. 2206. Similar to how the sun's heat revives life possible on the earth, God's teaching revives people's souls (19:7) and is a source of guidance, understanding, or insight ("light," 19:8).

19:10 *sweeter than honey:* Honey, a sweetener produced by bees from the nectar of flowers, existed in the ancient world in both wild and cultivated forms (see Deut 32:13; 1 Sam 14:25-27). It symbolized the richness of the land (Exod 3:17; 2 Chr 31:5). See also 119:103.

be pleasing in your sight,
O LORD, my Rock and my Redeemer.

Psalm 20

For the director of music. A psalm of David.

1 May the LORD answer you when you are in distress;
may the name of the God of Jacob protect you.
2 May he send you help from the sanctuary
and grant you support from Zion.
3 May he remember all your sacrifices
and accept your burnt offerings. *Selah*
4 May he give you the desire of your heart
and make all your plans succeed.
5 We will shout for joy when you are victorious
and will lift up our banners in the name of
our God.
May the LORD grant all your requests.

6 Now I know that the LORD saves his anointed;
he answers him from his holy heaven
with the saving power of his right hand.
7 Some trust in chariots and some in horses,
but we trust in the name of the LORD our God.
8 They are brought to their knees and fall,
but we rise up and stand firm.

9 O LORD, save the king!
Answer[a] us when we call!

Psalm 21

For the director of music. A psalm of David.

1 O LORD, the king rejoices in your strength.
How great is his joy in the victories you give!
2 You have granted him the desire of his heart
and have not withheld the request of his lips. *Selah*
3 You welcomed him with rich blessings
and placed a crown of pure gold on his head.
4 He asked you for life, and you gave it to him—
length of days, for ever and ever.
5 Through the victories you gave, his glory is great;
you have bestowed on him splendor and majesty.
6 Surely you have granted him eternal blessings
and made him glad with the joy of your presence.
7 For the king trusts in the LORD;
through the unfailing love of the Most High
he will not be shaken.

---

[a]9 Or *save! / O King, answer*

19:14 *my Rock:* See the note at 18:46.

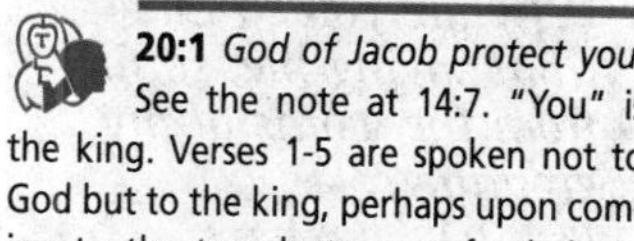

20:1 *God of Jacob protect you:* See the note at 14:7. "You" is the king. Verses 1-5 are spoken not to God but to the king, perhaps upon coming to the temple to pray for help in battle (see the note at 18:34-48).

20:2 *Zion:* See the note at 2:6.

20:6 *his anointed . . . right hand:* See the note at 2:2. "Right hand" is an image often used to describe the LORD's protection or power, especially in battle (Exod 14:21; 15:12, 16; Deut 5:15; Isa 14:26; 40:10). See the note at 16:11.

20:7 *trust in chariots:* The people of ancient Israel fought many battles, but they did not use chariots or horses like some of their enemies. They were not to put their trust in military equipment, but rather they were to trust God (see Josh 11:4-9; Ps 33:16-19; Isa 31:1).

21:1,2 *great is his joy in the victories:* Psalm 21 probably was used originally to celebrate the victories that the king prayed for in Psalm 20. These verses show that the prayers of 20:4, 5, 9 have been answered.

21:3-6 *rich blessings . . . length of days, for ever and ever:* "Length of days" here probably refers to the promise that the king's family line would continue and that the king would live on through his descendants. See also the mini-articles called "Son of God," p. 2044; "Messiah (Chosen One)," p. 1124; and "Kingship in Israel," p. 650.

19:4 Rom 10:18.

8 Your hand will lay hold on all your enemies;
your right hand will seize your foes.
9 At the time of your appearing
you will make them like a fiery furnace.
In his wrath the LORD will swallow them up,
and his fire will consume them.
10 You will destroy their descendants from the earth,
their posterity from mankind.
11 Though they plot evil against you
and devise wicked schemes, they cannot succeed;
12 for you will make them turn their backs
when you aim at them with drawn bow.

13 Be exalted, O LORD, in your strength;
we will sing and praise your might.

Psalm 22

For the director of music. To ⌞the tune of⌟ "The Doe of the Morning."
A psalm of David.

1 My God, my God, why have you forsaken me?
Why are you so far from saving me,
so far from the words of my groaning?
2 O my God, I cry out by day, but you do not answer,
by night, and am not silent.

3 Yet you are enthroned as the Holy One;
you are the praise of Israel.[a]
4 In you our fathers put their trust;
they trusted and you delivered them.
5 They cried to you and were saved;
in you they trusted and were not disappointed.

6 But I am a worm and not a man,
scorned by men and despised by the people.
7 All who see me mock me;
they hurl insults, shaking their heads:
8 "He trusts in the LORD;
let the LORD rescue him.
Let him deliver him,
since he delights in him."

9 Yet you brought me out of the womb;
you made me trust in you
even at my mother's breast.
10 From birth I was cast upon you;
from my mother's womb you have been my God.
11 Do not be far from me,

[a] **3** Or *Yet you are holy, / enthroned on the praises of Israel*

My God, my God, why have you forsaken me? Why are you so far from saving me, so far from the words of my groaning?
Ps 22:1

21:8–12 *right hand . . . fire will consume . . . make them turn their backs:* See the notes at 16:11 and 20:6. For "fire," see the note on 11:6. God will oppose their enemies and see that justice is done. See also the note at 18:34-48.

22:1 *My God . . . forsaken me:* This kind of question appears often in the prayers for help (13:1, 2). But trust, confidence, and praise (22:22-31) balance questions and complaints (22:1-21). According to writers of the Gospels, Jesus uttered the opening question of Psalm 22 from the cross (Matt 27:46; Mark 15:34).

22:3 *enthroned:* God's earthly throne in the temple was a symbol of God's heavenly throne. See the note at 11:4. Because God and God's people are opposed by enemies (22:12, 13), God's rule or "dominion" (22:28) is not the immediate enforcement of God's will (see the note at 5:10-12). This means that God's people can and will suffer, and that God is willing to share in the troubles of the afflicted (22:24).

22:4,5 *In you our fathers put their trust:* The psalmist remembers how God rescued the people from slavery in Egypt (Exod 2:23-25).

22:7 *All who see me mock me:* Being rejected by others is a common complaint in prayers for help (31:11; 69:7, 19, 20). Jesus also experienced this kind of rejection (Matt 27:39, 43; Mark 15:29; Luke 23:34, 35).

22:8 Matt 27:43.

for trouble is near
and there is no one to help.

12 Many bulls surround me;
strong bulls of Bashan encircle me.
13 Roaring lions tearing their prey
open their mouths wide against me.
14 I am poured out like water,
and all my bones are out of joint.
My heart has turned to wax;
it has melted away within me.
15 My strength is dried up like a potsherd,
and my tongue sticks to the roof of my mouth;
you lay me[a] in the dust of death.
16 Dogs have surrounded me;
a band of evil men has encircled me,
they have pierced[b] my hands and my feet.
17 I can count all my bones;
people stare and gloat over me.
18 They divide my garments among them
and cast lots for my clothing.

19 But you, O LORD, be not far off;
O my Strength, come quickly to help me.
20 Deliver my life from the sword,
my precious life from the power of the dogs.
21 Rescue me from the mouth of the lions;
save[c] me from the horns of the wild oxen.

22 I will declare your name to my brothers;
in the congregation I will praise you.
23 You who fear the LORD, praise him!
All you descendants of Jacob, honor him!
Revere him, all you descendants of Israel!
24 For he has not despised or disdained
the suffering of the afflicted one;
he has not hidden his face from him
but has listened to his cry for help.

25 From you comes the theme of my praise in the great assembly;
before those who fear you[d] will I fulfill my vows.
26 The poor will eat and be satisfied;
they who seek the LORD will praise him—
may your hearts live forever!
27 All the ends of the earth
will remember and turn to the LORD,

[a]15 Or/ *I am laid* [b]16 Some Hebrew manuscripts, Septuagint and Syriac; most Hebrew manuscripts / *like the lion,* [c]21 Or / *you have heard* [d]25 Hebrew *him*

22:12,13 *Many bulls . . . lions:* Here and in 22:16,20-22, enemies are compared to vicious animals. Animals sometimes symbolized demons, suggesting that the opposition seems more than human. See the mini-article called "Enemies (The Wicked)," p. 1084.

22:12 *Bashan:* This land, east of the Jordan River, was known for its rich pastures and strong cattle. See the map on p. 2465.

22:23 *descendants of Jacob:* Along with his grandfather Abraham and his father Isaac, Jacob was one of the ancestors of God's people. His name was changed to Israel at Peniel near the Jabbok River after he "struggled with God" there (Gen 32:28; 35:9-11).

22:24-26 *he has not despised or disdained:* Verse 24 appears to disagree with verse 2. Perhaps verses 22 to 31 were written later than verses 1 to 21, after the psalmist's prayers had been answered. More likely, the psalmist now realizes that God is present with him in his suffering. See the note at 13:5,6.

To show their thanks for God's presence, the psalmists regularly promise to continue to worship God and bring God offerings (56:12; 61:8). When someone brought a sacrifice to give thanks to God, the meat from the sacrificed animal (Lev 7:15) could be eaten, but not the fat. The psalmist intends to share his portion with "the poor." See the chart called "Sacrifices and Offerings," p. 219.

22:18 Matt 27:35; Mark 15:24; Luke 23:34; John 19:24. **22:22** Heb 2:12.

and all the families of the nations
will bow down before him,
28 for dominion belongs to the LORD
and he rules over the nations.

29 All the rich of the earth will feast and worship;
all who go down to the dust will kneel
before him—
those who cannot keep themselves alive.
30 Posterity will serve him;
future generations will be told about the Lord.
31 They will proclaim his righteousness
to a people yet unborn—
for he has done it.

Psalm 23

A psalm of David.

1 The LORD is my shepherd, I shall not be in want.
2 He makes me lie down in green pastures,
he leads me beside quiet waters,
3 he restores my soul.
He guides me in paths of righteousness
for his name's sake.
4 Even though I walk
through the valley of the shadow of death,[a]
I will fear no evil,
for you are with me;
your rod and your staff,
they comfort me.

5 You prepare a table before me
in the presence of my enemies.
You anoint my head with oil;
my cup overflows.
6 Surely goodness and love will follow me
all the days of my life,
and I will dwell in the house of the LORD
forever.

Psalm 24

Of David. A psalm.

1 The earth is the LORD's, and everything in it,
the world, and all who live in it;
2 for he founded it upon the seas
and established it upon the waters.

Surely goodness and love will follow me all the days of my life, and I will dwell in the house of the LORD forever.
Ps 23:6

22:28 *he rules over the nations:* See the notes at 22:3 and 8:1. The hope that all nations would recognize Israel's God as ruler is expressed by the prophets (Isa 56:6, 7; Zeph 3:8, 9; Zech 14:16). Much later, Jesus told his followers to gather a kingdom from "the ends of the earth" (compare 22:27 and Matt 28:19, 20).

23:1-3 *shepherd . . . paths:* God's kingship is a frequent subject in the psalms. Kings were known as the shepherds of their people. Their responsibility was to feed and protect their people (Ezek 34:1-16). This is what God does here, providing food, drink, guidance, and protection.

23:6 *dwell in the house of the LORD:* The LORD's "house" originally may have meant the tabernacle, and later the temple, where people went for protection. See also the notes at 17:1, 2 and 17:8. But it also can be a symbol for God's presence.

24:2 *upon the seas . . . the waters:* According to Genesis 1:1, 2, God established the world out of a watery chaos.

23:2 Rev 7:17. **24:1** 1 Cor 10:26.

[a]4 Or *through the darkest valley*

3 Who may ascend the hill of the LORD?
Who may stand in his holy place?
4 He who has clean hands and a pure heart,
who does not lift up his soul to an idol
or swear by what is false.[a]
5 He will receive blessing from the LORD
and vindication from God his Savior.
6 Such is the generation of those who seek him,
who seek your face, O God of Jacob.[b] *Selah*

7 Lift up your heads, O you gates;
be lifted up, you ancient doors,
that the King of glory may come in.
8 Who is this King of glory?
The LORD strong and mighty,
the LORD mighty in battle.
9 Lift up your heads, O you gates;
lift them up, you ancient doors,
that the King of glory may come in.
10 Who is he, this King of glory?
The LORD Almighty—
he is the King of glory. *Selah*

Psalm 25[c]

Of David.

1 To you, O LORD, I lift up my soul;
2 in you I trust, O my God.
Do not let me be put to shame,
nor let my enemies triumph over me.
3 No one whose hope is in you
will ever be put to shame,
but they will be put to shame
who are treacherous without excuse.

4 Show me your ways, O LORD,
teach me your paths;
5 guide me in your truth and teach me,
for you are God my Savior,
and my hope is in you all day long.
6 Remember, O LORD, your great mercy and love,
for they are from of old.
7 Remember not the sins of my youth
and my rebellious ways;
according to your love remember me,
for you are good, O LORD.

a4 Or *swear falsely* **b6** Two Hebrew manuscripts and Syriac (see also Septuagint); most Hebrew manuscripts *face, Jacob* **c** This psalm is an acrostic poem, the verses of which begin with the successive letters of the Hebrew alphabet.

24:3 *the hill of the LORD . . . his holy place:* The "hill" is Mount Zion (see the notes at 2:6 and 15:1). This psalm may have first been used in a ceremony as worshipers entered the temple.

24:7-10 *Who is this King of glory:* The questions and responses in these verses probably were part of an ancient liturgy (religious service) that was spoken as worshipers and Israel's priests brought the ark of the covenant into the temple. The ark was seen as the earthly throne of God, the King (see the note at 9:7). The title "LORD Almighty" often appears when the ark of the covenant is mentioned. It refers to God's rule over all creation. See also the mini-article called "Names of God," p. 243.

24:8 *mighty in battle:* Many nearby cultures saw creation as the result of a battle between two or more gods (74:12-14). This may be one reason why God is called "mighty in battle." Also, Israel's God fought for his people (Josh 10:8) and opposed the enemies of justice.

25:1 *lift up my soul:* The words "lift up" are sometimes used to describe the bringing of a sacrifice to God. Here, the psalmist offers not an animal but his own soul. See Rom 12:1,2.

25:4 *your paths:* God's "paths" (25:8-12) refer to the right way; that is, living and worshiping according to God's Law (see also 143:10; Prov 3:6; 4:10; 15:19,24). Note how the very first psalm begins by inviting people to be open to God's teaching (see 1:1,2 and the note).

24:4 Matt 5:8.

Girl Praying by George Tooker, 1977. PSALMS reflects the variety of feelings that are experienced by God's people. Jews and Christians continue to turn to this book of the Bible when looking for guidance and help. And many psalms, like Psalms 25–28, are really prayers to God with the heartfelt request: "Show me your ways, O LORD, teach me your paths; guide me in your truth and teach me" (Ps 25:4, 5).

8 Good and upright is the LORD;
therefore he instructs sinners in his ways.
9 He guides the humble in what is right
and teaches them his way.
10 All the ways of the LORD are loving and faithful
for those who keep the demands of his
covenant.
11 For the sake of your name, O LORD,
forgive my iniquity, though it is great.
12 Who, then, is the man that fears the LORD?
He will instruct him in the way chosen for him.
13 He will spend his days in prosperity,
and his descendants will inherit the land.
14 The LORD confides in those who fear him;
he makes his covenant known to them.

25:10 *keep the demands of his covenant:* "Covenant" here probably refers to the agreement based on God's Law. God will bless those who obey his Law. But the psalmist is also very aware of needing forgiveness (25:7, 11). He knows that while God wants obedience (25:4), God also forgives disobedience (25:11,18; compare Exod 34:6,7).

25:13 *inherit the land:* Because the land meant the opportunity to make a living, it became a symbol for life. Also, obedience to the Law meant being able to keep the promised land that God gave to Israel (Deut 7:6-15). See also the note at 37:3. See also the mini-article called "Land," p. 1751.

15 My eyes are ever on the LORD,
for only he will release my feet from the snare.

16 Turn to me and be gracious to me,
for I am lonely and afflicted.
17 The troubles of my heart have multiplied;
free me from my anguish.
18 Look upon my affliction and my distress
and take away all my sins.
19 See how my enemies have increased
and how fiercely they hate me!
20 Guard my life and rescue me;
let me not be put to shame,
for I take refuge in you.
21 May integrity and uprightness protect me,
because my hope is in you.

22 Redeem Israel, O God,
from all their troubles!

Psalm 26

Of David.

1 Vindicate me, O LORD,
for I have led a blameless life;
I have trusted in the LORD
without wavering.
2 Test me, O LORD, and try me,
examine my heart and my mind;
3 for your love is ever before me,
and I walk continually in your truth.
4 I do not sit with deceitful men,
nor do I consort with hypocrites;
5 I abhor the assembly of evildoers
and refuse to sit with the wicked.
6 I wash my hands in innocence,
and go about your altar, O LORD,
7 proclaiming aloud your praise
and telling of all your wonderful deeds.
8 I love the house where you live, O LORD,
the place where your glory dwells.

9 Do not take away my soul along with sinners,
my life with bloodthirsty men,
10 in whose hands are wicked schemes,
whose right hands are full of bribes.
11 But I lead a blameless life;
redeem me and be merciful to me.

12 My feet stand on level ground;
in the great assembly I will praise the LORD.

26:1,2 *Vindicate me . . . Test me:* The psalmist seems to have been falsely accused of a crime. The psalmist is so confident of remaining faithful to God that he is willing to be "tested." See the note at 7:3-5.

26:6 *wash my hands . . . go about your altar:* Priests had to wash their hands and feet before making a sacrifice at the altar (Exod 30:18-21).

26:8 *the house . . . where your glory dwells:* God was said to live in the tabernacle, and later in the temple in Jerusalem. See the notes at 5:7 (your house) and 9:7. God's "glory" refers to God's powerful presence (Exod 16:7, 10; Ps 63:2; Isa 60:1,2; Ezek 10:3-19; 11:22,23).

26:12 *stand on level ground . . . praise the LORD:* The prayers for help normally end with confidence and praise, often in the form of a promise. See the notes at 13:5,6 and 22:24-26.

The LORD *is my light and my salvation—whom shall I fear? The* LORD *is the stronghold of my life—of whom shall I be afraid?*
Ps 27:1

27:2 *enemies:* They are cruel and deceptive, threatening the psalmist's life (27:2,12). See the mini-article called "Enemies (The Wicked)," p. 1084.

27:4 *house . . . temple:* The temple in Jerusalem was known as God's "house" (see the notes at 5:7, your house; 9:7; and 26:8). Priests may have lived at the temple, and the psalmist desires the same source of security.

27:5 *tabernacle . . . rock:* When the people were in the desert, they worshiped God in the tabernacle (Exod 25:1-9). See the mini-article called "The Tabernacle," p. 2346. For "rock," see the note at 18:46.

27:6 *sacrifice:* When people came to the temple, they brought offerings to God, including animals to sacrifice. Some sacrifices were made especially to thank God for help and blessings. See the note at 22:24–26 and the chart called "Sacrifices and Offerings," p. 219.

27:8 *Seek his face:* See the notes at 11:7 and 17:15.

Psalm 27

Of David.

1 The LORD is my light and my salvation—
whom shall I fear?
The LORD is the stronghold of my life—
of whom shall I be afraid?
2 When evil men advance against me
to devour my flesh,[a]
when my enemies and my foes attack me,
they will stumble and fall.
3 Though an army besiege me,
my heart will not fear;
though war break out against me,
even then will I be confident.

4 One thing I ask of the LORD,
this is what I seek:
that I may dwell in the house of the LORD
all the days of my life,
to gaze upon the beauty of the LORD
and to seek him in his temple.
5 For in the day of trouble
he will keep me safe in his dwelling;
he will hide me in the shelter of his tabernacle
and set me high upon a rock.
6 Then my head will be exalted
above the enemies who surround me;
at his tabernacle will I sacrifice with shouts of joy;
I will sing and make music to the LORD.

7 Hear my voice when I call, O LORD;
be merciful to me and answer me.
8 My heart says of you, "Seek his[b] face!"
Your face, LORD, I will seek.
9 Do not hide your face from me,
do not turn your servant away in anger;
you have been my helper.
Do not reject me or forsake me,
O God my Savior.
10 Though my father and mother forsake me,
the LORD will receive me.
11 Teach me your way, O LORD;
lead me in a straight path
because of my oppressors.
12 Do not turn me over to the desire of my foes,
for false witnesses rise up against me,
breathing out violence.

---

[a]**2** Or *to slander me* [b]**8** Or *To you, O my heart, he has said, "Seek my*

13 I am still confident of this:
I will see the goodness of the LORD
in the land of the living.
14 Wait for the LORD;
be strong and take heart
and wait for the LORD.

Psalm 28

Of David.

1 To you I call, O LORD my Rock;
do not turn a deaf ear to me.
For if you remain silent,
I will be like those who have gone down to the pit.
2 Hear my cry for mercy
as I call to you for help,
as I lift up my hands
toward your Most Holy Place.

3 Do not drag me away with the wicked,
with those who do evil,
who speak cordially with their neighbors
but harbor malice in their hearts.
4 Repay them for their deeds
and for their evil work;
repay them for what their hands have done
and bring back upon them what they deserve.
5 Since they show no regard for the works of the LORD
and what his hands have done,
he will tear them down
and never build them up again.

6 Praise be to the LORD,
for he has heard my cry for mercy.
7 The LORD is my strength and my shield;
my heart trusts in him, and I am helped.
My heart leaps for joy
and I will give thanks to him in song.

8 The LORD is the strength of his people,
a fortress of salvation for his anointed one.
9 Save your people and bless your inheritance;
be their shepherd and carry them forever.

Psalm 29

A psalm of David.

1 Ascribe to the LORD, O mighty ones,
ascribe to the LORD glory and strength.

28:2 *I lift up my hands:* In ancient times, people lifted their hands when they prayed to the gods above, and lowered their hands when praying to the gods below. See 1 Kgs 8:38.

28:3-5 *the wicked . . . malice . . . Repay them:* The psalmist asks for help and protection from wicked people who are trying to hurt him or turn him away from God. See also the note at 3:5-8.

28:6,7 *Praise be to the LORD . . . give thanks:* The change from prayer to praise is sudden, but this is not unusual in the prayers for help. See the notes at 13:5, 6 and 22:24-26.

28:8 *his anointed one:* The "anointed one" may refer to the kings that God chose (see the note at 2:2).

28:9 *shepherd:* See the note at 23:1-3.

29:1,2 *mighty ones:* Referring to the angels. Those who live in heaven are invited to recognize God's kingship over all things. The same invitation is made to human beings in 96:7-9. See also the mini-article called "Angels," p. 88.

28:4 Rev 22:12.

29:3-9 *over the mighty waters . . . breaks the cedars:* God's power and glory are displayed in nature. Thunder is God's "voice" as when a heavy rain storm hits Canaan and Lebanon. The Canaanites believed that the god Baal brought rain and helped crops to grow. Here, the LORD is shown to be more powerful than Baal. See also the notes at 18:7-15 and 68:4.

29:5-8 *Lebanon . . . Sirion . . . Desert of Kadesh:* Mount Lebanon is a tall peak in the Lebanon Mountain range north of Palestine, though exactly which peak is uncertain. Sirion (another name for Mount Hermon) is the tallest peak (9,100 feet) in the Anti-Lebanon Mountains, a range to the east of the Lebanon Mountains. It was known for its abundant dew, and it was probably viewed as a home of Canaanite gods and goddesses. Lebanon was known for its cedar forests. The strong and aromatic timber from tall cedar trees was ideal for building palaces and was used to build the temple in Jerusalem. See the photographs on pp. 1103 and 1466. For Lebanon, see also the map on p. 2464.

The Desert of Kadesh may also be Kadesh Barnea (see the map on p. 2463).

29:9,10 *temple . . . enthroned:* Since beings in heaven are invited to praise God in 29:1, this probably refers to God's heavenly temple and throne. See the note at 11:4.

29:10 *the flood:* In ancient times the people of Israel believed that a mighty ocean surrounded all of creation, and that God could release the water to flood the earth. See also the note at 24:2. God's control of this "flood" showed God's kingship over everything.

30:2 *you healed me:* The psalmist may have been sick physically, emotionally, or spiritually. The LORD, however, is the source of all healing (see also Hos 14:4).

2 Ascribe to the LORD the glory due his name;
worship the LORD in the splendor of his[a] holiness.

3 The voice of the LORD is over the waters;
the God of glory thunders,
the LORD thunders over the mighty waters.
4 The voice of the LORD is powerful;
the voice of the LORD is majestic.
5 The voice of the LORD breaks the cedars;
the LORD breaks in pieces the cedars of Lebanon.
6 He makes Lebanon skip like a calf,
Sirion[b] like a young wild ox.
7 The voice of the LORD strikes
with flashes of lightning.
8 The voice of the LORD shakes the desert;
the LORD shakes the Desert of Kadesh.
9 The voice of the LORD twists the oaks[c]
and strips the forests bare.
And in his temple all cry, "Glory!"

10 The LORD sits[d] enthroned over the flood;
the LORD is enthroned as King forever.
11 The LORD gives strength to his people;
the LORD blesses his people with peace.

Psalm 30

A psalm. A song. For the dedication of the temple.[e] Of David.

1 I will exalt you, O LORD,
for you lifted me out of the depths
and did not let my enemies gloat over me.
2 O LORD my God, I called to you for help
and you healed me.
3 O LORD, you brought me up from the grave[f];
you spared me from going down into the pit.

4 Sing to the LORD, you saints of his;
praise his holy name.
5 For his anger lasts only a moment,
but his favor lasts a lifetime;
weeping may remain for a night,
but rejoicing comes in the morning.

6 When I felt secure, I said,
"I will never be shaken."
7 O LORD, when you favored me,
you made my mountain[g] stand firm;

[a]2 Or *LORD with the splendor of* [b]6 That is, Mount Hermon [c]9 Or *LORD makes the deer give birth* [d]10 Or *sat* [e]Title: Or *palace* [f]3 Hebrew *Sheol* [g]7 Or *hill country*

but when you hid your face,
I was dismayed.

[8] To you, O LORD, I called;
to the Lord I cried for mercy:
[9] "What gain is there in my destruction,[a]
in my going down into the pit?

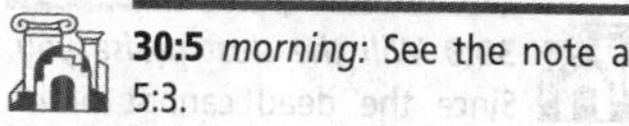
30:5 *morning:* See the note at 5:3.

[a]9 Or *there if I am silenced*

KINDS OF PSALMS

PSALMS is a collection of prayers and songs that were written to be used in private devotion, public worship, and for teaching. This chart identifies a variety of psalms according to some general categories and some specific topics they address. Many psalms can fit into more than one category. The ones listed here are just a sampling of the riches to be found in PSALMS.

LAMENTS	
Times of national crisis	44; 60; 74; 80; 83
Times of personal crisis or hardship	10; 22; 35; 42; 43; 102
PRAYERS AND PLEAS FOR HELP	
Help in times of trouble	6; 23; 25; 41; 57; 91
Deliverance from enemies	35; 68; 129; 137
Forgiveness	32; 38; 39; 51; 130
THANKSGIVING	
Deliverance	10; 70; 77; 98
Victory of enemies	21; 52; 108; 124
God's care and healing	30; 126; 127; 145
PRAISE	
God's goodness	100; 103
God as creator	8; 104; 148
God as Ruler (King) of all	29; 46; 93; 96; 99
God acts in world events	78; 105; 106; 114
Wisdom and God's law	1; 19; 37; 119
SONGS FOR WORSHIP	
In the holy temple	84; 87; 122; 134
For leader and congregation	24; 136; 149; 150

30:9 *Will the dust praise you:* Since the dead cannot praise God, the psalmist uses this familiar argument to bargain for his life. See also 28:1; 115:17; and the notes at 6:5 and 9:13.

30:11 *sackcloth:* This was a rough, dark-colored cloth made from goat or camel hair and used to make grain sacks. It was worn in times of trouble or sorrow. See the illustration on p. 1551.

31:2 *rock of refuge:* See the note at 18:46.

31:4 *trap:* Traps, snares, and pits were used to catch animals. They are used symbolically here and throughout PSALMS to refer to a variety of plots and schemes used by enemies to hurt God's people.

31:5 *Into your hands I commit my spirit:* LUKE reports Jesus speaking the words of this psalm from the cross (see Luke 23:46).

31:6 *worthless idols:* Those who worshiped idols were enemies of God and a threat to God's people. "Idols" were wooden, stone, or metal images of the gods worshiped by other nations. Above everything else, the people of Israel were to trust in and worship only the LORD God (Exod 20:1-6; Isa 44:6-20).

31:8 *enemy:* See the mini-article called "Enemies (The Wicked)," p. 1084 .

31:9,10 *distress . . . my strength fails:* Besides being a target of his enemies, the psalmist seems to be sick. But the language may be a symbol for any kind of suffering. See the note at 30:2.

31:11 Ps 22:6-8.

Will the dust praise you?
Will it proclaim your faithfulness?
10 Hear, O LORD, and be merciful to me;
O LORD, be my help."

11 You turned my wailing into dancing;
you removed my sackcloth and clothed me with joy,
12 that my heart may sing to you and not be silent.
O LORD my God, I will give you thanks forever.

Psalm 31

For the director of music. A psalm of David.

1 In you, O LORD, I have taken refuge;
let me never be put to shame;
deliver me in your righteousness.
2 Turn your ear to me,
come quickly to my rescue;
be my rock of refuge,
a strong fortress to save me.
3 Since you are my rock and my fortress,
for the sake of your name lead and guide me.
4 Free me from the trap that is set for me,
for you are my refuge.
5 Into your hands I commit my spirit;
redeem me, O LORD, the God of truth.

6 I hate those who cling to worthless idols;
I trust in the LORD.
7 I will be glad and rejoice in your love,
for you saw my affliction
and knew the anguish of my soul.
8 You have not handed me over to the enemy
but have set my feet in a spacious place.

9 Be merciful to me, O LORD, for I am in distress;
my eyes grow weak with sorrow,
my soul and my body with grief.
10 My life is consumed by anguish
and my years by groaning;
my strength fails because of my affliction,[a]
and my bones grow weak.
11 Because of all my enemies,
I am the utter contempt of my neighbors;
I am a dread to my friends—
those who see me on the street flee from me.
12 I am forgotten by them as though I were dead;
I have become like broken pottery.

[a]**10** Or *guilt*

13 For I hear the slander of many;
there is terror on every side;
they conspire against me
and plot to take my life.

14 But I trust in you, O LORD;
I say, "You are my God."
15 My times are in your hands;
deliver me from my enemies
and from those who pursue me.
16 Let your face shine on your servant;
save me in your unfailing love.
17 Let me not be put to shame, O LORD,
for I have cried out to you;
but let the wicked be put to shame
and lie silent in the grave.[a]
18 Let their lying lips be silenced,
for with pride and contempt
they speak arrogantly against the righteous.

19 How great is your goodness,
which you have stored up for those who fear you,
which you bestow in the sight of men
on those who take refuge in you.
20 In the shelter of your presence you hide them
from the intrigues of men;
in your dwelling you keep them safe
from accusing tongues.

21 Praise be to the LORD,
for he showed his wonderful love to me
when I was in a besieged city.
22 In my alarm I said,
"I am cut off from your sight!"
Yet you heard my cry for mercy
when I called to you for help.

23 Love the LORD, all his saints!
The LORD preserves the faithful,
but the proud he pays back in full.
24 Be strong and take heart,
all you who hope in the LORD.

Psalm 32

Of David. A *maskil.*[b]

1 Blessed is he
whose transgressions are forgiven,
whose sins are covered.

a17 Hebrew *Sheol* [b]Title: Probably a literary or musical term

31:13 *terror on every side:* This Hebrew saying also is found in Jeremiah 20 where the prophet Jeremiah has much the same experience that this psalm describes. Like the psalmist, Jeremiah complains to God (Jer 20:10, 14-18) and trusts God (Jer 20:11-13) at the same time. See the note at 31:19-22.

31:19-22 *How great is your goodness . . . you heard my cry:* The move from despair to praise and confidence is a regular part of the prayers for help. It usually happens toward the end of the psalm, but Psalm 31 has expressions of confidence and trust at several points (31:5,7,14,15). This suggests that, for the psalmist, suffering and praise cannot be separated. So he prays for help and celebrates at the same time, and he complains to God and trusts God at the same time. This constant trust in the midst of suffering may explain why 31:5 became Jesus' words from the cross (see the note at 31:5). See also the notes at 13:5, 6 and 22:24–26.

32:1,2 *blessed . . . forgiven:* Forgiveness is counted among God's blessings. In Psalm 1 people are said to receive God's blessing by obeying the Law. See the note at 1:1,2. The LORD demands obedience and promises blessing to those who obey his commands. But the LORD also is willing to forgive.

In the New Testament the apostle Paul quotes these verses to support his claim that God's blessings are never deserved and cannot be earned (Rom 4:7,8).

You are my hiding place; you will protect me from trouble and surround me with songs of deliverance.
Ps 32:7

32:4 *your hand was heavy upon me:* The psalmist's own sins are the cause of his suffering.

33:2 *ten-stringed lyre:* The psalmist encourages worshipers to use a musical instrument in singing praises to the LORD. Many psalms were sung as music was played. Other instruments also were used (see the illustration on p. 1190). See also 2 Sam 6:5; Ps 81:2,3; 150:3-5.

33:3 *Sing to him a new song:* New experiences of rescue and protection (see also 31:23; 32:10) call for new songs (40:3; 96:1; 98:1; 144:9; see also Isa 42:10). This psalm celebrates God's rule in creation (33:6-9) and history (33:10-19).

2 Blessed is the man
whose sin the LORD does not count
against him
and in whose spirit is no deceit.

3 When I kept silent,
my bones wasted away
through my groaning all day long.
4 For day and night
your hand was heavy upon me;
my strength was sapped
as in the heat of summer. *Selah*
5 Then I acknowledged my sin to you
and did not cover up my iniquity.
I said, "I will confess
my transgressions to the LORD"—
and you forgave
the guilt of my sin. *Selah*
6 Therefore let everyone who is godly pray
to you
while you may be found;
surely when the mighty waters rise,
they will not reach him.
7 You are my hiding place;
you will protect me from trouble
and surround me with songs of deliverance. *Selah*

8 I will instruct you and teach you in the way you
should go;
I will counsel you and watch over you.
9 Do not be like the horse or the mule,
which have no understanding
but must be controlled by bit and bridle
or they will not come to you.
10 Many are the woes of the wicked,
but the LORD's unfailing love
surrounds the man who trusts in him.

11 Rejoice in the LORD and be glad, you righteous;
sing, all you who are upright in heart!

Psalm 33

1 Sing joyfully to the LORD, you righteous;
it is fitting for the upright to praise him.
2 Praise the LORD with the harp;
make music to him on the ten-stringed lyre.
3 Sing to him a new song;
play skillfully, and shout for joy.

4 For the word of the LORD is right and true;
he is faithful in all he does.
5 The LORD loves righteousness and justice;
the earth is full of his unfailing love.

6 By the word of the LORD were the heavens made,
their starry host by the breath of his mouth.
7 He gathers the waters of the sea into jars[a];
he puts the deep into storehouses.
8 Let all the earth fear the LORD;
let all the people of the world revere him.
9 For he spoke, and it came to be;
he commanded, and it stood firm.
10 The LORD foils the plans of the nations;
he thwarts the purposes of the peoples.
11 But the plans of the LORD stand firm forever,
the purposes of his heart through all generations.

12 Blessed is the nation whose God is the LORD,
the people he chose for his inheritance.
13 From heaven the LORD looks down
and sees all mankind;
14 from his dwelling place he watches
all who live on earth—
15 he who forms the hearts of all,
who considers everything they do.
16 No king is saved by the size of his army;
no warrior escapes by his great strength.
17 A horse is a vain hope for deliverance;
despite all its great strength it cannot save.
18 But the eyes of the LORD are on those who fear him,
on those whose hope is in his unfailing love,
19 to deliver them from death
and keep them alive in famine.

20 We wait in hope for the LORD;
he is our help and our shield.
21 In him our hearts rejoice,
for we trust in his holy name.
22 May your unfailing love rest upon us, O LORD,
even as we put our hope in you.

Psalm 34[b]

Of David. When he pretended to be insane before Abimelech, who drove him away, and he left.

1 I will extol the LORD at all times;
his praise will always be on my lips.

[a]7 Or *sea as into a heap* [b]This psalm is an acrostic poem, the verses of which begin with the successive letters of the Hebrew alphabet.

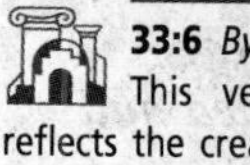

33:6 *By the word of the LORD:* This verse, as well as 33:9, reflects the creation story of Genesis 1 where God creates everything by speaking commands.

33:12 *Blessed:* See the note at 32:1,2.

33:14 *his dwelling place:* See the notes at 9:7 and 26:8.

33:16,17 *army . . . horse is a vain hope:* See the note at 20:7.

34 Title *David . . . Abimelech:* There is no one named Abimelech in the stories about David in 1 and 2 SAMUEL. A similar name, Ahimelech, does appear. The title recalls 1 Samuel 21:13-15. See also the mini-article called "David," p. 1028. Psalm 34 is another of the "acrostic" psalms (see the note at 119:1).

The LORD is close to the brokenhearted and saves those who are crushed in spirit.
Ps 34:18

2 My soul will boast in the LORD;
let the afflicted hear and rejoice.
3 Glorify the LORD with me;
let us exalt his name together.

4 I sought the LORD, and he answered me;
he delivered me from all my fears.
5 Those who look to him are radiant;
their faces are never covered with shame.
6 This poor man called, and the LORD heard him;
he saved him out of all his troubles.
7 The angel of the LORD encamps around those who
fear him,
and he delivers them.

8 Taste and see that the LORD is good;
blessed is the man who takes refuge in him.
9 Fear the LORD, you his saints,
for those who fear him lack nothing.
10 The lions may grow weak and hungry,
but those who seek the LORD lack no good thing.

11 Come, my children, listen to me;
I will teach you the fear of the LORD.
12 Whoever of you loves life
and desires to see many good days,
13 keep your tongue from evil
and your lips from speaking lies.
14 Turn from evil and do good;
seek peace and pursue it.
15 The eyes of the LORD are on the righteous
and his ears are attentive to their cry;
16 the face of the LORD is against those who do evil,
to cut off the memory of them from the earth.

17 The righteous cry out, and the LORD hears them;
he delivers them from all their troubles.
18 The LORD is close to the brokenhearted
and saves those who are crushed in spirit.

19 A righteous man may have many troubles,
but the LORD delivers him from them all;
20 he protects all his bones,
not one of them will be broken.

21 Evil will slay the wicked;
the foes of the righteous will be condemned.
22 The LORD redeems his servants;
no one will be condemned who takes refuge
in him.

34:2 *the afflicted:* The psalmists regularly describe themselves as "helpless," "poor," and "afflicted." See 37:11 and the note at 9:8,9.

34:7 *angel of the LORD:* Mysterious messengers sometimes appear in human form to do God's work. The angel of the LORD may have been a pre-incarnate appearance of Christ. See also the mini-article called "Angels," p. 88.

34:9 *those who fear him lack nothing:* Having been saved by God (34:4,6), the psalmist presents his experience as an example for others. Sayings like this one (see also 34:10,17) must be heard alongside 34:19. God's promises do not mean the end of suffering, but rather joy and protection even while suffering exists. See also the notes at 13:5, 6 and 31:19-22.

34:10 *lions:* In PSALMS, wild animals often stand for God's enemies. See also 10:9,10; 22:12,13.

34:11 *Come . . . listen to me:* In keeping with his intent to be an example for others (see the note at 34:9), the psalmist now speaks like a teacher to his students. See Prov 1:8; 3:1; 4:1.

34:16 *LORD is against . . . evil:* See the note at 5:10-12.

34:21 *wicked . . . condemned:* See the note at 1:4,5.

34:8 1 Pet 2:3. **34:12-16** 1 Pet 3:10-12. **34:20** John 19:36.

Psalm 35

Of David.

1 Contend, O LORD, with those who contend with me;
fight against those who fight against me.
2 Take up shield and buckler;
arise and come to my aid.
3 Brandish spear and javelin[a]
against those who pursue me.
Say to my soul,
"I am your salvation."

4 May those who seek my life
be disgraced and put to shame;
may those who plot my ruin
be turned back in dismay.
5 May they be like chaff before the wind,
with the angel of the LORD driving them away;
6 may their path be dark and slippery,
with the angel of the LORD pursuing them.
7 Since they hid their net for me without cause
and without cause dug a pit for me,
8 may ruin overtake them by surprise—
may the net they hid entangle them,
may they fall into the pit, to their ruin.
9 Then my soul will rejoice in the LORD
and delight in his salvation.
10 My whole being will exclaim,
"Who is like you, O LORD?
You rescue the poor from those too strong for them,
the poor and needy from those who rob them."

11 Ruthless witnesses come forward;
they question me on things I know nothing about.
12 They repay me evil for good
and leave my soul forlorn.
13 Yet when they were ill, I put on sackcloth
and humbled myself with fasting.
When my prayers returned to me unanswered,
14 I went about mourning
as though for my friend or brother.
I bowed my head in grief
as though weeping for my mother.
15 But when I stumbled, they gathered in glee;
attackers gathered against me when I was unaware.
They slandered me without ceasing.
16 Like the ungodly they maliciously mocked[b];

[a]3 Or *and block the way*
[b]16 Septuagint; Hebrew may mean *ungodly circle of mockers.*

35:1 *fight against those who fight against me:* The military language (see also 35:23) suggests a situation of conflict. The psalmist also seems to be the victim of false accusation (35:11,15,21,24), or perhaps he is sick (35:13). See also the notes at 3:5-8 and 18:34-48.

35:5 *chaff before the wind . . . angel of the LORD:* An angel of the LORD is sometimes sent to carry out God's punishment (1 Chr 21:14-17; Isa 37:36). See the notes at 34:7 and 1:4, 5.

35:13 *sackcloth . . . fasting:* See the note at 30:11. At this time, not eating (called "fasting") and wearing sackcloth were done to show sorrow. In this case, the psalmist's concern for his enemies contrasts sharply with their attitude toward him.

35:17 *lions:* See the note at 34:10.

35:19 *hate me without reason:* This is the psalmist's way of saying that his enemies' accusations are false (see 35:11,15,21,24). Centuries later, when Jesus was falsely accused and unfairly opposed, this and other psalms were recalled. See also Ps 69:4; John 15:25; and the note at 22:1.

35:21,22 *we have seen it:* The enemies do not tell the truth, and they fail to take into account that God's sight is greater than their own (10:11).

35:23,24 *rise to my defense . . . Vindicate me:* The purpose of this and similar requests (35:1, 4-6, 19, 26) is not merely revenge. For things to be set right for victims, their oppressors must be opposed. See the notes at 3:5-8; 5:10-12; and 18:34-48.

35:28 *speak . . . praises:* The prayers for help often end with a promise to praise God or to bring God an offering. See the note at 22:24-26. In this psalm, such promises also occur at 35:9,18.

36:1 *the sinfulness of the wicked:* "The wicked" here means those who never think about God, and so never ask for forgiveness (36:4). They are enemies of God and God's people. See also the mini-article called "Sin," p. 2181.

36:1 Rom 3:18.

they gnashed their teeth at me.
17 O Lord, how long will you look on?
Rescue my life from their ravages,
my precious life from these lions.
18 I will give you thanks in the great assembly;
among throngs of people I will praise you.

19 Let not those gloat over me
who are my enemies without cause;
let not those who hate me without reason
maliciously wink the eye.
20 They do not speak peaceably,
but devise false accusations
against those who live quietly in the land.
21 They gape at me and say, "Aha! Aha!
With our own eyes we have seen it."

22 O LORD, you have seen this; be not silent.
Do not be far from me, O Lord.
23 Awake, and rise to my defense!
Contend for me, my God and Lord.
24 Vindicate me in your righteousness, O LORD my God;
do not let them gloat over me.
25 Do not let them think, "Aha, just what we wanted!"
or say, "We have swallowed him up."

26 May all who gloat over my distress
be put to shame and confusion;
may all who exalt themselves over me
be clothed with shame and disgrace.
27 May those who delight in my vindication
shout for joy and gladness;
may they always say, "The LORD be exalted,
who delights in the well-being of his servant."
28 My tongue will speak of your righteousness
and of your praises all day long.

Psalm 36

For the director of music. Of David the servant of the LORD.

1 An oracle is within my heart
concerning the sinfulness of the wicked:[a]
There is no fear of God
before his eyes.
2 For in his own eyes he flatters himself
too much to detect or hate his sin.
3 The words of his mouth are wicked and deceitful;
he has ceased to be wise and to do good.

[a]1 Or *heart: / Sin proceeds from the wicked.*

[4]Even on his bed he plots evil;
he commits himself to a sinful course
and does not reject what is wrong.

[5]Your love, O LORD, reaches to the heavens,
your faithfulness to the skies.
[6]Your righteousness is like the mighty mountains,
your justice like the great deep.
O LORD, you preserve both man and beast.
[7] How priceless is your unfailing love!
Both high and low among men
find[a] refuge in the shadow of your wings.
[8]They feast on the abundance of your house;
you give them drink from your river of delights.
[9]For with you is the fountain of life;
in your light we see light.

[10]Continue your love to those who know you,
your righteousness to the upright in heart.
[11]May the foot of the proud not come against me,
nor the hand of the wicked drive me away.
[12]See how the evildoers lie fallen—
thrown down, not able to rise!

Psalm 37[b]

Of David.

[1]Do not fret because of evil men
or be envious of those who do wrong;
[2]for like the grass they will soon wither,
like green plants they will soon die away.

[3]Trust in the LORD and do good;
dwell in the land and enjoy safe pasture.
[4]Delight yourself in the LORD
and he will give you the desires of your heart.

[5]Commit your way to the LORD;
trust in him and he will do this:
[6]He will make your righteousness shine like the dawn,
the justice of your cause like the noonday sun.

[7]Be still before the LORD and wait patiently for him;
do not fret when men succeed in their ways,
when they carry out their wicked schemes.

[8]Refrain from anger and turn from wrath;
do not fret—it leads only to evil.

---

[a]7 Or *love, O God! / Men find*; or *love! / Both heavenly beings and men / find*
[b]This psalm is an acrostic poem, the stanzas of which begin with the successive letters of the Hebrew alphabet.

36:5,6 *Your love . . . mountains . . . the great deep:* These verses begin a celebration of God's love for the whole world, mentioning each major part of the world—skies, mountains, and sea (the deep). Because God loves the whole world, God's care extends beyond humanity. In keeping with this understanding, the final psalm invites "everything that has breath" to praise God (150:6).

36:7,8 *wings . . . house:* See the note at 17:8. The tabernacle (and later the temple) was known as God's "house" and as a place of shelter (see the note at 5:7). The psalmist may be describing a visit to the tabernacle or using it as a symbol for God's protection at all times. See also the note at 23:6.

36:11,12 *thrown down:* Even though he seems to suffer because of the wicked, the psalmist trusts that God's purposes (36:6) will win out in the end.

37:1 *those who do wrong:* The psalm deals with the question of why success comes to those who do wrong (37:7), while God's people suffer. See also the note at 10:5. This is another of the "acrostic" psalms (see the note at 119:1).

37:3 *dwell in the land:* God's promise of land to Israel is important throughout the Old Testament (see Gen 12:1-3; Exod 3:8; and the note at 25:13). This psalm may have been written during a time when national enemies threatened the land. Land meant the opportunity for life, so here it may be used symbolically. See also the mini-article called "Land," p. 1751.

37:11 *the meek will inherit the land:* The promise of land is also a promise of life (see note at 37:3). Centuries later, Jesus made a similar promise (Matt 5:5). See the mini-article called "The Poor," p. 2362.

37:13 *the Lord laughs:* God's laughter shows that God's rule of the world is not threatened by the wicked. See 2:4; 59:8.

37:26 *They . . . lend:* To give and lend were a way of helping the poor (37:21). God's people do this in response to God's own teachings and example (37:31; 41:1; Prov 14:31; 19:17). Deuteronomy 23:19, 20 adds that when God's people lend money to other Israelites, they are not to make money by charging interest.

37:15 Ps 34:21. **37:16** Prov 15:16; 16:8.

9 For evil men will be cut off,
but those who hope in the LORD will inherit the land.

10 A little while, and the wicked will be no more;
though you look for them, they will not be found.
11 But the meek will inherit the land
and enjoy great peace.

12 The wicked plot against the righteous
and gnash their teeth at them;
13 but the Lord laughs at the wicked,
for he knows their day is coming.

14 The wicked draw the sword
and bend the bow
to bring down the poor and needy,
to slay those whose ways are upright.
15 But their swords will pierce their own hearts,
and their bows will be broken.

16 Better the little that the righteous have
than the wealth of many wicked;
17 for the power of the wicked will be broken,
but the LORD upholds the righteous.

18 The days of the blameless are known to the LORD,
and their inheritance will endure forever.
19 In times of disaster they will not wither;
in days of famine they will enjoy plenty.

20 But the wicked will perish:
The LORD's enemies will be like the beauty of the fields,
they will vanish—vanish like smoke.

21 The wicked borrow and do not repay,
but the righteous give generously;
22 those the LORD blesses will inherit the land,
but those he curses will be cut off.

23 If the LORD delights in a man's way,
he makes his steps firm;
24 though he stumble, he will not fall,
for the LORD upholds him with his hand.

25 I was young and now I am old,
yet I have never seen the righteous forsaken
or their children begging bread.
26 They are always generous and lend freely;
their children will be blessed.

27 Turn from evil and do good;
then you will dwell in the land forever.

[28] For the LORD loves the just
and will not forsake his faithful ones.

They will be protected forever,
but the offspring of the wicked will be cut off;
[29] the righteous will inherit the land
and dwell in it forever.

[30] The mouth of the righteous man utters wisdom,
and his tongue speaks what is just.
[31] The law of his God is in his heart;
his feet do not slip.

[32] The wicked lie in wait for the righteous,
seeking their very lives;
[33] but the LORD will not leave them in their power
or let them be condemned when brought to trial.

[34] Wait for the LORD
and keep his way.
He will exalt you to inherit the land;
when the wicked are cut off, you will see it.

[35] I have seen a wicked and ruthless man
flourishing like a green tree in its native soil,
[36] but he soon passed away and was no more;
though I looked for him, he could not be found.

[37] Consider the blameless, observe the upright;
there is a future[a] for the man of peace.
[38] But all sinners will be destroyed;
the future[b] of the wicked will be cut off.

[39] The salvation of the righteous comes from the LORD;
he is their stronghold in time of trouble.
[40] The LORD helps them and delivers them;
he delivers them from the wicked and saves them,
because they take refuge in him.

Psalm 38

A psalm of David. A petition.

[1] O LORD, do not rebuke me in your anger
or discipline me in your wrath.
[2] For your arrows have pierced me,
and your hand has come down upon me.
[3] Because of your wrath there is no health in my body;
my bones have no soundness because of my sin.
[4] My guilt has overwhelmed me
like a burden too heavy to bear.

[a]37 Or *there will be posterity* [b]38 Or *posterity*

The mouth of the righteous man utters wisdom, and his tongue speaks what is just.
Ps 37:30

37:28 *the LORD loves the just:* Justice means exactly what the psalm promises: life for the poor and needy. See the notes at 9:8, 9 and 15:2-5.

37:30,31 *wisdom . . . law of his God:* See the note at 19:7,8. Openness to God's teaching means to experience life as God intends it (1:1,2).

37:33 *trial:* Several of the prayers for help seem to have been prayed originally by persons who had been falsely accused of something by their enemies. See the notes at 7:3-5; 17:1,2; 26:1,2; and 35:19. The Hebrew word for "trial" also means "justice." God's actions show that God "loves the just" (37:28).

37:39,40 *The LORD helps . . . take refuge in him:* Verse 39 shows that the psalmist clearly recognizes that God's people will have "times of disaster" (37:7, 19). But even during difficult times God's people can experience God's protection. God makes their steps firm (37:23), helps them to be patient (37:7, 8), to live right (37:16), and to gladly give to others (37:26). For more about God's power and mercy, see the note at 5:10-12.

38:2 *your arrows have pierced me:* The psalmist suggests that God caused his "wounds" (38:11) to punish him for his sins (38:3,4,18). See also Job 6:4; Lam 3:12.

38:5 *folly:* In Hebrew wisdom literature, folly, fools, and foolishness are opposed to God and his wisdom. See also the note at 14:1. The psalmist no longer opposes God, but instead looks to God for help (38:18, 20-22).

38:11 *my wounds:* This may refer to an actual physical illness (38:5-10) that was believed to be a punishment for sin (see the note at 38:1, 2). Or it may refer symbolically to his spiritual "sickness" caused by sin.

38:12 *Those who seek my life:* These people are the psalmist's "enemies" (38:19).

38:20 *repay my good with evil:* The enemies seem to be using the psalmist's suffering as an excuse to mistreat him. See the note at 35:13.

38:21,22 *Come quickly to help me:* The psalmist trusts that his suffering is not God's last word. Instead, it will be what leads God to help him. See also the note at 6:8,9.

39 Title *Jeduthun:* Jeduthun, a member of the Levite clan of Asaph, was appointed by David to play musical instruments during worship in the tabernacle (1 Chr 16:37-42; 25:1-3). The title may also mean that the music was to be played according to the style of Jeduthun of the Asaph clan.

39:1 *a muzzle on my mouth:* The psalmist wants to avoid accusing God of doing wrong. Also, he knows that evil people could use his words against him (39:8).

38:11 Ps 22:6,7.

5 My wounds fester and are loathsome
because of my sinful folly.
6 I am bowed down and brought very low;
all day long I go about mourning.
7 My back is filled with searing pain;
there is no health in my body.
8 I am feeble and utterly crushed;
I groan in anguish of heart.

9 All my longings lie open before you, O Lord;
my sighing is not hidden from you.
10 My heart pounds, my strength fails me;
even the light has gone from my eyes.
11 My friends and companions avoid me because of
my wounds;
my neighbors stay far away.
12 Those who seek my life set their traps,
those who would harm me talk of my ruin;
all day long they plot deception.

13 I am like a deaf man, who cannot hear,
like a mute, who cannot open his mouth;
14 I have become like a man who does not hear,
whose mouth can offer no reply.
15 I wait for you, O LORD;
you will answer, O Lord my God.
16 For I said, "Do not let them gloat
or exalt themselves over me when my foot slips."

17 For I am about to fall,
and my pain is ever with me.
18 I confess my iniquity;
I am troubled by my sin.
19 Many are those who are my vigorous enemies;
those who hate me without reason are numerous.
20 Those who repay my good with evil
slander me when I pursue what is good.

21 O LORD, do not forsake me;
be not far from me, O my God.
22 Come quickly to help me,
O Lord my Savior.

Psalm 39

For the director of music. For Jeduthun. A psalm of David.

1 I said, "I will watch my ways
and keep my tongue from sin;
I will put a muzzle on my mouth
as long as the wicked are in my presence."

[2] But when I was silent and still,
not even saying anything good,
my anguish increased.
[3] My heart grew hot within me,
and as I meditated, the fire burned;
then I spoke with my tongue:

[4] "Show me, O LORD, my life's end
and the number of my days;
let me know how fleeting is my life.
[5] You have made my days a mere handbreadth;
the span of my years is as nothing before you.
Each man's life is but a breath. *Selah*
[6] Man is a mere phantom as he goes to and fro:
He bustles about, but only in vain;
he heaps up wealth, not knowing who will get it.

[7] "But now, Lord, what do I look for?
My hope is in you.
[8] Save me from all my transgressions;
do not make me the scorn of fools.
[9] I was silent; I would not open my mouth,
for you are the one who has done this.
[10] Remove your scourge from me;
I am overcome by the blow of your hand.
[11] You rebuke and discipline men for their sin;
you consume their wealth like a moth—
each man is but a breath. *Selah*

[12] "Hear my prayer, O LORD,
listen to my cry for help;
be not deaf to my weeping.
For I dwell with you as an alien,
a stranger, as all my fathers were.
[13] Look away from me, that I may rejoice again
before I depart and am no more."

Psalm 40

For the director of music. Of David. A psalm.

[1] I waited patiently for the LORD;
he turned to me and heard my cry.
[2] He lifted me out of the slimy pit,
out of the mud and mire;
he set my feet on a rock
and gave me a firm place to stand.
[3] He put a new song in my mouth,
a hymn of praise to our God.
Many will see and fear
and put their trust in the LORD.

39:3 *the fire burned:* This is a symbol for something that cannot be resisted. See Jer 20:9.

39:4-6 *how fleeting is my life . . . Man is a mere phantom:* The psalmist does not complain about his sufferings but about the shortness of all human life. See also Job 7:7; 8:9; Ps 90:10; Eccl 5:10-17; 6:12.

39:12 *a stranger:* Non-Israelites living in the land were considered strangers. See also the mini-article called "Foreigners (Aliens)," p. 501. But Leviticus 25:23 says that since God really owns the land, even the Israelites are visitors. The idea of "visiting" could suggest the shortness of life (see 39:4-6), but David uses this idea to thank God for being so good to the people (1 Chr 29:15). Life may be short, but goodness is possible when people depend on God (39:7).

40:2 *pit:* The word is probably meant to be a symbol of danger and distress, but Jacob's son Joseph and the prophet Jeremiah were actually thrown into pits (cisterns) by their enemies (Gen 37:20; Jer 38:6). The word is also sometimes used for a grave or the land of the dead (see the note at 9:13).

40:3-5 *new song . . . Blessed . . . wonders:* The "new song" celebrates what God has done for the psalmist. See also the note at 33:3. Blessing or happiness comes from trusting God rather than other gods (see the note at 31:6).

40:6 *Sacrifice and offering ... you did not require:* To say that the LORD "did not require" sacrifices may seem confusing, since sacrifices were a regular, required part of worship at the temple. They were clearly described in God's Law (see especially LEVITICUS). But true obedience is not simply a matter of performing a ceremony. It is trusting God alone, being truly sorry for sins, and living as God wants, including treating others with justice (1 Sam 15:22; Ps 50:23; 51:16,17; Isa 1:12-17; Hos 6:6; Amos 5:21-24). For more on sacrifices, see the notes at 16:4 and 27:6. The writer later applied the words of verses 6-8 to Jesus (see Heb 10:5-7).

40:7 *the scroll:* The Bible refers to "books" or "scrolls" that contain the names of those who belong to God, or to a list of their deeds (Exod 32:32,33; Ps 69:28; 87:6; 139:16; Isa 34:16; Dan 12:1,4; Phil 4:3; Rev 3:5; 13:8; 17:8; 20:12,15; 21:27). The symbolism of a record book expresses that God knows everything about people.

40:8 *your law:* See the notes at 1:1, 2 and 19:7,8.

40:9,10 *proclaim righteousness in the great assembly:* The psalmist made a public testimony of faith, perhaps to fulfill a vow made earlier. See also the mini-article called "Making Vows," p. 328.

40:17 *poor and needy:* See the notes at 9:8,9 and 34:2. The prayers for help usually end with praise rather than a request, but the effect is the same. Praise and suffering are rarely separated entirely (see 40:13-16 and the notes at 13:5, 6 and 31:19-22).

40:6-8 Heb 10:5-7. **40:8** Jer 31:33.

4 Blessed is the man
who makes the LORD his trust,
who does not look to the proud,
to those who turn aside to false gods.[a]
5 Many, O LORD my God,
are the wonders you have done.
The things you planned for us
no one can recount to you;
were I to speak and tell of them,
they would be too many to declare.

6 Sacrifice and offering you did not desire,
but my ears you have pierced[b,c];
burnt offerings and sin offerings
you did not require.
7 Then I said, "Here I am, I have come—
it is written about me in the scroll.[d]
8 I desire to do your will, O my God;
your law is within my heart."

9 I proclaim righteousness in the great assembly;
I do not seal my lips,
as you know, O LORD.
10 I do not hide your righteousness in my heart;
I speak of your faithfulness and salvation.
I do not conceal your love and your truth
from the great assembly.

11 Do not withhold your mercy from me,
O LORD;
may your love and your truth always protect me.
12 For troubles without number surround me;
my sins have overtaken me, and I cannot see.
They are more than the hairs of my head,
and my heart fails within me.

13 Be pleased, O LORD, to save me;
O LORD, come quickly to help me.
14 May all who seek to take my life
be put to shame and confusion;
may all who desire my ruin
be turned back in disgrace.
15 May those who say to me, "Aha! Aha!"
be appalled at their own shame.
16 But may all who seek you
rejoice and be glad in you;

[a]**4** Or *to falsehood* [b]**6** Hebrew; Septuagint *but a body you have prepared for me* (see also Symmachus and Theodotion) [c]**6** Or *opened* [d]**7** Or *come / with the scroll written for me*

may those who love your salvation always say,
"The LORD be exalted!"

17 Yet I am poor and needy;
may the Lord think of me.
You are my help and my deliverer;
O my God, do not delay.

Psalm 41

For the director of music. A psalm of David.

1 Blessed is he who has regard for the weak;
the LORD delivers him in times of trouble.
2 The LORD will protect him and preserve his life;
he will bless him in the land
and not surrender him to the desire of his foes.
3 The LORD will sustain him on his sickbed
and restore him from his bed of illness.

4 I said, "O LORD, have mercy on me;
heal me, for I have sinned against you."
5 My enemies say of me in malice,
"When will he die and his name perish?"
6 Whenever one comes to see me,
he speaks falsely, while his heart gathers slander;
then he goes out and spreads it abroad.

41:1,2 *Blessed:* Like the first psalm in "Book I," this last one also begins with the ideas of blessing. See the note at 1:1,2 and the mini-article called "Blessed (Happy)," p. 1026. See also 10:17,18; 12:5; 14:6; 22:24-26; 37:11; 40:17.

41:2 *in the land:* See the note at 37:3.

41:2 *foes:* The "foes" and "enemies" appear regularly in the prayers for help. Here, the enemies try to take advantage of the psalmist's sickness (41:5,7,11).

41:4 *heal me . . . sinned:* The prayer may have been prayed originally by someone who was sick (41:3,7,10). It suggests that sickness is a punishment for sin, but it also suggests that God has helped or will help the one who suffers (41:10-12). See also the notes at 6:8,9 and 38:11.

QUESTIONS ABOUT PSALMS 1:1—41:13

1. Read Psalm 1 again along with the mini-articles called "Blessed (Happy)," p. 1026 and "Law," p. 1160. According to these, what is the source of enduring happiness? How does this differ from the ways people often pursue happiness today?
2. Read Psalm 2 along with the mini-article called "Messiah (Chosen One)," p. 1124. Who is the LORD's "Anointed One," and what was his responsibility? How is it that Jesus began to be called God's "Anointed One" in the New Testament?
3. A number of psalms in "Book I" are prayers for help (for example, Ps 3; 5; 10; 13; 28; 35; 38). In what situations do the psalmists ask for God's help? What "enemies" oppose God and God's people? How can the psalms help people today deal with opposition and trouble?
4. In many prayers for help, the psalmists ask God to punish or destroy their enemies (3:7; 5:10; 10:15; 28:4; 35:4-8; 41:10). How are these prayers more than simple requests for personal revenge? What do you make of the fact that God opposes evil, but evil still exists?
5. So far, what has reading PSALMS taught you about prayer?
6. Read Psalm 22. How does the first part of the psalm (22:1-21) differ from the second part? (22:22-31) What is the importance of this difference?
7. Read Psalm 15:1-3. What do these verses say about who should worship at God's temple? What do these words have to say about worshiping God today?
8. Write a psalm of your own in response to a situation in your life.

41:9 *close friend . . . lifted up his heel:* The psalmist is rejected even by his closest friend. See also the notes at 22:1 and 22:7.

41:10 *repay them:* See the notes at 3:5-8; 5:10-12; 7:6; and 17:13.

42 Title *Sons of Korah:* Korah was a Levite whose family served in areas of music and worship at the temple (1 Chr 6:33-38). Psalms 42 and 43 were originally one psalm with three stanzas that were united by the same refrain at 42:5; 42:11; and 43:5.

42:2 *meet with God:* See the notes at 11:7 and 17:15. The psalmist may have been wishing to visit the temple in Jerusalem to experience God's presence (42:4).

42:4 *house of God:* See the note at 5:7 (your house). The memory of a happier past causes sorrow (42:4) and discouragement (42:5).

42:5,6 *Why are you downcast . . . hope in God:* These lines are a good example of how the psalmists regularly trust God while they are suffering. See the notes at 13:5,6 and 22:24-26. See also 42:11 and 43:5.

41:9 Matt 26:23; Mark 14:18; Luke 22:21; John 13:18. **41:13** Ps 106:48.

7 All my enemies whisper together against me;
they imagine the worst for me, saying,
8 "A vile disease has beset him;
he will never get up from the place where he lies."
9 Even my close friend, whom I trusted,
he who shared my bread,
has lifted up his heel against me.

10 But you, O LORD, have mercy on me;
raise me up, that I may repay them.
11 I know that you are pleased with me,
for my enemy does not triumph over me.
12 In my integrity you uphold me
and set me in your presence forever.

13 Praise be to the LORD, the God of Israel,
from everlasting to everlasting.
Amen and Amen.

Book II (Psalms 42:1—72:20)

Book II opens with a collection of psalms "Of the Sons of Korah" (Ps 42-49; 43 probably was originally part of Psalm 42). These are followed by a single psalm of Asaph (50) and a collection of psalms of David (Ps 51-72).

Psalm 42[a]

For the director of music. A *maskil*[b] of the Sons of Korah.

1 As the deer pants for streams of water,
so my soul pants for you, O God.
2 My soul thirsts for God, for the living God.
When can I go and meet with God?
3 My tears have been my food
day and night,
while men say to me all day long,
"Where is your God?"
4 These things I remember
as I pour out my soul:
how I used to go with the multitude,
leading the procession to the house of God,
with shouts of joy and thanksgiving
among the festive throng.

5 Why are you downcast, O my soul?
Why so disturbed within me?

[a]In many Hebrew manuscripts Psalms 42 and 43 constitute one psalm. [b]Title: Probably a literary or musical term

Hinds Longing for Water, a mosaic from the Mausoleum of Galla Placidia, Ravenna, Italy, fifth century. Water is essential to all living creatures and often represents life itself. In Psalm 42, the psalmist compares his own longing for God to the longing of a deer thirsty for streams of fresh water. The psalmist then uses other water imagery to describe his turbulent emotions. "My tears," the psalmist says, "have been my food" (Ps 42:3); "pour out my soul" (Ps 42:4); and "waves and breakers have swept over me" (Ps 42:7).

Put your hope in God,
  for I will yet praise him,
  my Savior and 6my God.

My[a] soul is downcast within me;
  therefore I will remember you
from the land of the Jordan,
  the heights of Hermon—from Mount Mizar.
7 Deep calls to deep
  in the roar of your waterfalls;
all your waves and breakers
  have swept over me.

8 By day the LORD directs his love,
  at night his song is with me—
  a prayer to the God of my life.

9 I say to God my Rock,
  "Why have you forgotten me?
Why must I go about mourning,
  oppressed by the enemy?"
10 My bones suffer mortal agony
  as my foes taunt me,
saying to me all day long,
  "Where is your God?"

42:6 *the Jordan . . . Hermon . . . Mount Mizar:* The Jordan River begins to the north of Palestine near Mount Hermon (see the note at 29:5-8 and the map on p. 2464). It runs through the Sea of Galilee and south to the Dead Sea. The location of Mount Mizar is unknown.

42:7 *Deep . . . waterfalls . . . waves:* In contrast to 42:1, water here is a symbol of chaos, danger, and death. See the notes at 18:4,5 and 24:2.

42:9 *my Rock:* See the note at 18:46.

[a]**5,6** A few Hebrew manuscripts, Septuagint and Syriac; most Hebrew manuscripts *praise him for his saving help. / 6O my God, my*

Why are you downcast, O my soul? Why so disturbed within me? Put your hope in God, for I will yet praise him, my Savior and my God.
Ps 43:5

43:1,2 *ungodly nation ... deceitful and wicked men ... enemy:* These are names for the psalmist's "enemies." The psalmist may have been falsely accused of some crime.

43:3,4 *your holy mountain ... where you dwell ... altar of God:* See the notes at 42:4 and 2:6 (Zion). The temple was built on Mount Zion. Outside the temple was an altar for sacrificing animals (see the note at 27:6). In 42:1,2 the psalmist expressed the wish to visit the temple. These verses in Psalm 43 express the psalmist's joy at being able to worship God in the temple.

43:4 *harp:* See the note at 33:2.

44:1-3 *what you did ... your arm ... light of your face:* "What you did" refers to rescuing the people from slavery in Egypt (Exod 3–15) and leading them to the land of Canaan (44:2). According to NUMBERS, the LORD led and cared for the people in the desert. JOSHUA tells how the LORD fought for the people and helped them defeat powerful armies and "won the land." The image of God's powerful or mighty arm is often used to describe the LORD's protection or power, especially in battle (Exod 14:21; 15:12,16; Deut 5:15; Isa 14:26; 19:16; 40:10). For "light," see also the note at 18:28. See also the mini-article called "Holy War (The LORD's Battles)," p. 306.

11 Why are you downcast, O my soul?
Why so disturbed within me?
Put your hope in God,
for I will yet praise him,
my Savior and my God.

Psalm 43[a]

1 Vindicate me, O God,
and plead my cause against an ungodly nation;
rescue me from deceitful and wicked men.
2 You are God my stronghold.
Why have you rejected me?
Why must I go about mourning,
oppressed by the enemy?
3 Send forth your light and your truth,
let them guide me;
let them bring me to your holy mountain,
to the place where you dwell.
4 Then will I go to the altar of God,
to God, my joy and my delight.
I will praise you with the harp,
O God, my God.

5 Why are you downcast, O my soul?
Why so disturbed within me?
Put your hope in God,
for I will yet praise him,
my Savior and my God.

Psalm 44

For the director of music. Of the Sons of Korah. A *maskil.*[b]

1 We have heard with our ears, O God;
our fathers have told us
what you did in their days,
in days long ago.
2 With your hand you drove out the nations
and planted our fathers;
you crushed the peoples
and made our fathers flourish.
3 It was not by their sword that they won the land,
nor did their arm bring them victory;
it was your right hand, your arm,
and the light of your face, for you loved them.

[a]In many Hebrew manuscripts Psalms 42 and 43 constitute one psalm.
[b]Title: Probably a literary or musical term

[4] You are my King and my God,
who decrees[a] victories for Jacob.
[5] Through you we push back our enemies;
through your name we trample our foes.
[6] I do not trust in my bow,
my sword does not bring me victory;
[7] but you give us victory over our enemies,
you put our adversaries to shame.
[8] In God we make our boast all day long,
and we will praise your name forever. *Selah*

[9] But now you have rejected and humbled us;
you no longer go out with our armies.
[10] You made us retreat before the enemy,
and our adversaries have plundered us.
[11] You gave us up to be devoured like sheep
and have scattered us among the nations.
[12] You sold your people for a pittance,
gaining nothing from their sale.

[13] You have made us a reproach to our neighbors,
the scorn and derision of those around us.
[14] You have made us a byword among the nations;
the peoples shake their heads at us.
[15] My disgrace is before me all day long,
and my face is covered with shame
[16] at the taunts of those who reproach and revile me,
because of the enemy, who is bent on revenge.

[17] All this happened to us,
though we had not forgotten you
or been false to your covenant.
[18] Our hearts had not turned back;
our feet had not strayed from your path.
[19] But you crushed us and made us a haunt for jackals
and covered us over with deep darkness.

[20] If we had forgotten the name of our God
or spread out our hands to a foreign god,
[21] would not God have discovered it,
since he knows the secrets of the heart?
[22] Yet for your sake we face death all day long;
we are considered as sheep to be slaughtered.

[23] Awake, O Lord! Why do you sleep?
Rouse yourself! Do not reject us forever.
[24] Why do you hide your face
and forget our misery and oppression?

[a]**4** Septuagint, Aquila and Syriac; Hebrew *King, O God; / command*

44:4 *my King and my God:* See the note on p. 1024.

44:5 *our enemies:* This prayer for help is offered for the whole people. The "enemies" in this case are other nations that oppose God's people and threaten their future in the land (see 44:9-16).

44:9-11 *rejected . . . scattered:* Concerning God's leading the people into battle, see the notes at 18:34-48 and 44:1-3. Verses 10 and 11 suggest that the psalm was written in response to the loss of the land (44:2,3) following the destruction of Jerusalem in 586 B.C. It may have been written before that; but if so, it would have taken on new meaning at this time. In 586, the people were "scattered," and many were taken into exile in Babylon. See the mini-article called "Exile," p. 1541.

44:17 *your covenant:* Parts of the Old Testament interpret the exile in Babylon as the people's punishment for breaking their covenant with God (see the note at 44:9-11). The "covenant" is the one based on the Law (see the note at 25:10).

44:22 *sheep to be slaughtered:* If the people are innocent (44:17-21), then their suffering cannot be punishment. Rather, they suffer for God. This was an understanding of suffering that was very important following the exile (see Isa 53) and later as well. See also Rom 8:36.

44:23 *Awake . . . Why do you sleep:* Psalm 121:3 says that God "will not slumber." But to people who were suffering, it seemed that God was asleep. See also 1 Kgs 18:27.

25 We are brought down to the dust;
our bodies cling to the ground.
26 Rise up and help us;
redeem us because of your unfailing love.

Psalm 45

For the director of music. To ⌞the tune of⌟ "Lilies." Of the Sons of Korah. A *maskil.*[a] A wedding song.

1 My heart is stirred by a noble theme
as I recite my verses for the king;
my tongue is the pen of a skillful writer.

2 You are the most excellent of men
and your lips have been anointed with grace,
since God has blessed you forever.
3 Gird your sword upon your side, O mighty one;
clothe yourself with splendor and majesty.
4 In your majesty ride forth victoriously
in behalf of truth, humility and righteousness;
let your right hand display awesome deeds.
5 Let your sharp arrows pierce the hearts of the king's enemies;
let the nations fall beneath your feet.
6 Your throne, O God, will last for ever and ever;
a scepter of justice will be the scepter of your kingdom.
7 You love righteousness and hate wickedness;
therefore God, your God, has set you above your companions
by anointing you with the oil of joy.
8 All your robes are fragrant with myrrh and aloes and cassia;
from palaces adorned with ivory
the music of the strings makes you glad.
9 Daughters of kings are among your honored women;
at your right hand is the royal bride in gold of Ophir.

10 Listen, O daughter, consider and give ear:
Forget your people and your father's house.
11 The king is enthralled by your beauty;
honor him, for he is your lord.
12 The Daughter of Tyre will come with a gift,[b]
men of wealth will seek your favor.

13 All glorious is the princess within ⌞her chamber⌟;
her gown is interwoven with gold.
14 In embroidered garments she is led to the king;

[a]Title: Probably a literary or musical term [b]12 Or *A Tyrian robe is among the gifts*

45:1 *king:* The psalm was written for a royal wedding (45:9–15).

45:3-5 *Gird your sword upon your side:* As king of the whole universe, God desires justice. It was the job of the earthly king to do the "justice" God wants. This included fighting against the enemies of God and God's people.

45:6,7 *scepter . . . God . . . has set you above your companions:* Israel worshiped only one God, but the people understood the king to be related to God in a special way (see also the note at 21:3-6). As God's chosen one, the king would uphold God's concern for justice.

45:8,9 *myrrh and aloes and cassia . . . ivory . . . gold of Ophir:* Like spices, ivory also was imported and was considered a luxury (1 Kgs 10:18). See the chart called "Spices and Perfumes," p. 1278. Gold from Ophir was considered the very best.

45:12 *Tyre:* See the map on p. 2465. Many luxury items were imported through this important Mediterranean port city.

45:13 *her gown is interwoven with gold:* The gown was probably woven from the finest wool and linen and embroidered with golden threads. No expense would have been spared in making the wedding garments for the bride of the king.

her virgin companions follow her
and are brought to you.
15 They are led in with joy and gladness;
they enter the palace of the king.

16 Your sons will take the place of your fathers;
you will make them princes throughout the land.
17 I will perpetuate your memory through all generations;
therefore the nations will praise you for ever and ever.

Psalm 46

For the director of music. Of the Sons of Korah.
According to *alamoth*.[a] A song.

1 God is our refuge and strength,
an ever-present help in trouble.
2 Therefore we will not fear, though the earth give way
and the mountains fall into the heart of the sea,
3 though its waters roar and foam
and the mountains quake with their surging. *Selah*
4 There is a river whose streams make glad the city of God,
the holy place where the Most High dwells.
5 God is within her, she will not fall;
God will help her at break of day.
6 Nations are in uproar, kingdoms fall;
he lifts his voice, the earth melts.

7 The LORD Almighty is with us;
the God of Jacob is our fortress. *Selah*

8 Come and see the works of the LORD,
the desolations he has brought on the earth.
9 He makes wars cease to the ends of the earth;
he breaks the bow and shatters the spear,
he burns the shields[b] with fire.
10 "Be still, and know that I am God;
I will be exalted among the nations,
I will be exalted in the earth."

11 The LORD Almighty is with us;
the God of Jacob is our fortress. *Selah*

Psalm 47

For the director of music. Of the Sons of Korah. A psalm.

1 Clap your hands, all you nations;
shout to God with cries of joy.
2 How awesome is the LORD Most High,
the great King over all the earth!

[a]Title: Probably a musical term [b]9 Or *chariots*

45:16,17 *Your sons will take the place of your fathers . . . all generations:* See the notes on p. 1024 and at 45:6,7.

46:1 *refuge:* See the notes at 11:1 and 18:46.

46:4 *a river whose streams:* The river is a symbol of life (see Ezek 47:1-12; Rev 22:1-12).

46:6,7 *the earth melts . . . LORD Almighty:* The word "melts" does not mean destruction. Instead, it suggests that the whole world realizes the extent of God's power and its own powerlessness by comparison.

The title "Almighty" often is used for God when the ark of the covenant is mentioned. It refers to God's rule over all creation. The ark was kept in the temple in Jerusalem and was understood to be God's earthly throne (see 46:11 and the note at 132:6-8).

46:7 *Jacob:* See the note at 22:23.

46:9 *makes wars cease:* It is God's intention that all nations live in peace. This is possible because God rules the world from his throne (the temple) in Jerusalem (46:4,5). See Isa 2:1-4; Mic 4:1-4; and the note at 18:34-48. In fact, the last part of the name "Jerusalem" is similar to the Hebrew word for "peace."

47:2 *LORD Most High . . . great King over all the earth:* See the note at 18:13. God's universal rule is a major idea in the psalms, and it is especially celebrated in this psalm. See also the notes at 8:1 and 9:8,9; and the note on p. 1024.

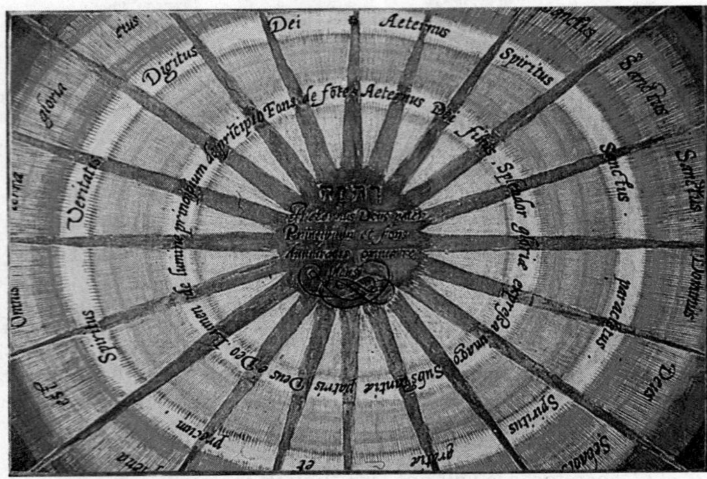

The Glory of God by Matthäus Merian, 1630. Praise is an important theme in many psalms. The *Tetragrammaton,* the four Hebrew letters that spell out the holy name of God, is found in the center of the sun in this hand-colored engraving. Hymns of praise to God are written in Latin in the circles that surround the sun. Psalms 46 and 48 are fine examples of psalms that try to express God's glory and majesty.

47:4 *Jacob:* See the note at 22:23.

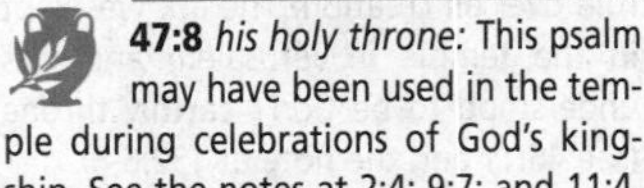

47:8 *his holy throne:* This psalm may have been used in the temple during celebrations of God's kingship. See the notes at 2:4; 9:7; and 11:4.

47:9 *God of Abraham:* God chose Abraham to be the father of his people (Gen 12:1-3). See also the note at 22:23 and the mini-article called "Abraham," p. 2254.

47:9 *the kings of the earth belong to God:* See the note at 46:9.

48:1,2 *city of our God, his holy mountain . . . Mount Zion:* See the notes at 2:6 and 15:1. Like Psalm 46, this psalm celebrates Jerusalem as the place where God rules.

47:3 Ps 18:47.

3 He subdued nations under us,
peoples under our feet.
4 He chose our inheritance for us,
the pride of Jacob, whom he loved. *Selah*

5 God has ascended amid shouts of joy,
the LORD amid the sounding of trumpets.
6 Sing praises to God, sing praises;
sing praises to our King, sing praises.
7 For God is the King of all the earth;
sing to him a psalm[a] of praise.
8 God reigns over the nations;
God is seated on his holy throne.
9 The nobles of the nations assemble
as the people of the God of Abraham,
for the kings[b] of the earth belong to God;
he is greatly exalted.

Psalm 48

A song. A psalm of the Sons of Korah.

1 Great is the LORD, and most worthy of praise,
in the city of our God, his holy mountain.

[a]7 Or *a maskil* (probably a literary or musical term) [b]9 Or *shields*

2 It is beautiful in its loftiness,
the joy of the whole earth.
Like the utmost heights of Zaphon[a] is Mount Zion,
the[b] city of the Great King.
3 God is in her citadels;
he has shown himself to be her fortress.

4 When the kings joined forces,
when they advanced together,
5 they saw ⌞her⌟ and were astounded;
they fled in terror.
6 Trembling seized them there,
pain like that of a woman in labor.
7 You destroyed them like ships of Tarshish
shattered by an east wind.

8 As we have heard,
so have we seen
in the city of the LORD Almighty,
in the city of our God:
God makes her secure forever. *Selah*

9 Within your temple, O God,
we meditate on your unfailing love.
10 Like your name, O God,
your praise reaches to the ends of the earth;
your right hand is filled with righteousness.
11 Mount Zion rejoices,
the villages of Judah are glad
because of your judgments.

12 Walk about Zion, go around her,
count her towers,
13 consider well her ramparts,
view her citadels,
that you may tell of them to the next generation.
14 For this God is our God for ever and ever;
he will be our guide even to the end.

Psalm 49

For the director of music. Of the Sons of Korah. A psalm.

1 Hear this, all you peoples;
listen, all who live in this world,
2 both low and high,
rich and poor alike:
3 My mouth will speak words of wisdom;
the utterance from my heart will give understanding.

[a]2 *Zaphon* can refer to a sacred mountain or the direction north. [b]2 Or *earth, / Mount Zion, on the northern side / of the*

48:2 *Great King:* See the note on p. 1024. See also Matt 5:35.

48:4-8 *kings . . . advanced . . . secure forever:* Jerusalem and its people did withstand many attacks by enemy armies and even destruction by the Babylonians (586 B.C.). Still, the people believed that the city would be "secure forever" as the place where God rules.

48:8 *LORD Almighty:* See the note at 46:6, 7.

48:11 *Mount Zion . . . Judah:* In this passage Mount Zion means Jerusalem (see the note at 2:6). Following the death of King Solomon, Israel split into two kingdoms. The northern kingdom was called Israel. The southern kingdom was called Judah after one of the twelve sons of Jacob. See also the mini-article called "Israel," p. 264.

48:11 *your judgments:* A main responsibility of kings was to establish justice. See the note at 9:8, 9.

48:12-14 *Walk about Zion:* The psalm may have been originally used by people when they visited Jerusalem. See also Ps 84 and 122. Experiencing the city put people in touch with the city's God (see 48:9,10).

49:3,4 *wisdom . . . proverb:* Unlike most psalms, this one is neither a prayer nor a song of praise. Instead, it teaches a lesson by exploring the question of poverty and wealth. Its message is similar to sayings found in other books of Hebrew Wisdom (for example, see Job 22:25; Prov 11:28; Eccl 5:10-17).

49:4 *the harp:* See the note at 33:2. The lesson could have been taught in the setting of worship.

49:7-9 *redeem the life of another:* In some situations, life could be "redeemed" (Exod 13:11-13; 21:29-31), but never in the sense that people won't someday die (49:9,12,19, 20). See also the mini-article called "Redeemer (Redemption)," p. 995.

49:10-12 *foolish and the senseless alike perish:* Wise and foolish, rich and poor—all people die. For people in ancient Israel, death was considered the end of existence (see the notes at 6:5 and 9:13).

49:15 *redeem my life from the grave:* This verse suggests a difference between what will happen to fools (49:13, 14) and to the psalmist. It is not clear if the psalmist is talking about being saved from something that might bring about his death, or if he is talking about living with God after death. See the notes at 9:13 and 16:10.

49:20 *perish:* The Hebrew of 49:20 differs from 49:12. This verse suggests that people "without understanding" die like animals. Those who "understand" will still die, but they know that God's power is greater than the power of death (49:15).

4 I will turn my ear to a proverb;
with the harp I will expound my riddle:

5 Why should I fear when evil days come,
when wicked deceivers surround me—
6 those who trust in their wealth
and boast of their great riches?
7 No man can redeem the life of another
or give to God a ransom for him—
8 the ransom for a life is costly,
no payment is ever enough—
9 that he should live on forever
and not see decay.

10 For all can see that wise men die;
the foolish and the senseless alike perish
and leave their wealth to others.
11 Their tombs will remain their houses[a] forever,
their dwellings for endless generations,
though they had[b] named lands after themselves.

12 But man, despite his riches, does not endure;
he is[c] like the beasts that perish.

13 This is the fate of those who trust in themselves,
and of their followers, who approve
their sayings. *Selah*
14 Like sheep they are destined for the grave,[d]
and death will feed on them.
The upright will rule over them in the morning;
their forms will decay in the grave,[d]
far from their princely mansions.
15 But God will redeem my life[e] from the grave;
he will surely take me to himself. *Selah*

16 Do not be overawed when a man grows rich,
when the splendor of his house increases;
17 for he will take nothing with him when he dies,
his splendor will not descend with him.
18 Though while he lived he counted himself
blessed—
and men praise you when you prosper—
19 he will join the generation of his fathers,
who will never see the light ⌞of life⌟.

20 A man who has riches without understanding
is like the beasts that perish.

[a]**11** Septuagint and Syriac; Hebrew *In their thoughts their houses will remain*
[b]**11** Or / *for they have* [c]**12** Hebrew; Septuagint and Syriac read verse 12 the same as verse 20. [d]**14** Hebrew *Sheol*; also in verse 15 [e]**15** Or *soul*

Psalm 50

A psalm of Asaph.

1 The Mighty One, God, the LORD,
speaks and summons the earth
from the rising of the sun to the place where it sets.
2 From Zion, perfect in beauty,
God shines forth.
3 Our God comes and will not be silent;
a fire devours before him,
and around him a tempest rages.
4 He summons the heavens above,
and the earth, that he may judge his people:
5 "Gather to me my consecrated ones,
who made a covenant with me by sacrifice."
6 And the heavens proclaim his righteousness,
for God himself is judge. *Selah*

7 "Hear, O my people, and I will speak,
O Israel, and I will testify against you:
I am God, your God.
8 I do not rebuke you for your sacrifices
or your burnt offerings, which are ever before me.
9 I have no need of a bull from your stall
or of goats from your pens,
10 for every animal of the forest is mine,
and the cattle on a thousand hills.
11 I know every bird in the mountains,
and the creatures of the field are mine.
12 If I were hungry I would not tell you,
for the world is mine, and all that is in it.
13 Do I eat the flesh of bulls
or drink the blood of goats?
14 Sacrifice thank offerings to God,
fulfill your vows to the Most High,
15 and call upon me in the day of trouble;
I will deliver you, and you will honor me."

16 But to the wicked, God says:

"What right have you to recite my laws
or take my covenant on your lips?
17 You hate my instruction
and cast my words behind you.
18 When you see a thief, you join with him;
you throw in your lot with adulterers.
19 You use your mouth for evil
and harness your tongue to deceit.
20 You speak continually against your brother
and slander your own mother's son.

50 Title *Asaph:* Asaph was from the tribe of Levi and was appointed by David to provide music and lead worship at the tabernacle and later at the temple (1 Chr 6:39-43; 16:4-7, 37). See also the note at 39 Title.

50:2,3 *a tempest:* God's appearances on earth are often described as a storm (Exod 19:16-18). God also appears in fire (Exod 3:2-4; 13:21, 22). See also the note at 18:7-15.

50:4,5 *judge his people . . . covenant:* As ruler of the world, God is concerned with justice (see the note at 9:8, 9). When God's people do not do God's will, they are called to account. The "covenant" here recalls Exodus 24:1-8, the ceremony where the people agree to obey God and live according to God's Law. See also the mini-articles called "Covenants (Agreements)," p. 386, and "Day of the LORD," p. 1727.

50:7-14 *my people . . . your sacrifices:* Here, God speaks directly to the people who have misunderstood the purpose of sacrifices. The people thought that God needed their "sacrifices" (50:8) for food (50:12,13), but God corrects this point of view. God wants thankful hearts, honesty, and loyalty (50:23). See also the notes at 40:6 and 51:16,17.

50:16-22 *the wicked . . . What right have you to recite my laws:* The wicked pretend to keep the covenant (obey God's Law), but their lives show that they don't really honor God or care for others. They will receive punishment from God (50:22). See also the mini-article called "Enemies (The Wicked)," p. 1084.

He who sacrifices thank offerings honors me, and he prepares the way so that I may show him the salvation of God.
Ps 50:23

51 Title *Nathan . . . Bathsheba:* David plotted to have Uriah the Hittite killed in battle so he could marry Uriah's wife Bathsheba who was already pregnant with David's child (2 Sam 11:1—12:15). David tried to hide his sin, but Nathan, the prophet, made it clear that God knew what David had done.

51:7 *hyssop:* This is a small bush with bunches of small, white flowers used to sprinkle blood or water in various ceremonies (Exod 12:22; Lev 14:49-52; Num 19:17, 18). Here, it is used to symbolize being cleansed from sin.

51:11 *Holy Spirit:* God's Spirit can create new things (51:10; see also Gen 1:2). Here the Spirit is God's enduring presence. See the mini-article called "Holy Spirit," p. 2082.

51:12-14 *Restore to me the joy of your salvation . . . God who saves me:* Joy or happiness comes from turning to God and being open to God's way (the Law; 51:13). See also the notes at 1:1,2 and 32:1,2. God "saves" from physical danger and also by forgiving sins. See also the mini-article called "Salvation," p. 2021.

51:16,17 *Offerings . . . broken spirit:* Offerings and sacrifices were to be a regular part of worship at the temple (51:19). But as the psalmists and prophets recognize, they are to be symbols of the worshipers' humility and gratitude, not the sole content of worship. See the notes at 40:6 and 50:7-14.

51:4 Luke 15:21; Rom 3:4.

21 These things you have done and I kept silent;
you thought I was altogether[a] like you.
But I will rebuke you
and accuse you to your face.

22 "Consider this, you who forget God,
or I will tear you to pieces, with none to rescue:
23 He who sacrifices thank offerings honors me,
and he prepares the way
so that I may show him[b] the salvation of God."

Psalm 51

For the director of music. A psalm of David. When the prophet Nathan came to him after David had committed adultery with Bathsheba.

1 Have mercy on me, O God,
according to your unfailing love;
according to your great compassion
blot out my transgressions.
2 Wash away all my iniquity
and cleanse me from my sin.

3 For I know my transgressions,
and my sin is always before me.
4 Against you, you only, have I sinned
and done what is evil in your sight,
so that you are proved right when you speak
and justified when you judge.
5 Surely I was sinful at birth,
sinful from the time my mother conceived me.
6 Surely you desire truth in the inner parts[c];
you teach[d] me wisdom in the inmost place.

7 Cleanse me with hyssop, and I will be clean;
wash me, and I will be whiter than snow.
8 Let me hear joy and gladness;
let the bones you have crushed rejoice.
9 Hide your face from my sins
and blot out all my iniquity.

10 Create in me a pure heart, O God,
and renew a steadfast spirit within me.
11 Do not cast me from your presence
or take your Holy Spirit from me.
12 Restore to me the joy of your salvation
and grant me a willing spirit, to sustain me.

[a]21 Or *thought the 'I AM' was* [b]23 Or *and to him who considers his way / I will show* [c]6 The meaning of the Hebrew for this phrase is uncertain. [d]6 Or *you desired . . . ; / you taught*

13 Then I will teach transgressors your ways,
and sinners will turn back to you.
14 Save me from bloodguilt, O God,
the God who saves me,
and my tongue will sing of your righteousness.
15 O Lord, open my lips,
and my mouth will declare your praise.
16 You do not delight in sacrifice, or I would bring it;
you do not take pleasure in burnt offerings.
17 The sacrifices of God are[a] a broken spirit;
a broken and contrite heart,
O God, you will not despise.

18 In your good pleasure make Zion prosper;
build up the walls of Jerusalem.
19 Then there will be righteous sacrifices,
whole burnt offerings to delight you;
then bulls will be offered on your altar.

Psalm 52

For the director of music. A *maskil*[b] of David.
When Doeg the Edomite had gone to Saul and told him:
"David has gone to the house of Ahimelech."

1 Why do you boast of evil, you mighty man?
Why do you boast all day long,
you who are a disgrace in the eyes of God?
2 Your tongue plots destruction;
it is like a sharpened razor,
you who practice deceit.
3 You love evil rather than good,
falsehood rather than speaking the truth. *Selah*
4 You love every harmful word,
O you deceitful tongue!

5 Surely God will bring you down to everlasting ruin:
He will snatch you up and tear you from your tent;
he will uproot you from the land of the
living. *Selah*
6 The righteous will see and fear;
they will laugh at him, saying,
7 "Here now is the man
who did not make God his stronghold
but trusted in his great wealth
and grew strong by destroying others!"

8 But I am like an olive tree
flourishing in the house of God;

a17 Or *My sacrifice, O God, is* **b**Title: Probably a literary or musical term

51:18 *Zion . . . build up the walls of Jerusalem:* See the notes at 2:6 and 15:1. Verses 18 and 19 may have been added to the psalm after the destruction of Jerusalem in 586 B.C. and before the rebuilding of its walls was completed in about 445 B.C. See the article called "After the Exile: God's People Return to Judea," p. 931.

52 Title *Doeg . . . Saul . . . David . . . Ahimelech:* Doeg the Edomite was one of King Saul's army officers. While trying to help Saul capture David, Doeg killed Ahimelech and many of Israel's priests and their families (1 Sam 22:9-19). The Edomites were descendants of Esau, Jacob's brother (Gen 36:1, 9-14, 40-43). The nation of Edom is usually described in the Bible as an enemy of Israel (Num 24:18; 1 Sam 14:47,48; 2 Sam 8:13,14). See the map on p. 2467. David entered the court of King Saul after defeating the Philistine giant Goliath in combat (1 Sam 17:55—18:5). He became king of Israel after Saul died and is remembered as Israel's greatest king. For more, see the mini-article called "David," p. 1028.

52:1-4 *you mighty man:* This psalm is unusual because here the psalmist speaks not to God but to the wicked.

52:5 *God will bring you down:* God acts for the sake of justice. See the note at 3:5-8. By opposing God, the wicked are responsible for their own destruction.

52:7 *trusted in his great wealth:* This is what the wicked often do (49:5, 6).

52:8 *olive tree:* Olive trees live a long time, and even when cut down, they sprout from the root. They are a good symbol for people whose foundation for life is their trust in God's love. Such people are the opposite of the wicked who have no roots (52:5). See also 1:3; 92:12-14.

52:8 *house of God:* This means the tabernacle and, later, the temple. See the notes at 5:7 (your house) and 26:8.

Giving Thanks by Horace Pippin, 1942. Giving thanks is one of the key themes of PSALMS. Some psalms give thanks to God for delivering people from their enemies (see Ps 18 and 30); others express the gratitude people feel for God's constant care and goodness (see Ps 23 and 52). "I will praise you forever for what you have done," says the psalmist. "I will praise you in the presence of your saints" (Ps 52:9).

53:1-4,6 *The fool says in his heart:* Psalm 53 is nearly the same as Psalm 14. See especially 14:1-4,7.

53:1-3 Rom 3:10-12.

I trust in God's unfailing love
    for ever and ever.
9 I will praise you forever for what you have done;
    in your name I will hope, for your name is good.
    I will praise you in the presence of your saints.

Psalm 53

For the director of music. According to *mahalath.*[a] A *maskil*[b] of David.

1 The fool says in his heart,
    "There is no God."
They are corrupt, and their ways are vile;
    there is no one who does good.

2 God looks down from heaven
    on the sons of men
to see if there are any who understand,
    any who seek God.
3 Everyone has turned away,
    they have together become corrupt;
there is no one who does good,
    not even one.

4 Will the evildoers never learn—
    those who devour my people as men eat bread
    and who do not call on God?

[a]Title: Probably a musical term [b]Title: Probably a literary or musical term

5 There they were, overwhelmed with dread,
where there was nothing to dread.
God scattered the bones of those who attacked you;
you put them to shame, for God despised them.

6 Oh, that salvation for Israel would come out of Zion!
When God restores the fortunes of his people,
let Jacob rejoice and Israel be glad!

Psalm 54

For the director of music. With stringed instruments.
A *maskil*[a] of David. When the Ziphites had gone to Saul
and said, "Is not David hiding among us?"

1 Save me, O God, by your name;
vindicate me by your might.
2 Hear my prayer, O God;
listen to the words of my mouth.

3 Strangers are attacking me;
ruthless men seek my life—
men without regard for God. *Selah*
4 Surely God is my help;
the Lord is the one who sustains me.

5 Let evil recoil on those who slander me;
in your faithfulness destroy them.

6 I will sacrifice a freewill offering to you;
I will praise your name, O LORD,
for it is good.
7 For he has delivered me from all my troubles,
and my eyes have looked in triumph on my foes.

Psalm 55

For the director of music. With stringed instruments.
A *maskil*[a] of David.

1 Listen to my prayer, O God,
do not ignore my plea;
2 hear me and answer me.
My thoughts trouble me and I am distraught
3 at the voice of the enemy,
at the stares of the wicked;
for they bring down suffering upon me
and revile me in their anger.

4 My heart is in anguish within me;
the terrors of death assail me.

[a]Title: Probably a literary or musical term

53:5 *scattered the bones:* See the note at 52:5.

53:6 *salvation for Israel would come out of Zion:* This is probably a cry for God to come from his home on Zion to save Israel. See the note at 14:7.

54 Title *Ziphites . . . Saul:* Like Doeg (52 Title), the people of Ziph tried to help King Saul kill David (1 Sam 23:19; 26:1). See also the mini-article called "David," p. 1028.

54:1 *Save me . . . vindicate me:* The psalmist asks God to defend and save him. See the notes at 26:1,2 and 51:12-14.

54:3 *ruthless men:* This is another name for the enemies (54:5,7). See also 38:12; 40:14.

54:5 *those who slander me:* See the mini-article called "Enemies (The Wicked)," p. 1084.

54:5 *destroy them:* See the notes at 3:5-8; 5:10-12; and 52:5.

54:6 *sacrifice a freewill offering:* The prayers for help often end with a promise (see the note at 22:24-26). A "freewill offering" was meant to show gratitude. See the notes at 4:5; 27:6; and 40:6.

55 Title *stringed instruments:* See the note at 33:2.

55:3 *enemy . . . wicked:* In this prayer for help, the enemies include the psalmist's closest friend (see the note at 55:13,20). But the problems mentioned in the prayer go beyond the personal. The city is filled with wicked people as well (see 55:9,10 and note). See the mini-article called "Enemies (The Wicked)," p. 1084.

55:9-11 *the city:* The "city" may be Jerusalem, but this is not certain. The concern about a violent and troubled city makes the psalm apply to many places and times. The prophets often warned that the corrupt leaders and wealthy people who cheated the poor would lead Jerusalem and the people of Judah to destruction (Isa 1:21-23; 3:10-15; Jer 5:7-13; Hab 1:2-4; 2:5-17). Similar concerns were raised against Samaria, the capital of the northern kingdom (Israel); see Hos 8:5, 14; Amos 3:9-12; 4:1-3.

5 Fear and trembling have beset me;
horror has overwhelmed me.
6 I said, "Oh, that I had the wings of a dove!
I would fly away and be at rest—
7 I would flee far away
and stay in the desert; *Selah*
8 I would hurry to my place of shelter,
far from the tempest and storm."

9 Confuse the wicked, O Lord, confound their speech,
for I see violence and strife in the city.
10 Day and night they prowl about on its walls;
malice and abuse are within it.
11 Destructive forces are at work in the city;
threats and lies never leave its streets.

ENEMIES (THE WICKED)

It is clear from the very beginning of PSALMS that both God and God's people have enemies. In Psalm 1, they are called "sinners" (Ps 1:1, 5) and "the wicked" (Ps 1:6). In Psalm 2, it is "the nations," "the peoples," and "the kings of the earth" who oppose God and God's purposes (Ps 2:1, 2). Psalm 3, the first prayer for help in PSALMS, begins, "O LORD, how many are my foes!" Almost all the prayers for help mention enemies, although other names for them are often used: "arrogant" (Ps 5:5), those "who do evil" (Ps 6:8), "ruthless men" (Ps 54:3), "liars" (Ps 63:11), and so on.

It is not always clear exactly who the enemies are or why they oppose God's people. Sometimes, they seem to make false accusations about the psalmist (Ps 7:3-5). At other times, they seem to be neighbors who are trying to take advantage of the psalmist's troubles in any way they can (Ps 55:12,13). At still other times, the enemies are other nations who oppose God's people (Ps 9:19, 20; 44:5). By including situations in David's life in the titles of some psalms, the collectors of the psalms suggest a way of understanding some of the enemies. See the mini-article called "David," p. 1028. Because it is not always obvious who the psalm writers are identifying as enemies, it is easy for the modern readers to use their imagination to suggest who best fills this role. Even so, the important thing to remember is that enemies are those people and forces who have set themselves against God, God's principles, and God's people.

What is clear about the enemies or the wicked is that they are selfish. They pursue happiness not by looking to God, but rather by trying to get what they want. They show no responsibility to God or to other people (Ps 10:3-11). Unfortunately, this suggests that most people are sometimes, if not most of the time, among the wicked (see the notes at Ps 119:176; 130:1-4).

The psalmists often pray for revenge as they ask God to punish their enemies. Such prayers should also be heard as prayers for justice. For things to be set right for victims, God must oppose oppressors (see the note at Ps 3:5-8).

It is striking to realize that God has enemies. This means that God does not force people to do his will. This in turn explains why the wicked sometimes succeed in opposing God and hurting God's people (Ps 73:3-11). The enemies' ultimate punishment is that they cut themselves off from God (Ps 28:4, 5). See also the notes at Ps 5:10-12; 22:3; and 37:39,40.

12 If an enemy were insulting me,
I could endure it;
if a foe were raising himself against me,
I could hide from him.
13 But it is you, a man like myself,
my companion, my close friend,
14 with whom I once enjoyed sweet fellowship
as we walked with the throng at the house of God.

15 Let death take my enemies by surprise;
let them go down alive to the grave,[a]
for evil finds lodging among them.

16 But I call to God,
and the LORD saves me.
17 Evening, morning and noon
I cry out in distress,
and he hears my voice.
18 He ransoms me unharmed
from the battle waged against me,
even though many oppose me.
19 God, who is enthroned forever,
will hear them and afflict them— *Selah*
men who never change their ways
and have no fear of God.

20 My companion attacks his friends;
he violates his covenant.
21 His speech is smooth as butter,
yet war is in his heart;
his words are more soothing than oil,
yet they are drawn swords.

22 Cast your cares on the LORD
and he will sustain you;
he will never let the righteous fall.
23 But you, O God, will bring down the wicked
into the pit of corruption;
bloodthirsty and deceitful men
will not live out half their days.

But as for me, I trust in you.

Psalm 56

For the director of music. To ⌞the tune of⌟ "A Dove on Distant Oaks." Of David. A *miktam.*[b] When the Philistines had seized him in Gath.

1 Be merciful to me, O God, for men hotly pursue me;
all day long they press their attack.

[a]**15** Hebrew *Sheol* [b]Title: Probably a literary or musical term

55:13,20 *companion, my close friend . . . violates his covenant:* In several prayers for help, friends and neighbors turn out to be enemies (31:11; 38:11; 88:8,18).

55:14 *house of God:* Meaning the tabernacle and temple (see the notes at 5:7, your house, and 23:6).

55:15 *go down alive to the grave:* See the note at 9:13. The psalmist may be thinking of what happened to Korah and others who were enemies of Moses and God (Num 16:30-33).

55:18 *the battle:* This and the mention of "drawn swords" in 55:21 suggest a military setting for the psalm. But the language also may be a symbol for the violence the psalmist experiences and sees all around him.

55:19 *enthroned forever:* The psalmists regularly say that God rules or that God is King, even when the enemies seem to be in control. See the note at 22:3 and the note on p. 1024.

5:22,23 *he will never let the righteous fall . . . pit of corruption:* The confidence that God will "never let the righteous fall" means that the psalmist does not let suffering separate himself from God. The "pit of corruption" refers to the world of the dead (see the note at 55:15).

56 Title *David . . . Philistines . . . Gath:* David ran to the Philistine city of Gath to get away from Saul (1 Sam 21:10-15). For Gath, see the map on p. 2465. The Philistines who lived to the west of Judah were traditional enemies of Israel from before the time of David and continued to be enemies long after David's death.

56:1-4 *men hotly pursue me . . . in God I trust:* See the note at 56 Title. Considering the threat from the enemies, the psalmist should be "afraid." But his trust in God is greater than his fear (see also 56:11). See also the note at 31:19-22.

56:8 *in your record:* This is a way of saying that God knows and cares about the psalmist. See also the note at 40:7.

56:13 *light of life:* See the note at 18:28. The psalmist is confident that God will protect him from "stumbling" if he keeps his promises to God (56:12), probably meaning obeying God's Law and remaining faithful to God alone.

57 Title *the cave:* This refers to another example of the jealous King Saul trying to find David (see 1 Sam 22:1, 2; 24:1-22).

57:1 *the shadow of your wings:* See the note at 17:8.

57:3 *sends from heaven:* God sees everything from "his heavenly throne" (11:4), and then acts to oppose "the wicked" (11:6). See also the description in 18:6-19 of God coming down from heaven to help the king.

56:4 Isa 41:10.

2 My slanderers pursue me all day long;
many are attacking me in their pride.

3 When I am afraid,
I will trust in you.
4 In God, whose word I praise,
in God I trust; I will not be afraid.
What can mortal man do to me?

5 All day long they twist my words;
they are always plotting to harm me.
6 They conspire, they lurk,
they watch my steps,
eager to take my life.

7 On no account let them escape;
in your anger, O God, bring down the nations.
8 Record my lament;
list my tears on your scroll[a]—
are they not in your record?

9 Then my enemies will turn back
when I call for help.
By this I will know that God is for me.
10 In God, whose word I praise,
in the LORD, whose word I praise—
11 in God I trust; I will not be afraid.
What can man do to me?

12 I am under vows to you, O God;
I will present my thank offerings to you.
13 For you have delivered me[b] from death
and my feet from stumbling,
that I may walk before God
in the light of life.[c]

Psalm 57

For the director of music. ⌊To the tune of⌋ "Do Not Destroy." Of David. A *miktam*.[d] When he had fled from Saul into the cave.

1 Have mercy on me, O God, have mercy on me,
for in you my soul takes refuge.
I will take refuge in the shadow of your wings
until the disaster has passed.

2 I cry out to God Most High,
to God, who fulfills ⌊his purpose⌋ for me.
3 He sends from heaven and saves me,
rebuking those who hotly pursue me; *Selah*
God sends his love and his faithfulness.

[a]**8** Or / *put my tears in your wineskin* [b]**13** Or *my soul* [c]**13** Or *the land of the living* [d]Title: Probably a literary or musical term

4 I am in the midst of lions;
I lie among ravenous beasts—
men whose teeth are spears and arrows,
whose tongues are sharp swords.

5 Be exalted, O God, above the heavens;
let your glory be over all the earth.

6 They spread a net for my feet—
I was bowed down in distress.
They dug a pit in my path—
but they have fallen into it themselves. *Selah*

7 My heart is steadfast, O God,
my heart is steadfast;
I will sing and make music.
8 Awake, my soul!
Awake, harp and lyre!
I will awaken the dawn.

9 I will praise you, O Lord, among the nations;
I will sing of you among the peoples.
10 For great is your love, reaching to the heavens;
your faithfulness reaches to the skies.

11 Be exalted, O God, above the heavens;
let your glory be over all the earth.

Psalm 58

For the director of music. ⌊To the tune of⌋ "Do Not Destroy." Of David. A *miktam*.[a]

1 Do you rulers indeed speak justly?
Do you judge uprightly among men?
2 No, in your heart you devise injustice,
and your hands mete out violence on the earth.
3 Even from birth the wicked go astray;
from the womb they are wayward and speak lies.
4 Their venom is like the venom of a snake,
like that of a cobra that has stopped its ears,
5 that will not heed the tune of the charmer,
however skillful the enchanter may be.

6 Break the teeth in their mouths, O God;
tear out, O LORD, the fangs of the lions!
7 Let them vanish like water that flows away;
when they draw the bow, let their arrows be
blunted.
8 Like a slug melting away as it moves along,
like a stillborn child, may they not see the sun.

[a]Title: Probably a literary or musical term

57:5 *your glory be over all the earth:* See the note at 26:8.

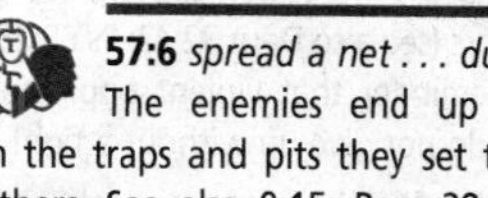

57:6 *spread a net . . . dug a pit:* The enemies end up caught in the traps and pits they set to catch others. See also 9:15; Prov 28:10; and the note at 7:14-16.

57:8 *awaken the dawn:* This phrase may be a poetic way of saying that the psalmist will get an early start or sing praises early in the morning.

58:5 *tune of the charmer:* Snake-charming was common in the ancient world (see also Eccl 10:11). Poisonous cobra snakes were and still are tamed by charmers. The word for "charmer" means "controller of the tongue." This may refer to the snake's tongue or to how the charmer used his voice to control the snake and make it move.

58:6-9 *Break the teeth in their mouths . . . swept away:* This prayer for personal revenge also seeks justice (58:11). See the notes at 3:5-8 and 5:10-12. Dried thorns make a fire that burns hot very quickly.

58:10 *bathe their feet in the blood of the wicked:* This violent picture is a symbol for the defeat of oppressors (see also Deut 32:42; Ps 68:23). It is a reminder that violent oppressors (58:1-5) do not give up without a fight.

58:11 *the righteous still are rewarded:* The Hebrew word for "are rewarded" means "are fruitful." If there is a "reward," it is the experience of being protected by God.

58:11 *a God who judges the earth:* The psalm ends as it began by talking about justice, the goal of God's rule. See the note at 9:8, 9.

59 Title *sent men to watch David's house:* This probably refers to the night Saul tried to kill David (1 Sam 19:9-11).

59:1-4 *protect me from those who rise up against me:* See also the note at 3:1, 2 and the mini-article called "Enemies (The Wicked)," p. 1084.

59:5 *the nations . . . wicked traitors:* The "wicked" are not always individuals (see the note at 44:5).

59:11-13 *do not kill them . . . my people will forget:* The psalmist wants the enemies to be left in ruin but not wiped out. Then his own people would see their enemies' humiliation and remember the power of their God. See also the note at 58:6-9.

59:11 *our shield:* Ancient warriors relied on shields for protection in close combat. They were made of wood covered by leather or metal. In this psalm, God is called a shield because of the protection he gives to his people.

9 Before your pots can feel ⌊the heat of⌋ the thorns—
whether they be green or dry—the wicked will be
swept away.[a]
10 The righteous will be glad when they are avenged,
when they bathe their feet in the blood of the wicked.
11 Then men will say,
"Surely the righteous still are rewarded;
surely there is a God who judges the earth."

Psalm 59

For the director of music. ⌊To the tune of⌋ "Do Not Destroy." Of David. A *miktam*.[b] When Saul had sent men to watch David's house in order to kill him.

1 Deliver me from my enemies, O God;
protect me from those who rise up against me.
2 Deliver me from evildoers
and save me from bloodthirsty men.

3 See how they lie in wait for me!
Fierce men conspire against me
for no offense or sin of mine, O LORD.
4 I have done no wrong, yet they are ready to attack me.
Arise to help me; look on my plight!
5 O LORD God Almighty, the God of Israel,
rouse yourself to punish all the nations;
show no mercy to wicked traitors. *Selah*

6 They return at evening,
snarling like dogs,
and prowl about the city.
7 See what they spew from their mouths—
they spew out swords from their lips,
and they say, "Who can hear us?"
8 But you, O LORD, laugh at them;
you scoff at all those nations.
9 O my Strength, I watch for you;
you, O God, are my fortress, 10 my loving God.

God will go before me
and will let me gloat over those who slander me.
11 But do not kill them, O Lord our shield,[c]
or my people will forget.
In your might make them wander about,
and bring them down.
12 For the sins of their mouths,
for the words of their lips,

[a]9 The meaning of the Hebrew for this verse is uncertain. [b]Title: Probably a literary or musical term [c]11 Or *sovereign*

let them be caught in their pride.
For the curses and lies they utter,
13 consume them in wrath,
consume them till they are no more.
Then it will be known to the ends of the earth
that God rules over Jacob. *Selah*

14 They return at evening,
snarling like dogs,
and prowl about the city.
15 They wander about for food
and howl if not satisfied.
16 But I will sing of your strength,
in the morning I will sing of your love;
for you are my fortress,
my refuge in times of trouble.

17 O my Strength, I sing praise to you;
you, O God, are my fortress, my loving God.

Psalm 60

For the director of music. To ⌊the tune of⌋ "The Lily of the Covenant." A *miktam*[a] of David. For teaching. When he fought Aram Naharaim[b] and Aram Zobah,[c] and when Joab returned and struck down twelve thousand Edomites in the Valley of Salt.

1 You have rejected us, O God, and burst forth upon us;
you have been angry—now restore us!
2 You have shaken the land and torn it open;
mend its fractures, for it is quaking.
3 You have shown your people desperate times;
you have given us wine that makes us stagger.

4 But for those who fear you, you have raised a banner
to be unfurled against the bow. *Selah*

5 Save us and help us with your right hand,
that those you love may be delivered.
6 God has spoken from his sanctuary:
"In triumph I will parcel out Shechem
and measure off the Valley of Succoth.
7 Gilead is mine, and Manasseh is mine;
Ephraim is my helmet,
Judah my scepter.
8 Moab is my washbasin,
upon Edom I toss my sandal;
over Philistia I shout in triumph."

[a]Title: Probably a literary or musical term [b]Title: That is, Arameans of Northwest Mesopotamia [c]Title: That is, Arameans of central Syria

59:17 *my loving God:* See the note at 13:5,6.

60 Title *fought Aram . . . Joab . . . Edomites:* The title describes the events of 2 Samuel 8:3-8,13; 10:15-19; 1 Chronicles 18:3-12. "Aram" is another name for Syria, Israel's traditional enemy to the northeast. Joab, David's nephew, was one of David's army commanders. Joab's defeat of the Edomites (see the note at 52 Title) is described in 2 Samuel 8:13; 1 Chronicles 18:12. The "Valley of Salt" probably refers to the area at the southern end of the Dead Sea (see the map on p. 2467).

60:1-3 *You have rejected us, O God . . . desperate times:* This psalm suggests that the people of Israel have been defeated by a foreign nation, perhaps Edom (60:9). The people of Israel experienced attacks by foreign armies and famines caused by drought or enemy invasions. Such things were seen as the LORD's punishment.

60:3 *given us wine that makes us stagger:* Drinking from the LORD's cup of wrath is a common symbol for God's punishment (Jer 25:15-29; Rev 16:19).

60:6-9 *Shechem . . . Edom:* The word from God may have been spoken during a worship service by a priest or prophet. The people have hope, because God controls the land of Israel and the lands of their neighbors. Shechem was in the territory of Manasseh west of the Jordan River. Succoth and Gilead were in the territory of Manasseh east of the Jordan. The Ephraim tribe settled in central Canaan. Its name sometimes stood for the whole northern kingdom. Judah was the name for the entire southern kingdom.

The people of Moab were descended from Lot, the nephew of Abraham. Moab and Israel had been enemies in the past (Num 22:2-11; 2 Sam 8:2,13,14; 2 Kgs 13:20). See also the notes at 52 Title. 137:7. and 56 Title. For all locations, see the map on p. 2464.

I long to dwell in your tent forever and take refuge in the shelter of your wings.
Ps 61:4

60:12 *we will gain the victory:* This prayer for help ends with trust in God. See the note at 13:5, 6.

61:2 *From the ends of the earth:* The psalmist may have been in exile, or this may be his way of symbolizing his distress. See also 42:2-6 and the note at 42:2.

61:2 *rock:* See the note at 18:46.

61:3 *strong tower:* Towers were important features built into the protective walls surrounding many ancient cities. See also the note at 11:1.

61:4 *shelter of your wings:* See the note at 17:8.

61:5,8 *my vows:* The promises of the psalmist probably include trusting in and worshiping God alone. See also the mini-article called "Making Vows," p. 328.

61:6,7 *Increase the days of the king's life . . . protect him:* This prayer for the king's health comes either from the king himself or a representative of the community.

62 Title *Jeduthun:* See the note at 39 Title.

62:2,6,7 *rock . . . fortress:* See the notes at 11:1 and 18:46.

62:3 *How long will you assault a man:* The psalmist is speaking to his enemies.

9 Who will bring me to the fortified city?
Who will lead me to Edom?
10 Is it not you, O God, you who have rejected us
and no longer go out with our armies?
11 Give us aid against the enemy,
for the help of man is worthless.
12 With God we will gain the victory,
and he will trample down our enemies.

Psalm 61

For the director of music. With stringed instruments. Of David.

1 Hear my cry, O God;
listen to my prayer.

2 From the ends of the earth I call to you,
I call as my heart grows faint;
lead me to the rock that is higher than I.
3 For you have been my refuge,
a strong tower against the foe.

4 I long to dwell in your tent forever
and take refuge in the shelter of your wings. *Selah*
5 For you have heard my vows, O God;
you have given me the heritage of those who fear
your name.

6 Increase the days of the king's life,
his years for many generations.
7 May he be enthroned in God's presence forever;
appoint your love and faithfulness to protect him.

8 Then will I ever sing praise to your name
and fulfill my vows day after day.

Psalm 62

For the director of music. For Jeduthun. A psalm of David.

1 My soul finds rest in God alone;
my salvation comes from him.
2 He alone is my rock and my salvation;
he is my fortress, I will never be shaken.

3 How long will you assault a man?
Would all of you throw him down—
this leaning wall, this tottering fence?
4 They fully intend to topple him
from his lofty place;
they take delight in lies.
With their mouths they bless,
but in their hearts they curse. *Selah*

[5] Find rest, O my soul, in God alone;
my hope comes from him.
[6] He alone is my rock and my salvation;
he is my fortress, I will not be shaken.
[7] My salvation and my honor depend on God[a];
he is my mighty rock, my refuge.
[8] Trust in him at all times, O people;
pour out your hearts to him,
for God is our refuge. *Selah*

[9] Lowborn men are but a breath,
the highborn are but a lie;
if weighed on a balance, they are nothing;
together they are only a breath.
[10] Do not trust in extortion
or take pride in stolen goods;
though your riches increase,
do not set your heart on them.

[11] One thing God has spoken,
two things have I heard:
that you, O God, are strong,
[12] and that you, O Lord, are loving.
Surely you will reward each person
according to what he has done.

Psalm 63

A psalm of David. When he was in the Desert of Judah.

[1] O God, you are my God,
earnestly I seek you;
my soul thirsts for you,
my body longs for you,
in a dry and weary land
where there is no water.
[2] I have seen you in the sanctuary
and beheld your power and your glory.
[3] Because your love is better than life,
my lips will glorify you.
[4] I will praise you as long as I live,
and in your name I will lift up my hands.
[5] My soul will be satisfied as with the richest of foods;
with singing lips my mouth will praise you.

[6] On my bed I remember you;
I think of you through the watches of the night.
[7] Because you are my help,
I sing in the shadow of your wings.

[a]7 Or / *God Most High is my salvation and my honor*

One thing God has spoken, two things have I heard: that you, O God, are strong, and that you, O Lord, are loving.
Ps 62:11,12

62:8-10 *Trust in him . . . riches:* The psalmists regularly show their trust in God, even as they suffer (62:3, 4). The wicked regularly trust in themselves or in their wealth (49:5, 6; 52:7).

62:12 *according to what he has done:* See the note at 7:14-16. God's "reward" does not mean a trouble-free life. Instead, it means "rest" (62:5) and protection (62:6, 7) during suffering.

63 Title *in the Desert of Judah:* This may refer either to Saul's attempt to kill David (1 Sam 23:14) or to Absalom's revolt (2 Sam 15–17). See also the notes at 3 Title; 52 Title; 56 Title; 57 Title; 59 Title.

63:7 *shadow of your wings:* See the note at 17:8.

63:11 *the king:* See the note at 61:6,7.

62:12 Job 34:11; Jer 17:10; Matt 16:27; Rom 2:6; Rev 2:23.

64:5,6 *snares:* See the note at 31:4.

64:6 *perfect plan:* Compare to 10:6-13.

64:7,8 *God will shoot them with arrows:* The enemies fail to realize that God also has arrows. God's response aims at establishing justice.

64:10 *rejoice in the Lord:* To find protection in God even while suffering causes rejoicing.

65:1 *Zion:* See the notes at 2:6 and 48:1, 2.

65:1 *our vows will be fulfilled:* The people kept their promises with correct worship, including offering prayers of thanks and bringing gifts and sacrifices.

64:3 Ps 57:4.

8 My soul clings to you;
your right hand upholds me.

9 They who seek my life will be destroyed;
they will go down to the depths of the earth.
10 They will be given over to the sword
and become food for jackals.

11 But the king will rejoice in God;
all who swear by God's name will praise him,
while the mouths of liars will be silenced.

Psalm 64

For the director of music. A psalm of David.

1 Hear me, O God, as I voice my complaint;
protect my life from the threat of the enemy.
2 Hide me from the conspiracy of the wicked,
from that noisy crowd of evildoers.

3 They sharpen their tongues like swords
and aim their words like deadly arrows.
4 They shoot from ambush at the innocent man;
they shoot at him suddenly, without fear.

5 They encourage each other in evil plans,
they talk about hiding their snares;
they say, "Who will see them[a]?"
6 They plot injustice and say,
"We have devised a perfect plan!"
Surely the mind and heart of man are cunning.

7 But God will shoot them with arrows;
suddenly they will be struck down.
8 He will turn their own tongues against them
and bring them to ruin;
all who see them will shake their heads in scorn.

9 All mankind will fear;
they will proclaim the works of God
and ponder what he has done.
10 Let the righteous rejoice in the Lord
and take refuge in him;
let all the upright in heart praise him!

Psalm 65

For the director of music. A psalm of David. A song.

1 Praise awaits[b] you, O God, in Zion;
to you our vows will be fulfilled.

---

[a]5 Or *us* [b]1 Or *befits*; the meaning of the Hebrew for this word is uncertain.

Springtime Blossoms in the Judean Desert. In PSALMS, God is often celebrated as the Creator and Ruler of all things. "You care for the land and water it; you enrich it abundantly," says the psalmist (Ps 65:9). There is no part of creation that God does not nurture. "You crown the year with your bounty, and your carts overflow with abundance. The grasslands of the desert overflow; the hills are clothed with gladness" (Ps 65:11,12).

2 O you who hear prayer,
to you all men will come.
3 When we were overwhelmed by sins,
you forgave[a] our transgressions.
4 Blessed are those you choose
and bring near to live in your courts!
We are filled with the good things of your house,
of your holy temple.

5 You answer us with awesome deeds of righteousness,
O God our Savior,
the hope of all the ends of the earth
and of the farthest seas,
6 who formed the mountains by your power,
having armed yourself with strength,
7 who stilled the roaring of the seas,
the roaring of their waves,
and the turmoil of the nations.
8 Those living far away fear your wonders;
where morning dawns and evening fades
you call forth songs of joy.

9 You care for the land and water it;
you enrich it abundantly.

[a]3 Or *made atonement for*

65:4 *Blessed are those you choose:* As in 32:1,2, God's blessing involves forgiveness. See 65:3 and the notes at 32:1, 2 and 28:8.

65:4 *your house . . . your holy temple:* See the notes at 5:7 and 27:4 . The psalmists often imagine living at or near the temple. For more about the temple in Jerusalem, see the article called "People of the Law: The Religion of Israel," p. 939.

65:5-8 *deeds of righteousness:* Celebrating God's rule over all creation and every nation. A primary purpose of God's rule is "righteousness."

65:9-13 *You care for the land and water it:* At this time Israel's neighbors, the Canaanites, believed that the god Baal sent the rain that made the crops grow. But this psalm says that it is God who sends the rain that brings rich harvests and fertile pastures for sheep and goats to graze in. See also the notes at 18:7-15 and 29:3-9. See also Ps 148.

Shout with joy to God, all the earth! Sing the glory of his name; make his praise glorious!
Ps 66:1,2

66:6 *turned the sea into dry land:* This refers to Hebrew people crossing the Red Sea on dry land after they escaped from Egypt (Exod 14:1—15:21; see also Josh 3:14-17).

66:7 *He rules forever:* God's kingship or rule is a major idea throughout PSALMS (see the note on p. 1024).

66:10-12 *tested us; you refined us like silver:* Gold and silver were melted in a hot fire, which burned off unwanted impurities such as dust. The events recall the troubles faced by the people in the desert after leaving Egypt and before entering Canaan. Those who survived the "testing" would be like the pure silver or gold that remains after being refined by fire. What the people experienced as a testing resulted in the gift of the promised land.

The streams of God are filled with water
to provide the people with grain,
for so you have ordained it.[a]
10 You drench its furrows
and level its ridges;
you soften it with showers
and bless its crops.
11 You crown the year with your bounty,
and your carts overflow with abundance.
12 The grasslands of the desert overflow;
the hills are clothed with gladness.
13 The meadows are covered with flocks
and the valleys are mantled with grain;
they shout for joy and sing.

Psalm 66

For the director of music. A song. A psalm.

1 Shout with joy to God, all the earth!
2 Sing the glory of his name;
make his praise glorious!
3 Say to God, "How awesome are your deeds!
So great is your power
that your enemies cringe before you.
4 All the earth bows down to you;
they sing praise to you,
they sing praise to your name." *Selah*

5 Come and see what God has done,
how awesome his works in man's behalf!
6 He turned the sea into dry land,
they passed through the waters on foot—
come, let us rejoice in him.
7 He rules forever by his power,
his eyes watch the nations—
let not the rebellious rise up against him. *Selah*

8 Praise our God, O peoples,
let the sound of his praise be heard;
9 he has preserved our lives
and kept our feet from slipping.
10 For you, O God, tested us;
you refined us like silver.
11 You brought us into prison
and laid burdens on our backs.
12 You let men ride over our heads;
we went through fire and water,
but you brought us to a place of abundance.

[a]9 Or *for that is how you prepare the land*

13 I will come to your temple with burnt offerings
and fulfill my vows to you—
14 vows my lips promised and my mouth spoke
when I was in trouble.
15 I will sacrifice fat animals to you
and an offering of rams;
I will offer bulls and goats. *Selah*

16 Come and listen, all you who fear God;
let me tell you what he has done for me.
17 I cried out to him with my mouth;
his praise was on my tongue.
18 If I had cherished sin in my heart,
the Lord would not have listened;
19 but God has surely listened
and heard my voice in prayer.
20 Praise be to God,
who has not rejected my prayer
or withheld his love from me!

Psalm 67

For the director of music. With stringed instruments.
A psalm. A song.

1 May God be gracious to us and bless us
and make his face shine upon us, *Selah*
2 that your ways may be known on earth,
your salvation among all nations.

3 May the peoples praise you, O God;
may all the peoples praise you.
4 May the nations be glad and sing for joy,
for you rule the peoples justly
and guide the nations of the earth. *Selah*
5 May the peoples praise you, O God;
may all the peoples praise you.

6 Then the land will yield its harvest,
and God, our God, will bless us.
7 God will bless us,
and all the ends of the earth will fear him.

Psalm 68

For the director of music. Of David. A psalm. A song.

1 May God arise, may his enemies be scattered;
may his foes flee before him.
2 As smoke is blown away by the wind,
may you blow them away;
as wax melts before the fire,
may the wicked perish before God.

66:13-15 *when I was in trouble:* The psalm has been talking about the whole people. But now the psalmist thanks God for a personal deliverance that he understands as a kind of new exodus.

67:1,2 *bless us . . . all nations:* God's blessing means that God provides everything needed for life, including teaching (see the note at 1:1, 2), forgiveness (see 32:1, 2), and material blessings (see 65:9-13; 67:6). When other nations see how God has blessed Israel, they will honor Israel's God. The psalmist also has in mind here the promise that God made to Abraham in Genesis 12:1-3. The blessings that Abraham's descendants receive will make them a blessing to others.

67:4 *rule the peoples justly and guide the nations:* The main purpose of God's rule is to judge fairly, which means to establish justice. See the note at 9:8,9.

67:6 *harvest:* The psalm may have been used originally at worship services during the harvest season.

68:1,2 *may his enemies be scattered:* Moses prays a similar prayer to ask God to lead the people from Sinai to the promised land (Num 10:35), where this journey is recalled in 68:6-18. See also the notes at 18:34-48 and 11:6.

66:13 Ps 22:25; 56:12.

68:3 *be happy:* See the notes at 1:1,2; 32:1,2 and 67:1,2.

68:4 *rides on the clouds:* The Canaanites believed that the god Baal brought rain to make crops grow. But this psalm says that God "rides on the clouds," meaning provides needed rain. See the notes at 18:7-15 and 29:3-9.

68:5 *fatherless . . . widows:* See the notes at 10:14 and 9:8,9. "Widows" are usually mentioned along with "orphans" as people who need God's protection.

68:5 *holy dwelling:* This could mean God's heavenly throne or the temple in Jerusalem, which was considered to be God's house. See the notes at 5:7 (your house) and 11:4.

68:6-8 *leads forth the prisoners:* These verses recall the exodus (see the note at 66:6) and the people's wandering in the desert after leaving Egypt. At Mount Sinai God gave Moses and the people the commandments and laws that they were to live by. See also Exod 19:18.

68:9-14 *inheritance . . . Zalmon:* After forty years of wandering, the people of Israel entered the land of Canaan (their "inheritance"). Verses 12-14 refer to the battles described in JOSHUA and JUDGES. The location of Mount Zalmon is not known.

68:13 *dove . . . silver . . . gold:* This may refer to a valuable object left by the retreating Canaanite armies (68:12). The Canaanite goddess Astarte was represented by a dove. See the mini-article called "Canaanite Gods and Goddesses," p. 469.

68:15,16 *Bashan . . . mountain where God chooses to reign:* See the note at 22:12. The "mountain" refers to Zion; see the notes at 2:6; and 48:1,2.

68:18 *ascended on high:* This refers to Zion, as does "there" later in the verse. God has traveled with the people from Sinai to Zion.

68:18 Eph 4:8.

3 But may the righteous be glad
    and rejoice before God;
    may they be happy and joyful.

4 Sing to God, sing praise to his name,
    extol him who rides on the clouds[a]—
his name is the LORD—
    and rejoice before him.
5 A father to the fatherless, a defender of widows,
    is God in his holy dwelling.
6 God sets the lonely in families,[b]
    he leads forth the prisoners with singing;
    but the rebellious live in a sun-scorched land.

7 When you went out before your people, O God,
    when you marched through the wasteland, *Selah*
8 the earth shook,
    the heavens poured down rain,
before God, the One of Sinai,
    before God, the God of Israel.
9 You gave abundant showers, O God;
    you refreshed your weary inheritance.
10 Your people settled in it,
    and from your bounty, O God, you provided for
        the poor.

11 The Lord announced the word,
    and great was the company of those who
        proclaimed it:
12 "Kings and armies flee in haste;
    in the camps men divide the plunder.
13 Even while you sleep among the campfires,[c]
    the wings of ⌞my⌟ dove are sheathed with silver,
    its feathers with shining gold."
14 When the Almighty[d] scattered the kings in the land,
    it was like snow fallen on Zalmon.

15 The mountains of Bashan are majestic mountains;
    rugged are the mountains of Bashan.
16 Why gaze in envy, O rugged mountains,
    at the mountain where God chooses to reign,
    where the LORD himself will dwell forever?
17 The chariots of God are tens of thousands
    and thousands of thousands;
    the Lord ⌞has come⌟ from Sinai into his
        sanctuary.
18 When you ascended on high,

[a]4 Or / *prepare the way for him who rides through the deserts* [b]6 Or *the desolate in a homeland* [c]13 Or *saddlebags* [d]14 Hebrew *Shaddai*

you led captives in your train;
you received gifts from men,
even from[a] the rebellious—
that you,[b] O LORD God, might dwell there.

19 Praise be to the Lord, to God our Savior,
who daily bears our burdens. *Selah*
20 Our God is a God who saves;
from the Sovereign LORD comes escape from death.

21 Surely God will crush the heads of his enemies,
the hairy crowns of those who go on in their sins.
22 The Lord says, "I will bring them from Bashan;
I will bring them from the depths of the sea,
23 that you may plunge your feet in the blood of your foes,
while the tongues of your dogs have their share."

24 Your procession has come into view, O God,
the procession of my God and King into the sanctuary.
25 In front are the singers, after them the musicians;
with them are the maidens playing tambourines.
26 Praise God in the great congregation;
praise the LORD in the assembly of Israel.
27 There is the little tribe of Benjamin, leading them,
there the great throng of Judah's princes,
and there the princes of Zebulun and of Naphtali.

28 Summon your power, O God[c];
show us your strength, O God, as you have done before.
29 Because of your temple at Jerusalem
kings will bring you gifts.
30 Rebuke the beast among the reeds,
the herd of bulls among the calves of the nations.
Humbled, may it bring bars of silver.
Scatter the nations who delight in war.
31 Envoys will come from Egypt;
Cush[d] will submit herself to God.

32 Sing to God, O kingdoms of the earth,
sing praise to the Lord, *Selah*
33 to him who rides the ancient skies above,
who thunders with mighty voice.
34 Proclaim the power of God,
whose majesty is over Israel,
whose power is in the skies.

a18 Or *gifts for men, / even* **b18** Or *they* **c28** Many Hebrew manuscripts, Septuagint and Syriac; most Hebrew manuscripts *Your God has summoned power for you* **d31** That is, the upper Nile region

68:19,20 *saves . . . escape from death:* Having been rescued from Egypt and other enemies and now settling in the land of promise, the people can celebrate. See also the note at 51:12-14.

68:21-23 *crush the heads of his enemies:* See the notes at 18:34-48 and 58:10.

68:24 *the sanctuary:* God's sanctuary is the "temple at Jerusalem" (68:29). The ceremony described in 68:24-29 is probably a celebration of God's kingship as worshipers entered the temple. See also the note on p. 1024.

68:27 *Benjamin . . . Judah . . . Zebulun . . . Naphtali:* These are four of the twelve tribes of Israel. Perhaps the tribes were to march to the temple in this particular order for the celebration of God's kingship (see the note at 68:24). See also the notes at 7 Title; 48:11 (Judah); and the map on p. 2464.

68:30,31 *beast among the reeds . . . bring bars of silver:* The "beast among the reeds" probably refers to Egypt, which had much marshy land near the Nile River. The prophets of Israel also said that Egypt and Ethiopia and other nations would bring gifts to honor Israel's God (Isa 18:7; 60:4-9; Zeph 3:10).

68:33,34 *rides the ancient skies:* See the note at 68:4.

69:1,2 *the waters . . . sink in the miry depths:* Drowning is a symbol of severe distress, and flooding was a major danger in ancient times and often a symbol of chaos and death. See also 69:14,15 and the note 18:16.

69:4 *hate me without reason:* See the note at 35:19.

69:4 *enemies without cause . . . I did not steal:* In this psalm, "enemies" are part of the threat to the psalmist's life. Here, they seem to have falsely accused the psalmist of stealing.

69:6 *the* L*ORD Almighty:* See the note at 46:6, 7.

69:7 *I endure scorn for your sake:* The psalmist does not view his suffering as punishment. Instead, he suffers for God's sake. This probably explains why parts of the psalm are used in the New Testament to suggest that Jesus lived out the experiences described here (see the notes at 69:9 and 69:21). See also the note at 22:1.

69:8 *stranger to my brothers:* The psalmists often complain about being rejected by those closest to them (see 38:11; 88:8,18). The prophet Jeremiah also complained that his family had rejected him (Jer 12:6).

69:9 *your house:* Loyalty to God's house, the temple (see the note at 5:7), was a sign of loyalty to God. See also John 2:17; Rom 15:3.

69:10 *weep and fast:* See the note at 35:13.

69:11 *sackcloth:* See the note at 30:11 and the illustration on p. 1551.

35 You are awesome, O God, in your sanctuary;
the God of Israel gives power and strength to his people.

Praise be to God!

Psalm 69

For the director of music. To ⌞the tune of⌟ "Lilies." Of David.

1 Save me, O God,
for the waters have come up to my neck.
2 I sink in the miry depths,
where there is no foothold.
I have come into the deep waters;
the floods engulf me.
3 I am worn out calling for help;
my throat is parched.
My eyes fail,
looking for my God.
4 Those who hate me without reason
outnumber the hairs of my head;
many are my enemies without cause,
those who seek to destroy me.
I am forced to restore
what I did not steal.

5 You know my folly, O God;
my guilt is not hidden from you.

6 May those who hope in you
not be disgraced because of me,
O Lord, the LORD Almighty;
may those who seek you
not be put to shame because of me,
O God of Israel.
7 For I endure scorn for your sake,
and shame covers my face.
8 I am a stranger to my brothers,
an alien to my own mother's sons;
9 for zeal for your house consumes me,
and the insults of those who insult you fall on me.
10 When I weep and fast,
I must endure scorn;
11 when I put on sackcloth,
people make sport of me.
12 Those who sit at the gate mock me,
and I am the song of the drunkards.

13 But I pray to you, O LORD,
in the time of your favor;
in your great love, O God,
answer me with your sure salvation.

[14] Rescue me from the mire,
do not let me sink;
deliver me from those who hate me,
from the deep waters.
[15] Do not let the floodwaters engulf me
or the depths swallow me up
or the pit close its mouth over me.
[16] Answer me, O LORD, out of the goodness of
your love;
in your great mercy turn to me.
[17] Do not hide your face from your servant;
answer me quickly, for I am in trouble.
[18] Come near and rescue me;
redeem me because of my foes.

[19] You know how I am scorned, disgraced and shamed;
all my enemies are before you.
[20] Scorn has broken my heart
and has left me helpless;
I looked for sympathy, but there was none,
for comforters, but I found none.
[21] They put gall in my food
and gave me vinegar for my thirst.

[22] May the table set before them become a snare;
may it become retribution and[a] a trap.
[23] May their eyes be darkened so they cannot see,
and their backs be bent forever.
[24] Pour out your wrath on them;
let your fierce anger overtake them.
[25] May their place be deserted;
let there be no one to dwell in their tents.
[26] For they persecute those you wound
and talk about the pain of those you hurt.
[27] Charge them with crime upon crime;
do not let them share in your salvation.
[28] May they be blotted out of the book of life
and not be listed with the righteous.

[29] I am in pain and distress;
may your salvation, O God, protect me.

[30] I will praise God's name in song
and glorify him with thankfursgiving.
[31] This will please the LORD more than an ox,
more than a bull with its horns and hoofs.
[32] The poor will see and be glad—
you who seek God, may your hearts live!

[a]22 Or *snare / and their fellowship become*

69:21 *gall in my food . . . vinegar for my thirst:* Gall is poisonous, symbolizing the deadly threats of the enemies. Vinegar is wine that has gone sour. The writers of the Gospels used this verse to describe the opposition to Jesus (see Matt 27:48; Mark 15:36; Luke 23:36; John 19:28,29).

69:22-27 *table set before them become a snare:* The psalmist's request for revenge is also a plea for justice. The psalmist wants God to make the enemies eat their own poisoned food (69:21). Enemies are often said to "snare" themselves by their own wickedness (see the notes at 31:4 and 57:6).

69:28 *blotted out of the book of life:* See the note at 40:7. See also Exod 32:32; Rev 3:5; 13:8; 17:8.

69:30,31 *glorify him with thanksgiving . . . please the LORD:* The prayers for help often end with praise and with expressions of thanks and trust (69:32,33). See also the notes at 13:5,6 and 22:24–26. The people were to worship God by offering animal sacrifices to show their thanks (see the note at 16:4). But here and in several other psalms a thankful heart will "please the LORD" (see the notes at 40:6 and 51:16,17).

69:14,15 Ps 69:1,2. **69:19** Ps 35:19; John 15:25. **69:22,23** Rom 11:9,10. **69:25** Acts 1:20.

69:33 *the needy . . . captive people:* See the note at 9:8, 9.

69:35,36 *God will save Zion:* These verses may have been added to make the psalm apply to the situation of the people in exile (see the note at 51:18).

70:1-5 *Hasten, O God, to save me:* Psalm 70 is almost exactly the same as 40:13-17. See also the notes at 51:12-14 and 40:17.

71:2 *in your righteousness:* For God, "righteousness" always involves doing justice and includes help and protection for people who are victims. See the note at 9:8, 9.

71:3 *rock . . . fortress:* See the notes at 18:46 and 11:1.

71:4 *cruel men:* See the note at 3:1,2 and the mini-article called "Enemies (The Wicked)," p. 1084.

33 The LORD hears the needy
and does not despise his captive people.

34 Let heaven and earth praise him,
the seas and all that move in them,
35 for God will save Zion
and rebuild the cities of Judah.
Then people will settle there and possess it;
36 the children of his servants will inherit it,
and those who love his name will dwell there.

Psalm 70

For the director of music. Of David. A petition.

1 Hasten, O God, to save me;
O LORD, come quickly to help me.
2 May those who seek my life
be put to shame and confusion;
may all who desire my ruin
be turned back in disgrace.
3 May those who say to me, "Aha! Aha!"
turn back because of their shame.
4 But may all who seek you
rejoice and be glad in you;
may those who love your salvation always say,
"Let God be exalted!"

5 Yet I am poor and needy;
come quickly to me, O God.
You are my help and my deliverer;
O LORD, do not delay.

Psalm 71

1 In you, O LORD, I have taken refuge;
let me never be put to shame.
2 Rescue me and deliver me in your righteousness;
turn your ear to me and save me.
3 Be my rock of refuge,
to which I can always go;
give the command to save me,
for you are my rock and my fortress.
4 Deliver me, O my God, from the hand of
the wicked,
from the grasp of evil and cruel men.

5 For you have been my hope, O Sovereign LORD,
my confidence since my youth.
6 From birth I have relied on you;
you brought me forth from my mother's womb.

I will ever praise you.
7 I have become like a portent to many,
but you are my strong refuge.
8 My mouth is filled with your praise,
declaring your splendor all day long.

9 Do not cast me away when I am old;
do not forsake me when my strength is gone.
10 For my enemies speak against me;
those who wait to kill me conspire together.
11 They say, "God has forsaken him;
pursue him and seize him,
for no one will rescue him."
12 Be not far from me, O God;
come quickly, O my God, to help me.
13 May my accusers perish in shame;
may those who want to harm me
be covered with scorn and disgrace.

14 But as for me, I will always have hope;
I will praise you more and more.
15 My mouth will tell of your righteousness,
of your salvation all day long,
though I know not its measure.
16 I will come and proclaim your mighty acts,
O Sovereign LORD;
I will proclaim your righteousness,
yours alone.
17 Since my youth, O God, you have taught me,
and to this day I declare your marvelous deeds.
18 Even when I am old and gray,
do not forsake me, O God,
till I declare your power to the next generation,
your might to all who are to come.

19 Your righteousness reaches to the skies, O God,
you who have done great things.
Who, O God, is like you?
20 Though you have made me see troubles, many
and bitter,
you will restore my life again;
from the depths of the earth
you will again bring me up.
21 You will increase my honor
and comfort me once again.

22 I will praise you with the harp
for your faithfulness, O my God;
I will sing praise to you with the lyre,
O Holy One of Israel.

71:6 *I will ever praise you:* The prayers for help regularly include expressions of trust and praise. See also 71:7,8,14-17,19-24 and the note at 31:19-22.

71:13 *scorn and disgrace:* The request is for justice as well as revenge. See also the notes at 71: 2 and 71:4.

71:15-19 *mighty acts . . . marvelous deeds:* The "mighty acts" and "marvelous deeds" probably refer to the way God helped the people of Israel in the past (see the note at 9:1), but they may also refer to the things God has done to help the psalmist. The psalmist wants future generations to know what God has done.

71:20 *troubles, many and bitter . . . depths of the earth:* See the notes at 6:1-4; 40:2; and 55:15.

71:22 *harp:* See the note at 33:2.

71:22 *Holy One:* To be holy means to be set apart. To call God the "Holy One" suggests God's greatness, and it is especially fitting after the psalmist has asked, "Who, O God, is like you?" (71:19). See also the mini-article called "Holiness," p. 1626.

71:23,24 *you have redeemed:* It is not clear whether the prayers of 71:1-4,12,13 have been answered or whether the psalmist is remembering past experiences when God has helped. In either case, the psalm suggests that suffering and celebration cannot be separated. See the notes at 13:5,6; 22:24-26; and 31:19-22.

72 Title *Solomon:* Solomon was David's son. For the account of his life and kingship, see 1 Kings 3–11 and the mini-article called "Solomon," p. 776.

72:1-3 *Endow the king with your justice:* This prayer for the king may have originally been used at times when a new king took office. The king was to serve God by being honest and fair and by taking care of the poor. Honesty and fairness are also called "justice." It is what God always wants. See the note at 9:8,9 and the mini-article called "Justice," p. 1721.

23 My lips will shout for joy
when I sing praise to you—
I, whom you have redeemed.
24 My tongue will tell of your righteous acts
all day long,
for those who wanted to harm me
have been put to shame and confusion.

Psalm 72

Of Solomon.

1 Endow the king with your justice, O God,
the royal son with your righteousness.
2 He will[a] judge your people in righteousness,
your afflicted ones with justice.
3 The mountains will bring prosperity to the people,
the hills the fruit of righteousness.
4 He will defend the afflicted among the people
and save the children of the needy;
he will crush the oppressor.

5 He will endure[b] as long as the sun,
as long as the moon, through all generations.

[a] 2 Or *May he*; similarly in verses 3-11 and 17 [b] 5 Septuagint; Hebrew *You will be feared*

QUESTIONS ABOUT PSALMS 42:1—72:20

1. Read Psalms 46 and 48. What do they say about the city of Jerusalem and about Mount Zion? Why and how were these places important for the people of God? What can they teach people today about the importance of sacred places?
2. Read Psalm 50. How had the people of God misunderstood sacrifice? What does the psalm say is a proper sacrifice?
3. What do Psalm 32 and Psalm 51 say about sin and forgiveness? Why is it important that God demands obedience but also forgives sin?
4. The "titles" of many psalms (Ps 51; 52; 54; 56; 57; 59; 60; and 63) mention David and things that happened in David's life. See also the notes and references to 1 SAMUEL. What do many of these events have in common? What do these "titles" add to the meaning of the psalms?
5. Read Psalm 55 and notice especially verses 12-14. Who is the psalmist's enemy in this case? How might people today have similar experiences, and how can this psalm help them in such situations?
6. Read Psalm 63 (see also Ps 57:1). What does it mean when the psalmist says to God that he finds help "in the shadow of your wings"?
7. It has been suggested that Psalm 71 is the prayer of an older person. Why might this be?

6 He will be like rain falling on a mown field,
like showers watering the earth.
7 In his days the righteous will flourish;
prosperity will abound till the moon is no more.

8 He will rule from sea to sea
and from the River[a] to the ends of the earth.[b]
9 The desert tribes will bow before him
and his enemies will lick the dust.
10 The kings of Tarshish and of distant shores
will bring tribute to him;
the kings of Sheba and Seba
will present him gifts.
11 All kings will bow down to him
and all nations will serve him.

12 For he will deliver the needy who cry out,
the afflicted who have no one to help.
13 He will take pity on the weak and the needy
and save the needy from death.
14 He will rescue them from oppression and
violence,
for precious is their blood in his sight.

15 Long may he live!
May gold from Sheba be given him.
May people ever pray for him
and bless him all day long.
16 Let grain abound throughout the land;
on the tops of the hills may it sway.
Let its fruit flourish like Lebanon;
let it thrive like the grass of the field.
17 May his name endure forever;
may it continue as long as the sun.

All nations will be blessed through him,
and they will call him blessed.

18 Praise be to the LORD God, the God of Israel,
who alone does marvelous deeds.
19 Praise be to his glorious name forever;
may the whole earth be filled with his glory.
Amen and Amen.

20 This concludes the prayers of David son of Jesse.

[a]8 That is, the Euphrates [b]8 Or *the end of the land*

72:8-12 *from sea to sea . . . desert tribes . . . Sheba and Seba:* Because God wants righteousness to "flourish" (72:7), the king needs to be recognized "from sea to sea," meaning all over the world. "The River" refers to the Euphrates River, located in Assyria and Mesopotamia to the north and east of Israel. "Desert tribes" probably refer to tribes to the south and southeast. Tarshish probably refers to a city far to the west in Spain. The "distant shores" may refer to the Greek islands, Crete, or Cyprus. Sheba may have been a place in what is now southwest Arabia, and Seba may have been in southern Arabia (1 Kgs 10:1-13). See the map on p. 2468.

72:16 *Lebanon:* The name "Lebanon" comes from the Hebrew word for "white" and refers to the snow that caps the mountain peaks of this range. See the note at 29:5-8.

72:17-19 *glorious name . . . filled with his glory:* The king's glory will shine if he rules with justice (see the note at 72:1-3). God's glory will be revealed not only in the life of the faithful king but in various miracles as well. See the notes at 26:8 and 9:1.

72:20 *This concludes the prayers of David son of Jesse:* For Jesse, see 1 Sam 16:1-22. This verse was probably added sometime after the psalm was written, and when the PSALMS was being collected, as a way to identify Books I and II as the prayers of David.

72:8 Zech 9:10.

Book III (Psalms 73:1—89:52)

Book III opens with a collection of psalms by Asaph (Ps 73–83). They are followed by psalms of the Sons of Korah (Ps 84; 85; 87; 88), David (Ps 86), and Ethan (Ps 89). Unlike the prayers for help in Books I and II, most of the prayers for help in Book III are offered by and for the whole nation. This suggests that the psalms in Book III may have been influenced by the destruction of Jerusalem in 586 B.C.

Psalm 73

A psalm of Asaph.

1 Surely God is good to Israel,
to those who are pure in heart.

2 But as for me, my feet had almost slipped;
I had nearly lost my foothold.
3 For I envied the arrogant
when I saw the prosperity of the wicked.

4 They have no struggles;
their bodies are healthy and strong.[a]
5 They are free from the burdens common to man;
they are not plagued by human ills.
6 Therefore pride is their necklace;
they clothe themselves with violence.
7 From their callous hearts comes iniquity[b];
the evil conceits of their minds know no limits.
8 They scoff, and speak with malice;
in their arrogance they threaten oppression.
9 Their mouths lay claim to heaven,
and their tongues take possession of the earth.
10 Therefore their people turn to them
and drink up waters in abundance.[c]
11 They say, "How can God know?
Does the Most High have knowledge?"

12 This is what the wicked are like—
always carefree, they increase in wealth.

13 Surely in vain have I kept my heart pure;
in vain have I washed my hands in innocence.
14 All day long I have been plagued;
I have been punished every morning.

15 If I had said, "I will speak thus,"
I would have betrayed your children.

---

[a]**4** With a different word division of the Hebrew; Masoretic Text *struggles at their death; / their bodies are healthy* [b]**7** Syriac (see also Septuagint); Hebrew *Their eyes bulge with fat* [c]**10** The meaning of the Hebrew for this verse is uncertain.

73 Title *Asaph:* See the note at 50 Title.

73:1 *pure in heart:* In Hebrew thought, the heart was not understood to be the seat of emotions so much as the place where a person's thoughts and intentions resided (see 51:10). To have a "pure heart," then, is to be obedient and loyal to God.

73:3-5 *arrogant . . . wicked . . . they are not plagued:* These people are selfish and deny God's claim on their lives (73:8-11). The psalmist wonders why the evil people seem to prosper and remain healthy, while those who are loyal to God are suffering. See also 37:1. Why good people suffer is the main question in Job. See the Introduction to Books of Wisdom and Poetry, p. 959.

73:11 *How can God know:* The proud often fail to believe that God knows everything they do (see 11:4 and 53:1).

73:13-17 *in vain have I kept my heart pure . . . till I entered the sanctuary of God:* The psalmist suffers and is confused. He is even tempted to join the wicked (73:13). But he remains loyal to God and visits the temple, where he finally understands what will happen to the wicked (73:17-20). It is not clear what experience at the temple led the psalmist to the new understanding, but he apparently discovers a deeper understanding as he prays and worships.

[16]When I tried to understand all this,
it was oppressive to me
[17]till I entered the sanctuary of God;
then I understood their final destiny.

[18]Surely you place them on slippery ground;
you cast them down to ruin.
[19]How suddenly are they destroyed,
completely swept away by terrors!
[20]As a dream when one awakes,
so when you arise, O Lord,
you will despise them as fantasies.

[21]When my heart was grieved
and my spirit embittered,
[22]I was senseless and ignorant;
I was a brute beast before you.

[23]Yet I am always with you;
you hold me by my right hand.
[24]You guide me with your counsel,
and afterward you will take me into glory.
[25]Whom have I in heaven but you?
And earth has nothing I desire besides you.
[26]My flesh and my heart may fail,
but God is the strength of my heart
and my portion forever.

[27]Those who are far from you will perish;
you destroy all who are unfaithful to you.
[28]But as for me, it is good to be near God.
I have made the Sovereign LORD my refuge;
I will tell of all your deeds.

Psalm 74

A *maskil*[a] of Asaph.

[1]Why have you rejected us forever, O God?
Why does your anger smolder against the sheep of your pasture?
[2]Remember the people you purchased of old,
the tribe of your inheritance, whom you redeemed—
Mount Zion, where you dwelt.
[3]Turn your steps toward these everlasting ruins,
all this destruction the enemy has brought on the sanctuary.

[4]Your foes roared in the place where you met with us;
they set up their standards as signs.

[a]Title: Probably a literary or musical term

73:18 *slippery ground:* The psalmist had "almost slipped" (73:2), but now he understands that the wicked will fall on slippery ground.

73:23 *hold me by my right hand:* To be held by the "right hand" means that God is always present, even during times of suffering.

73:27 *destroy ... unfaithful:* The wicked actually choose their own destruction by staying "far from" God. See the note at 1:4, 5.

73:28 *it is good to be near God:* Now the psalmist understands what is truly "good." It is to be near to God, which means protection even when things go wrong (73:14). See also the notes at 6:8, 9 and 13:5, 6.

74:2 *whom you redeemed:* This refers to God rescuing the Hebrew people from slavery in Egypt. See 74:13-15 and the note at 66:6.

74:2,3 *Mount Zion, where you dwelt:* The temple built on Mount Zion in Jerusalem was viewed as God's home. See the notes at 2:6 and 5:7 (your house).

74:3-7 *destruction ... burned your sanctuary to the ground:* This suggests that the psalm was written shortly after the temple and the city of Jerusalem were destroyed by the Babylonians in 586 B.C. (see 2 Kgs 25:1-17; 2 Chr 36:17-21). The people took this as a sign of rejection by God (74:1) and as a punishment for their sins (Jer 25:1-11). See also the note at 44:9-11.

74:4 *standards as signs:* The "standards" probably are victory flags put up by the enemy army. Foreign flags put up in Israel's most sacred place was a great disgrace against God and God's people.

74:9 *no prophets are left:* True prophets brought God's messages and helped to interpret God's will to the people, but they are silent at this time.

74:13 *split open the sea:* This recalls the people's crossing of the sea as they escaped from Egypt during the exodus. See Exod 14:21.

74:13,14 *monster in the waters . . . Leviathan:* The sea and its creatures represent the forces of chaos and opposition to God. God's defeat of the monsters and Leviathan show God's power over all creation (Job 41:1; Ps 104:26; Isa 27:1), as does God's victory over the Egyptians at the exodus.

74:15-17 *springs . . . summer and winter:* God created all things and rules every aspect of nature (Gen 1:9-18; 8:22). God gives his people the water they need to thrive (Exod 17:5, 6) and dries up rivers in order to help his people in times of need (Josh 3:14-17). En Gedi, a spring on the western shore of the Dead Sea, is typical of an oasis spring that provides much needed water for travelers in the desert (see 1 Samuel 24 for an interesting story about David and King Saul that happened at this spring).

74:21 *the poor and needy:* The exodus from Egypt is remembered as a moment when God helped the Hebrew people when they were oppressed. And now the people are oppressed again (see 74:3-7). The people beg for God to help them.

5 They behaved like men wielding axes
to cut through a thicket of trees.
6 They smashed all the carved paneling
with their axes and hatchets.
7 They burned your sanctuary to the ground;
they defiled the dwelling place of your Name.
8 They said in their hearts, "We will crush them completely!"
They burned every place where God was worshiped in the land.
9 We are given no miraculous signs;
no prophets are left,
and none of us knows how long this will be.

10 How long will the enemy mock you, O God?
Will the foe revile your name forever?
11 Why do you hold back your hand, your right hand?
Take it from the folds of your garment and destroy them!

12 But you, O God, are my king from of old;
you bring salvation upon the earth.
13 It was you who split open the sea by your power;
you broke the heads of the monster in the waters.
14 It was you who crushed the heads of Leviathan
and gave him as food to the creatures of the desert.
15 It was you who opened up springs and streams;
you dried up the ever flowing rivers.
16 The day is yours, and yours also the night;
you established the sun and moon.
17 It was you who set all the boundaries of the earth;
you made both summer and winter.

18 Remember how the enemy has mocked you, O LORD,
how foolish people have reviled your name.
19 Do not hand over the life of your dove to wild beasts;
do not forget the lives of your afflicted people forever.
20 Have regard for your covenant,
because haunts of violence fill the dark places of the land.
21 Do not let the oppressed retreat in disgrace;
may the poor and needy praise your name.

22 Rise up, O God, and defend your cause;
remember how fools mock you all day long.
23 Do not ignore the clamor of your adversaries,
the uproar of your enemies, which rises continually.

Psalm 75

For the director of music. ⌞To the tune of⌟ "Do Not Destroy."
A psalm of Asaph. A song.

1 We give thanks to you, O God,
we give thanks, for your Name is near;
men tell of your wonderful deeds.

2 You say, "I choose the appointed time;
it is I who judge uprightly.
3 When the earth and all its people quake,
it is I who hold its pillars firm. *Selah*
4 To the arrogant I say, 'Boast no more,'
and to the wicked, 'Do not lift up your horns.
5 Do not lift your horns against heaven;
do not speak with outstretched neck.' "

6 No one from the east or the west
or from the desert can exalt a man.
7 But it is God who judges:
He brings one down, he exalts another.
8 In the hand of the LORD is a cup
full of foaming wine mixed with spices;
he pours it out, and all the wicked of the earth
drink it down to its very dregs.

9 As for me, I will declare this forever;
I will sing praise to the God of Jacob.
10 I will cut off the horns of all the wicked,
but the horns of the righteous will be lifted up.

Psalm 76

For the director of music. With stringed instruments.
A psalm of Asaph. A song.

1 In Judah God is known;
his name is great in Israel.
2 His tent is in Salem,
his dwelling place in Zion.
3 There he broke the flashing arrows,
the shields and the swords, the weapons of war. *Selah*

4 You are resplendent with light,
more majestic than mountains rich with game.
5 Valiant men lie plundered,
they sleep their last sleep;
not one of the warriors
can lift his hands.
6 At your rebuke, O God of Jacob,
both horse and chariot lie still.
7 You alone are to be feared.

75:1 *wonderful deeds:* These include helping the Hebrew people escape from slavery in Egypt and cross the Red Sea on dry land (Exod 14:1—15:21), feeding the people in the desert (Exod 16), helping them cross the Jordan River (Josh 3:14-17), and helping them win many victories over their enemies. See also 74:13-15.

75:2 *judge uprightly:* Judging with fairness establishes justice, the goal of God's "wonderful deeds" (75:1). See also the note at 9:8,9.

75:3 *earth and all its people quake . . . firm:* The quaking earth may refer to a time of upheaval in the world, either brought on by war or natural disaster. The psalmist is confident that God will hold things together during the most severe threat.

75:4 *arrogant . . . wicked:* These are selfish people who oppose God and hurt others. See 75:10 and the mini-article called "Enemies (The Wicked)," p. 1084.

75:8 *a cup full of foaming wine:* In the Bible, God's "cup" sometimes stands for God's anger or judgment to be poured on evildoers. See also the note at 60:3.

75:9 *God of Jacob:* See the note at 22:23.

75:10 *the wicked:* God's destruction of "the wicked" is a matter of justice (75:2,7). See also the note at 3:5-8.

76:1-3 *Judah . . . Israel . . . Salem . . . Zion:* See the note at 48:11 (Mount Zion). Salem refers to Jerusalem, where Zion was located. The last part of the name "Jerusalem" is "Salem," which in Hebrew is similar to *shalom,* or "peace."

76:5 *Valiant men lie plundered:* This may recall the miraculous deliverance of Jerusalem in the year 701 B.C. (see 2 Kgs 19:35-37; Isa 37:36). See also the note at 48:4-8.

Jerusalem on Mount Zion. Many of the psalms speak of Jerusalem (the holy city), Mount Zion (God's holy hill), or the temple (God's house) and describe them as the place where God chose to dwell among his chosen people. "In Judah God is known; his name is great in Israel. His tent is in Salem, his dwelling place in Zion" (Ps 76:1, 2). Other psalms that speak of the importance of Mount Zion are Psalms 48; 78:67-72; and 125.

76:8,9 *pronounced judgment . . . rose up to judge, to save:* God is often described as a "judge" (see the note at 75:2). See also Eccl 3:17 and Isa 33:22. As "judge," God is concerned with justice, which means saving those in need and those who cannot defend themselves. See the note at 9:8, 9.

76:11 *Make vows . . . bring gifts:* See the note at 22:24-26.

76:12 *breaks the spirit of rulers:* This means that God is the real ruler and king of all. See the note on p. 1024.

77 Title *Jeduthun:* See the note at 39 Title.

77:2 *stretched out untiring hands:* See the note at 28:2.

Who can stand before you when you are angry?
8 From heaven you pronounced judgment,
and the land feared and was quiet—
9 when you, O God, rose up to judge,
to save all the afflicted of the land. *Selah*
10 Surely your wrath against men brings you praise,
and the survivors of your wrath are restrained.[a]
11 Make vows to the LORD your God and fulfill them;
let all the neighboring lands
bring gifts to the One to be feared.
12 He breaks the spirit of rulers;
he is feared by the kings of the earth.

Psalm 77

For the director of music. For Jeduthun. Of Asaph. A psalm.

1 I cried out to God for help;
I cried out to God to hear me.
2 When I was in distress, I sought the Lord;
at night I stretched out untiring hands
and my soul refused to be comforted.

3 I remembered you, O God, and I groaned;
I mused, and my spirit grew faint. *Selah*
4 You kept my eyes from closing;
I was too troubled to speak.

---

[a]**10** Or *Surely the wrath of men brings you praise, / and with the remainder of wrath you arm yourself*

5 I thought about the former days,
the years of long ago;
6 I remembered my songs in the night.
My heart mused and my spirit inquired:

7 "Will the Lord reject forever?
Will he never show his favor again?
8 Has his unfailing love vanished forever?
Has his promise failed for all time?
9 Has God forgotten to be merciful?
Has he in anger withheld his compassion?" *Selah*

10 Then I thought, "To this I will appeal:
the years of the right hand of the Most High."
11 I will remember the deeds of the LORD;
yes, I will remember your miracles of long ago.
12 I will meditate on all your works
and consider all your mighty deeds.

13 Your ways, O God, are holy.
What god is so great as our God?
14 You are the God who performs miracles;
you display your power among the peoples.
15 With your mighty arm you redeemed your people,
the descendants of Jacob and Joseph. *Selah*

16 The waters saw you, O God,
the waters saw you and writhed;
the very depths were convulsed.
17 The clouds poured down water,
the skies resounded with thunder;
your arrows flashed back and forth.
18 Your thunder was heard in the whirlwind,
your lightning lit up the world;
the earth trembled and quaked.
19 Your path led through the sea,
your way through the mighty waters,
though your footprints were not seen.

20 You led your people like a flock
by the hand of Moses and Aaron.

Psalm 78

A *maskil*[a] of Asaph.

1 O my people, hear my teaching;
listen to the words of my mouth.
2 I will open my mouth in parables,
I will utter hidden things, things from of old—

[a]Title: Probably a literary or musical term

77:5 *former days, the years of long ago:* The psalmist may be thinking back to the miraculous events in Israel's past (see the note at 75:1).

77:7-10 *reject forever . . . never show his favor:* In the past God helped the people by choosing leaders such as Moses and Aaron (77:20) and by rescuing Israel (see the note at 20:6). But the psalmist wonders if God has forgotten about the people. Such questions may suggest that this psalm comes from a time of severe national distress.

77:11-15 *remember the deeds . . . miracles of long ago:* Though he has questions, the psalmist remembers and praises God's saving acts and miracles (see the note at 77:5). Suffering and questions often are found next to statements of hope and celebration in the psalms (see the notes at 13:5,6 and 22:24-26).

77:15 *Jacob and Joseph:* See the note at 22:23. Joseph was one of Jacob's twelve sons (see Gen 37:39-50). The tribes of Ephraim and Manasseh descended from Joseph.

77:16-18 *waters . . . writhed . . . earth trembled and quaked:* In ancient times the ocean was seen as a symbol of chaos (see the note at 29:10). But God's power is stronger than the dangerous ocean. God's power is also revealed in the thunderstorm. God not only controls the waters on the earth, but the water above the earth that falls as rain (Gen 1:6). See the note at 18:7-15.

77:20 *Moses and Aaron:* These two brothers led the people out of slavery in Egypt (Exod 3–15). See the mini-article called "Moses," p. 2335, and the note at 90 Title.

78 Title *Asaph:* See the note at 50 Title.

78:1-4 *hear my teaching . . . tell the next generation:* Instead, it tells the story of God's people from the exodus to the time of David. Its purpose is to teach present and future generations about the past, so they will faithfully obey God (78:7,8).

78:4 *wonders:* See 77:11-16; 78:26-29, 43–52; and the note at 75:1.

78:5-7 *statutes . . . commands:* The "statues" and "commands" refer to the Law that was given to Moses on Mount Sinai where the people stopped on their way from Egypt to the promised land. See also the note at 1:1, 2 and the mini-article called "Law," p. 1160.

78:8 *their forefathers . . . stubborn and rebellious:* Besides telling of God's mighty miracles (78:4) the psalm also tells about the people's constant disobedience. In each case, God is angry (78:21-31,59-64), but God also forgives and restores (78:32-39; 65-72).

78:9 *Ephraim:* Ephraim was Joseph's youngest son. One of the twelve tribes was named after him, and the northern kingdom was also sometimes known as Ephraim. It is not known what specific battle is being described here.

78:10 *God's covenant:* See the note at 44:17.

78:12 *Egypt, in the region of Zoan:* Zoan is not mentioned in Exodus 7:8—12:32, which tells about God's miracles leading up to the exodus. Zoan is often identified with the city of Rameses that is mentioned in Exodus 1:11. See the map on p. 2463.

78:13,14 *divided the sea . . . fire all night:* This refers to the Red Sea crossing (Exod 14:21,22) and to the cloud and flame God used to guide the Hebrew people after leaving Egypt (Exod 13:21,22).

78:15,16 *He split rocks . . . streams out of a rocky crag:* When the people complained of thirst, God provided water. See Exod 17:1-7; Num 20:2-13.

78:5,6 Deut 6:4-9.

3 what we have heard and known,
what our fathers have told us.
4 We will not hide them from their children;
we will tell the next generation
the praiseworthy deeds of the LORD,
his power, and the wonders he has done.
5 He decreed statutes for Jacob
and established the law in Israel,
which he commanded our forefathers
to teach their children,
6 so the next generation would know them,
even the children yet to be born,
and they in turn would tell their children.
7 Then they would put their trust in God
and would not forget his deeds
but would keep his commands.
8 They would not be like their forefathers—
a stubborn and rebellious generation,
whose hearts were not loyal to God,
whose spirits were not faithful to him.

9 The men of Ephraim, though armed with bows,
turned back on the day of battle;
10 they did not keep God's covenant
and refused to live by his law.
11 They forgot what he had done,
the wonders he had shown them.
12 He did miracles in the sight of their fathers
in the land of Egypt, in the region of Zoan.
13 He divided the sea and led them through;
he made the water stand firm like a wall.
14 He guided them with the cloud by day
and with light from the fire all night.
15 He split the rocks in the desert
and gave them water as abundant as the seas;
16 he brought streams out of a rocky crag
and made water flow down like rivers.

17 But they continued to sin against him,
rebelling in the desert against the Most High.
18 They willfully put God to the test
by demanding the food they craved.
19 They spoke against God, saying,
"Can God spread a table in the desert?
20 When he struck the rock, water gushed out,
and streams flowed abundantly.
But can he also give us food?
Can he supply meat for his people?"
21 When the LORD heard them, he was very angry;

Israelites Passing through the Wilderness by William West, nineteenth century. Psalm 78 reminds the people of Israel of all the glorious things God had done for them—from the time God gave them the law (Ps 78:5) to the time God chose David to be their king (Ps 78:70). It describes how he led the Israelites out of slavery in Egypt and provided them with everything they needed during the time they wandered in the desert. During this time God "guided them with the cloud by day and with light from the fire all night" (Ps 78:14).

his fire broke out against Jacob,
and his wrath rose against Israel,
22 for they did not believe in God
or trust in his deliverance.
23 Yet he gave a command to the skies above
and opened the doors of the heavens;
24 he rained down manna for the people to eat,
he gave them the grain of heaven.
25 Men ate the bread of angels;
he sent them all the food they could eat.
26 He let loose the east wind from the heavens
and led forth the south wind by his power.
27 He rained meat down on them like dust,
flying birds like sand on the seashore.
28 He made them come down inside their camp,
all around their tents.
29 They ate till they had more than enough,
for he had given them what they craved.
30 But before they turned from the food they craved,
even while it was still in their mouths,
31 God's anger rose against them;
he put to death the sturdiest among them,
cutting down the young men of Israel.
32 In spite of all this, they kept on sinning;
in spite of his wonders, they did not believe.

78:18-28 *willfully put God to the test . . . manna . . . flying birds:* Though God had saved the people from slavery in Egypt, the people rebelled by complaining in the desert. God responded by giving the people a special kind of food to eat. It tasted like a wafer and was called "manna," which in Hebrew means "What is it?" (Exod 16:1-33; Num 11:4-23). Then the people whined about not having meat (Num 11:10-13), so God also provided birds (quail) to eat (Num 11:31-35).

78:31-34 *God's anger rose . . . put to death:* The people were to take only as much food as they needed each day as a sign of their ongoing trust in God. But some took more than they needed, and Moses became angry at their lack of faith (Exod 16:14-20). Some were put to death because of God's anger at them (Num 11:32-34). The people rebelled and sinned against God in many other ways while in the desert, so they received punishment (Exod 32; Num 14:1; 16; 25).

78:24 John 6:31.

78:35 *their Rock:* See the note at 18:46.

78:38,39 *Yet he was merciful:* Even though the people kept making God angry (78:31, 38), in his mercy he kept on forgiving their sins.

78:40,41 *rebelled . . . put God to the test:* See the notes at 78:18-28 and 78:31-34.

78:41 *Holy One of Israel:* See the note at 71:22 (Holy One).

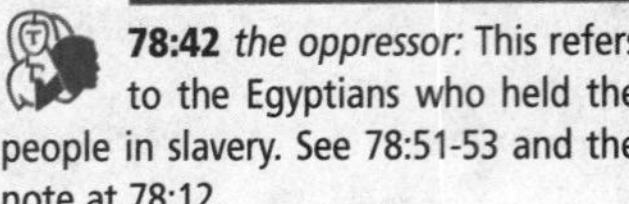

78:42 *the oppressor:* This refers to the Egyptians who held the people in slavery. See 78:51-53 and the note at 78:12.

78:43-53 *displayed his miraculous signs in Egypt . . . Zoan:* See the note at 78:12. The "miraculous signs" are the events that led up to the exodus, especially the terrible plagues. See the mini-article called "Disasters (Plagues)," p. 151.

78:37 Acts 8:21. **78:44** Exod 7:17-21. **78:45** Exod 8:1-6, 20-24. **78:46** Exod 10:12-15. **78:47,48** Exod 9:22-25. **78:49-51** Exod 12:29. **78:52** Exod 13:17-22. **78:53** Exod 14:26-28.

33 So he ended their days in futility
 and their years in terror.
34 Whenever God slew them, they would seek him;
 they eagerly turned to him again.
35 They remembered that God was their Rock,
 that God Most High was their Redeemer.
36 But then they would flatter him with their mouths,
 lying to him with their tongues;
37 their hearts were not loyal to him,
 they were not faithful to his covenant.
38 Yet he was merciful;
 he forgave their iniquities
 and did not destroy them.
Time after time he restrained his anger
 and did not stir up his full wrath.
39 He remembered that they were but flesh,
 a passing breeze that does not return.

40 How often they rebelled against him in the desert
 and grieved him in the wasteland!
41 Again and again they put God to the test;
 they vexed the Holy One of Israel.
42 They did not remember his power—
 the day he redeemed them from the oppressor,
43 the day he displayed his miraculous signs in Egypt,
 his wonders in the region of Zoan.
44 He turned their rivers to blood;
 they could not drink from their streams.
45 He sent swarms of flies that devoured them,
 and frogs that devastated them.
46 He gave their crops to the grasshopper,
 their produce to the locust.
47 He destroyed their vines with hail
 and their sycamore-figs with sleet.
48 He gave over their cattle to the hail,
 their livestock to bolts of lightning.
49 He unleashed against them his hot anger,
 his wrath, indignation and hostility—
 a band of destroying angels.
50 He prepared a path for his anger;
 he did not spare them from death
 but gave them over to the plague.
51 He struck down all the firstborn of Egypt,
 the firstfruits of manhood in the tents of Ham.
52 But he brought his people out like a flock;
 he led them like sheep through the desert.
53 He guided them safely, so they were unafraid;
 but the sea engulfed their enemies.

54 Thus he brought them to the border of his holy land,
to the hill country his right hand had taken.
55 He drove out nations before them
and allotted their lands to them as an inheritance;
he settled the tribes of Israel in their homes.

56 But they put God to the test
and rebelled against the Most High;
they did not keep his statutes.
57 Like their fathers they were disloyal and faithless,
as unreliable as a faulty bow.
58 They angered him with their high places;
they aroused his jealousy with their idols.
59 When God heard them, he was very angry;
he rejected Israel completely.
60 He abandoned the tabernacle of Shiloh,
the tent he had set up among men.
61 He sent ⌞the ark of⌟ his might into captivity,
his splendor into the hands of the enemy.
62 He gave his people over to the sword;
he was very angry with his inheritance.
63 Fire consumed their young men,
and their maidens had no wedding songs;
64 their priests were put to the sword,
and their widows could not weep.

65 Then the Lord awoke as from sleep,
as a man wakes from the stupor of wine.
66 He beat back his enemies;
he put them to everlasting shame.
67 Then he rejected the tents of Joseph,
he did not choose the tribe of Ephraim;
68 but he chose the tribe of Judah,
Mount Zion, which he loved.
69 He built his sanctuary like the heights,
like the earth that he established forever.
70 He chose David his servant
and took him from the sheep pens;
71 from tending the sheep he brought him
to be the shepherd of his people Jacob,
of Israel his inheritance.
72 And David shepherded them with integrity of heart;
with skillful hands he led them.

Psalm 79

A psalm of Asaph.

1 O God, the nations have invaded your inheritance;
they have defiled your holy temple,
they have reduced Jerusalem to rubble.

78:54,55 *border of his holy land:* The people entered the land God had promised them (Josh 3:14-17), and God helped them take it over (Josh 4:1—11:23).

78:56-58 *put God to the test . . . idols:* After taking over the land, the people were still rebellious (Judg 2:11-15). See the note at 31:6.

78:59 *rejected Israel:* Numerous times, God allowed Israel's enemies to make trouble for them.

78:60 *Shiloh:* Before Jerusalem became the center for worshiping God and before the temple was built on Mount Zion the people worshiped God in the tabernacle that was considered God's "home." See the note at 27:5,6. The tabernacle was once at Shiloh in the territory of Ephraim. See Josh 18:1; 1 Sam 1:3; Jer 7:12-14; 26:6. See also the map on p. 2464.

78:61 *ark of his might:* Referring to the ark of the covenant, made according to God's instructions to Moses (Exod 25:10-22). It was kept in the Most Holy Place in the tabernacle and later in the temple. See also the notes at 9:7 and 17:8. This verse and 78:62–64 probably describe the defeat of God's people by the Philistines (1 Sam 4:1-22).

78:67,68 *tents of Joseph . . . tribe of Ephraim . . . chose the tribe of Judah:* Shiloh was in the territory of Ephraim (see the note at 78:60). David chose Jerusalem in the territory of Judah to be Israel's capital. David brought the tabernacle there, and his son Solomon built the temple on Mount Zion (1 Kgs 5–8). These verses may reflect the destruction of the northern kingdom by the Assyrians in 722 B.C.

78:70 *He chose David:* See 1 Sam 16:1-13; 2 Sam 7:8,9; 1 Chr 17:7,8; and the mini-article called "David," p. 1028.

79:1 *the nations . . . reduced Jerusalem to rubble:* The psalm was written after the Babylonians destroyed Jerusalem in 586 B.C.

79:2,3 *bodies . . . blood:* The tragedy is made worse by the presence of unburied bodies. These were considered unclean and very shameful and made the land unholy.

79:6 *the nations:* This seems to refer especially to the Babylonians. See the note at 79:1.

79:7 *devoured Jacob:* Meaning the southern kingdom of Judah. See the note at 22:23.

79:8 *desperate need:* The people admit their sinfulness (79:9), but they also appeal to God's concern for the helpless. See the notes at 9:8, 9 and 34:2.

79:10 *avenge the outpoured blood:* The oppressors of the helpless must be opposed. See the notes at 3:5-8 and 5:10-12.

79:11 *prisoners . . . die:* After Jerusalem was destroyed, many of the survivors were taken to Babylon. These exiles had little hope of ever getting away. See the note at 79:1.

79:13 *your people, the sheep of your pasture:* Though the people ask God some serious questions (79:5), they trust that God will finally provide for them the way a good shepherd provides for his sheep. See 80:1 and the note at 23:1-3.

80:1 *Shepherd of Israel . . . cherubim:* "Shepherd" is a title used for kings (see the note at 79:13). See also the note at 17:8.

80:1,2 *lead Joseph . . . Ephraim, Benjamin and Manasseh:* See the note at 77:15 (Jacob and Joseph). Benjamin was Jacob's youngest son (see the note at 7 Title). Ephraim and Manasseh were Joseph's sons. Two of Israel's tribes were named for them. Because the northern kingdom was sometimes called "Ephraim," Psalm 80 may have been written shortly before or after its destruction in 722 B.C.

2 They have given the dead bodies of your servants
as food to the birds of the air,
the flesh of your saints to the beasts of the earth.
3 They have poured out blood like water
all around Jerusalem,
and there is no one to bury the dead.
4 We are objects of reproach to our neighbors,
of scorn and derision to those around us.

5 How long, O LORD? Will you be angry forever?
How long will your jealousy burn like fire?
6 Pour out your wrath on the nations
that do not acknowledge you,
on the kingdoms
that do not call on your name;
7 for they have devoured Jacob
and destroyed his homeland.
8 Do not hold against us the sins of the fathers;
may your mercy come quickly to meet us,
for we are in desperate need.

9 Help us, O God our Savior,
for the glory of your name;
deliver us and forgive our sins
for your name's sake.
10 Why should the nations say,
"Where is their God?"
Before our eyes, make known among the nations
that you avenge the outpoured blood of your
servants.
11 May the groans of the prisoners come before you;
by the strength of your arm
preserve those condemned to die.

12 Pay back into the laps of our neighbors seven times
the reproach they have hurled at you, O Lord.
13 Then we your people, the sheep of your pasture,
will praise you forever;
from generation to generation
we will recount your praise.

Psalm 80

For the director of music. To ⌊the tune of⌋ "The Lilies of the Covenant." Of Asaph. A psalm.

1 Hear us, O Shepherd of Israel,
you who lead Joseph like a flock;
you who sit enthroned between the cherubim,
shine forth

2 before Ephraim, Benjamin and Manasseh.
Awaken your might;
come and save us.

3 Restore us, O God;
make your face shine upon us,
that we may be saved.

4 O LORD God Almighty,
how long will your anger smolder
against the prayers of your people?
5 You have fed them with the bread of tears;
you have made them drink tears by the bowlful.
6 You have made us a source of contention to our neighbors,
and our enemies mock us.

7 Restore us, O God Almighty;
make your face shine upon us,
that we may be saved.

8 You brought a vine out of Egypt;
you drove out the nations and planted it.
9 You cleared the ground for it,
and it took root and filled the land.
10 The mountains were covered with its shade,
the mighty cedars with its branches.
11 It sent out its boughs to the Sea,[a]
its shoots as far as the River.[b]

12 Why have you broken down its walls
so that all who pass by pick its grapes?
13 Boars from the forest ravage it
and the creatures of the field feed on it.
14 Return to us, O God Almighty!
Look down from heaven and see!
Watch over this vine,
15 the root your right hand has planted,
the son[c] you have raised up for yourself.

16 Your vine is cut down, it is burned with fire;
at your rebuke your people perish.
17 Let your hand rest on the man at your right hand,
the son of man you have raised up for yourself.
18 Then we will not turn away from you;
revive us, and we will call on your name.

19 Restore us, O LORD God Almighty;
make your face shine upon us,
that we may be saved.

[a]11 Probably the Mediterranean [b]11 That is, the Euphrates [c]15 Or *branch*

80:4 *LORD God Almighty:* See the notes at 2:4 (LORD) and 46:6, 7.

80:6 *our enemies:* These are the opponents who cause the destruction described in 80:12, 13, 16.

80:8-11 *a vine . . . the River:* The grapevine represents the people of Israel. The "mountains" refer to Lebanon, the "Sea" is the Mediterranean Sea, and the "River" is probably the Euphrates. These formed the ideal western and northern boundaries for Israel. See the map on p. 2465.

80:12,13 *broken down its walls . . . Boars ravage it:* The picture of a vineyard is used for God's people Israel. Walls were sometimes built around vineyards to keep robbers and wild animals from trampling or stealing the grapes. Along with 80:16, these verses describe the destruction of the northern kingdom, and possibly the later destruction of the southern kingdom as well. See also Isa 5:1-7.

80:17 *at your right hand:* Since the right side was a place of honor, this "man" may refer to a future king who would help the people grow as David had done. See also the note at 2:2.

80:19 *be saved:* The people continued to trust God while they were suffering. See the note at 51:12-14.

79:10 Ps 42:3, 10; 115:2; Joel 2:17; Mic 7:10.

Psalm 81

For the director of music. According to *gittith.*[a] Of Asaph.

1 Sing for joy to God our strength;
shout aloud to the God of Jacob!
2 Begin the music, strike the tambourine,
play the melodious harp and lyre.

3 Sound the ram's horn at the New Moon,
and when the moon is full, on the day of our Feast;
4 this is a decree for Israel,
an ordinance of the God of Jacob.
5 He established it as a statute for Joseph
when he went out against Egypt,
where we heard a language we did not understand.[b]

6 He says, "I removed the burden from their shoulders;
their hands were set free from the basket.
7 In your distress you called and I rescued you,
I answered you out of a thundercloud;
I tested you at the waters of Meribah. *Selah*

8 "Hear, O my people, and I will warn you—
if you would but listen to me, O Israel!
9 You shall have no foreign god among you;
you shall not bow down to an alien god.
10 I am the LORD your God,
who brought you up out of Egypt.
Open wide your mouth and I will fill it.

11 "But my people would not listen to me;
Israel would not submit to me.
12 So I gave them over to their stubborn hearts
to follow their own devices.

13 "If my people would but listen to me,
if Israel would follow my ways,
14 how quickly would I subdue their enemies
and turn my hand against their foes!
15 Those who hate the LORD would cringe before him,
and their punishment would last forever.
16 But you would be fed with the finest of wheat;
with honey from the rock I would satisfy you."

Psalm 82

A psalm of Asaph.

1 God presides in the great assembly;
he gives judgment among the "gods":

[a]Title: Probably a musical term [b]5 Or / *and we heard a voice we had not known*

81:1 *Jacob:* Meaning Israel (see the note at 22:23).

81:3 *Sound the ram's horn at the New Moon . . . Feast:* Trumpets were blown on the first day of every month, which began with the "new moon" (Num 10:10; 28:11-15). Special sacrifices were offered on this day. This psalm may have been used originally at the New Moon Festival. But trumpets were also sounded for other festivals, including the Feast of Tabernacles celebrated in seventh month (Lev 23:23-44).

81:4,5 *this is a decree for Israel:* There are festival instructions in Leviticus 23:1-44; Numbers 28,29; and Deuteronomy 16:1-15. See also the chart called "Jewish Calendar and Festivals," p. 944.

81:5 *Joseph:* See the note at 77:15.

81:6,7 *removed the burden . . . waters of Meribah:* A priest or prophet may have spoken 81:6-16 during a festival. Removing the "burden" probably refers to rescuing the people from slavery in Egypt. The thundercloud may refer to the events at Mount Sinai (Exod 19:16). When the people complained of thirst in the desert, God told Moses to strike a rock with his walking stick and water came out. The place was called Massah ("test") and Meribah ("complaining"). See Exod 17:1-7; Num 20:2-13.

81:9,10 *no foreign god:* Because God saved the people from slavery in Egypt and gave them the Law, they were to be loyal to God alone (see Exod 20:1-3; Deut 5:6,7; and the note at 82:1).

81:14 *their enemies:* See the note at 80:6.

82:1 *among the "gods":* Psalm 82 describes a trial in heaven. The "gods" probably refers to the gods worshiped by the nations. But the Hebrew word translated "gods" may refer to God's angels or even to human rulers.

81:16 Deut 11:8-12; 32:13,14. **82:6** John 10:34.

2 "How long will you[a] defend the unjust
and show partiality to the wicked? *Selah*
3 Defend the cause of the weak and fatherless;
maintain the rights of the poor and oppressed.
4 Rescue the weak and needy;
deliver them from the hand of the wicked.

5 "They know nothing, they understand nothing.
They walk about in darkness;
all the foundations of the earth are shaken.

6 "I said, 'You are "gods";
you are all sons of the Most High.'
7 But you will die like mere men;
you will fall like every other ruler."

8 Rise up, O God, judge the earth,
for all the nations are your inheritance.

Psalm 83

A song. A psalm of Asaph.

1 O God, do not keep silent;
be not quiet, O God, be not still.
2 See how your enemies are astir,
how your foes rear their heads.
3 With cunning they conspire against your people;
they plot against those you cherish.
4 "Come," they say, "let us destroy them as a nation,
that the name of Israel be remembered no more."

5 With one mind they plot together;
they form an alliance against you—
6 the tents of Edom and the Ishmaelites,
of Moab and the Hagrites,
7 Gebal,[b] Ammon and Amalek,
Philistia, with the people of Tyre.
8 Even Assyria has joined them
to lend strength to the descendants of Lot. *Selah*

9 Do to them as you did to Midian,
as you did to Sisera and Jabin at the river
Kishon,
10 who perished at Endor
and became like refuse on the ground.
11 Make their nobles like Oreb and Zeeb,
all their princes like Zebah and Zalmunna,
12 who said, "Let us take possession
of the pasturelands of God."

[a]2 The Hebrew is plural. [b]7 That is, Byblos

82:5 *walk about in darkness . . . foundations of the earth are shaken:* See the note at 18:28. In ancient times it was believed that the earth was flat and supported by columns. These "foundations" are the mountains. When injustice exists, the whole world is threatened.

83:2-4 *your enemies . . . against your people:* God's "enemies" are also the people's "enemies." See the note at 44:5. The "enemies" are named in 83:6-8.

83:6-8 *Edom . . . Assyria:* These nations surrounded Israel (see the map on p. 2465). The Ishmaelites were generally known as nomads and caravan traders (Gen 16:1–16; 25:12). Lot's older daughter was the mother of the Moabites, and his younger daughter was the mother of the Ammonites (Gen 19:36-38). The land of the Hagrites was probably to the north of Ammon (1 Chr 5:10, 18, 19). Gebal, probably ancient Byblos, lies north of Tyre in Phoenicia. The Assyrians were a major power in the eighth and seventh centuries B.C. See the map on p. 2468 and the mini-article called "Assyria," p. 711. It is unlikely that these verses describe an actual alliance of all these nations against Israel. But each was a threat to Israel at different times.

83:9 *as you did to Midian:* God's defeat of Midian is described in Judges 6–8. Midian lies to the south of Edom (see the map on p. 2463).

83:9 *Sisera and Jabin:* Jabin was the King of Hazor (Judg 4:2), and Sisera was his army commander. Jabin and Sisera's army was defeated by Deborah and Barak, and Sisera was killed by Jael (Judg 4:1-24).

83:9,10 *Endor:* Sisera's defeat was just south of Mount Tabor near Endor (see the map on p. 2464).

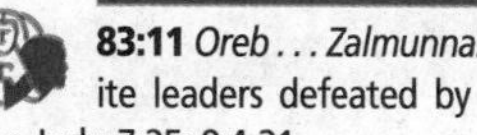

83:11 *Oreb . . . Zalmunna:* Midianite leaders defeated by Gideon. See Judg 7:25; 8:4-21.

13 Make them like tumbleweed, O my God,
like chaff before the wind.
14 As fire consumes the forest
or a flame sets the mountains ablaze,
15 so pursue them with your tempest
and terrify them with your storm.
16 Cover their faces with shame
so that men will seek your name, O LORD.

17 May they ever be ashamed and dismayed;
may they perish in disgrace.
18 Let them know that you, whose name is the LORD—
that you alone are the Most High over all the earth.

Psalm 84

For the director of music. According to *gittith.*[a]
Of the Sons of Korah. A psalm.

1 How lovely is your dwelling place,
O LORD Almighty!
2 My soul yearns, even faints,
for the courts of the LORD;
my heart and my flesh cry out
for the living God.

3 Even the sparrow has found a home,
and the swallow a nest for herself,
where she may have her young—
a place near your altar,
O LORD Almighty, my King and my God.
4 Blessed are those who dwell in your house;
they are ever praising you. *Selah*

5 Blessed are those whose strength is in you,
who have set their hearts on pilgrimage.
6 As they pass through the Valley of Baca,
they make it a place of springs;
the autumn rains also cover it with pools.[b]
7 They go from strength to strength,
till each appears before God in Zion.

8 Hear my prayer, O LORD God Almighty;
listen to me, O God of Jacob. *Selah*
9 Look upon our shield,[c] O God;
look with favor on your anointed one.

10 Better is one day in your courts
than a thousand elsewhere;

83:13-16 *flame . . . tempest . . . storm:* God's appearance in these forces usually signals a time of judgment (see Isa 66:15, 16; Amos 1:14; Nah 1:3). See also the note at 11:6 and the mini-article called "Fire," p. 2383.

83:18 *Most High:* See the notes at 2:4; 5:10-12; and 18:13.

84:1-3 *LORD Almighty . . . my King and my God:* See the note at 46:6, 7 and the note on p. 1024.

84:3 *a place near your altar:* The main altar of sacrifice was located in the courtyard outside the actual temple building. Perhaps the heat from the burning sacrifices helped to warm the birds' nests. See also the note at 16:4.

84:4,5 *Blessed are those who dwell in your house:* Blessing or happiness comes from depending on God (see 84:12 and the note at 1:1,2). On living in God's "house" (temple), see the note at 27:4.

84:6 *Valley of Baca:* The exact location is not known.

84:7 *Zion:* See the note at 2:6.

84:9 *your anointed one:* See the note at 2:2 and the mini-article called "Messiah (Chosen One)," p. 1124.

[a]Title: Probably a musical term [b]6 Or *blessings* [c]9 Or *sovereign*

I would rather be a doorkeeper in the house of my God
than dwell in the tents of the wicked.
11 For the LORD God is a sun and shield;
the LORD bestows favor and honor;
no good thing does he withhold
from those whose walk is blameless.

12 O LORD Almighty,
blessed is the man who trusts in you.

Psalm 85

For the director of music. Of the Sons of Korah. A psalm.

1 You showed favor to your land, O LORD;
you restored the fortunes of Jacob.
2 You forgave the iniquity of your people
and covered all their sins. *Selah*
3 You set aside all your wrath
and turned from your fierce anger.

4 Restore us again, O God our Savior,
and put away your displeasure toward us.
5 Will you be angry with us forever?
Will you prolong your anger through all generations?
6 Will you not revive us again,
that your people may rejoice in you?
7 Show us your unfailing love, O LORD,
and grant us your salvation.

8 I will listen to what God the LORD will say;
he promises peace to his people, his saints—
but let them not return to folly.
9 Surely his salvation is near those who fear him,
that his glory may dwell in our land.

10 Love and faithfulness meet together;
righteousness and peace kiss each other.
11 Faithfulness springs forth from the earth,
and righteousness looks down from heaven.
12 The LORD will indeed give what is good,
and our land will yield its harvest.
13 Righteousness goes before him
and prepares the way for his steps.

Psalm 86

A prayer of David.

1 Hear, O LORD, and answer me,
for I am poor and needy.
2 Guard my life, for I am devoted to you.
You are my God; save your servant
who trusts in you.

84:10 *the wicked:* See the mini-article called "Enemies (The Wicked)," p. 1084.

85:1-4 *Restore us again:* These verses suggest that the psalm was written about the time the people of Israel returned home to Judah from exile in Babylon (after 539 B.C.). See Isa 40:1-11 and the note at 74:3, 7.

85:1 *Jacob:* Meaning the people of Israel (see the note at 22:23).

85:5 *angry with us forever:* After the return from exile, new problems developed (see the Introduction to HAGGAI, p. 1787). The people found it necessary to pray again for deliverance.

85:8 *peace:* There is a relationship between peace and doing what is right (85:10).

86:1 *poor and needy:* See the note at 34:2. See also 88:4; 142:5.

86:2 *your servant:* As a "servant," the psalmist depends upon God's help (86:13, 17), and intends to do God's will (86:11).

O Lord, *the God who saves me, day and night I cry out before you. May my prayer come before you; turn your ear to my cry.*
Ps 88:1,2

86:8,10 *deeds . . . marvelous deeds:* See the notes at 75:1.

86:14 *ruthless men:* See the note at 3:1,2 and the mini-article called "Enemies (The Wicked)," p. 1084.

87:1-3 *holy mountain . . . Zion . . . city of God:* This refers to the hill on which the temple was built. See the notes at 2:6 and 48:1,2. Other psalms that praise Zion are 46; 48; 76; 84; and 122.

86:9 Rev 15:4.

3 Have mercy on me, O Lord,
for I call to you all day long.
4 Bring joy to your servant,
for to you, O Lord,
I lift up my soul.

5 You are forgiving and good, O Lord,
abounding in love to all who call to you.
6 Hear my prayer, O Lord;
listen to my cry for mercy.
7 In the day of my trouble I will call to you,
for you will answer me.

8 Among the gods there is none like you, O Lord;
no deeds can compare with yours.
9 All the nations you have made
will come and worship before you, O Lord;
they will bring glory to your name.
10 For you are great and do marvelous deeds;
you alone are God.

11 Teach me your way, O Lord,
and I will walk in your truth;
give me an undivided heart,
that I may fear your name.
12 I will praise you, O Lord my God, with all my heart;
I will glorify your name forever.
13 For great is your love toward me;
you have delivered me from the depths of the grave.[a]

14 The arrogant are attacking me, O God;
a band of ruthless men seeks my life—
men without regard for you.
15 But you, O Lord, are a compassionate and gracious God,
slow to anger, abounding in love and faithfulness.
16 Turn to me and have mercy on me;
grant your strength to your servant
and save the son of your maidservant.[b]
17 Give me a sign of your goodness,
that my enemies may see it and be put to shame,
for you, O Lord, have helped me and comforted me.

Psalm 87

Of the Sons of Korah. A psalm. A song.

1 He has set his foundation on the holy mountain;
2 the Lord loves the gates of Zion
more than all the dwellings of Jacob.

[a]**13** Hebrew *Sheol* [b]**16** Or *save your faithful son*

[3]Glorious things are said of you,
O city of God: *Selah*
[4]"I will record Rahab[a] and Babylon
among those who acknowledge me—
Philistia too, and Tyre, along with Cush[b]—
and will say, 'This[c] one was born in Zion.' "

[5]Indeed, of Zion it will be said,
"This one and that one were born in her,
and the Most High himself will establish her."
[6]The LORD will write in the register of the peoples:
"This one was born in Zion." *Selah*
[7]As they make music they will sing,
"All my fountains are in you."

Psalm 88

A song. A psalm of the Sons of Korah. For the director of music. According to *mahalath leannoth.*[d] A *maskil*[e] of Heman the Ezrahite.

[1]O LORD, the God who saves me,
day and night I cry out before you.

[a]**4** A poetic name for Egypt [b]**4** That is, the upper Nile region [c]**4** Or *"O Rahab and Babylon, / Philistia, Tyre and Cush, / I will record concerning those who acknowledge me: / 'This* [d]Title: Possibly a tune, "The Suffering of Affliction" [e]Title: Probably a literary or musical term

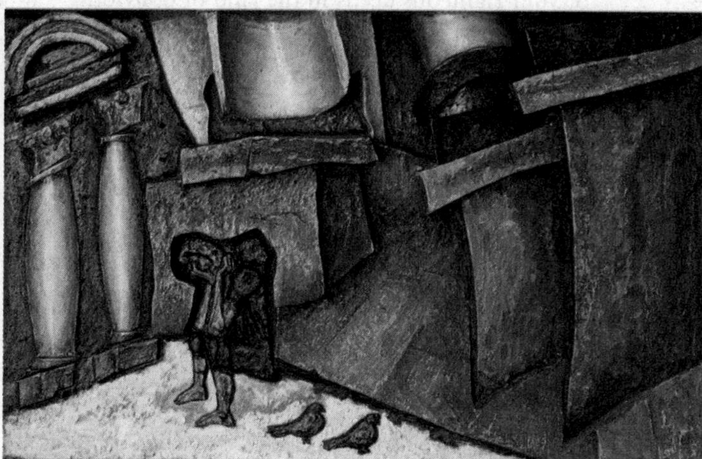

Lamentation Near the Temple's Wall by Alek Rapoport, 1976. Over a third of the psalms in the Bible can be classified as laments, or psalms of complaint. Some of these reflect national crises (see, for example, Ps 80), but most are complaints about the sufferings of individuals. In Psalm 88, the psalmist expresses a deep sense of despair and isolation. "My soul is full of trouble and my life draws near the grave . . . You have taken from me my closest friends and have made me repulsive to them. I am confined and cannot escape; my eyes are dim with grief" (Ps 88:3,8,9).

87:4 *Babylon . . . Philistia . . . Tyre . . . Cush:* These nations are usually presented as Israel's enemies. But here, God claims them, and they claim God's city as their hometown, indicating that God rules over and cares for all persons. It is also possible that this refers to Israelite people who have been scattered to these nations because of wars. Tyre was the capital of Phoenicia. The people of Phoenicia, located along the Mediterranean Sea north of Israel, were known for their sea travel and trading. Cush (Ethiopia) was a region south of Egypt (here called Rahab) that included parts of the present countries of Ethiopia and Sudan. See the maps on pp. 2467 and 2469.

88 Title *Sons of Korah . . . Heman the Ezrahite:* See the note at 42 Title (Korah). Heman was appointed by David to help in leading worship in the tabernacle and later at the temple (1 Chr 16:41,42; 25:1-8).

88:4 *without strength:* See the note at 34:2.

88:9 *spread out my hands:* See the note at 28:2.

88:10-12 *show your wonders to the dead:* The LORD's miracles are to be remembered and spoken of among the living (see 78:5,6). But the psalmist's questions are meant to prove a point: If the psalmist's suffering leads to death, how can he tell of God's miracles? See also the note at 9:13.

88:16-18 *Your wrath . . . darkness:* It is not unusual in the prayers for help for the psalmists to accuse God directly of causing suffering. Such complaints are usually balanced by expressions of trust in God (see the note at 13:5, 6). But here the psalmist remains in "darkness." He only trusts God enough to keep praying.

89 Title *Ethan the Ezrahite:* Ethan was known for his great wisdom (1 Kgs 4:30, 31).

89:20 1 Sam 13:14; 16:12; Acts 13:22; 1 Sam 16:12.

2 May my prayer come before you;
turn your ear to my cry.

3 For my soul is full of trouble
and my life draws near the grave.[a]
4 I am counted among those who go down to the pit;
I am like a man without strength.
5 I am set apart with the dead,
like the slain who lie in the grave,
whom you remember no more,
who are cut off from your care.

6 You have put me in the lowest pit,
in the darkest depths.
7 Your wrath lies heavily upon me;
you have overwhelmed me with all your waves. *Selah*
8 You have taken from me my closest friends
and have made me repulsive to them.
I am confined and cannot escape;
9 my eyes are dim with grief.

I call to you, O LORD, every day;
I spread out my hands to you.
10 Do you show your wonders to the dead?
Do those who are dead rise up and praise you? *Selah*
11 Is your love declared in the grave,
your faithfulness in Destruction[b]?
12 Are your wonders known in the place of darkness,
or your righteous deeds in the land of oblivion?

13 But I cry to you for help, O LORD;
in the morning my prayer comes before you.
14 Why, O LORD, do you reject me
and hide your face from me?

15 From my youth I have been afflicted and close to death;
I have suffered your terrors and am in despair.
16 Your wrath has swept over me;
your terrors have destroyed me.
17 All day long they surround me like a flood;
they have completely engulfed me.
18 You have taken my companions and loved ones from me;
the darkness is my closest friend.

Psalm 89

A *maskil*[c] of Ethan the Ezrahite.

1 I will sing of the LORD's great love forever;
with my mouth I will make your faithfulness known
through all generations.

[a]3 Hebrew *Sheol* [b]11 Hebrew *Abaddon* [c]Title: Probably a literary or musical term

[2]I will declare that your love stands firm forever,
that you established your faithfulness in heaven itself.

[3]You said, "I have made a covenant with my chosen one,
I have sworn to David my servant,
[4]'I will establish your line forever
and make your throne firm through all
generations.'" *Selah*

[5]The heavens praise your wonders, O LORD,
your faithfulness too, in the assembly of the holy ones.
[6]For who in the skies above can compare with the LORD?
Who is like the LORD among the heavenly beings?
[7]In the council of the holy ones God is greatly feared;
he is more awesome than all who surround him.
[8]O LORD God Almighty, who is like you?
You are mighty, O LORD, and your faithfulness
surrounds you.

[9]You rule over the surging sea;
when its waves mount up, you still them.
[10]You crushed Rahab like one of the slain;
with your strong arm you scattered your enemies.
[11]The heavens are yours, and yours also the earth;
you founded the world and all that is in it.
[12]You created the north and the south;
Tabor and Hermon sing for joy at your name.
[13]Your arm is endued with power;
your hand is strong, your right hand exalted.

[14]Righteousness and justice are the foundation of
your throne;
love and faithfulness go before you.
[15]Blessed are those who have learned to acclaim you,
who walk in the light of your presence, O LORD.
[16]They rejoice in your name all day long;
they exult in your righteousness.
[17]For you are their glory and strength,
and by your favor you exalt our horn.[a]
[18]Indeed, our shield[b] belongs to the LORD,
our king to the Holy One of Israel.

[19]Once you spoke in a vision,
to your faithful people you said:
"I have bestowed strength on a warrior;
I have exalted a young man from among the people.
[20]I have found David my servant;
with my sacred oil I have anointed him.

89:3,4 *covenant:* God's covenant with David is found in 2 Samuel 7:8-16 (see also 1 Chr 17:9-14; Ps 132:11). It includes the promise contained in 89:4. See also 18:50 and note. Years after the disappearance of the kingdom of David, Jesus fulfilled this promise (Acts 2:30).

89:3 *David my servant:* See the mini-article called "David," p. 1028.

89:5 *holy ones:* This may refer angels. See the notes at 29:1,2 and 34:7.

89:8 *Almighty:* See the note at 46:6,7.

89:10 *Rahab:* This probably refers to an ancient sea monster that stood for the power of the ocean (see Job 26:12,13). According to Isaiah 51:9, the LORD destroyed Rahab at the time of creation (compare Ps 74:12-14).

89:10 *scattered your enemies:* May refer to Rahab, or to people and nations that oppose God. See the notes at 44:5 and 80:6.

89:12 *Tabor and Hermon:* Tabor is located just southeast of the Sea of Galilee. For Hermon, see the note at 29:5-8. See also the map on p. 2464.

89:14 *Righteousness and justice:* See the note on p. 1024. God's rule involves "righteousness and justice" (see the note at 9:8, 9).

89:15 *blessed:* See the note at 1:1,2.

89:18 *Holy One of Israel:* See the note at 71:22 (Holy One).

89:19-37 *David my servant:* This long passage recalls 2 Samuel 7:8-16, which tells of God's promise to David that one of his descendants would always rule Israel. This message was delivered by Nathan, the prophet who may have received God's word in a "vision" (89:19).

[a]**17** *Horn* here symbolizes strong one. [b]**18** Or *sovereign*

89:26 *Rock:* See the note at 18:46.

89:27 *appoint him my firstborn:* David and his descendants who ruled as kings were known as God's "sons." See the notes at 2:2 and 2:7-9.

89:28 *my covenant:* Though a descendant of David continued on the throne for many years, the fall of Jerusalem put an end to the promise, at least until years later when a descendant of David (Joshua the high priest) ruled alongside the governor Zerubbabel (Zech 6:9-14). Because Jesus was from the family of David (Matt 1:1), Christians understand the covenant with David to be continued in Jesus, the Messiah.

89:27 Rev 1:5.

21 My hand will sustain him;
surely my arm will strengthen him.
22 No enemy will subject him to tribute;
no wicked man will oppress him.
23 I will crush his foes before him
and strike down his adversaries.
24 My faithful love will be with him,
and through my name his horn[a] will be exalted.
25 I will set his hand over the sea,
his right hand over the rivers.
26 He will call out to me, 'You are my Father,
my God, the Rock my Savior.'
27 I will also appoint him my firstborn,
the most exalted of the kings of the earth.
28 I will maintain my love to him forever,
and my covenant with him will never fail.

[a]24 *Horn* here symbolizes strength.

MESSIAH (CHOSEN ONE)

The Hebrew word "Messiah" means "anointed one." Anointing is the practice of pouring oil on the head of a person who is chosen to serve God and God's people. For example, priests were anointed (Lev 8:5-12; 1 Chr 29:22); prophets were sometimes anointed (1 Kgs 19:16); and Cyrus, a Persian king, was even called the LORD's "anointed" when God chose him to help the people return to Judea from their exile in Babylon (Isa 45:1).

In the Jewish Scriptures, it is the king who is most often called "the LORD's anointed" (1 Sam 16:6; 24:5-7). Several psalms about the king make it clear that as God's "Anointed One" (Ps 2:2) or "Son" (Ps 2:7), the king is responsible for establishing God's justice and peace on earth. See the notes at Ps 18:34-48 and 72:1-3. This means rescuing victims of oppression (see Ps 9:8,9).

God's covenant with King David was that one of his descendants would always be king (Ps 89:4). But when Jerusalem was destroyed and the exile began in 586 B.C., the kingdom of David and his descendants was ended (see Ps 89:38-45). After the exile, some people looked for the restoring of the kingship of David's line. Others suggested that all of God's people were now responsible for doing what the kings had done.

This matter was still being discussed hundreds of years later when the early Christians expressed their belief that Jesus was God's "anointed one." The early Christians saw in Jesus a "chosen one" who rescued the poor and established peace by inviting all people into God's kingdom. The Gospel of MARK uses the two titles for the king from Psalm 2 and applies them to Jesus: "Christ" (which is Greek for "anointed one") and "Son of God" (Mark 1:1; see Ps 2:2,7). MATTHEW identifies Jesus as a descendant of David and so places him in David's royal line (Matt 1:1). Jesus became known as "Jesus Messiah" (or Jesus Christ; Mark 8:29; 14:61,62), and confessing Jesus to be the Messiah set early Christians apart from their Jewish contemporaries (John 9:22,23; 1 John 2:22).

[29]I will establish his line forever,
his throne as long as the heavens endure.

[30]"If his sons forsake my law
and do not follow my statutes,
[31]if they violate my decrees
and fail to keep my commands,
[32]I will punish their sin with the rod,
their iniquity with flogging;
[33]but I will not take my love from him,
nor will I ever betray my faithfulness.
[34]I will not violate my covenant
or alter what my lips have uttered.
[35]Once for all, I have sworn by my holiness—
and I will not lie to David—
[36]that his line will continue forever
and his throne endure before me like the sun;
[37]it will be established forever like the moon,
the faithful witness in the sky." *Selah*

[38]But you have rejected, you have spurned,
you have been very angry with your anointed one.
[39]You have renounced the covenant with your servant
and have defiled his crown in the dust.
[40]You have broken through all his walls
and reduced his strongholds to ruins.
[41]All who pass by have plundered him;
he has become the scorn of his neighbors.
[42]You have exalted the right hand of his foes;
you have made all his enemies rejoice.
[43]You have turned back the edge of his sword
and have not supported him in battle.

The LORD said, *"I will establish his line forever, his throne as long as the heavens endure."*
Ps 89:29

89:30-32 *If his sons forsake my law:* David's descendants were to be "punished" but not rejected (2 Sam 7:14). A number of kings who descended from David did reject the Law (for example, see 2 Kgs 16:1-18; 21:1-16). See also the note at 1:1,2.

89:38-45 *you have rejected, you have spurned:* These verses mark a major shift in the psalm. The "covenant" that could "never fail" (89:28) has now been broken. This reflects the crisis of 586 B.C., when Jerusalem's city walls were broken through, and the kingdom of David and his descendants ended. See 2 Kgs 24–25 and the note at 44:9-11.

QUESTIONS ABOUT PSALMS 73:1—89:52

1. Several psalms in Book III are prayers spoken by the whole people. Read Psalms 74; 79; and 80. What trouble do the people pray about, and what do they ask God to do?
2. Read Psalm 78. What events from Israel's history does the psalm recall? Why was it important for the people to remember their past? How may it be important for people of faith today to remember their past? If you were to write a psalm describing your own "faith journey," what events would you be sure to include?
3. Read Psalm 86. What are "the gods" that are mentioned in verse 8? How does God's purpose differ from the behavior of the gods? How do people today sometimes worship what might be called "gods"?
4. How does Psalm 88 differ from almost all the other prayers for help in PSALMS? What is important about this difference?
5. Read Psalm 89. What covenant did God have with David and his descendants? What does it mean that God "rejected" the kingdom of his "anointed one"? (Ps 89:38,39) What crisis did this cause for the people of God?

89:46-51 *How long, O LORD:* The people ask God why their country has fallen and God's temple has been destroyed. In 89:50, 51 the defeated king asks God for help, but there seems to be no help in sight.

90 Title *Moses:* Moses led God's people out of Egypt, received God's teaching at Mount Sinai, and led the people to the borders of their new land. But Psalm 90 was really written much later in response to the crisis of 586 B.C. By assigning Psalm 90 to Moses, the collectors of the psalms suggest that Moses' prayers of long ago will still be helpful as the people face new troubles. See the mini-article called "Moses," p. 2335.

90:1 *you have been our dwelling:* This psalm most likely was written in response to the destruction of the temple in 586 B.C. Note how the psalmist calls the LORD "our dwelling." In previous psalms, "dwelling" or "home" usually referred to the LORD's temple (see the notes at 5:7 and 74:2,3).

90:2-8 *you brought forth the earth ... secret sins:* The psalmist confesses that God is the creator of the world and suggests that God controls human life and death ("turn men back to dust," see Gen 3:19). See also Prov 16:1, 9; Eccl 3:1-11. The idea that life is short and one should make the best of it (90:4-6,12) is found in other examples of Hebrew wisdom literature (Job 4:19-21; Eccl 3:12,13; 9:7-10).

God also knows everything, including people's most secret sins. This is another important theme in Hebrew Wisdom literature (see Job 34:21; Ps 139:16; Prov 15:3.

44 You have put an end to his splendor
and cast his throne to the ground.
45 You have cut short the days of his youth;
you have covered him with a mantle of shame. *Selah*

46 How long, O LORD? Will you hide yourself forever?
How long will your wrath burn like fire?
47 Remember how fleeting is my life.
For what futility you have created all men!
48 What man can live and not see death,
or save himself from the power of the grave[a]? *Selah*
49 O Lord, where is your former great love,
which in your faithfulness you swore to David?
50 Remember, Lord, how your servant has[b] been mocked,
how I bear in my heart the taunts of all the nations,
51 the taunts with which your enemies have mocked, O LORD,
with which they have mocked every step of your
anointed one.

52 Praise be to the LORD forever!
Amen and Amen.

Book IV (Psalms 90:1—106:48)

Book III ends with God's people asking questions (Ps 89:46-49) and God's "anointed one" complaining and asking for help (Ps 89:50,51). The people of Israel faced a terrible crisis. Jerusalem and the temple had been destroyed in 586 B.C. Many of the people, including the last in the line of kings from David's family, had been taken away into exile. Book IV seems to be organized to offer a response to this crisis. The first psalm is a prayer by Moses, who led the people out of slavery in Egypt. He was the great leader of Israel before they had a king, a temple, or a land of their own. In response to the disappearance of earthly kingship, Book IV offers the assurance that God rules the world (Ps 93; 95–99).

Psalm 90

A prayer of Moses the man of God.

1 Lord, you have been our dwelling place
throughout all generations.
2 Before the mountains were born
or you brought forth the earth and the world,
from everlasting to everlasting you are God.

3 You turn men back to dust,
saying, "Return to dust, O sons of men."

[a]**48** Hebrew *Sheol* [b]**50** Or *your servants have*

[4]For a thousand years in your sight
are like a day that has just gone by,
or like a watch in the night.
[5]You sweep men away in the sleep of death;
they are like the new grass of the morning—
[6]though in the morning it springs up new,
by evening it is dry and withered.

[7]We are consumed by your anger
and terrified by your indignation.
[8]You have set our iniquities before you,
our secret sins in the light of your presence.
[9]All our days pass away under your wrath;
we finish our years with a moan.
[10]The length of our days is seventy years—
or eighty, if we have the strength;
yet their span[a] is but trouble and sorrow,
for they quickly pass, and we fly away.

[11]Who knows the power of your anger?
For your wrath is as great as the fear that is due you.
[12]Teach us to number our days aright,
that we may gain a heart of wisdom.

[13]Relent, O LORD! How long will it be?
Have compassion on your servants.
[14]Satisfy us in the morning with your unfailing love,
that we may sing for joy and be glad all our days.
[15]Make us glad for as many days as you have afflicted us,
for as many years as we have seen trouble.
[16]May your deeds be shown to your servants,
your splendor to their children.

[17]May the favor[b] of the Lord our God rest upon us;
establish the work of our hands for us—
yes, establish the work of our hands.

Psalm 91

[1]He who dwells in the shelter of the Most High
will rest in the shadow of the Almighty.[c]
[2]I will say[d] of the LORD, "He is my refuge and my fortress,
my God, in whom I trust."

[3]Surely he will save you from the fowler's snare
and from the deadly pestilence.
[4]He will cover you with his feathers,
and under his wings you will find refuge;
his faithfulness will be your shield and rampart.

May the favor of the Lord our God rest upon us; establish the work of our hands for us— yes, establish the work of our hands.
Ps 90:17

90:12 *number our days aright:* This verse suggests that even though life is short (90:5,10), it can be lived wisely. This leads to the more hopeful interpretation of "time" in 90:13-17. See also the note at 19:7,8.

90:14 *Satisfy us . . . unfailing love:* Confidence in God's "love" is especially important after the people's questioning of God's "love" in 89:49.

91:1,9 *Most High . . . shadow . . . Almighty . . . refuge:* See the notes at 47:2 and 46:6,7. God's "shadow" is a symbol for "refuge." It is sometimes mentioned along with God's "wings" (see 91:4). See also the note at 11:1.

91:3 *fowler's snare . . . deadly pestilence:* See the note at 31:4. In the prayers for help, the psalmists often complain of sickness (91:6; see also 38:3-8; 41:3,4,7-10).

90:4 2 Pet 3:8.

a10 Or *yet the best of them* **b17** Or *beauty* **c1** Hebrew *Shaddai* **d2** Or *He says*

91:7 *A thousand may fall:* This could be from disease or from military conflict. The language is probably symbolic. See also the note at 35:1.

91:10 *no harm will befall you:* The promise is not that nothing bad will ever happen, but rather that God's protection will always be present for those who turn to God for help. See also 34:19 and the note at 37:39,40.

91:11 *angels:* In the Bible, angels act as both messengers and servants of God. See also the mini-article called "Angels," p. 88.

91:13 *lion . . . cobra:* Predatory animals are often symbols for enemies. See Luke 10:19.

91:16 *my salvation:* See the note at 51:12-14.

92 Title *Sabbath day:* The Sabbath was the seventh day of the week. It was a day for rest and worship. See Exod 20:8-11; Deut 5:12-15. See also the chart called "Jewish Calendar and Festivals," p. 944.

92:3 *harp:* See the note at 33:2 and the illustration on p. 897.

92:6 *fools:* See the note at 14:1.

92:7 *the wicked . . . forever destroyed:* Meaning the wicked will disappear. See the note at 3:1,2.

91:11,12 Matt 4:6; Luke 4:10, 11.

5 You will not fear the terror of night,
nor the arrow that flies by day,
6 nor the pestilence that stalks in the darkness,
nor the plague that destroys at midday.
7 A thousand may fall at your side,
ten thousand at your right hand,
but it will not come near you.
8 You will only observe with your eyes
and see the punishment of the wicked.

9 If you make the Most High your dwelling—
even the LORD, who is my refuge—
10 then no harm will befall you,
no disaster will come near your tent.
11 For he will command his angels concerning you
to guard you in all your ways;
12 they will lift you up in their hands,
so that you will not strike your foot against a stone.
13 You will tread upon the lion and the cobra;
you will trample the great lion and the serpent.

14 "Because he loves me," says the LORD, "I will rescue him;
I will protect him, for he acknowledges my name.
15 He will call upon me, and I will answer him;
I will be with him in trouble,
I will deliver him and honor him.
16 With long life will I satisfy him
and show him my salvation."

Psalm 92

A psalm. A song. For the Sabbath day.

1 It is good to praise the LORD
and make music to your name, O Most High,
2 to proclaim your love in the morning
and your faithfulness at night,
3 to the music of the ten-stringed lyre
and the melody of the harp.

4 For you make me glad by your deeds, O LORD;
I sing for joy at the works of your hands.
5 How great are your works, O LORD,
how profound your thoughts!
6 The senseless man does not know,
fools do not understand,
7 that though the wicked spring up like grass
and all evildoers flourish,
they will be forever destroyed.

[8]But you, O LORD, are exalted forever.

[9]For surely your enemies, O LORD,
surely your enemies will perish;
all evildoers will be scattered.
[10]You have exalted my horn[a] like that of a wild ox;
fine oils have been poured upon me.
[11]My eyes have seen the defeat of my adversaries;
my ears have heard the rout of my wicked foes.

[12]The righteous will flourish like a palm tree,
they will grow like a cedar of Lebanon;
[13]planted in the house of the LORD,
they will flourish in the courts of our God.
[14]They will still bear fruit in old age,
they will stay fresh and green,
[15]proclaiming, "The LORD is upright;
he is my Rock, and there is no wickedness
in him."

Psalm 93

[1]The LORD reigns, he is robed in majesty;
the LORD is robed in majesty
and is armed with strength.
The world is firmly established;
it cannot be moved.
[2]Your throne was established long ago;
you are from all eternity.

[3]The seas have lifted up, O LORD,
the seas have lifted up their voice;
the seas have lifted up their pounding waves.
[4]Mightier than the thunder of the great waters,
mightier than the breakers of the sea—
the LORD on high is mighty.

[5]Your statutes stand firm;
holiness adorns your house
for endless days, O LORD.

Psalm 94

[1]O LORD, the God who avenges,
O God who avenges, shine forth.
[2]Rise up, O Judge of the earth;
pay back to the proud what they deserve.
[3]How long will the wicked, O LORD,
how long will the wicked be jubilant?

[a]10 *Horn* here symbolizes strength.

92:8 *exalted forever:* To exalt is to lift up in praise. Here the psalmist contrasts God's exalted and eternal status with the low and dishonorable status of the wicked who will one day perish and be gone. See 93:1, 2.

92:12 *palm tree . . . cedar of Lebanon:* See the notes at 1:3 and 52:8 (olive tree), where trees are symbols for God's people. See also the note at 29:5-8 (Mount Lebanon). The palm trees shown here are from the Sinai Peninsula.

92:13 *house of the LORD:* God's "house" is the temple. See the notes at 5:7 and 27:4.

92:15 *Rock:* See the note at 18:46.

93:1,2 *The LORD reigns:* See the note on p. 1024. Psalms 93 and 95–99 may have been used in the temple to celebrate God's kingship.

93:3,4 *The seas . . . pounding waves:* The "seas" and "waves" are symbols for the power of chaos. See the notes at 18:16 and 24:2.

94:2 *O Judge of the earth:* The purpose of God's judging is justice. To establish justice for victims (94:6), God must oppose oppressors. See 94:15 and the note at 5:10-12.

94:3 *the wicked:* These are people who oppose God and hurt others (94:4-7,13). See also the note at 10:2,3.

When I said, "My foot is slipping," your love, O LORD, supported me.
Ps 94:18

94:5 *your inheritance:* This refers to the people of Israel (Exod 19:3-6; Deut 7:6-8). In this psalm the whole people of God are suffering. See the notes at 79:1 and 89:46-51.

94:6 *widow . . . alien . . . fatherless:* These are people who need help and who are given protection by God's law (Exod 22:21-24). See the note at 10:14.

94:7,8 *Jacob . . . fools:* See the notes at 22:23 and 14:1.

94:12 *Blessed . . . law:* See the note at 1:1, 2.

94:17 *dwelt in the silence of death:* This means death, often described as a place, the world of the dead (see the note at 9:13).

94:20,21 *corrupt throne . . . condemn the innocent:* The prophets of Israel often spoke out against those in power who ignored God's concern for justice and took advantage of the poor (see Isa 1:21-23; 5:8-24; Amos 2:6,7; 5:10-12; Mic 2:1,2).

94:22 *fortress . . . refuge:* See the note at 11:1.

95:1 *Rock of our salvation:* See the note at 18:46.

94:11 1 Cor 3:20.

[4]They pour out arrogant words;
all the evildoers are full of boasting.
[5]They crush your people, O LORD;
they oppress your inheritance.
[6]They slay the widow and the alien;
they murder the fatherless.
[7]They say, "The LORD does not see;
the God of Jacob pays no heed."

[8]Take heed, you senseless ones among the people;
you fools, when will you become wise?
[9]Does he who implanted the ear not hear?
Does he who formed the eye not see?
[10]Does he who disciplines nations not punish?
Does he who teaches man lack knowledge?
[11]The LORD knows the thoughts of man;
he knows that they are futile.

[12]Blessed is the man you discipline, O LORD,
the man you teach from your law;
[13]you grant him relief from days of trouble,
till a pit is dug for the wicked.
[14]For the LORD will not reject his people;
he will never forsake his inheritance.
[15]Judgment will again be founded on righteousness,
and all the upright in heart will follow it.

[16]Who will rise up for me against the wicked?
Who will take a stand for me against evildoers?
[17]Unless the LORD had given me help,
I would soon have dwelt in the silence of death.
[18]When I said, "My foot is slipping,"
your love, O LORD, supported me.
[19]When anxiety was great within me,
your consolation brought joy to my soul.

[20]Can a corrupt throne be allied with you—
one that brings on misery by its decrees?
[21]They band together against the righteous
and condemn the innocent to death.
[22]But the LORD has become my fortress,
and my God the rock in whom I take refuge.
[23]He will repay them for their sins
and destroy them for their wickedness;
the LORD our God will destroy them.

Psalm 95

[1]Come, let us sing for joy to the LORD;
let us shout aloud to the Rock of our salvation.

2 Let us come before him with thanksgiving
and extol him with music and song.

3 For the LORD is the great God,
the great King above all gods.
4 In his hand are the depths of the earth,
and the mountain peaks belong to him.
5 The sea is his, for he made it,
and his hands formed the dry land.

6 Come, let us bow down in worship,
let us kneel before the LORD our Maker;
7 for he is our God
and we are the people of his pasture,
the flock under his care.

Today, if you hear his voice,
8 do not harden your hearts as you did at Meribah,[a]
as you did that day at Massah[b] in the desert,
9 where your fathers tested and tried me,
though they had seen what I did.
10 For forty years I was angry with that generation;
I said, "They are a people whose hearts go
astray,
and they have not known my ways."
11 So I declared on oath in my anger,
"They shall never enter my rest."

Psalm 96

1 Sing to the LORD a new song;
sing to the LORD, all the earth.
2 Sing to the LORD, praise his name;
proclaim his salvation day after day.
3 Declare his glory among the nations,
his marvelous deeds among all peoples.

4 For great is the LORD and most worthy of praise;
he is to be feared above all gods.
5 For all the gods of the nations are idols,
but the LORD made the heavens.
6 Splendor and majesty are before him;
strength and glory are in his sanctuary.

7 Ascribe to the LORD, O families of nations,
ascribe to the LORD glory and strength.
8 Ascribe to the LORD the glory due his name;
bring an offering and come into his courts.

[a]8 *Meribah* means *quarreling*. [b]8 *Massah* means *testing*.

95:3 *King above all gods:* See the note at 82:1 and the note on p. 1024.

95:6,7 *our Maker . . . flock:* God is the Creator of the world but also one who takes care of his people as a shepherd. See also 100:3 and the notes at 23:1-3 and 80:1.

95:7 *hear his voice:* Sheep normally listen to their shepherd (John 10:4), but 95:8-11 tells how God's people did not listen. The psalmist uses this memory to call people to obey God "today." These verses may have been spoken in a worship service by a priest or prophet. See the note at 50:7-14.

95:8 *Meribah . . . Massah:* See the note at 81:6,7. See also Exod 17:1-7; Num 20:2-13.

95:9-11 *forty years . . . my rest:* What happened at Meribah and Massah was not unusual. As a result of the people's disobedience, God did not let the older generation of Israelites enter their "rest," the promised land of Canaan (Num 14:20-30; Deut 1:34-36; Heb 4:3, 5).

96:1 *a new song:* New songs celebrate new acts of deliverance by God. This "new song" could certainly have been sung in celebration of how God eventually restored the people following the crisis of 586 B.C. See also the note at 33:3.

96:5 *idols:* See the note at 31:6. Worship of idols was forbidden by God's Law (Exod 20:4-6; Deut 5:8-10).

96:8 *bring an offering:* See the notes at 22:24-26 and 27:6.

95:5 Gen 1:9,10. **95:7-11** Heb 3:7-11. **96:7-9** Ps 29:1,2.

Young Singers with a Book, marble Singing Gallery by Luca della Robbia, Florence Cathedral, Florence, Italy, around 1438. Many of the psalms in *The Psalter* (another name for PSALMS) were intended to be sung as part of the worship in the temple in Jerusalem. Some are even preceded by instructions to the music leader (see Ps 88, for example). Exactly how they were performed or what they sounded like is not known, but the words continue to inspire musicians today. Sung or chanted psalms are still an important part of Jewish and Christian worship services.

96:9,10 *the LORD . . . holiness . . . judge the peoples:* See the note at 71:22 (Holy One) and the note on p. 1024. See also 93:1,2 and note. Because God wants to establish justice for all people, his coming to "judge" could also be translated, "coming to establish justice."

96:11,12 *heavens rejoice . . . earth be glad:* All parts of the universe join humankind in praising God. This shows God's kingship over all things. See also 103:19-22; 148:13; and the note at 150:6.

9 Worship the LORD in the splendor of his[a] holiness;
tremble before him, all the earth.

10 Say among the nations, "The LORD reigns."
The world is firmly established, it cannot be moved;
he will judge the peoples with equity.
11 Let the heavens rejoice, let the earth be glad;
let the sea resound, and all that is in it;
12 let the fields be jubilant, and everything in them.

a9 Or *LORD with the splendor of*

Then all the trees of the forest will sing for joy;
13 they will sing before the LORD, for he comes,
he comes to judge the earth.
He will judge the world in righteousness
and the peoples in his truth.

Psalm 97

1 The LORD reigns, let the earth be glad;
let the distant shores rejoice.

2 Clouds and thick darkness surround him;
righteousness and justice are the foundation of
his throne.
3 Fire goes before him
and consumes his foes on every side.
4 His lightning lights up the world;
the earth sees and trembles.
5 The mountains melt like wax before the LORD,
before the Lord of all the earth.
6 The heavens proclaim his righteousness,
and all the peoples see his glory.

7 All who worship images are put to shame,
those who boast in idols—
worship him, all you gods!

8 Zion hears and rejoices
and the villages of Judah are glad
because of your judgments, O LORD.
9 For you, O LORD, are the Most High over all the earth;
you are exalted far above all gods.

10 Let those who love the LORD hate evil,
for he guards the lives of his faithful ones
and delivers them from the hand of the wicked.
11 Light is shed upon the righteous
and joy on the upright in heart.
12 Rejoice in the LORD, you who are righteous,
and praise his holy name.

Psalm 98

A psalm.

1 Sing to the LORD a new song,
for he has done marvelous things;
his right hand and his holy arm
have worked salvation for him.
2 The LORD has made his salvation known
and revealed his righteousness to the nations.
3 He has remembered his love

The heavens proclaim his righteousness, and all the peoples see his glory.
Ps 97:6

97:2-5 *Clouds and thick darkness . . . Fire:* God's appearance in these natural forces is meant to symbolize God's powerful presence. See also the notes at 18:7-15; 29:3-9; 46:6, 7; and 83:13-16.

For more about God's throne, see the note at 9:7.

97:2 *righteousness and justice:* See the notes at 9:8, 9.

97:7 *idols:* See the notes at 31:6 and 96:5.

97:8 *Zion . . . Judah:* See the notes at 2:6 and 48:11 (Mount Zion).

97:11 *the righteous:* See the note at 1:1, 2.

98:1 *new song:* See the notes at 33:3 and 96:1.

98:1 *marvelous things . . . his right hand and his holy arm:* For God's miracles, see the note at 75:1. See also the note at 20:6. The "marvelous things" probably recall what God did to free the people from their life of slavery in Egypt. But the people's return to Judah after the crisis of the exile in Babylon was also seen as a miracle of God's saving power (see Isa 43:14-20; 49:19-23).

98:2 *salvation:* See the notes at 51:12-14.

98:5,6 *harp . . . trumpets:* See the notes at 33:2 and 81:3, and the illustration on p. 1190. Trumpets were also used to announce the arrival of kings (1 Kgs 1:34; Ps 47:5).

98:7,8 *sea . . . rivers . . . mountains:* See the note at 96:11,12.

99:1 *The* LORD *reigns . . . cherubim:* Another psalm celebrating the kingship of God over Israel and all the world. For more about God's kingship, see the note on p. 1024 and the notes at 93:1,2 and 96:9,10. See also the notes at 11:4 and 17:8.

99:2 *Zion:* See the notes at 2:6 and 48:11 (Mount Zion).

99:5 *he is holy:* See the note at 71:22 (Holy One).

99:6 *Moses and Aaron . . . priests . . . Samuel:* See the note at 90 Title. Aaron was Moses' brother, and he and his sons became Israel's first priests. See Exod 28:1 and the mini-article called "Israel's Priests," p. 2344.

Samuel led the people of God after the time of the judges until Israel got its first king. See 1 Sam 1:1—12:25.

99:7 *pillar of cloud:* Before the temple was built, God appeared at the tabernacle in the form of a cloud. See Exod 19:9; 33:9-11.

98:4 Ps 96:11,12.

and his faithfulness to the house of Israel;
all the ends of the earth have seen
the salvation of our God.

4 Shout for joy to the LORD, all the earth,
burst into jubilant song with music;
5 make music to the LORD with the harp,
with the harp and the sound of singing,
6 with trumpets and the blast of the ram's horn—
shout for joy before the LORD, the King.

7 Let the sea resound, and everything in it,
the world, and all who live in it.
8 Let the rivers clap their hands,
let the mountains sing together for joy;
9 let them sing before the LORD,
for he comes to judge the earth.
He will judge the world in righteousness
and the peoples with equity.

Psalm 99

1 The LORD reigns,
let the nations tremble;
he sits enthroned between the cherubim,
let the earth shake.
2 Great is the LORD in Zion;
he is exalted over all the nations.
3 Let them praise your great and awesome name—
he is holy.

4 The King is mighty, he loves justice—
you have established equity;
in Jacob you have done
what is just and right.
5 Exalt the LORD our God
and worship at his footstool;
he is holy.

6 Moses and Aaron were among his priests,
Samuel was among those who called on his name;
they called on the LORD
and he answered them.
7 He spoke to them from the pillar of cloud;
they kept his statutes and the decrees he gave them.

8 O LORD our God,
you answered them;
you were to Israel[a] a forgiving God,

[a]8 Hebrew *them*

though you punished their misdeeds.[a]
9 Exalt the LORD our God
and worship at his holy mountain,
for the LORD our God is holy.

Psalm 100

A psalm. For giving thanks.

1 Shout for joy to the LORD, all the earth.
2 Worship the LORD with gladness;
come before him with joyful songs.
3 Know that the LORD is God.
It is he who made us, and we are his[b];
we are his people, the sheep of his pasture.

4 Enter his gates with thanksgiving
and his courts with praise;
give thanks to him and praise his name.
5 For the LORD is good and his love endures
forever;
his faithfulness continues through all generations.

Psalm 101

Of David. A psalm.

1 I will sing of your love and justice;
to you, O LORD, I will sing praise.
2 I will be careful to lead a blameless life—
when will you come to me?

I will walk in my house
with blameless heart.
3 I will set before my eyes
no vile thing.

The deeds of faithless men I hate;
they will not cling to me.
4 Men of perverse heart shall be far from me;
I will have nothing to do with evil.

5 Whoever slanders his neighbor in secret,
him will I put to silence;
whoever has haughty eyes and a proud heart,
him will I not endure.

6 My eyes will be on the faithful in the land,
that they may dwell with me;
he whose walk is blameless
will minister to me.

---

a8 Or / *an avenger of the wrongs done to them* b3 Or *and not we ourselves*

99:9 *his holy mountain:* This refers to Mount Zion in Jerusalem. See the notes at 2:6 and 48:1, 2.

100:3 *his people, the sheep of his pasture:* See 95:7 and the notes at 23:1-3 and 79:13.

100:5 *love endures forever:* This verse gives the basic reasons for praising God, and it is found in several other places in the Jewish Scriptures (Old Testament). See 1 Chr 16:34; 2 Chr 5:11-13; 7:3; Ezra 3:11; Ps 106:1; 107:1; 118:1; 136:1; Jer 33:11.

101:1,2 *lead a blameless life:* This psalm may have been spoken by the king, perhaps as an oath of office. The king promises to "lead a blameless life," meaning uphold God's concern for justice (see the note at 9:8, 9) and avoid being corrupt (101:3,4). After kingship came to an end in Israel, this psalm was heard as an expression of what God wants all people to do.

101:8 *Every morning . . . the city of the* Lord: The royal palace was in Jerusalem, also called the city of the Lord. The king may have heard and settled cases during the morning hours. See also Jer 21:12; Zeph 3:5.

102:3-5 *groaning . . . skin and bones:* It sounds like the psalmist is sick or experiencing great sadness (see 102:9). See also 42:3,4,10; 88:3-5.

102:9 *ashes as my food:* This probably refers to acts of mourning. People sometimes put dirt or ashes on themselves as a sign of deep sadness (see Esth 4:1-3; Job 2:8; Jer 6:26).

102:13-16 *rebuild Zion:* See the notes at 2:6 and 48:11. Verses 14 and 16 suggest that the psalm was written after Jerusalem was destroyed in 586 B.C. (see the note at 74:3,7).

7 No one who practices deceit
will dwell in my house;
no one who speaks falsely
will stand in my presence.

8 Every morning I will put to silence
all the wicked in the land;
I will cut off every evildoer
from the city of the Lord.

Psalm 102

A prayer of an afflicted man. When he is faint and pours out his lament before the Lord.

1 Hear my prayer, O Lord;
let my cry for help come to you.
2 Do not hide your face from me
when I am in distress.
Turn your ear to me;
when I call, answer me quickly.

3 For my days vanish like smoke;
my bones burn like glowing embers.
4 My heart is blighted and withered like grass;
I forget to eat my food.
5 Because of my loud groaning
I am reduced to skin and bones.
6 I am like a desert owl,
like an owl among the ruins.
7 I lie awake; I have become
like a bird alone on a roof.
8 All day long my enemies taunt me;
those who rail against me use my name as a curse.
9 For I eat ashes as my food
and mingle my drink with tears
10 because of your great wrath,
for you have taken me up and thrown me aside.
11 My days are like the evening shadow;
I wither away like grass.

12 But you, O Lord, sit enthroned forever;
your renown endures through all generations.
13 You will arise and have compassion on Zion,
for it is time to show favor to her;
the appointed time has come.
14 For her stones are dear to your servants;
her very dust moves them to pity.
15 The nations will fear the name of the Lord,
all the kings of the earth will revere your glory.
16 For the Lord will rebuild Zion

and appear in his glory.
17 He will respond to the prayer of the destitute;
he will not despise their plea.

18 Let this be written for a future generation,
that a people not yet created may praise the LORD:
19 "The LORD looked down from his sanctuary on high,
from heaven he viewed the earth,
20 to hear the groans of the prisoners
and release those condemned to death."
21 So the name of the LORD will be declared in Zion
and his praise in Jerusalem
22 when the peoples and the kingdoms
assemble to worship the LORD.

23 In the course of my life[a] he broke my strength;
he cut short my days.
24 So I said:
"Do not take me away, O my God, in the midst of
my days;
your years go on through all generations.
25 In the beginning you laid the foundations of the earth,
and the heavens are the work of your hands.
26 They will perish, but you remain;
they will all wear out like a garment.
Like clothing you will change them
and they will be discarded.
27 But you remain the same,
and your years will never end.
28 The children of your servants will live in your presence;
their descendants will be established before you."

Psalm 103

Of David.

1 Praise the LORD, O my soul;
all my inmost being, praise his holy name.
2 Praise the LORD, O my soul,
and forget not all his benefits—
3 who forgives all your sins
and heals all your diseases,
4 who redeems your life from the pit
and crowns you with love and compassion,
5 who satisfies your desires with good things
so that your youth is renewed like the eagle's.

6 The LORD works righteousness
and justice for all the oppressed.

[a]23 Or *By his power*

102:17 *the destitute:* This is another name used for victims in PSALMS (9:18; 69:33). But here "the destitute" seem to be people who were taken into exile after Jerusalem was destroyed. This suggests that 102:3-5 were heard as symbolic of the suffering of the whole people.

102:19 *his sanctuary on high:* God's "sanctuary" or "house" is sometimes understood to be in heaven, but the earthly temple in Jerusalem was also seen as God's home. See the notes at 9:7 and 11:4.

102:20 *prisoners . . . release those condemned:* "Prisoners" probably refers to people taken into exile (see the note at 102:17). But the psalm looks forward to the people's return from exile.

102:22 *the peoples and the kingdoms:* Some of Israel's prophets said that when Jerusalem and the temple were rebuilt after the exile, people from all nations would meet there to worship God (Isa 2:1-4; 56:6-8; Mic 4:1-3). See also the note at 87:4. The "second temple" was built in Jerusalem between 520 and 515 B.C.

102:25 *laid the foundations of the earth . . . heavens:* This brief description of the creation of the world recalls the longer account in GENESIS (see Gen 1:3-10). Mountains were viewed as the earth's "foundation" (see the note at 82:5).

102:28 *your presence:* This expression of trust means that the suffering described earlier in the psalm does not separate the psalmist from God. See also the note at 31:19-22.

103:2 *his benefits:* See the notes at 32:1,2 and 67:1,2.

103:6,7 *righteousness and justice:* A primary purpose of God's rule, which is celebrated in 103:19-22, is to establish "justice" (see the note at 9:8,9).

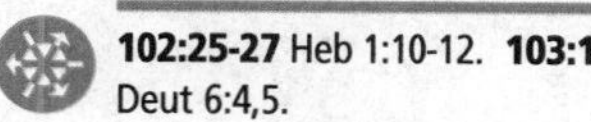

102:25-27 Heb 1:10-12. **103:1,2** Deut 6:4,5.

103:7 *Moses:* See the note at 90 Title.

103:8-10 *The* LORD *is compassionate and gracious:* See Exodus 34:6, which tells what God said when he appeared to Moses after the people had sinned (Exod 32:1-14). That the LORD is compassionate and gracious means that people will not be punished as their "sins deserve." See also Jas 5:11.

103:14-16 *we are dust . . . it is gone:* The psalmist comments on how short human life is when compared with the timeless God. See 90:2-6 and the notes at 90:2-8 and 90:12. It is possible that the crisis of 586 B.C. (see the note at 74:3-7) reminded people of the shortness of human life.

103:19 *throne in heaven . . . rules over all:* See the notes at 8:1,9 and 96:11,12.

103:20 *angels:* See the notes at 29:1,2 and 34:7.

104:1-3 *clothed with splendor and majesty . . . tent:* These verses suggest God's kingship or rule. God is "clothed" by splendor and wrapped in "light" (104:2) that comes from the heavens. In ancient times, people thought the sky was a dome that was held up by the mountains (Gen 1:6, 7). Here, God's home probably refers to the heavens, but see also the note at 9:7.

104:3,4 *clouds . . . wind . . . flames:* Clouds, wind, and flames" (lightning) are all parts of a thunderstorm. The Canaanites believed that their god Baal rode the clouds as lord of the storm and giver of the rain, but Israel claims this power belongs to God. See also the note at 18:7-15.

104:1 Ps 103:1.

7 He made known his ways to Moses,
his deeds to the people of Israel:
8 The LORD is compassionate and gracious,
slow to anger, abounding in love.
9 He will not always accuse,
nor will he harbor his anger forever;
10 he does not treat us as our sins deserve
or repay us according to our iniquities.
11 For as high as the heavens are above the earth,
so great is his love for those who fear him;
12 as far as the east is from the west,
so far has he removed our transgressions from us.
13 As a father has compassion on his children,
so the LORD has compassion on those who fear him;
14 for he knows how we are formed,
he remembers that we are dust.
15 As for man, his days are like grass,
he flourishes like a flower of the field;
16 the wind blows over it and it is gone,
and its place remembers it no more.
17 But from everlasting to everlasting
the LORD's love is with those who fear him,
and his righteousness with their children's children—
18 with those who keep his covenant
and remember to obey his precepts.

19 The LORD has established his throne in heaven,
and his kingdom rules over all.

20 Praise the LORD, you his angels,
you mighty ones who do his bidding,
who obey his word.
21 Praise the LORD, all his heavenly hosts,
you his servants who do his will.
22 Praise the LORD, all his works
everywhere in his dominion.

Praise the LORD, O my soul.

Psalm 104

1 Praise the LORD, O my soul.

O LORD my God, you are very great;
you are clothed with splendor and majesty.
2 He wraps himself in light as with a garment;
he stretches out the heavens like a tent
3 and lays the beams of his upper chambers on their waters.
He makes the clouds his chariot

and rides on the wings of the wind.
[4] He makes winds his messengers,[a]
flames of fire his servants.

[5] He set the earth on its foundations;
it can never be moved.
[6] You covered it with the deep as with a garment;
the waters stood above the mountains.
[7] But at your rebuke the waters fled,
at the sound of your thunder they took to flight;
[8] they flowed over the mountains,
they went down into the valleys,
to the place you assigned for them.
[9] You set a boundary they cannot cross;
never again will they cover the earth.

[10] He makes springs pour water into the ravines;
it flows between the mountains.
[11] They give water to all the beasts of the field;
the wild donkeys quench their thirst.
[12] The birds of the air nest by the waters;
they sing among the branches.
[13] He waters the mountains from his upper chambers;
the earth is satisfied by the fruit of his work.
[14] He makes grass grow for the cattle,
and plants for man to cultivate—
bringing forth food from the earth:
[15] wine that gladdens the heart of man,
oil to make his face shine,
and bread that sustains his heart.
[16] The trees of the LORD are well watered,
the cedars of Lebanon that he planted.
[17] There the birds make their nests;
the stork has its home in the pine trees.
[18] The high mountains belong to the wild goats;
the crags are a refuge for the coneys.[b]

[19] The moon marks off the seasons,
and the sun knows when to go down.
[20] You bring darkness, it becomes night,
and all the beasts of the forest prowl.
[21] The lions roar for their prey
and seek their food from God.
[22] The sun rises, and they steal away;
they return and lie down in their dens.
[23] Then man goes out to his work,
to his labor until evening.

104:5 *foundations:* These are the mountains. See the note at 102:25.

104:9 *set a boundary:* God's control over the chaotic waters shows God's rule over nature. See also Job 38:8-11; Prov 8:29.

104:16-18 *Lebanon . . . high mountains . . . coneys:* The Lebanon mountains (see the notes at 29:5-8 and 72:16) were well-known in ancient times for their tall cedars used for building palaces and temples and as a home for many types of animals (see also 2 Kgs 19:23; Isa 60:13; Song 4:8). The "coneys" are probably rock badgers.

104:19 *moon . . . sun:* In ancient times, people often worshiped the moon and the sun. Here it is clear that God created them, and so only God deserves to be worshiped.

104:4 Heb 1:7. **104:6** Gen 1:9, 10.

[a]4 Or *angels* [b]18 That is, the hyrax or rock badger

104:24 *In wisdom:* The word "wisdom" means both knowledge and creative power. In both senses of the word, God's creation shows God's wisdom. See also Prov 3:19; 8:12-31; and the note at Ps 19:7, 8.

104:26 *leviathan:* See the note at 74:13,14. See also Job 41:1; Isa 27:1.

104:30 *Spirit . . . created . . . renew:* The Spirit of God was present as the creative force at creation (Gen 1:1, 2). God's Spirit inspired Israel's prophets and their messages (Isa 48:16; Ezek 2:2; Mic 3:8). And God's Spirit was with those special "chosen ones" who were to lead Israel (Judg 6:34; 1 Sam 16:13; Isa 11:1-3). See also the mini-article called "Holy Spirit," p. 2082.

104:32 *earth . . . trembles . . . smoke:* See Exod 19:18 and the note at 97:2-5.

104:35 *may sinners vanish from the earth:* Those who disturb God's good creation are to be punished. See the notes at 3:5-8; 52:5; and the mini-article called "Enemies (The Wicked)," p. 1084.

105:1-15 *Give thanks to the LORD:* According to 1 Chronicles 16:7, David instructed Asaph and his associates to sing a song of praise that is similar to these verses.

105:2 *wonderful acts:* See the note at 75:1.

24 How many are your works, O LORD!
In wisdom you made them all;
the earth is full of your creatures.
25 There is the sea, vast and spacious,
teeming with creatures beyond number—
living things both large and small.
26 There the ships go to and fro,
and the leviathan, which you formed to
frolic there.
27 These all look to you
to give them their food at the proper time.
28 When you give it to them,
they gather it up;
when you open your hand,
they are satisfied with good things.
29 When you hide your face,
they are terrified;
when you take away their breath,
they die and return to the dust.
30 When you send your Spirit,
they are created,
and you renew the face of the earth.
31 May the glory of the LORD endure forever;
may the LORD rejoice in his works—
32 he who looks at the earth, and it trembles,
who touches the mountains, and they smoke.

33 I will sing to the LORD all my life;
I will sing praise to my God as long as I live.
34 May my meditation be pleasing to him,
as I rejoice in the LORD.
35 But may sinners vanish from the earth
and the wicked be no more.

Praise the LORD, O my soul.

Praise the LORD.[a]

Psalm 105

1 Give thanks to the LORD, call on his name;
make known among the nations what he has done.
2 Sing to him, sing praise to him;
tell of all his wonderful acts.
3 Glory in his holy name;
let the hearts of those who seek the LORD rejoice.

[a]35 Hebrew *Hallelu Yah*; in the Septuagint this line stands at the beginning of Psalm 105.

Hallah Cover, hand-dyed silk, by Hilde Zadigow, twentieth century. Many of the psalms reflect God's faithfulness to the people of Israel, the "sons of Jacob, his chosen ones" (Ps 105:6). This "nationalist" theme can be seen in Psalm 105, for instance. A Hallah cover is a decorated piece of cloth that is placed over the two loaves of bread (*hallah*) that are set out for the sabbath meal while a blessing is recited. The hallah cover shown here has a symbol for each of the twelve tribes of Israel.

4 Look to the LORD and his strength;
seek his face always.
5 Remember the wonders he has done,
his miracles, and the judgments he pronounced,
6 O descendants of Abraham his servant,
O sons of Jacob, his chosen ones.
7 He is the LORD our God;
his judgments are in all the earth.
8 He remembers his covenant forever,
the word he commanded, for a thousand generations,
9 the covenant he made with Abraham,
the oath he swore to Isaac.
10 He confirmed it to Jacob as a decree,
to Israel as an everlasting covenant:
11 "To you I will give the land of Canaan
as the portion you will inherit."

105:6 *descendants of Abraham . . . Jacob . . . chosen ones:* These all are names for the people of Israel. See the note at 47:9 (Abraham's God). "Chosen ones" usually refers to special leaders of the people (see the note at 2:2), but here it refers to the whole people (see the notes at 28:8 and 94:5). See also the note at 22:23.

105:7 *judgments:* See 98:2 and the note at 9:8,9.

105:8-11 *everlasting covenant:* In one covenant, God promised to give Abraham many descendants and land they could call their own (Gen 12:1-3,7; 15:4-6; 17:1-8; see also Exod 3:7,8). The promise was repeated for Abraham's son, Isaac (Gen 26:3), and for his grandson, Jacob (Gen 28:13). In another covenant, God gave the Law to Moses and the people at Sinai (see the note at 1:1,2). For their part, the people of Israel were to obey and worship only the LORD God (Deut 7:1-15). See also the mini-article called "Covenants (Agreements)," p. 386.

105:12-15 *wandered from nation to nation:* God told Abraham to leave his home (Gen 12:1), so he and his descendants were "wanderers" until they entered the land of Canaan. God's protection is seen in the story about Abraham and King Abimelech (Gen 20:3-7).

105:16-22 *famine on the land . . . Joseph:* Joseph, one of Jacob's twelve sons, was sold into slavery by his brothers (Gen 37:12-28). He ended up in Egypt where he earned his freedom and a position of authority by interpreting the dreams of Pharaoh (Gen 39:20—41:36). He was put in charge of Egypt's grain storage (Gen 41:39-49). When food became scarce in the region, including Canaan, Jacob sent his sons to Egypt to buy grain (Gen 41:53—42:8).

105:23-36 *Jacob . . . Moses . . . firstborn:* These verses tell what happened to the descendants of Jacob, who settled as foreigners in Egypt (Gen 46:1-7; 47:11). When the Israelites grew numerous, the Egyptians became their foes and enslaved them (Exod 1:7-14). In response to the oppression of the Hebrew people God chose Moses and his brother Aaron to speak to the Pharaoh and ask him to let the Hebrew people go (Exod 3:1—4:17). When the king refused, God sent a number of plagues upon Egypt. These plagues are listed in a different order here than in EXODUS. See the mini-article called "Disasters (Plagues)," p. 151.

105:37-41 *brought out Israel:* These verses describe the days immediately after the Hebrew people left Egypt. They left quickly (Exod 12:33-36), and God led them by a cloud and by a pillar of fire (Exod 13:21, 22). When they complained of hunger and thirst, God gave the people food (Exod 16:2-15) and water (Exod 17:1-7; Num 20:2-13).

105:42 *holy promise given to his servant Abraham:* See the note at 105:8-11.

105:28 Exod 10:21-23. **105:29** Exod 7:17-21. **105:30** Exod 8:1-6. **105:31** Exod 8:16,17,20-24. **105:32,33** Exod 9:22-25. **105:34,35** Exod 10:12-15.

12 When they were but few in number,
few indeed, and strangers in it,
13 they wandered from nation to nation,
from one kingdom to another.
14 He allowed no one to oppress them;
for their sake he rebuked kings:
15 "Do not touch my anointed ones;
do my prophets no harm."

16 He called down famine on the land
and destroyed all their supplies of food;
17 and he sent a man before them—
Joseph, sold as a slave.
18 They bruised his feet with shackles,
his neck was put in irons,
19 till what he foretold came to pass,
till the word of the LORD proved him true.
20 The king sent and released him,
the ruler of peoples set him free.
21 He made him master of his household,
ruler over all he possessed,
22 to instruct his princes as he pleased
and teach his elders wisdom.

23 Then Israel entered Egypt;
Jacob lived as an alien in the land of Ham.
24 The LORD made his people very fruitful;
he made them too numerous for their foes,
25 whose hearts he turned to hate his people,
to conspire against his servants.
26 He sent Moses his servant,
and Aaron, whom he had chosen.
27 They performed his miraculous signs among them,
his wonders in the land of Ham.
28 He sent darkness and made the land dark—
for had they not rebelled against his words?
29 He turned their waters into blood,
causing their fish to die.
30 Their land teemed with frogs,
which went up into the bedrooms of their rulers.
31 He spoke, and there came swarms of flies,
and gnats throughout their country.
32 He turned their rain into hail,
with lightning throughout their land;
33 he struck down their vines and fig trees
and shattered the trees of their country.
34 He spoke, and the locusts came,
grasshoppers without number;
35 they ate up every green thing in their land,
ate up the produce of their soil.

36 Then he struck down all the firstborn in their land,
the firstfruits of all their manhood.

37 He brought out Israel, laden with silver and gold,
and from among their tribes no one faltered.
38 Egypt was glad when they left,
because dread of Israel had fallen on them.
39 He spread out a cloud as a covering,
and a fire to give light at night.
40 They asked, and he brought them quail
and satisfied them with the bread of heaven.
41 He opened the rock, and water gushed out;
like a river it flowed in the desert.

42 For he remembered his holy promise
given to his servant Abraham.
43 He brought out his people with rejoicing,
his chosen ones with shouts of joy;
44 he gave them the lands of the nations,
and they fell heir to what others had toiled for—
45 that they might keep his precepts
and observe his laws.

Praise the LORD.[a]

Psalm 106

1 Praise the LORD.[b]

Give thanks to the LORD, for he is good;
his love endures forever.
2 Who can proclaim the mighty acts of the LORD
or fully declare his praise?
3 Blessed are they who maintain justice,
who constantly do what is right.
4 Remember me, O LORD, when you show favor to
your people,
come to my aid when you save them,
5 that I may enjoy the prosperity of your chosen ones,
that I may share in the joy of your nation
and join your inheritance in giving praise.

6 We have sinned, even as our fathers did;
we have done wrong and acted wickedly.
7 When our fathers were in Egypt,
they gave no thought to your miracles;
they did not remember your many kindnesses,
and they rebelled by the sea, the Red Sea.[c]

[a]45 Hebrew *Hallelu Yah* [b]1 Hebrew *Hallelu Yah*; also in verse 48 [c]7 Hebrew *Yam Suph*; that is, Sea of Reeds; also in verses 9 and 22

105:43 *rejoicing:* After God saved the people at the Red Sea (Exod 14:21-31), they celebrated with singing and dancing (Exod 15:1-21).

105:44,45 *gave them the lands of the nations . . . observe his laws:* After forty years of wandering in the desert, the LORD helped the people enter Canaan, the land God promised to give their ancestor Abraham (see the note at 105:8-11). See also Josh 11:16-23. The people received God's laws at Mount Sinai in the desert. To keep their new land, the people were to obey the laws and worship God alone. But Psalm 106 shows how the people failed to obey.

106:1 *love endures forever:* See the note at 100:5.

106:2 *mighty acts:* Like Psalm 105, this psalm retells Israel's story. But Psalm 106 calls attention to Israel's disobedience (106:6).

106:3 *Blessed:* Blessing comes from doing what God wants, including being just and doing right. See the note at 1:1,2.

106:5 *chosen ones:* See the note at 105:6.

106:6 *sinned . . . done wrong and acted wickedly:* The rest of the psalm tells how the people of Israel sinned, even though God kept rescuing them and showing them mercy.

106:7-12 *miracles . . . sang his praise:* For God's marvelous miracles in Egypt, see the note at 105:23-36. Even as God was preparing to deliver them from the Egyptians at the Red Sea, the people were complaining (Exod 14:10-12). The story of the crossing of the sea and God's defeat of the Egyptians, is found in Exodus 14:21-29. The people respond with trust (Exod 14:30,31) and praise (Exod 15:1-21). See also the map on p. 2463.

105:36 Exod 12:29. **106:1** 1 Chr 16:34; 2 Chr 5:11-13; 7:3; Ezra 3:11; Ps 100:5; 107:1; 118:1; 136:1; Jer 33:11.

106:13-15 *soon forgot . . . craving:* Despite the rescue at the Red Sea, the people began to grumble about being thirsty and hungry (Exod 15:22—16:3). God gave them water and food (Exod 16:4-34). Still, the people complained.

106:16-18 *envious . . . flame consumed the wicked:* The rebellion of Dathan and Abiram against Moses and Aaron is described in Numbers 16:1-35.

106:19-23 *At Horeb they made a calf and worshiped:* Horeb is another name for Mount Sinai where Moses received God's Law. While Moses was on Mount Sinai the people angered God by making and worshiping a golden statue of a bull. Moses talked God out of destroying all the people (Exod 32:1-14).

106:24-26 *did not believe his promise:* The people became afraid of entering Canaan, even though Joshua and Caleb gave a good report of the land. So, the people had to wander in the desert another thirty-nine years (see Num 14:1-35).

106:28-31 *yoked themselves to the Baal of Peor . . . Phinehas:* At the Shittim camp in Moab (see the map on p. 2463), some Israelite men had sex with Moabite women and worshiped the Moabite gods, including Baal of Peor (see the note at 29:3-9). Phinehas, grandson of Aaron, put to death two people who had been unfaithful. This led God to forgive the rest of the people and to honor Phinehas (Num 25:1-15).

106:32,33 *waters of Meribah:* This describes another rebellion against Moses. But Moses also got in trouble with God for speaking too quickly (Num 20:2-13). See also the note at 81:6, 7.

106:27 Lev 26:33.

8 Yet he saved them for his name's sake,
to make his mighty power known.
9 He rebuked the Red Sea, and it dried up;
he led them through the depths as through a desert.
10 He saved them from the hand of the foe;
from the hand of the enemy he redeemed them.
11 The waters covered their adversaries;
not one of them survived.
12 Then they believed his promises
and sang his praise.

13 But they soon forgot what he had done
and did not wait for his counsel.
14 In the desert they gave in to their craving;
in the wasteland they put God to the test.
15 So he gave them what they asked for,
but sent a wasting disease upon them.

16 In the camp they grew envious of Moses
and of Aaron, who was consecrated to the LORD.
17 The earth opened up and swallowed Dathan;
it buried the company of Abiram.
18 Fire blazed among their followers;
a flame consumed the wicked.

19 At Horeb they made a calf
and worshiped an idol cast from metal.
20 They exchanged their Glory
for an image of a bull, which eats grass.
21 They forgot the God who saved them,
who had done great things in Egypt,
22 miracles in the land of Ham
and awesome deeds by the Red Sea.
23 So he said he would destroy them—
had not Moses, his chosen one,
stood in the breach before him
to keep his wrath from destroying them.

24 Then they despised the pleasant land;
they did not believe his promise.
25 They grumbled in their tents
and did not obey the LORD.
26 So he swore to them with uplifted hand
that he would make them fall in the desert,
27 make their descendants fall among the nations
and scatter them throughout the lands.

28 They yoked themselves to the Baal of Peor
and ate sacrifices offered to lifeless gods;
29 they provoked the LORD to anger by their wicked deeds,
and a plague broke out among them.

[30] But Phinehas stood up and intervened,
and the plague was checked.
[31] This was credited to him as righteousness
for endless generations to come.

[32] By the waters of Meribah they angered the LORD,
and trouble came to Moses because of them;
[33] for they rebelled against the Spirit of God,
and rash words came from Moses' lips.[a]

[34] They did not destroy the peoples
as the LORD had commanded them,
[35] but they mingled with the nations
and adopted their customs.
[36] They worshiped their idols,
which became a snare to them.
[37] They sacrificed their sons
and their daughters to demons.
[38] They shed innocent blood,
the blood of their sons and daughters,
whom they sacrificed to the idols of Canaan,
and the land was desecrated by their blood.
[39] They defiled themselves by what they did;
by their deeds they prostituted themselves.

[40] Therefore the LORD was angry with his people
and abhorred his inheritance.
[41] He handed them over to the nations,
and their foes ruled over them.

[a]33 Or *against his spirit, / and rash words came from his lips*

106:34-39 *did not destroy the peoples . . . mingled . . . defiled:* The people's disobedience continued after they entered the promised land. They adopted the ways of the Canaanites, including worshiping their gods (see Judg 2:1-3; 3:5,6). For the destruction of enemies, see the mini-article called "Holy War (The LORD's Battles)," p. 306.

Sacrificing children was against God's instruction (Lev 18:21), but the people sometimes disobeyed (2 Kgs 17:17). The shedding of innocent blood was said to "defile" or pollute the land (Num 35:33,34).

106:40-46 *handed them over . . . heard their cry:* These verses describe a pattern found in JUDGES. The pattern is introduced in Judges 2:11-18. The other historical books (JUDGES through 2 CHRONICLES) also give many examples of Israel's sin and tell about the threats that came from neighboring nations. The prophets of Israel also told the people to remain faithful to the LORD and warned them of punishment if they turned away from God and God's Law (Isa 1:2-20, 27-31).

QUESTIONS ABOUT PSALMS 90:1—106:48

1. At the beginning of Book IV, the title of Psalm 90 mentions Moses. Who was Moses and what did he do? How would remembering what Moses had done hundreds of years earlier help the people face the crisis of seeing Jerusalem destroyed and many people being taken away into exile in Babylon in 586 B.C.? (see Ps 89:38-51)
2. According to a number of psalms in this section (Ps 93; 95–99), God is King. What sort of things does a king typically do for the people he rules? What sort of things does a king have a right to expect from his people? In what ways does God rule your life? How do you honor him in return?
3. Read Psalm 100. Why is God to be praised? Why is it important that "all the earth" is invited to praise God?
4. Read Psalms 103 and 104. How are they alike? How are they different? Why might it be especially important today to view all creation as coming from God and depending on God for its future?
5. Psalms 105 and 106 recall events from Israel's past. How are the two psalms different? What is the effect of reading the two psalms together? What can the events described in these psalms mean to our faith today?

42 Their enemies oppressed them
and subjected them to their power.
43 Many times he delivered them,
but they were bent on rebellion
and they wasted away in their sin.

44 But he took note of their distress
when he heard their cry;
45 for their sake he remembered his covenant
and out of his great love he relented.
46 He caused them to be pitied
by all who held them captive.

47 Save us, O LORD our God,
and gather us from the nations,
that we may give thanks to your holy name
and glory in your praise.

48 Praise be to the LORD, the God of Israel,
from everlasting to everlasting.
Let all the people say, "Amen!"

Praise the LORD.

Book V (Psalms 107:1—150:6)

Book V continues to announce God's kingship (Ps 145; 146; 149). Although it gives less direct attention to Moses than Book IV does, it gives greater attention to the law that Moses received from God. Psalm 119, the longest psalm, lies at the heart of Book V and praises the law of the LORD. Psalms collected in David's memory appear near the beginning and end of Book V (Ps 108–110; 138–145). This may suggest the hope that the kingdom of David and his descendants would be restored. But two psalms (Ps 144 and 149) appear to say that the duties and responsibilities of kingship belong to the whole people of God.

Psalm 107

1 Give thanks to the LORD, for he is good;
his love endures forever.
2 Let the redeemed of the LORD say this—
those he redeemed from the hand of the foe,
3 those he gathered from the lands,
from east and west, from north and south.[a]

4 Some wandered in desert wastelands,
finding no way to a city where they could settle.
5 They were hungry and thirsty,
and their lives ebbed away.

[a]3 Hebrew *north and the sea*

106:45 *remembered his covenant:* See the note at 105:8-11.

106:47,48 *Save us . . . gather us:* These verses end the song that David told Asaph and his relatives to sing (see 1 Chr 16:35, 36 and the note at 105:1–15). Clearly, the people are in exile in foreign lands and want to return home. See the note at 44:9-11. Psalm 107:3 suggests that the prayer of 106:47 has been answered.

107:1 *love endures forever:* See the note at 100:5.

107:2,3 *redeemed . . . gathered from the lands:* These verses suggest that the prayer of 106:47 has been answered and that the exile is over. People had been scattered not only to Babylon to the east, but to other nations as well (see Jer 41:16—43:8). See also the notes at 44:9-11 and 74:3-7.

107:1 1 Chr 16:34; 2 Chr 5:13; 7:3; Ezra 3:11; Ps 100:5; 105:1; 106:1; 118:1; 136:1; Jer 33:11.

[6]Then they cried out to the LORD in their trouble,
and he delivered them from their distress.
[7]He led them by a straight way
to a city where they could settle.
[8]Let them give thanks to the LORD for his unfailing love
and his wonderful deeds for men,
[9]for he satisfies the thirsty
and fills the hungry with good things.

[10]Some sat in darkness and the deepest gloom,
prisoners suffering in iron chains,
[11]for they had rebelled against the words of God
and despised the counsel of the Most High.
[12]So he subjected them to bitter labor;
they stumbled, and there was no one to help.
[13]Then they cried to the LORD in their trouble,
and he saved them from their distress.
[14]He brought them out of darkness and the deepest gloom
and broke away their chains.
[15]Let them give thanks to the LORD for his unfailing love
and his wonderful deeds for men,
[16]for he breaks down gates of bronze
and cuts through bars of iron.

[17]Some became fools through their rebellious ways
and suffered affliction because of their iniquities.
[18]They loathed all food
and drew near the gates of death.
[19]Then they cried to the LORD in their trouble,
and he saved them from their distress.
[20]He sent forth his word and healed them;
he rescued them from the grave.
[21]Let them give thanks to the LORD for his unfailing love
and his wonderful deeds for men.
[22]Let them sacrifice thank offerings
and tell of his works with songs of joy.

[23]Others went out on the sea in ships;
they were merchants on the mighty waters.
[24]They saw the works of the LORD,
his wonderful deeds in the deep.
[25]For he spoke and stirred up a tempest
that lifted high the waves.
[26]They mounted up to the heavens and went down to
the depths;
in their peril their courage melted away.
[27]They reeled and staggered like drunken men;
they were at their wits' end.
[28]Then they cried out to the LORD in their trouble,
and he brought them out of their distress.

107:7-9 *led them . . . wonderful deeds . . . satisfies the thirsty . . . fills the hungry:* This is the first of four examples of how God rescues people in "trouble" (107:6). The example recalls the experience of the people in the desert after God rescued them from Egypt (see the note at 105:37-41). The return from exile in Babylon also involved a trip through a "desert" (Isa 40:3).

107:10-16 *prisoners . . . broke away their chains . . . breaks down gates:* This is the second example of how God rescues people in "trouble" (107:13). It recalls the rescue from the "chains" of slavery in Egypt as well as the rescue from exile in Babylon. See also Isa 40:2; 49:7-12. "Darkness and the deepest gloom" (107:10,14) symbolize serious trouble.

107:17-22 *healed them . . . rescued them from the grave:* This third example of how God rescues people in "trouble" (107:19) involves healing from sickness, which may be a symbol for other kinds of distress, including "spiritual sickness" (sins). See the note at 38:11. Those who are healed and saved are to praise the LORD and offer sacrifices (107:21,22). See the notes at 22:24-26; 27:6; and 40:6.

For great is your love, higher than the heavens; your faithfulness reaches to the skies.
Ps 108:4

107:29-32 *stilled the storm . . . guided them to their desired haven:* This fourth example of how God rescues people in "trouble" (107:28) involves rescue from distress at sea. The sea and the ocean often were symbols for the deadly forces of chaos (see the notes at 18:16 and 69:1,2; see also Jonah 1:10—2:10). Again, those who are saved are encouraged to praise the LORD.

107:33-42 *lifted the needy:* These verses review the four examples in 107:4-32. They recall especially 107:4-9.

107:40 *pours contempt:* On the nature of God's "revenge," see the notes at 5:10-12 and 18:34-48. If the psalm is heard in light of the recent exile (see the note at 107:2,3), the conquerors would be the Babylonians. But the people of God regularly experience opposition from those who also oppose God and God's purposes.

107:42,43 *Whoever is wise:* To obey the LORD and live according to the Law of the LORD is wisdom (Prov 1:7; 9:10,11). See also the note at 1:1,2.

108:2 *awaken the dawn:* See the note at 57:8.

108:5 *your glory:* See the note at 26:8.

107:29 Mark 4:39. **108:1** Deut 6:4,5; Ps 103:1,2. **109:8** Acts 1:20.

29 He stilled the storm to a whisper;
the waves of the sea were hushed.
30 They were glad when it grew calm,
and he guided them to their desired haven.
31 Let them give thanks to the LORD for his unfailing love
and his wonderful deeds for men.
32 Let them exalt him in the assembly of the people
and praise him in the council of the elders.

33 He turned rivers into a desert,
flowing springs into thirsty ground,
34 and fruitful land into a salt waste,
because of the wickedness of those who lived there.
35 He turned the desert into pools of water
and the parched ground into flowing springs;
36 there he brought the hungry to live,
and they founded a city where they could settle.
37 They sowed fields and planted vineyards
that yielded a fruitful harvest;
38 he blessed them, and their numbers greatly increased,
and he did not let their herds diminish.

39 Then their numbers decreased, and they were humbled
by oppression, calamity and sorrow;
40 he who pours contempt on nobles
made them wander in a trackless waste.
41 But he lifted the needy out of their affliction
and increased their families like flocks.
42 The upright see and rejoice,
but all the wicked shut their mouths.

43 Whoever is wise, let him heed these things
and consider the great love of the LORD.

Psalm 108

A song. A psalm of David.

1 My heart is steadfast, O God;
I will sing and make music with all my soul.
2 Awake, harp and lyre!
I will awaken the dawn.
3 I will praise you, O LORD, among the nations;
I will sing of you among the peoples.
4 For great is your love, higher than the heavens;
your faithfulness reaches to the skies.
5 Be exalted, O God, above the heavens,
and let your glory be over all the earth.

6 Save us and help us with your right hand,
that those you love may be delivered.

[7] God has spoken from his sanctuary:
"In triumph I will parcel out Shechem
and measure off the Valley of Succoth.
[8] Gilead is mine, Manasseh is mine;
Ephraim is my helmet,
Judah my scepter.
[9] Moab is my washbasin,
upon Edom I toss my sandal;
over Philistia I shout in triumph."

[10] Who will bring me to the fortified city?
Who will lead me to Edom?
[11] Is it not you, O God, you who have rejected us
and no longer go out with our armies?
[12] Give us aid against the enemy,
for the help of man is worthless. ONLY W/ GOD
[13] With God we will gain the victory,
and he will trample down our enemies.

Psalm 109

For the director of music. Of David. A psalm.

[1] O God, whom I praise,
do not remain silent,
[2] for wicked and deceitful men
have opened their mouths against me;
they have spoken against me with lying tongues.
[3] With words of hatred they surround me;
they attack me without cause.
[4] In return for my friendship they accuse me,
but I am a man of prayer.
[5] They repay me evil for good,
and hatred for my friendship.
[6] Appoint[a] an evil man[b] to oppose him;
let an accuser[c] stand at his right hand.
[7] When he is tried, let him be found guilty,
and may his prayers condemn him.
[8] May his days be few;
may another take his place of leadership.
[9] May his children be fatherless
and his wife a widow.
[10] May his children be wandering beggars;
may they be driven[d] from their ruined homes.
[11] May a creditor seize all he has;
may strangers plunder the fruits of his labor.

108:6-13 *your right hand . . . helmet . . . scepter:* See the note at 44:1-3. These verses are similar to Psalm 60:5-12. For the locations and nations listed here, see the notes at 60 Title and 60:6–9. Also compare Psalm 108:1-5 to Psalm 57:7-11. Scholars have suggested that Psalm 57 and Psalm 60 were put together to form Psalm 108, perhaps to speak to the returned exiles in new ways.

The Ephraim tribe may have been known as strong warriors, and so were called God's "helmet." Helmets are protective headgear necessary for close combat. They were worn as early as the third millennium B.C. Although they varied in design, they were usually made of leather or metal (bronze or iron) and often included earflaps and neck guards. The one shown here is typical of Greek helmets from the fifth century B.C. Israel's kings ruled from Jerusalem in Judah, and so Judah is called God's "scepter," a symbol of royal power.

109:2,3 *lying tongues:* The psalmist is the victim of false accusation.

109:7-19 *let him be found guilty . . . condemn him:* Whether these words were spoken by the psalmist, or whether they were claimed by him after they were spoken by his enemies, they sound like a prayer for revenge. Such prayers appear often in the prayers for help. They show how people naturally respond when they are victims of injustice. "Let him be found guilty" in 109:7 could also be translated "bring him to justice." The psalmist asks that his enemies might experience the same bad things that they have done to others.

[a]**6** Or ⌞*They say:*⌟ "*Appoint* (with quotation marks at the end of verse 19) [b]**6** Or *the Evil One* [c]**6** Or *let Satan* [d]**10** Septuagint; Hebrew *sought*

David with His Musicians, illuminated page from the *Vespasian Psalter,* Canterbury, England, eighth century. When David served in King Saul's court, he was asked to play his harp in order to console the king whenever Saul was troubled. Many psalms which make up PSALMS were originally intended to be performed musically and have long been associated with King David. Other psalms celebrate David's military victories, and some are written as though spoken by the king. Psalm 108 is a beautiful example of one David's psalms.

109:16 *poor . . . needy . . . brokenhearted:* See the note at 9:8,9. The psalmist suggests that God's enemies do not care about those who are in need. The psalmist counts himself among the needy (109:22).

12 May no one extend kindness to him
or take pity on his fatherless children.
13 May his descendants be cut off,
their names blotted out from the next generation.
14 May the iniquity of his fathers be remembered before the LORD;
may the sin of his mother never be blotted out.
15 May their sins always remain before the LORD,
that he may cut off the memory of them from the earth.

16 For he never thought of doing a kindness,
but hounded to death the poor
and the needy and the brokenhearted.

17 He loved to pronounce a curse—
may it[a] come on him;
he found no pleasure in blessing—
may it be[b] far from him.
18 He wore cursing as his garment;
it entered into his body like water,
into his bones like oil.
19 May it be like a cloak wrapped about him,
like a belt tied forever around him.
20 May this be the LORD's payment to my accusers,
to those who speak evil of me.

21 But you, O Sovereign LORD,
deal well with me for your name's sake;
out of the goodness of your love, deliver me.
22 For I am poor and needy,
and my heart is wounded within me.
23 I fade away like an evening shadow;
I am shaken off like a locust.
24 My knees give way from fasting;
my body is thin and gaunt.
25 I am an object of scorn to my accusers;
when they see me, they shake their heads.

26 Help me, O LORD my God;
save me in accordance with your love.
27 Let them know that it is your hand,
that you, O LORD, have done it.
28 They may curse, but you will bless;
when they attack they will be put to shame,
but your servant will rejoice.
29 My accusers will be clothed with disgrace
and wrapped in shame as in a cloak.
30 With my mouth I will greatly extol the LORD;
in the great throng I will praise him.
31 For he stands at the right hand of the needy one,
to save his life from those who condemn him.

Psalm 110

Of David. A psalm.

1 The LORD says to my Lord:
"Sit at my right hand
until I make your enemies
a footstool for your feet."

2 The LORD will extend your mighty scepter from Zion;
you will rule in the midst of your enemies.

---

[a]17 Or *curse, / and it has* [b]17 Or *blessing, / and it is*

109:24 *fasting:* See the note at 35:13.

109:27 *done it:* That is, saved him. See the note at 51:12-14.

109:28,29 *put to shame ... clothed with disgrace:* Concerning God's punishment of the enemies, see the notes at 10:5 and 28:3-5.

109:31 *save his life:* The psalmist ends by expressing again his trust that God defends victims of injustice (see the note at 109:16). See also the note at 109:2, 3.

110:1 *right hand ... footstool:* The "right hand" is the side of power and authority. See also the notes at notes at 2:2 and 72:1-3. Footstools probably were commonly used with a throne (see 2 Chr 9:18). Some ancient throne footstools have been discovered with the pictures of defeated enemies painted on them. This may be what is behind the idea of a king making his enemies a footstool. See also Matt 22:44; Mark 12:36; Luke 20:42,43; Acts 2:34,35; 1 Cor 15:25; Eph 1:20-22; Col 3:1; Heb 1:13; 8:1; 10:12,13.

110:2 *Zion:* See the notes at 2:6 and 48:11 (Mount Zion).

109:25 Matt 27:39; Mark 15:29.

110:4 *a priest forever, in the order of Melchizedek:* God promised that one of David's descendants would always rule Israel (see 28:27-29 and the notes). But here the king also is called "priest." The kings of Israel were responsible for helping the priesthood provide for Israel's worship life (see 1 Kgs 5–7; 1 Chr 15:11-16; Neh 12:24,45). After the exile the royal throne of David was not restored. But the high priest named Joshua, one of David's descendants, was chosen to rule (see Zech 6:9-14). Melchizedek was king of Salem and he is also called a priest (Gen 14:18-20). See also Heb 5:6; 6:20; 7:17,20,21.

110:7 *drink from a brook:* Because of his authority (110:1), the king can choose to drink where he wishes. This also could be a reference to winning land in battles (110:5, 6).

111:4 *wonders:* See 77:11-16; 78:26-29, 43-52; and the note at 75:1

111:5 *provides food . . . remembers his covenant:* This recalls God's providing of "food" for the people in the desert after leaving Egypt. See the note at 105:37-41. For "covenant," see the notes at 44:17 and 105:8-11.

111:6 *giving them the lands of other nations:* See the note at 105:44,45.

111:7 *faithful and just . . . precepts:* God's laws (here called "precepts") serve the purpose of establishing justice among God's people. See the note at 1:1,2.

111:9 *holy and awesome:* God deserves respect. See also the note at 71:22 (Holy One).

111:10 Job 28:28; Prov 1:7; 9:10.

3 Your troops will be willing
on your day of battle.
Arrayed in holy majesty,
from the womb of the dawn
you will receive the dew of your youth.[a]

4 The LORD has sworn
and will not change his mind:
"You are a priest forever,
in the order of Melchizedek."

5 The Lord is at your right hand;
he will crush kings on the day of his wrath.
6 He will judge the nations, heaping up the dead
and crushing the rulers of the whole earth.
7 He will drink from a brook beside the way[b];
therefore he will lift up his head.

Psalm 111[c]

1 Praise the LORD.[d]

I will extol the LORD with all my heart
in the council of the upright and in the assembly.

2 Great are the works of the LORD;
they are pondered by all who delight in them.
3 Glorious and majestic are his deeds,
and his righteousness endures forever.
4 He has caused his wonders to be remembered;
the LORD is gracious and compassionate.
5 He provides food for those who fear him;
he remembers his covenant forever.
6 He has shown his people the power of his works,
giving them the lands of other nations.
7 The works of his hands are faithful and just;
all his precepts are trustworthy.
8 They are steadfast for ever and ever,
done in faithfulness and uprightness.
9 He provided redemption for his people;
he ordained his covenant forever—
holy and awesome is his name.

10 The fear of the LORD is the beginning of wisdom;
all who follow his precepts have good understanding.
To him belongs eternal praise.

---

[a]3 Or / *your young men will come to you like the dew* [b]7 Or / *The One who grants succession will set him in authority* [c]This psalm is an acrostic poem, the lines of which begin with the successive letters of the Hebrew alphabet. [d]1 Hebrew *Hallelu Yah*

Psalm 112[a]

1 Praise the LORD.[b]

Blessed is the man who fears the LORD,
who finds great delight in his commands.

2 His children will be mighty in the land;
the generation of the upright will be blessed.
3 Wealth and riches are in his house,
and his righteousness endures forever.
4 Even in darkness light dawns for the upright,
for the gracious and compassionate and righteous
man.[c]
5 Good will come to him who is generous and lends freely,
who conducts his affairs with justice.
6 Surely he will never be shaken;
a righteous man will be remembered forever.
7 He will have no fear of bad news;
his heart is steadfast, trusting in the LORD.
8 His heart is secure, he will have no fear;
in the end he will look in triumph on his foes.
9 He has scattered abroad his gifts to the poor,
his righteousness endures forever;
his horn[d] will be lifted high in honor.

10 The wicked man will see and be vexed,
he will gnash his teeth and waste away;
the longings of the wicked will come to nothing.

Psalm 113

1 Praise the LORD.[e]

Praise, O servants of the LORD,
praise the name of the LORD.
2 Let the name of the LORD be praised,
both now and forevermore.
3 From the rising of the sun to the place where it sets,
the name of the LORD is to be praised.

4 The LORD is exalted over all the nations,
his glory above the heavens.
5 Who is like the LORD our God,
the One who sits enthroned on high,
6 who stoops down to look
on the heavens and the earth?

---

[a]This psalm is an acrostic poem, the lines of which begin with the successive letters of the Hebrew alphabet. [b]1 Hebrew *Hallelu Yah* [c]4 Or / *for* ⌞*the LORD*⌟ *is gracious and compassionate and righteous* [d]9 *Horn* here symbolizes dignity. [e]1 Hebrew *Hallelu Yah*; also in verse 9

Let the name of the LORD be praised, both now and forevermore.
Ps 113:2

112:1 *Praise the LORD:* Psalm 111 and Psalm 112 are probably meant as a pair. Psalm 111 tells what God has done, and Psalm 112 describes the lives of those who follow the advice of 111:10. Both are acrostic poems (see the note at 119:1).

112:1,2 *Blessed:* Those who obey God's law will be blessed (see the note at 1:1, 2).

112:3,4 *Wealth and riches:* This does not mean that worshipers of God will have an easy life. But those who worship and obey God (112:1) will be like God—righteous. Doing what God desires is what it truly means to have great wealth.

112:5 *generous and lends freely:* See the note at 37:26.

112:6,7 *have no fear of bad news:* Those who obey God and do right will not be free of troubles, but the "bad news" they have to face won't defeat them because they trust in God. See also the note at 37:39, 40.

112:8-10 *his foes . . . The wicked:* See the note at 3:1,2.

113:4 *LORD . . . over all the nations:* See the note at 2:4 and the note on p. 1024.

113:5 *enthroned on high:* See the note at 9:7.

112:9 2 Cor 9:9.

113:7 *raises the poor . . . lifts the needy:* A primary purpose of God's rule over all (113:4-6) is to establish justice by helping the poor and needy. See the note at 9:8,9.

113:7 *dust . . . ash heap:* These are symbols of oppression.

113:9 *children:* Children are viewed in the Bible as a gift from God and a sign of God's blessing. See 128:3,4.

114:1,2 *out of Egypt . . . Judah became God's sanctuary:* God chose Moses to lead the Hebrew people out of slavery in Egypt (see Exod 12:51; Ps 105:37-41). Later, the people entered Canaan, the land God promised to give them (see the note at 105:44,45). Still later, David made Jerusalem in Judah the capital of all Israel. Because the temple (God's house) would be built there by David's son Solomon, Judah is called "God's sanctuary."

114:3,4 *sea . . . Jordan turned back . . . mountains skipped:* These verses tell in poetic terms of God's miraculous acts on behalf of Israel. The "sea" running away refers to the parting of the Red Sea to allow the Hebrews to flee Egypt (Exod 14:21,22). When the people crossed the Jordan River to enter the promised land, the river's waters flowed apart to let them pass (Josh 3:14-17). The skipping mountains may refer to God's thundering presence at Mount Sinai when God gave the Law (Exod 19:18).

114:8 *rock . . . springs:* This recalls God's providing for the people in the desert on their way to the promised land (Exod 17:1-7; Num 20:2-13).

115:2 *Where is their God:* In the ancient world, each nation had its own god or gods. When things went poorly for a nation, or if they were defeated in battle, it was thought to be a sign that the gods were angry or punishing them. Nations sometimes mocked the nations they defeated by asking this question. See also 42:3, 10; 79:10; Joel 2:17; Mic 7:10.

7 He raises the poor from the dust
and lifts the needy from the ash heap;
8 he seats them with princes,
with the princes of their people.
9 He settles the barren woman in her home
as a happy mother of children.

Praise the LORD.

Psalm 114

1 When Israel came out of Egypt,
the house of Jacob from a people of foreign tongue,
2 Judah became God's sanctuary,
Israel his dominion.

3 The sea looked and fled,
the Jordan turned back;
4 the mountains skipped like rams,
the hills like lambs.

5 Why was it, O sea, that you fled,
O Jordan, that you turned back,
6 you mountains, that you skipped like rams,
you hills, like lambs?

7 Tremble, O earth, at the presence of the Lord,
at the presence of the God of Jacob,
8 who turned the rock into a pool,
the hard rock into springs of water.

Psalm 115

1 Not to us, O LORD, not to us
but to your name be the glory,
because of your love and faithfulness.

2 Why do the nations say,
"Where is their God?"
3 Our God is in heaven;
he does whatever pleases him.
4 But their idols are silver and gold,
made by the hands of men.
5 They have mouths, but cannot speak,
eyes, but they cannot see;
6 they have ears, but cannot hear,
noses, but they cannot smell;
7 they have hands, but cannot feel,
feet, but they cannot walk;
nor can they utter a sound with their throats.

8 Those who make them will be like them,
and so will all who trust in them.

9 O house of Israel, trust in the LORD—
he is their help and shield.
10 O house of Aaron, trust in the LORD—
he is their help and shield.
11 You who fear him, trust in the LORD—
he is their help and shield.

12 The LORD remembers us and will bless us:
He will bless the house of Israel,
he will bless the house of Aaron,
13 he will bless those who fear the LORD—
small and great alike.

14 May the LORD make you increase,
both you and your children.
15 May you be blessed by the LORD,
the Maker of heaven and earth.

16 The highest heavens belong to the LORD,
but the earth he has given to man.
17 It is not the dead who praise the LORD,
those who go down to silence;
18 it is we who extol the LORD,
both now and forevermore.

Praise the LORD.[a]

Psalm 116

1 I love the LORD, for he heard my voice;
he heard my cry for mercy.
2 Because he turned his ear to me,
I will call on him as long as I live.

3 The cords of death entangled me,
the anguish of the grave[b] came upon me;
I was overcome by trouble and sorrow.
4 Then I called on the name of the LORD:
"O LORD, save me!"

5 The LORD is gracious and righteous;
our God is full of compassion.
6 The LORD protects the simplehearted;
when I was in great need, he saved me.

7 Be at rest once more, O my soul,
for the LORD has been good to you.

It is not the dead who praise the LORD, those who go down to silence; it is we who extol the LORD, both now and forevermore. Ps 115:17,18

115:4-8 *idols:* Unlike God (115:3), idols (images of foreign gods) are powerless (115:5-7). See also 135:15-18 and the note at 31:6.

115:10 *house of Aaron:* See the note at 99:6.

115:12,13 *LORD . . . will bless:* God's blessing comes to those who "trust" (115:9-11). See also the note at 1:1,2.

115:16 *earth he has given to man:* See the note at 8:5-8.

115:17 *not the dead who praise:* See the note at 9:13.

116:3 *cords of death entangled:* "Death" is described as a power that invades life. See the note at 18:4,5.

116:6 *when I was in great need, he saved me:* This psalm of thanks was prayed originally after a recovery from sickness. See 6:1-10 and the notes.

115:4-8 Rev 9:20. **115:13** Rev 11:18; 19:5.

[a]18 Hebrew *Hallelu Yah* [b]3 Hebrew *Sheol*

116:9 *land of the living:* In contrast to the "gates of death" (see the note at 9:13) the psalmist refers to life as a "land."

116:10 *believed ... afflicted:* The psalmist realizes that suffering does not separate him from God. See the note at 13:5,6. See also 2 Cor 4:13.

116:13 *cup of salvation:* Possibly lifted up to show thanks. Many cultures in the ancient Near East practiced some sort of drink offering (also called a "libation"). This Assyrian relief shows King Ashurbanipal of Assyria pouring oil or wine over the heads of slain lions.

116:14 *my vows to the LORD:* See 116:18 and the note at 22:24-26.

116:17 *sacrifice:* The psalmist's vow (116:14,18) involves the bringing of a sacrifice to give thanks for being healed. For more about sacrifices, see the note at 27:6.

117:1 *Praise the LORD:* The psalm invites all peoples to praise God. Paul uses this verse in Romans 15:11 to support his claim that the good news of Jesus Christ is for all people.

118:1 *love endures forever:* See the note at 100:5.

118:3 *house of Aaron:* See 115:10 and the note at 99:6.

118:1 1 Chr 16:34; 2 Chr 5:11-13; 7:3; Ezra 3:11; Ps 100:5; 106:1; 107:1; 136:1; Jer 33:11.

8 For you, O LORD, have delivered my soul from death,
my eyes from tears,
my feet from stumbling,
9 that I may walk before the LORD
in the land of the living.
10 I believed; therefore[a] I said,
"I am greatly afflicted."
11 And in my dismay I said,
"All men are liars."

12 How can I repay the LORD
for all his goodness to me?
13 I will lift up the cup of salvation
and call on the name of the LORD.
14 I will fulfill my vows to the LORD
in the presence of all his people.

15 Precious in the sight of the LORD
is the death of his saints.
16 O LORD, truly I am your servant;
I am your servant, the son of your maidservant[b];
you have freed me from my chains.

17 I will sacrifice a thank offering to you
and call on the name of the LORD.
18 I will fulfill my vows to the LORD
in the presence of all his people,
19 in the courts of the house of the LORD—
in your midst, O Jerusalem.

Praise the LORD.[c]

Psalm 117

1 Praise the LORD, all you nations;
extol him, all you peoples.
2 For great is his love toward us,
and the faithfulness of the LORD endures forever.

Praise the LORD.[c]

Psalm 118

1 Give thanks to the LORD, for he is good;
his love endures forever.

2 Let Israel say:
"His love endures forever."
3 Let the house of Aaron say:
"His love endures forever."

[a]**10** Or *believed even when* [b]**16** Or *servant, your faithful son* [c]**19,2** Hebrew *Hallelu Yah*

4 Let those who fear the LORD say:
"His love endures forever."

5 In my anguish I cried to the LORD,
and he answered by setting me free.
6 The LORD is with me; I will not be afraid.
What can man do to me?
7 The LORD is with me; he is my helper.
I will look in triumph on my enemies.

8 It is better to take refuge in the LORD
than to trust in man.

Cover for a Synagogue Reader's Desk, Turkey, early nineteenth century. Covers like this are sometimes placed on the *bimah* (reader's desk) in synagogues before the *Torah* scrolls are set down and opened for reading. This one features a stylized "gate of the LORD" in the center and includes the words of Psalm 118:20: "This is the gate of the LORD through which the righteous may enter."

Let those who fear the LORD say: "His love endures forever."
Ps 118:4

118:5-16 *answered by setting me free:* The psalmist's prayer has been answered, and he has been given "salvation" (118:14). Because verses 15 and 16 seem to describe a victory celebration, it is possible that the king spoke the psalm originally after a military victory.

118:7 *enemies:* See the note at 3:1,2. Here the enemies seem to be nations (118:10) that attacked the psalmist (see the note at 118:5-16).

118:6 Heb 13:6.

118:14 *The* Lord *is my strength and my song:* After he has been "helped" (118:13), the psalmist repeats part of the song that Moses, Miriam, and the people sang when God saved them from the Egyptians (Exod 15:2). See also Isa 12:2.

118:19,20 *gates of righteousness . . . gate of the* Lord*:* The references are to the entrance to the temple (see the note at 24:7-10). Because God wants people to be "righteous," the entrance to the temple is called "the gates of righteousness" (see the note at 9:8,9). These verses and those that follow may have been spoken during a ceremonial entry into the temple, "the house of the Lord" (118:26).

118:22 *capstone:* This would be the most important stone, at the top of the arch or, as it is sometimes translated, the "cornerstone" at the building's foundation. This capstone had been thrown away by builders.

Jesus said that, like such a stone, he too would be rejected by many, even though he alone is the foundation for faith. See Matt 21:42; Mark 12:10,11; Luke 20:17; Acts 4:11; 1 Pet 2:7.

118:25,26 *Blessed is he who comes:* Having seen the psalmist saved by God, the people now ask for help. They wait for help even as they celebrate. This also made the psalm useful in new situations. When Jesus entered Jerusalem, the crowds repeated 118:26 (see Matt 21:9; 23:39; Mark 11:9; Luke 13:35; 19:38; John 12:13).

118:27 *With boughs in hand, join in the festal procession:* The use of "boughs" (referring to palm branches) may suggest that the psalm was used originally during the Feast of Tabernacles (Lev 23:40). The altar is where sacrifices were offered, and the psalmist may have offered a sacrifice to show thanks to God.

9 It is better to take refuge in the Lord
than to trust in princes.

10 All the nations surrounded me,
but in the name of the Lord I cut them off.
11 They surrounded me on every side,
but in the name of the Lord I cut them off.
12 They swarmed around me like bees,
but they died out as quickly as burning thorns;
in the name of the Lord I cut them off.

13 I was pushed back and about to fall,
but the Lord helped me.
14 The Lord is my strength and my song;
he has become my salvation.

15 Shouts of joy and victory
resound in the tents of the righteous:
"The Lord's right hand has done mighty things!
16 The Lord's right hand is lifted high;
the Lord's right hand has done mighty things!"

17 I will not die but live,
and will proclaim what the Lord has done.
18 The Lord has chastened me severely,
but he has not given me over to death.

19 Open for me the gates of righteousness;
I will enter and give thanks to the Lord.
20 This is the gate of the Lord
through which the righteous may enter.
21 I will give you thanks, for you answered me;
you have become my salvation.

22 The stone the builders rejected
has become the capstone;
23 the Lord has done this,
and it is marvelous in our eyes.
24 This is the day the Lord has made;
let us rejoice and be glad in it.

25 O Lord, save us;
O Lord, grant us success.
26 Blessed is he who comes in the name of the Lord.
From the house of the Lord we bless you.[a]
27 The Lord is God,
and he has made his light shine upon us.
With boughs in hand, join in the festal procession
up[b] to the horns of the altar.

---

[a]**26** The Hebrew is plural. [b]**27** Or *Bind the festal sacrifice with ropes / and take it*

28 You are my God, and I will give you thanks;
you are my God, and I will exalt you.

29 Give thanks to the LORD, for he is good;
his love endures forever.

Psalm 119[a]

א Aleph

1 Blessed are they whose ways are blameless,
who walk according to the law of the LORD.
2 Blessed are they who keep his statutes
and seek him with all their heart.
3 They do nothing wrong;
they walk in his ways.
4 You have laid down precepts
that are to be fully obeyed.
5 Oh, that my ways were steadfast

119:1 *Blessed . . . walk according to the law of the LORD:* See the note at 1:1, 2. The word "law" and other related words ("commands," "teachings," "laws," "word," "instructions," and "rules") are repeated several times in Psalm 119. The repetition of these words makes the point that God's "law" is all-important. See also the note at 19:7,8.

In Hebrew, each eight-line stanza of Psalm 119 begins with the same letter. Verses 1 to 8 each begins with the first letter of the Hebrew alphabet; verses 9 to 16 each begins with the second letter of the Hebrew alphabet; and so forth. This kind of patterning supports the author's claim that God's law applies to everything (from "A to Z," as we would say in English).

[a] This psalm is an acrostic poem; the verses of each stanza begin with the same letter of the Hebrew alphabet.

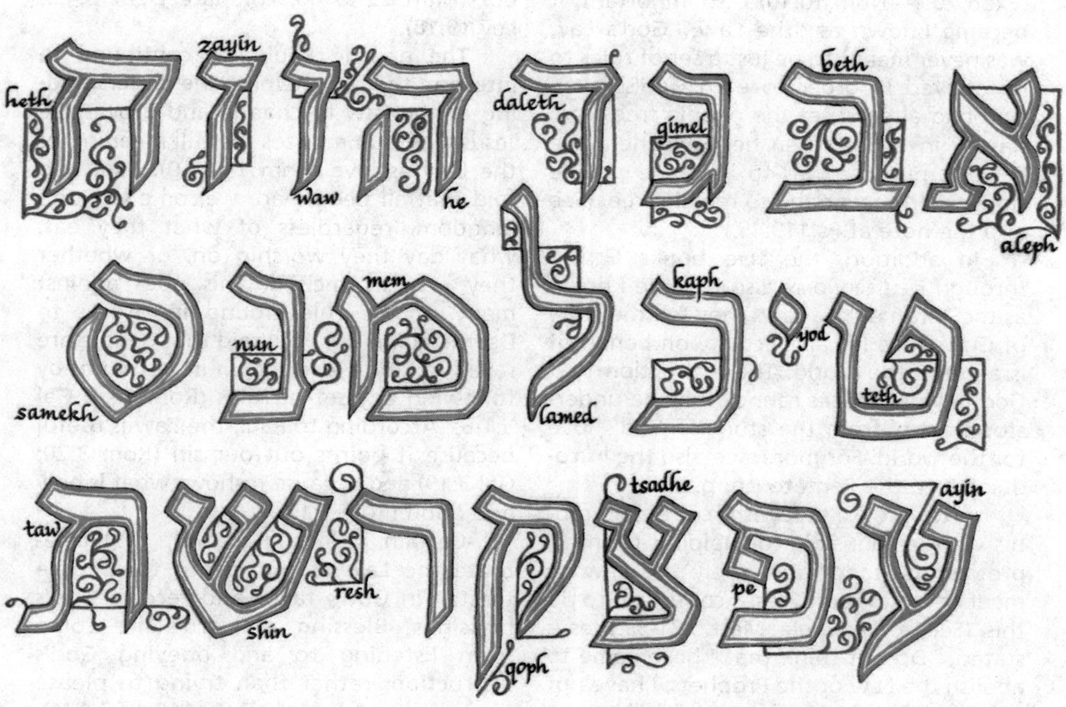

Hebrew Alphabet, calligraphy by Karen Silver. Psalm 119, the longest psalm in the Bible, celebrates the law of the LORD and is a beautiful example of Hebrew poetry. In Hebrew, the first word of each of the psalm's twenty-two sections begins with one of the letters of the Hebrew alphabet, using all of the letters from *aleph* to *taw.* Here, the psalmist creatively and literally celebrates the "letter of the law."

119:9 *keep his way pure:* God's law contains instructions about persons, animals, things, and situations that are "pure" or "impure." Here "pure" is a symbol for a life that is in keeping with God's will. See the mini-article called "Purity (Clean and Unclean)," p. 2125.

in obeying your decrees!
6 Then I would not be put to shame
when I consider all your commands.
7 I will praise you with an upright heart
as I learn your righteous laws.
8 I will obey your decrees;
do not utterly forsake me.

ב Beth

9 How can a young man keep his way pure?
By living according to your word.
10 I seek you with all my heart;
do not let me stray from your commands.

LAW

The Hebrew word that the NIV usually translates "Law" is *torah*. It means "teaching" or "instruction." Because the instruction that God gave Moses at Mount Sinai (Exod 20:1—Num 10:10) is so important, it became known as "the Law." God's Law was never meant to be just a set of rules to be obeyed in order to earn God's favor. God had already set the people free from slavery in Egypt when he gave them the Law. Its purpose was to help the people stay in God's favor and to remain free. (See also the note at Ps 119:45.)

In addition, the five books Genesis through Deuteronomy also became known as the *Torah* or the Law. They tell the story of God's love for and activity on behalf of Israel and the world. The instruction that God gave to Moses cannot fully be understood apart from the story of God's love for the world. For more, see also the Introduction to the Pentateuch, p. 35.

After the exile, Jewish scribes and rabbis were responsible for helping to interpret, understand, and apply the Law to meet new situations. Jesus continued to do this. (See, for example, Matt 5:21-39.) Jesus stated, "Do not think that I have come to abolish the Law or the Prophets; I have not come to abolish them but to fulfill them" (Matt 5:17). Jesus repudiated the Pharisees' emphasis on mere external obedience to the Law apart from a heart commitment to the underlying principles of the Law. Jesus summarized the full meaning of the Law as loving God and loving one's neighbor (Matt 22:37-40; compare Deut 6:4,5; Lev 19:18).

The apostle Paul also continued to interpret the Law, helping the understanding of the Law to change and grow. Like Jesus, Paul summarizes the full meaning of the Law as love (Rom 13:8-10). Paul also said that all people are welcome in God's kingdom, regardless of what they eat, what day they worship on, or whether they are circumcised. This goes against many of the rules found in Genesis to Deuteronomy. But Paul said that people are saved by God's love shown in Jesus, not by following any set of rules (Rom 10:4; Gal 5:1-6). According to Paul, the Law is useful because it points out our sin (Rom 3:20; Gal 3:19) and because it shows what is holy and good (Rom 7:12).

Certain psalms (Ps 1; 19; 119) celebrate the Law as the means for people to stay in God's favor and receive God's blessings. Blessing and true life come from listening to and obeying God's instruction, rather than trying to please oneself (Ps 1:1,2; 19:7,8; 119:1,92,174). See also the mini-article called "Blessed (Happy)," p. 1026.

11 I have hidden your word in my heart
that I might not sin against you.
12 Praise be to you, O LORD;
teach me your decrees.
13 With my lips I recount
all the laws that come from your mouth.
14 I rejoice in following your statutes
as one rejoices in great riches.
15 I meditate on your precepts
and consider your ways.
16 I delight in your decrees;
I will not neglect your word.

ג Gimel

17 Do good to your servant, and I will live;
I will obey your word.
18 Open my eyes that I may see
wonderful things in your law.
19 I am a stranger on earth;
do not hide your commands from me.
20 My soul is consumed with longing
for your laws at all times.
21 You rebuke the arrogant, who are cursed
and who stray from your commands.
22 Remove from me scorn and contempt,
for I keep your statutes.
23 Though rulers sit together and slander me,
your servant will meditate on your decrees.
24 Your statutes are my delight;
they are my counselors.

ד Daleth

25 I am laid low in the dust;
preserve my life according to your word.
26 I recounted my ways and you answered me;
teach me your decrees.
27 Let me understand the teaching of your precepts;
then I will meditate on your wonders.
28 My soul is weary with sorrow;
strengthen me according to your word.
29 Keep me from deceitful ways;
be gracious to me through your law.
30 I have chosen the way of truth;
I have set my heart on your laws.
31 I hold fast to your statutes, O LORD;
do not let me be put to shame.
32 I run in the path of your commands,
for you have set my heart free.

Open my eyes that I may see wonderful things in your law.
Ps 119:18

119:14 *great riches:* See the note at 112:3,4. True wealth means following God's teaching.

119:19 *stranger on earth:* See the note at 39:12.

119:21 *the arrogant:* Such people are usually called "enemies" or "the wicked." They oppose God and God's people. See the mini-article called "Enemies (The Wicked)," p. 1084. On God's punishment of the wicked, see the notes at 5:10-12 and 10:5.

119:25-28 *preserve my life . . . strengthen me:* These verses are like the complaints in the prayers for help. The psalmist's "sorrow" (119:28) shows that blessing or happiness (119:1) is not a matter of material reward. He calls on God's teachings (law) to strengthen him.

May your unfailing love come to me, O Lord, your salvation according to your promise.
Ps 119:41

119:36 *not toward selfish gain:* See the note at 119:14. See also Ps 37:16; Prov 15:16; 16:8.

119:41 *salvation:* The psalmist may be asking to be saved from "worthless things" (119:37), or from the attacks of enemies (119:39). See also the note at 51:12-14.

119:45 *in freedom:* God gave the law to Moses shortly after God had set the people free from slavery in Egypt. The law was intended to help people stay free by worshiping the Lord and living right, including treating one another with justice. This is what it means to serve God. The psalmist realizes that true "freedom" is to be a servant of God (119:38,49,65).

119:47 *commands . . . I love them:* See 119:1.

119:50 *comfort in my suffering:* See the note at 119:25-28.

119:51,53 *arrogant . . . the wicked:* See the note at 119:21.

ה He

33 Teach me, O Lord, to follow your decrees;
then I will keep them to the end.
34 Give me understanding, and I will keep your law
and obey it with all my heart.
35 Direct me in the path of your commands,
for there I find delight.
36 Turn my heart toward your statutes
and not toward selfish gain.
37 Turn my eyes away from worthless things;
preserve my life according to your word.[a]
38 Fulfill your promise to your servant,
so that you may be feared.
39 Take away the disgrace I dread,
for your laws are good.
40 How I long for your precepts!
Preserve my life in your righteousness.

ו Waw

41 May your unfailing love come to me, O Lord,
your salvation according to your promise;
42 then I will answer the one who taunts me,
for I trust in your word.
43 Do not snatch the word of truth from my mouth,
for I have put my hope in your laws.
44 I will always obey your law,
for ever and ever.
45 I will walk about in freedom,
for I have sought out your precepts.
46 I will speak of your statutes before kings
and will not be put to shame,
47 for I delight in your commands
because I love them.
48 I lift up my hands to[b] your commands, which I love,
and I meditate on your decrees.

ז Zayin

49 Remember your word to your servant,
for you have given me hope.
50 My comfort in my suffering is this:
Your promise preserves my life.
51 The arrogant mock me without restraint,
but I do not turn from your law.
52 I remember your ancient laws, O Lord,
and I find comfort in them.

[a]**37** Two manuscripts of the Masoretic Text and Dead Sea Scrolls; most manuscripts of the Masoretic Text *life in your way* [b]**48** Or *for*

[53] Indignation grips me because of the wicked,
who have forsaken your law.
[54] Your decrees are the theme of my song
wherever I lodge.
[55] In the night I remember your name, O LORD,
and I will keep your law.
[56] This has been my practice:
I obey your precepts.

ח Heth

[57] You are my portion, O LORD;
I have promised to obey your words.
[58] I have sought your face with all my heart;
be gracious to me according to your promise.
[59] I have considered my ways
and have turned my steps to your statutes.
[60] I will hasten and not delay
to obey your commands.
[61] Though the wicked bind me with ropes,
I will not forget your law.
[62] At midnight I rise to give you thanks
for your righteous laws.
[63] I am a friend to all who fear you,
to all who follow your precepts.
[64] The earth is filled with your love, O LORD;
teach me your decrees.

ט Teth

[65] Do good to your servant
according to your word, O LORD.
[66] Teach me knowledge and good judgment,
for I believe in your commands.
[67] Before I was afflicted I went astray,
but now I obey your word.
[68] You are good, and what you do is good;
teach me your decrees.
[69] Though the arrogant have smeared me with lies,
I keep your precepts with all my heart.
[70] Their hearts are callous and unfeeling,
but I delight in your law.
[71] It was good for me to be afflicted
so that I might learn your decrees.
[72] The law from your mouth is more precious to me
than thousands of pieces of silver and gold.

י Yodh

[73] Your hands made me and formed me;
give me understanding to learn your commands.

The law from your mouth is more precious to me than thousands of pieces of silver and gold.
Ps 119:72

119:62 *righteous laws:* The righteousness of God's laws means that they serve to establish justice. See the note at 9:8, 9.

119:64 *earth is filled with your love:* See the note at 36:5, 6.

119:66 *knowledge and good judgment:* Obeying the LORD's teachings brings protection and "good judgment," which could also be called "wisdom" (Ps 19:11; 111:10; Prov 1:7; 2:1-9). See also the mini-article called "Wisdom," p. 2206.

119:69,70 *arrogant . . . lies:* The liars who are attacking the reputation of the psalmist (119:21,22,39, 78) "are callous and unfeeling." They lack the wisdom that comes from following God's law. See the notes at 119:21 and 119:66. In contrast, the psalmist delights in God's law (see the note at 1:1, 2).

119:73 *give me understanding:* See the note at 119:66.

119:72 Ps 37:16; 119:36; Prov 15:16; 16:8.

Your word, O LORD, is eternal; it stands firm in the heavens.
Ps 119:89

119:78 *arrogant:* See the notes at 119:21 and 119:69,70.

119:82 *My eyes fail:* See the note at 119:123.

119:83 *a wineskin in the smoke:* In ancient times, bags were made from animal skins to hold wine, but when the bags dried up (by being hung too close to a fire, for instance) they cracked and could no longer be used. See the illustration on p. 1985.

119:84-87 *How long . . . persecutors:* These verses are like the complaints in the prayers for help. See also the note at 119:25-28. "Persecutors" and "arrogant" are names for the psalmist's enemies. See the note at 119:21.

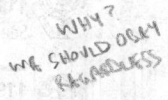

74 May those who fear you rejoice when they see me,
for I have put my hope in your word.
75 I know, O LORD, that your laws are righteous,
and in faithfulness you have afflicted me.
76 May your unfailing love be my comfort,
according to your promise to your servant.
77 Let your compassion come to me that I may live,
for your law is my delight.
78 May the arrogant be put to shame for wronging me
without cause;
but I will meditate on your precepts.
79 May those who fear you turn to me,
those who understand your statutes.
80 May my heart be blameless toward your decrees,
that I may not be put to shame.

כ Kaph

81 My soul faints with longing for your salvation,
but I have put my hope in your word.
82 My eyes fail, looking for your promise;
I say, "When will you comfort me?"
83 Though I am like a wineskin in the smoke,
I do not forget your decrees.
84 How long must your servant wait?
When will you punish my persecutors?
85 The arrogant dig pitfalls for me,
contrary to your law.
86 All your commands are trustworthy;
help me, for men persecute me without cause.
87 They almost wiped me from the earth,
but I have not forsaken your precepts.
88 Preserve my life according to your love,
and I will obey the statutes of your mouth.

ל Lamedh

89 Your word, O LORD, is eternal;
it stands firm in the heavens.
90 Your faithfulness continues through all generations;
you established the earth, and it endures.
91 Your laws endure to this day,
for all things serve you.
92 If your law had not been my delight,
I would have perished in my affliction.
93 I will never forget your precepts,
for by them you have preserved my life.
94 Save me, for I am yours;
I have sought out your precepts.
95 The wicked are waiting to destroy me,

but I will ponder your statutes.
[96]To all perfection I see a limit;
but your commands are boundless.

מ Mem

[97]Oh, how I love your law!
I meditate on it all day long.
[98]Your commands make me wiser than my enemies,
for they are ever with me.
[99]I have more insight than all my teachers,
for I meditate on your statutes.
[100]I have more understanding than the elders,
for I obey your precepts.
[101]I have kept my feet from every evil path
so that I might obey your word.
[102]I have not departed from your laws,
for you yourself have taught me.
[103]How sweet are your words to my taste,
sweeter than honey to my mouth!
[104]I gain understanding from your precepts;
therefore I hate every wrong path.

נ Nun

[105]Your word is a lamp to my feet
and a light for my path.
[106]I have taken an oath and confirmed it,
that I will follow your righteous laws.
[107]I have suffered much;
preserve my life, O LORD, according to your word.
[108]Accept, O LORD, the willing praise of my mouth,
and teach me your laws.
[109]Though I constantly take my life in my hands,
I will not forget your law.
[110]The wicked have set a snare for me,
but I have not strayed from your precepts.
[111]Your statutes are my heritage forever;
they are the joy of my heart.
[112]My heart is set on keeping your decrees
to the very end.

ס Samekh

[113]I hate double-minded men,
but I love your law.
[114]You are my refuge and my shield;
I have put my hope in your word.
[115]Away from me, you evildoers,
that I may keep the commands of my God!

Your word is a lamp to my feet and a light for my path.
Ps 119:105

119:98-100 *Your commands make me wiser than my enemies:* See the note at 119:66. Those who had grown old were considered wise because of their experience. But the psalmist suggests that true wisdom comes by studying God's Law.

119:103 *sweeter than honey:* See the note at 19:10.

119:106 *righteous laws:* See the note at 119:62.

119:110 *set a snare for me:* See 119:25-28,61,84-87; and the note at 31:4.

119:115,118 *evildoers . . . deceitfulness:* See the notes at 119:21 and 119:69,70.

119:122 *arrogant:* See the notes at 119:21 and 119:69, 70.

119:123 *My eyes fail, looking for your salvation:* The psalmist's many complaints (119:25-28, 84-87, 109, 110) show that God does not use his power to enforce his will immediately. So the psalmist is waiting. See also the notes at 5:10-12; 37:39, 40; and 126:5, 6.

119:127 *more than pure gold:* See 119:72 and the note at 112:3,4. See also Ps 37:16; 119:36; Prov 15:16; 16:8.

119:134 *oppression of men:* Oppression results from injustice, which in turn results from failing to do God's will. The psalmist is asking for protection from his enemies.

116 Sustain me according to your promise, and
I will live;
do not let my hopes be dashed.
117 Uphold me, and I will be delivered;
I will always have regard for your decrees.
118 You reject all who stray from your decrees,
for their deceitfulness is in vain.
119 All the wicked of the earth you discard like dross;
therefore I love your statutes.
120 My flesh trembles in fear of you;
I stand in awe of your laws.

ע Ayin

121 I have done what is righteous and just;
do not leave me to my oppressors.
122 Ensure your servant's well-being;
let not the arrogant oppress me.
123 My eyes fail, looking for your salvation,
looking for your righteous promise.
124 Deal with your servant according to your love
and teach me your decrees.
125 I am your servant; give me discernment
that I may understand your statutes.
126 It is time for you to act, O LORD;
your law is being broken.
127 Because I love your commands
more than gold, more than pure gold,
128 and because I consider all your precepts right,
I hate every wrong path.

פ Pe

129 Your statutes are wonderful;
therefore I obey them.
130 The unfolding of your words gives light;
it gives understanding to the simple.
131 I open my mouth and pant,
longing for your commands.
132 Turn to me and have mercy on me,
as you always do to those who love your name.
133 Direct my footsteps according to your word;
let no sin rule over me.
134 Redeem me from the oppression of men,
that I may obey your precepts.
135 Make your face shine upon your servant
and teach me your decrees.
136 Streams of tears flow from my eyes,
for your law is not obeyed.

צ Tsadhe

137 Righteous are you, O LORD,
and your laws are right.
138 The statutes you have laid down are righteous;
they are fully trustworthy.
139 My zeal wears me out,
for my enemies ignore your words.
140 Your promises have been thoroughly tested,
and your servant loves them.
141 Though I am lowly and despised,
I do not forget your precepts.
142 Your righteousness is everlasting
and your law is true.
143 Trouble and distress have come upon me,
but your commands are my delight.
144 Your statutes are forever right;
give me understanding that I may live.

ק Qoph

145 I call with all my heart; answer me, O LORD,
and I will obey your decrees.
146 I call out to you; save me
and I will keep your statutes.
147 I rise before dawn and cry for help;
I have put my hope in your word.
148 My eyes stay open through the watches of the
night,
that I may meditate on your promises.
149 Hear my voice in accordance with your love;
preserve my life, O LORD, according to your laws.
150 Those who devise wicked schemes are near,
but they are far from your law.
151 Yet you are near, O LORD,
and all your commands are true.
152 Long ago I learned from your statutes
that you established them to last forever.

ר Resh

153 Look upon my suffering and deliver me,
for I have not forgotten your law.
154 Defend my cause and redeem me;
preserve my life according to your promise.
155 Salvation is far from the wicked,
for they do not seek out your decrees.
156 Your compassion is great, O LORD;
preserve my life according to your laws.
157 Many are the foes who persecute me,

Your promises have been thoroughly tested, and your servant loves them.
Ps 119:140

119:137 *righteous:* See the note at 119:62.

119:139 *my enemies:* See the notes at 119:21 and 119:69,70.

119:147,148 *before dawn . . . watches of the night:* Morning was the usual time for prayer (see the note at 5:3), but the psalmist starts praying even before that. Since he also thinks about God during the night, he is always paying attention to God. See also 119:164.

119:153 *my suffering:* For more about how God responds to the complaints of the faithful, see the notes at 119:25-28 and 119:84-87.

119:155-158 *Salvation is far from the wicked:* Salvation is far from the wicked people because they cut themselves off from God. See the note at 119:21. See also the mini-article called "Salvation," p. 2021.

but I have not turned from your statutes.
158 I look on the faithless with loathing,
for they do not obey your word.
159 See how I love your precepts;
preserve my life, O LORD, according to your love.
160 All your words are true;
all your righteous laws are eternal.

ש Sin and Shin

161 Rulers persecute me without cause,
but my heart trembles at your word.
162 I rejoice in your promise
like one who finds great spoil.
163 I hate and abhor falsehood
but I love your law.
164 Seven times a day I praise you
for your righteous laws.
165 Great peace have they who love your law,
and nothing can make them stumble.
166 I wait for your salvation, O LORD,
and I follow your commands.
167 I obey your statutes,
for I love them greatly.
168 I obey your precepts and your statutes,
for all my ways are known to you.

ת Taw

169 May my cry come before you, O LORD;
give me understanding according to your word.
170 May my supplication come before you;
deliver me according to your promise.
171 May my lips overflow with praise,
for you teach me your decrees.
172 May my tongue sing of your word,
for all your commands are righteous.
173 May your hand be ready to help me,
for I have chosen your precepts.
174 I long for your salvation, O LORD,
and your law is my delight.
175 Let me live that I may praise you,
and may your laws sustain me.
176 I have strayed like a lost sheep.
Seek your servant,
for I have not forgotten your commands.

119:164 *Seven times a day:* The number seven was considered a perfect or complete number. So, it is probably a way of saying that the psalmist pays attention to God all the time.

119:165 *Great peace:* The goal of justice is peace. The psalmist says that he is experiencing "great peace." As the rest of the psalm makes clear, this peace of mind does not mean a life free of trouble and suffering. Instead, it means the ability to endure trouble and suffering.

119:172 *your word:* The psalmist has experienced troubles, but he still wants to praise God and sing about God's promise. The "word" may simply refer to the help the psalmist will receive. For a wider understanding of God's promises, see the note at 105:8-11.

119:174 *I long for your salvation:* See the note at 119:123.

119:176 *lost sheep:* After the psalmist has said so many times that he loves and obeys God's teaching, he ends by admitting that he has sinned. The psalmist's life does not finally depend on his ability to obey. Instead, it depends on God's willingness to forgive.

Psalm 120

A song of ascents.

1 I call on the LORD in my distress,
   and he answers me.
2 Save me, O LORD, from lying lips
   and from deceitful tongues.

3 What will he do to you,
   and what more besides, O deceitful tongue?
4 He will punish you with a warrior's sharp arrows,
   with burning coals of the broom tree.

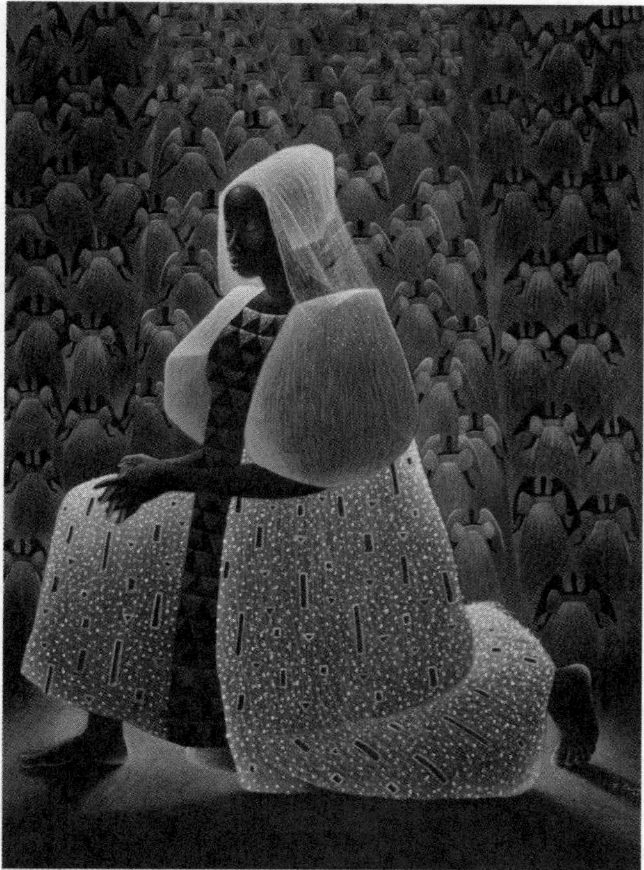

La Prière (The Prayer) by François Cauvin, twentieth century. Prayers asking for God's help, guidance, or protection occur frequently in PSALMS. In this painting, angels representing God's presence surround a woman kneeling in prayer. The psalmist could be speaking to her when he declares, "He will not let your foot slip—he who watches over you will not slumber . . . the LORD will watch over your coming and going both now and forevermore" (Ps 121:3,8).

120 Title *song of ascents:* The title "song of ascents" appears in the titles of Psalms 120–134. Jerusalem is built on hills, and the temple was located on the hill called Zion. This collection probably was used by worshipers as they were ascending to Jerusalem for one of the three pilgrimage festivals that all Israelite men were supposed to attend (Deut 16:16). Except for Psalm 132, all the psalms are very short and would have been easy to memorize. They often mention Jerusalem or Zion, the place where the people were going to celebrate the festival (122:2,3,6; 125:1; 126:1; 128:5; 129:5; 132:13,15; 133:3; 134:3). The order of the psalms also suggests their use by worshipers traveling to Jerusalem. Psalm 120 is spoken by someone who lives outside the land (120:5); Psalm 121 is about a journey; Psalm 122 talks about arriving at the temple in Jerusalem; Psalms 123–133 are prayers that could have been used at a festival; and Psalm 134 sounds like a blessing for the trip back home.

120:2,3 *deceitful tongue:* See the notes at 3:1,2; 7:3-5; and 119:21.

120:5 *Meshech . . . Kedar:* Meshech was a country near the Black Sea. Kedar was a tribe that lived on the edges of the Syrian desert (see the map on p. 2468). Meshech and Kedar may be symbols for "those who hate peace" (120:6).

120:6,7 *peace:* Peace results when justice is done. See the notes at 72:1-3 and 122:6,7. See also the mini-article called "Peace," p. 1337.

121 Title *A song of ascents:* See the note at 120 Title.

121:1 *to the hills:* Since this psalm was probably used originally by travelers to Jerusalem (see the note at 120 Title), "the hills" may include Mount Zion (see the note at 2:6).

121:3 *he who watches over you:* The LORD is the protector of those who travel to Jerusalem to celebrate the holy festivals.

121:6 *the sun . . . the moon:* For travelers on foot in this part of the world, the heat of the sun is clearly a danger. But people in ancient times also believed that the rays of the moon could cause sickness, especially mental disorders.

122 Title *A song of ascents. Of David:* See the notes at 120 Title and 122:5.

122:1-3 *the house of the LORD . . . Jerusalem:* The house of the LORD was the temple in Jerusalem. Travelers to Jerusalem probably used the psalm as they passed the city's gates or as they arrived in the temple area (see the map on p. 2466). See also the notes at 15:1; 9:14; 118:19,20; and 48:12-14.

122:4 *according to the statute:* All Israelite men were supposed to go to Jerusalem for the three major festivals of the year. See Deut 16:16 and the note at 120 Title. See also the chart called "Jewish Calendar and Festivals," p. 944.

5 Woe to me that I dwell in Meshech,
that I live among the tents of Kedar!
6 Too long have I lived
among those who hate peace.
7 I am a man of peace;
but when I speak, they are for war.

Psalm 121

A song of ascents.

1 I lift up my eyes to the hills—
where does my help come from?
2 My help comes from the LORD,
the Maker of heaven and earth.

3 He will not let your foot slip—
he who watches over you will not slumber;
4 indeed, he who watches over Israel
will neither slumber nor sleep.

5 The LORD watches over you—
the LORD is your shade at your right hand;
6 the sun will not harm you by day,
nor the moon by night.

7 The LORD will keep you from all harm—
he will watch over your life;
8 the LORD will watch over your coming and going
both now and forevermore.

Psalm 122

A song of ascents. Of David.

1 I rejoiced with those who said to me,
"Let us go to the house of the LORD."
2 Our feet are standing
in your gates, O Jerusalem.

3 Jerusalem is built like a city
that is closely compacted together.
4 That is where the tribes go up,
the tribes of the LORD,
to praise the name of the LORD
according to the statute given to Israel.
5 There the thrones for judgment stand,
the thrones of the house of David.

6 Pray for the peace of Jerusalem:
"May those who love you be secure.
7 May there be peace within your walls
and security within your citadels."
8 For the sake of my brothers and friends,

Pilgrims Going Up to Jerusalem. Jerusalem was the center of worship for the people of Israel from the time of King David. During major festivals (Passover and the Feast of Unleavened Bread and the Feast of Harvest in the spring, and the Feast of Tabernacles in the fall), the people would make pilgrimages to Jerusalem to celebrate, pray in the temple, and offer sacrifices to the LORD. PSALMS includes many examples of psalms that speak of the importance of Jerusalem (God's holy city) and the temple (God's house). See, for example, Psalm 122.

I will say, "Peace be within you."
9 For the sake of the house of the LORD our God,
I will seek your prosperity.

Psalm 123

A song of ascents.

1 I lift up my eyes to you,
to you whose throne is in heaven.
2 As the eyes of slaves look to the hand of their master,
as the eyes of a maid look to the hand of her mistress,

122:5 *thrones of the house of David:* The royal palace of King David and his descendants was in Jerusalem. As king of the universe, God wills justice. It was the responsibility of the earthly kings, David and his descendants, to establish justice on earth. See the notes at 9:8, 9 and 72:1-3.

122:6,7 *Jerusalem . . . peace:* The goal and result of justice is peace. In Hebrew, the final part of the name "Jerusalem" sounds like *shalom,* which means "peace."

123 Title *A song of ascents:* See the note at 120 Title.

123:1 *throne is in heaven:* See the note at 9:7.

123:3,4 *Have mercy . . . the proud:* This prayer for help for the whole people probably fits well into the period after the exile. See the note at 44:9-11. Although the people had returned to the land, other nations still ruled over them and caused them problems (see Neh 2:19; 4:4). See also the note at 119:21.

124 Title *A song of ascents. Of David:* See the note at 120 Title and 122:5.

124:2 *men attacked us:* See the note at 123:3,4. The circumstances of the "attack" are not known, but the prayer of 123:3,4 seems to have been answered.

125 Title *A song of ascents:* See the note at 120 Title.

125:1 *Mount Zion:* See the notes at 2:6 and 121:1.

125:2 *LORD surrounds his people:* See the note at 121:3.

125:3,5 *the wicked . . . banish:* See the note at 119:21.

125:5 *Peace be upon Israel:* See the note at 122:6,7.

126 Title *A song of ascents:* See the note at 120 Title.

126:1 *brought back the captives to Zion:* The psalm assumes the return from exile. See the notes at 44:9-11; 85:1-4; and 107:2, 3.

126:2,3 *great things:* The psalmist considers Israel's return from exile in Babylonia and the rebuilding of Jerusalem as "great things" done by God. Likewise, the people of Israel spoke of their escape from Egypt and safe crossing of the Red Sea as God's "wonderful deeds." See also the note at 75:1.

126:4 *streams in the Negev:* See the map on p. 2464. The Negev is a desert area south of Israel. In the rainy season, dry stream beds can suddenly become flowing streams, a wonderful and seemingly miraculous occurrence in the desert.

so our eyes look to the LORD our God,
till he shows us his mercy.

3 Have mercy on us, O LORD, have mercy on us,
for we have endured much contempt.
4 We have endured much ridicule from the proud,
much contempt from the arrogant.

Psalm 124

A song of ascents. Of David.

1 If the LORD had not been on our side—
let Israel say—
2 if the LORD had not been on our side
when men attacked us,
3 when their anger flared against us,
they would have swallowed us alive;
4 the flood would have engulfed us,
the torrent would have swept over us,
5 the raging waters
would have swept us away.

6 Praise be to the LORD,
who has not let us be torn by their teeth.
7 We have escaped like a bird
out of the fowler's snare;
the snare has been broken,
and we have escaped.
8 Our help is in the name of the LORD,
the Maker of heaven and earth.

Psalm 125

A song of ascents.

1 Those who trust in the LORD are like Mount Zion,
which cannot be shaken but endures forever.
2 As the mountains surround Jerusalem,
so the LORD surrounds his people
both now and forevermore.

3 The scepter of the wicked will not remain
over the land allotted to the righteous,
for then the righteous might use
their hands to do evil.

4 Do good, O LORD, to those who are good,
to those who are upright in heart.
5 But those who turn to crooked ways
the LORD will banish with the evildoers.

Peace be upon Israel.

Psalm 126

A song of ascents.

1 When the LORD brought back the captives to[a] Zion,
we were like men who dreamed.[b]
2 Our mouths were filled with laughter,
our tongues with songs of joy.
Then it was said among the nations,
"The LORD has done great things for them."
3 The LORD has done great things for us,
and we are filled with joy.

4 Restore our fortunes,[c] O LORD,
like streams in the Negev.
5 Those who sow in tears
will reap with songs of joy.
6 He who goes out weeping,
carrying seed to sow,
will return with songs of joy,
carrying sheaves with him.

Psalm 127

A song of ascents. Of Solomon.

1 Unless the LORD builds the house,
its builders labor in vain.
Unless the LORD watches over the city,
the watchmen stand guard in vain.
2 In vain you rise early
and stay up late,
toiling for food to eat—
for he grants sleep to[d] those he loves.

3 Sons are a heritage from the LORD,
children a reward from him.
4 Like arrows in the hands of a warrior
are sons born in one's youth.
5 Blessed is the man
whose quiver is full of them.
They will not be put to shame
when they contend with their enemies in the gate.

Psalm 128

A song of ascents.

1 Blessed are all who fear the LORD,
who walk in his ways.
2 You will eat the fruit of your labor;

[a]1 Or *LORD restored the fortunes of* [b]1 Or *men restored to health* [c]4 Or *Bring back our captives* [d]2 Or *eat— / for while they sleep he provides for*

Unless the LORD builds the house, its builders labor in vain. Unless the LORD watches over the city, the watchmen stand guard in vain.
Ps 127:1

126:5,6 *sow in tears . . . reap with songs of joy:* The people's crying shows the depth of their distress. But they both pray for and expect a joyful harvest. Such confidence while suffering suggests that the people of God always live in hopeful waiting.

127 Title *A song of ascents. Of Solomon:* See the notes at 120 Title and 72 Title. Solomon was responsible for building the temple.

127:1 *builds the house:* Building a house can mean constructing a house, but it can also mean starting and raising a family, which is the subject of 127:3-5. Either activity is vain without God.

127:3-5 *sons are a heritage . . . a reward:* In ancient times, having many children meant parents would have lots of help with daily tasks and would be cared for in old age. All parts of daily life—home, town, job, family—find their meaning as they are related to God.

128 Title *A song of ascents:* See the note at 120 Title.

128:1-4 *Blessed are all who fear the LORD:* The LORD's blessings are for those who obey the LORD and respect the LORD's Law. See the note at 1:1,2. The blessings include good harvests and many healthy children (see the note at 127:3-5). The promise that "blessings and prosperity will be yours" should not be understood to mean that those who obey God will never have troubles. See the note at 37:39,40.

128:5 *bless you from Zion:* The LORD's blessings were said to come from Zion, since that was where the LORD's temple was (see the notes at 27:4 and 43:3, 4). See also 125:5.

129 Title *A song of ascents:* See the note at 120 Title.

129:1 *They have greatly oppressed me:* See the note at 123:3,4.

129:3,4 *Plowmen have plowed my back . . . the wicked:* "The wicked" have hurt God's people in some way, but the people still exist. This shows that God aims to establish justice, including setting the captive Israelite people free. "Plowed my back" represents attacks and "cords" the pain of being a prisoner.

129:5-8 *all who hate Zion . . . shame:* This prayer for revenge against those "who hate Zion" includes a warning against giving them a blessing. Once spoken, such blessings could not be taken back. See also the mini-article called "Making Vows," p. 328.

130 Title *A song of ascents:* See the note at 120 Title.

130:1-4 *I cry to you . . . forgiveness:* It is clear that the psalmist's troubles are a result of his sins (130:3).

130:5,6 *my soul waits:* See the notes at 119:123 and 126:5, 6. The repeating of the sentences in 130:6 helps to create the effect of "waiting."

132:6-10 2 Chr 6:41,42.

blessings and prosperity will be yours.
3 Your wife will be like a fruitful vine
within your house;
your sons will be like olive shoots
around your table.
4 Thus is the man blessed
who fears the LORD.

5 May the LORD bless you from Zion
all the days of your life;
may you see the prosperity of Jerusalem,
6 and may you live to see your children's children.

Peace be upon Israel.

Psalm 129

A song of ascents.

1 They have greatly oppressed me from my youth—
let Israel say—
2 they have greatly oppressed me from my youth,
but they have not gained the victory over me.
3 Plowmen have plowed my back
and made their furrows long.
4 But the LORD is righteous;
he has cut me free from the cords of the wicked.

5 May all who hate Zion
be turned back in shame.
6 May they be like grass on the roof,
which withers before it can grow;
7 with it the reaper cannot fill his hands,
nor the one who gathers fill his arms.
8 May those who pass by not say,
"The blessing of the LORD be upon you;
we bless you in the name of the LORD."

Psalm 130

A song of ascents.

1 Out of the depths I cry to you, O LORD;
2 O Lord, hear my voice.
Let your ears be attentive
to my cry for mercy.

3 If you, O LORD, kept a record of sins,
O Lord, who could stand?
4 But with you there is forgiveness;
therefore you are feared.

5 I wait for the LORD, my soul waits,
and in his word I put my hope.

6 My soul waits for the Lord
more than watchmen wait for the morning,
more than watchmen wait for the morning.

7 O Israel, put your hope in the LORD,
for with the LORD is unfailing love
and with him is full redemption.
8 He himself will redeem Israel
from all their sins.

Psalm 131

A song of ascents. Of David.

1 My heart is not proud, O LORD,
my eyes are not haughty;
I do not concern myself with great matters
or things too wonderful for me.
2 But I have stilled and quieted my soul;
like a weaned child with its mother,
like a weaned child is my soul within me.

3 O Israel, put your hope in the LORD
both now and forevermore.

Psalm 132

A song of ascents.

1 O LORD, remember David
and all the hardships he endured.

2 He swore an oath to the LORD
and made a vow to the Mighty One of Jacob:
3 "I will not enter my house
or go to my bed—
4 I will allow no sleep to my eyes,
no slumber to my eyelids,
5 till I find a place for the LORD,
a dwelling for the Mighty One of Jacob."

6 We heard it in Ephrathah,
we came upon it in the fields of Jaar[a]:[b]
7 "Let us go to his dwelling place;
let us worship at his footstool—
8 arise, O LORD, and come to your resting place,
you and the ark of your might.
9 May your priests be clothed with righteousness;
may your saints sing for joy."

[a]**6** That is, Kiriath Jearim [b]**6** Or *heard of it in Ephrathah, / we found it in the fields of Jaar.* (And no quotes around verses 7-9)

130:7,8 *full redemption . . . redeem Israel from all their sins:* The understanding of God as giving full redemption is in keeping with God's message to Moses in Exodus 34:6, 7. See also Matt 1:21; Titus 2:14.

131 Title *A song of ascents. Of David:* See the notes at 120 Title and 122:5.

131:2,3 *like a weaned child:* Some scholars think Psalm 131 may have been written by a woman, perhaps one of the travelers to Jerusalem who brought her young child with her.

132 Title *A song of ascents:* Psalm 132 celebrates the key reason that people traveled to Jerusalem, to visit God's "chosen" dwelling in Zion (132:13) where David had ruled Israel (132:10). See the notes at 122:1-3 and 122:5.

132:1 *David . . . hardships:* David's suffering may refer to his attempt to take the ark of the covenant to Jerusalem (Ps 132:6-9; 2 Sam 6:1-19). But it probably refers to the end of the line of kings from David's family. See the note at 89:38-45.

132:2-5 *find a place for the LORD:* This promise refers either to David's goal of taking the ark of the covenant to Jerusalem or to David's desire to build a house (temple) for God (2 Sam 7:1,2).

132:6 *Ephrathah . . . Jaar:* Ephrathah probably refers to the region around Bethlehem. Jaar may be a poetic way of referring to Kiriath Jearim where the ark of the covenant was located in 1 Samuel 6:19—7:2.

132:6-8 *the ark:* See the mini-article called "The Ark of the Covenant," p. 513. The "we" and "us" in 132:6,7 could be people who followed David and the ark to its new dwelling place. Or they may be visitors to Jerusalem in later times who perhaps retraced David's journey. See the note at 120 Title.

132:10 *David . . . anointed one:* See the notes at 2:2 and 2:7, 9; see also the mini-article called "Messiah (Chosen One)," p. 1124.

132:11,12 *swore an oath . . . keep my covenant:* See the notes at 89:3,4 and 105:8-11. See also 2 Sam 7:12-16; 1 Chr 17:11-14; Acts 2:30.

132:17 *set up a lamp:* See 1 Kgs 11:36. See also the note at 18:28.

132:18 *his enemies:* See the notes at 18:3 and 44:5.

133 Title *A song of ascents:* See the note at 120 Title.

133:2 *precious oil . . . running down on Aaron's beard:* See the note at 99:6. Olive oil was poured on Aaron's head to show that God had chosen him to be the high priest. Oil used for such anointings was often stored in hollowed-out animal horns. See also the note at 2:2.

133:3 *Hermon . . . Mount Zion:* See the notes at 29:5-8 and 2:6.

134 Title *A song of ascents:* See the note at 120 Title.

134:2 *Lift up your hands:* See the note at 28:2.

10 For the sake of David your servant,
do not reject your anointed one.

11 The LORD swore an oath to David,
a sure oath that he will not revoke:
"One of your own descendants
I will place on your throne—
12 if your sons keep my covenant
and the statutes I teach them,
then their sons will sit
on your throne for ever and ever."

13 For the LORD has chosen Zion,
he has desired it for his dwelling:
14 "This is my resting place for ever and ever;
here I will sit enthroned, for I have desired it—
15 I will bless her with abundant provisions;
her poor will I satisfy with food.
16 I will clothe her priests with salvation,
and her saints will ever sing for joy.

17 "Here I will make a horn[a] grow for David
and set up a lamp for my anointed one.
18 I will clothe his enemies with shame,
but the crown on his head will be resplendent."

Psalm 133

A song of ascents. Of David.

1 How good and pleasant it is
when brothers live together in unity!
2 It is like precious oil poured on the head,
running down on the beard,
running down on Aaron's beard,
down upon the collar of his robes.
3 It is as if the dew of Hermon
were falling on Mount Zion.
For there the LORD bestows his blessing,
even life forevermore.

Psalm 134

A song of ascents.

1 Praise the LORD, all you servants of the LORD
who minister by night in the house of the LORD.
2 Lift up your hands in the sanctuary
and praise the LORD.

[a]17 *Horn* here symbolizes strong one, that is, king.

[3]May the LORD, the Maker of heaven and earth,
bless you from Zion.

Psalm 135

[1]Praise the LORD.[a]

Praise the name of the LORD;
praise him, you servants of the LORD,
[2]you who minister in the house of the LORD,
in the courts of the house of our God.

[3]Praise the LORD, for the LORD is good;
sing praise to his name, for that is pleasant.
[4]For the LORD has chosen Jacob to be his own,
Israel to be his treasured possession.

[5]I know that the LORD is great,
that our Lord is greater than all gods.
[6]The LORD does whatever pleases him,
in the heavens and on the earth,
in the seas and all their depths.
[7]He makes clouds rise from the ends of the earth;
he sends lightning with the rain
and brings out the wind from his storehouses.

[8]He struck down the firstborn of Egypt,
the firstborn of men and animals.
[9]He sent his signs and wonders into your midst,
O Egypt,
against Pharaoh and all his servants.
[10]He struck down many nations
and killed mighty kings—
[11]Sihon king of the Amorites,
Og king of Bashan
and all the kings of Canaan—
[12]and he gave their land as an inheritance,
an inheritance to his people Israel.

[13]Your name, O LORD, endures forever,
your renown, O LORD, through all generations.
[14]For the LORD will vindicate his people
and have compassion on his servants.

[15]The idols of the nations are silver and gold,
made by the hands of men.
[16]They have mouths, but cannot speak,
eyes, but they cannot see;
[17]they have ears, but cannot hear,

[a]1 Hebrew *Hallelu Yah*; also in verses 3 and 21

134:3 *Maker of heaven and earth, bless you from Zion:* These words may have been spoken by a priest to the worshipers, perhaps wishing them well as they prepared to travel home from Zion. See Ps 104 and the note at 95:6,7.

135:4 *chosen Jacob:* See the note at 22:23.

135:5 *greater than all gods:* See the note at 82:1.

135:7 *He makes clouds rise . . . lightning . . . wind:* See the notes at 29:3-9; 65:9-13; and 104:3, 4. God's "storehouses" refer to heaven.

135:8-12 *struck down . . . inheritance:* These verses recall Psalms 78; 105; and 106. See 136:10-22.

135:8,9 *signs and wonders:* See the note and cross-references at 78:43-53.

135:11 *Sihon . . . Og . . . king of Bashan:* Sihon refused to let the people pass through his land (Num 21:21-33; Deut 2:26-37). After defeating Sihon, the people also defeated Og (Num 21:33-35; Deut 3:1-11). For Bashan, see the note at 22:12.

135:11,12 *gave their land as an inheritance:* God helped the people enter Canaan (Josh 3:14-17) and take it over (Josh 4:1—11:23). See also the note at 105:44, 45.

135:14 *vindicate . . . compassion:* See the notes at 9:8,9 and 130:7,8.

135:15-18 *idols:* See the notes at 31:6 and 115:4-8. See also Rev 9:20.

135:6 Ps 115:3; Eccl 3:11.

135:19,20 *Aaron . . . house of Levi:* See the note at 99:6. Aaron was from the tribe of Levi, and all priests were from his family. The temple helpers, singers, and musicians were also from the tribe of Levi. See Num 3:5-13 and the note at 39 Title.

135:21 *Zion . . . dwells in Jerusalem:* See the notes at 2:6 and 9:7.

136:1 *His love endures forever:* See the note at 100:5. The repeated line may have been the people's response as the psalm was sung in worship.

136:4 *great wonders:* See the note at 75:1.

136:5-9 *by his understanding made the heavens:* On God's understanding and the creation, see the note at 104:24. See also Gen 1:1,2,16.

136:10-16 *struck down the firstborn of Egypt . . . led his people through the desert:* These verses describe events connected with the time God rescued the Hebrew people from their life of slavery in Egypt (Exod 3–19). See also 78:1-55 and the note at 106:7-12.

136:17-22 *struck down great kings . . . gave their land as an inheritance:* See Num 21:21-35 and the notes at 135:11 and 135:11,12.

136:24 *freed us from our enemies:* If the rescue intended here is the time God helped the Hebrew people escape from their life of slavery in Egypt, known as "the exodus," the enemies would be the Egyptians. If the rescue is the return from exile, the enemies would be the Babylonians (see 137:1-3). The return from exile was viewed as a new exodus. See also the notes at 44:5 and 123:3,4.

136:1 1 Chr 16:34; 2 Chr 5:11-13; 7:3; Ezra 3:11; Ps 100:5; 106:1; 107:1; 118:1; Jer 33:11. **136:10** Exod 12:29. **136:11** Exod 12:51. **136:13-15** Exod 14:21-29.

nor is there breath in their mouths.
18 Those who make them will be like them,
and so will all who trust in them.

19 O house of Israel, praise the LORD;
O house of Aaron, praise the LORD;
20 O house of Levi, praise the LORD;
you who fear him, praise the LORD.
21 Praise be to the LORD from Zion,
to him who dwells in Jerusalem.

Praise the LORD.

Psalm 136

1 Give thanks to the LORD, for he is good.
His love endures forever.
2 Give thanks to the God of gods.
His love endures forever.
3 Give thanks to the Lord of lords:
His love endures forever.

4 to him who alone does great wonders,
His love endures forever.
5 who by his understanding made the heavens,
His love endures forever.
6 who spread out the earth upon the waters,
His love endures forever.
7 who made the great lights—
His love endures forever.
8 the sun to govern the day,
His love endures forever.
9 the moon and stars to govern the night;
His love endures forever.

10 to him who struck down the firstborn of Egypt
His love endures forever.
11 and brought Israel out from among them
His love endures forever.
12 with a mighty hand and outstretched arm;
His love endures forever.

13 to him who divided the Red Sea[a] asunder
His love endures forever.
14 and brought Israel through the midst of it,
His love endures forever.
15 but swept Pharaoh and his army into the Red Sea;
His love endures forever.

[a]13 Hebrew *Yam Suph*; that is, Sea of Reeds; also in verse 15

[16]to him who led his people through the desert,
His love endures forever.
[17]who struck down great kings,
His love endures forever.
[18]and killed mighty kings—
His love endures forever.
[19]Sihon king of the Amorites
His love endures forever.
[20]and Og king of Bashan—
His love endures forever.
[21]and gave their land as an inheritance,
His love endures forever.
[22]an inheritance to his servant Israel;
His love endures forever.
[23]to the One who remembered us in our low estate
His love endures forever.
[24]and freed us from our enemies,
His love endures forever.
[25]and who gives food to every creature.
His love endures forever.
[26]Give thanks to the God of heaven.
His love endures forever.

Psalm 137

[1]By the rivers of Babylon we sat and wept
when we remembered Zion.
[2]There on the poplars
we hung our harps,
[3]for there our captors asked us for songs,
our tormentors demanded songs of joy;
they said, "Sing us one of the songs of Zion!"

[4]How can we sing the songs of the LORD
while in a foreign land?
[5]If I forget you, O Jerusalem,
may my right hand forget ⌊its skill⌋.
[6]May my tongue cling to the roof of my mouth
if I do not remember you,
if I do not consider Jerusalem
my highest joy.

[7]Remember, O LORD, what the Edomites did
on the day Jerusalem fell.
"Tear it down," they cried,
"tear it down to its foundations!"
[8]O Daughter of Babylon, doomed to destruction,
happy is he who repays you

How can we sing the songs of the LORD while in a foreign land?
Ps 137:4

137:1 *the rivers of Babylon:* The psalm probably was written between 586 and 539 B.C. while the people were in exile in Babylon. Or possibly it was written by a person remembering what it had been like to live there. See the note at 44:9-11 and the mini-article called "Babylon," p. 1363. The "rivers" probably refer to the canals that ran between the Tigris and the Euphrates Rivers (see the map on p. 2468).

137:2 *poplars:* The tree is probably the Euphrates poplar that often grows along streams in the Middle East.

137:3,4 *songs of Zion:* To torment God's people, the Babylonians tell them to sing about home. Several psalms are mainly about Zion (Ps 46; 48; 76; 87; 122).

137:7 *Edomites:* The Edomites seem to have rejoiced when the Babylonians destroyed Jerusalem. See Ezek 35:5-15; Obad 10-14.

137:8,9 *Babylon, doomed to destruction:* This disturbing prayer for revenge is also a cry for justice. See the notes at 3:5-8 and 5:10-12. Verse 9 reflects the cruelty of war that God's people had already experienced themselves.

136:25 Ps 104:27,28; 145:15,16.

Jerusalem and the Valley of Jehoshaphat from the Hill of the Evil Council by Thomas Seddon, 1854. Jerusalem continued to have great importance to the people of Judah even after they were taken into exile by the Babylonians. Psalm 137 is a lament over the destruction of Jerusalem by the Babylonians in 586 B.C. The psalmist promises to remember Jerusalem as he prays to the LORD to punish Israel's enemies.

for what you have done to us—
9 he who seizes your infants
and dashes them against the rocks.

Psalm 138

Of David.

1 I will praise you, O LORD, with all my heart;
before the "gods" I will sing your praise.
2 I will bow down toward your holy temple
and will praise your name
for your love and your faithfulness,
for you have exalted above all things
your name and your word.
3 When I called, you answered me;
you made me bold and stouthearted.

4 May all the kings of the earth praise you, O LORD,
when they hear the words of your mouth.
5 May they sing of the ways of the LORD,
for the glory of the LORD is great.

6 Though the LORD is on high, he looks upon the lowly,
but the proud he knows from afar.
7 Though I walk in the midst of trouble,
you preserve my life;

138:1 *before the "gods":* The psalmist comes to the temple to thank God for rescuing him from some distress (138:3). See the notes at 29:1,2 and 34:7.

138:6 *on high:* To say that God is "on high" is to say that God rules the world. Much like a good king, God does justice by helping the lowly and opposing the proud who oppress them. See the note at 113:7.

138:7 *midst of trouble . . . anger of my foes:* Although he reports being rescued in 138:1-3, the psalmist seems to be in trouble again. This may reflect the situation of the people of God after the return from exile (see the note at 123:3,4). Or, it may reflect difficulties that are a common part of the human condition. In any case, the psalmist trusts that God will protect him. See also the note at 3:1,2.

you stretch out your hand against the anger of my foes,
with your right hand you save me.
8 The LORD will fulfill ⌞his purpose⌟ for me;
your love, O LORD, endures forever—
do not abandon the works of your hands.

Psalm 139

For the director of music. Of David. A psalm.

1 O LORD, you have searched me
and you know me.
2 You know when I sit and when I rise;
you perceive my thoughts from afar.
3 You discern my going out and my lying down;
you are familiar with all my ways.
4 Before a word is on my tongue
you know it completely, O LORD.

5 You hem me in—behind and before;
you have laid your hand upon me.
6 Such knowledge is too wonderful for me,
too lofty for me to attain.

7 Where can I go from your Spirit?
Where can I flee from your presence?
8 If I go up to the heavens, you are there;
if I make my bed in the depths,[a] you are there.
9 If I rise on the wings of the dawn,
if I settle on the far side of the sea,
10 even there your hand will guide me,
your right hand will hold me fast.

11 If I say, "Surely the darkness will hide me
and the light become night around me,"
12 even the darkness will not be dark to you;
the night will shine like the day,
for darkness is as light to you.

13 For you created my inmost being;
you knit me together in my mother's womb.
14 I praise you because I am fearfully and wonderfully
made;
your works are wonderful,
I know that full well.
15 My frame was not hidden from you
when I was made in the secret place.
When I was woven together in the depths of the earth,
16 your eyes saw my unformed body.

[a]8 Hebrew *Sheol*

O LORD, you have searched me and you know me.
Ps 139:1

138:8 *your love, O LORD, endures forever:* See the note at 100:5.

139:1-3 *you know me:* The theme of this psalm is the psalmist's knowledge that God knows him completely. See also the note at 90:2-8.

139:7 *your Spirit:* See the note at 104:30.

139:8 *up to the heavens . . . the depths:* The psalmist refers to the two most distant places in the universe to declare that there is nowhere he could go that God could not care for him. For more about the depths, see the notes at 6:5 and 9:13.

139:15 *woven together in the depths of the earth:* The "depths of the earth" may be a symbol for the mother's womb (139:13). Or, this may be a poetic way of describing God as a weaver.

139:6 Rom 11:33.

139:16 *in your book:* See the note at 40:7.

139:18 *When I awake:* See the note at 17:15.

139:19-22 *slay the wicked:* The psalmist appears to be impatient with God, who allows evil people to threaten God's people and speak evil of God. But the prayer is also a prayer of loyalty to God. God's enemies are the psalmist's enemies as well (139:21,22). For there to be justice, God must oppose the "bloodthirsty men" who are adversaries of his purposes (139:20). See the notes at 3:1,2; 5:10-12; and 15:2-5.

140:1-4 *men of violence:* Enemies are also called "proud men" (140:5), "the wicked" (140:8), and "slanderers" (140:11). Their words and deeds threaten the psalmist's life. See also the note at 3:1,2 and the mini-article called "Enemies (The Wicked)," p. 1084.

140:5 *cords . . . traps:* See the note at 31:4.

140:7 *strong deliverer . . . battle:* See the notes at 51:12-14 and 35:1.

140:3 Rom 3:13.

All the days ordained for me
were written in your book
before one of them came to be.

17 How precious to[a] me are your thoughts, O God!
How vast is the sum of them!
18 Were I to count them,
they would outnumber the grains of sand.
When I awake,
I am still with you.

19 If only you would slay the wicked, O God!
Away from me, you bloodthirsty men!
20 They speak of you with evil intent;
your adversaries misuse your name.
21 Do I not hate those who hate you, O LORD,
and abhor those who rise up against you?
22 I have nothing but hatred for them;
I count them my enemies.

23 Search me, O God, and know my heart;
test me and know my anxious thoughts.
24 See if there is any offensive way in me,
and lead me in the way everlasting.

Psalm 140

For the director of music. A psalm of David.

1 Rescue me, O LORD, from evil men;
protect me from men of violence,
2 who devise evil plans in their hearts
and stir up war every day.
3 They make their tongues as sharp as a serpent's;
the poison of vipers is on their lips. *Selah*

4 Keep me, O LORD, from the hands of the wicked;
protect me from men of violence
who plan to trip my feet.
5 Proud men have hidden a snare for me;
they have spread out the cords of their net
and have set traps for me along my path. *Selah*

6 O LORD, I say to you, "You are my God."
Hear, O LORD, my cry for mercy.
7 O Sovereign LORD, my strong deliverer,
who shields my head in the day of battle—
8 do not grant the wicked their desires, O LORD;
do not let their plans succeed,
or they will become proud. *Selah*

---

[a]**17** Or *concerning*

9 Let the heads of those who surround me
be covered with the trouble their lips have caused.
10 Let burning coals fall upon them;
may they be thrown into the fire,
into miry pits, never to rise.
11 Let slanderers not be established in the land;
may disaster hunt down men of violence.

12 I know that the LORD secures justice for the poor
and upholds the cause of the needy.
13 Surely the righteous will praise your name
and the upright will live before you.

Psalm 141

A psalm of David.

1 O LORD, I call to you; come quickly to me.
Hear my voice when I call to you.
2 May my prayer be set before you like incense;
may the lifting up of my hands be like the evening sacrifice.

3 Set a guard over my mouth, O LORD;
keep watch over the door of my lips.
4 Let not my heart be drawn to what is evil,
to take part in wicked deeds
with men who are evildoers;
let me not eat of their delicacies.

5 Let a righteous man[a] strike me—it is a kindness;
let him rebuke me—it is oil on my head.
My head will not refuse it.

Yet my prayer is ever against the deeds of evildoers;
6 their rulers will be thrown down from the cliffs,
and the wicked will learn that my words were well spoken.
7 ⌊They will say,⌋ "As one plows and breaks up the earth,
so our bones have been scattered at the mouth of the grave.[b]"

8 But my eyes are fixed on you, O Sovereign LORD;
in you I take refuge—do not give me over to death.
9 Keep me from the snares they have laid for me,
from the traps set by evildoers.
10 Let the wicked fall into their own nets,
while I pass by in safety.

[a]5 Or *Let the Righteous One* [b]7 Hebrew *Sheol*

140:10 *burning coals . . . miry pits:* God's judgment is often accompanied by fire (see the note at 11:6). This also may be a reference to the battle tactics used against enemies in the ancient world. As enemies tried to crawl up the city walls, hot coals were dumped down on them. Deep pits were dug in the ground and covered with branches so that enemies would fall into the pits and be captured.

140:12 *justice for the poor . . . needy:* See the notes at 9:8,9 and 102:17.

140:13 *praise your name . . . upright:* The prayers for help regularly end with praise and trust, suggesting that suffering does not separate us from God. See the notes at 13:5,6 and 31:19-22. The "upright" are those who obey God's law and trust only in him.

141:2 *prayer . . . incense:* In Exodus 30:1, God instructs Moses to build an altar for burning incense, and Aaron is told to burn fragrant incense each evening (Exod 30:7). Incense was made of frankincense, other gums and spices, and a seasoning of salt, which together produced a sweet smell when burned. The smoke from the burning incense represented the prayers that went up to God. See also Rev 5:8.

141:2 *lifting up of my hands . . . evening sacrifice:* See the notes at 28:2 and 27:6. Sacrifices were offered each evening (Exod 29:38,39), sometimes followed by prayer (Ezra 9:5,6).

141:4 *drawn to what is evil . . . evildoers:* The psalmist prays to be delivered from temptation. On "evildoers" see the note at 140:1-4.

141:9,10 *snares:* See 140:5; 142:3; and the note at 31:4.

Psalm 142

A *maskil*[a] of David. When he was in the cave. A prayer.

1 I cry aloud to the LORD;
I lift up my voice to the LORD for mercy.
2 I pour out my complaint before him;
before him I tell my trouble.

3 When my spirit grows faint within me,
it is you who know my way.
In the path where I walk
men have hidden a snare for me.
4 Look to my right and see;
no one is concerned for me.
I have no refuge;
no one cares for my life.

5 I cry to you, O LORD;
I say, "You are my refuge,
my portion in the land of the living."
6 Listen to my cry,
for I am in desperate need;
rescue me from those who pursue me,
for they are too strong for me.
7 Set me free from my prison,
that I may praise your name.

Then the righteous will gather about me
because of your goodness to me.

Psalm 143

A psalm of David.

1 O LORD, hear my prayer,
listen to my cry for mercy;
in your faithfulness and righteousness
come to my relief.
2 Do not bring your servant into judgment,
for no one living is righteous before you.

3 The enemy pursues me,
he crushes me to the ground;
he makes me dwell in darkness
like those long dead.
4 So my spirit grows faint within me;
my heart within me is dismayed.

5 I remember the days of long ago;
I meditate on all your works
and consider what your hands have done.

[a]Title: Probably a literary or musical term

142 Title *David . . . cave:* David hid in caves to escape his enemies (1 Sam 22:1; 24:3). See also the note at 57 Title and the mini-article called "David," p. 1028.

142:5 *land of the living:* See the note at 116:9.

142:7 *prison . . . your goodness:* If not an actual prison, this probably refers to a very bad situation. Still the psalmist is confident. Like many other prayers for help, this psalm ends with praise and trust. See the note at 140:13.

143:2 *no one living is righteous:* When opposed by enemies, the psalmists usually say that they are innocent. For example, see 7:3-5. But here the psalmist says that all people are sinful. See also the note 130:1-4.

143:3,9 *enemy . . . enemies:* See the note at 140:1-4.

143:3 *dwell in darkness:* Since God and God's Word are described as "light," then "darkness" stands for evil and for times of deep despair. See also the note at 88:16-18.

143:2 Rom 3:20; Gal 2:16.

6 I spread out my hands to you;
    my soul thirsts for you like a parched land. *Selah*

7 Answer me quickly, O LORD;
    my spirit fails.
Do not hide your face from me
    or I will be like those who go down to the pit.
8 Let the morning bring me word of your unfailing love,
    for I have put my trust in you.
Show me the way I should go,
    for to you I lift up my soul.
9 Rescue me from my enemies, O LORD,
    for I hide myself in you.
10 Teach me to do your will,
    for you are my God;
may your good Spirit
    lead me on level ground.

11 For your name's sake, O LORD, preserve my life;
    in your righteousness, bring me out of trouble.
12 In your unfailing love, silence my enemies;
    destroy all my foes,
    for I am your servant.

Psalm 144

Of David.

1 Praise be to the LORD my Rock,
    who trains my hands for war,
    my fingers for battle.
2 He is my loving God and my fortress,
    my stronghold and my deliverer,
my shield, in whom I take refuge,
    who subdues peoples[a] under me.

3 O LORD, what is man that you care for him,
    the son of man that you think of him?
4 Man is like a breath;
    his days are like a fleeting shadow.

5 Part your heavens, O LORD, and come down;
    touch the mountains, so that they smoke.
6 Send forth lightning and scatter ⌞the enemies⌟;
    shoot your arrows and rout them.
7 Reach down your hand from on high;
    deliver me and rescue me
from the mighty waters,
    from the hands of foreigners

[a]2 Many manuscripts of the Masoretic Text, Dead Sea Scrolls, Aquila, Jerome and Syriac; most manuscripts of the Masoretic Text *subdues my people*

143:6 *spread out my hands:* See the note at 28:2.

143:8 *bring me word:* See the note at 17:15.

143:10 *Spirit:* See the note at 104:30.

143:12 *destroy all my foes:* The request is for justice. See the notes at 3:5-8 and 5:10-12.

144:1,2 *my Rock . . . my fortress:* See the notes at 18:46 and 11:1. The beginning of Psalm 144 is like the beginning of Psalm 18. There are other similarities as well (see the notes at 144:5-8 and 144:10). Psalm 144 seems to be a new version of Psalm 18 that takes into account the end of the kingdom of David and his descendants. See the note at 89:38-45.

144:3,4 *Man is like a breath:* The end of the kingdom of David called into question the meaning of life. Verse 3 recalls Psalm 8 (see especially Ps 8:4; see also Job 7:17,18). Verse 4 recalls Psalm 89 (see especially 89:47, 48 and the note at 89:38-45).

144:5-8 *come down . . . deliver me and rescue me:* Verse 5 recalls 18:9; verse 6 recalls 18:14; and verses 7,8 recall 18:16,17,43-45. What Psalm 18 describes as God's actions on David's behalf in Psalm 144 have become requests for God to act. This change suggests the new situation after the end of the kingdom of David. In this new situation, the enemies (144:6) and those who tell lies (144:8) are the nations that oppressed God's people during the exile and after their return. See the note at 123:3,4.

143:11 Ps 109:21.

144:9 *a new song . . . lyre:* See the notes at 33:2; 33:3; and 96:1.

144:10 *delivers his servant David:* This verse recalls the title of Psalm 18. But the prayer in 144:11 and the prayer for the nation in 144:12-14 suggests that David's kingdom did not last. See the note at 144:1, 2.

144:12-14 *no cry of distress:* This prayer for the nation looks back on the events of 586 B.C. when Jerusalem was breached, many people were taken into captivity, and there was much distress. The year 586 B.C. also marked the end of the kingdom of David. It is important that Psalm 144 ends with a prayer for and a promise to the nation (144:15). This suggests that it is the responsibility of the whole people to establish justice.

145:1 *King:* See the note on p. 1024. This is another one of the acrostic psalms (see the note at 119:1).

145:4 *One generation will commend your works to another:* See the notes at 71:15-19 and 75:1.

8 whose mouths are full of lies,
whose right hands are deceitful.

9 I will sing a new song to you, O God;
on the ten-stringed lyre I will make music to you,
10 to the One who gives victory to kings,
who delivers his servant David from the deadly sword.

11 Deliver me and rescue me
from the hands of foreigners
whose mouths are full of lies,
whose right hands are deceitful.

12 Then our sons in their youth
will be like well-nurtured plants,
and our daughters will be like pillars
carved to adorn a palace.
13 Our barns will be filled
with every kind of provision.
Our sheep will increase by thousands,
by tens of thousands in our fields;
14 our oxen will draw heavy loads.[a]
There will be no breaching of walls,
no going into captivity,
no cry of distress in our streets.

15 Blessed are the people of whom this is true;
blessed are the people whose God is the LORD.

Psalm 145[b]

A psalm of praise. Of David.

1 I will exalt you, my God the King;
I will praise your name for ever and ever.
2 Every day I will praise you
and extol your name for ever and ever.

3 Great is the LORD and most worthy of praise;
his greatness no one can fathom.
4 One generation will commend your works to another;
they will tell of your mighty acts.
5 They will speak of the glorious splendor of your majesty,
and I will meditate on your wonderful works.[c]
6 They will tell of the power of your awesome works,
and I will proclaim your great deeds.

---

[a]**14** Or *our chieftains will be firmly established* [b]This psalm is an acrostic poem, the verses of which (including verse 13b) begin with the successive letters of the Hebrew alphabet. [c]**5** Dead Sea Scrolls and Syriac (see also Septuagint); Masoretic Text *On the glorious splendor of your majesty / and on your wonderful works I will meditate*

7 They will celebrate your abundant goodness
and joyfully sing of your righteousness.
8 The LORD is gracious and compassionate,
slow to anger and rich in love.
9 The LORD is good to all;
he has compassion on all he has made.
10 All you have made will praise you, O LORD;
your saints will extol you.
11 They will tell of the glory of your kingdom
and speak of your might,
12 so that all men may know of your mighty acts
and the glorious splendor of your kingdom.
13 Your kingdom is an everlasting kingdom,
and your dominion endures through all
generations.

The LORD is faithful to all his promises
and loving toward all he has made.[a]
14 The LORD upholds all those who fall
and lifts up all who are bowed down.
15 The eyes of all look to you,
and you give them their food at the proper time.
16 You open your hand
and satisfy the desires of every living thing.

17 The LORD is righteous in all his ways
and loving toward all he has made.
18 The LORD is near to all who call on him,
to all who call on him in truth.
19 He fulfills the desires of those who fear him;
he hears their cry and saves them.
20 The LORD watches over all who love him,
but all the wicked he will destroy.

21 My mouth will speak in praise of the LORD.
Let every creature praise his holy name
for ever and ever.

Psalm 146

1 Praise the LORD.[b]

Praise the LORD, O my soul.
2 I will praise the LORD all my life;
I will sing praise to my God as long as I live.

3 Do not put your trust in princes,
in mortal men, who cannot save.

[a]13 One manuscript of the Masoretic Text, Dead Sea Scrolls and Syriac (see also Septuagint); most manuscripts of the Masoretic Text do not have the last two lines of verse 13. [b]1 Hebrew *Hallelu Yah*; also in verse 10

Praise the LORD, O my soul. I will praise the LORD all my life; I will sing praise to my God as long as I live.
Ps 146:1,2

145:7,8 *abundant goodness . . . rich in love:* See the notes at 130:7,8; 100:5; and 51:12-14.

145:9,10 *all he has made:* See the note at 96:11,12.

145:11-13 *glory of your kingdom:* The word "kingdom" appears three times. God's kingdom is where God rules and where his will and purposes are carried out. See also the notes at 9:8,9 and on p. 1024.

146:1 *Praise the LORD:* Psalms 146–150 all begin and end with this line.

146:3 *cannot save:* This verse reflects the strong message of Israel's prophets and the law that the people were to place their trust in the LORD God and not in earthly leaders, wealth, foreign powers, or idols. For example, see Exod 20:2-6; Isa 31:1-5; Hos 4:17-19; 14:1-3.

145:15,16 Ps 104:27,28; 136:25.

146:5 *Blessed:* See the note at 1:1, 2.

146:5 *Jacob:* See the note at 22:23.

146:7-9 *upholds the cause of the oppressed:* These verses emphasize God's concern for justice. See the notes at 9:8,9; 94:6; and 102:17.

146:9 *frustrates the ways of the wicked:* See the note at 104:35.

146:10 *LORD reigns forever . . . Zion:* See the notes at 8:1,9 and 2:6. See also 145:1,11-13.

147:2,3 *builds up Jerusalem . . . heals the brokenhearted:* These verses suggest that the psalm was written after the exile in Babylon was over (see the notes at 44:9-11 and 74:3,7). The people of Israel were allowed to return home after Cyrus of Persia defeated the Babylonians in 539 B.C. See also Isa 40:1-8; 44:28—45:4; and the mini-article called "Exile," p. 1541.

147:6 *sustains the humble:* This means that God establishes justice (see the note at 146:7-9). God, who names each star and understands everything (147:4, 5) reaches out to help the humble, who were judged unimportant by many in society.

147:8,9 *supplies the earth with rain . . . provides food:* See the note at 29:3-9. See also 135:7; 104:27,28; 136:25.

146:6 Acts 4:24; 14:15.

4 When their spirit departs, they return to
the ground;
on that very day their plans come to nothing.

5 Blessed is he whose help is the God of Jacob,
whose hope is in the LORD his God,
6 the Maker of heaven and earth,
the sea, and everything in them—
the LORD, who remains faithful forever.
7 He upholds the cause of the oppressed
and gives food to the hungry.
The LORD sets prisoners free,
8 the LORD gives sight to the blind,
the LORD lifts up those who are bowed down,
the LORD loves the righteous.
9 The LORD watches over the alien
and sustains the fatherless and the widow,
but he frustrates the ways of the wicked.

10 The LORD reigns forever,
your God, O Zion, for all generations.

Praise the LORD.

Psalm 147

1 Praise the LORD.[a]

How good it is to sing praises to our God,
how pleasant and fitting to praise him!

2 The LORD builds up Jerusalem;
he gathers the exiles of Israel.
3 He heals the brokenhearted
and binds up their wounds.

4 He determines the number of the stars
and calls them each by name.
5 Great is our Lord and mighty in power;
his understanding has no limit.
6 The LORD sustains the humble
but casts the wicked to the ground.

7 Sing to the LORD with thanksgiving;
make music to our God on the harp.
8 He covers the sky with clouds;
he supplies the earth with rain
and makes grass grow on the hills.
9 He provides food for the cattle
and for the young ravens when they call.

---

a1 Hebrew *Hallelu Yah;* also in verse 20

10 His pleasure is not in the strength of the horse,
nor his delight in the legs of a man;
11 the LORD delights in those who fear him,
who put their hope in his unfailing love.

12 Extol the LORD, O Jerusalem;
praise your God, O Zion,
13 for he strengthens the bars of your gates
and blesses your people within you.
14 He grants peace to your borders
and satisfies you with the finest of wheat.

15 He sends his command to the earth;
his word runs swiftly.
16 He spreads the snow like wool
and scatters the frost like ashes.
17 He hurls down his hail like pebbles.
Who can withstand his icy blast?
18 He sends his word and melts them;
he stirs up his breezes, and the waters flow.

19 He has revealed his word to Jacob,
his laws and decrees to Israel.
20 He has done this for no other nation;
they do not know his laws.

Praise the LORD.

Psalm 148

1 Praise the LORD.[a]

Praise the LORD from the heavens,
praise him in the heights above.
2 Praise him, all his angels,
praise him, all his heavenly hosts.
3 Praise him, sun and moon,
praise him, all you shining stars.
4 Praise him, you highest heavens
and you waters above the skies.
5 Let them praise the name of the LORD,
for he commanded and they were created.
6 He set them in place for ever and ever;
he gave a decree that will never pass away.

7 Praise the LORD from the earth,
you great sea creatures and all ocean depths,
8 lightning and hail, snow and clouds,
stormy winds that do his bidding,

[a]1 Hebrew *Hallelu Yah*; also in verse 14

147:10,11 *pleasure is not in the strength of the horse . . . hope in his unfailing love:* These verses emphasize the importance of trusting God rather than trusting human leaders or armies with chariots and horses (see the note at 20:7). These verses may also be suggesting that the power God cares about is love and not force (see also the note at 5:10-12).

147:13,14 *bars of your gates . . . finest of wheat:* God's blessings for Jerusalem and its people include secure gates (meaning peace), many children, and good harvests.

147:15-18 *sends his command to the earth:* The earth and forces of nature obey God's commands.

147:19,20 *laws and decrees:* God has spoken a personal word to his people. God's laws and decrees are given to Israel, and like nature (147:15-18), the people are expected to obey. Because Israel alone received God's teachings, Israel has both the privilege and the responsibility to pursue the justice and peace that God wants for the world.

148:2 *angels:* See the mini-article called "Angels," p. 88.

148:3,4 *sun and moon . . . stars . . . waters above the skies:* Some of Israel's neighbors worshiped the sun, moon, and stars as gods. Here these heavenly bodies worship the God who created them (see also 19:1).

It was believed that the sky was a dome that covered the flat earth. Above the sky were heavenly waters. It was also believed that an ocean of water was under the earth. See Gen 1:6-10.

148:7-12 *Praise the LORD:* These verses invite everyone and everything from the earth to praise God as Creator. The list recalls the parts of creation in Genesis 1,2. See also the note at 74:13,14. Because the LORD is King (see the note on p. 1024), all earthly rulers will also praise and honor the LORD God. See also 138:4,5.

Musical Instruments in the Ancient World. Music and musical instruments are mentioned frequently in the Bible, but unfortunately, no actual melodies are preserved and we can only guess at the exact sounds of the instruments. There are three categories of instruments: (1) those that are struck or shaken (bells, tambourines, gongs, drums); (2) those that are blown (flutes, pipes, trumpets, horns); (3) those that are plucked or strummed (lyres, harps, lutes, and other stringed instruments).

149:1 *a new song:* See 144:9 and the notes at 33:3 and 96:1.

149:2 *Zion:* Meaning the hill in Jerusalem where the temple was built. See the notes at 2:6 and 120 Title.

149:2 *King:* See the note at 96:9,10 and the note on p. 1024.

9 you mountains and all hills,
fruit trees and all cedars,
10 wild animals and all cattle,
small creatures and flying birds,
11 kings of the earth and all nations,
you princes and all rulers on earth,
12 young men and maidens,
old men and children.

13 Let them praise the name of the LORD,
for his name alone is exalted;
his splendor is above the earth and the heavens.
14 He has raised up for his people a horn,[a]
the praise of all his saints,
of Israel, the people close to his heart.

Praise the LORD.

[a]14 *Horn* here symbolizes strong one, that is, king.

Psalm 149

1 Praise the LORD.[a]

Sing to the LORD a new song,
his praise in the assembly of the saints.

2 Let Israel rejoice in their Maker;
let the people of Zion be glad in their King.
3 Let them praise his name with dancing
and make music to him with tambourine
and harp.
4 For the LORD takes delight in his people;
he crowns the humble with salvation.
5 Let the saints rejoice in this honor
and sing for joy on their beds.

6 May the praise of God be in their mouths
and a double-edged sword in their hands,
7 to inflict vengeance on the nations
and punishment on the peoples,
8 to bind their kings with fetters,
their nobles with shackles of iron,

[a]1 Hebrew *Hallelu Yah*; also in verse 9

149:3 *tambourine and harp:* See the note at 33:2.

149:4 *crowns the humble:* As King (149:2) God cares for and helps the humble. See the notes at 9:8, 9 and 146:7-9.

149:6-9 *sword . . . punishment:* The "sword" symbolizes God's concern for justice. Punishment is to serve the purpose of justice (see the notes at 3:5-8 and 5:10-12). God gave the king the responsibility for establishing justice on earth (see the note at 9:8, 9). But after the end of David's dynasty (see the note at 89:38-45) the responsibility for establishing justice was given to all God's people.

The New Testament writers do not speak about the sword of vengeance as much as the power of God at work within them (see 2 Cor 10:3-5; Eph 6:12-17; Heb 4:12). This power is God's Spirit, which helps them to be living examples of God's love.

QUESTIONS ABOUT PSALMS 107:1—150:6

1. Many of the prayers for help include requests for revenge against enemies. For example, see Psalms 109:6-20; 137:7-9; 149:6-9. How do these prayers for revenge strike you? Why? What does God's concern for justice have to do with the defeat of enemies or evildoers?
2. Read Psalms 111 and 112. How are they alike? How are they different? Compare especially Psalms 111:4 and 112:4. Why is this comparison important?
3. What does the Hebrew word translated "Law" mean? (See Ps 119 and the mini-article called "Law" on p. 1160.) Why is the Law so important for the psalmist? What can people today learn from Psalm 119 about obedience and forgiveness?
4. What are some common ideas found in the collection of psalms made up of Psalms 120–134? How were these psalms probably used in ancient times? What ideas found in these psalms may be important for people today?
5. What does Psalm 130 say about sin and forgiveness? Why is it important that "full redemption" is with God?
6. Read Psalms 140 and 142. What situations might have prompted these prayers for help? Our world today has its share of brutality, violence, and loneliness. How can prayers for help make a difference in dealing with such things?
7. Read Psalms 148 and 150. How are they alike? Why is it important that these psalms invite not only people, but also "everything that has breath" (Ps 150:6) and all creation (Ps 148) to praise God?
8. What images of God stand out for you in PSALMS?
9. Name at least three important themes you discovered in your reading and study of PSALMS. Do these themes affect your life and your faith? If so, how?

150:1 *in his sanctuary . . . mighty heavens:* "Sanctuary" probably refers to God's house in Jerusalem. People viewed the temple as the place where earth and heaven meet. See the notes at 5:7 (your house) and 11:4.

150:3,4 *trumpet . . . harp . . . flute:* Trumpets were used to welcome rulers and at festival times (see the note at 81:3). See the note at 33:2.

150:6 *everything that has breath:* The full orchestra of musical instruments is to be joined by a full choir of voices, as "everything that has breath" joins the song of praise. There is no better way to express the message that is found throughout PSALMS—God, the Creator and Ruler of the world, deserves the praise of everything and everybody. See 103:19-22; 148:13; and the note at 96:11,12.

9 to carry out the sentence written against them.
This is the glory of all his saints.

Praise the LORD.

Psalm 150

1 Praise the LORD.[a]

Praise God in his sanctuary;
praise him in his mighty heavens.
2 Praise him for his acts of power;
praise him for his surpassing greatness.
3 Praise him with the sounding of the trumpet,
praise him with the harp and lyre,
4 praise him with tambourine and dancing,
praise him with the strings and flute,
5 praise him with the clash of cymbals,
praise him with resounding cymbals.

6 Let everything that has breath praise the LORD.

Praise the LORD.

[a]1 Hebrew *Hallelu Yah*; also in verse 6

PROVERBS

Where does wisdom come from?
How can a person be truly "wise"?
Read Proverbs *to discover the answer*
to these questions and much more.

What makes Proverbs special?

Proverbs is a collection of wise sayings. It was originally included in that part of the Hebrew Scriptures known as the Writings, which includes some other "wisdom" books, such as Ecclesiastes and Job. Along with Song of Songs and Ecclesiastes, Proverbs has traditionally been credited to Israel's wise King Solomon.

Why was Proverbs written?

Proverbs 1:1-7 introduces the entire book and provides some clear statements about the purpose of the book's many proverbs: "for attaining wisdom and discipline; for understanding words of insight; for acquiring a disciplined and prudent life, doing what is right and just and fair." Above all, true knowledge (or wisdom) is discovered in respecting and obeying the Lord, who is the source of wisdom (2:6). Proverbs also describes wisdom as a gift from God. All of God's followers have this "gift" and are encouraged to use it. Those who are "wise" understand the importance of treating others with fairness and justice; of being humble, loyal, and hard-working; of respecting parents and others in authority; and of showing concern for the poor and needy.

Like other wisdom books, Proverbs says little about the history, laws, or religious life of Israel. But it provides a picture of the kind of practical teaching and instruction done in families, schools, and the royal palace. Generally, the proverbs in this collection give an uncomplicated picture of life. Certain actions are shown as always producing certain results. A wise person is able to recognize the right decision ahead of time and choose the "path" that leads to blessing, happiness, and even wealth. The foolish person always chooses incorrectly and receives punishment. This is why, for example, the ancient Hebrew proverbs encourage parents to be strict in disciplining their children. Foolish and disobedient children who do not learn wisdom when they are young may grow up to be "foolish" adults. Other wisdom books, such as Job and Ecclesiastes, deal with the more complicated matter of why good people sometimes suffer while bad people, including fools and criminals, sometimes prosper.

What's the story behind the scene?

Proverbs is said to be a collection of wise sayings, primarily from Israel's King Solomon (1:1; 10:1; 25:1), who was known as a very

King Solomon, David's son: Solomon was the son of Israel's King David and Bathsheba. After David's death, Solomon ruled Israel from about 970 to 931 B.C. He was known for his wisdom and for writing many wise sayings (1 Kgs 4:29–34), though near the end of his life he did not always live up to his reputation (see 1 Kgs 11:1-13). Books of wisdom were often named in honor of kings in the ancient Near East. Wise kings were those who ruled with honesty, justice, and fairness (1 Kgs 3:9-12; Prov 8:12-16; 28:15, 16; 29:14). For more, see the mini-articles called "Solomon," p. 776, and "David," p. 1028.

Foolishness and wisdom: An important theme in Proverbs is the idea that those who act foolishly or do evil things will be punished. But God will provide health and wealth for good (wise) people who obey his teachings. This concept—that a person gets what he or she deserves—is referred to as "just retribution." For more about this idea, see the Introduction to Job, p. 961.

Wisdom: In Proverbs, the idea of wisdom is frequently personified as a woman, or as a supernatural being (8:1-3) who was with God at the time of creation (8:22-31). The image of Wisdom as a woman may also reflect the influence of Israel's neighbors. For example, the Egyptian goddess Maat was described as the first creation of the creator god in Egyptian myth. She stood for justice and orderly life. Protective charm necklaces picturing Maat were worn by ancient Egyptian wise men. See also the mini-article called "Wisdom," p. 2206.

1:1 *proverbs:* Ancient proverbs are usually short statements that give advice or express some truth about human behavior. See also the chart called "Kinds of Proverbs," p. 1210.

1:1 *Solomon . . . David:* See the note on p. 1193 (King Solomon).

1:2 *wisdom:* "Wisdom" is knowledge and understanding of what is true, right, honest, and fair. Wisdom comes from the LORD, who gives understanding to those who respect and obey God (2:6; 9:10). For more, see the mini-article called "Wisdom," p. 2206.

wise man and the author of many wise sayings (1 Kgs 4:29-34). While a number of sayings in the book may have come from Solomon, other authors are quoted as well. The collection as we have it now probably was edited and put in its final form between three and four hundred years after Solomon died. A number of wise sayings probably came from a group of Israelites known as "the wise" (Jer 18:18). They were teachers of practical wisdom and were familiar with similar kinds of wisdom writings found in the literature of Israel's neighbors. For example, the thirty wise sayings in Proverbs 22:17—24:22 are similar in style and language to an ancient Egyptian collection known as Wisdom of Amenemope. Other wisdom sayings are similar to those found in Mesopotamian wisdom or the wisdom literature of Assyria.

The wise sayings in PROVERBS share a view of wisdom commonly held in the ancient world, but they differ from the wisdom of other nations on the key point of the source of wisdom. In PROVERBS, wisdom comes from the LORD God, and is said to have been with the LORD at the beginning of time (8:22-31).

HOW IS PROVERBS CONSTRUCTED?

PROVERBS is a collection of wise sayings that fall into several categories. Such a collection is difficult to outline, but a few general patterns can be seen. The first nine chapters have a number of short two-line sayings or "truth statements," and includes instructions of a parent to a child. Also, wisdom is pictured as a "woman" who invites all to live according to good sense and sound judgment (8:1—9:6).

The wise sayings in 10:1—22:16 are credited to Solomon (10:1). These include a variety of proverbs, especially many two-part sayings in which the second part contrasts with the first. See also the chart called "Kinds of Proverbs," p. 1210.

Thirty wise sayings credited to an unknown group of wise people (22:17—24:22) and further sayings of an unknown author (24:23-34) form another section. These are followed by a group of proverbs (25:1—29:27) credited to Solomon but copied in the time of Judah's King Hezekiah (715-687 B.C.). The final two chapters provide wise sayings of Agur (30:1) and the mother of King Lemuel (31:1). The final section (31:10-31) has been described as the book's ending (epilogue). It is an acrostic poem, which means the first word of each verse begins with a different letter of the Hebrew alphabet.

PROVERBS can be outlined in the following way:

Wisdom, advice, and instruction (1:1—9:18)
- An appeal (1:1-7)
- Seek wisdom and run away from foolishness (1:8—7:27)
- Wisdom's invitation to find life (8:1—9:18)

Many of Solomon's wise sayings (10:1—22:16)

Sayings of people with wisdom (22:17—24:34)

Solomon's proverbs copied by Hezekiah (25:1—29:27)

The wise sayings of Agur and of Lemuel's mother (30:1—31:31)

Wisdom, Advice, and Instruction

The first nine chapters of PROVERBS include a variety of wise sayings and instruction poems. Much of the advice sounds like a parent speaking to a child but can be applied to other relationships as well, such as elder to youth and teacher to student. Wisdom is described as a woman who will protect the wise and help them live right. Wisdom is portrayed as being present with the LORD at the beginning of creation and now inviting all people to her house to partake of her banquet.

AN APPEAL

The thesis of the entire book is summarized in Proverbs 1:2-7. The proverbs are meant to teach wisdom and self-control, and to help people learn what is right. Above all, wisdom is respecting and obeying the LORD.

PROLOGUE: PURPOSE AND THEME

1 The proverbs of Solomon son of David, king of Israel:

2 for attaining wisdom and discipline;
for understanding words of insight;
3 for acquiring a disciplined and prudent life,
doing what is right and just and fair;
4 for giving prudence to the simple,
knowledge and discretion to the young—
5 let the wise listen and add to their learning,
and let the discerning get guidance—
6 for understanding proverbs and parables,
the sayings and riddles of the wise.

7 The fear of the LORD is the beginning of knowledge,
but fools[a] despise wisdom and discipline.

SEEK WISDOM AND RUN AWAY FROM FOOLISHNESS

Readers are told how to be wise, to live right, and to keep from being foolish or wicked.

EXHORTATIONS TO EMBRACE WISDOM

Warning Against Enticement

8 Listen, my son, to your father's instruction
and do not forsake your mother's teaching.
9 They will be a garland to grace your head
and a chain to adorn your neck.

[a]7 The Hebrew words rendered *fool* in Proverbs, and often elsewhere in the Old Testament, denote one who is morally deficient.

1:3 *what is right . . . fair:* What is "right" means what is acceptable to God. According to Israel's law and prophets, those who do what is right are living according to God's commands and teachings. Right living includes treating others with justice and fairness. See also the mini-article called "Justice," p. 1721.

1:6 *proverbs . . . riddles:* See the notes at 1:1 (proverbs) and 1:2 (wisdom). A form of proverb called a "riddle" may be based on a difficult question (Judg 14:12-18), or it may refer to a saying that provides many answers to one of life's mysteries (30:15,16,18, 19,21-23,29-31). Asking and answering riddles was a form of entertainment in the ancient world. The ability to answer difficult riddles was considered a measure of one's wisdom.

1:7 *The fear of the LORD:* Wisdom and common sense were important in all ancient cultures. In PROVERBS wisdom is seen as directly related to the LORD's instruction. The truly wise person is the one who worships and honors the LORD and lives according to the LORD's commands.

"LORD" translates the Hebrew *Yahweh;* see the mini-article called "LORD (YHWH)," p. 140. See also Job 28:28; Ps 111:10; Prov 9:10.

1:8,9 *Listen, my son, to your father's instruction . . . a garland to grace your head:* Wisdom is passed to the young by older generations, especially from parent to child. To "wear" a parent's teachings is not meant in a literal way, in the way God's laws or teachings were worn in little leather pouches and tied around one's head and wrists (Deut 6:8,9). Rather, "wearing" the teachings is meant in a symbolic way (see also 3:3; 4:9).

1:10 *sinners:* This refers to those who turn their backs on God or refuse to obey God's teachings. Such people are often called "fools" in PROVERBS, because their sins lead to death (1:32; 9:13–18).

1:13 *fill our houses with plunder:* Stealing is a sin against the LORD's commands (Exod 20:15), but here it is used as an example of how committing a crime like robbery can eventually lead to other crimes, such as murder (1:16).

1:17 *a net . . . birds:* Birds and small animals were often caught in traps made of netting. The illustration of a "clap-net" style bird trap shown here is based on those shown in Egyptian wall paintings from the fifteenth century B.C. These were especially effective in capturing waterfowl that nested in marshes. Foolish or evil people are often compared to animals blindly walking into traps (7:23; Eccl 9:12).

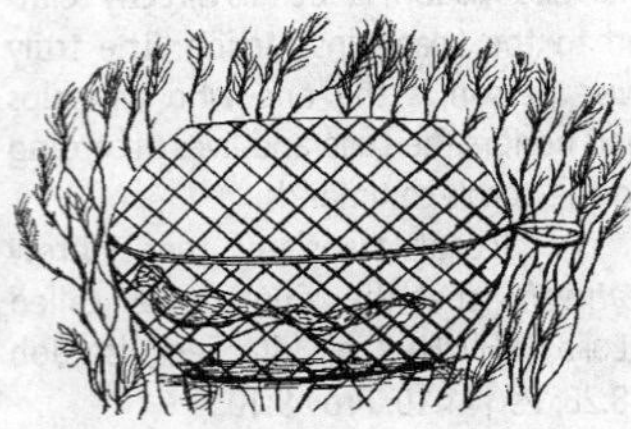

1:19 *takes away the lives:* See the note on p. 1193 (Foolishness and wisdom).

1:21 *noisy streets . . . gateways of the city:* These are places in ancient cities where large crowds were most likely to gather. City leaders judged court cases and made important decisions next to the city gates.

10 My son, if sinners entice you,
do not give in to them.
11 If they say, "Come along with us;
let's lie in wait for someone's blood,
let's waylay some harmless soul;
12 let's swallow them alive, like the grave,[a]
and whole, like those who go down to the pit;
13 we will get all sorts of valuable things
and fill our houses with plunder;
14 throw in your lot with us,
and we will share a common purse"—
15 my son, do not go along with them,
do not set foot on their paths;
16 for their feet rush into sin,
they are swift to shed blood.
17 How useless to spread a net
in full view of all the birds!
18 These men lie in wait for their own blood;
they waylay only themselves!
19 Such is the end of all who go after ill-gotten gain;
it takes away the lives of those who get it.

Warning Against Rejecting Wisdom

20 Wisdom calls aloud in the street,
she raises her voice in the public squares;
21 at the head of the noisy streets[b] she cries out,
in the gateways of the city she makes her speech:

22 "How long will you simple ones[c] love your simple ways?
How long will mockers delight in mockery
and fools hate knowledge?
23 If you had responded to my rebuke,
I would have poured out my heart to you
and made my thoughts known to you.
24 But since you rejected me when I called
and no one gave heed when I stretched out my hand,
25 since you ignored all my advice
and would not accept my rebuke,
26 I in turn will laugh at your disaster;
I will mock when calamity overtakes you—
27 when calamity overtakes you like a storm,
when disaster sweeps over you like a whirlwind,
when distress and trouble overwhelm you.

[a]**12** Hebrew *Sheol* [b]**21** Hebrew; Septuagint / *on the tops of the walls* [c]**22** The Hebrew word rendered *simple* in Proverbs generally denotes one without moral direction and inclined to evil.

28 "Then they will call to me but I will not answer;
they will look for me but will not find me.
29 Since they hated knowledge
and did not choose to fear the LORD,
30 since they would not accept my advice
and spurned my rebuke,
31 they will eat the fruit of their ways
and be filled with the fruit of their schemes.
32 For the waywardness of the simple will kill them,
and the complacency of fools will destroy them;
33 but whoever listens to me will live in safety
and be at ease, without fear of harm."

Moral Benefits of Wisdom

2 My son, if you accept my words
and store up my commands within you,
2 turning your ear to wisdom
and applying your heart to understanding,
3 and if you call out for insight
and cry aloud for understanding,
4 and if you look for it as for silver
and search for it as for hidden treasure,
5 then you will understand the fear of the LORD
and find the knowledge of God.
6 For the LORD gives wisdom,
and from his mouth come knowledge and understanding.
7 He holds victory in store for the upright,
he is a shield to those whose walk is blameless,
8 for he guards the course of the just
and protects the way of his faithful ones.

9 Then you will understand what is right and just
and fair—every good path.
10 For wisdom will enter your heart,
and knowledge will be pleasant to your soul.
11 Discretion will protect you,
and understanding will guard you.

12 Wisdom will save you from the ways of wicked men,
from men whose words are perverse,
13 who leave the straight paths
to walk in dark ways,
14 who delight in doing wrong
and rejoice in the perverseness of evil,
15 whose paths are crooked
and who are devious in their ways.

For the LORD gives wisdom, and from his mouth come knowledge and understanding.
Prov 2:6

1:31,32 *eat the fruit . . . complacency of fools will destroy them:* Those who reject Wisdom's warnings and advice will get what they deserve—destruction and death. But those who listen to Wisdom will be safe and live a happy life. See also 26:27; Isa 3:10,11; Gal 6:7,8.

2:1 *My son, if you accept my words:* See the note at 1:8,9.

2:7 *a shield to those whose walk is blameless:* People are encouraged to search for wisdom (2:4), and those who obey its teachings will be protected by the LORD.

2:8,9 *what is right and just and fair:* See the note at 1:3. Living right includes being honest and treating others with justice and fairness, especially those who are poor or less fortunate (see also 1:3; 3:27,28; 11:24,25; 22:9,22, 23; 28:27).

2:13 *walk in dark ways:* In the ancient world, the night was an especially frightening time. So, darkness often is used in the Bible to describe evil, stupidity, or death (4:19; 13:9; 20:20; Job 18:18). Compare this to the life of good (wise) people, whose lifestyle is like sunlight (4:18) and to the Law of the LORD, which is like a lamp (6:23).

2:16,17 *adulteress . . . wayward wife:* Having sex with an unfaithful woman (adulteress) is often used in the Bible as a symbol for being unfaithful to the LORD (Hos 1:2; Mal 2:10-16). Compare this "wayward wife" to the woman named "wisdom" (1:20-23).

2:18 *leads down to death:* See the note at 5:5.

2:21,22 *wicked will be cut off from the land:* This may simply refer to losing one's blessings (including land and possessions) because of foolish actions. It could also refer to Israel's being able to keep the land that the LORD had given them (Canaan). The people were warned that being disobedient or unfaithful to the LORD may cause them to lose the land (Deut 28:63).

3:3 *around your neck . . . tablet of your heart:* See the note at 1:8,9. The "heart" is the place where intentions and behavior were believed to come from. This is similar to the modern idea of taking advice "to heart."

3:6 *make your paths straight:* Being wise and obeying the LORD's teachings is often described as taking the straight path (4:10,11; 15:24; Ps 143:10).

3:9 *firstfruits of all your crops:* According to the Law of Moses, the Israelite people were required to give the first portion of their crops to the priests as a gift to the LORD (Lev 2:14; 23:9-14; Num 18:8-14). Those who follow this command are promised more blessings (3:10; see also Deut 28:1, 2, 8-13; Mal 3:10).

3:1 Prov 1:8; 2:1. **3:4** Luke 2:52. **3:7** Rom 12:16. **3:11,12** Job 5:17; Heb 12:5, 6; Rev 3:19.

16 It will save you also from the adulteress,
from the wayward wife with her seductive words,
17 who has left the partner of her youth
and ignored the covenant she made before God.[a]
18 For her house leads down to death
and her paths to the spirits of the dead.
19 None who go to her return
or attain the paths of life.

20 Thus you will walk in the ways of good men
and keep to the paths of the righteous.
21 For the upright will live in the land,
and the blameless will remain in it;
22 but the wicked will be cut off from the land,
and the unfaithful will be torn from it.

Further Benefits of Wisdom

3 My son, do not forget my teaching,
but keep my commands in your heart,
2 for they will prolong your life many years
and bring you prosperity.

3 Let love and faithfulness never leave you;
bind them around your neck,
write them on the tablet of your heart.
4 Then you will win favor and a good name
in the sight of God and man.

5 Trust in the LORD with all your heart
and lean not on your own understanding;
6 in all your ways acknowledge him,
and he will make your paths straight.[b]

7 Do not be wise in your own eyes;
fear the LORD and shun evil.
8 This will bring health to your body
and nourishment to your bones.

9 Honor the LORD with your wealth,
with the firstfruits of all your crops;
10 then your barns will be filled to overflowing,
and your vats will brim over with new wine.

11 My son, do not despise the LORD's discipline
and do not resent his rebuke,
12 because the LORD disciplines those he loves,
as a father[c] the son he delights in.

[a]**17** Or *covenant of her God* [b]**6** Or *will direct your paths* [c]**12** Hebrew; Septuagint / *and he punishes*

13 Blessed is the man who finds wisdom,
the man who gains understanding,
14 for she is more profitable than silver
and yields better returns than gold.
15 She is more precious than rubies;
nothing you desire can compare with her.
16 Long life is in her right hand;
in her left hand are riches and honor.
17 Her ways are pleasant ways,
and all her paths are peace.
18 She is a tree of life to those who embrace her;
those who lay hold of her will be blessed.

19 By wisdom the LORD laid the earth's foundations,
by understanding he set the heavens in place;
20 by his knowledge the deeps were divided,
and the clouds let drop the dew.

21 My son, preserve sound judgment and discernment,
do not let them out of your sight;
22 they will be life for you,
an ornament to grace your neck.
23 Then you will go on your way in safety,
and your foot will not stumble;
24 when you lie down, you will not be afraid;
when you lie down, your sleep will be sweet.
25 Have no fear of sudden disaster
or of the ruin that overtakes the wicked,
26 for the LORD will be your confidence
and will keep your foot from being snared.

27 Do not withhold good from those who deserve it,
when it is in your power to act.
28 Do not say to your neighbor,
"Come back later; I'll give it tomorrow"—
when you now have it with you.

29 Do not plot harm against your neighbor,
who lives trustfully near you.
30 Do not accuse a man for no reason—
when he has done you no harm.

31 Do not envy a violent man
or choose any of his ways,
32 for the LORD detests a perverse man
but takes the upright into his confidence.

33 The LORD's curse is on the house of the wicked,
but he blesses the home of the righteous.
34 He mocks proud mockers
but gives grace to the humble.

3:13-18 *wisdom . . . a tree of life:* See the notes at 1:2 and on p. 1193 (Foolishness and wisdom). These verses are a hymn that summarizes the benefits of Wisdom—long life, wealth, honor, safety, and happiness. The tree of life is a symbol of the LORD's blessing (Gen 2:9; Ezek 47:12; Rev 22:2). Those who follow the LORD's Law are also described as trees growing beside a stream (Ps 1:1-3).

3:19 *By wisdom the LORD laid the earth's foundations:* See the note at 8:24-26.

3:20 *the deeps were divided . . . dew:* The ancient Israelites believed the earth was flat. Under the earth was a huge ocean, and over the earth was a solid dome that held back the flood of water above. Rain and snow were said to fall when God opened windows in the sky (Gen 7:11,12; Ps 78:23). God's wisdom is compared to water which is essential for sustaining life.

3:27 *Do not withhold good:* See the note at 2:8, 9.

3:33-35 *curse . . . blesses:* This is a series of three sayings comparing positive and negative. The LORD will bless the home of the one who is wise but curse the home of the evil or foolish person. A wise person who is humble will be praised by neighbors, but the fool who sneers at the LORD will end up being disgraced. See also Jas 4:6; 1 Pet 5:5.

3:31 Prov 1:10-19.

[35] The wise inherit honor,
but fools he holds up to shame.

Wisdom Is Supreme

4 Listen, my sons, to a father's instruction;
pay attention and gain understanding.
[2] I give you sound learning,
so do not forsake my teaching.
[3] When I was a boy in my father's house,
still tender, and an only child of my mother,
[4] he taught me and said,
"Lay hold of my words with all your heart;
keep my commands and you will live.
[5] Get wisdom, get understanding;
do not forget my words or swerve from them.
[6] Do not forsake wisdom, and she will protect you;
love her, and she will watch over you.
[7] Wisdom is supreme; therefore get wisdom.
Though it cost all you have,[a] get understanding.
[8] Esteem her, and she will exalt you;
embrace her, and she will honor you.
[9] She will set a garland of grace on your head
and present you with a crown of splendor."

[10] Listen, my son, accept what I say,
and the years of your life will be many.
[11] I guide you in the way of wisdom
and lead you along straight paths.
[12] When you walk, your steps will not be hampered;
when you run, you will not stumble.
[13] Hold on to instruction, do not let it go;
guard it well, for it is your life.
[14] Do not set foot on the path of the wicked
or walk in the way of evil men.
[15] Avoid it, do not travel on it;
turn from it and go on your way.
[16] For they cannot sleep till they do evil;
they are robbed of slumber till they make
someone fall.
[17] They eat the bread of wickedness
and drink the wine of violence.

[18] The path of the righteous is like the first gleam of dawn,
shining ever brighter till the full light of day.
[19] But the way of the wicked is like deep darkness;
they do not know what makes them stumble.

4:4 *Lay hold of my words . . . keep my commands:* See the note at 3:3. "My words" refers to the instruction of a father.

4:6 *wisdom . . . love her:* See the note on p. 1193 (Foolishness and wisdom). Loving Wisdom, like faithfully obeying the LORD's teachings, is compared to the committed love of a husband for his wife (see also 2:16-19; 3:16-18; 5:15–19). Wisdom will protect the one who stays faithful to her.

4:9 *garland of grace . . . crown of splendor:* Headpieces made from flowers were worn at weddings and other special occasions (Song 3:11). See also the note at 1:8,9. In addition to wearing fancy headdresses, Israelite brides covered their faces with veils.

4:11 *straight paths:* See the note at 3:6.

4:17 *bread of wickedness . . . wine of violence:* In the Bible, drinking from the LORD's cup of anger means experiencing God's judgment and punishment (Job 21:20; Ps 60:3; Isa 51:22; Rev 14:10). But those who eat Wisdom's feast will live (9:1-6). See also 18:21; 26:22.

4:18,19 *gleam of dawn . . . deep darkness:* See the note at 2:13.

4:1 Prov 1:8; 2:1; 3:1. **4:14** Prov 3:31.

[a]7 Or *Whatever else you get*

[20] My son, pay attention to what I say;
listen closely to my words.
[21] Do not let them out of your sight,
keep them within your heart;
[22] for they are life to those who find them
and health to a man's whole body.
[23] Above all else, guard your heart,
for it is the wellspring of life.
[24] Put away perversity from your mouth;
keep corrupt talk far from your lips.
[25] Let your eyes look straight ahead,
fix your gaze directly before you.
[26] Make level[a] paths for your feet
and take only ways that are firm.
[27] Do not swerve to the right or the left;
keep your foot from evil.

Warning Against Adultery

5 My son, pay attention to my wisdom,
listen well to my words of insight,
[2] that you may maintain discretion
and your lips may preserve knowledge.
[3] For the lips of an adulteress drip honey,
and her speech is smoother than oil;
[4] but in the end she is bitter as gall,
sharp as a double-edged sword.
[5] Her feet go down to death;
her steps lead straight to the grave.[b]
[6] She gives no thought to the way of life;
her paths are crooked, but she knows it not.

[7] Now then, my sons, listen to me;
do not turn aside from what I say.
[8] Keep to a path far from her,
do not go near the door of her house,
[9] lest you give your best strength to others
and your years to one who is cruel,
[10] lest strangers feast on your wealth
and your toil enrich another man's house.
[11] At the end of your life you will groan,
when your flesh and body are spent.
[12] You will say, "How I hated discipline!
How my heart spurned correction!
[13] I would not obey my teachers
or listen to my instructors.

[a]26 Or *Consider the* **[b]5** Hebrew *Sheol*

4:25 *Let your eyes look straight ahead:* Another way of saying "make your paths straight" (see the note at 3:6). Most roads in the ancient Near East were curved and rocky. This made them difficult and dangerous to travel. A road as straight as the one shown here in Timna National Park in the Negev Desert, Israel, would have been a traveler's dream.

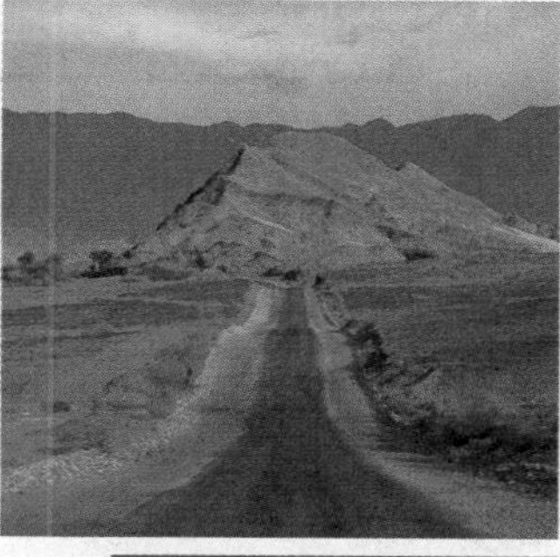

5:3 *adulteress . . . honey . . . oil:* See the note at 2:16,17. Honey was a prized food and olive oil was used in cooking, making healing ointments, and in special offerings for the LORD.

5:5 *go down to death . . . grave:* Death and the grave were considered to be a dark underground world where the souls of the dead were thought to go (Job 30:23; Ps 139:7, 8; Ezek 31:16-18; Acts 2:27). Death is described as being totally silent, a place where no one knows nor feels anything (Ps 88:12; 94:17).

5:10 *strangers:* Being unable to pass one's wealth to family members was considered a great tragedy (Eccl 5:13-16). Losing wealth to foreigners is a symbol for the Israelite people giving up their customs and worship for the customs of other nations and the worship of foreign gods.

4:26 Heb 12:13. **5:1,2** Prov 1:8; 2:1; 3:1; 4:1. **5:12** Prov 3:12.

5:15-18 *your own cistern . . . wife:* Taking water from another person's well or cistern was a serious crime. For more about the importance of faithfulness in marriage, see also Lev 20:10; Deut 22:22-27; and the note at 2:16,17.

5:22,23 *evil deeds of a wicked man ensnare him:* See the notes at 1:10 and 1:17.

6:1-3 *if you have put up security . . . press your plea:* These verses warn against co-signing a loan, meaning promising to pay off someone else's debt. This is dangerous because the person who does this may lose his own money or may have to become the lender's slave.

6:10,11 *a little folding of the hands to rest . . . poverty:* This is a warning about being lazy or careless about work that needs to be done (see also 10:4,5; 19:15; 20:4,13; 24:33,34). In contrast, hard work will be rewarded (12:11; 28:19).

5:18,19 Song 2:8,9; 7:1-3.

14 I have come to the brink of utter ruin
in the midst of the whole assembly."

15 Drink water from your own cistern,
running water from your own well.
16 Should your springs overflow in the streets,
your streams of water in the public squares?
17 Let them be yours alone,
never to be shared with strangers.
18 May your fountain be blessed,
and may you rejoice in the wife of your youth.
19 A loving doe, a graceful deer—
may her breasts satisfy you always,
may you ever be captivated by her love.
20 Why be captivated, my son, by an adulteress?
Why embrace the bosom of another man's wife?

21 For a man's ways are in full view of the LORD,
and he examines all his paths.
22 The evil deeds of a wicked man ensnare him;
the cords of his sin hold him fast.
23 He will die for lack of discipline,
led astray by his own great folly.

Warnings Against Folly

6 My son, if you have put up security for your neighbor,
if you have struck hands in pledge for another,
2 if you have been trapped by what you said,
ensnared by the words of your mouth,
3 then do this, my son, to free yourself,
since you have fallen into your neighbor's hands:
Go and humble yourself;
press your plea with your neighbor!
4 Allow no sleep to your eyes,
no slumber to your eyelids.
5 Free yourself, like a gazelle from the hand of the hunter,
like a bird from the snare of the fowler.

6 Go to the ant, you sluggard;
consider its ways and be wise!
7 It has no commander,
no overseer or ruler,
8 yet it stores its provisions in summer
and gathers its food at harvest.

9 How long will you lie there, you sluggard?
When will you get up from your sleep?
10 A little sleep, a little slumber,
a little folding of the hands to rest—

11 and poverty will come on you like a bandit
and scarcity like an armed man.[a]

12 A scoundrel and villain,
who goes about with a corrupt mouth,
13 who winks with his eye,
signals with his feet
and motions with his fingers,
14 who plots evil with deceit in his heart—
he always stirs up dissension.
15 Therefore disaster will overtake him in an instant;
he will suddenly be destroyed—without remedy.

16 There are six things the LORD hates,
seven that are detestable to him:
17 haughty eyes,
a lying tongue,
hands that shed innocent blood,
18 a heart that devises wicked schemes,
feet that are quick to rush into evil,
19 a false witness who pours out lies
and a man who stirs up dissension among brothers.

Warning Against Adultery

20 My son, keep your father's commands
and do not forsake your mother's teaching.
21 Bind them upon your heart forever;
fasten them around your neck.
22 When you walk, they will guide you;
when you sleep, they will watch over you;
when you awake, they will speak to you.
23 For these commands are a lamp,
this teaching is a light,
and the corrections of discipline
are the way to life,
24 keeping you from the immoral woman,
from the smooth tongue of the wayward wife.
25 Do not lust in your heart after her beauty
or let her captivate you with her eyes,
26 for the prostitute reduces you to a loaf of bread,
and the adulteress preys upon your very life.
27 Can a man scoop fire into his lap
without his clothes being burned?
28 Can a man walk on hot coals
without his feet being scorched?
29 So is he who sleeps with another man's wife;
no one who touches her will go unpunished.

[a]11 Or *like a vagrant / and scarcity like a beggar*

6:12,13 *scoundrel and villain . . . winks . . . signals:* This may refer to the deceitful attitude of liars and cheaters, or to specific hand or eye signals that business partners used to cheat a customer. See also 16:30.

6:23 *these commands are a lamp:* The Law of the LORD refers to the commandments and laws given to Moses and the people. See also the mini-article called "Law," p. 1160. These "commands" could also refer to the words of a parent (see 2:1 and 7:1). Lamps in the ancient world were small clay dishes that burned olive oil. See also Ps 19:8; 119:105; and the note at 2:13.

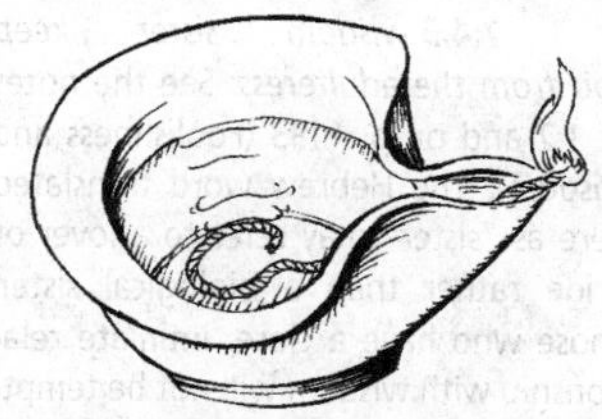

6:26 *the prostitute . . . preys upon your very life:* See also the mini-article called "Prostitution in the Bible," p. 1688. Having sex with another person's wife or husband was punishable by death (Lev 20:10). Jewish society was built on a man being able to pass on his inheritance to his children by his legal wife. But if she had sex with another man, she might get pregnant, and her husband might end up passing on part of his inheritance to a child that was not really his.

6:20-22 Deut 6:5-7.

6:31 *pay sevenfold:* The number "seven" stood for completeness. Here, seven is meant to symbolize full repayment, since the Law said a thief was to pay back no more than five times what he or she had stolen (Exod 22:1-9).

6:32 *destroys himself:* Sexual sins were considered especially dangerous (see 5:20-23; 6:26-29). A man and woman who committed adultery could be put to death (Lev 20:10). But here it sounds as if a husband could choose instead to beat and disgrace his wife and her lover in public.

7:3 *write them on the tablet of your heart:* See the note at 3:3.

7:4,5 *wisdom . . . sister . . . keep you from the adulteress:* See the notes at 1:2 and on p. 1193 (Foolishness and wisdom). The Hebrew word translated here as "sister" may refer to a lover or bride rather than a biological sister. Those who have a close, intimate relationship with wisdom will not be tempted to chase after "the adulteress."

7:10 *prostitute:* See the note at 6:26.

7:14 *fellowship offerings at home:* The sacrifice offered may have been given as part of an ancient Canaanite fertility ritual. That would mean that the woman's invitation also includes eating meat offered to an idol. But more likely the leftover meat is from a fellowship offering (Lev 7:11-36). Depending on the kind of sacrifice, the meat had to be eaten the same day (Lev 7:15).

7:1,2 Prov 2:1,2; 3:1,2; 4:1,10; 5:1,2; 6:20-22.

30 Men do not despise a thief if he steals
to satisfy his hunger when he is starving.
31 Yet if he is caught, he must pay sevenfold,
though it costs him all the wealth of his house.
32 But a man who commits adultery lacks judgment;
whoever does so destroys himself.
33 Blows and disgrace are his lot,
and his shame will never be wiped away;
34 for jealousy arouses a husband's fury,
and he will show no mercy when he takes revenge.
35 He will not accept any compensation;
he will refuse the bribe, however great it is.

Warning Against the Adulteress

7 My son, keep my words
and store up my commands within you.
2 Keep my commands and you will live;
guard my teachings as the apple of your eye.
3 Bind them on your fingers;
write them on the tablet of your heart.
4 Say to wisdom, "You are my sister,"
and call understanding your kinsman;
5 they will keep you from the adulteress,
from the wayward wife with her seductive words.

6 At the window of my house
I looked out through the lattice.
7 I saw among the simple,
I noticed among the young men,
a youth who lacked judgment.
8 He was going down the street near her corner,
walking along in the direction of her house
9 at twilight, as the day was fading,
as the dark of night set in.

10 Then out came a woman to meet him,
dressed like a prostitute and with crafty intent.
11 (She is loud and defiant,
her feet never stay at home;
12 now in the street, now in the squares,
at every corner she lurks.)
13 She took hold of him and kissed him
and with a brazen face she said:

14 "I have fellowship offerings[a] at home;
today I fulfilled my vows.
15 So I came out to meet you;

[a]**14** Traditionally *peace offerings*

I looked for you and have found you!
[16] I have covered my bed
with colored linens from Egypt.
[17] I have perfumed my bed
with myrrh, aloes and cinnamon.
[18] Come, let's drink deep of love till morning;
let's enjoy ourselves with love!
[19] My husband is not at home;
he has gone on a long journey.
[20] He took his purse filled with money
and will not be home till full moon."

[21] With persuasive words she led him astray;
she seduced him with her smooth talk.
[22] All at once he followed her
like an ox going to the slaughter,
like a deer[a] stepping into a noose[b]
[23] till an arrow pierces his liver,
like a bird darting into a snare,
little knowing it will cost him his life.

[24] Now then, my sons, listen to me;
pay attention to what I say.
[25] Do not let your heart turn to her ways
or stray into her paths.
[26] Many are the victims she has brought down;
her slain are a mighty throng.
[27] Her house is a highway to the grave,[c]
leading down to the chambers of death.

WISDOM'S INVITATION TO FIND LIFE

Wisdom invites all, including the world's rulers, to search for her. She is described as being present with God at the beginning of creation, so she symbolizes God's creative power. She also expresses the core of God's truth. The guests who come to Wisdom's feast will live (9:6, 11), but those who become the guests of Folly are as good as dead (9:13, 18).

Wisdom's Call

8 Does not wisdom call out?
Does not understanding raise her voice?
[2] On the heights along the way,
where the paths meet, she takes her stand;
[3] beside the gates leading into the city,
at the entrances, she cries aloud:

[a]**22** Syriac (see also Septuagint); Hebrew *fool* [b]**22** The meaning of the Hebrew for this line is uncertain. [c]**27** Hebrew *Sheol*

7:16,17 *colored linens . . . myrrh, aloes and cinnamon:* The cloth is expensive linen, a fine cloth woven out of the dried fibers of the flax plant. Egyptian linen was considered very valuable (Ezek 27:7). Myrrh and aloes had to be imported to Israel, so they were expensive. See also the chart called "Spices and Perfumes," p. 1278.

7:22 *ox:* This large animal was used for heavy work, such as plowing fields and pulling carts. They were also slaughtered and used for food.

7:23 *snare:* See the note and illustration at 1:17.

7:25 *Do not let your heart turn to her ways:* See the notes at 7:4,5 and 6:26.

7:27 *the grave . . . chambers of death:* See the note at 5:5.

8:1-3 *wisdom . . . heights . . . where the paths meet . . . gates:* See 1:20-33 and the note on p. 1193 (Foolishness and wisdom). Wisdom calls out from three of the busiest places in the ancient world—the heights where worship places were often set up, the crossroads where travelers and merchants met to talk and trade, and the city gates where important town business and court trials often took place.

Wisdom is more precious than rubies, and nothing you desire can compare with her.
Prov 8:11

8:6,7 *right . . . true:* Because Wisdom is from the LORD, she always tells what is right and true (see the note at 1:3). See also the mini-article called "Truth," p. 2087.

8:12 *I, wisdom:* See the notes at 8:1-3 and on p. 1193 (Foolishness and wisdom).

8:13 *fear the LORD:* See the note at 1:7.

8:14,15 *Counsel and sound judgment . . . kings . . . laws that are just:* Just as kings receive advice from counselors and advisers, Wisdom offers life-giving advice. Rulers who listen to wisdom rule with fairness and honesty. The wise king was the ideal king (Isa 9:6,7; 11:1-5).

8:18 *riches and honor . . . wealth and prosperity:* See the note on p. 1193 (Foolishness and wisdom).

8:24-26 *When there were no oceans, I was given birth:* Wisdom was present with God from the very beginning or was created before anything else was made (see also 3:19,20). The idea that Wisdom was one with and yet distinct from God probably had some influence on Christian understanding of Christ as God's Son, who was also said to be present with God at creation (John 1:1-3; Col 1:15-17). See also Rev 3:14.

8:10,11 Prov 3:14,15. **8:19** Ps 119:72, 127; Prov 3:14; 8:10.

4 "To you, O men, I call out;
I raise my voice to all mankind.
5 You who are simple, gain prudence;
you who are foolish, gain understanding.
6 Listen, for I have worthy things to say;
I open my lips to speak what is right.
7 My mouth speaks what is true,
for my lips detest wickedness.
8 All the words of my mouth are just;
none of them is crooked or perverse.
9 To the discerning all of them are right;
they are faultless to those who have knowledge.
10 Choose my instruction instead of silver,
knowledge rather than choice gold,
11 for wisdom is more precious than rubies,
and nothing you desire can compare with her.

12 "I, wisdom, dwell together with prudence;
I possess knowledge and discretion.
13 To fear the LORD is to hate evil;
I hate pride and arrogance,
evil behavior and perverse speech.
14 Counsel and sound judgment are mine;
I have understanding and power.
15 By me kings reign
and rulers make laws that are just;
16 by me princes govern,
and all nobles who rule on earth.[a]
17 I love those who love me,
and those who seek me find me.
18 With me are riches and honor,
enduring wealth and prosperity.
19 My fruit is better than fine gold;
what I yield surpasses choice silver.
20 I walk in the way of righteousness,
along the paths of justice,
21 bestowing wealth on those who love me
and making their treasuries full.

22 "The LORD brought me forth as the first of his works,[b,c]
before his deeds of old;
23 I was appointed[d] from eternity,
from the beginning, before the world began.
24 When there were no oceans, I was given birth,
when there were no springs abounding with water;

[a]16 Many Hebrew manuscripts and Septuagint; most Hebrew manuscripts *and nobles—all righteous rulers* [b]22 Or *way*; or *dominion* [c]22 Or *The LORD possessed me at the beginning of his work*; or *The LORD brought me forth at the beginning of his work* [d]23 Or *fashioned*

25 before the mountains were settled in place,
before the hills, I was given birth,
26 before he made the earth or its fields
or any of the dust of the world.
27 I was there when he set the heavens in place,
when he marked out the horizon on the face
of the deep,
28 when he established the clouds above
and fixed securely the fountains of the deep,
29 when he gave the sea its boundary
so the waters would not overstep his command,
and when he marked out the foundations of the earth.
30 Then I was the craftsman at his side.
I was filled with delight day after day,
rejoicing always in his presence,
31 rejoicing in his whole world
and delighting in mankind.

32 "Now then, my sons, listen to me;
blessed are those who keep my ways.
33 Listen to my instruction and be wise;
do not ignore it.
34 Blessed is the man who listens to me,
watching daily at my doors,
waiting at my doorway.
35 For whoever finds me finds life
and receives favor from the LORD.
36 But whoever fails to find me harms himself;
all who hate me love death."

Invitations of Wisdom and of Folly

9 Wisdom has built her house;
she has hewn out its seven pillars.
2 She has prepared her meat and mixed her wine;
she has also set her table.
3 She has sent out her maids, and she calls
from the highest point of the city.
4 "Let all who are simple come in here!"
she says to those who lack judgment.
5 "Come, eat my food
and drink the wine I have mixed.
6 Leave your simple ways and you will live;
walk in the way of understanding.

7 "Whoever corrects a mocker invites insult;
whoever rebukes a wicked man incurs abuse.
8 Do not rebuke a mocker or he will hate you;
rebuke a wise man and he will love you.

8:27,28 *set the heavens in place . . . fixed securely the fountains of the deep:* See Gen 1:1-19. The Hebrew people understood the sky to be a dome or bowl stretched over the flat earth and sea (see the note at 3:20). Lakes and oceans were thought to be filled by water springing up from the great ocean that was under the surface of land and sea.

8:29 *gave the sea its boundary:* In the Canaanite religion, the sea was a force of chaos and disorder. According to Job 38:8-11, God took the sea prisoner by setting its boundaries.

8:32-34 *my sons, listen to me . . . watching daily at my doors:* Wisdom continues the invitation that began in 8:1, but this time Wisdom uses the same words that have been used by human parents instructing their children (see 1:8; 2:1; 3:1; 4:1; 5:1,2). Wisdom's house is a place to find happiness and blessing, in contrast to the house of the adulteress, which leads to death (5:8; 7:27).

9:1 *seven pillars:* The seven columns may be a reference to the foundation or pillars that the LORD God in wisdom built at creation (see 8:29,30). Or, because seven was considered a perfect or complete number, this may mean that Wisdom's house is perfect, unlike the house of Folly (9:14).

9:2 *prepared her meat and mixed her wine:* The food of Wisdom is life-giving and provides strength for right living (see also the note at 4:17).

9:6 *Leave your simple ways:* This simple-minded foolishness includes hating knowledge (1:22); complacency (1:32); refusing to respect and obey the LORD (2:7); following an immoral woman (5:3-6; 7:6-23); and making evil plans, including stirring up trouble in a family (6:18,19).

9:9 *wiser still:* See the note at 2:8,9.

9:10 *fear of the* LORD*:* See the note at 1:7. See also Job 28:28; Ps 111:10.

9:10 *the Holy One:* This title describes how God is set apart from human beings and how God's wisdom is far greater than human understanding. Israel's LORD was also a personal God who chose them (Isa 41:8,9) and lived among them (Exod 25:18-22; 1 Kgs 8:6-13; Isa 6:1-8).

9:13-18 *Folly . . . sits at the door of her house . . . calling out:* Like Wisdom, Folly invites people into her house to lead them to self-destruction (compare this verse to 8:1-8; 9:1-6; see also 5:3-6; 7:6-23). Folly is like the adulteress, but her invitation is not limited to forbidden sex. Her invitation represents all forms of foolish behavior that eventually lead to death (see the note at 9:6).

9 Instruct a wise man and he will be wiser still;
teach a righteous man and he will add to his learning.

10 "The fear of the LORD is the beginning of wisdom,
and knowledge of the Holy One is understanding.
11 For through me your days will be many,
and years will be added to your life.
12 If you are wise, your wisdom will reward you;
if you are a mocker, you alone will suffer."

13 The woman Folly is loud;
she is undisciplined and without knowledge.
14 She sits at the door of her house,
on a seat at the highest point of the city,
15 calling out to those who pass by,
who go straight on their way.
16 "Let all who are simple come in here!"
she says to those who lack judgment.
17 "Stolen water is sweet;
food eaten in secret is delicious!"
18 But little do they know that the dead are there,
that her guests are in the depths of the grave.[a]

[a] **18** Hebrew *Sheol*

QUESTIONS ABOUT PROVERBS 1:1—9:18

1. What kinds of things are proverbs meant to teach? (1:1-6) What are some wise sayings or proverbs you heard as a child? How are they similar to or different from the proverbs you have read in these first few chapters of PROVERBS? What is the source of true wisdom? (1:7; 2:4-7)
2. Wisdom teaches what is right and just and fair (2:9). Explain what this statement means in your own words. In contrast, "fools" are described as living in darkness and headed for death. (1:32; 2:13; 9:13, 18) What does this mean?
3. Who or what is Wisdom? (1:20-33; 3:16-18; 4:6-9; 8:1—9:12) Who or what is the opposite of Wisdom? (2:16; 5:3-6; 7:6-27; 9:13-18)
4. In ancient Israelite society, who was responsible for passing on wisdom and instruction? (1:8,9; 2:1,2; 3:1,2; 5:1,2; 6:20-22) How are wisdom and understanding passed on in modern society? In your opinion, what value does modern society put on the wisdom of parents and elders?
5. To have wisdom means taking the path or road that leads to life. (4:10-13) When people have the option of going in many directions or taking many paths through life, how do they know which path to take? How do you find guidance when making important life decisions?
6. Quickly look over chapters 1–9 one more time. Which two sayings were especially meaningful to you? What truth or meaning do you find in these statements?

Many of Solomon's Wise Sayings

A collection of short sayings credited to Solomon (10:1) is found in 10:1—22:16. The majority of the sayings in this section are statements of truth, rather than being stated as instructions to follow or longer descriptive poems, as are found in Proverbs 1–9. This section includes 375 verses, which is also the number value of the Hebrew name "Solomon." The collection seems to be organized around types of wise sayings, such as opposite parallels (chapters 10–15) and sayings about wisdom and rulers (16).

The man of integrity
walks securely,
but he who takes
crooked paths will be
found out.
Prov 10:9

PROVERBS OF SOLOMON

10 The proverbs of Solomon:

A wise son brings joy to his father,
but a foolish son grief to his mother.

2 Ill-gotten treasures are of no value,
but righteousness delivers from death.

3 The LORD does not let the righteous go hungry
but he thwarts the craving of the wicked.

4 Lazy hands make a man poor,
but diligent hands bring wealth.

5 He who gathers crops in summer is a wise son,
but he who sleeps during harvest is a disgraceful son.

6 Blessings crown the head of the righteous,
but violence overwhelms the mouth of the wicked.[a]

7 The memory of the righteous will be a blessing,
but the name of the wicked will rot.

8 The wise in heart accept commands,
but a chattering fool comes to ruin.

9 The man of integrity walks securely,
but he who takes crooked paths will be found out.

10 He who winks maliciously causes grief,
and a chattering fool comes to ruin.

11 The mouth of the righteous is a fountain of life,
but violence overwhelms the mouth of the wicked.

12 Hatred stirs up dissension,
but love covers over all wrongs.

13 Wisdom is found on the lips of the discerning,
but a rod is for the back of him who lacks judgment.

14 Wise men store up knowledge,
but the mouth of a fool invites ruin.

[a]6 Or *but the mouth of the wicked conceals violence*; also in verse 11

10:1 *The proverbs of Solomon:* See the notes at 1:1.

10:3 *righteous . . . wicked:* See the note on p. 1193 (Foolishness and wisdom).

10:4 *Lazy hands:* Many proverbs praise effort but condemn laziness. See for example 6:6-11; 12:11,27; 13:4; 28:19.

10:5 *harvest:* Crops, fruits, and vegetables need to be picked when they are ripe, so harvest time is a very busy time. If crops are not picked in time, they will become too ripe to store or eat.

10:7 *memory of the righteous will be a blessing:* Having a good reputation is highly prized in Hebrew wisdom (22:1; see also Eccl 7:1).

10:8-14 *chattering fool . . . mouth of a fool invites ruin:* This group of sayings draws attention to the foolishness of pointless or evil talk. Words have the power to be a source of good or evil. Good words spoken wisely show a person has good sense, but wicked words may lead to the speaker's punishment (10:13). See also Eccl 10:12-14.

10:12 Jas 5:20; 1 Pet 4:8.

KINDS OF PROVERBS

The wise sayings found in PROVERBS can be grouped in a number of ways. At a very general level, the sayings can be described as statements of truth—"Pleasant words are a honeycomb" (16:24); or as instructions—"He who heeds discipline shows the way to life" (10:17). But the sayings can also be described by the form or pattern they take. One common pattern follows the form of Hebrew poetry known as "parallelism." In parallel statements, the second part either agrees with the first or provides its opposite. This chart gives some of the patterns or forms used in creating the proverbs.

FORM OR PATTERN OF PROVERB	EXAMPLES
1. **Opposite statements** The same statement or instruction is given twice, but in opposite ways.	Hatred stirs up dissension, but love covers over all wrongs. (10:12) The truly righteous man attains life, but he who pursues evil goes to his death. (11:19)
2. **Similar statements** The same statement or instruction is given twice in similar ways. The same idea is restated in different words. Sometimes, the second line makes the point more forcefully than the first line does.	The highway of the upright avoids evil; he who guards his way guards his life. (16:17) By wisdom a house is built and through understanding it is established; through knowledge its rooms are filled with rare and beautiful treasures. (24:3,4)
3. **Statement with an explanation** The first line is a concrete image which is then explained by the second line.	As iron sharpens iron, so one man sharpens another. (27:17) A king's wrath is like the roar of a lion; he who angers him forfeits his life. (20:2)
4. **Comparison** Some proverbs use striking images that compare one thing or person to another. These are called metaphors and similes.	Like a gold ring in a pig's snout is a beautiful woman who shows no discretion. (11:22) The lamp of the LORD searches the spirit of a man. (20:27) Like a roaring lion or a charging bear is a wicked man ruling over a helpless people. (28:15)
5. **Descriptive list** Usually three or four answers that follow a statement based on an unspoken question.	There are three things . . . four that I do not understand: the way of an eagle in the sky, the way of a snake on a rock, the way of a ship on the high seas, and the way of a man with a maiden. (30:18,19)
6. **"If . . . then" statement and "or else" instruction** The second part explains the consequences of doing or not doing something. The "or else" is usually implied but not stated.	My son, if you accept my words . . . then you will understand the fear of the LORD and find the knowledge of God. (2:1, 5) If a man pays back evil for good, evil will never leave his house. (17:13)

15 The wealth of the rich is their fortified city,
but poverty is the ruin of the poor.

16 The wages of the righteous bring them life,
but the income of the wicked brings them
punishment.

17 He who heeds discipline shows the way to life,
but whoever ignores correction leads others astray.

18 He who conceals his hatred has lying lips,
and whoever spreads slander is a fool.

19 When words are many, sin is not absent,
but he who holds his tongue is wise.

20 The tongue of the righteous is choice silver,
but the heart of the wicked is of little value.

21 The lips of the righteous nourish many,
but fools die for lack of judgment.

22 The blessing of the LORD brings wealth,
and he adds no trouble to it.

23 A fool finds pleasure in evil conduct,
but a man of understanding delights in wisdom.

24 What the wicked dreads will overtake him;
what the righteous desire will be granted.

25 When the storm has swept by, the wicked are gone,
but the righteous stand firm forever.

26 As vinegar to the teeth and smoke to the eyes,
so is a sluggard to those who send him.

27 The fear of the LORD adds length to life,
but the years of the wicked are cut short.

28 The prospect of the righteous is joy,
but the hopes of the wicked come to nothing.

29 The way of the LORD is a refuge for the righteous,
but it is the ruin of those who do evil.

30 The righteous will never be uprooted,
but the wicked will not remain in the land.

31 The mouth of the righteous brings forth wisdom,
but a perverse tongue will be cut out.

32 The lips of the righteous know what is fitting,
but the mouth of the wicked only what is perverse.

11 The LORD abhors dishonest scales,
but accurate weights are his delight.

10:15,16 *wealth . . . poverty . . . bring them life:* Wealth was considered a blessing or reward for good living (see also 3:16; 10:22), but the poor could expect suffering and difficulty (18:23; 19:7). However, those who rely on wealth and make it their protection will suffer in the end (11:28; 18:11, 12). Better than wealth is a good life, the reward for living right. See also the note at 1:3.

10:17 *heeds discipline:* This may refer to the LORD's correction (3:12), but more likely refers to parental instruction or wise teaching (4:10-13).

10:22 *LORD brings wealth:* See the note at 10:15,16.

10:27 *adds length to life . . . cut short:* See the notes at 1:7 and on p. 1193 (Foolishness and wisdom). This saying is difficult because life experience tells us that some faithful people will have their lives cut short by accident or disease, while some wrongdoers appear to lead a long and prosperous life. PROVERBS tends to describe the ideal situation, while other wisdom books such as JOB and ECCLESIASTES offer a more complicated view.

11:1 *dishonest scales . . . accurate weights:* In the Hebrew, this verse refers to the use of false and true balances when weighing goods to be bought or sold. Some merchants and traders used incorrect weights and balances to cheat people. See the illustration on p. 1732.

10:20 Prov 10:8-14; Eccl 10:12-14.

A gossip betrays a confidence, but a trustworthy man keeps a secret.
Prov 11:13

11:2 *pride . . . humility:* Pride is dangerous. It can cause a person to mock the LORD (3:34), disregard the LORD's commands, or trust in wealth (16:18,19) or one's own power instead of trusting in God (Isa 14:11-14). Being humble and being wise go hand in hand. To be humble is to recognize that wisdom is a gift from God.

11:4 *righteousness delivers from death:* God's wisdom and commands show the path to life (3:1,2; 6:23; 10:2). This is not a reference to life after death but a warning about unwise living that leads to the kind of death the wicked face (11:5).

11:11 *Through the blessing of the upright a city is exalted:* Those who live right and obey the LORD cause the whole community to be blessed (see also Isa 58:6-14).

11:15 *puts up security for another:* See the note at 6:1-3.

11:19 *truly righteous:* See the note at 1:3.

11:14 Prov 15:22; 24:6.

[2] When pride comes, then comes disgrace,
but with humility comes wisdom.

[3] The integrity of the upright guides them,
but the unfaithful are destroyed by their duplicity.

[4] Wealth is worthless in the day of wrath,
but righteousness delivers from death.

[5] The righteousness of the blameless makes a straight way for them,
but the wicked are brought down by their own wickedness.

[6] The righteousness of the upright delivers them,
but the unfaithful are trapped by evil desires.

[7] When a wicked man dies, his hope perishes;
all he expected from his power comes to nothing.

[8] The righteous man is rescued from trouble,
and it comes on the wicked instead.

[9] With his mouth the godless destroys his neighbor,
but through knowledge the righteous escape.

[10] When the righteous prosper, the city rejoices;
when the wicked perish, there are shouts of joy.

[11] Through the blessing of the upright a city is exalted,
but by the mouth of the wicked it is destroyed.

[12] A man who lacks judgment derides his neighbor,
but a man of understanding holds his tongue.

[13] A gossip betrays a confidence,
but a trustworthy man keeps a secret.

[14] For lack of guidance a nation falls,
but many advisers make victory sure.

[15] He who puts up security for another will surely suffer,
but whoever refuses to strike hands in pledge is safe.

[16] A kindhearted woman gains respect,
but ruthless men gain only wealth.

[17] A kind man benefits himself,
but a cruel man brings trouble on himself.

[18] The wicked man earns deceptive wages,
but he who sows righteousness reaps a sure reward.

[19] The truly righteous man attains life,
but he who pursues evil goes to his death.

20 The LORD detests men of perverse heart
but he delights in those whose ways are blameless.

21 Be sure of this: The wicked will not go unpunished,
but those who are righteous will go free.

22 Like a gold ring in a pig's snout
is a beautiful woman who shows no discretion.

23 The desire of the righteous ends only in good,
but the hope of the wicked only in wrath.

24 One man gives freely, yet gains even more;
another withholds unduly, but comes to poverty.

25 A generous man will prosper;
he who refreshes others will himself be refreshed.

26 People curse the man who hoards grain,
but blessing crowns him who is willing to sell.

27 He who seeks good finds goodwill,
but evil comes to him who searches for it.

28 Whoever trusts in his riches will fall,
but the righteous will thrive like a green leaf.

29 He who brings trouble on his family will inherit
only wind,
and the fool will be servant to the wise.

30 The fruit of the righteous is a tree of life,
and he who wins souls is wise.

31 If the righteous receive their due on earth,
how much more the ungodly and the sinner!

12 Whoever loves discipline loves knowledge,
but he who hates correction is stupid.

2 A good man obtains favor from the LORD,
but the LORD condemns a crafty man.

3 A man cannot be established through wickedness,
but the righteous cannot be uprooted.

4 A wife of noble character is her husband's crown,
but a disgraceful wife is like decay in his bones.

5 The plans of the righteous are just,
but the advice of the wicked is deceitful.

6 The words of the wicked lie in wait for blood,
but the speech of the upright rescues them.

7 Wicked men are overthrown and are no more,
but the house of the righteous stands firm.

11:24,25 *generous man will prosper:* Giving to others is rewarded, perhaps because a generous giver is remembered by those he or she helps. But a greedy person does not make friends and is cursed by the poor.

11:26 *curse the man who hoards grain:* Dishonest business practices eventually make people angry. This verse likely refers to merchants hoarding grain in order to cause a shortage. Then they can charge higher prices. See also the note at 11:1.

11:28 *Whoever trusts in his riches will fall:* See the note at 10:15,16.

11:30 *fruit of the righteous is a tree of life:* See the notes at 1:3 and 3:13-18.

12:1 *loves discipline:* See the note at 10:17.

12:2 *A good man obtains favor from the LORD:* See the note at 1:3.

12:4 *wife of noble character:* For a full description of such a wife, see 31:10-31. In ancient Hebrew society, the behavior of a man's wife and children affected his reputation and standing within the community.

11:31 1 Pet 4:18.

Reckless words pierce like a sword, but the tongue of the wise brings healing.
Prov 12:18

12:12 *the root of the righteous flourishes:* See the note at 3:13-18. Trees with deep roots can stand firm in stormy times. See also 11:30; 12:3.

12:14 *good things . . . rewards:* See the note on p. 1193 (Foolishness and wisdom).

12:19 *Truthful lips:* See the note at 8:6,7.

12:23 *keeps his knowledge to himself:* A common theme in PROVERBS is the importance of choosing words carefully when speaking. A wise person does not say more than is necessary and does not speak too quickly (10:13; 18:2,21).

8 A man is praised according to his wisdom,
but men with warped minds are despised.

9 Better to be a nobody and yet have a servant
than pretend to be somebody and have no food.

10 A righteous man cares for the needs of
his animal,
but the kindest acts of the wicked are cruel.

11 He who works his land will have abundant food,
but he who chases fantasies lacks judgment.

12 The wicked desire the plunder of evil men,
but the root of the righteous flourishes.

13 An evil man is trapped by his sinful talk,
but a righteous man escapes trouble.

14 From the fruit of his lips a man is filled with
good things
as surely as the work of his hands rewards him.

15 The way of a fool seems right to him,
but a wise man listens to advice.

16 A fool shows his annoyance at once,
but a prudent man overlooks an insult.

17 A truthful witness gives honest testimony,
but a false witness tells lies.

18 Reckless words pierce like a sword,
but the tongue of the wise brings healing.

19 Truthful lips endure forever,
but a lying tongue lasts only a moment.

20 There is deceit in the hearts of those who
plot evil,
but joy for those who promote peace.

21 No harm befalls the righteous,
but the wicked have their fill of trouble.

22 The LORD detests lying lips,
but he delights in men who are truthful.

23 A prudent man keeps his knowledge to himself,
but the heart of fools blurts out folly.

24 Diligent hands will rule,
but laziness ends in slave labor.

25 An anxious heart weighs a man down,
but a kind word cheers him up.

[26]A righteous man is cautious in friendship,[a]
but the way of the wicked leads them astray.

[27]The lazy man does not roast[b] his game,
but the diligent man prizes his possessions.

[28]In the way of righteousness there is life;
along that path is immortality.

13 A wise son heeds his father's instruction,
but a mocker does not listen to rebuke.

[2]From the fruit of his lips a man enjoys good things,
but the unfaithful have a craving for violence.

[3]He who guards his lips guards his life,
but he who speaks rashly will come to ruin.

[4]The sluggard craves and gets nothing,
but the desires of the diligent are fully satisfied.

[5]The righteous hate what is false,
but the wicked bring shame and disgrace.

[6]Righteousness guards the man of integrity,
but wickedness overthrows the sinner.

[7]One man pretends to be rich, yet has nothing;
another pretends to be poor, yet has great wealth.

[8]A man's riches may ransom his life,
but a poor man hears no threat.

[9]The light of the righteous shines brightly,
but the lamp of the wicked is snuffed out.

[10]Pride only breeds quarrels,
but wisdom is found in those who take advice.

[11]Dishonest money dwindles away,
but he who gathers money little by little
makes it grow.

[12]Hope deferred makes the heart sick,
but a longing fulfilled is a tree of life.

[13]He who scorns instruction will pay for it,
but he who respects a command is rewarded.

[14]The teaching of the wise is a fountain of life,
turning a man from the snares of death.

[15]Good understanding wins favor,
but the way of the unfaithful is hard.[c]

[a]**26** Or *man is a guide to his neighbor* [b]**27** The meaning of the Hebrew for this word is uncertain. [c]**15** Or *unfaithful does not endure*

12:28 *along that path:* See the note at 3:6.

13:1 *heeds his father's instruction:* See the note at 10:17.

13:4 *sluggard . . . diligent:* See the note at 6:10, 11.

13:6 *Righteousness guards the man of integrity:* See the note at 1:3. Living right comes from the Wisdom that comes from God. True Wisdom provides protection (2:12; 4:6).

13:9 *lamp:* This image is used here as a symbol for a person's life. See also the notes at 2:13 and 6:23.

13:10 *Pride:* See the note at 11:2.

13:12 *tree of life:* See the notes at 3:13-18 and 12:12.

13:13 *instruction . . . command:* See the note at 6:23.

13:14 *fountain of life:* Living things cannot survive without water. Sensible instruction (wisdom) is compared to a fountain of water, which was highly prized in the dry climate of the Middle East. See also 14:27; Ezek 47:1-12; John 7:37,38.

13:3 Prov 10:19,20.

He who walks with the wise grows wise, but a companion of fools suffers harm.
Prov 13:20

13:17 *A wicked messenger falls into trouble:* A bad messenger may cause problems by giving incorrect information or by treating the hearer with disrespect. A good messenger's gentle words and patience can help smooth out hard feelings and cause people, including rulers, to listen (12:18; 25:13).

13:21 *Misfortune . . . prosperity:* See the notes at 1:10 and 1:3. See also 11:29-31.

13:24 *discipline him:* See the note at 10:17. According to the Law of Moses a stubborn and disobedient son could be punished with death at the hands of the village elders (Deut 21:18-21). Obeying parents or elders was considered crucial to maintaining good order in ancient Hebrew society. Punishment and discipline were seen as a way to help children avoid foolish actions that would be harmful to them or others. See also Prov 19:18; 29:15, 17.

14:1 *wise woman builds her house . . . foolish one tears hers down:* This verse most likely refers to the important role a woman plays in teaching her family good values and respect for the LORD (14:2; 31:10-31).

14:4 *strength of an ox:* See the note at 7:22.

14:6 *wisdom:* See the note at 1:2.

14:5 Prov 6:16, 19.

16 Every prudent man acts out of knowledge,
but a fool exposes his folly.

17 A wicked messenger falls into trouble,
but a trustworthy envoy brings healing.

18 He who ignores discipline comes to poverty and shame,
but whoever heeds correction is honored.

19 A longing fulfilled is sweet to the soul,
but fools detest turning from evil.

20 He who walks with the wise grows wise,
but a companion of fools suffers harm.

21 Misfortune pursues the sinner,
but prosperity is the reward of the righteous.

22 A good man leaves an inheritance for his children's children,
but a sinner's wealth is stored up for the righteous.

23 A poor man's field may produce abundant food,
but injustice sweeps it away.

24 He who spares the rod hates his son,
but he who loves him is careful to discipline him.

25 The righteous eat to their hearts' content,
but the stomach of the wicked goes hungry.

14 The wise woman builds her house,
but with her own hands the foolish one tears hers down.

2 He whose walk is upright fears the LORD,
but he whose ways are devious despises him.

3 A fool's talk brings a rod to his back,
but the lips of the wise protect them.

4 Where there are no oxen, the manger is empty,
but from the strength of an ox comes an abundant harvest.

5 A truthful witness does not deceive,
but a false witness pours out lies.

6 The mocker seeks wisdom and finds none,
but knowledge comes easily to the discerning.

7 Stay away from a foolish man,
for you will not find knowledge on his lips.

8 The wisdom of the prudent is to give thought to their ways,
but the folly of fools is deception.

[9]Fools mock at making amends for sin,
but goodwill is found among the upright.

[10]Each heart knows its own bitterness,
and no one else can share its joy.

[11]The house of the wicked will be destroyed,
but the tent of the upright will flourish.

[12]There is a way that seems right to a man,
but in the end it leads to death.

[13]Even in laughter the heart may ache,
and joy may end in grief.

[14]The faithless will be fully repaid for their ways,
and the good man rewarded for his.

[15]A simple man believes anything,
but a prudent man gives thought to his steps.

[16]A wise man fears the LORD and shuns evil,
but a fool is hotheaded and reckless.

[17]A quick-tempered man does foolish things,
and a crafty man is hated.

[18]The simple inherit folly,
but the prudent are crowned with knowledge.

[19]Evil men will bow down in the presence of the good,
and the wicked at the gates of the righteous.

[20]The poor are shunned even by their neighbors,
but the rich have many friends.

[21]He who despises his neighbor sins,
but blessed is he who is kind to the needy.

[22]Do not those who plot evil go astray?
But those who plan what is good find[a] love and
faithfulness.

[23]All hard work brings a profit,
but mere talk leads only to poverty.

[24]The wealth of the wise is their crown,
but the folly of fools yields folly.

[25]A truthful witness saves lives,
but a false witness is deceitful.

[26]He who fears the LORD has a secure fortress,
and for his children it will be a refuge.

[a]22 Or *show*

He who despises his neighbor sins, but blessed is he who is kind to the needy.
Prov 14:21

14:9 *goodwill is found among the upright:* See the notes at 1:3 and 1:7.

14:11 *house of the wicked . . . tent of the upright:* Permanent houses made of brick and wood were meant to stand up to rain, wind, and heat better than tents. But the evil person's house (life) is more likely to be swept away because of the way he lives, while the tent of the upright person remains.

14:12 *a way that seems right:* See the note at 3:6. See also 16:25.

14:14 *fully repaid for their ways:* Meaning what one does and how one lives.

14:20 *poor . . . rich:* See the note at 10:15,16.

14:21 *blessed is he who is kind to the needy:* See the notes at 1:3 and 2:8,9. See also 14:31.

14:26,27 *fears the LORD . . . fortress:* See the note at 1:7. Fearing the LORD is closely connected to wisdom (1:7; 2:6-9).

14:23 Prov 6:6-11; 10:4, 8-14, 20; 12:11,27; 13:4; 28:19; Eccl 10:12-14.

14:27 *fountain of life:* See the note at 13:14.

14:31 *shows contempt for their Maker:* Meaning Israel's LORD God (see also Isa 43:1; 44:1,2,24). God's people were to share God's concern for the poor. Jesus made a similar statement when teaching his disciples about God's kingdom (see Matt 25:31-46).

14:34 *Righteousness exalts a nation . . . sin is a disgrace:* See the notes at 1:3 and 1:10.

15:3 *eyes of the LORD are everywhere:* Those who are foolish and evil cannot hide what they are doing. See also Job 31:4; 34:21; Prov 5:21; Jer 16:17; Zech 4:10.

15:5 *heeds correction:* See the notes at 10:17 and 13:24.

15:6 *righteous . . . great treasure . . . wicked . . . trouble:* See the note at 10:15,16.

15:8 *detests the sacrifice of the wicked:* This probably refers to the sacrifices offered in worship by those who do not live right (see the note at 1:3). These sacrifices are disgusting and worthless to the LORD. See also Isa 1:11-14.

27 The fear of the LORD is a fountain of life,
turning a man from the snares of death.

28 A large population is a king's glory,
but without subjects a prince is ruined.

29 A patient man has great understanding,
but a quick-tempered man displays folly.

30 A heart at peace gives life to the body,
but envy rots the bones.

31 He who oppresses the poor shows contempt for
their Maker,
but whoever is kind to the needy honors God.

32 When calamity comes, the wicked are brought down,
but even in death the righteous have a refuge.

33 Wisdom reposes in the heart of the discerning
and even among fools she lets herself be known.[a]

34 Righteousness exalts a nation,
but sin is a disgrace to any people.

35 A king delights in a wise servant,
but a shameful servant incurs his wrath.

15 A gentle answer turns away wrath,
but a harsh word stirs up anger.

2 The tongue of the wise commends knowledge,
but the mouth of the fool gushes folly.

3 The eyes of the LORD are everywhere,
keeping watch on the wicked and the good.

4 The tongue that brings healing is a tree of life,
but a deceitful tongue crushes the spirit.

5 A fool spurns his father's discipline,
but whoever heeds correction shows prudence.

6 The house of the righteous contains great treasure,
but the income of the wicked brings them trouble.

7 The lips of the wise spread knowledge;
not so the hearts of fools.

8 The LORD detests the sacrifice of the wicked,
but the prayer of the upright pleases him.

9 The LORD detests the way of the wicked
but he loves those who pursue righteousness.

[a]**33** Hebrew; Septuagint and Syriac / *but in the heart of fools she is not known*

[10] Stern discipline awaits him who leaves the path;
he who hates correction will die.

[11] Death and Destruction[a] lie open before the LORD—
how much more the hearts of men!

[12] A mocker resents correction;
he will not consult the wise.

[13] A happy heart makes the face cheerful,
but heartache crushes the spirit.

[14] The discerning heart seeks knowledge,
but the mouth of a fool feeds on folly.

[15] All the days of the oppressed are wretched,
but the cheerful heart has a continual feast.

[16] Better a little with the fear of the LORD
than great wealth with turmoil.

[17] Better a meal of vegetables where there is love
than a fattened calf with hatred.

[18] A hot-tempered man stirs up dissension,
but a patient man calms a quarrel.

[19] The way of the sluggard is blocked with thorns,
but the path of the upright is a highway.

[20] A wise son brings joy to his father,
but a foolish man despises his mother.

[21] Folly delights a man who lacks judgment,
but a man of understanding keeps a straight
course.

[22] Plans fail for lack of counsel,
but with many advisers they succeed.

[23] A man finds joy in giving an apt reply—
and how good is a timely word!

[24] The path of life leads upward for the wise
to keep him from going down to the grave.[b]

[25] The LORD tears down the proud man's house
but he keeps the widow's boundaries intact.

[26] The LORD detests the thoughts of the wicked,
but those of the pure are pleasing to him.

[27] A greedy man brings trouble to his family,
but he who hates bribes will live.

15:10 *leaves the path:* See the note at 3:6.

15:11 *Death and Destruction:* See the note at 5:5.

15:11 *open . . . hearts of men:* See the note at 3:3.

15:15-17 *Better a little . . . great wealth with turmoil:* Riches may help make one's life easier, but they are no substitute for being content and obeying the LORD. Here the rich are depicted as people who live difficult and complicated lives and who are forced to take their meals with people they can't trust.

15:19-21 *highway . . . straight course:* See the note at 3:6.

15:24 *The path of life leads upward:* See the note at 3:6.

15:25 *tears down the proud man's house . . . keeps the widow's boundaries intact:* See the note at 11:2. In the Bible, God is described as being especially concerned for widows and orphans (Deut 24:17; 27:14-26; Ps 68:5; Isa 1:16,17). Without adult male protection, they were powerless to defend themselves against those who wanted to steal from them. A widow's property might become stolen property by moving boundary markers. This was a crime forbidden in the Law (see Deut 19:14; Job 24:2-8; Prov 22:28).

15:20 Prov 10:1.

a11 Hebrew *Sheol and Abaddon* b24 Hebrew *Sheol*

15:28 *weighs its answers:* See the note at 12:23.

15:31 *life-giving rebuke:* See the note at 10:17.

15:33 *fear of the LORD:* See the note at 1:7.

16:1 *from the LORD:* The idea that the LORD controls all that happens in life is a common theme in wisdom literature (Prov 16:4, 9; Eccl 3:11-15).

16:4 *works out everything for his own ends:* Compare to Ecclesiastes 3:1-15. Those reasons may not always be clear to human minds.

16:5 *proud of heart:* See the note at 11:2. See also 15:25.

16:6 *Through love and faithfulness sin is atoned for:* "Love and faithfulness" here means to be faithful and loyal to God. Those who turn away from evil and back to God can be forgiven. See also Ps 51:1-14; Hos 14:1, 8, 9.

16:11 *Honest scales and balances:* See the note at 11:1.

16:12 *a throne is established through righteousness:* Those who rule with justice would have a large and faithful group of followers.

16:9 Prov 16:1,4.

28 The heart of the righteous weighs its answers,
but the mouth of the wicked gushes evil.

29 The LORD is far from the wicked
but he hears the prayer of the righteous.

30 A cheerful look brings joy to the heart,
and good news gives health to the bones.

31 He who listens to a life-giving rebuke
will be at home among the wise.

32 He who ignores discipline despises himself,
but whoever heeds correction gains understanding.

33 The fear of the LORD teaches a man wisdom,[a]
and humility comes before honor.

16 To man belong the plans of the heart,
but from the LORD comes the reply of the tongue.

2 All a man's ways seem innocent to him,
but motives are weighed by the LORD.

3 Commit to the LORD whatever you do,
and your plans will succeed.

4 The LORD works out everything for his own ends—
even the wicked for a day of disaster.

5 The LORD detests all the proud of heart.
Be sure of this: They will not go unpunished.

6 Through love and faithfulness sin is atoned for;
through the fear of the LORD a man avoids evil.

7 When a man's ways are pleasing to the LORD,
he makes even his enemies live at peace
with him.

8 Better a little with righteousness
than much gain with injustice.

9 In his heart a man plans his course,
but the LORD determines his steps.

10 The lips of a king speak as an oracle,
and his mouth should not betray justice.

11 Honest scales and balances are from the LORD;
all the weights in the bag are of his making.

12 Kings detest wrongdoing,
for a throne is established through righteousness.

---

[a]**33** Or *Wisdom teaches the fear of the LORD*

13 Kings take pleasure in honest lips;
they value a man who speaks the truth.

14 A king's wrath is a messenger of death,
but a wise man will appease it.

15 When a king's face brightens, it means life;
his favor is like a rain cloud in spring.

16 How much better to get wisdom than gold,
to choose understanding rather than silver!

17 The highway of the upright avoids evil;
he who guards his way guards his life.

18 Pride goes before destruction,
a haughty spirit before a fall.

19 Better to be lowly in spirit and among the oppressed
than to share plunder with the proud.

20 Whoever gives heed to instruction prospers,
and blessed is he who trusts in the LORD.

21 The wise in heart are called discerning,
and pleasant words promote instruction.[a]

22 Understanding is a fountain of life to those who have it,
but folly brings punishment to fools.

23 A wise man's heart guides his mouth,
and his lips promote instruction.[b]

24 Pleasant words are a honeycomb,
sweet to the soul and healing to the bones.

25 There is a way that seems right to a man,
but in the end it leads to death.

26 The laborer's appetite works for him;
his hunger drives him on.

27 A scoundrel plots evil,
and his speech is like a scorching fire.

28 A perverse man stirs up dissension,
and a gossip separates close friends.

29 A violent man entices his neighbor
and leads him down a path that is not good.

30 He who winks with his eye is plotting perversity;
he who purses his lips is bent on evil.

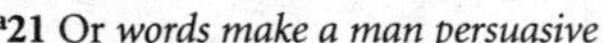

[a]21 Or *words make a man persuasive* [b]23 Or *mouth / and makes his lips persuasive*

Pride goes before destruction, a haughty spirit before a fall.
Prov 16:18

16:16 *better to get wisdom than gold:* See the note at 10:15,16.

16:18 *Pride goes before destruction:* See 13:10 and the note at 11:2.

16:22 *Understanding is a fountain of life:* See the note at 13:14.

16:26 *hunger drives him on:* Physical hunger can motivate a person to work hard at growing and harvesting food or earning money to buy it. See also 2 Thes 3:10.

16:30 *winks . . . purses his lips:* See 6:13 and the note at 6:12,13.

16:14 Esth 7:7-10; Prov 19:12; Rom 13:1-4. **16:19** Prov 3:34. **16:25** Prov 14:12. **16:27,28** Prov 10:10; 11:13.

31 Gray hair is a crown of splendor;
it is attained by a righteous life.

32 Better a patient man than a warrior,
a man who controls his temper than one who
takes a city.

33 The lot is cast into the lap,
but its every decision is from the LORD.

17 Better a dry crust with peace and quiet
than a house full of feasting,[a] with strife.

2 A wise servant will rule over a disgraceful son,
and will share the inheritance as one of the brothers.

3 The crucible for silver and the furnace for gold,
but the LORD tests the heart.

4 A wicked man listens to evil lips;
a liar pays attention to a malicious tongue.

5 He who mocks the poor shows contempt for their Maker;
whoever gloats over disaster will not go unpunished.

6 Children's children are a crown to the aged,
and parents are the pride of their children.

7 Arrogant[b] lips are unsuited to a fool—
how much worse lying lips to a ruler!

8 A bribe is a charm to the one who gives it;
wherever he turns, he succeeds.

9 He who covers over an offense promotes love,
but whoever repeats the matter separates close friends.

10 A rebuke impresses a man of discernment
more than a hundred lashes a fool.

11 An evil man is bent only on rebellion;
a merciless official will be sent against him.

12 Better to meet a bear robbed of her cubs
than a fool in his folly.

13 If a man pays back evil for good,
evil will never leave his house.

14 Starting a quarrel is like breaching a dam;
so drop the matter before a dispute breaks out.

15 Acquitting the guilty and condemning the innocent—
the LORD detests them both.

[a]1 Hebrew *sacrifices* [b]7 Or *Eloquent*

16:31 *Gray hair is a crown of splendor . . . righteous life:* Meaning that someone who has followed wisdom has lived right (see the note at 1:3) and has been blessed with a long life (3:16; 20:29).

16:33 *lot is cast . . . every decision is from the LORD:* In Hebrew, this verse refers to the practice of casting lots in order to make a decision. The lots could be sticks of different lengths or various kinds of stones. A decision was made based on which stick or stone was chosen. But this verse makes the point that even if lots are cast, the LORD determines which one is chosen, and so the LORD is in control of what happens (see the note at 16:1). See also Exod 28:30.

17:2 *A wise servant . . . share the inheritance:* Israelite law did not provide for servants to receive an inheritance. But a wise servant may receive more favorable treatment than a disobedient child (see also 12:24; 13:24 and the note).

17:3 *silver . . . gold . . . the LORD tests the heart:* Precious metals such as silver and gold were made more pure by a refining process called smelting. Metal ore was heated in a furnace at very high temperatures. When the ore melted, the precious metal could easily be separated from the impure materials (called slag) because they were different weights. In a similar way, the LORD tests the thoughts of his people (see also 15:11; 16:2; Isa 1:25; Ezek 22:18-22).

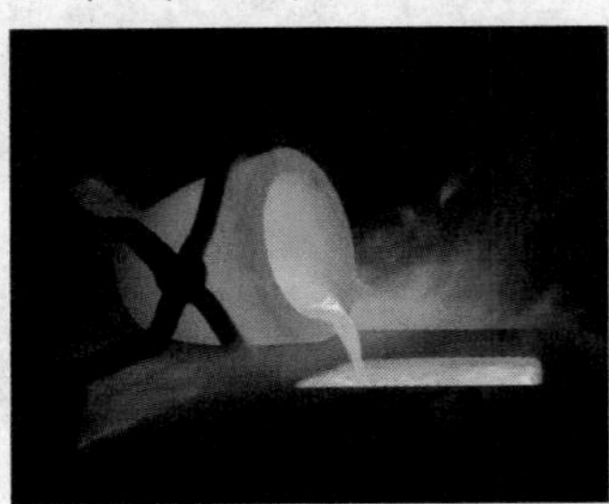

17:5 *mocks the poor shows contempt for their Maker:* See the notes at 2:8, 9 and 14:31.

17:1 Prov 15:17.

[16]Of what use is money in the hand of a fool,
since he has no desire to get wisdom?

[17]A friend loves at all times,
and a brother is born for adversity.

[18]A man lacking in judgment strikes hands in pledge
and puts up security for his neighbor.

[19]He who loves a quarrel loves sin;
he who builds a high gate invites destruction.

[20]A man of perverse heart does not prosper;
he whose tongue is deceitful falls into trouble.

[21]To have a fool for a son brings grief;
there is no joy for the father of a fool.

[22]A cheerful heart is good medicine,
but a crushed spirit dries up the bones.

[23]A wicked man accepts a bribe in secret
to pervert the course of justice.

[24]A discerning man keeps wisdom in view,
but a fool's eyes wander to the ends of the earth.

[25]A foolish son brings grief to his father
and bitterness to the one who bore him.

[26]It is not good to punish an innocent man,
or to flog officials for their integrity.

[27]A man of knowledge uses words with restraint,
and a man of understanding is even-tempered.

[28]Even a fool is thought wise if he keeps silent,
and discerning if he holds his tongue.

18 An unfriendly man pursues selfish ends;
he defies all sound judgment.

[2]A fool finds no pleasure in understanding
but delights in airing his own opinions.

[3]When wickedness comes, so does contempt,
and with shame comes disgrace.

[4]The words of a man's mouth are deep waters,
but the fountain of wisdom is a bubbling
brook.

[5]It is not good to be partial to the wicked
or to deprive the innocent of justice.

[6]A fool's lips bring him strife,
and his mouth invites a beating.

17:8 *bribe is a charm:* This verse is not meant to encourage secret bribes (as described in 17:23), but rather makes the point that the common practice of giving a gift in order to receive a favor in return was very effective. See also 18:16; 21:14.

17:10 *rebuke impresses a man of discernment:* See the notes at 10:17 and 13:24. See also 12:1; 13:1; 15:5, 31.

17:18 *A man lacking in judgment strikes hands . . . puts up security:* See 11:15 and the note at 6:1-3.

17:23 *wicked man accepts a bribe in secret:* It may have been common for those with money to bribe judges so they could escape punishment for a crime they committed or to get a ruling in their favor.

18:4 *fountain of wisdom:* See the note at 13:14.

18:6 *A fool's lips bring him strife:* See the note at 10:8-14.

17:21 Prov 10:1; 17:25. **17:25** Prov 10:1; 17:21. **17:27,28** Job 13:5; Prov 10:19; 12:23.

From the fruit of his mouth a man's stomach is filled; with the harvest from his lips he is satisfied.
Prov 18:20

18:10 *The name of the LORD is a strong tower:* The LORD is often described as a fortress or tower of protection (see also Ps 18:1,2; 91:2). The foolish rich rely on their money for protection rather than relying on the LORD (see the note at 10:15,16).

18:12 *proud . . . humility:* See the note at 11:2.

18:16 *A gift:* See the note at 17:8.

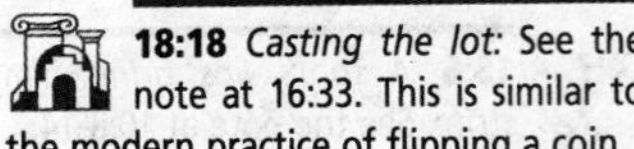

18:18 *Casting the lot:* See the note at 16:33. This is similar to the modern practice of flipping a coin.

18:22 *He who finds a wife finds what is good:* See the note at 12:4.

19:1 *poor man whose walk is blameless:* See 16:19 and the notes at 1:3 and 10:15,16.

18:8 Prov 26:22. **18:21** Prov 10:8-14; 18:6.

7 A fool's mouth is his undoing,
and his lips are a snare to his soul.

8 The words of a gossip are like choice morsels;
they go down to a man's inmost parts.

9 One who is slack in his work
is brother to one who destroys.

10 The name of the LORD is a strong tower;
the righteous run to it and are safe.

11 The wealth of the rich is their fortified city;
they imagine it an unscalable wall.

12 Before his downfall a man's heart is proud,
but humility comes before honor.

13 He who answers before listening—
that is his folly and his shame.

14 A man's spirit sustains him in sickness,
but a crushed spirit who can bear?

15 The heart of the discerning acquires knowledge;
the ears of the wise seek it out.

16 A gift opens the way for the giver
and ushers him into the presence of the great.

17 The first to present his case seems right,
till another comes forward and questions him.

18 Casting the lot settles disputes
and keeps strong opponents apart.

19 An offended brother is more unyielding than
a fortified city,
and disputes are like the barred gates of a citadel.

20 From the fruit of his mouth a man's stomach is filled;
with the harvest from his lips he is satisfied.

21 The tongue has the power of life and death,
and those who love it will eat its fruit.

22 He who finds a wife finds what is good
and receives favor from the LORD.

23 A poor man pleads for mercy,
but a rich man answers harshly.

24 A man of many companions may come to ruin,
but there is a friend who sticks closer than a brother.

19 Better a poor man whose walk is blameless
than a fool whose lips are perverse.

2 It is not good to have zeal without knowledge,
nor to be hasty and miss the way.

3 A man's own folly ruins his life,
yet his heart rages against the LORD.

4 Wealth brings many friends,
but a poor man's friend deserts him.

5 A false witness will not go unpunished,
and he who pours out lies will not go free.

6 Many curry favor with a ruler,
and everyone is the friend of a man who
gives gifts.

7 A poor man is shunned by all his relatives—
how much more do his friends avoid him!
Though he pursues them with pleading,
they are nowhere to be found.[a]

8 He who gets wisdom loves his own soul;
he who cherishes understanding prospers.

9 A false witness will not go unpunished,
and he who pours out lies will perish.

10 It is not fitting for a fool to live in luxury—
how much worse for a slave to rule over princes!

11 A man's wisdom gives him patience;
it is to his glory to overlook an offense.

12 A king's rage is like the roar of a lion,
but his favor is like dew on the grass.

13 A foolish son is his father's ruin,
and a quarrelsome wife is like a constant dripping.

14 Houses and wealth are inherited from parents,
but a prudent wife is from the LORD.

15 Laziness brings on deep sleep,
and the shiftless man goes hungry.

16 He who obeys instructions guards his life,
but he who is contemptuous of his ways will die.

17 He who is kind to the poor lends to the LORD,
and he will reward him for what he has done.

18 Discipline your son, for in that there is hope;
do not be a willing party to his death.

[a]7 The meaning of the Hebrew for this sentence is uncertain.

19:4 *Wealth brings many friends:* Some people become friends with rich people for selfish reasons.

19:7 *poor:* The poor were at or near the bottom of the social ladder in ancient Israel. People did not want to make friends with someone who had very little. See also the mini-article called "The Poor," p. 2362.

19:10 *fool . . . slave to rule:* Neither extreme fit with what was expected in Israelite society. A slave would not rule in place of a king, unless that king had foolishly given up his authority or mistreated others so that they rebelled.

19:14 *prudent wife:* See 18:22 and the note at 12:4.

19:15 *Laziness:* See the note at 6:10,11. See also 10:4,5; 20:13; 24:33,34.

19:16 *instructions:* See the notes at 1:8,9; 6:23; and 13:13.

19:17 *kind to the poor:* This was expected of those who wanted to do right (see the note at 2:8,9).

19:18 *Discipline your son:* See 3:12 and the note at 13:24.

19:13 Prov 10:1; 17:21, 25; 21:19.

Stop listening to instruction, my son, and you will stray from the words of knowledge.
Prov 19:27

19:20 *accept instruction:* See the note at 10:17.

19:21 *it is the LORD's purpose that prevails:* See the notes at 16:1 and 16:33.

19:23 *fear of the LORD:* See 9:10 and the note at 1:7.

19:28 *corrupt witness:* See the notes at 6:12,13 and 17:23.

20:4 *A sluggard does not plow in season:* See the note at 6:10,11.

20:7 *righteous man leads a blameless life:* See the note at 2:8,9.

19:24 Prov 6:10,11; 10:4,5; 19:15; 20:13; 24:33,34. **19:26** Prov 10:1; 17:21; 19:13. **20:2** Prov 19:12. **20:5** Prov 18:4.

19 A hot-tempered man must pay the penalty;
if you rescue him, you will have to do it again.

20 Listen to advice and accept instruction,
and in the end you will be wise.

21 Many are the plans in a man's heart,
but it is the LORD's purpose that prevails.

22 What a man desires is unfailing love[a];
better to be poor than a liar.

23 The fear of the LORD leads to life:
Then one rests content, untouched by trouble.

24 The sluggard buries his hand in the dish;
he will not even bring it back to his mouth!

25 Flog a mocker, and the simple will learn prudence;
rebuke a discerning man, and he will gain
knowledge.

26 He who robs his father and drives out his mother
is a son who brings shame and disgrace.

27 Stop listening to instruction, my son,
and you will stray from the words of knowledge.

28 A corrupt witness mocks at justice,
and the mouth of the wicked gulps down evil.

29 Penalties are prepared for mockers,
and beatings for the backs of fools.

20 Wine is a mocker and beer a brawler;
whoever is led astray by them is not wise.

2 A king's wrath is like the roar of a lion;
he who angers him forfeits his life.

3 It is to a man's honor to avoid strife,
but every fool is quick to quarrel.

DO NOT QUARREL

4 A sluggard does not plow in season;
so at harvest time he looks but finds nothing.

5 The purposes of a man's heart are deep waters,
but a man of understanding draws them out.

6 Many a man claims to have unfailing love,
but a faithful man who can find?

7 The righteous man leads a blameless life;
blessed are his children after him.

[a]22 Or *A man's greed is his shame*

8 When a king sits on his throne to judge,
he winnows out all evil with his eyes.

9 Who can say, "I have kept my heart pure;
I am clean and without sin"?

10 Differing weights and differing measures—
the LORD detests them both.

11 Even a child is known by his actions,
by whether his conduct is pure and right.

12 Ears that hear and eyes that see—
the LORD has made them both.

13 Do not love sleep or you will grow poor;
stay awake and you will have food to spare.

14 "It's no good, it's no good!" says the buyer;
then off he goes and boasts about his purchase.

15 Gold there is, and rubies in abundance,
but lips that speak knowledge are a rare jewel.

16 Take the garment of one who puts up security for a stranger;
hold it in pledge if he does it for a wayward woman.

17 Food gained by fraud tastes sweet to a man,
but he ends up with a mouth full of gravel.

18 Make plans by seeking advice;
if you wage war, obtain guidance.

19 A gossip betrays a confidence;
so avoid a man who talks too much.

20 If a man curses his father or mother,
his lamp will be snuffed out in pitch darkness.

21 An inheritance quickly gained at the beginning
will not be blessed at the end.

22 Do not say, "I'll pay you back for this wrong!"
Wait for the LORD, and he will deliver you.

23 The LORD detests differing weights,
and dishonest scales do not please him.

24 A man's steps are directed by the LORD.
How then can anyone understand his own way?

25 It is a trap for a man to dedicate something rashly
and only later to consider his vows.

26 A wise king winnows out the wicked;
he drives the threshing wheel over them.

20:9 *kept my heart pure . . . clean and without sin:* This form of question in Hebrew assumes a negative answer. See also Job 14:4 and Rom 3:23.

20:10 *Differing weights and differing measures:* See the note at 11:1.

20:16 *Take the garment . . . hold it in pledge:* See the note at 6:1-3. See also Amos 2:6-8.

20:20 *snuffed out in pitch darkness:* In Hebrew this literally is "their lamp will go out," meaning they will die prematurely. See the notes at 13:9 and 5:5.

20:24 *directed by the LORD:* See 19:21 and the notes at 16:1 and 16:33.

20:25 *dedicate something rashly:* Making a promise to God or in God's name was a serious commitment. This saying warns against making promises that one could not or did not intend to keep. See also the mini-article called "Making Vows," p. 328.

20:13 Prov 6:10,11; 10:4,5; 19:15; 19:24; 20:4; 24:33,34.

20:27 *the lamp of the* LORD *. . . inmost being:* The Law of the LORD was also called a lamp (see the note at 6:23; see also Ps 119:105). The "inmost being" here probably refers to the wisdom and common sense that the LORD gives (2:6). See also the note at 3:3.

20:29 *gray hair the splendor of the old:* See the note at 16:31.

21:1 *The king's heart is in the hand of the* LORD *. . . directs it:* Israel's LORD, the Creator of all things (14:31), is said to control the actions of rulers just as he controls the direction a river will flow. Not only did the LORD control Israel's rulers, but the rulers of other nations as well (see Isa 44:28—45:4). See also the notes at 16:1 and 16:33.

21:2 *the* LORD *weighs the heart:* See the note at 3:3. Outward actions are visible to everyone, but the LORD also knows secret thoughts and motives (Ps 139:15,16,23; Prov 16:2; 24:12).

21:3 *To do what is right and just is more acceptable . . . than sacrifice:* See the note at 2:8,9. Israel's prophets made it clear that offerings given to the LORD were worthless, if the people did not also live right (Isa 1:10-17; Amos 5:21-24; Mic 6:6-8).

21:12 *The Righteous One:* See the notes on p. 1193 (Foolishness and wisdom) and at 16:4. See also Job 34:10-13.

21:13 *shuts his ears to the cry of the poor:* See the note at 2:8,9.

20:30 Prov 10:13; 14:3; 19:29.

27 The lamp of the LORD searches the spirit of a man[a];
it searches out his inmost being.

28 Love and faithfulness keep a king safe;
through love his throne is made secure.

29 The glory of young men is their strength,
gray hair the splendor of the old.

30 Blows and wounds cleanse away evil,
and beatings purge the inmost being.

21 The king's heart is in the hand of the LORD;
he directs it like a watercourse wherever he pleases.

2 All a man's ways seem right to him,
but the LORD weighs the heart.

3 To do what is right and just
is more acceptable to the LORD than sacrifice.

4 Haughty eyes and a proud heart,
the lamp of the wicked, are sin!

5 The plans of the diligent lead to profit
as surely as haste leads to poverty.

6 A fortune made by a lying tongue
is a fleeting vapor and a deadly snare.[b]

7 The violence of the wicked will drag them away,
for they refuse to do what is right.

8 The way of the guilty is devious,
but the conduct of the innocent is upright.

9 Better to live on a corner of the roof
than share a house with a quarrelsome wife.

10 The wicked man craves evil;
his neighbor gets no mercy from him.

11 When a mocker is punished, the simple gain wisdom;
when a wise man is instructed, he gets knowledge.

12 The Righteous One[c] takes note of the house of the wicked
and brings the wicked to ruin.

13 If a man shuts his ears to the cry of the poor,
he too will cry out and not be answered.

---

[a]**27** Or *The spirit of man is the LORD's lamp* [b]**6** Some Hebrew manuscripts, Septuagint and Vulgate; most Hebrew manuscripts *vapor for those who seek death*
[c]**12** Or *The righteous man*

14 A gift given in secret soothes anger,
and a bribe concealed in the cloak pacifies great wrath.

15 When justice is done, it brings joy to the righteous
but terror to evildoers.

16 A man who strays from the path of understanding
comes to rest in the company of the dead.

17 He who loves pleasure will become poor;
whoever loves wine and oil will never be rich.

18 The wicked become a ransom for the righteous,
and the unfaithful for the upright.

19 Better to live in a desert
than with a quarrelsome and ill-tempered wife.

20 In the house of the wise are stores of choice food and oil,
but a foolish man devours all he has.

21 He who pursues righteousness and love
finds life, prosperity[a] and honor.

22 A wise man attacks the city of the mighty
and pulls down the stronghold in which they trust.

23 He who guards his mouth and his tongue
keeps himself from calamity.

24 The proud and arrogant man—"Mocker" is his name;
he behaves with overweening pride.

25 The sluggard's craving will be the death of him,
because his hands refuse to work.
26 All day long he craves for more,
but the righteous give without sparing.

27 The sacrifice of the wicked is detestable—
how much more so when brought with evil intent!

28 A false witness will perish,
and whoever listens to him will be destroyed forever.[b]

29 A wicked man puts up a bold front,
but an upright man gives thought to his ways.

30 There is no wisdom, no insight, no plan
that can succeed against the LORD.

31 The horse is made ready for the day of battle,
but victory rests with the LORD.

22 A good name is more desirable than great riches;
to be esteemed is better than silver or gold.

[a]21 Or *righteousness* [b]28 Or / *but the words of an obedient man will live on*

21:14 *a bribe concealed:* See the note at 17:8.

21:15 *justice:* See the note at 1:3. See also 10:27-29.

21:24 *proud and arrogant:* See the note at 11:2.

21:25 *his hands refuse to work:* See the note at 6:10, 11. See also 10:4, 5; 19:15; 24:33, 34.

21:27 *sacrifice of the wicked is detestable:* See the note at 21:3.

21:28 *A false witness will perish:* See the notes at 6:12, 13 and 17:23.

21:30 *no wisdom, no insight, no plan that can succeed against the LORD:* It is impossible to trick or outguess the LORD, who knows what is in every heart and mind (see the note at 21:2).

21:31 *horse is made ready for the day of battle:* Ancient armies that used horses for cavalry and chariots had an advantage in battle. When Israel first settled in Canaan they did not have horses to use in battle. Instead they were expected to rely on the LORD's help. See also the mini-article called "Holy War (The LORD's Battles)," p. 306.

22:1 *A good name:* See the note at 10:7.

21:21 Prov 3:3; 10:27-29; 14:21.
21:22 Prov 24:5; Eccl 9:13-16,18.

A prudent man sees danger and takes refuge, but the simple keep going and suffer for it.
Prov 22:3

22:4 *Humility and the fear of the* L*ORD* *bring wealth and honor and life:* See the note at 1:7.

22:5 *In the paths of the wicked lie thorns and snares:* See the note at 3:6.

22:6 *Train a child:* Teach children wisdom (4:1-5; 6:20-22) and correct them (3:12; 13:24) when necessary. See also Deut 6:4-9.

22:7 *the borrower is servant to the lender:* Some moneylenders charged high interest on loans, which made it hard for people to repay their debts in full. Sometimes people had to become slaves of their creditors in order to work off their debts.

2 Rich and poor have this in common:
The LORD is the Maker of them all.

3 A prudent man sees danger and takes refuge,
but the simple keep going and suffer for it.

4 Humility and the fear of the LORD
bring wealth and honor and life.

5 In the paths of the wicked lie thorns and snares,
but he who guards his soul stays far from them.

6 Train[a] a child in the way he should go,
and when he is old he will not turn from it.

7 The rich rule over the poor,
and the borrower is servant to the lender.

8 He who sows wickedness reaps trouble,
and the rod of his fury will be destroyed.

9 A generous man will himself be blessed,
for he shares his food with the poor.

10 Drive out the mocker, and out goes strife;
quarrels and insults are ended.

11 He who loves a pure heart and whose speech is gracious
will have the king for his friend.

[a]6 Or *Start*

QUESTIONS ABOUT PROVERBS 10:1—22:16

1. According to PROVERBS, how can riches be both a blessing (10:22) and a curse? (11:28; 13:8) What does it mean that one can become rich by being generous, or poor by being greedy? (11:24)
2. A number of proverbs mention foolish talk, gossip, and mean or hurtful comments. Why is it true that "he who holds his tongue is wise"? (10:19) In your opinion, does our modern society place enough emphasis on speaking respectfully and carefully? Why or why not?
3. A number of proverbs emphasize the importance of hard work. (10:4, 26; 12:11, 27) Why? What value is placed on hard work in modern society? Should more or less value be placed on work? Why?
4. How are the following images used in connection with wisdom and doing right: light (13:9); fountain (13:14); highway (15:19)? What other images might be used to describe "wisdom"?
5. The sayings in PROVERBS are over two thousand years old. It has been said that true wisdom is timeless. What does that mean? Give two or three examples of proverbs in this section (10:1—22:16) that may be described as "timeless wisdom." Explain. Which proverbs, if any, do you believe are not timeless, that do not make sense today?
6. Read 16:1-4, 33 and 21:1. What do these passages have in common? What do you think about the idea that God controls everything that happens?

[12]The eyes of the LORD keep watch over knowledge,
but he frustrates the words of the unfaithful.

[13]The sluggard says, "There is a lion outside!"
or, "I will be murdered in the streets!"

[14]The mouth of an adulteress is a deep pit;
he who is under the LORD's wrath will fall into it.

[15]Folly is bound up in the heart of a child,
but the rod of discipline will drive it far from him.

[16]He who oppresses the poor to increase his wealth
and he who gives gifts to the rich—both come to
poverty.

Sayings of People with Wisdom

The next section of PROVERBS (22:17—24:34) includes the wisdom of wise people, but is not credited to Solomon. Some of the thirty sayings (22:17—24:22) are similar in style to wise sayings found in the Egyptian collection known as Wisdom of Amenemope, which was divided into thirty sections, or "houses." Most of the sayings in this section are of the instruction type.

SAYINGS OF THE WISE

[17]Pay attention and listen to the sayings of the wise;
apply your heart to what I teach,
[18]for it is pleasing when you keep them in your heart
and have all of them ready on your lips.
[19]So that your trust may be in the LORD,
I teach you today, even you.
[20]Have I not written thirty[a] sayings for you,
sayings of counsel and knowledge,
[21]teaching you true and reliable words,
so that you can give sound answers
to him who sent you?

[22]Do not exploit the poor because they are poor
and do not crush the needy in court,
[23]for the LORD will take up their case
and will plunder those who plunder them.

[24]Do not make friends with a hot-tempered man,
do not associate with one easily angered,
[25]or you may learn his ways
and get yourself ensnared.

[26]Do not be a man who strikes hands in pledge
or puts up security for debts;

[a]**20** Or *not formerly written*; or *not written excellent*

22:9 *A generous man will himself be blessed:* See the notes at 2:8, 9 and 11:24,25.

22:15 *rod of discipline:* See 22:6 and the note at 10:17.

22:17 *sayings of the wise:* Exactly who these "wise" people are is uncertain. This phrase functions like a title for the section.

22:19 *your trust may be in the LORD:* Compare to the purposes stated in 1:7 and 9:10.

22:20,21 *thirty sayings . . . true and reliable words:* The Egyptian Wisdom of Amenemope also had thirty sections, or "houses." The purpose of that Egyptian work is similar to the purpose stated here. The introduction to Amenemope says the wise sayings are given to help the listener answer the one who has spoken, or to report to the one who has sent him and to show him the paths of life.

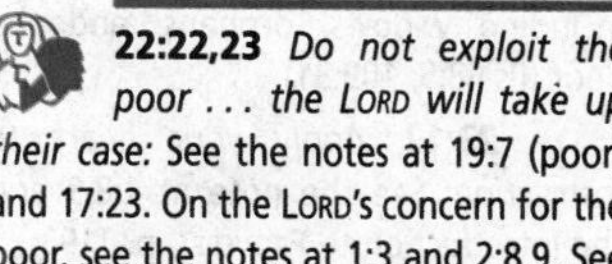

22:22,23 *Do not exploit the poor . . . the LORD will take up their case:* See the notes at 19:7 (poor) and 17:23. On the LORD's concern for the poor, see the notes at 1:3 and 2:8,9. See also 17:5; 22:9; Matt 25:31-46.

22:26 *strikes hands in pledge . . . security for debts:* See the note at 6:1-3. See also 17:18; 20:16.

22:28 *ancient boundary stone:* In ancient Israel, boundary stones were sacred because all property was a gift from the LORD. See Deut 19:14 and the note at Prov 15:25.

23:1-3 *dine with a ruler . . . put your knife to your throat:* How one acted at the table would be watched closely. This warns against gluttony. Verse 3 may also be a warning about how a feast might be used as a form of bribery to influence the guest.

23:10 *ancient boundary stone . . . fields of the fatherless:* See the notes at 15:25; 22:22,23; and 22:28.

23:11 *their Defender is strong:* According to Israelite law, a relative was supposed to step in and help a person who was having money trouble. This was done to make sure family land or property was not sold to nor taken by outsiders (Lev 25:25). A close relative could also take revenge for a relative's death (Num 35:16-19). In the same way, Israel's God would defend those who had no one else to stand up for them, including widows, orphans, and the poor (Ps 68:5; 109:31).

23:12 *Apply your heart to instruction:* See the note at 1:8,9 and the Introduction to PROVERBS, p. 1193.

23:13,14 *Do not withhold discipline:* See the notes at 10:17 and 13:24. See also 3:12 and 19:18.

22:29 Prov 12:24. **23:4,5** Prov 15:27; 28:20; Eccl 2:4-11, 18-24; Heb 13:5.

27 if you lack the means to pay,
your very bed will be snatched from under you.

28 Do not move an ancient boundary stone
set up by your forefathers.

29 Do you see a man skilled in his work?
He will serve before kings;
he will not serve before obscure men.

23 When you sit to dine with a ruler,
note well what[a] is before you,
2 and put a knife to your throat
if you are given to gluttony.
3 Do not crave his delicacies,
for that food is deceptive.

4 Do not wear yourself out to get rich;
have the wisdom to show restraint.
5 Cast but a glance at riches, and they are gone,
for they will surely sprout wings
and fly off to the sky like an eagle.

6 Do not eat the food of a stingy man,
do not crave his delicacies;
7 for he is the kind of man
who is always thinking about the cost.[b]
"Eat and drink," he says to you,
but his heart is not with you.
8 You will vomit up the little you have eaten
and will have wasted your compliments.

9 Do not speak to a fool,
for he will scorn the wisdom of your words.

10 Do not move an ancient boundary stone
or encroach on the fields of the fatherless,
11 for their Defender is strong;
he will take up their case against you.

12 Apply your heart to instruction
and your ears to words of knowledge.

13 Do not withhold discipline from a child;
if you punish him with the rod, he will not die.
14 Punish him with the rod
and save his soul from death.[c]

15 My son, if your heart is wise,
then my heart will be glad;

---

[a]**1** Or *who* [b]**7** Or *for as he thinks within himself, / so he is*; or *for as he puts on a feast, / so he is* [c]**14** Hebrew *Sheol*

16 my inmost being will rejoice
when your lips speak what is right.

17 Do not let your heart envy sinners,
but always be zealous for the fear of the LORD.
18 There is surely a future hope for you,
and your hope will not be cut off.

19 Listen, my son, and be wise,
and keep your heart on the right path.
20 Do not join those who drink too much wine
or gorge themselves on meat,
21 for drunkards and gluttons become poor,
and drowsiness clothes them in rags.

22 Listen to your father, who gave you life,
and do not despise your mother when she is old.
23 Buy the truth and do not sell it;
get wisdom, discipline and understanding.
24 The father of a righteous man has great joy;
he who has a wise son delights in him.
25 May your father and mother be glad;
may she who gave you birth rejoice!

26 My son, give me your heart
and let your eyes keep to my ways,
27 for a prostitute is a deep pit
and a wayward wife is a narrow well.
28 Like a bandit she lies in wait,
and multiplies the unfaithful among men.

29 Who has woe? Who has sorrow?
Who has strife? Who has complaints?
Who has needless bruises? Who has bloodshot
eyes?
30 Those who linger over wine,
who go to sample bowls of mixed wine.
31 Do not gaze at wine when it is red,
when it sparkles in the cup,
when it goes down smoothly!
32 In the end it bites like a snake
and poisons like a viper.
33 Your eyes will see strange sights
and your mind imagine confusing things.
34 You will be like one sleeping on the high seas,
lying on top of the rigging.
35 "They hit me," you will say, "but I'm not hurt!
They beat me, but I don't feel it!
When will I wake up
so I can find another drink?"

Buy the truth and do not sell it; get wisdom, discipline and understanding.
Prov 23:23

23:19 *the right path:* See the note at 3:6.

23:23 *truth . . . get wisdom, discipline and understanding:* See the notes at 8:6,7 and 1:2.

23:24 *righteous man:* See the note at 2:8,9.

23:27 *prostitute . . . wayward wife:* See the notes at 2:16,17 and 5:3. See also 5:1-23; 7:6-27.

23:29-35 *linger over wine . . . find another drink:* This section provides a graphic description of the effects of drinking too much. Wine may look good in the glass and taste good going down, but too much of it can cause a person to get sick or feel pain that's as bad as the effects of a snake bite. Drunkenness can cause a person to sleep as if on a rolling boat and to be bruised from bumping into things or falling down. Despite these bad effects, a person addicted to alcohol wants to start drinking again in the morning (23:35).

23:24,25 Prov 10:1; 27:11.

24 Do not envy wicked men,
do not desire their company;
2 for their hearts plot violence,
and their lips talk about making trouble.

3 By wisdom a house is built,
and through understanding it is established;
4 through knowledge its rooms are filled
with rare and beautiful treasures.

5 A wise man has great power,
and a man of knowledge increases strength;
6 for waging war you need guidance,
and for victory many advisers.

7 Wisdom is too high for a fool;
in the assembly at the gate he has nothing
to say.

8 He who plots evil
will be known as a schemer.
9 The schemes of folly are sin,
and men detest a mocker.

10 If you falter in times of trouble,
how small is your strength!

11 Rescue those being led away to death;
hold back those staggering toward
slaughter.
12 If you say, "But we knew nothing about this,"
does not he who weighs the heart perceive it?
Does not he who guards your life know it?
Will he not repay each person according to what he
has done?

13 Eat honey, my son, for it is good;
honey from the comb is sweet to your taste.
14 Know also that wisdom is sweet to your soul;
if you find it, there is a future hope for you,
and your hope will not be cut off.

15 Do not lie in wait like an outlaw against a righteous
man's house,
do not raid his dwelling place;
16 for though a righteous man falls seven times,
he rises again,
but the wicked are brought down by calamity.

17 Do not gloat when your enemy falls;
when he stumbles, do not let your heart
rejoice,

By wisdom a house is built, and through understanding it is established; through knowledge its rooms are filled with rare and beautiful treasures.
Prov 24:3,4

24:3 *By wisdom a house is built . . . established:* Compare this verse to the description of Wisdom building her house (see the note at 9:1).

24:5 *A wise man has great power:* See the note at 1:2.

24:12 *does not he who weighs the heart perceive it:* See the notes at 21:2 and on p. 1193 (Foolishness and wisdom).

24:16 *seven times:* Seven was considered a complete or perfect number. Here it stands for a very large number of times. Even good people, meaning those who obey the LORD, fall or experience hardship. See also Matt 18:21,22.

24:6 Prov 20:18.

18 or the LORD will see and disapprove
and turn his wrath away from him.

19 Do not fret because of evil men
or be envious of the wicked,
20 for the evil man has no future hope,
and the lamp of the wicked will be snuffed out.

21 Fear the LORD and the king, my son,
and do not join with the rebellious,
22 for those two will send sudden destruction
upon them,
and who knows what calamities they can bring?

FURTHER SAYINGS OF THE WISE

23 These also are sayings of the wise:

To show partiality in judging is not good:
24 Whoever says to the guilty, "You are innocent"—
peoples will curse him and nations denounce
him.
25 But it will go well with those who convict the guilty,
and rich blessing will come upon them.

26 An honest answer
is like a kiss on the lips.

27 Finish your outdoor work
and get your fields ready;
after that, build your house.

28 Do not testify against your neighbor without cause,
or use your lips to deceive.
29 Do not say, "I'll do to him as he has done to me;
I'll pay that man back for what he did."

30 I went past the field of the sluggard,
past the vineyard of the man who lacks
judgment;
31 thorns had come up everywhere,
the ground was covered with weeds,
and the stone wall was in ruins.
32 I applied my heart to what I observed
and learned a lesson from what I saw:
33 A little sleep, a little slumber,
a little folding of the hands to rest—
34 and poverty will come on you like a bandit
and scarcity like an armed man.[a]

24:20 *the lamp of the wicked will be snuffed out:* See the notes at 13:9 and 20:20.

24:21,22 *Fear the LORD and the king:* See the note at 1:7. Respecting and not rebelling against a king was sound advice, since an angry king had the authority to punish a disobedient person (16:14; 19:12). See also Rom 13:1-7.

24:23 *also are sayings of the wise:* The sayings in 24:23-34 are related to the sayings described in 22:17-21, but exactly who created these sayings is unclear.

24:23-25 *To show partiality in judging is not good:* Judges are to be honest and fair in their decisions (18:5) and not take bribe money (28:21). See also Lev 19:15; Deut 1:16,17; 16:18,19.

24:27 *get your fields ready:* This may refer to a young farmer working to build a livelihood before building a home, but it probably has the more general meaning of doing things in the proper order. A similar modern saying might be, "First things first."

24:30-34 *the field of the sluggard . . . scarcity:* See the note at 6:10,11.

24:33,34 Prov 6:10,11.

[a]**34** Or *like a vagrant / and scarcity like a beggar*

25:1 *proverbs of Solomon, copied by the men of Hezekiah king of Judah:* See the note on p. 1193 (King Solomon). After Solomon died, the united Israel divided into two separate kingdoms. The southern kingdom was named Judah, which Hezekiah ruled from 715 to 687 B.C., or over 200 years after the time of Solomon. Hezekiah was responsible for a religious reform in the country (2 Kgs 18:1-7). Such a time may have awakened interest in ancient wisdom, so that court officials and teachers researched ancient wisdom sayings and perhaps edited them or even added new ones of their own.

25:2,3 *glory of God to conceal a matter; to search out a matter is the glory of kings:* Human beings are to praise God, because God is beyond human understanding (Job 26:12-14; 37:14-24; Isa 40:12-26; Rom 11:33-36). The wise ruler who can explain certain mysteries is also to be highly respected. Knowing the mind of such a ruler is as difficult as trying to measure the extent of the heavens and earth.

25:4,5 *Remove the dross . . . remove the wicked:* See the note at 17:3. The LORD's purifying of the people is often compared to the process of purifying metal (Isa 48:9-11; Ezek 22:18-22; Mal 3:2,3). A just ruler will purify his or her country by removing evildoers (see also Isa 11:1-5).

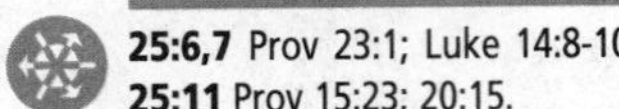

25:6,7 Prov 23:1; Luke 14:8-10.
25:11 Prov 15:23; 20:15.

Solomon's Proverbs Copied by Hezekiah

Chapters 25–29 include a number of proverbs connected to King Solomon but copied by officials who served King Hezekiah of Judah. While the sayings in chapters 25–27 are of various kinds of proverbs, most of the sayings in chapters 28 and 29 follow the "opposite parallel" form that is common in chapters 10–16.

MORE PROVERBS OF SOLOMON

25 These are more proverbs of Solomon, copied by the men of
Hezekiah king of Judah:

2 It is the glory of God to conceal a matter;
to search out a matter is the glory of kings.

3 As the heavens are high and the earth is deep,
so the hearts of kings are unsearchable.

4 Remove the dross from the silver,
and out comes material for[a] the silversmith;
5 remove the wicked from the king's presence,
and his throne will be established through righteousness.

6 Do not exalt yourself in the king's presence,
and do not claim a place among great men;
7 it is better for him to say to you, "Come up here,"
than for him to humiliate you before a nobleman.

What you have seen with your eyes
8 do not bring[b] hastily to court,
for what will you do in the end
if your neighbor puts you to shame?

9 If you argue your case with a neighbor,
do not betray another man's confidence,
10 or he who hears it may shame you
and you will never lose your bad reputation.

11 A word aptly spoken
is like apples of gold in settings of silver.

12 Like an earring of gold or an ornament of fine gold
is a wise man's rebuke to a listening ear.

13 Like the coolness of snow at harvest time
is a trustworthy messenger to those who send him;
he refreshes the spirit of his masters.

[a]**4** Or *comes a vessel from* [b]**7,8** Or *nobleman / on whom you had set your eyes. / 8 Do not go*

Serpentine Bracelet and Ring with Gold Stud, from around 350 to 300 B.C. All of the cultures in the ancient Near East valued gold and silver, and they all used these precious metals to make jewelry. Archaeologists, however, have found fewer examples of elaborate jewelry from the lands occupied by the Israelites than from among their neighbors (Persians, Greeks, and Egyptians). It is not surprising then for the Israelite authors of PROVERBS to contradict conventional values and to say that wisdom is more valuable than even the most beautiful piece of jewelry. (See 3:13-15; 25:11,12.)

14 Like clouds and wind without rain
is a man who boasts of gifts he does not give.

15 Through patience a ruler can be persuaded,
and a gentle tongue can break a bone.

16 If you find honey, eat just enough—
too much of it, and you will vomit.
17 Seldom set foot in your neighbor's house—
too much of you, and he will hate you.

18 Like a club or a sword or a sharp arrow
is the man who gives false testimony against
his neighbor.

19 Like a bad tooth or a lame foot
is reliance on the unfaithful in times of trouble.

20 Like one who takes away a garment on a cold day,
or like vinegar poured on soda,
is one who sings songs to a heavy heart.

21 If your enemy is hungry, give him food to eat;
if he is thirsty, give him water to drink.
22 In doing this, you will heap burning coals on his head,
and the LORD will reward you.

23 As a north wind brings rain,
so a sly tongue brings angry looks.

24 Better to live on a corner of the roof
than share a house with a quarrelsome wife.

25:14 *boasts of gifts he does not give:* See the note at 20:25.

25:15 *patience . . . a gentle tongue:* This is good advice, especially for those who negotiate or debate with a king. See also 15:1, 18; 24:21,22.

25:21,22 *enemy is hungry . . . heap burning coals:* The opposite of taking revenge or getting even (Lev 24:20), this saying shows the importance of being kind to one's enemy, or "turning the other cheek" (Matt 5:38-41). In an ancient Egyptian ritual, a person who had done wrong was to carry a bowl of hot coals on his head to show that he was sorry for what he had done. Perhaps this saying means that kindness will cause a guilty person to be sorry for the hurt he or she may have caused. See also Rom 12:20.

25:24 Prov 21:9.

25 Like cold water to a weary soul
is good news from a distant land.

26 Like a muddied spring or a polluted well
is a righteous man who gives way to the wicked.

27 It is not good to eat too much honey,
nor is it honorable to seek one's own honor.

28 Like a city whose walls are broken down
is a man who lacks self-control.

26 Like snow in summer or rain in harvest,
honor is not fitting for a fool.

2 Like a fluttering sparrow or a darting swallow,
an undeserved curse does not come to rest.

3 A whip for the horse, a halter for the donkey,
and a rod for the backs of fools!

4 Do not answer a fool according to his folly,
or you will be like him yourself.

5 Answer a fool according to his folly,
or he will be wise in his own eyes.

6 Like cutting off one's feet or drinking violence
is the sending of a message by the hand of
a fool.

7 Like a lame man's legs that hang limp
is a proverb in the mouth of a fool.

8 Like tying a stone in a sling
is the giving of honor to a fool.

9 Like a thornbush in a drunkard's hand
is a proverb in the mouth of a fool.

10 Like an archer who wounds at random
is he who hires a fool or any passer-by.

11 As a dog returns to its vomit,
so a fool repeats his folly.

12 Do you see a man wise in his own eyes?
There is more hope for a fool than for him.

13 The sluggard says, "There is a lion in the road,
a fierce lion roaming the streets!"

14 As a door turns on its hinges,
so a sluggard turns on his bed.

15 The sluggard buries his hand in the dish;
he is too lazy to bring it back to his mouth.

25:28 *a city whose walls are broken down:* Many ancient cities were surrounded by walls as a protection against enemies.

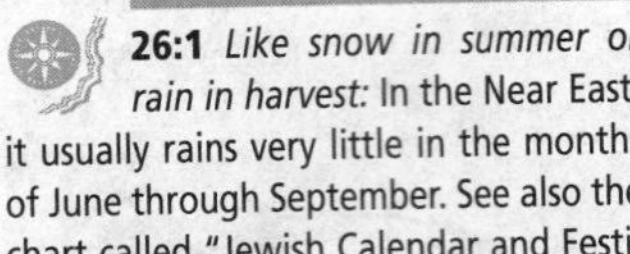

26:1 *Like snow in summer or rain in harvest:* In the Near East, it usually rains very little in the months of June through September. See also the chart called "Jewish Calendar and Festivals," p. 944.

26:3 *A whip . . . halter . . . rod:* Sticks or whips were sometimes used to get horses and donkeys to move faster, just as rods were sometimes used to beat fools (10:13). Then, as today, bridles made of strips of leather were placed over a horse's head, nose, and mouth as a way of guiding the animal. The bridle was attached to a wooden or metal bit that went in the horse's mouth. The rider controlled the horse by pulling on the reins that were attached to the bit. The marble fragment shown here is from the temple of Artemis at Ephesus, sixth century B.C.

26:8 *tying a stone in a sling:* A rock tied tightly in the loading area of a slingshot will not fly when the slingshot is released.

26:9 *thornbush in a drunkard's hand:* A drunken person's uncontrolled and unpredictable movements could easily cause harm to himself or others, especially if he is wildly waving a thorny bush.

26:12 *a man wise in his own eyes:* See the note at 11:2.

26:11 2 Pet 2:22.

16 The sluggard is wiser in his own eyes
than seven men who answer discreetly.

17 Like one who seizes a dog by the ears
is a passer-by who meddles in a quarrel not his own.

18 Like a madman shooting
firebrands or deadly arrows
19 is a man who deceives his neighbor
and says, "I was only joking!"

20 Without wood a fire goes out;
without gossip a quarrel dies down.

21 As charcoal to embers and as wood to fire,
so is a quarrelsome man for kindling strife.

22 The words of a gossip are like choice morsels;
they go down to a man's inmost parts.

23 Like a coating of glaze[a] over earthenware
are fervent lips with an evil heart.

24 A malicious man disguises himself with his lips,
but in his heart he harbors deceit.
25 Though his speech is charming, do not believe him,
for seven abominations fill his heart.
26 His malice may be concealed by deception,
but his wickedness will be exposed in the assembly.

27 If a man digs a pit, he will fall into it;
if a man rolls a stone, it will roll back on him.

28 A lying tongue hates those it hurts,
and a flattering mouth works ruin.

27 Do not boast about tomorrow,
for you do not know what a day may bring forth.

2 Let another praise you, and not your own mouth;
someone else, and not your own lips.

3 Stone is heavy and sand a burden,
but provocation by a fool is heavier than both.

4 Anger is cruel and fury overwhelming,
but who can stand before jealousy?

5 Better is open rebuke
than hidden love.

6 Wounds from a friend can be trusted,
but an enemy multiplies kisses.

[a]23 With a different word division of the Hebrew; Masoretic Text *of silver dross*

26:13-16 *sluggard . . . too lazy:* See the note at 6:10,11. To avoid being attacked by a lion is a sluggard's excuse for staying in bed rather than going to work (see also 22:13). He thinks this clever invention makes him smarter than others.

26:23 *coating of glaze over earthenware:* Clay pots were sometimes made smoother or fancier by a covering of transparent glaze, but the pot itself was not changed underneath. Smooth talk may be used as a cover-up for evil thoughts or plans.

27:1,2 *Do not boast about tomorrow:* See the note at 11:2. See also Jas 4:13-16.

26:22 Prov 18:8. **27:5,6** Prov 28:23.

27:9 *incense:* A sweet-scented substance that is burned or used in ointments and perfumes. Incense was burned to cover unpleasant odors and as a part of Israelite worship in the tabernacle and temple. Because the spices and resins used in making incense had to be imported from far-off lands, incense was a luxury item. See also the chart called "Spices and Perfumes," p. 1278.

27:10 *Do not forsake your friend and the friend of your father:* This is a caution about depending only on the help of family members, especially if a nearby friend can provide help more quickly.

27:11 *Be wise, my son:* Parents' reputations were judged by the behavior of their children. See also 10:1; 23:15,16.

27:13 *security . . . pledge:* Lending money to a stranger was considered risky. To reduce the risk, some item was given as a guarantee against the loan. See also the note at 6:1-3.

27:16 *restraining the wind . . . grasping oil:* The difference between a nagging wife and good wife is a common theme in PROVERBS (compare 21:9,19 and 25:24 to 31:10-31). "Restraining the wind" and "grasping oil" describe something that is impossible. See also Eccl 1:14,17; 2:26.

27:17 *iron sharpens iron:* A coarse piece of iron was often used to sharpen an iron blade.

27:12 Prov 22:3. **27:22** Prov 26:11.

7 He who is full loathes honey,
but to the hungry even what is bitter tastes sweet.

8 Like a bird that strays from its nest
is a man who strays from his home.

9 Perfume and incense bring joy to the heart,
and the pleasantness of one's friend springs from his
earnest counsel.

10 Do not forsake your friend and the friend of your father,
and do not go to your brother's house when disaster
strikes you—
better a neighbor nearby than a brother far away.

11 Be wise, my son, and bring joy to my heart;
then I can answer anyone who treats me with
contempt.

12 The prudent see danger and take refuge,
but the simple keep going and suffer for it.

13 Take the garment of one who puts up security for a
stranger;
hold it in pledge if he does it for a wayward woman.

14 If a man loudly blesses his neighbor early in the
morning,
it will be taken as a curse.

15 A quarrelsome wife is like
a constant dripping on a rainy day;
16 restraining her is like restraining the wind
or grasping oil with the hand.

17 As iron sharpens iron,
so one man sharpens another.

18 He who tends a fig tree will eat its fruit,
and he who looks after his master will be honored.

19 As water reflects a face,
so a man's heart reflects the man.

20 Death and Destruction[a] are never satisfied,
and neither are the eyes of man.

21 The crucible for silver and the furnace for gold,
but man is tested by the praise he receives.

22 Though you grind a fool in a mortar,
grinding him like grain with a pestle,
you will not remove his folly from him.

[a]**20** Hebrew *Sheol and Abaddon*

[23]Be sure you know the condition of your flocks,
give careful attention to your herds;
[24]for riches do not endure forever,
and a crown is not secure for all generations.
[25]When the hay is removed and new growth appears
and the grass from the hills is gathered in,
[26]the lambs will provide you with clothing,
and the goats with the price of a field.
[27]You will have plenty of goats' milk
to feed you and your family
and to nourish your servant girls.

28 The wicked man flees though no one pursues,
but the righteous are as bold as a lion.

[2]When a country is rebellious, it has many rulers,
but a man of understanding and knowledge
maintains order.

[3]A ruler[a] who oppresses the poor
is like a driving rain that leaves no crops.

[4]Those who forsake the law praise the wicked,
but those who keep the law resist them.
[5]Evil men do not understand justice,
but those who seek the LORD understand it fully.
[6]Better a poor man whose walk is blameless
than a rich man whose ways are perverse.
[7]He who keeps the law is a discerning son,
but a companion of gluttons disgraces his father.
[8]He who increases his wealth by exorbitant interest
amasses it for another, who will be kind to
the poor.
[9]If anyone turns a deaf ear to the law,
even his prayers are detestable.
[10]He who leads the upright along an evil path
will fall into his own trap,
but the blameless will receive a good inheritance.
[11]A rich man may be wise in his own eyes,
but a poor man who has discernment sees
through him.

[12]When the righteous triumph, there is great elation;
but when the wicked rise to power, men go into
hiding.

[a]3 Or *A poor man*

27:20 *Death . . . never satisfied:* The Hebrew words here translated as "Death" and "Destruction" refer to the dark world of the dead (see the note at 5:5). Death is often described as having a never-ending appetite for victims (30:15,16; Job 24:19; Isa 5:14; Hab 2:5). In the same way, human beings have a tendency not to be satisfied with what they have and to always desire more (Eccl 1:8; 4:8).

27:21 *silver . . . gold . . . tested by the praise he receives:* See the note at 17:3.

28:1 *the righteous:* See the notes at 1:3 and 2:8,9.

28:3 *oppresses the poor:* See the note at 19:7. To mistreat the poor was a direct insult against the LORD (see 14:31; 17:5; and the note at 2:8,9).

28:5 *justice:* See the note at 1:3.

28:7 *the law:* See the note at 6:23.

28:8 *exorbitant interest:* Moneylenders made a living by charging interest on loans. This proverb warns that those who charge an unfairly high interest rate will lose business to those who are charging a fair interest rate.

28:10 *evil path . . . blameless:* See the notes at 1:10 and 1:3.

28:6 Prov 19:1.

He who rebukes a man will in the end gain more favor than he who has a flattering tongue.
Prov 28:23

28:13 *conceals his sins does not prosper:* This proverb warns that those who keep on doing evil things or who try to cover them up will end up losing what they have (see also 3:33; 6:12-15; 10:16,28,29).

28:19 *works his land:* See the note at 6:10,11.

28:20 *richly blessed . . . not go unpunished:* See the notes on p. 1193 (Foolishness and wisdom) and the note at 10:15,16.

28:26 *walks in wisdom:* See the note at 1:2.

28:27 *gives to the poor:* See 22:9 and the notes at 1:3 and 2:8,9.

28:15 Prov 20:28; 28:3. **28:23** Prov 26:28; 27:5, 6. **28:28** Prov 28:12.

13 He who conceals his sins does not prosper,
but whoever confesses and renounces them
finds mercy.

14 Blessed is the man who always fears the LORD,
but he who hardens his heart falls into trouble.

15 Like a roaring lion or a charging bear
is a wicked man ruling over a helpless people.

16 A tyrannical ruler lacks judgment,
but he who hates ill-gotten gain will enjoy a long life.

17 A man tormented by the guilt of murder
will be a fugitive till death;
let no one support him.

18 He whose walk is blameless is kept safe,
but he whose ways are perverse will suddenly fall.

19 He who works his land will have abundant food,
but the one who chases fantasies will have his fill
of poverty.

20 A faithful man will be richly blessed,
but one eager to get rich will not go unpunished.

21 To show partiality is not good—
yet a man will do wrong for a piece of bread.

22 A stingy man is eager to get rich
and is unaware that poverty awaits him.

23 He who rebukes a man will in the end gain
more favor
than he who has a flattering tongue.

24 He who robs his father or mother
and says, "It's not wrong"—
he is partner to him who destroys.

25 A greedy man stirs up dissension,
but he who trusts in the LORD will prosper.

26 He who trusts in himself is a fool,
but he who walks in wisdom is kept safe.

27 He who gives to the poor will lack nothing,
but he who closes his eyes to them receives
many curses.

28 When the wicked rise to power, people go into hiding;
but when the wicked perish, the righteous thrive.

29

A man who remains stiff-necked after many rebukes
will suddenly be destroyed—without remedy.

2 When the righteous thrive, the people rejoice;
when the wicked rule, the people groan.

3 A man who loves wisdom brings joy to his father,
but a companion of prostitutes squanders his wealth.

4 By justice a king gives a country stability,
but one who is greedy for bribes tears it down.

5 Whoever flatters his neighbor
is spreading a net for his feet.

6 An evil man is snared by his own sin,
but a righteous one can sing and be glad.

7 The righteous care about justice for the poor,
but the wicked have no such concern.

8 Mockers stir up a city,
but wise men turn away anger.

9 If a wise man goes to court with a fool,
the fool rages and scoffs, and there is no peace.

10 Bloodthirsty men hate a man of integrity
and seek to kill the upright.

11 A fool gives full vent to his anger,
but a wise man keeps himself under control.

12 If a ruler listens to lies,
all his officials become wicked.

13 The poor man and the oppressor have this in common:
The LORD gives sight to the eyes of both.

14 If a king judges the poor with fairness,
his throne will always be secure.

15 The rod of correction imparts wisdom,
but a child left to himself disgraces his mother.

16 When the wicked thrive, so does sin,
but the righteous will see their downfall.

17 Discipline your son, and he will give you peace;
he will bring delight to your soul.

18 Where there is no revelation, the people cast off restraint;
but blessed is he who keeps the law.

19 A servant cannot be corrected by mere words;
though he understands, he will not respond.

20 Do you see a man who speaks in haste?
There is more hope for a fool than for him.

29:2 *When the righteous thrive, the people rejoice:* See the notes at 11:11 and 1:3. See also 29:12.

29:3 *prostitutes:* See the notes at 2:16, 17; 5:3; and 8:32-34. See also 5:1-23; 7:6-27.

29:4 *By justice a king gives a country stability:* See the notes at 2:8,9 and 8:14,15.

29:8 *Mockers stir up a city:* Attitudes and actions that create anger can spread quickly, but wise words and actions can stop anger from spreading. See also 6:12-14; 26:21.

29:13 *poor . . . oppressor . . . sight:* See the notes at 1:3 and 2:8,9.

29:15,17 *Discipline your son:* See 3:12; 19:18; and the note at 13:24.

29:18 *revelation . . . the law:* These are two ways that God's message and purposes are communicated to people. The message of God's prophets (revelation) was guided by God's Spirit, while the law was given to Moses and the people of Israel (see the note at 6:23).

29:5 Prov 26:28; 27:5,6. **29:11** Prov 12:16; 25:28.

A man's pride brings him low, but a man of lowly spirit gains honor.
Prov 29:23

29:26 *it is from the* LORD *that man gets justice:* See the notes at 1:3 and 1:7.

30:1 *sayings of Agur son of Jakeh:* The Hebrew word translated as "sayings" may also be a place name (*Massa*). If so, this could connect Agur with the ancestors of Ishmael who lived in northern Arabia (Gen 25:12-18). Exactly which or how many sayings are to be credited to this wise man is unclear.

30:2,3 *the most ignorant of men:* Agur says that his wisdom and understanding are nothing when compared to the wisdom and mystery of God. Compare his comments to Job 42:1-6. See also 9:10.

30:4 *Who has gone . . . gathered:* A series of questions that expect a negative answer. No human can do these things, but the LORD can. See also Job 38–41; Isa 40:12. Wrapping up the sea and marking the boundaries of the earth were done by God at creation (Gen 1:6-10; Ps 104:5-9).

29:22 Prov 12:16; 25:28; 29:11.

21 If a man pampers his servant from youth,
he will bring grief[a] in the end.

22 An angry man stirs up dissension,
and a hot-tempered one commits many sins.

23 A man's pride brings him low,
but a man of lowly spirit gains honor.

24 The accomplice of a thief is his own enemy;
he is put under oath and dare not testify.

25 Fear of man will prove to be a snare,
but whoever trusts in the LORD is kept safe.

26 Many seek an audience with a ruler,
but it is from the LORD that man gets justice.

27 The righteous detest the dishonest;
the wicked detest the upright.

The Wise Sayings of Agur and of Lemuel's Mother

The final chapters of PROVERBS *are collected sayings credited to two unknown authors, Agur and King Lemuel. A number of the proverbs in chapter 30 are "descriptive lists." Chapter 31 gives advice to a young king and describes what a good wife is like.*

SAYINGS OF AGUR

30 The sayings of Agur son of Jakeh—an oracle[b]:

This man declared to Ithiel,
to Ithiel and to Ucal:[c]

2 "I am the most ignorant of men;
I do not have a man's understanding.
3 I have not learned wisdom,
nor have I knowledge of the Holy One.
4 Who has gone up to heaven and come down?
Who has gathered up the wind in the hollow of his hands?
Who has wrapped up the waters in his cloak?
Who has established all the ends of the earth?
What is his name, and the name of his son?
Tell me if you know!

[a]21 The meaning of the Hebrew for this word is uncertain. [b]1 Or *Jakeh of Massa* [c]1 Masoretic Text; with a different word division of the Hebrew *declared, "I am weary, O God; / I am weary, O God, and faint.*

[5] "Every word of God is flawless;
he is a shield to those who take refuge in him.
[6] Do not add to his words,
or he will rebuke you and prove you a liar.

[7] "Two things I ask of you, O LORD;
do not refuse me before I die:
[8] Keep falsehood and lies far from me;
give me neither poverty nor riches,
but give me only my daily bread.
[9] Otherwise, I may have too much and disown you
and say, 'Who is the LORD?'
Or I may become poor and steal,
and so dishonor the name of my God.

[10] "Do not slander a servant to his master,
or he will curse you, and you will pay for it.

[11] "There are those who curse their fathers
and do not bless their mothers;
[12] those who are pure in their own eyes
and yet are not cleansed of their filth;
[13] those whose eyes are ever so haughty,
whose glances are so disdainful;
[14] those whose teeth are swords
and whose jaws are set with knives
to devour the poor from the earth,
the needy from among mankind.

[15] "The leech has two daughters.
'Give! Give!' they cry.

"There are three things that are never satisfied,
four that never say, 'Enough!':
[16] the grave,[a] the barren womb,
land, which is never satisfied with water,
and fire, which never says, 'Enough!'

[17] "The eye that mocks a father,
that scorns obedience to a mother,
will be pecked out by the ravens of the valley,
will be eaten by the vultures.

[18] "There are three things that are too amazing for me,
four that I do not understand:
[19] the way of an eagle in the sky,
the way of a snake on a rock,
the way of a ship on the high seas,
and the way of a man with a maiden.

[a]**16** Hebrew *Sheol*

Every word of God is flawless.
Prov 30:5

30:8 *give me neither poverty nor riches:* Both can present problems (see the note at 10:15,16).

30:9 *have too much:* God's people are to give the LORD credit for the things they have been given and for the help they have received (Deut 8:7-20; Ps 44).

30:11-14 *curse . . . pure in their own eyes . . . haughty . . . devour the poor:* Four types of people who are considered especially bad: those who curse their parents (Exod 20:12; Deut 27:14-26; Matt 15:4-6); those who do not recognize that they sin (16:2; Isa 65:1-7; Luke 18:9-14); those who are overly proud (11:2; 13:10; 16:5); and those who mistreat or rob the poor (28:3).

30:16 *the grave:* See the note at 5:5.

30:17 *mocks a father . . . mother:* See the note at 30:11-14. See also Deut 27:14-26.

30:17 *ravens . . . vultures:* Such disobedience will result in grotesque punishment.

30:22 *a servant who becomes king:* See the note at 19:10.

30:25-28 *Ants . . . lizard:* Four small animals admired for particular abilities: ants for their ability to work hard (6:6-8); coneys (badgers) for being able to survive among the rocks in the desert (Ps 104:18); locusts for their ability to swarm in large numbers (Joel 1:4); and lizards for their ability to sneak over a king's guarded palace walls.

30:33 *churning the milk produces butter:* Milk or cream poured into a barrel or a clay pot was stirred or beaten till it turned into butter.

31:1 *sayings of King Lemuel . . . mother:* Literature offering advice for young princes or kings is common in the ancient wisdom writings of Egypt and Mesopotamia. Here, advice comes from a mother. This follows the theme of the wise woman introduced earlier (see 1:20-33). A good wife and mother "speaks with wisdom, and faithful instruction is on her tongue" (31:26). See also the note at 30:1.

31:2 *son of my vows:* For a similar birth, see the prayer of Hannah (1 Sam 1:9-20).

31:3 *do not spend your strength on women:* For the potential problems that come from chasing after many women, see 5:1-23; 7:6-27.

31:4-7 *not for kings to drink wine:* Nations suffer when their leaders get drunk and can't handle their responsibilities (Eccl 10:16,17; Isa 5:21-24; 28:7-13). See also 20:1; 23:29-35. Though drinking is here approved for people in desperate situations (31:6,7) this is not to be taken as an excuse for giving in to despair.

20 "This is the way of an adulteress:
She eats and wipes her mouth
and says, 'I've done nothing wrong.'

21 "Under three things the earth trembles,
under four it cannot bear up:
22 a servant who becomes king,
a fool who is full of food,
23 an unloved woman who is married,
and a maidservant who displaces her mistress.

24 "Four things on earth are small,
yet they are extremely wise:
25 Ants are creatures of little strength,
yet they store up their food in the summer;
26 coneys[a] are creatures of little power,
yet they make their home in the crags;
27 locusts have no king,
yet they advance together in ranks;
28 a lizard can be caught with the hand,
yet it is found in kings' palaces.

29 "There are three things that are stately in their stride,
four that move with stately bearing:
30 a lion, mighty among beasts,
who retreats before nothing;
31 a strutting rooster, a he-goat,
and a king with his army around him.[b]

32 "If you have played the fool and exalted yourself,
or if you have planned evil,
clap your hand over your mouth!
33 For as churning the milk produces butter,
and as twisting the nose produces blood,
so stirring up anger produces strife."

SAYINGS OF KING LEMUEL

31 The sayings of King Lemuel—an oracle[c] his mother taught
him:

2 "O my son, O son of my womb,
O son of my vows,[d]
3 do not spend your strength on women,
your vigor on those who ruin kings.

4 "It is not for kings, O Lemuel—
not for kings to drink wine,
not for rulers to crave beer,

---

[a]26 That is, the hyrax or rock badger [b]31 Or *king secure against revolt* [c]1 Or *of Lemuel king of Massa, which* [d]2 Or */ the answer to my prayers*

[5]lest they drink and forget what the law decrees,
and deprive all the oppressed of their rights.
[6]Give beer to those who are perishing,
wine to those who are in anguish;
[7]let them drink and forget their poverty
and remember their misery no more.

[8]"Speak up for those who cannot speak for themselves,
for the rights of all who are destitute.
[9]Speak up and judge fairly;
defend the rights of the poor and needy."

EPILOGUE: THE WIFE OF NOBLE CHARACTER

[10][a]A wife of noble character who can find?
She is worth far more than rubies.
[11]Her husband has full confidence in her
and lacks nothing of value.
[12]She brings him good, not harm,
all the days of her life.
[13]She selects wool and flax
and works with eager hands.
[14]She is like the merchant ships,
bringing her food from afar.
[15]She gets up while it is still dark;
she provides food for her family
and portions for her servant girls.
[16]She considers a field and buys it;
out of her earnings she plants a vineyard.
[17]She sets about her work vigorously;
her arms are strong for her tasks.
[18]She sees that her trading is profitable,
and her lamp does not go out at night.
[19]In her hand she holds the distaff
and grasps the spindle with her fingers.
[20]She opens her arms to the poor
and extends her hands to the needy.
[21]When it snows, she has no fear for her household;
for all of them are clothed in scarlet.
[22]She makes coverings for her bed;
she is clothed in fine linen and purple.
[23]Her husband is respected at the city gate,
where he takes his seat among the elders of the land.
[24]She makes linen garments and sells them,
and supplies the merchants with sashes.
[25]She is clothed with strength and dignity;
she can laugh at the days to come.

[a]**10** Verses 10-31 are an acrostic, each verse beginning with a successive letter of the Hebrew alphabet.

31:8,9 *Speak up for those who cannot speak for themselves:* Not only did the king set general policies in his kingdom, but he could make decisions in favor of the poor (see 2 Sam 14:4-11). On kings ruling with justice, see 29:2, 14; the note on p. 1193 (King Solomon); and the notes at 2:8,9 and 16:12.

31:10 *wife of noble character:* In Hebrew, verses 10-31 form an acrostic poem. See the note at Ps 119:1. This is a poetic way of making a list of the qualities that make a "wife of noble character." The good wife described in the poem is like the personification of Wisdom (see 1:20-33; 8:1—9:12).

31:11 *husband has full confidence in her:* As a wise person depends on wisdom (8:12-21) and respects the LORD (1:7; 2:4,5; 28:25).

31:13,14 *selects wool and flax . . . bringing her food:* In most families, the mother and older daughters made clothing and prepared meals. These activities started early in the morning and continued throughout the day.

31:16-20 *considers a field and buys it . . . plants a vineyard . . . extends her hands to the needy:* The good wife and mother displays in her life many of the things connected with wisdom: see 10:4, 26; 12:11, 27; and the notes at 6:10,11 and 2:8,9.

31:23 *Her husband is respected:* Her husband's work is public and visible for all to see, but a woman's work in the home and family setting is equally important and will bring her praise and respect (31:31).

31:26 *speaks with wisdom:* Because she follows the wisdom that comes from the LORD (2:6,7). See also 1:8; 6:20-22; 31:8, 9.

31:27 *does not eat the bread of idleness:* See the note at 6:10, 11.

31:30 *Charm is deceptive, and beauty is fleeting . . . fears the LORD:* The beauty of one who honors and respects the LORD (see the note at 1:7) is more than skin-deep. It comes from the heart (see the note at 3:3). A woman who respects the LORD deserves respect and public recognition.

26 She speaks with wisdom,
and faithful instruction is on her tongue.
27 She watches over the affairs of her household
and does not eat the bread of idleness.
28 Her children arise and call her blessed;
her husband also, and he praises her:
29 "Many women do noble things,
but you surpass them all."
30 Charm is deceptive, and beauty is fleeting;
but a woman who fears the LORD is to be praised.
31 Give her the reward she has earned,
and let her works bring her praise at the city gate.

QUESTIONS ABOUT PROVERBS 22:17—31:31

1. Choose at least one of the thirty sayings in 22:17—24:22 and explain what it means in your own words. How does the saying apply to modern circumstances?
2. Match the following (see 25:1—29:27):

_____ boasts	a. multiplies kisses (27:6)
_____ good news	b. like a charging bear (28:15)
_____ fool speaking proverbs	c. stir up a city (29:8)
_____ wicked ruler	d. like a lame man's legs (26:7)
_____ an enemy	e. choice morsels (26:22)
_____ relying on the unfaithful	f. like cold water when you are weary (25:25)
_____ gossip	g. like a bad tooth (25:19)
_____ mockers	h. like rain clouds that don't bring rain (25:14)

3. Modern society puts a great deal of emphasis on wealth. What do you think of the prayer in 30:7-9? What do you ask God for when you pray?
4. Review the "descriptive list" type of proverbs in 30:15-31. Then create a wise saying of your own that follows this descriptive list pattern.
5. Why is the description of a good wife and mother (31:10-31) a fitting ending for PROVERBS? List some of the book's themes which can be found in this description.
6. Name two new things you discovered while reading and studying PROVERBS. How can these things be applied to your life?

ECCLESIASTES

What can people do to find satisfaction and happiness? Read ECCLESIASTES *to find out what one wise author says about the meaning of life.*

WHAT MAKES ECCLESIASTES SPECIAL?

The book's title comes from the ancient Greek translation of the Hebrew word *Qoheleth*, which means "one who assembles." The author is not known, but many suggest he was a teacher, preacher, or philosopher. The author is not telling a story, but is sharing his thoughts on the meaning of life. He uses sayings, proverbs, and poems to illustrate his point. A key phrase, "Everything is meaningless," begins and ends the book (1:2; 12:8), and is repeated in various forms throughout the book, emphasizing that the answers to many of life's questions are not easy to find.

WHY WAS ECCLESIASTES WRITTEN?

This book is a search for meaning in life. The writer sees that, from the human viewpoint, life is full of contradictions and mysteries. Hard work is a gift from God (5:19), but work can be painful and senseless (2:17), because after people die they won't have anything to show for their hard work (5:13-15), and others will get to enjoy their wealth (6:2). When people are poor, no one pays attention to them (9:16), but being wealthy doesn't guarantee happiness and satisfaction either (2:4-11; 5:10-12). Wisdom is better than foolishness, but whether a person is wise or foolish, everyone dies (2:13-16; 3:20), and knowing too much can be painful (1:18). Above all, human wisdom cannot help people understand the ways of God (8:17), who makes everything happen (3:11; 6:10; 7:13,14; 9:1). People are to respect and obey God (5:7; 8:12,13; 12:13), for God will judge what they do (3:17; 12:14). But the common destiny of death awaits all people, whether they live right or sin (9:2,3).

With life being so full of contradictions, where do humans find meaning? It is not surprising that some readers think the message of ECCLESIASTES lacks hope and gives no answers regarding the meaning of life. However, others see hope and answers in the author's repeated invitations to enjoy life as a gift from God (2:24-26). The author faces life's realities and sees how senseless life can seem to people with limited (human) understanding. But he also recognizes God's gifts and finds joy in them. He cannot understand God's mysterious ways, but he knows God holds the future. And so, he holds on to God and urges others to respect God and keep God's commandments, too.

WHAT'S THE STORY BEHIND THE SCENE?

The wise author is identified in 1:1 as being a son of David and a king in Jerusalem. While Solomon is not mentioned by name

son of David: David, Israel's greatest king, ruled in Jerusalem as king of Israel from about 1010 to 970 B.C. His son Solomon followed him as king and ruled from about 970 to 931 B.C. Solomon was known for his great wisdom (1 Kgs 4:29-34). The lives of David and Solomon are described in detail in 1 Samuel 16—1 Kings 11. See also the mini-articles called "David," p. 1028, and "Solomon," p. 776.

1:1 *the Teacher, son of David, king in Jerusalem:* The opening verse, called a superscription, provides the title for the book, and credits the words of the book to David's son, which probably means Solomon. This connects ECCLESIASTES with the "wisdom" literature of Solomon, who was called Israel's wisest person. For more about Solomon, see the note on p. 1249.

The word "Teacher," translates the Hebrew word *Qoheleth*, whose meaning is not certain. It may come from the word *kahal*, which means "assembly." So, this wise person is one who teaches in an assembly. It also may refer to someone who was a very wise leader or to someone who had become wise from collecting and studying sayings about wisdom.

anywhere in ECCLESIASTES, he is the only one of David's sons who was a king in Jerusalem (1 Kgs 1). Also, Solomon was known for his wisdom and was given credit for writing many wise sayings and songs (1 Kgs 3:5-12; 4:29-34; Prov 1:1).

It was not uncommon in ancient times to write "in the name" of an important person such as Solomon, and many scholars now think that Solomon may not have written ECCLESIASTES. One reason is that the Hebrew language of this book appears to come from a period many centuries after the time of Solomon, who ruled around 970 to 931 B.C. Also, the presence of Persian words suggests that the book was written sometime after the exile when the people returned to Judah from exile in Babylon (538 B.C.). From this time on, for nearly two hundred years, the Jewish people were strongly influenced by Persian language and culture. Another reason many scholars think Solomon may not have written this book personally is that the writer speaks as though he is not a king, but a subject (5:8,9; 8:2-5; 10:5-7,16,17,20).

HOW IS ECCLESIASTES CONSTRUCTED?

The following is just one of the dozens of different outlines that have been suggested for ECCLESIASTES. The book's title (also known as a "superscription") is given in 1:1, and a repeated theme phrase in 1:2 and 12:8 begins and ends the main body of the book. In the outline below, the main body has been divided into three sections. A conclusion (or "epilogue") is found in 12:9-14.

A wise person and the search for meaning in life (1:1—2:26)

One known to be very wise (1:1)

The search for meaning in life (1:2—2:26)

Life is puzzling, but it's a gift from God (3:1—11:6)

Enjoy life and remember God while you are young (11:7—12:8)

Conclusion (12:9-14)

A Wise Person and the Search for Meaning in Life

A key theme of the book is introduced at the very beginning (1:2; see also 12:8). The author says, "Everything is meaningless" and that life's meaning is not found in working hard, gaining wealth and property, or even in seeking wisdom. All these things are as difficult and impossible as chasing the wind.

ONE KNOWN TO BE VERY WISE

Everything Is Meaningless

1 The words of the Teacher,[a] son of David, king in Jerusalem:

[a]1 Or *leader of the assembly*; also in verses 2 and 12

Solomon, James Tissot, about 1880. ECCLESIASTES was written by a "Teacher" or someone known to be very wise. The author of 1 KINGS writes that King Solomon, one of King David's sons, "was wiser than any other man" (1 Kgs 4:31). Whether written by Solomon himself, or by a wise teacher wishing to honor the memory of this wise king, ECCLESIASTES is an examination of one of life's key questions: What is the meaning of life and the proper way to live?

THE SEARCH FOR MEANING IN LIFE

2 "Meaningless! Meaningless!"
says the Teacher.
"Utterly meaningless!
Everything is meaningless."

3 What does man gain from all his labor
at which he toils under the sun?
4 Generations come and generations go,
but the earth remains forever.
5 The sun rises and the sun sets,
and hurries back to where it rises.

1:2 *Everything is meaningless:* The traditional translation of this phrase is "Vanity of vanities." The Hebrew word used here is *hevel,* which means "breath." Human breath disappears quickly and has little substance, so the author seems to be saying that finding meaning in life is as difficult as trying to hold human breath in one's hand or "chasing after the wind" (1:14). Compare the note at 1:3-9. See also Job 7:7; Ps 39:4-6; 144:4.

1:3 *all his labor:* Work took up a great deal of one's day in ancient times. See also 2:11, 21; 5:15,16.

1:3-9 *under the sun . . . nothing new:* These phrases come from man's perspective apart from God. This provides understanding of the seemingly hopeless attitude that everything is "meaningless" (1:2; 12:8). If taken from a limited human perspective, much in life seems without meaning. See 1:13; 2:3, 11; 3:1, 11; 4:7.

1:4-7 *Generations come and generations go . . . sun rises and the sun sets . . . return again:* Individual people come and go, but the world continues on in the cycles of life. Ancient people often described the universe as being made up of the four key elements: earth (world), fire (sun), air (wind), and water (rivers and seas). Though the author goes on to describe the natural cycles of life as wearisome (1:8), it is these same cycles and elements that make all life possible. See Gen 8:22; Ps 104:1-30.

6 The wind blows to the south
and turns to the north;
round and round it goes,
ever returning on its course.
7 All streams flow into the sea,
yet the sea is never full.
To the place the streams come from,
there they return again.
8 All things are wearisome,
more than one can say.
The eye never has enough of seeing,
nor the ear its fill of hearing.
9 What has been will be again,
what has been done will be done again;
there is nothing new under the sun.
10 Is there anything of which one can say,
"Look! This is something new"?
It was here already, long ago;
it was here before our time.
11 There is no remembrance of men of old,
and even those who are yet to come
will not be remembered
by those who follow.

Wisdom Is Meaningless

12 I, the Teacher, was king over Israel in Jerusalem. 13 I devoted myself to study and to explore by wisdom all that is done under
heaven. What a heavy burden God has laid on men! 14 I have seen
all the things that are done under the sun; all of them are meaningless, a chasing after the wind.

15 What is twisted cannot be straightened;
what is lacking cannot be counted.

16 I thought to myself, "Look, I have grown and increased in
wisdom more than anyone who has ruled over Jerusalem before me;
I have experienced much of wisdom and knowledge." 17 Then I
applied myself to the understanding of wisdom, and also of madness and folly, but I learned that this, too, is a chasing after the wind.

18 For with much wisdom comes much sorrow;
the more knowledge, the more grief.

Pleasures Are Meaningless

2 I thought in my heart, "Come now, I will test you with pleasure
to find out what is good." But that also proved to be meaningless.
2 "Laughter," I said, "is foolish. And what does pleasure accomplish?" 3 I tried cheering myself with wine, and embracing folly—
my mind still guiding me with wisdom. I wanted to see what was

---

1:8-11 *All things are wearisome . . . will not be remembered:* The author's observation that the cycles of nature and life are boring and unsatisfying may grow out of his frustration at not understanding how God works. The author believes that God does make "everything beautiful in its time" (3:11), and that God decided long ago what will happen in the world (6:10). But even these beliefs seem to make the author feel powerless (8:7,8,16,17).

1:12,13 *king over Israel in Jerusalem . . . explore by wisdom:* See the Introduction to ECCLESIASTES and the note on p. 1249.

1:13,14 *God . . . chasing after the wind:* The only Hebrew word used for God in this book is *Elohim*, the name of God used in the creation story (Gen 1:1—2:4). See also the mini-article called "Names of God," p. 243.

The Hebrew verb translated as "chasing" (1:14) also may be related to a Hebrew word for taking care of sheep. "Shepherding" the wind would be even more impossible than catching it. See the note at 1:2.

1:16 *increased in wisdom more than anyone:* See the note at 1:1. See also the note on p. 1249.

1:17 *wisdom:* Wisdom often refers to the common sense and practical skill needed to solve everyday problems, but sometimes it involves trying to find answers to hard questions about the meaning of life. According to PROVERBS, true wisdom comes from God and is given to those who obey God (Prov 2:6,7; see also Eccl 12:13,14). See also the mini-article called "Wisdom," p. 2206.

1:15 Eccl 3:14; 7:13. **1:18** Eccl 7:4.

worthwhile for men to do under heaven during the few days of
their lives.
[4]I undertook great projects: I built houses for myself and
planted vineyards. [5]I made gardens and parks and planted all kinds
of fruit trees in them. [6]I made reservoirs to water groves of flourishing trees. [7]I bought male and female slaves and had other slaves
who were born in my house. I also owned more herds and flocks
than anyone in Jerusalem before me. [8]I amassed silver and gold for
myself, and the treasure of kings and provinces. I acquired men
and women singers, and a harem[a] as well—the delights of the
heart of man. [9]I became greater by far than anyone in Jerusalem
before me. In all this my wisdom stayed with me.

[10]I denied myself nothing my eyes desired;
  I refused my heart no pleasure.
My heart took delight in all my work,
  and this was the reward for all my labor.
[11]Yet when I surveyed all that my hands had done
  and what I had toiled to achieve,
everything was meaningless, a chasing after the wind;
  nothing was gained under the sun.

Wisdom and Folly Are Meaningless

[12]Then I turned my thoughts to consider wisdom,
  and also madness and folly.
What more can the king's successor do
  than what has already been done?
[13]I saw that wisdom is better than folly,
  just as light is better than darkness.
[14]The wise man has eyes in his head,
  while the fool walks in the darkness;
but I came to realize
  that the same fate overtakes them both.

[a]8 The meaning of the Hebrew for this phrase is uncertain.

2:4 *I:* It is not certain who this is. Some say that it is Solomon. Others think that it is the author imagining himself as a king like Solomon. In 2:3-11, the "king" tells of trying to find pleasure and enjoyment in the things he did and the wealth he owned (see list in 2:4-8). Like the king in these verses, Solomon was known for his great wealth (1 Kgs 10:10, 14-27; 2 Chr 9:22-27), huge flocks of sheep and cattle (1 Kgs 4:23), and for having many wives (1 Kgs 11:1-4). The author says that such things do bring delight to the heart (2:8,10), but they do not last and so they can't give lasting satisfaction or meaning (2:11).

2:9 *Jerusalem:* Jerusalem was Israel's political and religious capital. See the map on p. 575, and the mini-article called "Jerusalem," p. 574.

2:12 *consider wisdom, and also madness and folly:* See the note at 1:17. The author "considers" what he and the readers probably already know: wisdom is better than foolishness (see, for example, Prov 14:6-9). But because all face "the same fate," that is, everyone dies (2:14) and is eventually forgotten (2:16), it seems to make no difference whether one is wise or foolish. See also 3:19,20; 6:6; 9:2.

2:12 *the king's successor do:* See the note on p. 1249 (son of David). After Solomon's death, his son Rehoboam became king (1 Kgs 11:43).

2:8 1 Kgs 10:10,14-22. **2:9** 1 Chr 29:25.

QUESTIONS ABOUT ECCLESIASTES 1:1—2:26

1. How would you describe the author of ECCLESIASTES? (Introduction and note at 1:1)
2. How does the author describe life? (1:8-11) What do you think of this view?
3. Think about the statement in 1:18. Can you think of experiences in your own life or in the lives of others that show this to be true?
4. How did the author try to "find out what is good" and make himself happy? (2:1-10) What did he discover? (2:10,11)
5. How does the author describe "wisdom"? (2:13,14) According to the author, did being wise seem to make a difference? (2:15-19) Why or why not?
6. What conclusion does the author come to in 2:24,25?
7. What do you think of the author's view of God in 2:26?

15 Then I thought in my heart,

"The fate of the fool will overtake me also.
What then do I gain by being wise?"
I said in my heart,
"This too is meaningless."
16 For the wise man, like the fool, will not be long
remembered;
in days to come both will be forgotten.
Like the fool, the wise man too must die!

Toil Is Meaningless

17 So I hated life, because the work that is done under the sun
was grievous to me. All of it is meaningless, a chasing after the
wind. 18 I hated all the things I had toiled for under the sun,
because I must leave them to the one who comes after me. 19 And
who knows whether he will be a wise man or a fool? Yet he will
have control over all the work into which I have poured my effort
and skill under the sun. This too is meaningless. 20 So my heart
began to despair over all my toilsome labor under the sun. 21 For a
man may do his work with wisdom, knowledge and skill, and then
he must leave all he owns to someone who has not worked for it.
This too is meaningless and a great misfortune. 22 What does a man
get for all the toil and anxious striving with which he labors under
the sun? 23 All his days his work is pain and grief; even at night his
mind does not rest. This too is meaningless.
24 A man can do nothing better than to eat and drink and
find satisfaction in his work. This too, I see, is from the hand of
God, 25 for without him, who can eat or find enjoyment? 26 To the
man who pleases him, God gives wisdom, knowledge and happiness, but to the sinner he gives the task of gathering and storing
up wealth to hand it over to the one who pleases God. This too is
meaningless, a chasing after the wind.

Life Is Puzzling, but It's a Gift from God

The author uses observations of life, wise sayings, and proverbs to continue to explore life's meaning. Even though he knows God controls what happens in life and that God has power over everyone (3:11,17,18; 9:1-3), he still sees that there are many contradictions and mysteries in life. Because finding answers is so complicated, the author concludes once again that the best thing to do is to stop searching and enjoy life as a gift from God (5:18-20; 8:15; 9:7).

A Time for Everything

3 There is a time for everything,
and a season for every activity under heaven:

There is a time for everything, and a season for every activity under heaven.
Eccl 3:1

2:24-26 *do nothing better . . . To the man who pleases him, God gives wisdom, knowledge and happiness:* This is the first of several times that the author expresses the opinion in 2:24 (see also 3:13; 5:18; 9:7). Later, the author adds that eating, drinking, and working are gifts from God, but they can be enjoyed only if God allows this to happen (9:1). See also Luke 12:19; 1 Cor 15:32.

In 2:26, the author gives a common understanding of reward and punishment that can be found in many places in the Bible. God rewards those who are faithful and punishes those who are evil. Those who were wealthy were assumed to be favored by God (Job 8:20; Prov 13:22; 28:8). Later, however, the author says that good people are not always rewarded and that bad people sometimes live long and prosperous lives (7:15; 8:10-14; see also Job 9:22-24).

3:1-8 *a time for everything:* This phrase means that God controls what happens and when (3:11, 14, 15; 6:10; 8:6; 9:1; see also Prov 16:1-9). The number seven stood for completeness in ancient times. Note that each verse has a pair of opposites—seven sets in all. So, these were probably meant to represent the total life experience. See also the chart called "Numbers in the Bible," p. 2405.

2:18 Eccl 2:21; Ps 39:5, 6; Luke 12:20. **2:23** Job 5:6,7; 7:1-3; 14:1. **2:24** Isa 56:12. **2:26** Job 32:8; Prov 2:6.

Everything Has Its Time. Details from a multi-panel serigraph by John August Swanson, 1989. The endless changes of life are often bewildering. The author of ECCLESIASTES remembers that nothing lasts forever—that the time for sowing (planting seeds) is eventually followed by a time for bringing in the blessings of a harvest, and that the joy of embracing loved ones will one day be followed by a time of tearful partings. (See 3:1-8.)

2 a time to be born and a time to die,
a time to plant and a time to uproot,
3 a time to kill and a time to heal,
a time to tear down and a time to build,
4 a time to weep and a time to laugh,
a time to mourn and a time to dance,
5 a time to scatter stones and a time to gather
them,
a time to embrace and a time to refrain,
6 a time to search and a time to give up,
a time to keep and a time to throw away,
7 a time to tear and a time to mend,
a time to be silent and a time to speak,
8 a time to love and a time to hate,
a time for war and a time for peace.

9 What does the worker gain from his toil? 10 I have seen the
burden God has laid on men. 11 He has made everything beautiful
in its time. He has also set eternity in the hearts of men; yet they
cannot fathom what God has done from beginning to end. 12 I
know that there is nothing better for men than to be happy and
do good while they live. 13 That everyone may eat and drink,
and find satisfaction in all his toil—this is the gift of God. 14 I know
that everything God does will endure forever; nothing can be
added to it and nothing taken from it. God does it so that men will
revere him.

3:11 *made everything beautiful in its time . . . they cannot fathom what God has done:* The author says that God's actions and timing are always correct (see also the note at 3:1-8). But human beings cannot fully understand God's actions. The author's point is that people have limited knowledge, and this leads to questions that cannot be answered.

3:12,13 Eccl 2:24; 3:22; 5:18; 8:15; 9:7. **3:14** Eccl 1:15.

3:16,17 *something else . . . every deed:* The author seems to struggle with the fact that violence and injustice happen so often on the earth that God controls (3:11). Though life does not appear to be fair to humans (3:16), justice will be carried out when God judges the good and wicked. See also the mini-articles called "Justice," p. 1721, "Enemies (The Wicked)," p. 1084, and "Day of the LORD," p. 1727.

3:18-20 *God tests them . . . to dust all return:* It is not clear what the author means by "tests" (3:18). It may have to do with God showing human beings that their lives are limited and, like the animals, they will eventually die. And when they die, they will return to the dust from which they came. See also Gen 2:7; 3:19.

3:15 Eccl 1:9,10. **4:1** Eccl 3:16. **4:2** Eccl 6:3.

15 Whatever is has already been,
and what will be has been before;
and God will call the past to account.[a]

16 And I saw something else under the sun:

In the place of judgment—wickedness was there,
in the place of justice—wickedness was there.

17 I thought in my heart,

"God will bring to judgment
both the righteous and the wicked,
for there will be a time for every activity,
a time for every deed."

18 I also thought, "As for men, God tests them so that they
may see that they are like the animals. 19 Man's fate is like that
of the animals; the same fate awaits them both: As one dies, so dies
the other. All have the same breath[b]; man has no advantage over
the animal. Everything is meaningless. 20 All go to the same place;
all come from dust, and to dust all return. 21 Who knows if the
spirit of man rises upward and if the spirit of the animal[c] goes
down into the earth?"
22 So I saw that there is nothing better for a man than to
enjoy his work, because that is his lot. For who can bring him to
see what will happen after him?

Oppression, Toil, Friendlessness

4 Again I looked and saw all the oppression that was taking place under the sun:

I saw the tears of the oppressed—
and they have no comforter;
power was on the side of their oppressors—
and they have no comforter.
2 And I declared that the dead,
who had already died,
are happier than the living,
who are still alive.
3 But better than both
is he who has not yet been,
who has not seen the evil
that is done under the sun.

4 And I saw that all labor and all achievement spring from man's envy of his neighbor. This too is meaningless, a chasing after the wind.

[a]15 Or *God calls back the past* [b]19 Or *spirit* [c]21 Or *Who knows the spirit of man, which rises upward, or the spirit of the animal, which*

[5]The fool folds his hands
and ruins himself.
[6]Better one handful with tranquillity
than two handfuls with toil
and chasing after the wind.

[7]Again I saw something meaningless under the sun:
[8]There was a man all alone;
he had neither son nor brother.
There was no end to his toil,
yet his eyes were not content with his wealth.
"For whom am I toiling," he asked,
"and why am I depriving myself of enjoyment?"
This too is meaningless—
a miserable business!

[9]Two are better than one,
because they have a good return for their work:
[10]If one falls down,
his friend can help him up.
But pity the man who falls
and has no one to help him up!
[11]Also, if two lie down together, they will keep warm.
But how can one keep warm alone?
[12]Though one may be overpowered,
two can defend themselves.
A cord of three strands is not quickly broken.

Advancement Is Meaningless

[13]Better a poor but wise youth than an old but foolish king
who no longer knows how to take warning. [14]The youth may have
come from prison to the kingship, or he may have been born in
poverty within his kingdom. [15]I saw that all who lived and walked
under the sun followed the youth, the king's successor. [16]There was
no end to all the people who were before them. But those who
came later were not pleased with the successor. This too is meaningless, a chasing after the wind.

Stand in Awe of God

5 Guard your steps when you go to the house of God. Go near to
listen rather than to offer the sacrifice of fools, who do not know
that they do wrong.

[2]Do not be quick with your mouth,
do not be hasty in your heart
to utter anything before God.
God is in heaven
and you are on earth,

4:7 *meaningless:* See the notes at 1:2 and 1:3-9.

4:8 *There was a man all alone:* The author describes a person who spends so much time working to gather wealth that there is no time for friends or family. When the person dies, he won't even have anyone who can inherit his wealth.

4:9-12 *Two are better than one . . . cord of three strands:* Having a friend is an advantage in many situations, and a good friendship is as strong as a three-stranded rope. Rope made by weaving together long pieces (strands) of leather or some wool is much stronger than a rope made of a single strand.

4:13-16 *Better a poor but wise youth than an old but foolish king:* A young poor person who is wise is better off than an old king who has wealth but lacks wisdom. In the wisdom literature of the Jewish Scriptures, foolishness and making bad decisions are often connected to youth (Prov 7:6-23), while wisdom is connected to old age. But here the author reverses this expected pattern. The identity of the young leader in 4:15 is a mystery. The author makes the point that even the popular young leader's earthly achievements would be forgotten.

5:1 *house of God . . . sacrifice of fools:* This refers to proper ways to worship God at the temple in Jerusalem. According to the Law of Moses, people were to bring their best animals to the priests so that they could offer them as sacrifices to the LORD. According to Israelite wisdom, obeying God is much more important than showy and insincere worship (1 Sam 15:22). "Fools," says the author, are people who speak too much, pray without thinking, make promises to God they don't intend to keep, and offer sacrifices as an outward show of worship, while not living according to God's commands (5:2-7).

4:5,6 Prov 6:6-11; 24:30-34.

so let your words be few.
[3] As a dream comes when there are many cares,
so the speech of a fool when there are many words.

[4]When you make a vow to God, do not delay in fulfilling it.
He has no pleasure in fools; fulfill your vow. [5]It is better not to vow
than to make a vow and not fulfill it. [6]Do not let your mouth lead
you into sin. And do not protest to the ⌞temple⌟ messenger, "My
vow was a mistake." Why should God be angry at what you say and
destroy the work of your hands? [7]Much dreaming and many words
are meaningless. Therefore stand in awe of God. FEAR GOD

Whoever loves money never has money enough; whoever loves wealth is never satisfied with his income. This too is meaningless.
Eccl 5:10

5:8,9 *poor . . . official . . . increase from the land is taken:* In Israelite society, the king's officials collected taxes from everyone, including the poor. People were also expected to pay temple taxes to support those who were in charge of the temple. The author makes the point that dishonest officials, who make it difficult for the poor to receive fair treatment, often run these systems. See also 3:16,17; 4:1-3; and the mini-articles called "The Poor," p. 2362 and "Justice," p. 1721.

5:4 Ps 66:13,14. **5:7** Eccl 7:18; 12:13. **5:12** Matt 6:25-33. **5:15** Job 1:21; Ps 49:17; 1 Tim 6:7.

Riches Are Meaningless

[8]If you see the poor oppressed in a district, and justice and
rights denied, do not be surprised at such things; for one official is
eyed by a higher one, and over them both are others higher still.
[9]The increase from the land is taken by all; the king himself profits from the fields.

[10] Whoever loves money never has money enough;
whoever loves wealth is never satisfied with his
income.
This too is meaningless.

[11] As goods increase,
so do those who consume them.
And what benefit are they to the owner
except to feast his eyes on them?

[12] The sleep of a laborer is sweet,
whether he eats little or much,
but the abundance of a rich man
permits him no sleep.

[13]I have seen a grievous evil under the sun:

wealth hoarded to the harm of its owner,
[14] or wealth lost through some misfortune,
so that when he has a son
there is nothing left for him.
[15] Naked a man comes from his mother's womb,
and as he comes, so he departs.
He takes nothing from his labor
that he can carry in his hand.

[16]This too is a grievous evil:

As a man comes, so he departs,
and what does he gain,
since he toils for the wind?
[17] All his days he eats in darkness,
with great frustration, affliction and anger.

[18]Then I realized that it is good and proper for a man to eat
and drink, and to find satisfaction in his toilsome labor under the
sun during the few days of life God has given him—for this is his
lot. [19]Moreover, when God gives any man wealth and possessions,
and enables him to enjoy them, to accept his lot and be happy in
his work—this is a gift of God. [20]He seldom reflects on the days of
his life, because God keeps him occupied with gladness of heart.
6 I have seen another evil under the sun, and it weighs heavily
on men: [2]God gives a man wealth, possessions and honor, so that
he lacks nothing his heart desires, but God does not enable him to
enjoy them, and a stranger enjoys them instead. This is meaningless, a grievous evil.
[3]A man may have a hundred children and live many years;
yet no matter how long he lives, if he cannot enjoy his prosperity
and does not receive proper burial, I say that a stillborn child is
better off than he. [4]It comes without meaning, it departs in darkness, and in darkness its name is shrouded. [5]Though it never saw
the sun or knew anything, it has more rest than does that man—
[6]even if he lives a thousand years twice over but fails to enjoy his
prosperity. Do not all go to the same place?

[7]All man's efforts are for his mouth,
yet his appetite is never satisfied.

Still Life: An Allegory of the Vanities of Human Life by Harmen van Steenwyck, around 1640. Many of the things that the author of ECCLESIASTES describes as being pointless and making no more sense than chasing the wind are shown in this still life painting. These include the pursuit of power (symbolized by the sword) and knowledge (symbolized by the book). The skull is a reminder that everyone in the world, both rich and poor, comes to the same end. Wise or foolish, everyone will die (2:16).

5:18,19 *good and proper . . . find satisfaction . . . gift of God:* See the note at 2:24-26. Those who recognize that the good things of life—food, drink, and work—are a gift from God can truly enjoy them.

6:2 *God gives a man wealth, possessions and honor . . . God does not enable him to enjoy them:* God may give people wealth, but some who have received riches may not be allowed to enjoy them (2:18-23; 5:13-17). The author calls this situation senseless and unfair, but probably thinks that this is just one more example of how human beings cannot fully understand God's ways.

6:3,4 *have a hundred children . . . proper burial . . . departs in darkness:* Having children was considered a great gift from God. The more the children, the greater the blessing. But life is not worth living, and having many children and great wealth (6:1,2) aren't important, if one doesn't enjoy life or receive a decent burial (Jer 16:4-7; 22:18,19).

The author says that a child born dead will rest better in darkness than a person who lives in the world but does not enjoy life. In spite of the fact that everyone dies, life is meant to be enjoyed (3:16-22; 5:13-20).

6:7 Prov 16:26.

6:10 *Whatever exists has already been named:* See the notes at 1:8-11 and 3:11.

6:11 *The more the words:* The author may be repeating the idea that talking too much and talking without thinking are foolish (5:3; see also Prov 10:8, 19). Or, the author may be saying that people's talking will not change what God has already decided. The power of human talk is nothing when compared to God's power.

7:1 *good name:* A good reputation is highly prized in Israelite wisdom (Prov 22:1).

7:2-4 *better to go to a house of mourning . . . The heart of the wise is in the house of mourning:* The author makes the point that it is better to face life and death in a realistic way. Life is meant to be enjoyed (2:24), but people are not to ignore the reality of death. Someone who fills his or her life with parties and constant fun may not have the proper attitude about life and death. See also Prov 14:13.

7:6 *crackling of thorns:* The cackling of foolish laughter is like the loud crackling of dried thorns or thistles that are being burned. When other kinds of fuel were scarce, dry thorn branches were burned to cook food. Thorns burn fast, but they give little heat. See also Ps 58:9; Prov 26:9.

7:5 Prov 15:31,32; 17:10. **7:7** Deut 16:18,19. **7:8** Eccl 7:1; Prov 14:29. **7:9** Jas 1:19.

8 What advantage has a wise man
over a fool?
What does a poor man gain
by knowing how to conduct himself before others?
9 Better what the eye sees
than the roving of the appetite.
This too is meaningless,
a chasing after the wind.

10 Whatever exists has already been named,
and what man is has been known;
no man can contend
with one who is stronger than he.
11 The more the words,
the less the meaning,
and how does that profit anyone?

12 For who knows what is good for a man in life, during the
few and meaningless days he passes through like a shadow? Who
can tell him what will happen under the sun after he is gone?

Wisdom

7 A good name is better than fine perfume,
and the day of death better than the day of birth.
2 It is better to go to a house of mourning
than to go to a house of feasting,
for death is the destiny of every man;
the living should take this to heart.
3 Sorrow is better than laughter,
because a sad face is good for the heart.
4 The heart of the wise is in the house of mourning,
but the heart of fools is in the house of pleasure.
5 It is better to heed a wise man's rebuke
than to listen to the song of fools.
6 Like the crackling of thorns under the pot,
so is the laughter of fools.
This too is meaningless.

7 Extortion turns a wise man into a fool,
and a bribe corrupts the heart.

8 The end of a matter is better than its beginning,
and patience is better than pride.
9 Do not be quickly provoked in your spirit,
for anger resides in the lap of fools.

10 Do not say, "Why were the old days better than these?"
For it is not wise to ask such questions.

11 Wisdom, like an inheritance, is a good thing
and benefits those who see the sun.

12 Wisdom is a shelter
as money is a shelter,
but the advantage of knowledge is this:
that wisdom preserves the life of its possessor.

13 Consider what God has done:

Who can straighten
what he has made crooked?
14 When times are good, be happy;
but when times are bad, consider:
God has made the one
as well as the other.
Therefore, a man cannot discover
anything about his future.

15 In this meaningless life of mine I have seen both of these:
a righteous man perishing in his righteousness,
and a wicked man living long in his wickedness.
16 Do not be overrighteous,
neither be overwise—
why destroy yourself?
17 Do not be overwicked,
and do not be a fool—
why die before your time?
18 It is good to grasp the one
and not let go of the other.
The man who fears God will avoid all ⌊extremes⌋.[a]
19 Wisdom makes one wise man more powerful
than ten rulers in a city.

20 There is not a righteous man on earth
who does what is right and never sins.

21 Do not pay attention to every word people say,
or you may hear your servant cursing you—
22 for you know in your heart
that many times you yourself have cursed others.
23 All this I tested by wisdom and I said,

"I am determined to be wise"—
but this was beyond me.
24 Whatever wisdom may be,
it is far off and most profound—
who can discover it?
25 So I turned my mind to understand,
to investigate and to search out wisdom and the
scheme of things

[a]**18** Or *will follow them both*

Consider what God has done: Who can straighten what he has made crooked?
Eccl 7:13

7:16 *not be overrighteous . . . overwise:* The advice in this verse has been interpreted in various ways. The author may be saying that a person shouldn't try to be too good or too wise, because it may not be worth the effort, and besides, no one in the world always does the right thing anyway (7:20). Or, the author may be warning against pretending to be more wise or more good than one really is, because that can lead to disaster (Prov 16:18).

7:18 *grasp the one and not let go of the other . . . avoid all extremes:* The author encourages living life in a realistic way. Avoid evil and be good, but don't claim to be perfect. Avoid foolishness and be wise, but don't pretend to be wiser than you are. See also 5:7 and the note at 12:13,14.

7:24 *far off and most profound:* See 3:11 and the note.

7:12 Prov 16:16. **7:13,14** Eccl 1:15; 3:14. **7:15** Job 9:22-24; Eccl 3:16,17; 8:14. **7:20** Job 4:17; 9:2; Rom 3:9-18.

7:26 *woman who is a snare:* On one level, this woman is one who tries to tempt a man to commit adultery (Prov 2:16-19; 5:7-18; 9:13-18; 23:27, 28). But the bad woman here also stands for anything that tempts people to disobey God. In the Bible, both Wisdom and Folly are sometimes compared to a woman (Prov 3:15-18; 9:1-6, 13-18). Wisdom, like God's Law, is something to be followed. But unfaithfulness to God's Law, like a bad woman, is to be avoided.

7:28 *one upright man . . . not one upright woman:* The author says that finding a good man or woman is difficult. Some scholars suggest that this refers to Solomon and his hundreds of wives (see 1 Kgs 11:3, 4 and the note on p. 1249). King Solomon could not find one woman who was as good and precious as the one described in Proverbs 31:10-31.

8:2-4 *Obey the king's command:* Respecting the king's power and authority are stressed in Israelite wisdom (Prov 14:33-35; 16:14; 20:2; 24:21). But keeping a promise made to God is commanded as well (5:2-5; see also Num 30:2; Deut 23:21-23; Matt 5:33-37).

8:6 Eccl 3:1-8, 17.

and to understand the stupidity of wickedness
and the madness of folly.

26 I find more bitter than death
the woman who is a snare,
whose heart is a trap
and whose hands are chains.
The man who pleases God will escape her,
but the sinner she will ensnare.

27 "Look," says the Teacher,[a] "this is what I have discovered:

"Adding one thing to another to discover the scheme of things—
28 while I was still searching
but not finding—
I found one ⌊upright⌋ man among a thousand,
but not one ⌊upright⌋ woman among them all.
29 This only have I found:
God made mankind upright,
but men have gone in search of many schemes."

8 Who is like the wise man?
Who knows the explanation of things?
Wisdom brightens a man's face
and changes its hard appearance.

Obey the King

2 Obey the king's command, I say, because you took an oath
before God. 3 Do not be in a hurry to leave the king's presence. Do
not stand up for a bad cause, for he will do whatever he pleases.
4 Since a king's word is supreme, who can say to him, "What are
you doing?"

5 Whoever obeys his command will come to no harm,
and the wise heart will know the proper time and procedure.
6 For there is a proper time and procedure for every matter,
though a man's misery weighs heavily upon him.

7 Since no man knows the future,
who can tell him what is to come?
8 No man has power over the wind to contain it[b];
so no one has power over the day of his death.
As no one is discharged in time of war,
so wickedness will not release those who practice it.

9 All this I saw, as I applied my mind to everything done
under the sun. There is a time when a man lords it over others to

[a] **27** Or *leader of the assembly* [b] **8** Or *over his spirit to retain it*

his own[a] hurt. 10Then too, I saw the wicked buried—those who
used to come and go from the holy place and receive praise[b] in the
city where they did this. This too is meaningless.
11When the sentence for a crime is not quickly carried out,
the hearts of the people are filled with schemes to do wrong.
12Although a wicked man commits a hundred crimes and still
lives a long time, I know that it will go better with God-fearing
men, who are reverent before God. 13Yet because the wicked do not
fear God, it will not go well with them, and their days will not
lengthen like a shadow.
14There is something else meaningless that occurs on earth:
righteous men who get what the wicked deserve, and wicked men
who get what the righteous deserve. This too, I say, is meaningless.
15So I commend the enjoyment of life, because nothing is better
for a man under the sun than to eat and drink and be glad. Then
joy will accompany him in his work all the days of the life God has
given him under the sun.
16When I applied my mind to know wisdom and to observe
man's labor on earth—his eyes not seeing sleep day or night—
17then I saw all that God has done. No one can comprehend what
goes on under the sun. Despite all his efforts to search it out, man
cannot discover its meaning. Even if a wise man claims he knows,
he cannot really comprehend it.

A Common Destiny for All

9 So I reflected on all this and concluded that the righteous and
the wise and what they do are in God's hands, but no man knows
whether love or hate awaits him. 2All share a common destiny—
the righteous and the wicked, the good and the bad,[c] the clean and
the unclean, those who offer sacrifices and those who do not.

As it is with the good man,
  so with the sinner;
as it is with those who take oaths,
  so with those who are afraid to take them.

3This is the evil in everything that happens under the sun:
The same destiny overtakes all. The hearts of men, moreover, are
full of evil and there is madness in their hearts while they live, and
afterward they join the dead. 4Anyone who is among the living has
hope[d]—even a live dog is better off than a dead lion!

5For the living know that they will die,
  but the dead know nothing;

Despite all his efforts to search it out, man cannot discover its meaning. Even if a wise man claims he knows, he cannot really comprehend it.
Eccl 8:17

8:10-14 *wicked buried . . . righteous deserve:* A common belief in ancient times was that God provides health and wealth for everyone who lives right, but God punishes those who do evil (Job 4:7-9; Ps 94:1-3; Prov 10:27-29). The author is trying to figure out how God's justice works, but recognizes that there are certain situations he cannot understand (8:17). See also the notes at 2:24-26 and 3:11.

9:1 *what they do are in God's hands:* See the notes at 3:1-8 and 3:11.

9:2 *common destiny . . . take oaths:* See the notes at 3:18-20; 5:1; and 8:2-4. The "common destiny" that happens to everyone is that everyone dies.

---

[a]**9** Or *to their* [b]**10** Some Hebrew manuscripts and Septuagint (Aquila); most Hebrew manuscripts *and are forgotten* [c]**2** Septuagint (Aquila), Vulgate and Syriac; Hebrew does not have *and the bad.* [d]**4** Or *What then is to be chosen? With all who live, there is hope*

they have no further reward,
and even the memory of them is forgotten.
6 Their love, their hate
and their jealousy have long since vanished;
never again will they have a part
in anything that happens under the sun.

7 Go, eat your food with gladness, and drink your wine with
a joyful heart, for it is now that God favors what you do. 8 Always
be clothed in white, and always anoint your head with oil. 9 Enjoy
life with your wife, whom you love, all the days of this meaningless
life that God has given you under the sun— all your meaningless
days. For this is your lot in life and in your toilsome labor under
the sun. 10 Whatever your hand finds to do, do it with all your
might, for in the grave,[a] where you are going, there is neither
working nor planning nor knowledge nor wisdom.

11 I have seen something else under the sun:

The race is not to the swift
or the battle to the strong,
nor does food come to the wise
or wealth to the brilliant
or favor to the learned;
but time and chance happen to them all.

12 Moreover, no man knows when his hour will come:

As fish are caught in a cruel net,
or birds are taken in a snare,
so men are trapped by evil times
that fall unexpectedly upon them.

Wisdom Better Than Folly

13 I also saw under the sun this example of wisdom that
greatly impressed me: 14 There was once a small city with only a few
people in it. And a powerful king came against it, surrounded it
and built huge siegeworks against it. 15 Now there lived in that city
a man poor but wise, and he saved the city by his wisdom. But
nobody remembered that poor man. 16 So I said, "Wisdom is better than strength." But the poor man's wisdom is despised, and his
words are no longer heeded.

17 The quiet words of the wise are more to be heeded
than the shouts of a ruler of fools.
18 Wisdom is better than weapons of war,
but one sinner destroys much good.

10 As dead flies give perfume a bad smell,
so a little folly outweighs wisdom and honor.

[a]10 Hebrew *Sheol*

9:10 *the grave:* The underground world of the dead is described as a totally silent place where no one knows or feels anything (9:5,6; see also Job 10:21,22; Ps 88:12; 94:17). So, the author encourages people to enjoy life before they die and disappear forever. The idea of life after death was not a common belief in ancient times. For more, see the mini-articles called "Eternal Life," p. 2072, and "Hell," p. 1944.

9:11,12 *race is not to the swift . . . birds are taken in a snare:* A fish net or bird trap is quickly closed before the prey is aware of the danger. The author uses a wise saying (9:11) to say once again that life is unpredictable and often does not fit with human expectations. Here he seems to say that chance (good or bad luck) determines what happens, though earlier he stated that God determines everything (3:1-17; 7:14).

9:13-18 *example . . . saved the city . . . nobody remembered:* Teaching stories (parables) and wise sayings (proverbs) show the value of wisdom. The original Hebrew words of 9:15 can have different meanings: (1) the poor person offered wisdom that saved the town from attack, but he was soon forgotten because he was poor; or (2) the poor person gave wise advice that was ignored because he was poor. The second meaning seems to fit better with the conclusion in 9:16. An attitude of disrespect toward the poor can be found in other wisdom sayings (Prov 14:20; 18:23; 19:7). A wise person can outsmart a stronger opponent, but the actions of one fool can undo the good work someone else has done.

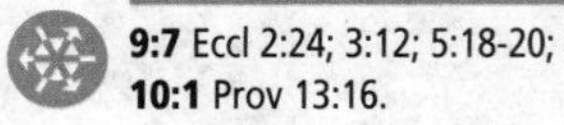

9:7 Eccl 2:24; 3:12; 5:18-20; 8:15.
10:1 Prov 13:16.

2 The heart of the wise inclines to the right,
but the heart of the fool to the left.
3 Even as he walks along the road,
the fool lacks sense
and shows everyone how stupid he is.
4 If a ruler's anger rises against you,
do not leave your post;
calmness can lay great errors to rest.

5 There is an evil I have seen under the sun,
the sort of error that arises from a ruler:
6 Fools are put in many high positions,
while the rich occupy the low ones.
7 I have seen slaves on horseback,
while princes go on foot like slaves.

8 Whoever digs a pit may fall into it;
whoever breaks through a wall may be bitten
by a snake.
9 Whoever quarries stones may be injured by them;
whoever splits logs may be endangered by them.
10 If the ax is dull
and its edge unsharpened,
more strength is needed
but skill will bring success.

11 If a snake bites before it is charmed,
there is no profit for the charmer.

12 Words from a wise man's mouth are gracious,
but a fool is consumed by his own lips.
13 At the beginning his words are folly;
at the end they are wicked madness—
14 and the fool multiplies words.

No one knows what is coming—
who can tell him what will happen after him?

15 A fool's work wearies him;
he does not know the way to town.

16 Woe to you, O land whose king was a servant[a]
and whose princes feast in the morning.
17 Blessed are you, O land whose king is of noble birth
and whose princes eat at a proper time—
for strength and not for drunkenness.

18 If a man is lazy, the rafters sag;
if his hands are idle, the house leaks.

[a]**16** Or *king is a child*

10:8 *digs a pit . . . bitten by a snake:* Walls of ancient houses were often made of stones or bricks with mud filling in the cracks between the stones. If some mud washed out, a snake could make a home inside the wall. See also Ps 7:14-16; Prov 26:27.

10:11 *snake bites before it is charmed:* Snake-charming was common in the ancient world (see Ps 58:4,5). Poisonous cobras were tamed by charmers, a practice that continues to this day. The word for "charmer" means "controller of the tongue." This may refer either to how the charmer used his voice to control the snake and make it move, or it may refer to the snake's tongue, which was thought to be the source of its poison. (See also Job 20:16; Ps 140:3.)

10:3 Prov 18:2. **10:4** Prov 19:2; 25:5. **10:5-7** Prov 30:21-23; Eccl 3:16; 4:1-3; 8:10,11,14. **10:12,13** Prov 14:3; 15:2; 18:7. **10:16** Isa 3:4,5, 12. **10:17** Prov 31:4. **10:18** Prov 20:4; 24:30-34.

10:19 *feast . . . money:* The first part of this verse restates a common theme of the book (see the note at 2:24-26). The author may mean the statement about money to be ironic. Elsewhere, he warns about relying on money and wealth to bring happiness (5:10-17; 6:1-3).

11:1,2 *Cast your bread upon the waters . . . seven, yes to eight:* Verse 1 is the translation of a difficult Hebrew phrase that literally means "Send out your bread on the waters." Some have taken this phrase to refer to giving gifts (alms) to the poor (see also Deut 15:10; Prov 19:17; Gal 6:9,10). Others have seen a reference to sending grain on trading ships. So, 11:2 may refer to gifts for the poor, or it may refer to dividing the grain into seven or eight different shipments. If all the grain is put in just one shipment, one disaster could wipe it all out. Dividing the grain into different shipments reduces the risk of losing everything. This interpretation would be like the modern saying, "Don't put all your eggs in one basket."

11:4 *watches the wind . . . looks at the clouds:* Since both life and the weather are unpredictable and under God's control (3:11, 15, 17; 6:10; 8:6-8; 9:1), a farmer must plant his crops and not worry about the future (11:6).

10:20 Exod 22:28; Acts 23:5.

Brass bowl with Arabic and Hebrew inscriptions, inlaid with silver, copper, and gold, from Damascus, around 1905. Among the many inscriptions on this bowl is a verse from Ecclesiastes that is somewhat difficult to translate: "Send your bread forth upon the water; for after many days you will find it" (11:1). The NIV renders it, "Cast your bread upon the waters, for after many days you will find it again." For more, see the note at 11:1,2.

19 A feast is made for laughter,
and wine makes life merry,
but money is the answer for everything.

20 Do not revile the king even in your thoughts,
or curse the rich in your bedroom,
because a bird of the air may carry your words,
and a bird on the wing may report what you say.

Bread Upon the Waters

11 Cast your bread upon the waters,
for after many days you will find it again.
2 Give portions to seven, yes to eight,
for you do not know what disaster may come
upon the land.

3 If clouds are full of water,
they pour rain upon the earth.
Whether a tree falls to the south or to the north,
in the place where it falls, there will it lie.
4 Whoever watches the wind will not plant;
whoever looks at the clouds will not reap.

5 As you do not know the path of the wind,
or how the body is formed[a] in a mother's womb,
so you cannot understand the work of God,
the Maker of all things.

6 Sow your seed in the morning,
and at evening let not your hands be idle,
for you do not know which will succeed,
whether this or that,
or whether both will do equally well.

Enjoy Life and Remember God While You Are Young

The author emphasizes the importance of enjoying life each day, because life will soon end in death (11:8). Remembering God and appreciating God's creation are especially important when young, since growing old causes physical problems that make enjoying life more difficult.

Remember Your Creator While Young

7 Light is sweet,
and it pleases the eyes to see the sun.
8 However many years a man may live,
let him enjoy them all.
But let him remember the days of darkness,
for they will be many.
Everything to come is meaningless.

9 Be happy, young man, while you are young,
and let your heart give you joy in the days of your youth.
Follow the ways of your heart
and whatever your eyes see,
but know that for all these things
God will bring you to judgment.
10 So then, banish anxiety from your heart
and cast off the troubles of your body,
for youth and vigor are meaningless.

12 Remember your Creator
in the days of your youth,
before the days of trouble come
and the years approach when you will say,
"I find no pleasure in them"—

[a]5 Or *know how life* (or *the spirit*) / *enters the body being formed*

11:7-10 *the sun . . . enjoy them all . . . banish anxiety:* The author acknowledges that there is great beauty in life (11:7). Whether the "sun" refers to the sun itself or to youth, the author says that it should be enjoyed when it is present, because death comes all too soon. See also the notes at 2:24-26; 3:18-20; 9:10.

11:9 *Follow the ways of your heart . . . God will bring you to judgment:* The first part of this verse sounds like the author's general philosophy of life (2:24-26; 3:12,13,22; 5:18-20; 9:7). But this is not intended to encourage reckless or foolish living (5:1-7; 7:17). Some scholars believe that the part of the verse concerning God's judgment may have been added by a later editor, so readers would not use the earlier part of the verse as an excuse to live in a selfish way or to disobey God (12:14). See the note at 3:16,17.

12:1 *Creator:* This refers to God (3:14,15; 9:1). See also Gen 1:27; 2:7, 21-23; Ps 8:3-5.

11:5 Ps 139:13-16; Job 10:9-11.
11:6 Eccl 9:10; 11:3,4.

12:2 *light . . . dark . . . rain:* The author compares old age to a gloomy and rainy day. See also Job 3:1-6.

12:5 *eternal home:* This probably refers to the world of the dead or the grave (see 12:7 and the note at 9:10).

12:6 *silver cord . . . wheel broken:* Light and water were important symbols of life. The author uses the spilling of oil and water to symbolize death. Oil was burned in a clay or metal bowl to make a lamp. Sometimes, these lamps were hung by metal cords. If the silver cord broke, the flame of life in the golden bowl would be extinguished. Similarly, a broken water pitcher, or a shattered wheel on the pulley at the well, will keep a person from life-giving water.

12:7 Gen 2:7; 3:19; Eccl 3:20.

2 before the sun and the light
and the moon and the stars grow dark,
and the clouds return after the rain;
3 when the keepers of the house tremble,
and the strong men stoop,
when the grinders cease because they are few,
and those looking through the windows
grow dim;
4 when the doors to the street are closed
and the sound of grinding fades;
when men rise up at the sound of birds,
but all their songs grow faint;
5 when men are afraid of heights
and of dangers in the streets;
when the almond tree blossoms
and the grasshopper drags himself along
and desire no longer is stirred.
Then man goes to his eternal home
and mourners go about the streets.

6 Remember him—before the silver cord is severed,
or the golden bowl is broken;
before the pitcher is shattered at the spring,
or the wheel broken at the well,
7 and the dust returns to the ground it came from,
and the spirit returns to God who gave it.

QUESTIONS ABOUT ECCLESIASTES 3:1—12:14

1. The author believes that everything on earth has its own time and season. (3:1-8) According to the author, who controls everything that happens and when? (3:11, 15) How might such a philosophy affect how a person lives his or her life?
2. What kinds of "oppression" is the author describing in 4:1-3? The author suggests that it would be better not to be born than to have seen these terrible things. But how might those who have been born respond to evil and injustice in the world?
3. What does the author say about proper worship and respect for God? (5:1-7)
4. The book says a wide variety of things about money and wealth (see 5:10-15; 6:2; 7:11; 10:19; 11:1). What is your reaction to these passages? How do you think the author's comments fit with modern understandings of wealth and money?
5. What do you think the author means when he says, "Do not be overrighteous, neither be overwise"? (7:16) Do you agree with this advice? Why or why not?
6. What is the author's view of growing old? (12:1-7) How does this compare with your own view?
7. For you, which of the following statements seems to be a better summary of the author's view of life in Ecclesiastes?
   "Everything is meaningless." (12:8)
   "Fear God and keep his commandments." (12:13)
   Explain your choice.
8. How would you summarize your own view of life in a short statement or wise saying?

[8]“Meaningless! Meaningless!” says the Teacher.[a]
“Everything is meaningless!”

Conclusion

The author’s mood and thoughts change suddenly as he concludes his book by saying that everything life is about boils down to respecting and obeying God.

The Conclusion of the Matter

[9]Not only was the Teacher wise, but also he imparted knowledge to the people. He pondered and searched out and set in order
many proverbs. [10]The Teacher searched to find just the right
words, and what he wrote was upright and true.
[11]The words of the wise are like goads, their collected sayings
like firmly embedded nails—given by one Shepherd. [12]Be warned,
my son, of anything in addition to them.

Of making many books there is no end, and much study wearies the body.

[13]Now all has been heard;
here is the conclusion of the matter:
Fear God and keep his commandments,
for this is the whole ⌊duty⌋ of man.
[14]For God will bring every deed into judgment,
including every hidden thing,
whether it is good or evil.

---

a8 Or *the leader of the assembly*; also in verses 9 and 10

12:8 *Everything is meaningless:* The book’s major theme, first stated in chapter 1, is repeated here. This forms a kind of “frame” around the rest of the author’s thoughts. See also the notes at 1:2 and 1:3-9.

12:9 *the Teacher wise:* See the note at 1:1.

12:13,14 *Fear God and keep his commandments . . . judgment:* In Hebrew wisdom, obeying God is often the best evidence that one is wise (see also the note at 1:17). These statements bring the author’s often conflicting observations more into line with the common viewpoint of Hebrew wisdom: Because human understanding is so limited and “everything is meaningless,” it is all right to enjoy life, but always within the framework of obedience to God. See 5:7; 7:17,18; 11:9; and the notes at 1:2; 1:3-9; 3:16,17; 7:18; 11:7-10.

SONG OF SONGS

Why is ancient love poetry included in the Holy Scriptures? Read this book that describes love as being "as strong as death."

mandrakes: SONG OF SONGS is rich in animal and plant imagery. The flowers, fruit, and root of the mandrake (see 7:13) were used in medicines. This plant was also thought to give sexual powers to people who possessed it (see Gen 30:14-16).

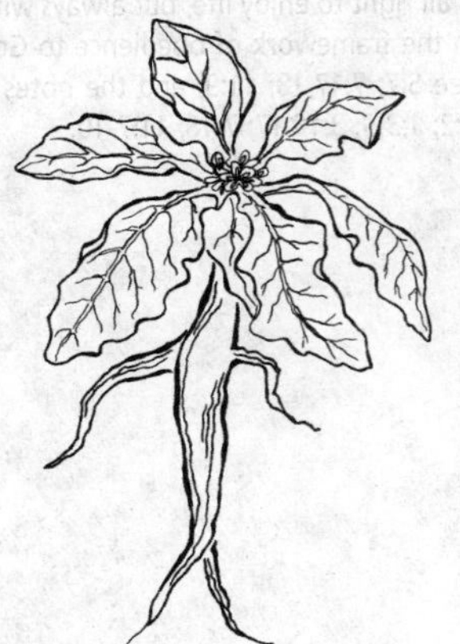

WHAT MAKES SONG OF SONGS SPECIAL?

The title of this book means "the most beautiful of songs," and in some translations it is called "The Song of Solomon" (see 1:1). In the Jewish Scriptures, this book is found in the section known as "The Writings" (see the article called "What Books Belong in the Bible?" p. 13). Why it was included in the Bible at all is a question that has prompted many debates among Jewish and Christian teachers for over two thousand years. Answers to this question have often been based on how the book is interpreted.

WHY WAS SONG OF SONGS WRITTEN?

On the surface, SONG OF SONGS is love poetry that celebrates the love between a man and a woman. Some consider the book to be a unified poem written by one author, while others think it is a collection of love songs or poems put together by an editor. Some people think SONG OF SONGS is a drama, while some scholars point out that parts of the book are very much like ancient Mesopotamian marriage songs or old Egyptian love poems. God is not mentioned in the book, and the poems seem only to provide a description of human love.

If SONG OF SONGS is simply a collection of poems that express the powerful love that a woman and a man can have for each other, why is it included in the Bible? Even as late as the second century A.D. Jewish rabbis debated whether or not SONG OF SONGS should be considered Holy Scripture. Early Christian writings reveal similar debates. Eventually, however, many Jewish teachers said the book symbolized God's love for the people of Israel. This interpretation may be based on passages from HOSEA (1–3) and JEREMIAH (2:20—3:5), which describe the relationship between God and Israel in terms of a marriage. Many Christian interpreters came to a similar conclusion, saying that the book symbolizes the kind of relationship that Jesus Christ (the bridegroom) has with the church (his bride). These interpretations helped the book gain acceptance as part of Scripture.

WHAT'S THE STORY BEHIND THE SCENE?

Scholars do not agree on who wrote this book or when. The first verse of the book (1:1) connects the book with King Solomon, who ruled Israel from 970 to 931 B.C. But the Hebrew in this verse can be translated various ways. The book may be "by," "according to," or "for" Solomon; or it may "belong to," or be "dedicated to" him. All that is clear is that the book was in some way owned by (or connected to) Solomon, who was known in ancient

Israel as the author of many wise sayings and poems (1 Kgs 4:32). As in the case of ECCLESIASTES (see the note at Eccl 1:1), having Solomon's name connected with the book added to its authority as true Israelite Wisdom.

HOW IS SONG OF SONGS CONSTRUCTED?

If the book is a collection of poems, an editor probably arranged them so that they would relate to each other as a whole. The romance between two lovers is the focus of the poem and provides a kind of connection between its various scenes or sections. But at some points it is hard to know who exactly is speaking, and it is not always easy to see how the sections of the poem relate to one another. When a new poem or speech begins, the NIV inserts "Beloved," "Lover," or "Friends" as a way of indicating who might be the speaker in the section that follows. The following outline suggests just one of many ways the book's sections may be grouped:

Solomon's Song (1:1)
Love blossoms (1:2—2:7)
Love dreams (2:8—3:5)
Love plans (3:6—6:10)
Love dances (6:11—8:4)
Powerful love is not for sale (8:5-14)

The beloved sang,
"Your name is like perfume poured out."
Song 1:3

1:1 *Solomon:* Solomon, the son of Israel's King David, ruled the united kingdom of Israel from 970 to 931 B.C. Under Solomon's leadership, Israel became a strong and wealthy nation. He supervised the building of the first temple in Jerusalem (1 Kgs 5–8), and he had a reputation as a wise man who wrote many wise sayings and songs (1 Kgs 4:29-34; Prov 1:1; Eccl 1:1). Even though his name is connected to SONG OF SONGS, it is not certain that Solomon is the author of any of the poems in the book. See also the mini-article called "Solomon," p. 776.

1:2,3 *kiss . . . your name . . . perfume:* His love is better than good wine, which was highly prized. His smell is like fragrant oil, and his name brings to mind the pouring out of expensive perfumed oil.

Solomon's Song

Verse 1 provides the book's title, or "superscription." In the Hebrew translation, the singular and plural forms of the same word ("song of songs") are combined to produce a phrase that means the "greatest" or "most beautiful" song.

1 Solomon's Song of Songs.

Love Blossoms

A young woman tells about her true love. She calls him her "king" (1:4). Then both the woman and man offer songs of love that are filled with images that excite the senses of sight, smell, and taste.

Beloved[a]

2 Let him kiss me with the kisses of his mouth—
for your love is more delightful than wine.
3 Pleasing is the fragrance of your perfumes;
your name is like perfume poured out.

[a]Primarily on the basis of the gender of the Hebrew pronouns used, male and female speakers are indicated by the captions *Lover* and *Beloved* respectively. The words of others are marked *Friends*. In some instances the divisions and their captions are debatable.

1:4,5 *king . . . daughters of Jerusalem:* "King" may refer to Solomon or simply to a man the young woman wants to marry. The "daughters of Jerusalem" are her friends. These friends appear later as well (2:7; 3:5; 5:8, 16; 8:4).

1:6 *darkened by the sun . . . my own vineyard I have neglected:* The word translated as "vineyard," refers to her neglecting her own body, her "vineyard" (see 8:12), while working in the grape vineyard.

In this society, brothers had authority over their sisters, and they expected a sister to ask for approval before getting romantically involved with a man. See also the note at 8:8,9.

1:7 *midday . . . a veiled woman:* The young woman does not want people to think she is like the prostitutes ("a veiled woman") who supposedly went to have sex with shepherds out in the pastures during the midday time of rest. She may be suggesting that she and her lover meet at noontime. But she also wants it known that unlike the "other women" who will go with any man, her desire grows only out of her love for her lover.

1:8 *tracks of the sheep:* The reply to the woman's question comes in a teasing way. A double meaning is probably intended in these references to grazing (feeding), which in the ancient Near East could also refer to having sex (see also 4:12—5:1).

1:12 *at his table . . . perfume:* See the note at 1:4,5. The "table" here may refer to a low table. In the ancient Near East, most people ate while lying on their sides next to a low table. "Perfume" probably refers to "spikenard" (or "nard"), a sweet-smelling ointment made from a plant that was imported from India. The ointment was sometimes used as a love charm.

No wonder the maidens love you!
4 Take me away with you—let us hurry!
Let the king bring me into his chambers.

Friends

We rejoice and delight in you[a];
we will praise your love more than wine.

Beloved

How right they are to adore you!

5 Dark am I, yet lovely,
O daughters of Jerusalem,
dark like the tents of Kedar,
like the tent curtains of Solomon.[b]
6 Do not stare at me because I am dark,
because I am darkened by the sun.
My mother's sons were angry with me
and made me take care of the vineyards;
my own vineyard I have neglected.
7 Tell me, you whom I love, where you graze your flock
and where you rest your sheep at midday.
Why should I be like a veiled woman
beside the flocks of your friends?

Friends

8 If you do not know, most beautiful of women,
follow the tracks of the sheep
and graze your young goats
by the tents of the shepherds.

Lover

9 I liken you, my darling, to a mare
harnessed to one of the chariots of Pharaoh.
10 Your cheeks are beautiful with earrings,
your neck with strings of jewels.
11 We will make you earrings of gold,
studded with silver.

Beloved

12 While the king was at his table,
my perfume spread its fragrance.
13 My lover is to me a sachet of myrrh
resting between my breasts.

[a]4 The Hebrew is masculine singular. [b]5 Or *Salma*

[14]My lover is to me a cluster of henna blossoms
from the vineyards of En Gedi.

Lover

[15]How beautiful you are, my darling!
Oh, how beautiful!
Your eyes are doves.

Beloved

[16]How handsome you are, my lover!
Oh, how charming!
And our bed is verdant.

Lover

[17]The beams of our house are cedars;
our rafters are firs.

Beloved[a]

2 I am a rose[b] of Sharon,
a lily of the valleys.

Lover

[2]Like a lily among thorns
is my darling among the maidens.

Beloved

[3]Like an apple tree among the trees of
the forest
is my lover among the young men.
I delight to sit in his shade,
and his fruit is sweet to my taste.
[4]He has taken me to the banquet hall,
and his banner over me is love.
[5]Strengthen me with raisins,
refresh me with apples,
for I am faint with love.
[6]His left arm is under my head,
and his right arm embraces me.
[7]Daughters of Jerusalem, I charge you
by the gazelles and by the does of
the field:
Do not arouse or awaken love
until it so desires.

[a]1 Or *Lover* [b]1 Possibly a member of the crocus family

1:14 *En Gedi:* En Gedi was an oasis on the western shore of the Dead Sea. Its fresh running water and many green plants contrasted sharply with the surrounding desert (see the map on p. 2464).

1:15 *doves:* The woman's eyes may be shaped like those of a dove. See also 4:1.

1:16,17 *our bed . . . cedars . . . firs:* Ancient Near Eastern love songs mention beds made of or decorated with fresh-cut branches. The cedar tree was highly valued throughout the ancient Near East and was used to build royal palaces, including the temple and palace of King Solomon (1 Kgs 5:3-9; 7:1-12). Fir, a form of pine, also was used for building. The imagery here implies the solidity and stability of their love.

2:1 *rose of Sharon . . . lily of the valleys:* The exact variety of the flower called a "rose" here is not known. Sharon is the fertile plain on the west side of the mountain ridge that stretches south from Mount Carmel (see the map on p. 2464). "Lily" may refer to a water lily or lotus.

2:3 *apple tree:* This refers to some kind of wild fruit tree whose exact identity is uncertain. Its "apples" were believed to add pleasure to making love (2:5).

2:4 *banquet hall:* This literally means a "house of wine." Wine symbolizes the joy of love (5:1).

2:7 *Daughters of Jerusalem:* See the note at 1:4,5.

2:7 *gazelles . . . does:* These were sacred animals in some religions of the ancient Near East, and were thought to have special powers.

The beloved sang,
"My lover is mine and I am his."
Song 2:16

2:11,12 *winter . . . cooing of doves:* The winter is a rainy season in the Near East. In spring, flowers bloom and doves that have flown away during winter return.

2:13 *fig tree . . . vines:* Figs are sweet fruits that are harvested twice a year in the late spring and in the fall. The early crop was eaten fresh, and the late crop often was dried for eating during the winter months. Grapevines produce grapes used to make wine, often connected with lovemaking in ancient poems.

2:14 *My dove:* See the note at 1:15. Doves are shy and often hide in rock openings in the side of cliffs.

2:15 *foxes . . . ruin the vineyards:* Here, vineyards refer to the lovers' own physical bodies (see the note at 1:6; see also 4:12—5:1). Foxes were known for damaging vineyards (see also Neh 4:3). No one really knows for sure who these foxes refer to, though many think they represent other young men who are also hoping to win the young woman for themselves. The young woman responds by promising that her love belongs to the young man alone (2:16).

2:16,17 *lilies . . . young stag:* See the notes at 2:1 and 2:7 (gazelles). Browsing among lilies and dancing on mountain slopes may refer to his enjoyment of her physical body.

Love Dreams

The young woman dreams of her lover coming to her window and singing of his love for her. She reaches for him as she lies in bed, but he is not there, so she goes out to the streets to search for him.

8 Listen! My lover!
Look! Here he comes,
leaping across the mountains,
bounding over the hills.
9 My lover is like a gazelle or a young stag.
Look! There he stands behind our wall,
gazing through the windows,
peering through the lattice.
10 My lover spoke and said to me,
"Arise, my darling,
my beautiful one, and come with me.
11 See! The winter is past;
the rains are over and gone.
12 Flowers appear on the earth;
the season of singing has come,
the cooing of doves
is heard in our land.
13 The fig tree forms its early fruit;
the blossoming vines spread their fragrance.
Arise, come, my darling;
my beautiful one, come with me."

Lover

14 My dove in the clefts of the rock,
in the hiding places on the mountainside,
show me your face,
let me hear your voice;
for your voice is sweet,
and your face is lovely.
15 Catch for us the foxes,
the little foxes
that ruin the vineyards,
our vineyards that are in bloom.

Beloved

16 My lover is mine and I am his;
he browses among the lilies.
17 Until the day breaks
and the shadows flee,
turn, my lover,
and be like a gazelle

Sacred Marriage by Meinrad Craighead, 1997. SONG OF SONGS contains beautiful and skillfully arranged love poems. Although God is not named in any of the poems, Jews and Christians throughout the ages have found pleasure and spiritual satisfaction in their portrayal of the power of love, passion, and commitment.

or like a young stag
  on the rugged hills.[a]

3 All night long on my bed
  I looked for the one my heart loves;
  I looked for him but did not find him.
2 I will get up now and go about the city,
  through its streets and squares;
I will search for the one my heart loves.
  So I looked for him but did not find him.
3 The watchmen found me
  as they made their rounds in the city.

---

[a]17 Or *the hills of Bether*

3:1-4 *my bed . . . my mother's house:* The young woman appears to be describing a dream. A young woman usually avoided being alone on the street after dark because she might be attacked, or people might think she was looking for men in order to have sex with them (see 5:2-7; Prov 7:6-12). Little is known about the "watchmen" who patrolled the city at night, but see Isaiah 62:6. The mother's house may refer to the mother's protective relationship with her unmarried daughter. See also 6:9; 8:2.

3:5 *Daughters of Jerusalem:* See the note at 1:4, 5.

3:6 *myrrh and incense:* See the chart called "Spices and Perfumes," p. 1278. Incense most likely refers to frankincense, made from the Boswellia shrub, shown below.

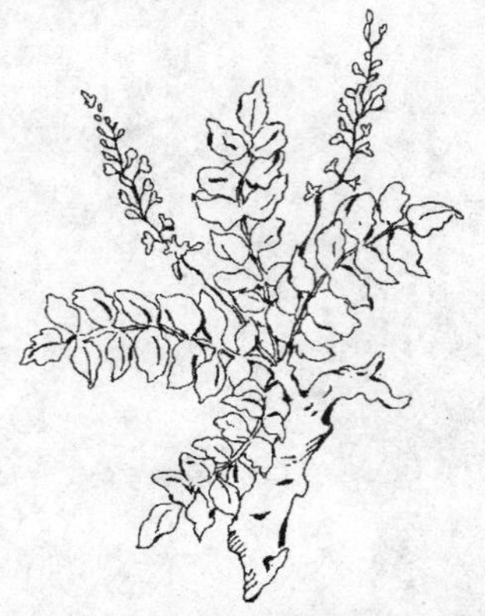

3.7 *Solomon's carriage:* See the note at 1:1. These verses may describe one of Solomon's weddings, and the approaching caravan may be one that is bringing one of his brides from a land beyond the desert. Solomon's "carriage" here is fancy and made of cedar (see the note at 1:16,17), silver, and gold. It may have had a chair that sat on a platform carried on poles by four or more men. Such a carriage (palanquin) probably had curtains around it that could be closed for privacy or to keep out flying dust.

3:11 *crown:* Probably a wedding crown made of flowers, rather than a royal crown.

"Have you seen the one my heart loves?"
4 Scarcely had I passed them
when I found the one my heart loves.
I held him and would not let him go
till I had brought him to my mother's house,
to the room of the one who conceived me.
5 Daughters of Jerusalem, I charge you
by the gazelles and by the does of the field:
Do not arouse or awaken love
until it so desires.

Love Plans

Images of a royal wedding begin this section (3:6-11), which continues with the adoring words of the young man (4:1-15). The young woman invites him to enter her "garden" and enjoy its fruits and spices (4:16—5:1). Then she dreams that her lover comes to her room, but when he is not there she wanders the street in search of him (5:2-8). Her adoring words (5:10-16) include her firm belief that she and her lover belong to each other (6:3). He praises her as the one he desires above all others (6:4-10).

6 Who is this coming up from the desert
like a column of smoke,
perfumed with myrrh and incense
made from all the spices of the merchant?
7 Look! It is Solomon's carriage,
escorted by sixty warriors,
the noblest of Israel,
8 all of them wearing the sword,
all experienced in battle,
each with his sword at his side,
prepared for the terrors of the night.
9 King Solomon made for himself the carriage;
he made it of wood from Lebanon.
10 Its posts he made of silver,
its base of gold.
Its seat was upholstered with purple,
its interior lovingly inlaid
by[a] the daughters of Jerusalem.
11 Come out, you daughters of Zion,
and look at King Solomon wearing the crown,
the crown with which his mother crowned him
on the day of his wedding,
the day his heart rejoiced.

[a] **10** Or *its inlaid interior a gift of love / from*

Lover

4 How beautiful you are, my darling!
Oh, how beautiful!
Your eyes behind your veil are doves.
Your hair is like a flock of goats
descending from Mount Gilead.
2 Your teeth are like a flock of sheep just shorn,
coming up from the washing.
Each has its twin;
not one of them is alone.
3 Your lips are like a scarlet ribbon;
your mouth is lovely.
Your temples behind your veil
are like the halves of a pomegranate.
4 Your neck is like the tower of David,
built with elegance[a];
on it hang a thousand shields,
all of them shields of warriors.
5 Your two breasts are like two fawns,
like twin fawns of a gazelle
that browse among the lilies.
6 Until the day breaks
and the shadows flee,
I will go to the mountain of myrrh
and to the hill of incense.
7 All beautiful you are, my darling;
there is no flaw in you.

8 Come with me from Lebanon, my bride,
come with me from Lebanon.
Descend from the crest of Amana,
from the top of Senir, the summit of Hermon,
from the lions' dens
and the mountain haunts of the leopards.
9 You have stolen my heart, my sister, my bride;
you have stolen my heart
with one glance of your eyes,
with one jewel of your necklace.
10 How delightful is your love, my sister, my bride!
How much more pleasing is your love than wine,
and the fragrance of your perfume than any spice!
11 Your lips drop sweetness as the honeycomb,
my bride;
milk and honey are under your tongue.
The fragrance of your garments is like that of
Lebanon.

[a]4 The meaning of the Hebrew for this word is uncertain.

4:1 *eyes . . . hair:* See the note at 1:15. The woman's hair flows like a flock of black goats moving down a hillside. The hills of Gilead had good pastures for raising sheep (see the map on p. 2467).

4:3 *temples . . . like the halves of a pomegranate:* Pomegranate fruit has red seeds surrounded by sweet-tasting pulp. If the round, red fruit were cut in half, each piece would look like a rosy cheek. See also Exod 28:33,34.

4:4 *tower of David:* What or where this "tower" may have been is unknown. The image suggests a neck that is made to look longer by adding rows of necklaces.

4:5,6 *two fawns . . . hill of incense:* The man describes the graceful curves of the young woman's body.

4:8 *Lebanon . . . Hermon:* See the map on p. 2464. Mount Hermon is over nine thousand feet high. These rugged Lebanon mountains were difficult to climb and dangerous lions and leopards lived in them. This poetic image may mean that for now—before they are married—the woman's body seems as unapproachable as these mountains.

4:10 *wine . . . perfume . . . spice:* His words echo her earlier words (see 1:2,3 and the note).

4:11 *tongue . . . fragrance of your garments is like that of Lebanon:* May refer to her kisses or to the sweet words that come from her mouth (see also 5:1). The cedar forests of Lebanon are very fragrant (see the note at 1:16,17).

4:2,3 Song 6:6,7. **4:9** Song 1:10.

SPICES AND PERFUMES

In the ancient Near East, most spices were considered to be valuable luxuries (1 Kgs 10:10, 25; Ezek 27:17-22), especially those that had to be imported by traders and merchants from lands far away. The following chart provides a description of the spices mentioned in Song of Songs 4:13,14 and lists some other Bible passages where they are mentioned.

SPICE	DESCRIPTION AND USE	SCRIPTURE PASSAGES
Henna	This small tree has light green spear-shaped leaves, thorny branches, and sweet-smelling flowers. Its leaves are dried, crushed, and mixed with warm water to make a dye used for coloring fingernails and toenails. The fragrant flowers of the henna plant were put in small bags and worn by women around the neck.	Song 1:14; 4:13
Nard	Also known as spikenard, this plant grows in the Himalayan countries of Bhutan, Nepal, and Kashmir. The fragrant root and lower stems were dried and used in a perfumed ointment.	Song 4:13, 14; Mark 14:3; John 12:3
Saffron	This probably came from the blue-flowered saffron crocus, which may have grown in Palestine in ancient times. Part of the flower was used to make a yellow dye for coloring food, clothing, and walls. It was also mixed with oil and used as a cooking spice, for perfumes, and medicines.	Song 4:14
Calamus	This probably refers to a fragrant long-stemmed reed or cane that was imported to Palestine. It was used in making the sweet-smelling anointing oil (Exod 30:23, "cane") used by Israel's holy priests.	Song 4:14; Isa 43:24; Jer 6:20; Ezek 27:19
Cinnamon	Cinnamon comes from the brown inner bark of an evergreen tree. It had to be imported to the Near East from countries as far away as Ceylon and Malaysia. It was used as a cooking spice, perfume fragrance, and as an ingredient in holy oil.	Exod 30:23; Prov 7:17; Song 4:14; Rev 18:13
Frankincense	Also called simply "incense," this white gummy resin comes from the wood of Boswellia shrubs or trees that grow in India, Somalia, and Arabia. It is uncertain whether these shrubs grew in Palestine. Frankincense resin was pounded into a valuable powder that was burned to make a sweet smell. It was a key ingredient in various ointments and in the holy incense burned by Israel's priests.	Exod 30:34-38; Song 4:14; Matt 2:11; Rev 18:13; probably also Lev 6:14,15
Myrrh	Some myrrh trees may have grown in Palestine, but most myrrh was imported from Arabia and East Africa. A light-colored sticky resin flows from its branches. After the resin is exposed to the air it hardens and turns brown. Myrrh resin was crushed and used in making expensive perfumes and ointments, including the holy oil for dedication ceremonies (Exod 30:23-33). Myrrh was also used for embalming the dead (John 19:39).	Esth 2:12; Ps 45:8; Prov 7:17; Song 1:13; 3:6; 4:6, 14; 5:1, 5, 13; Matt 2:11; probably also Mark 15:23
Aloes	Aloes may either refer to the fragrant resin from the tall eaglewood tree that grows in southeast Asia and northern India, or it may refer to the aloe plant, which has thick leaves that form a tight rose shape. Aloe resin has a pleasing smell but it tastes very bitter. It was used for making perfumes, medicines, and for embalming the dead.	Num 24:6; Ps 45:8; Prov 7:17; Song 4:14; John 19:39

12 You are a garden locked up, my sister,
my bride;
you are a spring enclosed, a sealed fountain.
13 Your plants are an orchard of pomegranates
with choice fruits,
with henna and nard,
14 nard and saffron,
calamus and cinnamon,
with every kind of incense tree,
with myrrh and aloes
and all the finest spices.
15 You are[a] a garden fountain,
a well of flowing water
streaming down from Lebanon.

Beloved

16 Awake, north wind,
and come, south wind!
Blow on my garden,
that its fragrance may spread abroad.
Let my lover come into his garden
and taste its choice fruits.

Lover

5 I have come into my garden, my sister, my bride;
I have gathered my myrrh with my spice.
I have eaten my honeycomb and my honey;
I have drunk my wine and my milk.

Friends

Eat, O friends, and drink;
drink your fill, O lovers.

Beloved

2 I slept but my heart was awake.
Listen! My lover is knocking:
"Open to me, my sister, my darling,
my dove, my flawless one.
My head is drenched with dew,
my hair with the dampness of the night."
3 I have taken off my robe—
must I put it on again?
I have washed my feet—
must I soil them again?

[a]15 Or *I am* (spoken by the *Beloved*)

The friends sang,
"Eat, O friends, and drink; drink your fill, O lovers."
Song 5:1

4:15 *flowing water streaming down from Lebanon:* Cool, clear streams ran down from the melting snows of Mount Lebanon (see the note at 4:8).

4:16 *my garden:* The young woman invites her lover into her "garden," her fragrant body, to enjoy the "fruits" of love. In 5:1, he claims this "garden" belongs to him alone. See also the note at 5:11-15.

5:2 *my dove, my flawless one:* See the notes at 1:15 and 2:14.

5:3-5 *washed my feet . . . hands dripped with myrrh:* These passages are suffused with poetic imagery as the, at first reluctant, then expectant, beloved anticipates the presence of her lover.

4:12 Song 4:15—5:1. **5:2-7** Song 2:8-17; 3:1-5.

5:7 *watchmen . . . beat me:* The young woman is so anxious to find her lover that she is willing to risk running through the dark streets, a very dangerous thing for a young woman to do (see the note at 3:1-4). Perhaps the watchmen thought she was a prostitute or an unfaithful wife, such as the one described in Proverbs 7:6-20. Either way, the watchmen's actions are harsh and wrong.

5:8 *faint with love:* The young woman may not want her friends to tell the one she loves about her search for him through the dark streets or about the way the guards treated her. But she does want them to give him the message that she is still "faint with love."

5:10 *radiant and ruddy, outstanding among ten thousand:* The same Hebrew word used to describe the healthy and good-looking young David (1 Sam 16:12; 17:42) is used here. "Ten thousand" is meant to symbolize a very large number (see also Ps 3:6).

5:11-15 *purest gold . . . choice as its cedars:* His head of "purest gold" may be another indication of his perfection. The eyes "like doves" could mean that his eyes are bright and clear. The water lily (lotus) was a flower that was connected with the pleasures of love. The dripping myrrh probably refers to his sweet and wet kisses. His body "like polished ivory" may refer to its color, smoothness, or its rare value. Legs like marble pillars suggest strength and stability. He is tall, like Mount Lebanon, and as strong as its cedars (see the notes at 4:8 and 1:16,17).

4 My lover thrust his hand through the latch-opening;
my heart began to pound for him.
5 I arose to open for my lover,
and my hands dripped with myrrh,
my fingers with flowing myrrh,
on the handles of the lock.
6 I opened for my lover,
but my lover had left; he was gone.
My heart sank at his departure.[a]
I looked for him but did not find him.
I called him but he did not answer.
7 The watchmen found me
as they made their rounds in the city.
They beat me, they bruised me;
they took away my cloak,
those watchmen of the walls!
8 O daughters of Jerusalem, I charge you—
if you find my lover,
what will you tell him?
Tell him I am faint with love.

Friends

9 How is your beloved better than others,
most beautiful of women?
How is your beloved better than others,
that you charge us so?

Beloved

10 My lover is radiant and ruddy,
outstanding among ten thousand.
11 His head is purest gold;
his hair is wavy
and black as a raven.
12 His eyes are like doves
by the water streams,
washed in milk,
mounted like jewels.
13 His cheeks are like beds of spice
yielding perfume.
His lips are like lilies
dripping with myrrh.
14 His arms are rods of gold
set with chrysolite.
His body is like polished ivory
decorated with sapphires.[b]

[a]**6** Or *heart had gone out to him when he spoke* [b]**14** Or *lapis lazuli*

[15]His legs are pillars of marble
set on bases of pure gold.
His appearance is like Lebanon,
choice as its cedars.
[16]His mouth is sweetness itself;
he is altogether lovely.
This is my lover, this my friend,
O daughters of Jerusalem.

Friends

6 Where has your lover gone,
most beautiful of women?
Which way did your lover turn,
that we may look for him with you?

Beloved

[2]My lover has gone down to his garden,
to the beds of spices,
to browse in the gardens
and to gather lilies.
[3]I am my lover's and my lover is mine;
he browses among the lilies.

Lover

[4]You are beautiful, my darling, as Tirzah,
lovely as Jerusalem,
majestic as troops with banners.
[5]Turn your eyes from me;
they overwhelm me.
Your hair is like a flock of goats
descending from Gilead.
[6]Your teeth are like a flock of sheep
coming up from the washing.
Each has its twin,
not one of them is alone.
[7]Your temples behind your veil
are like the halves of a pomegranate.
[8]Sixty queens there may be,
and eighty concubines,
and virgins beyond number;
[9]but my dove, my perfect one, is unique,
the only daughter of her mother,
the favorite of the one who bore her.
The maidens saw her and called her
blessed;
the queens and concubines praised her.

5:16 *daughters of Jerusalem:* See the note at 1:4,5.

6:2 *his garden . . . beds of spices . . . gather lilies:* See 4:13,14 and the note at 2:16,17. See also 1:8; 4:16—5:1.

6:4 *Tirzah . . . Jerusalem:* Jerusalem was the capital city of all Israel under kings David and Solomon, and of the southern kingdom (Judah) after the kingdom divided. Tirzah was chosen by Jeroboam (ruled 931 to 910 B.C.) as the first capital city of the northern kingdom (1 Kgs 14:17; 16:23,24). Tirzah means "beauty."

6:5 *goats . . . Gilead:* See the note at 4:1.

6:7 *temples:* See the note at 4:3.

6:8 *Sixty queens . . . beyond number:* This refers to Solomon's many wives and concubines (his harem), but the numbers are smaller than those mentioned in 1 Kings 11:3.

6:9,10 *my dove . . . majestic as the stars in procession:* See the notes at 1:15; 2:14; 4:1. The man would choose the young woman over thousands of other women. The women of the royal court are singing the young woman's praises as well (6:10).

6:1 Song 5:8. **6:6,7** Song 4:2,3.

Friends

10 Who is this that appears like the dawn,
fair as the moon, bright as the sun,
majestic as the stars in procession?

Love Dances

It is not clear whether the poem continues by describing a wedding dance, or if the woman is dancing to attract the eye of her lover. After he praises her beauty, she invites him to take a walk to her mother's house, where they prepare to fulfill their dreams of love (8:2-4).

Lover

11 I went down to the grove of nut trees
to look at the new growth in the valley,
to see if the vines had budded
or the pomegranates were in bloom.
12 Before I realized it,
my desire set me among the royal chariots of my people.[a]

Friends

13 Come back, come back, O Shulammite;
come back, come back, that we may gaze on you!

Lover

Why would you gaze on the Shulammite
as on the dance of Mahanaim?

7 How beautiful your sandaled feet,
O prince's daughter!
Your graceful legs are like jewels,
the work of a craftsman's hands.
2 Your navel is a rounded goblet
that never lacks blended wine.
Your waist is a mound of wheat
encircled by lilies.
3 Your breasts are like two fawns,
twins of a gazelle.
4 Your neck is like an ivory tower.
Your eyes are the pools of Heshbon
by the gate of Bath Rabbim.
Your nose is like the tower of Lebanon
looking toward Damascus.

[a]**12** Or *among the chariots of Amminadab*; or *among the chariots of the people of the prince*

6:11,12 *bloom . . . chariots:* These verses seem to return to the dialogue of 6:1-3. The young woman describes a walk or time spent searching in a garden filled with nut trees, vines, and pomegranate trees (see the notes at 2:3 and 2:13). In ancient Egypt, pomegranates were thought to add pleasure to making love.

The chariot reference is unclear. Either her lover was a wealthy man who owned a chariot, or he simply made her feel like a princess riding in a royal chariot.

6:13 *Shulammite:* This phrase is difficult. "Shulammite" is a feminine form of "Solomon," and it has been suggested that "Shulam" was a word that meant "Solomon's girl." Another suggestion is that she is "a woman from Shunem," a "Shunammite" (see 1 Kgs 1:3,4). Still others suggest the name may be connected with Shulmanitu, a Semitic goddess of war and love.

7:1-5 *feet . . . hair:* Compare the man's adoring words to those of the woman in 6:10-13. From her sandaled feet all the way to her hair (7:5), she is desirable.

Wheat (grain) stalks were often a symbol of female fertility. See the notes at 4:5,6 and 5:11-15.

For the mountains of Lebanon, see the note at 4:8. Mount Carmel refers to a forest-covered mountain range in northwestern Palestine. For the location of the places mentioned in 7:3-5, and Damascus in Syria, see the map on p. 2464.

5 Your head crowns you like Mount Carmel.
Your hair is like royal tapestry;
the king is held captive by its tresses.
6 How beautiful you are and how pleasing,
O love, with your delights!
7 Your stature is like that of the palm,
and your breasts like clusters of fruit.
8 I said, "I will climb the palm tree;
I will take hold of its fruit."
May your breasts be like the clusters of the vine,
the fragrance of your breath like apples,
9 and your mouth like the best wine.

Beloved

May the wine go straight to my lover,
flowing gently over lips and teeth.[a]
10 I belong to my lover,
and his desire is for me.
11 Come, my lover, let us go to the countryside,
let us spend the night in the villages.[b]
12 Let us go early to the vineyards
to see if the vines have budded,
if their blossoms have opened,
and if the pomegranates are in bloom—
there I will give you my love.
13 The mandrakes send out their fragrance,
and at our door is every delicacy,
both new and old,
that I have stored up for you, my lover.

8 If only you were to me like a brother,
who was nursed at my mother's breasts!
Then, if I found you outside,
I would kiss you,
and no one would despise me.
2 I would lead you
and bring you to my mother's house—
she who has taught me.
I would give you spiced wine to drink,
the nectar of my pomegranates.
3 His left arm is under my head
and his right arm embraces me.
4 Daughters of Jerusalem, I charge you:
Do not arouse or awaken love
until it so desires.

[a]9 Septuagint, Aquila, Vulgate and Syriac; Hebrew *lips of sleepers* [b]11 Or *henna bushes*

7:7-9 *palm . . . best wine:* The palm tree here is the tall date palm, whose fruit grows in clusters in the leafy tops of the tree. Again, lush imagery from nature describes their love for one another.

7:11 *countryside . . . villages:* The Hebrew word for village is similar to the word for "henna" (1:14; 4:13). Her desire to "spend the night in the villages," then could mean "sleep in the beds of henna flowers."

7:12,13 *vineyards . . . mandrakes:* See the notes at 2:3; 2:13; and 6:11,12. For more about mandrakes, see the note on p. 1270.

8:1,2 *brother . . . mother's house:* A sister could kiss her brother in public, but kissing a man who was not a close relative would have been shameful. To bring her beloved to the home of her mother would be another step in making their relationship public. See the note at 3:1-4.

8:4 *Daughters of Jerusalem:* See the note at 1:4,5.

7:10 Song 2:16; 6:3.

8:5 *Under the apple tree . . . there your mother conceived you:* See 2:3. Apple or fruit trees were often associated with sexual pleasure (see the notes at 2:3 and 2:6) and with giving birth.

8:6 *heart . . . a seal on your arm:* The seal on the arm may have been a bracelet that had a personalized design to be used as a seal. A seal was used to imprint a person's initials in wax on legal documents or to mark possessions to prove ownership (Jer 32:10,11).

8:6,7 *jealousy unyielding as the grave . . . Many waters:* In Hebrew "grave" refers to the underground world of the dead (Job 10:21, 22; Ps 88:12; 94:17). The "many waters" refer to the dark waters of chaos that God brought under control at creation (Gen 1:2; Ps 33:6,7; Job 38:8-10).

8:5 Song 3:6.

Powerful Love Is Not for Sale

The book comes to a close with the young woman's climactic words about the power of love (8:6,7). This is followed by a scene that seems to make clear why she says her love cannot be bought for "all the wealth of his house"—by the great King Solomon or anyone else. She will give her vineyard (her body) only to the one she loves.

Friends

5 Who is this coming up from the desert
leaning on her lover?

Beloved

Under the apple tree I roused you;
there your mother conceived you,
there she who was in labor gave you birth.
6 Place me like a seal over your heart,
like a seal on your arm;
for love is as strong as death,
its jealousy[a] unyielding as the grave.[b]
It burns like blazing fire,
like a mighty flame.[c]
7 Many waters cannot quench love;
rivers cannot wash it away.

[a]6 Or *ardor* [b]6 Hebrew *Sheol* [c]6 Or / *like the very flame of the* LORD

QUESTIONS ABOUT SONG OF SONGS

1. SONG OF SONGS has been described as a collection of loosely-related love poems, a drama, or a long poem that tells a story. Which of these descriptions, if any, best describes this book for you? Why? How else might this book be described?
2. If SONG OF SONGS is one long poem, who do you imagine the main characters in the poem to be? What can be known about the woman's relationships to people other than the man she loves? Her mother? Her brothers? The other young women of her town?
3. The man and the woman in this book use many images from nature (plants, animals, hills, etc.) to describe themselves and one another. Which images did you find most interesting? Which were difficult for you to understand or relate to? Try describing yourself (or a friend) using images from nature.
4. What does SONG OF SONGS have to say about love? About commitment? About God?
5. What does it mean to say that love is "as strong as death," "many waters cannot quench" it, and "all the wealth" someone has cannot buy it?
6. Some Jews have interpreted SONG OF SONGS as God's love for the people of Israel, and some Christians have seen it as Jesus' love for the church ("his bride"). Which verses, if any, seem to support this kind of interpretation? What do you think is the main purpose of this book?

If one were to give
all the wealth of his house for love,
it[a] would be utterly scorned.

Friends

8 We have a young sister,
and her breasts are not yet grown.
What shall we do for our sister
for the day she is spoken for?
9 If she is a wall,
we will build towers of silver on her.
If she is a door,
we will enclose her with panels of cedar.

Beloved

10 I am a wall,
and my breasts are like towers.
Thus I have become in his eyes
like one bringing contentment.
11 Solomon had a vineyard in Baal Hamon;
he let out his vineyard to tenants.
Each was to bring for its fruit
a thousand shekels[b] of silver.
12 But my own vineyard is mine to give;
the thousand shekels are for you, O Solomon,
and two hundred[c] are for those who tend its fruit.

Lover

13 You who dwell in the gardens
with friends in attendance,
let me hear your voice!

Beloved

14 Come away, my lover,
and be like a gazelle
or like a young stag
on the spice-laden mountains.

[a]7 Or *he* [b]11 That is, about 25 pounds (about 11.5 kilograms); also in verse 12
[c]12 That is, about 5 pounds (about 2.3 kilograms)

8:8,9 *young sister . . . a wall:* Most scholars interpret these verses to be the words of the young woman's brothers. They shared the family responsibility of protecting her and for approving who she married. See the note at 1:6.

8:10 *I am a wall . . . towers:* "Wall" may refer to her virginity or to her loyalty to her beloved. By describing her breasts as being like towers, she seems to be refuting her brothers who think she is too young to get married.

8:11 *Baal Hamon:* The location of Baal Hamon is unknown. The vineyard at Baal Hamon may have been an actual vineyard that Solomon allowed farmers to work for him in exchange for a share of the profits.

8:12 *my own vineyard is mine to give:* Most likely, this refers to her own body (see also 1:6; 4:16). Verse 12 seems to imply that she will not give herself even to the richest man in the world, even if he offered "all the wealth of his house" (8:7). Some scholars think the speaker of 8:11,12 is not the young woman, but is the young woman's lover who calls her his own vineyard, which he desires more than all of Solomon's vineyards (compare to 4:12; 5:1).

8:13 *gardens:* See the note at 4:16. The "friends" may refer to the man's companions.

8:14 *gazelle:* See the note at 2:7 (gazelles).

8:10 Song 2:6.

PROPHETIC BOOKS

THE BOOKS BEGINNING with ISAIAH and ending with MALACHI belong to a section of the Christian Bible called the Prophetic Books. These books record God's messages to the people of Israel and Judah in the form of speeches or sermons, visions, and life experiences of prophets who preached between about 750 and 450 B.C. Some of the messages are of judgment and warning, while others focus on forgiveness and renewal. The Hebrew Scriptures divide the Prophetic Books into the "Former Prophets" and the "Latter Prophets." The books of the "Former Prophets" (JOSHUA, JUDGES, 1 and 2 SAMUEL, 1 and 2 KINGS) are part of the Historical Books in the Old Testament or Christian Bible. The Prophetic Books in the Christian Bible are often divided into two categories: the "Major Prophets" and the "Book of the Twelve." The "Twelve" are sometimes referred to as the "Minor Prophets" because their speeches and sermons are much shorter than those of the "Major Prophets."

THE ROLE OF THE PROPHET. In the Bible, a "prophet" is a person called to speak for God and deliver God's messages to people. At times, this meant predicting the future. They observed what was going on around them and delivered God's messages for those situations. It must be noted, however, that the spoken or written words of the prophets were not necessarily driven by circumstances. Because the prophets were inspired by God's Spirit, their messages weren't dependent on human agendas or logic. The prophets often had to address difficult political, social, or religious situations, and so they sometimes spoke and acted in colorful ways to attract attention and make their messages clear. For example, Jeremiah placed a wooden yoke around his neck to represent the power of a foreign king (Jer 27:1-11). Ezekiel sketched a picture of Jerusalem on a clay tablet to warn the people of a coming attack on the city (Ezek 4:1-8). HOSEA uses the image of the prophet's marriage to a prostitute to compare Israel's relationship to God, who continually forgives an unfaithful wife (Israel).

The prophets usually introduced their speeches with the words "The LORD says." These words show that the prophets did not speak their own messages, but considered themselves messengers of God who had the authority to speak for God to the people. The prophets often referred to their words as the messages that God had given them for the people (see, for example, Isa 6:1-13; Ezek 2:1-10; Amos 1:1, 2; Hab 1:1; Zech 1:1). See also the article called "Prophets and Prophecy," p. 935.

The Message of the Prophet. Because some prophets spoke as early as 760 B.C. and others as late as 445 B.C., their messages are sometimes very different in what they emphasize. For example, Amos, Micah, and Zephaniah preached about the need for the people to change how they acted toward God and each other so that they could avoid being punished like the foreign nations around them. Others, like Jeremiah and Ezekiel, warned the people about the coming defeat of Jerusalem and the exile of its people to Babylon and promised a future time when God's people will be delivered and will return to Jerusalem. Still others, like Haggai, Zechariah, and Malachi preached to people who had returned from exile and were working to rebuild the temple in Jerusalem and begin the worship of God again. The messages of ISAIAH seem to address all these periods of Israel's history and span the events leading up to and following the return from exile in Babylon.

Many Bible scholars believe that some of the Prophetic Books, however, reflect historical settings much later than when the prophets themselves actually lived. According to this view, sometime after the prophets preached and wrote, their messages were adapted and edited by people who faced different social and religious situations. An example of this type of book is DANIEL which may have existed in a previous form as early as the sixth century B.C. but not put into its present form until the time when the Seleucid dynasty ruled Palestine (around 165 B.C.). This shows that the messages of the Prophetic Books address issues that are of continuing importance to God's people: proper worship of God, justice and equality, and caring for oppressed and mistreated people.

ISAIAH

It's a familiar phrase:
"I have some good news and some bad news."
Read this book to discover what the prophet
Isaiah has to say about the bad news of God's
judgment and the good news of God's love.

WHAT MAKES ISAIAH SPECIAL?

ISAIAH contains some of the most beautiful poetry and some of the best-known words of hope in the entire Bible. ISAIAH's message shows a deep understanding of God's Law as it relates to the history of God's chosen people, Israel. The people and their leaders disobeyed the Law of the LORD and so were punished. They were taken into exile in Babylon, but they returned home to Judah.

Their temple was rebuilt, as God had promised it would be, and the people looked forward to a brighter future.

The New Testament writers often quote from ISAIAH to show that Jesus Christ is the Messiah, the long-awaited king from the family of David. His coming fulfills God's promise to save all people and to create a future filled with promise. This Messiah is described as the one who will rule David's kingdom forever and bring everlasting peace (Isa 9:6,7; 11:1-9). Christian teachers also interpreted the suffering and death of Jesus as a fulfillment of the passages in ISAIAH that describe the work of God's special "Servant" (Isa 42:1-9; 49:1-7; 50:4-11; 52:13—53:12; see also Acts 8:32-35; Phil 2:6-11).

WHY WAS ISAIAH WRITTEN?

The meaning of Isaiah's own name reveals one of the key themes in the book. In Hebrew, Isaiah means "The LORD (*Yahweh*) saves." A major theme in the center section of the book (40–55) is comfort and hope for God's chosen people, who have been living in exile in Babylon. The LORD, the Holy One of Israel, will open a highway for the people to return home to Judah and will restore the temple on God's holy Mount Zion in Jerusalem. There, God will once again live among the people (Exod 25:8; 2 Sam 6:1, 2; 1 Kgs 8:1, 2, 10-13).

The first main section of ISAIAH (1–39) contains quite a bit of "bad news" about God's coming judgment. Many of Israel's people had rejected the LORD by worshiping other gods and sacrificing to idols made of wood and stone. Israel's leaders also made peace treaties with foreign powers and paid taxes to them. They did not trust in God alone to save them. They forgot that it was the LORD who saved them from slavery in Egypt, and they rejected the law that God had given to Moses and the people. That law commanded the people to worship the LORD God above all other gods and to work for justice by helping those in need (1:16,17;

Judah and Jerusalem: Jerusalem was the capital city of the southern kingdom (Judah). The temple of the people of Israel was located there. After the death of King Solomon, the Israelites were a divided nation consisting of the northern kingdom (Israel) and the southern kingdom (Judah). See the maps on pp. 2466 and 2467. See also the mini-articles called "Jerusalem," p. 574 and "Israel," p. 264, and the article called "From Joshua to the Exile: The People of Israel in the Promised Land," p. 924.

LORD Almighty: The Hebrew *Yahweh Sabaoth*, can also be translated "LORD of hosts." This term for Israel's God is used often in the first main section of ISAIAH (1–39). See for instance 1:9; 5:16; and 10:33. The "hosts" in this ancient name are either the armies of Israel, which the LORD led into battle (Ps 44:9); the heavenly stars, which God created (40:26); or the heavenly beings, such as angels (Ps 148:2). Isaiah makes it clear throughout the book that the powerful LORD of creation is also the God who has chosen Israel to be his special people (2:3; 10:20-23; 17:7; 21:10; 41:8-10,21; 44:24-28). See also Ps 89:6-8.

3:8-15). Because they turned their backs on the LORD and disobeyed him, the people of Jerusalem and Judah were punished. That punishment took the form of defeat at the hands of their enemies.

The final section of ISAIAH (56–66) provides a picture of the people of Israel who have been commanded to rebuild Zion and to live according to God's commands. The new people of Israel will be shining examples of the LORD's justice (60:1-3; 61:1-4). Foreign nations will recognize the power of Israel's God (62:1-3) and even serve God's people (60:10-18).

WHAT'S THE STORY BEHIND THE SCENE?

Isaiah lived in or near Jerusalem in Judah and brought his messages from the LORD during the time that four different kings ruled Judah (see the note at 1:1). Isaiah's work as a prophet began when he received a vision from the LORD in the temple. This was in 740 B.C., the year King Uzziah died (6:1). At this time, Assyria's armies had captured Aram (Syria) and threatened the northern kingdom (Israel). In 733 B.C., the kings of Aram and Israel invaded Judah and tried to force King Ahaz of Judah to join them in fighting against Assyria. Instead, Ahaz made a treaty with the Assyrian king, ignoring Isaiah's warning not to make such a treaty. Ahaz's strategy backfired when Assyria invaded and defeated the northern kingdom of Israel in 721 B.C. Israel's defeat meant that Judah was much more exposed to an attack from Assyria. In 701 B.C., King Sennacherib of Assyria threatened to capture Jerusalem, but King Hezekiah remained faithful to the LORD and Jerusalem was saved (36–38).

But Judah's troubles were not over. When some visitors from Babylon came to see Hezekiah, Isaiah said that one day the kingdom of Babylon would capture Jerusalem and take many of the Israelite people into exile along with the treasures of the palace and temple (39). Isaiah's words came true over one hundred years later when Babylon defeated Judah and destroyed Jerusalem. The final group of Israelite captives was taken to Babylon in 586 B.C. The prophecies in chapters 40–55 assume that this defeat has already taken place, so now the prophet's message is one of comfort and hope. The LORD would use King Cyrus of Persia to defeat the Babylonians (41:2-4), allowing the people of Judah to return home to rebuild Jerusalem and its temple (44:28; 45:13; Ezra 1:1-4). Cyrus did defeat Babylon in 539 B.C., and in 538 B.C. he gave an official order that allowed the Israelite people to return home.

After returning, the people rebuilt the temple, and it was rededicated in 515 B.C., even though Jerusalem's city walls were not yet rebuilt (Ezra 6:13-15; Neh 1–6). Though closely related to chapters 40–55, the final section of ISAIAH (56–66) seems to focus on this time after the return to Judah.

HOW IS ISAIAH CONSTRUCTED?

ISAIAH is often divided into three sections, based on the historic situation each section seems to address. The first section (1–39) deals primarily with the history of Israel and Judah from about 740 B.C. to some time shortly after 700 B.C. The message of judgment against Judah, Israel, and the surrounding nations is the main theme of this section, but words of hope and restoration also can be found here (11:1—12:6; 14:1,2; 24–27; 34; 35). The

LORD's punishment of Babylon, which took place about one hundred fifty years after the time of Isaiah, also is predicted in this section (13:1—14:22).

The second section of ISAIAH (40–55) focuses on the promises God made to the people of Judah that they would return home from exile in Babylon. But this section also includes strong words for those who trust in idols instead of the living God of Israel (44:12-20).

The final section of ISAIAH (56–66) focuses on the rebuilding of the temple on Mount Zion and a new start for Jerusalem and its people. But along with these promises, God's people are challenged to turn away from idols and obey God's commands. Promises of God's new creation (65:17-25) are mixed with threats of punishment for those who reject the LORD and God's Law (65:1-16).

Here is one way ISAIAH can be outlined:

ISAIAH, Part 1: Before the exile (1:1—39:8)
- Introduction (1:1-31)
- Prophecies concerning Judah and Jerusalem (2:1—12:6)
- Prophecies concerning foreign nations (13:1—23:18)
- A view of God's future judgment (24:1—27:13)
- Those who rebel against God will be punished (28:1—33:24)
- Visions of judgment and joy (34:1—35:10)
- In the days of King Hezekiah (36:1—39:8)

ISAIAH, Part 2: Good news for God's people in exile (40:1—55:13)
- Babylon is defeated and God's people are set free (40:1—48:22)
- Jerusalem will be rebuilt (49:1—55:13)

ISAIAH, Part 3: Warnings and promises for God's new people after the exile (56:1—66:24)
- Do right and obey God's laws (56:1—59:21)
- Celebrate, Jerusalem, for I have saved you (60:1—62:12)
- I will bless my servants but punish sinners (63:1—66:24)

ISAIAH, Part 1: Before the Exile

The first thirty-nine chapters of ISAIAH focus mainly on the prophet's messages to the people of Judah and its capital Jerusalem from about 742 B.C. to sometime shortly after 701 B.C. Isaiah warns of the LORD's judgment against his people, but he also provides some words of hope.

INTRODUCTION

Chapter 1 introduces Isaiah and tells when he preached (1:1). This chapter also introduces a number of themes that will be repeated throughout the book, including the nation's guilt, God's punishment and protection of Jerusalem, and God's special love for Zion.

1 The vision concerning Judah and Jerusalem that Isaiah son of Amoz saw during the reigns of Uzziah, Jotham, Ahaz and Hezekiah, kings of Judah.

1:1 *Judah and Jerusalem:* See the note on p. 1289 (Judah and Jerusalem).

1:1 *Isaiah son of Amoz . . . Uzziah . . . Hezekiah:* Isaiah brought God's messages of judgment and hope to Jerusalem and Judah (the southern kingdom) during the reigns of four kings of Judah, beginning in the last year of Uzziah's reign (6:1). Elsewhere, Isaiah is mentioned as the writer of a history of King Uzziah (2 Chr 26:22). For more about the historical context of this book, read the Introduction to ISAIAH. The approximate dates of the four kings are: Uzziah (781-740 B.C.); Jotham (740-736 B.C.); Ahaz (736-716 B.C.); Hezekiah (716-687 B.C.). See also 2 Kgs 15:1-7, 32-38; 16:1-20; 18:1—20:21; 2 Chr 26:1-23; 27:1-9; 28:1-27; 29:1—32:33.

The Prophet Isaiah by Philip Goul, fifteenth century. This detail from a mural in the Church of the Holy Cross, Paleochorio, Crete, depicts the great Hebrew prophet Isaiah, whose name means "The LORD (*Yahweh*) saves." Isaiah lived in Jerusalem, the capital of the southern kingdom (Judah), and prophesied during the reigns of King Uzziah, Jotham, Ahaz, and Hezekiah, from approximately 740 to 701 B.C.

1:2 *LORD:* In Hebrew, *Yahweh.* See also the mini-article called "LORD (YHWH)," p. 140.

1:2 *I reared children:* "Children" refers to the people of Israel. The LORD calls heaven and earth to be witnesses to Israel's sin (see also Deut 30:19; 31:28; Mic 6:1,2). The people have "rebelled against" the LORD by rejecting his law, by being dishonest and unjust (1:15-26), and by worshiping idols (1:29).

1:4 *sinful nation:* Probably refers to all God's people, not simply the northern kingdom. See also the mini-article called "Israel," p. 264. For their sins, see the note at 1:2 (children).

A Rebellious Nation

2 Hear, O heavens! Listen, O earth!
For the LORD has spoken:
"I reared children and brought them up,
but they have rebelled against me.
3 The ox knows his master,
the donkey his owner's manger,
but Israel does not know,
my people do not understand."

4 Ah, sinful nation,
a people loaded with guilt,
a brood of evildoers,
children given to corruption!
They have forsaken the LORD;

they have spurned the Holy One of Israel
and turned their backs on him.
[5]Why should you be beaten anymore?
Why do you persist in rebellion?
Your whole head is injured,
your whole heart afflicted.
[6]From the sole of your foot to the top of your head
there is no soundness—

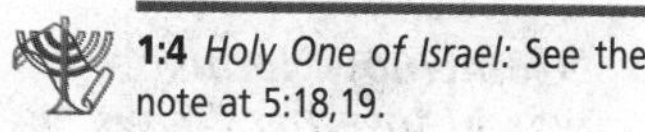

1:4 *Holy One of Israel:* See the note at 5:18,19.

HEZEKIAH

Hezekiah's name means "The LORD is my strength." He was the son of Ahaz and Abijah and the twelfth king of the southern kingdom (Judah), not counting the illegal reign of Athaliah. Based on the evidence given in the Bible, it is difficult to pinpoint the exact dates when Hezekiah ruled. For fourteen years, beginning about 729 B.C., Hezekiah ruled together with his father. From about 716 B.C., at the age of twenty-five, and continuing through 687 B.C., he ruled alone.

Hezekiah's time as king was notable for its religious reforms and steadfast resistance against the powerful Assyrian empire to the east. In addition to being the first Judean king to remove the local shrines to Canaanite gods and goddesses, he reopened the doors of the temple that his father had closed in Jerusalem (2 Chr 28:24). He also removed the Assyrian idols that his father had placed in the temple. He broke the bronze serpent Moses had lifted up in the wilderness (Num 21:4-9; 2 Kgs 18:4), because it had become an object of worship in itself and people were burning incense to it. Hezekiah brought back the holy vessels his father had removed, reorganized the Levite priesthood, and had the priests purify the altar so that they could make all the sacrifices commanded by the Law of Moses. In an honest gesture of concern, Hezekiah invited the people of the northern kingdom (Israel), who had been under Assyria's power, to join him in celebrating the Passover (2 Kgs 18:1-8; 2 Chr 29:1—31:21).

Ignoring the warnings of the prophet Isaiah, Hezekiah's father, Ahaz, had allowed Judah to become dependent upon the more powerful Assyria. Breaking with the policies of his father, Hezekiah organized a rebellion against the Assyrian control of Palestine and Aram. When Sargon II, who had conquered the northern kingdom in 721 B.C. (2 Kgs 17; Isa 20:1), captured the city of Ashdod, Hezekiah began to prepare Jerusalem for the next attack. He strengthened the walls, organized an army, and dug a tunnel through solid rock from the Gihon Spring to the waters of Shiloah to ensure the city's water supply. In 701 B.C., the Assyrian king Sennacherib, Sargon's son, crushed the rebellion and captured forty-six walled cities in Judah. Hezekiah paid a large sum of gold and silver in the hope that it would convince Sennacherib to spare Jerusalem. In spite of Hezekiah's gift of tribute, Sennacherib demanded Jerusalem's total surrender. But Jerusalem was saved by a plague that miraculously broke out among the Assyrian army (2 Kgs 18:17—19:37; 2 Chr 32:1-33; Isa 36–39).

The Bible tells us that shortly after these events, Hezekiah fell ill and was near death (2 Kgs 20:1; Isa 38:1). In his distress, he prayed to the LORD and his prayer was answered. The LORD sent the prophet Isaiah with a message for him, promising that Hezekiah and Jerusalem would be protected from the Assyrians. Isaiah instructed the king's servants to put a poultice of figs on Hezekiah's wounds and he recovered. Hezekiah then wrote the song of praise recorded in Isaiah 38:10-20.

> *"Come now, let us reason together," says the* LORD. *"Though your sins are like scarlet, they shall be as white as snow."*
> Isa 1:18

only wounds and welts
and open sores,
not cleansed or bandaged
or soothed with oil.
7 Your country is desolate,
your cities burned with fire;
your fields are being stripped by foreigners
right before you,
laid waste as when overthrown by strangers.
8 The Daughter of Zion is left
like a shelter in a vineyard,
like a hut in a field of melons,
like a city under siege.

1:6 *soothed with oil:* Olive oil was used to treat wounds (see Luke 10:34). See also the article called "Miracles, Magic, and Medicine," p. 1838. Here, Israel is described as a broken body.

ZION

The first mention of Zion in the Bible is 2 Samuel 5:7. It describes how Israel's King David captured the hilltop fortress known as Zion in the city of Jerusalem. At that time Jerusalem belonged to a group of people called the Jebusites and was thought to be unconquerable. David moved to Jerusalem and made it the capital of the united tribes of Israel. He had the ark of the covenant kept on Mount Zion, which also became known as the City of David (1 Kgs 8:1,2). See the photograph on p. 1108.

The exact meaning of the word Zion is uncertain. It may be related to a Hebrew word that means "dry place," or an Arabic word that means "hilltop" or "mountain ridge." Zion has come to stand for a number of different things. The first meaning has to do with its original location. Archaeological evidence and biblical descriptions point to the ridge immediately southeast of the Temple Mount area. By extension Zion also stands for the city of Jerusalem (Isa 51:3; 64:10, 11; Jer 3:14-17; Zeph 3:14, 15). The "people" of Zion are those who live in Jerusalem (Ps 149:2; Isa 1:27; Lam 4:2).

When David's son Solomon built the temple in Jerusalem, he moved the ark of the covenant from its original location on Mount Zion into the temple itself (1 Kgs 8:1,2). This may explain why Zion also became associated specifically with the temple area within Jerusalem. Israel's LORD is described as living on Mount Zion (Ps 74:1,2; Isa 8:18; Joel 3:17) and ruling there as Israel's "king" (Isa 24:23; Jer 8:19; Mic 4:6,7). Eventually, the LORD's dwelling place on Mount Zion was said to be in the Most Holy Place in the temple, the central place of worship for God's people (Ps 78:68,69; Jer 31:6,12; Mic 4:1,2).

In the New Testament, the apostle Paul compares Zion to the people of Israel (Rom 9:30-33), using the prophet Isaiah's words about a stone set in Zion to refer to Jesus as the Messiah (Christ). The book of 1 PETER uses these same words to compare Jesus to the living stone of Zion, and his followers to living stones that are being used to build a spiritual house, the church (1 Pet 2:4-6).

New Testament writers expanded the promise of God's new Zion found in the books of the prophets (Isa 59:20; 60:22; Zech 8:1-8). They describe the heavenly Jerusalem (Heb 12:22; Rev 14:1) as a place where God will live among God's faithful people forever (Rev 21:1-4).

See also the mini-article called "Jerusalem," p. 574, and the illustration of the temple, p. 942.

[9]Unless the LORD Almighty
had left us some survivors,
we would have become like Sodom,
we would have been like Gomorrah.

[10]Hear the word of the LORD,
you rulers of Sodom;
listen to the law of our God,
you people of Gomorrah!
[11]"The multitude of your sacrifices—
what are they to me?" says the LORD.
"I have more than enough of burnt offerings,
of rams and the fat of fattened animals;
I have no pleasure
in the blood of bulls and lambs and goats.
[12]When you come to appear before me,
who has asked this of you,
this trampling of my courts?
[13]Stop bringing meaningless offerings!
Your incense is detestable to me.
New Moons, Sabbaths and convocations—
I cannot bear your evil assemblies.
[14]Your New Moon festivals and your appointed feasts
my soul hates.
They have become a burden to me;
I am weary of bearing them.
[15]When you spread out your hands in prayer,
I will hide my eyes from you;
even if you offer many prayers,
I will not listen.
Your hands are full of blood;
[16]wash and make yourselves clean.
Take your evil deeds
out of my sight!
Stop doing wrong,
[17]learn to do right!
Seek justice,
encourage the oppressed.[a]
Defend the cause of the fatherless,
plead the case of the widow.

[18]"Come now, let us reason together,"
says the LORD.
"Though your sins are like scarlet,
they shall be as white as snow;
though they are red as crimson,

---

[a]**17** Or / *rebuke the oppressor*

1:7-9 *Your country is desolate ... hut ... Gomorrah:* The destruction probably refers to the invasion of the southern kingdom of Judah by the combined armies of Aram, the northern kingdom of Israel, Philistia, and Edom (see 2 Chr 28:5-18). It may refer to later invasions by the Assyrian armies led by Sennacherib, who surrounded Jerusalem in 701 B.C. (36:1—37:38). It could even refer to the Babylonian invasions of Judah (605-586 B.C.).

Watchtowers or huts were built either in trees or on piles of stones or bricks. The huts provided a place for guards to watch over fields or vineyards and to spot thieves or wild animals.

God destroyed the ancient cities of Sodom and Gomorrah, because their people were so wicked (Gen 19:1-29; Isa 13:19; Rom 9:29).

1:8 *Zion:* Here, "Zion" is another name for the city of Jerusalem. See the mini-article called "Zion," p. 1294.

1:9 *LORD Almighty:* See the note on p. 1289 (LORD).

1:11-14 *sacrifices ... New Moons, Sabbaths:* See the chart called "Sacrifices and Offerings," p. 219. See also Deut 14:22-29.

The Sabbath is the weekly day of rest. See also the chart called "Jewish Calendar and Festivals," p. 944. On the first day of every month (when there was a new moon) special sacrifices were offered (Num 28:11-15). See also Amos 4:1; 5:10-15, 21-24.

1:16,17 *evil deeds ... do right ... seek justice:* See the note at 1:2 (children). Living right means obeying the LORD's commands and treating others fairly. See the mini-article called "Justice," p. 1721.

1:17 *fatherless ... widow:* Orphans and widows were defenseless in ancient Near Eastern societies. The Law of Moses commanded the people of Israel to protect and care for them (Exod 22:22,23; Deut 24:17; 27:14-26).

they shall be like wool.
19 If you are willing and obedient,
you will eat the best from the land;
20 but if you resist and rebel,
you will be devoured by the sword."
For the mouth of the LORD has spoken.

21 See how the faithful city
has become a harlot!
She once was full of justice;
righteousness used to dwell in her—
but now murderers!
22 Your silver has become dross,
your choice wine is diluted with water.
23 Your rulers are rebels,
companions of thieves;
they all love bribes
and chase after gifts.
They do not defend the cause of the fatherless;
the widow's case does not come before
them.
24 Therefore the Lord, the LORD Almighty,
the Mighty One of Israel, declares:
"Ah, I will get relief from my foes
and avenge myself on my enemies.
25 I will turn my hand against you;
I will thoroughly purge away your dross
and remove all your impurities.
26 I will restore your judges as in days of old,
your counselors as at the beginning.
Afterward you will be called
the City of Righteousness,
the Faithful City."

27 Zion will be redeemed with justice,
her penitent ones with righteousness.
28 But rebels and sinners will both be broken,
and those who forsake the LORD will perish.

29 "You will be ashamed because of the sacred oaks
in which you have delighted;
you will be disgraced because of the gardens
that you have chosen.
30 You will be like an oak with fading leaves,
like a garden without water.
31 The mighty man will become tinder
and his work a spark;
both will burn together,
with no one to quench the fire."

1:21 *a harlot:* When the people of Judah turned their backs on God's Law and lived as they pleased, they were acting like an unfaithful wife, a description used by other prophets of Israel as well (Jer 3:6-10; Ezek 16; 23; Hos 1–3). See also the mini-article called "Prostitution in the Bible," p. 1688.

1:24 *LORD Almighty . . . Mighty One of Israel:* See note on p. 1289 (LORD).

1:25 *purge away your dross:* Precious metals such as silver and gold were made more pure by a process called refining. The metal was melted at high temperatures into a liquid to separate the impurities (called dross) from it. The result was pure, valuable metal. See the photo on p. 1222.

1:26 *restore your judges as in days of old:* This probably refers to the days of King David, when Jerusalem first became the capital city of Israel (2 Sam 5:1-12).

1:26,27 *justice . . . righteousness:* See the note at 1:16,17. See also 58:5-10; 59:1-17; 61:1-9.

1:27 *Zion:* Meaning the people of Jerusalem. See the note at 1:8.

1:29-31 *sacred oaks . . . gardens . . . fire:* Canaanite places of worship were usually built on a high place near a grove of trees (Deut 12:2; 1 Kgs 14:23; Jer 2:20). The people of Israel did not destroy all these places when they entered Canaan, so the fertility rituals honoring the Canaanite gods continued (Hos 4:12,13). Images of some of these gods were honored at these holy places. See also the mini-article called "Canaanite Gods and Goddesses," p. 469.

Fire is often a sign of punishment for those who turn away from God. See also the mini-article called "Fire," p. 2383.

1:19,20 Deut 8:10-20; Isa 65:13-15.

PROPHECIES CONCERNING JUDAH AND JERUSALEM

In chapters 2–12, Isaiah brings words of judgment against those who trust idols, those who turn to foreign nations for help instead of relying on the LORD, and those who treat others unfairly. But he also brings words of hope based on a person who will rule David's kingdom as Prince of Peace (9:6,7; 11:1-9).

The Mountain of the LORD

2 This is what Isaiah son of Amoz saw concerning Judah and
Jerusalem:

2 In the last days
the mountain of the LORD's temple will be established
as chief among the mountains;
it will be raised above the hills,
and all nations will stream to it.

3 Many peoples will come and say,

"Come, let us go up to the mountain of the LORD,
to the house of the God of Jacob.
He will teach us his ways,
so that we may walk in his paths."
The law will go out from Zion,
the word of the LORD from Jerusalem.
4 He will judge between the nations
and will settle disputes for many peoples.
They will beat their swords into plowshares
and their spears into pruning hooks.
Nation will not take up sword against nation,
nor will they train for war anymore.

5 Come, O house of Jacob,
let us walk in the light of the LORD.

The Day of the LORD

6 You have abandoned your people,
the house of Jacob.
They are full of superstitions from the East;
they practice divination like the Philistines
and clasp hands with pagans.
7 Their land is full of silver and gold;
there is no end to their treasures.
Their land is full of horses;
there is no end to their chariots.
8 Their land is full of idols;
they bow down to the work of their hands,

2:1 *Judah and Jerusalem:* See the note on p. 1289 (Judah and Jerusalem).

2:2 *mountain of the LORD's temple:* This refers to Zion (Jerusalem). See the note at 1:8. Zion is the "chief" because the temple of the LORD God of Israel is there, and the LORD will be recognized as the supreme judge of all the nations (2:4; see also Ps 48:1-3; Zech 14:7-11).

2:3 *LORD . . . the God of Jacob . . . law:* The people of Israel were descendants of Jacob, the grandson of Abraham. God changed Jacob's name to Israel (Gen 32:22-28) and chose the Israelites to be his own people (Deut 7:6-8; Isa 41:8,9; 43:1). See also the note at 1:2 (children). God gave the law to Moses and the people of Israel at Mount Sinai (see Exod 19–40), so they would know how God wanted them to live their lives. See also the mini-article called "Law," p. 1160.

2:5 *the light of the LORD:* In the Bible, "light" often symbolizes God or God's word (law). See Ps 119:105; Prov 13:9; Isa 60:1,19,20; John 8:12; 1 John 1:5-7.

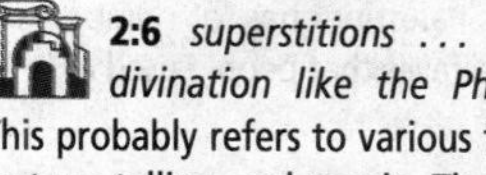

2:6 *superstitions . . . practice divination like the Philistines:* This probably refers to various forms of fortune-telling and magic. These practices were common in places such as Aram and Mesopotamia, but they were forbidden in the Law of Moses (Lev 19:26; Deut 18:9-12; see also 1 Sam 6:1-11; Ezek 21:21).

2:8 *land is full of idols:* See the note at 1:29-31.

2:2-4 Mic 4:1-3; Joel 3:10.
2:7 Deut 17:15-17.

to what their fingers have made.
9 So man will be brought low
and mankind humbled—
do not forgive them.[a]

10 Go into the rocks,
hide in the ground
from dread of the LORD
and the splendor of his majesty!
11 The eyes of the arrogant man will be humbled
and the pride of men brought low;
the LORD alone will be exalted in that day.

12 The LORD Almighty has a day in store
for all the proud and lofty,
for all that is exalted
(and they will be humbled),
13 for all the cedars of Lebanon, tall and lofty,
and all the oaks of Bashan,
14 for all the towering mountains
and all the high hills,
15 for every lofty tower
and every fortified wall,
16 for every trading ship[b]
and every stately vessel.
17 The arrogance of man will be brought low
and the pride of men humbled;
the LORD alone will be exalted in that day,
18 and the idols will totally disappear.

19 Men will flee to caves in the rocks
and to holes in the ground
from dread of the LORD
and the splendor of his majesty,
when he rises to shake the earth.
20 In that day men will throw away
to the rodents and bats
their idols of silver and idols of gold,
which they made to worship.
21 They will flee to caverns in the rocks
and to the overhanging crags
from dread of the LORD
and the splendor of his majesty,
when he rises to shake the earth.

22 Stop trusting in man,
who has but a breath in his nostrils.
Of what account is he?

[a]9 Or *not raise them up* [b]16 Hebrew *every ship of Tarshish*

Stop trusting in man, who has but a breath in his nostrils. Of what account is he?
Isa 2:22

2:11,12 *The LORD Almighty has a day in store:* On such a day of judgment the LORD will reward the faithful and punish those who have opposed him (2:17-22; see also Joel 2:1-11; 3:14-21; Amos 5:18-20; Zeph 1:14-18). See also the mini-article called "Day of the LORD," p. 1727.

2:13-16 *cedars of Lebanon . . . trading ship:* The tall cedar trees of Lebanon's forests were valued for their hardwood. Bashan, a region east of the Jordan River was famous for its oak trees. These impressive trees, high mountains, ships, and fortresses were all symbols of worldly strength.

2:18,19 *idols . . . caves:* ISAIAH often makes the point that Israel's LORD is stronger than the worthless idols made by people (30:22; 40:18-20, 25, 26; 44:9-20). Palestine has a number of limestone caves that people used as hiding places.

2:10,11 Rev 6:15; 2 Thes 1:9; 1 Sam 2:7, 8; Luke 1:51-53.

Judgment on Jerusalem and Judah

3 See now, the Lord,
the LORD Almighty,
is about to take from Jerusalem and Judah
both supply and support:
all supplies of food and all supplies of water,
2 the hero and warrior,
the judge and prophet,
the soothsayer and elder,
3 the captain of fifty and man of rank,
the counselor, skilled craftsman and clever
enchanter.

4 I will make boys their officials;
mere children will govern them.
5 People will oppress each other—
man against man, neighbor against neighbor.
The young will rise up against the old,
the base against the honorable.

6 A man will seize one of his brothers
at his father's home, and say,
"You have a cloak, you be our leader;
take charge of this heap of ruins!"
7 But in that day he will cry out,
"I have no remedy.
I have no food or clothing in my house;
do not make me the leader of the people."

8 Jerusalem staggers,
Judah is falling;
their words and deeds are against the LORD,
defying his glorious presence.
9 The look on their faces testifies against them;
they parade their sin like Sodom;
they do not hide it.
Woe to them!
They have brought disaster upon themselves.

10 Tell the righteous it will be well with them,
for they will enjoy the fruit of their deeds.
11 Woe to the wicked! Disaster is upon them!
They will be paid back for what their hands have done.

12 Youths oppress my people,
women rule over them.
O my people, your guides lead you astray;
they turn you from the path.

13 The LORD takes his place in court;
he rises to judge the people.

3:1 *LORD Almighty:* See the note on p. 1289 (LORD).

3:2-4 *hero and warrior . . . mere children will govern them:* The powerful people in Judah would one day be taken away from the land. See the mini-article called "Exile," p. 1541. As punishment the LORD promises to one day give lowly children power to rule over the evil adult leaders. See also the note at 3:12.

3:8,9 *Jerusalem . . . Sodom:* See the notes on p. 1289 (Judah and Jerusalem) and at 1:7-9.

3:10,11 *the righteous . . . Woe to the wicked:* These verses are like many of the ancient Israelite wisdom sayings about what will happen to the righteous (those who obey God) and to those who are wicked (those who disobey God). See also Job 18:5-21; Ps 37:16-20; Prov 10:27-30.

3:12 *Youths . . . women:* Like children ("youths"), women had less power and status in many ancient Near Eastern societies, including Israel. By turning away from the LORD, Judah's male leaders caused the usual social order to be turned upside down.

3:5 Isa 9:18-20; Mic 7:2-6; Mark 13:12.

14 The LORD enters into judgment
against the elders and leaders of his people:
"It is you who have ruined my vineyard;
the plunder from the poor is in your
houses.
15 What do you mean by crushing my people
and grinding the faces of the poor?"
declares the Lord, the LORD Almighty.

16 The LORD says,
"The women of Zion are haughty,
walking along with outstretched necks,
flirting with their eyes,
tripping along with mincing steps,
with ornaments jingling on their ankles.
17 Therefore the Lord will bring sores on the heads of the
women of Zion;
the LORD will make their scalps bald."

18 In that day the Lord will snatch away their finery: the ban-
gles and headbands and crescent necklaces, 19 the earrings and
bracelets and veils, 20 the headdresses and ankle chains and sashes,
the perfume bottles and charms, 21 the signet rings and nose rings,
22 the fine robes and the capes and cloaks, the purses 23 and mirrors,
and the linen garments and tiaras and shawls.

24 Instead of fragrance there will be a stench;
instead of a sash, a rope;
instead of well-dressed hair, baldness;
instead of fine clothing, sackcloth;
instead of beauty, branding.
25 Your men will fall by the sword,
your warriors in battle.
26 The gates of Zion will lament and mourn;
destitute, she will sit on the ground.

4 In that day seven women
will take hold of one man
and say, "We will eat our own food
and provide our own clothes;
only let us be called by your name.
Take away our disgrace!"

The Branch of the LORD

2 In that day the Branch of the LORD will be beautiful and glorious, and the fruit of the land will be the pride and glory of the
survivors in Israel. 3 Those who are left in Zion, who remain in
Jerusalem, will be called holy, all who are recorded among the
living in Jerusalem. 4 The Lord will wash away the filth of the
women of Zion; he will cleanse the bloodstains from Jerusalem by

3:14 *vineyard:* This refers to God's people, the nation of Israel (5:1-7).

3:16-24 *women of Zion . . . ornaments . . . snatch away their finery . . . sackcloth:* "Women" probably refers to the wives of Jerusalem's powerful and wealthy men. Their "ornaments" would have included anklets, necklaces, and rings. Some of the necklaces may have been in the shape of a crescent moon, which suggested worship of a popular moon-god. Other necklaces may have had charms with magic sayings written on them. Small boxes containing perfumed flower petals also may have been worn along with very fancy clothes.

Sackcloth (3:24) was dark, coarse cloth made from goat's wool. People wore sackcloth as a way of showing their deep sadness.

3:26—4:1 *sit on the ground . . . Take away our disgrace:* People sometimes rubbed dust on themselves or sat in dirt to show their sorrow or to show that they were sorry for their sins (Job 2:8, 12; Lam 4:5; Jonah 3:5, 6). In the ancient Near East, a woman was considered "disgraced" (4:1) if she did not have a husband and children.

4:4 *spirit of judgment and a spirit of fire:* Fire is often connected with the LORD's judgment against those who are evil or disobedient (Gen 19:23-29; Joel 2:1-3). Fire is also a symbol of purification (see 48:10 and the note at 1:25). See also the mini-article called "Fire," p. 2383.

Vineyard in Israel. Vineyards were a familiar sight to the people of ancient Israel and Judah. The grapes grown in Palestine were eaten fresh in the summer, dried for eating during the winter, or made into wine, which the people of Israel drank year-round and traded with its neighbors. In Isaiah's "Song of the Vineyard," the prophet told of the LORD's disappointment in the people he had chosen to be his own. "The vineyard of the LORD Almighty is the house of Israel, and the men of Judah are the garden of his delight. And he looked for justice, but saw bloodshed; for righteousness, but heard cries of distress." (See 5:1-7.)

a spirit[a] of judgment and a spirit[a] of fire. 5Then the LORD will create
over all of Mount Zion and over those who assemble there a cloud
of smoke by day and a glow of flaming fire by night; over all the
glory will be a canopy. 6It will be a shelter and shade from the heat
of the day, and a refuge and hiding place from the storm and rain.

The Song of the Vineyard

5 I will sing for the one I love
a song about his vineyard:
My loved one had a vineyard
on a fertile hillside.
2He dug it up and cleared it of stones
and planted it with the choicest vines.
He built a watchtower in it
and cut out a winepress as well.
Then he looked for a crop of good grapes,
but it yielded only bad fruit.

3"Now you dwellers in Jerusalem and men of Judah,
judge between me and my vineyard.
4What more could have been done for my vineyard
than I have done for it?

[a]**4** Or *the Spirit*

4:5 *cloud of smoke . . . flaming fire:* This is how the LORD led the people of Israel during the forty years they were in the desert (Exod 13:20-22; 40:36-38). For other appearances of the LORD in smoke and fire, see Exod 3:1-6; 19:16-19; 24:15-18. See also the note at 4:4.

5:1,2 *vineyard . . . watchtower . . . winepress:* The vineyard is Israel (5:7), but it is not clear whether this means the northern kingdom, or if it refers to all God's people, including those in Judah. See the note at 1:4 (nation). If it is the northern kingdom, this prophecy may refer to the time of King Ahaz of Judah when the Assyrians defeated and destroyed the northern kingdom in 721 B.C. (5:5, 6).

For "watchtower" see the note at 1:7-9. The "winepress" was a pit made of stone or plaster. Inside, people pressed grapes with their feet. See also the illustrations on pp. 1773 and 2046.

5:1,2 Matt 21:33; Mark 12:1; Luke 20:9.

5:4 *good grapes . . . bad:* A "fertile hillside" (5:1) that is well taken care of should produce sweet grapes. Here, God compares Israel with such a hill. Israel's sins were like bad grapes to the LORD and were described in detail by many of Israel's prophets, including Amos, Hosea, and Micah. See also Isa 9:8—10:34; 28:1-13.

5:5 *vineyard . . . trampled:* This may refer to Israel's fall to Assyria (see the note at 5:1,2). But the warning also applies to Judah, whose leaders were not being honest or fair (1:10-17,21-26; 3:1-15).

5:7 *LORD Almighty . . . justice:* See the notes on p. 1289 (LORD) and at 1:16,17.

5:8 *Woe to:* This phrase occurs a number of times in this chapter (5:8, 11,18,20,22). Isaiah announces judgments known as "woes."

5:8 *join field to field . . . you live alone in the land:* In ancient Israel, land was given or assigned to tribes and families. The ownership rights to these lands were to be passed on within the tribes, so every family could work the land and harvest crops or fruit. Land could be leased, but not bought or sold (Lev 25:23-28; Num 27:5-11; 1 Kgs 21:1-3). Isaiah describes some people in Israel buying or taking land away from the original family owners. This especially affected poor landowners.

5:11-13 *my people will go into exile:* This refers to wealthy persons. Instead of using their wealth to help others, they wasted it on parties. Eventually, these people would lose the land that the LORD gave them and be taken off to exile (see the note at 3:2-4).

When I looked for good grapes,
why did it yield only bad?
5 Now I will tell you
what I am going to do to my vineyard:
I will take away its hedge,
and it will be destroyed;
I will break down its wall,
and it will be trampled.
6 I will make it a wasteland,
neither pruned nor cultivated,
and briers and thorns will grow there.
I will command the clouds
not to rain on it."

7 The vineyard of the LORD Almighty
is the house of Israel,
and the men of Judah
are the garden of his delight.
And he looked for justice, but saw bloodshed;
for righteousness, but heard cries of distress.

Woes and Judgments

8 Woe to you who add house to house
and join field to field
till no space is left
and you live alone in the land.
9 The LORD Almighty has declared in my hearing:
"Surely the great houses will become desolate,
the fine mansions left without occupants.
10 A ten-acre[a] vineyard will produce only a bath[b]
of wine,
a homer[c] of seed only an ephah[d] of grain."
11 Woe to those who rise early in the morning
to run after their drinks,
who stay up late at night
till they are inflamed with wine.
12 They have harps and lyres at their banquets,
tambourines and flutes and wine,
but they have no regard for the deeds of the LORD,
no respect for the work of his hands.
13 Therefore my people will go into exile
for lack of understanding;

[a]10 Hebrew *ten-yoke,* that is, the land plowed by 10 yoke of oxen in one day [b]10 That is, probably about 6 gallons (about 22 liters) [c]10 That is, probably about 6 bushels (about 220 liters) [d]10 That is, probably about 3/5 bushel (about 22 liters)

their men of rank will die of hunger
and their masses will be parched with thirst.
14 Therefore the grave[a] enlarges its appetite
and opens its mouth without limit;
into it will descend their nobles and masses
with all their brawlers and revelers.
15 So man will be brought low
and mankind humbled,
the eyes of the arrogant humbled.
16 But the LORD Almighty will be exalted by his justice,
and the holy God will show himself holy by his
righteousness.
17 Then sheep will graze as in their own pasture;
lambs will feed[b] among the ruins of the rich.

18 Woe to those who draw sin along with cords of deceit,
and wickedness as with cart ropes,
19 to those who say, "Let God hurry,
let him hasten his work
so we may see it.
Let it approach,
let the plan of the Holy One of Israel come,
so we may know it."

20 Woe to those who call evil good
and good evil,
who put darkness for light
and light for darkness,
who put bitter for sweet
and sweet for bitter.

21 Woe to those who are wise in their own eyes
and clever in their own sight.

22 Woe to those who are heroes at drinking wine
and champions at mixing drinks,
23 who acquit the guilty for a bribe,
but deny justice to the innocent.
24 Therefore, as tongues of fire lick up straw
and as dry grass sinks down in the flames,
so their roots will decay
and their flowers blow away like dust;
for they have rejected the law of the LORD Almighty
and spurned the word of the Holy One of Israel.
25 Therefore the LORD's anger burns against his people;
his hand is raised and he strikes them down.
The mountains shake,
and the dead bodies are like refuse in the streets.

---

[a]14 Hebrew *Sheol*   [b]17 Septuagint; Hebrew / *strangers will eat*

5:14 *the grave enlarges its appetite:* This refers to the world of the dead. Elsewhere it is described as a totally silent place where no one knows or feels anything (Job 10:21, 22; Ps 88:12; 94:17). See also 14:9-17 and the mini-article called "Eternal Life," p. 2072.

5:16 *LORD Almighty . . . justice:* See the notes on p. 1289 (LORD) and at 1:16,17.

5:18,19 *draw sin along . . . Holy One of Israel:* The leaders, harnessed to their sins, drag the punishment for their lies behind them like a farmer forced to drag a cart by leather ropes.

Isaiah uses the name "Holy One of Israel" to show that God is both set apart from human beings (holy), but also close and personal. God chose Israel (41:8, 9) and lives among them (Exod 25:18-22; 1 Kgs 8:6-13; Isa 6:1-8). See also 5:24; 10:20; 12:6; 17:7; 31:1; 37:23.

5:23 *guilty for a bribe . . . deny justice to the innocent:* Some judges accepted gifts of money or goods in return for ruling in favor of the wealthy. That violated the rights of innocent people, such as poor people, widows, and children, who could not afford to bribe anyone (see also 1:23; Amos 5:10-12).

5:25,26 *mountains shake . . . distant nations:* The shaking mountains may refer to a violent earthquake that struck Israel in 760 B.C. (see Amos 1:1). Here, "distant nations" probably refers to Assyria. The powerful Assyrian army attacked the northern kingdom of Israel beginning about 738 B.C. and ending when Assyria finally captured and defeated Israel's capital of Samaria in 721 B.C. Some scholars believe that this section of ISAIAH (5:25-30) originally may have followed 9:8-21 because of the similar form and content.

5:28 *chariot wheels:* A chariot was a two-wheeled cart that was open at the back and that was pulled by horses. The Assyrian army was famous for its many battle chariots. See the illustration on p. 160.

5:30 *In that day . . . darkness and distress:* See the note at 2:11,12.

6:1 *the year that King Uzziah died:* About 742 B.C. (2 Kgs 15:7; 2 Chr 26:23).

6:1,2 *a throne . . . seraphs, each with six wings:* The lid of the ark of the covenant had two golden winged creatures (cherubim) on it and was considered God's throne among the people (Exod 25:10-22; 2 Sam 6:2). Much later, when King Solomon built Israel's great temple, he put two 15-foot cherubim in an area of the temple called the Most Holy Place (1 Kgs 6:19-29). The LORD's new throne was above the wings of these cherubim (2 Kgs 19:15). The cherubim probably looked like the winged lions or bulls that guarded other ancient Near Eastern temples. The "seraphs" probably looked like winged cobra snakes, since similar words are used in Numbers 21:6; and in Isaiah 14:29; 30:6 to refer to poisonous dragons or serpents. See also the mini-article called "The Ark of the Covenant," p. 513.

6:5 *I am ruined . . . seen the King, the LORD Almighty:* Isaiah thought he was doomed to die, because humans, being sinful, were not supposed to see God's face (Gen 16:13,14; Exod 33:19-23; Judg 13:20-22).

Israel's LORD is described as Israel's King (Isa 24:23; 41:21; Jer 8:19; Zeph 3:15; Mic 4:6, 7). See also the note on p. 1289 (LORD).

6:3 Rev 4:8. **6:4** Exod 19:18, 19; Rev 15:8. **6:9,10** Matt 13:14,15; Mark 4:12; Luke 8:10; John 12:40; Acts 28:26, 27.

Yet for all this, his anger is not turned away,
his hand is still upraised.

26 He lifts up a banner for the distant nations,
he whistles for those at the ends of the earth.
Here they come,
swiftly and speedily!
27 Not one of them grows tired or stumbles,
not one slumbers or sleeps;
not a belt is loosened at the waist,
not a sandal thong is broken.
28 Their arrows are sharp,
all their bows are strung;
their horses' hoofs seem like flint,
their chariot wheels like a whirlwind.
29 Their roar is like that of the lion,
they roar like young lions;
they growl as they seize their prey
and carry it off with no one to rescue.
30 In that day they will roar over it
like the roaring of the sea.
And if one looks at the land,
he will see darkness and distress;
even the light will be darkened by the clouds.

Isaiah's Commission

6 In the year that King Uzziah died, I saw the Lord seated on a
throne, high and exalted, and the train of his robe filled the temple. 2 Above him were seraphs, each with six wings: With two wings
they covered their faces, with two they covered their feet, and with
two they were flying. 3 And they were calling to one another:

"Holy, holy, holy is the LORD Almighty;
the whole earth is full of his glory."

4 At the sound of their voices the doorposts and thresholds shook
and the temple was filled with smoke.

5 "Woe to me!" I cried. "I am ruined! For I am a man of
unclean lips, and I live among a people of unclean lips, and my
eyes have seen the King, the LORD Almighty."

6 Then one of the seraphs flew to me with a live coal in his
hand, which he had taken with tongs from the altar. 7 With it he
touched my mouth and said, "See, this has touched your lips; your
guilt is taken away and your sin atoned for."

8 Then I heard the voice of the Lord saying, "Whom shall I
send? And who will go for us?"

And I said, "Here am I. Send me!"

9 He said, "Go and tell this people:

Isaiah's Vision and Call, by Reuven Rubin, 1970. In the year that King Uzziah died, Isaiah had a vision in the temple. Seraphs, each with six wings, appeared and proclaimed the holiness of the LORD. Isaiah immediately became aware of his own sinfulness. Then one of the seraphs used tongs to lift a burning coal from the altar. He touched Isaiah's lips with it and told the prophet, "See, this has touched your lips; your guilt is taken away and your sin atoned for." The LORD then chose Isaiah to take his message and warnings to the people. (See chapter 6.)

" 'Be ever hearing, but never understanding;
be ever seeing, but never perceiving.'
10 Make the heart of this people calloused;
make their ears dull
and close their eyes.[a]
Otherwise they might see with their eyes,
hear with their ears,
understand with their hearts,
and turn and be healed."

[a]9,10 Hebrew; Septuagint *'You will be ever hearing, but never understanding; / you will be ever seeing, but never perceiving.' / [10]This people's heart has become calloused; / they hardly hear with their ears, / and they have closed their eyes*

6:6,7 *live coal . . . tongs from the altar . . . touched my mouth:* On the Day of Atonement (Lev 16:11-14), the high priest took burning coals into the Most Holy Place as part of a ceremony to forgive the sins of the priest and the people. The "tongs" were probably a bronze tool used by the priests to offer sacrifices at the bronze altar (Exod 27:1-3). See also Jer 1:9.

6:11,12 *the cities lie ruined . . . sent everyone far away:* The Assyrians destroyed the northern kingdom (Israel) and took many of its people into exile in 721 B.C. Later, the Babylonians defeated and destroyed the southern kingdom (Judah) and took many of its people into exile.

7:1-3 *Ahaz . . . Pekah . . . Shear-Jashub:* Ahaz ruled Judah from 736 to 716 B.C., and Pekah ruled the northern kingdom of Israel from 737 to 732 B.C. Between 735 and 732 B.C., Israel and Aram invaded Judah (2 Kgs 15:27—16:20; 2 Chr 28:1-27). At first, Pekah and Rezin, the king of Aram, tried to force Ahaz to join them in their battles against Assyria. When Ahaz didn't cooperate, Pekah and Rezin tried to replace him with a king more friendly to their purpose (7:6). Against Isaiah's advice, Ahaz turned to the Assyrians for help, which later made things worse for Judah (2 Chr 28:16-20).

In Hebrew "Shear-Jashub" (7:3) means "a remnant will return." This probably refers to the small group that remained in Israel after it was defeated by Assyria (7:8, 9; 10:20-22).

7:3 *aqueduct of the Upper Pool:* This refers to a long tunnel that brought water to Jerusalem from a pool or cistern.

7:4-6 *don't be afraid . . . son of Tabeel:* God says that Ahaz would not be defeated by Israel and Aram nor replaced on the throne of Judah by the son of Tabeel.

7:8,9 *sixty-five years:* If this prophecy dates to around 735 B.C. (see the note at 7:1-3), sixty-five years later would be about 670 B.C., when Esarhaddon ruled Assyria (680-669 B.C.). He, along with King Ashurbanipal after him, brought foreigners in to settle the area around Samaria.

7:8,9 *Damascus . . . Samaria:* King Omri built the city of Samaria in the early ninth century B.C. and made it the capital of the northern kingdom of Israel (1 Kgs 16:24).

11 Then I said, "For how long, O Lord?"
And he answered:

"Until the cities lie ruined
and without inhabitant,
until the houses are left deserted
and the fields ruined and ravaged,
12 until the LORD has sent everyone far away
and the land is utterly forsaken.
13 And though a tenth remains in the land,
it will again be laid waste.
But as the terebinth and oak
leave stumps when they are cut down,
so the holy seed will be the stump in the land."

The Sign of Immanuel

7 When Ahaz son of Jotham, the son of Uzziah, was king of
Judah, King Rezin of Aram and Pekah son of Remaliah king of
Israel marched up to fight against Jerusalem, but they could not
overpower it.
2 Now the house of David was told, "Aram has allied itself
with[a] Ephraim"; so the hearts of Ahaz and his people were shaken,
as the trees of the forest are shaken by the wind.
3 Then the LORD said to Isaiah, "Go out, you and your son
Shear-Jashub,[b] to meet Ahaz at the end of the aqueduct of the
Upper Pool, on the road to the Washerman's Field. 4 Say to him, 'Be
careful, keep calm and don't be afraid. Do not lose heart because
of these two smoldering stubs of firewood—because of the fierce
anger of Rezin and Aram and of the son of Remaliah. 5 Aram,
Ephraim and Remaliah's son have plotted your ruin, saying, 6 "Let
us invade Judah; let us tear it apart and divide it among ourselves,
and make the son of Tabeel king over it." 7 Yet this is what the Sovereign LORD says:

" 'It will not take place,
it will not happen,
8 for the head of Aram is Damascus,
and the head of Damascus is only Rezin.
Within sixty-five years
Ephraim will be too shattered to be a people.
9 The head of Ephraim is Samaria,
and the head of Samaria is only Remaliah's son.
If you do not stand firm in your faith,
you will not stand at all.' "

10 Again the LORD spoke to Ahaz, 11 "Ask the LORD your God
for a sign, whether in the deepest depths or in the highest heights."

[a]2 Or *has set up camp in* [b]3 *Shear-Jashub* means *a remnant will return.*

12 But Ahaz said, "I will not ask; I will not put the LORD to the
test."
13 Then Isaiah said, "Hear now, you house of David! Is it not
enough to try the patience of men? Will you try the patience of my
God also? 14 Therefore the Lord himself will give you[a] a sign: The
virgin will be with child and will give birth to a son, and[b] will call
him Immanuel.[c] 15 He will eat curds and honey when he knows
enough to reject the wrong and choose the right. 16 But before the
boy knows enough to reject the wrong and choose the right, the
land of the two kings you dread will be laid waste. 17 The LORD will
bring on you and on your people and on the house of your father
a time unlike any since Ephraim broke away from Judah—he will
bring the king of Assyria."
18 In that day the LORD will whistle for flies from the distant
streams of Egypt and for bees from the land of Assyria. 19 They will
all come and settle in the steep ravines and in the crevices in the
rocks, on all the thornbushes and at all the water holes. 20 In that
day the Lord will use a razor hired from beyond the River[d]—the
king of Assyria—to shave your head and the hair of your legs, and
to take off your beards also. 21 In that day, a man will keep alive a
young cow and two goats. 22 And because of the abundance of the
milk they give, he will have curds to eat. All who remain in the
land will eat curds and honey. 23 In that day, in every place where
there were a thousand vines worth a thousand silver shekels,[e] there
will be only briers and thorns. 24 Men will go there with bow and
arrow, for the land will be covered with briers and thorns. 25 As for
all the hills once cultivated by the hoe, you will no longer go there
for fear of the briers and thorns; they will become places where
cattle are turned loose and where sheep run.

Assyria, the LORD's Instrument

8 The LORD said to me, "Take a large scroll and write on it with an
ordinary pen: Maher-Shalal-Hash-Baz.[f] 2 And I will call in Uriah the
priest and Zechariah son of Jeberekiah as reliable witnesses for me."
3 Then I went to the prophetess, and she conceived and gave
birth to a son. And the LORD said to me, "Name him Maher-Shalal-
Hash-Baz. 4 Before the boy knows how to say 'My father' or 'My
mother,' the wealth of Damascus and the plunder of Samaria will
be carried off by the king of Assyria."
5 The LORD spoke to me again:

6 "Because this people has rejected
the gently flowing waters of Shiloah

[a]**14** The Hebrew is plural. [b]**14** Masoretic Text; Dead Sea Scrolls *and he* or *and they* [c]**14** *Immanuel* means *God with us.* [d]**20** That is, the Euphrates [e]**23** That is, about 25 pounds (about 11.5 kilograms) [f]**1** *Maher-Shalal-Hash-Baz* means *quick to the plunder, swift to the spoil*; also in verse 3.

7:13 *house of David:* The LORD made a promise that one of David's descendants would always be king (2 Sam 7:8-29; Ps 132:10-18).

7:14 *Immanuel:* In Hebrew "Immanuel" means "God with us" (Matt 1:23). This name was meant to help convince Ahaz that God would protect him and Judah (see Ps 46:4-11; Isa 8:8-10). See the note at 8:3.

7:15-17 *the land of the two kings you dread will be laid waste:* In 732 B.C., Assyria invaded, robbed, and ruined much of Aram and the northern kingdom of Israel, which had broken away from the southern tribes known as Judah almost two hundred years earlier (1 Kgs 12:1-20). Ahaz of Judah sent gifts to the Assyrian king and tried to become friendly with him (2 Kgs 16:5-18). This meant a short time of relief for Judah, but eventually Assyria also invaded Judah (2 Kgs 18:13-37; Isa 8:6-8; 36:1).

7:20 *shave . . . beards:* To have one's beard, head, and body shaved brought great shame (2 Sam 10:4,5). The "razor" used to humble Judah was the Assyrian army.

8:1 *Maher-Shalal-Hash-Baz:* This means "suddenly attacked, quickly taken," and was the name of one of Isaiah's sons (see 8:3 and the note).

8:2 *Uriah . . . Zechariah:* Uriah served as priest under King Ahaz (2 Kgs 16:10-16). Zechariah may be Ahaz's father-in-law (2 Kgs 18:2).

8:3 *prophetess . . . son:* The "prophetess" refers to Isaiah's wife, and may be the same person as the "virgin" mentioned in 7:14. If this is so, the births of Immanuel (7:14) and Maher-Shalal-Hash-Baz (8:3) were not far apart, and their names refer to the same invasion of Israel and Aram by the Assyrians around 732 B.C. (see also 8:4; 7:15,16).

8:6,7 *Shiloah:* Shiloah was the canal that brought water from Gihon Spring to Jerusalem (see the note at 7:3).

and rejoices over Rezin
and the son of Remaliah,
7 therefore the Lord is about to bring against them
the mighty floodwaters of the River[a]—
the king of Assyria with all his pomp.
It will overflow all its channels,
run over all its banks
8 and sweep on into Judah, swirling over it,
passing through it and reaching up to the neck.
Its outspread wings will cover the breadth of your land,
O Immanuel[b]!"

9 Raise the war cry,[c] you nations, and be shattered!
Listen, all you distant lands.
Prepare for battle, and be shattered!
Prepare for battle, and be shattered!
10 Devise your strategy, but it will be thwarted;
propose your plan, but it will not stand,
for God is with us.[d]

Fear God

11 The LORD spoke to me with his strong hand upon me,
warning me not to follow the way of this people. He said:

12 "Do not call conspiracy
everything that these people call conspiracy[e];
do not fear what they fear,
and do not dread it.
13 The LORD Almighty is the one you are to regard as holy,
he is the one you are to fear,
he is the one you are to dread,
14 and he will be a sanctuary;
but for both houses of Israel he will be
a stone that causes men to stumble
and a rock that makes them fall.
And for the people of Jerusalem he will be
a trap and a snare.
15 Many of them will stumble;
they will fall and be broken,
they will be snared and captured."

16 Bind up the testimony
and seal up the law among my disciples.
17 I will wait for the LORD,
who is hiding his face from the house of Jacob.
I will put my trust in him.

---

[a]7 That is, the Euphrates [b]8 *Immanuel* means *God with us.* [c]9 Or *Do your worst* [d]10 Hebrew *Immanuel* [e]12 Or *Do not call for a treaty / every time these people call for a treaty*

"The LORD Almighty is the one you are to regard as holy, he is the one you are to fear, he is the one you are to dread, and he will be a sanctuary."
Isa 8:13,14

8:6 *Rezin:* The king of Aram. See the note at 7:1-3.

8:11 *The LORD spoke to me:* Meaning the prophet was about to receive a special message from the LORD (see also Ezek 1:3).

8:13 *The LORD Almighty . . . holy:* See the notes at 5:18,19 and on p. 1289 (LORD).

8:16 *seal up the law:* Isaiah's prophecies were written on scrolls and sealed with wax. The scrolls were to be kept sealed as long as the people remained disobedient. See also 29:11; Jer 32:8-15; and the mini-article called "Scrolls," p. 1491.

8:8 Deut 32:11; Ps 17:8; 61:4; 91:3,4. **8:9,10** Isa 17:12-14. **8:12,13** 1 Pet 3:14, 15. **8:14,15** Isa 28:16; 1 Pet 2:8. **8:17,18** Heb 2:13.

[18]Here am I, and the children the LORD has given me. We are
signs and symbols in Israel from the LORD Almighty, who dwells
on Mount Zion.
[19]When men tell you to consult mediums and spiritists, who
whisper and mutter, should not a people inquire of their God?
Why consult the dead on behalf of the living? [20]To the law and to
the testimony! If they do not speak according to this word, they
have no light of dawn. [21]Distressed and hungry, they will roam
through the land; when they are famished, they will become
enraged and, looking upward, will curse their king and their God.
[22]Then they will look toward the earth and see only distress and
darkness and fearful gloom, and they will be thrust into utter
darkness.

To Us a Child Is Born

9 Nevertheless, there will be no more gloom for those who were
in distress. In the past he humbled the land of Zebulun and the
land of Naphtali, but in the future he will honor Galilee of the
Gentiles, by the way of the sea, along the Jordan—

[2]The people walking in darkness
have seen a great light;
on those living in the land of the shadow of death[a]
a light has dawned.
[3]You have enlarged the nation
and increased their joy;
they rejoice before you
as people rejoice at the harvest,
as men rejoice
when dividing the plunder.
[4]For as in the day of Midian's defeat,
you have shattered
the yoke that burdens them,
the bar across their shoulders,
the rod of their oppressor.
[5]Every warrior's boot used in battle
and every garment rolled in blood
will be destined for burning,
will be fuel for the fire.
[6]For to us a child is born,
to us a son is given,
and the government will be on his shoulders.
And he will be called
Wonderful Counselor,[b] Mighty God,
Everlasting Father, Prince of Peace.

[a]2 Or *land of darkness* [b]6 Or *Wonderful, Counselor*

8:18 *Mount Zion:* See the note at 1:8.

8:19 *mediums and spiritists . . . consult the dead:* See the article called "Miracles, Magic, and Medicine," p. 1838.

9:1 *Zebulun . . . Naphtali . . . Galilee of the Gentiles:* Zebulun (Gen 30:19, 20) and Naphtali (Gen 30:7, 8) were the names of two of Israel's northern tribes (Josh 19:10-16, 32-39). In 733/32 B.C. Tiglath-Pileser of Assyria turned their lands into the Assyrian province known as Galilee. Gilead, the land east of the Jordan, and Dor, a city on the Mediterranean coast, also were incorporated into Assyrian provinces.

9:2 *walking in darkness . . . light:* Those living in the areas threatened or captured by Assyria. The "light" that gives them hope has to do with God's saving help, perhaps in the form of a new king.

9:4 *the day of Midian's defeat:* This refers to the time when Gideon defeated the people of Midian in Valley of Jezreel (Judg 6–8).

9:6 *Wonderful Counselor . . . Prince of Peace:* A king of Israel was compared to God's Son (Ps 2:7). The titles were similar to those given to an Egyptian king. "Wonderful Counselor" refers to a political leader; "Mighty God" to a warrior; "Everlasting Father" to one who cares for his people; and "Prince of Peace" to one who brings prosperity.

9:1 Matt 4:15.

9:7 *David's throne:* God promised that Israel's king would always come from the family of King David (2 Sam 7:8-29; Ps 132:10-18).

9:8,9 *Israel . . . Samaria:* Here Israel refers to the northern kingdom. See also the notes at 1:4 (nation) and 7:8,9 (Samaria).

9:10 *bricks . . . dressed stone . . . cedars:* Mud bricks and sycamore wood were common building materials. Dressed stones and cedar wood were more expensive and were used in building palaces. See also the illustrations on pp. 143 and 862.

9:11,12 *foes . . . Arameans . . . Philistines:* Arameans is another name for the people of Aram, Israel's enemy to the northeast. Israel's ongoing conflicts with the Philistines began before the time of King David and continued in Isaiah's day. Many scholars believe the prophecy in 9:8-21 actually fits with 5:25-30 and refers to the time before the war between Israel and Aram (see the notes at 5:25, 26 and 7:1-3).

9:15,16 *elders and prominent men . . . led astray:* See the notes at 1:29-31; 3:12; 5:18,19.

9:18 Eccl 7:6.

7 Of the increase of his government and peace
there will be no end.
He will reign on David's throne
and over his kingdom,
establishing and upholding it
with justice and righteousness
from that time on and forever.
The zeal of the LORD Almighty
will accomplish this.

The LORD's Anger Against Israel

8 The Lord has sent a message against Jacob;
it will fall on Israel.
9 All the people will know it—
Ephraim and the inhabitants of Samaria—
who say with pride
and arrogance of heart,
10 "The bricks have fallen down,
but we will rebuild with dressed stone;
the fig trees have been felled,
but we will replace them with cedars."
11 But the LORD has strengthened Rezin's foes against them
and has spurred their enemies on.
12 Arameans from the east and Philistines from the west
have devoured Israel with open mouth.

Yet for all this, his anger is not turned away,
his hand is still upraised.

13 But the people have not returned to him who struck them,
nor have they sought the LORD Almighty.
14 So the LORD will cut off from Israel both head and tail,
both palm branch and reed in a single day;
15 the elders and prominent men are the head,
the prophets who teach lies are the tail.
16 Those who guide this people mislead them,
and those who are guided are led astray.
17 Therefore the Lord will take no pleasure in the young men,
nor will he pity the fatherless and widows,
for everyone is ungodly and wicked,
every mouth speaks vileness.

Yet for all this, his anger is not turned away,
his hand is still upraised.

18 Surely wickedness burns like a fire;
it consumes briers and thorns,
it sets the forest thickets ablaze,
so that it rolls upward in a column of smoke.

[19] By the wrath of the LORD Almighty
the land will be scorched
and the people will be fuel for the fire;
no one will spare his brother.
[20] On the right they will devour,
but still be hungry;
on the left they will eat,
but not be satisfied.
Each will feed on the flesh of his own offspring[a]:
21 Manasseh will feed on Ephraim, and Ephraim
on Manasseh;
together they will turn against Judah.

Yet for all this, his anger is not turned away,
his hand is still upraised.

10 Woe to those who make unjust laws,
to those who issue oppressive decrees,
[2] to deprive the poor of their rights
and withhold justice from the oppressed of my people,
making widows their prey
and robbing the fatherless.
[3] What will you do on the day of reckoning,
when disaster comes from afar?
To whom will you run for help?
Where will you leave your riches?
[4] Nothing will remain but to cringe among the captives
or fall among the slain.

Yet for all this, his anger is not turned away,
his hand is still upraised.

God's Judgment on Assyria

[5] "Woe to the Assyrian, the rod of my anger,
in whose hand is the club of my wrath!
[6] I send him against a godless nation,
I dispatch him against a people who anger me,
to seize loot and snatch plunder,
and to trample them down like mud in the streets.
[7] But this is not what he intends,
this is not what he has in mind;
his purpose is to destroy,
to put an end to many nations.
[8] 'Are not my commanders all kings?' he says.
9 'Has not Calno fared like Carchemish?
Is not Hamath like Arpad,
and Samaria like Damascus?

[a]**20** Or *arm*

9:21 *Ephraim ... Manasseh:* These two northern tribes were named after the sons of Joseph (Gen 48:5,6). See also Judg 12:1-6; 2 Kgs 15:13-16,23-25.

10:1 *unjust laws ... oppressive decrees:* See the notes at 1:16, 17; 1:17; 5:23.

10:5 *the Assyrian, the rod of my anger:* Various kings of Assyria invaded and captured parts of Israel, Judah, and surrounding countries. The invasions took place from 738 to 701 B.C. See the note at 7:8,9 (sixty-five years).

10:9-12 *Calno ... Damascus ... Mount Zion and Jerusalem:* Assyrian king Tiglath-Pileser captured Calno twice, in 740 and in 738 B.C. He also captured Carchemish, which Sargon II of Assyria later recaptured in 717 B.C. The Assyrians captured Hamath in 738 B.C. and 720 B.C. Tiglath-Pileser captured Arpad in 740 B.C. Israel's capital, Samaria, fell to Assyria in 721 B.C. (2 Kgs 17:3-6). Damascus, capital of Aram, was captured by Tiglath-Pileser in 732 B.C. See also 29:1-8.

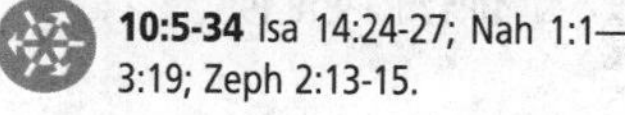

10:5-34 Isa 14:24-27; Nah 1:1—3:19; Zeph 2:13-15.

In that day the remnant of Israel, the survivors of the house of Jacob, will no longer rely on him who struck them down but will truly rely on the LORD, the Holy One of Israel.
Isa 10:20

10:12 *punish the king of Assyria . . . pride:* This refers to destruction of Sennacherib and his army (see 2 Kgs 19; Isa 36, 37).

10:16 *LORD Almighty:* See the note on p. 1289 (LORD).

10:17 *Holy One a flame:* See the notes at 5:18, 19 and 4:4.

10:20-22 *truly rely on the LORD . . . remnant will return:* See the note at 5:18,19. The nation "who struck them down" (10:20) is Assyria. King Ahaz of Judah had turned to Assyria for help instead of relying on the LORD's help (see the note at 7:1-3).

The "sand by the sea" refers to the many descendants that God promised to Abraham, Israel's ancestor (Gen 12:2; 22:17). Because of their sins, however, Isaiah warned that the LORD would punish the people of Israel and Judah and allow many to be carried off to foreign lands. Afterwards, a much smaller number would return to Judah.

10:17 Isa 9:18,19.

10 As my hand seized the kingdoms of the idols,
kingdoms whose images excelled those of Jerusalem
and Samaria—
11 shall I not deal with Jerusalem and her images
as I dealt with Samaria and her idols?' "

12 When the Lord has finished all his work against Mount
Zion and Jerusalem, he will say, "I will punish the king of Assyria
for the willful pride of his heart and the haughty look in his eyes.
13 For he says:

" 'By the strength of my hand I have done this,
and by my wisdom, because I have understanding.
I removed the boundaries of nations,
I plundered their treasures;
like a mighty one I subdued[a] their kings.
14 As one reaches into a nest,
so my hand reached for the wealth of the nations;
as men gather abandoned eggs,
so I gathered all the countries;
not one flapped a wing,
or opened its mouth to chirp.' "
15 Does the ax raise itself above him who swings it,
or the saw boast against him who uses it?
As if a rod were to wield him who lifts it up,
or a club brandish him who is not wood!
16 Therefore, the Lord, the LORD Almighty,
will send a wasting disease upon his sturdy warriors;
under his pomp a fire will be kindled
like a blazing flame.
17 The Light of Israel will become a fire,
their Holy One a flame;
in a single day it will burn and consume
his thorns and his briers.
18 The splendor of his forests and fertile fields
it will completely destroy,
as when a sick man wastes away.
19 And the remaining trees of his forests will be so few
that a child could write them down.

The Remnant of Israel

20 In that day the remnant of Israel,
the survivors of the house of Jacob,
will no longer rely on him
who struck them down
but will truly rely on the LORD,

[a]13 Or / *I subdued the mighty,*

the Holy One of Israel.
21 A remnant will return,[a] a remnant of Jacob
will return to the Mighty God.
22 Though your people, O Israel, be like the sand by the sea,
only a remnant will return.
Destruction has been decreed,
overwhelming and righteous.
23 The Lord, the LORD Almighty, will carry out
the destruction decreed upon the whole land.

24 Therefore, this is what the Lord, the LORD Almighty, says:

"O my people who live in Zion,
do not be afraid of the Assyrians,
who beat you with a rod
and lift up a club against you, as Egypt did.
25 Very soon my anger against you will end
and my wrath will be directed to their destruction."

26 The LORD Almighty will lash them with a whip,
as when he struck down Midian at the rock of Oreb;
and he will raise his staff over the waters,
as he did in Egypt.
27 In that day their burden will be lifted from your
shoulders,
their yoke from your neck;
the yoke will be broken
because you have grown so fat.[b]

28 They enter Aiath;
they pass through Migron;
they store supplies at Micmash.
29 They go over the pass, and say,
"We will camp overnight at Geba."
Ramah trembles;
Gibeah of Saul flees.
30 Cry out, O Daughter of Gallim!
Listen, O Laishah!
Poor Anathoth!
31 Madmenah is in flight;
the people of Gebim take cover.
32 This day they will halt at Nob;
they will shake their fist
at the mount of the Daughter of Zion,
at the hill of Jerusalem.
33 See, the Lord, the LORD Almighty,
will lop off the boughs with great power.

a21 Hebrew *shear-jashub*; also in verse 22 **b27** Hebrew; Septuagint *broken / from your shoulders*

10:24 *Assyrians . . . Egypt:* See the note at 10:5. The Egyptians treated the Hebrew people as slaves, but the LORD acted to free the people from them (Exod 12–15). The LORD will defeat the Assyrians, just as he defeated the Egyptians and the people of Midian at Oreb (Judg 6–8; Isa 9:4). Once God has used the Assyrians to punish the people (10:5), the Assyrians will not be a threat to the few who return.

10:28-32 *Aiath . . . Nob . . . Jerusalem:* Aiath probably is another name for the town of Ai (Josh 7:2). See the map on p. 1750, which includes the possible locations along the invasion route used by Sennacherib to reach Nob, probably Mount Scopus, just a mile to the northeast of Jerusalem.

10:32 *Zion . . . hill of Jerusalem:* See the note at 1:8.

10:33 *LORD Almighty . . . lofty trees:* See the note on p. 1289 (LORD). The LORD will protect Zion by cutting down the proud and powerful Assyrians like lumberjacks cut down trees (2:12, 13; 10:16-19). See the note at 2:13-16.

10:21,22 Rom 9:27; 11:1 Rev 5:5; 22:16.

11:1 *shoot . . . from the stump of Jesse . . . Branch will bear fruit:* Jesse was the father of King David (1 Sam 16:1-20). The image of the stump may mean that David's royal dynasty (2 Sam 7) has been threatened and reduced in power, as in the time of Ahaz (see the note at 7:1-3). Or it may refer to a future time when the line of Judah's kings descended from David would be removed from the throne by the Babylonians in 586 B.C.

11:2 *Spirit of the LORD:* Just as the LORD's Spirit came to David when he was chosen to be king of Israel (1 Sam 16:13), so this new king will receive the Spirit. See also the mini-article called "Holy Spirit," p. 2082.

11:2-5 *wisdom . . . understanding . . . justice:* The new king will be wise in his political dealings and wise in his respect of the LORD. In Israel, true wisdom came from the LORD, and the wise person obeyed the LORD's teachings (Prov 1:7; 2:6,7). The new king also would rule with justice and fairness, which God's law demanded (see the note at 1:16,17).

Tree of Jesse, by C. Terry Saul. Isaiah announced, "A shoot will come up from the stump of Jesse; from his roots a Branch will bear fruit. The Spirit of the LORD will rest on him—the Spirit of wisdom and of understanding, the Spirit of counsel and of power" (11:1, 2). This painting combines traditional "Tree of Jesse" imagery with Chickasaw/Choctaw spiritual symbols.

The lofty trees will be felled,
the tall ones will be brought low.
34 He will cut down the forest thickets with an ax;
Lebanon will fall before the Mighty One.

The Branch From Jesse

11 A shoot will come up from the stump of Jesse;
from his roots a Branch will bear fruit.
2 The Spirit of the LORD will rest on him—
the Spirit of wisdom and of understanding,
the Spirit of counsel and of power,
the Spirit of knowledge and of the fear of the LORD—
3 and he will delight in the fear of the LORD.

He will not judge by what he sees with his eyes,
or decide by what he hears with his ears;
4 but with righteousness he will judge the needy,
with justice he will give decisions for the poor of the earth.
He will strike the earth with the rod of his mouth;
with the breath of his lips he will slay the wicked.
5 Righteousness will be his belt
and faithfulness the sash around his waist.

6 The wolf will live with the lamb,
the leopard will lie down with the goat,
the calf and the lion and the yearling[a] together;
and a little child will lead them.
7 The cow will feed with the bear,
their young will lie down together,
and the lion will eat straw like the ox.
8 The infant will play near the hole of the cobra,
and the young child put his hand into the viper's nest.
9 They will neither harm nor destroy
on all my holy mountain,
for the earth will be full of the knowledge of the LORD
as the waters cover the sea.

10 In that day the Root of Jesse will stand as a banner for the
peoples; the nations will rally to him, and his place of rest will be
glorious. 11 In that day the Lord will reach out his hand a second
time to reclaim the remnant that is left of his people from Assyria,
from Lower Egypt, from Upper Egypt,[b] from Cush,[c] from Elam,
from Babylonia,[d] from Hamath and from the islands of the sea.

12 He will raise a banner for the nations
and gather the exiles of Israel;
he will assemble the scattered people of Judah
from the four quarters of the earth.
13 Ephraim's jealousy will vanish,
and Judah's enemies[e] will be cut off;
Ephraim will not be jealous of Judah,
nor Judah hostile toward Ephraim.
14 They will swoop down on the slopes of Philistia
to the west;
together they will plunder the people to the east.
They will lay hands on Edom and Moab,
and the Ammonites will be subject to them.
15 The LORD will dry up
the gulf of the Egyptian sea;
with a scorching wind he will sweep his hand

[a]6 Hebrew; Septuagint *lion will feed* [b]11 Hebrew *from Pathros* [c]11 That is, the upper Nile region [d]11 Hebrew *Shinar* [e]13 Or *hostility*

11:6-8 *leopard . . . viper's nest:* Dangerous animals no longer will be a threat. The vipers are the small, but deadly snakes known as adders. See also 2:2-4; 65:20-25.

11:9 *holy mountain . . . earth will be full of the knowledge of the LORD:* See the note at 2:2. See also Jer 24:7; 31:33,34.

11:10 *Root of Jesse:* See the note at 11:1. See also Rom 15:12.

11:11 *Assyria . . . Hamath:* See the notes at 6:11,12 and 10:9-12. For the location of these places, see the map on p. 2468.

Assyria captured and deported thousands of Israelite people from the northern kingdom (Israel) in 722-720 B.C. and from the southern kingdom (Judah) during the invasion of 701 B.C. Many probably ran away to Egypt and Ethiopia (Cush) at this time as well. Babylon captured Judah and deported many of its people from 596 to 586 B.C. Isaiah's prophecy refers to the return of many of their descendants to Judah.

11:14 *Philistia . . . Ammonites:* Once the Israelite people are reunited, they will defeat their old, traditional enemies and regain the lands captured during David's reign. See the map on p. 2467. See also Isa 60:10-14.

11:15 *Egyptian sea . . . Euphrates River:* The arm of the Red Sea is the Gulf of Suez. The Euphrates is the longest river in southwest Asia. After the Jordan and Nile Rivers it is the most frequently mentioned river in the Bible. It formed a natural boundary between Israel (at its greatest extent under Solomon) and the Mesopotamian superpowers to the east, Assyria and Babylon. The return of the exiled Israelite people is described as a new exodus. See also Jer 23:7,8; Rev 16:12.

11:4 2 Thes 2:8. **11:5** Eph 6:14. **11:13** Ezek 37:15-28.

In that day you will say . . . . "Surely God is my salvation; I will trust and not be afraid."
Isa 12:1,2

12:3 *water . . . wells of salvation:* This phrase may come from an ancient Israelite rite of worship. In it, water was taken from the spring of Gihon in Jerusalem and poured out on the altar in the temple in thanksgiving for the LORD's blessings. Or it simply may be meant to compare the LORD's life-giving power to a well, a very important source of life and refreshment. See also the mini-articles called "Water," p. 1647 and "Salvation," p. 2021.

12:2 Exod 15:2.

over the Euphrates River.[a]
He will break it up into seven streams
so that men can cross over in sandals.
16 There will be a highway for the remnant of his people
that is left from Assyria,
as there was for Israel
when they came up from Egypt.

Songs of Praise

12 In that day you will say:

"I will praise you, O LORD.
Although you were angry with me,
your anger has turned away
and you have comforted me.
2 Surely God is my salvation;
I will trust and not be afraid.
The LORD, the LORD, is my strength and my song;
he has become my salvation."
3 With joy you will draw water
from the wells of salvation.

4 In that day you will say:

"Give thanks to the LORD, call on his name;
make known among the nations what he has done,
and proclaim that his name is exalted.

[a]15 Hebrew *the River*

QUESTIONS ABOUT ISAIAH 1:1—12:6

1. When and where did Isaiah bring the LORD's message to the people? (1:1)
2. Isaiah 1 introduces some themes that will be repeated throughout the whole book. What are some of these key themes?
3. What had some of God's chosen people and their leaders done to bring God's judgment on themselves? (2:6—4:1; 5:1-25) How would Israel and Judah be punished? (3:1-5; 5:24-30; 7:18-25; 9:8—10:11)
4. According to ISAIAH, why is the future not completely bleak for God's people? (2:1-5; 4:2-6; 9:2-7; 10:20-25; 11:1—12:6)
5. Describe Isaiah's vision in the temple (chapter 6). When did it take place? As the LORD's prophet, what was Isaiah told to do? (6:8-10) What would make a prophet's life difficult?
6. What hope did Isaiah bring to Judah's King Ahaz? (7:1-9) What warning did he give to Ahaz? (7:8,9) What did Ahaz do, and how did his decision affect Judah? (See the notes at 7:1-3 and 7:15-17.)
7. Who were Isaiah's sons? How did their names reflect their father's messages from the LORD? (7:3; 8:3)
8. Who was "Immanuel"? (7:13-16) What, if any, connection do you think there is between Immanuel, the "child" (9:6,7), and the "shoot" from the stump of David's family? (11:1-9)
9. What passage in the first twelve chapters of ISAIAH is most memorable to you? Why?

[5]Sing to the LORD, for he has done glorious things;
let this be known to all the world.
[6]Shout aloud and sing for joy, people of Zion,
for great is the Holy One of Israel among you."

PROPHECIES CONCERNING FOREIGN NATIONS

In chapters 13–23, Isaiah speaks messages of warning and punishment against those foreign nations who have been the enemies of the LORD's chosen people. Sayings against the foreign nations can also be found in Jeremiah 46–51; Ezekiel 25–32; Amos 1:3—2:3.

A Prophecy Against Babylon

13 An oracle concerning Babylon that Isaiah son of Amoz saw:

[2]Raise a banner on a bare hilltop,
shout to them;
beckon to them
to enter the gates of the nobles.
[3]I have commanded my holy ones;
I have summoned my warriors to carry out
my wrath—
those who rejoice in my triumph.

[4]Listen, a noise on the mountains,
like that of a great multitude!
Listen, an uproar among the kingdoms,
like nations massing together!
The LORD Almighty is mustering
an army for war.
[5]They come from faraway lands,
from the ends of the heavens—
the LORD and the weapons of his wrath—
to destroy the whole country.

[6]Wail, for the day of the LORD is near;
it will come like destruction from the Almighty.[a]
[7]Because of this, all hands will go limp,
every man's heart will melt.
[8]Terror will seize them,
pain and anguish will grip them;
they will writhe like a woman in labor.
They will look aghast at each other,
their faces aflame.

[9]See, the day of the LORD is coming
—a cruel day, with wrath and fierce anger—

[a]6 Hebrew *Shaddai*

12:6 *people of Zion:* See the note at 1:8.

13:1 *An oracle:* This phrase is often used to introduce a prophetic saying. In Hebrew, the word translated as "oracle" means "to lift up the voice" or "to carry a burden." Here the message is a warning against Babylonia and Assyria (see the note at 13:1, Babylon). Note how a new message begins at 14:28. See also Jer 50:1—51:64.

13:1 *Babylon:* It is difficult to give the exact date and historical situation concerning this message about Babylon. In Isaiah's day, Babylon was under the Assyrian empire's control. Between 708 and 689 B.C. Assyria had to put down four different rebellions led by Babylon's rulers. During the last struggle in 689 B.C., Babylon suffered great destruction (see 13:19-22). This prophecy (13:1—14:27) could refer to Babylon as part of the Assyrian empire.

However, many argue that this message against Babylon points to the historical situation over one hundred years later in the middle of the sixth century B.C. after the Neo-Babylonian empire had captured Judah and had taken many of the Israelite people into exile. In 550 B.C., the Persian ruler Cyrus became king of the Medes (see 13:17) and threatened Babylon. In 539 B.C. Cyrus defeated Babylon (see Isa 45:1-4; 47:1-5), but the city was not destroyed, because its rulers surrendered peacefully. See also the mini-article called "Babylon," p. 1363.

13:4,6,10 *LORD Almighty . . . day . . . is near . . . darkened:* See the note on p. 1289 (LORD). The day that is coming (13:6) is the day when the LORD will bring judgment upon the people. See the note at 2:11,12. See also Joel 1:15. The disappearance of light (13:10) is often connected to visions of the LORD's day of judgment. See also Ezek 32:7; Matt 24:29; Mark 13:24,25; Luke 21:25; Rev 6:12,13; 8:12.

I will punish the world for its evil, the wicked for their sins. I will put an end to the arrogance of the haughty and will humble the pride of the ruthless.
Isa 13:11

13:17 *Medes:* The Medes were from Media, a nation northeast of Babylon. In Isaiah's day, the Medes were under the control of the Assyrians. Later, they joined the Babylonians in defeating Assyria (612-609 B.C.). Still later, they joined the Persians in defeating Babylon (see the note at 13:1, Babylon).

13:22 *Hyenas:* Hyenas are scavengers, eating dead things that they find or that have been killed by other animals. They usually hunt in packs at night. This verse pictures hyenas coming in from the desert and entering the ruins of Babylon to look for dead bodies.

13:13 Job 9:6,7; Joel 3:16. **13:17** Jer 51:11,12. **13:19** Gen 19:24 **13:21** Isa 34:11,13,15; Zeph 2:14; Rev 18:2. **13:22** Isa 34:14.

to make the land desolate
and destroy the sinners within it.
10 The stars of heaven and their constellations
will not show their light.
The rising sun will be darkened
and the moon will not give its light.
11 I will punish the world for its evil,
the wicked for their sins.
I will put an end to the arrogance of the haughty
and will humble the pride of the ruthless.
12 I will make man scarcer than pure gold,
more rare than the gold of Ophir.
13 Therefore I will make the heavens tremble;
and the earth will shake from its place
at the wrath of the LORD Almighty,
in the day of his burning anger.

14 Like a hunted gazelle,
like sheep without a shepherd,
each will return to his own people,
each will flee to his native land.
15 Whoever is captured will be thrust through;
all who are caught will fall by the sword.
16 Their infants will be dashed to pieces before
their eyes;
their houses will be looted and their wives ravished.

17 See, I will stir up against them the Medes,
who do not care for silver
and have no delight in gold.
18 Their bows will strike down the young men;
they will have no mercy on infants
nor will they look with compassion on children.
19 Babylon, the jewel of kingdoms,
the glory of the Babylonians'[a] pride,
will be overthrown by God
like Sodom and Gomorrah.
20 She will never be inhabited
or lived in through all generations;
no Arab will pitch his tent there,
no shepherd will rest his flocks there.
21 But desert creatures will lie there,
jackals will fill her houses;
there the owls will dwell,
and there the wild goats will leap about.
22 Hyenas will howl in her strongholds,
jackals in her luxurious palaces.

[a]**19** Or *Chaldeans'*

Her time is at hand,
and her days will not be prolonged.

14 The LORD will have compassion on Jacob;
once again he will choose Israel
and will settle them in their own land.
Aliens will join them
and unite with the house of Jacob.
2 Nations will take them
and bring them to their own place.
And the house of Israel will possess the nations
as menservants and maidservants in the LORD's land.
They will make captives of their captors
and rule over their oppressors.

3 On the day the LORD gives you relief from suffering and turmoil and cruel bondage, 4 you will take up this taunt against the
king of Babylon:

How the oppressor has come to an end!
How his fury[a] has ended!
5 The LORD has broken the rod of the wicked,
the scepter of the rulers,
6 which in anger struck down peoples
with unceasing blows,
and in fury subdued nations
with relentless aggression.
7 All the lands are at rest and at peace;
they break into singing.
8 Even the pine trees and the cedars of Lebanon
exult over you and say,
"Now that you have been laid low,
no woodsman comes to cut us down."
9 The grave[b] below is all astir
to meet you at your coming;
it rouses the spirits of the departed to greet you—
all those who were leaders in the world;
it makes them rise from their thrones—
all those who were kings over the nations.
10 They will all respond,
they will say to you,
"You also have become weak, as we are;
you have become like us."
11 All your pomp has been brought down to the grave,
along with the noise of your harps;

14:1,2 *house of Jacob . . . possess the nations:* See the notes at 1:4 (nation) and 2:3. See also 60:10-16; 61:5-7.

14:4 *king of Babylon:* If this poem is from Isaiah's time, this king may be either Assyrian King Sargon II, who died in battle against Tabal in Turkey in 705 B.C., or Sennacherib, whose Assyrian army suffered great losses in 701 B.C. while threatening Jerusalem (37:36). During Isaiah's time, these Assyrian kings were considered kings of Babylon, since Babylon was under Assyrian control. But the poem could also be referring to Nebuchadnezzar, the Babylonian king who would later force the people of Judah to go into exile in Babylon.

14:8 *pine trees . . . cedars of Lebanon:* Pine trees and the tall cedar trees which grew in the forests of Lebanon were used to build royal palaces, including the temple and palace of King Solomon (1 Kgs 5:3-9; 7:1-12). Assyrian and Babylonian kings also used cedars for building (37:24).

14:9,12-15 *grave . . . spirits of the departed to greet you . . . morning star, son of the dawn:* For "grave," see the note at 5:14. The great ruler who once cut down the mighty cedar trees has now been cut down by death (14:10,11). The shadowy spirits of other dead kings greet him.

The "morning star" that falls from the sky may refer to the Babylonian king and his descent into the world of the dead. The image would have reminded ancient readers of the Canaanite myth about "Day Star, son of Dawn." In it, Day Star, tries to climb above all the stars in the heavens to overthrow the Most High, who was said to live on Mount Zaphon in Aram. Day Star makes his move at daybreak, but the rays of the sun-god Shamash chase him and throw him back down to earth.

Some later writers interpreted this morning star as Satan, perhaps based on Jesus' words in Luke 10:18. In the Latin Vulgate Bible, the Hebrew for "Morning star" is translated "Lucifer," another name for Satan.

[a]4 Dead Sea Scrolls, Septuagint and Syriac; the meaning of the word in the Masoretic Text is uncertain. [b]9 Hebrew *Sheol*; also in verses 11 and 15

14:18,19 *cast out of your tomb:* The great pyramids in Egypt were tombs built to honor and provide a place of rest for those earthly leaders who had been servants of the gods, or were considered to be gods themselves. The spirit of a person left unburied was believed to wander around forever, unable to rest in peace. Both Sargon II and Sennacherib fit the description of kings who died but did not receive proper royal burials. Sargon's body was not found after he died in battle. Sennacherib was murdered by his own sons, and so did not receive a royal funeral. See also the mini-article called "Burial," p. 1998.

14:19 *the stones of the pit:* See the note at 14:9,12-15.

14:22 *cut off from Babylon her name and survivors:* See the note at 13:1 (Babylon). After Babylon fell to the Persians in 539 B.C., they never again were a great power.

14:25 *crush the Assyrian:* See the notes at 13:1 (Babylon) and 14:4.

14:28 *year King Ahaz died:* Probably 716 B.C. See also 2 Kgs 16:20; 2 Chr 28:27.

14:29-31 *Philistines . . . rod that struck you . . . smoke:* See the note at 9:11,12. Philistia was a prime target for attacks by the great empires, because it was on one of the main routes from Egypt to Mesopotamia. Shortly after Ahaz of Judah died, the Egyptians and Ethiopians helped the Philistines revolt against the Assyrians. The Philistines tried to get Judah to join the revolt (14:32), but Isaiah warned against this (20:1-6).

The "rod" likely refers to Assyria's King Sargon (20:1), whose troops would kick up lots of dust ("smoke") when they attacked from the north. See also Jer 47:1-7; Ezek 25:15-17; Joel 3:4-8; Amos 1:6-8; Zeph 2:4-7; Zech 9:5-7.

14:12 Rev 8:10; 9:1. **14:13-15** Matt 11:23; Luke 10:15.

maggots are spread out beneath you
and worms cover you.

12 How you have fallen from heaven,
O morning star, son of the dawn!
You have been cast down to the earth,
you who once laid low the nations!
13 You said in your heart,
"I will ascend to heaven;
I will raise my throne
above the stars of God;
I will sit enthroned on the mount of assembly,
on the utmost heights of the sacred mountain.[a]
14 I will ascend above the tops of the clouds;
I will make myself like the Most High."
15 But you are brought down to the grave,
to the depths of the pit.

16 Those who see you stare at you,
they ponder your fate:
"Is this the man who shook the earth
and made kingdoms tremble,
17 the man who made the world a desert,
who overthrew its cities
and would not let his captives go home?"

18 All the kings of the nations lie in state,
each in his own tomb.
19 But you are cast out of your tomb
like a rejected branch;
you are covered with the slain,
with those pierced by the sword,
those who descend to the stones of the pit.
Like a corpse trampled underfoot,
20 you will not join them in burial,
for you have destroyed your land
and killed your people.

The offspring of the wicked
will never be mentioned again.
21 Prepare a place to slaughter his sons
for the sins of their forefathers;
they are not to rise to inherit the land
and cover the earth with their cities.

22 "I will rise up against them,"
declares the LORD Almighty.

[a]13 Or *the north*; Hebrew *Zaphon*

"I will cut off from Babylon her name and survivors,
her offspring and descendants,"
declares the LORD.
23 "I will turn her into a place for owls
and into swampland;
I will sweep her with the broom of destruction,"
declares the LORD Almighty.

A Prophecy Against Assyria

24 The LORD Almighty has sworn,

"Surely, as I have planned, so it will be,
and as I have purposed, so it will stand.
25 I will crush the Assyrian in my land;
on my mountains I will trample him down.
His yoke will be taken from my people,
and his burden removed from their shoulders."
26 This is the plan determined for the whole world;
this is the hand stretched out over all nations.
27 For the LORD Almighty has purposed, and who can thwart him?
His hand is stretched out, and who can turn it back?

A Prophecy Against the Philistines

28 This oracle came in the year King Ahaz died:

29 Do not rejoice, all you Philistines,
that the rod that struck you is broken;
from the root of that snake will spring up a viper,
its fruit will be a darting, venomous serpent.
30 The poorest of the poor will find pasture,
and the needy will lie down in safety.
But your root I will destroy by famine;
it will slay your survivors.
31 Wail, O gate! Howl, O city!
Melt away, all you Philistines!
A cloud of smoke comes from the north,
and there is not a straggler in its ranks.
32 What answer shall be given
to the envoys of that nation?
"The LORD has established Zion,
and in her his afflicted people will find refuge."

A Prophecy Against Moab

15 An oracle concerning Moab:

Ar in Moab is ruined,
destroyed in a night!

14:32 *Zion:* See the note at 1:8.

15:1 *Moab:* According to Genesis 19:30-38, the people of Moab were descended from Lot, the nephew of Abraham. Moab and Israel had been enemies in the past (Num 22:2-11; 2 Sam 8:2,13,14; 2 Kgs 13:20). "Destroyed in a night" probably refers to the Assyrian invasion led by Sargon around 715 B.C.

Fourteen different locations in Moab are mentioned in 15:2-9. Dibon was probably a center for the worship of the Moabite god Chemosh. The destruction of Moab caused national sorrow and mourning. Zoar was probably located near the southern end of the Dead Sea. The verses seem to suggest that Moabite refugees from the north were fleeing to the south in order to escape the enemy attackers.

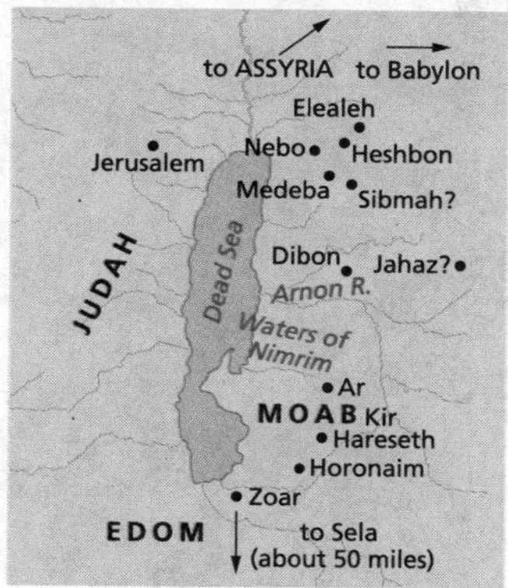

14:24-27 Isa 10:5-34; Nah 1:1—3:19; Zeph 2:13-15. **15:1—16:14** Isa 25:10-12; Jer 48:1-47; Ezek 25:8-11; Amos 2:1-3; Zeph 2:8-11.

16:1 *lambs as tribute:* Lambs were the main product of Moab. See 2 Kgs 3:4. Now, Judah's ruler will be offered lambs in the hope that he will then allow refugees from Moab to come into Judah.

16:1,2 *Sela . . . Zion . . . fords of the Arnon:* Sela, the capital of Edom, was located on a high plateau near the southern end of the Dead Sea. The Arnon River flows west into the Dead Sea, so the women were probably wading through the river from south to north in order to escape.

Kir in Moab is ruined,
destroyed in a night!
2 Dibon goes up to its temple,
to its high places to weep;
Moab wails over Nebo and Medeba.
Every head is shaved
and every beard cut off.
3 In the streets they wear sackcloth;
on the roofs and in the public squares
they all wail,
prostrate with weeping.
4 Heshbon and Elealeh cry out,
their voices are heard all the way to Jahaz.
Therefore the armed men of Moab cry out,
and their hearts are faint.

5 My heart cries out over Moab;
her fugitives flee as far as Zoar,
as far as Eglath Shelishiyah.
They go up the way to Luhith,
weeping as they go;
on the road to Horonaim
they lament their destruction.
6 The waters of Nimrim are dried up
and the grass is withered;
the vegetation is gone
and nothing green is left.
7 So the wealth they have acquired and stored up
they carry away over the Ravine of
the Poplars.
8 Their outcry echoes along the border of Moab;
their wailing reaches as far as Eglaim,
their lamentation as far as Beer Elim.
9 Dimon's[a] waters are full of blood,
but I will bring still more upon Dimon[a]—
a lion upon the fugitives of Moab
and upon those who remain in the land.

16 Send lambs as tribute
to the ruler of the land,
from Sela, across the desert,
to the mount of the Daughter of Zion.
2 Like fluttering birds
pushed from the nest,
so are the women of Moab
at the fords of the Arnon.

[a]9 Masoretic Text; Dead Sea Scrolls, some Septuagint manuscripts and Vulgate *Dibon*

[3]“Give us counsel,
render a decision.
Make your shadow like night—
at high noon.
Hide the fugitives,
do not betray the refugees.
[4]Let the Moabite fugitives stay with you;
be their shelter from the destroyer.”

The oppressor will come to an end,
and destruction will cease;
the aggressor will vanish from the land.
[5]In love a throne will be established;
in faithfulness a man will sit on it—
one from the house[a] of David—
one who in judging seeks justice
and speeds the cause of righteousness.
[6]We have heard of Moab's pride—
her overweening pride and conceit,
her pride and her insolence—
but her boasts are empty.
[7]Therefore the Moabites wail,
they wail together for Moab.
Lament and grieve
for the men[b] of Kir Hareseth.
[8]The fields of Heshbon wither,
the vines of Sibmah also.
The rulers of the nations
have trampled down the choicest vines,
which once reached Jazer
and spread toward the desert.
Their shoots spread out
and went as far as the sea.
[9]So I weep, as Jazer weeps,
for the vines of Sibmah.
O Heshbon, O Elealeh,
I drench you with tears!
The shouts of joy over your ripened fruit
and over your harvests have been stilled.
[10]Joy and gladness are taken away from the orchards;
no one sings or shouts in the vineyards;
no one treads out wine at the presses,
for I have put an end to the shouting.
[11]My heart laments for Moab like a harp,
my inmost being for Kir Hareseth.
[12]When Moab appears at her high place,

[a]5 Hebrew *tent* [b]7 Or “*raisin cakes*,” a wordplay

In love a throne will be established; in faithfulness a man will sit on it—one from the house of David—one who in judging seeks justice and speeds the cause of righteousness.
Isa 16:5

16:5 *one from the house of David:* See the notes at 9:6; 9:7; and 11:1. See also Amos 9:11, 12.

16:6,7 *Moab's pride . . . Lament and grieve:* See the note at 15:1.

16:7-9 *Kir Hareseth . . . Heshbon . . . Elealeh:* Kir Hareseth is probably the same as Kir (15:1, 2-9). Heshbon was located about eighteen miles east of the northern end of the Dead Sea (see also 15:4; Num 21:23-26; Jer 48:34). Elealeh was about one mile from Heshbon (Num 32:3).

16:9,10 *shouts of joy . . . harvests:* When the ripe grapes were picked, the people celebrated in the vineyards. See also the note at 5:1,2.

17:1,2 *Damascus . . . Aroer:* Damascus was the capital city of Aram (Syria). The Arameans had been enemies of Israel in the past (2 Sam 8:3-6; 1 Kgs 22:29-38), but in 735 B.C. they joined with Israel to invade Judah and to stand up to Assyrians (see the note at 7:1-3). Damascus fell to the Assyrians in 732 B.C. Aroer could be an unknown city near Damascus, or it could refer to Aroer in Moab, used here as an example of what will happen to Damascus.

17:3-5 *Ephraim . . . Valley of Rephaim:* Here meaning the northern kingdom. See the note at 1:4 (nation). Israel's prosperous people will be like the landless poor who survived by eating grain and fruit left behind in the fields after harvest (Deut 24:19-22; Ruth 2). The Valley of Rephaim was a few miles southwest of Jerusalem (Josh 15:5-9; 2 Sam 5:18). The city's poor probably would have picked clean any crops left in this valley after harvest time.

17:6 *olive tree:* Olives were a very important crop in ancient times and a key export of Israel (see the chart called "Trade in Old Testament Times," p. 949). See also the illustration on p. 1326.

17:8,9 *altars . . . Asherah poles . . . desolation:* Ancient Canaanite worship places and altars usually were built on high places near a grove of trees (Deut 12:2; Jer 2:20; 1 Kgs 14:23). Wooden poles symbolizing and honoring Asherah, goddess of fertility, were set up at these worship places. See Hos 4:12-19 and the mini-article called "Canaanite Gods and Goddesses," p. 469.

For the powerful Canaanite cities that were captured, see Deut 7:1-5; Josh 10:5-13; 11:1—12:24.

17:10 *the Rock, your fortress:* This phrase is used to compare the LORD to a mountain where his people can run for protection (Deut 32:4, 15; Ps 18:2; 19:14; Isa 26:4; 30:29; 44:8).

17:1-3 Jer 49:23-27; Amos 1:3-5; Zech 9:1.

she only wears herself out;
when she goes to her shrine to pray,
it is to no avail.

13 This is the word the LORD has already spoken concerning
Moab. 14 But now the LORD says: "Within three years, as a servant
bound by contract would count them, Moab's splendor and all her
many people will be despised, and her survivors will be very few
and feeble."

An Oracle Against Damascus

17 An oracle concerning Damascus:

"See, Damascus will no longer be a city
but will become a heap of ruins.
2 The cities of Aroer will be deserted
and left to flocks, which will lie down,
with no one to make them afraid.
3 The fortified city will disappear from Ephraim,
and royal power from Damascus;
the remnant of Aram will be
like the glory of the Israelites,"
declares the LORD Almighty.

4 "In that day the glory of Jacob will fade;
the fat of his body will waste away.
5 It will be as when a reaper gathers the standing grain
and harvests the grain with his arm—
as when a man gleans heads of grain
in the Valley of Rephaim.
6 Yet some gleanings will remain,
as when an olive tree is beaten,
leaving two or three olives on the topmost branches,
four or five on the fruitful boughs,"
declares the LORD, the God of Israel.

7 In that day men will look to their Maker
and turn their eyes to the Holy One of Israel.
8 They will not look to the altars,
the work of their hands,
and they will have no regard for the Asherah poles[a]
and the incense altars their fingers have made.

9 In that day their strong cities, which they left because of the
Israelites, will be like places abandoned to thickets and undergrowth. And all will be desolation.

10 You have forgotten God your Savior;
you have not remembered the Rock, your fortress.

[a]**8** That is, symbols of the goddess Asherah

Therefore, though you set out the finest plants
and plant imported vines,
11 though on the day you set them out, you make them grow,
and on the morning when you plant them, you bring them to bud,
yet the harvest will be as nothing
in the day of disease and incurable pain.

12 Oh, the raging of many nations—
they rage like the raging sea!
Oh, the uproar of the peoples—
they roar like the roaring of great waters!
13 Although the peoples roar like the roar of surging waters,
when he rebukes them they flee far away,
driven before the wind like chaff on the hills,
like tumbleweed before a gale.
14 In the evening, sudden terror!
Before the morning, they are gone!
This is the portion of those who loot us,
the lot of those who plunder us.

A Prophecy Against Cush

18 Woe to the land of whirring wings[a]
along the rivers of Cush,[b]
2 which sends envoys by sea
in papyrus boats over the water.

Go, swift messengers,
to a people tall and smooth-skinned,
to a people feared far and wide,
an aggressive nation of strange speech,
whose land is divided by rivers.

3 All you people of the world,
you who live on the earth,
when a banner is raised on the mountains,
you will see it,
and when a trumpet sounds,
you will hear it.
4 This is what the LORD says to me:
"I will remain quiet and will look on from my dwelling place,
like shimmering heat in the sunshine,
like a cloud of dew in the heat of harvest."
5 For, before the harvest, when the blossom is gone

[a]1 Or *of locusts* [b]1 That is, the upper Nile region

17:10 *finest plants:* This may refer to the planting of flowers in special garden pots to honor the Canaanite gods. These fast-growing plants (17:11) were believed to give life and fertility to those who planted them.

17:12-14 *nations . . . driven before the wind:* "Nations" refers to those who attack God's people in Judah (5:30; 7:1—8:8; 29:1-4).

18:1,2 *Cush . . . people tall and smooth-skinned . . . land is divided by rivers:* The long Nile River begins in Ethiopia (Cush) and runs north to the delta region on the Mediterranean Sea (see the note at 11:11).

In 715 B.C., an Cushite leader named Piye, formerly named Piankhi, gained control of Egypt and ended years of civil war. During this time Cushite ambassadors visited Jerusalem, perhaps at King Hezekiah's request. King Hezekiah twice rebelled against the Assyrians (713-711 B.C. and 705-701 B.C.). He considered getting help from Cush and Egypt. Isaiah warned the king not to (20:1-6; 30:1-7; 31:1-3).

18:2 *papyrus boats over the water:* Ancient Egypt was famous for the tall papyrus reeds that grew in the Nile River Delta. See also the article called "Trade and Travel," p. 948.

18:4,5 *my dwelling place . . . the blossom is gone:* "My dwelling place" may refer to the heavens or to Mount Zion (18:7). "The blossom is gone" means that the LORD's judgment against the Cushites will happen suddenly.

18:1-7 Zeph 2:12.

Olives and Olive Oil. Olives were very important to the diet and economy of ancient Israel. The fruit was eaten at almost every meal and the oil from olives was mixed with spices and other substances to make medicines and perfumes. Olive oil was also burned in lamps to provide light. At harvest time, olives were picked, or knocked out of the tree with a stick, and gathered into baskets. Those used for making oil were crushed by grinding a large round stone over them. The crushed olives were then pressed by weights that forced the juices to drip out of them into shallow pans. As the juice sat, the oil floated to the surface where it could be easily spooned off and stored in bottles.

18:7 *people tall and smooth-skinned . . . gifts will be brought to Mount Zion:* See the note at 18:1,2. Compare this verse to 45:14; 60:4-9.

and the flower becomes a ripening grape,
he will cut off the shoots with pruning knives,
and cut down and take away the spreading
branches.
6 They will all be left to the mountain birds of prey
and to the wild animals;
the birds will feed on them all summer,
the wild animals all winter.

7 At that time gifts will be brought to the LORD Almighty

from a people tall and smooth-skinned,
from a people feared far and wide,
an aggressive nation of strange speech,
whose land is divided by rivers—

the gifts will be brought to Mount Zion, the place of the Name of the LORD Almighty.

A Prophecy About Egypt

19 An oracle concerning Egypt:

See, the LORD rides on a swift cloud
and is coming to Egypt.
The idols of Egypt tremble before him,
and the hearts of the Egyptians melt within them.

2 "I will stir up Egyptian against Egyptian—
brother will fight against brother,
neighbor against neighbor,
city against city,
kingdom against kingdom.
3 The Egyptians will lose heart,
and I will bring their plans to nothing;
they will consult the idols and the spirits of the dead,
the mediums and the spiritists.
4 I will hand the Egyptians over
to the power of a cruel master,
and a fierce king will rule over them,"
declares the Lord, the LORD Almighty.

5 The waters of the river will dry up,
and the riverbed will be parched and dry.
6 The canals will stink;
the streams of Egypt will dwindle and dry up.
The reeds and rushes will wither,
7 also the plants along the Nile,
at the mouth of the river.
Every sown field along the Nile
will become parched, will blow away and be no more.
8 The fishermen will groan and lament,
all who cast hooks into the Nile;
those who throw nets on the water
will pine away.
9 Those who work with combed flax will despair,
the weavers of fine linen will lose hope.
10 The workers in cloth will be dejected,
and all the wage earners will be sick at heart.

11 The officials of Zoan are nothing but fools;
the wise counselors of Pharaoh give senseless advice.
How can you say to Pharaoh,
"I am one of the wise men,
a disciple of the ancient kings"?

12 Where are your wise men now?
Let them show you and make known
what the LORD Almighty
has planned against Egypt.

See, the LORD rides on a swift cloud and is coming to Egypt. The idols of Egypt tremble before him, and the hearts of the Egyptians melt within them.
Isa 19:1

19:1 *An oracle:* See the note at 13:1 (oracle).

19:1,2 *idols of Egypt . . . brother will fight against brother:* Although Egypt was a powerful nation, it often went through periods of civil war. From 720 to 716 B.C. Egypt experienced civil war while Osorkon IV was pharaoh. The war ended when the Ethiopian king Piye took over (see the note at 18:1,2).

19:4 *fierce king:* The identity of this king is unknown. The Assyrian king Esarhaddon defeated Egypt in 670 B.C.

19:5 *waters of the river:* During the yearly rainy season, the Nile River overflows its banks, and the flood waters fertilize fields of crops near the river. In Isaiah's time, a year or more without flooding was disastrous for ancient Egypt. Poor crops meant diminished food supplies and fewer plants that could be made into cloth.

19:11,13 *Zoan . . . Memphis:* Zoan, also called Tanis, was an important city in the northeastern delta region of Egypt (Num 13:22; Ps 78:9-12). Memphis, located on the Nile River about fifteen miles south of the delta, was the capital city of Egypt's Old Kingdom (2686-2160 B.C.). It is not clear what kind of "senseless advice" Egypt's leaders gave.

19:1-25 Jer 46:2-26; Ezek 29:1—32:32.

19:16 ***uplifted hand:*** This image is often used to describe the LORD's protection or power, especially in battle (Exod 14:21; 15:12,16; Deut 5:15; Isa 14:27; 40:10).

19:17-22 ***Judah . . . heal them:*** Why Egypt will fear Judah is not clear, nor is the identity of four of the five Egyptian cities. The "City of the Destruction," is also translated as "City of the Sun" or Heliopolis (Jer 43:13). In the time when Babylon threatened Judah, a number of Israelites migrated to Egypt to escape the coming destruction (Jer 44:1, 15). These cities near the eastern boundaries of Egypt may have been strongly influenced by the language and religion of the migrant Israelites (19:18-21).

20:1-3 ***Sargon king of Assyria . . . Ashdod . . . a sign and portent against Egypt and Cush:*** King Sargon II, who ruled Assyria from 721 to 705 B.C., captured the Philistine city of Ashdod in 711 B.C. after it had rebelled against Assyria in 713 B.C.

A number of Israel's prophets were told to act out the LORD's messages by doing something dramatic (see Hos 1–3; Jer 27; Ezek 24:15-27). Isaiah's nakedness (20:2) demonstrated how Egypt and Cush would be stripped of their power and taken prisoner. It gave the same warning to King Hezekiah and the leaders of Judah, who apparently decided to join Ashdod and the Cushites in their rebellion against Assyria (see the note at 18:1,2).

13 The officials of Zoan have become fools,
the leaders of Memphis[a] are deceived;
the cornerstones of her peoples
have led Egypt astray.
14 The LORD has poured into them
a spirit of dizziness;
they make Egypt stagger in all that she does,
as a drunkard staggers around in his vomit.
15 There is nothing Egypt can do—
head or tail, palm branch or reed.

16 In that day the Egyptians will be like women. They will
shudder with fear at the uplifted hand that the LORD Almighty
raises against them. 17 And the land of Judah will bring terror to the
Egyptians; everyone to whom Judah is mentioned will be terrified,
because of what the LORD Almighty is planning against them.

18 In that day five cities in Egypt will speak the language of
Canaan and swear allegiance to the LORD Almighty. One of them
will be called the City of Destruction.[b]

19 In that day there will be an altar to the LORD in the heart of
Egypt, and a monument to the LORD at its border. 20 It will be a sign
and witness to the LORD Almighty in the land of Egypt. When they
cry out to the LORD because of their oppressors, he will send them
a savior and defender, and he will rescue them. 21 So the LORD will
make himself known to the Egyptians, and in that day they will
acknowledge the LORD. They will worship with sacrifices and grain
offerings; they will make vows to the LORD and keep them. 22 The
LORD will strike Egypt with a plague; he will strike them and heal
them. They will turn to the LORD, and he will respond to their
pleas and heal them.

23 In that day there will be a highway from Egypt to Assyria.
The Assyrians will go to Egypt and the Egyptians to Assyria. The
Egyptians and Assyrians will worship together. 24 In that day Israel
will be the third, along with Egypt and Assyria, a blessing on the
earth. 25 The LORD Almighty will bless them, saying, "Blessed be
Egypt my people, Assyria my handiwork, and Israel my inheritance."

A Prophecy Against Egypt and Cush

20 In the year that the supreme commander, sent by Sargon king
of Assyria, came to Ashdod and attacked and captured it— 2 at that
time the LORD spoke through Isaiah son of Amoz. He said to him,
"Take off the sackcloth from your body and the sandals from your
feet." And he did so, going around stripped and barefoot.

3 Then the LORD said, "Just as my servant Isaiah has gone

[a]13 Hebrew *Noph* [b]18 Most manuscripts of the Masoretic Text; some manuscripts of the Masoretic Text, Dead Sea Scrolls and Vulgate *City of the Sun* (that is, Heliopolis)

stripped and barefoot for three years, as a sign and portent against
Egypt and Cush,[a] 4so the king of Assyria will lead away stripped
and barefoot the Egyptian captives and Cushite exiles, young and
old, with buttocks bared—to Egypt's shame. 5Those who trusted
in Cush and boasted in Egypt will be afraid and put to shame. 6In
that day the people who live on this coast will say, 'See what has
happened to those we relied on, those we fled to for help and
deliverance from the king of Assyria! How then can we escape?' "

A Prophecy Against Babylon

21 An oracle concerning the Desert by the Sea:

Like whirlwinds sweeping through the southland,
an invader comes from the desert,
from a land of terror.

2 A dire vision has been shown to me:
The traitor betrays, the looter takes loot.
Elam, attack! Media, lay siege!
I will bring to an end all the groaning she caused.

3 At this my body is racked with pain,
pangs seize me, like those of a woman in labor;
I am staggered by what I hear,
I am bewildered by what I see.
4 My heart falters,
fear makes me tremble;
the twilight I longed for
has become a horror to me.

5 They set the tables,
they spread the rugs,
they eat, they drink!
Get up, you officers,
oil the shields!

6 This is what the Lord says to me:

"Go, post a lookout
and have him report what he sees.
7 When he sees chariots
with teams of horses,
riders on donkeys
or riders on camels,
let him be alert,
fully alert."

8 And the lookout[b] shouted,

---

[a]3 That is, the upper Nile region; also in verse 5 [b]8 Dead Sea Scrolls and Syriac; Masoretic Text *A lion*

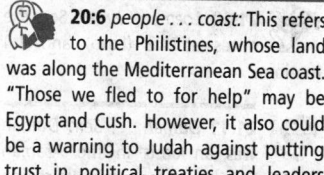

20:6 *people . . . coast:* This refers to the Philistines, whose land was along the Mediterranean Sea coast. "Those we fled to for help" may be Egypt and Cush. However, it also could be a warning to Judah against putting trust in political treaties and leaders instead of the LORD. See also Ps 118:6-10.

21:1 *An oracle:* See the note at 13:1 (oracle).

21:1 *Desert by the Sea . . . an invader comes from the desert:* The dry flatlands south of Babylon near the Persian Gulf were sometimes called "the Desert by the Sea." The invader from the desert is probably from the area between Egypt and southern Canaan. The attack on Babylon would be as sudden and destructive as the hot windstorms that blew in from the desert.

21:2,3 *Elam . . . Media . . . pain:* Elam and Media were located in the hill country to the east and northeast of Babylon. The Elamites and Medians battled Assyria in 691-689 B.C. before Assyria destroyed Babylon in 689 B.C. (see the note at 13:1, Babylon). But this prophecy could refer to the time about one hundred fifty years later when Elam and Media joined with Persia to attack Babylon in 540 B.C. If the earlier time is meant, Isaiah's "pain" may come from the fact that at this time Babylon was Judah's ally against Assyria (Isa 39:1-4). If the later time is intended, these verses seem to show some sympathy for Babylon, the country that eventually destroyed Jerusalem. See also the map on p. 2468.

21:6 *post a lookout:* Lookouts (watchmen) stood guard on the city wall, looking for approaching enemy troops. Isaiah himself may be the guard (see also 21:11; Ezek 3:17).

21:5 Dan 5:1-30.

21:10 *LORD . . . Israel:* See the notes at 1:2 (LORD) and 1:4 (nation).

21:11 *Dumah . . . Seir:* Dumah was an oasis in the Arabian Desert. Seir was a mountainous region of Edom southwest of the Dead Sea. The Assyrian army of Sennacherib probably went through these locations about the time it attacked Babylon (see the note at 21:1, desert; see also 34:5-15).

21:13-17 *Dedanites . . . Kedar:* The peoples living in the Arabian regions of Dedan (northwest), Tema (oasis in north), and Kedar (desert area) were told to provide food and shelter for the Edomite refugees who were running away from the advancing army. Note the phrase, "Within one year," and compare it to 16:14. If the Babylonian attack is meant, this prophecy was fulfilled at least a century after Isaiah lived.

22:1 *Valley of Vision:* The exact location of the Valley of Vision is not known. It may refer to the Babylonian land beside the sea (21:1) or to one of the many valleys surrounding Jerusalem.

22:1 *gone up on the roofs:* Flat roofs were common in the ancient Near East. Stairs on the outside of the house led up to the roof, which was made of wooden beams and boards covered with packed earth.

21:9 Rev 14:8; 18:2. **21:11-17** Jer 49:7-22; Ezek 25:12-14; Amos 1:11,12.

"Day after day, my lord, I stand on the watchtower;
every night I stay at my post.
9 Look, here comes a man in a chariot
with a team of horses.
And he gives back the answer:
'Babylon has fallen, has fallen!
All the images of its gods
lie shattered on the ground!' "

10 O my people, crushed on the threshing floor,
I tell you what I have heard
from the LORD Almighty,
from the God of Israel.

A Prophecy Against Edom

11 An oracle concerning Dumah[a]:

Someone calls to me from Seir,
"Watchman, what is left of the night?
Watchman, what is left of the night?"
12 The watchman replies,
"Morning is coming, but also the night.
If you would ask, then ask;
and come back yet again."

A Prophecy Against Arabia

13 An oracle concerning Arabia:

You caravans of Dedanites,
who camp in the thickets of Arabia,
14 bring water for the thirsty;
you who live in Tema,
bring food for the fugitives.
15 They flee from the sword,
from the drawn sword,
from the bent bow
and from the heat of battle.

16 This is what the Lord says to me: "Within one year, as a
servant bound by contract would count it, all the pomp of Kedar
will come to an end. 17 The survivors of the bowmen, the warriors
of Kedar, will be few." The LORD, the God of Israel, has spoken.

A Prophecy About Jerusalem

22 An oracle concerning the Valley of Vision:

What troubles you now,
that you have all gone up on the roofs,

[a] 11 *Dumah* means *silence* or *stillness,* a wordplay on *Edom.*

2 O town full of commotion,
O city of tumult and revelry?
Your slain were not killed by the sword,
nor did they die in battle.
3 All your leaders have fled together;
they have been captured without using the bow.
All you who were caught were taken prisoner together,
having fled while the enemy was still far away.
4 Therefore I said, "Turn away from me;
let me weep bitterly.
Do not try to console me
over the destruction of my people."

5 The Lord, the LORD Almighty, has a day
of tumult and trampling and terror
in the Valley of Vision,
a day of battering down walls
and of crying out to the mountains.
6 Elam takes up the quiver,
with her charioteers and horses;
Kir uncovers the shield.
7 Your choicest valleys are full of chariots,
and horsemen are posted at the city gates;
8 the defenses of Judah are stripped away.

And you looked in that day
to the weapons in the Palace of the Forest;
9 you saw that the City of David
had many breaches in its defenses;
you stored up water
in the Lower Pool.
10 You counted the buildings in Jerusalem
and tore down houses to strengthen the wall.
11 You built a reservoir between the two walls
for the water of the Old Pool,
but you did not look to the One who made it,
or have regard for the One who planned it long ago.

12 The Lord, the LORD Almighty,
called you on that day
to weep and to wail,
to tear out your hair and put on sackcloth.
13 But see, there is joy and revelry,
slaughtering of cattle and killing of sheep,
eating of meat and drinking of wine!
"Let us eat and drink," you say,
"for tomorrow we die!"

22:3-6 *leaders . . . captured . . . Elam . . . Kir:* These verses may be describing Assyria's attacks on Babylon under Sennacherib (see the note at 21:2,3). When Sennacherib attacked Babylon in 703-689 B.C., Babylon's king retreated from the battlefield. Elam (22:6), Babylon's ally at this time, was also defeated.

Some scholars suggest that these verses are describing the Babylonian King Nebuchadnezzar's attack on Jerusalem in 587 B.C. His army would likely have included warriors from Elam (see note at 21:2,3) and Kir.

22:8,9 *Palace of the Forest . . . Lower Pool:* Palace of the Forest was built centuries earlier in the days of King Solomon (1 Kgs 7:2-4). The Lower Pool may have been a natural pool located in the southern part of the Central Valley (Tyropean Valley) of Jerusalem (see the map on p. 2466).

22:10,11 *tore down houses . . . between the two walls:* Some ancient cities had two walls with a space between them. If the enemy broke through the outer wall, the city was still protected by the inner wall. The houses that were torn down to repair the outer wall were probably squatters' huts that had been built between the two walls.

22:13 *joy and revelry:* Judah's leaders did not mourn the disaster that was about to come upon their city. Instead, they decided to have one last big party, in case they died the next day.

14 The LORD Almighty has revealed this in my hearing: "Till
your dying day this sin will not be atoned for," says the Lord, the
LORD Almighty.

15 This is what the Lord, the LORD Almighty, says:

"Go, say to this steward,
to Shebna, who is in charge of the palace:
16 What are you doing here and who gave you permission
to cut out a grave for yourself here,
hewing your grave on the height
and chiseling your resting place in the rock?

17 "Beware, the LORD is about to take firm hold of you
and hurl you away, O you mighty man.
18 He will roll you up tightly like a ball
and throw you into a large country.
There you will die
and there your splendid chariots will remain—
you disgrace to your master's house!
19 I will depose you from your office,
and you will be ousted from your position.

20 "In that day I will summon my servant, Eliakim son of
Hilkiah. 21 I will clothe him with your robe and fasten your sash
around him and hand your authority over to him. He will be a
father to those who live in Jerusalem and to the house of Judah. 22 I
will place on his shoulder the key to the house of David; what he
opens no one can shut, and what he shuts no one can open. 23 I will
drive him like a peg into a firm place; he will be a seat[a] of honor
for the house of his father. 24 All the glory of his family will hang on
him: its offspring and offshoots—all its lesser vessels, from the
bowls to all the jars.

25 "In that day," declares the LORD Almighty, "the peg driven
into the firm place will give way; it will be sheared off and will fall,
and the load hanging on it will be cut down." The LORD has spoken.

A Prophecy About Tyre

23 An oracle concerning Tyre:

Wail, O ships of Tarshish!
For Tyre is destroyed
and left without house or harbor.
From the land of Cyprus[b]
word has come to them.

2 Be silent, you people of the island
and you merchants of Sidon,

22:15-21 *Shebna . . . Eliakim:* Shebna is mentioned only here and in 2 Kings 18:18 and Isaiah 36:3, where he is called a "secretary." He apparently overstepped his position of authority by ordering a tomb for himself to be carved out of the rocks where Judah's royalty had been buried.

Eliakim, whose name means "God will approve," would receive royal robes symbolizing his authority.

22:22,23 *key to the house of David . . . a peg:* Eliakim was in charge of the business of the royal palace and household, which in Judah remained in the hands of King David's descendants. Like a wooden tent peg hammered in hard dry earth, Eliakim would be hard to remove. But eventually he would lose his authority, too (22:25). See also Rev 3:7.

23:1-4 *Tyre . . . destroyed . . . Sidon:* Tyre was an important Phoenician seaport city built on the Mediterranean coast and on two islands near the shore. Sidon was a seacoast city about twenty-five miles north of Tyre (see the map on p. 2465).

The Assyrians did invade Phoenicia in 734 B.C. and again in 701 B.C. King Nebuchadnezzar of Babylon captured the mainland part of Tyre in 572 B.C. (Ezek 26:7-11), and Alexander the Great of Macedonia captured the whole city in 332 B.C. See also the mini-article called "Phoenicia," p. 1604.

23:1-18 Ezek 26:1—28:19; Joel 3:4-8; Amos 1:9,10; Zech 9:1-4; Matt 11:21,22; Luke 10:13,14.

[a]23 Or *throne* [b]1 Hebrew *Kittim*

whom the seafarers have enriched.
³On the great waters
came the grain of the Shihor;
the harvest of the Nile[a] was the revenue of Tyre,
and she became the marketplace of the nations.
⁴Be ashamed, O Sidon, and you, O fortress of the sea,
for the sea has spoken:
"I have neither been in labor nor given birth;
I have neither reared sons nor brought up daughters."
⁵When word comes to Egypt,
they will be in anguish at the report from Tyre.
⁶Cross over to Tarshish;
wail, you people of the island.
⁷Is this your city of revelry,
the old, old city,
whose feet have taken her
to settle in far-off lands?
⁸Who planned this against Tyre,
the bestower of crowns,
whose merchants are princes,
whose traders are renowned in the earth?
⁹The LORD Almighty planned it,
to bring low the pride of all glory
and to humble all who are renowned on the earth.

¹⁰Till[b] your land as along the Nile,
O Daughter of Tarshish,
for you no longer have a harbor.
¹¹The LORD has stretched out his hand over the sea
and made its kingdoms tremble.
He has given an order concerning Phoenicia[c]
that her fortresses be destroyed.
¹²He said, "No more of your reveling,
O Virgin Daughter of Sidon, now crushed!

"Up, cross over to Cyprus[d];
even there you will find no rest."
¹³Look at the land of the Babylonians,[e]
this people that is now of no account!
The Assyrians have made it
a place for desert creatures;
they raised up their siege towers,
they stripped its fortresses bare
and turned it into a ruin.

The LORD has stretched out his hand over the sea and made its kingdoms tremble.
Isa 23:11

23:5-10 *When word comes to Egypt . . . Till your land:* Egypt's leaders probably worried about what might happen to their economy, if they could no longer rely on Phoenician sailors to trade their crops and goods. Enemy attacks forced some Phoenicians to leave their cities and become farmers to make a living.

23:11-13 *cross over to Cyprus . . . Assyrians:* For the Assyrian threat, see the notes at 7:15-17 and 10:5. In 701 B.C., some leaders of Sidon escaped to Cyprus, perhaps to get away from Sennacherib's armies, who were also attacking Judah.

[a]**2,3** Masoretic Text; one Dead Sea Scroll *Sidon, / who cross over the sea; / your envoys* [3]*are on the great waters. / The grain of the Shihor, / the harvest of the Nile,* [b]**10** Dead Sea Scrolls and some Septuagint manuscripts; Masoretic Text *Go through* [c]**11** Hebrew *Canaan* [d]**12** Hebrew *Kittim* [e]**13** Or *Chaldeans*

23:15 *seventy years:* This may be a symbolic number, meaning a long time or a lifetime. Compare this to the time the prophet Jeremiah said Judah would be in exile in Babylon (Jer 25:11). See the chart called "Numbers in the Bible," on p. 2405.

23:17,18 *prostitute . . . ply her trade . . . profit:* Tyre's merchants, who would do anything to make a profit, are compared to a prostitute. But someday Tyre's wealth would be dedicated to the LORD God of Israel (60:5-13; 61:6). See also the mini-article called "Prostitution in the Bible," p. 1688.

24:1,2 *it will be the same:* All people, regardless of social standing, will be affected by the LORD's coming day of judgment. See also 3:1-4; Ezek 7:10-13.

14 Wail, you ships of Tarshish;
your fortress is destroyed!

15 At that time Tyre will be forgotten for seventy years, the span of a king's life. But at the end of these seventy years, it will happen to Tyre as in the song of the prostitute:

16 "Take up a harp, walk through the city,
O prostitute forgotten;
play the harp well, sing many a song,
so that you will be remembered."

17 At the end of seventy years, the LORD will deal with Tyre.
She will return to her hire as a prostitute and will ply her trade
with all the kingdoms on the face of the earth. 18 Yet her profit and
her earnings will be set apart for the LORD; they will not be stored
up or hoarded. Her profits will go to those who live before the
LORD, for abundant food and fine clothes.

A VIEW OF GOD'S FUTURE JUDGMENT

Chapters 24–27 of ISAIAH describe how God will act in the last days to judge the nations and win a victory over the forces of evil. The LORD will destroy the power of death (25:8), and his faithful people will rise from the grave to new life (26:19) to live in perfect peace (26:3). These themes are common in literature known as "Apocalyptic." So, this section of ISAIAH is sometimes called the "Apocalypse of Isaiah."

The LORD's Devastation of the Earth

24 See, the LORD is going to lay waste the earth
and devastate it;
he will ruin its face
and scatter its inhabitants—
2 it will be the same
for priest as for people,

QUESTIONS ABOUT ISAIAH 13:1—23:18

1. Chapters 13–23 provide messages about many of the neighboring nations. How would you describe the news given in most of these messages?
2. In what ways would God's judgment on Judah's neighbors affect Judah itself? (14:1-3, 25; 16:1-4; 19:16-25; 23:17,18)
3. Why will Israel and Judah not escape the LORD's judgment and punishment? (17:4-11; 22:7-25).
4. Isaiah's prophecies are based on the belief that the LORD of Israel has acted and will act at various times, using earthly rulers and armies to punish or to save. What do you think of the idea that God can or may be directing earthly events today?
5. If the prophet Isaiah were to deliver a "message" from the LORD to your nation today, what might the message be? Why?

for master as for servant,
for mistress as for maid,
for seller as for buyer,
for borrower as for lender,
for debtor as for creditor.
3 The earth will be completely laid waste
and totally plundered.
The LORD has spoken this word.

4 The earth dries up and withers,
the world languishes and withers,
the exalted of the earth languish.
5 The earth is defiled by its people;
they have disobeyed the laws,
violated the statutes
and broken the everlasting covenant.
6 Therefore a curse consumes the earth;
its people must bear their guilt.
Therefore earth's inhabitants are burned up,
and very few are left.
7 The new wine dries up and the vine withers;
all the merrymakers groan.
8 The gaiety of the tambourines is stilled,
the noise of the revelers has stopped,
the joyful harp is silent.
9 No longer do they drink wine with a song;
the beer is bitter to its drinkers.
10 The ruined city lies desolate;
the entrance to every house is barred.
11 In the streets they cry out for wine;
all joy turns to gloom,
all gaiety is banished from the earth.
12 The city is left in ruins,
its gate is battered to pieces.
13 So will it be on the earth
and among the nations,
as when an olive tree is beaten,
or as when gleanings are left after the grape harvest.

14 They raise their voices, they shout for joy;
from the west they acclaim the LORD's majesty.
15 Therefore in the east give glory to the LORD;
exalt the name of the LORD, the God of Israel,
in the islands of the sea.
16 From the ends of the earth we hear singing:
"Glory to the Righteous One."

But I said, "I waste away, I waste away!
Woe to me!

They raise their voices, they shout for joy. . . . From the ends of the earth we hear singing: "Glory to the Righteous One."
Isa 24:14,16

24:4,5 *earth dries up . . . broken the everlasting covenant:* Human sin can cause creation to suffer (see also 33:8, 9; Hos 4:1-3). The broken covenant seems to be a reference to how the people of Israel disobeyed God's Law (see the notes at 1:2, children, and 2:3). But some scholars have suggested that this prophecy is meant to describe all of humankind. In that case, the covenant mentioned here would be the covenant God made with Noah (Gen 9:8-17). See also the mini-article called "Covenants (Agreements)," p. 386.

24:8,9 *gaiety of the tambourines is stilled . . . silent:* Music and singing were often done in worship or in harvest celebrations (see the notes at 1:11-14 and 16:9,10). Such celebrating will end, because the land will no longer grow crops (24:7,11,13). Sweet-tasting wine made from grapes was considered a very important blessing. The loss of it would be a disaster (see the note at 5:4).

24:14-16 *shout for joy . . . The treacherous betray:* Though many in the world are praising the God of Israel, some are still dishonoring the LORD by being evil and treacherous.

24:18-20 *heavens . . . earth . . . rebellion:* Ancient people believed the sky was like a solid bowl set over the flat earth, and that high mountains held up the sky like columns (Job 9:5-10). This bowl or dome held back the flood of water above. Rain and snow were said to come through the dome when God opened windows or doors in the sky (Gen 7:11,12; Ps 78:23). God had the power to shake the foundations of the earth, probably meaning cause an earthquake. Natural disasters like floods and earthquakes were thought to be brought on by human sin (24:20; see also the note at 24:4,5).

24:21-23 *powers in the heavens . . . prison . . . moon . . . sun . . . Mount Zion:* In ancient times, the stars and moon were thought to be spiritual powers. They sometimes stood for other gods (see Deut 17:2, 3). These powers and evil human rulers would be punished by being thrown into the dark underworld prison (see the notes at 5:14 and 14:9,12-15). Their shame also might refer to how they will be overshadowed by the light of the LORD's glory when he comes to rule on Mount Zion (60:19,20; see also Rev 21:22-24; 22:5). See also the note at 1:8.

25:2 *foreigners' stronghold:* This is probably a general description of a city destroyed when the LORD judges it (see 24:10).

25:4 *poor . . . needy:* The God of justice offers them protection (1:17; 14:30,32; 58:6-8).

25:6 *this mountain . . . LORD Almighty . . . wines:* Mount Zion (see the note at 1:8) is the place where Israel's LORD will give a royal banquet for the nations. Zion, which represents both the people of God and the place where God will live among his people, is the source of the LORD's blessings (Ps 22:24-28; Ezek 47:1,2,12; Rev 22:1, 2). Certain New Testament texts also describe life in God's kingdom as a banquet (Matt 22:1-4; Luke 14:15-24; 22:14-17; Rev 19:6–10).

24:17,18 Jer 48:43,44.

The treacherous betray!
With treachery the treacherous betray!"
17 Terror and pit and snare await you,
O people of the earth.
18 Whoever flees at the sound of terror
will fall into a pit;
whoever climbs out of the pit
will be caught in a snare.

The floodgates of the heavens are opened,
the foundations of the earth shake.
19 The earth is broken up,
the earth is split asunder,
the earth is thoroughly shaken.
20 The earth reels like a drunkard,
it sways like a hut in the wind;
so heavy upon it is the guilt of its rebellion
that it falls—never to rise again.

21 In that day the LORD will punish
the powers in the heavens above
and the kings on the earth below.
22 They will be herded together
like prisoners bound in a dungeon;
they will be shut up in prison
and be punished[a] after many days.
23 The moon will be abashed, the sun ashamed;
for the LORD Almighty will reign
on Mount Zion and in Jerusalem,
and before its elders, gloriously.

Praise to the LORD

25 O LORD, you are my God;
I will exalt you and praise your name,
for in perfect faithfulness
you have done marvelous things,
things planned long ago.
2 You have made the city a heap of rubble,
the fortified town a ruin,
the foreigners' stronghold a city no more;
it will never be rebuilt.
3 Therefore strong peoples will honor you;
cities of ruthless nations will revere you.
4 You have been a refuge for the poor,
a refuge for the needy in his distress,
a shelter from the storm
and a shade from the heat.

[a]22 Or *released*

For the breath of the ruthless
is like a storm driving against a wall
5 and like the heat of the desert.
You silence the uproar of foreigners;
as heat is reduced by the shadow of a cloud,
so the song of the ruthless is stilled.

6 On this mountain the LORD Almighty will prepare
a feast of rich food for all peoples,

25:5 Ps 121:3-8.

PEACE

In modern society, "peace" usually means a time without war or an inner sense of calm. In the Bible, peace means more than that. The Hebrew word for peace is *shalom*, which means wholeness or well-being. So when people use the word *shalom* to greet others or to say good-bye, they are wishing them the best, including health and success.

In the Old Testament, peace is used to describe a time without war (Josh 10:1-4; 1 Sam 7:14; 1 Kgs 4:24) or a time of safety from attacks by wild animals or enemies (Lev 26:6-8). Prosperity is connected with the peace that God provides (Lev 26:3-13; Isa 60:17). God gives peace to those who live as God intends and who remain faithful (Isa 26:3,12,13; Mal 2:4-6). God also grants peace to those who live according to justice and truth (Isa 32:16,17; Zech 8:16, 19). But those who disobey God and do evil will never live in peace (Isa 48:22; 57:21).

God promised peace to the people of Israel as part of his covenants with them. Israel's priests were to include the blessing of peace as part of their duties (Num 6:22-26). Many sacrifices and offerings required by the Law were made in order to restore peace between people or between the people and God (Lev 4:1—7:10; 16:1-34). God's covenant with King David was to be fulfilled by a chosen leader (Messiah) from David's family who would be known as the Prince of Peace (Isa 9:6,7). Isaiah also announced the LORD's promise to give Israel peace that would last forever (Isa 54:10). Lasting peace is promised as part of the new future God will create for his people (Ezek 34:25-31; 37:24-28).

In the New Testament, peace has the usual meaning of the absence of conflict between people or nations (Luke 14:32; Acts 9:31; Rev 6:4). But the sense of *shalom* also appears in spoken and written greetings (Mark 5:34; Luke 7:50; John 20:19; also see Rom 1:7; 1 Cor 1:3; Gal 1:3). Many of Paul's letters encourage Christians to live in peace by accepting and loving each other in spite of their differences (Rom 14:19; 1 Cor 14:33; 2 Cor 13:11). Christians are to be at peace even with outsiders who try to do them harm, leaving the punishment of enemies up to God (Rom 12:18,19).

Christ was sent to earth to make peace between God and all people. This peace comes from forgiveness, and God's people are to carry this message of peace and forgiveness to others. Jesus makes peace with God possible (Rom 5:1) and makes it possible for the world's people to live together in peace (Gal 5:22,23; Eph 2:14,15).

The inner spiritual peace that comes to those who belong to Christ Jesus is described as being beyond human understanding, but powerful to control the way people think and feel (Phil 4:7). This kind of peace is not the kind that the world can give (John 14:27), but is connected to spiritual things rather than material well-being (1 Thes 5:23, Jas 3:17,18). The good news about Jesus is described as the good news of peace (Acts 10:36; Eph 6:15). And peacemakers will be blessed by God and will be called "sons of God" (Matt 5:9).

a banquet of aged wine—
the best of meats and the finest of wines.
7 On this mountain he will destroy
the shroud that enfolds all peoples,
the sheet that covers all nations;
8 he will swallow up death forever.
The Sovereign LORD will wipe away the tears
from all faces;
he will remove the disgrace of his people
from all the earth.
The LORD has spoken.

9 In that day they will say,

"Surely this is our God;
we trusted in him, and he saved us.
This is the LORD, we trusted in him;
let us rejoice and be glad in his salvation."

10 The hand of the LORD will rest on this mountain;
but Moab will be trampled under him
as straw is trampled down in the manure.
11 They will spread out their hands in it,
as a swimmer spreads out his hands to swim.
God will bring down their pride
despite the cleverness[a] of their hands.
12 He will bring down your high fortified walls
and lay them low;
he will bring them down to the ground,
to the very dust.

A Song of Praise

26 In that day this song will be sung in the land of Judah:

We have a strong city;
God makes salvation
its walls and ramparts.
2 Open the gates
that the righteous nation may enter,
the nation that keeps faith.
3 You will keep in perfect peace
him whose mind is steadfast,
because he trusts in you.
4 Trust in the LORD forever,
for the LORD, the LORD, is the Rock eternal.
5 He humbles those who dwell on high,
he lays the lofty city low;
he levels it to the ground

[a]11 The meaning of the Hebrew for this word is uncertain.

The Sovereign LORD will wipe away the tears from all faces; he will remove the disgrace of his people from all the earth.
Isa 25:8

25:7,8 *he will destroy the shroud that enfolds all peoples:* The "shroud" may refer to clothes worn by those who are in mourning, or to the strips of linen cloth used to wrap a dead body. If the people are in burial clothes, it is because Israel has been defeated by other nations. The image of God destroying the shroud also suggests bringing someone back to life from death. See the mini-articles called "Eternal Life," p. 2072 and "Resurrection," p. 2210. For God wiping away tears, see 51:11; 65:19; Rev 7:17; 21:4.

25:10 *Moab will be trampled:* See the note at 15:1.

26:1,2 *strong city . . . righteous nation:* This means Jerusalem, when the people have returned to the LORD and are obeying the laws of the LORD. See the note at 1:16,17.

26:3 *perfect peace:* The kind of inner peace that comes from confidence in God's promise. See also the mini-article called "Peace," p. 1337.

26:5 *dwell on high:* See the note at 25:2.

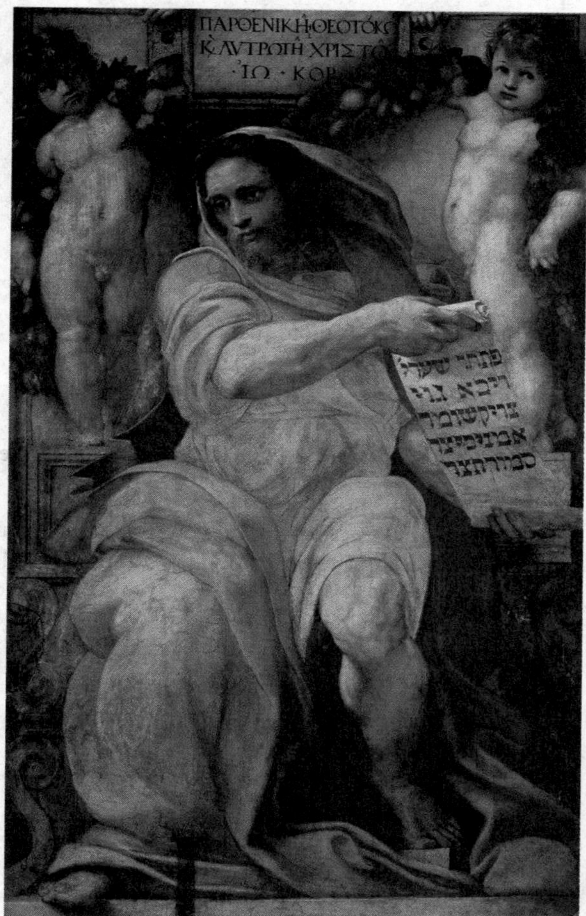

Prophet Isaiah, by Raphael, Sant'Agostino, Rome, around 1512. The Hebrew words on the prophet's scroll in this fresco are from Isaiah's song of praise (26:1-6): "Open the gates that the righteous nation may enter, the nation that keeps faith." Isaiah foresees a period when the LORD will judge the other nations and Judah will be victorious. Israel's enemies will be destroyed and God's people will be rewarded for their faithfulness.

and casts it down to the dust.
6 Feet trample it down—
the feet of the oppressed,
the footsteps of the poor.

7 The path of the righteous is level;
O upright One, you make the way of the righteous smooth.
8 Yes, LORD, walking in the way of your laws,[a]
we wait for you;

[a]8 Or *judgments*

26:7 *path of the righteous is level:* The path of the righteous is laid out by the LORD, who determines what is right and wrong. Those who obey the LORD (live right and do justice) will walk on the LORD's smooth and level path (see also Ps 1:1-6).

26:8,11,12 *be put to shame . . . fire reserved . . . establish peace:* See the notes at 1:16, 17 and 4:4. See also Heb 10:27. In the phrase "establish peace," the word translated "peace" is from the Hebrew *shalom*, which means calm, the absence of conflict, and a general sense of well-being and wholeness. This peace comes from receiving the LORD's blessings. All or any senses of the word can be meant here. See also the note at 26:3.

26:15-18 *enlarged the nation . . . disciplined them . . . have not given birth:* God promised to give Abraham's descendants, the people of Israel, their own land (Gen 15:18-21; 17:1-8). The promise of regaining their land provided great hope to the people of Israel and Judah who had been forced to leave (see the note at 6:11,12). See also the mini-article called "Land," p. 1751.

In these verses, Isaiah describes how God punished Israel in the past for being disobedient (see the notes at 1:7-9 and 1:21), but it's not clear which particular event he means. The complaint that there are no descendants recalls God's promise to their ancestor Abraham to have many descendants to populate and bless the earth (Gen 12:1-3; 17:4-6).

26:19—27:1 *bodies will rise . . . LORD . . . punish . . . Leviathan:* The phrase "bodies will rise" has been taken by some to refer to the rebirth of the Israelite nation from the dark period of the exile (Ezek 37:1-14). Others think it describes the promise of rising from death to new life (resurrection). See the note at 25:7,8.

The punishments described in 26:21 will take place on the LORD's day of judgment (see Isa 66:15,16 and the note at 2:11,12).

Leviathan (27:1) is the sea monster of chaos God conquered at the time of creation. In the Bible, it often symbolizes evil. Victory over this monster can stand for God's power over all creation or for defeat of his enemies, especially Egypt. See also Job 41:1-34; Ps 74:14; 104:26.

your name and renown
are the desire of our hearts.
9 My soul yearns for you in the night;
in the morning my spirit longs for you.
When your judgments come upon the earth,
the people of the world learn righteousness.
10 Though grace is shown to the wicked,
they do not learn righteousness;
even in a land of uprightness they go on doing evil
and regard not the majesty of the LORD.
11 O LORD, your hand is lifted high,
but they do not see it.
Let them see your zeal for your people and be put
to shame;
let the fire reserved for your enemies consume them.

12 LORD, you establish peace for us;
all that we have accomplished you have done for us.
13 O LORD, our God, other lords besides you have ruled
over us,
but your name alone do we honor.
14 They are now dead, they live no more;
those departed spirits do not rise.
You punished them and brought them to ruin;
you wiped out all memory of them.
15 You have enlarged the nation, O LORD;
you have enlarged the nation.
You have gained glory for yourself;
you have extended all the borders of the land.

16 LORD, they came to you in their distress;
when you disciplined them,
they could barely whisper a prayer.[a]
17 As a woman with child and about to give birth
writhes and cries out in her pain,
so were we in your presence, O LORD.
18 We were with child, we writhed in pain,
but we gave birth to wind.
We have not brought salvation to the earth;
we have not given birth to people of the world.

19 But your dead will live;
their bodies will rise.
You who dwell in the dust,
wake up and shout for joy.
Your dew is like the dew of the morning;
the earth will give birth to her dead.

[a]16 The meaning of the Hebrew for this clause is uncertain.

[20]Go, my people, enter your rooms
and shut the doors behind you;
hide yourselves for a little while
until his wrath has passed by.
[21]See, the LORD is coming out of his dwelling
to punish the people of the earth for their sins.
The earth will disclose the blood shed upon her;
she will conceal her slain no longer.

Deliverance of Israel

27 In that day,

the LORD will punish with his sword,
his fierce, great and powerful sword,
Leviathan the gliding serpent,
Leviathan the coiling serpent;
he will slay the monster of the sea.

[2]In that day—

"Sing about a fruitful vineyard:
[3] I, the LORD, watch over it;
I water it continually.
I guard it day and night
so that no one may harm it.
[4] I am not angry.
If only there were briers and thorns confronting me!
I would march against them in battle;
I would set them all on fire.
[5]Or else let them come to me for refuge;
let them make peace with me,
yes, let them make peace with me."

[6]In days to come Jacob will take root,
Israel will bud and blossom
and fill all the world with fruit.

[7]Has ⌞the LORD⌟ struck her
as he struck down those who struck her?
Has she been killed
as those were killed who killed her?
[8]By warfare[a] and exile you contend with her—
with his fierce blast he drives her out,
as on a day the east wind blows.
[9]By this, then, will Jacob's guilt be atoned for,
and this will be the full fruitage of the removal of
his sin:
When he makes all the altar stones

[a]**8** See Septuagint; the meaning of the Hebrew for this word is uncertain.

LORD, you establish peace for us; all that we have accomplished you have done for us. Isa 26:12

27:2-6 *fruitful vineyard:* See the notes at 5:1,2 and 5:4. The LORD promises to take care of his vineyard (the Israelites). However, if the vineyard produces briers and thorns (is disobedient), God will burn it (see 5:4-7). Israel's "fruit" is its people who are considered a blessing to the nations of the earth (Gen 12:3; Isa 60:1-3; 61:1-11).

27:9 *altar stones:* See the notes at 1:29-31 and 17:8,9. Getting rid of the worship places associated with other gods was a practical way of removing Israel's past sins.

27:10 *fortified city:* Which city is meant is uncertain. It could refer to Samaria (see the notes at 7:8,9, Samaria, and 10:5), Jerusalem, Babylon (13:19-22), or to any city that opposed the LORD (see the note at 25:2).

27:11 *twigs are dry . . . broken:* Those who opposed the LORD will be like broken sticks that have dried out. They will burn quickly when thrown into a fire (see also 27:4).

27:12,13 *Egypt . . . holy mountain in Jerusalem:* See the notes at 11:11 and 11:15. In that future day, God will gather his people from the lands where they had been taken or had escaped to avoid destruction. God will bring them back to worship on Mount Zion in Jerusalem (see the note at 1:8).

27:13 *trumpet:* The trumpet was used to call Israel's tribes together (Num 10:2-10), to prepare for battle (1 Sam 13:3), or to call the people to worship (Joel 2:15). In later writings, the trumpet is described as being blown in preparation for the LORD's coming day of judgment and salvation (Matt 24:30, 31; 1 Thes 4:16,17). See the illustration on p. 251.

28:1-3 *Woe to . . . Ephraim's drunkards:* The first message of judgment is against Ephraim, another name for the northern kingdom of Israel. The leaders of Israel (Ephraim) had become wealthy at the expense of others, and had allowed the worship of foreign gods. Isaiah warns that they will be crushed and eaten like a piece of ripe fruit. See the note at 10:9-12.

to be like chalk stones crushed to pieces,
no Asherah poles[a] or incense altars
will be left standing.
10 The fortified city stands desolate,
an abandoned settlement, forsaken like
the desert;
there the calves graze,
there they lie down;
they strip its branches bare.
11 When its twigs are dry, they are broken off
and women come and make fires with them.
For this is a people without understanding;
so their Maker has no compassion on them,
and their Creator shows them no favor.

12 In that day the LORD will thresh from the flowing
Euphrates[b] to the Wadi of Egypt, and you, O Israelites, will be gath-
ered up one by one. 13 And in that day a great trumpet will sound.
Those who were perishing in Assyria and those who were exiled in
Egypt will come and worship the LORD on the holy mountain in
Jerusalem.

THOSE WHO REBEL AGAINST GOD WILL BE PUNISHED

The next six chapters (28–33) present a series of judgment messages directed toward Judah in the time of King Hezekiah's revolt against Assyria's King Sennacherib in 705-701 B.C. The prophet warns Judah not to seek help from Egypt in this revolt.

Woe to Ephraim

28 Woe to that wreath, the pride of Ephraim's drunkards,
to the fading flower, his glorious beauty,
set on the head of a fertile valley—
to that city, the pride of those laid low by wine!
2 See, the Lord has one who is powerful and strong.
Like a hailstorm and a destructive wind,
like a driving rain and a flooding downpour,
he will throw it forcefully to the ground.
3 That wreath, the pride of Ephraim's drunkards,
will be trampled underfoot.
4 That fading flower, his glorious beauty,
set on the head of a fertile valley,
will be like a fig ripe before harvest—
as soon as someone sees it and takes it in his hand,
he swallows it.

[a]9 That is, symbols of the goddess Asherah [b]12 Hebrew *River*

5 In that day the LORD Almighty
will be a glorious crown,
a beautiful wreath
for the remnant of his people.
6 He will be a spirit of justice
to him who sits in judgment,
a source of strength
to those who turn back the battle at the gate.

7 And these also stagger from wine
and reel from beer:
Priests and prophets stagger from beer
and are befuddled with wine;
they reel from beer,
they stagger when seeing visions,
they stumble when rendering decisions.
8 All the tables are covered with vomit
and there is not a spot without filth.

9 "Who is it he is trying to teach?
To whom is he explaining his message?
To children weaned from their milk,
to those just taken from the breast?
10 For it is:
Do and do, do and do,
rule on rule, rule on rule[a];
a little here, a little there."

11 Very well then, with foreign lips and strange tongues
God will speak to this people,
12 to whom he said,
"This is the resting place, let the weary rest";
and, "This is the place of repose"—
but they would not listen.
13 So then, the word of the LORD to them will become:
Do and do, do and do,
rule on rule, rule on rule;
a little here, a little there—
so that they will go and fall backward,
be injured and snared and captured.

14 Therefore hear the word of the LORD, you scoffers
who rule this people in Jerusalem.
15 You boast, "We have entered into a covenant with death,
with the grave[b] we have made an agreement.
When an overwhelming scourge sweeps by,

[a]**10** Hebrew / *sav lasav sav lasav / kav lakav kav lakav* (possibly meaningless sounds; perhaps a mimicking of the prophet's words); also in verse 13
[b]**15** Hebrew *Sheol*; also in verse 18

28:5,6 *In that day . . . LORD Almighty . . . justice:* Here "that day" refers to the coming day of the LORD's judgment (see the note at 2:11, 12). For "LORD Almighty," see the note on p. 1289 (LORD). For "justice," see the note at 1:16,17. See also Isa 58:1-8; 60:1-3; 61:1-4.

28:7-9 *Priests and prophets . . . befuddled with wine:* Priests and prophets were to be spiritual leaders, but Isaiah says the priests and prophets are foolish and drunken, just like the political leaders (28:1; see also the note at 5:11-13).

28:11 *foreign lips and strange tongues:* This probably refers to the language of the Assyrian invaders. Because Judah's leaders treated Isaiah's message from the LORD as sound with no meaning, they will hear the language of Assyrian invaders, but not understand it.

28:15 *a covenant with death, with the grave:* This may refer to a treaty made with Egypt (30:1-5). Egypt's religion had a cult of the dead. This interest in the world of the dead would have been known in Judah. See also the note at 5:14.

28:11,12 1 Cor 14:21.

28:16,17 *precious cornerstone . . . plumb line:* The new people of Jerusalem will look to the LORD as their "cornerstone," their "sure foundation" (see the note at 17:10, Rock). See also 8:14,15. A "plumb line" is made of a long string with a weight tied to its end. The weight made it hang down in a straight line. Builders use plumb lines to make sure walls are perfectly vertical. See the illustration on p. 1730. God's new people will be built according to the measuring lines of justice and fairness. See also Ps 118:22, 23; Rom 9:33; 10:11; 1 Pet 2:6.

28:18,20 *covenant with death . . . bed is too short:* See the note at 28:15. Isaiah quotes a popular saying (28:20) as a way of warning that the treaty made with Egypt (28:15,18) cannot give Judah security.

28:21 *rise up . . . Mount Perazim . . . Valley of Gibeon . . . strange work:* The LORD helped Israel at these places in the past: David defeated the Philistines at Baal Perazim (2 Sam 5:17-21; 1 Chr 14:11), and Joshua defeated the Amorites at the Valley of Gibeon (Josh 10:1-11). The "strange work" is that the LORD will attack Jerusalem (see 29:1-3).

28:25-28 *caraway . . . cummin . . . wheat . . . barley:* These crops were grown in various types of soil at different times. After harvest, the spices caraway and cummin were pounded to remove the seeds. Because wheat and barley stalks were heavier, they had to be placed on a stone threshing floor and run over by something heavy in order to remove the husks from the grain. In the same way, Judah will face the LORD's "harvest," meaning they will be attacked (29:3) but not completely destroyed.

it cannot touch us,
for we have made a lie our refuge
and falsehood[a] our hiding place."

16 So this is what the Sovereign LORD says:

"See, I lay a stone in Zion,
a tested stone,
a precious cornerstone for a sure foundation;
the one who trusts will never be dismayed.
17 I will make justice the measuring line
and righteousness the plumb line;
hail will sweep away your refuge, the lie,
and water will overflow your hiding place.
18 Your covenant with death will be annulled;
your agreement with the grave will not stand.
When the overwhelming scourge sweeps by,
you will be beaten down by it.
19 As often as it comes it will carry you away;
morning after morning, by day and by night,
it will sweep through."

The understanding of this message
will bring sheer terror.
20 The bed is too short to stretch out on,
the blanket too narrow to wrap around you.
21 The LORD will rise up as he did at Mount Perazim,
he will rouse himself as in the Valley of Gibeon—
to do his work, his strange work,
and perform his task, his alien task.
22 Now stop your mocking,
or your chains will become heavier;
the Lord, the LORD Almighty, has told me
of the destruction decreed against the whole land.

23 Listen and hear my voice;
pay attention and hear what I say.
24 When a farmer plows for planting, does he plow
continually?
Does he keep on breaking up and harrowing the soil?
25 When he has leveled the surface,
does he not sow caraway and scatter cummin?
Does he not plant wheat in its place,[b]
barley in its plot,[b]
and spelt in its field?
26 His God instructs him
and teaches him the right way.

[a]15 Or *false gods* [b]25 The meaning of the Hebrew for this word is uncertain.

[27] Caraway is not threshed with a sledge,
nor is a cartwheel rolled over cummin;
caraway is beaten out with a rod,
and cummin with a stick.
[28] Grain must be ground to make bread;
so one does not go on threshing it forever.
Though he drives the wheels of his threshing cart
over it,
his horses do not grind it.
[29] All this also comes from the LORD Almighty,
wonderful in counsel and magnificent in wisdom.

Woe to David's City

29 Woe to you, Ariel, Ariel,
the city where David settled!
Add year to year
and let your cycle of festivals go on.
[2] Yet I will besiege Ariel;
she will mourn and lament,
she will be to me like an altar hearth.[a]
[3] I will encamp against you all around;
I will encircle you with towers
and set up my siege works against you.
[4] Brought low, you will speak from the ground;
your speech will mumble out of the dust.
Your voice will come ghostlike from the earth;
out of the dust your speech will whisper.

[5] But your many enemies will become like fine dust,
the ruthless hordes like blown chaff.
Suddenly, in an instant,
[6] the LORD Almighty will come
with thunder and earthquake and great noise,
with windstorm and tempest and flames of a
devouring fire.
[7] Then the hordes of all the nations that fight against Ariel,
that attack her and her fortress and besiege her,
will be as it is with a dream,
with a vision in the night—
[8] as when a hungry man dreams that he is eating,
but he awakens, and his hunger remains;
as when a thirsty man dreams that he is drinking,
but he awakens faint, with his thirst unquenched.
So will it be with the hordes of all the nations
that fight against Mount Zion.

29:1 *Ariel, the city where David settled:* Another name for Jerusalem. See the note on p. 1289 and the mini-article called "Zion," p. 1294.

29:1 *cycle of festivals:* For more about Israel's religious festivals see the note at 1:11-14 and the article called "People of the Law: The Religion of Israel," p. 939.

29:4-8 *speak from the ground . . . many enemies:* "Speak from the ground" is the place of the dead (see the note at 5:14). After punishing Jerusalem, the LORD will punish its enemies. See also 10:5-19; 24:17-22; 30:30-32.

[a]2 The Hebrew for *altar hearth* sounds like the Hebrew for *Ariel.*

29:9-11 *prophets . . . it is sealed:* See the note at 28:7-9. Because of their foolish actions, the LORD made Judah's false prophets unable to understand the meaning of the message given to Isaiah. See also Rom 11:8.

29:13 *honor me with their lips, but their hearts are far from me:* Judah's priests and people appeared to be following the laws and rituals of worship, but their devotion was false. Their show of faith did not come from the heart, and so they were not living right (see 1:10-17). See also Matt 15:8, 9; Mark 7:6,7.

29:14 *wisdom:* In Israel, true wisdom came from the LORD. The truly wise person was one who obeyed the LORD's teachings (Prov 1:7; 2:6,7). Judah's priests and leaders have not been obeying the LORD, so their wisdom is called into question. See also 1 Cor 1:19 and the mini-article called "Wisdom," p. 2206.

29:17 *fertile field:* This may represent how the whole creation will be fertile once again when the LORD brings a new future. Or this may represent God's people. They will be cut down like Assyria (see 10:15-19, 33, 34), but one day they will again be a thick field.

29:16 Isa 45:9; Rom 9:20.
29:18,19 Isa 35:5; 58:6-8.

9 Be stunned and amazed,
blind yourselves and be sightless;
be drunk, but not from wine,
stagger, but not from beer.
10 The LORD has brought over you a deep sleep:
He has sealed your eyes (the prophets);
he has covered your heads (the seers).

11 For you this whole vision is nothing but words sealed in a
scroll. And if you give the scroll to someone who can read, and say
to him, "Read this, please," he will answer, "I can't; it is sealed." 12 Or
if you give the scroll to someone who cannot read, and say, "Read
this, please," he will answer, "I don't know how to read."

13 The Lord says:

"These people come near to me with their mouth
and honor me with their lips,
but their hearts are far from me.
Their worship of me
is made up only of rules taught by men.[a]
14 Therefore once more I will astound these people
with wonder upon wonder;
the wisdom of the wise will perish,
the intelligence of the intelligent will vanish."
15 Woe to those who go to great depths
to hide their plans from the LORD,
who do their work in darkness and think,
"Who sees us? Who will know?"
16 You turn things upside down,
as if the potter were thought to be like the clay!
Shall what is formed say to him who formed it,
"He did not make me"?
Can the pot say of the potter,
"He knows nothing"?
17 In a very short time, will not Lebanon be turned into a
fertile field
and the fertile field seem like a forest?
18 In that day the deaf will hear the words of the scroll,
and out of gloom and darkness
the eyes of the blind will see.
19 Once more the humble will rejoice in the LORD;
the needy will rejoice in the Holy One of Israel.
20 The ruthless will vanish,
the mockers will disappear,
and all who have an eye for evil will be cut down—

[a]**13** Hebrew; Septuagint *They worship me in vain; / their teachings are but rules taught by men*

21 those who with a word make a man out to be guilty,
who ensnare the defender in court
and with false testimony deprive the innocent of justice.

22 Therefore this is what the LORD, who redeemed Abraham,
says to the house of Jacob:

"No longer will Jacob be ashamed;
no longer will their faces grow pale.
23 When they see among them their children,
the work of my hands,
they will keep my name holy;
they will acknowledge the holiness of the Holy One of Jacob,
and will stand in awe of the God of Israel.
24 Those who are wayward in spirit will gain understanding;
those who complain will accept instruction."

Woe to the Obstinate Nation

30 "Woe to the obstinate children,"
declares the LORD,
"to those who carry out plans that are not mine,
forming an alliance, but not by my Spirit,
heaping sin upon sin;
2 who go down to Egypt
without consulting me;
who look for help to Pharaoh's protection,
to Egypt's shade for refuge.
3 But Pharaoh's protection will be to your shame,
Egypt's shade will bring you disgrace.
4 Though they have officials in Zoan
and their envoys have arrived in Hanes,
5 everyone will be put to shame
because of a people useless to them,
who bring neither help nor advantage,
but only shame and disgrace."

6 An oracle concerning the animals of the Negev:

Through a land of hardship and distress,
of lions and lionesses,
of adders and darting snakes,
the envoys carry their riches on donkeys' backs,
their treasures on the humps of camels,
to that unprofitable nation,
7 to Egypt, whose help is utterly useless.
Therefore I call her
Rahab the Do-Nothing.

29:21 *false testimony:* Some people in Judah were using their power or wealth to bribe court officials to keep certain people, especially the poor, from getting a fair hearing. See also Amos 2:6-8; 5:10-12.

29:22 *redeemed Abraham . . . house of Jacob:* Redeeming Abraham probably refers to the LORD's choosing him to be the father of God's chosen people (Gen 12:1-3; Isa 51:2). Jacob was Abraham's grandson, and the tribes of Israel were named after Jacob's sons.

30:1,2 *carry out plans that are not mine . . . Pharaoh's protection:* This message probably was directed toward the leaders of Judah in 703-701 B.C. During that time, Sennacherib of Assyria was threatening to capture Jerusalem. By asking Egypt for help, Isaiah said that Judah's leaders showed a lack of trust in the LORD. See also 31:1-5 and the notes at 18:1,2; 20:1-3; 28:18,20.

30:4 *Zoan . . . Hanes:* See the note at 19:11,13. Hanes was to the south, about fifty miles south of Memphis.

30:6 *the Negev:* Also known as the Southern Desert. People traveling between Judah and Egypt had to travel through the Negev. Isaiah may be describing a caravan of goods and treasures that Judah is sending to Egypt to buy Egypt's help. "Unprofitable nation" refers to Egypt.

30:6,7 *adders and darting snakes . . . Rahab the Do-Nothing:* The adders and darting snakes may be poisonous snakes that lived in the frightening desert (Deut 8:15). In the Jewish Scriptures Egypt is frequently compared to Rahab, the monster that God was said to have defeated at the time of creation (Job 9:13; 26:12, 13; Ps 89:9, 10; Isa 51:9).

This is what the Sovereign LORD, the Holy One of Israel, says: "In repentance and rest is your salvation, in quietness and trust is your strength, but you would have none of it."
Isa 30:15

30:9 *rebellious people:* Refers to people of Judah who have rebelled against the LORD (30:1) by trusting in foreign powers.

30:11,12 *Holy One of Israel . . . you have rejected this message:* See the note at 5:18, 19. Some of Judah's leaders no longer wanted to hear the message (30:15) about how the LORD could protect Judah from its enemies.

30:17 Lev 26:36-38; Deut 32:30.

8 Go now, write it on a tablet for them,
inscribe it on a scroll,
that for the days to come
it may be an everlasting witness.
9 These are rebellious people, deceitful children,
children unwilling to listen to the LORD's
instruction.
10 They say to the seers,
"See no more visions!"
and to the prophets,
"Give us no more visions of what is right!
Tell us pleasant things,
prophesy illusions.
11 Leave this way,
get off this path,
and stop confronting us
with the Holy One of Israel!"

12 Therefore, this is what the Holy One of Israel says:

"Because you have rejected this message,
relied on oppression
and depended on deceit,
13 this sin will become for you
like a high wall, cracked and bulging,
that collapses suddenly, in an instant.
14 It will break in pieces like pottery,
shattered so mercilessly
that among its pieces not a fragment will
be found
for taking coals from a hearth
or scooping water out of a cistern."

15 This is what the Sovereign LORD, the Holy One of Israel,
says:

"In repentance and rest is your salvation,
in quietness and trust is your strength,
but you would have none of it.
16 You said, 'No, we will flee on horses.'
Therefore you will flee!
You said, 'We will ride off on swift horses.'
Therefore your pursuers will be swift!
17 A thousand will flee
at the threat of one;
at the threat of five
you will all flee away,
till you are left
like a flagstaff on a mountaintop,
like a banner on a hill."

18 Yet the LORD longs to be gracious to you;
he rises to show you compassion.
For the LORD is a God of justice.
Blessed are all who wait for him!

19 O people of Zion, who live in Jerusalem, you will weep no
more. How gracious he will be when you cry for help! As soon as he
hears, he will answer you. 20 Although the Lord gives you the bread of
adversity and the water of affliction, your teachers will be hidden no
more; with your own eyes you will see them. 21 Whether you turn to
the right or to the left, your ears will hear a voice behind you, saying,
"This is the way; walk in it." 22 Then you will defile your idols overlaid
with silver and your images covered with gold; you will throw them
away like a menstrual cloth and say to them, "Away with you!"

23 He will also send you rain for the seed you sow in the
ground, and the food that comes from the land will be rich and
plentiful. In that day your cattle will graze in broad meadows.
24 The oxen and donkeys that work the soil will eat fodder and
mash, spread out with fork and shovel. 25 In the day of great
slaughter, when the towers fall, streams of water will flow on every
high mountain and every lofty hill. 26 The moon will shine like the
sun, and the sunlight will be seven times brighter, like the light of
seven full days, when the LORD binds up the bruises of his people
and heals the wounds he inflicted.

27 See, the Name of the LORD comes from afar,
with burning anger and dense clouds of smoke;
his lips are full of wrath,
and his tongue is a consuming fire.
28 His breath is like a rushing torrent,
rising up to the neck.
He shakes the nations in the sieve of destruction;
he places in the jaws of the peoples
a bit that leads them astray.
29 And you will sing
as on the night you celebrate a holy festival;
your hearts will rejoice
as when people go up with flutes
to the mountain of the LORD,
to the Rock of Israel.
30 The LORD will cause men to hear his majestic voice
and will make them see his arm coming down
with raging anger and consuming fire,
with cloudburst, thunderstorm and hail.
31 The voice of the LORD will shatter Assyria;
with his scepter he will strike them down.
32 Every stroke the LORD lays on them
with his punishing rod

30:19 *Jerusalem . . . weep no more:* See the note on p. 1289 (Judah and Jerusalem). This message of promise regarding Jerusalem's future (30:18-26) interrupts Isaiah's messages of judgment (compare 29:17-24).

30:22,24 *idols overlaid with silver . . . gold . . . fodder:* For idols of silver and gold, see the note at 2:18,19. Usually oxen and donkeys ate hay or grass, not fodder and mash, which would be the finest grain. But in the future, Israel's land will produce so much food that even these animals will be able to eat grain.

30:25-27 *slaughter . . . light of seven full days . . . LORD comes . . . consuming fire:* The reference to people slaughtered may refer to Assyria's defeat. Then Judah's people will have a future filled with great brightness and joy. The LORD's coming judgment against Assyria (30:31) is described as a punishment by fire, smoke, and flood. See also 10:15-17 and the note at 4:4.

30:28 *a bit:* A piece of metal or wood that is put in the mouth of a horse or donkey and attached to reins. When riders pull on the reins they are able to make the animal turn or stop. In the same way the LORD will bridle the Assyrians and steer them to destruction (see also 37:29).

30:29 *holy festival:* Probably Passover. See the mini-article called "Passover and the Feast of Unleavened Bread," p. 2030.

30:29-31 *mountain of the LORD . . . Rock of Israel . . . thunderstorm . . . scepter:* See the note at 17:10 (Rock). The mountain of the LORD is "Zion" (see the note at 1:8). The LORD's voice often is connected with thunder (Exod 19:16; 20:18-20; Ps 29:3-9). Ancient rulers carried a staff or rod, also called a royal scepter, as a sign of their authority.

30:30 Isa 30:27.

will be to the music of tambourines and harps,
as he fights them in battle with the blows of his arm.
33 Topheth has long been prepared;
it has been made ready for the king.
Its fire pit has been made deep and wide,
with an abundance of fire and wood;
the breath of the LORD,
like a stream of burning sulfur,
sets it ablaze.

Woe to Those Who Rely on Egypt

31 Woe to those who go down to Egypt for help,
who rely on horses,
who trust in the multitude of their chariots
and in the great strength of their horsemen,
but do not look to the Holy One of Israel,
or seek help from the LORD.
2 Yet he too is wise and can bring disaster;
he does not take back his words.
He will rise up against the house of the wicked,
against those who help evildoers.
3 But the Egyptians are men and not God;
their horses are flesh and not spirit.
When the LORD stretches out his hand,
he who helps will stumble,
he who is helped will fall;
both will perish together.

4 This is what the LORD says to me:

"As a lion growls,
a great lion over his prey—
and though a whole band of shepherds
is called together against him,
he is not frightened by their shouts
or disturbed by their clamor—
so the LORD Almighty will come down
to do battle on Mount Zion and on its heights.
5 Like birds hovering overhead,
the LORD Almighty will shield Jerusalem;
he will shield it and deliver it,
he will 'pass over' it and will rescue it."

6 Return to him you have so greatly revolted against,
O Israelites. 7 For in that day every one of you will reject the idols
of silver and gold your sinful hands have made.

8 "Assyria will fall by a sword that is not of man;
a sword, not of mortals, will devour them.

Woe to those who go down to Egypt for help, who rely on horses, who trust in the multitude of their chariots . . . but do not look to the Holy One of Israel, or seek help from the LORD.
Isa 31:1

30:33 *Topheth:* The place where children were burned as sacrifices to the god Molech (2 Kgs 23:10; Jer 7:31; 19:4-7). The Hebrew word for "king" is similar to the name Molech. By making a pun on Molech's name, Isaiah is insulting the king of Assyria.

31:1-3 *go down to Egypt . . . the Holy One of Israel:* See 20:1-6 and the note at 20:1-3. See also the note at 5:18,19.

31:4 *lion growls . . . LORD Almighty . . . Mount Zion:* See Hos 11:10; Amos 3:8. See the notes on p. 1289 (LORD) and at 1:8.

31:7 *idols of silver and gold:* See the notes at 2:18, 19; 30:22, 24.

31:8,9 *Assyria will fall by a sword that is not of man:* The Assyrian army under Sennacherib suffered great losses in 701 B.C. (See 37:36-38.) In 612 B.C. the Assyrians were defeated, and their capital city of Nineveh was destroyed by the combined armies of the Medes and Babylonians.

They will flee before the sword
and their young men will be put to forced labor.
9 Their stronghold will fall because of terror;
at sight of the battle standard their commanders
will panic,"
declares the LORD,
whose fire is in Zion,
whose furnace is in Jerusalem.

The Kingdom of Righteousness

32 See, a king will reign in righteousness
and rulers will rule with justice.
2 Each man will be like a shelter from the wind
and a refuge from the storm,
like streams of water in the desert
and the shadow of a great rock in a thirsty land.

3 Then the eyes of those who see will no longer be closed,
and the ears of those who hear will listen.
4 The mind of the rash will know and understand,
and the stammering tongue will be fluent and clear.
5 No longer will the fool be called noble
nor the scoundrel be highly respected.
6 For the fool speaks folly,
his mind is busy with evil:
He practices ungodliness
and spreads error concerning the LORD;
the hungry he leaves empty
and from the thirsty he withholds water.
7 The scoundrel's methods are wicked,
he makes up evil schemes
to destroy the poor with lies,
even when the plea of the needy is just.
8 But the noble man makes noble plans,
and by noble deeds he stands.

The Women of Jerusalem

9 You women who are so complacent,
rise up and listen to me;
you daughters who feel secure,
hear what I have to say!
10 In little more than a year
you who feel secure will tremble;
the grape harvest will fail,
and the harvest of fruit will not come.
11 Tremble, you complacent women;
shudder, you daughters who feel secure!

31:9 *fire is in Zion . . . furnace is in Jerusalem:* Mount Zion in Jerusalem was the LORD's home on earth and the place where God was worshiped by Israel. Here, it is also described as the place of the LORD's judgment against Assyria. See the notes at 4:4 and 30:25-27.

32:2 *shelter . . . refuge . . . streams of water in the desert:* The same qualities used to describe these ideal rulers also are used to describe the LORD. See Isa 4:5,6; 25:4,5; 35:6,7; 41:17,18; 49:10; 2 Sam 22:2,3; Ps 121:5,6.

32:5 *the fool:* God's people have been suffering while fools and cruel people (enemies and unjust leaders) seemed to be prospering.

32:9-11 *You women . . . put sackcloth around your waists:* "You women" refers to the women of Jerusalem (see the note at 3:16-24). The poor grape harvest symbolizes the end of the wealthy and greedy lifestyle some of the women enjoyed. In times of sorrow or mourning, people wore sackcloth and pounded their chest. This message of judgment against the women of Jerusalem breaks up the message of promise which began in 32:1 and continues in 32:15.

32:1 Isa 1:16,17; 9:6; 11:2-5.

Strip off your clothes,
put sackcloth around your waists.
12 Beat your breasts for the pleasant fields,
for the fruitful vines
13 and for the land of my people,
a land overgrown with thorns and briers—
yes, mourn for all houses of merriment
and for this city of revelry.
14 The fortress will be abandoned,
the noisy city deserted;
citadel and watchtower will become a wasteland forever,
the delight of donkeys, a pasture for flocks,
15 till the Spirit is poured upon us from on high,
and the desert becomes a fertile field,
and the fertile field seems like a forest.
16 Justice will dwell in the desert
and righteousness live in the fertile field.
17 The fruit of righteousness will be peace;
the effect of righteousness will be quietness and
confidence forever.
18 My people will live in peaceful dwelling places,
in secure homes,
in undisturbed places of rest.
19 Though hail flattens the forest
and the city is leveled completely,
20 how blessed you will be,
sowing your seed by every stream,
and letting your cattle and donkeys range free.

Distress and Help

33 Woe to you, O destroyer,
you who have not been destroyed!
Woe to you, O traitor,
you who have not been betrayed!
When you stop destroying,
you will be destroyed;
when you stop betraying,
you will be betrayed.

2 O LORD, be gracious to us;
we long for you.
Be our strength every morning,
our salvation in time of distress.
3 At the thunder of your voice, the peoples flee;
when you rise up, the nations scatter.
4 Your plunder, O nations, is harvested as by young locusts;
like a swarm of locusts men pounce on it.

5 The LORD is exalted, for he dwells on high;
he will fill Zion with justice and righteousness.

The fruit of righteousness will be peace; the effect of righteousness will be quietness and confidence forever.
Isa 32:17

32:15-17 *Spirit . . . from on high . . . quietness and confidence forever:* See the note at 11:2. The time of judgment will be replaced with a time of peace, justice, and prosperity brought by God's Spirit. See also Isa 11:2-9; 44:3; 61:1; Ezek 39:29; Joel 2:28, 29; Acts 2:16-18.

33:1 *Woe to you:* This message of "woe" (see the note at 5:8, "woe to") is directed against one of Israel's enemies. It may be Assyria (10:5-12) or, more likely, Babylon (21:1-9).

33:4 *locusts:* These insects are similar to grasshoppers. They travel in swarms and cause great damage to crops. See the mini-article called "Locusts," p. 1708.

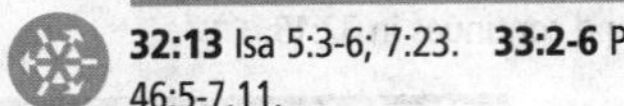

32:13 Isa 5:3-6; 7:23. **33:2-6** Ps 46:5-7,11.

[6] He will be the sure foundation for your times,
a rich store of salvation and wisdom and knowledge;
the fear of the LORD is the key to this treasure.[a]

[7] Look, their brave men cry aloud in the streets;
the envoys of peace weep bitterly.
[8] The highways are deserted,
no travelers are on the roads.
The treaty is broken,
its witnesses[b] are despised,
no one is respected.
[9] The land mourns[c] and wastes away,
Lebanon is ashamed and withers;
Sharon is like the Arabah,
and Bashan and Carmel drop their leaves.

[10] "Now will I arise," says the LORD.
"Now will I be exalted;
now will I be lifted up.
[11] You conceive chaff,
you give birth to straw;
your breath is a fire that consumes you.
[12] The peoples will be burned as if to lime;
like cut thornbushes they will be set ablaze."
[13] You who are far away, hear what I have done;
you who are near, acknowledge my power!
[14] The sinners in Zion are terrified;
trembling grips the godless:
"Who of us can dwell with the consuming fire?
Who of us can dwell with everlasting burning?"
[15] He who walks righteously
and speaks what is right,
who rejects gain from extortion
and keeps his hand from accepting bribes,
who stops his ears against plots of murder
and shuts his eyes against contemplating evil—
[16] this is the man who will dwell on the heights,
whose refuge will be the mountain fortress.
His bread will be supplied,
and water will not fail him.

[17] Your eyes will see the king in his beauty
and view a land that stretches afar.
[18] In your thoughts you will ponder the former terror:
"Where is that chief officer?
Where is the one who took the revenue?
Where is the officer in charge of the towers?"

[a] **6** Or *is a treasure from him* [b] **8** Dead Sea Scrolls; Masoretic Text / *the cities*
[c] **9** Or *dries up*

33:6 *wisdom and knowledge:* For the people of Israel, true wisdom is based on understanding and obeying God's law (see the note at 29:14).

33:7,8 *envoys of peace . . . treaty is broken:* This sorrowful prayer (lament) follows the prayer for help in 33:2-6. It describes the terrible conditions caused by the enemy invasion (33:1). The identity of the envoys of peace (33:7) is not certain. It could refer to those who met the Assyrian commander (Isa 36:2,3,21,22; 2 Kgs 18:13-37). The broken treaties could be military treaties, or they could be business agreements that had to be canceled because of war.

33:9 *Lebanon . . . Carmel:* These areas of Canaan were known for their beauty and rich pastures. See the note at 2:13-16. Mount Carmel was located near the Mediterranean Sea. It was just south of Phoenicia and just north of the fertile Sharon Valley. See the map on p. 2464.

33:10-13 *Now will I arise:* The LORD responds to Israel's prayer of sorrow, also called a lament. Israel's enemy (addressed as "You," see also 33:1) will be burned like thornbushes (10:16,17; 27:4; 30:27-30).

33:17 *the king in his beauty:* This may be the LORD himself, who lives with and rules the people on Zion (33:22). Or it may mean the king that the LORD will choose to rule in Zion.

33:18,19 *took the revenue . . . obscure speech:* This revenue (in the form of taxes) may actually be the huge amounts of silver and gold that Judah's King Hezekiah paid to Assyria's Sennacherib in 701 B.C. to keep him from attacking Jerusalem (2 Kgs 18:13-16). Or the payment of taxes may symbolize any enemy that terrified the people of Jerusalem and made them suffer (29:7, 8). When the "King" rules Zion, this taxation will end, and those who speak a strange language will no longer rule God's people.

33:20 *Zion . . . festivals:* See the notes at 1:8 and 29:1 (festivals).

33:21,23 *broad rivers . . . the sail is not spread:* Jerusalem did not have any broad rivers running by or through it. The image in 33:21 promises that Jerusalem will have plenty of "water" (spiritual blessings; see Ezek 47:1-12), and that it will be protected from the danger of attack by enemy ships. The identity of the "nation" that is compared to a ship in 33:23 is not certain, but it may be either Judah or Assyria.

34:4 *stars . . . scroll:* The stars and moon were worshiped as gods by some of Israel's neighbors (see the note at 24:21-23). Messages, including the Scriptures, were written on scrolls made of papyrus or thin leather. See the mini-article called "Scrolls," p. 1491. See also Matt 24:29; Mark 13:25; Luke 21:26; Rev 6:13,14.

33:20 Isa 22:23. **33:23,24** Isa 30:26; 35:5,6; 57:15. **34:2** Isa 26:21.

19 You will see those arrogant people no more,
those people of an obscure speech,
with their strange, incomprehensible tongue.

20 Look upon Zion, the city of our festivals;
your eyes will see Jerusalem,
a peaceful abode, a tent that will not be moved;
its stakes will never be pulled up,
nor any of its ropes broken.
21 There the LORD will be our Mighty One.
It will be like a place of broad rivers and streams.
No galley with oars will ride them,
no mighty ship will sail them.
22 For the LORD is our judge,
the LORD is our lawgiver,
the LORD is our king;
it is he who will save us.

23 Your rigging hangs loose:
The mast is not held secure,
the sail is not spread.
Then an abundance of spoils will be divided
and even the lame will carry off plunder.
24 No one living in Zion will say, "I am ill";
and the sins of those who dwell there will be forgiven.

VISIONS OF JUDGMENT AND JOY

Chapters 34 and 35 contain messages that probably refer to the same period as Isaiah 56–66, that is, after the exile (see the Introduction to Isaiah). They also have elements that are similar to ideas found in Isaiah 24–27. The nations are judged, and God's people return to Zion.

Judgment Against the Nations

34 Come near, you nations, and listen;
pay attention, you peoples!
Let the earth hear, and all that is in it,
the world, and all that comes out of it!
2 The LORD is angry with all nations;
his wrath is upon all their armies.
He will totally destroy[a] them,
he will give them over to slaughter.
3 Their slain will be thrown out,
their dead bodies will send up a stench;
the mountains will be soaked with their blood.
4 All the stars of the heavens will be dissolved

[a]2 The Hebrew term refers to the irrevocable giving over of things or persons to the LORD, often by totally destroying them; also in verse 5.

and the sky rolled up like a scroll;
all the starry host will fall
like withered leaves from the vine,
like shriveled figs from the fig tree.

5 My sword has drunk its fill in the heavens;
see, it descends in judgment on Edom,
the people I have totally destroyed.
6 The sword of the LORD is bathed in blood,
it is covered with fat—
the blood of lambs and goats,
fat from the kidneys of rams.
For the LORD has a sacrifice in Bozrah
and a great slaughter in Edom.
7 And the wild oxen will fall with them,
the bull calves and the great bulls.
Their land will be drenched with blood,
and the dust will be soaked with fat.

8 For the LORD has a day of vengeance,
a year of retribution, to uphold Zion's cause.
9 Edom's streams will be turned into pitch,
her dust into burning sulfur;
her land will become blazing pitch!
10 It will not be quenched night and day;
its smoke will rise forever.
From generation to generation it will lie desolate;
no one will ever pass through it again.
11 The desert owl[a] and screech owl[a] will possess it;
the great owl[a] and the raven will nest there.
God will stretch out over Edom
the measuring line of chaos
and the plumb line of desolation.
12 Her nobles will have nothing there to be called a kingdom,
all her princes will vanish away.
13 Thorns will overrun her citadels,
nettles and brambles her strongholds.
She will become a haunt for jackals,
a home for owls.
14 Desert creatures will meet with hyenas,
and wild goats will bleat to each other;
there the night creatures will also repose
and find for themselves places of rest.
15 The owl will nest there and lay eggs,
she will hatch them, and care for her young under the
shadow of her wings;

[a]**11** The precise identification of these birds is uncertain.

34:5 *Edom . . . destroyed:* The Edomites were descendants of Esau, Jacob's brother (Gen 36:1,9-14, 40-43). The nation of Edom is usually described in the Bible as an enemy of Israel (Num 24:18; 1 Sam 14:47,48; 2 Sam 8:13,14). See the map on p. 2467.

34:6 *blood . . . fat:* The LORD's blood-covered sword is used to make a holy sacrifice of the Edomites in Bozrah. They are compared to the lambs and goats that were sacrificed by Israel's priests. The fat, which was considered the best part of the sacrificed animal, was to be burned as an offering to the LORD (Lev 3:6-17).

34:6 *Bozrah:* This main city of Edom was located about twenty-five miles south of the Dead Sea. Its name means "grape gathering" (Isa 63:1-13). See also Jer 49:13,22 and the map on p. 2465.

34:8-10 *Zion's cause . . . Edom's streams . . . smoke will rise:* See the note at 1:8. In 34:8, Zion means God's people in Judah and Jerusalem. See also 61:2; 63:3,4. The LORD will use burning pitch and sulfur to destroy Edom in the same way the ancient cities of Sodom and Gomorrah were destroyed (Gen 19:24-28). See also 13:19.

34:5-17 Isa 63:1-16; Jer 49:7-22; Ezek 25:12-14; 35:1-15; Amos 1:11,12; Obad 1-14; Mal 1:2-5. **34:10** Rev 14:11; 19:3. **34:11-15** Isa 13:21,22; Zeph 2:13-15.

there also the falcons will gather,
each with its mate.

16 Look in the scroll of the LORD and read:

None of these will be missing,
not one will lack her mate.
For it is his mouth that has given the order,
and his Spirit will gather them together.
17 He allots their portions;
his hand distributes them by measure.
They will possess it forever
and dwell there from generation to generation.

Joy of the Redeemed

35 The desert and the parched land will be glad;
the wilderness will rejoice and blossom.
Like the crocus, 2 it will burst into bloom;
it will rejoice greatly and shout for joy.
The glory of Lebanon will be given to it,
the splendor of Carmel and Sharon;
they will see the glory of the LORD,
the splendor of our God.

3 Strengthen the feeble hands,
steady the knees that give way;
4 say to those with fearful hearts,
"Be strong, do not fear;
your God will come,
he will come with vengeance;
with divine retribution
he will come to save you."

5 Then will the eyes of the blind be opened
and the ears of the deaf unstopped.
6 Then will the lame leap like a deer,
and the mute tongue shout for joy.
Water will gush forth in the wilderness
and streams in the desert.
7 The burning sand will become a pool,
the thirsty ground bubbling springs.
In the haunts where jackals once lay,
grass and reeds and papyrus will grow.

8 And a highway will be there;
it will be called the Way of Holiness.
The unclean will not journey on it;
it will be for those who walk in that Way;
wicked fools will not go about on it.[a]

[a]8 Or / *the simple will not stray from it*

34:16 *the scroll of the LORD:* This book is unknown. It may refer to a scroll that included the judgment against Babylon (13:19-22). Or it may refer to a larger collection of prophetic books that include warning messages against Edom. See, for instance, Obad 1-14.

34:16,17 *None of these will be missing, not one will lack her mate:* Meaning the wild animals will inherit the land of Edom forever.

35:1 *desert and the parched land:* The land of God's people is pictured as blooming and rejoicing, because the LORD will bring his people back from exile to live in Zion (35:10). This image of a blooming desert is also found in parts of Isaiah 40–55; see, for example, 41:18-20; 43:19,20.

35:2 *Lebanon . . . Carmel:* See the note at 33:9.

35:5,6 *blind . . . ears . . . mute tongue:* This may refer to the healing of physical disabilities, or to God's opening of people's eyes, ears, and hearts to spiritual understanding (29:18; 32:3; 42:16, 18-20). See also Matt 11:5; Luke 7:22.

35:6,7 *Water . . . bubbling springs:* Water was the most precious natural resource in the dry lands where God's people lived. The image of a desert turning into wetland symbolizes abundance (41:17-19; Num 20:2-11).

35:8 *the Way of Holiness:* See also 11:16 and 40:3-5, which tell of a path or road that the LORD will make for his people to return to Judah following their time in exile. Here, the road is not just a path, but a "Way of Holiness." Only the people the LORD has saved can take this highway, which leads to Zion (35:10). For more about those who "walk in that Way," see the mini-article called "Redeemer (Redemption)," p. 995.

35:3,4 Josh 1:6-9; Isa 40:9,10; 41:10-14; 43:1-7; 44:1,2; 54:4,5; Heb 12:12.

9 No lion will be there,
nor will any ferocious beast get up on it;
they will not be found there.
But only the redeemed will walk there,
10 and the ransomed of the LORD will return.
They will enter Zion with singing;
everlasting joy will crown their heads.
Gladness and joy will overtake them,
and sorrow and sighing will flee away.

IN THE DAYS OF KING HEZEKIAH

Isaiah 36–39 includes much of the same material found in 2 Kings 18:13—20:19. This section was likely inserted into ISAIAH from 2 KINGS at a later date. It serves as a bridge between chapters 1–35, which focus primarily on the time of the Assyrian threat against Israel and Judah, and chapters 40–55, which focus on the period near the end of Israel's exile in Babylon. Only Hezekiah's prayer in 38:9-20 is new material not found in 2 KINGS.

Sennacherib Threatens Jerusalem

36 In the fourteenth year of King Hezekiah's reign, Sennacherib
king of Assyria attacked all the fortified cities of Judah and captured them. 2 Then the king of Assyria sent his field commander
with a large army from Lachish to King Hezekiah at Jerusalem.
When the commander stopped at the aqueduct of the Upper Pool,
on the road to the Washerman's Field, 3 Eliakim son of Hilkiah the
palace administrator, Shebna the secretary, and Joah son of Asaph
the recorder went out to him.

4 The field commander said to them, "Tell Hezekiah,

" 'This is what the great king, the king of Assyria, says:
On what are you basing this confidence of yours? 5 You say you
have strategy and military strength—but you speak only
empty words. On whom are you depending, that you rebel
against me? 6 Look now, you are depending on Egypt, that
splintered reed of a staff, which pierces a man's hand and
wounds him if he leans on it! Such is Pharaoh king of Egypt
to all who depend on him. 7 And if you say to me, "We are
depending on the LORD our God"—isn't he the one whose
high places and altars Hezekiah removed, saying to Judah and
Jerusalem, "You must worship before this altar"?

8 " 'Come now, make a bargain with my master, the king
of Assyria: I will give you two thousand horses—if you can put
riders on them! 9 How then can you repulse one officer of the
least of my master's officials, even though you are depending on
Egypt for chariots and horsemen? 10 Furthermore, have I come
to attack and destroy this land without the LORD? The LORD
himself told me to march against this country and destroy it.' "

35:10 *Zion:* See the note at 1:8.

36:1 *fourteenth year of King Hezekiah's reign, Sennacherib:* Ancient Assyrian records show that Sennacherib invaded Judah in 705 B.C. His army camped outside of Jerusalem in 701 B.C. This would mean Hezekiah became Judah's king about 715-716 B.C. However, other passages list the beginning of his reign as 729 B.C., or the third year of Hoshea's reign (see 2 Kgs 18:1). See also the map on p. 1311.

36:1,2 *fortified cities . . . Lachish:* Many towns had walls built around them for protection. According to Assyrian records, there were forty-six walled cities in Judah. Lachish, a fortress city in Judea, was located southwest of Jerusalem on the way to Gaza (see the map on p. 2464).

36:2 *aqueduct of the Upper Pool:* See the note at 7:3.

36:3 *Eliakim . . . Shebna . . . Joah:* Hezekiah sent these officials to meet the Assyrian commander. See the note at 22:15-21.

36:4-9 *king of Assyria . . . depending on Egypt:* The message from Sennacherib makes fun of Hezekiah's treaty with Egypt (see the notes at 20:1-3 and 30:1,2). Though Egypt had a strong army, the Assyrian army had the largest and most powerful chariot and cavalry forces at this time.

36:7 *high places and altars Hezekiah removed:* Actually, Hezekiah had torn down the places where idols were worshiped, and had told the people to worship the LORD at the temple in Jerusalem (2 Kgs 18:3-6; 2 Chr 29:3—31:21). In this verse, the Assyrian leader is confused and thinks all the places Hezekiah tore down were also places where the LORD was supposed to be worshiped (see 10:10, 11).

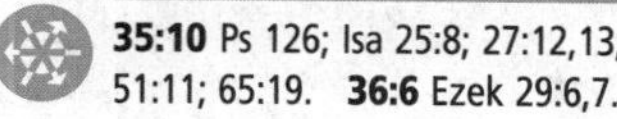

35:10 Ps 126; Isa 25:8; 27:12,13; 51:11; 65:19. **36:6** Ezek 29:6,7.

36:11 *Eliakim . . . Joah:* See the note at 22:15-21.

36:11 *Aramaic . . . Hebrew:* Aramaic was spoken by government officials and merchants throughout the region at this time. Hebrew, however, was the language spoken in Judah. Most of the people in Judah did not understand Aramaic.

36:13-17 *called out in Hebrew . . . eat from his own vine and fig tree:* The Assyrian commander ignored Hezekiah's officials (36:11) and yelled out in Hebrew, so all the people of Jerusalem could understand and be convinced to surrender. He promised that Sennacherib would let the people keep their land and water for a time before they were sent away to live in other lands held by the Assyrians. The Assyrian policy was to remove the peoples they defeated from their native lands and make them resettle in other places.

36:19 *Hamath . . . Samaria:* See the note at 10:9-12. Sepharvaim may be the "Sibraim" mentioned in Ezekiel 47:16. It was located in northern Aram. People who lived in Sepharvaim were sent to live in Israel, where they continued to worship their gods (2 Kgs 17:24-26,29-31).

Sennacherib's Siege of Lachish, Assyrian wall-relief, seventh century B.C. When Hezekiah was king of Judah, the Assyrians conquered the northern kingdom (Israel) and then invaded Judah in the south, capturing every walled city except Jerusalem. Lachish, one of Judah's strongholds, fell to Sennacherib's army around 701 B.C. The soldiers plundered the city, burned it to the ground, and took the people away into captivity.

[11]Then Eliakim, Shebna and Joah said to the field commander, "Please speak to your servants in Aramaic, since we
understand it. Don't speak to us in Hebrew in the hearing of the
people on the wall."
[12]But the commander replied, "Was it only to your master
and you that my master sent me to say these things, and not to the
men sitting on the wall—who, like you, will have to eat their own
filth and drink their own urine?"
[13]Then the commander stood and called out in Hebrew,
"Hear the words of the great king, the king of Assyria! [14]This is
what the king says: Do not let Hezekiah deceive you. He cannot
deliver you! [15]Do not let Hezekiah persuade you to trust in the
LORD when he says, 'The LORD will surely deliver us; this city will
not be given into the hand of the king of Assyria.'
[16]"Do not listen to Hezekiah. This is what the king of Assyria
says: Make peace with me and come out to me. Then every one of
you will eat from his own vine and fig tree and drink water from
his own cistern, [17]until I come and take you to a land like your
own—a land of grain and new wine, a land of bread and vineyards.
[18]"Do not let Hezekiah mislead you when he says, 'The LORD
will deliver us.' Has the god of any nation ever delivered his land
from the hand of the king of Assyria? [19]Where are the gods of
Hamath and Arpad? Where are the gods of Sepharvaim? Have they
rescued Samaria from my hand? [20]Who of all the gods of these
countries has been able to save his land from me? How then can
the LORD deliver Jerusalem from my hand?"

[21]But the people remained silent and said nothing in reply,
because the king had commanded, "Do not answer him."
[22]Then Eliakim son of Hilkiah the palace administrator,
Shebna the secretary, and Joah son of Asaph the recorder went to
Hezekiah, with their clothes torn, and told him what the field
commander had said.

Jerusalem's Deliverance Foretold

37 When King Hezekiah heard this, he tore his clothes and put
on sackcloth and went into the temple of the LORD. [2]He sent Eliakim
the palace administrator, Shebna the secretary, and the leading
priests, all wearing sackcloth, to the prophet Isaiah son of Amoz.
[3]They told him, "This is what Hezekiah says: This day is a day of distress and rebuke and disgrace, as when children come to the point of
birth and there is no strength to deliver them. [4]It may be that the
LORD your God will hear the words of the field commander, whom
his master, the king of Assyria, has sent to ridicule the living God,
and that he will rebuke him for the words the LORD your God has
heard. Therefore pray for the remnant that still survives."
[5]When King Hezekiah's officials came to Isaiah, [6]Isaiah said
to them, "Tell your master, 'This is what the LORD says: Do not be
afraid of what you have heard—those words with which the
underlings of the king of Assyria have blasphemed me. [7]Listen! I
am going to put a spirit in him so that when he hears a certain
report, he will return to his own country, and there I will have him
cut down with the sword.' "
[8]When the field commander heard that the king of Assyria
had left Lachish, he withdrew and found the king fighting against
Libnah.
[9]Now Sennacherib received a report that Tirhakah, the
Cushite[a] king ⌞of Egypt⌟, was marching out to fight against him.
When he heard it, he sent messengers to Hezekiah with this word:
[10]"Say to Hezekiah king of Judah: Do not let the god you depend
on deceive you when he says, 'Jerusalem will not be handed over to
the king of Assyria.' [11]Surely you have heard what the kings of
Assyria have done to all the countries, destroying them completely.
And will you be delivered? [12]Did the gods of the nations that were
destroyed by my forefathers deliver them—the gods of Gozan,
Haran, Rezeph and the people of Eden who were in Tel Assar?
[13]Where is the king of Hamath, the king of Arpad, the king of the
city of Sepharvaim, or of Hena or Ivvah?"

Hezekiah's Prayer

[14]Hezekiah received the letter from the messengers and read
it. Then he went up to the temple of the LORD and spread it out

a9 That is, from the upper Nile region

36:21—37:1 *clothes torn . . . sackcloth:* Tearing one's clothes and wearing sackcloth were ways people showed sadness or sorrow.

37:1 *temple:* This refers to the temple in Jerusalem, where Israel's priests offered sacrifices to the LORD.

37:2,3 *Eliakim . . . Isaiah:* See the note at 22:15-21. By sending his palace ministers to Isaiah, Hezekiah recognizes Isaiah as the LORD's prophet who speaks God's word.

37:7-9 *cut down with the sword:* Sennacherib's sons stabbed him to death (37:38) in 682 B.C., nearly twenty years after Sennacherib's siege of Jerusalem.

37:8,9 *Lachish . . . Libnah:* See the note at 36:1,2. The exact location of Libnah is not known.

37:11-13 *Gozan . . . Ivvah:* Gozan was in northern Mesopotamia (2 Kgs 17:6). Israel's ancestor Abraham lived at Haran west of Gozan on the Balikh River (Gen 11:26-32). Rezeph was located between Haran and the Euphrates River. Tel Assar was a city in the territory of Eden (modern Bit-adini) located between the Euphrates and Balikh rivers. See the maps on pp. 2462 and 2468. See the notes at 10:9-12 (Hamath, Arpad) and 36:19 (Sepharvaim). The locations of Hena and Ivvah are not known.

37:16 *Lord Almighty, God of Israel:* See the notes on p. 1289 (Lord) and at 5:18,19.

37:16 *cherubim:* These cherubim sat on top of the ark of the covenant in the Most Holy Place in the temple (see the note at 6:1,2). See also 40:26-28; 42:5; 45:12.

37:19 *thrown their gods into the fire:* See 36:20 and 37:12. The Assyrians destroyed the wood and metal idols worshiped by the peoples they defeated. Hezekiah asks the Lord to protect Jerusalem, to show that Israel's God is more powerful than the gods of the other nations.

37:21 *Sennacherib:* See the notes at 36:1 and 37:7-9.

37:24 *heaped insults on the Lord:* This refers to the message Sennacherib's commander shouted to the people outside the walls of Jerusalem (36:12-20).

37:26 *In days of old I planned it:* Though Sennacherib and other Assyrian leaders took credit for their many victories, it was Israel's Lord God who allowed them to happen (see also 10:5-14; 14:24-27).

37:16 Exod 25:22.

before the Lord. 15 And Hezekiah prayed to the Lord: 16 "O Lord
Almighty, God of Israel, enthroned between the cherubim, you
alone are God over all the kingdoms of the earth. You have made
heaven and earth. 17 Give ear, O Lord, and hear; open your eyes,
O Lord, and see; listen to all the words Sennacherib has sent to
insult the living God.

18 "It is true, O Lord, that the Assyrian kings have laid waste
all these peoples and their lands. 19 They have thrown their gods
into the fire and destroyed them, for they were not gods but only
wood and stone, fashioned by human hands. 20 Now, O Lord our
God, deliver us from his hand, so that all kingdoms on earth may
know that you alone, O Lord, are God.[a]"

Sennacherib's Fall

21 Then Isaiah son of Amoz sent a message to Hezekiah: "This
is what the Lord, the God of Israel, says: Because you have prayed
to me concerning Sennacherib king of Assyria, 22 this is the word
the Lord has spoken against him:

"The Virgin Daughter of Zion
  despises and mocks you.
The Daughter of Jerusalem
  tosses her head as you flee.
23 Who is it you have insulted and blasphemed?
  Against whom have you raised your voice
and lifted your eyes in pride?
  Against the Holy One of Israel!
24 By your messengers
  you have heaped insults on the Lord.
And you have said,
  'With my many chariots
I have ascended the heights of the mountains,
  the utmost heights of Lebanon.
I have cut down its tallest cedars,
  the choicest of its pines.
I have reached its remotest heights,
  the finest of its forests.
25 I have dug wells in foreign lands[b]
  and drunk the water there.
With the soles of my feet
  I have dried up all the streams of Egypt.'

26 "Have you not heard?
  Long ago I ordained it.
In days of old I planned it;

[a]20 Dead Sea Scrolls (see also 2 Kings 19:19); Masoretic Text *alone are the Lord*
[b]25 Dead Sea Scrolls (see also 2 Kings 19:24); Masoretic Text does not have *in foreign lands.*

now I have brought it to pass,
that you have turned fortified cities
into piles of stone.
27 Their people, drained of power,
are dismayed and put to shame.
They are like plants in the field,
like tender green shoots,
like grass sprouting on the roof,
scorched[a] before it grows up.

28 "But I know where you stay
and when you come and go
and how you rage against me.
29 Because you rage against me
and because your insolence has reached my ears,
I will put my hook in your nose
and my bit in your mouth,
and I will make you return
by the way you came.

30 "This will be the sign for you, O Hezekiah:

"This year you will eat what grows by itself,
and the second year what springs from that.
But in the third year sow and reap,
plant vineyards and eat their fruit.
31 Once more a remnant of the house of Judah
will take root below and bear fruit above.
32 For out of Jerusalem will come a remnant,
and out of Mount Zion a band of survivors.
The zeal of the LORD Almighty
will accomplish this.

33 "Therefore this is what the LORD says concerning the king of Assyria:

"He will not enter this city
or shoot an arrow here.
He will not come before it with shield
or build a siege ramp against it.
34 By the way that he came he will return;
he will not enter this city,"
declares the LORD.
35 "I will defend this city and save it,
for my sake and for the sake of David my servant!"

36 Then the angel of the LORD went out and put to death a
hundred and eighty-five thousand men in the Assyrian camp.

[a]27 Some manuscripts of the Masoretic Text, Dead Sea Scrolls and some Septuagint manuscripts (see also 2 Kings 19:26); most manuscripts of the Masoretic Text *roof / and terraced fields*

The LORD says, *"Once more a remnant of the house of Judah will take root below and bear fruit above."* Isa 37:31

37:27 *grass sprouting on the roof:* Many houses had flat roofs made of packed earth. Grass sometimes grew on the roof, but would die quickly because of the sun and hot winds.

37:29 *hook . . . bit:* See the note at 30:28. The Assyrians sometimes used metal hooks, rings, and bits to control their human prisoners, so now the LORD will treat Sennacherib the same way.

37:30 *This year . . . third year:* The Assyrian army controlled the farm land around Jerusalem for about three years, probably meaning 703-701 B.C. This caused hunger in Jerusalem.

37:35 *for the sake of David my servant:* See the note at 7:13.

37:36 *angel of the LORD . . . put to death:* The Hebrew word for "angel" also means "messenger." In the Bible, angels act both as messengers and servants of God. Sometimes they serve God's purpose by bringing plagues (Exod 12:23; 2 Sam 24:15-17). See also the mini-article called "Angels," p. 88. The death of the Assyrian soldiers relates to Isaiah's earlier prophecies (10:15-17; 30:27-32; 31:8).

37:33,34 Isa 37:38,39.

Babylon. Babylon, the capital of Babylonia, was famous for its size, beauty, and splendid architecture. An early Babylonian king, Hammurabi (ruled from 1792 to 1750 B.C.) was famous for his judgments and the laws he enacted. Some of these were carved onto a seven-foot pillar that survives to this day. A later king, Nebuchadnezzar, conquered Judah and led its citizens into exile. He built the Hanging Gardens, one of the "Seven Wonders" of the ancient world and refortified the seventeen miles of double-walls that surrounded the city. A half-mile long Processional Way led to the largest of eight gates, the Ishtar Gate, named for the temple behind it. Ishtar, a Babylonian goddess, was symbolized by the lion; 120 lions and 575 dragons decorated the glazed brick walls of the Processional Way. Nebuchadnezzar also rebuilt the terraced tower (called a ziggurat) in honor of the Babylonian god, Marduk.

37:37,38 *Sennacherib . . . Nisroch . . . sons:* In 701 B.C., after the disaster in Judah, Sennacherib and his army returned to Assyria. There, he continued to rule in the capital city of Nineveh until 682 B.C. when his own sons killed him. The murdering sons escaped to Ararat north of Assyria, so another son, Esarhaddon, became king. He ruled Assyria from 681 to 669 B.C. The identity and significance of the god Nisroch is uncertain.

When the people got up the next morning—there were all the
dead bodies! [37]So Sennacherib king of Assyria broke camp and
withdrew. He returned to Nineveh and stayed there.
[38]One day, while he was worshiping in the temple of his god
Nisroch, his sons Adrammelech and Sharezer cut him down with
the sword, and they escaped to the land of Ararat. And Esarhaddon his son succeeded him as king.

Hezekiah's Illness

38 In those days Hezekiah became ill and was at the point of
death. The prophet Isaiah son of Amoz went to him and said,
"This is what the LORD says: Put your house in order, because you
are going to die; you will not recover."
[2]Hezekiah turned his face to the wall and prayed to the
LORD, [3]"Remember, O LORD, how I have walked before you faith-

fully and with wholehearted devotion and have done what is good
in your eyes." And Hezekiah wept bitterly.
4 Then the word of the LORD came to Isaiah: 5 "Go and tell
Hezekiah, 'This is what the LORD, the God of your father David,
says: I have heard your prayer and seen your tears; I will add fifteen
years to your life. 6 And I will deliver you and this city from the
hand of the king of Assyria. I will defend this city.
7 " 'This is the LORD's sign to you that the LORD will do what

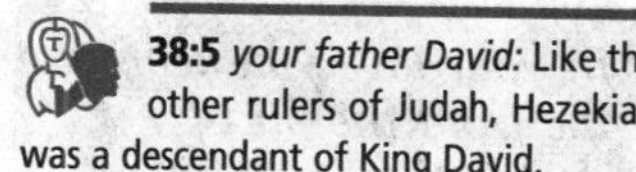

38:5 *your father David:* Like the other rulers of Judah, Hezekiah was a descendant of King David.

BABYLON

In the Bible, Babylon is the name for both the Mesopotamian region known as Babylonia and for its capital city. In the ancient language of Akkadian, Babylon means "the gate of the god." People lived in the region of Babylonia as early as 5000 B.C. However, the first written evidence of Babylon comes from around 2200 B.C.

Shortly after 2000 B.C. the Amorite people began to rule Babylon. The most famous Amorite king was Hammurabi (1792-1750 B.C.). He was a strong ruler who brought unity to the many small states in Babylonia. Hammurabi is most famous for a Law Code that still carries his name. While it resembles Hebrew law in form, style, and general content, there are also marked differences.

Babylon was famous in the ancient world as a center for writing and scholarly study. It was known as a place where ancient astrologers studied the stars and the movement of the planets, and made predictions about the future (Isa 47:13).

During the time of Israel's King Solomon (970-931 B.C.), Babylon was not a powerful military threat and carried on trade with countries to its west, including Egypt and Israel. Around 750 B.C. Babylon began to rise in fame and influence once again, beginning with the reign of King Nabonassar (747-734 B.C.). At this time, the strong Assyrian kingdom brought Babylon under its control, though certain local Babylonian leaders rebelled against the Assyrians (see the note at Isa 39:1). When Hezekiah ruled Judah, the Babylonian King Merodach-Baladan sent messengers to Jerusalem to ask for help. King Hezekiah welcomed these messengers and showed them the treasures of Israel's temple and palace. The prophet Isaiah then warned Hezekiah that someday Babylon would invade Jerusalem and send its people into exile (Isa 39:1-7).

The Babylonian King Nebuchadnezzar (also known as Nebuchadrezzar) came to power in 605 B.C. Under Nebuchadnezzar, the city of Babylon became a beautiful city. It had many impressive temples, a wide street for grand parades, and world-famous hanging gardens. He eventually led the invasion of Judah that Isaiah announced. The Babylonians destroyed Jerusalem and its temple, stole its treasures, and took many of its people into exile in Babylon (2 Kgs 24:10—25:21).

The final Babylonian king was Nabonidus (555-539 B.C.). His poor leadership and long periods of absence left the country weakened. In 539 B.C. the Persian ruler, Cyrus, defeated Babylon. He gave permission to the Israelite people living in Babylon to return home to Judah.

The Old Testament prophets describe the people's exile in Babylon as a punishment for sinning against the LORD (Isa 47:5, 6; Jer 13:15-27; 25:1-11). In the New Testament, Babylon is the name given to the evil kingdom and city that was opposed to God and God's people (Rev 14:8; 16:19; 17.5; 18:2, 10, 21). But Babylon was probably just a code name for Rome and the Roman empire (see 1 Pet 5:13 and the Introduction to REVELATION on p. 2403).

In your love you kept me from the pit of destruction; you have put all my sins behind your back.
Isa 38:17

38:8 *stairway of Ahaz:* See the note at 7:1-3. This may refer to a stairway in the palace courtyard, or perhaps some kind of sundial that was used to tell time according to the shadows made by the sun. See also Josh 10:12,13.

38:9 *A writing of Hezekiah:* Hezekiah's song does not appear in 2 KINGS or 2 CHRONICLES. It is similar to a number of psalms that give thanks for God's saving help (see Ps 18; 22; 30; 41).

38:10 *gates of death:* See the note at 5:14.

38:12 *the loom:* Threads of cloth were put on a loom and woven into clothing, blankets, curtains, or other items.

38:17,18 *pit of destruction . . . the grave:* See the note at 5:14.

38:13 Job 7:1-6; Ps 6:2; 32:3,4.

he has promised: [8]I will make the shadow cast by the sun go back
the ten steps it has gone down on the stairway of Ahaz.' " So the
sunlight went back the ten steps it had gone down.

[9]A writing of Hezekiah king of Judah after his illness and
recovery:

[10]I said, "In the prime of my life
must I go through the gates of death[a]
and be robbed of the rest of my years?"
[11]I said, "I will not again see the LORD,
the LORD, in the land of the living;
no longer will I look on mankind,
or be with those who now dwell in this world.[b]
[12]Like a shepherd's tent my house
has been pulled down and taken from me.
Like a weaver I have rolled up my life,
and he has cut me off from the loom;
day and night you made an end of me.
[13]I waited patiently till dawn,
but like a lion he broke all my bones;
day and night you made an end of me.
[14]I cried like a swift or thrush,
I moaned like a mourning dove.
My eyes grew weak as I looked to the heavens.
I am troubled; O Lord, come to my aid!"

[15]But what can I say?
He has spoken to me, and he himself has done this.
I will walk humbly all my years
because of this anguish of my soul.
[16]Lord, by such things men live;
and my spirit finds life in them too.
You restored me to health
and let me live.
[17]Surely it was for my benefit
that I suffered such anguish.
In your love you kept me
from the pit of destruction;
you have put all my sins
behind your back.
[18]For the grave[a] cannot praise you,
death cannot sing your praise;
those who go down to the pit
cannot hope for your faithfulness.
[19]The living, the living—they praise you,
as I am doing today;

[a]10,18 Hebrew *Sheol* [b]11 A few Hebrew manuscripts; most Hebrew manuscripts *in the place of cessation*

fathers tell their children
about your faithfulness.

20 The LORD will save me,
and we will sing with stringed instruments
all the days of our lives
in the temple of the LORD.

21 Isaiah had said, "Prepare a poultice of figs and apply it to
the boil, and he will recover."
22 Hezekiah had asked, "What will be the sign that I will go
up to the temple of the LORD?"

Envoys From Babylon

39 At that time Merodach-Baladan son of Baladan king of
Babylon sent Hezekiah letters and a gift, because he had heard of
his illness and recovery. 2 Hezekiah received the envoys gladly and
showed them what was in his storehouses—the silver, the gold, the
spices, the fine oil, his entire armory and everything found among
his treasures. There was nothing in his palace or in all his kingdom
that Hezekiah did not show them.
3 Then Isaiah the prophet went to King Hezekiah and asked,
"What did those men say, and where did they come from?"
"From a distant land," Hezekiah replied. "They came to me
from Babylon."
4 The prophet asked, "What did they see in your palace?"
"They saw everything in my palace," Hezekiah said. "There is
nothing among my treasures that I did not show them."

38:20 *stringed instruments . . . temple of the LORD:* The instruments probably refer to small hand-held harps. See also Ps 33:1-3; 149:3; 150. For "temple," see the note at 2:2.

38:21 *poultice of figs:* Figs were a common source of food. Here, they also are used to heal a wound. See the illustration on p. 1863.

39:1 *Merodach-Baladan . . . king of Babylon:* Merodach was originally the leader of the Chaldean Bit-Yakin clan on the east coast of the Persian Gulf. He led revolts against the Assyrians and for a time declared himself king of Babylon during the rule of Sargon II of Assyria (721-710 B.C.), and again later for a brief time during the rule of Sennacherib (703 B.C.). Here Isaiah reports that Merodach sent messengers to Hezekiah (39:1) to ask for Judah's help in defending Babylon against Assyria.

39:2 *silver . . . treasures:* It is not clear why Hezekiah showed the Babylonian messengers these treasures. Perhaps he saw the Babylonians as a possible ally against the Assyrians who were threatening Jerusalem.

QUESTIONS ABOUT ISAIAH 24:1—39:8

1. Name two or three reasons why Isaiah 24–27 is sometimes referred to as "apocalyptic."
2. What will happen to Israel's enemies? (25:2,3,10-12; 26:10-14)
3. What must the people of Israel do to receive complete forgiveness from their sin and guilt? (27:9; 30:15)
4. Why were Samaria and Jerusalem to be punished? (28, 29)
5. Why did Judah's leaders apparently want to make a treaty with Egypt? Why does Isaiah warn against this? (30:1-5; 31:1-5). What will happen if the people trust in the LORD? (30:15-33; 31:6—32:8)
6. How are people today like the rich women of Jerusalem in 32:9-13? Why may it seem to be easier to trust wealth, weapons, or political systems rather than to trust God?
7. Find a passage in chapters 24–39 that shows the LORD's concern for the poor or physically disabled. What does that passage say to us today?
8. Describe the situation in Judah when Sennacherib of Assyria invaded (36,37). Describe what role each of the following played: Sennacherib's commander, Hezekiah, Isaiah, the LORD. What eventually happened to Sennacherib?
9. Why did the Babylonians send messengers to see Hezekiah at this time? Why did Hezekiah show them his palace treasures and weapons? Did Isaiah approve or disapprove? Why?

39:5 *LORD Almighty:* See the note on p. 1289 (LORD).

39:6,7 *carried off to Babylon:* Isaiah likely refers to the events that were to occur about one hundred years later. See also the mini-article called "Exile," p. 1541.

39:8 *word of the LORD you have spoken is good:* Hezekiah's response seems shortsighted and unfeeling. But taken positively, Hezekiah's response shows that he accepts the disturbing prophecy about Judah's future while hoping for peace in his lifetime.

40:2 *Speak tenderly to Jerusalem . . . her sin has been paid for:* In 587 B.C., Babylon's armies completed their destruction of Jerusalem. In addition to stealing the treasures of the royal palace and temple, many of the people were forced to leave Judah and live in exile in Babylon (here called "her hard service"). The exile was seen as Judah's punishment for not remaining faithful to the LORD, but Judah's punishment ended when Babylon was defeated (see Jer 29:10-14). For more, see the mini-article called "Exile," p. 1541.

39:7 2 Kgs 24:10-16; 2 Chr 36:10; Dan 1:1-7.

5 Then Isaiah said to Hezekiah, "Hear the word of the LORD
Almighty: 6 The time will surely come when everything in your
palace, and all that your fathers have stored up until this day, will
be carried off to Babylon. Nothing will be left, says the LORD. 7 And
some of your descendants, your own flesh and blood who will be
born to you, will be taken away, and they will become eunuchs in
the palace of the king of Babylon."

8 "The word of the LORD you have spoken is good," Hezekiah
replied. For he thought, "There will be peace and security in my
lifetime."

ISAIAH, Part 2:
Good News for God's People in Exile

In chapters 40–55, the prophet delivers a message of comfort and hope to God's people who were at that time living in exile in Babylon. The LORD would use King Cyrus of Persia to defeat the Babylonians (41:2-4). Cyrus would allow the people of Judah to return home to rebuild Jerusalem and its temple (44:28; 45:13). This section also includes the passages known as the Servant Songs (42:1-4; 49:1-6; 50:4-9; 52:13—53:12).

BABYLON IS DEFEATED AND GOD'S PEOPLE ARE SET FREE

Chapters 40–48 announce the good news that the LORD is going to use the Persian leader Cyrus to defeat Babylon and allow the Israelite people to return home. The LORD created and chose Israel, and now he will deliver them from their enemies. This will show the nations that the LORD is more powerful than their gods.

Comfort for God's People

40 Comfort, comfort my people,
  says your God.
2 Speak tenderly to Jerusalem,
  and proclaim to her
that her hard service has been completed,
  that her sin has been paid for,
that she has received from the LORD's hand
  double for all her sins.

3 A voice of one calling:
"In the desert prepare
  the way for the LORD[a];
make straight in the wilderness
  a highway for our God.[b]

[a]3 Or *A voice of one calling in the desert: / "Prepare the way for the LORD*
[b]3 Hebrew; Septuagint *make straight the paths of our God*

[4]Every valley shall be raised up,
every mountain and hill made low;
the rough ground shall become level,
the rugged places a plain.
[5]And the glory of the LORD will be revealed,
and all mankind together will see it.
For the mouth of the LORD has spoken."

[6]A voice says, "Cry out."
And I said, "What shall I cry?"

"All men are like grass,
and all their glory is like the flowers of the field.
[7]The grass withers and the flowers fall,
because the breath of the LORD blows on them.
Surely the people are grass.
[8]The grass withers and the flowers fall,
but the word of our God stands forever."

[9]You who bring good tidings to Zion,
go up on a high mountain.
You who bring good tidings to Jerusalem,[a]
lift up your voice with a shout,
lift it up, do not be afraid;
say to the towns of Judah,
"Here is your God!"
[10]See, the Sovereign LORD comes with power,
and his arm rules for him.
See, his reward is with him,
and his recompense accompanies him.
[11]He tends his flock like a shepherd:
He gathers the lambs in his arms
and carries them close to his heart;
he gently leads those that have young.

[12]Who has measured the waters in the hollow of his hand,
or with the breadth of his hand marked off the
heavens?
Who has held the dust of the earth in a basket,
or weighed the mountains on the scales
and the hills in a balance?
[13]Who has understood the mind[b] of the LORD,
or instructed him as his counselor?
[14]Whom did the LORD consult to enlighten him,
and who taught him the right way?
Who was it that taught him knowledge
or showed him the path of understanding?

40:3 *In the desert prepare the way for the LORD:* The Babylonians were known for their parades during religious celebrations. Idols representing their gods often were carried in such parades. Isaiah uses the imagery of such a parade to describe the LORD's victory march back to Judah.

Those traveling from Babylon to Judah usually followed the river valleys north through Mesopotamia. They then headed east to Aram and then south from there. This path allowed them to avoid the hazards of the great Arabian Desert that lay directly between Babylon and Judah (see the map on p. 2468). But here the LORD leads the parade right through the desert. Several New Testament writers use Isaiah's prophecy to describe John the Baptist, who came from the desert to prepare the way for the LORD's Messiah, Jesus Christ (Matt 3:3; Mark 1:3; Luke 3:4-6; John 1:23).

40:6-8 *All men are like grass:* Human bodies, like flowers and grass, die and disappear, but God's word lasts forever. See also Jas 1:10,11; 1 Pet 1:24,25.

40:9 *Zion . . . Judah:* Refers to Jerusalem, the capital city of Judah. See the notes at 1:8 and on p. 1289 (LORD).

40:10 *his arm rules for him . . . his reward is with him:* See the note at 19:16. See also 62:11; Rev 22:12.

40:11 *like a shepherd:* Here, the LORD God of Israel is described as a loving shepherd leading his people (Israel) back to Judah. See also Jer 31:10; Ezek 34:15; John 10:11.

40:12 Job 38–41; Isa 24:18-20; 44:24; 48:13. **40:13** Rom 11:34; 1 Cor 2:16.

a9 Or *O Zion, bringer of good tidings, / go up on a high mountain. / O Jerusalem, bringer of good tidings* **b13** Or *Spirit*; or *spirit*

They Shall Mount Up with Wings as Eagles, by Lu Hsu Chia, around 1985. Throughout the ages, eagles have been admired for their strength and majesty, and for their ability to soar to great heights. The prophet Isaiah gives comfort to the people of Israel, who felt abandoned by the LORD, by telling them, "Those who hope in the LORD will renew their strength. They will soar on wings like eagles; they will run and not grow weary, they will walk and not be faint." (See 40:27-31.)

40:15,16 *dust on the scales:* Balance scales were used to weigh precious metals or grain. Dust would be too light to make a scale move at all. The message then is that no amount of cattle or even valuable cedar would be enough to equal God's greatness.

40:19 *idol:* An important theme in ISAIAH is how Israel's living LORD God is much greater than idols which are usually depicted as powerless objects, rather than as real gods (see the notes at 1:29-31 and 2:18,19). See also Isa 42:17; 45:16, 20; 46:1,2; Acts 17:29.

15 Surely the nations are like a drop in a bucket;
they are regarded as dust on the scales;
he weighs the islands as though they were fine dust.
16 Lebanon is not sufficient for altar fires,
nor its animals enough for burnt offerings.
17 Before him all the nations are as nothing;
they are regarded by him as worthless
and less than nothing.

18 To whom, then, will you compare God?
What image will you compare him to?
19 As for an idol, a craftsman casts it,
and a goldsmith overlays it with gold
and fashions silver chains for it.
20 A man too poor to present such an offering
selects wood that will not rot.
He looks for a skilled craftsman
to set up an idol that will not topple.

21 Do you not know?
Have you not heard?
Has it not been told you from the beginning?
Have you not understood since the earth was founded?
22 He sits enthroned above the circle of the earth,
and its people are like grasshoppers.

He stretches out the heavens like a canopy,
and spreads them out like a tent to live in.
23 He brings princes to naught
and reduces the rulers of this world to nothing.
24 No sooner are they planted,
no sooner are they sown,
no sooner do they take root in the ground,
than he blows on them and they wither,
and a whirlwind sweeps them away like chaff.

25 "To whom will you compare me?
Or who is my equal?" says the Holy One.
26 Lift your eyes and look to the heavens:
Who created all these?
He who brings out the starry host one by one,
and calls them each by name.
Because of his great power and mighty strength,
not one of them is missing.

27 Why do you say, O Jacob,
and complain, O Israel,
"My way is hidden from the LORD;
my cause is disregarded by my God"?
28 Do you not know?
Have you not heard?
The LORD is the everlasting God,
the Creator of the ends of the earth.
He will not grow tired or weary,
and his understanding no one can fathom.
29 He gives strength to the weary
and increases the power of the weak.
30 Even youths grow tired and weary,
and young men stumble and fall;
31 but those who hope in the LORD
will renew their strength.
They will soar on wings like eagles;
they will run and not grow weary,
they will walk and not be faint.

The Helper of Israel

41 "Be silent before me, you islands!
Let the nations renew their strength!
Let them come forward and speak;
let us meet together at the place of judgment.

2 "Who has stirred up one from the east,
calling him in righteousness to his service[a]?

[a]2 Or / *whom victory meets at every step*

Those who hope in the LORD will renew their strength. They will soar on wings like eagles; they will run and not grow weary, they will walk and not be faint. Isa 40:31

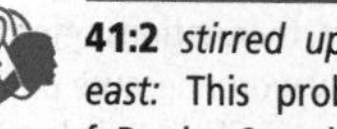

40:22 *stretches out the heavens like a canopy:* See the note at 24:18-20. See also Ps 19:4; Isa 42:5; 44:24; 51:13.

40:26 *brings out the starry host one by one:* Some people worshiped the stars as gods (see the note at 24:21-23). Isaiah's message is that the stars are not as great as the LORD, because the LORD actually created them and put them in place.

40:28 *everlasting God . . . Creator:* Compare God, who never gets weary, to the human being who makes idols in 44:12.

41:1 *let us meet together:* The nations are called into God's court to hear evidence concerning who controls human events (41:4).

41:2 *stirred up one from the east:* This probably refers to Cyrus of Persia. See the note at 13:1 (Babylon). See also 45:13 and 46:11.

40:23 Job 12:17-21; Isa 2:22; Dan 2:21.

41:5-7 *the ends of the earth tremble:* Nations in the path of Cyrus's advance were terrified. Although idol makers were proud of their idols and tried to take comfort in them, they felt they needed to nail them down just in case Cyrus's soldiers got close enough to pull them down. See the note at 1:29-31.

41:8 *Israel, my servant . . . Abraham:* See the note at 1:2 (children). The LORD's chosen "servant" refers to the whole people of Israel. As the LORD's "servant," the people were to trust only in the LORD and live according to his teachings (Exod 20:1-6; Deut 6:4-25). In the second section of ISAIAH (40–55), "servant" sometimes refers to the whole people of Israel and sometimes to just one person. See also 2 Chr 20:7; Jas 2:23.

41:10 *uphold you with my righteous right hand:* See the note at 19:16.

41:12 *enemies:* Meaning Assyria and Babylon, especially, but also others. See chapters 13–23. See also the mini-article called "Enemies (The Wicked)," p. 1084.

41:14 *worm Jacob . . . Holy One of Israel:* Other nations referred to Israel as a lowly worm because of the people's defeat and exile in Babylon (Ps 22:6-8). See also the note at 5:18,19.

41:4 Isa 43:10; 44:6; Rev 2:8; 22:13.

He hands nations over to him
    and subdues kings before him.
He turns them to dust with his sword,
    to windblown chaff with his bow.
3 He pursues them and moves on unscathed,
    by a path his feet have not traveled before.
4 Who has done this and carried it through,
    calling forth the generations from the beginning?
I, the LORD—with the first of them
    and with the last—I am he."

5 The islands have seen it and fear;
    the ends of the earth tremble.
They approach and come forward;
6
    each helps the other
    and says to his brother, "Be strong!"
7 The craftsman encourages the goldsmith,
    and he who smooths with the hammer
    spurs on him who strikes the anvil.
He says of the welding, "It is good."
    He nails down the idol so it will not topple.

8 "But you, O Israel, my servant,
    Jacob, whom I have chosen,
    you descendants of Abraham my friend,
9 I took you from the ends of the earth,
    from its farthest corners I called you.
I said, 'You are my servant';
    I have chosen you and have not rejected you.
10 So do not fear, for I am with you;
    do not be dismayed, for I am your God.
I will strengthen you and help you;
    I will uphold you with my righteous right hand.

11 "All who rage against you
    will surely be ashamed and disgraced;
those who oppose you
    will be as nothing and perish.
12 Though you search for your enemies,
    you will not find them.
Those who wage war against you
    will be as nothing at all.
13 For I am the LORD, your God,
    who takes hold of your right hand
and says to you, Do not fear;
    I will help you.
14 Do not be afraid, O worm Jacob,
    O little Israel,
for I myself will help you," declares the LORD,
    your Redeemer, the Holy One of Israel.

15 “See, I will make you into a threshing sledge,
new and sharp, with many teeth.
You will thresh the mountains and crush them,
and reduce the hills to chaff.
16 You will winnow them, the wind will pick them up,
and a gale will blow them away.
But you will rejoice in the LORD
and glory in the Holy One of Israel.

17 “The poor and needy search for water,
but there is none;
their tongues are parched with thirst.
But I the LORD will answer them;
I, the God of Israel, will not forsake them.
18 I will make rivers flow on barren heights,
and springs within the valleys.
I will turn the desert into pools of water,
and the parched ground into springs.
19 I will put in the desert
the cedar and the acacia, the myrtle and the olive.
I will set pines in the wasteland,
the fir and the cypress together,
20 so that people may see and know,
may consider and understand,
that the hand of the LORD has done this,
that the Holy One of Israel has created it.

21 “Present your case,” says the LORD.
“Set forth your arguments,” says Jacob’s King.
22 “Bring in ⌞your idols⌟ to tell us
what is going to happen.
Tell us what the former things were,
so that we may consider them
and know their final outcome.
Or declare to us the things to come,
23 tell us what the future holds,
so we may know that you are gods.
Do something, whether good or bad,
so that we will be dismayed and filled with fear.
24 But you are less than nothing
and your works are utterly worthless;
he who chooses you is detestable.

25 “I have stirred up one from the north, and he comes—
one from the rising sun who calls on my name.
He treads on rulers as if they were mortar,
as if he were a potter treading the clay.
26 Who told of this from the beginning, so we could know,
or beforehand, so we could say, ‘He was right’?

41:15 *threshing sledge . . . mountains . . . hills:* In ancient times this type of log or other heavy object was dragged over wheat or barley to separate the grain from the husk. The mountains and hills here stand for the power and pride of Israel’s enemies. So, like Cyrus (41:2), Israel will crush its enemies to dust.

41:17-19 *turn the desert into pools of water:* See the note at 35:6,7. See also 35:1,2; 55:12,13. The trees mentioned were not commonly found in desert areas. See the note at 2:13-16. The lumber from cypress and acacia trees were both used for building. The myrtle is a short evergreen tree or bush that usually grows in moist valley soil. The olive tree’s broad trunk is rough and twisted. Its fruit turns black when ripe and contains a large amount of oil. See the illustration on p. 1326.

41:21 *Set forth your arguments . . . Jacob’s King:* See the notes at 6:5 and 41:1.

41:22,23 *Bring in your idols to tell us what is going to happen:* See 41:5-7 and the note at 1:29-31. God challenges the idols to tell what will happen in the future or to do something amazing, but they cannot. Only the LORD, who is in control of history, can tell what will happen and then make it come true.

41:25 *one from the north:* Another reference to Cyrus of Persia (see the note at 41:2). The idols could not act. The LORD appointed Cyrus to honor the LORD by doing what the LORD wanted, which was to free his chosen people from Babylon. The “north” refers to the area to the north and east of Babylon (see the map on p. 2469).

41:25 *a potter treading the clay:* This was done to soften the clay and make it easier to shape. See also the illustration on p. 1467.

No one told of this,
no one foretold it,
no one heard any words from you.
27 I was the first to tell Zion, 'Look, here they are!'
I gave to Jerusalem a messenger of good tidings.
28 I look but there is no one—
no one among them to give counsel,
no one to give answer when I ask them.
29 See, they are all false!
Their deeds amount to nothing;
their images are but wind and confusion.

The Servant of the LORD

42 "Here is my servant, whom I uphold,
my chosen one in whom I delight;
I will put my Spirit on him
and he will bring justice to the nations.
2 He will not shout or cry out,
or raise his voice in the streets.
3 A bruised reed he will not break,
and a smoldering wick he will not snuff out.
In faithfulness he will bring forth justice;
4 he will not falter or be discouraged
till he establishes justice on earth.
In his law the islands will put their hope."

5 This is what God the LORD says—
he who created the heavens and stretched them out,
who spread out the earth and all that comes out of it,
who gives breath to its people,
and life to those who walk on it:
6 "I, the LORD, have called you in righteousness;
I will take hold of your hand.
I will keep you and will make you
to be a covenant for the people
and a light for the Gentiles,
7 to open eyes that are blind,
to free captives from prison
and to release from the dungeon those who sit in darkness.

8 "I am the LORD; that is my name!
I will not give my glory to another
or my praise to idols.
9 See, the former things have taken place,
and new things I declare;
before they spring into being
I announce them to you."

41:27 *tell Zion . . . good tidings:* The LORD announced that the people of Judah and Jerusalem (Zion) would return home from exile (40:9-11; 52:7-10).

42:1 *my servant . . . chosen one . . . justice:* Isaiah 42:1-9, is the first of four "servant songs." Scholars usually identify the "servant" in this song as Israel (41:8; 44:1,2; 45:4). But the servant also may be a ruler such as the one mentioned in 9:6,7 and 11:1-5. This ruler from the family of David will also receive the LORD's Spirit (see 11:2 and the note). Whether the servant is Israel or one chosen to lead Israel, the task of the servant is to bring "justice" to the nations. See the note at 1:16,17 and the mini-article called "Justice," p. 1721. See the mini-article called "The Servant Songs in Isaiah," p. 1398 for more about this and to see how Christian leaders in the early church understood the "servant" to be Jesus Christ, a descendant of David.

42:3-6 *bruised reed . . . smoldering wick . . . light:* The "bruised reed" and "smoldering wick" are symbols of those who are weak. In contrast to a warrior who crushes enemies (41:15), the just servant will not cut down or snuff out the weak but bring them help and healing. As Creator of the world and the source of all life, the LORD God gives the chosen servant power to bring justice and hope to the nations. See also Acts 17:24,25. Light (42:6) is an image for God's truth, justice, and saving power (49:6). Israel will be a visible example to all other nations. See Luke 2:32; Acts 13:47; 26:23.

42:1-4 Matt 12:18-21. **42:7** Isa 35:5, 6; 61:1; Luke 4:18.

Song of Praise to the LORD

10 Sing to the LORD a new song,
his praise from the ends of the earth,
you who go down to the sea, and all that is in it,
you islands, and all who live in them.
11 Let the desert and its towns raise their voices;
let the settlements where Kedar lives rejoice.
Let the people of Sela sing for joy;
let them shout from the mountaintops.
12 Let them give glory to the LORD
and proclaim his praise in the islands.
13 The LORD will march out like a mighty man,
like a warrior he will stir up his zeal;
with a shout he will raise the battle cry
and will triumph over his enemies.

14 "For a long time I have kept silent,
I have been quiet and held myself back.
But now, like a woman in childbirth,
I cry out, I gasp and pant.
15 I will lay waste the mountains and hills
and dry up all their vegetation;
I will turn rivers into islands
and dry up the pools.
16 I will lead the blind by ways they have not known,
along unfamiliar paths I will guide them;
I will turn the darkness into light before them
and make the rough places smooth.
These are the things I will do;
I will not forsake them.
17 But those who trust in idols,
who say to images, 'You are our gods,'
will be turned back in utter shame.

Israel Blind and Deaf

18 "Hear, you deaf;
look, you blind, and see!
19 Who is blind but my servant,
and deaf like the messenger I send?
Who is blind like the one committed to me,
blind like the servant of the LORD?
20 You have seen many things, but have paid no attention;
your ears are open, but you hear nothing."
21 It pleased the LORD
for the sake of his righteousness
to make his law great and glorious.
22 But this is a people plundered and looted,
all of them trapped in pits

"Here is my servant, whom I uphold, my chosen one in whom I delight; I will put my Spirit on him and he will bring justice to the nations."
Isa 42:1

42:16 *lead the blind . . . turn the darkness into light:* See the note at 42:3-6.

42:17 *trust in idols:* See the notes at 1:29-31 and 40:19.

42:18,19 *deaf . . . blind:* The LORD's people and their leaders were blind and deaf to the warnings of the prophets, a frequent theme in ISAIAH (1:2; 5:7; 6:9,10; 28:7-13; 29:9-14).

42:21,22 *make his law great and glorious:* As the LORD's chosen people, Israel is to be an example to all other nations by living according to the law that God gave to Moses and the people at Sinai (see the note at 2:3). But because they had turned away from God, the Israelites were now trapped in exile in Babylon, and all their wealth had been taken away. See also the mini-article called "Law," p. 1160.

42:24 *Israel:* Here "Israel" refers to all the LORD's people, not just to the northern kingdom. See also the mini-article called "Israel," p. 264.

42:25 *violence of war ... flames:* Fire often is used as a symbol of God's judgment (see the note at 4:4). See also 9:11-21; 30:30-33.

43:3 *LORD ... Holy One of Israel, your Savior:* See the notes at 1:2 (LORD) and 5:18, 19. The LORD saved the people from their enemies several times during their history. Especially important were the rescues from slavery in Egypt and from exile in Babylon. See Exod 1–15; Deut 7:6-8; Judg 2:16; Isa 25:9; 35:4; 43:11,12; 49:25,26.

43:3 *Egypt ... Cush ... Seba:* The Persians allowed the people of Judah to return home from exile and to rebuild their temple and their cities. But this did not mean that Judah was a free and independent country. Persia continued to control Judah as one of its provinces. Persia helped Judah in order to gain the favor of its leaders, so Judah would support Persia in its efforts to take over Egypt, Cush, and Seba, a region in southwest Arabia. See also the note at 11:11.

43:2 Ps 66:12; Dan 3:25–27.

or hidden away in prisons.
They have become plunder,
with no one to rescue them;
they have been made loot,
with no one to say, "Send them back."
23 Which of you will listen to this
or pay close attention in time to come?
24 Who handed Jacob over to become loot,
and Israel to the plunderers?
Was it not the LORD,
against whom we have sinned?
For they would not follow his ways;
they did not obey his law.
25 So he poured out on them his burning anger,
the violence of war.
It enveloped them in flames, yet they did not understand;
it consumed them, but they did not take it to heart.

Israel's Only Savior

43 But now, this is what the LORD says—
he who created you, O Jacob,
he who formed you, O Israel:
"Fear not, for I have redeemed you;
I have summoned you by name; you are mine.
2 When you pass through the waters,
I will be with you;
and when you pass through the rivers,
they will not sweep over you.
When you walk through the fire,
you will not be burned;
the flames will not set you ablaze.
3 For I am the LORD, your God,
the Holy One of Israel, your Savior;
I give Egypt for your ransom,
Cush[a] and Seba in your stead.
4 Since you are precious and honored in my sight,
and because I love you,
I will give men in exchange for you,
and people in exchange for your life.
5 Do not be afraid, for I am with you;
I will bring your children from the east
and gather you from the west.
6 I will say to the north, 'Give them up!'
and to the south, 'Do not hold them back.'
Bring my sons from afar

[a]3 That is, the upper Nile region

and my daughters from the ends of the earth—
7 everyone who is called by my name,
whom I created for my glory,
whom I formed and made."

8 Lead out those who have eyes but are blind,
who have ears but are deaf.
9 All the nations gather together
and the peoples assemble.
Which of them foretold this
and proclaimed to us the former things?
Let them bring in their witnesses to prove they were right,
so that others may hear and say, "It is true."
10 "You are my witnesses," declares the LORD,
"and my servant whom I have chosen,
so that you may know and believe me
and understand that I am he.
Before me no god was formed,
nor will there be one after me.
11 I, even I, am the LORD,
and apart from me there is no savior.
12 I have revealed and saved and proclaimed—
I, and not some foreign god among you.
You are my witnesses," declares the LORD, "that I am God.
13 Yes, and from ancient days I am he.
No one can deliver out of my hand.
When I act, who can reverse it?"

God's Mercy and Israel's Unfaithfulness

14 This is what the LORD says—
your Redeemer, the Holy One of Israel:
"For your sake I will send to Babylon
and bring down as fugitives all the Babylonians,[a]
in the ships in which they took pride.
15 I am the LORD, your Holy One,
Israel's Creator, your King."

16 This is what the LORD says—
he who made a way through the sea,
a path through the mighty waters,
17 who drew out the chariots and horses,
the army and reinforcements together,
and they lay there, never to rise again,
extinguished, snuffed out like a wick:
18 "Forget the former things;
do not dwell on the past.

---

[a]14 Or *Chaldeans*

43:6 *from the ends of the earth:* The return from Babylon is most important here. But God's people returned from other places as well after the Persians allowed Jerusalem and Judah to be resettled. See the note at 11:11 and the article called "After the Exile: God's People Return to Judea," p. 931.

43:8 *have eyes but are blind . . . have ears but are deaf:* See the note at 42:18,19.

43:10 *my servant whom I have chosen:* See the note at 41:8.

43:14 *Holy One of Israel:* See 43:3 and the note at 5:18,19.

43:14 *I will send to Babylon:* See the notes at 13:1 (Babylon) and 41:2.

43:15 *Israel's Creator, your King:* The LORD allowed the people of Israel to have kings (1 Sam 8:1-22). Still, the LORD was to be considered Israel's ruler (see 41:21; 52:7; and the note at 6:5).

43:16,17 *made a way through the sea . . . drew out the chariots and horses:* This refers to the Egyptian army, which was destroyed in the waters of the Red Sea while chasing after the Israelites (Exod 14).

43:7 Isa 43:1; 62:1-3.

43:19,20 *a way in the desert:* The LORD will help the people escape from exile in Babylon and return to Judah. The most direct path back to Judah from Babylon was through the desert (see the note at 40:3). A journey through a dry, barren desert would be very dangerous, but the LORD would provide water in the desert, just as God had done in the earlier exodus from Egypt (Exod 15:22-27; 17:1-7; Num 20:1-13).

43:20 *jackals:* Desert animal related to wolves, but smaller. See also the note at 13:22.

43:20 *my people, my chosen:* See the note at 41:8.

43:23,24 *sheep for burnt offerings . . . incense . . . calamus:* God's Law called for Israel's priests to offer sacrifices to honor the LORD (Lev 1–7). These included animal sacrifices, grain sacrifices, and sacrifices mixed with incense and spices ("calamus," in 43:24) that gave a pleasing smell when burned. More than these sacrifices, the LORD wants the people to trust and serve him by doing right (Isa 1:12-17,27; Mic 6:6-8). See also the chart called "Sacrifices and Offerings," p. 219.

43:25 *blots out your transgressions:* In spite of the people's sins, the LORD is willing to forgive (1:18; 44:22).

43:26 *state the case:* The LORD invites Israel to court, just as the nations were invited in 41:21-23. But Israel has no case. The people were guilty of sinning against God, so they were disgraced (43:28).

43:27 *first father sinned . . . spokesmen rebelled:* "First father" refers to Jacob (see the note at 2:3), who also had sinned against the LORD (Gen 27; 32:22-32; Hos 12:2, 3). The "spokesmen" could be any number of prophets, priests, or kings who led the people away from God (see the note at 28:7-9).

19 See, I am doing a new thing!
Now it springs up; do you not perceive it?
I am making a way in the desert
and streams in the wasteland.
20 The wild animals honor me,
the jackals and the owls,
because I provide water in the desert
and streams in the wasteland,
to give drink to my people, my chosen,
21 the people I formed for myself
that they may proclaim my praise.

22 "Yet you have not called upon me, O Jacob,
you have not wearied yourselves for me, O Israel.
23 You have not brought me sheep for burnt offerings,
nor honored me with your sacrifices.
I have not burdened you with grain offerings
nor wearied you with demands for incense.
24 You have not bought any fragrant calamus for me,
or lavished on me the fat of your sacrifices.
But you have burdened me with your sins
and wearied me with your offenses.

25 "I, even I, am he who blots out
your transgressions, for my own sake,
and remembers your sins no more.
26 Review the past for me,
let us argue the matter together;
state the case for your innocence.
27 Your first father sinned;
your spokesmen rebelled against me.
28 So I will disgrace the dignitaries of your temple,
and I will consign Jacob to destruction[a]
and Israel to scorn.

Israel the Chosen

44 "But now listen, O Jacob, my servant,
Israel, whom I have chosen.
2 This is what the LORD says—
he who made you, who formed you in the womb,
and who will help you:
Do not be afraid, O Jacob, my servant,
Jeshurun, whom I have chosen.
3 For I will pour water on the thirsty land,
and streams on the dry ground;

---

a28 The Hebrew term refers to the irrevocable giving over of things or persons to the LORD, often by totally destroying them.

"I will pour water on the thirsty land . . . ." Life cannot exist without water. And no one could have been more aware of this than the peoples who lived in and near the deserts in the ancient Near East. The life-giving power of water is a frequent theme in the Bible. Isaiah gives the people of Israel these comforting words from the LORD, "I will pour water on the thirsty land, and streams on the dry ground; I will pour out my Spirit on your offspring, and my blessing on your descendants." (See 44:3.)

I will pour out my Spirit on your offspring,
  and my blessing on your descendants.
4 They will spring up like grass in a meadow,
  like poplar trees by flowing streams.
5 One will say, 'I belong to the LORD';
  another will call himself by the name of Jacob;
still another will write on his hand, 'The LORD's,'
  and will take the name Israel.

The LORD, Not Idols

6 "This is what the LORD says—
  Israel's King and Redeemer, the LORD Almighty:
I am the first and I am the last;
  apart from me there is no God.
7 Who then is like me? Let him proclaim it.
  Let him declare and lay out before me
what has happened since I established my ancient people,
  and what is yet to come—
  yes, let him foretell what will come.
8 Do not tremble, do not be afraid.
  Did I not proclaim this and foretell it long ago?
You are my witnesses. Is there any God besides me?
  No, there is no other Rock; I know not one."

44:1-3 *servant . . . Spirit:* See the notes at 11:2 and 42:1.

44:5 *write on his hand:* An owner's name was sometimes tattooed or branded on a slave's hand. Israel belongs to the LORD. See also Exod 13:9-16; Isa 49:16; Rev 13:16,17.

44:6,8 *King . . . Redeemer . . . LORD Almighty . . . I am the first and I am the last . . . Rock:* These few verses include many terms that desribe God's greatness and love for his chosen people. For "King," see the notes at 6:5 and 43:15; for "Redeemer," see the mini-article called "Redeemer (Redemption)," p. 995. For "LORD Almighty," see the note on p. 1289. For "first and last," see 41:4; 43:10; 48:12 (compare Rev 1:17; 2:8; 22:13). For "Rock," see the note at 17:10.

44:9-20 *All who make idols are nothing:* These verses make fun of people who make and worship idols, because idols are powerless. Idol worship was forbidden by God's Law because Israel was commanded to trust in the LORD God alone (44:8; see also Exod 20:1-5). Earlier, God had called the nations (41:21-23) and Israel (43:26) into court. The LORD now tells idol makers to face him in court and try to defend their actions (44:11). See also 40:18-20; 41:21-29; 45:16; 46:5-7.

Archaeologists believe that the craft of metalworking began in the ancient Near East around 9000 B.C. The earliest evidence of metalworking, found at Shanidar cave in Iraq, are pieces of pure copper that have been shaped by hammers. Hammers were used then, as they are used today, to strengthen, shape, and decorate metal for a variety of uses. Metalworking is mentioned many times in the Bible. In Genesis 4:22, Tubal-Cain is described as having "forged all kinds of tools out of bronze and iron."

44:14 *cedars . . . pine:* See the notes at 2:13-16; 14:8; and 41:17-19.

44:18,19 Isa 44:9.

9 All who make idols are nothing,
and the things they treasure are worthless.
Those who would speak up for them are blind;
they are ignorant, to their own shame.
10 Who shapes a god and casts an idol,
which can profit him nothing?
11 He and his kind will be put to shame;
craftsmen are nothing but men.
Let them all come together and take their stand;
they will be brought down to terror and infamy.

12 The blacksmith takes a tool
and works with it in the coals;
he shapes an idol with hammers,
he forges it with the might of his arm.
He gets hungry and loses his strength;
he drinks no water and grows faint.
13 The carpenter measures with a line
and makes an outline with a marker;
he roughs it out with chisels
and marks it with compasses.
He shapes it in the form of man,
of man in all his glory,
that it may dwell in a shrine.
14 He cut down cedars,
or perhaps took a cypress or oak.
He let it grow among the trees of the forest,
or planted a pine, and the rain made it grow.
15 It is man's fuel for burning;
some of it he takes and warms himself,
he kindles a fire and bakes bread.
But he also fashions a god and worships it;
he makes an idol and bows down to it.
16 Half of the wood he burns in the fire;
over it he prepares his meal,
he roasts his meat and eats his fill.
He also warms himself and says,
"Ah! I am warm; I see the fire."
17 From the rest he makes a god, his idol;
he bows down to it and worships.
He prays to it and says,
"Save me; you are my god."
18 They know nothing, they understand nothing;
their eyes are plastered over so they cannot see,
and their minds closed so they cannot understand.
19 No one stops to think,
no one has the knowledge or understanding to say,
"Half of it I used for fuel;

I even baked bread over its coals,
I roasted meat and I ate.
Shall I make a detestable thing from what is left?
Shall I bow down to a block of wood?"
20 He feeds on ashes, a deluded heart misleads him;
he cannot save himself, or say,
"Is not this thing in my right hand a lie?"

21 "Remember these things, O Jacob,
for you are my servant, O Israel.
I have made you, you are my servant;
O Israel, I will not forget you.
22 I have swept away your offenses like a cloud,
your sins like the morning mist.
Return to me,
for I have redeemed you."

23 Sing for joy, O heavens, for the LORD has done this;
shout aloud, O earth beneath.
Burst into song, you mountains,
you forests and all your trees,
for the LORD has redeemed Jacob,
he displays his glory in Israel.

Jerusalem to Be Inhabited

24 "This is what the LORD says—
your Redeemer, who formed you in the womb:

I am the LORD,
who has made all things,
who alone stretched out the heavens,
who spread out the earth by myself,

25 who foils the signs of false prophets
and makes fools of diviners,
who overthrows the learning of the wise
and turns it into nonsense,
26 who carries out the words of his servants
and fulfills the predictions of his
messengers,
who says of Jerusalem, 'It shall be inhabited,'
of the towns of Judah, 'They shall be built,'
and of their ruins, 'I will restore them,'
27 who says to the watery deep, 'Be dry,
and I will dry up your streams,'
28 who says of Cyrus, 'He is my shepherd
and will accomplish all that I please;
he will say of Jerusalem, "Let it be rebuilt,"
and of the temple, "Let its foundations be laid." '

44:21 *Israel . . . my servant:* See the note at 41:8.

44:22 *swept away your offenses:* See the note at 43:25. See also the mini-article called "Redeemer (Redemption)," p. 995.

44:23 *LORD has redeemed Jacob:* Meaning from exile in Babylon (see the note at 43:19,20).

44:26 *Jerusalem . . . Judah:* See the note on p. 1289 (Judah and Jerusalem).

44:28—45:1 *Cyrus . . . his anointed:* The word translated as "anointed" in 45:1 is the Hebrew word for "messiah." Cyrus is the only non-Israelite in the Bible to be called the LORD'S "anointed." The title was usually given only to certain Israelite leaders. See the mini-article called "Messiah (Chosen One)," p. 1124. See also 2 Chr 36:22,23; Ezra 1:1-4. The great Persian empire lasted more than two hundred years. It began with the victories that Cyrus won over Media (549 B.C.), Lydia (546 B.C.), and Babylon (539 B.C.). Cyrus ruled until 530 (B.C.), when he died in battle. The policies of Cyrus allowed the conquered peoples of the empire to practice their own religion and rebuild their cities. For more, see the mini-article called "Persia," p. 859 and the article called "After the Exile: God's People Return to Judea," p. 931.

44:23 Ps 98:7-9; 148; Isa 35:1,2; 49:13; 55:12. **44:25** 1 Cor 1:20.

The LORD says, *"You heavens above, rain down righteousness; let the clouds shower it down. Let the earth open wide, let salvation spring up, let righteousness grow with it; I, the LORD, have created it."*
Isa 45:8

45:4 *Jacob my servant . . . Israel my chosen:* See the note at 41:8.

45:7,8 *form the light and create darkness . . . righteousness:* "Light" refers to hope and truth (see the notes at 2:5 and 9:2). "Darkness" refers to punishment or judgment (Exod 10:21-23; Joel 2:1,2). The people of Israel experienced both the LORD's light and darkness. See also Isa 1:27; 9:6,7; 42:1; 58:6-10; 61:1-3; Amos 5:21-24. See also the mini-article called "Hope," p. 2370.

45:6 Exod 20:1-5; Deut 5:6-9; Isa 44:8. **45:9** Isa 29:16; Rom 9:20.

45 "This is what the LORD says to his anointed,
to Cyrus, whose right hand I take hold of
to subdue nations before him
and to strip kings of their armor,
to open doors before him
so that gates will not be shut:
2 I will go before you
and will level the mountains[a];
I will break down gates of bronze
and cut through bars of iron.
3 I will give you the treasures of darkness,
riches stored in secret places,
so that you may know that I am the LORD,
the God of Israel, who summons you by name.
4 For the sake of Jacob my servant,
of Israel my chosen,
I summon you by name
and bestow on you a title of honor,
though you do not acknowledge me.
5 I am the LORD, and there is no other;
apart from me there is no God.
I will strengthen you,
though you have not acknowledged me,
6 so that from the rising of the sun
to the place of its setting
men may know there is none besides me.
I am the LORD, and there is no other.
7 I form the light and create darkness,
I bring prosperity and create disaster;
I, the LORD, do all these things.

8 "You heavens above, rain down righteousness;
let the clouds shower it down.
Let the earth open wide,
let salvation spring up,
let righteousness grow with it;
I, the LORD, have created it.

9 "Woe to him who quarrels with his Maker,
to him who is but a potsherd among the potsherds
on the ground.
Does the clay say to the potter,
'What are you making?'
Does your work say,
'He has no hands'?

[a]2 Dead Sea Scrolls and Septuagint; the meaning of the word in the Masoretic Text is uncertain.

10 Woe to him who says to his father,
'What have you begotten?'
or to his mother,
'What have you brought to birth?'
11 "This is what the LORD says—
the Holy One of Israel, and its Maker:
Concerning things to come,
do you question me about my children,
or give me orders about the work of my hands?
12 It is I who made the earth
and created mankind upon it.
My own hands stretched out the heavens;
I marshaled their starry hosts.
13 I will raise up Cyrus[a] in my righteousness:
I will make all his ways straight.
He will rebuild my city
and set my exiles free,
but not for a price or reward,
says the LORD Almighty."

14 This is what the LORD says:

"The products of Egypt and the merchandise of Cush,[b]
and those tall Sabeans—
they will come over to you
and will be yours;
they will trudge behind you,
coming over to you in chains.
They will bow down before you
and plead with you, saying,
'Surely God is with you, and there is no other;
there is no other god.'"
15 Truly you are a God who hides himself,
O God and Savior of Israel.
16 All the makers of idols will be put to shame and disgraced;
they will go off into disgrace together.
17 But Israel will be saved by the LORD
with an everlasting salvation;
you will never be put to shame or disgraced,
to ages everlasting.

18 For this is what the LORD says—
he who created the heavens,
he is God;
he who fashioned and made the earth,
he founded it;

[a]13 Hebrew *him* [b]14 That is, the upper Nile region

45:13 *raise up Cyrus . . . rebuild my city:* God used Cyrus to free the Israelite people from exile in Babylon so they could rebuild Jerusalem ("my city"). See the note at 44:28—45:1. EZRA and NEHEMIAH also tell how the people of Judah rebuilt Jerusalem. The sixth century marble bust shown here is of a Persian king, possibly Cyrus the Great.

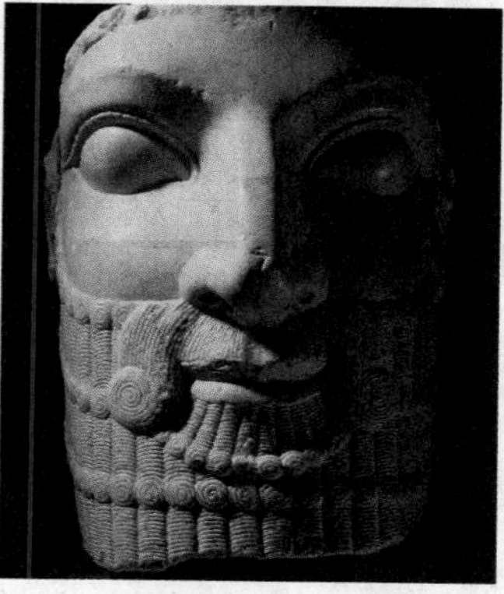

45:14 *Egypt . . . Cush . . . Sabeans:* See the notes at 11:11 and 43:3 (Egypt).

45:16 Isa 44:9-11. **45:17** Isa 41:10.

he did not create it to be empty,
but formed it to be inhabited—
he says:
"I am the LORD,
and there is no other.
19 I have not spoken in secret,
from somewhere in a land of darkness;
I have not said to Jacob's descendants,
'Seek me in vain.'
I, the LORD, speak the truth;
I declare what is right.

20 "Gather together and come;
assemble, you fugitives from the nations.
Ignorant are those who carry about idols of wood,
who pray to gods that cannot save.
21 Declare what is to be, present it—
let them take counsel together.
Who foretold this long ago,
who declared it from the distant past?
Was it not I, the LORD?
And there is no God apart from me,
a righteous God and a Savior;
there is none but me.

22 "Turn to me and be saved,
all you ends of the earth;
for I am God, and there is no other.
23 By myself I have sworn,
my mouth has uttered in all integrity
a word that will not be revoked:
Before me every knee will bow;
by me every tongue will swear.
24 They will say of me, 'In the LORD alone
are righteousness and strength.' "
All who have raged against him
will come to him and be put to shame.
25 But in the LORD all the descendants of Israel
will be found righteous and will exult.

Gods of Babylon

46 Bel bows down, Nebo stoops low;
their idols are borne by beasts of burden.[a]
The images that are carried about are burdensome,
a burden for the weary.
2 They stoop and bow down together;
unable to rescue the burden,
they themselves go off into captivity.

The LORD says, *"There is no God apart from me, a righteous God and a Savior; there is none but me."*
Isa 45:21

45:19 *Jacob's descendants:* See the note at 29:22.

45:21,22 *foretold this long ago:* This refers to Babylon's fall (41:25-29).

46:1,2 *Bel . . . Nebo:* Bel, meaning "lord," became another name for Marduk, the chief god of Babylon. Nebo is "Nabu," the son of Bel-Marduk and the chief god of the city of Borsippa.

Just before Cyrus invaded Babylon, King Nabonidus of Babylon had many images of the Babylonian gods brought from outlying areas in order to protect them. Isaiah mocks Babylon, saying that rather than the people bowing down to the images, the images bowed down to get out of the city. The Babylonian gods are helpless to protect their own images or the people who worship them.

45:23 Rom 14:11; Phil 2:10,11.

[a]1 Or *are but beasts and cattle*

3 “Listen to me, O house of Jacob,
all you who remain of the house of Israel,
you whom I have upheld since you were conceived,
and have carried since your birth.
4 Even to your old age and gray hairs
I am he, I am he who will sustain you.
I have made you and I will carry you;
I will sustain you and I will rescue you.

5 “To whom will you compare me or count me equal?
To whom will you liken me that we may be compared?
6 Some pour out gold from their bags
and weigh out silver on the scales;
they hire a goldsmith to make it into a god,
and they bow down and worship it.
7 They lift it to their shoulders and carry it;
they set it up in its place, and there it stands.
From that spot it cannot move.
Though one cries out to it, it does not answer;
it cannot save him from his troubles.

8 “Remember this, fix it in mind,
take it to heart, you rebels.
9 Remember the former things, those of long ago;
I am God, and there is no other;
I am God, and there is none like me.
10 I make known the end from the beginning,
from ancient times, what is still to come.
I say: My purpose will stand,
and I will do all that I please.
11 From the east I summon a bird of prey;
from a far-off land, a man to fulfill my purpose.
What I have said, that will I bring about;
what I have planned, that will I do.
12 Listen to me, you stubborn-hearted,
you who are far from righteousness.
13 I am bringing my righteousness near,
it is not far away;
and my salvation will not be delayed.
I will grant salvation to Zion,
my splendor to Israel.

The Fall of Babylon

47 “Go down, sit in the dust,
Virgin Daughter of Babylon;
sit on the ground without a throne,

46:6 *a god:* See 44:9-20 and the notes at 1:29-31 and 40:19.

46:8 *rebels:* Meaning the people of Israel. See the notes at 1:4 (nation) and 40:2.

46:9 *I am God, and there is no other:* See 44:8; 45:18.

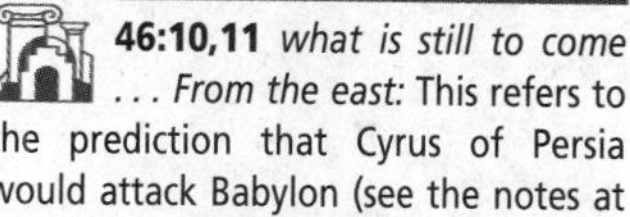

46:10,11 *what is still to come . . . From the east:* This refers to the prediction that Cyrus of Persia would attack Babylon (see the notes at 41:2; 41:22,23; and 44:28—45:1).

46:13 *Zion . . . Israel:* God will free the people of Israel from exile in Babylon and help them rebuild Jerusalem.

47:1,2 *Virgin Daughter of Babylon . . . your skirts:* See the note at 13:1 (Babylon). Here, Babylon is described as a queen reduced to the status of a servant.

Grinding flour was often done by servant women. “Take off your veil” may be a command to get ready for work. Or, it may be a warning that the “queen” (Babylon) will be taken away as a slave. “Wade through the streams” may mean that she will have to wade across the river herself to escape to safety rather than being carried or floated across the river.

46:3,4 Isa 40:10,11; 42:8,9; 43:1,2; 44:2. **47:1-15** Isa 13:1—14:23; Jer 50:1—51:64.

Thy Nakedness Shall Be Uncovered, Yea, Thy Shame Shall Be Seen, by Chaim Gross, 1979. The people of Judah were taken into captivity by the Babylonians. The prophet Isaiah, however, describes the city of Babylon as a proud and beautiful princess who will one day have to endure a humiliation of her own. Speaking for the LORD he says, " 'Sit in the dust . . . take off your veil. Lift up your skirts, bare your legs, and wade through the streams. Your nakedness will be exposed and your shame uncovered. I will take vengeance; I will spare no one.' Our Redeemer—the LORD Almighty is his name—is the Holy One of Israel." (See 47:1-4.)

47:4 *Our Redeemer:* The word "Redeemer" means that the LORD has saved Israel from its enemies and redeemed the people by forgiving their sins. See the mini-article called "Redeemer (Redemption)," p. 995.

Daughter of the Babylonians.[a]
No more will you be called
tender or delicate.
2 Take millstones and grind flour;
take off your veil.
Lift up your skirts, bare your legs,
and wade through the streams.
3 Your nakedness will be exposed
and your shame uncovered.
I will take vengeance;
I will spare no one."

4 Our Redeemer—the LORD Almighty is his name—
is the Holy One of Israel.

5 "Sit in silence, go into darkness,
Daughter of the Babylonians;
no more will you be called

[a]1 Or *Chaldeans*; also in verse 5

queen of kingdoms.
6 I was angry with my people
and desecrated my inheritance;
I gave them into your hand,
and you showed them no mercy.
Even on the aged
you laid a very heavy yoke.
7 You said, 'I will continue forever—
the eternal queen!'
But you did not consider these things
or reflect on what might happen.

8 "Now then, listen, you wanton creature,
lounging in your security
and saying to yourself,
'I am, and there is none besides me.
I will never be a widow
or suffer the loss of children.'
9 Both of these will overtake you
in a moment, on a single day:
loss of children and widowhood.
They will come upon you in full measure,
in spite of your many sorceries
and all your potent spells.
10 You have trusted in your wickedness
and have said, 'No one sees me.'
Your wisdom and knowledge mislead you
when you say to yourself,
'I am, and there is none besides me.'
11 Disaster will come upon you,
and you will not know how to conjure it away.
A calamity will fall upon you
that you cannot ward off with a ransom;
a catastrophe you cannot foresee
will suddenly come upon you.

12 "Keep on, then, with your magic spells
and with your many sorceries,
which you have labored at since childhood.
Perhaps you will succeed,
perhaps you will cause terror.
13 All the counsel you have received has only worn you out!
Let your astrologers come forward,
those stargazers who make predictions month by month,
let them save you from what is coming upon you.
14 Surely they are like stubble;
the fire will burn them up.
They cannot even save themselves
from the power of the flame.

47:6 *I was angry:* See the note at 40:2. See also 2 Kgs 25; 2 Chr 36:17-21; Isa 10:5-12; 37:26; 42:24.

47:9-15 *sorceries . . . spells . . . wisdom . . . astrologers:* The Babylonian leaders had advisers who used various means to predict the future, including reading drops of fluid in a cup, examining the inner organs of dead animals, and studying the movement of the stars. They also cast evil spells on their enemies (47:12), and performed special ceremonies to protect themselves. The wisdom and knowledge of Babylon was well known in the ancient world. However, "wisdom" here refers to advice and information given by these Babylonian magician-priests.

Present-day astrology is based in part on the ancient Babylonian study of the stars and planets. Fortunetellers would observe the positions of the stars and planets, and then would use them to predict Babylon's future. But here God says that trusting in such information is useless. It is like trying to stay warm with a fire fueled by straw (47:14), which burns quickly and then goes out.

47:7-9 Rev 18:7,8.

> The LORD says, *"For my own name's sake I delay my wrath; for the sake of my praise I hold it back from you, so as not to cut you off."*
> Isa 48:9

48:1 *house of Jacob . . . line of Judah:* See the notes at 1:4 (sinful nation) and 2:3. Those Israelites who returned from exile in Babylon were mainly from the southern tribes of Judah and Benjamin. See also the article called "After the Exile: God's People Return to Judah," p. 931.

48:8 *you were called a rebel from birth:* See the notes at 1:2 (children); 30:1,2; and 43:27.

48:10 *refined you . . . furnace of affliction:* See the note at 1:25. The LORD tested and refined Israel's faith by allowing Babylon to defeat them and make them live in exile.

Here are no coals to warm anyone;
here is no fire to sit by.
15 That is all they can do for you—
these you have labored with
and trafficked with since childhood.
Each of them goes on in his error;
there is not one that can save you.

Stubborn Israel

48 "Listen to this, O house of Jacob,
you who are called by the name of Israel
and come from the line of Judah,
you who take oaths in the name of the LORD
and invoke the God of Israel—
but not in truth or righteousness—
2 you who call yourselves citizens of the holy city
and rely on the God of Israel—
the LORD Almighty is his name:
3 I foretold the former things long ago,
my mouth announced them and I made them known;
then suddenly I acted, and they came to pass.
4 For I knew how stubborn you were;
the sinews of your neck were iron,
your forehead was bronze.
5 Therefore I told you these things long ago;
before they happened I announced them to you
so that you could not say,
'My idols did them;
my wooden image and metal god ordained them.'
6 You have heard these things; look at them all.
Will you not admit them?

"From now on I will tell you of new things,
of hidden things unknown to you.
7 They are created now, and not long ago;
you have not heard of them before today.
So you cannot say,
'Yes, I knew of them.'
8 You have neither heard nor understood;
from of old your ear has not been open.
Well do I know how treacherous you are;
you were called a rebel from birth.
9 For my own name's sake I delay my wrath;
for the sake of my praise I hold it back from you,
so as not to cut you off.
10 See, I have refined you, though not as silver;
I have tested you in the furnace of affliction.
11 For my own sake, for my own sake, I do this.

How can I let myself be defamed?
I will not yield my glory to another.

Israel Freed

12 "Listen to me, O Jacob,
Israel, whom I have called:
I am he;
I am the first and I am the last.
13 My own hand laid the foundations of the earth,
and my right hand spread out the heavens;
when I summon them,
they all stand up together.

14 "Come together, all of you, and listen:
Which of ⌞the idols⌟ has foretold these things?
The LORD's chosen ally
will carry out his purpose against Babylon;
his arm will be against the Babylonians.[a]
15 I, even I, have spoken;
yes, I have called him.
I will bring him,
and he will succeed in his mission.

16 "Come near me and listen to this:

"From the first announcement I have not spoken in secret;
at the time it happens, I am there."

And now the Sovereign LORD has sent me,
with his Spirit.

17 This is what the LORD says—
your Redeemer, the Holy One of Israel:
"I am the LORD your God,
who teaches you what is best for you,
who directs you in the way you should go.
18 If only you had paid attention to my commands,
your peace would have been like a river,
your righteousness like the waves of the sea.
19 Your descendants would have been like the sand,
your children like its numberless grains;
their name would never be cut off
nor destroyed from before me."

20 Leave Babylon,
flee from the Babylonians!
Announce this with shouts of joy
and proclaim it.

[a]**14** Or *Chaldeans*; also in verse 20

48:14,15 *chosen ally:* This probably refers to Cyrus (see the note at 44:28—45:1).

48:16 *sent me, with his Spirit:* See the note at 11:2. The message comes to the prophet Isaiah ("me") or to the servant (see 42:1 and the note at 61:1,2).

48:18,20 *my commands ... Leave Babylon:* The "commands" were the law (see the notes at 2:3 and 42:21,22). Becoming a great nation was only one of the LORD's blessings that would have resulted from obeying God's commands (48:19; Gen 17:1-8; Deut 6:4-25; Ps 1). For "leave Babylon," see the notes at 40:2 and 41:27.

48:12 Isa 44:6; Rev 1:17; 22:13.
48:20 Rev 18:4.

48:20 *servant Jacob:* See the note at 41:8.

49:1 *islands . . . distant nations:* This probably means those Gentile (non-Israelite) peoples who lived along the coastlands of the Mediterranean Sea, Red Sea, and Persian Gulf. This verse repeats the theme introduced in the first servant song (see 42:1-9 and the note at 42:1): Israel was chosen to bring justice, light, and hope to the nations (compare to 49:6).

49:2 *mouth like a sharpened sword:* God will help the servant speak the message of judgment and hope using piercing words that will cut to the heart. Arrows are sometimes used to describe the LORD's judgment (Deut 32:23,42). For God's protecting hand, see the note at 19:16.

49:3 *my servant, Israel:* See the note at 41:8.

49:4 *spent my strength in vain:* This refers to Israel's time in exile.

49:6,7 *light for the Gentiles . . . salvation . . . Redeemer and Holy One of Israel:* This describes the task the LORD's servant has been chosen to do. See also the notes at 2:5; 42:1; and 42:3-6. For "Redeemer and Holy One of Israel," see the mini-article called "Redeemer (Redemption)," p. 995 and the note at 5:18,19.

48:21 Exod 15:22-27; 17:1-7; Num 20:1-13. **48:22** Isa 57:21. **49:6** Isa 42:6; Luke 2:32; Acts 13:47; 26:23.

Send it out to the ends of the earth;
say, "The LORD has redeemed his servant Jacob."
21 They did not thirst when he led them through the deserts;
he made water flow for them from the rock;
he split the rock
and water gushed out.

22 "There is no peace," says the LORD, "for the wicked."

JERUSALEM WILL BE REBUILT

The focus in chapters 49–55 is on the new future that the LORD is creating for the people of Israel. Jerusalem lies in ruins, but it will be rebuilt, and the people will rejoice. God will bless and protect those who return from exile. This section also includes three more "songs" of the LORD's "suffering servant."

The Servant of the LORD

49 Listen to me, you islands;
hear this, you distant nations:
Before I was born the LORD called me;
from my birth he has made mention of my name.
2 He made my mouth like a sharpened sword,
in the shadow of his hand he hid me;
he made me into a polished arrow
and concealed me in his quiver.
3 He said to me, "You are my servant,
Israel, in whom I will display my splendor."
4 But I said, "I have labored to no purpose;
I have spent my strength in vain and for nothing.
Yet what is due me is in the LORD's hand,
and my reward is with my God."

5 And now the LORD says—
he who formed me in the womb to be his servant
to bring Jacob back to him
and gather Israel to himself,
for I am honored in the eyes of the LORD
and my God has been my strength—
6 he says:
"It is too small a thing for you to be my servant
to restore the tribes of Jacob
and bring back those of Israel I have kept.
I will also make you a light for the Gentiles,
that you may bring my salvation to the ends of the earth."

7 This is what the LORD says—
the Redeemer and Holy One of Israel—
to him who was despised and abhorred by the nation,
to the servant of rulers:
"Kings will see you and rise up,
princes will see and bow down,
because of the LORD, who is faithful,
the Holy One of Israel, who has chosen you."

Restoration of Israel

8 This is what the LORD says:

"In the time of my favor I will answer you,
and in the day of salvation I will help you;
I will keep you and will make you
to be a covenant for the people,
to restore the land
and to reassign its desolate inheritances,
9 to say to the captives, 'Come out,'
and to those in darkness, 'Be free!'

"They will feed beside the roads
and find pasture on every barren hill.
10 They will neither hunger nor thirst,
nor will the desert heat or the sun beat upon them.
He who has compassion on them will guide them
and lead them beside springs of water.
11 I will turn all my mountains into roads,
and my highways will be raised up.
12 See, they will come from afar—
some from the north, some from the west,
some from the region of Aswan.[a]"
13 Shout for joy, O heavens;
rejoice, O earth;
burst into song, O mountains!
For the LORD comforts his people
and will have compassion on his afflicted ones.

14 But Zion said, "The LORD has forsaken me,
the Lord has forgotten me."

15 "Can a mother forget the baby at her breast
and have no compassion on the child she has borne?
Though she may forget,
I will not forget you!
16 See, I have engraved you on the palms of my hands;
your walls are ever before me.

[a]12 Dead Sea Scrolls; Masoretic Text *Sinim*

49:7,8 *servant of rulers . . . restore the land:* The exile in Babylon is compared to the slavery the people's ancestors faced in Egypt (Exod 1:1-14). As long as the people of Israel are in exile, they are despised by the nations (53:2,3). But God promises that those who despise and enslave Israel will honor Israel's people and bring them gifts (49:23; 60:10-18). The people of Israel would rebuild the cities of Judah. See the article called "After the Exile: God's People Return to Judea," p. 931.

49:9-11 *Come out . . . my highways:* See the note at 43:19, 20.

49:12 *from afar . . . region of Aswan:* See the note at 43:6. The region of Aswan (now the name of a city) is in southern Egypt (see Ezek 29:10).

49:14 *Zion . . . forgotten:* See the note at 1:8. While in exile, many Israelites probably felt as if the LORD had forgotten about them forever.

49:16 *engraved you on the palms of my hands:* See the note at 44:5. Just as the people of Israel engraved the LORD's name on their hands, so Israel is said to be permanently engraved on the LORD's hand.

49:8 Isa 42:1,6; 49:6; 2 Cor 6:2. **49:9** Isa 42:7; 61:1. **49:10** Rev 7:16,17. **49:13** Ps 98:7-9; 148; Isa 35:1, 2; 44:23; 55:12.

49:19-22 *Though you were ruined . . . beckon to the Gentiles:* The temple and walls of Jerusalem were in ruins because of the Babylonians (see the notes at 40:2 and 49:7, 8). But when Jerusalem is rebuilt the population of the city will quickly grow. That is because many of Israel's "children," born in foreign countries during the years that Jerusalem was in ruins, will return (see the notes at 11:11; 43:6; 60:9). The LORD will "beckon" the nations to return Israel's children to Jerusalem.

49:26 *eat their own flesh:* The violent imagery in this verse is meant to emphasize the LORD as Israel's warrior-protector. Though the LORD did use Cyrus of Persia to defeat Babylon, Israel's return to Jerusalem was relatively peaceful. They did not have to fight their way back into the city.

49:18 Isa 52:1.

17 Your sons hasten back,
and those who laid you waste depart from you.
18 Lift up your eyes and look around;
all your sons gather and come to you.
As surely as I live," declares the LORD,
"you will wear them all as ornaments;
you will put them on, like a bride.

19 "Though you were ruined and made desolate
and your land laid waste,
now you will be too small for your people,
and those who devoured you will be far away.
20 The children born during your bereavement
will yet say in your hearing,
'This place is too small for us;
give us more space to live in.'
21 Then you will say in your heart,
'Who bore me these?
I was bereaved and barren;
I was exiled and rejected.
Who brought these up?
I was left all alone,
but these—where have they come from?' "

22 This is what the Sovereign LORD says:

"See, I will beckon to the Gentiles,
I will lift up my banner to the peoples;
they will bring your sons in their arms
and carry your daughters on their shoulders.
23 Kings will be your foster fathers,
and their queens your nursing mothers.
They will bow down before you with their faces to the ground;
they will lick the dust at your feet.
Then you will know that I am the LORD;
those who hope in me will not be disappointed."

24 Can plunder be taken from warriors,
or captives rescued from the fierce[a]?

25 But this is what the LORD says:

"Yes, captives will be taken from warriors,
and plunder retrieved from the fierce;
I will contend with those who contend with you,
and your children I will save.

[a]**24** Dead Sea Scrolls, Vulgate and Syriac (see also Septuagint and verse 25); Masoretic Text *righteous*

26 I will make your oppressors eat their own flesh;
they will be drunk on their own blood, as with wine.
Then all mankind will know
that I, the LORD, am your Savior,
your Redeemer, the Mighty One of Jacob."

Israel's Sin and the Servant's Obedience

50 This is what the LORD says:

"Where is your mother's certificate of divorce
with which I sent her away?
Or to which of my creditors
did I sell you?
Because of your sins you were sold;
because of your transgressions your mother was
sent away.
2 When I came, why was there no one?
When I called, why was there no one to answer?
Was my arm too short to ransom you?
Do I lack the strength to rescue you?
By a mere rebuke I dry up the sea,
I turn rivers into a desert;
their fish rot for lack of water
and die of thirst.
3 I clothe the sky with darkness
and make sackcloth its covering."

4 The Sovereign LORD has given me an instructed tongue,
to know the word that sustains the weary.
He wakens me morning by morning,
wakens my ear to listen like one being taught.
5 The Sovereign LORD has opened my ears,
and I have not been rebellious;
I have not drawn back.
6 I offered my back to those who beat me,
my cheeks to those who pulled out my beard;
I did not hide my face
from mocking and spitting.
7 Because the Sovereign LORD helps me,
I will not be disgraced.
Therefore have I set my face like flint,
and I know I will not be put to shame.
8 He who vindicates me is near.
Who then will bring charges against me?
Let us face each other!
Who is my accuser?
Let him confront me!
9 It is the Sovereign LORD who helps me.
Who is he that will condemn me?

50:1 *certificate of divorce . . . because of your transgressions:* The LORD seems to be answering an unspoken question from Israel: "Why did you divorce our mother?" God's Law did allow divorce under certain circumstances (Deut 24:1-4; Jer 3:1), and a husband could send his wife away. Israel is reminded that the LORD sent them away because of their sins. Israel, and not God, was responsible for the "divorce." See also Hos 2:2-8.

50:2,3 *rivers into a desert . . . clothe the sky with darkness:* The LORD called out to the people of Israel through the prophets, but many ignored the prophets' warnings. The dried up waters and darkened sky may be reminders of how the LORD rescued the Israelites from slavery in Egypt (Exod 14; 10:21-23).

50:3 *sackcloth:* See the note at 3:16-24.

50:4-11 *LORD has given me an instructed tongue . . . the word of his servant:* This is the third "servant song" (see the note at 42:1). In this song, the servant is usually identified as the prophet who wrote these words. Or the servant may be someone who had experiences like those of a prophet (for example, see Jer 11:18-21; 18:18-20; 20:10).

50:5,6 *not been rebellious . . . beat me . . . . spitting:* Unlike Israel, the servant (prophet) listened to God's teaching and did not rebel. The servant was beaten like a criminal or a fool (see Prov 10:13). Pulling out a man's beard and spitting in someone's face were both acts of extreme disrespect (2 Sam 10:4, 5; Neh 13:25; Job 30:9,10; Matt 26:67).

50:8,9 Rom 8:33,34.

50:10,11 *walks in the dark . . . fires:* Most of God's people did not listen to the prophet. They chose to turn away from the LORD (walk in the dark). They will get "burned" by their own evil ways and will face the LORD's judgment. See also the notes at 2:5; 4:4; 9:2; and 45:7,8.

51:2 *Abraham . . . Sarah:* Abraham and Sarah obeyed the LORD, who told them to leave their homeland and go to Canaan. Later generations would use Abraham's obedient action as an example of "righteousness" (Gen 12:1-5; 15:6; Hab 2:4; Rom 4:1-3; Gal 3:6). See the mini-article called "Abraham," p. 2254.

51:3 *Zion . . . Eden:* See the notes at 1:8 and 40:2. Eden was the garden God created in the beginning (Gen 2:4-15). The Bible often describes God's future for his faithful people as a return to a beautiful garden (Ezek 36:33-36; 47:1-12; Rev 22:1, 2). See also the mini-article called "Paradise," p. 2243.

51:4 *my people . . . my nation . . . justice:* See the notes at 41:8 and 42:1 (justice). See also the note at 42:3-6.

51:6 *heavens will vanish like smoke . . . salvation will last forever:* Though the earth and sky will change, God's saving power will go on forever (Isa 65:17-19; 2 Pet 3:10-13). For more, see the mini-article called "Salvation," p. 2021.

They will all wear out like a garment;
the moths will eat them up.

10 Who among you fears the LORD
and obeys the word of his servant?
Let him who walks in the dark,
who has no light,
trust in the name of the LORD
and rely on his God.
11 But now, all you who light fires
and provide yourselves with flaming torches,
go, walk in the light of your fires
and of the torches you have set ablaze.
This is what you shall receive from my hand:
You will lie down in torment.

Everlasting Salvation for Zion

51 "Listen to me, you who pursue righteousness
and who seek the LORD:
Look to the rock from which you were cut
and to the quarry from which you were hewn;
2 look to Abraham, your father,
and to Sarah, who gave you birth.
When I called him he was but one,
and I blessed him and made him many.
3 The LORD will surely comfort Zion
and will look with compassion on all her ruins;
he will make her deserts like Eden,
her wastelands like the garden of the LORD.
Joy and gladness will be found in her,
thanksgiving and the sound of singing.

4 "Listen to me, my people;
hear me, my nation:
The law will go out from me;
my justice will become a light to the nations.
5 My righteousness draws near speedily,
my salvation is on the way,
and my arm will bring justice to the
nations.
The islands will look to me
and wait in hope for my arm.
6 Lift up your eyes to the heavens,
look at the earth beneath;
the heavens will vanish like smoke,
the earth will wear out like a garment
and its inhabitants die like flies.
But my salvation will last forever,
my righteousness will never fail.

[7]"Hear me, you who know what is right,
you people who have my law in your
hearts:
Do not fear the reproach of men
or be terrified by their insults.
[8]For the moth will eat them up like a garment;
the worm will devour them like wool.
But my righteousness will last forever,
my salvation through all generations."

[9]Awake, awake! Clothe yourself with strength,
O arm of the LORD;
awake, as in days gone by,
as in generations of old.
Was it not you who cut Rahab to pieces,
who pierced that monster through?
[10]Was it not you who dried up the sea,
the waters of the great deep,
who made a road in the depths of the sea
so that the redeemed might cross over?
[11]The ransomed of the LORD will return.
They will enter Zion with singing;
everlasting joy will crown their heads.
Gladness and joy will overtake them,
and sorrow and sighing will flee away.

[12]"I, even I, am he who comforts you.
Who are you that you fear mortal men,
the sons of men, who are but grass,
[13]that you forget the LORD your Maker,
who stretched out the heavens
and laid the foundations of the earth,
that you live in constant terror every day
because of the wrath of the oppressor,
who is bent on destruction?
For where is the wrath of the oppressor?
[14]The cowering prisoners will soon be
set free;
they will not die in their dungeon,
nor will they lack bread.
[15]For I am the LORD your God,
who churns up the sea so that its waves roar—
the LORD Almighty is his name.
[16]I have put my words in your mouth
and covered you with the shadow of
my hand—
I who set the heavens in place,
who laid the foundations of the earth,
and who say to Zion, 'You are my people.' "

The ransomed of the LORD will return. They will enter Zion with singing; everlasting joy will crown their heads. Gladness and joy will overtake them, and sorrow and sighing will flee away.
Isa 51:11

51:7 *you who know what is right:* See the notes at 1:16,17; 26:7.

51:9,10 *Rahab . . . dried up the sea:* Rahab was said to be the chaos monster God defeated at creation (see the note at 30:6,7). Rahab may also be a symbol of Egypt at the time of the exodus. God saved the Hebrew people from the Egyptian army by making a dry path through the Red Sea (Exod 14).

51:13 *stretched out the heavens and laid the foundations of the earth:* An important theme in ISAIAH is that the God of Israel is the same God who created the world (see the note at 24:18-20).

51:15 *LORD Almighty:* See the note on p. 1289 (LORD).

51:8 Isa 50:9. **51:12** Isa 37:27; 40:6. **51:14** Isa 26:19; 49:8-10; 61:1-3. **51:16** Isa 40:22; 43:1; 44:21,24; 49:2; 51:13.

Awake, awake, O Zion, clothe yourself with strength. Put on your garments of splendor, O Jerusalem, the holy city.
Isa 52:1

51:17,18 *cup of his wrath . . . none to take her:* The people of Jerusalem have been punished for their sins (see the note at 40:2). Drinking from the LORD's "cup of wrath" is a common symbol for God's judgment and punishment (51:22; Jer 25:15-29; Rev 16:19). In 51:18; Jerusalem is pictured as a mother who has lost her children (see also 49:19-22).

51:21 *drunk, but not with wine:* See the note at 51:17,18. The cup of God's wrath will now be passed to Israel's enemies, and they will drink God's punishment.

52:1,2 *Zion . . . Jerusalem:* See the notes on p. 1289 and at 1:8. See also 51:17; Rev 21:2,27.

52:3 Isa 45:13; 50:1.

The Cup of the LORD's Wrath

17 Awake, awake!
Rise up, O Jerusalem,
you who have drunk from the hand of the LORD
the cup of his wrath,
you who have drained to its dregs
the goblet that makes men stagger.
18 Of all the sons she bore
there was none to guide her;
of all the sons she reared
there was none to take her by the hand.
19 These double calamities have come upon you—
who can comfort you?—
ruin and destruction, famine and sword—
who can[a] console you?
20 Your sons have fainted;
they lie at the head of every street,
like antelope caught in a net.
They are filled with the wrath of the LORD
and the rebuke of your God.

21 Therefore hear this, you afflicted one,
made drunk, but not with wine.
22 This is what your Sovereign LORD says,
your God, who defends his people:
"See, I have taken out of your hand
the cup that made you stagger;
from that cup, the goblet of my wrath,
you will never drink again.
23 I will put it into the hands of your tormentors,
who said to you,
'Fall prostrate that we may walk over you.'
And you made your back like the ground,
like a street to be walked over."

52 Awake, awake, O Zion,
clothe yourself with strength.
Put on your garments of splendor,
O Jerusalem, the holy city.
The uncircumcised and defiled
will not enter you again.
2 Shake off your dust;
rise up, sit enthroned, O Jerusalem.
Free yourself from the chains on your neck,
O captive Daughter of Zion.

3 For this is what the LORD says:

[a]19 Dead Sea Scrolls, Septuagint, Vulgate and Syriac; Masoretic Text / *how can I*

"You were sold for nothing,
and without money you will be redeemed."

4 For this is what the Sovereign LORD says:
"At first my people went down to Egypt to live;
lately, Assyria has oppressed them.

5 "And now what do I have here?" declares the LORD.

"For my people have been taken away for nothing,
and those who rule them mock,[a]"
declares the LORD.
"And all day long
my name is constantly blasphemed.
6 Therefore my people will know my name;
therefore in that day they will know
that it is I who foretold it.
Yes, it is I."
7 How beautiful on the mountains
are the feet of those who bring good news,
who proclaim peace,
who bring good tidings,
who proclaim salvation,
who say to Zion,
"Your God reigns!"
8 Listen! Your watchmen lift up their voices;
together they shout for joy.
When the LORD returns to Zion,
they will see it with their own eyes.
9 Burst into songs of joy together,
you ruins of Jerusalem,
for the LORD has comforted his people,
he has redeemed Jerusalem.
10 The LORD will lay bare his holy arm
in the sight of all the nations,
and all the ends of the earth will see
the salvation of our God.

11 Depart, depart, go out from there!
Touch no unclean thing!
Come out from it and be pure,
you who carry the vessels of the LORD.
12 But you will not leave in haste
or go in flight;
for the LORD will go before you,
the God of Israel will be your rear guard.

[a]5 Dead Sea Scrolls and Vulgate; Masoretic Text *wail*

52:4,5 *went down to Egypt . . . Assyria . . . taken away:* Around one thousand years earlier, Israel's ancestors (the family of Jacob) had gone to live in Egypt (Gen 46:1-4). The Israelite people were treated as slaves in Egypt, but the LORD saved them (Exod 1–15). Centuries later, Assyria defeated the northern kingdom of Israel (see the note at 6:11,12). The nation who took the people of Judah "away" was Babylon (see the notes at 11:11 and 40:2).

52:7 *those who bring good news:* In ancient times, messengers ran carrying news from place to place. They were especially important in times of battle (2 Sam 18:24-28).

52:7-10 *good news . . . God reigns . . . salvation of our God:* Those who guard Jerusalem's walls see a messenger coming with good news. The messenger says that the LORD is returning to Zion along with his people. See the notes at 41:27; 43:15; and 51:6.

52:11,12 *carry the vessels of the LORD:* See the notes at 40:2 and 43:19, 20. When Babylon defeated Jerusalem, they took many of Israel's treasures and temple items away (2 Kgs 25:13-17). As the Israelite people prepare to leave Babylon, God reminds them to gather the sacred items that had been stolen and bring them back to Jerusalem (Ezra 1:7-11). "Touch no unclean thing" probably refers to Babylonian religious items or idols. The new exodus from Babylon would be slow and orderly, not like the first exodus from Egypt, which was done in a hurry (Exod 12:31-34; 14:5-14).

52:5 Rom 2:24. **52:7** Nah 1:15; Rom 10:15; Eph 6:15. **52:11** 2 Cor 6:17.

52:13 *my servant:* This begins the fourth and last "servant song" in Isaiah (52:13—53:12). The servant could be the whole people of Israel (see the note at 41:8); a special, chosen leader (see the note at 42:1); or an individual, such as a prophet, who was treated badly because of what he said. The early church used this passage as a description for Jesus (Acts 8:32-35). The important thing is the message that God will help the servant succeed and will eventually reward the servant with honor and power (52:15; 53:12).

52:14,15 *appalled at him . . . shut their mouths because of him:* Israel certainly had become a despised nation (see the note at 49:7,8; also 50:4-10). But Isaiah promises that the LORD's deliverance of Israel will make other nations worship Israel's God. See also Rom 15:21; Phil 2:10,11.

53:2-5 *no beauty or majesty . . . despised and rejected:* It is not clear who is speaking these lines. Perhaps it is the other nations who are surprised to find out that Israel's suffering did not mean that the LORD had turned away from Israel forever. The LORD intended the suffering to be a step in God's plan to restore Israel and draw all people to worship Israel's God (see the note at 42:1). See also Matt 8:17; 1 Pet 2:22-24.

53:6,7 *sheep . . . shearers:* The speakers recognize that they have wandered away from the LORD's flock (see the note at 48:18,20). See also 1 Pet 2:25. The suffering servant is compared to a sheep that was quiet as it was being sheared. See also Rev 5:6.

53:1 John 12:38; Rom 10:16. **53:7,8** Acts 8:32, 33.

The Suffering and Glory of the Servant

13 See, my servant will act wisely[a];
he will be raised and lifted up and highly exalted.
14 Just as there were many who were appalled at him[b]—
his appearance was so disfigured beyond that of any man
and his form marred beyond human likeness—
15 so will he sprinkle many nations,[c]
and kings will shut their mouths because of him.
For what they were not told, they will see,
and what they have not heard, they will understand.

53 Who has believed our message
and to whom has the arm of the LORD been revealed?
2 He grew up before him like a tender shoot,
and like a root out of dry ground.
He had no beauty or majesty to attract us to him,
nothing in his appearance that we should desire him.
3 He was despised and rejected by men,
a man of sorrows, and familiar with suffering.
Like one from whom men hide their faces
he was despised, and we esteemed him not.

4 Surely he took up our infirmities
and carried our sorrows,
yet we considered him stricken by God,
smitten by him, and afflicted.
5 But he was pierced for our transgressions,
he was crushed for our iniquities;
the punishment that brought us peace was upon him,
and by his wounds we are healed.
6 We all, like sheep, have gone astray,
each of us has turned to his own way;
and the LORD has laid on him
the iniquity of us all.

7 He was oppressed and afflicted,
yet he did not open his mouth;
he was led like a lamb to the slaughter,
and as a sheep before her shearers is silent,
so he did not open his mouth.
8 By oppression[d] and judgment he was taken away.
And who can speak of his descendants?
For he was cut off from the land of the living;
for the transgression of my people he was stricken.[e]

[a]**13** Or *will prosper* [b]**14** Hebrew *you* [c]**15** Hebrew; Septuagint *so will many nations marvel at him* [d]**8** Or *From arrest* [e]**8** Or *away. / Yet who of his generation considered / that he was cut off from the land of the living / for the transgression of my people, / to whom the blow was due?*

[9]He was assigned a grave with the wicked,
and with the rich in his death,
though he had done no violence,
nor was any deceit in his mouth.

[10]Yet it was the LORD's will to crush him and
cause him to suffer,
and though the LORD makes[a] his life a guilt offering,
he will see his offspring and prolong his days,
and the will of the LORD will prosper in his hand.
[11]After the suffering of his soul,
he will see the light ⌞of life⌟[b] and be satisfied[c];
by his knowledge[d] my righteous servant will justify many,
and he will bear their iniquities.
[12]Therefore I will give him a portion among the great,[e]
and he will divide the spoils with the strong,[f]
because he poured out his life unto death,
and was numbered with the transgressors.
For he bore the sin of many,
and made intercession for the transgressors.

The Future Glory of Zion

54 "Sing, O barren woman,
you who never bore a child;
burst into song, shout for joy,
you who were never in labor;
because more are the children of the desolate woman
than of her who has a husband,"
says the LORD.
[2]"Enlarge the place of your tent,
stretch your tent curtains wide,
do not hold back;
lengthen your cords,
strengthen your stakes.
[3]For you will spread out to the right and to the left;
your descendants will dispossess nations
and settle in their desolate cities.

[4]"Do not be afraid; you will not suffer shame.
Do not fear disgrace; you will not be humiliated.
You will forget the shame of your youth
and remember no more the reproach of your
widowhood.
[5]For your Maker is your husband—

53:8,9 *he was taken away:* How the servant died is a mystery. Some have suggested this refers to someone who had a disease such as leprosy that eats away at the skin on a person's face and hands. His death is described as the result of the sins of others. See also 1 Pet 2:22 and the mini-article called "Burial," p. 1998.

53:10 *guilt offering:* The Law of Moses included instructions to Israel's priests for presenting burned offerings (sacrifices) to the LORD to remove guilt and sin (see Lev 4:1—6:7; 6:24—7:10). See also the chart called "Sacrifices and Offerings," p. 219. Here the servant gives his own life as a sacrifice to take away sins. See also Rom 3:21-26; Heb 9:25-28.

53:11 *suffering:* Just as Israel's faith was tested in order to make it pure (see the note at 48:10), the servant's suffering is said to lead to obedience.

54:1 *Sing, O barren woman:* Meaning that Jerusalem once again will be filled with Israelite people who will return from various nations. (See the notes at 49:19-22; 51:17,18.) See also Gal 4:27.

54:3 *dispossess nations and settle in their desolate cities:* Not only will Israel's people return to rebuild the towns of Judah, their descendants will occupy even more territory (see also the note at 26:15-18).

53:12 Luke 22:37; Phil 2:8,9.

[a]**10** Hebrew *though you make* [b]**11** Dead Sea Scrolls (see also Septuagint); Masoretic Text does not have *the light ⌞of life⌟*. [c]**11** Or (with Masoretic Text) *[11]He will see the result of the suffering of his soul / and be satisfied* [d]**11** Or *by knowledge of him* [e]**12** Or *many* [f]**12** Or *numerous*

"For a brief moment I abandoned you, but with deep compassion I will bring you back" . . . . says the LORD your Redeemer.
Isa 54:7,8

the LORD Almighty is his name—
the Holy One of Israel is your Redeemer;
he is called the God of all the earth.
6 The LORD will call you back
as if you were a wife deserted and distressed
in spirit—
a wife who married young,
only to be rejected," says your God.
7 "For a brief moment I abandoned you,
but with deep compassion I will bring you back.
8 In a surge of anger
I hid my face from you for a moment,
but with everlasting kindness
I will have compassion on you,"
says the LORD your Redeemer.

54:5 *LORD Almighty . . . Holy One of Israel:* See the notes on p. 1289 and at 5:18,19 (LORD).
54:8 *a wife:* The prophets often portrayed Israel as the LORD's wife. See Hos 1–3, for example.

THE SERVANT SONGS IN ISAIAH

Four passages in the book of Isaiah are often identified as "the Servant Songs" because they focus on the call and work of "the Servant of the LORD" (or "God's Servant"): Isa 42:1-9; 49:1-7; 50:4-11; and 52:13—53:12. These songs (or poems) describe the Servant as the one God chose to "bring justice to the nations" (42:1) and to lead the people of Israel back to God (49:5). But the Servant will also be "a light" so that other nations will recognize God's "salvation" (49:6). Unlike others in the Jewish Scriptures who are called the LORD's Servant (for example, Abraham, Jacob, and Moses), the Servant in Isaiah suffers physical pain and humiliation (50:6; 52:14; 53:3-7) in the work the LORD called him to do. The last of these songs, however, recognizes that the suffering of the Servant will help accomplish the work he was called to do. In other words, his own suffering will ultimately take away the sins and guilt of others (53:4-11), and the LORD will reward the Servant for sacrificing his life for others (53:12).

Scholars have different opinions about who this Servant might have been when the Songs were first written. Some believe the Servant was an important royal or religious individual in Israel's history who had the power to bring about change, such as King Hezekiah or Isaiah himself (see 61:1, 2). Other scholars believe the Servant was actually a reference to the people of Israel (see 49:3) to show that one day God will use Israel to bring hope and deliverance to the nations of the world. Still other scholars see the Servant Songs only as predictions of the future life and death of a Messiah (Chosen One) whose own servanthood and suffering would give life to people. See also the mini-article called "Messiah (Chosen One)," p. 1124.

As the early followers of Jesus read the Servant Songs, they clearly connected "the Servant" with Jesus the Messiah (Christ). For example, Matthew wrote that the predictions of Isaiah 42:1-4 were fulfilled in the life and work of Jesus (see Matt 12:18-21). Similarly, the early church leader Philip explained to an Ethiopian official that the words of Isaiah 53:7,8 referred to Jesus (Acts 8:26-35). Jesus identifies himself as the servant who will "give his life as a ransom for many" (Mark 10:45) and offers his work as a model of servanthood for his followers to practice. See also Phil 2:6-11; 1 Pet 2:22-25.

[9]"To me this is like the days of Noah,
when I swore that the waters of Noah would never
again cover the earth.
So now I have sworn not to be angry with you,
never to rebuke you again.
[10]Though the mountains be shaken
and the hills be removed,
yet my unfailing love for you will not be shaken
nor my covenant of peace be removed,"
says the LORD, who has compassion on you.

[11]"O afflicted city, lashed by storms and not comforted,
I will build you with stones of turquoise,[a]
your foundations with sapphires.[b]
[12]I will make your battlements of rubies,
your gates of sparkling jewels,
and all your walls of precious stones.
[13]All your sons will be taught by the LORD,
and great will be your children's peace.
[14]In righteousness you will be established:
Tyranny will be far from you;
you will have nothing to fear.
Terror will be far removed;
it will not come near you.
[15]If anyone does attack you, it will not be my doing;
whoever attacks you will surrender to you.

[16]"See, it is I who created the blacksmith
who fans the coals into flame
and forges a weapon fit for its work.
And it is I who have created the destroyer to work havoc;
[17]no weapon forged against you will prevail,
and you will refute every tongue that accuses you.
This is the heritage of the servants of the LORD,
and this is their vindication from me,"
declares the LORD.

Invitation to the Thirsty

55 "Come, all you who are thirsty,
come to the waters;
and you who have no money,
come, buy and eat!
Come, buy wine and milk
without money and without cost.
[2]Why spend money on what is not bread,
and your labor on what does not satisfy?

[a]11 The meaning of the Hebrew for this word is uncertain. [b]11 Or *lapis lazuli*

54:10 *my covenant:* The LORD's relationship with the people of Israel was based on a number of covenants. For more, see the mini-article called "Covenants (Agreements)," p. 386.

54:11,12 *afflicted city . . . sparkling jewels:* Jerusalem was left in ruins when the Babylonian armies destroyed the city. But now the LORD will help the people build a new Jerusalem even more beautiful than the old one. See also Rev 21:18-21 and the note on p. 1289 (Judah and Jerusalem).

54:14 *In righteousness you will be established:* See the notes at 1:16,17 and 28:16,17. In the new Jerusalem, the LORD's people will live according to the LORD's justice (58:5-10; 59:1-17; 61:1-9).

54:16,17 *blacksmith . . . the servants of the LORD:* Blacksmiths melted metal over hot coal fires and then poured the hot liquid metal into molds. After the metal cooled, the molded objects were pounded or trimmed into shape. This method was used to make weapons of iron, bronze or copper. For "servants," see the note at 41:8.

55:2 *what is not bread . . . richest of fare:* The offer in 55:1 probably is meant to be an invitation to "eat" the LORD's wisdom and promise of a new beginning (see also 25:6-8). Here, "what is not bread" refers to anything that does not really satisfy spiritual hunger. One example would be trusting in the promises of other gods. See also Prov 9:1-5; Jer 31:12-14.

54:9 Gen 9:8-17. **54:10** Ps 46; Isa 26:3. **54:13** John 6:45. **55:1** Rev 21:6; 22:17.

55:6,7 *wicked forsake his way:* The "way" the wicked should forsake means following other gods and treating the poor unfairly (see the note at 43:25).

55:3 2 Sam 7:4-17; Ps 89:20-37; Acts 13:34. **55:5** Ps 72:5-20; Isa 2:2-4; 60:10-18; 62:1-3. **55:8,9** Job 11:7-9; Ps 145:3; Isa 40:13-15.

Listen, listen to me, and eat what is good,
and your soul will delight in the richest of fare.
3 Give ear and come to me;
hear me, that your soul may live.
I will make an everlasting covenant with you,
my faithful love promised to David.
4 See, I have made him a witness to the peoples,
a leader and commander of the peoples.
5 Surely you will summon nations you know not,
and nations that do not know you will hasten to you,
because of the LORD your God,
the Holy One of Israel,
for he has endowed you with splendor."

6 Seek the LORD while he may be found;
call on him while he is near.
7 Let the wicked forsake his way
and the evil man his thoughts.
Let him turn to the LORD, and he will have mercy on him,
and to our God, for he will freely pardon.

8 "For my thoughts are not your thoughts,
neither are your ways my ways,"
declares the LORD.

QUESTIONS ABOUT ISAIAH 40:1—55:13

1. How does the end of chapter 39 serve as a kind of "bridge" between the first main section of ISAIAH (1–39) and the second main section (40–55)?
2. In chapter 40, the prophet announces good news to God's people (40:1) and to the city of Zion (40:9). What are these "good tidings"? Why is this announcement especially comforting for the people of Israel?
3. What images of God are presented in chapter 40? (See 40:10, 11, 22, 28, 29.) How do each of these images clarify the good news being announced to God's people?
4. Who is the "one from the east" who was chosen by the LORD to defeat Israel's enemies and free them from exile? (41:2; 44:28—45:4) What important ancient empire did this ruler establish?
5. Isaiah 40–55 often describes a "servant" chosen by the LORD. In the following passages, describe what the servant is chosen to do:
   - **a.** 41:8-11
   - **b.** 42:1-7,19
   - **c.** 44:1-5,21
   - **d.** 44:28—45:4
   - **e.** 49:1-6
   - **f.** 50:4-11
   - **g.** 52:1—53:12

   Who do you think the servant is?
6. How does Isaiah describe idols made of wood and stone in this section? How do they compare to the LORD? (40:12-26; 41:21-29; 44:9-20)
7. What was the LORD's message to Babylon? The Babylonians had been trusting in powers that would no longer be able to save them. What were these powers? (47:1-15) How does the warning given to Babylon also apply to the people of Israel? How does it apply to God's followers today?
8. What will the "new" Jerusalem look like? (52:7-10) What will happen there? (54:1—55:5)

9 "As the heavens are higher than the earth,
so are my ways higher than your ways
and my thoughts than your thoughts.
10 As the rain and the snow
come down from heaven,
and do not return to it
without watering the earth
and making it bud and flourish,
so that it yields seed for the sower and bread for the
eater,
11 so is my word that goes out from my mouth:
It will not return to me empty,
but will accomplish what I desire
and achieve the purpose for which I sent it.
12 You will go out in joy
and be led forth in peace;
the mountains and hills
will burst into song before you,
and all the trees of the field
will clap their hands.
13 Instead of the thornbush will grow the pine tree,
and instead of briers the myrtle will grow.
This will be for the LORD's renown,
for an everlasting sign,
which will not be destroyed."

The LORD says, *"You will go out in joy and be led forth in peace; the mountains and hills will burst into song before you, and all the trees of the field will clap their hands."*
Isa 55:12

55:11 *my word:* The LORD's "word" has power to create (Gen 1) and to save (Ps 107:20). Here the LORD's word promises to bring the people out of exile in Babylon (46:10) and to help them build a new Jerusalem (54:11-14).

55:12 *You will go out in joy:* In 538 B.C., Cyrus released the Israelites from exile in Babylon. See the notes at 40:2 and 43:19,20.

55:13 *pine tree . . . myrtle:* These trees will grow in areas that had earlier been turned into thorny desert by the LORD's judgment (5:5-7). See the note at 41:17-19.

56:1 *Maintain justice . . . salvation:* God's salvation will include nations who had not been part of God's people in the past (see 51:5). But this will happen only if God's people live right and treat others with justice (see the notes at 1:16,17 and 45:7,8).

ISAIAH, Part 3: Warnings and Promises for God's New People after the Exile

The final section of ISAIAH (56–66) focuses on the people of God living in the city of Jerusalem. The people are challenged to turn away from idols and obey God's commands, especially the command to bring justice to all people (59:7-15; 61:1-3). Promises of God's new creation (65:17-25) are mixed with threats of punishment for those who reject the LORD and the LORD's Law (65:1-16).

DO RIGHT AND OBEY GOD'S LAWS

Other nations will become part of God's people. Israel and its leaders are told to be examples to the nations by living according to the LORD's commands and treating all people with fairness and justice.

Salvation for Others

56 This is what the LORD says:

"Maintain justice
and do what is right,

56:2-6 *keeps the Sabbath . . . hold fast to my covenant:* Foreigners (non-Israelites) are welcome in the new Jerusalem. However, they must follow the same rules as the Israelites. They must keep the Sabbath (Exod 20:8-11; 31:12-17; Deut 5:12-15). They must refuse to worship idols and they must obey the Law of Moses (see the note at 2:3). Portions of the law had excluded foreigners and eunuchs (Deut 23:1-3), but these groups are now invited to take part in the new community of God's people.

56:5 *a memorial and a name:* If a man had no children to carry on his family name, a small sign or plaque could be placed in the temple so his name might be remembered (2 Sam 18:18).

56:7 *holy mountain . . . house of prayer:* Refers to the temple on Mount Zion in Jerusalem. See the notes at 1:8 and 2:2.

56:7 *offerings and sacrifices:* See the note at 1:11-14. The temple area would now be open to foreigners who came to worship Israel's LORD. See also Matt 21:13; Mark 11:17; Luke 19:46.

56:8 *I will gather still others to them:* The Israelites who were brought back to Jerusalem from exile (see the note at 11:11) would be joined by non-Israelites ("others") in worshiping the LORD (25:6-8; 45:22).

56:9,10 *beasts of the field . . . Israel's watchmen:* The "beasts" probably stand for foreign nations who invaded Israel and Judah (5:26-30). Israel's watchmen (prophets and priests) were to guard the people as watchdogs or shepherds guard a herd of sheep.

for my salvation is close at hand
and my righteousness will soon be revealed.
2 Blessed is the man who does this,
the man who holds it fast,
who keeps the Sabbath without desecrating it,
and keeps his hand from doing any evil."

3 Let no foreigner who has bound himself to the LORD say,
"The LORD will surely exclude me from his people."
And let not any eunuch complain,
"I am only a dry tree."

4 For this is what the LORD says:

"To the eunuchs who keep my Sabbaths,
who choose what pleases me
and hold fast to my covenant—
5 to them I will give within my temple and its walls
a memorial and a name
better than sons and daughters;
I will give them an everlasting name
that will not be cut off.
6 And foreigners who bind themselves to the LORD
to serve him,
to love the name of the LORD,
and to worship him,
all who keep the Sabbath without desecrating it
and who hold fast to my covenant—
7 these I will bring to my holy mountain
and give them joy in my house of prayer.
Their burnt offerings and sacrifices
will be accepted on my altar;
for my house will be called
a house of prayer for all nations."
8 The Sovereign LORD declares—
he who gathers the exiles of Israel:
"I will gather still others to them
besides those already gathered."

God's Accusation Against the Wicked

9 Come, all you beasts of the field,
come and devour, all you beasts of the forest!
10 Israel's watchmen are blind,
they all lack knowledge;
they are all mute dogs,
they cannot bark;
they lie around and dream,
they love to sleep.
11 They are dogs with mighty appetites;

they never have enough.
They are shepherds who lack understanding;
they all turn to their own way,
each seeks his own gain.
12 "Come," each one cries, "let me get wine!
Let us drink our fill of beer!
And tomorrow will be like today,
or even far better."

57 The righteous perish,
and no one ponders it in his heart;
devout men are taken away,
and no one understands
that the righteous are taken away
to be spared from evil.
2 Those who walk uprightly
enter into peace;
they find rest as they lie in death.
3 "But you—come here, you sons of a sorceress,
you offspring of adulterers and prostitutes!
4 Whom are you mocking?
At whom do you sneer
and stick out your tongue?
Are you not a brood of rebels,
the offspring of liars?
5 You burn with lust among the oaks
and under every spreading tree;
you sacrifice your children in the ravines
and under the overhanging crags.
6 ⌊The idols⌋ among the smooth stones of the ravines are
your portion;
they, they are your lot.
Yes, to them you have poured out drink offerings
and offered grain offerings.
In the light of these things, should I relent?
7 You have made your bed on a high and lofty hill;
there you went up to offer your sacrifices.
8 Behind your doors and your doorposts
you have put your pagan symbols.
Forsaking me, you uncovered your bed,
you climbed into it and opened it wide;
you made a pact with those whose beds you love,
and you looked on their nakedness.
9 You went to Molech[a] with olive oil
and increased your perfumes.

[a]9 Or *to the king*

57:1 *righteous perish . . . taken away:* Like lambs attacked by wild animals, God's people were killed or dragged away into exile. This happened because Israel's leaders turned away from trusting the LORD.

57:3 *offspring of adulterers and prostitutes:* See also the mini-article called "Prostitution in the Bible," p. 1688. See the notes at 1:29-31; 2:18,19.

57:5-7 *burn with lust . . . sacrifice your children . . . made your bed:* Ancient Canaanite worship sites were usually built on a high place (57:7), or near a grove of trees (57:5; see also Deut 12:2; 1 Kgs 14:23; Jer 2:20). The fertility rites and rituals honoring the Canaanite gods may have included worshipers having sex with cult prostitutes (Hos 4:11-14). The people of Israel were forbidden to sacrifice their children to honor the god Molech (Lev 18:21; Deut 18:10, 11). However, some followed this horrible practice anyway (2 Kgs 17:16-18; Ps 106:36-38; Jer 19:4-13).

57:8 *pagan symbols . . . those whose beds you love:* The "symbols" were small idols or good luck charms believed to provide protection. "Those whose beds you love" here are the foreign gods and the idols that represented them. The people have not literally "gone to bed" with these idols. But the peoples' unfaithfulness to God is like a person being unfaithful in marriage.

57:9 *Molech . . . olive oil:* See the note at 17:6. Olive oil was poured on the head of someone chosen to be a leader (1 Sam 10:1,2). Apparently, worshipers of Molech smeared themselves with olive oil and perfumed oils. Molech was the main god of the nation of Ammon (1 Kgs 11:7). Ceremonies honoring Molech sometimes included sacrificing children.

> *For this is what the high and lofty One says—he who lives forever, whose name is holy: "I live in a high and holy place, but also with him who is contrite and lowly in spirit."*
> Isa 57:15

57:9 *descended to the grave itself:* Probably referring to trying to contact the spirits of the dead.

57:13,14 *the land . . . my holy mountain . . . prepare the road:* "The land" and "my holy mountain" refer to Judah and Jerusalem's Mount Zion (see the note at 1:8). "The road" is the road that leads to Jerusalem from Babylon (see the note at 40:3).

57:15 *I live in a high and holy place:* The LORD's home was pictured as being in the heavens, far removed from human beings (18:4). However, God also promised to be near the people by living above the ark of the covenant in the Most Holy Place of the temple (see the note at 6:1, 2).

57:13 Isa 41:21-29; 44:9-22.
57:19 Eph 2:17.

You sent your ambassadors[a] far away;
  you descended to the grave[b] itself!
10 You were wearied by all your ways,
  but you would not say, 'It is hopeless.'
You found renewal of your strength,
  and so you did not faint.

11 "Whom have you so dreaded and feared
  that you have been false to me,
and have neither remembered me
  nor pondered this in your hearts?
Is it not because I have long been silent
  that you do not fear me?
12 I will expose your righteousness and your works,
  and they will not benefit you.
13 When you cry out for help,
  let your collection ⌞of idols⌟ save you!
The wind will carry all of them off,
  a mere breath will blow them away.
But the man who makes me his refuge
  will inherit the land
  and possess my holy mountain."

Comfort for the Contrite

14 And it will be said:

"Build up, build up, prepare the road!
  Remove the obstacles out of the way of my people."
15 For this is what the high and lofty One says—
  he who lives forever, whose name is holy:
"I live in a high and holy place,
  but also with him who is contrite and lowly in spirit,
to revive the spirit of the lowly
  and to revive the heart of the contrite.
16 I will not accuse forever,
  nor will I always be angry,
for then the spirit of man would grow faint before me—
  the breath of man that I have created.
17 I was enraged by his sinful greed;
  I punished him, and hid my face in anger,
  yet he kept on in his willful ways.
18 I have seen his ways, but I will heal him;
  I will guide him and restore comfort to him,
19 creating praise on the lips of the mourners in Israel.
Peace, peace, to those far and near,"
  says the LORD. "And I will heal them."

[a]9 Or *idols* [b]9 Hebrew *Sheol*

[20] But the wicked are like the tossing sea,
which cannot rest,
whose waves cast up mire and mud.
[21] "There is no peace," says my God, "for the wicked."

True Fasting

58 "Shout it aloud, do not hold back.
Raise your voice like a trumpet.
Declare to my people their rebellion
and to the house of Jacob their sins.
[2] For day after day they seek me out;
they seem eager to know my ways,
as if they were a nation that does what is right
and has not forsaken the commands of its God.
They ask me for just decisions
and seem eager for God to come near them.
[3] 'Why have we fasted,' they say,
'and you have not seen it?
Why have we humbled ourselves,
and you have not noticed?'

"Yet on the day of your fasting, you do as you please
and exploit all your workers.
[4] Your fasting ends in quarreling and strife,
and in striking each other with wicked fists.
You cannot fast as you do today
and expect your voice to be heard on high.
[5] Is this the kind of fast I have chosen,
only a day for a man to humble himself?
Is it only for bowing one's head like a reed
and for lying on sackcloth and ashes?
Is that what you call a fast,
a day acceptable to the LORD?

[6] "Is not this the kind of fasting I have chosen:
to loose the chains of injustice
and untie the cords of the yoke,
to set the oppressed free
and break every yoke?
[7] Is it not to share your food with the hungry
and to provide the poor wanderer with shelter—
when you see the naked, to clothe him,
and not to turn away from your own flesh and blood?
[8] Then your light will break forth like the dawn,
and your healing will quickly appear;
then your righteousness[a] will go before you,
and the glory of the LORD will be your rear guard.

---

[a]**8** Or *your righteous One*

58:1 *Declare to my people their rebellion:* See the notes at 1:2 (children) and 1:4 (nation).

58:2-5 *seek me out . . . fasted . . . sackcloth:* Outwardly, the people had continued to worship the LORD. They brought the required sacrifices and offerings. They fasted on special holy festival days. They even wore sackcloth and rubbed ashes on themselves to show that they were sorry for their sins (see also Job 2:8; Jonah 3:5,6; Joel 1:13,14). But these acts of worship were meaningless if the people did not treat each other with respect and justice.

58:6,7 *Is not this the kind of fasting I have chosen:* True worship was more than rituals and acts of honor or praise. Here, worship also means treating others with justice and fairness (see the note at 1:16,17). See also Matt 25:31-46.

58:8 *your light:* See 60:1-3 and the notes at 2:5 and 42:3-6.

58:8 *glory of the LORD:* This probably refers to how the LORD protected the people of ancient Israel as they fled from Egypt (Exod 13:21,22). The LORD's glory is often described as coming in thunder and lightning (see Exod 19:16-19, for example).

57:21 Isa 48:22.

"The LORD will guide you always; he will satisfy your needs in a sun-scorched land and will strengthen your frame."
Isa 58:11

58:10 *your light will rise in the darkness:* They will live according to the "light" of God's truth and justice, making the dark places of evil and injustice disappear. See also 61:1-3, 8-10.

58:13 *keep your feet from breaking the Sabbath:* See the notes at 1:11-14 and 56:2-6.

58:14 *your father Jacob:* See the note at 2:3.

59:2 *your iniquities:* See the notes at 1:2 (children) and 1:4 (nation).

59:4 *they conceive trouble and give birth to evil:* See the notes at 1:16,17 and 5:23. The people had become so sinful that it was as if they were giving birth to evil, itself. See also Job 15:34,35.

59:5 *vipers:* In the Bible, wicked people or evil in general is often represented by vipers, which are poisonous snakes (Ps 58:4; 140:3; Matt 3:7; 23:33; Jas 3:8).

58:11 Isa 35:1-7; 49:10.

9 Then you will call, and the LORD will answer;
you will cry for help, and he will say: Here am I.

"If you do away with the yoke of oppression,
with the pointing finger and malicious talk,
10 and if you spend yourselves in behalf of the hungry
and satisfy the needs of the oppressed,
then your light will rise in the darkness,
and your night will become like the noonday.
11 The LORD will guide you always;
he will satisfy your needs in a sun-scorched land
and will strengthen your frame.
You will be like a well-watered garden,
like a spring whose waters never fail.
12 Your people will rebuild the ancient ruins
and will raise up the age-old foundations;
you will be called Repairer of Broken Walls,
Restorer of Streets with Dwellings.

13 "If you keep your feet from breaking the Sabbath
and from doing as you please on my holy day,
if you call the Sabbath a delight
and the LORD's holy day honorable,
and if you honor it by not going your own way
and not doing as you please or speaking idle words,
14 then you will find your joy in the LORD,
and I will cause you to ride on the heights of the land
and to feast on the inheritance of your father Jacob."
The mouth of the LORD has spoken.

Sin, Confession and Redemption

59 Surely the arm of the LORD is not too short to save,
nor his ear too dull to hear.
2 But your iniquities have separated
you from your God;
your sins have hidden his face from you,
so that he will not hear.
3 For your hands are stained with blood,
your fingers with guilt.
Your lips have spoken lies,
and your tongue mutters wicked things.
4 No one calls for justice;
no one pleads his case with integrity.
They rely on empty arguments and speak lies;
they conceive trouble and give birth to evil.
5 They hatch the eggs of vipers
and spin a spider's web.
Whoever eats their eggs will die,
and when one is broken, an adder is hatched.

6 Their cobwebs are useless for clothing;
they cannot cover themselves with what they make.
Their deeds are evil deeds,
and acts of violence are in their hands.
7 Their feet rush into sin;
they are swift to shed innocent blood.
Their thoughts are evil thoughts;
ruin and destruction mark their ways.
8 The way of peace they do not know;
there is no justice in their paths.
They have turned them into crooked roads;
no one who walks in them will know peace.

9 So justice is far from us,
and righteousness does not reach us.
We look for light, but all is darkness;
for brightness, but we walk in deep shadows.
10 Like the blind we grope along the wall,
feeling our way like men without eyes.
At midday we stumble as if it were twilight;
among the strong, we are like the dead.
11 We all growl like bears;
we moan mournfully like doves.
We look for justice, but find none;
for deliverance, but it is far away.

12 For our offenses are many in your sight,
and our sins testify against us.
Our offenses are ever with us,
and we acknowledge our iniquities:
13 rebellion and treachery against the LORD,
turning our backs on our God,
fomenting oppression and revolt,
uttering lies our hearts have conceived.
14 So justice is driven back,
and righteousness stands at a distance;
truth has stumbled in the streets,
honesty cannot enter.
15 Truth is nowhere to be found,
and whoever shuns evil becomes a prey.

The LORD looked and was displeased
that there was no justice.
16 He saw that there was no one,
he was appalled that there was no one to intervene;
so his own arm worked salvation for him,
and his own righteousness sustained him.
17 He put on righteousness as his breastplate,
and the helmet of salvation on his head;
he put on the garments of vengeance

59:12,13 *our offenses . . . rebellion and treachery:* See the notes at 1:2 (children); 1:4 (nation); and 58:2-5.

59:16 *his own arm worked salvation:* See the note at 19:16 and the mini-article called "Salvation," p. 2021. See also 63:5.

59:17 *put on righteousness as his breastplate:* See the note at 1:16, 17. See also Eph 6:14, 17; 1 Thes 5:8.

59:7,8 Rom 3:15-17. **59:10** Job 5:12-14.

For Ye Shall Go Out with Joy . . . And All the Trees of the Field Shall Clap Their Hands by Chaim Gross, 1979. When the people of Judah were at last allowed to return home from their exile in Babylon, the joy of the people would be so great, Isaiah said, that all of nature will take part in the celebration. "The mountains and hills will burst into song before you, and all the trees of the field will clap their hands." (See 55:1-13.)

and wrapped himself in zeal as in a cloak.
18 According to what they have done,
so will he repay
wrath to his enemies
and retribution to his foes;
he will repay the islands their due.
19 From the west, men will fear the name of the LORD,
and from the rising of the sun, they will revere
his glory.
For he will come like a pent-up flood
that the breath of the LORD drives along.[a]
20 "The Redeemer will come to Zion,
to those in Jacob who repent of their sins,"
declares the LORD.

21 "As for me, this is my covenant with them," says the LORD.
"My Spirit, who is on you, and my words that I have put in your
mouth will not depart from your mouth, or from the mouths of
your children, or from the mouths of their descendants from this
time on and forever," says the LORD.

[a]**19** Or *When the enemy comes in like a flood, / the Spirit of the LORD will put him to flight*

59:18-20 *repay . . . retribution:* The LORD will punish Israel's enemies and bring his people back to Zion (Jerusalem) from distant lands (see the notes at 11:11 and 43:6). When Jerusalem is rebuilt and repopulated, foreign nations will see what has happened and honor Israel's LORD. See also the notes at 1:8 and 2:3.

59:21 *My Spirit . . . words that I have put in your mouth:* See the notes at 11:2 and 13:1 (oracle). See also 41:27. The LORD's message is brought by prophets like Isaiah, who have received the LORD's Spirit.

59:20 Rom 11:26.

CELEBRATE, JERUSALEM, FOR I HAVE SAVED YOU

Chapters 60–62 describe how foreigners will help rebuild Jerusalem and bring gifts to Israel's people and to the LORD. The LORD's people will live as shining examples of justice, and it will be clear to all that Israel is once again God's "Holy People" (62:12).

The Glory of Zion

60 "Arise, shine, for your light has come,
and the glory of the LORD rises upon you.
2 See, darkness covers the earth
and thick darkness is over the peoples,
but the LORD rises upon you
and his glory appears over you.
3 Nations will come to your light,
and kings to the brightness of your dawn.
4 "Lift up your eyes and look about you:
All assemble and come to you;
your sons come from afar,
and your daughters are carried on the arm.
5 Then you will look and be radiant,
your heart will throb and swell with joy;
the wealth on the seas will be brought to you,
to you the riches of the nations will come.
6 Herds of camels will cover your land,
young camels of Midian and Ephah.
And all from Sheba will come,
bearing gold and incense
and proclaiming the praise of the LORD.
7 All Kedar's flocks will be gathered to you,
the rams of Nebaioth will serve you;
they will be accepted as offerings on my altar,
and I will adorn my glorious temple.
8 "Who are these that fly along like clouds,
like doves to their nests?
9 Surely the islands look to me;
in the lead are the ships of Tarshish,[a]
bringing your sons from afar,
with their silver and gold,
to the honor of the LORD your God,
the Holy One of Israel,
for he has endowed you with splendor.

10 "Foreigners will rebuild your walls,
and their kings will serve you.

[a]9 Or *the trading ships*

60:1 *glory of the LORD rises upon you:* The future that the LORD has promised for Jerusalem is like a new day that dawns with a bright sunrise. See also the notes at 4:5 and 58:8 (light, LORD's glory). The glorious light of the LORD and of his people will draw nations to Jerusalem (2:2-5; 42:6,7).

60:4 *All assemble . . . come from afar:* God's people will return from exile. See the notes at 11:11 and 49:19-22.

60:6,7 *Midian . . . Ephah . . . Sheba . . . Nebaioth:* The Midianites were descendants of Midian, the son of Abraham and Keturah (Gen 25:1-4). They were a nomadic tribe of the Arabian Desert, east of the Gulf of Aqaba. Ephah was a clan within the tribe of Midian. Sheba may refer to a place in what is now southwest Arabia (see also 1 Kgs 10:1-13). Kedar (see the note at 21:13-17) and Nebaioth were regions in northern Arabia. See also 18:7; 45:14; 61:6; 66:12.

60:7 *my glorious temple:* This refers to the new temple that was rebuilt after the exile. It was rededicated in 515 B.C. See also the notes at 2:2 and 49:19-22.

60:9 *the islands:* This likely refers to Greek islands in the Mediterranean Sea, where some of the people of Judah had been sold as slaves (see the note at 11:11).

60:10 *rebuild your walls:* After many of the Israelite people returned from exile, Kings Cyrus and Darius of Persia helped them rebuild the temple (Ezra 3:7; 4:24—6:15). Later, King Artaxerxes of Persia helped the Israelite people rebuild the city walls (Neh 2:1-8).

Though in anger I struck you,
in favor I will show you compassion.
11 Your gates will always stand open,
they will never be shut, day or night,
so that men may bring you the wealth of the nations—
their kings led in triumphal procession.
12 For the nation or kingdom that will not serve you
will perish;
it will be utterly ruined.

13 "The glory of Lebanon will come to you,
the pine, the fir and the cypress together,
to adorn the place of my sanctuary;
and I will glorify the place of my feet.
14 The sons of your oppressors will come bowing
before you;
all who despise you will bow down at your feet
and will call you the City of the LORD,
Zion of the Holy One of Israel.

15 "Although you have been forsaken and hated,
with no one traveling through,
I will make you the everlasting pride
and the joy of all generations.
16 You will drink the milk of nations
and be nursed at royal breasts.
Then you will know that I, the LORD, am your
Savior,
your Redeemer, the Mighty One of Jacob.
17 Instead of bronze I will bring you gold,
and silver in place of iron.
Instead of wood I will bring you bronze,
and iron in place of stones.
I will make peace your governor
and righteousness your ruler.
18 No longer will violence be heard in your land,
nor ruin or destruction within your borders,
but you will call your walls Salvation
and your gates Praise.
19 The sun will no more be your light by day,
nor will the brightness of the moon shine on you,
for the LORD will be your everlasting light,
and your God will be your glory.
20 Your sun will never set again,
and your moon will wane no more;
the LORD will be your everlasting light,
and your days of sorrow will end.
21 Then will all your people be righteous
and they will possess the land forever.

60:13 *glory of Lebanon . . . pine, the fir and the cypress:* See the notes at 2:13-16 and 14:8. See also Ezra 3:7; Neh 2:8.

60:14 *City of the LORD . . . Zion:* See the note at 1:8.

60:14 *LORD . . . Holy One of Israel:* See the notes at 1:2 (LORD) and 5:18, 19.

60:17 *bronze:* This metal was made by melting and mixing copper and tin.

60:19 *LORD . . . everlasting light:* See the note at 60:1. See also Rev 21:23; 22:5.

60:21 *righteous . . . possess the land forever:* See the note at 1:16, 17. The LORD's ancient covenant with Israel's ancestor Abraham (Gen 17:7, 8) included a promise of land. But Israel could only keep the land if they were "righteous," that is, obeyed the Law and worshiped only the LORD God (Deut 6:10-25). See also the mini-article called "Land," p. 1751. God "planted" Israel in the land, so the people could be examples of the LORD's justice (see 5:2,7).

60:11 Rev 21:25,26. **60:14** Isa 49:7,23; Rev 3:9.

They are the shoot I have planted,
the work of my hands,
for the display of my splendor.
22 The least of you will become a thousand,
the smallest a mighty nation.
I am the LORD;
in its time I will do this swiftly."

The Year of the LORD's Favor

61 The Spirit of the Sovereign LORD is on me,
because the LORD has anointed me
to preach good news to the poor.
He has sent me to bind up the brokenhearted,
to proclaim freedom for the captives
and release from darkness for the prisoners,[a]
2 to proclaim the year of the LORD's favor
and the day of vengeance of our God,
to comfort all who mourn,
3 and provide for those who grieve in Zion—
to bestow on them a crown of beauty
instead of ashes,
the oil of gladness
instead of mourning,
and a garment of praise
instead of a spirit of despair.
They will be called oaks of righteousness,
a planting of the LORD
for the display of his splendor.

4 They will rebuild the ancient ruins
and restore the places long devastated;
they will renew the ruined cities
that have been devastated for generations.
5 Aliens will shepherd your flocks;
foreigners will work your fields and vineyards.
6 And you will be called priests of the LORD,
you will be named ministers of our God.
You will feed on the wealth of nations,
and in their riches you will boast.

7 Instead of their shame
my people will receive a double portion,
and instead of disgrace
they will rejoice in their inheritance;
and so they will inherit a double portion in their land,
and everlasting joy will be theirs.

[a]1 Hebrew; Septuagint *the blind*

61:1,2 *Spirit . . . anointed me . . . good news:* See the note at 11:2. It is not clear whether Isaiah or the "servant" is speaking here (see 42:1-4; 49:1-9). The speaker has been chosen to announce the good news (see the note at 41:27), which includes healing and freedom. The "year" (61:2) is likely a reference to the Year of Jubilee, which came every fifty years. During a Jubilee year, slaves were granted freedom and lands were returned to their original family owners (Lev 25:8-34). These verses were later quoted by Jesus as a way of describing the work he was chosen to do (Luke 4:16-19). See also Matt 11:5; Luke 7:22.

61:3 *oil of gladness instead of mourning:* See the note at 17:6. Because of its many uses, olive oil was considered a great blessing.

61:3 *oaks of righteousness:* See the notes at 1:16,17 and 60:21. See also Ps 1:1-3; Isa 27:2-6.

61:4 *rebuild the ancient ruins:* Meaning those cities destroyed when the armies of Assyria and Babylon invaded the land (see the notes at 40:2 and 60:10).

61:6 *priests . . . ministers:* The people of Israel will have a special place as the LORD's priests among the nations (Exod 19:6). See also 1 Pet 2:9.

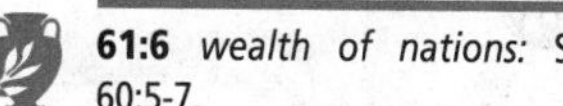

61:6 *wealth of nations:* See 60:5-7.

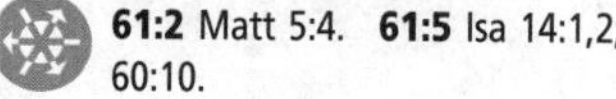

61:2 Matt 5:4. **61:5** Isa 14:1,2; 60:10.

The Sovereign LORD will make righteousness and praise spring up before all nations.
Isa 61:11

61:8 *justice:* See the note at 1:16,17.

61:8,9 *everlasting covenant . . . blessed:* See 54:9 and the note at 54:10. This covenant could be the new one the LORD promised to make with Israel (55:3-5; 59:21; also Jer 31:31-37). The covenant the LORD made with Israel's ancestor Abraham said that nations would be blessed by Abraham's descendants (Gen 12:1-3).

62:1 *salvation like a blazing torch:* See the notes at 2:5; 42:3-6; and 58:10.

62:4,5 *as a bridegroom rejoices over his bride:* The imagery here promises that the LORD will give Israel the attention a new husband gives his bride. The LORD's people will once again occupy the land they had been promised (see the note at 60:21).

62:6 *watchmen:* See the note at 21:6.

61:10 Isa 49:18; Rev 21:2.

8 "For I, the LORD, love justice;
I hate robbery and iniquity.
In my faithfulness I will reward them
and make an everlasting covenant with them.
9 Their descendants will be known among the nations
and their offspring among the peoples.
All who see them will acknowledge
that they are a people the LORD has blessed."

10 I delight greatly in the LORD;
my soul rejoices in my God.
For he has clothed me with garments of salvation
and arrayed me in a robe of righteousness,
as a bridegroom adorns his head like a priest,
and as a bride adorns herself with her jewels.
11 For as the soil makes the sprout come up
and a garden causes seeds to grow,
so the Sovereign LORD will make righteousness and praise
spring up before all nations.

Zion's New Name

62 For Zion's sake I will not keep silent,
for Jerusalem's sake I will not remain quiet,
till her righteousness shines out like the dawn,
her salvation like a blazing torch.
2 The nations will see your righteousness,
and all kings your glory;
you will be called by a new name
that the mouth of the LORD will bestow.
3 You will be a crown of splendor in the LORD's hand,
a royal diadem in the hand of your God.
4 No longer will they call you Deserted,
or name your land Desolate.
But you will be called Hephzibah,[a]
and your land Beulah[b];
for the LORD will take delight in you,
and your land will be married.
5 As a young man marries a maiden,
so will your sons[c] marry you;
as a bridegroom rejoices over his bride,
so will your God rejoice over you.
6 I have posted watchmen on your walls, O Jerusalem;
they will never be silent day or night.
You who call on the LORD,
give yourselves no rest,

[a]4 *Hephzibah* means *my delight is in her.* [b]4 *Beulah* means *married.*
[c]5 Or *Builder*

7 and give him no rest till he establishes Jerusalem
and makes her the praise of the earth.

8 The LORD has sworn by his right hand
and by his mighty arm:
"Never again will I give your grain
as food for your enemies,
and never again will foreigners drink the new wine
for which you have toiled;
9 but those who harvest it will eat it
and praise the LORD,
and those who gather the grapes will drink it
in the courts of my sanctuary."

10 Pass through, pass through the gates!
Prepare the way for the people.
Build up, build up the highway!
Remove the stones.
Raise a banner for the nations.

11 The LORD has made proclamation
to the ends of the earth:
"Say to the Daughter of Zion,
'See, your Savior comes!
See, his reward is with him,
and his recompense accompanies him.'"
12 They will be called the Holy People,
the Redeemed of the LORD;
and you will be called Sought After,
the City No Longer Deserted.

I WILL BLESS MY SERVANTS BUT PUNISH SINNERS

The final chapters of ISAIAH return to themes introduced in the rest of the book. The LORD will bless his people and take revenge on those nations that refuse to worship him. God repeats the promise of a new creation, but reminds the people that this promise depends on their trusting in God and living according to his commands.

God's Day of Vengeance and Redemption

63 Who is this coming from Edom,
from Bozrah, with his garments stained
crimson?
Who is this, robed in splendor,
striding forward in the greatness of his strength?

"It is I, speaking in righteousness,
mighty to save."

62:8,9 *sworn . . . those who gather the grapes will drink it:* The LORD's promise to Israel (62:8) meant that they would return to the promised land (see the note at 60:21). Wine was part of the harvest offerings to be brought to the temple (Deut 14:22-26).

62:10 *Raise a banner:* Banners were a kind of flag raised in battle to signal an attack (Ps 20:5). But this banner will guide nations to Jerusalem instead.

62:11 *Daughter of Zion . . . reward:* See the notes at 1:8; 60:1; and 60:10. See also Isa 40:10; Rev 22:12.

62:12 *the Redeemed of the LORD:* See the notes at 44:22 and 47:1-3. See also 62:4.

63:1 *Edom . . . Bozrah:* Bozrah was the main city in Edom, a nation that symbolizes the evil enemies of Israel. See the notes at 34:5 and 34:6 (Bozrah).

63:1-6 *garments stained crimson:* The LORD is pictured as a warrior taking revenge against the nations who attacked the people of Israel.

62:10 Isa 40:3; 49:11; 57:14. **63:1-6** Isa 34:5-17; Jer 49:7-22; Ezek 25:12-14; 35:1-15; Amos 1:11,12; Obad 1-14; Mal 1:2-5.

2 Why are your garments red,
like those of one treading the winepress?

3 "I have trodden the winepress alone;
from the nations no one was with me.
I trampled them in my anger
and trod them down in my wrath;
their blood spattered my garments,
and I stained all my clothing.
4 For the day of vengeance was in my heart,
and the year of my redemption has come.
5 I looked, but there was no one to help,
I was appalled that no one gave support;
so my own arm worked salvation for me,
and my own wrath sustained me.
6 I trampled the nations in my anger;
in my wrath I made them drunk
and poured their blood on the ground."

Praise and Prayer

7 I will tell of the kindnesses of the LORD,
the deeds for which he is to be praised,
according to all the LORD has done for us—
yes, the many good things he has done
for the house of Israel,
according to his compassion and many kindnesses.
8 He said, "Surely they are my people,
sons who will not be false to me";
and so he became their Savior.
9 In all their distress he too was distressed,
and the angel of his presence saved them.
In his love and mercy he redeemed them;
he lifted them up and carried them
all the days of old.
10 Yet they rebelled
and grieved his Holy Spirit.
So he turned and became their enemy
and he himself fought against them.

11 Then his people recalled[a] the days of old,
the days of Moses and his people—
where is he who brought them through the sea,
with the shepherd of his flock?
Where is he who set
his Holy Spirit among them,
12 who sent his glorious arm of power
to be at Moses' right hand,

a11 Or *But may he recall*

63:2-6 *treading the winepress . . . made them drunk:* Grapes were crushed by foot to extract juice. God punishes evildoers like a winemaker stamping grapes in a pit. The grape juice symbolizes the blood of those punished. See also Lam 1:15; Joel 3:13; Rev 14:18-20; 19:15. When evildoers are punished by God, they are said to "drink the cup of his wrath" and become drunk. See also the note at 51:17,18.

63:5 *my own arm worked salvation:* See the notes at 19:16 and 59:16.

63:7 *kindnesses:* This is a reminder of how the LORD had saved Israel in the past, especially at the time of the exodus from Egypt (63:11) and later when he helped them settle in the promised land of Canaan (63:14). See also the note at 43:19,20.

63:9 *the angel of his presence saved them:* This may refer to the death angel that passed over the homes of Israelites in Egypt (Exod 12:23), or to the presence of the LORD who went with the Israelites in the desert (Exod 33:14).

63:10 *they rebelled:* This probably refers to the times the people rebelled while they were in the desert (Exod 32; Num 20:1-13; 25:1-9).

63:10 *Holy Spirit:* See the note at 11:2.

63:11-14 *recalled the days of old . . . they were given rest:* This refers to how the LORD saved Moses and the people at the Red Sea at the time of the exodus (see Exod 14). After leaving Egypt and wandering in the desert for forty years, the Israelites finally settled in Canaan (Josh 21:43-45).

63:12 Exod 14:21.

who divided the waters before them,
to gain for himself everlasting renown,
13 who led them through the depths?
Like a horse in open country,
they did not stumble;
14 like cattle that go down to the plain,
they were given rest by the Spirit of the LORD.
This is how you guided your people
to make for yourself a glorious name.

15 Look down from heaven and see
from your lofty throne, holy and glorious.
Where are your zeal and your might?
Your tenderness and compassion are withheld
from us.
16 But you are our Father,
though Abraham does not know us
or Israel acknowledge us;
you, O LORD, are our Father,
our Redeemer from of old is your name.
17 Why, O LORD, do you make us wander from your ways
and harden our hearts so we do not revere you?
Return for the sake of your servants,
the tribes that are your inheritance.
18 For a little while your people possessed your holy place,
but now our enemies have trampled down your
sanctuary.
19 We are yours from of old;
but you have not ruled over them,
they have not been called by your name.[a]

64 Oh, that you would rend the heavens and come down,
that the mountains would tremble before you!
2 As when fire sets twigs ablaze
and causes water to boil,
come down to make your name known to your enemies
and cause the nations to quake before you!
3 For when you did awesome things that we did not expect,
you came down, and the mountains trembled
before you.
4 Since ancient times no one has heard,
no ear has perceived,
no eye has seen any God besides you,
who acts on behalf of those who wait for him.
5 You come to the help of those who gladly do right,
who remember your ways.

Look down from heaven and see from your lofty throne, holy and glorious. Where are your zeal and your might? Your tenderness and compassion are withheld from us.
Isa 63:15

63:16 *Abraham . . . Israel:* See the note at 29:22. See also 51:1, 2. Israel's ancestors may turn away from the people because they rebelled against the LORD, but the LORD will still claim the people as his own children.

63:17 *make us wander from your ways:* Some passages claim that Israel's rebellion was caused by the LORD making them stubborn (see Exod 4:21; Isa 6:10).

63:18 *your people possessed your holy place:* Israel's first temple was built while Solomon was king of Israel (970-931 B.C.). In 587 B.C., the Babylonians destroyed the temple and much of the city of Jerusalem. A second temple was rebuilt and rededicated in 515 B.C.

64:1 *rend the heavens . . . mountains would tremble:* The LORD's appearing is often marked by thunder, lightning, and earthquakes. See the notes at 30:25-27 and 58:8 (glory). See also Judg 5:4, 5; Hab 3:3-10.

64:4 1 Cor 2:9.

a19 Or *We are like those you have never ruled, / like those never called by your name*

64:8 *our Father . . . the potter:* The LORD created and formed Israel (43:1) as a potter shapes a piece of clay into something useful or beautiful. See also 45:9 and the illustration on p. 1467.

64:10,11 *sacred cities have become a desert . . . desolation . . . ruins:* This is another reference to the Babylonian army's destruction of Jerusalem and other towns of Judah. See also the notes at 40:2 and 2:2.

65:1,2 *those who did not ask for me:* This refers to the sinful people of Israel who turned their back on the LORD and were stubborn (see 30:8-17; 63:17).

65:3 *offering sacrifices in gardens and burning incense on altars:* For sacrificing to idols, see the notes at 1:29-31 and 57:5-7. Incense made of imported frankincense and other spices produced a sweet smell when burned. Here it was used in ceremonies honoring idols. But the Law of Moses commanded that incense was to be used by Israel's priests as they offered sacrifices to the LORD (see the note at 43:23,24). The smoke from the burning incense represented the prayers that went up to God (Ps 141:2; Rev 5:8).

65:4,5 *graves . . . flesh of pigs . . . smoke in my nostrils:* People sometimes went to graves to try to speak to the spirits of the dead. This was forbidden in the Law of Moses (Lev 19:26; Deut 18:11; 1 Sam 28:3). Some animals, such as pigs, were considered unclean and could not be touched or eaten according to the Law (Deut 14:8). See also the mini-article called "Purity (Clean and Unclean)," p. 2125.

Ironically, those who did these things claimed to be holy, perhaps so holy that they were actually above the Law. This was repugnant to God.

65:1,2 Rom 10:20,21.

But when we continued to sin against them,
you were angry.
How then can we be saved?
6 All of us have become like one who is unclean,
and all our righteous acts are like filthy rags;
we all shrivel up like a leaf,
and like the wind our sins sweep us away.
7 No one calls on your name
or strives to lay hold of you;
for you have hidden your face from us
and made us waste away because of our sins.

8 Yet, O LORD, you are our Father.
We are the clay, you are the potter;
we are all the work of your hand.
9 Do not be angry beyond measure, O LORD;
do not remember our sins forever.
Oh, look upon us, we pray,
for we are all your people.
10 Your sacred cities have become a desert;
even Zion is a desert, Jerusalem a desolation.
11 Our holy and glorious temple, where our fathers praised you,
has been burned with fire,
and all that we treasured lies in ruins.
12 After all this, O LORD, will you hold yourself back?
Will you keep silent and punish us beyond measure?

Judgment and Salvation

65 "I revealed myself to those who did not ask for me;
I was found by those who did not seek me.
To a nation that did not call on my name,
I said, 'Here am I, here am I.'
2 All day long I have held out my hands
to an obstinate people,
who walk in ways not good,
pursuing their own imaginations—
3 a people who continually provoke me
to my very face,
offering sacrifices in gardens
and burning incense on altars of brick;
4 who sit among the graves
and spend their nights keeping secret vigil;
who eat the flesh of pigs,
and whose pots hold broth of unclean meat;
5 who say, 'Keep away; don't come near me,
for I am too sacred for you!'

The Peaceable Kingdom by Edward Hicks, around 1845. The prophet Isaiah offered a vision of peace that will extend to all of creation. Not only will there be peace among people and nations, but even animals that appear to be natural enemies will learn to live in peace. The LORD said, "I will create new heavens and a new earth. . . . The wolf and the lamb will feed together, and the lion will eat straw like the ox, but dust will be the serpent's food. They will neither harm nor destroy on all my holy mountain" (65:17, 25). Compare this with the similar vision at 11:1-9.

Such people are smoke in my nostrils,
  a fire that keeps burning all day.

6 "See, it stands written before me:
  I will not keep silent but will pay back in full;
  I will pay it back into their laps—
7 both your sins and the sins of your fathers,"
  says the LORD.
"Because they burned sacrifices on the mountains
  and defied me on the hills,
I will measure into their laps
  the full payment for their former deeds."

8 This is what the LORD says:

"As when juice is still found in a cluster of grapes
  and men say, 'Don't destroy it,
  there is yet some good in it,'
so will I do in behalf of my servants;
  I will not destroy them all.
9 I will bring forth descendants from Jacob,
  and from Judah those who will possess my mountains;
my chosen people will inherit them,
  and there will my servants live.

65:7 *burned sacrifices on the mountains:* This refers to ceremonies honoring idols (see the note at 65:3).

65:9 *my chosen people:* See the notes on p. 1289 (Judah and Jerusalem) and at 1:4 (nation). See also the note at 41:8. God's people were promised many descendants (see the note at 10:20-22) and their own land (see the note at 60:21).

65:9,10 *possess my mountains . . . Valley of Achor:* The "mountains" are in Canaan. Canaan stretched from the Plain of Sharon on the Mediterranean coast in the west to the Valley of Achor near Jericho in the east. These two places stand for the whole country.

The LORD says, *"Behold, I will create new heavens and a new earth. The former things will not be remembered, nor will they come to mind."* Isa 65:17

65:11 *my holy mountain:* Meaning Mount Zion in Jerusalem (see the note at 1:8).

65:11 *Fortune . . . Destiny:* This probably refers to two Syrian and Arabian gods of fortune. Trusting in these gods and their "good luck charms" would lead to disaster (65:12).

65:16 *swear by the God of truth:* Prayers and promises were to be made (sworn) in the name of the LORD, who alone is the source of all blessings. To make a promise in the name of another god would be a sin. See also the mini-article called "Making Vows," p. 328.

65:17,18 *create new heavens and a new earth . . . Jerusalem:* Heaven and earth are included in the promise of a new future for Jerusalem and its people (see 26:2, 3, 19; 43:18-21; 52:7-10; 54:11-15; 60:1-3). See also Isa 66:22; 2 Pet 3:13; Rev 21:1.

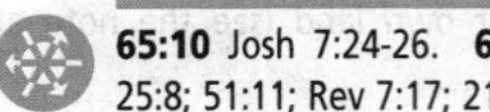

65:10 Josh 7:24-26. **65:19** Isa 25:8; 51:11; Rev 7:17; 21:4.

10 Sharon will become a pasture for flocks,
and the Valley of Achor a resting place for herds,
for my people who seek me.

11 "But as for you who forsake the LORD
and forget my holy mountain,
who spread a table for Fortune
and fill bowls of mixed wine for Destiny,
12 I will destine you for the sword,
and you will all bend down for the slaughter;
for I called but you did not answer,
I spoke but you did not listen.
You did evil in my sight
and chose what displeases me."

13 Therefore this is what the Sovereign LORD says:

"My servants will eat,
but you will go hungry;
my servants will drink,
but you will go thirsty;
my servants will rejoice,
but you will be put to shame.
14 My servants will sing
out of the joy of their hearts,
but you will cry out
from anguish of heart
and wail in brokenness of spirit.
15 You will leave your name
to my chosen ones as a curse;
the Sovereign LORD will put you to death,
but to his servants he will give another name.
16 Whoever invokes a blessing in the land
will do so by the God of truth;
he who takes an oath in the land
will swear by the God of truth.
For the past troubles will be forgotten
and hidden from my eyes.

New Heavens and a New Earth

17 "Behold, I will create
new heavens and a new earth.
The former things will not be remembered,
nor will they come to mind.
18 But be glad and rejoice forever
in what I will create,
for I will create Jerusalem to be a delight
and its people a joy.
19 I will rejoice over Jerusalem

and take delight in my people;
the sound of weeping and of crying
will be heard in it no more.

20 "Never again will there be in it
an infant who lives but a few days,
or an old man who does not live out his years;
he who dies at a hundred
will be thought a mere youth;
he who fails to reach[a] a hundred
will be considered accursed.
21 They will build houses and dwell in them;
they will plant vineyards and eat their fruit.
22 No longer will they build houses and others live
in them,
or plant and others eat.
For as the days of a tree,
so will be the days of my people;
my chosen ones will long enjoy
the works of their hands.
23 They will not toil in vain
or bear children doomed to misfortune;
for they will be a people blessed by the LORD,
they and their descendants with them.
24 Before they call I will answer;
while they are still speaking I will hear.
25 The wolf and the lamb will feed together,
and the lion will eat straw like the ox,
but dust will be the serpent's food.
They will neither harm nor destroy
on all my holy mountain,"
says the LORD.

Judgment and Hope

66 This is what the LORD says:

"Heaven is my throne,
and the earth is my footstool.
Where is the house you will build for me?
Where will my resting place be?
2 Has not my hand made all these things,
and so they came into being?"
declares the LORD.

"This is the one I esteem:
he who is humble and contrite in spirit,
and trembles at my word.
3 But whoever sacrifices a bull

[a]20 Or *I the sinner who reaches*

65:20-23 *he who dies at a hundred will be thought a mere youth:* The new Jerusalem will be a place of good health, long life, and prosperity. All these are signs of God's blessing and presence.

66:1 *Heaven is my throne . . . earth is my footstool:* See the note at 57:15. A throne is a type of chair used as a seat of judgment by a king or other ruler. The earliest known thrones were Egyptian, and before 600 B.C. thrones were largely used in royal ceremonies. This is the only passage in the Old Testament where the earth itself is called the LORD's footstool. This phrase proclaims God's rule over all things. In other places, the LORD's footstool is a name for the ark of the covenant in the Most Holy Place of the temple. The ark is also the LORD's throne on earth (see Exod 25:22; Ps 132:6-8; and the note at 6:1,2).

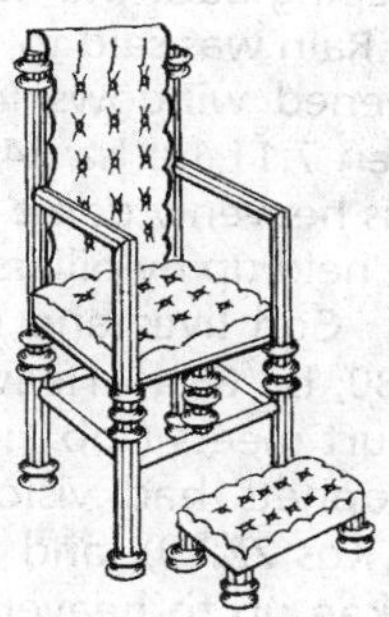

66:3 *sacrifices a bull:* The Law of Moses gave proper procedures for sacrificing animals and giving gifts. Incense was also burned as part of these offerings. But some of God's people also were honoring other gods with animal sacrifices and incense (see the notes at 65:3 and 65:4,5). This verse speaks against those who worshiped the LORD with these outward acts, but otherwise failed to obey him (see Isa 1:10-17 and the note at 1:11-14).

65:25 Isa 11:6-9. **66:1** Matt 5:34,35; 23:22. **66:1,2** Acts 7:49,50.

> The LORD says,
> *"When I called, no one answered, when I spoke, no one listened. They did evil in my sight and chose what displeases me."*
> Isa 66:4

is like one who kills a man,
and whoever offers a lamb,
like one who breaks a dog's neck;
whoever makes a grain offering
is like one who presents pig's blood,
and whoever burns memorial incense,
like one who worships an idol.
They have chosen their own ways,
and their souls delight in their abominations;
4 so I also will choose harsh treatment for them
and will bring upon them what they dread.
For when I called, no one answered,

HEAVEN

The ancient Hebrews spoke of heaven as a great ocean in the sky. A dome was said to cover the earth and was understood as keeping back the heavenly ocean (Gen 1:6, 7). Rain was said to fall on earth when God opened windows in the heavenly ceiling (Gen 7:11,12; Isa 24:18; Mal 3:10). Because this heavenly dome was so heavy, it had to be held up by pillars (Job 26:11).

God lives and rules in heaven (1 Kgs 8:30; Isa 66:1). Heaven is also where God's court meets (Job 1:6; 2:1). Some of Israel's prophets had visions of God in heaven (1 Kgs 22:19), and the prophet Elijah was taken up to heaven in a whirlwind (2 Kgs 2:1-12). The apostle Paul also spoke of being taken up into a "third heaven," where he heard wonderful things (2 Cor 12:1-4). John had a vision of heaven that revealed secrets about the future (Rev 1:1; 4:1).

The Old Testament does not describe heaven as a place where God's faithful will live with God after they die. In fact, it was only in the fifth or sixth century B.C. that we see the Israelites express a clear belief in eternal life after death. The prophet Daniel had a vision of the people whose names were written in *"the book."* These people were to rise from death and be given eternal life (Dan 12:1-3). But even this vision does not say that those who are raised from death will live in heaven.

The New Testament also describes heaven as the place where God lives and rules (Matt 5:34). The angels who announced the birth of Jesus praise God in heaven (Luke 2:14). When Jesus was baptized, God's voice came from heaven and called Jesus "my Son" (Luke 3:22). Jesus described God as a Father in heaven (Matt 6:1,9; 18:14; John 6:32). Jesus himself came from heaven (John 6:38-42) and returned there after death (Luke 24:50,51). And he will come back from heaven in the future (Matt 24:30,31; 1 Thes 4:16).

When Jesus spoke of the kingdom of heaven (Matt 4:17; 5:3; 13:44-47), he usually meant where God's will and purposes were done, rather than God's home. The promise of life after death is common in the New Testament (see the mini-article called "Eternal Life," p. 2072). Jesus told his disciples that he will go to his Father's house to prepare a place for them (John 14:1-3). The apostle Paul said that those who are raised from death will have new bodies like those who are in heaven (1 Cor 15:45-54). Paul also said that those who have faith in Christ are citizens of heaven. Christ will make their poor earthly bodies like his own glorious body (Phil 3:20, 21). Other New Testament books say that heaven and earth will be destroyed or replaced and made new (2 Pet 3:10-13; Rev 21:1—22:5). See also the mini-article called "Paradise," p. 2243.

when I spoke, no one listened.
They did evil in my sight
and chose what displeases me."

5 Hear the word of the LORD,
you who tremble at his word:
"Your brothers who hate you,
and exclude you because of my name, have said,
'Let the LORD be glorified,
that we may see your joy!'
Yet they will be put to shame.
6 Hear that uproar from the city,
hear that noise from the temple!
It is the sound of the LORD
repaying his enemies all they deserve.

7 "Before she goes into labor,
she gives birth;
before the pains come upon her,
she delivers a son.
8 Who has ever heard of such a thing?
Who has ever seen such things?
Can a country be born in a day
or a nation be brought forth in a moment?
Yet no sooner is Zion in labor
than she gives birth to her children.
9 Do I bring to the moment of birth
and not give delivery?" says the LORD.
"Do I close up the womb
when I bring to delivery?" says your God.
10 "Rejoice with Jerusalem and be glad for her,
all you who love her;
rejoice greatly with her,
all you who mourn over her.
11 For you will nurse and be satisfied
at her comforting breasts;
you will drink deeply
and delight in her overflowing abundance."

12 For this is what the LORD says:
"I will extend peace to her like a river,
and the wealth of nations like a flooding stream;
you will nurse and be carried on her arm
and dandled on her knees.
13 As a mother comforts her child,
so will I comfort you;
and you will be comforted over Jerusalem."
14 When you see this, your heart will rejoice
and you will flourish like grass;

66:4 *when I spoke, no one listened:* Meaning the LORD's law or the words of the prophets.

66:5 *they will be put to shame:* Some Israelites mocked those who trusted in the LORD's promises (5:19). See also Ps 22:7,8; Isa 36:13-20.

66:8 *Zion in labor:* Jerusalem is again pictured as a mother. With the LORD's help, she will give birth to new sons and daughters, and her labor will be short and nearly painless. The city will be a place of comfort. See 49:19-22 and the note at 51:17,18.

66:12 *wealth of nations:* See 60:5-7.

66:14 *servants . . . foes:* See 65:13-15.

66:7 Rev 12:5.

66:15,16 *fire . . . whirlwind:* To be caught in a desert whirlwind was very dangerous. Flaming chariots, fire, and a fiery sword all symbolize the LORD's punishment. See the notes at 4:4 and 30:25-27. See also 2 Kgs 2:11,12; 6:16,17.

66:17 *go into the gardens . . . eat the flesh of pigs and rats:* The "gardens" is where the idols were worshiped (see the notes at 1:29-31 and 65:3). The Law of Moses said that God's people could not eat meat from certain kinds of animals including pigs and rodents like rats (Lev 11:29,30). To eat such meat made a person ritually unclean. See also the note at 65:4, 5 and the mini-article called "Purity (Clean and Unclean)," p. 2125.

66:19 *Tarshish . . . Greece:* These locations were meant to represent all the known world. Tarshish may have been a Phoenician city in southern Spain. Tubal is south or southeast of the Black Sea.

66:20 *from all the nations, to my holy mountain in Jerusalem:* See the notes at 11:11; 1:8; and 2:2.

the hand of the LORD will be made known to his
servants,
but his fury will be shown to his foes.
15 See, the LORD is coming with fire,
and his chariots are like a whirlwind;
he will bring down his anger with fury,
and his rebuke with flames of fire.
16 For with fire and with his sword
the LORD will execute judgment upon all men,
and many will be those slain by the LORD.

17 "Those who consecrate and purify themselves to go into
the gardens, following the one in the midst of[a] those who eat the
flesh of pigs and rats and other abominable things—they will meet
their end together," declares the LORD.
18 "And I, because of their actions and their imaginations, am
about to come[b] and gather all nations and tongues, and they will
come and see my glory.
19 "I will set a sign among them, and I will send some of
those who survive to the nations—to Tarshish, to the Libyans[c] and
Lydians (famous as archers), to Tubal and Greece, and to the distant islands that have not heard of my fame or seen my glory. They
will proclaim my glory among the nations. 20 And they will bring
all your brothers, from all the nations, to my holy mountain in
Jerusalem as an offering to the LORD—on horses, in chariots and
wagons, and on mules and camels," says the LORD. "They will bring

[a]17 Or *gardens behind one of your temples, and* [b]18 The meaning of the Hebrew for this clause is uncertain. [c]19 Some Septuagint manuscripts *Put* (Libyans); Hebrew *Pul*

QUESTIONS ABOUT ISAIAH 56:1—66:24

1. What were foreigners required to do in order to be part of God's people in the new day that God was creating? (56:2-8)
2. List the reasons for Israel's punishment given in 57:3-13; 58:1-5; 59:1-15. Describe what these "sins" might look like today in our society.
3. According to 58:6-10 and 61:1-3, what is true worship of the LORD?
4. What does God promise regarding the rebuilding of Jerusalem? (60:10-22; 61:5-7; 62:1-12)
5. How is God described in the following passages: 59:16-19; 62:4,5; 63:1-6; 63:16; 64:8; 65:17,18; 66:15,16? Which of these images fits your understanding of God? What other images come to mind when you think about God?
6. Describe the "new heavens and new earth" the LORD is creating (65:17-25). If our world today could have a fresh new start, what would need to be different?
7. Choose a favorite passage from ISAIAH and explain why it is meaningful to you.
8. Name at least two new things you learned by reading and studying ISAIAH.

them, as the Israelites bring their grain offerings, to the temple of
the LORD in ceremonially clean vessels. 21And I will select some of
them also to be priests and Levites," says the LORD.

22"As the new heavens and the new earth that I make will
endure before me," declares the LORD, "so will your name and
descendants endure. 23From one New Moon to another and from
one Sabbath to another, all mankind will come and bow down
before me," says the LORD. 24"And they will go out and look upon
the dead bodies of those who rebelled against me; their worm will
not die, nor will their fire be quenched, and they will be loathsome
to all mankind."

66:22 *new heavens ... new earth:* See the note at 65:17,18.

66:23 *From one New Moon to another:* Trumpets were blown on the first day of every month, which began with the New Moon (Ps 81:3; Num 28:11-15). Special sacrifices were offered on this day, also known as the New Moon Festival. See also the notes at 1:11-14 and 56:2-6.

66:24 *worm ... fire:* The book ends with a picture of the LORD's eternal punishment for those who have turned against him (see 1:2, 31). Worms are constant companions in the world of the dead (14:11), and fire often appears as God's punishment of evildoers (see 34:9, 10 and the note at 4:4). In Mark 9:43-48, this verse is quoted in part as a description of hell. See the mini-article called "Hell," p. 1944.

JEREMIAH

Imagine being chosen for the awesome task of speaking God's word to the nations. How would you respond? Read this book to find out how the young prophet Jeremiah responded when God chose him. And discover the plans God has for his people.

What makes Jeremiah special?

The prophet Jeremiah lived during a time of great change for God's people. The tiny kingdom of Judah was caught in the middle of the struggle between old and new empires fighting to gain power over the region. Jeremiah began to serve as God's prophet in 627 B.C. when he was a young man, possibly less than 20 years old, and continued until shortly after the Babylonians captured Judah's capital city, Jerusalem, in 586 B.C. During Jeremiah's time as prophet he warned the kings, priests, and people of Judah of their coming doom.

We also know much about the feelings this prophet had for God's people. Jeremiah felt God's anger and sadness as the people turned away from God and stubbornly pursued their own ways. Jeremiah also was made to suffer in order to show the suffering that Judah would have to experience. During Jeremiah's lifetime Judah was conquered by the Babylonians from the east, and many of its leaders and people were taken into exile. But Judah's defeat was not God's last word. Jeremiah sent a message of comfort and hope to those who went into exile: God promises to make a new covenant with God's people in the future (chapters 30, 31).

Anathoth in the territory of Benjamin: Anathoth, Jeremiah's hometown, was over two miles northeast of Jerusalem. Benjamin was the youngest son of Jacob and Rachel (Gen 35:16-18). The Benjamin tribe, the smallest of Israel's tribes, was located in an area to the north of Judah (see the map on p. 2464). Together the tribes of Judah and Benjamin formed Israel's southern kingdom, also known as Judah.

Israel: After the nation was divided, the northern kingdom was called "Israel," and the southern kingdom was called "Judah" (see 1 Kgs 12:1-20 and the map on p. 2467). In 722 B.C. the Assyrians conquered the northern kingdom, and Judah was all that was left. And so in JEREMIAH the name "Israel" most often stands for the southern kingdom. See also the mini-article called "Israel," p. 264.

Why was Jeremiah written?

Jeremiah likely knew the message of Hosea, the prophet who had spoken to Israel over a hundred years earlier. Their messages are alike. Both Jeremiah and Hosea told the people to be faithful to the LORD, who had brought them out of slavery in Egypt and kept the promise to give them a land of their own. Jeremiah's message was a strong reminder that God's people were to base their lives on the covenant (agreement) the LORD God made with Moses and their ancestors at Mount Sinai. They were to obey God's Law above everything else.

But the people sinned by worshiping other gods. The leaders trusted their own military strength and the power of foreign countries rather than depending on the LORD to protect their nation. So, Jeremiah had two main messages for Judah. First, he warned that Judah would be defeated and its holy city Jerusalem would be destroyed. And second, because God continued to love the people, he would make a new covenant with the people after their punishment was over (31:31-34). Disaster is certain, but the future is filled with hope.

What's the story behind the scene?

Jeremiah's message was delivered during the reign of the last five kings of Judah, beginning in the "thirteenth year of the reign of Josiah son of Amon king of Judah" (627 B.C.). Josiah was considered a good king, who made a series of reforms that were based on a scroll containing parts of the book of DEUTERONOMY. This scroll, discovered in the Jerusalem temple around 621 B.C., prompted Josiah to get rid of foreign gods in the Jerusalem temple and to encourage the people to turn back to the LORD.

Josiah also wanted to reestablish the empire of Israel as it was in the days of David and Solomon. This meant trying to break free from the powerful Assyrian empire, which had defeated Israel's northern tribes in 722 B.C., and escape from the influence of Egypt, Judah's powerful neighbor to the west. However, Josiah was killed by the Egyptians in battle at Megiddo in 609 B.C. Josiah's son Jehoahaz ruled for three months in 609 B.C., but then the Egyptian ruler set Jehoiakim (ruled 609-598 B.C.) on the throne of Judah.

King Jehoiakim brought back the worship of foreign gods, which Josiah had banished from Judah. And he burned Jeremiah's message written on a scroll, which warned that God would use the new rising power, Babylon, to punish sinful Judah. Jehoiakim also refused to listen when Jeremiah encouraged him to submit to Nebuchadnezzar, king of Babylon, in order to keep Judah from being attacked by the powerful Babylonian army. It was at this low point in Jeremiah's ministry that he and his friend Baruch went into hiding and he wrote his "Confessions" (see 11:18-23; 12:1-6; 15:10,11,15-21; 17:14-18; 18:19-23; 20:7-18).

In 598 B.C. Nebuchadnezzar invaded Judah. He discovered that Jehoiakim had died, so he took Jehoiakim's young son Jehoiachin (who ruled for only three months in 598) into captivity along with many leaders of the land. Nebuchadnezzar then put Zedekiah on the throne as a puppet king, and Judah was forced to pay heavy taxes to its Babylonian overlords.

Over the next ten years the situation in Judah got worse as the leaders and lying prophets plotted against both Babylon and Jeremiah. Because of his message of doom and his opinion that Judah should submit to Babylon to avoid attack, Jeremiah was considered by many to be a traitor. Jeremiah was beaten, put in prison, and then placed under house arrest. Finally, when King Zedekiah made an agreement with Egypt and broke his treaty with Babylon, Nebuchadnezzar returned and destroyed Jerusalem in 586 B.C. He killed Zedekiah's sons, blinded the king, and took him along with many of the Jewish people back to exile in Babylon (Jer 39; 52; 2 Kgs 24:18—25:21).

Jeremiah stayed in Jerusalem, where he tried to help those who were left behind. It was at this time that his message changed from doom and destruction to hope and the promise of a new covenant between the LORD and his people. Jeremiah and his loyal friend Baruch were forced to flee to Egypt when some Jewish rebels killed Gedaliah, the ruler Nebuchadnezzar had chosen to rule Judah. These rebels still considered Jeremiah to be a traitor. This is the last we know of this great prophet, who suffered so much on behalf of his beloved Judah.

For more about this period of Israel's history, see the article called "From Joshua to the Exile: The People of Israel in the Promised Land," p. 924.

priests . . . leaders . . . prophets: The priests have ignored the terms of the covenant with God, which included obedience to God's commandments. The leaders have trusted in other nations and in their own power rather than in God. And some false prophets claimed to get messages from Baal, the Canaanite god of rain and fertility. Jeremiah will oppose all these people in power (1:18, 19). See the mini-articles called "Israel's Priests," p. 2344 and "Canaanite Gods and Goddesses," p. 469. See also the article called "Prophets and Prophecy," p. 935.

Egypt . . . Assyria: Judah could not win the game of power politics, but their leaders tried (see the note at 2:18). Jeremiah reminds the people that these neighboring superpowers will eventually let them down.

Nineveh, the capital of Assyria, fell to the Babylonians in 612 B.C. Egypt then tried to protect its own interests by entering into a treaty with Judah and other nations in the region. They hoped for ports and trade routes in return for military support.

HOW IS JEREMIAH CONSTRUCTED?

The message of JEREMIAH is one of doom before the fall of Judah and one of hope after the fall. During Jeremiah's career, many major events occurred. His messages, however, do not describe these events in order. They are roughly grouped by subject, not by dates. This makes it confusing to read the book straight through. Not only are the messages out of order, but we find different types of writing in this book. Many of the book's messages are written in a poetic form known as prophetic oracles. Other sections are sermon-like material similar to the speeches of Moses in DEUTERONOMY. Still other sections are narrative passages, which describe events in Jeremiah's life and report the destruction of Judah and Jerusalem by Nebuchadnezzar. Some of the writing was done by Jeremiah's friend Baruch, who wrote down parts of Jeremiah's message on at least two different scrolls (chapter 36).

The following is one way that JEREMIAH can be outlined:

Introducing Jeremiah, the LORD's prophet (1:1-19)

Words of warning and punishment (2:1—25:38)
- Jeremiah's early messages (2:1—6:30)
- Scenes from Jeremiah's life (7:1—13:27)
- A time of great sadness (14:1—17:27)
- Plots on Jeremiah's life and warnings to Judah (18:1—25:38)

Jeremiah against the lying prophets (26:1—29:32)

A homecoming and a new beginning (30:1—33:26)

Disaster for Judah and Jerusalem (34:1—44:30)
- Scenes from Jeremiah's ministry (34:1—38:28)
- The fall of Jerusalem and the escape to Egypt (39:1—44:30)

The LORD's judgment against the nations (45:1—51:64)

Another account of the fall of Jerusalem (52:1-34)

Introducing Jeremiah, the LORD's Prophet

Jeremiah introduces himself and tells how God has appointed him to speak to the nation of Judah. Jeremiah is unwilling, but God insists, telling Jeremiah that his task is to bring words of doom and words of hope. Then God promises to protect Jeremiah, even though this task will be difficult.

1 The words of Jeremiah son of Hilkiah, one of the priests at
Anathoth in the territory of Benjamin. 2 The word of the LORD
came to him in the thirteenth year of the reign of Josiah son of
Amon king of Judah, 3 and through the reign of Jehoiakim son of
Josiah king of Judah, down to the fifth month of the eleventh year
of Zedekiah son of Josiah king of Judah, when the people of Jerusalem went into exile.

1:1 *Anathoth ... territory of Benjamin:* See the note on p. 1424.

1:2,3 *thirteenth year of the reign of Josiah ... Zedekiah:* Josiah ruled from 640 to 609 B.C., so Jeremiah's career probably began around 627 B.C. Jehoiakim ruled from 609 to 598 B.C., and Zedekiah from 598 to 587 B.C. For more information about these kings and this troubled time, see the Introduction to JEREMIAH on p. 1424.

1:3 *fifth month ... went into exile:* Ab, the fifth month of the Hebrew calendar, fell from mid-July to mid-August. Zedekiah began to rule in 598 B.C., so the eleventh year of his reign was either 587 or 586 B.C. This is when the second group of Jews were taken to exile in Babylon by King Nebuchadnezzar.

1:2 2 Kgs 22:3—23:27; 2 Chr 34:8—35:19. **1:3 a** 2 Kgs 23:36—24:7; 2 Chr 36:5-8; **b** 2 Kgs 24:18—25:21; 2 Chr 36:11-21.

Jeremiah, sixth century mosaic in Church of San Vitale, Ravenna, Italy. Jeremiah was a prophet during the reigns of the last five kings of Judah: Josiah, Jehoahaz, Jehoiakim, Jehoiachin, and Zedekiah. Jeremiah's prophecies were written down by his friend and secretary, Baruch. When Jeremiah's prophecies were read to King Jehoiakim, the king had his servants burn the scroll, piece by piece. But the LORD told Jeremiah to make another copy, and to add to it even more warnings (see chapter 36).

The LORD said: *"Before I formed you in the womb I knew you, before you were born I set you apart; I appointed you as a prophet to the nations."* Jer 1:5

1:6 *I am only a child:* It is not clear just how old Jeremiah was. Compare his response to that of Moses (Exod 4:10) and Isaiah (Isa 6:8).

1:8 *I am with you:* Jeremiah's doubt and fear are reassured by the promise of the LORD's presence (Exod 3:12).

The Call of Jeremiah

4 The word of the LORD came to me, saying,

5 "Before I formed you in the womb I knew[a] you,
before you were born I set you apart;
I appointed you as a prophet to the nations."

6 "Ah, Sovereign LORD," I said, "I do not know how to speak;
I am only a child."
7 But the LORD said to me, "Do not say, 'I am only a child.'
You must go to everyone I send you to and say whatever I command you. 8 Do not be afraid of them, for I am with you and will
rescue you," declares the LORD.

[a]5 Or *chose*

1:10 *to destroy and overthrow, to build and to plant:* Jeremiah's message is twofold: God will destroy and overthrow Judah, and then God will restore and rebuild his people.

1:11 *branch of an almond tree:* Coupled with 1:12, this verse probably refers to how God will make sure that what he tells Jeremiah will actually happen.

1:13 *boiling pot, tilting away from the north:* The boiling pot stands for invading armies that will attack Judah and Jerusalem from the north. The exact identity of this enemy is not clear, though the Babylonians eventually did capture Jerusalem a few years after defeating the Assyrians, who had controlled the area to the north of Judah. See the map on p. 2468, which shows the Assyrian and Babylonian empires.

9 Then the LORD reached out his hand and touched my
mouth and said to me, "Now, I have put my words in your mouth.
10 See, today I appoint you over nations and kingdoms to uproot
and tear down, to destroy and overthrow, to build and to plant."
11 The word of the LORD came to me: "What do you see,
Jeremiah?"

"I see the branch of an almond tree," I replied.

12 The LORD said to me, "You have seen correctly, for I am
watching[a] to see that my word is fulfilled."
13 The word of the LORD came to me again: "What do
you see?"

"I see a boiling pot, tilting away from the north," I answered.

14 The LORD said to me, "From the north disaster will be
poured out on all who live in the land. 15 I am about to summon all
the peoples of the northern kingdoms," declares the LORD.

"Their kings will come and set up their thrones
  in the entrance of the gates of Jerusalem;
they will come against all her surrounding walls
  and against all the towns of Judah.
16 I will pronounce my judgments on my people
  because of their wickedness in forsaking me,
in burning incense to other gods
  and in worshiping what their hands have made.

17 "Get yourself ready! Stand up and say to them whatever I
command you. Do not be terrified by them, or I will terrify you
before them. 18 Today I have made you a fortified city, an iron pillar and a bronze wall to stand against the whole land—against the
kings of Judah, its officials, its priests and the people of the land.
19 They will fight against you but will not overcome you, for I am
with you and will rescue you," declares the LORD.

---

[a] **12** The Hebrew for *watching* sounds like the Hebrew for *almond tree.*

QUESTIONS ABOUT JEREMIAH 1:1-19

1. How does Jeremiah try to excuse himself from being the prophet that the LORD wants him to be? How does God respond to Jeremiah? (1:4-8)
2. Compare Jeremiah 1 with Exodus 4 and Isaiah 6. How are the situations in these passages similar? How are they different?
3. What is the twofold message that Jeremiah is told to preach? (1:10, 15, 16) How will the people respond to Jeremiah's message? (1:17, 19)
4. How might you, your community, or the nation react to a similar message today? Why?

Words of Warning and Punishment

In this long section (chapters 2–25), Jeremiah brings God's words of judgment to Judah and its capital city, Jerusalem. At times God pleads with the people; at other times God threatens them with terrible visions, and sometimes Jeremiah is told to act out God's message. Jeremiah's life will be a living expression of God's anger, disappointment, and sadness.

JEREMIAH'S EARLY MESSAGES

God's people have been worshiping other gods and ignoring the covenant God made with them in the time of Moses.

Israel Forsakes God

2 The word of the LORD came to me: [2]"Go and proclaim in the
hearing of Jerusalem:

" 'I remember the devotion of your youth,
how as a bride you loved me
and followed me through the desert,
through a land not sown.
[3]Israel was holy to the LORD,
the firstfruits of his harvest;
all who devoured her were held guilty,
and disaster overtook them,' "
declares the LORD.

[4]Hear the word of the LORD, O house of Jacob,
all you clans of the house of Israel.

[5]This is what the LORD says:

"What fault did your fathers find in me,
that they strayed so far from me?
They followed worthless idols
and became worthless themselves.
[6]They did not ask, 'Where is the LORD,
who brought us up out of Egypt
and led us through the barren wilderness,
through a land of deserts and rifts,
a land of drought and darkness,[a]
a land where no one travels and no one lives?'
[7]I brought you into a fertile land
to eat its fruit and rich produce.
But you came and defiled my land
and made my inheritance detestable.
[8]The priests did not ask,
'Where is the LORD?'

[a]**6** Or *and the shadow of death*

2:2,3 *Jerusalem . . . a bride . . . the firstfruits:* Jerusalem was the capital city of Judah, and the center of the religious life of the people of Israel. The LORD is often described as Israel's husband (Isa 54:5; Hos 2:16-20). God chose Israel, and Israel was to be devoted to God alone, just as a husband and wife promise to be faithful to one another. The people of Israel were supposed to offer the first part of the harvest as a gift to the LORD (Lev 23:10, 11). Like this best first part, the "firstfruits," Israel was considered the LORD's best.

2:4 *Israel:* See the note on p. 1424.

2:6,7 *brought us up out of Egypt . . . defiled my land:* God brought the people of Israel out of slavery in Egypt and helped them survive in the desert some seven hundred years before Jeremiah's time (see of EXODUS and NUMBERS). God had acted in history to keep the people safe and free. But in the desert (Exod 32; Num 25) and again after they settled the promised land of Canaan, the people worshiped false gods. The shrines and altars to these gods defiled God's holy land and people.

2:8 *priests . . . leaders . . . prophets:* See the note on p. 1425.

2:13 *spring of living water . . . broken cisterns:* In Judah, rainfall was scarce during the dry part of the year, so the people made cisterns, or pits in the ground, for holding water. A broken or cracked cistern was useless because it could not hold water. The idols are like cracked cisterns.

2:16 *Memphis and Tahpanhes:* See the map on p. 2463. Israelite leaders met with Egyptians in these cities to discuss a military alliance against the Assyrians (2:15). The Egyptian ruler Neco killed Judah's King Josiah at the Battle of Megiddo in 609 B.C. Judah remained under Egyptian control until the Battle of Carchemish in 605 B.C. when Egypt fell to Babylon.

2:18 *why go to Egypt . . . Assyria:* Israel's leaders begged for help from one of these two powerful empires, (see also Isa 30:1-3; Hos 8:9). King Jehoiakim of Judah made treaties with both Egypt and Assyria against Babylon (2:36).

2:9,10 Mic 6:1, 2.

Those who deal with the law did not know me;
the leaders rebelled against me.
The prophets prophesied by Baal,
following worthless idols.

9 "Therefore I bring charges against you again,"
declares the LORD.

"And I will bring charges against your
children's children.
10 Cross over to the coasts of Kittim[a] and look,
send to Kedar[b] and observe closely;
see if there has ever been anything like this:
11 Has a nation ever changed its gods?
(Yet they are not gods at all.)
But my people have exchanged their[c] Glory
for worthless idols.
12 Be appalled at this, O heavens,
and shudder with great horror,"
declares the LORD.
13 "My people have committed two sins:
They have forsaken me,
the spring of living water,
and have dug their own cisterns,
broken cisterns that cannot hold water.
14 Is Israel a servant, a slave by birth?
Why then has he become plunder?
15 Lions have roared;
they have growled at him.
They have laid waste his land;
his towns are burned and deserted.
16 Also, the men of Memphis[d] and Tahpanhes
have shaved the crown of your head.[e]
17 Have you not brought this on yourselves
by forsaking the LORD your God
when he led you in the way?
18 Now why go to Egypt
to drink water from the Shihor[f]?
And why go to Assyria
to drink water from the River[g]?
19 Your wickedness will punish you;
your backsliding will rebuke you.
Consider then and realize
how evil and bitter it is for you
when you forsake the LORD your God

[a]**10** That is, Cyprus and western coastlands [b]**10** The home of Bedouin tribes in the Syro-Arabian desert [c]**11** Masoretic Text; an ancient Hebrew scribal tradition *my* [d]**16** Hebrew *Noph* [e]**16** Or *have cracked your skull* [f]**18** That is, a branch of the Nile [g]**18** That is, the Euphrates

and have no awe of me,"
declares the Lord, the LORD Almighty.

20 "Long ago you broke off your yoke
and tore off your bonds;
you said, 'I will not serve you!'
Indeed, on every high hill
and under every spreading tree
you lay down as a prostitute.
21 I had planted you like a choice vine
of sound and reliable stock.
How then did you turn against me
into a corrupt, wild vine?
22 Although you wash yourself with soda
and use an abundance of soap,
the stain of your guilt is still before me,"
declares the Sovereign LORD.
23 "How can you say, 'I am not defiled;
I have not run after the Baals'?
See how you behaved in the valley;
consider what you have done.
You are a swift she-camel
running here and there,
24 a wild donkey accustomed to the desert,
sniffing the wind in her craving—
in her heat who can restrain her?
Any males that pursue her need not tire themselves;
at mating time they will find her.
25 Do not run until your feet are bare
and your throat is dry.
But you said, 'It's no use!
I love foreign gods,
and I must go after them.'

26 "As a thief is disgraced when he is caught,
so the house of Israel is disgraced—
they, their kings and their officials,
their priests and their prophets.
27 They say to wood, 'You are my father,'
and to stone, 'You gave me birth.'
They have turned their backs to me
and not their faces;
yet when they are in trouble, they say,
'Come and save us!'
28 Where then are the gods you made for yourselves?
Let them come if they can save you
when you are in trouble!
For you have as many gods
as you have towns, O Judah.

2:19 *LORD Almighty:* This Hebrew name, *Yahweh Sabaoth,* is also translated as "LORD of hosts." The "hosts" in this ancient name refer to the armies of Israel (1 Sam 4:4), or to the heavenly stars, which God created.

2:20 *every high hill . . . spreading tree . . . prostitute:* Ancient Canaanite worship places were usually built on a high place near a grove of trees (Deut 12:2; 1 Kgs 14:23). Fertility rituals honoring the Canaanite gods continued at these places. In some Canaanite religions, worshipers had sex with temple prostitutes who represented their gods. See also the mini-articles called "Prostitution in the Bible" p. 1688 and "Canaanite Gods and Goddesses," p. 469.

2:23 *Baals:* See the note at 2:8.

2:23 *in the valley:* Referring to the Valley of Ben Hinnom. This narrow valley, located south of Jerusalem, is mentioned in the Old Testament as a place where children were sometimes sacrificed to the god Molech by burning them to death (Lev 18:21; 20:1-5; 2 Kgs 23:10; Jer 7:30, 31; 19:1-6). See the map on p. 2466.

2:27,28 *wood . . . stone . . . gods you made:* People were praying to carved wooden and stone idols, which could be found in every city. But they ignored the LORD God who alone could help Israel. See the mini-article called "Canaanite Gods and Goddesses," p. 469.

2:31-34 *Have I been a desert to Israel . . . lifeblood of the innocent poor:* Though God saved the people from slavery in Egypt and did not abandon them in the desert, Israel worshiped idols and asked for help from foreign powers. In this way, they were like an unfaithful bride who acted like a prostitute (the worst of women). The people and their leaders also were guilty of treating others unfairly, especially the poor (see Isa 1:15-17; Amos 2:6-8; 5:10-12). See also the mini-article called "Justice," p. 1727.

2:35 *I will pass judgment:* God's judgment of Israel and other nations sometimes is described by the prophets in terms of a hearing or trial (Deut 30:19; Jer 2:9; Mic 6:1,2).

2:36 *Egypt . . . Assyria:* See the note on p. 1425 and at 2:18.

3:1 *If a man divorces his wife:* According to the Law of Moses, a woman could never return to the husband who had divorced her, even if she remarried and her second husband died or divorced her also (see Deut 24:1-4). This would cause the land to be defiled (not acceptable to God). Yet God was willing to be more merciful than this law and invited Israel to come back to him (3:12-14).

3:2 *barren heights . . . ravished:* See the note at 2:20. The people and the land of Canaan had been chosen and set apart to be holy (acceptable) to the LORD. But the people's unfaithfulness defiled not only themselves but the land as well.

29 "Why do you bring charges against me?
You have all rebelled against me,"
declares the LORD.
30 "In vain I punished your people;
they did not respond to correction.
Your sword has devoured your prophets
like a ravening lion.

31 "You of this generation, consider the word of the LORD:

"Have I been a desert to Israel
or a land of great darkness?
Why do my people say, 'We are free to roam;
we will come to you no more'?
32 Does a maiden forget her jewelry,
a bride her wedding ornaments?
Yet my people have forgotten me,
days without number.
33 How skilled you are at pursuing love!
Even the worst of women can learn from
your ways.
34 On your clothes men find
the lifeblood of the innocent poor,
though you did not catch them breaking in.
Yet in spite of all this
35 you say, 'I am innocent;
he is not angry with me.'
But I will pass judgment on you
because you say, 'I have not sinned.'
36 Why do you go about so much,
changing your ways?
You will be disappointed by Egypt
as you were by Assyria.
37 You will also leave that place
with your hands on your head,
for the LORD has rejected those you trust;
you will not be helped by them.

3 "If a man divorces his wife
and she leaves him and marries another man,
should he return to her again?
Would not the land be completely defiled?
But you have lived as a prostitute with many
lovers—
would you now return to me?"
declares the LORD.
2 "Look up to the barren heights and see.
Is there any place where you have not been ravished?
By the roadside you sat waiting for lovers,

sat like a nomad[a] in the desert.
You have defiled the land
with your prostitution and wickedness.
[3]Therefore the showers have been withheld,
and no spring rains have fallen.
Yet you have the brazen look of a prostitute;
you refuse to blush with shame.
[4]Have you not just called to me:
'My Father, my friend from my youth,
[5]will you always be angry?
Will your wrath continue forever?'
This is how you talk,
but you do all the evil you can."

Unfaithful Israel

[6]During the reign of King Josiah, the LORD said to me, "Have
you seen what faithless Israel has done? She has gone up on every
high hill and under every spreading tree and has committed adultery there. [7]I thought that after she had done all this she would
return to me but she did not, and her unfaithful sister Judah saw
it. [8]I gave faithless Israel her certificate of divorce and sent her
away because of all her adulteries. Yet I saw that her unfaithful sister Judah had no fear; she also went out and committed adultery.
[9]Because Israel's immorality mattered so little to her, she defiled
the land and committed adultery with stone and wood. [10]In spite
of all this, her unfaithful sister Judah did not return to me with all
her heart, but only in pretense," declares the LORD.
[11]The LORD said to me, "Faithless Israel is more righteous
than unfaithful Judah. [12]Go, proclaim this message toward the
north:

" 'Return, faithless Israel,' declares the LORD,
'I will frown on you no longer,
for I am merciful,' declares the LORD,
'I will not be angry forever.
[13]Only acknowledge your guilt—
you have rebelled against the LORD your God,
you have scattered your favors to foreign gods
under every spreading tree,
and have not obeyed me,' "
declares the LORD.

[14]"Return, faithless people," declares the LORD, "for I am
your husband. I will choose you—one from a town and two from
a clan—and bring you to Zion. [15]Then I will give you shepherds
after my own heart, who will lead you with knowledge and

[a]2 Or *an Arab*

3:6 *Josiah:* See the note at 1:2, 3 and the Introduction to JEREMIAH, p. 1424. Though the message comes to Jeremiah in the time of Josiah (about 627 B.C.), the message is about the unfaithfulness of the northern kingdom of Israel in the past (see the note at 3:6-10). See also 2 Kgs 22:1—23:30; 2 Chr 34:1—35:27.

3:6-10 *Israel . . . her unfaithful sister Judah:* This refers to the northern kingdom of Israel, which fell to Assyria in 722 B.C. (see the note at 2:4). Jeremiah uses the image of the unfaithful woman when speaking of Israel (see the note at 2:20). Many in Judah also worshiped idols, even while pretending to return to the LORD. "Pretense" may refer to Jeremiah's disappointment that Josiah's reforms didn't last and weren't taken to heart by the people of Judah.

3:12 *I am merciful:* God's kindness here is like the love of a parent who forgives a disobedient child.

3:14 *Zion:* Zion is the name of a hill in Jerusalem where God's temple was built. See also the mini-article called "Zion," p. 1294.

3:15 *shepherds after my own heart:* Israel's leaders did not live up to their responsibilities (Isa 56:10, 11; Jer 23:1, 2). See also the mini-article called "Shepherds," p. 1972.

understanding. 16 In those days, when your numbers have increased
greatly in the land," declares the LORD, "men will no longer say,
'The ark of the covenant of the LORD.' It will never enter their
minds or be remembered; it will not be missed, nor will another
one be made. 17 At that time they will call Jerusalem The Throne of
the LORD, and all nations will gather in Jerusalem to honor the
name of the LORD. No longer will they follow the stubbornness of
their evil hearts. 18 In those days the house of Judah will join the
house of Israel, and together they will come from a northern land
to the land I gave your forefathers as an inheritance.

19 "I myself said,

" 'How gladly would I treat you like sons
 and give you a desirable land,
 the most beautiful inheritance of any nation.'
I thought you would call me 'Father'
 and not turn away from following me.
20 But like a woman unfaithful to her husband,
 so you have been unfaithful to me, O house of Israel,"
 declares the LORD.

21 A cry is heard on the barren heights,
 the weeping and pleading of the people of Israel,
because they have perverted their ways
 and have forgotten the LORD their God.

22 "Return, faithless people;
 I will cure you of backsliding."

"Yes, we will come to you,
 for you are the LORD our God.
23 Surely the ⌊idolatrous⌋ commotion on the hills
 and mountains is a deception;
surely in the LORD our God
 is the salvation of Israel.
24 From our youth shameful gods have consumed
 the fruits of our fathers' labor—
their flocks and herds,
 their sons and daughters.
25 Let us lie down in our shame,
 and let our disgrace cover us.
We have sinned against the LORD our God,
 both we and our fathers;
from our youth till this day
 we have not obeyed the LORD our God."

4 "If you will return, O Israel,
 return to me,"
 declares the LORD.
"If you put your detestable idols out of my sight

3:16,17 *ark of the covenant . . . Throne of the LORD:* The ark of the covenant was kept in the Most Holy Place of the temple in Jerusalem (1 Kgs 8:1-13). It was thought to be God's throne on earth, the place where God lived among his people (Exod 25:22; 1 Sam 4:4; 2 Sam 6:2; Isa 6:1-5). See also the mini-article called "The Ark of the Covenant," p. 513.

3:18 *house of Judah will join the house of Israel:* The ten northern tribes of Israel broke away from the two southern tribes after the death of King Solomon (1 Kgs 12:1-19). See also the note at 2:4.

3:23,24 *idolatrous commotion on the hills . . . shameful gods:* See the notes at 2:8; 2:20; and 3:2. Some Israelites dedicated parts of their crops and livestock to Baal, the Canaanite god of fertility, instead of to the LORD as the law commanded. Israelite sons and daughters became involved in cultic prostitution connected to the worship of Baal. In Jeremiah's vision, God sees the people at last recognizing that the LORD is their true husband and parent (3:25).

4:1 *put your detestable idols out of my sight:* Getting rid of the worship places and objects connected to other gods was the only way to remove Israel's past guilt and sins (Isa 27:9).

3:18 Isa 11:11-14; Ezek 37:16-28. **3:19** Deut 8:7-9. **3:20** Jer 3:6.

and no longer go astray,
2 and if in a truthful, just and righteous way
you swear, 'As surely as the LORD lives,'
then the nations will be blessed by him
and in him they will glory."

3 This is what the LORD says to the men of Judah and to
Jerusalem:

"Break up your unplowed ground
and do not sow among thorns.
4 Circumcise yourselves to the LORD,
circumcise your hearts,
you men of Judah and people of Jerusalem,
or my wrath will break out and burn like fire
because of the evil you have done—
burn with no one to quench it.

Disaster From the North

5 "Announce in Judah and proclaim in Jerusalem and say:
'Sound the trumpet throughout the land!'
Cry aloud and say:
'Gather together!
Let us flee to the fortified cities!'
6 Raise the signal to go to Zion!
Flee for safety without delay!
For I am bringing disaster from the north,
even terrible destruction."

7 A lion has come out of his lair;
a destroyer of nations has set out.
He has left his place
to lay waste your land.
Your towns will lie in ruins
without inhabitant.
8 So put on sackcloth,
lament and wail,
for the fierce anger of the LORD
has not turned away from us.

9 "In that day," declares the LORD,
"the king and the officials will lose heart,
the priests will be horrified,
and the prophets will be appalled."

10 Then I said, "Ah, Sovereign LORD, how completely you have
deceived this people and Jerusalem by saying, 'You will have peace,'
when the sword is at our throats."

11 At that time this people and Jerusalem will be told, "A
scorching wind from the barren heights in the desert blows toward

4:2 *you swear . . . nations will be blessed:* To "swear," or make a vow in the name of the LORD was serious business, and the vow was to be kept. Making vows in the name of other gods was forbidden. See also the mini-article called "Making Vows," p. 328.

The idea of Israel being a blessing to other nations is first found in the promises to Abraham (Gen 12:1-3). See also 16:19-21; Zech 2:10-12; 8:20-23.

4:4 *circumcise your hearts:* The people are to be completely dedicated to following the laws and teachings that were part of the covenant the LORD made with their ancestors at Mount Sinai. The picture of circumcision meant that they were to "cut off" all sin and idolatry. See the note at 9:25,26.

4:6 *disaster from the north:* It is not clear who is meant. Assyria, Egypt, and Babylon are all possibilities (see the map on p. 2468). Most invasions of Israel came through the northern part of the country. Jeremiah knows that it is an agent of God, sent by God to punish the people for their sins. See the note at 1:13.

4:8 *sackcloth:* A rough, dark-colored cloth made from goat or camel hair and used to make grain sacks. It was worn in times of trouble or sorrow.

4:11,12 *scorching wind . . . too strong:* The LORD will send a sirocco, or strong burning wind from the desert, which carries off everything. This wind is too powerful to winnow grain. Farmers used a special shovel to pitch grain and husks into the air. A gentle wind would blow away the light husks, and the grain would fall back to the ground, where they could be gathered up.

4:3 Hos 10:12.

The LORD declares, *"O Jerusalem, wash the evil from your heart and be saved. How long will you harbor wicked thoughts?"* Jer 4:14

4:15 *Dan . . . Ephraim:* News of an invasion would travel from Dan in the far north to the hills of Ephraim, which were about twenty miles north of Jerusalem. Then the bad news would reach Jerusalem. See the map on p. 2464.

4:16 *besieging army . . . distant land:* The Babylonian army under King Nebuchadnezzar surrounded Jerusalem for eighteen months, from 588 to 586 B.C., and destroyed the surrounding towns and villages. When they finally left, the temple was robbed and destroyed, and the city was devastated (2 Kgs 25:1-21; 2 Chr 36:17-21). Many of the Jewish people and their leaders were taken away into exile in Babylon (see the map on p. 2468). Jeremiah predicts this destruction, which is Judah's punishment for repeatedly disobeying the covenant made with the LORD.

4:19 *My heart pounds:* Jeremiah feels the pain of his people (4:18; 10:19) and the pain of God. The anguish of Jeremiah is too deep to hold back. All will suffer—prophet, people, God—and everyone will be hurt. This shared heartache is a major theme of the poetic messages in JEREMIAH.

4:22 *fools . . . skilled in doing evil:* The people are morally stupid and too foolish to recognize that their sinful actions will lead to punishment. See the mini-article called "Sin," p. 2181.

my people, but not to winnow or cleanse; [12]a wind too strong for
that comes from me.[a] Now I pronounce my judgments against
them."

[13]Look! He advances like the clouds,
his chariots come like a whirlwind,
his horses are swifter than eagles.
Woe to us! We are ruined!
[14]O Jerusalem, wash the evil from your heart and be saved.
How long will you harbor wicked thoughts?
[15]A voice is announcing from Dan,
proclaiming disaster from the hills of Ephraim.
[16]"Tell this to the nations,
proclaim it to Jerusalem:
'A besieging army is coming from a distant land,
raising a war cry against the cities of Judah.
[17]They surround her like men guarding a field,
because she has rebelled against me,' "
declares the LORD.
[18]"Your own conduct and actions
have brought this upon you.
This is your punishment.
How bitter it is!
How it pierces to the heart!"

[19]Oh, my anguish, my anguish!
I writhe in pain.
Oh, the agony of my heart!
My heart pounds within me,
I cannot keep silent.
For I have heard the sound of the trumpet;
I have heard the battle cry.
[20]Disaster follows disaster;
the whole land lies in ruins.
In an instant my tents are destroyed,
my shelter in a moment.
[21]How long must I see the battle standard
and hear the sound of the trumpet?

[22]"My people are fools;
they do not know me.
They are senseless children;
they have no understanding.
They are skilled in doing evil;
they know not how to do good."

[23]I looked at the earth,
and it was formless and empty;

[a]12 Or *comes at my command*

and at the heavens,
and their light was gone.
24 I looked at the mountains,
and they were quaking;
all the hills were swaying.
25 I looked, and there were no people;
every bird in the sky had flown away.
26 I looked, and the fruitful land was a desert;
all its towns lay in ruins
before the LORD, before his fierce anger.

27 This is what the LORD says:

"The whole land will be ruined,
though I will not destroy it completely.
28 Therefore the earth will mourn
and the heavens above grow dark,
because I have spoken and will not relent,
I have decided and will not turn back."

29 At the sound of horsemen and archers
every town takes to flight.
Some go into the thickets;
some climb up among the rocks.
All the towns are deserted;
no one lives in them.

30 What are you doing, O devastated one?
Why dress yourself in scarlet
and put on jewels of gold?
Why shade your eyes with paint?
You adorn yourself in vain.
Your lovers despise you;
they seek your life.

31 I hear a cry as of a woman in labor,
a groan as of one bearing her first child—
the cry of the Daughter of Zion gasping
for breath,
stretching out her hands and saying,
"Alas! I am fainting;
my life is given over to murderers."

Not One Is Upright

5 "Go up and down the streets of Jerusalem,
look around and consider,
search through her squares.
If you can find but one person
who deals honestly and seeks the truth,
I will forgive this city.

4:23 *earth . . . formless and empty . . . heavens . . . light was gone:* This vision is the creation story in reverse. Jeremiah sees a world that has no life and no light (Gen 1:2). Darkness and destruction are commonly found in other prophetic visions of God's judgment (Joel 2:1-3, 10, 11; Amos 5:18-20; Zeph 1:14-18). See also the mini-article called "Day of the LORD," p. 1727.

4:27 *ruined . . . I will not destroy it completely:* God will bring something new out of this destruction. Devastation is not the last word. See also 5:10,18; 30:10,11.

4:30 *dress yourself in scarlet:* Referring to acting like a prostitute. See the notes at 2:20 and 2:31-34. Jerusalem is represented as a woman dressing up to make herself more beautiful to the approaching enemy. But nothing will change the fact that Jerusalem's enemies are out to destroy her.

5:1 *Go up and down the streets of Jerusalem:* God looked for ten people who were righteous in the evil city of Sodom (Gen 18:22-32). Here, Jeremiah searches for just one honest person but cannot find any. The leaders of the people are no better (5:5). The entire city and its people choose to disobey God. They are content with their rebellion and rottenness.

5:6 *lion . . . wolf . . . leopard:* The people are like sheep without a shepherd (see the note at 3:15) that can be attacked and torn to pieces by wild animals.

5:10 *vineyards:* Vineyards, where grapes are grown, are often used by the prophets as a symbol for Israel (Isa 5:1-7; Ezek 17:1-10). The vine branches are cut (pruned), but the main vine stalks are not destroyed, so the destruction is not final (see also 4:27).

5:12 *They have lied:* The prophets (5:13) deny that God will bring disaster, so the people get a false sense of security. But as God's true prophet, Jeremiah's words will be like a fire burning the false calm in Judah and Jerusalem (5:14). See also the article called "Prophets and Prophecy," p. 935.

2 Although they say, 'As surely as the LORD lives,'
still they are swearing falsely."

3 O LORD, do not your eyes look for truth?
You struck them, but they felt no pain;
you crushed them, but they refused correction.
They made their faces harder than stone
and refused to repent.
4 I thought, "These are only the poor;
they are foolish,
for they do not know the way of the LORD,
the requirements of their God.
5 So I will go to the leaders
and speak to them;
surely they know the way of the LORD,
the requirements of their God."
But with one accord they too had broken off
the yoke
and torn off the bonds.
6 Therefore a lion from the forest will attack them,
a wolf from the desert will ravage them,
a leopard will lie in wait near their towns
to tear to pieces any who venture out,
for their rebellion is great
and their backslidings many.

7 "Why should I forgive you?
Your children have forsaken me
and sworn by gods that are not gods.
I supplied all their needs,
yet they committed adultery
and thronged to the houses of prostitutes.
8 They are well-fed, lusty stallions,
each neighing for another man's wife.
9 Should I not punish them for this?"
declares the LORD.
"Should I not avenge myself
on such a nation as this?

10 "Go through her vineyards and ravage them,
but do not destroy them completely.
Strip off her branches,
for these people do not belong to the LORD.
11 The house of Israel and the house of Judah
have been utterly unfaithful to me,"
declares the LORD.

12 They have lied about the LORD;
they said, "He will do nothing!
No harm will come to us;

we will never see sword or famine.
13 The prophets are but wind
and the word is not in them;
so let what they say be done to them."

14 Therefore this is what the LORD God Almighty says:

"Because the people have spoken these words,
I will make my words in your mouth a fire
and these people the wood it consumes.
15 O house of Israel," declares the LORD,
"I am bringing a distant nation against you—
an ancient and enduring nation,
a people whose language you do not know,
whose speech you do not understand.
16 Their quivers are like an open grave;
all of them are mighty warriors.
17 They will devour your harvests and food,
devour your sons and daughters;
they will devour your flocks and herds,
devour your vines and fig trees.
With the sword they will destroy
the fortified cities in which you trust.

18 "Yet even in those days," declares the LORD, "I will not
destroy you completely. 19 And when the people ask, 'Why has the
LORD our God done all this to us?' you will tell them, 'As you have
forsaken me and served foreign gods in your own land, so now you
will serve foreigners in a land not your own.'

20 "Announce this to the house of Jacob
and proclaim it in Judah:
21 Hear this, you foolish and senseless people,
who have eyes but do not see,
who have ears but do not hear:
22 Should you not fear me?" declares the LORD.
"Should you not tremble in my presence?
I made the sand a boundary for the sea,
an everlasting barrier it cannot cross.
The waves may roll, but they cannot prevail;
they may roar, but they cannot cross it.
23 But these people have stubborn and rebellious
hearts;
they have turned aside and gone away.
24 They do not say to themselves,
'Let us fear the LORD our God,
who gives autumn and spring rains in season,
who assures us of the regular weeks of harvest.'
25 Your wrongdoings have kept these away;
your sins have deprived you of good.

5:15 *a distant nation against you:* This probably refers to Babylon (see the note at 4:16).

5:19 *when the people ask . . . serve foreigners in a land not your own:* Those who "ask" will be those who survive the destruction. After Babylon destroyed Jerusalem, some survivors, including Jeremiah, stayed in Jerusalem and the surrounding area. Others were taken away. Two or three different groups from Judah went to Babylon as prisoners: one group in 598 B.C.; another in 586 B.C.; and possibly a third in 582 B.C. See also the mini-article called "Exile," p. 1541.

5:22 *Should you not fear me . . . I made a boundary for the sea:* The idols that the people were worshiping were useless, but the LORD God is the powerful living God of creation who created the shores to hold back the earth's waters (Gen 1:9, 10; Job 38:8-11; Ps 104:5-9), which were viewed as dangerous and sometimes compared to a monster (Job 26:12,13).

5:18-20 Isa 6:11-13. **5:21** Isa 6:9, 10; Ezek 12:2; Mark 8:18.

5:26 *men ... snare birds ... catch men:* Bird catchers used large nets to catch birds. When a bird landed or flew close to where they were lying, the bird catcher threw the net over the bird and closed it by pulling on the cords. The birds were then placed in a basket or cage. The caging of birds is compared to the way some Israelites treated their neighbors unjustly and enslaved them.

5:28 *grown fat ... rights of the poor:* Moses had warned of the dangers of prosperity in Deuteronomy 8:10-20. When they became successful, the people forgot that their ancestors had once been slaves in Egypt (see the note at 2:6, 7) and they abandoned God's concern for justice to the poor (see the note at 2:31-34).

5:31 *prophets ... priests:* See 2:26-28; 5:12, 13; and the note at 2:8.

5:31 *what will you do in the end:* See the note at 4:23.

6:1 *Benjamin ... Tekoa ... Beth Hakkerem:* See the note at 1:1. Tekoa was in the hill country of Judah south of Jerusalem and Bethlehem (see 2 Sam 14:1-4; 2 Chr 11:5,6; Amos 1:1 and the map on p. 2467). Beth Hakkerem was west of Jerusalem. The warning keeps spreading south and west of the capital city. See also 4:15 and note.

6:3 *Shepherds ... pitch their tents:* Enemy kings and their troops camp outside the city just waiting for a chance to destroy the city and divide up its riches.

6:4,5 *attack at noon ... attack at night:* Invading kings decide that the midday time of rest or the cover of darkness are the best times to attack Jerusalem's walls.

6:6 *Lord Almighty ... build siege ramps against Jerusalem:* God's judgment against the people of Judah includes guiding their enemies to victory. See also Isa 9:11,12; 10:5-7.

26 "Among my people are wicked men
who lie in wait like men who snare birds
and like those who set traps to catch men.
27 Like cages full of birds,
their houses are full of deceit;
they have become rich and powerful
28 and have grown fat and sleek.
Their evil deeds have no limit;
they do not plead the case of the fatherless to win it,
they do not defend the rights of the poor.
29 Should I not punish them for this?"
declares the LORD.
"Should I not avenge myself
on such a nation as this?

30 "A horrible and shocking thing
has happened in the land:
31 The prophets prophesy lies,
the priests rule by their own authority,
and my people love it this way.
But what will you do in the end?

Jerusalem Under Siege

6 "Flee for safety, people of Benjamin!
Flee from Jerusalem!
Sound the trumpet in Tekoa!
Raise the signal over Beth Hakkerem!
For disaster looms out of the north,
even terrible destruction.
2 I will destroy the Daughter of Zion,
so beautiful and delicate.
3 Shepherds with their flocks will come against her;
they will pitch their tents around her,
each tending his own portion."

4 "Prepare for battle against her!
Arise, let us attack at noon!
But, alas, the daylight is fading,
and the shadows of evening grow long.
5 So arise, let us attack at night
and destroy her fortresses!"

6 This is what the LORD Almighty says:

"Cut down the trees
and build siege ramps against Jerusalem.
This city must be punished;
it is filled with oppression.

7 As a well pours out its water,
so she pours out her wickedness.
Violence and destruction resound in her;
her sickness and wounds are ever before me.
8 Take warning, O Jerusalem,
or I will turn away from you
and make your land desolate
so no one can live in it."

9 This is what the LORD Almighty says:

"Let them glean the remnant of Israel
as thoroughly as a vine;
pass your hand over the branches again,
like one gathering grapes."

10 To whom can I speak and give warning?
Who will listen to me?
Their ears are closed[a]
so they cannot hear.
The word of the LORD is offensive to them;
they find no pleasure in it.
11 But I am full of the wrath of the LORD,
and I cannot hold it in.

"Pour it out on the children in the street
and on the young men gathered together;
both husband and wife will be caught in it,
and the old, those weighed down with years.
12 Their houses will be turned over to others,
together with their fields and their wives,
when I stretch out my hand
against those who live in the land,"
declares the LORD.
13 "From the least to the greatest,
all are greedy for gain;
prophets and priests alike,
all practice deceit.
14 They dress the wound of my people
as though it were not serious.
'Peace, peace,' they say,
when there is no peace.
15 Are they ashamed of their loathsome conduct?
No, they have no shame at all;
they do not even know how to blush.
So they will fall among the fallen;
they will be brought down when I punish them,"
says the LORD.

[a]10 Hebrew *uncircumcised*

The LORD Almighty says, *"To whom can I speak and give warning? Who will listen to me?"* Jer 6:10

6:9 *like one gathering grapes:* See the note at 5:10.

6:11 *wrath:* Jeremiah feels God's anger, and neither God nor the prophet can hold the fury back any longer. The LORD is not "above" or beyond these very real emotions. God is deeply wounded by his disobedient children.

6:13,14 *prophets and priests . . . there is no peace:* These leaders deceive the people with peaceful words when peace is not at hand. See also Ezek 13:8-10.

6:12-15 Jer 8:10-12.

6:16 *the ancient paths . . . walk in it:* The "way" their ancestors took was based on the LORD's covenant with Moses, which was also the basis of the reforms made by King Josiah (see the Introduction to JEREMIAH, p. 1424 and 2 Kgs 22:1—23:30). In the end, Josiah's reforms didn't last because so many people in Judah continued to reject God's laws and do evil (6:19).

6:20 *incense from Sheba . . . burnt offerings:* Sheba was located in southwest Arabia. It was famous for the spices and incense it exported. Incense here probably is frankincense, which was burned to make a sweet smell. It was also an ingredient in ointments and in the holy incense burned at Israel's tabernacle and was mixed with sacrifices offered by the priests (Exod 30:34-38; Lev 6:14, 15). Calamus is a sweet-smelling reed or cane that was used in making sweet-smelling oil used by Israel's priests (Exod 30:23; Isa 43:24).

These sacrifices and the burnt offerings are not satisfying to God and cannot cover up the fact that the people have continued to disobey him. God desires a true change of heart that results in obedience and justice rather than meaningless ceremonies and rituals (Amos 5:21-24; Isa 1:12-17).

6:22,23 *the north . . . They are armed with bow and spear:* See the notes at 1:13 and 4:6.

16 This is what the LORD says:

"Stand at the crossroads and look;
ask for the ancient paths,
ask where the good way is, and walk in it,
and you will find rest for your souls.
But you said, 'We will not walk in it.'
17 I appointed watchmen over you and said,
'Listen to the sound of the trumpet!'
But you said, 'We will not listen.'
18 Therefore hear, O nations;
observe, O witnesses,
what will happen to them.
19 Hear, O earth:
I am bringing disaster on this people,
the fruit of their schemes,
because they have not listened to my words
and have rejected my law.
20 What do I care about incense from Sheba
or sweet calamus from a distant land?
Your burnt offerings are not acceptable;
your sacrifices do not please me."
21 Therefore this is what the LORD says:

"I will put obstacles before this people.
Fathers and sons alike will stumble over them;
neighbors and friends will perish."
22 This is what the LORD says:

"Look, an army is coming
from the land of the north;
a great nation is being stirred up
from the ends of the earth.
23 They are armed with bow and spear;
they are cruel and show no mercy.
They sound like the roaring sea
as they ride on their horses;
they come like men in battle formation
to attack you, O Daughter of Zion."

QUESTIONS ABOUT JEREMIAH 2:1—6:30

1. What pictures does God use in chapters 2 and 3 to show the people what their unfaithfulness looks like?
2. How can Israel return to the LORD?(4:1-4)
3. The vision of the day of the LORD in 4:23-26 is a powerful one. What in this description gets your attention the most? Why?
4. The Lord's anger is reported in 3:12 and 6:11. How do you react to a description of a God who is full of emotion? Why?

24 We have heard reports about them,
and our hands hang limp.
Anguish has gripped us,
pain like that of a woman in labor.
25 Do not go out to the fields
or walk on the roads,
for the enemy has a sword,
and there is terror on every side.
26 O my people, put on sackcloth
and roll in ashes;
mourn with bitter wailing
as for an only son,
for suddenly the destroyer
will come upon us.

27 "I have made you a tester of metals
and my people the ore,
that you may observe
and test their ways.
28 They are all hardened rebels,
going about to slander.
They are bronze and iron;
they all act corruptly.
29 The bellows blow fiercely
to burn away the lead with fire,
but the refining goes on in vain;
the wicked are not purged out.
30 They are called rejected silver,
because the LORD has rejected them."

SCENES FROM JEREMIAH'S LIFE

Jeremiah preaches in the temple and acts out God's message of doom. His life is threatened, and he complains to God. God's punishment of Judah is certain.

False Religion Worthless

7 This is the word that came to Jeremiah from the LORD: 2"Stand
at the gate of the LORD's house and there proclaim this message:
" 'Hear the word of the LORD, all you people of Judah who
come through these gates to worship the LORD. 3This is what the
LORD Almighty, the God of Israel, says: Reform your ways and your
actions, and I will let you live in this place. 4Do not trust in deceptive words and say, "This is the temple of the LORD, the temple of
the LORD, the temple of the LORD!" 5If you really change your ways
and your actions and deal with each other justly, 6if you do not
oppress the alien, the fatherless or the widow and do not shed
innocent blood in this place, and if you do not follow other gods
to your own harm, 7then I will let you live in this place, in the land

6:26 *sackcloth:* See the note at 4:8.

6:27-30 *tester of metals . . . the refining . . . rejected silver:* Jeremiah's testing is compared to the process of refining silver to make it more pure. In ancient times, lead or iron was placed in a container with silver ore. When taken to a white-hot heat, the lead oxidized and carried off impurities in the silver ore, leaving behind more pure silver. But the people are like hopelessly impure metal that cannot be purified by the refining process. See also Isa 1:22-26; 48:10.

7:2-4 *Stand at the gate of the LORD's house . . . the temple:* Chapter 7 has been described as a series of sermons. The first sermon (7:1-20) warns that the temple in Jerusalem will be destroyed just like the sanctuary that was built in the north at Shiloh if the people of Judah continue to worship false gods. It was after this temple sermon that Jeremiah's enemies began to oppose his message and persecute him. See also 26:1-6.

7:4 *temple:* Because of the promises made to David recorded in 2 Samuel 7, the people felt that the Jerusalem temple would never be destroyed, and it would keep them safe no matter what (7:10).

7:5-9 *deal with each other justly . . . burn incense to Baal:* The people of Judah have been unfair in their treatment of others, especially those less fortunate (see 2:31-34 and note), and they have worshiped idols, including the Canaanite god Baal (see the notes at 2:8; 3:23).

I gave your forefathers for ever and ever. 8But look, you are trusting in deceptive words that are worthless.
9" 'Will you steal and murder, commit adultery and perjury,[a]
burn incense to Baal and follow other gods you have not known,
10and then come and stand before me in this house, which bears
my Name, and say, "We are safe"—safe to do all these detestable
things? 11Has this house, which bears my Name, become a den of
robbers to you? But I have been watching! declares the LORD.
12" 'Go now to the place in Shiloh where I first made a
dwelling for my Name, and see what I did to it because of the
wickedness of my people Israel. 13While you were doing all these
things, declares the LORD, I spoke to you again and again, but you
did not listen; I called you, but you did not answer. 14Therefore,
what I did to Shiloh I will now do to the house that bears my
Name, the temple you trust in, the place I gave to you and your
fathers. 15I will thrust you from my presence, just as I did all your
brothers, the people of Ephraim.'
16"So do not pray for this people nor offer any plea or petition for them; do not plead with me, for I will not listen to you.
17Do you not see what they are doing in the towns of Judah and in
the streets of Jerusalem? 18The children gather wood, the fathers
light the fire, and the women knead the dough and make cakes of
bread for the Queen of Heaven. They pour out drink offerings to
other gods to provoke me to anger. 19But am I the one they are
provoking? declares the LORD. Are they not rather harming themselves, to their own shame?
20" 'Therefore this is what the Sovereign LORD says: My anger
and my wrath will be poured out on this place, on man and beast,
on the trees of the field and on the fruit of the ground, and it will
burn and not be quenched.
21" 'This is what the LORD Almighty, the God of Israel, says:
Go ahead, add your burnt offerings to your other sacrifices and eat
the meat yourselves! 22For when I brought your forefathers out of
Egypt and spoke to them, I did not just give them commands
about burnt offerings and sacrifices, 23but I gave them this command: Obey me, and I will be your God and you will be my people. Walk in all the ways I command you, that it may go well with
you. 24But they did not listen or pay attention; instead, they followed the stubborn inclinations of their evil hearts. They went
backward and not forward. 25From the time your forefathers left
Egypt until now, day after day, again and again I sent you my servants the prophets. 26But they did not listen to me or pay attention.
They were stiff-necked and did more evil than their forefathers.'
27"When you tell them all this, they will not listen to you;
when you call to them, they will not answer. 28Therefore say to
them, 'This is the nation that has not obeyed the LORD its God or

a9 Or *and swear by false gods*

7:10,11 *this house . . . a den of robbers:* The people are using the temple and worship there as a kind of "good-luck" charm. They are living immoral lives and not living up to God's laws (7:5-9). But then they go to the temple where they use worship as a cover-up for the way they are really living. See also Matt 21:13; Mark 11:17; Luke 19:46.

7:12 *Shiloh:* At Shiloh Joshua divided the land taken from the Canaanites (Josh 18:1-10; 19:51) and set up the tabernacle that housed the ark of the covenant. But it was destroyed by the Philistines in 1050 B.C. and never rebuilt. Jeremiah uses the destruction of Shiloh as a warning that God will destroy the Jerusalem temple. See Ps 78:60, 61; Jer 26:6; and the map on p. 2467.

7:18 *Queen of Heaven:* This is another name for the moon goddess Astarte, a fertility symbol along with Baal in Canaan. Here the entire family is involved in baking crescent-shaped cakes as gifts to the goddess. Wine offerings were also given to Astarte (44:17-19), as well as to other gods. See also Isa 57:6 and the mini-article called "Canaanite Gods and Goddesses," p. 469.

7:21 *burnt offerings:* Certain animal sacrifices burned on the altar by the priests to send up a pleasing smell to the LORD (Lev 1:1-17). But because the people have been so sinful, the LORD will not accept the burnt offerings of the priests. See also the chart called "Sacrifices and Offerings," p. 219.

7:23 *I will be your God:* God's most basic demand is obedience, not rituals. See also Deut 26:16-19.

7:27 *they will not listen:* Jeremiah persisted in trying to make the people hear the words of the LORD, even though he knew they would not listen and change their ways. He also continued to pray for his people, as we can gather from God's repeated protests in 6:14; 7:16; 11:14; 14:11.

responded to correction. Truth has perished; it has vanished from
their lips. 29 Cut off your hair and throw it away; take up a lament
on the barren heights, for the LORD has rejected and abandoned
this generation that is under his wrath.

The Valley of Slaughter

30 " 'The people of Judah have done evil in my eyes, declares
the LORD. They have set up their detestable idols in the house that
bears my Name and have defiled it. 31 They have built the high
places of Topheth in the Valley of Ben Hinnom to burn their sons
and daughters in the fire—something I did not command, nor did
it enter my mind. 32 So beware, the days are coming, declares the
LORD, when people will no longer call it Topheth or the Valley of
Ben Hinnom, but the Valley of Slaughter, for they will bury the
dead in Topheth until there is no more room. 33 Then the carcasses of this people will become food for the birds of the air and the
beasts of the earth, and there will be no one to frighten them away.
34 I will bring an end to the sounds of joy and gladness and to the
voices of bride and bridegroom in the towns of Judah and the
streets of Jerusalem, for the land will become desolate.
8 " 'At that time, declares the LORD, the bones of the kings and
officials of Judah, the bones of the priests and prophets, and the
bones of the people of Jerusalem will be removed from their
graves. 2 They will be exposed to the sun and the moon and all the
stars of the heavens, which they have loved and served and which
they have followed and consulted and worshiped. They will not be
gathered up or buried, but will be like refuse lying on the ground.
3 Wherever I banish them, all the survivors of this evil nation will
prefer death to life, declares the LORD Almighty.'

Sin and Punishment

4 "Say to them, 'This is what the LORD says:

" 'When men fall down, do they not get up?
    When a man turns away, does he not return?
5 Why then have these people turned away?
    Why does Jerusalem always turn away?
They cling to deceit;
    they refuse to return.
6 I have listened attentively,
    but they do not say what is right.
No one repents of his wickedness,
    saying, "What have I done?"
Each pursues his own course
    like a horse charging into battle.
7 Even the stork in the sky
    knows her appointed seasons,
and the dove, the swift and the thrush

7:29 *Cut off your hair:* Shaving the head was sometimes done as a sign of mourning or grief (Job 1:20; Ezek 7:18).

7:31 *Topheth in the Valley of Ben Hinnom:* Topheth probably comes from an Aramaic word meaning "fireplace." It was likely at Topheth that Israel's kings Ahaz (2 Kgs 16:2, 3) and Manasseh (2 Kgs 21:1, 6) sacrificed their sons to the god Molech. The practice of child sacrifice was forbidden by the Law of Moses (Lev 18:21; Deut 18:10, 11).

8:1,2 *bones . . . sun and the moon and all the stars:* Some of Judah's neighbors worshiped the sun, moon, and stars as gods. A number of God's people, including some of the leaders of Judah, followed these forbidden worship practices. The digging up and scattering of human bones was considered a terrible insult. But that is what Jeremiah warns will happen to the bones of the people who have worshiped false gods.

8:7 *stork . . . thrush:* These migratory birds have a strong homing instinct. The stork, shown below, spends winters in southeast Africa and summers in Europe and Asia. Jeremiah is criticizing Israel for not being as smart as the simple birds named here. The people have lost the instinct of self-preservation and their ability to obey the LORD.

7:34 Jer 16:9; 25:10; Rev 18:23.

8:8 *we have the law of the Lord:* King Josiah's reforms were based on the scroll found in the temple (see the Introduction to Jeremiah, p. 1424). Jeremiah saw that these "reforms" produced no real repentance. Possessing the written scroll has made them think they have wisdom, but they refuse to hear the words of God's prophet.

8:9 *The wise ... what kind of wisdom:* The "wise" are scribes, or professional interpreters of the law. In Israel, true wisdom came from respecting and obeying the Lord God (Prov 1:7), so it is ironic that the very ones who know God's Law the best don't live according to it. See also the mini-article called "Wisdom," p. 2206.

8:11 *Peace ... no peace:* See the note at 6:13, 14.

8:14 *given us poisoned water to drink:* The people will not actually "drink" poisoned water, but rather they will drink the poison of God's punishment (see also 9:15; 23:15). God's judgment is also described in the Bible as drinking the cup of the Lord's wrath (Ps 60:3; Isa 51:17, 22; Jer 25:15, 16; Rev 14:10; 16:19).

observe the time of their migration.
But my people do not know
the requirements of the Lord.

8 " 'How can you say, "We are wise,
for we have the law of the Lord,"
when actually the lying pen of the scribes
has handled it falsely?
9 The wise will be put to shame;
they will be dismayed and trapped.
Since they have rejected the word of the Lord,
what kind of wisdom do they have?
10 Therefore I will give their wives to other men
and their fields to new owners.
From the least to the greatest,
all are greedy for gain;
prophets and priests alike,
all practice deceit.
11 They dress the wound of my people
as though it were not serious.
"Peace, peace," they say,
when there is no peace.
12 Are they ashamed of their loathsome conduct?
No, they have no shame at all;
they do not even know how to blush.
So they will fall among the fallen;
they will be brought down when they are punished,
says the Lord.

13 " 'I will take away their harvest,
declares the Lord.
There will be no grapes on the vine.
There will be no figs on the tree,
and their leaves will wither.
What I have given them
will be taken from them.[a]' "

14 "Why are we sitting here?
Gather together!
Let us flee to the fortified cities
and perish there!
For the Lord our God has doomed us to perish
and given us poisoned water to drink,
because we have sinned against him.
15 We hoped for peace
but no good has come,
for a time of healing
but there was only terror.

[a]13 The meaning of the Hebrew for this sentence is uncertain.

16 The snorting of the enemy's horses
is heard from Dan;
at the neighing of their stallions
the whole land trembles.
They have come to devour
the land and everything in it,
the city and all who live there."

17 "See, I will send venomous snakes among you,
vipers that cannot be charmed,
and they will bite you,"
declares the LORD.

18 O my Comforter[a] in sorrow,
my heart is faint within me.
19 Listen to the cry of my people
from a land far away:
"Is the LORD not in Zion?
Is her King no longer there?"

"Why have they provoked me to anger with their images,
with their worthless foreign idols?"

20 "The harvest is past,
the summer has ended,
and we are not saved."

21 Since my people are crushed, I am crushed;
I mourn, and horror grips me.
22 Is there no balm in Gilead?
Is there no physician there?
Why then is there no healing
for the wound of my people?

9 1 Oh, that my head were a spring of water
and my eyes a fountain of tears!
I would weep day and night
for the slain of my people.
2 Oh, that I had in the desert
a lodging place for travelers,
so that I might leave my people
and go away from them;
for they are all adulterers,
a crowd of unfaithful people.

3 "They make ready their tongue
like a bow, to shoot lies;
it is not by truth
that they triumph[b] in the land.

[a]**18** The meaning of the Hebrew for this word is uncertain. [b]**3** Or *lies; / they are not valiant for truth*

8:16 *Dan:* See the note at 4:15.

8:17 *venomous snakes:* The enemy (Babylon).

8:18-21 *my heart is faint . . . I mourn:* In this poem Jeremiah identifies with the sorrow and suffering of his people. It appears as though the LORD has left Zion (see the note at 3:14) completely. Compare to the prophet Ezekiel's vision (Ezek 10, 11).

8:22 *balm in Gilead:* Trees in this region east of the Jordan River produced a resin that was used to make an ointment for wounds. But no medicine or ointment can heal Israel's deep wounds.

9:1 *weep day and night:* Jeremiah's sorrowful poem (8:18—9:2) expresses the heartache of God as well. God is not distant from the people's suffering. The people's pain is God's pain. Both Jeremiah and God are heartbroken over the spiritual illness that is killing and causing misery for the people of Judah.

9:3 Ps 64:3; Jer 9:8.

9:7 *I will refine and test them:* See the note at 6:27-30.

9:8 *arrow:* The lie of peace is as deadly as an arrow, because those who think peace will come are likely to be caught off guard when invading armies attack.

9:11 *jackals:* Jackals are desert animals that are related to wolves, but smaller. They survive by being scavengers, eating the flesh of dead animals or human beings. When Jerusalem and other cities are totally destroyed, the jackals will move in from the desert to feast on the dead.

9:14 *Baals:* See the notes at 2:8 and 3:23.

9:15 *eat bitter food and drink poisoned water:* See the note at 8:14.

9:17 *Call for the wailing women to come:* Two different practices may be in mind here: (1) Mourning was part of the ceremony of worshiping Baal. Each year at the end of the growing season, the god Baal was believed to die at the hands of Mot, the underworld god of barrenness. Some women would weep over the death of Baal at the places where Baal was worshiped. At the start of the next growing season Baal's female companion, Anat or Baalath, was thought to free Baal from death, so they could unite sexually and refertilize the earth and animal world. (2) Professional mourners, usually women, were hired to sing sad songs and wail in order to inspire grieving at funerals. The tears of these women were not a substitute for the tears of others, but a means of stirring the mourning process. See also the mini-article called "Burial," p. 1998.

They go from one sin to another;
  they do not acknowledge me,"
    declares the LORD.

4 "Beware of your friends;
  do not trust your brothers.
For every brother is a deceiver,[a]
  and every friend a slanderer.
5 Friend deceives friend,
  and no one speaks the truth.
They have taught their tongues to lie;
  they weary themselves with sinning.
6 You[b] live in the midst of deception;
  in their deceit they refuse to acknowledge me,"
    declares the LORD.

7 Therefore this is what the LORD Almighty says:

"See, I will refine and test them,
  for what else can I do
  because of the sin of my people?
8 Their tongue is a deadly arrow;
  it speaks with deceit.
With his mouth each speaks cordially to his neighbor,
  but in his heart he sets a trap for him.
9 Should I not punish them for this?"
  declares the LORD.
"Should I not avenge myself
  on such a nation as this?"

10 I will weep and wail for the mountains
  and take up a lament concerning the desert
    pastures.
They are desolate and untraveled,
  and the lowing of cattle is not heard.
The birds of the air have fled
  and the animals are gone.

11 "I will make Jerusalem a heap of ruins,
  a haunt of jackals;
and I will lay waste the towns of Judah
  so no one can live there."

12 What man is wise enough to understand this? Who has
been instructed by the LORD and can explain it? Why has the land
been ruined and laid waste like a desert that no one can cross?
13 The LORD said, "It is because they have forsaken my law,
which I set before them; they have not obeyed me or followed my
law. 14 Instead, they have followed the stubbornness of their hearts;

[a] **4** Or *a deceiving Jacob* [b] **6** That is, Jeremiah (the Hebrew is singular)

they have followed the Baals, as their fathers taught them."
15 Therefore, this is what the LORD Almighty, the God of Israel, says:
"See, I will make this people eat bitter food and drink poisoned
water. 16 I will scatter them among nations that neither they nor
their fathers have known, and I will pursue them with the sword
until I have destroyed them."

17 This is what the LORD Almighty says:

"Consider now! Call for the wailing women
to come;
send for the most skillful of them.
18 Let them come quickly
and wail over us
till our eyes overflow with tears
and water streams from our eyelids.
19 The sound of wailing is heard from Zion:
'How ruined we are!
How great is our shame!
We must leave our land
because our houses are in ruins.' "

20 Now, O women, hear the word of the LORD;
open your ears to the words of his mouth.
Teach your daughters how to wail;
teach one another a lament.
21 Death has climbed in through our windows
and has entered our fortresses;
it has cut off the children from the streets
and the young men from the public squares.

22 Say, "This is what the LORD declares:

" 'The dead bodies of men will lie
like refuse on the open field,
like cut grain behind the reaper,
with no one to gather them.' "

23 This is what the LORD says:

"Let not the wise man boast of his wisdom
or the strong man boast of his strength
or the rich man boast of his riches,
24 but let him who boasts boast about this:
that he understands and knows me,
that I am the LORD, who exercises kindness,
justice and righteousness on earth,
for in these I delight,"
declares the LORD.

25 "The days are coming," declares the LORD, "when I will
punish all who are circumcised only in the flesh— 26 Egypt, Judah,

9:19 *Zion:* See the note at 3:14.

9:20 *Teach your daughters how to wail:* The women who mourn at funerals are to teach their funeral songs to many others, because funeral songs and weeping will be in great demand in the coming time of destruction.

9:21 *Death has climbed in through our windows:* Mot, the Canaanite god of death, was believed to sneak in through windows to claim his victims. In this funeral song, death is pictured as a person. See also the mini-article called "Canaanite Gods and Goddesses," p. 469.

9:24 *boast about this:* Worshiping the LORD alone is the only kind of worship that one can brag about. But even this worship is meaningless, unless the people show their respect for the LORD by treating others with fairness and justice (Isa 1:16, 17; Amos 5:21-24; Mic 6:8; 1 Cor 1:31; 2 Cor 10:17).

9:25 *circumcised:* Circumcision was a common rite among many people in the ancient Near East. God commanded Abraham's male descendants to be circumcised as a physical sign that they were God's chosen people (see Gen 17:9-14; 34:21-23; Lev 12:3). The people of Judah continued to circumcise their sons as an outward sign of devotion to God, but the people were not spiritually devoted to God on the inside. See the mini-article called "Circumcision," p. 2251.

Edom, Ammon, Moab and all who live in the desert in distant places.[a] For all these nations are really uncircumcised, and even the whole house of Israel is uncircumcised in heart."

God and Idols

10 Hear what the LORD says to you, O house of Israel. 2 This is what the LORD says:

"Do not learn the ways of the nations
or be terrified by signs in the sky,
though the nations are terrified by them.
3 For the customs of the peoples are
worthless;
they cut a tree out of the forest,
and a craftsman shapes it with his chisel.
4 They adorn it with silver and gold;
they fasten it with hammer and nails
so it will not totter.
5 Like a scarecrow in a melon patch,
their idols cannot speak;
they must be carried
because they cannot walk.
Do not fear them;
they can do no harm
nor can they do any good."

6 No one is like you, O LORD;
you are great,
and your name is mighty in power.
7 Who should not revere you,
O King of the nations?
This is your due.
Among all the wise men of the nations
and in all their kingdoms,
there is no one like you.
8 They are all senseless and foolish;
they are taught by worthless wooden idols.
9 Hammered silver is brought from Tarshish
and gold from Uphaz.
What the craftsman and goldsmith have made
is then dressed in blue and purple—
all made by skilled workers.
10 But the LORD is the true God;
he is the living God, the eternal King.
When he is angry, the earth trembles;
the nations cannot endure his wrath.

[a]**26** Or *desert and who clip the hair by their foreheads*

"No one is like you, O LORD; you are great, and your name is mighty in power."
Jer 10:6

9:26 *Egypt . . . all who live in the desert:* See the map on p. 2468 for the location of these nations. Jeremiah preached the LORD's judgment against these nations (see the notes in 46:1—49:22). "All who live in the desert" probably refers to tribes who lived in the Arabian Desert.

10:2-5 *signs in the sky . . . cut a tree . . . adorn it:* Some of ancient Israel's neighbors explained lunar and solar eclipses and comets as signs from the gods. And they carved idols from wood and covered them with gold or silver. But the signs in the sky do not mean anything special, and the idols are shown for what they really are: motionless, speechless, lifeless, powerless.

10:9 *Tarshish . . . Uphaz:* The location of Uphaz is not known; it may be Ophir, famous for its gold. Tarshish was either far-away southern Spain or the island of Sardinia. The blue and purple clothes put on the idols are the color of royalty. But only the LORD God is the "King" of all the nations (10:7) and the living God (10:10) who alone created the heavens and the earth (10:11).

10:7 Rev 15:4.

11“Tell them this: ‘These gods, who did not make the heavens
and the earth, will perish from the earth and from under the
heavens.’ ”[a]

12 But God made the earth by his power;
he founded the world by his wisdom
and stretched out the heavens by his understanding.
13 When he thunders, the waters in the heavens roar;
he makes clouds rise from the ends of the earth.
He sends lightning with the rain
and brings out the wind from his storehouses.

14 Everyone is senseless and without knowledge;
every goldsmith is shamed by his idols.
His images are a fraud;
they have no breath in them.
15 They are worthless, the objects of mockery;
when their judgment comes, they will perish.
16 He who is the Portion of Jacob is not like these,
for he is the Maker of all things,
including Israel, the tribe of his inheritance—
the LORD Almighty is his name.

Coming Destruction

17 Gather up your belongings to leave the land,
you who live under siege.
18 For this is what the LORD says:
“At this time I will hurl out
those who live in this land;
I will bring distress on them
so that they may be captured.”

19 Woe to me because of my injury!
My wound is incurable!
Yet I said to myself,
“This is my sickness, and I must endure it.”
20 My tent is destroyed;
all its ropes are snapped.
My sons are gone from me and are no more;
no one is left now to pitch my tent
or to set up my shelter.
21 The shepherds are senseless
and do not inquire of the LORD;
so they do not prosper
and all their flock is scattered.
22 Listen! The report is coming—
a great commotion from the land of the north!

[a]11 The text of this verse is in Aramaic.

He is the Maker of all things, including Israel, the tribe of his inheritance—the LORD Almighty is his name.
Jer 10:16

10:12-16 *founded the world by his wisdom . . . Maker of all things:* This hymn to the one true God is very close in thought to Psalm 135. See also Gen 1; Job 38; Ps 104; Prov 8:12, 22-31. See also the mini-article called “Wisdom,” p. 2206.

10:16 *LORD Almighty:* See the note at 2:19.

10:17 *Gather up your belongings:* Apparently, the end is very near. This section (10:17-25) probably dates from the eve of the final destruction in 586 B.C. (see the Introduction to JEREMIAH, p. 1424). Jeremiah’s message is clear: “Get packed! Exile is at hand!”

10:22 *from the land of the north:* See the notes at 1:13 and 4:6.

10:22 *jackals:* See the note at 9:11.

10:25 *Pour out your wrath:* Except for chapters 46–51, this prayer for God to punish neighboring nations is rarely found in JEREMIAH. Compare to Psalm 79.

11:2-5 *Listen to the terms of this covenant . . . give them a land:* This entire chapter belongs to the time following Josiah's reforms, which were based on *The Book of the Law* found by Josiah's assistants in the temple (2 Kgs 22, 23). The laws in this scroll were based on the covenant God made with Moses and the Israelite people at Sinai (see Exod 19–23). In this covenant, God promised to be Israel's God and to give them "a land," the land of Canaan (Exod 23:20-31; Deut 1:6-8). In return, the people were to obey God's commands. God did give the land of Canaan to the people, but by Jeremiah's day many had turned their backs on God. Jeremiah saw that Josiah's reforms were completely dropped by Jehoiakim, the king who followed Josiah.

11:8 *all the curses of the covenant:* The covenant brings both blessings and curses—peace and plenty to the faithful, punishment on the unfaithful. See Deut 27:9—28:69.

11:10 *Israel . . . Judah:* See the note at 2:4.

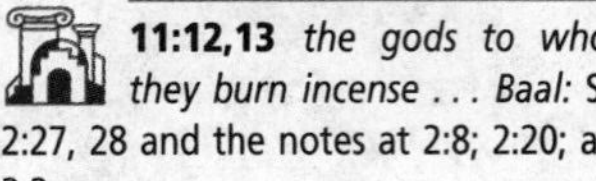

11:12,13 *the gods to whom they burn incense . . . Baal:* See 2:27, 28 and the notes at 2:8; 2:20; and 3:2.

10:23 Prov 20:24; Eccl 3:11,14, 17; Isa 28:23-29.

It will make the towns of Judah desolate,
a haunt of jackals.

Jeremiah's Prayer

23 I know, O LORD, that a man's life is not his own;
it is not for man to direct his steps.
24 Correct me, LORD, but only with justice—
not in your anger,
lest you reduce me to nothing.
25 Pour out your wrath on the nations
that do not acknowledge you,
on the peoples who do not call on your name.
For they have devoured Jacob;
they have devoured him completely
and destroyed his homeland.

The Covenant Is Broken

11 This is the word that came to Jeremiah from the LORD: 2 "Listen to the terms of this covenant and tell them to the people of
Judah and to those who live in Jerusalem. 3 Tell them that this is
what the LORD, the God of Israel, says: 'Cursed is the man who
does not obey the terms of this covenant— 4 the terms I commanded your forefathers when I brought them out of Egypt, out
of the iron-smelting furnace.' I said, 'Obey me and do everything I
command you, and you will be my people, and I will be your God.
5 Then I will fulfill the oath I swore to your forefathers, to give
them a land flowing with milk and honey'—the land you possess
today."

I answered, "Amen, LORD."

6 The LORD said to me, "Proclaim all these words in the towns
of Judah and in the streets of Jerusalem: 'Listen to the terms of this
covenant and follow them. 7 From the time I brought your forefathers up from Egypt until today, I warned them again and again,
saying, "Obey me." 8 But they did not listen or pay attention;
instead, they followed the stubbornness of their evil hearts. So I
brought on them all the curses of the covenant I had commanded
them to follow but that they did not keep.' "

9 Then the LORD said to me, "There is a conspiracy among
the people of Judah and those who live in Jerusalem. 10 They have
returned to the sins of their forefathers, who refused to listen to
my words. They have followed other gods to serve them. Both the
house of Israel and the house of Judah have broken the covenant I
made with their forefathers. 11 Therefore this is what the LORD says:
'I will bring on them a disaster they cannot escape. Although they
cry out to me, I will not listen to them. 12 The towns of Judah and
the people of Jerusalem will go and cry out to the gods to whom
they burn incense, but they will not help them at all when disaster

strikes. [13]You have as many gods as you have towns, O Judah; and
the altars you have set up to burn incense to that shameful god
Baal are as many as the streets of Jerusalem.'

[14]"Do not pray for this people nor offer any plea or petition
for them, because I will not listen when they call to me in the time
of their distress.

[15]"What is my beloved doing in my temple
as she works out her evil schemes
with many?
Can consecrated meat avert ⌞your punishment⌟?
When you engage in your wickedness,
then you rejoice.[a]"

[16]The LORD called you a thriving olive tree
with fruit beautiful in form.
But with the roar of a mighty storm
he will set it on fire,
and its branches will be broken.

[17]The LORD Almighty, who planted you, has decreed disaster for
you, because the house of Israel and the house of Judah have done
evil and provoked me to anger by burning incense to Baal.

Plot Against Jeremiah

[18]Because the LORD revealed their plot to me, I knew it, for at
that time he showed me what they were doing. [19]I had been like a
gentle lamb led to the slaughter; I did not realize that they had
plotted against me, saying,

"Let us destroy the tree and its fruit;
let us cut him off from the land of the living,
that his name be remembered no more."
[20]But, O LORD Almighty, you who judge
righteously
and test the heart and mind,
let me see your vengeance upon them,
for to you I have committed my cause.

[21]"Therefore this is what the LORD says about the men of
Anathoth who are seeking your life and saying, 'Do not prophesy
in the name of the LORD or you will die by our hands'— [22]there-
fore this is what the LORD Almighty says: 'I will punish them.
Their young men will die by the sword, their sons and daughters
by famine. [23]Not even a remnant will be left to them, because I
will bring disaster on the men of Anathoth in the year of their
punishment.' "

[a]15 Or *Could consecrated meat avert your punishment? / Then you would rejoice*

11:14 *Do not pray:* God's anger here is so strong that it overshadows his patience. See also the note at 7:27.

11:15 *Can consecrated meat avert your punishment:* See the notes at 6:20 and 7:21.

11:16 *olive tree:* Olive trees were very valuable because of the oil that was collected when the olives were crushed. The oil was used for cooking, for ointments, and in holy offerings to the LORD. Olive trees often live a long time. There are olive trees in Jerusalem today that date from the time of Jesus. But now Judah, God's precious olive tree, will be destroyed.

11:17 *burning incense to Baal:* See the note at 2:8 (Baal).

11:18-23 *their plot . . . their punishment:* This passage is the first of Jeremiah's personal laments (see also 12:1-6; 15:10-21; 17:14-18; 18:18-23; 20:7-13; 20:14-18). Also known as Jeremiah's "Confessions," they usually have two parts: Jeremiah's complaint to God, and God's response. These laments likely date from the time before the exile.

In this first lament (11:18–23), Jeremiah describes the plot on his life by some men from his hometown of Anathoth (see the note at 1:1). It is not clear why they are plotting to kill him. It may be because he has criticized the priesthood; it may be that Jeremiah's hometown folk are embarrassed by his message of doom against Judah and want to silence him. But the LORD's response is one of doom for the people of Anathoth. Families will be completely wiped out, making it impossible for children to carry on the family name (11:23).

12:1 *Why do all the faithless live at ease:* In the second of his laments, Jeremiah questions the LORD's sense of fairness. Why are the wicked successful while the innocent suffer? Jeremiah even goes so far as to claim that the LORD actually helps certain sinners prosper (12:2). Two themes from ancient Hebrew wisdom seem to be at work here. First, everything that happens is directed by the LORD (Prov 20:24; Eccl 3:11, 14, 17; Jer 10:23); second, the wicked deserve to be punished and the good rewarded. This is why Jeremiah feels justified in asking the LORD to "butcher" his evil enemies, who praise God but aren't really sincere (12:2), in particular, JOB especially struggles with these issues. If God is both good and powerful, the existence of evil in the world is a very real dilemma (Job 21; Ps 73; Hab 1:13).

12:5 *thickets by the Jordan:* In Jeremiah's time the Jordan River (see the map on p. 2467) was bordered by dense woods and thickets that sheltered wild animals. Jeremiah's task is more like a run through high grass and dense forest than a run through an open field. His task is hard and will get harder.

12:6 *your own family:* The plot to kill Jeremiah is being hatched by his own hometown relatives (see 11:18-23 and the note).

Jeremiah's Complaint

12 You are always righteous, O LORD,
when I bring a case before you.
Yet I would speak with you about your justice:
Why does the way of the wicked prosper?
Why do all the faithless live at ease?
2 You have planted them, and they have taken root;
they grow and bear fruit.
You are always on their lips
but far from their hearts.
3 Yet you know me, O LORD;
you see me and test my thoughts about you.
Drag them off like sheep to be butchered!
Set them apart for the day of slaughter!
4 How long will the land lie parched[a]
and the grass in every field be withered?
Because those who live in it are wicked,
the animals and birds have perished.
Moreover, the people are saying,
"He will not see what happens to us."

God's Answer

5 "If you have raced with men on foot
and they have worn you out,
how can you compete with horses?
If you stumble in safe country,[b]
how will you manage in the thickets by[c]
the Jordan?
6 Your brothers, your own family—
even they have betrayed you;
they have raised a loud cry against you.
Do not trust them,
though they speak well of you.

7 "I will forsake my house,
abandon my inheritance;
I will give the one I love
into the hands of her enemies.
8 My inheritance has become to me
like a lion in the forest.
She roars at me;
therefore I hate her.
9 Has not my inheritance become to me
like a speckled bird of prey
that other birds of prey surround and attack?

[a]4 Or *land mourn* [b]5 Or *If you put your trust in a land of safety* [c]5 Or *the flooding of*

Go and gather all the wild beasts;
bring them to devour.
10 Many shepherds will ruin my vineyard
and trample down my field;
they will turn my pleasant field
into a desolate wasteland.
11 It will be made a wasteland,
parched and desolate before me;
the whole land will be laid waste
because there is no one who cares.
12 Over all the barren heights in the desert
destroyers will swarm,
for the sword of the LORD will devour
from one end of the land to the other;
no one will be safe.
13 They will sow wheat but reap thorns;
they will wear themselves out but gain nothing.
So bear the shame of your harvest
because of the LORD's fierce anger."

14 This is what the LORD says: "As for all my wicked neighbors
who seize the inheritance I gave my people Israel, I will uproot
them from their lands and I will uproot the house of Judah from
among them. 15 But after I uproot them, I will again have compassion and will bring each of them back to his own inheritance and
his own country. 16 And if they learn well the ways of my people
and swear by my name, saying, 'As surely as the LORD lives'—even
as they once taught my people to swear by Baal—then they will be
established among my people. 17 But if any nation does not listen,
I will completely uproot and destroy it," declares the LORD.

A Linen Belt

13 This is what the LORD said to me: "Go and buy a linen belt
and put it around your waist, but do not let it touch water." 2 So I
bought a belt, as the LORD directed, and put it around my waist.
3 Then the word of the LORD came to me a second time:
4 "Take the belt you bought and are wearing around your waist,
and go now to Perath[a] and hide it there in a crevice in the rocks."
5 So I went and hid it at Perath, as the LORD told me.
6 Many days later the LORD said to me, "Go now to Perath
and get the belt I told you to hide there." 7 So I went to Perath and
dug up the belt and took it from the place where I had hidden it,
but now it was ruined and completely useless.
8 Then the word of the LORD came to me: 9 "This is what the
LORD says: 'In the same way I will ruin the pride of Judah and the
great pride of Jerusalem. 10 These wicked people, who refuse to

[a]4 Or possibly *the Euphrates*; also in verses 5-7

12:10 *ruin my vineyard:* Farming in Palestine was difficult and demanding. God had labored hard over Judah, his vineyard (see 2:21 and the note at 5:10), just as a farmer works hard to clear fields, plant crops, and care for grapevines. But because of the people's sins, God has allowed his beautiful land to be destroyed (12:12, 13).

12:15 *I will . . . have compassion:* Destruction is not the last word, even for the enemies of Israel, if they give up their worship of other gods and turn to the LORD God of Israel. God's people will teach the foreigners how to worship (Isa 56:1-8; see Jer 4:2 and the note).

13:1 *linen belt:* This belt was wrapped around the hips and reached about halfway down the thighs. Linen is fabric woven from yarn made from the flax plant. Israel's priests wore garments made of linen.

Here the LORD gets the message across to Jeremiah by having him do something (13:3-11; see also 18:1-8; 19:1-13; 27:1-11; 32:7-14).

13:4 *Perath:* Perath was a village northeast of Jerusalem, close to Jeremiah's hometown of Anathoth. In Hebrew, Perath may also refer to the Euphrates River.

13:9 *ruin the pride of Judah:* God's people were supposed to cling to the LORD as tightly as the LORD held on to them. But the people left God behind, trusting in other gods and in their own resources. So the LORD would use the exile to destroy their pride, just as Jeremiah's linen belt rotted and became useless.

13:12 *wineskin:* A wineskin was made of animal skin and used to store wine. The skin was flexible and could expand as the wine fermented.

13:12-14 *Every wineskin should be filled with wine . . . will smash them:* Someone who has drunk too much wine becomes wobbly and can't think straight. In the same way the people of Judah and Jerusalem have drunk from the cup of unfaithfulness, so they can no longer see straight. The LORD will destroy Judah's people like wineskins being smashed against each other, unless they return to God and give him glory (13:16).

13:16 *light . . . darkness:* Light is often used as a symbol for life and goodness in the Bible, while darkness is often an image for evil and death (Job 18:15, 18; Prov 13:9; 20:20; John 8:12). See also the note at 4:23.

13:17 *I will weep in secret . . . taken captive:* It is not clear who the speaker is. The heartache expressed in this verse applies both to Jeremiah and to God (see the notes at 4:19 and 9:1).

listen to my words, who follow the stubbornness of their hearts
and go after other gods to serve and worship them, will be like this
belt—completely useless! 11For as a belt is bound around a man's
waist, so I bound the whole house of Israel and the whole house of
Judah to me,' declares the LORD, 'to be my people for my renown
and praise and honor. But they have not listened.'

Wineskins

12"Say to them: 'This is what the LORD, the God of Israel,
says: Every wineskin should be filled with wine.' And if they say to
you, 'Don't we know that every wineskin should be filled with
wine?' 13then tell them, 'This is what the LORD says: I am going to
fill with drunkenness all who live in this land, including the kings
who sit on David's throne, the priests, the prophets and all those
living in Jerusalem. 14I will smash them one against the other,
fathers and sons alike, declares the LORD. I will allow no pity or
mercy or compassion to keep me from destroying them.' "

Threat of Captivity

15Hear and pay attention,
do not be arrogant,
for the LORD has spoken.
16Give glory to the LORD your God
before he brings the darkness,
before your feet stumble
on the darkening hills.
You hope for light,
but he will turn it to thick darkness
and change it to deep gloom.
17But if you do not listen,
I will weep in secret
because of your pride;

QUESTIONS ABOUT JEREMIAH 7:1—13:27

1. Compare 7:9 (in the temple sermon) with the Ten Commandments in Exodus 20:1-17. Which of these commandments does Jeremiah say have been violated?
2. What does God want most? (9:24) How do you think God feels when people do not respond in this way?
3. What is the most striking comparison you find in Jeremiah's comparison of false gods to the one true God? (10:1-16)
4. In his "Confessions," Jeremiah shows that prayer means talking to God (11:18-23; 12:1-6). This can include complaining to God and questioning God's ways. Does Jeremiah help you think differently about prayer? If so, in what ways? When have you had similar questions?
5. Looking back over this section. Where do you find evidence of Jeremiah's anger and sorrow? Of God's?

my eyes will weep bitterly,
overflowing with tears,
because the LORD's flock will be taken
captive.

18 Say to the king and to the queen mother,
"Come down from your thrones,
for your glorious crowns
will fall from your heads."
19 The cities in the Negev will be shut up,
and there will be no one to open them.
All Judah will be carried into exile,
carried completely away.

20 Lift up your eyes and see
those who are coming from the north.
Where is the flock that was entrusted to you,
the sheep of which you boasted?
21 What will you say when ⌊the LORD⌋ sets over you
those you cultivated as your special allies?
Will not pain grip you
like that of a woman in labor?
22 And if you ask yourself,
"Why has this happened to me?"—
it is because of your many sins
that your skirts have been torn off
and your body mistreated.
23 Can the Ethiopian[a] change his skin
or the leopard its spots?
Neither can you do good
who are accustomed to doing evil.

24 "I will scatter you like chaff
driven by the desert wind.
25 This is your lot,
the portion I have decreed for you,"
declares the LORD,
"because you have forgotten me
and trusted in false gods.
26 I will pull up your skirts over your face
that your shame may be seen—
27 your adulteries and lustful neighings,
your shameless prostitution!
I have seen your detestable acts
on the hills and in the fields.
Woe to you, O Jerusalem!
How long will you be unclean?"

[a]23 Hebrew *Cushite* (probably a person from the upper Nile region)

Can the Ethiopian change his skin or the leopard its spots? Neither can you do good who are accustomed to doing evil.
Jer 13:23

13:18 *king . . . queen mother:* This probably refers to Jehoiachin, the young king who ruled for only three months in 598 B.C. Jehoiachin and his mother Nehushta were sent into exile (2 Kgs 24:8-16). The king's mother usually had an important position in the royal court as the "First Lady."

13:19 *the Negev:* This refers to the desert region south of Judah (see the map on p. 2464).

13:20,21 *from the north . . . special allies:* See the notes at 1:13 and 2:18. A number of years before the time of Jeremiah, Judah's King Hezekiah (ruled 716-687 B.C.) had asked for help from the Babylonians in Judah's struggle against the Assyrians (Isa 36–39; 2 Kgs 18–20). In Jeremiah's day, King Jehoiakim made a secret alliance with the Babylonians against Egypt (see the note at 2:16). But now the Babylonians will defeat and rule over Judah.

13:22 *your skirts have been torn off:* The violence of the attack is compared to the violence of rape.

13:23 *Can the Ethiopian change his skin:* The question expects a negative answer. Judah has sinned so long that they are unable to change themselves.

13:24 *I will scatter you like chaff:* See the note at 4:16.

13:25-27 *trusted in false gods . . . prostitution:* See the notes at 2:20, 3:2, and 3:23. See also Hos 1–3.

14:1-3 *drought . . . cisterns:* Cisterns were pits dug into solid rock for collecting and storing rainwater (see the note at 2:13). The drought which dried up the land would soon lead to starvation. Even the animals would be confused and desperate to find food and water. This national emergency cannot be dated with certainty, but it probably occurred sometime just before the destruction of 586 B.C. (see the note at 4:16).

14:7 *do something for the sake of your name:* If the LORD allows Judah to be destroyed, Jeremiah argues, Judah's enemies will think that the LORD God is powerless. But if the LORD saves Judah, the nations will declare the LORD's greatness. See also 14:19-21.

A TIME OF GREAT SADNESS

Jeremiah sees that Judah will be destroyed because of its people's sins. The prophet grieves for his people and asks God to save them, even though God has made it clear that Judah will be punished.

Drought, Famine, Sword

14 This is the word of the LORD to Jeremiah concerning the drought:

2 "Judah mourns,
her cities languish;
they wail for the land,
and a cry goes up from Jerusalem.
3 The nobles send their servants for water;
they go to the cisterns
but find no water.
They return with their jars unfilled;
dismayed and despairing,
they cover their heads.
4 The ground is cracked
because there is no rain in the land;
the farmers are dismayed
and cover their heads.
5 Even the doe in the field
deserts her newborn fawn
because there is no grass.
6 Wild donkeys stand on the barren heights
and pant like jackals;
their eyesight fails
for lack of pasture."

7 Although our sins testify against us,
O LORD, do something for the sake of your name.
For our backsliding is great;
we have sinned against you.
8 O Hope of Israel,
its Savior in times of distress,
why are you like a stranger in the land,
like a traveler who stays only a night?
9 Why are you like a man taken by surprise,
like a warrior powerless to save?
You are among us, O LORD,
and we bear your name;
do not forsake us!

10 This is what the LORD says about this people:

"They greatly love to wander;
they do not restrain their feet.

So the LORD does not accept them;
he will now remember their wickedness
and punish them for their sins."

11Then the LORD said to me, "Do not pray for the well-being
of this people. 12Although they fast, I will not listen to their cry;
though they offer burnt offerings and grain offerings, I will not
accept them. Instead, I will destroy them with the sword, famine
and plague."

13But I said, "Ah, Sovereign LORD, the prophets keep telling
them, 'You will not see the sword or suffer famine. Indeed, I will
give you lasting peace in this place.' "

14Then the LORD said to me, "The prophets are prophesying
lies in my name. I have not sent them or appointed them or
spoken to them. They are prophesying to you false visions, divinations, idolatries[a] and the delusions of their own minds. 15There-
fore, this is what the LORD says about the prophets who are
prophesying in my name: I did not send them, yet they are saying,
'No sword or famine will touch this land.' Those same prophets
will perish by sword and famine. 16And the people they are prophesying to will be thrown out into the streets of Jerusalem because
of the famine and sword. There will be no one to bury them or
their wives, their sons or their daughters. I will pour out on them
the calamity they deserve.

17"Speak this word to them:

" 'Let my eyes overflow with tears
night and day without ceasing;
for my virgin daughter—my people—
has suffered a grievous wound,
a crushing blow.
18If I go into the country,
I see those slain by the sword;
if I go into the city,
I see the ravages of famine.
Both prophet and priest
have gone to a land they know not.' "
19Have you rejected Judah completely?
Do you despise Zion?
Why have you afflicted us
so that we cannot be healed?
We hoped for peace
but no good has come,
for a time of healing
but there is only terror.
20O LORD, we acknowledge our wickedness

[a]14 Or *visions, worthless divinations*

14:12 *fast . . . offer burnt offerings and grain offerings:* The people of Israel sometimes fasted (went without eating) to show sorrow for their sins. A main purpose of the burnt offering was to please the LORD with the smell of the sacrifice. A main purpose of the grain offering was to thank the LORD with a gift of grain. See also Lev 1,2 and the chart called "Sacrifices and Offerings," p. 219.

14:13 *the prophets*: Lying prophets say "You will not see the sword or suffer famine" (see also 1 Kgs 22:1-28) and give the people words they want to hear (Isa 30:8-11). See also the notes at 5:12 and 6:13, 14. Some of the lying prophets' messages are nothing more than fortunetelling or visions that supposedly came from idols (see 2:8 and note).

14:16 *no one to bury them:* Both the lying prophets and those who listen to them will suffer the double disgrace of dying and being left unburied.

14:11 Jer 7:16; 11:14. **14:19** Jer 8:15.

14:21 *your glorious throne:* God was thought to be enthroned in the Jerusalem temple (see the note at 3:16, 17), so the people of Israel worried that if the temple was destroyed and disgraced, their enemies might think God is powerless, like a warrior unable to save the day (14:9).

14:22 *bring rain:* Returning to the subject of 14:1-6, the people confess that God has control over the horrible dry spell. (See also Deut 28:12; 1 Kgs 18:1, 2; Job 5:10; Ps 68:8, 9.)

15:1 *Moses and Samuel:* Moses and Samuel were great leaders who successfully prayed to God on behalf of the people of Israel (Exod 32:11-14; Num 14:13-20; 1 Sam 7:5-10; 12:19-25; Ps 99:6). Even if they were to intercede for Judah, God would reject their prayer. Judah will go into exile.

15:4 *Manasseh:* Manasseh ruled Judah from 687 to 642 B.C. and died just two years before Josiah became king. Judah sank to an all-time low under Manasseh, who built altars to foreign gods and even sacrificed his own son (2 Kgs 21:1-16; 2 Chr 33:1-9).

15:6 *I can no longer show compassion:* As with the northern kingdom of Israel (Amos 7:1-9), God's patience has given out.

15:8 *widows more numerous than the sand of the sea:* Israel's sins will lead to a complete reversal of God's promise to Abraham (Gen 22:14-18).

15:9 *mother of seven:* Having seven sons is a sign of God's favor (Ruth 4:15; 1 Sam 2:5). In ancient times, "seven" also symbolized completeness or perfection. Seven sons, soon to be lost, emphasizes how severe and complete will be the loss of Jerusalem's mothers.

15:2 Rev 13:10.

and the guilt of our fathers;
we have indeed sinned against you.
21 For the sake of your name do not despise us;
do not dishonor your glorious throne.
Remember your covenant with us
and do not break it.
22 Do any of the worthless idols of the nations bring rain?
Do the skies themselves send down showers?
No, it is you, O LORD our God.
Therefore our hope is in you,
for you are the one who does all this.

15 Then the LORD said to me: "Even if Moses and Samuel were
to stand before me, my heart would not go out to this people. Send
them away from my presence! Let them go! 2 And if they ask you,
'Where shall we go?' tell them, 'This is what the LORD says:

" 'Those destined for death, to death;
those for the sword, to the sword;
those for starvation, to starvation;
those for captivity, to captivity.'

3 "I will send four kinds of destroyers against them," declares
the LORD, "the sword to kill and the dogs to drag away and the
birds of the air and the beasts of the earth to devour and destroy.
4 I will make them abhorrent to all the kingdoms of the earth
because of what Manasseh son of Hezekiah king of Judah did in
Jerusalem.

5 "Who will have pity on you, O Jerusalem?
Who will mourn for you?
Who will stop to ask how you are?
6 You have rejected me," declares the LORD.
"You keep on backsliding.
So I will lay hands on you and destroy you;
I can no longer show compassion.
7 I will winnow them with a winnowing fork
at the city gates of the land.
I will bring bereavement and destruction on my people,
for they have not changed their ways.
8 I will make their widows more numerous
than the sand of the sea.
At midday I will bring a destroyer
against the mothers of their young men;
suddenly I will bring down on them
anguish and terror.
9 The mother of seven will grow faint
and breathe her last.
Her sun will set while it is still day;
she will be disgraced and humiliated.

I will put the survivors to the sword
before their enemies,"
declares the LORD.

10 Alas, my mother, that you gave me birth,
a man with whom the whole land strives and
contends!
I have neither lent nor borrowed,
yet everyone curses me.

11 The LORD said,

"Surely I will deliver you for a good purpose;
surely I will make your enemies plead with you
in times of disaster and times of distress.

12 "Can a man break iron—
iron from the north—or bronze?
13 Your wealth and your treasures
I will give as plunder, without charge,
because of all your sins
throughout your country.
14 I will enslave you to your enemies
in[a] a land you do not know,
for my anger will kindle a fire
that will burn against you."

15 You understand, O LORD;
remember me and care for me.
Avenge me on my persecutors.
You are long-suffering—do not take me away;
think of how I suffer reproach for your sake.
16 When your words came, I ate them;
they were my joy and my heart's delight,
for I bear your name,
O LORD God Almighty.
17 I never sat in the company of revelers,
never made merry with them;
I sat alone because your hand was on me
and you had filled me with indignation.
18 Why is my pain unending
and my wound grievous and incurable?
Will you be to me like a deceptive brook,
like a spring that fails?

19 Therefore this is what the LORD says:

"If you repent, I will restore you
that you may serve me;

[a]**14** Some Hebrew manuscripts, Septuagint and Syriac (see also Jer. 17:4); most Hebrew manuscripts *I will cause your enemies to bring you / into*

You understand, O LORD; remember me and care for me.
Jer 15:15

15:10-21 *Alas, my mother, that you gave me birth . . . neither lent nor borrowed:* Another of Jeremiah's laments (see the note at 11:18-23). Compare his complaint to that of Job (Job 3:1-6). Lending money to others was considered risky, because it could lead to bad feelings (Prov 6:1-5), and moneylenders usually were not very popular. Jeremiah is disliked even more.

15:12 *iron from the north:* See the note at 1:13.

15:13,14 *all your sins . . . fire:* See 2:27, 28 and note. Fire is often connected with the LORD's judgment against those who are evil or disobedient (Gen 19:23-29; Lev 10:1, 2; Isa 4:4; Jer 17:4; Joel 2:1-3; Matt 13:36-42).

15:15-18 *think of how I suffer . . . pain unending:* Jeremiah complains bitterly about God's mistreatment of him. His task has made him an outcast, because he can't help speaking about the LORD's anger when he is with others. So he is ridiculed, hated, and alone. See also 11:20.

15:18 *a spring that fails:* Compare to 2:13, where God is the source of life-giving water.

if you utter worthy, not worthless, words,
you will be my spokesman.
Let this people turn to you,
but you must not turn to them.
20 I will make you a wall to this people,
a fortified wall of bronze;
they will fight against you
but will not overcome you,
for I am with you
to rescue and save you,”
declares the LORD.
21 “I will save you from the hands of the wicked
and redeem you from the grasp of the cruel.”

Day of Disaster

16 Then the word of the LORD came to me: 2“You must not
marry and have sons or daughters in this place.” 3For this is what
the LORD says about the sons and daughters born in this land and
about the women who are their mothers and the men who are
their fathers: 4“They will die of deadly diseases. They will not be
mourned or buried but will be like refuse lying on the ground.
They will perish by sword and famine, and their dead bodies will
become food for the birds of the air and the beasts of the earth.”
5For this is what the LORD says: “Do not enter a house where
there is a funeral meal; do not go to mourn or show sympathy,
because I have withdrawn my blessing, my love and my pity from
this people,” declares the LORD. 6“Both high and low will die in this
land. They will not be buried or mourned, and no one will cut
himself or shave his head for them. 7No one will offer food to
comfort those who mourn for the dead—not even for a father or
a mother—nor will anyone give them a drink to console them.
8“And do not enter a house where there is feasting and sit
down to eat and drink. 9For this is what the LORD Almighty, the
God of Israel, says: Before your eyes and in your days I will bring
an end to the sounds of joy and gladness and to the voices of bride
and bridegroom in this place.
10“When you tell these people all this and they ask you, ‘Why
has the LORD decreed such a great disaster against us? What wrong
have we done? What sin have we committed against the LORD our
God?’ 11then say to them, ‘It is because your fathers forsook me,’
declares the LORD, ‘and followed other gods and served and worshiped them. They forsook me and did not keep my law. 12But you
have behaved more wickedly than your fathers. See how each of
you is following the stubbornness of his evil heart instead of obeying me. 13So I will throw you out of this land into a land neither
you nor your fathers have known, and there you will serve other
gods day and night, for I will show you no favor.’
14“However, the days are coming,” declares the LORD, “when

15:20,21 *I will make you a wall . . . I will save you:* The LORD repeats the promise to keep Jeremiah safe from those who dislike his message (see 1:8, 18, 19).

16:2-8 *You must not marry . . . funeral meal . . . feasting:* Like the prophets of the eighth century B.C., Jeremiah is to be a living symbol of God's message (Isa 8:3, 4; Hos 1:2-9). Jeremiah was a young man of marriageable age, but he is told to remain single, a status almost unheard of during his time. By remaining single, Jeremiah will draw attention to God's warnings: In the near future all family life will be disrupted. The usual traditions regarding mourning for the dead will be useless now. There will be no need for ritual cutting of the flesh and head-shaving, customs practiced in some Canaanite religions and by some Israelites (41:5; Amos 8:10), though such rituals were forbidden by the Law of Moses (Lev 21:5; Deut 14:1, 2). Finally, Jeremiah is told not to attend feasts and joyful celebrations, as these too will end. All these actions are signs of the terrible future that awaits Judah. Jeremiah's task and the message he delivers make him a man set apart, and ultimately alone. See also the article called "Prophets and Prophecy," p. 935.

16:11-13 *your fathers forsook me . . . a land neither you nor your fathers have known:* See the notes at 2:6, 7 and 5:19.

16:14,15 *the days are coming . . . brought the Israelites up out of the land of the north:* Doom is not the last word. Just as God rescued Israel's ancestors from Egypt, God will again rescue the people of Judah from the exile in Babylon (see the note at 4:16). A time will come when the people will see both the exodus from Egypt and from the exile as evidence of God's concern. See also Isa 49:8-19; Jer 23:7, 8.

16:9 Jer 7:34; 25:10; Rev 18:23.

men will no longer say, 'As surely as the LORD lives, who brought
the Israelites up out of Egypt,' 15but they will say, 'As surely as the
LORD lives, who brought the Israelites up out of the land of the
north and out of all the countries where he had banished them.'
For I will restore them to the land I gave their forefathers.
16"But now I will send for many fishermen," declares the LORD,
"and they will catch them. After that I will send for many hunters,
and they will hunt them down on every mountain and hill and from
the crevices of the rocks. 17My eyes are on all their ways; they are not
hidden from me, nor is their sin concealed from my eyes. 18I will
repay them double for their wickedness and their sin, because they
have defiled my land with the lifeless forms of their vile images and
have filled my inheritance with their detestable idols."

19 O LORD, my strength and my fortress,
  my refuge in time of distress,
to you the nations will come
  from the ends of the earth and say,
"Our fathers possessed nothing but false gods,
  worthless idols that did them no good.
20 Do men make their own gods?
  Yes, but they are not gods!"

21 "Therefore I will teach them—
  this time I will teach them
  my power and might.
Then they will know
  that my name is the LORD.

17 "Judah's sin is engraved with an iron tool,
  inscribed with a flint point,
on the tablets of their hearts
  and on the horns of their altars.
2 Even their children remember
  their altars and Asherah poles[a]
beside the spreading trees
  and on the high hills.
3 My mountain in the land
  and your[b] wealth and all your treasures
I will give away as plunder,
  together with your high places,
  because of sin throughout your country.
4 Through your own fault you will lose
  the inheritance I gave you.
I will enslave you to your enemies
  in a land you do not know,

[a]2 That is, symbols of the goddess Asherah [b]2,3 Or *hills / [3]and the mountains of the land. / Your*

O LORD, my strength and my fortress, my refuge in time of distress.
Jer 16:19

16:15 *out of the land of the north:* See the note at 1:13.

16:18 *defiled my land:* See the notes at 2:6, 7 and 4:1.

16:19-21 *to you the nations will come . . . I will teach them:* For the idea of the nations turning to God in the future, see the note at 12:15. See also Isa 45:22-24; Zech 8:20-23.

17:1 *inscribed . . . on the tablets of their hearts and on the horns of their altars:* See the note at 4:4. The people's sins are permanently inscribed on their hearts like symbols carved in stone. When sacrifices were offered to the LORD to ask forgiveness for sins, some of the blood was smeared on the corners (called the "horns") of the altar (see Lev 4:7, 18-26, 30-35; 16:18). The "altars" here may refer to the altar in the temple where sacrifices are offered to the LORD, or to the "pagan altars" set up to worship idols.

17:2 *Asherah poles:* This goddess was also known by the name Astarte. See also the note at 7:18. Asherah was represented by wooden poles (see the note at 2:27, 28).

17:4 *lose the inheritance . . . enslave you:* See the note at 4:16.

17:4 *kindled my anger . . . burn forever:* See the note at 15:13, 14.

16:18 Isa 40:2.

for you have kindled my anger,
  and it will burn forever."

5 This is what the LORD says:

"Cursed is the one who trusts in man,
  who depends on flesh for his strength
  and whose heart turns away from the LORD.
6 He will be like a bush in the wastelands;
  he will not see prosperity when it comes.
He will dwell in the parched places of the desert,
  in a salt land where no one lives.

7 "But blessed is the man who trusts in the LORD,
  whose confidence is in him.
8 He will be like a tree planted by the water
  that sends out its roots by the stream.
It does not fear when heat comes;
  its leaves are always green.
It has no worries in a year of drought
  and never fails to bear fruit."

9 The heart is deceitful above all things
  and beyond cure.
  Who can understand it?

10 "I the LORD search the heart
  and examine the mind,
to reward a man according to his conduct,
  according to what his deeds deserve."

11 Like a partridge that hatches eggs it did not lay
  is the man who gains riches by unjust means.
When his life is half gone, they will desert him,
  and in the end he will prove to be a fool.

12 A glorious throne, exalted from the beginning,
  is the place of our sanctuary.
13 O LORD, the hope of Israel,
  all who forsake you will be put to shame.
Those who turn away from you will be written
    in the dust
  because they have forsaken the LORD,
  the spring of living water.

14 Heal me, O LORD, and I will be healed;
  save me and I will be saved,
  for you are the one I praise.
15 They keep saying to me,
  "Where is the word of the LORD?
  Let it now be fulfilled!"
16 I have not run away from being your shepherd;

17:5-8 *trusts in man . . . no worries in a year of drought:* Those who trust in God, the life-giving spring of water (2:13), will flourish, while those who do not trust in God will become dry as dust and be blown away (see also 17:13). Psalm 1 describes the person who happily obeys the Law of the LORD as a "tree planted by streams of water" (Ps 1:1-3).

17:10,11 *reward a man according to his conduct . . . Like a partridge that hatches eggs it did not lay:* These verses express the theme that is common in Israelite wisdom: God sees everything that happens and will hand out what each person deserves. Those who have cheated others to gain wealth will have it taken away (see also Job 1:10; 4:5-10). The proverb of the stolen eggs probably refers to how certain birds sit on and hatch the eggs of other birds. The newly hatched birds soon leave because they recognize that the bird is not their real mother. So it is with wealth gained falsely: it will fly away.

17:12 *A glorious throne . . . our sanctuary:* This refers to God's temple. See the notes at 3:16, 17 and 14:21.

17:14-18 *healed . . . saved . . . from terror:* Another of Jeremiah's personal laments (see the note at 11:18-23).

17:10 Ps 62:12; Rev 2:23.
17:14 Ps 6:2, 3.

you know I have not desired the day of despair.
What passes my lips is open before you.
17 Do not be a terror to me;
you are my refuge in the day of disaster.
18 Let my persecutors be put to shame,
but keep me from shame;
let them be terrified,
but keep me from terror.
Bring on them the day of disaster;
destroy them with double destruction.

Keeping the Sabbath Holy

19 This is what the LORD said to me: "Go and stand at the gate
of the people, through which the kings of Judah go in and out;
stand also at all the other gates of Jerusalem. 20 Say to them, 'Hear
the word of the LORD, O kings of Judah and all people of Judah
and everyone living in Jerusalem who come through these gates.
21 This is what the LORD says: Be careful not to carry a load on the
Sabbath day or bring it through the gates of Jerusalem. 22 Do not
bring a load out of your houses or do any work on the Sabbath,
but keep the Sabbath day holy, as I commanded your forefathers.
23 Yet they did not listen or pay attention; they were stiff-necked
and would not listen or respond to discipline. 24 But if you are careful to obey me, declares the LORD, and bring no load through the
gates of this city on the Sabbath, but keep the Sabbath day holy by
not doing any work on it, 25 then kings who sit on David's throne
will come through the gates of this city with their officials. They
and their officials will come riding in chariots and on horses,
accompanied by the men of Judah and those living in Jerusalem,
and this city will be inhabited forever. 26 People will come from the

17:18 *Bring on them the day of disaster:* If his enemies succeed, Jeremiah will not be alive to preach the second part of his message. See the note at 11:18-23.

17:19 *gate of the people:* Traders and visitors came and went through these busy entrances. City leaders met and held court hearings there. It was the most likely place for Jeremiah to get a large and influential audience.

17:24 *keep the Sabbath day holy:* The Sabbath day of rest began at sunset Friday and ended at sunset Saturday. The Sabbath law was to be obeyed (Exod 20:8-11; 23:12; Deut 5:12-14). Ignoring the Sabbath affected not only worship but the people's fair treatment of their hired workers and animals.

17:25 *kings who sit on David's throne:* The promises made to David in 2 Samuel 7 seemed to insure the continuation of his kingly line forever.

17:21-24 Neh 13:15-22.

QUESTIONS ABOUT JEREMIAH 14:1—17:27

1. When the people pray to God (14:7-9), what reason do they give for God saving them instead of punishing them? How sincere do you think their prayers are? Why? Are you surprised by the LORD's response? (14:10) Why or why not?
2. See what happened when Moses prayed for his people in Exodus 32:11-14. Then read Jeremiah 15:1, 2. What has happened since Moses' time? Why does the LORD say now, "My heart would not go out to this people"?
3. Jeremiah is told to live out his message in 16:1-10. What did this mean especially for his relationships with others? How do you think this made Jeremiah feel about being chosen as God's prophet? How might it make you feel?
4. Review Jeremiah's personal laments in 15:15-18 and 17:12-18. Note his honesty. Where do you see signs of his struggle with the LORD? Where do you see signs of his sadness?
5. Do you agree or disagree that difficult times can help us become stronger? Compare 17:5 to 17:17. From where can we find the better source of strength to face difficult times?

17:26 *offerings and sacrifices:* See the note at 14:12.

17:27 *not carrying any load:* This probably refers to trading and selling on the Sabbath. Compare to Amos 8:4-6.

18:3-6 *potter's house . . . clay in the hand of the potter:* The LORD can change his creation (Israel) and even destroy it and start over (18:4), just as a potter can quickly change the shape of a clay object on the wheel.

18:14 *snow of Lebanon . . . rocky slopes:* Mount Hermon in Lebanon, to the north of Israel, is 9,000 feet above sea level (see the map on p. 2467). Its melting snows form part of the source of the Jordan River. Streams fed by mountain snows never run dry, but Israel will be scattered like dust (18:17).

towns of Judah and the villages around Jerusalem, from the territory of Benjamin and the western foothills, from the hill country
and the Negev, bringing burnt offerings and sacrifices, grain offerings, incense and thank offerings to the house of the LORD. 27 But if
you do not obey me to keep the Sabbath day holy by not carrying
any load as you come through the gates of Jerusalem on the Sabbath day, then I will kindle an unquenchable fire in the gates of
Jerusalem that will consume her fortresses.' "

PLOTS ON JEREMIAH'S LIFE AND WARNINGS TO JUDAH

Jeremiah is threatened and eventually imprisoned for his messages. A collection of sayings against the leaders of Judah is also found in this section.

At the Potter's House

18 This is the word that came to Jeremiah from the LORD: 2 "Go
down to the potter's house, and there I will give you my message."
3 So I went down to the potter's house, and I saw him working at
the wheel. 4 But the pot he was shaping from the clay was marred
in his hands; so the potter formed it into another pot, shaping it as
seemed best to him.

5 Then the word of the LORD came to me: 6 "O house of Israel,
can I not do with you as this potter does?" declares the LORD. "Like
clay in the hand of the potter, so are you in my hand, O house of
Israel. 7 If at any time I announce that a nation or kingdom is to be
uprooted, torn down and destroyed, 8 and if that nation I warned
repents of its evil, then I will relent and not inflict on it the disaster I had planned. 9 And if at another time I announce that a nation
or kingdom is to be built up and planted, 10 and if it does evil in my
sight and does not obey me, then I will reconsider the good I had
intended to do for it.

11 "Now therefore say to the people of Judah and those living
in Jerusalem, 'This is what the LORD says: Look! I am preparing a
disaster for you and devising a plan against you. So turn from your
evil ways, each one of you, and reform your ways and your
actions.' 12 But they will reply, 'It's no use. We will continue with
our own plans; each of us will follow the stubbornness of his evil
heart.' "

13 Therefore this is what the LORD says:

"Inquire among the nations:
    Who has ever heard anything like this?
A most horrible thing has been done
    by Virgin Israel.
14 Does the snow of Lebanon
    ever vanish from its rocky slopes?

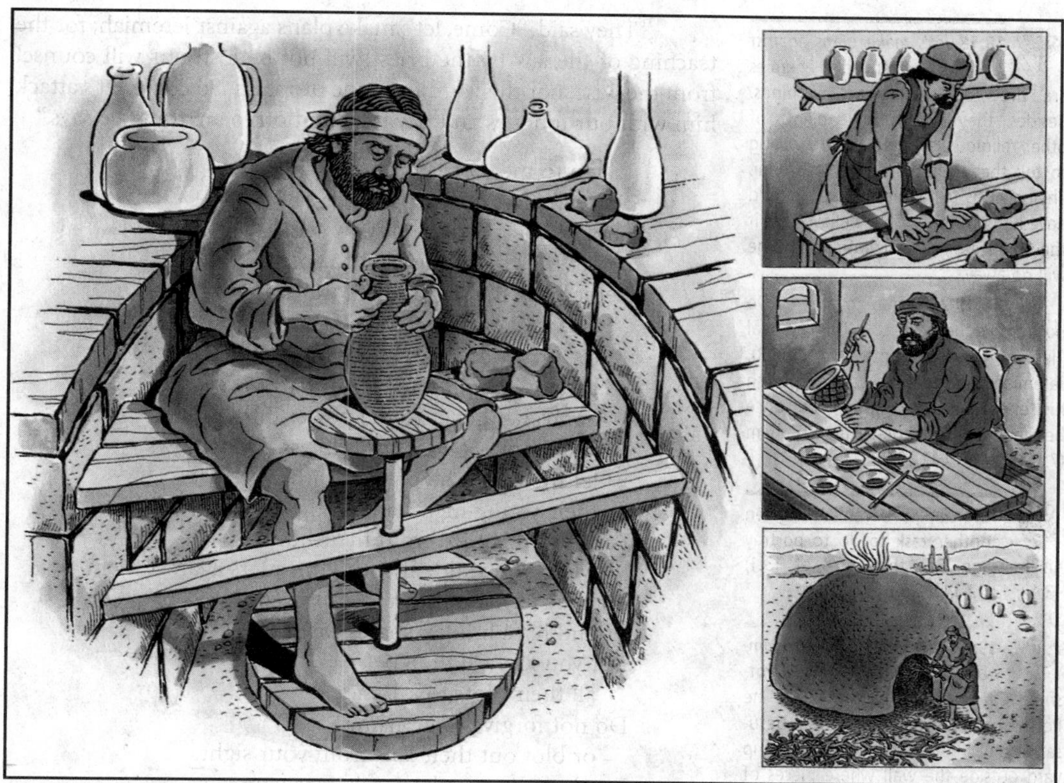

Making Pottery. Potters use soft clay to make pots and other useful items on a potter's wheel. The quickly spinning wheel helps the potter to create beautifully shaped and perfectly symmetrical round objects. The potters used a foot pedal to turn a lower wheel, which in turn drove a flat upper wheel. Once shaped, the objects were decorated with paints and glazes and then baked in a kiln (oven).

Do its cool waters from distant sources
ever cease to flow?[a]
15 Yet my people have forgotten me;
they burn incense to worthless idols,
which made them stumble in their ways
and in the ancient paths.
They made them walk in bypaths
and on roads not built up.
16 Their land will be laid waste,
an object of lasting scorn;
all who pass by will be appalled
and will shake their heads.
17 Like a wind from the east,
I will scatter them before their enemies;
I will show them my back and not my face
in the day of their disaster."

18:15 *burn incense to worthless idols:* See the notes at 6:20 and 3:23,24.

18:15 *ancient paths . . . bypaths:* The ancient path is the good road that the people's ancestors took (see 6:16 and note). This road of obedience is compared to the "bypath" of disobedience.

18:17 *wind from the east:* Hot, dry sirocco winds came from the desert areas to the east of Judah (see the note at 4:11,12).

[a]14 The meaning of the Hebrew for this sentence is uncertain.

18:18 *let's make plans against Jeremiah:* Jeremiah's enemies are tired of hearing his warnings. Besides, they already have plenty of other religious leaders who are willing to tell them what they want to hear. Their plan is to tell lies about him and have him put away. They believe that if they silence him, his irritating message will go away.

18:19-23 *Listen to me . . . Do not forgive their crimes:* In this personal "lament" (see the note at 11:18-23), Jeremiah now asks the LORD to punish his enemies, even though he once begged the LORD not to punish them (7:16; 11:14; 14:11,19-22).

19:1 *clay jar:* Jeremiah is given another task to do to portray his message. See the notes at 13:1; 13:12; 13:12-14; 18:3-6.

19:2 *Valley of Ben Hinnom, near the entrance of the Potsherd Gate:* See the note at 2:23. The Potsherd Gate was in southern Jerusalem, near Potters Street and a dump yard outside the wall where pieces of broken pottery (potsherds) were thrown away. See the map on p. 2466.

19:3-6 *a disaster on this place . . . the Valley of Slaughter:* The most gruesome of Israel's sins (child sacrifice) took place on a burning platform in Topheth (see the note at 7:31). The Valley of Ben Hinnom will be called the Valley of Slaughter because of the dead bodies that will be tossed or buried there after Jerusalem is invaded (7:32, 33).

19:9 *eat the flesh:* A common tactic in ancient warfare was surrounding a city until food and water supplies ran out. Before Nebuchadnezzar of Babylon attacked Jerusalem, his army surrounded the city for a year and a half, until all the food had run out (2 Kgs 25:1-5). See also 2 Kgs 6:24-29.

18:19 Jer 11:18-20.

18 They said, "Come, let's make plans against Jeremiah; for the teaching of the law by the priest will not be lost, nor will counsel from the wise, nor the word from the prophets. So come, let's attack him with our tongues and pay no attention to anything he says."

19 Listen to me, O LORD;
    hear what my accusers are saying!
20 Should good be repaid with evil?
    Yet they have dug a pit for me.
Remember that I stood before you
    and spoke in their behalf
    to turn your wrath away from them.
21 So give their children over to famine;
    hand them over to the power of the sword.
Let their wives be made childless and widows;
    let their men be put to death,
    their young men slain by the sword in battle.
22 Let a cry be heard from their houses
    when you suddenly bring invaders against them,
for they have dug a pit to capture me
    and have hidden snares for my feet.
23 But you know, O LORD,
    all their plots to kill me.
Do not forgive their crimes
    or blot out their sins from your sight.
Let them be overthrown before you;
    deal with them in the time of your anger.

19 This is what the LORD says: "Go and buy a clay jar from a
potter. Take along some of the elders of the people and of the
priests 2 and go out to the Valley of Ben Hinnom, near the entrance
of the Potsherd Gate. There proclaim the words I tell you, 3 and say,
'Hear the word of the LORD, O kings of Judah and people of
Jerusalem. This is what the LORD Almighty, the God of Israel, says:
Listen! I am going to bring a disaster on this place that will make
the ears of everyone who hears of it tingle. 4 For they have forsak-
en me and made this a place of foreign gods; they have burned
sacrifices in it to gods that neither they nor their fathers nor the
kings of Judah ever knew, and they have filled this place with the
blood of the innocent. 5 They have built the high places of Baal to
burn their sons in the fire as offerings to Baal—something I did
not command or mention, nor did it enter my mind. 6 So beware,
the days are coming, declares the LORD, when people will no longer
call this place Topheth or the Valley of Ben Hinnom, but the Valley of Slaughter.

7 " 'In this place I will ruin[a] the plans of Judah and Jerusalem.

---

[a]7 The Hebrew for *ruin* sounds like the Hebrew for *jar* (see verses 1 and 10).

I will make them fall by the sword before their enemies, at the
hands of those who seek their lives, and I will give their carcasses
as food to the birds of the air and the beasts of the earth. 8 I will
devastate this city and make it an object of scorn; all who pass by
will be appalled and will scoff because of all its wounds. 9 I will
make them eat the flesh of their sons and daughters, and they will
eat one another's flesh during the stress of the siege imposed on
them by the enemies who seek their lives.'
10 "Then break the jar while those who go with you are
watching, 11 and say to them, 'This is what the LORD Almighty says:
I will smash this nation and this city just as this potter's jar is

19:10 *break the jar:* Jeremiah again takes action to dramatize God's message (see also 13:1-11). His audience includes elders of the people and priests (19:1). Jeremiah's breaking of the jar was terrifying because it was understood as actually setting in motion God's destruction of Judah and Jerusalem. See 20:1, 2.

19:8 Jer 18:16.

NEBUCHADNEZZAR

The Babylonian king described in the Bible is Nebuchadnezzar II, the longest reigning and most successful king of the Neo-Babylonian empire. He ruled from 605 to 562 B.C. during the time when the Babylonian kingdom reached the peak of its power and influence in the region. Babylon's major competition for power during this time came from Media to the north (northwest Iran) and Egypt to the west. The Egyptians were interested in ports and trade in Aram (Syria) and Palestine so they stirred up rebellion against Babylonia whenever they could. At the Battle of Carchemish in 605 B.C., Pharaoh Neco of Egypt was defeated by Nebuchadnezzar and driven back to his country (2 Kgs 24:7; Jer 46:2).

Nebuchadnezzar sponsored many building projects in his capital city, Babylon. He fortified the city walls and built the famous Ishtar Gate as a grand entrance into his proud city. He also devoted himself to Marduk, the patron god of that city, and rebuilt Marduk's temple. See also the mini-article called "Babylon," p. 1363.

Nebuchadnezzar stopped at nothing when it came to conquering or punishing rebellious peoples. He invaded Judah twice. In 598 B.C., he punished Judah for refusing to pay tribute money to Babylon (a kind of bribe tax to keep Babylon from invading). Nebuchadnezzar deported Judah's King Jehoiachin and many of the nobles and craftsmen back to Babylon. In 587 B.C. Nebuchadnezzar responded to King Zedekiah's rebellion (2 Kgs 24:18-20) by surrounding Jerusalem and destroying many of the smaller towns in Judah. Judah's King Zedekiah tried to escape from Jerusalem in secret, but he and his family were arrested. Zedekiah was forced to watch as his sons were executed; then his own eyes were poked out and he was dragged off to Babylon (2 Kgs 25:1-7).

In August of 586 B.C., Nebuchadnezzar's army smashed through the walls of Jerusalem, and destroyed the city (see 2 Kgs 25:8-21). They burned down the temple, the king's palace, and much of the rest of the city. They also robbed the temple of many of its holy treasures, and carried them back to Babylon. Finally, still more of the Jewish people were sent to Babylon, where they lived as exiles until Babylon fell and Cyrus of Persia set them free in 539 B.C.

The prophet Jeremiah recognized two things about Nebuchadnezzar. For one, God was using him as an instrument of judgment for the sins of Judah. So, before Jerusalem fell, Jeremiah advised its leaders to give in to Nebuchadnezzar and surrender, in order to save the country and the city from horrible destruction. Second, after the fall of Jerusalem, Jeremiah foresaw that Babylon too would come under the judgment of God. Nebuchadnezzar's empire would face its day of reckoning as well (Jer 50,51).

19:13 *defiled like this place, Topheth . . . offerings to other gods:* See the notes at 7:31 and 19:3-6. Topheth was considered "defiled" (unacceptable to God) for two reasons: it was where sacrifice to idols took place, and it would become a place where the unburied dead rotted on the ground. According to God's Law, touching a dead body could make a person ritually unclean, as could an open grave (Lev 11; 21:1-4; Num 19:11-21; Deut 26:14). See also the mini-article called "Purity (Clean and Unclean)," p. 2125.

19:14 *court of the LORD's temple:* The temple courtyard was probably where Jeremiah delivered many of his messages of doom. See the diagram of Solomon's temple on p. 942.

19:15 *every disaster I pronounced:* In the eighth century B.C. the prophet Micah first delivered the message of doom to Jerusalem (Mic 3:12). This message was shocking because of God's promise that one of David's descendants would always be king (2 Sam 7:16). An eternal kingship implied that Jerusalem, where Israel's rulers lived, would always be safe from attack. So, any prophecy of disaster aimed against Jerusalem was thought to be a direct challenge to God's promise to David. Jeremiah points out that this message is not new, nor did he invent it. (See Amos 2:4, 5 and Hos 6:4-11).

20:1,2 *Pashhur . . . beaten and put in the stocks:* The temple police were to make sure that non-Israelites did not enter the holy temple. Pashhur, the chief officer of the temple, punishes Jeremiah for the message given in 19:15. This beating and public humiliation lasted until the next day. See also the mini-article called "Israel's Priests," p. 2344.

20:3-6 *Pashhur . . . you will die:* When he is released, Jeremiah gives Pashhur a new name. The curse will result in Pashhur and his family being taken into permanent exile to Babylon, where they will all eventually die. See also the note at 4:16.

smashed and cannot be repaired. They will bury the dead in
Topheth until there is no more room. [12]This is what I will do to
this place and to those who live here, declares the LORD. I will make
this city like Topheth. [13]The houses in Jerusalem and those of the
kings of Judah will be defiled like this place, Topheth—all the
houses where they burned incense on the roofs to all the starry
hosts and poured out drink offerings to other gods.' "

[14]Jeremiah then returned from Topheth, where the LORD had
sent him to prophesy, and stood in the court of the LORD's temple
and said to all the people, [15]"This is what the LORD Almighty, the
God of Israel, says: 'Listen! I am going to bring on this city and the
villages around it every disaster I pronounced against them,
because they were stiff-necked and would not listen to my words.' "

Jeremiah and Pashhur

20 When the priest Pashhur son of Immer, the chief officer in
the temple of the LORD, heard Jeremiah prophesying these things,
[2]he had Jeremiah the prophet beaten and put in the stocks at the
Upper Gate of Benjamin at the LORD's temple. [3]The next day, when
Pashhur released him from the stocks, Jeremiah said to him, "The
LORD's name for you is not Pashhur, but Magor-Missabib.[a] [4]For
this is what the LORD says: 'I will make you a terror to yourself and
to all your friends; with your own eyes you will see them fall by
the sword of their enemies. I will hand all Judah over to the king
of Babylon, who will carry them away to Babylon or put them to
the sword. [5]I will hand over to their enemies all the wealth of this
city—all its products, all its valuables and all the treasures of the
kings of Judah. They will take it away as plunder and carry it off to
Babylon. [6]And you, Pashhur, and all who live in your house will go
into exile to Babylon. There you will die and be buried, you and all
your friends to whom you have prophesied lies.' "

Jeremiah's Complaint

[7]O LORD, you deceived[b] me, and I was deceived[b];
    you overpowered me and prevailed.
I am ridiculed all day long;
    everyone mocks me.
[8]Whenever I speak, I cry out
    proclaiming violence and destruction.
So the word of the LORD has brought me
    insult and reproach all day long.
[9]But if I say, "I will not mention him
    or speak any more in his name,"
his word is in my heart like a fire,
    a fire shut up in my bones.

---

[a]3 *Magor-Missabib* means *terror on every side.* [b]7 Or *persuaded*

I am weary of holding it in;
indeed, I cannot.
10 I hear many whispering,
"Terror on every side!
Report him! Let's report him!"
All my friends
are waiting for me to slip, saying,
"Perhaps he will be deceived;
then we will prevail over him
and take our revenge on him."

11 But the LORD is with me like a mighty warrior;
so my persecutors will stumble and not prevail.
They will fail and be thoroughly disgraced;
their dishonor will never be forgotten.
12 O LORD Almighty, you who examine the righteous
and probe the heart and mind,
let me see your vengeance upon them,
for to you I have committed my cause.

13 Sing to the LORD!
Give praise to the LORD!
He rescues the life of the needy
from the hands of the wicked.

14 Cursed be the day I was born!
May the day my mother bore me not be blessed!
15 Cursed be the man who brought my father the news,
who made him very glad, saying,
"A child is born to you—a son!"
16 May that man be like the towns
the LORD overthrew without pity.
May he hear wailing in the morning,
a battle cry at noon.
17 For he did not kill me in the womb,
with my mother as my grave,
her womb enlarged forever.
18 Why did I ever come out of the womb
to see trouble and sorrow
and to end my days in shame?

God Rejects Zedekiah's Request

21 The word came to Jeremiah from the LORD when King
Zedekiah sent to him Pashhur son of Malkijah and the priest
Zephaniah son of Maaseiah. They said: 2 "Inquire now of the LORD
for us because Nebuchadnezzar[a] king of Babylon is attacking us.

[a]2 Hebrew *Nebuchadrezzar,* of which *Nebuchadnezzar* is a variant; here and often in Jeremiah and Ezekiel

20:4 *the king of Babylon:* See the Introduction to JEREMIAH, p. 1424, and the mini-article called "Nebuchadnezzar," p. 1469.

20:7-18 *you deceived me . . . Why did I ever come out of the womb:* This section (20:7-18) probably is made up of two different personal laments—20:7-13 and 20:14-18. See also the note at 11:18-23. Jeremiah expresses his deep pain. How difficult it was to be a prophet of doom to his own people, a people he loved! It hurt to be hated and ridiculed. Jeremiah's mood swings between confident faith in God (20:11, 13) and utter misery, cursing the day he was born (20:14-18). Not to live at all is better than the life he must lead as God's prophet (15:10).

20:16 *the towns the LORD overthrew:* This probably refers to the ancient cities of Sodom and Gomorrah (Gen 19:23-29).

21:1 *Zedekiah . . . Pashhur . . . Zephaniah:* See the notes at 1:2, 3 and 1:3 (Zedekiah). In 588 B.C., Zedekiah was encouraged by royal advisers and by promises of help from Egypt to break his treaty with Nebuchadnezzar of Babylon. The king sent two officials to ask Jeremiah to pray to the LORD for protection from Nebuchadnezzar. Pashhur was a member of the royal court who later tried to have Jeremiah killed for treason (38:1-4). Zephaniah, assistant to the chief priest, was not hostile to Jeremiah (37:3-5). Zephaniah was later executed by Nebuchadnezzar (52:24-27).

21:2 *Nebuchadnezzar . . . will withdraw from us:* See the mini-article called "Nebuchadnezzar," p. 1469. When the Babylonian army surrounded Jerusalem and prepared to attack, Pashhur and Zephaniah asked Jeremiah to pray for a miracle rescue like the one God provided in the prophet Isaiah's time (2 Kgs 18:13—19:37; Isa 36,37).

20:12,13 Ps 6:9,10; 22:24; 31:13-16; 109:30,31; Jer 11:20.

21:5 *I . . . will fight . . . you with an outstretched hand and a mighty arm:* The LORD's outstretched arm is an image often used to describe the LORD's protection or power, especially in battle (Exod 14:21; 15:12, 16; Deut 5:15; Isa 14:27; 19:16; 40:10). Here, the LORD is fighting against Judah, using the Babylonian army as an instrument of punishment against his sinful people.

21:9 *surrenders to the Babylonians . . . escape with his life:* This was the word of the LORD (see also 38:17). For this, Jeremiah will be accused of high treason. Zedekiah chose not to listen, and Jerusalem was destroyed.

21:11,12 *royal house . . . every morning:* The first part of each day was to be given to matters of justice (2 Sam 15:1-3). Israel's rulers were to defend the poor and rescue the homeless (Ps 72:1-4; Prov 16:11, 12; Isa 11:1-5). See also the mini-article called "Justice," p. 1721.

21:13 *Jerusalem . . . valley:* Three deep valleys were in or just outside Jerusalem's walls (see the map on p. 2466). The temple was built on a hill (Zion). It was believed that the valleys helped protect the city by providing a good view of armies attacking Jerusalem's high walls.

21:14 *kindle a fire . . . consume everything:* The king's palace was burned down along with the temple (2 Kgs 25:8, 9; Jer 39:8).

22:1 *king of Judah:* This probably refers to Zedekiah (see the note at 21:1).

21:3-7 2 Kgs 25:1-11; 2 Chr 36:17-21.

Perhaps the LORD will perform wonders for us as in times past so
that he will withdraw from us."
3 But Jeremiah answered them, "Tell Zedekiah, 4 'This is what
the LORD, the God of Israel, says: I am about to turn against you the
weapons of war that are in your hands, which you are using to fight
the king of Babylon and the Babylonians[a] who are outside the wall
besieging you. And I will gather them inside this city. 5 I myself will
fight against you with an outstretched hand and a mighty arm in
anger and fury and great wrath. 6 I will strike down those who live
in this city—both men and animals—and they will die of a terrible
plague. 7 After that, declares the LORD, I will hand over Zedekiah
king of Judah, his officials and the people in this city who survive
the plague, sword and famine, to Nebuchadnezzar king of Babylon
and to their enemies who seek their lives. He will put them to the
sword; he will show them no mercy or pity or compassion.'
8 "Furthermore, tell the people, 'This is what the LORD says:
See, I am setting before you the way of life and the way of death.
9 Whoever stays in this city will die by the sword, famine or plague.
But whoever goes out and surrenders to the Babylonians who are
besieging you will live; he will escape with his life. 10 I have determined to do this city harm and not good, declares the LORD. It will
be given into the hands of the king of Babylon, and he will destroy
it with fire.'
11 "Moreover, say to the royal house of Judah, 'Hear the word
of the LORD; 12 O house of David, this is what the LORD says:

" 'Administer justice every morning;
rescue from the hand of his oppressor
the one who has been robbed,
or my wrath will break out and burn like fire
because of the evil you have done—
burn with no one to quench it.
13 I am against you, ⌊Jerusalem,⌋
you who live above this valley
on the rocky plateau,
declares the LORD—
you who say, "Who can come against us?
Who can enter our refuge?"
14 I will punish you as your deeds deserve,
declares the LORD.
I will kindle a fire in your forests
that will consume everything around you.' "

Judgment Against Evil Kings

22 This is what the LORD says: "Go down to the palace of the
king of Judah and proclaim this message there: 2 'Hear the word of

a4 Or *Chaldeans*; also in verse 9

the LORD, O king of Judah, you who sit on David's throne—you,
your officials and your people who come through these gates.
3 This is what the LORD says: Do what is just and right. Rescue from
the hand of his oppressor the one who has been robbed. Do no
wrong or violence to the alien, the fatherless or the widow, and do
not shed innocent blood in this place. 4 For if you are careful to
carry out these commands, then kings who sit on David's throne
will come through the gates of this palace, riding in chariots and
on horses, accompanied by their officials and their people. 5 But if
you do not obey these commands, declares the LORD, I swear by
myself that this palace will become a ruin.'"

6 For this is what the LORD says about the palace of the king
of Judah:

"Though you are like Gilead to me,
like the summit of Lebanon,
I will surely make you like a desert,
like towns not inhabited.
7 I will send destroyers against you,
each man with his weapons,
and they will cut up your fine cedar beams
and throw them into the fire.

8 "People from many nations will pass by this city and will ask
one another, 'Why has the LORD done such a thing to this great city?'
9 And the answer will be: 'Because they have forsaken the covenant of
the LORD their God and have worshiped and served other gods.'"

10 Do not weep for the dead ⌞king⌟ or mourn his loss;
rather, weep bitterly for him who is exiled,
because he will never return
nor see his native land again.

11 For this is what the LORD says about Shallum[a] son of Josiah, who
succeeded his father as king of Judah but has gone from this place:
"He will never return. 12 He will die in the place where they have
led him captive; he will not see this land again."

13 "Woe to him who builds his palace by
unrighteousness,
his upper rooms by injustice,
making his countrymen work for nothing,
not paying them for their labor.
14 He says, 'I will build myself a great palace
with spacious upper rooms.'
So he makes large windows in it,
panels it with cedar
and decorates it in red.

22:3,4 *Do what is just and right . . . carry out these commands:* Zedekiah is encouraged to do what is right, that is, return to obeying God's Law and treating people with justice (see the note at 21:11, 12). If the king does right, then the kings from David's family will continue on Israel's throne, but disobedience will lead to destruction.

22:6,7 *Gilead . . . Lebanon . . . cedar beams:* Gilead was a forest-rich region east of the Jordan, and Lebanon, to the north of Israel, was famous for its magnificent tall cedar trees (see the map on p. 2467). King Solomon had imported cedar wood to make the temple and palace (1 Kgs 5:1—7:12). That is why the palace is compared to the tree-covered hills of Gilead and Lebanon.

22:10-12 *dead king . . . Shallum son of Josiah . . . captive:* The lament in these verses concerns the death of Josiah, who ruled from 640 to 609 B.C. Because Josiah was a good king who ruled a long time, his death is not to be mourned. The one to weep for instead is Josiah's son, Shallum (another name for Jehoahaz), who ruled only three months before being arrested by Egypt's King Neco. He was sent away to Egypt, where he died. See 2 Kgs 23:28-34; 2 Chr 35:20—36:4; Ezek 19:1-4.

22:13-18 *Woe to him . . . Jehoiakim . . . not mourn for him:* See the notes at 1:2, 3 and 2:18. During his eleven-year reign, Jehoiakim allied himself and the country first to Egypt and then to Babylon. He heavily taxed his people in order to pay off the Egyptians (2 Kgs 23:33-35). He also revived the practice of forced labor that Solomon had used and made workers build him a new palace in the Egyptian style (22:14) without paying them.

Jehoiakim may have been assassinated by members of his own royal court in 598 B.C. as a result of his rebellion against Nebuchadnezzar in 602 B.C. See 2 Kgs 23:36—24:6; 2 Chr 36:5-7.

22:5 Matt 23:38; Luke 13:35.

[a]**11** Also called *Jehoahaz*

22:20 *Lebanon . . . Bashan . . . Abarim:* These areas to the north (Lebanon), northeast (Bashan), and southeast (Abarim, also called Moab) have mountain ranges (see the map on p. 2467). From these high places the people of Jerusalem could look down on their land and mourn its destruction. These regions were also defeated and taken over by the Babylonians.

22:22 *The wind will drive all your shepherds away:* See the notes at 4:11, 12 and 18:17.

22:23 *cedar buildings:* A hall in the royal palace in Jerusalem was known as the Forest Hall, because its sides and ceiling were paneled with cedar wood from the forests of Lebanon (1 Kgs 7:2, 3).

22:24 *Jehoiachin . . . king of Judah:* Jehoiachin was eighteen years old when he followed Jehoiakim as ruler of Judah. But he ruled for only three months before being taken prisoner by Nebuchadnezzar in 598 B.C. He lived in Babylon the rest of his life, being made a "royal guest" of Babylon by Evil-Merodach after the death of Nebuchadnezzar in 562 B.C. (2 Kgs 24:8-15; 2 Chr 36:9, 10; Jer 52:31-34).

15 "Does it make you a king
to have more and more cedar?
Did not your father have food and drink?
He did what was right and just,
so all went well with him.
16 He defended the cause of the poor and needy,
and so all went well.
Is that not what it means to know me?"
declares the LORD.
17 "But your eyes and your heart
are set only on dishonest gain,
on shedding innocent blood
and on oppression and extortion."

18 Therefore this is what the LORD says about Jehoiakim son of Josiah king of Judah:

"They will not mourn for him:
'Alas, my brother! Alas, my sister!'
They will not mourn for him:
'Alas, my master! Alas, his splendor!'
19 He will have the burial of a donkey—
dragged away and thrown
outside the gates of Jerusalem."

20 "Go up to Lebanon and cry out,
let your voice be heard in Bashan,
cry out from Abarim,
for all your allies are crushed.
21 I warned you when you felt secure,
but you said, 'I will not listen!'
This has been your way from your youth;
you have not obeyed me.
22 The wind will drive all your shepherds away,
and your allies will go into exile.
Then you will be ashamed and disgraced
because of all your wickedness.
23 You who live in 'Lebanon,'[a]
who are nestled in cedar buildings,
how you will groan when pangs come upon you,
pain like that of a woman in labor!

24 "As surely as I live," declares the LORD, "even if you,
Jehoiachin[b] son of Jehoiakim king of Judah, were a signet ring on
my right hand, I would still pull you off. 25 I will hand you over to
those who seek your life, those you fear—to Nebuchadnezzar king
of Babylon and to the Babylonians.[c] 26 I will hurl you and the

[a] **23** That is, the palace in Jerusalem (see 1 Kings 7:2) [b] **24** Hebrew *Coniah,* a variant of *Jehoiachin;* also in verse 28 [c] **25** Or *Chaldeans*

mother who gave you birth into another country, where neither of
you was born, and there you both will die. [27]You will never come
back to the land you long to return to."

[28]Is this man Jehoiachin a despised, broken pot,
an object no one wants?
Why will he and his children be hurled out,
cast into a land they do not know?
[29]O land, land, land,
hear the word of the LORD!
[30]This is what the LORD says:
"Record this man as if childless,
a man who will not prosper in his lifetime,
for none of his offspring will prosper,
none will sit on the throne of David
or rule anymore in Judah."

The Righteous Branch

23 "Woe to the shepherds who are destroying and scattering the
sheep of my pasture!" declares the LORD. [2]Therefore this is what
the LORD, the God of Israel, says to the shepherds who tend my
people: "Because you have scattered my flock and driven them
away and have not bestowed care on them, I will bestow punishment on you for the evil you have done," declares the LORD. [3]"I
myself will gather the remnant of my flock out of all the countries
where I have driven them and will bring them back to their pasture, where they will be fruitful and increase in number. [4]I will
place shepherds over them who will tend them, and they will no
longer be afraid or terrified, nor will any be missing," declares the
LORD.

[5]"The days are coming," declares the LORD,
"when I will raise up to David[a] a righteous
Branch,
a King who will reign wisely
and do what is just and right in the land.
[6]In his days Judah will be saved
and Israel will live in safety.
This is the name by which he will be called:
The LORD Our Righteousness.

[7]"So then, the days are coming," declares the LORD, "when people
will no longer say, 'As surely as the LORD lives, who brought the
Israelites up out of Egypt,' [8]but they will say, 'As surely as the LORD
lives, who brought the descendants of Israel up out of the land of
the north and out of all the countries where he had banished
them.' Then they will live in their own land."

---

[a]5 Or *up from David's line*

The LORD declares, *"I myself will gather the remnant of my flock out of all the countries where I have driven them and will bring them back."* Jer 23:3

22:30 *Record this man as if childless:* None of Jehoiachin's seven sons (1 Chr 3:17, 18) ever became king of Judah. He was considered as good as childless, since his sons could not carry on his name as royalty. Though Jehoiachin's sons were disqualified from becoming king of Judah, his grandson Zerubbabel, son of Shealtiel, became governor of Judah after the time of the exile (see HAGGAI; Matt 1:12-16).

23:1 *shepherds:* See the note at 3:15. The leaders were supposed to care for their sheep (people), but they act like wolves instead. See also Ezekiel 34.

23:3 *gather the remnant of my flock:* This refers to the time after the people have been in exile. The Persian King Cyrus defeated Babylon in 539 B.C. and began to let the Jewish people return home in 538 B.C. (Isa 40:1-11; 45:1-8; Jer 50:4-9; Ezek 37:20-28).

23:5 *raise up to David a righteous Branch, a King:* These verses tell of the coming of an ideal king from the line of David, who will rule with justice. See also Isa 9:2—7; 11:1-5; Jer 33:14-16; Zech 3:8; and the mini-article called "Messiah (Chosen One)," p. 1124.

23:7,8 *the days are coming . . . live in their own land:* These verses date from the time of the exile. The living God will rescue the people from Babylon and restore them to the land of Israel. See 16:14,15.

23:10 *prophets . . . evil course:* Jeremiah refers to the lying prophets who spoke in the name of idols (see the note at 2:8) or who falsely preached that Judah was not in danger (6:13-15; 14:13-15). See also chapters 26–28, where Jeremiah's confrontation with some of these prophets is described.

23:11 *in my temple I find their wickedness:* Some of Judah's priests allowed idol worship and immoral rituals to take place in the temple (see 2 Kgs 23:6, 7; Ezek 8:1-18).

23:13,14 *prophets of Samaria . . . prophets of Jerusalem:* The city of Samaria was the capital of the northern kingdom of Israel for many years (see the map on p. 2467). Israel's King Ahab built an altar and temple to the Canaanite god Baal there (see 1 Kgs 16:29-33). A number of prophets of the northern kingdom served Baal (1 Kgs 18:1-40). Other prophets complained about the idol worship taking place in Israel (Hos 4:4-19; Mic 1:1-7). Like the prophets of Samaria before them, the prophets of Jerusalem in Jeremiah's day sinned against God and would suffer the LORD's punishment (23:15).

23:14 *Sodom . . . Gomorrah:* The LORD destroyed these ancient cities because their people were so evil (Gen 18:16—19:29; Ezek 16:48-50).

23:15 *drink poisoned water:* See the note at 8:14.

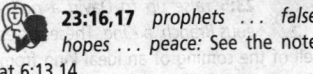

23:16,17 *prophets . . . false hopes . . . peace:* See the note at 6:13,14.

Lying Prophets

9 Concerning the prophets:

My heart is broken within me;
all my bones tremble.
I am like a drunken man,
like a man overcome by wine,
because of the LORD
and his holy words.
10 The land is full of adulterers;
because of the curse[a] the land lies parched[b]
and the pastures in the desert are withered.
The ⌞prophets⌟ follow an evil course
and use their power unjustly.

11 "Both prophet and priest are godless;
even in my temple I find their wickedness,"
declares the LORD.
12 "Therefore their path will become slippery;
they will be banished to darkness
and there they will fall.
I will bring disaster on them
in the year they are punished,"
declares the LORD.
13 "Among the prophets of Samaria
I saw this repulsive thing:
They prophesied by Baal
and led my people Israel astray.
14 And among the prophets of Jerusalem
I have seen something horrible:
They commit adultery and live a lie.
They strengthen the hands of evildoers,
so that no one turns from his wickedness.
They are all like Sodom to me;
the people of Jerusalem are like Gomorrah."

15 Therefore, this is what the LORD Almighty says concerning the prophets:

"I will make them eat bitter food
and drink poisoned water,
because from the prophets of Jerusalem
ungodliness has spread throughout the land."

16 This is what the LORD Almighty says:

"Do not listen to what the prophets are prophesying to you;
they fill you with false hopes.

[a]10 Or *because of these things* [b]10 Or *land mourns*

They speak visions from their own minds,
not from the mouth of the LORD.
17 They keep saying to those who despise me,
'The LORD says: You will have peace.'
And to all who follow the stubbornness of their hearts
they say, 'No harm will come to you.'
18 But which of them has stood in the council of the LORD
to see or to hear his word?
Who has listened and heard his word?
19 See, the storm of the LORD
will burst out in wrath,
a whirlwind swirling down
on the heads of the wicked.
20 The anger of the LORD will not turn back
until he fully accomplishes
the purposes of his heart.
In days to come
you will understand it clearly.
21 I did not send these prophets,
yet they have run with their message;
I did not speak to them,
yet they have prophesied.
22 But if they had stood in my council,
they would have proclaimed my words to my people
and would have turned them from their evil ways
and from their evil deeds.

23 "Am I only a God nearby,"
declares the LORD,
"and not a God far away?
24 Can anyone hide in secret places
so that I cannot see him?"
declares the LORD.
"Do not I fill heaven and earth?"
declares the LORD.

25 "I have heard what the prophets say who prophesy lies in
my name. They say, 'I had a dream! I had a dream!' 26 How long
will this continue in the hearts of these lying prophets, who prophesy the delusions of their own minds? 27 They think the dreams
they tell one another will make my people forget my name, just as
their fathers forgot my name through Baal worship. 28 Let the
prophet who has a dream tell his dream, but let the one who has
my word speak it faithfully. For what has straw to do with grain?"
declares the LORD. 29 "Is not my word like fire," declares the LORD,
"and like a hammer that breaks a rock in pieces?
30 "Therefore," declares the LORD, "I am against the prophets
who steal from one another words supposedly from me. 31 Yes,"
declares the LORD, "I am against the prophets who wag their own

"Do not I fill heaven and earth?" declares the LORD.
Jer 23:24

23:18 *the council of the LORD:* Sometimes, prophets had visions of the LORD meeting with the angels (1 Kgs 22:19-23; Isa 6:1-8). Here the LORD says that the false prophets never attended any such meeting; if they had, their message would be different (23:22).

23:23 *nearby . . . far away:* The LORD is not a small local god, as were the Canaanite idols, but rather the God of heaven and all the earth. God cannot be contained or confined to a single place. Therefore, nothing can be kept secret from him.

23:28 *dream . . . my word . . . straw . . . grain:* The dreams of the false prophets are one thing; God's word is another. The false prophets confuse the two, putting forth their dreams as God's truth. But these dreams are like worthless straw compared to God's real message (nutritious grain). Such is the difference between pleasing the people and declaring the truth. See also the article called "Prophets and Prophecy," p. 935.

23:33 *oracle . . . forsake you:* The people ask to hear the "oracle" of the LORD, expecting to hear good news—words of peace and prosperity—so the lying prophets give them what they want to hear. But they fill the people with their false optimism because God is already planning to forsake them.

24:1 *Jehoiachin . . . exile . . . Nebuchadnezzar:* For more about Nebuchadnezzar, see the notes at 20:4 and 21:2; for more about Jehoiachin, see the note at 22:24. Nebuchadnezzar invaded Judah twice: in 598 B.C. and again in 587 B.C. This parable is about the first invasion when Jehoiachin and many Jewish officials and skilled workers were forced to leave Judah and live in exile in Babylon. This group included the prophet Ezekiel (Ezek 1:1-3). See the map on p. 2468 and the mini-article called "Exile," p. 1541.

24:1 *two baskets of figs:* The people of Israel were to honor the LORD God by bringing the "first-fruits" of their harvest, not the leftovers (Lev 23:10,11; Deut 18:4). The two baskets represent two different groups (24:5-10).

24:5-8 *good figs . . . poor figs:* The future of Israel lies with the prisoners of war in Babylon. The "good figs" stood for those who would remain faithful to God while living in Babylon. They or their descendants would one day return to Judah (29:10-14) and return to the LORD with all their heart (31:31-34).

Many who were left behind in Judah after Nebuchadnezzar's first invasion in 598 B.C. thought that they were favored by God. They were wrong. These "poor figs" included Jehoiachin's uncle, King Zedekiah, and his royal officials. Some of these officials convinced Zedekiah to rebel against Nebuchadnezzar, which brought on the second invasion and destruction of Jerusalem in 586 B.C. See also the note at 21:1 and the mini-article called "Nebuchadnezzar," p. 1469.

tongues and yet declare, 'The LORD declares.' 32 Indeed, I am against
those who prophesy false dreams," declares the LORD. "They tell
them and lead my people astray with their reckless lies, yet I did
not send or appoint them. They do not benefit these people in the
least," declares the LORD.

False Oracles and False Prophets

33 "When these people, or a prophet or a priest, ask you, 'What
is the oracle[a] of the LORD?' say to them, 'What oracle?[b] I will forsake
you, declares the LORD.' 34 If a prophet or a priest or anyone else
claims, 'This is the oracle of the LORD,' I will punish that man and his
household. 35 This is what each of you keeps on saying to his friend
or relative: 'What is the LORD's answer?' or 'What has the LORD spoken?' 36 But you must not mention 'the oracle of the LORD' again,
because every man's own word becomes his oracle and so you distort the words of the living God, the LORD Almighty, our God. 37 This
is what you keep saying to a prophet: 'What is the LORD's answer to
you?' or 'What has the LORD spoken?' 38 Although you claim, 'This is
the oracle of the LORD,' this is what the LORD says: You used the
words, 'This is the oracle of the LORD,' even though I told you that
you must not claim, 'This is the oracle of the LORD.' 39 Therefore, I
will surely forget you and cast you out of my presence along with
the city I gave to you and your fathers. 40 I will bring upon you everlasting disgrace—everlasting shame that will not be forgotten."

Two Baskets of Figs

24 After Jehoiachin[c] son of Jehoiakim king of Judah and the
officials, the craftsmen and the artisans of Judah were carried into
exile from Jerusalem to Babylon by Nebuchadnezzar king of Babylon, the LORD showed me two baskets of figs placed in front of
the temple of the LORD. 2 One basket had very good figs, like those
that ripen early; the other basket had very poor figs, so bad they
could not be eaten.

3 Then the LORD asked me, "What do you see, Jeremiah?"

"Figs," I answered. "The good ones are very good, but the
poor ones are so bad they cannot be eaten."

4 Then the word of the LORD came to me: 5 "This is what the
LORD, the God of Israel, says: 'Like these good figs, I regard as good
the exiles from Judah, whom I sent away from this place to the
land of the Babylonians.[d] 6 My eyes will watch over them for their
good, and I will bring them back to this land. I will build them up
and not tear them down; I will plant them and not uproot them.
7 I will give them a heart to know me, that I am the LORD. They will

[a] 33 Or *burden* (see Septuagint and Vulgate) [b] 33 Hebrew; Septuagint and Vulgate *'You are the burden.* (The Hebrew for *oracle* and *burden* is the same.)
[c] 1 Hebrew *Jeconiah,* a variant of *Jehoiachin* [d] 5 Or *Chaldeans*

be my people, and I will be their God, for they will return to me
with all their heart.

8"'But like the poor figs, which are so bad they cannot be
eaten,' says the LORD, 'so will I deal with Zedekiah king of Judah,
his officials and the survivors from Jerusalem, whether they
remain in this land or live in Egypt. 9I will make them abhorrent
and an offense to all the kingdoms of the earth, a reproach and a
byword, an object of ridicule and cursing, wherever I banish them.
10I will send the sword, famine and plague against them until they
are destroyed from the land I gave to them and their fathers.' "

Seventy Years of Captivity

25 The word came to Jeremiah concerning all the people of
Judah in the fourth year of Jehoiakim son of Josiah king of Judah,
which was the first year of Nebuchadnezzar king of Babylon. 2So
Jeremiah the prophet said to all the people of Judah and to all
those living in Jerusalem: 3For twenty-three years—from the thirteenth year of Josiah son of Amon king of Judah until this very
day—the word of the LORD has come to me and I have spoken to
you again and again, but you have not listened.

4And though the LORD has sent all his servants the prophets
to you again and again, you have not listened or paid any attention. 5They said, "Turn now, each of you, from your evil ways and
your evil practices, and you can stay in the land the LORD gave to
you and your fathers for ever and ever. 6Do not follow other gods
to serve and worship them; do not provoke me to anger with what
your hands have made. Then I will not harm you."

7"But you did not listen to me," declares the LORD, "and you
have provoked me with what your hands have made, and you have
brought harm to yourselves."

8Therefore the LORD Almighty says this: "Because you have not
listened to my words, 9I will summon all the peoples of the north and
my servant Nebuchadnezzar king of Babylon," declares the LORD,
"and I will bring them against this land and its inhabitants and
against all the surrounding nations. I will completely destroy[a] them
and make them an object of horror and scorn, and an everlasting
ruin. 10I will banish from them the sounds of joy and gladness, the
voices of bride and bridegroom, the sound of millstones and the light
of the lamp. 11This whole country will become a desolate wasteland,
and these nations will serve the king of Babylon seventy years.

12"But when the seventy years are fulfilled, I will punish the
king of Babylon and his nation, the land of the Babylonians,[b] for
their guilt," declares the LORD, "and will make it desolate forever.
13I will bring upon that land all the things I have spoken against it,

[a]**9** The Hebrew term refers to the irrevocable giving over of things or persons to the LORD, often by totally destroying them. [b]**12** Or *Chaldeans*

25:1 *in the fourth year:* The date is 605 B.C., when the newly enthroned Nebuchadnezzar defeated the Egyptians at the Battle of Carchemish. Egypt's King Neco, who had placed Jehoiakim on the Judean throne four years earlier, was defeated at this battle. This was the same year that Jehoiakim burned Jeremiah's scroll (book) mentioned in 25:13 (see chapter 36). See also 2 Kgs 24:1; 2 Chr 36:5-7; Dan 1:1, 2; and the note at 13:20,21.

25:3 *Josiah:* See the note at 1:2,3 and the Introduction to JEREMIAH, p. 1424. See also 2 Kgs 22:1—23:30; 2 Chr 34:1—35:27.

25:5 *Turn . . . from your evil ways and your evil practices:* This is the heart of Jeremiah's message: turn back to God (repent), and God may allow you to stay in your own land. See also Isa 1:27; Ezek 14:4, 5; 18:25-32; Hos 14:1, 2, 8.

25:9 *peoples of the north and my servant Nebuchadnezzar:* See the notes at 1:13 and 20:4. The Babylonians also attacked and defeated many of the nations bordering Israel.

25:10 *sounds of joy and gladness . . . light of the lamp:* The comforting sights and sounds of the home will come to an end. See 7:34; 16:9; Rev 18:22,23.

25:11,12 *seventy years . . . punish the king of Babylon:* Seventy stands for a normal life-span (Ps 90:10). The point is that few can expect to witness the punishment of Babylon. The Babylonian exile actually lasted fifty years (586-538 B.C.) or at most sixty years. See the mini-article called "Exile," p. 1541.

all that are written in this book and prophesied by Jeremiah against all the nations. [14]They themselves will be enslaved by many nations and great kings; I will repay them according to their deeds and the work of their hands."

The Cup of God's Wrath

[15]This is what the LORD, the God of Israel, said to me: "Take from my hand this cup filled with the wine of my wrath and make all the nations to whom I send you drink it. [16]When they drink it, they will stagger and go mad because of the sword I will send among them."

[17]So I took the cup from the LORD's hand and made all the nations to whom he sent me drink it: [18]Jerusalem and the towns of Judah, its kings and officials, to make them a ruin and an object of horror and scorn and cursing, as they are today; [19]Pharaoh king of Egypt, his attendants, his officials and all his people, [20]and all the foreign people there; all the kings of Uz; all the kings of the Philistines (those of Ashkelon, Gaza, Ekron, and the people left at Ashdod); [21]Edom, Moab and Ammon; [22]all the kings of Tyre and Sidon; the kings of the coastlands across the sea; [23]Dedan, Tema, Buz and all who are in distant places[a]; [24]all the kings of Arabia and all the kings of the foreign people who live in the desert; [25]all the kings of Zimri, Elam and Media; [26]and all the kings of the north, near and far, one after the other—all the kingdoms on the face of the earth. And after all of them, the king of Sheshach[b] will drink it too.

[27]"Then tell them, 'This is what the LORD Almighty, the God of Israel, says: Drink, get drunk and vomit, and fall to rise no more because of the sword I will send among you.' [28]But if they refuse to take the cup from your hand and drink, tell them, 'This is what the LORD Almighty says: You must drink it! [29]See, I am beginning to bring disaster on the city that bears my Name, and will you indeed go unpunished? You will not go unpunished, for I am calling down a sword upon all who live on the earth, declares the LORD Almighty.'

[30]"Now prophesy all these words against them and say to them:

" 'The LORD will roar from on high;
  he will thunder from his holy dwelling
  and roar mightily against his land.
He will shout like those who tread the grapes,
  shout against all who live on the earth.
[31]The tumult will resound to the ends of the earth,
  for the LORD will bring charges against the nations;
he will bring judgment on all mankind
  and put the wicked to the sword,' "
    declares the LORD.

[a]23 Or *who clip the hair by their foreheads* [b]26 *Sheshach* is a cryptogram for Babylon.

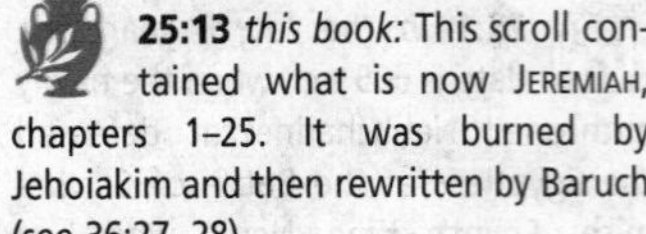

25:13 *this book:* This scroll contained what is now JEREMIAH, chapters 1–25. It was burned by Jehoiakim and then rewritten by Baruch (see 36:27, 28).

25:14 *many nations:* See the note at 23:3.

25:15 *cup filled with the wine of my wrath:* God's judgment on Judah will also affect surrounding nations when the Babylonian forces attack region (25:9). See also the note at 8:14.

25:18-26 *Judah . . . Egypt . . . Sheshach:* All nations must drink from the cup of God's wrath, beginning with Judah and including Egypt and Babylon (here called Sheshach). Egypt was defeated by Babylon in 605 B.C. Uz (25:20), the land where Job lived (Job 1:1), was probably east of Judah. The four key cities of Philistia (Ashkelon . . . Ashdod) were defeated by the Egyptians and by the Babylonians. Tyre and Sidon were Phoenician cities on the coast of the Mediterranean Sea. King Nebuchadnezzar of Babylon captured the mainland of Tyre in 572 B.C. (Ezek 26:7-11), and Alexander the Great captured the city in 332 B.C.

25:30 *The LORD will roar . . . tread the grapes:* For the image of God as the lion of judgment, see Amos 1:2. Treading grapes is used elsewhere as a symbol for God's judgment (Isa 63:3; Joel 3:11-13; Rev 14:18-20).

[32]This is what the LORD Almighty says:

"Look! Disaster is spreading
from nation to nation;
a mighty storm is rising
from the ends of the earth."

[33]At that time those slain by the LORD will be everywhere—from one end of the earth to the other. They will not be mourned or gathered up or buried, but will be like refuse lying on the ground.

[34]Weep and wail, you shepherds;
roll in the dust, you leaders of the flock.
For your time to be slaughtered has come;
you will fall and be shattered like fine pottery.
[35]The shepherds will have nowhere to flee,
the leaders of the flock no place to escape.
[36]Hear the cry of the shepherds,
the wailing of the leaders of the flock,
for the LORD is destroying their pasture.
[37]The peaceful meadows will be laid waste
because of the fierce anger of the LORD.
[38]Like a lion he will leave his lair,
and their land will become desolate
because of the sword[a] of the oppressor
and because of the LORD's fierce anger.

[a]38 Some Hebrew manuscripts and Septuagint (see also Jer. 46:16 and 50:16); most Hebrew manuscripts *anger*

25:32 *Disaster . . . mighty storm:* See the note at 25:9. God's anger and power are often depicted as a storm or whirlwind (23:19).

25:34 *leaders of the flock:* See the notes at 3:15 and 23:1. The leaders will be slaughtered along with the flocks (the people) they were supposed to protect and to lead as examples.

25:34 Jer 18:1-8; 19:1-13.

QUESTIONS ABOUT JEREMIAH 18:1—25:38

1. What does Jeremiah ask the LORD to do about his enemies? (18:19-23) What is your reaction to his request? How do you deal with anger and bitterness? Compare Jeremiah's prayer to Luke 6:27-29.
2. Compare what Jeremiah learns at the pottery shop in 18:1-8 with his "clay jar" message in chapter 19. What points do they have in common?
3. What do Jeremiah's complaints to the LORD in 20:7-18 tell you about the prophet? About prayer?
4. Why do you think the leaders had such a hard time hearing Jeremiah? In 21:3-10, what would they find very difficult to do?
5. Briefly summarize what you know so far about the kings who ruled during the time of Jeremiah: Josiah, Jehoahaz, Jehoiakim, Jehoiachin, and Zedekiah.
6. If you were the king of Judah, what would grab your attention in the prophecy of 22:13-30? Why?
7. How does Jeremiah describe the lying prophets in chapter 23? Why did the people have trouble telling the difference between true and false prophets?
8. How do Judah's sins affect nearby nations? (25:1-33) In what ways do you think evil affects our own nation today?

Jeremiah Against the Lying Prophets

In chapters 26–29 Jeremiah confronts Judah's leaders and the lying prophets. The first confrontation is his temple sermon delivered near the beginning of Jehoiakim's reign (609 B.C.). The other incidents occur during the reign of Zedekiah (probably in 594 B.C.). Though part of his original warning came true when Nebuchadnezzar invaded in 598 B.C., Jeremiah warns that Judah's punishment is not over and that the people in Judah and those taken to live in far-away Babylon must endure more punishment. This message brings him into conflict with the so-called "lying prophets," who argue that the worst is already over.

Jeremiah Threatened With Death

26 Early in the reign of Jehoiakim son of Josiah king of Judah,
this word came from the LORD: 2"This is what the LORD says: Stand
in the courtyard of the LORD's house and speak to all the people of
the towns of Judah who come to worship in the house of the LORD.
Tell them everything I command you; do not omit a word. 3Per-
haps they will listen and each will turn from his evil way. Then I
will relent and not bring on them the disaster I was planning
because of the evil they have done. 4Say to them, 'This is what the
LORD says: If you do not listen to me and follow my law, which I
have set before you, 5and if you do not listen to the words of my
servants the prophets, whom I have sent to you again and again
(though you have not listened), 6then I will make this house like
Shiloh and this city an object of cursing among all the nations of
the earth.' "

7The priests, the prophets and all the people heard Jeremiah
speak these words in the house of the LORD. 8But as soon as Jeremiah finished telling all the people everything the LORD had commanded him to say, the priests, the prophets and all the people
seized him and said, "You must die! 9Why do you prophesy in the
LORD's name that this house will be like Shiloh and this city will be
desolate and deserted?" And all the people crowded around Jeremiah in the house of the LORD.

10When the officials of Judah heard about these things, they
went up from the royal palace to the house of the LORD and took
their places at the entrance of the New Gate of the LORD's house.
11Then the priests and the prophets said to the officials and all the
people, "This man should be sentenced to death because he has
prophesied against this city. You have heard it with your own ears!"

12Then Jeremiah said to all the officials and all the people:
"The LORD sent me to prophesy against this house and this city all
the things you have heard. 13Now reform your ways and your
actions and obey the LORD your God. Then the LORD will relent
and not bring the disaster he has pronounced against you. 14As for
me, I am in your hands; do with me whatever you think is good

26:1 *Early in the reign of Jehoiakim:* The date is 609 B.C. The nation is still in a state of shock following the death of Jehoiakim's father, the good King Josiah. See 2 Kgs 23:36—24:6; 2 Chr 36:5–7; the note at 22:13-18 (Jehoiakim); and the Introduction to JEREMIAH, p. 1424.

26:2 *Stand in the courtyard of the LORD's house:* JEREMIAH has two accounts of the same event (see also 7:1-15). The emphasis in chapter 7 is on the message itself, while the emphasis here is on what happens after the message is delivered.

26:4-6 *If you do not listen . . . I will make this house like Shiloh:* See the note at 7:12. Jeremiah's word of doom against Jerusalem and its temple caused a riot (26:7-24), especially among those leaders connected with the temple and the king. If the temple were destroyed, it would mean that the LORD had abandoned Judah. And if the city were destroyed, that would likely mean that the line of rulers from David's family would come to an end. The priests and many of Judah's prophets could not imagine either of those possibilities. See also the note at 7:4.

26:8 *You must die:* The priests and prophets demand that Jeremiah be put to death for the message he proclaimed in the LORD's name. Messages spoken in the LORD's name were to be taken seriously, since they were considered powerful enough to make the events they described actually happen.

26:10 *officials . . . took their places . . . New Gate:* Next the city leaders and officers of the royal court set up a trial for Jeremiah. Public trials were often held in an open area near the gate of a city, palace, or temple.

26:11 *sentenced to death:* According to Deuteronomy 18:20, a prophet who lied or delivered a false message deserved death.

and right. 15Be assured, however, that if you put me to death, you
will bring the guilt of innocent blood on yourselves and on this
city and on those who live in it, for in truth the LORD has sent me
to you to speak all these words in your hearing."
16Then the officials and all the people said to the priests and
the prophets, "This man should not be sentenced to death! He has
spoken to us in the name of the LORD our God."
17Some of the elders of the land stepped forward and said to
the entire assembly of people, 18"Micah of Moresheth prophesied
in the days of Hezekiah king of Judah. He told all the people of
Judah, 'This is what the LORD Almighty says:

" 'Zion will be plowed like a field,
Jerusalem will become a heap of rubble,
the temple hill a mound overgrown with thickets.'[a]

19"Did Hezekiah king of Judah or anyone else in Judah put him to
death? Did not Hezekiah fear the LORD and seek his favor? And did
not the LORD relent, so that he did not bring the disaster he pronounced against them? We are about to bring a terrible disaster on
ourselves!"
20(Now Uriah son of Shemaiah from Kiriath Jearim was
another man who prophesied in the name of the LORD; he prophesied the same things against this city and this land as Jeremiah
did. 21When King Jehoiakim and all his officers and officials heard
his words, the king sought to put him to death. But Uriah heard
of it and fled in fear to Egypt. 22King Jehoiakim, however, sent
Elnathan son of Acbor to Egypt, along with some other men.
23They brought Uriah out of Egypt and took him to King
Jehoiakim, who had him struck down with a sword and his body
thrown into the burial place of the common people.)
24Furthermore, Ahikam son of Shaphan supported Jeremiah, and so he was not handed over to the people to be put to
death.

Judah to Serve Nebuchadnezzar

27 Early in the reign of Zedekiah[b] son of Josiah king of Judah,
this word came to Jeremiah from the LORD: 2This is what the LORD
said to me: "Make a yoke out of straps and crossbars and put it on
your neck. 3Then send word to the kings of Edom, Moab, Ammon,
Tyre and Sidon through the envoys who have come to Jerusalem to
Zedekiah king of Judah. 4Give them a message for their masters

[a]18 Micah 3:12 [b]1 A few Hebrew manuscripts and Syriac (see also Jer. 27:3, 12 and 28:1); most Hebrew manuscripts *Jehoiakim* (Most Septuagint manuscripts do not have this verse.)

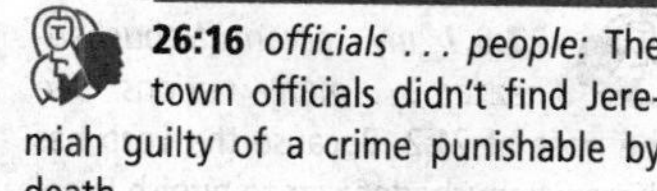

26:16 *officials . . . people:* The town officials didn't find Jeremiah guilty of a crime punishable by death.

26:18 *Micah . . . Hezekiah:* Hezekiah made many religious reforms (2 Kgs 18:1-4). Like Jeremiah, the prophet Micah had preached against Jerusalem, especially its unjust rulers and lying prophets (Mic 3:1-12).

26:20-24 *Uriah . . . Ahikam:* This is the only mention of the prophet Uriah in the Bible. His story shows how the situation might have turned out differently for Jeremiah. Jehoiakim showed no mercy toward Uriah. Ahikam and his father Shaphan were leaders of the reform under Josiah (2 Kgs 22:3, 12, 14). His son Gedaliah was appointed governor of Judah after the fall of Jerusalem (40:5—41:3).

27:1 *Early in the reign of Zedekiah:* About this time, royal officials convinced Zedekiah to rebel against Babylon (2 Kgs 24:18-20).

27:2 *a yoke:* The ox yoke is a wooden collar that fits around the neck of an ox. Using leather straps attached to the yoke, a driver can make the ox pull a cart or plow. Jeremiah is told to put on a yoke to symbolize the power of Nebuchadnezzar (27:8).

27:3 *Edom . . . Sidon:* The countries mentioned here had been enemies of the Israelite people in the past, but at this time they are meeting with Judah's leaders to form an alliance against Babylon. See also the notes at chapter 48 (Moab); 49:1-5 (Ammon); and 49:7,8 (Edom).

27:6,7 *my servant Nebuchadnezzar . . . many nations:* See the note at 21:2. Because the LORD has chosen Nebuchadnezzar to punish Israel and its neighbors, their alliance is pointless. Eventually, Babylon also will fall (see the note at 23:3).

27:9 *diviners . . . mediums . . . sorcerers:* See the note at 50:36. Telling fortunes or practicing witchcraft were forbidden by the Law of Moses (Exod 22:18; Lev 19:26, 31; Deut 18:14).

27:11 *bow its neck . . . remain in its own land:* Jeremiah's advice went against those who believed the lying prophets, who said that the LORD would protect Judah no matter what. Jeremiah saw a way for his nation and its neighbors to be spared total destruction.

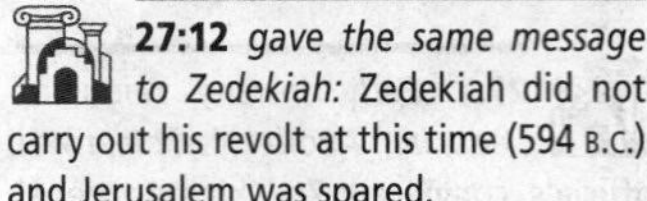

27:12 *gave the same message to Zedekiah:* Zedekiah did not carry out his revolt at this time (594 B.C.) and Jerusalem was spared.

27:14,15 *the prophets . . . are prophesying lies:* See 23:21-32 and the notes at 6:13, 14; 14:13.

27:19-21 *the pillars . . . things . . . left in the house of the LORD:* The pillars stood in front of the Jerusalem temple. The Sea was a huge bowl in the temple court (see Exod 30:17-21). See also 1 Kgs 7:15, 23–37; 2 Kgs 25:13-15; Jer 52:17-20.

and say, 'This is what the LORD Almighty, the God of Israel, says:
"Tell this to your masters: [5]With my great power and outstretched
arm I made the earth and its people and the animals that are on it,
and I give it to anyone I please. [6]Now I will hand all your countries over to my servant Nebuchadnezzar king of Babylon; I will
make even the wild animals subject to him. [7]All nations will serve
him and his son and his grandson until the time for his land
comes; then many nations and great kings will subjugate him.
[8]" ' "If, however, any nation or kingdom will not serve Nebuchadnezzar king of Babylon or bow its neck under his yoke, I will
punish that nation with the sword, famine and plague, declares the
LORD, until I destroy it by his hand. [9]So do not listen to your
prophets, your diviners, your interpreters of dreams, your mediums or your sorcerers who tell you, 'You will not serve the king of
Babylon.' [10]They prophesy lies to you that will only serve to remove
you far from your lands; I will banish you and you will perish.
[11]But if any nation will bow its neck under the yoke of the king of
Babylon and serve him, I will let that nation remain in its own
land to till it and to live there, declares the LORD." ' "
[12]I gave the same message to Zedekiah king of Judah. I said,
"Bow your neck under the yoke of the king of Babylon; serve him
and his people, and you will live. [13]Why will you and your people
die by the sword, famine and plague with which the LORD has
threatened any nation that will not serve the king of Babylon? [14]Do
not listen to the words of the prophets who say to you, 'You will
not serve the king of Babylon,' for they are prophesying lies to you.
[15]'I have not sent them,' declares the LORD. 'They are prophesying
lies in my name. Therefore, I will banish you and you will perish,
both you and the prophets who prophesy to you.' "
[16]Then I said to the priests and all these people, "This is what
the LORD says: Do not listen to the prophets who say, 'Very soon
now the articles from the LORD's house will be brought back from
Babylon.' They are prophesying lies to you. [17]Do not listen to them.
Serve the king of Babylon, and you will live. Why should this city
become a ruin? [18]If they are prophets and have the word of the
LORD, let them plead with the LORD Almighty that the furnishings
remaining in the house of the LORD and in the palace of the king
of Judah and in Jerusalem not be taken to Babylon. [19]For this is
what the LORD Almighty says about the pillars, the Sea, the movable stands and the other furnishings that are left in this city,
[20]which Nebuchadnezzar king of Babylon did not take away when
he carried Jehoiachin[a] son of Jehoiakim king of Judah into exile
from Jerusalem to Babylon, along with all the nobles of Judah and
Jerusalem— [21]yes, this is what the LORD Almighty, the God of
Israel, says about the things that are left in the house of the LORD

[a]**20** Hebrew *Jeconiah,* a variant of *Jehoiachin*

and in the palace of the king of Judah and in Jerusalem: 22“They
will be taken to Babylon and there they will remain until the day I
come for them,’ declares the LORD. ‘Then I will bring them back
and restore them to this place.’ ”

The False Prophet Hananiah

28 In the fifth month of that same year, the fourth year, early in
the reign of Zedekiah king of Judah, the prophet Hananiah son of
Azzur, who was from Gibeon, said to me in the house of the LORD
in the presence of the priests and all the people: 2“This is what the
LORD Almighty, the God of Israel, says: ‘I will break the yoke of the
king of Babylon. 3Within two years I will bring back to this place
all the articles of the LORD’s house that Nebuchadnezzar king of
Babylon removed from here and took to Babylon. 4I will also bring
back to this place Jehoiachin[a] son of Jehoiakim king of Judah and
all the other exiles from Judah who went to Babylon,’ declares the
LORD, ‘for I will break the yoke of the king of Babylon.’ ”
5Then the prophet Jeremiah replied to the prophet Hananiah before the priests and all the people who were standing in the
house of the LORD. 6He said, “Amen! May the LORD do so! May the
LORD fulfill the words you have prophesied by bringing the articles
of the LORD’s house and all the exiles back to this place from Babylon. 7Nevertheless, listen to what I have to say in your hearing and
in the hearing of all the people: 8From early times the prophets
who preceded you and me have prophesied war, disaster and
plague against many countries and great kingdoms. 9But the
prophet who prophesies peace will be recognized as one truly sent
by the LORD only if his prediction comes true.”
10Then the prophet Hananiah took the yoke off the neck of
the prophet Jeremiah and broke it, 11and he said before all the
people, “This is what the LORD says: ‘In the same way will I break
the yoke of Nebuchadnezzar king of Babylon off the neck of all the
nations within two years.’ ” At this, the prophet Jeremiah went on
his way.
12Shortly after the prophet Hananiah had broken the yoke
off the neck of the prophet Jeremiah, the word of the LORD came
to Jeremiah: 13“Go and tell Hananiah, ‘This is what the LORD says:
You have broken a wooden yoke, but in its place you will get a yoke
of iron. 14This is what the LORD Almighty, the God of Israel, says:
I will put an iron yoke on the necks of all these nations to make
them serve Nebuchadnezzar king of Babylon, and they will serve
him. I will even give him control over the wild animals.’ ”
15Then the prophet Jeremiah said to Hananiah the prophet,
“Listen, Hananiah! The LORD has not sent you, yet you have

[a]4 Hebrew *Jeconiah,* a variant of *Jehoiachin*

28:1 *In the fifth month of that same year:* As in chapter 27, the date is 594 B.C. King Zedekiah of Judah was on the verge of revolting against King Nebuchadnezzar. See also 2 Kgs 24:18-20; 2 Chr 36:11-13; and the notes at 1:2, 3 and 27:12.

28:1 *Hananiah son of Azzur:* Nothing else is known about the prophet Hananiah. Hananiah's prophecy in the temple (28:2-4) is nearly the opposite of Jeremiah's (27:1-15). So, Judah's leaders have to try to determine which prophet is false and which is true (see Deut 18:21, 22).

28:2,3 *break the yoke . . . Within two years:* See the note at 27:2 (yoke). Hananiah optimistically predicts that the LORD will smash Nebuchadnezzar by the fall of 592 B.C. and that King Jehoiachin would be allowed to return to Judah along with all the items Nebuchadnezzar had stolen during his first invasion of Jerusalem. Those who were putting together an alliance to rebel against Nebuchadnezzar (see the note at 27:3) probably were encouraged by Hananiah's prediction.

28:6-9 *May the LORD do so . . . prediction comes true:* Jeremiah hopes for good news and wishes for peace for his beloved country. But his and Hananiah's messages can't both be right—only one is truly from the LORD.

28:8 *prophets who preceded you and me:* Jeremiah is probably referring to Amos, Hosea, Micah, and Isaiah.

28:13,14 *wooden yoke . . . iron yoke:* The wooden yoke (27:1, 2) is replaced with a stronger iron yoke.

28:15-17 *The LORD has not sent you . . . died:* He who predicted good news in two years dies in two months. For the punishment of false prophets, see Deut 13:1-11; 18:20.

29:1 *letter . . . to the surviving elders:* Nebuchadnezzar had taken King Jehoiachin and many Judeans into exile in 598 B.C. Many others, including Jeremiah, were left behind in Judah. The year in which Jeremiah writes his letter is 594 B.C.

29:3 *Elasah . . . Gemariah . . . Zedekiah:* Elasah and possibly Gemariah were sons of Shaphan (see the note at 26:20-24).

29:5-7 *settle down . . . Pray to the LORD:* Jeremiah reminds the Jewish exiles that they are living in Babylon because the LORD made it happen. He also tells them to pray for Babylon. This request is a practical one: For the time being, Judah's welfare depends on Babylon's prosperity.

29:10 *seventy years:* See the note at 25:11, 12. The time between the rise of Babylon in 612 B.C. and Babylon's fall in 539 B.C. is seventy-three years; the time from the beginning of Nebuchadnezzar's rule (605 B.C.) to the fall of Babylon was sixty-six years.

29:13,14 *seek me . . . I will be found by you:* See Deut 4:29, 30 and the notes at Jer 4:4 and 24:5-8. According to tradition, the LORD's glory or presence was to be found in the tabernacle or in the temple (1 Kgs 8:11), but Jeremiah states that the LORD can be worshiped even in exile.

persuaded this nation to trust in lies. [16]Therefore, this is what the
LORD says: 'I am about to remove you from the face of the earth.
This very year you are going to die, because you have preached
rebellion against the LORD.' "
[17]In the seventh month of that same year, Hananiah the
prophet died.

A Letter to the Exiles

29 This is the text of the letter that the prophet Jeremiah sent
from Jerusalem to the surviving elders among the exiles and to the
priests, the prophets and all the other people Nebuchadnezzar had
carried into exile from Jerusalem to Babylon. [2](This was after King
Jehoiachin[a] and the queen mother, the court officials and the leaders of Judah and Jerusalem, the craftsmen and the artisans had
gone into exile from Jerusalem.) [3]He entrusted the letter to Elasah
son of Shaphan and to Gemariah son of Hilkiah, whom Zedekiah
king of Judah sent to King Nebuchadnezzar in Babylon. It said:

[4]This is what the LORD Almighty, the God of Israel, says
to all those I carried into exile from Jerusalem to Babylon:
[5]"Build houses and settle down; plant gardens and eat what
they produce. [6]Marry and have sons and daughters; find wives
for your sons and give your daughters in marriage, so that
they too may have sons and daughters. Increase in number
there; do not decrease. [7]Also, seek the peace and prosperity of
the city to which I have carried you into exile. Pray to the
LORD for it, because if it prospers, you too will prosper." [8]Yes,
this is what the LORD Almighty, the God of Israel, says: "Do
not let the prophets and diviners among you deceive you. Do
not listen to the dreams you encourage them to have. [9]They
are prophesying lies to you in my name. I have not sent them,"
declares the LORD.
[10]This is what the LORD says: "When seventy years are
completed for Babylon, I will come to you and fulfill my gracious promise to bring you back to this place. [11]For I know the
plans I have for you," declares the LORD, "plans to prosper you
and not to harm you, plans to give you hope and a future.
[12]Then you will call upon me and come and pray to me, and
I will listen to you. [13]You will seek me and find me when you
seek me with all your heart. [14]I will be found by you," declares
the LORD, "and will bring you back from captivity.[b] I will gather you from all the nations and places where I have banished
you," declares the LORD, "and will bring you back to the place
from which I carried you into exile."
[15]You may say, "The LORD has raised up prophets for us
in Babylon," [16]but this is what the LORD says about the king
who sits on David's throne and all the people who remain in

[a]2 Hebrew *Jeconiah,* a variant of *Jehoiachin* [b]14 Or *will restore your fortunes*

this city, your countrymen who did not go with you into
exile— [17]yes, this is what the LORD Almighty says: "I will send
the sword, famine and plague against them and I will make
them like poor figs that are so bad they cannot be eaten. [18]I
will pursue them with the sword, famine and plague and will
make them abhorrent to all the kingdoms of the earth and an
object of cursing and horror, of scorn and reproach, among
all the nations where I drive them. [19]For they have not listened
to my words," declares the LORD, "words that I sent to them
again and again by my servants the prophets. And you exiles
have not listened either," declares the LORD.
[20]Therefore, hear the word of the LORD, all you exiles
whom I have sent away from Jerusalem to Babylon. [21]This is
what the LORD Almighty, the God of Israel, says about Ahab
son of Kolaiah and Zedekiah son of Maaseiah, who are prophesying lies to you in my name: "I will hand them over to Nebuchadnezzar king of Babylon, and he will put them to death
before your very eyes. [22]Because of them, all the exiles from
Judah who are in Babylon will use this curse: 'The LORD treat
you like Zedekiah and Ahab, whom the king of Babylon
burned in the fire.' [23]For they have done outrageous things
in Israel; they have committed adultery with their neighbors'
wives and in my name have spoken lies, which I did not
tell them to do. I know it and am a witness to it," declares
the LORD.

Message to Shemaiah

[24]Tell Shemaiah the Nehelamite, [25]"This is what the LORD
Almighty, the God of Israel, says: You sent letters in your own
name to all the people in Jerusalem, to Zephaniah son of Maaseiah

29:16-19 *the people . . . like poor figs . . . not listened:* See the note at 24:5-8. Worse days are ahead for Jerusalem and Judah.

29:21-23 *Ahab . . . Zedekiah . . . spoken lies:* These Jewish prophets living in exile in Babylon were making the same false claims that Hananiah made (see 28:1-4).

29:21,22 *put them to death . . . burned in the fire:* They were probably executed because they predicted Babylon's immediate destruction. Their deaths show the LORD's judgment on them for their lies and immorality.

29:24,25 *Shemaiah . . . Zephaniah:* This is the only mention of Shemaiah, whose letters from Babylon are aimed at getting Jeremiah arrested. See also 21:1 and the note.

QUESTIONS ABOUT JEREMIAH 26:1—29:32

1. What was it about Jeremiah's message in the temple (chapter 26) that put him in such danger? What was it that made the angry crowds change their mind about arresting and killing him?
2. What good news did the future hold for Nebuchadnezzar in 27:4-11? For the people of Judah if they listened to Jeremiah? What bad news does the future hold for Nebuchadnezzar and for the people if they do not obey?
3. Read the promise made to the Jewish people living in exile. (29:10-14) What is important about this message, especially regarding worshiping the LORD? What made this message "good" news for the exiles? Why do you think some considered it bad news?
4. What is Hananiah's prophecy concerning Nebuchadnezzar and Babylon? (28:1-4) Jeremiah's reaction to Hananiah's message (28:5-9) is not a swift denial. Why? How do you think Jeremiah feels about the fate of his country? What is the relationship between his hopes and God's judgment?
5. Why does Jeremiah write letters to the people of Judah living in Babylon? (29:1-23, 30-32)

the priest, and to all the other priests. You said to Zephaniah,
26"The LORD has appointed you priest in place of Jehoiada to be in
charge of the house of the LORD; you should put any madman who
acts like a prophet into the stocks and neck-irons. 27So why have
you not reprimanded Jeremiah from Anathoth, who poses as a
prophet among you? 28He has sent this message to us in Babylon:
It will be a long time. Therefore build houses and settle down;
plant gardens and eat what they produce.' "
29Zephaniah the priest, however, read the letter to Jeremiah
the prophet. 30Then the word of the LORD came to Jeremiah:
31"Send this message to all the exiles: 'This is what the LORD says
about Shemaiah the Nehelamite: Because Shemaiah has prophesied
to you, even though I did not send him, and has led you to believe
a lie, 32this is what the LORD says: I will surely punish Shemaiah the
Nehelamite and his descendants. He will have no one left among
this people, nor will he see the good things I will do for my people,
declares the LORD, because he has preached rebellion against me.' "

A Homecoming and a New Beginning

Jeremiah's comforting words (30:1—31:40) declare that Judah's weeping will be replaced by singing, and joy will overtake grief. The LORD will rescue, heal, and rebuild his people. And the LORD will make a new covenant with them (31:31-34). Jeremiah buys a piece of land (32), even though Nebuchadnezzar is about to take over all of Judah. His land purchase symbolizes how God's people will one day be in charge of buying and selling their own land again (33).

Restoration of Israel

30 This is the word that came to Jeremiah from the LORD:
2"This is what the LORD, the God of Israel, says: 'Write in a book all
the words I have spoken to you. 3The days are coming,' declares the
LORD, 'when I will bring my people Israel and Judah back from
captivity[a] and restore them to the land I gave their forefathers to
possess,' says the LORD."
4These are the words the LORD spoke concerning Israel and
Judah: 5"This is what the LORD says:

" 'Cries of fear are heard—
terror, not peace.
6Ask and see:
Can a man bear children?
Then why do I see every strong man
with his hands on his stomach like a woman in labor,
every face turned deathly pale?

[a]3 Or *will restore the fortunes of my people Israel and Judah*

29:28 *sent this message:* This refers to Jeremiah's letter (29:3-23).

29:31,32 *prophesied . . . a lie . . . preached rebellion:* The message to Shemaiah is like the one Jeremiah gave to Hananiah (28:15,16).

30:2 *Write in a book:* In Jeremiah's time, texts were preserved in scrolls. (See the mini-article called "Scrolls," p. 1491). This book was written just after Jerusalem fell to Babylon in 586 B.C. At last, Jeremiah can fulfill the second part of his twofold task (1:10): to preach rescue and rebuilding.

30:3 *Israel and Judah:* Here, Israel refers to the northern kingdom. See also the note at 2:4 and the map on p. 2467.

30:5-7 *terror . . . saved out of it:* The suffering and destruction of Jerusalem and Judah will complete God's judgment (see the note at 4:16, 17). But the pain will end when the LORD rescues his people.

7 How awful that day will be!
None will be like it.
It will be a time of trouble for Jacob,
but he will be saved out of it.

8 " 'In that day,' declares the LORD Almighty,
'I will break the yoke off their necks
and will tear off their bonds;
no longer will foreigners enslave them.
9 Instead, they will serve the LORD their God
and David their king,
whom I will raise up for them.

10 " 'So do not fear, O Jacob my servant;
do not be dismayed, O Israel,'
declares the LORD.
'I will surely save you out of a distant place,
your descendants from the land of their exile.
Jacob will again have peace and security,
and no one will make him afraid.
11 I am with you and will save you,'
declares the LORD.
'Though I completely destroy all the nations
among which I scatter you,
I will not completely destroy you.
I will discipline you but only with justice;
I will not let you go entirely unpunished.'

12 "This is what the LORD says:

" 'Your wound is incurable,
your injury beyond healing.
13 There is no one to plead your cause,
no remedy for your sore,
no healing for you.
14 All your allies have forgotten you;
they care nothing for you.
I have struck you as an enemy would
and punished you as would the cruel,
because your guilt is so great
and your sins so many.
15 Why do you cry out over your wound,
your pain that has no cure?
Because of your great guilt and many sins
I have done these things to you.

16 " 'But all who devour you will be devoured;
all your enemies will go into exile.
Those who plunder you will be plundered;
all who make spoil of you I will despoil.

30:7 *Jacob:* Jacob represents the people and nation of Israel. See 30:10 and the note.

30:8,9 *break the yoke ... tear off their bonds ... David their king:* The people of Judah and Israel are like slaves in exile, but the LORD will end their exile and free them from the yoke of Babylon. Then the people will be free to serve the LORD again in their own land and have hope for a king or Messiah from the line of David (see the note at 23:5).

30:10 *Israel:* Refers to the people of both the northern and southern kingdoms. See also 46:27, 38.

30:12,13 *Your wound is incurable ... no one to plead your cause:* The "wound" of exile was caused by the people's disobedience. The LORD accused them and carried out their punishment (30:14). See also the notes at 2:35 and 8:22.

30:14 *your allies:* Refers to foreign nations, who acted as allies to the Judeans but later deserted them (see the notes at 2:36; 13:20, 21). For Israel's punishment, see Isa 1:5-9; Jer 10:17-22; 13:15-27.

30:16 *your enemies:* See the notes at 9:26; and 27:3.

30:18 *have compassion:* The Hebrew word translated as "compassion" can also be translated as "mercy" or "kind." See also 31:20; 33:26; and the note at 3:12.

30:18-21 *the city will be rebuilt . . . leader will be one of their own:* Because the people of Israel and Judah disobeyed the LORD, the promises made to their ancestors were endangered. But the LORD will renew these promises in the future, which include reclaiming their land and having many children (see Gen 12:1-3; 15:4-6; Exod 3:7-10). They are also promised that their new ruler will be an Israelite, not a foreigner (see 30:9). When the people returned to Judah, they were ruled by a governor and the high priest working together (Hag 1, 2). See also Deut 7:6-8; Jer 7:23; 11:4; 24:7.

30:24 *until he fully accomplishes the purposes of his heart:* Before the restoration can begin (30:18-22), the people of Israel must learn their lesson in exile. See also 23:19, 20.

31:1 *all the clans of Israel:* Israel was made up of twelve tribes (clans) named for the sons of Jacob (see Gen 49; Num 2). After King Solomon died, the ten northern tribes formed their own kingdom (Israel), while the two southernmost tribes formed the kingdom of Judah (see the notes at 23:13, 14; 30:3). Jeremiah envisions a time when all the tribes will be restored as one nation of God's people.

31:2 *find favor in the desert:* God recalls Israel's days of desert wandering. God will rescue God's people from Babylon, just as they were rescued from Egypt. See Exod 33:12-17; Jer 23:7, 8.

17 But I will restore you to health
and heal your wounds,'
declares the LORD,
'because you are called an outcast,
Zion for whom no one cares.'

18 "This is what the LORD says:

" 'I will restore the fortunes of Jacob's tents
and have compassion on his dwellings;
the city will be rebuilt on her ruins,
and the palace will stand in its proper place.
19 From them will come songs of thanksgiving
and the sound of rejoicing.
I will add to their numbers,
and they will not be decreased;
I will bring them honor,
and they will not be disdained.
20 Their children will be as in days of old,
and their community will be established
before me;
I will punish all who oppress them.
21 Their leader will be one of their own;
their ruler will arise from among them.
I will bring him near and he will come close
to me,
for who is he who will devote himself
to be close to me?'
declares the LORD.
22 " 'So you will be my people,
and I will be your God.' "

23 See, the storm of the LORD
will burst out in wrath,
a driving wind swirling down
on the heads of the wicked.
24 The fierce anger of the LORD will not turn back
until he fully accomplishes
the purposes of his heart.
In days to come
you will understand this.

31 "At that time," declares the LORD, "I will be the God of all the
clans of Israel, and they will be my people."
2 This is what the LORD says:

"The people who survive the sword
will find favor in the desert;
I will come to give rest to Israel."

Making Papyrus. The gummy stalks of the papyrus plant were used in the ancient world to make a durable, lightweight writing material that was easier to use, carry, and store than clay tablets, the other common writing material used at that time.

SCROLLS

In ancient times, writing was done on scrolls made of leather or papyrus. The papyrus plant, which grew in Egypt, provided the material for scrolls as early as 3000 B.C. Making scrolls involved a series of steps: (1) Strips were cut from the center of the papyrus plant's stalk, (2) soaked in water to soften them, (3) and laid in crisscrossed rows. (4) The sheets were pounded with a mallet to break down the fibers and force them to join together and then (5) rubbed smooth with shells. When the sheets were dry, they could be written on. Black ink made from carbon soot mixed with water and tree sap was applied with pens made from reeds. Errors in writing could be erased with water.

Papyrus scrolls are rare because moisture causes them to decay. Most surviving papyrus scrolls were discovered in dry, desert-like climates.

Leather scrolls were also used, and they eventually replaced papyrus as the preferred writing material. Leather scrolls were made from sheep, goat, or calf skins that had been scraped to remove the hair, stretched, and dried on a frame. Writing was done on the side where the hair had been removed. Texts written on leather could not be erased. Separate leather sheets were stitched together to make a long scroll. The Scroll of ISAIAH, found at Qumran by the Dead Sea, measures twenty-four feet long. It is made of seventeen sheets of sheepskin joined by linen thread.

31:3 *I have loved you with an everlasting love:* The patience of God has its limits and the judgment of God is sure, but the love of God cannot be exhausted. See also Isa 49:13-16; Hos 11:4.

31:5,6 *Samaria ... Ephraim ... Zion:* See the note at 23:13, 14. Samaria was the capital city and Ephraim was the leading tribe of the northern kingdom of Israel. Both names were used for the northern kingdom. Zion stands for Jerusalem, the capital city of Judah, and for the temple area there. See also the note at 3:14. See the map on p. 2467.

31:8,9 *from the land of the north ... on a level path:* In 539 B.C., Cyrus of Persia defeated Babylon and soon after allowed the people of Judah to return home (Ezra 1:1-3; Isa 45:1-4). Jeremiah pictures God bringing his people back to their homeland (Canaan) from all over the earth in a "new exodus." The later chapters of ISAIAH also echo this joyful theme (Isa 35:5-10; 40:3-5; 42:16; 43:1-7; 48:20-22; 49:8-12).

31:10 *watch over his flock like a shepherd:* For God as the good shepherd, see Ps 23; Isa 40:11. Compare to Jeremiah's description of Israel's leaders (23:1, 2).

31:12 *heights of Zion ... well-watered garden:* See the note at 3:14. The return from exile will be a new beginning, and God's people will again enjoy the blessings promised to their ancestors who first came to the promised land of Canaan (Exod 3:7; Deut 6:10-12).

3 The LORD appeared to us in the past,[a] saying:

"I have loved you with an everlasting love;
I have drawn you with loving-kindness.
4 I will build you up again
and you will be rebuilt, O Virgin Israel.
Again you will take up your tambourines
and go out to dance with the joyful.
5 Again you will plant vineyards
on the hills of Samaria;
the farmers will plant them
and enjoy their fruit.
6 There will be a day when watchmen cry out
on the hills of Ephraim,
'Come, let us go up to Zion,
to the LORD our God.' "

7 This is what the LORD says:

"Sing with joy for Jacob;
shout for the foremost of the nations.
Make your praises heard, and say,
'O LORD, save your people,
the remnant of Israel.'
8 See, I will bring them from the land of the north
and gather them from the ends of the earth.
Among them will be the blind and the lame,
expectant mothers and women in labor;
a great throng will return.
9 They will come with weeping;
they will pray as I bring them back.
I will lead them beside streams of water
on a level path where they will not stumble,
because I am Israel's father,
and Ephraim is my firstborn son.
10 "Hear the word of the LORD, O nations;
proclaim it in distant coastlands:
'He who scattered Israel will gather them
and will watch over his flock like a shepherd.'
11 For the LORD will ransom Jacob
and redeem them from the hand of those stronger
than they.
12 They will come and shout for joy on the heights of Zion;
they will rejoice in the bounty of the LORD—
the grain, the new wine and the oil,
the young of the flocks and herds.
They will be like a well-watered garden,

[a]3 Or *LORD has appeared to us from afar*

and they will sorrow no more.
[13] Then maidens will dance and be glad,
young men and old as well.
I will turn their mourning into gladness;
I will give them comfort and joy instead of sorrow.
[14] I will satisfy the priests with abundance,
and my people will be filled with my bounty,"
declares the LORD.

[15] This is what the LORD says:
"A voice is heard in Ramah,
mourning and great weeping,
Rachel weeping for her children
and refusing to be comforted,
because her children are no more."

[16] This is what the LORD says:
"Restrain your voice from weeping
and your eyes from tears,
for your work will be rewarded,"
declares the LORD.
"They will return from the land of the enemy.
[17] So there is hope for your future,"
declares the LORD.
"Your children will return to their own land.

[18] "I have surely heard Ephraim's moaning:
'You disciplined me like an unruly calf,
and I have been disciplined.
Restore me, and I will return,
because you are the LORD my God.
[19] After I strayed,
I repented;
after I came to understand,
I beat my breast.
I was ashamed and humiliated
because I bore the disgrace of my youth.'
[20] Is not Ephraim my dear son,
the child in whom I delight?
Though I often speak against him,
I still remember him.
Therefore my heart yearns for him;
I have great compassion for him,"
declares the LORD.

[21] "Set up road signs;
put up guideposts.
Take note of the highway,
the road that you take.

31:14 *satisfy the priests with abundance:* Priests were to take a portion of the choice meats and grains brought by the people to be offered as sacrifices (Lev 7:7-10; Lev 27:30; Deut 14:22-29).

31:15 *in Ramah . . . Rachel weeping:* Rachel was one of the wives of Jacob and the mother of Joseph and Benjamin (Gen 30:22-24; 35:16-19). She was buried near Ramah, a village to the north of Jerusalem (Gen 35:20; 1 Sam 10:2). Rachel's spirit weeps from the grave for her descendants, but God tells her that the people of these tribes will come back to her.

31:18 *disciplined me like an unruly calf . . . Restore me:* Wild bulls or oxen had to be broken (tamed) in order to be used as work animals. Israel acted like an unruly calf, but the LORD tamed them by disciplining them. And now, like the prodigal son (Luke 15:17-19), the people of Israel want to come home, so they admit their sin and beg for God's forgiveness.

31:20 *my dear son . . . I have great compassion:* God loves Rachel's children as strongly as their mother does. God is attached to the child (Israel) with unbreakable bonds of love. See also the note at 30:18.

31:21 *road signs . . . guideposts:* The first people who leave Babylon will set up signs and guideposts on the road leading back home to Israel so that others can more easily find their way back.

31:13 Isa 35:10. **31:15** Matt 2:18.

31:22 *create a new thing on earth:* This may be a reference to the age of peace promised by the prophet Isaiah (Isa 11:6-9).

31:23 *LORD Almighty . . . sacred mountain:* See the notes at 2:19 and 3:14.

31:23 *bring them back from captivity . . . Judah:* See the note at 31:8, 9. Now the message turns to the restoration of Judah (the southern kingdom).

31:28 *to uproot . . . to plant:* Judah's people were uprooted and taken into exile (see the notes at 4:16; 24:1). But God will replant the people in Judah (see the note at 31:8, 9).

31:29 *sour grapes:* In ancient times, children were thought to suffer because of their parents' evil actions. Applied to the situation in Judah and Israel, innocent children did suffer because of the disobedience of adults. But this new day for Israel means a new way of looking at sin: Children cannot suffer for the sins of their parents, and the nation will not be punished for the sins of earlier generations (see Ezek 18:2, 3; also Deut 24:16).

31:31 *a new covenant:* This is the high point of Jeremiah's message. God's new covenant with the people of Israel and Judah will not replace the earlier covenant made with Moses (see the note at 11:1-5), which the people broke. In the new covenant, God will write the laws directly on the hearts and minds of the people. The people will obey the LORD because they will realize that it is for their own good (32:39-41). They will understand that simply following rituals is not enough (see the note at 9:25, 26, circumcised). Also, in this new covenant, God will forgive and forget sins. See also 32:37-42; Hos 2:16-20; Heb 8:7-12; 10:16, 17, and the mini-article called Covenants (Agreements)," p. 386.

31:25 Isa 40:29-31.

Return, O Virgin Israel,
return to your towns.
22 How long will you wander,
O unfaithful daughter?
The LORD will create a new thing on earth—
a woman will surround[a] a man."

23 This is what the LORD Almighty, the God of Israel, says:
"When I bring them back from captivity,[b] the people in the land of
Judah and in its towns will once again use these words: 'The LORD
bless you, O righteous dwelling, O sacred mountain.' 24 People will
live together in Judah and all its towns—farmers and those who
move about with their flocks. 25 I will refresh the weary and satisfy
the faint."

26 At this I awoke and looked around. My sleep had been
pleasant to me.

27 "The days are coming," declares the LORD, "when I will
plant the house of Israel and the house of Judah with the offspring
of men and of animals. 28 Just as I watched over them to uproot
and tear down, and to overthrow, destroy and bring disaster, so I
will watch over them to build and to plant," declares the LORD.
29 "In those days people will no longer say,

'The fathers have eaten sour grapes,
and the children's teeth are set on edge.'

30 Instead, everyone will die for his own sin; whoever eats sour
grapes—his own teeth will be set on edge.

31 "The time is coming," declares the LORD,
"when I will make a new covenant
with the house of Israel
and with the house of Judah.
32 It will not be like the covenant
I made with their forefathers
when I took them by the hand
to lead them out of Egypt,
because they broke my covenant,
though I was a husband to[c] them,[d]"
declares the LORD.
33 "This is the covenant I will make with the house of Israel
after that time," declares the LORD.
"I will put my law in their minds
and write it on their hearts.
I will be their God,
and they will be my people.

[a]22 Or *will go about ⌊seeking⌋;* or *will protect* [b]23 Or *I restore their fortunes*
[c]32 Hebrew; Septuagint and Syriac / *and I turned away from* [d]32 Or *was their master*

[34]No longer will a man teach his neighbor,
or a man his brother, saying, 'Know the LORD,'
because they will all know me,
from the least of them to the greatest,"
declares the LORD.
"For I will forgive their wickedness
and will remember their sins no more."

[35]This is what the LORD says,

he who appoints the sun
to shine by day,
who decrees the moon and stars
to shine by night,
who stirs up the sea
so that its waves roar—
the LORD Almighty is his name:
[36]"Only if these decrees vanish from my sight,"
declares the LORD,
"will the descendants of Israel ever cease
to be a nation before me."

[37]This is what the LORD says:

"Only if the heavens above can be measured
and the foundations of the earth below be
searched out
will I reject all the descendants of Israel
because of all they have done,"
declares the LORD.

[38]"The days are coming," declares the LORD, "when this city
will be rebuilt for me from the Tower of Hananel to the Corner
Gate. [39]The measuring line will stretch from there straight to the
hill of Gareb and then turn to Goah. [40]The whole valley where
dead bodies and ashes are thrown, and all the terraces out to the
Kidron Valley on the east as far as the corner of the Horse Gate,
will be holy to the LORD. The city will never again be uprooted or
demolished."

Jeremiah Buys a Field

32 This is the word that came to Jeremiah from the LORD in the
tenth year of Zedekiah king of Judah, which was the eighteenth
year of Nebuchadnezzar. [2]The army of the king of Babylon was
then besieging Jerusalem, and Jeremiah the prophet was confined
in the courtyard of the guard in the royal palace of Judah.

[3]Now Zedekiah king of Judah had imprisoned him there,
saying, "Why do you prophesy as you do? You say, 'This is what the
LORD says: I am about to hand this city over to the king of Babylon, and he will capture it. [4]Zedekiah king of Judah will not

31:35,36 *appoints the sun . . . Only if these decrees vanish:* Just as God controls nature and makes sure the cycle of days and nights continues, so God will ensure Israel's future (see also 33:20, 25).

31:38-40 *Tower of Hananel . . . Horse Gate:* The Tower of Hananel was at the northeast corner of the city; Corner Gate was at the northwest. The hill of Gareb and Goah probably indicate the southwest and southeast corners. The valley of "dead bodies and ashes" refers to the Valley of Ben Hinnom outside the city (see the note at 2:23, valley). The Kidron Valley was on the city's eastern border; the Horse Gate was at the southeast corner of the city. See the map on p. 2466.

32:1-3 *the tenth year . . . Jeremiah . . . imprisoned:* The date is early in 587 B.C., and Jerusalem is surrounded by the Babylonian army (2 Kgs 25:1-7). Nebuchadnezzar invaded Judah a second time, because Zedekiah had participated in a rebellion against Babylon. Zedekiah had Jeremiah arrested because he had predicted that Babylon would conquer Jerusalem (see 21:3-10; 34:2-5). The action in this chapter actually should come after 37:11-21 where Jeremiah is arrested.

32:7 *Anathoth:* See the note at 1:1.

32:7 *Buy my field . . . nearest relative:* When a person was forced to sell land to pay a debt, the law required family members to have the first right to purchase or refuse the land (see Lev 25:25-32; Ruth 4:1-6). Jeremiah's cousin is selling at a terrible time. Why would anyone be so foolish as to invest in real estate near Jerusalem in 587 B.C. when the Babylonians might steal the land at any moment?

32:9-11 *seventeen shekels of silver . . . sealed copy:* An ancient business transaction is described. The silver pieces were not coins, but bars or rings known as shekels, which weighed about four-tenths of an ounce each. Two copies of the bill of sale were made and signed, probably on papyrus sheets (see the note at 30:2). Then one copy was rolled, tied, and sealed with hot wax. A carved clay stamp (called a "seal") or a signet ring was pressed into the hot wax, leaving the initials or personal symbol of the buyer and seller. The second copy was left unsealed, so it could be read more easily later.

32:12 *Baruch:* Baruch was Jeremiah's friend and secretary (see chapter 36). Baruch wrote down everything, both the messages from the LORD (36:1-32) and the stories about Jeremiah's life in Judah and Egypt.

32:14 *put them in a clay jar:* Certain items could be kept safe and would not decay in a sealed clay jar. In 1949, jars discovered in caves at Qumran in Palestine were found to contain readable scrolls dating back about 1900 years to the first century A.D. See the photograph on p. 933.

32:15 *fields . . . will again be bought in this land:* Jeremiah's purchase of land at such an unsettled time was a symbol of God's promise (32:43, 44) and a sign of hope for Judah's future.

escape out of the hands of the Babylonians[a] but will certainly be
handed over to the king of Babylon, and will speak with him face
to face and see him with his own eyes. 5He will take Zedekiah to
Babylon, where he will remain until I deal with him, declares the
LORD. If you fight against the Babylonians, you will not succeed.' "

6Jeremiah said, "The word of the LORD came to me: 7Han-
amel son of Shallum your uncle is going to come to you and say,
'Buy my field at Anathoth, because as nearest relative it is your
right and duty to buy it.'

8"Then, just as the LORD had said, my cousin Hanamel came
to me in the courtyard of the guard and said, 'Buy my field at
Anathoth in the territory of Benjamin. Since it is your right to
redeem it and possess it, buy it for yourself.'

"I knew that this was the word of the LORD; 9so I bought the
field at Anathoth from my cousin Hanamel and weighed out for
him seventeen shekels[b] of silver. 10I signed and sealed the deed, had
it witnessed, and weighed out the silver on the scales. 11I took the
deed of purchase—the sealed copy containing the terms and conditions, as well as the unsealed copy— 12and I gave this deed to
Baruch son of Neriah, the son of Mahseiah, in the presence of my
cousin Hanamel and of the witnesses who had signed the deed and
of all the Jews sitting in the courtyard of the guard.

13"In their presence I gave Baruch these instructions: 14"This
is what the LORD Almighty, the God of Israel, says: Take these documents, both the sealed and unsealed copies of the deed of purchase, and put them in a clay jar so they will last a long time. 15For
this is what the LORD Almighty, the God of Israel, says: Houses,
fields and vineyards will again be bought in this land.'

16"After I had given the deed of purchase to Baruch son of
Neriah, I prayed to the LORD:

17"Ah, Sovereign LORD, you have made the heavens and the
earth by your great power and outstretched arm. Nothing is
too hard for you. 18You show love to thousands but bring the
punishment for the fathers' sins into the laps of their children
after them. O great and powerful God, whose name is the
LORD Almighty, 19great are your purposes and mighty are your
deeds. Your eyes are open to all the ways of men; you reward
everyone according to his conduct and as his deeds deserve.
20You performed miraculous signs and wonders in Egypt and
have continued them to this day, both in Israel and among all
mankind, and have gained the renown that is still yours. 21You
brought your people Israel out of Egypt with signs and wonders, by a mighty hand and an outstretched arm and with
great terror. 22You gave them this land you had sworn to give

[a]4 Or *Chaldeans*; also in verses 5, 24, 25, 28, 29 and 43 [b]9 That is, about 7 ounces (about 200 grams)

their forefathers, a land flowing with milk and honey. [23]They
came in and took possession of it, but they did not obey you
or follow your law; they did not do what you commanded
them to do. So you brought all this disaster upon them.

[24]"See how the siege ramps are built up to take the city.
Because of the sword, famine and plague, the city will be
handed over to the Babylonians who are attacking it. What
you said has happened, as you now see. [25]And though the city
will be handed over to the Babylonians, you, O Sovereign
LORD, say to me, 'Buy the field with silver and have the transaction witnessed.' "

[26]Then the word of the LORD came to Jeremiah: [27]"I am the
LORD, the God of all mankind. Is anything too hard for me? [28]There-
fore, this is what the LORD says: I am about to hand this city over to
the Babylonians and to Nebuchadnezzar king of Babylon, who will
capture it. [29]The Babylonians who are attacking this city will come in
and set it on fire; they will burn it down, along with the houses
where the people provoked me to anger by burning incense on the
roofs to Baal and by pouring out drink offerings to other gods.

[30]"The people of Israel and Judah have done nothing but evil
in my sight from their youth; indeed, the people of Israel have
done nothing but provoke me with what their hands have made,
declares the LORD. [31]From the day it was built until now, this city
has so aroused my anger and wrath that I must remove it from my
sight. [32]The people of Israel and Judah have provoked me by all the
evil they have done—they, their kings and officials, their priests
and prophets, the men of Judah and the people of Jerusalem.
[33]They turned their backs to me and not their faces; though I
taught them again and again, they would not listen or respond to
discipline. [34]They set up their abominable idols in the house that
bears my Name and defiled it. [35]They built high places for Baal in
the Valley of Ben Hinnom to sacrifice their sons and daughters[a] to
Molech, though I never commanded, nor did it enter my mind,
that they should do such a detestable thing and so make Judah sin.

[36]"You are saying about this city, 'By the sword, famine and
plague it will be handed over to the king of Babylon'; but this is
what the LORD, the God of Israel, says: [37]I will surely gather them
from all the lands where I banish them in my furious anger and
great wrath; I will bring them back to this place and let them live
in safety. [38]They will be my people, and I will be their God. [39]I will
give them singleness of heart and action, so that they will always
fear me for their own good and the good of their children after
them. [40]I will make an everlasting covenant with them: I will never
stop doing good to them, and I will inspire them to fear me, so
that they will never turn away from me. [41]I will rejoice in doing

32:17-19 *outstretched arm . . . Your eyes are open:* See the note at 21:5. Jeremiah's prayer first points to God's power (10:12-16; 27:5). Nothing is hidden from God (Ps 139:1-16; Jer 17:10), so God's rewards and punishments are always correct.

32:20-23 *performed miraculous signs . . . in Egypt . . . they did not obey you:* Though the LORD God saved the people of Israel from slavery in Egypt and gave them the rich land of Canaan, the people did not obey God or remain faithful to him alone. See the note at 23:13, 14.

32:24,25 *siege ramps . . . Buy the field:* With Jerusalem under attack, Jeremiah wonders if he can really believe God's promise that things will return to normal in Judah in the future.

32:28 *Nebuchadnezzar . . . capture it:* See 2 Kgs 25:1-11; 2 Chr 36:17-21; and the notes at 21:2 and 27:6.

32:29 *burning incense on the roofs to Baal:* Houses in ancient Israel were often made with flat roofs. Some people went up on their roofs to make sacrifices and burn incense to honor Baal with the hope that they could please him. See the notes at 2:8; 3:23,24 and 6:20.

32:34,35 *idols in the house that bears my Name . . . Molech:* See 7:30, 31; 19:1-6; and the note at 7:31.

32:36,37 *famine and plague . . . banish them:* The people were starving and sick, because the Babylonian army had surrounded the city for months (see the note at 4:16).

32:38-41 *They will be my people, and I will be their God . . . everlasting covenant:* See 30:22; 31:1, 33 and the note at 31:31. See also Ezek 16:60-63; 37:26-28.

---

[a]35 Or *to make their sons and daughters pass through ⌞the fire⌟*

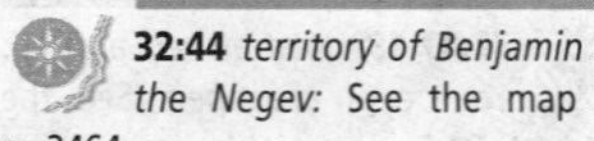

32:44 *territory of Benjamin . . . the Negev:* See the map on p. 2464.

33:1 *confined in the courtyard:* See 32:1-3 and note. Jeremiah is still imprisoned at Zedekiah's palace in Jerusalem. The destruction of Jerusalem is close at hand.

33:4 *houses . . . have been torn down:* Some houses and buildings on the palace grounds have been demolished and used for barricades and to plug gaps in the wall. Perhaps the Babylonian army has actually started to break through the outer walls of the city. See also Isa 22:8-10.

33:5,6 *I will slay . . . I will heal:* The destruction predicted in 21:3-7 and 37:6-10 is about to take place, but the LORD will not allow this destruction to be the last word. The LORD will eventually heal the people by forgiving them and heal the city by rebuilding it (31:31-40; 46:27, 28).

33:9 *all nations . . . tremble:* The destruction of Jerusalem will lead to Israel's enemies insulting and making fun of the LORD and his people (8:19; 33:24). But when the LORD helps the people of Judah rebuild their land and gives them prosperity and peace, other nations will have respect for Israel's God.

33:10,11 *desolate waste . . . restore the fortunes:* Verse 11 promises a reversal of the total destruction predicted in 7:34. The uninhabited places will one day be the sites for joyful occasions and grateful worship, and the land will once again produce crops.

33:11 1 Chr 16:34; 2 Chr 5:13; 7:3; Ezra 3:11; Ps 100:5; 106:1; 107:1; 118:1; 136:1.

them good and will assuredly plant them in this land with all my
heart and soul.
42“This is what the LORD says: As I have brought all this great
calamity on this people, so I will give them all the prosperity I have
promised them. 43Once more fields will be bought in this land of
which you say, ‘It is a desolate waste, without men or animals, for
it has been handed over to the Babylonians.’ 44Fields will be bought
for silver, and deeds will be signed, sealed and witnessed in the territory of Benjamin, in the villages around Jerusalem, in the towns
of Judah and in the towns of the hill country, of the western
foothills and of the Negev, because I will restore their fortunes,[a]
declares the LORD.”

Promise of Restoration

33 While Jeremiah was still confined in the courtyard of the
guard, the word of the LORD came to him a second time: 2“This is
what the LORD says, he who made the earth, the LORD who formed
it and established it—the LORD is his name: 3‘Call to me and I will
answer you and tell you great and unsearchable things you do not
know.’ 4For this is what the LORD, the God of Israel, says about the
houses in this city and the royal palaces of Judah that have been
torn down to be used against the siege ramps and the sword 5in
the fight with the Babylonians[b]: ‘They will be filled with the dead
bodies of the men I will slay in my anger and wrath. I will hide my
face from this city because of all its wickedness.
6“ ‘Nevertheless, I will bring health and healing to it; I will
heal my people and will let them enjoy abundant peace and security. 7I will bring Judah and Israel back from captivity[c] and will
rebuild them as they were before. 8I will cleanse them from all the
sin they have committed against me and will forgive all their sins
of rebellion against me. 9Then this city will bring me renown, joy,
praise and honor before all nations on earth that hear of all the
good things I do for it; and they will be in awe and will tremble at
the abundant prosperity and peace I provide for it.’
10“This is what the LORD says: ‘You say about this place, “It is
a desolate waste, without men or animals.” Yet in the towns of
Judah and the streets of Jerusalem that are deserted, inhabited by
neither men nor animals, there will be heard once more 11the
sounds of joy and gladness, the voices of bride and bridegroom,
and the voices of those who bring thank offerings to the house of
the LORD, saying,

“Give thanks to the LORD Almighty,
for the LORD is good;
his love endures forever.”

[a]44 Or *will bring them back from captivity* [b]5 Or *Chaldeans* [c]7 Or *will restore the fortunes of Judah and Israel*

For I will restore the fortunes of the land as they were before,' says
the LORD.
12"This is what the LORD Almighty says: 'In this place, desolate and without men or animals—in all its towns there will again
be pastures for shepherds to rest their flocks. 13In the towns of the
hill country, of the western foothills and of the Negev, in the territory of Benjamin, in the villages around Jerusalem and in the
towns of Judah, flocks will again pass under the hand of the one
who counts them,' says the LORD.
14" 'The days are coming,' declares the LORD, 'when I will fulfill the gracious promise I made to the house of Israel and to the
house of Judah.

15" 'In those days and at that time
I will make a righteous Branch sprout from David's line;
he will do what is just and right in the land.
16In those days Judah will be saved
and Jerusalem will live in safety.
This is the name by which it[a] will be called:
The LORD Our Righteousness.'

17For this is what the LORD says: 'David will never fail to have a
man to sit on the throne of the house of Israel, 18nor will the
priests, who are Levites, ever fail to have a man to stand before me
continually to offer burnt offerings, to burn grain offerings and to
present sacrifices.' "
19The word of the LORD came to Jeremiah: 20"This is what the
LORD says: 'If you can break my covenant with the day and my
covenant with the night, so that day and night no longer come at
their appointed time, 21then my covenant with David my servant—
and my covenant with the Levites who are priests ministering

[a]16 Or *he*

33:13 *towns of the hill country:* For the locations in these verses, see the map on p. 2464.

33:15 *righteous Branch sprout from David's line:* See the note at 23:5 and Isa 11:1-9.

33:16 *The LORD Our Righteousness:* Jerusalem is given a new name that emphasizes its concern for fair treatment of all people, especially the poor and homeless.

33:18 *Levites . . . offerings . . . sacrifices:* Levi was the son of Jacob and Leah (Gen 29:34). His descendants became the proper family line for Israel's priests (Num 3:5-10). See also the mini-article called "Israel's Priests," p. 2344. See also the note at 14:12.

33:21 *covenant with David . . . Levites:* The covenant made with David (2 Sam 7) and with the true priests (Deut 8:1-5) will never again be broken. The promise of many descendants in 33:22 echoes the covenant the LORD made with Abraham (Gen 15:5; Gen 22:17). See the mini-article called "Covenants (Agreements)," p. 386.

33:17 2 Sam 7:12-16; 1 Kgs 2:4; 9:5; 1 Chr 17:11-14.

QUESTIONS ABOUT JEREMIAH 30:1—33:26

1. Israel is described as God's "firstborn son" in 31:9, and in Exodus 4:22. What does this mean for Israel? What are the advantages of being the firstborn child in a family? The disadvantages? What responsibilities often come with being the oldest child?
2. Compare 31:19 with the words of the prodigal son in Luke 15:17-19. In what ways is Israel like the prodigal son? How is God like the father in Luke's story?
3. What is "new" about the new covenant in 31:31-34?
4. Imagine you are one of the witnesses to the sale of land in 32:1-14. How would you report this business transaction to someone else? What would you say about its timing? About Jeremiah?
5. Chapters 30–33 are full of remarkable and wonderful promises made to the people by God. What words of comfort do you think the exiled people would most cherish? What promises do you find most significant? Most comforting? Why?

before me—can be broken and David will no longer have a descendant to reign on his throne. [22]I will make the descendants of
David my servant and the Levites who minister before me as countless as the stars of the sky and as measureless as the sand on the
seashore.' "
[23]The word of the LORD came to Jeremiah: [24]"Have you not
noticed that these people are saying, 'The LORD has rejected the
two kingdoms[a] he chose'? So they despise my people and no longer
regard them as a nation. [25]This is what the LORD says: 'If I have not
established my covenant with day and night and the fixed laws of
heaven and earth, [26]then I will reject the descendants of Jacob and
David my servant and will not choose one of his sons to rule over
the descendants of Abraham, Isaac and Jacob. For I will restore
their fortunes[b] and have compassion on them.' "

Disaster for Judah and Jerusalem

This long section (chapters 34–44) includes scenes from Jeremiah's ministry before the fall of Jerusalem and the tragic story of the fall itself. It ends with Jeremiah in Egypt, among the exiles.

SCENES FROM JEREMIAH'S MINISTRY

Jeremiah and his message are attacked by people in power. He ends up in prison on the eve of the Babylonian attack of his beloved city, Jerusalem. Note that chapters 32 and 33 actually happen after Jeremiah is already imprisoned.

Warning to Zedekiah

34 While Nebuchadnezzar king of Babylon and all his army and
all the kingdoms and peoples in the empire he ruled were fighting
against Jerusalem and all its surrounding towns, this word came to
Jeremiah from the LORD: [2]"This is what the LORD, the God of Israel, says: Go to Zedekiah king of Judah and tell him, 'This is what
the LORD says: I am about to hand this city over to the king of
Babylon, and he will burn it down. [3]You will not escape from his
grasp but will surely be captured and handed over to him. You will
see the king of Babylon with your own eyes, and he will speak with
you face to face. And you will go to Babylon.
[4]" 'Yet hear the promise of the LORD, O Zedekiah king of
Judah. This is what the LORD says concerning you: You will not die
by the sword; [5]you will die peacefully. As people made a funeral
fire in honor of your fathers, the former kings who preceded you,
so they will make a fire in your honor and lament, "Alas, O master!" I myself make this promise, declares the LORD.' "
[6]Then Jeremiah the prophet told all this to Zedekiah king of

[a]24 Or *families* [b]26 Or *will bring them back from captivity*

33:26 *the descendants of Abraham, Isaac and Jacob:* The eternal promises are applied to all the people of Israel who descended from Abraham, his son Isaac, and his grandson Jacob (see the note at 31:1).

34:1,2 *Nebuchadnezzar . . . Zedekiah:* See the notes at 4:16 and 21:1. The date is late 588 B.C. and Zedekiah has already participated in a rebellion against the Babylonians (see the notes at 24:5-8 and 27:3). Nebuchadnezzar responded by sending his army to surround Jerusalem and destroy many neighboring towns. See also 2 Kgs 25:1-11; 2 Chr 36:17-21.

34:4 *You will not die by the sword:* Zedekiah is promised a peaceful death and a funeral fit for a king if he surrenders. But Zedekiah did not surrender, and he tried to sneak away before Jerusalem fell. He was captured, and sent to prison in Babylon where he died (52:6-11).

33:24 Jer 44:8; Hos 8:8; Joel 2:17.

Judah, in Jerusalem, [7]while the army of the king of Babylon was
fighting against Jerusalem and the other cities of Judah that were
still holding out—Lachish and Azekah. These were the only fortified cities left in Judah.

Freedom for Slaves

[8]The word came to Jeremiah from the LORD after King
Zedekiah had made a covenant with all the people in Jerusalem to
proclaim freedom for the slaves. [9]Everyone was to free his Hebrew
slaves, both male and female; no one was to hold a fellow Jew in
bondage. [10]So all the officials and people who entered into this
covenant agreed that they would free their male and female slaves
and no longer hold them in bondage. They agreed, and set them
free. [11]But afterward they changed their minds and took back the
slaves they had freed and enslaved them again.

[12]Then the word of the LORD came to Jeremiah: [13]"This is
what the LORD, the God of Israel, says: I made a covenant with
your forefathers when I brought them out of Egypt, out of the
land of slavery. I said, [14]'Every seventh year each of you must free
any fellow Hebrew who has sold himself to you. After he has
served you six years, you must let him go free.'[a] Your fathers, however, did not listen to me or pay attention to me. [15]Recently you
repented and did what is right in my sight: Each of you proclaimed freedom to his countrymen. You even made a covenant
before me in the house that bears my Name. [16]But now you have
turned around and profaned my name; each of you has taken back
the male and female slaves you had set free to go where they
wished. You have forced them to become your slaves again.

[17]"Therefore, this is what the LORD says: You have not
obeyed me; you have not proclaimed freedom for your fellow
countrymen. So I now proclaim 'freedom' for you, declares the
LORD—'freedom' to fall by the sword, plague and famine. I will
make you abhorrent to all the kingdoms of the earth. [18]The men
who have violated my covenant and have not fulfilled the terms of
the covenant they made before me, I will treat like the calf they
cut in two and then walked between its pieces. [19]The leaders of
Judah and Jerusalem, the court officials, the priests and all the
people of the land who walked between the pieces of the calf, [20]I
will hand over to their enemies who seek their lives. Their dead
bodies will become food for the birds of the air and the beasts of
the earth.

[21]"I will hand Zedekiah king of Judah and his officials over
to their enemies who seek their lives, to the army of the king of
Babylon, which has withdrawn from you. [22]I am going to give the
order, declares the LORD, and I will bring them back to this city.

---

[a]**14** Deut. 15:12

34:7 *Lachish and Azekah:* See the map on p. 2467. A broken piece of pottery dated just before the fall of Jerusalem was discovered in the outer gate tower at Lachish. On the pottery is a message from a town official named Hoshaiah to Yaosh, the military commander of Lachish. The message reads: "We are watching for the smoke signals of Lachish . . . because we do not see Azekah." No signal from Azekah probably meant the city had been captured. Both cities did fall to the Babylonians.

34:9 *free his Hebrew slaves:* "Hebrew" is an earlier term for Israelite and Jewish. The law called for the release of Hebrew slaves after six years of service (Exod 21:2; Deut 15:12; also Jer 34:14). It is not clear if Zedekiah called for the release of all slaves, or if he was enforcing the law that was being ignored by slave owners (see 34:11-16). Most likely the slaves were freed in order to make more people available to defend the city.

34:11 *changed their minds . . . took back the slaves:* Zedekiah may have made a covenant to free Hebrew slaves (34:8-10) in order to please the LORD. The Egyptian army marched east in 588 B.C., so Nebuchadnezzar had to stop his attack on Jerusalem to fight the Egyptians. Thinking that their Egyptian allies would save them and that the crisis had passed, the slave owners took the freed slaves back.

34:18 *covenant . . . calf they cut in two . . . walked between:* The ceremony involved cutting a calf in two and walking between the two parts to make a lasting covenant (see Gen 15:7-17). The point of the ceremony was to say: "May God do to me as has been done to this calf if I break the terms of this covenant."

34:21,22 *army . . . of Babylon . . . bring them back to this city:* The Egyptians pulled back, so the Babylonian army once again surrounded Jerusalem in January 587 B.C.

35:1 *during the reign of Jehoiakim:* The book now goes back in time to the last year of Jehoiakim's reign (598 B.C.) when the Babylonians first invaded Judah (see 35:11). The faithful Recabite clan (35:1-19) provides a clear contrast to the story of the unfaithful people of Judah in chapter 34.

35:2 *side rooms:* See the diagram of Solomon's temple on p. 942.

35:4 *Maaseiah:* Perhaps the father of Zephaniah (21:1) who held an important priestly office.

35:5 *the Recabite family . . . wine:* The Recabite clan descended from Jonadab, son of Recab. Jonadab's descendants followed his rules for living a simple shepherd life. They refused to drink wine, plant crops, or live in permanent houses. Instead, they wandered about with their herds and lived in tents, ready to move at God's command.

35:6 *Jonadab son of Recab:* This founder of the Recabite clan helped King Jehu kill the wicked descendants of Israel's King Ahab around 840 B.C. (see 2 Kgs 10:15-23).

35:11 *we must go to Jerusalem to escape:* The Recabites refused Jeremiah's wine, but they feel they must explain why they are living in the city, which also went against their clan rules. They are in Jerusalem because Nebuchadnezzar's army is taking over the countryside (see also 2 Kgs 23:36—24:6; 2 Chr 36:5-7).

35:13-16 *learn a lesson . . . descendants of Jonadab . . . carried out the command:* The point is not to become a Recabite (Jeremiah certainly was not one), but to be faithful to one's vows. It has been over two centuries since Jonadab's day, yet the Recabites have remained obedient. While they are faithful, Judah is not. Jeremiah's warning about disobedience fits equally well in 598 B.C. as it does later in 586 B.C.

They will fight against it, take it and burn it down. And I will lay
waste the towns of Judah so no one can live there."

The Recabites

35 This is the word that came to Jeremiah from the LORD during the reign of Jehoiakim son of Josiah king of Judah: 2"Go to the
Recabite family and invite them to come to one of the side rooms
of the house of the LORD and give them wine to drink."

3So I went to get Jaazaniah son of Jeremiah, the son of
Habazziniah, and his brothers and all his sons—the whole family
of the Recabites. 4I brought them into the house of the LORD, into
the room of the sons of Hanan son of Igdaliah the man of God. It
was next to the room of the officials, which was over that of Maaseiah son of Shallum the doorkeeper. 5Then I set bowls full of wine
and some cups before the men of the Recabite family and said to
them, "Drink some wine."

6But they replied, "We do not drink wine, because our forefather Jonadab son of Recab gave us this command: 'Neither you
nor your descendants must ever drink wine. 7Also you must never
build houses, sow seed or plant vineyards; you must never have
any of these things, but must always live in tents. Then you will live
a long time in the land where you are nomads.' 8We have obeyed
everything our forefather Jonadab son of Recab commanded us.
Neither we nor our wives nor our sons and daughters have ever
drunk wine 9or built houses to live in or had vineyards, fields or
crops. 10We have lived in tents and have fully obeyed everything
our forefather Jonadab commanded us. 11But when Nebuchadnezzar king of Babylon invaded this land, we said, 'Come, we must go
to Jerusalem to escape the Babylonian[a] and Aramean armies.' So
we have remained in Jerusalem."

12Then the word of the LORD came to Jeremiah, saying: 13"This
is what the LORD Almighty, the God of Israel, says: Go and tell the
men of Judah and the people of Jerusalem, 'Will you not learn a lesson and obey my words?' declares the LORD. 14'Jonadab son of Recab
ordered his sons not to drink wine and this command has been kept.
To this day they do not drink wine, because they obey their forefather's command. But I have spoken to you again and again, yet you
have not obeyed me. 15Again and again I sent all my servants the
prophets to you. They said, "Each of you must turn from your
wicked ways and reform your actions; do not follow other gods to
serve them. Then you will live in the land I have given to you and
your fathers." But you have not paid attention or listened to me. 16The
descendants of Jonadab son of Recab have carried out the command
their forefather gave them, but these people have not obeyed me.'

17"Therefore, this is what the LORD God Almighty, the God

---

[a]**11** Or *Chaldean*

of Israel, says: 'Listen! I am going to bring on Judah and on everyone living in Jerusalem every disaster I pronounced against them.
I spoke to them, but they did not listen; I called to them, but they
did not answer.' "
18 Then Jeremiah said to the family of the Recabites, "This is
what the LORD Almighty, the God of Israel, says: 'You have obeyed
the command of your forefather Jonadab and have followed all his
instructions and have done everything he ordered.' 19 Therefore,
this is what the LORD Almighty, the God of Israel, says: 'Jonadab
son of Recab will never fail to have a man to serve me.' "

Jehoiakim Burns Jeremiah's Scroll

36 In the fourth year of Jehoiakim son of Josiah king of Judah,
this word came to Jeremiah from the LORD: 2 "Take a scroll and
write on it all the words I have spoken to you concerning Israel,
Judah and all the other nations from the time I began speaking to
you in the reign of Josiah till now. 3 Perhaps when the people of
Judah hear about every disaster I plan to inflict on them, each of
them will turn from his wicked way; then I will forgive their
wickedness and their sin."
4 So Jeremiah called Baruch son of Neriah, and while Jeremiah dictated all the words the LORD had spoken to him, Baruch
wrote them on the scroll. 5 Then Jeremiah told Baruch, "I am
restricted; I cannot go to the LORD's temple. 6 So you go to the
house of the LORD on a day of fasting and read to the people from
the scroll the words of the LORD that you wrote as I dictated. Read
them to all the people of Judah who come in from their towns.
7 Perhaps they will bring their petition before the LORD, and each
will turn from his wicked ways, for the anger and wrath pronounced against this people by the LORD are great."
8 Baruch son of Neriah did everything Jeremiah the prophet
told him to do; at the LORD's temple he read the words of the LORD
from the scroll. 9 In the ninth month of the fifth year of Jehoiakim
son of Josiah king of Judah, a time of fasting before the LORD was
proclaimed for all the people in Jerusalem and those who had
come from the towns of Judah. 10 From the room of Gemariah son
of Shaphan the secretary, which was in the upper courtyard at the
entrance of the New Gate of the temple, Baruch read to all the
people at the LORD's temple the words of Jeremiah from the scroll.
11 When Micaiah son of Gemariah, the son of Shaphan,
heard all the words of the LORD from the scroll, 12 he went down to
the secretary's room in the royal palace, where all the officials were
sitting: Elishama the secretary, Delaiah son of Shemaiah, Elnathan
son of Acbor, Gemariah son of Shaphan, Zedekiah son of Hananiah, and all the other officials. 13 After Micaiah told them everything
he had heard Baruch read to the people from the scroll, 14 all the
officials sent Jehudi son of Nethaniah, the son of Shelemiah, the
son of Cushi, to say to Baruch, "Bring the scroll from which you

35:18,19 *Recabites . . . serve me:* The faithfulness of the Recabites remains an example for future generations.

36:1 *fourth year . . . Jehoiakim:* The date is 605 B.C. See the notes at 1:2,3 and 3:6 and the Introduction to JEREMIAH, p. 1424. The events in this chapter follow the message of 25:1-14 and the events of chapter 26. See also 2 Kgs 24:1; 2 Chr 36:5-7; Dan 1:1,2.

36:2 *scroll:* See the note at 30:2. Since about 627 B.C., Jeremiah has been receiving and speaking the LORD's messages of judgment (see the note at 1:2,3).

36:4 *Baruch:* Jeremiah's friend and secretary (scribe) will read the scroll, because the prophet is not allowed to enter the temple courtyard (36:5; see also 26:1-24). Scribes were governmental officials responsible for keeping records on papyrus scrolls which were closed and marked with an official seal like the one shown here.

36:6 *day of fasting:* Fasting was done to honor God and when asking for God's help in times of public or private distress (Esth 4:15,16).

36:9 *ninth month . . . fifth year of Jehoiakim:* The ninth month of the Hebrew calendar is Chislev, which lasts from about mid-November to mid-December. The year is 604 B.C. (see the note at 36:1). It has been either three or nine months since the LORD told Jeremiah to produce the scroll (36:2).

36:10 *courtyard . . . New Gate of the temple:* See the note at 26:10.

have read to the people and come." So Baruch son of Neriah went to them with the scroll in his hand. 15They said to him, "Sit down, please, and read it to us."

So Baruch read it to them. 16When they heard all these words, they looked at each other in fear and said to Baruch, "We must report all these words to the king." 17Then they asked Baruch, "Tell us, how did you come to write all this? Did Jeremiah dictate it?"

18"Yes," Baruch replied, "he dictated all these words to me, and I wrote them in ink on the scroll."

19Then the officials said to Baruch, "You and Jeremiah, go and hide. Don't let anyone know where you are."

20After they put the scroll in the room of Elishama the secretary, they went to the king in the courtyard and reported everything to him. 21The king sent Jehudi to get the scroll, and Jehudi brought it from the room of Elishama the secretary and read it to the king and all the officials standing beside him. 22It was the ninth month and the king was sitting in the winter apartment, with a fire burning in the firepot in front of him. 23Whenever Jehudi had read three or four columns of the scroll, the king cut them off with a scribe's knife and threw them into the firepot, until the entire scroll was burned in the fire. 24The king and all his attendants who heard all these words showed no fear, nor did they tear their clothes. 25Even though Elnathan, Delaiah and Gemariah urged the king not to burn the scroll, he would not listen to them. 26Instead, the king commanded Jerahmeel, a son of the king, Seraiah son of Azriel and Shelemiah son of Abdeel to arrest Baruch the scribe and Jeremiah the prophet. But the LORD had hidden them.

27After the king burned the scroll containing the words that Baruch had written at Jeremiah's dictation, the word of the LORD came to Jeremiah: 28"Take another scroll and write on it all the words that were on the first scroll, which Jehoiakim king of Judah burned up. 29Also tell Jehoiakim king of Judah, 'This is what the LORD says: You burned that scroll and said, "Why did you write on it that the king of Babylon would certainly come and destroy this land and cut off both men and animals from it?" 30Therefore, this is what the LORD says about Jehoiakim king of Judah: He will have no one to sit on the throne of David; his body will be thrown out and exposed to the heat by day and the frost by night. 31I will punish him and his children and his attendants for their wickedness; I will bring on them and those living in Jerusalem and the people of Judah every disaster I pronounced against them, because they have not listened.' "

32So Jeremiah took another scroll and gave it to the scribe Baruch son of Neriah, and as Jeremiah dictated, Baruch wrote on it all the words of the scroll that Jehoiakim king of Judah had burned in the fire. And many similar words were added to them.

36:23-25 *Jehudi . . . knife . . . burn the scroll:* The first scroll is read a third time. Jehudi, probably one of the king's scribes, reads aloud to the king while the officials stand nearby.

36:23-25 *cut them off . . . tear their clothes:* The same Hebrew word is used for both "tear" and "cut." The king had the scroll "cut" to pieces, but he did not "tear" his clothes in distress, though this would have been the proper response to Jeremiah's message.

36:26 *arrest Baruch . . . Jeremiah:* King Jehoiakim had executed the prophet Uriah for his message (26:20-23). He likely would have executed Jeremiah as well if God, with human help (36:19), had not hidden him safely. Elnathan, the official that Jehoiakim sent to fetch Uriah back from Egypt to be executed, here finds the courage to speak against the king's actions (36:25).

36:27,28 *burned the scroll . . . Take another scroll:* See 36:2. This second scroll (36:32) will replace the first scroll, which was burned (36:23-25). It contains everything the first scroll contained, and more! The text of JEREMIAH grew from this second scroll dictated to Baruch.

36:30 *have no one to sit on the throne . . . body will be thrown out:* See the notes at 22:13-18; 22:24; and 22:30. See also 2 Kgs 24:8-15; 2 Chr 36:9, 10; Jer 52:31-34.

Jeremiah in Prison

37 Zedekiah son of Josiah was made king of Judah by Nebuchadnezzar king of Babylon; he reigned in place of Jehoiachin[a]
son of Jehoiakim. [2]Neither he nor his attendants nor the people of
the land paid any attention to the words the LORD had spoken
through Jeremiah the prophet.
[3]King Zedekiah, however, sent Jehucal son of Shelemiah with
the priest Zephaniah son of Maaseiah to Jeremiah the prophet
with this message: "Please pray to the LORD our God for us."
[4]Now Jeremiah was free to come and go among the people,
for he had not yet been put in prison. [5]Pharaoh's army had
marched out of Egypt, and when the Babylonians[b] who were
besieging Jerusalem heard the report about them, they withdrew
from Jerusalem.
[6]Then the word of the LORD came to Jeremiah the prophet:
[7]"This is what the LORD, the God of Israel, says: Tell the king of
Judah, who sent you to inquire of me, 'Pharaoh's army, which has
marched out to support you, will go back to its own land, to Egypt.
[8]Then the Babylonians will return and attack this city; they will
capture it and burn it down.'
[9]"This is what the LORD says: Do not deceive yourselves,
thinking, 'The Babylonians will surely leave us.' They will not!
[10]Even if you were to defeat the entire Babylonian[c] army that is
attacking you and only wounded men were left in their tents, they
would come out and burn this city down."
[11]After the Babylonian army had withdrawn from Jerusalem
because of Pharaoh's army, [12]Jeremiah started to leave the city to
go to the territory of Benjamin to get his share of the property
among the people there. [13]But when he reached the Benjamin
Gate, the captain of the guard, whose name was Irijah son of
Shelemiah, the son of Hananiah, arrested him and said, "You are
deserting to the Babylonians!"
[14]"That's not true!" Jeremiah said. "I am not deserting to the
Babylonians." But Irijah would not listen to him; instead, he arrested Jeremiah and brought him to the officials. [15]They were angry
with Jeremiah and had him beaten and imprisoned in the house of
Jonathan the secretary, which they had made into a prison.
[16]Jeremiah was put into a vaulted cell in a dungeon, where
he remained a long time. [17]Then King Zedekiah sent for him and
had him brought to the palace, where he asked him privately, "Is
there any word from the LORD?"
"Yes," Jeremiah replied, "you will be handed over to the king
of Babylon."
[18]Then Jeremiah said to King Zedekiah, "What crime have I
committed against you or your officials or this people, that you

37:1 *Zedekiah . . . Nebuchadnezzar:* See the Introduction to JEREMIAH, p. 1424 and the note at 21:2. After removing Jehoiachin, Nebuchadnezzar placed Zedekiah on Judah's throne as a puppet king in 598 B.C. (2 Kgs 24:10-17; 2 Chr 36:9-12).

37:3-5 *Zedekiah . . . Egypt:* Zedekiah broke his treaty with Nebuchadnezzar in 588 B.C., hoping for support from the new Egyptian king, Hophra (also known as Apries). Nebuchadnezzar immediately sent an army to surround Jerusalem. In the summer of 588 B.C. the Egyptian army started marching east, so Nebuchadnezzar pulled his troops away from Jerusalem to face the Egyptians. It was at this time that King Zedekiah sent messengers to Jeremiah. (See also 34:8-16 and notes).

37:3 *Jehucal . . . Zephaniah:* Jehucal also appears in 38:1-4, where he calls for a death sentence on Jeremiah. Zephaniah is the assistant to the chief priest (29:24,25; 52:24).

37:8 *Babylonians will return . . . burn it down:* While everyone else is hopeful, Jeremiah is not. The Babylonians will return, and this time they won't leave till they capture and destroy the city (see 39:1-14 and the note at 4:16).

37:12,13 *territory of Benjamin... Benjamin Gate:* Jeremiah's hometown of Anathoth was there (see the note at 1:1 and the map on p. 2464). Jeremiah's share of the family land is probably not the field he bought from a family member (32:1-15). The Benjamin Gate was in the north wall of Jerusalem.

[a]**1** Hebrew *Coniah,* a variant of *Jehoiachin* [b]**5** Or *Chaldeans*; also in verses 8, 9, 13 and 14 [c]**10** Or *Chaldean*; also in verse 11

have put me in prison? [19]Where are your prophets who prophesied to you, 'The king of Babylon will not attack you or this land'? [20]But now, my lord the king, please listen. Let me bring my petition before you: Do not send me back to the house of Jonathan the secretary, or I will die there."

[21]King Zedekiah then gave orders for Jeremiah to be placed in the courtyard of the guard and given bread from the street of the bakers each day until all the bread in the city was gone. So Jeremiah remained in the courtyard of the guard.

Jeremiah Thrown Into a Cistern

38 Shephatiah son of Mattan, Gedaliah son of Pashhur, Jehucal[a] son of Shelemiah, and Pashhur son of Malkijah heard what Jeremiah was telling all the people when he said, [2]"This is what the LORD says: 'Whoever stays in this city will die by the sword, famine or plague, but whoever goes over to the Babylonians[b] will live. He will escape with his life; he will live.' [3]And this is what the LORD says: 'This city will certainly be handed over to the army of the king of Babylon, who will capture it.' "

[4]Then the officials said to the king, "This man should be put to death. He is discouraging the soldiers who are left in this city, as well as all the people, by the things he is saying to them. This man is not seeking the good of these people but their ruin."

[5]"He is in your hands," King Zedekiah answered. "The king can do nothing to oppose you."

[6]So they took Jeremiah and put him into the cistern of Malkijah, the king's son, which was in the courtyard of the guard. They lowered Jeremiah by ropes into the cistern; it had no water in it, only mud, and Jeremiah sank down into the mud.

[7]But Ebed-Melech, a Cushite,[c] an official[d] in the royal palace, heard that they had put Jeremiah into the cistern. While the king was sitting in the Benjamin Gate, [8]Ebed-Melech went out of the palace and said to him, [9]"My lord the king, these men have acted wickedly in all they have done to Jeremiah the prophet. They have thrown him into a cistern, where he will starve to death when there is no longer any bread in the city."

[10]Then the king commanded Ebed-Melech the Cushite, "Take thirty men from here with you and lift Jeremiah the prophet out of the cistern before he dies."

[11]So Ebed-Melech took the men with him and went to a room under the treasury in the palace. He took some old rags and worn-out clothes from there and let them down with ropes to Jeremiah in the cistern. [12]Ebed-Melech the Cushite said to Jeremiah, "Put these old rags and worn-out clothes under your arms to pad the ropes." Jeremiah did so, [13]and they pulled him up with the

[a]1 Hebrew *Jucal,* a variant of *Jehucal* [b]2 Or *Chaldeans;* also in verses 18, 19 and 23 [c]7 Probably from the upper Nile region [d]7 Or *a eunuch*

37:21 *courtyard of the guard . . . given bread:* The palace prison cells were not as bad as the dungeon in Jonathan's house, where he surely would have died (37:20). This house arrest was the setting of 32:1-15. During this time of emergency in Jerusalem, Jeremiah probably received the same amount of food that everyone else in the city received each day.

38:1 *Shephatiah . . . Pashhur:* This is a very different group than the officials who supported Jeremiah in the time of Jehoiakim (36:11-19, 23-25). The earlier group probably had been forced to leave Jerusalem during the first exile of 598 B.C. What was left in Jerusalem were the "poor figs" (see 24:5-8 and note), men who hated Jeremiah and disregarded his message from the LORD. King Zedekiah was unable to stop their plot against Jeremiah (38:5).

38:5 *The king can do nothing:* Nebuchadnezzar placed this puppet king on the throne in 598 B.C., probably because he knew Zedekiah was a weak leader and able to be controlled. Here in 587 B.C. these qualities show, as he is unable to stop his own men from doing whatever they wish.

38:6 *cistern:* Cisterns in the city captured water during the winter rainy season, so water would be available for use in the dry months from May to October. There was only mud in the cistern that Jeremiah was thrown into, so it seems likely that this happened in late summer.

38:7 *Ebed-Melech, a Cushite:* This court official came from the African region south of Egypt that included parts of the present countries of Ethiopia and Sudan. Jeremiah is delivered from his own countrymen by a foreigner, who recognizes their act as wrong.

38:7 *Benjamin Gate:* See the note at 37:12, 13. This is where the king went to hear complaints or to observe the defense of the city against the Babylonians.

ropes and lifted him out of the cistern. And Jeremiah remained in
the courtyard of the guard.

Zedekiah Questions Jeremiah Again

[14]Then King Zedekiah sent for Jeremiah the prophet and had
him brought to the third entrance to the temple of the LORD. "I am
going to ask you something," the king said to Jeremiah. "Do not
hide anything from me."
[15]Jeremiah said to Zedekiah, "If I give you an answer, will
you not kill me? Even if I did give you counsel, you would not listen to me."
[16]But King Zedekiah swore this oath secretly to Jeremiah: "As
surely as the LORD lives, who has given us breath, I will neither kill
you nor hand you over to those who are seeking your life."
[17]Then Jeremiah said to Zedekiah, "This is what the LORD
God Almighty, the God of Israel, says: 'If you surrender to the officers of the king of Babylon, your life will be spared and this city
will not be burned down; you and your family will live. [18]But if
you will not surrender to the officers of the king of Babylon, this
city will be handed over to the Babylonians and they will burn it
down; you yourself will not escape from their hands.' "
[19]King Zedekiah said to Jeremiah, "I am afraid of the Jews
who have gone over to the Babylonians, for the Babylonians may
hand me over to them and they will mistreat me."
[20]"They will not hand you over," Jeremiah replied. "Obey the
LORD by doing what I tell you. Then it will go well with you, and
your life will be spared. [21]But if you refuse to surrender, this is
what the LORD has revealed to me: [22]All the women left in the
palace of the king of Judah will be brought out to the officials of
the king of Babylon. Those women will say to you:

" 'They misled you and overcame you—
those trusted friends of yours.

38:14 *Zedekiah . . . brought to the third entrance:* See the note at 21:1. The "third entrance" may have been a private entrance to the temple, such as a secret passageway leading from the king's palace. Compare this interview to the one in 37:17-21.

38:15 *will you not kill me:* Jeremiah has a right to be suspicious (38:5, 6).

38:17 *surrender:* He repeats the message, "Surrender and live" (see 38:2, 3 and the notes at 21:9; 27:11).

38:19 *I am afraid of the Jews:* Zedekiah wants to hear the truth, but he cannot act on it. He fears that the Jewish people who have joined the Babylonians will torture him if Babylon gains control of Jerusalem. Some Jews had already taken Jeremiah's advice and surrendered to the Babylonians (39:9; 52:15). Perhaps these traitors think they will be put in power once Zedekiah is out of the way, or perhaps they will take their anger out on Zedekiah because he did not listen to Jeremiah's warnings.

38:21,22 *the LORD has revealed . . . sunk in the mud:* Jeremiah reports that he has seen the capture of Zedekiah's royal household (see the mini-article called "Nebuchadnezzar," p. 1469). The women of the palace speak of Zedekiah as the one stuck in the mud (see 38:6). The "friends" Zedekiah trusts (38:22) probably are the Egyptians.

QUESTIONS ABOUT JEREMIAH 34:1—38:28

1. Why did Zedekiah act to free Hebrew slaves in 587 B.C.? (34:8-18) What prompted slave owners to force the freed slaves back into slavery? What do the owners' actions tell you about their view of the Law? What happened because of the owners' actions?
2. What was the lesson to be learned from the Recabites in chapter 35? What, if anything, can be learned today from the Recabites' lifestyle and their attitude of keeping their vows no matter what?
3. What did King Jehoiakim do that disgusted Jeremiah so much? (36:20-26) If a prophet of God were to give a message to our political leaders today, what might his or her message be?
4. Compare and contrast the actions of Ebed-Melech (38:1-13) and King Zedekiah (38:14-28). How do you account for the differences between the two men?

Your feet are sunk in the mud;
your friends have deserted you.’

23“All your wives and children will be brought out to the Babylonians. You yourself will not escape from their hands but will be captured by the king of Babylon; and this city will[a] be burned down.”

24Then Zedekiah said to Jeremiah, “Do not let anyone know about this conversation, or you may die. 25If the officials hear that I talked with you, and they come to you and say, ‘Tell us what you said to the king and what the king said to you; do not hide it from us or we will kill you,’ 26then tell them, ‘I was pleading with the king not to send me back to Jonathan’s house to die there.’ ”

27All the officials did come to Jeremiah and question him, and he told them everything the king had ordered him to say. So they said no more to him, for no one had heard his conversation with the king.

28And Jeremiah remained in the courtyard of the guard until the day Jerusalem was captured.

THE FALL OF JERUSALEM AND THE ESCAPE TO EGYPT

Jerusalem is captured by the Babylonians, who take many of the people of Judah into exile. Jeremiah and others are left behind. But when another revolt occurs, the surviving Jewish refugees escape to Egypt, forcing Jeremiah to go with them.

The Fall of Jerusalem

39 This is how Jerusalem was taken: 1In the ninth year of Zedekiah king of Judah, in the tenth month, Nebuchadnezzar king of Babylon marched against Jerusalem with his whole army and laid siege to it. 2And on the ninth day of the fourth month of Zedekiah’s eleventh year, the city wall was broken through. 3Then all the officials of the king of Babylon came and took seats in the Middle Gate: Nergal-Sharezer of Samgar, Nebo-Sarsekim[b] a chief officer, Nergal-Sharezer a high official and all the other officials of the king of Babylon. 4When Zedekiah king of Judah and all the soldiers saw them, they fled; they left the city at night by way of the king’s garden, through the gate between the two walls, and headed toward the Arabah.[c]

5But the Babylonian[d] army pursued them and overtook Zedekiah in the plains of Jericho. They captured him and took him to Nebuchadnezzar king of Babylon at Riblah in the land of Hamath, where he pronounced sentence on him. 6There at Riblah the king of Babylon slaughtered the sons of Zedekiah before his

[a]23 Or *and you will cause this city to* [b]3 Or *Nergal-Sharezer, Samgar-Nebo, Sarsekim* [c]4 Or *the Jordan Valley* [d]5 Or *Chaldean*

38:24,25 *this conversation . . . If the officials hear . . . kill you:* The king has no real authority; he fears his own officials. By protecting Jeremiah, the king puts his own life at risk as well. See also 37:20, 21.

38:28 *the day Jerusalem was captured:* The Babylonian army captured Jerusalem in August 586 B.C.

39:1,2 *tenth month . . . fourth month:* (See the note at 1:2,3 Zedekiah). During the Babylonian army’s second invasion of Judah, Jerusalem was surrounded beginning in Tebeth, the tenth month of the Hebrew calendar, from about mid-December to mid-January 588/87 B.C. This siege continued, except for a brief time during the summer of 587 (see 37:3-5) until the summer of 586 B.C. (or Tammuz, the “fourth month” of the Hebrew calendar, from about mid-June to mid-July). The account in 39:1-10 is adapted from 2 Kings 25:1-12 by an editor who wanted to include the account of the fall of Jerusalem in Jeremiah’s book. The story of chapter 38 picks up again with 39:11.

39:1-3 *Nebuchadnezzar . . . Nergal-Sharezer:* See the note at 21:2. Nergal-Sharezer may have been Nebuchadnezzar’s son-in-law, who was king of Babylon from 560 to 556 B.C.

39:3 *Middle Gate:* The location of this gate is not known; but it may refer to the great eastern gate of the temple which is now called the Golden Gate (see the map on p. 2466). The rulers and leaders often sat in the broad open area at the gate of a city to take care of official business and hold trials. Taking their places here would show that the officials had set up a new government.

Jeremiah before Jerusalem in Flames By Master of Jean de Mandeville from *Bible Historiale,* Paris, around 1360. Jeremiah began his career as a prophet while still a young man. In this illuminated manuscript, the artist depicts the prophet as an old man, lamenting the destruction of Jerusalem after its fall around 586 B.C. when the people of Israel were taken into exile by the Babylonians. (See 39:1—40:6.)

eyes and also killed all the nobles of Judah. [7]Then he put out
Zedekiah's eyes and bound him with bronze shackles to take him
to Babylon.

[8]The Babylonians[a] set fire to the royal palace and the houses
of the people and broke down the walls of Jerusalem. [9]Neb-
uzaradan commander of the imperial guard carried into exile to
Babylon the people who remained in the city, along with those
who had gone over to him, and the rest of the people. [10]But Nebuzaradan the commander of the guard left behind in the land of
Judah some of the poor people, who owned nothing; and at that
time he gave them vineyards and fields.

[11]Now Nebuchadnezzar king of Babylon had given these
orders about Jeremiah through Nebuzaradan commander of the
imperial guard: [12]"Take him and look after him; don't harm him but
do for him whatever he asks." [13]So Nebuzaradan the commander of

[a]**8** Or *Chaldeans*

39:4,5 *king's garden . . . two walls . . . Riblah:* The same night that the Babylonians broke through the city walls, Zedekiah and his palace guards deserted the city. The name of the gate between the two city walls is not known, but their escape route may have started at the garden near the Pool of Siloam, in the southeast part of the city. They headed east toward the Arabah (the Jordan River Valley), but were captured near Jericho (see the map on p. 2467). Then Zedekiah, his sons, and guards were taken north to Riblah, a town on the Orontes River in Syria (see the map on p. 2465). There Nebuchadnezzar put them on trial.

39:6 *slaughtered the sons of Zedekiah:* The death of Zedekiah's sons meant that his descendants would not rule in the future when Judah and Israel are restored.

39:8 *set fire to the royal palace . . . houses of the people:* Jeremiah's prophecy (21:8-10) came true. In August of 586 B.C. Jerusalem was looted, torn apart, and burned. Breaking down the city walls made future resistance impossible.

39:9 *Nebuzaradan:* The commander of the occupying Babylonian army forced most of the people of Jerusalem to leave the city and go into exile in Babylon. Most of the Jewish people left behind in Judah were poor people who did not own land. They were given fields and vineyards, perhaps to encourage them to be loyal to the Babylonians.

39:12 *Take him . . . don't harm him:* Apparently, Jeremiah was considered a Babylonian sympathizer because of his message (see 21:8-10). He was high on the list of those who were to be kept safe while he remained in Jerusalem.

39:14 *Gedaliah:* Gedaliah's family members had befriended Jeremiah in 26:20 and 36:10. Gedaliah's ancestors are mentioned in 2 Kings 22:12, where they helped King Josiah with reforms in Jerusalem. Judah was made a province of the Babylonian empire, and Gedaliah was made its first governor (40:7-12). His family was not part of the royal family of David, however.

39:15,16 *Ebed-Melech the Cushite:* These verses continue the story from 38:27. In 38:7-13, this African official helped Jeremiah. Either Jeremiah sent the message to him, or Ebed-Melech came to see him while he was still being held prisoner.

39:17,18 *I will rescue . . . save you:* A similar blessing is given in 45:5 to Jeremiah's friend Baruch. Ebed-Melech is protected from the gang of four "officials" (38:1) he had boldly accused of wrongdoing (38:9).

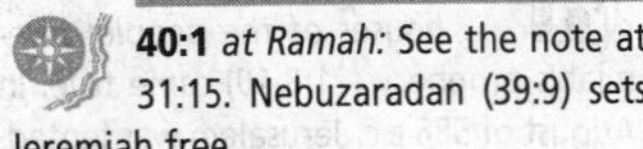

40:1 *at Ramah:* See the note at 31:15. Nebuzaradan (39:9) sets Jeremiah free.

40:5 *go anywhere else you please:* Jeremiah chooses to live in his beloved homeland. He is old, and his future lies with the exiled Jews (see 24:5-8 and the note).

40:6 *Mizpah:* Mizpah became the new capital after the fall of Jerusalem. Gedaliah (see 39:14 and note), the newly appointed governor of the Judah province, lived in Mizpah.

40:7,8 *army officers . . . Ishmael . . . Johanan:* Some Judean troops that were stationed outside of Jerusalem were not captured by the Babylonians. They went to see Gedaliah, perhaps to work out a military strategy to get rid of the Babylonians. Of the list of names in these verses, the two that stand out are Ishmael, who acts with deceit (41:1-3) and Johanan, who tries to stop Ishmael's plan to kill Gedaliah (40:13-16).

the guard, Nebushazban a chief officer, Nergal-Sharezer a high
official and all the other officers of the king of Babylon 14sent and
had Jeremiah taken out of the courtyard of the guard. They turned
him over to Gedaliah son of Ahikam, the son of Shaphan, to take
him back to his home. So he remained among his own people.
15While Jeremiah had been confined in the courtyard of the
guard, the word of the LORD came to him: 16"Go and tell Ebed-
Melech the Cushite, 'This is what the LORD Almighty, the God of
Israel, says: I am about to fulfill my words against this city through
disaster, not prosperity. At that time they will be fulfilled before
your eyes. 17But I will rescue you on that day, declares the LORD;
you will not be handed over to those you fear. 18I will save you; you
will not fall by the sword but will escape with your life, because
you trust in me, declares the LORD.' "

Jeremiah Freed

40 The word came to Jeremiah from the LORD after Nebuzaradan commander of the imperial guard had released him at
Ramah. He had found Jeremiah bound in chains among all the
captives from Jerusalem and Judah who were being carried into
exile to Babylon. 2When the commander of the guard found Jeremiah, he said to him, "The LORD your God decreed this disaster for
this place. 3And now the LORD has brought it about; he has done
just as he said he would. All this happened because you people
sinned against the LORD and did not obey him. 4But today I am
freeing you from the chains on your wrists. Come with me to
Babylon, if you like, and I will look after you; but if you do not
want to, then don't come. Look, the whole country lies before you;
go wherever you please." 5However, before Jeremiah turned to go,[a]
Nebuzaradan added, "Go back to Gedaliah son of Ahikam, the son
of Shaphan, whom the king of Babylon has appointed over the
towns of Judah, and live with him among the people, or go anywhere else you please."
Then the commander gave him provisions and a present and
let him go. 6So Jeremiah went to Gedaliah son of Ahikam at Mizpah and stayed with him among the people who were left behind
in the land.

Gedaliah Assassinated

7When all the army officers and their men who were still in
the open country heard that the king of Babylon had appointed
Gedaliah son of Ahikam as governor over the land and had put
him in charge of the men, women and children who were the
poorest in the land and who had not been carried into exile to
Babylon, 8they came to Gedaliah at Mizpah—Ishmael son of

[a]5 Or *Jeremiah answered*

Nethaniah, Johanan and Jonathan the sons of Kareah, Seraiah son
of Tanhumeth, the sons of Ephai the Netophathite, and Jaazaniah[a]
the son of the Maacathite, and their men. 9Gedaliah son of
Ahikam, the son of Shaphan, took an oath to reassure them and
their men. "Do not be afraid to serve the Babylonians,[b]" he said.
"Settle down in the land and serve the king of Babylon, and it will
go well with you. 10I myself will stay at Mizpah to represent you
before the Babylonians who come to us, but you are to harvest the
wine, summer fruit and oil, and put them in your storage jars, and
live in the towns you have taken over."

11When all the Jews in Moab, Ammon, Edom and all the
other countries heard that the king of Babylon had left a remnant
in Judah and had appointed Gedaliah son of Ahikam, the son of
Shaphan, as governor over them, 12they all came back to the land
of Judah, to Gedaliah at Mizpah, from all the countries where they
had been scattered. And they harvested an abundance of wine and
summer fruit.

13Johanan son of Kareah and all the army officers still in the
open country came to Gedaliah at Mizpah 14and said to him,
"Don't you know that Baalis king of the Ammonites has sent Ishmael son of Nethaniah to take your life?" But Gedaliah son of
Ahikam did not believe them.

15Then Johanan son of Kareah said privately to Gedaliah in
Mizpah, "Let me go and kill Ishmael son of Nethaniah, and no one
will know it. Why should he take your life and cause all the Jews
who are gathered around you to be scattered and the remnant of
Judah to perish?"

16But Gedaliah son of Ahikam said to Johanan son of
Kareah, "Don't do such a thing! What you are saying about Ishmael is not true."

41 In the seventh month Ishmael son of Nethaniah, the son of
Elishama, who was of royal blood and had been one of the king's
officers, came with ten men to Gedaliah son of Ahikam at Mizpah.
While they were eating together there, 2Ishmael son of Nethaniah
and the ten men who were with him got up and struck down
Gedaliah son of Ahikam, the son of Shaphan, with the sword,
killing the one whom the king of Babylon had appointed as governor over the land. 3Ishmael also killed all the Jews who were with
Gedaliah at Mizpah, as well as the Babylonian[c] soldiers who were
there.

4The day after Gedaliah's assassination, before anyone knew
about it, 5eighty men who had shaved off their beards, torn their
clothes and cut themselves came from Shechem, Shiloh and
Samaria, bringing grain offerings and incense with them to the
house of the LORD. 6Ishmael son of Nethaniah went out from

---

[a]8 Hebrew *Jezaniah,* a variant of *Jaazaniah* [b]9 Or *Chaldeans;* also in verse 10
[c]3 Or *Chaldean*

40:9 *Settle down . . . serve the king of Babylon:* Gedaliah tries to stop any further resistance to Babylon and rally the remaining Judean forces. He appears to have been influenced by Jeremiah's advice (24:4-8). See also 2 Kgs 25:22-24.

40:11,12 *the Jews in Moab, Ammon, Edom . . . came back:* During the Babylonian invasion of Judah, which lasted a year and a half, many of the people of Judah ran away to these surrounding countries (see the map on p. 2467). When Gedaliah was made ruler, these refugees felt safe enough to return to Judah and help with that year's abundant grape harvest.

40:13,14 *Johanan . . . came to Gedaliah . . . Baalis king of the Ammonites:* According to 2 Kings 25:25, the plot against Gedaliah occurred only two months after he was appointed governor. Baalis, king of Ammon, hired Ishmael, a Judean army officer, to kill Gedaliah. Baalis of Ammon probably thought that a successful revolt by Judah would weaken Babylonian authority over the region, including his own country of Ammon. Ishmael came from the royal family of Zedekiah, so he might have had some standing with the people of Judah.

41:1,2 *In the seventh month Ishmael . . . struck down Gedaliah:* Ishmael and his small rebel army came to Mizpah in the month of Tishri, also called Ethanim, the seventh month of the Hebrew calendar, from about mid-September to mid-October in 586 B.C. As Gedeliah's dinner guest, Ishmael took advantage of the situation and killed Gedaliah.

41:5 *shaved off their beards . . . came from Shechem, Shiloh and Samaria:* See the notes at 23:13,14 and 7:12. See also the note at 2:4 and the map on p. 2467. The men were heading south, through Mizpah, on their way to Jerusalem, where they were going to mourn the destruction of the temple. Shaving the beard, tearing one's clothes, and cutting the skin were done to show grief.

Mizpah to meet them, weeping as he went. When he met them, he said, "Come to Gedaliah son of Ahikam." 7When they went into the city, Ishmael son of Nethaniah and the men who were with him slaughtered them and threw them into a cistern. 8But ten of them said to Ishmael, "Don't kill us! We have wheat and barley, oil and honey, hidden in a field." So he let them alone and did not kill them with the others. 9Now the cistern where he threw all the bodies of the men he had killed along with Gedaliah was the one King Asa had made as part of his defense against Baasha king of Israel. Ishmael son of Nethaniah filled it with the dead.

10Ishmael made captives of all the rest of the people who were in Mizpah—the king's daughters along with all the others who were left there, over whom Nebuzaradan commander of the imperial guard had appointed Gedaliah son of Ahikam. Ishmael son of Nethaniah took them captive and set out to cross over to the Ammonites.

11When Johanan son of Kareah and all the army officers who were with him heard about all the crimes Ishmael son of Nethaniah had committed, 12they took all their men and went to fight Ishmael son of Nethaniah. They caught up with him near the great pool in Gibeon. 13When all the people Ishmael had with him saw Johanan son of Kareah and the army officers who were with him, they were glad. 14All the people Ishmael had taken captive at Mizpah turned and went over to Johanan son of Kareah. 15But Ishmael son of Nethaniah and eight of his men escaped from Johanan and fled to the Ammonites.

Flight to Egypt

16Then Johanan son of Kareah and all the army officers who were with him led away all the survivors from Mizpah whom he had recovered from Ishmael son of Nethaniah after he had assassinated Gedaliah son of Ahikam: the soldiers, women, children and court officials he had brought from Gibeon. 17And they went on, stopping at Geruth Kimham near Bethlehem on their way to Egypt 18to escape the Babylonians.[a] They were afraid of them because Ishmael son of Nethaniah had killed Gedaliah son of Ahikam, whom the king of Babylon had appointed as governor over the land.

42 Then all the army officers, including Johanan son of Kareah and Jezaniah[b] son of Hoshaiah, and all the people from the least to the greatest approached 2Jeremiah the prophet and said to him, "Please hear our petition and pray to the LORD your God for this entire remnant. For as you now see, though we were once many, now only a few are left. 3Pray that the LORD your God will tell us where we should go and what we should do."

4"I have heard you," replied Jeremiah the prophet. "I will

---

[a]**18** Or *Chaldeans* [b]**1** Hebrew; Septuagint (see also 43:2) *Azariah*

41:7-9 *threw them into a cistern . . . the one King Asa had made:* Ishmael makes a mass grave out of the cistern that had originally been dug in the time of Asa of Judah (911-870 B.C.).

41:10 *made captives of all . . . Nebuzaradan . . . Ammonites:* See the note at 39:9. Ishmael may have hoped to sell Zedekiah's daughters and others in Mizpah as slaves to King Baalis of Ammon (see the note at 40:13, 14).

41:12 *the great pool in Gibeon:* Gibeon was about six miles northwest of Jerusalem. The great pool was probably a cistern.

41:17 *Geruth Kimham near Bethlehem on their way to Egypt:* Afraid of what will happen when Nebuchadnezzar hears of Gedeliah's assassination, Johanan's group heads to Egypt to get as far as possible from any Babylonian retaliation. This group included Jeremiah, since he had been staying with Gedaliah near Mizpah (40:6). The location of Geruth Kimham is unknown. Bethlehem is a few miles south of Jerusalem (see the map on p. 2467).

42:3 *Pray that the LORD your God will tell us . . . what we should do:* The refugees are in a real dilemma and sincerely ask Jeremiah what the LORD wants them to do. If they stay in Judah and are accused of the rebellion (41:1-15), they might be killed or they might be cleared of any wrongdoing. If they flee to Egypt, it may look like they are admitting guilt, but they might be safe there. They promise to do whatever the LORD tells Jeremiah.

certainly pray to the LORD your God as you have requested; I will tell
you everything the LORD says and will keep nothing back from you.”
[5]Then they said to Jeremiah, “May the LORD be a true and
faithful witness against us if we do not act in accordance with
everything the LORD your God sends you to tell us. [6]Whether it is
favorable or unfavorable, we will obey the LORD our God, to whom
we are sending you, so that it will go well with us, for we will obey
the LORD our God.”
[7]Ten days later the word of the LORD came to Jeremiah. [8]So
he called together Johanan son of Kareah and all the army officers
who were with him and all the people from the least to the greatest. [9]He said to them, “This is what the LORD, the God of Israel, to
whom you sent me to present your petition, says: [10]‘If you stay in
this land, I will build you up and not tear you down; I will plant
you and not uproot you, for I am grieved over the disaster I have
inflicted on you. [11]Do not be afraid of the king of Babylon, whom
you now fear. Do not be afraid of him, declares the LORD, for I am
with you and will save you and deliver you from his hands. [12]I will
show you compassion so that he will have compassion on you and
restore you to your land.’
[13]“However, if you say, ‘We will not stay in this land,’ and so
disobey the LORD your God, [14]and if you say, ‘No, we will go and
live in Egypt, where we will not see war or hear the trumpet or be
hungry for bread,’ [15]then hear the word of the LORD, O remnant of
Judah. This is what the LORD Almighty, the God of Israel, says: ‘If
you are determined to go to Egypt and you do go to settle there,
[16]then the sword you fear will overtake you there, and the famine
you dread will follow you into Egypt, and there you will die.
[17]Indeed, all who are determined to go to Egypt to settle there will
die by the sword, famine and plague; not one of them will survive
or escape the disaster I will bring on them.’ [18]This is what the LORD
Almighty, the God of Israel, says: ‘As my anger and wrath have
been poured out on those who lived in Jerusalem, so will my wrath
be poured out on you when you go to Egypt. You will be an object
of cursing and horror, of condemnation and reproach; you will
never see this place again.’
[19]“O remnant of Judah, the LORD has told you, ‘Do not go to
Egypt.’ Be sure of this: I warn you today [20]that you made a fatal
mistake[a] when you sent me to the LORD your God and said, ‘Pray
to the LORD our God for us; tell us everything he says and we will
do it.’ [21]I have told you today, but you still have not obeyed the
LORD your God in all he sent me to tell you. [22]So now, be sure of
this: You will die by the sword, famine and plague in the place
where you want to go to settle.”
43 When Jeremiah finished telling the people all the words of
the LORD their God—everything the LORD had sent him to tell

[a]20 Or *you erred in your hearts*

42:7 *Ten days later:* God's word cannot be summoned at will. Ten days pass before Jeremiah has an answer.

42:10 *stay in this land, I will build you up:* This is a new message. Jeremiah had preached that the hope of Judah's future lay with the prisoners in Babylon (see 24:5-8 and note), but now God is saying that this small group of survivors will also be part of God's plan to rebuild Judah. And God will keep them safe from Nebuchadnezzar's revenge.

42:18 *my wrath . . . Egypt:* A large Jewish population eventually settled in Egypt. Alexandria, a major port, became an important center for Jewish literature and study until the second century A.D.

42:19-22 *Do not go to Egypt . . . You will die:* Jeremiah warns the people that running away from Judah to Egypt is a mistake, outright disobedience to God's will. Perhaps, in the ten-day wait for this message, the group had already made up their minds (43:1-5).

42:5,6 Josh 24:21,24.

43:2,3 *Azariah . . . Johanan . . . Baruch:* Johanan was the Jewish army officer who tried to stop Ishmael from assassinating Gedaliah (40:15). See the note at 32:12.

43:5 *led away all the remnant of Judah:* Jeremiah and Baruch probably had no choice but to go along with the group to Egypt. Perhaps Jeremiah felt responsible to continue preaching the LORD's messages, or perhaps the group wished to use Jeremiah as a "good luck charm" in Egypt. See 2 Kgs 25:26.

43:6 *left with Gedaliah:* After the fall of Jerusalem, Nebuzaradan had allowed Jeremiah and Baruch to live at Mizpah under the protection of Gedaliah (40:1-6). See also 41:10 and the note at 39:14.

43:7 *Tahpanhes:* Tahpanhes was the first Egyptian town the refugees reached after escaping from Israel (see the map on p. 2468).

43:9 *take some large stones . . . bury them:* Once again Jeremiah does a symbolic act (see also 16:1-7; 27:1, 2; 32:6-9) to show what the LORD will do. The message is especially for the Jews who think that escaping to Egypt has made them safe from Nebuchadnezzar.

43:10,11 *Nebuchadnezzar . . . will . . . attack Egypt:* Babylon's Nebuchadnezzar did invade Egypt in 568 B.C. as a warning to keep the Egyptians from trying to undermine Babylon's control over the region. This invasion did not lead to a decisive defeat of the Egyptians, and Nebuchadnezzar left the Egyptian king on the throne. See also Ezek 29:17-21.

43:13 *temple of the sun . . . demolish the sacred pillars:* Tall granite shafts (obelisks) were set up to honor the sun-god Re at the temple in Heliopolis (see the map on p. 2468).

them— 2 Azariah son of Hoshaiah and Johanan son of Kareah and
all the arrogant men said to Jeremiah, "You are lying! The LORD
our God has not sent you to say, 'You must not go to Egypt to settle there.' 3 But Baruch son of Neriah is inciting you against us to
hand us over to the Babylonians,[a] so they may kill us or carry us
into exile to Babylon."
4 So Johanan son of Kareah and all the army officers and all
the people disobeyed the LORD's command to stay in the land of
Judah. 5 Instead, Johanan son of Kareah and all the army officers led
away all the remnant of Judah who had come back to live in the
land of Judah from all the nations where they had been scattered.
6 They also led away all the men, women and children and the king's
daughters whom Nebuzaradan commander of the imperial guard
had left with Gedaliah son of Ahikam, the son of Shaphan, and
Jeremiah the prophet and Baruch son of Neriah. 7 So they entered
Egypt in disobedience to the LORD and went as far as Tahpanhes.
8 In Tahpanhes the word of the LORD came to Jeremiah:
9 "While the Jews are watching, take some large stones with you
and bury them in clay in the brick pavement at the entrance to
Pharaoh's palace in Tahpanhes. 10 Then say to them, 'This is what
the LORD Almighty, the God of Israel, says: I will send for my servant Nebuchadnezzar king of Babylon, and I will set his throne over
these stones I have buried here; he will spread his royal canopy
above them. 11 He will come and attack Egypt, bringing death to
those destined for death, captivity to those destined for captivity,
and the sword to those destined for the sword. 12 He[b] will set fire to
the temples of the gods of Egypt; he will burn their temples and
take their gods captive. As a shepherd wraps his garment around
him, so will he wrap Egypt around himself and depart from there
unscathed. 13 There in the temple of the sun[c] in Egypt he will
demolish the sacred pillars and will burn down the temples of the
gods of Egypt.' "

Disaster Because of Idolatry

44 This word came to Jeremiah concerning all the Jews living in
Lower Egypt—in Migdol, Tahpanhes and Memphis[d]—and in
Upper Egypt[e]: 2 "This is what the LORD Almighty, the God of Israel,
says: You saw the great disaster I brought on Jerusalem and on all
the towns of Judah. Today they lie deserted and in ruins 3 because
of the evil they have done. They provoked me to anger by burning
incense and by worshiping other gods that neither they nor you
nor your fathers ever knew. 4 Again and again I sent my servants
the prophets, who said, 'Do not do this detestable thing that I
hate!' 5 But they did not listen or pay attention; they did not turn

[a]3 Or *Chaldeans* [b]12 Or *I* [c]13 Or *in Heliopolis* [d]1 Hebrew *Noph*
[e]1 Hebrew *in Pathros*

from their wickedness or stop burning incense to other gods.
[6]Therefore, my fierce anger was poured out; it raged against the
towns of Judah and the streets of Jerusalem and made them the
desolate ruins they are today.

[7]"Now this is what the LORD God Almighty, the God of
Israel, says: Why bring such great disaster on yourselves by cutting
off from Judah the men and women, the children and infants, and
so leave yourselves without a remnant? [8]Why provoke me to anger
with what your hands have made, burning incense to other gods in
Egypt, where you have come to live? You will destroy yourselves
and make yourselves an object of cursing and reproach among all
the nations on earth. [9]Have you forgotten the wickedness committed by your fathers and by the kings and queens of Judah and the
wickedness committed by you and your wives in the land of Judah
and the streets of Jerusalem? [10]To this day they have not humbled
themselves or shown reverence, nor have they followed my law and
the decrees I set before you and your fathers.

[11]"Therefore, this is what the LORD Almighty, the God of
Israel, says: I am determined to bring disaster on you and to
destroy all Judah. [12]I will take away the remnant of Judah who were
determined to go to Egypt to settle there. They will all perish in
Egypt; they will fall by the sword or die from famine. From the
least to the greatest, they will die by sword or famine. They will
become an object of cursing and horror, of condemnation and
reproach. [13]I will punish those who live in Egypt with the sword,
famine and plague, as I punished Jerusalem. [14]None of the remnant of Judah who have gone to live in Egypt will escape or survive
to return to the land of Judah, to which they long to return and
live; none will return except a few fugitives."

[15]Then all the men who knew that their wives were burning
incense to other gods, along with all the women who were present—a large assembly—and all the people living in Lower and
Upper Egypt,[a] said to Jeremiah, [16]"We will not listen to the message you have spoken to us in the name of the LORD! [17]We will certainly do everything we said we would: We will burn incense to the
Queen of Heaven and will pour out drink offerings to her just as
we and our fathers, our kings and our officials did in the towns of
Judah and in the streets of Jerusalem. At that time we had plenty
of food and were well off and suffered no harm. [18]But ever since
we stopped burning incense to the Queen of Heaven and pouring
out drink offerings to her, we have had nothing and have been perishing by sword and famine."

[19]The women added, "When we burned incense to the
Queen of Heaven and poured out drink offerings to her, did not
our husbands know that we were making cakes like her image and
pouring out drink offerings to her?"

---

[a]15 Hebrew *in Egypt and Pathros*

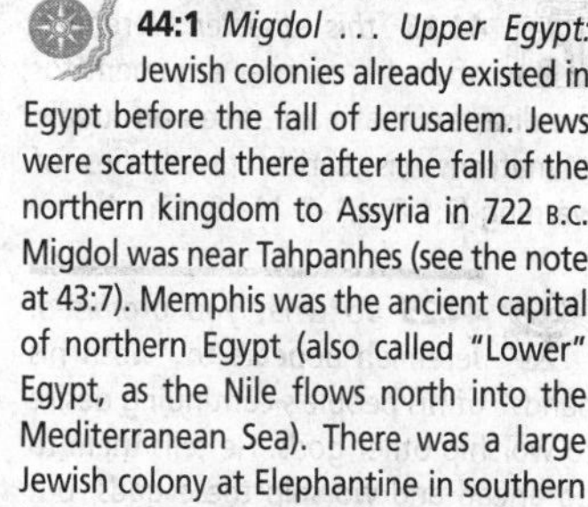

44:1 *Migdol . . . Upper Egypt:* Jewish colonies already existed in Egypt before the fall of Jerusalem. Jews were scattered there after the fall of the northern kingdom to Assyria in 722 B.C. Migdol was near Tahpanhes (see the note at 43:7). Memphis was the ancient capital of northern Egypt (also called "Lower" Egypt, as the Nile flows north into the Mediterranean Sea). There was a large Jewish colony at Elephantine in southern ("Upper") Egypt. See the maps on pp. 2463 and 2468.

44:2-4 *LORD Almighty . . . this detestable thing:* See the notes at 2:19; 2:6, 7; and 4:1.

44:7,8 *Why bring such great disaster on yourselves . . . other gods:* The Jewish people who escaped to Egypt were beginning to worship and burn incense to honor Egyptian gods and goddesses. This clearly violated the law commanding people to worship the LORD alone (Exod 20:3-6). It was as if they had not learned a lesson from the recent events of 586 B.C. (39:1-14).

44:15 *Lower and Upper Egypt:* See the note at 44:1.

44:17 *burn incense to the Queen of Heaven:* See the note at 7:18. The refugees in Egypt present a different view of recent history than Jeremiah. During the rule of King Manasseh (696-642 B.C.), Judah enjoyed a long period of peace. Manasseh allowed the worship of Asherah (2 Kgs 21:1–18). When Manasseh's grandson Josiah became king, he tried to stop the worship of idols (2 Kgs 23:4-14). But the refugees argue that it was during Josiah's reign, when they "stopped burning incense to the Queen of Heaven" (44:18), that Judah's serious troubles with war and hunger began.

44:19 *making cakes like her image:* The cakes were made in the shape of a crescent moon or stamped with a star shape for the "star" Venus.

44:12 Jer 41:16—43:7.

44:23 *this disaster:* Jeremiah offers his counter argument for the disasters that have fallen on Judah. It matches his earlier prophecies of warning (2:1-8; 4:1-4, 11-18; 17:1-4).

44:25 *do what you promised:* Jeremiah appears to "wash his hands" of his people's continuing desire to worship other gods. He tells them to go ahead and worship these gods, but be prepared to suffer the consequences (44:27,28). The people apparently keep hoping that they can worship God alongside other gods. But idol worship is unacceptable, even fatal.

[20]Then Jeremiah said to all the people, both men and
women, who were answering him, [21]"Did not the LORD remember
and think about the incense burned in the towns of Judah and the
streets of Jerusalem by you and your fathers, your kings and your
officials and the people of the land? [22]When the LORD could no
longer endure your wicked actions and the detestable things you
did, your land became an object of cursing and a desolate waste
without inhabitants, as it is today. [23]Because you have burned
incense and have sinned against the LORD and have not obeyed
him or followed his law or his decrees or his stipulations, this disaster has come upon you, as you now see."

[24]Then Jeremiah said to all the people, including the women,
"Hear the word of the LORD, all you people of Judah in Egypt.
[25]This is what the LORD Almighty, the God of Israel, says: You and
your wives have shown by your actions what you promised when
you said, 'We will certainly carry out the vows we made to burn
incense and pour out drink offerings to the Queen of Heaven.'

"Go ahead then, do what you promised! Keep your vows!
[26]But hear the word of the LORD, all Jews living in Egypt: 'I swear
by my great name,' says the LORD, 'that no one from Judah living
anywhere in Egypt will ever again invoke my name or swear, "As
surely as the Sovereign LORD lives." [27]For I am watching over them
for harm, not for good; the Jews in Egypt will perish by sword and
famine until they are all destroyed. [28]Those who escape the sword
and return to the land of Judah from Egypt will be very few. Then
the whole remnant of Judah who came to live in Egypt will know
whose word will stand—mine or theirs.

[29]" 'This will be the sign to you that I will punish you in this
place,' declares the LORD, 'so that you will know that my threats of

QUESTIONS ABOUT JEREMIAH 39:1—44:30

1. What in the account of the fall of Jerusalem (39:1-10) do you find most stunning? What do you think would be most distressing to the people of that time?
2. What do you think motivated Ishmael to take the evil and treacherous actions he did? (40:13—41:15) How did his actions violate the trust of others and the laws of God?
3. What did the Judean survivors fear might happen after Gedaliah's assassination? What was attractive about going to Egypt? (chapter 42) Why did the people ignore Jeremiah's advice?
4. Describe a time when you ignored good advice, when you "went to Egypt," or took the easy way out?
5. According to many of the Jewish refugees in Egypt, what events were the real cause for the destruction and fall of their homeland of Judah? (44:16-19) How did Jeremiah's interpretation differ from theirs? (44:2-14, 20-23)
6. Do you agree or disagree with the theory that "those who do not learn from the mistakes of the past are bound to repeat them"? Why? How might this be applied to the situation of the people of Judah in Jeremiah's day? How might this apply to your own life?

harm against you will surely stand.' [30]This is what the LORD says: 'I
am going to hand Pharaoh Hophra king of Egypt over to his enemies who seek his life, just as I handed Zedekiah king of Judah
over to Nebuchadnezzar king of Babylon, the enemy who was
seeking his life.'"

The LORD's Judgment Against the Nations

This section begins with a brief message to Jeremiah's friend Baruch. He is promised the LORD's protection in the midst of the disasters that will soon hit Judah and many other nations in the region. Then the nations near to and far from Judah are addressed in a series of prophecies of judgment preached in the fourth year of Jehoiakim's rule (about 605 B.C.). The LORD is God not only of Israel but of the whole world. God stands in judgment of all peoples.

A Message to Baruch

45 This is what Jeremiah the prophet told Baruch son of Neriah in the fourth year of Jehoiakim son of Josiah king of Judah,
after Baruch had written on a scroll the words Jeremiah was then
dictating: [2]"This is what the LORD, the God of Israel, says to you,
Baruch: [3]You said, 'Woe to me! The LORD has added sorrow to my
pain; I am worn out with groaning and find no rest.'"
[4]⌞The LORD said,⌟ "Say this to him: 'This is what the LORD says:
I will overthrow what I have built and uproot what I have planted,
throughout the land. [5]Should you then seek great things for yourself? Seek them not. For I will bring disaster on all people, declares
the LORD, but wherever you go I will let you escape with your life.'"

A Message About Egypt

46 This is the word of the LORD that came to Jeremiah the
prophet concerning the nations:

[2]Concerning Egypt:

This is the message against the army of Pharaoh Neco king of Egypt, which was defeated at Carchemish on the Euphrates River by Nebuchadnezzar king of Babylon in the fourth year of Jehoiakim son of Josiah king of Judah:

[3]"Prepare your shields, both large and small,
and march out for battle!
[4]Harness the horses,
mount the steeds!
Take your positions
with helmets on!

44:30 *Hophra . . . Zedekiah . . . Nebuchadnezzar:* Hophra, also known as Apries, ruled Egypt from 589 to 570 B.C. He was assassinated by an official in his own court by the name of Amasis, later known as Ahmosis II (ruled 570-526 B.C.). See also 2 Kgs 25:1-7 and the notes at 1:2, 3 and 21:2.

45:1 *fourth year of Jehoiakim:* This message to Baruch is from 605 B.C., when Jehoiakim burned the first scroll (see 36:23).

45:2-5 *Baruch . . . seek great things . . . I will let you escape:* See the note at 32:12. Like Jeremiah (20:7-18), Baruch was deeply disturbed by the message of doom (45:3). He was probably tired from the difficult work of copying all Jeremiah's prophecies by hand, and he was likely fearful about having to read the "bad news" contained in Jeremiah's scrolls. Baruch's work as Jeremiah's secretary would not allow him time for a personal life or to pursue any personal dreams ("don't seek great things," 45:5). But he is promised physical safety and the LORD's protection, no matter where he goes and no matter what disasters are going on around him.

46:1 *concerning the nations:* This verse provides a heading for the prophecies against the nations in chapters 46–51. While Jeremiah was a prophet of Judah, he was sent to speak to all the nations (1:10). This was also true of Isaiah (Isa 13–23), Ezekiel (Ezek 25–32), and Amos (Amos 1,2).

46:2 *Egypt . . . Carchemish:* The date is the summer of 605 B.C. Judah is caught in the middle of a power struggle between Egypt to their west and the rising power Babylon to their east. While Judah's King Jehoiakim trusted in Egypt as an ally, the Babylonians shattered the Egyptian forces at Carchemish on the Euphrates River (46:6) and later at Hamath in Syria. See the map on p. 2468 and the article called "The Ancient World: Peoples, Powers, and Politics," p. 919, which describes how ancient civilizations arose along the banks of these great rivers.

Polish your spears,
put on your armor!
5 What do I see?
They are terrified,
they are retreating,
their warriors are defeated.
They flee in haste
without looking back,
and there is terror on every side,"
declares the LORD.

6 "The swift cannot flee
nor the strong escape.
In the north by the River Euphrates
they stumble and fall.
7 "Who is this that rises like the Nile,
like rivers of surging waters?
8 Egypt rises like the Nile,
like rivers of surging waters.
She says, 'I will rise and cover the earth;
I will destroy cities and their people.'
9 Charge, O horses!
Drive furiously, O charioteers!
March on, O warriors—
men of Cush[a] and Put who carry shields,
men of Lydia who draw the bow.
10 But that day belongs to the Lord, the LORD Almighty—
a day of vengeance, for vengeance on his foes.
The sword will devour till it is satisfied,
till it has quenched its thirst with blood.
For the Lord, the LORD Almighty, will offer sacrifice
in the land of the north by the River Euphrates.

11 "Go up to Gilead and get balm,
O Virgin Daughter of Egypt.
But you multiply remedies in vain;
there is no healing for you.
12 The nations will hear of your shame;
your cries will fill the earth.
One warrior will stumble over another;
both will fall down together."

13 This is the message the LORD spoke to Jeremiah the prophet about the coming of Nebuchadnezzar king of Babylon to attack Egypt:

14 "Announce this in Egypt, and proclaim it in Migdol;
proclaim it also in Memphis[b] and Tahpanhes:

[a]9 That is, the upper Nile region [b]14 Hebrew *Noph*; also in verse 19

46:9 *Cush and Put . . . Lydia:* Cush is the Hebrew term for the modern area called Ethiopia (see the note at 38:7, Ebed-Melech, and the map on p. 2469). Put is modern day Libya, which is on the northern coast of Africa to the west of Egypt. Lydia may refer to an area in west-central Asia minor.

46:10 *that day belongs to the Lord, the LORD Almighty:* See the note at 2:19. The LORD is pictured here as a warrior who will kill the Egyptians and make them a sacrifice. See also Ezek 32:2-10 and the mini-article called "Holy War (the LORD's Battles)," p. 306.

46:11 *Go up to Gilead and get balm:* See the note at 8:22.

46:13,14 *Nebuchadnezzar . . . attack Egypt . . . Tahpanhes:* In 604 B.C., Nebuchadnezzar's army assembled on the plains of Philistia west of Judah and northeast of Egypt. The threat of the Babylonian army caused terror in Egypt, including the cities of Migdol, Memphis, and Tahpanhes (see the notes at 43:7; 44:1). Nebuchadnezzar did not actually invade Egypt until 568 B.C. Jeremiah saw Nebuchadnezzar as God's "servant" (43:10), so the Egyptians are actually fighting against the LORD, and not merely human armies.

'Take your positions and get ready,
for the sword devours those around you.'
15 Why will your warriors be laid low?
They cannot stand, for the LORD will push them down.
16 They will stumble repeatedly;
they will fall over each other.
They will say, 'Get up, let us go back
to our own people and our native lands,
away from the sword of the oppressor.'
17 There they will exclaim,
'Pharaoh king of Egypt is only a loud noise;
he has missed his opportunity.'

18 "As surely as I live," declares the King,
whose name is the LORD Almighty,
"one will come who is like Tabor among
the mountains,
like Carmel by the sea.
19 Pack your belongings for exile,
you who live in Egypt,
for Memphis will be laid waste
and lie in ruins without inhabitant.

20 "Egypt is a beautiful heifer,
but a gadfly is coming
against her from the north.
21 The mercenaries in her ranks
are like fattened calves.
They too will turn and flee together,
they will not stand their ground,
for the day of disaster is coming upon them,
the time for them to be punished.
22 Egypt will hiss like a fleeing serpent
as the enemy advances in force;
they will come against her with axes,
like men who cut down trees.
23 They will chop down her forest,"
declares the LORD,
"dense though it be.
They are more numerous than locusts,
they cannot be counted.
24 The Daughter of Egypt will be put to shame,
handed over to the people of the north."

25 The LORD Almighty, the God of Israel, says: "I am about to
bring punishment on Amon god of Thebes,[a] on Pharaoh, on Egypt
and her gods and her kings, and on those who rely on Pharaoh.

[a]**25** Hebrew *No*

46:17 *Pharaoh king of Egypt is only a loud noise:* The king of Egypt brags but never acts. See also Isa 19:1-15; 30:3-7.

46:18 *Tabor . . . Carmel:* These mountains in northern Israel are not especially tall, but both have steep slopes that rise above plains (see the map on p. 2464). Babylon will tower over (dominate) Egypt like mountains towering over the plains.

46:19 *Memphis:* See the note at 44:1.

46:20 *a gadfly is coming against her from the north:* The "gadfly" from the north is Nebuchadnezzar (see the notes at 21:2; 46:13,14), who will pester Egypt continuously, the way biting flies pester a cow.

46:23 *locusts:* This is a type of grasshopper that comes in swarms and causes great damage to plant life. See also the mini-article called "Locusts," p. 1708.

46:25 *Amon god of Thebes:* Amon was the king of all the Egyptian gods and the special god of Egyptian kings. Thebes was the ancient capital of Upper (southern) Egypt. Along with 46:19, the sense is that the devastation of Egypt will be complete from north to south. But see 46:26 and the note at 43:10,11.

26 I will hand them over to those who seek their lives, to Nebuchadnezzar king of Babylon and his officers. Later, however,
Egypt will be inhabited as in times past," declares the LORD.

27 "Do not fear, O Jacob my servant;
    do not be dismayed, O Israel.
I will surely save you out of a distant place,
    your descendants from the land of their exile.
Jacob will again have peace and security,
    and no one will make him afraid.
28 Do not fear, O Jacob my servant,
    for I am with you," declares the LORD.
"Though I completely destroy all the nations
    among which I scatter you,
    I will not completely destroy you.
I will discipline you but only with justice;
    I will not let you go entirely unpunished."

A Message About the Philistines

47 This is the word of the LORD that came to Jeremiah the
prophet concerning the Philistines before Pharaoh attacked Gaza:

2 This is what the LORD says:

"See how the waters are rising in the north;
    they will become an overflowing torrent.
They will overflow the land and everything in it,
    the towns and those who live in them.
The people will cry out;
    all who dwell in the land will wail
3 at the sound of the hoofs of galloping steeds,
    at the noise of enemy chariots
    and the rumble of their wheels.
Fathers will not turn to help their children;
    their hands will hang limp.
4 For the day has come
    to destroy all the Philistines
and to cut off all survivors
    who could help Tyre and Sidon.
The LORD is about to destroy the Philistines,
    the remnant from the coasts of Caphtor.[a]
5 Gaza will shave her head in mourning;
    Ashkelon will be silenced.
O remnant on the plain,
    how long will you cut yourselves?

6 " 'Ah, sword of the LORD,' ⌊you cry,⌋
    'how long till you rest?

[a]**4** That is, Crete

46:27 *do not be dismayed, O Israel:* "Israel" here refers to all God's people, both northern and southern kingdoms (see 30:10,11).

47:1 *Philistines . . . Gaza:* See the map on p. 2467. Pharaoh Neco II of Egypt captured Gaza on his return from the victory over King Josiah at Megiddo in 609 B.C. In 604 B.C. Nebuchadnezzar captured the Philistine city of Ashkelon (47:5). Three years later, after stopping the Babylonian attack at Migdol in Egypt, Pharaoh Neco of Egypt and his army pushed the Babylonian troops back to Philistia, where the Egyptians took over Gaza. Jeremiah's prophecy may refer to this occupation of Gaza in 601 B.C. (see 46:2 and the note).

47:2 *waters are rising in the north:* See the notes at 1:13; 46:20.

47:4 *Tyre and Sidon . . . coasts of Caphtor:* Caphtor is another name for Crete, an island south of Greece and the original homeland of the ancestors of the Philistines. Tyre and Sidon were Phoenician cities on the Mediterranean Sea coast north of Judah. The leaders of these city-states rebelled against Babylon in 594 B.C., and in 587 B.C. they formed an alliance with the Philistine cities against Babylon. See the map on p. 2468.

47:1-7 Isa 14:29-31; Ezek 25:15-17; Joel 3:4-8; Amos 1:6-8; Zeph 2:4-7; Zech 9:5-7.

Return to your scabbard;
cease and be still.'
7 But how can it rest
when the LORD has commanded it,
when he has ordered it
to attack Ashkelon and the coast?"

A Message About Moab

48 Concerning Moab:

This is what the LORD Almighty, the God of Israel, says:

"Woe to Nebo, for it will be ruined.
Kiriathaim will be disgraced and captured;
the stronghold[a] will be disgraced and
shattered.
2 Moab will be praised no more;
in Heshbon[b] men will plot her downfall:
'Come, let us put an end to that nation.'
You too, O Madmen,[c] will be silenced;
the sword will pursue you.
3 Listen to the cries from Horonaim,
cries of great havoc and destruction.
4 Moab will be broken;
her little ones will cry out.[d]
5 They go up the way to Luhith,
weeping bitterly as they go;
on the road down to Horonaim
anguished cries over the destruction are heard.
6 Flee! Run for your lives;
become like a bush[e] in the desert.
7 Since you trust in your deeds and riches,
you too will be taken captive,
and Chemosh will go into exile,
together with his priests and officials.
8 The destroyer will come against every town,
and not a town will escape.
The valley will be ruined
and the plateau destroyed,
because the LORD has spoken.
9 Put salt on Moab,
for she will be laid waste[f];
her towns will become desolate,
with no one to live in them.

47:7 *Ashkelon:* This is the Philistine city destroyed by Nebuchadnezzar and the Babylonians in 604 B.C.

48:1-3 *Moab . . . Nebo . . . Horonaim:* The people of Moab are often described as enemies of the Israelite people (Num 22–24; 1 Sam 14:47, 48; 2 Kgs 3:21-27). The defeat of Moabite cities probably refers to the invasion by Babylonian troops. When Jehoiakim of Judah rebelled against Babylon (see the note at 22:13-18), the Moabites raided Judah (2 Kgs 24:2). Later, in 595 B.C. the Moabites joined the alliance against Babylon (see 27:3). See the map on p. 1321 for the location of these places in Moab.

48:7 *Chemosh:* Chemosh, the national god of the Moabites, is mentioned in various Old Testament passages (1 Kgs 11:7, 33; 2 Kgs 23:13; Jer 48:45, 46). The national gods of Moab and other nations are useless against the living God of Israel (48:13; see also Isa 41:21-29).

48:9 *Put salt on Moab:* This may have been part of a ceremony to put a curse on a town. Salting farmland was an ancient military strategy to present the repopulation of defeated areas (see Judg 9:45). Crops cannot grow in soil that contains too much salt.

48:1-47 Isa 15:1—16:14; 25:10-12; Ezek 25:8-11; Amos 2:1-3; Zeph 2:8-11.

[a]1 Or / *Misgab* [b]2 The Hebrew for *Heshbon* sounds like the Hebrew for *plot.*
[c]2 The name of the Moabite town Madmen sounds like the Hebrew for *be silenced.* [d]4 Hebrew; Septuagint / *proclaim it to Zoar* [e]6 Or *like Aroer*
[f]9 Or *Give wings to Moab, / for she will fly away*

48:11 *wine . . . not poured from one jar to another:* Moab was famous for its vineyards (Isa 16:8-10). When bottled wine was not disturbed, some particles would settle to the bottom of the bottle. This "aging" process actually improved the quality of the wine. Unlike Judah, Moab was not destroyed by the Babylonians in 586 B.C. But eventually Moab was "poured out" (48:12) after it was invaded by Nebuchadnezzar's troops. Moab ceased to exist as a nation after an invasion of Arab tribes in the sixth century B.C.

48:13 *Bethel:* This may refer to the Phoenician or Canaanite god of that name, or it may refer to the town where people of the northern kingdom worshiped a golden calf at a local shrine (1 Kgs 12:26-30; Amos 3:13,14).

48:18-20 *Dibon . . . Aroer . . . Arnon:* Dibon (modern Dhiban), the capital city of Moab, was located 13 miles east of the Dead Sea (Isa 15:2,9). Aroer was located just north of the Arnon River, which flows east into the Dead Sea. See the map on p. 1321.

48:21 *Judgment has come to the plateau:* The complete destruction of Moab is described. Many of the places mentioned here are unknown. Bozrah is not the same Bozrah as in 49:13, where it is the capital of Edom. See also the note at 48:18-20.

10 "A curse on him who is lax in doing the LORD's work!
A curse on him who keeps his sword from bloodshed!

11 "Moab has been at rest from youth,
like wine left on its dregs,
not poured from one jar to another—
she has not gone into exile.
So she tastes as she did,
and her aroma is unchanged.
12 But days are coming,"
declares the LORD,
"when I will send men who pour from jars,
and they will pour her out;
they will empty her jars
and smash her jugs.
13 Then Moab will be ashamed of Chemosh,
as the house of Israel was ashamed
when they trusted in Bethel.

14 "How can you say, 'We are warriors,
men valiant in battle'?
15 Moab will be destroyed and her towns invaded;
her finest young men will go down in the slaughter,"
declares the King, whose name is the LORD Almighty.
16 "The fall of Moab is at hand;
her calamity will come quickly.
17 Mourn for her, all who live around her,
all who know her fame;
say, 'How broken is the mighty scepter,
how broken the glorious staff!'

18 "Come down from your glory
and sit on the parched ground,
O inhabitants of the Daughter of Dibon,
for he who destroys Moab
will come up against you
and ruin your fortified cities.
19 Stand by the road and watch,
you who live in Aroer.
Ask the man fleeing and the woman escaping,
ask them, 'What has happened?'
20 Moab is disgraced, for she is shattered.
Wail and cry out!
Announce by the Arnon
that Moab is destroyed.
21 Judgment has come to the plateau—
to Holon, Jahzah and Mephaath,
22 to Dibon, Nebo and Beth Diblathaim,
23 to Kiriathaim, Beth Gamul and Beth Meon,

24 to Kerioth and Bozrah—
to all the towns of Moab, far and near.
25 Moab's horn[a] is cut off;
her arm is broken,"
declares the LORD.

26 "Make her drunk,
for she has defied the LORD.
Let Moab wallow in her vomit;
let her be an object of ridicule.
27 Was not Israel the object of your ridicule?
Was she caught among thieves,
that you shake your head in scorn
whenever you speak of her?
28 Abandon your towns and dwell among the rocks,
you who live in Moab.
Be like a dove that makes its nest
at the mouth of a cave.

29 "We have heard of Moab's pride—
her overweening pride and conceit,
her pride and arrogance
and the haughtiness of her heart.
30 I know her insolence but it is futile,"
declares the LORD,
"and her boasts accomplish nothing.
31 Therefore I wail over Moab,
for all Moab I cry out,
I moan for the men of Kir Hareseth.
32 I weep for you, as Jazer weeps,
O vines of Sibmah.
Your branches spread as far as the sea;
they reached as far as the sea of Jazer.
The destroyer has fallen
on your ripened fruit and grapes.
33 Joy and gladness are gone
from the orchards and fields of Moab.
I have stopped the flow of wine from the presses;
no one treads them with shouts of joy.
Although there are shouts,
they are not shouts of joy.

34 "The sound of their cry rises
from Heshbon to Elealeh and Jahaz,
from Zoar as far as Horonaim and Eglath
Shelishiyah,
for even the waters of Nimrim are dried up.

[a]25 *Horn* here symbolizes strength.

48:26 *an object of ridicule:* Moab assisted Babylon in the attack on Judah in 598 B.C. (2 Kgs 24:1, 2). While once Moab had made fun of Judah, now Moab will be laughed at. For the wine of God's wrath see 25:15 and note.

48:28 *like a dove:* Like doves who made their nests in the rocks of high mountains, the Moabites will leave their lowland towns and take to the hills. See also Ezek 7:16.

48:31-34 *Kir Hareseth . . . waters of Nimrim:* More Moabite locations will be destroyed. Kir Hareseth was probably located about seventeen miles south of Ar. Sibmah is compared to a lush vineyard, heavy with riches and prosperity. The wine trade reached to Jazer, which was a center for the god Tammuz. Worship of Tammuz involved weeping over his death. Jazer was probably north of the Dead Sea near the southern border of Ammon. Elealeh was about one mile from Heshbon (see Num 32:3). Zoar was in southern Moab near the south end of the Dead Sea. The location of the waters of Nimrim may refer to Wadi Nimrim, which flows east into the Jordan River about eight miles north of the Dead Sea. See the map on p. 1321.

48:29-34 Isa 16:6-10.

48:36 *flute:* This ancient instrument was probably a pipe made from the tough stalk of a reed plant. It had a mournful sound that was especially suited for playing laments.

48:37 *head is shaved . . . sackcloth:* Here is a vivid picture of public mourning practices. See the notes at 4:8 and 41:5.

48:38 *broken Moab like a jar:* Compare this picture of Moab's destruction with the destruction of Judah (13:12-14) and of King Jehoiachin and his family (22:28).

48:43 *Terror and pit and snare:* For this triple threat see also Isa 24:17, 18 (compare Amos 5:19).

48:45 *a blaze from the midst of Sihon:* Sihon was the Amorite king who refused to let the Israelites pass through his country on their way to the promised land (Num 21:21-30).

48:40 Deut 28:49; Jer 49:22.

35 In Moab I will put an end
to those who make offerings on the high places
and burn incense to their gods,"
declares the LORD.

36 "So my heart laments for Moab like a flute;
it laments like a flute for the men of Kir Hareseth.
The wealth they acquired is gone.
37 Every head is shaved
and every beard cut off;
every hand is slashed
and every waist is covered with sackcloth.
38 On all the roofs in Moab
and in the public squares
there is nothing but mourning,
for I have broken Moab
like a jar that no one wants,"
declares the LORD.

39 "How shattered she is! How they wail!
How Moab turns her back in shame!
Moab has become an object of ridicule,
an object of horror to all those around her."

40 This is what the LORD says:

"Look! An eagle is swooping down,
spreading its wings over Moab.
41 Kerioth[a] will be captured
and the strongholds taken.
In that day the hearts of Moab's warriors
will be like the heart of a woman in labor.
42 Moab will be destroyed as a nation
because she defied the LORD.
43 Terror and pit and snare await you,
O people of Moab,"
declares the LORD.

44 "Whoever flees from the terror
will fall into a pit,
whoever climbs out of the pit
will be caught in a snare;
for I will bring upon Moab
the year of her punishment,"
declares the LORD.

45 "In the shadow of Heshbon
the fugitives stand helpless,
for a fire has gone out from Heshbon,
a blaze from the midst of Sihon;

[a]**41** Or *The cities*

it burns the foreheads of Moab,
the skulls of the noisy boasters.
46 Woe to you, O Moab!
The people of Chemosh are destroyed;
your sons are taken into exile
and your daughters into captivity.

47 "Yet I will restore the fortunes of Moab
in days to come,"
declares the LORD.

Here ends the judgment on Moab.

A Message About Ammon

49 Concerning the Ammonites:

This is what the LORD says:

"Has Israel no sons?
Has she no heirs?
Why then has Molech[a] taken possession of Gad?
Why do his people live in its towns?
2 But the days are coming,"
declares the LORD,
"when I will sound the battle cry
against Rabbah of the Ammonites;
it will become a mound of ruins,
and its surrounding villages will be set on fire.
Then Israel will drive out
those who drove her out,"
says the LORD.
3 "Wail, O Heshbon, for Ai is destroyed!
Cry out, O inhabitants of Rabbah!
Put on sackcloth and mourn;
rush here and there inside the walls,
for Molech will go into exile,
together with his priests and officials.
4 Why do you boast of your valleys,
boast of your valleys so fruitful?
O unfaithful daughter,
you trust in your riches and say,
'Who will attack me?'
5 I will bring terror on you
from all those around you,"
declares the Lord, the LORD Almighty.
"Every one of you will be driven away,
and no one will gather the fugitives.

---

[a]**1** Or *their king*; Hebrew *malcam*; also in verse 3

48:46 *Moab . . . Chemosh:* See the note at 48:7.

48:47 *I will restore the fortunes of Moab:* Compare to the last line of Jeremiah's message to Egypt (46:26).

49:1 *Ammonites:* Ammon and the people of Israel often battled (Judg 10:6—11:40; 1 Sam 11; 2 Sam 12:26-31). After the collapse of the northern kingdom of Israel in 722 B.C., Ammonites invaded portions of the territory of the Gad tribe. Finally, in Jeremiah's time, the Ammonite king Baalis hired Ishmael to assassinate the Jewish governor Gedaliah in 586 B.C. (40:13, 14). See the map on p. 2467.

49:1 *Molech:* Molech was the national god of Ammon (see the note at 7:31).

49:2,3 *Rabbah . . . Heshbon . . . Ai:* Rabbah is modern Amman, Jordan. Since Heshbon was near the border of Moab and Ammon, it was probably ruled by the country that was stronger at that time. The location of Ai is not known.

49:3 *sackcloth:* See the note at 4:8.

49:5 *you will be driven away:* The Ammonites came under Babylonian control when Babylon defeated Assyria (612 B.C.). They helped Babylon attack Judah during the rule of Jehoiakim (2 Kgs 24:2). But later they rebelled against Babylon (27:3; Ezek 21:18-23). Even after Judah fell, Ammon continued to support the Jewish rebel Ishmael (40:7-16). Because of their disloyalty to Babylon, Nebuchadnezzar invaded in 582 B.C.

49:1-6 Ezek 21:28-32; 25:1-7; Amos 1:13-15; Zeph 2:8-11.

49:6 *Yet afterward . . . restore:* See also 46:26 and 48:47.

49:7,8 *Edom . . . Esau:* The land of Edom, sometimes called Seir, was located south and southeast of the Dead Sea, which put it next to Judah's southwestern border (see the map on p. 2467). The people of Edom were descendants of Jacob's brother Esau (Gen 25:24-26; 36:1). The nation of Edom is usually described in the Bible as an enemy of Israel (Num 20:14-21; 24:18; 1 Sam 14:47, 48; 2 Sam 8:13, 14). The Edomites joined Nebuchadnezzar in defeating Jerusalem in 587 B.C. and is reported to have rejoiced when the city fell (Ps 137:7; Lam 4:21; Obad 10-16). The Edomites took advantage of Judah's defeat by settling in southern Judah.

49:7,8 *Teman . . . Dedan:* Teman was the name of a town in Edom, but here it probably stands for the whole nation. Dedan was the name of a town in northwest Arabia and was also used to describe the northwest region of Arabia along the Red Sea.

49:9 *grape pickers . . . leave a few grapes:* According to the Law of Moses, part of the harvest was to be left in the fields and vineyards to be gathered by the poor (Lev 19:9, 10; 23:22; Ruth 2:1-3).

49:12 *drink the cup:* See the note at 8:14.

49:13 *Bozrah:* The capital of northern Edom.

49:16 *clefts of the rocks:* Edom was noted for its rock fortresses built high in mountainous cliffs.

49:7-22 Isa 34:5-17; 63:1-6; Ezek 25:12-14; 35:1-15; Amos 1:11, 12; Obad 1-14; Mal 1:2-5. **49:14-16** Obad 1-4.

6 "Yet afterward, I will restore the fortunes of the
Ammonites,"
declares the LORD.

A Message About Edom

7 Concerning Edom:

This is what the LORD Almighty says:

"Is there no longer wisdom in Teman?
Has counsel perished from the prudent?
Has their wisdom decayed?
8 Turn and flee, hide in deep caves,
you who live in Dedan,
for I will bring disaster on Esau
at the time I punish him.
9 If grape pickers came to you,
would they not leave a few grapes?
If thieves came during the night,
would they not steal only as much as they wanted?
10 But I will strip Esau bare;
I will uncover his hiding places,
so that he cannot conceal himself.
His children, relatives and neighbors will perish,
and he will be no more.
11 Leave your orphans; I will protect their lives.
Your widows too can trust in me."

12 This is what the LORD says: "If those who do not deserve to
drink the cup must drink it, why should you go unpunished? You
will not go unpunished, but must drink it. 13 I swear by myself,"
declares the LORD, "that Bozrah will become a ruin and an object
of horror, of reproach and of cursing; and all its towns will be in
ruins forever."

14 I have heard a message from the LORD:
An envoy was sent to the nations to say,
"Assemble yourselves to attack it!
Rise up for battle!"

15 "Now I will make you small among the nations,
despised among men.
16 The terror you inspire
and the pride of your heart have deceived you,
you who live in the clefts of the rocks,
who occupy the heights of the hill.
Though you build your nest as high as the eagle's,
from there I will bring you down,"
declares the LORD.

17 “Edom will become an object of horror;
all who pass by will be appalled and will scoff
because of all its wounds.
18 As Sodom and Gomorrah were overthrown,
along with their neighboring towns,”
says the LORD,
“so no one will live there;
no man will dwell in it.

19 “Like a lion coming up from Jordan’s thickets
to a rich pastureland,
I will chase Edom from its land in an instant.
Who is the chosen one I will appoint for this?
Who is like me and who can challenge me?
And what shepherd can stand against me?”
20 Therefore, hear what the LORD has planned against Edom,
what he has purposed against those who live in Teman:
The young of the flock will be dragged away;
he will completely destroy their pasture because of them.
21 At the sound of their fall the earth will tremble;
their cry will resound to the Red Sea.[a]
22 Look! An eagle will soar and swoop down,
spreading its wings over Bozrah.
In that day the hearts of Edom’s warriors
will be like the heart of a woman in labor.

A Message About Damascus

23 Concerning Damascus:

“Hamath and Arpad are dismayed,
for they have heard bad news.
They are disheartened,
troubled like[b] the restless sea.
24 Damascus has become feeble,
she has turned to flee
and panic has gripped her;
anguish and pain have seized her,
pain like that of a woman in labor.
25 Why has the city of renown not been abandoned,
the town in which I delight?
26 Surely, her young men will fall in the streets;
all her soldiers will be silenced in that day,”
declares the LORD Almighty.
27 “I will set fire to the walls of Damascus;
it will consume the fortresses of Ben-Hadad.”

49:18 *As Sodom and Gomorrah were overthrown:* See the note at 23:14.

49:19-21 *Like a lion . . . earth will tremble:* In 50:44-46 this same phrase is used to describe Babylon. See also 4:7; 5:6; Hos 5:14; 13:4-8.

49:21 *Red Sea:* Referring to the Gulf of Aqaba, the northeastern arm of the Red Sea (see the map on p. 2463).

49:22 *An eagle will soar and swoop down:* Compare to 30:6 and 48:40. Note that there is no prophecy of the restoration of Edom as there is with other nations in this section (46:26, 27; 48:47; 49:6). The hatred between "brothers" Edom and Israel was deep and persistent.

49:23 *Damascus . . . Arpad:* The modern day capital of Syria, Damascus, fell to the Assyrian king Tiglath-Pileser II in 732 B.C., and little is known of its history in the next few centuries. Hamath and Arpad were two towns in Aram (Syria) that had been the capitals of small kingdoms allied with the more powerful kingdom whose capital was Damascus. Arpad was captured by the Assyrians in 740 B.C., and Hamath in 738 B.C. See the map on p. 2468.

49:27 *Ben-Hadad:* This was the name of several rulers of Damascus (1 Kgs 15:18-20; 20:1; 2 Kgs 6:24; 8:7; 13:24). See also Amos 1:4.

49:23-27 Isa 10:8, 9; 17:1-3; 37:13; Amos 1:3-5; Zech 9:1. **49:26** Jer 50:30.

[a] **21** Hebrew *Yam Suph*; that is, Sea of Reeds [b] **23** Hebrew *on* or *by*

49:28 *Kedar . . . kingdom of Hazor:* Kedar probably refers to the leading tribe of a group of nomadic tribes in the north Arabian desert east of Aram (see the map on p. 2468). Other desert peoples ("kingdom of Hazor") lived in villages and were not nomads. Neither the tent-dwelling tribes nor the desert villagers had cities with walls, so they were vulnerable to attack (49:31). Bedouin herders today live in tents made of animal skins much like the Kedar tribe described by Jeremiah.

49:28 *Nebuchadnezzar:* See the note at 21:2.

49:33 *jackals:* See the note at 9:11.

49:34 *early in the reign of Zedekiah:* Zedekiah became king in March 598 B.C. See also the note at 21:1.

49:35 *Elam:* This nation east of Babylon in modern southwest Iran was attacked by Nebuchadnezzar about 596 B.C. The Elamites later played a role in the overthrow of Babylon in 540 B.C. (Isa 21:2). See the map on p. 2468.

A Message About Kedar and Hazor

28 Concerning Kedar and the kingdoms of Hazor, which
Nebuchadnezzar king of Babylon attacked:

This is what the LORD says:

"Arise, and attack Kedar
and destroy the people of the East.
29 Their tents and their flocks will be taken;
their shelters will be carried off
with all their goods and camels.
Men will shout to them,
'Terror on every side!'

30 "Flee quickly away!
Stay in deep caves, you who live in Hazor,"
declares the LORD.
"Nebuchadnezzar king of Babylon has plotted
against you;
he has devised a plan against you.
31 "Arise and attack a nation at ease,
which lives in confidence,"
declares the LORD,
"a nation that has neither gates nor bars;
its people live alone.
32 Their camels will become plunder,
and their large herds will be booty.
I will scatter to the winds those who are in distant places[a]
and will bring disaster on them from every side,"
declares the LORD.
33 "Hazor will become a haunt of jackals,
a desolate place forever.
No one will live there;
no man will dwell in it."

A Message About Elam

34 This is the word of the LORD that came to Jeremiah the
prophet concerning Elam, early in the reign of Zedekiah king of
Judah:

35 This is what the LORD Almighty says:

"See, I will break the bow of Elam,
the mainstay of their might.
36 I will bring against Elam the four winds
from the four quarters of the heavens;
I will scatter them to the four winds,

---

[a] **32** Or *who clip the hair by their foreheads*

and there will not be a nation
where Elam's exiles do not go.
37 I will shatter Elam before their foes,
before those who seek their lives;
I will bring disaster upon them,
even my fierce anger,"
declares the LORD.
"I will pursue them with the sword
until I have made an end of them.
38 I will set my throne in Elam
and destroy her king and officials,"
declares the LORD.
39 "Yet I will restore the fortunes of Elam
in days to come,"
declares the LORD.

A Message About Babylon

50 This is the word the LORD spoke through Jeremiah the
prophet concerning Babylon and the land of the Babylonians[a]:

2 "Announce and proclaim among the nations,
lift up a banner and proclaim it;
keep nothing back, but say,
'Babylon will be captured;
Bel will be put to shame,
Marduk filled with terror.
Her images will be put to shame
and her idols filled with terror.'
3 A nation from the north will attack her
and lay waste her land.
No one will live in it;
both men and animals will flee away.

4 "In those days, at that time,"
declares the LORD,
"the people of Israel and the people of Judah together
will go in tears to seek the LORD their God.
5 They will ask the way to Zion
and turn their faces toward it.
They will come and bind themselves to the LORD
in an everlasting covenant
that will not be forgotten.

6 "My people have been lost sheep;
their shepherds have led them astray
and caused them to roam on the mountains.
They wandered over mountain and hill

[a]1 Or *Chaldeans*; also in verses 8, 25, 35 and 45

49:39 *Yet I will restore:* For similar promises, see 46:26; 48:47; 49:6.

50:2 *lift up a banner:* These banners were used to give orders on the battlefield.

50:2 *Marduk:* Marduk was the great cosmic god of the heavens and father of the family of gods in Babylon. He was worshiped with elaborate rituals and ceremonies led by priests, who carried images of Marduk through the streets in the New Year's procession. Marduk was also known by the names "Bel" and "Merodach." He is sometimes represented in art as a dragon or bull.

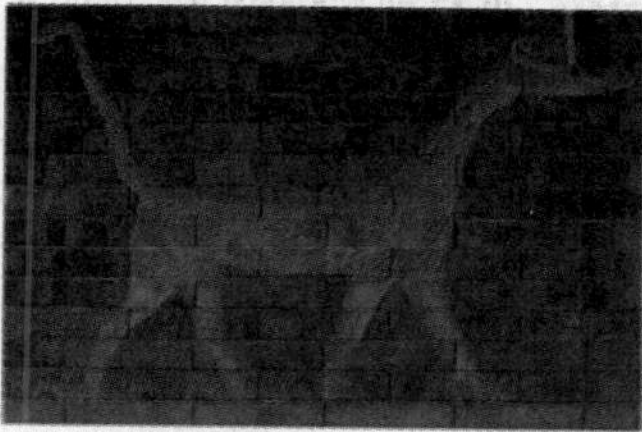

50:3 *A nation from the north will attack her . . . No one will live in it:* Elsewhere in JEREMIAH, Babylon and its king Nebuchadnezzar are called the LORD's "servant," chosen to be the instrument of God's judgment against the people of Judah and surrounding nations (25:9; 27:6,7; 29:7). But now the tone of the prophecies turns bitterly against Babylon.

Babylon fell to the Persian king Cyrus in October 539 B.C., but without a battle and with little damage to the city. The powerful priests of Marduk actually opened the city gates to Cyrus, because they were furious with their king, Nabonidus (556-539 B.C.), who tried to replace Marduk with the moon-god Sin. See the mini-articles called "Babylon," p. 1363, and "Persia," p. 859.

50:1—51:64 Isa 13:1—14:23; 47:1-15.

The LORD spoke,
"Flee out of Babylon;
leave the land of the
Babylonians, and be
like the goats that lead
the flock."
Jer 50:8

50:9 *alliance of great nations:* This refers to a group of kingdoms to the north of Babylon. For a list of these nations, see Jer 51:27,28 and the note.

50:13 *All who pass:* The Hebrew has "they will hiss." Hissing was thought to be a way to ward off the evil witnessed by those passing by an evil place.

50:8 Isa 48:20; Rev 18:4.

and forgot their own resting place.
7 Whoever found them devoured them;
their enemies said, 'We are not guilty,
for they sinned against the LORD, their true pasture,
the LORD, the hope of their fathers.'

8 "Flee out of Babylon;
leave the land of the Babylonians,
and be like the goats that lead the flock.
9 For I will stir up and bring against Babylon
an alliance of great nations from the land of the north.
They will take up their positions against her,
and from the north she will be captured.
Their arrows will be like skilled warriors
who do not return empty-handed.
10 So Babylonia[a] will be plundered;
all who plunder her will have their fill,"
declares the LORD.

11 "Because you rejoice and are glad,
you who pillage my inheritance,
because you frolic like a heifer threshing grain
and neigh like stallions,
12 your mother will be greatly ashamed;
she who gave you birth will be disgraced.
She will be the least of the nations—
a wilderness, a dry land, a desert.
13 Because of the LORD's anger she will not be inhabited
but will be completely desolate.
All who pass Babylon will be horrified and scoff
because of all her wounds.

14 "Take up your positions around Babylon,
all you who draw the bow.
Shoot at her! Spare no arrows,
for she has sinned against the LORD.
15 Shout against her on every side!
She surrenders, her towers fall,
her walls are torn down.
Since this is the vengeance of the LORD,
take vengeance on her;
do to her as she has done to others.
16 Cut off from Babylon the sower,
and the reaper with his sickle at harvest.
Because of the sword of the oppressor
let everyone return to his own people,
let everyone flee to his own land.

[a]**10** Or *Chaldea*

17 "Israel is a scattered flock
that lions have chased away.
The first to devour him
was the king of Assyria;
the last to crush his bones
was Nebuchadnezzar king of Babylon."

18 Therefore this is what the LORD Almighty, the God of Israel, says:

"I will punish the king of Babylon and his land
as I punished the king of Assyria.
19 But I will bring Israel back to his own pasture
and he will graze on Carmel and Bashan;
his appetite will be satisfied
on the hills of Ephraim and Gilead.
20 In those days, at that time,"
declares the LORD,
"search will be made for Israel's guilt,
but there will be none,
and for the sins of Judah,
but none will be found,
for I will forgive the remnant I spare.
21 "Attack the land of Merathaim
and those who live in Pekod.
Pursue, kill and completely destroy[a] them,"
declares the LORD.
"Do everything I have commanded you.
22 The noise of battle is in the land,
the noise of great destruction!
23 How broken and shattered
is the hammer of the whole earth!
How desolate is Babylon
among the nations!
24 I set a trap for you, O Babylon,
and you were caught before you knew it;
you were found and captured
because you opposed the LORD.
25 The LORD has opened his arsenal
and brought out the weapons of his wrath,
for the Sovereign LORD Almighty has work to do
in the land of the Babylonians.
26 Come against her from afar.
Break open her granaries;
pile her up like heaps of grain.
Completely destroy her

[a]21 The Hebrew term refers to the irrevocable giving over of things or persons to the LORD, often by totally destroying them; also in verse 26.

50:17-20 *Israel is a scattered flock . . . I will forgive the remnant I spare:* These verses give a condensed summary of the fall of Israel and Judah. The king of Assyria was either Shalmaneser V (ruled 726-722 B.C.), who conquered most of the northern kingdom and surrounded its capital city Samaria, or Sargon II (ruled 722-705 B.C.), who took thousands of prisoners back to Assyria. For Nebuchadnezzar's attack on the southern kingdom of Judah, see the note at 21:2. The punishment of Nebuchadnezzar is also described in 25:12. The places named in 50:19 were all in the territory of what was once the northern kingdom (see the map on p. 2467). See also the article called "From Joshua to the Exile: The People of Israel in the Promised Land," p. 924.

50:21 *Merathaim . . . Pekod:* Merathaim probably referred to lagoons near the mouth of the Tigris and Euphrates rivers or to the Persian Gulf (see the map on p. 2468), but in Hebrew it means "Twice as Rebellious." Pekod referred to a tribe of southeastern Babylon, but in Hebrew it means "Punishment." Thus, "Double Rebellion" will get its reward, and "Punishment" will see its own. The invitation to "completely destroy them" was part of the "ban" called for in Israel's "holy wars." See also the mini-article called "Holy War (The LORD's Battles)," p. 306.

50:28 *Zion . . . vengeance for his temple:* Those exiled in Babylon, set free at last, will tell how God took revenge on their captors in response to the destruction of the temple in Jerusalem. See the note at 3:14.

50:32 *The arrogant one will stumble and fall:* Babylon was an impressive and powerful city. But the pride of its people and leaders has turned into arrogance. So they will stumble and fall from their high position.

50:33,34 *captors . . . bring rest to their land:* In 586 B.C., thousands of Judeans were deported to Babylon. Now God will bring peace to Israel (Isa 32:18) and unrest for Babylon (see the note at 50:3).

50:34 *LORD Almighty:* See the note at 2:19.

50:36 *her false prophets:* Babylonian prophets and fortunetellers tried to predict the future by examining fluid in a cup, looking at the livers of animals, or trying to contact the spirits of the dead. The priests of Babylon also used astrology to chart a person's future based on the position of the stars and planets at the time of his or her birth. These prophets are called fools because they did not correctly predict Babylon's destruction.

50:29 Rev 18:6. **50:30** Jer 49:26.

and leave her no remnant.
27 Kill all her young bulls;
let them go down to the slaughter!
Woe to them! For their day has come,
the time for them to be punished.
28 Listen to the fugitives and refugees from Babylon
declaring in Zion
how the LORD our God has taken vengeance,
vengeance for his temple.

29 "Summon archers against Babylon,
all those who draw the bow.
Encamp all around her;
let no one escape.
Repay her for her deeds;
do to her as she has done.
For she has defied the LORD,
the Holy One of Israel.
30 Therefore, her young men will fall in the streets;
all her soldiers will be silenced in that day,"
declares the LORD.
31 "See, I am against you, O arrogant one,"
declares the Lord, the LORD Almighty,
"for your day has come,
the time for you to be punished.
32 The arrogant one will stumble and fall
and no one will help her up;
I will kindle a fire in her towns
that will consume all who are around her."

33 This is what the LORD Almighty says:

"The people of Israel are oppressed,
and the people of Judah as well.
All their captors hold them fast,
refusing to let them go.
34 Yet their Redeemer is strong;
the LORD Almighty is his name.
He will vigorously defend their cause
so that he may bring rest to their land,
but unrest to those who live in Babylon.

35 "A sword against the Babylonians!"
declares the LORD—
"against those who live in Babylon
and against her officials and wise men!
36 A sword against her false prophets!
They will become fools.
A sword against her warriors!
They will be filled with terror.

37 A sword against her horses and chariots
and all the foreigners in her ranks!
They will become women.
A sword against her treasures!
They will be plundered.
38 A drought on[a] her waters!
They will dry up.
For it is a land of idols,
idols that will go mad with terror.

39 "So desert creatures and hyenas will live there,
and there the owl will dwell.
It will never again be inhabited
or lived in from generation to generation.
40 As God overthrew Sodom and Gomorrah
along with their neighboring towns,"
declares the LORD,
"so no one will live there;
no man will dwell in it.

41 "Look! An army is coming from the north;
a great nation and many kings
are being stirred up from the ends of the earth.
42 They are armed with bows and spears;
they are cruel and without mercy.
They sound like the roaring sea
as they ride on their horses;
they come like men in battle formation
to attack you, O Daughter of Babylon.
43 The king of Babylon has heard reports about
them,
and his hands hang limp.
Anguish has gripped him,
pain like that of a woman in labor.
44 Like a lion coming up from Jordan's thickets
to a rich pastureland,
I will chase Babylon from its land in an instant.
Who is the chosen one I will appoint for this?
Who is like me and who can challenge me?
And what shepherd can stand against me?"
45 Therefore, hear what the LORD has planned
against Babylon,
what he has purposed against the land of the
Babylonians:
The young of the flock will be dragged away;
he will completely destroy their pasture because of
them.

[a]38 Or *A sword against*

50:37 *foreigners in her ranks:* When the defense of Babylon is necessary, these foreign soldiers will refuse to risk their lives.

50:38 *waters . . . dry up:* Babylon had two major rivers (Tigris and Euphrates), and it had developed a system of canals for transportation and irrigating crops.

50:40 *Sodom and Gomorrah:* See the note at 23:14.

50:41-43 *An army is coming from the north . . . pain like that of a woman in labor:* These verses echo 6:22-24, where they were addressed to Judah; here they are applied to Babylon. The enemy from the north here is Persia (see the map on p. 2469).

50:39 Rev 18:2. **50:44-46** Jer 49:19-21.

46 At the sound of Babylon's capture the earth will tremble;
its cry will resound among the nations.

51 This is what the LORD says:

"See, I will stir up the spirit of a destroyer
against Babylon and the people of Leb Kamai.[a]
2 I will send foreigners to Babylon
to winnow her and to devastate her land;
they will oppose her on every side
in the day of her disaster.
3 Let not the archer string his bow,
nor let him put on his armor.
Do not spare her young men;
completely destroy[b] her army.
4 They will fall down slain in Babylon,[c]
fatally wounded in her streets.
5 For Israel and Judah have not been forsaken
by their God, the LORD Almighty,
though their land[d] is full of guilt
before the Holy One of Israel.

6 "Flee from Babylon!
Run for your lives!
Do not be destroyed because of her sins.
It is time for the LORD's vengeance;
he will pay her what she deserves.
7 Babylon was a gold cup in the LORD's hand;
she made the whole earth drunk.
The nations drank her wine;
therefore they have now gone mad.
8 Babylon will suddenly fall and be broken.
Wail over her!
Get balm for her pain;
perhaps she can be healed.

9 " 'We would have healed Babylon,
but she cannot be healed;
let us leave her and each go to his own land,
for her judgment reaches to the skies,
it rises as high as the clouds.'

10 " 'The LORD has vindicated us;
come, let us tell in Zion
what the LORD our God has done.'

[a]1 *Leb Kamai* is a cryptogram for Chaldea, that is, Babylonia. [b]3 The Hebrew term refers to the irrevocable giving over of things or persons to the LORD, often by totally destroying them. [c]4 Or *Chaldea* [d]5 Or / *and the land ⌞of the Babylonians⌟*

51:1 *Babylon:* The theme of this chapter, and chapter 50 before it, is the end of Babylon's history. See the map on p. 2468 and the mini-article called "Babylon," p. 1363. The Hebrew of 51:1 uses a code name for Babylon. Codes (ciphers) were used as a means of protecting the writer and readers from punishment at the hands of an enemy. These codes were developed during the time of exile in Babylon. Code language was used frequently in REVELATION in New Testament times, when persecution of the churches in the Roman empire was widespread. In REVELATION, "Babylon" is the code name for the mighty Roman empire.

The defeat of Babylon is predicted. These verses seem to predict a bloody struggle, but the defeat of Babylon itself involved little fighting.

51:5 *Israel and Judah have not been forsaken:* Jeremiah's twofold task is restated (see 1:10). Israel and Judah turned away from the LORD, and so they were punished. Babylon was the instrument of God's judgment. Babylon crushed Judah, reduced Jerusalem to rubble, stole Israel's sacred objects while tearing down the temple, and took many of Judah's citizens into exile in Babylon. But this humiliating and dark time in the history of God's people will end with the defeat of Babylon, and the Jewish people will go home and be restored. See the note at 50:3.

51:7 *gold cup . . . drunk:* See the notes at 8:14 and 25:15. See also Rev 17:2-4; 18:3.

51:8 *Wail over her:* The words are those of a lament, but the tone is taunting, gloating. There is no hope for Babylon.

51:10 *Zion:* See the note at 3:14. The Jewish exiles in Babylon send the news back home to Judah: God is ready to destroy Babylon.

51:9 Jer 46:11.

11 "Sharpen the arrows,
take up the shields!
The LORD has stirred up the kings of the Medes,
because his purpose is to destroy Babylon.
The LORD will take vengeance,
vengeance for his temple.
12 Lift up a banner against the walls of Babylon!
Reinforce the guard,
station the watchmen,
prepare an ambush!
The LORD will carry out his purpose,
his decree against the people of Babylon.
13 You who live by many waters
and are rich in treasures,
your end has come,
the time for you to be cut off.
14 The LORD Almighty has sworn by himself:
I will surely fill you with men, as with
a swarm of locusts,
and they will shout in triumph over you.

15 "He made the earth by his power;
he founded the world by his wisdom
and stretched out the heavens by his understanding.
16 When he thunders, the waters in the heavens roar;
he makes clouds rise from the ends of the earth.
He sends lightning with the rain
and brings out the wind from his storehouses.

17 "Every man is senseless and without knowledge;
every goldsmith is shamed by his idols.
His images are a fraud;
they have no breath in them.
18 They are worthless, the objects of mockery;
when their judgment comes, they will perish.
19 He who is the Portion of Jacob is not like these,
for he is the Maker of all things,
including the tribe of his inheritance—
the LORD Almighty is his name.

20 "You are my war club,
my weapon for battle—
with you I shatter nations,
with you I destroy kingdoms,
21 with you I shatter horse and rider,
with you I shatter chariot and driver,
22 with you I shatter man and woman,
with you I shatter old man and youth,
with you I shatter young man and maiden,

51:11 *kings of the Medes:* Media was the ancient kingdom northeast of Babylon (see the map on p. 2468). The Median king Astyges was overthrown by Cyrus of Persia in 550 B.C. Then, Media was part of a coalition headed by Cyrus that brought Babylon down in 539 B.C. The "kings" here may also refer to the leaders of smaller kingdoms that were part of the Median empire (see 51:27, 28 and note). See also the mini-article called "Persia," p. 859.

51:12 *Lift up a banner:* See the note at 50:2 (banner). Like a general barking orders to the troops, the LORD rallies the coalition to destroy Babylon.

51:13 *by many waters:* See the note at 50:38.

51:14 *locusts:* See the note at 46:23. The enemy will descend on Babylon like a cloud of hungry insects.

51:15-17 *made the earth by his power . . . idols . . . are a fraud:* See the note at 10:12-16. See also Ps 104:2-4; 18:11-15; Job 28:25, 26. The LORD God of Israel, the Creator of all, is contrasted with the stupid and worthless idols (false gods) of Babylon. See also Isa 41:21-29. Israel, the nation of God, is marked as God's own forever (Isa 49:15, 16).

51:19 *the tribe of his inheritance:* The powerful God of creation is also Israel's personal God, who chose them (Isa 41:8, 9).

51:20 *You are my war club:* Once the LORD's chosen agent of judgment (25:9; 27:6, 7; 29:7), Babylon will soon be judged.

51:13 Rev 17:1.

23 with you I shatter shepherd and flock,
with you I shatter farmer and oxen,
with you I shatter governors and officials.

24 "Before your eyes I will repay Babylon and all who live in
Babylonia[a] for all the wrong they have done in Zion," declares the
LORD.

25 "I am against you, O destroying mountain,
you who destroy the whole earth,"
declares the LORD.

"I will stretch out my hand against you,
roll you off the cliffs,
and make you a burned-out mountain.
26 No rock will be taken from you for a cornerstone,
nor any stone for a foundation,
for you will be desolate forever,"
declares the LORD.

27 "Lift up a banner in the land!
Blow the trumpet among the nations!
Prepare the nations for battle against her;
summon against her these kingdoms:
Ararat, Minni and Ashkenaz.
Appoint a commander against her;
send up horses like a swarm of locusts.
28 Prepare the nations for battle against her—
the kings of the Medes,
their governors and all their officials,
and all the countries they rule.
29 The land trembles and writhes,
for the LORD's purposes against Babylon stand—
to lay waste the land of Babylon
so that no one will live there.
30 Babylon's warriors have stopped fighting;
they remain in their strongholds.
Their strength is exhausted;
they have become like women.
Her dwellings are set on fire;
the bars of her gates are broken.
31 One courier follows another
and messenger follows messenger
to announce to the king of Babylon
that his entire city is captured,
32 the river crossings seized,
the marshes set on fire,
and the soldiers terrified."

[a]**24** Or *Chaldea*; also in verse 35

51:24 *done in Zion:* See the notes at 3:14 and 39:8.

51:25 *a burned-out mountain:* Ancient Babylon was known for its towering brick temple (ziggurat) to the god Marduk and for beautiful cut stone palaces, walls, and roadways. The "burned-out mountain" may refer to the destruction of the towering temple of Marduk, which rose above the plains of Babylon like a mountain.

51:27,28 *Ararat, Minni and Ashkenaz . . . kings of the Medes:* These small kingdoms to the north of Babylon were defeated by the Medes between 600 and 575 B.C. and became part of the Median empire. They joined the Medes in the battle against Babylon (51:28).

Ararat (Urartu) peoples probably came from southeast Turkey, and the Minni from northern Iraq. The Ashkenaz, later called Scythians, came from the area of present-day Armenia. See the map on p. 2468.

51:30-32 *bars of her gates are broken . . . marshes set on fire:* The Babylonian king receives one message of doom after another. Once Babylon's important waterways have been captured, the country is in deep trouble (see 51:36 and note at 50:38). The tall grass in marshes surrounding Babylon could have provided hiding places for people trying to escape from Babylon. But they are set on fire to cut off escape and to smoke out enemy troops.

[33]This is what the LORD Almighty, the God of Israel, says:

"The Daughter of Babylon is like a threshing floor
at the time it is trampled;
the time to harvest her will soon come."

[34]"Nebuchadnezzar king of Babylon has devoured us,
he has thrown us into confusion,
he has made us an empty jar.
Like a serpent he has swallowed us
and filled his stomach with our delicacies,
and then has spewed us out.
[35]May the violence done to our flesh[a] be upon Babylon,"
say the inhabitants of Zion.
"May our blood be on those who live in Babylonia,"
says Jerusalem.

[36]Therefore, this is what the LORD says:

"See, I will defend your cause
and avenge you;
I will dry up her sea
and make her springs dry.
[37]Babylon will be a heap of ruins,
a haunt of jackals,
an object of horror and scorn,
a place where no one lives.
[38]Her people all roar like young lions,
they growl like lion cubs.
[39]But while they are aroused,
I will set out a feast for them
and make them drunk,
so that they shout with laughter—
then sleep forever and not awake,"
declares the LORD.
[40]"I will bring them down
like lambs to the slaughter,
like rams and goats.

[41]"How Sheshach[b] will be captured,
the boast of the whole earth seized!
What a horror Babylon will be
among the nations!
[42]The sea will rise over Babylon;
its roaring waves will cover her.
[43]Her towns will be desolate,
a dry and desert land,

[a]35 Or *done to us and to our children* [b]41 *Sheshach* is a cryptogram for Babylon.

51:33 *threshing floor:* In preparation for harvest, a dirt surface for threshing the grain was made level and packed down to make it hard and smooth. After the grain was threshed (separated from the stalk), the place was swept clean. So will Babylon be pounded and then swept away by war.

51:34 *Nebuchadnezzar . . . swallowed us . . . our delicacies:* See the note at 21:2. During the destruction of Jerusalem in 586 B.C., Nebuchadnezzar's army stole the temple treasures and captured many of Judah's people. The treasures and people were carried off to Babylon.

51:36 *dry up her sea . . . make her springs dry:* The "sea" is probably the Euphrates River. Cutting off the water supply is cutting off Babylon's life, as the city depended on the river and springs (see also 51:32 and the note at 50:38).

51:37 *jackals:* See the note at 9:11. Babylon will become a scorched desert, fit for only wild desert animals. See also Isa 13:19-22.

51:38-40 *young lions . . . slaughter:* See 50:44-46 and the note at 49:19-21. The Babylonian leaders will devour other countries the way young lions devour their prey. But their banquet of conquest will make them drunk (51:39) as if they have drunk God's cup of wrath (see 51:7). While in a drunken sleep they will be dragged to the butcher to be slaughtered.

"Remember the LORD in a distant land, and think on Jerusalem."
Jer 51:50

51:44 *I will punish Bel:* The fall of Babylon is described as a cosmic battle between Israel's LORD God and Babylon's god Bel (also called Marduk, see the note at 50:2). Bel will be forced to vomit up everything that Babylon's armies took from Judah (see 51:34 and note). The people of Judah will leave Babylon and return home with the temple treasures (Ezra 1:1-11).

51:45-50 *Run for your lives . . . Babylon must fall . . . do not linger:* Many political upheavals and changes on the throne occurred in Babylon after Nebuchadnezzar's death in 562 B.C. These changes and the rumors of the Persian advance on Babylon around 540 B.C. would make the Judean prisoners living there fearful. God's people are told to run away because Babylon's destruction is coming. But God will protect the people of Judah when the Persians attack Babylon. In reality, the Persian takeover of Babylon was not violent. And Cyrus of Persia allowed the people of Judah to return home in peace. See also the mini-article called "Exile," p. 1541, and the article called "After the Exile: God's People Return to Judea," p. 931.

51:53 *Even if Babylon reaches the sky:* See the note at 51:25.

51:48,49 Rev 18:20; 18:24.

a land where no one lives,
    through which no man travels.
44 I will punish Bel in Babylon
    and make him spew out what he has swallowed.
The nations will no longer stream to him.
    And the wall of Babylon will fall.

45 "Come out of her, my people!
    Run for your lives!
    Run from the fierce anger of the LORD.
46 Do not lose heart or be afraid
    when rumors are heard in the land;
one rumor comes this year, another the next,
    rumors of violence in the land
    and of ruler against ruler.
47 For the time will surely come
    when I will punish the idols of Babylon;
her whole land will be disgraced
    and her slain will all lie fallen within her.
48 Then heaven and earth and all that is in them
    will shout for joy over Babylon,
for out of the north
    destroyers will attack her,"
        declares the LORD.

49 "Babylon must fall because of Israel's slain,
    just as the slain in all the earth
    have fallen because of Babylon.
50 You who have escaped the sword,
    leave and do not linger!
Remember the LORD in a distant land,
    and think on Jerusalem."

51 "We are disgraced,
    for we have been insulted
    and shame covers our faces,
because foreigners have entered
    the holy places of the LORD's house."

52 "But days are coming," declares the LORD,
    "when I will punish her idols,
and throughout her land
    the wounded will groan.
53 Even if Babylon reaches the sky
    and fortifies her lofty stronghold,
    I will send destroyers against her,"
        declares the LORD.

54 "The sound of a cry comes from Babylon,
    the sound of great destruction

from the land of the Babylonians.[a]
55 The LORD will destroy Babylon;
he will silence her noisy din.
Waves ⌊of enemies⌋ will rage like great waters;
the roar of their voices will resound.
56 A destroyer will come against Babylon;
her warriors will be captured,
and their bows will be broken.
For the LORD is a God of retribution;
he will repay in full.
57 I will make her officials and wise men drunk,
her governors, officers and warriors as well;
they will sleep forever and not awake,"
declares the King, whose name is the LORD Almighty.

58 This is what the LORD Almighty says:

"Babylon's thick wall will be leveled
and her high gates set on fire;
the peoples exhaust themselves for nothing,
the nations' labor is only fuel for the flames."

59 This is the message Jeremiah gave to the staff officer Seraiah son of Neriah, the son of Mahseiah, when he went to Babylon
with Zedekiah king of Judah in the fourth year of his reign. 60 Jeremiah had written on a scroll about all the disasters that would
come upon Babylon—all that had been recorded concerning
Babylon. 61 He said to Seraiah, "When you get to Babylon, see that
you read all these words aloud. 62 Then say, 'O LORD, you have said

[a]54 Or *Chaldeans*

51:57 *make her officials and wise men drunk:* See the note at 51:38-40.

51:58 *high gates set on fire:* A wide avenue known as the Processional Way led through the heart of ancient Babylon. Its entrance was the famous Ishtar Gate, made of brick and decorated with some 575 bulls and serpent-headed dragons. It was an impressive entryway into a proud city. All the effort that Nebuchadnezzar put into building projects to beautify and fortify the city would become as nothing. See also Hab 2:13 and the mini-article called "Babylon," p. 1363.

51:59 *Seraiah . . . Zedekiah . . . fourth year:* See the note at 1:2,3. Zedekiah's fourth year was 594 B.C. Why he went to Babylon is not known. Seraiah was the brother of Jeremiah's friend Baruch, who wrote down Jeremiah's messages (see 32:12 and the note).

51:55 Jer 51:42.

QUESTIONS ABOUT JEREMIAH 45:1—51:64

1. Review what you know about Jeremiah's friend Baruch (see 32:12-14; 36:4-32). Then look at the message to Baruch in chapter 45. What is he promised there? Why might it have been difficult to be Jeremiah's friend?
2. Review what the LORD says about the Egyptians, Philistines, and Moabites in chapters 46–48. Why do you think these foreign nations are included in Jeremiah's prophecy? What images do you find particularly powerful? What hope is given in a number of these prophecies?
3. What were the sources of power for the nations addressed in chapter 49? In what did these nations trust? What will happen to them?
4. Babylon is addressed in chapters 50, 51. Compare the future of this great city with the future promised to Israel and Judah. How is it that Babylon can be both God's chosen instrument of judgment (27:6) and the target of God's revenge (chapters 50, 51)?
5. In the New Testament book of REVELATION, "Babylon" was the code name used for the Roman empire, enemy to Christian churches at that time. What made Babylon such a long-lasting symbol of evil? In what ways, if any, are some nations like "Babylon"?

51:63 *scroll, tie a stone to it . . . throw it into the Euphrates:* The prophecy is acted out as in 13:1-11. The message is given emphasis by the action. Compare this action also to the purchase of the field in 32:1-14. There the message is hope for Judah; here the message is doom for Babylon. See also Rev 18:21.

51:64 *The words of Jeremiah end here:* This is probably an editor's comment to show that what follows in chapter 52 was added to the end of the book by another editor to give further background for the events described in Jeremiah's prophecies and in the episodes from his life.

52:1-3 *Zedekiah . . . rebelled against the king of Babylon:* Chapter 52 was added by an editor (see the note at 51:64). By repeating the historic records dealing with portions of Zedekiah's reign, the siege and capture of Jerusalem, the destruction of the temple, and the exile of the Jews, the editor is showing how Jeremiah's prophecies came true.

52:1 *Hamutal daughter of Jeremiah:* Zedekiah's mother (Hamutal) was not the daughter of Jeremiah the prophet, but of a different Jeremiah.

52:3 *because of the* L*ORD's anger:* Worship of foreign idols, unfair treatment of the poor, and making treaties with foreign powers were Judah's primary acts of disobedience. See especially 2:1-28 and the notes.

52:4-6 *tenth month . . . fourth month:* See 39:1,2. See also Ezek 24:1,2.

52:8-11 *Zedekiah . . . took him to Babylon:* See 39:6 and note. The last thing Zedekiah saw was the execution of his own sons. See 2 Kgs 25:7; Ezek 12:13.

52:12 *in the nineteenth year of Nebuchadnezzar:* See the note at 21:2.

52:7 Ezek 33:21.

you will destroy this place, so that neither man nor animal will live
in it; it will be desolate forever.' [63]When you finish reading this
scroll, tie a stone to it and throw it into the Euphrates. [64]Then say,
'So will Babylon sink to rise no more because of the disaster I will
bring upon her. And her people will fall.'"

The words of Jeremiah end here.

Another Account of the Fall of Jerusalem

This chapter supports Jeremiah's prophecy as history bears witness to the truth of his message.

The Fall of Jerusalem

52 Zedekiah was twenty-one years old when he became king,
and he reigned in Jerusalem eleven years. His mother's name was
Hamutal daughter of Jeremiah; she was from Libnah. [2]He did evil
in the eyes of the LORD, just as Jehoiakim had done. [3]It was because
of the LORD's anger that all this happened to Jerusalem and Judah,
and in the end he thrust them from his presence.

Now Zedekiah rebelled against the king of Babylon.

[4]So in the ninth year of Zedekiah's reign, on the tenth day of
the tenth month, Nebuchadnezzar king of Babylon marched
against Jerusalem with his whole army. They camped outside the
city and built siege works all around it. [5]The city was kept under
siege until the eleventh year of King Zedekiah.

[6]By the ninth day of the fourth month the famine in the city
had become so severe that there was no food for the people to eat.
[7]Then the city wall was broken through, and the whole army fled.
They left the city at night through the gate between the two walls
near the king's garden, though the Babylonians[a] were surrounding
the city. They fled toward the Arabah,[b] [8]but the Babylonian[c] army
pursued King Zedekiah and overtook him in the plains of Jericho.
All his soldiers were separated from him and scattered, [9]and he was
captured.

He was taken to the king of Babylon at Riblah in the land of
Hamath, where he pronounced sentence on him. [10]There at Riblah
the king of Babylon slaughtered the sons of Zedekiah before his
eyes; he also killed all the officials of Judah. [11]Then he put out
Zedekiah's eyes, bound him with bronze shackles and took him to
Babylon, where he put him in prison till the day of his death.

[12]On the tenth day of the fifth month, in the nineteenth year
of Nebuchadnezzar king of Babylon, Nebuzaradan commander of

---

[a]7 Or *Chaldeans*; also in verse 17 [b]7 Or *the Jordan Valley* [c]8 Or *Chaldean*; also in verse 14

the imperial guard, who served the king of Babylon, came to
Jerusalem. 13He set fire to the temple of the LORD, the royal palace
and all the houses of Jerusalem. Every important building he
burned down. 14The whole Babylonian army under the commander of the imperial guard broke down all the walls around
Jerusalem. 15Nebuzaradan the commander of the guard carried
into exile some of the poorest people and those who remained in
the city, along with the rest of the craftsmen[a] and those who had
gone over to the king of Babylon. 16But Nebuzaradan left behind
the rest of the poorest people of the land to work the vineyards
and fields.
17The Babylonians broke up the bronze pillars, the movable

[a]15 Or *populace*

52:12-15 *Nebuzaradan . . . carried into exile:* See 39:9 and note. Nebuchadnezzar had also taken away some of Judah's skilled workers eleven years before (2 Kgs 24:14-16).

52:17-20 *broke up the bronze pillars . . . the Sea:* Nebuzaradan had his men take from the temple the sacred objects that Israel's priests used to offer sacrifices to the LORD. For detailed descriptions of these objects, see 1 Kings 7:13-50.

52:13 1 Kgs 9:8.

EXILE

"Exile" is the term used for the captivity of a number of Judah's people taken to Babylon during the invasions of King Nebuchadnezzar of Babylon. Nebuchadnezzar first invaded Judah in 598 B.C. and took King Jehoiachin and a number of Judah's leaders back to Babylon. In 587 B.C. Judah's King Zedekiah rebelled and Nebuchadnezzar again invaded Judah. This time Nebuchadnezzar's army smashed the walls of Jerusalem and took many sacred objects from the temple there. Once again, many of Jerusalem's leaders and skilled workers were taken away into exile.

Judah was made a Babylonian province under a governor appointed by Nebuchadnezzar. No longer would a king from the family of David sit on the throne of Israel. Counting the deportations of 597 and 586 B.C. and perhaps a later one in 582 B.C., Jeremiah 52:28-30 puts the total number of persons exiled at 4,600, while 2 Kings 24:14 says ten thousand were deported in 597 B.C. alone. The lower figure in JEREMIAH may include only adult males.

Little is known about life in Judah for those who were left behind or about life in Babylon for the exiles. There is no evidence that life in Babylon was unusually harsh, though some Judeans struggled to hang on to their beliefs in the face of pressure from Babylonian culture and religion. And many longed to return home to the promised land (Ps 137). Others probably established themselves as part of the Babylonian community, taking advantage of business opportunities there. There is evidence that a number of Jews stayed behind in Babylon, even after Cyrus of Persia captured it and allowed the Jews to return home to Judea.

The experience of the exile had a profound impact on the Jewish people. Having no temple where the priests could offer sacrifices, the people began to gather in groups for prayer and to study the Scriptures—which was perhaps the origin of the Jewish synagogues. It is possible that during this time many of the Jewish Scriptures were written down and compiled by editors and scribes. These Scriptures made clear why the people of Israel suffered the great humiliation of the exile. The Jews learned that the exile did not happen by accident. The LORD God allowed it to happen because the people turned away from God and sinned, forgetting especially the commandment of Exodus 20:3: "You shall have no other gods before me." When it was time to return to the homeland in 539 B.C., the Judeans (or Jews) were ready to rebuild Jerusalem and its temple and to renew their earlier covenant with the LORD.

52:21,22 *pillars . . . pomegranates:* These hollow bronze columns were over half the height of the temple itself, which was forty-five feet high. A pomegranate is a small red fruit that looks like an apple on the outside. It is full of seeds and has very sweet-tasting juice.

52:24 *Seraiah . . . Zephaniah:* This Seraiah may be the same as the one mentioned in 36:26 but not the one in 51:59. Seraiah was the grandfather of Joshua, the high priest when the temple was rebuilt after the exile. See 21:1; 29:29; 37:3-5.

52:25-27 *those still in the city . . . Riblah . . . executed:* The seventy-four arrested men are taken to the Babylonian camp at Riblah and killed as a representative punishment and warning to the rest who survived. See the note at 39:4, 5.

52:28-30 *This is the number . . . taken into exile:* Nebuchadnezzar's seventh year was 598 B.C., when Jehoiachin was king of Judah (compare the number in 2 Kgs 24:14). His eighteenth year (compare 52:12) was 586 B.C., when Zedekiah reigned and Jerusalem was destroyed. The twenty-third year would have been 582 B.C., which probably refers to the time of troubles following the assassination of Gedaliah (41:1-3). These numbers for exiled Jews are not found in 2 KINGS; perhaps they come from a Babylonian record. What happened to the rest of the people? The poorest were left behind (52:16); others chose to relocate to Egypt and nearby lands.

stands and the bronze Sea that were at the temple of the LORD and
they carried all the bronze to Babylon. [18]They also took away the
pots, shovels, wick trimmers, sprinkling bowls, dishes and all the
bronze articles used in the temple service. [19]The commander of
the imperial guard took away the basins, censers, sprinkling bowls, pots, lampstands, dishes and bowls used for drink offerings—all that were made of pure gold or silver.

[20]The bronze from the two pillars, the Sea and the twelve bronze bulls under it, and the movable stands, which King Solomon had made for the temple of the LORD, was more than
could be weighed. [21]Each of the pillars was eighteen cubits high and twelve cubits in circumference[a]; each was four fingers thick,
and hollow. [22]The bronze capital on top of the one pillar was five cubits[b] high and was decorated with a network and pomegranates of bronze all around. The other pillar, with its pomegranates, was
similar. [23]There were ninety-six pomegranates on the sides; the total number of pomegranates above the surrounding network was a hundred.

[24]The commander of the guard took as prisoners Seraiah the chief priest, Zephaniah the priest next in rank and the three door-
keepers. [25]Of those still in the city, he took the officer in charge of the fighting men, and seven royal advisers. He also took the secretary who was chief officer in charge of conscripting the people of
the land and sixty of his men who were found in the city. [26]Neb-
uzaradan the commander took them all and brought them to the
king of Babylon at Riblah. [27]There at Riblah, in the land of
Hamath, the king had them executed.

So Judah went into captivity, away from her land. [28]This is
the number of the people Nebuchadnezzar carried into exile:

in the seventh year, 3,023 Jews;

[29]in Nebuchadnezzar's eighteenth year,

832 people from Jerusalem;

[30]in his twenty-third year,

[a]21 That is, about 27 feet (about 8.1 meters) high and 18 feet (about 5.4 meters) in circumference [b]22 That is, about 7 1/2 feet (about 2.3 meters)

QUESTIONS ABOUT JEREMIAH 52

1. Why do you think JEREMIAH ends with the account of the capture of Jerusalem? What does 52:2,3 tell you about the people? about the LORD?
2. The last verses of the book are concerned with the exiled king, Jehoiachin. How did his life mirror that of all God's people?
3. Choose several images from JEREMIAH that especially help you remember and understand the book's message. Explain your choices.
4. How is the experience of "exile" painful? How can this experience or idea of exile be helpful to the life of faith?

745 Jews taken into exile by Nebuzaradan the commander
of the imperial guard.
There were 4,600 people in all.

Jehoiachin Released

31In the thirty-seventh year of the exile of Jehoiachin king of
Judah, in the year Evil-Merodach[a] became king of Babylon, he
released Jehoiachin king of Judah and freed him from prison on
the twenty-fifth day of the twelfth month. 32He spoke kindly to
him and gave him a seat of honor higher than those of the other
kings who were with him in Babylon. 33So Jehoiachin put aside his
prison clothes and for the rest of his life ate regularly at the king's
table. 34Day by day the king of Babylon gave Jehoiachin a regular
allowance as long as he lived, till the day of his death.

[a]31 Also called *Amel-Marduk*

52:31-34 *Jehoiachin ... Evil-Merodach:* Jehoiachin was exiled after the first rebellion in 598 B.C. See 22:24 and the note. Nebuchadnezzar died in 562, and his son Evil-Merodach succeeded him. His Babylonian name was "Amel-Marduk," meaning "man of the god Marduk." The twelfth month of the Hebrew calendar is Adar, from about mid-February to mid-March. After thirty-seven years of imprisonment, Jehoiachin was set free by Evil-Merodach. Jehoiachin's freedom was a hopeful sign of the coming restoration of Judah (see the note at 50:3). A year after he became king, Evil-Merodach was murdered by Nergal-Sharezer (who ruled from 560 to 556 B.C.).

LAMENTATIONS

Grief and sadness are part of the human experience. Read Lamentations to see how eyewitnesses responded to the tragic destruction of Jerusalem and its temple.

Jerusalem: Jerusalem was the capital of the united Israelite kingdom under kings David and Solomon (from around 1010 to 931 B.C.). It became the capital of the southern kingdom (Judah) when the kingdom divided after the death of Solomon. David originally captured the city from the Jebusites around 1000 B.C. (2 Sam 5:6-12) and had the ark of the covenant brought there (2 Sam 6:1-19), making it the religious and spiritual center, as well as the political capital, of the nation. Later, David's son, Solomon, expanded the city, built a glorious royal palace for himself and a temple for worshiping the LORD (1 Kgs 5,6). Even after the kingdom divided, and after being conquered several times by foreigners, Jerusalem retained special significance for the Jewish people, who would continue to think of it as God's city for God's people. See the mini-article called "Jerusalem," on p. 574.

What makes Lamentations special?

LAMENTATIONS is actually a collection of five separate poems, printed here as chapters. These poems, sometimes called "laments," express deep sadness and share a common theme and a common use in worship. In synagogues today, LAMENTATIONS is read aloud on the ninth day of Ab (late July), a day of fasting that commemorates the destruction of the Jerusalem temple in 586 B.C., and of the second temple in A.D. 70. Many Christian churches include readings from LAMENTATIONS in their worship services during Holy Week, the week before Easter. The expression of the people's grief and agony is timeless, as is the hope for restoration and renewal that is based on God's mercy. In LAMENTATIONS we find deep sorrow, much complaint, but also hope and trust in God's mercy.

Why was Lamentations written?

The five poems are presented as eyewitness accounts to one of the greatest tragedies in Jewish history. God's special city (Jerusalem) and God's special place (the temple) were robbed and destroyed by Israel's enemies. The poems are written to lament this destruction, but also as a way of finding some meaning in it for God's people. Sometimes tragedy reveals God's purpose. God punished the people for their sins, but did not abandon them completely.

What's the story behind the scene?

The small southern kingdom of Judah fell to the powerful forces of Babylon in 586 B.C. after years of repression following an unsuccessful rebellion in 597 B.C. The capture and destruction, described in 2 Kings 25, was swift, terrible, and total. King Zedekiah, who ruled Judah from 598 to 586 B.C., was taken prisoner and exiled to Babylon along with many of Jerusalem, and Judah's leading citizens, priests, and craftsmen. The poor and the peasants were left behind. For more information, see the mini-articles called "Babylon," p. 1363, and "Exile," p. 1541; see also the article called "From Joshua to the Exile: The People of Israel in the Promised Land," p. 924.

The Septuagint, the Greek translation of the Jewish Scriptures, calls this book the "Lamentations of Jeremiah." The poems are similar in tone and mood, and include phrases similar to those used by that prophet.

SECOND CHRONICLES speaks of a lament written by Jeremiah (see 2 Chr 35:25). That song, however, was written to commemorate the death of King Josiah (609 B.C.) rather than the destruction of Jerusalem (586 B.C.). The oldest and best Hebrew texts of LAMENTATIONS do not name an author.

Many scholars believe that the collection is not the work of a single author. The poems—whether composed by the people of Judah who had been taken into captivity by the Babylonians, or by those who were left behind—were no doubt written by eyewitnesses to this terrible tragedy.

HOW IS LAMENTATIONS CONSTRUCTED?

The five poems are presented here as being spoken by either the author or by the city of Jerusalem itself. Chapters 1, 2, and 4 are public expressions of grief over the loss of Jerusalem. Chapter 3 is a personal lament, similar to the Servant's Song in Isaiah 53, which ends in a prayer of thanksgiving and trust. Chapter 5 is a public prayer for mercy.

The poems were carefully constructed to make them easier to remember. Chapters 1 through 4 are called "alphabetic acrostics," meaning that each stanza (verse) begins with a letter of the Hebrew alphabet and follows the order of the alphabet. Chapters 1, 2, and 4 have twenty-two stanzas, one for each of the twenty-two letters of the alphabet. Chapter 3 has sixty-six stanzas, three for each letter. Chapter 5 also has twenty-two stanzas, but is not an acrostic.

The careful structure of these poems shows that the expression of grief is measured and conscious, and it is well-suited to a public worship service where LAMENTATIONS would be spoken aloud by the congregation or worship leader. The special treatment of chapter 3 also highlights its important message. Placed at the center of the book, it is constructed on the basis of the number three, which in the ancient world had the meaning of completeness. This special chapter speaks of God's unending love and desire to rescue people from their enemies.

First lament: Lonely Jerusalem (1:1-22)
Second lament: The LORD is like an enemy (2:1-22)
Third lament: There is still hope (3:1-66)
Fourth lament: The punishment of Jerusalem (4:1-22)
Fifth lament: A prayer for mercy (5:1-22)

1:1 *the city:* Referring to Jerusalem, the capital of the southern kingdom, Judah. See the note on p. 1544. The author of this poem describes the city as if it were a woman. At the height of its fame it was "queen among the provinces," now it is an abandoned widow who can do nothing but grieve for her losses.

1:1,2 *become a slave . . . lovers:* Jerusalem's king, court officials, priests, and leading citizens were led into captivity by King Nebuchadnezzar in 586 B.C. They were taken to Babylon, some five hundred miles away (see the map on p. 2468).

The poet speaks of Judah's former allies as "lovers" and "friends" who were not trustworthy. Judah relied on other nations, in particular Egypt, for support in its rebellion against Babylon, rather than relying on the LORD. For evidence that they should have known better, see Isa 31:1-3.

First Lament: Lonely Jerusalem

The writer speaks of the punishment of the city, and Jerusalem speaks of sorrow and loneliness.

1[a] How deserted lies the city,
once so full of people!
How like a widow is she,
who once was great among the nations!

[a]This chapter is an acrostic poem, the verses of which begin with the successive letters of the Hebrew alphabet.

The LORD has brought her grief because of her many sins. Her children have gone into exile, captive before the foe.
Lam 1:5

1:3 *All who pursue her have overtaken her:* This refers to the Babylonian army. The burning, robbing, and destruction of the city is described in 2 Kgs 25:1-21. See also the note at 1:14.

1:4 *Zion:* The hill where the temple stood; Zion was also used as a name for the city of Jerusalem. The only proper place for sacrifices was the temple, and pilgrims traveled long distances to celebrate important feast days there. See also the mini-article called "Zion," p. 1294.

Western Wall in Jerusalem, nineteenth century photograph. Nothing remains of the temple Solomon built in Jerusalem in the tenth century B.C. which was destroyed by the Babylonians in 586 B.C. The five poems that make up LAMENTATIONS express great sadness for the destruction of Jerusalem and the temple. The temple was rebuilt after the Jews returned from exile in the sixth century (dedicated in 516 B.C.). Later it was enlarged under Herod the Great (who ruled Palestine from 37 B.C. to 4 B.C.). This second temple was destroyed in A.D. 70 when the Romans suppressed a Jewish revolt. The Western Wall is from Herod's temple. By the sixteenth century, it became an important place for Jewish prayer.

She who was queen among the provinces
  has now become a slave.

2 Bitterly she weeps at night,
  tears are upon her cheeks.
Among all her lovers
  there is none to comfort her.
All her friends have betrayed her;
  they have become her enemies.

3 After affliction and harsh labor,
  Judah has gone into exile.
She dwells among the nations;
  she finds no resting place.
All who pursue her have overtaken her
  in the midst of her distress.

4 The roads to Zion mourn,
  for no one comes to her appointed feasts.
All her gateways are desolate,
  her priests groan,

her maidens grieve,
    and she is in bitter anguish.

5 Her foes have become her masters;
    her enemies are at ease.
The LORD has brought her grief
    because of her many sins.
Her children have gone into exile,
    captive before the foe.

6 All the splendor has departed
    from the Daughter of Zion.
Her princes are like deer
    that find no pasture;
in weakness they have fled
    before the pursuer.

7 In the days of her affliction and wandering
    Jerusalem remembers all the treasures
    that were hers in days of old.
When her people fell into enemy hands,
    there was no one to help her.
Her enemies looked at her
    and laughed at her destruction.

8 Jerusalem has sinned greatly
    and so has become unclean.
All who honored her despise her,
    for they have seen her nakedness;
she herself groans
    and turns away.

9 Her filthiness clung to her skirts;
    she did not consider her future.
Her fall was astounding;
    there was none to comfort her.
"Look, O LORD, on my affliction,
    for the enemy has triumphed."

10 The enemy laid hands
    on all her treasures;
she saw pagan nations
    enter her sanctuary—
those you had forbidden
    to enter your assembly.

11 All her people groan
    as they search for bread;
they barter their treasures for food
    to keep themselves alive.
"Look, O LORD, and consider,
    for I am despised."

1:6 *Daughter of Zion:* Jerusalem is sometimes personified as a woman (see Isa 1:8). In Hebrew, the word city has a feminine gender. See also the note at 1:1.

1:6 *like deer that find no pasture:* At one time there were at least three species of deer living in Palestine. The most common were roe deer, which were the smallest of the three species. They didn't graze and travel in herds, and were best adapted to the landscape and climate.

1:7 *the days of her affliction and wandering:* Many Judeans fled to the neighboring nations of Edom, Moab, and Ammon for safety in the turbulent years between the "first exile" of 597 B.C. and the "last exile" of 586 B.C. Large numbers of people from Judah also settled in Egypt during this period. Edom and Moab did not come to Judah's aid; instead, these nations assisted Babylon in the destruction of Judah.

1:8 *sinned greatly:* The destruction was not an accident, but rather a punishment for the sins of the people. Placing their trust in false gods, or idols, was their greatest sins.

1:9 *Her filthiness clung to her skirts:* For a discussion of this concept, see the mini-article called "Purity (Clean and Unclean)," p. 2125.

1:10 *enemy laid hands on all her treasures:* For a list of the treasures taken and melted down for transport back to Babylon, see Jer 52:17-23.

1:13 *he sent fire . . . spread a net:* The author of this lament is clearly saying that the destruction is God's doing. Jerusalem is painfully learning what the prophets Jeremiah and Ezekiel had been trying to tell her: Sin has consequences, and it is God who does the punishing. See Jer 1:16; 30:14; Ezek 7:2-4.

1:14 *those I cannot withstand:* The Babylonian forces invaded Judah and leveled the towns surrounding Jerusalem in 587 B.C., then proceeded to lay siege to Jerusalem with a blockade that lasted a year and a half. In 586 B.C., the walls of Jerusalem fell. The temple was robbed and its treasure sent back to Babylon (2 Kgs 25:9-17; Jer 52:17-23). King Zedekiah was blinded after seeing his sons put to death (2 Kgs 25:6,7). Finally, still more people of Judah were sent to Babylon, where they lived as slaves.

See also the mini-articles called "Nebuchadnezzar," p. 1469, "Exile," p. 1541, and "Enemies (The Wicked)," p. 1084.

1:15 *In his winepress:* Other prophets were also drawn to this vivid image of God's punishment; see Isaiah 63:3; Joel 3:13. For an explanation about winemaking, see the illustration and mini-article called "Wine," p. 2047.

1:17 *Jacob:* Jacob was the grandson of Abraham and father to twelve sons who are named as the ancestors of the twelve tribes of Israel. See also the mini-article called "Israel," p. 264.

12 "Is it nothing to you, all you who pass by?
Look around and see.
Is any suffering like my suffering
that was inflicted on me,
that the LORD brought on me
in the day of his fierce anger?

13 "From on high he sent fire,
sent it down into my bones.
He spread a net for my feet
and turned me back.
He made me desolate,
faint all the day long.

14 "My sins have been bound into a yoke[a];
by his hands they were woven together.
They have come upon my neck
and the Lord has sapped my strength.
He has handed me over
to those I cannot withstand.

15 "The Lord has rejected
all the warriors in my midst;
he has summoned an army against me
to[b] crush my young men.
In his winepress the Lord has trampled
the Virgin Daughter of Judah.

16 "This is why I weep
and my eyes overflow with tears.
No one is near to comfort me,
no one to restore my spirit.
My children are destitute
because the enemy has prevailed."

17 Zion stretches out her hands,
but there is no one to comfort her.
The LORD has decreed for Jacob
that his neighbors become his foes;
Jerusalem has become
an unclean thing among them.

18 "The LORD is righteous,
yet I rebelled against his command.
Listen, all you peoples;
look upon my suffering.
My young men and maidens
have gone into exile.

---

[a]**14** Most Hebrew manuscripts; Septuagint *He kept watch over my sins*
[b]**15** Or *has set a time for me / when he will*

19 "I called to my allies
but they betrayed me.
My priests and my elders
perished in the city
while they searched for food
to keep themselves alive.

20 "See, O LORD, how distressed I am!
I am in torment within,
and in my heart I am disturbed,
for I have been most rebellious.
Outside, the sword bereaves;
inside, there is only death.

21 "People have heard my groaning,
but there is no one to comfort me.
All my enemies have heard of my distress;
they rejoice at what you have done.
May you bring the day you have announced
so they may become like me.

22 "Let all their wickedness come before you;
deal with them
as you have dealt with me
because of all my sins.
My groans are many
and my heart is faint."

Second Lament: The LORD Is Like an Enemy

The LORD has shown anger and brought heartache to Jerusalem; no one can comfort her.

2[a] How the Lord has covered the Daughter of Zion
with the cloud of his anger[b]!
He has hurled down the splendor of Israel
from heaven to earth;
he has not remembered his footstool
in the day of his anger.

2 Without pity the Lord has swallowed up
all the dwellings of Jacob;

1:19 *allies . . . betrayed me:* See the note at 1:1, 2.

1:20 *in my heart I am disturbed:* The author of this lament continues to speak of Jerusalem as if it were a woman (see the note at 1:1). After listing the terrible hardships she has experienced, Jerusalem is able to confess her guilt to God. This is the first step toward turning back to the LORD.

1:22 *deal with them as you have dealt with me:* Jerusalem asks God to punish her enemies. Jerusalem has suffered but her enemies should also suffer. See 3:64-66.

2:1 *Daughter of Zion:* See the note at 1:6.

2:1 *He has hurled down the splendor of Israel:* An image applied to enemy rulers in Isaiah 14:12 and Ezekiel 28:17. Here it is used to describe God's anger toward the people. For Zion, see the note at 1:4.

2:1 *the day of his anger:* God's anger at the people was justified. God's people are finally realizing that what happened to them was not an accident, but an expression of God's righteous character.

[a]This chapter is an acrostic poem, the verses of which begin with the successive letters of the Hebrew alphabet. [b]1 Or *How the Lord in his anger / has treated the Daughter of Zion with contempt*

2:2 *torn down the strongholds:* In the ancient Near East almost all cities were enclosed by a wall for protection. The best walls were made of stone but sometimes bricks made from mud were used. Archaeologists have found the ruins of some ancient walls that were as much as fifteen feet thick.

2:3 *cut off every horn of Israel:* This refers to the Assyrian victory over the northern kingdom, also called Israel, resulting in its fall in 722 B.C.

2:6 *his dwelling . . . feasts . . . Sabbaths:* The temple, God's "dwelling," is destroyed as if it were a temporary shelter set up at harvest time. Everything that God is destroying here was originally given to the people of Israel as something holy and good. But because of the people's sins, God is now punishing them and taking these good things away from them, including the monarchy and priesthood.

2:7 *raised a shout:* The roar of battle replaces the happy shouts of giving thanks to God.

in his wrath he has torn down
the strongholds of the Daughter of Judah.
He has brought her kingdom and its princes
down to the ground in dishonor.

3 In fierce anger he has cut off
every horn[a] of Israel.
He has withdrawn his right hand
at the approach of the enemy.
He has burned in Jacob like a flaming fire
that consumes everything around it.

4 Like an enemy he has strung his bow;
his right hand is ready.
Like a foe he has slain
all who were pleasing to the eye;
he has poured out his wrath like fire
on the tent of the Daughter of Zion.

5 The Lord is like an enemy;
he has swallowed up Israel.
He has swallowed up all her palaces
and destroyed her strongholds.
He has multiplied mourning and lamentation
for the Daughter of Judah.

6 He has laid waste his dwelling like a garden;
he has destroyed his place of meeting.
The LORD has made Zion forget
her appointed feasts and her Sabbaths;
in his fierce anger he has spurned
both king and priest.

7 The Lord has rejected his altar
and abandoned his sanctuary.
He has handed over to the enemy
the walls of her palaces;
they have raised a shout in the house of the LORD
as on the day of an appointed feast.

8 The LORD determined to tear down
the wall around the Daughter of Zion.
He stretched out a measuring line
and did not withhold his hand from destroying.
He made ramparts and walls lament;
together they wasted away.

9 Her gates have sunk into the ground;
their bars he has broken and destroyed.

[a]3 Or *all the strength*; or *every king*; *horn* here symbolizes strength.

Her king and her princes are exiled among the nations,
the law is no more,
and her prophets no longer find
visions from the LORD.

10 The elders of the Daughter of Zion
sit on the ground in silence;
they have sprinkled dust on their heads
and put on sackcloth.
The young women of Jerusalem
have bowed their heads to the ground.

11 My eyes fail from weeping,
I am in torment within,
my heart is poured out on the ground
because my people are destroyed,
because children and infants faint
in the streets of the city.

12 They say to their mothers,
"Where is bread and wine?"
as they faint like wounded men
in the streets of the city,
as their lives ebb away
in their mothers' arms.

13 What can I say for you?
With what can I compare you,
O Daughter of Jerusalem?
To what can I liken you,
that I may comfort you,
O Virgin Daughter of Zion?
Your wound is as deep as the sea.
Who can heal you?

14 The visions of your prophets
were false and worthless;
they did not expose your sin
to ward off your captivity.
The oracles they gave you
were false and misleading.

15 All who pass your way
clap their hands at you;
they scoff and shake their heads
at the Daughter of Jerusalem:
"Is this the city that was called
the perfection of beauty,
the joy of the whole earth?"

16 All your enemies open their mouths
wide against you;

2:9 *king . . . the law . . . prophets:* The leadership of God's people. The Babylonians took King Zedekiah into exile in Babylon in 586 B.C. Responsibility for teaching the law to the people belonged to the priests (Lev 10:11; 2 Kgs 17:28; Jer 18:18; Mal 2:7). The prophets had failed to look after the needs of God's people and God was no longer sending them visions (see the note at 2:14).

2:10 *sprinkled dust . . . put on sackcloth:* This is how people expressed grief and mourning. The picture the writer is creating here is of guests at a funeral, where the only proper response is to sit silently. See also 2 Sam 13:19; Job 2:12, 13; Jer 6:26.

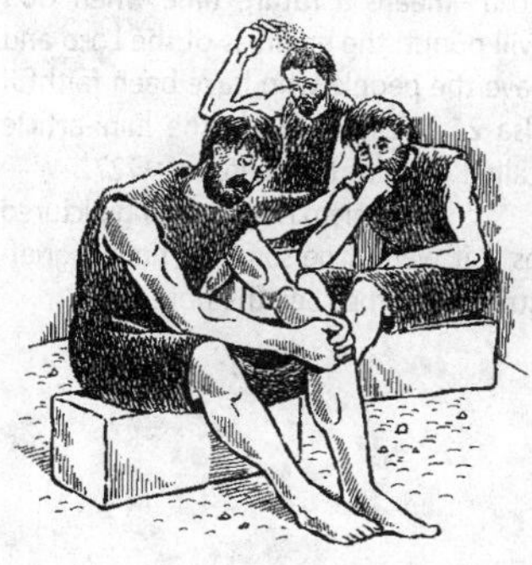

2:11 *My eyes fail from weeping . . . children and infants faint:* Two powerful pictures of unspeakable grief and suffering.

2:13 *Your wound is as deep as the sea:* No one can comfort Zion; her pain is too enormous.

2:14 *prophets . . . false and misleading:* Jeremiah and Ezekiel were obedient prophets who spoke for the LORD, but there were many other prophets in Judah in the sixth century B.C. who did not. These false prophets told the kings and people what they wanted to hear, giving them false hopes (see Jer 14:13-16; 23:25-32; Ezek 13:1-7). See also the article called "Prophets and Prophecy," p. 935.

Pour out your heart like water in the presence of the Lord.
Lam 2:19

2:20 *Should women eat their offspring:* The disaster of 586 B.C. caused starvation, a punishment predicted in Leviticus 26:29 and Ezekiel 5:10.

2:22 *you summoned against me terrors . . . the day of the LORD's anger:* For many of the prophets in the Bible, "the day" or "the day of the LORD" means a future time when God will punish the enemies of the LORD and save the people who have been faithful (Isa 24:21-23). See also the mini-article called "Day of the LORD," p. 1727.

Jerusalem is again being pictured as if it were a person, this time a grief-stricken mother. See the note at 1:1.

they scoff and gnash their teeth
 and say, "We have swallowed her up.
This is the day we have waited for;
 we have lived to see it."

17 The LORD has done what he planned;
 he has fulfilled his word,
 which he decreed long ago.
He has overthrown you without pity,
 he has let the enemy gloat over you,
 he has exalted the horn[a] of your foes.

18 The hearts of the people
 cry out to the Lord.
O wall of the Daughter of Zion,
 let your tears flow like a river
 day and night;
give yourself no relief,
 your eyes no rest.

19 Arise, cry out in the night,
 as the watches of the night begin;
pour out your heart like water
 in the presence of the Lord.
Lift up your hands to him
 for the lives of your children,
who faint from hunger
 at the head of every street.

20 "Look, O LORD, and consider:
 Whom have you ever treated like this?
Should women eat their offspring,
 the children they have cared for?
Should priest and prophet be killed
 in the sanctuary of the Lord?

21 "Young and old lie together
 in the dust of the streets;
my young men and maidens
 have fallen by the sword.
You have slain them in the day of your anger;
 you have slaughtered them without pity.

22 "As you summon to a feast day,
 so you summoned against me terrors on every side.
In the day of the LORD's anger
 no one escaped or survived;
those I cared for and reared,
 my enemy has destroyed."

[a]**17** *Horn* here symbolizes strength.

Third Lament: There Is Still Hope

The writer's lament is both personal (3:1-24) and universal (3:25-66). His own experience speaks to everyone who suffers.

3[a] I am the man who has seen affliction
by the rod of his wrath.
2 He has driven me away and made me walk
in darkness rather than light;
3 indeed, he has turned his hand against me
again and again, all day long.

4 He has made my skin and my flesh grow old
and has broken my bones.
5 He has besieged me and surrounded me
with bitterness and hardship.
6 He has made me dwell in darkness
like those long dead.

7 He has walled me in so I cannot escape;
he has weighed me down with chains.
8 Even when I call out or cry for help,
he shuts out my prayer.
9 He has barred my way with blocks of stone;
he has made my paths crooked.

10 Like a bear lying in wait,
like a lion in hiding,
11 he dragged me from the path and mangled me
and left me without help.
12 He drew his bow
and made me the target for his arrows.

13 He pierced my heart
with arrows from his quiver.
14 I became the laughingstock of all my people;
they mock me in song all day long.
15 He has filled me with bitter herbs
and sated me with gall.

16 He has broken my teeth with gravel;
he has trampled me in the dust.
17 I have been deprived of peace;
I have forgotten what prosperity is.
18 So I say, "My splendor is gone
and all that I had hoped from the LORD."

[a]This chapter is an acrostic poem; the verses of each stanza begin with the successive letters of the Hebrew alphabet, and the verses within each stanza begin with the same letter.

3:1 *the man who has seen affliction:* The deep personal sense of anguish in this poem has much in common with psalms of lamentation; see, for example, Ps 6; 56; 140.

3:10 *Like a bear . . . lion:* The LORD is compared to a predatory animal, who waits patiently for the prey and then attacks fiercely.

3:14 *I became the laughingstock:* Being mocked by neighbors or enemies is another kind of pain frequently addressed in the Bible. (See, for example, Job 30:9; Ps 22:6,7; 44:12-16; Jer 15:15.) The author of this lament repeats this complaint in 3:63. See also the mini-article called "Enemies (The Wicked)," p. 1084.

3:4 Job 7:5; 30:30. **3:6** Job 23:17. **3:16-18** Job 19:10,11; 30:19.

Because of the LORD's great love we are not consumed, for his compassions never fail. They are new every morning; great is your faithfulness.
Lam 3:22,23

3:21 *Yet this I call to mind:* It is not until after the author has finished describing his suffering (3:1-20) that he is able to say what it is that fills the heart with hope (3:21-24). The shift from anguish to hope is based on the author's trust and faith in God. Once he acknowledges this for himself, the author can then proclaim it to other suffering people (3:25-40).

3:22,23 *the LORD's great love . . . his faithfulness:* A similar message is found in many of the Psalms; see, for example, Ps 78:38; 86:15; 111:4; 145:8.

3:24 *The LORD is my portion:* The author ends his personal lament confident that God has heard him and can be trusted. The author's words apply as well to all the people of Judah who have experienced loss. Though they too will raise their voices in sad cries of lamentation, the people will also find hope. God will act to save as surely as God has acted to punish.

3:29,30 *bury his face in the dust . . . offer his cheek:* The Hebrew can be read "mouth in the dust." To accept the reality of the situation is the important first step. Like a loving parent, God punishes the people to teach them valuable lessons, not merely to inflict pain.

3:32 *compassion:* See the note at 3:22, 23.

3:40 *examine our ways:* Honest self-examination is the first step in repentance.

3:26 Isa 40:29-31. **3:38** Isa 45:7; Amos 3:6.

19 I remember my affliction and my wandering,
the bitterness and the gall.
20 I well remember them,
and my soul is downcast within me.
21 Yet this I call to mind
and therefore I have hope:

22 Because of the LORD's great love we are not consumed,
for his compassions never fail.
23 They are new every morning;
great is your faithfulness.
24 I say to myself, "The LORD is my portion;
therefore I will wait for him."

25 The LORD is good to those whose hope is in him,
to the one who seeks him;
26 it is good to wait quietly
for the salvation of the LORD.
27 It is good for a man to bear the yoke
while he is young.

28 Let him sit alone in silence,
for the LORD has laid it on him.
29 Let him bury his face in the dust—
there may yet be hope.
30 Let him offer his cheek to one who would strike him,
and let him be filled with disgrace.

31 For men are not cast off
by the Lord forever.
32 Though he brings grief, he will show compassion,
so great is his unfailing love.
33 For he does not willingly bring affliction
or grief to the children of men.

34 To crush underfoot
all prisoners in the land,
35 to deny a man his rights
before the Most High,
36 to deprive a man of justice—
would not the Lord see such things?

37 Who can speak and have it happen
if the Lord has not decreed it?
38 Is it not from the mouth of the Most High
that both calamities and good things come?
39 Why should any living man complain
when punished for his sins?

40 Let us examine our ways and test them,
and let us return to the LORD.

[41] Let us lift up our hearts and our hands
to God in heaven, and say:
[42] "We have sinned and rebelled
and you have not forgiven.

[43] "You have covered yourself with anger and pursued us;
you have slain without pity.
[44] You have covered yourself with a cloud
so that no prayer can get through.
[45] You have made us scum and refuse
among the nations.

[46] "All our enemies have opened their mouths
wide against us.
[47] We have suffered terror and pitfalls,
ruin and destruction."
[48] Streams of tears flow from my eyes
because my people are destroyed.

[49] My eyes will flow unceasingly,
without relief,
[50] until the LORD looks down
from heaven and sees.
[51] What I see brings grief to my soul
because of all the women of my city.

[52] Those who were my enemies without cause
hunted me like a bird.
[53] They tried to end my life in a pit
and threw stones at me;
[54] the waters closed over my head,
and I thought I was about to be cut off.

[55] I called on your name, O LORD,
from the depths of the pit.
[56] You heard my plea: "Do not close your ears
to my cry for relief."
[57] You came near when I called you,
and you said, "Do not fear."

[58] O Lord, you took up my case;
you redeemed my life.
[59] You have seen, O LORD, the wrong done to me.
Uphold my cause!
[60] You have seen the depth of their vengeance,
all their plots against me.

[61] O LORD, you have heard their insults,
all their plots against me—
[62] what my enemies whisper and mutter
against me all day long.

3:41 *lift up our hearts and our hands:* This was a common way to pray to God in the ancient world. See also Ps 77:2; 88:9; 134:2; 143:6; and the mini-article called "Prayer," p. 2289. In Christian art, these figures are sometimes called "orants." The praying figure shown below is from the Catacomb of Priscilla, Rome, Italy (around A.D. 150). This Priscilla may have been a woman very active in the early church (See Acts 18:2).

3:53 *pit:* This was a cistern or deep well for holding fresh water. In Judah, rainfall was scarce, and the people dug deep pits for holding water and preventing it from evaporating too quickly in the hot sun. See also the mini-article called "Water," p. 1647.

3:57 *Do not fear:* See also Isa 41:10.

3:61 Ps 137:1-3.

3:64 *Pay them back:* The author expresses confidence that God will also punish the enemies of the people of Judah, an attitude also frequently expressed in the Psalms (see, for example, Ps 3:7; 17:13; 35:26; 59:10-13). See also Jeremiah's cry for vengeance on his enemies in Jeremiah 11:20; 18:19-23.

4:1,2 *sacred gems . . . sons of Zion:* The temple treasures have been thrown into the streets by the enemy. God's people living in Zion (Jerusalem) are thrown out of their homes.

4:3 *jackals . . . ostriches:* Jackals are desert animals related to wolves. They were seen as pests because they ate crops and bothered livestock. Ostriches are large birds that run swiftly but cannot fly. They were thought to be foolish and neglectful of their young (see Job 39:13-16).

4:5 *destitute in the streets:* A horrible famine occurred in Jerusalem as a result of the long siege by the Babylonians in 587-586 B.C. (see 2 Kgs 25:2, 3). The author's other references to eating human flesh (2:20 and 4:10) are further evidence of the horror of the famine.

4:6 *Sodom:* This ancient city was destroyed along with its sister city Gomorrah because of the sin of its inhabitants (Gen 19:24, 25). This destruction was God's work. But while Sodom's destruction was swift, Jerusalem's death will be slow and painful.

63 Look at them! Sitting or standing,
they mock me in their songs.

64 Pay them back what they deserve, O LORD,
for what their hands have done.
65 Put a veil over their hearts,
and may your curse be on them!
66 Pursue them in anger and destroy them
from under the heavens of the LORD.

Fourth Lament: The Punishment of Jerusalem

This lament echoes the themes of the second lament, showing the contrast between the past glory of Jerusalem and the present sufferings of the "sons of Zion" at the hands of the Babylonians.

4[a] How the gold has lost its luster,
the fine gold become dull!
The sacred gems are scattered
at the head of every street.

2 How the precious sons of Zion,
once worth their weight in gold,
are now considered as pots of clay,
the work of a potter's hands!

3 Even jackals offer their breasts
to nurse their young,
but my people have become heartless
like ostriches in the desert.

4 Because of thirst the infant's tongue
sticks to the roof of its mouth;
the children beg for bread,
but no one gives it to them.

5 Those who once ate delicacies
are destitute in the streets.
Those nurtured in purple
now lie on ash heaps.

6 The punishment of my people
is greater than that of Sodom,
which was overthrown in a moment
without a hand turned to help her.

[a] This chapter is an acrostic poem, the verses of which begin with the successive letters of the Hebrew alphabet.

7 Their princes were brighter than snow
and whiter than milk,
their bodies more ruddy than rubies,
their appearance like sapphires.[a]

8 But now they are blacker than soot;
they are not recognized in the streets.
Their skin has shriveled on their bones;
it has become as dry as a stick.

9 Those killed by the sword are better off
than those who die of famine;
racked with hunger, they waste away
for lack of food from the field.

10 With their own hands compassionate women
have cooked their own children,
who became their food
when my people were destroyed.

11 The LORD has given full vent to his wrath;
he has poured out his fierce anger.
He kindled a fire in Zion
that consumed her foundations.

12 The kings of the earth did not believe,
nor did any of the world's people,
that enemies and foes could enter
the gates of Jerusalem.

13 But it happened because of the sins of her prophets
and the iniquities of her priests,
who shed within her
the blood of the righteous.

14 Now they grope through the streets
like men who are blind.
They are so defiled with blood
that no one dares to touch their garments.

15 "Go away! You are unclean!" men cry to them.
"Away! Away! Don't touch us!"
When they flee and wander about,
people among the nations say,
"They can stay here no longer."

16 The LORD himself has scattered them;
he no longer watches over them.
The priests are shown no honor,
the elders no favor.

a7 Or *lapis lazuli*

4:7,8 *whiter than milk . . . blacker than soot:* Jerusalem's leading citizens are transformed from health to sickness by the famine.

4:11,12 *kindled a fire in Zion . . . the gates of Jerusalem:* In the eighth century B.C., the prophet Micah first delivered the message of doom to Jerusalem (Mic 3:12). God promised David, "Your throne will be established forever" (2 Sam 7:16). Thus to promise disaster on Jerusalem, David's city, was blasphemy. Jeremiah echoed this prophecy and was beaten and arrested for it (Jer 19:15—20:2). The poem repeats an idea popular in Judah—that no earthly power could overcome the great capital (see also Isa 37:33,34).

4:13,14 *prophets . . . priests . . . defiled with blood:* It was the practice of priests to sacrifice animals at the temple as a way of giving thanks to God and asking the LORD for forgiveness. Here, however, the blood on their clothes is not from a proper sacrifice, but is evidence of their guilt. This blood makes them defiled (unclean). See also the mini-articles called "Blood," p. 180 and "Purity (Clean and Unclean)," p. 2125.

For more about God's judgment of dishonest priests and false prophets, see Isa 28:7-10; Jer 6:13,14; 23:11-22; Ezek 22:26,28.

4:10 Deut 28:56,57; Ezek 5:10.

4:17 *a nation that could not save us:* Egypt had been an ally of Judah against their common enemy, the Babylonians. See Jer 37:6-10.

4:20 *The LORD's anointed:* A reference to King Zedekiah, the last king of Judah, who was taken away to Babylon in 586 B.C. (2 Kgs 25:2-7). The people believed in an eternal kingdom that would be ruled by someone from David's line (see also the note at 4:11,12).

4:21 *Daughter of Edom:* This is a personification of the people of Edom, neighbor of Judah to the southeast of the Dead Sea (see the map on p. 2468). Edom took advantage of Judah after the Babylonian invasion. Because of this betrayal, the author calls down punishment on Edom. See also Jer 49:7-22 and Obad 8-14.

5:1 *what has happened to us:* See the note at 1:14.

5:4 *water . . . wood:* Water and firewood were necessities of life in the ancient world. But now the land and its resources belong to others. After the invasion of 586 B.C., Judah became a province of the Babylonian empire and the poor people of Judah who were not taken into exile were forced to depend on their conquerors.

5:6 *Egypt and Assyria:* People from Judah looked to these areas for help, and fled there because of the terrible conditions in Judah. See the map on p. 2468. See also the mini-articles called "Egypt," p. 135 and "Assyria," p. 711.

17 Moreover, our eyes failed,
looking in vain for help;
from our towers we watched
for a nation that could not save us.

18 Men stalked us at every step,
so we could not walk in our streets.
Our end was near, our days were numbered,
for our end had come.

19 Our pursuers were swifter
than eagles in the sky;
they chased us over the mountains
and lay in wait for us in the desert.

20 The LORD's anointed, our very life breath,
was caught in their traps.
We thought that under his shadow
we would live among the nations.

21 Rejoice and be glad, O Daughter of Edom,
you who live in the land of Uz.
But to you also the cup will be passed;
you will be drunk and stripped naked.

22 O Daughter of Zion, your punishment will end;
he will not prolong your exile.
But, O Daughter of Edom, he will punish your sin
and expose your wickedness.

Fifth Lament: A Prayer for Mercy

Perhaps written for a public occasion of lamentation after the fall of Jerusalem in 586 B.C., this is a prayer in which the people ask God to remember them and have mercy.

5 Remember, O LORD, what has happened to us;
look, and see our disgrace.
2 Our inheritance has been turned over to aliens,
our homes to foreigners.
3 We have become orphans and fatherless,
our mothers like widows.
4 We must buy the water we drink;
our wood can be had only at a price.
5 Those who pursue us are at our heels;
we are weary and find no rest.
6 We submitted to Egypt and Assyria
to get enough bread.

7 Our fathers sinned and are no more,
and we bear their punishment.
8 Slaves rule over us,
and there is none to free us from their hands.
9 We get our bread at the risk of our lives
because of the sword in the desert.
10 Our skin is hot as an oven,
feverish from hunger.
11 Women have been ravished in Zion,
and virgins in the towns of Judah.
12 Princes have been hung up by their hands;
elders are shown no respect.
13 Young men toil at the millstones;
boys stagger under loads of wood.
14 The elders are gone from the city gate;
the young men have stopped their music.
15 Joy is gone from our hearts;
our dancing has turned to mourning.
16 The crown has fallen from our head.
Woe to us, for we have sinned!
17 Because of this our hearts are faint,
because of these things our eyes grow dim
18 for Mount Zion, which lies desolate,
with jackals prowling over it.
19 You, O LORD, reign forever;
your throne endures from generation to generation.
20 Why do you always forget us?
Why do you forsake us so long?
21 Restore us to yourself, O LORD, that we may return;
renew our days as of old
22 unless you have utterly rejected us
and are angry with us beyond measure.

5:7 *Our fathers sinned . . . we bear their punishment:* It was a common understanding in the ancient world that God not only punished people for the sins they committed, but he also punished the descendants of these sinners. The prophet Ezekiel announced that God would not punish children for the sins of their parents (Ezek 18; Jer 31:29, 30). See also the mini-article called "Sin," p. 2181.

5:8 *Slaves rule over us:* Important jobs were sometimes given to high-ranking slaves of foreign kings. The Israelites, the ancestors of the people of Judah, were once slaves in Egypt, but now they were being ruled by slaves. This situation is devastating to the people of Judah who were left behind after 586 B.C.

5:9 *the sword in the desert:* Desert nomads may have been raiding the countryside and preventing the remaining people of Judah from bringing in their crops. The result would have been starvation and illness (5:10).

5:16-18 *Crown has fallen . . . Zion . . . desolate:* The line of David, thought to be a never-ending kingship, is over (see the note at 4:11, 12). Yet God is King forever (5:19).

5:21,22 *Restore us . . . rejected us:* The fifth lament ends on a note of hope mixed with doubts about the future.

5:20-22 Ps 74:1-3; 79:5-9; 80:4-7.

QUESTIONS ABOUT LAMENTATIONS

1. The poems in LAMENTATIONS were written not simply to lament the destruction of Jerusalem, but to interpret its meaning for God's people. What did the people of Judah learn about themselves and God from this tragic event? (1:5; 3:39, 40; 4:13)
2. Read 3:21-24. Which statements in this short passage give you hope? What is the relationship between hope and dependence on the LORD?
3. What seem to be some of the key characteristics and themes of the five poems (laments) that make up this book? What is the relationship of sadness and hope in a lament? If you were to write a lament, what key ideas would you include?

EZEKIEL

Visions of God's bright glory, dry bones that come back to life, and a life-giving river that flows out of God's new temple. Read about these and other prophecies of the prophet Ezekiel.

King Jehoiachin . . . Ezekiel the priest: Ezekiel was not only a prophet, but also a priest, most likely from the Zadokite clan. He was probably serving in Jerusalem's temple when the Babylonian army first invaded the city in 597 B.C. In order to keep Judah under control, the Babylonians took King Jehoiachin and many others of Jerusalem's religious and political leaders into exile in Babylon (see also 2 Kgs 24:1-16; 2 Chr 36:9,10). Ezekiel was among those forced to leave Jerusalem in 597 B.C. See also the mini-article called "Israel's Priests," p. 2344.

What makes Ezekiel special?

EZEKIEL is unique among the prophetic books because the Hebrew text is written completely in the first person. That is, the prophet Ezekiel's visions, prophecies, and strange actions are described from Ezekiel's own point of view. The book has traditionally been thought to be difficult to interpret, and even dangerous. Some early Jewish teachers were troubled by Ezekiel's vision of the new temple (40–48) because it seemed to contradict parts of the Law of Moses. They were also afraid that Ezekiel's graphic visions of God's glory (1:1-28; 10:1-22) might lead to controversial beliefs about the mystery of God. Some even thought a person could be seriously troubled by thinking about the visions too deeply. For these reasons, some taught that EZEKIEL should only be read by people over the age of thirty.

Why was Ezekiel written?

In the years just before Ezekiel was chosen to be a prophet, the kingdom known as Judah was caught up in the power struggle between Egypt and Babylon. Eventually, Babylon invaded Judah and took over Jerusalem in 597 B.C. Many of Judah's leaders, including King Jehoiachin and Ezekiel himself, were taken as prisoners to live in exile in Babylon. Ten years later, when Judah rebelled, King Nebuchadnezzar of Babylon put down the rebellion, destroyed Jerusalem and its temple, and took more people into exile. Ezekiel's visions and prophecies were meant to explain why the Sovereign LORD of Israel had allowed such a terrible thing to happen. Ezekiel spoke the LORD's messages of doom and warning to the people of Judah and Jerusalem because they had sinned against God. They had worshiped idols, turned to foreign powers instead of God in times of need, and not lived according to God's Law. The people had made their land and God's temple impure by their sin and rebellion. Because of this, the "glory of the LORD" left the temple in Jerusalem. The LORD's people were defeated by the Babylonians and forced to live as captives in exile.

But Ezekiel's message also included promises of hope for the future. The LORD would free the people from exile and lead them back to Jerusalem where they would worship the LORD in a new, holy temple and once again live according to God's Law. The glory of the LORD would shine brightly again in Jerusalem, and both the people of Israel and the surrounding nations would recognize that there is no other God but Israel's LORD.

What's the story behind the scene?

Some prophetic books give little or no information that helps place the time of the prophet or the prophet's message, but many of Ezekiel's messages (oracles) begin with specific dates (for example, see 1:1-3; 8:1; and 40:1). According to these dates, Ezekiel's work as a prophet probably began in late June or early July of 593 B.C. At the time he received his first vision, Ezekiel was living by the Kebar River in Babylon. He and a number of Israel's leading families had been forced to leave Jerusalem when Babylon first took over the city in 597 B.C. While Ezekiel and others lived as refugees there, the king of Babylon made Jehoiachin's uncle Zedekiah the king in Judah (see 2 Kgs 24:8-17).

At first, Zedekiah was loyal to Babylon, but eventually Zedekiah rebelled against Nebuchadnezzar (2 Kgs 24:18-20). That's when King Nebuchadnezzar once again invaded Judah and destroyed Jerusalem and its temple (587 or 586 B.C.). Most of Ezekiel's prophecies date to the time between 593 and 586 B.C. and provide warnings to the people of Judah about the LORD's coming judgment—their defeat at the hands of the Babylonians because of their sin and unfaithfulness. Ezekiel's prophecy about the future temple in Jerusalem is dated 573 B.C. His last prophecy, an oracle against Egypt (29:17-21), is given a date of 571 B.C.

How is Ezekiel constructed?

The final form of EZEKIEL appears to be carefully structured around several dates. These dates relate to the events in the years just before and after the fall of Jerusalem to the Babylonians. The general themes of Ezekiel's prophecies also relate to this defeat. Chapters 1–32 include Ezekiel's messages of judgment and doom against Judah and the nations. Chapters 33–48 focus on how the LORD will restore Judah and bring a bright new future for God's people.

The division of the book into these two main sections is also reflected in the two accounts of Ezekiel's call to be a prophet. The first section begins with the LORD calling Ezekiel to be a watchman for the people of Israel (3:16-21). This call is repeated in 33:1-9. Ezekiel's speaking voice is taken away at the beginning of the first section (3:22-27) and is restored at the beginning of the second section (33:22). Here is one way EZEKIEL can be outlined:

The LORD will judge Judah and Jerusalem (1:1—24:27)
- Ezekiel is chosen to be a prophet (1:1—3:27)
- Disaster is coming (4:1—7:27)
- The LORD's glory leaves Jerusalem (8:1—11:25)
- Messages of doom for Judah and Jerusalem (12:1—24:27)

Prophesies against foreign nations (25:1—32:32)

The LORD will restore Jerusalem and Israel (33:1—39:29)
- Watchman and shepherd (33:1—34:31)
- Preparing the way for Judah's new future (35:1—39:29)

The LORD's glory returns to Judah and Jerusalem (40:1—48:35)
- A new temple (40:1—43:27)
- Laws and rules for God's people (44:1—46:24)
- Dividing the land (47:1—48:35)

throne of sapphire: Two views of where God lives come together in Ezekiel's vision in chapter 1. First, Israel's God lives in the heavens, separated from the world he created and rules (Isa 18:4; 57:15). But the LORD also was said to live above the ark of the covenant in the most holy place of the temple (1 Sam 4:4; 2 Sam 6:2). Winged creatures, called cherubim, like those in Ezekiel's vision were also connected to the LORD's place above the ark (see Exod 25:22; Isa 6:1-5). The image of cherubim holding up the throne of a god was common in the ancient Near East. And woodcarvings of cherubim decorated the inside walls and doors of the temple in Jerusalem. The LORD's throne was made of something like precious blue sapphire stone similar to the bright sapphire pavement described in Exodus 24:9,10. See also Ezek 10:1; Rev 4:2,3.

The LORD Will Judge Judah and Jerusalem

The first twenty-four chapters of EZEKIEL deal mostly with the LORD's coming judgment against Judah and Jerusalem because their people had turned away from the LORD. Ezekiel sees a vision of the LORD's glory and is chosen to be the LORD's prophet (1–3). The LORD gives Ezekiel the difficult task of telling and showing (with pictures or by his own actions) how Jerusalem and Judah will be punished. In a second vision (8–11), Ezekiel actually sees the LORD's glory leave Jerusalem.

EZEKIEL IS CHOSEN TO BE A PROPHET

In 593 B.C., while living in exile in Babylon, Ezekiel receives a vision of the LORD's glory and is chosen to be a prophet to the rebellious people of Israel (2:3).

The Living Creatures and the Glory of the LORD

1 In the[a] thirtieth year, in the fourth month on the fifth day,
while I was among the exiles by the Kebar River, the heavens were
opened and I saw visions of God.
2 On the fifth of the month—it was the fifth year of the exile
of King Jehoiachin— 3 the word of the LORD came to Ezekiel the
priest, the son of Buzi,[b] by the Kebar River in the land of the Babylonians.[c] There the hand of the LORD was upon him.
4 I looked, and I saw a windstorm coming out of the north—
an immense cloud with flashing lightning and surrounded by brilliant light. The center of the fire looked like glowing metal, 5 and in
the fire was what looked like four living creatures. In appearance
their form was that of a man, 6 but each of them had four faces and
four wings. 7 Their legs were straight; their feet were like those of a
calf and gleamed like burnished bronze. 8 Under their wings on
their four sides they had the hands of a man. All four of them had
faces and wings, 9 and their wings touched one another. Each one
went straight ahead; they did not turn as they moved.
10 Their faces looked like this: Each of the four had the face of
a man, and on the right side each had the face of a lion, and on
the left the face of an ox; each also had the face of an eagle. 11 Such
were their faces. Their wings were spread out upward; each had
two wings, one touching the wing of another creature on either
side, and two wings covering its body. 12 Each one went straight
ahead. Wherever the spirit would go, they would go, without turning as they went. 13 The appearance of the living creatures was like
burning coals of fire or like torches. Fire moved back and forth
among the creatures; it was bright, and lightning flashed out of it.
14 The creatures sped back and forth like flashes of lightning.

[a]1 Or ⌞*my*⌟ [b]3 Or *Ezekiel son of Buzi the priest* [c]3 Or *Chaldeans*

1:1,2 *In the thirtieth year . . . fifth year of the exile:* The fifth year of the first exile (see the note on p. 1560) would have been 593 B.C. The "fourth month on the fifth day" of the Jewish calendar refers to late June. The event on which the "thirtieth year" is based is unknown. Some have suggested that "thirtieth" refers to Ezekiel's age at the time of the vision.

1:2,3 *King Jehoiachin . . . Ezekiel the priest:* See the note on p. 1560.

1:1,3 *Kebar River:* A canal of the Euphrates River near Nippur, southeast of Babylon (see the map on p. 2468).

1:3 *hand of the LORD was upon him:* A sign that the LORD had chosen Ezekiel.

1:4 *an immense cloud with flashing lightning:* Fire, lightning, and clouds are often connected with appearances of the LORD (see Exod 3:1-6; 13:20-22; 19:16-19; Ps 18:9-14; Isa 4:5).

1:5-9 *four living creatures:* The number four symbolized completeness and meant that the creatures could move together in any direction (1:9). These creatures probably looked something like the man-beast statues that guarded some ancient Near Eastern temples and palaces. In chapter 10, these creatures are called "cherubim."

1:10 *the face of a man . . . eagle:* The creatures and their faces were arranged so that they could see in all directions at all times. Christian sculpture and art used the human, bull, ox, and eagle faces to represent each of the four Gospels (for example, see p. 2414). See also 10:14; Rev 4:6,7.

1:1-3 Rev 19:11.

Lamentation and Mourning and Woe, Alex Rapoport, 1990, triptych, relief, tempera and oil on canvas. While in exile in Babylon, Ezekiel was given a vision of God's glory and chosen to preach the LORD's message to the people of Israel. Ezekiel saw a hand stretched toward him holding a scroll. The LORD then ordered Ezekiel to open his mouth and eat the scroll. Although both sides were filled with words of lament, mourning and woe, "it tasted as sweet as honey." (See 2:1—3:3.)

15As I looked at the living creatures, I saw a wheel on the
ground beside each creature with its four faces. 16This was the
appearance and structure of the wheels: They sparkled like chrysolite, and all four looked alike. Each appeared to be made like a
wheel intersecting a wheel. 17As they moved, they would go in any
one of the four directions the creatures faced; the wheels did not
turn about[a] as the creatures went. 18Their rims were high and awesome, and all four rims were full of eyes all around.

19When the living creatures moved, the wheels beside them
moved; and when the living creatures rose from the ground, the
wheels also rose. 20Wherever the spirit would go, they would go,
and the wheels would rise along with them, because the spirit of
the living creatures was in the wheels. 21When the creatures
moved, they also moved; when the creatures stood still, they also
stood still; and when the creatures rose from the ground, the
wheels rose along with them, because the spirit of the living creatures was in the wheels.

22Spread out above the heads of the living creatures was

[a]17 Or *aside*

1:13,14 *burning coals . . . lightning:* See the note at 1:4. When the prophet Isaiah was chosen, he also had a vision, in which flying creatures touched his lips with burning coals (see Isa 6:1-7). See also Rev 4:5.

1:16-21 *wheels . . . chrysolite:* Chrysolite is a precious stone that has an olive green color. The wheels could move with the "creatures" in any direction much more easily than any chariot or wagon made by human hands. See also 10:9-18. "Full of eyes all around" are probably meant to symbolize God's all-seeing nature.

1:22 *an expanse:* Ancient Hebrews understood the sky to be like a solid bowl or dome set over the flat earth (Gen 1:6-8; Job 9:5-10; 26:11) that held back the waters above. Rain and snow were said to come through only when God opened gates or doors in the sky (Gen 7:11; Ps 78:23). Here the expanse seems to separate the living creatures from God who sits on a throne above the expanse (1:25-28). See also Rev 4:6.

1:18 Rev 4:8.

what looked like an expanse, sparkling like ice, and awesome.
[23]Under the expanse their wings were stretched out one toward the
other, and each had two wings covering its body. [24]When the creatures moved, I heard the sound of their wings, like the roar of
rushing waters, like the voice of the Almighty,[a] like the tumult of
an army. When they stood still, they lowered their wings.
[25]Then there came a voice from above the expanse over their
heads as they stood with lowered wings. [26]Above the expanse over
their heads was what looked like a throne of sapphire,[b] and high
above on the throne was a figure like that of a man. [27]I saw that
from what appeared to be his waist up he looked like glowing
metal, as if full of fire, and that from there down he looked like fire;
and brilliant light surrounded him. [28]Like the appearance of a rainbow in the clouds on a rainy day, so was the radiance around him.

This was the appearance of the likeness of the glory of the
LORD. When I saw it, I fell facedown, and I heard the voice of one
speaking.

Ezekiel's Call

2 He said to me, "Son of man, stand up on your feet and I will
speak to you." [2]As he spoke, the Spirit came into me and raised me
to my feet, and I heard him speaking to me.
[3]He said: "Son of man, I am sending you to the Israelites, to
a rebellious nation that has rebelled against me; they and their
fathers have been in revolt against me to this very day. [4]The people to whom I am sending you are obstinate and stubborn. Say to
them, 'This is what the Sovereign LORD says.' [5]And whether they
listen or fail to listen—for they are a rebellious house—they will
know that a prophet has been among them. [6]And you, son of man,
do not be afraid of them or their words. Do not be afraid, though
briers and thorns are all around you and you live among scorpions. Do not be afraid of what they say or terrified by them, though
they are a rebellious house. [7]You must speak my words to them,
whether they listen or fail to listen, for they are rebellious. [8]But
you, son of man, listen to what I say to you. Do not rebel like that
rebellious house; open your mouth and eat what I give you."
[9]Then I looked, and I saw a hand stretched out to me. In it
was a scroll, [10]which he unrolled before me. On both sides of it
were written words of lament and mourning and woe.
3 And he said to me, "Son of man, eat what is before you, eat this
scroll; then go and speak to the house of Israel." [2]So I opened my
mouth, and he gave me the scroll to eat.
[3]Then he said to me, "Son of man, eat this scroll I am giving
you and fill your stomach with it." So I ate it, and it tasted as sweet
as honey in my mouth.

---

[a]24 Hebrew *Shaddai* [b]26 Or *lapis lazuli*

1:24 *the Almighty:* Translation for *Shaddai,* one of the ancient names for Israel's God. See the mini-article called "Names of God," p. 243. See also Rev 1:4-15; 19:6.

1:26 *throne of sapphire:* See the note on p. 1561.

1:27,28 *full of fire . . . glory of the LORD:* God's glory is often connected with bright light or fire (see the note at 1:4; see also Isa 60:19, 20). The "rainbow" is a reminder of God's promise in Genesis 9:9-16 that God would not destroy humankind. Also important here is the location of Ezekiel's vision. According to traditions connected to Israel's priests, the LORD's glory or presence was to be found in the tabernacle or in the Most Holy Place in the temple (Exod 25:22; 40:34; Lev 9:22-24; Num 14:10; 1 Kgs 8:11). But here the LORD's glory is seen outside the temple and in a foreign land (Babylon). See also Ezek 8:2.

2:1 *Son of man:* See the note at 4:1.

2:2 *the Spirit:* Probably the LORD's Spirit (11:5; 37:1). See also the mini-article called "Holy Spirit," p. 2082.

2:3 *the Israelites . . . a rebellious nation:* Here "Israelites" refers to both the northern and southern kingdoms of Israel. See also the mini-article called "Israel," p. 264. The people rebelled by worshiping foreign gods (6:1-10; 8:10-15; 16:16-22), by being unfair in their dealings with each other (7:10-13; 8:17), and by entering into treaties with foreign nations instead of relying on the LORD for help (16:28-43).

2:8—3:3 *eat . . . this scroll:* The scroll, a roll of papyrus or special leather used for writing, contained the LORD's message. Touching the mouth was an important symbolic part of being chosen as a prophet of the LORD (see also Isa 6:6,7; Jer 1:9). But only Ezekiel actually ate God's words. Even though these words were filled with bad news, they tasted sweet to Ezekiel. See also Ps 119:101-104; Rev 5:1; 10:9,10.

[4]He then said to me: "Son of man, go now to the house of
Israel and speak my words to them. [5]You are not being sent to a
people of obscure speech and difficult language, but to the house
of Israel— [6]not to many peoples of obscure speech and difficult
language, whose words you cannot understand. Surely if I had sent
you to them, they would have listened to you. [7]But the house of
Israel is not willing to listen to you because they are not willing to
listen to me, for the whole house of Israel is hardened and obstinate. [8]But I will make you as unyielding and hardened as they are.
[9]I will make your forehead like the hardest stone, harder than flint.
Do not be afraid of them or terrified by them, though they are a
rebellious house."

[10]And he said to me, "Son of man, listen carefully and take to
heart all the words I speak to you. [11]Go now to your countrymen
in exile and speak to them. Say to them, 'This is what the Sovereign
LORD says,' whether they listen or fail to listen."

[12]Then the Spirit lifted me up, and I heard behind me a loud
rumbling sound—May the glory of the LORD be praised in his
dwelling place!— [13]the sound of the wings of the living creatures
brushing against each other and the sound of the wheels beside
them, a loud rumbling sound. [14]The Spirit then lifted me up and
took me away, and I went in bitterness and in the anger of my spirit, with the strong hand of the LORD upon me. [15]I came to the
exiles who lived at Tel Abib near the Kebar River. And there, where
they were living, I sat among them for seven days—overwhelmed.

Warning to Israel

[16]At the end of seven days the word of the LORD came to me:
[17]"Son of man, I have made you a watchman for the house of
Israel; so hear the word I speak and give them warning from me.
[18]When I say to a wicked man, 'You will surely die,' and you do not
warn him or speak out to dissuade him from his evil ways in order
to save his life, that wicked man will die for[a] his sin, and I will hold
you accountable for his blood. [19]But if you do warn the wicked
man and he does not turn from his wickedness or from his evil
ways, he will die for his sin; but you will have saved yourself.

[20]"Again, when a righteous man turns from his righteousness
and does evil, and I put a stumbling block before him, he will die.
Since you did not warn him, he will die for his sin. The righteous
things he did will not be remembered, and I will hold you
accountable for his blood. [21]But if you do warn the righteous man
not to sin and he does not sin, he will surely live because he took
warning, and you will have saved yourself."

[22]The hand of the LORD was upon me there, and he said to
me, "Get up and go out to the plain, and there I will speak to you."

[a]**18** Or *in*; also in verses 19 and 20

3:9 *make your forehead like the hardest stone:* Ezekiel's message would not be popular, especially to those who had rebelled against the LORD (2:5-7). Also, those living in exile in Babylon were probably convinced that God had forgotten about them.

3:11 *your countrymen in exile:* Refers to the first group of Israelites who had been taken away into exile in Babylon (see the Introduction and the note on p. 1560). See also the mini-article called "Babylon," p. 1363.

3:12 *glory of the LORD:* See the note at 1:27,28.

3:14 *in bitterness . . . anger:* Probably meaning that Ezekiel identified with the LORD's anger.

3:15 *Tel Abib . . . Kebar River:* See the note at 1:1-3 (Kebar River). Tel Abib meant "mound of the flood," and may have been destroyed earlier by flooding.

3:15 *sat . . . seven days—overwhelmed:* Ezekiel was made speechless by the experience of seeing the LORD's glory. Compare this to the experiences of Job (Job 2:11-13) and Saul (Acts 9:1-9). The number "seven" symbolized completeness, and it was the length of time the ancient ordination ceremony for Israel's priests was supposed to last (Lev 8:31-33).

3:17-21 *Son of man . . . watchman . . . saved yourself:* Ezekiel (called "son of man," see the note at 4:1) is appointed to be a watchman for the people of Israel. This includes warning the people to turn away from their sins (see the note at 2:3). If Ezekiel doesn't warn the people, he will be responsible for their death. See also 33:1-9.

3:22 *the plain:* Probably the flat plains that made up the river basin near Babylon's major rivers, the Tigris and the Euphrates.

3:12,13 Ezek 1:24.

[23]So I got up and went out to the plain. And the glory of the LORD
was standing there, like the glory I had seen by the Kebar River,
and I fell facedown.
[24]Then the Spirit came into me and raised me to my feet. He
spoke to me and said: "Go, shut yourself inside your house. [25]And
you, son of man, they will tie with ropes; you will be bound so that
you cannot go out among the people. [26]I will make your tongue
stick to the roof of your mouth so that you will be silent and
unable to rebuke them, though they are a rebellious house. [27]But
when I speak to you, I will open your mouth and you shall say to
them, 'This is what the Sovereign LORD says.' Whoever will listen
let him listen, and whoever will refuse let him refuse; for they are
a rebellious house.

DISASTER IS COMING

Ezekiel draws a picture of Jerusalem's coming destruction and lies down on his side for over a year as a sign of the suffering Jerusalem's people will face. Then he tells the people of Israel that they are doomed because they have sinned against the LORD.

Siege of Jerusalem Symbolized

4 "Now, son of man, take a clay tablet, put it in front of you and
draw the city of Jerusalem on it. [2]Then lay siege to it: Erect siege
works against it, build a ramp up to it, set up camps against it and
put battering rams around it. [3]Then take an iron pan, place it as
an iron wall between you and the city and turn your face toward it.
It will be under siege, and you shall besiege it. This will be a sign
to the house of Israel.
[4]"Then lie on your left side and put the sin of the house
of Israel upon yourself.[a] You are to bear their sin for the number of
days you lie on your side. [5]I have assigned you the same number of
days as the years of their sin. So for 390 days you will bear the sin
of the house of Israel.
[6]"After you have finished this, lie down again, this time on
your right side, and bear the sin of the house of Judah. I have
assigned you 40 days, a day for each year. [7]Turn your face toward
the siege of Jerusalem and with bared arm prophesy against her. [8]I
will tie you up with ropes so that you cannot turn from one side to
the other until you have finished the days of your siege.
[9]"Take wheat and barley, beans and lentils, millet and spelt;
put them in a storage jar and use them to make bread for yourself.
You are to eat it during the 390 days you lie on your side. [10]Weigh
out twenty shekels[b] of food to eat each day and eat it at set times.
[11]Also measure out a sixth of a hin[c] of water and drink it at set

[a]**4** Or *your side* [b]**10** That is, about 8 ounces (about 0.2 kilogram) [c]**11** That is, about 2/3 quart (about 0.6 liter)

3:23,24 *glory of the LORD . . . Spirit:* See the notes at 1:27, 28 and 2:2.

3:24-27 *shut yourself inside your house . . . you will be silent . . . open your mouth:* These verses have been difficult for interpreters. Why is Ezekiel to be locked in his house and made not to speak right after he has been told (3:17-21) to warn the Israelite people? If his silence is meant to last until the city of Jerusalem is destroyed about seven years later (see 33:21,22), why does he tell the people many messages of doom beginning in chapter 4? Some have suggested that Ezekiel wrote down his messages or acted them out, rather than speaking them out loud. Others believe his inability to speak was only temporary or symbolic. Still others think that Ezekiel's silence meant that during this time he was not supposed to pray for his people, but could only deliver his messages of doom.

4:1 *son of man:* This phrase is often used in this book when the LORD speaks directly to Ezekiel. It means that Ezekiel is a mere human, yet he is the one the LORD has chosen to speak for him to the people of Israel.

4:1-3 *clay tablet . . . siege works . . . iron pan:* Ezekiel drew a picture of Jerusalem's walls on the clay tablet and then built a mound of dirt (siege works) next to it. Ancient armies often piled up dirt ramps to make it easier to get over a city's walls and attack the people inside. They also used large wooden log battering rams to break through the city gates. The iron pan was meant to symbolize the barrier that separated God and his people and showed that Jerusalem would not get any help from the LORD until after it had been destroyed.

Ezekiel lying on his side, ninth century illuminated manuscript. The LORD ordered Ezekiel to lie on his left side for three hundred-ninety days as a sign of Israel's punishment, then for another forty days on his right side as a sign of Judah's punishment. Each day represented a year of suffering. (See 4:1-6.)

times. 12Eat the food as you would a barley cake; bake it in the
sight of the people, using human excrement for fuel." 13The LORD
said, "In this way the people of Israel will eat defiled food among
the nations where I will drive them."
14Then I said, "Not so, Sovereign LORD! I have never defiled
myself. From my youth until now I have never eaten anything
found dead or torn by wild animals. No unclean meat has ever
entered my mouth."
15"Very well," he said, "I will let you bake your bread over
cow manure instead of human excrement."
16He then said to me: "Son of man, I will cut off the supply
of food in Jerusalem. The people will eat rationed food in anxiety
and drink rationed water in despair, 17for food and water will be

4:4,5 *Israel . . . days . . . years:* Israel here means the northern kingdom, which was invaded and destroyed by the Assyrians in 722-721 B.C. It is unclear exactly what period of time the 390 years refers to. Israel's "sin" possibly refers to the time when the northern and southern kingdoms first split apart after the death of King Solomon. See also the article called "From Joshua to the Exile: The People of Israel in the Promised Land," p. 924, and the mini-article called "Israel," p. 264.

4:6 *Judah . . . a day for each year:* The southern kingdom known as Judah was defeated in 586 B.C. Forty years of exile would be 546 B.C., but Cyrus of Persia actually defeated the Babylonians in 539 B.C. and allowed the people of Judah to begin returning home in 538 B.C.

4:9 *wheat and barley . . . bread:* These were common grains in Israel's diet, so mixing them together would only have been done in times when there was not enough of any one of them to make a loaf. The scarcity of grain during a time of attack forced people to mix together different grains.

4:12,15 *human excrement . . . cow manure:* Cooking food over a fire made from dried human waste would have made the food unclean, since human waste was considered ritually unclean (Deut 23:12-14). Because he was a priest and did not want to become impure (unacceptable to God) by eating food cooked over burning human waste, Ezekiel protested and begged the LORD to use cow manure as fuel for the fire. See also the mini-article called "Purity (Clean and Unclean)," p. 2125.

4:13 *defiled food . . . nations where I will drive them:* Many of the people of Israel and Judah were taken away to live in foreign nations, where they sometimes had to eat things that were considered unclean. For example, see Dan 1:8.

4:17 *waste away because of their sin:* See the note at 2:3.

5:1-4 *shave your head and your beard:* Having one's hair or beard cut off was considered a great embarrassment and a loss of personal identity (see 2 Sam 10:3-5). Ezekiel's haircut with a sword was meant to symbolize Jerusalem's embarrassment when they are defeated in battle. Next the hair was divided into three piles to show that a third of Jerusalem's people would die by fire, a third would be killed by the sword, and a third would be scattered, that is, sent away into exile. The few hairs Ezekiel kept in the hem of his clothes symbolized those in exile in Babylon. Some of them would also die violently (5:4). Compare Ezekiel's symbolic action with the prophet Isaiah's threatening message in Isaiah 7:20.

5:5 *Jerusalem:* In the traditions connected to Israel's priests, Jerusalem and the LORD's holy temple there were the center of all the other nations of the world.

5:6 *rejected my laws:* See the note at 2:3. For more, see the mini-article called "Law," p. 1160 and the article called "People of the Law: The Religion of Israel," p. 939.

5:8-17 *inflict punishment:* These verses explain the scene that Ezekiel was supposed to draw and act out (4:1-3; 5:1-4). Because of their sins against the LORD (see the note at 2:3), some of the people of Jerusalem would suffer starvation (5:10,12,16,17); others would be killed in battle (5:12); and still others would be scattered, that is, sent into exile in foreign lands (5:12).

5:16 *deadly and destructive arrows:* A common description of suffering or of the LORD's punishment of those who are disobedient (see also Job 6:4; Lam 3:12,13).

5:10 Lam 4:10. **5:17** Rev 6:8.

scarce. They will be appalled at the sight of each other and will
waste away because of[a] their sin.
5 "Now, son of man, take a sharp sword and use it as a barber's
razor to shave your head and your beard. Then take a set of scales
and divide up the hair. [2]When the days of your siege come to an end,
burn a third of the hair with fire inside the city. Take a third and
strike it with the sword all around the city. And scatter a third to the
wind. For I will pursue them with drawn sword. [3]But take a few
strands of hair and tuck them away in the folds of your garment.
[4]Again, take a few of these and throw them into the fire and burn
them up. A fire will spread from there to the whole house of Israel.

[5]"This is what the Sovereign LORD says: This is Jerusalem,
which I have set in the center of the nations, with countries all
around her. [6]Yet in her wickedness she has rebelled against my laws
and decrees more than the nations and countries around her. She
has rejected my laws and has not followed my decrees.

[7]"Therefore this is what the Sovereign LORD says: You have
been more unruly than the nations around you and have not followed my decrees or kept my laws. You have not even[b] conformed
to the standards of the nations around you.

[8]"Therefore this is what the Sovereign LORD says: I myself am
against you, Jerusalem, and I will inflict punishment on you in the
sight of the nations. [9]Because of all your detestable idols, I will do
to you what I have never done before and will never do again.
[10]Therefore in your midst fathers will eat their children, and children will eat their fathers. I will inflict punishment on you and will
scatter all your survivors to the winds. [11]Therefore as surely as I live,
declares the Sovereign LORD, because you have defiled my sanctuary
with all your vile images and detestable practices, I myself will
withdraw my favor; I will not look on you with pity or spare you.
[12]A third of your people will die of the plague or perish by famine
inside you; a third will fall by the sword outside your walls; and a
third I will scatter to the winds and pursue with drawn sword.

[13]"Then my anger will cease and my wrath against them will
subside, and I will be avenged. And when I have spent my wrath
upon them, they will know that I the LORD have spoken in my zeal.

[14]"I will make you a ruin and a reproach among the nations
around you, in the sight of all who pass by. [15]You will be a
reproach and a taunt, a warning and an object of horror to the
nations around you when I inflict punishment on you in anger
and in wrath and with stinging rebuke. I the LORD have spoken.
[16]When I shoot at you with my deadly and destructive arrows of
famine, I will shoot to destroy you. I will bring more and more
famine upon you and cut off your supply of food. [17]I will send
famine and wild beasts against you, and they will leave you child-

---

[a]17 Or *away in* [b]7 Most Hebrew manuscripts; some Hebrew manuscripts and Syriac *You have*

less. Plague and bloodshed will sweep through you, and I will bring the sword against you. I the LORD have spoken.”

A Prophecy Against the Mountains of Israel

6 The word of the LORD came to me: 2“Son of man, set your face against the mountains of Israel; prophesy against them 3and say: ‘O mountains of Israel, hear the word of the Sovereign LORD. This is what the Sovereign LORD says to the mountains and hills, to the ravines and valleys: I am about to bring a sword against you, and I will destroy your high places. 4Your altars will be demolished and your incense altars will be smashed; and I will slay your people in front of your idols. 5I will lay the dead bodies of the Israelites in front of their idols, and I will scatter your bones around your altars. 6Wherever you live, the towns will be laid waste and the high places demolished, so that your altars will be laid waste and devastated, your idols smashed and ruined, your incense altars broken down, and what you have made wiped out. 7Your people will fall slain among you, and you will know that I am the LORD.

8“ ‘But I will spare some, for some of you will escape the sword when you are scattered among the lands and nations. 9Then in the nations where they have been carried captive, those who escape will remember me—how I have been grieved by their adulterous hearts, which have turned away from me, and by their eyes, which have lusted after their idols. They will loathe themselves for the evil they have done and for all their detestable practices. 10And they will know that I am the LORD; I did not threaten in vain to bring this calamity on them.

11“ ‘This is what the Sovereign LORD says: Strike your hands together and stamp your feet and cry out “Alas!” because of all the wicked and detestable practices of the house of Israel, for they will fall by the sword, famine and plague. 12He that is far away will die of the plague, and he that is near will fall by the sword, and he that survives and is spared will die of famine. So will I spend my wrath upon them. 13And they will know that I am the LORD, when their people lie slain among their idols around their altars, on every high hill and on all the mountaintops, under every spreading tree and every leafy oak—places where they offered fragrant incense to all their idols. 14And I will stretch out my hand against them and make the land a desolate waste from the desert to Diblah[a]—wherever they live. Then they will know that I am the LORD.’ ”

The End Has Come

7 The word of the LORD came to me: 2“Son of man, this is what the Sovereign LORD says to the land of Israel: The end! The end has come upon the four corners of the land. 3The end is now upon you

[a]14 Most Hebrew manuscripts; a few Hebrew manuscripts *Riblah*

6:2 *Son of man:* See the note at 4:1.

6:3-6 *high places . . . idols . . . altars:* Ancient Canaanite worship places were usually built on high places near a grove of trees (Deut 12:2; 1 Kgs 14:23; Jer 2:20). The people of Israel did not destroy all these places when they settled in Canaan, so some Israelites started worshiping the Canaanite gods. One of these was Asherah, the goddess of fertility. Wooden poles symbolizing and honoring Asherah were set up at these worship places. Other idols were made out of metal or stone. See Isa 44:12-20; Hos 4:12-19; and the mini-article called "Canaanite Gods and Goddesses," p. 469.

6:5 *dead bodies . . . bones:* Compare this death scene with 37:1-14.

6:9 *lusted after their idols:* Worshiping idols was forbidden by the Law of Moses (Exod 20:3-5; Deut 5:7-9).

6:13 *high hill . . . fragrant incense . . . idols:* See the note at 6:3-6. Incense made of sweet-smelling spices was burned to honor the LORD (Exod 30:1-10). But incense was also used in the worship of idols.

6:14 *the desert to Diblah:* "The desert" refers to the wilderness area south of Judah (see the map on p. 2465). Diblah was a town in Syria near the Orontes River. Though this area was much larger than the territory of Judah, it was meant to emphasize how the LORD's punishment would cover every area ever considered part of Israel's territory.

7:2 *Israel:* Ezekiel is primarily speaking to the people of Judah and Jerusalem (see the note at 2:3).

6:7-9 Ezek 5:7-17.

7:3 *detestable practices:* See the note at 2:3.

7:9,10 *your conduct . . . arrogance:* See 8:6-17 and the note at 2:3. For examples of injustice being done in Israel, see Amos 2:6-8; 4:1; 5:10-13; Isa 1:16, 17, 21-23; 5:8-23. See also the mini-article called "Justice," p. 1721.

7:12 *The time has come:* The LORD's coming day of judgment is described by many of Israel's prophets. Here Ezekiel is referring to the day when Babylon will capture and destroy Jerusalem. For more, see the mini-article called "Day of the LORD," p. 1727.

7:14 *blow the trumpet:* Trumpets shaped like bugles measuring about one foot long were blown as a signal to prepare for battle (Num 10:9). Though Jerusalem's people were called to battle, they would not successfully defeat the Babylonians because of the LORD's anger.

7:15 *sword . . . plague and famine:* All will occur when the Babylonians invade the land. See also 5:7-17; 6:7-14.

7:18 *sackcloth . . . heads will be shaved:* Sackcloth was a rough, dark-colored cloth made of goat or camel hair and used to make grain sacks. Wearing sackcloth and shaving one's head were done in times of trouble or sorrow.

7:20 *jewelry . . . idols:* Some in Israel may have made jewelry and necklaces in the shape of a crescent moon, which suggested worship of a popular moon-god (see Isa 3:16-23). Other necklaces may have had sayings written on them that were supposed to protect the wearer.

7:22 *desecrate my treasured place:* The Babylonians destroyed much of the temple area in Jerusalem and took many of its holy furnishings and treasures back to Babylon (2 Kgs 25:8-17; Dan 1:2; 5:1, 2). The people were likely surprised that the LORD allowed foreigners to enter the holy temple and make it unfit for worship.

and I will unleash my anger against you. I will judge you according to your conduct and repay you for all your detestable practices. 4 I will not look on you with pity or spare you; I will surely repay you for your conduct and the detestable practices among you. Then you will know that I am the LORD.

5 "This is what the Sovereign LORD says: Disaster! An unheard-of[a] disaster is coming. 6 The end has come! The end has come! It has roused itself against you. It has come! 7 Doom has come upon you—you who dwell in the land. The time has come, the day is near; there is panic, not joy, upon the mountains. 8 I am about to pour out my wrath on you and spend my anger against you; I will judge you according to your conduct and repay you for all your detestable practices. 9 I will not look on you with pity or spare you; I will repay you in accordance with your conduct and the detestable practices among you. Then you will know that it is I the LORD who strikes the blow.

10 "The day is here! It has come! Doom has burst forth, the rod has budded, arrogance has blossomed! 11 Violence has grown into[b] a rod to punish wickedness; none of the people will be left, none of that crowd—no wealth, nothing of value. 12 The time has come, the day has arrived. Let not the buyer rejoice nor the seller grieve, for wrath is upon the whole crowd. 13 The seller will not recover the land he has sold as long as both of them live, for the vision concerning the whole crowd will not be reversed. Because of their sins, not one of them will preserve his life. 14 Though they blow the trumpet and get everything ready, no one will go into battle, for my wrath is upon the whole crowd.

15 "Outside is the sword, inside are plague and famine; those in the country will die by the sword, and those in the city will be devoured by famine and plague. 16 All who survive and escape will be in the mountains, moaning like doves of the valleys, each because of his sins. 17 Every hand will go limp, and every knee will become as weak as water. 18 They will put on sackcloth and be clothed with terror. Their faces will be covered with shame and their heads will be shaved. 19 They will throw their silver into the streets, and their gold will be an unclean thing. Their silver and gold will not be able to save them in the day of the LORD's wrath. They will not satisfy their hunger or fill their stomachs with it, for it has made them stumble into sin. 20 They were proud of their beautiful jewelry and used it to make their detestable idols and vile images. Therefore I will turn these into an unclean thing for them. 21 I will hand it all over as plunder to foreigners and as loot to the wicked of the earth, and they will defile it. 22 I will turn my face away from them, and they will desecrate my treasured place; robbers will enter it and desecrate it.

[a]5 Most Hebrew manuscripts; some Hebrew manuscripts and Syriac *Disaster after* [b]11 Or *The violent one has become*

23“Prepare chains, because the land is full of bloodshed and
the city is full of violence. 24I will bring the most wicked of the
nations to take possession of their houses; I will put an end to the
pride of the mighty, and their sanctuaries will be desecrated.
25When terror comes, they will seek peace, but there will be none.
26Calamity upon calamity will come, and rumor upon rumor.
They will try to get a vision from the prophet; the teaching of the
law by the priest will be lost, as will the counsel of the elders. 27The
king will mourn, the prince will be clothed with despair, and the
hands of the people of the land will tremble. I will deal with them
according to their conduct, and by their own standards I will judge
them. Then they will know that I am the LORD.”

THE LORD’S GLORY LEAVES JERUSALEM

In a second vision, Ezekiel is carried to Jerusalem in the fall of 592 B.C. There he watches disgusting things happening in the LORD's temple and sees the glory of the LORD leave the Most Holy Place of the temple. He also sees a vision of horrible punishment for Jerusalem's people and leaders because of their sins against the LORD.

Idolatry in the Temple

8 In the sixth year, in the sixth month on the fifth day, while I
was sitting in my house and the elders of Judah were sitting before
me, the hand of the Sovereign LORD came upon me there. 2I
looked, and I saw a figure like that of a man.[a] From what appeared
to be his waist down he was like fire, and from there up his appearance was as bright as glowing metal. 3He stretched out what looked
like a hand and took me by the hair of my head. The Spirit lifted
me up between earth and heaven and in visions of God he took
me to Jerusalem, to the entrance to the north gate of the inner
court, where the idol that provokes to jealousy stood. 4And there
before me was the glory of the God of Israel, as in the vision I had
seen in the plain.

5Then he said to me, “Son of man, look toward the north.”
So I looked, and in the entrance north of the gate of the altar I saw
this idol of jealousy.

6And he said to me, “Son of man, do you see what they are
doing—the utterly detestable things the house of Israel is doing
here, things that will drive me far from my sanctuary? But you will
see things that are even more detestable.”

7Then he brought me to the entrance to the court. I looked,
and I saw a hole in the wall. 8He said to me, “Son of man, now dig
into the wall.” So I dug into the wall and saw a doorway there.

9And he said to me, “Go in and see the wicked and detestable

[a]2 Or *saw a fiery figure*

7:26 *teaching of the law . . . will be lost:* Many of Israel's leaders, including many priests who served in the temple, were sent away into exile. Without a temple, the priests had no place to offer sacrifices or to teach the people about the law. The destruction of Jerusalem and resulting exile also stripped Judah and its rulers of any political power (7:27). Finally, many of Israel's prophets would receive no messages from the LORD or the LORD's Spirit (see also Mic 3:6,7).

8:1 *sixth year . . . sixth month:* Probably August of 592 B.C. See also the note on p. 1560. Ezekiel met with the elders of Judah in his house in Babylon. Apparently Ezekiel was often asked for advice or for a message from the LORD (see also 14:1; 20:1; 33:30-32).

8:2 *figure like that of a man . . . fire:* This figure is similar to the one described in Ezekiel's first vision (see the note at 1:27,28).

8:3 *The Spirit . . . took me to Jerusalem:* See the note at 2:2. Jerusalem, Ezekiel's home city, was the capital of Judah. It was about 600 miles west of where Ezekiel lived in Babylon (see the map on p. 2468).

8:3-5 *inner court . . . idol:* For a picture of the temple area, see the article called “People of the Law: The Religion of Israel,” p. 939. The idol mentioned here and in 8:5 may have been a statue of the Canaanite goddess Asherah. Judah's King Manasseh had set up an Asherah pole in the temple area (2 Kgs 21:1-7) almost one hundred years earlier, but King Josiah had taken all the idols out of the temple after discovering the Book of the Covenant (2 Kgs 23:1-4). Perhaps one of Judah's kings after Josiah had allowed images of the Canaanite gods back into the temple area (see 2 Kgs 23:31,32; 24:8,9).

8:4 *glory of the God of Israel:* See the notes at 1:4 and 1:27,28.

8:4 *in the plain:* See the note at 3:22.

8:10 *crawling things . . . idols:* Pictures of animals that were considered ritually impure (see Lev 11:9-19) were placed in the temple along with idols.

8:11-13 *seventy elders . . . incense:* Jaazaniah was the son of Shaphan, who had helped discover the lost Book of the Law (2 Kgs 22:8-13). But now he and the others were using incense (see the note at 6:13) while performing a worship ritual to honor the idol of a foreign god. See also the note at 6:3-6.

8:14 *Tammuz:* A god of plant growth and fertility who was thought to die in the dry season. During the Hebrew month of Tammuz (from about mid-June to mid-July), some Israelite women were mourning the death of this god.

8:16 *inner court . . . bowing down to the sun in the east:* Ezekiel is in the temple courtyard, near the doorway to the temple. The men bowing toward the rising sun may have been worshiping the Babylonian sun god Shamash. By turning their backs on the temple and facing east to worship this god, they were showing they believed that the LORD was helpless against the mighty sun god of Babylon.

9:1,2 *weapon . . . six men . . . linen:* These six figures may have been angels the LORD had sent to bring about destruction. These verses may also reflect the idea that some of the Babylonian gods were associated with their own weapons. For example, Hadad used lightening and an ax, Marduk used a bow and net, and Sin used a curved sword. Israel's priests wore linen robes (Exod 28:39-42), so the seventh figure "in linen" was perhaps meant to be a priest or an angel (see Dan 10:4-9).

9:2 *upper gate . . . bronze altar:* The destroyers came in the north gate where the large idol (8:5) stood near the bronze altar used for offering sacrifices to the LORD (Exod 27:1-8; Lev 1:1-4).

things they are doing here." 10So I went in and looked, and I saw portrayed all over the walls all kinds of crawling things and detestable animals and all the idols of the house of Israel. 11In front of them stood seventy elders of the house of Israel, and Jaazaniah son of Shaphan was standing among them. Each had a censer in his hand, and a fragrant cloud of incense was rising.

12He said to me, "Son of man, have you seen what the elders of the house of Israel are doing in the darkness, each at the shrine of his own idol? They say, 'The LORD does not see us; the LORD has forsaken the land.' " 13Again, he said, "You will see them doing things that are even more detestable."

14Then he brought me to the entrance to the north gate of the house of the LORD, and I saw women sitting there, mourning for Tammuz. 15He said to me, "Do you see this, son of man? You will see things that are even more detestable than this."

16He then brought me into the inner court of the house of the LORD, and there at the entrance to the temple, between the portico and the altar, were about twenty-five men. With their backs toward the temple of the LORD and their faces toward the east, they were bowing down to the sun in the east.

17He said to me, "Have you seen this, son of man? Is it a trivial matter for the house of Judah to do the detestable things they are doing here? Must they also fill the land with violence and continually provoke me to anger? Look at them putting the branch to their nose! 18Therefore I will deal with them in anger; I will not look on them with pity or spare them. Although they shout in my ears, I will not listen to them."

Idolaters Killed

9 Then I heard him call out in a loud voice, "Bring the guards of the city here, each with a weapon in his hand." 2And I saw six men coming from the direction of the upper gate, which faces north, each with a deadly weapon in his hand. With them was a man clothed in linen who had a writing kit at his side. They came in and stood beside the bronze altar.

3Now the glory of the God of Israel went up from above the cherubim, where it had been, and moved to the threshold of the temple. Then the LORD called to the man clothed in linen who had the writing kit at his side 4and said to him, "Go throughout the city of Jerusalem and put a mark on the foreheads of those who grieve and lament over all the detestable things that are done in it."

5As I listened, he said to the others, "Follow him through the city and kill, without showing pity or compassion. 6Slaughter old men, young men and maidens, women and children, but do not touch anyone who has the mark. Begin at my sanctuary." So they began with the elders who were in front of the temple.

7Then he said to them, "Defile the temple and fill the courts with the slain. Go!" So they went out and began killing throughout

the city. 8While they were killing and I was left alone, I fell facedown, crying out, "Ah, Sovereign LORD! Are you going to destroy
the entire remnant of Israel in this outpouring of your wrath on
Jerusalem?"

9He answered me, "The sin of the house of Israel and Judah
is exceedingly great; the land is full of bloodshed and the city is full
of injustice. They say, 'The LORD has forsaken the land; the LORD
does not see.' 10So I will not look on them with pity or spare them,
but I will bring down on their own heads what they have done."

11Then the man in linen with the writing kit at his side
brought back word, saying, "I have done as you commanded."

The Glory Departs From the Temple

10 I looked, and I saw the likeness of a throne of sapphire[a]
above the expanse that was over the heads of the cherubim. 2The
LORD said to the man clothed in linen, "Go in among the wheels
beneath the cherubim. Fill your hands with burning coals from
among the cherubim and scatter them over the city." And as I
watched, he went in.

3Now the cherubim were standing on the south side of the
temple when the man went in, and a cloud filled the inner court.
4Then the glory of the LORD rose from above the cherubim and
moved to the threshold of the temple. The cloud filled the temple,
and the court was full of the radiance of the glory of the LORD.
5The sound of the wings of the cherubim could be heard as far
away as the outer court, like the voice of God Almighty[b] when he
speaks.

6When the LORD commanded the man in linen, "Take fire
from among the wheels, from among the cherubim," the man went
in and stood beside a wheel. 7Then one of the cherubim reached
out his hand to the fire that was among them. He took up some of
it and put it into the hands of the man in linen, who took it and
went out. 8(Under the wings of the cherubim could be seen what
looked like the hands of a man.)

9I looked, and I saw beside the cherubim four wheels, one
beside each of the cherubim; the wheels sparkled like chrysolite.
10As for their appearance, the four of them looked alike; each was
like a wheel intersecting a wheel. 11As they moved, they would go
in any one of the four directions the cherubim faced; the wheels
did not turn about[c] as the cherubim went. The cherubim went in
whatever direction the head faced, without turning as they went.
12Their entire bodies, including their backs, their hands and their
wings, were completely full of eyes, as were their four wheels. 13I
heard the wheels being called "the whirling wheels." 14Each of the
cherubim had four faces: One face was that of a cherub, the second

---

a1 Or *lapis lazuli* **b5** Hebrew *El-Shaddai* **c11** Or *aside*

9:3 *glory of the God of Israel . . . cherubim:* See the notes on p. 1561 and at 1:27,28. Cherubim were placed on the lid of the ark of the covenant, which was kept in the Most Holy Place in the temple (Exod 25:10-22; 1 Kgs 6:19-28). The LORD's glory now moves out of the Most Holy Place to the door of the temple.

9:4 *put a mark on the foreheads:* These allowed the destroyers to know which people to kill and which not to harm. See also Rev 7:3; 9:4; 14:1.

9:7 *Defile the temple . . . the slain:* According to God's Law, touching a dead body could make one ritually impure (Num 19:11-22). Dead bodies lying around the temple could make the temple impure.

9:9 *The sin of . . . Israel . . . is exceedingly great:* Including the horrible things being done in Ezekiel's temple vision. See also the notes at 2:3 and 7:9,10.

10:1 *throne of sapphire . . . cherubim:* See the note on p. 1561, and the notes at 9:3 and 1:22,23.

10:2 *man clothed in linen . . . wheels . . . burning coals:* See the notes at 9:1,2; 1:16-21; and 1:13,14. Coals from the temple altar had the power to purify (Isa 6:6, 7), but here the coals are to be dropped all over the city, probably to cause a judgment fire that would destroy the city. See also Rev 8:5.

10:4,5 *glory of the LORD . . . God Almighty:* See the notes at 1:27,28 and 1:24.

10:9,10 *chrysolite . . . a wheel intersecting a wheel:* See the note at 1:16-21.

10:14 *four faces:* See the note at 1:10-12. See also Rev 4:7.

10:9-13 Ezek 1:15-21. **10:12** Rev 4:8.

10:15 *Kebar River:* See the note at 1:1,3 (Kebar River).

10:18,19 *glory . . . east gate of the Lord's house:* Ezekiel watches as the Lord's glory is carried by the cherubim away from the doorway of the temple (9:3; 10:4) to the east gate of the temple courtyard, a main entrance to the temple area also known as "the gate of the Lord" (see Ps 118:20).

11:1 *the Spirit:* See the note at 2:2.

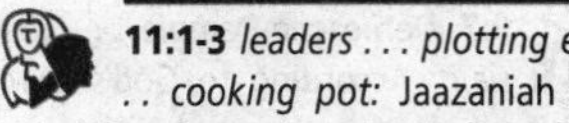

11:1-3 *leaders . . . plotting evil . . . cooking pot:* Jaazaniah and Pelatiah are mentioned only here. They are probably not priests but city officials who are trying to get the people of the city to ignore the danger of being invaded. They were trying to convince the people of Jerusalem that they were secure and told them to keep building new houses in the city. The men promised that the city walls will protect them from enemy attacks, just as a cooking pot protects meat from a blazing fire.

11:5 *the Spirit of the Lord came upon me:* In the middle of his vision, the Lord's Spirit gives Ezekiel a message that he is to tell the leaders.

11:8-10 *the sword . . . hand you over to foreigners:* The "foreigners" that will attack Jerusalem are the Babylonians (see the note at 4:6). They will complete the job of killing people in Jerusalem, which Judah's evil leaders had begun (11:7).

the face of a man, the third the face of a lion, and the fourth the
face of an eagle.
15 Then the cherubim rose upward. These were the living
creatures I had seen by the Kebar River. 16 When the cherubim
moved, the wheels beside them moved; and when the cherubim
spread their wings to rise from the ground, the wheels did not
leave their side. 17 When the cherubim stood still, they also stood
still; and when the cherubim rose, they rose with them, because
the spirit of the living creatures was in them.
18 Then the glory of the Lord departed from over the threshold of the temple and stopped above the cherubim. 19 While I
watched, the cherubim spread their wings and rose from the
ground, and as they went, the wheels went with them. They
stopped at the entrance to the east gate of the Lord's house, and
the glory of the God of Israel was above them.
20 These were the living creatures I had seen beneath the God
of Israel by the Kebar River, and I realized that they were cherubim. 21 Each had four faces and four wings, and under their wings
was what looked like the hands of a man. 22 Their faces had the
same appearance as those I had seen by the Kebar River. Each one
went straight ahead.

Judgment on Israel's Leaders

11 Then the Spirit lifted me up and brought me to the gate of
the house of the Lord that faces east. There at the entrance to the
gate were twenty-five men, and I saw among them Jaazaniah son of
Azzur and Pelatiah son of Benaiah, leaders of the people. 2 The Lord
said to me, "Son of man, these are the men who are plotting evil
and giving wicked advice in this city. 3 They say, 'Will it not soon be
time to build houses?[a] This city is a cooking pot, and we are the
meat.' 4 Therefore prophesy against them; prophesy, son of man."
5 Then the Spirit of the Lord came upon me, and he told me
to say: "This is what the Lord says: That is what you are saying,
O house of Israel, but I know what is going through your mind.
6 You have killed many people in this city and filled its streets with
the dead.
7 "Therefore this is what the Sovereign Lord says: The bodies
you have thrown there are the meat and this city is the pot, but I
will drive you out of it. 8 You fear the sword, and the sword is what
I will bring against you, declares the Sovereign Lord. 9 I will drive
you out of the city and hand you over to foreigners and inflict
punishment on you. 10 You will fall by the sword, and I will execute
judgment on you at the borders of Israel. Then you will know that
I am the Lord. 11 This city will not be a pot for you, nor will you be
the meat in it; I will execute judgment on you at the borders of

[a] **3** Or *This is not the time to build houses.*

Israel. [12]And you will know that I am the LORD, for you have not
followed my decrees or kept my laws but have conformed to the
standards of the nations around you."

[13]Now as I was prophesying, Pelatiah son of Benaiah died.
Then I fell facedown and cried out in a loud voice, "Ah, Sovereign
LORD! Will you completely destroy the remnant of Israel?"

[14]The word of the LORD came to me: [15]"Son of man, your
brothers—your brothers who are your blood relatives[a] and the
whole house of Israel—are those of whom the people of Jerusalem
have said, 'They are[b] far away from the LORD; this land was given
to us as our possession.'

Promised Return of Israel

[16]"Therefore say: 'This is what the Sovereign LORD says:
Although I sent them far away among the nations and scattered
them among the countries, yet for a little while I have been a sanctuary for them in the countries where they have gone.'

[17]"Therefore say: 'This is what the Sovereign LORD says: I will
gather you from the nations and bring you back from the countries where you have been scattered, and I will give you back the
land of Israel again.'

[18]"They will return to it and remove all its vile images and
detestable idols. [19]I will give them an undivided heart and put a
new spirit in them; I will remove from them their heart of stone
and give them a heart of flesh. [20]Then they will follow my decrees
and be careful to keep my laws. They will be my people, and I will
be their God. [21]But as for those whose hearts are devoted to their

[a]**15** Or *are in exile with you* (see Septuagint and Syriac) [b]**15** Or *those to whom the people of Jerusalem have said, 'Stay*

11:12 *not . . . kept my laws . . . the standards of the nations:* The "standards of the nations" refers to following their religious practices (5:7; 8:3-16). "Decrees" and "laws" refers to the law that the LORD gave to Moses and the Israelite people (see the note at 5:6, 7).

11:13 *Pelatiah:* Though Ezekiel had said the leaders would die when their nation was invaded, Pelatiah died immediately, as if to put an exclamation point on Ezekiel's words. This causes Ezekiel to act in the role of a priest and speak in defense of his people.

11:16-21 *I sent them far away . . . idols:* Some who were left in Judah after the Babylonians' first attack on Jerusalem (see the note on p. 1560) thought that the land of Judah belonged to them (11:15). Some leaders, both those in Jerusalem and those in exile in Babylon, apparently believed that the LORD could not be worshiped properly outside of Judah. But the LORD tells those in exile that he is with them (11:16), so they can worship him even if they are far away from the temple. See also the mini-article called "Exile," p. 1541.

11:19,20 Ezek 36:26-28.

QUESTIONS ABOUT EZEKIEL 1:1—11:25

1. Where and when did Ezekiel receive his first vision? (1:1-3) What was the historical situation in Israel at this time?
2. Briefly describe Ezekiel's vision (1:4—3:14). Why was Ezekiel chosen, and what did the LORD want him to do? (2:3—3:11; 3:16-21) What could make this assignment difficult? Recall a difficult task or decision you have had to make. What made the decision or task difficult? Recall a time when you felt the need to speak out about injustice. What did you do?
3. Ezekiel was an unusual prophet because he not only spoke the LORD's messages, he also had to act out events that would happen to God's people. How did he act out the coming destruction of Jerusalem? (4:1—5:4) Why were Jerusalem and its people facing God's punishment? (5:7—6:13)
4. How would Jerusalem and its people be punished and disgraced? (7:15-27)
5. Where was Ezekiel taken in his second vision? (8:1—11:23) What terrible things did he see there? Where did the LORD's glory "live"? (9:3) Why did the LORD's glory leave that place?
6. What is significant about the fact that Ezekiel the prophet probably came from a family of priests?

vile images and detestable idols, I will bring down on their own
heads what they have done, declares the Sovereign LORD."
22 Then the cherubim, with the wheels beside them, spread their
wings, and the glory of the God of Israel was above them. 23 The glory
of the LORD went up from within the city and stopped above the
mountain east of it. 24 The Spirit lifted me up and brought me to the
exiles in Babylonia[a] in the vision given by the Spirit of God.
Then the vision I had seen went up from me, 25 and I told the
exiles everything the LORD had shown me.

MESSAGES OF DOOM FOR JUDAH AND JERUSALEM

In the following chapters (12–24), Ezekiel delivers a number of judgment messages and stories (allegories) warning of the destruction and death that was coming to Jerusalem, Judah, and many of Judah's leaders. Even the death of Ezekiel's wife (24:15-24) and Ezekiel's mourning draw attention to Jerusalem's coming punishment.

The Exile Symbolized

12 The word of the LORD came to me: 2 "Son of man, you are living among a rebellious people. They have eyes to see but do not see
and ears to hear but do not hear, for they are a rebellious people.
3 "Therefore, son of man, pack your belongings for exile and
in the daytime, as they watch, set out and go from where you are
to another place. Perhaps they will understand, though they are a
rebellious house. 4 During the daytime, while they watch, bring out
your belongings packed for exile. Then in the evening, while they
are watching, go out like those who go into exile. 5 While they
watch, dig through the wall and take your belongings out through
it. 6 Put them on your shoulder as they are watching and carry
them out at dusk. Cover your face so that you cannot see the land,
for I have made you a sign to the house of Israel."
7 So I did as I was commanded. During the day I brought out
my things packed for exile. Then in the evening I dug through the
wall with my hands. I took my belongings out at dusk, carrying
them on my shoulders while they watched.
8 In the morning the word of the LORD came to me: 9 "Son of
man, did not that rebellious house of Israel ask you, 'What are you
doing?'
10 "Say to them, 'This is what the Sovereign LORD says: This
oracle concerns the prince in Jerusalem and the whole house of
Israel who are there.' 11 Say to them, 'I am a sign to you.'
"As I have done, so it will be done to them. They will go into
exile as captives.

[a]24 Or *Chaldea*

11:22,23 *cherubim . . . glory of the LORD:* See the notes at 9:3 and 1:27,28. Finally, the LORD's glory leaves Jerusalem completely (see 9:3; 10:4,18, 19). See also Ezek 43:2-5.

11:24 *the vision:* The Spirit carried Ezekiel to Jerusalem (8:1-3). When he comes back to himself at home in Babylon, he explains his vision to his visitors.

12:2 *Son of man:* See the note at 4:1.

12:2 *rebellious people:* See the note at 2:3. Ezekiel knows his words and actions may have no effect on his people, but he had no choice but to do as the LORD told him (2:4-8; 3:10,11,17-21). See also Isa 6:9,10; Jer 5:21; Mark 8:18.

12:3-7 *pack . . . dig through the wall . . . dusk:* Ezekiel is told to act out a night-time escape, as one might do to avoid being taken prisoner. Most houses in Babylon were made of mud bricks that had been dried in the sun, so a hole could easily have been dug through these bricks. Though many watched Ezekiel's strange pantomime, no one asked what it meant.

12:10-13 *prince in Jerusalem . . . go into exile . . . die:* Ezekiel's pantomime was intended to show what was going to happen to Zedekiah, the leader that Nebuchadnezzar had put in charge of Judah after Judah's King Jehoiachin (see the note on p. 1560). When Zedekiah rebelled against Babylon, Nebuchadnezzar's army returned to Jerusalem and surrounded the city (587/86 B.C.). Zedekiah and his family managed to escape, but they were captured on the plains near Jericho and taken to Nebuchadnezzar at Riblah. There Zedekiah's sons were killed, and Zedekiah's eyes were poked out before he was taken away as a prisoner to Babylon (2 Kgs 24:18—25:7; Jer 52:1-11). About a month later, the Babylonians burned down the temple and king's palace in Jerusalem, tore down the city's walls, and took all but the poorest people away into exile (Jer 52:12-16).

12“The prince among them will put his things on his shoulder at dusk and leave, and a hole will be dug in the wall for him to
go through. He will cover his face so that he cannot see the land.
13I will spread my net for him, and he will be caught in my snare;
I will bring him to Babylonia, the land of the Chaldeans, but he
will not see it, and there he will die. 14I will scatter to the winds all
those around him—his staff and all his troops—and I will pursue
them with drawn sword.
15“They will know that I am the LORD, when I disperse them
among the nations and scatter them through the countries. 16But I
will spare a few of them from the sword, famine and plague, so
that in the nations where they go they may acknowledge all their
detestable practices. Then they will know that I am the LORD.”
17The word of the LORD came to me: 18“Son of man, tremble
as you eat your food, and shudder in fear as you drink your water.
19Say to the people of the land: ‘This is what the Sovereign LORD
says about those living in Jerusalem and in the land of Israel: They
will eat their food in anxiety and drink their water in despair, for
their land will be stripped of everything in it because of the violence of all who live there. 20The inhabited towns will be laid waste
and the land will be desolate. Then you will know that I am the
LORD.’ ”
21The word of the LORD came to me: 22“Son of man, what is
this proverb you have in the land of Israel: ‘The days go by and
every vision comes to nothing’? 23Say to them, ‘This is what the
Sovereign LORD says: I am going to put an end to this proverb, and
they will no longer quote it in Israel.’ Say to them, ‘The days are
near when every vision will be fulfilled. 24For there will be no more
false visions or flattering divinations among the people of Israel.
25But I the LORD will speak what I will, and it shall be fulfilled
without delay. For in your days, you rebellious house, I will fulfill
whatever I say, declares the Sovereign LORD.’ ”
26The word of the LORD came to me: 27“Son of man, the
house of Israel is saying, ‘The vision he sees is for many years from
now, and he prophesies about the distant future.’
28“Therefore say to them, ‘This is what the Sovereign LORD
says: None of my words will be delayed any longer; whatever I say
will be fulfilled, declares the Sovereign LORD.’ ”

False Prophets Condemned

13 The word of the LORD came to me: 2“Son of man, prophesy
against the prophets of Israel who are now prophesying. Say to
those who prophesy out of their own imagination: ‘Hear the word
of the LORD! 3This is what the Sovereign LORD says: Woe to the foolish[a] prophets who follow their own spirit and have seen nothing!

---

[a]3 Or *wicked*

> *“I the LORD will speak what I will, and it shall be fulfilled without delay.”*
> Ezek 12:25

12:16 *the nations . . . detestable practices:* Though many of Jerusalem’s people were taken away to Babylon, some escaped to other nations as well. As they looked back at what happened, they would realize that their sins against the LORD had led to Jerusalem’s destruction. See also the note at 2:3.

12:18 *shudder in fear:* Ezekiel’s shaking was meant to show how fearful the people of Jerusalem would be when they came under attack by the Babylonians. Shaking could also be caused by extreme starvation (see 5:7-12).

12:22-28 *every vision . . . whatever I say will be fulfilled:* Even though the threat to Jerusalem was very real, many people had begun to distrust the messages of their prophets. Perhaps rival prophets gave opposite messages, or perhaps messages about Jerusalem’s coming destruction had been spoken so often and for so long that the people had come to think that it wouldn’t really happen, or that it would happen in the distant future (12:26, 27). So the people probably felt they had no reason to believe Ezekiel’s messages and pantomimes of doom. See also the article called “Prophets and Prophecy,” p. 935.

13:2-6 *Son of man . . . Their visions are false:* See the note at 4:1. While Israel’s false prophets made up messages from their own imaginations, Ezekiel’s messages were from the LORD, who had chosen him (2:3-5; 3:17). See also Jer 14:11-18; 23:9-32.

4 Your prophets, O Israel, are like jackals among ruins. 5 You have not gone up to the breaks in the wall to repair it for the house of Israel so that it will stand firm in the battle on the day of the LORD. 6 Their visions are false and their divinations a lie. They say, "The LORD declares," when the LORD has not sent them; yet they expect their words to be fulfilled. 7 Have you not seen false visions and uttered lying divinations when you say, "The LORD declares," though I have not spoken?

8 " 'Therefore this is what the Sovereign LORD says: Because of your false words and lying visions, I am against you, declares the Sovereign LORD. 9 My hand will be against the prophets who see false visions and utter lying divinations. They will not belong to the council of my people or be listed in the records of the house of Israel, nor will they enter the land of Israel. Then you will know that I am the Sovereign LORD.

10 " 'Because they lead my people astray, saying, "Peace," when there is no peace, and because, when a flimsy wall is built, they cover it with whitewash, 11 therefore tell those who cover it with whitewash that it is going to fall. Rain will come in torrents, and I will send hailstones hurtling down, and violent winds will burst forth. 12 When the wall collapses, will people not ask you, "Where is the whitewash you covered it with?"

13 " 'Therefore this is what the Sovereign LORD says: In my wrath I will unleash a violent wind, and in my anger hailstones and torrents of rain will fall with destructive fury. 14 I will tear down the wall you have covered with whitewash and will level it to the ground so that its foundation will be laid bare. When it[a] falls, you will be destroyed in it; and you will know that I am the LORD. 15 So I will spend my wrath against the wall and against those who covered it with whitewash. I will say to you, "The wall is gone and so are those who whitewashed it, 16 those prophets of Israel who prophesied to Jerusalem and saw visions of peace for her when there was no peace, declares the Sovereign LORD." '

17 "Now, son of man, set your face against the daughters of your people who prophesy out of their own imagination. Prophesy against them 18 and say, 'This is what the Sovereign LORD says: Woe to the women who sew magic charms on all their wrists and make veils of various lengths for their heads in order to ensnare people. Will you ensnare the lives of my people but preserve your own? 19 You have profaned me among my people for a few handfuls of barley and scraps of bread. By lying to my people, who listen to lies, you have killed those who should not have died and have spared those who should not live.

20 " 'Therefore this is what the Sovereign LORD says: I am against your magic charms with which you ensnare people like birds and I will tear them from your arms; I will set free the peo-

---

[a]**14** Or *the city*

13:4 *jackals:* Desert animals related to wolves, but smaller. Jackals were scavengers who would search for food, including dead and rotting flesh, in a ruined city or on a deserted battlefield.

13:10-16 *they lead my people astray . . . there was no peace:* The false prophets are deceiving the people by claiming that the city will soon have peaceful times, but the Babylonian threat is real. They are like builders who try to cover dangerous cracks in a wall simply by painting over them with whitewash. But cracked walls, especially those made with mud bricks, will fall apart when they are hit with hard rain, hail, and wind. The prophets also tried to overlook the evil going on in Jerusalem and in the temple itself (see the notes at 2:3; 5:6, 7; and in chapter 8). When Jerusalem is destroyed, the false prophets will be killed along with many of the people they deceived.

13:17-23 *the daughters of your people . . . charms . . . divination:* Some women were also giving false prophecies while claiming their messages came from the LORD. They apparently made and wore charm bracelets and special scarves that were supposed to give them power to predict the future. They may have sold these charms and their messages to people for a few handfuls of barley or a couple of pieces of bread. This price would have seemed very cheap for such important information. Perhaps these false prophetesses also were asked to hear cases and decide whether a person should go free or be punished. Because the people believed the women had special powers, their decisions were accepted, no matter what the actual evidence was. But when the LORD tears the bracelets and magic scarves off these women, their spell over the people will be broken.

13:10 Jer 6:14; 8:11.

The Three Righteous Men of the Old Testament, stained glass window from Canterbury Cathedral, England, late twelfth century. The Israelites were sinning against the LORD and worshiping idols. They were so unfaithful that the LORD told Ezekiel that even if Noah, Daniel and Job were living, their faithfulness would not save anyone but themselves. These three "righteous men" are depicted in this window being crowned by angels. (See 14:1-14.)

ple that you ensnare like birds. [21]I will tear off your veils and save
my people from your hands, and they will no longer fall prey to
your power. Then you will know that I am the LORD. [22]Because you
disheartened the righteous with your lies, when I had brought
them no grief, and because you encouraged the wicked not to turn
from their evil ways and so save their lives, [23]therefore you will no
longer see false visions or practice divination. I will save my people from your hands. And then you will know that I am the
LORD.' "

Idolaters Condemned

14 Some of the elders of Israel came to me and sat down in
front of me. [2]Then the word of the LORD came to me: [3]"Son of
man, these men have set up idols in their hearts and put wicked
stumbling blocks before their faces. Should I let them inquire of
me at all? [4]Therefore speak to them and tell them, 'This is what the
Sovereign LORD says: When any Israelite sets up idols in his heart
and puts a wicked stumbling block before his face and then goes to

14:1 *elders of Israel came to me:* These are leaders of the Jewish people living in exile in Babylon. Once again (see also 8:1) they come to Ezekiel for a message from the LORD.

14:3 *Son of man, these men:* See the note at 4:1. Why the elders have come to Ezekiel is not clear, but Ezekiel is warned not to give them a message because they have started worshiping idols, probably meaning gods worshiped by the Babylonians.

 **14:2** Rev 6:8.

14:4 *answer him . . . with his great idolatry:* No message that Ezekiel would tell the elders is as important as pointing out their sins against the LORD by worshiping idols. If they don't stop doing this, no other message matters, because they will no longer be God's people.

14:9 *I the LORD have enticed that prophet:* A prophet who gives the people a message, though they have been worshiping idols, will be in trouble. The LORD will not stop the prophet from doing this, so the prophet will be destroyed. Compare 1 Kgs 22:18-23; Ezek 3:20.

14:14 *Noah, Daniel and Job:* These men were known in the ancient Near East for being righteous even though they and their children suffered under difficult circumstances. See Genesis 6–9 and Job 1,2; 42. Daniel may refer to an ancient hero or ruler named Dan'el described in the tale of Aqhat, (a Ugaritic legend from about 1500 B.C.) or to the Daniel in the Bible. Even the presence of such righteous men could not save a sinful nation from the LORD's destruction.

14:21,22 *four dreadful judgments . . . disaster:* Ezekiel repeats the four ways the people of Jerusalem will be punished for their sins (see also 5:11-17). Those who survive will be taken as captives into exile in Babylon. This refers to the second group taken into exile after Jerusalem is destroyed in 587/86 B.C. (see the note at 12:10-13). All of these events are to take place so that Ezekiel and the people will recognize the LORD's power and that the LORD is the only real God (compare Isa 45:9-25).

15:2 *wood of a vine:* Vines are thin and flexible, so they are not strong enough to use as pegs to hang things on. When they no longer grow fruit, grapevines are cut down and burned. Israel is described as the LORD's vine in other books of the Bible (Ps 80:8-13; Isa 5; Hos 10:1). See also John 15:1-17.

a prophet, I the LORD will answer him myself in keeping with his great idolatry. 5 I will do this to recapture the hearts of the people of Israel, who have all deserted me for their idols.'

6 "Therefore say to the house of Israel, 'This is what the Sovereign LORD says: Repent! Turn from your idols and renounce all your detestable practices!

7 " 'When any Israelite or any alien living in Israel separates himself from me and sets up idols in his heart and puts a wicked stumbling block before his face and then goes to a prophet to inquire of me, I the LORD will answer him myself. 8 I will set my face against that man and make him an example and a byword. I will cut him off from my people. Then you will know that I am the LORD.

9 " 'And if the prophet is enticed to utter a prophecy, I the LORD have enticed that prophet, and I will stretch out my hand against him and destroy him from among my people Israel. 10 They will bear their guilt—the prophet will be as guilty as the one who consults him. 11 Then the people of Israel will no longer stray from me, nor will they defile themselves anymore with all their sins. They will be my people, and I will be their God, declares the Sovereign LORD.' "

Judgment Inescapable

12 The word of the LORD came to me: 13 "Son of man, if a country sins against me by being unfaithful and I stretch out my hand against it to cut off its food supply and send famine upon it and kill its men and their animals, 14 even if these three men—Noah, Daniel[a] and Job—were in it, they could save only themselves by their righteousness, declares the Sovereign LORD.

15 "Or if I send wild beasts through that country and they leave it childless and it becomes desolate so that no one can pass through it because of the beasts, 16 as surely as I live, declares the Sovereign LORD, even if these three men were in it, they could not save their own sons or daughters. They alone would be saved, but the land would be desolate.

17 "Or if I bring a sword against that country and say, 'Let the sword pass throughout the land,' and I kill its men and their animals, 18 as surely as I live, declares the Sovereign LORD, even if these three men were in it, they could not save their own sons or daughters. They alone would be saved.

19 "Or if I send a plague into that land and pour out my wrath upon it through bloodshed, killing its men and their animals, 20 as surely as I live, declares the Sovereign LORD, even if Noah, Daniel and Job were in it, they could save neither son nor

[a] **14** Or *Danel*; the Hebrew spelling may suggest a person other than the prophet Daniel; also in verse 20.

daughter. They would save only themselves by their righteousness.
21"For this is what the Sovereign LORD says: How much
worse will it be when I send against Jerusalem my four dreadful
judgments—sword and famine and wild beasts and plague—to kill
its men and their animals! 22Yet there will be some survivors—sons
and daughters who will be brought out of it. They will come to
you, and when you see their conduct and their actions, you will be
consoled regarding the disaster I have brought upon Jerusalem—
every disaster I have brought upon it. 23You will be consoled when
you see their conduct and their actions, for you will know that I
have done nothing in it without cause, declares the Sovereign
LORD."

Jerusalem, A Useless Vine

15 The word of the LORD came to me: 2"Son of man, how is the
wood of a vine better than that of a branch on any of the trees in
the forest? 3Is wood ever taken from it to make anything useful?
Do they make pegs from it to hang things on? 4And after it is
thrown on the fire as fuel and the fire burns both ends and chars
the middle, is it then useful for anything? 5If it was not useful for
anything when it was whole, how much less can it be made into
something useful when the fire has burned it and it is charred?
6"Therefore this is what the Sovereign LORD says: As I have
given the wood of the vine among the trees of the forest as fuel for
the fire, so will I treat the people living in Jerusalem. 7I will set my
face against them. Although they have come out of the fire, the fire
will yet consume them. And when I set my face against them, you
will know that I am the LORD. 8I will make the land desolate
because they have been unfaithful, declares the Sovereign LORD."

An Allegory of Unfaithful Jerusalem

16 The word of the LORD came to me: 2"Son of man, confront
Jerusalem with her detestable practices 3and say, 'This is what the
Sovereign LORD says to Jerusalem: Your ancestry and birth were in
the land of the Canaanites; your father was an Amorite and your
mother a Hittite. 4On the day you were born your cord was not
cut, nor were you washed with water to make you clean, nor were
you rubbed with salt or wrapped in cloths. 5No one looked on you
with pity or had compassion enough to do any of these things for
you. Rather, you were thrown out into the open field, for on the
day you were born you were despised.
6" 'Then I passed by and saw you kicking about in your
blood, and as you lay there in your blood I said to you, "Live!"[a]
7I made you grow like a plant of the field. You grew up and

[a]6 A few Hebrew manuscripts, Septuagint and Syriac; most Hebrew manuscripts *"Live!" And as you lay there in your blood I said to you, "Live!"*

15:7 *the fire will yet consume them:* Though Jerusalem and many of its people survived the first invasion of the Babylonians in 597 B.C. (see the note on p. 1560), the city was destroyed by fire when it was invaded a second time in 587/86 B.C. (see 2 Kgs 25:8-12 and the note at 12:10-13).

16:2 *Son of man:* See the note at 4:1.

16:2 *detestable practices:* See the notes at 2:3; 5:6, 7; and in chapter 8.

16:3 *Jerusalem: Your ancestry and birth:* In chapter 16, Jerusalem is pictured as an abandoned baby that the LORD God found and took care of. Later the city is compared to a prostitute who did not remain faithful to the one who loved her and cared for her, namely the LORD.

16:3 *Canaanites . . . Amorite . . . Hittite:* The Canaanites, descendants of Noah's son Ham (Gen 10:6-20), settled mainly in cities or villages near the Jordan River and the Mediterranean Sea northwest of Jerusalem. The Amorites lived in the hill country of Canaan at the time the Israelites invaded it (Num 21:21-35; Josh 2:10). The Hittites were a powerful people who were descendants of Heth, grandson of Ham (Gen 10:6-20). They established an empire in Asia Minor and were a dominant force in Canaan from the time of Abraham to the twelfth century B.C. God perhaps used these names to remind the people of Jerusalem that as descendants of foreigners, they were also foreigners in the land.

16:4 *rubbed with salt:* People believed that this toughened the skin of babies. The salt may have also helped to prevent infection.

developed and became the most beautiful of jewels.[a] Your breasts
were formed and your hair grew, you who were naked and bare.
8 “ ‘Later I passed by, and when I looked at you and saw that
you were old enough for love, I spread the corner of my garment
over you and covered your nakedness. I gave you my solemn oath
and entered into a covenant with you, declares the Sovereign LORD,
and you became mine.
9 “ ‘I bathed[b] you with water and washed the blood from you
and put ointments on you. 10 I clothed you with an embroidered
dress and put leather sandals on you. I dressed you in fine linen
and covered you with costly garments. 11 I adorned you with jewelry: I put bracelets on your arms and a necklace around your neck,
12 and I put a ring on your nose, earrings on your ears and a beautiful crown on your head. 13 So you were adorned with gold and silver; your clothes were of fine linen and costly fabric and
embroidered cloth. Your food was fine flour, honey and olive oil.
You became very beautiful and rose to be a queen. 14 And your
fame spread among the nations on account of your beauty,
because the splendor I had given you made your beauty perfect,
declares the Sovereign LORD.
15 “ ‘But you trusted in your beauty and used your fame to
become a prostitute. You lavished your favors on anyone who
passed by and your beauty became his.[c] 16 You took some of your
garments to make gaudy high places, where you carried on your
prostitution. Such things should not happen, nor should they ever
occur. 17 You also took the fine jewelry I gave you, the jewelry made
of my gold and silver, and you made for yourself male idols and
engaged in prostitution with them. 18 And you took your embroidered clothes to put on them, and you offered my oil and incense
before them. 19 Also the food I provided for you—the fine flour,
olive oil and honey I gave you to eat—you offered as fragrant
incense before them. That is what happened, declares the
Sovereign LORD.
20 “ ‘And you took your sons and daughters whom you bore
to me and sacrificed them as food to the idols. Was your prostitution not enough? 21 You slaughtered my children and sacrificed
them[d] to the idols. 22 In all your detestable practices and your prostitution you did not remember the days of your youth, when you
were naked and bare, kicking about in your blood.
23 “ ‘Woe! Woe to you, declares the Sovereign LORD. In addition to all your other wickedness, 24 you built a mound for yourself
and made a lofty shrine in every public square. 25 At the head of
every street you built your lofty shrines and degraded your beauty, offering your body with increasing promiscuity to anyone who

16:8 *spread ... my garment over you:* When a man spread his robe over a woman, he was showing his intention to marry her. The LORD here promises to make Jerusalem his bride and take care of her.

16:9-14 *bathed you ... clothed you .... jewelry ... beauty:* The LORD took care of Jerusalem and gave her the finest clothes and jewelry. Especially during the time of Israel's King Solomon, Jerusalem was known for its riches and for the beautiful temple Solomon had constructed.

16:15-19 *prostitute ... olive oil:* Though Jerusalem had been chosen as the LORD's holy city and the place where the LORD lived in the Most Holy Place in the temple, Jerusalem's people built shrines and idols to honor other gods (see the notes at 6:3-6 and 6:13; see also Isa 2:6-9). Olive oil mixed with fine flour was to be offered along with sweet-smelling incense as a sacrifice to give thanks to the LORD (Lev 2:1-3). But some in Jerusalem were also offering these items in ceremonies honoring other gods.

16:20,21 *sons and daughters ... sacrificed:* Child sacrifice was forbidden (see Lev 18:21; 20:2-5; Deut 12:31; 18:10, 11), but some Israelites did this anyway in and near Jerusalem (see 2 Kgs 21:4-7; 23:10; Jer 7:31; 32:35).

16:22 *your prostitution:* Jerusalem is pictured as a prostitute having "sex" with foreign nations and their gods, meaning its people worshiped those gods and Jerusalem's leaders made treaties with foreign nations (16:26-29), instead of trusting in the LORD for help.

[a] **7** Or *became mature* [b] **9** Or *I had bathed* [c] **15** Most Hebrew manuscripts; one Hebrew manuscript (see some Septuagint manuscripts) *by. Such a thing should not happen* [d] **21** Or *and made them pass through ⌊the fire⌋*

passed by. 26 You engaged in prostitution with the Egyptians, your lustful neighbors, and provoked me to anger with your increasing promiscuity. 27 So I stretched out my hand against you and reduced your territory; I gave you over to the greed of your enemies, the daughters of the Philistines, who were shocked by your lewd conduct. 28 You engaged in prostitution with the Assyrians too, because you were insatiable; and even after that, you still were not satisfied. 29 Then you increased your promiscuity to include Babylonia,[a] a land of merchants, but even with this you were not satisfied.

30 “‘How weak-willed you are, declares the Sovereign LORD, when you do all these things, acting like a brazen prostitute! 31 When you built your mounds at the head of every street and made your lofty shrines in every public square, you were unlike a prostitute, because you scorned payment.

32 “‘You adulterous wife! You prefer strangers to your own husband! 33 Every prostitute receives a fee, but you give gifts to all your lovers, bribing them to come to you from everywhere for your illicit favors. 34 So in your prostitution you are the opposite of others; no one runs after you for your favors. You are the very opposite, for you give payment and none is given to you.

35 “‘Therefore, you prostitute, hear the word of the LORD! 36 This is what the Sovereign LORD says: Because you poured out your wealth[b] and exposed your nakedness in your promiscuity with your lovers, and because of all your detestable idols, and because you gave them your children's blood, 37 therefore I am going to gather all your lovers, with whom you found pleasure, those you loved as well as those you hated. I will gather them against you from all around and will strip you in front of them, and they will see all your nakedness. 38 I will sentence you to the punishment of women who commit adultery and who shed blood; I will bring upon you the blood vengeance of my wrath and jealous anger. 39 Then I will hand you over to your lovers, and they will tear down your mounds and destroy your lofty shrines. They will strip you of your clothes and take your fine jewelry and leave you naked and bare. 40 They will bring a mob against you, who will stone you and hack you to pieces with their swords. 41 They will burn down your houses and inflict punishment on you in the sight of many women. I will put a stop to your prostitution, and you will no longer pay your lovers. 42 Then my wrath against you will subside and my jealous anger will turn away from you; I will be calm and no longer angry.

43 “‘Because you did not remember the days of your youth but enraged me with all these things, I will surely bring down on your head what you have done, declares the Sovereign LORD. Did you not add lewdness to all your other detestable practices?

44 “‘Everyone who quotes proverbs will quote this proverb

a 29 Or *Chaldea* b 36 Or *lust*

16:26-29 *engaged in prostitution . . . Egyptians . . . Assyrians . . . Babylonia:* Jerusalem and the land of Judah were located along major trade routes connecting Egypt to the west and Assyria and Babylonia to the northeast and east. At various times in their history, Judah's leaders made treaties with and paid bribe money to Egypt, Assyria, or Babylonia for protection against one of the other powers (see Isa 7; 20; 31; 39 and notes). The Philistines, who lived along the Mediterranean Sea directly to the west of Judah, had been enemies of Israel from the time of the judges, King Saul, and King David. This trouble continued into Ezekiel's time.

16:32-34 *adulterous wife . . . prostitute . . . you give payment:* See the notes at 16:22 and 16:26-29. Jerusalem not only acted like an unfaithful wife and prostitute, but it also paid those nations it had "sex" with. This payment probably refers to the money its leaders paid to other countries for protection.

16:36 *detestable idols . . . children's blood:* See the notes at 16:15-19 and 16:20, 21.

16:38 *sentence you . . . adultery:* According to the Law of Moses, the penalty for having sex with another's wife or husband could be death by stoning (Lev 20:10). Jerusalem's coming punishment (see 5:11-17; 14:21-23) is here described as that kind of punishment, because its people have been unfaithful to their husband, the LORD. See also the note at 15:7.

16:43 *lewdness . . . detestable practices:* See the notes at 16:22 and 2:3.

16:45 *Hittite . . . Amorite:* See the note at 16:3.

16:46-52 *sister was Samaria . . . Sodom . . . disgrace:* Shortly after King Solomon died (931 B.C.), the northern kingdom of Israel was formed when ten of Israel's tribes broke away from the southern tribes. The southern tribes were known as Judah (see 1 Kgs 12). King Omri of Israel built the city of Samaria and made it the capital of the northern kingdom of Israel (1 Kgs 16:23, 24). Samaria became known as an evil place, because many of its kings allowed and even encouraged the people to worship Baal, the Canaanite god of rain and fertility. Because of this sin, the LORD allowed Samaria and the northern kingdom to be destroyed by the Assyrians (see 2 Kgs 17:1-23). The ancient city of Sodom was destroyed because of its wicked people (Gen 18:16—19:29), and it became a symbol of evil for Israel (Isa 3:8,9; 13:19). Ezekiel says that Jerusalem's wickedness is even greater than that of these two evil cities.

16:53 *restore . . . Sodom . . . Samaria:* Jerusalem and its evil sister cities are to be restored, so that Jerusalem can be ashamed that it sneered at Sodom and Samaria while being terribly evil itself.

16:57 *Edom . . . Philistines:* These traditional enemies of Israel and Judah will join other countries in making fun of Jerusalem, even after it is restored.

16:59-63 *breaking the covenant . . . you will remember:* The covenant (agreement) mentioned in verses 59 and 60 may refer to the ancient covenant the LORD made with Moses and the people of Israel at Sinai (Exod 19–40; see also Deut 6:1—7:15), or it may refer to the marriage covenant described in Ezekiel 16:8. Even though Jerusalem and its people did not hold up their part of this covenant, the LORD now makes a promise that will last forever. This new covenant begins with the LORD forgiving Jerusalem's sins (see Jer 31:31-34). See also the mini-article called "Covenants (Agreements)," p. 386.

about you: "Like mother, like daughter." 45 You are a true daughter
of your mother, who despised her husband and her children; and
you are a true sister of your sisters, who despised their husbands
and their children. Your mother was a Hittite and your father an
Amorite. 46 Your older sister was Samaria, who lived to the north
of you with her daughters; and your younger sister, who lived to
the south of you with her daughters, was Sodom. 47 You not only
walked in their ways and copied their detestable practices, but in
all your ways you soon became more depraved than they. 48 As
surely as I live, declares the Sovereign LORD, your sister Sodom and
her daughters never did what you and your daughters have done.

49 " 'Now this was the sin of your sister Sodom: She and her
daughters were arrogant, overfed and unconcerned; they did not
help the poor and needy. 50 They were haughty and did detestable
things before me. Therefore I did away with them as you have
seen. 51 Samaria did not commit half the sins you did. You have
done more detestable things than they, and have made your sisters
seem righteous by all these things you have done. 52 Bear your disgrace, for you have furnished some justification for your sisters.
Because your sins were more vile than theirs, they appear more
righteous than you. So then, be ashamed and bear your disgrace,
for you have made your sisters appear righteous.

53 " 'However, I will restore the fortunes of Sodom and her
daughters and of Samaria and her daughters, and your fortunes
along with them, 54 so that you may bear your disgrace and be
ashamed of all you have done in giving them comfort. 55 And your
sisters, Sodom with her daughters and Samaria with her daughters, will return to what they were before; and you and your
daughters will return to what you were before. 56 You would not
even mention your sister Sodom in the day of your pride, 57 before
your wickedness was uncovered. Even so, you are now scorned by
the daughters of Edom[a] and all her neighbors and the daughters of
the Philistines—all those around you who despise you. 58 You will
bear the consequences of your lewdness and your detestable practices, declares the LORD.

59 " 'This is what the Sovereign LORD says: I will deal with you
as you deserve, because you have despised my oath by breaking the
covenant. 60 Yet I will remember the covenant I made with you in
the days of your youth, and I will establish an everlasting covenant
with you. 61 Then you will remember your ways and be ashamed
when you receive your sisters, both those who are older than you
and those who are younger. I will give them to you as daughters,
but not on the basis of my covenant with you. 62 So I will establish
my covenant with you, and you will know that I am the LORD.
63 Then, when I make atonement for you for all you have done, you

[a]57 Many Hebrew manuscripts and Syriac; most Hebrew manuscripts, Septuagint and Vulgate *Aram*

will remember and be ashamed and never again open your mouth
because of your humiliation, declares the Sovereign LORD.’ ”

Two Eagles and a Vine

17 The word of the LORD came to me: 2“Son of man, set forth an
allegory and tell the house of Israel a parable. 3Say to them, ‘This
is what the Sovereign LORD says: A great eagle with powerful
wings, long feathers and full plumage of varied colors came to
Lebanon. Taking hold of the top of a cedar, 4he broke off its topmost shoot and carried it away to a land of merchants, where he
planted it in a city of traders.
5“ ‘He took some of the seed of your land and put it in fertile soil. He planted it like a willow by abundant water, 6and it
sprouted and became a low, spreading vine. Its branches turned
toward him, but its roots remained under it. So it became a vine
and produced branches and put out leafy boughs.
7“ ‘But there was another great eagle with powerful wings
and full plumage. The vine now sent out its roots toward him from
the plot where it was planted and stretched out its branches to him
for water. 8It had been planted in good soil by abundant water so
that it would produce branches, bear fruit and become a splendid
vine.’
9“Say to them, ‘This is what the Sovereign LORD says: Will it
thrive? Will it not be uprooted and stripped of its fruit so that it
withers? All its new growth will wither. It will not take a strong
arm or many people to pull it up by the roots. 10Even if it is trans-
planted, will it thrive? Will it not wither completely when the east
wind strikes it—wither away in the plot where it grew?’ ”
11Then the word of the LORD came to me: 12“Say to this
rebellious house, ‘Do you not know what these things mean?’ Say
to them: ‘The king of Babylon went to Jerusalem and carried off
her king and her nobles, bringing them back with him to Babylon.
13Then he took a member of the royal family and made a treaty
with him, putting him under oath. He also carried away the leading men of the land, 14so that the kingdom would be brought low,
unable to rise again, surviving only by keeping his treaty. 15But the
king rebelled against him by sending his envoys to Egypt to get
horses and a large army. Will he succeed? Will he who does such
things escape? Will he break the treaty and yet escape?
16“ ‘As surely as I live, declares the Sovereign LORD, he shall
die in Babylon, in the land of the king who put him on the throne,
whose oath he despised and whose treaty he broke. 17Pharaoh with
his mighty army and great horde will be of no help to him in war,
when ramps are built and siege works erected to destroy many
lives. 18He despised the oath by breaking the covenant. Because he
had given his hand in pledge and yet did all these things, he shall
not escape.
19“ ‘Therefore this is what the Sovereign LORD says: As surely

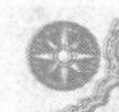

16:61 *your sisters:* See the note at 16:46-52

17:2 *Son of man:* See the note at 4:1.

17:2 *parable:* The parable is an allegory, in which the actions of animals and plants are compared to historical human actions or events.

17:3-6 *great eagle ... Lebanon ... top of a cedar ... toward him:* The great eagle is Nebuchadnezzar, the king of Babylon (17:12) who put down a rebellion in Jerusalem in 597 B.C. The cedar is a very majestic tree that grew in the forests of Lebanon. Israel's King Solomon used cedars to build the temple and his palace in Jerusalem. The "topmost shoot" refers to Judah's King Jehoiachin, who was taken captive to Babylon, "a land of merchants." The "seed" planted by the eagle refers to Zedekiah (see the Introduction to Ezekiel and the note at 12:10-13).

17:7-10 *another great eagle ... vine ... east wind:* This second eagle refers to the ruler of Egypt (probably Pharaoh Psammetichus II). The seed (Zedekiah of Israel) turned into a vine and turned toward this new eagle for help. This represents Zedekiah's rebellion against the Babylonians (see the note at 12:10-13).

17:12-15 *king of Babylon ... king rebelled:* Babylon's king invaded Judah and captured King Jehoiachin and took him and many of Jerusalem's leaders into exile in Babylon (see 2 Kgs 24:10-16 and the note on p. 1560). Then Zedekiah was put in charge in Jerusalem and signed a treaty with Babylon, but later he asked Egypt to help him rebel against the Babylonians (see 2 Kgs 24:15-20 and 2 Chr 36:9-13).

17:16-21 *die in Babylon ... scattered:* Refers to Zedekiah, who made a sacred promise in the name of Israel's LORD to keep his treaty with Babylon. When he asked for Egypt's help, he broke this promise and disgraced the LORD's name. The Bible does not report exactly where or when Zedekiah died, but it does describe the terrible things that happened to him (2 Kgs 25:2-7).

as I live, I will bring down on his head my oath that he despised and my covenant that he broke. [20]I will spread my net for him, and he will be caught in my snare. I will bring him to Babylon and execute judgment upon him there because he was unfaithful to me. [21]All his fleeing troops will fall by the sword, and the survivors will be scattered to the winds. Then you will know that I the LORD have spoken.

[22]" 'This is what the Sovereign LORD says: I myself will take a shoot from the very top of a cedar and plant it; I will break off a tender sprig from its topmost shoots and plant it on a high and lofty mountain. [23]On the mountain heights of Israel I will plant it; it will produce branches and bear fruit and become a splendid cedar. Birds of every kind will nest in it; they will find shelter in the shade of its branches. [24]All the trees of the field will know that I the LORD bring down the tall tree and make the low tree grow tall. I dry up the green tree and make the dry tree flourish.

" 'I the LORD have spoken, and I will do it.' "

The Soul Who Sins Will Die

18 The word of the LORD came to me: [2]"What do you people mean by quoting this proverb about the land of Israel:

" 'The fathers eat sour grapes,
and the children's teeth are set on edge'?

[3]"As surely as I live, declares the Sovereign LORD, you will no longer quote this proverb in Israel. [4]For every living soul belongs to me, the father as well as the son—both alike belong to me. The soul who sins is the one who will die.

[5]"Suppose there is a righteous man
who does what is just and right.
[6]He does not eat at the mountain shrines
or look to the idols of the house of Israel.
He does not defile his neighbor's wife
or lie with a woman during her period.
[7]He does not oppress anyone,
but returns what he took in pledge for a loan.
He does not commit robbery
but gives his food to the hungry
and provides clothing for the naked.
[8]He does not lend at usury
or take excessive interest.[a]
He withholds his hand from doing wrong
and judges fairly between man and man.
[9]He follows my decrees
and faithfully keeps my laws.

[a]8 Or *take interest*; similarly in verses 13 and 17

"Every living soul belongs to me, the father as well as the son—both alike belong to me."
Ezek 18:4

17:22-24 *the Sovereign LORD . . . will take a shoot . . . plant it:* Meaning that the LORD will choose someone from Judah's royal family (the cedar tree) and put him back on the throne in Jerusalem. Jerusalem's Mount Zion was not Israel's tallest mountain, but it was more important than all the others because the LORD's holy temple was located there. See also Isa 11:1-10; Jer 23:5,6 and the mini-article called "Zion," p. 1294.

18:2-4 *sour grapes . . . The soul who sins:* This popular saying meant that children suffered because of the actions of their parents. Some of the Israelites living in exile blamed their situation on the sins of their ancestors and did not take full responsibility for their own sins. But that old saying will no longer be true. Each person—young and old alike—will be judged by his or her sins and not the sins of another generation. See also Jer 31:29.

18:6-9 *does not eat at the mountain shrines . . . faithfully keeps my laws:* Ezekiel describes a man who obeys a number of different laws in the Law of Moses. Eating food at mountain shrines refers to eating food offered to idols, which probably implied taking part in ceremonies honoring foreign gods (see Hos 4:13). This broke the first commandment in the Law (Exod 20:3-5). For the other sins mentioned, see Lev 20:10; 18:19,20; Lev 25:17; Exod 22:22-25.

18:9 Lev 18:4,5.

That man is righteous;
he will surely live,
declares the Sovereign LORD.

10“Suppose he has a violent son, who sheds blood or does any
of these other things[a] 11(though the father has done none of them):

“He eats at the mountain shrines.
He defiles his neighbor’s wife.
12He oppresses the poor and needy.
He commits robbery.
He does not return what he took in pledge.
He looks to the idols.
He does detestable things.
13He lends at usury and takes excessive interest.

Will such a man live? He will not! Because he has done all these
detestable things, he will surely be put to death and his blood will
be on his own head.

14“But suppose this son has a son who sees all the sins his
father commits, and though he sees them, he does not do such things:

15“He does not eat at the mountain shrines
or look to the idols of the house of Israel.
He does not defile his neighbor’s wife.
16He does not oppress anyone
or require a pledge for a loan.
He does not commit robbery
but gives his food to the hungry
and provides clothing for the naked.
17He withholds his hand from sin[b]
and takes no usury or excessive interest.
He keeps my laws and follows my decrees.

He will not die for his father’s sin; he will surely live. 18But his
father will die for his own sin, because he practiced extortion,
robbed his brother and did what was wrong among his people.

19“Yet you ask, ‘Why does the son not share the guilt of his
father?’ Since the son has done what is just and right and has been
careful to keep all my decrees, he will surely live. 20The soul who
sins is the one who will die. The son will not share the guilt of the
father, nor will the father share the guilt of the son. The righteousness of the righteous man will be credited to him, and the
wickedness of the wicked will be charged against him.

21“But if a wicked man turns away from all the sins he has
committed and keeps all my decrees and does what is just and
right, he will surely live; he will not die. 22None of the offenses he

[a]10 Or *things to a brother the poor*

[b]17 Septuagint (see also verse 8); Hebrew *from the poor*

18:10-13 *violent son . . . looks to the idols . . . blood will be on his own head:* The good man’s son disobeys the laws described above (see 18:6-9 and note). The evil son can’t rely on his father’s good reputation, so the son will die because of his own evil actions.

18:14-18 *this son has a son . . . keeps my laws:* The first man’s grandson does not follow the evil example his father set, so the grandson will be not die because of his father’s sins.

18:20-23 *The soul who sins . . . will die . . . turn from their ways:* While those who sin will suffer for their sins and die, those who turn away from sinning and live right will be forgiven.

18:20 Deut 24:16.

has committed will be remembered against him. Because of the
righteous things he has done, he will live. [23]Do I take any pleasure
in the death of the wicked? declares the Sovereign LORD. Rather,
am I not pleased when they turn from their ways and live?
[24]"But if a righteous man turns from his righteousness and
commits sin and does the same detestable things the wicked man
does, will he live? None of the righteous things he has done will be
remembered. Because of the unfaithfulness he is guilty of and
because of the sins he has committed, he will die.
[25]"Yet you say, 'The way of the Lord is not just.' Hear,
O house of Israel: Is my way unjust? Is it not your ways that are
unjust? [26]If a righteous man turns from his righteousness and
commits sin, he will die for it; because of the sin he has committed he will die. [27]But if a wicked man turns away from the wickedness he has committed and does what is just and right, he will save
his life. [28]Because he considers all the offenses he has committed
and turns away from them, he will surely live; he will not die. [29]Yet
the house of Israel says, 'The way of the Lord is not just.' Are my
ways unjust, O house of Israel? Is it not your ways that are unjust?
[30]"Therefore, O house of Israel, I will judge you, each one
according to his ways, declares the Sovereign LORD. Repent! Turn
away from all your offenses; then sin will not be your downfall. [31]Rid
yourselves of all the offenses you have committed, and get a new
heart and a new spirit. Why will you die, O house of Israel? [32]For I
take no pleasure in the death of anyone, declares the Sovereign LORD.
Repent and live!

A Lament for Israel's Princes

19 "Take up a lament concerning the princes of Israel [2]and say:

" 'What a lioness was your mother
among the lions!
She lay down among the young lions
and reared her cubs.
[3]She brought up one of her cubs,
and he became a strong lion.
He learned to tear the prey
and he devoured men.
[4]The nations heard about him,
and he was trapped in their pit.
They led him with hooks
to the land of Egypt.

[5]" 'When she saw her hope unfulfilled,
her expectation gone,
she took another of her cubs
and made him a strong lion.
[6]He prowled among the lions,

"Do I take any pleasure in the death of the wicked?" declares the Sovereign LORD. "Rather, am I not pleased when they turn from their ways and live?"
Ezek 18:23

18:30-32 *Repent . . . and live!:* Though most of Ezekiel's messages predict destruction and death for the people of Israel, this message opens the door for the people to come back to the LORD and receive forgiveness. To repent means to turn away from sin and live right. See also Isa 1:27; Jer 35:15; Ezek 14:6; Hos 14:1, 2.

19:1 *a lament:* Though the verses in chapter 19 are in the form of a Hebrew lament, or funeral song, they are really an allegory used to explain historical events.

19:1-4 *princes of Israel . . . lioness . . . Egypt:* The first of the two princes (cubs) probably refers to Jehoahaz, the son of King Josiah and wife Hamutal (2 Kgs 23:28-32). Jehoahaz ruled Israel for only three months in 609 B.C. before Egypt's King Neco defeated Israel in battle and took Jehoahaz as a prisoner to Egypt, where he died. (See also 2 Kgs 23:33, 34.) The "lioness" may refer to Hamutal the mother of Zedekiah (see the note at 19:5-9), or more likely to the tribe of Judah. Judah is elsewhere symbolized as a lion (Gen 49:8-10).

19:5-9 *another of her cubs . . . Babylon:* The second lion cub may refer to Jehoiachin (grandson of King Josiah), who ruled Judah for only three months before he was taken as a prisoner to Babylon (see 2 Kgs 24:8-16 and the note on p. 1560). Or it may mean Zedekiah (son of King Josiah and Hamutal), who was captured and taken prisoner to Babylon in 587/86 B.C. (see the note at 12:10-13).

for he was now a strong lion.
He learned to tear the prey
and he devoured men.
7 He broke down[a] their strongholds
and devastated their towns.
The land and all who were in it
were terrified by his roaring.
8 Then the nations came against him,
those from regions round about.
They spread their net for him,
and he was trapped in their pit.
9 With hooks they pulled him into a cage
and brought him to the king of Babylon.
They put him in prison,
so his roar was heard no longer
on the mountains of Israel.

10 " 'Your mother was like a vine in your vineyard[b]
planted by the water;
it was fruitful and full of branches
because of abundant water.
11 Its branches were strong,
fit for a ruler's scepter.
It towered high
above the thick foliage,
conspicuous for its height
and for its many branches.
12 But it was uprooted in fury
and thrown to the ground.
The east wind made it shrivel,
it was stripped of its fruit;
its strong branches withered
and fire consumed them.
13 Now it is planted in the desert,
in a dry and thirsty land.
14 Fire spread from one of its main[c] branches
and consumed its fruit.
No strong branch is left on it
fit for a ruler's scepter.'

This is a lament and is to be used as a lament."

Rebellious Israel

20 In the seventh year, in the fifth month on the tenth day, some of the elders of Israel came to inquire of the LORD, and they sat down in front of me.

[a]7 Targum (see Septuagint); Hebrew *He knew* [b]10 Two Hebrew manuscripts; most Hebrew manuscripts *your blood* [c]14 Or *from under its*

19:8 *net:* In the ancient world, nets were sometimes used as weapons to capture enemy soldiers and their weapons.

19:10-14 *Your mother was like a vine . . . stripped of its fruit . . . . Fire spread:* This second allegory is probably meant to be related to the lion allegory (19:1-9) and the eagle and vine allegory in chapter 17. The vine probably refers to Judah or more generally to the line of kings that descended from King David. The strong branches (19:11) probably refer to a number of strong kings who ruled Judah and helped its reputation grow among neighboring nations. But the vine was pulled up and dried out by the desert winds that blew across the land of Judah from the east toward Babylon (compare 17:7-10). The transplanting in a hot, dry desert (19:13) refers to the Israelite people being forced to live in exile in Babylon or to the capture of Judah's kings (see the notes at 19:1-4 and 19:5-9). There the entire vine burns up, referring to the people's punishment or to the death of Jehoiachin or Zedekiah.

20:1 *seventh year . . . fifth month:* Probably late July 591 B.C. Once again Ezekiel is visited by some of Israel's elders living in exile (see 8:1; 14:1).

20:3 *Son of man:* See the note at 4:1.

20:5-8 *chose Israel . . . in Egypt . . . they rebelled:* The LORD chose Moses to lead the Hebrew people out of Egypt, where they were living as slaves. The LORD repeated his earlier promise to make the descendants of Abraham and Sarah a great nation and give them their own land, Canaan (see Gen 12:1-3; 17:1-8; Exod 6:2-8). But some continued to worship the old Egyptian gods or to keep idols or other objects intended to honor those gods. Even so, the LORD kept his promise and led them out of Egypt (Exod 14, 15).

20:10,11 *the desert . . . my laws:* After leaving Egypt, the Hebrew people wandered in the desert for many years. Early in their wandering, the LORD gave the Law to Moses and the people at Mount Sinai (Exod 19–40). See also Lev 18:5 and the mini-article called "Law," p. 1160.

20:12 *Sabbaths:* The Sabbath is the weekly day of rest that began at sunset on Friday when a ram's horn (shofar) was blown. It ended with a blessing (benediction) at sunset on Saturday. No work was to be done on the Sabbath, which means to "rest" or "stop working" (see also Exod 20:8-11; 31:12-17; Deut 5:12-15).

20:13-16 *rebelled . . . idols:* Even while Moses was receiving the LORD's Commandments, the people rebelled (Exod 32:1-35). But many other rebellions are also reported (see, for example, Lev 10:1-5; Num 11:1-10; 14:1-10). Because they rebelled, the LORD did not let the older generation of Hebrews who left Egypt enter the promised land of Canaan (see Num 14:26-38).

20:18-22 *said to their children . . . rebelled against me . . . withheld my hand:* Though the second generation of Hebrews who came out of Egypt were allowed to enter Canaan, they and their descendants also rebelled. This rebellion took many forms in the centuries between the time the people entered the land and the time of the prophets, including Ezekiel.

[2]Then the word of the LORD came to me: [3]"Son of man,
speak to the elders of Israel and say to them, 'This is what the
Sovereign LORD says: Have you come to inquire of me? As surely as
I live, I will not let you inquire of me, declares the Sovereign LORD.'
[4]"Will you judge them? Will you judge them, son of man?
Then confront them with the detestable practices of their fathers
[5]and say to them: 'This is what the Sovereign LORD says: On the
day I chose Israel, I swore with uplifted hand to the descendants of
the house of Jacob and revealed myself to them in Egypt. With
uplifted hand I said to them, "I am the LORD your God." [6]On that
day I swore to them that I would bring them out of Egypt into a
land I had searched out for them, a land flowing with milk and
honey, the most beautiful of all lands. [7]And I said to them, "Each
of you, get rid of the vile images you have set your eyes on, and do
not defile yourselves with the idols of Egypt. I am the LORD your
God."
[8]" 'But they rebelled against me and would not listen to me;
they did not get rid of the vile images they had set their eyes on,
nor did they forsake the idols of Egypt. So I said I would pour out
my wrath on them and spend my anger against them in Egypt.
[9]But for the sake of my name I did what would keep it from being
profaned in the eyes of the nations they lived among and in whose
sight I had revealed myself to the Israelites by bringing them out of
Egypt. [10]Therefore I led them out of Egypt and brought them into
the desert. [11]I gave them my decrees and made known to them my
laws, for the man who obeys them will live by them. [12]Also I gave
them my Sabbaths as a sign between us, so they would know that
I the LORD made them holy.
[13]" 'Yet the people of Israel rebelled against me in the desert.
They did not follow my decrees but rejected my laws—although the
man who obeys them will live by them—and they utterly desecrated my Sabbaths. So I said I would pour out my wrath on them and
destroy them in the desert. [14]But for the sake of my name I did
what would keep it from being profaned in the eyes of the nations
in whose sight I had brought them out. [15]Also with uplifted hand I
swore to them in the desert that I would not bring them into the
land I had given them—a land flowing with milk and honey, most
beautiful of all lands— [16]because they rejected my laws and did not
follow my decrees and desecrated my Sabbaths. For their hearts
were devoted to their idols. [17]Yet I looked on them with pity and
did not destroy them or put an end to them in the desert. [18]I said
to their children in the desert, "Do not follow the statutes of your
fathers or keep their laws or defile yourselves with their idols. [19]I am
the LORD your God; follow my decrees and be careful to keep my
laws. [20]Keep my Sabbaths holy, that they may be a sign between us.
Then you will know that I am the LORD your God."
[21]" 'But the children rebelled against me: They did not follow
my decrees, they were not careful to keep my laws—although the

man who obeys them will live by them—and they desecrated my Sabbaths. So I said I would pour out my wrath on them and spend my anger against them in the desert. [22]But I withheld my hand, and for the sake of my name I did what would keep it from being profaned in the eyes of the nations in whose sight I had brought them out. [23]Also with uplifted hand I swore to them in the desert that I would disperse them among the nations and scatter them through the countries, [24]because they had not obeyed my laws but had rejected my decrees and desecrated my Sabbaths, and their eyes ⌞lusted⌟ after their fathers' idols. [25]I also gave them over to statutes that were not good and laws they could not live by; [26]I let them become defiled through their gifts—the sacrifice of every firstborn[a]—that I might fill them with horror so they would know that I am the LORD.'

[27]"Therefore, son of man, speak to the people of Israel and say to them, 'This is what the Sovereign LORD says: In this also your fathers blasphemed me by forsaking me: [28]When I brought them into the land I had sworn to give them and they saw any high hill or any leafy tree, there they offered their sacrifices, made offerings that provoked me to anger, presented their fragrant incense and poured out their drink offerings. [29]Then I said to them: What is this high place you go to?' " (It is called Bamah[b] to this day.)

Judgment and Restoration

[30]"Therefore say to the house of Israel: 'This is what the Sovereign LORD says: Will you defile yourselves the way your fathers did and lust after their vile images? [31]When you offer your gifts—the sacrifice of your sons in[c] the fire—you continue to defile yourselves with all your idols to this day. Am I to let you inquire of me, O house of Israel? As surely as I live, declares the Sovereign LORD, I will not let you inquire of me.

[32]" 'You say, "We want to be like the nations, like the peoples of the world, who serve wood and stone." But what you have in mind will never happen. [33]As surely as I live, declares the Sovereign LORD, I will rule over you with a mighty hand and an outstretched arm and with outpoured wrath. [34]I will bring you from the nations and gather you from the countries where you have been scattered—with a mighty hand and an outstretched arm and with outpoured wrath. [35]I will bring you into the desert of the nations and there, face to face, I will execute judgment upon you. [36]As I judged your fathers in the desert of the land of Egypt, so I will judge you, declares the Sovereign LORD. [37]I will take note of you as you pass under my rod, and I will bring you into the bond of the covenant. [38]I will purge you of those who revolt and rebel against

[a]**26** Or *—making every firstborn pass through ⌞the fire⌟* [b]**29** *Bamah* means *high place.* [c]**31** Or *—making your sons pass through*

20:23-26 *disperse them . . . not obeyed my laws . . . defiled:* For their sins, the people of Israel were punished by losing their land and by being scattered to other nations (see Amos 2:4—3:2; Hos 11:12—12:14; Isa 5:7-13; 6:11, 12; Lev 26:33; and the notes at Ezek 4:13; 5:8-17). See also the notes at 16:15-19 and 16:20, 21.

20:27-32 *blasphemed . . . lust after their vile images . . . serve wood and stone:* Another summary of Israel's disobedience (see the notes at 6:3-6; 6:13; 16:15-19).

20:33 *as I live... mighty hand . . . outstretched arm:* Israel's LORD was "living," and not like the idols made of wood and stone, which were lifeless and could not help the people (see Isa 41:21-29; 44:9-20). The LORD's mighty hand and powerful arm are images often used to describe the LORD's protection or power (see Exod 14:21; 15:12, 16; Deut 5:15; Isa 14:27; 40:10).

20:35,36 *desert . . . judged your fathers . . . judge you:* May refer to the Israelite's journey through the desert on their way back from exile in Babylon. The LORD will punish the Israelites for their sins, just as he had punished their ancestors in the Desert of Sinai when they made an idol in the shape of a bull (Exod 32:25-35).

20:40-44 *on my holy mountain . . . know that I am the* L*ORD:* The time of judgment (exile) would not last forever. Some of the Israelite people who had been scattered among the nations would be allowed to return to rebuild the temple on Mount Zion in Jerusalem. Then the people and their priests could once again offer holy sacrifices to honor the LORD. The restoration did begin in 538 B.C. when the Persian ruler named Cyrus defeated Babylon and allowed the Israelite people living in exile to return home to Judah. The rebuilt temple was dedicated in 515 B.C. See also Isa 40:9-11; 44:28—45:13; and the article called "After the Exile: God's People Return to Judea," p. 931.

When Israel and Jerusalem are restored, the nations will recognize the power of Israel's LORD, and the people will recognize their horrible sins.

20:46-47 *toward the south . . . fire:* The locations in this short message about the burning forests are unclear. In Hebrew, the region known as the Negev is mentioned, but it is a dry area to the south of Judah with few trees. Perhaps the far southern and northern borders of Israel are intended to emphasize the LORD's complete destruction of the land (see the note at 6:14; see also 21:4).

21:2,3 *set your face against Jerusalem . . . sword:* This judgment message focuses on the idol worship going on in Jerusalem (see the notes at 6:3-6 and in chapter 8). But instead of fire (20:47) the LORD will punish with a sword (see also Isa 34:6; 66:16).

me. Although I will bring them out of the land where they are living, yet they will not enter the land of Israel. Then you will know
that I am the LORD.
39“ ‘As for you, O house of Israel, this is what the Sovereign
LORD says: Go and serve your idols, every one of you! But afterward you will surely listen to me and no longer profane my holy
name with your gifts and idols. 40For on my holy mountain, the
high mountain of Israel, declares the Sovereign LORD, there in the
land the entire house of Israel will serve me, and there I will accept
them. There I will require your offerings and your choice gifts,[a]
along with all your holy sacrifices. 41I will accept you as fragrant
incense when I bring you out from the nations and gather you
from the countries where you have been scattered, and I will show
myself holy among you in the sight of the nations. 42Then you will
know that I am the LORD, when I bring you into the land of Israel,
the land I had sworn with uplifted hand to give to your fathers.
43There you will remember your conduct and all the actions by
which you have defiled yourselves, and you will loathe yourselves
for all the evil you have done. 44You will know that I am the LORD,
when I deal with you for my name's sake and not according to
your evil ways and your corrupt practices, O house of Israel,
declares the Sovereign LORD.' ”

Prophecy Against the South

45The word of the LORD came to me: 46“Son of man, set your
face toward the south; preach against the south and prophesy
against the forest of the southland. 47Say to the southern forest:
'Hear the word of the LORD. This is what the Sovereign LORD says:
I am about to set fire to you, and it will consume all your trees,
both green and dry. The blazing flame will not be quenched, and
every face from south to north will be scorched by it. 48Everyone
will see that I the LORD have kindled it; it will not be quenched.' ”
49Then I said, “Ah, Sovereign LORD! They are saying of me,
'Isn't he just telling parables?' ”

Babylon, God's Sword of Judgment

21 The word of the LORD came to me: 2“Son of man, set your
face against Jerusalem and preach against the sanctuary. Prophesy
against the land of Israel 3and say to her: 'This is what the LORD
says: I am against you. I will draw my sword from its scabbard and
cut off from you both the righteous and the wicked. 4Because I am
going to cut off the righteous and the wicked, my sword will be
unsheathed against everyone from south to north. 5Then all people will know that I the LORD have drawn my sword from its scabbard; it will not return again.'

[a]**40** Or *and the gifts of your firstfruits*

6 “Therefore groan, son of man! Groan before them with
broken heart and bitter grief. 7 And when they ask you, ‘Why are
you groaning?’ you shall say, ‘Because of the news that is coming.
Every heart will melt and every hand go limp; every spirit will
become faint and every knee become as weak as water.’ It is coming! It will surely take place, declares the Sovereign LORD.”
8 The word of the LORD came to me: 9 “Son of man, prophesy
and say, ‘This is what the Lord says:

“ ‘A sword, a sword,
sharpened and polished—
10 sharpened for the slaughter,
polished to flash like lightning!

“ ‘Shall we rejoice in the scepter of my son ⌞Judah⌟? The
sword despises every such stick.

11 “ ‘The sword is appointed to be polished,
to be grasped with the hand;
it is sharpened and polished,
made ready for the hand of the slayer.
12 Cry out and wail, son of man,
for it is against my people;
it is against all the princes of Israel.
They are thrown to the sword
along with my people.
Therefore beat your breast.

13 “ ‘Testing will surely come. And what if the scepter ⌞of
Judah⌟, which the sword despises, does not continue? declares the
Sovereign LORD.’

14 “So then, son of man, prophesy
and strike your hands together.
Let the sword strike twice,
even three times.
It is a sword for slaughter—
a sword for great slaughter,
closing in on them from every side.
15 So that hearts may melt
and the fallen be many,
I have stationed the sword for slaughter[a]
at all their gates.
Oh! It is made to flash like lightning,
it is grasped for slaughter.
16 O sword, slash to the right,
then to the left,
wherever your blade is turned.

---

[a] **15** Septuagint; the meaning of the Hebrew for this word is uncertain.

21:6 *Groan before them with broken heart and bitter grief:* Ezekiel was told to wail loudly, the way mourners did during funeral processions in ancient Israel. His wailing was meant to attract attention so he could give a message about the LORD's coming judgment against Judah, which would happen soon or in about four years (see 20:1 and the note at 12:10-13).

21:12-17 *Cry out and wail . . . sword . . . strike my hands together:* Ezekiel continues to groan (see 21:6), perhaps as he acts out or tells about the LORD's vicious attack on Jerusalem's people. The LORD will swing his sword in every direction, killing people with every stroke. Ezekiel is to clap his hands to celebrate the LORD's slaughter of Jerusalem's people (21:14), just as the LORD will (21:17).

21:19 *mark out two roads:* Next, Ezekiel is to draw a map in the dirt showing two roads leading west from Babylon, one going to Rabbah in Ammon and the other going to Jerusalem in Judah.

21:21,22 *cast lots with arrows . . . sound the battle cry:* Babylon's leaders often tried to find out what their gods wanted them to do by divining (examining fluid in a cup or looking at the liver of a sacrificed animal), by astrology (telling the future by observing the movement of the stars and planets), or by trying to contact the spirits of the dead (see Isa 47:12-15). Here Nebuchadnezzar also seems to put the names "Rabbah" and "Jerusalem" on different arrows (21:20). The direction he went also would be determined by the luck of the draw, though the LORD is actually directing Nebuchadnezzar to choose the Jerusalem arrow (21:22).

21:23 *sworn allegiance to him:* After Babylon first defeated Jerusalem in 597 B.C. (see the note on p. 1560), Zedekiah was put on the throne. He signed a treaty promising to be loyal to Babylon, but then he turned to Egypt for help in rebelling against the Babylonians (see the note at 17:12-15).

21:25 *wicked prince of Israel:* Meaning Zedekiah.

21:27 *to whom it rightfully belongs:* King Nebuchadnezzar of Babylon, Israel's enemy, is also the LORD's chosen one to punish Jerusalem.

21:28,29 *Ammonites . . . punishment:* Ancient enemies of Israel (Judg 10:11-18; 1 Sam 14:47, 48). Located east of Israel, Ammon's people were not chosen to be attacked at this time (21:22), but Ezekiel gives them a warning about the LORD's coming judgment. See also Jer 49:1-6; Ezek 25:1-7; Amos 1:13–15; Zeph 2:8-11.

21:30 *Return the sword to its scabbard:* May refer to the swords of Nebuchadnezzar's soldiers being put away when he defeated Jerusalem and the Ammonites. Or it may refer to the LORD's judgment against Ammon.

17 I too will strike my hands together,
and my wrath will subside.
I the LORD have spoken."

18 The word of the LORD came to me: 19 "Son of man, mark
out two roads for the sword of the king of Babylon to take, both
starting from the same country. Make a signpost where the road
branches off to the city. 20 Mark out one road for the sword to
come against Rabbah of the Ammonites and another against Judah
and fortified Jerusalem. 21 For the king of Babylon will stop at the
fork in the road, at the junction of the two roads, to seek an omen:
He will cast lots with arrows, he will consult his idols, he will
examine the liver. 22 Into his right hand will come the lot for
Jerusalem, where he is to set up battering rams, to give the command to slaughter, to sound the battle cry, to set battering rams
against the gates, to build a ramp and to erect siege works. 23 It will
seem like a false omen to those who have sworn allegiance to him,
but he will remind them of their guilt and take them captive.

24 "Therefore this is what the Sovereign LORD says: 'Because
you people have brought to mind your guilt by your open rebellion, revealing your sins in all that you do—because you have done
this, you will be taken captive.

25 " 'O profane and wicked prince of Israel, whose day has
come, whose time of punishment has reached its climax, 26 this is
what the Sovereign LORD says: Take off the turban, remove the
crown. It will not be as it was: The lowly will be exalted and the
exalted will be brought low. 27 A ruin! A ruin! I will make it a ruin!
It will not be restored until he comes to whom it rightfully
belongs; to him I will give it.'

28 "And you, son of man, prophesy and say, 'This is what the
Sovereign LORD says about the Ammonites and their insults:

" 'A sword, a sword,
drawn for the slaughter,
polished to consume
and to flash like lightning!
29 Despite false visions concerning you
and lying divinations about you,
it will be laid on the necks
of the wicked who are to be slain,
whose day has come,
whose time of punishment has reached its climax.
30 Return the sword to its scabbard.
In the place where you were created,
in the land of your ancestry,
I will judge you.
31 I will pour out my wrath upon you
and breathe out my fiery anger against you;
I will hand you over to brutal men,

men skilled in destruction.
32You will be fuel for the fire,
your blood will be shed in your land,
you will be remembered no more;
for I the LORD have spoken.' "

Jerusalem's Sins

22 The word of the LORD came to me: 2"Son of man, will you
judge her? Will you judge this city of bloodshed? Then confront
her with all her detestable practices 3and say: 'This is what the
Sovereign LORD says: O city that brings on herself doom by shedding blood in her midst and defiles herself by making idols, 4you
have become guilty because of the blood you have shed and have
become defiled by the idols you have made. You have brought your
days to a close, and the end of your years has come. Therefore I
will make you an object of scorn to the nations and a laughingstock to all the countries. 5Those who are near and those who are
far away will mock you, O infamous city, full of turmoil.
6" 'See how each of the princes of Israel who are in you uses
his power to shed blood. 7In you they have treated father and
mother with contempt; in you they have oppressed the alien and
mistreated the fatherless and the widow. 8You have despised my
holy things and desecrated my Sabbaths. 9In you are slanderous
men bent on shedding blood; in you are those who eat at the
mountain shrines and commit lewd acts. 10In you are those who
dishonor their fathers' bed; in you are those who violate women
during their period, when they are ceremonially unclean. 11In you
one man commits a detestable offense with his neighbor's wife,
another shamefully defiles his daughter-in-law, and another violates his sister, his own father's daughter. 12In you men accept
bribes to shed blood; you take usury and excessive interest[a] and
make unjust gain from your neighbors by extortion. And you have
forgotten me, declares the Sovereign LORD.
13" 'I will surely strike my hands together at the unjust gain
you have made and at the blood you have shed in your midst. 14Will
your courage endure or your hands be strong in the day I deal with
you? I the LORD have spoken, and I will do it. 15I will disperse you
among the nations and scatter you through the countries; and I will
put an end to your uncleanness. 16When you have been defiled[b] in
the eyes of the nations, you will know that I am the LORD.' "
17Then the word of the LORD came to me: 18"Son of man, the
house of Israel has become dross to me; all of them are the copper,
tin, iron and lead left inside a furnace. They are but the dross of
silver. 19Therefore this is what the Sovereign LORD says: 'Because
you have all become dross, I will gather you into Jerusalem. 20As

[a]**12** Or *usury and interest* [b]**16** Or *When I have allotted you your inheritance*

22:2-4 *city of bloodshed . . . the idols you have made:* The blood they have "shed" probably refers to all forms of evil done to people (22:6-9), while worshiping idols refers to evil done against the LORD (see also the notes at 2:3; 6:3-6; 16:15-19).

22:7-12 *treated father and mother with contempt . . . take usury and excessive interest:* The people of Jerusalem had disobeyed many of God's laws, including: dishonoring parents (Exod 20:12; Deut 5:16); cheating foreigners, widows, and orphans, who were protected by the law (Exod 22:21, 22; Deut 24:17; Isa 1:17); not respecting the temple by worshiping idols in the temple area (see the notes in chapter 8); ignoring the Sabbath (see the note at 20:12; also Lev 19:30; 26:2); eating meat sacrificed to idols (see the note at 18:6-9); improper sexual behavior (see the note at 16:38; also Lev 18:7-20); accepting murder payoffs and charging high interest (see Exod 22:25; 23:8; Lev 25:36, 37; Deut 16:19; 23:19).

22:15 *I will . . . scatter you:* See the notes at 4:13; 5:1-4; 20:23-26.

22:18-22 *dross . . . silver is melted in a furnace:* Precious metals such as silver were purified by a process called refining or smelting. Metal ore was melted into a liquid, and the particles that were not pure were separated out. This leftover metal (dross) was thrown away. The prophet Isaiah said that the LORD would purify the people of Israel by getting rid of the leftover metal, the evil people and sinful activities (see Isa 1:22-25), but Ezekiel says that all of Jerusalem's people will be melted down and destroyed. See also Jer 9:7; Zech 13:9.

men gather silver, copper, iron, lead and tin into a furnace to melt
it with a fiery blast, so will I gather you in my anger and my wrath
and put you inside the city and melt you. 21 I will gather you and I
will blow on you with my fiery wrath, and you will be melted
inside her. 22 As silver is melted in a furnace, so you will be melted
inside her, and you will know that I the LORD have poured out my
wrath upon you.' "
23 Again the word of the LORD came to me: 24 "Son of man,
say to the land, 'You are a land that has had no rain or showers[a] in
the day of wrath.' 25 There is a conspiracy of her princes[b] within her
like a roaring lion tearing its prey; they devour people, take treasures and precious things and make many widows within her. 26 Her
priests do violence to my law and profane my holy things; they do
not distinguish between the holy and the common; they teach that
there is no difference between the unclean and the clean; and they
shut their eyes to the keeping of my Sabbaths, so that I am profaned among them. 27 Her officials within her are like wolves tearing their prey; they shed blood and kill people to make unjust
gain. 28 Her prophets whitewash these deeds for them by false
visions and lying divinations. They say, 'This is what the
Sovereign LORD says'—when the LORD has not spoken. 29 The people of the land practice extortion and commit robbery; they
oppress the poor and needy and mistreat the alien, denying them
justice.
30 "I looked for a man among them who would build up the
wall and stand before me in the gap on behalf of the land so I
would not have to destroy it, but I found none. 31 So I will pour out
my wrath on them and consume them with my fiery anger, bringing down on their own heads all they have done, declares the
Sovereign LORD."

Two Adulterous Sisters

23 The word of the LORD came to me: 2 "Son of man, there were
two women, daughters of the same mother. 3 They became prostitutes in Egypt, engaging in prostitution from their youth. In that
land their breasts were fondled and their virgin bosoms caressed.
4 The older was named Oholah, and her sister was Oholibah. They
were mine and gave birth to sons and daughters. Oholah is
Samaria, and Oholibah is Jerusalem.
5 "Oholah engaged in prostitution while she was still mine;
and she lusted after her lovers, the Assyrians—warriors 6 clothed in
blue, governors and commanders, all of them handsome young
men, and mounted horsemen. 7 She gave herself as a prostitute to
all the elite of the Assyrians and defiled herself with all the idols of

[a]24 Septuagint; Hebrew *has not been cleansed or rained on* [b]25 Septuagint; Hebrew *prophets*

22:25 *princes . . . take treasures:* Apparently some leaders used their political power to take land and property that rightly belonged to others (see also Isa 3:10-15; 5:8-13).

22:26 *priests do violence to my law:* Israel's priests were responsible for offering correct sacrifices and for making sure that no unacceptable things were sacrificed or brought into the holy spaces in and around the temple (see Lev 10:10). But the priests here in EZEKIEL were not keeping the temple area free of impure or unclean things (see the notes in chapter 8). See also the mini-articles called "Israel's Priests," p. 2344, and "Purity (Clean and Unclean)," p. 2125.

22:27-29 *officials . . . prophets . . . people:* The "officials" probably refer to political leaders who were especially guilty of being unfair in deciding cases (see the notes at 7:9, 10; 11:1-3; see also Isa 1:23; Mic 2:1-10). See the notes at 7:26; 12:22-28; and 22:7-12.

23:2-4 *two women, daughters of the same mother . . . Samaria . . . Jerusalem:* Ezekiel uses the image of the two cities as prostitutes (see also the notes at 16:22 and 16:26-29) to describe their unfaithfulness and their worship of foreign gods and idols. The names "Oholah" and "Oholibah" are based on the Hebrew word for "tent," but it is not clear what this image is meant to portray.

23:5-10 *Oholah . . . killed her:* During the time of Assyria's control in the ancient Near East, they threatened Israel and its capital Samaria. Some of the northern kingdom's rulers made treaties with and paid bribe money to Assyria to keep from being attacked (2 Kgs 15:19, 20; 17:3). Even worse, however, was the fact that Samaria's leaders allowed the people to worship foreign gods. Ezekiel is saying that Israel's dependence on Assyria (her "lovers") instead of on the LORD is as bad as the worst sexual sins. Eventually, Assyria's army destroyed Samaria (722-721 B.C.) and forced many people in Israel to leave their homes and live in foreign lands (see 2 Kgs 17:5-23).

everyone she lusted after. 8She did not give up the prostitution she began in Egypt, when during her youth men slept with her, caressed her virgin bosom and poured out their lust upon her.

9"Therefore I handed her over to her lovers, the Assyrians, for whom she lusted. 10They stripped her naked, took away her sons and daughters and killed her with the sword. She became a byword among women, and punishment was inflicted on her.

11"Her sister Oholibah saw this, yet in her lust and prostitution she was more depraved than her sister. 12She too lusted after the Assyrians—governors and commanders, warriors in full dress, mounted horsemen, all handsome young men. 13I saw that she too defiled herself; both of them went the same way.

14"But she carried her prostitution still further. She saw men portrayed on a wall, figures of Chaldeans[a] portrayed in red, 15with belts around their waists and flowing turbans on their heads; all of them looked like Babylonian chariot officers, natives of Chaldea.[b] 16As soon as she saw them, she lusted after them and sent messengers to them in Chaldea. 17Then the Babylonians came to her, to the bed of love, and in their lust they defiled her. After she had been defiled by them, she turned away from them in disgust. 18When she carried on her prostitution openly and exposed her nakedness, I turned away from her in disgust, just as I had turned away from her sister. 19Yet she became more and more promiscuous as she recalled the days of her youth, when she was a prostitute in Egypt. 20There she lusted after her lovers, whose genitals were like those of donkeys and whose emission was like that of horses. 21So you longed for the lewdness of your youth, when in Egypt your bosom was caressed and your young breasts fondled.[c]

22"Therefore, Oholibah, this is what the Sovereign LORD says: I will stir up your lovers against you, those you turned away from in disgust, and I will bring them against you from every side— 23the Babylonians and all the Chaldeans, the men of Pekod and Shoa and Koa, and all the Assyrians with them, handsome young men, all of them governors and commanders, chariot officers and men of high rank, all mounted on horses. 24They will come against you with weapons,[d] chariots and wagons and with a throng of people; they will take up positions against you on every side with large and small shields and with helmets. I will turn you over to them for punishment, and they will punish you according to their standards. 25I will direct my jealous anger against you, and they will deal with you in fury. They will cut off your noses and your ears, and those of you who are left will fall by the sword. They will take away your sons and daughters, and those of you who are left will be consumed by fire. 26They will also strip you of your clothes

[a]**14** Or *Babylonians* [b]**15** Or *Babylonia*; also in verse 16 [c]**21** Syriac (see also verse 3); Hebrew *caressed because of your young breasts* [d]**24** The meaning of the Hebrew for this word is uncertain.

23:11-18 *Oholibah . . . lusted after the Assyrians . . . her prostitution:* To protect themselves, the southern kingdom of Israel (Judah) also made treaties with foreign countries, such as Assyria (see 2 Kgs 16:5-9; 18:1-37) and Babylon (see 2 Kgs 20:12-19; and the note at Ezek 17:12-15).

23:19 *when she was a prostitute in Egypt:* See the notes at 20:5-8 and 23:5-10.

23:20 *lusted after her lovers:* The danger in Ezekiel's day was that the people of Judah who had been taken into exile in Babylon would start worshiping the gods of the Babylonians.

23:23 *Babylonians . . . Chaldeans . . . Assyrians:* The Babylonians were sometimes referred to as Chaldeans (see also Job 1:17). The Pekod tribe lived east of Babylon, but the exact identity of the Shoa and Koa tribes is unknown. Babylonian and Assyrian armies attacked Judah and Jerusalem from the north, using the best routes from Mesopotamia.

23:25 *fall by the sword:* Because Jerusalem had acted like a prostitute and was not a faithful wife to the LORD, it would be put to death, the usual penalty for adultery, according to the Law of Moses (see the note at 16:38).

23:27 *began in Egypt:* See the notes at 20:5-8 and 23:5-10.

23:29,30 *shame of your prostitution . . . nations:* See the notes in chapter 16; see also 23:11-18.

23:32-34 *drink your sister's cup . . . drain it dry:* Drinking from the LORD's cup of anger is a common symbol for God's judgment and punishment (Job 21:20; Ps 60:3; Isa 51:22; Jer 25:15-29; Rev 14:10; 16:19). Jerusalem will drink until it is drunk. Drinking the cup dry means receiving the full amount of God's anger.

23:36-39 *Oholah and Oholibah . . . my Sabbaths . . . idols:* Jerusalem did not learn from its sister city Samaria, which was destroyed because of idol worship and because people did not treat one another with fairness and justice. See the notes at 2:3; 6:3-6; 16:15-19; 16:20, 21. See also the notes at 20:12 and 22:7-12 (Sabbath).

23:40 *sent messengers for men:* May refer to actual messengers who traveled to foreign nations asking for help, as in the case of seeking help from the Egyptians and Cushites (Ethiopians) against Assyria (see Isa 18:1, 2; 20:2-5 and notes) and Babylon (see the notes at 17:7-10 and 17:12-15). Or it may refer to the worship of foreign idols in shrines set up in Jerusalem and in the temple itself (see the notes in chapter 8 and at 16:15-19).

and take your fine jewelry. 27 So I will put a stop to the lewdness
and prostitution you began in Egypt. You will not look on these
things with longing or remember Egypt anymore.

28 "For this is what the Sovereign LORD says: I am about to
hand you over to those you hate, to those you turned away from in
disgust. 29 They will deal with you in hatred and take away everything you have worked for. They will leave you naked and bare,
and the shame of your prostitution will be exposed. Your lewdness
and promiscuity 30 have brought this upon you, because you lusted
after the nations and defiled yourself with their idols. 31 You have
gone the way of your sister; so I will put her cup into your hand.

32 "This is what the Sovereign LORD says:

"You will drink your sister's cup,
a cup large and deep;
it will bring scorn and derision,
for it holds so much.
33 You will be filled with drunkenness and sorrow,
the cup of ruin and desolation,
the cup of your sister Samaria.
34 You will drink it and drain it dry;
you will dash it to pieces
and tear your breasts.

I have spoken, declares the Sovereign LORD.

35 "Therefore this is what the Sovereign LORD says: Since you
have forgotten me and thrust me behind your back, you must bear
the consequences of your lewdness and prostitution."

36 The LORD said to me: "Son of man, will you judge Oholah
and Oholibah? Then confront them with their detestable practices,
37 for they have committed adultery and blood is on their hands.
They committed adultery with their idols; they even sacrificed
their children, whom they bore to me,[a] as food for them. 38 They
have also done this to me: At that same time they defiled my sanctuary and desecrated my Sabbaths. 39 On the very day they sacrificed their children to their idols, they entered my sanctuary and
desecrated it. That is what they did in my house.

40 "They even sent messengers for men who came from far
away, and when they arrived you bathed yourself for them, painted your eyes and put on your jewelry. 41 You sat on an elegant
couch, with a table spread before it on which you had placed the
incense and oil that belonged to me.

42 "The noise of a carefree crowd was around her; Sabeans[b]
were brought from the desert along with men from the rabble, and
they put bracelets on the arms of the woman and her sister and
beautiful crowns on their heads. 43 Then I said about the one worn

---

[a] **37** Or *even made the children they bore to me pass through ⌞the fire⌟* [b] **42** Or *drunkards*

out by adultery, 'Now let them use her as a prostitute, for that is all
she is.' 44 And they slept with her. As men sleep with a prostitute, so
they slept with those lewd women, Oholah and Oholibah. 45 But
righteous men will sentence them to the punishment of women
who commit adultery and shed blood, because they are adulterous
and blood is on their hands.

46 "This is what the Sovereign LORD says: Bring a mob against
them and give them over to terror and plunder. 47 The mob will
stone them and cut them down with their swords; they will kill
their sons and daughters and burn down their houses.

48 "So I will put an end to lewdness in the land, that all
women may take warning and not imitate you. 49 You will suffer the
penalty for your lewdness and bear the consequences of your sins
of idolatry. Then you will know that I am the Sovereign LORD."

The Cooking Pot

24 In the ninth year, in the tenth month on the tenth day, the
word of the LORD came to me: 2 "Son of man, record this date, this
very date, because the king of Babylon has laid siege to Jerusalem
this very day. 3 Tell this rebellious house a parable and say to them:
'This is what the Sovereign LORD says:

" 'Put on the cooking pot; put it on
and pour water into it.
4 Put into it the pieces of meat,
all the choice pieces—the leg and the shoulder.
Fill it with the best of these bones;
5 take the pick of the flock.
Pile wood beneath it for the bones;
bring it to a boil
and cook the bones in it.

6 " 'For this is what the Sovereign LORD says:

" 'Woe to the city of bloodshed,
to the pot now encrusted,
whose deposit will not go away!
Empty it piece by piece
without casting lots for them.
7 " 'For the blood she shed is in her midst:
She poured it on the bare rock;
she did not pour it on the ground,
where the dust would cover it.
8 To stir up wrath and take revenge
I put her blood on the bare rock,
so that it would not be covered.

9 " 'Therefore this is what the Sovereign LORD says:

" 'Woe to the city of bloodshed!
I, too, will pile the wood high.

23:44 *Oholah and Oholibah:* Meaning the sister cities, Samaria and Jerusalem, had been unfaithful to the LORD (see the notes at 23:5-10 and 23:11-18).

23:46 *a mob:* Meaning the nations that will defeat and destroy Israel and Judah (see 23:22-26).

23:48 *end to lewdness:* Actual prostitution was to be outlawed because it was a sin, and because it was a reminder of the spiritual unfaithfulness of Samaria and Jerusalem. See also the mini-article called "Prostitution in the Bible," p. 1688.

24:1,2 *ninth year . . . tenth month . . . siege to Jerusalem:* Probably late December of 589 B.C. See the note on p. 1560. King Nebuchadnezzar of Babylon returned to attack Jerusalem when Zedekiah rebelled (see the note at 12:10-13). See also 2 Kgs 25:1; Jer 52:4.

24:2 *Son of man:* See the note at 4:1.

24:6-12 *the city . . . pot now encrusted . . . heavy deposit:* A rusty pot pollutes everything that is put into it. Like the pot, Jerusalem had polluted the people who live there with the blood of many innocent victims. According to the Law of Moses, blood was not to be eaten (Lev 7:26, 27; 19:26; Deut 12:23, 24; 15:23), and the shedding of blood polluted the land (Num 35:33, 34). Penalties had to be paid and sacrifices made to make up for the shedding of blood and to make the person and the land clean again (see Exod 21:12-36; Lev 4:1—5:19).

To make Jerusalem clean once again, its pollution had to be burned away like the cooking pot and all its contents. Heating a metal pot to red-hot burns away the deposit. Jerusalem's destruction occurred in 587/86 B.C. (see the notes at 12:10-13; 14:21,22).

24:16 *the delight of your eyes:* Ezekiel's wife (24:18), who had suddenly become so sick that she was close to death.

24:17 *Groan quietly . . . Keep your turban fastened . . . food of mourners:* The usual way people mourned was to remove anything worn on the head, to go barefoot, to cover their faces, and to eat special food. Loud wailing and crying was also common, especially during the funeral procession.

10 So heap on the wood
    and kindle the fire.
Cook the meat well,
    mixing in the spices;
    and let the bones be charred.
11 Then set the empty pot on the coals
    till it becomes hot and its copper glows
so its impurities may be melted
    and its deposit burned away.
12 It has frustrated all efforts;
    its heavy deposit has not been removed,
    not even by fire.

13 " 'Now your impurity is lewdness. Because I tried to cleanse
you but you would not be cleansed from your impurity, you will
not be clean again until my wrath against you has subsided.

14 " 'I the LORD have spoken. The time has come for me to
act. I will not hold back; I will not have pity, nor will I relent. You
will be judged according to your conduct and your actions,
declares the Sovereign LORD.' "

Ezekiel's Wife Dies

15 The word of the LORD came to me: 16 "Son of man, with one
blow I am about to take away from you the delight of your eyes. Yet
do not lament or weep or shed any tears. 17 Groan quietly; do not

QUESTIONS ABOUT EZEKIEL 12:1 — 24:27

1. What did Ezekiel act out in chapter 12? What was the reaction of his neighbors? What did his pantomime mean? Who is the "prince" mentioned in 12:12?
2. Who were the "false" prophets? (13:1-16) What was false about their messages? Why is it difficult for people to give and believe bad news? If you were a prophet, what important message might you give to your city or town? To your friends? Why?
3. To what does Ezekiel compare Jerusalem in chapter 16? What relationship does the LORD have with Jerusalem, according to this chapter? In what way(s), was Jerusalem guilty of being unfaithful to the LORD?
4. Who were Jerusalem's two sisters? (16:44-58) What did these "sisters" do that was evil in the sight of God? How was Jerusalem like these sisters?
5. In the story of two eagles and a vine (17:1-24), what were the eagles, the seed, and the vine?
6. According to chapter 18, who is responsible for a person's sins? What is the good news about sin in this chapter?
7. Even though the LORD chose the people of Israel to be his own while they were in Egypt (20:5), they kept on rebelling against the LORD. How? How would their rebellion come to an end? (21:1-27)
8. Why did Jerusalem have to be purified? (22:17-31; 24:6-8). How would it be purified? (24:2-5, 9-14)
9. Even the death of Ezekiel's wife became an opportunity for him to give a message about Jerusalem. What was the message, and how was this message confirmed? (24:20-26)

mourn for the dead. Keep your turban fastened and your sandals
on your feet; do not cover the lower part of your face or eat the
customary food ⌞of mourners⌟."
18 So I spoke to the people in the morning, and in the
evening my wife died. The next morning I did as I had been commanded.
19 Then the people asked me, "Won't you tell us what these
things have to do with us?"
20 So I said to them, "The word of the LORD came to me: 21 Say
to the house of Israel, 'This is what the Sovereign LORD says: I am
about to desecrate my sanctuary—the stronghold in which you
take pride, the delight of your eyes, the object of your affection.
The sons and daughters you left behind will fall by the sword.
22 And you will do as I have done. You will not cover the lower part
of your face or eat the customary food ⌞of mourners⌟. 23 You will
keep your turbans on your heads and your sandals on your feet.
You will not mourn or weep but will waste away because of[a] your
sins and groan among yourselves. 24 Ezekiel will be a sign to you;
you will do just as he has done. When this happens, you will know
that I am the Sovereign LORD.'
25 "And you, son of man, on the day I take away their stronghold, their joy and glory, the delight of their eyes, their heart's
desire, and their sons and daughters as well— 26 on that day a fugitive will come to tell you the news. 27 At that time your mouth will
be opened; you will speak with him and will no longer be silent. So
you will be a sign to them, and they will know that I am the LORD."

Prophecies Against Foreign Nations

In chapters 25–32, Ezekiel gives messages of judgment against many of Israel's neighbors, including Ammon, Moab, Edom, and Philistia. Three whole chapters focus on the destruction coming to Tyre and Sidon in Phoenicia, and four chapters focus on how Egypt and its king will be defeated by Babylon as part of the LORD's judgment against them.

A Prophecy Against Ammon

25 The word of the LORD came to me: 2 "Son of man, set your
face against the Ammonites and prophesy against them. 3 Say to
them, 'Hear the word of the Sovereign LORD. This is what the
Sovereign LORD says: Because you said "Aha!" over my sanctuary
when it was desecrated and over the land of Israel when it was laid
waste and over the people of Judah when they went into exile,
4 therefore I am going to give you to the people of the East as a

[a]23 Or *away in*

24:21-25 *desecrate my sanctuary . . . the delight of their eyes:* The Babylonians returned to destroy Jerusalem and its temple in 587/86 B.C. (see the note at 12:10-13). By not mourning in the "expected" way, Ezekiel got the attention of his neighbors. He warned that they would soon mourn for Jerusalem the way he mourned for his wife. The people living in exile in Babylon would be so shocked when they heard about the temple's destruction (see also the note at 7:22) and about the deaths of the children they had left behind in 597 B.C. that they would only be able to walk around and groan. They would realize that their sins had caused this terrible tragedy.

24:26,27 *a fugitive will come . . . your mouth will be opened:* The LORD told Ezekiel that one of the people who escapes Jerusalem's destruction in 587/86 B.C. will reach Babylon with the bad news. When Ezekiel heard the news, he would be able to speak again (see the note at 3:24-27; see also 33:21,22). Ezekiel's prophecies and actions in the first part of the book have focused on the coming destruction of Jerusalem. After the Jerusalem tragedy is reported, Ezekiel continues to be a warning sign for his people, but the focus of his message changes.

25:2 *Son of man:* See the note at 4:1.

25:2-5 *Ammonite . . . Rabbah:* See the note at 21:28, 29. Ammon would be punished by "people of the East" (meaning Babylon or Persia), because Ammon celebrated when the Babylonians destroyed the temple in Jerusalem. According to 2 Kgs 24:2 some troops from Ammon and Moab joined the Babylonian troops when they first invaded Judah in 597 B.C. For other prophecies against Ammon, see Jer 49:1-6; Ezek 21:28-32; Amos 1:13-15; Zeph 2:8-11.

25:8-11 *Moab:* Like the Ammonites, the people of Moab were traditional enemies of Israel (see Num 22–25; Judg 3:12-30; 1 Sam 14:47, 48; 2 Kgs 3:21-27; 2 Chr 20:10, 11). In Ezekiel's day, the Moabites were to be punished because they said that Judah and its people were not really special to the LORD. They would also be invaded by the same eastern desert tribes (see the note at 25:2-5).

25:12,13 *Edom . . . Dedan:* The nation of Edom is usually described in the Bible as an enemy of Israel (see Num 24:18; 1 Sam 14:47, 48; 2 Sam 8:13, 14; Isa 34:5-17). At the time Babylon invaded Judah and destroyed Jerusalem, the people of Edom celebrated Babylon's victory and then raided southern Judah themselves (Obad 1-14). The locations of Teman and Dedan are not certain, but Dedan may have been the southern territory of Edom.

25:15 *Philistines:* People who lived on a strip of land bordered by the Mediterranean Sea on the west and Judah on the east. The Philistine people often battled the people of Israel (for example, see Judg 13–16; 1 Sam 14:52; 17:1–54). It is not clear how, but it is possible that the Philistines profited in some way from the destruction of Judah and Jerusalem.

26:1 *eleventh year:* Probably late in 587 B.C., the year Jerusalem was destroyed by the Babylonians. See also the note on p. 1560.

26:2 *Tyre:* Tyre was an important seaport city in Phoenicia. The city was built on the mainland and on two islands near the shore. The people of Phoenicia were famous for their shipbuilding and sailing, which made them a very important part of the trading business throughout the region surrounding the Mediterranean Sea. Tyre celebrated Jerusalem's destruction for economic reasons. If Jerusalem was no longer a major center for trade, more nations would come to Tyre to do business. See also the mini-article called "Phoenicia," p. 1604.

possession. They will set up their camps and pitch their tents
among you; they will eat your fruit and drink your milk. [5]I will
turn Rabbah into a pasture for camels and Ammon into a resting
place for sheep. Then you will know that I am the LORD. [6]For this
is what the Sovereign LORD says: Because you have clapped your
hands and stamped your feet, rejoicing with all the malice of your
heart against the land of Israel, [7]therefore I will stretch out my
hand against you and give you as plunder to the nations. I will cut
you off from the nations and exterminate you from the countries.
I will destroy you, and you will know that I am the LORD.' "

A Prophecy Against Moab

[8]"This is what the Sovereign LORD says: 'Because Moab and
Seir said, "Look, the house of Judah has become like all the other
nations," [9]therefore I will expose the flank of Moab, beginning at
its frontier towns—Beth Jeshimoth, Baal Meon and Kiriathaim—
the glory of that land. [10]I will give Moab along with the
Ammonites to the people of the East as a possession, so that the
Ammonites will not be remembered among the nations; [11]and I
will inflict punishment on Moab. Then they will know that I am
the LORD.' "

A Prophecy Against Edom

[12]"This is what the Sovereign LORD says: 'Because Edom took
revenge on the house of Judah and became very guilty by doing so,
[13]therefore this is what the Sovereign LORD says: I will stretch out my
hand against Edom and kill its men and their animals. I will lay it
waste, and from Teman to Dedan they will fall by the sword. [14]I will
take vengeance on Edom by the hand of my people Israel, and they
will deal with Edom in accordance with my anger and my wrath;
they will know my vengeance, declares the Sovereign LORD.' "

A Prophecy Against Philistia

[15]"This is what the Sovereign LORD says: 'Because the
Philistines acted in vengeance and took revenge with malice in
their hearts, and with ancient hostility sought to destroy Judah,
[16]therefore this is what the Sovereign LORD says: I am about to
stretch out my hand against the Philistines, and I will cut off the
Kerethites and destroy those remaining along the coast. [17]I will
carry out great vengeance on them and punish them in my wrath.
Then they will know that I am the LORD, when I take vengeance
on them.' "

A Prophecy Against Tyre

26 In the eleventh year, on the first day of the month, the word
of the LORD came to me: [2]"Son of man, because Tyre has said of

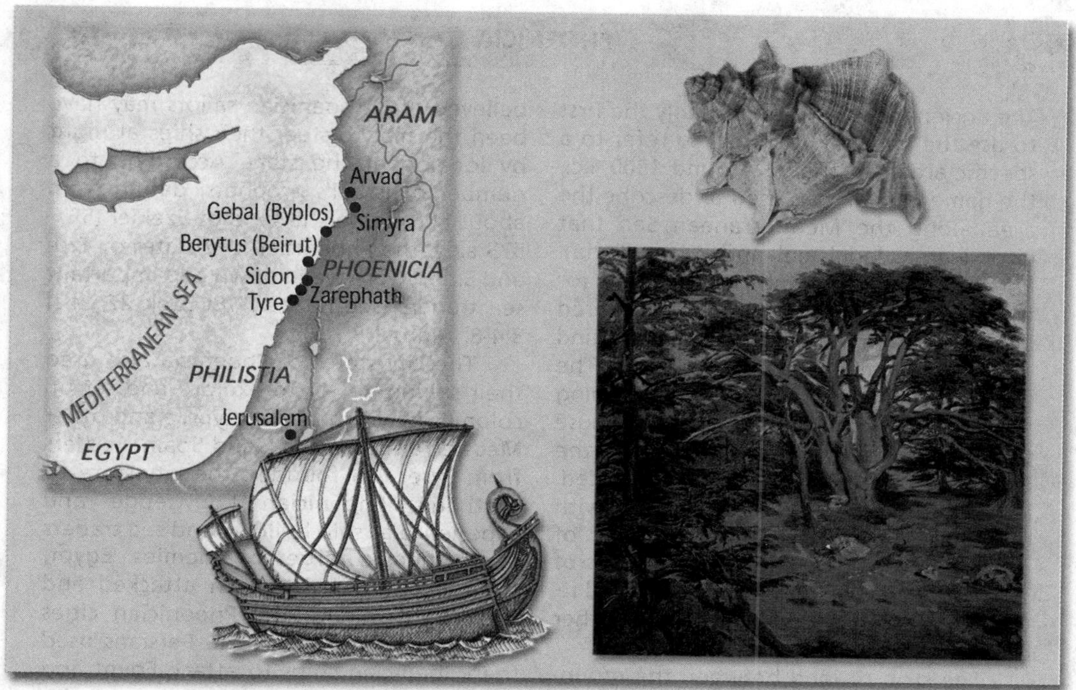

Phoenicia. Phoenicia refers to the area along the Mediterranean coast that is now modern Lebanon. The Bible usually mentions the names of its most important city-states such as Tyre, Sidon, and Zarephath. Pictured at top right is the "mollusk hexaplex trunculus," which provided the region's famous purple dye. At the lower right is a painting of a cedar tree like the ones Solomon imported from Tyre to build his temple. These cedars also provided the masts for the trading ships the Phoenicians sent all over the Mediterranean.

Jerusalem, 'Aha! The gate to the nations is broken, and its doors
have swung open to me; now that she lies in ruins I will prosper,'
3therefore this is what the Sovereign LORD says: I am against you,
O Tyre, and I will bring many nations against you, like the sea casting up its waves. 4They will destroy the walls of Tyre and pull down
her towers; I will scrape away her rubble and make her a bare rock.
5Out in the sea she will become a place to spread fishnets, for I have
spoken, declares the Sovereign LORD. She will become plunder for
the nations, 6and her settlements on the mainland will be ravaged
by the sword. Then they will know that I am the LORD.

7"For this is what the Sovereign LORD says: From the north I
am going to bring against Tyre Nebuchadnezzar[a] king of Babylon,
king of kings, with horses and chariots, with horsemen and a great
army. 8He will ravage your settlements on the mainland with the
sword; he will set up siege works against you, build a ramp up to
your walls and raise his shields against you. 9He will direct the

26:3–14 *bring many nations against you . . . spread fishnets:* The Assyrians had invaded Phoenicia in 734 B.C. and again in 701 B.C. King Nebuchadnezzar of Babylon surrounded and tried to blockade the city for thirteen years. He finally captured the mainland part of the city of Tyre in 572 B.C., but he didn't capture the island parts of the city (see 29:18). Even so, the long Babylonian invasion caused many deaths and the loss of much property. Alexander the Great of Macedonia captured Tyre in 332 B.C. For more prophecies against Tyre, see Isa 23:1-18; Joel 3:4-8; Amos 1:9,10; Zech 9:1-4; Matt 11:21,22; Luke 10:13,14.

[a]7 Hebrew *Nebuchadrezzar,* of which *Nebuchadnezzar* is a variant; here and often in Ezekiel and Jeremiah

PHOENICIA

The ancient Greeks were probably the first to use the name "Phoenicia" to refer to a specific area of Canaan. Around 1300 B.C., the name Canaan was used to describe the area along the Mediterranean Sea that later was called Israel and Aram (Syria). Phoenicia was used more specifically for the long and narrow region bordered by the Lebanon Mountains on the east and the Mediterranean Sea on the west. The Greeks used the word *phoinix,* meaning "red-purple," to refer to this area because the people there were famous for the expensive purple dye they produced. Phoenicia was not a unified country with one government, but had a number of city-states, including the seacoast cities of Tyre, Sidon, Gebal, and Arvad. Each had its own king and carried on trade with other countries.

The strip of land between the mountains and the sea was fertile, and people grew plants, shrubs, vegetables, and fruits there. But most of the rest of the land was mountainous and covered with great cedars and pine forests. These trees were cut down and exported to many countries, including Egypt and Israel. King Solomon of Israel traded with Tyre's King Hiram for many cedar logs and skilled builders to construct his temple and palace (1 Kgs 5–7). Eventually, much of the Lebanon forests disappeared.

Because the land to the east was so rugged, the Phoenician cities turned to the Mediterranean Sea to make a living. The main product of Phoenicia was the purple dye made from the large sea snail murex, found in the Mediterranean. The huge mounds of crushed snails produced by their dye factories probably made Phoenician cities smell bad. But this was probably easy to overlook because the dye business brought so much income to the Phoenician cities. The Phoenicians also made a lot of money transporting goods all over the Mediterranean world on ships they built, and they became experts at sailing. It is believed that Phoenician sailors may have been the first to steer their ships at night by looking at the stars. According to a number of Israel's prophets, dating from about 800 B.C. to the time of Ezekiel (597-573 B.C.), the Phoenician city-states of Tyre and Sidon were well-known and important sea traders (see Isa 23:1-18; Ezek 27; Joel 3:4-8; Amos 1:9, 10).

The city-states of Phoenicia also used their sailing ability to explore and set up colonies in North Africa, Cyprus and other Mediterranean islands, and Spain. Settlers from Tyre also founded the city-state of Carthage. Phoenician knowledge and experience as ship builders and sea traders made them a target of enemies. Egypt, Assyria, and Babylon each attacked and tried to dominate the Phoenician cities through the centuries. The Persians used the Phoenician ships to attack Egypt and Greece, but eventually the Greek empire defeated the Persians (about 333 B.C.) and destroyed Tyre. As the cities of Phoenicia became more and more influenced by Greek customs and culture, the power and influence of the old Phoenicia came to an end.

Religion in Phoenicia was influenced early on by the Semitic peoples, meaning they worshiped many of the Canaanite gods and goddesses, such as El, Baal, and Asherah (see the mini-article called "Canaanite Gods and Goddesses," p. 469). Ashtoreth (Astarte) was also worshiped along with Tammuz (Adonis), the god of vegetation and fertility, who supposedly died each year when the summer dry season began. Ashtoreth was believed to go down to the world of the dead to bring Tammuz back to life at the beginning of the next planting season. There is some evidence in ancient texts that the Phoenicians offered human sacrifices. King Ahab of Israel married Jezebel, a princess from Phoenicia. She brought Baal worship into Israel, which eventually sealed the fate of the northern kingdom.

blows of his battering rams against your walls and demolish your
towers with his weapons. [10]His horses will be so many that they
will cover you with dust. Your walls will tremble at the noise of the
war horses, wagons and chariots when he enters your gates as men
enter a city whose walls have been broken through. [11]The hoofs of
his horses will trample all your streets; he will kill your people with
the sword, and your strong pillars will fall to the ground. [12]They
will plunder your wealth and loot your merchandise; they will
break down your walls and demolish your fine houses and throw
your stones, timber and rubble into the sea. [13]I will put an end to
your noisy songs, and the music of your harps will be heard no
more. [14]I will make you a bare rock, and you will become a place
to spread fishnets. You will never be rebuilt, for I the LORD have
spoken, declares the Sovereign LORD.

[15]"This is what the Sovereign LORD says to Tyre: Will not the
coastlands tremble at the sound of your fall, when the wounded
groan and the slaughter takes place in you? [16]Then all the princes of
the coast will step down from their thrones and lay aside their robes
and take off their embroidered garments. Clothed with terror, they
will sit on the ground, trembling every moment, appalled at you.
[17]Then they will take up a lament concerning you and say to you:

" 'How you are destroyed, O city of renown,
 peopled by men of the sea!
You were a power on the seas,
 you and your citizens;
you put your terror
 on all who lived there.
[18]Now the coastlands tremble
 on the day of your fall;
the islands in the sea
 are terrified at your collapse.'

[19]"This is what the Sovereign LORD says: When I make you a
desolate city, like cities no longer inhabited, and when I bring the
ocean depths over you and its vast waters cover you, [20]then I will
bring you down with those who go down to the pit, to the people
of long ago. I will make you dwell in the earth below, as in ancient
ruins, with those who go down to the pit, and you will not return
or take your place[a] in the land of the living. [21]I will bring you to a
horrible end and you will be no more. You will be sought, but you
will never again be found, declares the Sovereign LORD."

A Lament for Tyre

27 The word of the LORD came to me: [2]"Son of man, take up a
lament concerning Tyre. [3]Say to Tyre, situated at the gateway to the

[a]**20** Septuagint; Hebrew *return, and I will give glory*

26:15-18 *coastlands tremble . . . day of your fall:* The destruction of Tyre would have caused problems for the nations surrounding the Mediterranean Sea. They relied on trade with the merchants of Tyre, as well as transportation and cargo-hauling on Phoenician ships. Hard economic times could cause kings to worry and fret about how they would keep business and money flowing in their countries. See also Rev 18:9, 10.

26:19,20 *ocean depths . . . down to the pit:* The ocean itself will cover the city and take its people to the "pit," the underground world inhabited by the dead. This is a place of total silence where no one knows or feels anything (Job 10:21,22; Ps 88:12; 94:17). Tyre's destruction was not as complete as Ezekiel's prophecy suggests, but its power and freedom were greatly reduced.

27:2 *Son of man:* See the note at 4:1.

27:2-4 *Tyre . . . Your domain was on the high seas:* See the note at 26:2.

26:13 Rev 18:22. **26:21** Rev 18:21.

sea, merchant of peoples on many coasts, 'This is what the Sovereign LORD says:

" 'You say, O Tyre,
"I am perfect in beauty."
4 Your domain was on the high seas;
your builders brought your beauty to perfection.
5 They made all your timbers
of pine trees from Senir[a];
they took a cedar from Lebanon
to make a mast for you.
6 Of oaks from Bashan
they made your oars;
of cypress wood[b] from the coasts of Cyprus[c]
they made your deck, inlaid with ivory.
7 Fine embroidered linen from Egypt was your sail
and served as your banner;
your awnings were of blue and purple
from the coasts of Elishah.
8 Men of Sidon and Arvad were your oarsmen;
your skilled men, O Tyre, were aboard as your seamen.
9 Veteran craftsmen of Gebal[d] were on board
as shipwrights to caulk your seams.
All the ships of the sea and their sailors
came alongside to trade for your wares.

10 " 'Men of Persia, Lydia and Put
served as soldiers in your army.
They hung their shields and helmets on your walls,
bringing you splendor.
11 Men of Arvad and Helech
manned your walls on every side;
men of Gammad
were in your towers.
They hung their shields around your walls;
they brought your beauty to perfection.

12 " 'Tarshish did business with you because of your great
wealth of goods; they exchanged silver, iron, tin and lead for your
merchandise.
13 " 'Greece, Tubal and Meshech traded with you; they
exchanged slaves and articles of bronze for your wares.
14 " 'Men of Beth Togarmah exchanged work horses, war
horses and mules for your merchandise.
15 " 'The men of Rhodes[e] traded with you, and many coastlands
were your customers; they paid you with ivory tusks and ebony.

---

[a]5 That is, Hermon [b]6 Targum; the Masoretic Text has a different division of the consonants. [c]6 Hebrew *Kittim* [d]9 That is, Byblos [e]15 Septuagint; Hebrew *Dedan*

27:5,6 *trees . . . wood:* The ships built in Tyre used the best woods from all over the ancient Near East. Cypress (a form of pine) and the tall cedar trees which grew in the forests of Lebanon were used to build royal palaces, including the temple and palace of King Solomon (1 Kgs 5:3-9; 7:1-12). Assyrian and Babylonian kings also cut down cedars and used them for building (Isa 37:24). Bashan, a region east of the Jordan River and north of Gilead, was famous for its large oak trees, which were a source of valuable wood. Cyprus is a large island in the Mediterranean Sea to the northwest of Tyre.

27:7 *Fine embroidered linen from Egypt . . . blue and purple:* The ships of Tyre made their sails out of linen, a fine cloth woven out of the dried fibers of the flax plant, and cloth from the island of Cyprus (Elishah) that had been dyed purple, using "ink" from the crushed shells of large sea snails.

27:8-11 *Sidon and Arvad . . . Gammad:* Tyre's merchant navy also attracted workers, sailors, and soldiers from all over. Sidon, Arvad, and Gebal (also known as Byblos) were important coastal cities of Phoenicia, located north of Tyre. Soldiers came from the northeast (Persia, or modern-day Iraq), the north (Lydia, a province in Asia Minor), and the southwest (Put, or Libya, a province in northern Africa). Helech is a region in southeast Asia Minor. The location of Gammad is uncertain, but may be in northern Asia Minor.

27:12-25 *did business with you . . . heavy cargo:* Tyre's merchants made money by transporting and selling goods between the many nations that surrounded the Mediterranean Sea. See the map on p. 2271.

27:15 *ivory tusks and ebony:* Ivory is from the tusks of various animals, such as elephants. Ebony is a valuable black wood.

16“ ‘Aram[a] did business with you because of your many
products; they exchanged turquoise, purple fabric, embroidered
work, fine linen, coral and rubies for your merchandise.
17“ ‘Judah and Israel traded with you; they exchanged wheat
from Minnith and confections,[b] honey, oil and balm for your wares.
18“ ‘Damascus, because of your many products and great
wealth of goods, did business with you in wine from Helbon and
wool from Zahar.
19“ ‘Danites and Greeks from Uzal bought your merchandise;
they exchanged wrought iron, cassia and calamus for your wares.
20“ ‘Dedan traded in saddle blankets with you.
21“ ‘Arabia and all the princes of Kedar were your customers;
they did business with you in lambs, rams and goats.
22“ ‘The merchants of Sheba and Raamah traded with you;
for your merchandise they exchanged the finest of all kinds of
spices and precious stones, and gold.
23“ ‘Haran, Canneh and Eden and merchants of Sheba,
Asshur and Kilmad traded with you. 24In your marketplace they
traded with you beautiful garments, blue fabric, embroidered work
and multicolored rugs with cords twisted and tightly knotted.

25“ ‘The ships of Tarshish serve
as carriers for your wares.
You are filled with heavy cargo
in the heart of the sea.
26 Your oarsmen take you
out to the high seas.
But the east wind will break you to pieces
in the heart of the sea.
27 Your wealth, merchandise and wares,
your mariners, seamen and shipwrights,
your merchants and all your soldiers,
and everyone else on board
will sink into the heart of the sea
on the day of your shipwreck.
28 The shorelands will quake
when your seamen cry out.
29 All who handle the oars
will abandon their ships;
the mariners and all the seamen
will stand on the shore.
30 They will raise their voice
and cry bitterly over you;
they will sprinkle dust on their heads
and roll in ashes.

[a]**16** Most Hebrew manuscripts; some Hebrew manuscripts and Syriac *Edom*
[b]**17** The meaning of the Hebrew for this word is uncertain.

27:29-31 *abandon their ships . . . put on sackcloth:* The crew members from Tyre’s sunken ships mourn in the traditional way by putting dust on their heads, smearing themselves with ashes, and cutting their hair. See the note at 7:18.

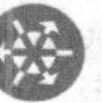

27:25-36 Rev 18:11-19.

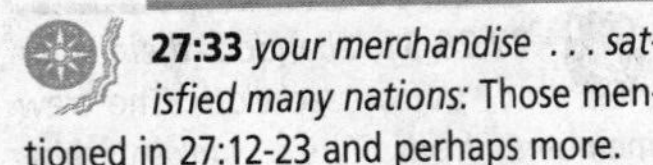

27:33 *your merchandise . . . satisfied many nations:* Those mentioned in 27:12-23 and perhaps more.

28:2-10 *ruler of Tyre . . . a god . . . will die:* Tyre (see the note at 26:2) was a city-state and had its own king, but just which ruler is meant here is not clear. The king will be punished because he is arrogant and acts like a god. The people of Tyre worshiped the Canaanite gods, including the chief god known as El, who was described as living in a place where rivers and deep waters come together. Tyre comes close to fitting such a description. The king will drown in a watery grave, just the way the city will be covered by the ocean's depths (26:19-21). Some think this judgment message also has to do with Israel's LORD overthrowing the gods of Tyre.

27:32 Ezek 26:19,20.

[31]They will shave their heads because of you
and will put on sackcloth.
They will weep over you with anguish of soul
and with bitter mourning.
[32]As they wail and mourn over you,
they will take up a lament concerning you:
"Who was ever silenced like Tyre,
surrounded by the sea?"
[33]When your merchandise went out on the seas,
you satisfied many nations;
with your great wealth and your wares
you enriched the kings of the earth.
[34]Now you are shattered by the sea
in the depths of the waters;
your wares and all your company
have gone down with you.
[35]All who live in the coastlands
are appalled at you;
their kings shudder with horror
and their faces are distorted with fear.
[36]The merchants among the nations hiss at you;
you have come to a horrible end
and will be no more.' "

A Prophecy Against the King of Tyre

28 The word of the LORD came to me: [2]"Son of man, say to the ruler of Tyre, 'This is what the Sovereign LORD says:

" 'In the pride of your heart
you say, "I am a god;
I sit on the throne of a god
in the heart of the seas."
But you are a man and not a god,
though you think you are as wise as a god.
[3]Are you wiser than Daniel[a]?
Is no secret hidden from you?
[4]By your wisdom and understanding
you have gained wealth for yourself
and amassed gold and silver
in your treasuries.
[5]By your great skill in trading
you have increased your wealth,
and because of your wealth
your heart has grown proud.

[6]" 'Therefore this is what the Sovereign LORD says:

[a]3 Or *Danel*; the Hebrew spelling may suggest a person other than the prophet Daniel.

“ ‘Because you think you are wise,
as wise as a god,
7 I am going to bring foreigners against you,
the most ruthless of nations;
they will draw their swords against your beauty and wisdom
and pierce your shining splendor.
8 They will bring you down to the pit,
and you will die a violent death
in the heart of the seas.
9 Will you then say, “I am a god,”
in the presence of those who kill you?
You will be but a man, not a god,
in the hands of those who slay you.
10 You will die the death of the uncircumcised
at the hands of foreigners.

I have spoken, declares the Sovereign LORD.’ ”

11 The word of the LORD came to me: 12 “Son of man, take up
a lament concerning the king of Tyre and say to him: ‘This is what
the Sovereign LORD says:

“ ‘You were the model of perfection,
full of wisdom and perfect in beauty.
13 You were in Eden,
the garden of God;
every precious stone adorned you:
ruby, topaz and emerald,
chrysolite, onyx and jasper,
sapphire,[a] turquoise and beryl.[b]
Your settings and mountings[c] were made of gold;
on the day you were created they were prepared.
14 You were anointed as a guardian cherub,
for so I ordained you.
You were on the holy mount of God;
you walked among the fiery stones.
15 You were blameless in your ways
from the day you were created
till wickedness was found in you.
16 Through your widespread trade
you were filled with violence,
and you sinned.
So I drove you in disgrace from the mount of God,
and I expelled you, O guardian cherub,
from among the fiery stones.

[a]**13** Or *lapis lazuli* [b]**13** The precise identification of some of these precious stones is uncertain. [c]**13** The meaning of the Hebrew for this phrase is uncertain.

28:12-19 *a lament concerning the king of Tyre . . . will be no more:* See the notes at 26:2 and 28:2-10. The downfall of Tyre's king is described in a way that recalls the way the first human beings sinned and were forced to leave the Garden of Eden (see Gen 2:4—3:24). Though he was good at birth, he started doing evil things, so he was forced to leave "the mount of God," a phrase that described the home of the gods in the Canaanite religion.

Some believe that Ezekiel meant this allegory about Tyre's fallen ruler to have a double meaning. In the Hebrew text of 28:13, all the precious stones are named individually, and they match the stones in the breastpiece worn by Israel's high priest (see Exod 28:15-21). The "guardian cherub" is similar to the creatures that guarded the Garden of Eden (Gen 3:24), but it also is similar to the cherubim on the ark of the covenant in the Most Holy Place in the temple (see the note at 9:3). Finally, because the "mount of God" could also be Zion, some think this allegory is also about the downfall of Israel's high priest in Jerusalem. Taken this way, Ezekiel's Jewish neighbors living in exile may have heard this message about Tyre's king and recognized their own sins and resulting downfall.

28:21 *Sidon:* A Phoenician seaport city north of Tyre that also depended on sea trading. The reason for the LORD's judgment against Sidon is likely similar to those of Tyre (see the note at 26:2). See also Joel 3:4-8; Zech 9:1, 2; Matt 11:21, 22; Luke 10:13, 14.

28:22 *show myself holy:* Many events are described in EZEKIEL as happening in order that people will recognize the sacred power of the LORD (see also 7:27; 20:44; 28:25).

28:25 *my servant Jacob:* Another name for the people of Israel. Jacob's name was changed to Israel after he wrestled with God (Gen 32:22-28). The people of Israel were descendants of Jacob's sons and two of his grandsons. The God of Jacob is the LORD (*Yahweh*), who chose the Israelite people to be his own people (Deut 7:6-8; Isa 2:3; 41:8, 9).

29:1 *the tenth year . . . tenth month:* Late December 588 B.C. See also the note on p. 1560.

29:2 *Son of man . . . Pharaoh king of Egypt:* See the note at 4:1. At the time of this prophecy's date, Hophra was pharaoh in Egypt. See the mini-article called "King of Egypt (Pharaoh)," p. 110.

29:1—32:32 Isa 19:1-25; Jer 46:2-26.

17 Your heart became proud
on account of your beauty,
and you corrupted your wisdom
because of your splendor.
So I threw you to the earth;
I made a spectacle of you before kings.
18 By your many sins and dishonest trade
you have desecrated your sanctuaries.
So I made a fire come out from you,
and it consumed you,
and I reduced you to ashes on the ground
in the sight of all who were watching.
19 All the nations who knew you
are appalled at you;
you have come to a horrible end
and will be no more.' "

A Prophecy Against Sidon

20 The word of the LORD came to me: 21 "Son of man, set your
face against Sidon; prophesy against her 22 and say: 'This is what the
Sovereign LORD says:

" 'I am against you, O Sidon,
and I will gain glory within you.
They will know that I am the LORD,
when I inflict punishment on her
and show myself holy within her.
23 I will send a plague upon her
and make blood flow in her streets.
The slain will fall within her,
with the sword against her on every side.
Then they will know that I am the LORD.

24 " 'No longer will the people of Israel have malicious neighbors who are painful briers and sharp thorns. Then they will know that I am the Sovereign LORD.

25 " 'This is what the Sovereign LORD says: When I gather the
people of Israel from the nations where they have been scattered,
I will show myself holy among them in the sight of the nations.
Then they will live in their own land, which I gave to my servant
Jacob. 26 They will live there in safety and will build houses and
plant vineyards; they will live in safety when I inflict punishment
on all their neighbors who maligned them. Then they will know
that I am the LORD their God.' "

A Prophecy Against Egypt

29 In the tenth year, in the tenth month on the twelfth day, the
word of the LORD came to me: 2 "Son of man, set your face against

Pharaoh king of Egypt and prophesy against him and against all
Egypt. 3Speak to him and say: 'This is what the Sovereign LORD
says:

" 'I am against you, Pharaoh king of Egypt,
you great monster lying among your streams.
You say, "The Nile is mine;
I made it for myself."
4But I will put hooks in your jaws
and make the fish of your streams stick to your scales.
I will pull you out from among your streams,
with all the fish sticking to your scales.
5I will leave you in the desert,
you and all the fish of your streams.
You will fall on the open field
and not be gathered or picked up.
I will give you as food
to the beasts of the earth and the birds of the air.

6Then all who live in Egypt will know that I am the LORD.

" 'You have been a staff of reed for the house of Israel.
7When they grasped you with their hands, you splintered and you
tore open their shoulders; when they leaned on you, you broke and
their backs were wrenched.[a]

8" 'Therefore this is what the Sovereign LORD says: I will
bring a sword against you and kill your men and their animals.
9Egypt will become a desolate wasteland. Then they will know that
I am the LORD.

" 'Because you said, "The Nile is mine; I made it," 10therefore
I am against you and against your streams, and I will make the land
of Egypt a ruin and a desolate waste from Migdol to Aswan, as far as
the border of Cush.[b] 11No foot of man or animal will pass through
it; no one will live there for forty years. 12I will make the land of
Egypt desolate among devastated lands, and her cities will lie desolate forty years among ruined cities. And I will disperse the Egyptians among the nations and scatter them through the countries.

13" 'Yet this is what the Sovereign LORD says: At the end of
forty years I will gather the Egyptians from the nations where they
were scattered. 14I will bring them back from captivity and return
them to Upper Egypt,[c] the land of their ancestry. There they will
be a lowly kingdom. 15It will be the lowliest of kingdoms and will
never again exalt itself above the other nations. I will make it so
weak that it will never again rule over the nations. 16Egypt will no
longer be a source of confidence for the people of Israel but will be

29:3-5 *great monster . . . fish . . . fall on the open field:* Egypt's ruler is compared to one of the large crocodiles that lived along the banks of the Nile River (see also Job 41:1-34). Egypt's ruler will be punished for being too proud, that is, thinking that the great Nile River was the property and creation of the king rather than of the LORD. See 28:2-10 and the note there. The "fish" that stick to the monster probably refer to the king's officials and priests who will be removed from power and destroyed along with the king himself. Ancient kings in Egypt were usually honored as gods with big funerals and placed in huge tombs, such as the pyramids. But this king would suffer the terrible humiliation of being left unburied.

29:6,7 *staff of reed . . . you broke:* Egypt did support Judah in its rebellion against Babylon, but they were ineffective (Jer 37:6-10). Egypt was like one of the tall reeds that grew by the Nile River. When Judah leaned on this "reed" for support, it bent in half (Isa 36:6).

29:8-12 *bring a sword against you . . . Egypt a ruin . . . forty years:* Probably refers to the Babylonian troops under the command of Nebuchadnezzar. Though the Babylonians likely battled and won a victory over the Egyptians around the time of Jerusalem's fall, there is no record of a full-scale invasion and destruction of Egypt by the Babylonians. But the idea of Egypt's destruction from Migdol in the northern delta region to Aswan in Cush in the far south compares to the total destruction that was to occur in Israel (see 6:14 and note). The number "forty" symbolizes a long time of exile or suffering (Gen 7:4, 17-21; Num 14:33; Ezek 4:6; Matt 4:2).

29:13,14 *gather the Egyptians . . . lowly kingdom:* It is not clear if a major exile occurred in Egypt. War in ancient times often caused defeated people to be captured as slaves or to become refugees. Egypt's end would not be total. Like Israel (11:17; 28:25), its people would come back. Yet, Egypt never regained its status as a world power.

[a]**7** Syriac (see also Septuagint and Vulgate); Hebrew *and you caused their backs to stand* [b]**10** That is, the upper Nile region [c]**14** Hebrew *to Pathros*

a reminder of their sin in turning to her for help. Then they will
know that I am the Sovereign LORD.' "

17 In the twenty-seventh year, in the first month on the first
day, the word of the LORD came to me: 18 "Son of man, Nebuchadnezzar king of Babylon drove his army in a hard campaign against
Tyre; every head was rubbed bare and every shoulder made raw.
Yet he and his army got no reward from the campaign he led
against Tyre. 19 Therefore this is what the Sovereign LORD says: I am
going to give Egypt to Nebuchadnezzar king of Babylon, and he
will carry off its wealth. He will loot and plunder the land as pay
for his army. 20 I have given him Egypt as a reward for his efforts
because he and his army did it for me, declares the Sovereign
LORD.

21 "On that day I will make a horn[a] grow for the house of
Israel, and I will open your mouth among them. Then they will
know that I am the LORD."

A Lament for Egypt

30 The word of the LORD came to me: 2 "Son of man, prophesy
and say: 'This is what the Sovereign LORD says:

" 'Wail and say,
"Alas for that day!"
3 For the day is near,
the day of the LORD is near—
a day of clouds,
a time of doom for the nations.
4 A sword will come against Egypt,
and anguish will come upon Cush.[b]
When the slain fall in Egypt,
her wealth will be carried away
and her foundations torn down.

5 Cush and Put, Lydia and all Arabia, Libya[c] and the people of the
covenant land will fall by the sword along with Egypt.

6 " 'This is what the LORD says:

" 'The allies of Egypt will fall
and her proud strength will fail.
From Migdol to Aswan
they will fall by the sword within her,
declares the Sovereign LORD.
7 " 'They will be desolate
among desolate lands,
and their cities will lie
among ruined cities.

[a] 21 *Horn* here symbolizes strength. [b] 4 That is, the upper Nile region; also in verses 5 and 9 [c] 5 Hebrew *Cub*

29:17 *twenty-seventh year . . . first month:* The middle of March of 571 B.C. See also the note on p. 1560. This message against Egypt (29:17-21) is the latest of Ezekiel's dated prophecies.

29:18-20 *Nebuchadnezzar . . . Tyre . . . Egypt as a reward:* This prophecy takes place just a year or two after Nebuchadnezzar's attack on Tyre (see the note at 26:3-14). Nebuchadnezzar did send raids into Egypt, but Babylon did not destroy all of Egypt. Egypt's defeat opened the way for Israel to become strong again (29:21). Ezekiel apparently did not live to see Jerusalem and its temple rebuilt.

30:3 *the day of the LORD:* The day of the LORD is often accompanied by clouds and darkness. The judgment day of the LORD is a common theme in many of the prophets (see Isa 2:11,12,17-22; 4:1,2; Joel 2:1-11; 3:14-21; Amos 5:18-20; Zeph 1:14-18). See also the mini-article called "Day of the LORD," p. 1727.

30:5 *Cush . . . Libya . . . Egypt:* These countries may refer to Egypt's allies in battle against the enemy Babylon (30:10). See the note at 27:8-11 (Libya and Lydia). Arabia probably refers to the desert areas south of Judah and east of Egypt, stretching all the way to the Persian Gulf. "The people of the covenant land" may refer to Israelites living in Egypt (see Isa 11:11; Jer 44:1).

30:6,7 *From Migdol to Aswan:* See the note at 29:8-12.

8 Then they will know that I am the LORD,
when I set fire to Egypt
and all her helpers are crushed.

9 " 'On that day messengers will go out from me in ships to
frighten Cush out of her complacency. Anguish will take hold of
them on the day of Egypt's doom, for it is sure to come.

10 " 'This is what the Sovereign LORD says:

" 'I will put an end to the hordes of Egypt
by the hand of Nebuchadnezzar king of Babylon.
11 He and his army—the most ruthless of nations—
will be brought in to destroy the land.
They will draw their swords against Egypt
and fill the land with the slain.
12 I will dry up the streams of the Nile
and sell the land to evil men;
by the hand of foreigners
I will lay waste the land and everything in it.

I the LORD have spoken.

13 " 'This is what the Sovereign LORD says:

" 'I will destroy the idols
and put an end to the images in Memphis.[a]
No longer will there be a prince in Egypt,
and I will spread fear throughout the land.
14 I will lay waste Upper Egypt,[b]
set fire to Zoan
and inflict punishment on Thebes.[c]
15 I will pour out my wrath on Pelusium,[d]
the stronghold of Egypt,
and cut off the hordes of Thebes.
16 I will set fire to Egypt;
Pelusium will writhe in agony.
Thebes will be taken by storm;
Memphis will be in constant distress.
17 The young men of Heliopolis[e] and Bubastis[f]
will fall by the sword,
and the cities themselves will go into captivity.
18 Dark will be the day at Tahpanhes
when I break the yoke of Egypt;
there her proud strength will come to an end.
She will be covered with clouds,
and her villages will go into captivity.

[a]**13** Hebrew *Noph*; also in verse 16 [b]**14** Hebrew *waste Pathros* [c]**14** Hebrew *No*; also in verses 15 and 16 [d]**15** Hebrew *Sin*; also in verse 16 [e]**17** Hebrew *Awen* (or *On*) [f]**17** Hebrew *Pi Beseth*

30:9 *Cush:* The Cushites (Ethiopians) lived to the south of Egypt. Isaiah 18:7 describes them as "tall and smooth-skinned" who were feared throughout the world as strong warriors.

30:10-12 *Nebuchadnezzar . . . dry up the streams of the Nile:* Nebuchadnezzar of Babylon is the one who was to bring destruction to Egypt (see also the notes at 29:8-12 and 29:18-20). But the death caused by the troops won't be any worse than the death and starvation that will occur when the Nile River dries up. The waters of the Nile were used to water Egypt's crops, for drinking, and for transporting goods from one part of the country to another. The sale of Egyptian land may refer to foreigners buying up land from owners in hard times, such as a major drought.

30:13 *idols . . . images:* Many different people worshiped particular gods and goddesses. The Hebrew words here may also refer to "leaders."

30:13-18 *Memphis . . . Tahpanhes:* A number of Egypt's major cities will be destroyed. See the map on p. 2468 for the possible location of these cities. Memphis had been the capital of Egypt and its largest city (see also Isa 19:13). Heliopolis was named for the sun-god On and meant "city of the sun." Tahpanhes was a frontier fortress city to the northeast of the Nile delta region (see Jer 43:4-7). See also the mini-article called "Egypt," p. 135.

30:18 *Dark . . . covered with clouds . . . captivity:* See the notes at 30:3 and 29:13,14.

30:20 *eleventh year . . . first month:* Late March of 587 B.C. See also the note on p. 1560.

30:21 *Son of man:* See the note at 4:1.

30:21-26 *I . . . against Pharaoh king of Egypt . . . scatter them:* When the Babylonian army surrounded Jerusalem in 588 B.C., Pharaoh Hophra of Egypt sent troops to help Judah rebel against Babylon (Jer 37:1-5), but the powerful Babylonian army fought and turned away the Egyptians. The Egyptian king's "broken arms" are a symbol for his army's total defeat. It is likely that Egyptian soldiers captured in battle would have been taken as prisoners and forced to live in lands controlled by the Babylonians. See also the notes at 29:8-12; 29:13, 14; 29:18-20.

31:1 *eleventh year . . . third month:* Late May of 587 B.C. See also the notes at 30:20 and on p. 1560.

31:2-9 *Pharaoh king of Egypt . . . a cedar in Lebanon . . . beautiful:* Ezekiel's message to the Egyptian pharaoh and people begins as a story (allegory) about a tall cedar tree that grew in the forests of Lebanon (see the notes at 17:3-6; 27:5, 6). Verse 9 makes it clear that it was the LORD who made the tree beautiful and strong.

19 So I will inflict punishment on Egypt,
and they will know that I am the LORD.' "

20 In the eleventh year, in the first month on the seventh day,
the word of the LORD came to me: 21 "Son of man, I have broken
the arm of Pharaoh king of Egypt. It has not been bound up for
healing or put in a splint so as to become strong enough to hold a
sword. 22 Therefore this is what the Sovereign LORD says: I am
against Pharaoh king of Egypt. I will break both his arms, the good
arm as well as the broken one, and make the sword fall from his
hand. 23 I will disperse the Egyptians among the nations and scatter them through the countries. 24 I will strengthen the arms of the
king of Babylon and put my sword in his hand, but I will break the
arms of Pharaoh, and he will groan before him like a mortally
wounded man. 25 I will strengthen the arms of the king of Babylon,
but the arms of Pharaoh will fall limp. Then they will know that I
am the LORD, when I put my sword into the hand of the king of
Babylon and he brandishes it against Egypt. 26 I will disperse the
Egyptians among the nations and scatter them through the countries. Then they will know that I am the LORD."

A Cedar in Lebanon

31 In the eleventh year, in the third month on the first day, the
word of the LORD came to me: 2 "Son of man, say to Pharaoh king
of Egypt and to his hordes:

" 'Who can be compared with you in majesty?
3 Consider Assyria, once a cedar in Lebanon,
with beautiful branches overshadowing the forest;
it towered on high,
its top above the thick foliage.
4 The waters nourished it,
deep springs made it grow tall;
their streams flowed
all around its base
and sent their channels
to all the trees of the field.
5 So it towered higher
than all the trees of the field;
its boughs increased
and its branches grew long,
spreading because of abundant waters.
6 All the birds of the air
nested in its boughs,
all the beasts of the field
gave birth under its branches;
all the great nations
lived in its shade.

7 It was majestic in beauty,
with its spreading boughs,
for its roots went down
to abundant waters.
8 The cedars in the garden of God
could not rival it,
nor could the pine trees
equal its boughs,
nor could the plane trees
compare with its branches—
no tree in the garden of God
could match its beauty.
9 I made it beautiful
with abundant branches,
the envy of all the trees of Eden
in the garden of God.

10 “ ‘Therefore this is what the Sovereign LORD says: Because
it towered on high, lifting its top above the thick foliage, and
because it was proud of its height, 11 I handed it over to the ruler of
the nations, for him to deal with according to its wickedness. I cast
it aside, 12 and the most ruthless of foreign nations cut it down and
left it. Its boughs fell on the mountains and in all the valleys; its
branches lay broken in all the ravines of the land. All the nations
of the earth came out from under its shade and left it. 13 All the
birds of the air settled on the fallen tree, and all the beasts of
the field were among its branches. 14 Therefore no other trees by
the waters are ever to tower proudly on high, lifting their tops
above the thick foliage. No other trees so well-watered are ever to
reach such a height; they are all destined for death, for the earth
below, among mortal men, with those who go down to the pit.

15 “ ‘This is what the Sovereign LORD says: On the day it was
brought down to the grave[a] I covered the deep springs with
mourning for it; I held back its streams, and its abundant waters
were restrained. Because of it I clothed Lebanon with gloom, and
all the trees of the field withered away. 16 I made the nations tremble at the sound of its fall when I brought it down to the grave
with those who go down to the pit. Then all the trees of Eden, the
choicest and best of Lebanon, all the trees that were well-watered,
were consoled in the earth below. 17 Those who lived in its shade,
its allies among the nations, had also gone down to the grave with
it, joining those killed by the sword.

18 “ ‘Which of the trees of Eden can be compared with you in
splendor and majesty? Yet you, too, will be brought down with the
trees of Eden to the earth below; you will lie among the uncircumcised, with those killed by the sword.

[a]15 Hebrew *Sheol*; also in verses 16 and 17

31:10-13 *towered on high . . . proud of its height . . . cut it down:* The cedar tree, which stands for Egypt and its king. The tree became arrogant and proud (see 29:3-5 and note), so the LORD allowed a foreign ruler to cut it down (see the notes at 29:8-12; 30:10-12). The nations who enjoyed the tree's shade probably stand for Egypt's allies, who relied on Egypt's army for help (see 30:5 and the note).

At one time, cedars, like the one shown here, covered the slopes of the Lebanon Mountains. They were highly valued for their beautiful and fragrant lumber which was used to build royal palaces and the temple in Jerusalem (see 1 Kgs 5).

31:14-17 *the earth below . . . down to the grave:* The dark underground place of death (see the note at 26:19, 20). The LORD would send the tree down to the grave along with those who relied on the tree for protection.

31:18 *trees of Eden . . . earth below . . . Pharaoh and all his hordes:* Egypt's destruction will be complete. The Egyptian king, who was considered a god in Egyptian religion (see 31:10 and the note at 29:3-5), would end up in the world of the dead, where he would discover that he was human after all.

32:1 *twelfth year . . . twelfth month:* Probably February of 586 B.C. See also the note on p. 1560.

32:2 *Son of man:* See the note at 4:1.

32:2,3 *Pharaoh king of Egypt . . . monster in the seas . . . my net:* See the note at 29:3-5. The Hebrew word translated "monster" is *tannin,* a great sea monster like Leviathan (Isa 27:1) or Rahab (Job 7:12). The image of the LORD catching the water monster (king) in a net is similar to the battle scene from Babylonian mythology in which Marduk, the Babylonian god of creation, catches the great sea monster Tiamat in a net, kills her, and then chops her up.

32:4-6 *throw you on the land . . . flowing blood:* The Egyptian king will not receive a royal burial (see also the note at 29:3-5). Further, the king's rotting body and blood will pollute the land and water (see the note at 24:6-12).

32:7,8 *cover the heavens . . . darkness:* See the note at 30:3. The darkness that is part of the LORD's coming judgment is like the terrible darkness the LORD sent upon Egypt in the time of Moses (Exod 10:21-23).

32:10 *brandish my sword:* A symbol for the LORD's punishment (see also the notes at 21:2, 3 and 21:12-17).

32:7 Isa 13:10; Matt 24:29; Mark 13:24, 25; Luke 21:25; Rev 6:12, 13; 8:12.

" 'This is Pharaoh and all his hordes, declares the Sovereign LORD.' "

A Lament for Pharaoh

32 In the twelfth year, in the twelfth month on the first day, the
word of the LORD came to me: [2]"Son of man, take up a lament
concerning Pharaoh king of Egypt and say to him:

" 'You are like a lion among the nations;
you are like a monster in the seas
thrashing about in your streams,
churning the water with your feet
and muddying the streams.

[3]" 'This is what the Sovereign LORD says:

" 'With a great throng of people
I will cast my net over you,
and they will haul you up in my net.
[4]I will throw you on the land
and hurl you on the open field.
I will let all the birds of the air settle on you
and all the beasts of the earth gorge themselves on you.
[5]I will spread your flesh on the mountains
and fill the valleys with your remains.
[6]I will drench the land with your flowing blood
all the way to the mountains,
and the ravines will be filled with your flesh.
[7]When I snuff you out, I will cover the heavens
and darken their stars;
I will cover the sun with a cloud,
and the moon will not give its light.
[8]All the shining lights in the heavens
I will darken over you;
I will bring darkness over your land,
declares the Sovereign LORD.
[9]I will trouble the hearts of many peoples
when I bring about your destruction among the nations,
among[a] lands you have not known.
[10]I will cause many peoples to be appalled at you,
and their kings will shudder with horror because of you
when I brandish my sword before them.
On the day of your downfall

[a]9 Hebrew; Septuagint *bring you into captivity among the nations, / to*

each of them will tremble
every moment for his life.

11" 'For this is what the Sovereign LORD says:

" 'The sword of the king of Babylon
will come against you.
12 I will cause your hordes to fall
by the swords of mighty men—
the most ruthless of all nations.
They will shatter the pride of Egypt,
and all her hordes will be overthrown.
13 I will destroy all her cattle
from beside abundant waters
no longer to be stirred by the foot of man
or muddied by the hoofs of cattle.
14 Then I will let her waters settle
and make her streams flow like oil,
declares the Sovereign LORD.
15 When I make Egypt desolate
and strip the land of everything in it,
when I strike down all who live there,
then they will know that I am the LORD.'

16"This is the lament they will chant for her. The daughters
of the nations will chant it; for Egypt and all her hordes they will
chant it, declares the Sovereign LORD."

17 In the twelfth year, on the fifteenth day of the month, the
word of the LORD came to me: 18"Son of man, wail for the hordes
of Egypt and consign to the earth below both her and the daughters of mighty nations, with those who go down to the pit. 19 Say to
them, 'Are you more favored than others? Go down and be laid
among the uncircumcised.' 20 They will fall among those killed by
the sword. The sword is drawn; let her be dragged off with all her
hordes. 21 From within the grave[a] the mighty leaders will say of
Egypt and her allies, 'They have come down and they lie with the
uncircumcised, with those killed by the sword.'

22"Assyria is there with her whole army; she is surrounded
by the graves of all her slain, all who have fallen by the sword.
23 Their graves are in the depths of the pit and her army lies around
her grave. All who had spread terror in the land of the living are
slain, fallen by the sword.

24"Elam is there, with all her hordes around her grave. All of
them are slain, fallen by the sword. All who had spread terror in
the land of the living went down uncircumcised to the earth
below. They bear their shame with those who go down to the pit.

32:11-15 *king of Babylon . . . abundant waters . . . Egypt desolate:* Probably refers to Nebuchadnezzar of Babylon (see the notes at 29:8-12; 29:18-20). The "abundant waters" possibly refers to the Nile River (see the note at 30:10-12).

32:17 *twelfth year . . . fifteenth day of the month:* The same month as 32:1.

32:18-21 *hordes of Egypt . . . pit . . . the grave:* Referring to death. See the notes at 31:14-17 and 31:18.

32:22,23 *Assyria is there with her whole army . . . depths of the pit:* Assyria was the most powerful nation in the Near East for over two hundred years until it was defeated at Nineveh in 612 B.C. by the Babylonians, who then took over as the main power in the region. See also the note at 23:5-10. The Egyptians would join the Assyrians in the world of the dead (see the note at 32:18-21).

32:24-27 *Elam . . . bear their shame Meshech and Tubal:* Elam was a kingdom to the east of Babylon and the Tigris River. It was defeated by the Assyrians around 650 B.C. Meshech and Tubal probably refer to areas of Asia Minor. Soldiers from all these warring countries would die in battle and not receive proper burial. To be unburied was considered a terrible thing. Some believed the spirits of the unburied dead could never rest in peace.

[a]**21** Hebrew *Sheol;* also in verse 27

32:29 *Edom:* See the note at 25:12, 13.

32:30 *princes of the north . . . Sidonians:* The "princes of the north" may refer to Phoenician rulers, such as those from Tyre (see the notes at 26:2; 26:3-14). The Sidonians were from the Phoenician city of Sidon (see the note at 27:8-11).

32:31,32 *Pharaoh . . . and all his hordes:* See the note at 31:18.

25 A bed is made for her among the slain, with all her hordes
around her grave. All of them are uncircumcised, killed by the
sword. Because their terror had spread in the land of the living,
they bear their shame with those who go down to the pit; they are
laid among the slain.
26 "Meshech and Tubal are there, with all their hordes around
their graves. All of them are uncircumcised, killed by the sword
because they spread their terror in the land of the living. 27 Do they
not lie with the other uncircumcised warriors who have fallen,
who went down to the grave with their weapons of war, whose
swords were placed under their heads? The punishment for their
sins rested on their bones, though the terror of these warriors had
stalked through the land of the living.
28 "You too, O Pharaoh, will be broken and will lie among the
uncircumcised, with those killed by the sword.
29 "Edom is there, her kings and all her princes; despite their
power, they are laid with those killed by the sword. They lie with
the uncircumcised, with those who go down to the pit.
30 "All the princes of the north and all the Sidonians are
there; they went down with the slain in disgrace despite the terror
caused by their power. They lie uncircumcised with those killed
by the sword and bear their shame with those who go down to
the pit.
31 "Pharaoh—he and all his army—will see them and he will
be consoled for all his hordes that were killed by the sword,
declares the Sovereign LORD. 32 Although I had him spread terror
in the land of the living, Pharaoh and all his hordes will be laid
among the uncircumcised, with those killed by the sword, declares
the Sovereign LORD."

QUESTIONS ABOUT EZEKIEL 25:1—32:32

1. Why were the lands of Ammon, Moab, Edom, and Philistia to be punished? (25:1-17)
2. For what was the city of Tyre famous? Why would Tyre be punished by the LORD? Who attacked and nearly destroyed the city of Tyre? What effect would the destruction of Tyre have on other nations?
3. What was to happen to the kings of Tyre and Egypt? (28:1-19; 29:16) Why?
4. Who was going to be sent to attack Egypt? How would the land of Egypt suffer?
5. What is the "pit"? Who would be sent there? What kind of proper burial was usually given to the Egyptian kings? What was so bad about not receiving such a burial, or about being left to rot on the field of battle?

The LORD Will Restore Jerusalem and Israel

After many chapters of telling and showing how the LORD is going to punish Israel and many of its enemies, Ezekiel's prophecy takes a turn, beginning in chapter 33. News of Jerusalem's fall reaches Ezekiel in Babylon, and his voice is restored. Though he continues to tell his people to turn away from their sins, he also offers good news about how the LORD will help breathe new life into his people (37:1-14) and restore them once again in Jerusalem, where the LORD's glory will return to a new temple (40:1—47:12). Finally, after years of living in exile, the people will also regain their land (47:13—48:35).

WATCHMAN AND SHEPHERD

Once again, Ezekiel is appointed to be a watchman (see also 3:17-21) to warn the people of Israel to turn from their sins. He criticizes Israel's leaders as bad shepherds, but reminds the people that the LORD is their good shepherd, and they are still the LORD's sheep.

Ezekiel a Watchman

33 The word of the LORD came to me: 2“Son of man, speak to
your countrymen and say to them: ‘When I bring the sword
against a land, and the people of the land choose one of their men
and make him their watchman, 3and he sees the sword coming
against the land and blows the trumpet to warn the people, 4then
if anyone hears the trumpet but does not take warning and the
sword comes and takes his life, his blood will be on his own head.
5Since he heard the sound of the trumpet but did not take warning, his blood will be on his own head. If he had taken warning, he
would have saved himself. 6But if the watchman sees the sword
coming and does not blow the trumpet to warn the people and the
sword comes and takes the life of one of them, that man will be
taken away because of his sin, but I will hold the watchman
accountable for his blood.’

7“Son of man, I have made you a watchman for the house of
Israel; so hear the word I speak and give them warning from me.
8When I say to the wicked, ‘O wicked man, you will surely die,’ and
you do not speak out to dissuade him from his ways, that wicked
man will die for[a] his sin, and I will hold you accountable for his
blood. 9But if you do warn the wicked man to turn from his ways
and he does not do so, he will die for his sin, but you will have
saved yourself.

10“Son of man, say to the house of Israel, ‘This is what you
are saying: “Our offenses and sins weigh us down, and we are wasting away because of[b] them. How then can we live?” ’ 11Say to them,

[a]**8** Or *in*; also in verse 9 [b]**10** Or *away in*

33:2 *Son of man:* See the note at 4:1.

33:2-7 *watchman . . . house of Israel:* Watchmen stood on the walls of cities and warned people if they saw an enemy approaching. If the watchman sounded the warning signal and the people ignored it, then the people themselves were to blame. But if the watchman didn't sound the warning, it was his fault. The LORD appointed Ezekiel as Israel's watchman (see also 3:16-21) to warn the people of their sins.

33:8 *wicked man will die for his sin:* For Israel's sins, see the notes at 2:3; 7:9,10 and in chapter 8.

33:10 *Our offenses and sins weigh us down:* The people who had been forced to leave their homes and live in exile in Babylon no doubt complained that the loss of their homeland was a severe punishment for their sins. Many must have felt powerless, with no chance of regaining their land or rebuilding what had been destroyed.

33:11 *turn from their ways and live:* The people of Israel living in exile have already suffered for their sins, but Ezekiel is told to continue telling the present generation to turn back to the LORD.

33:11 Lam 3:33; Ezek 18:23; 1 Tim 2:4.

33:15 *pledge for a loan . . . follows the decrees:* Charging interest or taking something in exchange for loaning money, especially when dealing with the poor, was against the Law of Moses (see Exod 22:25-27). Any kind of stealing was also wrong, and stolen objects were to be replaced (Exod 20:15; 22:1-15; Lev 6:1-7). See also chapter 18 and the notes.

33:21 *twelfth year of our exile . . . tenth month:* Late December 586 B.C. See also the note on p. 1560. The news of Jerusalem's fall reaches Ezekiel about six months after the city's actual destruction (see the note at 12:10-13). See also 2 Kgs 25:2-10; Jer 39:1-8; 52:4-14.

33:22 *I was no longer silent:* See 3:27 and the note at 3:24-27.

33:24 *Abraham . . . possessed the land:* The LORD made a covenant with Israel's first ancestor, Abraham. If Abraham trusted the LORD and did as he was told to do, he and his descendants would receive their own land, namely Canaan (Gen 12:1-3; 17:1-8). This promise was repeated to Moses (Exod 6:2-8). Later, this promise of the land was also tied to a second covenant that the LORD made with Moses and the people at Sinai. If the people obeyed God's Law, they would keep their land (see Deut 6:10-25; 7:6-15). See also the mini-article called "Land," p. 1751.

33:25-29 *eat meat with the blood still in it . . . all the detestable things:* For the sins listed in 33:25, 26, see the notes at 24:6-12 (eating blood); 6:3-6 and 6:9 (worshiping idols); 22:2-4 (murder, violence and injustice); and 16:32-34 and 16:38 (unfaithfulness in marriage). Because they continued to sin, those who remained in Judah would also be punished.

33:12,13 Ezek 18:21–24.

'As surely as I live, declares the Sovereign LORD, I take no pleasure
in the death of the wicked, but rather that they turn from their
ways and live. Turn! Turn from your evil ways! Why will you die,
O house of Israel?'
12"Therefore, son of man, say to your countrymen, 'The
righteousness of the righteous man will not save him when he disobeys, and the wickedness of the wicked man will not cause him to
fall when he turns from it. The righteous man, if he sins, will not
be allowed to live because of his former righteousness.' 13If I tell
the righteous man that he will surely live, but then he trusts in his
righteousness and does evil, none of the righteous things he has
done will be remembered; he will die for the evil he has done.
14And if I say to the wicked man, 'You will surely die,' but he then
turns away from his sin and does what is just and right— 15if he
gives back what he took in pledge for a loan, returns what he has
stolen, follows the decrees that give life, and does no evil, he will
surely live; he will not die. 16None of the sins he has committed
will be remembered against him. He has done what is just and
right; he will surely live.
17"Yet your countrymen say, 'The way of the Lord is not just.'
But it is their way that is not just. 18If a righteous man turns from
his righteousness and does evil, he will die for it. 19And if a wicked
man turns away from his wickedness and does what is just and
right, he will live by doing so. 20Yet, O house of Israel, you say, 'The
way of the Lord is not just.' But I will judge each of you according
to his own ways."

Jerusalem's Fall Explained

21In the twelfth year of our exile, in the tenth month on the
fifth day, a man who had escaped from Jerusalem came to me and
said, "The city has fallen!" 22Now the evening before the man
arrived, the hand of the LORD was upon me, and he opened my
mouth before the man came to me in the morning. So my mouth
was opened and I was no longer silent.
23Then the word of the LORD came to me: 24"Son of man, the
people living in those ruins in the land of Israel are saying, 'Abraham was only one man, yet he possessed the land. But we are
many; surely the land has been given to us as our possession.'
25Therefore say to them, 'This is what the Sovereign LORD says:
Since you eat meat with the blood still in it and look to your idols
and shed blood, should you then possess the land? 26You rely on
your sword, you do detestable things, and each of you defiles his
neighbor's wife. Should you then possess the land?'
27"Say this to them: 'This is what the Sovereign LORD says: As
surely as I live, those who are left in the ruins will fall by the sword,
those out in the country I will give to the wild animals to be
devoured, and those in strongholds and caves will die of a plague.
28I will make the land a desolate waste, and her proud strength will

come to an end, and the mountains of Israel will become desolate
so that no one will cross them. 29Then they will know that I am the
LORD, when I have made the land a desolate waste because of all
the detestable things they have done.'
30"As for you, son of man, your countrymen are talking
together about you by the walls and at the doors of the houses,
saying to each other, 'Come and hear the message that has come
from the LORD.' 31My people come to you, as they usually do, and
sit before you to listen to your words, but they do not put them
into practice. With their mouths they express devotion, but their
hearts are greedy for unjust gain. 32Indeed, to them you are nothing more than one who sings love songs with a beautiful voice and
plays an instrument well, for they hear your words but do not put
them into practice.
33"When all this comes true—and it surely will—then they
will know that a prophet has been among them."

Shepherds and Sheep

34 The word of the LORD came to me: 2"Son of man, prophesy
against the shepherds of Israel; prophesy and say to them: 'This is
what the Sovereign LORD says: Woe to the shepherds of Israel who
only take care of themselves! Should not shepherds take care of the
flock? 3You eat the curds, clothe yourselves with the wool and
slaughter the choice animals, but you do not take care of the flock.
4You have not strengthened the weak or healed the sick or bound
up the injured. You have not brought back the strays or searched
for the lost. You have ruled them harshly and brutally. 5So they
were scattered because there was no shepherd, and when they were
scattered they became food for all the wild animals. 6My sheep
wandered over all the mountains and on every high hill. They were
scattered over the whole earth, and no one searched or looked for
them.
7" 'Therefore, you shepherds, hear the word of the LORD: 8As
surely as I live, declares the Sovereign LORD, because my flock lacks
a shepherd and so has been plundered and has become food for
all the wild animals, and because my shepherds did not search for
my flock but cared for themselves rather than for my flock, 9there-
fore, O shepherds, hear the word of the LORD: 10This is what the
Sovereign LORD says: I am against the shepherds and will hold
them accountable for my flock. I will remove them from tending
the flock so that the shepherds can no longer feed themselves. I
will rescue my flock from their mouths, and it will no longer be
food for them.
11" 'For this is what the Sovereign LORD says: I myself will
search for my sheep and look after them. 12As a shepherd looks
after his scattered flock when he is with them, so will I look after
my sheep. I will rescue them from all the places where they were
scattered on a day of clouds and darkness. 13I will bring them out

The LORD says, *"As a shepherd looks after his scattered flock when he is with them, so will I look after my sheep."* Ezek 34:12

33:30-33 *your countrymen . . . a prophet has been among them:* If the people left in Judah will die because of their sins, perhaps the only hope for a restored Judah is with the people living in exile in Babylon. They like to hear Ezekiel's prophecies, but they treat them as entertainment and don't really do what Ezekiel says. So, the exiles are also in danger of further punishment (compare to 33:1-9).

34:2-10 *prophesy against the shepherds of Israel . . . rescue my flock:* Shepherds protected their flocks from being stolen, killed by wild animals, or wandering into danger. But many of Israel's leaders had not been good shepherds, and because of their evil and neglectful ways, the sheep (the people of Israel) were killed or scattered across the earth. These leaders included kings, priests, and city officials (see the notes at 11:1-3; 16:22; 16:26-29; 16:46-52; 22:25; 22:26; 22:27-29). The LORD will punish those shepherds (leaders) who failed to be good shepherds.

34:11-13 *my sheep . . . scattered . . . I will pasture them:* The people of Israel ("my sheep," see 34:17) were led away as prisoners on the day of "darkness" when the Babylonians defeated Jerusalem (see the note on p. 1560 and the note at 12:10-13). But Ezekiel now offers some good news: The LORD will rescue the people and bring them home from exile (see the note at 4:6), as a good shepherd rescues sheep that have become lost or have wandered into danger. The image of the LORD as a shepherd is common in the Bible (see also Gen 49:24; Ps 23; 80:1; Isa 40:11; John 10:11; Heb 13:20).

34:5 Num 27:17; 1 Kgs 22:17; Matt 9:36; Mark 6:34.

from the nations and gather them from the countries, and I will bring them into their own land. I will pasture them on the mountains of Israel, in the ravines and in all the settlements in the land. [14]I will tend them in a good pasture, and the mountain heights of Israel will be their grazing land. There they will lie down in good grazing land, and there they will feed in a rich pasture on the mountains of Israel. [15]I myself will tend my sheep and have them lie down, declares the Sovereign LORD. [16]I will search for the lost and bring back the strays. I will bind up the injured and strengthen the weak, but the sleek and the strong I will destroy. I will shepherd the flock with justice.

[17]" 'As for you, my flock, this is what the Sovereign LORD says: I will judge between one sheep and another, and between rams and goats. [18]Is it not enough for you to feed on the good pasture? Must you also trample the rest of your pasture with your feet? Is it not enough for you to drink clear water? Must you also muddy the rest with your feet? [19]Must my flock feed on what you have trampled and drink what you have muddied with your feet?

[20]" 'Therefore this is what the Sovereign LORD says to them: See, I myself will judge between the fat sheep and the lean sheep. [21]Because you shove with flank and shoulder, butting all the weak sheep with your horns until you have driven them away, [22]I will save my flock, and they will no longer be plundered. I will judge between one sheep and another. [23]I will place over them one shepherd, my servant David, and he will tend them; he will tend them and be their shepherd. [24]I the LORD will be their God, and my servant David will be prince among them. I the LORD have spoken.

[25]" 'I will make a covenant of peace with them and rid the land of wild beasts so that they may live in the desert and sleep in the forests in safety. [26]I will bless them and the places surrounding my hill.[a] I will send down showers in season; there will be showers of blessing. [27]The trees of the field will yield their fruit and the ground will yield its crops; the people will be secure in their land. They will know that I am the LORD, when I break the bars of their yoke and rescue them from the hands of those who enslaved them. [28]They will no longer be plundered by the nations, nor will wild animals devour them. They will live in safety, and no one will make them afraid. [29]I will provide for them a land renowned for its crops, and they will no longer be victims of famine in the land or bear the scorn of the nations. [30]Then they will know that I, the LORD their God, am with them and that they, the house of Israel, are my people, declares the Sovereign LORD. [31]You my sheep, the sheep of my pasture, are people, and I am your God, declares the Sovereign LORD.' "

34:20 *judge between the fat sheep and the lean sheep:* Some leaders and rich people ("fat sheep") used their wealth and influence to cheat the poor. But the LORD promises to rescue the weak (see also Ps 37:11; Isa 11:4; 29:19; 61:1).

34:23,24 *one shepherd . . . my servant David:* God had promised that Israel's true king would always come from the family of King David (2 Sam 7:8-29; Ps 132:10-18). Once the people were restored to their land, the LORD would also restore Israel's king to the throne. These verses mean that the new king would also be a descendant of King David's family. See also Isa 11:1-5; Rev 7:17.

34:25 *a covenant of peace:* The Hebrew word here translated as "peace" is *shalom,* which means "well-being." It means the absence of war, but also includes good health and blessings. See also the mini-article called "Peace," p. 1337. See also Isa 26:3; 54:10; Mal 2:5.

34:26 *my hill:* That is, Mount Zion in Jerusalem (see the note at 17:22-24).

34:26-30 *showers of blessing . . . they will know . . . the LORD:* Ezekiel's promise of a time of peace and blessing contrasts with his earlier prophecies of doom and punishment. Once again, the LORD will protect Israel in order to show other nations that the LORD is Israel's shepherd.

---

[a]**26** Or *I will make them and the places surrounding my hill a blessing*

PREPARING THE WAY FOR JUDAH'S NEW FUTURE

Ezekiel warns Edom that it is doomed and he tells the mountains of Israel to rejoice. Though the LORD's people have sinned, the LORD will bring them home in order to honor his name. They will receive the LORD's Spirit and a new heart, so they can obey his laws and teachings. Ezekiel sees a vision of dry bones (the people of Israel) coming to life, so they can return home, and he sees the LORD defeat a great army of Israel's enemies led by Gog of Magog.

A Prophecy Against Edom

35 The word of the LORD came to me: 2"Son of man, set your
face against Mount Seir; prophesy against it 3and say: 'This is what
the Sovereign LORD says: I am against you, Mount Seir, and I will
stretch out my hand against you and make you a desolate waste. 4I
will turn your towns into ruins and you will be desolate. Then you
will know that I am the LORD.

5" 'Because you harbored an ancient hostility and delivered
the Israelites over to the sword at the time of their calamity, the
time their punishment reached its climax, 6therefore as surely as I
live, declares the Sovereign LORD, I will give you over to bloodshed
and it will pursue you. Since you did not hate bloodshed, bloodshed will pursue you. 7I will make Mount Seir a desolate waste and
cut off from it all who come and go. 8I will fill your mountains
with the slain; those killed by the sword will fall on your hills and
in your valleys and in all your ravines. 9I will make you desolate
forever; your towns will not be inhabited. Then you will know that
I am the LORD.

10" 'Because you have said, "These two nations and countries
will be ours and we will take possession of them," even though I
the LORD was there, 11therefore as surely as I live, declares the
Sovereign LORD, I will treat you in accordance with the anger and
jealousy you showed in your hatred of them and I will make
myself known among them when I judge you. 12Then you will
know that I the LORD have heard all the contemptible things you
have said against the mountains of Israel. You said, "They have
been laid waste and have been given over to us to devour." 13You
boasted against me and spoke against me without restraint, and I
heard it. 14This is what the Sovereign LORD says: While the whole
earth rejoices, I will make you desolate. 15Because you rejoiced
when the inheritance of the house of Israel became desolate, that
is how I will treat you. You will be desolate, O Mount Seir, you and
all of Edom. Then they will know that I am the LORD.' "

A Prophecy to the Mountains of Israel

36 "Son of man, prophesy to the mountains of Israel and say,
'O mountains of Israel, hear the word of the LORD. 2This is what
the Sovereign LORD says: The enemy said of you, "Aha! The ancient
heights have become our possession." ' 3Therefore prophesy and
say, 'This is what the Sovereign LORD says: Because they ravaged

35:2 *Son of man:* See the note at 4:1.

35:2 *Mount Seir:* This refers to a mountainous region southeast of the land of Canaan inhabited by the Edomites.

35:2-15 *Mount Seir . . . You will be desolate:* See the note at 25:12, 13. After Israel was defeated by the Babylonians, some Edomites apparently thought they could walk in and take over parts of the land that belonged to the people of Israel (35:10). So, just as Edom celebrated when Israel was destroyed, so everyone on earth will celebrate the destruction of Edom.

35:10 *These two nations and countries will be ours:* Referring to Judah and Israel. See the notes at 16:46-52 and 35:2-15.

36:1-3 *mountains of Israel . . . ravaged and hounded you from every side:* The mountains here probably are meant to refer to the land of Israel (see 35:12), which enemies both claimed (36:2; also 35:10) and captured (see the notes at 4:4, 5 and 12:10-13).

35:1-15 Isa 34:5-17; 63:1-6; Jer 49:7-22; Amos 1:11,12; Obad 1-14; Mal 1:2-5.

and hounded you from every side so that you became the possession of the rest of the nations and the object of people's malicious talk and slander, 4therefore, O mountains of Israel, hear the word of the Sovereign LORD: This is what the Sovereign LORD says to the mountains and hills, to the ravines and valleys, to the desolate ruins and the deserted towns that have been plundered and ridiculed by the rest of the nations around you— 5this is what the Sovereign LORD says: In my burning zeal I have spoken against the rest of the nations, and against all Edom, for with glee and with malice in their hearts they made my land their own possession so that they might plunder its pastureland.' 6Therefore prophesy concerning the land of Israel and say to the mountains and hills, to the ravines and valleys: 'This is what the Sovereign LORD says: I speak in my jealous wrath because you have suffered the scorn of the nations. 7Therefore this is what the Sovereign LORD says: I swear with uplifted hand that the nations around you will also suffer scorn.

8" 'But you, O mountains of Israel, will produce branches and fruit for my people Israel, for they will soon come home. 9I am concerned for you and will look on you with favor; you will be plowed and sown, 10and I will multiply the number of people upon you, even the whole house of Israel. The towns will be inhabited and the ruins rebuilt. 11I will increase the number of men and animals upon you, and they will be fruitful and become numerous. I will settle people on you as in the past and will make you prosper more than before. Then you will know that I am the LORD. 12I will cause people, my people Israel, to walk upon you. They will possess you, and you will be their inheritance; you will never again deprive them of their children.

13" 'This is what the Sovereign LORD says: Because people say to you, "You devour men and deprive your nation of its children," 14therefore you will no longer devour men or make your nation childless, declares the Sovereign LORD. 15No longer will I make you hear the taunts of the nations, and no longer will you suffer the scorn of the peoples or cause your nation to fall, declares the Sovereign LORD.' "

16Again the word of the LORD came to me: 17"Son of man, when the people of Israel were living in their own land, they defiled it by their conduct and their actions. Their conduct was like a woman's monthly uncleanness in my sight. 18So I poured out my wrath on them because they had shed blood in the land and because they had defiled it with their idols. 19I dispersed them among the nations, and they were scattered through the countries; I judged them according to their conduct and their actions. 20And wherever they went among the nations they profaned my holy name, for it was said of them, 'These are the LORD's people, and yet they had to leave his land.' 21I had concern for my holy name, which the house of Israel profaned among the nations where they had gone.

36:5 *I have spoken against . . . the nations:* Foreign nations had invaded Israel's land, including the holy city of Jerusalem. The blood of those who died polluted the land, as did the presence of those nations who did not honor Israel's LORD (see the note at 24:6-12). So the LORD promised to take revenge on those who had destroyed Israel's mountains and made the land barren.

36:8-15 *mountains of Israel . . . no longer will you suffer:* The mountains (land) of Israel, ruined by Israel's enemies, will once again bear fruit and provide a home for God's people when they return from exile. Israel's population had been reduced by war, famine, and forced exile but it would increase when the people returned to live in the fertile mountains of Israel (36:11).

36:17-20 *people of Israel . . . leave his land:* Israel's sins included murder, injustice, and worshiping idols. These verses say that their sins defiled the land and made it ritually unclean, just as the blood flow of a women's monthly period made her temporarily unclean (see Lev 15:19-31 and the note at Ezek 24:6-12). See also the mini-article called "Purity (Clean and Unclean)," p. 2125.

36:22-24 *my holy name . . . bring you back:* The sinful actions of the people of Israel (see 36:17–20 and note) made the land unclean. For these sins, they were defeated and sent into exile. This humiliation of the LORD's people disgraced the name of the LORD. Israel's enemies believed that their LORD was not powerful enough to save them (see also the note at 20:40-44). But the LORD now promises to bring the people home so that the LORD's name can once again be honored among the nations.

36:25 *sprinkle clean water on you:* In ancient Israel, water was used in a ceremony to wash away sin and in other cleansing rituals (see Exod 30:18-21; Lev 14:51; Num 19:1-21). The LORD promised to make the people ritually clean again, especially by removing the idols they had been worshiping.

22“Therefore say to the house of Israel, ‘This is what the
Sovereign LORD says: It is not for your sake, O house of Israel, that
I am going to do these things, but for the sake of my holy name,
which you have profaned among the nations where you have gone.
23I will show the holiness of my great name, which has been profaned among the nations, the name you have profaned among
them. Then the nations will know that I am the LORD, declares
the Sovereign LORD, when I show myself holy through you before
their eyes.
24“ ‘For I will take you out of the nations; I will gather you
from all the countries and bring you back into your own land. 25I
will sprinkle clean water on you, and you will be clean; I will
cleanse you from all your impurities and from all your idols. 26I
will give you a new heart and put a new spirit in you; I will remove
from you your heart of stone and give you a heart of flesh. 27And
I will put my Spirit in you and move you to follow my decrees and
be careful to keep my laws. 28You will live in the land I gave your
forefathers; you will be my people, and I will be your God. 29I will
save you from all your uncleanness. I will call for the grain and
make it plentiful and will not bring famine upon you. 30I will
increase the fruit of the trees and the crops of the field, so that you
will no longer suffer disgrace among the nations because of
famine. 31Then you will remember your evil ways and wicked
deeds, and you will loathe yourselves for your sins and detestable
practices. 32I want you to know that I am not doing this for your
sake, declares the Sovereign LORD. Be ashamed and disgraced for
your conduct, O house of Israel!
33“ ‘This is what the Sovereign LORD says: On the day I
cleanse you from all your sins, I will resettle your towns, and the
ruins will be rebuilt. 34The desolate land will be cultivated instead
of lying desolate in the sight of all who pass through it. 35They will
say, “This land that was laid waste has become like the garden of
Eden; the cities that were lying in ruins, desolate and destroyed, are
now fortified and inhabited.” 36Then the nations around you that
remain will know that I the LORD have rebuilt what was destroyed
and have replanted what was desolate. I the LORD have spoken, and
I will do it.’
37“This is what the Sovereign LORD says: Once again I will
yield to the plea of the house of Israel and do this for them: I will
make their people as numerous as sheep, 38as numerous as the
flocks for offerings at Jerusalem during her appointed feasts. So
will the ruined cities be filled with flocks of people. Then they will
know that I am the LORD.”

The Valley of Dry Bones

37 The hand of the LORD was upon me, and he brought me out
by the Spirit of the LORD and set me in the middle of a valley; it

The Lord said, *“I will give you a new heart and put a new spirit in you; I will remove from you your heart of stone and give you a heart of flesh.”*
Ezek 36:26

36:27 *put my Spirit in you:* See the note at 2:2. The LORD’s Spirit would help the people obey the LORD’s teachings. Their obedience would help the land from becoming ritually unclean again.

36:33-38 *cleanse you . . . resettle your towns . . . flocks for offerings:* The cleansing of the land of Israel begins the process of restoring the people and renewing the land. Fields and trees will grow plenty of food, and cities will be rebuilt and repopulated. Then God’s people will once again be able to bring sacrifices to honor the LORD during regular festivals, such as the New Moon festival (Ps 81:3; Num 28:11-15). See the chart “Sacrifices and Offerings, p. 219, and the chart called “Jewish Calendar and Festivals,” p. 944. For more about Israel’s sacrifices and religious festivals, see LEVITICUS and the article called “People of the Law: The Religion of Israel,” p. 939.

37:1 *hand of the LORD . . . Spirit . . . valley . . . full of bones:* See the note at 2:2. The date of Ezekiel’s vision of the dry bones is not known, but it probably happened after many of the people of Israel had been in exile for a time and had begun to lose hope (37:11). The valley of dry bones may be the same valley where he had his first vision (1:1—3:15). An important word that occurs in the following verses is the Hebrew word *ruach.* This word means either “wind,” “breath,” or “Spirit.” These three meanings are all used in the vision of dry bones coming back to life.

36:26-28 Ezek 11:19,20.

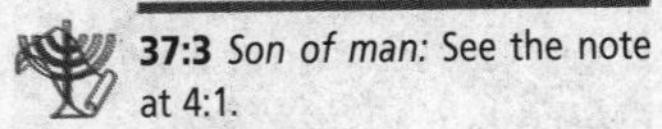

37:3 *Son of man:* See the note at 4:1.

was full of bones. [2]He led me back and forth among them, and I
saw a great many bones on the floor of the valley, bones that were
very dry. [3]He asked me, "Son of man, can these bones live?"
I said, "O Sovereign LORD, you alone know."
[4]Then he said to me, "Prophesy to these bones and say to
them, 'Dry bones, hear the word of the LORD! [5]This is what the

HOLINESS

Generally, the word "holiness" describes something that is considered sacred, godly, or spiritual. In the Old Testament, the words for holiness have more specific meanings. One meaning emphasizes the difference between what is holy or sacred and what is considered common or ritually unclean (Ezek 22:8). Holy things (such as priests' clothes; sacrifices) were not to come into contact with common people or things. The holy things could become defiled (no longer holy or acceptable to the LORD), and that person could be harmed.

Another meaning for holiness has to do with "setting apart" or "devoting" something for a special purpose. Things or people were to be devoted or set apart for complete destruction as a holy gift for the LORD (Lev 27:28; Josh 6:15—7:13). People were also chosen for special duties or for holy purposes. The priests were chosen and set apart for doing the sacred work in the temple. (See the mini-article called "Israel's Priests," p. 2344.) People known as Nazirites took vows of holiness, which meant that they would act in a certain way or do certain things that set them apart from other people (Num 6:1-21). Before giving the Israelite people the law that would set them apart from other people, the LORD told Moses that he had chosen Israel to be his holy nation (Exod 19:5, 6; see also Isa 43:21). One New Testament writer uses these same words in describing Christ's followers on earth (1 Pet 2:9).

Things connected to the LORD or the LORD's presence are considered holy. For example, the LORD was said to live in the Most Holy Place in the temple located on Mount Zion in Jerusalem. For this reason Jerusalem was called the "holy city" and Zion was called the LORD's "holy mountain." The LORD is often referred to as the "Holy One," meaning God is set apart from human beings, but is also Israel's personal God, who chose them and lives among them (Exod 25:18-22; 1 Kgs 8:6-13; Isa 6:1-8). Often in the Old Testament the holy and awe-inspiring LORD appears in fire or a cloud, a sign of either the LORD's protection or his judgment (Exod 3:2,3; 19:18; Deut 5:22-27; Isa 4:4; Ezek 1:4-28). The LORD's fire is also said to purify in the same way a hot fire is used to make a precious metal more pure (Ezek 22:18-22). And those who survive the LORD's "fiery wrath" are seen as the ones who are holy or chosen to live holy lives. See also the mini-article called "Fire," p. 2383.

In the New Testament, the Holy Spirit is given to those who believe in Jesus. The Spirit both teaches and guides (Rom 15:13-16; 1 Cor 2:13), making it possible for the followers of Jesus to live holy lives and be holy, just as God is holy (Gal 5:16-25; 1 Pet 1:16). The law and many of Israel's prophets emphasized that holiness came from living according to the LORD's commands. The New Testament writers also recognize the holiness of God's Law, but for them holiness is not based on following the rituals connected to worship at the temple. Instead, holiness comes from the presence of God's Spirit living among Christ's followers, the church (see Eph 2:19-22; 1 Pet 2:4,5).

Ezekiel's vision of dry bones, wall painting at Dura-Europos, third century synagogue on the Euphrates River. In the valley full of dry bones, the LORD commanded Ezekiel to say to the bones: "I will put breath in you, and you will come to life." This wall-painting shows the hand of the LORD upon Ezekiel as he fulfills the LORD's command. The bones begin putting on flesh, and the bodies receive the breath of life. (See 37: 1-14.)

Sovereign LORD says to these bones: I will make breath[a] enter you, and you will come to life. 6I will attach tendons to you and make flesh come upon you and cover you with skin; I will put breath in you, and you will come to life. Then you will know that I am the LORD.' "

7So I prophesied as I was commanded. And as I was prophesying, there was a noise, a rattling sound, and the bones came together, bone to bone. 8I looked, and tendons and flesh appeared on them and skin covered them, but there was no breath in them.

9Then he said to me, "Prophesy to the breath; prophesy, son of man, and say to it, 'This is what the Sovereign LORD says: Come from the four winds, O breath, and breathe into these slain, that they may live.' " 10So I prophesied as he commanded me, and breath entered them; they came to life and stood up on their feet—a vast army.

11Then he said to me: "Son of man, these bones are the whole house of Israel. They say, 'Our bones are dried up and our hope is gone; we are cut off.' 12Therefore prophesy and say to them: 'This is what the Sovereign LORD says: O my people, I am going to open your graves and bring you up from them; I will bring you back to the land of Israel. 13Then you, my people, will know that I am the LORD, when I open your graves and bring you up from them. 14I will put my Spirit in you and you will live, and I will settle you in your own land. Then you will know that I the LORD have spoken, and I have done it, declares the LORD.' "

[a]5 The Hebrew for this word can also mean *wind* or *spirit* (see verses 6-14).

37:3-10 *bones . . . breath enter you . . . they came to life:* Ezekiel's reply to the LORD's question in 37:3 is not a simple "no," as might be expected, but he recognizes that the power of the holy LORD makes anything possible. Then the LORD invites Ezekiel to take part in bringing the bones back to life. He calls on the wind (or breath) to give the bones life. Ezekiel calls this life-force wind from the four corners of the earth, but it is not an ordinary wind. It contains the LORD's life-giving breath (see also Gen 2:7) and Spirit which gives new life (37:14).

37:11-14 *Our bones are dried up . . . will settle you in your own land:* These verses interpret the vision. The people of Israel living in exile are feeling as if their hopes have dried up. But the LORD offers hopeful news. Like the army of dry bones that rose from death, the people of Israel will stand up and return home (see Isa 40:1-11; 49:8-12; and the note at 4:6).

37:10 Rev 11:11.

One Nation Under One King

[15]The word of the LORD came to me: [16]"Son of man, take a stick of wood and write on it, 'Belonging to Judah and the Israelites associated with him.' Then take another stick of wood, and write on it, 'Ephraim's stick, belonging to Joseph and all the house of Israel associated with him.' [17]Join them together into one stick so that they will become one in your hand.

[18]"When your countrymen ask you, 'Won't you tell us what you mean by this?' [19]say to them, 'This is what the Sovereign LORD says: I am going to take the stick of Joseph—which is in Ephraim's hand—and of the Israelite tribes associated with him, and join it to Judah's stick, making them a single stick of wood, and they will become one in my hand.' [20]Hold before their eyes the sticks you have written on [21]and say to them, 'This is what the Sovereign LORD says: I will take the Israelites out of the nations where they have gone. I will gather them from all around and bring them back into their own land. [22]I will make them one nation in the land, on the mountains of Israel. There will be one king over all of them and they will never again be two nations or be divided into two kingdoms. [23]They will no longer defile themselves with their idols and vile images or with any of their offenses, for I will save them from all their sinful backsliding,[a] and I will cleanse them. They will be my people, and I will be their God.

[24]" 'My servant David will be king over them, and they will all have one shepherd. They will follow my laws and be careful to keep my decrees. [25]They will live in the land I gave to my servant Jacob, the land where your fathers lived. They and their children and their children's children will live there forever, and David my servant will be their prince forever. [26]I will make a covenant of peace with them; it will be an everlasting covenant. I will establish them and increase their numbers, and I will put my sanctuary among them forever. [27]My dwelling place will be with them; I will be their God, and they will be my people. [28]Then the nations will know that I the LORD make Israel holy, when my sanctuary is among them forever.' "

A Prophecy Against Gog

38 The word of the LORD came to me: [2]"Son of man, set your face against Gog, of the land of Magog, the chief prince of[b] Meshech and Tubal; prophesy against him [3]and say: 'This is what the Sovereign LORD says: I am against you, O Gog, chief prince of[c] Meshech and Tubal. [4]I will turn you around, put hooks in your jaws and bring you out with your whole army—your horses, your horsemen fully armed, and a great horde with large and small

[a]23 Many Hebrew manuscripts (see also Septuagint); most Hebrew manuscripts *all their dwelling places where they sinned* [b]2 Or *the prince of Rosh,* [c]3 Or *Gog, prince of Rosh,*

37:16-22 *Judah ... Israelite tribes ... one nation:* About three centuries before the time of Ezekiel, the tribes of Israel divided into two kingdoms (see the note at 16:46-52). In 722/21 B.C. the northern kingdom (Israel) was defeated by Assyria (see the note at 23:5-10). Later, the southern kingdom (Judah) was defeated by the Babylonians (see the note at 12:10-13). But the LORD will bring the people home from exile and make the two kingdoms into one kingdom with one ruler, as in the days of King David.

37:24,25 *servant David . . . servant Jacob:* See the notes at 34:23,24; 28:25; and 33:24.

37:26 *covenant of peace ... everlasting covenant:* The LORD repeats his new covenant with the people of Israel (see also 36:24-38).

37:28 *my sanctuary:* The first temple built by Solomon was destroyed by the Babylonians in 587/86 B.C. The people who returned to Jerusalem from exile built a new temple, dedicated in 515 B.C. The rebuilt temple would once again stand as a reminder to the nations that the LORD was Israel's God.

38:2 *Gog . . . land of Magog . . . Meshech and Tubal:* The exact identity of Gog is unknown, though the name has been linked with King Gyges, who ruled the kingdom of Lydia in Asia Minor around 600 B.C. Meshech and Tubal probably refer to areas of Asia Minor (see the note at 32:24-27), so Magog likely is meant to refer to Asia Minor, north of Israel. Magog was the name of one of Japheth's sons (see Gen 10:2).

38:4 *put hooks in your jaws and bring you out:* Though Gog leads a powerful army, the LORD controls what will happen to Gog.

shields, all of them brandishing their swords. 5 Persia, Cush[a] and
Put will be with them, all with shields and helmets, 6 also Gomer
with all its troops, and Beth Togarmah from the far north with all
its troops—the many nations with you.

7 " 'Get ready; be prepared, you and all the hordes gathered
about you, and take command of them. 8 After many days you will
be called to arms. In future years you will invade a land that has
recovered from war, whose people were gathered from many
nations to the mountains of Israel, which had long been desolate.
They had been brought out from the nations, and now all of them
live in safety. 9 You and all your troops and the many nations with
you will go up, advancing like a storm; you will be like a cloud covering the land.

10 " 'This is what the Sovereign LORD says: On that day
thoughts will come into your mind and you will devise an evil
scheme. 11 You will say, "I will invade a land of unwalled villages; I
will attack a peaceful and unsuspecting people—all of them living
without walls and without gates and bars. 12 I will plunder and loot
and turn my hand against the resettled ruins and the people gathered from the nations, rich in livestock and goods, living at the center of the land." 13 Sheba and Dedan and the merchants of Tarshish
and all her villages[b] will say to you, "Have you come to plunder?
Have you gathered your hordes to loot, to carry off silver and gold,
to take away livestock and goods and to seize much plunder?" '

14 "Therefore, son of man, prophesy and say to Gog: 'This is
what the Sovereign LORD says: In that day, when my people Israel
are living in safety, will you not take notice of it? 15 You will come
from your place in the far north, you and many nations with you,
all of them riding on horses, a great horde, a mighty army. 16 You
will advance against my people Israel like a cloud that covers the
land. In days to come, O Gog, I will bring you against my land, so
that the nations may know me when I show myself holy through
you before their eyes.

17 " 'This is what the Sovereign LORD says: Are you not the
one I spoke of in former days by my servants the prophets of
Israel? At that time they prophesied for years that I would bring
you against them. 18 This is what will happen in that day: When
Gog attacks the land of Israel, my hot anger will be aroused,
declares the Sovereign LORD. 19 In my zeal and fiery wrath I declare
that at that time there shall be a great earthquake in the land of
Israel. 20 The fish of the sea, the birds of the air, the beasts of the
field, every creature that moves along the ground, and all the people on the face of the earth will tremble at my presence. The
mountains will be overturned, the cliffs will crumble and every
wall will fall to the ground. 21 I will summon a sword against Gog

[a]5 That is, the upper Nile region [b]13 Or *her strong lions*

38:5,6 *Persia . . . Beth Togarmah:* The Persians defeated the Babylonians in 539 B.C. See also the mini-article called "Persia," p. 859. Gomer is the name of one of Japheth's sons (see Gen 10:2), and Togarmah is a child of Gomer (Gen 10:3). The descendants of both were said to come from northern Asia Minor. See also the map on p. 1603.

38:8-12 *called to arms . . . against the resettled ruins:* A huge attack on Israel did not occur shortly after the people of Israel returned to their land, and Ezekiel's message began to be interpreted as describing a battle between the LORD and Israel's enemies at the end of time.

38:13 *Sheba and Dedan:* Sheba may refer to what is now southwest Arabia (see also 1 Kgs 10:1-13). See also the note at 25:12,13 (Dedan).

38:16-23 *against my people Israel . . . my holiness:* The LORD allows Gog's army to invade Israel in order that Gog's defeat (38:21-23) will show that the LORD is holy. See also the notes at 20:40-44; 28:22; 36:22-24. Gog's army is defeated by earthquakes, Israel's mountains, disease, hail, and burning sulfur rain, all sent by the LORD.

39:1 *Son of man:* See the note at 4:1.

39:1 *Gog ... chief prince of Meshech and Tubal:* See the note at 38:2.

39:6 *send fire on Magog:* See the note at 38:2. Fire is often used as a weapon of the LORD's judgment against those who are evil or disobedient (Gen 19:23-29; Lev 10:1, 2; Ezek 5:1-5; 10:2; 20:45-47; Joel 2:1-3; Matt 13:36-42).

39:7 *my holy name ... Holy One:* See the note at 36:22-24 and the mini-article called "Holiness," p. 1626.

39:9 *weapons for fuel ... seven years:* So many weapons will be collected from the dead soldiers of Gog's army that they can be burned as firewood for seven years. In the ancient world, the number "seven" symbolized perfection or completeness.

39:11 *the valley of those who travel east ... the Valley of Hamon Gog:* The location of this burial valley is not certain, but probably refers to an area east of the Dead Sea.

39:12-15 *burying them ... gravediggers:* According to the Law of Moses, touching the body or bones of a corpse could make a person ritually unclean (Lev 21:1, 11; Num 6:6-12; 19:16), and the blood of the dead bodies could make the land itself ritually unclean (Num 35:33, 34; see also the note at 24:6-12). To make the land clean (ritually pure) again, the bodies had to be buried. Burying the bodies of Gog's army outside the land of Israel was a way to make certain the land was cleansed.

39:2 Ezek 38:4.

on all my mountains, declares the Sovereign LORD. Every man's
sword will be against his brother. 22 I will execute judgment upon
him with plague and bloodshed; I will pour down torrents of rain,
hailstones and burning sulfur on him and on his troops and on
the many nations with him. 23 And so I will show my greatness and
my holiness, and I will make myself known in the sight of many
nations. Then they will know that I am the LORD.'

39 "Son of man, prophesy against Gog and say: 'This is what the
Sovereign LORD says: I am against you, O Gog, chief prince of[a]
Meshech and Tubal. 2 I will turn you around and drag you along. I
will bring you from the far north and send you against the mountains of Israel. 3 Then I will strike your bow from your left hand
and make your arrows drop from your right hand. 4 On the mountains of Israel you will fall, you and all your troops and the nations
with you. I will give you as food to all kinds of carrion birds and
to the wild animals. 5 You will fall in the open field, for I have
spoken, declares the Sovereign LORD. 6 I will send fire on Magog
and on those who live in safety in the coastlands, and they will
know that I am the LORD.

7 " 'I will make known my holy name among my people
Israel. I will no longer let my holy name be profaned, and the
nations will know that I the LORD am the Holy One in Israel. 8 It is
coming! It will surely take place, declares the Sovereign LORD. This
is the day I have spoken of.

9 " 'Then those who live in the towns of Israel will go out and
use the weapons for fuel and burn them up—the small and large
shields, the bows and arrows, the war clubs and spears. For seven
years they will use them for fuel. 10 They will not need to gather
wood from the fields or cut it from the forests, because they will
use the weapons for fuel. And they will plunder those who plundered them and loot those who looted them, declares the
Sovereign LORD.

11 " 'On that day I will give Gog a burial place in Israel, in the
valley of those who travel east toward[b] the Sea.[c] It will block the
way of travelers, because Gog and all his hordes will be buried
there. So it will be called the Valley of Hamon Gog.[d]

12 " 'For seven months the house of Israel will be burying
them in order to cleanse the land. 13 All the people of the land will
bury them, and the day I am glorified will be a memorable day for
them, declares the Sovereign LORD.

14 " 'Men will be regularly employed to cleanse the land.
Some will go throughout the land and, in addition to them, others
will bury those that remain on the ground. At the end of the seven
months they will begin their search. 15 As they go through the land
and one of them sees a human bone, he will set up a marker beside

[a]1 Or *Gog, prince of Rosh,* [b]11 Or *of* [c]11 That is, the Dead Sea
[d]11 *Hamon Gog* means *hordes of Gog.*

it until the gravediggers have buried it in the Valley of Hamon
Gog. 16 (Also a town called Hamonah[a] will be there.) And so they
will cleanse the land.'

17 "Son of man, this is what the Sovereign LORD says: Call out
to every kind of bird and all the wild animals: 'Assemble and come
together from all around to the sacrifice I am preparing for you,
the great sacrifice on the mountains of Israel. There you will eat
flesh and drink blood. 18 You will eat the flesh of mighty men and
drink the blood of the princes of the earth as if they were rams and
lambs, goats and bulls—all of them fattened animals from Bashan.
19 At the sacrifice I am preparing for you, you will eat fat till you
are glutted and drink blood till you are drunk. 20 At my table you
will eat your fill of horses and riders, mighty men and soldiers of
every kind,' declares the Sovereign LORD.

21 "I will display my glory among the nations, and all the
nations will see the punishment I inflict and the hand I lay upon
them. 22 From that day forward the house of Israel will know that I
am the LORD their God. 23 And the nations will know that the people of Israel went into exile for their sin, because they were
unfaithful to me. So I hid my face from them and handed them
over to their enemies, and they all fell by the sword. 24 I dealt with
them according to their uncleanness and their offenses, and I hid
my face from them.

25 "Therefore this is what the Sovereign LORD says: I will now
bring Jacob back from captivity[b] and will have compassion on all
the people of Israel, and I will be zealous for my holy name. 26 They
will forget their shame and all the unfaithfulness they showed
toward me when they lived in safety in their land with no one to

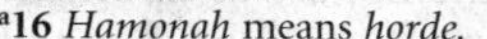

[a]16 *Hamonah* means *horde.* [b]25 Or *now restore the fortunes of Jacob*

39:15,16 *Valley of Hamon Gog:* See the note at 39:11.

39:17-20 *Call out . . . the great sacrifice . . . eat your fill:* The LORD will sacrifice Gog's army and make the dead bodies a feast for wild animals. See Rev 19:17, 18 and the note at 22:26.

39:21 *display my glory:* See the note at 1:27, 28.

39:23 *their sin . . . unfaithful to me . . . handed them over to their enemies:* For Israel's sins, see the notes at 2:3; 6:3-6; chapter 8; 22:2-4; 22:7-12. See also the note at 37:16-22 (Israel attacked).

39:25 *bring Jacob back:* The people of Israel (see the note at 28:25).

39:25 *my holy name:* See the notes at 20:40-44; 28:22; 36:22-24.

QUESTIONS ABOUT EZEKIEL 33:1 — 39:29

1. As a watchman for Israel, what message was Ezekiel supposed to give the people? (33:7-12)
2. What important news came to Ezekiel? (33:21). What happened to Ezekiel after he heard this news? (33:22)
3. In chapter 34, who are the following: the bad shepherds; the sheep; Israel's good shepherd; the strong sheep; the weak sheep? In 34:25-31, what promise is made? What made this such a hopeful message for the people of Israel?
4. What was the LORD's message to Edom (35), and why? What message was given to Israel's mountains? (36:1-15)
5. Explain why it was important that the land and the people of Israel be "cleansed" at the time they returned from exile (36:16-38). What does the modern phrase "clean up your act" mean? How might this modern saying apply to Ezekiel's message to his Israelite neighbors?
6. How was the vision of the dry bones coming to life again related to the people of Israel returning home from exile? (37:1-14)
7. Describe Gog and what will happen to him (38:1—39:20). Why was it considered so important to bury the dead bodies of Gog's army?

39:27 *brought them back from the nations:* See the notes at 34:11-13 and 36:22-24.

39:29 *pour out my Spirit:* See 36:26-28 and the note at 36:27.

40:1 *twenty-fifth year . . . beginning . . . fourteenth year after the fall:* Probably late March 573 B.C. See also the note on p. 1560 and 12:10-13.

40:2 *a very high mountain:* Probably meaning Mount Zion (see the note at 17:22-24). Ezekiel is carried to Jerusalem from Babylon (compare 8:1-3). See also Rev 21:10.

40:3 *man . . . like bronze:* The man is described as appearing "like" bronze to show that he is some kind of heavenly being, and not human. Bronze is made by melting and mixing copper and tin. See also Rev 11:1; 21:15.

40:4 *Son of man:* See the note at 4:1.

40:5,6 *wall . . . gate facing east:* The temple area was surrounded completely by a wall that was about ten feet high and ten feet thick. Steps led up to the east gate entrance to the temple area. In the passageway connecting the outer entrance and inner entrance to the temple area were six guard rooms (alcoves), three on each side and each ten feet square. See the temple diagram on p. 1633.

40:5—42:20 1 Kgs 6:1-38; 2 Chr 3:1-9.

make them afraid. [27]When I have brought them back from the
nations and have gathered them from the countries of their enemies, I will show myself holy through them in the sight of many
nations. [28]Then they will know that I am the LORD their God, for
though I sent them into exile among the nations, I will gather
them to their own land, not leaving any behind. [29]I will no longer
hide my face from them, for I will pour out my Spirit on the house
of Israel, declares the Sovereign LORD."

The LORD's Glory Returns to Judah and Jerusalem

Ezekiel's final vision provides a detailed description of the restored temple in Jerusalem (40–43). Ezekiel sees the LORD's glory return to the temple (43:1-5), and the LORD teaches him the rules that are to guide the work of Israel's priests and the life of God's people. The book concludes with a description of how the repopulated land of Israel would be divided among Israel's tribes (47, 48).

A NEW TEMPLE

Ezekiel is shown a vision of a new temple, which is to be kept sacred. Some details of the temple in Ezekiel's vision match the temple built by Solomon, but other details are new.

The New Temple Area

40 In the twenty-fifth year of our exile, at the beginning of the
year, on the tenth of the month, in the fourteenth year after the fall
of the city—on that very day the hand of the LORD was upon me
and he took me there. [2]In visions of God he took me to the land of
Israel and set me on a very high mountain, on whose south side
were some buildings that looked like a city. [3]He took me there, and
I saw a man whose appearance was like bronze; he was standing in
the gateway with a linen cord and a measuring rod in his hand.
[4]The man said to me, "Son of man, look with your eyes and hear
with your ears and pay attention to everything I am going to show
you, for that is why you have been brought here. Tell the house of
Israel everything you see."

The East Gate to the Outer Court

[5]I saw a wall completely surrounding the temple area. The
length of the measuring rod in the man's hand was six long cubits,
each of which was a cubit[a] and a handbreadth.[b] He measured the
wall; it was one measuring rod thick and one rod high.

[a]5 The common cubit was about 1 1/2 feet (about 0.5 meter). [b]5 That is, about 3 inches (about 8 centimeters)

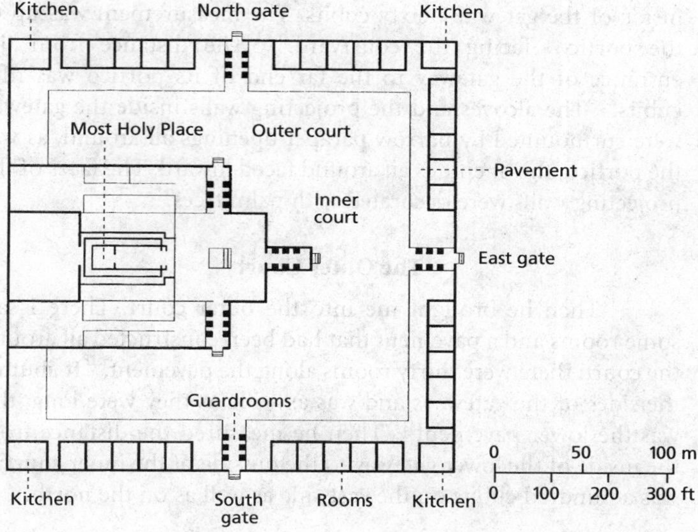

Ezekiel's Vision of the Restored Temple. In Ezekiel's plan for the restored temple the security of the Most Holy Place is the main element in the design. Ezekiel carefully keeps different areas of the temple separate from one another to ensure that there was no accidental entry into the Most Holy Place. As a priest, he was concerned with the difference between what is sacred and what is common.

6Then he went to the gate facing east. He climbed its steps
and measured the threshold of the gate; it was one rod deep.[a] 7The
alcoves for the guards were one rod long and one rod wide, and
the projecting walls between the alcoves were five cubits thick. And
the threshold of the gate next to the portico facing the temple was
one rod deep.

8Then he measured the portico of the gateway; 9it[b] was eight
cubits deep and its jambs were two cubits thick. The portico of the
gateway faced the temple.
10Inside the east gate were three alcoves on each side; the
three had the same measurements, and the faces of the projecting
walls on each side had the same measurements. 11Then he measured the width of the entrance to the gateway; it was ten cubits
and its length was thirteen cubits. 12In front of each alcove was a
wall one cubit high, and the alcoves were six cubits square. 13Then
he measured the gateway from the top of the rear wall of one
alcove to the top of the opposite one; the distance was twenty-five
cubits from one parapet opening to the opposite one. 14He
measured along the faces of the projecting walls all around the

[a]**6** Septuagint; Hebrew *deep, the first threshold, one rod deep* [b]**8,9** Many Hebrew manuscripts, Septuagint, Vulgate and Syriac; most Hebrew manuscripts *gateway facing the temple; it was one rod deep. 9Then he measured the portico of the gateway; it*

40:16 *decorated with palm trees:* The palm mentioned here is probably the date palm which could grow taller than sixty feet and live up to two hundred years. Palm tree carvings also were used to decorate Israel's first temple built by King Solomon (see 1 Kgs 6:29-35).

40:17 *outer court . . . thirty rooms:* The outer court area inside the outside walls was surrounded on three sides by a number of rooms. These rooms were probably used as storage rooms and as places where worshipers could meet and share sacrificial meals (see Neh 13:4-13; Jer 35:2-4).

40:19 *gateway to the outside of the inner court:* Three gated entrances lead to the inner court that surrounded the sanctuary. These gated entrances were located directly across from the three gated entrances that opened onto the outer court.

40:20-22 *the gate facing north:* The description is similar to the east gate entrance (see the note at 40:5,6).

40:24-27 *a gate facing south:* The description is similar to the east and north gate entrances.

40:28-37 *into the inner court . . . eight steps:* The gates leading into the inner court were similar in design and size to the gates leading into the outer court, though they had eight steps rather than seven leading into them.

40:38 *burnt offerings:* In these offerings, the whole animal was burned on the altar. A main purpose of such a sacrifice was to please the LORD with the smell of the sacrifices. See Lev 1:1-17.

inside of the gateway—sixty cubits. The measurement was up to
the portico[a] facing the courtyard.[b] 15The distance from the
entrance of the gateway to the far end of its portico was fifty
cubits. 16The alcoves and the projecting walls inside the gateway
were surmounted by narrow parapet openings all around, as was
the portico; the openings all around faced inward. The faces of the
projecting walls were decorated with palm trees.

The Outer Court

17Then he brought me into the outer court. There I saw
some rooms and a pavement that had been constructed all around
the court; there were thirty rooms along the pavement. 18It abutted
the sides of the gateways and was as wide as they were long; this
was the lower pavement. 19Then he measured the distance from
the inside of the lower gateway to the outside of the inner court; it
was a hundred cubits on the east side as well as on the north.

The North Gate

20Then he measured the length and width of the gate facing
north, leading into the outer court. 21Its alcoves—three on each
side—its projecting walls and its portico had the same measurements as those of the first gateway. It was fifty cubits long and
twenty-five cubits wide. 22Its openings, its portico and its palm tree
decorations had the same measurements as those of the gate facing east. Seven steps led up to it, with its portico opposite them.
23There was a gate to the inner court facing the north gate, just as
there was on the east. He measured from one gate to the opposite
one; it was a hundred cubits.

The South Gate

24Then he led me to the south side and I saw a gate facing
south. He measured its jambs and its portico, and they had the
same measurements as the others. 25The gateway and its portico
had narrow openings all around, like the openings of the others. It
was fifty cubits long and twenty-five cubits wide. 26Seven steps led
up to it, with its portico opposite them; it had palm tree decorations on the faces of the projecting walls on each side. 27The inner
court also had a gate facing south, and he measured from this gate
to the outer gate on the south side; it was a hundred cubits.

Gates to the Inner Court

28Then he brought me into the inner court through the
south gate, and he measured the south gate; it had the same meas-

[a]14 Septuagint; Hebrew *projecting wall* [b]14 The meaning of the Hebrew for this verse is uncertain.

urements as the others. [29]Its alcoves, its projecting walls and its
portico had the same measurements as the others. The gateway
and its portico had openings all around. It was fifty cubits long
and twenty-five cubits wide. [30](The porticoes of the gateways
around the inner court were twenty-five cubits wide and five
cubits deep.) [31]Its portico faced the outer court; palm trees decorated its jambs, and eight steps led up to it.

[32]Then he brought me to the inner court on the east side,
and he measured the gateway; it had the same measurements as
the others. [33]Its alcoves, its projecting walls and its portico had the
same measurements as the others. The gateway and its portico had
openings all around. It was fifty cubits long and twenty-five cubits
wide. [34]Its portico faced the outer court; palm trees decorated the
jambs on either side, and eight steps led up to it.

[35]Then he brought me to the north gate and measured it. It
had the same measurements as the others, [36]as did its alcoves, its
projecting walls and its portico, and it had openings all around. It
was fifty cubits long and twenty-five cubits wide. [37]Its portico[a]
faced the outer court; palm trees decorated the jambs on either
side, and eight steps led up to it.

The Rooms for Preparing Sacrifices

[38]A room with a doorway was by the portico in each of the
inner gateways, where the burnt offerings were washed. [39]In the
portico of the gateway were two tables on each side, on which the
burnt offerings, sin offerings and guilt offerings were slaughtered.
[40]By the outside wall of the portico of the gateway, near the steps
at the entrance to the north gateway were two tables, and on the
other side of the steps were two tables. [41]So there were four tables
on one side of the gateway and four on the other—eight tables in
all—on which the sacrifices were slaughtered. [42]There were also
four tables of dressed stone for the burnt offerings, each a cubit
and a half long, a cubit and a half wide and a cubit high. On them
were placed the utensils for slaughtering the burnt offerings and
the other sacrifices. [43]And double-pronged hooks, each a handbreadth long, were attached to the wall all around. The tables were
for the flesh of the offerings.

Rooms for the Priests

[44]Outside the inner gate, within the inner court, were two
rooms, one[b] at the side of the north gate and facing south, and
another at the side of the south[c] gate and facing north. [45]He said
to me, "The room facing south is for the priests who have charge
of the temple, [46]and the room facing north is for the priests who

---

[a]**37** Septuagint (see also verses 31 and 34); Hebrew *jambs* [b]**44** Septuagint; Hebrew *were rooms for singers, which were* [c]**44** Septuagint; Hebrew *east*

40:39 *portico ... two tables:* Tables probably made of stone where animals that were offered as sacrifices were prepared and killed by Israel's priests.

40:39 *sin offerings:* Sin offerings were given in order to purify one who had intentionally sinned by disobeying God's laws or who had accidentally done something God told them not to do. Different objects of sacrifice were used for different individuals and for the whole people. See Lev 4:1—5:13; 6:1-7; and the chart called "Sacrifices and Offerings," p. 219.

40:39 *guilt offerings:* This offering was like a sacrifice to ask forgiveness, except that the offender also paid a fine for the damages. This payment included the cost of fixing or replacing the broken object plus twenty percent extra. See Lev 5:14-19; 7:1-10.

40:42,43 *the utensils for slaughtering ... hooks:* These lay on stone shelves or hung on pegs next to the sacrifice tables.

40:44,45 *two rooms:* Two rooms for the priests who served in the temple area. They were located just to the west of the north inner gate and the south inner gate.

40:45,46 *priests ... sons of Zadok:* Only priests of the Levi tribe were allowed to serve in the temple area, preparing and making sacrifices. Zadok was a priest at the time of King David (2 Sam 20:25). He supported David during a time of civil war in Israel and then supported David's son Solomon when he became king (1 Kgs 1:8, 32-45). The Zadok family was in charge of Israel's priests from the time of Solomon till the time of the exile. Ezekiel's vision supported the Zadok family of priests continuing to serve in the temple. Other Levite families could do the work of cleaning and helping in the temple area, but could not offer sacrifices (44:10-14). See also the article called "Israel's Priests," p. 2344.

40:47 *the altar:* A large square altar in the inner court area where meat from the sacrificial animals was to be burned (43:13-17).

40:48,49 *portico of the temple:* The area at the top of the steps served as an entrance to the temple sanctuary.

41:1,2 *outer sanctuary:* An area similar to the Holy Place in the original tabernacle (Exod 25:1-9; 26:31-35). Compare also to the description of King Solomon's temple (1 Kgs 6:15-35).

41:3,4 *inner sanctuary . . . Most Holy Place:* This area, separated from the main room of the temple sanctuary, contained Israel's ark of the covenant and was considered God's dwelling place among the people (Exod 25:22). Notice that Ezekiel does not walk with the man back to measure the Most Holy Place. Only Israel's high priest was allowed to enter the Most Holy Place, and only on the Day of Atonement (see Lev 16:1-28; Heb 9:7).

41:5-7 *side rooms:* Against the outer walls of the temple were ninety storage rooms (compare to 1 Kgs 6:5-10). It is unclear what these rooms were used for, but they may have been for storing the grain and oil given to the priests by the people and used for offerings.

have charge of the altar. These are the sons of Zadok, who are the only Levites who may draw near to the LORD to minister before him."

47 Then he measured the court: It was square—a hundred cubits long and a hundred cubits wide. And the altar was in front of the temple.

The Temple

48 He brought me to the portico of the temple and measured the jambs of the portico; they were five cubits wide on either side. The width of the entrance was fourteen cubits and its projecting walls were[a] three cubits wide on either side. 49 The portico was twenty cubits wide, and twelve[b] cubits from front to back. It was reached by a flight of stairs,[c] and there were pillars on each side of the jambs.

41 Then the man brought me to the outer sanctuary and measured the jambs; the width of the jambs was six cubits[d] on each side.[e] 2 The entrance was ten cubits wide, and the projecting walls on each side of it were five cubits wide. He also measured the outer sanctuary; it was forty cubits long and twenty cubits wide.

3 Then he went into the inner sanctuary and measured the jambs of the entrance; each was two cubits wide. The entrance was six cubits wide, and the projecting walls on each side of it were seven cubits wide. 4 And he measured the length of the inner sanctuary; it was twenty cubits, and its width was twenty cubits across the end of the outer sanctuary. He said to me, "This is the Most Holy Place."

5 Then he measured the wall of the temple; it was six cubits thick, and each side room around the temple was four cubits wide. 6 The side rooms were on three levels, one above another, thirty on each level. There were ledges all around the wall of the temple to serve as supports for the side rooms, so that the supports were not inserted into the wall of the temple. 7 The side rooms all around the temple were wider at each successive level. The structure surrounding the temple was built in ascending stages, so that the rooms widened as one went upward. A stairway went up from the lowest floor to the top floor through the middle floor.

8 I saw that the temple had a raised base all around it, forming the foundation of the side rooms. It was the length of the rod, six long cubits. 9 The outer wall of the side rooms was five cubits thick. The open area between the side rooms of the temple 10 and the ⌞priests'⌟ rooms was twenty cubits wide all around the temple. 11 There were entrances to the side rooms from the open area, one

[a]48 Septuagint; Hebrew *entrance was* [b]49 Septuagint; Hebrew *eleven* [c]49 Hebrew; Septuagint *Ten steps led up to it* [d]1 The common cubit was about 1 1/2 feet (about 0.5 meter). [e]1 One Hebrew manuscript and Septuagint; most Hebrew manuscripts *side, the width of the tent*

on the north and another on the south; and the base adjoining the open area was five cubits wide all around.

12 The building facing the temple courtyard on the west side was seventy cubits wide. The wall of the building was five cubits thick all around, and its length was ninety cubits.

13 Then he measured the temple; it was a hundred cubits long, and the temple courtyard and the building with its walls were also a hundred cubits long. 14 The width of the temple courtyard on the east, including the front of the temple, was a hundred cubits.

15 Then he measured the length of the building facing the courtyard at the rear of the temple, including its galleries on each side; it was a hundred cubits.

The outer sanctuary, the inner sanctuary and the portico facing the court, 16 as well as the thresholds and the narrow windows and galleries around the three of them—everything beyond and including the threshold was covered with wood. The floor, the wall up to the windows, and the windows were covered. 17 In the space above the outside of the entrance to the inner sanctuary and on the walls at regular intervals all around the inner and outer sanctuary 18 were carved cherubim and palm trees. Palm trees alternated with cherubim. Each cherub had two faces: 19 the face of a man toward the palm tree on one side and the face of a lion toward the palm tree on the other. They were carved all around the whole temple. 20 From the floor to the area above the entrance, cherubim and palm trees were carved on the wall of the outer sanctuary.

21 The outer sanctuary had a rectangular doorframe, and the one at the front of the Most Holy Place was similar. 22 There was a wooden altar three cubits high and two cubits square[a]; its corners, its base[b] and its sides were of wood. The man said to me, "This is the table that is before the LORD." 23 Both the outer sanctuary and the Most Holy Place had double doors. 24 Each door had two leaves—two hinged leaves for each door. 25 And on the doors of the outer sanctuary were carved cherubim and palm trees like those carved on the walls, and there was a wooden overhang on the front of the portico. 26 On the sidewalls of the portico were narrow windows with palm trees carved on each side. The side rooms of the temple also had overhangs.

Rooms for the Priests

42 Then the man led me northward into the outer court and brought me to the rooms opposite the temple courtyard and opposite the outer wall on the north side. 2 The building whose door faced north was a hundred cubits[c] long and fifty cubits wide.

[a]22 Septuagint; Hebrew *long* [b]22 Septuagint; Hebrew *length* [c]2 The common cubit was about 1 1/2 feet (about 0.5 meter).

41:12-15 *building . . . west side . . . galleries:* The foundation of the west building was the same size as that of the temple, but what this west building was for is unclear. It could have been a dormitory for priests who were on duty or a stable for animals that were to be sacrificed.

41:16-20 *threshold was covered with wood . . . cherubim . . . palm trees:* This is like Solomon's temple, which had a pine floor and cedar wood planks covering the inside walls (1 Kgs 6:15-36). The cherubim (winged creatures) carved into the walls were probably intended to be heavenly guards. These cherubim only had two faces, unlike the creatures in Ezekiel's earlier vision, which had four faces (see 1:5-9 and note). See also the note at 40:16 (palm trees).

41:22 *wooden altar:* Located at the back end of the main room of the temple and just in front of the entrance to the Most Holy Place. Though the altar is described here as a reminder of the LORD's presence in the temple, it probably was meant to serve as a table for the bread of the Presence placed in the temple each week (see Exod 25:23-30; Lev 24:5-9; 1 Kgs 7:48).

41:25 *doors . . . carved:* See the note at 41:16-20.

42:1-10 *rooms opposite the temple courtyard . . . north side . . . south side:* See the note at 41:12-15. Because of the difficult Hebrew text, the location of these rooms is not completely clear, but they probably were located on each side of the west building and could only be entered from the east, or the inner court, where only priests could come and go. This was so the holy offerings and sacred priestly clothes would not be in an area where other people (non-priests) could touch them and make them ritually unclean (42:14).

42:3 *the section opposite the pavement of the outer court:* See 41:10 and 40:17.

42:13 *priests . . . eat the most holy offerings:* The priests who served in the temple were allowed to eat a portion of the grain and meat offerings sacrificed to the LORD (see Exod 29:22-34; Lev 6:14-18, 29; 7:5-10). See also the notes at 40:38 and 40:39.

42:14 *the garments . . . are holy:* The priests and the high priests wore special clothes that were to be worn while they were performing their sacred duties. To keep these clothes from becoming ritually unclean, they could not be worn outside the temple area, where they could come into contact with people or "unclean" objects. For a description of this sacred clothing, see Exodus 28 and the mini-article called "Israel's Priests," p. 2344.

42:20 *wall . . . separate the holy from the common:* All the objects and activities inside the wall separating the inner court, temple, and sacred rooms from the outer court were to remain sacred, or holy. Sacred or holy things were not to come into contact with unholy (common) things because the sacred things could become ritually unclean. See also the mini-article called "Purity (Clean and Unclean)," p. 2125.

43:1 *the gate facing east:* See the note at 40:5,6.

43:2-4 *the glory of the God of Israel . . . gate facing east:* See the note at 1:27, 28. The east gate is the same gate the LORD's glory went through when it left Jerusalem (see also 10:3, 4, 18, 19; 11:22, 23). The glory left because Israel's priests had brought unclean things into the temple (chapter 8). The return of the LORD's glory meant that the land and the temple were ritually clean, and they would stay that way, if Israel's priests and people obeyed God's Law.

[3]Both in the section twenty cubits from the inner court and in the section opposite the pavement of the outer court, gallery faced gallery at the three levels. [4]In front of the rooms was an inner passageway ten cubits wide and a hundred cubits[a] long. Their doors were on the north. [5]Now the upper rooms were narrower, for the galleries took more space from them than from the rooms on the lower and middle floors of the building. [6]The rooms on the third floor had no pillars, as the courts had; so they were smaller in floor space than those on the lower and middle floors. [7]There was an outer wall parallel to the rooms and the outer court; it extended in front of the rooms for fifty cubits. [8]While the row of rooms on the side next to the outer court was fifty cubits long, the row on the side nearest the sanctuary was a hundred cubits long. [9]The lower rooms had an entrance on the east side as one enters them from the outer court.

[10]On the south side[b] along the length of the wall of the outer court, adjoining the temple courtyard and opposite the outer wall, were rooms [11]with a passageway in front of them. These were like the rooms on the north; they had the same length and width, with similar exits and dimensions. Similar to the doorways on the north [12]were the doorways of the rooms on the south. There was a doorway at the beginning of the passageway that was parallel to the corresponding wall extending eastward, by which one enters the rooms.

[13]Then he said to me, "The north and south rooms facing the temple courtyard are the priests' rooms, where the priests who approach the LORD will eat the most holy offerings. There they will put the most holy offerings—the grain offerings, the sin offerings and the guilt offerings—for the place is holy. [14]Once the priests enter the holy precincts, they are not to go into the outer court until they leave behind the garments in which they minister, for these are holy. They are to put on other clothes before they go near the places that are for the people."

[15]When he had finished measuring what was inside the temple area, he led me out by the east gate and measured the area all around: [16]He measured the east side with the measuring rod; it was five hundred cubits.[c] [17]He measured the north side; it was five hundred cubits[d] by the measuring rod. [18]He measured the south side; it was five hundred cubits by the measuring rod. [19]Then he turned to the west side and measured; it was five hundred cubits by the measuring rod. [20]So he measured the area on all four sides. It had a wall around it, five hundred cubits long and five hundred cubits wide, to separate the holy from the common.

---

[a]**4** Septuagint and Syriac; Hebrew *and one cubit* [b]**10** Septuagint; Hebrew *Eastward* [c]**16** See Septuagint of verse 17; Hebrew *rods;* also in verses 18 and 19. [d]**17** Septuagint; Hebrew *rods*

The Glory Returns to the Temple

43 Then the man brought me to the gate facing east, [2]and I saw
the glory of the God of Israel coming from the east. His voice was
like the roar of rushing waters, and the land was radiant with his
glory. [3]The vision I saw was like the vision I had seen when he[a]
came to destroy the city and like the visions I had seen by the
Kebar River, and I fell facedown. [4]The glory of the LORD entered
the temple through the gate facing east. [5]Then the Spirit lifted me
up and brought me into the inner court, and the glory of the LORD
filled the temple.

[6]While the man was standing beside me, I heard someone
speaking to me from inside the temple. [7]He said: "Son of man, this
is the place of my throne and the place for the soles of my feet.
This is where I will live among the Israelites forever. The house of
Israel will never again defile my holy name—neither they nor their
kings—by their prostitution[b] and the lifeless idols[c] of their kings at
their high places. [8]When they placed their threshold next to my
threshold and their doorposts beside my doorposts, with only a
wall between me and them, they defiled my holy name by their
detestable practices. So I destroyed them in my anger. [9]Now let
them put away from me their prostitution and the lifeless idols of
their kings, and I will live among them forever.

[10]"Son of man, describe the temple to the people of Israel,
that they may be ashamed of their sins. Let them consider the
plan, [11]and if they are ashamed of all they have done, make known
to them the design of the temple—its arrangement, its exits and
entrances—its whole design and all its regulations[d] and laws. Write
these down before them so that they may be faithful to its design
and follow all its regulations.

[12]"This is the law of the temple: All the surrounding area on
top of the mountain will be most holy. Such is the law of the
temple.

The Altar

[13]"These are the measurements of the altar in long cubits,
that cubit being a cubit[e] and a handbreadth[f]: Its gutter is a cubit
deep and a cubit wide, with a rim of one span[g] around the edge.
And this is the height of the altar: [14]From the gutter on the ground
up to the lower ledge it is two cubits high and a cubit wide, and
from the smaller ledge up to the larger ledge it is four cubits high
and a cubit wide. [15]The altar hearth is four cubits high, and four

[a]3 Some Hebrew manuscripts and Vulgate; most Hebrew manuscripts *I*
[b]7 Or *their spiritual adultery*; also in verse 9 [c]7 Or *the corpses*; also in verse 9 [d]11 Some Hebrew manuscripts and Septuagint; most Hebrew manuscripts *regulations and its whole design* [e]13 The common cubit was about 1 1/2 feet (about 0.5 meter). [f]13 That is, about 3 inches (about 8 centimeters) [g]13 That is, about 9 inches (about 22 centimeters)

43:3 *like the vision I had seen:* See the visions in Ezek 1–3; 8–11.

43:5 *the Spirit:* See the note at 2:2.

43:5 *the glory of the LORD filled the temple:* The LORD's glory had earlier filled the tabernacle in the desert (Exod 40:34-38) and Solomon's temple in Jerusalem (1 Kgs 8:10-13).

43:6 *the man:* See the note at 40:3.

43:7 *this is the place of my throne:* See the note on p. 1560. See also Jer 3:16, 17; Rev 21:1-4.

43:7-9 *defile my holy name . . . lifeless idols of their kings:* See the notes at 6:3-6 and chapter 8. The "idols of their kings" may refer to actual burial sites or to monuments set up in the temple area. Some of these kings did evil things, including encouraging the worship of foreign gods. In the new temple and in the restored community of God's people, there was to be no trace of these evil kings or any kind of idols.

43:10-12 *ashamed of their sins . . . design of the temple . . . most holy:* For Israel's sins against the LORD, see the note at 2:3. If the people admit their sins, then Ezekiel can reveal the plans for the new temple and any new rules for worship.

43:13-17 *altar:* Probably refers to the altar located in the inner court in front of the temple (40:42,43, 47). Steps were needed to reach the top level where sacrifices were burned. Horns have been discovered attached to the top level of other ancient altars. A person accused of a crime was safe from punishment until proven guilty, as long as he held onto the horns of an altar (see Exod 21:12-14).

horns project upward from the hearth. [16]The altar hearth is square,
twelve cubits long and twelve cubits wide. [17]The upper ledge also is
square, fourteen cubits long and fourteen cubits wide, with a rim
of half a cubit and a gutter of a cubit all around. The steps of the
altar face east."

[18]Then he said to me, "Son of man, this is what the
Sovereign LORD says: These will be the regulations for sacrificing
burnt offerings and sprinkling blood upon the altar when it is
built: [19]You are to give a young bull as a sin offering to the priests,
who are Levites, of the family of Zadok, who come near to minister before me, declares the Sovereign LORD. [20]You are to take some
of its blood and put it on the four horns of the altar and on the
four corners of the upper ledge and all around the rim, and so
purify the altar and make atonement for it. [21]You are to take the
bull for the sin offering and burn it in the designated part of the
temple area outside the sanctuary.

[22]"On the second day you are to offer a male goat without
defect for a sin offering, and the altar is to be purified as it was
purified with the bull. [23]When you have finished purifying it, you
are to offer a young bull and a ram from the flock, both without
defect. [24]You are to offer them before the LORD, and the priests are
to sprinkle salt on them and sacrifice them as a burnt offering to
the LORD.

[25]"For seven days you are to provide a male goat daily for a
sin offering; you are also to provide a young bull and a ram from
the flock, both without defect. [26]For seven days they are to make
atonement for the altar and cleanse it; thus they will dedicate it.
[27]At the end of these days, from the eighth day on, the priests are
to present your burnt offerings and fellowship offerings[a] on the
altar. Then I will accept you, declares the Sovereign LORD."

LAWS AND RULES FOR GOD'S PEOPLE

The LORD instructs Ezekiel about who can and can't be in the temple area and provides rules for those who serve in the temple. Other rules describe the LORD's sacred land and land that will belong to the prince. Finally, the LORD gives laws describing how Israel's prince and people are to celebrate their religious festivals.

The Prince, the Levites, the Priests

44 Then the man brought me back to the outer gate of the sanctuary, the one facing east, and it was shut. [2]The LORD said to me,
"This gate is to remain shut. It must not be opened; no one may
enter through it. It is to remain shut because the LORD, the God of
Israel, has entered through it. [3]The prince himself is the only one
who may sit inside the gateway to eat in the presence of the LORD.

[a]27 Traditionally *peace offerings*

43:18 *regulations for . . . burnt offerings . . . sprinkling blood:* See the notes at 36:33-38 and 40:38, 39. Blood sprinkled on the altar or on the people had cleansing power and showed that something or someone was dedicated to God (43:20,22; see also Exod 29:10-21). See also the mini-article called "Blood," p. 180.

43:19 *sin offering:* See the note at 40:39 (sin offerings).

43:19 *priests . . . Levites . . . family of Zadok:* See the note at 40:45, 46.

43:20 *blood . . . put it on . . . of the altar:* See the note at 43:18.

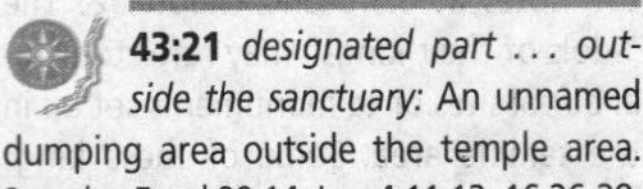

43:21 *designated part . . . outside the sanctuary:* An unnamed dumping area outside the temple area. See also Exod 29:14; Lev 4:11,12; 16:26-28.

43:24 *sprinkle salt . . . burnt offering:* Salt was normally used with grain or vegetable offerings (see Lev 2:13), but here it is included in the animal sacrifices. See the note at 40:38 (burnt offerings).

43:27 *burnt offerings and fellowship offerings:* See the note at 40:38 (burnt offerings). For more on the fellowship offering, see Leviticus 3.

44:1 *the man:* See the note at 40:3.

44:1,2 *outer gate . . . the one facing east . . . remain shut:* See the notes at 40:5,6 and 40:17 and the diagram on p. 1633. The east gate, where the LORD reentered the temple area (43:1,2), was closed forever as a sign that the LORD had returned to stay.

43:18-27 Exod 29:35-37.

He is to enter by way of the portico of the gateway and go out the same way."

[4]Then the man brought me by way of the north gate to the front of the temple. I looked and saw the glory of the LORD filling the temple of the LORD, and I fell facedown.

[5]The LORD said to me, "Son of man, look carefully, listen closely and give attention to everything I tell you concerning all the regulations regarding the temple of the LORD. Give attention to the entrance of the temple and all the exits of the sanctuary.
[6]Say to the rebellious house of Israel, 'This is what the Sovereign LORD says: Enough of your detestable practices, O house of Israel!
[7]In addition to all your other detestable practices, you brought foreigners uncircumcised in heart and flesh into my sanctuary, desecrating my temple while you offered me food, fat and blood, and
you broke my covenant. [8]Instead of carrying out your duty in regard to my holy things, you put others in charge of my sanctu-
ary. [9]This is what the Sovereign LORD says: No foreigner uncircumcised in heart and flesh is to enter my sanctuary, not even the foreigners who live among the Israelites.

[10]" 'The Levites who went far from me when Israel went astray and who wandered from me after their idols must bear the
consequences of their sin. [11]They may serve in my sanctuary, having charge of the gates of the temple and serving in it; they may slaughter the burnt offerings and sacrifices for the people and
stand before the people and serve them. [12]But because they served them in the presence of their idols and made the house of Israel fall into sin, therefore I have sworn with uplifted hand that they must bear the consequences of their sin, declares the Sovereign
LORD. [13]They are not to come near to serve me as priests or come near any of my holy things or my most holy offerings; they must
bear the shame of their detestable practices. [14]Yet I will put them in charge of the duties of the temple and all the work that is to be done in it.

[15]" 'But the priests, who are Levites and descendants of Zadok and who faithfully carried out the duties of my sanctuary when the Israelites went astray from me, are to come near to minister before me; they are to stand before me to offer sacrifices of
fat and blood, declares the Sovereign LORD. [16]They alone are to enter my sanctuary; they alone are to come near my table to minister before me and perform my service.

[17]" 'When they enter the gates of the inner court, they are to wear linen clothes; they must not wear any woolen garment while ministering at the gates of the inner court or inside the temple.
[18]They are to wear linen turbans on their heads and linen undergarments around their waists. They must not wear anything that
makes them perspire. [19]When they go out into the outer court where the people are, they are to take off the clothes they have been ministering in and are to leave them in the sacred rooms, and

44:3 *prince . . . eat in the presence of the LORD:* The "prince" in the new community of the LORD's people is in charge of civil matters, but he is not a priest and does not do the work of a priest. The prince would probably eat a portion of the fellowship offering.

44:4 *the glory of the LORD:* See the note at 1:27, 28.

44:7-9 *brought foreigners . . . uncircumcised in heart and flesh:* In the past, Israel's priests had apparently allowed foreigners (non-Jews) to help in the temple area (44:8). This increased the chance that the temple and sacrifices to the LORD might be defiled by those who did not fully understand Israel's laws, especially those laws regarding ritual purity. (See also Deut 23:2; Ezra 9,10; Neh 13:1-3,23-29).

44:10-14 *Levites . . . duties of the temple:* God chose the men of one Levite family, the descendants of Aaron, to be Israel's priests. However, in Ezekiel's vision of the new temple, only the Levites from the family of Zadok could offer sacrifices (see the note at 40:45,46). See also the mini-article called "Israel's Priests," p. 2344.

44:15 *descendants of Zadok:* See the note at 40:45,46.

44:17-19 *linen clothes . . . other clothes:* Linen was light cloth made from the fibers of the flax plant. Common people were forbidden to touch sacred things, for fear they might be harmed. See also the note at 42:14.

44:17-19 Exod 28:39-43; Lev 16:4,23,24.

44:20-22 *not shave their heads . . . marry only virgins:* These laws emphasized how Israel's priests were holy, that is, set apart from the rest of the people. See also Lev 21:5; 10:9; 21:7, 13, 14.

44:25-27 *defile himself . . . sin offering:* A dead body was considered "unclean," and could make those who touched it unclean. If a priest touched a body, he would become ritually unclean. He could not do his temple duties until he had gone through a seven-day cleansing ritual to be acceptable to the LORD again. See Lev 21:1-4.

44:28-30 *priests . . . no possession . . . special gifts:* The priests were from the Levi tribe, which did not receive a share of the land of Canaan (Num 18:20; Deut 10:9), but they were given towns and nearby pasture lands (see Num 35:1-8; Josh 21:1-42). The priests and their families received food gifts from the people and were allowed to eat portions of certain sacrifices (see Num 18:8-19). See also the notes at 40:38 and 40:39.

44:29 *devoted to the LORD:* This translates a Hebrew word that describes property and things that were taken from humans and given to God. In the early history of Israel, such things had to be destroyed (see Josh 6:15-19). Now the priests were to receive these things along with a part of other offerings. See also the mini-article called "Holy War" (The LORD's Battles), p. 306.

45:1-5 *allot the land . . . inheritance . . . Levites:* The tribes of Israel were named for the sons of Jacob (also known as "Israel," Gen 32:27, 28). The new allotment of the land for the exiles who have returned to the land was to include a large sacred area. One half of the area included the temple and space for the priests' houses, while the other half was reserved for the Levite towns (see Num 35:1-8; Josh 21:1-42).

44:31 Lev 22:8.

put on other clothes, so that they do not consecrate the people by means of their garments.

20“ ‘They must not shave their heads or let their hair grow long, but they are to keep the hair of their heads trimmed. 21No priest is to drink wine when he enters the inner court. 22They must not marry widows or divorced women; they may marry only virgins of Israelite descent or widows of priests. 23They are to teach my people the difference between the holy and the common and show them how to distinguish between the unclean and the clean.

24“ ‘In any dispute, the priests are to serve as judges and decide it according to my ordinances. They are to keep my laws and my decrees for all my appointed feasts, and they are to keep my Sabbaths holy.

25“ ‘A priest must not defile himself by going near a dead person; however, if the dead person was his father or mother, son or daughter, brother or unmarried sister, then he may defile himself. 26After he is cleansed, he must wait seven days. 27On the day he goes into the inner court of the sanctuary to minister in the sanctuary, he is to offer a sin offering for himself, declares the Sovereign LORD.

28“ ‘I am to be the only inheritance the priests have. You are to give them no possession in Israel; I will be their possession. 29They will eat the grain offerings, the sin offerings and the guilt offerings; and everything in Israel devoted[a] to the LORD will belong to them. 30The best of all the firstfruits and of all your special gifts will belong to the priests. You are to give them the first portion of your ground meal so that a blessing may rest on your household. 31The priests must not eat anything, bird or animal, found dead or torn by wild animals.

Division of the Land

45 “ ‘When you allot the land as an inheritance, you are to present to the LORD a portion of the land as a sacred district, 25,000 cubits long and 20,000[b] cubits wide; the entire area will be holy. 2Of this, a section 500 cubits square is to be for the sanctuary, with 50 cubits around it for open land. 3In the sacred district, measure off a section 25,000 cubits[c] long and 10,000 cubits[d] wide. In it will be the sanctuary, the Most Holy Place. 4It will be the sacred portion of the land for the priests, who minister in the sanctuary and who draw near to minister before the LORD. It will be a place for their houses as well as a holy place for the sanctuary. 5An area 25,000 cubits long and 10,000 cubits wide will belong to the

[a]**29** The Hebrew term refers to the irrevocable giving over of things or persons to the LORD. [b]**1** Septuagint (see also verses 3 and 5 and 48:9); Hebrew *10,000* [c]**3** That is, about 7 miles (about 12 kilometers) [d]**3** That is, about 3 miles (about 5 kilometers)

Levites, who serve in the temple, as their possession for towns to
live in.[a]
6“ ‘You are to give the city as its property an area 5,000 cubits
wide and 25,000 cubits long, adjoining the sacred portion; it will
belong to the whole house of Israel.
7“ ‘The prince will have the land bordering each side of the
area formed by the sacred district and the property of the city. It
will extend westward from the west side and eastward from the
east side, running lengthwise from the western to the eastern border parallel to one of the tribal portions. 8This land will be his possession in Israel. And my princes will no longer oppress my people
but will allow the house of Israel to possess the land according to
their tribes.
9“ ‘This is what the Sovereign LORD says: You have gone far
enough, O princes of Israel! Give up your violence and oppression
and do what is just and right. Stop dispossessing my people,
declares the Sovereign LORD. 10You are to use accurate scales, an
accurate ephah[b] and an accurate bath.[c] 11The ephah and the bath
are to be the same size, the bath containing a tenth of a homer[d] and
the ephah a tenth of a homer; the homer is to be the standard measure for both. 12The shekel[e] is to consist of twenty gerahs. Twenty
shekels plus twenty-five shekels plus fifteen shekels equal one mina.[f]

Offerings and Holy Days

13“ ‘This is the special gift you are to offer: a sixth of an
ephah from each homer of wheat and a sixth of an ephah from
each homer of barley. 14The prescribed portion of oil, measured by
the bath, is a tenth of a bath from each cor (which consists of ten
baths or one homer, for ten baths are equivalent to a homer).
15Also one sheep is to be taken from every flock of two hundred
from the well-watered pastures of Israel. These will be used for the
grain offerings, burnt offerings and fellowship offerings[g] to make
atonement for the people, declares the Sovereign LORD. 16All the
people of the land will participate in this special gift for the use of
the prince in Israel. 17It will be the duty of the prince to provide
the burnt offerings, grain offerings and drink offerings at the festivals, the New Moons and the Sabbaths—at all the appointed
feasts of the house of Israel. He will provide the sin offerings, grain
offerings, burnt offerings and fellowship offerings to make atonement for the house of Israel.
18“ ‘This is what the Sovereign LORD says: In the first month
on the first day you are to take a young bull without defect and

[a]5 Septuagint; Hebrew *temple; they will have as their possession 20 rooms*
[b]10 An ephah was a dry measure. [c]10 A bath was a liquid measure. [d]11 A homer was a dry measure. [e]12 A shekel weighed about 2/5 ounce (about 11.5 grams). [f]12 That is, 60 shekels; the common mina was 50 shekels.
[g]15 Traditionally *peace offerings*; also in verse 17

45:6 *the city . . . sacred portion:* In Ezekiel's vision of the new land, the temple would no longer be in Jerusalem, which would be sacred land belonging to all the people of Israel and not just the tribe of Judah, which had claimed it in the past.

45:7,8 *land . . . princes:* Israel's ruler received a large share of the land, perhaps so he did not become greedy or tax the people in order to pay his share of the temple offerings (see 45:17).

45:10-12 *use accurate scales . . . mina:* Israel's leaders were not to treat the people unfairly, as had been done in the past (see 1 Kgs 21:1-19; Isa 5:8; and the notes at 22:25; 34:20). See the chart on p. 1644 for a list of standard measures and their modern equivalents.

45:15 *offerings:* See the notes at 40:38 and 40:39.

45:17 *New Moons . . . appointed feasts:* Special sacrifices were offered on the first day of a new month, known as the New Moon festival (Num 28:11-15; Ps 81:3). See also the note at 20:12. For more about Israel's sacrifices and religious festivals, see LEVITICUS and the article called "People of the Law: The Religion of Israel," p. 939.

45:18 *first month:* Abib (also called Nisan), the first month of the Hebrew calendar, from about mid-March to mid-April.

45:18-20 *purify the sanctuary . . . do the same:* The ceremony to purify the temple described here appears to be a new rule, similar to but not exactly the same as the yearly Day of Atonement on the tenth day of the seventh month (Lev 16:29-34). See also Lev 16:1-28; 23:26-32.

45:10 Lev 19:35,36.

WEIGHTS AND MEASURES IN ANCIENT ISRAEL

KIND OF MEASURE	FRACTIONS	STANDARD	MULTIPLES
Dry (grain)	omer 1/10 ephah	ephah (about 3/5 bushel)	homer = 10 ephahs (about 6 bushels)
Liquid (olive oil)	hin 1/6 bath	bath (about 6 gallons)	cor = 10 baths (about 60 gallons)
Weight	gerah = 1/20 shekel	shekel (about 2/5 ounce)	mina = 50 shekels (about 20 ounces)

45:21 *observe the Passover . . . eat bread made without yeast:* The Passover festival was a celebration of how God acted to save the Israelite people in Egypt when the angel of death "passed over" them (Exod 12:1-20, 23, 27). The Feast of Unleavened Bread began the day after Passover and lasted seven days (see Num 28:16–25). The bread made without yeast was eaten as a reminder of how quickly the people had to leave Egypt. They did not have time to let the dough for their bread rise, so they made bread dough without yeast, the tiny yellowish fungus that causes dough to rise when mixed with water and flour. See also the mini-article called "Passover and the Feast of Unleavened Bread," p. 2030.

45:23 *seven:* The number "seven" symbolized completeness or perfection.

45:23 *burnt offering . . . sin offering:* See the notes at 40:38 and 40:39.

45:25 *the seven days of the Feast . . . seventh month:* The Feast of Tabernacles took place at the end of the fall harvest (Deut 16:13-17). In addition to giving thanks to God for the fall harvest, the people were to build and live in shelters made of tree branches to remember the temporary shelters they lived in after they left Egypt and wandered in the desert (Lev 23:33-36,42, 43). See also Num 29:12-38; Neh 8. The seventh month is Tishri (also called Ethanim), the seventh month of the Hebrew calendar, from about mid-September to mid-October.

purify the sanctuary. 19 The priest is to take some of the blood of
the sin offering and put it on the doorposts of the temple, on the
four corners of the upper ledge of the altar and on the gateposts of
the inner court. 20 You are to do the same on the seventh day of the
month for anyone who sins unintentionally or through ignorance;
so you are to make atonement for the temple.

21 " 'In the first month on the fourteenth day you are to
observe the Passover, a feast lasting seven days, during which you
shall eat bread made without yeast. 22 On that day the prince is to
provide a bull as a sin offering for himself and for all the people of
the land. 23 Every day during the seven days of the Feast he is to
provide seven bulls and seven rams without defect as a burnt
offering to the LORD, and a male goat for a sin offering. 24 He is to
provide as a grain offering an ephah for each bull and an ephah
for each ram, along with a hin[a] of oil for each ephah.

25 " 'During the seven days of the Feast, which begins in the
seventh month on the fifteenth day, he is to make the same provision for sin offerings, burnt offerings, grain offerings and oil.

46 " 'This is what the Sovereign LORD says: The gate of the inner
court facing east is to be shut on the six working days, but on the
Sabbath day and on the day of the New Moon it is to be opened.
2 The prince is to enter from the outside through the portico of the
gateway and stand by the gatepost. The priests are to sacrifice his
burnt offering and his fellowship offerings.[b] He is to worship at the
threshold of the gateway and then go out, but the gate will not be
shut until evening. 3 On the Sabbaths and New Moons the people
of the land are to worship in the presence of the LORD at the
entrance to that gateway. 4 The burnt offering the prince brings to
the LORD on the Sabbath day is to be six male lambs and a ram, all
without defect. 5 The grain offering given with the ram is to be an
ephah,[c] and the grain offering with the lambs is to be as much as
he pleases, along with a hin[a] of oil for each ephah. 6 On the day of

[a]24,5 That is, probably about 4 quarts (about 4 liters) [b]2 Traditionally *peace offerings*; also in verse 12 [c]5 That is, probably about 3/5 bushel (about 22 liters)

Blessing said for the appearance of the New Moon, oil painting, unknown artist, around 1911. The last section of EZEKIEL is devoted to the restoration of proper worship after the return from the Babylonian exile. This section of the book describes the responsibilities of the people and their leaders on festival and feast days, like the New Moon festival. On the first day of each lunar month, special sacrifices were to be made and prayers offered to the LORD. (See 46: 1-14.)

the New Moon he is to offer a young bull, six lambs and a ram, all
without defect. 7He is to provide as a grain offering one ephah
with the bull, one ephah with the ram, and with the lambs as
much as he wants to give, along with a hin of oil with each ephah.
8When the prince enters, he is to go in through the portico of the
gateway, and he is to come out the same way.
9" 'When the people of the land come before the LORD at the
appointed feasts, whoever enters by the north gate to worship is to
go out the south gate; and whoever enters by the south gate is to
go out the north gate. No one is to return through the gate by
which he entered, but each is to go out the opposite gate. 10The
prince is to be among them, going in when they go in and going
out when they go out.
11" 'At the festivals and the appointed feasts, the grain offering is to be an ephah with a bull, an ephah with a ram, and with
the lambs as much as one pleases, along with a hin of oil for each
ephah. 12When the prince provides a freewill offering to the
LORD—whether a burnt offering or fellowship offerings—the gate
facing east is to be opened for him. He shall offer his burnt offering or his fellowship offerings as he does on the Sabbath day. Then
he shall go out, and after he has gone out, the gate will be shut.
13" 'Every day you are to provide a year-old lamb without
defect for a burnt offering to the LORD; morning by morning you
shall provide it. 14You are also to provide with it morning by
morning a grain offering, consisting of a sixth of an ephah with a
third of a hin of oil to moisten the flour. The presenting of this

46:1-3 *Sabbath . . . The prince . . . gateway:* The east gate's outer entrance was closed permanently (see 44:1, 2), but the entrance leading to the outer court was to be opened every Sabbath. Because the gateway was raised, the ruler could look west and see the sacrifice performed by the priests on the altar in the inner court in front of the temple. The people could be in the outer court area, but they were not allowed to stand in the raised east gate entrance. See the notes at 40:38 and 40:39.

46:6-8 *day of the New Moon . . . portico of the gateway:* See the note at 45:17. The ruler followed the same procedure as on the Sabbath.

46:9 *go out the opposite gate:* The people could enter the outer court area by the north or south gates. But they had to leave by the opposite gate, probably to make sure traffic flowed smoothly and to avoid overcrowding at either entrance.

46:11 *the festivals and the appointed feasts:* See also the article called "People of the Law: The Religion of Israel," p. 939, for a description of the Jewish festivals.

46:12 *offerings . . . Sabbath day:* See the note at 46:1-3.

46:13-15 *Every day . . . morning by morning:* For more on the daily offering, see Numbers 28:3-8.

46:16,17 *property by inheritance . . . the year of freedom:* Land could be sold or given away in Israel, but during the sacred "year of freedom" (called the Year of Jubilee) property was to be returned to its original owners (see Lev 25:8-34). This was done so that each Israelite tribe could hold on to the land they were given when they first entered the land of Canaan (Num 34:1-29; Josh 15:1-14).

46:18 *prince must not take any . . . property:* Because he received a large share of the land (45:7, 8 and note), the prince was not to take land from anyone else.

46:20 *offering:* See the notes at 40:38 and 40:39. If common people touched a sacred sacrifice, they could be harmed. That is why sacrifice offerings had to be prepared in kitchens attached to the inner sacred temple area.

46:21-24 *outer court . . . four corners . . . kitchens:* In each corner of the outer court were cooking areas where the temple helpers (Levites who were not allowed to offer sacrifices at the altar by the temple) could help prepare offerings brought by the people (see 2 Chr 35:11-13).

47:1 *The man:* See the note at 40:3. Ezekiel's vision now returns to the sort of vision that was described in chapters 40–43.

47:1-5 *water . . . river:* Water was an especially important resource in the ancient Near East (see the mini-article called "Water," p. 1647). The water that flows from the temple may be a reference to the LORD as the source of life and fertility. Compare the water springing up out of the temple to the river that watered God's garden in Eden (Gen 2:10-14). Other Old Testament writings also mention a life-giving fountain flowing from the temple (see Ps 46:4; Joel 3:18; Zech 13:1; 14:8). See also John 7:38; Rev 22:1.

grain offering to the LORD is a lasting ordinance. [15]So the lamb and the grain offering and the oil shall be provided morning by morning for a regular burnt offering.

[16]" 'This is what the Sovereign LORD says: If the prince makes a gift from his inheritance to one of his sons, it will also belong to his descendants; it is to be their property by inheritance. [17]If, however, he makes a gift from his inheritance to one of his servants, the servant may keep it until the year of freedom; then it will revert to the prince. His inheritance belongs to his sons only; it is theirs. [18]The prince must not take any of the inheritance of the people, driving them off their property. He is to give his sons their inheritance out of his own property, so that none of my people will be separated from his property.' "

[19]Then the man brought me through the entrance at the side of the gate to the sacred rooms facing north, which belonged to the priests, and showed me a place at the western end. [20]He said to me, "This is the place where the priests will cook the guilt offering and the sin offering and bake the grain offering, to avoid bringing them into the outer court and consecrating the people."

[21]He then brought me to the outer court and led me around to its four corners, and I saw in each corner another court. [22]In the four corners of the outer court were enclosed[a] courts, forty cubits long and thirty cubits wide; each of the courts in the four corners was the same size. [23]Around the inside of each of the four courts was a ledge of stone, with places for fire built all around under the ledge. [24]He said to me, "These are the kitchens where those who minister at the temple will cook the sacrifices of the people."

DIVIDING THE LAND

Ezekiel now sees a vision of a life-giving river flowing from the temple across the land and emptying into the Dead Sea. Then he is told how the land of Israel will be divided among Israel's tribes. The new division of land will be based on equal shares for all the tribes, unlike the earlier division when the Israelites first settled in the land of Canaan.

The River From the Temple

47 The man brought me back to the entrance of the temple, and I saw water coming out from under the threshold of the temple toward the east (for the temple faced east). The water was coming down from under the south side of the temple, south of the altar. [2]He then brought me out through the north gate and led me around the outside to the outer gate facing east, and the water was flowing from the south side.

[3]As the man went eastward with a measuring line in his

---

[a]22 The meaning of the Hebrew for this word is uncertain.

WATER

In the ancient Near East, great civilizations grew up in the areas close to rivers, such as the Nile in Egypt and the Tigris and Euphrates Rivers in Mesopotamia. These rivers provided water for drinking, fishing, transportation, and even for early forms of watering crops. But many areas of the lands described in the Bible were dry or received rain only at certain times of the year. Some ancient peoples survived by wandering from place to place to find water for their herds. Others who settled down to a life of growing grains, fruits, and vegetables had to learn how to store rain water in pits dug in the ground (cisterns), dig wells, or bring water from nearby streams or springs by using water tunnels known as aqueducts. Having enough water meant survival and life, but a lack of water led to crop failure, food shortages, and death.

Water is often at the center of the Bible. In GENESIS, God creates the heavens and the earth by bringing under control the waters that surrounded the earth (Gen 1:2). In the creation stories of Israel's Mesopotamian and Canaanite neighbors, creation happened when the waters of chaos, sometimes pictured as a monster, were killed. Hints of this idea can be found in some Old Testament texts in which Israel's God of creation kills or imprisons a water monster known as Leviathan or Rahab (Job 9:13; Ps 89:8-10; Isa 27:1). Rain is considered a direct blessing from God (Job 5:10; Isa 44:1-4; Joel 2:23). God saves the people of Israel by making the waters of the Red Sea open for them so they can get away from Pharaoh's army (Exod 14), and by giving them water from a rock as they wander in the desert (Exod 17:1-7).

Water is dangerous and a source of fear in many Bible stories. For example, God uses a great flood to wipe out the earth's sinful people (Gen 6–9). A shortage of water causes rival herders to fight with one another (Gen 26:17-22). Those who are suffering or in distress say they feel like they are being drowned in deep water (Ps 69:1, 2; Lam 3:54), and being saved from an enemy is like being pulled out of the waters of death (Ps 18:16). Sometimes the LORD holds back the rain as a punishment when the Israelite people disobey him (Amos 4:6-8; Hag 1:9-11). The people of Israel were severely punished when they openly worshiped the Canaanite gods which were thought to bring rain to fertilize crops (Jer 2:18-28; Hos 5:10; 6:3), and when they forgot that God alone was to be their "spring of living water" (Jer 2:13).

Water was also used in religious ceremonies to make people clean after being healed of certain kinds of diseases (Lev 14, 15), after touching certain kinds of animals that were said to be unclean (Lev 11), or after touching dead bodies (Num 19). If a husband thought his wife had been unfaithful, she was to drink holy water mixed with dust from the floor of the Holy Place and ink from a scroll on which a curse had been written (Num 5:11-31).

In the New Testament, Jesus claims to be a source of life-giving water, like "a spring of water welling up to eternal life" (John 4:10-14). Christian baptism brings together two symbolic meanings for water that echo Old Testament themes. The water of baptism is a symbol of being made ritually clean, or cleansed from sin (Matt 3:11; Rom 6:3, 4), and the water of baptism is compared to the waters of the great flood that God used to save Noah and his family (1 Pet 3:20, 21). Baptism waters are a source of both death and life. In the waters of baptism, Christ's followers die (are drowned or buried) with Christ who died to defeat the power of sin, but they also are raised up out of the water to new life (Rom 6:3-11).

Water is also important in hope-filled visions of the future. John's vision of a river filled with life-giving water flowing from God's throne in the New Jerusalem (Rev 22:1, 2) is similar to the life-giving river that flows from the temple in the prophet Ezekiel's vision (Ezek 47:1-12). And both are reminders of the river that God made flow out of the ground to water the beautiful garden of creation (Gen 2:10-14).

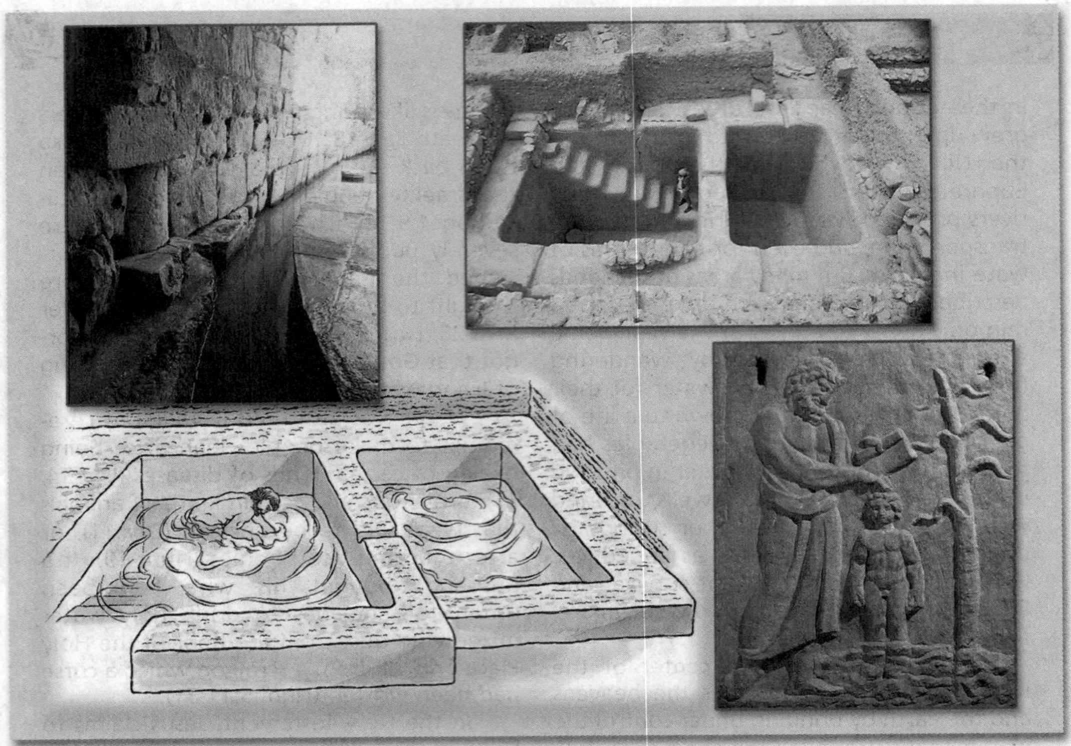

Ritual Bath and Baptism. Water was necessary to the people of Israel not just for physical survival but also to maintain ritual cleanliness (see the mini-article called "Purity (Clean and Unclean)," p. 2125). Jewish law required the person who had become unclean to take a ritual bath, or Mikvah, before rejoining the community. (See photo top right; illustration bottom.) EZEKIEL reflects the ancient understanding that water can bring about spiritual renewal (see 36:25). The Christian ritual of baptism (bottom right) was probably borrowed from the Mikvah. Because Jerusalem, the center of worship, was not located near a river, it depended for its water on two local springs. In the time of King Hezekiah, a tunnel from the Gihon spring to the Pool of Siloam was dug so that water would still be available when the city was attacked. (See 47:1.)

47:8-10 *the Arabah . . . the Sea . . . the Great Sea:* The "Arabah" is the Jordan River Valley. The Jordan River flows south from the Sea of Galilee and empties into the Dead Sea (here called "the Sea"). The stream from the temple would purify the salty water of the Dead Sea so that fish could live in it. En Gedi was a small valley oasis on the western side of the Dead Sea. The location of En Eglaim is uncertain. The "Great Sea" is the Mediterranean Sea. For the area described see the map on p. 2464.

hand, he measured off a thousand cubits[a] and then led me through
water that was ankle-deep. 4He measured off another thousand
cubits and led me through water that was knee-deep. He measured
off another thousand and led me through water that was up to the
waist. 5He measured off another thousand, but now it was a river
that I could not cross, because the water had risen and was deep
enough to swim in—a river that no one could cross. 6He asked me,
"Son of man, do you see this?"

Then he led me back to the bank of the river. 7When I
arrived there, I saw a great number of trees on each side of the
river. 8He said to me, "This water flows toward the eastern region
and goes down into the Arabah,[b] where it enters the Sea.[c] When it

[a]**3** That is, about 1,500 feet (about 450 meters) [b]**8** Or *the Jordan Valley*

empties into the Sea,[a] the water there becomes fresh. 9Swarms of
living creatures will live wherever the river flows. There will be
large numbers of fish, because this water flows there and makes the
salt water fresh; so where the river flows everything will live.
10Fishermen will stand along the shore; from En Gedi to En Eglaim
there will be places for spreading nets. The fish will be of many
kinds—like the fish of the Great Sea.[b] 11But the swamps and
marshes will not become fresh; they will be left for salt. 12Fruit
trees of all kinds will grow on both banks of the river. Their leaves
will not wither, nor will their fruit fail. Every month they will bear,
because the water from the sanctuary flows to them. Their fruit
will serve for food and their leaves for healing."

The Boundaries of the Land

13This is what the Sovereign LORD says: "These are the boundaries by which you are to divide the land for an inheritance among
the twelve tribes of Israel, with two portions for Joseph. 14You are to
divide it equally among them. Because I swore with uplifted hand
to give it to your forefathers, this land will become your inheritance.

15"This is to be the boundary of the land:

"On the north side it will run from the Great Sea by the Hethlon
road past Lebo[c] Hamath to Zedad, 16Berothah[d] and Sibraim
(which lies on the border between Damascus and
Hamath), as far as Hazer Hatticon, which is on the border
of Hauran. 17The boundary will extend from the sea to
Hazar Enan,[e] along the northern border of Damascus, with
the border of Hamath to the north. This will be the north
boundary.

18 "On the east side the boundary will run between Hauran and
Damascus, along the Jordan between Gilead and the land
of Israel, to the eastern sea and as far as Tamar.[f] This will be
the east boundary.

19 "On the south side it will run from Tamar as far as the waters of
Meribah Kadesh, then along the Wadi ⌊of Egypt⌋ to the
Great Sea. This will be the south boundary.

20 "On the west side, the Great Sea will be the boundary to a point
opposite Lebo[g] Hamath. This will be the west boundary.

21"You are to distribute this land among yourselves according to the tribes of Israel. 22You are to allot it as an inheritance for
yourselves and for the aliens who have settled among you and who

---

[a]**8** That is, the Dead Sea [b]**10** That is, the Mediterranean; also in verses 15, 19 and 20 [c]**15** Or *past the entrance to* [d]**15,16** See Septuagint and Ezekiel 48:1; Hebrew *road to go into Zedad, 16Hamath, Berothah* [e]**17** Hebrew *Enon*, a variant of *Enan* [f]**18** Septuagint and Syriac; Hebrew *Israel. You will measure to the eastern sea* [g]**20** Or *opposite the entrance to*

47:11 *salt:* Salt was for flavoring food and for preserving meat and fish, as well as in preparing sacrifices (43:24; also Lev 2:13).

47:13,14 *divide the land . . . two portions for Joseph . . . equally:* That is, the tribes of Manasseh and Ephraim, Joseph's sons. Each received a share of land in Canaan (see Gen 48:5,6). The tribe of Levi was given special duties but did not receive a share of the land (Num 1:47-53). The rest of the land was divided between Jacob's other sons (see Josh 13–19). See also the note at 28:25.

47:15-21 *the boundary of the land . . . to distribute:* The area described is much larger than the territory that belonged to Israel at the time of the exile. Also, the new land division does not include any of the land east of the Jordan River and Dead Sea, which had been given to some of Israel's tribes (see the map on p. 2464). The new boundaries ran from the Mediterranean Sea east to around Damascus on the north, and then ran south through the Jordan Valley to the south end of the Dead Sea. From there it ran southwest to Meribah Kadesh (probably the same as Kadesh Barnea, see Num 34:4), where it turned northwest along the Wadi of Egypt (a gorge) that emptied into the Mediterranean Sea. The map on p. 2465 shows many of the key locations mentioned. Some of the locations listed are uncertain.

47:22 *for the aliens who have settled among you:* A surprisingly generous rule, especially considering the rule about foreigners mentioned in 44:9 (see also the note at 44:7-9). See also Lev 19:33,34; 24:22; Deut 23:2-8.

48:1-7 *northern frontier, Dan . . . Judah:* Seven tribes, including Dan in the far north to Judah in the south, were to receive land north of the sacred land reserved for the temple, the priests, the ruler, and Jerusalem (see 45:1-8; 48:8-14).

48:8-20 *special gift . . . property of the city:* See 45:1-6 and notes. The special section of land running through the middle of the tribal lands would include a section for the temple and the priests (48:8-12), land for the Levites (48:13,14), and regions to include Jerusalem and adjoining farmland (48:15-20).

have children. You are to consider them as native-born Israelites; along with you they are to be allotted an inheritance among the tribes of Israel. [23]In whatever tribe the alien settles, there you are to give him his inheritance," declares the Sovereign LORD.

The Division of the Land

48 "These are the tribes, listed by name: At the northern frontier, Dan will have one portion; it will follow the Hethlon road to Lebo[a] Hamath; Hazar Enan and the northern border of Damascus next to Hamath will be part of its border from the east side to the west side.

[2]"Asher will have one portion; it will border the territory of Dan from east to west.

[3]"Naphtali will have one portion; it will border the territory of Asher from east to west.

[4]"Manasseh will have one portion; it will border the territory of Naphtali from east to west.

[5]"Ephraim will have one portion; it will border the territory of Manasseh from east to west.

[6]"Reuben will have one portion; it will border the territory of Ephraim from east to west.

[7]"Judah will have one portion; it will border the territory of Reuben from east to west.

[8]"Bordering the territory of Judah from east to west will be the portion you are to present as a special gift. It will be 25,000 cubits[b] wide, and its length from east to west will equal one of the tribal portions; the sanctuary will be in the center of it.

[9]"The special portion you are to offer to the LORD will be 25,000 cubits long and 10,000 cubits[c] wide. [10]This will be the sacred portion for the priests. It will be 25,000 cubits long on the north side, 10,000 cubits wide on the west side, 10,000 cubits wide on the east side and 25,000 cubits long on the south side. In the center of it will be the sanctuary of the LORD. [11]This will be for the consecrated priests, the Zadokites, who were faithful in serving me and did not go astray as the Levites did when the Israelites went astray. [12]It will be a special gift to them from the sacred portion of the land, a most holy portion, bordering the territory of the Levites.

[13]"Alongside the territory of the priests, the Levites will have an allotment 25,000 cubits long and 10,000 cubits wide. Its total length will be 25,000 cubits and its width 10,000 cubits. [14]They must not sell or exchange any of it. This is the best of the land and must not pass into other hands, because it is holy to the LORD.

[15]"The remaining area, 5,000 cubits wide and 25,000 cubits long, will be for the common use of the city, for houses and for

[a]**1** Or *to the entrance to* [b]**8** That is, about 7 miles (about 12 kilometers)
[c]**9** That is, about 3 miles (about 5 kilometers)

pastureland. The city will be in the center of it [16]and will have
these measurements: the north side 4,500 cubits, the south side
4,500 cubits, the east side 4,500 cubits, and the west side 4,500
cubits. [17]The pastureland for the city will be 250 cubits on the
north, 250 cubits on the south, 250 cubits on the east, and 250
cubits on the west. [18]What remains of the area, bordering on the
sacred portion and running the length of it, will be 10,000 cubits
on the east side and 10,000 cubits on the west side. Its produce will
supply food for the workers of the city. [19]The workers from the city
who farm it will come from all the tribes of Israel. [20]The entire
portion will be a square, 25,000 cubits on each side. As a special
gift you will set aside the sacred portion, along with the property
of the city.

[21]"What remains on both sides of the area formed by the
sacred portion and the city property will belong to the prince. It
will extend eastward from the 25,000 cubits of the sacred portion
to the eastern border, and westward from the 25,000 cubits to the
western border. Both these areas running the length of the tribal
portions will belong to the prince, and the sacred portion with the
temple sanctuary will be in the center of them. [22]So the property of
the Levites and the property of the city will lie in the center of the
area that belongs to the prince. The area belonging to the prince
will lie between the border of Judah and the border of Benjamin.

[23]"As for the rest of the tribes: Benjamin will have one portion; it will extend from the east side to the west side.

[24]"Simeon will have one portion; it will border the territory
of Benjamin from east to west.

48:21,22 *the area . . . will belong to the prince . . . border of Benjamin:* See also 45:7, 8 and note. The ruler's land would be two long narrow sections on the east and west sides of the sacred lands. The northern border would be the southern border of Judah's land, and the southern border of the ruler's land would be the northern border of the Benjamin tribe.

48:23-27 *the rest of the tribes . . . Gad:* Five of Israel's tribes would occupy the land to the south of the sacred lands, with Gad being the southernmost tribe. See the note at 47:15-21.

QUESTIONS ABOUT EZEKIEL 40:1—48:35

1. Why was it important for the people of Israel to hear Ezekiel's vision of the future temple in Jerusalem?
2. Through how many gates could people enter the outer court of the temple grounds? (40:1-27) Through which of these gates did the LORD's glory return to the temple? (43:1-5)
3. Who was allowed into the inner court and into the temple itself? Why did a wall separate the inner area from the outer court?
4. What kinds of sacrifices were Israel's priests to offer on the altar near the entrance of the temple? (43:18-27) Does anything in worship today compare to the sacrifices offered by Israel's priests?
5. Explain the difference between the things that were considered sacred and common, clean and unclean, especially as they relate to the temple, the priests, and the people of Israel.
6. Why did the prince of Israel receive his own share of land in the new Israel? (45:7-9)
7. Why was the river flowing from the temple such a hopeful vision? (47:1-12)
8. How did the division of the land in the new Israel differ from the old division of the land?
9. What image, vision, or statement in EZEKIEL is especially meaningful to you, and why?

[25]“Issachar will have one portion; it will border the territory of Simeon from east to west.

[26]“Zebulun will have one portion; it will border the territory of Issachar from east to west.

[27]“Gad will have one portion; it will border the territory of Zebulun from east to west.

[28]“The southern boundary of Gad will run south from Tamar to the waters of Meribah Kadesh, then along the Wadi ⌞of Egypt⌟ to the Great Sea.[a]

[29]“This is the land you are to allot as an inheritance to the tribes of Israel, and these will be their portions,” declares the Sovereign LORD.

The Gates of the City

[30]“These will be the exits of the city: Beginning on the north side, which is 4,500 cubits long, [31]the gates of the city will be named after the tribes of Israel. The three gates on the north side will be the gate of Reuben, the gate of Judah and the gate of Levi.

[32]“On the east side, which is 4,500 cubits long, will be three gates: the gate of Joseph, the gate of Benjamin and the gate of Dan.

[33]“On the south side, which measures 4,500 cubits, will be three gates: the gate of Simeon, the gate of Issachar and the gate of Zebulun.

[34]“On the west side, which is 4,500 cubits long, will be three gates: the gate of Gad, the gate of Asher and the gate of Naphtali.

[35]“The distance all around will be 18,000 cubits.

“And the name of the city from that time on will be:

THE LORD IS THERE.”

[a]**28** That is, the Mediterranean

48:31-34 *the gates of the city will be named after the tribes of Israel:* There will be twelve gates. Twelve was considered a complete number. The twelve gates, three on each of the city's four sides, were to be named for the tribes of Israel. Compare the arrangement and names of the gates to the arrangement of Israel's tribes as they camped in the desert many centuries earlier (see Num 2:1-31 and the chart on p. 288). Notice that Jerusalem's gates are named for Jacob's sons and do not include Joseph's sons, Manasseh and Ephraim, who each received land when it was decided the Levi tribe would not own a share. See also Rev 21:12,13.

48:35 *name . . . THE LORD IS THERE:* A translation of the Hebrew *Yahweh-Shammah* which emphasizes the return of the LORD's glory to Jerusalem (43:1-5) and ends the book on a very hopeful note.

DANIEL

How does the message of Daniel bring hope to God's faithful people in times of hardship and persecution?

What makes Daniel special?

In the Hebrew Scriptures, Daniel is listed in the section called the Writings. In the Greek translation of the Old Testament made during the third and second centuries B.C. (called the Septuagint), it is listed among the prophetical books. Daniel has been described both as prophecy and as an apocalypse, a kind of literature that uses symbols, signs, and interpretations of the underlying meaning of events in current history in order to describe how God will triumph over his enemies and the enemies of God's people (see the mini-article called "Apocalyptic Writing," p. 1656).

The first six chapters of Daniel are a collection of stories about Daniel and his friends, young Jewish men who were taken into exile in Babylon where they became important government officials and where their faith in God was severely tested. The second half of the book, chapters 7–12, reports a number of visions that Daniel had. These visions show God's control of historical events and provide hope for those who remain faithful in times of persecution.

One other fact makes Daniel unique. Just over half the book (2:4—7:28) is written in Aramaic; the rest is in Hebrew. Why this is so is not clear, though it is a factor that has led some scholars to conclude that Daniel was written at a date much later than the time of the historic events described in chapters 1–6. The traditional view, however, holds that the prophet Daniel received the visions described in this book and wrote them down during the time of the exile some time in the sixth century B.C. (see the mini-article called "Exile," p. 1541).

Why was Daniel written?

The book of Daniel was written to provide hope and encouragement to God's people. Daniel and his friends were heroes and role models for the Jewish people because they were faithful to God while serving foreign kings who often persecuted them.

What's the story behind the scene?

At various times in their history, the Jewish people were tempted to turn away from God and abandon the religious practices that were based on the Law of Moses. This happened to some degree while they lived in their own land, but the pressure grew in the time of the exile in Babylon (from around 606 to 538 B.C.), when they were forced by the Babylonians to leave their home in Palestine and live in other

The Ptolemies and the Seleucids: When Alexander the Great died in 323 B.C. his vast empire (based in Greek culture and language) split into four parts, each ruled by one of his generals. Two parts of Alexander's empire are often mentioned in Daniel. These are the southern kingdom (Egypt), ruled by the Ptolemies, and the northern kingdom (Syria), ruled by the Seleucids. These two kingdoms fought for control of Palestine. From 323 to 198 B.C. the Ptolemies controlled Palestine, including Jerusalem. The Seleucids controlled Palestine from 198 to 142 B.C.

During the rule of the Ptolemies and the Seleucids, Greek culture had a strong influence in the cities and among the ruling classes of the ancient Near East. Although the majority of the people continued to speak their native language, much of the important business of the day was now done in the Greek language. Greek literature and philosophical ideas became widely known. During this period, many Hebrew texts were translated into Greek, the most important being the Septuagint, the Greek translation of the Hebrew Bible.

For the most part, the Jewish people lived peacefully under the rule of the Seleucids and Ptolemies. However, when the Seleucid ruler Antiochus IV Epiphanes tried to force the Jewish people to accept Greek religious customs, a civil war broke out. This war eventually brought Jewish independence from Seleucid rule. The Jewish people who experienced the persecution of Antiochus IV would likely have received encouragement from the stories and visions in Daniel.

Maccabees and Hasmoneans: These terms refer to the same Jewish family who lived in Palestine during the time when the Seleucids (see the note on p. 1653) were in power. An account of how the early generations of this family started a revolt against Antiochus IV Epiphanes is given in books called *1* and *2 Maccabees* which are found in editions of the Bible that include the Deuterocanonical (Apocryphal) books (see the article called "What Books Belong in the Bible?" p. 13).

Mattathias began the revolt around 167 B.C. when he killed a fellow Jew and a royal official when the Jew tried to make a sacrifice to Zeus on the altar in the Jewish temple. Mattathias and his five sons fled into the Judean hills, but Mattathias was soon killed. His son Judas, known as Maccabeus (meaning "hammer"), and his brothers continued the revolt. Eventually, they captured the temple and removed the altar to Zeus. This rededication of the temple is still celebrated annually in the Jewish festival of Hanukkah.

The notes for DANIEL in the Learning Bible occasionally refer to the books of *1* and *2 Maccabees*. Although these books are not included in the Learning Bible, most readers will find them interesting and informative. Chapter and verse citations are given to help the reader find the passages most relevant to an understanding of DANIEL.

1:1 *third year . . . Jehoiakim . . . Nebuchadnezzar:* The third year would have been 606 B.C., since Jehoiakim ruled Judah from around 609 to 598 B.C. This report of Jehoiakim's capture is reported in 2 Kings 24:1 and 2 Chronicles 36:5-7. According to 2 Kings 24:8-16, Nebuchadnezzar II captured Jerusalem in 587 or 586 B.C. during the reign of Jehoiachin, Jehoiakim's son (see also 2 Chr 36:9,10). See the mini-article called "Nebuchadnezzar," p. 1469.

parts of the Babylonian empire. This meant they had to live among people who had different gods and observed different religious practices. (For more about this, see the article called "From Joshua to the Exile: The People of Israel in the Promised Land," p. 924.) Around 538 B.C. Cyrus II of Persia conquered the Babylonians and allowed its captive people to return to their homelands. Many Jews began to return to Judah, the area around Jerusalem. Hundreds of years later, they suffered even more severe persecution under Antiochus IV Epiphanes (ruled 175-164 B.C.). Their sacred books were burned, worship at the temple in Jerusalem was forbidden, the people were forced to eat food that was considered ritually "unclean," and many faithful Jews were put to death.

These horrible events are described in the books of *1* and *2 Maccabees,* which are included in some editions of the Bible. (Roman Catholic editions of the Bible usually place these with other historical books, after ESTHER and before JOB, and refer to them as "deuterocanonical." Protestant editions of the Bible that include these books place them in a section called the Apocrypha, either at the end of the Bible or between the Old and New Testaments. For more about this, see the article called "What Books Belong in the Bible?" p. 13.)

Even though scholars are divided as to when DANIEL was written, most agree that much of what is described in its visions applies to the cruel treatment of the Jewish people by Antiochus IV, who pressured the Jews living in Judea to abandon their faith in God. Scholars who believe DANIEL was written during the exile (sixth century B.C.) understand the prophet's visions as predictions of events to come centuries later. Scholars who conclude that DANIEL was written during the reign of Antiochus IV (middle of the second century B.C.), believe Daniel's visions were based on the author's experience of ongoing historical events. Either way, DANIEL is a strong testimony to the strength God gives to people of faith during times of difficulty and persecution.

How is Daniel constructed?

DANIEL can be divided into two main parts: chapters 1–6 include stories of Daniel and his friends set during the time of the Babylonian exile (606-538 B.C.). Chapters 7–12 describe a number of visions Daniel had and how these visions were explained to him by angels. The outline of DANIEL below shows how these stories and visions are collected and arranged. Note that the final vision spans three chapters.

The stories of Daniel in Babylon (1:1—6:28)
God is with Daniel and his friends (1:1—3:30)
The dream, the writing on the wall, and the den of lions (4:1—6:28)

The visions of Daniel (7:1—12:13)
Two visions and a prayer (7:1—9:27)
The final vision (10:1—12:13)

The Stories of Daniel in Babylon

Daniel and three of his friends from Judah become important officials in the government of Babylon, but their faith is tested a number of times. They remain completely faithful to the LORD, even when it means risking their lives. Whether facing death in a fiery furnace or in a den of lions, or being challenged to interpret the dreams of the king, Daniel and his friends are clearly helped by God.

GOD IS WITH DANIEL AND HIS FRIENDS

Daniel and his friends prosper when they refuse the king's food and faithfully eat food that is acceptable according to the Law of Moses. Daniel is promoted within the king's court after interpreting the king's dream. And God helps Daniel's friends survive the fiery furnace.

Daniel's Training in Babylon

1 In the third year of the reign of Jehoiakim king of Judah, Nebuchadnezzar king of Babylon came to Jerusalem and besieged it.
[2]And the Lord delivered Jehoiakim king of Judah into his hand,
along with some of the articles from the temple of God. These he
carried off to the temple of his god in Babylonia[a] and put in the
treasure house of his god.
[3]Then the king ordered Ashpenaz, chief of his court officials,
to bring in some of the Israelites from the royal family and the
nobility— [4]young men without any physical defect, handsome,
showing aptitude for every kind of learning, well informed, quick
to understand, and qualified to serve in the king's palace. He was
to teach them the language and literature of the Babylonians.[b]
[5]The king assigned them a daily amount of food and wine from
the king's table. They were to be trained for three years, and after
that they were to enter the king's service.
[6]Among these were some from Judah: Daniel, Hananiah,
Mishael and Azariah. [7]The chief official gave them new names: to
Daniel, the name Belteshazzar; to Hananiah, Shadrach; to Mishael,
Meshach; and to Azariah, Abednego.
[8]But Daniel resolved not to defile himself with the royal food
and wine, and he asked the chief official for permission not to
defile himself this way. [9]Now God had caused the official to show
favor and sympathy to Daniel, [10]but the official told Daniel, "I am
afraid of my lord the king, who has assigned your[c] food and drink.
Why should he see you looking worse than the other young men
your age? The king would then have my head because of you."
[11]Daniel then said to the guard whom the chief official had
appointed over Daniel, Hananiah, Mishael and Azariah, [12]"Please

[a]2 Hebrew *Shinar* [b]4 Or *Chaldeans* [c]10 The Hebrew for *your* and *you* in this verse is plural.

1:2 *the Lord delivered:* The people of Judah were deported to Babylon (this event is sometimes called the exile) because they had failed to remain loyal to God (9:3-14; Jer 25:1-11).

1:2 *temple of God . . . house of his god:* Nebuchadnezzar removed sacred items used for worship from the temple in Jerusalem (see 1 Kgs 7:13—8:9) and took them back to Babylon. He placed them in the temple of the chief Babylonian god Marduk, also known as Bel. See also 2 Kgs 20:17,18; 24:10-16; 2 Chr 36:10; Isa 39:7,8.

1:3 *royal family and the nobility:* The Babylonians drafted young men from the leading Jewish families to learn the Babylonian language and culture, and then assigned them jobs in the royal palace and court of Babylon. They did this thinking that if young men from leading Jewish families worked for the Babylonian government, it might encourage all Jewish people to be loyal to Babylon and eventually adopt Babylonian customs and religion.

1:6,7 *Daniel . . . Abednego:* Daniel's Hebrew name means "God is judge" or "God is my judge"; Hananiah means "The LORD shows grace"; Mishael means "Who is what God is?"; and Azariah means "The LORD helps." These names are contrasted with the Babylonian names they were given, which include references to Babylonian gods. Daniel's new Babylonian name, Belteshazzar, meant something like "Bel protect him."

1:8 *not to defile himself with the royal food and wine:* Daniel wanted to obey the Law of Moses, which said that some foods were "unclean," that is, unfit for the Jewish people to eat (see Lev 11). Daniel may also have wanted to avoid meat prepared in a way that left blood in it (see Lev 17:10-14). Some food served on the king's table may also have been used in sacrifices made to the Babylonian gods, so Daniel did not want to be disloyal to God by eating it. See the mini-article called "Purity (Clean and Unclean)," p. 2125.

APOCALYPTIC WRITING

The word "apocalyptic" comes from a Greek word *apokalypsis*, meaning revealing or unveiling. In the Bible, DANIEL in the Old Testament and REVELATION in the New Testament are the most clear examples of apocalypses. But there are many other books from the Jewish and Christian world that can be classified as apocalypses. In addition, other books of the Bible contain apocalyptic passages.

What makes a particular writing an apocalypse? Apocalypses are stories that use symbols and visions to describe how people received understanding of spiritual realities from heavenly beings. Human beings are given this knowledge by a vision that reveals the truth God wants them to know. Often, the meanings of these visions are difficult to grasp and are explained by an angel.

Apocalyptic visions reveal hidden truths about God, the course of human life, and the spiritual world. These visions often express or describe the meaning of human history, show insights about the nature of life after death, or tell of God's coming judgment on humanity. An important part of God's judgment is a final confrontation between the forces of evil and the forces of good. In this final battle, God defeats the evil forces forever, and brings about a world ruled by justice and mercy. See Revelation 20–22, and the mini-article called "Day of the LORD," p. 1727.

Many parts of the Bible contain elements of apocalyptic writing. Sometimes the visions God gives to people have to be interpreted by those inspired by God, as Joseph does in Genesis 40,41. When the king of Egypt says that Joseph can interpret dreams, Joseph replies "I cannot do it, but God will give Pharaoh the answer he desires" (Gen 41:16). To help the people of Jerusalem, the LORD gives Zechariah eight symbolic visions (Zech 1–6).

Apocalyptic literature has features in common with both prophecy and poetry. Like prophecy, apocalyptic literature may speak to the future of God's people and a coming day of judgment. Like poetry, apocalyptic literature uses symbols and intense images to describe realities that cannot be communicated any other way.

But apocalyptic writings are not the same thing as prophetic writings. The prophets were recognized religious authorities of Israel who spoke the messages that the LORD gave them. These prophecies could be predictions of the future, but were more often warnings to purify Israel's religion or messages urging the people to help the poor and oppressed. See the article called "Prophets and Prophecy," p. 935.

In apocalyptic visions, on the other hand, seers or visionaries (those who see apocalyptic visions) are not as concerned about the present world, but look to heaven or the end of history through a vision that God has granted them. Sometimes an angel acts as the seer's guide and interprets the vision. In Daniel 7–12, for example, Daniel (the seer in this book) receives visions in the night which are explained to him by an angel.

Apocalyptic visions take two major forms. In one kind of apocalyptic vision, the seer is given a new understanding of human history and sees God's hidden purpose and final plan for what happens to the created world. In Daniel 10, for example, the angel Gabriel comes to Daniel to "explain to you what will happen to your people in the future" (Dan 10:14).

In the other kind of apocalyptic vision, the seer travels to heaven and is shown secrets of God's kingdom in heaven. In Revelation 4, for example, John sees a door open in heaven and sees heavenly beings worshiping the LORD (Rev 4).

Even though biblical scholars may disagree about the specific meanings of some of the symbols and visions in various apocalyptic writings, they agree that apocalyptic writings serve to give hope to God's people in times of crisis. By seeing that God is in control of events and has a plan for human history, the faithful are encouraged to look beyond death and the struggles of this life toward a time of justice under God's future rule.

test your servants for ten days: Give us nothing but vegetables to
eat and water to drink. [13]Then compare our appearance with that
of the young men who eat the royal food, and treat your servants
in accordance with what you see." [14]So he agreed to this and tested
them for ten days.
[15]At the end of the ten days they looked healthier and better
nourished than any of the young men who ate the royal food. [16]So
the guard took away their choice food and the wine they were to
drink and gave them vegetables instead.
[17]To these four young men God gave knowledge and understanding of all kinds of literature and learning. And Daniel could
understand visions and dreams of all kinds.
[18]At the end of the time set by the king to bring them in, the
chief official presented them to Nebuchadnezzar. [19]The king talked
with them, and he found none equal to Daniel, Hananiah, Mishael
and Azariah; so they entered the king's service. [20]In every matter
of wisdom and understanding about which the king questioned
them, he found them ten times better than all the magicians and
enchanters in his whole kingdom.
[21]And Daniel remained there until the first year of King
Cyrus.

Nebuchadnezzar's Dream

2 In the second year of his reign, Nebuchadnezzar had dreams;
his mind was troubled and he could not sleep. [2]So the king summoned the magicians, enchanters, sorcerers and astrologers[a] to tell

[a]2 Or *Chaldeans*; also in verses 4, 5 and 10

1:17 *God gave knowledge and understanding:* Through God's help, Daniel and his friends receive wisdom and rise in power in the Babylonian government (1:19,20; 2:27-29,47).

1:18 *Nebuchadnezzar:* See the note at 1:1.

1:21 *first year of King Cyrus:* This would be around 539 B.C.; but see the note at 6:28. Although this marks the end of Daniel's time in the king's court, he continued to serve in some capacity beyond this point (see 10:1).

2:1 *second year:* 604 or 603 B.C. It is hard to make this date agree with the date of Nebuchadnezzar's reign given in 1:1 and 1:18. Those verses suggest that Nebuchadnezzar was already king during the training period of Daniel and his friends.

2:2 *magicians . . . astrologers:* See the note at 2:10.

APOCALYPTIC WRITINGS

A brief list of some apocalyptic writings is given below. Apocalyptic writings appear not only in some of the books of the Bible, but also in other Near Eastern writings from the centuries just before and after the birth of Christ.

Jewish Apocalypses not included in the Hebrew Bible	Old Testament books with apocalyptic elements	New Testament books with apocalyptic elements	Jewish or Christian Apocalypses not included in the New Testament	Writings from other cultures with apocalyptic elements
1 Enoch	Daniel	Revelation	*Apocalypse of Peter*	*Dynastic Prophecy; Uruk Prophecy* (ancient Babylon)
4 Ezra; 2 and 3 Baruch	Ezekiel; Isaiah	Matthew (24, 25); Mark (13)	*Shepherd of Hermas*	*Vision of the Netherworld* (ancient Assyrian)
Apocalypse of Abraham	Joel; Zechariah	Luke (21); 1 Thessalonians (4:13-18)	*Ascension of Isaiah*	*Sibylline Oracles* (ancient Greek)

Daniel said, *"Praise be to the name of God for ever and ever; wisdom and power are his."*
Dan 2:20

2:4 *Aramaic ... live forever:* This section (2:4—7:28) is written in Aramaic, a language which was used in the ancient Near East as a common language of trade and official business between nations. The greeting in this verse was the royal greeting used for Persian kings for many centuries.

2:10 *magician or enchanter or astrologer:* The groups mentioned probably had slightly different functions, but here they are all asked to use their "powers" to interpret the king's dream. "Astrologers" is sometimes translated as "Chaldeans," the name of a group known for studying the stars (astrology) to tell the future. See also the article called "Miracles, Magic, and Medicine," p. 1838.

2:14 *Arioch:* The meaning of his name is uncertain, but the probable meaning is "servant of the moon god."

2:18 *God of heaven:* This name for God is common in writings from the Persian period, about 539 to 333 B.C. Of the twenty-two uses of this name in the Old Testament, seventeen come from EZRA, NEHEMIAH, and DANIEL. See Ezra 1:2; 5:11; 6:9,10; Neh 1:5. See also the mini-article called "Names of God," p. 243.

him what he had dreamed. When they came in and stood before
the king, 3 he said to them, "I have had a dream that troubles me
and I want to know what it means.[a]"
4 Then the astrologers answered the king in Aramaic,[b]
"O king, live forever! Tell your servants the dream, and we will
interpret it."
5 The king replied to the astrologers, "This is what I have
firmly decided: If you do not tell me what my dream was and
interpret it, I will have you cut into pieces and your houses turned
into piles of rubble. 6 But if you tell me the dream and explain it,
you will receive from me gifts and rewards and great honor. So tell
me the dream and interpret it for me."
7 Once more they replied, "Let the king tell his servants the
dream, and we will interpret it."
8 Then the king answered, "I am certain that you are trying to
gain time, because you realize that this is what I have firmly decided: 9 If you do not tell me the dream, there is just one penalty for
you. You have conspired to tell me misleading and wicked things,
hoping the situation will change. So then, tell me the dream, and I
will know that you can interpret it for me."
10 The astrologers answered the king, "There is not a man on
earth who can do what the king asks! No king, however great and
mighty, has ever asked such a thing of any magician or enchanter or
astrologer. 11 What the king asks is too difficult. No one can reveal it
to the king except the gods, and they do not live among men."
12 This made the king so angry and furious that he ordered
the execution of all the wise men of Babylon. 13 So the decree was
issued to put the wise men to death, and men were sent to look for
Daniel and his friends to put them to death.
14 When Arioch, the commander of the king's guard, had
gone out to put to death the wise men of Babylon, Daniel spoke to
him with wisdom and tact. 15 He asked the king's officer, "Why did
the king issue such a harsh decree?" Arioch then explained the
matter to Daniel. 16 At this, Daniel went in to the king and asked
for time, so that he might interpret the dream for him.
17 Then Daniel returned to his house and explained the matter to his friends Hananiah, Mishael and Azariah. 18 He urged them
to plead for mercy from the God of heaven concerning this mystery, so that he and his friends might not be executed with the rest
of the wise men of Babylon. 19 During the night the mystery was
revealed to Daniel in a vision. Then Daniel praised the God of
heaven 20 and said:

"Praise be to the name of God for ever and ever;
wisdom and power are his.
21 He changes times and seasons;

[a]3 Or *was* [b]4 The text from here through chapter 7 is in Aramaic.

he sets up kings and deposes them.
He gives wisdom to the wise
and knowledge to the discerning.
22 He reveals deep and hidden things;
he knows what lies in darkness,
and light dwells with him.
23 I thank and praise you, O God of my fathers:
You have given me wisdom and power,
you have made known to me what we asked of you,
you have made known to us the dream of the king."

Daniel Interprets the Dream

24 Then Daniel went to Arioch, whom the king had appointed to execute the wise men of Babylon, and said to him, "Do not
execute the wise men of Babylon. Take me to the king, and I will
interpret his dream for him."

25 Arioch took Daniel to the king at once and said, "I have
found a man among the exiles from Judah who can tell the king
what his dream means."

26 The king asked Daniel (also called Belteshazzar), "Are you
able to tell me what I saw in my dream and interpret it?"

27 Daniel replied, "No wise man, enchanter, magician or
diviner can explain to the king the mystery he has asked about,
28 but there is a God in heaven who reveals mysteries. He has shown
King Nebuchadnezzar what will happen in days to come. Your
dream and the visions that passed through your mind as you lay
on your bed are these:

29 "As you were lying there, O king, your mind turned to
things to come, and the revealer of mysteries showed you what is
going to happen. 30 As for me, this mystery has been revealed to
me, not because I have greater wisdom than other living men, but
so that you, O king, may know the interpretation and that you
may understand what went through your mind.

31 "You looked, O king, and there before you stood a large
statue—an enormous, dazzling statue, awesome in appearance.
32 The head of the statue was made of pure gold, its chest and arms
of silver, its belly and thighs of bronze, 33 its legs of iron, its feet
partly of iron and partly of baked clay. 34 While you were watching,
a rock was cut out, but not by human hands. It struck the statue
on its feet of iron and clay and smashed them. 35 Then the iron, the
clay, the bronze, the silver and the gold were broken to pieces at
the same time and became like chaff on a threshing floor in the
summer. The wind swept them away without leaving a trace. But
the rock that struck the statue became a huge mountain and filled
the whole earth.

36 "This was the dream, and now we will interpret it to the
king. 37 You, O king, are the king of kings. The God of heaven has
given you dominion and power and might and glory; 38 in your

2:21,22 *wisdom . . . light dwells with him:* PROVERBS makes two things clear about the nature of wisdom. First, true wisdom comes from God (Prov 2:6,7). Second, God's Law offers wisdom and guidance for daily life (Prov 6:23). For more, see the mini-article called "Law," p. 1160. God's wisdom lights up the darkness and unlocks mysteries (Ps 139:12; Eccl 2:13,14; John 1:4-8; Rev 22:5).

2:28-30 *God . . . mysteries:* See the note at 2:18. The word for "mysteries" came into the Aramaic from the Persian language and means something secret that can only be revealed by God, not by human wisdom. This particular word is found only in DANIEL (see also 2:19; 4:9), but it is also found in the writings known as the Dead Sea Scrolls, which date from the third century B.C. to the first century A.D. (See the photographs on p. 933.)

2:31-35 *statue:* The materials used to make the statue decrease in value from head (gold), to chest (silver), to belly and thighs (bronze), to feet (iron and clay). These different materials relate to different historic kingdoms (2:38-45).

2:35 *broken in pieces . . . threshing floor:* In ancient times, wheat stalks were threshed by having oxen walk over them or drag a heavy stone over them. This separated the seeds from the husks. When the wheat was then thrown into the air the wind blew the light husks away, but the heavier seeds fell back down to the threshing floor where they could be easily scooped up. See the illustration on p. 730.

2:37 *given you dominion and power:* In the Bible, God is said to give power to earthly rulers, even to those who do not worship him (see Isa 45:1-4; Jer 27:5-7; Rom 13:1).

hands he has placed mankind and the beasts of the field and the birds of the air. Wherever they live, he has made you ruler over them all. You are that head of gold.

39“After you, another kingdom will rise, inferior to yours. Next, a third kingdom, one of bronze, will rule over the whole earth. 40Finally, there will be a fourth kingdom, strong as iron—for iron breaks and smashes everything—and as iron breaks things to pieces, so it will crush and break all the others. 41Just as you saw that the feet and toes were partly of baked clay and partly of iron, so this will be a divided kingdom; yet it will have some of the strength of iron in it, even as you saw iron mixed with clay. 42As the toes were partly iron and partly clay, so this kingdom will be partly strong and partly brittle. 43And just as you saw the iron mixed with baked clay, so the people will be a mixture and will not remain united, any more than iron mixes with clay.

44“In the time of those kings, the God of heaven will set up a kingdom that will never be destroyed, nor will it be left to another people. It will crush all those kingdoms and bring them to an end, but it will itself endure forever. 45This is the meaning of the vision of the rock cut out of a mountain, but not by human hands—a rock that broke the iron, the bronze, the clay, the silver and the gold to pieces.

“The great God has shown the king what will take place in the future. The dream is true and the interpretation is trustworthy.”

46Then King Nebuchadnezzar fell prostrate before Daniel and paid him honor and ordered that an offering and incense be presented to him. 47The king said to Daniel, “Surely your God is the God of gods and the Lord of kings and a revealer of mysteries, for you were able to reveal this mystery.”

48Then the king placed Daniel in a high position and lavished many gifts on him. He made him ruler over the entire province of Babylon and placed him in charge of all its wise men. 49Moreover, at Daniel’s request the king appointed Shadrach, Meshach and Abednego administrators over the province of Babylon, while Daniel himself remained at the royal court.

The Image of Gold and the Fiery Furnace

3 King Nebuchadnezzar made an image of gold, ninety feet high and nine feet[a] wide, and set it up on the plain of Dura in the province of Babylon. 2He then summoned the satraps, prefects, governors, advisers, treasurers, judges, magistrates and all the other provincial officials to come to the dedication of the image he had set up. 3So the satraps, prefects, governors, advisers, treasurers, judges, magistrates and all the other provincial officials assembled

[a]1 Aramaic *sixty cubits high and six cubits wide* (about 27 meters high and 2.7 meters wide)

2:39-45 *fourth kingdom ... never be destroyed:* Some scholars have suggested that the first kingdom, represented by the gold head, was the Babylonian kingdom ruled by Nebuchadnezzar II and that this kingdom was followed by the Medo-Persian, Greek, and Roman empires. Other scholars believe the first kingdom (Babylon) was followed by the kingdoms of Media, Persia, and Greece. Whichever understanding is preferred, the rule of the mysterious "Darius the Mede" (5:31) falls between the rules of Babylon's Nebuchadnezzar and Persia's Cyrus (see the note at 1:21). For the political "mixture" that led to the fourth kingdom, see the note at 11:6,7.

2:46 *Nebuchadnezzar fell prostrate:* Since Daniel probably would not have allowed the king to worship him as if he were a god, it has been suggested that Nebuchadnezzar came to worship Daniel's God after he saw that Daniel was able to interpret his dream (2:47). The Jewish readers would have understood this scene as a symbol of the eventual triumph of God's people over Babylon (see also Isa 49:23; 60:14).

2:46 *incense be presented to him:* Incense was a substance made of frankincense, other gums and spices, and salt. It produced a sweet smell when burned.

3:1 *image of gold:* According to the Babylonian measuring system, the statue was 60 cubits high and 6 cubits wide. Sources outside the Bible dating to both the first and fifth centuries B.C. report a golden statue of Zeus in Babylon. This statue may have originally represented the Babylonian god Bel. See also the note at 1:2 (temple of God).

3:1 *plain of Dura ... Babylon:* The location of this plain is not certain. In Aramaic, the word *dura* means "fortress" or "city wall," so this verse could mean that the statue was set up outside the city walls of Babylon. See the note at 4:28-30.

Adoration of the Statue and the Three Hebrews in the Furnace, illuminated page from a Spanish *Apocalypse* painted by the monk Maius, tenth century. King Nebuchadnezzar ordered a gold statue to be built that was 90 feet high and 9 feet wide. He had it set up on the plain of Dura near Babylon and commanded everyone to worship it. When the three Jewish court officials, Shadrach, Meshach, and Abednego, refused to do this, Nebuchadnezzar had them thrown into a furnace seven times hotter than usual. When the king looked in, he could see four men walking around in the furnace. The fourth one, he said, "looks like a son of the gods." (See chapter 3.)

for the dedication of the image that King Nebuchadnezzar had set
up, and they stood before it.
4 Then the herald loudly proclaimed, "This is what you are
commanded to do, O peoples, nations and men of every language:
5 As soon as you hear the sound of the horn, flute, zither, lyre, harp,
pipes and all kinds of music, you must fall down and worship the
image of gold that King Nebuchadnezzar has set up. 6 Whoever
does not fall down and worship will immediately be thrown into a
blazing furnace."
7 Therefore, as soon as they heard the sound of the horn,

3:4 *peoples, nations and men of every language:* A common introduction to an official statement intended to give the announcement more importance. See also 3:29; 4:1; 7:14; Esth 1:22; 8:9; Rev 5:9; 7:9.

3:5 *sound of the horn, flute, zither, lyre, harp, pipes:* Musical instruments were an important part of religious celebrations and worship in many cultures of the ancient Near East. See the illustration on p. 1190.

3:6 *Whoever does not fall down and worship:* As faithful Jews, Daniel and his friends lived by the laws Moses received from the LORD in the Sinai desert (see Exod 20:2-17), especially the commandment "You shall have no other gods before me." When the king asked them to worship the statue, he was really asking them to turn their back on their faith and the Law.

3:6 *blazing furnace:* The furnace was probably a large stone kiln with an opening at the top (see 3:23) and an opening at the bottom, where items could be put into and removed from the fire.

> The three men replied, *"The God we serve is able to save us from it, and he will rescue us from your hand, O king. But even if he does not, we want you to know, O king, that we will not serve your gods or worship the image of gold you have set up."*
> Dan 3:17,18

3:17 *God . . . is able to save us:* God's ability to save his chosen people is an important theme in DANIEL. See also 6:16,26,27; 12:1,2. See also Heb 11:33,34 and the mini-article called "Salvation," p. 2021.

3:19 *seven times hotter:* See the note at 3:6 (furnace). The heat of the fire was controlled by a series of bellows, and it is possible that there were seven such bellows. However, it is more likely that "seven times hotter" simply is meant to signify the hottest fire possible, since seven was a number symbolizing completeness. See also the chart called "Numbers in the Bible," p. 2405.

3:21-23 *Shadrach . . . Abednego:* See the note at 1:6,7.

flute, zither, lyre, harp and all kinds of music, all the peoples, nations and men of every language fell down and worshiped the image of gold that King Nebuchadnezzar had set up.

[8]At this time some astrologers[a] came forward and denounced the Jews. [9]They said to King Nebuchadnezzar, "O king, live forever! [10]You have issued a decree, O king, that everyone who hears the sound of the horn, flute, zither, lyre, harp, pipes and all kinds of music must fall down and worship the image of gold, [11]and that whoever does not fall down and worship will be thrown into a blazing furnace. [12]But there are some Jews whom you have set over the affairs of the province of Babylon—Shadrach, Meshach and Abednego—who pay no attention to you, O king. They neither serve your gods nor worship the image of gold you have set up."

[13]Furious with rage, Nebuchadnezzar summoned Shadrach, Meshach and Abednego. So these men were brought before the king, [14]and Nebuchadnezzar said to them, "Is it true, Shadrach, Meshach and Abednego, that you do not serve my gods or worship the image of gold I have set up? [15]Now when you hear the sound of the horn, flute, zither, lyre, harp, pipes and all kinds of music, if you are ready to fall down and worship the image I made, very good. But if you do not worship it, you will be thrown immediately into a blazing furnace. Then what god will be able to rescue you from my hand?"

[16]Shadrach, Meshach and Abednego replied to the king, "O Nebuchadnezzar, we do not need to defend ourselves before you in this matter. [17]If we are thrown into the blazing furnace, the God we serve is able to save us from it, and he will rescue us from your hand, O king. [18]But even if he does not, we want you to know, O king, that we will not serve your gods or worship the image of gold you have set up."

[19]Then Nebuchadnezzar was furious with Shadrach, Meshach and Abednego, and his attitude toward them changed. He ordered the furnace heated seven times hotter than usual [20]and commanded some of the strongest soldiers in his army to tie up Shadrach, Meshach and Abednego and throw them into the blazing furnace. [21]So these men, wearing their robes, trousers, turbans and other clothes, were bound and thrown into the blazing furnace. [22]The king's command was so urgent and the furnace so hot that the flames of the fire killed the soldiers who took up Shadrach, Meshach and Abednego, [23]and these three men, firmly tied, fell into the blazing furnace.

[24]Then King Nebuchadnezzar leaped to his feet in amazement and asked his advisers, "Weren't there three men that we tied up and threw into the fire?"

They replied, "Certainly, O king."

---

[a]**8** Or *Chaldeans*

25 He said, “Look! I see four men walking around in the fire,
unbound and unharmed, and the fourth looks like a son of
the gods.”
26 Nebuchadnezzar then approached the opening of the
blazing furnace and shouted, “Shadrach, Meshach and Abednego,
servants of the Most High God, come out! Come here!”
So Shadrach, Meshach and Abednego came out of the fire,
27 and the satraps, prefects, governors and royal advisers crowded
around them. They saw that the fire had not harmed their bodies,
nor was a hair of their heads singed; their robes were not scorched,
and there was no smell of fire on them.
28 Then Nebuchadnezzar said, “Praise be to the God of
Shadrach, Meshach and Abednego, who has sent his angel and rescued his servants! They trusted in him and defied the king’s command
and were willing to give up their lives rather than serve or worship any
god except their own God. 29 Therefore I decree that the people of any
nation or language who say anything against the God of Shadrach,
Meshach and Abednego be cut into pieces and their houses be turned
into piles of rubble, for no other god can save in this way.”
30 Then the king promoted Shadrach, Meshach and Abednego in the province of Babylon.

THE DREAM, THE WRITING ON THE WALL, AND THE DEN OF LIONS

Daniel interprets another of Nebuchadnezzar’s dreams and gives the meaning of strange writing that appears on the wall at Belshazzar’s banquet. Later, God helps Daniel survive in a den of lions, where he is thrown because he will not turn his back on God and worship King Darius.

Nebuchadnezzar’s Dream of a Tree

4 King Nebuchadnezzar,

To the peoples, nations and men of every language, who
live in all the world:

May you prosper greatly!

2 It is my pleasure to tell you about the miraculous signs
and wonders that the Most High God has performed for me.

3 How great are his signs,
how mighty his wonders!
His kingdom is an eternal kingdom;
his dominion endures from generation to
generation.

4 I, Nebuchadnezzar, was at home in my palace, contented and prosperous. 5 I had a dream that made me afraid. As I
was lying in my bed, the images and visions that passed

Nebuchadnezzar said, *“They trusted in him and defied the king’s command and were willing to give up their lives rather than serve or worship any god except their own God.”* Dan 3:28

3:25 *fourth looks like a son of the gods:* Nebuchadnezzar may have been referring to one of the “angels” or “mighty ones” which the Bible says are members of God’s heavenly council (Job 1:6; 38:7; Ps 29:1). In verse 28, Nebuchadnezzar calls this being an “angel.”

3:26 *Most High God:* Nebuchadnezzar here is using the term to refer to Daniel’s God, a title used in the Bible both by the people of Israel and by other nations. Abram (Abraham) identifies “God Most High” with Israel’s LORD (Gen 14:22). See also Num 24:16; Deut 32:8; Ps 46:4; Acts 16:17. See also the mini-article called “Names of God,” p. 243.

3:28 *angel:* See the note at 3:25. In Hebrew the word for “angel” also means “messenger.” In the Bible, angels act both as messengers and as servants of God. See also the mini-article called “Angels,” p. 88.

4:1 *Nebuchadnezzar . . . peoples, nations and men of every language:* See the notes at 1:1 and 3:4.

4:2 *Most High God:* See the note at 3:26.

4:4 *contented and prosperous:* During Nebuchadnezzar’s reign, the Babylonian empire had a renewed interest in art and culture, and many important building projects were completed. Because they didn’t have to face an ongoing threat of war, the Babylonians could concentrate their energy and wealth on peacetime activities.

4:6 *wise men:* See the note at 2:10.

4:8 *Belteshazzar:* See the note at 1:6, 7.

4:8 *name of my god . . . holy gods:* The "holy gods" refers to Babylonian gods worshiped by King Nebuchadnezzar. Perhaps he considered Daniel's God the chief god over all the others (4:2,34). See the note at 1:2 (temple of God).

4:10-12 *tree . . . fruit abundant:* A tree filled with fruit located at the center of the world was a common image in many ancient Near Eastern stories. See also Gen 2:9; 3:3; Rev 22:2.

4:13 *a messenger, a holy one:* See the note at 3:28.

4:14,15 *Cut down the tree . . . stump and its roots:* Nebuchadnezzar was to be stripped of his power for a time. But just as the stump of a tree left in the ground will later grow again, so Nebuchadnezzar's power would one day return. See also Isa 14:4-20; Ezek 31.

4:16 *seven:* A number symbolizing completeness in the ancient world. See also 4:25 and the note at 3:19.

4:17 *gives them to anyone he wishes:* See the note at 2:37.

4:18 *Belteshazzar:* See the note at 1:6,7.

4:18 *holy gods:* See the note at 4:8 (holy gods).

through my mind terrified me. [6]So I commanded that all the
wise men of Babylon be brought before me to interpret the
dream for me. [7]When the magicians, enchanters, astrologers[a]
and diviners came, I told them the dream, but they could not
interpret it for me. [8]Finally, Daniel came into my presence and
I told him the dream. (He is called Belteshazzar, after the
name of my god, and the spirit of the holy gods is in him.)
[9]I said, "Belteshazzar, chief of the magicians, I know that
the spirit of the holy gods is in you, and no mystery is too difficult for you. Here is my dream; interpret it for me. [10]These
are the visions I saw while lying in my bed: I looked, and there
before me stood a tree in the middle of the land. Its height was
enormous. [11]The tree grew large and strong and its top
touched the sky; it was visible to the ends of the earth. [12]Its
leaves were beautiful, its fruit abundant, and on it was food for
all. Under it the beasts of the field found shelter, and the birds
of the air lived in its branches; from it every creature was fed.
[13]"In the visions I saw while lying in my bed, I looked,
and there before me was a messenger,[b] a holy one, coming
down from heaven. [14]He called in a loud voice: 'Cut down the
tree and trim off its branches; strip off its leaves and scatter its
fruit. Let the animals flee from under it and the birds from its
branches. [15]But let the stump and its roots, bound with iron
and bronze, remain in the ground, in the grass of the field.

" 'Let him be drenched with the dew of heaven, and let
him live with the animals among the plants of the earth. [16]Let
his mind be changed from that of a man and let him be given
the mind of an animal, till seven times[c] pass by for him.
[17]" 'The decision is announced by messengers, the holy
ones declare the verdict, so that the living may know that the
Most High is sovereign over the kingdoms of men and gives
them to anyone he wishes and sets over them the lowliest
of men.'
[18]"This is the dream that I, King Nebuchadnezzar, had.
Now, Belteshazzar, tell me what it means, for none of the wise
men in my kingdom can interpret it for me. But you can,
because the spirit of the holy gods is in you."

Daniel Interprets the Dream

[19]Then Daniel (also called Belteshazzar) was greatly
perplexed for a time, and his thoughts terrified him. So the
king said, "Belteshazzar, do not let the dream or its meaning
alarm you."

Belteshazzar answered, "My lord, if only the dream

[a]7 Or *Chaldeans* [b]13 Or *watchman*; also in verses 17 and 23 [c]16 Or *years*; also in verses 23, 25 and 32

applied to your enemies and its meaning to your adversaries!
[20]The tree you saw, which grew large and strong, with its top
touching the sky, visible to the whole earth, [21]with beautiful
leaves and abundant fruit, providing food for all, giving shelter to the beasts of the field, and having nesting places in its
branches for the birds of the air— [22]you, O king, are that tree!
You have become great and strong; your greatness has grown
until it reaches the sky, and your dominion extends to distant
parts of the earth.

[23]"You, O king, saw a messenger, a holy one, coming
down from heaven and saying, 'Cut down the tree and destroy
it, but leave the stump, bound with iron and bronze, in the
grass of the field, while its roots remain in the ground. Let
him be drenched with the dew of heaven; let him live like the
wild animals, until seven times pass by for him.'

[24]"This is the interpretation, O king, and this is the
decree the Most High has issued against my lord the king:
[25]You will be driven away from people and will live with the
wild animals; you will eat grass like cattle and be drenched
with the dew of heaven. Seven times will pass by for you until
you acknowledge that the Most High is sovereign over the
kingdoms of men and gives them to anyone he wishes. [26]The
command to leave the stump of the tree with its roots means
that your kingdom will be restored to you when you acknowledge that Heaven rules. [27]Therefore, O king, be pleased to
accept my advice: Renounce your sins by doing what is right,
and your wickedness by being kind to the oppressed. It may
be that then your prosperity will continue."

The Dream Is Fulfilled

[28]All this happened to King Nebuchadnezzar. [29]Twelve
months later, as the king was walking on the roof of the royal
palace of Babylon, [30]he said, "Is not this the great Babylon I
have built as the royal residence, by my mighty power and for
the glory of my majesty?"

[31]The words were still on his lips when a voice came
from heaven, "This is what is decreed for you, King Nebuchadnezzar: Your royal authority has been taken from you.
[32]You will be driven away from people and will live with the
wild animals; you will eat grass like cattle. Seven times will
pass by for you until you acknowledge that the Most High is
sovereign over the kingdoms of men and gives them to anyone he wishes."

[33]Immediately what had been said about Nebuchadnezzar was fulfilled. He was driven away from people and ate
grass like cattle. His body was drenched with the dew of
heaven until his hair grew like the feathers of an eagle and his
nails like the claws of a bird.

> Daniel said to the king, *"Therefore, O king, be pleased to accept my advice: Renounce your sins by doing what is right."*
> Dan 4:27

4:22 *dominion extends to distant parts of the earth:* The Babylonian kingdom covered a large area of the ancient Near East. The language is exaggerated to emphasize just how powerful Nebuchadnezzar was. See also the note at 3:4 and the map on p. 2468.

4:23 *Cut down the tree . . . seven times:* See the notes at 4:14,15 and 4:16.

4:25 *Most High is sovereign . . . gives them to anyone he wishes:* See the notes at 3:26 and 2:37.

4:27 *Renounce your sins:* Sin is turning away from God and disobeying God's Law. To renounce your sin is to "repent." The king's repentance was to be carried out in acts of justice and mercy. See also the mini-article called "Sin," p. 2181.

4:28-30 *royal palace of Babylon:* Under Nebuchadnezzar the great city of Babylon was rebuilt. In honor of the city's chief god Marduk, the king built a huge palace and a large temple, which he had surrounded by a double wall for protection. The wall was so wide that a chariot team four-horses wide could ride around on top of it. Ancient Babylon also had one of the Seven Wonders of the ancient world, the Hanging Gardens, and a temple tower known as a ziggurat that was nearly 300 feet high. See the illustration on p. 1362. See also Gen 11:1-9.

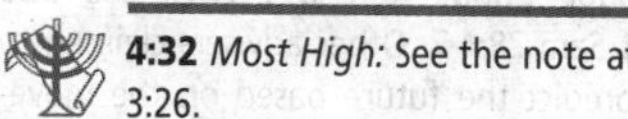

4:32 *Most High:* See the note at 3:26.

4:36 *sanity was restored:* Nebuchadnezzar's prayer was answered, and he was restored to power because he came to recognize that God, and not he himself, was the true ruler of all the earth.

5:1,2 *King Belshazzar . . . father . . . wives:* Belshazzar's name in Babylonian means "Bel, protect the king." Bel was another name for Marduk, Babylon's chief god. Belshazzar was actually the son of King Nabonidus (ruled 556 to 539 B.C.) who was not from Nebuchadnezzar's family. In ancient times, it was possible to refer to the previous king as the "father" of the present ruler. No Babylonian records say that Belshazzar was a "full king," but some ancient inscriptions have been discovered which tell of King Nabonidus being away from Babylon for long periods. While he was gone, his son Belshazzar acted as king on his behalf.

Following ancient customs Belshazzar had many wives, and many of them were at the banquet. The "wives" probably included women called "concubines," who, though legally bound to a man, did not have the full privileges of a primary wife.

5:2-4 *goblets . . . praised the gods:* The goblets were some of the holy objects taken from the Jerusalem temple (see the note at 1:2, temple), and were intended to be used only for the rituals involving the sacrifices offered by Israel's priests. But Belshazzar and his guests drank wine out of these sacred goblets while praising and toasting their own gods. Using the sacred vessels of the temple in this way greatly dishonored Israel's God.

5:7 *astrologers and diviners:* See the note at 2:10. Some of the king's advisers claimed to have the power to speak to the spirits of the dead who were said to have special knowledge about coming events. See also 1 Sam 28:4-7. Other advisers claimed to predict the future based on the movement of the stars. The king apparently hoped these advisers were wise enough to understand the very strange writing.

34 At the end of that time, I, Nebuchadnezzar, raised my
eyes toward heaven, and my sanity was restored. Then I
praised the Most High; I honored and glorified him who lives
forever.

His dominion is an eternal dominion;
his kingdom endures from generation to generation.
35 All the peoples of the earth
are regarded as nothing.
He does as he pleases
with the powers of heaven
and the peoples of the earth.
No one can hold back his hand
or say to him: "What have you done?"

36 At the same time that my sanity was restored, my
honor and splendor were returned to me for the glory of my
kingdom. My advisers and nobles sought me out, and I was
restored to my throne and became even greater than before.
37 Now I, Nebuchadnezzar, praise and exalt and glorify the King
of heaven, because everything he does is right and all his ways
are just. And those who walk in pride he is able to humble.

The Writing on the Wall

5 King Belshazzar gave a great banquet for a thousand of his
nobles and drank wine with them. 2 While Belshazzar was drinking
his wine, he gave orders to bring in the gold and silver goblets that
Nebuchadnezzar his father[a] had taken from the temple in Jerusalem,
so that the king and his nobles, his wives and his concubines
might drink from them. 3 So they brought in the gold goblets
that had been taken from the temple of God in Jerusalem, and the
king and his nobles, his wives and his concubines drank from
them. 4 As they drank the wine, they praised the gods of gold and
silver, of bronze, iron, wood and stone.
5 Suddenly the fingers of a human hand appeared and wrote on
the plaster of the wall, near the lampstand in the royal palace. The
king watched the hand as it wrote. 6 His face turned pale and he was
so frightened that his knees knocked together and his legs gave way.
7 The king called out for the enchanters, astrologers[b] and
diviners to be brought and said to these wise men of Babylon,
"Whoever reads this writing and tells me what it means will be
clothed in purple and have a gold chain placed around his neck,
and he will be made the third highest ruler in the kingdom."
8 Then all the king's wise men came in, but they could not
read the writing or tell the king what it meant. 9 So King Belshaz-

[a]2 Or *ancestor*; or *predecessor*; also in verses 11, 13 and 18 [b]7 Or *Chaldeans*; also in verse 11

Belshazzar's Feast by Rembrandt van Rijn, around 1635. King Belshazzar gave a great feast for his highest officials and ordered that the gold and silver goblets which had been taken from the temple in Jerusalem be used. During the banquet a hand was seen writing the words "mene," "tekel," and "parsin" on the wall. The king was frightened by the message, which he could not read or understand. At the queen's urging, Belshazzar sent for Daniel, one of the captives from Judah who had been in charge of all of Nebuchadnezzar's wise men and advisers. Although the message foretold the end of Belshazzar's kingdom, the king honored Daniel by making him the third most powerful man in his kingdom. (See chapter 5.)

zar became even more terrified and his face grew more pale. His
nobles were baffled.
10The queen,[a] hearing the voices of the king and his nobles,
came into the banquet hall. "O king, live forever!" she said. "Don't
be alarmed! Don't look so pale! 11There is a man in your kingdom
who has the spirit of the holy gods in him. In the time of your
father he was found to have insight and intelligence and wisdom
like that of the gods. King Nebuchadnezzar your father—your
father the king, I say—appointed him chief of the magicians,
enchanters, astrologers and diviners. 12This man Daniel, whom the
king called Belteshazzar, was found to have a keen mind and
knowledge and understanding, and also the ability to interpret
dreams, explain riddles and solve difficult problems. Call for
Daniel, and he will tell you what the writing means."
13So Daniel was brought before the king, and the king said to
him, "Are you Daniel, one of the exiles my father the king brought
from Judah? 14I have heard that the spirit of the gods is in you
and that you have insight, intelligence and outstanding wisdom.

5:10,11 *queen ... man:* The queen was most likely the wife of Nebuchadnezzar (but possibly of Nabonidus), and not the wife of Belshazzar. The man she described is Daniel who had been put in charge of Nebuchadnezzar's advisers. These advisers practiced magic, sorcery, fortune telling, and speaking to the spirits of the dead, all of which were forbidden in the Law of Moses (Lev 19:26; Deut 18:10-14). However, Daniel's ability to interpret dreams came from God.

5:11 *holy gods:* See the note at 4:8 (holy gods).

---

[a]**10** Or *queen mother*

5:15 *wise men and enchanters:* See the notes at 2:10 and 5:7.

5:16 *clothed in purple . . . third highest ruler:* Daniel would be third most powerful after Belshazzar and the king. The purple dye that was used for the royal robes given to Daniel was made from the shells of sea snails. Because it took thousands of shells to make a small amount of purple dye, purple was the most expensive dye used in cloth production. Only very wealthy people, like kings, could afford purple cloth.

5:18,19 *Most High God . . . all the peoples and nations:* See the notes at 3:26 and 3:4.

5:22 *Belshazzar:* See the note at 5:1,2.

5:25-28 *MENE, MENE, TEKEL, PARSIN:* Daniel gave these mysterious words a meaning that was based on the roots of similar-sounding Aramaic words. These words may literally refer to three different coins: the mina, shekel (*tekel* being its Aramaic spelling), and half mina (*parsin*). The Babylonian kingdom was defeated and divided between the Persians and Medes. "Peres," the singular of "parsin" may be a pun on "paras" meaning "Persia." See also the note at 2:39-45.

5:25-28 *Medes and Persians:* The Medes came from Media, a land about 400 miles north of the Persian Gulf. The Medes helped Babylon defeat the Assyrians in 612 B.C. Media became a province of the Persian empire in 549 B.C. The Persians came from the area that corresponds to modern-day Iran. After defeating the Medes in 549 B.C., they defeated Babylon in 539 B.C. Their empire influenced much of the ancient Near East until they were defeated by Alexander the Great of Macedonia (Greece) in 331 B.C. See the map on p. 2469.

15 The wise men and enchanters were brought before me to read
this writing and tell me what it means, but they could not explain
it. 16 Now I have heard that you are able to give interpretations and
to solve difficult problems. If you can read this writing and tell me
what it means, you will be clothed in purple and have a gold chain
placed around your neck, and you will be made the third highest
ruler in the kingdom."

17 Then Daniel answered the king, "You may keep your gifts
for yourself and give your rewards to someone else. Nevertheless,
I will read the writing for the king and tell him what it means.

18 "O king, the Most High God gave your father Nebuchadnezzar sovereignty and greatness and glory and splendor.
19 Because of the high position he gave him, all the peoples and
nations and men of every language dreaded and feared him. Those
the king wanted to put to death, he put to death; those he wanted
to spare, he spared; those he wanted to promote, he promoted; and
those he wanted to humble, he humbled. 20 But when his heart
became arrogant and hardened with pride, he was deposed from
his royal throne and stripped of his glory. 21 He was driven away
from people and given the mind of an animal; he lived with the
wild donkeys and ate grass like cattle; and his body was drenched
with the dew of heaven, until he acknowledged that the Most High
God is sovereign over the kingdoms of men and sets over them
anyone he wishes.

22 "But you his son,[a] O Belshazzar, have not humbled yourself, though you knew all this. 23 Instead, you have set yourself up
against the Lord of heaven. You had the goblets from his temple
brought to you, and you and your nobles, your wives and your
concubines drank wine from them. You praised the gods of silver
and gold, of bronze, iron, wood and stone, which cannot see or
hear or understand. But you did not honor the God who holds in
his hand your life and all your ways. 24 Therefore he sent the hand
that wrote the inscription.

25 "This is the inscription that was written:

MENE, MENE, TEKEL, PARSIN[b]

26 "This is what these words mean:

Mene[c]: God has numbered the days of your reign and
brought it to an end.

27 *Tekel*[d]: You have been weighed on the scales and found
wanting.

28 *Peres*[e]: Your kingdom is divided and given to the
Medes and Persians."

---

[a]22 Or *descendant*; or *successor* [b]25 Aramaic *UPARSIN* (that is, *AND PARSIN*) [c]26 *Mene* can mean *numbered* or *mina* (a unit of money). [d]27 *Tekel* can mean *weighed* or *shekel.* [e]28 *Peres* (the singular of *Parsin*) can mean *divided* or *Persia* or *a half mina* or *a half shekel.*

[29]Then at Belshazzar's command, Daniel was clothed in purple, a gold chain was placed around his neck, and he was proclaimed the third highest ruler in the kingdom.

[30]That very night Belshazzar, king of the Babylonians,[a] was slain, [31]and Darius the Mede took over the kingdom, at the age of sixty-two.

Daniel in the Den of Lions

6 It pleased Darius to appoint 120 satraps to rule throughout the kingdom, [2]with three administrators over them, one of whom was Daniel. The satraps were made accountable to them so that the king might not suffer loss. [3]Now Daniel so distinguished himself among the administrators and the satraps by his exceptional qualities that the king planned to set him over the whole kingdom. [4]At this, the administrators and the satraps tried to find grounds for charges against Daniel in his conduct of government affairs, but they were unable to do so. They could find no corruption in him, because he was trustworthy and neither corrupt nor negligent. [5]Finally these men said, "We will never find any basis for charges against this man Daniel unless it has something to do with the law of his God."

[6]So the administrators and the satraps went as a group to the king and said: "O King Darius, live forever! [7]The royal administrators, prefects, satraps, advisers and governors have all agreed that the king should issue an edict and enforce the decree that anyone who prays to any god or man during the next thirty days, except to you, O king, shall be thrown into the lions' den. [8]Now, O king, issue the decree and put it in writing so that it cannot be altered—in accordance with the laws of the Medes and Persians, which cannot be repealed." [9]So King Darius put the decree in writing.

[10]Now when Daniel learned that the decree had been published, he went home to his upstairs room where the windows opened toward Jerusalem. Three times a day he got down on his knees and prayed, giving thanks to his God, just as he had done before. [11]Then these men went as a group and found Daniel praying and asking God for help. [12]So they went to the king and spoke to him about his royal decree: "Did you not publish a decree that during the next thirty days anyone who prays to any god or man except to you, O king, would be thrown into the lions' den?"

The king answered, "The decree stands—in accordance with the laws of the Medes and Persians, which cannot be repealed."

[13]Then they said to the king, "Daniel, who is one of the exiles from Judah, pays no attention to you, O king, or to the decree you put in writing. He still prays three times a day." [14]When the king heard this, he was greatly distressed; he was determined to rescue Daniel and made every effort until sundown to save him.

[a]**30** Or *Chaldeans*

5:31 *Darius the Mede:* There is no mention of this Darius outside of the Bible. Darius I was a Persian king who ruled from 522 to 486 B.C. and may not be the ruler intended here. Babylon was conquered by Cyrus of Persia, not by the Medes, though certain prophecies suggest that the Medes would be involved in defeating Babylon (see Isa 13:17,18; 21:1,2; Jer 51:11,12). The Medes likely were part of the Persian armies that attacked Babylon, and the Persians may have put some of the conquered Babylonian territory under Median governors.

6:1,2 *satraps . . . administrators . . . king:* Darius I of Persia organized the empire into areas called "satrapies." Persian records tell of twenty to thirty such satrapies, so the 120 states mentioned here may refer to the smaller divisions that made up the satrapies, each of which was ruled by a satrap (or governor). Daniel was one of three administrators put in charge of the satraps. His power probably made his fellow administrators and the satraps jealous, and they wanted to take over his position of authority.

6:7 *lions' den:* Records from the Persian empire and much ancient art show that lions were hunted and trapped in pits (Ezek 19:4-9). Then they were moved to cages or dens where they could be more easily watched and fed.

6:8 *cannot be altered:* Once signed, an official decree must be carried out (see also Esth 1:19). Note that in 6:16 Darius hopes Daniel will not be killed, although it is Darius's own decree that puts Daniel in danger.

6:10 *Three times a day . . . prayed:* During and after the time of the exile, facing west toward Jerusalem during prayer was important for the Jewish people (see 1 Kgs 8:38-45; 2 Chr 6:37-39). Prayers were not required three times a day, but Jewish custom did call for morning and evening prayers (1 Chr 23:30). See also the mini-article called "Prayer," p. 2289.

Daniel and the Lions, a stone carving from Duomo, Oristano, Italy. Daniel was one of King Darius's favorite and most trusted officials. The king was so pleased with Daniel that he let him rule the whole kingdom. This made the other officials in Darius's government jealous. They plotted against Daniel and succeeded in having Daniel thrown into a lions' den. The next day, when the cover to the den was unsealed, the king found that Daniel had not been harmed, and he knew that Daniel had been innocent. The king then threw Daniel's accusers into the same den, and the lions ripped them to pieces. (See chapter 6.)

[15]Then the men went as a group to the king and said to him,
"Remember, O king, that according to the law of the Medes and
Persians no decree or edict that the king issues can be changed."
[16]So the king gave the order, and they brought Daniel and
threw him into the lions' den. The king said to Daniel, "May your
God, whom you serve continually, rescue you!"
[17]A stone was brought and placed over the mouth of the
den, and the king sealed it with his own signet ring and with
the rings of his nobles, so that Daniel's situation might not be
changed. [18]Then the king returned to his palace and spent the
night without eating and without any entertainment being
brought to him. And he could not sleep.
[19]At the first light of dawn, the king got up and hurried to
the lions' den. [20]When he came near the den, he called to Daniel in
an anguished voice, "Daniel, servant of the living God, has your
God, whom you serve continually, been able to rescue you from
the lions?"
[21]Daniel answered, "O king, live forever! [22]My God sent his

6:17 *den:* See the note at 6:7 (lions' den).

6:17 *sealed it . . . signet ring:* Royal seals were often made by pressing the king's or queen's ring (called a signet ring) into clay or wax. These seals were used on official documents and letters. See 1 Kings 21:8-10 and the illustration on p. 908.

6:21 *O king, live forever:* See the note at 2:4.

6:22 *angel:* See the note at 3:28.

angel, and he shut the mouths of the lions. They have not hurt me,
because I was found innocent in his sight. Nor have I ever done
any wrong before you, O king."
23 The king was overjoyed and gave orders to lift Daniel out
of the den. And when Daniel was lifted from the den, no wound
was found on him, because he had trusted in his God.
24 At the king's command, the men who had falsely accused
Daniel were brought in and thrown into the lions' den, along with
their wives and children. And before they reached the floor of the
den, the lions overpowered them and crushed all their bones.
25 Then King Darius wrote to all the peoples, nations and
men of every language throughout the land:

"May you prosper greatly!

26 "I issue a decree that in every part of my kingdom
people must fear and reverence the God of Daniel.

"For he is the living God
and he endures forever;
his kingdom will not be destroyed,
his dominion will never end.
27 He rescues and he saves;
he performs signs and wonders
in the heavens and on the earth.

King Darius wrote to all the peoples. . . . "The God of Daniel. . . . is the living God and he endures forever; his kingdom will not be destroyed, his dominion will never end."
Dan 6:25,26

6:24 *men . . . wives and children:* Sometimes in the ancient world, the family of a person who had broken the law was also put to death (see, for example, Josh 7:20-26; Esth 9:24,25). This may have been done as a way of making sure that no one in the executed person's family could take revenge or cause trouble for the king.

6:26 *living God:* The LORD, Daniel's God, was a living God who participates in real-life events. See also Deut 5:26; Josh 3:10; 1 Sam 17:26; and Jer 10:6-16.

QUESTIONS ABOUT DANIEL 1:1—6:28

1. At the beginning of DANIEL, what major event had recently happened in the history of the Jewish people? Besides their homes, what else were the Israelites in danger of losing when they were driven into exile?
2. Why were Daniel and his friends chosen by the king's official? (1:3-5) Why did Daniel object to eating the king's food? What do you think it took for Daniel and his friends to avoid this food? (1:8-16)
3. What special power or gift was Daniel given? According to Daniel, where did that power come from? (1:17, 20; 2:27-30) What opportunities did Daniel have to use this special gift and what was the result of Daniel using this power successfully? (2:46; 4:37; 5:29)
4. What was the meaning of Nebuchadnezzar's two dreams? (2:26-45 and 4:19-37) What did they help him to understand about Daniel's God?
5. Who was Belshazzar, and how did he and his party guests mock the God of Israel? What strange event occurred at the party? What role did Daniel play in the story?
6. On what grounds did Daniel's fellow officials try to get the king to get rid of Daniel? (6:1-13) What was King Darius's reaction to the news that Daniel had broken his new decree? (6:14-20) What was his reaction to Daniel being saved in the den of lions? (6:23-27)
7. If you had been a Jewish person living in a time of persecution, how may the stories in Daniel 1–6 have affected you? Think of a friend or someone in your family who may be going through a difficult time. What might you say to encourage them and show them they are not alone?

He has rescued Daniel
from the power of the lions."

28So Daniel prospered during the reign of Darius and the reign of Cyrus[a] the Persian.

The Visions of Daniel

The second half of the book records the visions of Daniel. They belong to a kind of literature known as "apocalyptic" writing. Apocalyptic literature uses symbols, signs, and interpretations of history to describe how God will triumph over the enemies of his people. The names of key persons and events are hidden by the symbolic language, but many agree that Daniel's visions focus on the time of Antiochus IV Epiphanes, the Seleucid ruler who was in charge of Palestine from 175 to 164 B.C.

TWO VISIONS AND A PRAYER

Daniel's visions of the four beasts and of the ram and the goat provide an understanding of the kingdoms that controlled the ancient Near East from the sixth to the second centuries B.C. Daniel's visions are interrupted by his prayer for the Jewish people in chapter 9.

Daniel's Dream of Four Beasts

7 In the first year of Belshazzar king of Babylon, Daniel had a dream, and visions passed through his mind as he was lying on his bed. He wrote down the substance of his dream.

2Daniel said: "In my vision at night I looked, and there before me were the four winds of heaven churning up the great sea. 3Four great beasts, each different from the others, came up out of the sea.

4"The first was like a lion, and it had the wings of an eagle. I watched until its wings were torn off and it was lifted from the ground so that it stood on two feet like a man, and the heart of a man was given to it.

5"And there before me was a second beast, which looked like a bear. It was raised up on one of its sides, and it had three ribs in its mouth between its teeth. It was told, 'Get up and eat your fill of flesh!'

6"After that, I looked, and there before me was another beast, one that looked like a leopard. And on its back it had four wings like those of a bird. This beast had four heads, and it was given authority to rule.

7"After that, in my vision at night I looked, and there before me was a fourth beast—terrifying and frightening and very powerful. It had large iron teeth; it crushed and devoured its victims and trampled underfoot whatever was left. It was different from all the former beasts, and it had ten horns.

[a]**28** Or *Darius, that is, the reign of Cyrus*

6:28 *Cyrus the Persian:* Cyrus of Persia defeated Babylon and brought it under Persian rule in 539 B.C. He ruled from 539 to 530 B.C. The prophet Isaiah spoke of Cyrus as God's "anointed" and "chosen" (Isa 45:1,4) who would help the Jewish people to be released from captivity in Babylon. An ancient Persian document called the Cyrus Cylinder (see the photograph on p. 854) describes how Cyrus defeated the Babylonians and treated foreign captives there with generosity. See also the article called "After the Exile: God's People Return to Judea," p. 931.

7:1,2 *first year of Belshazzar:* This would be 554 or 553 B.C. See the note at 5:1,2 (Belshazzar). The events described in chapter 7 happened before the events in chapter 5.

7:1,2 *four winds of heaven churning up the great sea:* Early readers of DANIEL would have recognized the four winds and the sea as characters in an ancient Babylonian myth about Marduk (see the note at 1:2, temple).

7:3-7 *Four great beasts:* The beasts that come from the sea are different ancient kingdoms (see also Rev 13:1; 17:8). The first refers to the Babylonian empire (see 2:36-38). The second beast represents the kingdom of Media (see the note at 2:39-45). The Medes' attack on Babylon had been predicted but did not happen (see the note at 5:31). The third beast represents the kingdom of Persia. See also the note at 5:31. The fourth beast refers to the empire founded by Alexander the Great, who defeated the Persians in 331 B.C. Eventually, Alexander's kingdom was divided between his generals and two ruling families, the Ptolemies and the Seleucids (see the note on p. 1653). Seleucid coins pictured certain Seleucid kings wearing horned crowns. See also Rev 13:2; 12:3; 13:1. Some scholars suggest that the second kingdom was that of Medo-Persia, the third, Greek, and the fourth, Roman.

Daniel's Vision of the Four Great Beasts by Matthäus Merian, 1627. Daniel had a dream, in which he saw four powerful beasts coming out of the sea. One looked like a lion, one like a bear, and one like a leopard with four heads. The fourth beast was stronger and more terrifying than the others. In this print, the artist has labeled these beasts to say that they represent four powerful kingdoms: Assyria, Persia, Greece, and Rome. See the note at 7:3-7 for another explanation. DANIEL, like all apocalyptic writings, contains many such examples of vivid symbolic imagery.

8 "While I was thinking about the horns, there before me was
another horn, a little one, which came up among them; and three
of the first horns were uprooted before it. This horn had eyes like
the eyes of a man and a mouth that spoke boastfully.

9 "As I looked,

"thrones were set in place,
  and the Ancient of Days took his seat.
His clothing was as white as snow;
  the hair of his head was white like wool.
His throne was flaming with fire,
  and its wheels were all ablaze.
10 A river of fire was flowing,
  coming out from before him.
Thousands upon thousands attended him;
  ten thousand times ten thousand stood before him.

7:8 *another horn:* Probably Antiochus IV Epiphanes, the Seleucid ruler who controlled Palestine from 175 to 164 B.C. He tried to get the Jewish people to abandon their worship and customs and adopt the Greek lifestyle. Some traditions interpret the smaller horn as the antichrist (see 2 Thes 2:4; Rev 13:5,6).

7:9 *thrones:* One is for the Eternal God (see Rev 20:4) and another for "a son of man" (7:13).

7:10 *books:* Books of judgment containing the record of good and evil that each person has done.

7:10 Acts 9:3; 22:6-9; Rev 5:11; 20:12.

7:11,12 *the beast was slain . . . other beasts:* These verses may refer to the fact that the fourth kingdom receives God's harshest judgment, while the earlier three just have their power stripped away.

7:13 *son of man:* The human being is contrasted with the beasts representing the earthly kingdoms. The "son" is crowned as king over an eternal kingdom (see also 2:44,45). In the New Testament, Jesus refers to himself as the Son of Man to emphasize his humanity and his role as the one who will save all of God's people (see Matt 24:30; 26:64; Mark 13:26; 14:62; Luke 21:27; Rev 1:7, 13; 14:14). See also the mini-article called "Son of Man," p. 1866.

7:16 *one of those standing there:* The "one" probably refers to an angel sent to interpret the visions or to one of those thousands attending him mentioned in 7:10.

7:17-19 *four great beasts . . . saints . . . Most High . . . fourth beast:* See the notes at 7:3-7 and 3:26. "The saints" here means the Jewish people (see 7:21). See the note at 7:8.

7:21,22 *horn was waging war against the saints:* See the note at 7:8. God comes to rescue his saints and judge the "horn." See also Rev 13:7; 20:4.

7:23,24 *fourth beast . . . fourth kingdom . . . ten . . . three kings:* See the note at 7:3-7. The ten kings, or horns, probably refers to the Seleucid rulers who came before Antiochus IV. Each of his three nephews was in line to be king before him, but he managed to cheat them out of their rights and become king himself. See 2:44; Rev 17:12.

7:25 *speak against the Most High . . . change the set times and the laws:* Antiochus IV Epiphanes banned the Jewish people from observing the Sabbath and from celebrating the yearly Jewish festivals (see Rev 12:14; 13:5,6; and *1 Maccabees* 1:41-53 in the Apocrypha). See also the notes on p. 1653 and p. 1654 (Maccabees).

7:18 Rev 22:5.

The court was seated,
and the books were opened.

[11]"Then I continued to watch because of the boastful words
the horn was speaking. I kept looking until the beast was slain and
its body destroyed and thrown into the blazing fire. [12](The other
beasts had been stripped of their authority, but were allowed to
live for a period of time.)

[13]"In my vision at night I looked, and there before me was
one like a son of man, coming with the clouds of heaven. He
approached the Ancient of Days and was led into his presence.
[14]He was given authority, glory and sovereign power; all peoples,
nations and men of every language worshiped him. His dominion
is an everlasting dominion that will not pass away, and his kingdom is one that will never be destroyed.

The Interpretation of the Dream

[15]"I, Daniel, was troubled in spirit, and the visions that
passed through my mind disturbed me. [16]I approached one of
those standing there and asked him the true meaning of all this.

"So he told me and gave me the interpretation of these
things: [17]'The four great beasts are four kingdoms that will rise
from the earth. [18]But the saints of the Most High will receive the
kingdom and will possess it forever—yes, for ever and ever.'

[19]"Then I wanted to know the true meaning of the fourth
beast, which was different from all the others and most terrifying,
with its iron teeth and bronze claws—the beast that crushed and
devoured its victims and trampled underfoot whatever was left. [20]I
also wanted to know about the ten horns on its head and about
the other horn that came up, before which three of them fell—the
horn that looked more imposing than the others and that had eyes
and a mouth that spoke boastfully. [21]As I watched, this horn was
waging war against the saints and defeating them, [22]until the
Ancient of Days came and pronounced judgment in favor of the
saints of the Most High, and the time came when they possessed
the kingdom.

[23]"He gave me this explanation: 'The fourth beast is a fourth
kingdom that will appear on earth. It will be different from all the
other kingdoms and will devour the whole earth, trampling it
down and crushing it. [24]The ten horns are ten kings who will come
from this kingdom. After them another king will arise, different
from the earlier ones; he will subdue three kings. [25]He will speak
against the Most High and oppress his saints and try to change the
set times and the laws. The saints will be handed over to him for a
time, times and half a time.[a]

[26]" 'But the court will sit, and his power will be taken away

[a]**25** Or *for a year, two years and half a year*

and completely destroyed forever. [27]Then the sovereignty, power
and greatness of the kingdoms under the whole heaven will be
handed over to the saints, the people of the Most High. His kingdom will be an everlasting kingdom, and all rulers will worship
and obey him.'
[28]"This is the end of the matter. I, Daniel, was deeply troubled by my thoughts, and my face turned pale, but I kept the matter to myself."

Daniel's Vision of a Ram and a Goat

8 In the third year of King Belshazzar's reign, I, Daniel, had a
vision, after the one that had already appeared to me. [2]In my vision
I saw myself in the citadel of Susa in the province of Elam; in the
vision I was beside the Ulai Canal. [3]I looked up, and there before
me was a ram with two horns, standing beside the canal, and the
horns were long. One of the horns was longer than the other but
grew up later. [4]I watched the ram as he charged toward the west
and the north and the south. No animal could stand against him,
and none could rescue from his power. He did as he pleased and
became great.
[5]As I was thinking about this, suddenly a goat with a prominent horn between his eyes came from the west, crossing the whole
earth without touching the ground. [6]He came toward the two-
horned ram I had seen standing beside the canal and charged at
him in great rage. [7]I saw him attack the ram furiously, striking the
ram and shattering his two horns. The ram was powerless to stand
against him; the goat knocked him to the ground and trampled on
him, and none could rescue the ram from his power. [8]The goat
became very great, but at the height of his power his large horn
was broken off, and in its place four prominent horns grew up
toward the four winds of heaven.
[9]Out of one of them came another horn, which started small
but grew in power to the south and to the east and toward the
Beautiful Land. [10]It grew until it reached the host of the heavens,
and it threw some of the starry host down to the earth and trampled on them. [11]It set itself up to be as great as the Prince of the
host; it took away the daily sacrifice from him, and the place of his
sanctuary was brought low. [12]Because of rebellion, the host ⌞of the
saints⌟[a] and the daily sacrifice were given over to it. It prospered in
everything it did, and truth was thrown to the ground.
[13]Then I heard a holy one speaking, and another holy one
said to him, "How long will it take for the vision to be fulfilled—
the vision concerning the daily sacrifice, the rebellion that causes
desolation, and the surrender of the sanctuary and of the host that
will be trampled underfoot?"

[a]12 Or *rebellion, the armies*

7:27 *saints, the people of the Most High:* See the notes at 7:17-19 and 3:26. See also Rev 20:4; 22:5.

8:1 *third year:* See the note at 7:1,2 (first year). Beginning with this verse, the rest of DANIEL is written in Hebrew.

8:2 *Susa:* Susa was a fortress city located east of Babylon in the province of Elam. See the map on p. 2469.

8:3-7 *ram with two horns . . . goat:* The ram with two horns refers to the Medes and Persians who were pictured as being together in one kingdom (see 6:8,12). The longer horn stands for Persia, which controlled lands to its west, north, and south, including Palestine. The goat from the west represents the Macedonians (Greeks), first led by Alexander the Great, who conquered Persia in 331 B.C.

8:8 *large horn was broken off:* Alexander the Great died in 323 B.C. His large empire was divided among four generals. The four horns most likely refer to these four men. The descendants of Ptolemy and Seleucus fought each other for control of the Near East and Egypt. See the note on p. 1653.

8:9-12 *horn, which started small . . . trampled on them . . . host of the saints:* The little horn is Antiochus IV Epiphanes, who was a descendant of Seleucus (see note at 8:8). His attack on the Jewish people is pictured as a direct attack on the "host of the saints," a term that could refer to angels or to God's people. The army's "Prince" may refer to an angel-prince or to the high priest of Israel.

During the last years of his rule, Antiochus IV tried to destroy Jewish worship and customs. He challenged the authority of the Jewish priests, interfered with daily offerings and sacrifices in the temple (8:13), and set up an altar honoring a foreign god in the temple of Jerusalem (see the note at 9:27).

8:10 Rev 12:4.

14 He said to me, "It will take 2,300 evenings and mornings; then the sanctuary will be reconsecrated."

The Interpretation of the Vision

15 While I, Daniel, was watching the vision and trying to understand it, there before me stood one who looked like a man. 16 And I heard a man's voice from the Ulai calling, "Gabriel, tell this man the meaning of the vision."

17 As he came near the place where I was standing, I was terrified and fell prostrate. "Son of man," he said to me, "understand that the vision concerns the time of the end."

18 While he was speaking to me, I was in a deep sleep, with my face to the ground. Then he touched me and raised me to my feet. 19 He said: "I am going to tell you what will happen later in the time of wrath, because the vision concerns the appointed time of the end.[a] 20 The two-horned ram that you saw represents the kings of Media and Persia. 21 The shaggy goat is the king of Greece, and the large horn between his eyes is the first king. 22 The four horns that replaced the one that was broken off represent four kingdoms that will emerge from his nation but will not have the same power.

23 "In the latter part of their reign, when rebels have become completely wicked, a stern-faced king, a master of intrigue, will arise. 24 He will become very strong, but not by his own power. He will cause astounding devastation and will succeed in whatever he does. He will destroy the mighty men and the holy people. 25 He will cause deceit to prosper, and he will consider himself superior. When they feel secure, he will destroy many and take his stand against the Prince of princes. Yet he will be destroyed, but not by human power.

26 "The vision of the evenings and mornings that has been given you is true, but seal up the vision, for it concerns the distant future."

27 I, Daniel, was exhausted and lay ill for several days. Then I got up and went about the king's business. I was appalled by the vision; it was beyond understanding.

Daniel's Prayer

9 In the first year of Darius son of Xerxes[b] (a Mede by descent), who was made ruler over the Babylonian[c] kingdom— 2 in the first year of his reign, I, Daniel, understood from the Scriptures, according to the word of the LORD given to Jeremiah the prophet, that the desolation of Jerusalem would last seventy years. 3 So I turned to the Lord God and pleaded with him in prayer and petition, in fasting, and in sackcloth and ashes.

---

a19 Or *because the end will be at the appointed time* **b1** Hebrew *Ahasuerus*
c1 Or *Chaldean*

8:14 *It will take 2,300 evenings and mornings:* Or 1,150 days. There were to be two daily sacrifices in the temple, one in the morning and one at dusk (Exod 29:38-42). Antiochus IV stopped these sacrifices and set up the foreign altar in 167 B.C. The Jewish people led by Judas Maccabeus eventually defeated Antiochus and rededicated the temple on Chislev 25, 164 B.C. (around mid-December). The 1,150 days roughly correspond to the three and a half years mentioned in *1 Maccabees* 1:54—4:52 (in the Apocrypha).

8:16 *Gabriel:* An angel whose name means "God is Mighty." See also 9:21; Luke 1:19,26.

8:17 *the time of the end:* Here this phrase refers to the end of the persecution of God's people, not to the final end of time (see 7:14,18,27; 12:1-4).

8:20,21 *ram . . . Media and Persia . . . goat . . . Greece:* See the notes at 5:25-28 (Medes and Persians); 8:3-7; and 8:8. The conquest of Alexander began the spread of Greek culture and religion, which often conflicted with Jewish customs and religion.

8:23 *a stern-faced king:* Antiochus IV Epiphanes. See the notes at 7:25 and 8:9-12. Record of Antiochus's sneak attack on Jerusalem is reported in the Apocrypha, *1 Maccabees* 1:29,30.

8:27 *king's business:* Referring to Belshazzar (8:1).

9:1,2 *Darius son of Xerxes (a Mede by descent):* See the note at 5:31. The identities of the Darius and Xerxes named here are unclear.

9:2 *seventy years:* See Jer 25:11; 29:10. The "seventy years" in JEREMIAH is probably counted from the capture of Jerusalem by Nebuchadnezzar in 587/586 B.C. The rebuilt temple was dedicated in 515 B.C. Most likely, the "seventy years" here symbolizes a whole lifetime.

4 I prayed to the LORD my God and confessed:
"O Lord, the great and awesome God, who keeps his
covenant of love with all who love him and obey his commands, 5 we have sinned and done wrong. We have been
wicked and have rebelled; we have turned away from your
commands and laws. 6 We have not listened to your servants
the prophets, who spoke in your name to our kings, our
princes and our fathers, and to all the people of the land.
7 "Lord, you are righteous, but this day we are covered
with shame—the men of Judah and people of Jerusalem and
all Israel, both near and far, in all the countries where you
have scattered us because of our unfaithfulness to you.
8 O LORD, we and our kings, our princes and our fathers are
covered with shame because we have sinned against you. 9 The
Lord our God is merciful and forgiving, even though we have
rebelled against him; 10 we have not obeyed the LORD our God
or kept the laws he gave us through his servants the prophets.
11 All Israel has transgressed your law and turned away, refusing to obey you.
"Therefore the curses and sworn judgments written in
the Law of Moses, the servant of God, have been poured out
on us, because we have sinned against you. 12 You have fulfilled
the words spoken against us and against our rulers by bringing upon us great disaster. Under the whole heaven nothing
has ever been done like what has been done to Jerusalem.
13 Just as it is written in the Law of Moses, all this disaster has
come upon us, yet we have not sought the favor of the LORD
our God by turning from our sins and giving attention to
your truth. 14 The LORD did not hesitate to bring the disaster
upon us, for the LORD our God is righteous in everything he
does; yet we have not obeyed him.
15 "Now, O Lord our God, who brought your people out
of Egypt with a mighty hand and who made for yourself a
name that endures to this day, we have sinned, we have done
wrong. 16 O Lord, in keeping with all your righteous acts, turn
away your anger and your wrath from Jerusalem, your city,
your holy hill. Our sins and the iniquities of our fathers have
made Jerusalem and your people an object of scorn to all
those around us.
17 "Now, our God, hear the prayers and petitions of your
servant. For your sake, O Lord, look with favor on your desolate sanctuary. 18 Give ear, O God, and hear; open your eyes
and see the desolation of the city that bears your Name. We
do not make requests of you because we are righteous, but
because of your great mercy. 19 O Lord, listen! O Lord, forgive!
O Lord, hear and act! For your sake, O my God, do not delay,
because your city and your people bear your Name."

9:3,4 *fasting . . . sackcloth and ashes:* To show deep sadness or to express sorrow for sinning, Israelites went without eating (called fasting), rubbed ashes on their clothes and body, and wore clothes made of sackcloth (a rough cloth made from goat or camel hair). See the illustration on p. 1551. See the note at 4:27.

9:5 *sinned . . . rebelled:* Refers to the many ways the people of Israel and their leaders disobeyed God's Laws by following other gods, ignoring the warnings of God's prophets, and making bad alliances out of fear (see Neh 1:4-7; 9:16-35; Isa 30:8-13).

9:12-14 *great disaster:* Refers either to the destruction of Jerusalem and the temple and the exile that followed in Babylon in the sixth century B.C., or the pollution of the Jerusalem temple under Antiochus IV in the second century B.C. See the notes at 7:25; 8:9-12; and 9:27.

9:16 *holy hill:* The temple in Jerusalem was built on an area of high ground known as Mount Zion (see Ps 48:1-3). It was considered holy because God was present there in the temple (Ps 9:11; Joel 3:21). See also the mini-article called "Zion," p. 1294.

9:11 Lev 26:14-46; Deut 28:15-68; 29:9-29. **9:15** Exod 12–14; Deut 6:21-23; Jer 32:20-22.

The Seventy "Sevens"

20 While I was speaking and praying, confessing my sin and the sin of my people Israel and making my request to the LORD my God for his holy hill— 21 while I was still in prayer, Gabriel, the man I had seen in the earlier vision, came to me in swift flight about the time of the evening sacrifice. 22 He instructed me and said to me, "Daniel, I have now come to give you insight and understanding. 23 As soon as you began to pray, an answer was given, which I have come to tell you, for you are highly esteemed. Therefore, consider the message and understand the vision:

24 "Seventy 'sevens'[a] are decreed for your people and your holy city to finish[b] transgression, to put an end to sin, to atone for wickedness, to bring in everlasting righteousness, to seal up vision and prophecy and to anoint the most holy.[c]

25 "Know and understand this: From the issuing of the decree[d] to restore and rebuild Jerusalem until the Anointed One,[e] the ruler, comes, there will be seven 'sevens,' and sixty-two 'sevens.' It will be rebuilt with streets and a trench, but in times of trouble. 26 After the sixty-two 'sevens,' the Anointed One will be cut off and will have nothing.[f] The people of the ruler who will come will destroy the city and the sanctuary. The end will come like a flood: War will continue until the end, and desolations have been decreed. 27 He will confirm a covenant with many for one 'seven.'[g] In the middle of the 'seven'[g] he will put an end to sacrifice and offering. And on a wing ⌞of the temple⌟ he will set up an abomination that causes desolation, until the end that is decreed is poured out on him.[h][i]"

THE FINAL VISION

In these final chapters, an angel gives Daniel a four-part message about a conflict between Persian and Greek rulers. This conflict, the angel tells Daniel, will take place before God comes to deliver the chosen people from the time of persecution and to give them eternal life. The angel concludes his message by instructing Daniel to remain faithful.

Daniel's Vision of a Man

10 In the third year of Cyrus king of Persia, a revelation was given to Daniel (who was called Belteshazzar). Its message was true and it concerned a great war.[j] The understanding of the message came to him in a vision.

[a]24 Or *'weeks'*; also in verses 25 and 26 [b]24 Or *restrain* [c]24 Or *Most Holy Place*; or *most holy One* [d]25 Or *word* [e]25 Or *an anointed one*; also in verse 26 [f]26 Or *off and will have no one*; or *off, but not for himself* [g]27 Or *'week'* [h]27 Or *it* [i]27 Or *And one who causes desolation will come upon the pinnacle of the abominable ⌞temple⌟, until the end that is decreed is poured out on the desolated ⌞city⌟* [j]1 Or *true and burdensome*

9:24 *Seventy 'sevens' . . . anoint the most holy:* This time of suffering is also translated as seventy weeks of years, or 490 years. See also the note at 9:2.

9:25 *Anointed One, the ruler:* The "Anointed One" here may refer to Zerubbabel or to the high priest Joshua, who were leaders of the Jewish people when the temple in Jerusalem was rebuilt (see Hag 1:1-14; 2:21-23; Zech 4:1-14; 6:9-14). Christian leaders would later identify Jesus Christ as the "Anointed One."

9:25 *seven 'sevens' . . . sixty-two 'sevens':* The first seven "sevens" may mean "seven times seven years" (or forty-nine) years. This period could represent the time from 586 B.C., the final exile from Jerusalem, to 538 B.C. when Cyrus's decree allowed the Jewish people to return to Judah to restore the temple (see Ezra 1:2-4). The sixty-two "sevens" may mean "weeks" of years (or 434 years) represent a difficult time for Jerusalem, probably under the rule of the Persians and then the Greeks.

9:26 *Anointed One . . . the ruler who will come:* This refers to another "Anointed One" many years after the one mentioned in 9:25. Most likely it is Onias III, the high priest when Antiochus IV came to power. The "ruler who will come" refers to Antiochus IV (see the notes at 7:8; 8:9-12). For Christians, the reference to an Anointed One who would be cut off refers to Jesus' death on the cross.

9:27 *end to sacrifice and offering . . . abomination that causes desolation:* Antiochus did a number of things to try to wipe out Jewish worship (see the notes at 8:9-12 and 8:14). The "abomination" has been identified as an altar used to make sacrifices to foreign gods or as some kind of statue honoring one of the Greek gods (see in the Apocrypha *1 Maccabees* 1:11,15,54). It remained in the temple for the three and a half years until 25 Chislev 164 B.C. when the temple was purified and rededicated (see the note at 8:14). See also 11:31; 12:11; Matt 24:15; Mark 13:14.

[2]At that time I, Daniel, mourned for three weeks. [3]I ate no
choice food; no meat or wine touched my lips; and I used no
lotions at all until the three weeks were over.
[4]On the twenty-fourth day of the first month, as I was standing on the bank of the great river, the Tigris, [5]I looked up and there
before me was a man dressed in linen, with a belt of the finest gold
around his waist. [6]His body was like chrysolite, his face like lightning, his eyes like flaming torches, his arms and legs like the gleam
of burnished bronze, and his voice like the sound of a multitude.
[7]I, Daniel, was the only one who saw the vision; the men
with me did not see it, but such terror overwhelmed them that
they fled and hid themselves. [8]So I was left alone, gazing at this
great vision; I had no strength left, my face turned deathly pale and
I was helpless. [9]Then I heard him speaking, and as I listened to
him, I fell into a deep sleep, my face to the ground.
[10]A hand touched me and set me trembling on my hands
and knees. [11]He said, "Daniel, you who are highly esteemed, consider carefully the words I am about to speak to you, and stand up,
for I have now been sent to you." And when he said this to me, I
stood up trembling.
[12]Then he continued, "Do not be afraid, Daniel. Since the
first day that you set your mind to gain understanding and to
humble yourself before your God, your words were heard, and I
have come in response to them. [13]But the prince of the Persian
kingdom resisted me twenty-one days. Then Michael, one of the
chief princes, came to help me, because I was detained there with
the king of Persia. [14]Now I have come to explain to you what will
happen to your people in the future, for the vision concerns a time
yet to come."
[15]While he was saying this to me, I bowed with my face
toward the ground and was speechless. [16]Then one who looked like
a man[a] touched my lips, and I opened my mouth and began to
speak. I said to the one standing before me, "I am overcome with
anguish because of the vision, my lord, and I am helpless. [17]How
can I, your servant, talk with you, my lord? My strength is gone
and I can hardly breathe."
[18]Again the one who looked like a man touched me and gave
me strength. [19]"Do not be afraid, O man highly esteemed," he said.
"Peace! Be strong now; be strong."

When he spoke to me, I was strengthened and said, "Speak,
my lord, since you have given me strength."
[20]So he said, "Do you know why I have come to you? Soon I
will return to fight against the prince of Persia, and when I go, the
prince of Greece will come; [21]but first I will tell you what is written

---

a16 Most manuscripts of the Masoretic Text; one manuscript of the Masoretic Text, Dead Sea Scrolls and Septuagint *Then something that looked like a man's hand*

10:1 *third year of Cyrus:* Or, 536 B.C. See the note at 6:28.

10:2,3 *mourned . . . lotions:* See the note at 9:3,4. Oils and lotions were put on one's face and hair as a normal part of grooming, but in times of sorrow this was not done (see Isa 61:3).

10:4 *first month:* Nisan (also known as Abib), the first month of the Hebrew calendar, from about mid-March to mid-April.

10:4 *the great river, the Tigris:* A river in Babylonia that joined the Euphrates River forming a wide fertile area. See the map on p. 2469. See also 8:2; Ezek 1:1-3.

10:5,6 *a man dressed in linen . . . burnished bronze:* Daniel saw an angel, perhaps Gabriel (see 8:16). Fine linen, a symbol of purity, was used for priestly garments. Compare to 2:31-35. See also Ezek 1; 9–11; Rev 1:13-15; 2:18; 19:12.

10:13 *prince of the Persian kingdom . . . Michael:* In ancient Near Eastern stories, battles between the gods or angel-princes who represented different countries were common. See also Josh 5:13-15. Michael was the guardian angel of the Jewish people (10:21; 12:1; Rev 12:7).

10:13 *Persian kingdom:* See the note at 5:25-28 (Medes and Persians). See also the mini-article called "Persia," p. 859.

10:20,21 *prince of Persia . . . Greece . . . Book of Truth . . . Michael:* See the notes at 10:13 (prince); 5:25-28 (Medes and Persians); and 8:20, 21 (ram). Alexander the Great defeated the Persians in 331 B.C. (see the note at 8:3-7). The "Book of Truth" may refer to God's record of the names of people who belonged to God, or to a record of the good and evil that people have done (see Exod 32:32,33; Dan 12:1). See also the note at 7:10.

11:1 *Darius the Mede:* See the note at 5:31.

11:2-4 *fourth . . . mighty king . . . empire will be uprooted:* The four kings are kings of Persia, which may include Darius and Xerxes (see the note at 9:1, 2), Darius II and Artaxerxes, but this is uncertain. The "mighty king" is most likely Alexander the Great (see the notes at 5:25-28 and 8:20,21). After his death, Alexander's empire was divided into four kingdoms (see the note at 8:8).

11:5 *king of the South . . . one of his commanders:* This may refer to Ptolemy I of Egypt and Seleucus I, who established an even greater empire to the north in Syria.

11:6,7 *daughter . . . family line:* Berenice, daughter of Ptolemy II Philadelphus (285-246 B.C.), the king of the South, was married to Antiochus II Theos (261-246 B.C.) of Syria, the king of the north, to create a treaty. But Antiochus II's wife Laodice plotted to have Berenice and Antiochus II killed. Berenice's brother Ptolemy III Euergetes (246-222 B.C.) then attacked the northern kingdom and carried away many of its precious treasures back to Egypt.

11:9,10 *king of the North . . . sons:* Seleucus II Callinicus (246-226 B.C.) tried to invade the southern kingdom but was defeated. His sons, Seleucus III (226-223 B.C.) and Antiochus III (called "the Great"; 223-187 B.C.), could not defeat the southern kingdom either.

11:11 *king of the South . . . North:* Ptolemy IV Philopator (221-203 B.C.), king of the South, defeated Antiochus III, king of the North, in 217 B.C. at Raphia. Later Antiochus III was joined by some of the Jewish people (11:14) to fight against Ptolemy V Epiphanes (203-181 B.C.), king of the South, but this rebellion was also defeated. Eventually Antiochus III did defeat the forces of the South at Paneas in 200 B.C. (11:15). Then he took control of Palestine by 197 B.C. In order to make peace, Antiochus III gave his daughter Cleopatra I to marry Ptolemy V of Egypt, king of the South. A Roman general defeated Antiochus III at Magnesia in Asia Minor in 190 B.C.

in the Book of Truth. (No one supports me against them except
11 Michael, your prince. [1]And in the first year of Darius the
Mede, I took my stand to support and protect him.)

The Kings of the South and the North

[2]"Now then, I tell you the truth: Three more kings will
appear in Persia, and then a fourth, who will be far richer than all
the others. When he has gained power by his wealth, he will stir up
everyone against the kingdom of Greece. [3]Then a mighty king will
appear, who will rule with great power and do as he pleases. [4]After
he has appeared, his empire will be broken up and parceled out
toward the four winds of heaven. It will not go to his descendants,
nor will it have the power he exercised, because his empire will be
uprooted and given to others.

[5]"The king of the South will become strong, but one of his
commanders will become even stronger than he and will rule his
own kingdom with great power. [6]After some years, they will
become allies. The daughter of the king of the South will go to the
king of the North to make an alliance, but she will not retain her
power, and he and his power[a] will not last. In those days she will be
handed over, together with her royal escort and her father[b] and the
one who supported her.

[7]"One from her family line will arise to take her place. He
will attack the forces of the king of the North and enter his
fortress; he will fight against them and be victorious. [8]He will also
seize their gods, their metal images and their valuable articles of
silver and gold and carry them off to Egypt. For some years he will
leave the king of the North alone. [9]Then the king of the North will
invade the realm of the king of the South but will retreat to his
own country. [10]His sons will prepare for war and assemble a great
army, which will sweep on like an irresistible flood and carry the
battle as far as his fortress.

[11]"Then the king of the South will march out in a rage and
fight against the king of the North, who will raise a large army, but
it will be defeated. [12]When the army is carried off, the king of the
South will be filled with pride and will slaughter many thousands,
yet he will not remain triumphant. [13]For the king of the North will
muster another army, larger than the first; and after several years,
he will advance with a huge army fully equipped.

[14]"In those times many will rise against the king of the
South. The violent men among your own people will rebel in fulfillment of the vision, but without success. [15]Then the king of the
North will come and build up siege ramps and will capture a fortified city. The forces of the South will be powerless to resist; even
their best troops will not have the strength to stand. [16]The invader
will do as he pleases; no one will be able to stand against him. He

[a]**6** Or *offspring* [b]**6** Or *child* (see Vulgate and Syriac)

will establish himself in the Beautiful Land and will have the power to destroy it. [17]He will determine to come with the might of his entire kingdom and will make an alliance with the king of the South. And he will give him a daughter in marriage in order to overthrow the kingdom, but his plans[a] will not succeed or help him. [18]Then he will turn his attention to the coastlands and will take many of them, but a commander will put an end to his insolence and will turn his insolence back upon him. [19]After this, he will turn back toward the fortresses of his own country but will stumble and fall, to be seen no more.

[20]"His successor will send out a tax collector to maintain the royal splendor. In a few years, however, he will be destroyed, yet not in anger or in battle.

[21]"He will be succeeded by a contemptible person who has not been given the honor of royalty. He will invade the kingdom when its people feel secure, and he will seize it through intrigue. [22]Then an overwhelming army will be swept away before him; both it and a prince of the covenant will be destroyed. [23]After coming to an agreement with him, he will act deceitfully, and with only a few people he will rise to power. [24]When the richest provinces feel secure, he will invade them and will achieve what neither his fathers nor his forefathers did. He will distribute plunder, loot and wealth among his followers. He will plot the overthrow of fortresses—but only for a time.

[25]"With a large army he will stir up his strength and courage against the king of the South. The king of the South will wage war with a large and very powerful army, but he will not be able to stand because of the plots devised against him. [26]Those who eat from the king's provisions will try to destroy him; his army will be swept away, and many will fall in battle. [27]The two kings, with their hearts bent on evil, will sit at the same table and lie to each other, but to no avail, because an end will still come at the appointed time. [28]The king of the North will return to his own country with great wealth, but his heart will be set against the holy covenant. He will take action against it and then return to his own country.

[29]"At the appointed time he will invade the South again, but this time the outcome will be different from what it was before. [30]Ships of the western coastlands[b] will oppose him, and he will lose heart. Then he will turn back and vent his fury against the holy covenant. He will return and show favor to those who forsake the holy covenant.

[31]"His armed forces will rise up to desecrate the temple fortress and will abolish the daily sacrifice. Then they will set up the abomination that causes desolation. [32]With flattery he will corrupt those who have violated the covenant, but the people who know their God will firmly resist him.

[a]**17** Or *but she* [b]**30** Hebrew *of Kittim*

11:20 *His successor:* Antiochus III's son, Seleucus IV Philopator (187-175 B.C.). He sent his finance minister Heliodorus to take money from the treasury of the Jewish temple in Jerusalem (see in the Apocrypha *1 Maccabees* 3:1–40). Seleucus IV was assassinated by supporters of Heliodorus.

11:21 *a contemptible person:* Antiochus IV Epiphanes (175-164 B.C.), the brother of Seleucus IV. The sons of Seleucus IV were next in line to be king when their father was killed, but because they were still young Antiochus stepped in and took the throne.

11:22-24 *distribute plunder, loot and wealth:* Antiochus IV removed the Jewish high priest Onias III (see the note at 9:26) and made a treaty with Pergamum, which allowed Antiochus to take it over with a small force. One of the "richest provinces" may have been Egypt.

11:25-27 *against the king of the South . . . lie to each other:* Antiochus IV attacked Egypt, which was ruled by the young Ptolemy VI Philometor. The "lies" they tell each other may refer to Antiochus IV trying to trick Ptolemy VI into giving Antiochus control over Egypt.

11:28 *return . . . take action against it:* Before Antiochus left Egypt, the city of Alexandria declared its support for Ptolemy Euergetes and Cleopatra (brother and sister of Philometor). Antiochus tried to take the city but couldn't, so he returned home by way of Palestine in 169 B.C. He entered the temple in Jerusalem and stole large amounts of gold (see in the Apocrypha *1 Maccabees* 1:20).

11:29,30 *invade the South . . . Ships of the western coastlands:* Antiochus IV's next invasion of Egypt in 168 B.C. was stopped by Roman troops that came on ships from the west.

11:31-33 *desecrate the temple . . . Those who are wise:* See the notes at 8:9-12; 8:14; and 9:27. See also 12:11; Matt 24:15; Mark 13:14. A number of faithful Jews died during Antiochus IV's reign (see in the Apocrypha *1 Maccabees* 1:63).

33“Those who are wise will instruct many, though for a time
they will fall by the sword or be burned or captured or plundered.
34When they fall, they will receive a little help, and many who are
not sincere will join them. 35Some of the wise will stumble, so that
they may be refined, purified and made spotless until the time of
the end, for it will still come at the appointed time.

The King Who Exalts Himself

36“The king will do as he pleases. He will exalt and magnify
himself above every god and will say unheard-of things against the
God of gods. He will be successful until the time of wrath is completed, for what has been determined must take place. 37He will
show no regard for the gods of his fathers or for the one desired by
women, nor will he regard any god, but will exalt himself above
them all. 38Instead of them, he will honor a god of fortresses; a god
unknown to his fathers he will honor with gold and silver, with
precious stones and costly gifts. 39He will attack the mightiest
fortresses with the help of a foreign god and will greatly honor
those who acknowledge him. He will make them rulers over many
people and will distribute the land at a price.[a]
40“At the time of the end the king of the South will engage
him in battle, and the king of the North will storm out against him
with chariots and cavalry and a great fleet of ships. He will invade
many countries and sweep through them like a flood. 41He will
also invade the Beautiful Land. Many countries will fall, but Edom,
Moab and the leaders of Ammon will be delivered from his hand.
42He will extend his power over many countries; Egypt will not
escape. 43He will gain control of the treasures of gold and silver
and all the riches of Egypt, with the Libyans and Nubians in submission. 44But reports from the east and the north will alarm him,
and he will set out in a great rage to destroy and annihilate many.
45He will pitch his royal tents between the seas at[b] the beautiful
holy mountain. Yet he will come to his end, and no one will help
him.

The End Times

12 “At that time Michael, the great prince who protects your
people, will arise. There will be a time of distress such as has not
happened from the beginning of nations until then. But at that
time your people—everyone whose name is found written in the
book—will be delivered. 2Multitudes who sleep in the dust of the
earth will awake: some to everlasting life, others to shame and
everlasting contempt. 3Those who are wise[c] will shine like the
brightness of the heavens, and those who lead many to righteousness, like the stars for ever and ever. 4But you, Daniel, close up and

[a]39 Or *land for a reward* [b]45 Or *the sea and* [c]3 Or *who impart wisdom*

11:36 *say unheard-of things against the God of gods:* Antiochus claimed the name “Epiphanes,” which in Greek means god “revealed.” See also 2 Thes 2:3,4; Rev 13:5,6.

11:37,38 *gods of his fathers or for the one desired by women:* It is unclear which gods Antiochus IV rejected, but the god desired by women probably is Tammuz (Adonis), the Mesopotamian god of vegetation. The “god of fortresses” likely refers to Zeus, the Greek equivalent of the Canaanite god Baal Shamem (see in the Apocrypha *1 Maccabees* 1:54–59; *2 Maccabees* 6:2). Antiochus rewarded those who worshiped Zeus and encouraged the spread of the Zeus cult.

11:40-45 *king of the South . . . king of the North . . . Ammon:* These verses describe the hoped-for end of Antiochus IV, but the historical records apart from the Bible do not clearly show the details mentioned here. The king of the North is identified as Antiochus IV. Edom, Moab, and Ammon escape the northern king’s massacre, but the people of the holy land do not. Verse 44 shows a reaction similar to that of Antiochus IV in 11:30,31. The destruction of the evil king is said to come in a battle taking place between the Mediterranean Sea and Mount Zion (see the note at 9:16). See also Ezek 38,39; Rev 16:13-16. Other ancient sources say Antiochus IV actually died in Persia during an invasion in 164 B.C.

12:1 *Michael . . . the book:* See the note at 10:13 (Michael). The earthly battles of chapter 11 now become a battle fought by God’s heavenly messenger who will come during the time of terrible suffering. It is not clear whether this means during the time of Antiochus IV or some other future time (see also Jer 30:7; Joel 2:1-27; Rev 12:7). For more on the “book,” see the notes at 7:10 and 10:20, 21.

12:2 *everlasting life:* See the mini-articles called “Eternal Life,” p. 2072 and “Resurrection,” p. 2210. See also Isa 26:19; Matt 25:46; John 5:29.

12:4 Rev 22:10.

seal the words of the scroll until the time of the end. Many will go
here and there to increase knowledge."

5Then I, Daniel, looked, and there before me stood two others, one on this bank of the river and one on the opposite bank.
6One of them said to the man clothed in linen, who was above the
waters of the river, "How long will it be before these astonishing
things are fulfilled?"
7The man clothed in linen, who was above the waters of the
river, lifted his right hand and his left hand toward heaven, and I
heard him swear by him who lives forever, saying, "It will be for a
time, times and half a time.[a] When the power of the holy people
has been finally broken, all these things will be completed."
8I heard, but I did not understand. So I asked, "My lord,
what will the outcome of all this be?"
9He replied, "Go your way, Daniel, because the words are
closed up and sealed until the time of the end. 10Many will be purified, made spotless and refined, but the wicked will continue to be
wicked. None of the wicked will understand, but those who are
wise will understand.
11"From the time that the daily sacrifice is abolished and the
abomination that causes desolation is set up, there will be 1,290
days. 12Blessed is the one who waits for and reaches the end of the
1,335 days.
13"As for you, go your way till the end. You will rest, and then at
the end of the days you will rise to receive your allotted inheritance."

[a]7 Or *a year, two years and half a year*

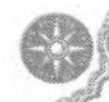

12:5 *the river:* See the note at 10:4 (Tigris).

12:5,6 *two others . . . man clothed in linen:* The two people are witnesses to the angel's proclamation (12:7). According to the Law of Moses, two witnesses were needed to confirm an event (Deut 19:15).

12:11 *daily sacrifice . . . abomination that causes desolation:* This number of days may refer to the number of days that Antiochus IV's persecutions will continue, or they may refer to some other future period connected with the end. See the notes at 8:9-12 and 9:27. See also 11:31; Matt 24:15; Mark 13:14.

12:13 *you will rise:* This one of only a few explicit references to "resurrection" in the Old Testament. See the mini-article called "Resurrection," p. 2210.

12:7 Rev 10:5; 12:14. **12:10** Rev 22:11.

QUESTIONS ABOUT DANIEL 7:1—12:13

1. Summarize the meaning of Daniel's vision in 7:1-27. What would such a vision mean to people who were going through a time of persecution and suffering?
2. Who are the "ram," the "goat," and the "little horn"? How will the little horn attack God and his people? (8:1-14)
3. What was the main purpose behind Daniel's prayer for his people? (9:1-19) What are some of the reasons God has allowed his people to endure suffering, such as the exile or later persecutions?
4. What is the "abomination" that a foreign ruler will bring to Jerusalem? (9:26, 27) Name some ways God is dishonored today.
5. How did Daniel prepare to receive the vision given in chapters 11 and 12? How can we receive God's messages today?
6. What great promise is given in Daniel's final vision? (12:1-13) Who will benefit from this promise?
7. Reflecting on DANIEL may show you that it was written to offer comfort to God's people who were enduring persecution. Think of a situation in your own life when you were made to feel bad for doing the right thing. How could thinking about God's saving power help you?

HOSEA

A strong marriage is built on trust and commitment. But trust is broken when one partner is unfaithful. Keep this image in mind as you read the prophet Hosea's message to Israel.

What makes Hosea special?

Hosea is a short version of the Hebrew name *Hoshaiah,* which means "the LORD has saved." Hosea lived and wrote in the northern kingdom (Israel). Some scholars believe that when the Assyrians invaded Israel, Hosea may have escaped to the southern kingdom (Judah), taking his prophecies with him. The first three chapters of HOSEA tell of Hosea's marriage to Gomer, a woman who may have been a temple prostitute in the cult of Baal, a Canaanite fertility god. Hosea's family life became a living picture of the message he preached. HOSEA uses language and images from the Canaanite religion to fight against Baal worship.

Why was Hosea written?

Hosea told the people of Israel and Judah to be faithful to the LORD, who had brought them out of slavery in Egypt and kept his promise to give them a land of their own. But the people sinned by worshiping other gods. Their leaders trusted in their own military strength and in the power of allied foreign countries rather than depending on the LORD to protect their nation. Hosea told the people of Israel that they were to be punished because they had not been loyal to the LORD. However, he also offers the hope that God would forgive them and give them a fresh start as God's chosen people.

What's the story behind the scene?

Why would the people turn away from the LORD God after becoming rich and wealthy in the land of promise (Canaan)? When the people of Israel settled in Canaan, they did not force all of the Canaanite people out the land. Instead, they settled among the Canaanites and began to adopt some of their ways. The Canaanite gods were believed to be responsible for giving rain and making the land fertile for good crops. In order to have good crops some of the Israelite people began to participate in religious ceremonies honoring the Canaanite gods. These ceremonies included the practice of ritual prostitution (see the note at 1:2). Also at this time (750-722 B.C.) Israel was threatened by the powerful Assyrian empire. Various kings of Israel paid tribute money to the Assyrian leaders to keep them from taking over the land. At other times, they asked countries such as Egypt to help them stand up against the Assyrians. Eventually, these political attempts to save the land backfired. Assyria defeated the northern kingdom (Israel) in 722 B.C. and forced many of its people to

Hosea and the kings of Judah and Israel: Little is known about the prophet Hosea except what is told in the first three chapters of this book about his wife and children. Hosea's prophecies date to the time when Uzziah (781-740 B.C.), Jotham (740-736 B.C.), Ahaz (736-716 B.C.), and Hezekiah (716-687 B.C.) were kings in Judah and Jeroboam II (783-743 B.C.) was king in Israel. Hosea's work as a prophet began around 750 B.C. during the reign of Jeroboam II and probably ended just before Israel fell to the Assyrians in 722 B.C. Why Jeroboam II is the only northern ruler mentioned is a mystery, since a number of Israel's other kings played key roles in the downfall of the northern kingdom. To read what the Bible has to say about these rulers, see 2 Kgs 15:1-7 and 2 Chr 26:1-23 (Uzziah, also called Azariah); 2 Kgs 15:32-38 and 2 Chr 27:1-8 (Jotham); 2 Kgs 16:1-20 and 2 Chr 28:1-27 (Ahaz); 2 Kgs 18:1—20:21 and 2 Chr 29:1—32:33 (Hezekiah) and 2 Kgs 14:23-29 (Jeroboam II).

marriage and betrothal: Hosea uses the image of marriage between a man and a woman as a way of describing God's relationship with his chosen people, Israel. And when the people offer sacrifices to and worship other gods, Hosea says, this is like a wife who is being unfaithful to her husband.

One custom in the ancient Near East was for a man to pay a "bride price" to the father of the woman he wanted to marry (Gen 34:12). If accepted, the exchange marked the beginning of the couple's betrothal. The LORD tells Hosea how much more than a bride price he is willing to give to show the people the kind of husband he intends to be (2:19).

leave their homeland. See also the article called "From Joshua to the Exile: The People of Israel in the Promised Land," p. 924.

Most of the prophecies in the book are directed toward the northern kingdom (Israel). But the southern kingdom (Judah) is also named in a few places (5:5, 10-15; 6:4-11; 12:2). Some scholars have suggested that the prophecies naming Judah may have been added at a later time, so that Hosea's strong message about remaining faithful to the LORD could apply to all God's people.

HOW IS HOSEA CONSTRUCTED?

HOSEA has two clear sections. The first section (chapters 1–3) compares Hosea's marriage with the LORD's relationship with the people of Israel. The second section contains Hosea's messages to the people and leaders of Israel and Judah. His words describe God's anger and judgment as well as God's promise to forgive the people.

Hosea's family compared to unfaithful Israel (1:1—3:5)

Hosea's message to Israel, Judah, and their leaders (4:1—14:9)

- Israel and Judah are unfaithful to the LORD (4:1—5:15)
- The people try to trust the LORD but fail (6:1—8:14)
- The LORD will punish Israel (9:1—13:16)
- Those who return to the LORD will be forgiven (14:1-9)

Hosea's Family Compared to Unfaithful Israel

The LORD tells Hosea to marry an unfaithful woman as a way of showing how unfaithful Israel has been. Then the LORD tells Hosea what to name his children. The chosen names are reminders that Israel is going to be punished. Hosea is told to love his unfaithful wife, and his love for her is to be a picture of the LORD's continuing love for unfaithful Israel.

1 The word of the LORD that came to Hosea son of Beeri during
the reigns of Uzziah, Jotham, Ahaz and Hezekiah, kings of Judah,
and during the reign of Jeroboam son of Jehoash[a] king of Israel:

Hosea's Wife and Children

2When the LORD began to speak through Hosea, the LORD
said to him, "Go, take to yourself an adulterous wife and children
of unfaithfulness, because the land is guilty of the vilest adultery in
departing from the LORD." 3So he married Gomer daughter of
Diblaim, and she conceived and bore him a son.
4Then the LORD said to Hosea, "Call him Jezreel, because I
will soon punish the house of Jehu for the massacre at Jezreel, and
I will put an end to the kingdom of Israel. 5In that day I will break
Israel's bow in the Valley of Jezreel."

a1 Hebrew *Joash,* a variant of *Jehoash*

1:1 *Hosea . . . kings of Judah . . . king of Israel:* See the note on p. 1684 (Hosea).

1:2 *an adulterous wife . . . the land is guilty of the vilest adultery:* "The land" here refers to the northern kingdom, which broke away from the southern tribes known as Judah (1 Kgs 12). See also the mini-article called "Israel," p. 264.

The Canaanite worship of the fertility god Baal included ritual prostitution. Worshipers of Baal believed that this practice would bring rain and make their crops grow.

It is not clear whether the woman Hosea was told to marry was a temple prostitute, a woman who had been unfaithful to her husband, or a woman who was faithful to Hosea at first but then became unfaithful. In any case, Hosea's marriage was to draw attention to Israel's own unfaithfulness: the nation had turned from the LORD to worship idols. See also the mini-article called "Prostitution in the Bible," p. 1688.

1:4 *Jezreel . . . house of Jehu:* In Hebrew "Jezreel" means "God scatters (seed)." Here the name is used as a threat—the LORD will punish Israel by scattering its people as a farmer scatters seeds. In 1:11 "Jezreel" is used as a promise—the LORD will bless Israel by giving the nation many people, just as a big harvest comes when many seeds are scattered in a field. For more about King Jehu, see 2 Kgs 9:1—10:14.

1:6-9 *Lo-Ruhamah . . . Lo-Ammi:* In Hebrew "Lo-Ruhamah" means "No Mercy," or "Not Loved," and "Lo-Ammi" means "Not My People." The names of Hosea's children were meant to be a reminder that the LORD would punish Israel for being unfaithful.

1:7 *Judah:* Hosea's prophecies were directed mainly at Israel. This reference to the southern kingdom of Judah may point to how Jerusalem escaped being destroyed by the Assyrian leader Sennacherib in 701 B.C. (2 Kgs 19:32-37).

1:10,11 *the Israelites . . . people of Judah and the people of Israel will be reunited:* Hosea foresees a time when God will restore Israel and Judah and bring them together under one leader. This promise echoes the ancient promise the LORD had made to the Israelite ancestors, Abraham and Jacob (Gen 22:17; 32:12). See also the note at 1:4.

The prophet Hosea, a twelfth century enamel plaque. Many of Israel's prophets used dramatic methods for communicating the messages God wanted them to deliver. Hosea used his marriage to Gomer, a woman who may have served as a prostitute at the temple of Baal, as a way of depicting Israel's unfaithfulness to the LORD. This striking image helped Hosea to show the people how great God's love was for his chosen people. The LORD says of his people, "I will heal their waywardness and love them freely, for my anger has turned away from them" (14:4).

[6]Gomer conceived again and gave birth to a daughter. Then
the LORD said to Hosea, "Call her Lo-Ruhamah,[a] for I will no
longer show love to the house of Israel, that I should at all forgive
them. [7]Yet I will show love to the house of Judah; and I will save
them—not by bow, sword or battle, or by horses and horsemen,
but by the LORD their God."

[8]After she had weaned Lo-Ruhamah, Gomer had another
son. [9]Then the LORD said, "Call him Lo-Ammi,[b] for you are not my
people, and I am not your God.

[10]"Yet the Israelites will be like the sand on the seashore,
which cannot be measured or counted. In the place where it was

[a]6 *Lo-Ruhamah* means *not loved.* [b]9 *Lo-Ammi* means *not my people.*

said to them, 'You are not my people,' they will be called 'sons of
the living God.' 11 The people of Judah and the people of Israel will
be reunited, and they will appoint one leader and will come up out
of the land, for great will be the day of Jezreel.
2 "Say of your brothers, 'My people,' and of your sisters, 'My
loved one.'

Israel Punished and Restored

2 "Rebuke your mother, rebuke her,
for she is not my wife,
and I am not her husband.
Let her remove the adulterous look from her face
and the unfaithfulness from between her breasts.
3 Otherwise I will strip her naked
and make her as bare as on the day she was born;
I will make her like a desert,
turn her into a parched land,
and slay her with thirst.
4 I will not show my love to her children,
because they are the children of adultery.
5 Their mother has been unfaithful
and has conceived them in disgrace.
She said, 'I will go after my lovers,
who give me my food and my water,
my wool and my linen, my oil and my drink.'
6 Therefore I will block her path with thornbushes;
I will wall her in so that she cannot find her way.
7 She will chase after her lovers but not catch them;
she will look for them but not find them.
Then she will say,
'I will go back to my husband as at first,
for then I was better off than now.'
8 She has not acknowledged that I was the one
who gave her the grain, the new wine and oil,
who lavished on her the silver and gold—
which they used for Baal.
9 "Therefore I will take away my grain when it ripens,
and my new wine when it is ready.
I will take back my wool and my linen,
intended to cover her nakedness.
10 So now I will expose her lewdness
before the eyes of her lovers;
no one will take her out of my hands.
11 I will stop all her celebrations:
her yearly festivals, her New Moons,
her Sabbath days—all her appointed feasts.
12 I will ruin her vines and her fig trees,
which she said were her pay from her lovers;

2:2 *adulterous . . . unfaithfulness:* See the note at 1:2.

2:5 *my lovers:* "Lovers" here may refer to the practice of having sex with the worshipers of the Canaanite gods, or it may simply refer to the gods themselves. See the note at 2:8.

2:5 *linen . . . oil:* Linen cloth was made from fibers of the flax plant. Olive oil was used for cooking, as fuel for lamps, for making ointments, and for religious ceremonies (Exod 30:23-31; 1 Sam 16:12,13).

2:8 *I was the one . . . used for Baal:* Israel was to thank the LORD for a good harvest (Deut 26:1-11). In Hosea's time, many of the people were honoring Baal instead, because he was believed to fertilize the earth with rain. For more, see the mini-article called "Canaanite Gods and Goddesses," p. 469.

2:11 *New Moons . . . Sabbath days . . . feasts:* The New Moon Festival was celebrated on the first day of each month when the new moon came out (Num 28:11-15). The Sabbath began at sunset on Friday and ended at sunset on Saturday. No work was to be done on the Sabbath, which means "rest" or to "stop working" (Exod 20:8-11; Deut 5:12-15). For more, see the chart called "Jewish Calendar and Festivals," p. 944.

2:12 *her lovers:* See the note at 2:5.

2:13 *burned incense:* Incense was a substance made of aromatic spices and gums that was burned on a special altar in Israel's temple (Exod 30:7,8,34,35). Here incense is being burned to honor Baal. See also Isa 65:3.

2:14,15 *Valley of Achor:* The location of the Valley of Achor (meaning the Valley of Trouble) is uncertain. It is somewhere near Jericho and Ai (see Josh 7:24-26).

2:16 *my husband . . . my master:* "Master" probably refers to Baal (see the note at 2:8). In ancient Israel, a man could have, in addition to a wife who had full legal rights, a wife known as a "concubine." A concubine was legally bound to the man but did not have the full privileges of the primary wife. The LORD will be Israel's true husband and not merely her master.

2:18 Lev 25:18, 19; Ezek 34:25-31.

I will make them a thicket,
and wild animals will devour them.
13 I will punish her for the days
she burned incense to the Baals;
she decked herself with rings and jewelry,
and went after her lovers,
but me she forgot,"
declares the LORD.

14 "Therefore I am now going to allure her;
I will lead her into the desert
and speak tenderly to her.
15 There I will give her back her vineyards,
and will make the Valley of Achor[a] a door of hope.
There she will sing[b] as in the days of her youth,
as in the day she came up out of Egypt.

16 "In that day," declares the LORD,
"you will call me 'my husband';
you will no longer call me 'my master.[c]'
17 I will remove the names of the Baals from her lips;
no longer will their names be invoked.
18 In that day I will make a covenant for them

[a]15 *Achor* means *trouble.* [b]15 Or *respond* [c]16 Hebrew *baal*

PROSTITUTION IN THE BIBLE

Two different kinds of prostitutes are found in biblical stories. First are those who offered to have sex with men to earn money or to get some personal favor. Some women may have become prostitutes as a way to survive when they no longer were under the protection or care of a husband, father, or other family members. Prostitutes wore fancy clothes and jewels to attract men (Ezek 16:8-26). One prostitute named Rahab was best known for helping Joshua's spies escape from Jericho after they had sneaked into the city (Josh 2).

A second kind of prostitute may have been a female or a male who had sex with worshipers of a god or goddess in a temple. Many of these gods or goddesses were thought to make the land and its people fertile. In Canaan, there were pairs of such gods: Baal and Asherah, and later, Osiris and Isis. The prophet Hosea seems to be warning the people of Israel against having sex with temple prostitutes in rituals honoring these Canaanite fertility gods (Hos 4:10-19). Some time later, Judah's King Josiah (639-609 B.C.) tore down buildings that housed "male shrine prostitutes" (2 Kgs 23:7) who may have served in the worship of Canaanite gods. In the Old Testament, Israel's unfaithfulness is often compared with being a prostitute or chasing after prostitutes (Isa 23:16; Jer 3:6; Ezek 16; Nah 3:4). In the New Testament, the book of REVELATION calls Babylon, meaning the Roman empire, a shameless prostitute who tempts people and nations into relations with her (Rev 17).

The Law of Moses (Lev 19:29) forbade prostitution. A priest's daughter who became a prostitute was to be burned to death (Lev 21:9). No money earned by prostitutes was to be accepted as a gift to the temple (Deut 23:18).

with the beasts of the field and the birds of the air
and the creatures that move along the ground.
Bow and sword and battle
I will abolish from the land,
so that all may lie down in safety.
19 I will betroth you to me forever;
I will betroth you in[a] righteousness and justice,
in[b] love and compassion.
20 I will betroth you in faithfulness,
and you will acknowledge the LORD.

21 "In that day I will respond,"
declares the LORD—
"I will respond to the skies,
and they will respond to the earth;
22 and the earth will respond to the grain,
the new wine and oil,
and they will respond to Jezreel.[c]
23 I will plant her for myself in the land;
I will show my love to the one I called
'Not my loved one.[d]'
I will say to those called 'Not my people,[e]'
'You are my people';
and they will say, 'You are my God.' "

Hosea's Reconciliation With His Wife

3 The LORD said to me, "Go, show your love to your wife again,
though she is loved by another and is an adulteress. Love her as the
LORD loves the Israelites, though they turn to other gods and love
the sacred raisin cakes."

2 So I bought her for fifteen shekels[f] of silver and about a
homer and a lethek[g] of barley. 3 Then I told her, "You are to live

[a]19 Or *with*; also in verse 20 [b]19 Or *with* [c]22 *Jezreel* means *God plants.*
[d]23 Hebrew *Lo-Ruhamah* [e]23 Hebrew *Lo-Ammi* [f]2 That is, about 6 ounces (about 170 grams) [g]2 That is, probably about 10 bushels (about 330 liters)

2:19 *betroth you to me:* See the note on p. 1684 (marriage).

2:22 *Jezreel:* See the note at 1:4.

2:23 *Not my loved one . . . Not my people:* See the note at 1:6-9. See also Rom 9:25; 1 Pet 2:10.

3:1,2 *your wife:* Probably refers to Hosea's wife Gomer (see the note at 1:2). As in chapter 1, Hosea's act of loving such a woman is meant to symbolize how Israel rejected its true husband (the LORD) to worship foreign idols, but how God continued to love her. Compare the price Hosea paid for Gomer to Exodus 21:32 and Leviticus 27:1-7.

3:1 *sacred raisin cakes:* Made of pressed grapes or raisins, these cakes were eaten at religious rituals honoring the Canaanite gods. See also Jer 7:18; 44:19.

QUESTIONS ABOUT HOSEA 1:1—3:5

1. Who was Hosea, and what did the LORD tell him to do? (1:2; 3:1) Who was Gomer? What did the names of Hosea's children have to do with the relationship between the LORD and Israel at this time? (1:3-9)
2. Why did the LORD promise to punish Israel? (2:2-13)
3. The LORD's harsh words of punishment were balanced by his promise to help Israel in the future (2:14-23). What did this hopeful future look like? How could Israel regain the LORD's help and blessings?
4. Why is King David mentioned in 3:5?
5. Complete these sentences:
A strong marriage is based on . . .
A strong relationship with God is based on . . .

3:5 *David their king:* David ruled over the united Israelite kingdom (1010-970 B.C.). See also the mini-article called "David," p. 1028. The people of Israel would have to live for a time without a temple to worship the LORD and without a government (3:4), but the LORD promised to restore the kingdom to the level it had reached under King David.

4:1 *Israelites:* Referring to the people of the northern kingdom. See the note at 1:2.

4:2 *cursing . . . adultery:* The people have turned away from worshiping the LORD, and so they are breaking many of the LORD's commands (Exod 20:3-17; Deut 5:7-21).

4:3 *the land mourns . . . waste away:* The sins of the people are causing the land to "mourn" and causing suffering for its creatures (Lev 18:25-27).

4:4,5 *priest . . . prophets:* Israel's priests served as God's representatives for all the people. But some of the priests allowed the worship of idols and they encouraged people to sin so they could get rich from increased sin offerings (see the note at 4:8).

The prophets of the Bible delivered God's messages. Apparently, some who called themselves prophets were associated with the unfaithful priests and caused the people to turn away from God. See also the mini-article called "Israel's Priests," p. 2344, and the article called "Prophets and Prophecy," p. 935.

with[a] me many days; you must not be a prostitute or be intimate
with any man, and I will live with[a] you."
4 For the Israelites will live many days without king or prince,
without sacrifice or sacred stones, without ephod or idol. 5 Afterward the Israelites will return and seek the LORD their God and
David their king. They will come trembling to the LORD and to his
blessings in the last days.

Hosea's Message to Israel, Judah, and Their Leaders

This second part of HOSEA records the prophet's messages to the people of Israel and Judah and to their leaders. Most of Hosea's words describe God's anger and judgment against the people who have sinned in many ways, but his message also includes the hope that the people will be restored to their land sometime in the future.

ISRAEL AND JUDAH ARE UNFAITHFUL TO THE LORD

Hosea tells the people of Israel and Judah that the LORD accuses them of being unfaithful by worshiping the Canaanite idols and by turning to foreign kings for help.

The Charge Against Israel

4 Hear the word of the LORD, you Israelites,
because the LORD has a charge to bring
against you who live in the land:
"There is no faithfulness, no love,
no acknowledgment of God in the land.
2 There is only cursing,[b] lying and murder,
stealing and adultery;
they break all bounds,
and bloodshed follows bloodshed.
3 Because of this the land mourns,[c]
and all who live in it waste away;
the beasts of the field and the birds of the air
and the fish of the sea are dying.

4 "But let no man bring a charge,
let no man accuse another,
for your people are like those
who bring charges against a priest.
5 You stumble day and night,
and the prophets stumble with you.
So I will destroy your mother—
6 my people are destroyed from lack of knowledge.

[a]3 Or *wait for* [b]2 That is, to pronounce a curse upon [c]3 Or *dries up*

"Because you have rejected knowledge,
I also reject you as my priests;
because you have ignored the law of your God,
I also will ignore your children.
7 The more the priests increased,
the more they sinned against me;
they exchanged[a] their[b] Glory for something disgraceful.
8 They feed on the sins of my people
and relish their wickedness.
9 And it will be: Like people, like priests.
I will punish both of them for their ways
and repay them for their deeds.

10 "They will eat but not have enough;
they will engage in prostitution but not increase,
because they have deserted the LORD
to give themselves 11 to prostitution,
to old wine and new,
which take away the understanding 12 of my people.
They consult a wooden idol
and are answered by a stick of wood.
A spirit of prostitution leads them astray;
they are unfaithful to their God.
13 They sacrifice on the mountaintops
and burn offerings on the hills,
under oak, poplar and terebinth,
where the shade is pleasant.
Therefore your daughters turn to prostitution
and your daughters-in-law to adultery.

14 "I will not punish your daughters
when they turn to prostitution,
nor your daughters-in-law
when they commit adultery,
because the men themselves consort with harlots
and sacrifice with shrine prostitutes—
a people without understanding will come to ruin!

15 "Though you commit adultery, O Israel,
let not Judah become guilty.

"Do not go to Gilgal;
do not go up to Beth Aven.[c]
And do not swear, 'As surely as the LORD lives!'
16 The Israelites are stubborn,
like a stubborn heifer.

[a]7 Syriac and an ancient Hebrew scribal tradition; Masoretic Text *I will exchange* [b]7 Masoretic Text; an ancient Hebrew scribal tradition *my* [c]15 *Beth Aven* means *house of wickedness* (a name for Bethel, which means *house of God*).

4:8 *feed on the sins of my people:* Sin offerings (Lev 4:1—6:7) were actually done in order to purify someone who had sinned by disobeying God's laws or who had accidentally done something God told them not to do. Some of the meat from the offerings was given to the priests to eat. The priests were "feeding" on the people's sins by relishing the fact that the people kept sinning, had to bring offerings, and thus gave the priests more food. See also the chart called "Sacrifices and Offerings," p. 219.

4:10 *engage in prostitution:* See the note at 1:2.

4:12 *wooden idol . . . stick of wood:* Wooden poles were set up to honor the Canaanite goddess Asherah (Deut 16:21; Judg 6:25). Wooden sticks or staffs were thrown in an ancient practice called divination. Which stick was chosen or how the sticks landed was thought to reveal a god's wishes.

4:13,14 *sacrifice on the mountaintops . . . men themselves consort with harlots:* Ancient Canaanite worship places were usually built on a high place near a grove of trees (Deut 12:2; 1 Kgs 14:23; Jer 2:20). The people of Israel did not destroy all these places when they settled in Canaan, so the fertility rituals honoring the Canaanite gods continued. Some Israelite men and women joined in these rituals.

4:15 *Judah . . . Gilgal . . . Beth Aven:* See the Introduction to HOSEA and the note at 1:7. Gilgal was an Israelite worship place in the Jordan Valley (Josh 4:19-23).

"Beth Aven" is what Hosea calls Bethel. Bethel was a sacred place to the people of Israel because their ancestor Jacob had a special dream there (Gen 28:10-22). Jacob named the place "Bethel," which means "house of God." To show how the people have fallen away from God, Hosea calls this same place "Beth Aven," meaning "house of sin" or "house of wickedness." See 1 Kgs 12:25—13:10.

How then can the LORD pasture them
like lambs in a meadow?
17 Ephraim is joined to idols;
leave him alone!
18 Even when their drinks are gone,
they continue their prostitution;
their rulers dearly love shameful ways.
19 A whirlwind will sweep them away,
and their sacrifices will bring them shame.

Judgment Against Israel

5 "Hear this, you priests!
Pay attention, you Israelites!
Listen, O royal house!
This judgment is against you:
You have been a snare at Mizpah,
a net spread out on Tabor.
2 The rebels are deep in slaughter.
I will discipline all of them.
3 I know all about Ephraim;
Israel is not hidden from me.
Ephraim, you have now turned to prostitution;
Israel is corrupt.

4 "Their deeds do not permit them
to return to their God.
A spirit of prostitution is in their heart;
they do not acknowledge the LORD.
5 Israel's arrogance testifies against them;
the Israelites, even Ephraim, stumble in their sin;
Judah also stumbles with them.
6 When they go with their flocks and herds
to seek the LORD,
they will not find him;
he has withdrawn himself from them.
7 They are unfaithful to the LORD;
they give birth to illegitimate children.
Now their New Moon festivals
will devour them and their fields.

8 "Sound the trumpet in Gibeah,
the horn in Ramah.
Raise the battle cry in Beth Aven[a];
lead on, O Benjamin.
9 Ephraim will be laid waste
on the day of reckoning.

[a]**8** *Beth Aven* means *house of wickedness* (a name for Bethel, which means *house of God*).

4:19 *their sacrifices:* Along with participating in ritual prostitution, people also brought sacrifices to honor the Canaanite gods.

5:1 *priests . . . Israelites . . . royal house:* See the note at 4:4,5. "Israelites" here probably means the tribal leaders of Israel. The royal house is the family and attendants of whoever was king of Israel at this time.

5:1 *Mizpah . . . Tabor:* Jacob and Laban made a covenant at Mizpah (Gen 31:43-49), perhaps because it was an ancient holy place. Mount Tabor was located between Nazareth and the Sea of Galilee near the Valley of Jezreel (see the map on p. 2467). A god called Baal of Tabor was worshiped there.

5:6 *go with their flocks and herds to seek the LORD:* In ancient times, offering animal sacrifices was a way to worship God and to restore or celebrate the relationship between the giver and God. Israel's laws for sacrifice usually called for the sacrifice of cattle or sheep. See LEVITICUS; and the chart called "Sacrifices and Offerings," p. 219.

5:7 *illegitimate children:* See 4:14 and the note at 1:2.

5:7 *New Moon festivals:* See the note at 2:11.

5:8 *Gibeah . . . Ramah . . . Beth Aven:* See the note at 4:15. These three towns string northward from Jerusalem across the tribal land of Benjamin. See the map on p. 2464. An attack from the south would put the entire land of Benjamin (belonging to Israel) in danger.

Among the tribes of Israel
I proclaim what is certain.
10 Judah's leaders are like those
who move boundary stones.
I will pour out my wrath on them
like a flood of water.
11 Ephraim is oppressed,
trampled in judgment,
intent on pursuing idols.[a]
12 I am like a moth to Ephraim,
like rot to the people of Judah.
13 "When Ephraim saw his sickness,
and Judah his sores,
then Ephraim turned to Assyria,
and sent to the great king for help.
But he is not able to cure you,
not able to heal your sores.
14 For I will be like a lion to Ephraim,
like a great lion to Judah.
I will tear them to pieces and go away;
I will carry them off, with no one to rescue them.
15 Then I will go back to my place
until they admit their guilt.
And they will seek my face;
in their misery they will earnestly seek me."

THE PEOPLE TRY TO TRUST THE LORD BUT FAIL

At first, Hosea's message causes the people to encourage one another to return to the LORD, but their change of heart only lasts a little while. Soon they return to worshiping idols, killing each other to gain power, and asking foreign powers for help.

Israel Unrepentant

6 "Come, let us return to the LORD.
He has torn us to pieces
but he will heal us;
he has injured us
but he will bind up our wounds.
2 After two days he will revive us;
on the third day he will restore us,
that we may live in his presence.
3 Let us acknowledge the LORD;
let us press on to acknowledge him.
As surely as the sun rises,
he will appear;

[a]11 The meaning of the Hebrew for this word is uncertain.

5:10 *Judah's leaders . . . boundary stones:* Judah's invasion of Israel is compared to moving boundary markers, a practice forbidden in Israel's law (Deut 19:14; 27:14-26; Prov 22:28). People used things such as large rocks to mark the boundaries of the land they owned.

5:13 *turned to Assyria:* This passage may refer either to King Menahem trying to buy an alliance with the Assyrian king, Tiglath-Pileser, in 738 B.C. (2 Kgs 15:19, 20; he is also called Pul, see 1 Chron 5:26). Or it may refer to King Hoshea of Israel (see the note at 7:3) who paid taxes to King Shalmaneser of Assyria and then asked King So of Egypt to help him rebel against Assyria (2 Kgs 17:1-6). See the map on p. 2468.

5:15 *go back to my place:* The word translated as "place" can refer to the LORD's place in the heavens. The point is that the LORD is withdrawing from the land and its people. The LORD will not return to be with them until they have confessed their guilt.

6:1-3 *let us return . . . acknowledge him:* This time of conflict between Israel and Judah and the threat from Assyria must have made the people feel as if their land was being torn apart. So, they turned to the LORD for help and healing. But their return probably did not include a true confession of their guilt, which the LORD required (5:15). Perhaps the priests did return to making sacrifices to the LORD God of Israel (6:6), but they did not try to stop the people from worshiping the Canaanite gods of the land.

6:5 *my prophets:* See the note at 4:4,5.

6:6 *I desire mercy, not sacrifice:* Treating one another with justice and kindness was far more important than simply the rituals of offering sacrifices (Isa 1:12-17; Amos 5:21-24; Mic 6:6-8). See also Matt 9:13; 12:7.

6:7-9 *Adam ... Gilead ... Shechem:* Which of God's laws the people broke at Adam is not clear (Josh 3:14-17). Gilead most likely refers to the mountainous region southeast of the Sea of Galilee. The blood may refer to child sacrifices, or it may refer to a political revolt (see 2 Kgs 15:25). Shechem had been a place to worship the LORD for many years (Josh 24). Perhaps the priests from towns such as Bethel, where the Canaanite gods continued to be worshiped, attacked people who were going to worship God at Shechem. See also Num 35:9-13; Josh 20:1-9; and the map on p. 2464.

6:11 *Judah:* See the note at 1:7. The southern kingdom is warned that its people will also turn to idol worship, and their leaders will rely on the protection of foreign kings.

7:1 *Israel ... Samaria:* See the note at 1:2. King Omri (ruled 885-874 B.C.) built the city of Samaria and made it the capital of the northern kingdom of Israel (1 Kgs 16:24). See the map on p. 2467.

7:3 *king:* This may refer to King Hoshea. He took Israel's throne by murdering King Pekah (2 Kgs 15:30) and then ruled for nine years (2 Kgs 17:1-4). See also the note at 5:13.

7:5 *On the day ... inflamed with wine:* The "day" here probably refers to the day Hoshea's friends got King Pekah drunk and killed him, and then crowned Hoshea.

he will come to us like the winter rains,
like the spring rains that water the earth."

4 "What can I do with you, Ephraim?
What can I do with you, Judah?
Your love is like the morning mist,
like the early dew that disappears.
5 Therefore I cut you in pieces with my prophets,
I killed you with the words of my mouth;
my judgments flashed like lightning upon you.
6 For I desire mercy, not sacrifice,
and acknowledgment of God rather than burnt offerings.
7 Like Adam,[a] they have broken the covenant—
they were unfaithful to me there.
8 Gilead is a city of wicked men,
stained with footprints of blood.
9 As marauders lie in ambush for a man,
so do bands of priests;
they murder on the road to Shechem,
committing shameful crimes.
10 I have seen a horrible thing
in the house of Israel.
There Ephraim is given to prostitution
and Israel is defiled.

11 "Also for you, Judah,
a harvest is appointed.

"Whenever I would restore the fortunes of my people,
7 1 whenever I would heal Israel,
the sins of Ephraim are exposed
and the crimes of Samaria revealed.
They practice deceit,
thieves break into houses,
bandits rob in the streets;
2 but they do not realize
that I remember all their evil deeds.
Their sins engulf them;
they are always before me.

3 "They delight the king with their wickedness,
the princes with their lies.
4 They are all adulterers,
burning like an oven
whose fire the baker need not stir
from the kneading of the dough till it rises.
5 On the day of the festival of our king

[a]7 Or *As at Adam*; or *Like men*

the princes become inflamed with wine,
and he joins hands with the mockers.
[6] Their hearts are like an oven;
they approach him with intrigue.
Their passion smolders all night;
in the morning it blazes like a flaming fire.
[7] All of them are hot as an oven;
they devour their rulers.
All their kings fall,
and none of them calls on me.

[8] "Ephraim mixes with the nations;
Ephraim is a flat cake not turned over.
[9] Foreigners sap his strength,
but he does not realize it.
His hair is sprinkled with gray,
but he does not notice.
[10] Israel's arrogance testifies against him,
but despite all this
he does not return to the LORD his God
or search for him.

[11] "Ephraim is like a dove,
easily deceived and senseless—
now calling to Egypt,
now turning to Assyria.
[12] When they go, I will throw my net over them;
I will pull them down like birds of the air.
When I hear them flocking together,
I will catch them.
[13] Woe to them,
because they have strayed from me!
Destruction to them,
because they have rebelled against me!
I long to redeem them
but they speak lies against me.
[14] They do not cry out to me from their hearts
but wail upon their beds.
They gather together[a] for grain and new wine
but turn away from me.
[15] I trained them and strengthened them,
but they plot evil against me.
[16] They do not turn to the Most High;
they are like a faulty bow.
Their leaders will fall by the sword
because of their insolent words.

Woe to them, because they have strayed from me! Destruction to them, because they have rebelled against me! I long to redeem them but they speak lies against me.
Hos 7:13

7:7 *hot as an oven . . . All their kings fall:* During a twelve-year period (745-732 B.C.), four of Israel's kings were murdered by those who replaced them in power (2 Kgs 15:8-30).

7:8 *the nations:* Israel has not kept its traditions and its identity separate from the foreigners living in the land. In 7:9, foreigners may refer to Egypt and Aram (Syria) who helped Israel in its rebellion against Assyria, or it may refer to how some of Israel's kings paid heavy taxes to keep the Assyrians from taking over all of Israel (2 Kgs 15:17-20; 17:1-4).

7:11 *like a dove, easily deceived and senseless . . . Egypt . . . Assyria:* See the notes at 5:13 and 7:8.

[a]**14** Most Hebrew manuscripts; some Hebrew manuscripts and Septuagint *They slash themselves*

8:1 *eagle:* Probably refers to Assyria. Enemies are often compared to attacking birds (Deut 28:49; Jer 4:13; Lam 4:18, 19; Hab 1:6-8).

8:3 *rejected what is good:* This refers to the covenant that the LORD made with Moses and the people at Sinai (Exod 19–40; Lev 26:1-13).

8:4 *set up kings:* After Israel's tribes split into two kingdoms the northern kingdom (Israel) experienced periods of civil war. A number of men became king by revolting against, and often murdering, the king in power (see the note at 7:7). By seizing power rather than waiting to be appointed by one of the LORD's prophets, many of Israel's kings showed a lack of trust in the LORD.

8:4 *idols:* Making idols was forbidden in the Law of Moses (Exod 20:3-6, 23; Lev 19:3,4; Deut 5:7-9). One of the most common Canaanite idols was a golden statue in the shape of a bull that symbolized Baal. See 1 Kgs 12:26-30.

8:9 *Assyria . . . sold herself to lovers:* See the Introduction to HOSEA and the note at 5:13.

8:11-13 *many altars . . . offer sacrifices . . . eat the meat:* Israel's priests had built many altars for offering sacrifices. But the sacrifices and meals made from the meat of the sacrificed animals were not done according to the LORD's instructions and so were unacceptable. The proper procedures for the offerings can be found in Leviticus 4:1—6:7.

8:13 *return to Egypt:* This may refer to going to Egypt to find help against Assyria, or it may refer to being slaves there as Israel's ancestors had been in the past (Exod 1:8-14).

For this they will be ridiculed
in the land of Egypt.

Israel to Reap the Whirlwind

8 "Put the trumpet to your lips!
An eagle is over the house of the LORD
because the people have broken my covenant
and rebelled against my law.
2 Israel cries out to me,
'O our God, we acknowledge you!'
3 But Israel has rejected what is good;
an enemy will pursue him.
4 They set up kings without my consent;
they choose princes without my approval.
With their silver and gold
they make idols for themselves
to their own destruction.
5 Throw out your calf-idol, O Samaria!
My anger burns against them.
How long will they be incapable of purity?
6 They are from Israel!
This calf—a craftsman has made it;
it is not God.
It will be broken in pieces,
that calf of Samaria.

7 "They sow the wind
and reap the whirlwind.
The stalk has no head;
it will produce no flour.
Were it to yield grain,
foreigners would swallow it up.
8 Israel is swallowed up;
now she is among the nations
like a worthless thing.
9 For they have gone up to Assyria
like a wild donkey wandering alone.
Ephraim has sold herself to lovers.
10 Although they have sold themselves among the nations,
I will now gather them together.
They will begin to waste away
under the oppression of the mighty king.

11 "Though Ephraim built many altars for sin offerings,
these have become altars for sinning.
12 I wrote for them the many things of my law,
but they regarded them as something alien.
13 They offer sacrifices given to me

and they eat the meat,
but the LORD is not pleased with them.
Now he will remember their wickedness
and punish their sins:
They will return to Egypt.
14 Israel has forgotten his Maker
and built palaces;
Judah has fortified many towns.
But I will send fire upon their cities
that will consume their fortresses."

THE LORD WILL PUNISH ISRAEL

The next five chapters focus on the LORD's judgment and punishment of Israel. Mixed in with these warnings and words of doom are reminders of the LORD's care for Israel in the past.

Punishment for Israel

9 Do not rejoice, O Israel;
do not be jubilant like the other nations.
For you have been unfaithful to your God;
you love the wages of a prostitute
at every threshing floor.
2 Threshing floors and winepresses will not feed
the people;
the new wine will fail them.
3 They will not remain in the LORD's land;
Ephraim will return to Egypt
and eat unclean[a] food in Assyria.
4 They will not pour out wine offerings to the LORD,
nor will their sacrifices please him.
Such sacrifices will be to them like the bread
of mourners;
all who eat them will be unclean.
This food will be for themselves;
it will not come into the temple of the LORD.
5 What will you do on the day of your appointed feasts,
on the festival days of the LORD?
6 Even if they escape from destruction,
Egypt will gather them,
and Memphis will bury them.
Their treasures of silver will be taken over by briers,
and thorns will overrun their tents.
7 The days of punishment are coming,
the days of reckoning are at hand.
Let Israel know this.

[a]3 That is, ceremonially unclean

8:14 *Judah has fortified many towns . . . fortresses:* See the Introduction to HOSEA and the note at 1:7. Judah's leaders did this because they no longer trusted the LORD to protect them.

9:1 *threshing floor:* In threshing, stalks of grain are beaten by hand or walked on by large animals in order to separate the kernels from the husks (see the note at 10:11). Then the light husks are thrown in the air so the wind can blow them away while the heavier grain kernels fall back down and can be gathered up. Threshing was done on hills or other windy places. See also the note at 10:11. People also met at these places to worship Baal, the god they thought had given them the grain harvest.

9:1 *prostitute:* See the note at 1:2.

9:3 *the LORD's land:* Meaning Canaan, the land the LORD gave to the Israelites. By 733 B.C. some of the people of Israel had already been taken into exile in Assyria. Others ran away to hide in Egypt. When they worshiped Baal as the lord of the land, they gave up their rights as God's chosen people.

9:3 *eat unclean food:* See the mini-article called "Purity (Clean and Unclean)," p. 2125.

9:5 *festival days of the LORD:* This probably refers to the Feast of Tabernacles (Lev 23:33-44; Num 29:12-39). See also the chart called "Jewish Calendar and Festivals," p. 944.

9:6 *Memphis:* Memphis was an Egyptian city with a famous cemetery. God brought the Israelite people out of Egypt about 500 years earlier (Exod 12:23—13:22).

9:7 Luke 21:22.

The prophet, along with my God, is the watchman over Ephraim.
Hos 9:8

9:8 *the house of his God:* This may refer to the LORD's land (see 9:3) or to the sanctuary where the people faithfully worshiped the LORD.

9:9 *days of Gibeah:* See the note at 5:8. During the time when Israel was ruled by leaders called judges, the men of Gibeah raped and murdered a woman (Judg 19:1-30).

9:10 *grapes . . . fig tree:* Grapes were a prized fruit that could be eaten or made into wine. Figs are sweet fruits from bushy trees. Both grapes and figs can be dried in the sun and eaten months after being picked. It would be especially surprising to find these fruits in a barren desert.

9:10 *Baal Peor:* Some Israelites had worshiped the idol Baal Peor even before entering Canaan (Num 25:1-5).

9:11 *no birth:* Israel's women will be unable to have children, because Israel worshiped the Canaanite fertility gods.

9:15 *wickedness in Gilgal:* See the notes at 4:15 and 4:19.

9:15 *my house:* Meaning the land of Canaan (see 9:3 and 9:8)

Because your sins are so many
and your hostility so great,
the prophet is considered a fool,
the inspired man a maniac.
8 The prophet, along with my God,
is the watchman over Ephraim,[a]
yet snares await him on all his paths,
and hostility in the house of his God.
9 They have sunk deep into corruption,
as in the days of Gibeah.
God will remember their wickedness
and punish them for their sins.

10 "When I found Israel,
it was like finding grapes in the desert;
when I saw your fathers,
it was like seeing the early fruit on the fig tree.
But when they came to Baal Peor,
they consecrated themselves to that shameful idol
and became as vile as the thing they loved.
11 Ephraim's glory will fly away like a bird—
no birth, no pregnancy, no conception.
12 Even if they rear children,
I will bereave them of every one.
Woe to them
when I turn away from them!
13 I have seen Ephraim, like Tyre,
planted in a pleasant place.
But Ephraim will bring out
their children to the slayer."

14 Give them, O LORD—
what will you give them?
Give them wombs that miscarry
and breasts that are dry.

15 "Because of all their wickedness in Gilgal,
I hated them there.
Because of their sinful deeds,
I will drive them out of my house.
I will no longer love them;
all their leaders are rebellious.
16 Ephraim is blighted,
their root is withered,
they yield no fruit.
Even if they bear children,
I will slay their cherished offspring."

[a]**8** Or *The prophet is the watchman over Ephraim, / the people of my God*

[17]My God will reject them
because they have not obeyed him;
they will be wanderers among the nations.

10 Israel was a spreading vine;
he brought forth fruit for himself.
As his fruit increased,
he built more altars;
as his land prospered,
he adorned his sacred stones.
[2]Their heart is deceitful,
and now they must bear their guilt.
The LORD will demolish their altars
and destroy their sacred stones.

[3]Then they will say, "We have no king
because we did not revere the LORD.
But even if we had a king,
what could he do for us?"
[4]They make many promises,
take false oaths
and make agreements;
therefore lawsuits spring up
like poisonous weeds in a plowed field.
[5]The people who live in Samaria fear
for the calf-idol of Beth Aven.[a]
Its people will mourn over it,
and so will its idolatrous priests,
those who had rejoiced over its splendor,
because it is taken from them into exile.
[6]It will be carried to Assyria
as tribute for the great king.
Ephraim will be disgraced;
Israel will be ashamed of its wooden idols.[b]
[7]Samaria and its king will float away
like a twig on the surface of the waters.
[8]The high places of wickedness[c] will be destroyed—
it is the sin of Israel.
Thorns and thistles will grow up
and cover their altars.
Then they will say to the mountains, "Cover us!"
and to the hills, "Fall on us!"

[9]"Since the days of Gibeah, you have sinned, O Israel,
and there you have remained.[d]

9:17 *wanderers among the nations:* The people of Israel will lose their identity as God's people when they are forced to leave the land that the LORD has given them.

10:1 *prospered . . . sacred stones:* After the united Israelite kingdom split in two (see note at 1:2), the wealth of the northern kingdom (Israel) grew. But they used some of their new riches to build shrines to honor the Canaanite gods, because they believed these gods had helped them grow rich.

10:5 *Samaria . . . calf-idol of Beth Aven:* See the notes at 7:1 and 4:15.

10:6,7 *carried to Assyria . . . Samaria and its king:* Pekah was king of Israel from 737 to 732 B.C. During Pekah's reign, the Assyrian king Tiglath-Pileser invaded Israel and forced a number of Israelites into exile in Assyria (2 Kgs 15:27-29). Pekah's palace was in the city of Samaria, the capital of Israel. In 722 B.C. the Assyrian King Shalmaneser captured Samaria (2 Kgs 17:5-23). Sargon, the king who followed Shalmaneser, took many of the remaining people of Israel as prisoners to Assyria.

10:8 *high places . . . Cover us:* See the note at 4:15. See also the notes at 4:13, 14 and 10:1. Also see Luke 23:30; Rev 6:16.

10:9 *Gibeah:* See the notes at 5:8 and 9:9.

---

a5 *Beth Aven* means *house of wickedness* (a name for Bethel, which means *house of God*). **b6** Or *its counsel* **c8** Hebrew *aven,* a reference to Beth Aven (a derogatory name for Bethel) **d9** Or *there a stand was taken*

10:11 *trained heifer that loves to thresh:* Calves sometimes threshed (separated) the grain kernels from their outer husks by walking on the grain (see the note at 9:1). As the calf stomped on the grain, it was also allowed to eat some of the fresh grain, (Deut 25:4). Israel will no longer enjoy such an easy life, but will be made to do the harder work of plowing.

10:13 *planted wickedness ... reaped evil ... depended on your own strength:* See the notes at 6:6 and 5:13. See also Amos 2:6-8; 5:6-13.

10:14 *battle will rise ... Shalman:* Israel was threatened by the Assyrians. See the Introduction to HOSEA and the note at 10:6, 7. There is no other record in the Bible of what happened at Beth Arbel. "Shalman" may refer to the Moabite king known as Salamanu, who paid taxes to Tiglath-Pileser III of Assyria around 735 to 733 B.C. Or, it may be a shortened version of Shalmaneser, referring to one of the Assyrian kings by this name. At least two of them led military attacks on Israel.

11:2 *the further they went ... burned incense to images:* See the notes at 2:8 and 4:13,14.

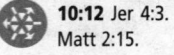

10:12 Jer 4:3. **11:1** Exod 4:22; Matt 2:15.

Did not war overtake
the evildoers in Gibeah?
10 When I please, I will punish them;
nations will be gathered against them
to put them in bonds for their double sin.
11 Ephraim is a trained heifer
that loves to thresh;
so I will put a yoke
on her fair neck.
I will drive Ephraim,
Judah must plow,
and Jacob must break up the ground.
12 Sow for yourselves righteousness,
reap the fruit of unfailing love,
and break up your unplowed ground;
for it is time to seek the LORD,
until he comes
and showers righteousness on you.
13 But you have planted wickedness,
you have reaped evil,
you have eaten the fruit of deception.
Because you have depended on your own strength
and on your many warriors,
14 the roar of battle will rise against your people,
so that all your fortresses will be devastated—
as Shalman devastated Beth Arbel on the day of battle,
when mothers were dashed to the ground
with their children.
15 Thus will it happen to you, O Bethel,
because your wickedness is great.
When that day dawns,
the king of Israel will be completely destroyed.

God's Love for Israel

11 "When Israel was a child, I loved him,
and out of Egypt I called my son.
2 But the more I[a] called Israel,
the further they went from me.[b]
They sacrificed to the Baals
and they burned incense to images.
3 It was I who taught Ephraim to walk,
taking them by the arms;
but they did not realize
it was I who healed them.
4 I led them with cords of human kindness,
with ties of love;

[a]2 Some Septuagint manuscripts; Hebrew *they* [b]2 Septuagint; Hebrew *them*

I lifted the yoke from their neck
and bent down to feed them.

5 “Will they not return to Egypt
and will not Assyria rule over them
because they refuse to repent?
6 Swords will flash in their cities,
will destroy the bars of their gates
and put an end to their plans.
7 My people are determined to turn from me.
Even if they call to the Most High,
he will by no means exalt them.

8 “How can I give you up, Ephraim?
How can I hand you over, Israel?
How can I treat you like Admah?
How can I make you like Zeboiim?
My heart is changed within me;
all my compassion is aroused.
9 I will not carry out my fierce anger,
nor will I turn and devastate Ephraim.
For I am God, and not man—
the Holy One among you.
I will not come in wrath.[a]
10 They will follow the LORD;
he will roar like a lion.
When he roars,
his children will come trembling from the west.
11 They will come trembling
like birds from Egypt,
like doves from Assyria.
I will settle them in their homes,”
declares the LORD.

Israel’s Sin

12 Ephraim has surrounded me with lies,
the house of Israel with deceit.
And Judah is unruly against God,
even against the faithful Holy One.

12 1 Ephraim feeds on the wind;
he pursues the east wind all day
and multiplies lies and violence.
He makes a treaty with Assyria
and sends olive oil to Egypt.
2 The LORD has a charge to bring against Judah;
he will punish Jacob[b] according to his ways

[a]9 Or *come against any city* [b]2 *Jacob* means *he grasps the heel* (figuratively, *he deceives*).

11:5 *return to Egypt . . . Assyria rule over them:* See the Introduction to HOSEA and the notes at 5:13 and 7:8.

11:8 *Admah . . . Zeboiim:* These towns were destroyed (Deut 29:23) when the LORD destroyed Sodom and Gomorrah (Gen 19:23-29).

11:10 *roar like a lion:* Other passages describe the LORD as a lion who will attack Israel (5:14; 13:7). Here the roaring lion is a picture of Israel’s God as a protector, who roars to announce that he is coming to help Israel. See also Joel 3:16; Amos 3:8.

11:9-11 *his children will come trembling from the west:* The LORD will not allow Israel to be punished forever. They will eventually return to Canaan (1:10,11). As the “Holy One,” the LORD is set apart from human beings and has great power and majesty (Num 23:19; Isa 31:3).

12:1 *treaty with Assyria . . . Egypt:* See the Introduction to HOSEA and the notes at 5:13 and 7:8.

12:1 *olive oil:* Olive oil was one of Israel’s important exports. See the note at 2:5, the article called “Trade and Travel,” p. 948, and the illustration on p. 1326.

12:2-4 *Judah . . . Jacob:* See the note at 1:7. In Hebrew, “Jacob” sounds like the words for “cheat” and “heel” (Gen 25:26). The Israelites who heard Hosea’s prophecy would have recalled the stories in GENESIS about their sometimes sneaky ancestor Jacob (Gen 25:29-34; 27:1-40; 32:22-28). See also the mini-article called “Israel,” p. 264.

12:5 *LORD God Almighty:* "LORD" is a translation of *Yahweh,* the Hebrew word used as God's personal name (see Exod 3:14,15). The Hebrew word translated here as "God" is *Elohim.* See also the mini-articles called "Names of God," p. 243, and "LORD (YHWH)," p. 140.

12:9 *live in tents again:* The people of Israel lived in tents in the desert for 40 years after they left Egypt (see the Introduction to NUMBERS). The tents could also refer to the "shelters" the Israelites lived in during the Feast of Tabernacles (see the note at 9:5).

12:10 *prophets:* See the note at 4:4,5.

12:11 *Gilead . . . Gilgal:* See the notes at 6:7-9 and 4:15.

12:11 *bulls . . . altars:* See the note at 8:11-13.

12:12,13 *Jacob . . . a prophet:* See the note at 12:2-4. Jacob worked for Laban for fourteen years so he could marry Laban's daughters Leah and Rachel (Gen 29:1-30). The "prophet" who brought Israel up from Egypt was Moses. See the mini-article called "Moses," p. 2335.

12:12 *Aram:* See the map on p. 2470.

13:1,2 *Baal worship . . . idols . . . calf-idols:* See the notes at 2:8 and 8:4 (idols).

12:8 Deut 8:17-20. **12:9** Lev 23:42,43.

and repay him according to his deeds.
3 In the womb he grasped his brother's heel;
as a man he struggled with God.
4 He struggled with the angel and overcame him;
he wept and begged for his favor.
He found him at Bethel
and talked with him there—
5 the LORD God Almighty,
the LORD is his name of renown!
6 But you must return to your God;
maintain love and justice,
and wait for your God always.

7 The merchant uses dishonest scales;
he loves to defraud.
8 Ephraim boasts,
"I am very rich; I have become wealthy.
With all my wealth they will not find in me
any iniquity or sin."

9 "I am the LORD your God,
⌊who brought you⌋ out of[a] Egypt;
I will make you live in tents again,
as in the days of your appointed feasts.
10 I spoke to the prophets,
gave them many visions
and told parables through them."
11 Is Gilead wicked?
Its people are worthless!
Do they sacrifice bulls in Gilgal?
Their altars will be like piles of stones
on a plowed field.
12 Jacob fled to the country of Aram[b];
Israel served to get a wife,
and to pay for her he tended sheep.
13 The LORD used a prophet to bring Israel up from Egypt,
by a prophet he cared for him.
14 But Ephraim has bitterly provoked him to anger;
his Lord will leave upon him the guilt
of his bloodshed
and will repay him for his contempt.

The LORD's Anger Against Israel

13 When Ephraim spoke, men trembled;
he was exalted in Israel.
But he became guilty of Baal worship and died.

[a]9 Or *God / ever since you were in*   [b]12 That is, Northwest Mesopotamia

2 Now they sin more and more;
they make idols for themselves from their silver,
cleverly fashioned images,
all of them the work of craftsmen.
It is said of these people,
"They offer human sacrifice
and kiss[a] the calf-idols."
3 Therefore they will be like the morning mist,
like the early dew that disappears,
like chaff swirling from a threshing floor,
like smoke escaping through a window.

4 "But I am the LORD your God,
⌞who brought you⌟ out of[b] Egypt.
You shall acknowledge no God but me,
no Savior except me.
5 I cared for you in the desert,
in the land of burning heat.
6 When I fed them, they were satisfied;
when they were satisfied, they became proud;
then they forgot me.
7 So I will come upon them like a lion,
like a leopard I will lurk by the path.
8 Like a bear robbed of her cubs,
I will attack them and rip them open.
Like a lion I will devour them;
a wild animal will tear them apart.

9 "You are destroyed, O Israel,
because you are against me, against your helper.
10 Where is your king, that he may save you?
Where are your rulers in all your towns,
of whom you said,
'Give me a king and princes'?
11 So in my anger I gave you a king,
and in my wrath I took him away.
12 The guilt of Ephraim is stored up,
his sins are kept on record.
13 Pains as of a woman in childbirth come to him,
but he is a child without wisdom;
when the time arrives,
he does not come to the opening of the womb.

14 "I will ransom them from the power of the grave[c];
I will redeem them from death.
Where, O death, are your plagues?
Where, O grave,[c] is your destruction?

---

[a]2 Or *"Men who sacrifice / kiss*
[b]4 Or *God / ever since you were in*
[c]14 Hebrew *Sheol*

I am the LORD your God, who brought you out of Egypt. You shall acknowledge no God but me, no Savior except me.
Hos 13:4

13:3 *morning mist . . . . chaff:* Just as Israel's faith in the LORD disappeared like the morning mist (6:4), Israel will vanish. See also the note at 9:1 (threshing floor).

13:4-6 *Egypt . . . desert . . . fed them:* The LORD helped the Israelites escape slavery in Egypt (Exod 12–14). During the forty years that Israel wandered through the desert, the LORD fed them (Exod 16; Num 11:7-9, 31, 32) and provided them with water (Exod 17:1-7; Num 20:1-13). See also Deut 8:11-17. But the people of Hosea's generation have forgotten how the LORD saved and took care of their ancestors.

13:10,11 *Give me a king . . . I took him away:* When the people of Israel begged for a king, God granted their request (1 Sam 8:4-22; 10:17-26). For more, see the mini-article called "Kingship in Israel," p. 650. The king who has been taken "away" may refer to Israel's king Hoshea who was arrested by Shalmaneser when the Assyrians captured Samaria, the capital of Israel (2 Kgs 17:1-9).

13:12 *guilt . . . stored up . . . on record:* The sins here refer to Israel's worshiping Canaanite gods and trusting in foreign powers rather than trusting the LORD. Ancient documents were rolled and stored in a dry place. For more, see the mini-article called "Scrolls," p. 1491.

13:7 Hos 5:14. **13:14** 1 Cor 15:55.

13:15 *blowing in from the desert . . . plundered of all its treasures:* The translation of this verse is difficult. The desert wind may refer to the Assyrians who will invade from the desert east of Canaan. They will kill and capture many Israelites and take Israel's jewels and gold from the royal treasury.

13:16 *Samaria must bear their guilt:* See the notes at 7:1 and 10:6, 7.

14:2 *offer the fruit of our lips:* Israel's requests for God's forgiveness are sincere and not like the unacceptable sacrifices described in the note at 8:11-13. See also Ps 50:7-23; 51:15-17.

14:1 Hos 6:1-3.

"I will have no compassion,
15 even though he thrives among his brothers.
An east wind from the LORD will come,
blowing in from the desert;
his spring will fail
and his well dry up.
His storehouse will be plundered
of all its treasures.
16 The people of Samaria must bear their guilt,
because they have rebelled against their God.
They will fall by the sword;
their little ones will be dashed to the ground,
their pregnant women ripped open."

THOSE WHO RETURN TO THE LORD WILL BE FORGIVEN

This final chapter begins by calling Israel to turn away from sin and return to the LORD. It ends with the LORD's promise to forgive and heal Israel. If the people of Israel obey the LORD, the LORD will take care of them. But if they return to their sinful ways they will fall again.

Repentance to Bring Blessing

14 Return, O Israel, to the LORD your God.
Your sins have been your downfall!
2 Take words with you
and return to the LORD.
Say to him:

QUESTIONS ABOUT HOSEA 4:1—14:9

1. Of what specific sins did the LORD accuse Israel? What role did Israel's priests play in Israel's sins? (4:1—5:7)
2. Why was Bethel chosen to receive the LORD's warning? (5:8, 9) What did King Jeroboam do at Bethel? (See 1 Kgs 12:26-29.)
3. How did the people respond to Hosea's warnings? (6:1-3) Was their response honest and sincere? Why or why not?
4. In terms of Israel's history, what is the meaning of Hosea 7:11?
5. Why were the Israelites drawn toward worshiping Baal and the other Canaanite gods and goddesses? (7:14-16)
6. How were the people of Israel punished for their sins? Name at least three ways. (8:1—11:6; 12:9—13:16)
7. Why are Judah and Israel compared to their ancestor Jacob? (11:12—12:8)
8. How were the people of Israel supposed to return to the LORD? (14:1-3) For you, what does the phrase "return to the LORD" mean?
9. What warning and what promises are found in 14:8, 9?
10. Hosea describes idols as images made of wood, metal, or stone that represent gods. What or who might be considered "idols" in society today? How could these "idols" challenge faithfulness or trust in God?

"Forgive all our sins
and receive us graciously,
that we may offer the fruit of our lips.[a]
3 Assyria cannot save us;
we will not mount war-horses.
We will never again say 'Our gods'
to what our own hands have made,
for in you the fatherless find compassion."

4 "I will heal their waywardness
and love them freely,
for my anger has turned away from them.
5 I will be like the dew to Israel;
he will blossom like a lily.
Like a cedar of Lebanon
he will send down his roots;
6 his young shoots will grow.
His splendor will be like an olive tree,
his fragrance like a cedar of Lebanon.
7 Men will dwell again in his shade.
He will flourish like the grain.
He will blossom like a vine,
and his fame will be like the wine from Lebanon.
8 O Ephraim, what more have I[b] to do with idols?
I will answer him and care for him.
I am like a green pine tree;
your fruitfulness comes from me."
9 Who is wise? He will realize these things.
Who is discerning? He will understand them.
The ways of the LORD are right;
the righteous walk in them,
but the rebellious stumble in them.

[a]2 Or *offer our lips as sacrifices of bulls* [b]8 Or *What more has Ephraim*

14:3 *Assyria . . . war-horses:* See the Introduction to HOSEA and the note at 5:13. The Assyrian army's skillful use of war-horses and chariots helped make it the leading military force of the period. Although Israel's army also used war-horses, Hosea declares that winning a military battle was not the way out of Israel's troubles. For images of Assyrian warfare, see the illustration on p. 772.

14:5 *blossom like a lily:* Lilies are plants with delicate and fragrant flowers. Only one kind is known to have grown in Palestine, though it is unlikely it was ever very common. This kind has a white blossom. Even rare plants like lilies will bloom because God's love (dew) is so plentiful.

14:6 *a cedar of Lebanon:* Lebanon means "white," referring to its snow-capped mountains (Jer 18:14). In the ancient world, Lebanon was famous for cedar, cypress, and other timber trees (1 Kgs 4:33; 2 Chr 2:8,16; Ezra 3:7; Ps 29:5; Isa 2:13).

14:7 *a vine:* A vineyard filled with grapes was considered a sign of God's blessing.

14:8 *I am like a green pine tree:* This is the only place in the Old Testament where the LORD is compared to a tree. Hosea reminds the people that the LORD is the source of life, rather than the Canaanite gods and goddesses that are worshiped under trees at the local shrines.

14:9 Ps 1; 107:43; Jer 9:12.

JOEL

The prophet Joel watched a hungry swarm of locusts cover the land of Israel, destroying crops and causing starvation. Read his vivid description and see why he compares this disaster to the LORD's coming day of judgment.

the day of the LORD: This is an important theme in the message of Joel (see 2:1). It is a future time when the LORD will interrupt history and judge the nations. Often this day is described as being accompanied by destruction, darkness, and unusual events taking place in nature (2:10; Amos 5:18-20). Joel sees the locust invasion as a sign of the coming day of judgment. Besides Joel, other prophets spoke about a judgment day of the LORD (Isa 13:6,9; Ezek 13:5; 30:2,3; Obad 15; Zeph 1:7,14; Mal 3:2,3). See also the mini-article called "Day of the LORD," p. 1727.

WHAT MAKES JOEL SPECIAL?

The book of JOEL belongs to the writings in the Bible called the books of the prophets. All we know for certain about the prophet Joel is his name, which in Hebrew means "The LORD (*Yahweh*) is God." Joel describes in very lively language the effects of a locust plague—an attack by so many locusts flying over the land that they block out the sun. Joel goes on to compare the resulting darkness with the day of the LORD, a special event he refers to several more times. On that day God will judge and punish the nations that have hurt Israel. See also the mini-article called "Day of the LORD," p. 1727.

Joel prays to God and warns the people that the LORD will send his army to fight for justice. He compares the locusts to horses in battle that make loud noises as they charge and are frightening to look at. But there is hope if people will turn to the LORD with all their hearts. The LORD will listen to them and save them from the destruction, not only by restoring the harvest, but by assuring everyone that he is indeed their God. The LORD will even help them to understand the future through his Spirit (prophecy). Those who call on the name of the LORD will receive salvation and deliverance (2:28-32).

WHY WAS JOEL WRITTEN?

Joel brings to the people of Israel a message from God that the day of the LORD is near. He points to the swarm of locusts destroying the land as a sign that God is punishing Israel for its sins, and warns that a real army is going to attack. But Joel also wants the people to know that it's not too late to turn to the LORD, to ask for forgiveness, and to receive his blessings again.

WHAT'S THE STORY BEHIND THE SCENE?

A number of books of prophecy in the Bible tell who was king at the time the prophet preached (for example, see Hos 1:1; Amos 1:1; Mic 1:1). This helps to give modern readers a sense of when the prophet was most active by matching what the prophet said with specific historical situations. Since the book of JOEL does not mention any specific king or ruler, the exact dating of the book continues to be a mystery. It has been placed in time as early as 800 B.C. and as late as 300 B.C.

There are a few clues in the book about who Joel was and when he preached. He speaks of Judah and Jerusalem and the

LORD's temple. He mentions no king, but refers to the priests and elders as Israel's leaders. The invading army mentioned in the book is sometimes thought to be from Assyria, which defeated Israel (northern kingdom) in 721 B.C., or Babylon, which defeated Judah (southern kingdom) in 586 B.C. and took many of its leading citizens into exile. Some scholars suggest that Joel lived and preached in Judah sometime after the people returned from exile and rebuilt the temple in 515 B.C. See also the article called "After the Exile: God's People Return to Judea," p. 931.

HOW IS JOEL CONSTRUCTED?

Although JOEL has been divided into three chapters, it has two main parts: The first (1:1—2:17) tells of an invasion of locusts, the invasion of the LORD's unstoppable army, and includes Joel's message telling the people to return to the LORD. The second part (2:18—3:21) describes how the LORD will rescue the people of Israel and bring a future day of judgment when the enemies of Israel will be punished.

The LORD's invitation to Israel (1:1—2:17)

The LORD's blessings and judgment of nations (2:18—3:21)

The LORD's Invitation to Israel

Joel watches a huge swarm of locusts invade Israel and destroy its crops. He compares this invasion to an invasion of Israel by an unknown enemy army. These invasions are just a taste of the coming judgment day of the LORD. Joel exhorts the people of Israel to turn away from sin and return to the LORD, so they can be saved when that day of judgment comes.

1 The word of the LORD that came to Joel son of Pethuel.

An Invasion of Locusts

2 Hear this, you elders;
listen, all who live in the land.
Has anything like this ever happened in your days
or in the days of your forefathers?
3 Tell it to your children,
and let your children tell it to their children,
and their children to the next generation.
4 What the locust swarm has left
the great locusts have eaten;
what the great locusts have left
the young locusts have eaten;
what the young locusts have left
other locusts[a] have eaten.

[a]4 The precise meaning of the four Hebrew words used here for locusts is uncertain.

1:1 *Joel son of Pethuel:* For more about Joel, see the Introduction to JOEL. The Hebrew meaning of the name Pethuel is not certain. Joel is a prophet because the LORD gives him a message. See also the article called "Prophets and Prophecy," p. 935.

1:2 *Hear:* Compare Joel's invitation to "hear" to similar invitations at the beginning of other prophetic books (Isa 1:2; Hos 4:1; Mic 1:2). Everyone (the elders and their children) is asked to hear the words of the prophet, not just one specific leader or a king. After they understand his message, everyone in the nation will have the LORD's Spirit (see 2:28).

1:2 *elders:* "Elders" here refers to the leaders of Israel, not a ruling king. The elders were men whose age and wisdom made them respected leaders.

1:4 *locusts:* See the mini-article called "Locusts," p. 1708.

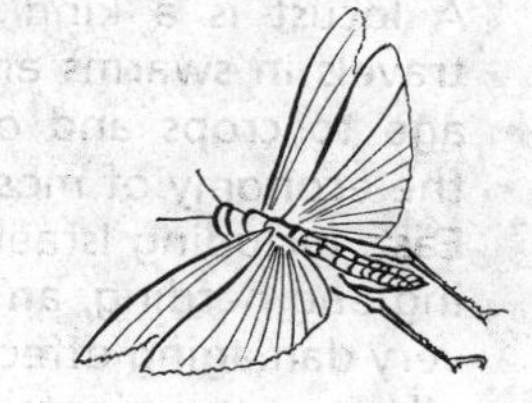

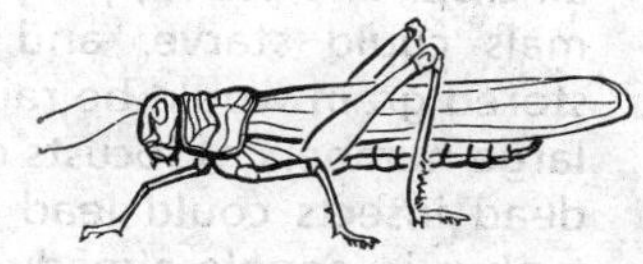

1:5 *Wake up, you drunkards:* The abundance of wine in the ancient world was seen as evidence of God's blessings. But being drunk was seen as a sign of foolishness that could lead to a person's destruction. Here, the prophet is both giving a warning and making a statement of fact. Those who often got drunk, he says, would have no choice but to sober up. The locust swarm would eat all the grapevines, and there would be no new grapes for making wine. See also Prov 20:1; 23:20,21.

1:6 *A nation has invaded my land:* Meaning the swarms of locusts.

1:6 Rev 9:8.

5 Wake up, you drunkards, and weep!
Wail, all you drinkers of wine;
wail because of the new wine,
for it has been snatched from your lips.
6 A nation has invaded my land,
powerful and without number;
it has the teeth of a lion,
the fangs of a lioness.
7 It has laid waste my vines
and ruined my fig trees.
It has stripped off their bark
and thrown it away,
leaving their branches white.
8 Mourn like a virgin[a] in sackcloth
grieving for the husband[b] of her youth.
9 Grain offerings and drink offerings
are cut off from the house of the LORD.

[a]8 Or *young woman* [b]8 Or *betrothed*

LOCUSTS

A locust is a kind of grasshopper that travels in swarms and causes great damage to crops and other plants. Because the economy of most of the ancient Near East, including Israel, was based on farming and herding, an attack by locusts had very damaging effects. If locusts devoured all crops and plants, people and their animals could starve, and prices for any stored grain would be raised very high. If large numbers of locusts died, the rotting dead insects could lead to diseases like typhus in people already weakened from hunger, and could cause disease in animals too.

Locusts continue to be a problem in modern times. They hatch in fields where each female insect can lay hundreds of eggs that hatch and grow in four stages: the youngest "hopper" stage without wings; the "jumper" stage when wings begin to develop; the "biter," or "cutter" stage which describes the nearly full-grown locust; and finally the sexually mature stage. These adult locusts can fly great distances. Swarms of flying locusts can be huge. In 1881, workers in Cyprus tried to stop a locust swarm attack by digging up and destroying the locust eggs, which weighed a total of thirteen hundred tons. A swarm that was seen crossing the Red Sea in 1889 was estimated as having at least 120 million locusts and covered two thousand square miles.

It is easy to imagine, then, why the locust disaster plague that the LORD sent upon Egypt (Exod 10:4-19) was so horrible and why such swarms could actually block out the sun and seem to turn the day into night (Joel 2:10). Israel's King Solomon prayed that the LORD would listen to his prayers during locust attacks (1 Kgs 8:37-40; 2 Chr 6:28-31). Because the devastation caused by locusts could be so great, the prophet Joel used such an attack as a way of describing the invasion of Israel by enemy soldiers (Joel 2:1-11), although some scholars believe the book of JOEL refers to an actual plague of locusts. In the Bible, locust swarms are described as one way the LORD punishes those who have rejected him (Deut 28:36-42; Amos 4:9; 7:1).

The priests are in mourning,
those who minister before the LORD.
10 The fields are ruined,
the ground is dried up[a];
the grain is destroyed,
the new wine is dried up,
the oil fails.
11 Despair, you farmers,
wail, you vine growers;
grieve for the wheat and the barley,
because the harvest of the field is destroyed.
12 The vine is dried up
and the fig tree is withered;
the pomegranate, the palm and the apple tree—
all the trees of the field—are dried up.
Surely the joy of mankind
is withered away.

A Call to Repentance

13 Put on sackcloth, O priests, and mourn;
wail, you who minister before the altar.
Come, spend the night in sackcloth,
you who minister before my God;
for the grain offerings and drink offerings
are withheld from the house of your God.
14 Declare a holy fast;
call a sacred assembly.
Summon the elders
and all who live in the land
to the house of the LORD your God,
and cry out to the LORD.

15 Alas for that day!
For the day of the LORD is near;
it will come like destruction from the Almighty.[b]

16 Has not the food been cut off
before our very eyes—
joy and gladness
from the house of our God?
17 The seeds are shriveled
beneath the clods.[c]
The storehouses are in ruins,
the granaries have been broken down,
for the grain has dried up.
18 How the cattle moan!

[a]10 Or *ground mourns* [b]15 Hebrew *Shaddai* [c]17 The meaning of the Hebrew for this word is uncertain.

1:7 *vines . . . fig trees:* Grapes could be eaten fresh, dried to make raisins, or made into wine. Figs are a sweet fruit harvested two times during the year.

1:8 *Mourn . . . grieving:* Harvest time was a time of great joy and celebration, but the locust invasion would make Israel mourn instead.

1:9 *Offerings . . . house of the LORD:* The LORD's temple refers to the temple in Jerusalem, where Israel's priests made offerings. See the mini-article called "Israel's Priests," p. 2344, the chart called "Sacrifices and Offerings," p. 219, and the article called "People of the Law: The Religion of Israel," p. 939.

1:12 *pomegranate:* A red fruit that has a rind that encloses a juicy middle with many seeds.

1:13,14 *sackcloth . . . mourn . . . fast:* Sackcloth was a rough cloth worn in times of sorrow and trouble. People also showed their sadness and sorrow by going for a period of time without eating, called fasting.

1:15 *the Almighty:* See the mini-article called "Names of God," p. 243.

1:17 *storehouses . . . grain has dried up:* If enough grain was stored, a community could survive one or two years of bad harvests. Grain was stored in large clay jars in storehouses, and in grain silos (pits) like this one from the eighth century B.C., discovered by archaeologists at Megiddo. It could hold up to 12,000 bushels of grain.

2:1 *Zion:* Another name for Jerusalem. See the mini-article called "Zion," p. 1294.

2:1 *day of the* LORD*:* See the note on p. 1706.

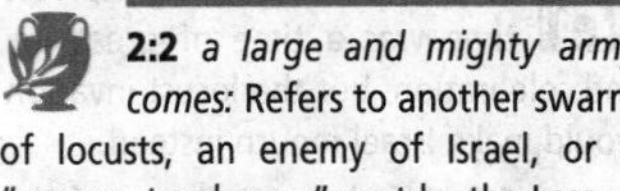

2:2 *a large and mighty army comes:* Refers to another swarm of locusts, an enemy of Israel, or a "supernatural army" sent by the LORD.

2:3 *Eden:* Before the first man and woman, Adam and Eve, rebelled against God, they lived in the beautiful and fertile garden of Eden (Gen 2:4-15). By choosing this metaphor Joel is reminding the people of Israel that their suffering is due, in part, to their rebellion against God.

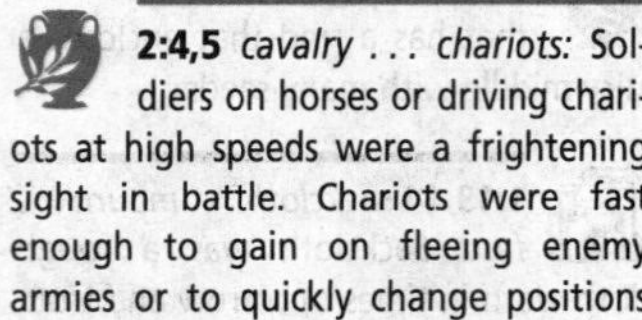

2:4,5 *cavalry . . . chariots:* Soldiers on horses or driving chariots at high speeds were a frightening sight in battle. Chariots were fast enough to gain on fleeing enemy armies or to quickly change positions and attack their enemies from another direction.

2:7-9 *scale walls . . . climb into the houses:* The LORD's army cannot be stopped. It will go over city walls and come into homes like the locusts that entered the homes of the Egyptians (Exod 10:6).

2:4,5 Rev 9:7-9.

The herds mill about
because they have no pasture;
even the flocks of sheep are suffering.

19 To you, O LORD, I call,
for fire has devoured the open pastures
and flames have burned up all the trees of the field.
20 Even the wild animals pant for you;
the streams of water have dried up
and fire has devoured the open pastures.

An Army of Locusts

2 Blow the trumpet in Zion;
sound the alarm on my holy hill.
Let all who live in the land tremble,
for the day of the LORD is coming.
It is close at hand—
2
a day of darkness and gloom,
a day of clouds and blackness.
Like dawn spreading across the mountains
a large and mighty army comes,
such as never was of old
nor ever will be in ages to come.

3 Before them fire devours,
behind them a flame blazes.
Before them the land is like the garden of Eden,
behind them, a desert waste—
nothing escapes them.
4 They have the appearance of horses;
they gallop along like cavalry.
5 With a noise like that of chariots
they leap over the mountaintops,
like a crackling fire consuming stubble,
like a mighty army drawn up for battle.

6 At the sight of them, nations are in anguish;
every face turns pale.
7 They charge like warriors;
they scale walls like soldiers.
They all march in line,
not swerving from their course.
8 They do not jostle each other;
each marches straight ahead.
They plunge through defenses
without breaking ranks.
9 They rush upon the city;
they run along the wall.

They climb into the houses;
like thieves they enter through the windows.

10 Before them the earth shakes,
the sky trembles,
the sun and moon are darkened,
and the stars no longer shine.
11 The LORD thunders
at the head of his army;
his forces are beyond number,
and mighty are those who obey his command.
The day of the LORD is great;
it is dreadful.
Who can endure it?

Rend Your Heart

12 "Even now," declares the LORD,
"return to me with all your heart,
with fasting and weeping and mourning."

13 Rend your heart
and not your garments.
Return to the LORD your God,
for he is gracious and compassionate,
slow to anger and abounding in love,
and he relents from sending calamity.
14 Who knows? He may turn and have pity
and leave behind a blessing—
grain offerings and drink offerings
for the LORD your God.

15 Blow the trumpet in Zion,
declare a holy fast,
call a sacred assembly.
16 Gather the people,
consecrate the assembly;
bring together the elders,
gather the children,
those nursing at the breast.
Let the bridegroom leave his room
and the bride her chamber.
17 Let the priests, who minister before the LORD,
weep between the temple porch and the altar.
Let them say, "Spare your people, O LORD.
Do not make your inheritance
an object of scorn,
a byword among the nations.
Why should they say among the peoples,
'Where is their God?' "

2:10 *sun and moon are darkened:* May be a reference to the swarms of locusts blocking out the sun during the day and the moon and stars at night (Exod 10:13-15). But this kind of darkness is also commonly used to describe what happens when the judgment day of the LORD is near (Isa 13:9, 10; Amos 5:18-20; Zeph 1:14-16; Mark 13:24,25; Rev 8:12).

2:11 *The day of the LORD:* See the note on p. 1706. See also Rev 6:17.

2:12,13 *return to me . . . Rend your heart:* Though the judgment day is coming, the LORD says that it is not too late for the people of Israel to return to obeying him. This returning is sometimes called "repenting." Joel doesn't say what the people's specific sins are, but in order to be forgiven, they need to show an honest attitude of sadness (rending their hearts) and admit that they are guilty (see also Prov 4:23; Jer 31:31-34; 1 John 3:18). The people are to show their sadness by performing acts of mourning (see the note at 1:13,14).

2:14 *offerings:* Turning back to the LORD will cause the LORD to restore the land and its crops. With plenty of food, the people can again make sacrifices at the temple (see the note at 1:9).

2:15 *Zion:* See the note at 2:1 (Zion).

2:16 *consecrate the assembly:* The people of Israel performed certain rituals in order to "consecrate" themselves and be "clean" enough for worship (see Lev 7; 15; Num 19). See also the mini-article called "Purity (Clean and Unclean)," p. 2125.

2:17 *priests:* See the note at 1:9 and the mini-article called "Israel's Priests," p. 2344.

2:15 Joel 1:14; 2:12. **2:17** Ps 22:1,7; 79:4,10; 115:2; Ezek 22:4.

2:19 *grain . . . oil:* Wheat was the most common grain used for eating and for offering as a sacrifice. Olive oil was made by crushing olives. It was used for cooking, as fuel for lamps, and for pouring on the head of someone chosen for a special task such as a king or priest (1 Sam 16:12,13).

2:20 *northern army:* See the note at 2:2. It is not clear what army is being described here. If it is the locust "army," the smell of rotting locusts covers the whole land. If it is one of Israel's enemies, it is not clear which one, since even enemies from the east and the west would have used the trade routes from the north to attack Israel.

2:20 *eastern sea . . . western sea:* The eastern sea refers to the Dead Sea; the western sea to the Mediterranean Sea. Both were large bodies of water that served as boundaries for Israel. See the map on p. 2467.

2:22 *fig tree . . . vine:* See the note at 1:7.

2:23 *Zion:* See the note at 2:1 (Zion).

2:24 *threshing floors:* Harvested grain was carried to dry, open places called threshing floors. There, the dried stalks were beaten with something like a whip or crushed by a heavy board with sharp stones in it (a sledge). The board was dragged across the threshing floor by an ox or a donkey to loosen the chaff (husks) from the grain. Then the grain and husks were thrown into the air. Wind blew away the light husks, while the heavier grain kernels fell to the ground and were gathered up.

2:25 *locusts:* See the mini-article called "Locusts," p. 1708.

The LORD's Blessings and Judgment of Nations

The LORD promises to bless the people by making the land produce food again and by rescuing them from the locust attack. As the day of the LORD's judgment comes closer, the LORD will send his Spirit to work wonders in nature. Then the LORD will gather the nations and judge them. Those who have been guilty of attacking and robbing the LORD's people will be punished.

The LORD's Answer

18 Then the LORD will be jealous for his land
and take pity on his people.

19 The LORD will reply[a] to them:

"I am sending you grain, new wine and oil,
enough to satisfy you fully;
never again will I make you
an object of scorn to the nations.

20 "I will drive the northern army far from you,
pushing it into a parched and barren land,
with its front columns going into the eastern sea[b]
and those in the rear into the western sea.[c]
And its stench will go up;
its smell will rise."

Surely he has done great things.[d]
21 Be not afraid, O land;
be glad and rejoice.
Surely the LORD has done great things.
22 Be not afraid, O wild animals,
for the open pastures are becoming green.
The trees are bearing their fruit;
the fig tree and the vine yield their riches.
23 Be glad, O people of Zion,
rejoice in the LORD your God,
for he has given you
the autumn rains in righteousness.[e]
He sends you abundant showers,
both autumn and spring rains, as before.
24 The threshing floors will be filled with grain;
the vats will overflow with new wine and oil.

25 "I will repay you for the years the locusts have eaten—
the great locust and the young locust,

---

[a]**18,19** Or *LORD was jealous . . . / and took pity . . . /* [19]*The LORD replied* [b]**20** That is, the Dead Sea [c]**20** That is, the Mediterranean [d]**20** Or *rise. / Surely it has done great things."* [e]**23** Or */ the teacher for righteousness:*

the other locusts and the locust swarm[a]—
my great army that I sent among you.
[26] You will have plenty to eat, until you are full,
and you will praise the name of the LORD your God,
who has worked wonders for you;
never again will my people be shamed.
[27] Then you will know that I am in Israel,
that I am the LORD your God,
and that there is no other;
never again will my people be shamed.

The Day of the LORD

[28] "And afterward,
I will pour out my Spirit on all people.
Your sons and daughters will prophesy,
your old men will dream dreams,
your young men will see visions.
[29] Even on my servants, both men and women,
I will pour out my Spirit in those days.
[30] I will show wonders in the heavens
and on the earth,
blood and fire and billows of smoke.
[31] The sun will be turned to darkness
and the moon to blood
before the coming of the great and dreadful day
of the LORD.
[32] And everyone who calls
on the name of the LORD will be saved;
for on Mount Zion and in Jerusalem
there will be deliverance,
as the LORD has said,
among the survivors
whom the LORD calls.

The Nations Judged

3 "In those days and at that time,
when I restore the fortunes of Judah and Jerusalem,
[2] I will gather all nations
and bring them down to the Valley of Jehoshaphat.[b]
There I will enter into judgment against them
concerning my inheritance, my people Israel,
for they scattered my people among the nations
and divided up my land.
[3] They cast lots for my people

[a]25 The precise meaning of the four Hebrew words used here for locusts is uncertain. [b]2 *Jehoshaphat* means *the LORD judges*; also in verse 12.

2:28 *Spirit:* The Spirit brings the LORD's power and special gifts. See also the mini-article called "Holy Spirit," p. 2082.

2:30,31 *wonders . . . dreadful day:* See the note at 2:10. These wonders are common in the "apocalyptic" writings of the Bible (see the mini-article called "Apocalyptic Writing," p. 1656). The "dreadful day" is the judgment day of the LORD. See the note on p. 1706.

2:32 *Mount Zion . . . Jerusalem:* See the note at 2:1.

3:1,2 *Judah and Jerusalem . . . Valley of Jehoshaphat . . . enter into judgment:* Joel's mention of Judah and Jerusalem is another clue that his prophecy was given after the rebuilding of the temple, when the people of Israel's future and hopes were centered on Jerusalem. The location of the Valley of Jehoshaphat is unknown, but apparently was named after an early king of Judah (1 Kgs 22:41-50). It is mentioned here and in 3:12, but nowhere else in the Bible.

3:2-8 *nations . . . Sabeans:* Babylon and Assyria, who had defeated Israel and Judah, are not named here (see the mini-article called "Exile," p. 1541). Tyre and Sidon were important coastal cities in Phoenicia (see the mini-article called "Phoenicia," p. 1604); the Philistines were ancient enemies of Israel; the Greeks lived mostly on the western coast of Asia Minor; and the Sabeans were people from southwest Arabia.

2:27 Exod 20:3,4; Deut 5:6,7; Amos 3:1,2. **2:28-32** Acts 2:17-21. **2:31** Matt 24:29; Mark 13:24,25; Luke 21:25; Rev 6:12,13. **2:32** Rom 10:13.

"In that day the mountains will drip with new wine, and the hills will flow with milk; all the ravines of Judah will run with water."
Joel 3:18

3:10 *Beat your plowshares into swords:* Compare Joel's war-like image to the image presented in Isa 2:4 and Mic 4:3.

3:12 *Valley of Jehoshaphat:* See the note at 3:1,2.

3:13 *trample the grapes:* People trampled grapes with their bare feet to squeeze out the juice, which then was made into wine. See the mini-article called "Wine," p. 2047.

3:14 *valley of decision . . . day of the LORD:* The valley of decision is not mentioned anywhere else in the Bible. It is may be another name for the Valley of Jehoshaphat (3:2,12). See also the note on p. 1706.

3:16 *The LORD will roar from Zion:* This phrase is nearly identical to one used by the prophet Amos (Amos 1:2). If Joel preached sometime after the people returned from their exile in Babylonia (538 B.C.), then he is most likely quoting Amos, whose prophecy is from 760 to 750 B.C.

3:13 Rev 14:14-20. **3:15** Joel 2:2,10,31.

and traded boys for prostitutes;
they sold girls for wine
that they might drink.

4 "Now what have you against me, O Tyre and Sidon and all
you regions of Philistia? Are you repaying me for something I have
done? If you are paying me back, I will swiftly and speedily return
on your own heads what you have done. 5 For you took my silver
and my gold and carried off my finest treasures to your temples.
6 You sold the people of Judah and Jerusalem to the Greeks, that
you might send them far from their homeland.

7 "See, I am going to rouse them out of the places to which
you sold them, and I will return on your own heads what you have
done. 8 I will sell your sons and daughters to the people of Judah,
and they will sell them to the Sabeans, a nation far away." The
LORD has spoken.

9 Proclaim this among the nations:
Prepare for war!
Rouse the warriors!
Let all the fighting men draw near and attack.
10 Beat your plowshares into swords
and your pruning hooks into spears.
Let the weakling say,
"I am strong!"
11 Come quickly, all you nations from every side,
and assemble there.

Bring down your warriors, O LORD!

12 "Let the nations be roused;
let them advance into the Valley
of Jehoshaphat,
for there I will sit
to judge all the nations on every side.
13 Swing the sickle,
for the harvest is ripe.
Come, trample the grapes,
for the winepress is full
and the vats overflow—
so great is their wickedness!"

14 Multitudes, multitudes
in the valley of decision!
For the day of the LORD is near
in the valley of decision.
15 The sun and moon will be darkened,
and the stars no longer shine.
16 The LORD will roar from Zion
and thunder from Jerusalem;
the earth and the sky will tremble.

But the LORD will be a refuge for his people,
a stronghold for the people of Israel.

Blessings for God's People

17 "Then you will know that I, the LORD your God,
dwell in Zion, my holy hill.
Jerusalem will be holy;
never again will foreigners invade her.
18 "In that day the mountains will drip new wine,
and the hills will flow with milk;
all the ravines of Judah will run with water.
A fountain will flow out of the LORD's house
and will water the valley of acacias.[a]
19 But Egypt will be desolate,
Edom a desert waste,
because of violence done to the people of Judah,
in whose land they shed innocent blood.
20 Judah will be inhabited forever
and Jerusalem through all generations.
21 Their bloodguilt, which I have not pardoned,
I will pardon."

The LORD dwells in Zion!

[a]**18** Or *Valley of Shittim*

3:17 *Zion:* See the note at 2:1 (Zion).

3:18 *that day . . . A fountain will flow out of the LORD's house:* "That day" means the time following the LORD's day of judgment when the LORD will restore the people of Judah. They will have plenty to eat and trade with others, and won't be bothered by enemies (3:17). Compare Joel's message here with these other hopeful prophecies: Isa 66:10-14; Hos 14:4-9; Amos 9:11-15; Mic 7:8-20; Zeph 3:14-20. The fountain that comes from the LORD's house (the temple) is like the river that runs from the temple in Ezekiel 47:1-12. See also Rev 22:1-5.

3:17 Joel 2:27.

QUESTIONS ABOUT JOEL

1. What astonishing event did Joel witness? Why was this event so devastating for the people? Why did the people and the temple priests mourn? (1:4-20)
2. What is the "day of the LORD," and what hints does nature give that this day is about to happen? (2:1-12)
3. Who or what are the troops and army compared to? (2:2-11) Do you think knowing about Joel's message in advance could have helped the people? How?
4. What important thing does the LORD invite the people to do? (2:12-17) What does the LORD promise if the people do what he asks? (2:18-27; 3:17-21) Can you think of someone you might want to make things right with? How would the person respond to an apology?
5. Why does the LORD judge the nations? (3:1-13)
6. Create a newspaper front-page headline for each chapter of JOEL. How do your headlines sum up the key events and themes of this book?

AMOS

"Away with the noise of your songs! . . . But let justice roll on like a river" (Amos 5:23,24). Read this book to find out why God told the prophet Amos to speak these powerful words to the people of Israel.

What makes Amos special?

Amos wasn't a professional prophet like the members of a prophetic guild (2 Kgs 4:38) or those who served the king (1 Chr 21:9; 25:5). He was a shepherd (1:1) and took care of sycamore-fig trees (7:14) near the small town of Tekoa, located south of Jerusalem in the southern kingdom (Judah). But the LORD gave Amos messages to preach to the people and leaders of the northern kingdom (Israel).

Although Israel had many prophets before the time of Amos (1 Sam 9:9-13; 2 Sam 12), his prophecies were quite possibly the first to be written down and preserved as a book of the Bible.

Why was Amos written?

Amos was sent to tell the people of Israel that the LORD was going to punish them because the rich and powerful people of the country were robbing the poor and treating them unjustly. Also, many of the people and their priests worshiped other gods besides the LORD at new worship places built by Israel's kings. Amos preached his messages at the city of Bethel (7:10), where Israel's Jeroboam I had earlier built a worship place (1 Kgs 12:25—13:10). Amos's message also included words of judgment against several countries that were neighbors of Israel and Judah.

What's the story behind the scene?

The first verse of the book says that Amos preached during the time Uzziah was king in Judah (781-740 B.C.) and Jeroboam II was king of Israel (786-746 B.C.). It is not clear which earthquake he is referring to in the same verse, but it may be one that happened in 760 B.C. So, Amos likely preached his message for about one year somewhere between 762 and 750 B.C. Jeroboam II ruled Israel during a fairly peaceful time. Without having to worry about a major military threat, Israel became a fairly wealthy nation. Many people became rich, built fancy homes (3:15), and had all they wanted to eat and drink (4:1). But the rich people did not use their wealth or influence to help others. Instead they were greedy for more, so they cheated honest people and made the poor pay heavy taxes. The people continued to celebrate the religious festivals, but the LORD grew tired of their insincere rituals. What the LORD really wanted them to do was to treat others with justice and fairness and to be faithful to the LORD alone. For more, see the article called "From

1:1 *Amos . . . Uzziah . . . Jeroboam:* All that we now know about Amos is what is mentioned in this book of the Bible (see 7:14, 15). Amos lived in the Judean hills in the town of Tekoa and made his living by raising sheep and taking care of fig trees. Though Amos was from the south (Judah), his message was for the people of the northern kingdom (Israel). He appears to have been a prophet for only a short time and preached his messages just a few years before the prophets Isaiah, Hosea, and Micah began their work. See also the article called "Prophets and Prophecy," p. 935.

Uzziah ruled Judah (781-740 B.C.) at about the same time Jeroboam II ruled Israel (783-743 B.C.). See also 2 Kgs 14:23-29; 15:1-7 (Azariah is another spelling of the Hebrew name Uzziah); 2 Chr 26:1-23.

1:1,2 *Tekoa . . . top of Carmel:* Tekoa was in the hill country of Judah south of Jerusalem (2 Sam 14:1-4; 2 Chr 11:5, 6). When King Solomon died (about 931 B.C.), Israel's ten northern tribes broke away from the two remaining southern tribes (1 Kgs 12). Two kingdoms were formed—Israel (northern kingdom) and Judah (southern kingdom). Jerusalem remained the capital of Judah and the traditional center of worship.

Mount Carmel was located in Israel about 70 miles to the northwest of Jerusalem (see the map on p. 2467).

Joshua to the Exile: The People of Israel in the Promised Land," p. 924.

How is Amos constructed?

Amos can be divided into two main sections: The first section (1:1—6:14) includes Amos's messages of judgment against Israel and neighboring nations. The second section (7:1—9:15) includes Amos's visions, which tell of the Lord's coming judgment against Israel, and also describes a future time when the Lord would help Israel rebuild its kingdom and prosper once again (9:11-15).

Messages of judgment against Israel and its neighbors (1:1—6:14)
- Amos preaches against Israel's neighbors (1:1—2:5)
- Amos announces the Lord's judgment against Israel (2:6—6:14)

Visions of Israel's punishment and renewal (7:1—9:15)
- The punishment visions (7:1—9:10)
- The Lord will rebuild Israel (9:11-15)

Messages of Judgment Against Israel and Its Neighbors

Amos, the shepherd farmer from Judah, goes to Israel to preach the Lord's messages of judgment against Israel and its neighbors, including Judah. The nations are to be punished because their ancestors treated the Israelite people badly in the past. Israel will be punished because the nation's rich and powerful people are taking advantage of the poor and worshiping foreign gods.

AMOS PREACHES AGAINST ISRAEL'S NEIGHBORS

1 The words of Amos, one of the shepherds of Tekoa—what he
saw concerning Israel two years before the earthquake, when Uzziah was king of Judah and Jeroboam son of Jehoash[a] was king of
Israel.

2 He said:

"The Lord roars from Zion
and thunders from Jerusalem;
the pastures of the shepherds dry up,[b]
and the top of Carmel withers."

Judgment on Israel's Neighbors

3 This is what the Lord says:

[a]1 Hebrew *Joash,* a variant of *Jehoash* [b]2 Or *shepherds mourn*

1:1 *earthquake:* This may refer to the violent earthquake that happened about 760 B.C., according to evidence discovered by archaeologists in the ruins of Hazor, an ancient city in Israel.

1:3 *threshed Gilead with sledges:* Sledges were dragged over grain stalks to separate the grain from the chaff.

1:3-5 *Damascus ... Kir:* For these locations, see the map. Damascus was the capital of Aram (Syria). "Valley of Aven" means Valley of Wickedness and may refer to a valley in Lebanon. "Beth Eden" may refer to a city-state on the banks of the Euphrates River. Gilead was controlled by Israel. "Kir" is identified in Amos 9:7 as the original home of the Arameans, the ancestors of the people of Aram. So this verse may mean that the Arameans would lose all that they had gained since the days their ancestors lived in Kir.

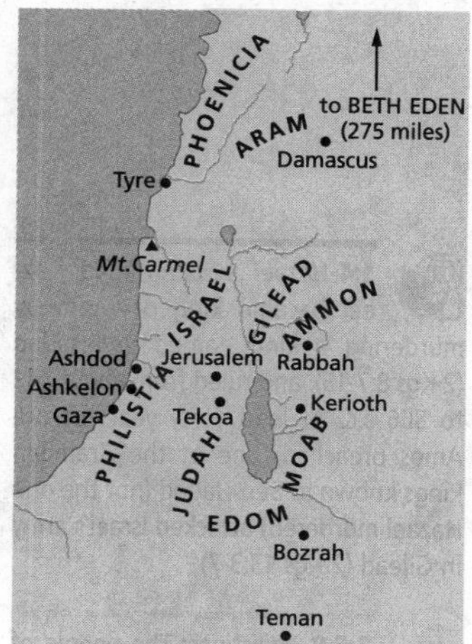

1:2 Joel 3:16. **1:3-5** Isa 17:1-3; Jer 49:23-27; Zech 9:1.

The Prophet Amos with Goats, illuminated page from an English "Workshop Bestiary," about 1187. Amos may have been the first of the prophets in the Bible to have his sayings written down. He was a simple farmer and shepherd with no formal training in prophecy. But when the LORD gave Amos messages about Israel and the surrounding nations, he left his herds and preached to the people of Israel (7:14-16).

"For three sins of Damascus,
    even for four, I will not turn back ⌞my wrath⌟.
Because she threshed Gilead
    with sledges having iron teeth,
4 I will send fire upon the house of Hazael
    that will consume the fortresses of Ben-Hadad.
5 I will break down the gate of Damascus;
    I will destroy the king who is in[a] the Valley of Aven[b]
and the one who holds the scepter in Beth Eden.
    The people of Aram will go into exile to Kir,"
        says the LORD.

6 This is what the LORD says:

"For three sins of Gaza,
    even for four, I will not turn back ⌞my wrath⌟.
Because she took captive whole communities
    and sold them to Edom,
7 I will send fire upon the walls of Gaza

[a]5 Or *the inhabitants of* [b]5 *Aven* means *wickedness.*

1:4 *Hazael . . . Ben-Hadad:* Hazael became king of Aram by murdering a king named Ben-Hadad (2 Kgs 8:7-15), and ruled from about 842 to 806 B.C. At least forty years before Amos preached, one of the Aramean kings known as Ben-Hadad (not the one Hazael murdered) attacked Israel's army in Gilead (2 Kgs 13:3-7).

1:6-8 *Philistines:* The people of Philistia often battled the people of Israel (for example, see 1 Sam 14:52; 17:1-54). The cities mentioned here are some of the main Philistine cities. The Philistines probably kidnapped people in one of the border towns of Judah and sold them to the Edomites.

1:6-8 Isa 14:29-31; Jer 47:1-7; Ezek 25:15-17; Joel 3:4-8; Zeph 2:4-7; Zech 9:5-7.

that will consume her fortresses.
8 I will destroy the king[a] of Ashdod
and the one who holds the scepter in Ashkelon.
I will turn my hand against Ekron,
till the last of the Philistines is dead,"
says the Sovereign LORD.

9 This is what the LORD says:

"For three sins of Tyre,
even for four, I will not turn back ⌊my wrath⌋.
Because she sold whole communities of captives
to Edom,
disregarding a treaty of brotherhood,
10 I will send fire upon the walls of Tyre
that will consume her fortresses."

11 This is what the LORD says:

"For three sins of Edom,
even for four, I will not turn back ⌊my wrath⌋.
Because he pursued his brother with a sword,
stifling all compassion,[b]
because his anger raged continually
and his fury flamed unchecked,
12 I will send fire upon Teman
that will consume the fortresses of Bozrah."

13 This is what the LORD says:

"For three sins of Ammon,
even for four, I will not turn back ⌊my wrath⌋.
Because he ripped open the pregnant women
of Gilead
in order to extend his borders,
14 I will set fire to the walls of Rabbah
that will consume her fortresses
amid war cries on the day of battle,
amid violent winds on a stormy day.
15 Her king[c] will go into exile,
he and his officials together,"
says the LORD.

2 This is what the LORD says:

"For three sins of Moab,
even for four, I will not turn back ⌊my wrath⌋.
Because he burned, as if to lime,
the bones of Edom's king,

---

[a]8 Or *inhabitants* [b]11 Or *sword / and destroyed his allies* [c]15 Or / *Molech;* Hebrew *malcam*

1:9,10 *Tyre . . . treaty:* What treaty the Phoenicians broke is not clear, but their other crime is similar to that of the Philistines (see the note at 1:6-8). Tyre was the leading city of Phoenicia at the time of Amos. See the mini-article called "Phoenicia," p. 1604.

1:11,12 *Edom . . . Bozrah:* The Edomites were descendants of Esau (Gen 36:1, 9-14, 40-43), whose brother Jacob was the ancestor of the Israelites (Gen 32:22-28; 49:1-28). The LORD's judgment would cover all of Edom, from the city or region of Teman in the south to the northern fortress city of Bozrah.

1:13,14 *Ammon . . . Gilead . . . Rabbah:* The event mentioned in 1:13 probably refers to a border war Ammon fought to try to take over some of Israel's land in Gilead. In mentioning the murder of innocent pregnant women, Amos calls attention to the horrible nature of war (2 Kgs 8:12; 15:14-16). Rabbah was the capital city of Ammon.

2:1,2 *Moab . . . Kerioth:* See the map on p. 1717. Though Moab and Israel had been enemies in the past (Num 22:2-11; 2 Sam 8:2, 13, 14), Moab's crime here is digging up the body of an Edomite king and burning his bones until they became lime powder. The powder was mixed with water and used to whitewash (paint) the walls of their houses. An ancient stone monument called the Mesha stele names Kerioth as a center for the worship of Chemosh, chief god of Moab.

1:9,10 Isa 23:1-18; Ezek 26:1—28:19; Joel 3:4-8; Zech 9:1-4; Matt 11:21, 22; Luke 10:13, 14. **1:11,12** Isa 34:5-17; 63:1-6; Jer 49:7-22; Ezek 25:12-14; 35:1-15; Obad 1-14; Mal 1:2-5. **1:13-15** Jer 49:1-6; Ezek 21:28-32; 25:1-7; Zeph 2:8-11. **2:1-3** Isa 15:1—16:14; 25:10-12; Jer 48:1-47; Ezek 25:8-11; Zeph 2:8-11.

2:4,5 *Judah . . . Jerusalem:* Over 150 years after Amos preached, the LORD's judgment against Judah took place when the armies of Babylon destroyed its capital city Jerusalem (587 or 586 B.C.). Many people from Judah were forced into exile (2 Kgs 25). The phrase, "rejected the law of the LORD," is similar to language used in DEUTERONOMY, which was completed in its final form sometime after the people returned to Jerusalem from exile. This has led some scholars to conclude that these words of judgment against Judah may have been added well after the time of Amos.

2:6,7 *sell the righteous . . . deny justice:* Honest people who owed debts were being sold as slaves when they could not pay their debts on time. Poor or debt-ridden people were being sold into slavery for the price of a pair of sandals. "Deny justice to the oppressed" probably refers to bribing court officials to keep certain people from getting a fair hearing.

2:7,8 *Father and son use the same girl . . . garments . . . wine:* According the Law of Moses, improper sexual relations were forbidden (Lev 18:6-17; 20:11, 12). The actions of the fathers and sons certainly dishonored God. A coat taken as security to repay a loan was to be returned to the owner before sunset in case the coat was the only way the owner was able to keep warm during the night (Exod 22:26, 27). Similarly, the wine they drank in the temple may have been wine received as a payment for a debt or may have been bought with money received from fines.

2:9 *Amorite:* "Amorites" is the name often used for all the people who lived in Canaan at the time Israel took over the land. Amorites lived in Canaan in the area that would later be claimed by the tribe of Judah (Exod 3:8; Deut 1:19-27; 3:8-11; 1 Chr 1:14) and in the hill country east of the Jordan River. They were Israel's enemies until King Solomon defeated them (1 Kgs 9:20,21).

2 I will send fire upon Moab
that will consume the fortresses of Kerioth.[a]
Moab will go down in great tumult
amid war cries and the blast of the trumpet.
3 I will destroy her ruler
and kill all her officials with him,"
says the LORD.

4 This is what the LORD says:

"For three sins of Judah,
even for four, I will not turn back ⌞my wrath⌟.
Because they have rejected the law of the LORD
and have not kept his decrees,
because they have been led astray by false gods,[b]
the gods[c] their ancestors followed,
5 I will send fire upon Judah
that will consume the fortresses of Jerusalem."

AMOS ANNOUNCES THE LORD'S JUDGMENT AGAINST ISRAEL

The longest of AMOS's judgment messages is against Israel, whose wealthy and powerful people are being greedy and using their power to cheat the poor.

Judgment on Israel

6 This is what the LORD says:

"For three sins of Israel,
even for four, I will not turn back ⌞my wrath⌟.
They sell the righteous for silver,
and the needy for a pair of sandals.
7 They trample on the heads of the poor
as upon the dust of the ground
and deny justice to the oppressed.
Father and son use the same girl
and so profane my holy name.
8 They lie down beside every altar
on garments taken in pledge.
In the house of their god
they drink wine taken as fines.

9 "I destroyed the Amorite before them,
though he was tall as the cedars
and strong as the oaks.
I destroyed his fruit above
and his roots below.

[a] 2 Or *of her cities* [b] 4 Or *by lies* [c] 4 Or *lies*

[10]"I brought you up out of Egypt,
and I led you forty years in the desert
to give you the land of the Amorites.
[11]I also raised up prophets from among your sons
and Nazirites from among your young men.
Is this not true, people of Israel?"
declares the LORD.
[12]"But you made the Nazirites drink wine
and commanded the prophets not to prophesy.

2:11 *prophets . . . Nazirites:* See the article called "Prophets and Prophecy," p. 935. Nazirites showed their dedication to the LORD by refusing to eat or drink certain things, and by promising not to cut their hair or touch a dead body (Num 6:1-8).

2:10 Exod 12:31-41; Lev 26:44, 45; Amos 3:1, 2.

JUSTICE

In modern society, justice is most often described as fairness according to the law. When people receive justice, they receive the penalty they deserve, or they are repaid for the damages done to them. In the Bible, justice is related to the Law of Moses, which the LORD gave to the people of Israel as a gift for their protection and well-being. But God's justice goes beyond simply obeying the law; it is mainly concerned with doing what is right in all relationships. Here is a modern example: A company's manufacturing process creates poisonous waste that flows into a nearby river. The company is following the law by keeping the waste flow to the limit set by the law. But that means some poisonous waste still flows into the river. This company is following the law, but is it doing all it can to protect and care for the environment and the people who use the river?

Justice in the Bible is not simply obeying the law. It means living in relationships of love and caring. Justice begins with God and flows from God's overwhelming love. God wants justice for all of creation (Ps 9:7-9) and chose the people of Israel to be living examples of God's justice (Deut 10:17-19; Isa 1:16,17; Hos 12:6).

In the New Testament, the apostle Paul describes how God's justice comes from God's overwhelming love, which flows through God's followers to the poor and needy (2 Cor 9:7-11). Responding to a question about which of the commandments was most important, Jesus answered in a way that emphasized God's justice: "Love the Lord your God with all your heart and with all your soul and with all your mind and with all your strength . . . Love your neighbor as yourself" (Mark 12:30,31; see also Lev 19:18). When Jesus announced the purpose for his work on earth, he said it was to bring the good news to the poor, the prisoners, the blind, and the oppressed (Luke 4:18; Isa 61:1,2). Justice brings protection and freedom to all. When a person's desperate needs are taken care of by acts of justice, they are set free from the painful effects of their need.

Justice is so important to God that if God's people don't do justice in their relationships with others, their worship and other acts of devotion toward God are meaningless (Isa 1:10-17; Jer 9:23,24; Amos 5:21-24). While all of God's people are expected to be just, those who have power and wealth are especially responsible for being living examples of God's justice (2 Sam 8:15; Ps 45:6, 7; Prov 16:12; Jer 21:11, 12). Those who use power and wealth to take advantage of others will suffer the LORD's judgment (Amos 2:6-8). This means that some will not see God's justice as an advantage for them. All people, especially the poor and oppressed, have a right to have their basic needs met. As those in need are given what they deserve, those who have made them needy in the first place may suddenly have less, or may even become oppressed and needy themselves (Amos 5:7-15; Luke 1:51-53; 6:20-25).

3:2 *chosen . . . your sins:* The people of Israel were chosen to have a special relationship with the LORD, and they were chosen for a purpose—to be living examples of the LORD's justice and goodness. But many in Israel turned their backs on the LORD and refused to live according to this purpose. Being the LORD's chosen people did not protect Israel from being judged for these sins. Rather, the LORD judged them even more strictly.

3:3-8 *Do two walk together . . . The lion has roared:* Amos asks a series of questions about events that don't happen simply by chance. These lead to the final key point of his argument: The LORD can do whatever he wants to do, including bringing disaster on a city. The LORD's voice is like a lion's terrifying roar that can turn ordinary people—including Amos himself—into prophets (7:12-16). See also 1:2.

3:9 *Ashdod . . . Egypt . . . Samaria:* Ashdod was a town of the Philistines (see the note at 1:6-8). The ancestors of the Israelite people had once been slaves in Egypt. The Egyptians saw the LORD work miracles and lead the people out of slavery (Exod 6–14; Amos 3:1). Now, because of Israel's lawlessness, the leaders of Egypt and Philistia were going to see the LORD punish Samaria, Israel's capital city. The northern kingdom of Israel was also known as Samaria.

3:9-11 *do not know how to do right . . . plunder your fortresses:* See the notes at 2:6,7 and 2:7,8. In 722 B.C., the Assyrians invaded Israel and captured the city of Samaria. Israel's treasures were stolen by the Assyrians who took many Israelite people away into exile in Assyrian lands in 720 B.C. (2 Kgs 17:1-23).

3:12 *shepherd saves:* When a wild animal killed a sheep, the shepherd had to rescue part of the sheep and take it to the owner as proof that it had been killed by an animal. Otherwise, the shepherd had to pay the owner for the cost of the sheep. See also the mini-article called "Shepherds," p. 1972.

13 "Now then, I will crush you
as a cart crushes when loaded with grain.
14 The swift will not escape,
the strong will not muster their strength,
and the warrior will not save his life.
15 The archer will not stand his ground,
the fleet-footed soldier will not get away,
and the horseman will not save his life.
16 Even the bravest warriors
will flee naked on that day,"
declares the LORD.

Witnesses Summoned Against Israel

3 Hear this word the LORD has spoken against you, O people of
Israel—against the whole family I brought up out of Egypt:

2 "You only have I chosen
of all the families of the earth;
therefore I will punish you
for all your sins."

3 Do two walk together
unless they have agreed to do so?
4 Does a lion roar in the thicket
when he has no prey?
Does he growl in his den
when he has caught nothing?
5 Does a bird fall into a trap on the ground
where no snare has been set?
Does a trap spring up from the earth
when there is nothing to catch?
6 When a trumpet sounds in a city,
do not the people tremble?
When disaster comes to a city,
has not the LORD caused it?

7 Surely the Sovereign LORD does nothing
without revealing his plan
to his servants the prophets.

8 The lion has roared—
who will not fear?
The Sovereign LORD has spoken—
who can but prophesy?

9 Proclaim to the fortresses of Ashdod
and to the fortresses of Egypt:
"Assemble yourselves on the mountains of Samaria;
see the great unrest within her
and the oppression among her people."

10 "They do not know how to do right," declares the LORD,
"who hoard plunder and loot in their fortresses."

11 Therefore this is what the Sovereign LORD says:

"An enemy will overrun the land;
he will pull down your strongholds
and plunder your fortresses."

12 This is what the LORD says:

"As a shepherd saves from the lion's mouth
only two leg bones or a piece of an ear,
so will the Israelites be saved,
those who sit in Samaria
on the edge of their beds
and in Damascus on their couches.[a]"

13 "Hear this and testify against the house of Jacob," declares
the Lord, the LORD God Almighty.

14 "On the day I punish Israel for her sins,
I will destroy the altars of Bethel;
the horns of the altar will be cut off
and fall to the ground.
15 I will tear down the winter house
along with the summer house;
the houses adorned with ivory will be destroyed
and the mansions will be demolished,"
declares the LORD.

Israel Has Not Returned to God

4 Hear this word, you cows of Bashan on Mount Samaria,
you women who oppress the poor and crush the needy
and say to your husbands, "Bring us some drinks!"
2 The Sovereign LORD has sworn by his holiness:
"The time will surely come
when you will be taken away with hooks,
the last of you with fishhooks.
3 You will each go straight out
through breaks in the wall,
and you will be cast out toward Harmon,[b]"
declares the LORD.

4 "Go to Bethel and sin;
go to Gilgal and sin yet more.
Bring your sacrifices every morning,

[a]12 The meaning of the Hebrew for this line is uncertain. [b]3 Masoretic Text; with a different word division of the Hebrew (see Septuagint) *out, O mountain of oppression*

3:13 *LORD God Almighty:* "LORD" is a translation of *Yahweh,* the Hebrew word used as God's personal name (see Exod 3:14,15). The Hebrew word translated here as "God" is *Elohim.* Used together these names describe Israel's one true God, the almighty ruler of all creation. See also the mini-articles called "Names of God," p. 243, and "LORD (YHWH)," p. 140.

3:14,15 *destroy the altars of Bethel . . . mansions:* Canaanite gods were worshiped at the altars of Bethel, a religious shrine built by Jeroboam I (1 Kgs 12:25—13:10). Bethel's altars represented Israel's unfaithfulness to the LORD, and the mansions represented Israel's greed (2:6-8; 4:1; 6:4-6). People whose lives were in danger could grab the "horns of the altar" and no one could kill them (1 Kgs 1:50; 2:28). Amos warns that Israel's sinful people would not be protected from the LORD's punishment by holding on to altars or by hiding out in their fancy homes. See also 2 Kgs 23:15-17.

4:1 *cows of Bashan . . . women:* Samaria's wealthy women were compared to the cows of Bashan. Bashan was a fertile plain east of the Jordan River famous for its rich pastures and well-fed cattle.

4:4 *Bethel . . . Gilgal:* Bethel (see the note at 3:14, 15) and Gilgal were two of the most important centers of worship in northern Israel. Gilgal was located in the Jordan Valley (Josh 4:19). See also Hos 4:15 and Amos 5:5.

4:4,5 *sacrifices . . . tithes . . . offerings:* The things mentioned here are simply things the LORD expected the Israelites to do, such as offering sacrifices (Lev 3; 7:11-38), bringing a tithe (a tenth) of their harvest and the firstborn of their flocks (Deut 14:22-29), and bringing offerings (Lev 22:29,30). But Amos is saying that these outward acts of worship have no meaning because the people are ignoring what the LORD really wants them to do—stop worshiping other gods and start treating all people with justice.

He who forms the mountains, creates the wind, and reveals his thoughts to man, he who turns dawn to darkness, and treads the high places of the earth—the LORD God Almighty is his name.
Amos 4:13

4:6-11 *lack of bread . . . snatched from the fire . . . you have not returned:* The LORD had often punished the people of Israel for being unfaithful. Rains were held back and crops dried up, probably by hot winds from the Arabian desert. Locusts similar to the ones the LORD sent on Egypt (Exod 10:1-20) came and ate up valuable olive and fig trees. See the mini-article called "Locusts," p. 1708. The people suffered terrible military defeats and were nearly destroyed like the people of Sodom and Gomorrah (Gen 19:12-29). Even after the LORD rescued them, the people rejected the LORD. See also Deut 28:15-26.

4:13 *LORD God Almighty:* See the note at 3:13.

your tithes every three years.[a]
5 Burn leavened bread as a thank offering
and brag about your freewill offerings—
boast about them, you Israelites,
for this is what you love to do,"
declares the Sovereign LORD.

6 "I gave you empty stomachs[b] in every city
and lack of bread in every town,
yet you have not returned to me,"
declares the LORD.

7 "I also withheld rain from you
when the harvest was still three months away.
I sent rain on one town,
but withheld it from another.
One field had rain;
another had none and dried up.
8 People staggered from town to town for water
but did not get enough to drink,
yet you have not returned to me,"
declares the LORD.

9 "Many times I struck your gardens and vineyards,
I struck them with blight and mildew.
Locusts devoured your fig and olive trees,
yet you have not returned to me,"
declares the LORD.

10 "I sent plagues among you
as I did to Egypt.
I killed your young men with the sword,
along with your captured horses.
I filled your nostrils with the stench of your camps,
yet you have not returned to me,"
declares the LORD.

11 "I overthrew some of you
as I[c] overthrew Sodom and Gomorrah.
You were like a burning stick snatched from the fire,
yet you have not returned to me,"
declares the LORD.

12 "Therefore this is what I will do to you, Israel,
and because I will do this to you,
prepare to meet your God, O Israel."

13 He who forms the mountains,
creates the wind,

---

[a] **4** Or *tithes on the third day* [b] **6** Hebrew *you cleanness of teeth*
[c] **11** Hebrew *God*

and reveals his thoughts to man,
he who turns dawn to darkness,
and treads the high places of the earth—
the LORD God Almighty is his name.

A Lament and Call to Repentance

5 Hear this word, O house of Israel, this lament I take up concerning you:

2 "Fallen is Virgin Israel,
never to rise again,
deserted in her own land,
with no one to lift her up."

3 This is what the Sovereign LORD says:

"The city that marches out a thousand strong
for Israel
will have only a hundred left;
the town that marches out a hundred strong
will have only ten left."

4 This is what the LORD says to the house of Israel:

"Seek me and live;
5 do not seek Bethel,
do not go to Gilgal,
do not journey to Beersheba.
For Gilgal will surely go into exile,
and Bethel will be reduced to nothing.[a]"
6 Seek the LORD and live,
or he will sweep through the house of Joseph
like a fire;
it will devour,
and Bethel will have no one to quench it.

7 You who turn justice into bitterness
and cast righteousness to the ground
8 (he who made the Pleiades and Orion,
who turns blackness into dawn
and darkens day into night,
who calls for the waters of the sea
and pours them out over the face of the land—
the LORD is his name—
9 he flashes destruction on the stronghold
and brings the fortified city to ruin),
10 you hate the one who reproves in court
and despise him who tells the truth.

[a]5 Or *grief*; or *wickedness*; Hebrew *aven*, a reference to Beth Aven (a derogatory name for Bethel)

5:1 *lament:* Laments, songs of mourning, were sung at funerals in ancient Israel. Amos is trying to shock the Israelites by singing a lament (5:2,3) even before Israel had fallen and been defeated. See also the note at 3:9-11.

5:5-7 *Bethel . . . Gilgal . . . Beersheba:* See the notes at 3:14,15 and 4:4. Beersheba was an ancient place of worship in the southern part of Judea going back to the days of Israel's ancestors, Abraham (Gen 21:30-33), Isaac (Gen 26:23-25), and Jacob (Gen 46:1-4). But the LORD warns the people not to go to these places, because they will be destroyed. Rather they are to turn to the LORD (5:4,6) in true prayer and by living according to the LORD's purpose for them (5:7; see also the note at 3:2).

5:6 *house of Joseph:* Joseph was one of Jacob's twelve sons. Two of Israel's tribes were named after Joseph's sons, Ephraim and Manasseh (Gen 48). By the time of Amos, Ephraim was the most influential tribe in the northern kingdom and so "house of Joseph" is here used as another name for "Israel."

5:8 *he who made the Pleiades and Orion:* As Creator of the stars, the LORD controls the seasons that are signaled by the different positions of the stars. Also, the stars are created objects and should not be worshiped. Some ancient religions were based on worshiping stars, the sun, and the moon. See also Job 9:8,9; 38:31.

5:10-12 *hate the one who reproves in court . . . deprive the poor of justice:* Once again Amos lists the ways many of Israel's rich and powerful people have ignored the LORD's concern for justice. They get angry at witnesses who accuse them and at judges who rule against them at the city gate (the "court"), where town leaders listened to disputes and settled them. See also the notes at 2:6,7; 3:2; and 3:14,15.

5:14,15 *Seek good, not evil . . . remnant of Joseph:* See the notes at 3:2 and 5:6.

5:16 *summoned to weep:* In ancient times, some people were paid to mourn and make loud cries at funerals. See also the mini-article called "Burial," p. 1998.

5:17 *vineyards:* Joyful celebrations took place in vineyards after the grapes were harvested, but the LORD's judgment would turn vineyards into places of sadness. See also the mini-article called "Wine," p. 2047.

5:18-20 *the day of the LORD:* Amos is the first prophet to speak about a specific day in the future when the LORD would come to judge. For more, see the mini-article called "Day of the LORD," p. 1727.

5:21-24 *despise your religious feasts . . . let justice roll:* The LORD's message is now spoken clearly and directly (compare to 4:4,5). Religious feasts, worship, and music meant to honor the LORD are meaningless if the people don't act with justice and fairness. The word translated as "justice" here is often translated as "righteousness," a word that means "living right." See also Isa 1:11-14.

11 You trample on the poor
and force him to give you grain.
Therefore, though you have built stone mansions,
you will not live in them;
though you have planted lush vineyards,
you will not drink their wine.
12 For I know how many are your offenses
and how great your sins.

You oppress the righteous and take bribes
and you deprive the poor of justice in the courts.
13 Therefore the prudent man keeps quiet in such times,
for the times are evil.

14 Seek good, not evil,
that you may live.
Then the LORD God Almighty will be with you,
just as you say he is.
15 Hate evil, love good;
maintain justice in the courts.
Perhaps the LORD God Almighty will have mercy
on the remnant of Joseph.

16 Therefore this is what the Lord, the LORD God Almighty, says:

"There will be wailing in all the streets
and cries of anguish in every public square.
The farmers will be summoned to weep
and the mourners to wail.
17 There will be wailing in all the vineyards,
for I will pass through your midst,"
says the LORD.

The Day of the LORD

18 Woe to you who long
for the day of the LORD!
Why do you long for the day of the LORD?
That day will be darkness, not light.
19 It will be as though a man fled from a lion
only to meet a bear,
as though he entered his house
and rested his hand on the wall
only to have a snake bite him.
20 Will not the day of the LORD be darkness,
not light—
pitch-dark, without a ray of brightness?

21 "I hate, I despise your religious feasts;
I cannot stand your assemblies.

DAY OF THE LORD

The "day of the LORD" refers to a future time when the LORD will act in history to punish his enemies and to save those who have been faithful. In the Old Testament, the day of the LORD (or simply, "the day") is described most often in the books of the prophets. It usually refers to some future historical event, rather than to a final judgment when God's enemies receive eternal punishment and God's faithful people receive eternal life. This idea of a final judgment day is more common in the New Testament (see below).

Perhaps the oldest passage in the Bible that mentions the day of the LORD is found in AMOS (Amos 5:18-20). This and other passages from the prophets describe the day of the LORD as a dark day of disaster when the LORD will punish the wicked. The "wicked" may be other nations (Isa 13:1-6; Amos 1:3—2:3; Obad 15), the people from Israel and Judah (Ezek 7:2-13; Joel 1:15), or the people of the earth in general (Isa 2:12-22; Zeph 1:14-18). Punishment connected with the day of the LORD can take the form of an invasion by an enemy nation (Isa 10:5-12; Hos 10:10-15) or natural disasters such as swarms of locusts (Joel 1:4-7; Amos 7:1, 2), earthquakes and darkness (Joel 2:10; Amos 8:9), and famine (Ezek 5:13-17).

The day of the LORD also is described as a time when God will restore the people of Israel and Judah and save those who have been faithful. This time of restoration follows a time of punishment. For example, the prophets Isaiah, Jeremiah, and Ezekiel each warned the people that their exile in Babylon was punishment for being unfaithful to the LORD. But the LORD would forgive them and lead them back to Jerusalem, where they could once again be a "light" among the other nations (Isa 40:1-11; 49:8-13; Jer 23:7, 8; Ezek 37:15-23; see also Amos 9:11-15). Often this time of restoration is described as time of peace when the people would once again be ruled by an anointed ruler (Messiah) from the family of David (Isa 11).

A few Old Testament passages hint that God's salvation and judgment affect more than events in this life. For example, the prophet Daniel speaks of a time when the dead will rise from death. At this time, some people will receive eternal life and others will receive eternal shame (Dan 12:1-3; see also Job 19:25-27; Isa 26:19). These passages and later passages that come from writings dating to the period between the Testaments (first and second century B.C.) laid the foundation for the many New Testament passages that describe a coming day of judgment.

Jesus refers to a day of judgment (Matt 10:15; 11:22,24; 12:36), and describes a time of coming judgment that sounds a great deal like the disastrous day of the LORD described above (Mark 13). But his words introduce the idea that the coming time of disaster is a warning that the end of time is near and soon the Son of Man will return and gather his chosen ones (Mark 13:27); see also the mini-article called "Second Coming," p. 2277. One of Jesus' parables describes a coming time of judgment that is meant to encourage people to help their neighbors in this lifetime (Matt 25:31-46).

When the apostle Paul speaks of the coming day of the Lord, he connects it to the return of Christ (1 Cor 1:8; 5:5; Phil 1:9, 10; 2:16; 1 Thes 5:2). REVELATION describes the future day when God will finally defeat the forces of evil as "the battle on the great day of God Almighty" (Rev 16:14). Death itself will be thrown into the lake of fire along with all those whose names are not written in the book of life (Rev 20:14,15). Then God will create a new heaven and new earth (Rev 21:1-7). Some New Testament passages suggest that people face judgment or reward immediately after they die (Luke 16:19-24; 23:39-43).

But let justice roll on like a river, righteousness like a never-failing stream!
Amos 5:24

5:25-27 *beyond Damascus:* The people will be forced to leave their land and march beyond Damascus in Aram, where Israel had extended its borders by victories in war (2 Kgs 14:28). See the note at 3:9-11. See also Acts 7:42,43.

6:1,2 *Zion . . . Samaria . . . Philistia:* Zion is another name for Jerusalem. See the mini-article called "Jerusalem," p. 574, and the note at 3:9. Calneh, Hamath and Gath were captured by the Assyrians about 711 B.C.

6:3 *the evil day:* See the note at 5:18-20.

6:4-6 *lounge on your couches . . . finest lotions:* The rich and powerful in Israel ignored their nation's problems and its needy people. Ancient Israelites usually ate while sitting on the floor, but these wealthy Israelites were imitating neighboring peoples who ate while lying on their sides.

6:6 *the ruin of Joseph:* The northern kingdom. See the note at 5:6.

22 Even though you bring me burnt offerings
and grain offerings,
I will not accept them.
Though you bring choice fellowship offerings,[a]
I will have no regard for them.
23 Away with the noise of your songs!
I will not listen to the music of your harps.
24 But let justice roll on like a river,
righteousness like a never-failing stream!

25 "Did you bring me sacrifices and offerings
forty years in the desert, O house of Israel?
26 You have lifted up the shrine of your king,
the pedestal of your idols,
the star of your god[b]—
which you made for yourselves.
27 Therefore I will send you into exile beyond
Damascus,"
says the LORD, whose name is God Almighty.

Woe to the Complacent

6 Woe to you who are complacent in Zion,
and to you who feel secure on Mount Samaria,
you notable men of the foremost nation,
to whom the people of Israel come!
2 Go to Calneh and look at it;
go from there to great Hamath,
and then go down to Gath in Philistia.
Are they better off than your two kingdoms?
Is their land larger than yours?
3 You put off the evil day
and bring near a reign of terror.
4 You lie on beds inlaid with ivory
and lounge on your couches.
You dine on choice lambs
and fattened calves.
5 You strum away on your harps like David
and improvise on musical instruments.
6 You drink wine by the bowlful
and use the finest lotions,
but you do not grieve over the ruin of Joseph.
7 Therefore you will be among the first to go
into exile;
your feasting and lounging will end.

---

[a]**22** Traditionally *peace offerings* [b]**26** Or *lifted up Sakkuth your king / and Kaiwan your idols, / your star-gods*; Septuagint *lifted up the shrine of Molech / and the star of your god Rephan, / their idols*

The LORD Abhors the Pride of Israel

[8]The Sovereign LORD has sworn by himself—the LORD God
Almighty declares:

"I abhor the pride of Jacob
and detest his fortresses;
I will deliver up the city
and everything in it."

[9]If ten men are left in one house, they too will die. [10]And if a
relative who is to burn the bodies comes to carry them out of the
house and asks anyone still hiding there, "Is anyone with you?" and
he says, "No," then he will say, "Hush! We must not mention the
name of the LORD."

[11]For the LORD has given the command,
and he will smash the great house into pieces
and the small house into bits.
[12]Do horses run on the rocky crags?
Does one plow there with oxen?
But you have turned justice into poison
and the fruit of righteousness into bitterness—
[13]you who rejoice in the conquest of Lo Debar[a]
and say, "Did we not take Karnaim[b] by our own
strength?"

[14]For the LORD God Almighty declares,
"I will stir up a nation against you, O house of Israel,

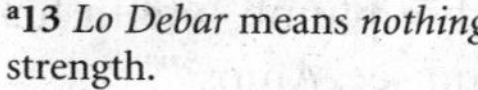

[a]13 *Lo Debar* means *nothing.* [b]13 *Karnaim* means *horns; horn* here symbolizes strength.

6:8 *LORD God Almighty:* See the note at 3:13 (LORD God Almighty).

6:8 *pride of Jacob . . . deliver up the city:* Israel's tribes were named for the sons of Jacob (Gen 49). For more about the defeat of Samaria, see the note at 3:9-11.

6:10 *We must not mention:* One relative warns the other to be careful not to mention the name of the LORD for fear that mentioning it will cause the LORD to cause more suffering for them.

6:13,14 *Lo Debar . . . Karnaim . . . Lebo Hamath . . . Arabah:* Israel's Jeroboam II captured the cities of Lo Debar and Karnaim, located east of the Jordan River. Lebo Hamath and the valley of the Arabah are the northern and southern boundaries of the northern kingdom of Israel. Israel was later captured by Assyria (see the note at 3:9-11), which fits the description in this verse.

QUESTIONS ABOUT AMOS 1:1—6:14

1. What does 1:1 tell about who Amos was? What was Amos supposed to do with what the LORD gave him? What was unusual about Amos being chosen by the LORD? Some additional information about Amos is given in 7:12-15. How does this add to your understanding of who Amos was?
2. For what reasons did the LORD judge many of the nations bordering Israel? (1:3—2:3)
3. What was the relationship between Israel and Judah at the time of Amos's preaching? See the Introduction to AMOS and various notes.
4. For what reasons did Amos preach the LORD's words of judgment against Israel? (2:6—6:14) How would Israel be punished?
5. How does the following statement connect with Amos's message to the people of Israel: "Being chosen means being judged"? Which of the following words do you think is closest to the idea of being chosen—privilege, task, or commitment? Why?
6. After reading the first six chapters of AMOS, how would you define the kind of "justice" the LORD wants? What pictures of this kind of justice come to mind?
7. Where do you see examples of true justice in today's world? Where do you see injustice?

7:1 *locusts:* See the note at 4:6-11.

7:1 *king's share had been harvested:* The king may have had first choice of the grain to feed his troops and animals. A swarm of hungry locusts would have been especially bad at the time described. The non-grain crops such as onions and other vegetables were just beginning to sprout, and the spring grain harvest was beginning. The people needed the food produced by this first harvest to survive until the second harvest in the fall.

7:4 *judgment by fire:* The LORD's judgment fire is described as being so huge that it burns up the whole earth and dries up the oceans, which here means more than waters on the surface of the earth. They are also the waters that many ancient peoples called the "great deep," which was believed to run under the surface of the earth and feed the earth's rivers and springs (Gen 1:2; 7:11,12; Isa 51:10).

7:7,8 *plumb line:* Amos sees a long string with a weight tied to it. Builders used such a measuring line, sometimes called a "plumb line," to make sure walls were being built straight up and down. The LORD is using the measuring device to see if the people of Israel are measuring up to their role as the LORD's chosen people. See the note at 3:2 and Deut 7:6-15.

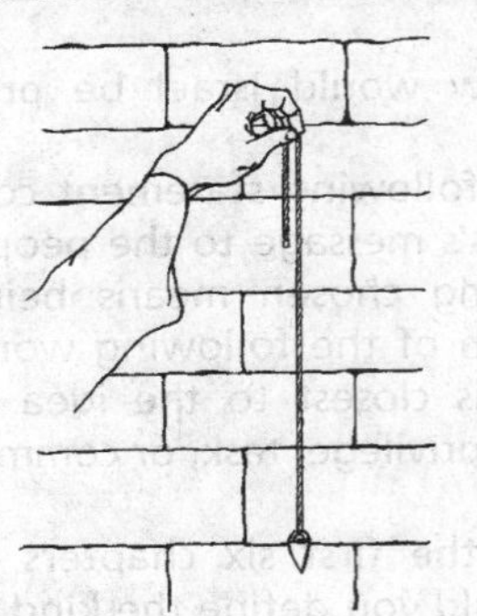

7:9 *Jeroboam:* See the Introduction to AMOS and the note at 1:1.

that will oppress you all the way
from Lebo[a] Hamath to the valley of the Arabah."

Visions of Israel's Punishment and Renewal

THE PUNISHMENT VISIONS

In spite of Amos's prayers, the LORD will destroy Israel because of its wicked ways.

Locusts, Fire and a Plumb Line

7 This is what the Sovereign LORD showed me: He was preparing
swarms of locusts after the king's share had been harvested and
just as the second crop was coming up. 2 When they had stripped
the land clean, I cried out, "Sovereign LORD, forgive! How can
Jacob survive? He is so small!"

3 So the LORD relented.

"This will not happen," the LORD said.

4 This is what the Sovereign LORD showed me: The Sovereign
LORD was calling for judgment by fire; it dried up the great deep
and devoured the land. 5 Then I cried out, "Sovereign LORD, I beg
you, stop! How can Jacob survive? He is so small!"

6 So the LORD relented.

"This will not happen either," the Sovereign LORD said.

7 This is what he showed me: The Lord was standing by a
wall that had been built true to plumb, with a plumb line in his
hand. 8 And the LORD asked me, "What do you see, Amos?"

"A plumb line," I replied.

Then the Lord said, "Look, I am setting a plumb line among my people Israel; I will spare them no longer.

9 "The high places of Isaac will be destroyed
and the sanctuaries of Israel will be ruined;
with my sword I will rise against the house of Jeroboam."

Amos and Amaziah

10 Then Amaziah the priest of Bethel sent a message to Jeroboam king of Israel: "Amos is raising a conspiracy against you in
the very heart of Israel. The land cannot bear all his words. 11 For
this is what Amos is saying:

" 'Jeroboam will die by the sword,
and Israel will surely go into exile,
away from their native land.' "

[a]14 Or *from the entrance to*

[12]Then Amaziah said to Amos, "Get out, you seer! Go back to the land of Judah. Earn your bread there and do your prophesying there. [13]Don't prophesy anymore at Bethel, because this is the king's sanctuary and the temple of the kingdom."

[14]Amos answered Amaziah, "I was neither a prophet nor a prophet's son, but I was a shepherd, and I also took care of sycamore-fig trees. [15]But the LORD took me from tending the flock and said to me, 'Go, prophesy to my people Israel.' [16]Now then, hear the word of the LORD. You say,

" 'Do not prophesy against Israel,
 and stop preaching against the house of Isaac.'

[17]"Therefore this is what the LORD says:

" 'Your wife will become a prostitute in the city,
 and your sons and daughters will fall
 by the sword.
Your land will be measured and divided up,
 and you yourself will die in a pagan[a] country.
And Israel will certainly go into exile,
 away from their native land.' "

A Basket of Ripe Fruit

8 This is what the Sovereign LORD showed me: a basket of ripe fruit. [2]"What do you see, Amos?" he asked.

"A basket of ripe fruit," I answered.

Then the LORD said to me, "The time is ripe for my people Israel; I will spare them no longer.

[3]"In that day," declares the Sovereign LORD, "the songs in the temple will turn to wailing.[b] Many, many bodies—flung everywhere! Silence!"

[4]Hear this, you who trample the needy
 and do away with the poor of the land,

[5]saying,

"When will the New Moon be over
 that we may sell grain,
and the Sabbath be ended
 that we may market wheat?"—
skimping the measure,
 boosting the price
 and cheating with dishonest scales,
[6]buying the poor with silver
 and the needy for a pair of sandals,
 selling even the sweepings with the wheat.

[a]17 Hebrew *an unclean* [b]3 Or *"the temple singers will wail*

7:10-13 *Amaziah the priest of Bethel . . . Don't prophesy anymore:* Amaziah was probably the head priest of Israel's temple at Bethel (see the note at 3:14,15). Amaziah saw Amos's message as a direct threat to Israel's king. He does not want Amos preaching his messages in Israel's royal sanctuary where the king worships.

7:14 *neither a prophet nor a prophet's son:* See also the note at 1:1. Amos emphasizes that he is not a prophet, especially one who serves a king. He is a shepherd and fig grower, but he serves the LORD, who has chosen him and has given him authority to preach.

7:17 *prostitute . . . go into exile:* Two kinds of prostitutes were common during Amos's time—those who accepted payment for sex as a way of making a living and those who had sex as part of religious rituals. See also the mini-article called "Prostitution in the Bible," p. 1688. For Israel's defeat and exile, see the note at 3:9-11.

8:4 *trample the needy:* See the notes at 2:6,7 and 5:10-12.

8:5 *New Moon . . . Sabbath:* Selling grain and other kinds of work were forbidden on the first day of every month, which began with the "New Moon" (Ps 81:3; Num 28:11-15). This was also true on the weekly day of rest called the Sabbath, which means "rest" or to "stop working" (Exod 20:8-11; 31:12-17; Deut 5:12-15).

8:5 *dishonest scales:* See the illustration and description on p. 1732. The cheating that Amos describes here was forbidden by the Law of Moses (Exod 20:15; Deut 25:13-16; see also Prov 20:10).

8:6 Amos 2:6, 7; 5:10-12.

Merchants Weighing Grain. Some merchants became wealthy in Israel by buying up large amounts of grain and selling it at high prices. A standard price was to be paid for a certain amount of grain measured on a balance scale. When they sold grain, dishonest merchants added dust to the grain in a smaller than legal basket and used a heavier than legal weight to measure it, so people got less for their money. When they bought grain, they used lighter weights to balance it, so they got more grain for their money.

7 The LORD has sworn by the Pride of Jacob: "I will never forget anything they have done.

8 "Will not the land tremble for this,
and all who live in it mourn?
The whole land will rise like the Nile;
it will be stirred up and then sink
like the river of Egypt.

9 "In that day," declares the Sovereign LORD,

"I will make the sun go down at noon
and darken the earth in broad daylight.
10 I will turn your religious feasts into mourning
and all your singing into weeping.
I will make all of you wear sackcloth
and shave your heads.
I will make that time like mourning for an only son
and the end of it like a bitter day.

8:7 *the Pride of Jacob:* See the note at 1:11, 12.

8:8 *tremble . . . the Nile:* This probably refers to an earthquake. The Nile River flooded over its banks each year (like ground pushed up and down by an earthquake).

8:9 *sun go down at noon:* This probably refers to some kind of eclipse, an event that often caused great fear for ancient people. A major solar eclipse had been seen in this region of the world in both 784 and 763 B.C.

[11]“The days are coming,” declares the Sovereign LORD,
“when I will send a famine through the land—
not a famine of food or a thirst for water,
but a famine of hearing the words of the LORD.
[12]Men will stagger from sea to sea
and wander from north to east,
searching for the word of the LORD,
but they will not find it.

[13]“In that day

“the lovely young women and strong young men
will faint because of thirst.
[14]They who swear by the shame[a] of Samaria,
or say, ‘As surely as your god lives, O Dan,’
or, ‘As surely as the god[b] of Beersheba lives’—
they will fall,
never to rise again.”

Israel to Be Destroyed

9 I saw the Lord standing by the altar, and he said:

“Strike the tops of the pillars
so that the thresholds shake.
Bring them down on the heads of all the people;
those who are left I will kill with the sword.
Not one will get away,
none will escape.
[2]Though they dig down to the depths of the grave,[c]
from there my hand will take them.
Though they climb up to the heavens,
from there I will bring them down.
[3]Though they hide themselves on the top of Carmel,
there I will hunt them down and seize them.
Though they hide from me at the bottom of the sea,
there I will command the serpent to bite them.
[4]Though they are driven into exile by their enemies,
there I will command the sword to slay them.
I will fix my eyes upon them
for evil and not for good.”

[5]The Lord, the LORD Almighty,
he who touches the earth and it melts,
and all who live in it mourn—
the whole land rises like the Nile,
then sinks like the river of Egypt—
[6]he who builds his lofty palace[d] in the heavens

[a]**14** Or *by Ashima*; or *by the idol* [b]**14** Or *power* [c]**2** Hebrew *to Sheol*
[d]**6** The meaning of the Hebrew for this phrase is uncertain.

8:10 *wear sackcloth and shave your heads:* Sackcloth was a rough, dark-colored cloth made from goat or camel hair. It was worn in times of sorrow and trouble. Shaving one's head was also done in times of extreme sadness (Job 1:20).

8:12-14 *searching for the word of the LORD . . . Dan:* See the note at 3:9. Jeroboam I built a shrine for worshiping the LORD at Dan in the northern part of Israel.

8:14 *the shame of Samaria:* Probably refers to one of the Aramean or Canaanite goddesses that some Israelites worshiped. See also Deut 16:21; Judg 6:25; Jer 7:18; 44:19. See also the mini-article called "Canaanite Gods and Goddesses," p. 469.

9:1 *the altar:* This refers to the altar at Bethel, not Jerusalem. See the note at 7:10-13.

9:2 *dig down to the depths of the grave:* Meaning down to the world of the dead underground (Job 30:23; Ps 139:7,8; Ezek 31:16-18; Acts 2:27).

9:3 *the top of Carmel:* See the note at 1:1,2.

9:5 *LORD Almighty:* See the note at 3:13 (LORD).

9:5 Amos 8:8.

9:7 *Cushites . . . Philistines . . . Arameans:* Cush was a region south of Egypt that included parts of the present-day countries of Ethiopia and Sudan. See the note at 1:6-8. In the twelfth century B.C., the people who came to be known as Philistines migrated from the island of Crete to the area west of Canaan. The Arameans migrated from Kir (see the note at 1:3-5). Amos compares the migrations of Israel's enemies to Israel's own migration from Egypt to Canaan described in Exodus 13—Numbers 36, which occurred at about the same time. God's people think their migration was special, but Amos makes the point that the LORD cares for others, too.

9:8 *the house of Jacob:* See the note at 1:11,12.

9:9 *as grain is shaken in a sieve:* After grain kernels were separated from chaff they fell to the ground or onto a stone threshing floor. Rocks or other pieces of debris were scooped up along with the kernels of grain. The grain was then put in a sieve with holes large enough to let the good grain fall through but small enough to catch the larger stones and other debris. Those who have been faithful to the LORD will escape disaster but still be scattered among the nations. The unfaithful people will be trapped and killed.

9:11,12 Acts 15:16-18.

and sets its foundation[a] on the earth,
who calls for the waters of the sea
and pours them out over the face of the land—
the LORD is his name.

7 "Are not you Israelites
the same to me as the Cushites[b]?"
declares the LORD.
"Did I not bring Israel up from Egypt,
the Philistines from Caphtor[c]
and the Arameans from Kir?

8 "Surely the eyes of the Sovereign LORD
are on the sinful kingdom.
I will destroy it
from the face of the earth—
yet I will not totally destroy
the house of Jacob,"
declares the LORD.
9 "For I will give the command,
and I will shake the house of Israel
among all the nations
as grain is shaken in a sieve,
and not a pebble will reach the ground.
10 All the sinners among my people
will die by the sword,
all those who say,
'Disaster will not overtake or meet us.'

THE LORD WILL REBUILD ISRAEL

Amos's messages of doom are followed by this message of hope for a new beginning.

Israel's Restoration

11 "In that day I will restore
David's fallen tent.
I will repair its broken places,
restore its ruins,
and build it as it used to be,
12 so that they may possess the remnant of Edom
and all the nations that bear my name,[d]"
declares the LORD, who will
do these things.

13 "The days are coming," declares the LORD,

[a]6 The meaning of the Hebrew for this word is uncertain. [b]7 That is, people from the upper Nile region [c]7 That is, Crete [d]12 Hebrew; Septuagint *so that the remnant of men / and all the nations that bear my name may seek ⌞the Lord⌟*

"when the reaper will be overtaken by the plowman
and the planter by the one treading grapes.
New wine will drip from the mountains
and flow from all the hills.
14 I will bring back my exiled[a] people Israel;
they will rebuild the ruined cities and live in them.
They will plant vineyards and drink their wine;
they will make gardens and eat their fruit.
15 I will plant Israel in their own land,
never again to be uprooted
from the land I have given them,"

says the LORD your God.

[a]14 Or *will restore the fortunes of my*

9:11 *David's fallen tent:* David, Israel's great king, ruled the united kingdom of Israel from around 1010 to 970 B.C. Later, around 931 B.C., the kingdom split in two (see the note at 1:1,2). Eventually the northern kingdom (Israel) was defeated by the Assyrians (see the note at 3:9-11). Afterward, Judah was defeated by the Babylonians, as Amos had warned (see the note at 2:4,5). Amos 9:11-15 seems to imply that both Israel and Judah have already been defeated. This vision of a reunited Israel has led some scholars to suggest that these final verses of AMOS were added to the book during the time of the Babylonian exile (597-539 B.C.), a number of years after Amos lived. See also the articles called "From Joshua to the Exile: The People of Israel in the Promised Land," p. 924, and "After the Exile: God's People Return to Judea" p. 931.

9:12 *Edom:* See the note at 1:11,12.

QUESTIONS ABOUT AMOS 7:1—9:15

1. What did Amos see in the first four visions of the LORD's judgment against Israel? (7:1—8:3) How did the first two visions differ from the last two visions?
2. Who was Amaziah, and why did he tell Amos to stop preaching in Israel? (7:10-13) How did Amos respond to Amaziah's request? (7:14-17)
3. Why were the rich grain merchants impatient during the Sabbath and New Moon festival? (8:4-6) What affect did their dishonest business practices have on their country and its people? How did the LORD respond to these practices? (8:7-14; 9:1-4)
4. What, if anything, is surprising about the last verses of the book? (9:11-15) Why is it difficult to live without hope?
5. Has your understanding or picture of God changed by reading AMOS? If so, how? Name two new things you have learned while reading and studying AMOS. In what way are these things important for you?

OBADIAH

Injustice! Betrayal! Tragedy! Even if you don't cause it, should you still be blamed if you watch it happen and do nothing to prevent it? Read OBADIAH's prophecy about Edom to find out.

The day of the LORD: See verse 15. The "day" Obadiah mentions is a coming day of judgment (see the mini-article called "Day of the LORD," p. 1727). Edom's punishments fit the sins its people committed. Obadiah prophesied that the Edomites would be tricked and trapped by their best friends (verse 7), just as the Edomites had been cruel to Judah, their own relatives (verse 10). The Edomites would be despised and "brought down" (verses 2, 4), just as they had looked down on God's people by celebrating Judah's disaster (verses 12,13). Everything Edom treasured most would be taken from them (verses 5, 6), just as they had stolen from God's people (verse 13). Edom would find no friends that they could trust (verse 7), just as they had been untrustworthy and had ambushed refugees (verse 14).

WHAT MAKES OBADIAH SPECIAL?

OBADIAH is the shortest book in the Old Testament—so short that it has no chapter divisions. The name "Obadiah" was a common one in ancient Israel and means "worshiper of the LORD." All that we know about Obadiah the person comes from this book, which was probably written some time after the Babylonians invaded Jerusalem in 587 B.C. Other prophetic books, such as ISAIAH and JEREMIAH, have passages condemning the sins of many nations (see Isa 13; 15–21; Jer 46–51), but OBADIAH singles out the sins of just one nation. That nation is Edom, which bordered the land of Judah on the south near the Dead Sea.

WHY WAS OBADIAH WRITTEN?

Obadiah condemns Edom, the descendants of Esau (verse 9), because of the way they mistreated their own relatives (Israel), descendants of Esau's brother Jacob (verses 10, 12). More than that, Obadiah speaks out against Edom's pride. Even though Edom was a small nation, it felt confident that no enemy could destroy its fortress cities built high on rocky, mountainous land. But Obadiah made it clear that no nation which disobeyed God, including Edom, could be protected against God's judgment. Obadiah's prophecy also describes a future victory for the LORD's people, who will capture and rule over many neighboring lands, including Edom (verse 21).

WHAT'S THE STORY BEHIND THE SCENE?

OBADIAH is part of the story of a long-lasting bitterness between two families: the family of Jacob (the ancestor of the Israelites) and the family of Esau (the ancestor of the Edomites). Hundreds of years before Obadiah's time, Jacob had cheated his brother Esau out of his inheritance (Gen 25:27-34; 27:1-41; 36:1,9-14). Esau hated Jacob, but forgave him in later life (Gen 33:1-16). But trouble between the descendants of Jacob and Esau started again in the time of Moses (Num 20:14-21). It continued in the time of King David when Edom was conquered by Israel (2 Sam 8:13,14), and in the time of King Ahaz (736-716 B.C.), when the Edomites regained their independence from Judah. Israel's troubles with Edom are also mentioned in the writings of other prophets (Isa 34:5-15; Jer 49:7-22; Ezek 25:12-14; Amos 1:11,12; Mal 1:2-4).

No historical date or name is given in OBADIAH to provide a clue about when Obadiah lived. But the invasion of Jerusalem mentioned in verse 11 is most likely the Babylonian invasion of Jerusalem in 587 or 586 B.C. The Edomites did nothing to help

Judah, but stood by and celebrated the enemy victory. More than that, the Edomites moved north into southern Judah and took land and property (verse 13), and they captured Judean refugees and handed them over to the Babylonians (verse 14). Obadiah declared that no natural defenses or treaties with friends could preserve Edom from God's coming judgment. One day Edom would be destroyed (verses 9,15,18) and Israel would capture Edom's land (verse 19). By the fourth century B.C., the land of Edom had been taken over by the Nabateans, an Arab people who lived in the northwestern Arabian Desert.

How is Obadiah constructed?

This short book can be divided into two main sections:

God's judgment on Edom and the nations (1-16)
Israel's expansion and victory (17-21)

God's Judgment on Edom and the Nations

Obadiah announces God's plan to judge Edom, and then lists Edom's sins. Obadiah sees God's judgment on both Edom and Judah (God's own people), as a warning to every nation: Those who remain disobedient will face the judgment of God.

1 The vision of Obadiah.

This is what the Sovereign LORD says about Edom—

We have heard a message from the LORD:
An envoy was sent to the nations to say,
"Rise, and let us go against her for battle"—
2 "See, I will make you small among the nations;
you will be utterly despised.
3 The pride of your heart has deceived you,
you who live in the clefts of the rocks[a]
and make your home on the heights,
you who say to yourself,
'Who can bring me down to the ground?'
4 Though you soar like the eagle
and make your nest among the stars,
from there I will bring you down,"
declares the LORD.

5 "If thieves came to you,
if robbers in the night—
Oh, what a disaster awaits you—

[a]3 Or *of Sela*

1 *The vision of Obadiah . . . Sovereign LORD:* LORD is used for the Hebrew term, *Yahweh.* See also the mini-article called "LORD (YHWH)," p. 140. The message given to God's prophets is often described as a "vision."

1 *Edom:* The land of Edom, sometimes called Seir, was located southeast of the Dead Sea, which put it next to Judah's southern border (see the map on p. 2467). The people of Edom were descendants of Jacob's brother Esau (Gen 25:24-26; 36:1) and spoke a language similar to Hebrew. But Edom is usually described in the Bible as an enemy of Israel (Num 20:14-21; 24:18; 1 Sam 14:47, 48; 2 Sam 8:13,14).

1 *We have heard:* The "we" may refer to Obadiah and the people of Israel, or to Obadiah and other prophets, who had a similar message for Edom.

3 *clefts of the rocks and make your home on the heights:* The Edomites built fortified cities in the mountains, which they thought would protect them from enemy attacks. But the pride they take in these fortresses is wrong. They will be brought down (verse 4).

1-14 Isa 34:5-17; 63:1-6; Jer 49:7-22; Ezek 25:12-14; 35:1-15; Amos 1:11, 12; Mal 1:2-5. **4** Isa 14:11-15; Jer 49:16, 22; Amos 9:2.

5 *grape pickers . . . leave a few grapes:* According to the law of Moses, some of the ripe grapes and stalks of grain were not to be picked at harvest time, so poor people and foreigners living in Israel could take what they needed (Lev 19:10; Deut 24:21).

7 *your allies will force you to the border:* Edom's "allies" here may refer to the Babylonians, who defeated Judah with Edom's help. It could also refer to the Nabateans, who took over the land of Edom some time after 400 B.C.

8 *will I not destroy the wise men of Edom:* Edom also took pride in its wise men, but they would be destroyed along with the mountain fortresses (see the note at verse 3).

9 *Teman:* With Bozrah (Amos 1:12), Teman was one of the two main cities in Edom. Teman was fortified and controlled the fertile region of Edom.

9,10 *violence against your brother Jacob:* The people of Edom were descendants of Esau, the brother of Jacob (Israel). See Gen 36:1; Obad 12.

11 *foreigners entered his gates:* The story of Babylon's capture of Jerusalem is told in 2 Kgs 24:15—25:21 and 2 Chr 36:17-21. Edom reportedly rejoiced when the city fell (Ps 137:7; Lam 4:21; Obad 12).

12-14 *rejoice . . . day of their destruction . . . hand over their survivors:* In addition to celebrating Jerusalem's capture, the Edomites took advantage of Judah's defeat by settling in southern Judah and they apparently mistreated refugees and even handed them over to the Babylonians.

The rocky landscape near Petra, Jordan. The name "Edom" comes from a Semitic word that means "red" and was probably given to this area located between the Dead and Red Seas because of the red sandstone that makes up the landscape. Obadiah gave the people of Edom a strong message from the LORD: "The pride of your heart has deceived you, you who live in the clefts of the rocks" (verse 3). The monastery shown here was probably originally a shrine built by the Nabateans, the people who occupied this land after the Edomites left (around the fourth century B.C.).

would they not steal only as much as they wanted?
If grape pickers came to you,
would they not leave a few grapes?
6 But how Esau will be ransacked,
his hidden treasures pillaged!
7 All your allies will force you to the border;
your friends will deceive and overpower you;
those who eat your bread will set a trap for you,[a]
but you will not detect it.

8 "In that day," declares the LORD,
"will I not destroy the wise men of Edom,
men of understanding in the mountains of Esau?
9 Your warriors, O Teman, will be terrified,
and everyone in Esau's mountains
will be cut down in the slaughter.
10 Because of the violence against your brother Jacob,
you will be covered with shame;
you will be destroyed forever.
11 On the day you stood aloof
while strangers carried off his wealth
and foreigners entered his gates
and cast lots for Jerusalem,

[a]7 The meaning of the Hebrew for this clause is uncertain.

you were like one of them.
[12]You should not look down on your brother
in the day of his misfortune,
nor rejoice over the people of Judah
in the day of their destruction,
nor boast so much
in the day of their trouble.
[13]You should not march through the gates of my people
in the day of their disaster,
nor look down on them in their calamity
in the day of their disaster,
nor seize their wealth
in the day of their disaster.
[14]You should not wait at the crossroads
to cut down their fugitives,
nor hand over their survivors
in the day of their trouble.
[15]"The day of the LORD is near
for all nations.
As you have done, it will be done to you;
your deeds will return upon your own head.
[16]Just as you drank on my holy hill,
so all the nations will drink continually;
they will drink and drink
and be as if they had never been.

The day of the LORD is near for all nations. As you have done, it will be done to you.
Obad 15

15 *day of the LORD is near:* See the note on p. 1736.

16 *my holy hill . . . drink continually:* God's judgment on Judah came in 587 B.C. when the Babylonian army destroyed Jerusalem (his "holy hill"). Drinking the LORD's wine or from his cup of wrath is a symbol for God's judgment and punishment (Ps 60:3; Isa 51:22; Jer 25:15-29; Rev 14:10; 16:19).

17 *on Mount Zion will be deliverance:* Israel's King David captured the hilltop fortress known as Zion in the Jebusite city of Jerusalem (2 Sam 5:6-9). He later had the ark of the covenant kept on Mount Zion. God was present on the ark (Exod 25:22), and that made Zion God's "holy hill" (verse 16). See also the mini-article called "Zion," p. 1294.

"Deliverance" probably refers to those who will be freed from captivity in Babylon. They will return to Zion, because it is their holy mountain.

Israel's Expansion and Victory

Edom's judgment will come at the hands of Israel, which will not only conquer the land of Edom to the south, but other surrounding lands. Jerusalem will become the center of God's new kingdom.

[17]But on Mount Zion will be deliverance;
it will be holy,

QUESTIONS ABOUT OBADIAH

1. What did Edom do (or not do) to God's people that was worthy of judgment? (10-14)
2. Why did Edom think that it was safe from any harm? (4, 8) Why did Obadiah say that Edom was not safe at all?
3. The Babylonians defeated Judah, destroyed Jerusalem, and took many of Judah's people away into exile. According to Obadiah, how would this situation be reversed? What would happen to God's people (Israel) and to their enemies, such as Edom? (17-21)
4. Summarize the key message of OBADIAH in one or two sentences.

18 *house of Jacob will be a fire . . . the house of Esau will be stubble:* Fire is an important symbol in the Bible for the presence of God (Exod 3:2; 13:21,22; 19:18; Acts 2:3). It also represented the purity of God and God's activity in destroying evil (Ps 11:6; 21:9; 140:8-10; 1 Cor 3:13-15). Obadiah believed that God would use Israel as his instrument to destroy Edom as easily as fire destroys stubble. See also Isa 33:10-14 and the mini-article called "Fire," p. 2383.

19,20 *Negev . . . Sepharad:* For the locations mentioned in these verses, see the maps on pp. 2464 and 2467. Obadiah describes the expansion of Israel in every direction: south, to the Negev; west, to the lands of Israel's ancient enemy, Philistia, on the Mediterranean Sea; east, to Gilead on the eastern side of the Jordan River; north, to Phoenicia and the city of Zarephath (1 Kgs 5:1; 17:8-16); and finally south again. In the two southern expansions, Obadiah mentions the involvement of both those who had remained in Judah during the exile (verse 19) and those who returned from Sepharad in the far north after the exile (verse 20). Sepharad possibly refers to the city of Sardis, the capital of Lydia, in south central Asia Minor (see the map on p. 2469).

21 *the kingdom will be the* LORD*'s:* Obadiah looked for the day when God's rule would be restored on Zion, and the suffering and shame God's people had suffered would be reversed. The LORD would rule over all people, including Edom. See also Isa 60:10-14.

and the house of Jacob
will possess its inheritance.
18 The house of Jacob will be a fire
and the house of Joseph a flame;
the house of Esau will be stubble,
and they will set it on fire and consume it.
There will be no survivors
from the house of Esau."
The LORD has spoken.

19 People from the Negev will occupy
the mountains of Esau,
and people from the foothills will possess
the land of the Philistines.
They will occupy the fields of Ephraim and Samaria,
and Benjamin will possess Gilead.
20 This company of Israelite exiles who are in Canaan
will possess ⌞the land⌟ as far as Zarephath;
the exiles from Jerusalem who are in Sepharad
will possess the towns of the Negev.
21 Deliverers will go up on[a] Mount Zion
to govern the mountains of Esau.
And the kingdom will be the LORD's.

[a]21 Or *from*

JONAH

God uses prophets to deliver messages of both doom and hope. But what happens if the prophet disobeys God and fails to deliver these important messages? Read Jonah and find out.

What makes Jonah special?

All the other prophetic books primarily contain speeches of the prophets they are named after. Jonah has only one verse of prophecy (3:4). A few prophetic books also contain historical information about the prophets. But Jonah reads more like a story from beginning to end.

Why was Jonah written?

In recounting the reign of Jeroboam II, 2 Kings 14:25 mentions a prophet by the name of "Jonah son of Amittai"—the same person identified in the first verse of the book of Jonah. Since Jeroboam II ruled over the northern kingdom (Israel) from 783 to 743 B.C., the prophet Jonah's life can be dated to that time period as well. Tradition has credited the authorship of Jonah to the prophet himself, although the book doesn't name its author. Regardless of authorship, some scholars believe the book was written before Israel was conquered by Assyria in 722 B.C.

Other scholars think that the message of Jonah reflects the situation for Israel during or after the time of the exile in Babylon, which lasted from 597 to 539 B.C. The exile was viewed as a time of punishment because the people had turned away from the Lord. In the time after the exile, Israel struggled with how they could keep their identity as God's chosen people. Some suggested that the best way to do this was to separate themselves from people of other nations. This led to a self-centered and unforgiving attitude toward those who were not Jewish. Many forgot that God had chosen the people of Israel to be a blessing to everyone on earth (Gen 12:3) and a light to other nations (Isa 49:6). No matter when Jonah was written, the book challenges the Israelites by showing how foolish it is to try to keep God to yourself, because God is the God of all, and God can show mercy to everyone, even enemies.

What's the story behind the scene?

Assyria was an aggressive and destructive power in the ancient Near East. When it conquered nations, families were often split apart and sent to different regions of the empire. As a result, Assyria was hated by many of the peoples of the ancient world. This was certainly true for the people of Israel, who were threatened by the prospect of Assyrian invasion. In 722 B.C., the ten tribes of Israel would indeed be completely destroyed by Assyria—taken from their homes, never to be heard from again. By sending Jonah to Assyria's "great city" of Nineveh, God's

Nineveh, Tarshish, and Joppa: Nineveh, traditionally known as the "great city" (1:2), was a large and "very important city" (3:3) in the powerful nation of Assyria, a hated enemy of Israel. It was located in northeastern Mesopotamia (modern-day Iraq) on the Tigris River. Nineveh's wickedness is described in Nahum 2:10—3:4. See the map on p. 2462 and the mini-article called "Assyria," p. 711.

Joppa was a busy seaport on the Mediterranean coast in Palestine. Tarshish may be another name for Tartessus, a city on the coast of Spain. Spain was far in the opposite direction from Nineveh and one of the most distant places one could sail to at the time. By naming Nineveh and Tarshish in the opening of Jonah (1:2,3), the author is preparing the reader to learn one of the key messages of this short book—that God rules the entire world from one end to the other. For Tarshish, see the map on p. 2471.

overwhelming love and mercy are revealed. Jonah's anger at God for forgiving Israel's hated enemy is probably meant to reflect a similar attitude in Israel. Israel was jealous of its special relationship with God and was unwilling to allow this relationship to be extended to other nations, especially nations that were clearly enemies of God and God's people.

How is Jonah constructed?

Jonah tries to run away from the Lord (1:1-17)
The Lord saves Jonah (2:1-10)
Jonah in Nineveh (3:1—4:11)

Jonah Tries to Run Away from the Lord

The Lord tells Jonah to go to Nineveh, an important city of Israel's great enemy Assyria, to tell its people they are doomed. But Jonah tries to run away from the Lord. Of all the places God could have sent Jonah, Nineveh may have been the hardest place for Jonah to go. To Jonah, the danger isn't simply that Nineveh is an evil, wicked city. Jonah has an even bigger fear, which will become clear later in the story.

Jonah Flees From the Lord

1 The word of the Lord came to Jonah son of Amittai: 2“Go to
the great city of Nineveh and preach against it, because its wickedness has come up before me.”
3But Jonah ran away from the Lord and headed for Tarshish.
He went down to Joppa, where he found a ship bound for that
port. After paying the fare, he went aboard and sailed for Tarshish
to flee from the Lord.
4Then the Lord sent a great wind on the sea, and such a violent storm arose that the ship threatened to break up. 5All the
sailors were afraid and each cried out to his own god. And they
threw the cargo into the sea to lighten the ship.
But Jonah had gone below deck, where he lay down and fell
into a deep sleep. 6The captain went to him and said, “How can
you sleep? Get up and call on your god! Maybe he will take notice
of us, and we will not perish.”
7Then the sailors said to each other, “Come, let us cast lots to
find out who is responsible for this calamity.” They cast lots and
the lot fell on Jonah.
8So they asked him, “Tell us, who is responsible for making

1:1 *Lord:* “Lord” is used for the Hebrew *Yahweh,* which is God's personal name in the Jewish Scriptures (Old Testament). Jonah clearly shows God's power over all of creation. In Jonah's time, many people believed there was more than one god (1:5). See also the mini-article called “Lord (YHWH),” p. 140.

1:1 *Jonah son of Amittai:* A prophet with this name lived at the time of Jeroboam II, who ruled the northern kingdom of Israel from 783 to 743 B.C. (see 2 Kgs 14:25).

1:2,3 *Nineveh . . . Tarshish . . . Joppa:* See the note on p. 1741.

1:5,6 *sailors . . . captain:* The Hebrew text refers to the sailors as “salts” and the captain as the “chief rope puller.” Notice that when the storm comes up, it is the sailors who pray to their gods, while Jonah, God's prophet, is fast asleep.

Scenes from the Story of Jonah, mosaic in the Basilica at Aquileia, Italy, fourth or fifth century. Jonah has been called "the reluctant prophet" because he did not immediately take God's message to the people of Nineveh like the LORD wanted him to. It was only after Jonah was swallowed by a great fish and vomited onto the shore that Jonah did as the LORD commanded. This mosaic also shows Jonah resting under a vine as he waits to see what will happen to the city of Nineveh (4:1-11).

all this trouble for us? What do you do? Where do you come from? What is your country? From what people are you?"

9He answered, "I am a Hebrew and I worship the LORD, the God of heaven, who made the sea and the land."

10This terrified them and they asked, "What have you done?" (They knew he was running away from the LORD, because he had already told them so.)

11The sea was getting rougher and rougher. So they asked him, "What should we do to you to make the sea calm down for us?"

12"Pick me up and throw me into the sea," he replied, "and it will become calm. I know that it is my fault that this great storm has come upon you."

13Instead, the men did their best to row back to land. But
they could not, for the sea grew even wilder than before. 14Then
they cried to the LORD, "O LORD, please do not let us die for taking this man's life. Do not hold us accountable for killing an innocent
man, for you, O LORD, have done as you pleased." 15Then they took
Jonah and threw him overboard, and the raging sea grew calm.
16At this the men greatly feared the LORD, and they offered a sacrifice to the LORD and made vows to him.

17But the LORD provided a great fish to swallow Jonah, and Jonah was inside the fish three days and three nights.

1:9 *Hebrew . . . LORD, the God of heaven:* Israelites called themselves "Hebrews" when identifying themselves to foreigners. See also the note at 1:1 (LORD). To say that the LORD is God of heaven, sea, and land is to claim he is the God of all creation, the one supreme God.

1:16 *the men greatly feared the LORD . . . offered a sacrifice:* Fearing that they will be punished for throwing Jonah overboard, the sailors offer a sacrifice to Jonah's LORD. See the chart called "Sacrifices and Offerings," p. 219.

1:17 *great fish:* The type of fish is unknown. It is used to save Jonah and to return him to dry land. See also Matt 12:40.

2:2-6 *depths of the grave . . . pit:* The ancient Hebrews believed that a deep sea was located under the surface of the earth. The world of the dead, the "pit," lay beneath this great sea. The Bible describes the grave as a totally silent place where no one knows or feels anything (Job 10:21,22; Ps 88:12; 94:17). Jonah uses this imagery to show that he felt both physically and spiritually separated from God.

2:4 *your holy temple:* Jonah believed God was present in a special way in the temple in Jerusalem (Exod 25:10-22; 2 Sam 6:2; 1 Kgs 8:6-13; Ezek 10:1-5). Jonah was tossed into the "pit" below the deepest part of the sea, and far from God's temple. But no physical distance was great enough to keep God from hearing Jonah's prayers.

2:9 *sacrifice to you . . . Salvation:* Compare 2:9 to 1:16 and the note. When Jonah is the one being saved, he is happy to state his belief in God's ability to do so. Later in the story, Jonah will not be so happy to witness God's mercy (see 4:1-3). See also the mini-article called "Salvation," p. 2021.

3:3 *a very important city . . . three days:* Nineveh was a large city, but archaeological evidence indicates that the city's size is exaggerated in the story for effect. Nineveh was only three miles across and a mile and a half wide (see the map on p. 1766).

3:4 *Forty more days:* A period of time often associated with times of testing in the Bible, (Gen 6:17; Exod 34:28).

3:5, 6 *declared a fast . . . sackcloth . . . dust:* To go without eating (fasting) was done in times of sadness or sorrow. Sackcloth was a rough, dark-colored cloth made from goat or camel hair. Sometimes people wore sackcloth and sat in dust to show how sorry they were for their sins. See also Job 2:8; Lam 2:10; Matt 12:41; Luke 11:32.

The LORD Saves Jonah

Two verses tell how God rescues Jonah from the depths of the sea (1:17 and 2:10). The verses in between (2:1-9) are Jonah's prayer of thanksgiving. In this prayer Jonah speaks as though his rescue has already taken place.

Jonah's Prayer

2 From inside the fish Jonah prayed to the LORD his God.
2 He said:

"In my distress I called to the LORD,
and he answered me.
From the depths of the grave[a] I called
for help,
and you listened to my cry.
3 You hurled me into the deep,
into the very heart of the seas,
and the currents swirled about me;
all your waves and breakers
swept over me.
4 I said, 'I have been banished
from your sight;
yet I will look again
toward your holy temple.'
5 The engulfing waters threatened me,[b]
the deep surrounded me;
seaweed was wrapped around my head.
6 To the roots of the mountains
I sank down;
the earth beneath barred me in forever.
But you brought my life up from the pit,
O LORD my God.
7 "When my life was ebbing away,
I remembered you, LORD,
and my prayer rose to you,
to your holy temple.
8 "Those who cling to worthless idols
forfeit the grace that could be theirs.
9 But I, with a song of thanksgiving,
will sacrifice to you.
What I have vowed I will make good.
Salvation comes from the LORD."

10 And the LORD commanded the fish, and it vomited Jonah
onto dry land.

[a]2 Hebrew *Sheol* [b]5 Or *waters were at my throat*

Jonah in Nineveh

Again, God tells Jonah to go to Nineveh and preach. This time Jonah goes, but he still does not like his task. We hear no beautiful language or long, pleading passages when Jonah speaks to the people. Jonah wastes as few words as possible on these people (see 3:4). When the message is effective and the people stop doing evil things, Jonah becomes angry and pouts. The story ends with a question (4:11) meant not only for Jonah but for all who read the book.

Jonah Goes to Nineveh

3 Then the word of the LORD came to Jonah a second time: 2"Go to the great city of Nineveh and proclaim to it the message I give you."

3Jonah obeyed the word of the LORD and went to Nineveh. Now Nineveh was a very important city—a visit required three days. 4On the first day, Jonah started into the city. He proclaimed: "Forty more days and Nineveh will be overturned." 5The Ninevites believed God. They declared a fast, and all of them, from the greatest to the least, put on sackcloth.

6When the news reached the king of Nineveh, he rose from his throne, took off his royal robes, covered himself with sackcloth and sat down in the dust. 7Then he issued a proclamation in Nineveh:

"By the decree of the king and his nobles:

Do not let any man or beast, herd or flock, taste anything; do not let them eat or drink. 8But let man and beast be covered with sackcloth. Let everyone call urgently on God. Let them give up their evil ways and their violence. 9Who knows? God may yet relent and with compassion turn from his fierce anger so that we will not perish."

10When God saw what they did and how they turned from their evil ways, he had compassion and did not bring upon them the destruction he had threatened.

Jonah's Anger at the LORD's Compassion

4 But Jonah was greatly displeased and became angry. 2He prayed to the LORD, "O LORD, is this not what I said when I was still at home? That is why I was so quick to flee to Tarshish. I knew that you are a gracious and compassionate God, slow to anger and abounding in love, a God who relents from sending calamity. 3Now, O LORD, take away my life, for it is better for me to die than to live."

4But the LORD replied, "Have you any right to be angry?"

5Jonah went out and sat down at a place east of the city. There he made himself a shelter, sat in its shade and waited to see

Jonah prayed, saying, *"I knew that you are a gracious and compassionate God, slow to anger and abounding in love, a God who relents from sending calamity."* Jonah 4:2

3:6 *king of Nineveh:* This probably refers to the king of Assyria, whose palace was in Nineveh. His actions show in a public way that he, too, is not above having to obey God, who rules all people. The king orders the people to pray to Jonah's God (3:7-9), though the people of Nineveh normally worshiped other gods and goddesses. Compare their actions to those of the sailors (1:14).

3:10 *God . . . did not bring upon them the destruction he had threatened:* God's compassion and the Ninevites' repentance resulted in God's judgment being averted. Later, however, the people of Nineveh returned to their wickedness and cruelty, as demonstrated by the destruction of Israel in 722 B.C. In 612 B.C., Nineveh itself was destroyed.

4:1-3 *Jonah was greatly displeased . . . take away my life:* Now it becomes more clear why Jonah wanted to run away from the LORD. He knew that the LORD was merciful (4:2) and may forgive the people of Nineveh. But like many in Israel, Jonah probably thought the Assyrians deserved the LORD's punishment, not his forgiveness.

4:2 Exod 34:6; 2 Chr 30:9; Neh 9:17; Ps 86:15; 111:4; Isa 54:10.
4:3 1 Kgs 19:4.

4:6 *vine:* The Hebrew word translated here as "vine" is *kikayon,* which would indicate a plant with wide leaves, such as a castor bean (shown here) or cucumber plant.

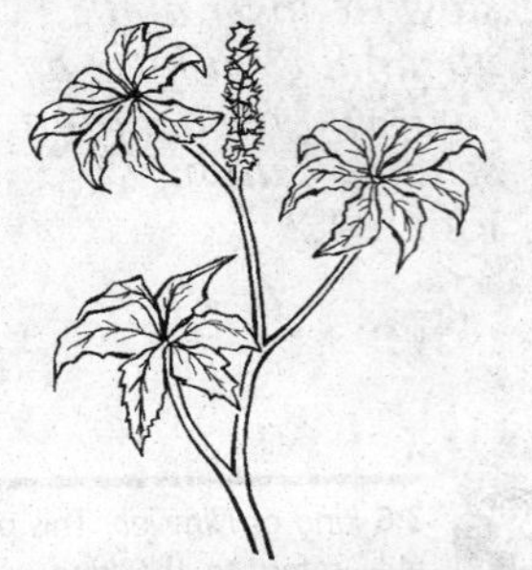

4:6 *shade for his head:* Once again God protects Jonah, in spite of his anger at God (see 1:17; see also the note at 2:9).

4:11 *cannot tell their right hand from their left . . . many cattle:* This phrase means that they do not know right from wrong; it may refer to infants and young children (see also Isa 7:15,16). If so, that would mean that there were many more than 120,000 people in Nineveh (but see the note at 3:3). Even the cattle of Nineveh wore sackcloth (3:7-9). The fact that the LORD was concerned about the cattle further drove home the point that the LORD's mercy was not just for the people of Israel.

what would happen to the city. [6]Then the LORD God provided a
vine and made it grow up over Jonah to give shade for his head to
ease his discomfort, and Jonah was very happy about the vine. [7]But
at dawn the next day God provided a worm, which chewed the
vine so that it withered. [8]When the sun rose, God provided a
scorching east wind, and the sun blazed on Jonah's head so that he
grew faint. He wanted to die, and said, "It would be better for me
to die than to live."

[9]But God said to Jonah, "Do you have a right to be angry
about the vine?"

"I do," he said. "I am angry enough to die."

[10]But the LORD said, "You have been concerned about this
vine, though you did not tend it or make it grow. It sprang up
overnight and died overnight. [11]But Nineveh has more than a hundred and twenty thousand people who cannot tell their right hand
from their left, and many cattle as well. Should I not be concerned
about that great city?"

QUESTIONS ABOUT JONAH

1. Why did Jonah find going to Nineveh such a hateful task? Have you ever felt that way about something you had to do? Did you do it? Why or why not? What happened?
2. Compare the attitudes and actions of the non-Israelites (the sailors, ship captain, and people of Nineveh) to the actions of Jonah. How do they differ? How does this contrast reflect the overall theme of the book?
3. Read Jonah's prayer again (2:2-9). What qualities does it have that you expect to find in a prayer? Think of a situation in your life when God came to your rescue, and write a prayer of thanksgiving using Jonah's prayer as a model.
4. What aspects of Jonah's personality are revealed in the story? Which ones do you admire? Which ones are troubling? Which remind you of yourself?
5. What aspects of God are revealed in the story? Which ones give you comfort or strength? Which ones trouble you?
6. What can the story of Jonah teach us about trying to understand God's will for the world?

MICAH

What does God want from his people more than anything else? Read* MICAH *to find out what happened to the people of Israel when they forgot the answer to this important question.

WHAT MAKES MICAH SPECIAL?

In Hebrew, the name "Micah" means "who is like the LORD." This phrase is more of an exclamation than a question, for in this book the prophet Micah proclaims that no one is as powerful as the LORD God of Israel. God judges earthly leaders and nations who oppose God and ignore God's concern for justice, but God also saves those who confess their sins and return to him (7:9,18,19).

It did not matter to Micah that he came from a small town in the country. He found courage to criticize leaders in the capital cities of Israel and Judah. Micah's courage was so great it was still famous over one hundred years later in the time of the prophet Jeremiah (Jer 26:18).

One brief passage in MICAH (5:2-5) has become an important passage for Christians. It tells of a shepherd from Bethlehem who will take care of his sheep (his people) and bring peace to the world. The Gospel of MATTHEW identified this "shepherd" with Jesus of Nazareth (Matt 2:1-6).

WHY WAS MICAH WRITTEN?

The LORD God had made covenants with the ancestors of the people of Israel: Abraham and Jacob (Gen 12:1-3; 15:4-6; 35:9-12; Mic 7:20), and Moses (Exod 3:7, 8; 20–24; Deut 5–7). God promised to bless Israel with land and many descendants if they worshiped him alone and obeyed his laws. Micah said that many of God's people had turned their backs on God's Law and were in danger of losing out on God's promises. The messages in the book were especially for Samaria, the capital of the northern kingdom (Israel), and for Jerusalem, the capital of the southern kingdom (Judah). Instead of worshiping and obeying the LORD, the leaders and the people of these cities were worshiping other gods, as well as cheating and robbing the poor. And so the LORD was going to punish Israel and Judah.

But Micah also announced that God would rescue the people in the future. God would lead them home to worship once again in Jerusalem (4:1-13) and choose a leader who would care for the people like a shepherd and bring them peace (5:2-5). Micah shared a hope with the prophet Isaiah that one day the LORD's Law would be obeyed by all nations and all weapons of war would be remade into "plowshares and pruning hooks" (Isa 2:1-5; Mic 4:1-5). Though God's people (Israel) had suffered at the hands of nations such as Assyria (5:5,6) and Babylon (4:10), the LORD would forgive Israel and renew the promises the LORD made to their ancestors (7:18-20).

Bethlehem Ephrathah: Bethlehem was a small town located in the farming region five miles south of Jerusalem (see the map on p. 2467). Ephrathah is a name for the region around Bethlehem (Ruth 1:2; 4:11; 1 Sam 17:12) and may have been another name for the town. Bethlehem was the hometown of Israel's King David (1 Sam 16:1). In the New Testament, Jesus' birth in Bethlehem is seen as the fulfillment of Micah's prophecy in 5:2-5 (Matt 2:1-6; Luke 2:4-7; John 7:42).

Moresheth, Samaria, and Jerusalem: Micah's hometown of Moresheth (1:1) was a small town in southern Judah not far from Gath. In 1:14 it is called Moresheth Gath. Samaria was the capital of the northern kingdom (Israel), and Jerusalem was the capital of the southern kingdom (Judah). See the map on p. 2467 and the article called "From Joshua to the Exile: The People of Israel in the Promised Land," p. 924, which explains how the ten northern tribes of Israel broke away from the two southern tribes and formed their own nation after the death of King Solomon (1 Kgs 12).

1:1 *Jotham, Ahaz and Hezekiah:* Jotham, the son of Uzziah, ruled Judah 740-736 B.C. (2 Kgs 15:32-38; 2 Chr 27:1-7); Ahaz, the son of Jotham, ruled 736-716 B.C. (2 Kgs 16:1-20; 2 Chr 28:1-27); Hezekiah, the son of Ahaz, ruled 716-687 B.C. (2 Kgs 18:1—20:21; 2 Chr 29:1—32:33).

1:2 *the Sovereign LORD may witness against you:* God's judgment of Israel and other nations sometimes is described by the prophets in terms of a hearing or trial (Deut 30:19; Jer 2:9, 35; Mic 6:1,2). God, the judge, says the whole earth will suffer (1:2,4) because the people have worshiped idols (1:5-7).

See also the mini-articles called "Covenants (Agreements)," p. 386, and "Justice," p. 1721.

WHAT'S THE STORY BEHIND THE SCENE?

Micah came from a small town in the country called Moresheth, which was probably located about twenty-five miles southwest of Jerusalem. According to 1:1, he preached during the time that Jotham (740-736 B.C.), Ahaz (736-716 B.C.), and Hezekiah (716-687 B.C.) ruled in Judah. Micah criticized the leaders of Samaria and Jerusalem, repeating the warnings of the earlier prophets Amos and Hosea. The leaders and people of Samaria would be judged because they were worshiping other gods and treating the poor unjustly (Hos 2:2-13; Amos 5:10-27; Mic 1:2-7). These warnings were fulfilled in 722-21 B.C. when Assyria invaded Israel and conquered Samaria. Many of the people of Israel's northern kingdom were forced to leave their land and live in other parts of the Assyrian empire.

Micah warned the leaders of Jerusalem that they would suffer a similar punishment because they were doing some of the same evil things (1:8—2:11; 3:8-12). In 701 B.C., the Assyrians passed through the area of Micah's hometown, Moresheth, while destroying many towns in Judah. Jerusalem was surrounded but escaped destruction when Hezekiah prayed for God's help (2 Kgs 18:13—19:37; Isa 36:37). In 586 B.C. another enemy, the Babylonians, did capture Jerusalem and many of its leading citizens were taken away into captivity in Babylon (2 Kgs 25:1-21).

But the destruction of Samaria and Jerusalem was not Micah's final word from God. Even though God acted as a judge, he still cared for his people. One day, the people would return to Jerusalem and worship the LORD in the temple, and a new ruler would lead God's people like a faithful shepherd and bring in a time of peace. In 539 B.C., the Persians conquered Babylonia and allowed many of Judah's people to return home and rebuild Jerusalem and the temple (2 Chr 36:22, 23). The new temple was dedicated in 515 B.C. (Ezra 6:13-18). Micah's words of hope echo the great promises of a number of Israel's prophets (Isa 45:1-13; 52:1-12; 59:9-21; Jer 46:27, 28; Ezek 37; Zech 9:9-17).

HOW IS MICAH CONSTRUCTED?

The prophecies in MICAH alternate between doom and hope. Scholars have pointed out many similarities between the lifestyle and messages of Micah and Isaiah, especially the first part of ISAIAH (chapters 1-39). A number of these are identified in the notes that follow. See also the Introduction to ISAIAH, p. 1289.

The book can be outlined as follows:

Messages of judgment against Israel and Judah (1:1—3:12)

Messages of hope for God's people (4:1—5:15)

The LORD puts the people of Israel on trial for their sins (6:1—7:7)

The LORD forgives those who confess their sins (7:8-20)

Messages of Judgment against Israel and Judah

Micah announces the LORD*'s judgment of Israel and Judah. Their leaders are allowing the worship of idols and ignoring God's concern for justice. God will use enemy armies to destroy Samaria and Jerusalem, and the leaders will feel the same pain and powerlessness that they have caused their own people. A message of hope (2:12,13) proclaims that those who survive the days of judgment will once again be gathered together as God's people.*

1 The word of the LORD that came to Micah of Moresheth during the reigns of Jotham, Ahaz and Hezekiah, kings of Judah—the vision he saw concerning Samaria and Jerusalem.

2 Hear, O peoples, all of you,
listen, O earth and all who are in it,
that the Sovereign LORD may witness against you,
the Lord from his holy temple.

Judgment Against Samaria and Jerusalem

3 Look! The LORD is coming from his dwelling place;
he comes down and treads the high places of the earth.
4 The mountains melt beneath him
and the valleys split apart,
like wax before the fire,
like water rushing down a slope.
5 All this is because of Jacob's transgression,
because of the sins of the house of Israel.
What is Jacob's transgression?
Is it not Samaria?
What is Judah's high place?
Is it not Jerusalem?

6 "Therefore I will make Samaria a heap of rubble,
a place for planting vineyards.
I will pour her stones into the valley
and lay bare her foundations.
7 All her idols will be broken to pieces;
all her temple gifts will be burned with fire;
I will destroy all her images.
Since she gathered her gifts from the wages of prostitutes,
as the wages of prostitutes they will again be used."

Weeping and Mourning

8 Because of this I will weep and wail;
I will go about barefoot and naked.
I will howl like a jackal
and moan like an owl.

1:2 *holy temple:* Here "temple" may mean God's throne in heaven (Ps 11:4), or may refer to the Jerusalem temple, where God was said to live (1 Kgs 8:1-13; Isa 6:1-4). If the "temple" here refers to heaven, then Micah may be saying that the Jerusalem temple is no longer the center of God's rule on earth. It has become a center of idolatry (2 Kgs 16:7-18), and God will judge (1:3, 5) and purify it until it is fit to be used again (4:1-4).

1:4 *mountains . . . valleys:* God's presence and power are often described in terms of their effect on the world's land and waters (Exod 19:18; Judg 5:4, 5; Ps 18:6-15).

1:5 *Jacob's transgression:* "Jacob" is used as a name for the people of Israel (Gen 32:28). Here Micah is probably referring to the northern kingdom rather than to the entire nation of Israel, but he also uses the name "Jacob" for the southern kingdom of Judah (2:7) or for the whole people of Israel (5:7). See also the mini-article called "Israel," p. 264.

1:7 *her idols . . . wages of prostitutes:* At pagan temples, people had sex with prostitutes as a way of worshiping idols, such as Baal and Asherah. The money earned in this way was used to support the pagan religion. The worship of Canaanite gods and goddesses had become a big problem in Israel (Hos 4:9-19). As a fitting punishment, God will smash Israel's idols, and foreigners will use the gold and silver from the idols to pay temple prostitutes once again. See also the mini-articles called "Prostitution in the Bible," p. 1688, and "Canaanite Gods and Goddesses," p. 469.

1:8 *Because of this:* "This" refers to either the destruction of Samaria (1:6, 7) or to the coming destruction of Judah and Jerusalem (1:9-16).

1:10-12 *Gath . . . Beth Ophrah . . . Maroth:* Gath was a Philistine city; Beth Ophrah is unknown, but in Hebrew it sounds like "House of Dust." Shaphir, Zaanan, Beth Ezel and Maroth are mentioned only here in the Old Testament. These towns form the path of the invading army approaching Jerusalem from the coastal plain.

1:13 *Lachish:* This important fortified city of southwest Judah was the base for the Assyrian attack on Jerusalem about 701 B.C. (2 Kgs 18:13-17).

1:14 *parting gifts:* The gift described here is called a "dowry," which is what a bride's father gave her when she left home to live with the family of her husband. In Hebrew the word for "bride" or "fiancee" sounds like "Moresheth" (see the note on p. 1747).

1:14,15 *Aczib . . . Mareshah . . . Adullam:* Aczib, whose name means "deception," was near the cave of Adullam, where David hid from King Saul (1 Sam 22:1, 2). Micah probably means that the people of Israel (including their king) will have to run for their lives, but will find that all hope for escape is merely a lie.

1:16 *children . . . go from you into exile:* The smaller towns mentioned in 1:10-15 were like children to the "mother" city of Jerusalem. This prophecy was fulfilled when many of Judah's leading citizens were dragged off to live in exile after the Babylonian army destroyed Jerusalem in 586 B.C. See 4:10 and the mini-article called "Exile," p. 1541.

9 For her wound is incurable;
it has come to Judah.
It[a] has reached the very gate of my people,
even to Jerusalem itself.
10 Tell it not in Gath[b];
weep not at all.[c]
In Beth Ophrah[d]
roll in the dust.
11 Pass on in nakedness and shame,
you who live in Shaphir.[e]
Those who live in Zaanan[f]
will not come out.
Beth Ezel is in mourning;
its protection is taken from you.
12 Those who live in Maroth[g] writhe in pain,
waiting for relief,
because disaster has come from the LORD,
even to the gate of Jerusalem.
13 You who live in Lachish,[h]
harness the team to the chariot.
You were the beginning of sin
to the Daughter of Zion,
for the transgressions of Israel
were found in you.
14 Therefore you will give parting gifts
to Moresheth Gath.
The town of Aczib[i] will prove deceptive
to the kings of Israel.
15 I will bring a conqueror against you
who live in Mareshah.[j]
He who is the glory of Israel
will come to Adullam.
16 Shave your heads in mourning
for the children in whom you delight;
make yourselves as bald as the vulture,
for they will go from you into exile.

Man's Plans and God's

2 Woe to those who plan iniquity,
to those who plot evil on their beds!
At morning's light they carry it out
because it is in their power to do it.

[a]9 Or *He* [b]10 *Gath* sounds like the Hebrew for *tell.* [c]10 Hebrew; Septuagint may suggest *not in Acco.* The Hebrew for *in Acco* sounds like the Hebrew for *weep.* [d]10 *Beth Ophrah* means *house of dust.* [e]11 *Shaphir* means *pleasant.* [f]11 *Zaanan* sounds like the Hebrew for *come out.* [g]12 *Maroth* sounds like the Hebrew for *bitter.* [h]13 *Lachish* sounds like the Hebrew for *team.* [i]14 *Aczib* means *deception.* [j]15 *Mareshah* sounds like the Hebrew for *conqueror.*

[2]They covet fields and seize them,
and houses, and take them.
They defraud a man of his home,
a fellowman of his inheritance.

[3]Therefore, the LORD says:

"I am planning disaster against this people,
from which you cannot save yourselves.
You will no longer walk proudly,
for it will be a time of calamity.
[4]In that day men will ridicule you;
they will taunt you with this mournful song:
'We are utterly ruined;
my people's possession is divided up.
He takes it from me!
He assigns our fields to traitors.'"

2:2 *covet fields and seize them:* According to a number of prophets, leaders and rich people in both Israel and Judah were treating the poor unjustly (Isa 5:8-10; Hos 5:10; Amos 2:6-8; 4:1; 5:10-13; Zeph 1:9). The taking of family land and grabbing land as a payment for a debt were against God's Law (Lev 24:14).

2:4 *mournful song:* This means the kind of song (lament) sung by professional mourners at funerals. See also Jer 9:17-22; Amos 5:16.

LAND

The people of Israel believed that God was the creator and owner of all land (Gen 1, 2). God promised Abraham that the land of Canaan would one day belong to his descendants, the people of Israel (Gen 15:7-21). That promise was repeated to Moses (Exod 3:7-10), the great leader who led the people out of slavery in Egypt and to the border of Canaan. See also the articles called "The Ancient World: Peoples, Powers, and Politics," p. 919, and "From Joshua to the Exile: The People of Israel in the Promised Land," p. 924.

Each tribe in Israel, except the Levi tribe, was given land by God as an inheritance (see Josh 13:8—21:45 and the map on p. 2464). Land belonging to each tribe (Num 36:5-9) was to be passed to future generations through daughters as well as sons (Num 27:2-11). Land bought or sold was to be returned to the family that originally owned it in the "Year of Jubilee," which was to occur every forty-nine years (Lev 25:8-28). This law was not always kept, but it reminded people that all land belonged to God. The law was intended to limit the number of people who could become powerful by owning land and to decrease the number of poor people who could not provide for their families because they had no land.

Since the true owner of all land was God, land was to be treated with great respect (Lev 25:1-7). Those who had land were to use it to supply the needs of others (Exod 23:10,11; Lev 19:9,10; 23:22; Deut 24:19-22). In this way the land provided an opportunity for people to show kindness to others, just as God had shown kindness to them.

When people disobeyed God, their actions were sometimes understood as polluting or defiling the land (Num 35:33, 34). Penalties had to be paid and sacrifices made to make up for the shedding of blood and to make the person and the land clean again (Exod 21:12-36; Lev 4:1—5:19). The prophet Ezekiel said that Israel's sins defiled the land and made it ritually unclean (Ezek 36:17-20). These sins were interpreted by a number of the prophets as the reason Israel and Judah would lose their land and suffer a time of exile (Isa 1:2-9; Jer 7:7-17; 10:17-21; Ezek 5:4-12; Hos 9:1-3; Mic 1:16). See also the mini-article called "Exile," p. 1541.

2:6 *Do not prophesy:* Micah kept preaching even though his message was unpopular with those who were cheating others (2:2, 8, 9). See also 1 Kgs 18:17; Jer 38:1-6; Hos 9:7; Amos 7:12-17; Luke 4:16-30; Acts 7:54-60.

2:7 *whose ways are upright:* It is unclear exactly who is speaking. It may be Micah's enemies challenging those who agree with Micah. They may have thought of themselves as those "whose ways are upright" and didn't believe that Micah's words of judgment applied to them. But the questions may be the prophet's. In verse 8 Micah clearly is presenting the LORD's case again.

2:9 *homes ... my blessing:* In ancient Israel, land ownership rights were to be passed on within families (Lev 25:23-28; Num 27:5-11; 1 Kgs 21:1-3). But some rich people in Israel and Judah were buying up the rights to land or stealing it outright, making many people homeless with little means of making a living. See also Isa 5:8-10, and the mini-article called "Land," p. 1751.

2:12,13 *I will surely gather ... remnant ... sheep ... king:* Micah adds a hopeful promise. God will gather together those who survive the difficult days ahead (the "remnant") as a shepherd gathers his flock. In contrast to the leaders who were abusing their power (Jer 23:1, 2; Ezek 34:1-10; Mic 3:9-11), God would be a good shepherd and take care of the faithful ones who return to Judah. God's ideal rulers were to be like shepherds, looking out for the needs of their people (Jer 23:4-6; Ezek 34:2-10). See also Ps 23; John 10:14.

3:1,2 *leaders ... love evil:* The rulers of Israel (3:1,11) were to provide justice on the basis of God's Law (Exod 18:24-26; Isa 1:21-23,26; Jer 23:1, 2). But they treated others unjustly and broke God's Law in many other ways, including worshiping idols (1:7), cheating in court (7:3), murder (3:10), stealing (2:2, 8), lying (2:11; 3:5), and using dishonest scales to cheat (6:11).

5 Therefore you will have no one in the assembly
of the LORD
to divide the land by lot.

False Prophets

6 "Do not prophesy," their prophets say.
"Do not prophesy about these things;
disgrace will not overtake us."
7 Should it be said, O house of Jacob:
"Is the Spirit of the LORD angry?
Does he do such things?"

"Do not my words do good
to him whose ways are upright?
8 Lately my people have risen up
like an enemy.
You strip off the rich robe
from those who pass by without a care,
like men returning from battle.
9 You drive the women of my people
from their pleasant homes.
You take away my blessing
from their children forever.
10 Get up, go away!
For this is not your resting place,
because it is defiled,
it is ruined, beyond all remedy.
11 If a liar and deceiver comes and says,
'I will prophesy for you plenty of wine and beer,'
he would be just the prophet for this people!

Deliverance Promised

12 "I will surely gather all of you, O Jacob;
I will surely bring together the remnant of Israel.
I will bring them together like sheep in a pen,
like a flock in its pasture;
the place will throng with people.
13 One who breaks open the way will go up before them;
they will break through the gate and go out.
Their king will pass through before them,
the LORD at their head."

Leaders and Prophets Rebuked

3 Then I said,

"Listen, you leaders of Jacob,
you rulers of the house of Israel.

Should you not know justice,
[2] you who hate good and love evil;
who tear the skin from my people
and the flesh from their bones;
[3] who eat my people's flesh,
strip off their skin
and break their bones in pieces;
who chop them up like meat for the pan,
like flesh for the pot?"

[4] Then they will cry out to the LORD,
but he will not answer them.
At that time he will hide his face from them
because of the evil they have done.

[5] This is what the LORD says:

"As for the prophets
who lead my people astray,
if one feeds them,
they proclaim 'peace';
if he does not,
they prepare to wage war against him.
[6] Therefore night will come over you, without
visions,
and darkness, without divination.
The sun will set for the prophets,
and the day will go dark for them.
[7] The seers will be ashamed
and the diviners disgraced.
They will all cover their faces
because there is no answer from God."

[8] But as for me, I am filled with power,
with the Spirit of the LORD,
and with justice and might,
to declare to Jacob his transgression,
to Israel his sin.
[9] Hear this, you leaders of the house of Jacob,
you rulers of the house of Israel,
who despise justice
and distort all that is right;
[10] who build Zion with bloodshed,
and Jerusalem with wickedness.
[11] Her leaders judge for a bribe,
her priests teach for a price,
and her prophets tell fortunes for money.
Yet they lean upon the LORD and say,
"Is not the LORD among us?
No disaster will come upon us."

3:5-7 *the prophets who lead my people astray . . . seers:* The prophets were to remind the people how God wanted them to live. The priests and prophets could receive money or goods in return for doing their religious duties (Num 18:8-13; 1 Sam 9:6-8; Amos 7:12). Some prophets took payments but were not willing to speak out against injustice or encourage the leaders to do what was right. For not speaking out against the evil in Israel, they would be silenced (3:7).

3:8 *filled with power, with the Spirit:* In contrast to the prophets who preached what people wanted to hear in order to get paid, Micah's prophecies came directly from the LORD's "Spirit," which is God's presence and power. God's Spirit guided other true prophets in Israel (Isa 6:1-13; Jer 1:1-19; Ezek 2:1-8; Amos 7:14-16). See also the mini-article called "Holy Spirit," p. 2082.

3:11,12 *leaders . . . prophets . . . temple:* See the note at 1:2 (temple). Judah's leaders believed that no harm could come to them while the temple was in Jerusalem, since God lived there among them. But Micah warned that the temple itself would be destroyed (see the note at 1:16).

[12] Therefore because of you,
Zion will be plowed like a field,
Jerusalem will become a heap of rubble,
the temple hill a mound overgrown with thickets.

Messages of Hope for God's People

Micah promises that, in the future, people of all nations will worship the LORD in Jerusalem. Peace will come when they live according to God's Law. God's people will return home to Judah and rebuild the city after a time of punishment. God will appoint a ruler to take care of the people and to bring them peace. Enemies will be defeated and idols honoring other gods will be destroyed.

The Mountain of the LORD

4 In the last days

the mountain of the LORD's temple will be established
as chief among the mountains;
it will be raised above the hills,
and peoples will stream to it.

[2] Many nations will come and say,

"Come, let us go up to the mountain of the LORD,
to the house of the God of Jacob.
He will teach us his ways,
so that we may walk in his paths."
The law will go out from Zion,
the word of the LORD from Jerusalem.
[3] He will judge between many peoples
and will settle disputes for strong nations far and wide.
They will beat their swords into plowshares
and their spears into pruning hooks.
Nation will not take up sword against nation,
nor will they train for war anymore.
[4] Every man will sit under his own vine
and under his own fig tree,
and no one will make them afraid,
for the LORD Almighty has spoken.
[5] All the nations may walk
in the name of their gods;
we will walk in the name of the LORD
our God for ever and ever.

The LORD's Plan

[6] "In that day," declares the LORD,

"I will gather the lame;
I will assemble the exiles

4:1 *In the last days:* The prophet describes a future time when Judah's people will return home and rebuild Jerusalem and the temple (2 Chr 36:22, 23). The new temple was dedicated in 515 B.C. (Ezra 6:13-18).

4:1 *mountain of the LORD's temple:* The temple in Jerusalem was located on a hill known as Mount Zion. See also the mini-article called "Zion," p. 1294.

4:2 *Jacob:* Meaning Israel. See the note at 1:5.

4:2 *The law will go out from Zion:* Here "law" refers to the Law of Moses. See also the mini-articles called "Law," p. 1160, and "Wisdom," p. 2206.

4:5 *walk in the name of their gods:* See the note at 1:7.

4:6 *In that day:* See the note at 4:1 (last days).

4:6,7 *lame:* People who were born with birth defects or who had suffered physical injuries were not allowed to serve in the temple (Lev 21:18), and were often considered to be of little value in ancient Israelite society. But in the future, God will include these along with other outsiders ("exiles") as fully part of God's people. See also the mini-article called "Justice," p. 1721.

3:12 Jer 26:18. **4:1-3** Isa 2:1-4. **4:3** Isa 2:4; Joel 3:10. **4:4** Zech 3:10; Matt 11:28; Heb 4:1-10.

World Peace, by Gai Muo-seng, 1984. The prophet Micah speaks of a day when the LORD will settle all arguments between powerful nations. In that time weapons of war will be turned into peaceful tools and "nation will not take up sword against nation, nor will they train for war anymore" (see 4:1-5). The prophet Isaiah who lived at the same time as Micah shared this hope (see Isa 2:1-5).

Many nations will come and say, "Come, let us go up to the mountain of the LORD, to the house of the God of Jacob. He will teach us his ways, so that we may walk in his paths."
Mic 4:2

and those I have brought to grief.
7 I will make the lame a remnant,
those driven away a strong nation.
The LORD will rule over them in Mount Zion
from that day and forever.
8 As for you, O watchtower of the flock,
O stronghold[a] of the Daughter of Zion,
the former dominion will be restored to you;
kingship will come to the Daughter of Jerusalem."

[a]**8** Or *hill*

4:9,10 *a woman in labor . . . go to Babylon . . . redeem you:* The pain the people will have to endure is like the pain of a woman in childbirth. The pain won't last forever and will lead to new life.

4:11-13 *Zion . . . like sheaves to the threshing floor . . . horns of iron . . . hoofs of bronze:* The LORD will punish the nations who made fun of Judah's fall (4:2; 5:15; also Obad 10-12). The picture of Zion (Jerusalem) as a metal bull, stomping on its enemies, is probably meant to mock the foreign gods worshiped by Judah's neighbors. For example, idols honoring the Canaanite god Baal were made in the shape of a wooden or metal bull.

In ancient Israel, ripe grain stalks were cut and put on a hard surface called the threshing floor. Then oxen trampled on the grain or pulled a sledge across it (Amos 1:3). This separated the grain kernels from the stalks. Micah uses this image to describe God's judgment (see also Jer 51:33; Matt 3:12).

4:13 *their wealth to the Lord of all the earth:* When God's people defeated an enemy, it was understood that all wealth gained in battle belonged to God, who gave them the victory. This is why the wealth of defeated nations is to be given to him. See Lev 27:28,29; Deut 20:16-18; Isa 23:18. See also the mini-article called "Holy War (The LORD's Battles)," p. 306.

5:2 *Bethlehem Ephrathah:* See the note on p. 1747.

5:3,4 *shepherd his flock in the strength of the LORD:* The leader described will come from the hometown of Israel's greatest king, David (1 Sam 16:1). He will rule like the ideal shepherd-king, bringing justice and peace to his people (Ps 72:1-4, 12-14; see also Isa 9:6, 7; 11:1-5). New Testament writers understood this ruler to be God's Messiah, Jesus Christ (Matt 2:6-17; John 7:40-42). See also the note at 2:12, 13 and the mini-article called "Messiah (Chosen One)," p. 1124.

9 Why do you now cry aloud—
have you no king?
Has your counselor perished,
that pain seizes you like that of a woman in labor?
10 Writhe in agony, O Daughter of Zion,
like a woman in labor,
for now you must leave the city
to camp in the open field.
You will go to Babylon;
there you will be rescued.
There the LORD will redeem you
out of the hand of your enemies.

11 But now many nations
are gathered against you.
They say, "Let her be defiled,
let our eyes gloat over Zion!"
12 But they do not know
the thoughts of the LORD;
they do not understand his plan,
he who gathers them like sheaves to the threshing floor.

13 "Rise and thresh, O Daughter of Zion,
for I will give you horns of iron;
I will give you hoofs of bronze
and you will break to pieces many nations."

You will devote their ill-gotten gains to the LORD,
their wealth to the Lord of all the earth.

A Promised Ruler From Bethlehem

5 Marshal your troops, O city of troops,[a]
for a siege is laid against us.
They will strike Israel's ruler
on the cheek with a rod.

2 "But you, Bethlehem Ephrathah,
though you are small among the clans[b] of Judah,
out of you will come for me
one who will be ruler over Israel,
whose origins[c] are from of old,
from ancient times.[d]"

3 Therefore Israel will be abandoned
until the time when she who is in labor gives birth
and the rest of his brothers return
to join the Israelites.

---

[a]1 Or *Strengthen your walls, O walled city* [b]2 Or *rulers* [c]2 Hebrew *goings out*
[d]2 Or *from days of eternity*

4 He will stand and shepherd his flock
in the strength of the LORD,
in the majesty of the name of the LORD his God.
And they will live securely, for then his greatness
will reach to the ends of the earth.
5 And he will be their peace.

Deliverance and Destruction

When the Assyrian invades our land
and marches through our fortresses,
we will raise against him seven shepherds,
even eight leaders of men.
6 They will rule[a] the land of Assyria with the sword,
the land of Nimrod with drawn sword.[b]
He will deliver us from the Assyrian
when he invades our land
and marches into our borders.
7 The remnant of Jacob will be
in the midst of many peoples
like dew from the LORD,
like showers on the grass,
which do not wait for man
or linger for mankind.
8 The remnant of Jacob will be among the nations,
in the midst of many peoples,
like a lion among the beasts of the forest,
like a young lion among flocks of sheep,
which mauls and mangles as it goes,
and no one can rescue.
9 Your hand will be lifted up in triumph
over your enemies,
and all your foes will be destroyed.

10 "In that day," declares the LORD,

"I will destroy your horses from among you
and demolish your chariots.
11 I will destroy the cities of your land
and tear down all your strongholds.
12 I will destroy your witchcraft
and you will no longer cast spells.
13 I will destroy your carved images
and your sacred stones from among you;
you will no longer bow down
to the work of your hands.

[a]6 Or *crush* [b]6 Or *Nimrod in its gates*

The Ruler of Israel will stand and shepherd his flock in the strength of the LORD, in the majesty of the name of the LORD his God. And they will live securely, for then his greatness will reach to the ends of the earth.
Mic 5:4

5:6 *He will deliver us from the Assyrian:* The old leaders of Israel had been of no help to their people (see the notes at 3:1, 2 and 3:11, 12). Influenced by the new shepherd-ruler (5:4), the new leaders become strong enough to stop the attack of their powerful enemy, Assyria. In 701 B.C. the Assyrians surrounded Jerusalem, but the city escaped destruction when Hezekiah prayed for God's help (2 Kgs 18:13—19:37).

5:7 *remnant of Jacob . . . showers on the grass:* See the note at 1:5. When the northern kingdom of Israel was defeated, many of its people were scattered throughout the Assyrian empire. The same thing happened to many in Judah when the Babylonians captured Jerusalem over one hundred years later. Here, Micah pictures the descendants of the exiled survivors growing in numbers (covering the ground like showers on the grass) and then returning in the future to defeat their enemies. See also the note at 2:12, 13.

5:10-14 *I will destroy . . . your carved images . . . Asherah poles:* When God's people return to their land, God will do away with witchcraft, idol worship, and battle chariots, which are symbols of Israel's trust in things other than God. See the note at 1:7. "Asherah poles" carved from wood were used in the worship of Asherah, the Canaanite fertility goddess.

5:15 *nations:* The LORD will punish on any nation, including Israel (5:10-14), that refuses to obey him.

6:1 *plead your case:* See the note at 1:2 (witness against you).

6:2 *mountains . . . foundations of the earth:* In this court scene, God calls on mountains and earth to be witnesses in the trial against Israel (compare to Isa 1:2; Ezek 6:3).

6:4,5 *brought you up out of Egypt . . . Balak king of Moab:* God rescued Israel repeatedly, beginning in the time of the exodus from Egypt (Exod 3–15). Moses' brother Aaron was appointed the first high priest of Israel (Exod 28:1-4), and his sister Miriam was called a prophetess (Exod 15:20).

King Balak of Moab wanted to get rid of the people of Israel who were passing through his land, so he hired Balaam the prophet to place a curse on them (Num 22:2—24:25).

6:5 *Shittim to Gilgal:* The Israelites camped at Shittim on the east side of the Jordan River just before entering the land God had promised them (Num 25:1; Josh 2:1; 3:1). After crossing the river, they camped at Gilgal before attacking Jericho (Josh 3:1—5:12).

6:6,7 *burnt offerings . . . offer my firstborn:* The people of Israel assume that they can restore their broken relationship with God by making some kind of offering to please God (Lev 1:1-4; Num 28, 29). See the chart called "Sacrifices and Offerings," p. 219. The numbers of sheep and amount of oil go far beyond the amount required in the law and reflect what only a king might be able to afford (1 Kgs 3:4; 8:62-64). The ultimate suggestion, child sacrifice, was forbidden in the law (Lev 18:21; 20:2-5; Deut 18:10) and was condemned by the prophets (Isa 57:5; Jer 19:5; Ezek 16:20). The suggested sacrifices reveal a sense of panic or desperation.

6:4 Exod 4:10-16; 12:50, 51; 15:20.

14 I will uproot from among you your Asherah poles[a]
and demolish your cities.
15 I will take vengeance in anger and wrath
upon the nations that have not obeyed me."

The LORD Puts the People of Israel on Trial for Their Sins

The LORD God invites the people of Israel to explain their evil actions. They have forgotten how the LORD saved them in the past, and now they are sinning against God, forgetting what is right and what it is that God really wants (6:8). Jerusalem and its people will be punished (6:16), but Micah holds out hope that God will save them and hear the prayers of his people (7:7).

The LORD's Case Against Israel

6 Listen to what the LORD says:

"Stand up, plead your case before the mountains;
let the hills hear what you have to say.
2 Hear, O mountains, the LORD's accusation;
listen, you everlasting foundations of the earth.
For the LORD has a case against his people;
he is lodging a charge against Israel.

3 "My people, what have I done to you?
How have I burdened you? Answer me.
4 I brought you up out of Egypt
and redeemed you from the land of slavery.
I sent Moses to lead you,
also Aaron and Miriam.
5 My people, remember
what Balak king of Moab counseled
and what Balaam son of Beor answered.
Remember ⌞your journey⌟ from Shittim to Gilgal,
that you may know the righteous acts of the LORD."

6 With what shall I come before the LORD
and bow down before the exalted God?
Shall I come before him with burnt offerings,
with calves a year old?
7 Will the LORD be pleased with thousands of rams,
with ten thousand rivers of oil?
Shall I offer my firstborn for my transgression,
the fruit of my body for the sin of my soul?
8 He has showed you, O man, what is good.
And what does the LORD require of you?
To act justly and to love mercy
and to walk humbly with your God.

a14 That is, symbols of the goddess Asherah

Israel's Guilt and Punishment

9 Listen! The LORD is calling to the city—
and to fear your name is wisdom—
"Heed the rod and the One who appointed it.[a]
10 Am I still to forget, O wicked house,
your ill-gotten treasures
and the short ephah,[b] which is accursed?
11 Shall I acquit a man with dishonest scales,
with a bag of false weights?
12 Her rich men are violent;
her people are liars
and their tongues speak deceitfully.
13 Therefore, I have begun to destroy you,
to ruin you because of your sins.
14 You will eat but not be satisfied;
your stomach will still be empty.[c]
You will store up but save nothing,
because what you save I will give to the sword.
15 You will plant but not harvest;
you will press olives but not use the oil on yourselves,
you will crush grapes but not drink the wine.
16 You have observed the statutes of Omri
and all the practices of Ahab's house,
and you have followed their traditions.
Therefore I will give you over to ruin
and your people to derision;
you will bear the scorn of the nations.[d]"

Israel's Misery

7 What misery is mine!
I am like one who gathers summer fruit
at the gleaning of the vineyard;
there is no cluster of grapes to eat,
none of the early figs that I crave.
2 The godly have been swept from the land;
not one upright man remains.
All men lie in wait to shed blood;
each hunts his brother with a net.
3 Both hands are skilled in doing evil;
the ruler demands gifts,
the judge accepts bribes,
the powerful dictate what they desire—
they all conspire together.

[a]**9** The meaning of the Hebrew for this line is uncertain. [b]**10** An ephah was a dry measure. [c]**14** The meaning of the Hebrew for this word is uncertain. [d]**16** Septuagint; Hebrew *scorn due my people*

6:8 *act justly . . . love mercy . . . walk humbly:* Micah reminds the people that God doesn't want their sacrifices if people refuse to do what is most important—treat each other with justice and love. (See 1 Sam 15:22; Isa 1:10-17; Hos 6:6; Amos 5:21-24.) See also Mark 12:28-31; Rom 12:1; and the mini-article called "Justice," p. 1721.

6:10-12 *dishonest scales . . . violent:* A standard price was to be paid for grain measured on a balance scale. When dishonest merchants sold grain, they added dust to the grain in a smaller than legal basket and used a heavier than legal weight to measure it, so people got less for their money. When the merchants bought grain they used lighter weights to balance it, so they got more grain for their money. These dishonest practices were forbidden by the Law of Moses (Exod 20:15; Lev 19:35, 36; Deut 25:13-16; Prov 20:10). See the illustration on p. 1732.

6:16 *statutes of Omri . . . practices of Ahab's house:* Omri encouraged the people of Israel to worship idols (1 Kgs 16:25-28). His son Ahab also encouraged the worship of idols (1 Kgs 16:29-33) and plotted with his wife Jezebel to kill Naboth so they could steal his vineyard (1 Kgs 21:1-16). The prophet Elijah spoke out against the sinful things that Ahab did (1 Kgs 16:21-34; 18:1-26; 21:17-24).

7:1-7 *What misery is mine . . . I watch in hope:* A sad song (lament) is spoken by the prophet, who feels alone. No one is loyal to God in his land, and dishonest people are everywhere (see the notes at 3:1,2; 3:5-7; 6:10-12). No one can be trusted, not even friends or family members (7:5, 6). Justice, mercy, and humble obedience (6:8) are absent both in public and in private relationships. In spite of this, the prophet continues to trust the LORD to save him and his people (7:7). See also Ps 38; 42.

7:3 Amos 2:6; 5:10,12.

7:8-10 *my enemy:* The exact identity of the "enemy" is uncertain. It may be Assyria, who threatened Jerusalem in 701 B.C. (see the note at 5:6). Its leaders claimed that Israel's God was helpless (2 Kgs 18:27-36). Or it may refer to Edom, who rejoiced when the Babylonians defeated Jerusalem in 586 B.C. (Isa 34:8-14; Obad 10-15).

7:8 *darkness . . . light:* Darkness often is used in the Bible to describe evil, ignorance, and death (Job 18:18; Prov 4:19; 13:9; 20:20). Judah recognizes that it has sinned by turning away from God and God's Law. They have been living in darkness. But the LORD God can take away the darkness by forgiving their sins and by helping them to live according to the LORD's teachings, which are like a "light" to guide them as they go through life (Ps 119:105). See also Ps 27:1; Isa 9:2; John 1:4-9; 3:19-21; 1 John 1:5-7; 2:9-11; Rev 22:5. See also the mini-article called "Sin," p. 2181.

7:11 *building your walls:* The rebuilt towns would include those mentioned in 1:8-16. Jerusalem was rebuilt after the people of Judah were allowed to return from their exile in Babylon. See also Neh 1:3; 3:1; Ps 69:35; 102:16; Isa 60:10; Jer 31:38-40. See also the mini-article called "Exile," p. 1541.

7:12 *Assyria . . . Egypt . . . Euphrates:* The people had gone into exile in Assyria and beyond the Euphrates (in Babylon). People ran away to Egypt when the Babylonians invaded Judah (Jer 43:1-8). Micah's vision depicts God's scattered people returning to Judah's towns (as in 4:7). See also 2 Kgs 17:5-23; 2 Kgs 25:1-12; and the Introduction to MICAH.

7:6 Matt 10:35, 36; Luke 12:53.

4 The best of them is like a brier,
the most upright worse than a thorn hedge.
The day of your watchmen has come,
the day God visits you.
Now is the time of their confusion.
5 Do not trust a neighbor;
put no confidence in a friend.
Even with her who lies in your embrace
be careful of your words.
6 For a son dishonors his father,
a daughter rises up against her mother,
a daughter-in-law against her mother-in-law—
a man's enemies are the members of his own household.

7 But as for me, I watch in hope for the LORD,
I wait for God my Savior;
my God will hear me.

The LORD Forgives Those Who Confess Their Sins

The two poems in the final part of MICAH combine to show hope in the future. First, the people confess their sins and declare their trust in the LORD, looking forward to the day when Judah will be restored and strong (7:8-13). Secondly, the people of Judah acknowledge the LORD as their shepherd and praise God for forgiving them and for keeping the promises made to their ancestors (7:14-20).

Israel Will Rise

8 Do not gloat over me, my enemy!
Though I have fallen, I will rise.
Though I sit in darkness,
the LORD will be my light.
9 Because I have sinned against him,
I will bear the LORD's wrath,
until he pleads my case
and establishes my right.
He will bring me out into the light;
I will see his righteousness.
10 Then my enemy will see it
and will be covered with shame,
she who said to me,
"Where is the LORD your God?"
My eyes will see her downfall;
even now she will be trampled underfoot
like mire in the streets.

11 The day for building your walls will come,
the day for extending your boundaries.
12 In that day people will come to you
from Assyria and the cities of Egypt,
even from Egypt to the Euphrates
and from sea to sea
and from mountain to mountain.
13 The earth will become desolate because of its inhabitants,
as the result of their deeds.

Prayer and Praise

14 Shepherd your people with your staff,
the flock of your inheritance,
which lives by itself in a forest,
in fertile pasturelands.[a]
Let them feed in Bashan and Gilead
as in days long ago.

15 "As in the days when you came out of Egypt,
I will show them my wonders."

16 Nations will see and be ashamed,
deprived of all their power.
They will lay their hands on their mouths
and their ears will become deaf.
17 They will lick dust like a snake,
like creatures that crawl on the ground.
They will come trembling out of their dens;
they will turn in fear to the LORD our God
and will be afraid of you.

---

[a]**14** Or *in the middle of Carmel*

7:14 *Shepherd your people:* See the note at 2:12,13.

7:14 *Bashan and Gilead:* These two regions had belonged to Israel "long ago" in the days of King David. See the map on p. 2467.

7:15,16 *show them my wonders ... Nations will see and be ashamed:* The people of Israel would return to Judah from exile because the LORD would help them. This return would be like a "second exodus," similar to the first exodus when the LORD miraculously helped Israel escape from slavery in Egypt (Exod 12–14; Mic 6:4). As at the time of the first exodus, the power of God will bring shame and shock to Israel's enemies (Exod 15:11-16; Isa 25:1-3; Jer 32:20, 21).

QUESTIONS ABOUT MICAH

1. What kind of sins committed in Israel and Judah led to God's judgment? (1:3-7, 13; 2:8-11; 3:1-11) Where do you see evidence of such sins in society today?
2. According to Micah, who was going to suffer God's punishment? (1–3; 5:10—6:16) Do God's judgments seem fair or unfair? Why?
3. In what ways would God show mercy to and restore the people of Israel? (4:1—5:5; 7:11-20)
4. Micah speaks a great deal about good and bad rulers. How does Micah think a ruler influences people? Micah uses the image of "shepherd" to describe a leader. How can leaders in government and the church be more like shepherds?
5. Read Micah 6:6-8 and Amos 5:21-24. In your own words, describe what God "wants" more than anything else. How easy or difficult is it to do this? Why?
6. Name one new thing you learned from reading and studying MICAH.

7:18,19 *Who is a God like you . . . hurl all our iniquities into the depths of the sea:* These words of praise are similar in meaning to the Hebrew name "Micah," which means "who is like the LORD." The people who have survived the time of exile (2:12) praise God for forgiving the sins of the nation. They have confessed their guilt (7:9), and now God forgives them. Their sins are thrown into the sea, far out of sight and out of reach (Ps 103:12).

7:20 *as you pledged on oath to our fathers:* Starting with forgiveness, God will completely restore the people of Israel by helping them return to the land God promised to give their ancestors so they can rebuild it (Gen 22:17; 26:3,4; 50:24; Exod 13:5,11; Deut 7:1-16; Jer 32:22).

18 Who is a God like you,
who pardons sin and forgives the transgression
of the remnant of his inheritance?
You do not stay angry forever
but delight to show mercy.
19 You will again have compassion on us;
you will tread our sins underfoot
and hurl all our iniquities into the depths of the sea.
20 You will be true to Jacob,
and show mercy to Abraham,
as you pledged on oath to our fathers
in days long ago.

NAHUM

You've probably heard it said: "I hope that bully gets what's coming to them!" Read NAHUM *to find out what harsh words God's prophet had for a powerful nation that "bullied" God's people and many other nations as well.*

WHAT MAKES NAHUM SPECIAL?

Little is known about the prophet Nahum. Even the location of his hometown of Elkosh (1:1) is not known for certain, though it was somewhere in the nation of Judah. In Hebrew, Nahum means "comfort," but the prophet spoke harsh words of judgment against the nation of Assyria that were anything but comforting (although they certainly would have brought comfort to the Israelites). Nahum's severe message of judgment against Assyria's capital, Nineveh, is often compared and contrasted with the message of JONAH, which describes the people of Nineveh turning away from their wicked ways and being forgiven by God.

WHY WAS NAHUM WRITTEN?

NAHUM announces the coming downfall of the Assyrian empire and its capital city, Nineveh. The powerful Assyrians caused great suffering for a number of other nations, including the people of Israel. In fact, Assyria invaded and defeated the northern kingdom of Israel in 722 B.C., taking many of its people into exile. During the following one hundred years, Assyria continued to be a threat to the southern kingdom of Judah as well. But Nahum reassures the people of Judah that God will soon set them free from the shackles of the Assyrians (1:13), so they can once again enjoy peace and celebrate their festivals (1:15). The LORD is "a refuge in times of trouble" (1:7). NAHUM's message of doom for Assyria was comforting for those nations who had been threatened and injured by Assyria. And it repeated a theme that was common in the message of Israel's prophets: The LORD is concerned with justice and will punish those nations or individuals who use their power to mistreat others.

WHAT'S THE STORY BEHIND THE SCENE?

In 853 B.C. at Qarqar, Assyria defeated a coalition of nations that included the northern kingdom of Israel. That decisive victory helped make Assyria the most powerful force in the ancient Near East (see the map on p. 2468). Assyria conquered many nations and made others pay heavy taxes, including Israel and Judah (2 Kgs 15:19,20,29; 16:5-18; 17:1-6; 18:7-21).

It is uncertain when the prophet Nahum lived and preached. But it was sometime after 663 B.C., when Assyria defeated the Egyptian city of Thebes (3:8-10), and before 612 B.C., when Assyria's capital city Nineveh was destroyed by a group of

Nineveh: The ancient city of Nineveh was located on the Tigris River in northern Mesopotamia (see the map on p. 2468). People probably lived on the site of Nineveh even before 3000 B.C. It was rebuilt and resettled many times in the centuries before Sennacherib made Nineveh the capital of the growing Assyrian empire in 705 B.C. Beginning in the time when Akkadian kings ruled Assyria (about 1750 B.C.), the city of Nineveh was dedicated to the goddess known as "Ishtar." Considered a child of the moon god Sin and goddess of fertility, Ishtar probably was similar to the Canaanite goddess Astarte, referred to as the "Queen of Heaven" (Jer 7:18; 44:17-19).

Under kings Esarhaddon (681-669 B.C.) and Ashurbanipal (669-627 B.C.), Assyria continued to grow in strength and pushed its influence all the way to Egypt. Assyria was a hated enemy of Israel. Nineveh, as the capital city of Assyria, was the most powerful city in the world and a center for trade and culture. Ashurbanipal established a great library there that was discovered by archaeologists 2500 years after he lived.

In 612 B.C. the power of the Assyrian empire decreased greatly when the city of Nineveh was conquered by the combined armies of the Babylonians and Medes. For more, see the mini-article called "Assyria," p. 711.

Nahum the Elkoshite: The location of Elkosh is not known. For Nahum, see the Introduction.

nations that included the Babylonians and Medes. Most likely, Nahum's message comes from the time of Judah's king Josiah (640-609 B.C.), which means he lived and preached at the same time as the prophets Zephaniah and the young Jeremiah.

How is Nahum constructed?

NAHUM can be divided into two main sections: the first is a psalm describing the power of the LORD God and how he will deliver Judah from the shackles of Assyrian influence; the second part of the book includes prophecies announcing the downfall of Nineveh, the capital of Assyria.

Hope for Judah: The LORD will break the power of Assyria (1:1-15)

Nahum's strong words of judgment for Nineveh (2:1—3:19)

Hope for Judah: The LORD Will Break the Power of Assyria

Nahum announces that the powerful LORD God will destroy his enemies (1:8), including Assyria (1:11-14). Then the LORD's people in Judah will be free from Assyria's evil plans and cruel shackles (1:11-13), so they can live in peace and celebrate their religious festivals once again (1:15).

1 An oracle concerning Nineveh. The book of the vision of Nahum the Elkoshite.

The LORD's Anger Against Nineveh

2 The LORD is a jealous and avenging God;
the LORD takes vengeance and is filled with wrath.
The LORD takes vengeance on his foes
and maintains his wrath against his enemies.
3 The LORD is slow to anger and great in power;
the LORD will not leave the guilty unpunished.
His way is in the whirlwind and the storm,
and clouds are the dust of his feet.
4 He rebukes the sea and dries it up;
he makes all the rivers run dry.
Bashan and Carmel wither
and the blossoms of Lebanon fade.
5 The mountains quake before him
and the hills melt away.
The earth trembles at his presence,
the world and all who live in it.
6 Who can withstand his indignation?

The LORD is slow to anger and great in power.
Nah 1:3

1:2 *LORD . . . God:* LORD is used for the Hebrew term *Yahweh.* For a full explanation, see the mini-article called "LORD (YHWH)," p. 140. The word "God" translated the Hebrew word for the God of Israel who is holy, but who also is Israel's personal God. The LORD God chose the Israelites to be his special people (Isa 41:8,9) and lives among them (Exod 25:18-22; 1 Kgs 8:6-13; Isa 6:1-8).

1:3-6 *slow to anger and great in power . . . rocks are shattered:* Nahum uses a number of images found elsewhere in the Old Testament to describe the LORD's patience, power, and anger. Storms and whirlwinds are powerful evidence of the LORD's presence (Exod 14:21; Job 38:1; Ps 50:3; 104:1-4). The LORD can command waters to dry up (Exod 14:22; Josh 3:14-17), fertile lands to wither (Hag 1:10, 11), and mountains and hills to shake (Job 9:5, 6; Ezek 38:20). The LORD God is angered by evil and will act to destroy his enemies. But the LORD is also patient (Neh 9:17) and willing to protect those who seek the LORD's protection (1:7). For the LORD's anger compared to fire, see Isa 5:24; 66:15,16,24; and the mini-article called "Fire," p. 2383. No doubt some people in Judah wondered why it was taking the LORD so long to free them from the power of Assyria, but Nahum assured the people that the LORD would act when the time was right, and the "guilty" would be punished (1:3).

1:4 *Bashan and Carmel . . . Lebanon fade:* These regions in the north and east were noted for their trees, flowers, and fertile pastures. See also Isa 33:9 and the map on p. 2467.

Assyrian War Chariot, bas-relief from the palace of Ashurbanipal, sixth century B.C. The Assyrians were a major power in the ancient Near East. Their armies were known for their cruelty and their chariots were famous for their speed. The prophet Nahum describes how Assyria and its famous capital, Nineveh, will one day be defeated: "Although they have allies and are numerous, they will be cut off and pass away" (1:12).

Who can endure his fierce anger?
His wrath is poured out like fire;
the rocks are shattered before him.

7 The LORD is good,
a refuge in times of trouble.
He cares for those who trust in him,
8 but with an overwhelming flood
he will make an end of ⌞Nineveh⌟;
he will pursue his foes into darkness.

9 Whatever they plot against the LORD
he[a] will bring to an end;
trouble will not come a second time.
10 They will be entangled among thorns
and drunk from their wine;
they will be consumed like dry stubble.[b]
11 From you, ⌞O Nineveh,⌟ has one come forth
who plots evil against the LORD
and counsels wickedness.

12 This is what the LORD says:

"Although they have allies and are numerous,
they will be cut off and pass away.

[a]**9** Or *What do you foes plot against the LORD? / He* [b]**10** The meaning of the Hebrew for this verse is uncertain.

1:8-10 *with an overwhelming flood . . . drunk from their wine:* God's judgment against Assyria will be as unstoppable as flood waters, just as Assyrian soldiers once covered Judah like a flood (Isa 8:7, 8). Those who drink from the LORD's cup of wrath become helpless to stop God's judgment and punishment (Ps 60:3; Isa 51:22; Jer 25:15-29; Obad 16; Rev 14:10; 16:19).

1:11 *Nineveh:* See the Introduction to NAHUM and the note on p. 1763 (Nineveh).

1:11 *has one come forth who plots evil:* Exactly who has "come forth" is uncertain. Most likely this refers to a ruler. It could refer to Sennacherib, who surrounded Jerusalem in 701 B.C. (2 Kgs 18:13—19:37), but any of the kings that followed Sennacherib would also have been regarded as a threat to God's people in Judah.

1:12,13 *Judah . . . tear your shackles away:* Judah was the name for the southern kingdom of Israel (see the map on p. 2467). As their empire expanded, Assyria became increasingly dependent on captive labor and taxes paid by weaker nations. When the Assyrians destroyed Samaria in 722 B.C., they forced many people from Israel's northern kingdom to leave their homeland and live as servants in other parts of the Assyrian empire (2 Kgs 17:6). The "shackles" mentioned in verse 13 may refer to this captivity, or they may represent the heavy taxes Judah was forced to pay Assyria (2 Kgs 15:19, 20, 29; 16:5-11).

1:14 *no descendants to bear your name:* In the ancient world, it was considered a great tragedy when one did not have children to carry on a family name. Posterity was seen as a form of life after death, because a man's descendants were a constant reminder to the community that he had existed. When Nahum said that Assyria's name would be forgotten, it meant that Assyria had no future. Not only would it be destroyed, it would be forgotten by future generations. See also 1 Sam 24:21; Job 18:14-21.

1:15 *peace . . . festivals:* Nahum is the messenger of peace. When Assyria threatened Judah, the yearly festivals may not have been celebrated because of the threat of invasion. This verse may refer to renewing the Passover celebration in the "eighteenth year of King Josiah" (2 Kgs 23:21-23), which would be 622 B.C., ten years before the downfall of Nineveh in 612 B.C.

2:1 *Nineveh . . . fortress:* Nineveh was like a fortress. The city was protected by outer walls and a moat that guarded it on the east. High city walls, canals, and the Tigris River guarded Nineveh on the west. See also the note at 2:6-8.

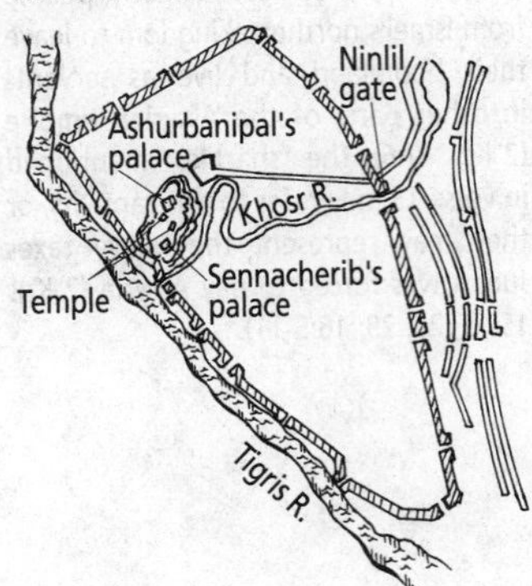

Although I have afflicted you, ⌞O Judah,⌟
I will afflict you no more.
13 Now I will break their yoke from your neck
and tear your shackles away."

14 The LORD has given a command concerning you, ⌞Nineveh⌟:
"You will have no descendants to bear your name.
I will destroy the carved images and cast idols
that are in the temple of your gods.
I will prepare your grave,
for you are vile."

15 Look, there on the mountains,
the feet of one who brings good news,
who proclaims peace!
Celebrate your festivals, O Judah,
and fulfill your vows.
No more will the wicked invade you;
they will be completely destroyed.

Nahum's Strong Words of Judgment for Nineveh

Nineveh is doomed! Nahum proclaims that Assyria's capital city Nineveh will be destroyed because the LORD Almighty is against it. Nothing can stop Assyria's enemies from capturing Nineveh: not the walls of the city, not the surrounding river system, not Assyria's armies. When Nineveh's destruction is complete, those who have been treated cruelly by Assyria will clap for joy.

Nineveh to Fall

2 An attacker advances against you, ⌞Nineveh⌟.
Guard the fortress,
watch the road,
brace yourselves,
marshal all your strength!

2 The LORD will restore the splendor of Jacob
like the splendor of Israel,
though destroyers have laid them waste
and have ruined their vines.

3 The shields of his soldiers are red;
the warriors are clad in scarlet.
The metal on the chariots flashes
on the day they are made ready;
the spears of pine are brandished.[a]
4 The chariots storm through the streets,

[a]3 Hebrew; Septuagint and Syriac / *the horsemen rush to and fro*

rushing back and forth through the squares.
They look like flaming torches;
they dart about like lightning.

5 He summons his picked troops,
yet they stumble on their way.
They dash to the city wall;
the protective shield is put in place.
6 The river gates are thrown open
and the palace collapses.
7 It is decreed[a] that ⌞the city⌟
be exiled and carried away.
Its slave girls moan like doves
and beat upon their breasts.
8 Nineveh is like a pool,
and its water is draining away.
"Stop! Stop!" they cry,
but no one turns back.
9 Plunder the silver!
Plunder the gold!
The supply is endless,
the wealth from all its treasures!
10 She is pillaged, plundered, stripped!
Hearts melt, knees give way,
bodies tremble, every face grows pale.

11 Where now is the lions' den,
the place where they fed their young,
where the lion and lioness went,
and the cubs, with nothing to fear?
12 The lion killed enough for his cubs
and strangled the prey for his mate,
filling his lairs with the kill
and his dens with the prey.

13 "I am against you,"
declares the LORD Almighty.
"I will burn up your chariots in smoke,
and the sword will devour your young lions.
I will leave you no prey on the earth.
The voices of your messengers
will no longer be heard."

Woe to Nineveh

3 Woe to the city of blood,
full of lies,
full of plunder,
never without victims!

[a]7 The meaning of the Hebrew for this word is uncertain.

2:5 *dash to the city wall . . . protective shield is put in place:* When enemies tried to climb over the walls around the city, the people often threw large rocks down on them. This may be the "protective shield" to which Nahum refers. Or this may be a call to the attackers to dash to the wall and hold up their shields against rocks thrown down from above.

2:6-8 *river gates . . . Nineveh is like a pool:* Canals from the Tigris River brought water into Nineveh (see the note at 2:1). Enemy troops rushing into the city would cause panic, and people would start to "spill" out of the city like water draining out of a flooded pool. Compare to 1:8.

2:9 *treasures:* Treasures stolen or collected as taxes from other nations by Assyria would have been taken to the royal palace in Nineveh (2 Kgs 15:19, 20; 16:5-11). Attacking soldiers would rob Nineveh of these treasures, and some countries would get back what was stolen from them.

2:11-13 *Where now is the lions' den:* The Assyrian forces are compared to a powerful lion that attacks and rips up its prey.

2:13 *LORD Almighty:* In Hebrew this name for God is *Yahweh Sabaoth.*

2:13 *your messengers will no longer be heard:* Many years earlier, King Sennacherib of Assyria sent a messenger to threaten the people of Jerusalem (2 Chr 32:1-19; Isa 36:1-22).

3:4 *prostitution . . . witchcraft:* Nineveh is pictured as a prostitute, attracting nations to itself so it can steal their treasures. The reference to magic and witchcraft may be a reference to the influence of Assyrian religion and gods upon those nations they defeated. See also Ezekiel's description of Assyria's influence on Israel (Ezek 23:1-13) and the mini-article called "Prostitution in the Bible," p. 1688.

3:5 *lift your skirts . . . nakedness:* To the people of Israel, having one's nakedness exposed was considered shameful (Gen 3:10,21; Isa 47:3). The LORD had also given Moses Laws forbidding sexual relationships outside of marriage (Lev 18:6-23). Pictured here as a prostitute or unfaithful wife, Nineveh will be attacked and shamed by the "lovers" (nations) she had attracted (3:4). Compare to Ezek 16:35-38.

3:8 *Thebes:* Thebes was the prosperous capital of Egypt for over one thousand years until 663 B.C. when the Assyrian king Ashurbanipal captured it. The city was built on the Nile River with magnificent temples and palaces on both sides of the river.

3:9 *Cush and Egypt . . . Put and Libya: Cush* was the region south of Egypt that included parts of the present countries of Ethiopia and Sudan. Put was in Africa, possibly part of the present country of Libya. A Cushite king ruled over Thebes between 712 and 663 B.C.

3:12-14 *fig trees . . . ripe fruit . . . repair the brickwork:* Figs were a common food in the ancient Near East. When ripe, figs can be easily shaken from the tree. Nineveh's fortresses will fall as easily as ripe figs. The people will try to strengthen the walls of the city with newly-made bricks (see the note and illustration on brickmaking on p. 143).

2 The crack of whips,
the clatter of wheels,
galloping horses
and jolting chariots!
3 Charging cavalry,
flashing swords
and glittering spears!
Many casualties,
piles of dead,
bodies without number,
people stumbling over the corpses—
4 all because of the wanton lust of a harlot,
alluring, the mistress of sorceries,
who enslaved nations by her prostitution
and peoples by her witchcraft.

5 "I am against you," declares the LORD Almighty.
"I will lift your skirts over your face.
I will show the nations your nakedness
and the kingdoms your shame.
6 I will pelt you with filth,
I will treat you with contempt
and make you a spectacle.
7 All who see you will flee from you and say,
'Nineveh is in ruins—who will mourn for her?'
Where can I find anyone to comfort you?"

8 Are you better than Thebes,[a]
situated on the Nile,
with water around her?
The river was her defense,
the waters her wall.
9 Cush[b] and Egypt were her boundless strength;
Put and Libya were among her allies.
10 Yet she was taken captive
and went into exile.
Her infants were dashed to pieces
at the head of every street.
Lots were cast for her nobles,
and all her great men were put in chains.
11 You too will become drunk;
you will go into hiding
and seek refuge from the enemy.

12 All your fortresses are like fig trees
with their first ripe fruit;
when they are shaken,
the figs fall into the mouth of the eater.

[a]8 Hebrew *No Amon* [b]9 That is, the upper Nile region

13 Look at your troops—
they are all women!
The gates of your land
are wide open to your enemies;
fire has consumed their bars.

14 Draw water for the siege,
strengthen your defenses!
Work the clay,
tread the mortar,
repair the brickwork!
15 There the fire will devour you;
the sword will cut you down
and, like grasshoppers, consume you.
Multiply like grasshoppers,
multiply like locusts!
16 You have increased the number of your merchants
till they are more than the stars of the sky,
but like locusts they strip the land
and then fly away.
17 Your guards are like locusts,
your officials like swarms of locusts
that settle in the walls on a cold day—
but when the sun appears they fly away,
and no one knows where.
18 O king of Assyria, your shepherds[a] slumber;
your nobles lie down to rest.
Your people are scattered on the mountains
with no one to gather them.
19 Nothing can heal your wound;
your injury is fatal.
Everyone who hears the news about you
claps his hands at your fall,
for who has not felt
your endless cruelty?

---

[a]**18** Or *rulers*

3:12-17 *fortresses . . . guards . . . officials:* Nahum lists many things that made Assyria a great power: its fortresses, its army, its city gates, its water supply and defenses, its ability to build, its many merchants and government leaders. But none of these, Nahum believes, will be of any value when the enemy comes.

3:15-17 *locusts:* Locusts are flying insects that are known for their ability to move in and devour crops quickly. For more, see the mini-article called "Locusts," p. 1708.

3:18 *your shepherds slumber:* This probably refers to the death of the Assyrian leaders.

3:18 *Your people are scattered on the mountains:* This pictures a scattered flock of sheep without a shepherd. In the Bible, kings and rulers are often compared to shepherds because they are responsible for leading and protecting the people of their nations. See also Num 27:17; Ps 78:70-72; Ezek 34; John 10:1-18. See also the mini-article called "Shepherds," p. 1972.

QUESTIONS ABOUT NAHUM

1. Most of NAHUM speaks about God's judgment. In which verses does Nahum speak about God's kindness and mercy? What is the message of these verses, and who are they directed toward?
2. In the years before and during the time of Nahum, why was Assyria hated and feared by other nations in the ancient Near East? According to the prophet, why will Assyria and its capital city Nineveh fall? (1:11, 14; 2:12, 13; 3:1-4, 10) Describe the city's destruction.
3. What can people expect from God? (1:3, 7) Do you find these expectations to be challenging, comforting, frightening, or something else? Why?

HABAKKUK

How do you keep trusting in God when it seems that God's ways make no sense? That's what the prophet Habakkuk wondered. Read this book to find out how God answered Habakkuk's questions.

Habakkuk the prophet: Nothing is known about Habakkuk, except that he was a prophet. He probably lived in the southern kingdom (Judah) and may have served in the temple, perhaps as a priest, but this is uncertain. An apocryphal book called *Bel and the Dragon*, (see the article called "What Books Belong in the Bible," p. 13), claims to be a "prophecy of Habakkuk ... of the tribe of Levi." The priests of Israel were from the Levi tribe. Another Jewish tradition says Habakkuk lived during the reign of King Manasseh of Judah (687-642 B.C.), but it is most likely that Habakkuk worked as a prophet in Judah late in the reign of King Josiah (640-609 B.C.) or during the reign of Jehoiakim, who ruled from 609 to 598 B.C. See the article called "Prophets and Prophecy," p. 935.

The writings of the prophets are often introduced as "oracles," "visions," or "the word of the LORD" (see also Isa 1:1; 13:1; Joel 1:1).

WHAT MAKES HABAKKUK SPECIAL?

This short book records a prayer-filled conversation between the prophet Habakkuk and the LORD God. Habakkuk was not afraid to ask God serious questions about events he did not understand. He was especially troubled that God would use the cruel Babylonians to punish the people of Judah. Comments on HABAKKUK were discovered among the Jewish Dead Sea Scrolls, written during the century before Christ. New Testament writers, such as the apostle Paul (Rom 1:17; Gal 3:11) and the writer of HEBREWS (10:38), quoted Habakkuk 2:4.

WHY WAS HABAKKUK WRITTEN?

Habakkuk complained that the LORD had not acted quickly enough to stop cruelty and injustice in Judah. But Habakkuk became even more upset when the LORD told him that Judah's punishment would be carried out by the army of Babylon. To Habakkuk, this solution was worse than the crime because the behavior of the Babylonians was worse than the behavior of the leaders and people of Judah!

HABAKKUK is a good example of how the prayers of a faithful person can include both complaint and praise, questioning and trust. The Babylonians may punish Judah, but Babylon will eventually fall because its leaders worship their own strength (1:11). The LORD does not accept the proud, but rather accepts those who live by faith (2:4). Faith will be tested by tough times, but HABAKKUK shows the importance of continuing to praise God, the "Savior," who is the one true source of strength (3:17-19).

WHAT'S THE STORY BEHIND THE SCENE?

Little is known about Habakkuk except what we learn from his book. He calls himself a prophet, a person who speaks for God. Some ancient traditions suggest that Habakkuk was also a priest who served in the Jerusalem temple. Certain terms or directions ("For the director of music," 3:19) suggest to many scholars that the prayer in chapter 3 was a formal prayer used in Israel's worship.

Habakkuk writes of a time of violence, terrible injustice, and lawlessness among God's people (1:2-4). This situation was often repeated in Israel's history, but the reference to "raising up the Babylonians" (1:6) seems to indicate that Habakkuk wrote this book shortly before or after 600 B.C. It was at this time that the Babylonians became the strongest power in the ancient Near East. They defeated the Assyrian city of Nineveh in 612 B.C. before defeating the Egyptians at the battle of Carchemish in 605 B.C. Judah's King Jehoiakim forced his own people to pay heavy taxes, and much of this money went to Babylon's king so he would not attack Judah. Eventually, Jehoiakim rebelled against Babylon in 602 B.C., and in 598 B.C. Babylon invaded Judah and surrounded Jerusalem. Jehoiakim died and the new king, Jehoiachin, was taken away as a prisoner to Babylon (2 Kgs 24:1-12). Eleven years later, the Babylonians captured and destroyed the city of Jerusalem and its temple following another revolt. Habakkuk's book may have been used for worship in the temple before it was destroyed in 586 B.C. In Jewish tradition, chapter 3 of HABAKKUK is one of the readings for the second day of the Shavuoth (Feast of Pentecost), which has become a celebration of God's giving of the law at Mount Sinai.

HOW IS HABAKKUK CONSTRUCTED?

HABAKKUK has two major sections. The first section (1:1—2:20) contains two conversations between Habakkuk and God. In the second section (3:1-19), Habakkuk's formal prayer or hymn praises God for helping the people of Israel in the past. And the prophet declares his trust in God in spite of the difficult times Habakkuk and God's people are facing.

Habakkuk's conversations with God (1:1—2:20)

Habakkuk's prayer of praise and trust (3:1-19)

Why do you make me look at injustice? Why do you tolerate wrong?
Hab 1:3

1:1 *Habakkuk the prophet:* See the note on p. 1770.

1:2 *How long:* Habakkuk's prayer begins with the kind of question commonly found in other prayers asking for God's help (Ps 6:3-6; 13:1, 2; 89:46; 90:13; 94:3).

1:2-4 *Violence ... injustice:* Habakkuk is likely complaining about violence and lawlessness in his own nation of Judah. According to the Law of Moses, the people of Israel were to treat each other with honesty and justice. But many of the LORD's prophets accused the people and their leaders of being unjust in their treatment of others (Isa 1:4, 15-17; 5:7-25; Hos 4:1-3; Amos 5:10-13). For many years God's Law had been ignored in the nation of Judah. The law was rediscovered in the days of King Josiah (2 Kgs 22, 23). For a time, the kind of lawlessness described by Habakkuk diminished. But the law was soon forgotten by the leading people in Judah during the reign of Josiah's son, Jehoiakim (609-598 B.C.). As a result, injustice, violence, crime, and cruelty followed (Jer 6:6-15; 25:1-9). See also the mini-article called "Justice," p. 1721.

Habakkuk's Conversations with God

Habakkuk complains to the LORD about the violence and injustice within his own nation of Judah. He does not understand why the LORD is so slow to deal with this evil. God surprises Habakkuk by saying that the armies of Babylon will bring an end to the evil in Judah. Then Habakkuk complains that Judah's sin are less serious than the sins of the Babylonians. Habakkuk is reminded that one day in the future God will punish the proud, including Babylon, and accept all people who live by faith (2:4).

1 The oracle that Habakkuk the prophet received.

Habakkuk's Complaint

2 How long, O LORD, must I call for help,
but you do not listen?
Or cry out to you, "Violence!"
but you do not save?
3 Why do you make me look at injustice?
Why do you tolerate wrong?
Destruction and violence are before me;
there is strife, and conflict abounds.

1:5-8 *be utterly amazed . . . raising up the Babylonians:* In the time of Habakkuk, Babylon was a rising political power. The Babylonian army was "ruthless" (1:6) and attacked with the speed of leopards or wolves (1:8). The LORD "amazes" Habakkuk by sending the Babylonians to conquer "the whole earth," including Judah. See the mini-article called "Babylon," p. 1363.

1:9,10 *gather prisoners . . . build earthen ramps:* When the Babylonians defeated another nation, they arrested that nation's leaders and leading citizens and forced them to leave their homeland and live in Babylon. Attacking armies often built up dirt mounds or ramps against city walls to make it easier for them to get over the wall and capture the city.

1:12 *my Holy One . . . LORD . . . Rock:* "LORD" is frequently used in English translations of the Old Testament for the Hebrew term *Yahweh.* For a more complete explanation of what this term means, see the mini-article called "LORD (YHWH)," p. 140. When combined with "God," this name refers to the God of Israel who is holy (set apart from human beings and awesome in power) but who also is Israel's personal God, who chose them (Isa 41:8,9). "Rock" was sometimes used as a name for God, to compare the LORD to a mountain where his people can run for protection from their enemies (Deut 32:4,15; Ps 18:2; Isa 17:10).

1:13 *you cannot tolerate wrong:* Habakkuk wonders how the "Holy One" who hates sin can use the sinful Babylonians to punish God's people. From Habakkuk's perspective, the sins of the ones who attack God's chosen people will always be greater than the sins of Israel.

1:14-16 *men like fish in the sea . . . catches them in his net:* Ancient Mesopotamian drawings symbolically picture Babylonian rulers capturing their enemies in fishnets.

1:5 Acts 13:41 **1:6** 2 Kgs 24:2. **2:4** Rom 1:17; Gal 3:11; Heb 10:38.

4 Therefore the law is paralyzed,
and justice never prevails.
The wicked hem in the righteous,
so that justice is perverted.

The LORD's Answer

5 "Look at the nations and watch—
and be utterly amazed.
For I am going to do something in your days
that you would not believe,
even if you were told.
6 I am raising up the Babylonians,[a]
that ruthless and impetuous people,
who sweep across the whole earth
to seize dwelling places not their own.
7 They are a feared and dreaded people;
they are a law to themselves
and promote their own honor.
8 Their horses are swifter than leopards,
fiercer than wolves at dusk.
Their cavalry gallops headlong;
their horsemen come from afar.
They fly like a vulture swooping to devour;
9 they all come bent on violence.
Their hordes[b] advance like a desert wind
and gather prisoners like sand.
10 They deride kings
and scoff at rulers.
They laugh at all fortified cities;
they build earthen ramps and capture them.
11 Then they sweep past like the wind and go on—
guilty men, whose own strength is their god."

Habakkuk's Second Complaint

12 O LORD, are you not from everlasting?
My God, my Holy One, we will not die.
O LORD, you have appointed them to execute judgment;
O Rock, you have ordained them to punish.
13 Your eyes are too pure to look on evil;
you cannot tolerate wrong.
Why then do you tolerate the treacherous?
Why are you silent while the wicked
swallow up those more righteous than themselves?
14 You have made men like fish in the sea,
like sea creatures that have no ruler.

[a]**6** Or *Chaldeans* [b]**9** The meaning of the Hebrew for this word is uncertain.

[15]The wicked foe pulls all of them up with hooks,
he catches them in his net,
he gathers them up in his dragnet;
and so he rejoices and is glad.
[16]Therefore he sacrifices to his net
and burns incense to his dragnet,
for by his net he lives in luxury
and enjoys the choicest food.
[17]Is he to keep on emptying his net,
destroying nations without mercy?

2

I will stand at my watch
and station myself on the ramparts;
I will look to see what he will say to me,
and what answer I am to give to this complaint.[a]

The LORD's Answer

[2]Then the LORD replied:

"Write down the revelation
and make it plain on tablets
so that a herald[b] may run with it.
[3]For the revelation awaits an appointed time;
it speaks of the end
and will not prove false.
Though it linger, wait for it;
it[c] will certainly come and will not delay.

[4]"See, he is puffed up;
his desires are not upright—
but the righteous will live by his faith[d]—
[5]indeed, wine betrays him;
he is arrogant and never at rest.
Because he is as greedy as the grave[e]
and like death is never satisfied,
he gathers to himself all the nations
and takes captive all the peoples.

[6]"Will not all of them taunt him with ridicule and scorn,
saying,

" 'Woe to him who piles up stolen goods
and makes himself wealthy by extortion!
How long must this go on?'
[7]Will not your debtors[f] suddenly arise?

2:1 *watch . . . ramparts:* Habakkuk waits for the LORD to answer his question as he stands at his "watch" and stations himself "on the ramparts" (2:1). Watchtowers were placed in city walls to help watch for enemies, and built in fields to protect crops from thieves and wild animals at harvest time. Habakkuk pictures himself as a guard waiting for the LORD's answer to his questions. See also Isa 5:2; 21:8; Ezek 3:17-21; Matt 21:33.

2:3 *it will certainly come and will not delay:* God will act when the time is right. See also Ps 90:1-4; Jer 33:20, 25; Dan 11:35; Heb 10:37.

2:4 *he is puffed up:* "Puffed up" refers to pride. The Babylonians proudly worshiped their own strength as their god (1:11). This also refers to those who take pride in their own abilities, power, or wealth above trusting in God.

2:5 *greedy as the grave: Sheol,* the Hebrew word for the underground world of the dead, is described as a realm of silent oblivion (Job 10:21,22; Ps 88:12; 94:17). Death's hunger for human beings is never satisfied (Prov 30:15,16; Isa 14:9-11).

2:6 *Woe to him:* This phrase introduces a series of prophetic messages of doom. These are likely aimed at the arrogant Babylonians who will be punished according to their actions: robbing and cheating (2:6-8); providing for one's own family (or nation) at the expense of others (2:9-11); building cities with money and labor gained by violence (2:12-14); disgracing friends and ruining the land (2:15-17).

---

a1 Or *and what to answer when I am rebuked* b2 Or *so that whoever reads it*
c3 Or *Though he linger, wait for him; / he* d4 Or *faithfulness* e5 Hebrew *Sheol*
f7 Or *creditors*

2:8 *plundered many nations . . . shed man's blood:* Babylon invaded and destroyed many cities in Judah (2 Kgs 24:8—25:21). See also the mini-articles called "Babylon," p. 1363, and "Nebuchadnezzar," p. 1469.

2:10 *plotted the ruin of many peoples:* The Babylonians destroyed Jerusalem in 586 B.C. and stole the treasures of Israel's temple. By 539 B.C., Babylonia had become so weak that King Cyrus of Persia was able to capture Babylon without a fight. The city itself was never destroyed in war. A ruler in the Intertestamental Period relocated the population of Babylon, and the ancient city was said to be in ruins by the late first century A.D.

2:13 *the LORD Almighty . . . fuel for the fire:* The title "Almighty" is often used in the Old Testament to describe God as the commander, either of the armies of Israel or of all the angels in heaven. The "Almighty" LORD is entirely different from the powerless idols worshiped by the Babylonians (2:18,19).

2:17 *violence you have done to Lebanon . . . destruction of animals:* The mountains of Lebanon (see the map on p. 2465) were covered with cedar and cypress trees that provided lumber for royal palaces (1 Kgs 5:3-9; 7:1-12; Isa 37:24). Few cedars remain today. The removal of many trees also may have destroyed the natural habitat of some of the animals that lived in the forests of Lebanon (2 Kgs 14:9; Ps 104:16-18).

2:18,19 *what value is an idol:* Ancient idols were often made of carved wood or stone, and sometimes covered with silver or gold. These gods would be taken away to foreign countries when Babylon fell to its enemies (Isa 46:1-10).

2:14 Isa 11:9.

Will they not wake up and make you tremble?
Then you will become their victim.
8 Because you have plundered many nations,
the peoples who are left will plunder you.
For you have shed man's blood;
you have destroyed lands and cities and everyone
in them.

9 "Woe to him who builds his realm by unjust gain
to set his nest on high,
to escape the clutches of ruin!
10 You have plotted the ruin of many peoples,
shaming your own house and forfeiting your life.
11 The stones of the wall will cry out,
and the beams of the woodwork will echo it.

12 "Woe to him who builds a city with bloodshed
and establishes a town by crime!
13 Has not the LORD Almighty determined
that the people's labor is only fuel for the fire,
that the nations exhaust themselves for nothing?
14 For the earth will be filled with the knowledge of the
glory of the LORD,
as the waters cover the sea.

15 "Woe to him who gives drink to his neighbors,
pouring it from the wineskin till they are drunk,
so that he can gaze on their naked bodies.
16 You will be filled with shame instead of glory.
Now it is your turn! Drink and be exposed[a]!
The cup from the LORD's right hand is coming around
to you,
and disgrace will cover your glory.
17 The violence you have done to Lebanon will overwhelm
you,
and your destruction of animals will terrify you.
For you have shed man's blood;
you have destroyed lands and cities and everyone
in them.

18 "Of what value is an idol, since a man has carved it?
Or an image that teaches lies?
For he who makes it trusts in his own creation;
he makes idols that cannot speak.
19 Woe to him who says to wood, 'Come to life!'
Or to lifeless stone, 'Wake up!'

[a]16 Masoretic Text; Dead Sea Scrolls, Aquila, Vulgate and Syriac (see also Septuagint) *and stagger*

Can it give guidance?
It is covered with gold and silver;
there is no breath in it.
20 But the LORD is in his holy temple;
let all the earth be silent before him."

Habakkuk's Prayer of Praise and Trust

Habakkuk's prayer in chapter 3 begins with a request for the LORD to be merciful to the people of Judah (3:2) and then continues with a description of the LORD's presence and power in the world (3:3-15). Habakkuk is overwhelmed by the LORD's awesome power, which makes him confident that the LORD will save the people of Judah, even though they face difficulties at the present time.

Habakkuk's Prayer

3 A prayer of Habakkuk the prophet. On *shigionoth*.[a]
2 LORD, I have heard of your fame;
I stand in awe of your deeds, O LORD.
Renew them in our day,
in our time make them known;
in wrath remember mercy.

3 God came from Teman,
the Holy One from Mount Paran. *Selah*[b]
His glory covered the heavens
and his praise filled the earth.
4 His splendor was like the sunrise;
rays flashed from his hand,
where his power was hidden.
5 Plague went before him;
pestilence followed his steps.
6 He stood, and shook the earth;
he looked, and made the nations tremble.
The ancient mountains crumbled
and the age-old hills collapsed.
His ways are eternal.
7 I saw the tents of Cushan in distress,
the dwellings of Midian in anguish.
8 Were you angry with the rivers, O LORD?
Was your wrath against the streams?

[a]1 Probably a literary or musical term [b]3 A word of uncertain meaning; possibly a musical term; also in verses 9 and 13

2:20 *holy temple . . . be silent:* This verse could be an ending to the final "woe" (2:18,19). All people who trust in lifeless idols should remain silent and worship before the holy LORD who is present in Israel's temple in Jerusalem (Ps 11:4; 46:10; Mic 4:1-4; Zeph 1:7; Rev 8:1). This verse also looks ahead to Habakkuk's psalm of praise in chapter 3: The LORD has not abandoned his people and will save them from the present trouble.

3:2 *stand in awe of your deeds . . . in wrath remember mercy:* The LORD acted in the past in various ways (see 3:3-15) to save the people of Israel. Habakkuk now asks the LORD to turn away from his anger (see 1:2-10, 13) and save them again.

3:4 *His splendor was like the sunrise; rays flashed:* Fire, thunder, and lightening are often connected with the appearance of God in the Bible (Exod 3:1-6; 13:20-22; Isa 4:5). This verse probably celebrates God's appearance to Moses and the people at Sinai (Exod 19:16-19; 24:15-18).

3:5 *Plague . . . pestilence:* The LORD used terrible plagues against Egypt (Exod 7:14—12:32) to get the king of Egypt to set the Israelite people free. The LORD also used diseases to punish the Israelites who rebelled against the LORD in the desert (Num 16:41-49; 25:1-9).

3:7 *Cushan . . . Midian:* These tribes of the desert south of Edom were enemies of Israel (Num 31:1-12).

3:8 *rivers . . . streams . . . sea:* God controls the forces of nature. Habakkuk may also have in mind the LORD parting the waters to let the people of Israel escape from the Egyptian army (Exod 14). This event is the focus of Psalm 77, which is very similar to Habakkuk 3:8-15.

3:6 Exod 15:14-16; 19:18; Ps 18:7,8; Jer 10:10.

3:9 *many arrows:* God's "arrows" probably refers to lightning (Hab 3:11). See also 2 Sam 22:15; Ps 18:14; 77:16-18; 144:6; Ezek 1:13, 14.

3:12,13 *threshed the nations . . . save your anointed one:* A number of God's acts on behalf of Israel may be in mind here: the LORD's victory over Egypt (Exod 7–14); Israel's victories when they entered Canaan (Josh 3–12); or even the victories of God's chosen ruler King David over many surrounding nations (2 Sam 5–8).

3:16 *I heard . . . my legs trembled:* Having heard God's mighty acts (3:3-15) recited in the psalm in worship, or having seen these things in a vision, Habakkuk has learned to trust God. His renewed faith erases any concern that God will do nothing about evil. His fear of God's magnificent, overwhelming power shows his deep respect for God and for God's ability to defeat evil.

Did you rage against the sea
when you rode with your horses
and your victorious chariots?
9 You uncovered your bow,
you called for many arrows. *Selah*
You split the earth with rivers;
10 the mountains saw you and writhed.
Torrents of water swept by;
the deep roared
and lifted its waves on high.

11 Sun and moon stood still in the heavens
at the glint of your flying arrows,
at the lightning of your flashing spear.
12 In wrath you strode through the earth
and in anger you threshed the nations.
13 You came out to deliver your people,
to save your anointed one.
You crushed the leader of the land of wickedness,
you stripped him from head to foot. *Selah*
14 With his own spear you pierced his head
when his warriors stormed out to scatter us,
gloating as though about to devour
the wretched who were in hiding.
15 You trampled the sea with your horses,
churning the great waters.

16 I heard and my heart pounded,
my lips quivered at the sound;
decay crept into my bones,
and my legs trembled.

QUESTIONS ABOUT HABAKKUK

1. What is Habakkuk's first complaint about? (1:2-4) What is the LORD's surprising response to this complaint? (1:5-11) The LORD's response leads to Habakkuk's second complaint. What is it? (1:12-17)
2. In chapter 1, who seems to be weak and who seems to be strong? What warning is given to the seeming "strong" ones, the "proud"? (1:11)
3. Habakkuk 2:4 is used by a number of New Testament writers (see Rom 1:17; Gal 3:11; Heb 10:38). The translation of 2:4 is uncertain (see the footnote). What do you think Habakkuk most likely meant by this verse? Why?
4. Habakkuk speaks about those who are doomed (2:6,9). In a column, list the actions that lead to their punishment. Next to these make a second column listing the punishments for each of the evil actions. How do the punishments fit the actions?
5. In your opinion, does Habakkuk's view of God change from the beginning of the book to the end? Why or why not? What have you learned about God by reading and studying HABAKKUK?

Yet I will wait patiently for the day of calamity
to come on the nation invading us.
17 Though the fig tree does not bud
and there are no grapes on the vines,
though the olive crop fails
and the fields produce no food,
though there are no sheep in the pen
and no cattle in the stalls,
18 yet I will rejoice in the LORD,
I will be joyful in God my Savior.

19 The Sovereign LORD is my strength;
he makes my feet like the feet of a deer,
he enables me to go on the heights.

For the director of music. On my stringed instruments.

3:17 *Fig tree . . . cattle in the stalls:* Figs, grapes, and olives were an important sources of food, wine, and oil. Cattle and sheep also were a source of food, as well as wool and hides. The loss or scarcity of these things was seen as a sign of God's punishment for disobedience (Deut 28:38-51; Amos 4:9; Mic 6:13-15; Hag 1:9-11; 2:16-19).

3:18,19 *rejoice . . . go on the heights:* Even though judgment would bring suffering to God's people, Habakkuk trusted that all would not be lost. This trust allows him to celebrate in the midst of defeat and have confidence like that of a sure-footed deer climbing on a dangerous rocky mountain slope. Though he questioned God (1:2-4, 12-17), Habakkuk did not stop trusting in God's power to save (1:12). It is this kind of "faith" that makes one acceptable to God (2:4).

3:19 2 Sam 22:34; Ps 18:33.

ZEPHANIAH

What can one person say or do to change the hearts, minds, and actions of society's most powerful people? Armed with God's Word, a young prophet named Zephaniah faced this question.

Hezekiah . . . Josiah . . . king of Judah: The "Hezekiah" mentioned in 1:1 probably refers to the king who ruled Judah from 716 to 687 B.C. (2 Kgs 18:1—20:21; 2 Chr 29:1—32:33). Hezekiah was 25 years old when he became king (2 Kgs 18:2). Figuring about 25 years for each generation (1:1) from the beginning of Hezekiah's rule, Zephaniah would have been born around 666 B.C. That means Zephaniah would have been in his mid-twenties when King Josiah began to rule Judah in 640 B.C.

Manasseh and Amon, the kings before Josiah, were known for following foreign customs and building shrines to worship foreign idols (2 Kgs 21). Manasseh also practiced magic and witchcraft and had his own son sacrificed. Amon ruled only two years before being killed in a plot by palace officials (2 Kgs 21:23). Josiah began to rule Judah when he was only eight years old (2 Kgs 22:1). Judah and its capital city Jerusalem were badly in need of reform. If things didn't change soon, the people of Judah would become just like their neighbors who worshiped pagan gods.

Eighteen years after Josiah became king, the high priest Hilkiah found the *Book of the Law* in the temple in Jerusalem (2 Kgs 22). Josiah read this book and followed its teachings. He reformed Judah by tearing down shrines built to honor pagan gods. But the kings who followed Josiah did not continue the reforms he had begun, so Judah was punished (2 Kgs 23:31—25:21). It was during and, perhaps, after Josiah's reign that Zephaniah preached his messages.

What makes Zephaniah special?

In Hebrew, the name "Zephaniah" means "The LORD protects." Zephaniah is the only prophet who traces his family ancestry back four generations (1:1). As a great-great-grandson of Judah's King Hezekiah (ruled 716-687 B.C.), Zephaniah probably came from a family that had some wealth and social standing. And he was very familiar with the customs and the politics of the royal court in Jerusalem. Zephaniah may have known the prophets Nahum and Jeremiah, who lived about the same time.

Why was Zephaniah written?

ZEPHANIAH has two key messages. The first is to announce that a "great day of the LORD" is coming soon. The people of Judah believed that one day the LORD was going to make them powerful and wipe out their enemies. But Zephaniah told the people that when the day of the LORD did come, the LORD would punish those who had not obeyed him. And this included Judah, as well as other nations. Zephaniah described how the people and their leaders had disobeyed the LORD: Many worshiped idols (1:5); the king and other leaders were following foreign customs (1:8) and abusing their power (1:9; 3:3); false prophets told the people not to worry about what the LORD demanded and said the LORD wouldn't do anything about it anyway (1:12); and priests were disgracing the temple and abusing God's Law (3:4). Zephaniah tells the people to be humble, obey the LORD, and worship only God (2:3; 3:12). If they do this, they could still avoid the terrible punishment that would destroy them.

ZEPHANIAH's second message is one of mercy and hope. The LORD wants to create a new people who will do no wrong (3:13) and will sing and shout (3:14) because the LORD has given them victory and refreshes their lives with his love (3:15-17). The LORD will bring home to Judah those who have been scattered or exiled by war. They will once again worship the LORD in Jerusalem, and other nations will see how the LORD has blessed them (3:18-20).

What's the story behind the scene?

Zephaniah probably preached his message from the LORD near the beginning of the reign of Judah's King Josiah (640-609 B.C.).

The people of Judah were greatly influenced by the powerful Assyrians during the reigns of Manasseh (687-642 B.C.) and Amon (642-640 B.C.). Apparently, these kings and other royal leaders of Judah followed Assyrian customs and dressed in Assyrian clothing (1:8). People were allowed to worship the stars and foreign gods such as Baal and Molech (1:4, 5). Zephaniah's message was clear: Judah and its leaders must reform and turn back to the LORD. This was also the message that King Josiah would later give to the people in 621 B.C. after the *Book of the Law* was discovered in the temple in Jerusalem (see 2 Kgs 22,23). Josiah got rid of foreign gods in the temple and encouraged the people to live according to the Law given to them by Moses. But Josiah was killed by the Egyptians in a battle at Megiddo in 609 B.C., and Jerusalem's leaders fell back into their old evil ways. See 2 Kgs 23:31—24:20 and 2 Chr 34:1—35:27 and the Introduction to JEREMIAH, p. 1424.

It is possible that some of Zephaniah's criticism of Jerusalem took place after Josiah's attempt to reform Jerusalem and its leaders. If that is the case, after the reformer Josiah died, Zephaniah reports that the people were "still eager to act corruptly in all they did" (3:7). Eventually, Zephaniah's warnings of a day of punishment came true when the Babylonians captured and destroyed Jerusalem in 587 or 586 B.C. It took nearly fifty years before the people taken as prisoners to Babylon were allowed to return home to Judah and begin to rebuild Jerusalem and the temple, a hopeful time that seems to be described in 3:8-20.

HOW IS ZEPHANIAH CONSTRUCTED?

ZEPHANIAH has three main sections. The first two focus on God's judgment. The final section focuses on a time of restoration and celebration after the day of judgment has passed.

A day of judgment for Judah (1:1—2:3)

A day of judgment for all people (2:4—3:7)

A new day of celebration promised (3:8-20)

Moab ... the Ammonites ... Sodom ... Gomorrah: See 2:8-11. The people of Moab and Ammon had been enemies of Israel in the past (Num 22:2-11; 2 Sam 8:2,13,14). Moab was located south and east of Judah, and Ammon bordered Israel's lands east of the Jordan River (see the map on p. 2465). Zephaniah warns that Moab and Ammon will end up like the cities of Sodom and Gomorrah, which God destroyed because of the evil people who lived there (Gen 19:23-29).

Cushites ... Assyria: See 2:12-15. Cush was the region south of Egypt that included parts of the present countries of Ethiopia and Sudan. At one time, the king of Cush also controlled Egypt. Zephaniah probably used this name to refer to Egypt as well. The prophet Isaiah had once warned Judah's King Hezekiah not to make a treaty with Cush and Egypt against Assyria, Judah's enemy to the north (Isa 20:1-6; 30:1-7; 31:1-3).

For many years, Assyria was the most powerful nation in ancient Near East. It defeated the northern kingdom of Israel in 721 B.C. and threatened the southern kingdom of Judah during Zephaniah's lifetime. Its capital city, Nineveh, was protected by high walls and by a moat filled with water from the nearby Tigris River. Even so, Nineveh fell to the Babylonians and Medes in 612 B.C., and Assyria was powerless after 609 B.C. For more, see the Introduction to NAHUM and the mini-article called "Assyria," p. 711.

1:1 *Cushi ... Gedaliah ... Amariah:* Nothing is known about these members of Zephaniah's family. For more about Zephaniah, see the Introduction to ZEPHANIAH and the note on p. 1778.

1:1 *Hezekiah ... Josiah ... king of Judah:* See the note on p. 1778.

A Day of Judgment for Judah

Zephaniah introduces himself and brings a message from the LORD, who is angry with the people and leaders of Judah. They are worshiping the idols of foreign gods, following foreign customs, and treating one another badly. He warns that a "great" and "terrible" day is coming when no one will escape God's judgment (1:2-18). But Zephaniah also says that those who humbly obey and worship the LORD will be safe on that day (2:3).

1 The word of the LORD that came to Zephaniah son of Cushi, the son of Gedaliah, the son of Amariah, the son of Hezekiah, during the reign of Josiah son of Amon king of Judah:

1:2 *LORD:* God's special name. See the mini-article called "LORD (YHWH)," p. 140.

1:2,3 *sweep away everything from the face of the earth:* Compare Zephaniah's strong words of judgment to the promise God made to Noah (Gen 9:15). The coming judgment Zephaniah describes is as serious as the ancient flood.

1:4 *Judah . . . Jerusalem:* After the death of King Solomon about 931 B.C., the united kingdom of Israel divided into two nations. The northern kingdom was named Israel, and the southern kingdom was called Judah (see the map on p. 2467). Some of Judah's kings allowed the worship of foreign gods. Altars to foreign gods were even built in Jerusalem and in the temple area. See also the notes on p. 1778 and at 1:4,5.

1:4,5 *Baal . . . Molech:* Baal was a Canaanite fertility god often worshiped in Israel and Judah (Judg 2:13; 6:25-32; 1 Kgs 18:16-40; Jer 7:8-11; Hos 2:8). Molech was an Ammonite fertility god (1 Kgs 11:5; Jer 49:3). In Zephaniah's day, Molech was worshiped in the Valley of Ben Hinnom near Jerusalem (see the map on p. 2466). The worship of Molech included human sacrifice (2 Kgs 23:10; Lev 18:21). Some people in Judah also worshiped the moon and stars, a religion popular among some of Judah's neighbors. See also the mini-article called "Canaanite Gods and Goddesses," p. 469.

1:7,8 *the day of the LORD is near . . . On the day:* The "day of the LORD" Zephaniah mentions is when the LORD will judge all the nations (see the notes at 1:14-18 and 3:8). Zephaniah's message was shocking: The LORD would punish his own people and "sacrifice" them.

1:5 Exod 20:3-7; Deut 4:19, 35-39; 5:7-11.

Warning of Coming Destruction

2 "I will sweep away everything
from the face of the earth,"
declares the LORD.
3 "I will sweep away both men and animals;
I will sweep away the birds of the air
and the fish of the sea.
The wicked will have only heaps of rubble[a]
when I cut off man from the face of the earth,"
declares the LORD.

Against Judah

4 "I will stretch out my hand against Judah
and against all who live in Jerusalem.
I will cut off from this place every remnant of Baal,
the names of the pagan and the idolatrous priests—
5 those who bow down on the roofs
to worship the starry host,
those who bow down and swear by the LORD
and who also swear by Molech,[b]
6 those who turn back from following the LORD
and neither seek the LORD nor inquire of him.
7 Be silent before the Sovereign LORD,
for the day of the LORD is near.
The LORD has prepared a sacrifice;
he has consecrated those he has invited.
8 On the day of the LORD's sacrifice
I will punish the princes
and the king's sons
and all those clad
in foreign clothes.
9 On that day I will punish
all who avoid stepping on the threshold,[c]
who fill the temple of their gods
with violence and deceit.

10 "On that day," declares the LORD,
"a cry will go up from the Fish Gate,
wailing from the New Quarter,
and a loud crash from the hills.
11 Wail, you who live in the market district[d];
all your merchants will be wiped out,
all who trade with[e] silver will be ruined.
12 At that time I will search Jerusalem with lamps
and punish those who are complacent,

---

[a]3 The meaning of the Hebrew for this line is uncertain. [b]5 Hebrew *Malcam*, that is, Milcom [c]9 See 1 Samuel 5:5. [d]11 Or *the Mortar* [e]11 Or *in*

who are like wine left on its dregs,
who think, 'The LORD will do nothing,
either good or bad.'
13 Their wealth will be plundered,
their houses demolished.
They will build houses
but not live in them;
they will plant vineyards
but not drink the wine.

The Great Day of the LORD

14 "The great day of the LORD is near—
near and coming quickly.
Listen! The cry on the day of the LORD will be bitter,
the shouting of the warrior there.
15 That day will be a day of wrath,
a day of distress and anguish,
a day of trouble and ruin,
a day of darkness and gloom,
a day of clouds and blackness,
16 a day of trumpet and battle cry
against the fortified cities
and against the corner towers.
17 I will bring distress on the people
and they will walk like blind men,
because they have sinned against the LORD.
Their blood will be poured out like dust
and their entrails like filth.
18 Neither their silver nor their gold
will be able to save them
on the day of the LORD's wrath.
In the fire of his jealousy
the whole world will be consumed,
for he will make a sudden end
of all who live in the earth."

2 Gather together, gather together,
O shameful nation,
2 before the appointed time arrives
and that day sweeps on like chaff,
before the fierce anger of the LORD comes upon you,
before the day of the LORD's wrath comes upon
you.
3 Seek the LORD, all you humble of the land,
you who do what he commands.
Seek righteousness, seek humility;
perhaps you will be sheltered
on the day of the LORD's anger.

1:8,9 *foreign clothes . . . avoid stepping on the threshold . . . violence and deceit:* Judah's royal officials probably were wearing the kind of clothes worn by Assyrian officials, and they were allowing the worship of foreign gods. (To avoid stepping on the threshold was a custom that had to do with idol worship; see 1 Sam 5:4,5.) Zephaniah joined a number of Israel's prophets in warning its leaders and the wealthy to treat all people, especially the poor, with justice and fairness. See also Isa 41:17; Amos 2:6-8; 5:10-12; Mic 4:6,7; and the mini-article called "Justice," p. 1721.

1:10,11 *Fish Gate . . . New Quarter . . . market district:* These sections of Jerusalem were probably centers of the city's business activity. The cries and wails heard from these places are probably meant to be the cries of the merchants and wealthy people who had been cheating their neighbors and robbing them of their property (see also Isa 5:8-13; Mic 6:9-16). Zephaniah is warning these people that their possessions, homes, and vineyards will be destroyed.

1:14-18 *great day of the LORD . . . fire:* In powerful terms, Zephaniah describes how the LORD will act like a great warrior who was not going to fight for his people as in times past, but was going fight against them. God's judgment is also compared to a raging fire (Isa 4:4; Joel 2:1-3; Matt 13:36-42). See also the note at 1:7,8 and the mini-articles called "Fire," p. 2383, and the "Day of the LORD," p. 1727.

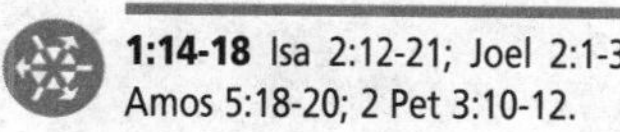

1:14-18 Isa 2:12-21; Joel 2:1-3; Amos 5:18-20; 2 Pet 3:10-12.

A Day of Judgment for All People

Zephaniah declares that the LORD *will also punish Judah's enemies (2:4-15) on every side. But this does not mean that the people of Jerusalem are pardoned for their sins. The* LORD*'s judgment will also fall on all in Jerusalem who "profane the sanctuary and do violence to the law" (3:4).*

The LORD *their God will care for them; he will restore their fortunes.*
Zeph 2:7

Against Philistia

4 Gaza will be abandoned
 and Ashkelon left in ruins.
At midday Ashdod will be emptied
 and Ekron uprooted.
5 Woe to you who live by the sea,
 O Kerethite people;
the word of the LORD is against you,
 O Canaan, land of the Philistines.

"I will destroy you,
 and none will be left."

6 The land by the sea, where the Kerethites[a] dwell,
 will be a place for shepherds and sheep pens.
7 It will belong to the remnant of the house of Judah;
 there they will find pasture.
In the evening they will lie down
 in the houses of Ashkelon.
The LORD their God will care for them;
 he will restore their fortunes.[b]

Against Moab and Ammon

8 "I have heard the insults of Moab
 and the taunts of the Ammonites,
who insulted my people
 and made threats against their land.
9 Therefore, as surely as I live,"
 declares the LORD Almighty, the God of Israel,
"surely Moab will become like Sodom,
 the Ammonites like Gomorrah—
a place of weeds and salt pits,
 a wasteland forever.
The remnant of my people will plunder them;
 the survivors of my nation will inherit their land."
10 This is what they will get in return for their pride,
 for insulting and mocking the people of
 the LORD Almighty.

2:4,5 *land of the Philistines:* Gaza, Ashkelon, Ashdod, Ekron, and Gath (not mentioned because it was already destroyed) were the five major Philistine towns (see the map on p. 2467). The Philistine people often battled the people of Israel. See 1 Sam 14:52; 17:1-54; Isa 14:29-31; Jer 47:1-7; Ezek 25:15-17; Joel 3:4-8; Amos 1:6-8; Zech 9:5-7.

2:7 *the remnant:* Zephaniah believed that some of God's people would survive judgment and would rule over other nations. See also Isa 10:20-27; 46:3, 4; Joel 2:32—3:7; Mic 5:7, 8; Zeph 2:9; 3:13; Zech 8:12, 13.

2:8-11 *Moab . . . the Ammonites . . . Sodom . . . Gomorrah:* See the note on p. 1779 (Moab . . . Gomorrah).

2:8-11 Gen 19:24; Isa 15:1—16:14; 25:10-12; Jer 48:1-47; 49:1-6; Ezek 21:28-32; 25:1-11; Amos 1:13-15.

[a]**6** The meaning of the Hebrew for this word is uncertain. [b]**7** Or *will bring back their captives*

[11]The LORD will be awesome to them
when he destroys all the gods of the land.
The nations on every shore will worship him,
every one in its own land.

Against Cush

[12]"You too, O Cushites,[a]
will be slain by my sword."

Against Assyria

[13]He will stretch out his hand against the north
and destroy Assyria,
leaving Nineveh utterly desolate
and dry as the desert.
[14]Flocks and herds will lie down there,
creatures of every kind.
The desert owl and the screech owl
will roost on her columns.
Their calls will echo through the windows,
rubble will be in the doorways,
the beams of cedar will be exposed.
[15]This is the carefree city
that lived in safety.
She said to herself,
"I am, and there is none besides me."
What a ruin she has become,
a lair for wild beasts!
All who pass by her scoff
and shake their fists.

The Future of Jerusalem

3 Woe to the city of oppressors,
rebellious and defiled!
[2]She obeys no one,
she accepts no correction.
She does not trust in the LORD,
she does not draw near to her God.
[3]Her officials are roaring lions,
her rulers are evening wolves,
who leave nothing for the morning.
[4]Her prophets are arrogant;
they are treacherous men.
Her priests profane the sanctuary
and do violence to the law.

[a]12 That is, people from the upper Nile region

2:12-15 *Cushites ... Assyria:* See the note on p. 1779.

2:14 *desert owl . . . screech owl:* Owls were considered unclean animals because they eat raw flesh (Lev 11:13-19). Because owls live in ruins, their presence in cities indicates that the Assyrian capital that once thrived is now a lonely and abandoned place. (See also Isa 34:11,15.)

3:1 *the city of oppressors:* Zephaniah's message of judgment now turns to Jerusalem. It was supposed to be the center of worship for God's people and the place where the rulers of God's people governed with justice according to God's Law. But it had become corrupt See the notes at 1:4,5; 1:8,9; 1:10,11.

3:3,4 *officials . . . rulers . . . prophets . . . priests:* Judah's officials and rulers acted like hungry animals, gobbling up the property and possessions of the poor and taking bribes in court (see Isa 1:21-23; 3:8-15.) Prophets were to deliver messages from God and priests were to lead worship in the temple according to God's Law. But some prophets ignored the truth and told the leaders and the people what they wanted to hear (Jer 6:13-15; Mic 3:5-12). The priests allowed the worship of idols in the temple (Jer 2:26-28; Ezek 8:1-18).

3:5 *justice:* See the mini-article called "Justice," p. 1721.

2:12 Isa 18:1-7. **2:13-15** Isa 10:5-34; 14:24-27; Nah 1:1—3:19.

3:6 *cut off nations:* This may refer to the defeat of the Assyrian capital city, Nineveh.

3:7 *Surely you will fear me . . . act corruptly:* Some scholars have suggested that the prophecy in 3:1-7 follows the reforms of King Josiah. The discovery of the *Book of the Law* in the temple and Josiah's reforms may have given hope that Jerusalem would turn away from evil and once again obey the Law of Moses. But after Josiah died in battle against the Egyptians in 609 B.C., the leaders and people abandoned Josiah's reforms.

3:8 *the day . . . world will be consumed by the fire:* See the note at 1:14-18. God's judgment both destroys and purifies. Surviving judgment is like being purified in a metal refiner's fire. The survivors will live right and have nothing to fear (3:13).

3:9,10 *purify the lips of the peoples . . . From beyond the rivers of Cush:* Compare the purifying of languages which brings unity, to the story of Genesis 11:1-9, where God punishes proud people by confusing their languages and scattering the people all over the earth. During the Babylonian invasion of Judah, some people of Judah ran away to Egypt (Jer 41:16—43:7). Zephaniah sees both the ancient scattering and the exile of God's people being reversed. See also Acts 2:1-13.

5 The LORD within her is righteous;
he does no wrong.
Morning by morning he dispenses his justice,
and every new day he does not fail,
yet the unrighteous know no shame.

6 "I have cut off nations;
their strongholds are demolished.
I have left their streets deserted,
with no one passing through.
Their cities are destroyed;
no one will be left—no one at all.
7 I said to the city,
'Surely you will fear me
and accept correction!'
Then her dwelling would not be cut off,
nor all my punishments come upon her.
But they were still eager
to act corruptly in all they did.

8 Therefore wait for me," declares the LORD,
"for the day I will stand up to testify.[a]
I have decided to assemble the nations,
to gather the kingdoms
and to pour out my wrath on them—
all my fierce anger.
The whole world will be consumed
by the fire of my jealous anger.

9 "Then will I purify the lips of the peoples,
that all of them may call on the name of the LORD
and serve him shoulder to shoulder.
10 From beyond the rivers of Cush[b]
my worshipers, my scattered people,
will bring me offerings.
11 On that day you will not be put to shame
for all the wrongs you have done to me,
because I will remove from this city
those who rejoice in their pride.
Never again will you be haughty
on my holy hill.
12 But I will leave within you
the meek and humble,
who trust in the name of the LORD.
13 The remnant of Israel will do no wrong;
they will speak no lies,

[a]**8** Septuagint and Syriac; Hebrew *will rise up to plunder* [b]**10** That is, the upper Nile region

nor will deceit be found in their mouths.
They will eat and lie down
and no one will make them afraid."

A New Day of Celebration Promised

The nations have been punished and purified, and some of the people scattered to other lands are returning home to Judah and Jerusalem. The LORD's punishment has ended, and the people can celebrate. The LORD will bless the people once again and make them famous everywhere on earth (3:20).

14 Sing, O Daughter of Zion;
shout aloud, O Israel!
Be glad and rejoice with all your heart,
O Daughter of Jerusalem!
15 The LORD has taken away your punishment,
he has turned back your enemy.
The LORD, the King of Israel, is with you;
never again will you fear any harm.
16 On that day they will say to Jerusalem,
"Do not fear, O Zion;
do not let your hands hang limp.
17 The LORD your God is with you,
he is mighty to save.
He will take great delight in you,
he will quiet you with his love,
he will rejoice over you with singing."
18 "The sorrows for the appointed feasts
I will remove from you;
they are a burden and a reproach to you.[a]

---

[a]**18** Or *"I will gather you who mourn for the appointed feasts; / your reproach is a burden to you*

Zephaniah announced,
"The LORD your God is with you, he is mighty to save. He will take great delight in you, he will quiet you with his love, he will rejoice over you with singing."
Zeph 3:17

3:11 *my holy hill:* This refers to Mount Zion in Jerusalem, where the temple was built. See the note at 3:15, 16.

3:15,16 *Zion:* Zion is the hill in Jerusalem where the temple was built. Because of this, the name "Zion" is also used poetically to represent Jerusalem, its people, or the whole people of Judah. The punishment described here is the time of exile suffered by the people of Judah, because they had disobeyed the LORD (see the Introduction to ZEPHANIAH, p. 1778). See also the mini-article called "Zion," p. 1294.

3:12 Zeph 2:3. **3:13** Rev 14:5. **3:18** Isa 40:1,2.

QUESTIONS ABOUT ZEPHANIAH

1. What sins described in 1:2-13 led to Judah being punished by the LORD?
2. How could the people escape the LORD's anger? (2:3)
3. According to Zephaniah, how will Judah's neighbors be affected by the day of the LORD? Why? (2:4-15)
4. What does Zephaniah say about the leaders of the people and what they have done to misuse their powers? What will happen to Jerusalem as a result? (3:1-7)
5. Why will Jerusalem and the people of Judah celebrate once again? (3:8-20)
6. Briefly describe the historical situation in Judah shortly before and during Zephaniah's lifetime. For example, how might the reforms of King Josiah fit with Zephaniah's prophecies?
7. What, if anything, in our society today needs to be "reformed"? Why?

3:19 *lame . . . those who have been scattered:* The LORD is concerned for the "lame" and the "scattered," not only in Judah but in all the world. One sign of God's future rule would be that the lame, the scattered, and other persons needing help will receive it. See Isa 35:5,6; Jer 31:7,8; Mic 4:6,7; Matt 11:2-5; 15:30,31. But the scattered may also refer specifically to the people of Judah who had been scattered from their homeland during the Babylonian invasion. They will receive the LORD's blessings once again and be restored to a place of honor in the world (3:20).

19 At that time I will deal
with all who oppressed you;
I will rescue the lame
and gather those who have been scattered.
I will give them praise and honor
in every land where they were put to shame.
20 At that time I will gather you;
at that time I will bring you home.
I will give you honor and praise
among all the peoples of the earth
when I restore your fortunes[a]
before your very eyes,"
says the LORD.

[a]**20** Or *I bring back your captives*

HAGGAI

Life is filled with choices. As you read HAGGAI, think about the choices the people of Jerusalem were making and how this affected their relationship with God. What can you learn about the choices you make?

WHAT MAKES HAGGAI SPECIAL?

Haggai is the first prophet God sent to the Jewish people after they returned to Judah from exile in Babylon. His language is plain and direct, not poetic like many of the prophets. And while his name means "festive," Haggai's message is serious.

WHY WAS HAGGAI WRITTEN?

This book was written to record Haggai's tireless activity in encouraging the people of Judah to rebuild the temple in Jerusalem. Haggai told the people that they were experiencing hard times because they stopped working on the temple (1:6-11). But if they began to work again and rebuilt the temple, God would once again fill the temple and bless the people with peace (2:7-9). Haggai also prophesied that Zerubbabel governor of Judah would rule over a restored kingdom (2:21-23). These promises were especially meaningful to the Jewish people, who had suffered through a time of exile in Babylon and were now living under Persian rule.

WHAT'S THE STORY BEHIND THE SCENE?

In 538 B.C., King Cyrus of Persia gave an order that allowed the Jews who had been captive in Babylon for seventy years to return home to Jerusalem (Ezra 1:2-4). About forty thousand people returned with Zerubbabel governor of Judah and Joshua the high priest, and they began to rebuild Jerusalem and the temple that had been destroyed in 587 B.C. The foundations of the temple were laid right away. However, a group of neighboring peoples opposed the rebuilding of the temple and interfered with its construction because they didn't want the people of Judah to become a strong nation again (Ezra 3:1—4:23). Fifteen years later, no progress had been made on the temple.

In 522 B.C., Darius, the next Persian king, encouraged the Jews to begin building again (Ezra 4:24). But the people complained that they couldn't continue rebuilding because of poor harvests, little food, and lack of money (Hag 1:1-6). In 520 B.C., the prophet Haggai warned the people that time was running out. God's people had delayed rebuilding the LORD's temple long enough. Haggai and the prophet Zechariah (Ezra 5:1,2) challenged and encouraged the people to complete the rebuilding of the temple. Construction started up again, and in

Darius . . . Zerubbabel . . . Joshua: After the death of King Cyrus' son Cambyses, Darius became king of Persia in 522 B.C. and ruled until 486 B.C. The Persians defeated the Babylonians in 539 B.C., and controlled a large part of the ancient Near East at this time (see the map on p. 2469). Judah and its capital city Jerusalem were part of the Persian empire. The Persians allowed those they ruled to practice their own religions, so Persia's king let the people of Judah rebuild their temple.

Zerubbabel (called Sheshbazzar in Ezra 1:8) was the grandson of King Jehoiachin of Judah. Zerubbabel and the high priest Joshua were among the leaders in charge of the people who returned to Judah from Babylon in 538 B.C. (Ezra 2:1-20). They rebuilt the altar of Israel's God and began to offer sacrifices again even before work on the temple began (Ezra 3:1-6). Work on the foundation of the new temple began early in the second year after the people returned to Judah (Ezra 3:7-13). But the work slowed and was probably at a standstill in 522 B.C. when Darius became the Persian king. It likely was Darius who officially named Zerubbabel as governor of Judah, which by this time was a small province of Persia consisting of little more than the villages and land around Jerusalem. See also the Introduction to ZECHARIAH, p. 1792.

For more about this time in Israel's history, see the article called "After the Exile: God's People Return to Judea," p. 931.

> *"Is it a time for you yourselves to be living in your paneled houses, while this house remains a ruin?"*
> Hag 1:4

1:1 *second year . . . sixth month:* This refers to Elul, the month of the Hebrew calendar that runs, from about mid-August to mid-September. Haggai's messages are given over a four-month period in 520 B.C., the second year that Darius ruled Persia (see also 2:10).

1:1 *Darius . . . Zerubbabel . . . Joshua:* See the note on p. 1787.

1:2-5 *paneled houses . . . this house remains a ruin:* The temple was burned and almost entirely destroyed in 587 B.C. In the twenty years or so since the people had returned to Judah from Babylon, some people had built expensive houses for themselves, while only the foundation of the temple had been completed.

515 B.C. the newly rebuilt temple was dedicated (Ezra 6:13-15). It is not clear whether or not Haggai was alive to see the new temple completed.

How is Haggai constructed?

Haggai can be divided into two sections:

Neglect and rebuilding of the temple (1:1-15)

The Lord will bless Judah and its leader, Zerubbabel (2:1-23)

Neglect and Rebuilding of the Temple

God's people have been back in Jerusalem from exile in Babylon for nearly twenty years, but they still have not kept their promise to God to rebuild the temple. Haggai warns the people that their excuses and apathy have led to hard times that won't end until they begin work again. Haggai's message stirs the people to action. The people enthusiastically begin to rebuild the temple.

A Call to Build the House of the Lord

1 In the second year of King Darius, on the first day of the sixth
month, the word of the Lord came through the prophet Haggai to
Zerubbabel son of Shealtiel, governor of Judah, and to Joshua[a] son
of Jehozadak, the high priest:
2This is what the Lord Almighty says: "These people say,
'The time has not yet come for the Lord's house to be built.'"
3Then the word of the Lord came through the prophet Haggai: 4"Is it a time for you yourselves to be living in your paneled
houses, while this house remains a ruin?"
5Now this is what the Lord Almighty says: "Give careful
thought to your ways. 6You have planted much, but have harvested little. You eat, but never have enough. You drink, but never have
your fill. You put on clothes, but are not warm. You earn wages,
only to put them in a purse with holes in it."
7This is what the Lord Almighty says: "Give careful thought
to your ways. 8Go up into the mountains and bring down timber
and build the house, so that I may take pleasure in it and be honored," says the Lord. 9"You expected much, but see, it turned out
to be little. What you brought home, I blew away. Why?" declares
the Lord Almighty. "Because of my house, which remains a ruin,
while each of you is busy with his own house. 10Therefore, because
of you the heavens have withheld their dew and the earth its crops.
11I called for a drought on the fields and the mountains, on the

[a]1 A variant of *Jeshua*; here and elsewhere in Haggai

grain, the new wine, the oil and whatever the ground produces, on
men and cattle, and on the labor of your hands."

12Then Zerubbabel son of Shealtiel, Joshua son of Jehozadak,
the high priest, and the whole remnant of the people obeyed the
voice of the LORD their God and the message of the prophet Haggai, because the LORD their God had sent him. And the people
feared the LORD.
13Then Haggai, the LORD's messenger, gave this message of
the LORD to the people: "I am with you," declares the LORD. 14So
the LORD stirred up the spirit of Zerubbabel son of Shealtiel, governor of Judah, and the spirit of Joshua son of Jehozadak, the high
priest, and the spirit of the whole remnant of the people. They
came and began to work on the house of the LORD Almighty, their
God, 15on the twenty-fourth day of the sixth month in the second
year of King Darius.

The LORD Will Bless Judah and Its Leader, Zerubbabel

The LORD tells Haggai to encourage the people by telling them how the new temple will possess a special glory and how the nations will bring their treasures to the temple. The LORD will bless the people of Judah for their obedience. Zerubbabel, a descendant of David, will rule in God's name and with God's authority.

The Promised Glory of the New House

2 On the twenty-first day of the seventh month, the word of the
LORD came through the prophet Haggai: 2"Speak to Zerubbabel
son of Shealtiel, governor of Judah, to Joshua son of Jehozadak, the
high priest, and to the remnant of the people. Ask them, 3'Who of
you is left who saw this house in its former glory? How does it look
to you now? Does it not seem to you like nothing? 4But now be
strong, O Zerubbabel,' declares the LORD. 'Be strong, O Joshua son
of Jehozadak, the high priest. Be strong, all you people of the land,'
declares the LORD, 'and work. For I am with you,' declares the LORD
Almighty. 5'This is what I covenanted with you when you came out
of Egypt. And my Spirit remains among you. Do not fear.'
6"This is what the LORD Almighty says: 'In a little while I will
once more shake the heavens and the earth, the sea and the dry
land. 7I will shake all nations, and the desired of all nations will
come, and I will fill this house with glory,' says the LORD Almighty.
8'The silver is mine and the gold is mine,' declares the LORD
Almighty. 9'The glory of this present house will be greater than the
glory of the former house,' says the LORD Almighty. 'And in this
place I will grant peace,' declares the LORD Almighty."

1:6-11 *purse with holes in it . . . build the house:* Haggai tells the people that they are having bad times because they abandoned work on the LORD's temple. Harvests have been poor, so there is less food. When food is scarce, food prices rise, so money may disappear as quickly as if it were kept in a "purse with holes in it." The LORD will cause the bad times to continue (1:11) until the people once again gather wood and begin rebuilding the temple (1:8).

1:12 *Zerubbabel . . . the whole remnant of the people:* See the note at 1:1 (Darius). At three different times —598 B.C., 587 B.C., and 582 B.C.—the Babylonians forced groups of people living in Judah to move out of their homeland. In 538 B.C., the Persian king, Cyrus, allowed the Jewish people to return to Judah. See also the mini-article called "Exile," p. 1541.

1:15 *twenty-fourth day:* See the note at 1:1 (sixth month).

2:1,2 *the seventh month:* This is Tishri (which was called Ethanim before the exile), the seventh month of the Hebrew calendar, from about mid-September to mid-October. See the note at 1:1 and (sixth month).

2:3 *saw this house in its former glory:* The first temple was built when Solomon was king of Israel. It took seven years to build (1 Kgs 6:38) and was finished in 951 B.C. (1 Kgs 5:1—8:13). The Babylonians destroyed the temple in 587 B.C. (2 Kgs 25:1-12). Some older people living in 520 B.C. may have been alive when the first temple was destroyed. They would have remembered what it looked like and mourned its loss (Ezra 3:12). See the illustration of Solomon's temple on p. 942.

2:7 *I will shake all nations:* The phrase "shake all nations" refers to God's judgment of the unfaithful, both past and future (2:21,22). See also Isa 14:16,17; Heb 12:26.

2:5 Exod 29:45,46.

Rebuilding the Wall around Jerusalem, engraving by Matthäus Merian, seventeenth century. After Cyrus the Great conquered the Babylonians in 539 B.C., he allowed the Jewish people to return to their home in Judah. The people immediately began building houses and planting farms and vineyards. But the prophet Haggai warned them that they would not receive the LORD's blessings until they rebuilt the temple that the Babylonians had destroyed years before.

Blessings for a Defiled People

10On the twenty-fourth day of the ninth month, in the second year of Darius, the word of the LORD came to the prophet
Haggai: 11"This is what the LORD Almighty says: 'Ask the priests
what the law says: 12If a person carries consecrated meat in the fold
of his garment, and that fold touches some bread or stew, some
wine, oil or other food, does it become consecrated?' "

The priests answered, "No."

13Then Haggai said, "If a person defiled by contact with a
dead body touches one of these things, does it become defiled?"

"Yes," the priests replied, "it becomes defiled."

14Then Haggai said, " 'So it is with this people and this
nation in my sight,' declares the LORD. 'Whatever they do and
whatever they offer there is defiled.

15" 'Now give careful thought to this from this day on[a]—consider how things were before one stone was laid on another in the
LORD's temple. 16When anyone came to a heap of twenty measures,
there were only ten. When anyone went to a wine vat to draw fifty
measures, there were only twenty. 17I struck all the work of your
hands with blight, mildew and hail, yet you did not turn to me,'
declares the LORD. 18'From this day on, from this twenty-fourth

[a]15 Or *to the days past*

2:10 *ninth month:* This is Chislev, the ninth month of the Hebrew calendar, from about mid-November to mid-December. See the note at 1:1 (sixth month).

2:11 *priests:* Israel's priests were responsible for offering sacrifices to the LORD and for blessing the people. In addition, they taught the people God's Law and how they should live according to it. See also the mini-article called "Israel's Priests," p. 2344.

2:12-14 *consecrated . . . defiled:* The rules that defied ritual purity and consecrated sacrifices were especially important in Jewish worship and culture. The example Haggai presents to the priests is a reminder that it is much easier to pass on uncleanness than cleanness (Num 19:11-22). In times past, the sacrifices of Judah's priests were sometimes defiled because of all the evil things the people were doing (Isa 1:10-17, 21-25; Mic 6:6-16). See also the mini-article called "Purity (Clean and Unclean)," p. 2125.

day of the ninth month, give careful thought to the day when the
foundation of the LORD's temple was laid. Give careful thought:
19 Is there yet any seed left in the barn? Until now, the vine and the
fig tree, the pomegranate and the olive tree have not borne fruit.
" 'From this day on I will bless you.' "

Zerubbabel the LORD's Signet Ring

20 The word of the LORD came to Haggai a second time on
the twenty-fourth day of the month: 21 "Tell Zerubbabel governor
of Judah that I will shake the heavens and the earth. 22 I will over-
turn royal thrones and shatter the power of the foreign kingdoms.
I will overthrow chariots and their drivers; horses and their riders
will fall, each by the sword of his brother.
23 " 'On that day,' declares the LORD Almighty, 'I will take you,
my servant Zerubbabel son of Shealtiel,' declares the LORD, 'and I
will make you like my signet ring, for I have chosen you,' declares
the LORD Almighty."

2:19 *fig tree . . . pomegranate:* A fig is a small, seedy fruit that is harvested twice a year. A pomegranate is a bright red fruit that was prized for its juice.

2:21,22 *shake the heavens and the earth . . . overthrow chariots:* See the note at 2:4-7. The LORD will fight for Judah and save the people from their enemies, just as the LORD overturned the chariots of Egypt at the Red Sea (Exod 14:26-28).

2:23 *my servant Zerubbabel . . . my signet ring:* The words "my servant" mean someone God has chosen for a special role or task (Num 12:7, 8; Isa 22:20; Jer 27:6, 7). God had once called Israel's King David his "servant" and promised that someone from his family would always rule over Israel (2 Sam 7:4, 10-16). The prophets said that a special chosen leader would come from the line of David (Isa 11:1-9; Mic 5:2-5), bringing justice and peace. Zerubbabel was a descendant of David. See also the mini-article called "Messiah (Chosen One)," p. 1124.

The marking on a signet ring made impressions on clay or wax which were used as a signature, usually to guarantee ownership or payment. Making Zerubbabel God's "signet ring" suggests the restoration of God's covenant with his people. See also Jer 22:24.

QUESTIONS ABOUT HAGGAI

1. When Haggai preached his messages in 520 B.C. many of the Jewish people had been back in Jerusalem for almost twenty years. Why hadn't they finished rebuilding God's temple? (1:1-11 and the notes)
2. What encouraging promises did Haggai give to the people and their leader, Zerubbabel? 2:3-9,18-23)
3. What important "unfinished work" do you have to do? What stops your work? What or who encourages you to keep going?
4. Most of us will never be involved in building a temple, cathedral, or church. But what other things can we "build" for God? What can you do to make sure that God's work has top priority in your life?

ZECHARIAH

A person with "vision" understands how to make plans for a better future. The prophet Zechariah was a person of "vision." In fact, he actually had visions about Israel's future. Read Zechariah to find out what he had to say.

What makes Zechariah special?

Zechariah is made up of a number of different kinds of writings found in prophetic literature, including visions, speeches of prophets (oracles), and apocalyptic writings. Apocalyptic writings often focus on the "end of time" when God will defeat evil and bring about a new creation. This type of writing commonly includes visions and symbolic imagery using animals, angels, demons, and numbers. They were often meant to comfort and encourage people who were experiencing oppression by promising them the final victory over their enemies. See also mini-article called "Apocalyptic Writing," p. 1656.

New Testament Gospel writers quote Zechariah (Matt 21:5; Mark 14:27; John 12:15) or refer to certain passages indirectly (compare, for instance, Matt 26:15 and Zech 11:12; Matt 26:28 and Zech 9:11) to show that Jesus is the fulfillment of prophecies of a coming Messiah. Many references to Zechariah also appear in Revelation because both books have visions of God's victory over all enemies and the creation of a new Jerusalem where God will bless and give new life to all who are faithful (compare Rev 22:1 and Zech 14:8; Rev 22:3 and Zech 14:10, 11).

Why was Zechariah written?

The people of Judah returned to Jerusalem from exile in Babylon in 538 B.C. They soon laid the foundation for a new temple to replace the one destroyed by the Babylonians in 586 B.C. But the work stopped, so in 520 B.C., Zechariah joined the prophet Haggai in encouraging the people of Jerusalem to complete the work of rebuilding the temple. Why was rebuilding the temple so important? It was to be the center of worship and a symbol of God's renewed blessings for the restored people of God.

In addition, Zechariah focuses on other concerns that the people of Judah had after the exile. Because Judah was now only a small province in the Persian empire and there were no more kings in Israel, what kind of political leadership could they expect? What about God's promise to King David that one of his descendants would always rule over Israel (2 Sam 7:12-16)—was this still to be expected? Would God continue to protect them now that they were back in their homeland? God had punished them in the past by letting their enemies take over their land and send many of them into exile. Would God punish them in this way again? What could they expect to happen in the near

Zechariah: Zechariah means "The Lord remembers." Zechariah urged the people to rebuild God's temple (see also the Introduction to Haggai, p. 1787). He was active in the period of 520-518 B.C., or about twenty years after the exile in Babylon ended. (See the mini-article called "Exile," p. 1541.)

Zechariah is called the son of Berekiah here, but in other places he is identified as the son of Iddo (Neh 12:16). Iddo was the head of a priestly family and so Zechariah also may have been a priest. See also the mini-article "Israel's Priests," p. 2344.

Darius: Darius ruled Persia from 522 to 486 B.C. The empire of Persia was a powerful nation and controlled large areas of the ancient Near East at this time (see the map on p. 2469). This empire made major contributions to civilization in the areas of law, religion, politics, and economics. For more, see the mini-article called "Persia," p. 859.

When Darius came to power in 522 B.C. he encouraged the Jews to continue their efforts to rebuild the temple. His interest in seeing Judah prosper may have resulted from a desire to see the Jewish nation act as a "buffer" between Persia and Egypt.

future? Where did they fit in God's plans for the rest of the world?

Zechariah said that David's descendant, Zerubbabel the governor of Judah and Joshua the high priest would be empowered and enabled by the LORD to perform their duties. Zechariah also said that in the future, Judah and Jerusalem will be attacked by enemies, but the LORD will appear and rescue his people. The people will turn back to the LORD and he will forgive them. The mountains around Jerusalem will be flattened, while Jerusalem remains on the mountain towering high above the land around it. Living water will flow from Jerusalem, and all people on earth will worship the LORD (14:8-11).

WHAT'S THE STORY BEHIND THE SCENE?

ZECHARIAH is a book in two parts. The first book (chapters 1–8) was written undoubtedly by the prophet Zechariah himself. Like the prophet Haggai, Zechariah encouraged the people to trust in God and rebuild the temple (see also the Introduction to HAGGAI, p. 1787). Unlike Haggai's simple and direct message, however, Zechariah's message comes through eight visions, as well as prophetic speeches. The visions describe who will end up ruling Judah. What seems to come out of these visions is a partnership between the civil leader, Zerubbabel governor of Judah, and the religious leader, the high priest Joshua.

It is difficult to pinpoint the historical setting of the second part of the book (chapters 9–14), which appears to be divided into two units. Some scholars believe the second part of ZECHARIAH is a collection of oracles from a later period. However other scholars believe the differences in the two sections can be explained and see no need to question the authorship of the book. The first unit (chapters 9–11) speaks of the LORD's judgment against Israel's enemies and against Israel's own worthless "shepherds" (leaders) who had been unfaithful. It also describes how the LORD will bring home captives scattered to other lands and tells of a king who will bring peace to the nations. A reference to Greece (9:13) may refer to the Hellenistic kings who ruled Judah after Alexander the Great conquered the Persians in 333 B.C. The second unit (chapters 12–14) focuses on an unknown future time. Jerusalem and Judah will be attacked by all nations and many of Jerusalem's people will die. But the LORD will come to the rescue and create a new holy Jerusalem where the LORD will rule as King.

HOW IS ZECHARIAH CONSTRUCTED?

Based on the two-fold development described above, ZECHARIAH can be divided into the following sections:

Zechariah preaches to the people of Israel in the days of Darius, King of Persia (1:1—8:23)
- Introduction (1:1-6)
- Zechariah's eight visions (1:7—6:8)
- Joshua the high priest is given a crown (6:9-15)
- Questions and promises (7:1—8:23)

Visions of Israel's future (9:1—14:21)
- Punishment and victory (9:1—11:17)
- The LORD will rule as King in Jerusalem (12:1—14:21)

1:1 *eighth month . . . second year . . . Darius:* The eighth month of the Hebrew calendar is Bul, from about mid-October to mid-November. See the chart called "Jewish Calendar and Festivals," p. 944. The second year of the rule of Darius was 520 B.C. See also Ezra 4:14—5:1; 6:14. Zechariah's first prophecy came about two months after Haggai preached to the people (Hag 1:1).

1:1-3 *the word of the LORD came . . . LORD Almighty:* In ancient Hebrew, "The word of the LORD came" is literally "the word of the LORD happened to me." The prophets regularly use dramatic language like this to emphasize the powerful way they experienced what God wanted them to say. "The LORD Almighty" is literally "The LORD of Hosts." This refers to both the army of Israel and to the "heavenly host"—either the angels or the sun, moon, stars, and planets that the LORD created. The whole phrase, then, means that God is the LORD of all earthly and heavenly forces.

1:1 *Darius . . . Zechariah:* See the notes on p. 1792.

1:1 *word of the* L*ORD:* See the note on p. 1793.

1:2-6 *tell the people . . . just as he determined:* The people of Israel were God's chosen people (see the mini-article called "Israel," p. 264). Only two months before, the prophet Haggai had warned the Israelites that the LORD was angry, so the people had begun to rebuild God's temple in Jerusalem (Hag 1:1-15). In these verses, the people are reminded that when they disobey God, they bring disaster upon themselves. Earlier prophets warned the people of Judah that they would be punished for their sins, as happened when Jerusalem fell to Babylon in 586 B.C.

1:7,8 *Shebat . . . the second year of Darius:* This is still the second year of Darius (see also 1:1). Shebat is the eleventh month of the Hebrew calendar, from about mid-January to mid-February. The year is 520 B.C.

1:7,8 *myrtle trees:* These evergreen shrubs were symbols of fertility, peace, and renewal. Myrtle branches (shown below) were used during the Feast of Tabernacles to make temporary shelters (see the note at 14:16).

1:7-9 *I had a vision . . . angel:* Zechariah's first vision of horsemen on patrol is similar to the last of his eight visions (6:1-8). See also Rev 6:2-4. Angels deliver God's messages, praise God, or complete a task for God. See also the mini-article called "Angels," p. 88.

Zechariah Preaches to the People of Israel in the Days of Darius, King of Persia

The first part of Z*ECHARIAH (chapters 1–8) records the prophetic messages and visions of the prophet Zechariah during 520 to 518 B.C. Zechariah encourages the people of Jerusalem to rebuild their city and the temple. Joshua, the high priest, will be chosen to lead the people of Judah, perhaps alongside the civil governor, Zerubbabel. Those who have returned to Jerusalem from exile are to see that justice is done and to be kind and merciful to one another. If they do this, the* L*ORD will make them a blessing to the nations.*

INTRODUCTION

Zechariah delivers a message to the people of Jerusalem in the eighth month of 520 B.C.

A Call to Return to the LORD

1 In the eighth month of the second year of Darius, the word of
the LORD came to the prophet Zechariah son of Berekiah, the son
of Iddo:
2"The LORD was very angry with your forefathers. 3Therefore
tell the people: This is what the LORD Almighty says: 'Return to
me,' declares the LORD Almighty, 'and I will return to you,' says the
LORD Almighty. 4Do not be like your forefathers, to whom the earlier prophets proclaimed: This is what the LORD Almighty says:
'Turn from your evil ways and your evil practices.' But they would
not listen or pay attention to me, declares the LORD. 5Where are
your forefathers now? And the prophets, do they live forever? 6But
did not my words and my decrees, which I commanded my servants the prophets, overtake your forefathers?
"Then they repented and said, 'The LORD Almighty has done
to us what our ways and practices deserve, just as he determined
to do.' "

ZECHARIAH'S EIGHT VISIONS

During one evening in the eleventh month of 520 B.C., Zechariah has eight visions, which are recorded in chapters 1–6. Each description follows a common pattern. First, the prophet describes the vision (what he has seen). Then Zechariah asks a question about the vision, and an angel answers the question.

The Man Among the Myrtle Trees

7On the twenty-fourth day of the eleventh month, the
month of Shebat, in the second year of Darius, the word of the
LORD came to the prophet Zechariah son of Berekiah, the son of
Iddo.

8 During the night I had a vision—and there before me was
a man riding a red horse! He was standing among the myrtle trees
in a ravine. Behind him were red, brown and white horses.
9 I asked, "What are these, my lord?"
The angel who was talking with me answered, "I will show
you what they are."
10 Then the man standing among the myrtle trees explained,
"They are the ones the LORD has sent to go throughout the earth."
11 And they reported to the angel of the LORD, who was
standing among the myrtle trees, "We have gone throughout the
earth and found the whole world at rest and in peace."
12 Then the angel of the LORD said, "LORD Almighty, how long
will you withhold mercy from Jerusalem and from the towns of
Judah, which you have been angry with these seventy years?" 13 So
the LORD spoke kind and comforting words to the angel who
talked with me.
14 Then the angel who was speaking to me said, "Proclaim
this word: This is what the LORD Almighty says: 'I am very jealous
for Jerusalem and Zion, 15 but I am very angry with the nations
that feel secure. I was only a little angry, but they added to the
calamity.'
16 "Therefore, this is what the LORD says: 'I will return to
Jerusalem with mercy, and there my house will be rebuilt. And the
measuring line will be stretched out over Jerusalem,' declares the
LORD Almighty.
17 "Proclaim further: This is what the LORD Almighty says:
'My towns will again overflow with prosperity, and the LORD will
again comfort Zion and choose Jerusalem.' "

Four Horns and Four Craftsmen

18 Then I looked up—and there before me were four horns!
19 I asked the angel who was speaking to me, "What are these?"
He answered me, "These are the horns that scattered Judah,
Israel and Jerusalem."
20 Then the LORD showed me four craftsmen. 21 I asked, "What
are these coming to do?"
He answered, "These are the horns that scattered Judah so
that no one could raise his head, but the craftsmen have come to
terrify them and throw down these horns of the nations who lifted up their horns against the land of Judah to scatter its people."

A Man With a Measuring Line

2 Then I looked up—and there before me was a man with a
measuring line in his hand! 2 I asked, "Where are you going?"
He answered me, "To measure Jerusalem, to find out how
wide and how long it is."
3 Then the angel who was speaking to me left, and another

1:11-16 *world at rest and in peace . . . seventy years . . . my house will be rebuilt:* The time of peace could refer to the fact that Darius had stopped many of the revolts that were present in the Persian kingdom when he began his rule two years earlier. The seventy years of the LORD's anger is a round number that refers to 586-520 B.C. This period included the time known as the exile in Babylon. The exile ended in 538 B.C., and many of the Jewish people returned home to Judah. But the people did not follow through on their promise to rebuild the temple in Jerusalem. Instead of bringing more punishment, the LORD promises to help the people rebuild the city and the temple.

1:14 *LORD Almighty:* See the note on p. 1793.

1:17 *Zion . . . Jerusalem:* See the mini-articles called "Zion," p. 1294 and "Jerusalem," p. 574.

1:18 *four horns:* Horns, especially horns from bulls, were symbols of power in ancient times. The number "four" shows completeness, representing each of the four directions—north, south, east, and west.

1:18-21 *four craftsmen . . . throw down these horns:* In this second vision, four animal horns symbolize four major enemies that threatened Israel and Judah from the time of King David (about 1000 B.C.) to the time of Zechariah. These powerful nations probably are Egypt, Assyria, Babylon, and Medo-Persia. The craftsmen symbolize the power God will use to crush those enemies.

2:1-5 *measure Jerusalem . . . I myself will be a wall of fire:* In this vision someone is about to measure the city of Jerusalem so that walls can be built to protect it. The angel says that Jerusalem will grow too large to stay within its walls, but that God promises to live in and protect the city. God's promise to be Jerusalem's "glory within" could refer to the rebuilt temple (Isa 49:19; Ezek 43:1-5).

2:6,7 *land of the north . . . Babylon:* The land to the north is often the location of Israel's enemies (Jer 1:13-15; Joel 2:20). Here, the enemy is Babylon, which is east of Judah. The Babylonians and other enemies from the east could not easily cross the Arabian Desert, but had to follow the Euphrates River Valley and then attack Israel and Judah from the north (see the map on p. 2468). The Israelites were captives in Babylon during the exile (see the note at 1:11-16).

2:6-13 *this is what the* LORD *Almighty . . . his holy dwelling:* See the note on p. 1793. The LORD says that Zion (Jerusalem) is as precious as his eyes (2:8). In the Hebrew the expression is literally "apple of his eye," meaning the pupil of the eye. God promises to live in the city of Zion and speak from "his holy dwelling," probably meaning the temple (2:13). See also Deut 26:15; Isa 63:15; Jer 25:30; Hab 2:20.

3:1 *Joshua the high priest:* As the high priest, Joshua was the spiritual leader of the people. He was one of the leaders in charge of those returning to Judah from Babylon in 538 B.C. In Ezra 2:1-20, he is called Jeshua. See also the mini-article called "Israel's Priests," p. 2344.

3:1,2 *Satan standing at his right side to accuse him:* In this vision Joshua stands before God's council of angels, which includes Satan, who was pointing out Joshua's weaknesses. See also Job 1:6-12 and the mini-article called "Satan," p. 963.

3:3-5 *filthy clothes . . . rich garments:* See Exodus 28:1-39.

3:8 *my servant, the Branch:* This may refer to Zerubbabel (see the note at 6:12-15). See also the mini-article called "Messiah (Chosen One)," p. 1124.

3:1 Ezra 5:2; Rev 12:10.
3:2 Jude 9.

angel came to meet him 4and said to him: "Run, tell that young
man, 'Jerusalem will be a city without walls because of the great
number of men and livestock in it. 5And I myself will be a
wall of fire around it,' declares the LORD, 'and I will be its glory
within.'

6"Come! Come! Flee from the land of the north," declares
the LORD, "for I have scattered you to the four winds of heaven,"
declares the LORD.

7"Come, O Zion! Escape, you who live in the Daughter of
Babylon!" 8For this is what the LORD Almighty says: "After he has
honored me and has sent me against the nations that have plundered you—for whoever touches you touches the apple of his
eye— 9I will surely raise my hand against them so that their slaves
will plunder them.[a] Then you will know that the LORD Almighty
has sent me.

10"Shout and be glad, O Daughter of Zion. For I am coming,
and I will live among you," declares the LORD. 11"Many nations will
be joined with the LORD in that day and will become my people. I
will live among you and you will know that the LORD Almighty has
sent me to you. 12The LORD will inherit Judah as his portion in the
holy land and will again choose Jerusalem. 13Be still before the LORD,
all mankind, because he has roused himself from his holy dwelling."

Clean Garments for the High Priest

3 Then he showed me Joshua[b] the high priest standing before
the angel of the LORD, and Satan[c] standing at his right side to
accuse him. 2The LORD said to Satan, "The LORD rebuke you, Satan!
The LORD, who has chosen Jerusalem, rebuke you! Is not this man
a burning stick snatched from the fire?"

3Now Joshua was dressed in filthy clothes as he stood before
the angel. 4The angel said to those who were standing before him,
"Take off his filthy clothes."

Then he said to Joshua, "See, I have taken away your sin, and
I will put rich garments on you."

5Then I said, "Put a clean turban on his head." So they put a
clean turban on his head and clothed him, while the angel of the
LORD stood by.

6The angel of the LORD gave this charge to Joshua: 7"This is
what the LORD Almighty says: 'If you will walk in my ways and
keep my requirements, then you will govern my house and have
charge of my courts, and I will give you a place among these standing here.

8" 'Listen, O high priest Joshua and your associates seated
before you, who are men symbolic of things to come: I am going

---

a8,9 Or *says after . . . eye:* 9"*I . . . plunder them."* **b1** A variant of *Jeshua*; here and elsewhere in Zechariah **c1** *Satan* means *accuser.*

to bring my servant, the Branch. 9See, the stone I have set in front
of Joshua! There are seven eyes[a] on that one stone, and I will
engrave an inscription on it,' says the LORD Almighty, 'and I will
remove the sin of this land in a single day.
10" 'In that day each of you will invite his neighbor to sit
under his vine and fig tree,' declares the LORD Almighty."

The Gold Lampstand and the Two Olive Trees

4 Then the angel who talked with me returned and wakened me, as
a man is wakened from his sleep. 2He asked me, "What do you see?"
I answered, "I see a solid gold lampstand with a bowl at the
top and seven lights on it, with seven channels to the lights. 3Also
there are two olive trees by it, one on the right of the bowl and the
other on its left."
4I asked the angel who talked with me, "What are these, my
lord?"
5He answered, "Do you not know what these are?"
"No, my lord," I replied.
6So he said to me, "This is the word of the LORD to Zerubbabel: 'Not by might nor by power, but by my Spirit,' says the LORD
Almighty.
7"What[b] are you, O mighty mountain? Before Zerubbabel
you will become level ground. Then he will bring out the capstone
to shouts of 'God bless it! God bless it!' "
8Then the word of the LORD came to me: 9"The hands of
Zerubbabel have laid the foundation of this temple; his hands will
also complete it. Then you will know that the LORD Almighty has
sent me to you.
10"Who despises the day of small things? Men will rejoice
when they see the plumb line in the hand of Zerubbabel.
"(These seven are the eyes of the LORD, which range
throughout the earth.)"
11Then I asked the angel, "What are these two olive trees on
the right and the left of the lampstand?"
12Again I asked him, "What are these two olive branches
beside the two gold pipes that pour out golden oil?"
13He replied, "Do you not know what these are?"
"No, my lord," I said.
14So he said, "These are the two who are anointed to[c] serve
the Lord of all the earth."

The Flying Scroll

5 I looked again—and there before me was a flying scroll!
2He asked me, "What do you see?"

[a]9 Or *facets* [b]7 Or *Who* [c]14 Or *two who bring oil and*

3:9,10 *stone:* Refers to the final stone to be laid in the building of the temple. It probably also refers to a jewel that Joshua is to wear as part of his priestly clothing (Exod 28:11,12,36-38).

4:2-14 *gold lampstand . . . olive trees . . . the two who are anointed:* In this vision, the lampstand (4:2) symbolizes the eyes of the LORD that watch over the earth (4:10; Rev 5:6). The two olive trees (4:3,11-14) most likely represent the chosen leaders, Joshua and Zerubbabel. Olive oil was burned in lamps to give light. This shows how the LORD's Spirit guides the two anointed leaders. The lampstand (menorah) is a very ancient symbol for the Jewish people. This comtemporary painting by Mark Ari captures the spirit of the symbol.

4:6 *Zerubbabel:* Zerubbabel was governor of Judah (see Hag 1:1). He and Joshua the high priest encouraged the people to rebuild the temple (Ezra 5:2). Zerubbabel was also a descendant of David.

4:7 *mighty mountain . . . capstone:* The "mountain" that Zerubbabel faced may have been opposition from outsiders (Ezra 4:1-5) or the apathy of the people of Judah (Hag 1:1-11). The capstone may refer to the final stone to be put in place in the rebuilt temple, or it may refer to a stone taken from the rubble of the old temple that would be placed in the new temple.

4:11 Rev 11:4.

I answered, "I see a flying scroll, thirty feet long and fifteen
feet wide.[a]"
3And he said to me, "This is the curse that is going out over
the whole land; for according to what it says on one side, every
thief will be banished, and according to what it says on the other,
everyone who swears falsely will be banished. 4The LORD Almighty
declares, 'I will send it out, and it will enter the house of the thief
and the house of him who swears falsely by my name. It will
remain in his house and destroy it, both its timbers and its
stones.' "

The Woman in a Basket

5Then the angel who was speaking to me came forward and
said to me, "Look up and see what this is that is appearing."
6I asked, "What is it?"
He replied, "It is a measuring basket.[b]" And he added, "This
is the iniquity[c] of the people throughout the land."
7Then the cover of lead was raised, and there in the basket
sat a woman! 8He said, "This is wickedness," and he pushed her
back into the basket and pushed the lead cover down over its
mouth.
9Then I looked up—and there before me were two women,
with the wind in their wings! They had wings like those of a stork,
and they lifted up the basket between heaven and earth.
10"Where are they taking the basket?" I asked the angel who
was speaking to me.
11He replied, "To the country of Babylonia[d] to build a house
for it. When it is ready, the basket will be set there in its place."

Four Chariots

6 I looked up again—and there before me were four chariots
coming out from between two mountains—mountains of bronze!
2The first chariot had red horses, the second black, 3the third
white, and the fourth dappled—all of them powerful. 4I asked the
angel who was speaking to me, "What are these, my lord?"
5The angel answered me, "These are the four spirits[e] of heav-
en, going out from standing in the presence of the Lord of the
whole world. 6The one with the black horses is going toward the
north country, the one with the white horses toward the west,[f] and
the one with the dappled horses toward the south."
7When the powerful horses went out, they were straining to
go throughout the earth. And he said, "Go throughout the earth!"
So they went throughout the earth.

5:5-11 *the angel . . . the basket will be set there in its place:* This vision continues the ideas of the last vision (5:1-4). The woman in the basket represents all the sins of the people of Judah. She is taken to Babylonia, the same country the people of Judah were sent to because of their sins (2 Kgs 25:8-21).

6:1 *chariots:* Two-wheeled carts that were open at the back and pulled by one or more horses. See the illustration on p. 2119.

6:1-5 *mountains of bronze . . . horses . . . four spirits of heaven:* Compare to Zechariah's first vision (1:7-11). The chariots come from an opening between two bronze mountains, which some scholars think represents the opening to the place where God lives.

In Zechariah's first vision, things were calm. In this vision, God begins to act. The "north country" is Babylon (see the note at 2:6,7).

6:2,3 Rev 6:2-5. **6:5** Rev 7:1,2.

[a]2 Hebrew *twenty cubits long and ten cubits wide* (about 9 meters long and 4.5 meters wide) [b]6 Hebrew *an ephah*; also in verses 7-11 [c]6 Or *appearance* [d]11 Hebrew *Shinar* [e]5 Or *winds* [f]6 Or *horses after them*

The Vision of the Four Chariots, an engraving by Gustave Doré, around 1860. Zechariah's visions are similar in style to the apocalyptic imagery of Ezekiel's four living creatures (Ezek 1). The vision of the four chariots is the last of Zechariah's visions and shows the power of God at work at the farthest edges of the universe. (See 6:1-15.)

[8]Then he called to me, "Look, those going toward the north
country have given my Spirit[a] rest in the land of the north."

JOSHUA THE HIGH PRIEST IS GIVEN A CROWN

Zechariah's fourth and fifth visions focused on Joshua the high priest and Zerubbabel the governor. Now the message is related to the coming Messiah-King.

A Crown for Joshua

[9]The word of the LORD came to me: [10]"Take ⌞silver and gold⌟
from the exiles Heldai, Tobijah and Jedaiah, who have arrived from
Babylon. Go the same day to the house of Josiah son of Zephaniah.

[a]8 Or *spirit*

6:9 *The word of the LORD came to me:* See the note on p. 1793.

6:10,11 *Heldai, Tobijah and Jedaiah . . . Joshua son of Jehozadak:* Nothing more is known about the first three men, who are told to make a crown to put on Joshua's head. For Joshua, see the note at 3:1. Josiah most likely was a wealthy homeowner in Jerusalem. Josiah's father Zephaniah should not be confused with the prophet of the same name.

6:12-15 *whose name is the Branch:* Although earlier, Zerubbabel was identified as the one to complete the rebuilding of the temple (3:8; 4:6-10), these verses suggest that Joshua the high priest would wear the crown. The term "Branch" was used to show that the LORD had chosen Joshua to be a ruler. This passage may reflect the growing importance of priests after the rebuilding of the temple. See also Jer 23:5; 33:15; Zech 3:8.

6:15 *Those who are far away:* This may refer to some people of Judah who were still living in other lands.

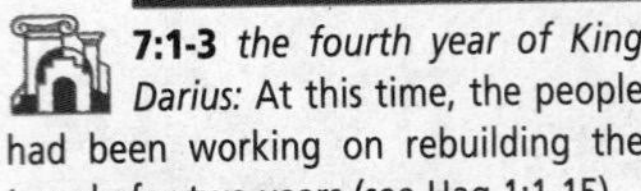

7:1-3 *the fourth year of King Darius:* At this time, the people had been working on rebuilding the temple for two years (see Hag 1:1-15).

7:2,3 *Bethel:* Bethel was an important city in the religious history of the Israelites. Abraham built an altar here when he entered Canaan (Gen 12:8). Jacob, Abraham's grandson, built an altar at Bethel after God appeared to him there at two different times (Gen 28:10-22; 35:1-16). The ark of the covenant was kept in Bethel for a period of time (Judg 20:26, 27). Deborah (Judg 4:5) and Samuel (1 Sam 7:16) served as judges in Bethel. People worshiped God properly in Bethel until Jeroboam built two golden calf statues and began worshiping idols there (1 Kgs 12:29-33). Bethel was destroyed during the exile, but some Israelites returned there after being released by the Persians. See the map on p. 2467.

7:2-9 *mourn and fast . . . Administer true justice:* The people of Judah had observed a time of fasting (going without eating) during the fifth and seventh months of every year since the temple in Jerusalem was destroyed (see the note at 1:11-16). The men from Bethel ask Zechariah whether they need to continue this custom as a way to remember the destruction of the temple. Zechariah answers that fasting does not take the place of obeying God's law and treating each other with justice, mercy, and compassion.

11 Take the silver and gold and make a crown, and set it on the head
of the high priest, Joshua son of Jehozadak. 12 Tell him this is what
the LORD Almighty says: 'Here is the man whose name is the
Branch, and he will branch out from his place and build the temple of the LORD. 13 It is he who will build the temple of the LORD,
and he will be clothed with majesty and will sit and rule on his
throne. And he will be a priest on his throne. And there will be
harmony between the two.' 14 The crown will be given to Heldai,[a]
Tobijah, Jedaiah and Hen[b] son of Zephaniah as a memorial in the
temple of the LORD. 15 Those who are far away will come and help
to build the temple of the LORD, and you will know that the LORD
Almighty has sent me to you. This will happen if you diligently
obey the LORD your God."

QUESTIONS AND PROMISES

This section has three parts. Zechariah answers a question about what is necessary for proper worship of God (7:1-14). Zechariah delivers seven promises of future happiness for Jerusalem and Judah (8:1-17). Then, Zechariah delivers God's promise that the time of mourning and fasting to remember the old temple will become a time of joy and celebration.

Justice and Mercy, Not Fasting

7 In the fourth year of King Darius, the word of the LORD came
to Zechariah on the fourth day of the ninth month, the month of
Kislev. 2 The people of Bethel had sent Sharezer and Regem-
Melech, together with their men, to entreat the LORD 3 by asking
the priests of the house of the LORD Almighty and the prophets,
"Should I mourn and fast in the fifth month, as I have done for so
many years?"

4 Then the word of the LORD Almighty came to me: 5 "Ask all
the people of the land and the priests, 'When you fasted and
mourned in the fifth and seventh months for the past seventy
years, was it really for me that you fasted? 6 And when you were eating and drinking, were you not just feasting for yourselves? 7 Are
these not the words the LORD proclaimed through the earlier
prophets when Jerusalem and its surrounding towns were at rest
and prosperous, and the Negev and the western foothills were settled?' "

8 And the word of the LORD came again to Zechariah: 9 "This
is what the LORD Almighty says: 'Administer true justice; show
mercy and compassion to one another. 10 Do not oppress the
widow or the fatherless, the alien or the poor. In your hearts do
not think evil of each other.'

11 "But they refused to pay attention; stubbornly they turned

[a]**14** Syriac; Hebrew *Helem* [b]**14** Or *and the gracious one, the*

their backs and stopped up their ears. 12They made their hearts as
hard as flint and would not listen to the law or to the words that
the LORD Almighty had sent by his Spirit through the earlier
prophets. So the LORD Almighty was very angry.
13“ ‘When I called, they did not listen; so when they called, I
would not listen,’ says the LORD Almighty. 14‘I scattered them with
a whirlwind among all the nations, where they were strangers. The
land was left so desolate behind them that no one could come or
go. This is how they made the pleasant land desolate.’ ”

The LORD Promises to Bless Jerusalem

8 Again the word of the LORD Almighty came to me. 2This is
what the LORD Almighty says: “I am very jealous for Zion; I am
burning with jealousy for her.”
3This is what the LORD says: “I will return to Zion and dwell
in Jerusalem. Then Jerusalem will be called the City of Truth, and
the mountain of the LORD Almighty will be called the Holy Mountain.”
4This is what the LORD Almighty says: “Once again men and
women of ripe old age will sit in the streets of Jerusalem, each with
cane in hand because of his age. 5The city streets will be filled with
boys and girls playing there.”
6This is what the LORD Almighty says: “It may seem marvelous to the remnant of this people at that time, but will it seem
marvelous to me?” declares the LORD Almighty.
7This is what the LORD Almighty says: “I will save my people
from the countries of the east and the west. 8I will bring them back
to live in Jerusalem; they will be my people, and I will be faithful
and righteous to them as their God.”
9This is what the LORD Almighty says: “You who now hear
these words spoken by the prophets who were there when the
foundation was laid for the house of the LORD Almighty, let your
hands be strong so that the temple may be built. 10Before that time
there were no wages for man or beast. No one could go about his
business safely because of his enemy, for I had turned every man
against his neighbor. 11But now I will not deal with the remnant of
this people as I did in the past,” declares the LORD Almighty.
12“The seed will grow well, the vine will yield its fruit, the
ground will produce its crops, and the heavens will drop their dew.
I will give all these things as an inheritance to the remnant of this
people. 13As you have been an object of cursing among the
nations, O Judah and Israel, so will I save you, and you will be a
blessing. Do not be afraid, but let your hands be strong.”
14This is what the LORD Almighty says: “Just as I had determined to bring disaster upon you and showed no pity when your
fathers angered me,” says the LORD Almighty, 15“so now I have
determined to do good again to Jerusalem and Judah. Do not be

8:1 *the LORD Almighty:* See the note on p. 1793.

8:2-7 *Zion ... Jerusalem ... the east and the west:* See the note at 1:17. The lands in the east probably refer to Babylon (see the note at 2:6,7). The lands in the west refer to Egypt. The LORD promises to bring back to Jerusalem the people of Judah who were scattered to other lands when Judah was defeated by the Babylonians (8:8).

8:9,10 *when the foundation was laid for the house of the LORD Almighty:* These verses seem to describe the situation in 520 B.C. The foundation of the temple had been laid soon after the people returned to Jerusalem from exile in Babylon in about 538 B.C., but work on the temple stopped, so harvests went bad and everyone suffered (Hag 1:1-11). But if the people finished the work of building the temple the LORD would bless them once again (Hag 2:18,19; Zech 8:11,12).

8:13 *Judah and Israel:* After King Solomon died about 930 B.C., the united kingdom of Israel was divided into two nations. The northern tribes were known as Israel, while the southern tribes were known as Judah (see the map on p. 2467). Israel was defeated by the Assyrians in 722 B.C., and Judah was defeated by the Babylonians in 586 B.C., because the people had made the LORD angry (8:14). The nations made fun of God's people, but now the LORD promises to save a "remnant" (8:11) who have survived the time of punishment and to make them a blessing to the same nations that had cursed them (see also Gen 12:3).

8:19 *fasts . . . happy festivals:* The men from Bethel asked only about going without eating (fasting) in order to remember the destruction of the temple (7:2, 3). Here, Zechariah says that all times of fasting will now be times of joy. Other nations will notice how God is blessing his people in Jerusalem and will ask to join them (8:20-23).

9:1-6 *Hadrach . . . Damascus . . . Philistines:* The cities and nations mentioned in these verses had been enemies of Israel and Judah. Hadrach was located north of both Damascus and Hamath (see also Isa 17:1-3; Jer 49:23-27). Tyre and Sidon were Phoenician cities. Other prophets also spoke of the LORD's judgment against these cities (Isa 23:1-18; Ezek 26:1—28:26; Joel 3:4-8; Amos 1:9,10). Ashkelon, Gaza, Ekron, and Ashdod were Philistine cities. The Philistines settled in the area west of Judah and often battled with the people of Israel (see also Isa 14:29-31; Jer 47:1-7; Ezek 25:15-17; Joel 3:4-8; Amos 1:6-8; Zeph 2:4-7). See the maps on pp. 2467 and 2469.

9:1 *tribes of Israel:* The nation of Israel was divided into twelve tribes, which were descended from the twelve sons of Jacob (Gen 48,49). Though the tribes of Levi and Joseph did not get land in Canaan, the tribes of Joseph's two sons, Ephraim and Manasseh, each received land, so that is why the number of Israel's tribes is twelve.

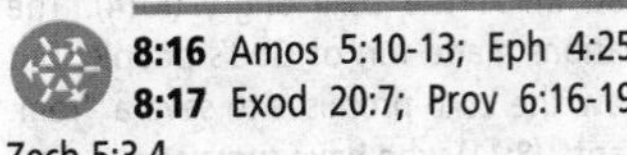

8:16 Amos 5:10-13; Eph 4:25. **8:17** Exod 20:7; Prov 6:16-19; Zech 5:3,4.

afraid. [16]These are the things you are to do: Speak the truth to each
other, and render true and sound judgment in your courts; [17]do not
plot evil against your neighbor, and do not love to swear falsely.
I hate all this," declares the LORD.

[18]Again the word of the LORD Almighty came to me. [19]This is
what the LORD Almighty says: "The fasts of the fourth, fifth, seventh and tenth months will become joyful and glad occasions and
happy festivals for Judah. Therefore love truth and peace."

[20]This is what the LORD Almighty says: "Many peoples and
the inhabitants of many cities will yet come, [21]and the inhabitants
of one city will go to another and say, 'Let us go at once to entreat
the LORD and seek the LORD Almighty. I myself am going.' [22]And
many peoples and powerful nations will come to Jerusalem to seek
the LORD Almighty and to entreat him."

[23]This is what the LORD Almighty says: "In those days ten
men from all languages and nations will take firm hold of one Jew
by the hem of his robe and say, 'Let us go with you, because we
have heard that God is with you.' "

Visions of Israel's Future

The second part of ZECHARIAH (chapters 9–14) presents two messages about the future of the people of Israel (see 9:1; 12:1). These messages tell of the LORD defeating Israel's enemies and punishing worthless shepherds (leaders). Jerusalem will be attacked, but the LORD will save the city and create a new future for Jerusalem and its people.

PUNISHMENT AND VICTORY

Israel's enemies will be punished. The LORD will send a new king to bring peace to the nations. The LORD will protect Israel and Judah but bring disaster to the leaders who caused the people to sin.

Judgment on Israel's Enemies

An Oracle

9 The word of the LORD is against the land of Hadrach
and will rest upon Damascus—
for the eyes of men and all the tribes of Israel
are on the LORD—[a]
[2]and upon Hamath too, which borders on it,
and upon Tyre and Sidon, though they are very
skillful.
[3]Tyre has built herself a stronghold;

[a]1 Or *Damascus. / For the eye of the LORD is on all mankind, / as well as on the tribes of Israel,*

she has heaped up silver like dust,
and gold like the dirt of the streets.
4 But the Lord will take away her possessions
and destroy her power on the sea,
and she will be consumed by fire.
5 Ashkelon will see it and fear;
Gaza will writhe in agony,
and Ekron too, for her hope will wither.
Gaza will lose her king
and Ashkelon will be deserted.
6 Foreigners will occupy Ashdod,
and I will cut off the pride of the Philistines.
7 I will take the blood from their mouths,
the forbidden food from between their teeth.
Those who are left will belong to our God
and become leaders in Judah,
and Ekron will be like the Jebusites.
8 But I will defend my house
against marauding forces.
Never again will an oppressor overrun my people,
for now I am keeping watch.

The Coming of Zion's King

9 Rejoice greatly, O Daughter of Zion!
Shout, Daughter of Jerusalem!
See, your king[a] comes to you,
righteous and having salvation,
gentle and riding on a donkey,
on a colt, the foal of a donkey.
10 I will take away the chariots from Ephraim
and the war-horses from Jerusalem,
and the battle bow will be broken.
He will proclaim peace to the nations.
His rule will extend from sea to sea
and from the River[b] to the ends of the earth.[c]
11 As for you, because of the blood of my covenant with you,
I will free your prisoners from the waterless pit.
12 Return to your fortress, O prisoners of hope;
even now I announce that I will restore twice as much
to you.
13 I will bend Judah as I bend my bow
and fill it with Ephraim.
I will rouse your sons, O Zion,
against your sons, O Greece,
and make you like a warrior's sword.

a9 Or *King* **b10** That is, the Euphrates **c10** Or *the end of the land*

9:6,7 *Foreigners . . . blood . . . forbidden food:* The term "foreigners" may refer to a group of half-Jewish people, or it may refer to settlers from other nations who will come to Ashdod and take the place of its citizens after God has destroyed it. The Philistines (9:7) will become part of Judah and obey the Law of Moses, which forbids eating meat with blood in it and eating some other kinds of foods (Lev 11:1-23; Deut 14:3-21). Because blood was thought to be the source of life, it was to be returned to God when meat was eaten (Lev 17:10-14). See also the mini-article called "Blood," p. 180.

9:7 *Jebusites:* These people lived near Jerusalem in Canaan before it was captured by Israel's King David (2 Sam 5:6-10).

9:9,10 *your king comes to you, righteous and having salvation, gentle and riding on a donkey:* Israel's new king rides a donkey rather than a war chariot. This is a sign of the peace that he will bring to Jerusalem and the nations. The exact identity of this king is not certain, but he sounds like the chosen king (Messiah) described by other prophets (Isa 9:6, 7; 11:1-9; Mic 5:2-5; see also Ps 72:8). In reality, no earthly leader of Judah ever again ruled over a large nation that stretched from the Mediterranean Sea east to the Euphrates River.

New Testament writers understood Jesus to be the one God chose to bring peace and to restore Israel and the nations (Matt 21:5; John 12:15).

9:13 *Greece:* The Greeks ruled the land of Israel beginning in 333 B.C. with Alexander the Great's conquest of the region, long after Zechariah lived. At the time of Zechariah, Judah was not threatened by the Greeks, so some scholars believe this message refers to this future time of Greek rule. Other scholars suggest that the later chapters of ZECHARIAH (9–14) were written long after Zechariah lived.

The LORD Will Appear

14 Then the LORD will appear over them;
his arrow will flash like lightning.
The Sovereign LORD will sound the trumpet;
he will march in the storms of the south,
15 and the LORD Almighty will shield them.
They will destroy
and overcome with slingstones.
They will drink and roar as with wine;
they will be full like a bowl
used for sprinkling[a] the corners of the altar.
16 The LORD their God will save them on that day
as the flock of his people.
They will sparkle in his land
like jewels in a crown.
17 How attractive and beautiful they will be!
Grain will make the young men thrive,
and new wine the young women.

The LORD Will Care for Judah

10 Ask the LORD for rain in the springtime;
it is the LORD who makes the storm clouds.
He gives showers of rain to men,
and plants of the field to everyone.
2 The idols speak deceit,
diviners see visions that lie;
they tell dreams that are false,
they give comfort in vain.
Therefore the people wander like sheep
oppressed for lack of a shepherd.

3 "My anger burns against the shepherds,
and I will punish the leaders;
for the LORD Almighty will care
for his flock, the house of Judah,
and make them like a proud horse
in battle.
4 From Judah will come the cornerstone,
from him the tent peg,
from him the battle bow,
from him every ruler.
5 Together they[b] will be like mighty men
trampling the muddy streets in battle.
Because the LORD is with them,
they will fight and overthrow the horsemen.

[a] 15 Or *bowl, / like* [b] 4,5 Or *ruler, all of them together. / [5] They*

9:14-17 *lightning . . . storms of the south:* The LORD's appearance in a cloud and sounding a trumpet is similar to the description of his appearance in Exodus 19:16-20. God is telling Zechariah that even though the people will have a part in destroying their enemies (9:13), the power to do so will come from God.

10:1,2 *Ask the LORD for rain . . . idols speak deceit:* The people are to pray to God if they need rain, instead of offering sacrifices to idols or relying on fortunetellers and witchcraft. See also Ps 104; Isa 44:1-21. They are compared to sheep without a shepherd, because they have not looked to God for help.

10:3 *leaders:* The leaders may be the leaders of enemy nations or the leaders of Judah who have failed to be good shepherds of the people (11:4-17). See also Ezek 34:1-10.

10:6 *house of Judah . . . house of Joseph:* "House of Joseph" refers to Israel. See the note at 8:13.

10:9,10 *distant lands . . . Egypt . . . Assyria:* The people of Israel and Judah were scattered to distant countries after being defeated by the Assyrians and Babylonians (see the note at 8:13). Egypt and Assyria were two of the nations where the people ran.

10:10 *Gilead and Lebanon:* Gilead bordered Israel on the east across the Jordan River. Lebanon was the area along Israel's northern border (see the map on p. 2467). So many people will return to Israel that they will overflow its old borders.

10:11 *sea of trouble . . . depths of the Nile will dry up:* This probably refers to the period of punishment that led to the exile (see the notes at 1:11-16; 2:6,7). But the LORD would punish Israel's enemies, symbolized by the drying up of Egypt's main source of fresh water, the Nile River, and by the eventual defeat of Assyria (Nah 1:7—3:19).

10:2 Matt 9:36; Mark 6:34.

[6]“I will strengthen the house of Judah
and save the house of Joseph.
I will restore them
because I have compassion on them.
They will be as though
I had not rejected them,
for I am the LORD their God
and I will answer them.
[7]The Ephraimites will become like mighty men,
and their hearts will be glad as with wine.
Their children will see it and be joyful;
their hearts will rejoice in the LORD.
[8]I will signal for them
and gather them in.
Surely I will redeem them;
they will be as numerous as before.
[9]Though I scatter them among the peoples,
yet in distant lands they will remember me.
They and their children will survive,
and they will return.
[10]I will bring them back from Egypt
and gather them from Assyria.
I will bring them to Gilead and Lebanon,
and there will not be room enough for them.
[11]They will pass through the sea of trouble;
the surging sea will be subdued
and all the depths of the Nile will dry up.
Assyria's pride will be brought down
and Egypt's scepter will pass away.
[12]I will strengthen them in the LORD
and in his name they will walk,”
declares the LORD.

11 Open your doors, O Lebanon,
so that fire may devour your cedars!
[2]Wail, O pine tree, for the cedar has fallen;
the stately trees are ruined!
Wail, oaks of Bashan;
the dense forest has been cut down!
[3]Listen to the wail of the shepherds;
their rich pastures are destroyed!
Listen to the roar of the lions;
the lush thicket of the Jordan is ruined!

Two Shepherds

[4]This is what the LORD my God says: “Pasture the flock
marked for slaughter. [5]Their buyers slaughter them and go unpunished. Those who sell them say, ‘Praise the LORD, I am rich!’ Their

11:1-3 *cedar . . . forest:* The images in 11:1-3 show the losses that Israel's enemies will feel. Trees as wonderful as Lebanon's cedars will fall and rot. Shepherds will have no pastures for their sheep, and lions will have no forests to roam. Lebanon's tall cedars were used to build Solomon's temple (1 Kgs 5:10-18) and probably the new temple built at the time of Zechariah (see the note at 1:2-6).

11:4-17 *shepherds . . . worthless shepherd:* This difficult passage appears to be a warning to the people and their leaders to obey God, so that God won't abandon them. The person asked to represent God and be a shepherd to the people may be the prophet Zechariah himself, but this is not certain. The people are in danger of being destroyed because the sheep buyers (perhaps community leaders) care more about money than they do about the people (11:4,5,7). The shepherd names the sticks he uses to tend the sheep "Favor" and "Union" (11:7). These names represent the kind of relationships God wanted the people to have with him and with each other (8:14-17). The warning is made clear when the shepherd breaks the two sticks. The people see that the breaking of "Favor" is a sign that God is breaking the covenant with them (11:8-10). The breaking of "Union" may suggest a despair that the restoration of the kingdoms of Judah and Israel into one kingdom will never come about (11:14).

The final verses of this passage (11:15-17) tell how the same shepherd will then become a "worthless" leader who will be cursed for his mistreatment of the sheep. This shepherd may also be the one referred to in 13:7.

See Ezekiel 34:1–10 for a similar description of Israel's leaders as worthless shepherds.

12:1 *stretches out the heavens . . . forms the spirit of man within him:* The LORD God of Israel is the creator of the earth (Gen 1:1-31; Isa 42:5; Jer 10:12).

12:2,3 *a cup . . . an immovable rock:* A cup of wine is often used as a symbol of God's judgment (Isa 51:17,22; Jer 25:15-29; Rev 14:10; 16:19).

12:6 *flaming torch . . . sheaves:* Here, those nations that attack Judah will get burned like dry hay. See also the mini-article called "Fire," p. 2383.

12:7 *house of David:* David was Israel's greatest king. The LORD promised David that one of his descendants would always rule Israel (2 Sam 7:11-16). But in this vision of the future, all of God's people will be as strong as David, and David's kingdom won't simply be led by an earthly ruler. God and God's angel will rule (12:8).

12:10-13 *house of David . . . the one they have pierced:* Here, the "house of David" probably refers to the kingdom of David (12:7). The identity of "the one they have pierced" is not certain and neither is it clear who killed him. It may refer to the prophet Zechariah or someone from the future. New Testament writers saw the suffering and death of Jesus as a fulfillment of the death of this unknown person (John 19:37; Rev 1:7). See also Isa 52:13—53:12.

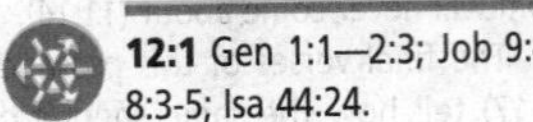
12:1 Gen 1:1—2:3; Job 9:4-9; Ps 8:3-5; Isa 44:24.

own shepherds do not spare them. 6For I will no longer have pity
on the people of the land," declares the LORD. "I will hand everyone
over to his neighbor and his king. They will oppress the land, and
I will not rescue them from their hands."

7So I pastured the flock marked for slaughter, particularly
the oppressed of the flock. Then I took two staffs and called one
Favor and the other Union, and I pastured the flock. 8In one
month I got rid of the three shepherds.

The flock detested me, and I grew weary of them 9and said,
"I will not be your shepherd. Let the dying die, and the perishing
perish. Let those who are left eat one another's flesh."

10Then I took my staff called Favor and broke it, revoking
the covenant I had made with all the nations. 11It was revoked on
that day, and so the afflicted of the flock who were watching me
knew it was the word of the LORD.

12I told them, "If you think it best, give me my pay; but if
not, keep it." So they paid me thirty pieces of silver.

13And the LORD said to me, "Throw it to the potter"—the
handsome price at which they priced me! So I took the thirty
pieces of silver and threw them into the house of the LORD to the
potter.

14Then I broke my second staff called Union, breaking the
brotherhood between Judah and Israel.

15Then the LORD said to me, "Take again the equipment of a
foolish shepherd. 16For I am going to raise up a shepherd over the
land who will not care for the lost, or seek the young, or heal the
injured, or feed the healthy, but will eat the meat of the choice
sheep, tearing off their hoofs.

17"Woe to the worthless shepherd,
who deserts the flock!
May the sword strike his arm and his right eye!
May his arm be completely withered,
his right eye totally blinded!"

THE LORD WILL RULE AS KING IN JERUSALEM

Nations will attack Jerusalem, but the attack will give the LORD an opportunity to punish Judah's enemies and protect Judah. Many people of Judah will suffer and die, but the LORD's final victory will do away with idols. Those who survive will be purified and dedicated to the LORD. Living water will flow from Jerusalem, and everyone on earth will worship the LORD as King.

Jerusalem's Enemies to Be Destroyed

An Oracle

12 This is the word of the LORD concerning Israel. The LORD,
who stretches out the heavens, who lays the foundation of the

earth, and who forms the spirit of man within him, declares: 2“I
am going to make Jerusalem a cup that sends all the surrounding
peoples reeling. Judah will be besieged as well as Jerusalem. 3On
that day, when all the nations of the earth are gathered against her,
I will make Jerusalem an immovable rock for all the nations. All
who try to move it will injure themselves. 4On that day I will strike
every horse with panic and its rider with madness,” declares the
LORD. “I will keep a watchful eye over the house of Judah, but I will
blind all the horses of the nations. 5Then the leaders of Judah will
say in their hearts, ‘The people of Jerusalem are strong, because the
LORD Almighty is their God.’

6“On that day I will make the leaders of Judah like a firepot
in a woodpile, like a flaming torch among sheaves. They will consume right and left all the surrounding peoples, but Jerusalem will
remain intact in her place.

7“The LORD will save the dwellings of Judah first, so that the
honor of the house of David and of Jerusalem's inhabitants may
not be greater than that of Judah. 8On that day the LORD will shield
those who live in Jerusalem, so that the feeblest among them will
be like David, and the house of David will be like God, like the
Angel of the LORD going before them. 9On that day I will set out to
destroy all the nations that attack Jerusalem.

Mourning for the One They Pierced

10“And I will pour out on the house of David and the inhabitants of Jerusalem a spirit[a] of grace and supplication. They will
look on[b] me, the one they have pierced, and they will mourn for
him as one mourns for an only child, and grieve bitterly for him as
one grieves for a firstborn son. 11On that day the weeping in
Jerusalem will be great, like the weeping of Hadad Rimmon in the
plain of Megiddo. 12The land will mourn, each clan by itself, with
their wives by themselves: the clan of the house of David and their
wives, the clan of the house of Nathan and their wives, 13the clan
of the house of Levi and their wives, the clan of Shimei and their
wives, 14and all the rest of the clans and their wives.

Cleansing From Sin

13 “On that day a fountain will be opened to the house of
David and the inhabitants of Jerusalem, to cleanse them from sin
and impurity.

2“On that day, I will banish the names of the idols from the
land, and they will be remembered no more,” declares the LORD
Almighty. “I will remove both the prophets and the spirit of impurity from the land. 3And if anyone still prophesies, his father and
mother, to whom he was born, will say to him, ‘You must die,

[a]10 Or *the Spirit* [b]10 Or *to*

12:12,13 *house of Nathan . . . Levi . . . Shimei:* Nathan here probably refers to the prophet during the rule of King David (2 Sam 7), but it might also refer to David's son by the same name (2 Sam 5:14). Levi was the son of Jacob and Leah (Gen 29:34). God chose the tribe of Levi to be Israel's priests (Num 3:11-13). Here, the family of Levi may refer to the priests as a group. Shimei was Levi's grandson (Exod 6:17) and one of David's temple musicians (1 Chr 6:32-43). Here, the family of Shimei may refer to others who worked in the temple.

12:11 *Hadad Rimmon:* Hadad Rimmon is a foreign god who is not mentioned anywhere else in the Old Testament. In some ancient religions, it was believed that certain gods died and could be brought back to life if people cried and mourned for them. See also the mini-article called "Canaanite Gods and Goddesses," p. 469.

12:11 *Megiddo:* Megiddo was a famous battle site (Judg 5:19; 2 Kgs 23:29). See the map on p. 2464.

13:2-5 *banish the names of the idols . . . not a prophet:* Worshiping idols was one of the sins that defiled the land of Judah and made it ritually "unclean" (Ezek 36:17-19). Restoring Judah and Jerusalem meant getting rid of all idols.

The false prophets claimed to have received messages from their gods in dreams or visions (13:4). Such prophets may have "wounded" themselves (13:6) by slashing their bodies as part of a worship ceremony (1 Kgs 18:28). For other examples of false prophets, see Jer 14:11-18; 23:9-32; Ezek 13:1-16.

because you have told lies in the LORD's name.' When he prophesies, his own parents will stab him.

[4]"On that day every prophet will be ashamed of his prophetic vision. He will not put on a prophet's garment of hair in order to deceive. [5]He will say, 'I am not a prophet. I am a farmer; the land has been my livelihood since my youth.[a]' [6]If someone asks him, 'What are these wounds on your body[b]?' he will answer, 'The wounds I was given at the house of my friends.'

The Shepherd Struck, the Sheep Scattered

[7]"Awake, O sword, against my shepherd,
against the man who is close to me!"
declares the LORD Almighty.
"Strike the shepherd,
and the sheep will be scattered,
and I will turn my hand against the little ones.
[8]In the whole land," declares the LORD,
"two-thirds will be struck down and perish;
yet one-third will be left in it.
[9]This third I will bring into the fire;
I will refine them like silver
and test them like gold.
They will call on my name
and I will answer them;
I will say, 'They are my people,'
and they will say, 'The LORD is our God.'"

The LORD Comes and Reigns

14 A day of the LORD is coming when your plunder will be divided among you.

[2]I will gather all the nations to Jerusalem to fight against it; the city will be captured, the houses ransacked, and the women raped. Half of the city will go into exile, but the rest of the people will not be taken from the city.

[3]Then the LORD will go out and fight against those nations, as he fights in the day of battle. [4]On that day his feet will stand on the Mount of Olives, east of Jerusalem, and the Mount of Olives will be split in two from east to west, forming a great valley, with half of the mountain moving north and half moving south. [5]You will flee by my mountain valley, for it will extend to Azel. You will flee as you fled from the earthquake[c] in the days of Uzziah king of Judah. Then the LORD my God will come, and all the holy ones with him.

[a]5 Or *farmer; a man sold me in my youth* [b]6 Or *wounds between your hands*
[c]5 Or [5]*My mountain valley will be blocked and will extend to Azel. It will be blocked as it was blocked because of the earthquake*

13:7 *sword . . . LORD Almighty . . . sheep:* See the note at 1:1-3. Here, the sword is used as a weapon to bring about God's justice. See also Isa 34:6.

The "shepherd" appears to be a faithful leader who suffers even though he has been faithful. The sheep are God's people. Only a third of them will survive the time of testing (13:8). See the note at 11:4-17; see also Matt 26:31; Mark 14:27.

13:9 *refine them like silver and test them like gold:* Around 1000 B.C., the people in the ancient world had discovered a process of purifying precious metals known as "smelting." In smelting, gold and silver are melted in a hot fire, which burns off unwanted metals and impurities such as dust. Zechariah is saying that the survivors of the destruction (13:7,8) will be like the pure silver and gold that remain after being tested (smelted) by fire.

14:1-7 *A day of the LORD . . . Jerusalem to fight:* Here, the day of the LORD brings an attack against Jerusalem and its people. Though many will die or be dragged off, this final attack is not a dark day because the LORD will take charge and turn the battle around (14:5), just as he has done in the past (Judg 5:4,5; 1 Sam 7:9,10; 2 Kgs 19:35). See also the mini-article called "Day of the LORD," p. 1727.

14:4,5 *Mount of Olives . . . Azel:* See the map on p. 2466. The location of Azel is unknown.

14:5 *earthquake in the days of Uzziah:* Uzziah was king of Judah from 792 to 740 B.C. The earthquake is probably the earthquake of 760 B.C., which seems to have been very destructive (Amos 1:1).

[6]On that day there will be no light, no cold or frost. [7]It will
be a unique day, without daytime or nighttime—a day known to
the LORD. When evening comes, there will be light.
[8]On that day living water will flow out from Jerusalem, half
to the eastern sea[a] and half to the western sea,[b] in summer and in
winter.
[9]The LORD will be king over the whole earth. On that day
there will be one LORD, and his name the only name.
[10]The whole land, from Geba to Rimmon, south of Jerusalem, will become like the Arabah. But Jerusalem will be raised up
and remain in its place, from the Benjamin Gate to the site of the
First Gate, to the Corner Gate, and from the Tower of Hananel to
the royal winepresses. [11]It will be inhabited; never again will it be
destroyed. Jerusalem will be secure.
[12]This is the plague with which the LORD will strike all the
nations that fought against Jerusalem: Their flesh will rot while
they are still standing on their feet, their eyes will rot in their sockets, and their tongues will rot in their mouths. [13]On that day men
will be stricken by the LORD with great panic. Each man will seize
the hand of another, and they will attack each other. [14]Judah too
will fight at Jerusalem. The wealth of all the surrounding nations
will be collected—great quantities of gold and silver and clothing.
[15]A similar plague will strike the horses and mules, the camels and
donkeys, and all the animals in those camps.
[16]Then the survivors from all the nations that have attacked
Jerusalem will go up year after year to worship the King, the LORD
Almighty, and to celebrate the Feast of Tabernacles. [17]If any of the

[a]8 That is, the Dead Sea [b]8 That is, the Mediterranean

14:8-11 *living water will flow out from Jerusalem . . . from Geba to Rimmon:* God's victory will even change nature. Living water will flow from Jerusalem, and the hilly land from Geba to Rimmon will be flattened out. Geba and Rimmon mark the northern and southern borders of Judah before the exile (2 Kgs 23:8).

14:10,11 *Benjamin Gate . . . royal winepresses:* The Benjamin Gate was in the north wall, and the Corner Gate was on the northwest wall. It is not known where the First Gate was. The Tower of Hananel was near the Benjamin Gate (Neh 3:1). The royal winepresses were probably in the southeast corner of the city.

14:16 *worship the King . . . Feast of Tabernacles:* The whole world will worship the LORD and recognize the LORD as King (14:9,16). The Feast of Tabernacles took place at the end of the fall harvest (Exod 23:16; Deut 16:13-7). In addition to giving thanks to God for the fall harvest, the people were to build and live in shelters made of tree branches during the celebration (Lev 23:39-43; Neh 8).

14:10,11 Rev 22:3.

QUESTIONS ABOUT ZECHARIAH

1. What was the situation in Judah at the time of Zechariah's visions? (1:1—6:8) Take a moment to read the short book of HAGGAI, beginning on p. 1787. What parts of Zechariah's message are like the message of the prophet Haggai?
2. Who were Joshua and Zerubbabel? (3:1—4:14; 6:9-15) What roles were they to play in the future of the people of Israel, according to Zechariah's visions and messages?
3. How might our society be different today if religious leaders were in charge of leading our country and government? In your opinion, would this be a good change or not? Explain your answer.
4. Summarize what Zechariah says will happen to Jerusalem and its people in the future (9:1—14:21). What part will the LORD play in future events? How will the nations of the earth respond to the LORD? (14:9,16)
5. Choose one vision or image from ZECHARIAH and tell why it was especially meaningful to you.
6. The name Zechariah means "The LORD remembers." (See the note on p. 1792.) In what ways does God remember you? How would you like to be remembered by others?

14:20,21 *Holy to the Lord:* These words are the same ones that were written on a strip of gold worn by the high priest (Exod 28:36-38).

14:20,21 *cooking pots . . . sacred bowls:* Merchants sold special metal pots that were acceptable for offering sacrifices to the LORD. But after the LORD's victory purifies Jerusalem (13:9), all pots and bowls will be considered acceptable for use in the temple, and all God's people will truly be a "holy nation" and serve the LORD as priests (Exod 19:5, 6). The shapes of the bowl, cooking pot, and jug shown below are similar to those used in Palestine in the fifth and sixth centuries B.C.

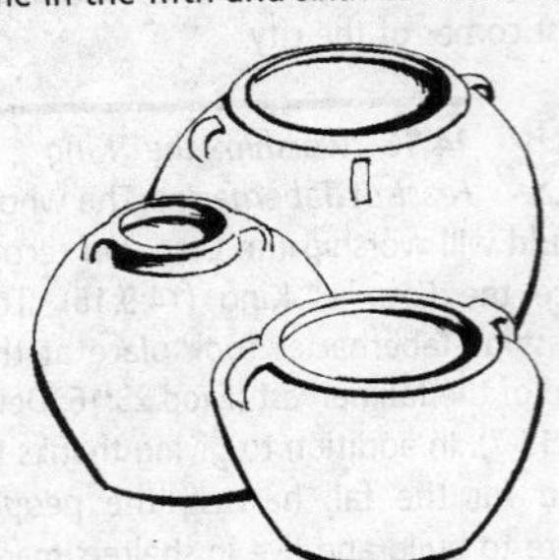

peoples of the earth do not go up to Jerusalem to worship the
King, the LORD Almighty, they will have no rain. [18]If the Egyptian
people do not go up and take part, they will have no rain. The
LORD[a] will bring on them the plague he inflicts on the nations that
do not go up to celebrate the Feast of Tabernacles. [19]This will be
the punishment of Egypt and the punishment of all the nations
that do not go up to celebrate the Feast of Tabernacles.

[20]On that day HOLY TO THE LORD will be inscribed on the
bells of the horses, and the cooking pots in the LORD's house will
be like the sacred bowls in front of the altar. [21]Every pot in
Jerusalem and Judah will be holy to the LORD Almighty, and all
who come to sacrifice will take some of the pots and cook in them.
And on that day there will no longer be a Canaanite[b] in the house
of the LORD Almighty.

---

[a]**18** Or *part, then the LORD* [b]**21** Or *merchant*

MALACHI

How does the LORD respond to those who grow careless about how they worship, break important promises, fail to make proper gifts to God, and ignore the needs of their neighbors? Read MALACHI to find out!

WHAT MAKES MALACHI SPECIAL?

MALACHI is the last book of the "Scroll of the Twelve" in the Hebrew Bible (and what Christians sometimes call the "Minor Prophets"). See the chart on p. 13 and the Introduction to the Prophetic Books, p. 1287. The name "Malachi" means "my messenger." This may be the name of the author, or it may simply be a description of the author as a "messenger" of God. This is how the word is used in the Hebrew text of Malachi 3:1.

Malachi may have intended to write his book as if he was reporting a legal case in court. His message takes the form of an argument, with charges and responses being traded back and forth between God and the people of Judah.

WHY WAS MALACHI WRITTEN?

In love, God chose the people of Israel to be his precious children. In love, God promised to bless the people if they would obey his commands, which included rules for right living and proper worship. God longed for the people to respond to his love with joyful obedience. But the people kept forgetting that God loved them, so God's rules and rituals seemed to be hard and demanding—sacrificial animals had to be perfect, offerings to support worship in the temple were supposed to be generous, and a husband's marriage promises to his wife were meant to last forever.

As the people forgot about God's love, or no longer believed in it, they also lost their desire to keep God's rules and rituals. The priests and the people simply ignored some of them and were careless about the way they carried out others. MALACHI was written to remind the people of God's love, and to call them back to a joyful obedience to God.

WHAT'S THE STORY BEHIND THE SCENE?

In 586 B.C., Jerusalem and its temple were destroyed by the Babylonians. Many of the leading citizens of Judah were taken as captives to Babylon. In 538 B.C., after the Persians defeated the Babylonians, some of the Israelites who had been taken into captivity returned to Judah and its capital city Jerusalem. The prophets Haggai and Zechariah encouraged the people to rebuild the temple in Jerusalem. They promised that a new day of success and prosperity would follow. The new temple in Jerusalem was

---

defiled food on my altar: According to God's Law, daily offerings of sheep, grain, and wine were to be made to God (Exod 29:38-43; Num 28:1-8). These offerings were meant to represent a fine meal prepared in honor of a great king (1:14). The animals offered to God were to be without defect (not blind, crippled, or sick) and would not have been acceptable if they were stolen (Lev 4:32; 22:21-24; see also 1:8,13). By offering less than the best animals for sacrifice ("defiled food"), the priests did not show proper respect for God. See also Exod 12:4,5; Deut 15:21; and the mini-article called "Temple Offerings," p. 2027.

The temple altar that Malachi would have been familiar with would have been positioned in the temple courtyard and most likely was made of acacia wood covered with bronze. Like the altars of other ancient peoples (the stone altar shown here is from Megiddo, around 1000 B.C., the temple altar had "horns" in each corner.

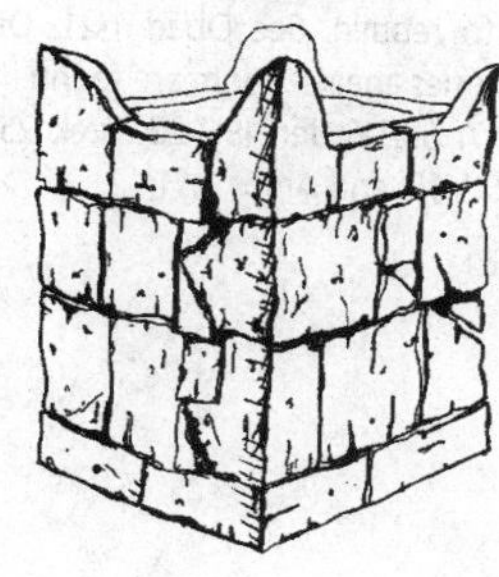

completed and dedicated in 516 B.C. But Judah did not gain its independence from Persia, nor did it become prosperous. The Jews, as the people who returned from Babylon came to be called in this period, remained a small nation and were under the control of more powerful nations (by Persia until around 333 B.C. and then by Greece until the time of Roman rule in the first century B.C.). See also the article called "After the Exile: God's People Return to Judea," p. 931.

MALACHI was probably written around 470-430 B.C., after the rebuilding of the temple and around the time of Ezra and Nehemiah (see Ezra 7:1-25; Neh 1:1-11; 8:1-13). At this time, Judah was under Persian control. Taxes were probably high (1:8), and it is likely that periods of drought and crop damage caused by locust swarms had brought about famine (3:10, 11). Life was difficult. Many people in Judah, including the spiritual leaders, began to question whether the LORD God really was concerned about them. Perhaps they wondered if it made any difference at all if they lived as God expected or worshiped God in the proper way.

HOW IS MALACHI CONSTRUCTED?

MALACHI is written as a series of questions and responses between God and the people of Israel. The message can only be understood clearly if the reader keeps asking "what is the question?" and "who is speaking now?" Some of the questions are stated clearly in the text, but sometimes the reader has to figure out the questions that prompt Malachi's messages. The following outline is a general overview of the book:

Malachi declares God's love for Israel (1:1-5)

Unfaithful priests and broken promises (1:6—2:16)

God promises to judge evil and reward good (2:17—4:6)

Malachi Declares God's Love for Israel

The people of Israel can find no evidence that God loves them. Malachi reminds them of God's love by comparing their situation to that of their relatives, the Edomites.

1 An oracle: The word of the LORD to Israel through Malachi.[a]

Jacob Loved, Esau Hated

2"I have loved you," says the LORD.
"But you ask, 'How have you loved us?'
"Was not Esau Jacob's brother?" the LORD says. "Yet I have
loved Jacob, 3but Esau I have hated, and I have turned his mountains into a wasteland and left his inheritance to the desert jackals."

[a]1 *Malachi* means *my messenger.*

1:1,2 *Israel . . . Esau . . . Jacob:* Here "Israel" refers to the people of Judah and their leaders. Specifically, it probably refers to the descendants of the people who returned to Judah after the time of exile in Babylon. For more, see the mini-article called "Israel," p. 264.

Esau and Jacob were twin grandsons of Abraham. God chose Jacob rather than Esau to be the one to receive the blessings promised to Abraham, even though Jacob was younger than Esau (Gen 25:23). Esau's descendants were the "Edomites" (see the note at 1:4). Jacob was given a new name, "Israel" (Gen 32:28), and his descendants came to be known as the Israelites. See also Rom 9:13.

1:2 *I have loved you:* Questions about God's purposes and love for Israel are often found in the Bible (Exod 5:22; Ps 22:1; 44:23,24; 74:11; 79:5,10; Jer 15:18). The people of Israel often are reminded that God loves them and has a purpose for them (Deut 7:6-8; 8:16; Isa 5:1-7; 43:4; Jer 31:3,4; Ezek 16:1-14; Hos 11:1-4).

1:3 *jackals:* Desert animals related to wolves, but smaller.

1:4 *Edom . . . we have been crushed:* See the map on p. 2463. The Edomites took advantage of the Babylonian victory over God's people in 586 B.C. by invading the conquered land of Judah (Ps 137:7; Lam 4:21,22). However, the Nabatean Arabs later drove the Edomites out of Edom and left it "crushed." The Edomites were never able to rebuild. See Obad 1-21. Other prophecies against Edom are found in Isa 34:5-17; 63:1-6; Jer 49:7-22; Ezek 25:12-14; 35:1-15; and Amos 1:11,12.

[4]Edom may say, "Though we have been crushed, we will rebuild the ruins."

But this is what the LORD Almighty says: "They may build, but I will demolish. They will be called the Wicked Land, a people always under the wrath of the LORD. [5]You will see it with your own eyes and say, 'Great is the LORD—even beyond the borders of Israel!'

Unfaithful Priests and Broken Promises

The people of Israel have forgotten how to love and honor both God and each other. God questions the priests because they do not make sacrifices in the proper way, and their false teachings are leading people to do sinful things. God also questions those who break their marriage vows.

Blemished Sacrifices

[6]"A son honors his father, and a servant his master. If I am a father, where is the honor due me? If I am a master, where is the respect due me?" says the LORD Almighty. "It is you, O priests, who show contempt for my name.

"But you ask, 'How have we shown contempt for your name?'

[7]"You place defiled food on my altar.

"But you ask, 'How have we defiled you?'

"By saying that the LORD's table is contemptible. [8]When you bring blind animals for sacrifice, is that not wrong? When you sacrifice crippled or diseased animals, is that not wrong? Try offering them to your governor! Would he be pleased with you? Would he accept you?" says the LORD Almighty.

[9]"Now implore God to be gracious to us. With such offerings from your hands, will he accept you?"—says the LORD Almighty.

[10]"Oh, that one of you would shut the temple doors, so that you would not light useless fires on my altar! I am not pleased with you," says the LORD Almighty, "and I will accept no offering from your hands. [11]My name will be great among the nations, from the rising to the setting of the sun. In every place incense and pure offerings will be brought to my name, because my name will be great among the nations," says the LORD Almighty.

[12]"But you profane it by saying of the Lord's table, 'It is defiled,' and of its food, 'It is contemptible.' [13]And you say, 'What a burden!' and you sniff at it contemptuously," says the LORD Almighty.

"When you bring injured, crippled or diseased animals and offer them as sacrifices, should I accept them from your hands?"

1:4 *the LORD Almighty:* "LORD" translates the Hebrew *Yahweh,* the personal name for Israel's God. See also the mini-article called "LORD (YHWH)," p. 140. Malachi uses the name "LORD Almighty" often to remind people that their God is not just the God of Israel, but of all people.

1:6 *priests:* Priests were responsible to help people honor and worship God. This responsibility included offering animal sacrifices to God in the way commanded by the Law of Moses. See also the mini-article called "Israel's Priests," p. 2344.

1:6-8 *father . . . master . . . governor:* The priests would have agreed that masters, fathers, and the governor were worthy of respect (see Exod 20:12). Malachi's comparison clearly reminds them that God, the LORD Almighty, is even more worthy of respect. See 3:17.

1:7 *defiled food on my altar:* See the note on p. 1811.

1:8 *governor:* The Persians appointed governors to rule the provinces of their empire. The Bible mentions four of these governors by name: Tattenai, Sheshbazzar, Nehemiah, and Zerubbabel (Ezra 5:3,13-15; Neh 5:14; Hag 1:1).

1:11 *among the nations . . . pure offerings:* Malachi tries to shame the people of Israel into action by comparing them with other nations who have no special relationship with God. Malachi says that other nations make "pure offerings," while God's people bring offerings that are far from pure.

1:10 Isa 1:11-13.

2:3 *spread on your faces the offal from your festival sacrifices:* Rubbing offal (the waste, such as entrails, from butchered animals) in the priests' faces was likely intended to disgrace the priests because of their disgraceful behavior shown toward God (1:10-14). Malachi may also have had in mind that touching the offal would have made the priests ritually "unclean." This uncleanness would have made them unfit to conduct worship.

2:4 *covenant with Levi may continue:* The Bible does not mention a covenant between God and Levi. "Levi" may refer to the whole tribe of Levi (Num 3:11-13; 8:20-26; Deut 33:8-11). Or it may refer to Phinehas, a descendant of Levi, who had been loyal to the LORD (Num 25:10-13; Ps 106:30,31).

2:7 *from his mouth men should seek instruction:* The role of both prophets and priests (Neh 8:1-8; Jer 18:18).

2:9 *shown partiality:* The priests kept a portion of the offerings the people made to God. They may have been giving preference to those who could afford large offerings rather than small ones.

2:11 *Judah . . . Jerusalem:* Jerusalem was the capital city of Judah, the name given to the southern part of Israel and to the people who returned there from exile in Babylon.

2:11 *broken faith:* To Malachi, "faithfulness" meant keeping promises and covenants. It also meant being completely loyal to God or to a partner in marriage (2:11,14-16).

2:11 *marrying the daughter of a foreign god:* Marrying foreigners was forbidden (Gen 24:2,3; 28:1,6; Josh 23:12,13). Israelites who married foreigners might be tempted to worship the foreign gods worshiped by their non-Israelite spouses.

says the LORD. 14"Cursed is the cheat who has an acceptable male in his flock and vows to give it, but then sacrifices a blemished animal to the Lord. For I am a great king," says the LORD Almighty, "and my name is to be feared among the nations.

Admonition for the Priests

2 "And now this admonition is for you, O priests. 2If you do not listen, and if you do not set your heart to honor my name," says the LORD Almighty, "I will send a curse upon you, and I will curse your blessings. Yes, I have already cursed them, because you have not set your heart to honor me.

3"Because of you I will rebuke[a] your descendants[b]; I will spread on your faces the offal from your festival sacrifices, and you will be carried off with it. 4And you will know that I have sent you this admonition so that my covenant with Levi may continue," says the LORD Almighty. 5"My covenant was with him, a covenant of life and peace, and I gave them to him; this called for reverence and he revered me and stood in awe of my name. 6True instruction was in his mouth and nothing false was found on his lips. He walked with me in peace and uprightness, and turned many from sin.

7"For the lips of a priest ought to preserve knowledge, and from his mouth men should seek instruction—because he is the messenger of the LORD Almighty. 8But you have turned from the way and by your teaching have caused many to stumble; you have violated the covenant with Levi," says the LORD Almighty. 9"So I have caused you to be despised and humiliated before all the people, because you have not followed my ways but have shown partiality in matters of the law."

Judah Unfaithful

10Have we not all one Father[c]? Did not one God create us? Why do we profane the covenant of our fathers by breaking faith with one another?

11Judah has broken faith. A detestable thing has been committed in Israel and in Jerusalem: Judah has desecrated the sanctuary the LORD loves, by marrying the daughter of a foreign god. 12As for the man who does this, whoever he may be, may the LORD cut him off from the tents of Jacob[d]—even though he brings offerings to the LORD Almighty.

13Another thing you do: You flood the LORD's altar with tears. You weep and wail because he no longer pays attention to your offerings or accepts them with pleasure from your hands. 14You ask, "Why?" It is because the LORD is acting as the witness between you and the wife of your youth, because you have broken

[a]**3** Or *cut off* (see Septuagint) [b]**3** Or *will blight your grain* [c]**10** Or *father*
[d]**12** Or 12*May the LORD cut off from the tents of Jacob anyone who gives testimony in behalf of the man who does this*

faith with her, though she is your partner, the wife of your marriage covenant.
15 Has not ⌞the LORD⌟ made them one? In flesh and spirit they
are his. And why one? Because he was seeking godly offspring.[a] So
guard yourself in your spirit, and do not break faith with the wife
of your youth.
16 "I hate divorce," says the LORD God of Israel, "and I hate a
man's covering himself[b] with violence as well as with his garment,"
says the LORD Almighty.

So guard yourself in your spirit, and do not break faith.

God Promises to Judge Evil and Reward Good

God's people see no immediate reward for obeying God and giving generous gifts to support God's temple. They question God's concern to do what is right. But Malachi says that God will send a special messenger to destroy evil. God's slowness to act has been an act of kindness: God is giving the people of Israel another chance. If they will keep his law and give generous offerings they will see God provide "so much blessing" that they will not have room enough for it (3:10). MALACHI *concludes with a final reminder of God's coming judgment. God will trample evil but reward those who obey his laws.*

The Day of Judgment

17 You have wearied the LORD with your words.
"How have we wearied him?" you ask.
By saying, "All who do evil are good in the eyes of the LORD,
and he is pleased with them" or "Where is the God of justice?"
3 "See, I will send my messenger, who will prepare the way
before me. Then suddenly the Lord you are seeking will come to
his temple; the messenger of the covenant, whom you desire, will
come," says the LORD Almighty.
2 But who can endure the day of his coming? Who can stand
when he appears? For he will be like a refiner's fire or a launderer's
soap. 3 He will sit as a refiner and purifier of silver; he will purify
the Levites and refine them like gold and silver. Then the LORD will
have men who will bring offerings in righteousness, 4 and the offerings of Judah and Jerusalem will be acceptable to the LORD, as in
days gone by, as in former years.
5 "So I will come near to you for judgment. I will be quick to
testify against sorcerers, adulterers and perjurers, against those
who defraud laborers of their wages, who oppress the widows and

[a]15 Or *15But the one ⌞who is our father⌟ did not do this, not as long as life remained in him. And what was he seeking? An offspring from God* [b]16 Or *his wife*

2:16 *I hate divorce:* Malachi sees marriage as the same kind of permanent covenant as the covenant that united God and the people of Israel. See the note at 2:11 (broken faith). See also Matt 5:31,32; 19:4-6; Mark 10:6-9.

3:1 *my messenger:* For Malachi, the "messenger" is a person who would prepare the people for the LORD's coming or return. He would prepare them by making sure that the priests and the people brought proper gifts and sacrifices to the temple and that they got rid of any foreign idols. Many years later, the early Christians described John the Baptist as this "messenger" (Matt 11:10; Mark 1:2; Luke 7:27).

3:2 *the day of his coming . . . refiner's fire or a launderer's soap:* A coming day of the LORD's judgment is a common theme in the prophets. It is usually described as a day of darkness and destruction when the LORD judges and punishes evildoers (Joel 2:1-11; Amos 5:18-20). Here, the "day" is a time when the LORD will purify or clean the descendants of Levi (3:3). See the note at 4:1 and the mini-article called "Day of the LORD," p. 1727. See also Matt 3:11,12; Luke 3:16,17; Rev 6:17.

3:3 *the Levites:* See the note at 2:4.

3:5 *sorcerers . . . do not fear me:* Each activity in this list is condemned by God's Law: sorcery (Exod 22:18; Lev 20:27); adultery (Exod 20:14); perjury (Exod 20:16; Deut 19:16-21); fraud against laborers (Deut 24:14,15); oppression of orphans and widows (Exod 22:22-24; Deut 24:17,18); injustice toward foreigners (Exod 20:10; 23:12; Deut 14:29; 24:14; 26:12,13); disrespect toward God (Exod 20:1-7).

3:1 Matt 24:42-44; 25:13; Mark 13:32-37; 1 Thes 5:3. **3:2** Isa 2:12-21; Zeph 1:8, 14; Rom 2:5; 1 Cor 1:8; Phil 1:6; 2:16; 2 Tim 1:18; 1 Pet 2:12; 2 Pet 2:9; 3:7; 1 John 4:17.

the fatherless, and deprive aliens of justice, but do not fear me,”
says the LORD Almighty.

Robbing God

6“I the LORD do not change. So you, O descendants of Jacob,
are not destroyed. 7Ever since the time of your forefathers you have
turned away from my decrees and have not kept them. Return to
me, and I will return to you,” says the LORD Almighty.
“But you ask, ‘How are we to return?’
8“Will a man rob God? Yet you rob me.
“But you ask, ‘How do we rob you?’
“In tithes and offerings. 9You are under a curse—the whole
nation of you—because you are robbing me. 10Bring the whole
tithe into the storehouse, that there may be food in my house. Test
me in this,” says the LORD Almighty, “and see if I will not throw
open the floodgates of heaven and pour out so much blessing that
you will not have room enough for it. 11I will prevent pests from

3:8 *tithes:* The people of Israel were supposed to give to the LORD a tenth (tithe) of everything they harvested, as well as animals from their flocks and herds (Lev 27:30-33; Num 18:21-24; Deut 12:5-19; 14:22-29; Neh 13:12). The ten percent belonged to God, meaning it was to be used in temple sacrifices and to support the temple priests and their families. Choosing not to give the required offerings was like "robbing" God and failing to support God's servants, the priests.

3:10 *throw open the floodgates of heaven:* This probably refers to rain, since there seems to have been a terrible drought during Malachi's time.

ELIJAH

The prophet Elijah lived in Israel from around 899 to 850 B.C. after the Israelite kingdom of David and Solomon had divided into northern (Israel) and southern (Judah) kingdoms. In Elijah's day, many people in the northern kingdom were worshiping foreign gods such as Baal and Asherah (see the mini-article called "Canaanite Gods and Goddesses," p. 469). The worship of these gods was encouraged by Israel's King Ahab and his Phoenician queen, Jezebel (1 Kgs 16:30-33). At this time, Elijah seems to have been the only prophet who had the courage to challenge the influence of powerful people.

Elijah challenged the priests of Baal to see whose god was stronger (1 Kgs 18:15-40). He confronted Ahab and Jezebel because they killed a man named Naboth just so they could take his land and vineyard (1 Kgs 21). After this, he challenged Ahab's son, Ahaziah, when Ahaziah turned to the god Baal-Zebub for guidance instead of turning to the LORD (2 Kgs 1:1-4). And finally, Elijah challenged the false worship and cruel behavior of Jehoram, king of the southern kingdom, Judah (2 Chr 21:12-15).

Elijah was also known for his miracles. He predicted a drought (1 Kgs 17:1), provided food that would not run out (1 Kgs 17:14), raised a dead boy back to life (1 Kgs 17:17-24), and called for fire to come from heaven (1 Kgs 18:36-38; 2 Kgs 1:12).

Elijah did not die but was taken to heaven in a whirlwind (2 Kgs 2:11). Many centuries later, some people believed that John the Baptist was Elijah himself come back from heaven (John 1:21), which John clearly denied. Others thought Jesus was Elijah (Matt 16:13,14; Luke 9:8). The people's identification with them as the prophet Elijah was due to the prophet Malachi's prediction that "Elijah" would come to prepare God's people for the coming of the Messiah (Mal 4:5). Jesus identified John the Baptist not as the returned Elijah himself, but as the one prophesied by Malachi who would be like Elijah (Matt 17:10-13, see also Luke 1:17). Elijah and Moses appeared on the Mount of Transfiguration with Jesus (Matt 17:3,4; Mark 9:4, 5; Luke 9:30-33).

Elijah Cup by Michel Schwartz, silver and gold, 1989. Every year at the Passover meal (Seder), Jews set out a special cup of wine for Elijah and open the front door of their homes so that the prophet can come in. According to the author of 2 KINGS, Elijah did not die but was taken up to heaven (2 Kgs 2:11). Elijah is mentioned in the final verses of the last book of the Old Testament (4:5, 6). The first book of the New Testament, MATTHEW, begins with an account of the ministry of John the Baptist who announces the coming of someone greater than himself (Jesus) who will baptize people with the Holy Spirit and fire (Matt 3:11). In Jesus' day, some people thought John, or even Jesus himself, was actually the prophet Elijah returned to announce the coming of God's judgment. See also Matt 11:13, 14; 16:14; 17:1-13.

devouring your crops, and the vines in your fields will not cast
their fruit," says the LORD Almighty. 12"Then all the nations will call
you blessed, for yours will be a delightful land," says the LORD
Almighty.
13"You have said harsh things against me," says the LORD.
"Yet you ask, 'What have we said against you?'
14"You have said, 'It is futile to serve God. What did we gain by
carrying out his requirements and going about like mourners before
the LORD Almighty? 15But now we call the arrogant blessed. Certainly the evildoers prosper, and even those who challenge God escape.' "
16Then those who feared the LORD talked with each other,
and the LORD listened and heard. A scroll of remembrance was

3:11 *pests:* Probably referring to locusts that travel in swarms and cause great damage to plant life. For more, see the mini-article called "Locusts," p. 1708.

3:16 *A scroll of remembrance:* The Bible refers to "books" or "scrolls" that contain the names of those who belong to God or to a list of their deeds (see Exod 32:32,33; Ps 40:7, 8; 69:28; 87:6; 139:16; Isa 34:16; Dan 12:1,4; Phil 4:3; Rev 3:5; 13:8; 17:8; 20:12,15; 21:27). The "book" mentioned by Malachi probably refers to the book that records good deeds.

3:15 Job 21:7-13; Ps 10:1-13; 37:1; 73:1-14; Jer 12:1; Hab 1:13.

written in his presence concerning those who feared the LORD and
honored his name.
[17]"They will be mine," says the LORD Almighty, "in the day
when I make up my treasured possession.[a] I will spare them, just as
in compassion a man spares his son who serves him. [18]And you
will again see the distinction between the righteous and the
wicked, between those who serve God and those who do not.

The Day of the LORD

4 "Surely the day is coming; it will burn like a furnace. All the
arrogant and every evildoer will be stubble, and that day that is
coming will set them on fire," says the LORD Almighty. "Not a root
or a branch will be left to them. [2]But for you who revere my name,
the sun of righteousness will rise with healing in its wings. And
you will go out and leap like calves released from the stall. [3]Then
you will trample down the wicked; they will be ashes under the
soles of your feet on the day when I do these things," says the LORD
Almighty.
[4]"Remember the law of my servant Moses, the decrees and
laws I gave him at Horeb for all Israel.
[5]"See, I will send you the prophet Elijah before that great
and dreadful day of the LORD comes. [6]He will turn the hearts of
the fathers to their children, and the hearts of the children to their
fathers; or else I will come and strike the land with a curse."

[a]17 Or *Almighty, "my treasured possession, in the day when I act*

4:1 *day is coming . . . set them on fire:* The LORD's coming day of judgment is often described as a time when the LORD will punish evil people using fire (Joel 2:1-3; Matt 13:36-42). See also the note at 3:2 and the mini-article called "Fire," p. 2383.

4:3 *trample down the wicked:* Malachi and other prophets believed that the faithful people of Israel would be God's helpers on the day of judgment (Isa 11:10-14; Mic 4:13; see also 1 Cor 6:2).

4:4 *Horeb:* Another name for Mount Sinai. See the map on p. 2463. God gave the law to Moses and the people of Israel while they camped at Sinai (Exod 19:1—20:17; 31:18; 34:29-32; Lev 26:46; 27:34; Neh 9:13). Mount Sinai was also the place where the prophet Elijah later experienced the presence of God (1 Kgs 19:7-18).

4:5 *Elijah:* See the mini-article called "Elijah," p. 1816.

3:17 Isa 43:4; Jer 31:20.

QUESTIONS ABOUT MALACHI

1. Some of God's people doubted God's love for them (1:2). What did Malachi say to respond to their doubts?
2. What were the priests doing wrong that made God wish that all their acts of worship would stop? (1:6—2:12)
3. What did Malachi say about divorce? (2:14-16) How is marriage like the relationship that the people were to have with God?
4. Keeping promises is an important theme in MALACHI. List all references to promises that you can find. What promises does God make? How are these promises related to the behavior of God's people?
5. Choose one passage from MALACHI and explain why it is meaningful to you.

The New Testament

THE WORLD OF JESUS: PEOPLES, POWERS, AND POLITICS

Jesus was born in the town of Bethlehem in the province of Judea during the reign of Augustus Caesar, the first Roman ruler called emperor. About sixty years earlier, the Romans had invaded Palestine as they continued expanding their great empire throughout the lands surrounding the Mediterranean Sea and beyond (see the map, p. 2471). At the time of Augustus, the Roman Empire ruled over fifty million people from many different nationalities—from Palestine and Syria in the east to Spain in the west, including most of northern Africa and much of Europe. Because the Romans were well-organized and had a strong army, their empire was actually very stable. Travel and trade between areas was easier than it had ever been. Historians have observed that the international peace brought by Roman rule and the superior system of Roman roads helped disciples to spread a new religion based on Jesus' teachings.

Palestine before Roman Rule

The centuries leading up to Jesus' birth were not politically stable in the area known as Palestine. The Jewish people who returned to Judah from exile in Babylonia had been allowed to rebuild their cities and the temple in Jerusalem, but they were ruled by the Persians. (See the article called "After the Exile: God's People Return to Judea," p. 931.) Then the Greeks, led by Alexander the Great, defeated the Persians and drove them out of Palestine. Alexander's generals and their descendants ruled the land for many years, bringing with them Greek (Hellenistic) culture. One Greek ruler from the Seleucid family (Antiochus IV Epiphanes) tried to force the Hellenistic way of life on the Jewish people in Palestine. When he put up a statue of a pagan god in the holy Jewish temple in 168 B.C., the Jewish people were enraged and rebelled. Led by Judas Maccabeus, the people defeated the Seleucids, reclaimed the temple, and created their own government.

When Jesus began preaching the gospel of the kingdom of God to the people of Galilee and Judea in the first century A.D. the Romans were in control of the entire Mediterranean world.

For nearly one hundred years the Jewish people were again in charge of the land, led by members of Judas Maccabeus' family (the Hasmoneans), who took over as kings and priests of Israel. Yet many thought that the Hasmonean rulers were as selfish and cruel as the foreign kings who had ruled before them, so Jews did not fight back when the Romans invaded the country in 63 B.C.

During these two centuries before Jesus was born, a number of different Jewish religious groups were formed, each having different ideas about how to interpret the Scriptures and live the Jewish faith. These groups with their competing ideas appear in the New Testament and will be discussed individually later in this article.

Roman Rule in Palestine

Though many peoples and cultures contributed to the cultural life in Palestine in Jesus' day, the Romans were by far the most powerful. They controlled the land with strong, well-trained armies. The Roman emperor appointed a governor (procurator) who was in charge of collecting taxes and preventing the people from rebelling against Rome. The Romans placed heavy taxes on land, on goods and food that were bought and sold, and on inheritances. They also charged tolls for people traveling through the areas they controlled. The taxes went to support the Roman army and to maintain control of Palestine. Farmers and the poor suffered the most under this system of taxes.

The Romans made contracts with local people in order to collect taxes. These local tax collectors would often collect much more than the amount they were supposed to turn over to the Romans. They kept the rest. In Palestine, this led to bad feelings between the Jewish people and their neighbors who agreed to collect taxes for the Romans. Tax collectors were often seen as traitors by the Jewish religious leaders. Some called them sinners, and said they were not welcome to be part of the Jewish people or to worship with them. When Jesus ate with tax collectors and welcomed them (Luke 5:27-32; 19:1-10), he offended those who wanted to keep the tax collectors apart from Jewish social life.

Roman policy was to respect local customs and the laws of the peoples they ruled. They let local people form councils to control local affairs. In Judea the local ruling council (Sanhedrin) was made up of the high priest and chief priests and wealthy supporters of the Roman government. Their participation in the work of the council made them become even wealthier.

The Romans also set up rulers in the areas that were under their control. These local kings and governors reported to the Roman senate or to the emperor's representatives. For example, in 37 B.C. the Romans appointed Herod the Great as king of Palestine, partly because Herod's father had helped the Romans take control of the region. Herod ruled until 4 B.C. and was responsible for rebuilding the temple in Jerusalem, which attracted many worshipers and visitors from all over the Roman empire during the days of Jesus. The outer court of the temple, called the Court of the Gentiles, was a place where non-Jews (Gentiles) could come to see the beauty of this great building. The high priest was the person in charge of the temple. He was able to hold this position because of the support of the Roman authorities. The income from gifts and offerings to the temple was the major source of money for the whole people of Israel.

When Herod died, his three sons were appointed by the Romans to rule Galilee and Perea, the land east of the Jordan River. The map on p. 2472 shows the lands ruled by each son. Under the Herods, the priests and their supporters on the council gained greater power and wealth. Although John the Baptist and Jesus were born during the time of Herod the Great, it was Herod's son, Herod Antipas, who was in power when they came to trial. Herod Antipas ordered the death of John the Baptist (Matt 14:1-12). During Jesus' trial, the Roman governor, Pontius Pilate, sent Jesus to see Herod Antipas because Jesus was from Galilee, the area under this Herod's rule. Usually, the Roman governors did not want to get mixed up in local problems and arguments. This is why Pilate sentenced Jesus to death only after the leaders of the people almost started a riot and argued that Jesus claimed to be a king of the Jews. This claim meant Jesus was considered guilty of rebellion against Rome and could therefore be put to death according to Roman law.

Class and Rank in the Roman Empire

The Roman Empire had a class structure based on wealth, birth, and citizenship. At the very top of Roman society was the emperor, who was considered the empire's "first citizen." Some emperors even declared themselves to be equal with the gods. Below the emperor were six hundred senators, who were the empire's wealthiest citizens. Next came a group known as "knights," who had reached a certain level of wealth. They were well-educated and often were recruited to serve in the government of the empire. Beneath them were wealthy local citizens, known as "honorable men," who formed city councils. The upper classes in Roman society wore special clothes and got the best seats at special events.

Below these top groups came the large group of ordinary working people. They were divided into levels. First came those who were not wealthy but still had the privileges of Roman citizenship. Rome recognized only a small group of its subjects as full citizens. Citizens had the freedom and protection of their personal rights. For example, the apostle Paul was able to have his trial in Rome because he was a Roman citizen (Acts 16:37; 22:27). Jesus was not a Roman citizen, so he could be condemned to death without a formal trial by the personal decision of the Roman governor, Pontius Pilate.

Below citizens in the class structure was a large group of non-citizens who were free but did not have the special privileges allowed to Roman citizens. And beneath these non-citizens, at the very bottom of the class structure, were slaves, who could legally be bought or sold, beaten or tortured, as their owners saw fit. Slaves worked mostly as household servants for the rich. At the time of Jesus, almost one-third of the population of Italy were slaves. Slavery was very common and accepted throughout the Roman Empire in Jesus' day. For more, see the mini-article called "Slaves and Servants in the Time of Jesus," p. 2006.

Jewish Groups in Palestine

As mentioned above, the Romans allowed the various peoples in their empire to develop their own local councils. These councils usually included the wealthy and powerful people in a region, who were

The Jewish people in Palestine had different opinions about the best way to deal with the Roman authorities who had control of their land. Even though they may have had different outlooks on these kinds of matters, they all turned to the Law of Moses and discussed it passionately in public and in their synagogues.

free to make laws and to force the people in that region to obey them. The chief priests and the rich people who worked with the Roman authorities formed the Jewish council based in Jerusalem. The Greek word for this council was the *synedrion.* The Jews began to use this name spelled in Hebrew (*Sanhedrin*) for the group that replaced the priests as the organizers and lawmakers of the Jewish people in Jerusalem. It was the Sanhedrin who began to write down formulas for applying the Law of Moses. These interpretations developed into what today are known as the "Mishnah" and "Talmud."

The Jews in the time of Jesus had different opinions about what it meant to be the people of God. Here is a summary of some of the key groups that formed and how each one interpreted the Law of Moses:

Zealots. The Maccabees, as discussed

EMPEROR
600 Senators
Wealthy Knights
Honorable Men
Common Workers (citizens)
Common Workers (non-citizens)
Slaves

earlier, insisted that the Jewish people have their own king. They were defeated when the Romans took over the land in 63 B.C. Later attempts to win freedom and create an independent Jewish state failed in A.D. 70 and again in A.D. 135. The Jewish nationalists who tried to organize the revolt against the Romans were called Zealots. Scholars disagree about whether this term applies to a single, well-organized group or to any number of groups of dissatisfied Jews who wanted to be rid of their Roman rulers. At one time, this term also meant "someone who was strongly devoted to God and God's law." In the New Testament the term is even applied to one of the followers of Jesus (Luke 6:15; Acts 1:13).

Pharisees. By Jesus' day, it was common for Jewish people to meet in private homes for worship and to study the Scriptures. This practice had begun in the later second century B.C. and continued in the first century A.D. One group that did this would become very powerful within the Jewish community. They called themselves "Pharisees," which meant "The Separate Ones" in Hebrew. They wanted to renew and protect Judaism by having all Jewish people strictly follow the laws concerning the Sabbath, fasting, and the purity of food. Most Pharisees had regular jobs and were involved in the Roman culture of the day. But their special meetings and the strict way they followed the Sabbath law forbidding work on the seventh day of the week set them apart. As a result, they had a strong sense of group identity. There were also Pharisaic groups in cities outside Palestine. The apostle Paul, who was from Tarsus in southeastern Asia Minor, said he was once a Pharisee who strictly observed the law (Phil 3:5).

The Pharisees taught the Law of Moses as well as other traditional laws not found in the Scriptures. Their interpretation of traditional laws are included in the Mishnah and Talmud. The Pharisees were popular with the common people and established synagogues (Jewish meeting places) and schools. Unlike some other Jewish groups, they believed in life after death (resurrection) and future rewards and punishments (see Acts 23:6).

Sadducees. This group's name may come from Zadok, the high priest of Israel at the time of King David. The Sadducees also may have been descendants of the Zadokites, who had controlled the temple as high priests for many years until the middle of the second century B.C., when they were forced from power by Jonathan, the first Maccabean high priest. The Sadducees stayed close to the priestly families and tried to influence the business of the temple. They were willing to work with the Romans when they came to rule Palestine. Unlike the Pharisees, the Sadducees did not accept interpretations of the Law, but believed in following only the Law of Moses. They also did not believe that the dead were raised to life (Mark 12:18; Acts 23:8). As long as the Sadducees followed the main teachings of the Law and stayed friendly with the Romans, they expected to continue in positions of power and wealth among their people. After the Jewish revolt led to the destruction of the temple in A.D. 70, the Sadducees no longer existed as a group.

Essenes. The Essenes may have been formed as a group at about the same time as the Sadducees. Instead of trying to influence the priesthood and religion of Israel from the inside, they withdrew from Jewish society, met secretly to study, and had their own special interpretation of the Jewish Scriptures. As a group, they disagreed completely with the priests and other official leaders of the Jews, and like the Pharisees, they believed in life after death.

The Essene communities were very structured. Each group had a leader who controlled who was allowed into the group, decided how property and belongings would be shared among group members, and made rulings concerning the law. Some scholars think that the Dead Sea community was an

Essene group. Whether they were or not, the Essenes' beliefs show how deeply disappointed many Jews were with their religious leaders. The Dead Sea group withdrew from Jewish society and lived on a bluff overlooking the Dead Sea until the Roman army invaded the land in A.D. 66 to put down the Jewish revolt and completely destroyed the community there. For more about the Dead Sea community, see the article called "Archaeology and the Bible," p. 27.

Scribes. The earliest scribes in the Jewish Scriptures (Old Testament) served kings as secretaries, such as Shebna under Hezekiah (2 Kgs 18:18, where the Hebrew word for "scribe" is translated "secretary"). Because they could read and write in a time when many people could not, scribes were very valuable to kings and governments. They had the authority to write legal papers and served as keepers of official records. Like Jeremiah's scribe, Baruch, they took dictation and then read it aloud for people to hear (Jer 36:4-18).

From the exilic period on, the scribes were scholars who studied, interpreted, and taught the Jewish Scriptures. In the New Testament, they are referred to as "teachers of the law" and addressed as rabbis (Matt 23:7). The scribes were not the same as the Pharisees, but most of these teachers belonged to the party of the Pharisees. They sometimes argued with Jesus about the meaning of traditional Jewish laws (Matt 9:3; 15:1,2; Mark 2:16; 7:1,2; Luke 5:30; 6:7).

Samaritans. Another group mentioned a few times in the New Testament are the Samaritans. The ancestors of the Samaritans came from the ten Israelite tribes that rebelled against King Solomon's son Rehoboam and formed a separate kingdom known as Israel, or the northern kingdom. They had their own temple on Mount Gerizim near Shechem, and their own priests. They followed the laws about the Sabbath in a very strict way, and they said that their holy Mount Gerizim was more important than Mount Zion, where the temple in Jerusalem was located. The Jewish people did not like the Samaritans and believed they were not really part of God's chosen people. The writers of the Gospels, however, record that Jesus reached out to them (Luke 17:11-19; John 4:3-9), and used one as a positive example when explaining to an expert in the law what it means to have compassion and be a neighbor (Luke 10:25-37).

Jesus faced this complicated situation as he tried to preach his message of good news. When he defended the poor and reached out to accept people such as tax collectors, Samaritans, and prostitutes, he offended the local religious leaders. The arguments described by the New Testament writers are mainly between different groups who have different ideas about who could or could not be part of God's people. The Romans controlled Palestine but were not very interested in getting involved in these local arguments, unless they led to rebellion against Roman authority.

HOW PEOPLE MADE A LIVING IN THE TIME OF JESUS

The Bible describes a wide range of cultures and lifestyles. The time from Abraham to the time of the early church spans a period of about two thousand years. How people made a living varied depending on when and where they lived. Some people were "nomads," living in small groups, keeping flocks of sheep and goats, and traveling from place to place in order to feed and protect their animals. Others lived more settled lives, growing crops or providing services to people in towns and urban areas. Most of the "jobs" described in this article were still practiced by at least some part of the population of Palestine at the time of Jesus.

From the time of Abraham to the present day, the herding of sheep and goats has been an important occupation throughout much of the Near East.

Living Off the Land: Herding and Farming

The Bible describes the many different kinds of jobs people had in the ancient world, but caring for land and animals are two of the central jobs mentioned. Genesis reports that one of Adam and Eve's sons herded sheep while the other farmed the land (Gen 4:2). The earliest ancestors of the people of Israel, including Abraham and Sarah, traveled from place to place and survived by keeping herds and flocks of animals (Gen 13:1-3). Another piece of evidence for the importance of herding and farming in ancient Israelite society is that the Bible gives special instructions about eating (Lev 11), sacrificing animals (Lev 1), and offering grain (Lev 2).

Keeping herds of animals like sheep and goats was common among the many generations of the people of Israel. At first, these herders (shepherds) were wandering nomads who lived in tents and had very little personal property. They moved from place to place, always trying to find food and water for their animals. They survived by eating the meat and drinking the milk produced by their flocks. They used the animals' wool and hides to make clothes and other things, including the tents they lived in.

Closer to the time of Jesus, when urban life was more developed, shepherds may also have lived in or near villages. They had the right to let their flocks feed in nearby pastures and would have been hired by landowners who needed help to harvest their fields. When food supplies got scarce near the villages, shepherds would move their herds to mountain pastures in the hot summer, or to warmer valleys in the winter.

A shepherd's life was not easy. Shepherds spent most of their time outside watching over the herd, no matter what the weather. They often slept near their flock to protect it from robbers or wild animals. The shepherd's tools and weapons were a rod, a staff, and a sling. Each night, the shepherds would gather their flocks into places called "sheepfolds." These could be stone walls made by the shepherds or natural enclosures, such as a cave. Shepherds used their rods to help count their animals each evening when they brought them into the fold and again in the morning when they left for the pastures. For more, see mini-article called "Shepherds," p. 1972.

When the Israelites settled in Canaan after leaving their life of slavery in Egypt, farming became a more important way of making a living for them. Grains, such as wheat and barley, were used for making bread, and were the most important crop. Grains, as well as lentils and peas, are known to have been cultivated in Palestine since prehistoric times. Unlike farmers in Egypt and Mesopotamia, Israelite farmers did not need to depend on irrigation for water. Even though the rainy season in Palestine was rather short and the soil was often rocky, the farmers' know-how in clearing and fertilizing the land usually produced fine crops. The Israelite farmers learned how to grow crops according to the yearly cycle of

Planting and Growing Grain. *Bread made from grains like wheat and barley was a daily food for people in Jesus' day. To grow grain, farmers had to first plow the soil to break it up and make it suitable for planting. Here, two yoked oxen pull a plow while the farmer guides it from behind. Next, seeds are scattered (sown) in the field, though sowing was sometimes done before plowing. Planting was done after the first rains in autumn. Barley was harvested in late April or early May, and wheat was harvested about a month later. At harvest time, the standing grain was cut with sickles that had flint or iron blades and was then tied into sheaves that could easily be gathered and carried to a threshing floor.*

rainy and dry spells. They also learned to adjust the crops to what was best for the different kinds of land: fertile plains, rocky hills, and semi-barren areas. As time went on, their knowledge as farmers helped them to grow fruits, including melons, figs, dates, grapes, and olives.

Growing crops affected the economy and social life of the people. For example, some of the major religious festivals in Israel—the Feast of Pentecost and the Feast of Tabernacles—were coordinated with the farming cycle. The Feast of Pentecost, also called the Feast of Weeks or Feast of Harvest, celebrated the beginning of the wheat harvest in the spring (Exod 23:16; 34:22; Lev 23:15-22; Num 28:26-31; Deut 16:9). The Feast of Tabernacles (or Booths) is an autumn holiday for the occasion of the planting and gathering of crops, and the annual harvest (Exod 23:16; 34:22; Lev 23:33-43; Num 29:12-39; Deut 16:13-17; Ezek 45:25).

An amazing feature of the life of Israel was the sabbatical year, the one year in every seven when farmers would let the land rest. This followed the pattern of working only six days out of each week according to God's command to rest on the seventh day, called the Sabbath (Exod 23:10-12). This sabbatical rest for fields also had practical benefits, since it increased the long-term fertility of the land.

The people may also have practiced crop rotation, further improving the soil (Isa 28:23-29). The orderly way in which the farmers grew their crops was to match God's plan for the Israelite people and for the good of creation. From a religious perspective, however, DEUTERONOMY makes it clear that a large harvest also depended on how the people of Israel obeyed God's commandments (Deut 11:10-17).

Fishing

Fishing was a far less important source of food and income for the people of Israel, since the Philistines and others controlled the seacoast. What fish were available usually came from the Sea of Galilee and the Jordan River. The most common fish was a type of sardine. According to the Law of Moses, the Israelite people were not to eat fish that lacked fins or scales (Deut 14:9), but the Bible does not mention specific kinds of fish. Since fishing is mentioned so little in the Jewish Scriptures (Old Testament), some scholars think it was not important to the economy of Israel. It is possible that the fishing industry was more prosperous in the time of Jesus than it had been earlier, since when Jesus called James

In Jesus' time carpenters prepared lumber for shipbuilders and architects, made their own tools, and provided ironsmiths with wooden handles for farm implements like axes, plows, and sickles. Carpenters built furniture and even structural elements of houses, like doors and window frames.

and John to be his disciples, they left the family fishing business to their father and the "hired men" (Mark 1:19,20). For more, see the mini-article called "Fish and Fishing," p. 1922.

Special Skills and Crafts

As the Israelites became more settled in and near cities, they became involved in many other types of work. Some men and women became skilled workers, or artisans, who worked on various crafts, very often at home. Many times parents taught their children these skills so they could also use them to make a living. Skilled workers were highly respected, since people needed their skills and products to live comfortably. After the time of the exile (around 538 B.C.; see the mini-article called "Exile," p. 1541), artisans in the same type of craft began to form into professional groups. Such groups of people in the same business were still present in New Testament times (see Acts 19:24-27). Those who worked on special crafts were builders, stonemasons (stonecutters), carpenters, woodcarvers, boatbuilders, and silversmiths, glass workers, potters, leather workers, weavers, and fullers, who worked with cleaning and texturing old and new cloth.

The Bible tells us that Jesus grew up helping his father Joseph, who was a carpenter (Matt 13:55). And the apostle Paul apparently made a living at the craft of

Cloth Making. *Cloth was made from both plant and animal fibers. Fibers from the flax plant (top left) were spun into the fine thread used to weave linen, a luxury fabric often used for priests' robes. Wool shorn from sheep (top right) was the most commonly used animal fiber. It was used to make ordinary, everyday kinds of fabric. After wool was spun into yarn (left), the yarn could be dyed (center) before being woven into fabric on a loom. Stripes and other patterns could be created by using different colored yarns.*

tentmaking (Acts 18:3). Some crafts like baking, cooking, and sewing were done in the everyday work of keeping a household, but some people used these skills to create businesses as well.

Servants and Slaves

Many people, free and slave, provided personal services as laborers. These servants included household servants, employed by royalty and other wealthy people. Such servants might work as cooks, maids, grounds keepers, tutors, or in helping to care for children. Loyal household workers were highly valued. A royal servant called a cupbearer (Gen 40:11; Neh 1:11) brought food and drink to a ruler. Others served as midwives (Gen 35:16-18), doctors (2 Chr 16:12; Mark 5:25, 26), nurses (usually a woman who fed another woman's baby), money changers (Matt 21:12), innkeepers (Luke 2:7; 10:35), and prostitutes (Gen 38:14-18; Josh 2:1).

Often the Bible is not clear when describing the work of servants, because the word "servant" may mean either a slave or a person hired to do some task. Slavery in many forms was fairly common in Bible times. Some people sold themselves into slavery to pay back a debt, or because they were desperately poor and that was the only way they could get food and shelter. Many slaves in Bible times were prisoners of war. Most slaves performed household work rather than field work or manual labor. There are some rules regarding slavery in the Bible, including ones that put a limit on the customs for slavery and recommended when a term of slavery should come to an end (Exod 21:2-6; Lev 25:10,38-41). There was also some expectation that slaves would be treated fairly and without cruelty (Deut 23:15,16). For more, see the mini-article called "Slaves and Servants in the Time of Jesus," p. 2006.

Military and Government Work

A number of jobs were related to maintaining governments and kingdoms. At the top of the social structure were kings, queens and emperors, diplomats and ambassadors, senators and governors (Acts 23:33). Within the palace there were deputies, counselors, interpreters (Gen 42:23), and messengers (Num 20:14; 1 Kgs 20:5; 2 Chr 32:31). The interests of the leaders and the nation were protected by armies which were made up of military officers (Matt 8:9; Acts 21:32), soldiers, and armor-bearers (Judg 9:54; 1 Sam 14:6). To maintain the government, additional workers were needed, such as tax collectors (Luke 19:1,2), keepers of records and secretaries (2 Sam 8:16,17), and lawyers (Acts 24:1; Titus 3:13). Some rulers hired musicians (1 Sam 16:14-23) and others paid for advice from astrologers or fortune-tellers (Isa 19:3).

The Jewish people in Jesus' day were ruled by the Roman government, which appointed a Roman governor (or procurator) to oversee the collection of taxes and keep order in the land (Matt 27:2; Acts 24:1). On the local level, the Romans allowed a council of religious and business leaders to handle certain problems and concerns, especially those related to maintaining the temple and worship (Acts 22:5).

Special Servants of God

For years, the temple in Jerusalem was the center of the religious life of the people of Israel. It took many people to see that its important work was carried out properly. According to the Law of Moses, the members of the tribe of Levi were to work as priests, serving all the people of God. Since the Levites were not given their own land, they were allowed to keep a portion of the sacrifices that the Israelite people offered to God (Josh 13:14). A high priest was in charge of the temple, and supported by chief priests, gatekeepers (1 Chr 9:17-32), temple workers (Ezra 2:43-54), and guards (1 Chr 9:17-32). For more, see the mini-article called "Israel's Priests," p. 2344.

Most of Israel's neighbors had their own temples and religious practices. These employed temple priests and various kinds of workers as well, and some even used women to serve as "sacred prostitutes." All religions supported many artisans, such as architects, builders, goldsmiths, silversmiths, and sculptors, who used their skills to build and decorate temples and shrines (1 Kgs 5:13-18).

Although the tabernacle and the temple were the center of religious life for the people of Israel, many of the kings of Israel and Judah also employed prophets, or seers (1 Chr 21:9; 2 Chr 35:15) who helped them make decisions based on God's will, and who warned them of the consequences of their actions. Other prophets worked independently as preachers (1 Sam 9:6-21). By the time of Jesus, a growing number of teachers known as scribes and Pharisees earned money as teachers of the law.

Other Occupations

Unskilled workers were often poor and did difficult jobs like mining, cutting rocks, digging wells, building roads, cleaning streets, training and driving camels, loading and unloading goods along trade routes, working as a crew member or rower on a boat, and tending and harvesting crops. Still others worked as dancers, musicians, and even as professional mourners. Some of these mourners were paid to cry and wail during funeral processions (Jer 9:17; Matt 9:23); others played sad music on flutes, beat their chests with their hands, and wore rough clothing called sackcloth (Gen 37:34). Merchants and traders bought and sold all sorts of items, carrying them from town to town to offer for sale in outdoor marketplaces. Some wealthy merchants owned ships or large numbers of camels, which they used to transport goods across long distances. For more about merchants, see the article called "Trade and Travel," p. 948.

Wages and Pay

The Bible does speak of people being paid for certain kinds of work (Gen 29:15; Mic 3:11; Matt 20:1-15; Luke 3:14), but it is difficult to determine just how much people were paid early in Israel's history. Most likely they received goods or food for the work they did. During the time of the kings, some people were paid in weighed pieces of gold or silver. Later, around 600 B.C., the Persian empire began making coins, which were sometimes used to pay workers. (See the chart called "Banking and Money in the Ancient World," p. 951.) By the time of Jesus, various kinds of coins were commonly used to pay for goods and the services of workers. The story Jesus told in Matthew 20:1-16 describes vineyard workers being paid the amount of one day's wage, which was one denarius. How much that one coin could buy is not clear, so it is hard to determine what a person's wage would have been when compared to a worker's salary today.

RELIGIONS AND PHILOSOPHIES IN BIBLE TIMES

Both the faith of Israel and the faith of the early Christians developed in cultural contexts steeped in other religious traditions. The people of Israel encountered religions with many similar beliefs and rituals in Palestine and Egypt. Christianity came into being as one among many religions and philosophies spread around the Mediterranean world by merchants and soldiers.

The People of Israel and Canaanite Religions

The people of Israel believed in one God. This belief is known as "monotheism." Many of the other religions in the ancient Mediterranean world recognized a number of different gods. When the Israelite people entered Canaan well over one thousand years before Jesus was born, they came into contact with the various gods of their neighbors. The Law of Moses commanded God's people to remain loyal to the one true God, *Yahweh,* who had led them out of slavery in Egypt and into the promised land of Canaan (Exod 20:1-5). Once they settled there, they were often tempted to follow the other gods, and often did.

The Gods of Israel's Neighbors. Among the Canaanites, one of the most common names for god was El. The Canaanites did not believe that El was the only god, but they did believe that El was the one who ruled over all the other gods. They believed El was the creator of the universe and the kind, compassionate father of the whole human race. El was worshiped in Palestine before the Israelites took over the land. In the Jewish Scriptures, "El" also frequently refers to the God of Israel. Some examples of the use of this name are found in the Old Testament.

Some of the enemies of El were known as Yamm (the sea), Mot (death), and Leviathan (the sea monster). See Psalm 104:26 and Isaiah 27:1.

Another name for a god in the ancient Near East was Baal, which means "master," "husband," and "lord." Baal was worshiped by the Canaanites as a god of fertility who ensured good and abundant crops. Baal was also connected to storms that came into Syria and Palestine from the sea in the winter and early spring. Since rain was essential for the growth of crops, people believed that the storms that came from the sea were powerful gods. Some ancient people believed that parts of nature itself were filled with god-like spirits, so they worshiped things like trees, rivers, fountains, and caves.

Some people in the ancient world believed goddesses provided fertility for crops and flocks and helped human beings to have children. The Canaanite goddess Asherah was pictured as the mother of the gods. She was identified as the wife of El. King Manasseh of Judah had a carved image of Asherah placed in the temple of the LORD in Jerusalem (2 Kgs 21:7). Asherah poles were put up on hilltops as symbols of fertility (1 Kgs 14:23; 16:33).

The goddess Anath was also a fertility

NAMES OF GOD

NAME	SCRIPTURE PASSAGES
El Elyon (God Most High)	Gen 14:18-20
El Olam (Eternal God)	Gen 21:33
El Elohe Israel (God of Israel)	Gen 33:20
El Shaddai (God Almighty or God of the Mountains)	Gen 17:1; 35:9-11; Exod 6:3

goddess. She was famous for performing acts of violence against those who opposed her. An important city in Israel, Anathoth, was named for her (Josh 21:18; Jer 1:1; 11:21). This means that she was probably worshiped in this town at an earlier time. Even during the time when Nehemiah (about 445 B.C.) was helping restore Israel to the land and reminding the people to practice God's law after the exile in Babylon, the city's name remained Anathoth (Neh 7:27; 11:32).

The Philistine people who lived in the narrow strip of land between Judah and the Mediterranean Sea often battled with Israel. Their chief god was Dagon (1 Sam 5:1-5). The people of Moab, another of Israel's enemies when the Israelites were settling in Canaan, worshiped the god named Chemosh.

When the people of Israel worshiped other gods, God punished them. Ahab, the king of Israel, married Jezebel, the daughter of the king Ethbaal of Sidon. Part of Jezebel's name, *Zebul*, was a form of Baal's name. Ahab went against the Law of Moses when he built a temple with an altar to worship Baal in his capital city, Samaria (1 Kgs 16:31,32), and when he allowed Jezebel to encourage him to support hundreds of prophets of Asherah (1 Kgs 18:19). Many of the people of Israel were led to worship *Yahweh,* Israel's God, as well as Baal and Asherah. This worship broke the commandment God had given to Moses: "You shall have no other gods before me" (Exod 20:3). Because of their sins, God allowed Israel's neighbors to defeat them and carry many of the people into exile (2 Kgs 17).

Other Religions Outside of Palestine. In the ancient world, many cities or city-states had their own gods. Often people would build altars and places of worship (shrines) where they could bring sacrifices for their gods. These sacrifices were intended to please the gods in the hope that they would then protect the people of the city and give them good crops. In ancient Babylonia, for example, each city built temples to its protector gods.

Astrology, the belief that the sun and the stars control human life, came out of Babylonia and had a great influence throughout the Greek and Roman empires. The people of Israel rejected this belief in the influence of the stars as contrary to monotheism. They believed that God created the sun, moon, and stars (Gen 1:14-19; Ps 8:3; 147:4). Since these heavenly bodies are created, they cannot be gods.

In Egypt the cults of Isis, Osiris, and Serapis were popular. In Syria (also called Aram), Israel's northern neighbor, people worshiped the great sky-god named Hadad, and helped spread the belief in astrology, common in Babylon, to the Greeks. From Persia, a nation that conquered the Babylonians and ruled Palestine before the Greeks invaded the land, came the cult of Mazdaism. This was connected to the religion taught by Zoroaster, a teacher whose ideas would later influence Gnostic beliefs (see below). The most important of the cults popular in Asia Minor was the cult of Cybele, also known as the Great Mother. The Greeks identified Cybele with Rhea, the mother of the Greek gods, and with Artemis, who is mentioned in the Bible as the goddess of the Ephesians (Acts 19:21-41).

The Christian Church in the Greek World

Greek Religions. In the centuries before Jesus was born, the number of religions, cults, and forms of philosophy in the Mediterranean world had grown rapidly. The letters of the New Testament provide glimpses of how various religions, philosophies, and cult teachings opposed Christian followers. (For examples, see 1 Cor 8; 10; Gal 1:6-9; 1 John 2:26,27; Rev 2:2-6, 14-16, 20-25).

The greatest religious influences and new philosophies came from the ancient Greeks. When Alexander the Great and his heirs took over Syria and Palestine after

330 B.C., they gave new names to the local gods and goddesses and introduced new deities. There was the Greek god of time, Chronos, and Zeus, the chief of the Greek gods. The Greeks also worshiped goddesses, such as Artemis, goddess of the hunt, and the Egyptian goddess Isis. Isis is not mentioned in the New Testament, but it is known that many people in the Mediterranean world at this time believed in her as the one who made crops and flocks fertile every year. Belief in Isis was spread by merchants and soldiers and became a very important religion. The worship of Isis competed with the spread of Christianity in the first three centuries A.D. Asklepios, the god of healing, was also popular. The desire of Christians to show the superiority of Jesus over this god may have influenced the way some of the miracle stories about Jesus' power to heal were shaped by the writers of the New Testament.

Various "mystery cults" were popular throughout the Greek world as well. Mystery cults had secret beliefs, so becoming a member usually required going through initiation ceremonies or practicing specific kinds of rites or sacraments. Participants in these cults believed that the ceremonies brought a person into the very life of the gods. The most popular Greek mystery cults were the cults of Demeter and Dionysus. Demeter was the goddess of grain and of the tamed or cultured aspects of nature. Dionysus was the god of wine and of the wild, untamed aspects of nature. The spirit of Dionysus was said to be in the animal (and possibly human) flesh that was eaten as part of the cult rituals. Members who participated in the rite believed they were consuming part of Dionysus when they ate. To many people at this time, Christians also seemed to be a mystery cult, because when they celebrated the Lord's Supper, Christians ate the bread and drank the wine that Jesus described as his body and blood (Mark 14:22-24). Dionysus was also believed to make new birth possible for his followers. These beliefs would have seemed similar to the Christians' claim that Jesus had the power to renew the life of his people (John 3:1-21).

The Egyptian fertility goddess Isis holding her son Horus. Although this goddess is never mentioned in the Bible, she was worshiped throughout the Greek and Roman world in the time of Jesus and his apostles.

Other religions in the first century were based on fate, fortune, astrology, and magic. Some people believed that the supreme god was Tyche ("Fortune"), who ruled the lives of human beings. If someone became rich, it was because of Fortune; if that person suddenly lost his or her wealth, that was because of Fortune, too. Similarly, some people believed in a ruler known as "Fate." Fate was thought to determine everything that would happen in the universe, including the actions of all people. Good things and bad things alike were caused by Fate, and human beings were simply thought to be the means Fate used to carry out present and future events already determined.

This type of thinking opened the way for the religions based on astrology. In astrology, it was believed that the movement of the sun, moon, and planets determined a person's life. In Greece, astrology was combined with science in order to develop "horoscopes" (maps of the positions of planets) for predicting the future of individuals. Those who did not like the idea that their lives were controlled by the planets or by fate turned to magic. They wore charms or amulets and recited spells in order to hold off the power of evil.

Greek Philosophies. In Greece during the third and fourth centuries before Christ, the Greek philosophers Socrates, Plato, and Aristotle were concerned with how people could live a virtuous life that was in harmony with their city, their culture, and the natural world. Disciples of these great teachers would later form a number of schools of philosophy. By the time of the early Christian church, the teachings of these schools had spread throughout the Mediterranean world. Plato and Aristotle especially had a profound effect on later Christian writers and thinkers.

Originally worshiped as a goddess of fertility and successful childbearing, Fortuna was believed to control both good and bad luck. She is often represented holding a cornucopia and a steering oar.

Socrates of Athens lived from about 469 to 399 B.C. The Greek philosophers who lived before Socrates were concerned with trying to discover what the world was made of, but Socrates believed that philosophy could also tell people how to live a good life. To do this, Socrates developed two forms of gathering and presenting information, called induction (to suggest general conclusions from specific examples) and definition (to try to clearly describe what is meant by the general quality of a thing), and a method of using logic in discussions called "dialectic," which involved asking and answering questions. Because of his interest in virtue, Socrates is usually considered the founder of ethics.

Plato, a student of Socrates, lived from about 428 to 348 B.C. and started a school called the "Academy," which continued for more than nine hundred years. Plato's teachings, written in his *Dialogues,* have been among the most influential in the history of Western Civilization. Plato believed that Reason (in Greek, called *logos*) was the nature of the universe, controlling things from within. When he thought about how the world was constantly changing, Plato looked for things that do not change, which are represented in the things that do change. He called these "Forms" or "Ideas." Plato thought that when we call things by a general name, such as Beauty or Courage, we do so because there is a permanent Idea or Form of Beauty or Courage underlying each individual example of it. He believed that these Ideas or Forms, which are the meanings behind physical laws and material things, are what is truly real. Plato also believed that the human soul was immortal, and that the soul is superior to the body. According to Plato, it is the soul that makes us what we are, and that the highest responsibility of people is to "tend the soul," so that it is acceptable to the gods.

Aristotle lived from about 384 to 322 B.C. and was a student of Plato at the "Academy." When Plato died, Aristotle left Athens and became a teacher of Alexander the Great. When Aristotle returned to Athens, he began a school called the "Lyceum," where he taught that the knowledge of a thing requires an understanding of what caused it. Unlike Plato, he believed that form caused matter to move, and that the only pure form was God, who was the cause and goal of all motion. Aristotle's teachings, recorded by his students, cover many fields, including ethics and logic, the natural sciences, politics, physics, and poetry.

Cynics were followers of the Greek philosophical school founded by Antisthenes, a student of Socrates who lived from about 444 to 370 B.C. The most famous Cynic philosopher was Diogenes of Sinope (a town on the shore of the Black Sea). Diogenes believed that happiness came from following virtue for its own sake, and by living a life free from grasping after material possessions and pleasures. It is not clear why the Cynic school (from the Greek word *kyon* meaning "dog") was given its name. It may be a reference to their harshly critical style, in response to what they thought was a corrupt society. Or it may refer to the "Cynosarges," a school where the followers met to discuss philosophy. Cynic philosophers were not tied to one place and their wandering style was copied by some early Christian apostles. This is evidenced when Paul preached at the Areopagus in Athens, and his audience thought he was a wandering philosopher (Acts 17:16-34).

Stoicism was founded by Zeno of Citium (a town in Cyprus), who lived from around 336 to 261 B.C. The name "stoicism" comes from the Greek word *stoa.* Zeno and his students used to meet regularly at a pillared porch, the *Stoa Poikile,* on the north side of the marketplace in Athens (see the illustration). The Stoics thought that the whole universe was a divine being, and that the gods were simply various names of the one cosmic God. They believed that virtue was living in harmony with the rational force of nature. To find peace of mind, the Stoics said, people should learn what is in their power and what isn't, and should concern themselves only with the things in their power. The Stoics concluded that people had the power to live in harmony with the cosmic God, which they called virtue. They believed that people should live according to virtue (the rational force of all nature) and be indifferent (the Greek word *apatheia*) to all things—like wealth, pleasure, good or bad fortune—that might prevent them from living a virtuous life. (In English today, the word "stoic" has come to mean patient, disciplined, or self-restrained.) Like all Stoics who would come after him, Zeno preached the equality of the sexes and was strongly opposed to slavery. Stoics had many beliefs in common with early Christians. Most significantly, however, they did not believe in the divinity of Christ, his resurrection, or the judgment of the world. Stoic influences can be found in the writings of the Jewish teacher Philo of Alexandria (who lived from around 25 B.C. to A.D. 50). The apostle Paul also uses Stoic terms to communicate with his Greek-speaking audience. (See Acts 17:28; 1 Cor 7:32-35; Phil 4:11-13.)

Porch-like structures called "stoas" were gathering places for people in the Greek and Roman worlds. A group of philosophers came to be known as the Stoics because they met in the stoa in Athens.

Epicureanism was founded in Athens by Epicurus, who lived from about 342 to 270 B.C. The main goal of life for Epicureans was to find true happiness. They believed true happiness was gained by encouraging serenity (the Greek word *ataraxia*) and by avoiding pain. They did not believe that fate or destiny ruled their lives; instead, they believed in free will. Since they did not believe that the gods influenced a person's life, they were considered by some to be atheists. For them, true pleasure came from living nobly and justly and with a healthy lifestyle. They believed intellectual pleasure was superior to bodily pleasure. The Epicureans valued friendship as a way for people to support each other in the search for happiness. They believed death was the end of existence, but that it was not to be feared because it brought peace and an end to pain. Epicureanism was probably most popular among the upper classes of the Roman Empire.

Gnostics is a term historians have given to a number of religious groups in the second and third centuries A.D. Some of the letters of the New Testament, such as COLOSSIANS and 1 JOHN, seem to be battling early forms of Gnosticism. *Gnosis* is the Greek word for knowledge, and Gnostics believed they possessed a special or secret knowledge. Many sects who have been identified as Gnostics believed that the world was ruled by evil forces (called "archons"). Among these evil forces, they included the God of the Old Testament. Archons held humanity captive in a state of ignorance and suffering. Gnostics believed that Jesus was a godlike being (rather than a living person) who had been sent to restore people's knowledge of their origin in the true God. People, they said, were made of body, soul, and spirit. People who lived only the life of the body could not be saved. Christians might achieve a lower form of salvation through their faith, but real salvation came through a superior knowledge *(gnosis)* of the life of the spirit and soul, which is the divine element in human beings. In the early centuries after Christ, Gnosticism was a serious challenge, leading to the rise of elitist sects within Christianity. Gnostics were a very diverse group of sects, but some of their general characteristics have been described by historians.

Emperor Worship. The Jews and early Christians faced the problem of emperor worship in the centuries just before and after Jesus was born. Beginning in the fourth century B.C., Alexander the Great (356-323 B.C.), the Macedonian king who conquered much of the Near East, claimed that he was divine. Rulers who took over after he died made similar claims. They demanded that all their subjects honor them as gods. One of these rulers, Antiochus IV Epiphanes put up a statue of Zeus in the Jerusalem temple. This set off the Maccabean revolt of 168-165 B.C., in which the Jewish people reclaimed the temple and gained their freedom for a brief period of time.

Roman emperors, whose armies conquered Palestine in 63 B.C., also claimed that they were gods. The Roman emperor Gaius Caligula (ruled A.D. 37-41) wanted to put up a statue of himself in the temple, but he died before he could make this happen. Around the end of the first century, the emperor Domitian ordered people to address him as "Lord and God." REVELATION pictures a prostitute and a horrible beast which likely symbolized the Roman Empire's attempt to destroy God's people and their worship of "the Lamb" (Christ), and to force Christians to honor the emperor as divine instead (Rev 17).

The Bible and the Beliefs of the Ancient World

As Jews and Christians moved away from Jerusalem after the destruction of the temple in A.D. 70 and settled in other parts of the Roman Empire, they encountered the various religions and philosophies described in this article, and many others as well. Many of these systems of belief were not compatible with the monotheism of Judaism and Christianity. Sometimes, however, they adapted some of the teachings from these other systems of thought in response to the situations they faced. In light of these situations, both the Jewish Scriptures (Old Testament) and the New Testament contain direct and indirect references to these other forms of belief. It is, therefore, important to become aware of these other beliefs in order to understand the Bible more fully.

MIRACLES, MAGIC, AND MEDICINE

The Bible is a book of faith, telling the story of how God acted in history to protect and save humankind. Miracles are an important part of that story. God's actions in miracles on behalf of the faithful are contrasted with the situation of those who looked to other gods and relied on magic, reading the stars, or calling on the spirits of the dead. Throughout the Bible, the miracles of God are extraordinary acts. These miracles are often unexplainable by the expectations, common at the time, of how nature works. Many of these miracles can be described in the categories shown on the chart below.

The people praised God for these miracles, including God's amazing actions in Israel's history (Deut 7:19; 11:1-4; 34:10-12). The writers of the PSALMS and the later teachers of the Law of Moses saw God working in these miracles to preserve and reward the Israelite people, and to keep them living in God's ways (Ps 105; 107; 136; see also Neh 9).

Throughout the Bible, miracles are presented as signs that point to a larger meaning. This is evident, for example, in the descriptions of the Israelites' experiences in the Desert of Sinai, which show God's special purpose for the people. Not only do they survive their ordeal, but they are brought into the land God promised to them so that they can worship the LORD (Deut 4:23-34; 6:21-25; 26:5-11; Josh 24:17). Miracles also helped the Israelites believe God's promises because the Israelites could see them being fulfilled. Even a Babylonian king came to believe that Israel's God had miraculous power after he saw how God preserved the three faithful young Israelite men in the fiery furnace (Dan 3).

HOW GOD USES MIRACLES

TYPE OF MIRACLE	SCRIPTURE PASSAGES
God's power revealed to the people	Gen 15:17; Exod 3:1-6; Josh 3:14-17; 1 Kgs 18:16-39; Luke 8:22-25; John 2:1-12; 6:16-21; Acts 2
God helps women unable to have children	Gen 17:15-22; Judg 13; 1 Sam 1; Luke 1:5-25
God's power used to judge evildoers and rebellious people	Gen 6–9; 19:1-29; Exod 7:14—12:30; 1 Kgs 18:1-40; Jer 18; Acts 5:1-11
God helps Israel in battle	Josh 5:13—6:27; 10:1-15; Judg 6:33—8:21; 1 Sam 17:41-54
God saves or delivers people from trouble	Exod 14; Dan 3,6; Acts 12:6-17; 16:16-34
God provides food and other blessings	Exod 16:1—17:7; 2 Kgs 4:1-7; Luke 5:1-11; John 6:5-15; 21:1-14
God heals and restores health	Num 21:4-9; 2 Kgs 5:1-14; Mark 5:21-43; Luke 18:35-43; Acts 3:1-10
God's purposes and glory revealed in a vision	Isa 6; Ezek 1; Zech 1:7—5:11; Acts 9:1-19; 10:1-48
God overcomes death	2 Kgs 4:18-37; Matt 28:1-7; Luke 7:11-17; John 11:1-44; Acts 9:36-43
God chooses servants and gives them special gifts	Gen 41; Exod 4:1-17; Judg 6:11-24; 1 Sam 3:1-18; Dan 2; Luke 1:26-38; Acts 2:1-13; 1 Cor 12:1-11

Jesus' Miracles Show God's Love and Power

The New Testament reports Jesus' many miracles (see the chart below). Yet, when Jesus' opponents tried to test him by making him perform a miracle to prove that God was with him, Jesus refused (Matt 16:1-4; Mark 8:11,12; John 6:30, 31). Also, Jesus sometimes warned people not to tell anyone about his miracles (Mark 1:44; 5:43), possibly because non-believers would have thought Jesus was just a magician. Often, it seemed that Jesus' miracles only worked for people who believed (Mark 2:5-12; 5:34). His miracles were not for showing off. Instead, they demonstrated God's love for the people (Luke 4:18-21) and announced the presence of the kingdom of God.

Miracles in the Early Church

At the time of the early church, public miracles helped people recognize that God was at work (Acts 2:19-22, 43; 4:30; 5:12; 8:13). At the same time, some people wrongly thought that the ability to heal and do miracles was a result of magical powers. In Acts 8:9-24 a magician named Simon claimed to be converted to Christianity, but he still had to learn that God's power was a gift, and not some magic power that could be bought. The apostle Paul claimed that God helped him perform miracles to confirm the good news about Jesus and Paul's own role as an apostle (Rom 15:15-19; 2 Cor 12:12).

Magic, Sorcery, and Witchcraft

In the ancient world, the belief in magic, sorcery, and witchcraft were common. The people of Israel claimed that the miracles performed by their prophets and leaders were different from these things because they were based on God's power. The writers of the Scriptures often contrasted these "true" miracles with unusual acts done by

SOME WELL-KNOWN MIRACLES OF JESUS

MIRACLE	SCRIPTURE PASSAGE
Turns water into wine in Cana	John 2:1-11
Orders the wind and waves to be quiet	Mark 4:35-41
Walks on the water of the Sea of Galilee	Matthew 14:22-33
With five loaves and two fishes, feeds a crowd of more than 5,000 people	Matthew 14:13-21
Raises his friend Lazarus to life	John 11:17-44
Raises a dead girl to life	Matthew 9:18-26
Gives sight to a man born blind	John 9:1-41
Cures the woman who had been bleeding for twelve years	Matthew 9:20-22
Cures a man of evil spirits and sends the spirits into a herd of pigs	Mark 5:1-20
Heals ten men with leprosy	Luke 17:11-19
Heals a crippled man in Capernaum	Mark 2:1-12
Heals a man who was deaf and could hardly talk	Mark 7:31-37
Heals the high priest's servant after the man's ear is cut off	Luke 22:49-51

the prophets and priests of other peoples and religions. For example, Joseph used God's help to interpret the dreams of the king of Egypt after the king's own magicians and wise men could not (Gen 41:1-36). Later, when the Egyptian king's magicians turned their walking sticks into snakes, Moses and his brother Aaron used God's power to do the same thing, and their snake ate the snakes created by the Egyptians (Exod 7:8-13). This showed the superiority of the God of Israel. See also the chart called "Key Events in Moses' Life," p. 2336. In another case, Elijah showed that the power of Israel's God was greater than that of the god Baal when God helped Elijah win a contest against the prophets of Baal (1 Kgs 18:16-40). For more about Elijah see the mini-article called "Elijah," p. 1816.

Witchcraft was forbidden by the Law of Moses (Lev 19:26), because relying on spirits or powers other than God showed a lack of faith and trust in the one true God. Disobeying the command against witchcraft could lead to harsh punishment (Exod 22:18; Deut 18:10-13). When King Saul, Israel's first king, was afraid of the approaching Philistine army, he did not pray to God for help. Instead, he broke the law forbidding witchcraft and asked a woman from Endor who talked to spirits to call on Samuel, who died some time before (1 Sam 28:4-20). In another example, when the people of the northern kingdom (Israel) disobeyed God by worshiping the stars and using magic, or by worshiping idols like Asherah and Baal, God became so furious with them that he allowed them to be defeated by the Assyrians and carried away as prisoners (2 Kgs 17:16-18). Later, King Manasseh of the southern kingdom (Judah) sinned against God by worshiping the stars and planets, by practicing magic and witchcraft, and by asking fortune-tellers for advice. Apparently, the advice he received included offering his own child as a sacrifice (2 Kgs 21:4-7). For Manasseh's terrible sins, the whole nation suffered God's judgment and punishment (2 Kgs 21:8-16). In another example, King Balak of Moab hired Balaam to put a curse on the Israelites, but Balaam would not do it (Num 22–24).

Parts of the New Testament make clear that sorcery and fortune-telling were caused by evil spirits. In one case, a slave girl lost her power to tell fortunes after Paul ordered an evil spirit to leave her. This angered her owners because she could no longer make money for them by telling fortunes (Acts 16:16-19). In GALATIANS, Paul includes witchcraft on the list of acts done by those who obey their own selfish desires instead of obeying God's Spirit (Gal 5:20). And in REVELATION, a beast fooled people into believing in the beast who opposed God by doing magical miracles, such as making an idol speak as if it were alive (Rev 13:11-15).

Medicine and Healing

What does the Bible reveal about doctors in the ancient world? In one part of the Old Testament, it says that King Asa's death may have been from depending only on human physicians, and not asking for God's help (2 Chr 16:12,13). God is seen as the main healer in the Old Testament (Exod 15:26; Ps 41:1-4; Jer 17:14; Hos 6:1). In fact, often the priests were seen as healers on God's behalf (Lev 13:1-3; 14:1-32). That is perhaps one reason why Hannah went to the temple to pray for God's help once she realized that she could not have children (1 Sam 1:1-18). (In ancient times, this was seen as a sickness in a woman.)

Some parts of the Bible reflect the belief that disease and sickness are caused by failing to live according to God's Law (Deut 28:21-23,27-29,34,35), while health and well-being were seen as the reward for trusting God (Exod 15:26; Deut 7:12-15). Other parts of the Bible temper this perspective (Job 2; 42:7; Eccl 8:10-13, 9:2; John 9:1-7). People with certain diseases were set apart from the rest of God's people because they were considered unclean (Lev 13; Num 12:9-14). While this was done primarily for religious reasons, those who had these diseases were not allowed to worship or be among their friends and neighbors until they were cured and had gone through a ritual cleansing ceremony (Lev 14).

Jesus knew these laws about sickness and being cleansed, but he also showed himself to be a great healer. Many of Jesus' miracles included healing people considered unclean (see the chart on p. 1839). He encouraged the ten men he healed of leprosy to show themselves to the priests, probably so they could go through the ritual cleansing and be welcomed back into the community of God's people (Luke 17:11-14). Another time, Jesus' power healed a woman who had spent all her money and had gone to many doctors without finding a cure (Mark 5:25-34). Jesus offered his healing also to those who were not part of the Jewish people (Luke 4:23-29), just as the prophets before him had done (1 Kgs 17:1-24; 2 Kgs 5:14). This was surely amazing to many people, and was a way of showing that God's love is for everyone.

Around the time of Jesus, Greeks and Romans went to the shrines of a god of healing, hoping to be cured of their ailments. The early stages of modern medicine began in these shrines, but some of the cures developed there, like eating the liver of a fox or drinking juice from an iris plant, had no connection with the cause of the diseases.

The Bible tends to teach trust in God and prayer and fasting as the way to be healed from illness, rather than trusting solely in human doctors or medicine. The Bible is not always against doctors and medicine though, and biblical authors were not aware of modern scientific techniques. After all, Luke, a companion of the apostle Paul, was said to be a physician (Col 4:14). Also, modern medicine can be seen in light of the biblical command to love one's neighbor (Luke 10:25-37). Jesus instructed his followers to go heal the sick (Luke 10:9). The Bible also stresses the value and dignity of human life, teaching that all human beings are created by God and in God's likeness (Gen 1:26,27). This belief has probably influenced the practice and ethics of modern medicine as well.

In conclusion, the Bible's accounts of miracles, magic, and medicine are all stories about God's power and love. They are not scientific explanations of supernatural events, but a faithful witness to the all-powerful nature of God, the Creator.

Healing was an important part of Jesus' ministry on earth. The apostle Paul listed healing as one of the gifts the Spirit gives the church so that God's people can take care of one another (1 Cor 12:9) and grow stronger in their faith.

THE NEW TESTAMENT

THE "NEW TESTAMENT" is the second part of the Christian Bible. Its twenty-seven books continue the story of God's people begun in the Old Testament (the Jewish Scriptures). The word "testament" comes from a Latin word that means "will," which was used to translate the Greek word *diatheke,* which means "will" or "agreement," or "covenant." The Old Testament tells of the covenant God made with the people of Israel. This covenant was based, in large part, on the Law of Moses. Those who obeyed God and lived according to this Law were God's people. But about six hundred years before the time of Jesus, the prophet Jeremiah announced a "new covenant" based on an inward relationship with God (Jer 31:31-34). Jesus used the language of a "new covenant" to describe what God was doing through him (Luke 22:20; 1 Cor 11:25), and other New Testament writers did the same (2 Cor 3:6; Heb 8:8; 9:15; 12:24). The apostle Paul says that this new covenant is not based on written law but comes from God's Spirit and brings new life (Gal 3:10-14).

The books of the New Testament were written during a period of about one hundred years following the time of Jesus. Many of the books focus on Jesus of Nazareth, who was born to Jewish parents and declared by Christians to be the Christ (Messiah), or Savior (Mark 8:29; 14:61, 62; Luke 2:11; John 20:30, 31; Acts 3:18-21). The four Gospels (MATTHEW, MARK, LUKE, and JOHN) tell about the life and teachings of Jesus, each from a different perspective. ACTS tells how the earliest apostles preached about Jesus and spread his message in the decades following Jesus. The Letters of the New Testament provide an understanding of the ways the message of Jesus was being preached and interpreted during the first years of the early Church as the good news about Jesus was being taken to new lands. They also give some clues about what the earliest Christians were experiencing. REVELATION, the last book in the New Testament, ends with the hope of a future in which God will bring a new heaven and a new earth.

It is impossible to give an exact date for the writings of the New Testament books, but most scholars now agree that some of the Letters of Paul are the oldest of the New Testament writings. The Gospels and ACTS actually were written later. MARK, probably the first Gospel to be put in writing, was most likely written sometime after A.D. 60.

Though Jesus and his disciples spoke Aramaic, the books of the New Testament were first written in the "everyday" Greek of that time. The New Testament writers also were familiar with the Greek translation of the Jewish Scriptures (called the Septuagint). A number of quotations found in the New Testament come directly from this Greek translation, while others were translated into Greek from the Hebrew of the Jewish Scriptures. The original manuscripts of the New Testament deteriorated or were destroyed long ago. But hand-made copies of the text of these books were made repeatedly down through the centuries. The earliest copy of the entire Greek New Testament dates from the fourth century, and the earliest fragment of a New Testament book dates from around A.D. 125. Also of value to biblical scholars are early translations of New Testament writings into Coptic, Syriac, and Latin. It took over three hundred years before the twenty-seven books that make up the New Testament became the accepted list followed in our Bibles today (see also the article called "How the Bible Came to Us," p. 9). Ever since that time, the Church has regarded these writings as equal in authority to the Old Testament Scriptures.

THE GOSPELS AND ACTS

THE FOUR GOSPELS (MATTHEW, MARK, LUKE, and JOHN) present various accounts of the life and teachings of Jesus Christ. ACTS gives a detailed report of what happened to some of Jesus' early followers as they carried the message about Jesus from Jerusalem to the other areas of the Roman empire.

The word "Gospel" comes from an Old English word that means "good news." The Greek word that is translated as "gospel" or "good news" is *euangelion* (see Mark 1:1). The English words "evangelist" and "evangelism" also come from this word. An evangelist is one who tells good news.

The Gospels were probably written down in their present form between thirty and sixty years after Jesus' crucifixion. Since Jesus himself left no writings, the Gospels record stories and eyewitness descriptions that had been passed on by word of mouth for a number of years. At first, Jesus' followers were so eager to tell the message about him that they didn't think it was necessary to write down what he had said and done. But as Jesus' first followers and eyewitnesses grew older and died, it became more important to have a written record of what Jesus did and taught, and to describe his death and resurrection.

Although other "gospels" about Jesus were written and circulated, the only ones accepted as reliable by the whole church were MATTHEW, MARK, LUKE, and JOHN. It is not certain who actually wrote these Gospels, since the names of the authors are never given in the books themselves. Traditionally, Matthew and John, two of the 12 apostles, have been held as the authors of MATTHEW and JOHN; and the authors of MARK and LUKE are considered to be early followers of Christ who heard about Jesus from one or more of Jesus' first disciples. Some biblical scholars believe that all four of the Gospels were written by followers of Christ who heard about Jesus from his first disciples. For more about how these four Gospels became part of the New Testament, see the article called "What Books Belong in the Bible? " p. 13.

Many sources were used to write the Gospels. These sources probably included various collections of Jesus' sayings and stories that were available to the Gospel writers. For example, a number of Jesus' sayings are similar in MATTHEW and LUKE, so they may have been working with the same source. Both of them also appear to have used MARK for their basic outlines. But MATTHEW and LUKE also used different sources to describe the events surrounding Jesus' birth, since MARK has nothing to say about Jesus' childhood. MATTHEW, MARK, and LUKE have so much material in common and follow the same basic outline, that they are sometimes referred to as the "Synoptic" Gospels (from the Greek word *synopsis*, which means "seeing together").

The three Synoptic Gospels are more like each other than any of them is like JOHN. While MATTHEW, MARK, and LUKE focus on Jesus' public teaching and miracle working in Galilee, JOHN contains information about Jesus' early work in Judea. JOHN also contains some of Jesus' sayings that are not found in the other Gospels. These include the so-called "I am" sayings, such as "I am the bread of life" (John 6:35) and "I am the light of the world" (John 8:12). The order of events in JOHN does not follow the order shared by the Synoptic Gospels. And JOHN does not include any of Jesus' parables that are found in the other three Gospels. For more about what makes each of these accounts of Jesus' life and ministry unique, see the Introductions to each Gospel.

Although the author of ACTS is not identified in the book, scholars agree that it was written by the same person who wrote LUKE. Besides being addressed to someone known as Theophilus (Luke 1:1-4; Acts 1:1), these books share a written style of Greek that is more formal than the Greek used in the other Gospels or in any other book of the New Testament. A number of common themes also tie these two books together as the work of one author. These themes are listed in the Introductions to the individual books of LUKE and ACTS.

MATTHEW

Promises are meant to be kept. Read the book of MATTHEW to find out how God kept an ancient promise by sending Jesus to be the Savior of the whole world.

WHAT MAKES MATTHEW SPECIAL?

Like the other Gospels, MATTHEW tells about the life and teachings of Jesus. It also describes what it means to be part of God's people and includes instructions on how God expects them to live.

WHY WAS MATTHEW WRITTEN?

The writer of MATTHEW was writing for people who knew the Jewish Scriptures, which Christians call the Old Testament. The writer often points out how these earlier texts look forward to Jesus as the Christ (the Messiah) sent from God.

WHAT'S THE STORY BEHIND THE SCENE?

MATTHEW shows that the message Jesus taught was based on the laws and teachings found in the Old Testament. On Mount Sinai God gave Moses the laws that the people of Israel were to follow. In the Sermon on the Mount found in Matthew's Gospel, Jesus goes up on a mountain and tells his followers how God wants them to live. As seen in the outline below, the lengthy section of MATTHEW that tells about Jesus' work and teachings (4:12—25:46) is arranged in five parts, just like the Law of Moses contains five parts in the Old Testament — GENESIS, EXODUS, LEVITICUS, NUMBERS, and DEUTERONOMY. Matthew also wanted to show that much of what Jesus said and did was predicted hundreds of years earlier by the prophets of Israel, and that Jesus expresses in a new way the hope that all nations will share the faith of Israel (for example, Isa 2:2, 3). Jesus' message was new and was offered to all people, not just to the Jews. Jesus invited everyone to trust and serve God and to love their neighbors.

HOW IS MATTHEW CONSTRUCTED?

MATTHEW can be outlined in the following way:

God sends Jesus, the Christ (1:1—4:11)
Where Jesus came from (1:1—2:23)
Preparing the way for Jesus (3:1—4:11)

Jesus teaches the good news in Galilee and Judea (4:12—25:46)
Jesus preaches and chooses his first disciples (4:12-25)
Jesus teaches the crowds from a mountain (5:1—7:29)
Jesus heals many and works miracles (8:1—9:38)
Jesus instructs the twelve disciples (10:1-42)

Bethlehem in Judea: Bethlehem was known as King David's hometown (Luke 2:4) and the village where Jesus was born (Matt 2:1). A similar connection between King David and Jesus is made by including David in the list of Jesus' ancestors (1:1). In Hebrew, Bethlehem means "house of bread" or "house of food." Bethlehem is located about 2,500 feet above sea level. To the west of Bethlehem are fertile slopes and plains and the Mediterranean Sea; to the east are the dry valleys and hills that slope down to the Dead Sea.

1:1 *son of David, the son of Abraham:* Jesus was born into a Jewish family with several famous ancestors. King David was considered Israel's greatest ruler. Some prophets said that the Christ, or Messiah, would come from David's family (Isa 11:1-5). Abraham lived hundreds of years before David. Abraham obeyed God, and so God promised Abraham and Sarah that their descendants would become a great nation. Their descendants were called Israelites. See also the mini-articles called "David," p. 1028 and "Abraham," p. 2254.

1:2-11 *Abraham ... Jeconiah:* Stories about some of Jesus' ancestors can be found in Genesis 12–38; RUTH 4:13-22; 1 Sam 16-30; 2 SAMUEL; 1 and 2 KINGS.

Jesus faces opponents and their questions (11:1—12:50)
Jesus tells parables about the kingdom of heaven (13:1-58)
Jesus is the Christ (14:1—17:27)
Jesus instructs his followers (18:1-35)
Jesus faces opponents in Judea (19:1—23.39)
Jesus teaches about God's coming kingdom (24:1—25:46)

Jesus dies and is raised to life to fulfill God's plan (26:1—28:20)

God Sends Jesus, the Christ

MATTHEW begins by listing the ancestors of Jesus to make it clear that Jesus is from the family of King David and Abraham. This is followed by the story of Jesus' birth and early life. Then the story of Jesus moves ahead to when he is about thirty years of age. He meets John the Baptist, who baptizes him, and then he faces the devil's temptations in the desert. These events helped to prepare Jesus to serve as the one God chose to save the people of the world.

WHERE JESUS CAME FROM

Jesus' ancestors are listed, and his birth is described.

The Genealogy of Jesus

1 A record of the genealogy of Jesus Christ the son of David, the son of Abraham:

2 Abraham was the father of Isaac,
Isaac the father of Jacob,
Jacob the father of Judah and his brothers,
3 Judah the father of Perez and Zerah, whose mother was Tamar,
Perez the father of Hezron,
Hezron the father of Ram,
4 Ram the father of Amminadab,
Amminadab the father of Nahshon,
Nahshon the father of Salmon,
5 Salmon the father of Boaz, whose mother was Rahab,
Boaz the father of Obed, whose mother was Ruth,
Obed the father of Jesse,
6 and Jesse the father of King David.

David was the father of Solomon, whose mother had been Uriah's wife,
7 Solomon the father of Rehoboam,

Rehoboam the father of Abijah,
Abijah the father of Asa,
8 Asa the father of Jehoshaphat,
Jehoshaphat the father of Jehoram,
Jehoram the father of Uzziah,
9 Uzziah the father of Jotham,
Jotham the father of Ahaz,
Ahaz the father of Hezekiah,
10 Hezekiah the father of Manasseh,
Manasseh the father of Amon,
Amon the father of Josiah,
11 and Josiah the father of Jeconiah[a] and his brothers at the time of the exile to Babylon.

12 After the exile to Babylon:
Jeconiah was the father of Shealtiel,
Shealtiel the father of Zerubbabel,
13 Zerubbabel the father of Abiud,
Abiud the father of Eliakim,
Eliakim the father of Azor,
14 Azor the father of Zadok,
Zadok the father of Akim,
Akim the father of Eliud,
15 Eliud the father of Eleazar,
Eleazar the father of Matthan,
Matthan the father of Jacob,
16 and Jacob the father of Joseph, the husband of Mary, of whom was born Jesus, who is called Christ.

17 Thus there were fourteen generations in all from Abraham
to David, fourteen from David to the exile to Babylon, and fourteen from the exile to the Christ.[b]

---

a11 That is, Jehoiachin; also in verse 12 **b17** Or *Messiah.* "The Christ" (Greek) and "the Messiah" (Hebrew) both mean "the Anointed One."

1:11 *the time of the exile to Babylon:* In 587 or 586 B.C. the Babylonian army captured and destroyed the city of Jerusalem. The Babylonians took sacred objects from the Jewish temple and sent many of the Jewish people living in and around Jerusalem to live in Babylon. This exile lasted until 538 B.C. when the Persians defeated the Babylonians and allowed the Jewish people to return to their homeland of Judah.

1:16 *Joseph, the husband of Mary, of whom was born Jesus:* MATTHEW does not identify Joseph as "the father of Jesus," as in the pattern of the rest of this genealogy. Rather, Joseph is identified as the husband of Mary—who, as a virgin, gave birth to Jesus (1:18-25).

1:17 *Christ:* This word in Greek is *Christos.* Both *Christos* and the Hebrew word *Messiah* mean "the Anointed One" or "the Chosen One." See the mini-article called "Messiah (Chosen One)," p. 1124. Anointing was done by putting oil on someone's head to show that the person was chosen for a special duty, like a high office (1 Sam 16:13). Anointing was also considered to be a sign that God's power had come upon the person.

DATES IN B.C. AND A.D.

The initials B.C. have traditionally been an abbreviation for "Before Christ." If Luke's dating (in Luke 2:1, 2) is correct, then Jesus was born at least four years before the years known as A.D. began. (A.D. stands for the Latin phrase "in the year of our Lord".) Christian dating was actually not introduced until A.D. 526 by a monk named Dionysius Exiguus. He was given the job of creating a calendar for the feasts of the church. He fixed the birth of Jesus in the Roman year 754, which was selected as the first year of the Christian era beginning on January 1. Dionysius apparently misjudged Herod's reign by about five years.

The initials B.C.E. (Before the Common Era) and C.E. (in the Common Era) are sometimes used for the traditional B.C. and A.D.

Ethiopian Nativity from an eighteenth century illuminated manuscript called The Road to Bethlehem, artist unknown. In this picture the Magi, or Wise Men, are depicted as kings who have removed their crowns as a sign of respect. See 2:1-12.

An angel of the Lord said, *"The virgin will be with child and will give birth to a son, and they will call him Immanuel"—which means, "God with us."* Matt 1:23

1:18 *Holy Spirit:* The Holy Spirit represents the power of God at work in the world. See the mini-article called "Holy Spirit," p. 2082.

1:21 *give him the name Jesus:* The Hebrew name Joshua, which is translated as "Jesus," means "the LORD saves." See also Luke 1:31.

1:18 Luke 1:27. **1:23** Isa 7:14. **1:25** Luke 2:21.

The Birth of Jesus Christ

18This is how the birth of Jesus Christ came about: His
mother Mary was pledged to be married to Joseph, but before they
came together, she was found to be with child through the Holy
Spirit. 19Because Joseph her husband was a righteous man and did
not want to expose her to public disgrace, he had in mind to
divorce her quietly.

20But after he had considered this, an angel of the Lord
appeared to him in a dream and said, "Joseph son of David, do not
be afraid to take Mary home as your wife, because what is conceived in her is from the Holy Spirit. 21She will give birth to a son,
and you are to give him the name Jesus,[a] because he will save his
people from their sins."

22All this took place to fulfill what the Lord had said through
the prophet: 23"The virgin will be with child and will give birth to
a son, and they will call him Immanuel"[b]—which means, "God
with us."

24When Joseph woke up, he did what the angel of the Lord
had commanded him and took Mary home as his wife. 25But he
had no union with her until she gave birth to a son. And he gave
him the name Jesus.

[a]**21** *Jesus* is the Greek form of *Joshua,* which means *the LORD saves.* [b]**23** Isaiah 7:14

The Visit of the Magi

2 After Jesus was born in Bethlehem in Judea, during the time of
King Herod, Magi[a] from the east came to Jerusalem 2 and asked,
"Where is the one who has been born king of the Jews? We saw his
star in the east[b] and have come to worship him."
3 When King Herod heard this he was disturbed, and all
Jerusalem with him. 4 When he had called together all the people's
chief priests and teachers of the law, he asked them where the
Christ[c] was to be born. 5 "In Bethlehem in Judea," they replied, "for
this is what the prophet has written:

6 " 'But you, Bethlehem, in the land of Judah,
are by no means least among the rulers of Judah;
for out of you will come a ruler
who will be the shepherd of my people Israel.'[d]"

7 Then Herod called the Magi secretly and found out from
them the exact time the star had appeared. 8 He sent them to Bethlehem and said, "Go and make a careful search for the child. As
soon as you find him, report to me, so that I too may go and worship him."
9 After they had heard the king, they went on their way, and
the star they had seen in the east[e] went ahead of them until it
stopped over the place where the child was. 10 When they saw the
star, they were overjoyed. 11 On coming to the house, they saw the
child with his mother Mary, and they bowed down and worshiped
him. Then they opened their treasures and presented him with
gifts of gold and of incense and of myrrh. 12 And having been
warned in a dream not to go back to Herod, they returned to their
country by another route.

The Escape to Egypt

13 When they had gone, an angel of the Lord appeared to
Joseph in a dream. "Get up," he said, "take the child and his mother and escape to Egypt. Stay there until I tell you, for Herod is
going to search for the child to kill him."
14 So he got up, took the child and his mother during the
night and left for Egypt, 15 where he stayed until the death of
Herod. And so was fulfilled what the Lord had said through the
prophet: "Out of Egypt I called my son."[f]
16 When Herod realized that he had been outwitted by the
Magi, he was furious, and he gave orders to kill all the boys in
Bethlehem and its vicinity who were two years old and under, in
accordance with the time he had learned from the Magi. 17 Then
what was said through the prophet Jeremiah was fulfilled:

a1 Traditionally *Wise Men* **b2** Or *star when it rose* **c4** Or *Messiah*
d6 Micah 5:2 **e9** Or *seen when it rose* **f15** Hosea 11:1

2:1 *King Herod:* Also known as Herod the Great, he was first made governor of Galilee when the Romans occupied Palestine. Herod became king of Judea, Galilee, Samaria and the area east of the Jordan River in about 37 B.C. Historical records report that he died in 4 B.C. (see also 2:19). Herod rebuilt cities like Caesarea and Jericho, and he tried to become popular with the Jewish people by rebuilding the temple in Jerusalem (see the illustration on p. 1902).

2:1 *Magi from the east:* These men, identified in Greek as *magoi,* and sometimes called "Wise Men," may have been astrologers who came from a land to the east. Like others who studied the stars, they believed that when a great leader was about to be born, a new star would appear in the sky.

2:4 *chief priests and teachers of the law:* Chief priests were members of the group in charge of the temple in Jerusalem. The teachers of the law were Jewish scholars who studied the first five books of the Jewish Scriptures and explained how to live by what these books taught. See also the mini-article called "Law," p. 1160.

2:8 *so that I too may go and worship him:* Herod did not really want to worship the child, as 2:3 and 2:16 show.

2:11 *gold . . . incense . . . myrrh:* The "incense" was probably frankincense, a white gummy substance produced by certain trees in Arabia. The valuable powder made from this substance had a sweet smell and was used in Jewish worship ceremonies (Exod 30:34-38). Myrrh is a dark red gum with a strong smell and a bitter taste that comes from a bush in Arabia and Africa. It was crushed into powder and used to make expensive perfumes and ointments.

2:6 Mic 5:2. **2:15** Hos 11:1.

[18]"A voice is heard in Ramah,
weeping and great mourning,
Rachel weeping for her children
and refusing to be comforted,
because they are no more."[a]

The Return to Nazareth

[19]After Herod died, an angel of the Lord appeared in a
dream to Joseph in Egypt [20]and said, "Get up, take the child and
his mother and go to the land of Israel, for those who were trying
to take the child's life are dead."
[21]So he got up, took the child and his mother and went to
the land of Israel. [22]But when he heard that Archelaus was reigning
in Judea in place of his father Herod, he was afraid to go there.
Having been warned in a dream, he withdrew to the district of
Galilee, [23]and he went and lived in a town called Nazareth. So was
fulfilled what was said through the prophets: "He will be called a
Nazarene."

PREPARING THE WAY FOR JESUS

John tells people to repent, turn back to God, and get ready for the one God will send (Jesus). Jesus is baptized by John and faces the devil's temptations in the desert.

John the Baptist Prepares the Way

3 In those days John the Baptist came, preaching in the Desert of
Judea [2]and saying, "Repent, for the kingdom of heaven is near."
[3]This is he who was spoken of through the prophet Isaiah:

"A voice of one calling in the desert,
'Prepare the way for the Lord,
make straight paths for him.' "[b]

[4]John's clothes were made of camel's hair, and he had a
leather belt around his waist. His food was locusts and wild honey.
[5]People went out to him from Jerusalem and all Judea and the
whole region of the Jordan. [6]Confessing their sins, they were baptized by him in the Jordan River.
[7]But when he saw many of the Pharisees and Sadducees
coming to where he was baptizing, he said to them: "You brood of
vipers! Who warned you to flee from the coming wrath? [8]Produce
fruit in keeping with repentance. [9]And do not think you can say to
yourselves, 'We have Abraham as our father.' I tell you that out of
these stones God can raise up children for Abraham. [10]The ax is

[a]**18** Jer. 31:15 [b]**3** Isaiah 40:3

2:22 *Archelaus . . . his father Herod:* Archelaus was one of the sons of Herod the Great. The Romans made him governor of southern and central Palestine. See the map on p. 2472. He ruled this area from the time his father died in 4 B.C. until A.D. 6. Because Archelaus had no authority in Galilee, Joseph could live there safely with Mary and Jesus.

2:22,23 *Galilee . . . Nazareth:* Galilee was the area west of the Sea of Galilee. The area was once part of the northern kingdom of Israel. Later, it was ruled by the Assyrians, Babylonians, Persians, Greeks, and Syrians. In 63 B.C., the Romans made it part of their empire and ruled it during the time Jesus lived. Nazareth was a small town that is never mentioned in the Old Testament. See the map on p. 2473.

2:23 *Nazarene:* The exact meaning of this name is unclear. It may come from the Hebrew word meaning "branch" or "root" (Isa 11:1). MATTHEW could have been saying that Jesus would be known as a "Branch of Jesse," the father of David.

3:1 *Desert of Judea:* This is an area that stretched about twenty miles eastward from the Jerusalem-Bethlehem plateau down to the Jordan River and the Dead Sea.

3:2 *kingdom of heaven:* This term refers to the eternal rule of God, who lives in heaven, but whose kingdom will include everything that happens on earth. Jesus talks about how God's rule will be complete at some time in the future (24:14, 30). In MARK and LUKE, "kingdom of God" has the same meaning.

3:7 *Pharisees and Sadducees:* See the note at 16:1. See also 12:38.

2:23 Mark 1:24; Luke 2:39; John 1:45. **3:4** 2 Kgs 1:8. **3:7** Matt 12:34; 23:33. **3:9,10** John 8:33; Matt 7:19.

already at the root of the trees, and every tree that does not produce good fruit will be cut down and thrown into the fire.
11 “I baptize you with[a] water for repentance. But after me will
come one who is more powerful than I, whose sandals I am not fit
to carry. He will baptize you with the Holy Spirit and with fire.
12 His winnowing fork is in his hand, and he will clear his threshing floor, gathering his wheat into the barn and burning up the
chaff with unquenchable fire.”

The Baptism of Jesus

13 Then Jesus came from Galilee to the Jordan to be baptized
by John. 14 But John tried to deter him, saying, “I need to be baptized by you, and do you come to me?”
15 Jesus replied, “Let it be so now; it is proper for us to do this
to fulfill all righteousness.” Then John consented.
16 As soon as Jesus was baptized, he went up out of the water.
At that moment heaven was opened, and he saw the Spirit of God
descending like a dove and lighting on him. 17 And a voice from
heaven said, “This is my Son, whom I love; with him I am well
pleased.”

3:11 *whose sandals I am not fit to carry:* Carrying another person's sandals was one of the duties of a servant or slave.

3:12 *winnowing fork . . . chaff:* A large fork to throw the grain and husks into the air. Wind would blow away the chaff, which was lighter; and the grain would fall to the floor and be gathered up.

3:16 *Jesus was baptized:* John preached and baptized in order to encourage people to repent of their sins, turn back to God, and be forgiven (Luke 3:3). Even though John insisted that Jesus didn't need this, Jesus said he should be baptized because God wanted him to be. See also the mini-article called "Baptism," p. 1976.

3:17 Gen 22:2; Ps 2:7; Isa 42:1; Matt 12:18; 17:5; Mark 1:11; Luke 9:35.

---

[a] 11 Or *in*

JOHN THE BAPTIST

John is sometimes called the "last Old Testament prophet" because of the warnings he brought about God's judgment and because he announced the coming of God's "Anointed One" (Christ, the Messiah). LUKE reports that John was born to an old couple named Elizabeth and Zechariah, who had learned from the angel Gabriel that God was going to give them a son. This son would have special work to do in preparing the way for Christ (see Luke 1:13-17, 57-66). In the Gospels, John is described as a prophet who preached in the desert and warned people that they should get ready for the new thing God was going to do (Matt 3:1-12; Mark 1:4-8; Luke 3:1-20). John wore clothes made of camel hair (see 2 Kgs 1:8), and he ate locusts and wild honey (see Lev 11:20-23). He told the people of Israel that they could not count on being accepted by God simply because they were descendants of Abraham. They had to realize how they were disobeying God, and they needed to know how they could get ready to accept the new powerful messenger God was going to send to live among them (Luke 3:16).

John baptized people who were sorry for their sins. Many people thought he was the Christ (Luke 3:15). But John told everyone that the Messiah would be more powerful than he was (Matt 3:11, 12; Luke 3:16, 17). Jesus compared John with Elijah, the prophet who many believed would come back before God judged the world (Matt 11:14), and he said that John's work was to prepare people for the coming of the kingdom of God (Matt 11:10; Luke 7:27). Herod Antipas, a son of Herod the Great and brother of Archelaus (Matt 2:19-22), ordered that John the Baptist be killed (Matt 14:1-12; Mark 6:14-29).

Jesus answered, "It is written: 'Man does not live on bread alone, but on every word that comes from the mouth of God.'" Matt 4:4

4:1 *the Spirit . . . devil:* See the note at 1:18. The devil is the leader of the evil forces that are against God and God's people. See the mini-article called "Satan," p. 963.

4:1 *desert:* This was probably the Desert of Judea. See the note at 3:1.

4:2 *fasting forty days and forty nights:* On special occasions the Jewish people went without eating to show sorrow for their sins. In this case, Jesus probably fasted to show his dedication to God, just as Moses had done (Deut 9:9,18). The number forty has special meaning in the Bible. See also the chart called "Numbers in the Bible," p. 2405.

4:3 *tell these stones to become bread:* The devil was taking advantage of Jesus' hunger to try to make him act disloyally toward God.

4:1 Heb 2:18; 4:15.

The Temptation of Jesus

4 Then Jesus was led by the Spirit into the desert to be tempted
by the devil. [2]After fasting forty days and forty nights, he was hungry. [3]The tempter came to him and said, "If you are the Son of
God, tell these stones to become bread."
[4]Jesus answered, "It is written: 'Man does not live on bread
alone, but on every word that comes from the mouth of God.'[a]"
[5]Then the devil took him to the holy city and had him stand
on the highest point of the temple. [6]"If you are the Son of God," he
said, "throw yourself down. For it is written:

" 'He will command his angels concerning you,
and they will lift you up in their hands,
so that you will not strike your foot against a stone.'[b]"

[7]Jesus answered him, "It is also written: 'Do not put the Lord
your God to the test.'[c]"
[8]Again, the devil took him to a very high mountain and
showed him all the kingdoms of the world and their splendor. [9]"All
this I will give you," he said, "if you will bow down and worship me."
[10]Jesus said to him, "Away from me, Satan! For it is written:
'Worship the Lord your God, and serve him only.'[d]"
[11]Then the devil left him, and angels came and attended
him.

[a]**4** Deut. 8:3 [b]**6** Psalm 91:11,12 [c]**7** Deut. 6:16 [d]**10** Deut. 6:13

QUESTIONS ABOUT MATTHEW 1:1—4:11

1. Matthew begins with a genealogy of Jesus (1:1-17). Who were Jesus' most important ancestors? What special meaning did his birth have?
2. How did Joseph, the Magi, and King Herod react to the birth of Jesus? (1:18—2:18) Why did Herod react the way he did?
3. Think of ways in which people mistreat others because they want to hold on to power. Have there been times when you have misused power? Have you ever been mistreated by someone who wanted to hold on to power? If so, describe the situation.
4. What was John the Baptist's message and why was it important? (3:1-12) What does it mean to "repent"?
5. After Jesus was baptized by John, the Holy Spirit led him into the desert (4:1-11). What happened there? How did Jesus respond to the things the devil suggested?

Jesus Teaches the Good News in Galilee and Judea

The next major section of MATTHEW *tells about what Jesus did and what he taught, first in his home region of Galilee (4:12—18:35), and then in the area of Judea (19:1—25:46). Jesus has predicted that he will have to go to Jerusalem and face his enemies (16:21).*

JESUS PREACHES AND CHOOSES HIS FIRST DISCIPLES

Jesus Begins to Preach

[12]When Jesus heard that John had been put in prison, he
returned to Galilee. [13]Leaving Nazareth, he went and lived in
Capernaum, which was by the lake in the area of Zebulun and
Naphtali— [14]to fulfill what was said through the prophet Isaiah:

[15]"Land of Zebulun and land of Naphtali,
the way to the sea, along the Jordan,
Galilee of the Gentiles—
[16]the people living in darkness
have seen a great light;
on those living in the land of the shadow of death
a light has dawned."[a]

[17]From that time on Jesus began to preach, "Repent, for the
kingdom of heaven is near."

The Calling of the First Disciples

[18]As Jesus was walking beside the Sea of Galilee, he saw two
brothers, Simon called Peter and his brother Andrew. They were
casting a net into the lake, for they were fishermen. [19]"Come, follow me," Jesus said, "and I will make you fishers of men." [20]At once
they left their nets and followed him.
[21]Going on from there, he saw two other brothers, James son
of Zebedee and his brother John. They were in a boat with their
father Zebedee, preparing their nets. Jesus called them, [22]and
immediately they left the boat and their father and followed
him.

Jesus Heals the Sick

[23]Jesus went throughout Galilee, teaching in their synagogues, preaching the good news of the kingdom, and healing
every disease and sickness among the people. [24]News about him
spread all over Syria, and people brought to him all who were ill

[a]**16** Isaiah 9:1,2

4:13 *Capernaum ... by the lake:* An important fishing town on the northern shore of the Sea of Galilee (here called "the lake") located on a major trade route between Egypt and Syria. In Jesus' day, Capernaum was a base for Roman soldiers who enforced the collection of taxes. Jesus moved to Capernaum from Nazareth. The Sea of Galilee is also known as the Lake of Gennesaret (Luke 5:1) and the Sea of Tiberias (John 6:1; 21:1). See the map on p. 2473.

4:13 *Zebulun and Naphtali:* In Old Testament times these Israelite tribes settled in northern Palestine. In New Testament times, many Gentiles (non-Jews) lived where these tribes had once been.

4:18 *casting a net into the lake ... fishermen:* Fishing on the Sea of Galilee was often done by spinning a circular net overhead and throwing (casting) it into shallow water. The outside of the net had weights tied to it so the net would sink in the shape of a dome. When the fish swam into this dome, the fisherman would pull the net closed with a line attached to its center. For more, see the mini-article called "How People Made a Living in the Time of Jesus," p. 1826, and "Fish and Fishing," p. 1922.

4:23,24 *synagogue ... those having seizures:* For "synagogues," see the mini-article on p. 1857. In ancient times people who had convulsions or seizures (uncontrolled shaking) caused by diseases like epilepsy were thought to be crazy or under the influence of the moon or evil spirits. However, in many cases demon-possession was real, for Jesus did indeed cast out demons from many people. See the note at 8:16.

4:12 Matt 14:3; Mark 6:17; Luke 3:19,20. **4:23** Matt 9:35; Mark 1:39.

4:25 *Decapolis:* A group of ten Gentile cities east of Samaria and Galilee. The buildings in these cities were designed according to Greek architecture, and each city was laid out in the style of a typical Greek city. The people who lived in them followed the Greek way of life. See the illustration on p. 1858.

5:1 *mountainside:* In MATTHEW, Jesus often went up on the side of a mountain to teach or to pray or to be alone (14:23; 15:29; 17:1, 2; 24:3; 28:16). This makes him like Moses, who went up on Mount Sinai to learn from God what he should teach the people of Israel (see Exod 19).

5:1 *sat down:* Teachers in the ancient world, including Jewish teachers, usually sat down when they taught.

5:13 *salt:* Salt was used to flavor food and to keep it from spoiling. Jesus was telling his followers to help others, just as salt helps the taste of food. See also Mark 9:50; Luke 14:34, 35.

5:14,15 *light . . . lamp:* In Jesus' day, people used small clay lamps that burned olive oil. In the Old Testament, God's Word is compared to a "lamp" and a "light" (Ps 119:105). See also John 8:12; 9:5.

5:4-6 Isa 61:2; Ps 37:11; Isa 55:1,2. **5:8** Ps 24:3,4. **5:10,11** 1 Pet 3:14; 4:14. **5:12** 2 Chr 36:16; Acts 7:52. **5:15** Mark 4:21; Luke 8:16; 11:33.

with various diseases, those suffering severe pain, the demon-
possessed, those having seizures, and the paralyzed, and he healed
them. 25 Large crowds from Galilee, the Decapolis,[a] Jerusalem,
Judea and the region across the Jordan followed him.

JESUS TEACHES THE CROWDS FROM A MOUNTAIN

In this long section (chapters 5–7), Jesus teaches about practical matters like prayer, marriage and divorce, money, and dealing with worry.

The Beatitudes

5 Now when he saw the crowds, he went up on a mountainside
and sat down. His disciples came to him, 2 and he began to teach
them, saying:

3 "Blessed are the poor in spirit,
for theirs is the kingdom of heaven.
4 Blessed are those who mourn,
for they will be comforted.
5 Blessed are the meek,
for they will inherit the earth.
6 Blessed are those who hunger and thirst for righteousness,
for they will be filled.
7 Blessed are the merciful,
for they will be shown mercy.
8 Blessed are the pure in heart,
for they will see God.
9 Blessed are the peacemakers,
for they will be called sons of God.
10 Blessed are those who are persecuted because of righteousness,
for theirs is the kingdom of heaven.

11 "Blessed are you when people insult you, persecute you
and falsely say all kinds of evil against you because of me. 12 Rejoice
and be glad, because great is your reward in heaven, for in the
same way they persecuted the prophets who were before you.

Salt and Light

13 "You are the salt of the earth. But if the salt loses its saltiness, how can it be made salty again? It is no longer good for anything, except to be thrown out and trampled by men.
14 "You are the light of the world. A city on a hill cannot be
hidden. 15 Neither do people light a lamp and put it under a bowl.

[a]25 That is, the Ten Cities

Instead they put it on its stand, and it gives light to everyone in the
house. 16 In the same way, let your light shine before men, that they
may see your good deeds and praise your Father in heaven.

The Fulfillment of the Law

17 "Do not think that I have come to abolish the Law or the
Prophets; I have not come to abolish them but to fulfill them. 18 I
tell you the truth, until heaven and earth disappear, not the smallest letter, not the least stroke of a pen, will by any means disappear
from the Law until everything is accomplished. 19 Anyone who
breaks one of the least of these commandments and teaches others to do the same will be called least in the kingdom of heaven,
but whoever practices and teaches these commands will be called

5:17 *the Law or the Prophets:* As a phrase, this can mean all of the Jewish Scriptures, including the section known as the "writings." Specifically, the "Law" refers to the first five books of the Jewish Scriptures: GENESIS, EXODUS, LEVITICUS, NUMBERS, and DEUTERONOMY. The "Prophets" refers to the books of JOSHUA, JUDGES, SAMUEL, KINGS, ISAIAH, JEREMIAH, EZEKIEL, and the twelve minor prophets. See the article called "What Books Belong in the Bible?" p. 13.

5:16 1 Pet 2:12. **5:18** Luke 16:17.

SYNAGOGUES

Synagogue comes directly from a Greek word that means "gathering." In the broad sense, a "synagogue" was any group of people who met together. Just when the Jewish synagogue meetings began is not certain, but they may have begun after the Babylonians defeated Judah and took many of the Jewish people away in 586 B.C. While in Babylon, the people could not worship or offer sacrifices to God at the temple in Jerusalem, so they were forced to find different ways to worship.

Later, the Jewish people began moving to other parts of the world, especially to Egypt, Greece, and areas known today as Turkey and southern Russia. They also began meeting together for worship, study, and to keep their group identity. These meetings were called synagogues. In their own land, Jews continued to have these meetings even when Seleucid kings tried to force them to worship Greek gods. One of these kings, Antiochus IV Epiphanes, who ruled Palestine from 175-164 B.C., claimed that he himself was a god, just as Alexander the Great had done years before him. Jewish priests from the family known as the Maccabees led a revolt against the Greek leader. They gained freedom for the Jews and ruled the land, but the actions of the Maccabean leaders later caused divisions among their own people. Some of the people were not content just to go to the temple for worship. They met in homes and public rooms to study the Scriptures and find the real meaning of their lives as God's people.

This was the situation during the lifetime of Jesus (Matt 4:23; 9:35) and the apostles (Acts 1:12-14; 9:2, 20; 13:5). Under Jewish law, a synagogue could be formed only if there were at least ten male heads of families. In locations where there weren't enough Jews to have a synagogue, the meeting places were known as "places of prayer" (Acts 16:13). After the Roman military forces destroyed the Jerusalem temple in A.D. 70, the temple's priests no longer had a place to lead the people in worship of God. With the loss of the temple, synagogues became the most important feature of Jewish worship and community experience throughout the Mediterranean world. The Jewish people continued to meet in homes or public halls, as was the case when Paul was in Ephesus (Acts 19:8-10). It wasn't until the second and third centuries A.D. that houses were remodeled or new meeting places were built to serve as formal settings for worshiping God. These meeting places were also called synagogues. The remains of many have been found in various parts of the land of Israel and throughout the countries that border the Mediterranean Sea.

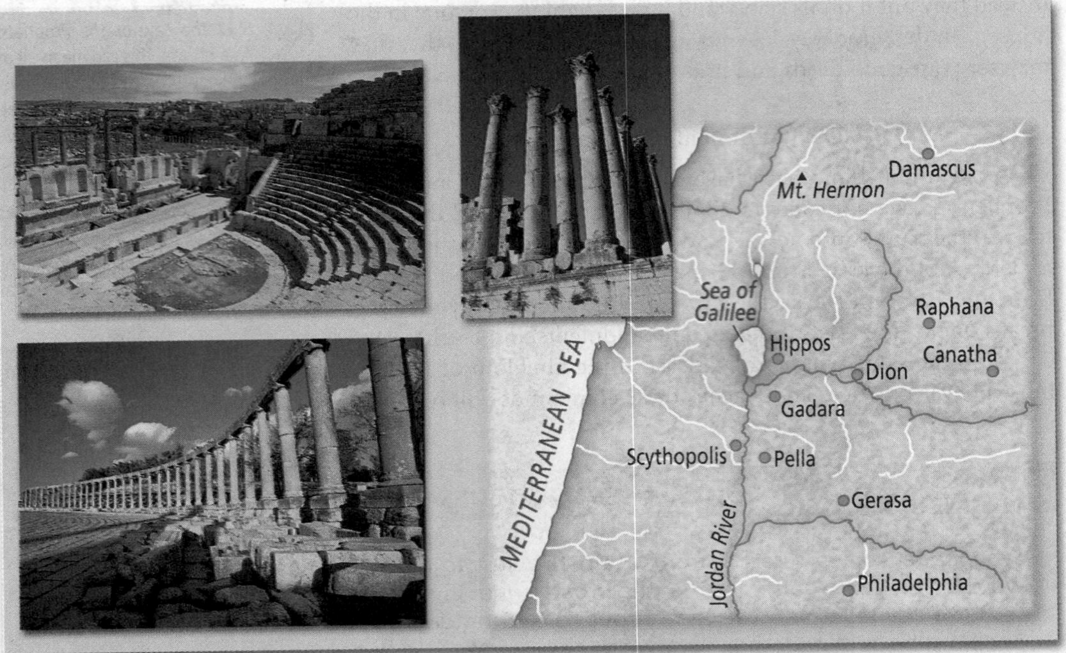

Cities of the Decapolis. A Greek term meaning "Ten Cities," Decapolis describes a region east of the Sea of Galilee and the Jordan Valley (Matt 4:25). Damascus is almost 70 miles northeast of Hippos on the Sea of Galilee's eastern shore; Philadelphia, the southeasternmost city, is within 25 miles of the Dead Sea. All ten cities (see map) were strongly influenced by the Greek culture that was brought to Palestine after its conquest by Alexander the Great (late fourth century B.C.). The ruins of Gerasa (modern Jerash) show features that would have been typical of many Greek-influenced Roman cities of the first century A.D.: an amphitheater, a forum (marketplace), and one or more temples to pagan gods and goddesses (the one shown here was built in honor of Artemis).

great in the kingdom of heaven. [20]For I tell you that unless your
righteousness surpasses that of the Pharisees and the teachers of
the law, you will certainly not enter the kingdom of heaven.

Murder

[21]"You have heard that it was said to the people long ago, 'Do
not murder,[a] and anyone who murders will be subject to judgment.' [22]But I tell you that anyone who is angry with his brother[b]
will be subject to judgment. Again, anyone who says to his brother, 'Raca,[c]' is answerable to the Sanhedrin. But anyone who says,
'You fool!' will be in danger of the fire of hell.
[23]"Therefore, if you are offering your gift at the altar and
there remember that your brother has something against you,
[24]leave your gift there in front of the altar. First go and be reconciled to your brother; then come and offer your gift.

5:22 *Sanhedrin:* See the note at 26:3.

5:22 *fire of hell:* In Greek, the word for hell is *gehenna*, from the Hebrew words that mean "Valley of Ben Hinnom," a valley near Jerusalem where children were once burned as sacrifices to the god Molech (Jer 32:35; Lev 20:2-5). It later became a place for burning garbage. In the century before Jesus was born, some Jewish teachers taught that the place where wicked people go when they die is like the burning Valley of Ben Hinnom. So the New Testament pictures the place of judgment as one of fiery torture (Luke 16:23, 24; Rev 20:14). See also the mini-article called "Hell," p. 1944.

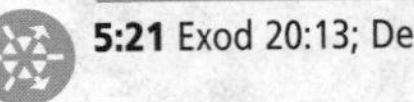

5:21 Exod 20:13; Deut 5:17.

[a]**21** Exodus 20:13 [b]**22** Some manuscripts *brother without cause* [c]**22** An Aramaic term of contempt

[25]"Settle matters quickly with your adversary who is taking
you to court. Do it while you are still with him on the way, or he
may hand you over to the judge, and the judge may hand you over
to the officer, and you may be thrown into prison. [26]I tell you the
truth, you will not get out until you have paid the last penny.[a]

Adultery

[27]"You have heard that it was said, 'Do not commit adultery.'[b] [28]But I tell you that anyone who looks at a woman lustfully
has already committed adultery with her in his heart. [29]If your
right eye causes you to sin, gouge it out and throw it away. It is better for you to lose one part of your body than for your whole body
to be thrown into hell. [30]And if your right hand causes you to sin,
cut it off and throw it away. It is better for you to lose one part of
your body than for your whole body to go into hell.

Divorce

[31]"It has been said, 'Anyone who divorces his wife must give
her a certificate of divorce.'[c] [32]But I tell you that anyone who
divorces his wife, except for marital unfaithfulness, causes her to

[a]**26** Greek *kodrantes* [b]**27** Exodus 20:14 [c]**31** Deut. 24:1

Sermon on the Mount, Fra Angelico (died 1455). This fresco from the Museum of San Marco, Florence, Italy, shows Jesus giving his famous sermon sitting down (see Matt 5:1). In Jesus' day this is the way a teacher (rabbi) would have taught his followers.

Jesus said, *"If you are offering your gift at the altar and there remember that your brother has something against you, leave your gift there in front of the altar. First go and be reconciled to your brother; then come and offer your gift."* Matt 5:23,24

5:24 *gift there in front of the altar:* While the temple in Jerusalem was still standing, Jewish people offered to God gifts called "sacrifices." Jesus told people not to offer their gifts to God until after they have made peace with others who might be angry at them.

5:31 *a certificate of divorce:* The Law of Moses required a man to write out legal papers before divorcing his wife. The purpose of this was to make it harder for a man to divorce his wife. Before this, a man could simply send his wife away and say that she was no longer his wife. The Law of Moses did not allow women to divorce their husbands. See also 19:7 and Mark 10:4.

5:27 Deut 5:18. **5:29** Matt 18:9; Mark 9:47. **5:30** Matt 18:8; Mark 9:43. **5:32** Matt 19:9; Mark 10:11, 12; Luke 16:18; 1 Cor 7:10,11.

Jesus taught,
"Love your enemies and pray for those who persecute you."
Matt 5:43

5:39 *strikes you on the right cheek:* A slap on the cheek was a serious insult.

5:41 *one mile ... two miles:* Under Roman law a soldier had the right to force a person to carry his pack as far as one mile.

5:46 *tax collectors:* The Romans hired local people to collect taxes for them. These tax collectors often collected much more than they needed to pay the Romans, keeping the rest for themselves. The Jewish tax collectors in Palestine were hated by their own people, who considered them traitors to their country and to their religion. Also, their work and associations with the Romans made them "unclean" according to Jewish laws.

6:1 *acts of righteousness:* This refers to the three acts of devotion that the Jewish people thought were most important: giving gifts to the poor, praying, and fasting (not eating during certain periods of time). In 6:1-18, Jesus reminds people not to misuse these good deeds by doing them in a way that draws attention to themselves.

6:2,5 *hypocrites:* Jesus is not opposed to sincere acts of public devotion, but warns against becoming a religious "showoff." See also the note at 23:5.

5:34,35 Jas 5:12; Isa 66:1; Matt 3:22. **5:48** Lev 19:2; Deut 18:13.

become an adulteress, and anyone who marries the divorced woman commits adultery.

Oaths

[33]"Again, you have heard that it was said to the people long ago, 'Do not break your oath, but keep the oaths you have made to the Lord.' [34]But I tell you, Do not swear at all: either by heaven, for it is God's throne; [35]or by the earth, for it is his footstool; or by Jerusalem, for it is the city of the Great King. [36]And do not swear by your head, for you cannot make even one hair white or black. [37]Simply let your 'Yes' be 'Yes,' and your 'No,' 'No'; anything beyond this comes from the evil one.

An Eye for an Eye

[38]"You have heard that it was said, 'Eye for eye, and tooth for tooth.'[a] [39]But I tell you, Do not resist an evil person. If someone strikes you on the right cheek, turn to him the other also. [40]And if someone wants to sue you and take your tunic, let him have your cloak as well. [41]If someone forces you to go one mile, go with him two miles. [42]Give to the one who asks you, and do not turn away from the one who wants to borrow from you.

Love for Enemies

[43]"You have heard that it was said, 'Love your neighbor[b] and hate your enemy.' [44]But I tell you: Love your enemies[c] and pray for those who persecute you, [45]that you may be sons of your Father in heaven. He causes his sun to rise on the evil and the good, and sends rain on the righteous and the unrighteous. [46]If you love those who love you, what reward will you get? Are not even the tax collectors doing that? [47]And if you greet only your brothers, what are you doing more than others? Do not even pagans do that? [48]Be perfect, therefore, as your heavenly Father is perfect.

Giving to the Needy

6 "Be careful not to do your 'acts of righteousness' before men, to be seen by them. If you do, you will have no reward from your Father in heaven.

[2]"So when you give to the needy, do not announce it with trumpets, as the hypocrites do in the synagogues and on the streets, to be honored by men. I tell you the truth, they have received their reward in full. [3]But when you give to the needy, do not let your left hand know what your right hand is doing, [4]so that your giving may be in secret. Then your Father, who sees what is done in secret, will reward you.

[a]**38** Exodus 21:24; Lev. 24:20; Deut. 19:21 [b]**43** Lev. 19:18 [c]**44** Some late manuscripts *enemies, bless those who curse you, do good to those who hate you*

Prayer

5“And when you pray, do not be like the hypocrites, for
they love to pray standing in the synagogues and on the street
corners to be seen by men. I tell you the truth, they have received
their reward in full. 6But when you pray, go into your room, close
the door and pray to your Father, who is unseen. Then your
Father, who sees what is done in secret, will reward you. 7And
when you pray, do not keep on babbling like pagans, for they
think they will be heard because of their many words. 8Do not
be like them, for your Father knows what you need before you
ask him.

9“This, then, is how you should pray:

“ ‘Our Father in heaven,
hallowed be your name,
10your kingdom come,
your will be done
on earth as it is in heaven.
11Give us today our daily bread.
12Forgive us our debts,
as we also have forgiven our debtors.
13And lead us not into temptation,
but deliver us from the evil one.[a]’

14For if you forgive men when they sin against you, your heavenly
Father will also forgive you. 15But if you do not forgive men their
sins, your Father will not forgive your sins.

Fasting

16“When you fast, do not look somber as the hypocrites do,
for they disfigure their faces to show men they are fasting. I tell
you the truth, they have received their reward in full. 17But when
you fast, put oil on your head and wash your face, 18so that it will
not be obvious to men that you are fasting, but only to your
Father, who is unseen; and your Father, who sees what is done in
secret, will reward you.

Treasures in Heaven

19“Do not store up for yourselves treasures on earth, where
moth and rust destroy, and where thieves break in and steal. 20But
store up for yourselves treasures in heaven, where moth and rust
do not destroy, and where thieves do not break in and steal. 21For
where your treasure is, there your heart will be also.

22“The eye is the lamp of the body. If your eyes are good,
your whole body will be full of light. 23But if your eyes are bad,

[a]**13** Or *from evil;* some late manuscripts *one, / for yours is the kingdom and the power and the glory forever. Amen.*

Jesus taught,
“Store up for yourselves treasures in heaven, where moth and rust do not destroy, and where thieves do not break in and steal. For where your treasure is, there your heart will be also.”
Matt 6:20,21

6:5 *pray:* The Jewish people usually prayed in public at the temple or in their synagogues, normally while standing with their arms raised. They also prayed while kneeling or lying down. Jesus wanted people to see that it was wrong to pray just to be seen by others. See also the mini-article called “Prayer,” p. 2289.

6:9 *hallowed be your name:* This means “let your name be regarded as holy.” This is not so much a prayer of petition as it is an act of worship.

6:16-18 *When you fast . . . disfigure your faces:* Going without eating, wearing sackcloth (garments made out of coarse material), and putting ashes on one’s head were three ways people in the ancient world showed they were sorry for their sins (see Lev 16:29-31; Dan 9:3; Jonah 3:5-8). People also fasted when asking for God’s protection (Ezra 8:21) or as a way of preparing to do God’s work (Matt 4:2). Sitting in ashes or putting ashes on one’s head was also done during times of deep mourning (Job 2:8; Jer 6:26). Like Jesus, the Old Testament prophets were aware that fasting was not always sincere (Isa 58:3-5).

6:14,15 Mark 11:25,26. **6:16** Matt 4:2. **6:19** Jas 5:2,3.

> Jesus said,
> *"Do not worry about tomorrow, for tomorrow will worry about itself. Each day has enough trouble of its own."*
> Matt 6:34

6:29 *Solomon in all his splendor:* Solomon, son of the great King David, ruled Israel at a time when the country was very rich. Solomon collected taxes from his own people to train a large army, to build the first temple in Jerusalem, and to construct a huge palace for himself. He had dealings with the leaders of many of Israel's neighbors. According to Jewish tradition, Solomon was the wisest and richest person who had ever lived. See 1 Kgs 10:4-7; 2 Chr 9:3-6.

7:12 *the Law and the Prophets:* See the note at 5:17.

7:2 Mark 4:24.

your whole body will be full of darkness. If then the light within you is darkness, how great is that darkness!

[24]"No one can serve two masters. Either he will hate the one and love the other, or he will be devoted to the one and despise the other. You cannot serve both God and Money.

Do Not Worry

[25]"Therefore I tell you, do not worry about your life, what you will eat or drink; or about your body, what you will wear. Is not life more important than food, and the body more important than clothes? [26]Look at the birds of the air; they do not sow or reap or store away in barns, and yet your heavenly Father feeds them. Are you not much more valuable than they? [27]Who of you by worrying can add a single hour to his life[a]?

[28]"And why do you worry about clothes? See how the lilies of the field grow. They do not labor or spin. [29]Yet I tell you that not even Solomon in all his splendor was dressed like one of these. [30]If that is how God clothes the grass of the field, which is here today and tomorrow is thrown into the fire, will he not much more clothe you, O you of little faith? [31]So do not worry, saying, 'What shall we eat?' or 'What shall we drink?' or 'What shall we wear?' [32]For the pagans run after all these things, and your heavenly Father knows that you need them. [33]But seek first his kingdom and his righteousness, and all these things will be given to you as well. [34]Therefore do not worry about tomorrow, for tomorrow will worry about itself. Each day has enough trouble of its own.

Judging Others

7 "Do not judge, or you too will be judged. [2]For in the same way you judge others, you will be judged, and with the measure you use, it will be measured to you.

[3]"Why do you look at the speck of sawdust in your brother's eye and pay no attention to the plank in your own eye? [4]How can you say to your brother, 'Let me take the speck out of your eye,' when all the time there is a plank in your own eye? [5]You hypocrite, first take the plank out of your own eye, and then you will see clearly to remove the speck from your brother's eye.

[6]"Do not give dogs what is sacred; do not throw your pearls to pigs. If you do, they may trample them under their feet, and then turn and tear you to pieces.

Ask, Seek, Knock

[7]"Ask and it will be given to you; seek and you will find; knock and the door will be opened to you. [8]For everyone who asks

[a]27 Or *single cubit to his height*

receives; he who seeks finds; and to him who knocks, the door will be opened.
[9]"Which of you, if his son asks for bread, will give him a stone? [10]Or if he asks for a fish, will give him a snake? [11]If you, then, though you are evil, know how to give good gifts to your children, how much more will your Father in heaven give good gifts to those who ask him! [12]So in everything, do to others what you would have them do to you, for this sums up the Law and the Prophets.

The Narrow and Wide Gates

[13]"Enter through the narrow gate. For wide is the gate and broad is the road that leads to destruction, and many enter through it. [14]But small is the gate and narrow the road that leads to life, and only a few find it.

A Tree and Its Fruit

[15]"Watch out for false prophets. They come to you in sheep's clothing, but inwardly they are ferocious wolves. [16]By their fruit you will recognize them. Do people pick grapes from thornbushes, or figs from thistles? [17]Likewise every good tree bears good fruit, but a bad tree bears bad fruit. [18]A good tree cannot bear bad fruit, and a bad tree cannot bear good fruit. [19]Every tree that does not bear good fruit is cut down and thrown into the fire. [20]Thus, by their fruit you will recognize them.
[21]"Not everyone who says to me, 'Lord, Lord,' will enter the kingdom of heaven, but only he who does the will of my Father who is in heaven. [22]Many will say to me on that day, 'Lord, Lord, did we not prophesy in your name, and in your name drive out demons and perform many miracles?' [23]Then I will tell them plainly, 'I never knew you. Away from me, you evildoers!'

7:15 *false prophets:* Those who claim to speak for God but actually lead God's people away from the truth into trouble.

7:16 *figs:* Figs are sweet fruits from bushy trees that grow as high as 30 feet. A fig tree can produce two crops each year. The early fig crop ripens in June and is eaten fresh. The second crop is harvested in August or September. Many families covered the roofs of their homes with this second crop of figs so they could dry in the sun, and then be eaten during the winter months.

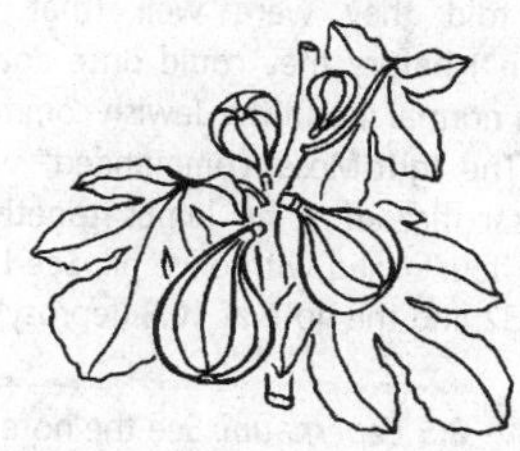

7:22 *on that day:* Refers to the coming day of judgment when God will examine how people have lived and judge whether they have been faithful and obedient to him. This is an important theme in MATTHEW. See also the mini-article called "Day of the LORD," p. 1727.

7:12 Lev 19:18; Luke 6:31. **7:19** Matt 3:10; Luke 3:9. **7:20** Matt 12:33. **7:23** Ps 6:8.

QUESTIONS ABOUT MATTHEW 4:12—7:29

1. Who did Jesus choose to be his first followers? (4:18-22) What do you think Jesus meant when he told them they would be "fishers of men"? How can Jesus' followers today be fishers of men and women?
2. Read through the list of beatitudes found in 5:3-12. Which ones do you find most comforting? Which are most puzzling to you? Why?
3. In this section known as the Sermon on the Mount, Jesus taught about many things. Choose five of Jesus' teachings that you find most challenging. How can applying these lessons improve your life and strengthen your faith?
4. What is the purpose of prayer? (6:5-15) What sorts of things does Jesus want his followers to pray for? What is the relationship of prayer and forgiveness? What do you pray about?
5. What was the most important thing you learned while reading the Sermon on the Mount? Why?

The Wise and Foolish Builders

24"Therefore everyone who hears these words of mine and puts them into practice is like a wise man who built his house on the rock. 25The rain came down, the streams rose, and the winds blew and beat against that house; yet it did not fall, because it had its foundation on the rock. 26But everyone who hears these words of mine and does not put them into practice is like a foolish man who built his house on sand. 27The rain came down, the streams rose, and the winds blew and beat against that house, and it fell with a great crash."

28When Jesus had finished saying these things, the crowds were amazed at his teaching, 29because he taught as one who had authority, and not as their teachers of the law.

JESUS HEALS MANY AND WORKS MIRACLES

Jesus continues his ministry in Galilee by healing many people and working a number of miracles. He also chooses Matthew to be one of his disciples.

The Man With Leprosy

8 When he came down from the mountainside, large crowds followed him. 2A man with leprosy[a] came and knelt before him and said, "Lord, if you are willing, you can make me clean."

3Jesus reached out his hand and touched the man. "I am willing," he said. "Be clean!" Immediately he was cured[b] of his leprosy. 4Then Jesus said to him, "See that you don't tell anyone. But go, show yourself to the priest and offer the gift Moses commanded, as a testimony to them."

The Faith of the Centurion

5When Jesus had entered Capernaum, a centurion came to him, asking for help. 6"Lord," he said, "my servant lies at home paralyzed and in terrible suffering."

7Jesus said to him, "I will go and heal him."

8The centurion replied, "Lord, I do not deserve to have you come under my roof. But just say the word, and my servant will be healed. 9For I myself am a man under authority, with soldiers under me. I tell this one, 'Go,' and he goes; and that one, 'Come,' and he comes. I say to my servant, 'Do this,' and he does it."

10When Jesus heard this, he was astonished and said to those following him, "I tell you the truth, I have not found anyone in Israel with such great faith. 11I say to you that many will come from the east and the west, and will take their places at the feast

[a]2 The Greek word was used for various diseases affecting the skin—not necessarily leprosy. [b]3 Greek *made clean*

7:28 *When Jesus had finished saying these things:* This phrase or one like it is repeated five times in MATTHEW (7:28; 11:1; 13:53; 19:1; 26:1). These phrases give the reader a clue about how MATTHEW is organized. Matthew 4–25 can be divided into five sections, each of which ends with this phrase. Each section has two smaller parts—one telling what Jesus did, and the other giving some of Jesus' teachings.

8:2-4 *leprosy . . . go, show yourself to the priest:* People with leprosy had to be examined by a priest and told they were well (that is, "clean") before they could once again live a normal life in the Jewish community. The "gift Moses commanded" was the sacrifice of some lambs together with flour mixed with olive oil. See Lev 14:1-32 and the note at 10:8 (leprosy).

8:5 *Capernaum:* See the note at 4:13 (Capernaum).

8:5 *centurion:* A Roman military officer who commanded and trained one hundred men. Centurions were expected to serve in the army for twenty-five years.

8:11 *feast . . . kingdom of heaven:* This refers to a future event when God will bring together all who trust in Jesus, not only those from the people of Israel but from every nation. Jesus compares this event to a feast, a time of celebration. See also Isa 25:6-8; Luke 13:29.

7:28,29 Mark 1:22; Luke 4:32. **8:12** Luke 13:28.

with Abraham, Isaac and Jacob in the kingdom of heaven. 12But
the subjects of the kingdom will be thrown outside, into the darkness, where there will be weeping and gnashing of teeth."
13Then Jesus said to the centurion, "Go! It will be done just
as you believed it would." And his servant was healed at that very
hour.

Jesus Heals Many

14When Jesus came into Peter's house, he saw Peter's mother-
in-law lying in bed with a fever. 15He touched her hand and the
fever left her, and she got up and began to wait on him.
16When evening came, many who were demon-possessed
were brought to him, and he drove out the spirits with a word and
healed all the sick. 17This was to fulfill what was spoken through
the prophet Isaiah:

> "He took up our infirmities
> and carried our diseases."[a]

The Cost of Following Jesus

18When Jesus saw the crowd around him, he gave orders to
cross to the other side of the lake. 19Then a teacher of the law came
to him and said, "Teacher, I will follow you wherever you go."
20Jesus replied, "Foxes have holes and birds of the air have
nests, but the Son of Man has no place to lay his head."
21Another disciple said to him, "Lord, first let me go and
bury my father."
22But Jesus told him, "Follow me, and let the dead bury their
own dead."

Jesus Calms the Storm

23Then he got into the boat and his disciples followed him.
24Without warning, a furious storm came up on the lake, so that
the waves swept over the boat. But Jesus was sleeping. 25The disciples went and woke him, saying, "Lord, save us! We're going to
drown!"
26He replied, "You of little faith, why are you so afraid?" Then
he got up and rebuked the winds and the waves, and it was completely calm.
27The men were amazed and asked, "What kind of man is
this? Even the winds and the waves obey him!"

The Healing of Two Demon-possessed Men

28When he arrived at the other side in the region of the
Gadarenes,[b] two demon-possessed men coming from the tombs

[a]17 Isaiah 53:4 [b]28 Some manuscripts *Gergesenes*; others *Gerasenes*

8:12 *into the darkness:* This is a description of the place of punishment for those who do evil. See also 22:13; 25:30; and the note at 5:22.

8:14 *Peter's house:* See the note at 10:2.

8:16 *demon-possessed . . . drove out the spirits:* Demons are evil spirits that work for the devil. They were understood to be the cause of many kinds of sickness and mental illness.

8:19 *teacher of the law:* Another name for this kind of teacher was *scribe,* which means one who was an expert in the sacred writings. These scribes studied the Jewish Scriptures and interpreted the law in order to help people know how they should live.

8:20 *Son of Man:* When Jesus calls himself the Son of Man here, he may be drawing attention to the fact that he is a human being. For more, see the mini-article called "Son of Man," p. 1866.

8:22 *let the dead bury their own dead:* For more about Jewish burial customs, see the mini-article called "Burial," p. 1998. It is not clear if the disciple's father is sick and dying, or if he is already dead. In either case, Jesus seems to be saying that other friends and relatives who are spiritually "dead" can fulfill the burial obligation while the disciple joins in Jesus' ministry.

8:28 *region of the Gadarenes:* The city of Gadara was located east of the Jordan River and to the south of the Sea of Galilee. Its population, architecture, and style of life were mostly Greek. See the map on p. 1858.

8:28 *tombs:* In Palestine, tombs were usually carved out of the soft limestone hillsides. For more, see the mini-article called "Burial," p. 1998.

8:29 *Son of God:* The demons knew that Jesus was God's Son, even if people did not fully believe, or understand who Jesus was. See the mini-article called "Son of God," p. 2044.

8:30 *large herd of pigs:* According to the Law of Moses, pigs were considered "unclean" animals and were not to be eaten (Lev 11:4-8; Deut 14:8). The fact that a large herd of pigs was near Gadara makes it clear that this was a Gentile area where few Jews lived. See also the mini-article called "Purity (Clean and Unclean)," p. 2125.

9:1 *his own town:* Referring to Capernaum. Although Jesus grew up in Nazareth, more recently he had been living in Capernaum (see 4:13).

met him. They were so violent that no one could pass that way.
29"What do you want with us, Son of God?" they shouted. "Have
you come here to torture us before the appointed time?"
30Some distance from them a large herd of pigs was feeding.
31The demons begged Jesus, "If you drive us out, send us into the
herd of pigs."
32He said to them, "Go!" So they came out and went into the
pigs, and the whole herd rushed down the steep bank into the lake
and died in the water. 33Those tending the pigs ran off, went into
the town and reported all this, including what had happened to
the demon-possessed men. 34Then the whole town went out
to meet Jesus. And when they saw him, they pleaded with him to
leave their region.

Jesus Heals a Paralytic

9 Jesus stepped into a boat, crossed over and came to his own
town. 2Some men brought to him a paralytic, lying on a mat.
When Jesus saw their faith, he said to the paralytic, "Take heart,
son; your sins are forgiven."
3At this, some of the teachers of the law said to themselves,
"This fellow is blaspheming!"

SON OF MAN

In the Jewish Scriptures (Old Testament), the expression "Son of Man" often refers simply to a human being. This is clear from EZEKIEL where the LORD's prophet is called "son of man" nearly one hundred times. In this way, the LORD reminded Ezekiel that he was a mere human being, and that he must accept God's power and purpose in the world.

The prophet Daniel also uses the expression, but with a slightly different meaning. Daniel says he saw in a vision "one like a son of man, coming with the clouds of heaven" (Dan 7:13). Here "son of man" refers to a savior—the person God will choose to rule over all the world and its people. Like this son of man, Jesus comes as God's Anointed One (Christ, the Messiah).

In the Gospels, Jesus speaks of himself as the Son of Man. Sometimes he uses the term to express his humanity (Matt 8:20) or to emphasize his role as the one who will suffer and die to forgive sins (Mark 8:31; 9:31; 10:45). But this expression is used as well when referring to Jesus' future glory, when God's people will be gathered together and God's kingdom (rule) will be set up (Mark 8:38—9:1). People will see the Son of Man sitting at the right hand of God (Mark 14:62). Also, he will be seen returning to earth with great power and authority (Matt 24:30). It seems clear that in some instances Jesus was using the expression in the same way Daniel was.

People are called to decide and publicly acknowledge who the Son of Man is (Luke 12:8). Those who believe that he was sent by God to renew God's people and to bring all creation under God's control will be part of God's family. They will also be rewarded for what they have done (Matt 16:27, 28).

See also the mini-articles called "Son of God," p. 2044 and "Messiah (Chosen One)," p. 1124.

Jesus Calls Matthew, Ryohei Koiso (twentieth century). This watercolor painting shows Jesus (center) having dinner with tax collectors and sinners in the home of Matthew. Jesus chose Matthew to be one of his disciples, even though Matthew was a tax collector (see Matt 9:9) and would have been despised by many other Jews.

4Knowing their thoughts, Jesus said, "Why do you entertain evil
thoughts in your hearts? 5Which is easier: to say, 'Your sins are forgiv-
en,' or to say, 'Get up and walk'? 6But so that you may know that the
Son of Man has authority on earth to forgive sins . . ." Then he said to
the paralytic, "Get up, take your mat and go home." 7And the man got
up and went home. 8When the crowd saw this, they were filled with
awe; and they praised God, who had given such authority to men.

The Calling of Matthew

9As Jesus went on from there, he saw a man named Matthew
sitting at the tax collector's booth. "Follow me," he told him, and
Matthew got up and followed him.
10While Jesus was having dinner at Matthew's house, many
tax collectors and "sinners" came and ate with him and his disciples. 11When the Pharisees saw this, they asked his disciples, "Why
does your teacher eat with tax collectors and 'sinners'?"
12On hearing this, Jesus said, "It is not the healthy who need
a doctor, but the sick. 13But go and learn what this means: 'I desire
mercy, not sacrifice.'[a] For I have not come to call the righteous, but
sinners."

[a]**13** Hosea 6:6

Jesus said,
"It is not the healthy who need a doctor, but the sick. . . . I have not come to call the righteous, but sinners."
Matt 9:12,13

9:2 *your sins are forgiven:* Sin occurs when people rebel against God and disobey God's Law. The Law of Moses taught that sins could be taken away by the sacrifice of a young goat on the Day of Atonement (Lev 16:1-22). In Jesus' day, the teachers of the Law taught that only God could forgive sins. So when Jesus told the man that his sins were forgiven, the teachers were shocked and angry. They thought Jesus had no respect for God or God's power.

9:9 *Matthew . . . tax collector's booth:* See the note at 5:46 for more information about tax collectors. Matthew was one of Jesus' twelve closest disciples. Though many scholars follow the early church fathers, who unanimously held that Matthew is the author of the Gospel bearing his name, some scholars believe it is not possible to identify the author for certain.

9:10,11 Luke 15:1,2. **9:13** Matt 12:7; Hos 6:6.

9:14 *fast:* See the notes at 4:2 and 6:16-18.

9:17 *skins will burst:* The juice from grapes turns to wine during a process called fermentation. During fermentation, a gas is produced that swells and stretches the fresh goatskins in which the wine is stored. If new wine was put into old skins that had become stiff, the skins would burst when the new wine began to ferment.

9:23 *flute players . . . noisy crowd:* The family of a dead person often hired musicians and mourners for funerals. A few hours before a body was to be brought to a tomb, family members, neighbors, and hired mourners would begin to wail. They often beat on their chests or tore their clothes to express their sadness.

9:27 *Son of David:* Many of the prophets of Israel said that the Messiah would come from the family of King David, and for this reason the Messiah was often called the "Son of David" (see the note at 1:1).

9:34 *prince of demons:* Also known as Beelzebul or Beelzebub (see Matt 10:25; 12:24; Mark 3:22; Luke 11:15). The first title is from the name of the Canaanite god Baal. The second is from a Hebrew pun on that title, which means "lord of the flies." The "prince of demons" was also known as Satan, and the devil.

10:1,2 *twelve disciples . . . apostles:* A disciple is a follower who learns from a master teacher, and the term "apostle" refers to those who carry to others the teacher's actions and message.

Although this is the only time the word "apostle" is found in MATTHEW, in ACTS and the letters of the New Testament the twelve disciples where commonly referred to as apostles, as were a few others such as the apostle Paul. Jesus gave his disciples the power to heal people and drive out evil spirits. A list of disciples is also given, with slight changes, in Mark 3:16-19 and Luke 6:13-16. See the chart on the next page.

Jesus Questioned About Fasting

14 Then John's disciples came and asked him, "How is it that we and the Pharisees fast, but your disciples do not fast?"

15 Jesus answered, "How can the guests of the bridegroom mourn while he is with them? The time will come when the bridegroom will be taken from them; then they will fast.

16 "No one sews a patch of unshrunk cloth on an old garment, for the patch will pull away from the garment, making the tear worse. 17 Neither do men pour new wine into old wineskins. If they do, the skins will burst, the wine will run out and the wineskins will be ruined. No, they pour new wine into new wineskins, and both are preserved."

A Dead Girl and a Sick Woman

18 While he was saying this, a ruler came and knelt before him and said, "My daughter has just died. But come and put your hand on her, and she will live." 19 Jesus got up and went with him, and so did his disciples.

20 Just then a woman who had been subject to bleeding for twelve years came up behind him and touched the edge of his cloak. 21 She said to herself, "If I only touch his cloak, I will be healed."

22 Jesus turned and saw her. "Take heart, daughter," he said, "your faith has healed you." And the woman was healed from that moment.

23 When Jesus entered the ruler's house and saw the flute players and the noisy crowd, 24 he said, "Go away. The girl is not dead but asleep." But they laughed at him. 25 After the crowd had been put outside, he went in and took the girl by the hand, and she got up. 26 News of this spread through all that region.

Jesus Heals the Blind and Mute

27 As Jesus went on from there, two blind men followed him, calling out, "Have mercy on us, Son of David!"

28 When he had gone indoors, the blind men came to him, and he asked them, "Do you believe that I am able to do this?"

"Yes, Lord," they replied.

29 Then he touched their eyes and said, "According to your faith will it be done to you"; 30 and their sight was restored. Jesus warned them sternly, "See that no one knows about this." 31 But they went out and spread the news about him all over that region.

32 While they were going out, a man who was demon-possessed and could not talk was brought to Jesus. 33 And when the demon was driven out, the man who had been mute spoke. The crowd was amazed and said, "Nothing like this has ever been seen in Israel."

34 But the Pharisees said, "It is by the prince of demons that he drives out demons."

JESUS' TWELVE DISCIPLES

The twelve disciples of Jesus are listed in three of the four Gospels. See how the disciples named in MARK and LUKE compare to the list in MATTHEW.

MATTHEW 10:2-4	MARK 3:14-19	LUKE 6:13-16
Simon (Peter)	Simon (Peter)	Simon (Peter)
Andrew, Peter's brother	Andrew	Andrew, Peter's brother
James, son of Zebedee	James, son of Zebedee (Boanerges)	James
John, son of Zebedee	John, son of Zebedee (Boanerges)	John
Philip	Philip	Philip
Bartholomew	Bartholomew	Bartholomew
Thomas	Thomas	Thomas
Matthew, the tax collector	Matthew	Matthew
James, son of Alphaeus	James, son of Alphaeus	James, son of Alphaeus
Thaddaeus	Thaddaeus	Judas, son of James
Simon the Zealot	Simon the Zealot	Simon the Zealot
Judas Iscariot	Judas Iscariot	Judas Iscariot

The Workers Are Few

35 Jesus went through all the towns and villages, teaching in
their synagogues, preaching the good news of the kingdom and
healing every disease and sickness. 36 When he saw the crowds, he
had compassion on them, because they were harassed and helpless, like sheep without a shepherd. 37 Then he said to his disciples,
"The harvest is plentiful but the workers are few. 38 Ask the Lord of
the harvest, therefore, to send out workers into his harvest field."

JESUS INSTRUCTS THE TWELVE DISCIPLES

Jesus Sends Out the Twelve

10 He called his twelve disciples to him and gave them authority to drive out evil[a] spirits and to heal every disease and sickness.
2 These are the names of the twelve apostles: first, Simon
(who is called Peter) and his brother Andrew; James son of
Zebedee, and his brother John; 3 Philip and Bartholomew;

10:2 *Simon (who is called Peter):* Simon, one of the first disciples chosen by Jesus (4:18-22), would become better known by the name Jesus gave him—Peter (John 1:42). The Greek form of his new name (*Petros*) and the Aramaic form (*Cephas*) both mean "rock" (see 16:18). In 8:14, Jesus heals Peter's mother-in-law. MARK and LUKE tell about the healing of Peter's mother-in-law, too. In those stories, Peter is called Simon.

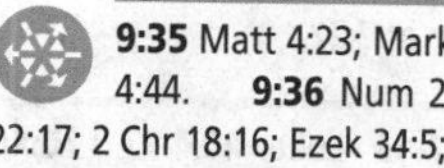

9:35 Matt 4:23; Mark 1:39; Luke 4:44. **9:36** Num 27:17; 1 Kgs 22:17; 2 Chr 18:16; Ezek 34:5; Mark 6:34. **9:37,38** Luke 10:2.

a1 Greek *unclean*

Thomas and Matthew the tax collector; James son of Alphaeus,
and Thaddaeus; [4]Simon the Zealot and Judas Iscariot, who
betrayed him.

[5]These twelve Jesus sent out with the following instructions: "Do not go among the Gentiles or enter any town of the
Samaritans. [6]Go rather to the lost sheep of Israel. [7]As you go,
preach this message: 'The kingdom of heaven is near.' [8]Heal the
sick, raise the dead, cleanse those who have leprosy,[a] drive out
demons. Freely you have received, freely give. [9]Do not take along
any gold or silver or copper in your belts; [10]take no bag for the
journey, or extra tunic, or sandals or a staff; for the worker is
worth his keep.

[11]"Whatever town or village you enter, search for some worthy person there and stay at his house until you leave. [12]As you
enter the home, give it your greeting. [13]If the home is deserving,
let your peace rest on it; if it is not, let your peace return to you.
[14]If anyone will not welcome you or listen to your words, shake the
dust off your feet when you leave that home or town. [15]I tell you
the truth, it will be more bearable for Sodom and Gomorrah on
the day of judgment than for that town. [16]I am sending you out
like sheep among wolves. Therefore be as shrewd as snakes and as
innocent as doves.

[17]"Be on your guard against men; they will hand you over to
the local councils and flog you in their synagogues. [18]On my
account you will be brought before governors and kings as witnesses to them and to the Gentiles. [19]But when they arrest you, do
not worry about what to say or how to say it. At that time you will
be given what to say, [20]for it will not be you speaking, but the Spirit of your Father speaking through you.

[21]"Brother will betray brother to death, and a father his
child; children will rebel against their parents and have them put
to death. [22]All men will hate you because of me, but he who stands
firm to the end will be saved. [23]When you are persecuted in one
place, flee to another. I tell you the truth, you will not finish going
through the cities of Israel before the Son of Man comes.

[24]"A student is not above his teacher, nor a servant above his
master. [25]It is enough for the student to be like his teacher, and
the servant like his master. If the head of the house has been
called Beelzebub,[b] how much more the members of his household!

[26]"So do not be afraid of them. There is nothing concealed
that will not be disclosed, or hidden that will not be made known.
[27]What I tell you in the dark, speak in the daylight; what is whispered in your ear, proclaim from the roofs. [28]Do not be afraid of
those who kill the body but cannot kill the soul. Rather, be afraid

[a]8 The Greek word was used for various diseases affecting the skin—not necessarily leprosy. [b]25 Greek *Beezeboul* or *Beelzeboul*

10:3 *Matthew the tax collector:* See the note at 5:46. Jesus choosing a tax collector to be one of his disciples is one example of his reaching out to people despised by the religious establishment (see also 15:21-28; 26:6-13).

10:4 *Iscariot:* This probably means "a man from Kerioth" (a place in Judea).

10:5 *Gentiles ... Samaritans:* See the mini-article called "Gentiles," p. 2127. Samaritans, whose distant ancestors included Jews, lived in the area of Palestine near the city of Samaria (see the map on p. 2472). Most Jews in Jesus' day believed they should have nothing to do with Gentiles and Samaritans.

10:8 *leprosy:* In biblical times the word translated "leprosy" was used for several different kinds of skin diseases. According to Leviticus 13:1—14:32, certain skin diseases made a person "unclean." Anyone who touched an unclean person or thing had to go through a cleansing ritual in order to be fit to join the worshiping community again. When Jesus touched the man with leprosy (8:3), he made himself ritually unclean according to the Law of Moses.

10:14 *shake the dust off your feet:* This was a way of showing rejection. See also Acts 13:51.

10:15 *Sodom and Gomorrah:* According to Genesis 19:1-29, God destroyed these cities because they were so evil. The location of ancient Sodom is not known, but it was probably southeast of the Dead Sea. See 11:24.

10:15 *day of judgment:* See the note at 7:22.

10:7-15 Luke 10:4-12. **10:10** 1 Cor 9:14; 1 Tim 5:18. **10:16** Luke 10:3. **10:17-20** Mark 13:9-11; Luke 12:11,12; 21:12-15. **10:21** Mark 13:12; Luke 21:16. **10:22** Matt 24:9,13; Mark 13:13; Luke 21:17. **10:24** Luke 6:40; John 13:16; 15:20. **10:25** Matt 9:34; 12:24; Mark 3:22; Luke 11:15. **10:26** Mark 4:22; Luke 8:17.

of the One who can destroy both soul and body in hell. [29]Are not two sparrows sold for a penny[a]? Yet not one of them will fall to the ground apart from the will of your Father. [30]And even the very hairs of your head are all numbered. [31]So don't be afraid; you are worth more than many sparrows.

[32]"Whoever acknowledges me before men, I will also acknowledge him before my Father in heaven. [33]But whoever disowns me before men, I will disown him before my Father in heaven.

[34]"Do not suppose that I have come to bring peace to the earth. I did not come to bring peace, but a sword. [35]For I have come to turn

" 'a man against his father,
a daughter against her mother,
a daughter-in-law against her mother-in-law—
36 a man's enemies will be the members of his own household.'[b]

[37]"Anyone who loves his father or mother more than me is not worthy of me; anyone who loves his son or daughter more than me is not worthy of me; [38]and anyone who does not take his cross and follow me is not worthy of me. [39]Whoever finds his life will lose it, and whoever loses his life for my sake will find it.

[40]"He who receives you receives me, and he who receives me receives the one who sent me. [41]Anyone who receives a prophet because he is a prophet will receive a prophet's reward, and anyone who receives a righteous man because he is a righteous man will receive a righteous man's reward. [42]And if anyone gives even a cup of cold water to one of these little ones because he is my disciple, I tell you the truth, he will certainly not lose his reward."

[a]**29** Greek *an assarion* [b]**36** Micah 7:6

Jesus said,
Whoever acknowledges me before men, I will also acknowledge him before my Father in heaven."
Matt 10:32

10:20 *Spirit:* See the note at 1:18.

10:23 *Son of Man:* See the mini-article called "Son of Man," p. 1866.

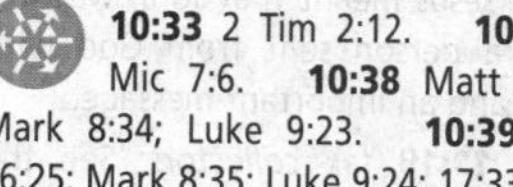

10:41 *Anyone who receives:* According to the Law of Moses, the Jewish people were expected to be kind and generous to strangers and to welcome them into their homes to rest or to eat. This kind of welcoming is called hospitality. One way people showed hospitality to guests was to wash their feet, because most people went barefoot or wore open sandals.

10:33 2 Tim 2:12. **10:35,36** Mic 7:6. **10:38** Matt 16:24; Mark 8:34; Luke 9:23. **10:39** Matt 16:25; Mark 8:35; Luke 9:24; 17:33; John 12:25. **10:40** Mark 9:37; Luke 9:48; 10:16; John 13:20.

QUESTIONS ABOUT MATTHEW 8:1—10:42

1. In chapters 8 and 9, MATTHEW gives several accounts of Jesus healing people. Which of these stories moved you most? Why? What did these stories teach you about Jesus?
2. Jesus chose Matthew, a tax collector, to be one of his disciples (9:9-13). Why was this considered unusual? What did Jesus say to the Pharisees who criticized him for this? How do you treat people that society calls "sinners"?
3. What are some of the instructions and warnings Jesus gave his twelve disciples? (10:5-42) What qualities does Jesus seem to require of his followers? In today's world, what does it mean for a person to "take his cross" and follow Jesus? (10:38)

JESUS FACES OPPONENTS AND THEIR QUESTIONS

Jesus' teaching and work begin to attract lots of attention. Some people, especially the Jewish religious authorities, question why he does things like healing on the Sabbath.

Jesus and John the Baptist

11 After Jesus had finished instructing his twelve disciples, he went on from there to teach and preach in the towns of Galilee.[a] [2]When John heard in prison what Christ was doing, he sent his disciples [3]to ask him, "Are you the one who was to come, or should we expect someone else?"

[4]Jesus replied, "Go back and report to John what you hear and see: [5]The blind receive sight, the lame walk, those who have leprosy[b] are cured, the deaf hear, the dead are raised, and the good news is preached to the poor. [6]Blessed is the man who does not fall away on account of me."

[7]As John's disciples were leaving, Jesus began to speak to the crowd about John: "What did you go out into the desert to see? A reed swayed by the wind? [8]If not, what did you go out to see? A man dressed in fine clothes? No, those who wear fine clothes are in kings' palaces. [9]Then what did you go out to see? A prophet? Yes, I tell you, and more than a prophet. [10]This is the one about whom it is written:

> " 'I will send my messenger ahead of you,
> who will prepare your way before you.'[c]

[11]I tell you the truth: Among those born of women there has not risen anyone greater than John the Baptist; yet he who is least in the kingdom of heaven is greater than he. [12]From the days of John the Baptist until now, the kingdom of heaven has been forcefully advancing, and forceful men lay hold of it. [13]For all the Prophets and the Law prophesied until John. [14]And if you are willing to accept it, he is the Elijah who was to come. [15]He who has ears, let him hear.

[16]"To what can I compare this generation? They are like children sitting in the marketplaces and calling out to others:

> [17]" 'We played the flute for you,
> and you did not dance;
> we sang a dirge,
> and you did not mourn.'

[18]For John came neither eating nor drinking, and they say, 'He has a demon.' [19]The Son of Man came eating and drinking, and they say, 'Here is a glutton and a drunkard, a friend of tax collectors and "sinners." ' But wisdom is proved right by her actions."

[a]1 Greek *in their towns* [b]5 The Greek word was used for various diseases affecting the skin—not necessarily leprosy. [c]10 Mal. 3:1

11:2 *John:* This refers to John the Baptist. See the mini-article called "John the Baptist," p. 1853.

11:2 *Christ:* This is the Greek word that translates the Hebrew word *Messiah.* (See the note at 1:17.) The Jewish people believed that God would choose and give power to a leader who would renew the faith of the people and fulfill God's purposes for them.

11:5 *leprosy:* See the note at 10:8.

11:13 *the Prophets and the Law:* See the note at 5:17.

11:14 *Elijah:* Elijah was a prophet in Israel over 800 years before Jesus was born. Some later prophets expected God to send Elijah back to earth to warn people of God's judgment (Mal 3:1-4; 4:5, 6). Some people thought John the Baptist was Elijah (Matt 17:10-13; Mark 9:11-13). By saying that John "is the Elijah who was to come," Jesus meant that John was like Elijah, a person sent from God with power and an important message.

11:19 *tax collectors:* See the note at 5:46.

11:19 *wisdom:* True wisdom was said to come from obeying God's Law (Ps 19:7). But Jesus seems to be saying that wisdom is more than this. Wisdom finds a way to help a neighbor, even if that person is a Gentile or someone who doesn't live by the Law of Moses. See the mini-article called "Wisdom," p. 2206.

11:5 Isa 35:5, 6; 61:1. **11:10** Mal 3:1. **11:12,13** Luke 16:16. **11:21** Isa 23:1-18; Ezek 26:1—28:26; Joel 3:4-8; Amos 1:9, 10; Zech 9:3, 4. **11:24** Matt 10:15; Luke 10:12. **11:27** John 1:18; 3:35; 10:15. **12:5** Num 28:9, 10. **12:11** Luke 14:5.

Woe on Unrepentant Cities

20Then Jesus began to denounce the cities in which most of
his miracles had been performed, because they did not repent.
21"Woe to you, Korazin! Woe to you, Bethsaida! If the miracles that
were performed in you had been performed in Tyre and Sidon,
they would have repented long ago in sackcloth and ashes. 22But I
tell you, it will be more bearable for Tyre and Sidon on the day of
judgment than for you. 23And you, Capernaum, will you be lifted
up to the skies? No, you will go down to the depths.[a] If the miracles that were performed in you had been performed in Sodom, it
would have remained to this day. 24But I tell you that it will be
more bearable for Sodom on the day of judgment than for you."

Rest for the Weary

25At that time Jesus said, "I praise you, Father, Lord of heav-
en and earth, because you have hidden these things from the wise
and learned, and revealed them to little children. 26Yes, Father, for
this was your good pleasure.

27"All things have been committed to me by my Father. No
one knows the Son except the Father, and no one knows the Father
except the Son and those to whom the Son chooses to reveal him.

28"Come to me, all you who are weary and burdened, and I
will give you rest. 29Take my yoke upon you and learn from me, for
I am gentle and humble in heart, and you will find rest for your
souls. 30For my yoke is easy and my burden is light."

Lord of the Sabbath

12 At that time Jesus went through the grainfields on the Sabbath. His disciples were hungry and began to pick some heads of
grain and eat them. 2When the Pharisees saw this, they said to him,
"Look! Your disciples are doing what is unlawful on the Sabbath."

3He answered, "Haven't you read what David did when he
and his companions were hungry? 4He entered the house of God,
and he and his companions ate the consecrated bread—which was
not lawful for them to do, but only for the priests. 5Or haven't you
read in the Law that on the Sabbath the priests in the temple desecrate the day and yet are innocent? 6I tell you that one[b] greater
than the temple is here. 7If you had known what these words
mean, 'I desire mercy, not sacrifice,'[c] you would not have condemned the innocent. 8For the Son of Man is Lord of the Sabbath."

9Going on from that place, he went into their synagogue,
10and a man with a shriveled hand was there. Looking for a reason
to accuse Jesus, they asked him, "Is it lawful to heal on the Sabbath?"

11He said to them, "If any of you has a sheep and it falls into

---

11:21 *Korazin . . . Bethsaida . . . Tyre and Sidon:* Korazin and Bethsaida were Jewish towns just north of the Sea of Galilee. Tyre and Sidon were important Phoenician port cities on the Mediterranean Sea. While the people in the Jewish towns often did not respond to Jesus' message and miracles, Jesus says that non-Jewish people in cities like Tyre and Sidon were more willing to turn to God. See the maps on p. 1981 and 2473.

11:21 *in sackcloth and ashes:* See the note at 6:16-18.

11:23 *Capernaum . . . Sodom:* See the notes at 4:13 (Capernaum) and 10:15 (Sodom). See also Isa 14:13-15; Gen 19:24-28.

11:29 *yoke:* Yokes were wooden frames put on the necks of work animals so that they could pull a plow or wagon. A yoke was a symbol of obedience and hard work (see also Jer 27:2-11). Jesus may be using this symbol ironically (see 16:24-26 for another metaphor for following Jesus).

12:1 *Sabbath:* In Hebrew, "Sabbath" means to rest or to stop working. Sabbath is the Jewish day of rest that begins at sunset on Friday and ends at sunset on Saturday. All Jewish people must observe this holy day (Exod 20:8-11). In this story, some Pharisees considered picking grain to be work and a violation of the Sabbath law.

12:1 *pick some heads of grain:* It was the custom in Israel to let hungry travelers pick grains of wheat as they passed by a field (Deut 24:19-22).

12:3 *what David did:* Jesus is referring to a time when David and his followers received special bread from the priests in the tabernacle (Lev 24:5-9; 1 Sam 21:1-6).

---

[a]**23** Greek *Hades* [b]**6** Or *something*; also in verses 41 and 42 [c]**7** Hosea 6:6

12:14 *Pharisees . . . plotted how they might kill Jesus:* The Pharisees were respected by many of the Jewish people because they studied God's Law and helped the people see how to live according to it. When Jesus challenged their teachings and authority, some Pharisees decided to try to get rid of him because they thought he was becoming a threat to their position and power.

12:16 *warning them not to tell who he was:* When Jesus healed people, he often told them not to tell what he had done for them. He probably said this so that others would not come to him simply for miracles of healing and nothing more. He also likely didn't want to encourage the popular understanding of the Messiah as a political and military leader.

12:24 *Beelzebub, the prince of demons:* See 10:25 and the note at 9:34.

12:31 *blasphemy against the Spirit:* The sin of blasphemy, or speaking against the Holy Spirit, is a complete turning away from God. Those who reject God also reject God's forgiveness.

12:18-21 Isa 42:1-4. **12:30** Mark 9:40.

a pit on the Sabbath, will you not take hold of it and lift it out?
[12]How much more valuable is a man than a sheep! Therefore it is
lawful to do good on the Sabbath."
[13]Then he said to the man, "Stretch out your hand." So he
stretched it out and it was completely restored, just as sound as the
other. [14]But the Pharisees went out and plotted how they might kill
Jesus.

God's Chosen Servant

[15]Aware of this, Jesus withdrew from that place. Many followed
him, and he healed all their sick, [16]warning them not to tell who he
was. [17]This was to fulfill what was spoken through the prophet Isaiah:

[18]"Here is my servant whom I have chosen,
the one I love, in whom I delight;
I will put my Spirit on him,
and he will proclaim justice to the nations.
[19]He will not quarrel or cry out;
no one will hear his voice in the streets.
[20]A bruised reed he will not break,
and a smoldering wick he will not snuff out,
till he leads justice to victory.
[21]In his name the nations will put their hope."[a]

Jesus and Beelzebub

[22]Then they brought him a demon-possessed man who was
blind and mute, and Jesus healed him, so that he could both talk
and see. [23]All the people were astonished and said, "Could this be
the Son of David?"
[24]But when the Pharisees heard this, they said, "It is only by
Beelzebub,[b] the prince of demons, that this fellow drives out demons."
[25]Jesus knew their thoughts and said to them, "Every kingdom divided against itself will be ruined, and every city or household divided against itself will not stand. [26]If Satan drives out
Satan, he is divided against himself. How then can his kingdom
stand? [27]And if I drive out demons by Beelzebub, by whom do
your people drive them out? So then, they will be your judges.
[28]But if I drive out demons by the Spirit of God, then the kingdom
of God has come upon you.
[29]"Or again, how can anyone enter a strong man's house and
carry off his possessions unless he first ties up the strong man?
Then he can rob his house.
[30]"He who is not with me is against me, and he who does
not gather with me scatters. [31]And so I tell you, every sin and blasphemy will be forgiven men, but the blasphemy against the Spirit

[a]**21** Isaiah 42:1-4 [b]**24** Greek *Beezeboul* or *Beelzeboul*; also in verse 27

will not be forgiven. 32 Anyone who speaks a word against the Son
of Man will be forgiven, but anyone who speaks against the Holy
Spirit will not be forgiven, either in this age or in the age to come.
33 "Make a tree good and its fruit will be good, or make a tree
bad and its fruit will be bad, for a tree is recognized by its fruit.
34 You brood of vipers, how can you who are evil say anything good?
For out of the overflow of the heart the mouth speaks. 35 The good
man brings good things out of the good stored up in him, and the
evil man brings evil things out of the evil stored up in him. 36 But I
tell you that men will have to give account on the day of judgment
for every careless word they have spoken. 37 For by your words you
will be acquitted, and by your words you will be condemned."

The Sign of Jonah

38 Then some of the Pharisees and teachers of the law said to
him, "Teacher, we want to see a miraculous sign from you."
39 He answered, "A wicked and adulterous generation asks for
a miraculous sign! But none will be given it except the sign of the
prophet Jonah. 40 For as Jonah was three days and three nights in
the belly of a huge fish, so the Son of Man will be three days and
three nights in the heart of the earth. 41 The men of Nineveh will
stand up at the judgment with this generation and condemn it; for
they repented at the preaching of Jonah, and now one[a] greater
than Jonah is here. 42 The Queen of the South will rise at the judgment with this generation and condemn it; for she came from the
ends of the earth to listen to Solomon's wisdom, and now one
greater than Solomon is here.
43 "When an evil[b] spirit comes out of a man, it goes through
arid places seeking rest and does not find it. 44 Then it says, 'I will
return to the house I left.' When it arrives, it finds the house unoc-
cupied, swept clean and put in order. 45 Then it goes and takes with
it seven other spirits more wicked than itself, and they go in and
live there. And the final condition of that man is worse than the
first. That is how it will be with this wicked generation."

Jesus' Mother and Brothers

46 While Jesus was still talking to the crowd, his mother and
brothers stood outside, wanting to speak to him. 47 Someone told
him, "Your mother and brothers are standing outside, wanting to
speak to you."[c]
48 He replied to him, "Who is my mother, and who are my
brothers?" 49 Pointing to his disciples, he said, "Here are my mother
and my brothers. 50 For whoever does the will of my Father in
heaven is my brother and sister and mother."

---

a41 Or *something*; also in verse 42 **b43** Greek *unclean* **c47** Some manuscripts do not have verse 47.

Jesus said,
"Whoever does the will of my Father in heaven is my brother and sister and mother."
Matt 12:50

12:32 *Son of Man:* See the mini-article called "Son of Man," p. 1866.

12:36 *day of judgment:* See the note at 7:22.

12:39-41 *prophet Jonah . . . Nineveh:* God chose the prophet Jonah to go to Nineveh, the capital of Assyria, and tell the people of Nineveh to repent of their sins and ask for God's forgiveness. Jonah did not want God to forgive Israel's Assyrian enemies, so he tried to run away from God in a ship (Jonah 1:3). But God sent a storm, Jonah was thrown into the water, and a great fish swallowed him (Jonah 1:12-17). He stayed inside the fish for three days before being spit out (Jonah 2:10). Jesus is comparing the time he would spend in the grave with the time Jonah spent inside the fish. See also Matt 16:4; Mark 8:12.

12:42 *Queen of the South . . . listen to Solomon's wisdom:* This refers to the Queen of Sheba, a country in southern Arabia. The queen traveled north to listen to the wisdom of Israel's King Solomon (see 1 Kgs 10:1-10; 2 Chr 9:1-12). Jesus is making the point that if a Gentile like the Queen of Sheba could learn from a Jewish king in the past, why can't the leaders of the Jewish people recognize God's message from one of their own people, namely Jesus?

12:32,33 Luke 12:10; Matt 7:20; Luke 6:44. **12:34** Matt 3:7; 15:18; 23:33; Luke 3:7; 6:45. **12:38** Matt 16:1; Mark 8:11; Luke 11:16.

13:1-3 *Jesus . . . sat by the lake . . . parables:* Jewish teachers usually sat while they taught. Jesus often used stories called parables to teach something important. See also the mini-article called "Parables," p. 1876.

13:4 *scattering the seed:* After breaking up the ground, a farmer planted seeds by scattering them a handful at a time. Some seed was quickly eaten by birds. Other seed dried out in the sun or landed among weeds. After sowing the seeds, the farmer would plow the seed into the ground along with the stubble from the previous crop, which would act as fertilizer as it decayed.

13:2 Luke 5:1–3.

JESUS TELLS PARABLES ABOUT THE KINGDOM OF HEAVEN

The Parable of the Sower

13 That same day Jesus went out of the house and sat by the
lake. 2 Such large crowds gathered around him that he got into a
boat and sat in it, while all the people stood on the shore. 3 Then he
told them many things in parables, saying: "A farmer went out to
sow his seed. 4 As he was scattering the seed, some fell along the
path, and the birds came and ate it up. 5 Some fell on rocky places,
where it did not have much soil. It sprang up quickly, because the
soil was shallow. 6 But when the sun came up, the plants were
scorched, and they withered because they had no root. 7 Other seed
fell among thorns, which grew up and choked the plants. 8 Still
other seed fell on good soil, where it produced a crop—a hundred,
sixty or thirty times what was sown. 9 He who has ears, let him
hear."

10 The disciples came to him and asked, "Why do you speak
to the people in parables?"

11 He replied, "The knowledge of the secrets of the kingdom

PARABLES

Parable comes from the Greek word which means "to put things together in order to compare them." Parables are usually short stories told to teach a lesson. Sometimes they are just short sayings that compare something people do with something in the world of nature or some common human experience. For example, Proverbs 6:7, 8 compares an ant, which on its own collects food and plans for the future, and human beings who should be dependable and carry out their own responsibilities. The prophet Isaiah compared the people of Israel in his day with a vineyard that failed to produce grapes (Isa 5:1-5), so the owner quit taking care of the vineyard. In the same way, Isaiah says, God will not keep taking care of the people of Israel if their lives do not produce good fruit (do what is right).

In MATTHEW, MARK, and LUKE, Jesus often uses parables to describe God and tell how God expects people to live in the kingdom. Some are only short sayings, such as the blind leading the blind (Matt 15:14), the family that fights and destroys itself (Matt 12:25), throwing pearls to pigs (Matt 7:6), and the eye as the lamp of the body (Matt 6:22, 23). More than forty parables are short stories, such as when Jesus compares the coming kingdom of heaven with a farmer planting seed (Matt 13:1-23), with hidden treasure (Matt 13:44), and with weeds mixed with wheat (Matt 13:24-30). In some of these, an explanation of the parable has been added to the story itself, as in Matthew 13:36-43. These explanations helped new followers of Jesus better understand his message.

Other well-known parables are the Good Samaritan (Luke 10:25-37), the Rich Fool (Luke 12:13-21), the Persistent Widow (Luke 18:1-8), the Wedding Banquet (Matt 22:1-14), and the Lost Son (Luke 15:11-32).

of heaven has been given to you, but not to them. 12Whoever has
will be given more, and he will have an abundance. Whoever does
not have, even what he has will be taken from him. 13This is why I
speak to them in parables:

> "Though seeing, they do not see;
>   though hearing, they do not hear or understand.

14In them is fulfilled the prophecy of Isaiah:

> " 'You will be ever hearing but never under
>   standing;
>   you will be ever seeing but never perceiving.
> 15For this people's heart has become calloused;
>   they hardly hear with their ears,
>   and they have closed their eyes.
> Otherwise they might see with their eyes,
>   hear with their ears,
>   understand with their hearts
> and turn, and I would heal them.'[a]

16But blessed are your eyes because they see, and your ears because
they hear. 17For I tell you the truth, many prophets and righteous
men longed to see what you see but did not see it, and to hear
what you hear but did not hear it.
18"Listen then to what the parable of the sower means:
19When anyone hears the message about the kingdom and does
not understand it, the evil one comes and snatches away what was
sown in his heart. This is the seed sown along the path. 20The one
who received the seed that fell on rocky places is the man who
hears the word and at once receives it with joy. 21But since he has
no root, he lasts only a short time. When trouble or persecution
comes because of the word, he quickly falls away. 22The one who
received the seed that fell among the thorns is the man who hears
the word, but the worries of this life and the deceitfulness of
wealth choke it, making it unfruitful. 23But the one who received
the seed that fell on good soil is the man who hears the word and
understands it. He produces a crop, yielding a hundred, sixty or
thirty times what was sown."

The Parable of the Weeds

24Jesus told them another parable: "The kingdom of heaven
is like a man who sowed good seed in his field. 25But while everyone was sleeping, his enemy came and sowed weeds among the
wheat, and went away. 26When the wheat sprouted and formed
heads, then the weeds also appeared.

[a]**15** Isaiah 6:9,10

Jesus explained,
"The one who received the seed that fell on good soil is the man who hears the word and understands it. He produces a crop, yielding a hundred, sixty or thirty times what was sown."
Matt 13:23

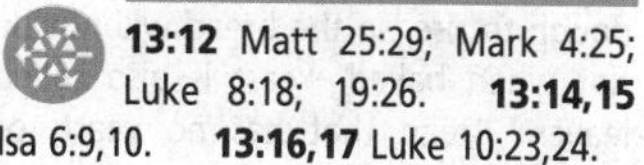

13:11 *secrets of the kingdom of heaven:* For "Kingdom of heaven," see the note at 3:2. The good news that Jesus would proclaim and that his disciples would proclaim after him was previously hidden from the world. Although this message was for all, only those with faith would be able to understand this "secret."

13:12 Matt 25:29; Mark 4:25; Luke 8:18; 19:26. **13:14,15** Isa 6:9,10. **13:16,17** Luke 10:23,24.

13:31 *mustard seed:* This tiny black seed was used to flavor food and to keep it fresh. It contained oil and was used as a medicine. The mustard plant does not usually grow as tall as most trees, but this treelike shrub can grow taller than a human being. Sometimes the stem can be as thick as a person's arm.

13:33 *yeast:* Yeast is a tiny yellowish fungus. When it is mixed with water and flour, it causes the dough to rise, so the bread will not be flat when baked. Yeast is also called leaven. Bread that has no yeast, or leaven, is flat and is called unleavened bread. Unleavened bread was served at special times, such as Passover. See also the note at 26:2.

13:37 *Son of Man:* See the mini-article called "Son of Man," p. 1866.

13:39 *end of the age:* This refers to the day of judgment (see the note at 7:22). MATTHEW describes it as a future time when God will judge and separate those who have been faithful from those who have not been faithful.

27“The owner's servants came to him and said, ‘Sir, didn't you
sow good seed in your field? Where then did the weeds come from?’
28“ ‘An enemy did this,’ he replied.
“The servants asked him, ‘Do you want us to go and pull
them up?’
29“ ‘No,’ he answered, ‘because while you are pulling the
weeds, you may root up the wheat with them. 30Let both grow
together until the harvest. At that time I will tell the harvesters:
First collect the weeds and tie them in bundles to be burned; then
gather the wheat and bring it into my barn.’ ”

The Parables of the Mustard Seed and the Yeast

31He told them another parable: “The kingdom of heaven is
like a mustard seed, which a man took and planted in his field.
32Though it is the smallest of all your seeds, yet when it grows, it is
the largest of garden plants and becomes a tree, so that the birds of
the air come and perch in its branches.”
33He told them still another parable: “The kingdom of heav-
en is like yeast that a woman took and mixed into a large amount[a]
of flour until it worked all through the dough.”
34Jesus spoke all these things to the crowd in parables; he did
not say anything to them without using a parable. 35So was fulfilled
what was spoken through the prophet:

“I will open my mouth in parables,
I will utter things hidden since the creation of
the world.”[b]

The Parable of the Weeds Explained

36Then he left the crowd and went into the house. His disciples came to him and said, “Explain to us the parable of the weeds
in the field.”
37He answered, “The one who sowed the good seed is the
Son of Man. 38The field is the world, and the good seed stands for
the sons of the kingdom. The weeds are the sons of the evil one,
39and the enemy who sows them is the devil. The harvest is the end
of the age, and the harvesters are angels.
40“As the weeds are pulled up and burned in the fire, so it
will be at the end of the age. 41The Son of Man will send out his
angels, and they will weed out of his kingdom everything that
causes sin and all who do evil. 42They will throw them into the
fiery furnace, where there will be weeping and gnashing of teeth.
43Then the righteous will shine like the sun in the kingdom of their
Father. He who has ears, let him hear.

[a]33 Greek *three satas* (probably about 1/2 bushel or 22 liters)
[b]35 Psalm 78:2

The Parables of the Hidden Treasure and the Pearl

44“The kingdom of heaven is like treasure hidden in a field.
When a man found it, he hid it again, and then in his joy went and
sold all he had and bought that field.
45“Again, the kingdom of heaven is like a merchant looking
for fine pearls. 46When he found one of great value, he went away
and sold everything he had and bought it.

The Parable of the Net

47“Once again, the kingdom of heaven is like a net that was let
down into the lake and caught all kinds of fish. 48When it was full,
the fishermen pulled it up on the shore. Then they sat down and
collected the good fish in baskets, but threw the bad away. 49This is
how it will be at the end of the age. The angels will come and separate the wicked from the righteous 50and throw them into the fiery
furnace, where there will be weeping and gnashing of teeth.
51“Have you understood all these things?” Jesus asked.
“Yes,” they replied.
52He said to them, “Therefore every teacher of the law who has
been instructed about the kingdom of heaven is like the owner of a
house who brings out of his storeroom new treasures as well as old.”

A Prophet Without Honor

53When Jesus had finished these parables, he moved on from
there. 54Coming to his hometown, he began teaching the people in
their synagogue, and they were amazed. “Where did this man get
this wisdom and these miraculous powers?” they asked. 55“Isn’t
this the carpenter’s son? Isn’t his mother’s name Mary, and aren’t
his brothers James, Joseph, Simon and Judas? 56Aren’t all his sisters
with us? Where then did this man get all these things?” 57And they
took offense at him.
But Jesus said to them, “Only in his hometown and in his
own house is a prophet without honor.”
58And he did not do many miracles there because of their
lack of faith.

Jesus said, *“The kingdom of heaven is like a merchant looking for fine pearls. When he found one of great value, he went away and sold everything he had and bought it.”* Matt 13:45,46

13:47 *a net that was let down into the lake:* See the note at 4:18.

13:50 *fiery furnace:* Another way of describing the place of punishment for evildoers. See the notes at 5:22 and 8:12.

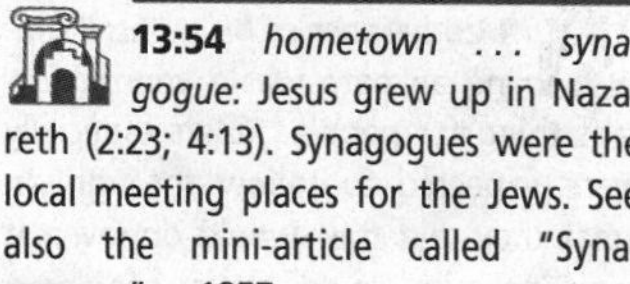

13:54 *hometown . . . synagogue:* Jesus grew up in Nazareth (2:23; 4:13). Synagogues were the local meeting places for the Jews. See also the mini-article called “Synagogues,” p. 1857.

13:57 John 4:44.

QUESTIONS ABOUT MATTHEW 11:1—13:58

1. What is the good news that Jesus talks about in 11:2-5? Who are messengers of the good news today? What message do they tell, and why is it good news?
2. When Jesus did work on the Sabbath, how did the Pharisees react? (12:1-14) When the Pharisees accused Jesus of serving Satan, what was his reply? (12:22-37)
3. Jesus uses a number of images and parables to describe what the kingdom of heaven is like (13:1-52). Choose one of these and explain what you think it means.
4. Using an example from your everyday life, complete the following sentence: I think the kingdom of heaven is like . . .

14:1 *Herod the tetrarch:* This is Herod Antipas, one of several sons of Herod the Great (see the note at 2:1). After Herod the Great died in 4 B.C., the area he had ruled was divided among three of his sons. Herod Antipas ruled over Galilee and Perea from 4 B.C. to A.D. 39. His formal title was tetrarch, which meant someone who ruled part of a province. But the people sometimes also called him a king (see 14:9).

14:3,4 *Herodias, his brother Philip's wife:* Herodias was a granddaughter of Herod the Great. She married Herod's son Philip, who (like Herod Antipas) was her uncle. Once when Herod Antipas was visiting in Philip's house in Rome, he talked Herodias into leaving Philip and marrying him. The Law of Moses did not allow a man to marry his brother's wife while the brother was still living (see Lev 18:16; 20:21). That's why John the Baptist told Herod Antipas that marrying Herodias was wrong. See also Luke 3:19, 20.

14:9 *because of his oaths:* Keeping an oath was a very important thing for people. Rulers especially were expected to follow through on what they said they would do, even if their promise could cause problems. When Herod swore to his step-daughter in the presence of important guests, he could not take it back.

14:13 *he withdrew by boat privately to a solitary place:* Meaning that Jesus crossed the Sea of Galilee (see John 6:1), which is located in the northern part of the Jordan River valley. Storms often sweep across the lake because it is surrounded by mountains. See the map on p. 2473.

JESUS IS THE CHRIST

This next section reports the death of John the Baptist, whose message was rejected by the Jewish leaders, just as Jesus had been rejected by the people in Nazareth. Then Jesus performs a number of miracles and tells his disciples what will happen to him in the future.

John the Baptist Beheaded

14 At that time Herod the tetrarch heard the reports about Jesus, 2and he said to his attendants, "This is John the Baptist; he has risen from the dead! That is why miraculous powers are at work in him."

3Now Herod had arrested John and bound him and put him in prison because of Herodias, his brother Philip's wife, 4for John had been saying to him: "It is not lawful for you to have her." 5Herod wanted to kill John, but he was afraid of the people, because they considered him a prophet.

6On Herod's birthday the daughter of Herodias danced for them and pleased Herod so much 7that he promised with an oath to give her whatever she asked. 8Prompted by her mother, she said, "Give me here on a platter the head of John the Baptist." 9The king was distressed, but because of his oaths and his dinner guests, he ordered that her request be granted 10and had John beheaded in the prison. 11His head was brought in on a platter and given to the girl, who carried it to her mother. 12John's disciples came and took his body and buried it. Then they went and told Jesus.

Jesus Feeds the Five Thousand

13When Jesus heard what had happened, he withdrew by boat privately to a solitary place. Hearing of this, the crowds followed him on foot from the towns. 14When Jesus landed and saw a large crowd, he had compassion on them and healed their sick.

15As evening approached, the disciples came to him and said, "This is a remote place, and it's already getting late. Send the crowds away, so they can go to the villages and buy themselves some food."

16Jesus replied, "They do not need to go away. You give them something to eat."

17"We have here only five loaves of bread and two fish," they answered.

18"Bring them here to me," he said. 19And he directed the people to sit down on the grass. Taking the five loaves and the two fish and looking up to heaven, he gave thanks and broke the loaves. Then he gave them to the disciples, and the disciples gave them to the people. 20They all ate and were satisfied, and the disciples picked up twelve basketfuls of broken pieces that were left

The Beheading of St. John the Baptist, Ferdinand Bol (died 1680). This drawing shows a guard presenting the head of John the Baptist to Herodias's daughter. This is the "gift" she requested when her stepfather Herod wanted to reward her for her dancing at his birthday celebration (see 14:1-12).

over. [21]The number of those who ate was about five thousand men,
besides women and children.

Jesus Walks on the Water

[22]Immediately Jesus made the disciples get into the boat and
go on ahead of him to the other side, while he dismissed the
crowd. [23]After he had dismissed them, he went up on a mountainside by himself to pray. When evening came, he was there alone,
[24]but the boat was already a considerable distance[a] from land, buf-
feted by the waves because the wind was against it.
[25]During the fourth watch of the night Jesus went out to
them, walking on the lake. [26]When the disciples saw him walking
on the lake, they were terrified. "It's a ghost," they said, and cried
out in fear.

14:17 *five loaves of bread:* These would have been flat and round or in the shape of a bun.

14:19 *he gave thanks and broke the loaves:* This same language is used when Jesus later shares his last supper with his disciples (26:26).

14:20 *twelve basketfuls:* Twelve may be a significant number here because there were twelve tribes that made up the whole people of Israel. See also the chart called "Numbers in the Bible," p. 2405.

[a]**24** Greek *many stadia*

14:34 *Gennesaret:* This town was located on the northwestern side of the Sea of Galilee, southwest of Capernaum, where Jesus had been living. It was probably located on a narrow plain, also known as Gennesaret, which was about four miles long and about two miles wide. This plain had rich soil and plenty of rainfall, so it was very good for farming. See the map on p. 2473.

15:1 *Pharisees and teachers of the law:* See the notes at 8:19 and 16:1.

15:2 *wash their hands:* According to the Law of Moses, if people touched something impure before they ate, any food they touched would also be ritually impure.

15:5 *devoted to God:* According to Jewish custom, when people said something was devoted to God, it belonged to God and could not be used for anyone else. The teachers said that they had devoted to God many of the things they owned. That is why they would not even use these things to help their parents.

15:11 *unclean:* The Law of Moses taught that what people ate and touched could make them unclean and therefore unfit to worship God. The Jewish people tried to keep their relationship with God clean and pure by eating only foods that the law allowed. But Jesus said that what people eat doesn't make them unclean. Rather, it is what they think and say that does so.

27 But Jesus immediately said to them: "Take courage! It is I.
Don't be afraid."

28 "Lord, if it's you," Peter replied, "tell me to come to you on
the water."

29 "Come," he said.

Then Peter got down out of the boat, walked on the water
and came toward Jesus. 30 But when he saw the wind, he was afraid
and, beginning to sink, cried out, "Lord, save me!"

31 Immediately Jesus reached out his hand and caught him.
"You of little faith," he said, "why did you doubt?"

32 And when they climbed into the boat, the wind died down.
33 Then those who were in the boat worshiped him, saying, "Truly
you are the Son of God."

34 When they had crossed over, they landed at Gennesaret.
35 And when the men of that place recognized Jesus, they sent word
to all the surrounding country. People brought all their sick to him
36 and begged him to let the sick just touch the edge of his cloak,
and all who touched him were healed.

Clean and Unclean

15 Then some Pharisees and teachers of the law came to Jesus
from Jerusalem and asked, 2 "Why do your disciples break the tradition of the elders? They don't wash their hands before they eat!"

3 Jesus replied, "And why do you break the command of God
for the sake of your tradition? 4 For God said, 'Honor your father
and mother'[a] and 'Anyone who curses his father or mother must
be put to death.'[b] 5 But you say that if a man says to his father or
mother, 'Whatever help you might otherwise have received from
me is a gift devoted to God,' 6 he is not to 'honor his father[c]' with
it. Thus you nullify the word of God for the sake of your tradition.
7 You hypocrites! Isaiah was right when he prophesied about you:

> 8 " 'These people honor me with their lips,
> but their hearts are far from me.
> 9 They worship me in vain;
> their teachings are but rules taught by men.'[d]"

10 Jesus called the crowd to him and said, "Listen and understand. 11 What goes into a man's mouth does not make him
'unclean,' but what comes out of his mouth, that is what makes
him 'unclean.' "

12 Then the disciples came to him and asked, "Do you know
that the Pharisees were offended when they heard this?"

13 He replied, "Every plant that my heavenly Father has not
planted will be pulled up by the roots. 14 Leave them; they are blind

---

[a] **4** Exodus 20:12; Deut. 5:16 [b] **4** Exodus 21:17; Lev. 20:9 [c] **6** Some manuscripts *father or his mother* [d] **9** Isaiah 29:13

guides.[a] If a blind man leads a blind man, both will fall into a pit."
15Peter said, "Explain the parable to us."
16"Are you still so dull?" Jesus asked them. 17"Don't you see
that whatever enters the mouth goes into the stomach and then out
of the body? 18But the things that come out of the mouth come from
the heart, and these make a man 'unclean.' 19For out of the heart
come evil thoughts, murder, adultery, sexual immorality, theft, false
testimony, slander. 20These are what make a man 'unclean'; but eating with unwashed hands does not make him 'unclean.' "

The Faith of the Canaanite Woman

21Leaving that place, Jesus withdrew to the region of Tyre
and Sidon. 22A Canaanite woman from that vicinity came to him,
crying out, "Lord, Son of David, have mercy on me! My daughter
is suffering terribly from demon-possession."
23Jesus did not answer a word. So his disciples came to him
and urged him, "Send her away, for she keeps crying out after us."
24He answered, "I was sent only to the lost sheep of Israel."
25The woman came and knelt before him. "Lord, help me!"
she said.
26He replied, "It is not right to take the children's bread and
toss it to their dogs."
27"Yes, Lord," she said, "but even the dogs eat the crumbs
that fall from their masters' table."
28Then Jesus answered, "Woman, you have great faith! Your
request is granted." And her daughter was healed from that very hour.

Jesus Feeds the Four Thousand

29Jesus left there and went along the Sea of Galilee. Then he
went up on a mountainside and sat down. 30Great crowds came to
him, bringing the lame, the blind, the crippled, the mute and many
others, and laid them at his feet; and he healed them. 31The people
were amazed when they saw the mute speaking, the crippled made
well, the lame walking and the blind seeing. And they praised the
God of Israel.
32Jesus called his disciples to him and said, "I have compassion for these people; they have already been with me three days
and have nothing to eat. I do not want to send them away hungry,
or they may collapse on the way."
33His disciples answered, "Where could we get enough bread
in this remote place to feed such a crowd?"
34"How many loaves do you have?" Jesus asked.
"Seven," they replied, "and a few small fish."
35He told the crowd to sit down on the ground. 36Then he
took the seven loaves and the fish, and when he had given thanks,

a14 Some manuscripts *guides of the blind*

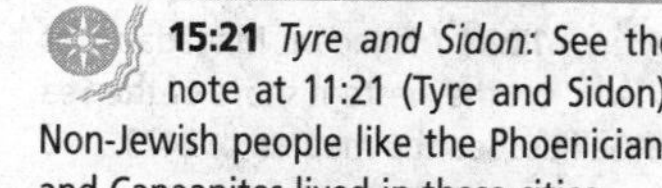

15:21 *Tyre and Sidon:* See the note at 11:21 (Tyre and Sidon). Non-Jewish people like the Phoenicians and Canaanites lived in these cities.

15:22 *Canaanite woman:* This woman was not Jewish. Her Canaanite ancestors had lived in the area before the tribes of Israel took it over and settled there hundreds of years earlier.

15:22 *Son of David:* See the note at 9:27.

15:26 *toss it to their dogs:* Jewish people in Jesus' day considered dogs to be unclean animals because they ate garbage and the carcasses of dead animals. They did not keep them as pets and some Jews even referred to people they didn't like as "dogs" (Ps 22:16).

15:34 *How many loaves:* See the note at 14:17.

15:36 *loaves . . . when he had given thanks he broke them:* See the note at 14:19.

15:39 *Magadan:* Magadan was on the western shore of the Sea of Galilee. See the map on p. 2473.

16:1 *Pharisees and Sadducees:* The name *Pharisee* comes from Hebrew words that may mean "separate ones" or "pure ones," though the exact meaning is not clear. Pharisees dedicated themselves to studying and teaching the Jewish Scriptures. The Sadducees were a wealthy group of Jews whose name probably comes from Zadok, a major priestly family (see 2 Sam 20:25; 1 Kgs 1:39-45). They taught that the most important thing was going to the temple and offering sacrifices there. For more, see the article called "The World of Jesus: People, Powers, and Politics," p. 1821.

16:4 *the sign of Jonah:* See the note at 12:39-41.

16:6-12 *yeast of the Pharisees and Sadducees:* Jesus was saying that the corrupt teaching of the Pharisees and Sadducees affected the whole people of Israel the way a little bit of yeast makes a whole batch of bread dough rise. See also Luke 12:1.

16:13 *Caesarea Philippi:* A city about 25 miles north of the Sea of Galilee. The Roman emperor Caesar Augustus gave the town to Herod the Great. Later, Herod's son Philip rebuilt the city and named it in honor of the emperor and of himself. See the map on p. 2472.

16:14 *Elijah . . . Jeremiah:* For "Elijah," see the note at 11:14. Jeremiah served as a prophet in Judah from about 626 to 586 B.C. During this time King Josiah tried to make some important religious reforms. Many people did not like Jeremiah; he said that the people of Judah would be defeated and punished because they had sinned against God.

16:16 *the Christ:* See the note at 1:17. See also John 6:68,69.

he broke them and gave them to the disciples, and they in turn to the people. 37 They all ate and were satisfied. Afterward the disciples picked up seven basketfuls of broken pieces that were left over. 38 The number of those who ate was four thousand, besides women and children. 39 After Jesus had sent the crowd away, he got into the boat and went to the vicinity of Magadan.

The Demand for a Sign

16 The Pharisees and Sadducees came to Jesus and tested him by asking him to show them a sign from heaven.

2 He replied,[a] "When evening comes, you say, 'It will be fair weather, for the sky is red,' 3 and in the morning, 'Today it will be stormy, for the sky is red and overcast.' You know how to interpret the appearance of the sky, but you cannot interpret the signs of the times. 4 A wicked and adulterous generation looks for a miraculous sign, but none will be given it except the sign of Jonah." Jesus then left them and went away.

The Yeast of the Pharisees and Sadducees

5 When they went across the lake, the disciples forgot to take bread. 6 "Be careful," Jesus said to them. "Be on your guard against the yeast of the Pharisees and Sadducees."

7 They discussed this among themselves and said, "It is because we didn't bring any bread."

8 Aware of their discussion, Jesus asked, "You of little faith, why are you talking among yourselves about having no bread? 9 Do you still not understand? Don't you remember the five loaves for the five thousand, and how many basketfuls you gathered? 10 Or the seven loaves for the four thousand, and how many basketfuls you gathered? 11 How is it you don't understand that I was not talking to you about bread? But be on your guard against the yeast of the Pharisees and Sadducees." 12 Then they understood that he was not telling them to guard against the yeast used in bread, but against the teaching of the Pharisees and Sadducees.

Peter's Confession of Christ

13 When Jesus came to the region of Caesarea Philippi, he asked his disciples, "Who do people say the Son of Man is?"

14 They replied, "Some say John the Baptist; others say Elijah; and still others, Jeremiah or one of the prophets."

15 "But what about you?" he asked. "Who do you say I am?"

16 Simon Peter answered, "You are the Christ,[b] the Son of the living God."

[a] **2** Some early manuscripts do not have the rest of verse 2 and all of verse 3.
[b] **16** Or *Messiah;* also in verse 20

17 Jesus replied, "Blessed are you, Simon son of Jonah, for this
was not revealed to you by man, but by my Father in heaven. 18 And
I tell you that you are Peter,[a] and on this rock I will build my
church, and the gates of Hades[b] will not overcome it.[c] 19 I will give
you the keys of the kingdom of heaven; whatever you bind on
earth will be[d] bound in heaven, and whatever you loose on earth
will be[d] loosed in heaven." 20 Then he warned his disciples not to
tell anyone that he was the Christ.

Jesus Predicts His Death

21 From that time on Jesus began to explain to his disciples
that he must go to Jerusalem and suffer many things at the hands
of the elders, chief priests and teachers of the law, and that he must
be killed and on the third day be raised to life.
22 Peter took him aside and began to rebuke him. "Never,
Lord!" he said. "This shall never happen to you!"
23 Jesus turned and said to Peter, "Get behind me, Satan! You
are a stumbling block to me; you do not have in mind the things
of God, but the things of men."
24 Then Jesus said to his disciples, "If anyone would come
after me, he must deny himself and take up his cross and follow
me. 25 For whoever wants to save his life[e] will lose it, but whoever
loses his life for me will find it. 26 What good will it be for a man if
he gains the whole world, yet forfeits his soul? Or what can a man
give in exchange for his soul? 27 For the Son of Man is going to
come in his Father's glory with his angels, and then he will reward
each person according to what he has done. 28 I tell you the truth,
some who are standing here will not taste death before they see the
Son of Man coming in his kingdom."

The Transfiguration

17 After six days Jesus took with him Peter, James and John the
brother of James, and led them up a high mountain by themselves.
2 There he was transfigured before them. His face shone like the
sun, and his clothes became as white as the light. 3 Just then there
appeared before them Moses and Elijah, talking with Jesus.
4 Peter said to Jesus, "Lord, it is good for us to be here. If you
wish, I will put up three shelters—one for you, one for Moses and
one for Elijah."
5 While he was still speaking, a bright cloud enveloped them,
and a voice from the cloud said, "This is my Son, whom I love;
with him I am well pleased. Listen to him!"
6 When the disciples heard this, they fell facedown to the
ground, terrified. 7 But Jesus came and touched them. "Get up," he

[a]18 *Peter* means *rock.* [b]18 Or *hell* [c]18 Or *not prove stronger than it* [d]19 Or *have been* [e]25 The Greek word means either *life* or *soul*; also in verse 26.

16:18 *church:* MATTHEW is the only Gospel that uses the word "church." The Greek word for church means "a group of people who are called together"; that is to say, they have a common purpose. The church was the new people of God that Jesus was "building."

16:20 *not to tell anyone that he was the Christ:* See the note at 12:16.

16:21 *Jerusalem:* The capital city of Judea. From the time of King David, Jerusalem was the center of the Jewish religion. In Jesus' day, the Romans controlled Jerusalem, but the Jewish people were allowed to worship at the temple, which had been rebuilt twice since being built by Solomon. Jesus went to Jerusalem to preach his message, knowing that he would face opposition from the Jewish religious leaders. See the mini-article called "Jerusalem," p. 574.

16:23 *Satan:* This word means "adversary." Satan was also known as the devil ("accuser") and the prince of demons (see 4:1 and 9:34).

16:27 *Son of Man:* See the mini-article called "Son of Man," p. 1866.

17:3 *Moses and Elijah:* Two of Israel's most important leaders. They called God's people to live a new way of life, and are used here to represent the two main sections of the Hebrew Scriptures. Moses represents the Law, while Elijah represents the Prophets. MATTHEW seems to suggest that Jesus is the fulfillment of the Hebrew Scriptures. For more, see the mini-article called "Moses," p. 2335 and the note on Elijah at 11:14.

16:19 Matt 18:18; John 20:23. **16:24** Matt 10:38; Luke 14:27. **16:25** Matt 10:39; Luke 17:33; John 12:25. **16:27** Matt 25:31; Ps 62:12; Rom 2:6. **17:1-5** 2 Pet 1:17,18. **17:5** Gen 22:2; Deut 18:15; Ps 2:7; Isa 42:1; Matt 3:17; 12:18; Mark 1:11; Luke 3:22.

Jesus replied to his disciples, *"If you have faith as small as a mustard seed, you can say to this mountain, 'Move from here to there' and it will move."*
Matt 17:20

17:9 *Son of Man:* See the mini-article called "Son of Man," p. 1866.

17:10 *Elijah must come first:* Many Jews in Jesus' day believed that the prophet Elijah must come back and appear before the Christ, or Messiah, could appear. This belief was based on the Old Testament prophecy in Mal 4:5, 6. They wondered: If Jesus was the Christ, why hadn't they seen Elijah?

17:18 *demon:* It was generally understood in Jesus' day that seizures were caused by demons. See the notes at 4:23,24 and 8:16.

17:24 *Capernaum:* See the note at 4:13 (Capernaum).

17:24 *temple tax:* The temple tax was required according to the Law of Moses (Exod 30:11-16; 38:26). The tax was two drachmas (Greek coins), the equivalent of half a shekel in the Jewish monetary system. This amounted on average to what a laborer got paid for working two days.

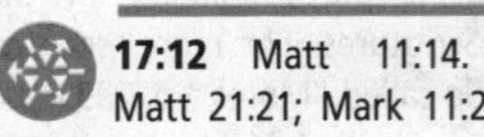

17:12 Matt 11:14. **17:20** Matt 21:21; Mark 11:23; 1 Cor 13:2.

said. "Don't be afraid." 8When they looked up, they saw no one
except Jesus.
9As they were coming down the mountain, Jesus instructed
them, "Don't tell anyone what you have seen, until the Son of Man
has been raised from the dead."
10The disciples asked him, "Why then do the teachers of the
law say that Elijah must come first?"
11Jesus replied, "To be sure, Elijah comes and will restore all
things. 12But I tell you, Elijah has already come, and they did not
recognize him, but have done to him everything they wished. In
the same way the Son of Man is going to suffer at their hands."
13Then the disciples understood that he was talking to them about
John the Baptist.

The Healing of a Boy With a Demon

14When they came to the crowd, a man approached Jesus
and knelt before him. 15"Lord, have mercy on my son," he said. "He
has seizures and is suffering greatly. He often falls into the fire or
into the water. 16I brought him to your disciples, but they could
not heal him."
17"O unbelieving and perverse generation," Jesus replied,
"how long shall I stay with you? How long shall I put up with you?
Bring the boy here to me." 18Jesus rebuked the demon, and it came
out of the boy, and he was healed from that moment.
19Then the disciples came to Jesus in private and asked,
"Why couldn't we drive it out?"
20He replied, "Because you have so little faith. I tell you the
truth, if you have faith as small as a mustard seed, you can say to
this mountain, 'Move from here to there' and it will move. Nothing will be impossible for you.[a]"
22When they came together in Galilee, he said to them, "The
Son of Man is going to be betrayed into the hands of men. 23They
will kill him, and on the third day he will be raised to life." And the
disciples were filled with grief.

The Temple Tax

24After Jesus and his disciples arrived in Capernaum, the collectors of the two-drachma tax came to Peter and asked, "Doesn't
your teacher pay the temple tax[b]?"
25"Yes, he does," he replied.
When Peter came into the house, Jesus was the first to speak.
"What do you think, Simon?" he asked. "From whom do the kings
of the earth collect duty and taxes—from their own sons or from
others?"

[a]**20** Some manuscripts *you.* 21*But this kind does not go out except by prayer and fasting.* [b]**24** Greek *the two drachmas*

26"From others," Peter answered.
"Then the sons are exempt," Jesus said to him. 27"But so that
we may not offend them, go to the lake and throw out your line.
Take the first fish you catch; open its mouth and you will find a
four-drachma coin. Take it and give it to them for my tax and
yours."

JESUS INSTRUCTS HIS FOLLOWERS

Jesus tells his disciples and other followers how to love and forgive one another.

The Greatest in the Kingdom of Heaven

18 At that time the disciples came to Jesus and asked, "Who is
the greatest in the kingdom of heaven?"
2He called a little child and had him stand among them.
3And he said: "I tell you the truth, unless you change and become
like little children, you will never enter the kingdom of heaven.
4Therefore, whoever humbles himself like this child is the greatest
in the kingdom of heaven.
5"And whoever welcomes a little child like this in my name
welcomes me. 6But if anyone causes one of these little ones who
believe in me to sin, it would be better for him to have a large millstone hung around his neck and to be drowned in the depths of
the sea.
7"Woe to the world because of the things that cause people
to sin! Such things must come, but woe to the man through whom
they come! 8If your hand or your foot causes you to sin, cut it off
and throw it away. It is better for you to enter life maimed or crippled than to have two hands or two feet and be thrown into eternal fire. 9And if your eye causes you to sin, gouge it out and throw
it away. It is better for you to enter life with one eye than to have
two eyes and be thrown into the fire of hell.

The Parable of the Lost Sheep

10"See that you do not look down on one of these little ones.
For I tell you that their angels in heaven always see the face of my
Father in heaven.[a]
12"What do you think? If a man owns a hundred sheep, and
one of them wanders away, will he not leave the ninety-nine on the
hills and go to look for the one that wandered off? 13And if he
finds it, I tell you the truth, he is happier about that one sheep
than about the ninety-nine that did not wander off. 14In the same
way your Father in heaven is not willing that any of these little
ones should be lost.

[a]**10** Some manuscripts *heaven.* [11]*The Son of Man came to save what was lost.*

Jesus said to his disciples, *"Whoever humbles himself like this child is the greatest in the kingdom of heaven."*
Matt 18:4

18:1 *kingdom of heaven:* See the note at 3:2. See also Luke 22:24.

18:3 *become like little children:* Children were considered a gift from God because they cared for older parents and carried on the family name when the parents died. Yet children had little power and were to obey their parents completely and do as they were told. Jesus used children as an example to show that being powerful is not the way to get into God's kingdom. What God wants is obedience.

18:8,9 *your hand . . . your eye . . . throw it away:* Sometimes Jesus used very difficult and unpopular sayings to emphasize the truth. He wanted to make it clear that the physical pain of losing a hand or an eye is nothing compared to the pain of being in the fire of hell. See also 5:29,30.

18:3 Mark 10:15; Luke 18:17.
18:10,11 Luke 19:10.

> Jesus told his disciples, *"Where two or three come together in my name, there am I with them."*
> Matt 18:20

18:17 *church:* In the four Gospels, the word "church" is found only here and at Matthew 16:18 (see the note there).

18:17 *tax collector:* See the note at 5:46.

18:22 *seventy-seven:* The large number means that one follower of Christ should never stop forgiving another. For more, see the chart called "Numbers in the Bible," p. 2405.

18:15 Luke 17:3. **18:16** Deut 19:15. **18:18** Matt 16:19; John 20:23. **18:21,22** Luke 17:3,4; Gen 4:24.

A Brother Who Sins Against You

15 "If your brother sins against you,[a] go and show him his
fault, just between the two of you. If he listens to you, you have
won your brother over. 16 But if he will not listen, take one or two
others along, so that 'every matter may be established by the testimony of two or three witnesses.'[b] 17 If he refuses to listen to them,
tell it to the church; and if he refuses to listen even to the church,
treat him as you would a pagan or a tax collector.

18 "I tell you the truth, whatever you bind on earth will be[c]
bound in heaven, and whatever you loose on earth will be[c] loosed
in heaven.

19 "Again, I tell you that if two of you on earth agree about
anything you ask for, it will be done for you by my Father in heav-
en. 20 For where two or three come together in my name, there am
I with them."

The Parable of the Unmerciful Servant

21 Then Peter came to Jesus and asked, "Lord, how many
times shall I forgive my brother when he sins against me? Up to
seven times?"
22 Jesus answered, "I tell you, not seven times, but seventy-
seven times.[d]
23 "Therefore, the kingdom of heaven is like a king who wanted to settle accounts with his servants. 24 As he began the settlement,
a man who owed him ten thousand talents[e] was brought to him.
25 Since he was not able to pay, the master ordered that he and his
wife and his children and all that he had be sold to repay the debt.
26 "The servant fell on his knees before him. 'Be patient
with me,' he begged, 'and I will pay back everything.' 27 The serv-

---

a15 Some manuscripts do not have *against you.* b16 Deut. 19:15 c18 Or *have been* d22 Or *seventy times seven* e24 That is, millions of dollars

QUESTIONS ABOUT MATTHEW 14:1—18:35

1. Jesus asked his disciples, "Who do you say I am?" (16:15). Why did Peter answer as he did? How would you answer? Why?
2. In this section, Jesus speaks twice about his coming death (16:21-28; 17:22, 23). How do the disciples react? Has someone ever told you something you did not want to believe was true? How did you react?
3. This section contains some of Jesus' "hard sayings." Which of these teachings do you find difficult to follow? Why? Which ones do you find most comforting? How would following these teachings build up the church and strengthen people's faith?
4. Why does Jesus say that it is important to forgive others? Have you ever had to forgive someone for something? Did your willingness to forgive improve your relationship with that person? What would the world be like without forgiveness?

ant’s master took pity on him, canceled the debt and let him go.
28“But when that servant went out, he found one of his
fellow servants who owed him a hundred denarii.[a] He grabbed
him and began to choke him. ‘Pay back what you owe me!’ he
demanded.
29“His fellow servant fell to his knees and begged him, ‘Be
patient with me, and I will pay you back.’
30“But he refused. Instead, he went off and had the man
thrown into prison until he could pay the debt. 31When the other
servants saw what had happened, they were greatly distressed and
went and told their master everything that had happened.
32“Then the master called the servant in. ‘You wicked servant,’ he said, ‘I canceled all that debt of yours because you begged
me to. 33Shouldn’t you have had mercy on your fellow servant just
as I had on you?’ 34In anger his master turned him over to the jail-
ers to be tortured, until he should pay back all he owed.
35“This is how my heavenly Father will treat each of you
unless you forgive your brother from your heart.”

19:1 *the other side of the Jordan:* This area was later known as Transjordan or Perea. Today this area is in Jordan.

19:3-9 *divorce:* See the note at 5:31.

19:4,5 Gen 1:27; 5:2; 2:24. **19:7** Deut 24:1-4; Matt 5:31. **19:9** Matt 5:32; 1 Cor 7:10,11.

JESUS FACES OPPONENTS IN JUDEA

As Jesus continues teaching, his enemies are often in the crowd, listening.

Divorce

19 When Jesus had finished saying these things, he left Galilee
and went into the region of Judea to the other side of the Jordan.
2Large crowds followed him, and he healed them there.
3Some Pharisees came to him to test him. They asked, “Is it
lawful for a man to divorce his wife for any and every reason?”
4“Haven’t you read,” he replied, “that at the beginning the
Creator ‘made them male and female,’[b] 5and said, ‘For this reason a
man will leave his father and mother and be united to his wife, and
the two will become one flesh’[c]? 6So they are no longer two, but
one. Therefore what God has joined together, let man not separate.”
7“Why then,” they asked, “did Moses command that a man
give his wife a certificate of divorce and send her away?”
8Jesus replied, “Moses permitted you to divorce your wives
because your hearts were hard. But it was not this way from the beginning. 9I tell you that anyone who divorces his wife, except for marital
unfaithfulness, and marries another woman commits adultery.”
10The disciples said to him, “If this is the situation between a
husband and wife, it is better not to marry.”
11Jesus replied, “Not everyone can accept this word, but only
those to whom it has been given. 12For some are eunuchs because

[a]**28** That is, a few dollars [b]**4** Gen. 1:27 [c]**5** Gen. 2:24

19:16 *eternal life:* By the time of Jesus, many Jewish people had come to believe in life after death. Some thought that life after death would be like on earth. Others like the Sadducees, did not accept the concept of eternal life because they said that it was not mentioned in the Law of Moses. Jesus compares the future kingdom of God to a feast (see 8:11). See the mini-article called "Eternal Life," p. 2072.

19:24 *camel:* Camels are used in the Middle East for transporting goods over long distances and have been called the "ships of the desert." The camel's stomach holds water in cells that help it go with little or no water for days at a time, and the camel's hump stores fat. Camel hair was used to make tents and clothes.

they were born that way; others were made that way by men; and others have renounced marriage[a] because of the kingdom of heaven. The one who can accept this should accept it."

The Little Children and Jesus

13 Then little children were brought to Jesus for him to place his hands on them and pray for them. But the disciples rebuked those who brought them.
14 Jesus said, "Let the little children come to me, and do not hinder them, for the kingdom of heaven belongs to such as these."
15 When he had placed his hands on them, he went on from there.

The Rich Young Man

16 Now a man came up to Jesus and asked, "Teacher, what good thing must I do to get eternal life?"
17 "Why do you ask me about what is good?" Jesus replied. "There is only One who is good. If you want to enter life, obey the commandments."
18 "Which ones?" the man inquired.
Jesus replied, " 'Do not murder, do not commit adultery, do not steal, do not give false testimony,
19 honor your father and mother,'[b] and 'love your neighbor as yourself.'[c]"
20 "All these I have kept," the young man said. "What do I still lack?"
21 Jesus answered, "If you want to be perfect, go, sell your

[a]12 Or *have made themselves eunuchs* [b]19 Exodus 20:12-16; Deut. 5:16-20 [c]19 Lev. 19:18

AT THE MARKET

In Jesus' day, every village in Palestine had a marketplace, which was usually located in an open area or where streets crossed. The marketplace had many stalls or booths where foods or spices could be measured and sold. A visitor would find things like wheat or barley, bread, fish, olives, and figs.

The market was filled with sights and sounds and smells. Sellers would often shout at buyers to try to get them to look at their food or other items. Animals like sheep, goats, or birds that were being sold also made lots of noise. The smell of animals, cooking food, and spices filled the air.

As is shown in Jesus' parable about the man who went to the marketplace to hire workers for his vineyard (20:1-16), the market was also a place where people might meet to talk or just to spend some time. Others went there because they knew that landowners often came to the market looking for workers.

Friday, the day before the Sabbath, was an especially busy day in the marketplace. This was when Jewish people came to buy the special things they needed to celebrate the weekly holy day of rest, which began at sunset on Friday evening and lasted until sunset on Saturday.

A Typical Marketplace in the Time of Jesus. *(See 20:1-7.)*

possessions and give to the poor, and you will have treasure in
heaven. Then come, follow me."
22 When the young man heard this, he went away sad,
because he had great wealth.
23 Then Jesus said to his disciples, "I tell you the truth, it is
hard for a rich man to enter the kingdom of heaven. 24 Again I tell
you, it is easier for a camel to go through the eye of a needle than
for a rich man to enter the kingdom of God."
25 When the disciples heard this, they were greatly astonished
and asked, "Who then can be saved?"
26 Jesus looked at them and said, "With man this is impossible, but with God all things are possible."
27 Peter answered him, "We have left everything to follow
you! What then will there be for us?"
28 Jesus said to them, "I tell you the truth, at the renewal of all
things, when the Son of Man sits on his glorious throne, you who
have followed me will also sit on twelve thrones, judging the twelve
tribes of Israel. 29 And everyone who has left houses or brothers or
sisters or father or mother[a] or children or fields for my sake will

19:24 *through the eye of a needle:* By contrasting the smallest of openings with the largest animal found in Palestine, the camel, Jesus emphasizes the need for God's grace in salvation. See also the note on Mark 10:23.

19:28 *sit on twelve thrones, judging the twelve tribes of Israel:* See the mini-article called "Israel," p. 264. Here "judging" is best understood as "ruling" or "governing." See also Matt 25:31; Luke 22:30.

19:18 Exod 20:13-16; Deut 5:17-20. **19:19** Exod 20:12; Lev 19:18; Deut 5:16.

a29 Some manuscripts *mother or wife*

receive a hundred times as much and will inherit eternal life. 30But
many who are first will be last, and many who are last will be first.

The Parable of the Workers in the Vineyard

20 "For the kingdom of heaven is like a landowner who went
out early in the morning to hire men to work in his vineyard. 2He
agreed to pay them a denarius for the day and sent them into his
vineyard.

3"About the third hour he went out and saw others standing
in the marketplace doing nothing. 4He told them, 'You also go and
work in my vineyard, and I will pay you whatever is right.' 5So they
went.

"He went out again about the sixth hour and the ninth hour
and did the same thing. 6About the eleventh hour he went out and
found still others standing around. He asked them, 'Why have you
been standing here all day long doing nothing?'

7" 'Because no one has hired us,' they answered.

"He said to them, 'You also go and work in my vineyard.'

8"When evening came, the owner of the vineyard said to his
foreman, 'Call the workers and pay them their wages, beginning
with the last ones hired and going on to the first.'

9"The workers who were hired about the eleventh hour came
and each received a denarius. 10So when those came who were
hired first, they expected to receive more. But each one of them
also received a denarius. 11When they received it, they began to
grumble against the landowner. 12'These men who were hired last
worked only one hour,' they said, 'and you have made them equal
to us who have borne the burden of the work and the heat of the
day.'

13"But he answered one of them, 'Friend, I am not being
unfair to you. Didn't you agree to work for a denarius? 14Take your
pay and go. I want to give the man who was hired last the same as
I gave you. 15Don't I have the right to do what I want with my own
money? Or are you envious because I am generous?'

16"So the last will be first, and the first will be last."

Jesus Again Predicts His Death

17Now as Jesus was going up to Jerusalem, he took the twelve
disciples aside and said to them, 18"We are going up to Jerusalem,
and the Son of Man will be betrayed to the chief priests and the
teachers of the law. They will condemn him to death 19and will
turn him over to the Gentiles to be mocked and flogged and crucified. On the third day he will be raised to life!"

A Mother's Request

20Then the mother of Zebedee's sons came to Jesus with her
sons and, kneeling down, asked a favor of him.

20:1 *vineyard:* The place where grapes are grown. A vineyard was usually located on a stony hillside and was often surrounded by a wall to protect the vines. A watchtower was sometimes built nearby so a worker could watch for robbers and animals. Grapes grow on vines that require a lot of special care, so an owner needed many workers to work in the vineyard.

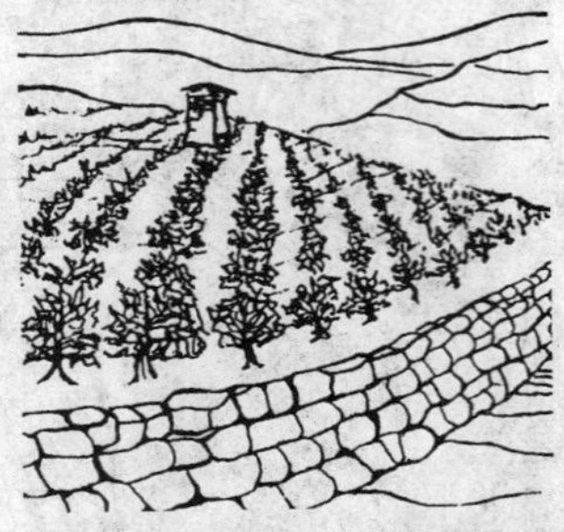

20:2 *a denarius:* This silver Roman coin was the usual amount of pay for a day's work. See the note at 22:19.

20:3 *marketplace:* See the mini-article called "At the Market," on p. 1890 and the illustration on p. 1891.

20:18 *chief priests:* These men were assigned special duties connected to the temple and to worship, like preparing sacrifices, collecting donations, blessing the people, and taking care of the building itself. For most of the first century, the Romans appointed one priest to be in charge of the others; he was called the high priest (see 26:57). For more, see the article called "People of the Law: The Religion of Israel," p. 939.

20:19 *the Gentiles:* This refers to the Romans, who ruled Judea at this time.

19:30 Matt 20:16; Luke 13:30. **20:8** Lev 19:13; Deut 24:15. **20:16** Matt 19:30; Mark 10:31; Luke 13:30.

21“What is it you want?” he asked.
She said, “Grant that one of these two sons of mine may sit
at your right and the other at your left in your kingdom.”
22“You don’t know what you are asking,” Jesus said to them.
“Can you drink the cup I am going to drink?”
“We can,” they answered.
23Jesus said to them, “You will indeed drink from my cup,
but to sit at my right or left is not for me to grant. These places
belong to those for whom they have been prepared by my Father.”
24When the ten heard about this, they were indignant with
the two brothers. 25Jesus called them together and said, “You know
that the rulers of the Gentiles lord it over them, and their high
officials exercise authority over them. 26Not so with you. Instead,
whoever wants to become great among you must be your servant,
27and whoever wants to be first must be your slave— 28just as the
Son of Man did not come to be served, but to serve, and to give his
life as a ransom for many.”

Two Blind Men Receive Sight

29As Jesus and his disciples were leaving Jericho, a large
crowd followed him. 30Two blind men were sitting by the roadside,
and when they heard that Jesus was going by, they shouted, “Lord,
Son of David, have mercy on us!”
31The crowd rebuked them and told them to be quiet, but they
shouted all the louder, “Lord, Son of David, have mercy on us!”
32Jesus stopped and called them. “What do you want me to
do for you?” he asked.
33“Lord,” they answered, “we want our sight.”
34Jesus had compassion on them and touched their eyes.
Immediately they received their sight and followed him.

The Triumphal Entry

21 As they approached Jerusalem and came to Bethphage on
the Mount of Olives, Jesus sent two disciples, 2saying to them, “Go
to the village ahead of you, and at once you will find a donkey tied
there, with her colt by her. Untie them and bring them to me. 3If
anyone says anything to you, tell him that the Lord needs them,
and he will send them right away.”
4This took place to fulfill what was spoken through the
prophet:

5“Say to the Daughter of Zion,
‘See, your king comes to you,
gentle and riding on a donkey,
on a colt, the foal of a donkey.’ ”[a]

[a]5 Zech. 9:9

Jesus said, *“Whoever wants to become great among you must be your servant . . . just as the Son of Man did not come to be served, but to serve, and to give his life as a ransom for many.”* Matt 20:26,28

20:21 *sit at your right . . . left:* The most powerful people in the kingdom sat directly at the right and left side of the ruler.

20:22 *drink the cup:* In the Scriptures a cup is sometimes used as a symbol of shared suffering. Here, to “drink the cup” is to suffer.

20:28 *ransom:* This is a term that refers to the cost of buying a slave’s freedom. The Law of Moses describes the terms by which Jews could buy back relatives who had become slaves (Lev 25:25-34, 47-55). See also the mini-article called “Redeemer (Redemption),” p. 995.

20:30 *Son of David:* See the note at 9:27. See also Ps 118:25,26.

20:25,26 Luke 22:25, 26. **20:26,27** Matt 23:11; Mark 9:35; Luke 22:26. **21:5** Isa 62:11; Zech 9:9.

21:7 *donkey:* The Israelite people rode on donkeys and used them to carry and move things much more often than they used horses or camels. Sometimes donkeys were used to do farm work, like pulling a grinding wheel that crushed grain into flour.

21:8 *spread their cloaks . . . branches:* This was one way that Jewish people welcomed a person in Jesus' day.

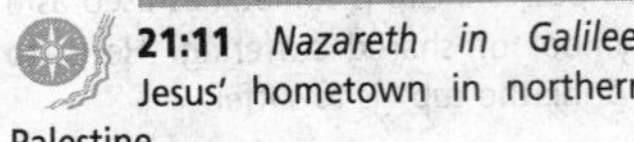

21:11 *Nazareth in Galilee:* Jesus' hometown in northern Palestine.

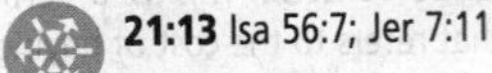

21:13 Isa 56:7; Jer 7:11.

6 The disciples went and did as Jesus had instructed them.
7 They brought the donkey and the colt, placed their cloaks on
them, and Jesus sat on them. 8 A very large crowd spread their
cloaks on the road, while others cut branches from the trees and
spread them on the road. 9 The crowds that went ahead of him and
those that followed shouted,

"Hosanna[a] to the Son of David!"
"Blessed is he who comes in the name of the Lord!"[b]
"Hosanna[a] in the highest!"

10 When Jesus entered Jerusalem, the whole city was stirred
and asked, "Who is this?"
11 The crowds answered, "This is Jesus, the prophet from
Nazareth in Galilee."

Jesus at the Temple

12 Jesus entered the temple area and drove out all who were
buying and selling there. He overturned the tables of the money
changers and the benches of those selling doves. 13 "It is written," he

[a]9 A Hebrew expression meaning "Save!" which became an exclamation of praise; also in verse 15 [b]9 Psalm 118:26

MONEY CHANGING IN THE TEMPLE

People came to Jerusalem at the time of the yearly celebration of Passover and for other religious holidays. Part of the celebration and worship involved sacrificing animals and making offerings of grain to God. Different sacrifices required different types of animals (for example, see Lev 3:1-13; 14:10, 21; Num 28:16-25), so many merchants set up animal pens and cages in the outer court of the temple, which was called the Court of the Gentiles. This court was the only part of the temple that Gentiles (non-Jewish people) were allowed to enter. It was also here that money changers often set up money tables where out-of-town Jewish visitors could change their money into the special kind of money used at the temple. The people used this money to pay the annual temple tax (see the note at 17:24). Jesus became angry that these merchants had turned the Court of the Gentiles into a place not of worship but of merchandising. Even worse, sometimes, these merchants overcharged people, and the money changers did not give a fair amount of money back to people in return for the foreign money they had exchanged. Jesus accused these merchants and money changers of being robbers (Mark 11:17). He was also making the point that Amos the prophet had made eight centuries earlier: Offering sacrifices was not as important as worshiping God and being fair to people (see Amos 5:21-24). The chief priests and other temple officials, as well as their families, made money from the activity of selling and buying at the temple, so they didn't like it when Jesus attacked this system.

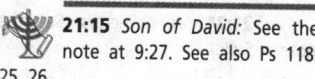

Christ Driving the Money Changers from the Temple, El Greco (1541-1614). El Greco was a painter and sculptor who was born in Crete but who lived much of his life in Toledo, Spain. He produced church altarpieces and many paintings on religious and biblical subjects, like the one shown here. (See 21:12-17.)

said to them, " 'My house will be called a house of prayer,'[a] but you
are making it a 'den of robbers.'[b]"
14The blind and the lame came to him at the temple, and he
healed them. 15But when the chief priests and the teachers of the law
saw the wonderful things he did and the children shouting in the
temple area, "Hosanna to the Son of David," they were indignant.
16"Do you hear what these children are saying?" they asked
him.

"Yes," replied Jesus, "have you never read,

" 'From the lips of children and infants
you have ordained praise'[c]?"

17And he left them and went out of the city to Bethany,
where he spent the night.

[a]13 Isaiah 56:7 [b]13 Jer. 7:11 [c]16 Psalm 8:2

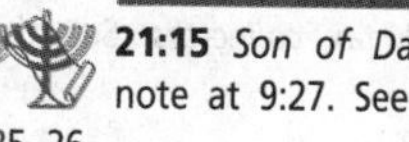

21:15 *Son of David:* See the note at 9:27. See also Ps 118: 25, 26.

21:17 *Bethany:* This is a small town about two miles east of Jerusalem, below the slope of the Mount of Olives. See the map on p. 2473 for its exact location. Jesus' friends Mary, Martha, and their brother Lazarus lived in Bethany where Jesus raised Lazarus back to life (see John 11). Today it is known as El-'Azariyeh, named after Lazarus, whose tomb is still said to be there.

21:16 Ps 8:2.

Jesus said,
"If you believe, you will receive whatever you ask for in prayer."
Matt 21:22

21:19-22 *Seeing a fig tree . . . the tree withered . . . whatever you ask:* Figs were an important food for people in the Middle East (see the note at 7:16). Healthy fig trees that were carefully tended (pruned and watered) produced two crops a year. This event from Jesus' life shows the power of the spoken word and faith. Besides demonstrating to his disciples the power of prayer, Jesus may have cursed the fig tree in order to show that God expects people to "bear fruit." Prophets often performed dramatic acts as a way of showing people what God expects of them. See the article called "Prophets and Prophecy," p. 935.

21:23 *chief priests and the elders of the people:* See the note at 20:18 and the article called "The World of Jesus: Peoples, Powers, and Politics," p. 1821.

21:25 *John's baptism:* Referring to John the Baptist. See the mini-article called "John the Baptist," p. 1853.

21:31 *tax collectors:* See the note at 5:46.

21:21 Matt 17:20; 1 Cor 13:2.
21:32 Luke 3:12; 7:29,30.

The Fig Tree Withers

18 Early in the morning, as he was on his way back to the city,
he was hungry. 19 Seeing a fig tree by the road, he went up to it but
found nothing on it except leaves. Then he said to it, "May you
never bear fruit again!" Immediately the tree withered.
20 When the disciples saw this, they were amazed. "How did
the fig tree wither so quickly?" they asked.
21 Jesus replied, "I tell you the truth, if you have faith and do
not doubt, not only can you do what was done to the fig tree, but
also you can say to this mountain, 'Go, throw yourself into the sea,'
and it will be done. 22 If you believe, you will receive whatever you
ask for in prayer."

The Authority of Jesus Questioned

23 Jesus entered the temple courts, and, while he was teaching, the chief priests and the elders of the people came to him. "By
what authority are you doing these things?" they asked. "And who
gave you this authority?"
24 Jesus replied, "I will also ask you one question. If you
answer me, I will tell you by what authority I am doing these
things. 25 John's baptism—where did it come from? Was it from
heaven, or from men?"
They discussed it among themselves and said, "If we say,
'From heaven,' he will ask, 'Then why didn't you believe him?'
26 But if we say, 'From men'—we are afraid of the people, for they
all hold that John was a prophet."
27 So they answered Jesus, "We don't know."
Then he said, "Neither will I tell you by what authority I am
doing these things.

The Parable of the Two Sons

28 "What do you think? There was a man who had two sons.
He went to the first and said, 'Son, go and work today in the vineyard.'
29 " 'I will not,' he answered, but later he changed his mind
and went.
30 "Then the father went to the other son and said the same
thing. He answered, 'I will, sir,' but he did not go.
31 "Which of the two did what his father wanted?"
"The first," they answered.
Jesus said to them, "I tell you the truth, the tax collectors and
the prostitutes are entering the kingdom of God ahead of you.
32 For John came to you to show you the way of righteousness,
and you did not believe him, but the tax collectors and the prostitutes did. And even after you saw this, you did not repent and
believe him.

The Parable of the Vineyard, Zelda Fitzgerald (1900-1948). This painting (gouache on paper) shows a vineyard tenant stoning the landowner's servants who were sent to collect his share of the harvest (see 21:33-40).

The Parable of the Tenants

33"Listen to another parable: There was a landowner who
planted a vineyard. He put a wall around it, dug a winepress in it
and built a watchtower. Then he rented the vineyard to some
farmers and went away on a journey. 34When the harvest time
approached, he sent his servants to the tenants to collect his fruit.
35"The tenants seized his servants; they beat one, killed
another, and stoned a third. 36Then he sent other servants to them,
more than the first time, and the tenants treated them the same
way. 37Last of all, he sent his son to them. 'They will respect my
son,' he said.
38"But when the tenants saw the son, they said to each other,
'This is the heir. Come, let's kill him and take his inheritance.' 39So
they took him and threw him out of the vineyard and killed him.
40"Therefore, when the owner of the vineyard comes, what
will he do to those tenants?"
41"He will bring those wretches to a wretched end," they
replied, "and he will rent the vineyard to other tenants, who will
give him his share of the crop at harvest time."

21:33 *vineyard:* See the note at 20:1. See also Isa 5:1,2.

22:2 *wedding banquet:* In most Jewish weddings, the families and friends of both the bride and the groom would gather at different locations and then march to the same place. Very often, music and dancing went on while they marched. The wedding banquet most often took place in the home of the groom, where food and wine would be served, and people would celebrate with more music and dancing.

22:11,12 *not wearing wedding clothes:* It was customary to wear the finest clothes for a wedding. It may have been a custom that the groom's father would even provide wedding clothes to guests who didn't have the right kind of clothes. If a guest didn't accept the host's wedding clothes, the host would be insulted.

22:13 *darkness:* This is another word for the place where those who do evil will be punished. See the note at 5:22. See also 8:12; 25:30.

22:16 *the Herodians:* People who were political followers of the family of Herod the Great (2:1) and his son Herod Antipas (14:1). They wanted Herod to be king in Jerusalem.

22:17 *pay taxes to Caesar:* Jewish people had to pay taxes to the Roman government that controlled their land. The highest Roman official, the emperor, was called Caesar. Had Jesus said that people should not pay taxes, the Jewish leaders could have accused him of being disloyal to the Roman rulers.

21:42 Ps 118:22,23

42 Jesus said to them, "Have you never read in the Scriptures:

" 'The stone the builders rejected
has become the capstone[a];
the Lord has done this,
and it is marvelous in our eyes'[b]?

43 "Therefore I tell you that the kingdom of God will be taken
away from you and given to a people who will produce its fruit.
44 He who falls on this stone will be broken to pieces, but he on
whom it falls will be crushed."[c]

45 When the chief priests and the Pharisees heard Jesus' parables, they knew he was talking about them. 46 They looked for a way
to arrest him, but they were afraid of the crowd because the people held that he was a prophet.

The Parable of the Wedding Banquet

22 Jesus spoke to them again in parables, saying: 2 "The kingdom of heaven is like a king who prepared a wedding banquet for
his son. 3 He sent his servants to those who had been invited to the
banquet to tell them to come, but they refused to come.

4 "Then he sent some more servants and said, 'Tell those who
have been invited that I have prepared my dinner: My oxen and
fattened cattle have been butchered, and everything is ready. Come
to the wedding banquet.'

5 "But they paid no attention and went off—one to his field,
another to his business. 6 The rest seized his servants, mistreated
them and killed them. 7 The king was enraged. He sent his army
and destroyed those murderers and burned their city.

8 "Then he said to his servants, 'The wedding banquet is ready,
but those I invited did not deserve to come. 9 Go to the street corners
and invite to the banquet anyone you find.' 10 So the servants went
out into the streets and gathered all the people they could find, both
good and bad, and the wedding hall was filled with guests.

11 "But when the king came in to see the guests, he noticed a man
there who was not wearing wedding clothes. 12 'Friend,' he asked, 'how
did you get in here without wedding clothes?' The man was speechless.

13 "Then the king told the attendants, 'Tie him hand and
foot, and throw him outside, into the darkness, where there will be
weeping and gnashing of teeth.'

14 "For many are invited, but few are chosen."

Paying Taxes to Caesar

15 Then the Pharisees went out and laid plans to trap him in
his words. 16 They sent their disciples to him along with the Hero-

[a]42 Or *cornerstone* [b]42 Psalm 118:22,23 [c]44 Some manuscripts do not have verse 44.

dians. "Teacher," they said, "we know you are a man of integrity
and that you teach the way of God in accordance with the truth.
You aren't swayed by men, because you pay no attention to who
they are. 17 Tell us then, what is your opinion? Is it right to pay taxes
to Caesar or not?"
18 But Jesus, knowing their evil intent, said, "You hypocrites,
why are you trying to trap me? 19 Show me the coin used for paying the tax." They brought him a denarius, 20 and he asked them,
"Whose portrait is this? And whose inscription?"
21 "Caesar's," they replied.
Then he said to them, "Give to Caesar what is Caesar's, and
to God what is God's."
22 When they heard this, they were amazed. So they left him
and went away.

Marriage at the Resurrection

23 That same day the Sadducees, who say there is no resurrection, came to him with a question. 24 "Teacher," they said, "Moses
told us that if a man dies without having children, his brother must
marry the widow and have children for him. 25 Now there were seven
brothers among us. The first one married and died, and since he had
no children, he left his wife to his brother. 26 The same thing happened to the second and third brother, right on down to the seventh.
27 Finally, the woman died. 28 Now then, at the resurrection, whose
wife will she be of the seven, since all of them were married to her?"
29 Jesus replied, "You are in error because you do not know
the Scriptures or the power of God. 30 At the resurrection people
will neither marry nor be given in marriage; they will be like the
angels in heaven. 31 But about the resurrection of the dead—have
you not read what God said to you, 32 'I am the God of Abraham,
the God of Isaac, and the God of Jacob'[a]? He is not the God of the
dead but of the living."
33 When the crowds heard this, they were astonished at his
teaching.

The Greatest Commandment

34 Hearing that Jesus had silenced the Sadducees, the Pharisees got together. 35 One of them, an expert in the law, tested him
with this question: 36 "Teacher, which is the greatest commandment
in the Law?"
37 Jesus replied: " 'Love the Lord your God with all your heart
and with all your soul and with all your mind.'[b] 38 This is the first
and greatest commandment. 39 And the second is like it: 'Love your
neighbor as yourself.'[c] 40 All the Law and the Prophets hang on
these two commandments."

[a]**32** Exodus 3:6 [b]**37** Deut. 6:5 [c]**39** Lev. 19:18

22:19 *denarius:* In the time of Jesus, a denarius had a picture of Tiberius Caesar on one side. This is the coin that was used to pay taxes to Caesar.

22:23 *Sadducees:* See the notes at 16:1 and 19:16. The Sadducees didn't believe that God brought people back to life after they had died because they did not think that was directly taught in the Law of Moses. They thought their question to Jesus would show how foolish it was to believe that people came back to life after they died. See also Acts 23:8.

22:32 *I am the God of Abraham . . . Isaac, and . . . Jacob:* Jesus quotes Exodus 3:6, where the Lord used the present tense in speaking to Moses about his ancestors. His point is that if God is still worshiped by these three (because God uses the present tense of the verb, "I am"), who entered into a covenant with God in ancient times, then they must in some way still be alive. Therefore, God is the God of the living because he brings his followers back to life. Jesus relies on a quotation from the book of Exodus—because the Sadducees only considered the Torah (Pentateuch) to be sacred Scripture.

22:40 *the Law and the Prophets:* See the note at 5:17.

22:24 Deut 25:5. **22:35-40** Luke 10:25-28. **22:37** Deut 6:5. **22:39** Lev 19:18.

22:42 *son of David:* See the note at 9:27.

22:44 *my right hand:* This was the place of power and honor. See the note at 20:21.

22:45 *David . . . Lord:* Jesus asked a question that even the Pharisees could not answer. That is, how could a person be both David's son and David's Lord? In other words, how could the Christ, or Messiah, be descended from David and be more important than David? See the notes at 1:1; 1:17; 9:27.

23:4 *tie up heavy loads and put them on men's shoulders:* The Pharisees and teachers of the law taught people how to follow the law as the way to serve God. These rules were a big burden for some. Jesus was saying that these teachers liked to lay down rules but were not willing to help others keep them.

23:5 *phylacteries . . . tassels:* Many Jewish people literally obeyed Deuteronomy 11:18 by wearing Scripture verses in small leather boxes called phylacteries. See the illustration on p. 356. Some Pharisees in Jesus' day may have tried to show off by making the boxes bigger than they had to be. Tassels were worn on the four corners of some clothing as a sign of belonging to God. See also Deut 6:8; Num 15:38.

22:44 Ps 110:1. **23:11** Matt 20:26, 27; Mark 9:35; 10:43, 44; Luke 22:26 **23:12** Luke 14:11; 18:14. **23:17** Exod 30:23-29. **23:22** Isa 66:1; Matt 5:34. **23:33** Matt 3:7; 12:34; Luke 3:7.

Whose Son Is the Christ?

[41]While the Pharisees were gathered together, Jesus asked them, [42]"What do you think about the Christ[a]? Whose son is he?"

"The son of David," they replied.

[43]He said to them, "How is it then that David, speaking by the Spirit, calls him 'Lord'? For he says,

[44]" 'The Lord said to my Lord:
"Sit at my right hand
until I put your enemies
under your feet." '[b]

[45]If then David calls him 'Lord,' how can he be his son?" [46]No one could say a word in reply, and from that day on no one dared to ask him any more questions.

Seven Woes

23 Then Jesus said to the crowds and to his disciples: [2]"The teachers of the law and the Pharisees sit in Moses' seat. [3]So you must obey them and do everything they tell you. But do not do what they do, for they do not practice what they preach. [4]They tie up heavy loads and put them on men's shoulders, but they themselves are not willing to lift a finger to move them.

[5]"Everything they do is done for men to see: They make their phylacteries[c] wide and the tassels on their garments long; [6]they love the place of honor at banquets and the most important seats in the synagogues; [7]they love to be greeted in the marketplaces and to have men call them 'Rabbi.'

[8]"But you are not to be called 'Rabbi,' for you have only one Master and you are all brothers. [9]And do not call anyone on earth 'father,' for you have one Father, and he is in heaven. [10]Nor are you to be called 'teacher,' for you have one Teacher, the Christ.[a] [11]The greatest among you will be your servant. [12]For whoever exalts himself will be humbled, and whoever humbles himself will be exalted.

[13]"Woe to you, teachers of the law and Pharisees, you hypocrites! You shut the kingdom of heaven in men's faces. You yourselves do not enter, nor will you let those enter who are trying to.[d]

[15]"Woe to you, teachers of the law and Pharisees, you hypocrites! You travel over land and sea to win a single convert, and when he becomes one, you make him twice as much a son of hell as you are.

[16]"Woe to you, blind guides! You say, 'If anyone swears by

---

[a]**42,10** Or *Messiah* [b]**44** Psalm 110:1 [c]**5** That is, boxes containing Scripture verses, worn on forehead and arm [d]**13** Some manuscripts *to.* [14]*Woe to you, teachers of the law and Pharisees, you hypocrites! You devour widows' houses and for a show make lengthy prayers. Therefore you will be punished more severely.*

the temple, it means nothing; but if anyone swears by the gold
of the temple, he is bound by his oath.' 17You blind fools! Which
is greater: the gold, or the temple that makes the gold sacred?
18You also say, 'If anyone swears by the altar, it means nothing;
but if anyone swears by the gift on it, he is bound by his oath.'
19You blind men! Which is greater: the gift, or the altar that
makes the gift sacred? 20Therefore, he who swears by the altar
swears by it and by everything on it. 21And he who swears by the
temple swears by it and by the one who dwells in it. 22And he
who swears by heaven swears by God's throne and by the one
who sits on it.

23"Woe to you, teachers of the law and Pharisees, you hypocrites! You give a tenth of your spices—mint, dill and cummin.
But you have neglected the more important matters of the law—
justice, mercy and faithfulness. You should have practiced the latter, without neglecting the former. 24You blind guides! You strain
out a gnat but swallow a camel.

25"Woe to you, teachers of the law and Pharisees, you hypocrites! You clean the outside of the cup and dish, but inside they
are full of greed and self-indulgence. 26Blind Pharisee! First clean
the inside of the cup and dish, and then the outside also will be
clean.

27"Woe to you, teachers of the law and Pharisees, you hypocrites! You are like whitewashed tombs, which look beautiful on
the outside but on the inside are full of dead men's bones and
everything unclean. 28In the same way, on the outside you appear
to people as righteous but on the inside you are full of hypocrisy
and wickedness.

29"Woe to you, teachers of the law and Pharisees, you hypocrites! You build tombs for the prophets and decorate the
graves of the righteous. 30And you say, 'If we had lived in the
days of our forefathers, we would not have taken part with them
in shedding the blood of the prophets.' 31So you testify against
yourselves that you are the descendants of those who murdered
the prophets. 32Fill up, then, the measure of the sin of your forefathers!

33"You snakes! You brood of vipers! How will you escape
being condemned to hell? 34Therefore I am sending you prophets
and wise men and teachers. Some of them you will kill and crucify; others you will flog in your synagogues and pursue from town
to town. 35And so upon you will come all the righteous blood that
has been shed on earth, from the blood of righteous Abel to the
blood of Zechariah son of Berekiah, whom you murdered between
the temple and the altar. 36I tell you the truth, all this will come
upon this generation.

37"O Jerusalem, Jerusalem, you who kill the prophets and
stone those sent to you, how often I have longed to gather your

23:23 *You give a tenth of your spices:* The teachers followed the law about giving one-tenth of everything back to the Lord (see Lev 27:30; Deut 14:22), even one-tenth of the spices in their gardens. But Jesus says helping others is more important.

23:24 *gnat . . . camel:* Gnats were the smallest of unclean animals (see Lev 11), while camels were one of the largest.

23:25 *clean the outside of the cup and dish:* Jesus was referring to one of the many purification rituals followed by the Pharisees and teachers. See also Mark 7:3, 4.

23:27 *whitewashed tombs:* Tombs were whitewashed to make them stand out so people would not accidentally touch them. A person who touched a tomb was considered unclean (see Num 19:16) and had to go through ritual cleansing before worshiping again with the rest of the Jewish people. See also Acts 23:3.

23:29 *You build tombs for the prophets:* Archaeologists have found that, in the time of Jesus, people in Palestine were building funeral monuments to honor the prophets.

23:35 *Abel . . . Zechariah:* GENESIS, the first book in the Jewish Scriptures, tells that Abel was the first person to be murdered (Gen 4:1-16). SECOND CHRONICLES is the last book in the Hebrew Scriptures. (See the chart called "Books of the Hebrew Scriptures, or 'Tanak'," p. 13.) The last murder it tells about is that of Zechariah, the son of the high priest Jehoiada (2 Chr 24:17-22).

23:37 *kill the prophets and stone those sent to you:* It is unclear what prophets Jesus had in mind, but see 1 Kgs 19:10; Jer 2:30; 26:20-23. Stoning was done by dropping heavy stones on a condemned person. This was a common form of capital punishment in Israelite society.

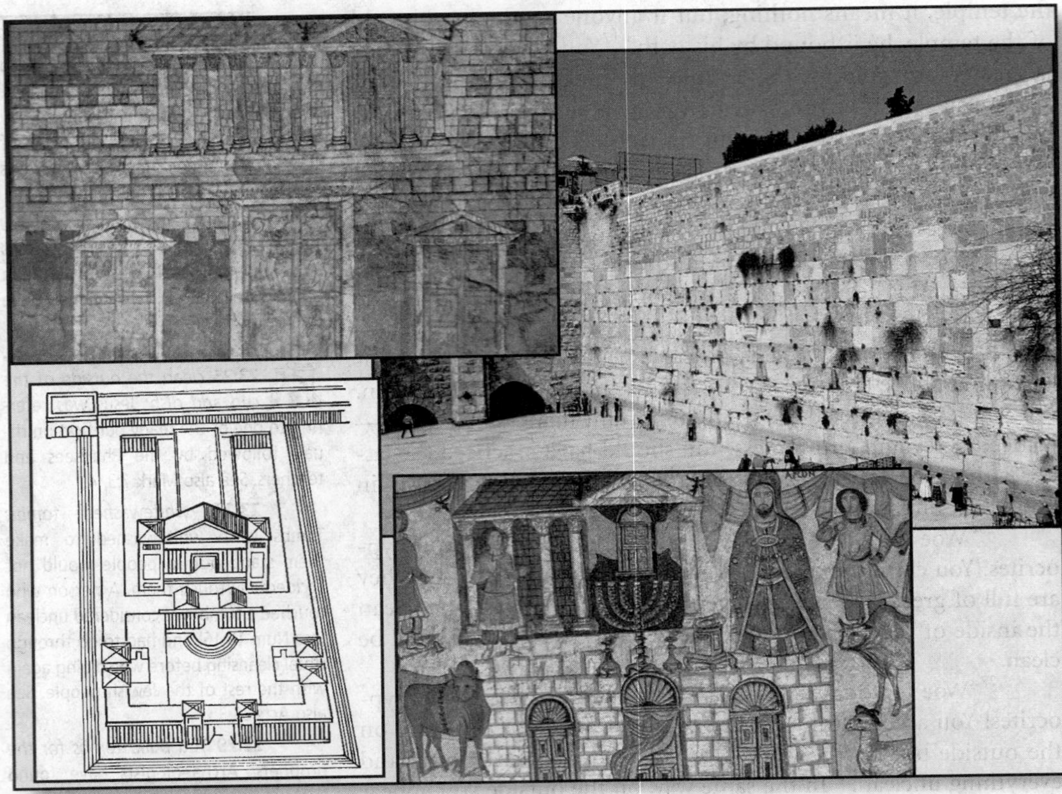

Herod's temple was destroyed by the Romans in A.D. 70. (SEE 24:1,2.) The "Wailing Wall" (right) is all that remains today. The wall-paintings from the synagogue at Dura-Europos (around A.D. 200) show that the memory of the temple continued to be important to Jews for many years.

children together, as a hen gathers her chicks under her wings, but
you were not willing. 38 Look, your house is left to you desolate.
39 For I tell you, you will not see me again until you say, 'Blessed is
he who comes in the name of the Lord.'[a]"

JESUS TEACHES ABOUT GOD'S COMING KINGDOM

Jesus uses parables to challenge his opponents and to tell his listeners how to be ready for God's coming kingdom.

Signs of the End of the Age

24 Jesus left the temple and was walking away when his disciples came up to him to call his attention to its buildings. 2 "Do you

[a]**39** Psalm 118:26

24:1,2 *temple . . . not one stone here will be left on another:* This is the temple that Herod built in Jerusalem. It was made of large blocks of stone, some over thirty feet long and sat on a foundation nearly a mile around at the base. In A.D. 70 the Romans attacked Jerusalem and destroyed Herod's temple.

24:3 *Mount of Olives:* The Mount of Olives is a ridge over two miles long that is part of a larger mountain range running through Palestine. It is located just east of the temple area in Jerusalem. See the map on p. 2474.

23:38,39 Jer 22:5; Ps 118:26; Matt 21:9.

see all these things?" he asked. "I tell you the truth, not one stone
here will be left on another; every one will be thrown down."
3As Jesus was sitting on the Mount of Olives, the disciples
came to him privately. "Tell us," they said, "when will this happen,
and what will be the sign of your coming and of the end of the age?"
4Jesus answered: "Watch out that no one deceives you. 5For
many will come in my name, claiming, 'I am the Christ,'[a] and will
deceive many. 6You will hear of wars and rumors of wars, but see
to it that you are not alarmed. Such things must happen, but the
end is still to come. 7Nation will rise against nation, and kingdom
against kingdom. There will be famines and earthquakes in various
places. 8All these are the beginning of birth pains.
9"Then you will be handed over to be persecuted and put to
death, and you will be hated by all nations because of me. 10At that
time many will turn away from the faith and will betray and hate
each other, 11and many false prophets will appear and deceive
many people. 12Because of the increase of wickedness, the love of
most will grow cold, 13but he who stands firm to the end will be
saved. 14And this gospel of the kingdom will be preached in the
whole world as a testimony to all nations, and then the end will
come.
15"So when you see standing in the holy place 'the abomination that causes desolation,'[b] spoken of through the prophet
Daniel—let the reader understand— 16then let those who are in
Judea flee to the mountains. 17Let no one on the roof of his house
go down to take anything out of the house. 18Let no one in the
field go back to get his cloak. 19How dreadful it will be in those
days for pregnant women and nursing mothers! 20Pray that your
flight will not take place in winter or on the Sabbath. 21For then
there will be great distress, unequaled from the beginning of the
world until now—and never to be equaled again. 22If those days
had not been cut short, no one would survive, but for the sake of
the elect those days will be shortened. 23At that time if anyone says
to you, 'Look, here is the Christ!' or, 'There he is!' do not believe it.
24For false Christs and false prophets will appear and perform
great signs and miracles to deceive even the elect—if that were
possible. 25See, I have told you ahead of time.
26"So if anyone tells you, 'There he is, out in the desert,' do
not go out; or, 'Here he is, in the inner rooms,' do not believe it.
27For as lightning that comes from the east is visible even in the
west, so will be the coming of the Son of Man. 28Wherever there is
a carcass, there the vultures will gather.
29"Immediately after the distress of those days

" 'the sun will be darkened,
and the moon will not give its light;

---

[a]5 Or *Messiah*; also in verse 23 [b]15 Daniel 9:27; 11:31; 12:11

24:15 *the abomination that causes desolation:* Jesus repeated Daniel's prophecy (see Dan 9:27; 11:31; 12:11). In 168 B.C., a Syrian ruler named Antiochus IV Epiphanes set up an altar to the Greek god Zeus in the temple. Within three years the people of Judea got rid of this altar and reclaimed the temple. This event was celebrated in the Feast of Dedication (John 10:22), known today as Hanukkah.

24:17 *roof:* In Palestine the houses usually had flat roofs. Stairs or a ladder on the outside led up to the roof, which was made of beams and boards covered with packed earth. When people wanted to get fresh air, they often went out into their courtyard or up on the roof.

24:20 *in winter or on the Sabbath:* In Palestine the winters have long periods of cold and rain that make travel difficult. According to the law, the Jews who wanted to keep the Sabbath holy should not travel much over half a mile on the Sabbath. For these reasons it was hard for them to escape from their enemies in the winter or on the Sabbath.

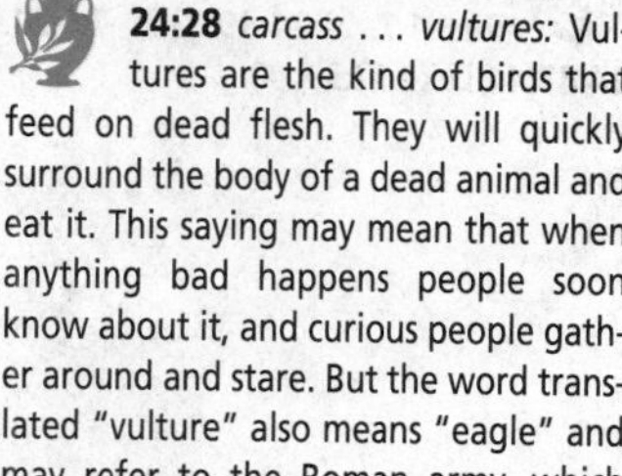

24:28 *carcass . . . vultures:* Vultures are the kind of birds that feed on dead flesh. They will quickly surround the body of a dead animal and eat it. This saying may mean that when anything bad happens people soon know about it, and curious people gather around and stare. But the word translated "vulture" also means "eagle" and may refer to the Roman army, which had an eagle as its symbol. See also Luke 17:37.

24:9,13 Matt 10:22 **24:17,18** Luke 17:31. **24:21** Dan 12:1; Rev 7:14. **24:26,27** Luke 17:23,24. **24:29** Isa 13:10; 34:4; Ezek 32:7; Joel 2:10,31; 3:15; Rev 6:12,13.

Jesus taught,
"So you also must be ready, because the Son of Man will come at an hour when you do not expect him."
Matt 24:44

24:29 *the stars will fall from the sky:* In ancient times many people thought that the stars were divine powers.

24:30 *Son of Man:* See the mini-article "Son of Man," on p. 1866.

24:32 *fig tree:* See the notes at 7:16 and 21:19-22.

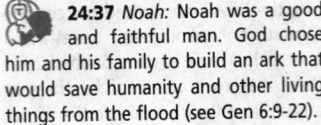

24:37 *Noah:* Noah was a good and faithful man. God chose him and his family to build an ark that would save humanity and other living things from the flood (see Gen 6:9-22).

24:30 Dan 7:13; Zech 12:10-14; Rev 1:7. **24:39** Gen 7:6-24. **24:43,44** Luke 12:39, 40.

the stars will fall from the sky,
and the heavenly bodies will be shaken.'[a]

30"At that time the sign of the Son of Man will appear in the sky, and all the nations of the earth will mourn. They will see the Son of Man coming on the clouds of the sky, with power and great glory. 31And he will send his angels with a loud trumpet call, and they will gather his elect from the four winds, from one end of the heavens to the other.

32"Now learn this lesson from the fig tree: As soon as its twigs get tender and its leaves come out, you know that summer is near. 33Even so, when you see all these things, you know that it[b] is near, right at the door. 34I tell you the truth, this generation[c] will certainly not pass away until all these things have happened. 35Heaven and earth will pass away, but my words will never pass away.

The Day and Hour Unknown

36"No one knows about that day or hour, not even the angels in heaven, nor the Son,[d] but only the Father. 37As it was in the days of Noah, so it will be at the coming of the Son of Man. 38For in the days before the flood, people were eating and drinking, marrying and giving in marriage, up to the day Noah entered the ark; 39and they knew nothing about what would happen until the flood came and took them all away. That is how it will be at the coming of the Son of Man. 40Two men will be in the field; one will be taken and the other left. 41Two women will be grinding with a hand mill; one will be taken and the other left.

42"Therefore keep watch, because you do not know on what day your Lord will come. 43But understand this: If the owner of the house had known at what time of night the thief was coming, he would have kept watch and would not have let his house be broken into. 44So you also must be ready, because the Son of Man will come at an hour when you do not expect him.

45"Who then is the faithful and wise servant, whom the master has put in charge of the servants in his household to give them their food at the proper time? 46It will be good for that servant whose master finds him doing so when he returns. 47I tell you the truth, he will put him in charge of all his possessions. 48But suppose that servant is wicked and says to himself, 'My master is staying away a long time,' 49and he then begins to beat his fellow servants and to eat and drink with drunkards. 50The master of that servant will come on a day when he does not expect him and at an hour he is not aware of. 51He will cut him to pieces and assign him a place with the hypocrites, where there will be weeping and gnashing of teeth.

[a]**29** Isaiah 13:10; 34:4 [b]**33** Or *he* [c]**34** Or *race* [d]**36** Some manuscripts do not have *nor the Son.*

The Parable of the Ten Virgins

25 "At that time the kingdom of heaven will be like ten virgins
who took their lamps and went out to meet the bridegroom.
2 Five of them were foolish and five were wise. 3 The foolish ones
took their lamps but did not take any oil with them. 4 The wise,
however, took oil in jars along with their lamps. 5 The bridegroom was a long time in coming, and they all became drowsy
and fell asleep.
6 "At midnight the cry rang out: 'Here's the bridegroom!
Come out to meet him!'
7 "Then all the virgins woke up and trimmed their lamps.
8 The foolish ones said to the wise, 'Give us some of your oil; our
lamps are going out.'
9 " 'No,' they replied, 'there may not be enough for both us
and you. Instead, go to those who sell oil and buy some for yourselves.'
10 "But while they were on their way to buy the oil, the bridegroom arrived. The virgins who were ready went in with him to
the wedding banquet. And the door was shut.
11 "Later the others also came. 'Sir! Sir!' they said. 'Open the
door for us!'
12 "But he replied, 'I tell you the truth, I don't know you.'
13 "Therefore keep watch, because you do not know the day
or the hour.

Ten Maidens—Five Foolish, Five Wise, Gui-jie Zhang (twentieth century). This artist used a traditional Chinese art form, cut paper, to depict the Parable of the Ten Virgins (see 25:1-13).

25:1-4 *ten virgins who took their lamps . . . to meet the bridegroom:* It was the custom for the groom to go to the home of the bride's parents to get the bride. Young girls and other guests would then go with them to the home of the groom's parents, where the wedding feast would take place. Since lamps needed oil to burn, some of the young girls were prepared, having brought extra oil. See also Luke 12:35.

25:11,12 Luke 13:25.

25:14 *Again, it will be like:* As in the previous parable, Jesus is teaching about the kingdom of heaven (25:1). See the note at 3:2.

25:27 *bankers:* Bankers in Jesus' day changed foreign money for the local money. They helped businesses by investing money and giving out loans. They took in money at low interest rates for some of their investments. Wealthy people usually invested their money with bankers, hoping to make a profit. Most people, however, did not give their money to bankers. They often buried or hid it. As a result, they didn't earn any profit or interest.

25:30 *darkness:* See the notes at 5:22 and 8:12. See also Matt 22:13; Luke 13:28.

25:31 *Son of Man:* See the mini-article called "Son of Man," on p. 1866. See also 16:27; 19:28.

25:32 *shepherd separates the sheep from the goats:* A shepherd's flock sometimes had both sheep and goats. Sheep need lots of attention and care. Goats are more daring and independent. They like to climb the steep and rocky slopes to feed. The wool of sheep and the hair of goats were useful for making blankets and clothing. In addition, female goats provided milk. At the end of each day, the shepherds would count their flocks while separating the sheep and goats.

25:14-30 Luke 19:11-27. **25:29** Matt 13:12; Mark 4:25; Luke 8:18.

The Parable of the Talents

14"Again, it will be like a man going on a journey, who called
his servants and entrusted his property to them. 15To one he gave
five talents[a] of money, to another two talents, and to another one
talent, each according to his ability. Then he went on his journey.
16The man who had received the five talents went at once and put
his money to work and gained five more. 17So also, the one with
the two talents gained two more. 18But the man who had received
the one talent went off, dug a hole in the ground and hid his master's money.

19"After a long time the master of those servants returned
and settled accounts with them. 20The man who had received the
five talents brought the other five. 'Master,' he said, 'you entrusted
me with five talents. See, I have gained five more.'

21"His master replied, 'Well done, good and faithful servant!
You have been faithful with a few things; I will put you in charge
of many things. Come and share your master's happiness!'

22"The man with the two talents also came. 'Master,' he said,
'you entrusted me with two talents; see, I have gained two more.'

23"His master replied, 'Well done, good and faithful servant!
You have been faithful with a few things; I will put you in charge
of many things. Come and share your master's happiness!'

24"Then the man who had received the one talent came.
'Master,' he said, 'I knew that you are a hard man, harvesting where
you have not sown and gathering where you have not scattered
seed. 25So I was afraid and went out and hid your talent in the
ground. See, here is what belongs to you.'

26"His master replied, 'You wicked, lazy servant! So you knew
that I harvest where I have not sown and gather where I have not
scattered seed? 27Well then, you should have put my money on
deposit with the bankers, so that when I returned I would have
received it back with interest.

28" 'Take the talent from him and give it to the one who has
the ten talents. 29For everyone who has will be given more, and he
will have an abundance. Whoever does not have, even what he has
will be taken from him. 30And throw that worthless servant outside, into the darkness, where there will be weeping and gnashing
of teeth.'

The Sheep and the Goats

31"When the Son of Man comes in his glory, and all the
angels with him, he will sit on his throne in heavenly glory. 32All
the nations will be gathered before him, and he will separate the
people one from another as a shepherd separates the sheep from

[a]15 A talent was worth more than a thousand dollars.

the goats. 33He will put the sheep on his right and the goats on
his left.
34"Then the King will say to those on his right, 'Come, you
who are blessed by my Father; take your inheritance, the kingdom
prepared for you since the creation of the world. 35For I was hungry and you gave me something to eat, I was thirsty and you gave
me something to drink, I was a stranger and you invited me in, 36I
needed clothes and you clothed me, I was sick and you looked
after me, I was in prison and you came to visit me.'
37"Then the righteous will answer him, 'Lord, when did we
see you hungry and feed you, or thirsty and give you something to
drink? 38When did we see you a stranger and invite you in, or
needing clothes and clothe you? 39When did we see you sick or in
prison and go to visit you?'
40"The King will reply, 'I tell you the truth, whatever you did
for one of the least of these brothers of mine, you did for me.'
41"Then he will say to those on his left, 'Depart from me, you
who are cursed, into the eternal fire prepared for the devil and his
angels. 42For I was hungry and you gave me nothing to eat, I was
thirsty and you gave me nothing to drink, 43I was a stranger and
you did not invite me in, I needed clothes and you did not clothe
me, I was sick and in prison and you did not look after me.'
44"They also will answer, 'Lord, when did we see you hungry
or thirsty or a stranger or needing clothes or sick or in prison, and
did not help you?'
45"He will reply, 'I tell you the truth, whatever you did not
do for one of the least of these, you did not do for me.'
46"Then they will go away to eternal punishment, but the
righteous to eternal life."

Jesus said,
"I tell you the truth, whatever you did for one of the least of these brothers of mine, you did for me."
Matt 25:40

25:41 *eternal fire prepared for the devil and his angels:* See the notes at 5:22 and 9:34.

25:46 *eternal life:* See the note at 19:16. See also Dan 12:2.

QUESTIONS ABOUT MATTHEW 19:1—25:46

1. What is your reaction to Jesus' words about marriage and divorce? (19:1-12) About children? (19:13-15) About following him? (19:16-30)
2. Read the story of how Jesus enters Jerusalem riding on a donkey (21:1-11). What does it mean for the crowd to praise Jesus as the Son of David? Do you think Jesus was the kind of king they were expecting? Why or why not?
3. How did Jesus respond to those who were seeking to trap him with their questions about taxes and marriage? (22:15-33)
4. Read what Jesus had to say about the Law of Moses (22:34-40). Explain what you think Jesus means in 22:40.
5. Jesus and the Pharisees did not see eye to eye. What do you think was the reason for this? Have you ever had to disagree with someone over something you believed in? If so, how did you handle it?
6. Jesus told his disciples to "keep watch" (25:13). How does one "keep watch" for Jesus' return?
7. How does Jesus describe the final judgment? (25:31-46) What does this say to you about living your life today? According to Jesus, in what ways can people show God's love to others? In what ways do you show love to others?

Jesus Dies and Is Raised to Life To Fulfill God's Plan

Just as Jesus had predicted (see 16:21), those who are against his teachings make a plot to get rid of him. Jesus is betrayed by one of his own disciples and has to stand trial, first in front of the high priest and the Jewish leaders in Jerusalem, and then before the Roman governor, Pilate, who sentences Jesus to death on a cross as one who claimed to be King of the Jews. Jesus dies, but after three days God brings him back to life in order to fulfill God's plan to destroy the power of sin and death. This leads to Jesus' final meeting with his disciples in Galilee.

The Plot Against Jesus

26 When Jesus had finished saying all these things, he said to his
disciples, 2"As you know, the Passover is two days away—and the
Son of Man will be handed over to be crucified."
3Then the chief priests and the elders of the people assembled in the palace of the high priest, whose name was Caiaphas,
4and they plotted to arrest Jesus in some sly way and kill him.
5"But not during the Feast," they said, "or there may be a riot
among the people."

Jesus Anointed at Bethany

6While Jesus was in Bethany in the home of a man known as
Simon the Leper, 7a woman came to him with an alabaster jar of
very expensive perfume, which she poured on his head as he was
reclining at the table.
8When the disciples saw this, they were indignant. "Why this
waste?" they asked. 9"This perfume could have been sold at a high
price and the money given to the poor."
10Aware of this, Jesus said to them, "Why are you bothering
this woman? She has done a beautiful thing to me. 11The poor you
will always have with you, but you will not always have me.
12When she poured this perfume on my body, she did it to prepare
me for burial. 13I tell you the truth, wherever this gospel is
preached throughout the world, what she has done will also be
told, in memory of her."

Judas Agrees to Betray Jesus

14Then one of the Twelve—the one called Judas Iscariot—
went to the chief priests 15and asked, "What are you willing to give
me if I hand him over to you?" So they counted out for him thirty silver coins. 16From then on Judas watched for an opportunity
to hand him over.

26:2 *Passover:* Passover celebrates how God helped the people of Israel escape from slavery in Egypt (Exod 12:1-27). It was to be celebrated on the fourteenth day of the first month, starting at twilight. The Feast of Unleavened Bread began the next day and lasted for seven days (Lev 23:4-8; Num 28:16-25). See also the mini-article called "Passover and the Feast of Unleavened Bread," p. 2030.

26:3 *chief priests and the elders of the people . . . high priest . . . Caiaphas:* The Romans appointed Caiaphas to be the high priest in Jerusalem, and he served from A.D. 18-36. Besides overseeing the work of the priests who served at the temple, the high priest also was in charge of the powerful council called the Sanhedrin, made up of the chief priests and other Jewish leaders. The Romans gave the Sanhedrin the authority to make most decisions about local matters. For more on the role of the priests, see the article called "People of the Law: The Religion of Israel," p. 939.

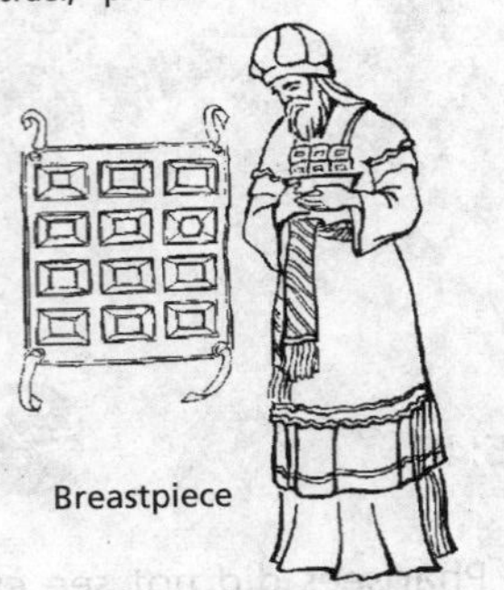
Breastpiece

26:5 *not during the Feast:* Many people who liked Jesus and his teachings would have been in the city to celebrate Passover. The leaders didn't want so many people to see Jesus arrested. They were afraid that the followers of Jesus might riot against them.

26:6 *Bethany:* See the note at 21:17.

26:7 Luke 7:37, 38. **26:11** Deut 15:11. **26:15** Zech 11:12.

The Lord's Supper

17 On the first day of the Feast of Unleavened Bread, the disciples came to Jesus and asked, "Where do you want us to make
preparations for you to eat the Passover?"
18 He replied, "Go into the city to a certain man and tell him,
'The Teacher says: My appointed time is near. I am going to celebrate the Passover with my disciples at your house.'" 19 So the disciples did as Jesus had directed them and prepared the Passover.
20 When evening came, Jesus was reclining at the table with
the Twelve. 21 And while they were eating, he said, "I tell you the
truth, one of you will betray me."
22 They were very sad and began to say to him one after the
other, "Surely not I, Lord?"
23 Jesus replied, "The one who has dipped his hand into the
bowl with me will betray me. 24 The Son of Man will go just as it is
written about him. But woe to that man who betrays the Son of
Man! It would be better for him if he had not been born."
25 Then Judas, the one who would betray him, said, "Surely
not I, Rabbi?"
Jesus answered, "Yes, it is you."[a]
26 While they were eating, Jesus took bread, gave thanks and
broke it, and gave it to his disciples, saying, "Take and eat; this is
my body."
27 Then he took the cup, gave thanks and offered it to them,
saying, "Drink from it, all of you. 28 This is my blood of the[b]
covenant, which is poured out for many for the forgiveness of sins.
29 I tell you, I will not drink of this fruit of the vine from now on until
that day when I drink it anew with you in my Father's kingdom."
30 When they had sung a hymn, they went out to the Mount
of Olives.

Jesus Predicts Peter's Denial

31 Then Jesus told them, "This very night you will all fall away
on account of me, for it is written:

"'I will strike the shepherd,
and the sheep of the flock will be scattered.'[c]

32 But after I have risen, I will go ahead of you into Galilee."
33 Peter replied, "Even if all fall away on account of you, I
never will."
34 "I tell you the truth," Jesus answered, "this very night,
before the rooster crows, you will disown me three times."
35 But Peter declared, "Even if I have to die with you, I will
never disown you." And all the other disciples said the same.

[a] **25** Or *"You yourself have said it"* [b] **28** Some manuscripts *the new*
[c] **31** Zech. 13:7

Jesus took the cup, gave thanks and offered it to them, saying, "Drink from it, all of you. This is my blood of the covenant, which is poured out for many for the forgiveness of sins."
Matt 26:27,28

26:6 *the Leper:* See the note at 10:8. Evidently Simon had been healed of his leprosy, or he would not have been part of the community.

26:12 *poured this perfume . . . prepare me for burial:* Giving someone a proper burial was very important. Pouring oil or perfume on someone was called anointing (see the note at 1:17). Sometimes people anointed the dead with oil and put spices on the body to help preserve it. Jesus said the woman was preparing his body for burial, but what she did is also a reminder that Jesus is God's Anointed One.

26:14 *Judas Iscariot:* See the note at 10:4.

26:17 *Feast of Unleavened Bread . . . eat the Passover:* See the note at 26:2.

26:26-28 *this is my body . . . my blood:* A young lamb was sacrificed and eaten at Passover. Jesus used the bread and wine to show how his life would be sacrificed to forgive sins. This sacrifice was the basis for the new covenant between God and God's new people. Christians celebrate this event in the Lord's Supper.

26:30 *Mount of Olives:* See the note at 24:3.

26:23 Ps 41:9. **26:28** Exod 24:8; Jer 31:31-34. **26:32** Matt 28:16.

Gethsemane

36 Then Jesus went with his disciples to a place called Gethsemane, and he said to them, "Sit here while I go over there and
pray." 37 He took Peter and the two sons of Zebedee along with
him, and he began to be sorrowful and troubled. 38 Then he said to
them, "My soul is overwhelmed with sorrow to the point of death.
Stay here and keep watch with me."
39 Going a little farther, he fell with his face to the ground and
prayed, "My Father, if it is possible, may this cup be taken from
me. Yet not as I will, but as you will."
40 Then he returned to his disciples and found them sleeping.
"Could you men not keep watch with me for one hour?" he asked
Peter. 41 "Watch and pray so that you will not fall into temptation.
The spirit is willing, but the body is weak."
42 He went away a second time and prayed, "My Father, if it is
not possible for this cup to be taken away unless I drink it, may
your will be done."
43 When he came back, he again found them sleeping,
because their eyes were heavy. 44 So he left them and went away
once more and prayed the third time, saying the same thing.
45 Then he returned to the disciples and said to them, "Are
you still sleeping and resting? Look, the hour is near, and the Son
of Man is betrayed into the hands of sinners. 46 Rise, let us go! Here
comes my betrayer!"

Jesus Arrested

47 While he was still speaking, Judas, one of the Twelve,
arrived. With him was a large crowd armed with swords and clubs,
sent from the chief priests and the elders of the people. 48 Now the
betrayer had arranged a signal with them: "The one I kiss is the
man; arrest him." 49 Going at once to Jesus, Judas said, "Greetings,
Rabbi!" and kissed him.
50 Jesus replied, "Friend, do what you came for."[a]
Then the men stepped forward, seized Jesus and arrested
him. 51 With that, one of Jesus' companions reached for his sword,
drew it out and struck the servant of the high priest, cutting off
his ear.
52 "Put your sword back in its place," Jesus said to him, "for
all who draw the sword will die by the sword. 53 Do you think I
cannot call on my Father, and he will at once put at my disposal
more than twelve legions of angels? 54 But how then would the
Scriptures be fulfilled that say it must happen in this way?"
55 At that time Jesus said to the crowd, "Am I leading a rebellion, that you have come out with swords and clubs to capture me?
Every day I sat in the temple courts teaching, and you did not

[a]**50** Or *"Friend, why have you come?"*

Jesus fell with his face to the ground and prayed, "My Father, if it is possible, may this cup be taken from me. Yet not as I will, but as you will."
Matt 26:39

26:36 *Gethsemane:* Gethsemane means "a press for squeezing oil out of olives." The exact location of this place is not known, but it was probably on the east side of the Kidron Valley in the area near the Mount of Olives. See the map on p. 2474 for the most likely location.

26:39 *may this cup be taken from me:* See the note at 20:22.

26:48 *The one I kiss is the man:* It was the custom for friends to greet each other with a kiss on the cheek.

26:55 Luke 19:47; 21:37.

arrest me. 56But this has all taken place that the writings of the
prophets might be fulfilled." Then all the disciples deserted him
and fled.

Before the Sanhedrin

57Those who had arrested Jesus took him to Caiaphas, the
high priest, where the teachers of the law and the elders had
assembled. 58But Peter followed him at a distance, right up to the
courtyard of the high priest. He entered and sat down with the
guards to see the outcome.
59The chief priests and the whole Sanhedrin were looking for
false evidence against Jesus so that they could put him to death.
60But they did not find any, though many false witnesses came forward.
Finally two came forward 61and declared, "This fellow said,
'I am able to destroy the temple of God and rebuild it in three
days.' "
62Then the high priest stood up and said to Jesus, "Are you
not going to answer? What is this testimony that these men are
bringing against you?" 63But Jesus remained silent.
The high priest said to him, "I charge you under oath by the
living God: Tell us if you are the Christ,[a] the Son of God."
64"Yes, it is as you say," Jesus replied. "But I say to all of you:
In the future you will see the Son of Man sitting at the right hand
of the Mighty One and coming on the clouds of heaven."
65Then the high priest tore his clothes and said, "He has
spoken blasphemy! Why do we need any more witnesses? Look,
now you have heard the blasphemy. 66What do you think?"
"He is worthy of death," they answered.
67Then they spit in his face and struck him with their
fists. Others slapped him 68and said, "Prophesy to us, Christ. Who
hit you?"

Peter Disowns Jesus

69Now Peter was sitting out in the courtyard, and a servant
girl came to him. "You also were with Jesus of Galilee," she said.
70But he denied it before them all. "I don't know what you're
talking about," he said.
71Then he went out to the gateway, where another girl saw
him and said to the people there, "This fellow was with Jesus of
Nazareth."
72He denied it again, with an oath: "I don't know the man!"
73After a little while, those standing there went up to Peter
and said, "Surely you are one of them, for your accent gives you
away."

[a]**63** Or *Messiah*; also in verse 68

26:57,58 *took him to Caiaphas, the high priest . . . courtyard:* See the note at 26:3. The action in these verses is taking place at the same location, not two different ones.

26:59,60 *Sanhedrin . . . false witnesses . . . two:* In addition to the chief priests, the Sanhedrin was made up of Jewish religious and political leaders. They had the authority to decide cases of local matters and to see that people obeyed laws. The Law of Moses taught that two witnesses were needed before a person could be put to death (see Num 35:30). The Sanhedrin followed the Law of Moses regarding the need for two witnesses, while disobeying it by using those known to be false witnesses (Exod 20:16).

26:63 *the Christ, the Son of God:* See the note at 1:17 and the mini-article called "Son of God," on p. 2044.

26:64 *at the right hand:* See the note at 20:21.

26:65 *high priest tore his clothes:* The Law of Moses said that the high priest was not allowed to tear his clothes to show his sorrow (see Lev 10:6; 21:10). But this was an extreme situation. The high priest thought Jesus was claiming to be God, a very terrible sin. A person who claimed to be God was guilty of blasphemy (shaming God's name) and could be sentenced to death (Lev 24:16).

26:61 John 2:19. **26:64** Dan 7:13; Ps 110:1. **26:67** Isa 50:6.

27:1 *chief priests and the elders of the people:* See the note at 26:3.

27:2 *handed him over to Pilate, the governor:* Pontius Pilate was the Roman governor in charge of Judea from A.D. 26 to 36. His official residence was in Caesarea on the Mediterranean coast. When he was in Jerusalem, he lived at the Fortress Antonia (called the Praetorium), which overlooked the temple area from the northwest. See the map on p. 2474. The Sanhedrin agreed that Jesus should be put to death, but only the Romans could legally pronounce the death sentence. See also the mini-article called "Pontius Pilate," p. 2091.

27:6 *against the law to put this into the treasury ... blood money:* The money given to Judas as payment for betraying Jesus may have been considered unclean.

27:10 *potter's field:* Perhaps a field owned by someone who made clay pots. But it may have been a field where potters came to get clay to make pots or to throw away their broken pieces of pottery.

27:3-8 Acts 1:18,19. **27:9,10** Zech 11:12, 13; Jer 18:2,3; 32:6-15.

[74]Then he began to call down curses on himself and he swore to them, "I don't know the man!"

Immediately a rooster crowed. [75]Then Peter remembered the word Jesus had spoken: "Before the rooster crows, you will disown me three times." And he went outside and wept bitterly.

Judas Hangs Himself

27 Early in the morning, all the chief priests and the elders of the people came to the decision to put Jesus to death. [2]They bound him, led him away and handed him over to Pilate, the governor.

[3]When Judas, who had betrayed him, saw that Jesus was condemned, he was seized with remorse and returned the thirty silver coins to the chief priests and the elders. [4]"I have sinned," he said, "for I have betrayed innocent blood."

"What is that to us?" they replied. "That's your responsibility."

[5]So Judas threw the money into the temple and left. Then he went away and hanged himself.

[6]The chief priests picked up the coins and said, "It is against the law to put this into the treasury, since it is blood money." [7]So they decided to use the money to buy the potter's field as a burial place for foreigners. [8]That is why it has been called the Field of Blood to this day. [9]Then what was spoken by Jeremiah the prophet was fulfilled: "They took the thirty silver coins, the price set on him by the people of Israel, [10]and they used them to buy the potter's field, as the Lord commanded me."[a]

Jesus Before Pilate

[11]Meanwhile Jesus stood before the governor, and the governor asked him, "Are you the king of the Jews?"

"Yes, it is as you say," Jesus replied.

[12]When he was accused by the chief priests and the elders, he gave no answer. [13]Then Pilate asked him, "Don't you hear the testimony they are bringing against you?" [14]But Jesus made no reply, not even to a single charge—to the great amazement of the governor.

[15]Now it was the governor's custom at the Feast to release a prisoner chosen by the crowd. [16]At that time they had a notorious prisoner, called Barabbas. [17]So when the crowd had gathered, Pilate asked them, "Which one do you want me to release to you: Barabbas, or Jesus who is called Christ?" [18]For he knew it was out of envy that they had handed Jesus over to him.

[19]While Pilate was sitting on the judge's seat, his wife sent him this message: "Don't have anything to do with that innocent man, for I have suffered a great deal today in a dream because of him."

[a]**10** See Zech. 11:12,13; Jer. 19:1-13; 32:6-9.

Pilate Washes His Hands, artist unknown (African, twentieth century). Jesus is sentenced to death at the request of the crowd. Pilate, the governor of Judea, washes his hands in front of the people to show them that the decision to kill Jesus was theirs and not his (see 27:24).

20 But the chief priests and the elders persuaded the crowd to
ask for Barabbas and to have Jesus executed.
21 "Which of the two do you want me to release to you?"
asked the governor.
"Barabbas," they answered.
22 "What shall I do, then, with Jesus who is called Christ?"
Pilate asked.
They all answered, "Crucify him!"
23 "Why? What crime has he committed?" asked Pilate.
But they shouted all the louder, "Crucify him!"
24 When Pilate saw that he was getting nowhere, but that
instead an uproar was starting, he took water and washed his
hands in front of the crowd. "I am innocent of this man's blood,"
he said. "It is your responsibility!"
25 All the people answered, "Let his blood be on us and on
our children!"
26 Then he released Barabbas to them. But he had Jesus
flogged, and handed him over to be crucified.

The Soldiers Mock Jesus

27 Then the governor's soldiers took Jesus into the Praetorium and gathered the whole company of soldiers around him.
28 They stripped him and put a scarlet robe on him, 29 and then
twisted together a crown of thorns and set it on his head. They put
a staff in his right hand and knelt in front of him and mocked
him. "Hail, king of the Jews!" they said. 30 They spit on him, and
took the staff and struck him on the head again and again. 31 After
they had mocked him, they took off the robe and put his own
clothes on him. Then they led him away to crucify him.

27:24 *Pilate . . . washed his hands:* He did this to claim that he felt he was innocent of sentencing Jesus to death. He wanted to show that it was the leaders' decision to put Jesus to death on a cross, not his, though the execution would not have happened without his final approval. See also Deut 21:6-9.

27:27 *Praetorium:* Where the Roman governor stayed when in Jerusalem. His normal residence was in Caesarea. Roman soldiers were also stationed here. See the map on p. 2474.

27:28 *scarlet robe:* This was probably a Roman soldier's cloak or cape.

A condemned man carries the crosspiece to the place of execution.

Some criminals were nailed to crosses and some were tied with ropes.

A condemned man's crime was written on a sign and nailed to the cross.

CRUCIFIXION

Crucifixion was a common way to punish criminals and to publicly humiliate them in the ancient world. In Jesus' day, the Romans used crucifixion to put criminals to death. A person was tied with cords or nailed to a wooden cross that was shaped like a T or like a plus sign (+). Usually the worst criminals, slaves who had done wrong, and those who had led revolts were crucified.

After a criminal was sentenced to die on the cross, he had to carry his cross to the crucifixion site. Sometimes he carried only the crosspiece. Before being put on the cross, he would be stripped and beaten. Then he would be fastened on the cross with his arms stretched out. This painful position made it difficult for the condemned man to breathe, and eventually he would die from suffocation. He might use his legs to push up for breath, so the legs would eventually be broken to speed up death (John 19:31).

In God's Law, execution was usually by stoning (Lev 24:23; Num 15:36). Sometimes the Romans (who ruled Palestine at this time), allowed for executions (such as Stephen, Acts 7:59), but normally they retained the right to give the death penalty. That was why the Jewish leaders went to Pilate when they wanted Jesus to die (Matt 27:22). Crucifixion of Jesus would remove the blame from themselves, as well as provide a method of execution that, according to their law, would carry a curse (Deut 21:22, 23). So Jesus was accused of starting a revolt against the Romans by allowing himself to be called "King of the Jews." A sign with this title was placed on his cross (Matt 27:37).

God overcame the death of Jesus by bringing him back to life after he died on the cross. That's why the cross became the major symbol for God's power to forgive sins and give new life to people (1 Cor 1:18-24).

The Crucifixion

32 As they were going out, they met a man from Cyrene, named
Simon, and they forced him to carry the cross. 33 They came to a place
called Golgotha (which means The Place of the Skull). 34 There they
offered Jesus wine to drink, mixed with gall; but after tasting it, he
refused to drink it. 35 When they had crucified him, they divided up
his clothes by casting lots.[a] 36 And sitting down, they kept watch over
him there. 37 Above his head they placed the written charge against
him: THIS IS JESUS, THE KING OF THE JEWS. 38 Two robbers were crucified
with him, one on his right and one on his left. 39 Those who passed by
hurled insults at him, shaking their heads 40 and saying, "You who are
going to destroy the temple and build it in three days, save yourself!
Come down from the cross, if you are the Son of God!"
41 In the same way the chief priests, the teachers of the law
and the elders mocked him. 42 "He saved others," they said, "but he
can't save himself! He's the King of Israel! Let him come down now
from the cross, and we will believe in him. 43 He trusts in God. Let
God rescue him now if he wants him, for he said, 'I am the Son of
God.'" 44 In the same way the robbers who were crucified with him
also heaped insults on him.

The Death of Jesus

45 From the sixth hour until the ninth hour darkness came
over all the land. 46 About the ninth hour Jesus cried out in a loud
voice, *"Eloi, Eloi,*[b] *lama sabachthani?"*—which means, "My God,
my God, why have you forsaken me?"[c]
47 When some of those standing there heard this, they said,
"He's calling Elijah."
48 Immediately one of them ran and got a sponge. He filled it
with wine vinegar, put it on a stick, and offered it to Jesus to drink.
49 The rest said, "Now leave him alone. Let's see if Elijah comes to
save him."
50 And when Jesus had cried out again in a loud voice, he
gave up his spirit.
51 At that moment the curtain of the temple was torn in two
from top to bottom. The earth shook and the rocks split. 52 The
tombs broke open and the bodies of many holy people who had
died were raised to life. 53 They came out of the tombs, and after
Jesus' resurrection they went into the holy city and appeared to
many people.
54 When the centurion and those with him who were guarding Jesus saw the earthquake and all that had happened, they were
terrified, and exclaimed, "Surely he was the Son[d] of God!"

---

[a]**35** A few late manuscripts *lots that the word spoken by the prophet might be fulfilled: "They divided my garments among themselves and cast lots for my clothing"* (Psalm 22:18) [b]**46** Some manuscripts *Eli, Eli* [c]**46** Psalm 22:1 [d]**54** Or *a son*

27:32 *a man from Cyrene, named Simon:* Cyrene was a city in North Africa. Simon was probably a Jew who came to Jerusalem to celebrate the Passover.

27:33 *Golgotha . . . The Place of the Skull:* The place was probably given this name because it was near a large rock shaped like a human skull. The Latin translation of Golgotha is *calvaria*, which entered the English language as Calvary.

27:34 *wine . . . mixed with gall:* Gall was a drug that helped ease pain. It likely made the dying person unconscious and may even have hastened death. Offering Jesus this mixture may have been an act of compassion. Jesus most likely refused to drink it because he wanted to remain conscious to the very moment of death.

27:46 *Eloi . . . sabachthani:* This statement comes from Psalm 22:1 and others but is quoted here in Aramaic, the language spoken by Jews in the Middle East at this time.

27:47-49 *see if Elijah comes:* The name "Elijah" sounds like "Eloi," which means "my God." The Jewish people expected the prophet Elijah to come and prepare the way for the Christ, or Messiah (see Mal 4:5, 6), so many thought Jesus was calling for Elijah. See the note at 11:14.

27:51 *curtain of the temple:* There were two curtains in the temple. One was at the entrance to the Holy Place, where only the priests could go. The other curtain separated the Holy Place from the Most Holy Place, which only the high priest could go past, and then only once a year. The second curtain is probably the one that is meant here.

27:34,35 Ps 69:21. **27:39** Ps 22:7; 109:25. **27:40** Matt 26:61; John 2:19. **27:43** Ps 22:8. **27:48** Ps 69:21.

55 Many women were there, watching from a distance. They
had followed Jesus from Galilee to care for his needs. 56 Among
them were Mary Magdalene, Mary the mother of James and Joses,
and the mother of Zebedee's sons.

The Burial of Jesus

57 As evening approached, there came a rich man from Arimathea, named Joseph, who had himself become a disciple of
Jesus. 58 Going to Pilate, he asked for Jesus' body, and Pilate ordered
that it be given to him. 59 Joseph took the body, wrapped it in a
clean linen cloth, 60 and placed it in his own new tomb that he had
cut out of the rock. He rolled a big stone in front of the entrance
to the tomb and went away. 61 Mary Magdalene and the other Mary
were sitting there opposite the tomb.

The Guard at the Tomb

62 The next day, the one after Preparation Day, the chief
priests and the Pharisees went to Pilate. 63 "Sir," they said, "we
remember that while he was still alive that deceiver said, 'After
three days I will rise again.' 64 So give the order for the tomb to be
made secure until the third day. Otherwise, his disciples may come
and steal the body and tell the people that he has been raised from
the dead. This last deception will be worse than the first."
65 "Take a guard," Pilate answered. "Go, make the tomb as
secure as you know how." 66 So they went and made the tomb
secure by putting a seal on the stone and posting the guard.

The Resurrection

28 After the Sabbath, at dawn on the first day of the week, Mary
Magdalene and the other Mary went to look at the tomb.
2 There was a violent earthquake, for an angel of the Lord
came down from heaven and, going to the tomb, rolled back the
stone and sat on it. 3 His appearance was like lightning, and his
clothes were white as snow. 4 The guards were so afraid of him that
they shook and became like dead men.
5 The angel said to the women, "Do not be afraid, for I know
that you are looking for Jesus, who was crucified. 6 He is not here;
he has risen, just as he said. Come and see the place where he lay.
7 Then go quickly and tell his disciples: 'He has risen from the dead
and is going ahead of you into Galilee. There you will see him.'
Now I have told you."
8 So the women hurried away from the tomb, afraid yet filled
with joy, and ran to tell his disciples. 9 Suddenly Jesus met them.
"Greetings," he said. They came to him, clasped his feet and worshiped him. 10 Then Jesus said to them, "Do not be afraid. Go and
tell my brothers to go to Galilee; there they will see me."

27:56 *Mary Magdalene:* Her name probably means that she was from Magdala, a town on the western shore of the Sea of Galilee. Other Gospels tell how Jesus healed her (see Mark 16:9; Luke 8:2, 3). As a follower of Jesus she may have traveled with a group of Jesus' closest friends.

27:57 *a rich man from Arimathea, named Joseph:* Arimathea was a small village in the hilly area called Ephraim, about 20 miles northwest of Jerusalem. We know from Luke 23:50,51 that Joseph was a member of the Sanhedrin who had not agreed with that council's decision to put Jesus to death (see the note at 26:3). Because Joseph was rich, he probably had money to pay Pilate and the guards so he could take the body.

27:60 *tomb . . . cut out of the rock:* Some of the Jewish people of this time buried their dead in rooms carved out of solid rock. These tombs had a small square entrance about a yard high and a yard wide. A groove was cut on the outside of the tomb, and a large round stone that looked like a millstone was used to cover the entrance.

27:64 *This last deception will be worse than the first:* The first deception, according to the religious authorities was probably the belief that Jesus is the Christ or Messiah.

28:1 *After the Sabbath:* The Jewish Sabbath lasted from sundown on Friday until sundown on Saturday. When daylight arrived the next morning, which was Sunday, the women could walk to the tomb and put spices on Jesus' body.

28:7 *Galilee:* This is the home area of Jesus in northern Palestine. See the note at 2:22,23 and the map on p. 2473.

27:63 Matt 16:21; 17:23; 20:19; Mark 8:31; 9:31; 10:33,34; Luke 9:22; 18:31-33.

The Guards' Report

[11]While the women were on their way, some of the guards
went into the city and reported to the chief priests everything that
had happened. [12]When the chief priests had met with the elders
and devised a plan, they gave the soldiers a large sum of money,
[13]telling them, "You are to say, 'His disciples came during the night
and stole him away while we were asleep.' [14]If this report gets
to the governor, we will satisfy him and keep you out of trouble."
[15]So the soldiers took the money and did as they were instructed.
And this story has been widely circulated among the Jews to this
very day.

Jesus said,
"Go and make disciples of all nations, baptizing them in the name of the Father and of the Son and of the Holy Spirit."
Matt 28:19

28:14 *governor:* See the note at 27:2.

28:19 *baptizing them:* People who were baptized were usually dunked in a pool or stream of water. Jesus says that this was to be done in the name of God—the Father, Son, and Holy Spirit. Baptism was done to show that a person was now part of God's new people. Other New Testament writers describe baptism as dying to the old self and being born to a new life in Christ (see Rom 6:3, 4). See also the mini-article called "Baptism," p. 1976.

The Great Commission

[16]Then the eleven disciples went to Galilee, to the mountain
where Jesus had told them to go. [17]When they saw him, they worshiped him; but some doubted. [18]Then Jesus came to them and
said, "All authority in heaven and on earth has been given to me.
[19]Therefore go and make disciples of all nations, baptizing them
in[a] the name of the Father and of the Son and of the Holy Spirit,
[20]and teaching them to obey everything I have commanded you.
And surely I am with you always, to the very end of the age."

28:16 Matt 26:32; Mark 14:28.
28:19 Acts 1:8.

[a]**19** Or *into*; see Acts 8:16; 19:5; Romans 6:3; 1 Cor. 1:13; 10:2 and Gal. 3:27.

QUESTIONS ABOUT MATTHEW 26:1—28:20

1. These last chapters tell of Jesus' arrest, trial, and execution by the Roman authorities. How did Jesus react to the violent ways people treated him? What does that say about how we are to relate to others?
2. Jesus was betrayed by Judas, and after Jesus was arrested "all the disciples deserted him and fled" (26:56). Have you ever felt betrayed by someone or abandoned by your friends at a time when you needed them most? Have you ever stayed away from someone who may have needed you?
3. It may seem easy to judge the disciples for leaving Jesus during his time of need because it happened so many years ago. Think about your own relationship with Jesus. What are the ways you may sometimes betray, deny, or abandon Jesus today?
4. Re-read the mini-article called "Crucifixion," p. 1914. What does the fact that Jesus willingly let himself be executed in this manner say about his love for his disciples? How can you best show your gratitude for the sacrifice Jesus made on your behalf?
5. After God raised Jesus to life, what did Jesus tell his disciples to do? (28:18-20) What does this message mean for Jesus' followers today?

MARK

Sometimes good news needs to be kept secret until the time is right. The big secret in MARK is the answer to the question, "Who is Jesus?"

WHAT MAKES MARK SPECIAL?

MARK is the shortest and probably the oldest of the four Gospels included in the New Testament. Its language is simple, but the story it tells is powerful. MATTHEW and LUKE include most of what is in MARK, but arrange the material differently and add more to it. MARK is full of action and tells about many of Jesus' miracles and healings. But according to MARK, the most powerful miracles of Jesus are his suffering and death. The first person in the Gospel who appears to understand this miracle is the Roman centurion who saw Jesus die on the cross and says, "Surely this man was the Son of God!" (15:39).

MARK provides answers to some important questions about Jesus, like:

- How does Jesus fulfill the prophecies made in the Jewish Scriptures (Old Testament)?
- How is Jesus the Son of God, and how will he be seen in the future as the Son of Man?
- How and why did Jesus die, and how will he return?
- How are the new people of God to live?

WHY WAS MARK WRITTEN?

The very first verse says that the subject of MARK is "the gospel about Jesus Christ, the Son of God." In the rest of the book, Jesus shows by his words and by his actions that he truly is the Son of God.

WHAT'S THE STORY BEHIND THE SCENE?

The explanations of Aramaic words and Jewish customs in this book suggest that Mark wrote the Gospel so that Gentiles or non-Jewish Christians could understand it. Since Peter is especially important in this Gospel, and since Mark is connected with Peter in 1 Peter 5:13, it was believed by the second century A.D. that it was Mark, also known as John Mark (Acts 12:12, 25; 2 Tim 4:11) who wrote the Gospel.

HOW IS MARK CONSTRUCTED?

At various places in the Gospel, Jesus reminds different people and even the demons not to tell anyone about who he is or what he has done (1:41-44; 3:10-12; 7:34-36; 8:30). Finally, in 15:39, a Roman centurion identifies Jesus as the Son of God, which is how Mark describes Jesus in the very first verse of the Gospel. This makes reading the Gospel a little like reading a mystery. Clues are given throughout the story to help people discover Jesus' true identity.

1:1 *the gospel about Jesus Christ, the Son of God:* The Greek word for "gospel" can also be translated as "good news." MARK tells about who Jesus is. The king God chose to rule over the people of Israel was described as God's Son (Ps 2:6-8). By calling Jesus the Son of God, MARK is claiming that Jesus is the one God has chosen to rule over Israel, as well as the entire world. See also the mini-article called "Son of God," p. 2044.

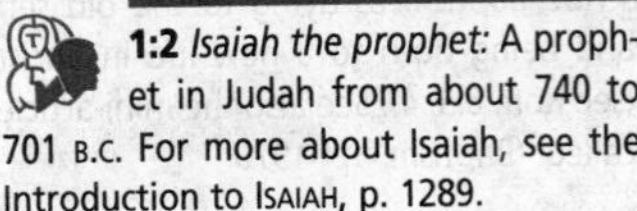

1:2 *Isaiah the prophet:* A prophet in Judah from about 740 to 701 B.C. For more about Isaiah, see the Introduction to ISAIAH, p. 1289.

1:4 *John:* This was John the Baptist. The name John means "The LORD is gracious." Some people believed that he was the prophet Elijah who had come back to life. See also the mini-articles called "John the Baptist," p. 1853 and "Elijah," p. 1816.

When you read chapter 16 you will notice that the ending of Mark is somewhat of a mystery. The NIV translators included verses 9-20 with a notation that the earliest known Greek manuscripts do not include those verses. Mark's original Gospel likely ended at 16:8 or else its original ending has been lost.

Mark can be outlined in the following way:

Jesus prepares for his work (1:1-20)

Jesus does the work of God's kingdom in Galilee (1:21—9:50)
- Healings, miracles, and parables (1:21—8:26)
- Jesus is the Messiah (8:27—9:13)
- More work in Galilee (9:14-50)

Jesus ministers in Judea (10:1-52)

Jesus in Jerusalem (11:1—15:47)
- Teachings in the temple (11:1—12:44)
- God's coming kingdom (13:1-37)
- Jesus prepares for his death (14:1-42)
- The final hours (14:43—15:47)

Jesus lives (16:1-20)

Jesus Prepares for His Work

Jesus is already an adult, and he is ready to begin the work God has sent him to do. To prepare for this work, Jesus is baptized by John, faces Satan in the desert, and chooses the first four of his closest disciples.

John the Baptist Prepares the Way

1 The beginning of the gospel about Jesus Christ, the Son of God.[a]

2 It is written in Isaiah the prophet:

"I will send my messenger ahead of you,
who will prepare your way"[b]—
3 "a voice of one calling in the desert,
'Prepare the way for the Lord,
make straight paths for him.'"[c]

4 And so John came, baptizing in the desert region and preaching a
baptism of repentance for the forgiveness of sins. 5 The whole
Judean countryside and all the people of Jerusalem went out to
him. Confessing their sins, they were baptized by him in the Jordan River. 6 John wore clothing made of camel's hair, with a leather
belt around his waist, and he ate locusts and wild honey. 7 And this

[a] 1 Some manuscripts do not have *the Son of God.* [b] 2 Mal. 3:1 [c] 3 Isaiah 40:3

1:4 *desert region:* Probably the Desert of Judea (Matt 3:1), which stretched about twenty miles eastward from the Jerusalem-Bethlehem plateau down to the Jordan River and the Dead Sea. See the map on p. 2473.

1:4 *baptism of repentance for the forgiveness of sins:* John baptized people with water, symbolizing the old way of life being washed away. John encouraged people to turn back to God and to be forgiven for their sins (Luke 3:3). See also the mini-article called "Baptism," p. 1976. People "sin" when they turn away from God and disobey God's commands. Forgiveness is God's way of pardoning those who are sorry for their sins.

1:5 *Judean countryside . . . Jerusalem . . . Jordan River:* Judea was in the southern part of Palestine. Many centuries earlier, one of Israel's twelve tribes, Judah, settled in this area of Canaan. Jerusalem was the most important center of worship in Jesus' day, because the temple was located there. The Jordan River, the longest river in Palestine, flows from the slopes of Mount Hermon through Lake Huleh and the Sea of Galilee to the Dead Sea. See the map on p. 2464.

1:6 *clothing made of camel's hair . . . wild honey:* John's clothes were similar to those worn by the prophet Elijah (2 Kgs 1:8). Because he lived in the desert, John had to find food wherever he could.

1:2 Mal 3:1. **1:3** Isa 40:3.

1:7 *sandals . . . not worthy to stoop down and untie:* This was the duty of a slave. John was saying he was not even worthy to be the slave of this one who was to come.

1:8 *baptize . . . Holy Spirit:* Baptism in the name of Jesus would make people completely new by giving them the gift of the Holy Spirit. See also the mini-articles called "Baptism," p. 1976 and "Holy Spirit," p. 2082.

1:10 *the Spirit . . . like a dove:* In the New Testament, God's Spirit is often described as a Counselor or helper (John 14:16).

1:11 *You are my Son, whom I love:* The voice of God identifies Jesus as the Son (1:1).

1:12 *the desert:* See the note at 1:4 (desert region).

1:13 *Satan . . . angels:* The word "satan" means "adversary." Satan was also known as the devil ("accuser") or Beelzebub, the prince of the demons (3:22). The word "angel" is based on the Greek word *angelos*, which means "messenger." Angels act as messengers and servants of God. See also the mini-articles called "Satan," p. 963 and "Angels," p. 88.

1:15 *kingdom of God:* The kingdom of God refers to the eternal rule of God, and this rule includes instructions on how to live in obedience to God.

1:16 *Sea of Galilee:* A freshwater lake located in the northern part of the Jordan River Valley. It is also known as the Lake of Gennesaret (Luke 5:1), and the Romans called it the Sea of Tiberias (John 6:1; 21:1). See the map on p. 2473.

1:16 *Simon and his brother Andrew:* Simon was best known by his nicknames, *Cephas* in Aramaic (1 Cor 1:12; 9:5) and *Peter* in Greek (Matt 16:18). Both of these names mean "rock." JOHN indicates that Andrew was a disciple of John the Baptist before becoming one of Jesus' first disciples (John 1:35-42).

The Baptism of Jesus, artist unknown. John the Baptist said, "I baptize you with water, but he will baptize you with the Holy Spirit." This thirteenth century Byzantine-style mosaic is located in the Baptistery of St. Mark's Cathedral in Venice, Italy. It depicts the heavens opening at the moment of Jesus' baptism and the Holy Spirit coming down upon him in the form of a dove. (See 1:8-10.)

was his message: "After me will come one more powerful than I,
the thongs of whose sandals I am not worthy to stoop down and
untie. [8]I baptize you with[a] water, but he will baptize you with the
Holy Spirit."

The Baptism and Temptation of Jesus

[9]At that time Jesus came from Nazareth in Galilee and was
baptized by John in the Jordan. [10]As Jesus was coming up out of
the water, he saw heaven being torn open and the Spirit descending on him like a dove. [11]And a voice came from heaven: "You are
my Son, whom I love; with you I am well pleased."

[12]At once the Spirit sent him out into the desert, [13]and he
was in the desert forty days, being tempted by Satan. He was with
the wild animals, and angels attended him.

The Calling of the First Disciples

[14]After John was put in prison, Jesus went into Galilee, proclaiming the good news of God. [15]"The time has come," he said.
"The kingdom of God is near. Repent and believe the good news!"
[16]As Jesus walked beside the Sea of Galilee, he saw Simon

[a]**8** Or *in*

and his brother Andrew casting a net into the lake, for they were
fishermen. 17"Come, follow me," Jesus said, "and I will make you
fishers of men." 18At once they left their nets and followed him.
19When he had gone a little farther, he saw James son of
Zebedee and his brother John in a boat, preparing their nets.
20Without delay he called them, and they left their father Zebedee
in the boat with the hired men and followed him.

Jesus Does the Work of God's Kingdom in Galilee

This long section of MARK (1:21—9:50) tells how Jesus traveled around Galilee healing people, working miracles, and teaching about the kingdom of God. Near the end of the section, he tells his disciples what will happen to him in the future (8:31, 32), and God reveals Jesus' true glory (9:2-8).

HEALINGS, MIRACLES, AND PARABLES

Jesus displays the power of God by healing many people and working miracles.

Jesus Drives Out an Evil Spirit

21They went to Capernaum, and when the Sabbath came,
Jesus went into the synagogue and began to teach. 22The people
were amazed at his teaching, because he taught them as one who
had authority, not as the teachers of the law. 23Just then a man in
their synagogue who was possessed by an evil[a] spirit cried out,
24"What do you want with us, Jesus of Nazareth? Have you come
to destroy us? I know who you are—the Holy One of God!"
25"Be quiet!" said Jesus sternly. "Come out of him!" 26The
evil spirit shook the man violently and came out of him with a
shriek.
27The people were all so amazed that they asked each other,
"What is this? A new teaching—and with authority! He even gives
orders to evil spirits and they obey him." 28News about him spread
quickly over the whole region of Galilee.

Jesus Heals Many

29As soon as they left the synagogue, they went with James
and John to the home of Simon and Andrew. 30Simon's mother-
in-law was in bed with a fever, and they told Jesus about her. 31So
he went to her, took her hand and helped her up. The fever left her
and she began to wait on them.

[a]23 Greek *unclean*; also in verses 26 and 27

1:19 *James son of Zebedee and his brother John:* Jesus nicknamed these two brothers Boanerges, which means "Sons of Thunder" (3:17). The nickname may refer to the time when they wanted Jesus to call fire down from heaven (Luke 9:54).

1:21 *Capernaum:* Although Jesus grew up in Nazareth, he now lived in this important fishing town on the northern shore of the Sea of Galilee. It was located on the "high road," the major trade route between Egypt to the southwest and Syria to the northeast. In Jesus' day, Capernaum was a base for Roman soldiers who enforced the collection of taxes. See the map on p. 2473.

1:21 *Sabbath . . . synagogue:* The Sabbath was the seventh day of the week, the day that God rested after the work of creation (Gen 2:2, 3). Sabbath means "rest," and the Jewish people were commanded not to work on the Sabbath (Exod 20:8-11; Deut 5:12-15). The synagogues were the local meeting places for the Jews. See also the note at 5:22 (synagogue).

1:22 *the teachers of the law:* See the note at 12:38.

1:23 *evil spirit:* See the note at 3:30.

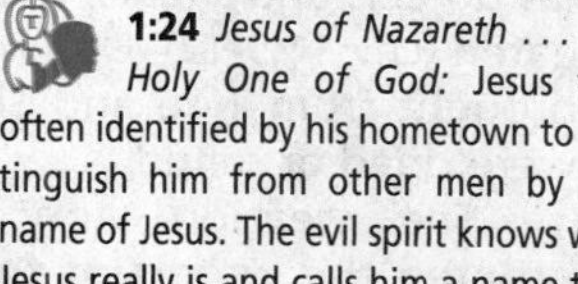

1:24 *Jesus of Nazareth . . . the Holy One of God:* Jesus was often identified by his hometown to distinguish him from other men by the name of Jesus. The evil spirit knows who Jesus really is and calls him a name that identifies Jesus as the Christ or Messiah (see the note at 8:29).

1:28 *Galilee:* See the note at 9:30.

1:29 *James and John . . . Simon and Andrew:* See the notes at 1:19 and 1:16 (Simon).

1:11 Gen 22:2; Ps 2:7; Isa 42:1; Matt 3:17; 12:18; Mark 9:7; Luke 3:22. **1:22** Matt 7:28,29.

1:32 *after sunset:* The Sabbath was now over, as a new day began at sunset.

1:32 *demon-possessed:* See the note at 3:30.

1:39 *Galilee:* See the note at 9:30.

1:39 *synagogues:* See the note at 5:22 (synagogue).

1:39 Matt 4:23; 9:35.

32That evening after sunset the people brought to Jesus all
the sick and demon-possessed. 33The whole town gathered at the
door, 34and Jesus healed many who had various diseases. He also
drove out many demons, but he would not let the demons speak
because they knew who he was.

Jesus Prays in a Solitary Place

35Very early in the morning, while it was still dark, Jesus got
up, left the house and went off to a solitary place, where he prayed.
36Simon and his companions went to look for him, 37and when
they found him, they exclaimed: "Everyone is looking for you!"
38Jesus replied, "Let us go somewhere else—to the nearby
villages—so I can preach there also. That is why I have come." 39So
he traveled throughout Galilee, preaching in their synagogues and
driving out demons.

FISH AND FISHING

In Jesus' time, fishing took place mostly on the Sea of Galilee (also called the Sea of Tiberias or the Lake of Gennesaret) because the Jewish people could not use many of the harbors along the coast of the Mediterranean Sea, since these harbors were often controlled by unfriendly neighbors. The most common fish in the Sea of Galilee were carp and catfish. The Law of Moses allowed people to eat any fish with fins and scales, but since catfish lack scales (as do eels and sharks) they were not to be eaten (Lev 11:9-12). Fish were also probably brought from Tyre and Sidon, where they were dried or salted.

The creation story tells that God ordered the waters of the earth to bring forth fish along with all kinds of creatures that live in the water (Gen 1:20-22). God gave human beings control over the creation, including fish (Gen 1:28; Ps 8:6-8), but people are forbidden to make or worship an image of any created thing, including fish (Deut 4:15-18). When God renews the creation, the salty Dead Sea will become fresh water and will be filled with fish (Ezek 47:7-10).

Fishing was also an important source of jobs and income in Galilee, and several of Jesus' disciples were fishermen. Jesus told them that they were going to "fish for people" instead of fish (Mark 1:16, 17; Matt 4:18, 19; Luke 5:10). When Jesus fed the hungry crowd that followed him out of town, the food he provided was bread and fish (Mark 6:30-44; Matt 14:14-21; Luke 9:10-17). Jesus used fishing to show his disciples the amazing results they could expect from having faith in him and sharing the good news with others. The net the apostles threw into the lake became so full of fish they could not pull it into their boat (John 21:4-12).

Among early Christians, the fish was a favorite image for Jesus, because the Greek word for fish (*ichthus*) consists of the first letters of the Greek words that tell who Jesus is:

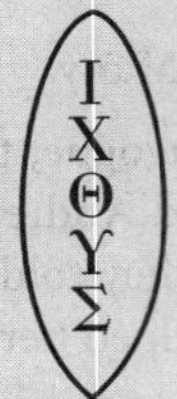

I hsous	Jesus
Ch ristos	Christ
Th eou	of God
U ios	the Son
S wthr	Savior

Fishing in the Sea of Galilee. The book of MARK tells how Jesus called four fishermen to follow him—Simon (also called Peter), Andrew, James, and John (See 1:16-20). Although many fishermen cast nets in the shallow waters along the shore, fishing from boats was also common in the Sea of Galilee. Those who fished from boats needed to hire additional workers to help them pull in the heavy nets. Carp, catfish, and other small freshwater fish were plentiful in the Sea of Galilee.

A Man With Leprosy

40 A man with leprosy[a] came to him and begged him on his
knees, "If you are willing, you can make me clean."
41 Filled with compassion, Jesus reached out his hand and
touched the man. "I am willing," he said. "Be clean!" 42 Immediately the leprosy left him and he was cured.
43 Jesus sent him away at once with a strong warning: 44 "See
that you don't tell this to anyone. But go, show yourself to the
priest and offer the sacrifices that Moses commanded for your
cleansing, as a testimony to them." 45 Instead he went out and
began to talk freely, spreading the news. As a result, Jesus could no
longer enter a town openly but stayed outside in lonely places. Yet
the people still came to him from everywhere.

[a]40 The Greek word was used for various diseases affecting the skin—not necessarily leprosy.

1:40 *leprosy:* In biblical times the word "leprosy" was used for several different kinds of skin diseases. When Jesus touched the man with leprosy (1:41), he not only risked being infected but he also was making himself "unclean" (unfit to worship with other Jews) according to the law.

1:44 *don't tell . . . priest:* Jesus often told the people he helped not to tell what he had done for them (3:10-12; 7:34-36) in order to avoid crowds of people who merely wanted to be healed. People with leprosy had to be examined by a priest and told that they were well ("clean") before they could once again live a normal life in the community.

2:1 *Capernaum:* See the note at 1:21 (Capernaum).

2:4 *roof:* In villages in Palestine, houses usually had flat roofs. A set of stairs on the outside of the house led up to the roof, which was made of beams and boards covered with packed earth. See illustration below.

2:5 *your sins are forgiven:* The teachers of the law were surprised to hear Jesus say this, since they believed that only God could forgive sins (2:7; Isa 43:25). See also the note at 1:4 (baptism of repentance).

2:10 *Son of Man:* See the mini-article called "Son of Man," p. 1866.

Jesus Heals a Paralytic

2 A few days later, when Jesus again entered Capernaum, the
people heard that he had come home. 2So many gathered that
there was no room left, not even outside the door, and he preached
the word to them. 3Some men came, bringing to him a paralytic,
carried by four of them. 4Since they could not get him to Jesus
because of the crowd, they made an opening in the roof above
Jesus and, after digging through it, lowered the mat the paralyzed
man was lying on. 5When Jesus saw their faith, he said to the paralytic, "Son, your sins are forgiven."

6Now some teachers of the law were sitting there, thinking
to themselves, 7"Why does this fellow talk like that? He's blaspheming! Who can forgive sins but God alone?"

8Immediately Jesus knew in his spirit that this was what they
were thinking in their hearts, and he said to them, "Why are you
thinking these things? 9Which is easier: to say to the paralytic,

Typical Residence in Palestine in the Time of Jesus. Most people in Jesus' day lived in simple one-room houses that sometimes included an area where animals were kept and fed. Roofs were flat and made of layers of branches packed with mud. Because the roofs were used for some kinds of gardening and as a place to sleep when it was hot, a first-century house often had a set of stairs leading to the roof. It was probably easy for the friends of the paralyzed man to make a hole in the roof of the house where Jesus was teaching, and lower their friend inside so he could be healed (see 2:1-12).

'Your sins are forgiven,' or to say, 'Get up, take your mat and walk'?
10But that you may know that the Son of Man has authority on
earth to forgive sins . . ." He said to the paralytic, 11"I tell you, get
up, take your mat and go home." 12He got up, took his mat and
walked out in full view of them all. This amazed everyone and they
praised God, saying, "We have never seen anything like this!"

The Calling of Levi

13Once again Jesus went out beside the lake. A large crowd
came to him, and he began to teach them. 14As he walked along, he
saw Levi son of Alphaeus sitting at the tax collector's booth. "Follow me," Jesus told him, and Levi got up and followed him.
15While Jesus was having dinner at Levi's house, many tax
collectors and "sinners" were eating with him and his disciples, for
there were many who followed him. 16When the teachers of the law
who were Pharisees saw him eating with the "sinners" and tax collectors, they asked his disciples: "Why does he eat with tax collectors and 'sinners'?"
17On hearing this, Jesus said to them, "It is not the healthy
who need a doctor, but the sick. I have not come to call the righteous, but sinners."

Jesus Questioned About Fasting

18Now John's disciples and the Pharisees were fasting. Some
people came and asked Jesus, "How is it that John's disciples and
the disciples of the Pharisees are fasting, but yours are not?"
19Jesus answered, "How can the guests of the bridegroom
fast while he is with them? They cannot, so long as they have him
with them. 20But the time will come when the bridegroom will be
taken from them, and on that day they will fast.
21"No one sews a patch of unshrunk cloth on an old garment. If he does, the new piece will pull away from the old, making the tear worse. 22And no one pours new wine into old
wineskins. If he does, the wine will burst the skins, and both the
wine and the wineskins will be ruined. No, he pours new wine into
new wineskins."

Lord of the Sabbath

23One Sabbath Jesus was going through the grainfields, and
as his disciples walked along, they began to pick some heads of
grain. 24The Pharisees said to him, "Look, why are they doing what
is unlawful on the Sabbath?"
25He answered, "Have you never read what David did when
he and his companions were hungry and in need? 26In the days of
Abiathar the high priest, he entered the house of God and ate the
consecrated bread, which is lawful only for priests to eat. And he
also gave some to his companions."
27Then he said to them, "The Sabbath was made for man,

2:16 *teachers of the law who were Pharisees:* The name *Pharisee* comes from Hebrew words that may mean "separate ones" or "pure ones." They believed in following the Law of Moses as closely as possible.

2:19 *bridegroom:* Since weddings were times of celebration, it would have been considered rude for the friends of a bridegroom to fast. Jesus is the bridegroom, and while he is with the people they are free from the practice of fasting.

2:21,22 *unshrunk cloth . . . new wineskins:* A patch made of new, unshrunk cloth could shrink after being washed. If it had been used to patch a hole in an old piece of clothing, it could tear away and make a bigger hole.

When the juice from grapes is becoming wine, gas is produced from a process that is called fermentation. As wine fermented, the gas would swell and stretch the new wineskins. If new wine was put into old wineskins that had become stiff, the skins could burst.

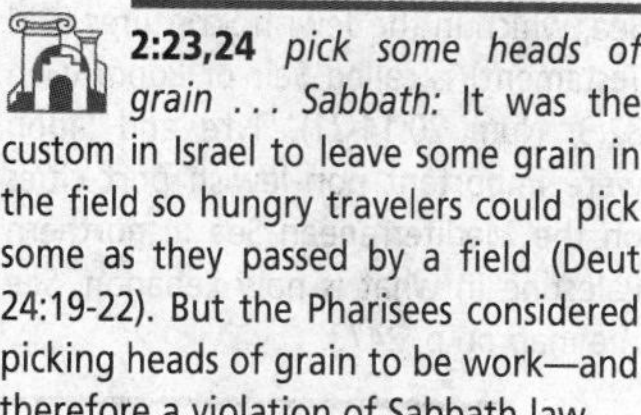

2:23,24 *pick some heads of grain . . . Sabbath:* It was the custom in Israel to leave some grain in the field so hungry travelers could pick some as they passed by a field (Deut 24:19-22). But the Pharisees considered picking heads of grain to be work—and therefore a violation of Sabbath law.

2:28 *the Son of Man is Lord even of the Sabbath:* See the mini-article called "Son of Man," p. 1866. For more on the Sabbath, see the note at 1:21 (Sabbath). What Jesus, the Son of Man, teaches and does has more authority than even the Law of Moses, which includes the laws about the Sabbath.

3:1 *synagogue:* See the note at 5:22 (synagogue).

3:2 *heal him on the Sabbath:* See the note at 1:21 (Sabbath). Healing the man on the Sabbath would have been considered work, which was a violation of the Sabbath laws.

3:6 *Herodians:* Political followers of Herod Antipas, the son of Herod the Great. Herod Antipas ruled over Galilee and Perea from 4 B.C. to A.D. 39. The formal name for his title was tetrarch, but the people sometimes also called him a king (Matt 14:9).

3:7,8 *Galilee . . . Sidon:* See the notes at 9:30 and 1:5. Idumea was the hill country south of the Dead Sea, which in the Jewish Scriptures (Old Testament) is called Seir or Edom (Gen 32:3; Num 20:14-21). Tyre and Sidon were important non-Jewish port cities on the Mediterranean Sea in northern Palestine in what is now Lebanon. See the map on p. 2473.

3:11 *evil spirits:* See the note at 3:30.

3:11 *Son of God:* See the note at 1:1.

3:12 *not to tell who he was:* See the note at 1:44.

3:14-19 *twelve . . . apostles:* A *disciple* means a follower who learns from a master teacher, and the term *apostle* refers to a person chosen and sent by a leader to do a special job. The number of apostles (twelve) is the same number as the tribes of Israel. Jesus gave these disciples the power to preach and drive out evil spirits. See also Matt 10:1, 2 and Luke 6:13-16.

3:9,10 Mark 4:1; Luke 5:1-3.

not man for the Sabbath. 28 So the Son of Man is Lord even of the
Sabbath."

3 Another time he went into the synagogue, and a man with a
shriveled hand was there. 2 Some of them were looking for a reason
to accuse Jesus, so they watched him closely to see if he would heal
him on the Sabbath. 3 Jesus said to the man with the shriveled
hand, "Stand up in front of everyone."

4 Then Jesus asked them, "Which is lawful on the Sabbath: to
do good or to do evil, to save life or to kill?" But they remained silent.
5 He looked around at them in anger and, deeply distressed at
their stubborn hearts, said to the man, "Stretch out your hand." He
stretched it out, and his hand was completely restored. 6 Then the
Pharisees went out and began to plot with the Herodians how they
might kill Jesus.

Crowds Follow Jesus

7 Jesus withdrew with his disciples to the lake, and a large
crowd from Galilee followed. 8 When they heard all he was doing,
many people came to him from Judea, Jerusalem, Idumea, and the
regions across the Jordan and around Tyre and Sidon. 9 Because of
the crowd he told his disciples to have a small boat ready for him,
to keep the people from crowding him. 10 For he had healed many,
so that those with diseases were pushing forward to touch him.
11 Whenever the evil[a] spirits saw him, they fell down before him
and cried out, "You are the Son of God." 12 But he gave them strict
orders not to tell who he was.

The Appointing of the Twelve Apostles

13 Jesus went up on a mountainside and called to him those he
wanted, and they came to him. 14 He appointed twelve—designating
them apostles[b]—that they might be with him and that he might send
them out to preach 15 and to have authority to drive out demons.
16 These are the twelve he appointed: Simon (to whom he gave the
name Peter); 17 James son of Zebedee and his brother John (to them he
gave the name Boanerges, which means Sons of Thunder); 18 Andrew,
Philip, Bartholomew, Matthew, Thomas, James son of Alphaeus,
Thaddaeus, Simon the Zealot 19 and Judas Iscariot, who betrayed him.

Jesus and Beelzebub

20 Then Jesus entered a house, and again a crowd gathered, so
that he and his disciples were not even able to eat. 21 When his family
heard about this, they went to take charge of him, for they said,
"He is out of his mind."

[a]11 Greek *unclean*; also in verse 30 [b]14 Some manuscripts do not have *designating them apostles.*

[22]And the teachers of the law who came down from
Jerusalem said, "He is possessed by Beelzebub[a]! By the prince of
demons he is driving out demons."
[23]So Jesus called them and spoke to them in parables: "How
can Satan drive out Satan? [24]If a kingdom is divided against itself,
that kingdom cannot stand. [25]If a house is divided against itself,
that house cannot stand. [26]And if Satan opposes himself and is
divided, he cannot stand; his end has come. [27]In fact, no one can
enter a strong man's house and carry off his possessions unless he
first ties up the strong man. Then he can rob his house. [28]I tell you
the truth, all the sins and blasphemies of men will be forgiven
them. [29]But whoever blasphemes against the Holy Spirit will never
be forgiven; he is guilty of an eternal sin."
[30]He said this because they were saying, "He has an evil
spirit."

Jesus' Mother and Brothers

[31]Then Jesus' mother and brothers arrived. Standing outside,
they sent someone in to call him. [32]A crowd was sitting around
him, and they told him, "Your mother and brothers are outside
looking for you."
[33]"Who are my mother and my brothers?" he asked.
[34]Then he looked at those seated in a circle around him and
said, "Here are my mother and my brothers! [35]Whoever does God's
will is my brother and sister and mother."

The Parable of the Sower

4 Again Jesus began to teach by the lake. The crowd that gathered around him was so large that he got into a boat and sat in it
out on the lake, while all the people were along the shore at the
water's edge. [2]He taught them many things by parables, and in his
teaching said: [3]"Listen! A farmer went out to sow his seed. [4]As he
was scattering the seed, some fell along the path, and the birds
came and ate it up. [5]Some fell on rocky places, where it did not
have much soil. It sprang up quickly, because the soil was shallow.
[6]But when the sun came up, the plants were scorched, and they
withered because they had no root. [7]Other seed fell among thorns,
which grew up and choked the plants, so that they did not bear
grain. [8]Still other seed fell on good soil. It came up, grew and produced a crop, multiplying thirty, sixty, or even a hundred times."
[9]Then Jesus said, "He who has ears to hear, let him hear."
[10]When he was alone, the Twelve and the others around him
asked him about the parables. [11]He told them, "The secret of the
kingdom of God has been given to you. But to those on the outside everything is said in parables [12]so that,

[a]22 Greek *Beezeboul* or *Beelzeboul*

3:22 *Beelzebub . . . prince of demons:* Also known as the devil and Satan.

3:23 *parables:* Short stories told to teach a lesson. See also the mini-article called "Parables," p. 1876.

3:29 *Holy Spirit:* See the note at 1:8. The sin of blaspheming or speaking against the Holy Spirit is a complete turning away from God. Those who reject God also reject God's forgiveness.

3:30 *evil spirit:* Evil spirits were understood to work for Satan (see the note at 1:13). In Jesus' day, evil spirits or demons were understood to be the cause of many kinds of sickness and mental illness. A Jewish person who had an evil spirit was considered "unclean" and was not allowed to eat or worship with other Jews. People were afraid that the illness caused by the evil spirit would "rub off" on them, so the unclean person was isolated.

3:31 *Jesus' mother and brothers:* Jesus' mother is Mary (Luke 1:26—2:52). Jesus' family came to take charge of him because they thought he was out of his mind (3:21). Mark 6:3 mentions the names of four brothers and says that he also had sisters.

4:1 *by the lake:* By the Sea of Galilee (see the note at 1:16).

4:1 *got into a boat and sat in it:* Jesus probably went in the boat because the crowd was pushing so close to him.

4:3 *farmer went out to sow his seed:* Farmers planted seeds by scattering them a handful at a time. After sowing the seeds, they plowed them into the ground. Before some of the seeds could be covered, birds would quickly eat them. Other seeds would fall on rocks and dry out in the sun, and still others might be thrown among weeds.

3:22 Matt 9:34; 10:25.
4:12 Isa 6:9,10.

4:14 *the word:* The "word" refers to the gospel, or good news, about the Kingdom of God. See the notes at 1:1 and 1:15.

4:15 *Satan:* See the note at 1:13.

4:21 *lamp . . . bowl:* In Jesus' day, people used small clay lamps that burned olive oil. The oil was drawn up from the clay lamp by a wick and like a candle, gave off light as it burned. In the Jewish Scriptures (Old Testament), God's Word is compared to "a lamp to my feet and a light for my path" (Ps 119:105). Putting a bowl over the lamp would put the lamp out or keep its light from being seen.

4:26,30 *kingdom of God:* See the note at 1:15.

4:29 *sickle:* A sickle is a knife with a long curved blade, used to cut grain and other crops.

4:31 *mustard seed:* In Jesus' day, the smallest quantity of something was compared with the tiny black "mustard seed." This seed was used to flavor food and to keep it fresh. It also contained oil and was used as a medicine. The mustard plant does not usually grow as tall as most trees, but this tree-like shrub can grow taller than a human being. The stem can be as thick as a person's arm.

4:21 Matt 5:15; Luke 11:33. **4:22** Matt 10:26; Luke 12:2. **4:24** Matt 7:2; Luke 6:38. **4:25** Matt 13:12; 25:29; Luke 19:26. **4:29** Joel 3:13.

" 'they may be ever seeing but never perceiving,
and ever hearing but never understanding;
otherwise they might turn and be forgiven!'[a]"

13 Then Jesus said to them, "Don't you understand this parable? How then will you understand any parable? 14 The farmer sows
the word. 15 Some people are like seed along the path, where the
word is sown. As soon as they hear it, Satan comes and takes away
the word that was sown in them. 16 Others, like seed sown on rocky
places, hear the word and at once receive it with joy. 17 But since they
have no root, they last only a short time. When trouble or persecution comes because of the word, they quickly fall away. 18 Still others, like seed sown among thorns, hear the word; 19 but the worries
of this life, the deceitfulness of wealth and the desires for other
things come in and choke the word, making it unfruitful. 20 Others,
like seed sown on good soil, hear the word, accept it, and produce
a crop—thirty, sixty or even a hundred times what was sown."

A Lamp on a Stand

21 He said to them, "Do you bring in a lamp to put it under a
bowl or a bed? Instead, don't you put it on its stand? 22 For whatever is hidden is meant to be disclosed, and whatever is concealed
is meant to be brought out into the open. 23 If anyone has ears to
hear, let him hear."

24 "Consider carefully what you hear," he continued. "With
the measure you use, it will be measured to you—and even more.
25 Whoever has will be given more; whoever does not have, even
what he has will be taken from him."

The Parable of the Growing Seed

26 He also said, "This is what the kingdom of God is like. A
man scatters seed on the ground. 27 Night and day, whether he
sleeps or gets up, the seed sprouts and grows, though he does not
know how. 28 All by itself the soil produces grain—first the stalk,
then the head, then the full kernel in the head. 29 As soon as the
grain is ripe, he puts the sickle to it, because the harvest has come."

The Parable of the Mustard Seed

30 Again he said, "What shall we say the kingdom of God is
like, or what parable shall we use to describe it? 31 It is like a mustard seed, which is the smallest seed you plant in the ground. 32 Yet
when planted, it grows and becomes the largest of all garden
plants, with such big branches that the birds of the air can perch in
its shade."

33 With many similar parables Jesus spoke the word to them,

[a]12 Isaiah 6:9,10

The Storm at Sea, from an early eleventh century illuminated manuscript, artist unknown. Jesus is shown sleeping, his arm resting casually over the edge of the boat. As Jesus slept through the storm, the disciples became frightened that the boat would sink. When they woke him, Jesus ordered the wind and the waves to be still. (See 4:35-41.)

as much as they could understand. [34]He did not say anything to them without using a parable. But when he was alone with his own disciples, he explained everything.

Jesus Calms the Storm

[35]That day when evening came, he said to his disciples, "Let
us go over to the other side." [36]Leaving the crowd behind, they took
him along, just as he was, in the boat. There were also other boats
with him. [37]A furious squall came up, and the waves broke over the
boat, so that it was nearly swamped. [38]Jesus was in the stern, sleeping on a cushion. The disciples woke him and said to him,
"Teacher, don't you care if we drown?"

The disciples said to each other, *"Who is this? Even the wind and the waves obey him!"*
Mark 4:41

4:35 *go over to the other side:* Mark has described Jesus' ministry thus far as being largely in Galilee and its neighboring areas (1:14,45; 3:13), especially along the shore (1:16; 2:13; 4:1), and centering in Capernaum (1:21; 2:1). Now Jesus wants to cross to the eastern side of the Sea of Galilee. See the note at 1:16 (Sea of Galilee).

[39]He got up, rebuked the wind and said to the waves, "Quiet!
Be still!" Then the wind died down and it was completely calm.
[40]He said to his disciples, "Why are you so afraid? Do you
still have no faith?"
[41]They were terrified and asked each other, "Who is this?
Even the wind and the waves obey him!"

The Healing of a Demon-possessed Man

5 They went across the lake to the region of the Gerasenes.[a]
[2]When Jesus got out of the boat, a man with an evil[b] spirit came
from the tombs to meet him. [3]This man lived in the tombs, and
no one could bind him any more, not even with a chain. [4]For he
had often been chained hand and foot, but he tore the chains apart
and broke the irons on his feet. No one was strong enough to subdue him. [5]Night and day among the tombs and in the hills he
would cry out and cut himself with stones.
[6]When he saw Jesus from a distance, he ran and fell on his
knees in front of him. [7]He shouted at the top of his voice, "What
do you want with me, Jesus, Son of the Most High God? Swear to
God that you won't torture me!" [8]For Jesus had said to him,
"Come out of this man, you evil spirit!"
[9]Then Jesus asked him, "What is your name?"
"My name is Legion," he replied, "for we are many." [10]And he
begged Jesus again and again not to send them out of the area.
[11]A large herd of pigs was feeding on the nearby hillside.
[12]The demons begged Jesus, "Send us among the pigs; allow us to
go into them." [13]He gave them permission, and the evil spirits
came out and went into the pigs. The herd, about two thousand in
number, rushed down the steep bank into the lake and were
drowned.
[14]Those tending the pigs ran off and reported this in the
town and countryside, and the people went out to see what had
happened. [15]When they came to Jesus, they saw the man who had
been possessed by the legion of demons, sitting there, dressed and
in his right mind; and they were afraid. [16]Those who had seen it
told the people what had happened to the demon-possessed
man—and told about the pigs as well. [17]Then the people began to
plead with Jesus to leave their region.
[18]As Jesus was getting into the boat, the man who had been
demon-possessed begged to go with him. [19]Jesus did not let him,
but said, "Go home to your family and tell them how much the
Lord has done for you, and how he has had mercy on you." [20]So
the man went away and began to tell in the Decapolis[c] how much
Jesus had done for him. And all the people were amazed.

---

a1 Some manuscripts *Gadarenes*; other manuscripts *Gergesenes* **b2** Greek *unclean*; also in verses 8 and 13 **c20** That is, the Ten Cities

5:1 *across the lake to the region of the Gerasenes:* See the note at 1:16 (Sea). The region of the Gerasenes was located east of the Jordan River and to the south of the Sea of Galilee. The area's population, architecture, and style of life were mostly Greek (non-Jewish).

5:2 *evil spirit:* Also called "demons" (5:12). See the note at 3:30.

5:3 *lived in the tombs:* It was thought evil spirits lived in areas surrounding tombs.

5:7 *Son of the Most High God:* The demons know who Jesus is. See also the notes at 1:1 and 1:24. The title "Most High God" was used by both Jews (Dan 5:18) and Gentiles (Acts 16:17).

5:9 *My name is Legion:* A Roman army legion was made up of 6000 men. This man was possessed by many evil spirits.

5:11 *large herd of pigs:* Jewish people considered the pig an unclean animal; see the mini-article called "Purity (Clean and Unclean)," p. 2125. Since Jews in Palestine would never have raised pigs, the fact that a large herd of pigs was in this region shows that this was likely a Gentile area where few Jews lived.

5:19 *the Lord:* The Greek word for "Lord" is *kyrios*, which may mean master or may be used to address someone as "sir." When it is used for Jesus, it emphasizes his authority and power. See also the mini-article called "Lord (Title for Jesus)," p. 2106.

5:20 *the Decapolis:* A group of ten Gentile cities east of Samaria and Galilee. The buildings in the cities were designed according to Greek architecture, and each city was laid out in the style of a typical Greek city. The people who lived in these cities followed the Greek way of life. See the illustration on p. 1858.

A Dead Girl and a Sick Woman

21When Jesus had again crossed over by boat to the other side
of the lake, a large crowd gathered around him while he was by the
lake. 22Then one of the synagogue rulers, named Jairus, came there.
Seeing Jesus, he fell at his feet 23and pleaded earnestly with him,
"My little daughter is dying. Please come and put your hands on
her so that she will be healed and live." 24So Jesus went with him.
A large crowd followed and pressed around him. 25And a
woman was there who had been subject to bleeding for twelve years.
26She had suffered a great deal under the care of many doctors and
had spent all she had, yet instead of getting better she grew worse.
27When she heard about Jesus, she came up behind him in the
crowd and touched his cloak, 28because she thought, "If I just touch
his clothes, I will be healed." 29Immediately her bleeding stopped and
she felt in her body that she was freed from her suffering.
30At once Jesus realized that power had gone out from him. He
turned around in the crowd and asked, "Who touched my clothes?"
31"You see the people crowding against you," his disciples
answered, "and yet you can ask, 'Who touched me?' "
32But Jesus kept looking around to see who had done it.
33Then the woman, knowing what had happened to her, came and
fell at his feet and, trembling with fear, told him the whole truth.
34He said to her, "Daughter, your faith has healed you. Go in peace
and be freed from your suffering."
35While Jesus was still speaking, some men came from the

The Raising of Jairus's Daughter, bas-relief carving, fourth century sarcophagus, artist unknown. The importance of faith is emphasized in this representation of two healing miracles: Jesus is shown raising Jairus's daughter from death, while the woman who had been bleeding is healed by touching Jesus' cloak. (See 5:21-43.)

Jesus said to her, *"Daughter, your faith has healed you. Go in peace and be freed from your suffering."* Mark 5:34

5:21 *crossed over by boat to the other side of the lake:* They crossed to the west side of the Sea of Galilee (see the note at 4:35).

5:22 *synagogue:* This was a Jewish meeting place. The word in Greek means "gathering." In the Bible, a synagogue consisted of a group of Jewish people who met together to worship and to study the Scriptures. See also the mini-article called "Synagogues," p. 1857.

5:22 *Jairus:* As a synagogue ruler, he likely made arrangements for meetings and worship.

5:26 *doctors:* In New Testament times there were doctors who helped people when they were sick or injured. Though they had many skills, their knowledge of what causes diseases was limited. See also the article called "Miracles, Magic, and Medicine," p. 1838.

5:33 *fell at his feet:* This was a way of showing great respect for someone in Jesus' day.

5:38 *crying and wailing loudly:* It was a common Jewish custom in Jesus' day to hire mourners to cry out in sorrow during the procession to the tomb. Burial often took place on the same day that a person died.

5:39 *not dead but asleep:* In the New Testament, the dead are sometimes described as being asleep (see John 11:11-14; Eph 5:14; 1 Thes 5:10).

5:41,42 *Talitha koum:* These words are in the Aramaic language. Aramaic had gained widespread use in the Near East as the diplomatic language of the Persian empire, which had controlled the area centuries before the time of Jesus.

5:43 *strict orders not to let anyone know:* See the note at 1:44.

6:1 *his hometown:* Nazareth (see the note at 1:24).

house of Jairus, the synagogue ruler. "Your daughter is dead," they
said. "Why bother the teacher any more?"
36 Ignoring what they said, Jesus told the synagogue ruler,
"Don't be afraid; just believe."
37 He did not let anyone follow him except Peter, James and
John the brother of James. 38 When they came to the home of the synagogue ruler, Jesus saw a commotion, with people crying and wailing
loudly. 39 He went in and said to them, "Why all this commotion and
wailing? The child is not dead but asleep." 40 But they laughed at him.
After he put them all out, he took the child's father and
mother and the disciples who were with him, and went in where
the child was. 41 He took her by the hand and said to her, "*Talitha
koum!*" (which means, "Little girl, I say to you, get up!"). 42 Immediately the girl stood up and walked around (she was twelve years
old). At this they were completely astonished. 43 He gave strict
orders not to let anyone know about this, and told them to give
her something to eat.

A Prophet Without Honor

6 Jesus left there and went to his hometown, accompanied by his
disciples. 2 When the Sabbath came, he began to teach in the synagogue, and many who heard him were amazed.

FAITH

In the Bible, faith often means trust in God, but it can also refer to a set of beliefs or religious ideas. A Hebrew word sometimes translated as "faith" is *Amen*, which is used in English in prayers and hymns. It means to rely on what is firm and dependable, especially on God, whose words and works are completely reliable.

The importance of this trust relationship with God is shown powerfully in Genesis 15:1-6, where God tells Abraham that he will have a son and heir, even though he and his wife have not been able to have any children. God had earlier promised to bless all the families of the earth because of Abraham and his descendants (Gen 12:3; 17:3-7). These promises were not based on what Abraham could accomplish, but on what God would provide out of love and overwhelming kindness. Abraham's only response was to trust God's promises. This is what God's people are called to do: trust God's promises no matter what their problems and difficulties (Ps 25:5; 32:10; Prov 16:20; Jer 39:17, 18).

In the Gospels, the charge that Jesus' disciples and others do not have faith (Mark 4:40; 6:6) is not a matter of their lack of correct beliefs, but their failure to trust God's power at work in Jesus. But those who do trust in Jesus experience that power, as did the father of the dying girl and the sick woman who reached out to touch Jesus (Mark 5:21-43).

After Jesus died and later was resurrected, his disciples and the apostle Paul urge men and women everywhere to put their trust ("have faith") in Jesus, who acts as a sacrifice to bring forgiveness of sins (Rom 1:3-6; 3:22-26) and is raised from death to bring God's promise of eternal life (Acts 2:36-39; 1 Cor 15:12-24; Eph 1:15-23). Those who trust in what Jesus has done are considered part of God's family (Gal 3:23-29).

"Where did this man get these things?" they asked. "What's this wisdom that has been given him, that he even does miracles!
[3]Isn't this the carpenter? Isn't this Mary's son and the brother of James, Joseph,[a] Judas and Simon? Aren't his sisters here with us?" And they took offense at him.

[4]Jesus said to them, "Only in his hometown, among his relatives and in his own house is a prophet without honor." [5]He could not do any miracles there, except lay his hands on a few sick people and heal them. [6]And he was amazed at their lack of faith.

Jesus Sends Out the Twelve

Then Jesus went around teaching from village to village.
[7]Calling the Twelve to him, he sent them out two by two and gave them authority over evil[b] spirits.

[8]These were his instructions: "Take nothing for the journey except a staff—no bread, no bag, no money in your belts. [9]Wear sandals but not an extra tunic. [10]Whenever you enter a house, stay there until you leave that town. [11]And if any place will not welcome you or listen to you, shake the dust off your feet when you leave, as a testimony against them."

[12]They went out and preached that people should repent.
[13]They drove out many demons and anointed many sick people with oil and healed them.

John the Baptist Beheaded

[14]King Herod heard about this, for Jesus' name had become well known. Some were saying,[c] "John the Baptist has been raised from the dead, and that is why miraculous powers are at work in him."

[15]Others said, "He is Elijah."

And still others claimed, "He is a prophet, like one of the prophets of long ago."

[16]But when Herod heard this, he said, "John, the man I beheaded, has been raised from the dead!"

[17]For Herod himself had given orders to have John arrested, and he had him bound and put in prison. He did this because of Herodias, his brother Philip's wife, whom he had married. [18]For John had been saying to Herod, "It is not lawful for you to have your brother's wife." [19]So Herodias nursed a grudge against John and wanted to kill him. But she was not able to, [20]because Herod feared John and protected him, knowing him to be a righteous and holy man. When Herod heard John, he was greatly puzzled[d]; yet he liked to listen to him.

[21]Finally the opportune time came. On his birthday Herod

[a]**3** Greek *Joses*, a variant of *Joseph* [b]**7** Greek *unclean* [c]**14** Some early manuscripts *He was saying* [d]**20** Some early manuscripts *he did many things*

6:3 *Mary's son . . . . brother:* See the note at 3:31. Little is known about Jesus' brothers and sisters, except for James, who became an important leader in the church. James saw Jesus after Jesus had been raised from death (1 Cor 15:7) and was head of the Jewish-Christian church in Jerusalem (Acts 15:13; 21:18; Gal 1:19). Church tradition says that James was the author of the book of JAMES, and that he was put to death some time before A.D. 70.

6:11 *shake the dust off your feet:* This was a way of showing rejection. See Acts 13:51.

6:13 *demons:* Another word for evil spirits. See the note at 3:30.

6:13 *anointed many sick people with oil:* In Jesus' day olive oil was used as part of healing rituals (see Jas 5:4).

6:14 *King Herod . . . John the Baptist:* This refers to Herod Antipas. See the notes at 3:6 and 1:4 (John).

6:15 *Elijah:* Elijah was a prophet in Israel over 800 years before Jesus was born. Later prophets expected God to send Elijah back to earth to warn people of God's judgment (Mal 3:1-4; 4:5,6) and prepare the way for the Messiah. See also the mini-article called "Elijah," p. 1816.

6:17,18 *Herodias, his brother Philip's wife:* Herodias was a granddaughter of Herod the Great. She married Herod's son Philip, who was her uncle. Herod Antipas (also her uncle) later talked Herodias into leaving Philip and marrying him. The Law of Moses did not allow a man to marry his brother's wife while the brother was still living (Lev 18:6).

6:4 John 4:44. **6:8-11** Luke 10:4-11. **6:14,15** Matt 16:14; Mark 8:28; Luke 9:19.

6:21 *high officials . . . military commanders . . . leading men:* Even though the Romans ruled the area, Herod had some officials and a small army. The leading men of Galilee could have been local Jewish officials or the Roman leaders in the area, or both.

6:26 *because of his oaths:* Rulers were expected to do what they said they would do. So when Herod made a promise to his stepdaughter in the presence of important guests, he could not take it back.

6:29 *tomb:* Tombs were usually carved out of the soft limestone hillsides in Palestine. Many times a large circular stone was used to seal the entrance to the tomb.

gave a banquet for his high officials and military commanders and
the leading men of Galilee. 22When the daughter of Herodias came
in and danced, she pleased Herod and his dinner guests.

The king said to the girl, "Ask me for anything you want, and
I'll give it to you." 23And he promised her with an oath, "Whatever
you ask I will give you, up to half my kingdom."

24She went out and said to her mother, "What shall I
ask for?"

"The head of John the Baptist," she answered.

25At once the girl hurried in to the king with the request: "I
want you to give me right now the head of John the Baptist on a
platter."

26The king was greatly distressed, but because of his oaths
and his dinner guests, he did not want to refuse her. 27So he immediately sent an executioner with orders to bring John's head. The
man went, beheaded John in the prison, 28and brought back his
head on a platter. He presented it to the girl, and she gave it to her
mother. 29On hearing of this, John's disciples came and took his
body and laid it in a tomb.

The Multiplication of the Loaves, Pablo Mayorga, Nicaraguan, about 1982. Many people through the ages have taken comfort from the miracle story of Jesus feeding more than five thousand men, women, and children who had come to hear him teach (see 6:30-44). Jesus is shown as a compassionate leader who cares for people's physical needs as well as for their spiritual needs.

Jesus Feeds the Five Thousand

30 The apostles gathered around Jesus and reported to him all
they had done and taught. 31 Then, because so many people were
coming and going that they did not even have a chance to eat, he
said to them, "Come with me by yourselves to a quiet place and
get some rest."
32 So they went away by themselves in a boat to a solitary
place. 33 But many who saw them leaving recognized them and ran
on foot from all the towns and got there ahead of them. 34 When
Jesus landed and saw a large crowd, he had compassion on them,
because they were like sheep without a shepherd. So he began
teaching them many things.
35 By this time it was late in the day, so his disciples came to
him. "This is a remote place," they said, "and it's already very late.
36 Send the people away so they can go to the surrounding countryside and villages and buy themselves something to eat."
37 But he answered, "You give them something to eat."
They said to him, "That would take eight months of a man's
wages[a]! Are we to go and spend that much on bread and give it to
them to eat?"
38 "How many loaves do you have?" he asked. "Go and see."
When they found out, they said, "Five—and two fish."
39 Then Jesus directed them to have all the people sit down
in groups on the green grass. 40 So they sat down in groups of hundreds and fifties. 41 Taking the five loaves and the two fish and looking up to heaven, he gave thanks and broke the loaves. Then he
gave them to his disciples to set before the people. He also divided
the two fish among them all. 42 They all ate and were satisfied, 43 and
the disciples picked up twelve basketfuls of broken pieces of bread
and fish. 44 The number of the men who had eaten was five thousand.

Jesus Walks on the Water

45 Immediately Jesus made his disciples get into the boat and
go on ahead of him to Bethsaida, while he dismissed the crowd.
46 After leaving them, he went up on a mountainside to pray.
47 When evening came, the boat was in the middle of the
lake, and he was alone on land. 48 He saw the disciples straining at
the oars, because the wind was against them. About the fourth
watch of the night he went out to them, walking on the lake. He
was about to pass by them, 49 but when they saw him walking on
the lake, they thought he was a ghost. They cried out, 50 because
they all saw him and were terrified.
Immediately he spoke to them and said, "Take courage! It is
I. Don't be afraid." 51 Then he climbed into the boat with them, and

[a]37 Greek *take two hundred denarii*

6:30 *apostles . . . reported:* These are the twelve apostles Jesus had earlier sent on a mission (6:7-13). See also the note at 3:14-19.

6:34 *sheep without a shepherd:* Sheep are easygoing animals that need lots of attention and care. Sheep become familiar with the voice of their shepherd and follow him when he calls.

6:35 *remote place:* Jesus' feeding of the five thousand people in this remote place would have reminded Mark's readers of how God fed the Israelite people as they wandered in the desert many centuries earlier, after leaving Egypt (Exod 16; Num 11).

6:37 *eight months of a man's wages:* The Greek text has "two hundred denari" (silver coins). Each coin was the average day's wage for a worker.

6:38 *loaves:* These would have been flat and round or in the shape of a bun. See the mini-article called "Bread," p. 2058.

6:41 *gave thanks and broke the loaves:* This same language is used when Jesus later shares a final meal with his disciples (14:22-26).

6:43 *twelve basketfuls:* Twelve is an important number in Jewish culture and religion. See also the chart called "Numbers in the Bible," p. 2405.

6:45 *Bethsaida:* A Jewish town just east of where the Jordan River empties into the northern end of the Sea of Galilee.

6:47 *the lake:* The Sea of Galilee. See the note at 1:16 (Sea of Galilee).

6:34 Num 27:17; 1 Kgs 22:17; 2 Chr 18:16; Ezek 34:5; Matt 9:36.

the wind died down. They were completely amazed, 52 for they had
not understood about the loaves; their hearts were hardened.
53 When they had crossed over, they landed at Gennesaret
and anchored there. 54 As soon as they got out of the boat, people
recognized Jesus. 55 They ran throughout that whole region and
carried the sick on mats to wherever they heard he was. 56 And
wherever he went—into villages, towns or countryside—they
placed the sick in the marketplaces. They begged him to let them
touch even the edge of his cloak, and all who touched him were
healed.

Clean and Unclean

7 The Pharisees and some of the teachers of the law who had
come from Jerusalem gathered around Jesus and 2 saw some of his
disciples eating food with hands that were "unclean," that is,
unwashed. 3 (The Pharisees and all the Jews do not eat unless they
give their hands a ceremonial washing, holding to the tradition of
the elders. 4 When they come from the marketplace they do not eat
unless they wash. And they observe many other traditions, such as
the washing of cups, pitchers and kettles.[a])
5 So the Pharisees and teachers of the law asked Jesus, "Why
don't your disciples live according to the tradition of the elders
instead of eating their food with 'unclean' hands?"
6 He replied, "Isaiah was right when he prophesied about you
hypocrites; as it is written:

" 'These people honor me with their lips,
but their hearts are far from me.
7 They worship me in vain;
their teachings are but rules taught by men.'[b]

8 You have let go of the commands of God and are holding on to
the traditions of men."
9 And he said to them: "You have a fine way of setting aside the
commands of God in order to observe[c] your own traditions! 10 For
Moses said, 'Honor your father and your mother,'[d] and, 'Anyone who
curses his father or mother must be put to death.'[e] 11 But you say that
if a man says to his father or mother: 'Whatever help you might
otherwise have received from me is Corban' (that is, a gift devoted to
God), 12 then you no longer let him do anything for his father or
mother. 13 Thus you nullify the word of God by your tradition that
you have handed down. And you do many things like that."
14 Again Jesus called the crowd to him and said, "Listen to
me, everyone, and understand this. 15 Nothing outside a man can

---

[a]4 Some early manuscripts *pitchers, kettles and dining couches* [b]6,7 Isaiah 29:13 [c]9 Some manuscripts *set up* [d]10 Exodus 20:12; Deut. 5:16 [e]10 Exodus 21:17; Lev. 20:9

6:52 *had not understood about the loaves:* Even though the disciples witnessed Jesus' miracles, they did not yet understand who he really was.

6:53 *Gennesaret:* This town was located on the northwestern side of the Sea of Galilee, southwest of Capernaum (see the note at 1:21).

6:56 *marketplaces:* In Jesus' day, every village in Palestine had a market, usually located on a street or in an open area. See also the mini-article called "At the Market," p. 1890.

7:1 *Pharisees . . . teachers of the law . . . Jerusalem:* See the notes at 2:16; 12:38; and 1:5. Jesus was attracting attention among the Jewish leaders in Jerusalem, who were willing to travel many miles to the north to hear him.

7:2 *eating food with hands that were "unclean":* According to the Law of Moses, if people touched something impure before they ate, any food they touched would also be ritually impure. So the Law required them to wash their hands before eating.

7:4 *washing of cups, pitchers and kettles:* Traditional Jewish teaching said that anything that had been bought in the market or things that had the chance of being made impure by coming into contact with impure things needed to be washed. See also the mini-article called "Purity (Clean and Unclean)," p. 2125.

7:6 *Isaiah:* See the note at 1:2.

7:11 *devoted to God:* According to Jewish custom, when people said something was devoted to God, it belonged solely to God and could not then be given to anyone else. The teachers of the law said that everything they owned had been devoted to God. That's why they wouldn't use what they had given to God to help their parents. By adhering to this custom they were breaking one of the Ten Commandments (see Deut 5:16).

make him 'unclean' by going into him. Rather, it is what comes out of a man that makes him 'unclean.'[a]"

17After he had left the crowd and entered the house, his disciples asked him about this parable. 18"Are you so dull?" he asked. "Don't you see that nothing that enters a man from the outside can make him 'unclean'? 19For it doesn't go into his heart but into his stomach, and then out of his body." (In saying this, Jesus declared all foods "clean.")

20He went on: "What comes out of a man is what makes him 'unclean.' 21For from within, out of men's hearts, come evil thoughts, sexual immorality, theft, murder, adultery, 22greed, malice, deceit, lewdness, envy, slander, arrogance and folly. 23All these evils come from inside and make a man 'unclean.'"

The Faith of a Syrophoenician Woman

24Jesus left that place and went to the vicinity of Tyre.[b] He entered a house and did not want anyone to know it; yet he could not keep his presence secret. 25In fact, as soon as she heard about him, a woman whose little daughter was possessed by an evil[c] spirit came and fell at his feet. 26The woman was a Greek, born in Syrian Phoenicia. She begged Jesus to drive the demon out of her daughter.

27"First let the children eat all they want," he told her, "for it is not right to take the children's bread and toss it to their dogs."

28"Yes, Lord," she replied, "but even the dogs under the table eat the children's crumbs."

29Then he told her, "For such a reply, you may go; the demon has left your daughter."

30She went home and found her child lying on the bed, and the demon gone.

The Healing of a Deaf and Mute Man

31Then Jesus left the vicinity of Tyre and went through Sidon, down to the Sea of Galilee and into the region of the Decapolis.[d] 32There some people brought to him a man who was deaf and could hardly talk, and they begged him to place his hand on the man.

33After he took him aside, away from the crowd, Jesus put his fingers into the man's ears. Then he spit and touched the man's tongue. 34He looked up to heaven and with a deep sigh said to him, "*Ephphatha!*" (which means, "Be opened!"). 35At this, the man's ears were opened, his tongue was loosened and he began to speak plainly.

36Jesus commanded them not to tell anyone. But the more

---

[a]15 Some early manuscripts *'unclean.'* **16***If anyone has ears to hear, let him hear.*
[b]24 Many early manuscripts *Tyre and Sidon* **[c]25** Greek *unclean* **[d]31** That is, the Ten Cities

7:15,16 *unclean:* The Law of Moses taught that what people ate and touched could make them unclean, and therefore unfit to worship God. But Jesus said that what people eat doesn't make them unclean. Rather, it's what they say, because their words reflect what they believe. See the mini-article called "Purity (Clean and Unclean)," p. 2125.

7:24 *vicinity of Tyre:* See the note at 3:7, 8 and the map on p. 2473.

7:25 *evil spirit:* See the note at 3:30.

7:26 *Greek . . . Syrian Phoenicia:* The woman was a Gentile (not Jewish). Phoenicia was a narrow strip of land along the eastern coast of the Mediterranean Sea. Most of the people who lived there were non-Jews, and many made their living as sailors, merchants, and fishermen. See the map on p. 2473.

7:27 *toss it to their dogs:* Some Jewish people in the time of Jesus unkindly referred to Gentiles as dogs.

7:29 *demon:* See the note at 3:30.

7:31 *Sidon:* For more about Sidon, see the note at 3:7,8 and on the map on p. 1603.

7:31 *Decapolis:* See the note at 5:20.

7:34 *Ephphatha:* This word is in Aramaic, a language spoken in Palestine during the time of Jesus (see the note at 5:41, 42).

7:36 *not to tell anyone:* See the note at 1:44.

7:6,7 Isa 29:13. **7:10** Exod 20:12; 21:17; Lev 20:9; Deut 5:16.

8:4 *remote place . . . four thousand men:* See the note at 6:35. This is a separate event from that recorded in 6:30-44, and is perhaps included to show how slow Jesus' disciples were to learn who Jesus was and what he could do. This is a separate event from that recorded in 6:30-44.

8:5 *loaves:* See the note at 6:38.

8:6 *given thanks . . . broke them:* See the note at 6:41.

8:8,9 *seven basketfuls:* Seven was a sacred number in the ancient Near East. It symbolized completeness or perfection. See also the chart called "Numbers in the Bible," p. 2405.

8:10 *Dalmanutha:* Probably located on the west coast of the Sea of Galilee, though its exact location is not known.

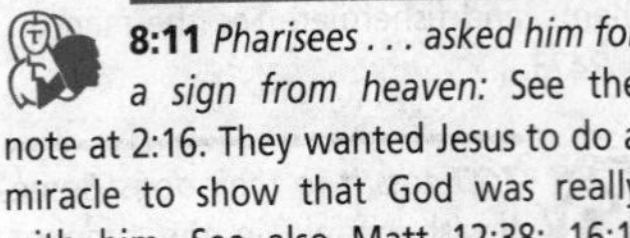

8:11 *Pharisees . . . asked him for a sign from heaven:* See the note at 2:16. They wanted Jesus to do a miracle to show that God was really with him. See also Matt 12:38; 16:1; Luke 11:16.

8:15 *the yeast of the Pharisees and that of Herod:* Yeast (Leaven) is a tiny yellowish fungus. When it is mixed with water and flour, it causes the dough to rise, so the bread will not be flat when baked. Bread that has no yeast, or leaven, is called unleavened bread.

Jesus was saying that the teaching of the Pharisees and the actions of Herod Antipas (see the notes at 2:16 and 3:6) affect the whole people of God just as yeast affects a whole batch of dough. See also Luke 12:1.

8:22 *Bethsaida:* See the note at 6:45.

8:12 Matt 12:39; Luke 11:29. **8:18** Jer 5:21; Ezek 12:2; Mark 4:12.

he did so, the more they kept talking about it. 37People were overwhelmed with amazement. "He has done everything well," they
said. "He even makes the deaf hear and the mute speak."

Jesus Feeds the Four Thousand

8 During those days another large crowd gathered. Since they
had nothing to eat, Jesus called his disciples to him and said, 2"I
have compassion for these people; they have already been with me
three days and have nothing to eat. 3If I send them home hungry,
they will collapse on the way, because some of them have come a
long distance."

4His disciples answered, "But where in this remote place can
anyone get enough bread to feed them?"

5"How many loaves do you have?" Jesus asked.

"Seven," they replied.

6He told the crowd to sit down on the ground. When he had
taken the seven loaves and given thanks, he broke them and gave
them to his disciples to set before the people, and they did so.
7They had a few small fish as well; he gave thanks for them also
and told the disciples to distribute them. 8The people ate and were
satisfied. Afterward the disciples picked up seven basketfuls of broken pieces that were left over. 9About four thousand men were
present. And having sent them away, 10he got into the boat with his
disciples and went to the region of Dalmanutha.

11The Pharisees came and began to question Jesus. To test
him, they asked him for a sign from heaven. 12He sighed deeply
and said, "Why does this generation ask for a miraculous sign? I
tell you the truth, no sign will be given to it." 13Then he left them,
got back into the boat and crossed to the other side.

The Yeast of the Pharisees and Herod

14The disciples had forgotten to bring bread, except for one
loaf they had with them in the boat. 15"Be careful," Jesus warned
them. "Watch out for the yeast of the Pharisees and that of Herod."

16They discussed this with one another and said, "It is
because we have no bread."

17Aware of their discussion, Jesus asked them: "Why are you
talking about having no bread? Do you still not see or understand?
Are your hearts hardened? 18Do you have eyes but fail to see, and
ears but fail to hear? And don't you remember? 19When I broke the
five loaves for the five thousand, how many basketfuls of pieces did
you pick up?"

"Twelve," they replied.

20"And when I broke the seven loaves for the four thousand,
how many basketfuls of pieces did you pick up?"

They answered, "Seven."

21He said to them, "Do you still not understand?"

The Healing of a Blind Man at Bethsaida

[22]They came to Bethsaida, and some people brought a blind
man and begged Jesus to touch him. [23]He took the blind man by
the hand and led him outside the village. When he had spit on the
man's eyes and put his hands on him, Jesus asked, "Do you see
anything?"
[24]He looked up and said, "I see people; they look like trees
walking around."
[25]Once more Jesus put his hands on the man's eyes. Then his
eyes were opened, his sight was restored, and he saw everything
clearly. [26]Jesus sent him home, saying, "Don't go into the village.[a]"

JESUS IS THE MESSIAH

The focus in this section (8:27—9:13) is on how Jesus identifies himself and his mission, and on how God identifies Jesus as his Son while glorifying him on the mountain.

Peter's Confession of Christ

[27]Jesus and his disciples went on to the villages around Caesarea Philippi. On the way he asked them, "Who do people say
I am?"
[28]They replied, "Some say John the Baptist; others say Elijah;
and still others, one of the prophets."
[29]"But what about you?" he asked. "Who do you say I am?"
Peter answered, "You are the Christ.[b]"
[30]Jesus warned them not to tell anyone about him.

Jesus Predicts His Death

[31]He then began to teach them that the Son of Man must
suffer many things and be rejected by the elders, chief priests and
teachers of the law, and that he must be killed and after three days
rise again. [32]He spoke plainly about this, and Peter took him aside
and began to rebuke him.
[33]But when Jesus turned and looked at his disciples, he
rebuked Peter. "Get behind me, Satan!" he said. "You do not have
in mind the things of God, but the things of men."
[34]Then he called the crowd to him along with his disciples
and said: "If anyone would come after me, he must deny himself
and take up his cross and follow me. [35]For whoever wants to save
his life[c] will lose it, but whoever loses his life for me and for the
gospel will save it. [36]What good is it for a man to gain the whole
world, yet forfeit his soul? [37]Or what can a man give in exchange

[a]**26** Some manuscripts *Don't go and tell anyone in the village* [b]**29** Or *Messiah.* "The Christ" (Greek) and "the Messiah" (Hebrew) both mean "the Anointed One." [c]**35** The Greek word means either *life* or *soul*; also in verse 36.

8:27 *Caesarea Philippi:* This city was located about twenty-five miles north of the Sea of Galilee.

8:28 *John the Baptist . . . Elijah . . . one of the prophets:* See the notes at 1:4 (John) and 6:15. See also Mark 6:14,15; Luke 9:7,8. For more on the "prophets," see the article called "Prophets and Prophecy," p. 935.

8:29 *Christ:* This word in Greek is *Christos.* Both *Christos* and the Hebrew word *Messiah* mean "Anointed One" or "Chosen One." See the mini-article called "Messiah (Chosen One)," p. 1124. When Peter calls Jesus the Christ, this means that Jesus was the Messiah, God's Chosen One. Compare this passage with John 6:66- 69.

8:30 *warned them not to tell anyone about him:* Even though Peter has identified Jesus as the Messiah, Jesus does not want the disciples to tell this to others. For "teachers of the law," see the note at 1:44.

8:31 *Son of Man . . . rejected . . . killed . . . rise again:* See the mini-article called "Son of Man," p. 1866. Jesus was talking about his trial, his death on a cross, and the fact that God would bring him back to life.

8:31 *rejected by the elders, chief priests and teachers of the law:* The chief priests and other leaders, like the Pharisees and Sadducees, formed a council called the Sanhedrin, which the Romans gave the right to make decisions about local matters (14:53,55). See the note at 12:38.

8:32 *Peter:* See the note at 1:16 (Simon).

8:33 *Satan:* See the note at 1:13. Jesus uses strong language to make his point—to avoid doing God's will would be to do the work of Satan.

8:34 *cross:* See the note at 15:13.

8:34 Matt 10:38; Luke 14:27.
8:35 Matt 10:39; Luke 17:33; John 12:25.

8:38 *sinful generation:* See the note at 1:4 (baptism).

8:38 *Son of Man . . . comes in his Father's glory with the holy angels:* See the mini-article called "Son of Man," p. 1866. See also the note at 1:13 (angels). Jesus referred to the God of Israel as his "Father."

9:1 *some who are standing here will not taste death before they see the kingdom of God:* See the note at 1:15. Jesus may be referring to how God would reveal Jesus in all his glory on the mountain (9:2-8), or to Jesus' death and resurrection followed by the coming of the Holy Spirit with power (Acts 2:1-4).

9:2 *Peter, James and John:* See the notes at 1:16 (Simon) and 1:19. These three disciples are often with Jesus at important times (5:37; 13:3; 14:33).

9:4 *Elijah and Moses:* God chose Moses to lead the Hebrew people out of slavery in Egypt (Exod 3–14) and to receive the Ten Commandments. See also the mini-article called "Moses," p. 2335. Elijah was a prophet who encouraged the people of Israel to worship God. See the mini-article called "Elijah," p. 1816. Moses and Elijah represented the most important parts of the Jewish Scriptures: the Law and the Prophets. These two leaders were chosen to tell God's people to live a new way of life, just as Jesus was telling his disciples.

9:5 *shelters:* Peter wanted the moment of glory on the mountain to continue.

9:2-7 2 Pet 1:17,18.

Transfiguration, Fra Angelico, about 1448. There are around fifty frescoes of New Testament subjects by Fra Angelico in the Museum of San Marco, Florence, Italy (see also the illustration on p. 1859). In this painting of the Transfiguration, three apostles, Peter, James, and John, see Jesus' true glory as he talks with two of the greatest Old Testament prophets, Moses and Elijah (see 9:2-4). In addition, the artist took the liberty of including Jesus' mother Mary and an unidentified church figure in his interpretation of this biblical event.

for his soul? 38 If anyone is ashamed of me and my words in this adulterous and sinful generation, the Son of Man will be ashamed of him when he comes in his Father's glory with the holy angels."

9 And he said to them, "I tell you the truth, some who are standing here will not taste death before they see the kingdom of God come with power."

The Transfiguration

2 After six days Jesus took Peter, James and John with him and led them up a high mountain, where they were all alone. There he was transfigured before them. 3 His clothes became dazzling white, whiter than anyone in the world could bleach them.
4 And there appeared before them Elijah and Moses, who were talking with Jesus.

5 Peter said to Jesus, "Rabbi, it is good for us to be here. Let us
put up three shelters—one for you, one for Moses and one for Elijah." 6 (He did not know what to say, they were so frightened.)
7 Then a cloud appeared and enveloped them, and a voice
came from the cloud: "This is my Son, whom I love. Listen to him!"
8 Suddenly, when they looked around, they no longer saw
anyone with them except Jesus.
9 As they were coming down the mountain, Jesus gave them
orders not to tell anyone what they had seen until the Son of Man
had risen from the dead. 10 They kept the matter to themselves, discussing what "rising from the dead" meant.
11 And they asked him, "Why do the teachers of the law say
that Elijah must come first?"
12 Jesus replied, "To be sure, Elijah does come first, and
restores all things. Why then is it written that the Son of Man must
suffer much and be rejected? 13 But I tell you, Elijah has come, and
they have done to him everything they wished, just as it is written
about him."

MORE WORK IN GALILEE

The Healing of a Boy With an Evil Spirit

14 When they came to the other disciples, they saw a large
crowd around them and the teachers of the law arguing with them.
15 As soon as all the people saw Jesus, they were overwhelmed with
wonder and ran to greet him.
16 "What are you arguing with them about?" he asked.
17 A man in the crowd answered, "Teacher, I brought you my
son, who is possessed by a spirit that has robbed him of speech.
18 Whenever it seizes him, it throws him to the ground. He foams at
the mouth, gnashes his teeth and becomes rigid. I asked your disciples to drive out the spirit, but they could not."
19 "O unbelieving generation," Jesus replied, "how long shall
I stay with you? How long shall I put up with you? Bring the boy
to me."
20 So they brought him. When the spirit saw Jesus, it immediately threw the boy into a convulsion. He fell to the ground and
rolled around, foaming at the mouth.
21 Jesus asked the boy's father, "How long has he been like
this?"
"From childhood," he answered. 22 "It has often thrown him
into fire or water to kill him. But if you can do anything, take pity
on us and help us."
23 " 'If you can'?" said Jesus. "Everything is possible for him
who believes."
24 Immediately the boy's father exclaimed, "I do believe; help
me overcome my unbelief!"

Then a cloud appeared and enveloped them, and a voice came from the cloud: "This is my Son, whom I love. Listen to him!"
Mark 9:7

9:9 *not to tell . . . until the Son of Man had risen:* See the notes at 1:44 and the mini-article called "Son of Man," p. 1866. Jesus knew that the Jewish people expected the Messiah to be a political leader who would rule the country, or who would be a miracle-worker. But Jesus' true mission would only be completed when he died to defeat sin and overcame death by being raised to life.

9:11 *Elijah must come first:* See the note at 6:15. Since the prophet Elijah was expected to return before God's Messiah appeared, many may have wondered: If Jesus is the Messiah, why haven't we seen Elijah?

9:12 *Why then is it written:* In the Jewish Scriptures, which Christians call the Old Testament.

9:12,13 *Elijah does come first . . . Elijah has come:* See the note at 6:15. When Jesus says that Elijah has already come and been mistreated (9:13), he was talking about John the Baptist (Matt 11:14). See also 1 Kgs 19:2, 10.

9:14 *the other disciples:* Only Peter, James, and John had gone up on the mountain with Jesus (see 9:2). Now they are returning to the rest of the twelve disciples.

9:17 *possessed by a spirit:* See the note at 3:30. The boy appears to have been having some kind of epileptic seizures.

9:7 Matt 3:17; Mark 1:11; Luke 3:22.

9:30 *Galilee:* Galilee was the northern part of Palestine west of the Jordan River (see the note at 1:5) and the Sea of Galilee. The area was part of the northern kingdom of Israel that the Assyrians conquered in 722 B.C. Later, it was ruled by the Babylonians, Persians, Greeks, and Syrians. In 63 B.C., the Romans made it part of their empire and ruled it during the time Jesus lived. Jesus grew up in Nazareth (Matt 2:19-23), a small town that is never mentioned in the Old Testament. See the map on p. 2472 for the location of Nazareth in Galilee. See the note at 1:5.

9:31 *Son of Man:* See the mini-article called "Son of Man," p. 1866. Compare this passage to 8:31. The disciples did not understand why Jesus had to die (9:32).

9:33 *Capernaum:* See the note at 1:21 (Capernaum).

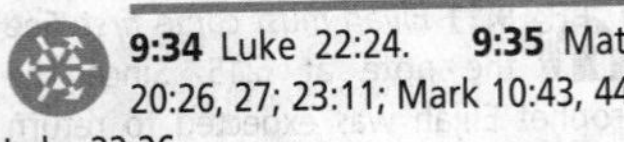

9:34 Luke 22:24. **9:35** Matt 20:26, 27; 23:11; Mark 10:43, 44; Luke 22:26.

25 When Jesus saw that a crowd was running to the scene, he
rebuked the evil[a] spirit. "You deaf and mute spirit," he said, "I command you, come out of him and never enter him again."
26 The spirit shrieked, convulsed him violently and came out. The
boy looked so much like a corpse that many said, "He's dead." 27 But
Jesus took him by the hand and lifted him to his feet, and he stood up.
28 After Jesus had gone indoors, his disciples asked him privately, "Why couldn't we drive it out?"
29 He replied, "This kind can come out only by prayer.[b]"
30 They left that place and passed through Galilee. Jesus did
not want anyone to know where they were, 31 because he was teaching his disciples. He said to them, "The Son of Man is going to be betrayed into the hands of men. They will kill him, and after three
days he will rise." 32 But they did not understand what he meant and were afraid to ask him about it.

Who Is the Greatest?

33 They came to Capernaum. When he was in the house, he
asked them, "What were you arguing about on the road?" 34 But
they kept quiet because on the way they had argued about who was the greatest.
35 Sitting down, Jesus called the Twelve and said, "If anyone wants to be first, he must be the very last, and the servant of all."

[a]25 Greek *unclean* [b]29 Some manuscripts *prayer and fasting*

QUESTIONS ABOUT MARK 1:1—9:50

1. MARK begins with the words, "The beginning of the gospel about Jesus Christ." What exactly is this "gospel"? Give two or three examples from the first nine chapters to support your definition.
2. MARK tells how Jesus healed many people. For example, read 1:40-45. Whom did Jesus heal? What did he tell the man not to do? Why? What happened anyway?
3. Read 3:1-6. What did Jesus do that made the Pharisees angry? What is the answer to Jesus' question in 3:4? Why?
4. Jesus used parables (stories) to teach the good news. Chapter 4 has three parables about seeds and planting. How is the message similar in each story? What is the key message? Why did Jesus use an example like planting seeds to teach his message? Think about where you live: What images or examples from everyday life could Jesus use to teach his message effectively to you and your friends?
5. Why was it difficult for Jesus to teach in his hometown of Nazareth? (6:1-6) Do you think it is still difficult today for religious leaders to be effective teachers or preachers in their home area? Why or why not?
6. Read 8:31-38. What surprising news did Jesus tell the disciples? What was Peter's reaction? Why do you think he reacted the way he did? What was Jesus' response to Peter? Share the meaning of 8:34, 35 in your own words.
7. Read 9:33-35. How does Jesus' teaching go against what our modern world often teaches? Is Jesus' teaching easy or difficult to follow? Why?

[36]He took a little child and had him stand among them. Taking him in his arms, he said to them, [37]"Whoever welcomes one of
these little children in my name welcomes me; and whoever welcomes me does not welcome me but the one who sent me."

Whoever Is Not Against Us Is for Us

[38]"Teacher," said John, "we saw a man driving out demons in
your name and we told him to stop, because he was not one of us."
[39]"Do not stop him," Jesus said. "No one who does a miracle
in my name can in the next moment say anything bad about me,
[40]for whoever is not against us is for us. [41]I tell you the truth, anyone who gives you a cup of water in my name because you belong
to Christ will certainly not lose his reward.

Causing to Sin

[42]"And if anyone causes one of these little ones who believe in
me to sin, it would be better for him to be thrown into the sea with a
large millstone tied around his neck. [43]If your hand causes you to sin,
cut it off. It is better for you to enter life maimed than with two hands
to go into hell, where the fire never goes out.[a] [45]And if your foot causes
you to sin, cut it off. It is better for you to enter life crippled than to
have two feet and be thrown into hell.[b] [47]And if your eye causes you
to sin, pluck it out. It is better for you to enter the kingdom of God
with one eye than to have two eyes and be thrown into hell, [48]where

" 'their worm does not die,
and the fire is not quenched.'[c]

[49]Everyone will be salted with fire.
[50]"Salt is good, but if it loses its saltiness, how can you make
it salty again? Have salt in yourselves, and be at peace with each
other."

Jesus Ministers in Judea

The scene now shifts to Judea as Jesus prepares to go to Jerusalem, where he knows he must suffer and die. Before this happens, there is more teaching and miracle-working to be done.

Divorce

10 Jesus then left that place and went into the region of Judea
and across the Jordan. Again crowds of people came to him, and as
was his custom, he taught them.

[a]**43** Some manuscripts *out,* **44***where /* " *'their worm does not die, / and the fire is not quenched.'* [b]**45** Some manuscripts *hell,* **46***where /* " *'their worm does not die, / and the fire is not quenched.'* [c]**48** Isaiah 66:24

9:35 *the Twelve:* See the note at 3:14-19.

9:36 *a little child:* See the note at 10:13.

9:38 *demons:* See the note at 3:30. Jesus had given his twelve apostles power over the demons (3:14, 15; 6:7).

9:42 *sin:* See the note at 1:4 (baptism of repentance).

9:42 *large millstone:* This refers to a heavy stone that was pulled by a mule in order to crush grain stalks and separate the grain (seeds) from the chaff.

9:43-48 *hand . . . cut it off . . . eye . . . pluck it out . . . fire is not quenched:* Sometimes Jesus used bold expressions to emphasize the truth of what he was saying. He wanted to make it clear that the physical pain of losing a hand or an eye is nothing compared to the pain of being in the fires of hell. See also Matt 5:30.

In the New Testament, the place of judgment for evildoers is often pictured as a place of fiery torture (Matt 5:22; Luke 16:23, 24; Rev 20:14). See also the mini-articles called "Fire," p. 2383 and "Hell," p. 1944.

9:50 *Salt:* Salt was used to preserve foods and add flavor to them. "Have salt in yourselves" could refer to how Christ's followers add the flavor of peace to their lives together. See also Matt 5:13.

10:1 *Judea . . . Jordan:* See the note at 1:5.

9:37 Matt 10:40; Luke 10:16; John 13:20. **9:40** Matt 12:30; Luke 11:23. **9:41** Matt 10:42. **9:47** Matt 5:29. **9:48** Isa 66:24. **9:50** Matt 5:13.

10:4 *certificate of divorce:* The Law of Moses allowed a man to write out legal papers to divorce his wife if she became "displeasing to him" (Deut 24:1-4; Matt 5:31). Writing these papers was designed to make it harder for a man to divorce his wife. Jesus uses the creation story to explain how important marriage is (Gen 1:27, 28; 2:18-24).

10:11,12 *Anyone who divorces his wife . . . if she divorces her husband:* Roman law let a woman divorce her husband, but the Law of Moses did not.

10:6 Gen 1:27; 5:2. **10:7,8** Gen 2:24. **10:11,12** Matt 5:32; 1 Cor 7:10, 11.

2 Some Pharisees came and tested him by asking, "Is it lawful
for a man to divorce his wife?"
3 "What did Moses command you?" he replied.
4 They said, "Moses permitted a man to write a certificate of
divorce and send her away."
5 "It was because your hearts were hard that Moses wrote you
this law," Jesus replied. 6 "But at the beginning of creation God
'made them male and female.'[a] 7 'For this reason a man will leave
his father and mother and be united to his wife,[b] 8 and the two will
become one flesh.'[c] So they are no longer two, but one. 9 Therefore
what God has joined together, let man not separate."
10 When they were in the house again, the disciples asked
Jesus about this. 11 He answered, "Anyone who divorces his wife and

[a] **6** Gen. 1:27 [b] **7** Some early manuscripts do not have *and be united to his wife.*
[c] **8** Gen. 2:24

HELL

The word "hell" only appears in the New Testament and is almost always a translation of the Greek word *Gehenna*, which comes from the Hebrew word *Gehinnom* found in the Old Testament. *Gehinnom* means "Valley of Ben Hinnom." This narrow valley is located south and west of Jerusalem and runs into the Kidron Valley. During the time of Israel's kings, this valley became the site of a worship place known as *Topheth*, which in Aramaic means "fireplace." Some Israelites and their kings disobeyed God and worshiped the god Molech at this place. This worship of Molech included sacrificing children by throwing them into the fire and burning them to death (Lev 18:21; 20:2-5; Jer 32:35). For this terrible sin, the prophet Jeremiah said that this place would one day be known as the Valley of Slaughter (Jer 7:31, 32; 19:6).

In the two hundred years before Jesus was born, some Jewish teachers said that the place where wicked people go when they die is like the burning Valley of Ben Hinnom. The Greek word used to describe this place is *Gehenna*. Because the word *Gehenna* (hell) is always used in the New Testament to describe a place of fiery death and punishment, it has a different meaning than the Hebrew *Sheol* or the Greek *Hades*. These words refer to the dark place where all the dead go (Job 30:23; Ezek 31:16-18; Acts 2:27), or where the dead wait for God's final judgment (Rev 20:13). *Sheol* (*Hades*) is a place somewhere under the earth that is totally silent and where no one knows or feels anything (Job 10:21, 22; Ps 88:12; 94:17). Punishment and torture are not connected with *Sheol*.

In the New Testament, hell (*Gehenna*) is the place of judgment where God sends evildoers to face fiery torture and everlasting punishment (Matt 5:22; Luke 16:23, 24; Rev 20:14, 15). It is pictured as a fiery furnace (Matt 13:42, 50), a fire that never goes out (Mark 9:43, 44), a lake of fire (Rev 20:14, 15), and an eternal fire prepared for the devil and his angels (Matt 25:41). Jesus warned people that they might end up in hell for their sins (Matt 23:13-15, 29-33; Mark 9:45-48; Luke 12:5), and the book of JAMES warns that the human tongue can be used to speak evil, setting a person's entire life on fire with flames that come from hell (Jas 3:6).

marries another woman commits adultery against her. [12]And if she divorces her husband and marries another man, she commits adultery."

The Little Children and Jesus

[13]People were bringing little children to Jesus to have him touch them, but the disciples rebuked them. [14]When Jesus saw this, he was indignant. He said to them, "Let the little children come to me, and do not hinder them, for the kingdom of God belongs to such as these. [15]I tell you the truth, anyone who will not receive the kingdom of God like a little child will never enter it." [16]And he took the children in his arms, put his hands on them and blessed them.

The Rich Young Man

[17]As Jesus started on his way, a man ran up to him and fell on his knees before him. "Good teacher," he asked, "what must I do to inherit eternal life?"

[18]"Why do you call me good?" Jesus answered. "No one is good—except God alone. [19]You know the commandments: 'Do not murder, do not commit adultery, do not steal, do not give false testimony, do not defraud, honor your father and mother.'[a]"

[20]"Teacher," he declared, "all these I have kept since I was a boy."

[21]Jesus looked at him and loved him. "One thing you lack," he said. "Go, sell everything you have and give to the poor, and you will have treasure in heaven. Then come, follow me."

[22]At this the man's face fell. He went away sad, because he had great wealth.

[23]Jesus looked around and said to his disciples, "How hard it is for the rich to enter the kingdom of God!"

[24]The disciples were amazed at his words. But Jesus said again, "Children, how hard it is[b] to enter the kingdom of God! [25]It is easier for a camel to go through the eye of a needle than for a rich man to enter the kingdom of God."

[26]The disciples were even more amazed, and said to each other, "Who then can be saved?"

[27]Jesus looked at them and said, "With man this is impossible, but not with God; all things are possible with God."

[28]Peter said to him, "We have left everything to follow you!"

[29]"I tell you the truth," Jesus replied, "no one who has left home or brothers or sisters or mother or father or children or fields for me and the gospel [30]will fail to receive a hundred times as much in this present age (homes, brothers, sisters, mothers,

[a]**19** Exodus 20:12-16; Deut. 5:16-20 [b]**24** Some manuscripts *is for those who trust in riches*

10:13 *children:* Jesus used children as an example because they were not considered powerful or wise like adults. Jesus wanted to show that being wise or powerful is not the way to get into the kingdom of God. Being humble and faithful is (10:15).

10:16 *put his hands on them and blessed them:* By holding the children and touching them, Jesus showed that they were full members of God's family.

10:17 *eternal life:* By the time of Jesus, many Jewish people had come to believe in and hope for life after death. But some, like the Sadducees, did not accept the concept of eternal life, because they believed that it was not specifically mentioned in the Law of Moses. For more, see the mini-article called "Eternal Life," p. 2072.

10:23 *How hard it is for the rich to enter the kingdom of God:* The wealthy were considered to be blessed by God, especially if they had lived according to the Law of Moses. But Jesus warns that having wealth can actually make it harder for people to get into God's kingdom, especially for those who trust their wealth instead of God. See the note at 1:15.

10:25 *a camel to go through the eye of a needle:* Camels are large animals used to transport heavy loads of valuable merchandise long distances. Jesus' outlandish statement emphasized the point he was making.

10:26,27 *saved . . . With man this is impossible, but not with God:* Salvation is a gift from God. It cannot be bought with wealth but comes through the sacrifice Jesus made to redeem sinners (see the note at 10:45). See also the mini-article called "Salvation," p. 2021.

10:15 Matt 18:3. **10:19 a** Exod 20:13; Deut 5:17; **b** Exod 20:14; Deut 5:18; **c** Exod 20:15; Deut 5:19; **d** Exod 20:16; Deut 5:20; **e** Exod 20:12; Deut 5:16.

10:29,30 *the age to come:* The "age to come" may be heaven, or it may be a future time when Jesus returns to gather his chosen ones from all over the earth (13:26,27).

10:32 *Jerusalem:* See the note at 1:5.

10:32 *the disciples:* See the note at 3:14-19.

10:33 *Son of Man will be betrayed . . . chief priests and teachers of the law . . . Gentiles:* See the notes at 8:31 and 12:38. "Gentiles" here refers to the Romans who then ruled Judea.

10:35 *James and John, the sons of Zebedee:* See the notes at 1:19 and 9:2.

10:37 *at your right . . . left:* The most powerful people in the kingdom sat closest to the king.

10:38 *drink the cup . . . the baptism I am baptized with:* In the Scriptures a "cup" is sometimes used as a symbol of suffering. To "drink the cup" means to suffer. Baptism is used with the same meaning that "cup" has in this verse. See also Luke 12:50.

10:44 *slave:* See the mini-article called "Slaves and Servants in the Time of Jesus," p. 2006.

10:45 *ransom:* The cost of redeeming or buying back someone who had been sold into slavery. See the mini-article called "Redeemer (Redemption)," p. 995. Jesus is saying that the sacrifice he would make for sinful humanity would redeem them from their slavery to sin.

10:46 *Jericho:* Jericho is located about thirty miles northeast of Jerusalem and about six miles north of the Dead Sea. See the map on p. 2473.

10:47 *Son of David:* The Jewish people expected the Messiah to be from the family of King David. For this reason the Messiah was often referred to as the "Son of David."

children and fields—and with them, persecutions) and in the age
to come, eternal life. 31 But many who are first will be last, and the
last first."

Jesus Again Predicts His Death

32 They were on their way up to Jerusalem, with Jesus leading
the way, and the disciples were astonished, while those who followed
were afraid. Again he took the Twelve aside and told them what was
going to happen to him. 33 "We are going up to Jerusalem," he said,
"and the Son of Man will be betrayed to the chief priests and teachers of the law. They will condemn him to death and will hand him
over to the Gentiles, 34 who will mock him and spit on him, flog him
and kill him. Three days later he will rise."

The Request of James and John

35 Then James and John, the sons of Zebedee, came to him.
"Teacher," they said, "we want you to do for us whatever we ask."
36 "What do you want me to do for you?" he asked.
37 They replied, "Let one of us sit at your right and the other
at your left in your glory."
38 "You don't know what you are asking," Jesus said. "Can you
drink the cup I drink or be baptized with the baptism I am baptized with?"
39 "We can," they answered.
Jesus said to them, "You will drink the cup I drink and be
baptized with the baptism I am baptized with, 40 but to sit at my
right or left is not for me to grant. These places belong to those for
whom they have been prepared."
41 When the ten heard about this, they became indignant
with James and John. 42 Jesus called them together and said, "You
know that those who are regarded as rulers of the Gentiles lord it
over them, and their high officials exercise authority over them.
43 Not so with you. Instead, whoever wants to become great among
you must be your servant, 44 and whoever wants to be first must be
slave of all. 45 For even the Son of Man did not come to be served,
but to serve, and to give his life as a ransom for many."

Blind Bartimaeus Receives His Sight

46 Then they came to Jericho. As Jesus and his disciples,
together with a large crowd, were leaving the city, a blind man,
Bartimaeus (that is, the Son of Timaeus), was sitting by the roadside begging. 47 When he heard that it was Jesus of Nazareth, he
began to shout, "Jesus, Son of David, have mercy on me!"
48 Many rebuked him and told him to be quiet, but he shouted all the more, "Son of David, have mercy on me!"
49 Jesus stopped and said, "Call him."
So they called to the blind man, "Cheer up! On your feet!

He's calling you." [50]Throwing his cloak aside, he jumped to his feet
and came to Jesus.
[51]"What do you want me to do for you?" Jesus asked him.
The blind man said, "Rabbi, I want to see."
[52]"Go," said Jesus, "your faith has healed you." Immediately
he received his sight and followed Jesus along the road.

Jesus in Jerusalem

As he had earlier predicted three times (8:31; 9:31; and 10:32-34), Jesus now enters Jerusalem, knowing that he will face suffering and death. Before this happens, he spends time teaching his followers about many things and gives his closest disciples a vision of what will happen in the future (13:1-37).

TEACHINGS IN THE TEMPLE

After entering Jerusalem to the shouts of an excited crowd, Jesus spends time teaching in the temple area.

The Triumphal Entry

11 As they approached Jerusalem and came to Bethphage and
Bethany at the Mount of Olives, Jesus sent two of his disciples, [2]say-
ing to them, "Go to the village ahead of you, and just as you enter it,
you will find a colt tied there, which no one has ever ridden. Untie
it and bring it here. [3]If anyone asks you, 'Why are you doing this?'
tell him, 'The Lord needs it and will send it back here shortly.' "
[4]They went and found a colt outside in the street, tied at a
doorway. As they untied it, [5]some people standing there asked,
"What are you doing, untying that colt?" [6]They answered as Jesus
had told them to, and the people let them go. [7]When they brought
the colt to Jesus and threw their cloaks over it, he sat on it. [8]Many
people spread their cloaks on the road, while others spread
branches they had cut in the fields. [9]Those who went ahead and
those who followed shouted,

"Hosanna![a]"

"Blessed is he who comes in the name of the Lord!"[b]

[10]"Blessed is the coming kingdom of our father David!"

"Hosanna in the highest!"

[11]Jesus entered Jerusalem and went to the temple. He looked
around at everything, but since it was already late, he went out to
Bethany with the Twelve.

---

a9 A Hebrew expression meaning "Save!" which became an exclamation of praise; also in verse 10 **b9** Psalm 118:25,26

10:51 *Rabbi:* The blind man used the Aramaic term *Rabboni*, which in English means "my teacher."

10:52 *faith:* See 5:34 and the mini-article called "Faith," p. 1932.

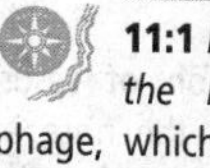

11:1 *Bethphage and Bethany at the Mount of Olives:* Bethphage, which means "house of figs," was a little village on the road from Jericho approaching Jerusalem. Bethany, a small village about two miles east of Jerusalem, is on the slopes of the Mount of Olives.

The Mount of Olives is a ridge about two and a half miles long and is part of a larger mountain range that runs north and south through central and southern Palestine. Its name comes from the olive trees that grew on its slopes. It is located about half a mile east of the temple area in Jerusalem. Because it was about 300 to 500 feet higher than the temple area, it was a perfect place for Jesus to show his disciples the temple area while he taught them what was going to happen to the temple (13:3). See the maps on pp. 2473 and 2474.

11:2 *a colt:* See Zechariah 9:9, which predicts the coming of Israel's king on "a colt, the foal of a donkey."

11:8 *spread their cloaks . . . spread branches:* This was one way that the Jewish people welcomed a famous person.

11:10 *coming kingdom of our father David:* See the note at 10:47.

11:11 *Jerusalem . . . temple:* See the note at 13:1.

10:31 Matt 20:16; Luke 13:30. **10:33,34** Mark 8:31; 9:31. **10:42,43** Luke 22:25,26. **10:43,44** Matt 23:11; Mark 9:35; Luke 22:26. **11:9** Ps 118:25,26.

11:13,14 *fig tree . . . no one ever eat fruit from you again:* In Jesus' day the fruit (figs) that grew on this tree was an important source of food. The first fig crop ripens in June and is eaten fresh. The second crop is harvested about two months later and is usually dried in the sun and eaten during the winter months.

For an explanation of Jesus' cursing the fig tree, see the note at Matt 21:18,19. See 11:20-26 for the effects of Jesus' words and Jesus' teaching about the power of faith.

11:15 *temple . . . buying and selling . . . money changers:* See the note at 13:1. Jewish people came to the temple to buy animals to make a sacrifice to God. Many sellers set up animal pens and cages in the outer court of the temple, and money changers set up tables for those who needed to exchange their money. Sometimes the people selling animals and the money changers cheated their customers. For more, see the mini-article called "Money Changing in the Temple," p. 1894.

11:18 *chief priests and the teachers of the law:* See the notes at 8:31 (elders) and 12:38.

11:17 Isa 56:7; Jer 7:11. **11:23** Matt 17:20; 1 Cor 13:2.

Jesus Clears the Temple

12 The next day as they were leaving Bethany, Jesus was hungry. 13 Seeing in the distance a fig tree in leaf, he went to find out if
it had any fruit. When he reached it, he found nothing but leaves,
because it was not the season for figs. 14 Then he said to the tree,
"May no one ever eat fruit from you again." And his disciples
heard him say it.
15 On reaching Jerusalem, Jesus entered the temple area and
began driving out those who were buying and selling there. He
overturned the tables of the money changers and the benches of
those selling doves, 16 and would not allow anyone to carry merchandise through the temple courts. 17 And as he taught them, he
said, "Is it not written:

" 'My house will be called
a house of prayer for all nations'[a]?

But you have made it 'a den of robbers.'[b]"
18 The chief priests and the teachers of the law heard this and
began looking for a way to kill him, for they feared him, because
the whole crowd was amazed at his teaching.
19 When evening came, they[c] went out of the city.

The Withered Fig Tree

20 In the morning, as they went along, they saw the fig tree
withered from the roots. 21 Peter remembered and said to Jesus,
"Rabbi, look! The fig tree you cursed has withered!"
22 "Have[d] faith in God," Jesus answered. 23 "I tell you the truth, if
anyone says to this mountain, 'Go, throw yourself into the sea,' and
does not doubt in his heart but believes that what he says will happen, it will be done for him. 24 Therefore I tell you, whatever you ask
for in prayer, believe that you have received it, and it will be yours.
25 And when you stand praying, if you hold anything against anyone,
forgive him, so that your Father in heaven may forgive you your sins.[e]"

The Authority of Jesus Questioned

27 They arrived again in Jerusalem, and while Jesus was walking in the temple courts, the chief priests, the teachers of the law
and the elders came to him. 28 "By what authority are you doing
these things?" they asked. "And who gave you authority to do this?"
29 Jesus replied, "I will ask you one question. Answer me, and
I will tell you by what authority I am doing these things. 30 John's
baptism—was it from heaven, or from men? Tell me!"
31 They discussed it among themselves and said, "If we say,

[a]**17** Isaiah 56:7 [b]**17** Jer. 7:11 [c]**19** Some early manuscripts *he* [d]**22** Some early manuscripts *If you have* [e]**25** Some manuscripts *sins.* [26]*But if you do not forgive, neither will your Father who is in heaven forgive your sins.*

Entry into Jerusalem, German, thirteenth century, artist unknown. This painted wooden sculpture on wheels is life-sized and was probably pulled through city streets in Palm Sunday celebrations. Jesus is shown holding a palm leaf in his left hand. His right arm is raised to bless the crowd, just as he might have done when he entered Jerusalem the week before his death. (See 11:1-11.)

'From heaven,' he will ask, 'Then why didn't you believe him?'
32But if we say, 'From men' . . ." (They feared the people, for everyone held that John really was a prophet.)
33So they answered Jesus, "We don't know."

Jesus said, "Neither will I tell you by what authority I am doing these things."

The Parable of the Tenants

12 He then began to speak to them in parables: "A man planted
a vineyard. He put a wall around it, dug a pit for the winepress and
built a watchtower. Then he rented the vineyard to some farmers
and went away on a journey. 2At harvest time he sent a servant to
the tenants to collect from them some of the fruit of the vineyard.

11:20 *fig tree:* See the note at 11:13.

11:21 *Peter:* See the note at 1:16 (Simon).

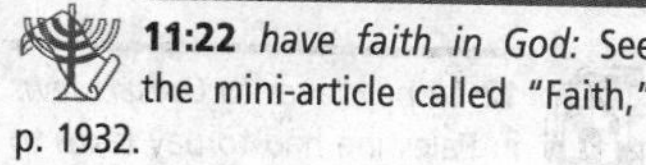

11:22 *have faith in God:* See the mini-article called "Faith," p. 1932.

11:25,26 *when you stand praying:* People in Jesus' day usually prayed in public at the temple or in their synagogues. It was traditional to stand with arms raised when praying to God. Jesus emphasized the importance of praying for forgiveness. See also the mini-article called "Prayer," p. 2289.

11:25,26 *forgive you your sins:* See the note at 1:4 (baptism of repentance). See also Matt 6:14,15.

11:27 *Jerusalem . . . temple:* See the notes at 1:5 and 13:1.

11:27 *chief priests, the teachers of the law and the elders:* See the notes at 8:31 (elders) and 12:38.

11:30 *John's baptism:* Referring to John the Baptist. See the note at 1:4 (John).

11:32 *prophet:* See the note at 8:28.

12:1 *parables:* See the note at 4:2.

12:1 *vineyard:* A vineyard is where grapes are grown. Grapevines need lots of special care. Branches that aren't producing need to be cut off, and the soil around the vines needs to be loosened and weeded. Many workers were required to care for and protect the grapevines. Vineyards were usually located on stony hillsides and enclosed by walls for protection. Many had a high tower where someone could watch over the valuable fruit. See also the mini-article called "Wine," p. 2047.

12:1 Isa 5:1,2.

12:12 *he had spoken the parable against them:* Referring to Israel's leaders. See 11:27 and the note at 8:31 (elders).

12:13 *Pharisees and Herodians:* See the notes at 2:16 and 3:6.

12:14 *pay taxes to Caesar:* Jews in Palestine had to pay taxes to the Romans, who controlled their land. The emperor, known as Caesar, was the highest Roman official. If Jesus answered that the Jews should not pay taxes, the religious leaders could accuse him of rebelling against the Romans.

12:15 *denarius:* In the time of Jesus, a denarius had a picture of the emperor Tiberius on one side. On the other side were the words: "Tiberius Caesar Augustus, son of the divine Augustus." The coin was used to pay taxes to Caesar.

12:18 *Sadducees:* The Sadducees were a wealthy group of Jews who worked closely with the priests. Their name probably comes from "Zadok," the name of a major priestly family (2 Sam 20:25; 1 Kgs 1:39-45). They taught that the most important act was to go to the temple and offer sacrifices there. The Pharisees believed in the possibility of life after death, but the Sadducees did not (Acts 23:8), since they did not find it specifically mentioned in the Law of Moses (see the note at 10:17).

12:19 *the man must marry the widow:* When a married man died and left no children, it was the custom in Israel in ancient times for one of his brothers to marry his widow. Their first son would be considered the son of the dead brother, so that his family line could continue. By the time of Jesus, this law was not followed as strictly as it once had been. Even so, the Sadducees tried to use this law (based on Deut 25:5-10) to question whether life after death was a possibility.

12:10,11 Ps 118:22,23.

3 But they seized him, beat him and sent him away empty-handed.
4 Then he sent another servant to them; they struck this man on
the head and treated him shamefully. 5 He sent still another, and
that one they killed. He sent many others; some of them they beat,
others they killed.

6 "He had one left to send, a son, whom he loved. He sent
him last of all, saying, 'They will respect my son.'

7 "But the tenants said to one another, 'This is the heir.
Come, let's kill him, and the inheritance will be ours.' 8 So they took
him and killed him, and threw him out of the vineyard.

9 "What then will the owner of the vineyard do? He will
come and kill those tenants and give the vineyard to others.
10 Haven't you read this scripture:

" 'The stone the builders rejected
has become the capstone[a];
11 the Lord has done this,
and it is marvelous in our eyes'[b]?"

12 Then they looked for a way to arrest him because they
knew he had spoken the parable against them. But they were afraid
of the crowd; so they left him and went away.

Paying Taxes to Caesar

13 Later they sent some of the Pharisees and Herodians to
Jesus to catch him in his words. 14 They came to him and said,
"Teacher, we know you are a man of integrity. You aren't swayed by
men, because you pay no attention to who they are; but you teach
the way of God in accordance with the truth. Is it right to pay taxes
to Caesar or not? 15 Should we pay or shouldn't we?"

But Jesus knew their hypocrisy. "Why are you trying to trap
me?" he asked. "Bring me a denarius and let me look at it." 16 They
brought the coin, and he asked them, "Whose portrait is this? And
whose inscription?"

"Caesar's," they replied.

17 Then Jesus said to them, "Give to Caesar what is Caesar's
and to God what is God's."

And they were amazed at him.

Marriage at the Resurrection

18 Then the Sadducees, who say there is no resurrection, came
to him with a question. 19 "Teacher," they said, "Moses wrote for us
that if a man's brother dies and leaves a wife but no children, the
man must marry the widow and have children for his brother.
20 Now there were seven brothers. The first one married and died
without leaving any children. 21 The second one married the

a10 Or *cornerstone* **b11** Psalm 118:22,23

widow, but he also died, leaving no child. It was the same with the third. 22In fact, none of the seven left any children. Last of all, the woman died too. 23At the resurrection[a] whose wife will she be, since the seven were married to her?”

24Jesus replied, “Are you not in error because you do not know the Scriptures or the power of God? 25When the dead rise, they will neither marry nor be given in marriage; they will be like the angels in heaven. 26Now about the dead rising—have you not read in the book of Moses, in the account of the bush, how God said to him, ‘I am the God of Abraham, the God of Isaac, and the God of Jacob’[b]? 27He is not the God of the dead, but of the living. You are badly mistaken!”

The Greatest Commandment

28One of the teachers of the law came and heard them debating. Noticing that Jesus had given them a good answer, he asked him, “Of all the commandments, which is the most important?”

29“The most important one,” answered Jesus, “is this: ‘Hear, O Israel, the Lord our God, the Lord is one.[c] 30Love the Lord your God with all your heart and with all your soul and with all your mind and with all your strength.’[d] 31The second is this: ‘Love your neighbor as yourself.’[e] There is no commandment greater than these.”

32“Well said, teacher,” the man replied. “You are right in saying that God is one and there is no other but him. 33To love him with all your heart, with all your understanding and with all your strength, and to love your neighbor as yourself is more important than all burnt offerings and sacrifices.”

34When Jesus saw that he had answered wisely, he said to him, “You are not far from the kingdom of God.” And from then on no one dared ask him any more questions.

Whose Son Is the Christ?

35While Jesus was teaching in the temple courts, he asked, “How is it that the teachers of the law say that the Christ[f] is the son of David? 36David himself, speaking by the Holy Spirit, declared:

“The Lord said to my Lord:
“Sit at my right hand
until I put your enemies
under your feet.” ’[g]

37David himself calls him ‘Lord.’ How then can he be his son?”

The large crowd listened to him with delight.

[a]23 Some manuscripts *resurrection, when men rise from the dead,*
[b]26 Exodus 3:6 [c]29 Or *the Lord our God is one Lord* [d]30 Deut. 6:4,5
[e]31 Lev. 19:18 [f]35 Or *Messiah* [g]36 Psalm 110:1

12:25 *When the dead rise . . . angels:* See the notes at 10:17 and 1:13 (angels). Jesus says that life after death will be very different than the life people live on earth. Believers will be "like angels" in that there will be no marriage, procreation, or death.

12:27 *He is not the God of the dead, but of the living:* Jesus argues that if God is worshiped by Abraham, Isaac, and Jacob (God said to Moses: "I *am*," not "I *was*"), who entered into a covenant with God in ancient times, then they must in some way still be alive. Notice that Jesus quotes from EXODUS, one of the books of the Pentateuch the only books the Sadducees viewed as Scripture.

12:28 *One of the teachers of the law:* See the note at 12:38.

12:33 *burnt offerings and sacrifices:* Before the destruction of Jerusalem by the Romans in A.D. 70, faithful Jews were to bring offerings and make sacrifices at the temple there. See the chart called "Sacrifices and Offerings," p. 219. But several of Israel's prophets also spoke of the importance of helping others (doing justice). See Isa 1:10-17; Hos 6:6; and Amos 5:21-24.

12:34 *kingdom of God:* See the note at 1:15.

12:35 *temple:* See the note at 13:1.

12:35 *teachers of the law:* See the note at 12:38.

12:35 *the Christ is the son of David:* See the notes at 8:29 and 10:47.

12:36 *Holy Spirit . . . right hand:* See the notes at 1:8 and 10:37.

12:37 *David himself calls him 'Lord':* Jesus is saying that the Messiah is more than David's son—he is also David's Lord. See also the mini-article called "David," p. 1028.

12:26 Exod 3:6. **12:28-34** Luke 10:25-28. **12:29-31** Deut 6:4,5; Lev 19:18. **12:36** Ps 110:1.

12:38 *the teachers of the law:* These teachers were Jewish scholars who studied the Law of Moses and tried to teach others how to live by what the law taught. The law was found in the Torah, the first five books of the Jewish Scriptures (GENESIS through DEUTERONOMY).

12:38-40 *flowing robes . . . lengthy prayers:* Jesus lists a number of things that showed how the teachers of the law liked to be noticed for what they were doing. Since they were financially dependent on others, widows were particularly vulnerable to exploitation.

12:42 *two very small copper coins . . . fraction of a penny:* The coins were the Greek *lepton,* the smallest Greek coin. The point is that the widow's small offering was all she had.

13:1 *temple:* The temple mentioned here was built in Jerusalem under the leadership of Herod the Great. See the illustration on p. 1902. Work began in 20 B.C., and construction continued in Jesus' day (John 2:20). The temple sat on a huge stone platform that was nearly a mile around at the base. It was built above the bedrock where King Solomon had built the first temple over 900 years earlier. Jesus' prophecy (13:2) came true when the Romans headed by General Titus (later Emperor) captured Jerusalem from Jewish rebels and destroyed the temple in A.D. 70.

38As he taught, Jesus said, "Watch out for the teachers of the
law. They like to walk around in flowing robes and be greeted in
the marketplaces, 39and have the most important seats in the synagogues and the places of honor at banquets. 40They devour widows' houses and for a show make lengthy prayers. Such men will
be punished most severely."

The Widow's Offering

41Jesus sat down opposite the place where the offerings were
put and watched the crowd putting their money into the temple
treasury. Many rich people threw in large amounts. 42But a poor
widow came and put in two very small copper coins,[a] worth only
a fraction of a penny.[b]

43Calling his disciples to him, Jesus said, "I tell you the truth,
this poor widow has put more into the treasury than all the others.
44They all gave out of their wealth; but she, out of her poverty, put
in everything—all she had to live on."

GOD'S COMING KINGDOM

Jesus explains to the disciples what will happen to the temple and to his followers in the future.

Signs of the End of the Age

13 As he was leaving the temple, one of his disciples said to him,
"Look, Teacher! What massive stones! What magnificent buildings!"

2"Do you see all these great buildings?" replied Jesus. "Not
one stone here will be left on another; every one will be thrown
down."

3As Jesus was sitting on the Mount of Olives opposite the
temple, Peter, James, John and Andrew asked him privately, 4"Tell
us, when will these things happen? And what will be the sign that
they are all about to be fulfilled?"

5Jesus said to them: "Watch out that no one deceives you.
6Many will come in my name, claiming, 'I am he,' and will deceive
many. 7When you hear of wars and rumors of wars, do not be
alarmed. Such things must happen, but the end is still to come.
8Nation will rise against nation, and kingdom against kingdom.
There will be earthquakes in various places, and famines. These are
the beginning of birth pains.

9"You must be on your guard. You will be handed over to the
local councils and flogged in the synagogues. On account of me
you will stand before governors and kings as witnesses to them.
10And the gospel must first be preached to all nations. 11Whenever

[a]42 Greek *two lepta* [b]42 Greek *kodrantes*

The Widow's Mite, T'oros Taronec'i, about 1304, Armenian illuminated manuscript. The widow's coin (or "mite") is small compared to the larger coins filling the offering cup. But Jesus tells his disciples that her small offering was worth more than all the others, because she gave the money she needed to live on. (See 12:41-44.)

you are arrested and brought to trial, do not worry beforehand
about what to say. Just say whatever is given you at the time, for it
is not you speaking, but the Holy Spirit.
[12]"Brother will betray brother to death, and a father his
child. Children will rebel against their parents and have them put
to death. [13]All men will hate you because of me, but he who stands
firm to the end will be saved.
[14]"When you see 'the abomination that causes desolation'[a]
standing where it[b] does not belong—let the reader understand—
then let those who are in Judea flee to the mountains. [15]Let no one
on the roof of his house go down or enter the house to take anything out. [16]Let no one in the field go back to get his cloak. [17]How
dreadful it will be in those days for pregnant women and nursing
mothers! [18]Pray that this will not take place in winter, [19]because
those will be days of distress unequaled from the beginning, when
God created the world, until now—and never to be equaled again.
[20]If the Lord had not cut short those days, no one would survive.
But for the sake of the elect, whom he has chosen, he has shortened them. [21]At that time if anyone says to you, 'Look, here is the
Christ[c]!' or, 'Look, there he is!' do not believe it. [22]For false Christs
and false prophets will appear and perform signs and miracles to

13:3 *Mount of Olives:* See the note at 11:1.

13:10 *the gospel:* See the note at 1:1.

13:11 *Holy Spirit:* See the notes at 1:8 and 1:10.

13:12 *Brother will betray brother:* Some who would try to follow the teachings of Jesus would be considered traitors to their own people.

13:13 *will be saved:* This means "will receive eternal life" (see the note at 10:17).

13:14 *'the abomination that causes desolation' standing where it does not belong:* Jesus was probably referring to the prophecy that someone would set up an idol in the Holy Place in the temple and make people worship it instead of God (Dan 9:27; 11:31; 12:11). In 168 B.C., the Syrian ruler Antiochus IV Epiphanes, had done just that. Jesus is saying that a similar abomination is going to occur again, probably in the temple.

13:15 *on the roof:* See the note at 2:4.

13:18 *in winter:* In Palestine the winters are cold and rainy and make travel difficult.

13:21 *the Christ:* See the note at 8:29.

13:9-11 Matt 10:17-20; Luke 12:11,12. **13:15,16** Luke 17:31. **13:19** Dan 12:1; Rev 7:14. **13:22** 1 John 2:18; 2 Pet 2:1,2; Rev 13:1-16.

[a]**14** Daniel 9:27; 11:31; 12:11 [b]**14** Or *he*; also in verse 29 [c]**21** Or *Messiah*

13:25 *the stars will fall from the sky:* Many people believed that the stars were spiritual powers.

13:32 *angels in heaven . . . Son . . . Father:* See the notes at 1:13; 1:1; and 8:38 (Son of Man). Jesus is saying that no one can predict when he will return, so people need to be ready at all times.

14:1 *Passover and the Feast of Unleavened Bread:* An important pilgrimage festival when Jewish men were expected to go to the temple in Jerusalem and to make sacrifices and celebrate. See the mini-article called "Passover and the Feast of Unleavened Bread," p. 2030, and the chart called "Jewish Calendar and Festivals," p. 944.

14:1 *chief priests and the teachers of the law:* See the notes at 8:31 (elders) and 12:38.

14:3 *expensive perfume, made of pure nard:* The Greek text has "perfume made of pure spikenard." In ancient times perfumed ointment and oil were kept in sealed jars or flasks, which could be opened only by breaking the jar's long neck. See also the chart called "Spices and Perfumes," p. 1278. The woman's action shows her devotion to Jesus.

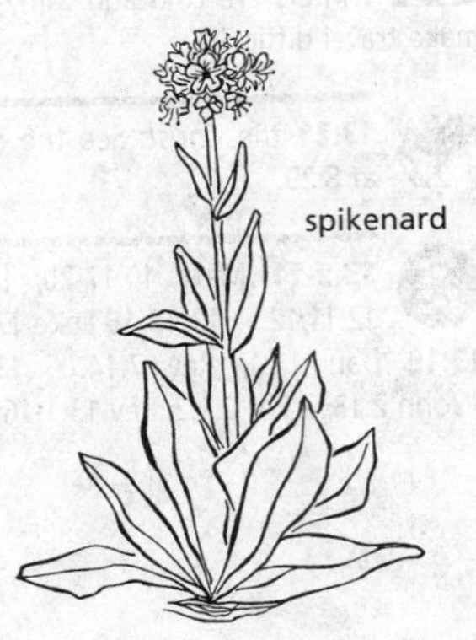

13:24 Isa 13:10; Ezek 32:7; Joel 2:10,31; 3:15; Rev 6:12. **13:25** Isa 34:4; Joel 2:10; Rev 6:13. **13:32** Matt 24:36. **13:34,35** Luke 12:36-38. **14:3** Luke 7:37,38.

deceive the elect—if that were possible. 23So be on your guard; I
have told you everything ahead of time.

24"But in those days, following that distress,

" 'the sun will be darkened,
and the moon will not give its light;
25the stars will fall from the sky,
and the heavenly bodies will be shaken.'[a]

26"At that time men will see the Son of Man coming in
clouds with great power and glory. 27And he will send his angels
and gather his elect from the four winds, from the ends of the
earth to the ends of the heavens.

28"Now learn this lesson from the fig tree: As soon as its twigs
get tender and its leaves come out, you know that summer is near.
29Even so, when you see these things happening, you know that it is
near, right at the door. 30I tell you the truth, this generation[b] will certainly not pass away until all these things have happened. 31Heav-
en and earth will pass away, but my words will never pass away.

The Day and Hour Unknown

32"No one knows about that day or hour, not even the angels
in heaven, nor the Son, but only the Father. 33Be on guard! Be alert[c]!
You do not know when that time will come. 34It's like a man going
away: He leaves his house and puts his servants in charge, each with
his assigned task, and tells the one at the door to keep watch.

35"Therefore keep watch because you do not know when the
owner of the house will come back—whether in the evening, or at
midnight, or when the rooster crows, or at dawn. 36If he comes
suddenly, do not let him find you sleeping. 37What I say to you, I
say to everyone: 'Watch!' "

JESUS PREPARES FOR HIS DEATH

These verses focus on Jesus' last hours with his disciples.

Jesus Anointed at Bethany

14 Now the Passover and the Feast of Unleavened Bread were
only two days away, and the chief priests and the teachers of the
law were looking for some sly way to arrest Jesus and kill him.
2"But not during the Feast," they said, "or the people may riot."

3While he was in Bethany, reclining at the table in the home
of a man known as Simon the Leper, a woman came with an
alabaster jar of very expensive perfume, made of pure nard. She
broke the jar and poured the perfume on his head.

4Some of those present were saying indignantly to one
another, "Why this waste of perfume? 5It could have been sold for

[a]25 Isaiah 13:10; 34:4 [b]30 Or *race* [c]33 Some manuscripts *alert and pray*

more than a year's wages[a] and the money given to the poor." And
they rebuked her harshly.
6“Leave her alone,” said Jesus. “Why are you bothering her?
She has done a beautiful thing to me. 7The poor you will always
have with you, and you can help them any time you want. But you
will not always have me. 8She did what she could. She poured perfume on my body beforehand to prepare for my burial. 9I tell you
the truth, wherever the gospel is preached throughout the world,
what she has done will also be told, in memory of her.”
10Then Judas Iscariot, one of the Twelve, went to the chief
priests to betray Jesus to them. 11They were delighted to hear this
and promised to give him money. So he watched for an opportunity to hand him over.

The Lord's Supper

12On the first day of the Feast of Unleavened Bread, when it
was customary to sacrifice the Passover lamb, Jesus' disciples asked
him, “Where do you want us to go and make preparations for you
to eat the Passover?”
13So he sent two of his disciples, telling them, “Go into the
city, and a man carrying a jar of water will meet you. Follow him.
14Say to the owner of the house he enters, ‘The Teacher asks:
Where is my guest room, where I may eat the Passover with my
disciples?’ 15He will show you a large upper room, furnished and
ready. Make preparations for us there.”
16The disciples left, went into the city and found things just
as Jesus had told them. So they prepared the Passover.
17When evening came, Jesus arrived with the Twelve. 18While
they were reclining at the table eating, he said, “I tell you the truth,
one of you will betray me—one who is eating with me.”
19They were saddened, and one by one they said to him,
“Surely not I?”
20“It is one of the Twelve,” he replied, “one who dips bread
into the bowl with me. 21The Son of Man will go just as it is written about him. But woe to that man who betrays the Son of Man!
It would be better for him if he had not been born.”
22While they were eating, Jesus took bread, gave thanks and
broke it, and gave it to his disciples, saying, “Take it; this is my body.”
23Then he took the cup, gave thanks and offered it to them,
and they all drank from it.
24“This is my blood of the[b] covenant, which is poured out
for many,” he said to them. 25“I tell you the truth, I will not drink
again of the fruit of the vine until that day when I drink it anew in
the kingdom of God.”
26When they had sung a hymn, they went out to the Mount
of Olives.

[a]5 Greek *than three hundred denarii* [b]24 Some manuscripts *the new*

14:8 *prepare for my burial:* Perfumes and spices were used to prepare bodies for burial. See also the mini-article called “Burial,” p. 1998.

14:9 *the gospel:* See the note at 1:1.

14:10 *Judas Iscariot . . . chief priests:* See the notes at 3:14-19 and 8:31 (elders).

14:12 *Feast of Unleavened Bread . . . eat the Passover:* See the note at 14:1 (Passover). On the fifteenth of the Jewish month called Nisan, all yeast was to be removed from homes (Exod 12:15-20), and the Passover lambs were to be killed. The Passover meal took place after sunset and included the offering and eating of the sacrificial lamb, unleavened bread and other special foods, and drinking wine.

14:13 *a man carrying a jar of water:* Since this was considered “women's work,” a man carrying water would have stood out.

14:21 *Son of Man will go just as it is written about him:* See the note at 8:31 (Son of Man). Jesus likely had in mind “the suffering servant” passage of Isaiah 53.

14:22-24 *my body . . . my blood of the covenant:* Jesus used the bread and wine to show how his body would be killed and his blood poured out as a sacrifice to forgive sins. Jesus' death would be the basis for a new covenant between God and God's new people.

14:25 *drink it anew in the kingdom of God:* See the note at 1:15. Jesus spoke of the Kingdom of God as both a present reality and a coming hope. Here he is looking to the future, when his return will bring in the Kingdom of God in its fullness.

14:7 Deut 15:11. **14:18** Ps 41:9. **14:24** Exod 24:8; Jer 31:31-34.

Jesus Predicts Peter's Denial

[27]"You will all fall away," Jesus told them, "for it is written:

" 'I will strike the shepherd,
and the sheep will be scattered.'[a]

[28]But after I have risen, I will go ahead of you into Galilee."
[29]Peter declared, "Even if all fall away, I will not."
[30]"I tell you the truth," Jesus answered, "today—yes,
tonight—before the rooster crows twice[b] you yourself will disown
me three times."
[31]But Peter insisted emphatically, "Even if I have to die with
you, I will never disown you." And all the others said the same.

Gethsemane

[32]They went to a place called Gethsemane, and Jesus said to
his disciples, "Sit here while I pray." [33]He took Peter, James and
John along with him, and he began to be deeply distressed and
troubled. [34]"My soul is overwhelmed with sorrow to the point of
death," he said to them. "Stay here and keep watch."
[35]Going a little farther, he fell to the ground and prayed that
if possible the hour might pass from him. [36]"*Abba*,[c] Father," he
said, "everything is possible for you. Take this cup from me. Yet not
what I will, but what you will."
[37]Then he returned to his disciples and found them sleeping.
"Simon," he said to Peter, "are you asleep? Could you not keep
watch for one hour? [38]Watch and pray so that you will not fall into
temptation. The spirit is willing, but the body is weak."
[39]Once more he went away and prayed the same thing.
[40]When he came back, he again found them sleeping, because their
eyes were heavy. They did not know what to say to him.
[41]Returning the third time, he said to them, "Are you still
sleeping and resting? Enough! The hour has come. Look, the Son
of Man is betrayed into the hands of sinners. [42]Rise! Let us go!
Here comes my betrayer!"

THE FINAL HOURS

Jesus is arrested, tried, and put to death on a cross.

Jesus Arrested

[43]Just as he was speaking, Judas, one of the Twelve, appeared.
With him was a crowd armed with swords and clubs, sent from the
chief priests, the teachers of the law, and the elders.

[a]27 Zech. 13:7 [b]30 Some early manuscripts do not have *twice*. [c]36 Aramaic for *Father*

Jesus prayed, *"Abba, Father, everything is possible for you. Take this cup from me. Yet not what I will, but what you will."* Mark 14:36

14:28 *Galilee:* See the note at 9:30.

14:29 *Peter:* See the note at 1:16 (Simon).

14:30 *rooster crows:* Since roosters crow at dawn, Jesus is saying that Peter will deny that he knows Jesus three times before the next sunrise.

14:32 *Gethsemane:* The exact location is not known, but it was probably on the east side of the Kidron Valley in an area near the Mount of Olives. See the map on p. 2474 for the most likely location.

14:33 *Peter, James and John:* See the note at 9:2.

14:35,36 *Take this cup from me:* See the note at 10:38.

14:41 *Son of Man . . . sinners:* See the notes at 8:31 and 2:17. Here Jesus is talking about how he will be handed over to Jewish and Roman authorities.

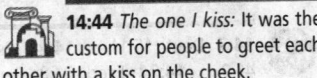

14:43 *Judas, one of the twelve:* See the note at 3:14-19. See also 14:10, 11.

14:43 *sent from the chief priests, the teachers of the law, and the elders:* See the notes at 8:31 (elders) and 12:38.

14:44 *The one I kiss:* It was the custom for people to greet each other with a kiss on the cheek.

14:27 Zech 13:7. **14:28** Matt 28:16. **14:58** John 2:19. **14:62** Dan 7:13; Ps 110:1; Mark 13:26.

44Now the betrayer had arranged a signal with them: "The
one I kiss is the man; arrest him and lead him away under guard."
45Going at once to Jesus, Judas said, "Rabbi!" and kissed him. 46The
men seized Jesus and arrested him. 47Then one of those standing
near drew his sword and struck the servant of the high priest, cutting off his ear.
48"Am I leading a rebellion," said Jesus, "that you have come
out with swords and clubs to capture me? 49Every day I was with
you, teaching in the temple courts, and you did not arrest me. But
the Scriptures must be fulfilled." 50Then everyone deserted him
and fled.
51A young man, wearing nothing but a linen garment, was
following Jesus. When they seized him, 52he fled naked, leaving his
garment behind.

Before the Sanhedrin

53They took Jesus to the high priest, and all the chief priests,
elders and teachers of the law came together. 54Peter followed him
at a distance, right into the courtyard of the high priest. There he
sat with the guards and warmed himself at the fire.
55The chief priests and the whole Sanhedrin were looking for
evidence against Jesus so that they could put him to death, but
they did not find any. 56Many testified falsely against him, but their
statements did not agree.
57Then some stood up and gave this false testimony against
him: 58"We heard him say, 'I will destroy this man-made temple
and in three days will build another, not made by man.'" 59Yet even
then their testimony did not agree.
60Then the high priest stood up before them and asked Jesus,
"Are you not going to answer? What is this testimony that these
men are bringing against you?" 61But Jesus remained silent and
gave no answer.
Again the high priest asked him, "Are you the Christ,[a] the
Son of the Blessed One?"
62"I am," said Jesus. "And you will see the Son of Man sitting
at the right hand of the Mighty One and coming on the clouds of
heaven."
63The high priest tore his clothes. "Why do we need any
more witnesses?" he asked. 64"You have heard the blasphemy. What
do you think?"
They all condemned him as worthy of death. 65Then some
began to spit at him; they blindfolded him, struck him with their
fists, and said, "Prophesy!" And the guards took him and beat
him.

[a]**61** Or *Messiah*

14:47 *sword . . . servant:* John 18:10 names Peter as the one who struck the high priest's servant.

14:51 *young man:* Only MARK mentions this young man, whose identity is not known. Some feel that this may have been John Mark, the author of this Gospel

14:53 *high priest . . . teachers of the law:* Caiaphas was the high priest in Jerusalem from A.D. 18 to 36. See the notes at 8:31 (elders) and 12:38.

14:54 *the courtyard of the high priest:* According to tradition, Caiaphas the high priest lived in the upper part of the city, probably near the temple. See also the map on p. 2474.

14:55 *chief priests and the whole Sanhedrin:* See the note at 8:31 (elders).

14:55,56 *looking for evidence . . . statement did not agree:* The Law of Moses stated that two witnesses were needed before a person could be put to death (Num 35:30).

14:61 *the Christ, the Son of the Blessed One:* See the note at 8:29. The "Blessed One" was a way that the high priest could refer to God without actually saying God's name.

14:62 *Son of Man sitting at the right hand:* See the mini-article called "Son of Man," p. 1866, and the note at 10:37.

14:63,64 *high priest tore his clothes:* The Law of Moses said that the high priest was not allowed to tear his clothes to show sorrow (Lev 10:6; 21:10). Even so, the high priest used this dramatic gesture to show that he thought Jesus' statement about himself was a great sin. A person who claimed to be God was considered guilty of blasphemy (shaming God's name) and could be put to death by stoning (Lev 24:16).

14:67 *that Nazarene, Jesus:* See the note at 1:24.

14:70 *a Galilean:* Peter may have had an accent that helped the servant girl notice that he was from the northern area of Palestine.

15:1 *chief priests . . . whole Sanhedrin:* See the note at 8:31 (elders).

15:1 *Pilate:* Pontius Pilate was the Roman governor in charge of Judea from A.D. 26 to 36. The Jewish leaders wanted Pilate to find Jesus guilty of breaking Roman law and to sentence Jesus to death on a cross. See also the mini-article called "Pontius Pilate," p. 2091.

15:2 *king of the Jews:* Someone who claimed to rule without the support of the Romans would be considered a rebel. The Jewish leaders did not think that Jesus was a king, although many Jewish people believed he was the long-awaited Messiah (see the notes at 8:29 and 11:10).

15:6 *release a prisoner:* According to tradition, the Romans set one prisoner free during the celebration of Passover.

15:7 *Barabbas:* His name means "son of Abba." Barabbas was known as a violent criminal who committed murder while taking part in riots against the Romans, hoping to gain freedom for the Jewish people.

15:9,10 *king of the Jews . . . chief priests:* See the notes at 15:2 and 8:31 (elders).

15:13 *Crucify him:* This was the most common way the Romans used to put criminals and other troublemakers to death. Dying on a cross was a very slow and painful death. See the mini-article called "Crucifixion," p. 1914.

14:72 Mark 14:30.

Peter Disowns Jesus

66 While Peter was below in the courtyard, one of the servant
girls of the high priest came by. 67 When she saw Peter warming
himself, she looked closely at him.

"You also were with that Nazarene, Jesus," she said.

68 But he denied it. "I don't know or understand what you're
talking about," he said, and went out into the entryway.[a]

69 When the servant girl saw him there, she said again to
those standing around, "This fellow is one of them." 70 Again he
denied it.

After a little while, those standing near said to Peter, "Surely
you are one of them, for you are a Galilean."

71 He began to call down curses on himself, and he swore to
them, "I don't know this man you're talking about."

72 Immediately the rooster crowed the second time.[b] Then
Peter remembered the word Jesus had spoken to him: "Before the
rooster crows twice[c] you will disown me three times." And he
broke down and wept.

Jesus Before Pilate

15 Very early in the morning, the chief priests, with the elders,
the teachers of the law and the whole Sanhedrin, reached a decision. They bound Jesus, led him away and handed him over to
Pilate.

2 "Are you the king of the Jews?" asked Pilate.

"Yes, it is as you say," Jesus replied.

3 The chief priests accused him of many things. 4 So again
Pilate asked him, "Aren't you going to answer? See how many
things they are accusing you of."

5 But Jesus still made no reply, and Pilate was amazed.

6 Now it was the custom at the Feast to release a prisoner
whom the people requested. 7 A man called Barabbas was in prison
with the insurrectionists who had committed murder in the uprising. 8 The crowd came up and asked Pilate to do for them what he
usually did.

9 "Do you want me to release to you the king of the Jews?"
asked Pilate, 10 knowing it was out of envy that the chief priests had
handed Jesus over to him. 11 But the chief priests stirred up the
crowd to have Pilate release Barabbas instead.

12 "What shall I do, then, with the one you call the king of the
Jews?" Pilate asked them.

13 "Crucify him!" they shouted.

14 "Why? What crime has he committed?" asked Pilate.

---

[a]**68** Some early manuscripts *entryway and the rooster crowed* [b]**72** Some early manuscripts do not have *the second time.* [c]**72** Some early manuscripts do not have *twice.*

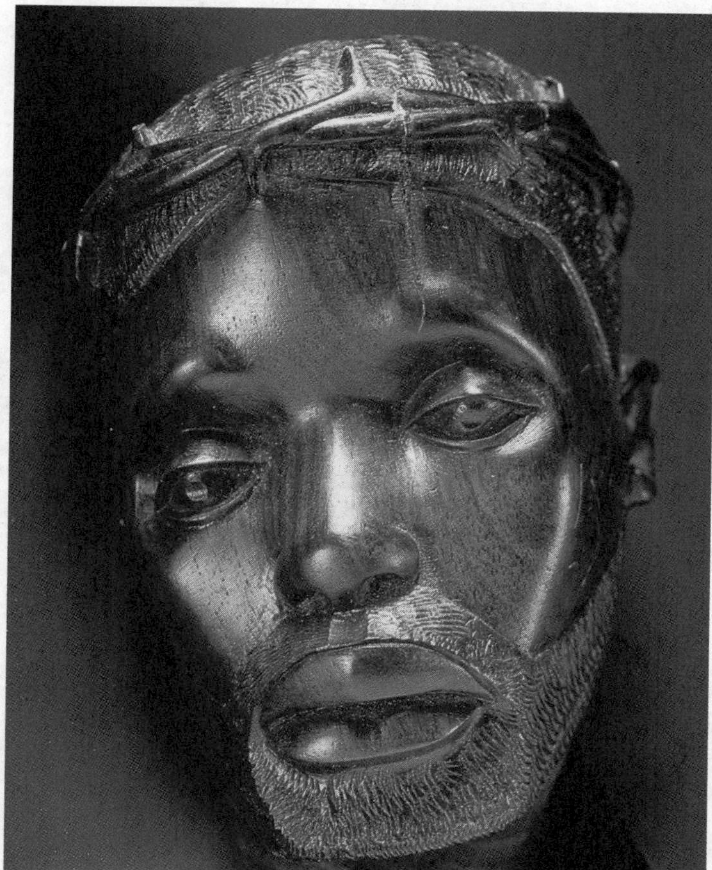

Christ with the Crown of Thorns, artist unknown. The Gospels tell the story of the life and teachings of Jesus Christ. This African wood carving depicts Jesus at the time of his death on the cross. Before Jesus was taken to Golgotha, "The Place of the Skull," where he was crucified, the Roman soldiers mocked him by putting a purple robe on him and by making him wear a crown made out of thorns (see 15:16-20).

But they shouted all the louder, "Crucify him!"
15Wanting to satisfy the crowd, Pilate released Barabbas to
them. He had Jesus flogged, and handed him over to be crucified.

The Soldiers Mock Jesus

16The soldiers led Jesus away into the palace (that is, the
Praetorium) and called together the whole company of soldiers.
17They put a purple robe on him, then twisted together a crown of
thorns and set it on him. 18And they began to call out to him,
"Hail, king of the Jews!" 19Again and again they struck him on the

15:16 *the Praetorium:* Also called the Antonia Fortress, where the Roman governor stayed when in Jerusalem.

15:17 *purple robe:* This was probably a Roman soldier's robe.

15:21 *man from Cyrene, Simon, the father of Alexander and Rufus:* Cyrene was a city in North Africa. Simon was probably a Jew who was in Jerusalem to celebrate Passover. Alexander and Rufus may have been known by the first readers of MARK.

15:22 *Golgotha:* Probably located outside Jerusalem near a large rock resembling a human skull. See John 19:20.

15:32 *this Christ, this King of Israel:* See the notes at 8:29 and 15:2. Because Jesus did not save himself, many didn't believe he could be the Christ.

15:34 *Eloi . . . sabachthani:* These words are in Aramaic, a language spoken in Palestine during the time of Jesus (see the note at 5:41,42).

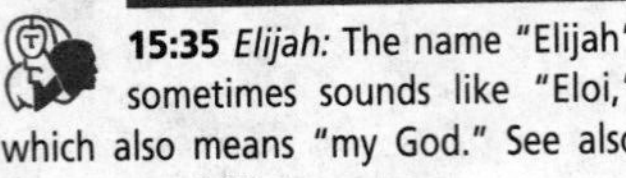

15:35 *Elijah:* The name "Elijah" sometimes sounds like "Eloi," which also means "my God." See also the note at 6:15.

15:38 *curtain of the temple was torn:* This curtain separated the Holy Place from the Most Holy Place which was thought of as God's home on earth (Exod 26:31-33). Only the high priest could go past this curtain. That it was torn when Jesus died meant that Jesus' death was the sacrifice that made it possible for all people to enter into God's presence.

15:39 *the centurion . . . Son of God:* This Roman centurion was a Gentile. It is significant that a Gentile was the first person after Jesus' death to recognize Jesus as the "Son of God." The good news that Jesus died as a sacrifice for the sins of human beings is for all people.

15:40,41 *Mary Magdalene, Mary the mother of James . . . Salome:* See the note at 16:9.

15:24 Ps 22:18. **15:28** Isa 53:12. **15:29** Ps 22:7; 109:25; Mark 14:58; John 2:19. **15:34** Ps 22:1. **15:36** Ps 69:21. **15:40,41** Luke 8:2,3.

head with a staff and spit on him. Falling on their knees, they paid
homage to him. [20]And when they had mocked him, they took off
the purple robe and put his own clothes on him. Then they led
him out to crucify him.

The Crucifixion

[21]A certain man from Cyrene, Simon, the father of Alexander and Rufus, was passing by on his way in from the country, and
they forced him to carry the cross. [22]They brought Jesus to the
place called Golgotha (which means The Place of the Skull).
[23]Then they offered him wine mixed with myrrh, but he did not
take it. [24]And they crucified him. Dividing up his clothes, they cast
lots to see what each would get.

[25]It was the third hour when they crucified him. [26]The written notice of the charge against him read: THE KING OF THE JEWS.
[27]They crucified two robbers with him, one on his right and one
on his left.[a] [29]Those who passed by hurled insults at him, shaking
their heads and saying, "So! You who are going to destroy the temple and build it in three days, [30]come down from the cross and save
yourself!"

[31]In the same way the chief priests and the teachers of the
law mocked him among themselves. "He saved others," they said,
"but he can't save himself! [32]Let this Christ,[b] this King of Israel,
come down now from the cross, that we may see and believe."
Those crucified with him also heaped insults on him.

The Death of Jesus

[33]At the sixth hour darkness came over the whole land until
the ninth hour. [34]And at the ninth hour Jesus cried out in a loud
voice, "*Eloi, Eloi, lama sabachthani?*"—which means, "My God, my
God, why have you forsaken me?"[c]

[35]When some of those standing near heard this, they said,
"Listen, he's calling Elijah."

[36]One man ran, filled a sponge with wine vinegar, put it on
a stick, and offered it to Jesus to drink. "Now leave him alone. Let's
see if Elijah comes to take him down," he said.

[37]With a loud cry, Jesus breathed his last.

[38]The curtain of the temple was torn in two from top to bottom. [39]And when the centurion, who stood there in front of Jesus,
heard his cry and[d] saw how he died, he said, "Surely this man was
the Son[e] of God!"

[40]Some women were watching from a distance. Among them
were Mary Magdalene, Mary the mother of James the younger and

[a]**27** Some manuscripts *left,* **[28]***and the scripture was fulfilled which says, "He was counted with the lawless ones"* (Isaiah 53:12) [b]**32** Or *Messiah* [c]**34** Psalm 22:1 [d]**39** Some manuscripts do not have *heard his cry and* [e]**39** Or *a son*

of Joses, and Salome. [41]In Galilee these women had followed him and cared for his needs. Many other women who had come up with him to Jerusalem were also there.

The Burial of Jesus

[42]It was Preparation Day (that is, the day before the Sabbath). So as evening approached, [43]Joseph of Arimathea, a prominent member of the Council, who was himself waiting for the kingdom of God, went boldly to Pilate and asked for Jesus' body. [44]Pilate was surprised to hear that he was already dead. Summoning the centurion, he asked him if Jesus had already died. [45]When he learned from the centurion that it was so, he gave the body to Joseph. [46]So Joseph bought some linen cloth, took down the body, wrapped it in the linen, and placed it in a tomb cut out of rock. Then he rolled a stone against the entrance of the tomb. [47]Mary Magdalene and Mary the mother of Joses saw where he was laid.

Jesus Lives

As Jesus predicted, God raises Jesus to life after three days. As in other Gospel accounts, the women are the first to learn of his resurrection. An angel appears to the women who have come to the tomb and tells them to deliver a message to Peter and the other disciples, instructing them to go to Galilee where Jesus will meet them.

The Resurrection

16 When the Sabbath was over, Mary Magdalene, Mary the mother of James, and Salome bought spices so that they might go to anoint Jesus' body. [2]Very early on the first day of the week, just after sunrise, they were on their way to the tomb [3]and they asked each other, "Who will roll the stone away from the entrance of the tomb?"

[4]But when they looked up, they saw that the stone, which was very large, had been rolled away. [5]As they entered the tomb, they saw a young man dressed in a white robe sitting on the right side, and they were alarmed.

[6]"Don't be alarmed," he said. "You are looking for Jesus the Nazarene, who was crucified. He has risen! He is not here. See the place where they laid him. [7]But go, tell his disciples and Peter, 'He is going ahead of you into Galilee. There you will see him, just as he told you.' "

[8]Trembling and bewildered, the women went out and fled from the tomb. They said nothing to anyone, because they were afraid.

15:42 *Sabbath:* See the note at 1:21 (Sabbath). Since the Sabbath begins at sundown, it was important that Jesus' body be prepared for burial before then. Otherwise removing his body and preparing it for burial would have broken Sabbath laws.

15:43 *Joseph of Arimathea:* Arimathea was a small village about twenty miles northwest of Jerusalem. Joseph was a respected member of the Sanhedrin, and had not consented to the decision to put Jesus to death (Luke 23:50,51). Now he further risks his reputation by helping to give Jesus a good burial.

15:46 *linen cloth:* In Jesus' day, dead bodies were usually wrapped in strips of linen cloth. See also the mini-article called "Burial," p. 1998.

16:1 *the Sabbath:* The Sabbath lasted from sundown on Friday till sundown Saturday. When daylight came on the next morning (Sunday), the women could walk to the tomb and put spices on Jesus' body.

16:1 *Mary Magdalene, Mary the mother of James, and Salome:* See the note at 16:9.

16:1 *spices:* Probably myrrh and aloes (John 19:39). See the chart called "Spices and Perfumes," p. 1278.

16:5 *a young man dressed in a white robe:* Identified in MATTHEW as an angel (Matt 28:2). See the mini-article called "Angels," p. 88.

16:6 *He has risen:* God brought Jesus back to life from death. This act is also called the resurrection. See the mini-article called "Resurrection," p. 2210.

16:7 *disciples . . . Peter . . . Galilee:* See the notes at 1:16 (Simon); 3:14-19; and 9:30.

16:7 Matt 26:32; Mark 14:28.

Jesus said, *"Go into all the world and preach the good news to all creation. Whoever believes and is baptized will be saved, but whoever does not believe will be condemned."*
Mark 16:15,16

16:9 *Mary Magdalene:* Mary Magdalene's name probably means that she was from Magdala, a town on the western shore of the Sea of Galilee. As a follower of Jesus, she may have traveled with a group of Jesus' closest friends.

The Gospel of MARK states that Mary Magdalene was one of several women who had witnessed Jesus' death on the cross (see 15:40, 41). With her were Mary the mother of James and Joses, and Salome. The other Mary and her sons are hard to identify, though they were probably known to many of MARK's earliest readers. James may be the disciple James who is mentioned as the son of Alphaeus (Mark 3:18; Acts 1:13), but this is not certain. Salome may have been the wife of one of Jesus' disciples or the mother of the disciples James and John (11:19; Matt 27:56).

16:12 *two of them:* This is a brief account of the two unnamed followers of Jesus who met him on their way to Emmaus, as reported in Luke 24:13-35.

16:14 *the Eleven:* See the note at 3:14-19. Judas Iscariot was no longer part of the group at this time. Other New Testament books report that Judas committed suicide after Jesus was arrested (Matt 27:3-10; Acts 1:16-20).

16:16 *will be saved:* See 10:17 and John 3:16. See also the note at 13:13 and mini-article called "Salvation," p. 2021.

16:15 Acts 1:8. **16:19** Acts 1:9-11.

The Marys at the Tomb, sixth century Byzantine mosaic, artist unknown. This unusual mosaic in the Church of Sant'Apollinare Nuovo, Ravenna, Italy, shows two of the women who went to put spiced oils on Jesus' body in the tomb, a common way of preparing a body for burial in ancient times. The winged figure on the left is the young man, depicted here as an angel, who told them "He has risen!" (See 16:1-8.)

[The earliest manuscripts and some other ancient witnesses do not have Mark 16:9-20.]

9 When Jesus rose early on the first day of the week, he
appeared first to Mary Magdalene, out of whom he had driven
seven demons. 10 She went and told those who had been with him
and who were mourning and weeping. 11 When they heard that
Jesus was alive and that she had seen him, they did not believe it.
12 Afterward Jesus appeared in a different form to two of
them while they were walking in the country. 13 These returned and
reported it to the rest; but they did not believe them either.
14 Later Jesus appeared to the Eleven as they were eating; he
rebuked them for their lack of faith and their stubborn refusal to
believe those who had seen him after he had risen.
15 He said to them, "Go into all the world and preach the
good news to all creation. 16 Whoever believes and is baptized will
be saved, but whoever does not believe will be condemned. 17 And
these signs will accompany those who believe: In my name they

will drive out demons; they will speak in new tongues; [18]they will pick up snakes with their hands; and when they drink deadly poison, it will not hurt them at all; they will place their hands on sick people, and they will get well."

[19]After the Lord Jesus had spoken to them, he was taken up into heaven and he sat at the right hand of God. [20]Then the disciples went out and preached everywhere, and the Lord worked with them and confirmed his word by the signs that accompanied it.

16:17 *drive out demons . . . speak in new tongues:* See the notes at 3:30 and 9:38. The ability to speak in new languages without having learned them is one of the gifts of the Holy Spirit (Acts 2:4-6; 1 Cor 12:10).

16:18 *place their hands on sick people, and they will get well:* Jesus often touched people when he healed them. In the early church, laying hands on sick people and annointing them with oil was an important part of healing ceremonies (see Acts 28:8; Jas 5:14).

16:19 *right hand of God:* See the note at 10:37.

QUESTIONS ABOUT MARK 10:1—16:20

1. Describe the meeting between Jesus and the rich young man (10:17-22). What happened at the end of their meeting? Why?
2. Why did Jesus throw the money changers and merchants out of the temple area? (11:15-18) Why did his actions anger the chief priests and teachers of the law? In your opinion, what are the three most important reasons why churches or synagogues exist today?
3. What did Jesus say are the two most important commandments? (12:28-31)
4. Summarize Jesus' teachings about the future (13:1-37). Are his words comforting or frightening, or both? Why?
5. What promise did Peter make to Jesus? (14:27-31) Was he able to keep it? Why or why not? What does it mean to disown Jesus? How does such disowning take place in today's world?
6. What did the Roman centurion guarding Jesus' cross realize? (15:39) What makes this important in MARK?
7. Why was Joseph of Arimathea's burial of Jesus (15:42-47) an act of courage? What is the most courageous thing you have ever done? Why did you do it? Does it take courage to be a follower of Christ? Explain.

LUKE

"Timing is everything," so the saying goes. Read LUKE to find out how God sent Jesus to earth when the time was right.

WHAT MAKES LUKE SPECIAL?

LUKE is the first part of a two-volume work that includes ACTS. This is clear from the introductions to both books (see Luke 1:1-4 and Acts 1:1-5). These books together tell about the life of Jesus from his birth until he was taken to heaven (LUKE). Then they report how the early followers of Jesus continued to spread the teachings of Jesus and tell about his life (ACTS).

WHY WAS LUKE WRITTEN?

The author of LUKE says that "since I myself have carefully investigated everything from the beginning, it seemed good also to me to write an orderly account for you" (1:3) concerning Jesus. The book is dedicated to Theophilus, a friend or supporter.

WHAT'S THE STORY BEHIND THE SCENE?

LUKE was likely created from at least three different sources: (1) the book of MARK; (2) a collection of Jesus' sayings, which MATTHEW also used; and (3) a collection of stories not included in any other Gospel. Many scholars believe that Luke probably wrote this Gospel sometime after A.D. 70, the year the Romans destroyed Jerusalem and the temple while putting down a Jewish revolt. LUKE's stories about the birth of Jesus are more detailed than those of any other New Testament book. And some familiar stories told by Jesus are found only in LUKE: "The Good Samaritan" (10:25-37), "The Lost Sheep" (15:1-7), and "The Lost Son" (15:11-32). LUKE is the only Gospel that tells how Jesus visited the home of the hated tax collector named Zacchaeus (19:1-10) and promised life in paradise to a dying criminal (23:39-43).

LUKE, like the book of ACTS, often mentions the Holy Spirit (1:15, 35; 4:1, 14, 18; 10:21; 11:13). LUKE also shows how important prayer was to Jesus (3:21; 6:12; 9:18; 23:34, 46). From LUKE we learn of three parables that Jesus used in teaching about prayer (11:5-10; 18:1-8, 9-14).

Jesus' concern for the poor is an important theme in LUKE. The good news is preached to them (4:18; 7:22); they receive God's blessings (6:20); they are invited to a great banquet (14:13, 21); the poor beggar named Lazarus is taken to heaven by angels (16:20, 22); and Jesus commands his disciples to sell what they have and give the money to the poor (12:33).

Traditionally, the writer of LUKE and ACTS has been identified as Luke the doctor, the companion and co-worker of Paul (Phlm 24; Col 4:14). He wrote in the style of the Greek and Roman historians and biographers of his day. Many think that he

Holy Spirit: The Holy Spirit is very important in both LUKE and ACTS as God's power at work in the world. The Holy Spirit does miraculous things like causing the virgin Mary to become pregnant. The Holy Spirit leads people (Luke 4:1, 14; Acts 8:29, 39) and gives them special power, such as the ability to preach about Jesus (Acts 2:1-11). The Holy Spirit gave the first apostles courage to preach and helped the church grow and become stronger (Acts 9:31). See also the mini-article called "Holy Spirit," on p. 2002.

Elijah: Elijah was a prophet in Israel more than 800 years before Jesus was born. Elijah was known for his power to work miracles and for his strong desire for people to worship only the Lord. Later prophets spoke of God sending Elijah back to earth to warn people of God's judgment (Mal 3:1-4; 4:5, 6). Some people thought John the Baptist was Elijah come back again, which John himself clearly denied (John 1:21). In Luke 1:17, the angel Gabriel tells John's father that John will minister "in the spirit and power of Elijah." Rather than Elijah returning in the flesh, John was sent to serve a similar role as that earlier prophet of repentance. In that respect, John fulfilled Malachi 4:5,6. For more, see the mini-article called "Elijah," p. 1816.

was not Jewish and lived outside of Judea, and that he was writing for a Gentile audience (see the mini-article called "Gentiles," p. 2127). This is supported by a key theme in LUKE: God sent Jesus to be the Savior of all people, both Jews and Gentiles.

How is Luke constructed?

Note in the following outline how LUKE is organized around important events in Jesus' life and the places where these events happen.

- **Preparing the way for Jesus (1:1—4:13)**
  - Introduction: Why Luke wrote this book (1:1-4)
  - Two miraculous births (1:5—2:20)
  - Jesus as a child (2:21-52)
  - Jesus is God's own Son (3:1—4:13)
- **Jesus preaches and heals in Galilee (4:14—9:50)**
  - Mixed reactions toward Jesus (4:14-37)
  - Jesus heals many people and calls his first disciples (4:38—5:32)
  - Jesus continues his work in Galilee (5:33—9:17)
  - Who Jesus is and what he must do (9:18-50)
- **Jesus journeys toward Jerusalem (9:51—19:27)**
  - Followers and unbelievers (9:51—10:42)
  - Jesus teaches many things (11:1—12:59)
  - Teachings about the kingdom of God (13:1—14:35)
  - The lost are found (15:1-32)
  - Faithful servants (16:1—19:27)
- **Jesus' final week in Jerusalem (19:28—23:56)**
  - Jesus teaches in Jerusalem (19:28—21:38)
  - The last days of Jesus: his trial and death (22:1—23:56)
- **Jesus rises from death and appears to the disciples (24:1-53)**

1:1 *the things that have been fulfilled among us:* In this brief introduction (1:1-4), the author of LUKE shows that he is aware that others have tried to tell the story about Jesus' miracles and teachings and about how Jesus died and was raised to life. Such stories are called "Gospels," an Old English word that is a translation of the Greek word *euangelion*, meaning "good news." For more, see the Introduction to the Gospels and Acts, p. 1845.

Preparing the Way for Jesus

The writer of LUKE begins by explaining why he has written this Gospel. Then the focus shifts to events surrounding Jesus' birth. One important event is the birth of John the Baptist who, as an adult, preaches a message that is intended to get people ready to receive Jesus. The last part of this section tells about John baptizing Jesus and how the devil tempts Jesus in the desert.

INTRODUCTION: WHY LUKE WROTE THIS BOOK

Introduction

1 Many have undertaken to draw up an account of the things
that have been fulfilled[a] among us, 2 just as they were handed down

[a] 1 Or *been surely believed*

1:3 *Theophilus:* The name means "friend of God" in Greek. Some think this name stands for anyone who is a friend or follower of Jesus. Others think Theophilus was a Roman official or someone of importance who paid for the writing and copying of LUKE.

1:5 *Herod king of Judea:* Also known as Herod the Great, he was made governor of Galilee when the Romans occupied Palestine. He became king in 37 B.C. and died shortly after Jesus was born (Matt 2:19). Even though he was an Idumean and not actually Jewish, he tried to become popular with the Jewish people by rebuilding the temple in Jerusalem.

1:5 *Zechariah . . . Elizabeth:* Both Zechariah and his wife Elizabeth were from priestly families. King David divided the male descendants of Aaron, the first high priest, into twenty-four divisions of priests. Each division took a turn serving in the temple. Abijah was head of the eighth division (1 Chr 24:10). See also the mini-article called "Israel's Priests," p. 2344.

1:9 *custom . . . burn incense:* Priests placed fresh incense on an altar in the temple after the morning and evening sacrifices were made. Incense was made of frankincense, other gums and spices, and salt.

1:13 *John:* The name John means "The Lord is gracious." See the mini-article called "John the Baptist," p. 1853.

1:15 *never to take wine or other fermented drink:* In ancient Israel, a group called the Nazirites made a vow never to drink alcohol (Num 6:1-4). Some people think that John was a Nazirite.

1:17 *Elijah:* See the note on p. 1964.

1:19 *Gabriel:* This angel first appears in DANIEL as a messenger who brings Daniel the wisdom to understand a vision (Dan 8:16; 9:21).

to us by those who from the first were eyewitnesses and servants of
the word. 3Therefore, since I myself have carefully investigated
everything from the beginning, it seemed good also to me to write
an orderly account for you, most excellent Theophilus, 4so that you
may know the certainty of the things you have been taught.

TWO MIRACULOUS BIRTHS

Angels announce the births of both John and Jesus. Elizabeth, John's mother, and Mary, the mother of Jesus, both become pregnant in miraculous ways. This section includes Mary's famous song of praise and events surrounding the births of John and Jesus.

The Birth of John the Baptist Foretold

5In the time of Herod king of Judea there was a priest named
Zechariah, who belonged to the priestly division of Abijah; his wife
Elizabeth was also a descendant of Aaron. 6Both of them were
upright in the sight of God, observing all the Lord's commandments and regulations blamelessly. 7But they had no children,
because Elizabeth was barren; and they were both well along in
years.

8Once when Zechariah's division was on duty and he was
serving as priest before God, 9he was chosen by lot, according to
the custom of the priesthood, to go into the temple of the Lord
and burn incense. 10And when the time for the burning of incense
came, all the assembled worshipers were praying outside.

11Then an angel of the Lord appeared to him, standing at the
right side of the altar of incense. 12When Zechariah saw him, he
was startled and was gripped with fear. 13But the angel said to him:
"Do not be afraid, Zechariah; your prayer has been heard. Your
wife Elizabeth will bear you a son, and you are to give him the
name John. 14He will be a joy and delight to you, and many will
rejoice because of his birth, 15for he will be great in the sight of the
Lord. He is never to take wine or other fermented drink, and he
will be filled with the Holy Spirit even from birth.[a] 16Many of the
people of Israel will he bring back to the Lord their God. 17And he
will go on before the Lord, in the spirit and power of Elijah, to
turn the hearts of the fathers to their children and the disobedient
to the wisdom of the righteous—to make ready a people prepared
for the Lord."

18Zechariah asked the angel, "How can I be sure of this? I am
an old man and my wife is well along in years."

19The angel answered, "I am Gabriel. I stand in the presence
of God, and I have been sent to speak to you and to tell you this
good news. 20And now you will be silent and not able to speak

[a]**15** Or *from his mother's womb*

until the day this happens, because you did not believe my words,
which will come true at their proper time."
21Meanwhile, the people were waiting for Zechariah and
wondering why he stayed so long in the temple. 22When he came
out, he could not speak to them. They realized he had seen a vision
in the temple, for he kept making signs to them but remained
unable to speak.
23When his time of service was completed, he returned
home. 24After this his wife Elizabeth became pregnant and for five
months remained in seclusion. 25"The Lord has done this for me,"
she said. "In these days he has shown his favor and taken away my
disgrace among the people."

The Birth of Jesus Foretold

26In the sixth month, God sent the angel Gabriel to
Nazareth, a town in Galilee, 27to a virgin pledged to be married to
a man named Joseph, a descendant of David. The virgin's name
was Mary. 28The angel went to her and said, "Greetings, you who
are highly favored! The Lord is with you."
29Mary was greatly troubled at his words and wondered what
kind of greeting this might be. 30But the angel said to her, "Do not
be afraid, Mary, you have found favor with God. 31You will be with
child and give birth to a son, and you are to give him the name
Jesus. 32He will be great and will be called the Son of the Most
High. The Lord God will give him the throne of his father David,
33and he will reign over the house of Jacob forever; his kingdom
will never end."
34"How will this be," Mary asked the angel, "since I am a
virgin?"
35The angel answered, "The Holy Spirit will come upon you,
and the power of the Most High will overshadow you. So the holy
one to be born will be called[a] the Son of God. 36Even Elizabeth
your relative is going to have a child in her old age, and she who
was said to be barren is in her sixth month. 37For nothing is
impossible with God."
38"I am the Lord's servant," Mary answered. "May it be to me
as you have said." Then the angel left her.

Mary Visits Elizabeth

39At that time Mary got ready and hurried to a town in the
hill country of Judea, 40where she entered Zechariah's home and
greeted Elizabeth. 41When Elizabeth heard Mary's greeting, the
baby leaped in her womb, and Elizabeth was filled with the Holy
Spirit. 42In a loud voice she exclaimed: "Blessed are you among
women, and blessed is the child you will bear! 43But why am I so

[a]35 Or *So the child to be born will be called holy,*

1:23 *time of service:* Each priest spent some time each year working in the temple. See the note at 1:5 (Zechariah) and the mini-article called "Israel's Priests," p. 2344.

1:26 *Nazareth, a town in Galilee:* This small town is never mentioned in the Old Testament. In 63 B.C., the Romans made Galilee part of their empire and ruled it during the time Jesus lived. See the map on p. 2473.

1:27 *Joseph, a descendant of David:* Joseph was from the family of David, who was considered Israel's greatest king. Israelite prophets said the Messiah would come from David's family (2 Sam 7:12-16; Isa 11:1-3).

1:31 *Jesus:* In Hebrew *Jesus* means "the LORD saves."

1:32 *the Most High:* This name for God goes back to the time of Abraham (Gen 14:17-22). See also the mini-article called "Names of God," p. 243.

1:35 *Holy Spirit:* See the note on p. 1964.

1:35 *Son of God:* The result of the Holy Spirit coming upon the virgin Mary was the miraculous birth of Jesus, the Son of God. See the mini-article called "Son of God," p. 2044.

1:39 *hill country of Judea:* Judea was an area in the southern part of Palestine. Since many parts of Judea are hilly, it's not clear exactly where in Judea Zechariah and Elizabeth lived.

1:41 *Holy Spirit:* See the note on p. 1964 (Holy Spirit).

1:32,33 2 Sam 7:12,13,16; Isa 9:7. **1:37** Gen 18:14.

The Annunciation, Visitation, and Nativity, page from an illuminated Psalter, thirteenth century. Psalters are devotional books containing some or all of the psalms from the Old Testament. This one from France includes images from the life of Jesus' mother Mary. Immediately after an angel tells Mary that she is pregnant (Annunciation, top left), Mary visits her cousin Elizabeth (Visitation, top right), who is pregnant with John the Baptist. The bottom panel (Nativity) shows the baby Jesus lying in a manger as her husband Joseph and two animals look on. (See 1:26-45; 2:1-7.)

favored, that the mother of my Lord should come to me? 44 As soon
as the sound of your greeting reached my ears, the baby in my
womb leaped for joy. 45 Blessed is she who has believed that what
the Lord has said to her will be accomplished!"

1:46-55 *My soul glorifies the Lord . . . even as he said to our fathers:* Mary's song is a prayer that praises God and is like the song that Hannah sang when God gave her a son (1 Sam 2:1-10). Mary's song is also known by some Christians as the *Magnificat*, which in Latin means "magnify." This song introduces an important theme in LUKE: God is a friend of poor people.

Mary's Song

46 And Mary said:

"My soul glorifies the Lord
47 and my spirit rejoices in God my Savior,

[48] for he has been mindful
of the humble state of his servant.
From now on all generations will call me blessed,
[49] for the Mighty One has done great things
for me—
holy is his name.
[50] His mercy extends to those who fear him,
from generation to generation.
[51] He has performed mighty deeds with his arm;
he has scattered those who are proud in their inmost
thoughts.
[52] He has brought down rulers from their thrones
but has lifted up the humble.
[53] He has filled the hungry with good things
but has sent the rich away empty.
[54] He has helped his servant Israel,
remembering to be merciful
[55] to Abraham and his descendants forever,
even as he said to our fathers."

[56] Mary stayed with Elizabeth for about three months and then returned home.

The Birth of John the Baptist

[57] When it was time for Elizabeth to have her baby, she gave
birth to a son. [58] Her neighbors and relatives heard that the Lord
had shown her great mercy, and they shared her joy.
[59] On the eighth day they came to circumcise the child, and
they were going to name him after his father Zechariah, [60] but his
mother spoke up and said, "No! He is to be called John."
[61] They said to her, "There is no one among your relatives
who has that name."
[62] Then they made signs to his father, to find out what he
would like to name the child. [63] He asked for a writing tablet, and
to everyone's astonishment he wrote, "His name is John." [64] Immediately his mouth was opened and his tongue was loosed, and he
began to speak, praising God. [65] The neighbors were all filled with
awe, and throughout the hill country of Judea people were talking
about all these things. [66] Everyone who heard this wondered about
it, asking, "What then is this child going to be?" For the Lord's
hand was with him.

Zechariah's Song

[67] His father Zechariah was filled with the Holy Spirit and prophesied:

[68] "Praise be to the Lord, the God of Israel,
because he has come and has redeemed his people.

Mary said: "My soul glorifies the Lord and my spirit rejoices in God my Savior, for he has been mindful of the humble state of his servant."
Luke 1:46-48

1:55 *to Abraham and his descendants forever:* This refers to the people of Israel, all of whom can trace their families back to Abraham and Sarah. God made a covenant with Abraham many centuries before Jesus was born (Gen 12:1-3; 17:4-8). Abraham agreed to follow God, and God promised Abraham that he and Sarah would be the parents of a great nation (Gen 15:1-6). See also the mini-articles called "Abraham," p. 2254, and "Israel," p. 264.

1:56 *three months . . . returned home:* Mary likely stayed with her relative Elizabeth until John was born (see 1:36). Mary then returned to her home in Nazareth (1:26).

1:59 *eighth day they came to circumcise the child:* The Law of Moses commanded that all Jewish boys be circumcised eight days after they were born to show that they belonged to the Lord (Gen 17:9-14; Lev 12:3). See also the mini-article called "Circumcision," p. 2251.

1:67 *Holy Spirit:* See the note on p. 1964.

1:68-79 *Praise be to the Lord . . . path of peace:* Zechariah praised God and offered a prophecy or vision of what his son, John, would do. Zechariah's song is in the form of a blessing much like those found in PSALMS. See Ps 41:13; 106:48.

1:48 1 Sam 1:11. **1:52** Job 5:11; 12:19.

1:69 *his servant David:* This refers to Israel's King David. See also the mini-article called "David," p. 1028.

1:70 *holy prophets:* The prophets of Israel were special messengers who spoke for God. They told about God's promise to send a Messiah who would save the people (see Isa 7:14; 9:6, 7; Mic 5:2). See the article called "Prophets and Prophecy," p. 935.

1:73 *our father Abraham:* See the note at 1:55.

1:80 *desert:* John probably lived in the Desert of Judea, which is between Jerusalem and the Dead Sea. See the map on p. 2473.

1:80 *appeared publicly to Israel:* The time between John's birth and his preaching in the desert was about thirty years.

2:1 *Caesar Augustus:* The Roman emperor at the time Jesus was born. His actual name was Octavian, but he was better known by his title, Caesar Augustus. Under the rule of Augustus, Rome controlled almost all the land surrounding the Mediterranean Sea. See the article called "The World of Jesus: Peoples, Powers, and Politics," p. 1821.

1:76 Mal 3:1. **1:79** Isa 9:2.

69 He has raised up a horn[a] of salvation for us
in the house of his servant David
70 (as he said through his holy prophets of long ago),
71 salvation from our enemies
and from the hand of all who hate us—
72 to show mercy to our fathers
and to remember his holy covenant,
73 the oath he swore to our father Abraham:
74 to rescue us from the hand of our enemies,
and to enable us to serve him without fear
75 in holiness and righteousness before him all our days.

76 And you, my child, will be called a prophet of the Most High;
for you will go on before the Lord to prepare the way for him,
77 to give his people the knowledge of salvation
through the forgiveness of their sins,
78 because of the tender mercy of our God,
by which the rising sun will come to us from heaven
79 to shine on those living in darkness
and in the shadow of death,
to guide our feet into the path of peace."

80 And the child grew and became strong in spirit; and he
lived in the desert until he appeared publicly to Israel.

The Birth of Jesus

2 In those days Caesar Augustus issued a decree that a census
should be taken of the entire Roman world. 2 (This was the first
census that took place while Quirinius was governor of Syria.)
3 And everyone went to his own town to register.
4 So Joseph also went up from the town of Nazareth in
Galilee to Judea, to Bethlehem the town of David, because he
belonged to the house and line of David. 5 He went there to register with Mary, who was pledged to be married to him and was
expecting a child. 6 While they were there, the time came for the
baby to be born, 7 and she gave birth to her firstborn, a son. She
wrapped him in cloths and placed him in a manger, because there
was no room for them in the inn.

The Shepherds and the Angels

8 And there were shepherds living out in the fields nearby,
keeping watch over their flocks at night. 9 An angel of the Lord
appeared to them, and the glory of the Lord shone around them,

[a] 69 *Horn* here symbolizes strength.

Judean Desert. The deserts in Palestine are dry areas of land that support little plant or animal life, but where flash flooding sometimes occurs during the winter months. LUKE says that John lived in the desert until the time he was sent to tell the people to repent, turn back to God, and be baptized (1:80; 3:3). He wore clothes made out of camel's hair and ate locusts and wild honey (see Mark 1:6).

and they were terrified. 10But the angel said to them, "Do not be
afraid. I bring you good news of great joy that will be for all the
people. 11Today in the town of David a Savior has been born to
you; he is Christ[a] the Lord. 12This will be a sign to you: You will
find a baby wrapped in cloths and lying in a manger."
13Suddenly a great company of the heavenly host appeared
with the angel, praising God and saying,

14"Glory to God in the highest,
and on earth peace to men on whom his favor rests."

15When the angels had left them and gone into heaven, the
shepherds said to one another, "Let's go to Bethlehem and see this
thing that has happened, which the Lord has told us about."
16So they hurried off and found Mary and Joseph, and the
baby, who was lying in the manger. 17When they had seen him,
they spread the word concerning what had been told them about

[a]**11** Or *Messiah.* "The Christ" (Greek) and "the Messiah" (Hebrew) both mean "the Anointed One"; also in verse 26.

2:1 *a census:* This was done so that everyone living in Roman-held territories could be made to pay taxes to the Roman emperor. All the people were supposed to register in their hometowns (2:3).

2:2 *Quirinius:* A distinguished military leader who may have begun serving as governor of Syria around 12 B.C. Herod the Great made him governor of Judea in 6 B.C. The census he conducted was for tax purposes. He would conduct another census in A.D. 6 (see Acts 5:37). Quirinius died in A.D. 21.

2:4 *Nazareth . . . Bethlehem:* See the note at 1:26. In Hebrew, Bethlehem means "house of bread." It is located south of Jerusalem and stands about 2,500 feet above sea level. See the map on p. 2473.

2:7 *firstborn, a son:* See the note at 2:23.

2:7 *a manger:* This refers to an animal's feedbox, probably filled with soft hay.

2:11 *town of David:* Referring to Bethlehem; see the note at 2:4. See also 1 Sam 17:12.

2:11 *Savior . . . Christ:* A savior is one who rescues or sets people free. See Isa 43:11; Matt 1:21. "Christ" is from the Greek *Christos.* Both *Christos* and the Hebrew word *Messiah* mean "Anointed One" or "Chosen One." See the mini-article called "Messiah (Chosen One)," p. 1124.

2:13-15 *angels:* The word "angel" means "messenger." In the Bible, angels act both as messengers and as servants of God. See also the mini-article called "Angels," p. 88.

SHEPHERDS

In Jesus' day, shepherds either wandered from place to place living in tents, or lived in villages. Peasant shepherds who lived in a village had the right to let their flocks feed in the pastures near the village. When food supplies got scarce, they would move their herds to higher pastures in the hot summer or to warmer valleys in the winter.

Life was often difficult for shepherds. They spent most of their time outside watching over the herd and often slept near their flock to protect it from robbers and wild animals. At night, they gathered their flocks into places called sheepfolds. These could be stone walls made by the shepherds or natural enclosures like a cave. Shepherds counted their flocks when they came into the fold at night by separating the sheep from the goats with a walking stick. They counted them again in the morning when they left for the pastures.

A flock often included both sheep and goats. Sheep are timid animals that need constant protection. Goats are harder to handle because they like to climb up the rocky hillsides. Sheep produce wool for clothing and meat for special meals. Many sheep were also used for sacrifices at the temple in Jerusalem. It is likely that some of the sheep in the fields near Bethlehem at the time of Jesus' birth (Luke 2:3) were intended to be offered as temple sacrifices on one of the important Jewish festivals.

Jesus identified with shepherds, even though many in society looked down on them. Jesus called himself the Good Shepherd who would lay down his life for his sheep (John 10:11-16). The writers of the Psalms (Ps 23:1; 100:3) and the prophet Ezekiel pictured God as a shepherd who would save his flock, the Israelite people (Ezek 34:11-16).

this child, [18]and all who heard it were amazed at what the shepherds said to them. [19]But Mary treasured up all these things and pondered them in her heart. [20]The shepherds returned, glorifying and praising God for all the things they had heard and seen, which were just as they had been told.

JESUS AS A CHILD

LUKE is the only one of the four Gospels that tells about Jesus' childhood or youth.

Jesus Presented in the Temple

[21]On the eighth day, when it was time to circumcise him, he was named Jesus, the name the angel had given him before he had been conceived.

[22]When the time of their purification according to the Law of Moses had been completed, Joseph and Mary took him to Jerusalem to present him to the Lord [23](as it is written in the Law of the Lord, "Every firstborn male is to be consecrated to the Lord"[a]), [24]and to offer a sacrifice in keeping with what is said in the Law of the Lord: "a pair of doves or two young pigeons."[b]

[25]Now there was a man in Jerusalem called Simeon, who was righteous and devout. He was waiting for the consolation of Israel, and the Holy Spirit was upon him. [26]It had been revealed to him by the Holy Spirit that he would not die before he had seen the Lord's Christ. [27]Moved by the Spirit, he went into the temple courts. When the parents brought in the child Jesus to do for him what the custom of the Law required, [28]Simeon took him in his arms and praised God, saying:

[29]"Sovereign Lord, as you have promised,
you now dismiss[c] your servant in peace.
[30]For my eyes have seen your salvation,
[31] which you have prepared in the sight of all people,
[32]a light for revelation to the Gentiles
and for glory to your people Israel."

[33]The child's father and mother marveled at what was said about him. [34]Then Simeon blessed them and said to Mary, his mother: "This child is destined to cause the falling and rising of many in Israel, and to be a sign that will be spoken against, [35]so that the thoughts of many hearts will be revealed. And a sword will pierce your own soul too."

[36]There was also a prophetess, Anna, the daughter of Phanuel, of the tribe of Asher. She was very old; she had lived with her husband seven years after her marriage, [37]and then was a

[a]**23** Exodus 13:2,12 [b]**24** Lev. 12:8 [c]**29** Or *promised, / now dismiss*

2:21 *circumcise . . . was named Jesus:* See 1:31 and the note at 1:59.

2:22 *time of their purification:* After a Jewish mother gave birth to a child, she was considered ritually "unclean" (Lev 12:1-8). When a woman gave birth to a son, she had to stay home for seven days, and on the eighth day the boy was circumcised. Then the mother had to stay home for another thirty-three days. After this period apart from society, she offered a sacrifice to the Lord to make herself "clean" again (2:24).

2:23 *firstborn male:* According to the Law of Moses, the firstborn males of both Israelite families and their livestock belonged to the Lord (Exod 13:2). The firstborn animals were sacrificed, whereas an additional animal sacrifice was made on behalf of firstborn sons, who were dedicated to serve God all their lives (Exod 13:12,13).

2:28-32 *Simeon . . . praised God:* Simeon's song is also known by some Christians as the *Nunc Dimittis,* which in Latin means "Now you let [me] leave."

2:32 *a light for revelation to the Gentiles:* Simeon was referring to Isaiah 42:6; 49:6; 52:10. See also Acts 13:46,47, where Paul and Barnabas say that they have been chosen to carry on the work of Jesus by taking his message to the Gentiles (non-Jews). See also the mini-article called "Gentiles," p. 2127.

2:36 *prophetess, Anna . . . tribe of Asher:* Little is known about the prophetess Anna or her father Phanuel. Though most prophets were male, LUKE has a number of examples of women who, like Anna, spoke God's messages or participated as Jesus' followers. One of the twelve tribes of Israel was named for Asher, one of Jacob's twelve sons (Gen 30:9-13; Num 2:27).

widow until she was eighty-four.[a] She never left the temple but
worshiped night and day, fasting and praying. 38Coming up to
them at that very moment, she gave thanks to God and spoke
about the child to all who were looking forward to the redemption
of Jerusalem.

39When Joseph and Mary had done everything required by
the Law of the Lord, they returned to Galilee to their own town of
Nazareth. 40And the child grew and became strong; he was filled
with wisdom, and the grace of God was upon him.

The Boy Jesus at the Temple

41Every year his parents went to Jerusalem for the Feast of
the Passover. 42When he was twelve years old, they went up to the
Feast, according to the custom. 43After the Feast was over, while his
parents were returning home, the boy Jesus stayed behind in
Jerusalem, but they were unaware of it. 44Thinking he was in their
company, they traveled on for a day. Then they began looking for
him among their relatives and friends. 45When they did not find
him, they went back to Jerusalem to look for him. 46After three
days they found him in the temple courts, sitting among the teachers, listening to them and asking them questions. 47Everyone who
heard him was amazed at his understanding and his answers.
48When his parents saw him, they were astonished. His mother
said to him, "Son, why have you treated us like this? Your father
and I have been anxiously searching for you."

49"Why were you searching for me?" he asked. "Didn't you
know I had to be in my Father's house?" 50But they did not understand what he was saying to them.

51Then he went down to Nazareth with them and was obedient to them. But his mother treasured all these things in her
heart. 52And Jesus grew in wisdom and stature, and in favor with
God and men.

JESUS IS GOD'S OWN SON

John preaches in the desert, preparing people for the coming of the Messiah, Jesus. Jesus is baptized by John and identified as God's Son, and a list of Jesus' ancestors is given. Jesus then goes into the desert where he is tempted by the devil.

John the Baptist Prepares the Way

3 In the fifteenth year of the reign of Tiberius Caesar—when
Pontius Pilate was governor of Judea, Herod tetrarch of Galilee, his
brother Philip tetrarch of Iturea and Traconitis, and Lysanias
tetrarch of Abilene— 2during the high priesthood of Annas and

[a]37 Or *widow for eighty-four years*

2:41 *Feast of the Passover:* Passover celebrated the people's escape from slavery in Egypt (Exod 12:1-27; Deut 16:1-8). See also the mini-article called "Passover and the Feast of Unleavened Bread," p. 2030.

2:42 *twelve years old:* At this age, Jewish boys prepared to take their full place in the religious community when they turned thirteen.

2:46 *teachers:* Probably refers to men who taught the Law of Moses and the other Jewish Scriptures.

3:1,2 *Tiberius Caesar . . . Annas and Caiaphas:* Tiberius Claudius Caesar ruled the Roman empire from A.D. 14 to 37. The fifteenth year of his rule would be A.D. 28 or 29. Tiberius appointed Pontius Pilate governor of Judea in A.D. 26. Herod Antipas, the son of Herod the Great, ruled Galilee at this time. After Herod the Great died, his kingdom was divided between his sons. As rulers of a portion of a region, they were known as "tetrarchs." Herod Antipas was the tetrarch of Galilee from 4 B.C. to A.D. 39. The Romans appointed Philip, Herod Antipas's brother, as tetrarch of Iturea and Traconitis. Little is known about Lysanias, tetrarch of Abilene who was not a son of Herod the Great. See the map on p. 2473 for the locations mentioned here. Annas was the Jewish high priest from A.D. 6 to 15, although the Jewish people continued to recognize him as high priest even after the Romans removed him from office. His son-in-law Caiaphas was high priest from A.D. 18 to 37. See also the mini-article called "Israel's Priests," p. 2344.

3:8 *children for Abraham:* John warned the Jewish people not to think that they could live any way they wanted, just because they were descendants of Abraham and Sarah. See also John 8:33.

2:52 1 Sam 2:26; Prov 3:4.

Caiaphas, the word of God came to John son of Zechariah in the
desert. [3]He went into all the country around the Jordan, preaching
a baptism of repentance for the forgiveness of sins. [4]As is written
in the book of the words of Isaiah the prophet:

"A voice of one calling in the desert,
'Prepare the way for the Lord,
make straight paths for him.
[5]Every valley shall be filled in,
every mountain and hill made low.
The crooked roads shall become straight,
the rough ways smooth.
[6]And all mankind will see God's salvation.'"[a]

[7]John said to the crowds coming out to be baptized by him,
"You brood of vipers! Who warned you to flee from the coming
wrath? [8]Produce fruit in keeping with repentance. And do not
begin to say to yourselves, 'We have Abraham as our father.' For I
tell you that out of these stones God can raise up children for
Abraham. [9]The ax is already at the root of the trees, and every tree
that does not produce good fruit will be cut down and thrown into
the fire."

[10]"What should we do then?" the crowd asked.

[11]John answered, "The man with two tunics should share
with him who has none, and the one who has food should do the
same."

[12]Tax collectors also came to be baptized. "Teacher," they
asked, "what should we do?"

[13]"Don't collect any more than you are required to," he told
them.

[14]Then some soldiers asked him, "And what should we do?"

He replied, "Don't extort money and don't accuse people
falsely—be content with your pay."

[15]The people were waiting expectantly and were all wondering in their hearts if John might possibly be the Christ.[b]
[16]John answered them all, "I baptize you with[c] water. But one
more powerful than I will come, the thongs of whose sandals I
am not worthy to untie. He will baptize you with the Holy Spirit and with fire. [17]His winnowing fork is in his hand to clear his
threshing floor and to gather the wheat into his barn, but he will
burn up the chaff with unquenchable fire." [18]And with many
other words John exhorted the people and preached the good
news to them.

[19]But when John rebuked Herod the tetrarch because of
Herodias, his brother's wife, and all the other evil things he had
done, [20]Herod added this to them all: He locked John up in
prison.

[a]**6** Isaiah 40:3-5 [b]**15** Or *Messiah* [c]**16** Or *in*

3:12 *Tax collectors:* The Romans issued contracts for the right to collect taxes. These contracts were usually given to wealthy foreigners, who hired local people to collect taxes. These collectors usually took from people more than was actually demanded by Rome. Most Jews in Jesus' day hated tax collectors, considered them ritually unclean, and treated them as traitors.

3:15 *the Christ:* See the note at 2:11 (Savior).

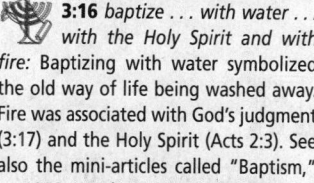

3:16 *baptize . . . with water . . . with the Holy Spirit and with fire:* Baptizing with water symbolized the old way of life being washed away. Fire was associated with God's judgment (3:17) and the Holy Spirit (Acts 2:3). See also the mini-articles called "Baptism," p. 1976, "Holy Spirit," p. 2082, and "Fire," p. 2383.

3:16 *sandals . . . untie:* This was the duty of a slave.

3:17 *winnowing fork:* Farmers used a winnowing fork to pick up the grain and husks and pitch them into the air. The light husks would blow away, but the heavier grain would fall back to the ground to be gathered up. This separated the worthless chaff from the valuable grain.

3:19 *Herodias:* Herodias was Herod's niece and the former wife of his brother Philip (see Matt 14:3,4).

3:4-6 Isa 40:3-5. **3:7** Matt 12:34; 23:33. **3:9** Matt 7:19.

The Baptism and Genealogy of Jesus

A voice came from heaven: "You are my Son, whom I love; with you I am well pleased." Luke 3:22

21When all the people were being baptized, Jesus was baptized too. And as he was praying, heaven was opened 22and the
Holy Spirit descended on him in bodily form like a dove. And a
voice came from heaven: "You are my Son, whom I love; with you
I am well pleased."
23Now Jesus himself was about thirty years old when he
began his ministry. He was the son, so it was thought, of Joseph,

the son of Heli, 24the son of Matthat,
the son of Levi, the son of Melki,
the son of Jannai, the son of Joseph,

3:22 Gen 22:2; Ps 2:7; Isa 42:1; Matt 3:17; Mark 1:11; Luke 9:35.

BAPTISM

The English word "baptism" comes from the Greek verb that means "to dip in water." In the Jewish Scriptures there were laws that required priests to wash themselves before they could offer sacrifices to God (Exod 40:12-15). The high priest had to bathe himself before and after he went into the Most Holy Place inside the tabernacle or the temple to make the sacrifice on the Day of Atonement (Lev 16:4,23,24).

The prophets of Israel instructed the people to "wash" themselves, symbolically speaking, by turning from their sins and doing what God wanted them to do (Isa 1:15-17; Jer 4:14). At the site of the religious community in Qumran, archaeologists discovered a pool that members used to wash themselves as a way of showing that they wanted their lives to be pure. During the same period in Israel's history John the Baptist began preaching. John told people to be baptized as a way of preparing themselves for the coming of someone who would be more powerful than he was, and who would bring the Holy Spirit to God's people (Luke 3:15-17). Jesus was also baptized by John at this time (Luke 3:21,22), an event which confirmed that he was the Son of God.

Jesus did not baptize anyone himself during his earthly ministry, but his disciples did baptize people with Jesus' approval (John 3:22; 4:1,2). And later, before Jesus was taken up to heaven, he told his disciples to teach and to baptize people of all nations (Matt 28:18-20). His disciples obeyed his command, and Acts is full of accounts of how Jesus' disciples baptized new believers as they became part of the Christian church. These new members were baptized to show that they wanted to stop sinning, turn away from their old way of life, and show that they were ready to enter a new life of obedience to God (Rom 6:1-4).

Acts begins with the story of how the Holy Spirit was sent to the church on the Day of Pentecost and how 3,000 new Christians were baptized (Acts 2:41). As the gospel of Jesus spread throughout Judea and across Asia Minor, new Christians were baptized, including many who were not Jews: Samaritans (Acts 8:12), an Ethiopian official (Acts 8:38), a Roman centurion (Acts 10:47, 48), and a wealthy Greek woman (Acts 16:15). The apostle Paul wrote letters to local churches explaining that those who are baptized should make a break with their past life and become part of the people of faith (Rom 6:1-4; Col 2:11,12). Just as God saved Noah from the flood, and just as God raised Jesus from the dead, so baptism signifies that God's new people are saved from the power of death, made acceptable to God, and welcomed into God's family (1 Pet 3:18-22).

25 the son of Mattathias, the son of Amos,
the son of Nahum, the son of Esli,
the son of Naggai, 26 the son of Maath,
the son of Mattathias, the son of Semein,
the son of Josech, the son of Joda,
27 the son of Joanan, the son of Rhesa,
the son of Zerubbabel, the son of Shealtiel,
the son of Neri, 28 the son of Melki,
the son of Addi, the son of Cosam,

Temptation of Christ, from a fifteenth century illuminated *Book of Hours* by the Limbourg brothers. After Jesus was baptized by John, he went into the desert to pray. The devil appeared to him and tempted him three times. The devil took Jesus to a high place and offered him "authority and splendor," but Jesus answered him by quoting the Scriptures: "Worship the Lord your God and serve him only." (See 4:1-13.)

3:21 *Jesus was baptized too . . . as he was praying:* Although Jesus did not need to be cleansed from sin, he was baptized as a way to identify with people. His baptism also served as an example to his followers. See the mini-article called "Baptism" on p. 1976.

This is the only Gospel that mentions Jesus praying when he was baptized. LUKE often pictures Jesus in prayer.

3:22 *Holy Spirit descended . . . "You are my Son, whom I love":* See the note on p. 1964 (Holy Spirit). The voice of God identifies Jesus as the Son of God. See the mini-article called "Son of God," p. 2044.

3:23 *so it was thought:* LUKE reinforces that Joseph was not Jesus' biological father (see 1:34,35).

3:23-38 *son of:* Family roots were very important to the Jewish people. They believed that the Messiah would come from the family of David (Isa 3:31; 11:1-11). LUKE traces Jesus' personal history all the way back to Adam and to God. Compare this genealogy with the one at Matthew 1:1-17.

> *The devil said to him, "If you are the Son of God, tell this stone to become bread."*
> *Jesus answered, "It is written: 'Man does not live on bread alone.'"*
> Luke 4:3,4

the son of Elmadam, the son of Er,
29 the son of Joshua, the son of Eliezer,
the son of Jorim, the son of Matthat,
the son of Levi, 30 the son of Simeon,
the son of Judah, the son of Joseph,
the son of Jonam, the son of Eliakim,
31 the son of Melea, the son of Menna,
the son of Mattatha, the son of Nathan,
the son of David, 32 the son of Jesse,
the son of Obed, the son of Boaz,
the son of Salmon,[a] the son of Nahshon,
33 the son of Amminadab, the son of Ram,[b]
the son of Hezron, the son of Perez,
the son of Judah, 34 the son of Jacob,
the son of Isaac, the son of Abraham,
the son of Terah, the son of Nahor,
35 the son of Serug, the son of Reu,
the son of Peleg, the son of Eber,
the son of Shelah, 36 the son of Cainan,
the son of Arphaxad, the son of Shem,
the son of Noah, the son of Lamech,
37 the son of Methuselah, the son of Enoch,
the son of Jared, the son of Mahalalel,
the son of Kenan, 38 the son of Enosh,
the son of Seth, the son of Adam,
the son of God.

---

[a]32 Some early manuscripts *Sala* [b]33 Some manuscripts *Amminadab, the son of Admin, the son of Arni*; other manuscripts vary widely.

QUESTIONS ABOUT LUKE 1:1—4:13

1. What message did the angel Gabriel bring to Zechariah? to Mary? (1:5-38) How did each of them respond to the angel's message?
2. Why did Mary visit Elizabeth? (1:39-45) Mary sings about the promises God has made (1:46-55). What are these promises? Where do you see signs of these promises in the world today? What are some of these signs?
3. Describe how each of the following reacted to the birth of Jesus: (a) the shepherds, (b) Simeon, (c) Anna (2:1-38). What is the promise that Simeon sings about? What would you say is special about Jesus' birth?
4. What was John's main message? (3:1-20) What does John's message have for people today? John was later killed for speaking the truth about God and how God wants people to live. What situations can you think of in the world today that might be like what happened to John?
5. In what ways does the devil tempt Jesus? (4:1-13) How does Jesus challenge these temptations? Has anyone ever tried to persuade you to do something that you knew was wrong? How did you handle it? Where do you turn for help in facing temptations or times of testing?

The Temptation of Jesus

4 Jesus, full of the Holy Spirit, returned from the Jordan and was
led by the Spirit in the desert, 2 where for forty days he was tempted by the devil. He ate nothing during those days, and at the end
of them he was hungry.
3 The devil said to him, "If you are the Son of God, tell this
stone to become bread."
4 Jesus answered, "It is written: 'Man does not live on bread
alone.'[a]"
5 The devil led him up to a high place and showed him in an
instant all the kingdoms of the world. 6 And he said to him, "I will
give you all their authority and splendor, for it has been given to
me, and I can give it to anyone I want to. 7 So if you worship me, it
will all be yours."
8 Jesus answered, "It is written: 'Worship the Lord your God
and serve him only.'[b]"
9 The devil led him to Jerusalem and had him stand on the
highest point of the temple. "If you are the Son of God," he said,
"throw yourself down from here. 10 For it is written:

" 'He will command his angels concerning you
to guard you carefully;
11 they will lift you up in their hands,
so that you will not strike your foot against a stone.'[c]"

12 Jesus answered, "It says: 'Do not put the Lord your God to
the test.'[d]"
13 When the devil had finished all this tempting, he left him
until an opportune time.

Jesus Preaches and Heals in Galilee

Led by the Spirit, Jesus returns to Galilee to teach, work miracles, and choose his disciples. He also runs into trouble from teachers and experts in the Law of Moses. Twice in this section Jesus talks about his coming death, but it is clear that the disciples don't yet know why this needs to happen.

MIXED REACTIONS TOWARD JESUS

Jesus is rejected in his hometown
but gains a big following in other places.

Jesus Rejected at Nazareth

14 Jesus returned to Galilee in the power of the Spirit, and
news about him spread through the whole countryside. 15 He
taught in their synagogues, and everyone praised him.

4:1 *Jordan . . . desert:* The Desert of Judea stretched about twenty miles eastward from the highlands around Jerusalem down to the Jordan River and the Dead Sea. See the map on p. 2473.

4:2 *forty days:* The forty days and nights Jesus spent in the desert are the same number of days that Moses (Exod 24:18; 34:28) and Elijah (1 Kgs 19:8) spent preparing for the important work they had to do among God's people. See also the chart called "Numbers in the Bible," p. 2405.

On special occasions the Jewish people went without eating (called "fasting") to show sorrow for their sins or to prepare themselves to serve God in some special way (see Deut 9:9,18).

4:3 *devil:* The devil, also known as Satan, is the leader of the forces that are against God and God's people. For more, see the mini-article called "Satan," p. 963.

4:10-12 *it is written . . . It says:* Jesus responded to all three temptations by quoting from the Jewish Scripture (Old Testament). In presenting his third temptation, the devil also quotes Scripture (Ps 91:11,12).

4:14 *Galilee:* Jesus' home region. See the note at 1:26.

4:14 *power of the Spirit:* See the note on p. 1964 (Holy Spirit). LUKE often notes that God's Spirit is at work directing Jesus and others.

4:15 *synagogues:* Jewish meeting places. See also the mini-article called "Synagogues," p. 1857.

4:4 Deut 8:3. **4:8** Deut 6:13 **4:10,11** Ps 91:11,12. **4:12** Deut 6:16.

[a]**4** Deut. 8:3 [b]**8** Deut. 6:13 [c]**11** Psalm 91:11,12 [d]**12** Deut. 6:16

4:16 *Sabbath:* Seventh day of the week, the Jewish day of rest.

4:17 *Isaiah:* A prophet in Judah from about 740 to 701 B.C. See the Introduction to ISAIAH, p. 1289.

4:20 *the scroll:* Jewish Scriptures were written on long parchment or leather scrolls. See also the mini-article called "Scrolls," p. 1491.

4:23 *Capernaum:* This was an important fishing town on the northern shore of the Sea of Galilee. Jesus moved to Capernaum from Nazareth when he began his ministry.

4:25-27 *widows in Zarepath . . . Naaman the Syrian:* See 1 Kgs 17:1-15 and 2 Kgs 5:1-14. This widow and Naaman were Gentiles. Jesus shows how God cares about all people.

4:27 *leprosy:* The word translated as "leprosy" described several kinds of skin diseases.

4:33 *a demon, an evil spirit:* Demons work for the devil and were understood to be the cause of many kinds of physical and mental illness. This demon recognized who Jesus was.

4:18,19 Isa 61:1,2. **4:24** John 4:44. **4:32** Matt 7:28,29.

16 He went to Nazareth, where he had been brought up, and
on the Sabbath day he went into the synagogue, as was his custom.
And he stood up to read. 17 The scroll of the prophet Isaiah was
handed to him. Unrolling it, he found the place where it is written:

18 "The Spirit of the Lord is on me,
because he has anointed me
to preach good news to the poor.
He has sent me to proclaim freedom for the
prisoners
and recovery of sight for the blind,
to release the oppressed,
19 to proclaim the year of the Lord's favor."[a]

20 Then he rolled up the scroll, gave it back to the attendant
and sat down. The eyes of everyone in the synagogue were fastened
on him, 21 and he began by saying to them, "Today this scripture is
fulfilled in your hearing."

22 All spoke well of him and were amazed at the gracious
words that came from his lips. "Isn't this Joseph's son?" they
asked.

23 Jesus said to them, "Surely you will quote this proverb to
me: 'Physician, heal yourself! Do here in your hometown what we
have heard that you did in Capernaum.'"

24 "I tell you the truth," he continued, "no prophet is accepted in his hometown. 25 I assure you that there were many widows
in Israel in Elijah's time, when the sky was shut for three and a half
years and there was a severe famine throughout the land. 26 Yet Elijah was not sent to any of them, but to a widow in Zarephath in
the region of Sidon. 27 And there were many in Israel with leprosy[b]
in the time of Elisha the prophet, yet not one of them was
cleansed—only Naaman the Syrian."

28 All the people in the synagogue were furious when they
heard this. 29 They got up, drove him out of the town, and took him
to the brow of the hill on which the town was built, in order to
throw him down the cliff. 30 But he walked right through the crowd
and went on his way.

Jesus Drives Out an Evil Spirit

31 Then he went down to Capernaum, a town in Galilee, and
on the Sabbath began to teach the people. 32 They were amazed at
his teaching, because his message had authority.

33 In the synagogue there was a man possessed by a demon,
an evil[c] spirit. He cried out at the top of his voice, 34 "Ha! What do
you want with us, Jesus of Nazareth? Have you come to destroy us?
I know who you are—the Holy One of God!"

---

[a]**19** Isaiah 61:1,2 [b]**27** The Greek word was used for various diseases affecting the skin—not necessarily leprosy. [c]**33** Greek *unclean;* also in verse 36

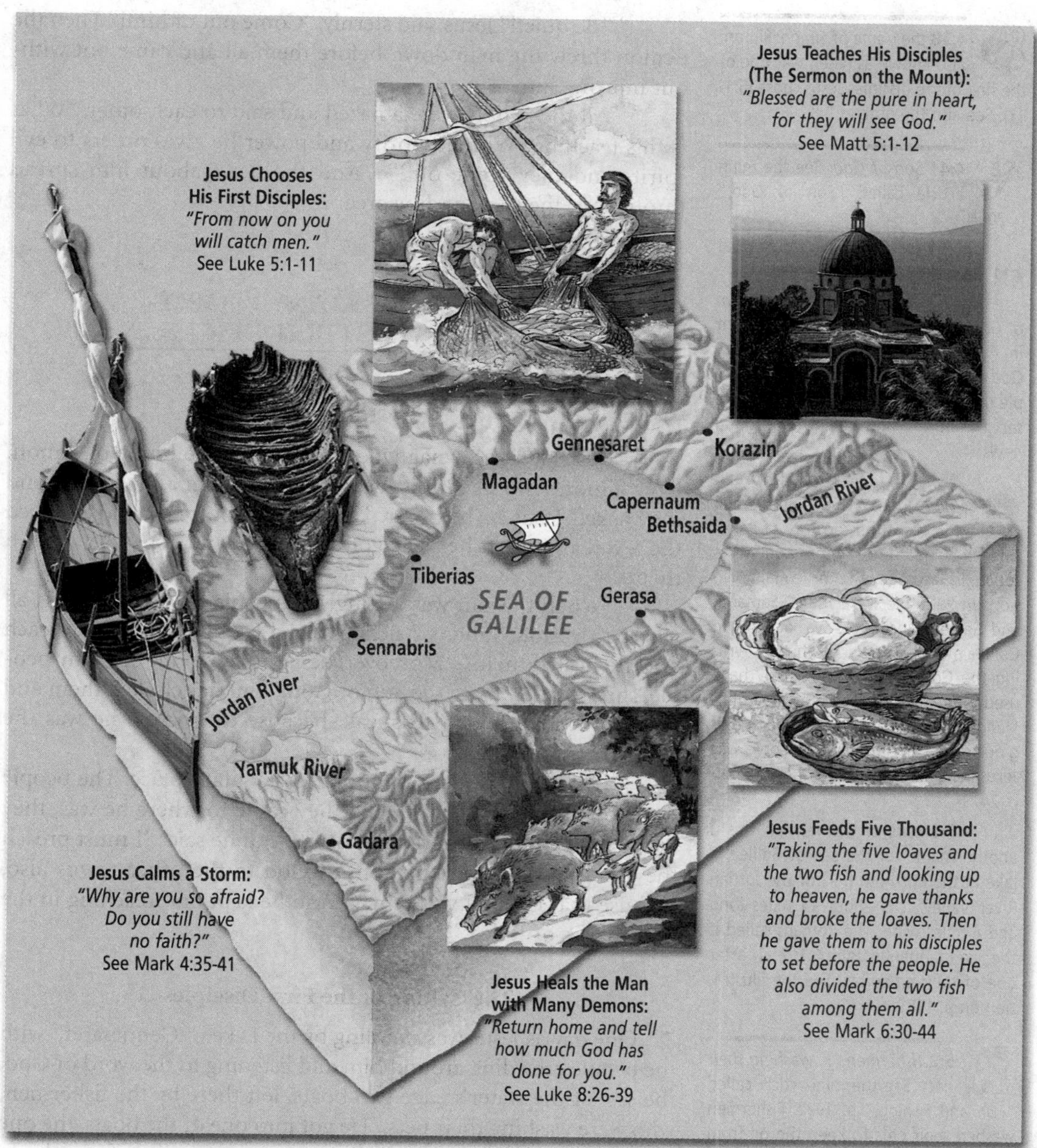
Jesus Teaches His Disciples
(The Sermon on the Mount):
"Blessed are the pure in heart,
for they will see God."
See Matt 5:1-12
Jesus Chooses
His First Disciples:
"From now on you
will catch men."
See Luke 5:1-11
Gennesaret
Korazin
Magadan
Capernaum
Jordan River
Bethsaida
Tiberias
SEA OF
GALILEE
Gerasa
Sennabris
Jordan River
Yarmuk River
Gadara
Jesus Calms a Storm:
"Why are you so afraid?
Do you still have
no faith?"
See Mark 4:35-41
Jesus Heals the Man
with Many Demons:
"Return home and tell
how much God has
done for you."
See Luke 8:26-39
Jesus Feeds Five Thousand:
"Taking the five loaves and
the two fish and looking up
to heaven, he gave thanks
and broke the loaves. Then
he gave them to his disciples
to set before the people. He
also divided the two fish
among them all."
See Mark 6:30-44

Jesus at the Sea of Galilee. Jesus was born and died in Judea, the Roman province to the west of the Dead Sea, and he grew up in Nazareth in the province of Galilee in the north. Most of his healing and preaching ministry took place in the small towns around the large, freshwater lake called the Sea of Galilee. On the shores of this lake Jesus chose his first disciples and gave his famous "Sermon on the Mount." (The Church of the Beatitudes, shown here, marks the traditional site of the sermon.) The Gospels describe many miracles Jesus performed in this area. Once, Jesus commanded a storm on the sea to stop, and the wind and the water obeyed him. (Shown above is a 2000-year-old fishing boat discovered in 1986 in the mud of the Sea of Galilee. This discovery has given archaeologists a better understanding of what boats from Jesus' day looked like; see the reconstructed model to the left.) In one of the towns near the Sea of Galilee (perhaps Gadara or Gerasa), Jesus ordered demons to come out of a man and then commanded them to go into a herd of pigs who rushed off the cliffs into the lake. In one of Jesus' most famous miracles, a crowd who had gathered to hear him preach became hungry, and Jesus fed all five thousand of them with just five loaves of bread and two fish.

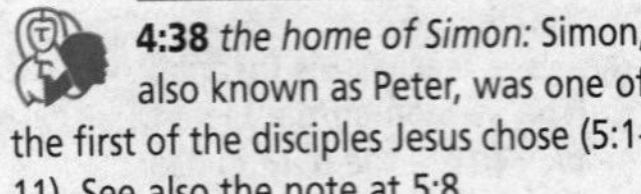

4:38 *the home of Simon:* Simon, also known as Peter, was one of the first of the disciples Jesus chose (5:1-11). See also the note at 5:8.

4:41 *Son of God:* See the mini-article called "Son of God," p. 2044.

4:41 *the Christ:* See the note at 2:11 (Savior).

4:43 *good news of the kingdom of God:* Jesus first told why he was sent in 4:18,19. This is the "good news." God's kingdom is anywhere God's people do what God wants them to do, like serving others and telling the good news.

4:44 *Judea:* This is the Greek name for the territory of Palestine that had once been known as Judah. In Jesus' day the three main divisions in Palestine were Judea, Samaria, and Galilee. Since Jesus was actually in Galilee at this time, Luke, who was writing the Gospel for Gentiles, may have used "Judea" in the sense of the entire "land of the Jews." The capital and religious center for the Jewish people was Jerusalem, in Judea. See the map on p. 2473.

5:1 *Lake of Gennesaret:* This is another name for the Sea of Galilee, a lake in the northern part of the Jordan River Valley. It is about 14 miles long and 6 miles wide. The Romans called it the Sea of Tiberias (John 6:1; 21:1) after one of their emperors. See the illustration on p. 1981.

5:2 *fishermen . . . washing their nets:* See the mini-article called "Fish and Fishing," p. 1922. Fishermen washed their nets to keep the oil from the fish from drying and making the nets brittle.

5:3 *he sat down:* Teachers in the ancient world usually sat down when they taught (see also Matt 5:1).

5:5,6 John 21:3,6.

[35]"Be quiet!" Jesus said sternly. "Come out of him!" Then the
demon threw the man down before them all and came out without injuring him.
[36]All the people were amazed and said to each other, "What
is this teaching? With authority and power he gives orders to evil
spirits and they come out!" [37]And the news about him spread
throughout the surrounding area.

JESUS HEALS MANY PEOPLE AND CALLS HIS FIRST DISCIPLES

Jesus Heals Many

[38]Jesus left the synagogue and went to the home of Simon.
Now Simon's mother-in-law was suffering from a high fever, and
they asked Jesus to help her. [39]So he bent over her and rebuked
the fever, and it left her. She got up at once and began to wait on
them.
[40]When the sun was setting, the people brought to Jesus all
who had various kinds of sickness, and laying his hands on each
one, he healed them. [41]Moreover, demons came out of many people, shouting, "You are the Son of God!" But he rebuked them and
would not allow them to speak, because they knew he was the
Christ.[a]
[42]At daybreak Jesus went out to a solitary place. The people
were looking for him and when they came to where he was, they
tried to keep him from leaving them. [43]But he said, "I must preach
the good news of the kingdom of God to the other towns also,
because that is why I was sent." [44]And he kept on preaching in the
synagogues of Judea.[b]

The Calling of the First Disciples

5 One day as Jesus was standing by the Lake of Gennesaret,[c] with
the people crowding around him and listening to the word of God,
[2]he saw at the water's edge two boats, left there by the fishermen,
who were washing their nets. [3]He got into one of the boats, the one
belonging to Simon, and asked him to put out a little from shore.
Then he sat down and taught the people from the boat.
[4]When he had finished speaking, he said to Simon, "Put
out into deep water, and let down[d] the nets for a catch."
[5]Simon answered, "Master, we've worked hard all night and
haven't caught anything. But because you say so, I will let down
the nets."

[a]41 Or *Messiah* [b]44 Or *the land of the Jews*; some manuscripts *Galilee*
[c]1 That is, Sea of Galilee [d]4 The Greek verb is plural.

Jesus Calls His First Disciples, mosaic from Sant'Apollinare Nuovo, Ravenna, Italy, around A.D. 530. Jesus did not choose priests or other established religious leaders to be his disciples. Instead, he chose people like Simon (Peter) and his business partners, James and John, who were simple fishermen. Jesus told Peter where to cast his net so that he would catch so many fish he wouldn't be able to pull in the net alone. Then he told the amazed fisherman, "From now on you will catch men." (See 5:1-11.)

6When they had done so, they caught such a large number of
fish that their nets began to break. 7So they signaled their partners
in the other boat to come and help them, and they came and filled
both boats so full that they began to sink.
8When Simon Peter saw this, he fell at Jesus' knees and said,
"Go away from me, Lord; I am a sinful man!" 9For he and all his
companions were astonished at the catch of fish they had taken,
10and so were James and John, the sons of Zebedee, Simon's partners.

Then Jesus said to Simon, "Don't be afraid; from now on
you will catch men." 11So they pulled their boats up on shore, left
everything and followed him.

The Man With Leprosy

12While Jesus was in one of the towns, a man came along
who was covered with leprosy.[a] When he saw Jesus, he fell with his
face to the ground and begged him, "Lord, if you are willing, you
can make me clean."
13Jesus reached out his hand and touched the man. "I am

[a]12 The Greek word was used for various diseases affecting the skin—not necessarily leprosy.

5:8 *Simon Peter:* Simon would become better known by the new name Jesus gave him—Peter (John 1:42). Both the Greek form of his new name (*Petros*) and the Aramaic form (*Cephas*) mean "rock," (see Matt 16:18).

5:8 *I am a sinful man:* Genesis 3 tells how sin entered the world. See also Rom 3:23. Peter recognized God's glory in Jesus. This made Peter realize that he himself was sinful. See also the mini-article called "Sin," p. 2181.

5:10 *James and John, the sons of Zebedee:* James and John became disciples of Jesus (5:11; 6:14). He nicknamed them "Boanerges," which means "Sons of Thunder" (Mark 3:17).

5:12 *leprosy:* See the note at 4:27.

willing," he said. "Be clean!" And immediately the leprosy left him.

[14]Then Jesus ordered him, "Don't tell anyone, but go, show yourself to the priest and offer the sacrifices that Moses commanded for your cleansing, as a testimony to them."

[15]Yet the news about him spread all the more, so that crowds of people came to hear him and to be healed of their sicknesses. [16]But Jesus often withdrew to lonely places and prayed.

Jesus Heals a Paralytic

[17]One day as he was teaching, Pharisees and teachers of the law, who had come from every village of Galilee and from Judea and Jerusalem, were sitting there. And the power of the Lord was present for him to heal the sick. [18]Some men came carrying a paralytic on a mat and tried to take him into the house to lay him before Jesus. [19]When they could not find a way to do this because of the crowd, they went up on the roof and lowered him on his mat through the tiles into the middle of the crowd, right in front of Jesus.

[20]When Jesus saw their faith, he said, "Friend, your sins are forgiven."

[21]The Pharisees and the teachers of the law began thinking to themselves, "Who is this fellow who speaks blasphemy? Who can forgive sins but God alone?"

[22]Jesus knew what they were thinking and asked, "Why are you thinking these things in your hearts? [23]Which is easier: to say, 'Your sins are forgiven,' or to say, 'Get up and walk'? [24]But that you may know that the Son of Man has authority on earth to forgive sins . . ." He said to the paralyzed man, "I tell you, get up, take your mat and go home." [25]Immediately he stood up in front of them, took what he had been lying on and went home praising God. [26]Everyone was amazed and gave praise to God. They were filled with awe and said, "We have seen remarkable things today."

The Calling of Levi

[27]After this, Jesus went out and saw a tax collector by the name of Levi sitting at his tax booth. "Follow me," Jesus said to him, [28]and Levi got up, left everything and followed him.

[29]Then Levi held a great banquet for Jesus at his house, and a large crowd of tax collectors and others were eating with them. [30]But the Pharisees and the teachers of the law who belonged to their sect complained to his disciples, "Why do you eat and drink with tax collectors and 'sinners'?"

[31]Jesus answered them, "It is not the healthy who need a doctor, but the sick. [32]I have not come to call the righteous, but sinners to repentance."

Jesus answered them, "It is not the healthy who need a doctor, but the sick."
Luke 5:31

5:14 *Don't tell anyone:* Jesus often told people he helped not to tell what he had done for them (Mark 3:10-12; 7:34-36). He may have wanted the miracle to speak for itself. Or he may have wanted to avoid drawing crowds of people who were more interested in miracles than in hearing about God's new kingdom.

5:14 *show yourself to the priest:* People with leprosy had to be examined by a priest to have their healing confirmed before they could once again live in the Jewish community (Lev 13). The gift that was required for this was the sacrifice of some lambs and flour mixed with olive oil (Lev 14:1-32).

5:17 *Pharisees and teachers of the law:* The Pharisees met in homes to pray and to study the Jewish Scriptures. The teachers of the law (meaning the Law of Moses) studied the first five books of the Jewish Scriptures. Like the Pharisees, they believed that only God could forgive sins. See also the article called "The World of Jesus: Peoples, Powers, and Politics," p. 1821.

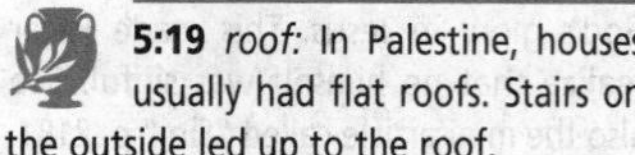

5:19 *roof:* In Palestine, houses usually had flat roofs. Stairs on the outside led up to the roof.

5:24 *Son of Man:* See the mini-article called "Son of Man," p. 1866.

5:27 *tax collector . . . Levi:* Levi is also called Matthew (Matt 9:9-13). He was probably collecting taxes from people and merchants as they traveled past him on a major highway.

5:21 Isa 43:25.

JESUS CONTINUES HIS WORK IN GALILEE

Jesus continues to do his work of teaching, healing, and working miracles. He also chooses his twelve disciples and has to face many questions about his actions and his message.

Jesus Questioned About Fasting

[33]They said to him, "John's disciples often fast and pray, and so do the disciples of the Pharisees, but yours go on eating and drinking."

[34]Jesus answered, "Can you make the guests of the bridegroom fast while he is with them? [35]But the time will come when the bridegroom will be taken from them; in those days they will fast."

[36]He told them this parable: "No one tears a patch from a new garment and sews it on an old one. If he does, he will have torn the new garment, and the patch from the new will not match the old. [37]And no one pours new wine into old wineskins. If he does, the new wine will burst the skins, the wine will run out and the wineskins will be ruined. [38]No, new wine must be poured into new wineskins. [39]And no one after drinking old wine wants the new, for he says, 'The old is better.'"

Lord of the Sabbath

6 One Sabbath Jesus was going through the grainfields, and his disciples began to pick some heads of grain, rub them in their hands and eat the kernels. [2]Some of the Pharisees asked, "Why are you doing what is unlawful on the Sabbath?"

[3]Jesus answered them, "Have you never read what David did when he and his companions were hungry? [4]He entered the house of God, and taking the consecrated bread, he ate what is lawful only for priests to eat. And he also gave some to his companions." [5]Then Jesus said to them, "The Son of Man is Lord of the Sabbath."

[6]On another Sabbath he went into the synagogue and was teaching, and a man was there whose right hand was shriveled. [7]The Pharisees and the teachers of the law were looking for a reason to accuse Jesus, so they watched him closely to see if he would heal on the Sabbath. [8]But Jesus knew what they were thinking and said to the man with the shriveled hand, "Get up and stand in front of everyone." So he got up and stood there.

[9]Then Jesus said to them, "I ask you, which is lawful on the Sabbath: to do good or to do evil, to save life or to destroy it?"

[10]He looked around at them all, and then said to the man, "Stretch out your hand." He did so, and his hand was completely restored. [11]But they were furious and began to discuss with one another what they might do to Jesus.

5:34,35 *bridegroom will be taken:* Jesus was referring to himself. See also 9:22 and 17:22.

5:36-38 *patch . . . wineskins:* A patch made of new, unwashed cloth could shrink after being washed. If it had been used to patch a hole in an old piece of clothing, it could tear away from the garment and make a bigger tear.

Similarly, as grape juice becomes wine, gas is produced which swells and stretches the wineskins used for storing it. If new wine was put into old skins that had become stiff, rather than into flexible new skins, the skins could burst. See also the mini-article called "Wine," p. 2047.

6:1 *going through the grainfields:* It was the custom among the Jewish people to let hungry travelers pick grains of wheat (Deut 23:25).

6:3,4 *David . . . lawful only for priests to eat:* This story is recorded in 1 Samuel 21:1-6.

6:5 *Son of Man:* See the mini-article called "Son of Man," p. 1866. What Jesus teaches and does has more authority than the Law of Moses, which includes the laws about the Sabbath. See also Heb 2:1—3:6.

6:9 *lawful on the Sabbath:* Since any work done on the Sabbath was forbidden by the Jewish law, the Pharisees and teachers of the law thought that Jesus was breaking the law when he healed the man. Jesus showed by his actions that doing a good deed on the Sabbath is not against God's law.

The Twelve Apostles

12One of those days Jesus went out to a mountainside to
pray, and spent the night praying to God. 13When morning came,
he called his disciples to him and chose twelve of them, whom he
also designated apostles: 14Simon (whom he named Peter), his
brother Andrew, James, John, Philip, Bartholomew, 15Matthew,
Thomas, James son of Alphaeus, Simon who was called the Zealot,
16Judas son of James, and Judas Iscariot, who became a traitor.

Blessings and Woes

17He went down with them and stood on a level place.
A large crowd of his disciples was there and a great number of
people from all over Judea, from Jerusalem, and from the coast of
Tyre and Sidon, 18who had come to hear him and to be healed
of their diseases. Those troubled by evil[a] spirits were cured, 19and
the people all tried to touch him, because power was coming from
him and healing them all.

20Looking at his disciples, he said:

"Blessed are you who are poor,
for yours is the kingdom of God.
21Blessed are you who hunger now,
for you will be satisfied.
Blessed are you who weep now,
for you will laugh.
22Blessed are you when men hate you,
when they exclude you and insult you
and reject your name as evil,
because of the Son of Man.

23"Rejoice in that day and leap for joy, because great is your
reward in heaven. For that is how their fathers treated the
prophets.

24"But woe to you who are rich,
for you have already received your comfort.
25Woe to you who are well fed now,
for you will go hungry.
Woe to you who laugh now,
for you will mourn and weep.
26Woe to you when all men speak well of you,
for that is how their fathers treated the false prophets.

Love for Enemies

27"But I tell you who hear me: Love your enemies, do good
to those who hate you, 28bless those who curse you, pray for those

a18 Greek *unclean*

Jesus said, *"Love your enemies, do good to those who hate you."* Luke 6:27

6:12 *mountainside:* Jesus went to a mountain to pray before selecting his apostles. In Luke, mountains are often associated with important moments in Jesus' ministry (see also 4:5; 9:28; and 19:29).

6:13 *disciples . . . twelve . . . apostles:* A *disciple* is a follower who learns from a master teacher, and an *apostle* is someone who is sent to others to carry the teacher's actions and message. The number of disciples (twelve) is the same number as the tribes of Israel. These twelve were later commonly called apostles, as were a few others such as the apostle Paul (1 Cor 9:1). See also the chart, called "Jesus' Twelve Disciples," p. 1869.

6:17 *went down with them . . . level place:* It is not clear exactly where this was. What Jesus teaches in 6:20-49 is sometimes called the "Sermon on the Plain." Notice that many of the things that Jesus says here are similar to what he says in the "Sermon on the Mount" in Matthew 5:1—7:29.

6:22 *Son of Man:* See the mini-article called "Son of Man," p. 1866.

6:23 *heaven:* Living under God's rule in heaven will be the reward for those who are faithful. See also the mini-article called "Heaven," p. 1420.

6:22 1 Pet 4:14. **6:22,23** 2 Chr 36:16; Acts 7:52.

who mistreat you. 29 If someone strikes you on one cheek, turn to
him the other also. If someone takes your cloak, do not stop him
from taking your tunic. 30 Give to everyone who asks you, and if
anyone takes what belongs to you, do not demand it back. 31 Do to
others as you would have them do to you.
32 "If you love those who love you, what credit is that to you?
Even 'sinners' love those who love them. 33 And if you do good to
those who are good to you, what credit is that to you? Even 'sinners' do that. 34 And if you lend to those from whom you expect
repayment, what credit is that to you? Even 'sinners' lend to 'sinners,' expecting to be repaid in full. 35 But love your enemies, do
good to them, and lend to them without expecting to get anything
back. Then your reward will be great, and you will be sons of the
Most High, because he is kind to the ungrateful and wicked. 36 Be
merciful, just as your Father is merciful.

Judging Others

37 "Do not judge, and you will not be judged. Do not condemn, and you will not be condemned. Forgive, and you will be
forgiven. 38 Give, and it will be given to you. A good measure,
pressed down, shaken together and running over, will be poured
into your lap. For with the measure you use, it will be measured
to you."
39 He also told them this parable: "Can a blind man lead a
blind man? Will they not both fall into a pit? 40 A student is not
above his teacher, but everyone who is fully trained will be like his
teacher.
41 "Why do you look at the speck of sawdust in your brother's
eye and pay no attention to the plank in your own eye? 42 How can
you say to your brother, 'Brother, let me take the speck out of your
eye,' when you yourself fail to see the plank in your own eye? You
hypocrite, first take the plank out of your eye, and then you will
see clearly to remove the speck from your brother's eye.

A Tree and Its Fruit

43 "No good tree bears bad fruit, nor does a bad tree bear
good fruit. 44 Each tree is recognized by its own fruit. People do not
pick figs from thornbushes, or grapes from briers. 45 The good man
brings good things out of the good stored up in his heart, and the
evil man brings evil things out of the evil stored up in his heart.
For out of the overflow of his heart his mouth speaks.

The Wise and Foolish Builders

46 "Why do you call me, 'Lord, Lord,' and do not do what I
say? 47 I will show you what he is like who comes to me and hears
my words and puts them into practice. 48 He is like a man building

Jesus said: *"Do not judge, and you will not be judged. Do not condemn, and you will not be condemned. Forgive, and you will be forgiven."*
Luke 6:37

6:22 *sinner:* See the note at 15:1 and the mini-article called "Sin," p. 2181.

6:29 *someone strikes you on one cheek:* A slap on the cheek was a very bad insult.

6:35,36 *sons of the Most High:* "Sons" is used to describe members of God's family, both men and women, no matter how young or old they are. Jesus says that the true sons of God will act like God by loving their enemies, being generous, and by being merciful toward others.

6:41 *plank in your own eye:* Jesus uses this exaggeration to emphasize how important it is not to judge others before looking closely at one's own life.

6:44 *figs . . . grapes:* Figs are sweet fruits from bushy trees that can grow quite tall. In Jesus' day they were an important source of food. A large fig tree produced two crops each year. Grapes were also an important food. They were eaten fresh or dried, but most were used for making wine. Grapes grow on vines that have to be watered, weeded, and trimmed so that they will produce good grapes. See also Matt 12:33.

6:31 Matt 7:12. **6:39** Matt 15:14. **6:40** Matt 10:24,25; John 13:16; 15:20. **6:45** Matt 12:34.

7:1 *Capernaum:* See the note at 4:23.

7:2 *centurion's servant:* A centurion was a leader of one hundred soldiers. He commanded and trained his men to fight and die at his command. Since this story takes place in Galilee, it is possible that this centurion served in the army of Herod Antipas. Although he was a Gentile, the centurion was admired by the Jews (7:4,5) and affirmed by Jesus (7:9).

7:3 *some elders of the Jews:* These were probably respected local leaders who worked with the government authorities in Capernaum.

7:5 *built our synagogue:* See the note at 4:15. In recent years, archaeologists have examined the remains of the ancient synagogue at Capernaum. They have found that it was originally a private house that was rebuilt to serve as a meeting place. Later, it was completely rebuilt as a formal place of worship. This type of religious building began to be erected by Jews in the second century A.D.

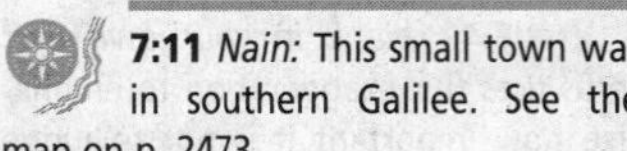

7:11 *Nain:* This small town was in southern Galilee. See the map on p. 2473.

7:12 *a dead person was being carried out:* The Jewish people usually took the dead body to a tomb on the same day the person died. The family of a dead person often hired professional mourners for funerals. The family and other mourners would wail (cry out loud) and beat on their chests or tear their clothes to show their sadness (see Gen 37:34; Deut 34:8; 1 Sam 31:13).

7:14,15 *touched the coffin . . . gave him back to his mother:* Jewish people in the crowd would have been reminded of the prophet Elijah who used God's power to raise a widow's dead son (1 Kgs 17:8-24). The Gospels tell of two other times Jesus raised people from the dead: the daughter of Jairus (Luke 8:40-56) and Lazarus (John 11:38-44).

a house, who dug down deep and laid the foundation on rock. When a flood came, the torrent struck that house but could not shake it, because it was well built. 49 But the one who hears my words and does not put them into practice is like a man who built a house on the ground without a foundation. The moment the torrent struck that house, it collapsed and its destruction was complete."

The Faith of the Centurion

7 When Jesus had finished saying all this in the hearing of the people, he entered Capernaum. 2 There a centurion's servant, whom his master valued highly, was sick and about to die. 3 The centurion heard of Jesus and sent some elders of the Jews to him, asking him to come and heal his servant. 4 When they came to Jesus, they pleaded earnestly with him, "This man deserves to have you do this, 5 because he loves our nation and has built our synagogue." 6 So Jesus went with them.

He was not far from the house when the centurion sent friends to say to him: "Lord, don't trouble yourself, for I do not deserve to have you come under my roof. 7 That is why I did not even consider myself worthy to come to you. But say the word, and my servant will be healed. 8 For I myself am a man under authority, with soldiers under me. I tell this one, 'Go,' and he goes; and that one, 'Come,' and he comes. I say to my servant, 'Do this,' and he does it."

9 When Jesus heard this, he was amazed at him, and turning to the crowd following him, he said, "I tell you, I have not found such great faith even in Israel." 10 Then the men who had been sent returned to the house and found the servant well.

Jesus Raises a Widow's Son

11 Soon afterward, Jesus went to a town called Nain, and his disciples and a large crowd went along with him. 12 As he approached the town gate, a dead person was being carried out—the only son of his mother, and she was a widow. And a large crowd from the town was with her. 13 When the Lord saw her, his heart went out to her and he said, "Don't cry."

14 Then he went up and touched the coffin, and those carrying it stood still. He said, "Young man, I say to you, get up!" 15 The dead man sat up and began to talk, and Jesus gave him back to his mother.

16 They were all filled with awe and praised God. "A great prophet has appeared among us," they said. "God has come to help his people." 17 This news about Jesus spread throughout Judea[a] and the surrounding country.

---

[a]**17** Or *the land of the Jews*

Jesus and John the Baptist

[18]John's disciples told him about all these things. Calling two of them, [19]he sent them to the Lord to ask, "Are you the one who was to come, or should we expect someone else?"

[20]When the men came to Jesus, they said, "John the Baptist sent us to you to ask, 'Are you the one who was to come, or should we expect someone else?' "

[21]At that very time Jesus cured many who had diseases, sicknesses and evil spirits, and gave sight to many who were blind. [22]So he replied to the messengers, "Go back and report to John what you have seen and heard: The blind receive sight, the lame walk, those who have leprosy[a] are cured, the deaf hear, the dead are raised, and the good news is preached to the poor. [23]Blessed is the man who does not fall away on account of me."

[24]After John's messengers left, Jesus began to speak to the crowd about John: "What did you go out into the desert to see? A reed swayed by the wind? [25]If not, what did you go out to see? A man dressed in fine clothes? No, those who wear expensive clothes and indulge in luxury are in palaces. [26]But what did you go out to see? A prophet? Yes, I tell you, and more than a prophet. [27]This is the one about whom it is written:

> " 'I will send my messenger ahead of you,
> who will prepare your way before you.'[b]

[28]I tell you, among those born of women there is no one greater than John; yet the one who is least in the kingdom of God is greater than he."

[29](All the people, even the tax collectors, when they heard Jesus' words, acknowledged that God's way was right, because they had been baptized by John. [30]But the Pharisees and experts in the law rejected God's purpose for themselves, because they had not been baptized by John.)

[31]"To what, then, can I compare the people of this generation? What are they like? [32]They are like children sitting in the marketplace and calling out to each other:

> " 'We played the flute for you,
> and you did not dance;
> we sang a dirge,
> and you did not cry.'

[33]For John the Baptist came neither eating bread nor drinking wine, and you say, 'He has a demon.' [34]The Son of Man came eating and drinking, and you say, 'Here is a glutton and a drunkard, a friend of tax collectors and "sinners." ' [35]But wisdom is proved right by all her children."

[a]**22** The Greek word was used for various diseases affecting the skin—not necessarily leprosy. [b]**27** Mal. 3:1

7:20 *John the Baptist:* See the note at 1:13.

7:22 *leprosy:* See the note at 4:27.

7:27 *I will send my messenger:* Jesus says that John is a messenger sent from God (Mal 3:1) to prepare the way for Jesus.

7:29,30 *tax collectors . . . Pharisees and experts in the law:* For "tax collectors," see the notes at 3:12 and 15:1; for "Pharisees and experts in the law," see the note at 5:17. See also Matt 21:32.

7:32-34 *children sitting in the marketplace:* Jesus said that some of the Jewish people and their religious leaders were like quarreling children. Some children wanted to play a joyful game, but others wanted to play a sad game. Jesus is saying that some leaders didn't agree with John's ways, because they were so strict. And they didn't like Jesus' ways, because they weren't strict enough.

7:35 *wisdom:* Wise people were honored in Jewish society. True wisdom was said to come from God's Law (Ps 19:7). Here Jesus is saying that wisdom is made visible by the good we do for others. See the mini-article called "Wisdom," p. 2206.

7:22,23: Isa 35:5, 6; 61:1; Luke 4:18. **7:28** Matt 11:11.

Jesus Anointed by a Sinful Woman

36Now one of the Pharisees invited Jesus to have dinner
with him, so he went to the Pharisee's house and reclined at the
table. 37When a woman who had lived a sinful life in that town
learned that Jesus was eating at the Pharisee's house, she brought
an alabaster jar of perfume, 38and as she stood behind him at his
feet weeping, she began to wet his feet with her tears. Then she
wiped them with her hair, kissed them and poured perfume on
them.

39When the Pharisee who had invited him saw this, he said
to himself, "If this man were a prophet, he would know who is
touching him and what kind of woman she is—that she is a sinner."

40Jesus answered him, "Simon, I have something to tell you."

"Tell me, teacher," he said.

41"Two men owed money to a certain moneylender. One
owed him five hundred denarii,[a] and the other fifty. 42Neither of
them had the money to pay him back, so he canceled the debts of
both. Now which of them will love him more?"

43Simon replied, "I suppose the one who had the bigger debt
canceled."

"You have judged correctly," Jesus said.

44Then he turned toward the woman and said to Simon,
"Do you see this woman? I came into your house. You did not
give me any water for my feet, but she wet my feet with her tears
and wiped them with her hair. 45You did not give me a kiss, but
this woman, from the time I entered, has not stopped kissing my
feet. 46You did not put oil on my head, but she has poured perfume on my feet. 47Therefore, I tell you, her many sins have been
forgiven—for she loved much. But he who has been forgiven little loves little."

48Then Jesus said to her, "Your sins are forgiven."

49The other guests began to say among themselves, "Who is
this who even forgives sins?"

50Jesus said to the woman, "Your faith has saved you; go in
peace."

The Parable of the Sower

8 After this, Jesus traveled about from one town and village to
another, proclaiming the good news of the kingdom of God. The
Twelve were with him, 2and also some women who had been cured
of evil spirits and diseases: Mary (called Magdalene) from whom
seven demons had come out; 3Joanna the wife of Cuza, the manager of Herod's household; Susanna; and many others. These
women were helping to support them out of their own means.

[a]41 A denarius was a coin worth about a day's wages.

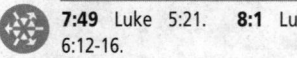

7:36 *reclined at the table:* The Jewish people often followed the Greek and Roman custom of lying on their left side while eating with the right hand. This is what Jesus was doing when the woman washed his feet (7:38).

7:37 *an alabaster jar of perfume:* The bottle was made out of a very soft and beautiful stone.

7:39 *would know who is touching him:* The woman was likely a prostitute. According to Jewish law, someone who touched a sinner like her would become unclean and unable to go to worship. Simon was a Pharisee who always tried to avoid contact with anyone who could make him unclean. Therefore, he was surprised that Jesus let the woman touch him.

7:41 *denarii*: The plural of denarius, a coin which was equal to about the daily pay of a common laborer (see Matt 20:9).

7:44-46 *water for my feet . . . a kiss . . . oil on my head:* The Jewish people believed that it was very important to be friendly to guests. Since most people wore open sandals, guests in a home were usually offered water so they could wash their feet. Guests were also greeted with a kiss on the cheek and often had olive oil poured on their head.

8:2 *Mary (called Magdalene):* Her name means that she was from Magdala, a small town on the shore of the Sea of Galilee. Some say that she was the sinful woman in 7:36-50, but the Bible gives no hint that this is true. She was present when Jesus died on a cross (Luke 23:49; Mark 15:40, 41) and saw where he was buried (Luke 23:55; Mark 15:47). She brought spices to the tomb to use in preparing Jesus' body for burial (Luke 24:1; Mark 16:1) and so became the first person to see Jesus after he was raised from death (Luke 24:9, 10; Mark 16:9).

7:49 Luke 5:21. **8:1** Luke 6:12-16.

4While a large crowd was gathering and people were coming to Jesus from town after town, he told this parable: 5"A farmer went out to sow his seed. As he was scattering the seed, some fell along the path; it was trampled on, and the birds of the air ate it up. 6Some fell on rock, and when it came up, the plants withered because they had no moisture. 7Other seed fell among thorns, which grew up with it and choked the plants. 8Still other seed fell on good soil. It came up and yielded a crop, a hundred times more than was sown."

When he said this, he called out, "He who has ears to hear, let him hear."

9His disciples asked him what this parable meant. 10He said, "The knowledge of the secrets of the kingdom of God has been given to you, but to others I speak in parables, so that,

" 'though seeing, they may not see;
though hearing, they may not understand.'[a]

11"This is the meaning of the parable: The seed is the word of God. 12Those along the path are the ones who hear, and then the devil comes and takes away the word from their hearts, so that they may not believe and be saved. 13Those on the rock are the ones who receive the word with joy when they hear it, but they have no root. They believe for a while, but in the time of testing they fall away. 14The seed that fell among thorns stands for those who hear, but as they go on their way they are choked by life's worries, riches and pleasures, and they do not mature. 15But the seed on good soil stands for those with a noble and good heart, who hear the word, retain it, and by persevering produce a crop.

A Lamp on a Stand

16"No one lights a lamp and hides it in a jar or puts it under a bed. Instead, he puts it on a stand, so that those who come in can see the light. 17For there is nothing hidden that will not be disclosed, and nothing concealed that will not be known or brought out into the open. 18Therefore consider carefully how you listen. Whoever has will be given more; whoever does not have, even what he thinks he has will be taken from him."

Jesus' Mother and Brothers

19Now Jesus' mother and brothers came to see him, but they were not able to get near him because of the crowd. 20Someone told him, "Your mother and brothers are standing outside, wanting to see you."

21He replied, "My mother and brothers are those who hear God's word and put it into practice."

a10 Isaiah 6:9

8:3 *Joanna . . . Cuza . . . Susanna:* Joanna and Susanna probably traveled with Jesus and helped in his ministry. This is the only mention of Susanna in the Bible. Joanna is mentioned again in 24:10. Cuza was a manager who worked for Herod Antipas (see the note at 3:1,2).

8:5 *A farmer went out to sow his seed:* Farmers prepared the ground by breaking up the surface, and then scattered seeds on the ground a handful at a time. The farmer plowed the seed into the ground along with the stubble from the previous crop, which acted as fertilizer as it decayed. Of course, some seeds stayed on the surface. See also the article called "How People Made a Living in the Time of Jesus," p. 1826.

8:10 *secrets of the kingdom of God:* See the note at 4:43. In the New Testament a "secret" is a truth that people can understand only by revelation from God.

8:10 *though seeing, they may not see:* Jesus quotes Isaiah 6:9 to make the point that for those who were not willing to receive the message Jesus brought about God's kingdom, the good news would remain hidden. Although Jesus' message is for everyone, not everyone would be open to it.

8:12 *devil:* See the note at 4:3.

8:16 *lamp:* In Jesus' day, people used small clay lamps that burned olive oil. They were small enough to hold in one's hand. See Matt 5:15; Luke 11:33.

8:19 *Jesus' mother and brothers:* Mark 6:3 gives the names of four brothers and says that Jesus also had sisters.

8:10 Isa 6:9. **8:17** Matt 10:26; Luke 12:2. **8:18** Matt 25:29; Luke 19:26.

8:22 *the other side of the lake:* They were going to go to the eastern shore of the Sea of Galilee, where most people were not Jewish. The Jewish area of Galilee (8:26) was west of the Sea of Galilee. See the map on p. 2473.

8:26 *region of the Gerasenes:* Gerasa was probably located about twenty miles east of the Jordan River. It was one of the ten cities that formed what was known as the Decapolis, or "ten towns." Its population, architecture, and style of life were mostly Greek. See the illustration on p. 1858 (Decapolis Map).

8:27 *a demon-possessed man:* See the note at 4:33-35.

8:27 *tombs:* It was thought that demons lived in tombs. See also the mini-article called "Burial," p. 1998.

8:28 *Son of the Most High God:* The demons knew that Jesus was God's Son, even if people didn't fully believe or understand who Jesus was. Compare this verse to 4:34. See the mini-article called "Son of God," p. 2044.

8:30 *Legion:* A Roman army legion was made up of 6000 men. This man was possessed by many demons.

8:31 *the Abyss:* The place where evil spirits were kept and punished. The Abyss may be the place later described as "hell" (see the note at 12:5).

8:32 *herd of pigs:* Jewish people did not have pigs, since the Law of Moses said they could not eat pork. This shows that the area was Gentile, not Jewish.

8:37 *region of the Gerasenes:* See the note at 8:26 (Gerasenes).

Jesus Calms the Storm

22 One day Jesus said to his disciples, "Let's go over to the
other side of the lake." So they got into a boat and set out. 23 As
they sailed, he fell asleep. A squall came down on the lake, so that
the boat was being swamped, and they were in great danger.
24 The disciples went and woke him, saying, "Master, Master,
we're going to drown!"
He got up and rebuked the wind and the raging waters; the
storm subsided, and all was calm. 25 "Where is your faith?" he asked
his disciples.
In fear and amazement they asked one another, "Who
is this? He commands even the winds and the water, and they
obey him."

The Healing of a Demon-possessed Man

26 They sailed to the region of the Gerasenes,[a] which is across
the lake from Galilee. 27 When Jesus stepped ashore, he was met by
a demon-possessed man from the town. For a long time this man
had not worn clothes or lived in a house, but had lived in the
tombs. 28 When he saw Jesus, he cried out and fell at his feet, shouting at the top of his voice, "What do you want with me, Jesus, Son
of the Most High God? I beg you, don't torture me!" 29 For Jesus
had commanded the evil[b] spirit to come out of the man. Many
times it had seized him, and though he was chained hand and foot
and kept under guard, he had broken his chains and had been
driven by the demon into solitary places.
30 Jesus asked him, "What is your name?"
"Legion," he replied, because many demons had gone into
him. 31 And they begged him repeatedly not to order them to go
into the Abyss.
32 A large herd of pigs was feeding there on the hillside. The
demons begged Jesus to let them go into them, and he gave them
permission. 33 When the demons came out of the man, they went
into the pigs, and the herd rushed down the steep bank into the
lake and was drowned.
34 When those tending the pigs saw what had happened, they
ran off and reported this in the town and countryside, 35 and the
people went out to see what had happened. When they came to
Jesus, they found the man from whom the demons had gone out,
sitting at Jesus' feet, dressed and in his right mind; and they were
afraid. 36 Those who had seen it told the people how the demon-
possessed man had been cured. 37 Then all the people of the region
of the Gerasenes asked Jesus to leave them, because they were
overcome with fear. So he got into the boat and left.

---

[a] **26** Some manuscripts *Gadarenes*; other manuscripts *Gergesenes*; also in verse 37
[b] **29** Greek *unclean*

[38]The man from whom the demons had gone out begged to go with him, but Jesus sent him away, saying, [39]"Return home and tell how much God has done for you." So the man went away and told all over town how much Jesus had done for him.

A Dead Girl and a Sick Woman

[40]Now when Jesus returned, a crowd welcomed him, for they were all expecting him. [41]Then a man named Jairus, a ruler of the synagogue, came and fell at Jesus' feet, pleading with him to come to his house [42]because his only daughter, a girl of about twelve, was dying.

As Jesus was on his way, the crowds almost crushed him. [43]And a woman was there who had been subject to bleeding for twelve years,[a] but no one could heal her. [44]She came up behind him and touched the edge of his cloak, and immediately her bleeding stopped.

[45]"Who touched me?" Jesus asked.

When they all denied it, Peter said, "Master, the people are crowding and pressing against you."

[46]But Jesus said, "Someone touched me; I know that power has gone out from me."

[47]Then the woman, seeing that she could not go unnoticed, came trembling and fell at his feet. In the presence of all the people, she told why she had touched him and how she had been instantly healed. [48]Then he said to her, "Daughter, your faith has healed you. Go in peace."

[49]While Jesus was still speaking, someone came from the house of Jairus, the synagogue ruler. "Your daughter is dead," he said. "Don't bother the teacher any more."

[50]Hearing this, Jesus said to Jairus, "Don't be afraid; just believe, and she will be healed."

[51]When he arrived at the house of Jairus, he did not let anyone go in with him except Peter, John and James, and the child's father and mother. [52]Meanwhile, all the people were wailing and mourning for her. "Stop wailing," Jesus said. "She is not dead but asleep."

[53]They laughed at him, knowing that she was dead. [54]But he took her by the hand and said, "My child, get up!" [55]Her spirit returned, and at once she stood up. Then Jesus told them to give her something to eat. [56]Her parents were astonished, but he ordered them not to tell anyone what had happened.

Jesus Sends Out the Twelve

9 When Jesus had called the Twelve together, he gave them power and authority to drive out all demons and to cure diseases,

[a]**43** Many manuscripts *years, and she had spent all she had on doctors*

Jesus said to her, *"Daughter, your faith has healed you. Go in peace."*
Luke 8:48

8:41 *synagogue:* See the note at 4:15.

8:43 *bleeding for twelve years; but no one could heal her:* In Jesus' day there were physicians who helped people when they were sick or injured. Though they had many skills, their knowledge of what causes diseases was limited. See the article called "Miracles, Magic, and Medicine," p. 1838.

8:51 *Peter, John and James:* Three of the twelve apostles (see the note at 6:13). All three of them were fishermen when Jesus called them to follow him. James and John were brothers (5:10). All three would see Jesus' true glory (transfiguration) on a mountaintop (9:28-36), and all of them were with Jesus when he prayed in Gethsemane before his arrest (Mark 14:33).

8:55 *give her something to eat:* Eating was a sign that the girl was alive and not just a spirit. Compare this with 24:30-43. After God raised Jesus from the dead, he met two of his followers on the road to Emmaus. They recognized him when he shared a meal with them. Later, when he appeared to his disciples, he also ate with them.

8:56 *ordered them not to tell:* See the note at 5:14 (Don't tell anyone).

9:1 *the Twelve together:* See the note at 6:13.

8:55 Luke 7:14,15.

2 and he sent them out to preach the kingdom of God and to heal the sick. 3 He told them: "Take nothing for the journey—no staff, no bag, no bread, no money, no extra tunic. 4 Whatever house you enter, stay there until you leave that town. 5 If people do not welcome you, shake the dust off your feet when you leave their town, as a testimony against them." 6 So they set out and went from village to village, preaching the gospel and healing people everywhere.

7 Now Herod the tetrarch heard about all that was going on. And he was perplexed, because some were saying that John had been raised from the dead, 8 others that Elijah had appeared, and still others that one of the prophets of long ago had come back to life. 9 But Herod said, "I beheaded John. Who, then, is this I hear such things about?" And he tried to see him.

Jesus Feeds the Five Thousand

10 When the apostles returned, they reported to Jesus what they had done. Then he took them with him and they withdrew by themselves to a town called Bethsaida, 11 but the crowds learned about it and followed him. He welcomed them and spoke to them about the kingdom of God, and healed those who needed healing.

12 Late in the afternoon the Twelve came to him and said, "Send the crowd away so they can go to the surrounding villages and countryside and find food and lodging, because we are in a remote place here."

13 He replied, "You give them something to eat."

They answered, "We have only five loaves of bread and two fish—unless we go and buy food for all this crowd." 14 (About five thousand men were there.)

But he said to his disciples, "Have them sit down in groups of about fifty each." 15 The disciples did so, and everybody sat down. 16 Taking the five loaves and the two fish and looking up to heaven, he gave thanks and broke them. Then he gave them to the disciples to set before the people. 17 They all ate and were satisfied, and the disciples picked up twelve basketfuls of broken pieces that were left over.

WHO JESUS IS AND WHAT HE MUST DO

Jesus wants to make it clear to his disciples who he is and what he must do. Peter, John, and James get to see Jesus' true glory and hear God identify Jesus as "my Son, whom I have chosen" (9:35). This is similar to the statement God made when Jesus was baptized (3:22).

Peter's Confession of Christ

18 Once when Jesus was praying in private and his disciples were with him, he asked them, "Who do the crowds say I am?"

9:5 *shake the dust off your feet:* This was a customary way of rejecting someone. See Acts 13:51.

9:7 *Herod the tetrarch:* This is Herod Antipas, one of the sons of Herod the Great (see the note at 3:1, 2). The formal name for Herod's title was "tetrarch," which meant someone who ruled a fourth of a province. Jesus called Herod a fox (13:32), because he thought Herod was clever and dangerous.

9:8 *Elijah had appeared:* See the note on p. 1964 (Elijah). See also Matt 16:14; Mark 8:28; Luke 9:19.

9:10 *Bethsaida:* Bethsaida was a Jewish town just east of where the Jordan River empties into the Sea of Galilee. See the map on p. 2473.

9:11 *kingdom of God:* See the note at 4:43.

9:13 *five loaves of bread:* These would have been flat like a pancake, or plump and round like a bun.

9:17 *twelve basketfuls:* The Jewish people believed that twelve was an especially sacred number. See the chart called "Numbers in the Bible," p. 2405.

9:19 *John the Baptist . . . Elijah:* See the notes at 1:13 and on p. 1964 (Elijah). See also Matt 14:1,2; Mark 6:14,15; Luke 9:7,8.

9:20 *Peter:* See the notes at 4:38 and 5:8 (Simon Peter).

9:20 *The Christ:* See the note at 2:11 (Savior). See also John 6:68,69.

9:3-5 Luke 10:4-11. **9:9** Matt 14:1-12.

19 They replied, "Some say John the Baptist; others say Elijah;
and still others, that one of the prophets of long ago has come
back to life."
20 "But what about you?" he asked. "Who do you say I am?"
Peter answered, "The Christ[a] of God."
21 Jesus strictly warned them not to tell this to anyone. 22 And
he said, "The Son of Man must suffer many things and be rejected
by the elders, chief priests and teachers of the law, and he must be
killed and on the third day be raised to life."
23 Then he said to them all: "If anyone would come after me,
he must deny himself and take up his cross daily and follow me.
24 For whoever wants to save his life will lose it, but whoever loses
his life for me will save it. 25 What good is it for a man to gain the
whole world, and yet lose or forfeit his very self? 26 If anyone is
ashamed of me and my words, the Son of Man will be ashamed of
him when he comes in his glory and in the glory of the Father and
of the holy angels. 27 I tell you the truth, some who are standing
here will not taste death before they see the kingdom of God."

The Transfiguration

28 About eight days after Jesus said this, he took Peter, John
and James with him and went up onto a mountain to pray. 29 As he
was praying, the appearance of his face changed, and his clothes
became as bright as a flash of lightning. 30 Two men, Moses and Elijah, 31 appeared in glorious splendor, talking with Jesus. They spoke
about his departure, which he was about to bring to fulfillment at
Jerusalem. 32 Peter and his companions were very sleepy, but when
they became fully awake, they saw his glory and the two men
standing with him. 33 As the men were leaving Jesus, Peter said to
him, "Master, it is good for us to be here. Let us put up three shelters—one for you, one for Moses and one for Elijah." (He did not
know what he was saying.)
34 While he was speaking, a cloud appeared and enveloped
them, and they were afraid as they entered the cloud. 35 A voice
came from the cloud, saying, "This is my Son, whom I have chosen; listen to him." 36 When the voice had spoken, they found that
Jesus was alone. The disciples kept this to themselves, and told no
one at that time what they had seen.

The Healing of a Boy With an Evil Spirit

37 The next day, when they came down from the mountain, a
large crowd met him. 38 A man in the crowd called out, "Teacher, I
beg you to look at my son, for he is my only child. 39 A spirit seizes
him and he suddenly screams; it throws him into convulsions so
that he foams at the mouth. It scarcely ever leaves him and is

[a]**20** Or *Messiah*

9:22 *Son of Man must suffer:* See the mini-article called "Son of Man," p. 1866. This is the first of seven times in LUKE that Jesus predicts his suffering and death (9:44; 12:50; 17:25; 18:31-33).

9:22 *elders, chief priests and teachers of the law:* Representatives of these three groups formed a council called the Sanhedrin that was given some authority by the Romans to make decisions about the local affairs of the Jewish people. The elders were wealthy older men who had ties to the chief priests. See also the note at 5:17.

9:26 *the Father . . . holy angels:* Jesus often referred to God as "Father" (see John 15–17). See also the note at 2:13-15.

9:28 *Peter, John and James:* See the note at 8:51.

9:28 *mountain:* The exact location of this mountain is not clear.

9:30 *Moses and Elijah:* God revealed his name, "I Am," to Moses and chose him to lead the people out of slavery in Egypt. Moses' face glowed with light when he met God on Mount Sinai (Exod 34:29,30). For more, see the mini-article called "Moses," p. 2335.

See also the note on p. 1964 (Elijah). Both Moses and Elijah were chosen to call God's people to live a new way of life, just as Jesus was.

9:39 *A spirit:* See the note at 4:33-35. The boy appears to be having some kind of epileptic seizures. See the article called "Miracles, Magic, and Medicine," p. 1838.

9:23 Matt 10:38; Luke 14:27. **9:24** Matt 10:39; Luke 17:33; John 12:25. **9:28-35** 2 Pet 1:17,18. **9:35** Luke 3:22.

> Jesus said to his disciples, *"He who is least among you all—he is the greatest."*
> Luke 9:48

9:44 *Son of Man . . . betrayed into the hands of men:* See the mini-article called "Son of Man," p. 1866. See also the note at 9:22.

9:49 *demons:* See the note at 4:33.

9:48 Matt 10:40; Luke 10:16; John 13:20.

destroying him. [40]I begged your disciples to drive it out, but they could not."

[41]"O unbelieving and perverse generation," Jesus replied, "how long shall I stay with you and put up with you? Bring your son here."

[42]Even while the boy was coming, the demon threw him to the ground in a convulsion. But Jesus rebuked the evil[a] spirit, healed the boy and gave him back to his father. [43]And they were all amazed at the greatness of God.

While everyone was marveling at all that Jesus did, he said to his disciples, [44]"Listen carefully to what I am about to tell you: The Son of Man is going to be betrayed into the hands of men." [45]But they did not understand what this meant. It was hidden from them, so that they did not grasp it, and they were afraid to ask him about it.

Who Will Be the Greatest?

[46]An argument started among the disciples as to which of them would be the greatest. [47]Jesus, knowing their thoughts, took a little child and had him stand beside him. [48]Then he said to them, "Whoever welcomes this little child in my name welcomes me; and whoever welcomes me welcomes the one who sent me. For he who is least among you all—he is the greatest."

[49]"Master," said John, "we saw a man driving out demons in your name and we tried to stop him, because he is not one of us."

[50]"Do not stop him," Jesus said, "for whoever is not against you is for you."

[a]**42** Greek *unclean*

QUESTIONS ABOUT LUKE 4:14—9:50

1. What did Jesus mean when he said, "Today this scripture is fulfilled in your hearing"? (4:21) What was Jesus announcing? How did the people of his hometown of Nazareth react to his announcement? (4:22-30) Why? What is your reaction to Jesus' announcement?
2. In this section, LUKE gives two accounts of Jesus calling people to follow him (5:1-11; 5:27-32). How are these two stories different? How are they similar? What do they show about the kind of teacher Jesus was? Also in this section, LUKE gives the names of the disciples Jesus called to be apostles (6:12-16). What were their names? What did Jesus do before choosing them?
3. What can we learn from Jesus' teachings about loving our enemies and about judging others? (6:27-42) When are these teachings hard to follow? Explain.
4. This section contains a number of stories about people Jesus healed (4:31-41; 5:12-26; 6:6-11; 7:1-17; 8:26-56; 9:37-43). Who are some of these people? Which story moved you the most? Why? What took place after each healing described?

Jesus Journeys toward Jerusalem

Jesus gives his disciples special powers and prepares them for what is going to happen to him. He has made up his mind to go to Jerusalem. All that he says and does along the way has a purpose. Jesus now prepares his disciples for his death and helps them understand how they can continue the work that he has begun.

FOLLOWERS AND UNBELIEVERS

On his way to Jerusalem Jesus encounters many people. Some understand his teachings and decide to follow Jesus. Some do not understand or are unwilling to do what is required to be a follower.

Samaritan Opposition

51 As the time approached for him to be taken up to heaven,
Jesus resolutely set out for Jerusalem. 52 And he sent messengers on
ahead, who went into a Samaritan village to get things ready for
him; 53 but the people there did not welcome him, because he was
heading for Jerusalem. 54 When the disciples James and John saw
this, they asked, "Lord, do you want us to call fire down from heav-
en to destroy them[a]?" 55 But Jesus turned and rebuked them, 56 and[b]
they went to another village.

The Cost of Following Jesus

57 As they were walking along the road, a man said to him, "I
will follow you wherever you go."
58 Jesus replied, "Foxes have holes and birds of the air have
nests, but the Son of Man has no place to lay his head."
59 He said to another man, "Follow me."
But the man replied, "Lord, first let me go and bury my father."
60 Jesus said to him, "Let the dead bury their own dead, but
you go and proclaim the kingdom of God."
61 Still another said, "I will follow you, Lord; but first let me
go back and say good-by to my family."
62 Jesus replied, "No one who puts his hand to the plow and
looks back is fit for service in the kingdom of God."

Jesus Sends Out the Seventy-two

10 After this the Lord appointed seventy-two[c] others and sent
them two by two ahead of him to every town and place where he
was about to go. 2 He told them, "The harvest is plentiful, but the
workers are few. Ask the Lord of the harvest, therefore, to send out

---

[a]**54** Some manuscripts *them, even as Elijah did* [b]**55,56** Some manuscripts *them. And he said, "You do not know what kind of spirit you are of, for the Son of Man did not come to destroy men's lives, but to save them."* 56*And* [c]**1** Some manuscripts *seventy*; also in verse 17

9:51 *Jerusalem:* Jerusalem was the religious center for the Jewish people. Although the Romans controlled Jerusalem in Jesus' day, the Jewish people were still allowed to worship at the temple. Jesus went to the temple to face the Jewish religious leaders who were against him, and to preach his message to the Jewish people who worshiped there. See also the article called "People of the Law: The Religion of Israel," p. 939 and the mini-article called "Jerusalem," p. 574.

9:52 *Samaritan village:* The exact location of this village is not known. Samaria was a region north of Jerusalem. In Jesus' day the Jews and the Samaritans despised one another. Luke 17:11-19 records another encounter Jesus had with a Samaritan, and Jesus' well-known parable of the Good Samaritan is found in Luke 10:25-37.

9:54 *James and John . . . call fire down from heaven:* See the note at 5:10. See also 1 Kgs 18:16-39; 2 Kgs 1:9-15.

9:58 *Son of Man:* See the mini-article called "Son of Man," p. 1866.

9:60 *Let the dead bury their dead:* For more about Jewish burial customs, see the mini-article called "Burial," p. 1998. It is not clear if the disciple's father is sick and dying or if he is already dead. In either case, Jesus seems to be saying that other friends and relatives who are spiritually "dead" can fulfill the burial obligation while the disciple joins in Jesus' ministry.

9:60 *kingdom of God:* See the note at 4:43.

10:1 *seventy-two:* According to Genesis 10, where the descendants of Noah are listed, there were seventy nations on earth. (But the Septuagint, the ancient Greek translation of the Old Testament, has "seventy-two" in place of seventy.) Jesus probably chose this number to show that his message was for everyone in the world.

9:61 1 Kgs 19:20. **10:2** Matt 9:37,38.

10:13-15 *Korazin ... Bethsaida ... Tyre and Sidon ... Capernaum:* While the people in the Jewish towns did not respond to Jesus' message and miracles, Jesus says that the people in Gentile cities like Tyre and Sidon would be more willing to turn to God.

10:13 *sackcloth and ashes:* People wore sackcloth or put ashes on their heads in times of deep sadness.

10:3 Matt 10:16. **10:4-11** Matt 10:7-14; Mark 6:8-11; Luke 9:3-5. **10:7** 1 Cor 9:14; 1 Tim 5:18. **10:12** Gen 19:24-28; Matt 10:15; 11:24. **10:13** Isa 23:1-18; Ezek 26:1—28:26; Joel 3:4-8; Amos 1:9, 10; Zech 9:2-4.

workers into his harvest field. [3]Go! I am sending you out like
lambs among wolves. [4]Do not take a purse or bag or sandals; and
do not greet anyone on the road.

[5]"When you enter a house, first say, 'Peace to this house.' [6]If
a man of peace is there, your peace will rest on him; if not, it will
return to you. [7]Stay in that house, eating and drinking whatever
they give you, for the worker deserves his wages. Do not move
around from house to house.

[8]"When you enter a town and are welcomed, eat what is set
before you. [9]Heal the sick who are there and tell them, 'The kingdom of God is near you.' [10]But when you enter a town and are not
welcomed, go into its streets and say, [11]'Even the dust of your town
that sticks to our feet we wipe off against you. Yet be sure of this:
The kingdom of God is near.' [12]I tell you, it will be more bearable
on that day for Sodom than for that town.

[13]"Woe to you, Korazin! Woe to you, Bethsaida! For if the

BURIAL

The people of Israel and the other countries of the ancient Near East considered it very important to honor those who had died by giving them a proper burial (Luke 9:59). - Because of the warm climate in Palestine, it was important to bury people within twenty-four hours after they died. In fact, Jewish law required that a dead person should be buried before sunset (Deut 21:23). To let a loved-one's body decay above ground where vultures and dogs could eat it was considered a serious dishonor.

There is no complete description in the Bible of how Jewish people prepared a body for burial. However, it is known that the body was washed (Acts 9:37), anointed with spices (Luke 24:1), and wrapped in cloth (Matt 27:59; John 11:44).

Most ancient Hebrews were buried in caves or in trenches dug in the ground. Sarah and Abraham were buried in the cave of Machpelah near Hebron (Gen 23:19; 25:9, 10). Later, tombs cut out of rock were used for burying the dead. Some tombs could only hold one body, others could hold several and were used by families. Because touching a corpse, even accidentally, made a person ceremonially unclean according to Jewish law, tombs were clearly marked. After the flesh had rotted away in the tomb, the bones would be collected in a box (called an *ossuary*). Then the level place where the dead body had been could be used to receive the body of another person who died.

Greeks, Romans, and Canaanites often burned (cremated) the bodies of people who died. Jewish people saw this as a dishonor and did this only if a body was already in an advanced state of decay. The bodies of Saul and his sons were burned probably to prevent further abuse by the Philistines (1 Sam 31:12). The dead bodies of people who had disobeyed God's law were sometimes burned (Josh 7:25).

Burial ceremonies centered on the family's mourning for the dead person and the carrying of the body to the place of burial. The bodies of the dead were put on wooden frames and carried to the place of burial (2 Sam 3:31; Luke 7:11-15). After the burial, those who handled the body were considered unclean and had to undergo a cleansing ceremony in order to be part of the community again (Num 19:11-20). There is no evidence that the Jewish people of Jesus' day performed funeral services to honor the dead.

Left: Perfume bottles from burial caves in Jerusalem, 6th to 5th centuries B.C.
Right: First-century tomb near Jerusalem.

miracles that were performed in you had been performed in Tyre
and Sidon, they would have repented long ago, sitting in sackcloth
and ashes. [14]But it will be more bearable for Tyre and Sidon at the
judgment than for you. [15]And you, Capernaum, will you be lifted
up to the skies? No, you will go down to the depths.[a]

[16]"He who listens to you listens to me; he who rejects you
rejects me; but he who rejects me rejects him who sent me."

[17]The seventy-two returned with joy and said, "Lord, even
the demons submit to us in your name."

[18]He replied, "I saw Satan fall like lightning from heaven. [19]I
have given you authority to trample on snakes and scorpions and
to overcome all the power of the enemy; nothing will harm you.
[20]However, do not rejoice that the spirits submit to you, but rejoice
that your names are written in heaven."

[21]At that time Jesus, full of joy through the Holy Spirit, said,
"I praise you, Father, Lord of heaven and earth, because you have
hidden these things from the wise and learned, and revealed them
to little children. Yes, Father, for this was your good pleasure.

[22]"All things have been committed to me by my Father. No
one knows who the Son is except the Father, and no one knows
who the Father is except the Son and those to whom the Son
chooses to reveal him."

[a]15 Greek *Hades*

10:14 *at the judgment:* On the day of judgment God will judge the people of the world. Those who put their trust in Christ will be saved, but those who did not will experience God's anger and punishment (see Matt 13:47-50; 25:31-46; John 12:44-50). See also the mini-article called "Day of the LORD," p. 1727.

10:16 *him who sent me:* Jesus is referring to God. See also Matt 10:40; Mark 9:37; Luke 9:48; John 13:20.

10:17 *demons:* See the note at 4:33.

10:18 *Satan:* See the note at 4:3.

10:20 *names are written in heaven:* Eternal life in heaven will be the reward for those who are faithful. Hebrews 12:23 also says that the names of the faithful are written in heaven. References to a book of life can be found in Ps 69:28; Dan 12:1; Phil 4:3; Rev 3:5.

10:18 Isa 14:12. **10:19** Ps 91:13. **10:22** John 3:35; 10:15.

The Good Samaritan by Vincent Van Gogh, 1890. When an expert in the law asked Jesus who was his "neighbor" that he should love like himself, Jesus answered by telling him a parable. In the parable, a man was beaten and robbed and left along the side of the road. The person who helped this man was not a priest or Levite, as the expert in the law would have expected, but a Samaritan. This would have been astonishing because Jews and Samaritans hated each other in Jesus' day. (See 10:25-37.)

23 Then he turned to his disciples and said privately, "Blessed
are the eyes that see what you see. 24 For I tell you that many
prophets and kings wanted to see what you see but did not see it,
and to hear what you hear but did not hear it."

The Parable of the Good Samaritan

25 On one occasion an expert in the law stood up to test Jesus.
"Teacher," he asked, "what must I do to inherit eternal life?"
26 "What is written in the Law?" he replied. "How do you
read it?"
27 He answered: " 'Love the Lord your God with all your heart
and with all your soul and with all your strength and with all your
mind'[a]; and, 'Love your neighbor as yourself.'[b]"

---

[a]27 Deut. 6:5 [b]27 Lev. 19:18

10:25 *expert in the law:* See the note at 5:17.

10:25 *eternal life:* By the time of Jesus, many Jewish people had come to believe in and hope for life after death. But some, like the Sadducees, did not accept the concept of eternal life, because it was not specifically mentioned in the Law of Moses (see the article called "The World of Jesus: Peoples, Powers, and Politics," p. 1821). Jesus says that all who have faith in him will have eternal life. For more, see the mini-article called "Eternal Life," p. 2072.

10:26 *the Law:* See the note at 4:16 (read). Specifically the first five books of the Jewish Scriptures (Old Testament). See also the mini-article called "Law," p. 1160.

10:25-28 Matt 22:35-40; Mark 12:28-34. **10:27,28** Deut 6:5; Lev 18:5; 19:18.

[28]"You have answered correctly," Jesus replied. "Do this and
you will live."
[29]But he wanted to justify himself, so he asked Jesus, "And
who is my neighbor?"
[30]In reply Jesus said: "A man was going down from Jerusalem
to Jericho, when he fell into the hands of robbers. They stripped
him of his clothes, beat him and went away, leaving him half dead.
[31]A priest happened to be going down the same road, and when he
saw the man, he passed by on the other side. [32]So too, a Levite,
when he came to the place and saw him, passed by on the other
side. [33]But a Samaritan, as he traveled, came where the man was;
and when he saw him, he took pity on him. [34]He went to him and
bandaged his wounds, pouring on oil and wine. Then he put the
man on his own donkey, took him to an inn and took care of him.
[35]The next day he took out two silver coins[a] and gave them to the
innkeeper. 'Look after him,' he said, 'and when I return, I will reim-
burse you for any extra expense you may have.'
[36]"Which of these three do you think was a neighbor to the
man who fell into the hands of robbers?"
[37]The expert in the law replied, "The one who had mercy on
him."
Jesus told him, "Go and do likewise."

At the Home of Martha and Mary

[38]As Jesus and his disciples were on their way, he came to a village where a woman named Martha opened her home to him. [39]She
had a sister called Mary, who sat at the Lord's feet listening to what
he said. [40]But Martha was distracted by all the preparations that had
to be made. She came to him and asked, "Lord, don't you care that
my sister has left me to do the work by myself? Tell her to help me!"
[41]"Martha, Martha," the Lord answered, "you are worried and
upset about many things, [42]but only one thing is needed.[b] Mary has
chosen what is better, and it will not be taken away from her."

JESUS TEACHES MANY THINGS

In this section, Jesus teaches about prayer, evil, being a follower of God, the importance of trust, and the proper use of money. He also criticizes the Pharisees and teachers of the law.

Jesus' Teaching on Prayer

11 One day Jesus was praying in a certain place. When he finished, one of his disciples said to him, "Lord, teach us to pray, just
as John taught his disciples."

[a]35 Greek *two denarii* [b]42 Some manuscripts *but few things are needed—or only one*

10:30 *down from Jerusalem to Jericho:* Jericho is eight hundred feet below sea level and is located about sixteen miles northeast of Jerusalem. Since Jerusalem is 2,500 feet above sea level, the route to Jericho is downhill. See the map on p. 2473. The road passed through a rocky wilderness, which enabled robbers to ambush vulnerable travelers.

10:31,32 *priest . . . Levite:* Jewish priests were descendants of Moses' brother Aaron (see Num 18:20-32). A priest knew that touching a dead body or the blood of an injured man would make him unclean according to the Law of Moses. If he became unclean, he would have to go through a cleansing ceremony before he could serve in the temple again. Levites assisted the priests at the temple. This Levite was also afraid of becoming unclean. See also the mini-articles called "Israel's Priests," p. 2344, and "Purity, (Clean and Unclean)," p. 2125.

10:33 *Samaritan:* People from Samaria were known as Samaritans. See the note at 9:52.

10:34 *oil and wine:* In Jesus' day these were used as medicine. Sometimes olive oil was used in healing ceremonies (Jas 5:14).

10:38 *village:* This is the village of Bethany, where Mary and Martha lived with their brother Lazarus (John 11:1). Bethany was about two miles east of Jerusalem.

10:38-40 *Martha . . . sister called Mary:* Martha was concerned with practical matters like preparing food and offering hospitality to a traveler. Mary was more interested in listening to Jesus teach. In JOHN, Martha did not understand what Jesus said about rising from the dead (John 11:17-27).

10:33,34 2 Chr 28:15.

11:2 *hallowed be your name:* This means "let your name be regarded as holy." This is not so much a prayer of petition as it is an act of worship.

11:2 *your kingdom:* See the note at 4:43.

11:4 *sins:* Sin occurs when people rebel against God and disobey God's Word. Forgiveness removes the sin. According to the Jewish Scriptures, those who disobeyed God's commandments could be forgiven if they turned back to God and stopped committing the sinful acts (repented). The Jewish teachers taught that only God could forgive sin. See also the mini-article called "Sin," p. 2181.

11:13,14 *Holy Spirit:* See the notes on p. 1964.

11:14 *demon . . . mute:* See the note at 4:33.

11:15 *Beelzebub, the prince of demons:* The name Beelzebub comes from a title of the Canaanite god Baal and means "prince Baal" or "lord of power." See also Matt 9:34; 12:24. Beelzebub came to be used for Satan. For more, see the mini-article called "Satan," p. 963.

11:23 *gather with me:* Jesus is referring to the harvest of believers. Those who don't join with Jesus in this task are against him and his message. See also Mark 9:40.

11:24 *evil spirit:* See the note at 4:33-35.

11:16 Matt 12:38; 16:1; Mark 8:11.

2 He said to them, "When you pray, say:

" 'Father,[a]
hallowed be your name,
your kingdom come.[b]
3 Give us each day our daily bread.
4 Forgive us our sins,
for we also forgive everyone who sins against us.[c]
And lead us not into temptation.[d] ' "

5 Then he said to them, "Suppose one of you has a friend,
and he goes to him at midnight and says, 'Friend, lend me three
loaves of bread, 6 because a friend of mine on a journey has come
to me, and I have nothing to set before him.'

7 "Then the one inside answers, 'Don't bother me. The door
is already locked, and my children are with me in bed. I can't get
up and give you anything.' 8 I tell you, though he will not get up
and give him the bread because he is his friend, yet because of the
man's boldness[e] he will get up and give him as much as he needs.

9 "So I say to you: Ask and it will be given to you; seek and
you will find; knock and the door will be opened to you. 10 For
everyone who asks receives; he who seeks finds; and to him who
knocks, the door will be opened.

11 "Which of you fathers, if your son asks for[f] a fish, will give
him a snake instead? 12 Or if he asks for an egg, will give him a
scorpion? 13 If you then, though you are evil, know how to give
good gifts to your children, how much more will your Father in
heaven give the Holy Spirit to those who ask him!"

Jesus and Beelzebub

14 Jesus was driving out a demon that was mute. When the
demon left, the man who had been mute spoke, and the crowd was
amazed. 15 But some of them said, "By Beelzebub,[g] the prince of
demons, he is driving out demons." 16 Others tested him by asking
for a sign from heaven.

17 Jesus knew their thoughts and said to them: "Any kingdom
divided against itself will be ruined, and a house divided against
itself will fall. 18 If Satan is divided against himself, how can his
kingdom stand? I say this because you claim that I drive out
demons by Beelzebub. 19 Now if I drive out demons by Beelzebub,
by whom do your followers drive them out? So then, they will be
your judges. 20 But if I drive out demons by the finger of God, then
the kingdom of God has come to you.

---

[a] **2** Some manuscripts *Our Father in heaven* [b] **2** Some manuscripts *come. May your will be done on earth as it is in heaven.* [c] **4** Greek *everyone who is indebted to us* [d] **4** Some manuscripts *temptation but deliver us from the evil one* [e] **8** Or *persistence* [f] **11** Some manuscripts *for bread, will give him a stone; or if he asks for* [g] **15** Greek *Beezeboul* or *Beelzeboul*; also in verses 18 and 19

[21]"When a strong man, fully armed, guards his own house, his possessions are safe. [22]But when someone stronger attacks and overpowers him, he takes away the armor in which the man trusted and divides up the spoils.

[23]"He who is not with me is against me, and he who does not gather with me, scatters.

[24]"When an evil[a] spirit comes out of a man, it goes through arid places seeking rest and does not find it. Then it says, 'I will return to the house I left.' [25]When it arrives, it finds the house swept clean and put in order. [26]Then it goes and takes seven other spirits more wicked than itself, and they go in and live there. And the final condition of that man is worse than the first."

[27]As Jesus was saying these things, a woman in the crowd called out, "Blessed is the mother who gave you birth and nursed you."

[28]He replied, "Blessed rather are those who hear the word of God and obey it."

The Sign of Jonah

[29]As the crowds increased, Jesus said, "This is a wicked generation. It asks for a miraculous sign, but none will be given it except the sign of Jonah. [30]For as Jonah was a sign to the Ninevites, so also will the Son of Man be to this generation. [31]The Queen of the South will rise at the judgment with the men of this generation and condemn them; for she came from the ends of the earth to listen to Solomon's wisdom, and now one[b] greater than Solomon is here. [32]The men of Nineveh will stand up at the judgment with this generation and condemn it; for they repented at the preaching of Jonah, and now one greater than Jonah is here.

The Lamp of the Body

[33]"No one lights a lamp and puts it in a place where it will be hidden, or under a bowl. Instead he puts it on its stand, so that those who come in may see the light. [34]Your eye is the lamp of your body. When your eyes are good, your whole body also is full of light. But when they are bad, your body also is full of darkness. [35]See to it, then, that the light within you is not darkness. [36]Therefore, if your whole body is full of light, and no part of it dark, it will be completely lighted, as when the light of a lamp shines on you."

Six Woes

[37]When Jesus had finished speaking, a Pharisee invited him to eat with him; so he went in and reclined at the table. [38]But the

[a]**24** Greek *unclean* [b]**31** Or *something*; also in verse 32

Jesus said, *"Blessed rather are those who hear the word of God and obey it."* Luke 11:28

11:29,30 *Jonah was a sign to the Ninevites:* After the prophet Jonah refused God's command to bring a message to the people of Nineveh, Israel's enemies, God sent a great fish to swallow Jonah. He stayed inside the fish for three days before being spit out. Jesus is comparing the time he would spend in the grave (23:50—24:12) with the time Jonah spent inside the fish. See also Matt 16:4; Mark 8:12; Jonah 1:17—3:4.

11:31,32 *The Queen of the South:* This refers to the Queen of Sheba. Sheba was a country in southern Arabia, or possibly northeast Africa. Jesus is saying that if Gentiles like the people of Nineveh (Jonah 3:5) or the Queen of Sheba (1 Kgs 10:1-10; 2 Chr 9:1-12) could learn from Jewish prophets and kings, why can't the current Jewish leaders recognize God's message from one of their own people, namely Jesus?

11:33 *lamp:* See the note at 8:16. See also Matt 5:15; Mark 4:21; Luke 8:16.

11:37 *Pharisee:* See the note at 5:17.

11:37 *reclined at the table:* See the note at 7:36.

11:38,39 *did not first wash before the meal:* The Jewish law taught that what people ate and touched could make them unfit to worship God. This is why they washed their hands and cleaned their dishes before eating. See also the mini-article called "Purity (Clean and Unclean)," p. 2125.

11:42 *give God a tenth:* The Pharisees were meticulous about obeying the law requiring tithing (Lev 27:30; Deut 14:22). Jesus told them that helping others was just as important.

11:43 *love the most important seats . . . greetings:* The Pharisees usually sat in the most important seats in the synagogues because they often taught the Scriptures.

11:44 *unmarked graves:* Tombs were whitewashed so that people would notice them and not touch them. A person who touched a dead body or a tomb had to go through a cleansing ceremony before worshiping again with the rest of the Jewish people.

11:46 *burdens they can hardly carry:* Refers to the laws that the Pharisees and teachers of the law taught people to follow. Jesus suggests that these teachers liked to lay down rules, but weren't willing to help those who struggled to keep them.

11:49 *God in his wisdom said:* Jesus is quoting from an unknown source. God sent messengers (prophets) before Jesus, but the Jewish people turned their backs on them or even killed some of them.

11:51 *Abel . . . Zechariah:* Jesus is giving the names of the first and last persons that the Jewish Scriptures say were murdered. For Abel, see Gen 4:1-16; for Zechariah see 2 Chr 24:17-22. SECOND CHRONICLES is the last book in the Hebrew Bible Jesus would have known (see the chart called "Books of the Hebrew Scriptures or Tanak," p. 13).

11:52 *experts in the law:* See the note at 5:17.

Pharisee, noticing that Jesus did not first wash before the meal, was
surprised.
39Then the Lord said to him, "Now then, you Pharisees clean
the outside of the cup and dish, but inside you are full of greed
and wickedness. 40You foolish people! Did not the one who made
the outside make the inside also? 41But give what is inside ⸤the
dish⸥[a] to the poor, and everything will be clean for you.
42"Woe to you Pharisees, because you give God a tenth of
your mint, rue and all other kinds of garden herbs, but you neglect
justice and the love of God. You should have practiced the latter
without leaving the former undone.
43"Woe to you Pharisees, because you love the most important seats in the synagogues and greetings in the marketplaces.
44"Woe to you, because you are like unmarked graves, which
men walk over without knowing it."
45One of the experts in the law answered him, "Teacher,
when you say these things, you insult us also."
46Jesus replied, "And you experts in the law, woe to you,
because you load people down with burdens they can hardly carry,
and you yourselves will not lift one finger to help them.
47"Woe to you, because you build tombs for the prophets,
and it was your forefathers who killed them. 48So you testify that
you approve of what your forefathers did; they killed the prophets,
and you build their tombs. 49Because of this, God in his wisdom
said, 'I will send them prophets and apostles, some of whom they
will kill and others they will persecute.' 50Therefore this generation
will be held responsible for the blood of all the prophets that has
been shed since the beginning of the world, 51from the blood of
Abel to the blood of Zechariah, who was killed between the altar
and the sanctuary. Yes, I tell you, this generation will be held
responsible for it all.
52"Woe to you experts in the law, because you have taken
away the key to knowledge. You yourselves have not entered, and
you have hindered those who were entering."
53When Jesus left there, the Pharisees and the teachers of the
law began to oppose him fiercely and to besiege him with questions, 54waiting to catch him in something he might say.

Warnings and Encouragements

12 Meanwhile, when a crowd of many thousands had gathered,
so that they were trampling on one another, Jesus began to speak
first to his disciples, saying: "Be on your guard against the yeast of
the Pharisees, which is hypocrisy. 2There is nothing concealed that
will not be disclosed, or hidden that will not be made known.
3What you have said in the dark will be heard in the daylight, and

[a]41 Or *what you have*

what you have whispered in the ear in the inner rooms will be proclaimed from the roofs.
4"I tell you, my friends, do not be afraid of those who kill the
body and after that can do no more. 5But I will show you whom
you should fear: Fear him who, after the killing of the body, has
power to throw you into hell. Yes, I tell you, fear him. 6Are not five
sparrows sold for two pennies[a]? Yet not one of them is forgotten by
God. 7Indeed, the very hairs of your head are all numbered. Don't
be afraid; you are worth more than many sparrows.
8"I tell you, whoever acknowledges me before men, the Son
of Man will also acknowledge him before the angels of God. 9But
he who disowns me before men will be disowned before the angels
of God. 10And everyone who speaks a word against the Son of Man
will be forgiven, but anyone who blasphemes against the Holy
Spirit will not be forgiven.
11"When you are brought before synagogues, rulers and
authorities, do not worry about how you will defend yourselves or
what you will say, 12for the Holy Spirit will teach you at that time
what you should say."

The Parable of the Rich Fool

13Someone in the crowd said to him, "Teacher, tell my brother to divide the inheritance with me."
14Jesus replied, "Man, who appointed me a judge or an
arbiter between you?" 15Then he said to them, "Watch out! Be on
your guard against all kinds of greed; a man's life does not consist
in the abundance of his possessions."
16And he told them this parable: "The ground of a certain
rich man produced a good crop. 17He thought to himself, 'What
shall I do? I have no place to store my crops.'
18"Then he said, 'This is what I'll do. I will tear down my
barns and build bigger ones, and there I will store all my grain and
my goods. 19And I'll say to myself, "You have plenty of good things
laid up for many years. Take life easy; eat, drink and be merry." '
20"But God said to him, 'You fool! This very night your life
will be demanded from you. Then who will get what you have prepared for yourself?'
21"This is how it will be with anyone who stores up things
for himself but is not rich toward God."

Do Not Worry

22Then Jesus said to his disciples: "Therefore I tell you, do
not worry about your life, what you will eat; or about your body,
what you will wear. 23Life is more than food, and the body more
than clothes. 24Consider the ravens: They do not sow or reap, they

[a]6 Greek *two assaria*

12:5 *power to throw you into hell:* See the mini-article called "Hell," p. 1944. Only God has the power to cast a person into hell. We should "fear" God in the sense of having a deep respect for God's character and authority. Even before Jesus was born, some Jewish teachers said that the place where wicked people go when they die is like the burning Valley of Ben Hinnom.

12:6 *five sparrows . . . two pennies:* The Roman coin referred to here is an assarius, which equals only about one-sixteenth of what a common laborer earned for one day's work. The Law of Moses did not forbid the eating of sparrows. Because they were so cheap, the ordinary person could afford them.

12:8 *Son of Man . . . angels:* See the mini-articles called "Son of Man," p. 1866, and "Angels," p. 88.

12:10 *blasphemes against the Holy Spirit:* See the note at Mark 3:29.

12:11 *synagogues:* See the note at 4:15.

12:1 Matt 16:6; Mark 8:15. **12:2** Mark 4:22; Luke 8:17. **12:10** Matt 12:32; Mark 3:29. **12:11,12** Matt 10:19,20; Mark 13:11; Luke 21:14,15.

Jesus said, "*Where your treasure is, there your heart will be also.*" Luke 12:34

12:27 *Solomon in all his splendor:* The Jewish people thought that King Solomon was the richest person who had ever lived. See also 1 Kgs 10:4-7; 2 Chr 9:3-6; and the mini-article called "Solomon," p. 776.

12:30 *your Father:* Jesus is referring to God.

12:32 *the kingdom:* See the note at 4:43.

12:33 *heaven:* See the note at 6:23.

12:35 Matt 25:1-13. **12:36** Mark 13:34-36.

have no storeroom or barn; yet God feeds them. And how much
more valuable you are than birds! [25]Who of you by worrying can
add a single hour to his life[a]? [26]Since you cannot do this very little
thing, why do you worry about the rest?
[27]"Consider how the lilies grow. They do not labor or spin. Yet
I tell you, not even Solomon in all his splendor was dressed like one of
these. [28]If that is how God clothes the grass of the field, which is here
today, and tomorrow is thrown into the fire, how much more will he
clothe you, O you of little faith! [29]And do not set your heart on what
you will eat or drink; do not worry about it. [30]For the pagan world
runs after all such things, and your Father knows that you need them.
[31]But seek his kingdom, and these things will be given to you as well.
[32]"Do not be afraid, little flock, for your Father has been
pleased to give you the kingdom. [33]Sell your possessions and give
to the poor. Provide purses for yourselves that will not wear out, a
treasure in heaven that will not be exhausted, where no thief
comes near and no moth destroys. [34]For where your treasure is,
there your heart will be also.

Watchfulness

[35]"Be dressed ready for service and keep your lamps burning, [36]like men waiting for their master to return from a wedding

[a]25 Or *single cubit to his height*

SLAVES AND SERVANTS IN THE TIME OF JESUS

The word in the New Testament usually translated as "servant" actually means "slave," and refers to someone who was owned or controlled by someone else, not just a servant hired to do a certain job. Some slaves performed common household tasks. Others, called "managers," supervised the work of lesser servants or managed the master's finances (Luke 12:42-46). In Jesus' day, some people were slaves because they were born to slave parents. Others were captured in war and forced to become slaves. Some people actually sold themselves as slaves because they could have a higher standard of living as a slave than if they had to keep struggling to find housing or food on their own.

Some slaves were better educated than their masters and served as teachers of their masters' children. Slaves of rich masters had all kinds of opportunities that they would never have had on their own. But slaves had no freedom, and their owners could do with them whatever they wanted, including selling them to someone else. After slaves became 30 years old, many would become "freedmen," now employed by the former master. Some slaves earned enough money to buy their own freedom, which would mean that their children could be free also.

Both the Old and New Testaments give regulations for treatment of slaves. Such regulations were not condoning slavery, but were God-given practical ways to deal with a cultural reality. When Paul gives advice to slaves and masters, he does not condone slavery nor does he recommend revolt against the system. Instead, he calls on slaves and masters to show Christian principles in their relationship (Eph 6:5; Col 3:22—4:1).

banquet, so that when he comes and knocks they can immediately open the door for him. 37 It will be good for those servants whose
master finds them watching when he comes. I tell you the truth, he
will dress himself to serve, will have them recline at the table and
will come and wait on them. 38 It will be good for those servants
whose master finds them ready, even if he comes in the second or
third watch of the night. 39 But understand this: If the owner of the
house had known at what hour the thief was coming, he would
not have let his house be broken into. 40 You also must be ready,
because the Son of Man will come at an hour when you do not
expect him."

41 Peter asked, "Lord, are you telling this parable to us, or to
everyone?"

42 The Lord answered, "Who then is the faithful and wise
manager, whom the master puts in charge of his servants to give
them their food allowance at the proper time? 43 It will be good for
that servant whom the master finds doing so when he returns. 44 I
tell you the truth, he will put him in charge of all his possessions.
45 But suppose the servant says to himself, 'My master is taking a
long time in coming,' and he then begins to beat the menservants
and maidservants and to eat and drink and get drunk. 46 The master of that servant will come on a day when he does not expect
him and at an hour he is not aware of. He will cut him to pieces
and assign him a place with the unbelievers.

47 "That servant who knows his master's will and does not get
ready or does not do what his master wants will be beaten with
many blows. 48 But the one who does not know and does things
deserving punishment will be beaten with few blows. From everyone
who has been given much, much will be demanded; and from the
one who has been entrusted with much, much more will be asked.

Not Peace but Division

49 "I have come to bring fire on the earth, and how I wish it
were already kindled! 50 But I have a baptism to undergo, and how
distressed I am until it is completed! 51 Do you think I came to
bring peace on earth? No, I tell you, but division. 52 From now on
there will be five in one family divided against each other, three
against two and two against three. 53 They will be divided, father
against son and son against father, mother against daughter and
daughter against mother, mother-in-law against daughter-in-law
and daughter-in-law against mother-in-law."

Interpreting the Times

54 He said to the crowd: "When you see a cloud rising in the
west, immediately you say, 'It's going to rain,' and it does. 55 And
when the south wind blows, you say, 'It's going to be hot,' and it is.
56 Hypocrites! You know how to interpret the appearance of the

12:37 *servants . . . have them recline at the table:* See the mini-article called "Slaves and Servants in the Time of Jesus" on the previous page. See also the note at 7:36.

12:40 *Son of Man:* See the mini-article called "Son of Man," p. 1866.

12:41 *Peter:* See the notes at 4:38 and 5:8 (Simon Peter).

12:42 *manager:* See the mini-article called "Slaves and Servants in the Time of Jesus," on the previous page.

12:50 *baptism:* Jesus is referring to his coming suffering of being rejected and sacrificed. See also the note at 9:22 (Son of Man Must Suffer).

12:54 *a cloud rising in the west:* Weather systems usually travel from west to east. This is true in Palestine, where there are occasional heavy rainstorms in the winter.

12:39,40 Matt 24:43,44. **12:50** Mark 10:38. **12:53** Mic 7:6.

earth and the sky. How is it that you don't know how to interpret
this present time?
57"Why don't you judge for yourselves what is right? 58As you
are going with your adversary to the magistrate, try hard to be reconciled to him on the way, or he may drag you off to the judge,
and the judge turn you over to the officer, and the officer throw
you into prison. 59I tell you, you will not get out until you have
paid the last penny.[a]"

TEACHINGS ABOUT THE KINGDOM OF GOD

Jesus teaches about living in the kingdom of God and heals two more people on the Sabbath.

Repent or Perish

13 Now there were some present at that time who told Jesus
about the Galileans whose blood Pilate had mixed with their sacrifices. 2Jesus answered, "Do you think that these Galileans were worse
sinners than all the other Galileans because they suffered this way? 3I
tell you, no! But unless you repent, you too will all perish. 4Or those
eighteen who died when the tower in Siloam fell on them—do you
think they were more guilty than all the others living in Jerusalem?
5I tell you, no! But unless you repent, you too will all perish."
6Then he told this parable: "A man had a fig tree, planted in
his vineyard, and he went to look for fruit on it, but did not find
any. 7So he said to the man who took care of the vineyard, 'For
three years now I've been coming to look for fruit on this fig tree
and haven't found any. Cut it down! Why should it use up the soil?'
8"'Sir,' the man replied, 'leave it alone for one more year, and
I'll dig around it and fertilize it. 9If it bears fruit next year, fine! If
not, then cut it down.'"

A Crippled Woman Healed on the Sabbath

10On a Sabbath Jesus was teaching in one of the synagogues,
11and a woman was there who had been crippled by a spirit for eighteen years. She was bent over and could not straighten up at all.
12When Jesus saw her, he called her forward and said to her, "Woman,
you are set free from your infirmity." 13Then he put his hands on
her, and immediately she straightened up and praised God.
14Indignant because Jesus had healed on the Sabbath, the
synagogue ruler said to the people, "There are six days for work. So
come and be healed on those days, not on the Sabbath."
15The Lord answered him, "You hypocrites! Doesn't each of
you on the Sabbath untie his ox or donkey from the stall and lead
it out to give it water? 16Then should not this woman, a daughter

[a]59 Greek *lepton*

13:1 *Pilate:* The Roman governor in charge of Judea from A.D. 26 to 36. When Pilate was in Jerusalem, he lived at the Praetorium, a fortress that overlooked the temple area. Several Jewish historians reported that Pilate was a cruel leader who was disrespectful of Jewish religious customs. Normally, however, Romans did not interfere with the everyday work and worship at the temple. See also the mini-article called "Pontius Pilate," p. 2091. This inscription from a pagan temple in Caesarea includes Pilate's name.

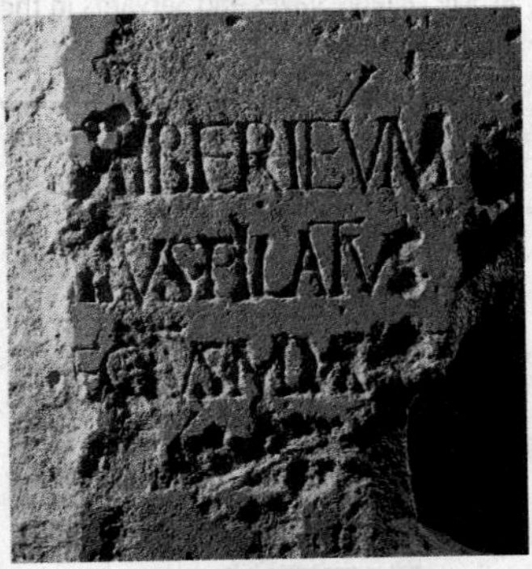

13:2 *sinners:* Those who rebel against God and disobey God's Word. People in Jesus' day generally believed that bad things happened to someone who was sinful. Jesus is saying that all people are sinful and need to turn to God. See also the note at 11:4.

13:14 *healed on the Sabbath:* Doing any kind of work on the Sabbath, including healing someone, was against the Jewish Law. See the note at 6:9 and the chart called "Jewish Calendar and Festivals," p. 944.

13:15 *ox or donkey:* Both animals were very valuable to the agricultural society of Jesus' day. The ox was used for heavy work like plowing. Donkeys were used as pack animals and for transportation.

13:16 *Satan:* See the note at 4:3. In Jesus' day, Satan and demons were often thought to be responsible for sickness and other physical and mental problems.

of Abraham, whom Satan has kept bound for eighteen long years,
be set free on the Sabbath day from what bound her?"
[17]When he said this, all his opponents were humiliated, but the
people were delighted with all the wonderful things he was doing.

The Parables of the Mustard Seed and the Yeast

[18]Then Jesus asked, "What is the kingdom of God like? What
shall I compare it to? [19]It is like a mustard seed, which a man took
and planted in his garden. It grew and became a tree, and the birds
of the air perched in its branches."
[20]Again he asked, "What shall I compare the kingdom of
God to? [21]It is like yeast that a woman took and mixed into a large
amount[a] of flour until it worked all through the dough."

The Narrow Door

[22]Then Jesus went through the towns and villages, teaching
as he made his way to Jerusalem. [23]Someone asked him, "Lord, are
only a few people going to be saved?"
He said to them, [24]"Make every effort to enter through the
narrow door, because many, I tell you, will try to enter and will not
be able to. [25]Once the owner of the house gets up and closes the
door, you will stand outside knocking and pleading, 'Sir, open the
door for us.'
"But he will answer, 'I don't know you or where you come
from.'
[26]"Then you will say, 'We ate and drank with you, and you
taught in our streets.'
[27]"But he will reply, 'I don't know you or where you come
from. Away from me, all you evildoers!'
[28]"There will be weeping there, and gnashing of teeth, when
you see Abraham, Isaac and Jacob and all the prophets in the kingdom of God, but you yourselves thrown out. [29]People will come
from east and west and north and south, and will take their places
at the feast in the kingdom of God. [30]Indeed there are those who
are last who will be first, and first who will be last."

Jesus' Sorrow for Jerusalem

[31]At that time some Pharisees came to Jesus and said to him,
"Leave this place and go somewhere else. Herod wants to kill you."
[32]He replied, "Go tell that fox, 'I will drive out demons and
heal people today and tomorrow, and on the third day I will reach
my goal.' [33]In any case, I must keep going today and tomorrow and
the next day—for surely no prophet can die outside Jerusalem!
[34]"O Jerusalem, Jerusalem, you who kill the prophets and

---

[a]**21** Greek *three satas* (probably about 1/2 bushel or 22 liters)

13:18 *kingdom of God:* See the note at 4:43.

13:19 *mustard seed:* This tiny seed was used to flavor food and to keep it fresh. The mustard plant does not grow as tall as most trees, but it can grow taller than a human being.

13:21 *yeast:* Yeast is a tiny yellowish fungus. When it is mixed with water and flour, it causes the dough to rise, so the bread will not be flat when baked. Yeast is also called leaven.

13:28 *Abraham, Isaac and Jacob:* The Jewish people Jesus was talking to would have known that God made a covenant with Abraham, the ancestor of all Jewish people (Gen 12:1-3; 17:1-9). See also the mini-article called "Abraham," p. 2254. Isaac was Abraham's son and Jacob was Isaac's son.

13:29 *feast in the kingdom of God:* This feast refers to a future time when God will bring together faithful people not only from the people of Israel but from every nation. Jesus compares this time to a feast because a feast was a time of celebration.

13:31 *Pharisees:* See the note at 5:17.

13:31 *Herod:* See the notes at 3:1,2 and 9:7. The Pharisees may have been trying to scare Jesus into leaving for Judea.

13:32 *fox:* The Greeks, like many people throughout the ages, thought of foxes as sly or clever animals.

13:33 *Jerusalem:* See the note at 9:51. A number of the prophets had also been killed when they brought unpopular messages to Jerusalem.

13:27 Ps 6:8. **13:30** Matt 19:30; 20:16; Mark 10:31.

stone those sent to you, how often I have longed to gather your children together, as a hen gathers her chicks under her wings, but you were not willing! [35]Look, your house is left to you desolate. I tell you, you will not see me again until you say, 'Blessed is he who comes in the name of the Lord.'[a]"

Jesus at a Pharisee's House

14 One Sabbath, when Jesus went to eat in the house of a prominent Pharisee, he was being carefully watched. [2]There in front of him was a man suffering from dropsy. [3]Jesus asked the Pharisees and experts in the law, "Is it lawful to heal on the Sabbath or not?" [4]But they remained silent. So taking hold of the man, he healed him and sent him away.

[5]Then he asked them, "If one of you has a son[b] or an ox that falls into a well on the Sabbath day, will you not immediately pull him out?" [6]And they had nothing to say.

[7]When he noticed how the guests picked the places of honor at the table, he told them this parable: [8]"When someone invites you to a wedding feast, do not take the place of honor, for a person more distinguished than you may have been invited. [9]If so, the host who invited both of you will come and say to you, 'Give this man your seat.' Then, humiliated, you will have to take the least important place. [10]But when you are invited, take the lowest place, so that when your host comes, he will say to you, 'Friend, move up to a better place.' Then you will be honored in the presence of all your fellow guests. [11]For everyone who exalts himself will be humbled, and he who humbles himself will be exalted."

[12]Then Jesus said to his host, "When you give a luncheon or dinner, do not invite your friends, your brothers or relatives, or your rich neighbors; if you do, they may invite you back and so you will be repaid. [13]But when you give a banquet, invite the poor, the crippled, the lame, the blind, [14]and you will be blessed. Although they cannot repay you, you will be repaid at the resurrection of the righteous."

The Parable of the Great Banquet

[15]When one of those at the table with him heard this, he said to Jesus, "Blessed is the man who will eat at the feast in the kingdom of God."

[16]Jesus replied: "A certain man was preparing a great banquet and invited many guests. [17]At the time of the banquet he sent his servant to tell those who had been invited, 'Come, for everything is now ready.'

[18]"But they all alike began to make excuses. The first said, 'I have just bought a field, and I must go and see it. Please excuse me.'

---

[a]35 Psalm 118:26 [b]5 Some manuscripts *donkey*

13:35 *your house:* Referring to God's "house," the temple in Jerusalem. This is the temple that Herod the Great built in Jerusalem. Work began in 20 B.C. and continued in Jesus' day (see John 2:20). The temple sat on a huge stone platform that was nearly a mile around at the base. Some of the huge blocks of stone in Herod's original foundation wall are still in place, but the temple itself was completely destroyed when the Romans, headed by Titus, attacked Jerusalem in A.D. 70. See also the article called "People of the Law: The Religion of Israel," p. 939, which includes diagrams of the Jewish temple.

14:1-3 *Pharisee . . . experts in the law:* See the note at 5:17.

14:3 *heal on the Sabbath:* See the notes at 4:16 (Sabbath); 6:9; and 13:14.

14:8 *wedding feast:* In Jesus' day, wedding feasts could be elaborate affairs, sometimes lasting for an entire week. Before marriage, couples had a betrothal (agreement to marry in the future), and there was a celebration to recognize the betrothal. A document called a *tena'im* was also drawn up. This document spelled out the date, place, and size of the wedding to come. The wedding itself was a very important ceremony and celebration. Both the bride and the bridegroom were beautifully dressed and ornamented. There was a procession from the house of the bride to the bridegroom's house, and this was followed by dancing, music, and poetry in which the whole community took part.

14:14 *resurrection of the righteous:* Jesus is talking about the future time when God will bring his faithful followers back from death to live under God's everlasting rule (Dan 12:2; John 5:28,29; 1 Thes 4:16; Rev 20:11-15). See also the mini-article called "Resurrection," p. 2210.

14:15 *the feast in the kingdom of God:* See the note at 13:29.

19“Another said, ‘I have just bought five yoke of oxen, and I’m on my way to try them out. Please excuse me.’

20“Still another said, ‘I just got married, so I can’t come.’

21“The servant came back and reported this to his master. Then the owner of the house became angry and ordered his servant, ‘Go out quickly into the streets and alleys of the town and bring in the poor, the crippled, the blind and the lame.’

22“ ‘Sir,’ the servant said, ‘what you ordered has been done, but there is still room.’

23“Then the master told his servant, ‘Go out to the roads and country lanes and make them come in, so that my house will be full. 24I tell you, not one of those men who were invited will get a taste of my banquet.’ ”

The Cost of Being a Disciple

25Large crowds were traveling with Jesus, and turning to them he said: 26“If anyone comes to me and does not hate his father and mother, his wife and children, his brothers and sisters—yes, even his own life—he cannot be my disciple. 27And anyone who does not carry his cross and follow me cannot be my disciple.

28“Suppose one of you wants to build a tower. Will he not first sit down and estimate the cost to see if he has enough money to complete it? 29For if he lays the foundation and is not able to finish it, everyone who sees it will ridicule him, 30saying, ‘This fellow began to build and was not able to finish.’

31“Or suppose a king is about to go to war against another king. Will he not first sit down and consider whether he is able with ten thousand men to oppose the one coming against him with twenty thousand? 32If he is not able, he will send a delegation while the other is still a long way off and will ask for terms of peace. 33In the same way, any of you who does not give up everything he has cannot be my disciple.

34“Salt is good, but if it loses its saltiness, how can it be made salty again? 35It is fit neither for the soil nor for the manure pile; it is thrown out.

“He who has ears to hear, let him hear.”

THE LOST ARE FOUND

This chapter includes three parables about how God cares for people who are lost. In LUKE’s Gospel, the “lost” are sinners and tax collectors who were considered to be outcasts by many in the Jewish community in Jesus’ day.

The Parable of the Lost Sheep

15 Now the tax collectors and “sinners” were all gathering around to hear him. 2But the Pharisees and the teachers of the law muttered, “This man welcomes sinners and eats with them.”

Jesus said to the crowd, *“Anyone who does not carry his cross and follow me cannot be my disciple.”* Luke 14:27

14:26 *hate his father and mother, his wife and children:* Jesus was using a figure of speech that made a point through an exaggerated contrast. Jesus’ followers must love him even more than they love their immediate families. The Bible clearly teaches people to honor their families and love others (see Luke 10:26-28; Eph 6:1-4).

14:27 *cross:* The cross was a symbol for suffering, since the Romans used it as a way to put criminals or rebels to death. Death on a cross was usually slow and painful, and was most often the result of suffocation. See also Matt 10:38; 16:24; Mark 8:34; Luke 9:23. See also the mini-article called “Crucifixion,” p. 1914.

14:34 *salt:* Salt was used to flavor food. It was also used to preserve food, especially meat and fish. Salt that had lost its taste was no longer useful.

15:1 *tax collectors and “sinners”:* See the notes at 3:12. “Sinners” was the name given to people who were unclean or disobedient according to the Law of Moses. Jesus wanted to show how much God cared for these social outcasts and wanted to welcome them into the community of God’s people.

15:2 *Pharisees and the teachers of the law:* See the note at 5:17.

13:35 Ps 118:26; Luke 19:38. **14:5** Luke 13:15; Matt 12:11. **14:8-10** Prov 25:6,7. **14:11** Matt 23:12; Luke 18:14. **14:26** Matt 10:37. **15:1,2** Luke 5:29,30.

[3]Then Jesus told them this parable: [4]"Suppose one of you has
a hundred sheep and loses one of them. Does he not leave the
ninety-nine in the open country and go after the lost sheep until
he finds it? [5]And when he finds it, he joyfully puts it on his shoulders [6]and goes home. Then he calls his friends and neighbors
together and says, 'Rejoice with me; I have found my lost sheep.'
[7]I tell you that in the same way there will be more rejoicing in
heaven over one sinner who repents than over ninety-nine righteous persons who do not need to repent.

The Parable of the Lost Coin

[8]"Or suppose a woman has ten silver coins[a] and loses one.
Does she not light a lamp, sweep the house and search carefully
until she finds it? [9]And when she finds it, she calls her friends and
neighbors together and says, 'Rejoice with me; I have found my
lost coin.' [10]In the same way, I tell you, there is rejoicing in the
presence of the angels of God over one sinner who repents."

The Parable of the Lost Son

[11]Jesus continued: "There was a man who had two sons.
[12]The younger one said to his father, 'Father, give me my share of
the estate.' So he divided his property between them.
[13]"Not long after that, the younger son got together all he
had, set off for a distant country and there squandered his wealth
in wild living. [14]After he had spent everything, there was a severe
famine in that whole country, and he began to be in need. [15]So
he went and hired himself out to a citizen of that country, who
sent him to his fields to feed pigs. [16]He longed to fill his stomach with the pods that the pigs were eating, but no one gave him
anything.
[17]"When he came to his senses, he said, 'How many of my
father's hired men have food to spare, and here I am starving to
death! [18]I will set out and go back to my father and say to him:
Father, I have sinned against heaven and against you. [19]I am no
longer worthy to be called your son; make me like one of your
hired men.' [20]So he got up and went to his father.

"But while he was still a long way off, his father saw him and
was filled with compassion for him; he ran to his son, threw his
arms around him and kissed him.
[21]"The son said to him, 'Father, I have sinned against heaven
and against you. I am no longer worthy to be called your son.[b]'
[22]"But the father said to his servants, 'Quick! Bring the best
robe and put it on him. Put a ring on his finger and sandals on his
feet. [23]Bring the fattened calf and kill it. Let's have a feast and cel-

[a]8 Greek *ten drachmas,* each worth about a day's wages [b]21 Some early manuscripts *son. Make me like one of your hired men.*

15:4 *go after the lost sheep:* A good shepherd in Jesus' time would not have been likely to leave his whole herd unattended in open country in order to go search for one lost sheep. See also the mini-article called "Shepherds," p. 1972.

15:7 *heaven . . . sinner . . . righteous persons who do not need to repent:* See the notes at 6:23 and 13:2. Jesus' comment about the "righteous persons who do not need to repent" was probably a reference to the Pharisees and teachers of the Law (15:2). They thought they were righteous and had no need to repent.

15:12 *my share of the estate:* In a Jewish family, the sons inherited the family's goods and property from their father. The older son was to receive a greater share, often twice as much as his younger brothers.

15:15 *feed pigs:* The Law of Moses taught that pigs were not fit to eat or even to touch (Deut 14:8). A Jewish man would have felt terribly insulted if he had to feed pigs, much less eat with them. See also the mini-article called "Purity (Clean and Unclean)," p. 2125.

15:16 *the pods that the pigs were eating:* These pods, which came from a tree in Palestine called the carob tree. Ripe carob pods have a rich syrup-like juice that is very nourishing. Carob pods are still used to feed animals today, and many poor people continue to rely on them for nourishment.

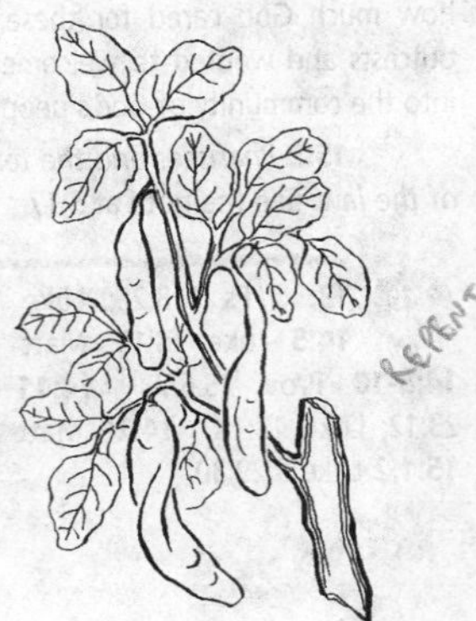

The Prodigal Son by Marc Chagall, around 1975. When the religious leaders grumbled because Jesus was friendly with tax collectors and sinners, Jesus told them three parables about things that had been lost but were then found. (See chapter 15.) The third parable tells of a son who asked his father for his inheritance. After he spent it all and was desperate, he returned to his father's estate. The father rejoiced at his son's return, saying, "This son of mine was dead and is alive again; he was lost and is found" (15:24).

ebrate. 24For this son of mine was dead and is alive again; he was
lost and is found.' So they began to celebrate.
25"Meanwhile, the older son was in the field. When he came
near the house, he heard music and dancing. 26So he called one of
the servants and asked him what was going on. 27'Your brother has
come,' he replied, 'and your father has killed the fattened calf
because he has him back safe and sound.'
28"The older brother became angry and refused to go in. So
his father went out and pleaded with him. 29But he answered his
father, 'Look! All these years I've been slaving for you and never
disobeyed your orders. Yet you never gave me even a young goat so
I could celebrate with my friends. 30But when this son of yours

The father said, *"Bring the fattened calf and kill it. Let's have a feast and celebrate. For this son of mine was dead and is alive again; he was lost and is found."* Luke 15:23, 24

15:22 *a ring on his finger and sandals on his feet:* These show that the young man's father fully accepted him as his son. A ring was a sign of high position in the family. Sandals showed that he was a son instead of a slave, since slaves did not usually wear sandals.

who has squandered your property with prostitutes comes home,
you kill the fattened calf for him!'
31 " 'My son,' the father said, 'you are always with me, and
everything I have is yours. 32 But we had to celebrate and be glad,
because this brother of yours was dead and is alive again; he was
lost and is found.' "

FAITHFUL SERVANTS

As Jesus continues his journey toward Jerusalem, he heals more people and talks to his disciples and others about what it means to be faithful servants of God.

The Parable of the Shrewd Manager

16 Jesus told his disciples: "There was a rich man whose manager was accused of wasting his possessions. 2 So he called him in
and asked him, 'What is this I hear about you? Give an account of
your management, because you cannot be manager any longer.'
3 "The manager said to himself, 'What shall I do now? My
master is taking away my job. I'm not strong enough to dig, and
I'm ashamed to beg— 4 I know what I'll do so that, when I lose my
job here, people will welcome me into their houses.'
5 "So he called in each one of his master's debtors. He asked
the first, 'How much do you owe my master?'
6 " 'Eight hundred gallons[a] of olive oil,' he replied.
"The manager told him, 'Take your bill, sit down quickly,
and make it four hundred.'
7 "Then he asked the second, 'And how much do you owe?'
" 'A thousand bushels[b] of wheat,' he replied.
"He told him, 'Take your bill and make it eight hundred.'
8 "The master commended the dishonest manager because
he had acted shrewdly. For the people of this world are more
shrewd in dealing with their own kind than are the people of the
light. 9 I tell you, use worldly wealth to gain friends for yourselves,
so that when it is gone, you will be welcomed into eternal
dwellings.
10 "Whoever can be trusted with very little can also be trusted with much, and whoever is dishonest with very little will also be
dishonest with much. 11 So if you have not been trustworthy in
handling worldly wealth, who will trust you with true riches?
12 And if you have not been trustworthy with someone else's property, who will give you property of your own?
13 "No servant can serve two masters. Either he will hate the

[a]6 Greek *one hundred batous* (probably about 3 kiloliters) [b]7 Greek *one hundred korous* (probably about 35 kiloliters)

Jesus said, *"No servant can serve two masters. Either he will hate the one and love the other, or he will be devoted to the one and despise the other. You cannot serve both God and Money."* Luke 16:13

16:8 *people of this world . . . people of the light:* The "people of this world" do not follow God or are opposed to God's purposes. In the New Testament, the "world" is sometimes pictured as being evil and opposed to God (Rom 12:2; Gal 4:3; Jas 1:27; 1 John 5:19). In the Bible, "light" is used to describe those people or things that reveal God's truth (see Isa 49:6; John 1:3, 4). The followers of Jesus are also called "children of light" (Eph 5:8).

16:9 *worldly wealth:* Jesus is not saying that money is evil in and of itself, but that people sometimes get money by cheating others. Money and possessions can also be used to make friends and to serve others. Money can run out, but God offers something more valuable: an eternal home (living with God forever). And Christians who give generously can look forward to being gratefully "welcomed" into heaven by some of those whom they helped.

16:14 *Pharisees:* See the note at 5:17.

16:13 Matt 6:24. **16:17** Matt 5:18. **16:18** Matt 5:32; 1 Cor 7:10,11.

The Rich Man and Lazarus, portal of Abbey Church, Moissac, France. Only Luke, of all the Gospel writers, tells the parable of the poor beggar Lazarus who lay outside the gate of a rich man's house. Dogs licked his sores as he longed to eat the scraps that fell from the rich man's table. When he died, he received a place of honor next to Abraham (shown here as being cradled in Abraham's lap like a baby), but the rich man went to hell and suffered terribly. (See 16:19-31.)

one and love the other, or he will be devoted to the one and
despise the other. You cannot serve both God and Money."
14The Pharisees, who loved money, heard all this and were
sneering at Jesus. 15He said to them, "You are the ones who justify
yourselves in the eyes of men, but God knows your hearts. What is
highly valued among men is detestable in God's sight.

Additional Teachings

16"The Law and the Prophets were proclaimed until John.
Since that time, the good news of the kingdom of God is being
preached, and everyone is forcing his way into it. 17It is easier for
heaven and earth to disappear than for the least stroke of a pen to
drop out of the Law.
18"Anyone who divorces his wife and marries another
woman commits adultery, and the man who marries a divorced
woman commits adultery.

The Rich Man and Lazarus

19"There was a rich man who was dressed in purple and fine
linen and lived in luxury every day. 20At his gate was laid a beggar
named Lazarus, covered with sores 21and longing to eat what fell
from the rich man's table. Even the dogs came and licked his sores.
22"The time came when the beggar died and the angels carried him to Abraham's side. The rich man also died and was buried.
23In hell,[a] where he was in torment, he looked up and saw Abraham
far away, with Lazarus by his side. 24So he called to him, 'Father
Abraham, have pity on me and send Lazarus to dip the tip of his finger in water and cool my tongue, because I am in agony in this fire.'

[a]**23** Greek *Hades*

16:16 *The Law and the Prophets:* See the mini-article called "Law," p. 1160. The Law of Moses refers to the first five books of the Bible. The Law gives the early history of God's people and lists the rules that God gave the people through Moses about how to live right.

The Prophets include those books written by God's special messengers. See the articles called "Prophets and Prophecy," p. 935 and "What Books Belong in the Bible," p. 13. See also Matt 11:12,13.

16:16 *John:* Referring to John the Baptist. See chapter 3.

16:22 *Abraham's side:* Some Jewish people thought that the life to come would be like a feast that God would give for them. Abraham would be the most important person there, and the guest of honor would sit next to him. See also the mini-article called "Eternal Life," p. 2072.

16:23 *hell:* The Jewish people often thought of hell, or Hades, as the place where the dead wait for final punishment. See also the note at 12:5 and the mini-article called "Hell," p. 1944.

> Jesus said, *"If you have faith as small as a mustard seed, you can say to this mulberry tree, 'Be uprooted and planted in the sea,' and it will obey you."*
> Luke 17:6

16:29 *Moses and the Prophets:* This was a way of referring to all the Jewish Scriptures, the entire Old Testament. The rich man had not heeded the teaching of Scripture and was afraid that his brothers wouldn't either.

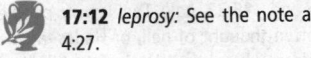

16:31 *even if someone rises from the dead:* Jesus is saying that some people, including many of the Pharisees he is referring to, will not be convinced by his message even after he is raised from death.

17:1 *sin:* See the note at 11:4.

17:6 *mustard seed . . . mulberry tree:* See the note at 13:19. The mulberry tree was first grown in Persia. It can grow to a height of about 20 feet and is usually very wide at the top. Its berries turn black when ripe and contain a sweet red juice.

17:7 *servant:* See the mini-article called "Slaves and Servants in the Time of Jesus," p. 2006.

17:11 *Jerusalem . . . Samaria and Galilee:* See the notes at 9:51; 9:52; and 1:26. See also map on p. 2473.

17:12 *leprosy:* See the note at 4:27.

17:3 Matt 18:15.

[25]"But Abraham replied, 'Son, remember that in your lifetime you received your good things, while Lazarus received bad
things, but now he is comforted here and you are in agony. [26]And
besides all this, between us and you a great chasm has been fixed,
so that those who want to go from here to you cannot, nor can
anyone cross over from there to us.'

[27]"He answered, 'Then I beg you, father, send Lazarus to my
father's house, [28]for I have five brothers. Let him warn them, so
that they will not also come to this place of torment.'

[29]"Abraham replied, 'They have Moses and the Prophets; let
them listen to them.'

[30]" 'No, father Abraham,' he said, 'but if someone from the
dead goes to them, they will repent.'

[31]"He said to him, 'If they do not listen to Moses and the
Prophets, they will not be convinced even if someone rises from
the dead.' "

Sin, Faith, Duty

17 Jesus said to his disciples: "Things that cause people to sin
are bound to come, but woe to that person through whom they
come. [2]It would be better for him to be thrown into the sea with a
millstone tied around his neck than for him to cause one of these
little ones to sin. [3]So watch yourselves.

"If your brother sins, rebuke him, and if he repents, forgive
him. [4]If he sins against you seven times in a day, and seven times
comes back to you and says, 'I repent,' forgive him."

[5]The apostles said to the Lord, "Increase our faith!"

[6]He replied, "If you have faith as small as a mustard seed,
you can say to this mulberry tree, 'Be uprooted and planted in the
sea,' and it will obey you.

[7]"Suppose one of you had a servant plowing or looking after
the sheep. Would he say to the servant when he comes in from the
field, 'Come along now and sit down to eat'? [8]Would he not rather
say, 'Prepare my supper, get yourself ready and wait on me while I
eat and drink; after that you may eat and drink'? [9]Would he thank
the servant because he did what he was told to do? [10]So you also,
when you have done everything you were told to do, should say,
'We are unworthy servants; we have only done our duty.' "

Ten Healed of Leprosy

[11]Now on his way to Jerusalem, Jesus traveled along the border between Samaria and Galilee. [12]As he was going into a village,
ten men who had leprosy[a] met him. They stood at a distance [13]and
called out in a loud voice, "Jesus, Master, have pity on us!"

---

[a]**12** The Greek word was used for various diseases affecting the skin—not necessarily leprosy.

Christ Healing the Sick, stone roof carving from Norwich Cathedral, England, around 1500. Like the other Gospels, the book of LUKE tells of the many people Jesus healed as he traveled through Galilee and Judea preaching the good news (4:38-44). He healed a paralytic (5:17-26), a sick woman (8:43-48), ten men with leprosy (17:11-19), a blind beggar (18:35-43), and many others.

14 When he saw them, he said, "Go, show yourselves to the
priests." And as they went, they were cleansed.
15 One of them, when he saw he was healed, came back,
praising God in a loud voice. 16 He threw himself at Jesus' feet and
thanked him—and he was a Samaritan.
17 Jesus asked, "Were not all ten cleansed? Where are the other
nine? 18 Was no one found to return and give praise to God except
this foreigner?" 19 Then he said to him, "Rise and go; your faith has
made you well."

The Coming of the Kingdom of God

20 Once, having been asked by the Pharisees when the kingdom of God would come, Jesus replied, "The kingdom of God does
not come with your careful observation, 21 nor will people say, 'Here
it is,' or 'There it is,' because the kingdom of God is within[a] you."
22 Then he said to his disciples, "The time is coming when

[a]21 Or *among*

17:14 *show yourselves to the priests:* See the note at 5:14 (show yourself to the priest).

17:16 *a Samaritan:* See the note at 9:52. Those who heard this story may have been surprised that it was the Samaritan who thanked Jesus. But like other non-Jews ("Gentiles") in LUKE, he is healed because of his faith (see also 7:1-10).

17:20 *Pharisees:* See the note at 5:17.

17:20 *kingdom of God:* See the note at 4:43.

17:14 Lev 14:1-32.

17:22 *Son of Man:* Throughout this passage, Jesus talks about the coming time when he will return in glory and deliver his followers from distress. See also the mini-article called "Son of Man," p. 1866.

17:26,27 *Noah:* God chose the good and faithful Noah to build an ark that would save his family and other living things from the flood (see Gen 6–9).

17:28,29 *Lot . . . Sodom:* Lot, the nephew of Abraham, ran into trouble in Sodom, which was a very evil city (see Gen 18:16—19:29). God destroyed the evil people who lived there, but rescued Lot and his family. The location of Sodom is not known, but it may have been near the south end of the Dead Sea.

17:31 *on the roof of his house:* See the note at 5:19.

17:32 *Remember Lot's wife:* She turned into a pillar of salt when she disobeyed God by turning around to look at the destruction of Sodom (see Gen 19:26).

17:35,36 *grinding grain:* Usually women sifted the harvested wheat grains and crushed (ground) them in a mill to make flour. A simple mill would have had a flat rock surface where grain could be pounded or rolled with a rock or wooden tool.

17:37 *a dead body . . . vultures:* Vultures are birds that feed on dead flesh. They will quickly surround a dead animal and eat it. This saying may mean that when anything bad happens, people soon know about it, and curious people gather around and stare.

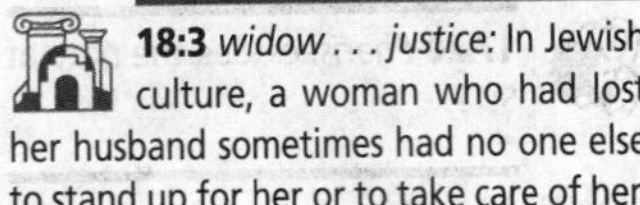

18:3 *widow . . . justice:* In Jewish culture, a woman who had lost her husband sometimes had no one else to stand up for her or to take care of her.

17:26,27 Gen 6:5-8; Gen 7:6-24. **17:31** Matt 24:17,18; Mark 13:15,16. **17:33** Matt 10:39; 16:25; Mark 8:35; Luke 9:24; John 12:25.

you will long to see one of the days of the Son of Man, but you
will not see it. 23Men will tell you, 'There he is!' or 'Here he is!' Do
not go running off after them. 24For the Son of Man in his day[a]
will be like the lightning, which flashes and lights up the sky from
one end to the other. 25But first he must suffer many things and be
rejected by this generation.

26"Just as it was in the days of Noah, so also will it be in the
days of the Son of Man. 27People were eating, drinking, marrying
and being given in marriage up to the day Noah entered the ark.
Then the flood came and destroyed them all.

28"It was the same in the days of Lot. People were eating and
drinking, buying and selling, planting and building. 29But the day
Lot left Sodom, fire and sulfur rained down from heaven and
destroyed them all.

30"It will be just like this on the day the Son of Man is
revealed. 31On that day no one who is on the roof of his house,
with his goods inside, should go down to get them. Likewise, no
one in the field should go back for anything. 32Remember Lot's
wife! 33Whoever tries to keep his life will lose it, and whoever loses
his life will preserve it. 34I tell you, on that night two people will be
in one bed; one will be taken and the other left. 35Two women will
be grinding grain together; one will be taken and the other left.[b]"

37"Where, Lord?" they asked.

He replied, "Where there is a dead body, there the vultures will gather."

The Parable of the Persistent Widow

18 Then Jesus told his disciples a parable to show them that
they should always pray and not give up. 2He said: "In a certain
town there was a judge who neither feared God nor cared about
men. 3And there was a widow in that town who kept coming to
him with the plea, 'Grant me justice against my adversary.'

4"For some time he refused. But finally he said to himself,
'Even though I don't fear God or care about men, 5yet because this
widow keeps bothering me, I will see that she gets justice, so that
she won't eventually wear me out with her coming!' "

6And the Lord said, "Listen to what the unjust judge says.
7And will not God bring about justice for his chosen ones, who cry
out to him day and night? Will he keep putting them off? 8I tell
you, he will see that they get justice, and quickly. However, when
the Son of Man comes, will he find faith on the earth?"

The Parable of the Pharisee and the Tax Collector

9To some who were confident of their own righteousness
and looked down on everybody else, Jesus told this parable: 10"Two

[a]24 Some manuscripts do not have *in his day.* [b]35 Some manuscripts *left.* 36*Two men will be in the field; one will be taken and the other left.*

men went up to the temple to pray, one a Pharisee and the other a
tax collector. 11The Pharisee stood up and prayed about[a] himself:
'God, I thank you that I am not like other men—robbers, evildoers, adulterers—or even like this tax collector. 12I fast twice a
week and give a tenth of all I get.'
13"But the tax collector stood at a distance. He would not
even look up to heaven, but beat his breast and said, 'God, have
mercy on me, a sinner.'
14"I tell you that this man, rather than the other, went home
justified before God. For everyone who exalts himself will be humbled, and he who humbles himself will be exalted."

The Little Children and Jesus

15People were also bringing babies to Jesus to have him
touch them. When the disciples saw this, they rebuked them.
16But Jesus called the children to him and said, "Let the little children come to me, and do not hinder them, for the kingdom of
God belongs to such as these. 17I tell you the truth, anyone who
will not receive the kingdom of God like a little child will never
enter it."

The Rich Ruler

18A certain ruler asked him, "Good teacher, what must I do
to inherit eternal life?"
19"Why do you call me good?" Jesus answered. "No one is
good—except God alone. 20You know the commandments: 'Do
not commit adultery, do not murder, do not steal, do not give false
testimony, honor your father and mother.'[b]"
21"All these I have kept since I was a boy," he said.
22When Jesus heard this, he said to him, "You still lack one
thing. Sell everything you have and give to the poor, and you will
have treasure in heaven. Then come, follow me."
23When he heard this, he became very sad, because he was a
man of great wealth. 24Jesus looked at him and said, "How hard it
is for the rich to enter the kingdom of God! 25Indeed, it is easier
for a camel to go through the eye of a needle than for a rich man
to enter the kingdom of God."
26Those who heard this asked, "Who then can be saved?"
27Jesus replied, "What is impossible with men is possible
with God."
28Peter said to him, "We have left all we had to follow you!"
29"I tell you the truth," Jesus said to them, "no one who has
left home or wife or brothers or parents or children for the sake of
the kingdom of God 30will fail to receive many times as much in
this age and, in the age to come, eternal life."

---

[a]**11** Or *to* [b]**20** Exodus 20:12-16; Deut. 5:16-20

18:8 *Son of Man:* See the note at 17:22.

18:10 *went up to the temple to pray:* People usually went to the temple for prayer early in the morning and about three o'clock in the afternoon.

18:10 *Pharisee . . . tax collector:* See the notes at 5:17 and 3:12.

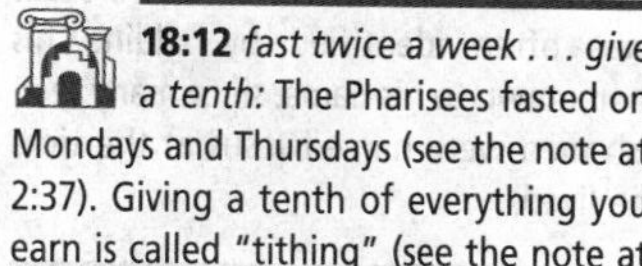

18:12 *fast twice a week . . . give a tenth:* The Pharisees fasted on Mondays and Thursdays (see the note at 2:37). Giving a tenth of everything you earn is called "tithing" (see the note at 11:42).

18:13 *sinner:* See the note at 13:2.

18:16,17 *kingdom of God . . . a little child:* See the note at 4:43.

18:18 *eternal life:* See the note at 10:25 (eternal life).

18:19,20 *the commandments:* The five commandments Jesus recites here are part of the Ten Commandments that God gave to Moses on Mount Sinai. See Exod 20:1-17 and Deut 5:1-21.

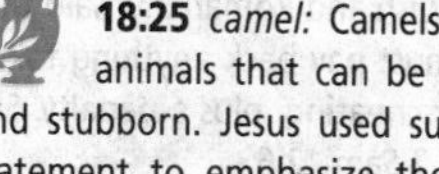

18:25 *camel:* Camels are large animals that can be very nasty and stubborn. Jesus used such a bold statement to emphasize the truth of what he was saying. See also the notes at Matt 19:24.

18:28 *Peter:* See the notes at 4:38 and 5:8 (Peter).

18:14 Matt 23:12; Luke 14:11. **18:20** Exod 20:14; Deut 5:18; Exod 20:13; Deut 5:17; Exod 20:15; Deut 5:19; Exod 20:16; Deut 5:20; Exod 20:12; Deut 5:16. **18:28** Luke 5:1-11.

Jesus Again Predicts His Death

31Jesus took the Twelve aside and told them, "We are going up to Jerusalem, and everything that is written by the prophets about the Son of Man will be fulfilled. 32He will be handed over to the Gentiles. They will mock him, insult him, spit on him, flog him and kill him. 33On the third day he will rise again."

34The disciples did not understand any of this. Its meaning was hidden from them, and they did not know what he was talking about.

A Blind Beggar Receives His Sight

35As Jesus approached Jericho, a blind man was sitting by the roadside begging. 36When he heard the crowd going by, he asked what was happening. 37They told him, "Jesus of Nazareth is passing by."

38He called out, "Jesus, Son of David, have mercy on me!"

39Those who led the way rebuked him and told him to be quiet, but he shouted all the more, "Son of David, have mercy on me!"

40Jesus stopped and ordered the man to be brought to him. When he came near, Jesus asked him, 41"What do you want me to do for you?"

"Lord, I want to see," he replied.

42Jesus said to him, "Receive your sight; your faith has healed you." 43Immediately he received his sight and followed Jesus, praising God. When all the people saw it, they also praised God.

Zacchaeus the Tax Collector

19 Jesus entered Jericho and was passing through. 2A man was there by the name of Zacchaeus; he was a chief tax collector and was wealthy. 3He wanted to see who Jesus was, but being a short man he could not, because of the crowd. 4So he ran ahead and climbed a sycamore-fig tree to see him, since Jesus was coming that way.

5When Jesus reached the spot, he looked up and said to him, "Zacchaeus, come down immediately. I must stay at your house today." 6So he came down at once and welcomed him gladly.

7All the people saw this and began to mutter, "He has gone to be the guest of a 'sinner.'"

8But Zacchaeus stood up and said to the Lord, "Look, Lord! Here and now I give half of my possessions to the poor, and if I have cheated anybody out of anything, I will pay back four times the amount."

9Jesus said to him, "Today salvation has come to this house,

18:32 *Gentiles:* The Romans, who ruled Judea at this time.

18:35 *Jericho:* See the note at 10:30. Joshua 5:13—6:26 describes how the people of Israel destroyed Jericho after crossing the Jordan River into the land of Canaan.

18:35 *blind man:* He is called Bartimaeus in Mark 10:46.

18:37 *Jesus of Nazareth:* Jesus was often identified by adding his hometown to his name, since many Jewish men were named Jesus at the time he lived.

18:38 *Son of David:* The Jewish people expected the Messiah to be from the family of King David (Isa 11:1-11). For this reason the Messiah was often called the "Son of David."

19:1 *Jericho:* See the notes at 10:30 and 18:35.

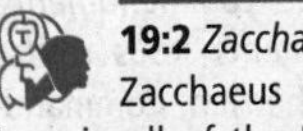

19:2 *Zacchaeus . . . tax collector:* Zacchaeus is mentioned only here in all of the New Testament. See the note at 3:12.

19:8 *pay back four times:* Both Jewish and Roman law said that a person must pay back anything taken by theft or cheating, plus a penalty. See Exod 22:1; 2 Sam 12:6.

19:9 *salvation:* After admitting his sin, Zacchaeus is rescued and placed under God's care. See the mini-article called "Salvation," on the next page.

19:9 *son of Abraham:* The Jewish people were also called the sons and daughters of Abraham. Here, Jesus says Zacchaeus is truly one of God's special people.

18:31 Ps 22; Isa 53; Zech 13:7.

because this man, too, is a son of Abraham. 10For the Son of Man
came to seek and to save what was lost."

The Parable of the Ten Minas

11While they were listening to this, he went on to tell them a
parable, because he was near Jerusalem and the people thought
that the kingdom of God was going to appear at once. 12He said: "A
man of noble birth went to a distant country to have himself
appointed king and then to return. 13So he called ten of his servants and gave them ten minas.[a] 'Put this money to work,' he said,
'until I come back.'
14"But his subjects hated him and sent a delegation after him
to say, 'We don't want this man to be our king.'
15"He was made king, however, and returned home. Then he

[a]13 A mina was about three months' wages.

19:10 *Son of Man:* See the mini-article called "Son of Man," p. 1866.

19:11 *kingdom of God was going to appear at once:* See the note at 4:43. Some thought a great earthly king like David would defeat the Romans and restore Israel's land and freedom. Others thought the whole world would be changed when the kingdom of God came.

19:13 *servants:* See the mini-article called "Slaves and Servants in the Time of Jesus," p. 2006.

19:11-27 Matt 25:14-30.

SALVATION

In the Bible, the term "salvation" refers to what God has done and is still doing to free humans from sin, sorrow, sickness, death, and the powers of evil. God wants human beings to live as God created them to live in the beginning (Gen 1,2). When sin entered the world (Gen 3), people needed to "be saved" from the power that death now had over them.

The people of Israel knew that God acted to save them (Exod 12:17; Deut 6:20-24; Ps 44:1-8; 78:4). God saved the Israelites from slavery in Egypt, and then helped them defeat their enemies and settle in the land of Canaan. God also saved some of them many centuries later after they had been forced to go and live in Babylon (Isa 43:14-16). For a full description of these events, read the articles called "From Joshua to the Exile: The People of Israel in the Promised Land," p. 924 and "After the Exile: God's People Return to Judea," p. 931.

Israel's worship also centers on what God has done to save them from the suffering they had to face (Deut 26:6-10). They offered sacrifices in the temple to show that they were sorry for breaking God's laws and to ask for God's saving help, so they could continue to be God's holy people.

God also promised to give new life to them and to the whole earth, bringing peace and taking care of all their needs (Isa 65:17-25). The prophets of Israel said that a savior would bring good news to those who were brokenhearted or imprisoned or poor. This savior would also make a new covenant with God's people in the presence of all the nations of the world (Isa 61:1-11). And God would overcome the powers of evil and make his rule over the world last forever (Dan 7:27).

The New Testament describes Jesus as the one who "will save his people from their sins" (Matt 1:21). He is the one who has been sent "to seek and to save what was lost" (Luke 19:10). His healings and his telling about God's forgiveness are signs that he is bringing salvation (Luke 7:50; 19:9; Mark 5:34). Jesus' death saves human beings and sets them free from their sins (Mark 10:45). By rising from death, he saves and frees people from the power of death (Rom 4:25; 5:10).

> *"Well done, my good servant!" his master replied. "Because you have been trustworthy in a very small matter, take charge of ten cities."*
> Luke 19:17

sent for the servants to whom he had given the money, in order to
find out what they had gained with it.
16"The first one came and said, 'Sir, your mina has earned
ten more.'
17" 'Well done, my good servant!' his master replied. 'Because
you have been trustworthy in a very small matter, take charge of
ten cities.'
18"The second came and said, 'Sir, your mina has earned five
more.'
19"His master answered, 'You take charge of five cities.'
20"Then another servant came and said, 'Sir, here is your
mina; I have kept it laid away in a piece of cloth. 21I was afraid of
you, because you are a hard man. You take out what you did not
put in and reap what you did not sow.'
22"His master replied, 'I will judge you by your own words,
you wicked servant! You knew, did you, that I am a hard man, taking out what I did not put in, and reaping what I did not sow?
23Why then didn't you put my money on deposit, so that when I
came back, I could have collected it with interest?'
24"Then he said to those standing by, 'Take his mina away
from him and give it to the one who has ten minas.'
25" 'Sir,' they said, 'he already has ten!'
26"He replied, 'I tell you that to everyone who has, more will
be given, but as for the one who has nothing, even what he has will
be taken away. 27But those enemies of mine who did not want me
to be king over them—bring them here and kill them in front
of me.' "

19:23 *interest:* Bankers used the money given to them to make more money by buying and selling. Some of the bankers' profits were returned as interest to the people who gave the banker money to invest.

19:26 Matt 13:12; Mark 4:25; Luke 8:18.

QUESTIONS ABOUT LUKE 9:51—19:27

1. How is love expressed in the parable of the Good Samaritan? (10:25-37) How would you respond to the question, "Who is your neighbor?"
2. Describe what Jesus says about being his disciple (14:25-35). What do you think this means for the way you live your life?
3. What do you see as the main point in Jesus' parables about the lost sheep, the lost coin, and the lost son? (15:1-32)
4. Jesus healed ten men who had leprosy (17:11-19). What are your thoughts about the nine who did not return to thank Jesus? Why is it important to say thank you to people who help us? What people in society today might be considered "lepers" or outcasts? What is your attitude toward such persons? Why?
5. Compare the story of the rich ruler (18:18-30) with the story of Zacchaeus (19:1-10). What strikes you about each man and his meeting with Jesus?
6. Choose one verse or passage from this section of LUKE that has special meaning for you and explain why you chose it.

Jesus' Final Week in Jerusalem

After a long journey, Jesus is finally ready to enter Jerusalem. He knows that he must face his enemies in order to fulfill God's plan. Before he is arrested and put on trial, he has a few days to teach in the temple and to prepare his disciples for what will happen after he dies.

JESUS TEACHES IN JERUSALEM

The Triumphal Entry

28After Jesus had said this, he went on ahead, going up to
Jerusalem. 29As he approached Bethphage and Bethany at the hill
called the Mount of Olives, he sent two of his disciples, saying to
them, 30"Go to the village ahead of you, and as you enter it, you
will find a colt tied there, which no one has ever ridden. Untie it
and bring it here. 31If anyone asks you, 'Why are you untying it?'
tell him, 'The Lord needs it.' "

32Those who were sent ahead went and found it just as he
had told them. 33As they were untying the colt, its owners asked
them, "Why are you untying the colt?"

34They replied, "The Lord needs it."

35They brought it to Jesus, threw their cloaks on the colt and
put Jesus on it. 36As he went along, people spread their cloaks on
the road.

37When he came near the place where the road goes down
the Mount of Olives, the whole crowd of disciples began joyfully to
praise God in loud voices for all the miracles they had seen:

38"Blessed is the king who comes in the name of the
Lord!"[a]

"Peace in heaven and glory in the highest!"

39Some of the Pharisees in the crowd said to Jesus, "Teacher,
rebuke your disciples!"

40"I tell you," he replied, "if they keep quiet, the stones will
cry out."

41As he approached Jerusalem and saw the city, he wept over
it 42and said, "If you, even you, had only known on this day what
would bring you peace—but now it is hidden from your eyes.
43The days will come upon you when your enemies will build an
embankment against you and encircle you and hem you in on
every side. 44They will dash you to the ground, you and the children within your walls. They will not leave one stone on another,
because you did not recognize the time of God's coming to you."

[a]**38** Psalm 118:26

19:28,29 *Jerusalem . . . Bethphage and Bethany . . . Mount of Olives:* See the note at 9:51. Bethphage, which means "house of figs," was a little village on the road between Jericho and Jerusalem. Bethany is on the slopes of the Mount of Olives and was the place where Jesus was taken up into heaven after his resurrection (24:50,51). The Mount of Olives is a ridge about two and a half miles long to the east of the Kidron Valley and Jerusalem. It rises about 300 to 500 feet above the temple area in Jerusalem. See the map on p. 2474 and the mini-article called "Jerusalem," p. 574.

19:36 *spread their cloaks on the road:* This is one way that people welcomed a famous person (2 Kgs 9:13).

19:37 *Mount of Olives:* See the note at 19:28, 29. If Jesus entered the city by way of the temple gate (see the map on p. 2474), crowds could have been lined up for over a mile. People in the temple area could have watched Jesus ride down from the Mount of Olives, across the Kidron Valley, and back up the road that led to the temple gate.

19:43 *The days will come upon you:* Jesus' predictions came true. In A.D. 70, the Romans put down a Jewish revolt in Jerusalem. In the process, they destroyed many of the city walls and the temple.

19:44 *you did not recognize the time of God's coming:* The Jewish people looked for the time when God would rescue them from their enemies. But when Jesus came, many did not recognize him as their "savior." See also the mini-article called "Salvation," p. 2021.

19:38 Ps 118:26

Jesus at the Temple

45Then he entered the temple area and began driving out those who were selling. 46"It is written," he said to them, " 'My house will be a house of prayer'[a]; but you have made it 'a den of robbers.'[b]"

47Every day he was teaching at the temple. But the chief priests, the teachers of the law and the leaders among the people were trying to kill him. 48Yet they could not find any way to do it, because all the people hung on his words.

The Authority of Jesus Questioned

20 One day as he was teaching the people in the temple courts and preaching the gospel, the chief priests and the teachers of the law, together with the elders, came up to him. 2"Tell us by what authority you are doing these things," they said. "Who gave you this authority?"

3He replied, "I will also ask you a question. Tell me, 4John's baptism—was it from heaven, or from men?"

5They discussed it among themselves and said, "If we say, 'From heaven,' he will ask, 'Why didn't you believe him?' 6But if we say, 'From men,' all the people will stone us, because they are persuaded that John was a prophet."

7So they answered, "We don't know where it was from."

8Jesus said, "Neither will I tell you by what authority I am doing these things."

The Parable of the Tenants

9He went on to tell the people this parable: "A man planted a vineyard, rented it to some farmers and went away for a long time. 10At harvest time he sent a servant to the tenants so they would give him some of the fruit of the vineyard. But the tenants beat him and sent him away empty-handed. 11He sent another servant, but that one also they beat and treated shamefully and sent away empty-handed. 12He sent still a third, and they wounded him and threw him out.

13"Then the owner of the vineyard said, 'What shall I do? I will send my son, whom I love; perhaps they will respect him.'

14"But when the tenants saw him, they talked the matter over. 'This is the heir,' they said. 'Let's kill him, and the inheritance will be ours.' 15So they threw him out of the vineyard and killed him.

"What then will the owner of the vineyard do to them? 16He will come and kill those tenants and give the vineyard to others."

When the people heard this, they said, "May this never be!"

17Jesus looked directly at them and asked, "Then what is the meaning of that which is written:

[a]**46** Isaiah 56:7 [b]**46** Jer. 7:11

19:47 *chief priests, the teachers of the law and the leaders among the people:* The "leaders among the people" are likely those whom LUKE calls "elders" (see 9:22 and the note; 20:1; 22:52). These three groups had the most to lose if the people accepted Jesus and his teachings. Jesus challenged their authority and power, which made them so angry they wanted to kill Jesus. See also the articles called "People of the Law: The Religion of Israel," p. 939, and "The World of Jesus: Peoples, Powers, and Politics," p. 1821.

20:4 *John's baptism:* Referring to John the Baptist. See the note at 1:13.

20:9 *vineyard:* The place where grapes are grown, often on a hillside. Many vineyards had walls around them and a watchtower where someone could keep an eye out for robbers or stray animals.

20:10 *servant:* See the mini-article called "Slaves and Servants in the Time of Jesus," p. 2006. In this parable, Jesus was likely comparing the vineyard to Israel (Isa 5:1-7); the servant to Israel's past prophets (Neh 9:26; Jer 7:25,26); the son to Jesus himself (20:13); and the tenants to the Jewish religious leaders (20:19).

20:17,18 *The stone the builders rejected:* Jesus was describing himself as this important stone.

20:20 *the governor:* Referring to Pontius Pilate. See the note at 13:1.

20:22 *pay taxes to Caesar:* In Jesus' time, Judea was part of the Roman empire, so the people in Judea had to pay taxes to the Roman government. The highest Roman leader was called Caesar, who ruled from Rome.

"'The stone the builders rejected
has become the capstone[a]'[b]?

18 Everyone who falls on that stone will be broken to pieces, but he on whom it falls will be crushed."

19 The teachers of the law and the chief priests looked for a way to arrest him immediately, because they knew he had spoken this parable against them. But they were afraid of the people.

Paying Taxes to Caesar

20 Keeping a close watch on him, they sent spies, who pretended to be honest. They hoped to catch Jesus in something he said so that they might hand him over to the power and authority of the governor. 21 So the spies questioned him: "Teacher, we know that you speak and teach what is right, and that you do not show partiality but teach the way of God in accordance with the truth. 22 Is it right for us to pay taxes to Caesar or not?"

23 He saw through their duplicity and said to them, 24 "Show me a denarius. Whose portrait and inscription are on it?"

25 "Caesar's," they replied.

He said to them, "Then give to Caesar what is Caesar's, and to God what is God's."

26 They were unable to trap him in what he had said there in public. And astonished by his answer, they became silent.

The Resurrection and Marriage

27 Some of the Sadducees, who say there is no resurrection, came to Jesus with a question. 28 "Teacher," they said, "Moses wrote for us that if a man's brother dies and leaves a wife but no children, the man must marry the widow and have children for his brother. 29 Now there were seven brothers. The first one married a woman and died childless. 30 The second 31 and then the third married her, and in the same way the seven died, leaving no children. 32 Finally, the woman died too. 33 Now then, at the resurrection whose wife will she be, since the seven were married to her?"

34 Jesus replied, "The people of this age marry and are given in marriage. 35 But those who are considered worthy of taking part in that age and in the resurrection from the dead will neither marry nor be given in marriage, 36 and they can no longer die; for they are like the angels. They are God's children, since they are children of the resurrection. 37 But in the account of the bush, even Moses showed that the dead rise, for he calls the Lord 'the God of Abraham, and the God of Isaac, and the God of Jacob.'[c] 38 He is not the God of the dead, but of the living, for to him all are alive."

39 Some of the teachers of the law responded, "Well said, teacher!" 40 And no one dared to ask him any more questions.

---

a17 Or *cornerstone* **b17** Psalm 118:22 **c37** Exodus 3:6

Jesus said, *"Give to Caesar what is Caesar's, and to God what is God's."*
Luke 20:25

20:24 *denarius:* This coin was roughly the wages for a day's work. In the time of Jesus, a denarius had a picture of Emperor Tiberius on one side. On the other side were the words: "Tiberius Caesar Augustus, son of the divine Augustus." This coin was used to pay taxes to Caesar. If Jesus had said the Jewish people should refuse to pay the taxes, the Jewish religious leaders could accuse him of rebelling against the Romans.

20:27 *Sadducees:* The Sadducees were a wealthy group of Jews who worked closely with the priests in the temple. They taught that the most important thing in life was going to the temple and offering sacrifices there. The Sadducees didn't believe that God brought people back to life from death, because it was not directly taught in the Law of Moses (the first five books of Jewish Scriptures). See also the article called "The World of Jesus: Peoples, Powers, and Politics," p. 1821.

20:35,36 *resurrection . . . God's children:* Jesus taught that eternal life, for God's children who have been resurrected, is not like the life of this world. For more, see the mini-articles called "Resurrection," p. 2210 and "Eternal Life," p. 2072.

20:37 *the God of Abraham, and the God of Isaac, and the God of Jacob:* See the note at 1:55. Jesus argues that if God is worshiped by Abraham, Isaac, and Jacob, who entered into a covenant with God in ancient times, then they must still be alive, because God is the God of the living.

19:46 Isa 56:7; Jer 7:11. **20:9** Isa 5:1. **20:17** Ps 118:22. **20:28** Deut 25:5,6. **20:37** Exod 3:6.

20:41 *Christ . . . Son of David:* See the notes at 2:11 (Savior) and 18:38.

20:42 *right hand:* The place of power and honor.

20:44 *'Lord' . . . son:* Jesus asks how a person could be both David's son and David's Lord. The implied answer is that the Messiah is more than David's son—he is also David's Lord.

20:46,47 *Beware of the teachers of the law . . . walk around in flowing robes . . . make lengthy prayers:* See the note at 5:17. Jesus lists a number of things that show how teachers of the law liked to be noticed for what they were doing. Since widows were financially dependent on others, they were particularly vulnerable to exploitation.

21:1 *temple treasury:* These funnel-shaped boxes were located in the court of women in the temple area.

21:2 *copper coins:* The coins were the Greek *lepton,* which was the smallest Greek coin. It was worth only half of the smallest Roman coin. The point is that the widow's small offering was generous because it was all she had.

21:6 *the time will come:* See the note at 19:43.

21:8 *I am he:* Referring to the Messiah, the Anointed One. See the note at 2:11 (Savior).

21:12 *synagogues:* See the note at 4:15. What Jesus said later came true. The book of Acts tells about how some of Jesus' disciples were put on trial in the Jewish synagogues and at the temple (see Acts 4:1-22; 5:17-42; 6:8—8:2; 17:1-9; 21:27—26:32).

20:42,43 Ps 110:1. **21:14,15** Luke 12:11,12.

Whose Son Is the Christ?

41 Then Jesus said to them, "How is it that they say the Christ[a]
is the Son of David? 42 David himself declares in the Book of Psalms:

" 'The Lord said to my Lord:
"Sit at my right hand
43 until I make your enemies
a footstool for your feet." '[b]

44 David calls him 'Lord.' How then can he be his son?"
45 While all the people were listening, Jesus said to his disciples, 46 "Beware of the teachers of the law. They like to walk around
in flowing robes and love to be greeted in the marketplaces and
have the most important seats in the synagogues and the places of
honor at banquets. 47 They devour widows' houses and for a show
make lengthy prayers. Such men will be punished most severely."

The Widow's Offering

21 As he looked up, Jesus saw the rich putting their gifts into
the temple treasury. 2 He also saw a poor widow put in two very
small copper coins.[c] 3 "I tell you the truth," he said, "this poor
widow has put in more than all the others. 4 All these people gave
their gifts out of their wealth; but she out of her poverty put in all
she had to live on."

Signs of the End of the Age

5 Some of his disciples were remarking about how the temple
was adorned with beautiful stones and with gifts dedicated to God.
But Jesus said, 6 "As for what you see here, the time will come when
not one stone will be left on another; every one of them will be
thrown down."
7 "Teacher," they asked, "when will these things happen? And
what will be the sign that they are about to take place?"
8 He replied: "Watch out that you are not deceived. For many
will come in my name, claiming, 'I am he,' and, 'The time is near.'
Do not follow them. 9 When you hear of wars and revolutions, do
not be frightened. These things must happen first, but the end will
not come right away."
10 Then he said to them: "Nation will rise against nation, and
kingdom against kingdom. 11 There will be great earthquakes,
famines and pestilences in various places, and fearful events and
great signs from heaven.
12 "But before all this, they will lay hands on you and persecute you. They will deliver you to synagogues and prisons, and you
will be brought before kings and governors, and all on account of
my name. 13 This will result in your being witnesses to them. 14 But
make up your mind not to worry beforehand how you will defend

[a]41 Or *Messiah* [b]43 Psalm 110:1 [c]2 Greek *two lepta*

yourselves. 15 For I will give you words and wisdom that none of your adversaries will be able to resist or contradict. 16 You will be betrayed even by parents, brothers, relatives and friends, and they will put some of you to death. 17 All men will hate you because of me. 18 But not a hair of your head will perish. 19 By standing firm you will gain life.

20 "When you see Jerusalem being surrounded by armies, you will know that its desolation is near. 21 Then let those who are in Judea flee to the mountains, let those in the city get out, and let those in the country not enter the city. 22 For this is the time of punishment in fulfillment of all that has been written. 23 How dreadful it will be in those days for pregnant women and nursing mothers! There will be great distress in the land and wrath against this people. 24 They will fall by the sword and will be taken as prisoners to all the nations. Jerusalem will be trampled on by the Gentiles until the times of the Gentiles are fulfilled.

25 "There will be signs in the sun, moon and stars. On the earth, nations will be in anguish and perplexity at the roaring and tossing of the sea. 26 Men will faint from terror, apprehensive of what is coming on the world, for the heavenly bodies will be shaken. 27 At that time they will see the Son of Man coming in a cloud with power

21:20 *When you see Jerusalem being surrounded:* See the note at 19:43.

21:21 *Judea:* Hills can be found in various parts of Judea, especially north and southeast of Jerusalem. See the map on p. 2473 and the note at 1:39.

21:26 *heavenly bodies will be shaken:* In ancient times, some thought that the stars were spiritual powers. Others compared the stars to nations on earth. So this verse may mean that God would shake earthly powers (nations) or the spiritual powers that opposed God.

21:22-24 Isa 63:4; Jer 5:29; Hos 9:7. **21:25** Isa 13:10; Ezek 32:7; Joel 2:31; Rev 6:12,13. **21:27** Dan 7:13; Rev 1:7.

TEMPLE OFFERINGS

In Jesus' day, Jewish people went to worship and to make sacrifices to God at the temple in Jerusalem. Sacrifices required by the Law of Moses included the killing of certain animals and the burning of grains and incense. Some kinds of sacrifices could be made any day of the year, while others were only made on special days like the Day of Atonement. See the article called "People of the Law: The Religion of Israel," p. 939. Some of the meat that people offered in the temple was eaten by the priests and Levites who devoted their lives to serving God and making sacrifices for the people of Israel.

In addition to bringing animals and grain to be sacrificed for the forgiveness of sin, the Jewish people also gave vegetables they had grown, valuable items, and money to help with the cost of running the temple and providing for the needs of the priests and Levites. The Law of Moses also stated that the people should give to the LORD one-tenth of what they grew or earned (Lev 27:30-33; Num 18:21-32). This practice was called tithing.

The Jewish people believed that God was present among them in the Most Holy Place in the temple. Offerings were given to God each day in the same way servants might bring gifts or food to their masters. The size of the gift offered was based on who offered the gift. A poor person, for example, was not expected to offer as much as someone who was wealthy.

Some offerings were presented to God in order to confess guilt and to ask for forgiveness of sins (Lev 4:1—6:7; 6:24-30; 7:1-6; 8:14-17; 16:3-22). Other offerings were presented as a way of worshiping God, giving thanks to God, and showing commitment to God (Lev 1–3; 6:8-23; 7:11-34). Compare the praise Jesus had for the poor widow who gave her last two coins (Luke 21:1-4) with the warning he has for people who make a big show of their generosity while neglecting important matters of the law, such as justice, mercy, and faithfulness (Matt 23:23,24).

and great glory. [28]When these things begin to take place, stand up
and lift up your heads, because your redemption is drawing near."
[29]He told them this parable: "Look at the fig tree and all the
trees. [30]When they sprout leaves, you can see for yourselves and
know that summer is near. [31]Even so, when you see these things
happening, you know that the kingdom of God is near.

[32]"I tell you the truth, this generation[a] will certainly not pass
away until all these things have happened. [33]Heaven and earth will
pass away, but my words will never pass away.

[34]"Be careful, or your hearts will be weighed down with dissipation, drunkenness and the anxieties of life, and that day will
close on you unexpectedly like a trap. [35]For it will come upon all
those who live on the face of the whole earth. [36]Be always on the
watch, and pray that you may be able to escape all that is about to
happen, and that you may be able to stand before the Son of Man."

[37]Each day Jesus was teaching at the temple, and each
evening he went out to spend the night on the hill called the
Mount of Olives, [38]and all the people came early in the morning to
hear him at the temple.

THE LAST DAYS OF JESUS: HIS TRIAL AND DEATH

During the Feast of Unleavened Bread, some of the chief priests and teachers of the law plot to arrest Jesus. Jesus is betrayed by his disciple Judas after Jesus and the other disciples share a Passover meal. His arrest is followed by a trial in front of the Jewish leaders. Later, the Roman governor Pilate sentences Jesus to die on a cross.

Judas Agrees to Betray Jesus

22 Now the Feast of Unleavened Bread, called the Passover, was
approaching, [2]and the chief priests and the teachers of the law
were looking for some way to get rid of Jesus, for they were afraid
of the people. [3]Then Satan entered Judas, called Iscariot, one of the
Twelve. [4]And Judas went to the chief priests and the officers of the
temple guard and discussed with them how he might betray Jesus.
[5]They were delighted and agreed to give him money. [6]He consented, and watched for an opportunity to hand Jesus over to them
when no crowd was present.

The Last Supper

[7]Then came the day of Unleavened Bread on which the
Passover lamb had to be sacrificed. [8]Jesus sent Peter and John, saying, "Go and make preparations for us to eat the Passover."

[a]32 Or *race*

21:36 *Son of Man:* See the mini-article called "Son of Man," p. 1866.

21:37 *temple . . . Mount of Olives:* See 19:47 and the notes at 19:28,29 and 19:37.

22:1 *Feast of Unleavened Bread, called the Passover:* By the time of Jesus these two terms were virtually synonymous. See the mini-article called "Passover and the Feast of Unleavened Bread," p. 2030.

22:2 *chief priests and the teachers of the law:* See the note at 19:47.

22:3 *Satan:* See the note at 4:3.

22:3 *Satan entered Judas, called Iscariot:* Judas is the Greek spelling of the Hebrew name "Judah," which could mean that he was from Judea. There are many possible meanings of his second name, "Iscariot." It may mean "a man from Kerioth" (a place in Judea) or it may mean "a man who was a betrayer" or "a man who was a liar." Some scholars believe "Iscariot" comes from "Sicarii," a group of assassins who used knives, and that Judas was a member of a group called Zealots who fought against the Romans. Judas acted as treasurer for Jesus and the Twelve (John 12:5, 6). LUKE says here that Satan has entered Judas' heart. Having left Jesus until an opportune time (Luke 4:13), the devil is now back, and will lead Judas to betray Jesus.

22:4 *chief priests and the officers of the temple guard:* The chief priests consisted of the former high priest, Annas; the current high priest, Caiaphas (see the note at 3:1,2); and the high priestly families. The temple guard were Jewish men who guarded the temple and helped keep order in the temple area.

22:7 *Unleavened Bread . . . Passover lamb:* See the note at 22:1.

9“Where do you want us to prepare for it?” they asked.
10He replied, “As you enter the city, a man carrying a jar of water
will meet you. Follow him to the house that he enters, 11and say to the
owner of the house, ‘The Teacher asks: Where is the guest room,
where I may eat the Passover with my disciples?’ 12He will show you a
large upper room, all furnished. Make preparations there.”
13They left and found things just as Jesus had told them. So
they prepared the Passover.
14When the hour came, Jesus and his apostles reclined at the
table. 15And he said to them, “I have eagerly desired to eat this
Passover with you before I suffer. 16For I tell you, I will not eat it
again until it finds fulfillment in the kingdom of God.”
17After taking the cup, he gave thanks and said, “Take this
and divide it among you. 18For I tell you I will not drink again of
the fruit of the vine until the kingdom of God comes.”
19And he took bread, gave thanks and broke it, and gave it to
them, saying, “This is my body given for you; do this in remembrance of me.”
20In the same way, after the supper he took the cup, saying,
“This cup is the new covenant in my blood, which is poured out
for you. 21But the hand of him who is going to betray me is with
mine on the table. 22The Son of Man will go as it has been decreed,
but woe to that man who betrays him.” 23They began to question
among themselves which of them it might be who would do this.
24Also a dispute arose among them as to which of them was
considered to be greatest. 25Jesus said to them, “The kings of the
Gentiles lord it over them; and those who exercise authority over
them call themselves Benefactors. 26But you are not to be like that.
Instead, the greatest among you should be like the youngest, and
the one who rules like the one who serves. 27For who is greater, the
one who is at the table or the one who serves? Is it not the one who
is at the table? But I am among you as one who serves. 28You are
those who have stood by me in my trials. 29And I confer on you a
kingdom, just as my Father conferred one on me, 30so that you
may eat and drink at my table in my kingdom and sit on thrones,
judging the twelve tribes of Israel.
31“Simon, Simon, Satan has asked to sift you[a] as wheat. 32But
I have prayed for you, Simon, that your faith may not fail. And
when you have turned back, strengthen your brothers.”
33But he replied, “Lord, I am ready to go with you to prison
and to death.”
34Jesus answered, “I tell you, Peter, before the rooster crows
today, you will deny three times that you know me.”
35Then Jesus asked them, “When I sent you without purse,
bag or sandals, did you lack anything?”

[a]31 The Greek is plural.

22:10 *man carrying a jar of water:* Usually this kind of work was done by a woman, so the man would have been easy to see.

22:14 *reclined at the table:* See the note at 7:36.

22:16 *kingdom of God:* See the notes at 4:43 and 13:29.

22:19 *bread:* This probably would have been the unleavened bread that was made for the Passover meal.

22:20 *new covenant in my blood:* God made a covenant with Moses when God gave him the laws the Israelites were to live by. Here Jesus is saying that God is about to create a new covenant (see Jer 31:31-34; Exod 24:8). This new covenant is for all people. See also the mini-articles called “Salvation,” p. 2021 and “Covenants (Agreements),” p. 386.

22:30 *twelve tribes of Israel:* Originally the twelve tribes of Israel referred to the Hebrew descendants of Jacob's twelve sons (see Gen 32:20-32; 35:23-26). Because the priestly line of Levi did not hold land (Num 1:47-53), it was no longer considered one of the twelve tribes. Joseph's descendants formed two separate tribes (Ephraim and Manasseh). See also the article called “From Joshua to the Exile: The People of Israel in the Promised Land,” p. 924.

22:31 *Simon:* Referring to Peter. See the notes at 4:38 and 5:8 (Peter).

22:31 *sift you as wheat:* See the note at 3:17.

22:21 Ps 41:9. **22:24** Matt 18:1; Mark 9:34; Luke 9:46. **22:25,26** Matt 20:25-27; Mark 10:42-44. **22:26** Matt 23:11; Mark 9:35. **22:27** John 13:12-15. **22:35** Matt 10:9,10; Mark 6:8,9; Luke 9:3; 10:4.

22:36 *purse . . . bag . . . sword:* Things that someone would take on a dangerous journey. Jesus was telling his disciples to be ready for anything that might happen.

22:37 *he was numbered with the transgressors:* In fulfillment of Scripture, Jesus was about to be tried as a criminal, and his disciples would also be in danger.

22:39 *Mount of Olives:* See the notes at 19:28,29 and 19:37.

22:37 Isa 53:12.

"Nothing," they answered.
36 He said to them, "But now if you have a purse, take it, and
also a bag; and if you don't have a sword, sell your cloak and buy
one. 37 It is written: 'And he was numbered with the transgressors'[a];
and I tell you that this must be fulfilled in me. Yes, what is written
about me is reaching its fulfillment."
38 The disciples said, "See, Lord, here are two swords."
"That is enough," he replied.

Jesus Prays on the Mount of Olives

39 Jesus went out as usual to the Mount of Olives, and his disciples followed him. 40 On reaching the place, he said to them,
"Pray that you will not fall into temptation." 41 He withdrew about
a stone's throw beyond them, knelt down and prayed, 42 "Father, if

[a]**37** Isaiah 53:12

PASSOVER AND THE FEAST OF UNLEAVENED BREAD

These two special spring festivals were brought together in the Jewish calendar long before the time of Jesus. Passover was celebrated to remind the people of Israel how God rescued them from slavery in Egypt (Exod 12,13). It was to be celebrated on the fourteenth day of the first month, Abib (later called Nisan), a month that overlaps March and April on modern calendars. Passover started at sunset. The Feast of Unleavened Bread began the next day, the fifteenth day of the first month, and lasted for seven days (Lev 23:4-8; Num 28:17-25).

During the Passover festival, a lamb was to be killed, roasted, and eaten. The blood of the lamb was a reminder of the blood that the Israelites put on their doorframes before God sent a final plague on Egypt. God's angel of death "passed over" the Israelite homes that were marked by the blood, but the death angel killed the firstborn in the families of Egypt (Exod 12:1-27). The unleavened bread that was to be eaten during Passover and during the seven days of the Feast of Unleavened Bread was a reminder of how quickly the people had to leave Egypt. They did not have time to let the dough for their bread rise, so they made bread without using yeast (leaven). Bread made this way will always be flat, like a cracker.

The Feast of Unleavened Bread also became a time to give thanks to God for the annual harvest of grain, which provided food for all the people. Later, these two feasts were joined and celebrated partly at the temple in Jerusalem and partly in people's homes. Jewish people came from all over the world to be in Jerusalem to take part in these yearly feasts. Here they recalled with thanks what God had done for them in the past and celebrated their life together in the present.

The reports of the celebration of these meals in the time of Jesus includes both the offering and eating of the sacrificial lamb, eating unleavened bread and drinking wine. (See Luke 22:7-10.) Children were taught the meaning of the meal as they ate it. Jews throughout the world continue to celebrate these important festivals in much the same manner.

See also the chart called "Jewish Calendar and Festivals" in the article called "People of the Law: The Religion of Israel," p. 939.

Family gathered to celebrate the Passover meal. In Jesus' day, only men had to take part in this ritual pilgrimage festival. On the first day of the festival, a Passover meal was celebrated in which the men reclined around a low table. Today, men and women alike take part in the ritual, called a Seder. The photograph shows a Seder plate, a later addition to the ritual dinner, with foods that have symbolic meanings connected to the story of the exodus from Egypt.

you are willing, take this cup from me; yet not my will, but yours
be done." 43 An angel from heaven appeared to him and strengthened him. 44 And being in anguish, he prayed more earnestly, and
his sweat was like drops of blood falling to the ground.[a]
45 When he rose from prayer and went back to the disciples,
he found them asleep, exhausted from sorrow. 46 "Why are you
sleeping?" he asked them. "Get up and pray so that you will not fall
into temptation."

Jesus Arrested

47 While he was still speaking a crowd came up, and the man
who was called Judas, one of the Twelve, was leading them. He
approached Jesus to kiss him, 48 but Jesus asked him, "Judas, are
you betraying the Son of Man with a kiss?"
49 When Jesus' followers saw what was going to happen,

[a]**44** Some early manuscripts do not have verses 43 and 44.

22:42 *take this cup from me:* Here the "cup" refers to the suffering Jesus must experience. Jesus knew that God had planned that he would have to suffer and die to fulfill God's purposes (see 9:22; 18:31-33; 22:20-22).

22:43 *An angel from heaven:* See the note at 2:13-15.

22:47 *Judas:* See the note at 22:3 (Judas).

22:47,48 *kiss:* It was customary for people to greet each other with a kiss on the cheek.

Peter Repentant, Mary and John, an illuminated page from an early fifteenth century Ethiopian book containing the Pentateuch, JOSHUA, JUDGES, RUTH, and the four Gospels. At the Last Supper, Jesus warned Peter that he would be tested by Satan, told him to be strong, and instructed him to help others. Peter assured Jesus that he would be willing to die for him, but Jesus told him "Before the rooster crows today, you will deny three times that you know me" (22:34). When what Jesus predicted happened, Peter "went outside and wept bitterly." (See 22:54-62.)

22:50 *one of them struck the servant of the high priest:* John 18:10 states that Simon Peter struck the servant, whose name was Malchus.

22:52 *chief priests, the officers of the temple guard, and the elders:* See the notes at 22:4 and 19:47.

22:53 *darkness:* Darkness stands for the power of the devil and evil. See also the note at 16:8.

22:54 *house of the high priest:* See the note at 3:1,2. The council of the elders (the Sanhedrin) who questioned Jesus (22:66-71) may have met at the house of Caiaphas. See also the article called "People of the Law: The Religion of Israel," p. 939.

22:53 Luke 19:47; 21:37.

they said, "Lord, should we strike with our swords?" 50And one
of them struck the servant of the high priest, cutting off his
right ear.

51But Jesus answered, "No more of this!" And he touched the
man's ear and healed him.

52Then Jesus said to the chief priests, the officers of the temple guard, and the elders, who had come for him, "Am I leading a
rebellion, that you have come with swords and clubs? 53Every day
I was with you in the temple courts, and you did not lay a hand on
me. But this is your hour—when darkness reigns."

Peter Disowns Jesus

54Then seizing him, they led him away and took him into the
house of the high priest. Peter followed at a distance. 55But when
they had kindled a fire in the middle of the courtyard and had sat
down together, Peter sat down with them. 56A servant girl saw him

seated there in the firelight. She looked closely at him and said,
"This man was with him."
57 But he denied it. "Woman, I don't know him," he said.
58 A little later someone else saw him and said, "You also are
one of them."
"Man, I am not!" Peter replied.
59 About an hour later another asserted, "Certainly this fellow
was with him, for he is a Galilean."
60 Peter replied, "Man, I don't know what you're talking
about!" Just as he was speaking, the rooster crowed. 61 The Lord
turned and looked straight at Peter. Then Peter remembered the
word the Lord had spoken to him: "Before the rooster crows today,
you will disown me three times." 62 And he went outside and wept
bitterly.

The Guards Mock Jesus

63 The men who were guarding Jesus began mocking and
beating him. 64 They blindfolded him and demanded, "Prophesy!
Who hit you?" 65 And they said many other insulting things to him.

Jesus Before Pilate and Herod

66 At daybreak the council of the elders of the people, both
the chief priests and teachers of the law, met together, and Jesus
was led before them. 67 "If you are the Christ,[a]" they said, "tell us."
Jesus answered, "If I tell you, you will not believe me, 68 and
if I asked you, you would not answer. 69 But from now on, the Son
of Man will be seated at the right hand of the mighty God."
70 They all asked, "Are you then the Son of God?"
He replied, "You are right in saying I am."
71 Then they said, "Why do we need any more testimony? We
have heard it from his own lips."
23 Then the whole assembly rose and led him off to Pilate. 2 And
they began to accuse him, saying, "We have found this man sub-
verting our nation. He opposes payment of taxes to Caesar and
claims to be Christ,[b] a king."
3 So Pilate asked Jesus, "Are you the king of the Jews?"
"Yes, it is as you say," Jesus replied.
4 Then Pilate announced to the chief priests and the crowd, "I
find no basis for a charge against this man."
5 But they insisted, "He stirs up the people all over Judea[c] by
his teaching. He started in Galilee and has come all the way here."
6 On hearing this, Pilate asked if the man was a Galilean.
7 When he learned that Jesus was under Herod's jurisdiction, he
sent him to Herod, who was also in Jerusalem at that time.

[a] 67 Or *Messiah* [b] 2 Or *Messiah*; also in verses 35 and 39 [c] 5 Or *over the land of the Jews*

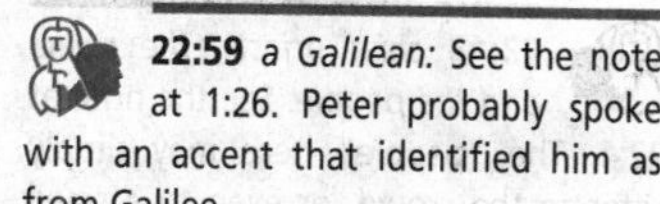

22:59 *a Galilean:* See the note at 1:26. Peter probably spoke with an accent that identified him as from Galilee.

22:66 *At daybreak . . . council:* The council mentioned here (also called the Sanhedrin) was made up of representatives of various Jewish groups (see the notes at 9:22; 19:47; 22:54). The Romans allowed this council to hear cases that involved crimes against Jewish religious laws. Since the Jewish laws did not allow the officials to do any business at night, Jesus was brought before them first thing in the morning. The Law of Moses taught that two witnesses were needed before a person could be put to death (Deut 19:15).

22:67 *the Christ:* See the note at 2:11 (Savior).

22:69 *Son of Man:* See the mini-article called "Son of Man," p. 1866.

22:70 *Son of God:* See the mini-article called "Son of God," p. 2044.

23:1 *Pilate:* See the note at 13:1.

23:2 *opposes payment of taxes to Caesar:* See the notes at 20:22 and 20:24. Jesus had not done what the council accused him of doing, but they were trying to get him in trouble with the Roman rulers.

23:2 *Christ, a king:* See the note at 2:11 (Savior). Because the Romans were in charge of the land, no one could declare himself to be a king. Only the Roman authorities could give someone such a powerful position.

23:6,7 *Galilean . . . Herod's jurisdiction:* Herod Antipas, the son of King Herod the Great, ruled Galilee at this time. See the notes at 3:1, 2 and 9:7. Pilate didn't want to handle this case, so he sent Jesus to Herod. Although Herod's main headquarters were in the city of Tiberias by the Sea of Galilee, he was in Jerusalem because of the Passover celebration.

23:13 *chief priests, the rulers and the people:* See the note at 22:4. The "people" here may simply refer to the crowd, or even to a small mob that had gathered. It does not mean everyone in Jerusalem or all the Jewish people. In the narrow streets of Jerusalem it probably didn't take many to make a crowd.

23:18 *Barabbas:* His name means "son of Abba." He was a violent criminal who apparently caused riots and murdered people (see also Matt 27:15-20; Mark 15:6-11).

23:21 *Crucify him:* The people wanted Jesus to die by means of the Roman method of execution called crucifixion. Jesus was put to death on a cross for political reasons, not because he had broken the Law of Moses. See the mini-article called "Crucifixion," p. 1914.

23:26 *Simon from Cyrene:* Cyrene was a city in North Africa (see the map on p. 2475). Simon was probably in Jerusalem to celebrate the Passover and Feast of Unleavened Bread.

23:31 *if men do these things when the tree is green . . . dry:* This saying possibly means, "If this can happen to an innocent person, what do you think will happen to one who is guilty?" See also the note at 19:43.

[8]When Herod saw Jesus, he was greatly pleased, because for
a long time he had been wanting to see him. From what he had
heard about him, he hoped to see him perform some miracle. [9]He
plied him with many questions, but Jesus gave him no answer.
[10]The chief priests and the teachers of the law were standing there,
vehemently accusing him. [11]Then Herod and his soldiers ridiculed
and mocked him. Dressing him in an elegant robe, they sent him
back to Pilate. [12]That day Herod and Pilate became friends—
before this they had been enemies.

[13]Pilate called together the chief priests, the rulers and the
people, [14]and said to them, "You brought me this man as one who
was inciting the people to rebellion. I have examined him in your
presence and have found no basis for your charges against him.
[15]Neither has Herod, for he sent him back to us; as you can see, he
has done nothing to deserve death. [16]Therefore, I will punish him
and then release him.[a]"

[18]With one voice they cried out, "Away with this man!
Release Barabbas to us!" [19](Barabbas had been thrown into prison
for an insurrection in the city, and for murder.)

[20]Wanting to release Jesus, Pilate appealed to them again.
[21]But they kept shouting, "Crucify him! Crucify him!"

[22]For the third time he spoke to them: "Why? What crime
has this man committed? I have found in him no grounds for the
death penalty. Therefore I will have him punished and then release
him."

[23]But with loud shouts they insistently demanded that he be
crucified, and their shouts prevailed. [24]So Pilate decided to grant
their demand. [25]He released the man who had been thrown into
prison for insurrection and murder, the one they asked for, and
surrendered Jesus to their will.

The Crucifixion

[26]As they led him away, they seized Simon from Cyrene, who
was on his way in from the country, and put the cross on him and
made him carry it behind Jesus. [27]A large number of people followed him, including women who mourned and wailed for him.
[28]Jesus turned and said to them, "Daughters of Jerusalem, do not
weep for me; weep for yourselves and for your children. [29]For the
time will come when you will say, 'Blessed are the barren women,
the wombs that never bore and the breasts that never nursed!'
[30]Then

" 'they will say to the mountains, "Fall on us!"
and to the hills, "Cover us!" '[b]

[a]**16** Some manuscripts *him." [17]Now he was obliged to release one man to them at the Feast.* [b]**30** Hosea 10:8

Mount Calvary by William H. Johnson, 1939. In LUKE's version of the death of Jesus, the Gospel writer tells how two criminals were nailed to crosses next to Jesus. One criminal insulted Jesus, but the other answered him saying, "We are punished justly, for we are getting what our deeds deserve. But this man has done nothing wrong." Jesus then said to the criminal who feared God, "I tell you the truth, today you will be with me in paradise." (See 23:26-43.)

31 For if men do these things when the tree is green, what will happen when it is dry?"
32 Two other men, both criminals, were also led out with him
to be executed. 33 When they came to the place called the Skull,
there they crucified him, along with the criminals—one on his
right, the other on his left. 34 Jesus said, "Father, forgive them, for
they do not know what they are doing."[a] And they divided up his
clothes by casting lots.
35 The people stood watching, and the rulers even sneered at
him. They said, "He saved others; let him save himself if he is the
Christ of God, the Chosen One."

23:33 *the Skull:* This place was Golgotha, which may have gotten its name because it was near a large rock shaped like a human skull or from the fact that the Romans performed executions there. See the map on p. 2474 for its probable location.

23:35 *the Christ . . . the Chosen One:* See the note at 2:11 (Savior).

23:30 Hos 10:8; Rev 6:16.
23:34,35 Ps 22:7,18.

[a]**34** Some early manuscripts do not have this sentence.

23:36 *wine vinegar:* This may have been wine mixed with a bitter and poisonous herb called gall (Matt 27:34). Such a mixture may have deadened pain. See also Ps 69:21.

23:38 *a written notice above him:* Usually Roman soldiers would put a sign above the condemned person's head to tell what the person was accused of doing. Since Jesus was not really found guilty of any crime, they put up the words, "THIS IS THE KING OF THE JEWS."

23:43 *paradise:* See the mini-article called "Paradise," p. 2243.

23:45 *curtain of the temple:* The curtain referred to here was the one that separated the Holy Place from the Most Holy Place (Exod 26:31-33). Only the high priest could go past this curtain. The tearing of the curtain showed that Jesus' death was the sacrifice that made it possible for all people to enter into God's presence.

23:50,51 *Joseph . . . from the Judean town of Arimathea:* Arimathea was a small village about twenty miles from Jerusalem. Joseph risked his reputation as a member of the Jewish Sanhedrin by giving Jesus a decent burial.

23:53 *tomb:* Some of the Jewish people buried their dead in rooms carved into soft limestone rock. These tombs had a small square entrance about a yard high and a yard wide. A groove was cut on the outside of the tomb and a large round stone that looked like a millstone was rolled down to cover the entrance.

23:54 *Preparation Day . . . Sabbath:* Preparation Day was Friday, leading up to Friday at sunset when the Sabbath would officially begin. No work was to be done on the Sabbath.

23:56 *they rested on the Sabbath:* After preparing the spices, the women could not walk to the tomb and prepare the body because the Law of Moses did not allow this work on the Sabbath (see Exod 20:10; Deut 5:14). They waited until Sunday morning.

[36]The soldiers also came up and mocked him. They offered
him wine vinegar [37]and said, "If you are the king of the Jews, save
yourself."
[38]There was a written notice above him, which read: THIS IS
THE KING OF THE JEWS.
[39]One of the criminals who hung there hurled insults at him:
"Aren't you the Christ? Save yourself and us!"
[40]But the other criminal rebuked him. "Don't you fear God,"
he said, "since you are under the same sentence? [41]We are punished
justly, for we are getting what our deeds deserve. But this man has
done nothing wrong."
[42]Then he said, "Jesus, remember me when you come into
your kingdom.[a]"
[43]Jesus answered him, "I tell you the truth, today you will be
with me in paradise."

Jesus' Death

[44]It was now about the sixth hour, and darkness came over
the whole land until the ninth hour, [45]for the sun stopped shining.
And the curtain of the temple was torn in two. [46]Jesus called out
with a loud voice, "Father, into your hands I commit my spirit."
When he had said this, he breathed his last.
[47]The centurion, seeing what had happened, praised God
and said, "Surely this was a righteous man." [48]When all the people
who had gathered to witness this sight saw what took place, they
beat their breasts and went away. [49]But all those who knew him,
including the women who had followed him from Galilee, stood
at a distance, watching these things.

Jesus' Burial

[50]Now there was a man named Joseph, a member of the
Council, a good and upright man, [51]who had not consented to
their decision and action. He came from the Judean town of Arimathea and he was waiting for the kingdom of God. [52]Going to
Pilate, he asked for Jesus' body. [53]Then he took it down, wrapped
it in linen cloth and placed it in a tomb cut in the rock, one in
which no one had yet been laid. [54]It was Preparation Day, and the
Sabbath was about to begin.
[55]The women who had come with Jesus from Galilee followed Joseph and saw the tomb and how his body was laid in
it. [56]Then they went home and prepared spices and perfumes.
But they rested on the Sabbath in obedience to the commandment.

[a]**42** Some manuscripts *come with your kingly power*

Jesus Rises from Death and Appears to the Disciples

The women discover that Jesus has risen from the dead and tell the disciples. Later, two followers of Jesus meet him on the road to Emmaus. After sharing a meal with him, they realize that he is Jesus raised from death and go to share this good news with the others.

The Resurrection

24 On the first day of the week, very early in the morning, the
women took the spices they had prepared and went to the tomb.
[2]They found the stone rolled away from the tomb, [3]but when they
entered, they did not find the body of the Lord Jesus. [4]While they
were wondering about this, suddenly two men in clothes that
gleamed like lightning stood beside them. [5]In their fright the
women bowed down with their faces to the ground, but the men
said to them, "Why do you look for the living among the dead?
[6]He is not here; he has risen! Remember how he told you, while he
was still with you in Galilee: [7]'The Son of Man must be delivered
into the hands of sinful men, be crucified and on the third day be
raised again.' " [8]Then they remembered his words.
[9]When they came back from the tomb, they told all these
things to the Eleven and to all the others. [10]It was Mary Magdalene, Joanna, Mary the mother of James, and the others with them
who told this to the apostles. [11]But they did not believe the
women, because their words seemed to them like nonsense.
[12]Peter, however, got up and ran to the tomb. Bending over, he saw
the strips of linen lying by themselves, and he went away, wondering to himself what had happened.

On the Road to Emmaus

[13]Now that same day two of them were going to a village
called Emmaus, about seven miles[a] from Jerusalem. [14]They were
talking with each other about everything that had happened. [15]As
they talked and discussed these things with each other, Jesus himself came up and walked along with them; [16]but they were kept
from recognizing him.
[17]He asked them, "What are you discussing together as you
walk along?"
They stood still, their faces downcast. [18]One of them, named
Cleopas, asked him, "Are you only a visitor to Jerusalem and do
not know the things that have happened there in these days?"
[19]"What things?" he asked.
"About Jesus of Nazareth," they replied. "He was a prophet,
powerful in word and deed before God and all the people. [20]The

[a]**13** Greek *sixty stadia* (about 11 kilometers)

24:1 *the first day of the week, very early in the morning:* The Sabbath ended at sunset on Saturday evening, so they went to the tomb early on Sunday morning when it was light.

24:4 *two men in clothes that gleamed like lightning:* Other accounts specify that these were angels (24:23; John 20:12).

24:7 *Son of Man:* See the mini-article called "Son of Man," p. 1866. Jesus had predicted his death (9:22).

24:9 *the Eleven:* These are Jesus' hand-picked followers (see 6:12-16). There are only eleven because Judas, who betrayed Jesus, is no longer with them. Matthew 27:3-5 reports that Judas committed suicide.

24:10 *Mary Magdalene, Joanna, Mary the mother of James:* See the notes at 8:2 and 8:3. Mary the mother of James is also mentioned in Mark 16:1. Who she was, or which James was her son, is not clear. She may have been the mother of one of the two disciples whose names were James.

24:13 *two of them:* These were followers of Jesus but not two of his twelve chosen disciples. One of them was Cleopas (24:18); the other wasn't identified.

24:13 *Emmaus:* Emmaus was a small village in Judea about seven miles from Jerusalem. Its exact location is not certain.

24:18 *Cleopas:* He was a follower of Jesus mentioned only here in LUKE, and nothing else is known about him.

23:49 Luke 8:2,3. **24:6,7** Matt 16:21; 17:22,23; 20:18,19; Mark 8:31; 9:31; 10:33,34; Luke 9:22; 18:31-33.

Road to Emmaus by Karl Schmidt-Rottluff, 1918, woodcut. On the same day that Jesus was raised to life, two of his followers were going to the town of Emmaus, not far from Jerusalem. As they made their way, Jesus began walking with them. He talked with them, and they told him about how Jesus had been put to death and how the women had found his tomb empty that morning. But they did not recognize Jesus. Only later, when they sat down to eat with Jesus, did they realize that he was their risen Lord. (See 24:13-35.)

24:26 *the Christ:* See the note at 2:11 (Savior).

24:27 *Moses and all the Prophets:* See the note at 16:29.

24:32 *Scriptures:* These are the Jewish Scriptures, which Christians call the Old Testament.

chief priests and our rulers handed him over to be sentenced to
death, and they crucified him; [21]but we had hoped that he was the
one who was going to redeem Israel. And what is more, it is the
third day since all this took place. [22]In addition, some of our
women amazed us. They went to the tomb early this morning
[23]but didn't find his body. They came and told us that they had
seen a vision of angels, who said he was alive. [24]Then some of our
companions went to the tomb and found it just as the women had
said, but him they did not see."

[25]He said to them, "How foolish you are, and how slow of
heart to believe all that the prophets have spoken! [26]Did not the
Christ[a] have to suffer these things and then enter his glory?" [27]And
beginning with Moses and all the Prophets, he explained to them
what was said in all the Scriptures concerning himself.

[28]As they approached the village to which they were going,
Jesus acted as if he were going farther. [29]But they urged him
strongly, "Stay with us, for it is nearly evening; the day is almost
over." So he went in to stay with them.

[30]When he was at the table with them, he took bread, gave

[a]**26** Or *Messiah*; also in verse 46

thanks, broke it and began to give it to them. 31Then their eyes
were opened and they recognized him, and he disappeared from
their sight. 32They asked each other, "Were not our hearts burning
within us while he talked with us on the road and opened the
Scriptures to us?"
33They got up and returned at once to Jerusalem. There they
found the Eleven and those with them, assembled together 34and
saying, "It is true! The Lord has risen and has appeared to Simon."
35Then the two told what had happened on the way, and how Jesus
was recognized by them when he broke the bread.

Jesus Appears to the Disciples

36While they were still talking about this, Jesus himself stood
among them and said to them, "Peace be with you."
37They were startled and frightened, thinking they saw a
ghost. 38He said to them, "Why are you troubled, and why do
doubts rise in your minds? 39Look at my hands and my feet. It is I
myself! Touch me and see; a ghost does not have flesh and bones,
as you see I have."
40When he had said this, he showed them his hands and feet.
41And while they still did not believe it because of joy and amazement, he asked them, "Do you have anything here to eat?" 42They
gave him a piece of broiled fish, 43and he took it and ate it in their
presence.
44He said to them, "This is what I told you while I was still
with you: Everything must be fulfilled that is written about me in
the Law of Moses, the Prophets and the Psalms."

Jesus said to his disciples, *"Look at my hands and my feet. It is I myself!"*
Luke 24:39

24:39 *my hands and my feet:* Sometimes large nails were driven through the wrists and feet of a person who was being crucified. Jesus wanted them to see his wounds so that they would realize who he was.

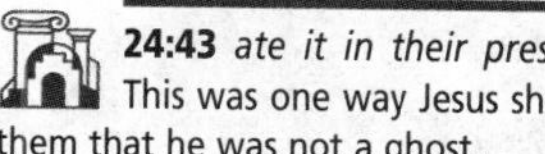

24:43 *ate it in their presence:* This was one way Jesus showed them that he was not a ghost.

24:44 *Law of Moses . . . Psalms:* The Jewish Scriptures are made up of three parts: 1) the Law of Moses; 2) the Books of the Prophets; 3) and the Writings, which include the Psalms. See the article called "Different Kinds of Literature in the Bible," p. 19.

QUESTIONS ABOUT LUKE 19:28—24:53

1. Why did Jesus weep as he approached Jerusalem? (19:41-44) Compare this passage with 21:5-24. What does Jesus say is going to happen?
2. Jesus tells about things that will happen when he comes again (21:25-36). What warning does he give? How does this warning affect the way you live your life?
3. How did Jesus settle the argument among the disciples who were discussing which one of them was the greatest? (22:24-30) Think of situations today where people want to be "Number 1." What can be learned from Jesus' teachings about power and service? (See also 9:46-48.)
4. Jesus asked God to forgive his enemies while he was on the cross (23:34). Why is it difficult to forgive those who hurt or make fun of us? Someone I need to forgive or to ask for forgiveness is . . .
5. How did the disciples react to what they were told by the women who had gone to the tomb? (24:1-12) Why do you think they acted that way? Do you find the women's story hard to believe or not? Why?
6. Why didn't the two followers who met Jesus on the road to Emmaus recognize him right away? (24:13-35) At what point do they recognize him? Why? How does one recognize Jesus today? Explain.
7. What does Jesus tell his followers to do? (24:45-49) What does he promise will happen?
8. Complete this sentence: I think being a follower of Jesus means . . .

24:49 *what my Father has promised:* Jesus is talking about the Holy Spirit. Acts 2 tells how this promise came true on the day of Pentecost. See also Acts 1:1-11 and the note on p. 1964 (Holy Spirit).

24:50 *Bethany:* See the note at 19:28,29.

24:53 *temple:* The temple in Jerusalem (see the note at 13:35).

24:46,47 Ps 22; Isa 53; 50:6; Hos 6:2. **24:50,51** Acts 1:9-11.

45 Then he opened their minds so they could understand the
Scriptures. 46 He told them, "This is what is written: The Christ will
suffer and rise from the dead on the third day, 47 and repentance
and forgiveness of sins will be preached in his name to all nations,
beginning at Jerusalem. 48 You are witnesses of these things. 49 I am
going to send you what my Father has promised; but stay in the
city until you have been clothed with power from on high."

The Ascension

50 When he had led them out to the vicinity of Bethany, he
lifted up his hands and blessed them. 51 While he was blessing
them, he left them and was taken up into heaven. 52 Then they worshiped him and returned to Jerusalem with great joy. 53 And they
stayed continually at the temple, praising God.

JOHN

Signs point us in the right direction.
As you read JOHN, watch for the signs (miracles)
that point out how Jesus is God's powerful Son.

WHAT MAKES JOHN SPECIAL?

JOHN tells about the life and words of Jesus in a way that is different from the Gospels of MATTHEW, MARK, and LUKE. Although the key events in Jesus' life are mentioned, JOHN pays a lot more attention to three questions:

1. *Who is Jesus?* In the first chapter, the author calls Jesus the "Word," who was present with God from the beginning and participated with God in creating everything. This Word became a human being (1:14), so people could see what God is really like. John the Baptist calls Jesus the "Lamb of God, who takes away the sin of the world" (1:29). Philip soon believed Jesus to be "the one Moses wrote about in the Law" (1:45). Nathanael says to Jesus, "You are the Son of God; you are the King of Israel" (1:49). In this Gospel, Jesus describes himself as: the Messiah (4:25,26); the bread of life (6:35); the source of living water (7:37-39); the good shepherd (10:14); the resurrection and the life (11:25); the way, the truth, and the life (14:6); and the true vine (15:1). JOHN also reports that when Jesus explains who he is and what God is doing through him, he uses the words "I am." These are the same words God told Moses to use when referring to God (Exod 3:13-15).
2. *What did Jesus do that proves that he is God's Son?* JOHN describes many miracles ("signs") that point to the deeper meaning of Jesus' actions and words. When Jesus changes water into wine, calms the storm on the lake, feeds the hungry crowd, heals the sick, and brings the dead to life, he shows that he is God's Son and that he is doing what God sent him to do: bring new life to all people.
3. *What was the relationship between Jesus and his followers and those who were against him?* This Gospel helps us to better understand the struggle between Jesus and those who followed his new teachings and those who felt they could not do that and still remain loyal to the teachings of the Law of Moses.

WHY WAS JOHN WRITTEN?

The author, identified by tradition as Jesus' apostle John, clearly states why the Gospel was written: "These are written that you may believe that Jesus is the Christ, the Son of God, and that by believing you may have life in his name" (20:31).

light and darkness: Light and darkness are important images in JOHN. The first thing God created was light (Gen 1:3). In the Bible, light is used to describe God or God's word (1 John 1:5; Ps 119:105) and those people or things that reveal God's truth (Isa 49:6). Darkness refers to places of pain and suffering (Ps 107:10) or confusion (Eccl 2:14). God's opponents are called the rulers of darkness (Eph 6:12), and those who do not do what God expects may be thrown "into the darkness" (Matt 22:13). JOHN uses the opposites "light" and "darkness" to refer to the struggle between those who accept Jesus and those who refuse to believe (see, for example, 1:4-9; 8:12-20).

Jesus of Nazareth, the son of Joseph: This is how Philip, who became one of Jesus' twelve disciples, identified Jesus when he first met him (1:45). Both MATTHEW and LUKE report that Mary was a virgin when she became pregnant with Jesus (Matt 1:18; Luke 1:30-35). Mary's husband, Joseph, was a carpenter (Matt 13:55) from Nazareth (Matt 1:18—2:23). MATTHEW gives a list of his ancestors (Matt 1:1-17) and explains that everyone thought Joseph was Jesus' father. (See also Luke 3:23).

Nazareth was a small village in the hills of Galilee overlooking caravan routes through Palestine. Since the Christ (the Messiah) was expected to come from David's family, whose hometown was Bethlehem in Judea, some people wondered if Jesus from Nazareth could be the one the Jewish people expected (see, for example, 1:46).

Lamb of God: John the Baptist said that Jesus was like the lamb that would be silently led to be slaughtered in order to take away the sin of the world (1:29; see also Isa 53:4-12). "The Lamb" also refers to the lambs that were killed at the Passover Feast (Exod 12), which was celebrated each spring to remind the people how God had set Israel free from slavery in Egypt. The apostle Paul also refers to Jesus as "our Passover lamb, [who] has been sacrificed" (1 Cor 5:7). See also Rom 3:24, 25; Rev 5:6-13.

In the beginning was the Word, and the Word was with God, and the Word was God. He was with God in the beginning.
John 1:1,2

1:1-3 *In the beginning . . . the Word:* This same phrase is used to begin Genesis 1, which describes how God created all things. The Greek word translated here as "Word" also means "reason" or "purpose." In the Jewish Scriptures (Old Testament), God used Wisdom to create the world (Prov 8:12,22-31). The Word also shows God's power, a power that was able to create simply by speaking (see "God said" repeatedly in Gen 1). The Word refers to Jesus Christ, who brings God's message to all people and reveals God's power and purpose. These verses show that even though Jesus is God's Son born as a human being, he is also truly God, because he has existed with God from the beginning of time.

1:4,5 *light . . . darkness:* See the note on p. 2041 (light and darkness).

1:6 *John:* See the mini-article called "John the Baptist," p. 1853.

1:7 *that light:* Here, "light" refers to Jesus. See also verse 9.

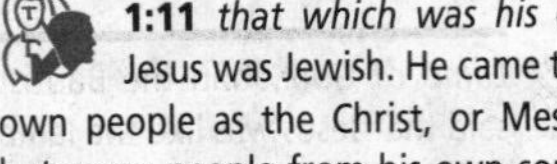

1:11 *that which was his own:* Jesus was Jewish. He came to his own people as the Christ, or Messiah, but many people from his own country did not believe in him or accept his message.

1:12 *children of God:* This phrase is used to describe those who trust Jesus as God's true light.

1:14 *The Word became flesh:* Jesus lived as a human being in order to show God's glory. Sometimes this is referred to as the "incarnation."

WHAT'S THE STORY BEHIND THE SCENE?

The Gospel seems to have been written down a number of years after Jesus died and was raised from death, and probably after the Romans destroyed the temple and ended a Jewish uprising in A.D. 70.

HOW IS JOHN CONSTRUCTED?

The action in JOHN shifts back and forth quickly between Galilee and the area in and around Jerusalem. Time is also marked by certain Jewish festivals. The basic outline of JOHN can be described in the following way:

Who Jesus is (1:1-51)

Jesus' seven miracles (2:1—11:44)

- These miracles caused people to see Jesus as either the Christ or an enemy.
  - *Miracle one—Jesus at a wedding in Cana (2:1-11)*
- Jesus in Judea and Samaria (2:12—4:42)
  - *Miracle two—Jesus heals a royal official's son (4:43-54)*
  - *Miracle three—Jesus heals an invalid (5:1-47)*
  - *Miracle four—Jesus feeds five thousand (6:1-15)*
  - *Miracle five—Jesus walks on the water (6:16-24)*
- Jesus teaches in Galilee and Judea (6:25—8:59)
  - *Miracle six—Jesus heals a blind man (9:1-41)*
- The good shepherd and the true flock (10:1-42)
  - *Miracle seven—Jesus brings Lazarus to life (11:1-44)*

Jesus' final days (11:45—19:42)

- Preparations for Jesus' death (11:45—12:50)
- Jesus prepares his followers (13:1—17:26)
- Jesus' arrest, trial, and death on a cross (18:1—19:42)

Jesus appears to his followers (20:1—21:25)

Who Jesus Is

The first chapter of JOHN makes it clear from the start just who Jesus is. An opening hymn (1:1-14) identifies Jesus as the Word in human form. John the Baptist and some of Jesus' first disciples recognize that Jesus is the Lamb of God, Christ, Rabbi, and Son of God.

The Word Became Flesh

1 In the beginning was the Word, and the Word was with God,
and the Word was God. 2He was with God in the beginning.
3Through him all things were made; without him nothing
was made that has been made. 4In him was life, and that life was
the light of men. 5The light shines in the darkness, but the darkness has not understood[a] it.
6There came a man who was sent from God; his name was
John. 7He came as a witness to testify concerning that light, so that

[a] 5 Or *darkness, and the darkness has not overcome*

through him all men might believe. 8He himself was not the light;
he came only as a witness to the light. 9The true light that gives
light to every man was coming into the world.[a]
10He was in the world, and though the world was made
through him, the world did not recognize him. 11He came to that
which was his own, but his own did not receive him. 12Yet to all who
received him, to those who believed in his name, he gave the right to
become children of God— 13children born not of natural descent,[b]
nor of human decision or a husband's will, but born of God.
14The Word became flesh and made his dwelling among us.
We have seen his glory, the glory of the One and Only,[c] who came
from the Father, full of grace and truth.
15John testifies concerning him. He cries out, saying, "This
was he of whom I said, 'He who comes after me has surpassed me
because he was before me.'" 16From the fullness of his grace we
have all received one blessing after another. 17For the law was given
through Moses; grace and truth came through Jesus Christ. 18No
one has ever seen God, but God the One and Only,[c, d] who is at the
Father's side, has made him known.

John the Baptist Denies Being the Christ

19Now this was John's testimony when the Jews of Jerusalem
sent priests and Levites to ask him who he was. 20He did not fail to
confess, but confessed freely, "I am not the Christ.[e]"
21They asked him, "Then who are you? Are you Elijah?"
He said, "I am not."
"Are you the Prophet?"
He answered, "No."
22Finally they said, "Who are you? Give us an answer to take
back to those who sent us. What do you say about yourself?"
23John replied in the words of Isaiah the prophet, "I am the
voice of one calling in the desert, 'Make straight the way for the
Lord.'"[f]
24Now some Pharisees who had been sent 25questioned him,
"Why then do you baptize if you are not the Christ, nor Elijah, nor
the Prophet?"
26"I baptize with[g] water," John replied, "but among you
stands one you do not know. 27He is the one who comes after me,
the thongs of whose sandals I am not worthy to untie."
28This all happened at Bethany on the other side of the Jordan, where John was baptizing.

[a] **9** Or *This was the true light that gives light to every man who comes into the world* [b] **13** Greek *of bloods* [c] **14,18** Or *the Only Begotten* [d] **18** Some manuscripts *but the only* (or *only begotten*) *Son* [e] **20** Or *Messiah.* "The Christ" (Greek) and "the Messiah" (Hebrew) both mean "the Anointed One"; also in verse 25. [f] **23** Isaiah 40:3 [g] **26** Or *in*; also in verses 31 and 33

1:17 *the law . . . grace and truth:* Jesus did not intend to throw out the law of Moses, but he wanted to show how people can fill their lives with "grace and truth." See also the mini-article called "Law," p. 1160.

1:18 *God the One and Only, who is at the Father's side:* This is one of the strongest affirmations of Jesus' divinity in the Bible.

1:19 *the Jews:* Here, "the Jews of Jerusalem" may refer to the ruling council called the Sanhedrin (see the notes at 7:50 and 2:18).

1:19 *priests and Levites:* Along with their duties in the temple, both the priests and the Levites (priests' assistants) had teaching responsibilities. They were sent to assess the ministry of John the Baptist. See also the mini-article called "Israel's Priests," p. 2344.

1:20 *the Christ:* See the mini-article called "Messiah (Chosen One)," p. 1124.

1:21 *Elijah . . . the Prophet:* See the mini-article called "Elijah," p. 1816. See also Mal 4:5. The "Prophet" had been spoken of by Moses (Deut 18:15).

1:23 *Isaiah:* A prophet in Judah from about 740 to 701 B.C. See the Introduction to ISAIAH, p. 1289.

1:24 *Pharisees:* See the article called "The World of Jesus: Peoples, Powers, and Politics," p. 1821.

1:26 *I baptize with water:* See the mini-article called "Baptism," p. 1976.

1:27 *thongs of whose sandals I am not worthy to untie:* One of the duties of a servant or slave.

1:28 *Bethany:* Not to be confused with the village near Jerusalem where Jesus' friends Mary, Martha, and Lazarus lived (11:1). This Bethany was located somewhere east of the Jordan.

1:6 Matt 3:1; Mark 1:4; Luke 3:1, 2. **1:23** Isa 40:3.

1:29 *Lamb of God:* See the note on p. 2041.

1:32 *Spirit:* See the mini-article called "Holy Spirit," p. 2082.

1:33 *baptize with the Holy Spirit:* Just as God poured the Spirit on Jesus (1:32), Jesus will pour out the Spirit on those who follow him.

1:34 *Son of God:* John the Baptist is claiming that Jesus is Israel's Messiah, the Son of God. See also the mini-article called "Son of God," below.

1:40 *Andrew:* Andrew was a fisherman who came from Bethsaida (1:44), but he lived in Capernaum (Mark 1:21, 29) with his brother Simon Peter. Before following Jesus, Andrew was a disciple of John the Baptist (1:35).

Jesus the Lamb of God

29 The next day John saw Jesus coming toward him and said,
"Look, the Lamb of God, who takes away the sin of the world!
30 This is the one I meant when I said, 'A man who comes after me
has surpassed me because he was before me.' 31 I myself did not
know him, but the reason I came baptizing with water was that he
might be revealed to Israel."
32 Then John gave this testimony: "I saw the Spirit come
down from heaven as a dove and remain on him. 33 I would not
have known him, except that the one who sent me to baptize with
water told me, 'The man on whom you see the Spirit come down
and remain is he who will baptize with the Holy Spirit.' 34 I have
seen and I testify that this is the Son of God."

Jesus' First Disciples

35 The next day John was there again with two of his disciples.
36 When he saw Jesus passing by, he said, "Look, the Lamb of God!"
37 When the two disciples heard him say this, they followed
Jesus. 38 Turning around, Jesus saw them following and asked,
"What do you want?"

SON OF GOD

Many passages in the Old Testament describe the people of Israel as God's son or child (Exod 4:22, 23; Jer 31:19, 20; Hos 11:1), but the title "Son of God" is given to an unnamed king of Israel (Ps 2:7). God said that King David is "my firstborn, the most exalted of the kings of the earth" (Ps 89:27). David is also told that one of his offspring would be God's son (2 Sam 7:12-16). The prophets spoke of the faithful members of the people of Israel as God's children (Isa 43:6; Hos 1:10). Only in later Jewish writings is the Messiah spoken of as Son of God (*Enoch* 105:2; *2 Esdras* 7:28, 29). See "What Books Belong in the Bible?" p. 13.

In the Gospels, Jesus is the only true Son of God, as is declared by the voice from heaven at his baptism (Mark 1:11). The religious leaders who wanted to have him put to death asked him if he was the Son of God, and he said that he was (Mark 14:61, 62). The devil recognizes Jesus as the Son of God (Luke 4:1-12), and the demons do so as well (Mark 3:11; 5:7).

Most important is the direct claim of Jesus in Luke 10:21,22 to be the Son of God who has been given God's wisdom, which he shares with those who trust him as one sent by God. Before Jesus was born, he was identified by the angel as the Son of God (Luke 1:32-35). Matthew 2:15 quotes Hosea 11:1, which speaks of God bringing his Son back from Egypt. Paul wrote that Jesus as to his human nature was a descendant of David but by his resurrection was declared to be the Son of God (Rom 1:3,4). John wrote that Jesus is the Son of God (1:12-14) who was sent by God into the world to save people from their sins (3:16,17). He does God's work in the world (10:34-36) and is one with God (17:1,22).

John begins his Gospel by claiming that Jesus is truly God and has existed from the beginning. Before closing he affirms his purpose for writing: "that you may believe that Jesus is the Christ, the Son of God, and that by believing you may have life in his name" (20:31).

They said, "Rabbi" (which means Teacher), "where are you
staying?"
39 "Come," he replied, "and you will see."
So they went and saw where he was staying, and spent that
day with him. It was about the tenth hour.
40 Andrew, Simon Peter's brother, was one of the two who
heard what John had said and who had followed Jesus. 41 The first
thing Andrew did was to find his brother Simon and tell him, "We
have found the Messiah" (that is, the Christ). 42 And he brought
him to Jesus.
Jesus looked at him and said, "You are Simon son of John.
You will be called Cephas" (which, when translated, is Peter[a]).

Jesus Calls Philip and Nathanael

43 The next day Jesus decided to leave for Galilee. Finding
Philip, he said to him, "Follow me."
44 Philip, like Andrew and Peter, was from the town of Bethsaida. 45 Philip found Nathanael and told him, "We have found the
one Moses wrote about in the Law, and about whom the prophets
also wrote—Jesus of Nazareth, the son of Joseph."
46 "Nazareth! Can anything good come from there?"
Nathanael asked.
"Come and see," said Philip.
47 When Jesus saw Nathanael approaching, he said of him,
"Here is a true Israelite, in whom there is nothing false."
48 "How do you know me?" Nathanael asked.
Jesus answered, "I saw you while you were still under the fig
tree before Philip called you."
49 Then Nathanael declared, "Rabbi, you are the Son of God;
you are the King of Israel."
50 Jesus said, "You believe[b] because I told you I saw you under
the fig tree. You shall see greater things than that." 51 He then
added, "I tell you[c] the truth, you[c] shall see heaven open, and the
angels of God ascending and descending on the Son of Man."

[a] **42** Both *Cephas* (Aramaic) and *Peter* (Greek) mean *rock.* [b] **50** Or *Do you believe . . . ?*
[c] **51** The Greek is plural.

1:41 *Messiah . . . Christ:* Two words meaning "anointed one." See the note at 1:20.

1:42 *Simon . . . Cephas . . . Peter:* Simon was a common Jewish name at this time. The nickname Jesus gives this disciple means "rock." *Cephas* is the Aramaic form, *Peter,* the Greek.

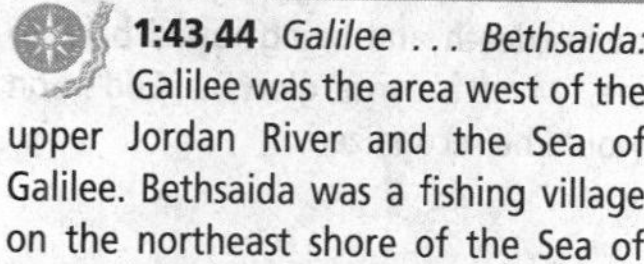

1:43,44 *Galilee . . . Bethsaida:* Galilee was the area west of the upper Jordan River and the Sea of Galilee. Bethsaida was a fishing village on the northeast shore of the Sea of Galilee. See the map on p. 2473.

1:44,45 *Philip . . . Nathanael . . . Joseph:* Philip was from Bethsaida and probably knew Andrew and Peter. Nathanael's name means "God has given." He recognizes Jesus as God's Son and the King of Israel (1:49).

See also the note on p. 2041 (Jesus of Nazareth).

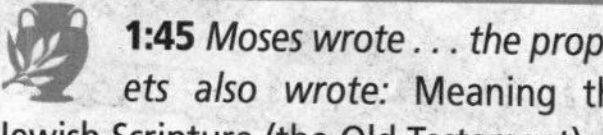

1:45 *Moses wrote . . . the prophets also wrote:* Meaning the Jewish Scripture (the Old Testament).

1:51 *the angels of God ascending and descending on the Son of Man:* Jacob had a dream about angels going up and down on a ladder from earth to heaven (Gen 28:10-17). See also the mini-articles called "Son of Man," p. 1866, and "Angels," p. 88.

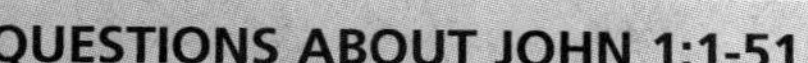

QUESTIONS ABOUT JOHN 1:1-51

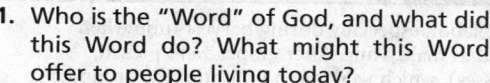

1. Who is the "Word" of God, and what did this Word do? What might this Word offer to people living today?
2. What other titles for Jesus are suggested in the first chapter of John's Gospel? What makes each of these titles important?
3. What do you think is the main purpose of this chapter? Why? Which verses support your point of view?

2:1 *Cana in Galilee:* See the map on p. 2473.

2:1 *Jesus' mother:* This was Mary. See Luke 1:26-56; 2:1-52. Mary lived in Nazareth, which was about ten miles south of Cana.

2:4 *My time has not yet come:* Jesus was referring to the time of his death and being raised back to life, when his true glory as God's Son would be recognized.

Jesus' Seven Miracles

This lengthy section of JOHN *(2:1—11:44) includes seven key miracles that Jesus performed. Each of these miracles (signs) point to Jesus as the true Messiah (the Christ), the Son of God. This section also includes people Jesus met and things that Jesus taught about himself.*

MIRACLE ONE—JESUS AT A WEDDING IN CANA

Jesus Changes Water to Wine

2 On the third day a wedding took place at Cana in Galilee. Jesus'
mother was there, 2 and Jesus and his disciples had also been invited to the wedding. 3 When the wine was gone, Jesus' mother said to
him, "They have no more wine."
4 "Dear woman, why do you involve me?" Jesus replied. "My
time has not yet come."

Making Wine. Vineyards required much care and intensive labor, especially during harvest time when extra workers were needed to gather the ripened grapes and to make wine. After grapes were picked, they were crushed under foot in stone pits (called winepresses), which were often built into the ground. Sometimes, the workers held onto straps for balance. As they trampled the grapes, they danced and gave expression to their belief that wine was one of life's blessings.

5His mother said to the servants, "Do whatever he tells you."
6Nearby stood six stone water jars, the kind used by the Jews
for ceremonial washing, each holding from twenty to thirty gallons.[a]
7Jesus said to the servants, "Fill the jars with water"; so they
filled them to the brim.
8Then he told them, "Now draw some out and take it to the
master of the banquet."
They did so, 9and the master of the banquet tasted the water
that had been turned into wine. He did not realize where it had
come from, though the servants who had drawn the water knew.
Then he called the bridegroom aside 10and said, "Everyone brings
out the choice wine first and then the cheaper wine after the guests
have had too much to drink; but you have saved the best till now."

[a] **6** Greek *two to three metretes* (probably about 75 to 115 liters)

2:6 *jars . . . for ceremonial washing:* According to the Law of Moses, if people touched something unclean before they ate, any food they touched would also be made unclean. See also the mini-article called "Purity (Clean and Unclean)," p. 2125.

2:10 *Everyone brings out the choice wine first:* The best wine was served early in the celebration, because people would be more aware of the wine's quality and taste. As they drank more wine, their senses would become dull, making it more difficult to appreciate good wine. See the mini-article called "Wine" below.

WINE

In the Middle East, wine is made from grapes that are picked late in the summer and then spread out on the ground for a while before they are pressed to get out the juice. The annual Feast of Tabernacles, which celebrated Israel's journey through the desert on their way to the promised land, took place in the early fall. It was at this time that grapes were gathered (Deut 16:13-15).

Pits or vats were dug out of the rock or out of rocky ground. The pits were joined together in pairs, so that when the grapes were pressed in the upper pit, the juice would flow down into the lower pit. Workers squeezed the juice out of the grapes by walking back and forth on them in the pit (Isa 16:10). The juice was collected from the lower pit in clay jars or in bags made from animal skins. These containers had to have an opening to let out the gas that was created as the wine fermented (Job 32:19). Skins that had become old and stiff would often burst when new wine was stored in them (Matt 9:17).

Palestine and Syria produced large quantities of excellent wine. Even before the people of Israel settled in Canaan they knew the land was fertile. When Moses sent spies to inspect the land, they brought back a cluster of grapes so large it had to be carried on a pole (Num 13:21-27). Other reports of the things produced in Canaan often mention grain, olive oil, and wine (Gen 27:28; Deut 7:13; 18:4; 2 Kgs 18:32; Jer 31:12).

Since water was scarce in Palestine, people drank wine at both ordinary meals and banquets, and especially at wedding banquets (John 2:1-11). Wine was also used as medicine (Luke 10:34; 1 Tim 5:23). Jewish people visiting the temple brought wine with them (1 Sam 1:24) and drank it when they celebrated Passover.

Because wine and winemaking were so familiar to people in Israel and Judah, the prophets could use them as metaphors when trying to explain God's attitude toward the people. Joel, for instance, compares God's coming judgment of the wicked with the trampling of grapes (Joel 3:13). He also says wine is one of the good things God will give the people to bless them (Joel 3:18).

In the New Testament, wine is the symbol of Jesus' blood, which was poured out when he died in order to save people from their sins (Mark 14:23-25). Jesus compared the new life he brings to new wine put in fresh wineskins (Matt 9:17). And REVELATION uses the image of grapes being trampled in a winepress to describe how God will judge the wicked (Rev 14:19,20).

[11]This, the first of his miraculous signs, Jesus performed at
Cana in Galilee. He thus revealed his glory, and his disciples put
their faith in him.

JESUS IN JUDEA AND SAMARIA

The scene now quickly shifts from Galilee in the north to the southern and middle parts of Palestine known as Judea and Samaria. Jesus throws the merchants and money changers out of the temple in Jerusalem and talks to Nicodemus and a Samaritan woman.

Jesus Clears the Temple

[12]After this he went down to Capernaum with his mother
and brothers and his disciples. There they stayed for a few days.
[13]When it was almost time for the Jewish Passover, Jesus
went up to Jerusalem. [14]In the temple courts he found men selling
cattle, sheep and doves, and others sitting at tables exchanging
money. [15]So he made a whip out of cords, and drove all from the
temple area, both sheep and cattle; he scattered the coins of the
money changers and overturned their tables. [16]To those who sold
doves he said, "Get these out of here! How dare you turn my
Father's house into a market!"
[17]His disciples remembered that it is written: "Zeal for your
house will consume me."[a]
[18]Then the Jews demanded of him, "What miraculous sign
can you show us to prove your authority to do all this?"
[19]Jesus answered them, "Destroy this temple, and I will raise
it again in three days."
[20]The Jews replied, "It has taken forty-six years to build this
temple, and you are going to raise it in three days?" [21]But the temple he had spoken of was his body. [22]After he was raised from the
dead, his disciples recalled what he had said. Then they believed
the Scripture and the words that Jesus had spoken.
[23]Now while he was in Jerusalem at the Passover Feast, many
people saw the miraculous signs he was doing and believed in his
name.[b] [24]But Jesus would not entrust himself to them, for he knew
all men. [25]He did not need man's testimony about man, for he
knew what was in a man.

Jesus Teaches Nicodemus

3 Now there was a man of the Pharisees named Nicodemus, a member of the Jewish ruling council. [2]He came to Jesus at night and said,

[a] **17** Psalm 69:9 [b] **23** Or *and believed in him*

2:11 *miraculous signs:* In JOHN the Greek word *semeia* ("sign") is used in reference to miracles. The significance of these miraculous signs is emphasized, as JOHN points to Jesus as the Messiah and the Son of God.

2:12,13 *Capernaum . . . Jerusalem:* Capernaum was a base for Roman soldiers and tax collectors. Jesus moved there from Nazareth when he began his ministry.

2:13 *Jerusalem:* The capital city of Judea in southern Palestine. See also the mini-article called "Jerusalem," p. 574.

2:13 *Passover:* See the mini-article called "Passover and the Feast of Unleavened Bread," p. 2030.

2:14 *selling cattle . . . exchanging money:* In the Court of the Gentiles at the temple, people profited from exchanging foreign money and selling animals for the temple sacrifices. See also the mini-article called "Money Changing in the Temple," p. 1894.

2:18 *the Jews:* See the note at 1:19 (the Jews).

2:19 *I will raise it again in three days:* Jesus was claiming that his body—not the actual temple—would be destroyed and that God would raise him from death in three days (2:22).

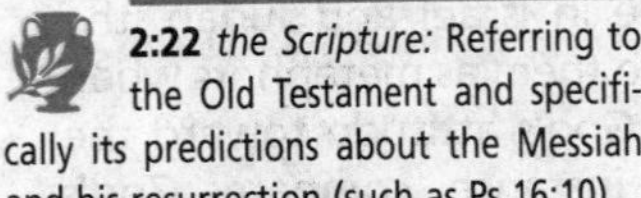

2:22 *the Scripture:* Referring to the Old Testament and specifically its predictions about the Messiah and his resurrection (such as Ps 16:10).

3:1 *Nicodemus:* Perhaps Nicodemus came to Jesus at night because he didn't want to be seen. Nicodemus is only mentioned in JOHN (7:50; 19:39). See also the notes at 1:24 and 7:50.

3:3 *kingdom of God:* God's kingdom is not simply a place. It is what happens when God rules and people serve God's will.

"Rabbi, we know you are a teacher who has come from God. For no
one could perform the miraculous signs you are doing if God were
not with him."
3 In reply Jesus declared, "I tell you the truth, no one can see
the kingdom of God unless he is born again.[a]"
4 "How can a man be born when he is old?" Nicodemus
asked. "Surely he cannot enter a second time into his mother's
womb to be born!"
5 Jesus answered, "I tell you the truth, no one can enter the
kingdom of God unless he is born of water and the Spirit. 6 Flesh
gives birth to flesh, but the Spirit[b] gives birth to spirit. 7 You should
not be surprised at my saying, 'You[c] must be born again.' 8 The
wind blows wherever it pleases. You hear its sound, but you cannot
tell where it comes from or where it is going. So it is with everyone
born of the Spirit."
9 "How can this be?" Nicodemus asked.
10 "You are Israel's teacher," said Jesus, "and do you not
understand these things? 11 I tell you the truth, we speak of what
we know, and we testify to what we have seen, but still you people
do not accept our testimony. 12 I have spoken to you of earthly
things and you do not believe; how then will you believe if I speak
of heavenly things? 13 No one has ever gone into heaven except the
one who came from heaven—the Son of Man.[d] 14 Just as Moses lifted up the snake in the desert, so the Son of Man must be lifted up,
15 that everyone who believes in him may have eternal life.[e]
16 "For God so loved the world that he gave his one and only
Son,[f] that whoever believes in him shall not perish but have eternal life. 17 For God did not send his Son into the world to condemn
the world, but to save the world through him. 18 Whoever believes
in him is not condemned, but whoever does not believe stands
condemned already because he has not believed in the name of
God's one and only Son.[g] 19 This is the verdict: Light has come into
the world, but men loved darkness instead of light because their
deeds were evil. 20 Everyone who does evil hates the light, and will
not come into the light for fear that his deeds will be exposed.
21 But whoever lives by the truth comes into the light, so that it may
be seen plainly that what he has done has been done through
God."[h]

John the Baptist's Testimony About Jesus

22 After this, Jesus and his disciples went out into the Judean
countryside, where he spent some time with them, and baptized.

[a] 3 Or *born from above*; also in verse 7 [b] 6 Or *but spirit* [c] 7 The Greek is plural. [d] 13 Some manuscripts *Man, who is in heaven* [e] 15 Or *believes may have eternal life in him* [f] 16 Or *his only begotten Son* [g] 18 Or *God's only begotten Son* [h] 21 Some interpreters end the quotation after verse 15.

3:5 *born of water and the Spirit:* See the notes at 1:26; 1:32 and 1:33.

3:6 *the Spirit gives birth to spirit:* The Holy Spirit produces spiritual children—God's children. This is what Jesus means about being born again (3:3,7). Jesus is saying that being a child of God no longer has to do simply with being born into a Jewish family or following the Law of Moses. See also Gal 3:1-5, 26-29.

3:10 *Israel's teacher:* As a Pharisee, Nicodemus was also a teacher of the Jewish Scriptures.

3:13 *heaven . . . Son of Man:* See the mini-article called "Heaven," p. 1420, and "Son of Man," p. 1866.

3:14,15 *Just as Moses lifted up the snake:* Jesus is saying that he would be lifted up like the bronze snake Moses lifted up to cure the people of poisonous snake bites in the desert (Num 21:4-9). Jesus would be nailed to a cross, and whoever believed in him would be saved from sin and death.

3:16 *God so loved the world:* The motivation for God's giving his Son, as a sacrifice for sin. See also the mini-articles called "Son of God," p. 2044, and "Eternal Life," p. 2072.

3:19 *Light . . . darkness:* See the note on p. 2041 (light and darkness).

3:22 *Judean countryside:* "Judea" is the Latin name for the territory previously called "Judah." In the time of Jesus, Judea was under Roman rule. See the map on p. 2473.

3:22 *baptized:* See the note at 1:26. John 4:2 makes it clear that the disciples, rather than Jesus himself, were baptizing people.

2:12 Matt 4:13. **2:17** Ps 69:9. **2:19** Matt 26:61; 27:40; Mark 14:58; 15:29. **2:22** John 20:1-23. **3:17** Matt 1:21; John 5:36,38; 12:47.

23Now John also was baptizing at Aenon near Salim, because there was plenty of water, and people were constantly coming to be baptized. 24(This was before John was put in prison.) 25An argument developed between some of John's disciples and a certain Jew[a] over the matter of ceremonial washing. 26They came to John and said to him, "Rabbi, that man who was with you on the other side of the Jordan—the one you testified about—well, he is baptizing, and everyone is going to him."

27To this John replied, "A man can receive only what is given him from heaven. 28You yourselves can testify that I said, 'I am not the Christ[b] but am sent ahead of him.' 29The bride belongs to the bridegroom. The friend who attends the bridegroom waits and listens for him, and is full of joy when he hears the bridegroom's voice. That joy is mine, and it is now complete. 30He must become greater; I must become less.

31"The one who comes from above is above all; the one who is from the earth belongs to the earth, and speaks as one from the earth. The one who comes from heaven is above all. 32He testifies to what he has seen and heard, but no one accepts his testimony. 33The man who has accepted it has certified that God is truthful. 34For the one whom God has sent speaks the words of God, for God[c] gives the Spirit without limit. 35The Father loves the Son and has placed everything in his hands. 36Whoever believes in the Son has eternal life, but whoever rejects the Son will not see life, for God's wrath remains on him."[d]

Jesus Talks With a Samaritan Woman

4 The Pharisees heard that Jesus was gaining and baptizing more disciples than John, 2although in fact it was not Jesus who baptized, but his disciples. 3When the Lord learned of this, he left Judea and went back once more to Galilee.

4Now he had to go through Samaria. 5So he came to a town in Samaria called Sychar, near the plot of ground Jacob had given to his son Joseph. 6Jacob's well was there, and Jesus, tired as he was from the journey, sat down by the well. It was about the sixth hour. 7When a Samaritan woman came to draw water, Jesus said to her, "Will you give me a drink?" 8(His disciples had gone into the town to buy food.)

9The Samaritan woman said to him, "You are a Jew and I am a Samaritan woman. How can you ask me for a drink?" (For Jews do not associate with Samaritans.[e])

10Jesus answered her, "If you knew the gift of God and who it is that asks you for a drink, you would have asked him and he would have given you living water."

[a] **25** Some manuscripts *and certain Jews* [b] **28** Or *Messiah* [c] **34** Greek *he* [d] **36** Some interpreters end the quotation after verse 30. [e] **9** Or *do not use dishes Samaritans have used*

3:23 *Aenon near Salim:* The exact location of this place is not known, though it probably was west of the Jordan River at a place where there were springs.

3:25 *ceremonial washing:* The Jewish people had rules about washing themselves and their dishes, in order to make themselves fit to worship God. See also the mini-article called "Purity (Clean and Unclean)," p. 2125.

3:28 *the Christ:* See the note at 1:20.

3:31 *The one who comes from above . . . the one who is from earth:* John the Baptist is comparing Jesus, and his heavenly origin to himself. John clearly affirms the superiority of Jesus, the Messiah (3:30,38).

3:36 *whoever believes in the Son has eternal life:* See the mini-articles called "Son of God," p. 2044, and "Eternal Life," p. 2072.

4:1 *Pharisees:* See the note at 1:24.

4:3,4 *Judea . . . Galilee . . . Samaria:* See the notes at 3:22 and 1:43,44. Samaria was an area in central Palestine between Judea and Galilee (see the map on p. 2473). In 722 B.C. the Assyrians attacked the Israelite people living in the northern kingdom (Israel) and took many of them away (2 Kgs 17:5-23). Some of the Israelites who were left behind married Gentiles brought in by the Assyrians. Their descendants known as the Samaritans, set up their own temple, chose their own priests, and followed their own version of the Law of Moses. The Jews in Jesus' day despised Samaritans, because they thought the Samaritans were not faithful to the God of Israel.

4:5 *Sychar:* This refers to Shechem, the place where Abraham stayed when he first came to Palestine (Gen 12:6) and where Jacob bought land and built an altar (Gen 33:18-20). Before he died, Jacob gave the hillside near Shechem to his son Joseph (Gen 48:22). See also Josh 24:32.

[11]"Sir," the woman said, "you have nothing to draw with and the well is deep. Where can you get this living water? [12]Are you greater than our father Jacob, who gave us the well and drank from it himself, as did also his sons and his flocks and herds?"

[13]Jesus answered, "Everyone who drinks this water will be thirsty again, [14]but whoever drinks the water I give him will never thirst. Indeed, the water I give him will become in him a spring of water welling up to eternal life."

[15]The woman said to him, "Sir, give me this water so that I won't get thirsty and have to keep coming here to draw water."

[16]He told her, "Go, call your husband and come back."

[17]"I have no husband," she replied.

Woman at the Well by Hatigammana Uttarananda. In Jesus' day, great tension existed between Jews and Samaritans. When Jesus was resting at Jacob's well he asked a Samaritan woman for water. She was surprised because she knew he was Jewish. But Jesus showed her that God cares for all people by telling her about the water that will become "a spring of water welling up to eternal life." (See 4:3-29.)

4:6 *Jacob's well:* This well, which was cut into the rock, can still be seen near the ruins of ancient Shechem. The woman mentioned here went to the well about noon (the sixth hour), during the hottest part of the day when few other people would do so.

4:9 *Jews do not associate with Samaritans:* See the note at 4:3, 4. Jewish people who were strict about following certain purity laws were not supposed to come in contact with Samaritans, and certainly were not supposed to drink from a Samaritan's cup or bucket.

4:12 *our father Jacob:* See the note at 4:5. Like the Jews living in Judea and Galilee, the Samaritans were descendants of the earliest ancestors of Israel. The woman wonders if Jesus is claiming to be greater than Jacob, one of the most important of all their ancestors.

4:14 *a spring of water welling up to eternal life:* The "living water" (4:10) Jesus offers is life-full, satisfying, and eternal. See also 10:10 and the mini-article called "Eternal Life," p. 2072.

4:14 *eternal life:* See the note at 3:15.

4:15 *give me this water:* The woman thinks Jesus is going to give her a private supply of water that will never run out. Then she wouldn't have to go to the well each day in the hot sun.

4:16 *call your husband:* Jesus knew that the woman had lived with many men and that she currently had no husband (either because she was divorced or her last husband had died).

3:23,24 Matt 14:3; Mark 6:17, 18; Luke 3:19,20. **3:35** Matt 11:27; Luke 10:22. **3:36** John 3:16-18. **4:9** Ezra 4:1-5; Neh 4:1,2.

Jesus said to her, "You are right when you say you have no husband. [18]The fact is, you have had five husbands, and the man you now have is not your husband. What you have just said is quite true."

[19]"Sir," the woman said, "I can see that you are a prophet. [20]Our fathers worshiped on this mountain, but you Jews claim that the place where we must worship is in Jerusalem."

[21]Jesus declared, "Believe me, woman, a time is coming when you will worship the Father neither on this mountain nor in Jerusalem. [22]You Samaritans worship what you do not know; we worship what we do know, for salvation is from the Jews. [23]Yet a time is coming and has now come when the true worshipers will worship the Father in spirit and truth, for they are the kind of worshipers the Father seeks. [24]God is spirit, and his worshipers must worship in spirit and in truth."

[25]The woman said, "I know that Messiah" (called Christ) "is coming. When he comes, he will explain everything to us."

[26]Then Jesus declared, "I who speak to you am he."

The Disciples Rejoin Jesus

[27]Just then his disciples returned and were surprised to find him talking with a woman. But no one asked, "What do you want?" or "Why are you talking with her?"

[28]Then, leaving her water jar, the woman went back to the town and said to the people, [29]"Come, see a man who told me everything I ever did. Could this be the Christ[a]?" [30]They came out of the town and made their way toward him.

[31]Meanwhile his disciples urged him, "Rabbi, eat something."

[32]But he said to them, "I have food to eat that you know nothing about."

[33]Then his disciples said to each other, "Could someone have brought him food?"

[34]"My food," said Jesus, "is to do the will of him who sent me and to finish his work. [35]Do you not say, 'Four months more and then the harvest'? I tell you, open your eyes and look at the fields! They are ripe for harvest. [36]Even now the reaper draws his wages, even now he harvests the crop for eternal life, so that the sower and the reaper may be glad together. [37]Thus the saying 'One sows and another reaps' is true. [38]I sent you to reap what you have not worked for. Others have done the hard work, and you have reaped the benefits of their labor."

Many Samaritans Believe

[39]Many of the Samaritans from that town believed in him because of the woman's testimony, "He told me everything I ever did." [40]So when the Samaritans came to him, they urged him to

[a] **29** Or *Messiah*

4:19 *a prophet:* Prophets sometimes had visions about things that would happen in the future. More often prophets were faithful people who observed what was happening around them and brought a message from God that fit the situation. See the article called "Prophets and Prophecy," p. 935.

4:20 *Our fathers worshiped on this mountain:* The Samaritans worshiped God in a temple they built on Mount Gerizim near the city of Shechem, while Jews worshiped in the temple in Jerusalem. See the map on p. 2473.

4:23 *true worshipers will worship the Father in spirit and truth:* Jesus is saying that true worship does not depend on being at a certain place. Rather, true worship happens when people are led by God's Spirit.

4:25 *Messiah . . . Christ:* See the note at 1:41. This is the only time, before his trial, when Jesus explicitly claims to be the Messiah.

4:34 *My food . . . is to do the will of him who sent me:* In John, Jesus often talks about doing the work that God sent him to do. Here he calls this work his "food." See also 3:16,17,34; 5:26; 6:27, 33-35; 17:1,2. Later, Jesus describes doing what God wants him to do as "drinking the cup" (18:11), an image that is often used in the Bible as a symbol of suffering (Isa 51:17, 22; Jer 25:15, 17).

4:35 *Four months more and then the harvest:* Jesus quotes a proverb. The grain harvest for the area was still months away, but Jesus says that the harvest (gathering) of many new followers is ready right away.

4:37 *One sows and another reaps:* Those who sow the seed are those who tell God's message to others; those who reap are those who help others trust in Jesus.

4:39 *Samaritans:* See the note at 4:3,4. Many believed that Jesus was the "Savior of the world" (4:42) because of what the woman told them she learned at the well, and many more believed because of Jesus' own words.

stay with them, and he stayed two days. [41]And because of his words
many more became believers.
[42]They said to the woman, "We no longer believe just
because of what you said; now we have heard for ourselves, and we
know that this man really is the Savior of the world."

MIRACLE TWO— JESUS HEALS A ROYAL OFFICIAL'S SON

Jesus Heals the Official's Son

[43]After the two days he left for Galilee. [44](Now Jesus himself
had pointed out that a prophet has no honor in his own country.)
[45]When he arrived in Galilee, the Galileans welcomed him. They
had seen all that he had done in Jerusalem at the Passover Feast,
for they also had been there.
[46]Once more he visited Cana in Galilee, where he had turned
the water into wine. And there was a certain royal official whose
son lay sick at Capernaum. [47]When this man heard that Jesus had
arrived in Galilee from Judea, he went to him and begged him to
come and heal his son, who was close to death.
[48]"Unless you people see miraculous signs and wonders,"
Jesus told him, "you will never believe."
[49]The royal official said, "Sir, come down before my child
dies."
[50]Jesus replied, "You may go. Your son will live."
The man took Jesus at his word and departed. [51]While he
was still on the way, his servants met him with the news that his
boy was living. [52]When he inquired as to the time when his son got
better, they said to him, "The fever left him yesterday at the seventh hour."
[53]Then the father realized that this was the exact time at
which Jesus had said to him, "Your son will live." So he and all his
household believed.
[54]This was the second miraculous sign that Jesus performed,
having come from Judea to Galilee.

MIRACLE THREE— JESUS HEALS AN INVALID

The Healing at the Pool

5 Some time later, Jesus went up to Jerusalem for a feast of the
Jews. [2]Now there is in Jerusalem near the Sheep Gate a pool, which
in Aramaic is called Bethesda[a] and which is surrounded by five
covered colonnades. [3]Here a great number of disabled people used

[a] 2 Some manuscripts *Bethzatha*; other manuscripts *Bethsaida*

4:43,46 *Galilee . . . Cana:* For Galilee, see the note at 1:43,44. For Cana, see the note at 2:1.

4:44 *a prophet:* See the note at 4:19. Many Samaritans in the area around Sychar believed Jesus was God's chosen Messiah, but Jesus knew that many people in his own home area of Nazareth in Galilee would not accept him as the Messiah.

4:46 *royal official whose son lay sick at Capernaum:* The Greek word describing this man suggests that he was an officer who served the king (Herod Antipas). See the note at 2:12. Because Jesus healed the boy at the very moment he said he would, the official and his whole family put their faith in Jesus (4:53).

5:1 *Jerusalem . . . feast of the Jews:* See the note at 2:13. The feast was evidently either the Feast of Tabernacles or Passover. The Feast of Tabernacles takes place at the end of the fall harvest (Lev 23:33-36; Deut 16:13-17). To celebrate this feast the people built temporary shelters to remind themselves of how God provided for the people of Israel when they wandered in the desert after leaving Egypt. See also the mini-article called "Passover and the Feast of Unleavened Bread," p. 2030, and the chart called "Jewish Calendar and Festivals," p. 944.

5:2 *near the Sheep Gate a pool . . . called Bethesda . . . surrounded by five covered colonnades:* This pool was just north of the temple area. A pool that fits this description has been found. See the map on p. 2474 for its possible location.

4:43,44 Matt 13:57; Mark 6:4; Luke 4:24. **4:45** John 2:23. **5:3,4** Isa 35:5,6; Luke 4:16-20.

5:7 *when the water is stirred:* The water may have been stirred once in a while by a spring. Some believed an angel of God stirred the waters.

5:9 *Sabbath:* The Sabbath is the seventh day of the week, the day that God rested after the work of creation (Gen 2:2, 3). Jewish law forbade Jews and their servants from working on the Sabbath (Exod 20:8-11; Deut 5:12-15).

5:10 *the Jews . . . the law forbids you to carry your mat:* See the note at 1:19 (the Jews). The Jewish leaders went beyond the Law of Moses by considering carrying loads of any kind to be work. In their view, the man who was healed was breaking the Sabbath by carrying his mat.

5:14 *Stop sinning:* See the mini-article called "Sin," p. 2181. See also the note at 9:2 and the article called "Miracles, Magic, and Medicine," p. 1838.

5:16 *doing these things on the Sabbath:* Doing any kind of work on the Sabbath was a capital offense according to the Law of Moses (Exod 31:14, 15; 35:2). However, during Jesus' day when the Roman Empire controlled Judea, Jewish leaders did not have the authority to execute people for this crime. It is not clear exactly how the Jewish leaders, who wrongly viewed Jesus as a lawbreaker, "persecuted" him.

5:17 *My Father:* In this Gospel, Jesus often refers to God as his Father (3:35; 5:20-30; 15:1, 16; 17). For Jesus to call God his Father was to claim a special relationship with God and authority in relation to God's people (Ps 2:6, 7). Since the Jewish leaders believed no human being could be equal with God, they thought Jesus was dishonoring the Law of Moses by saying God was his Father (5:18).

5:10 Neh 13:19; Jer 17:21-24.

to lie—the blind, the lame, the paralyzed.[a] 5One who was there had
been an invalid for thirty-eight years. 6When Jesus saw him lying
there and learned that he had been in this condition for a long
time, he asked him, "Do you want to get well?"

7"Sir," the invalid replied, "I have no one to help me into the
pool when the water is stirred. While I am trying to get in, someone else goes down ahead of me."

8Then Jesus said to him, "Get up! Pick up your mat and walk."
9At once the man was cured; he picked up his mat and walked.

The day on which this took place was a Sabbath, 10and so the
Jews said to the man who had been healed, "It is the Sabbath; the
law forbids you to carry your mat."

11But he replied, "The man who made me well said to me,
'Pick up your mat and walk.'"

12So they asked him, "Who is this fellow who told you to
pick it up and walk?"

13The man who was healed had no idea who it was, for Jesus
had slipped away into the crowd that was there.

14Later Jesus found him at the temple and said to him, "See,
you are well again. Stop sinning or something worse may happen
to you." 15The man went away and told the Jews that it was Jesus
who had made him well.

Life Through the Son

16So, because Jesus was doing these things on the Sabbath,
the Jews persecuted him. 17Jesus said to them, "My Father is always
at his work to this very day, and I, too, am working." 18For this reason the Jews tried all the harder to kill him; not only was he breaking the Sabbath, but he was even calling God his own Father,
making himself equal with God.

19Jesus gave them this answer: "I tell you the truth, the Son
can do nothing by himself; he can do only what he sees his Father
doing, because whatever the Father does the Son also does. 20For
the Father loves the Son and shows him all he does. Yes, to your
amazement he will show him even greater things than these. 21For
just as the Father raises the dead and gives them life, even so the
Son gives life to whom he is pleased to give it. 22Moreover, the
Father judges no one, but has entrusted all judgment to the Son,
23that all may honor the Son just as they honor the Father. He who
does not honor the Son does not honor the Father, who sent him.

24"I tell you the truth, whoever hears my word and believes
him who sent me has eternal life and will not be condemned; he
has crossed over from death to life. 25I tell you the truth, a time is

[a] **3** Some less important manuscripts *paralyzed—and they waited for the moving of the waters. 4From time to time an angel of the Lord would come down and stir up the waters. The first one into the pool after each such disturbance would be cured of whatever disease he had.*

coming and has now come when the dead will hear the voice of the
Son of God and those who hear will live. 26 For as the Father has life
in himself, so he has granted the Son to have life in himself. 27 And
he has given him authority to judge because he is the Son of Man.
28 "Do not be amazed at this, for a time is coming when all
who are in their graves will hear his voice 29 and come out—those
who have done good will rise to live, and those who have done evil
will rise to be condemned. 30 By myself I can do nothing; I judge
only as I hear, and my judgment is just, for I seek not to please
myself but him who sent me.

Testimonies About Jesus

31 "If I testify about myself, my testimony is not valid. 32 There
is another who testifies in my favor, and I know that his testimony
about me is valid.
33 "You have sent to John and he has testified to the truth.
34 Not that I accept human testimony; but I mention it that you
may be saved. 35 John was a lamp that burned and gave light, and
you chose for a time to enjoy his light.
36 "I have testimony weightier than that of John. For the very
work that the Father has given me to finish, and which I am doing,
testifies that the Father has sent me. 37 And the Father who sent me has
himself testified concerning me. You have never heard his voice nor
seen his form, 38 nor does his word dwell in you, for you do not believe
the one he sent. 39 You diligently study[a] the Scriptures because you
think that by them you possess eternal life. These are the Scriptures
that testify about me, 40 yet you refuse to come to me to have life.
41 "I do not accept praise from men, 42 but I know you. I know
that you do not have the love of God in your hearts. 43 I have come
in my Father's name, and you do not accept me; but if someone
else comes in his own name, you will accept him. 44 How can you
believe if you accept praise from one another, yet make no effort to
obtain the praise that comes from the only God[b]?
45 "But do not think I will accuse you before the Father. Your
accuser is Moses, on whom your hopes are set. 46 If you believed
Moses, you would believe me, for he wrote about me. 47 But since
you do not believe what he wrote, how are you going to believe
what I say?"

MIRACLE FOUR— JESUS FEEDS FIVE THOUSAND

Jesus Feeds the Five Thousand

6 Some time after this, Jesus crossed to the far shore of the Sea of
Galilee (that is, the Sea of Tiberias), 2 and a great crowd of people

[a] **39** Or *Study diligently* (the imperative) [b] **44** Some early manuscripts *the Only One*

5:19 *Son . . . Father:* Jesus calls himself God's Son (1:1-3,18). See also the mini-article called "Son of God," p. 2044.

5:21 *the Father raises the dead and gives them life:* Jesus was referring here to eternal life (see the note at 4:14).

5:25 *a time is coming and has now come:* Jesus is saying that those who hear his message of forgiveness and new life have life that will never end. This includes those who have already died as faithful people. See also 1 Cor 15:12-57; 1 Thes 4:13-18.

5:27 *Son of Man:* See the mini-article called "Son of Man," p. 1866.

5:35 *John was a lamp that burned and gave light:* See the notes at 1:6 and on p. 2041 (light and darkness).

5:39,40 *You diligently study the Scriptures . . . come to me to have life:* The Scriptures are the Jewish Scriptures, which Christians call the Old Testament. The teachers followed the teachings of Scripture as a guide to living as God expected. Jesus is saying that those same Scriptures point to him as the way to eternal life (14:6). See also the note at 3:15.

5:45-47 *Moses, on whom your hopes are set:* Jesus was referring to the Law of Moses (see the note at 1:17), which was an important part of the Jewish Scriptures. Moses was the great leader who led the Israelite people out of slavery in Egypt and received from God the laws that the Israelite people were to live by. When Jesus says that Moses "wrote about me," he is referring to the overall message of the first five books of the Jewish Scriptures, traditionally called the Books of Moses.

6:1 *Sea of Galilee (that is, the Sea of Tiberias):* Jesus apparently crossed the lake from west to east. The Sea of Galilee is also known as the Lake of Gennesaret (Luke 5:1); and the Romans called it the Sea of Tiberias (also 21:1), after the Roman emperor Tiberius.

5:24 John 3:16,17. **5:29** Dan 12:2. **5:33** John 1:19-27; 3:27-30.

6:4 *Jewish Passover Feast:* See the mini-article called "Passover and the Feast of Unleavened Bread," p. 2030.

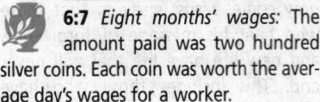

6:5 *Philip:* See the note at 1:44,45 (Philip).

6:7 *Eight months' wages:* The amount paid was two hundred silver coins. Each coin was worth the average day's wages for a worker.

6:8 *Andrew, Simon Peter's brother:* See the notes at 1:40 and 1:42.

6:9 *five small barley loaves:* Barley was a very cheap source of food in Palestine. It was mainly used to feed cattle, but it was also used for making bread in times of emergency. See also the mini-article called "Bread," p. 2058.

6:11 *Jesus then took the loaves:* Over a thousand years earlier, God miraculously fed the Israelite people in the desert with bread (manna) that came down from heaven (Exod 16:1-35; Num 11:7-9). Those who saw Jesus' miracle of feeding five thousand may have been reminded of God's earlier miracle.

6:13 *twelve baskets:* Twelve is a very significant number to the Jewish people because Israel was made up of twelve tribes. See the chart called "Numbers in the Bible," p. 2405.

6:14 *miraculous sign:* See the note at 2:11.

6:14 *the Prophet:* See the note at 1:21.

6:16 *lake:* Meaning the Sea of Galilee. See the note at 6:1. Storms often sweep across this lake because it is surrounded on nearly every side by mountains.

6:17 *Capernaum:* See the note at 2:12. The disciples and Jesus had been on the east side of the Sea of Galilee.

followed him because they saw the miraculous signs he had performed on the sick. 3 Then Jesus went up on a mountainside and
sat down with his disciples. 4 The Jewish Passover Feast was near.
5 When Jesus looked up and saw a great crowd coming
toward him, he said to Philip, "Where shall we buy bread for these
people to eat?" 6 He asked this only to test him, for he already had
in mind what he was going to do.
7 Philip answered him, "Eight months' wages[a] would not buy
enough bread for each one to have a bite!"
8 Another of his disciples, Andrew, Simon Peter's brother,
spoke up, 9 "Here is a boy with five small barley loaves and two
small fish, but how far will they go among so many?"
10 Jesus said, "Have the people sit down." There was plenty of
grass in that place, and the men sat down, about five thousand of
them. 11 Jesus then took the loaves, gave thanks, and distributed to
those who were seated as much as they wanted. He did the same
with the fish.
12 When they had all had enough to eat, he said to his disciples, "Gather the pieces that are left over. Let nothing be wasted."
13 So they gathered them and filled twelve baskets with the pieces of
the five barley loaves left over by those who had eaten.
14 After the people saw the miraculous sign that Jesus did, they
began to say, "Surely this is the Prophet who is to come into the
world." 15 Jesus, knowing that they intended to come and make him
king by force, withdrew again to a mountain by himself.

MIRACLE FIVE—JESUS WALKS ON THE WATER

Jesus Walks on the Water

16 When evening came, his disciples went down to the lake,
17 where they got into a boat and set off across the lake for Capernaum. By now it was dark, and Jesus had not yet joined them. 18 A
strong wind was blowing and the waters grew rough. 19 When they
had rowed three or three and a half miles,[b] they saw Jesus
approaching the boat, walking on the water; and they were terrified. 20 But he said to them, "It is I; don't be afraid." 21 Then they
were willing to take him into the boat, and immediately the boat
reached the shore where they were heading.
22 The next day the crowd that had stayed on the opposite
shore of the lake realized that only one boat had been there, and
that Jesus had not entered it with his disciples, but that they had
gone away alone. 23 Then some boats from Tiberias landed near the
place where the people had eaten the bread after the Lord had

[a] **7** Greek *two hundred denarii* [b] **19** Greek *rowed twenty-five or thirty stadia* (about 5 or 6 kilometers)

Christ at the Sea of Galilee by Jacopo Tintoretto, painted around 1575-1580. The evening after Jesus had fed over five thousand people with only five loaves of bread and two fish, Jesus' disciples got into a boat on the east side of the Sea of Galilee and began sailing for Capernaum on the west side. While they were out on the lake the water began to get rough. In the storm they saw Jesus coming toward them, walking on the water. Jesus said to them, "It is I; don't be afraid." (See 6:16-21.)

given thanks. 24Once the crowd realized that neither Jesus nor his
disciples were there, they got into the boats and went to Capernaum in search of Jesus.

JESUS TEACHES IN GALILEE AND JUDEA

In this section (6:25—8:59), Jesus teaches many important things. He describes himself as the bread of life, the source of living water, and the light of the world. His words and his actions continue to cause conflicts with the Jewish leaders.

Jesus the Bread of Life

25When they found him on the other side of the lake, they
asked him, "Rabbi, when did you get here?"
26Jesus answered, "I tell you the truth, you are looking for me,
not because you saw miraculous signs but because you ate the
loaves and had your fill. 27Do not work for food that spoils, but for
food that endures to eternal life, which the Son of Man will give
you. On him God the Father has placed his seal of approval."

6:19 *Jesus . . . walking on the water:* Jesus' miracle of walking on the water may have reminded the disciples of two miracles God had done earlier: controlling the waters of creation (Gen 1:1-13) and saving the Israelite people when Moses parted the waters of the Red Sea (Exod 14:21-31).

6:23,24 *Tiberias . . . Capernaum:* Tiberias was a city on the west coast of the Sea of Galilee, built around A.D. 20 by Herod Antipas to honor the emperor, Tiberius Caesar. See the map on p. 2470. When the people didn't find Jesus on the east side of the lake, they sailed back to Capernaum (see the note at 2:12).

6:27 *eternal life . . . Son of Man:* See the mini-articles called "Eternal Life," p. 2072 and "Son of Man" p. 1866.

6:31 *manna:* See the note at 6:11.

6:35 *I am:* This is the first of several occasions in JOHN where Jesus describes himself with a phrase beginning with "I am" (8:12; 9:5; 10:7,9; 10:11,14; 11:25; 14:6; 15:1,5). See the mini-article called "I Am," p. 2081.

6:35 *the bread of life:* Jesus compares himself to the gift of manna that God sent from heaven. Just as God sent the manna, God sends Jesus to bring life. See also the mini-article called "Bread," below.

6:31 Exod 16:4,15; Ps 78:24.

28 Then they asked him, "What must we do to do the works
God requires?"
29 Jesus answered, "The work of God is this: to believe in the
one he has sent."
30 So they asked him, "What miraculous sign then will you
give that we may see it and believe you? What will you do? 31 Our
forefathers ate the manna in the desert; as it is written: 'He gave
them bread from heaven to eat.'[a] "
32 Jesus said to them, "I tell you the truth, it is not Moses who
has given you the bread from heaven, but it is my Father who gives
you the true bread from heaven. 33 For the bread of God is he who
comes down from heaven and gives life to the world."
34 "Sir," they said, "from now on give us this bread."
35 Then Jesus declared, "I am the bread of life. He who comes
to me will never go hungry, and he who believes in me will never
be thirsty. 36 But as I told you, you have seen me and still you do
not believe. 37 All that the Father gives me will come to me, and
whoever comes to me I will never drive away. 38 For I have come
down from heaven not to do my will but to do the will of him who

[a] **31** Exodus 16:4; Neh. 9:15; Psalm 78:24,25

BREAD

Bread has always been an important and basic food for people. Bread was made at home by wives (Gen 18:6) and daughters (2 Sam 13:7,8). It was usually made fresh each day, but because it could last for several days without going bad, it could also be given to those setting out on a long journey (Gen 45:23). Bread was offered to strangers who passed through the land (Gen 14:18), and when God's people were disobedient, God warned them that their supply of daily bread would be taken away as punishment (Lev 26:23-26).

Most bread was made in flat cakes on flat stones or in pans. Some was baked into larger, thicker loaves that were placed on a special table in the temple and offered to God as "the bread of the Presence" (Exod 25:23-30). Only priests could eat this bread, but David and his supporters were once given some by priests when they were hungry (1 Sam 21:1-6). God provided bread for the Israelite people as they were wandering through the desert of Sinai on the way from Egypt to the promised land. They called this bread *manna*, which in Hebrew means, "What is it?" This bread is also referred to as the "bread from heaven" (Exod 16:4).

Ancient documents discovered in the twentieth century known as the Dead Sea Scrolls reveal that Jews in the community at Qumran shared meals of bread and wine. These meals were both a celebration of good times in the present and a celebration of the day when God would defeat their enemies and send the Messiah. Jesus' followers believed that he was God's chosen Messiah and the true bread from heaven that gives life (John 6:32-35). Jesus told his followers to ask God to give them the basic food (bread) they needed to live from day to day (Luke 11:3). After Jesus was taken to heaven, they continued to celebrate their new life together as God's people by "breaking bread" in ordinary meals (Acts 2:42-46), and by sharing in the bread of communion, which Jesus said was his body (Mark 14:22-25; 1 Cor 11:23-26).

Making Bread in Jesus' Day. Bread-baking, a daily chore, was almost always done by women and girls. Wheat or barley grain was ground into a coarse flour in hand-mills. The flour was then mixed with water, salt, and unbaked dough from the day before. This left-over dough contained the yeast needed to make the new batch of dough rise. The yeast was massaged into the dough (a process called "kneading") to distribute it throughout the batch, and the batches were set aside until the gasses produced by the yeast made the dough rise. The dough was then shaped into round, flat loaves that baked quickly in outdoor ovens.

sent me. 39 And this is the will of him who sent me, that I shall lose
none of all that he has given me, but raise them up at the last day.
40 For my Father's will is that everyone who looks to the Son and
believes in him shall have eternal life, and I will raise him up at the
last day."
41 At this the Jews began to grumble about him because he
said, "I am the bread that came down from heaven." 42 They said,
"Is this not Jesus, the son of Joseph, whose father and mother we
know? How can he now say, 'I came down from heaven'?"
43 "Stop grumbling among yourselves," Jesus answered. 44 "No
one can come to me unless the Father who sent me draws him, and
I will raise him up at the last day. 45 It is written in the Prophets:
'They will all be taught by God.'[a] Everyone who listens to the Father
and learns from him comes to me. 46 No one has seen the Father
except the one who is from God; only he has seen the Father. 47 I tell
you the truth, he who believes has everlasting life. 48 I am the bread

[a] **45** Isaiah 54:13

6:39 *the last day:* Jesus is referring to the time when God will judge all people. Those who have faith in Jesus, the Son, will be raised up to life (6:40), that is, have eternal life. See also the mini-articles called "Eternal Life," p. 2072 and "Day of the LORD," p. 1727.

6:42 *the son of Joseph:* See the note on p. 2041 (Jesus of Nazareth).

6:44 *raise him up at the last day:* See the note at 6:39.

6:45 Isa 54:13; Jer 31:33,34.

of life. 49 Your forefathers ate the manna in the desert, yet they died.
50 But here is the bread that comes down from heaven, which a man
may eat and not die. 51 I am the living bread that came down from
heaven. If anyone eats of this bread, he will live forever. This bread
is my flesh, which I will give for the life of the world."
52 Then the Jews began to argue sharply among themselves,
"How can this man give us his flesh to eat?"
53 Jesus said to them, "I tell you the truth, unless you eat the
flesh of the Son of Man and drink his blood, you have no life in
you. 54 Whoever eats my flesh and drinks my blood has eternal life,
and I will raise him up at the last day. 55 For my flesh is real food
and my blood is real drink. 56 Whoever eats my flesh and drinks my
blood remains in me, and I in him. 57 Just as the living Father sent
me and I live because of the Father, so the one who feeds on me
will live because of me. 58 This is the bread that came down from
heaven. Your forefathers ate manna and died, but he who feeds on
this bread will live forever." 59 He said this while teaching in the
synagogue in Capernaum.

Many Disciples Desert Jesus

60 On hearing it, many of his disciples said, "This is a hard
teaching. Who can accept it?"
61 Aware that his disciples were grumbling about this, Jesus
said to them, "Does this offend you? 62 What if you see the Son of
Man ascend to where he was before! 63 The Spirit gives life; the flesh
counts for nothing. The words I have spoken to you are spirit[a] and
they are life. 64 Yet there are some of you who do not believe." For
Jesus had known from the beginning which of them did not believe
and who would betray him. 65 He went on to say, "This is why I told
you that no one can come to me unless the Father has enabled him."
66 From this time many of his disciples turned back and no
longer followed him.
67 "You do not want to leave too, do you?" Jesus asked the
Twelve.
68 Simon Peter answered him, "Lord, to whom shall we go?
You have the words of eternal life. 69 We believe and know that you
are the Holy One of God."
70 Then Jesus replied, "Have I not chosen you, the Twelve? Yet
one of you is a devil!" 71 (He meant Judas, the son of Simon Iscariot, who, though one of the Twelve, was later to betray him.)

Jesus Goes to the Feast of Tabernacles

7 After this, Jesus went around in Galilee, purposely staying away
from Judea because the Jews there were waiting to take his life.
2 But when the Jewish Feast of Tabernacles was near, 3 Jesus' broth-

[a] **63** Or *Spirit*

6:53 *eat the flesh of the Son of Man and drink his blood:* Some see this as a reference to the Lord's Supper, which Jesus' followers share in response to his command (Matt 26:26-30; Mark 14:22-26; Luke 22:14-23; 1 Cor 11:23-29). Others think Jesus is emphasizing the need for people to activate, through their own faith, the spiritual benefits of Jesus' sacrificial death. See also the mini-article called "Son of Man," p. 1866.

6:58 *bread that came down from heaven:* See the notes at 6:11 and 6:35 (the bread of life).

6:59 *the synagogue in Capernaum:* The Greek word that is translated here as *synagogue* means "gathering." See also the mini-article called "Synagogues," p. 1857.

See the note at 2:12. A Roman army officer built a synagogue for the Jewish people in Capernaum (Luke 7:5).

6:63 *Spirit:* See the mini-article called "Holy Spirit," p. 2082.

6:67 *the Twelve:* These are the ones whom Jesus called to be his special apostles (Matt 10:1-4).

6:68 *Simon Peter:* See the note at 1:42.

6:68 *eternal life:* See the note at 4:14.

6:70,71 *a devil ... Judas ... Iscariot:* Judas would be Satan's instrument for opposing Jesus. Jesus knew that Judas, one of Jesus' twelve special disciples, would betray him. "Iscariot" may mean "a man from Kerioth" (a place in Judea); or, "a man who was a liar," or "a man who was a betrayer" (Matt 10:4).

7:1 *Galilee ... Judea:* See the notes at 1:43,44 and 3:22 (Judean countryside).

7:1 *the Jews:* See the note at 1:19 (the Jews).

ers said to him, "You ought to leave here and go to Judea, so that your disciples may see the miracles you do. [4]No one who wants to become a public figure acts in secret. Since you are doing these things, show yourself to the world." [5]For even his own brothers did not believe in him.

[6]Therefore Jesus told them, "The right time for me has not yet come; for you any time is right. [7]The world cannot hate you, but it hates me because I testify that what it does is evil. [8]You go to the Feast. I am not yet[a] going up to this Feast, because for me the right time has not yet come." [9]Having said this, he stayed in Galilee.

[10]However, after his brothers had left for the Feast, he went also, not publicly, but in secret. [11]Now at the Feast the Jews were watching for him and asking, "Where is that man?"

[12]Among the crowds there was widespread whispering about him. Some said, "He is a good man."

Others replied, "No, he deceives the people." [13]But no one would say anything publicly about him for fear of the Jews.

Jesus Teaches at the Feast

[14]Not until halfway through the Feast did Jesus go up to the temple courts and begin to teach. [15]The Jews were amazed and asked, "How did this man get such learning without having studied?"

[16]Jesus answered, "My teaching is not my own. It comes from him who sent me. [17]If anyone chooses to do God's will, he will find out whether my teaching comes from God or whether I speak on my own. [18]He who speaks on his own does so to gain honor for himself, but he who works for the honor of the one who sent him is a man of truth; there is nothing false about him. [19]Has not Moses given you the law? Yet not one of you keeps the law. Why are you trying to kill me?"

[20]"You are demon-possessed," the crowd answered. "Who is trying to kill you?"

[21]Jesus said to them, "I did one miracle, and you are all astonished. [22]Yet, because Moses gave you circumcision (though actually it did not come from Moses, but from the patriarchs), you circumcise a child on the Sabbath. [23]Now if a child can be circumcised on the Sabbath so that the law of Moses may not be broken, why are you angry with me for healing the whole man on the Sabbath? [24]Stop judging by mere appearances, and make a right judgment."

Is Jesus the Christ?

[25]At that point some of the people of Jerusalem began to ask, "Isn't this the man they are trying to kill? [26]Here he is, speaking publicly, and they are not saying a word to him. Have the authorities really

[a]**8** Some early manuscripts do not have *yet.*

7:2 *Feast of Tabernacles:* See the note at 5:1.

7:3 *Jesus' brothers:* These were most likely Jesus' half-brothers —other children of Mary and Joseph after Jesus was born.

7:6 *The right time for me has not yet come:* See the note at 2:4.

7:10 *he went also, not publicly, but in secret:* Jesus goes in secret rather than attracting attention to himself. He knows that there is danger in having people believe in him just because of his miracles.

7:14 *temple:* The center of Jewish worship in Jerusalem. Herod greatly expanded this important building as a way of trying to win the favor of the Jewish people. During the time of the festivals many visitors came to Jerusalem to offer sacrifices at the temple, so Jesus would have been able to speak to large crowds of people. See also the article called "People of the Law: The Religion of Israel," p. 939.

7:16 *him who sent me:* Jesus was referring to God, the Father. See the notes at 5:17 and 5:19.

7:19 *Yet not one of you keeps the law:* See the note at 1:17. Jesus tells his listeners that they have not really understood what God was saying in the law.

7:21 *I did one miracle:* Jesus is talking about his healing of the man who was crippled (5:1-16).

7:22 *you circumcise a child on the Sabbath:* See the mini-article called "Circumcision," p. 2251. Jesus is arguing that if it is acceptable to circumcise on the Sabbath, then it should be acceptable to treat the whole body, as he did when he healed the man who was crippled (5:1-16).

6:68,69 Matt 16:16; Mark 8:29; Luke 9:20. **7:2** Lev 23:34; Deut 16:13-15.

7:26 *the Christ:* See the note at 1:20.

7:30 *his time had not yet come:* See the note at 2:4.

7:31 *miraculous signs:* See the note at 2:11.

7:32 *Pharisees . . . chief priests . . . temple guards:* See the note at 1:24. The chief priests were members of a group in charge of the temple in Jerusalem. The temple guards policed the temple area and helped the council of Jewish leaders in Jerusalem (the Sanhedrin) keep order among the Jewish people.

7:35 *The Jews . . . the Greeks:* The "Jews" refers to the Jewish leaders; see the note at 1:19 (the Jews). "Greeks" may refer to Gentiles (non-Jews) or to Jews who followed Greek customs.

7:37 *On the last and greatest day:* On each of the seven days of the festival, a group of priests would go to the Pool of Siloam (see the note at 9:7) to fill a container of water to bring back to the temple. People would follow the priests to the pool and back up the steps to the temple. It may have been at the Pool of Siloam or somewhere along the ceremonial route to the temple that Jesus stood up and shouted that he was the source of living water (7:38; see the note at 4:14). See also Ezek 47:1-12; Zech 14:16, 17; and the mini-article called "Water," p. 1647.

7:39 *the Spirit:* See the notes at 1:32 and 1:33.

7:39 *Jesus had not yet been glorified:* John speaks of Jesus being given his full glory, when he is crucified and raised from death. See the note at 12:27.

7:40 *the Prophet:* See the note at 1:21.

7:41,42 *can the Christ come from Galilee . . . from Bethlehem:* See the note at 1:20, and the note on p. 2041 (Jesus of Nazareth). Bethlehem was known as King David's hometown (Luke 2:4).

concluded that he is the Christ[a] ? 27 But we know where this man is
from; when the Christ comes, no one will know where he is from."
28 Then Jesus, still teaching in the temple courts, cried out,
"Yes, you know me, and you know where I am from. I am not here
on my own, but he who sent me is true. You do not know him,
29 but I know him because I am from him and he sent me."
30 At this they tried to seize him, but no one laid a hand on
him, because his time had not yet come. 31 Still, many in the crowd
put their faith in him. They said, "When the Christ comes, will he
do more miraculous signs than this man?"
32 The Pharisees heard the crowd whispering such things
about him. Then the chief priests and the Pharisees sent temple
guards to arrest him.
33 Jesus said, "I am with you for only a short time, and then I
go to the one who sent me. 34 You will look for me, but you will not
find me; and where I am, you cannot come."
35 The Jews said to one another, "Where does this man intend
to go that we cannot find him? Will he go where our people live
scattered among the Greeks, and teach the Greeks? 36 What did he
mean when he said, 'You will look for me, but you will not find
me,' and 'Where I am, you cannot come'?"
37 On the last and greatest day of the Feast, Jesus stood and
said in a loud voice, "If anyone is thirsty, let him come to me and
drink. 38 Whoever believes in me, as[b] the Scripture has said, streams
of living water will flow from within him." 39 By this he meant the
Spirit, whom those who believed in him were later to receive. Up
to that time the Spirit had not been given, since Jesus had not yet
been glorified.
40 On hearing his words, some of the people said, "Surely this
man is the Prophet."
41 Others said, "He is the Christ."
Still others asked, "How can the Christ come from Galilee?
42 Does not the Scripture say that the Christ will come from David's
family[c] and from Bethlehem, the town where David lived?" 43 Thus
the people were divided because of Jesus. 44 Some wanted to seize
him, but no one laid a hand on him.

Unbelief of the Jewish Leaders

45 Finally the temple guards went back to the chief priests and
Pharisees, who asked them, "Why didn't you bring him in?"
46 "No one ever spoke the way this man does," the guards
declared.
47 "You mean he has deceived you also?" the Pharisees retorted.
48 "Has any of the rulers or of the Pharisees believed in him? 49 No! But

[a] **26** Or *Messiah*; also in verses 27, 31, 41 and 42 [b] **37, 38** Or / *If anyone is thirsty, let him come to me. / And let him drink,* 38 *who believes in me. / As* [c] **42** Greek *seed*

this mob that knows nothing of the law—there is a curse on them."
50Nicodemus, who had gone to Jesus earlier and who was
one of their own number, asked, 51"Does our law condemn anyone without first hearing him to find out what he is doing?"
52They replied, "Are you from Galilee, too? Look into it, and
you will find that a prophet[a] does not come out of Galilee."

[The earliest manuscripts and many other ancient witnesses do not have John 7:53—8:11.]

53Then each went to his own home.
8 But Jesus went to the Mount of Olives. 2At dawn he appeared
again in the temple courts, where all the people gathered around

[a] 52 Two early manuscripts *the Prophet*

Christ and the Woman Taken in Adultery by Max Beckmann, 1917. When Jesus was teaching in the temple courtyard, some Pharisees and teachers of the Law of Moses brought in a woman who had been caught in the act of adultery. The Pharisees and teachers, testing Jesus, said she should be put to death, a punishment commanded by the Law (Lev 20:10). But Jesus challenged their narrow understanding of sin and told the woman, "Neither do I condemn you . . . Go now and leave your life of sin." (See 8:1-11.)

7:50 *Nicodemus . . . one of their own number:* See the note at 3:1. "Their own number" refers to the Jewish ruling council (also called the Sanhedrin), which was made up of religious and civic leaders, including representatives of the chief priests, Pharisees, and Sadducees. The Romans, who ruled Palestine, allowed the local leaders in each part of their empire to decide cases against those who broke religious laws and to make people obey local laws.

7:51 *our law:* The Law of Moses taught that two witnesses were needed before a person could be convicted of a crime (Deut 17:6; 19:15) and put to death (Num 35:30).

7:52 *a prophet does not come out of Galilee:* Since Jesus is from Nazareth in Galilee, they don't believe he could be the Messiah. What the leaders didn't realize was that Jesus was born in Bethlehem in Judea, the hometown of King David, and that he was a descendant of David. It was from the family of King David that a Messiah was to come (2 Sam 7:16, 17; Isa 11:1).

8:1 *Mount of Olives:* The Mount of Olives is a ridge about two and a half miles long that is located about one-half mile east of the temple area in Jerusalem, across the Kidron Valley. It got its name because of all the olive trees that grew on its slopes. See the map on p. 2474.

8:2 *temple:* See the note at 7:14.

7:23 John 5:9. **7:34** John 14:1-6. **7:37** Lev 23:36. **7:38** Ezek 47:1; Zech 14:8. **7:42** 1 Sam 16:1; Mic 5:2.

him, and he sat down to teach them. [3]The teachers of the law and the Pharisees brought in a woman caught in adultery. They made her stand before the group [4]and said to Jesus, "Teacher, this woman was caught in the act of adultery. [5]In the Law Moses commanded us to stone such women. Now what do you say?" [6]They were using this question as a trap, in order to have a basis for accusing him.

But Jesus bent down and started to write on the ground with his finger. [7]When they kept on questioning him, he straightened up and said to them, "If any one of you is without sin, let him be the first to throw a stone at her." [8]Again he stooped down and wrote on the ground.

[9]At this, those who heard began to go away one at a time, the older ones first, until only Jesus was left, with the woman still standing there. [10]Jesus straightened up and asked her, "Woman, where are they? Has no one condemned you?"

[11]"No one, sir," she said.

"Then neither do I condemn you," Jesus declared. "Go now and leave your life of sin."

The Validity of Jesus' Testimony

[12]When Jesus spoke again to the people, he said, "I am the light of the world. Whoever follows me will never walk in darkness, but will have the light of life."

[13]The Pharisees challenged him, "Here you are, appearing as your own witness; your testimony is not valid."

[14]Jesus answered, "Even if I testify on my own behalf, my testimony is valid, for I know where I came from and where I am going. But you have no idea where I come from or where I am going. [15]You judge by human standards; I pass judgment on no one. [16]But if I do judge, my decisions are right, because I am not alone. I stand with the Father, who sent me. [17]In your own Law it is written that the testimony of two men is valid. [18]I am one who testifies for myself; my other witness is the Father, who sent me."

[19]Then they asked him, "Where is your father?"

"You do not know me or my Father," Jesus replied. "If you knew me, you would know my Father also." [20]He spoke these words while teaching in the temple area near the place where the offerings were put. Yet no one seized him, because his time had not yet come.

[21]Once more Jesus said to them, "I am going away, and you will look for me, and you will die in your sin. Where I go, you cannot come."

[22]This made the Jews ask, "Will he kill himself? Is that why he says, 'Where I go, you cannot come'?"

[23]But he continued, "You are from below; I am from above. You are of this world; I am not of this world. [24]I told you that you

8:2 *sat down:* Teachers in the ancient world usually sat down to teach. This was a sign of their authority.

8:3 *The teachers of the law and the Pharisees:* The teachers of the law studied the Law of Moses and explained it to others. See the notes at 1:17 and 1:24.

8:5 *the Law . . . stone such women:* According to the Law of Moses, a woman caught in adultery and the man she slept with were to be killed by stoning (Lev 20:10; Deut 22:22-24). The witnesses are supposed to be the first ones to throw the stones. The woman's partner is conspicuously absent in this story.

8:12 *I am the light of the world:* Jesus is saying that he has come into the world to help people see who God really is and to show them that God wants to give them new life. See the notes at 6:35 (I am) and 1:7; and the note on p. 2041 (light and darkness). See also Matt 5:14; John 9:5.

8:16 *Father:* See the note at 5:17. Jesus has come from the Father and will go back to rule beside the Father (8:14).

8:17 *your own Law . . . testimony of two men:* See the note at 7:51.

8:20 *the temple area near the place where the offerings were put:* Refers to the part of the temple known as "the court of the women," where offering boxes for the temple treasury were located (Mark 12:41). See also the mini-article called "Temple Offerings," p. 2027.

8:20 *his time had not yet come:* See the note at 2:4.

8:23 *You are from below; I am from above:* Jesus is referring to the fact that he was sent from God in heaven (above). When he uses the word "below" he is referring to "the world," which is often described in the Scriptures as being opposed to God (15:18, 19; Gal 6:14).

would die in your sins; if you do not believe that I am ⌞the one I
claim to be⌟,[a] you will indeed die in your sins."
25"Who are you?" they asked.
"Just what I have been claiming all along," Jesus replied. 26"I
have much to say in judgment of you. But he who sent me is reliable, and what I have heard from him I tell the world."
27They did not understand that he was telling them about
his Father. 28So Jesus said, "When you have lifted up the Son of
Man, then you will know that I am ⌞the one I claim to be⌟ and that
I do nothing on my own but speak just what the Father has taught
me. 29The one who sent me is with me; he has not left me alone,
for I always do what pleases him." 30Even as he spoke, many put
their faith in him.

The Children of Abraham

31To the Jews who had believed him, Jesus said, "If you hold
to my teaching, you are really my disciples. 32Then you will know
the truth, and the truth will set you free."
33They answered him, "We are Abraham's descendants[b] and
have never been slaves of anyone. How can you say that we shall be
set free?"
34Jesus replied, "I tell you the truth, everyone who sins is a
slave to sin. 35Now a slave has no permanent place in the family,
but a son belongs to it forever. 36So if the Son sets you free, you
will be free indeed. 37I know you are Abraham's descendants. Yet
you are ready to kill me, because you have no room for my word.
38I am telling you what I have seen in the Father's presence, and
you do what you have heard from your father.[c]"
39"Abraham is our father," they answered.
"If you were Abraham's children," said Jesus, "then you
would[d] do the things Abraham did. 40As it is, you are determined
to kill me, a man who has told you the truth that I heard from
God. Abraham did not do such things. 41You are doing the things
your own father does."
"We are not illegitimate children," they protested. "The only
Father we have is God himself."

The Children of the Devil

42Jesus said to them, "If God were your Father, you would
love me, for I came from God and now am here. I have not come
on my own; but he sent me. 43Why is my language not clear to
you? Because you are unable to hear what I say. 44You belong to
your father, the devil, and you want to carry out your father's

---

[a] **24** Or *I am he*; also in verse 28 [b] **33** Greek *seed*; also in verse 37 [c] **38** Or *presence. Therefore do what you have heard from the Father.* [d] **39** Some early manuscripts *"If you are Abraham's children," said Jesus, "then*

> Jesus said, *"You will know the truth, and the truth will set you free."* John 8:32

8:24 *if you do not believe that I am the one I claim to be:* Jesus refers to himself using the phrase "I Am." See the note at 6:35 (I am) and the mini-article called "I Am," p. 2081. Those who don't have faith in him as God's Son will be cutting themselves off from the forgiveness that God offers.

8:27 *his Father:* See the note at 5:17.

8:28 *lifted up the Son of Man:* See the note at 3:14,15 and the mini-article called "Son of Man," p. 1866.

8:33 *Abraham's descendants . . . never been slaves of anyone:* See the mini-article called "Abraham," p. 2254. God chose Abraham (Gen 12:1-3; 15:1-6; 17:1-8), and so it was believed that anyone who was a descendant of Abraham was also a child of God. The people of Israel had once been slaves in Egypt (Exod 1–14), and they were presently ruled by the Romans. Still, they believed that because they were descendants of Abraham, they would never be enslaved by anyone.

8:34 *a slave to sin:* Meaning sin is the master. See also the mini-articles called "Sin," p. 2181 and "Salvation," p. 2021.

8:44 *devil:* The devil, sometimes called Satan, is the leader of all the forces that are against God and God's people. One of the reasons God sent Jesus was to defeat the devil and all the devil has done (1 John 3:7, 8). See also the mini-article called "Satan," p. 963.

8:13 John 5:31. **8:33** Matt 3:9; Luke 3:8.

desire. He was a murderer from the beginning, not holding to the truth, for there is no truth in him. When he lies, he speaks his native language, for he is a liar and the father of lies. [45]Yet because I tell the truth, you do not believe me! [46]Can any of you prove me guilty of sin? If I am telling the truth, why don't you believe me? [47]He who belongs to God hears what God says. The reason you do not hear is that you do not belong to God."

The Claims of Jesus About Himself

[48]The Jews answered him, "Aren't we right in saying that you are a Samaritan and demon-possessed?"

[49]"I am not possessed by a demon," said Jesus, "but I honor my Father and you dishonor me. [50]I am not seeking glory for myself; but there is one who seeks it, and he is the judge. [51]I tell you the truth, if anyone keeps my word, he will never see death."

[52]At this the Jews exclaimed, "Now we know that you are demon-possessed! Abraham died and so did the prophets, yet you say that if anyone keeps your word, he will never taste death. [53]Are you greater than our father Abraham? He died, and so did the prophets. Who do you think you are?"

[54]Jesus replied, "If I glorify myself, my glory means nothing. My Father, whom you claim as your God, is the one who glorifies me. [55]Though you do not know him, I know him. If I said I did not, I would be a liar like you, but I do know him and keep his word. [56]Your father Abraham rejoiced at the thought of seeing my day; he saw it and was glad."

[57]"You are not yet fifty years old," the Jews said to him, "and you have seen Abraham!"

[58]"I tell you the truth," Jesus answered, "before Abraham was born, I am!" [59]At this, they picked up stones to stone him, but Jesus hid himself, slipping away from the temple grounds.

MIRACLE SIX— JESUS HEALS A BLIND MAN

Jesus heals a man born with physical blindness, but the central message behind this event is that Jesus is the light that has power over the darkness of the world.

Jesus Heals a Man Born Blind

9 As he went along, he saw a man blind from birth. [2]His disciples asked him, "Rabbi, who sinned, this man or his parents, that he was born blind?"

[3]"Neither this man nor his parents sinned," said Jesus, "but this happened so that the work of God might be displayed in his

8:48 *The Jews . . . you are a Samaritan:* See the note at 1:19 (the Jews). Regarding Samaritans, see the notes at 4:3, 4 and 4:9. Jesus' opponents probably called Jesus a Samaritan because they felt he failed to keep the Law of Moses.

8:49 *demon:* Demons are evil spirits that work for the devil (Satan). In Jesus' day, demons were understood to be the cause of many kinds of physical and mental illness. A Jewish person who was demon-possessed was considered "unclean" and was not allowed to eat or worship with other Jews.

8:52 *Abraham died and so did the prophets:* The Jewish leaders don't understand what Jesus means when he tells them that they will never die if they obey him (8:51). At this time, there were differing opinions about eternal life. See the mini-article called "Eternal Life," p. 2072.

8:56 *Abraham rejoiced at the thought of seeing my day:* Jesus is saying that Abraham was able to see how the promises God made to Abraham would be fulfilled.

8:58 *before Abraham was born, I am!:* See the note at 1:1-3 and the mini-article called "I Am," p. 2081.

8:59 *picked up stones to stone him:* Because of Jesus' claim in 8:58 (see the note), the Jewish leaders felt that Jesus was guilty of blasphemy. The punishment for this serious sin was death by stoning (Lev 24:16). See also the notes at 10:31 and 10:33.

9:2 *who sinned, this man or his parents:* At the time of Jesus, the teachers of the law commonly taught that a person who was blind was being punished by God for sinning, or for the sin of his or her parents (Exod 20:5). See the note at 5:14.

9:4 *Night is coming:* Night brings darkness, which symbolizes a lack of understanding. See the note on p. 2041 (light and darkness). Jesus may also be referring to a time of judgment.

life. 4As long as it is day, we must do the work of him who sent me.
Night is coming, when no one can work. 5While I am in the world,
I am the light of the world."
6Having said this, he spit on the ground, made some mud
with the saliva, and put it on the man's eyes. 7"Go," he told him,
"wash in the Pool of Siloam" (this word means Sent). So the man
went and washed, and came home seeing.
8His neighbors and those who had formerly seen him begging asked, "Isn't this the same man who used to sit and beg?"
9Some claimed that he was.
Others said, "No, he only looks like him."
But he himself insisted, "I am the man."
10"How then were your eyes opened?" they demanded.
11He replied, "The man they call Jesus made some mud and
put it on my eyes. He told me to go to Siloam and wash. So I went
and washed, and then I could see."
12"Where is this man?" they asked him.
"I don't know," he said.

The Pharisees Investigate the Healing

13They brought to the Pharisees the man who had been
blind. 14Now the day on which Jesus had made the mud and
opened the man's eyes was a Sabbath. 15Therefore the Pharisees
also asked him how he had received his sight. "He put mud on my
eyes," the man replied, "and I washed, and now I see."
16Some of the Pharisees said, "This man is not from God, for
he does not keep the Sabbath."
But others asked, "How can a sinner do such miraculous
signs?" So they were divided.
17Finally they turned again to the blind man, "What have
you to say about him? It was your eyes he opened."
The man replied, "He is a prophet."
18The Jews still did not believe that he had been blind and
had received his sight until they sent for the man's parents. 19"Is
this your son?" they asked. "Is this the one you say was born blind?
How is it that now he can see?"
20"We know he is our son," the parents answered, "and we
know he was born blind. 21But how he can see now, or who
opened his eyes, we don't know. Ask him. He is of age; he will
speak for himself." 22His parents said this because they were afraid
of the Jews, for already the Jews had decided that anyone who
acknowledged that Jesus was the Christ[a] would be put out of the
synagogue. 23That was why his parents said, "He is of age; ask him."
24A second time they summoned the man who had been blind.
"Give glory to God,[b]" they said. "We know this man is a sinner."

[a] 22 Or *Messiah* [b] 24 A solemn charge to tell the truth (see Joshua 7:19)

9:5 *I am the light of the world:* See the notes at 6:35 (I am) and 8:12.

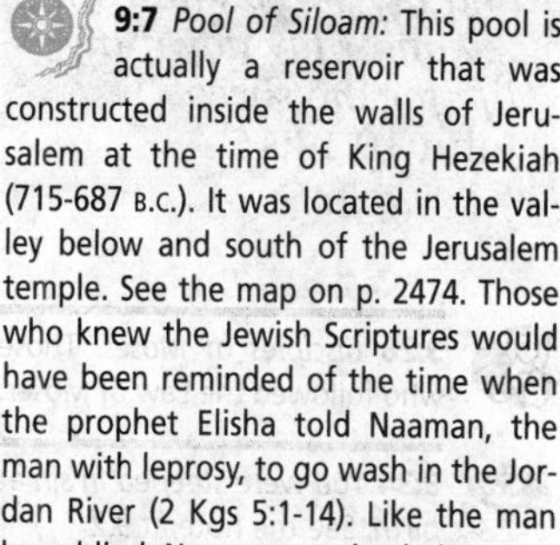

9:7 *Pool of Siloam:* This pool is actually a reservoir that was constructed inside the walls of Jerusalem at the time of King Hezekiah (715-687 B.C.). It was located in the valley below and south of the Jerusalem temple. See the map on p. 2474. Those who knew the Jewish Scriptures would have been reminded of the time when the prophet Elisha told Naaman, the man with leprosy, to go wash in the Jordan River (2 Kgs 5:1-14). Like the man born blind, Naaman was healed.

9:13 *Pharisees:* See the note at 1:24.

9:14 *Sabbath:* See the note at 5:9. When Jesus healed the blind man, he was accused of violating the Sabbath law (9:16).

9:16 *miraculous signs:* See the note at 2:11.

9:17 *He is a prophet:* See the note at 4:19. Prophets like Elijah and Elisha had worked miracles, so those who heard Jesus and saw him do miracles would have been reminded of what the Jewish Scriptures said about the prophets.

9:18 *The Jews:* See the note at 1:19 (the Jews).

9:22 *the Christ:* See the note at 1:20 (the Christ).

9:22 *put out of the synagogue:* The Jewish leaders were going to put out of the Jewish community and Jewish meeting places (9:34) anyone who became a follower of Jesus. See also the Introduction to JOHN, p. 2041.

9:24 *this man is a sinner:* The leaders thought Jesus was a sinner because he did not follow the Law of Moses.

9:5 Matt 5:14; John 1:4,5; 8:12.

Jesus said,
"I am the good shepherd; I know my sheep and my sheep know me . . . and I lay down my life for the sheep."
John 10:14,15

9:28 *disciples of Moses:* Those who followed the Law of Moses.

9:34 *You were steeped in sin at birth:* See the note at 9:2.

9:34 *they threw him out:* See the note at 9:22 (put out of the synagogue). See also the note at 6:59 (synagogue).

9:35 *Son of Man:* See the mini-article called "Son of Man," p. 1866.

9:38 *"Lord, I believe . . . worshiped him:* Believing in Jesus (placing trust and faith in him) is a key theme in JOHN (see the note at 20:31 and the mini-article called "Faith," p. 1932). The man Jesus had healed of blindness put his faith in Jesus and worshiped him as God.

9:41 *If you were blind:* Jesus is saying that those who are blind spiritually but respond to his message will not be guilty. But those who claim they understand the truth (based on the Law of Moses), but will not trust Jesus, continue to be guilty.

10:1 *sheep pen . . . thief and a robber:* A sheep pen was an enclosed area for keeping sheep safe at night.

10:2,3 *gate . . . shepherd . . . watchman:* The watchman decided who or what got into the sheep pen. Often the watchman was the shepherd himself, who counted the sheep as they entered the pen for the night. The gate was the only way to go into or out of the pen.

9:39 Matt 13:11; Luke 4:16-19.

The Good Shepherd, unknown Nigerian artist, 1978. Shepherds were a familiar sight in Palestine in Jesus' day. The crowds that gathered to hear Jesus speak knew that looking after sheep was difficult, and sometimes dangerous, work. Even so, it probably surprised some of them to hear Jesus say, "I am the good shepherd; I know my sheep and my sheep know me . . . and I lay down my life for the sheep." (See 10:7-21.)

25 He replied, "Whether he is a sinner or not, I don't know.
One thing I do know. I was blind but now I see!"
26 Then they asked him, "What did he do to you? How did he
open your eyes?"
27 He answered, "I have told you already and you did not listen. Why do you want to hear it again? Do you want to become his
disciples, too?"
28 Then they hurled insults at him and said, "You are this fellow's disciple! We are disciples of Moses! 29 We know that God
spoke to Moses, but as for this fellow, we don't even know where
he comes from."
30 The man answered, "Now that is remarkable! You don't
know where he comes from, yet he opened my eyes. 31 We know
that God does not listen to sinners. He listens to the godly man
who does his will. 32 Nobody has ever heard of opening the eyes of
a man born blind. 33 If this man were not from God, he could do
nothing."
34 To this they replied, "You were steeped in sin at birth; how
dare you lecture us!" And they threw him out.

Spiritual Blindness

35 Jesus heard that they had thrown him out, and when he
found him, he said, "Do you believe in the Son of Man?"
36 "Who is he, sir?" the man asked. "Tell me so that I may
believe in him."

37 Jesus said, "You have now seen him; in fact, he is the one
speaking with you."
38 Then the man said, "Lord, I believe," and he worshiped him.
39 Jesus said, "For judgment I have come into this world, so
that the blind will see and those who see will become blind."
40 Some Pharisees who were with him heard him say this and
asked, "What? Are we blind too?"
41 Jesus said, "If you were blind, you would not be guilty of
sin; but now that you claim you can see, your guilt remains.

THE GOOD SHEPHERD AND THE TRUE FLOCK

In chapter 10, Jesus uses the images of the shepherd, flock, and thieves to describe the relationship between himself, his true followers, and those who want to come between God and God's people.

The Shepherd and His Flock

10 "I tell you the truth, the man who does not enter the sheep
pen by the gate, but climbs in by some other way, is a thief and a
robber. 2 The man who enters by the gate is the shepherd of his
sheep. 3 The watchman opens the gate for him, and the sheep listen
to his voice. He calls his own sheep by name and leads them out.
4 When he has brought out all his own, he goes on ahead of them,
and his sheep follow him because they know his voice. 5 But they
will never follow a stranger; in fact, they will run away from him
because they do not recognize a stranger's voice." 6 Jesus used this
figure of speech, but they did not understand what he was telling
them.
7 Therefore Jesus said again, "I tell you the truth, I am the
gate for the sheep. 8 All who ever came before me were thieves and
robbers, but the sheep did not listen to them. 9 I am the gate; whoever enters through me will be saved.[a] He will come in and go out,
and find pasture. 10 The thief comes only to steal and kill and
destroy; I have come that they may have life, and have it to the full.
11 "I am the good shepherd. The good shepherd lays down
his life for the sheep. 12 The hired hand is not the shepherd who
owns the sheep. So when he sees the wolf coming, he abandons the
sheep and runs away. Then the wolf attacks the flock and scatters
it. 13 The man runs away because he is a hired hand and cares nothing for the sheep.
14 "I am the good shepherd; I know my sheep and my sheep
know me— 15 just as the Father knows me and I know the Father—
and I lay down my life for the sheep. 16 I have other sheep that are
not of this sheep pen. I must bring them also. They too will listen

[a] 9 Or *kept safe*

10:3 *the sheep listen to his voice:* In the Scriptures, sheep and flocks of sheep are symbols for God's people (Ps 23:1; 77:20; Isa 53:6; Ezek 34:11-16). See also the mini-article called "Shepherds," p. 1972. The Good Shepherd was an early Christian symbol for Christ, as in this stone carving from a catacomb in Rome (third century).

10:7 *I am the gate for the sheep:* See the notes at 6:35 (I am) and 10:2,3. As the gate for the sheep (his followers), Jesus stands guard and protects them. He also determines who will go through the gate.

10:8 *thieves and robbers:* Jesus is talking about those who had been teaching the people (God's sheep) in a way that led them away from the truth.

10:11 *I am . . . good shepherd lays down his life:* See the note at 6:35 (I am). See also 10:15; 15:13; and the note on p. 2041 (Lamb of God).

10:13 *a hired hand:* This may be a reference to Israel's leaders, but the key point is that the real shepherd (Jesus) who "owns" the sheep would never run away when danger threatened.

10:16 *other sheep . . . one flock:* Jesus will help his followers become "one" in spite of their differences (see also Gal 3:26-29).

10:15 Matt 11:27; Luke 10:22.

10:17,18 *take it up again:* Jesus is referring to his resurrection.

10:21 *demon:* See the note at 8:49.

10:22 *Feast of Dedication:* This was a celebration of how God freed the Jewish people from foreign rule. This feast is also known as Hanukkah.

10:23 *Solomon's Colonnade:* This was a public place, made from huge stone columns, on the east and south sides of the temple area. See the map on p. 2474.

10:24 *The Jews . . . the Christ:* See the notes at 1:19 (the Jews) and 1:20.

10:30 *I and the Father are one:* Jesus boldly proclaims that he is equal with God the Father. This reality is the basis of his "I am" statements (see the mini-article called "I Am," p. 2081) and his claim to be God's Son (see 10:36 and the mini-article called "Son of God," p. 2044.

10:31 *picked up stones:* Anyone who disobeyed the Law of Moses in a way that threatened the purity of the community was to be put to death (Lev 24:15,16; Deut 21:18-21; 22:20-22). The group would throw big stones to crush and bury the one who was accused of being a threat to all of God's people.

10:33 *you, a mere man, claim to be God:* The Jewish leaders accused Jesus of claiming he was God. Since they believed he was only a man, and not God, they said that Jesus was guilty of one of the most horrible offenses against God (blasphemy), which was punishable by death. See also 8:58,59.

10:34,35 *in your Law . . . Scripture cannot be broken:* The Law refers to the Jewish Scriptures (Old Testament). By saying that "Scripture cannot be broken," Jesus asserts their total reliability and authority.

to my voice, and there shall be one flock and one shepherd. [17]The
reason my Father loves me is that I lay down my life—only to take
it up again. [18]No one takes it from me, but I lay it down of my own
accord. I have authority to lay it down and authority to take it up
again. This command I received from my Father."
[19]At these words the Jews were again divided. [20]Many of them
said, "He is demon-possessed and raving mad. Why listen to him?"
[21]But others said, "These are not the sayings of a man possessed by a demon. Can a demon open the eyes of the blind?"

The Unbelief of the Jews

[22]Then came the Feast of Dedication[a] at Jerusalem. It was winter, [23]and Jesus was in the temple area walking in Solomon's Colonnade. [24]The Jews gathered around him, saying, "How long will you
keep us in suspense? If you are the Christ,[b] tell us plainly."
[25]Jesus answered, "I did tell you, but you do not believe. The
miracles I do in my Father's name speak for me, [26]but you do not
believe because you are not my sheep. [27]My sheep listen to my
voice; I know them, and they follow me. [28]I give them eternal life,
and they shall never perish; no one can snatch them out of my
hand. [29]My Father, who has given them to me, is greater than all[c];
no one can snatch them out of my Father's hand. [30]I and the
Father are one."
[31]Again the Jews picked up stones to stone him, [32]but Jesus
said to them, "I have shown you many great miracles from the
Father. For which of these do you stone me?"
[33]"We are not stoning you for any of these," replied the Jews,
"but for blasphemy, because you, a mere man, claim to be God."
[34]Jesus answered them, "Is it not written in your Law, 'I have
said you are gods'[d] ? [35]If he called them 'gods,' to whom the word
of God came—and the Scripture cannot be broken— [36]what about
the one whom the Father set apart as his very own and sent into
the world? Why then do you accuse me of blasphemy because I
said, 'I am God's Son'? [37]Do not believe me unless I do what my
Father does. [38]But if I do it, even though you do not believe me,
believe the miracles, that you may know and understand that the
Father is in me, and I in the Father." [39]Again they tried to seize
him, but he escaped their grasp.
[40]Then Jesus went back across the Jordan to the place where
John had been baptizing in the early days. Here he stayed [41]and
many people came to him. They said, "Though John never performed a miraculous sign, all that John said about this man was
true." [42]And in that place many believed in Jesus.

[a]**22** That is, Hanukkah [b]**24** Or *Messiah* [c]**29** Many early manuscripts *What my Father has given me is greater than all* [d]**34** Psalm 82:6

MIRACLE SEVEN—
JESUS BRINGS LAZARUS TO LIFE

The Death of Lazarus

11 Now a man named Lazarus was sick. He was from Bethany,
the village of Mary and her sister Martha. [2]This Mary, whose
brother Lazarus now lay sick, was the same one who poured perfume on the Lord and wiped his feet with her hair. [3]So the sisters
sent word to Jesus, "Lord, the one you love is sick."

[4]When he heard this, Jesus said, "This sickness will not end
in death. No, it is for God's glory so that God's Son may be glorified through it." [5]Jesus loved Martha and her sister and Lazarus.
[6]Yet when he heard that Lazarus was sick, he stayed where he was
two more days.

[7]Then he said to his disciples, "Let us go back to Judea."

[8]"But Rabbi," they said, "a short while ago the Jews tried to
stone you, and yet you are going back there?"

[9]Jesus answered, "Are there not twelve hours of daylight? A
man who walks by day will not stumble, for he sees by this world's
light. [10]It is when he walks by night that he stumbles, for he has no
light."

[11]After he had said this, he went on to tell them, "Our friend
Lazarus has fallen asleep; but I am going there to wake him up."

[12]His disciples replied, "Lord, if he sleeps, he will get better."
[13]Jesus had been speaking of his death, but his disciples thought he
meant natural sleep.

[14]So then he told them plainly, "Lazarus is dead, [15]and for
your sake I am glad I was not there, so that you may believe. But
let us go to him."

[16]Then Thomas (called Didymus) said to the rest of the disciples, "Let us also go, that we may die with him."

Jesus Comforts the Sisters

[17]On his arrival, Jesus found that Lazarus had already been
in the tomb for four days. [18]Bethany was less than two miles[a] from
Jerusalem, [19]and many Jews had come to Martha and Mary to
comfort them in the loss of their brother. [20]When Martha heard
that Jesus was coming, she went out to meet him, but Mary stayed
at home.

[21]"Lord," Martha said to Jesus, "if you had been here, my
brother would not have died. [22]But I know that even now God will
give you whatever you ask."

[23]Jesus said to her, "Your brother will rise again."

[a] **18** Greek *fifteen stadia* (about 3 kilometers)

10:40 *across the Jordan:* Jesus escaped and traveled east, crossing the Jordan River near where John had been baptizing (see 1:28).

11:1,2 *Lazarus . . . Mary . . . Martha:* The name Lazarus in Hebrew means "God helps." Martha and Mary are mentioned in Luke 10:38-42. Jesus had a very close relationship with this family (11:3,5).

11:1 *Bethany:* A small village about two miles east of Jerusalem, on the slopes of the Mount of Olives. Today it is known as El-'Azariyeh, after Lazarus, whose tomb is still said to be here. See also the map on p. 2473.

11:6 *he stayed . . . two more days:* As elsewhere in John, Jesus acts at the time he knows to be right (see 2:3,4; 7:6-8).

11:7 *go back to Judea:* Jesus apparently got the message about Lazarus while on the east side of the Jordan River (10:40).

11:11 *Lazarus has fallen asleep:* Jesus meant that Lazarus was dead (11:13). Jesus would "wake him up" by bringing him back to life from the dead.

11:16 *Thomas:* Thomas was one of Jesus' twelve close apostles (disciples). Both his Hebrew name and Greek nickname Didymus, mean "Twin." Thomas is mentioned in the lists of the twelve apostles (Matt 10:3; Mark 3:18; and Luke 6:15). He is sometimes known as "doubting Thomas," because he refused at first to believe that Jesus had been raised from death (20:24-29).

11:17 *tomb:* In Palestine, tombs were usually carved out of the soft limestone hillsides.

10:33 Lev 24:16. **10:34** Ps 82:6. **11:1** Luke 10:38,39.

11:24 *rise again in the resurrection at the last day:* Martha apparently believed in the hope of life after death. See the mini-article called "Eternal Life," below. See also the note at 6:39 (the last day).

11:25 *I am the resurrection and the life:* See the notes at 6:35 (I am) and 4:14.

24 Martha answered, "I know he will rise again in the resurrection at the last day."
25 Jesus said to her, "I am the resurrection and the life. He
who believes in me will live, even though he dies; 26 and whoever
lives and believes in me will never die. Do you believe this?"
27 "Yes, Lord," she told him, "I believe that you are the Christ,[a]
the Son of God, who was to come into the world."

[a] 27 Or *Messiah*

ETERNAL LIFE

In ancient times, the people of Israel based their hope for life beyond death on the lives of their descendants. It was considered a tragedy when a man died without having a son to carry on the family line. Most people expected that their bodies would rot and turn to dust after they died (Eccl 12:7; Ps 104:29; Job 7:9, 10). Some believed that the souls of the dead went to a special place, but these souls had no thoughts or feelings there (Eccl 9:10; Isa 38:10). The Bible reports that a few people did not die but were taken up to be with God (Gen 5:21-24; 2 Kgs 2:1-14).

The idea of people being raised from death appears in the book of the prophet Daniel, who said that both good and bad people would be raised from death to new life. The good would experience eternal life, while the bad would have eternal shame (Dan 12:1-3). Other passages express confidence that God would not send faithful people to the world of the dead, but would save them from death (Ps 16:10, 11; 49:13-15; Isa 26:19).

The people of Israel were taken into exile in Babylon around 586 B.C. Later, the Persians defeated Babylon and let the people of Israel begin to return home (538 B.C.). Some Israelites were influenced by Persians who believed that God's enemy, Satan, would be defeated and that the souls and bodies of faithful people who had died would be brought back to life. During the four centuries before the birth of Christ, the Jewish people were also influenced by some Greek thinkers who believed that the physical human body had no lasting value and would rot away, but the invisible soul or spirit would live forever. The apostle Paul told the church in Corinth that the physical bodies of Christ's followers will die, but when God raises them to new life, their bodies will change into "spiritual bodies" (1 Cor 15:35-54). This is different from the belief that only the soul would live on after the body decayed. Paul says that the whole person—both soul and body—will be new and experience life after death (eternal life).

Jesus called himself "the resurrection and the life" (John 11:25, 26) and promises that all who believe in him will have eternal life (John 3:16). One group of religious Jews called Sadducees questioned Jesus' teachings about life after death (Luke 20:27). Jesus told them that when God's people rise from death they will not marry but their new lives will be like those of the angels in heaven (Mark 12:18-27). Jesus also gave a surprising parable in Luke 14:15-24 about which people would be part of God's future kingdom.

Early Christians believed that God's people would be raised to new life because God raised Jesus from death to new life (Acts 2:22-24, 29-32; 1 Cor 15:20-28; 1 Thes 4:13-17). Revelation 21 describes the new Jerusalem, where God will live among people on earth and where God will feed and protect his followers forever. (See also Ezek 37:26, 27; Matt 1:23; 2 Cor 4:16—5:5.)

28And after she had said this, she went back and called her
sister Mary aside. "The Teacher is here," she said, "and is asking for
you." 29When Mary heard this, she got up quickly and went to him.
30Now Jesus had not yet entered the village, but was still at the
place where Martha had met him. 31When the Jews who had been
with Mary in the house, comforting her, noticed how quickly she
got up and went out, they followed her, supposing she was going
to the tomb to mourn there.

32When Mary reached the place where Jesus was and saw
him, she fell at his feet and said, "Lord, if you had been here, my
brother would not have died."

33When Jesus saw her weeping, and the Jews who had come
along with her also weeping, he was deeply moved in spirit and
troubled. 34"Where have you laid him?" he asked.

"Come and see, Lord," they replied.

35Jesus wept.

36Then the Jews said, "See how he loved him!"

37But some of them said, "Could not he who opened the eyes
of the blind man have kept this man from dying?"

Jesus Raises Lazarus From the Dead

38Jesus, once more deeply moved, came to the tomb. It was a
cave with a stone laid across the entrance. 39"Take away the stone,"
he said.

"But, Lord," said Martha, the sister of the dead man, "by this
time there is a bad odor, for he has been there four days."

40Then Jesus said, "Did I not tell you that if you believed, you
would see the glory of God?"

41So they took away the stone. Then Jesus looked up and
said, "Father, I thank you that you have heard me. 42I knew that
you always hear me, but I said this for the benefit of the people
standing here, that they may believe that you sent me."

Jesus said . . . "I am the resurrection and the life. He who believes in me will live, even though he dies; and whoever lives and believes in me will never die."
John 11:25,26

11:27 *the Christ, the Son of God:* See the notes at 1:20 and 1:34, and the mini-article called "Son of God," p. 2044.

11:39 *a bad odor:* A body that had been dead for four days would have begun to decay, causing a bad odor to come from the tomb. Martha was concerned with the practical fact that the body would smell when Jesus goes in to look at it.

QUESTIONS ABOUT JOHN 2:1—11:44

1. What do the many miracles in chapters 2–11 say about Jesus? What effect did Jesus' miracles have on people?
2. What did Jesus mean when he described himself as "the bread of life"? (6:35) As "the light of the world"? (8:12) As "the good shepherd"? (10:14) As "the resurrection and the life"? (11:25)
3. What was remarkable about Jesus' meeting with the Samaritan woman at the well? (4:3-42) What point did Jesus make about worship? (4:21-24)
4. What did Jesus do that made the leaders angry enough to kill him? (5:16-18) Why did they want to get rid of Jesus?
5. What did Jesus mean when he said, "If the Son sets you free, you will be free indeed"? (8:36) In what areas of your life do you feel you are not "free"?
6. When Jesus says he has come to give sight to the blind and make blind everyone who can see, what does he mean? (9:39) In your life, what would you like to "see" more clearly? Why?

11:44 *grave clothes:* In Jesus' day, dead bodies were usually wrapped in strips of linen cloth. Sometimes sweet-smelling spices and ointments were also put on the body. A single piece of cloth was used to cover the face of the person who had died. See also the mini-article called "Burial," p. 1998.

11:46,47 *chief priests and the Pharisees . . . Sanhedrin:* See the notes at 1:24; 7:32 (chief priests), and 7:50.

11:47 *miraculous signs:* See the note at 2:11.

11:48 *the Romans will come and take away both our place and our nation:* "Our place" likely refers to the temple in Jerusalem. The Jewish leaders were afraid that Jesus would lead his followers to rebel against Rome and that the Roman army would then destroy their nation and the temple. They were also afraid that if many people started to follow Jesus and his teachings, their own power would be lessened.

11:49 *Caiaphas:* Caiaphas was the high priest in Jerusalem from A.D. 18 to 37. He was in charge of the priests who served in the temple. He had great power among the religious and political leaders of Israel.

11:51 *he prophesied that Jesus would die:* See the article called "Prophets and Prophecy," p. 935. The office of the high priest did not typically carry prophetic powers. Caiaphas, like other opponents of Jesus in JOHN's Gospel, spoke more truly than he realized.

11:52 *the scattered children of God, to bring them together:* Though God had chosen Israel (the Jewish nation), people of all nations are invited to be part of God's new family.

The Resurrection of Lazarus by Henry Ossawa Tanner, 1896. All of the Gospels tell of Jesus' raising to life someone who had died, but only JOHN tells about Jesus raising his good friend, Lazarus, back to life. Lazarus had been dead and buried for four days when Jesus came to Lazarus's tomb, prayed to God, and shouted, "Lazarus, come out!" (See 11:1-44.) This miracle, the last one reported in JOHN, upset the chief priests so much that they began to make plans to kill Lazarus. (See 12:9-11.)

43 When he had said this, Jesus called in a loud voice,
"Lazarus, come out!" 44 The dead man came out, his hands and feet
wrapped with strips of linen, and a cloth around his face.

Jesus said to them, "Take off the grave clothes and let him go."

Jesus' Final Days

This section (11:45—19:42) describes the final days before Jesus' death on the cross, which in JOHN is the time when his full glory is to be revealed (7:39). First, the plot to arrest and kill Jesus is revealed. Then Jesus visits Bethany where Mary pours expensive perfume on him in preparation for his upcoming burial (12:7). Later, Jesus prepares his own disciples for his death and prays for them just before he is arrested, put on trial, and put to death.

PREPARATIONS FOR JESUS' DEATH

The Plot to Kill Jesus

45 Therefore many of the Jews who had come to visit Mary,
and had seen what Jesus did, put their faith in him. 46 But some of
them went to the Pharisees and told them what Jesus had done.

47Then the chief priests and the Pharisees called a meeting of the
Sanhedrin.
"What are we accomplishing?" they asked. "Here is this man
performing many miraculous signs. 48If we let him go on like this,
everyone will believe in him, and then the Romans will come and
take away both our place[a] and our nation."
49Then one of them, named Caiaphas, who was high priest
that year, spoke up, "You know nothing at all! 50You do not realize
that it is better for you that one man die for the people than that
the whole nation perish."
51He did not say this on his own, but as high priest that year
he prophesied that Jesus would die for the Jewish nation, 52and not
only for that nation but also for the scattered children of God, to
bring them together and make them one. 53So from that day on
they plotted to take his life.
54Therefore Jesus no longer moved about publicly among the
Jews. Instead he withdrew to a region near the desert, to a village
called Ephraim, where he stayed with his disciples.
55When it was almost time for the Jewish Passover, many
went up from the country to Jerusalem for their ceremonial
cleansing before the Passover. 56They kept looking for Jesus, and as
they stood in the temple area they asked one another, "What do
you think? Isn't he coming to the Feast at all?" 57But the chief
priests and Pharisees had given orders that if anyone found out
where Jesus was, he should report it so that they might arrest him.

Jesus Anointed at Bethany

12 Six days before the Passover, Jesus arrived at Bethany, where
Lazarus lived, whom Jesus had raised from the dead. 2Here a dinner was given in Jesus' honor. Martha served, while Lazarus was
among those reclining at the table with him. 3Then Mary took
about a pint[b] of pure nard, an expensive perfume; she poured it
on Jesus' feet and wiped his feet with her hair. And the house was
filled with the fragrance of the perfume.
4But one of his disciples, Judas Iscariot, who was later to
betray him, objected, 5"Why wasn't this perfume sold and the
money given to the poor? It was worth a year's wages.[c]" 6He did
not say this because he cared about the poor but because he was a
thief; as keeper of the money bag, he used to help himself to what
was put into it.
7"Leave her alone," Jesus replied. "⌊It was intended⌋ that she
should save this perfume for the day of my burial. 8You will always
have the poor among you, but you will not always have me."
9Meanwhile a large crowd of Jews found out that Jesus was
there and came, not only because of him but also to see Lazarus,

[a] **48** Or *temple* [b] **3** Greek *a litra* (probably about 0.5 liter) [c] **5** Greek *three hundred denarii*

11:53 *plotted to take his life:* They probably hoped to arrest and kill Jesus during the time of the upcoming Passover Feast.

11:54 *Ephraim:* This village was probably north of Jerusalem on the border of the Judean desert toward the Jordan River.

11:55 *Passover:* See the mini-article called "Passover and the Feast of Unleavened Bread," p. 2030.

11:55 *ceremonial cleansing:* The Jewish people had to purify themselves with certain cleansing rituals in order to prepare to worship God and to celebrate the feast.

11:57 *chief priests and Pharisees:* See the notes at 1:24 and 7:32.

12:1,2 *Bethany . . . Lazarus . . . Martha:* See the notes at 11:1,2.

12:2 *reclining at the table:* See the note at 13:23 (reclining).

12:3 *pure nard, an expensive perfume:* This perfume was made from the spikenard plant. See the chart called "Spices and Perfumes," p. 1278. In ancient times perfumed ointment and oil were kept in sealed jars, which could be opened only by breaking the jar's neck.

12:4 *Judas Iscariot:* Judas was the disciple in charge of the money bag that was used to support Jesus and the disciples and to give to the poor. See also the note at 6:70,71.

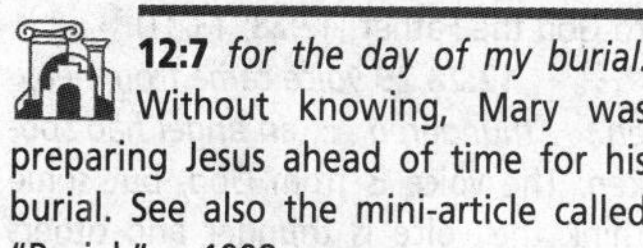

12:7 *for the day of my burial:* Without knowing, Mary was preparing Jesus ahead of time for his burial. See also the mini-article called "Burial," p. 1998.

12:8 Deut 15:11.

whom he had raised from the dead. [10]So the chief priests made
plans to kill Lazarus as well, [11]for on account of him many of the
Jews were going over to Jesus and putting their faith in him.

The Triumphal Entry

[12]The next day the great crowd that had come for the Feast
heard that Jesus was on his way to Jerusalem. [13]They took palm
branches and went out to meet him, shouting,

> "Hosanna![a]"
>
> "Blessed is he who comes in the name of the Lord!"[b]
>
> "Blessed is the King of Israel!"

[14]Jesus found a young donkey and sat upon it, as it is written,

> [15]"Do not be afraid, O Daughter of Zion;
> see, your king is coming,
> seated on a donkey's colt."[c]

[16]At first his disciples did not understand all this. Only after
Jesus was glorified did they realize that these things had been written about him and that they had done these things to him.
[17]Now the crowd that was with him when he called Lazarus
from the tomb and raised him from the dead continued to spread
the word. [18]Many people, because they had heard that he had given
this miraculous sign, went out to meet him. [19]So the Pharisees said
to one another, "See, this is getting us nowhere. Look how the
whole world has gone after him!"

Jesus Predicts His Death

[20]Now there were some Greeks among those who went up to
worship at the Feast. [21]They came to Philip, who was from Bethsaida in Galilee, with a request. "Sir," they said, "we would like to
see Jesus." [22]Philip went to tell Andrew; Andrew and Philip in turn
told Jesus.
[23]Jesus replied, "The hour has come for the Son of Man to
be glorified. [24]I tell you the truth, unless a kernel of wheat falls to
the ground and dies, it remains only a single seed. But if it dies, it
produces many seeds. [25]The man who loves his life will lose it,
while the man who hates his life in this world will keep it for eternal life. [26]Whoever serves me must follow me; and where I am, my
servant also will be. My Father will honor the one who serves me.
[27]"Now my heart is troubled, and what shall I say? 'Father,
save me from this hour'? No, it was for this very reason I came to
this hour. [28]Father, glorify your name!"

---

[a]**13** A Hebrew expression meaning "Save!" which became an exclamation of praise
[b]**13** Psalm 118:25,26 [c]**15** Zech. 9:9

12:10 *chief priests made plans to kill Lazarus:* See the note at 7:32. They wanted to kill Lazarus because he was living proof of Jesus' power (12:11).

12:12 *the Feast . . . Jerusalem:* The "Feast" (also in 12:20) refers to the Jewish Passover.

12:13 *palm branches:* In the ancient world, palm branches were regularly used to welcome visiting rulers or famous people.

12:14,15 *donkey's colt:* See Zechariah 9:9, which predicts the coming of Israel's Messianic king on a donkey. Roman leaders usually rode large horses when they entered a city in a parade.

12:16 *after Jesus was glorified:* See the note at 7:39 (glorified).

12:16 *these things had been written:* In the Jewish Scriptures, which Christians call the Old Testament.

12:19 *Pharisees:* See the note at 1:24.

12:20 *Greeks:* Perhaps Gentiles who worshiped with Jews; they were also known as "God-fearers".

12:21,22 *Philip . . . Andrew:* See the notes at 1:44,45 (Philip) and 1:40.

12:23 *the Son of Man to be glorified:* See the mini-article called "Son of Man," p. 1866, and the note at 7:39 (glorified).

12:25 *eternal life:* See the mini-article called "Eternal Life," p. 2072.

12:27 *for this very reason I came:* Jesus knows that he will fulfill God's purposes by suffering death on a cross. His death would also bring glory to God the Father (12:28; 13:31).

12:28,29 *voice came from heaven . . . thundered . . . an angel had spoken:* The voice is from God, but some think the voice is thunder and others think it is an angel. Thunder is linked with God's voice in the Bible (Exod 20:18; 1 Sam 7:9, Ps 29:3; 10; Rev 14:2).

Then a voice came from heaven, "I have glorified it, and will
glorify it again." 29 The crowd that was there and heard it said it had
thundered; others said an angel had spoken to him.
30 Jesus said, "This voice was for your benefit, not mine.
31 Now is the time for judgment on this world; now the prince of
this world will be driven out. 32 But I, when I am lifted up from the
earth, will draw all men to myself." 33 He said this to show the kind
of death he was going to die.
34 The crowd spoke up, "We have heard from the Law that the
Christ[a] will remain forever, so how can you say, 'The Son of Man
must be lifted up'? Who is this 'Son of Man'?"
35 Then Jesus told them, "You are going to have the light just
a little while longer. Walk while you have the light, before darkness
overtakes you. The man who walks in the dark does not know
where he is going. 36 Put your trust in the light while you have it, so
that you may become sons of light." When he had finished speaking, Jesus left and hid himself from them.

The Jews Continue in Their Unbelief

37 Even after Jesus had done all these miraculous signs in
their presence, they still would not believe in him. 38 This was to
fulfill the word of Isaiah the prophet:

"Lord, who has believed our message
and to whom has the arm of the Lord been
revealed?"[b]

39 For this reason they could not believe, because, as Isaiah
says elsewhere:

40 "He has blinded their eyes
and deadened their hearts,
so they can neither see with their eyes,
nor understand with their hearts,
nor turn—and I would heal them."[c]

41 Isaiah said this because he saw Jesus' glory and spoke about him.
42 Yet at the same time many even among the leaders believed
in him. But because of the Pharisees they would not confess their
faith for fear they would be put out of the synagogue; 43 for they
loved praise from men more than praise from God.
44 Then Jesus cried out, "When a man believes in me, he does
not believe in me only, but in the one who sent me. 45 When he
looks at me, he sees the one who sent me. 46 I have come into the
world as a light, so that no one who believes in me should stay in
darkness.

[a] **34** Or *Messiah* [b] **38** Isaiah 53:1 [c] **40** Isaiah 6:10

12:31 *prince of this world:* This is one of John's names for the devil, sometimes called Satan, who is the leader of the forces in the world that are against God and God's people (8:44; 14:30; 16:11). In JOHN, "world" sometimes refers to the people who live in this world and to the evil forces that seek to control their lives (see the note at 8:23).

12:32 *lifted up from the earth:* Jesus used these words to refer both to the time when he would be crucified (12:33) and when he would be raised from death and ascended to heaven.

12:34 *the Christ will remain forever:* No specific passage in the Jewish Scriptures says this, but the people may be referring to the promise that the family of King David would rule forever (2 Chron 21:7; Ps 89:36; Isa 9:7). See the note at 1:20 (the Christ). If Jesus was the Christ, the people didn't understand why he, the Son of Man, would have to be "lifted up," which here means put to death on a cross.

12:35,36 *light . . . darkness:* See the notes on p. 2041 (light and darkness) and at 1:7.

12:42 *Pharisees . . . put out of the synagogue:* The Pharisees (see the note at 1:24) were in charge of many of the Jewish synagogues. Some Jewish leaders had secretly put their faith in Jesus, but they were afraid to be open about this for fear that they would be thrown out of the synagogues by the Pharisees. See the notes at 6:59 and 9:22 (put out of the synagogue).

12:44 *When a man believes in me . . . in the one who sent me:* Jesus is saying that when people put their trust in him they are putting their trust in God. See also the mini-article called "Faith," p. 1932.

12:46 *light . . . darkness:* See the note at 12:35,36.

12:13 Ps 118:25, 26. **12:25** Matt 10:39; 16:25; Mark 8:35; Luke 9:24; 17:33. **12:34** Ps 110:4; Isa 9:7; Ezek 37:25; Dan 7:14. **12:38** Isa 53:1. **12:40** Isa 6:9,10.

47"As for the person who hears my words but does not keep
them, I do not judge him. For I did not come to judge the world,
but to save it. 48There is a judge for the one who rejects me and
does not accept my words; that very word which I spoke will condemn him at the last day. 49For I did not speak of my own accord,
but the Father who sent me commanded me what to say and how
to say it. 50I know that his command leads to eternal life. So whatever I say is just what the Father has told me to say."

JESUS PREPARES HIS FOLLOWERS

Jesus Washes His Disciples' Feet

13 It was just before the Passover Feast. Jesus knew that the time
had come for him to leave this world and go to the Father. Having
loved his own who were in the world, he now showed them the full
extent of his love.[a]

2The evening meal was being served, and the devil had
already prompted Judas Iscariot, son of Simon, to betray Jesus.
3Jesus knew that the Father had put all things under his power, and
that he had come from God and was returning to God; 4so he got
up from the meal, took off his outer clothing, and wrapped a towel
around his waist. 5After that, he poured water into a basin and
began to wash his disciples' feet, drying them with the towel that
was wrapped around him.

6He came to Simon Peter, who said to him, "Lord, are you
going to wash my feet?"

7Jesus replied, "You do not realize now what I am doing, but
later you will understand."

8"No," said Peter, "you shall never wash my feet."

Jesus answered, "Unless I wash you, you have no part with me."

9"Then, Lord," Simon Peter replied, "not just my feet but my
hands and my head as well!"

10Jesus answered, "A person who has had a bath needs only
to wash his feet; his whole body is clean. And you are clean, though
not every one of you." 11For he knew who was going to betray him,
and that was why he said not every one was clean.

12When he had finished washing their feet, he put on his
clothes and returned to his place. "Do you understand what I have
done for you?" he asked them. 13"You call me 'Teacher' and 'Lord,'
and rightly so, for that is what I am. 14Now that I, your Lord and
Teacher, have washed your feet, you also should wash one another's
feet. 15I have set you an example that you should do as I have done
for you. 16I tell you the truth, no servant is greater than his master,
nor is a messenger greater than the one who sent him. 17Now that
you know these things, you will be blessed if you do them.

[a] 1 Or *he loved them to the last*

12:48 *condemn him at the last day:* See the note at 6:39.

12:50 *eternal life:* See the mini-article called "Eternal Life," p. 2072.

13:1 *before the Passover Feast:* See the note at 2:13. It is not clear just how long before the Passover this is. In the other Gospels, Jesus' last supper with the disciples is the Passover meal (see Mark 14:12, for example).

13:2 *devil had already prompted Judas Iscariot:* See the note at 8:44; the mini-article called "Satan," p. 963; and the notes at 6:70,71, and 12:4. For more about Judas, see Mark 14:10,11 and Luke 22:3-6.

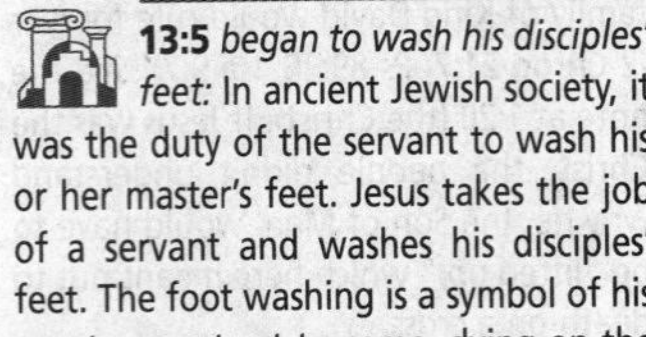

13:5 *began to wash his disciples' feet:* In ancient Jewish society, it was the duty of the servant to wash his or her master's feet. Jesus takes the job of a servant and washes his disciples' feet. The foot washing is a symbol of his great servant act to come, dying on the cross for the sins of the world.

13:6 *Simon Peter:* See the note at 1:42. Peter's argument (13:8) is understandable, since Jesus was the master.

13:11 *not every one was clean:* Jesus was talking about Judas (13:2).

13:13 *Lord:* The Greek word for "Lord" is *kyrios,* which may mean master or may be used to address someone as "sir." When it is used for Jesus, it emphasizes his authority and power. See also the note at 20:28 and the mini-article called "Lord (Title for Jesus)," p. 2106.

13:12-15 Luke 22:27. **13:16** Matt 10:24; Luke 6:40; John 15:20.

Jesus Predicts His Betrayal

[18]"I am not referring to all of you; I know those I have chosen. But this is to fulfill the scripture: 'He who shares my bread has lifted up his heel against me.'[a]

[19]"I am telling you now before it happens, so that when it does happen you will believe that I am He. [20]I tell you the truth, whoever accepts anyone I send accepts me; and whoever accepts me accepts the one who sent me."

[21]After he had said this, Jesus was troubled in spirit and testified, "I tell you the truth, one of you is going to betray me."

[22]His disciples stared at one another, at a loss to know which of them he meant. [23]One of them, the disciple whom Jesus loved, was reclining next to him. [24]Simon Peter motioned to this disciple and said, "Ask him which one he means."

[a] **18** Psalm 41:9

Washing the Feet by Jyoti Sahi, twentieth century. At Jesus' last supper with his disciples, he removed his outer garment, wrapped a towel around his waist, and began washing his disciples' feet. When he was finished he explained to them, "Now that I, your Lord and Teacher, have washed your feet, you also should wash one another's feet. I have set you an example that you should do as I have done for you." (See 13:1-17.)

Jesus knew that the time had come for him to leave this world and go to the Father. Having loved his own who were in the world, he now showed them the full extent of his love. John 13:1

13:18 *shares my bread . . . lifted up his heel:* Sharing a meal with another was an indication of a deep bond of fellowship in the ancient world. To lift up one's heel against someone suggests betrayal, perhaps in the manner that a domestic animal might strike its owner when its hoofs are being scraped.

13:19 *I am he:* See the note at 8:24.

13:21 *one of you is going to betray me:* See the notes at 13:2 and 13:11.

13:23 *the disciple whom Jesus loved:* In John, one disciple is singled out in this way (19:26; 20:2). Although the identity of this disciple is never expressly stated, it traditionally has been assumed that this is John, the author of this Gospel. Obviously, this expression doesn't mean that Jesus didn't love the other disciples, but rather that there was a special bond between Jesus and this individual. See also the note at 21:24.

13:23 *reclining:* On special occasions the Jewish people followed the Greek and Roman custom of lying down on their side and leaning on their left elbow, while eating with their right hand.

13:18 Ps 41:9. **13:20** Matt 10:40; Mark 9:37; Luke 9:48; 10:16.

Jesus said to his disciples, *"A new command I give you: Love one another."* John 13:34

13:26,27 *Judas . . . Satan:* See the note at 13:2.

13:29 *the Feast:* The Feast of Passover (see the note at 2:13).

13:30 *it was night:* See the note on p. 2041 (light and darkness).

13:31 *Son of Man glorified:* See the notes at 12:23 and 12:27.

13:34 *new command . . . so you must love one another:* Jesus' love for his followers is to be the standard for how they will love one another (15:12,17; 1 John 3:23; 2 John 5).

13:36 *Simon Peter:* See the note at 1:42.

13:38 *before the rooster crows:* Since roosters crowed at dawn, Jesus is saying that Peter will deny that he knows Jesus three times before the next sunrise.

14:2 *In my Father's house are many rooms:* Jesus is talking about heaven. See the mini-article called "Heaven," p. 1420.

14:5 *Thomas:* See the note at 11:16.

14:6 *I am the way and the truth and the life:* See the note at 6:35 (I am). Jesus here claims that he is the "way" people can learn the "truth" about God and find "life" with God. See the mini-articles called "I Am," on the next page, and "Truth" on p. 2087.

13:29 John 12:6. **13:33** John 7:34.

[25]Leaning back against Jesus, he asked him, "Lord, who is it?"
[26]Jesus answered, "It is the one to whom I will give this piece of bread when I have dipped it in the dish." Then, dipping the piece of bread, he gave it to Judas Iscariot, son of Simon. [27]As soon as Judas took the bread, Satan entered into him.

"What you are about to do, do quickly," Jesus told him, [28]but no one at the meal understood why Jesus said this to him. [29]Since Judas had charge of the money, some thought Jesus was telling him to buy what was needed for the Feast, or to give something to the poor. [30]As soon as Judas had taken the bread, he went out. And it was night.

Jesus Predicts Peter's Denial

[31]When he was gone, Jesus said, "Now is the Son of Man glorified and God is glorified in him. [32]If God is glorified in him,[a] God will glorify the Son in himself, and will glorify him at once.

[33]"My children, I will be with you only a little longer. You will look for me, and just as I told the Jews, so I tell you now: Where I am going, you cannot come.

[34]"A new command I give you: Love one another. As I have loved you, so you must love one another. [35]By this all men will know that you are my disciples, if you love one another."

[36]Simon Peter asked him, "Lord, where are you going?"

Jesus replied, "Where I am going, you cannot follow now, but you will follow later."

[37]Peter asked, "Lord, why can't I follow you now? I will lay down my life for you."

[38]Then Jesus answered, "Will you really lay down your life for me? I tell you the truth, before the rooster crows, you will disown me three times!

Jesus Comforts His Disciples

14 "Do not let your hearts be troubled. Trust in God[b] ; trust also in me. [2]In my Father's house are many rooms; if it were not so, I would have told you. I am going there to prepare a place for you. [3]And if I go and prepare a place for you, I will come back and take you to be with me that you also may be where I am. [4]You know the way to the place where I am going."

Jesus the Way to the Father

[5]Thomas said to him, "Lord, we don't know where you are going, so how can we know the way?"

[6]Jesus answered, "I am the way and the truth and the life. No one comes to the Father except through me. [7]If you really knew

[a] **32** Many early manuscripts do not have *If God is glorified in him.* [b] **1** Or *You trust in God*

me, you would know[a] my Father as well. From now on, you do
know him and have seen him."
8Philip said, "Lord, show us the Father and that will be
enough for us."
9Jesus answered: "Don't you know me, Philip, even after I have
been among you such a long time? Anyone who has seen me has seen
the Father. How can you say, 'Show us the Father'? 10Don't you
believe that I am in the Father, and that the Father is in me? The
words I say to you are not just my own. Rather, it is the Father, living
in me, who is doing his work. 11Believe me when I say that I am in the
Father and the Father is in me; or at least believe on the evidence of
the miracles themselves. 12I tell you the truth, anyone who has faith in
me will do what I have been doing. He will do even greater things
than these, because I am going to the Father. 13And I will do whatever you ask in my name, so that the Son may bring glory to the
Father. 14You may ask me for anything in my name, and I will do it.

Jesus Promises the Holy Spirit

15"If you love me, you will obey what I command. 16And I
will ask the Father, and he will give you another Counselor to be
with you forever— 17the Spirit of truth. The world cannot accept
him, because it neither sees him nor knows him. But you know

[a] 7 Some early manuscripts *If you really have known me, you will know*

14:8 *Philip:* See the note at 1:44,45 (Philip).

14:9,10 *Father:* See the note at 5:17.

14:11 *believe on the evidence of the miracles:* See the note at 2:11.

14:12 *even greater things than these:* Jesus is saying that Philip and the other disciples will be able to preach the good news and work miracles (14:12) because of the gift of the Holy Spirit (14:16).

14:16,17 *Counselor . . . the Spirit of truth:* Jesus uses a legal term to describe the Holy Spirit. It refers to an advocate who helps someone accused of breaking the law. The Holy Spirit stands up for Jesus' followers as their counselor, helper, and defender. "Spirit of truth" is another way that Jesus refers to the Holy Spirit. The fundamental nature of the Holy Spirit is truth. People are brought to God's truth by the work of the Holy Spirit. See the mini-article called "Holy Spirit," p. 2082, and "Truth," p. 2087.

I AM

When God commanded Moses to lead Israel out of slavery in Egypt into the promised land (Canaan), God had declared, "I am the God of your father, the God of Abraham, the God of Isaac and the God of Jacob" (Exod 3:1-6). When Moses asked what God's name was, God replied, "I AM WHO I AM" (Exod 3:13-15).

The Hebrew name *Yahweh* is most likely related to the Hebrew verb "to be" and so may mean "I am the one who is" or "I will be what I will be" or "I am the one who causes to be." These possible meanings of the sacred name show that Yahweh is the God who *is, will be, and causes to be*. Yahweh, God, is the source of all that is and will fulfill his purpose for the people of God and for the whole creation.

In JOHN, Jesus uses the term "I am" to proclaim his divinity. He connects himself to these aspects of God's nature and with God's eternal existence, and he also describes the work God has given him to do. Jesus identifies himself as the one who supplies all needs ("I am the bread of life," John 6:35) and who brings the knowledge about God to people ("I am the light of the world," John 8:12). Jesus also uses this "*I am*" language to identify himself as the way for people to find God and become God's people ("I am the gate for the sheep," John 10:7-16; and "I am the way and the truth and the life," John 14:6). Using imagery from ISAIAH, Jesus says "I am the true vine" and that his people are "the branches," sharing in the common life of the new people of God (John 15:1,5; see also Isa 5:1-7). By making these comparisons to the Jewish Scriptures, Jesus shows that he has always existed as the Son of God and has been in God's plan from the beginning: "Before Abraham was born, I am!" (John 8:58).

HOLY SPIRIT

The Christian church believes that the Bible asserts that one God eternally exists in three persons. Christians are more familiar with the Father and the Son, but the Bible also contains a wealth of teaching about the Holy Spirit. The Holy Spirit represents the presence of God at work in the world. The Jewish Scriptures (Old Testament) declare that the Spirit of God was at work in the creation of the world (Gen 1:2), giving life to plants, animals, and humans (Ps 104:27-30). The leaders of Israel were given power and direction by the Spirit, including Moses and the seventy-two leaders chosen to help him (Num 11:24-30), Gideon (Judg 6:34), and Kings Saul and David (1 Sam 10:6-13; 11:6; 16:13; 2 Sam 23:1-4). The prophets were guided by the Spirit of God and given messages for the people (Isa 61:1; Ezek 2:2; 3:12-27; Mic 3:8; Zech 7:12).

The LORD promised to give his Spirit and message to his people so that they would become eager to obey his law and teachings (Isa 59:21; Ezek 36:24-29). The prophet Isaiah reminded the people that it was by the Spirit that God guided the history of Israel from the beginning (Isa 63:10-14). If God's people disobey the Spirit, they will be punished (Isa 63:10), but when they follow the Spirit, their lives and hearts will be transformed and purified (Ezek 36:26, 27). And ultimately, their hope for the future is that God's Spirit will renew them and their relationship with God (Isa 44:3-5; Ezek 11:19, 20), and send them a new ruler filled with wisdom and justice (Isa 11:2-5).

For the writers of the New Testament, Jesus is seen as the one who fulfills the vision that inspired the prophets. LUKE reports that an angel told Mary that the Holy Spirit would come upon her, and God's power would overshadow her and that her holy child, Jesus, would be called the Son of God (Luke 1:35). Jesus' relationship with God is again emphasized at his baptism when "the Holy Spirit descended on him in bodily form like a dove" (Luke 3:22). Jesus' baptism clearly involves the Father, the Son, and the Holy Spirit. At the beginning of his ministry Jesus read a passage from ISAIAH and declared that the Spirit of the Lord had come on him and had anointed him to preach the good news to the poor (Luke 4:16-19). Although Jesus' enemies accused him of having an evil spirit (Mark 3:28-30), Jesus claimed that it was by God's Spirit, not by Satan, that he was able to drive out demons (Matt 12:28). MATTHEW also claimed that Jesus was the chosen servant who the prophet Isaiah had said would be given the Spirit of God and would bring justice to the nations (Matt 12:15-21; see also Isa 42:1-4).

In JOHN, Jesus tells his disciples he will send the Holy Spirit to help them; to teach them everything and remind them of what Jesus had already taught them; to show them what is true; and to guide them into all truth (John 14:15-17,25,26; 15:26; 16:4-15).

After Jesus died and was raised to life, he spent forty days with his apostles. He told them that they would be baptized with the Holy Spirit (Acts 1:3-5) and that the Spirit would give them the power to be Jesus' witnesses "to the ends of the earth" (Acts 1:8). Then, on the day of Pentecost, the Spirit came to the apostles who were gathered in Jerusalem (Acts 2:1-12). ACTS goes on to tell of the many ways the Holy Spirit guided and strengthened the apostles as they took the good news about Jesus to other lands and people (for example, see Acts 4:8,31; 6:3-5; 8:29; 13:2-12; 20:22-28).

For Paul, it is the Spirit who sets free God's new people and who changes their lives so that they can have peace and be obedient to God (Rom 8:1-17). The Spirit gives them the ability to understand God's will, to live together in love, to see what the future will bring, and to carry out the different kinds of work that need to be done in the churches (1 Cor 12–14). The Spirit produces within them the love and the lifestyle that God wants for his people (Rom 8:9-13; Gal 5:22,23).

him, for he lives with you and will be[a] in you. [18]I will not leave you as orphans; I will come to you. [19]Before long, the world will not see me anymore, but you will see me. Because I live, you also will live. [20]On that day you will realize that I am in my Father, and you are in me, and I am in you. [21]Whoever has my commands and obeys them, he is the one who loves me. He who loves me will be loved by my Father, and I too will love him and show myself to him."

[22]Then Judas (not Judas Iscariot) said, "But, Lord, why do you intend to show yourself to us and not to the world?"

[23]Jesus replied, "If anyone loves me, he will obey my teaching. My Father will love him, and we will come to him and make our home with him. [24]He who does not love me will not obey my teaching. These words you hear are not my own; they belong to the Father who sent me.

[25]"All this I have spoken while still with you. [26]But the Counselor, the Holy Spirit, whom the Father will send in my name, will teach you all things and will remind you of everything I have said to you. [27]Peace I leave with you; my peace I give you. I do not give to you as the world gives. Do not let your hearts be troubled and do not be afraid.

[28]"You heard me say, 'I am going away and I am coming back to you.' If you loved me, you would be glad that I am going to the Father, for the Father is greater than I. [29]I have told you now before it happens, so that when it does happen you will believe. [30]I will not speak with you much longer, for the prince of this world is coming. He has no hold on me, [31]but the world must learn that I love the Father and that I do exactly what my Father has commanded me.

"Come now; let us leave.

The Vine and the Branches

15 "I am the true vine, and my Father is the gardener. [2]He cuts off every branch in me that bears no fruit, while every branch that does bear fruit he prunes[b] so that it will be even more fruitful. [3]You are already clean because of the word I have spoken to you. [4]Remain in me, and I will remain in you. No branch can bear fruit by itself; it must remain in the vine. Neither can you bear fruit unless you remain in me.

[5]"I am the vine; you are the branches. If a man remains in me and I in him, he will bear much fruit; apart from me you can do nothing. [6]If anyone does not remain in me, he is like a branch that is thrown away and withers; such branches are picked up, thrown into the fire and burned. [7]If you remain in me and my

[a] **17** Some early manuscripts *and is* [b] **2** The Greek for *prunes* also means *cleans.*

14:22 *Judas (not Judas Iscariot):* This Judas is "Judas son of James," mentioned in Luke 6:16 and Acts 1:13.

14:26 *Counselor:* See the note at 14:16,17.

14:27 *Peace . . . my peace:* The peace that Jesus gives is more than simple contentment or the absence of conflict. It is complete well-being and wholeness of mind, body, and spirit.

14:28 *I am going to the Father:* Jesus is talking about going back to heaven to rule beside God the Father (Luke 24:50,51).

14:30 *prince of this world is coming:* To influence the people who would take Jesus' life. See the note at 12:31.

15:1,2 *I am the true vine:* See the note at 6:35 (I am). Jesus says that he is the main vine of the plant, which produces many smaller branches. A farmer who takes care of fruit-bearing vines needs to trim away branches that are not giving fruit. If the vine is not pruned, the plant won't produce as much fruit. Only those branches that stay connected to the vine (Jesus) can produce fruit (15:5). The kind of "fruit" Jesus wants his followers to produce is based on loving God and other people. God's people, Israel, are sometimes pictured in the Jewish Scriptures as a vineyard that did not produce the kind of grapes the owner expected (Isa 5:1-7).

words remain in you, ask whatever you wish, and it will be given
you. 8This is to my Father's glory, that you bear much fruit, showing yourselves to be my disciples.
9"As the Father has loved me, so have I loved you. Now
remain in my love. 10If you obey my commands, you will remain
in my love, just as I have obeyed my Father's commands and
remain in his love. 11I have told you this so that my joy may be in
you and that your joy may be complete. 12My command is this:
Love each other as I have loved you. 13Greater love has no one than
this, that he lay down his life for his friends. 14You are my friends
if you do what I command. 15I no longer call you servants, because
a servant does not know his master's business. Instead, I have
called you friends, for everything that I learned from my Father I
have made known to you. 16You did not choose me, but I chose
you and appointed you to go and bear fruit—fruit that will last.
Then the Father will give you whatever you ask in my name. 17This
is my command: Love each other.

The World Hates the Disciples

18"If the world hates you, keep in mind that it hated me first.
19If you belonged to the world, it would love you as its own. As it
is, you do not belong to the world, but I have chosen you out of
the world. That is why the world hates you. 20Remember the words
I spoke to you: 'No servant is greater than his master.'[a] If they persecuted me, they will persecute you also. If they obeyed my teaching, they will obey yours also. 21They will treat you this way
because of my name, for they do not know the One who sent me.
22If I had not come and spoken to them, they would not be guilty
of sin. Now, however, they have no excuse for their sin. 23He who
hates me hates my Father as well. 24If I had not done among them
what no one else did, they would not be guilty of sin. But now they
have seen these miracles, and yet they have hated both me and my
Father. 25But this is to fulfill what is written in their Law: 'They
hated me without reason.'[b]
26"When the Counselor comes, whom I will send to you
from the Father, the Spirit of truth who goes out from the Father,
he will testify about me. 27And you also must testify, for you have
been with me from the beginning.
16 "All this I have told you so that you will not go astray. 2They
will put you out of the synagogue; in fact, a time is coming when
anyone who kills you will think he is offering a service to God.
3They will do such things because they have not known the Father
or me. 4I have told you this, so that when the time comes you will
remember that I warned you. I did not tell you this at first because
I was with you.

[a] 20 John 13:16 [b] 25 Psalms 35:19; 69:4

15:8 *bear much fruit:* See the note at 15:1,2.

15:15 *servants . . . friends:* The word in the New Testament usually translated as "servant" actually means a slave who was owned or controlled by someone else, not a servant hired to do a certain job. Slaves or servants were not considered to be equal to their masters, and masters would not have talked with them as equals, the way two friends would talk together. See also the mini-article called "Slaves and Servants in the Time of Jesus," p. 2006.

15:16 *bear fruit—fruit that will last:* See the note at 15:1,2.

15:18 *world:* See the notes at 8:23 and 12:31.

15:21 *They will treat you this way because of my name:* Jesus is saying that some people of the "world" who are not followers of Jesus will treat Jesus' followers badly. Some of Jesus' followers will be persecuted and even put to death, just as Jesus was (15:20; 16:2).

15:22 *sin:* See the note at 5:14. Jesus came to offer all people a chance to turn to God and believe the truth. Many chose not to believe in Jesus' new message.

15:24 *they have seen these miracles:* See the note at 2:11.

15:26 *Counselor . . . the Spirit of truth:* See the note at 14:16,17.

16:2 *put you out of the synagogue:* See the notes at 9:22 (put out) and 12:42.

15:12 John 13:34; 15:17; 1 John 3:23; 2 John 5. **15:20** Matt 10:24; Luke 6:40; John 13:16. **15:25** Ps 35:19; 69:4.

The Work of the Holy Spirit

[5]"Now I am going to him who sent me, yet none of you asks
me, 'Where are you going?' [6]Because I have said these things, you
are filled with grief. [7]But I tell you the truth: It is for your good
that I am going away. Unless I go away, the Counselor will not
come to you; but if I go, I will send him to you. [8]When he comes,
he will convict the world of guilt[a] in regard to sin and righteousness and judgment: [9]in regard to sin, because men do not believe
in me; [10]in regard to righteousness, because I am going to the
Father, where you can see me no longer; [11]and in regard to judgment, because the prince of this world now stands condemned.
[12]"I have much more to say to you, more than you can now
bear. [13]But when he, the Spirit of truth, comes, he will guide you
into all truth. He will not speak on his own; he will speak only what
he hears, and he will tell you what is yet to come. [14]He will bring
glory to me by taking from what is mine and making it known to
you. [15]All that belongs to the Father is mine. That is why I said the
Spirit will take from what is mine and make it known to you.
[16]"In a little while you will see me no more, and then after a
little while you will see me."

The Disciples' Grief Will Turn to Joy

[17]Some of his disciples said to one another, "What does he
mean by saying, 'In a little while you will see me no more, and
then after a little while you will see me,' and 'Because I am going to
the Father'?" [18]They kept asking, "What does he mean by 'a little
while'? We don't understand what he is saying."
[19]Jesus saw that they wanted to ask him about this, so he said
to them, "Are you asking one another what I meant when I said, 'In
a little while you will see me no more, and then after a little while
you will see me'? [20]I tell you the truth, you will weep and mourn
while the world rejoices. You will grieve, but your grief will turn to
joy. [21]A woman giving birth to a child has pain because her time
has come; but when her baby is born she forgets the anguish
because of her joy that a child is born into the world. [22]So with
you: Now is your time of grief, but I will see you again and you
will rejoice, and no one will take away your joy. [23]In that day you
will no longer ask me anything. I tell you the truth, my Father will
give you whatever you ask in my name. [24]Until now you have not
asked for anything in my name. Ask and you will receive, and your
joy will be complete.
[25]"Though I have been speaking figuratively, a time is coming
when I will no longer use this kind of language but will tell you
plainly about my Father. [26]In that day you will ask in my name. I am
not saying that I will ask the Father on your behalf. [27]No, the Father

[a] **8** Or *will expose the guilt of the world*

Jesus told his disciples, *"It is for your good that I am going away. Unless I go away, the Counselor will not come to you; but if I go, I will send him to you."*
John 16:7

16:5 *I am going to him who sent me:* See the note at 14:28.

16:7 *Counselor:* See the note at 14:16,17. The Holy Spirit will show how wrong the world is about sin and reveal the right way to live (16:8). The Spirit teaches the truth about God and God's purposes.

16:8 *convict the world of guilt in regard to sin and righteousness and judgment:* Many believed that the laws and rules based on the Law of Moses were the whole truth about the righteousness God expected of God's people. Jesus made it clear that some had missed the true message of the Law and misunderstood what God expected. God's righteousness was meant for all people, not just a chosen few from Israel. Those who did not believe Jesus would have to face God's judgment.

16:11 *prince of this world:* See the note at 12:31.

16:13 *the Spirit of truth:* See the note at 14:16,17.

16:20 *you will weep and mourn while the world rejoices:* Jesus was talking about the sadness and fear his followers would feel when he was put to death on a cross (19:17-30). This sadness would be severe, like the pain a woman feels before she gives birth to a baby (16:21). However, those who do not have faith in Jesus ("the world"), will be happy to get rid of him.

16:7 Luke 24:47-49; Acts 1:4,5.

himself loves you because you have loved me and have believed that I came from God. [28]I came from the Father and entered the world; now I am leaving the world and going back to the Father."

[29]Then Jesus' disciples said, "Now you are speaking clearly and without figures of speech. [30]Now we can see that you know all things and that you do not even need to have anyone ask you questions. This makes us believe that you came from God."

[31]"You believe at last!"[a] Jesus answered. [32]"But a time is coming, and has come, when you will be scattered, each to his own home. You will leave me all alone. Yet I am not alone, for my Father is with me.

[33]"I have told you these things, so that in me you may have peace. In this world you will have trouble. But take heart! I have overcome the world."

Jesus Prays for Himself

17 After Jesus said this, he looked toward heaven and prayed:

"Father, the time has come. Glorify your Son, that your Son may glorify you. [2]For you granted him authority over all people that he might give eternal life to all those you have given him. [3]Now this is eternal life: that they may know you, the only true God, and Jesus Christ, whom you have sent. [4]I have brought you glory on earth by completing the work you gave me to do. [5]And now, Father, glorify me in your presence with the glory I had with you before the world began.

Jesus Prays for His Disciples

[6]"I have revealed you[b] to those whom you gave me out of the world. They were yours; you gave them to me and they have obeyed your word. [7]Now they know that everything you have given me comes from you. [8]For I gave them the words you gave me and they accepted them. They knew with certainty that I came from you, and they believed that you sent me. [9]I pray for them. I am not praying for the world, but for those you have given me, for they are yours. [10]All I have is yours, and all you have is mine. And glory has come to me through them. [11]I will remain in the world no longer, but they are still in the world, and I am coming to you. Holy Father, protect them by the power of your name—the name you gave me—so that they may be one as we are one. [12]While I was with them, I protected them and kept them safe by that name you gave

[a] **31** Or *"Do you now believe?"* [b] **6** Greek *your name*; also in verse 26

Jesus said, *"I have told you these things, so that in me you may have peace. In this world you will have trouble. But take heart! I have overcome the world."*
John 16:33

16:32 *you will be scattered . . . You will leave me all alone:* Even though the disciples said they knew who Jesus really was, his trial and death would test their courage and faith. Jesus tells them that they will not, at first, stand by him in his suffering (18:15-27; Mark 14:50,51).

16:33 *I have overcome the world:* See the notes at 8:23 and 12:31.

17:1 *the time has come. Glorify your Son:* See the notes at 2:4 and 7:39 (glorified).

17:2 *eternal life:* See the mini-article called "Eternal Life," p. 2072.

17:5 *before the world began:* See the note at 1:1-3.

17:9 *I am not praying for the world:* See the note at 12:31.

16:28 John 1:1-3; 13:3; 14:28.

me. None has been lost except the one doomed to
destruction so that Scripture would be fulfilled.
13"I am coming to you now, but I say these things
while I am still in the world, so that they may have the
full measure of my joy within them. 14I have given them
your word and the world has hated them, for they are
not of the world any more than I am of the world. 15My
prayer is not that you take them out of the world but
that you protect them from the evil one. 16They are not
of the world, even as I am not of it. 17Sanctify[a] them by
the truth; your word is truth. 18As you sent me into the
world, I have sent them into the world. 19For them I
sanctify myself, that they too may be truly sanctified.

[a] 17 Greek *hagiazo (set apart for sacred use* or *make holy)*; also in verse 19

17:12 *the one doomed to destruction:* Jesus was talking about Judas Iscariot. See the notes at 6:70,71 and 13:2.

17:15 *the evil one:* Satan (the devil). See the notes at 8:44 and 12:31; and the mini-article called "Satan," p. 963.

17:17 *Sanctify them by the truth; your word is truth:* Sanctification, or holiness, comes by the truth of God's word. See also the mini-articles called "Truth," (below), and "Holiness," p. 1626.

17:12 Ps 41:9; John 13:18.

TRUTH

In the Bible, truth refers to what is dependable, tested, and trustworthy. It is firm and never changes. This contrasts with some Greek philosophies, where truth is an idea or a principle that exists apart from the physical world that gets old and decays. Truth in the Bible is based on God's unchanging purpose for the world and all the people God created. The proper response to the truth of God, therefore, is trust in God's promises.

Trust is the basis for the special relationship between God and people throughout human history. Abraham trusted God's promises (Gen 15:6). Jacob gave thanks for the ongoing love and faithfulness that God showed him in spite of his disobedience (Gen 32:9-12). Moses praised God on Mount Sinai because God's love was continuing through each generation of his people (Exod 34:8,9). God is always faithful, and God's promises and plans are true and trustworthy (Deut 32:3,4). Just as plants always grow and the sun and stars always shine, so God's love and promises are forever dependable (Ps 85:10,11).

In the New Testament, Jesus claimed that the prophet Isaiah's words were coming true because of the work the Spirit had anointed Jesus to do (Luke 4:16-21). In his teaching, Jesus frequently used the Hebrew word *amen* (translated in the NIV, "I tell you *the truth*") to emphasize that what he says about God's will for his people is completely true and reliable (Matthew 5:18; 6:2; 8:10; 18:18; 19:23; 24:2; 25:12). Jesus tells his disciples that his death on a cross and his resurrection fulfill promises recorded in the Jewish Scriptures, and so are surely true (Luke 24:27, 45-47).

In JOHN, Jesus is the true light (John 1:9) who brings God's true word. He is also the true bread (John 6:32), the true vine (John 15:1), and the true way to God (John 14:6), who brings the Spirit of truth (John 16:13). And Jesus is the truth of God (John 14:6). His people live by the actions and promises of God, and as a result, they are the people of truth (John 18:37) who hear and trust him as the living word of God.

In the later letters of the New Testament, truth comes to be understood in the more usual modern sense—as what is correct, in contrast to what is false. There are warnings against false teaching (1 Tim 1:3, 4; 2 Tim 2:16-18) and against those who are enemies of the truth (2 Tim 3:6-9) and who tell senseless stories (Titus 1:10-14). These letters say the church should fight for the true faith (1 Tim 6:11-21) and should see itself as "the pillar and foundation of the truth" (1 Tim 3:14,15), which here means "right belief."

17:23 *let the world know that you sent me:* Jesus prays that his followers will be one with God and one with each other. The unity that Jesus' followers show will help convince the world (unbelievers) that Jesus really did come from God.

17:24 *loved me before the creation of the world:* See the note at 1:1-3.

18:1 *Kidron Valley:* This valley runs just east of the temple mount in Jerusalem. Across the Kidron Valley to the east is a high hill known as the Mount of Olives. Near the bottom of that slope was a grove of olive trees, which other Gospels call Gethsemane (Matt 26:36; Mark 14:32). See the map on p. 2474.

This hill is where the prophet Zechariah said God would appear and defeat his enemies (Zech 14:1-4). It is in this place that Jesus' enemies arrest him.

18:2 *Judas . . . his disciples:* For more about Judas, see the notes at 6:70,71 and 12:4. For more about "disciples," see the note at 6:67.

18:3-5 *a detachment of soldiers . . . chief priests and Pharisees . . . Jesus of Nazareth:* Roman soldiers were stationed in the Fortress Antonia near the temple. They were in charge of keeping order in the city. The chief priests and Pharisees may have persuaded the Roman soldiers to make the arrest by saying that Jesus was a dangerous rebel. The "officials" who accompanied them were likely temple guards. See the notes at 1:24 and 7:32.

18:5 *Jesus of Nazareth:* Jesus was often identified by adding his hometown (Nazareth) to his name, since there were probably many Jewish men named Jesus at the time he lived.

18:5 *I am he:* See the mini-article called "I Am," p. 2081. Jesus' use of these divine words inspired a reverential response (they "fell to the ground") from his opponents.

Jesus Prays for All Believers

20 "My prayer is not for them alone. I pray also
for those who will believe in me through their message, 21 that all of them may be one, Father, just as you
are in me and I am in you. May they also be in us so
that the world may believe that you have sent me. 22 I
have given them the glory that you gave me, that they
may be one as we are one: 23 I in them and you in me.
May they be brought to complete unity to let the
world know that you sent me and have loved them
even as you have loved me.

24 "Father, I want those you have given me to be
with me where I am, and to see my glory, the glory
you have given me because you loved me before the
creation of the world.

25 "Righteous Father, though the world does not
know you, I know you, and they know that you have
sent me. 26 I have made you known to them, and will
continue to make you known in order that the love
you have for me may be in them and that I myself may
be in them."

JESUS' ARREST, TRIAL, AND DEATH ON A CROSS

The action in the next two chapters takes place in less than 24 hours. Shortly after Jesus is finished praying for his disciples he is arrested and brought to trial. The Roman governor, Pontius Pilate, sentences Jesus to be crucified in order to keep the crowd from starting a riot. Jesus' death comes quickly as he completes the work God has sent him to do.

Jesus Arrested

18 When he had finished praying, Jesus left with his disciples and
crossed the Kidron Valley. On the other side there was an olive
grove, and he and his disciples went into it.

2 Now Judas, who betrayed him, knew the place, because
Jesus had often met there with his disciples. 3 So Judas came to the
grove, guiding a detachment of soldiers and some officials from
the chief priests and Pharisees. They were carrying torches,
lanterns and weapons.

4 Jesus, knowing all that was going to happen to him, went
out and asked them, "Who is it you want?"

5 "Jesus of Nazareth," they replied.

"I am he," Jesus said. (And Judas the traitor was standing
there with them.) 6 When Jesus said, "I am he," they drew back and
fell to the ground.

7Again he asked them, "Who is it you want?"
And they said, "Jesus of Nazareth."
8"I told you that I am he," Jesus answered. "If you are looking for me, then let these men go." 9This happened so that the
words he had spoken would be fulfilled: "I have not lost one of
those you gave me."[a]
10Then Simon Peter, who had a sword, drew it and struck the
high priest's servant, cutting off his right ear. (The servant's name
was Malchus.)
11Jesus commanded Peter, "Put your sword away! Shall I not
drink the cup the Father has given me?"

Jesus Taken to Annas

12Then the detachment of soldiers with its commander and
the Jewish officials arrested Jesus. They bound him 13and brought
him first to Annas, who was the father-in-law of Caiaphas, the

[a] 9 John 6:39

St. Peter Cuts Off Malchus's Ear, a painted ceiling panel from St. Martin's Church, Zillis, Switzerland, twelfth century. After praying for his disciples, Jesus went with them to a garden. Judas knew where they would be and brought Roman soldiers and temple police to arrest Jesus. Although Jesus let himself be arrested, Simon Peter reacted by cutting off the right ear of the servant of the high priest. But Jesus told Peter, "Put your sword away! Shall I not drink the cup the Father has given me?" (See 18:1-11.)

18:10 *Simon Peter . . . Malchus:* See the note at 1:42. The sword that Peter used to strike the high priest's servant was actually a dagger, which is like a short, straight sword.

The name Malchus means "king." He may have come from Nabatea. He served Caiaphas, the high priest, but his exact position is not known.

18:11 *Shall I not drink the cup:* In the Scriptures a cup is sometimes used as a symbol of suffering (Isa 51:17; Jer 25:15; Rev 14:10; 16:19). To "drink the cup" is to suffer. See also the note at 4:34.

18:12 *detachment of soldiers with its commander and the Jewish officials:* The commander is a Roman tribune, who commanded 1000 soldiers. The "Jewish officials" likely refers to the temple guards (see the note at 7:32).

18:13 *Annas . . . father-in-law of Caiaphas:* Annas was the high priest of the Jewish people when Jesus was a child, but his sons and son-in-law, Caiaphas, were appointed by the Romans after Annas was forced to leave that position. Annas kept the title of high priest even though others took over the job from him. He was asked to give his advice on certain major problems, such as what to do with Jesus. See the note at 11:49.

18:11 Matt 26:39; Mark 14:35, 36; Luke 22:42.

18:15 *Simon Peter and another disciple:* See the note at 1:42. The other disciple who follows Jesus and the arrest party to the home of the high priest is probably the same as "the disciple whom Jesus loved" (see the note at 13:23), who stood at the foot of the cross (19:25-27) and who went with Peter to the tomb (20:1-10).

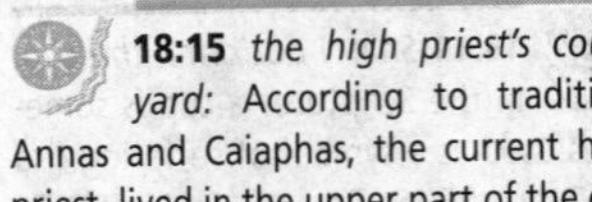

18:15 *the high priest's courtyard:* According to tradition, Annas and Caiaphas, the current high priest, lived in the upper part of the city, probably near the temple.

18:18 *the servants and officials:* The "officials" (18:22 also) are likely part of the temple guard. See the note at 7:32.

18:19 *high priest:* See the notes at 11:49 and 18:13. In the other Gospels, Jesus goes on trial in front of the high priest and a whole council of Jewish leaders (see Matt 26:57-68; Mark 14:55-65; Luke 22:66-71).

18:20 *synagogues:* See the note at 6:59 and the mini-article called "Synagogues," p. 1857.

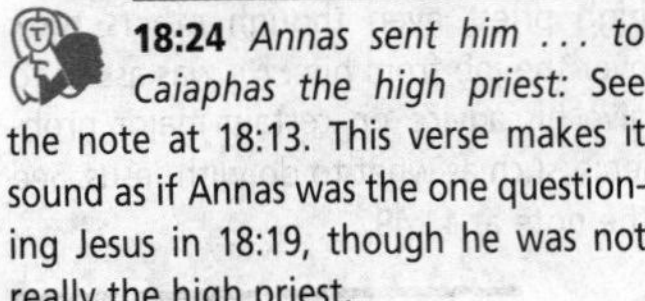

18:24 *Annas sent him . . . to Caiaphas the high priest:* See the note at 18:13. This verse makes it sound as if Annas was the one questioning Jesus in 18:19, though he was not really the high priest.

18:27 *Again Peter denied it:* This is the third time Peter denies knowing Jesus (see the note at 13:38).

18:28 *the palace of the Roman governor:* Pilate's official home was Caesarea on the Mediterranean coast. When he was in Jerusalem, he lived at the Antonia, a fortress that overlooked the temple area from the northwest. See the map on p. 2474. See also the mini-article called "Pontius Pilate" on the next page.

18:14 John 11:49,50. **18:17** John 13:38. **18:26** John 18:10.

high priest that year. 14Caiaphas was the one who had advised the
Jews that it would be good if one man died for the people.

Peter's First Denial

15Simon Peter and another disciple were following Jesus.
Because this disciple was known to the high priest, he went with
Jesus into the high priest's courtyard, 16but Peter had to wait out-
side at the door. The other disciple, who was known to the high
priest, came back, spoke to the girl on duty there and brought
Peter in.

17"You are not one of his disciples, are you?" the girl at the
door asked Peter.

He replied, "I am not."

18It was cold, and the servants and officials stood around a
fire they had made to keep warm. Peter also was standing with
them, warming himself.

The High Priest Questions Jesus

19Meanwhile, the high priest questioned Jesus about his
disciples and his teaching.

20"I have spoken openly to the world," Jesus replied. "I always
taught in synagogues or at the temple, where all the Jews come
together. I said nothing in secret. 21Why question me? Ask those
who heard me. Surely they know what I said."

22When Jesus said this, one of the officials nearby struck him
in the face. "Is this the way you answer the high priest?" he
demanded.

23"If I said something wrong," Jesus replied, "testify as to
what is wrong. But if I spoke the truth, why did you strike me?"
24Then Annas sent him, still bound, to Caiaphas the high priest.[a]

Peter's Second and Third Denials

25As Simon Peter stood warming himself, he was asked, "You
are not one of his disciples, are you?"

He denied it, saying, "I am not."

26One of the high priest's servants, a relative of the man
whose ear Peter had cut off, challenged him, "Didn't I see you with
him in the olive grove?" 27Again Peter denied it, and at that
moment a rooster began to crow.

Jesus Before Pilate

28Then the Jews led Jesus from Caiaphas to the palace of the
Roman governor. By now it was early morning, and to avoid ceremonial uncleanness the Jews did not enter the palace; they wanted

[a] **24** Or *(Now Annas had sent him, still bound, to Caiaphas the high priest.)*

to be able to eat the Passover. 29 So Pilate came out to them and
asked, "What charges are you bringing against this man?"
30 "If he were not a criminal," they replied, "we would not
have handed him over to you."
31 Pilate said, "Take him yourselves and judge him by your
own law."
"But we have no right to execute anyone," the Jews objected.
32 This happened so that the words Jesus had spoken indicating the
kind of death he was going to die would be fulfilled.
33 Pilate then went back inside the palace, summoned Jesus
and asked him, "Are you the king of the Jews?"
34 "Is that your own idea," Jesus asked, "or did others talk to
you about me?"

18:31 *we have no right to execute anyone:* The Roman authorities normally did not allow the Jewish officials to put anyone to death. That right was reserved for the Roman government. As a result, Jesus died by the Roman means of execution, crucifixion, rather than by the Jewish method of stoning—just as Jesus had said would happen (18:32; see 12:32,33 and the note at 12:32).

18:33 *king of the Jews:* If Jesus admitted to being a real king, he could be put on trial as a political rebel. This crime against Roman authority was punishable by death on a cross.

PONTIUS PILATE

Pontius Pilate was governor (prefect) of Judea from A.D. 26 to 36, during the time that Tiberius was the Roman emperor (A.D. 14-37) and Herod Antipas was governor (tetrarch) of Galilee (4 B.C. to A.D. 39). Pilate is mentioned by Roman, Jewish, and Christian writers. The Roman historian, Tacitus, tells in his Annals that Jesus was put to death by Pilate during the reign of Tiberius. Philos, a Jewish scholar from Alexandria, wrote that Pilate angered the Jews in Jerusalem by displaying metal shields at the governor's palace that bore the image and name of the emperor as though he were a god. The Jewish historian Josephus tells about the public outcry Pilate caused when he brought standards (images carried on poles) into Jerusalem picturing the emperor as a god, and when he took funds from the temple treasury to pay for an aqueduct to bring water into Jerusalem.

In the New Testament, Pilate is mentioned several times (Acts 3:13; 4:27; 13:28; 1 Tim 6:13), but he is most important in the Gospel accounts of Jesus' trial and execution. Mark 15:1-15, probably the oldest of these stories, says that when Pilate asked Jesus if he was the king of the Jews, Jesus answered, "Yes, it is as you say." Pilate saw no reason to put Jesus to death and was warned by his wife, because of a dream she had experienced, not to do so (Matt 27:19). But when the crowd demanded that Jesus be crucified, Pilate gave in to their demands and ordered Jesus' death. Pilate washed his hands in public to show he did not intend to take the blame for Jesus' death. Luke is the only Gospel that mentions Pilate sending Jesus to Herod Antipas (Luke 23:7). In each of the Gospel accounts, Pilate gave in to the demands of the crowd that Jesus be crucified, and ordered Jesus' death. Pilate was in a political bind. When the chief priests shouted, "We have no king but Caesar" (John 19:15), they pointed out the dilemma. With his claim to be a king, Jesus was a threat to the empire. If Pilate let Jesus go, it could end his political career, and perhaps his life.

The Gospel accounts put the blame for Jesus' death on the Jews and their leaders. If Jesus had been put to death for breaking the Jewish law, his execution under Jewish authority would have been done by crushing him to death with stones. This was the form of punishment commanded in the Law of Moses and that was later used to kill the church's "first martyr," Stephen, (Acts 7:54-60; Deut 13:9,10; 21:18-21). But Pilate had him put to death by crucifixion, the Roman method of execution. And the sign he had put on Jesus' cross identified Jesus as the "King of the Jews" (Matt 27:37; Mark 15:26; John 19:19).

18:36 *My kingdom is not of this world:* See the note at 3:3.

18:40 *Barabbas had taken part in a rebellion:* Rebels like Barabbas stirred up trouble against the Romans in the hope of gaining freedom for the Jewish people.

19:1,2 *flogged . . . crown of thorns:* In the Roman empire, often before a condemned person was nailed to a cross (crucified) he would be mocked and beaten with a whip ("flogged"). The "crown of thorns" that the soldiers placed on Jesus' head may have been made from the branches of the spiny burnet plant that grows in Palestine.

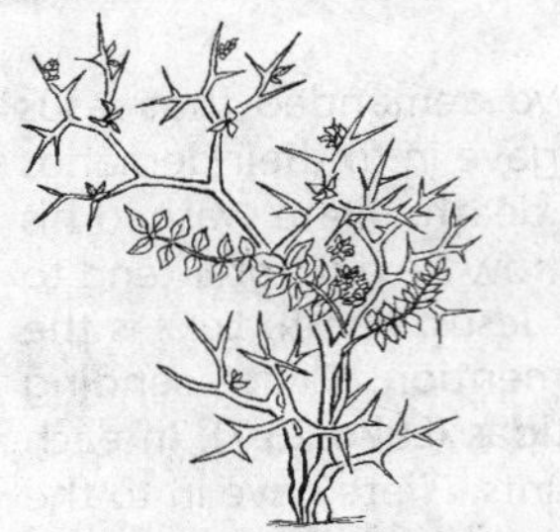

19:4 *I find no basis for a charge against him:* According to Matthew 27:24, Pilate washed his hands in front of the crowd as a sign that he was not responsible for Jesus' death. See also the note at 18:28.

19:6 *chief priests and their officials:* The "officials" were most likely temple guards. See the note at 7:32.

19:6 *Crucify:* See the mini-article called "Crucifixion," p. 1914.

19:7 *according to that law he must die . . . claimed to be the Son of God:* See the mini-article called "Son of God" on p. 2044. See also the note at 10:33 (claim).

19:11 *the one who handed me over to you:* The "one" mentioned here may be Judas, Caiaphas, or even Satan.

35 "Am I a Jew?" Pilate replied. "It was your people and your
chief priests who handed you over to me. What is it you have done?"
36 Jesus said, "My kingdom is not of this world. If it were, my
servants would fight to prevent my arrest by the Jews. But now my
kingdom is from another place."
37 "You are a king, then!" said Pilate.
Jesus answered, "You are right in saying I am a king. In fact,
for this reason I was born, and for this I came into the world, to
testify to the truth. Everyone on the side of truth listens to me."
38 "What is truth?" Pilate asked. With this he went out again
to the Jews and said, "I find no basis for a charge against him. 39 But
it is your custom for me to release to you one prisoner at the time
of the Passover. Do you want me to release 'the king of the Jews'?"
40 They shouted back, "No, not him! Give us Barabbas!" Now
Barabbas had taken part in a rebellion.

Jesus Sentenced to Be Crucified

19 Then Pilate took Jesus and had him flogged. 2 The soldiers twisted together a crown of thorns and put it on his head. They clothed
him in a purple robe 3 and went up to him again and again, saying,
"Hail, king of the Jews!" And they struck him in the face.
4 Once more Pilate came out and said to the Jews, "Look, I
am bringing him out to you to let you know that I find no basis for
a charge against him." 5 When Jesus came out wearing the crown of
thorns and the purple robe, Pilate said to them, "Here is the man!"
6 As soon as the chief priests and their officials saw him, they
shouted, "Crucify! Crucify!"
But Pilate answered, "You take him and crucify him. As for
me, I find no basis for a charge against him."
7 The Jews insisted, "We have a law, and according to that law
he must die, because he claimed to be the Son of God."
8 When Pilate heard this, he was even more afraid, 9 and he
went back inside the palace. "Where do you come from?" he asked
Jesus, but Jesus gave him no answer. 10 "Do you refuse to speak to
me?" Pilate said. "Don't you realize I have power either to free you
or to crucify you?"
11 Jesus answered, "You would have no power over me if it
were not given to you from above. Therefore the one who handed
me over to you is guilty of a greater sin."
12 From then on, Pilate tried to set Jesus free, but the Jews
kept shouting, "If you let this man go, you are no friend of Caesar.
Anyone who claims to be a king opposes Caesar."
13 When Pilate heard this, he brought Jesus out and sat down
on the judge's seat at a place known as the Stone Pavement (which
in Aramaic is Gabbatha). 14 It was the day of Preparation of
Passover Week, about the sixth hour.
"Here is your king," Pilate said to the Jews.

15 But they shouted, "Take him away! Take him away! Crucify
him!"
"Shall I crucify your king?" Pilate asked.
"We have no king but Caesar," the chief priests answered.
16 Finally Pilate handed him over to them to be crucified.

The Crucifixion

So the soldiers took charge of Jesus. 17 Carrying his own
cross, he went out to the place of the Skull (which in Aramaic is
called Golgotha). 18 Here they crucified him, and with him two
others—one on each side and Jesus in the middle.
19 Pilate had a notice prepared and fastened to the cross. It
read: JESUS OF NAZARETH, THE KING OF THE JEWS. 20 Many of the Jews
read this sign, for the place where Jesus was crucified was near the
city, and the sign was written in Aramaic, Latin and Greek. 21 The

The Crucifixion, a painting on parchment, Coptic, fifth century. When Jesus was crucified he looked down and saw the disciple whom he loved, standing near his mother. He said to the disciple, "Here is your mother." From that time on, the disciple took Jesus' mother into his home. (See 19:26, 27.)

19:12 *Pilate . . . Caesar:* See the mini-article called "Pontius Pilate," p. 2091. At this time the Roman emperor was Tiberius Caesar, who ruled the Roman empire from A.D. 14 to 37.

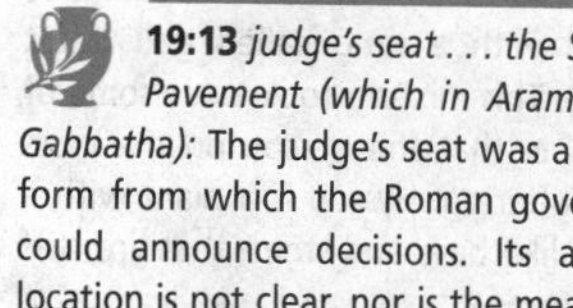

19:13 *judge's seat . . . the Stone Pavement (which in Aramaic is Gabbatha):* The judge's seat was a platform from which the Roman governor could announce decisions. Its actual location is not clear, nor is the meaning of the Aramaic word, *Gabbatha*. Normally, Pilate would have sat down there to make his pronouncements.

19:14 *the day of Preparation of Passover Week, about the sixth hour:* This would refer to noon on the day before Passover. At the time Jesus was being put on trial and sentenced to die on the cross, the Passover lambs were being slaughtered and prepared for the next day's Passover meal. See also the note on p. 2041 (Lamb of God).

19:15 *We have no king but Caesar:* Though the chief priests are supposed to serve God, they showed their loyalty to the Roman emperor in order to get Pilate to sentence Jesus to death.

19:17 *the Skull (which in Aramaic is called Golgotha):* The place was probably given this name because it was near a large rock in the shape of a human skull. See the map on p. 2474.

19:18 *crucified him:* See the mini-article called "Crucifixion," p. 1914.

19:20 *Aramaic, Latin and Greek:* The sign over Jesus was written in all these languages so that nearly everyone could read it. The Jewish people spoke Aramaic (a Semitic language similar to Hebrew). The official Roman language was Latin, though many Romans probably spoke Greek. Greek was the language of commerce commonly spoken throughout the Mediterranean world by many different peoples.

19:26 *the disciple whom he loved:* See the note at 13:23.

19:29 *jar of wine vinegar . . . a stalk of the hyssop plant:* Sometimes inexpensive wine or vinegar was mixed with a drug called gall (Matt 27:34). This mixture took away some of the pain that the person on the cross was suffering. Hyssop is a plant with a shrub-like base and stems that are stiff and strong.

19:30 *It is finished:* Jesus' words show not only that his earthly life was done, but that the work God had sent him to do, to sacrifice himself for the sins of the world (1:29), had been completed.

19:31 *a special Sabbath:* Since the Passover was set by the phase of the moon (see the note at 2:13), it could be on any day of the week. In Israel a day began at sundown. Here, the next day was also the Sabbath, so it was important that the dead body of Jesus not be left to decay on that doubly holy day. And anyone who touched a dead body would have to go through purification rites before being able to celebrate the Passover.

19:31 *have the legs broken:* This is the way that the Romans sometimes speeded up the death of a person who had been nailed to a cross. See the mini-article called "Crucifixion," p. 1914.

chief priests of the Jews protested to Pilate, "Do not write 'The
King of the Jews,' but that this man claimed to be king of the Jews."
22 Pilate answered, "What I have written, I have written."
23 When the soldiers crucified Jesus, they took his clothes,
dividing them into four shares, one for each of them, with the
undergarment remaining. This garment was seamless, woven in
one piece from top to bottom.
24 "Let's not tear it," they said to one another. "Let's decide by
lot who will get it."

This happened that the scripture might be fulfilled which said,

"They divided my garments among them
and cast lots for my clothing."[a]

So this is what the soldiers did.
25 Near the cross of Jesus stood his mother, his mother's sister, Mary the wife of Clopas, and Mary Magdalene. 26 When Jesus
saw his mother there, and the disciple whom he loved standing
nearby, he said to his mother, "Dear woman, here is your son,"
27 and to the disciple, "Here is your mother." From that time on,
this disciple took her into his home.

The Death of Jesus

28 Later, knowing that all was now completed, and so that the
Scripture would be fulfilled, Jesus said, "I am thirsty." 29 A jar of
wine vinegar was there, so they soaked a sponge in it, put the
sponge on a stalk of the hyssop plant, and lifted it to Jesus' lips.
30 When he had received the drink, Jesus said, "It is finished." With
that, he bowed his head and gave up his spirit.
31 Now it was the day of Preparation, and the next day was to
be a special Sabbath. Because the Jews did not want the bodies left

[a] **24** Psalm 22:18

QUESTIONS ABOUT JOHN 12:1—19:42

1. Shortly before he was put to death, Jesus visited Mary and Martha in Bethany (12:1-8). What did Mary do and what did it have to do with Jesus' death? What was Judas' complaint? How did Jesus respond to his complaint? What did Jesus mean? (12:7,8)
2. Read 12:23-26. What is the meaning of Jesus' words? Is anything worth risking death? If so, what?
3. Why did Jesus wash the feet of his disciples? (13:1-17) Why is this surprising? How can Christians serve one another?
4. What is the "new command" Jesus gave his followers? (13:34,35) How can this command be followed?
5. Read 14:6 and 15:1-5. Explain what Jesus means by these statements.
6. How did Jesus promise to help his followers after he left to be with the Father? (16:5-15)
7. How did Jesus reply to Pilate's questions? (18:33-37) What is Jesus' kingdom?

on the crosses during the Sabbath, they asked Pilate to have the
legs broken and the bodies taken down. 32 The soldiers therefore
came and broke the legs of the first man who had been crucified
with Jesus, and then those of the other. 33 But when they came to
Jesus and found that he was already dead, they did not break his
legs. 34 Instead, one of the soldiers pierced Jesus' side with a spear,
bringing a sudden flow of blood and water. 35 The man who saw it
has given testimony, and his testimony is true. He knows that he
tells the truth, and he testifies so that you also may believe. 36 These
things happened so that the scripture would be fulfilled: "Not one
of his bones will be broken,"[a] 37 and, as another scripture says,
"They will look on the one they have pierced."[b]

The Burial of Jesus

38 Later, Joseph of Arimathea asked Pilate for the body of
Jesus. Now Joseph was a disciple of Jesus, but secretly because he
feared the Jews. With Pilate's permission, he came and took the
body away. 39 He was accompanied by Nicodemus, the man who
earlier had visited Jesus at night. Nicodemus brought a mixture of
myrrh and aloes, about seventy-five pounds.[c] 40 Taking Jesus' body,
the two of them wrapped it, with the spices, in strips of linen. This
was in accordance with Jewish burial customs. 41 At the place where
Jesus was crucified, there was a garden, and in the garden a new
tomb, in which no one had ever been laid. 42 Because it was the
Jewish day of Preparation and since the tomb was nearby, they laid
Jesus there.

Jesus Appears to His Followers

The last two chapters of JOHN *focus on Jesus' appearances to a number of his disciples after God has raised him from death. This final miracle shows God's power over death.*

The Empty Tomb

20 Early on the first day of the week, while it was still dark, Mary
Magdalene went to the tomb and saw that the stone had been
removed from the entrance. 2 So she came running to Simon Peter
and the other disciple, the one Jesus loved, and said, "They have
taken the Lord out of the tomb, and we don't know where they
have put him!"

3 So Peter and the other disciple started for the tomb. 4 Both
were running, but the other disciple outran Peter and reached the

[a] **36** Exodus 12:46; Num. 9:12; Psalm 34:20 [b] **37** Zech. 12:10 [c] **39** Greek *a hundred litrai* (about 34 kilograms)

19:34 *pierced Jesus' side with a spear:* Like the breaking of victims' legs, this may have been done to hasten death. See also 20:27.

19:38 *Joseph of Arimathea:* Arimathea was a small village twenty miles northwest of Jerusalem. Because Joseph was rich (Matt 27:57), he had enough money to prepare Jesus' body for a proper burial.

19:39 *Nicodemus:* See the note at 3:1.

19:39 *myrrh and aloes:* See the chart called "Spices and Perfumes," p. 1278.

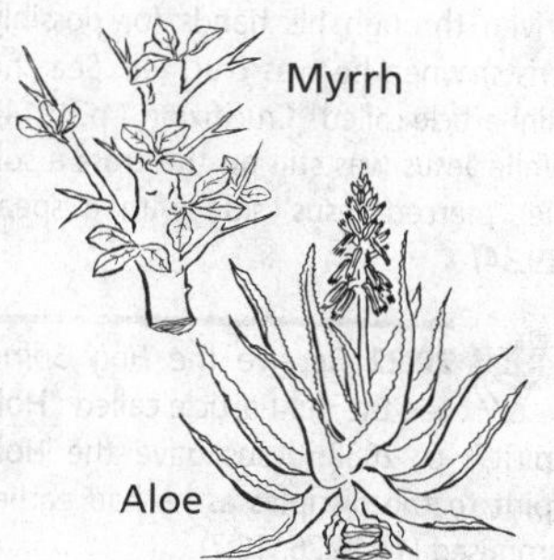

19:40 *wrapped it . . . strips of linen:* See the note at 11:44.

19:41 *in the garden a new tomb:* See the note at 11:17 (tomb). The tomb and garden must have been near Golgotha (see the note at 19:17). This would have made it easier to finish the task of preparing and burying the body before the Sabbath.

19:42 *Jewish day of Preparation:* See the note at 19:31.

20:1 *Early on the first day of the week:* This would be Sunday.

20:1 *Mary Magdalene:* Other Gospels tell how Jesus healed this woman from the town of Magdala (Mark 16:9; Luke 8:2). See also 19:25.

20:2 *Simon Peter and the other disciple, the one Jesus loved:* See the notes at 1:42 and 13:23.

19:24 Ps 22:18. **19:28** Ps 22:15. **19:39** John 3:1,2.

20:5 *strips of linen:* See the note at 11:44.

20:12 *two angels:* See the mini-article called "Angels," p. 88.

20:16 *Rabboni:* See 1:38.

20:19 *disciples . . . the doors locked for fear of the Jews:* See the note at 1:19 (the Jews). Jesus' followers were afraid that they would be identified and harassed for their beliefs, so they hid out in a locked room.

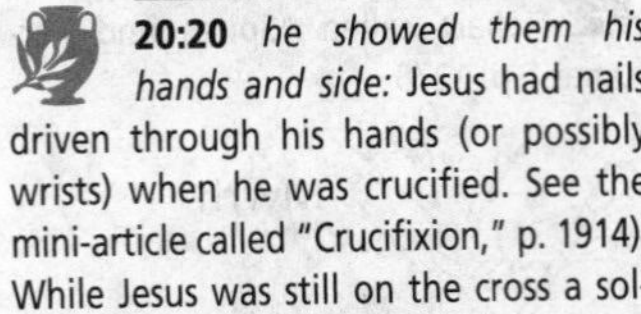
20:20 *he showed them his hands and side:* Jesus had nails driven through his hands (or possibly wrists) when he was crucified. See the mini-article called "Crucifixion," p. 1914). While Jesus was still on the cross a soldier pierced Jesus' side with a spear (19:34).

20:22 *Receive the Holy Spirit:* See the mini-article called "Holy Spirit," p. 2082. Jesus gave the Holy Spirit to the disciples as he had earlier promised (14:16,26; 16:7).

20:23 *forgive anyone his sins, they are forgiven:* In giving the Holy Spirit, Jesus gave the disciples the power to preach the good news about Jesus so that their sins might be forgiven. The Christian church has been "sent" by the Christ (20:21) with the authority to proclaim that people's sins can be forgiven because of what Jesus has done.

tomb first. 5He bent over and looked in at the strips of linen lying
there but did not go in. 6Then Simon Peter, who was behind him,
arrived and went into the tomb. He saw the strips of linen lying
there, 7as well as the burial cloth that had been around Jesus' head.
The cloth was folded up by itself, separate from the linen. 8Finally
the other disciple, who had reached the tomb first, also went
inside. He saw and believed. 9(They still did not understand from
Scripture that Jesus had to rise from the dead.)

Jesus Appears to Mary Magdalene

10Then the disciples went back to their homes, 11but Mary
stood outside the tomb crying. As she wept, she bent over to look
into the tomb 12and saw two angels in white, seated where Jesus'
body had been, one at the head and the other at the foot.
13They asked her, "Woman, why are you crying?"
"They have taken my Lord away," she said, "and I don't know
where they have put him." 14At this, she turned around and saw
Jesus standing there, but she did not realize that it was Jesus.
15"Woman," he said, "why are you crying? Who is it you are
looking for?"
Thinking he was the gardener, she said, "Sir, if you have carried him away, tell me where you have put him, and I will get him."
16Jesus said to her, "Mary."
She turned toward him and cried out in Aramaic, "Rabboni!" (which means Teacher).
17Jesus said, "Do not hold on to me, for I have not yet
returned to the Father. Go instead to my brothers and tell them, 'I am returning to my Father and your Father, to my God and your God.'"
18Mary Magdalene went to the disciples with the news: "I have seen the Lord!" And she told them that he had said these things to her.

Jesus Appears to His Disciples

19On the evening of that first day of the week, when the disciples were together, with the doors locked for fear of the Jews, Jesus came and stood among them and said, "Peace be with you!"
20After he said this, he showed them his hands and side. The disciples were overjoyed when they saw the Lord.
21Again Jesus said, "Peace be with you! As the Father has sent
me, I am sending you." 22And with that he breathed on them and
said, "Receive the Holy Spirit. 23If you forgive anyone his sins, they
are forgiven; if you do not forgive them, they are not forgiven."

Jesus Appears to Thomas

[24]Now Thomas (called Didymus), one of the Twelve, was not
with the disciples when Jesus came. [25]So the other disciples told
him, "We have seen the Lord!"

But he said to them, "Unless I see the nail marks in his hands
and put my finger where the nails were, and put my hand into his
side, I will not believe it."

[26]A week later his disciples were in the house again, and
Thomas was with them. Though the doors were locked, Jesus came
and stood among them and said, "Peace be with you!" [27]Then he
said to Thomas, "Put your finger here; see my hands. Reach out
your hand and put it into my side. Stop doubting and believe."

[28]Thomas said to him, "My Lord and my God!"

[29]Then Jesus told him, "Because you have seen me, you have
believed; blessed are those who have not seen and yet have
believed."

[30]Jesus did many other miraculous signs in the presence of
his disciples, which are not recorded in this book. [31]But these are
written that you may[a] believe that Jesus is the Christ, the Son of
God, and that by believing you may have life in his name.

Jesus and the Miraculous Catch of Fish

21 Afterward Jesus appeared again to his disciples, by the Sea of
Tiberias.[b] It happened this way: [2]Simon Peter, Thomas (called

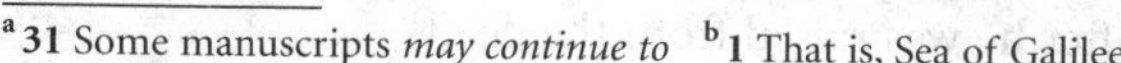

[a] **31** Some manuscripts *may continue to* [b] **1** That is, Sea of Galilee

20:24 *Thomas (called Didymus):* See the note at 11:16.

20:28 *My Lord and my God:* See the note at 13:13. Once doubtful, Thomas now boldly proclaims that Jesus is indeed "God" (see the note at 9:38).

20:31 *these are written:* Verses 30 and 31 have often been called the "theme verses" of JOHN. John tells about Jesus' miraculous signs (see the note at 2:11) so that people who were not able to see and hear Jesus in person (20:29) would have faith in Jesus.

21:1 *Sea of Tiberias:* See the note at 6:1.

21:2 *Simon Peter, Thomas (called Didymus), Nathanael . . . the sons of Zebedee, and two other disciples:* See the notes at 1:42; 11:16; and 1:44,45 (Nathanael). James and John were the "sons of Zebedee" (Mark 3:17). The "two other disciples" are simply not named.

Doubting Thomas by Michael Smither, twentieth century. Thomas the Twin was not with the other disciples when Jesus appeared to them after God had raised him to life. Thomas told them he would not believe what they were telling him unless he could see and touch Jesus' wounds for himself. Later, Jesus appeared to the disciples again and invited Thomas to touch his wounds. Thomas immediately recognized Jesus, but Jesus said to him, "Because you have seen me, you have believed; blessed are those who have not seen and yet have believed." (See 20:24-29.)

Jesus did many other things as well. If every one of them were written down, I suppose that even the whole world would not have room for the books that would be written.
John 21:25

21:7 *the disciple whom Jesus loved:* See the note at 13:23.

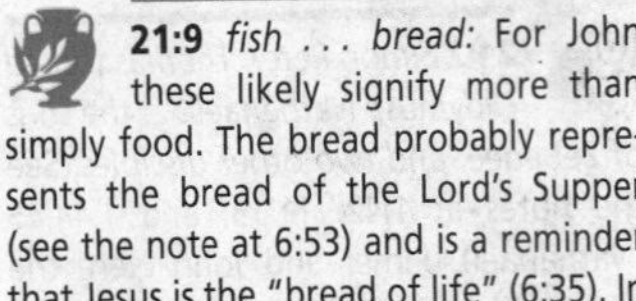

21:9 *fish . . . bread:* For John these likely signify more than simply food. The bread probably represents the bread of the Lord's Supper (see the note at 6:53) and is a reminder that Jesus is the "bread of life" (6:35). In the early church a favorite symbol for Jesus was the fish.

21:3,6 Luke 5:4-6.

Didymus), Nathanael from Cana in Galilee, the sons of Zebedee,
and two other disciples were together. 3"I'm going out to fish,"
Simon Peter told them, and they said, "We'll go with you." So they
went out and got into the boat, but that night they caught nothing.
4Early in the morning, Jesus stood on the shore, but the disciples did not realize that it was Jesus.
5He called out to them, "Friends, haven't you any fish?"
"No," they answered.
6He said, "Throw your net on the right side of the boat and you will find some." When they did, they were unable to haul the net in because of the large number of fish.
7Then the disciple whom Jesus loved said to Peter, "It is the
Lord!" As soon as Simon Peter heard him say, "It is the Lord," he
wrapped his outer garment around him (for he had taken it off)
and jumped into the water. 8The other disciples followed in the
boat, towing the net full of fish, for they were not far from shore,
about a hundred yards.[a] 9When they landed, they saw a fire of
burning coals there with fish on it, and some bread.
10Jesus said to them, "Bring some of the fish you have just caught."
11Simon Peter climbed aboard and dragged the net ashore.
It was full of large fish, 153, but even with so many the net was not
torn. 12Jesus said to them, "Come and have breakfast." None of the
disciples dared ask him, "Who are you?" They knew it was the
Lord. 13Jesus came, took the bread and gave it to them, and did the
same with the fish. 14This was now the third time Jesus appeared to
his disciples after he was raised from the dead.

Jesus Reinstates Peter

15When they had finished eating, Jesus said to Simon Peter, "Simon son of John, do you truly love me more than these?"
"Yes, Lord," he said, "you know that I love you."

[a] **8** Greek *about two hundred cubits* (about 90 meters)

QUESTIONS ABOUT JOHN 20:1—21:25

1. Who were the first persons to go to Jesus' tomb on Sunday morning? (20:1-9) What did they find, and what were their reactions?
2. What task did Jesus give to his disciples when he met them after he was raised from death? (20:21-23) What does this mean for the church today?
3. According to 20:30,31, why did John write this Gospel? Compare this to Jesus' words in 20:29. How do people living two thousand years after Jesus come to have faith in Jesus as God's Son and the Messiah?
4. What commands did Jesus give to Peter? (21:15-19) What did that mean for Peter? What does it mean for Jesus' followers (the church) today?

Jesus said, "Feed my lambs."
16 Again Jesus said, "Simon son of John, do you truly love
me?"
He answered, "Yes, Lord, you know that I love you."
Jesus said, "Take care of my sheep."
17 The third time he said to him, "Simon son of John, do you
love me?"
Peter was hurt because Jesus asked him the third time, "Do
you love me?" He said, "Lord, you know all things; you know that
I love you."
Jesus said, "Feed my sheep. 18 I tell you the truth, when you
were younger you dressed yourself and went where you wanted;
but when you are old you will stretch out your hands, and someone
else will dress you and lead you where you do not want to go."
19 Jesus said this to indicate the kind of death by which Peter would
glorify God. Then he said to him, "Follow me!"
20 Peter turned and saw that the disciple whom Jesus loved
was following them. (This was the one who had leaned back
against Jesus at the supper and had said, "Lord, who is going to
betray you?") 21 When Peter saw him, he asked, "Lord, what about
him?"
22 Jesus answered, "If I want him to remain alive until I
return, what is that to you? You must follow me." 23 Because of this,
the rumor spread among the brothers that this disciple would not
die. But Jesus did not say that he would not die; he only said, "If I
want him to remain alive until I return, what is that to you?"
24 This is the disciple who testifies to these things and who
wrote them down. We know that his testimony is true.
25 Jesus did many other things as well. If every one of them
were written down, I suppose that even the whole world would not
have room for the books that would be written.

21:15-17 *Feed my lambs . . . Take care of my sheep . . . Feed my sheep:* Jesus called himself the good shepherd (10:14). His followers are his flock of lambs (sheep). Jesus tells Peter to take care of his sheep by feeding them the message of Jesus, which includes offering the message of forgiveness of sins through Jesus (20:23).

21:18,19 *you will stretch out your hands . . . lead you where you do not want to go . . . glorify God:* The phrase "stretch out your hands" probably means that Peter would die on a cross just as Jesus had. Peter's freedom would be taken away and he would be led where he does not want to go. Even so, his death would glorify God, just as Jesus' death glorified God (see the note at 12:27).

21:20 *the disciple whom Jesus loved:* See the note at 13:23.

21:24 *This is the disciple who testifies to these things and who wrote them down:* According to this verse, "the disciple whom Jesus loved" (21:20) is the one who wrote this true account of Jesus' words and works, though he had to choose them from the many stories and memories of what Jesus said and did (21:25).

21:20 John 13:25.

ACTS

What is the first thing you do when you hear good news? Read Acts to discover how the good news about Jesus was spread far and wide!

What makes Acts special?

Acts is the second volume of a two-part work written by the same person who wrote Luke. In Luke, the writer told "all that Jesus began to do and to teach until the day he was taken up to heaven" (Acts 1:1,2). And this is where Acts begins. Before Jesus goes up to heaven, he tells his disciples, "You will be my witnesses in Jerusalem, and in all Judea and Samaria, and to the ends of the earth." To help them with this, Jesus promises to send the Holy Spirit (1:8).

Why was Acts written?

The writer of Acts wanted to show that nothing could keep the good news about Jesus from spreading everywhere. Acts also tells about how the earliest followers struggled to decide who could belong to God's people. Since Jesus' first followers were Jews, it was only natural for many of them to think Jesus' message was only for Jews. But the Spirit showed them that Jesus came to invite people from every nation and race to be part of God's people. Acts 15 tells about the important meeting in Jerusalem where early church leaders agreed that the Spirit of God was leading them to reach out to both Jews and Gentiles with the gospel.

What's the story behind the scene?

The writer of Luke and Acts used the same style of writing used by historians and public speakers of the time. He knows many details about the people and places the apostles visited and about how those who spread the gospel did miracles in Jesus' name. Traditionally, the writer of Luke and Acts has been identified as Luke the doctor, the co-worker of Paul (Col 4:14; Phlm 24).

Acts tells about the man named Saul (Paul), a loyal Jew who had been working to put an end to the Jesus movement (8:1-3; 9:1-2). While he was on a trip to arrest some of Jesus' followers, Jesus himself appeared to Saul in a way that radically changed Saul's life. He became a devout follower of Jesus. Much of the second half of Acts tells how Paul began preaching the gospel and making missionary journeys throughout the Mediterranean world. He eventually took the message about Jesus as far as Rome, the world's most important city at that time (28:16-31). See the map on p. 2477.

Holy Spirit: The Holy Spirit is very important in both Acts and Luke, the Gospel written by the same author. The Holy Spirit does amazing things, like causing the virgin Mary to become pregnant (Luke 1:35) and showing the apostle Paul which cities he should avoid or go to next on his missionary journeys (Acts 16:6-8; 20:22). The Holy Spirit leads people (Luke 4:1,14; Acts 8:29,39) and gives them special gifts, like the ability to preach about Jesus and be understood in different languages (Acts 2:1-11). The Holy Spirit also gave the first apostles courage to preach and to heal. This power helped the church grow and become stronger (Acts 9:31). See also the mini-article called "Holy Spirit," p. 2082.

The Holy Spirit is frequently depicted in art as a descending dove, because all four Gospel writers state that when Jesus was baptized by John "the Holy Spirit descended on him in bodily form like a dove" (Luke 3:22; see also Matt 3:16; Mark 1:10; John 1:32).

HOW IS ACTS CONSTRUCTED?

The following outline shows how ACTS can be divided into major sections according to how the gospel spread throughout the known world, starting in Jerusalem and going out all the way to Rome, in ever-widening circles.

The Spirit gives power to Jesus' followers (1:1—2:47)
The apostles prepare to receive God's power (1:1-26)
God sends the Holy Spirit (2:1-47)

The church in Jerusalem (3:1—8:1a)
Peter and John (3:1—4:22)
Life among the early followers in Jerusalem (4:23—5:42)
Leaders for the new church (6:1—8:1a)

The gospel is preached in Judea and Samaria (8:1b—9:31)
Philip, Peter, and John in Samaria (8:1b-40)
God chooses Saul (9:1-31)

The gospel goes out to the Gentile world (9:32—15:35)
Peter preaches and lives the gospel (9:32—11:18)
The growing church faces persecution (11:19—12:25)
Saul (Paul) and Barnabas journey to share the gospel (13:1—14:28)
An important meeting in Jerusalem (15:1-35)

The gospel reaches Asia Minor, Greece, and Rome (15:36—28:31)
Paul's second journey (15:36—18:22)
Paul's third journey (18:23—21:16)
Paul in Jerusalem (21:17—23:22)
Paul in Caesarea (23:23—26:32)
Paul brings the gospel to Rome (27:1—28:31)

The Spirit Gives Power to Jesus' Followers

Jesus is about to go up to heaven and is giving his disciples some final instructions. He tells them to wait in Jerusalem until God gives them the Holy Spirit. The Spirit will give them power to preach the gospel to the world. As promised, the Holy Spirit comes to the disciples on Pentecost.

THE APOSTLES PREPARE TO RECEIVE GOD'S POWER

Jesus Taken Up Into Heaven

1 In my former book, Theophilus, I wrote about all that Jesus
began to do and to teach 2until the day he was taken up to heaven,
after giving instructions through the Holy Spirit to the apostles he

1:1 *In my former book, Theophilus, I wrote:* The author's "former book" refers to LUKE (see Luke 1:1-4). For more, see the Introduction to LUKE on p. 1964.

The name Theophilus means "friend of God" in Greek, so some think Theophilus stands for anyone who is a friend or follower of Jesus. More likely, Theophilus was a Roman official or a wealthy and important person who paid for the writing and copying of Luke's Gospel. Such a person is called a patron.

1:2 *taken up to heaven:* Jesus' going up to heaven is sometimes called the "Ascension." See also the mini-article called "Heaven," p. 1420.

1:2 *Holy Spirit:* See the note on p. 2100.

1:2 *apostles he had chosen:* An "apostle" is someone chosen for a special mission, such as carrying to others the message of a teacher or a group. Here "apostles" refers to the group of disciples Jesus chose. See Luke 6:12-16; Acts 1:12,13.

had chosen. 3After his suffering, he showed himself to these men
and gave many convincing proofs that he was alive. He appeared to
them over a period of forty days and spoke about the kingdom of
God. 4On one occasion, while he was eating with them, he gave
them this command: "Do not leave Jerusalem, but wait for the gift
my Father promised, which you have heard me speak about. 5For
John baptized with[a] water, but in a few days you will be baptized
with the Holy Spirit."

6So when they met together, they asked him, "Lord, are you
at this time going to restore the kingdom to Israel?"

7He said to them: "It is not for you to know the times or
dates the Father has set by his own authority. 8But you will receive
power when the Holy Spirit comes on you; and you will be my
witnesses in Jerusalem, and in all Judea and Samaria, and to the
ends of the earth."

9After he said this, he was taken up before their very eyes,
and a cloud hid him from their sight.

10They were looking intently up into the sky as he was going,
when suddenly two men dressed in white stood beside them.
11"Men of Galilee," they said, "why do you stand here looking into
the sky? This same Jesus, who has been taken from you into heav-
en, will come back in the same way you have seen him go into
heaven."

Matthias Chosen to Replace Judas

12Then they returned to Jerusalem from the hill called the
Mount of Olives, a Sabbath day's walk[b] from the city. 13When they
arrived, they went upstairs to the room where they were staying.
Those present were Peter, John, James and Andrew; Philip and
Thomas, Bartholomew and Matthew; James son of Alphaeus and
Simon the Zealot, and Judas son of James. 14They all joined togeth-
er constantly in prayer, along with the women and Mary the moth-
er of Jesus, and with his brothers.

15In those days Peter stood up among the believers[c] (a group
numbering about a hundred and twenty) 16and said, "Brothers, the
Scripture had to be fulfilled which the Holy Spirit spoke long ago
through the mouth of David concerning Judas, who served as
guide for those who arrested Jesus— 17he was one of our number
and shared in this ministry."

18(With the reward he got for his wickedness, Judas bought
a field; there he fell headlong, his body burst open and all his
intestines spilled out. 19Everyone in Jerusalem heard about this, so
they called that field in their language Akeldama, that is, Field of
Blood.)

20"For," said Peter, "it is written in the book of Psalms,

[a]5 Or *in* [b]12 That is, about 3/4 mile (about 1,100 meters) [c]15 Greek *brothers*

1:3 *forty days:* Forty is a number that has special meaning for the Jewish people. See the chart called "Numbers in the Bible," p. 2405.

1:4 *Jerusalem:* See Luke 24:49 and the mini-article called "Jerusalem," p. 574.

1:4 *wait for the gift my Father promised:* The "gift" was the Holy Spirit. See the note on p. 2100.

1:5 *John:* This is John the Baptist. See also the mini-article called "John the Baptist," p. 1853.

1:5 *baptized with water:* John baptized people with water to show how their old way of life had been washed away when they turned from their sin (see Luke 3:3). See the mini-article called "Baptism," p. 1976.

1:8 *Jerusalem . . . Judea . . . Samaria:* See the map on p. 2473.

1:10 *two men dressed in white:* These "men" were probably angels. See also Luke 24:4.

1:11 *Men of Galilee:* The apostles came from this region in northern Palestine. See the map on p. 2473.

1:14 *women . . . Mary the mother of Jesus . . . his brothers:* Women often traveled along with the group of Jesus' followers. For Mary, see Luke 1:26-56; 2:1-52. The "brothers" were probably sons of Mary and Joseph, younger half-brothers of Jesus. See Mark 6:3.

1:18 *Judas bought a field:* Judas was paid 30 silver coins to betray Jesus (Matt 26:15). Since he gave the coins back (Matt 27:3-8), he didn't personally buy the field. The priests used the money to buy it.

1:5 Matt 3:11; Mark 1:8; Luke 3:16; John 1:33. **1:9** Mark 16:19; Luke 24:50,51. **1:12,13** Matt 10:2-4; Mark 3:16-19; Luke 6:14-16.

" 'May his place be deserted;
let there be no one to dwell in it,'[a]

and,

" 'May another take his place of leadership.'[b]

21 Therefore it is necessary to choose one of the men who have been
with us the whole time the Lord Jesus went in and out among us,
22 beginning from John's baptism to the time when Jesus was taken
up from us. For one of these must become a witness with us of his
resurrection."
23 So they proposed two men: Joseph called Barsabbas (also
known as Justus) and Matthias. 24 Then they prayed, "Lord, you
know everyone's heart. Show us which of these two you have chosen 25 to take over this apostolic ministry, which Judas left to go
where he belongs." 26 Then they cast lots, and the lot fell to
Matthias; so he was added to the eleven apostles.

GOD SENDS THE HOLY SPIRIT

As promised, God sends the Holy Spirit to give power and courage to the apostles. They begin to declare the wonders of God which people hear in many different languages, and three thousand new followers are baptized in one day.

The Holy Spirit Comes at Pentecost

2 When the day of Pentecost came, they were all together in one
place. 2 Suddenly a sound like the blowing of a violent wind came
from heaven and filled the whole house where they were sitting.
3 They saw what seemed to be tongues of fire that separated and came
to rest on each of them. 4 All of them were filled with the Holy Spirit
and began to speak in other tongues[c] as the Spirit enabled them.
5 Now there were staying in Jerusalem God-fearing Jews from
every nation under heaven. 6 When they heard this sound, a crowd
came together in bewilderment, because each one heard them
speaking in his own language. 7 Utterly amazed, they asked: "Are
not all these men who are speaking Galileans? 8 Then how is it that
each of us hears them in his own native language? 9 Parthians,
Medes and Elamites; residents of Mesopotamia, Judea and Cappadocia, Pontus and Asia, 10 Phrygia and Pamphylia, Egypt and the
parts of Libya near Cyrene; visitors from Rome 11 (both Jews and
converts to Judaism); Cretans and Arabs—we hear them declaring
the wonders of God in our own tongues!" 12 Amazed and perplexed, they asked one another, "What does this mean?"
13 Some, however, made fun of them and said, "They have
had too much wine.[d]"

[a]**20** Psalm 69:25 [b]**20** Psalm 109:8 [c]**4** Or *languages*; also in verse 11
[d]**13** Or *sweet wine*

1:20 *another take his place:* Twelve was considered a holy number. Jesus had called twelve apostles, the same number as the tribes in ancient Israel. So the apostles felt they needed to appoint someone to take the place of Judas in order to make their number complete again. See also the chart called "Numbers in the Bible," p. 2405.

1:26 *they cast lots:* They used a process called "casting lots," a custom widely used in the ancient Near East. The apostles probably used marked stones or small twigs. They used this method in order to be sure that God, not they, chose the person to replace Judas.

2:1 *the day of Pentecost:* Pentecost, also known as the Feast of Harvest or Feast of Weeks, is a Jewish festival that came fifty days after the Sabbath of Passover week and celebrated the wheat harvest (see Lev 23:15-21; Deut 16:9-11). Jesus had been put to death on a cross earlier, on the day before the Passover Sabbath. See the chart called "Jewish Calendar and Festivals," p. 944.

2:5 *God-fearing Jews from every nation:* Because Jerusalem was still the most important center for the Jewish religion, many faithful Jews lived there. In addition, Jews from other lands would have been in the city for the Pentecost celebration, an important pilgrimage festival.

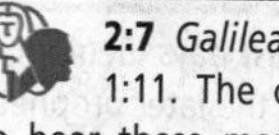

2:7 *Galileans:* See the note at 1:11. The crowd was surprised to hear these men speaking so many different languages.

2:11 *Jews and converts to Judaism:* Most people who followed the Jewish religion were born to Jewish parents. Men who converted to Judaism had to go through the ceremony called circumcision (see the note at 7:8) in order to be accepted as Jews.

1:21,22 Matt 3:16; Mark 1:9; 16:19; Luke 3:21; 24:51.

Pentecost, illuminated page from a bishop's book of religious ceremonies, called a *Pontifical,* English, late tenth century. Before Jesus was taken into heaven he told the apostles that the Holy Spirit would come and give them power to tell the whole world the gospel of Jesus. When Jesus' followers were together in Jerusalem for the feast of Pentecost, there was suddenly "a sound like the blowing of a violent wind . . . They saw what seemed to be tongues of fire that separated and came to rest on each of them." Other Jews who were in Jerusalem celebrating the holiday were confused by what they saw and heard, but Peter explained to everyone there what God was doing. (See 2:1-41.)

2:14 *Peter:* This is Simon, one of the first disciples Jesus chose (Matt 4:18-22). The Greek form of his name (Petros) and the Aramaic form (Cephas) both mean "rock."

2:17 *In the last days:* Beginning with some of the later prophets, some in Israel believed that God would come to judge the world one day. This would mark the last days of the present age, since when the Lord returned (2:20) he would make life and the world completely new. See the mini-articles called "Day of the LORD," p. 1727, and "End Times," p. 2295.

2:17-21 Joel 2:28-32.

Peter Addresses the Crowd

14Then Peter stood up with the Eleven, raised his voice and
addressed the crowd: "Fellow Jews and all of you who live in
Jerusalem, let me explain this to you; listen carefully to what I say.
15These men are not drunk, as you suppose. It's only nine in the
morning! 16No, this is what was spoken by the prophet Joel:

17" 'In the last days, God says,
  I will pour out my Spirit on all people.
 Your sons and daughters will prophesy,

your young men will see visions,
your old men will dream dreams.
18 Even on my servants, both men and women,
I will pour out my Spirit in those days,
and they will prophesy.
19 I will show wonders in the heaven above
and signs on the earth below,
blood and fire and billows of smoke.
20 The sun will be turned to darkness
and the moon to blood
before the coming of the great and glorious day
of the Lord.
21 And everyone who calls
on the name of the Lord will be saved.'[a]

22 "Men of Israel, listen to this: Jesus of Nazareth was a man
accredited by God to you by miracles, wonders and signs, which
God did among you through him, as you yourselves know. 23 This
man was handed over to you by God's set purpose and foreknowledge; and you, with the help of wicked men,[b] put him to death by
nailing him to the cross. 24 But God raised him from the dead, freeing him from the agony of death, because it was impossible for
death to keep its hold on him. 25 David said about him:

" 'I saw the Lord always before me.
Because he is at my right hand,
I will not be shaken.
26 Therefore my heart is glad and my tongue rejoices;
my body also will live in hope,
27 because you will not abandon me to the grave,
nor will you let your Holy One see decay.
28 You have made known to me the paths of life;
you will fill me with joy in your presence.'[c]

29 "Brothers, I can tell you confidently that the patriarch
David died and was buried, and his tomb is here to this day. 30 But
he was a prophet and knew that God had promised him on oath
that he would place one of his descendants on his throne. 31 Seeing
what was ahead, he spoke of the resurrection of the Christ,[d] that
he was not abandoned to the grave, nor did his body see decay.
32 God has raised this Jesus to life, and we are all witnesses of the
fact. 33 Exalted to the right hand of God, he has received from the
Father the promised Holy Spirit and has poured out what you now
see and hear. 34 For David did not ascend to heaven, and yet he said,

" 'The Lord said to my Lord:
"Sit at my right hand

[a]**21** Joel 2:28-32 [b]**23** Or *of those not having the law* (that is, Gentiles)
[c]**28** Psalm 16:8-11 [d]**31** Or *Messiah.* "The Christ" (Greek) and "the Messiah" (Hebrew) both mean "the Anointed One"; also in verse 36.

2:21 *the name of the Lord ... saved:* See the mini-article called "Lord (Title for Jesus)," on the next page. Being "saved" refers to how God rescues people from sin and death. Salvation comes to those who have faith in Jesus Christ as God's Son and as the Savior of the world. See the mini-article called "Salvation," p. 2021.

2:22 *Jesus of Nazareth:* Jesus was often identified by adding his hometown to his name, since there were many Jewish men named Jesus at the time he lived.

2:29-31 *the patriarch David ... Seeing what was ahead:* David was considered Israel's greatest ruler. People in Israel believed that the Messiah (Chosen One) would come from David's family (Ps 132:11; 2 Sam 7:12, 13). When Peter says David was a prophet, he means that David spoke God's message in the PSALMS, and that Jesus being raised to life illustrates what David had spoken about many centuries earlier. See also the mini-article called "David," p. 1028.

2:33 *the right hand of God:* Being at a ruler's or dignitary's right side was the place of honor and power.

2:34-35 *The Lord said to my Lord:* In quoting these verses from Psalm 110, Peter is using them in much the same way as Jesus did: to point out that the Messiah (Christ) has a special relationship with God and shares God's authority in heaven (see Luke 20:41-44). See also Heb 1:13.

2:23 Matt 27:35; Mark 15:24; Luke 23:33; John 19:18. **2:24** Matt 28:5,6; Mark 16:6; Luke 24:5. **2:25-28** Ps 16:8-11. **2:34,35** Ps 110:1.

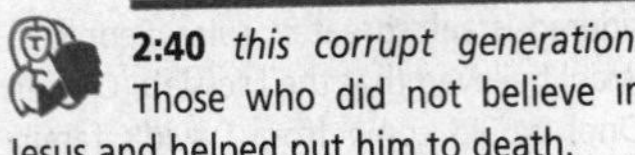

2:36 *Lord and Christ:* See the mini-article called "Lord (Title for Jesus)," below. "Christ" comes from the Greek word, *christos*, which means "Chosen One" or "Anointed One," as does the Hebrew title *Messiah*. See also the mini-article called "Messiah (Chosen One)," p. 1124.

2:38 *Repent:* This means to turn away from sin and turn back to God.

2:38 *forgiveness of your sins:* Sin occurs when people turn away from God and disobey God's Word. Forgiveness takes away the guilt that comes from the sin. See also the mini-article called "Sin," p. 2181.

2:40 *this corrupt generation:* Those who did not believe in Jesus and helped put him to death.

35 until I make your enemies
a footstool for your feet." '[a]

36 "Therefore let all Israel be assured of this: God has made
this Jesus, whom you crucified, both Lord and Christ."
37 When the people heard this, they were cut to the heart and
said to Peter and the other apostles, "Brothers, what shall we do?"
38 Peter replied, "Repent and be baptized, every one of you,
in the name of Jesus Christ for the forgiveness of your sins. And
you will receive the gift of the Holy Spirit. 39 The promise is for you
and your children and for all who are far off—for all whom the
Lord our God will call."
40 With many other words he warned them; and he pleaded
with them, "Save yourselves from this corrupt generation." 41 Those
who accepted his message were baptized, and about three thousand were added to their number that day.

[a]35 Psalm 110:1

LORD (TITLE FOR JESUS)

The Greek word for "Lord" is *kyrios,* which ordinarily meant "master" or "sir." "Lord" should not be confused with "LORD," the word which is printed in capital letters and used to represent God's special name *Yahweh* in the Old Testament. See the mini-article called "LORD (YHWH)," p. 140. In the Roman empire, "Lord" was used for Caesar and indicated his absolute power as monarch, but did not mean that he was a god. "Lord" appears as a title for Jesus in the New Testament and declares his royal authority as the one who has been raised from the dead to sit at God's right hand. Practically speaking, "Lord" functions in the same way as "Christ," another royal title. When Peter addressed the crowd on the day of Pentecost, he said, "Let all Israel be assured of this: God has made this Jesus, whom you crucified, both Lord and Christ" (Acts 2:36). Another example of the royal meaning of this title is found in its Aramaic form, *maran,* which means "Our Lord," and was used to designate the king in the royal courts. In two places in the New Testament (1 Cor 16:22; Rev 22:20), the Christian community calls upon Jesus to return soon by using the expression *marana tha* ("Come, O Lord").

The apostle Paul repeatedly refers to Jesus as "Lord," and twice his letters contain the specific expression "Jesus is Lord" (Rom 10:9; 1 Cor 12:3). It is one of the shortest and oldest statements of belief (called creeds) in the New Testament. Since "Lord" is used in the Septuagint (the Greek translation of the Hebrew Scriptures) to translate *Yahweh,* Paul was undoubtedly asserting Christ's deity and his authority over every other power. To affirm Christ as Lord gave great confidence to the early Christians who suffered for their belief that God raised Jesus from death, gave him the highest place, and honored his name above all others. As one ancient hymn that Paul quoted said, "Therefore God exalted him to the highest place and gave him the name that is above every name, that at the name of Jesus every knee should bow, in heaven and on earth and under the earth, and every tongue confess that Jesus Christ is Lord, to the glory of God the Father" (Phil 2:9-11).

The Fellowship of the Believers

[42]They devoted themselves to the apostles' teaching and to
the fellowship, to the breaking of bread and to prayer. [43]Everyone
was filled with awe, and many wonders and miraculous signs were
done by the apostles. [44]All the believers were together and had
everything in common. [45]Selling their possessions and goods, they
gave to anyone as he had need. [46]Every day they continued to meet
together in the temple courts. They broke bread in their homes
and ate together with glad and sincere hearts, [47]praising God and
enjoying the favor of all the people. And the Lord added to their
number daily those who were being saved.

The Church in Jerusalem

Chapters 3–7 tell how the apostles first spread the gospel in Jerusalem, the center of the Jewish religion.

PETER AND JOHN

Peter and John, two of Jesus' first apostles, heal a man and preach about Jesus at the temple in Jerusalem. Their actions cause them to be brought before the same Jewish council that had arrested Jesus. Peter and John bravely defend themselves and the good news about Jesus.

Peter Heals the Crippled Beggar

3 One day Peter and John were going up to the temple at the
time of prayer—at three in the afternoon. [2]Now a man crippled
from birth was being carried to the temple gate called Beautiful,
where he was put every day to beg from those going into the temple courts. [3]When he saw Peter and John about to enter, he asked
them for money. [4]Peter looked straight at him, as did John. Then
Peter said, "Look at us!" [5]So the man gave them his attention,
expecting to get something from them.

2:42 *breaking of bread:* Jesus used the bread and wine to show how his life would be sacrificed to forgive sins, which was the basis for a new covenant between God and God's new people (Matt 26:26-29; Luke 22:14-22; 1 Cor 11:23-26). Christians celebrate this event in a ceremony called the Lord's Supper (Holy Communion).

2:45 *selling their possessions . . . they gave:* See the note at 4:34,35.

2:47 *those who were being saved:* See the note at 2:21.

3:1 *Peter and John:* See the note at 2:14. Like Peter, John and his brother James were fishermen who became disciples of Jesus (Luke 5:11; 6:14). See also Mark 3:17; Luke 9:54.

3:1 *temple:* This is the temple built by Herod the Great. The apostles went to the temple to pray just like other loyal Jews. See also the article called "People of the Law: The Religion of Israel, " p. 939.

3:1 *the time of prayer:* Jewish people prayed in homes at regular times each day (Dan 6:10).

3:2 *the temple gate called Beautiful:* Perhaps the Nicanor Gate. People with physical problems, who were considered ritually unclean, were not allowed into the temple. But they could sit by its gates and beg for money.

2:44 Acts 4:32-35.

QUESTIONS ABOUT ACTS 1:1—2:47

1. What instructions did Jesus give the apostles before he went up to heaven? (1:3-9) How can followers of Jesus today carry out these instructions?
2. Describe the coming of the Holy Spirit (2:1-13). What happened as a result? How is the Holy Spirit at work in the world today?
3. When Peter preached, what did he say about the prophet Joel's prophecy? About Jesus? About David? (2:14-41) How did the crowd react to Peter's message? How do you respond to Peter's message?
4. Describe life among the Lord's followers as described in 2:42-47. Is this a good model that the church could follow today? Why or why not?

6Then Peter said, "Silver or gold I do not have, but what I have I give you. In the name of Jesus Christ of Nazareth, walk." 7Taking him by the right hand, he helped him up, and instantly the man's feet and ankles became strong. 8He jumped to his feet and began to walk. Then he went with them into the temple courts, walking and jumping, and praising God. 9When all the people saw him walking and praising God, 10they recognized him as the same man who used to sit begging at the temple gate called Beautiful, and they were filled with wonder and amazement at what had happened to him.

Peter Speaks to the Onlookers

11While the beggar held on to Peter and John, all the people were astonished and came running to them in the place called Solomon's Colonnade. 12When Peter saw this, he said to them: "Men of Israel, why does this surprise you? Why do you stare at us as if by our own power or godliness we had made this man walk? 13The God of Abraham, Isaac and Jacob, the God of our fathers, has glorified his servant Jesus. You handed him over to be killed, and you disowned him before Pilate, though he had decided to let him go. 14You disowned the Holy and Righteous One and asked that a murderer be released to you. 15You killed the author of life, but God raised him from the dead. We are witnesses of this. 16By faith in the name of Jesus, this man whom you see and know was made strong. It is Jesus' name and the faith that comes through him that has given this complete healing to him, as you can all see.

17"Now, brothers, I know that you acted in ignorance, as did your leaders. 18But this is how God fulfilled what he had foretold through all the prophets, saying that his Christ[a] would suffer. 19Repent, then, and turn to God, so that your sins may be wiped out, that times of refreshing may come from the Lord, 20and that he may send the Christ, who has been appointed for you—even Jesus. 21He must remain in heaven until the time comes for God to restore everything, as he promised long ago through his holy prophets. 22For Moses said, 'The Lord your God will raise up for you a prophet like me from among your own people; you must listen to everything he tells you. 23Anyone who does not listen to him will be completely cut off from among his people.'[b]

24"Indeed, all the prophets from Samuel on, as many as have spoken, have foretold these days. 25And you are heirs of the prophets and of the covenant God made with your fathers. He said to Abraham, 'Through your offspring all peoples on earth will be blessed.'[c] 26When God raised up his servant, he sent him first to you to bless you by turning each of you from your wicked ways."

3:6 *In the name of Jesus Christ of Nazareth:* Since there were other people who practiced healing in the name of other gods, Peter wanted everyone present to know the true source of this man's healing.

3:11 *Solomon's Colonnade:* A public place with tall columns along the east side of the temple, it was named for King Solomon, who built the first Jewish temple in Jerusalem.

3:13 *The God of Abraham:* Peter was talking about *Yahweh*, the God of Israel, who made a covenant with Abraham and his descendants. See the mini-article called "LORD (YHWH)," p. 140.

3:13 *Pilate:* See Luke 23:1-4, 13-25 and the mini-article called "Pontius Pilate," p. 2091.

3:14 *a murderer:* Peter is talking about Barabbas. See Matt 27:15-26; Mark 15:6-15; Luke 23:13-23.

3:18 *foretold through all the prophets . . . Christ would suffer:* See Isa 53:7, 8; Luke 9:22, 44; 18:31-33; and the mini-article called "Messiah (Chosen One)," p. 1124.

3:19 *Repent, then, and turn to God, so that your sins may be wiped out:* See the notes at 2:38.

3:20 *the Christ:* See also the note at 2:36.

3:21 *heaven:* See the mini-article called "Heaven," p. 1420.

3:24 *all the prophets from Samuel on:* Samuel's life is described in 1 Samuel 1–12; 19:18-24; 25:1. He was mainly known as a judge (leader), though Peter calls him a prophet. Samuel anointed the first two kings of Israel, Saul and David. See also the article called "Prophets and Prophecy," p. 935.

3:25 *covenant:* See the mini-article called "Covenants (Agreements)," p. 386.

[a]**18** Or *Messiah*; also in verse 20 [b]**23** Deut. 18:15,18,19 [c]**25** Gen. 22:18; 26:4

Peter and John Before the Sanhedrin

4 The priests and the captain of the temple guard and the Sadducees came up to Peter and John while they were speaking to the
people. 2 They were greatly disturbed because the apostles were
teaching the people and proclaiming in Jesus the resurrection of the
dead. 3 They seized Peter and John, and because it was evening, they
put them in jail until the next day. 4 But many who heard the message believed, and the number of men grew to about five thousand.
5 The next day the rulers, elders and teachers of the law met
in Jerusalem. 6 Annas the high priest was there, and so were
Caiaphas, John, Alexander and the other men of the high priest's
family. 7 They had Peter and John brought before them and began
to question them: "By what power or what name did you do this?"
8 Then Peter, filled with the Holy Spirit, said to them: "Rulers
and elders of the people! 9 If we are being called to account today
for an act of kindness shown to a cripple and are asked how he was
healed, 10 then know this, you and all the people of Israel: It is by
the name of Jesus Christ of Nazareth, whom you crucified but
whom God raised from the dead, that this man stands before you
healed. 11 He is

" 'the stone you builders rejected,
which has become the capstone.'[a] [b]

12 Salvation is found in no one else, for there is no other name
under heaven given to men by which we must be saved."
13 When they saw the courage of Peter and John and realized
that they were unschooled, ordinary men, they were astonished
and they took note that these men had been with Jesus. 14 But since
they could see the man who had been healed standing there with
them, there was nothing they could say. 15 So they ordered them to
withdraw from the Sanhedrin and then conferred together.
16 "What are we going to do with these men?" they asked. "Everybody living in Jerusalem knows they have done an outstanding
miracle, and we cannot deny it. 17 But to stop this thing from
spreading any further among the people, we must warn these men
to speak no longer to anyone in this name."
18 Then they called them in again and commanded them not
to speak or teach at all in the name of Jesus. 19 But Peter and John
replied, "Judge for yourselves whether it is right in God's sight to
obey you rather than God. 20 For we cannot help speaking about
what we have seen and heard."
21 After further threats they let them go. They could not
decide how to punish them, because all the people were praising
God for what had happened. 22 For the man who was miraculously healed was over forty years old.

---

[a] **11** Or *cornerstone* [b] **11** Psalm 118:22

4:1 *priests . . . captain of the temple guard . . . Sadducees:* The priests were assigned to perform religious rites in the temple. See the mini-article called "Israel's Priests," p. 2344. The Jewish leaders were allowed to employ men as temple guards. Their duties were to keep order and to make sure no one broke the laws that governed the temple. The captain of the temple guard came from a priestly family and was close in rank to the high priest.

The Sadducees were a wealthy group of Jews who worked closely with the priests. They taught that the most important thing in life was going to the temple and offering sacrifices there. This sometimes caused the Sadducees to oppose the Pharisees, a group who thought that obeying the Law of Moses was more important than following all the rules about temple worship and sacrifice. The Pharisees believed in life after death, but the Sadducees didn't. For more, see the article called "The World of Jesus: Peoples, Powers, and Politics," p. 1821.

4:5 *rulers, elders and teachers of the law:* These three groups comprised the Sanhedrin (4:15; see the note at 5:21). The rulers were a group of wealthy men connected to the priests and the temple. The elders may have been a highly respected group of teachers who were very familiar with the Law of Moses. The teachers of the Law carefully studied the first five books of the Jewish Scriptures, called the *Torah*.

4:6 *Annas the high priest . . . Caiaphas:* Annas had been the high priest from A.D. 6 to 15, but he was removed by the Romans. His son Eleazar was appointed in his place. Eventually, Annas's son-in-law Caiaphas was made high priest and served in this position from A.D. 18 to 36.

4:8 *filled with the Holy Spirit:* This refers to how the Holy Spirit gives power, courage, and special gifts to Jesus' followers. See the note on p. 2100.

4:11 Ps 118:22; Luke 20:17,18.

4:23 *chief priests . . . elders:* The chief priests included Caiaphas, the current ruling high priest; his father-in-law Annas, the previous high priest; and the high priestly families. See the note at 4:6. For "elders," see the note at 4:5.

4:25 *our father David:* See the note at 2:29-31.

4:27 *Herod and Pontius Pilate:* Herod Antipas, the son of Herod the Great, ruled over Galilee from 4 B.C. to A.D. 39. See also the note at 3:13 (Pilate).

4:27 *your holy servant Jesus, whom you anointed:* See the note at 2:36.

4:31 *spoke the word of God boldly:* Despite the threats of the Jewish religious leaders, the believers continued to share the gospel.

4:33 *grace:* "Grace" is the undeserved kindness and favor that God extends to people.

4:34,35 *those who owned lands . . . put it at the apostles' feet:* These acts of sharing were voluntary. Believers were inspired to make sure that "there were no needy among them." Putting the money "at the apostles' feet" meant giving it "with no strings attached."

4:36,37 *Joseph . . . called Barnabas:* Joseph was from the Levite tribe. The Levites did not actually own inherited land in Palestine, but since this man lived on the island of Cyprus he probably was allowed to purchase land there. See the map on p. 2474. Barnabas became an important leader in the early church. He went with Paul on Paul's first missionary trip (13:1—15:2). Barnabas was "a good man, full of the Holy Spirit and faith" (11:24; see the note at 4:8).

4:24 Exod 20:11; Neh 9:6; Ps 146:6. **4:25,26** Ps 2:1,2. **4:27a** Luke 23:7-11; **b** Matt 27:1,2; Mark 15:1; Luke 23:1; John 18:28,29. **4:32** Acts 2:44,45.

LIFE AMONG THE EARLY FOLLOWERS IN JERUSALEM

At the very beginning, the followers of Jesus met together often to pray and to break bread. They also shared their possessions so no one would be in need.

The Believers' Prayer

23 On their release, Peter and John went back to their own people and reported all that the chief priests and elders had said to them.
24 When they heard this, they raised their voices together in prayer to
God. "Sovereign Lord," they said, "you made the heaven and the earth
and the sea, and everything in them. 25 You spoke by the Holy Spirit
through the mouth of your servant, our father David:

" 'Why do the nations rage
and the peoples plot in vain?
26 The kings of the earth take their stand
and the rulers gather together
against the Lord
and against his Anointed One.[a]'[b]

27 Indeed Herod and Pontius Pilate met together with the Gentiles
and the people[c] of Israel in this city to conspire against your holy
servant Jesus, whom you anointed. 28 They did what your power
and will had decided beforehand should happen. 29 Now, Lord,
consider their threats and enable your servants to speak your word
with great boldness. 30 Stretch out your hand to heal and perform
miraculous signs and wonders through the name of your holy
servant Jesus."

31 After they prayed, the place where they were meeting was
shaken. And they were all filled with the Holy Spirit and spoke the
word of God boldly.

The Believers Share Their Possessions

32 All the believers were one in heart and mind. No one
claimed that any of his possessions was his own, but they shared
everything they had. 33 With great power the apostles continued to
testify to the resurrection of the Lord Jesus, and much grace was
upon them all. 34 There were no needy persons among them. For
from time to time those who owned lands or houses sold them,
brought the money from the sales 35 and put it at the apostles' feet,
and it was distributed to anyone as he had need.

36 Joseph, a Levite from Cyprus, whom the apostles called
Barnabas (which means Son of Encouragement), 37 sold a field he
owned and brought the money and put it at the apostles' feet.

[a]**26** That is, Christ or Messiah [b]**26** Psalm 2:1,2 [c]**27** The Greek is plural.

Ananias and Sapphira

5 Now a man named Ananias, together with his wife Sapphira,
also sold a piece of property. 2With his wife's full knowledge he
kept back part of the money for himself, but brought the rest and
put it at the apostles' feet.
3Then Peter said, "Ananias, how is it that Satan has so filled
your heart that you have lied to the Holy Spirit and have kept for
yourself some of the money you received for the land? 4Didn't it
belong to you before it was sold? And after it was sold, wasn't the
money at your disposal? What made you think of doing such a
thing? You have not lied to men but to God."
5When Ananias heard this, he fell down and died. And great
fear seized all who heard what had happened. 6Then the young
men came forward, wrapped up his body, and carried him out and
buried him.
7About three hours later his wife came in, not knowing what
had happened. 8Peter asked her, "Tell me, is this the price you and
Ananias got for the land?"
"Yes," she said, "that is the price."
9Peter said to her, "How could you agree to test the Spirit of
the Lord? Look! The feet of the men who buried your husband are
at the door, and they will carry you out also."
10At that moment she fell down at his feet and died. Then
the young men came in and, finding her dead, carried her out and
buried her beside her husband. 11Great fear seized the whole
church and all who heard about these events.

The Apostles Heal Many

12The apostles performed many miraculous signs and wonders among the people. And all the believers used to meet together in Solomon's Colonnade. 13No one else dared join them, even
though they were highly regarded by the people. 14Nevertheless,
more and more men and women believed in the Lord and were
added to their number. 15As a result, people brought the sick into
the streets and laid them on beds and mats so that at least Peter's
shadow might fall on some of them as he passed by. 16Crowds
gathered also from the towns around Jerusalem, bringing their sick
and those tormented by evil[a] spirits, and all of them were healed.

The Apostles Persecuted

17Then the high priest and all his associates, who were members of the party of the Sadducees, were filled with jealousy. 18They
arrested the apostles and put them in the public jail. 19But during
the night an angel of the Lord opened the doors of the jail and

[a]16 Greek *unclean*

5:1 *Ananias, together with his wife Sapphira:* All we know about this couple is what we read in ACTS. They are shown as a bad example of sharing, while Barnabas was a good example. Their actions would likely have reminded the believers of the sin of Achan, who stole things that had been set aside for the LORD (Josh 7).

5:3 *Satan:* Satan, which means "adversary," is the leader of the forces in the world that are against God and God's people. See also the mini-article called "Satan," p. 963.

5:9 *test the Spirit of the Lord:* Another way of saying "lying to God's Spirit." It was important that the believers could trust each other. If Ananias and Sapphira had gotten away with their lie, it might have tempted others to do the same. Keeping the money was not a sin, since it was rightfully their money. Lying in order to appear more generous was the sin.

5:11 *the whole church:* The Greek word for "church" is *ekklesia*, which means "assembly" and can refer to any kind of gathering of people. See also the mini-article called "Church," p. 2264.

5:12 *Solomon's Colonnade:* See the note at 3:11.

5:16 *tormented by evil spirits:* Evil spirits, or demons, work for the devil. Demons were thought to be the primary cause of many kinds of sickness and mental illness.

5:17 *high priest . . . Sadducees:* At this time Caiaphas would have been the high priest. See the note at 4:6. See also the mini-article called "Israel's Priests," p. 2344. For more about Sadducees see the note at 4:1.

5:19 *an angel of the Lord:* In the Bible, angels frequently play an important part in seeing that God's will is carried out. See also the mini-article called "Angels," p. 88.

5:21 *Sanhedrin:* The chief priests and other prominent Jewish citizens formed a council of Jewish leaders called the Sanhedrin. The Roman rulers gave this council the right to make decisions about some local matters that affected the Jewish people. See also the note at 4:5.

5:24 *captain of the temple guard . . . chief priests:* See the notes at 4:1 and 4:23.

5:26 *stone them:* See the note at 7:58.

5:30 *The God of our fathers:* See the note at 3:13.

5:31 *Prince and Savior:* These are two titles for Jesus. The Greek word for savior means "deliverer," or one who brings salvation (see the note at 2:21).

5:34 *Pharisee named Gamaliel:* Pharisees believed in following God's law as closely as possible and separating themselves from those who did not. Gamaliel I, also known as Gamaliel the Elder, was a member of the Sanhedrin in Jerusalem. See Acts 22:3.

5:36,37 *Theudas . . . Judas the Galilean:* Theudas probably led a revolt against the Roman rulers occupying Palestine. Judas the Galilean, possibly the founder of the Zealots, led a rebellion against Rome in A.D. 6. For more about Zealots see the article called "The World of Jesus: Peoples, Powers, and Politics," p. 1821.

5:40 *flogged:* Jewish law allowed for a beating of no more than forty lashes with a whip. Therefore, the practice was to stop the flogging at thirty-nine lashes (see 2 Cor 11:24).

5:41 *the Name:* Referring to the name of Jesus.

5:42 *good news that Jesus is the Christ:* The good news is the message Jesus brought about God's kingdom and the message Jesus' followers brought about what Jesus did.

5:28 Matt 27:25.

brought them out. 20"Go, stand in the temple courts," he said, "and
tell the people the full message of this new life."
21At daybreak they entered the temple courts, as they had
been told, and began to teach the people.
When the high priest and his associates arrived, they called
together the Sanhedrin—the full assembly of the elders of Israel—
and sent to the jail for the apostles. 22But on arriving at the jail, the
officers did not find them there. So they went back and reported,
23"We found the jail securely locked, with the guards standing at
the doors; but when we opened them, we found no one inside."
24On hearing this report, the captain of the temple guard and the
chief priests were puzzled, wondering what would come of this.
25Then someone came and said, "Look! The men you put in
jail are standing in the temple courts teaching the people." 26At
that, the captain went with his officers and brought the apostles.
They did not use force, because they feared that the people would
stone them.
27Having brought the apostles, they made them appear
before the Sanhedrin to be questioned by the high priest. 28"We
gave you strict orders not to teach in this name," he said. "Yet you
have filled Jerusalem with your teaching and are determined to
make us guilty of this man's blood."
29Peter and the other apostles replied: "We must obey God
rather than men! 30The God of our fathers raised Jesus from the
dead—whom you had killed by hanging him on a tree. 31God
exalted him to his own right hand as Prince and Savior that he
might give repentance and forgiveness of sins to Israel. 32We are
witnesses of these things, and so is the Holy Spirit, whom God has
given to those who obey him."
33When they heard this, they were furious and wanted to put
them to death. 34But a Pharisee named Gamaliel, a teacher of the
law, who was honored by all the people, stood up in the Sanhedrin
and ordered that the men be put outside for a little while. 35Then
he addressed them: "Men of Israel, consider carefully what you
intend to do to these men. 36Some time ago Theudas appeared,
claiming to be somebody, and about four hundred men rallied to
him. He was killed, all his followers were dispersed, and it all came
to nothing. 37After him, Judas the Galilean appeared in the days of
the census and led a band of people in revolt. He too was killed,
and all his followers were scattered. 38Therefore, in the present case
I advise you: Leave these men alone! Let them go! For if their purpose or activity is of human origin, it will fail. 39But if it is from
God, you will not be able to stop these men; you will only find
yourselves fighting against God."
40His speech persuaded them. They called the apostles in and
had them flogged. Then they ordered them not to speak in the
name of Jesus, and let them go.
41The apostles left the Sanhedrin, rejoicing because they had

been counted worthy of suffering disgrace for the Name. [42]Day
after day, in the temple courts and from house to house, they never
stopped teaching and proclaiming the good news that Jesus is the
Christ.[a]

LEADERS FOR THE NEW CHURCH

The believers in Jerusalem select leaders to help administrate their community life. One bold leader named Stephen is put to death for preaching about Christ.

The Choosing of the Seven

6 In those days when the number of disciples was increasing, the
Grecian Jews among them complained against the Hebraic Jews
because their widows were being overlooked in the daily distribution of food. [2]So the Twelve gathered all the disciples together and
said, "It would not be right for us to neglect the ministry of the
word of God in order to wait on tables. [3]Brothers, choose seven
men from among you who are known to be full of the Spirit and
wisdom. We will turn this responsibility over to them [4]and will
give our attention to prayer and the ministry of the word."
[5]This proposal pleased the whole group. They chose
Stephen, a man full of faith and of the Holy Spirit; also Philip,
Procorus, Nicanor, Timon, Parmenas, and Nicolas from Antioch, a
convert to Judaism. [6]They presented these men to the apostles,
who prayed and laid their hands on them.
[7]So the word of God spread. The number of disciples in
Jerusalem increased rapidly, and a large number of priests became
obedient to the faith.

Stephen Seized

[8]Now Stephen, a man full of God's grace and power, did
great wonders and miraculous signs among the people. [9]Opposi-
tion arose, however, from members of the Synagogue of the Freedmen (as it was called)—Jews of Cyrene and Alexandria as well as
the provinces of Cilicia and Asia. These men began to argue with
Stephen, [10]but they could not stand up against his wisdom or the
Spirit by whom he spoke.
[11]Then they secretly persuaded some men to say, "We have
heard Stephen speak words of blasphemy against Moses and
against God."
[12]So they stirred up the people and the elders and the teachers of the law. They seized Stephen and brought him before the
Sanhedrin. [13]They produced false witnesses, who testified, "This
fellow never stops speaking against this holy place and against the

[a]**42** Or *Messiah*

6:1 *Grecian Jews . . . Hebraic Jews:* When Alexander the Great (356-323 B.C.) conquered the Near East, Greek culture began to spread throughout the ancient world and Greek became a kind of universal language. The "Grecian Jews" were born outside Palestine, spoke Greek as their first language, and were heavily influenced by Greek culture. The "Hebraic Jews" spoke primarily Hebrew or Aramaic (similar to Hebrew).

6:2 *the Twelve . . . wait on tables:* This would mean that the twelve apostles would be in charge either of distributing the food to the widows or handling the money.

6:3 *seven men:* The Greek word that describes their work is related to the word often translated as "deacon."

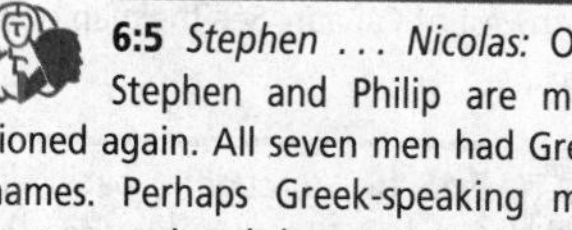

6:5 *Stephen . . . Nicolas:* Only Stephen and Philip are mentioned again. All seven men had Greek names. Perhaps Greek-speaking men were appointed because it was the Greek-speaking believers who had been complaining (6:1).

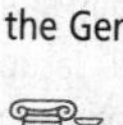

6:5 *Antioch:* This Greek city in Syria became an important center for the early Christian outreach to the Gentiles (11:19-30).

6:6 *laid their hands on them:* See the note at 8:17.

6:7 *priests:* This statement is noteworthy because these leaders generally opposed the new followers of Jesus. See the note at 4:1.

6:9 *Synagogue of the Freedmen:* A group of Jews who had once been slaves but were now free.

6:9 *Cyrene and Alexandria . . . provinces of Cilicia and Asia:* See the map on p. 2471.

6:11-13 *blasphemy against Moses . . . God . . . this holy place . . . the law:* The trumped-up charges were that Stephen slandered the things Jews held most sacred.

7:2 *our father Abraham:* See the mini-article called "Abraham," p. 2254.

7:2-4 *Mesopotamia . . . Haran:* See Gen 11:26—12:9 and the map on p. 2462.

7:8 *covenant of circumcision:* See Gen 17:9-14; 21:2-4 and the mini-article called "Circumcision," p. 2251.

7:9 *Joseph:* Joseph was Jacob's first son by his favorite wife, Rachel, and a great-grandson of Abraham. See Genesis 37–50 for the entire story of this famous ancestor.

7:9 *Egypt:* At this time Egypt was a powerful country to the southwest of Canaan. See the map on p. 2463.

7:15,16 *brought back to Shechem:* Late in his life, the Jewish patriarch Jacob moved from Canaan to Egypt (Gen 46:1-7). Before he died, he instructed his sons to take his body back to Canaan for burial (Gen 49:29-33). Abraham had actually bought land at Hebron (Gen 23:3-18) where he (Gen 25:9-11), Isaac (Gen 35:28, 29), and Jacob (Gen 50:7-13) were buried. Jacob bought land at Shechem and built an altar to the LORD there (Gen 33:19). His son Joseph was later buried there (Josh 24:32). Stephen actually has summarized all this history to make the point that Israel's earliest ancestors were buried in Canaan, not in Egypt. However, most of Jacob's descendants did remain in Egypt for many years (see 7:6 and Exod 1,2).

7:5 Gen 12:7; 13:15; 15:18; 17:8. **7:6,7** Gen 15:13-15. **7:7** Exod 3:12. **7:8** Gen 17:10-14; 21:2-4; 25:26; 29:31—35:18 **7:9** Gen 37:11, 28; 39:2, 21. **7:10,11** Gen 41:39-41; 42:1,2. **7:13** Gen 45:1,4,16. **7:14** Gen 45:9,10, 17,18; 46:27. **7:17-29** Exod 1:1—2:15.

law. 14For we have heard him say that this Jesus of Nazareth will
destroy this place and change the customs Moses handed down
to us."

15All who were sitting in the Sanhedrin looked intently at
Stephen, and they saw that his face was like the face of an angel.

Stephen's Speech to the Sanhedrin

7 Then the high priest asked him, "Are these charges true?"
2To this he replied: "Brothers and fathers, listen to me! The
God of glory appeared to our father Abraham while he was still in
Mesopotamia, before he lived in Haran. 3'Leave your country and
your people,' God said, 'and go to the land I will show you.'[a]
4"So he left the land of the Chaldeans and settled in Haran.
After the death of his father, God sent him to this land where you
are now living. 5He gave him no inheritance here, not even a foot
of ground. But God promised him that he and his descendants
after him would possess the land, even though at that time Abraham had no child. 6God spoke to him in this way: 'Your descendants will be strangers in a country not their own, and they will be
enslaved and mistreated four hundred years. 7But I will punish the
nation they serve as slaves,' God said, 'and afterward they will come
out of that country and worship me in this place.'[b] 8Then he gave
Abraham the covenant of circumcision. And Abraham became the
father of Isaac and circumcised him eight days after his birth. Later
Isaac became the father of Jacob, and Jacob became the father of
the twelve patriarchs.
9"Because the patriarchs were jealous of Joseph, they sold
him as a slave into Egypt. But God was with him 10and rescued him
from all his troubles. He gave Joseph wisdom and enabled him to
gain the goodwill of Pharaoh king of Egypt; so he made him ruler
over Egypt and all his palace.
11"Then a famine struck all Egypt and Canaan, bringing
great suffering, and our fathers could not find food. 12When Jacob
heard that there was grain in Egypt, he sent our fathers on their
first visit. 13On their second visit, Joseph told his brothers who he
was, and Pharaoh learned about Joseph's family. 14After this,
Joseph sent for his father Jacob and his whole family, seventy-five
in all. 15Then Jacob went down to Egypt, where he and our fathers
died. 16Their bodies were brought back to Shechem and placed in
the tomb that Abraham had bought from the sons of Hamor at
Shechem for a certain sum of money.
17"As the time drew near for God to fulfill his promise to
Abraham, the number of our people in Egypt greatly increased.
18Then another king, who knew nothing about Joseph, became
ruler of Egypt. 19He dealt treacherously with our people and

[a]3 Gen. 12:1 [b]7 Gen. 15:13,14

oppressed our forefathers by forcing them to throw out their newborn babies so that they would die.
20"At that time Moses was born, and he was no ordinary
child.[a] For three months he was cared for in his father's house.
21When he was placed outside, Pharaoh's daughter took him and
brought him up as her own son. 22Moses was educated in all the
wisdom of the Egyptians and was powerful in speech and action.
23"When Moses was forty years old, he decided to visit his
fellow Israelites. 24He saw one of them being mistreated by an
Egyptian, so he went to his defense and avenged him by killing the
Egyptian. 25Moses thought that his own people would realize that
God was using him to rescue them, but they did not. 26The next
day Moses came upon two Israelites who were fighting. He tried
to reconcile them by saying, 'Men, you are brothers; why do you
want to hurt each other?'
27"But the man who was mistreating the other pushed Moses
aside and said, 'Who made you ruler and judge over us? 28Do you
want to kill me as you killed the Egyptian yesterday?'[b] 29When
Moses heard this, he fled to Midian, where he settled as a foreigner and had two sons.
30"After forty years had passed, an angel appeared to Moses
in the flames of a burning bush in the desert near Mount Sinai.
31When he saw this, he was amazed at the sight. As he went over to
look more closely, he heard the Lord's voice: 32'I am the God of
your fathers, the God of Abraham, Isaac and Jacob.'[c] Moses trembled with fear and did not dare to look.
33"Then the Lord said to him, 'Take off your sandals; the
place where you are standing is holy ground. 34I have indeed seen
the oppression of my people in Egypt. I have heard their groaning and have come down to set them free. Now come, I will send you back to Egypt.'[d]
35"This is the same Moses whom they had rejected with the words, 'Who made you ruler and judge?' He was sent to be their ruler and deliverer by God himself, through the angel who
appeared to him in the bush. 36He led them out of Egypt and did
wonders and miraculous signs in Egypt, at the Red Sea[e] and for forty years in the desert.
37"This is that Moses who told the Israelites, 'God will send
you a prophet like me from your own people.'[f] 38He was in the
assembly in the desert, with the angel who spoke to him on Mount Sinai, and with our fathers; and he received living words to pass on to us.
39"But our fathers refused to obey him. Instead, they rejected him and in their hearts turned back to Egypt. 40They told
Aaron, 'Make us gods who will go before us. As for this fellow

[a]20 Or *was fair in the sight of God* [b]28 Exodus 2:14 [c]32 Exodus 3:6
[d]34 Exodus 3:5,7,8,10 [e]36 That is, Sea of Reeds [f]37 Deut. 18:15

7:20 *Moses:* For many Jews, Moses was the most important person in their history. He led the Hebrew people out of slavery in Egypt, and God chose to give him the laws which the Israelite people were to live by. The story of Moses that Stephen tells in 7:20-44 is given in the books of EXODUS, LEVITICUS, NUMBERS, and DEUTERONOMY. See also the mini-article called "Moses," p. 2335.

7:29 *Midian:* See Exod 2:15. Midian was the land east of the Gulf of Aqabah. See the map on p. 2463.

7:29 *two sons:* Moses' sons were Gershom and Eliezer (Exod 18:2-4).

7:30 *the desert near Mount Sinai:* See the map on p. 133 for the possible location of Mount Sinai, the place where God gave the Ten Commandments and the Law to Moses and the people of Israel (Exod 19–40).

7:33 *Take off your sandals:* This was considered an act of respect for God and God's holy place. See also Josh 5:15.

7:35 *angel:* See the note at 5:19. See also Exod 3:2.

7:36 *out of Egypt and did wonders and miraculous signs:* See the chart called "Disasters (Plagues)," p. 151, for a list of the plagues that the LORD brought upon the Egyptians. See Exodus 14:1-31 for the story of how the LORD parted the Red Sea for Moses and the people. The miracles in the desert are described in Exodus 15:22—17:7 and Numbers 20:1-13.

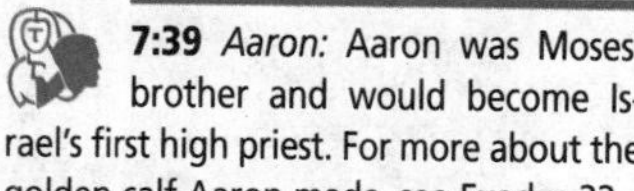

7:39 *Aaron:* Aaron was Moses' brother and would become Israel's first high priest. For more about the golden calf Aaron made, see Exodus 32.

7:30-34 Exod 3:1-10. **7:36** Exod 7:3,4; 14:21; Num 14:33. **7:37** Deut 18:15,18. **7:38** Exod 19:1—20:17; Deut 5:1-33. **7:40,41** Exod 32:1-6.

7:42,43 *God turned away . . . Babylon:* See Ezek 20:1-29. The Old Testament prophets often told the people of Israel how they had turned their back on God. Stephen's quote from Amos 5:25-27 recalled that the people had worshiped idols.

When the people of the northern kingdom (Israel) turned their backs on God and were defeated by the Assyrians in 721 B.C., many of them were carried off to Damascus and other parts of Assyria. About 130 years later, the southern kingdom (Judah) was defeated by the Babylonians who took many of its people into exile in Babylon. See also the mini-article called "Exile," p. 1541.

7:44 *tabernacle of the Testimony:* See the mini-article called "The Tabernacle," p. 2346. "The Testimony" is the name given to the two stone tablets upon which the Ten Commandments were inscribed. These were placed in the ark of the covenant, which was kept in the Most Holy Place in the tabernacle, and later the temple (Exod 25:16).

7:47 *Solomon who built the house:* Solomon, David's son, was a wise and wealthy king who built the first temple (house of God). See 1 Kgs 6:1-38; 2 Chr 3:1-17.

7:45 Josh 3:14-17. **7:46** 2 Sam 7:1-16; 1 Chr 17:1-14. **7:49,50** Isa 66:1,2. **7:51** Isa 63:10.

Moses who led us out of Egypt—we don't know what has happened to him!'[a] 41That was the time they made an idol in the form
of a calf. They brought sacrifices to it and held a celebration in
honor of what their hands had made. 42But God turned away and
gave them over to the worship of the heavenly bodies. This agrees
with what is written in the book of the prophets:

" 'Did you bring me sacrifices and offerings
forty years in the desert, O house of Israel?
43You have lifted up the shrine of Molech
and the star of your god Rephan,
the idols you made to worship.
Therefore I will send you into exile'[b] beyond Babylon.

44"Our forefathers had the tabernacle of the Testimony with
them in the desert. It had been made as God directed Moses,
according to the pattern he had seen. 45Having received the tabernacle, our fathers under Joshua brought it with them when they
took the land from the nations God drove out before them. It
remained in the land until the time of David, 46who enjoyed God's

[a]**40** Exodus 32:1 [b]**43** Amos 5:25-27

Saint Stephen Being Led Outside the Walls of Jerusalem, from an ornamented box for holding remains of a saint (called a "reliquary"), Limoges enamel, late twelfth century. Stephen was an important church leader. God gave him the power to work great miracles and to preach. Some people who heard Stephen speaking about Jesus were upset by what Stephen was saying and dragged him before the Sanhedrin. After Stephen preached to the council about the law and called the Jewish leaders "stiff-necked," the angry crowd dragged Stephen outside the city and stoned him to death. Stephen was the first martyr of the church. (See 6:8—7:60.)

favor and asked that he might provide a dwelling place for the God
of Jacob.[a] 47 But it was Solomon who built the house for him.
48 "However, the Most High does not live in houses made by
men. As the prophet says:

49 " 'Heaven is my throne,
and the earth is my footstool.
What kind of house will you build for me?
says the Lord.
Or where will my resting place be?
50 Has not my hand made all these things?'[b]

51 "You stiff-necked people, with uncircumcised hearts and
ears! You are just like your fathers: You always resist the Holy Spirit! 52 Was there ever a prophet your fathers did not persecute? They
even killed those who predicted the coming of the Righteous One.
And now you have betrayed and murdered him— 53 you who have
received the law that was put into effect through angels but have
not obeyed it."

The Stoning of Stephen

54 When they heard this, they were furious and gnashed their
teeth at him. 55 But Stephen, full of the Holy Spirit, looked up to

[a]**46** Some early manuscripts *the house of Jacob* [b]**50** Isaiah 66:1,2

7:48 *Most High:* This name for God was very old. In Israel's history, it went all the way back to the time of Abraham. Abraham met the King of Salem named Melchizedek who was called "priest of God Most High" (Gen 14:17-22). See also the mini-article called "Names of God," p. 243.

7:51 *uncircumcised hearts and ears:* Though physically circumcised according to the Jewish custom, they were acting like the uncircumcised pagan nations around them. They were not truly consecrated to the Lord. See also the note at 7:8.

7:52 *the Righteous One:* That is, Jesus.

7:53 *the law . . . through angels:* This refers to the law that God gave to Moses. See 7:38 and the notes at 7:20 and 5:19.

7:55 *full of the Holy Spirit:* See 6:3 and the note at 4:8.

QUESTIONS ABOUT ACTS 3:1—7:60

1. What happened to Peter and John as a result of healing the crippled man at the temple? (3:1—4:31) What did they say when they were told that they must not "speak or teach at all in the name of Jesus"? (4:18) Why did the Sanhedrin give them this warning? Can you think of places where it is considered dangerous to speak or teach about Jesus today? Why is this? What can a Christian do in these situations?
2. Complete this statement: "For me, speaking about Jesus is _________ because . . ."
3. Describe how the early followers of Jesus lived and worshiped (4:32-37). What does this say to you about the purpose of possessions? What happened to Ananias and Sapphira? (5:1-11) Why?
4. In what ways are churches today like the early church? In what ways are they different?
5. Why did the religious leaders in Jerusalem continue to persecute the apostles? (5:12-42) Has anyone ever opposed you for doing something you knew was right? How did you handle the situation?
6. What special problem that the early church faced is described in 6:1-7? How did the apostles deal with it? How does your church handle conflicts and differences of opinion?
7. Describe the situation in which the church leader Stephen found himself in 6:8-15. Stephen was allowed to address the Sanhedrin. What were the main points of his speech? (7:1-53) How did the people who heard him react? (7:54-60) How did Stephen act in this difficult situation? ACTS describes Stephen as someone with great wisdom and filled with the Spirit (6:10; 7:55). Do you know someone like that? Describe that person. Where does his or her wisdom come from?

7:55 *Jesus standing at the right hand of God:* The "right hand" is the place of honor and power. "Standing" may mean that Jesus is welcoming Stephen (see 7:59).

7:56 *heaven . . . Son of Man:* See the mini-articles called "Heaven," p. 1420, and "Son of Man," p. 1866.

7:58 *began to stone him . . . laid their clothes at the feet of . . . Saul:* According to the Law of Moses, stoning was the prescribed method of execution, at least in part because God held the entire community of Israel responsible for maintaining its purity (see Lev 24:10-16).

It is not clear why the witnesses put their coats at Saul's feet. Some think it shows that Saul was in charge of the execution. For more about Saul, see the note at 8:3.

7:60 *fell asleep:* This expression means that Stephen died..

8:1 *Judea and Samaria:* See the map on p. 2473 for the location of these places.

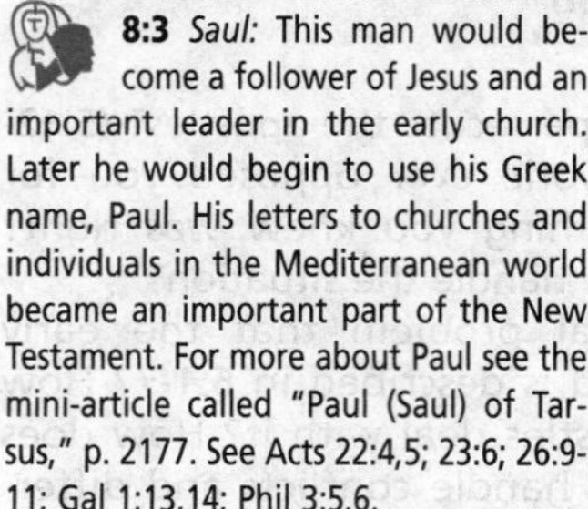

8:3 *Saul:* This man would become a follower of Jesus and an important leader in the early church. Later he would begin to use his Greek name, Paul. His letters to churches and individuals in the Mediterranean world became an important part of the New Testament. For more about Paul see the mini-article called "Paul (Saul) of Tarsus," p. 2177. See Acts 22:4,5; 23:6; 26:9-11; Gal 1:13,14; Phil 3:5,6.

8:5 *Philip:* Philip was one of the seven men chosen to be a leader in the new church (6:5).

8:5 *a city in Samaria:* Samaria in Jesus' day was the region south of Galilee and north of Judea. See the map on p. 2473. It is not clear which city Philip went to though it could have been the territory's capital, also called Samaria.

7:60 Luke 23:34,35.

heaven and saw the glory of God, and Jesus standing at the right
hand of God. 56"Look," he said, "I see heaven open and the Son of
Man standing at the right hand of God."
57At this they covered their ears and, yelling at the top of
their voices, they all rushed at him, 58dragged him out of the city
and began to stone him. Meanwhile, the witnesses laid their
clothes at the feet of a young man named Saul.
59While they were stoning him, Stephen prayed, "Lord Jesus,
receive my spirit." 60Then he fell on his knees and cried out, "Lord,
do not hold this sin against them." When he had said this, he fell
asleep.
8 And Saul was there, giving approval to his death.

The Gospel Is Preached in Judea and Samaria

The followers of Jesus begin to preach the gospel outside of Jerusalem, taking it to the rest of Judea, into Samaria, and even to Damascus in Syria. This section also tells about the work of Philip and introduces Saul, whose life is dramatically changed when Jesus meets him on the road to Damascus and chooses him to preach the gospel about Jesus to the Gentiles.

PHILIP, PETER, AND JOHN IN SAMARIA

The Church Persecuted and Scattered

On that day a great persecution broke out against the church
at Jerusalem, and all except the apostles were scattered throughout
Judea and Samaria. 2Godly men buried Stephen and mourned
deeply for him. 3But Saul began to destroy the church. Going from
house to house, he dragged off men and women and put them in
prison.

Philip in Samaria

4Those who had been scattered preached the word wherever
they went. 5Philip went down to a city in Samaria and proclaimed
the Christ[a] there. 6When the crowds heard Philip and saw the
miraculous signs he did, they all paid close attention to what he
said. 7With shrieks, evil[b] spirits came out of many, and many par-
alytics and cripples were healed. 8So there was great joy in that city.

[a]5 Or *Messiah* [b]7 Greek *unclean*

Simon the Sorcerer

[9]Now for some time a man named Simon had practiced sorcery in the city and amazed all the people of Samaria. He boasted
that he was someone great, [10]and all the people, both high and low,
gave him their attention and exclaimed, "This man is the divine
power known as the Great Power." [11]They followed him because he
had amazed them for a long time with his magic. [12]But when they
believed Philip as he preached the good news of the kingdom of
God and the name of Jesus Christ, they were baptized, both men
and women. [13]Simon himself believed and was baptized. And he
followed Philip everywhere, astonished by the great signs and miracles he saw.

[14]When the apostles in Jerusalem heard that Samaria had
accepted the word of God, they sent Peter and John to them.
[15]When they arrived, they prayed for them that they might receive
the Holy Spirit, [16]because the Holy Spirit had not yet come upon
any of them; they had simply been baptized into[a] the name of the
Lord Jesus. [17]Then Peter and John placed their hands on them, and
they received the Holy Spirit.

[18]When Simon saw that the Spirit was given at the laying on
of the apostles' hands, he offered them money [19]and said, "Give me
also this ability so that everyone on whom I lay my hands may
receive the Holy Spirit."

[20]Peter answered: "May your money perish with you, because
you thought you could buy the gift of God with money! [21]You have
no part or share in this ministry, because your heart is not right
before God. [22]Repent of this wickedness and pray to the Lord. Perhaps he will forgive you for having such a thought in your heart.
[23]For I see that you are full of bitterness and captive to sin."

[24]Then Simon answered, "Pray to the Lord for me so that
nothing you have said may happen to me."

[25]When they had testified and proclaimed the word of the
Lord, Peter and John returned to Jerusalem, preaching the gospel
in many Samaritan villages.

Philip and the Ethiopian

[26]Now an angel of the Lord said to Philip, "Go south to the
road—the desert road—that goes down from Jerusalem to Gaza."
[27]So he started out, and on his way he met an Ethiopian[b] eunuch,
an important official in charge of all the treasury of Candace,
queen of the Ethiopians. This man had gone to Jerusalem to worship, [28]and on his way home was sitting in his chariot reading the
book of Isaiah the prophet. [29]The Spirit told Philip, "Go to that
chariot and stay near it."

[30]Then Philip ran up to the chariot and heard the man

a16 Or *in* **b27** That is, from the upper Nile region

8:9 *Simon . . . practiced sorcery:* Simon's witchcraft was to call up the spirits of the dead or to tell fortunes. He apparently believed what Philip taught (8:13), but later he wanted to try to buy the gift of the Holy Spirit (8:18,19). When Peter rebuked Simon for his greed, Simon asked for forgiveness. See also the article called "Miracles, Magic, and Medicine," p. 1838.

8:17 *placed their hands on them:* This gesture was used in healing or giving a blessing (Mark 1:41; 10:16), choosing someone for a special task (Acts 6:6; 1 Tim 5:22), or when passing on the gifts of the Holy Spirit (Acts 19:6; 1 Tim 4:14). See also Gen 48:13-20.

8:26 *an angel of the Lord:* See the note at 5:19.

8:26 *from Jerusalem to Gaza:* A distance of about fifty miles.

8:27 *Ethiopian eunuch . . . official . . . Candace:* Ethiopia at this time was the name for the Upper Nile River region, south of Egypt. This official handled the money for the Candace, which was the title for the queen mother, who took care of the everyday duties of the king.

8:28 *book of Isaiah:* The scroll called ISAIAH that is found in the Jewish Scriptures (Old Testament). See also the mini-article called "Scrolls," p. 1491.

8:29 *chariot:* A chariot was a basket-shaped vehicle with two wheels that was pulled by either horses or oxen.

8:32 *a lamb before the shearer is silent:* This refers to the lamb that was sacrificed in the temple on Passover, and it also points to Christ, who was executed by the Romans during this festival. See the mini-article called "Passover and the Feast of Unleavened Bread," p. 2030, and Rom 3:24,25; Heb 10:12-14; Rev 5:6-13.

8:36-38 *here is water . . . and Philip baptized him:* See the mini-article called "Baptism," p. 1976.

8:40 *Azotus . . . Caesarea:* Caesarea was about forty miles north of Azotus on the Mediterranean coast (see the map on p. 2473). Herod named this city in honor of the Roman emperor Caesar Augustus, who had made Herod "king" of Judea. Herod, who was famous for his building projects, built an aqueduct (shown here) and a fortress in Caesarea, and turned the harbor into a major seaport.

Philip Baptizes the Ethiopian Official, stained glass window from the Church in Bury St. Edmunds, England, nineteenth century. Philip was one of the seven leaders of the church at Jerusalem chosen to be in charge of the needs of the church. An angel of the Lord sent Philip south on the desert road that leads to Gaza. Along the way an important Ethiopian official passed by in his chariot. He was reading the book of the prophet Isaiah but did not understand it. Philip explained the text to him and told him the good news about Jesus. The official believed and asked to be baptized immediately. (See 8:26-39.)

reading Isaiah the prophet. "Do you understand what you are reading?" Philip asked.

31"How can I," he said, "unless someone explains it to me?" So he invited Philip to come up and sit with him.

32The eunuch was reading this passage of Scripture:

"He was led like a sheep to the slaughter,
and as a lamb before the shearer is silent,
so he did not open his mouth.
33In his humiliation he was deprived of justice.
Who can speak of his descendants?
For his life was taken from the earth."[a]

34The eunuch asked Philip, "Tell me, please, who is the prophet talking about, himself or someone else?" 35Then Philip

[a]**33** Isaiah 53:7,8

began with that very passage of Scripture and told him the good
news about Jesus.
[36]As they traveled along the road, they came to some water
and the eunuch said, “Look, here is water. Why shouldn’t I be baptized?”[a] [38]And he gave orders to stop the chariot. Then both Philip
and the eunuch went down into the water and Philip baptized
him. [39]When they came up out of the water, the Spirit of the Lord
suddenly took Philip away, and the eunuch did not see him again,
but went on his way rejoicing. [40]Philip, however, appeared at Azotus and traveled about, preaching the gospel in all the towns until
he reached Caesarea.

GOD CHOOSES SAUL

Saul, a faithful follower of the Law of Moses, is on his way to Damascus to persecute those who had accepted "the Way." But Jesus stops him on the road and chooses him to preach the gospel.

Saul's Conversion

9 Meanwhile, Saul was still breathing out murderous threats
against the Lord’s disciples. He went to the high priest [2]and asked
him for letters to the synagogues in Damascus, so that if he found
any there who belonged to the Way, whether men or women, he
might take them as prisoners to Jerusalem. [3]As he neared Damascus on his journey, suddenly a light from heaven flashed around
him. [4]He fell to the ground and heard a voice say to him, “Saul,
Saul, why do you persecute me?”
[5]“Who are you, Lord?” Saul asked.
“I am Jesus, whom you are persecuting,” he replied. [6]“Now
get up and go into the city, and you will be told what you must do.”
[7]The men traveling with Saul stood there speechless; they
heard the sound but did not see anyone. [8]Saul got up from the
ground, but when he opened his eyes he could see nothing. So they
led him by the hand into Damascus. [9]For three days he was blind,
and did not eat or drink anything.
[10]In Damascus there was a disciple named Ananias. The
Lord called to him in a vision, “Ananias!”
“Yes, Lord,” he answered.
[11]The Lord told him, “Go to the house of Judas on Straight
Street and ask for a man from Tarsus named Saul, for he is praying. [12]In a vision he has seen a man named Ananias come and
place his hands on him to restore his sight.”
[13]“Lord,” Ananias answered, “I have heard many reports
about this man and all the harm he has done to your saints in

[a]**36** Some late manuscripts *baptized?” [37]Philip said, “If you believe with all your heart, you may.” The eunuch answered, “I believe that Jesus Christ is the Son of God.”*

9:1 *Saul . . . high priest:* See the notes at 8:3 and 5:17. The high priest had authority over the Jewish synagogues both in Judea and outside of Judea, such as in Damascus.

9:2 *Damascus:* One of the oldest continuously inhabited cities in the Near East. Under the Romans it became one of the major cities in the Greek-style confederacy called the Decapolis (Matt 4:25). At the time of Saul, Damascus was a major center for trade between Palestine and many other parts of the Mediterranean world. Saul knew that if he didn't stop the Christians and their message in Damascus, the message had a good chance of spreading everywhere.

9:2 *the Way:* In ACTS, "the Way" refers to the group of people who had became followers of Jesus Christ. See also 18:25,26; 19:9,23; 22:4; 24:14,22.

9:8 *Damascus:* See the note at 9:2 (Damascus).

9:10 *Ananias:* This Ananias is mentioned again at 22:12. His name is probably the Greek version of the Hebrew name *Hananiah,* which means "The Lord is gracious."

9:11 *Straight Street . . . Tarsus:* Still today Damascus has one long straight street running through it from east to west. Many of its other streets are narrow and crooked.

Saul grew up in Tarsus, which was located in the Roman province in Asia Minor called Cilicia (see the map on p. 2473). Its location on a trade route through the Tarsus Mountains allowed for a mix of cultures and ideas. Tarsus was famous as a center of learning, on the level of Athens in Greece and Alexandria in Egypt.

9:7 Dan 10:7; Acts 22:6-9.

9:14 *chief priests:* Chief priests were members of the group in charge of the temple in Jerusalem. See also the note at 4:23 and the article called "The World of Jesus: Peoples, Powers, and Politics," p. 1821.

9:15 *Gentiles . . . kings . . . people of Israel:* Gentiles are non-Jews. See also the mini-article called "Gentiles," p. 2127. Even though Saul's preaching would be done mostly among the Gentiles, he would also tell the good news about Jesus to Jewish people ("the people of Israel") and to kings (25:22,23; 26:1).

9:17 *Placing his hands on Saul . . . the Lord . . . filled with the Holy Spirit:* See the notes at 4:8; 8:17; and the mini-article called "Lord (Title for Jesus)," p. 2106.

9:18 *baptized:* See the note at 1:5 (baptized).

9:20 *synagogues:* "Synagogue" comes from a Greek word that means "gathering." In the Bible, a synagogue was a group of Jewish people who met together to worship the Lord and study the Scriptures. These gatherings usually took place in someone's home. See also the mini-article called "Synagogues," p. 1857.

Saint Paul Fleeing Damascus, enamel plaque from the eleventh century. Saul, who would later be known as Paul, had gone to Damascus to arrest any Jews who had become followers of Jesus. On the way, the Lord appeared to Saul, and Saul's life was changed forever. He became a follower of Jesus and began to preach about Jesus in the synagogues. Some people were so upset by what Saul was now saying that they made plans to kill him. Saul's followers heard about this and helped Saul escape by lowering him over the city wall in a large basket. (See 9:20-25.)

Jerusalem. 14And he has come here with authority from the chief
priests to arrest all who call on your name."
15But the Lord said to Ananias, "Go! This man is my chosen
instrument to carry my name before the Gentiles and their kings
and before the people of Israel. 16I will show him how much he
must suffer for my name."
17Then Ananias went to the house and entered it. Placing his
hands on Saul, he said, "Brother Saul, the Lord—Jesus, who
appeared to you on the road as you were coming here—has sent
me so that you may see again and be filled with the Holy Spirit."
18Immediately, something like scales fell from Saul's eyes, and he

QUESTIONS ABOUT ACTS 8:1—9:31

1. What was the situation in the city of Samaria described in 8:1b-25? How did the apostles in Jerusalem respond to this situation? Who was the "Simon" described in this passage and what did he want? What was his motive? How did Peter respond to Simon's request? What does this tell you about what it means to be a follower of Jesus?
2. What happened when Philip explained the good news about Jesus to the Ethiopian official? (8:26-40) Have you ever told anyone about Jesus? If so, what did you say? How did the person react?
3. Do you agree or disagree with the following statement: "I believe that telling people about Jesus is very important." Explain your response.
4. Why was Saul going to Damascus? What happened to change his plans? (9:1-19) How did Ananias help Saul?
5. What did Saul do next? (9:20-31) What caused the change in Saul's attitude? How does God change lives today?

could see again. He got up and was baptized, 19 and after taking
some food, he regained his strength.

Saul in Damascus and Jerusalem

Saul spent several days with the disciples in Damascus. 20 At
once he began to preach in the synagogues that Jesus is the Son of
God. 21 All those who heard him were astonished and asked, "Isn't
he the man who raised havoc in Jerusalem among those who call
on this name? And hasn't he come here to take them as prisoners to
the chief priests?" 22 Yet Saul grew more and more powerful and baffled the Jews living in Damascus by proving that Jesus is the Christ.[a]
23 After many days had gone by, the Jews conspired to kill him,
24 but Saul learned of their plan. Day and night they kept close watch
on the city gates in order to kill him. 25 But his followers took him by
night and lowered him in a basket through an opening in the wall.
26 When he came to Jerusalem, he tried to join the disciples,
but they were all afraid of him, not believing that he really was a
disciple. 27 But Barnabas took him and brought him to the apostles. He told them how Saul on his journey had seen the Lord and
that the Lord had spoken to him, and how in Damascus he had
preached fearlessly in the name of Jesus. 28 So Saul stayed with
them and moved about freely in Jerusalem, speaking boldly in the
name of the Lord. 29 He talked and debated with the Grecian Jews,
but they tried to kill him. 30 When the brothers learned of this, they
took him down to Caesarea and sent him off to Tarsus.
31 Then the church throughout Judea, Galilee and Samaria
enjoyed a time of peace. It was strengthened; and encouraged by
the Holy Spirit, it grew in numbers, living in the fear of the Lord.

9:20-22 *Jesus is the Son of God . . . Jesus is the Christ:* See the mini-article called "Son of God," p. 2044, and the note at 2:36.

9:23 *After many days:* From Paul's letters we know that Paul stayed in Damascus or the area just east of it, which he calls "Arabia," for three years (2 Cor 11:32,33; Gal 1:17,18).

9:26 *Jerusalem:* Most of the apostles and many other followers of Jesus were still in Jerusalem, the center of the Jewish religion.

9:27 *Barnabas:* See the note at 4:36,37.

9:30 *Caesarea . . . Tarsus:* See the notes at 8:40 and 9:11.

9:31 *church:* See the note at 5:11. The church here refers not to a single congregation but to all the followers of Jesus wherever they lived.

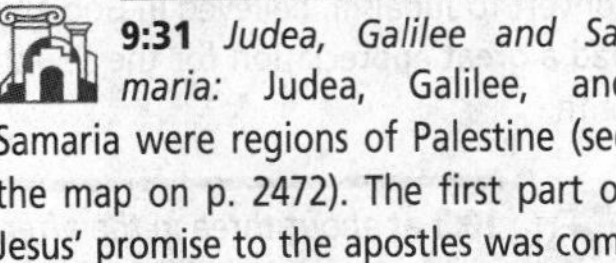

9:31 *Judea, Galilee and Samaria:* Judea, Galilee, and Samaria were regions of Palestine (see the map on p. 2472). The first part of Jesus' promise to the apostles was coming to pass (see 1:8).

9:32 *Peter:* See the note at 2:14.

9:32 *Lydda:* Lydda was about thirty-five miles northwest of Jerusalem and eleven miles southeast of Joppa. It was a commercially important town that had been controlled by different powers at different times in its long history. Since around 145 B.C. it had been a Jewish town. The fact that there were followers of the Lord here shows that the church was spreading to the northwest of Jerusalem as well as to the northeast (Damascus). See the map on p. 2473.

9:27 Acts 9:3-6, 20-22.

The Gospel Goes out to the Gentile World

This section focuses on how the church faced the question of who could be part of God's new people. First, God shows Peter in a vision that the gospel is also for the Gentiles. Then Paul and Barnabas are chosen and sent by the church to bring the gospel to Gentiles outside of Palestine.

PETER PREACHES AND LIVES THE GOSPEL

Aeneas and Dorcas

32 As Peter traveled about the country, he went to visit the
saints in Lydda. 33 There he found a man named Aeneas, a paralytic

[a]22 Or *Messiah*

9:35 *Sharon:* Sharon was a fertile strip of land that stretched fifty miles along the Mediterranean Sea coast between Mount Carmel in the north and Joppa in the south.

9:36 *Joppa:* When Peter arrived in the port city of Joppa, there was already a Christian community living there. Joppa dates back to the eighteenth century B.C. For a time, it was controlled by the Egyptians (around 1500 to 1225 B.C.). Later, it became a Phoenician city and was the port where lumber from the mountains of Lebanon was shipped before being taken overland to Jerusalem (see 2 Chr 2:16). Today, this city is called Jaffa and is a suburb of Tel Aviv, Israel.

9:43 *a tanner named Simon:* A tanner was a leather maker.

10:1,2 *Cornelius, a centurion . . . God-fearing:* A Roman centurion was in charge of about one-sixth of an army regiment, or about 100 men. The expression "God-fearing" referred to someone who, although not a formal convert to Judaism, believed in God and had a great appreciation for the Jewish faith.

10:3 *at about three in the afternoon:* Probably while he was praying. See the note at 3:1 (prayer).

10:3,10 *vision . . . trance:* A vision is like a dream, but the person having the vision may or may not be asleep. In the Bible, visions happen when God's Spirit or a messenger of God, such as an angel, speaks to the deepest thoughts of a person and provides a clear picture of something they are to do or say. See 2:17. When Peter received a vision, God caused him to fall into a trance (10:10) in order to reveal a message to him.

who had been bedridden for eight years. 34“Aeneas,” Peter said to
him, “Jesus Christ heals you. Get up and take care of your mat.”
Immediately Aeneas got up. 35All those who lived in Lydda and
Sharon saw him and turned to the Lord.
36In Joppa there was a disciple named Tabitha (which, when
translated, is Dorcas[a]), who was always doing good and helping the
poor. 37About that time she became sick and died, and her body
was washed and placed in an upstairs room. 38Lydda was near
Joppa; so when the disciples heard that Peter was in Lydda, they
sent two men to him and urged him, “Please come at once!”
39Peter went with them, and when he arrived he was taken
upstairs to the room. All the widows stood around him, crying and
showing him the robes and other clothing that Dorcas had made
while she was still with them.
40Peter sent them all out of the room; then he got down on
his knees and prayed. Turning toward the dead woman, he said,
“Tabitha, get up.” She opened her eyes, and seeing Peter she sat up.
41He took her by the hand and helped her to her feet. Then he
called the believers and the widows and presented her to them
alive. 42This became known all over Joppa, and many people
believed in the Lord. 43Peter stayed in Joppa for some time with a
tanner named Simon.

Cornelius Calls for Peter

10 At Caesarea there was a man named Cornelius, a centurion
in what was known as the Italian Regiment. 2He and all his family
were devout and God-fearing; he gave generously to those in need
and prayed to God regularly. 3One day at about three in the afternoon he had a vision. He distinctly saw an angel of God, who
came to him and said, “Cornelius!”
4Cornelius stared at him in fear. “What is it, Lord?” he asked.
The angel answered, “Your prayers and gifts to the poor
have come up as a memorial offering before God. 5Now send
men to Joppa to bring back a man named Simon who is called
Peter. 6He is staying with Simon the tanner, whose house is by the
sea.”
7When the angel who spoke to him had gone, Cornelius
called two of his servants and a devout soldier who was one of his
attendants. 8He told them everything that had happened and sent
them to Joppa.

Peter's Vision

9About noon the following day as they were on their journey and approaching the city, Peter went up on the roof to pray.
10He became hungry and wanted something to eat, and while the

[a]**36** Both *Tabitha* (Aramaic) and *Dorcas* (Greek) mean *gazelle.*

meal was being prepared, he fell into a trance. [11]He saw heaven
opened and something like a large sheet being let down to earth
by its four corners. [12]It contained all kinds of four-footed animals,
as well as reptiles of the earth and birds of the air. [13]Then a voice
told him, "Get up, Peter. Kill and eat."
[14]"Surely not, Lord!" Peter replied. "I have never eaten anything impure or unclean."
[15]The voice spoke to him a second time, "Do not call anything impure that God has made clean."
[16]This happened three times, and immediately the sheet was taken back to heaven.
[17]While Peter was wondering about the meaning of the
vision, the men sent by Cornelius found out where Simon's house
was and stopped at the gate. [18]They called out, asking if Simon
who was known as Peter was staying there.
[19]While Peter was still thinking about the vision, the Spirit
said to him, "Simon, three[a] men are looking for you. [20]So get up

[a]19 One early manuscript *two*; other manuscripts do not have the number.

10:4 *angel:* See the note at 5:19.

10:5 *Joppa:* Joppa was about thirty miles south of Caesarea. See the note at 9:36.

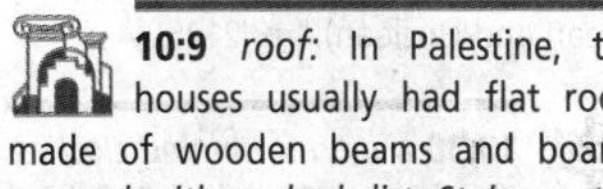

10:9 *roof:* In Palestine, the houses usually had flat roofs made of wooden beams and boards covered with packed dirt. Stairs on the outside led up to the roof. See the illustration on p. 1924.

10:14 *impure or unclean:* The Law of Moses taught that some foods were not fit to eat. See the mini-article called "Purity (Clean and Unclean)," below.

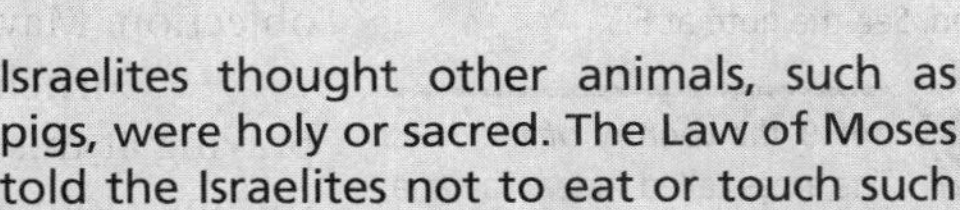

PURITY (CLEAN AND UNCLEAN)

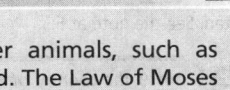

Ancient Israel defined being pure in three ways: (1) to be free of dirt or pollution; (2) to have no contact with anything that was unfit for a religious person to touch; (3) to be free of actions that were evil or that hurt others and went against God's commands.

According to the Law of Moses, different things could be clean or unclean (pure or impure). People could become unclean if they had certain kinds of diseases, when they touched a dead body, or when they ate certain foods—like pork or certain kinds of fish. The law told the people what to avoid so they wouldn't become unclean (see especially Lev 11–18). It also told them how they could become clean again by waiting for a period of time and then being washed and making the right kind of sacrifice.

God's priests also showed the people how to take care of who or what was unclean. Other people who lived in the ancient Near East believed that evil powers or spirits lived in certain kinds of animals and plants. Some of the nations that lived around the Israelites thought other animals, such as pigs, were holy or sacred. The Law of Moses told the Israelites not to eat or touch such animals.

Once a year, on the Day of Atonement, all of the people were made pure. On this day, an animal was killed and its blood was sprinkled in the Most Holy Place of the tabernacle or temple. This was an offering to God as a sacrifice for the sins of the people. Another animal (a scapegoat) was driven out into the desert and carried Israel's sins away (see Lev 16; 23:26-32; Num 29:7-11). See the charts called "Jewish Calendar and Festivals," p. 944, and "Sacrifices and Offerings," p. 219.

The early Christians understood that the sacrifice that made them pure and clean was the death of Jesus Christ (Mark 10:45). Jesus' blood was poured out for the forgiveness of sins (Matt 26:28), and it cleanses his people from all sin (1 John 1:7). The death of Jesus, they affirmed, makes it possible for his followers to be with God, and it makes their hearts and minds pure (Heb 10:19-22).

10:23,24 *Joppa ... Caesarea:* See the notes at 9:36 and 8:40.

10:28 *against our law for a Jew to associate with a Gentile ... impure or unclean:* See the note at 11:3 and the mini-article called "Purity (Clean and Unclean)," p. 2125.

10:30 *a man in shining clothes:* This is how Cornelius described the angel. See also 1:10 and Luke 24:4.

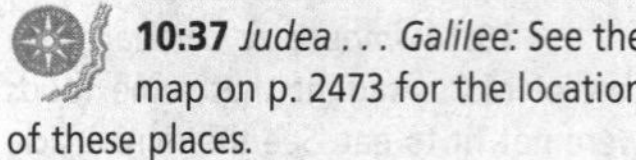

10:37 *Judea ... Galilee:* See the map on p. 2473 for the location of these places.

10:37 *John:* This is John the Baptist. See Luke 3:3-17.

10:38 *Jesus of Nazareth:* See the note at 2:22.

10:38 *Holy Spirit:* See the note on p. 2082.

10:38 *devil:* Also known as Satan. See the note at 5:3.

10:39 *the country of the Jews:* The areas called Judea, Samaria, and Galilee that had once been part of the nation of Israel.

10:43 *All the prophets:* Israel's prophets lived hundreds of years before Jesus. None of them mentioned Jesus by name, but many talked about how God would restore the Israelite people or make a new start with them. Others talked about one who would be the Christ or Messiah, the Anointed One.

10:34 Deut 10:17. **10:40,41** Luke 23:26—24:50; Acts 1:1-11.

and go downstairs. Do not hesitate to go with them, for I have sent
them."
21Peter went down and said to the men, "I'm the one you're
looking for. Why have you come?"
22The men replied, "We have come from Cornelius the centurion. He is a righteous and God-fearing man, who is respected
by all the Jewish people. A holy angel told him to have you come
to his house so that he could hear what you have to say." 23Then
Peter invited the men into the house to be his guests.

Peter at Cornelius's House

The next day Peter started out with them, and some of the
brothers from Joppa went along. 24The following day he arrived in
Caesarea. Cornelius was expecting them and had called together
his relatives and close friends. 25As Peter entered the house, Cornelius met him and fell at his feet in reverence. 26But Peter made
him get up. "Stand up," he said, "I am only a man myself."
27Talking with him, Peter went inside and found a large gathering of people. 28He said to them: "You are well aware that it is
against our law for a Jew to associate with a Gentile or visit him.
But God has shown me that I should not call any man impure or
unclean. 29So when I was sent for, I came without raising any
objection. May I ask why you sent for me?"
30Cornelius answered: "Four days ago I was in my house
praying at this hour, at three in the afternoon. Suddenly a man in
shining clothes stood before me 31and said, 'Cornelius, God has
heard your prayer and remembered your gifts to the poor. 32Send
to Joppa for Simon who is called Peter. He is a guest in the home
of Simon the tanner, who lives by the sea.' 33So I sent for you
immediately, and it was good of you to come. Now we are all here
in the presence of God to listen to everything the Lord has commanded you to tell us."
34Then Peter began to speak: "I now realize how true it is
that God does not show favoritism 35but accepts men from every
nation who fear him and do what is right. 36You know the message
God sent to the people of Israel, telling the good news of peace
through Jesus Christ, who is Lord of all. 37You know what has happened throughout Judea, beginning in Galilee after the baptism
that John preached— 38how God anointed Jesus of Nazareth with
the Holy Spirit and power, and how he went around doing good
and healing all who were under the power of the devil, because
God was with him.
39"We are witnesses of everything he did in the country of
the Jews and in Jerusalem. They killed him by hanging him on a
tree, 40but God raised him from the dead on the third day and
caused him to be seen. 41He was not seen by all the people, but by
witnesses whom God had already chosen—by us who ate and
drank with him after he rose from the dead. 42He commanded us

to preach to the people and to testify that he is the one whom God
appointed as judge of the living and the dead. 43All the prophets
testify about him that everyone who believes in him receives forgiveness of sins through his name."
44While Peter was still speaking these words, the Holy Spirit
came on all who heard the message. 45The circumcised believers
who had come with Peter were astonished that the gift of the Holy
Spirit had been poured out even on the Gentiles. 46For they heard
them speaking in tongues[a] and praising God.
Then Peter said, 47"Can anyone keep these people from
being baptized with water? They have received the Holy Spirit just
as we have." 48So he ordered that they be baptized in the name of
Jesus Christ. Then they asked Peter to stay with them for a few
days.

[a]46 Or *other languages*

10:44 *the Holy Spirit came on all:* See 2:1-4 and the note at 4:8.

10:45 *circumcised believers:* See the note at 7:8. Most of the very earliest followers of Jesus were Jewish, as were Jesus and his first disciples.

10:45 *Gentiles:* See the mini-article called "Gentiles," below.

10:47 *baptized:* See the note at 1:5 (baptized).

10:46 Acts 2:4-12.

GENTILES

The English word "gentile" comes from the Latin word for "people." In the Bible, Gentiles are all the peoples who are not Jews. The descendants of Noah and his family spread out over the world and became divided into many different nations or peoples (Gen 10). God divided these nations by giving them different languages because they had acted in evil ways (Gen 11). But then God chose Abraham and Sarah and told them that he would use them and their descendants to bring God's blessing to "all peoples on earth" (Gen 12:1-3). Later, at the dedication of the temple, Israel's King Solomon prayed that when foreigners came to Jerusalem that God would hear and answer their prayers—"so that all the peoples of the earth may know your name and fear you" (1 Kgs 8:41-43).

The prophets of Israel kept telling the people that God was eager to have other nations honor him (Jer 4:2) and know the God of Israel (Isa 42:1-4; 51:4, 5). If the people of God were obedient, they would be a model and witness to all the nations of the world (Isa 61). The story of Jonah shows how God reached out with mercy to a nation that was Israel's enemy. God will one day be the single ruler over all nations, and they will join to honor God (Ps 47:8, 9; 86:8, 9). In the kingdom that God will establish, "all peoples, nations and men of every language" will worship the LORD (Dan 7:14).

In the New Testament Simeon blesses the child Jesus, and says that he will be a light for the Gentiles (Luke 2:29-32). Jesus reaches out to heal people who are not Jewish, like the man with the demon in the Gentile region of the Gerasanes (Mark 5), the deaf man in the region of Tyre and Sidon (Mark 7:31-37), and the young servant of a Roman centurion (Matt 8:5-13). In ACTS, God gives the apostle Peter a startling vision to show the new believers that God accepts people "from every nation who fear him and do what is right" (Acts 10:35). Paul says that both Jews and Gentiles who trust what God has done through Jesus are accepted into the life of his new people (Gal 2:11-16). The book of REVELATION celebrates the fact that Jesus was willing to die for the sins of the *whole* world and make it possible for people from every tribe and nation, language and race to share in the kingdom of God (Rev 5:6-10). They can share the privilege that only Israel's priests were previously allowed to enjoy—they can enter into God's presence.

Peter Explains His Actions

11 The apostles and the brothers throughout Judea heard that the
Gentiles also had received the word of God. 2So when Peter went up
to Jerusalem, the circumcised believers criticized him 3and said, "You
went into the house of uncircumcised men and ate with them."

4Peter began and explained everything to them precisely as it
had happened: 5"I was in the city of Joppa praying, and in a trance
I saw a vision. I saw something like a large sheet being let down
from heaven by its four corners, and it came down to where I was.
6I looked into it and saw four-footed animals of the earth, wild
beasts, reptiles, and birds of the air. 7Then I heard a voice telling
me, 'Get up, Peter. Kill and eat.'

8"I replied, 'Surely not, Lord! Nothing impure or unclean has
ever entered my mouth.'

9"The voice spoke from heaven a second time, 'Do not call
anything impure that God has made clean.' 10This happened three
times, and then it was all pulled up to heaven again.

11"Right then three men who had been sent to me from
Caesarea stopped at the house where I was staying. 12The Spirit
told me to have no hesitation about going with them. These six
brothers also went with me, and we entered the man's house. 13He
told us how he had seen an angel appear in his house and say,
'Send to Joppa for Simon who is called Peter. 14He will bring you a
message through which you and all your household will be saved.'

15"As I began to speak, the Holy Spirit came on them as he
had come on us at the beginning. 16Then I remembered what the
Lord had said: 'John baptized with[a] water, but you will be baptized
with the Holy Spirit.' 17So if God gave them the same gift as he
gave us, who believed in the Lord Jesus Christ, who was I to think
that I could oppose God?"

18When they heard this, they had no further objections and
praised God, saying, "So then, God has granted even the Gentiles
repentance unto life."

THE GROWING CHURCH FACES PERSECUTION

The persecution the early followers of Christ face is painful, but it forces them to go to other areas and take with them the good news about Jesus.

The Church in Antioch

19Now those who had been scattered by the persecution in
connection with Stephen traveled as far as Phoenicia, Cyprus and
Antioch, telling the message only to Jews. 20Some of them, however, men from Cyprus and Cyrene, went to Antioch and began to

[a]16 Or *in*

11:1 *apostles and the brothers throughout Judea:* These are the rest of the twelve apostles and other believers who lived in and around Jerusalem. At this time, Jerusalem was still the center for the followers of Jesus.

11:2 *circumcised believers:* See the note at 10:45.

11:3 *house of uncircumcised men and ate with them:* The Law of Moses said Jewish people were not to spend time with Gentiles (non-Jews) or eat food Gentiles had touched. They were shocked that Peter had done this and thought this had made Peter unclean. See also the mini-article called "Purity (Clean and Unclean)," p. 2125.

11:12,13 *the man's house . . . He told us:* Peter is referring to Cornelius. See 10:1-4, 29-33.

11:17 *gave them the same gift as he gave us:* God gave the Holy Spirit to the Gentile believers just as he had to the Jewish believers. See 2:1-4 and the mini-article called "Gentiles," p. 2127.

11:19 *persecution in connection with Stephen:* See Acts 6:8—8:4. The killing of Stephen created fear among the early Christians. Jewish leaders, like Saul, persucted them so the Christians began to move out of Jerusalem and Judea to places where they could gather and worship in peace.

11:19 *Phoenicia, Cyprus and Antioch:* Phoenicia was an area that stretched about 120 miles along the northeastern Mediterranean coast. Its most important cities were Tyre and Sidon. Cyprus is an island in the northeastern Mediterranean Sea, about 100 miles west of the coast of Syria. At this time, it was part of the Roman empire. A Jewish colony started on Cyprus as early as the middle of the second century B.C. Paul and Barnabas preached in the synagogue on Cyprus (13:4-12). For more about Antioch, see the note at 6:5 (Antioch).

11:16 Acts 1:5.

speak to Greeks also, telling them the good news about the Lord Jesus. 21The Lord's hand was with them, and a great number of people believed and turned to the Lord.

22News of this reached the ears of the church at Jerusalem, and they sent Barnabas to Antioch. 23When he arrived and saw the evidence of the grace of God, he was glad and encouraged them all to remain true to the Lord with all their hearts. 24He was a good man, full of the Holy Spirit and faith, and a great number of people were brought to the Lord.

25Then Barnabas went to Tarsus to look for Saul, 26and when he found him, he brought him to Antioch. So for a whole year Barnabas and Saul met with the church and taught great numbers of people. The disciples were called Christians first at Antioch.

27During this time some prophets came down from Jerusalem to Antioch. 28One of them, named Agabus, stood up and through the Spirit predicted that a severe famine would spread over the entire Roman world. (This happened during the reign of Claudius.) 29The disciples, each according to his ability, decided to provide help for the brothers living in Judea. 30This they did, sending their gift to the elders by Barnabas and Saul.

Peter's Miraculous Escape From Prison

12 It was about this time that King Herod arrested some who belonged to the church, intending to persecute them. 2He had James, the brother of John, put to death with the sword. 3When he saw that this pleased the Jews, he proceeded to seize Peter also. This happened during the Feast of Unleavened Bread. 4After arresting him, he put him in prison, handing him over to be guarded by four squads of four soldiers each. Herod intended to bring him out for public trial after the Passover.

5So Peter was kept in prison, but the church was earnestly praying to God for him.

6The night before Herod was to bring him to trial, Peter was sleeping between two soldiers, bound with two chains, and sentries stood guard at the entrance. 7Suddenly an angel of the Lord appeared and a light shone in the cell. He struck Peter on the side and woke him up. "Quick, get up!" he said, and the chains fell off Peter's wrists.

8Then the angel said to him, "Put on your clothes and sandals." And Peter did so. "Wrap your cloak around you and follow me," the angel told him. 9Peter followed him out of the prison, but he had no idea that what the angel was doing was really happening; he thought he was seeing a vision. 10They passed the first and second guards and came to the iron gate leading to the city. It opened for them by itself, and they went through it. When they had walked the length of one street, suddenly the angel left him.

11Then Peter came to himself and said, "Now I know without a doubt that the Lord sent his angel and rescued me from

11:21 *The Lord's hand:* Referring to the power of the Holy Spirit.

11:22 *Barnabas:* See the note at 4:36,37.

11:28 *Agabus:* He is a follower of Jesus who had received the gift of prophecy from the Holy Spirit (1 Cor 12:7-11). In ACTS, prophets usually encourage Christ's followers with special messages from God (15:32), but here Agabus warns them about a coming famine and later predicts that Paul would go to prison (see 21:10-12).

11:28 *during the reign of Claudius:* Claudius was the emperor of the Roman empire from A.D. 41 to 54. Under Claudius, the empire was stable, which meant the early church could more easily grow and expand throughout the empire.

12:1 *King Herod:* This is Herod Agrippa I, the grandson of Herod the Great. He was appointed king of Judea in A.D. 37 and died in A.D. 44 (see 12:21-23). He was a smart politician who observed Jewish customs even though he wasn't born a Jew.

12:2 *James, the brother of John:* James and John were two of the apostles, the sons of Zebedee (see Matt 4:21). Jesus had earlier predicted that the brothers would drink from the cup that he must soon drink from (Matt 20:22,23), which meant they would also face suffering at the hands of people who hated them.

12:3 *the Jews:* This refers to the Jewish people who resisted becoming followers of Jesus.

12:3,4 *Feast of Unleavened Bread . . . Passover:* See Exodus 12:1-27 and the mini-article called "Passover and the Feast of Unleavened Bread," p. 2030.

12:7 *an angel of the Lord:* See the note at 5:19.

12:12 *Mary the mother of John . . . Mark:* This Mary was likely the aunt of Barnabas (Col 4:10). Her home was probably a meeting place for the followers of Jesus. John Mark is mentioned again in 12:25. For a time, he would become a co-worker of Paul (13:5; 15:37-39).

12:13 *Rhoda:* This is the only place she is mentioned.

12:15 *his angel:* They probably mean his personal or "guardian" angel.

Herod's clutches and from everything the Jewish people were anticipating."

12When this had dawned on him, he went to the house of
Mary the mother of John, also called Mark, where many people had
gathered and were praying. 13Peter knocked at the outer entrance,
and a servant girl named Rhoda came to answer the door. 14When
she recognized Peter's voice, she was so overjoyed she ran back
without opening it and exclaimed, "Peter is at the door!"

15"You're out of your mind," they told her. When she kept
insisting that it was so, they said, "It must be his angel."

16But Peter kept on knocking, and when they opened the
door and saw him, they were astonished. 17Peter motioned with his
hand for them to be quiet and described how the Lord had

Early Christian Symbols. The cross was not the earliest image used by Christians to identify themselves. Early Christians spread the gospel of Jesus by retelling the stories they had heard from Jesus' first disciples. Many early Christian symbols reflect these stories: The loaves of bread and fishes represented Jesus' miraculous feeding of the five thousand (Mark 6:30-44); Jesus as the "good shepherd" who looks after his sheep (John 10:7-21); Jesus as the true "vine" who helps his followers to produce much fruit (John 15:1-17). The grapes would also have reminded early Christians of the wine that was shared at their special meals (called the Lord's Supper; see 1 Cor 11:23-26). Other familiar images were a person with hands raised in prayer and an anchor (perhaps a sign of security and hope). Another symbol, perhaps an early form of the cross, was made up of the Greek letters Chi (which looks like an X) and Rho (which looks like a P). These are the first two letters of the Greek word for "Christ." For more about the cross, see the illustration on p. 2257.

brought him out of prison. "Tell James and the brothers about
this," he said, and then he left for another place.
[18]In the morning, there was no small commotion among
the soldiers as to what had become of Peter. [19]After Herod had a
thorough search made for him and did not find him, he cross-
examined the guards and ordered that they be executed.

Herod's Death

Then Herod went from Judea to Caesarea and stayed there a
while. [20]He had been quarreling with the people of Tyre and Sidon;
they now joined together and sought an audience with him. Having secured the support of Blastus, a trusted personal servant of
the king, they asked for peace, because they depended on the king's
country for their food supply.
[21]On the appointed day Herod, wearing his royal robes, sat
on his throne and delivered a public address to the people. [22]They
shouted, "This is the voice of a god, not of a man." [23]Immediately,
because Herod did not give praise to God, an angel of the Lord
struck him down, and he was eaten by worms and died.
[24]But the word of God continued to increase and spread.
[25]When Barnabas and Saul had finished their mission, they
returned from[a] Jerusalem, taking with them John, also called
Mark.

SAUL (PAUL) AND BARNABAS JOURNEY TO SHARE THE GOSPEL

Saul (Paul) and Barnabas are appointed to share the gospel in cities in the Gentile world. Both men would later make other journeys like this one, but not together.

Barnabas and Saul Sent Off

13 In the church at Antioch there were prophets and teachers:
Barnabas, Simeon called Niger, Lucius of Cyrene, Manaen (who
had been brought up with Herod the tetrarch) and Saul. [2]While
they were worshiping the Lord and fasting, the Holy Spirit said,
"Set apart for me Barnabas and Saul for the work to which I have
called them." [3]So after they had fasted and prayed, they placed
their hands on them and sent them off.

On Cyprus

[4]The two of them, sent on their way by the Holy Spirit, went
down to Seleucia and sailed from there to Cyprus. [5]When they
arrived at Salamis, they proclaimed the word of God in the Jewish
synagogues. John was with them as their helper.

[a]25 Some manuscripts *to*

12:17 *James:* The brother of Jesus (Matt 13:55; Mark 6:3). Later, he became the leader of the church in Jerusalem (Acts 15:13; 21:18; Gal 1:19), where he helped work out an understanding between the Jewish and Gentile Christians (15:22-29; see also Gal 2:9).

12:19,20 *Caesarea . . . Tyre and Sidon:* See the note at 8:40 (Caesarea). Tyre and Sidon were the leading cities of Phoenicia. Herod (see the note at 12:1) ruled an area that included Judea, Samaria, and parts of Galilee. He died in A.D. 44 (12:23).

12:25 *Barnabas and Saul:* See the notes at 4:36,37 and 8:3. For "their mission," see 11:27-30.

13:1 *church at Antioch:* See 11:20-26 and the note at 6:5 (Antioch).

13:1 *Simeon . . . Niger . . . Lucius . . . Manaen:* Simeon is a Jewish name, but Niger is Latin, meaning "black." This may mean that he had dark skin. Lucius came to teach in Antioch from his home in Cyrene (see 11:20). Manaen grew up as the foster brother of Herod Antipas, who had ruled Galilee at the time of Jesus.

13:2 *Holy Spirit:* See the note on p. 2100.

13:3 *placed their hands on:* See the note at 8:17.

13:4 *Seleucia . . . Cyprus:* Seleucia was Antioch's port city. See the note at 11:19 (Cyprus) and the map on p. 2476.

13:5 *Salamis:* Many Jews had formed a colony in this city on the eastern coast of the island of Cyprus. See the map on p. 2477.

13:5 *synagogues:* See the note at 9:20.

13:5 *John:* This is John Mark (see 12:25 and the note at 12:12).

13:6 *Paphos:* Paphos became the capital of the Roman province of Cyprus in 22 B.C. Paul and Barnabas visited the city around A.D. 46. See the map on p. 2476.

13:6 *Jewish sorcerer:* The name Bar-Jesus means "son of Jesus" (Jesus was a common name at the time). His other name, Elymas, means "sorcerer" or "wise man." The sorcery he practiced probably included casting spells, telling fortunes, and doing magic.

13:7 *Sergius Paulus:* He was the Roman proconsul (a type of governor) of Cyprus.

13:9 *Saul, who was also called Paul:* Saul was his Jewish name. Paul was his Greek name. In Greek-speaking areas, he would likely be better received by using his Greek name.

13:10 *child of the devil:* This was Paul's way of saying that Elymas's deceitful ways made him closely related to the devil.

13:13 *Perga in Pamphylia:* Perga had Greek temples and a Greek city plan, though the conquering Romans probably remodeled the city, building wide-columned streets, a stadium, and a theater that may have held as many as 12,000 people.

13:13 *John left them:* See the note at 12:12. Why he left is not certain. See also 15:36-40.

13:14 *Pisidian Antioch:* This is not the same Antioch that was mentioned previously in Acts. (See the note at 6:5.) This city was located in the district of Pisidia in Asia Minor, about 110 miles northeast of Perga.

13:14 *Sabbath:* The weekly day of rest when Jews gathered to read and discuss the Scriptures. See also the note at 9:20 (synagogues).

13:17 Gen 12:1-3; Exod 1:7; 12:51. **13:18** Num 14:34; Deut 1:31. **13:19** Deut 7:1; Josh 14:1-5. **13:22** 1 Sam 13:14; 16:12; Ps 89:20. **13:23** 2 Sam 7:11-16; Isa 11:1-16; **13:25** John 1:19, 20; Matt 3:11; Mark 1:7; Luke 3:16; John 1:27.

[6]They traveled through the whole island until they came to Paphos. There they met a Jewish sorcerer and false prophet named Bar-Jesus, [7]who was an attendant of the proconsul, Sergius Paulus. The proconsul, an intelligent man, sent for Barnabas and Saul because he wanted to hear the word of God. [8]But Elymas the sorcerer (for that is what his name means) opposed them and tried to turn the proconsul from the faith. [9]Then Saul, who was also called Paul, filled with the Holy Spirit, looked straight at Elymas and said, [10]"You are a child of the devil and an enemy of everything that is right! You are full of all kinds of deceit and trickery. Will you never stop perverting the right ways of the Lord? [11]Now the hand of the Lord is against you. You are going to be blind, and for a time you will be unable to see the light of the sun."

Immediately mist and darkness came over him, and he groped about, seeking someone to lead him by the hand. [12]When the proconsul saw what had happened, he believed, for he was amazed at the teaching about the Lord.

In Pisidian Antioch

[13]From Paphos, Paul and his companions sailed to Perga in Pamphylia, where John left them to return to Jerusalem. [14]From Perga they went on to Pisidian Antioch. On the Sabbath they entered the synagogue and sat down. [15]After the reading from the Law and the Prophets, the synagogue rulers sent word to them, saying, "Brothers, if you have a message of encouragement for the people, please speak."

[16]Standing up, Paul motioned with his hand and said: "Men of Israel and you Gentiles who worship God, listen to me! [17]The God of the people of Israel chose our fathers; he made the people prosper during their stay in Egypt, with mighty power he led them out of that country, [18]he endured their conduct[a] for about forty years in the desert, [19]he overthrew seven nations in Canaan and gave their land to his people as their inheritance. [20]All this took about 450 years.

"After this, God gave them judges until the time of Samuel the prophet. [21]Then the people asked for a king, and he gave them Saul son of Kish, of the tribe of Benjamin, who ruled forty years. [22]After removing Saul, he made David their king. He testified concerning him: 'I have found David son of Jesse a man after my own heart; he will do everything I want him to do.'

[23]"From this man's descendants God has brought to Israel the Savior Jesus, as he promised. [24]Before the coming of Jesus, John preached repentance and baptism to all the people of Israel. [25]As John was completing his work, he said: 'Who do you think I am? I am not that one. No, but he is coming after me, whose sandals I am not worthy to untie.'

---

[a]**18** Some manuscripts *and cared for them*

26"Brothers, children of Abraham, and you God-fearing
Gentiles, it is to us that this message of salvation has been sent.
27The people of Jerusalem and their rulers did not recognize Jesus,
yet in condemning him they fulfilled the words of the prophets
that are read every Sabbath. 28Though they found no proper
ground for a death sentence, they asked Pilate to have him executed. 29When they had carried out all that was written about him,
they took him down from the tree and laid him in a tomb. 30But
God raised him from the dead, 31and for many days he was seen by
those who had traveled with him from Galilee to Jerusalem. They
are now his witnesses to our people.

32"We tell you the good news: What God promised our
fathers 33he has fulfilled for us, their children, by raising up Jesus.
As it is written in the second Psalm:

> " 'You are my Son;
> today I have become your Father.'[a,b]

34The fact that God raised him from the dead, never to decay, is
stated in these words:

> " 'I will give you the holy and sure blessings promised
> to David.'[c]

35So it is stated elsewhere:

> " 'You will not let your Holy One see decay.'[d]

36"For when David had served God's purpose in his own
generation, he fell asleep; he was buried with his fathers and his
body decayed. 37But the one whom God raised from the dead did
not see decay.

38"Therefore, my brothers, I want you to know that through
Jesus the forgiveness of sins is proclaimed to you. 39Through him
everyone who believes is justified from everything you could not
be justified from by the law of Moses. 40Take care that what the
prophets have said does not happen to you:

> 41" 'Look, you scoffers,
> wonder and perish,
> for I am going to do something in your days
> that you would never believe,
> even if someone told you.'[e]"

42As Paul and Barnabas were leaving the synagogue, the people invited them to speak further about these things on the next
Sabbath. 43When the congregation was dismissed, many of the Jews
and devout converts to Judaism followed Paul and Barnabas, who
talked with them and urged them to continue in the grace of God.

---

[a] **33** Or *have begotten you* [b] **33** Psalm 2:7 [c] **34** Isaiah 55:3 [d] **35** Psalm 16:10
[e] **41** Hab. 1:5

13:16 *Men of Israel and you Gentiles who worship God:* "Men of Israel" refers to the Jewish people. Gentiles who worshiped the God of Israel but who hadn't become full members of the Jewish community by being circumcised were also there to listen to the teaching (see also 13:26).

13:19,20 *overthrew seven nations ... judges ... Samuel:* Deuteronomy 7:1 names the people who were living in Canaan before the Israelites settled there. When the Israelites were later oppressed by these people, God sent them leaders called judges who made decisions and acted as military leaders (Judg 2:16). Samuel was the last of these judges (1 Sam 7:15; see the note at 3:24).

13:21 *the people asked for a king:* See 1 Sam 8:5 and 10:21. When the people asked for a king like the nations around them, the LORD chose Saul to be Israel's first king. The history of his time as king of Israel is told in 1 Samuel 9–31.

13:22 *David:* See the mini-article called "David," p. 1028.

13:24 *John:* This is John the Baptist. See the mini-article called "John the Baptist," p. 1853; see also Mark 1:4; Luke 3:3.

13:26 *children of Abraham:* The Jewish people, descendants of Abraham.

13:26 *salvation:* See the note at 2:21.

13:32 *good news:* See the note at 5:42.

13:38 *through Jesus the forgiveness of sins:* See the note at 2:38 (forgiveness).

13:39 *law of Moses:* See the note at 7:20. See also Rom 3:20; Gal 2:15,16.

13:28 Matt 27:22, 23; Mark 15:13,14; Luke 23:21-23; John 19:15 **13:29** Matt 27:57-61; Mark 15:42-47; Luke 23:50-56; John 19:38-42. **13:31** Acts 1:3. **13:33** Ps 2:7. **13:34** Isa 55:3. **13:35** Ps 16:10. **13:41** Hab 1:5.

13:45 *the Jews:* This does not mean all the Jewish people, since some Jews had invited Paul and Barnabas back to the next Sabbath meeting (13:42). But it refers to Jewish people who did not believe what Paul was saying about Jesus. They thought he was trying to destroy the Law of Moses and the Jewish beliefs.

13:48 *eternal life:* A reference to the belief that those who trust in Christ will be resurrected and live with God forever. For more, see the mini-article called "Eternal Life," p. 2072.

13:50 *God-fearing women of high standing:* These were probably wealthy Gentiles (non-Jews) who were interested in the Jewish faith.

13:51 *shook the dust from their feet:* This was a way of showing that Paul and Barnabas renounced those who persecuted them and their responsibility for those people. See also Matt 10:14; Mark 6:11; Luke 9:5; 10:11.

13:52 *filled with joy and with the Holy Spirit:* See the note at 4:8.

14:1 *Iconium:* Iconium was an important commercial city in the province of Galatia in Asia Minor. It was about 100 miles east of Antioch in Pisidia. See the map on p. 2476. Highways from Syria to Ephesus and Rome went through Iconium.

14:5 *a plot . . . to mistreat them and stone them:* This is similar to what happened in Antioch (13:50), with the added threat of stoning (see the note at 7:58).

14:6,7 *Lycaonian cities of Lystra and Derbe:* Lycaonia was a district in the province of Galatia. It was east of the district of Pisidia and north of the Taurus Mountains. Lystra was about twenty miles southwest of Iconium. Derbe was about sixty miles southeast of Lystra. See the map on p. 2477.

13:47 Isa 42:6; 49:6.

44On the next Sabbath almost the whole city gathered to hear the word of the Lord. 45When the Jews saw the crowds, they were filled with jealousy and talked abusively against what Paul was saying.

46Then Paul and Barnabas answered them boldly: "We had to speak the word of God to you first. Since you reject it and do not consider yourselves worthy of eternal life, we now turn to the Gentiles. 47For this is what the Lord has commanded us:

> " 'I have made you[a] a light for the Gentiles,
> that you[a] may bring salvation to the ends of the earth.'[b]"

48When the Gentiles heard this, they were glad and honored the word of the Lord; and all who were appointed for eternal life believed.

49The word of the Lord spread through the whole region. 50But the Jews incited the God-fearing women of high standing and the leading men of the city. They stirred up persecution against Paul and Barnabas, and expelled them from their region. 51So they shook the dust from their feet in protest against them and went to Iconium. 52And the disciples were filled with joy and with the Holy Spirit.

In Iconium

14 At Iconium Paul and Barnabas went as usual into the Jewish synagogue. There they spoke so effectively that a great number of Jews and Gentiles believed. 2But the Jews who refused to believe stirred up the Gentiles and poisoned their minds against the brothers. 3So Paul and Barnabas spent considerable time there, speaking boldly for the Lord, who confirmed the message of his grace by enabling them to do miraculous signs and wonders. 4The people of the city were divided; some sided with the Jews, others with the apostles. 5There was a plot afoot among the Gentiles and Jews, together with their leaders, to mistreat them and stone them. 6But they found out about it and fled to the Lycaonian cities of Lystra and Derbe and to the surrounding country, 7where they continued to preach the good news.

In Lystra and Derbe

8In Lystra there sat a man crippled in his feet, who was lame from birth and had never walked. 9He listened to Paul as he was speaking. Paul looked directly at him, saw that he had faith to be healed 10and called out, "Stand up on your feet!" At that, the man jumped up and began to walk.

11When the crowd saw what Paul had done, they shouted in

---

[a]**47** The Greek is singular. [b]**47** Isaiah 49:6

the Lycaonian language, "The gods have come down to us in
human form!" 12 Barnabas they called Zeus, and Paul they called
Hermes because he was the chief speaker. 13 The priest of Zeus,
whose temple was just outside the city, brought bulls and wreaths
to the city gates because he and the crowd wanted to offer sacrifices to them.

14 But when the apostles Barnabas and Paul heard of this,
they tore their clothes and rushed out into the crowd, shouting:
15 "Men, why are you doing this? We too are only men, human like
you. We are bringing you good news, telling you to turn from these
worthless things to the living God, who made heaven and earth
and sea and everything in them. 16 In the past, he let all nations go
their own way. 17 Yet he has not left himself without testimony: He
has shown kindness by giving you rain from heaven and crops in
their seasons; he provides you with plenty of food and fills your
hearts with joy." 18 Even with these words, they had difficulty keeping the crowd from sacrificing to them.

19 Then some Jews came from Antioch and Iconium and won
the crowd over. They stoned Paul and dragged him outside the
city, thinking he was dead. 20 But after the disciples had gathered

14:12 *Zeus . . . Hermes:* Zeus was the chief Greek god. A temple was built in his honor in Lystra (14:13). Hermes was considered the messenger of the other gods. Since Paul was the one who talked the most, people would compare him to Hermes. See the mini-article below and the chart called "Greek and Roman Gods and Goddesses," p. 2136.

14:14 *tore their clothes:* A way of showing sadness and anger.

14:15 *the living God:* Paul was talking about Israel's God (Deut 5:26; Ps 42:2). He was comparing the one true, living God to "worthless" gods like Zeus, which were imaginary or simply made of stone.

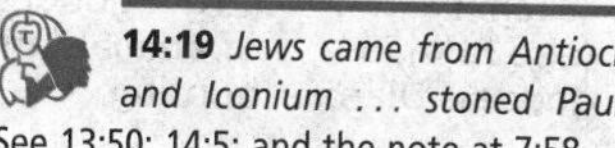

14:19 *Jews came from Antioch and Iconium . . . stoned Paul:* See 13:50; 14:5; and the note at 7:58.

RELIGION IN THE ROMAN WORLD

At the time Christianity was beginning to spread throughout the Roman empire, most Romans believed that there were many gods and goddesses who were at work controlling every aspect of their lives and the world of nature. Each deity was thought to be in control of one or more areas of life—such as the sun or moon, the weather, plant life and crops, the fertility of animals and people, success in battle—and even specific professions, like sailing, teaching, or weaving. Which deity a worshiper chose to honor usually depended on what that person did for a living. Particular gods and goddesses were also thought to give protection to specific towns and cities.

Many of the gods and goddesses that were worshiped by the Romans were "borrowed" from the cultures they had conquered, such as the Greeks and Egyptians. That is why many deities have both Greek and Latin (Roman) names. The Roman god Jupiter, for instance, was considered the greatest god. He controlled the forces of nature as well as the events in human history. Many of the myths associated with him are based on the myths originally associated with the Greek god Zeus. See the chart on p. 2136 for a list of some gods and goddesses worshiped in the Roman world.

In addition, emperor worship became common practice in the first century A.D. After Caesar Augustus died (A.D. 14), the Roman senate declared that he was a god. Sacrifices were made to him in order to make sure the empire remained prosperous. The emperors who came after Augustus also claimed to be gods or declared that those who had lived before them were gods. For example, Caligula (ruled from A.D. 37 to 41) ordered a statue depticting himself as a god to be set up in the Jewish temple in Jerusalem. By A.D. 100, all the people in the Roman empire were required to offer prayers and sacrifices to the emperors. This was said to be necessary so the empire would survive and remain stable. Christians who refused to worship the emperor in this way were subject to persecution. Some were even put to death.

GREEK AND ROMAN GODS AND GODDESSES

The ancient Greeks worshiped many gods and goddesses and believed these deities controlled aspects of the natural world. The responsibility of worshipers was to believe in the gods and goddesses and to make ritual sacrifices to them. The ancient Romans also worshiped many god and goddesses, some modeled after the Greek deities. The Romans believed that it did not matter what the worshipers thought of the gods as long as they performed the proper rituals.

GOD	WORSHIPED AS	RELATION TO OTHER GODS	BELIEFS ABOUT	SYMBOLS
Zeus (also Roman god Jupiter)	Chief god	Father of many gods and goddesses	Ruled clouds and rain, hurled thunderbolts, decided outcomes of battles; celebrated in Olympic Games	The eagle, the color white, the element tin
Apollo	God of music, archery, poetry, prophecy, and healing	Son of Zeus, brother of Artemis, father of Asclepios	Killed mythical monsters, leader of Muses (spirits of art), sometimes pictured as Helios, the sun god	The laurel, bow and arrow, lyre, lions
Artemis (also Roman goddess Diana)	Virgin goddess of animals and hunting	Daughter of Zeus, sister of Apollo	Presided over nature, helped Hera give birth to Apollo	Bow and arrow, wild animals, the moon
Asclepios (also Roman god Aesculapius)	Mortal who became a god of physicians and healing	Son of Apollo and a mortal woman	Lived as a mortal, killed by Zeus for bringing a human back to life	A rod with twin snakes coiled around it
Athena (also Roman goddess Minerva)	Chief goddess, goddess of war	Daughter of Zeus, born without a mother	Symbol of discipline and self-control, helped legendary heroes in battle, brought olive tree to humankind	The owl, the skin of a sacrificial goat
Hera (also Roman goddess Juno)	Goddess of marriage and childbirth	Wife and sister of Zeus, mother of Hephaestus	Took revenge against Zeus's lovers, celebrated in the *Heraia* and Olympic Women's Games	The cow, the peacock, the cuckoo
Hermes (also Roman god Mercury)	Messenger of the gods; also god of boundaries, shepherds, and thieves	Son of Zeus, brother of Apollo	Only god able to travel to the underworld (Hades) and back	Winged sandals, magical herald's staff
Hephaestus (also Roman god Vulcan)	God of fire and blacksmiths	Son of Zeus and Hera	Made shields and weapons for other gods and heroes; only disabled (lame) god	Fire, volcanoes
Demeter (also Roman goddess Ceres)	Goddess of agriculture	Sister of Zeus	Searched for her daughter Persephone, who had been kidnapped by Hades and taken into the underworld	Pigs, a basket filled with flowers, fruit, and grain
Dionysus (also Roman god Bacchus or Liber)	God of fruitfulness, wine, and intoxication	Son of Zeus	Lavish drinking and sexual rites (Bacchanalia) held in his honor	The ivy wreath and the *kantharos* (large goblet)
Hades (also Roman god Pluto)	God of the dead and ruler of the underworld	Brother of Zeus and Poseidon	Supervised the trial and punishment of the wicked after death, would not respond to prayer or sacrifice	A black chariot drawn by horses, a two-pronged harpoon, a key
Poseidon (also Roman god Neptune)	God of the sea, water, and earthquakes	Brother of Zeus and Hades	Ruled the oceans from a palace at the bottom of the sea	The trident, the dolphin, the tuna

around him, he got up and went back into the city. The next day he and Barnabas left for Derbe.

The Return to Antioch in Syria

21 They preached the good news in that city and won a large number of disciples. Then they returned to Lystra, Iconium and Antioch, 22 strengthening the disciples and encouraging them to remain true to the faith. "We must go through many hardships to enter the kingdom of God," they said. 23 Paul and Barnabas appointed elders[a] for them in each church and, with prayer and fasting, committed them to the Lord, in whom they had put their trust. 24 After going through Pisidia, they came into Pamphylia, 25 and when they had preached the word in Perga, they went down to Attalia.

26 From Attalia they sailed back to Antioch, where they had been committed to the grace of God for the work they had now completed. 27 On arriving there, they gathered the church together and reported all that God had done through them and how he had opened the door of faith to the Gentiles. 28 And they stayed there a long time with the disciples.

AN IMPORTANT MEETING IN JERUSALEM

While still in Antioch, Paul and Barnabas argue with Jewish believers who have come from Judea and were insisting that new male Gentile Christians be circumcised according to the Law of Moses. This leads to a meeting in Jerusalem where church leaders discuss who could be a part of God's new people.

The Council at Jerusalem

15 Some men came down from Judea to Antioch and were teaching the brothers: "Unless you are circumcised, according to the custom taught by Moses, you cannot be saved." 2 This brought Paul and Barnabas into sharp dispute and debate with them. So Paul and Barnabas were appointed, along with some other believers, to go up to Jerusalem to see the apostles and elders about this question. 3 The church sent them on their way, and as they traveled through Phoenicia and Samaria, they told how the Gentiles had been converted. This news made all the brothers very glad. 4 When they came to Jerusalem, they were welcomed by the church and the apostles and elders, to whom they reported everything God had done through them.

5 Then some of the believers who belonged to the party of the Pharisees stood up and said, "The Gentiles must be circumcised and required to obey the law of Moses."

[a]**23** Or *Barnabas ordained elders*; or *Barnabas had elders elected*

14:21 *good news:* See the note at 5:42.

14:21 *that city . . . Lystra, Iconium and Antioch:* "That city" refers to Derbe. This Antioch is Pisidian Antioch. See the note at 13:14 and the map on p. 2477. Paul and Barnabas had the courage to go back to the cities where they had been mistreated, in order to encourage the new followers of Jesus.

14:23 *fasting:* Fasting means to go without eating in order to focus on prayer.

14:24 *Pisidia . . . Pamphylia:* Pisidia was a district in the province of Galatia. Pisidian Antioch was in this district. Pamphylia was a smaller district located south of Pisidia. See the maps on p. 2476 and 2477.

14:25,26 *Perga . . . Attalia . . . Antioch:* See the note at 13:13 (Perga). Attalia was a seaport on the coast of Pamphylia. This Antioch was the one in Syria (as opposed to the Antioch in Pisidia). See also the note at 6:5 (Antioch).

15:1 *Judea:* Judea was the area around Jerusalem. Many of the apostles and church leaders still lived there.

15:1 *Unless you are circumcised . . . you cannot be saved:* See the mini-article called "Circumcision," p. 2251. Paul and Barnabas argued that this outward sign was not necessary for anyone to be part of God's new people.

15:5 *believers who belonged to the party of the Pharisees:* These strict followers of the Law of Moses wanted to follow Jesus, but they also wanted to make people hold on to Jewish traditions like circumcision.

15:5 *Gentiles must be circumcised:* This is an argument that Paul faced many times (see Gal 2:3,11-21; 5:1-18).

6 The apostles and elders met to consider this question. 7 After much discussion, Peter got up and addressed them: "Brothers, you know that some time ago God made a choice among you that the Gentiles might hear from my lips the message of the gospel and believe. 8 God, who knows the heart, showed that he accepted them by giving the Holy Spirit to them, just as he did to us. 9 He made no distinction between us and them, for he purified their hearts by faith. 10 Now then, why do you try to test God by putting on the necks of the disciples a yoke that neither we nor our fathers have been able to bear? 11 No! We believe it is through the grace of our Lord Jesus that we are saved, just as they are."

12 The whole assembly became silent as they listened to Barnabas and Paul telling about the miraculous signs and wonders God had done among the Gentiles through them. 13 When they finished, James spoke up: "Brothers, listen to me. 14 Simon[a] has described to us how God at first showed his concern by taking from the Gentiles a people for himself. 15 The words of the prophets are in agreement with this, as it is written:

16 " 'After this I will return
  and rebuild David's fallen tent.
 Its ruins I will rebuild,
  and I will restore it,
17 that the remnant of men may seek the Lord,
  and all the Gentiles who bear my name,
 says the Lord, who does these things'[b]
  18 that have been known for ages.[c]

19 "It is my judgment, therefore, that we should not make it difficult for the Gentiles who are turning to God. 20 Instead we should write to them, telling them to abstain from food polluted by idols, from sexual immorality, from the meat of strangled animals and from blood. 21 For Moses has been preached in every city from the earliest times and is read in the synagogues on every Sabbath."

The Council's Letter to Gentile Believers

22 Then the apostles and elders, with the whole church, decided to choose some of their own men and send them to Antioch with Paul and Barnabas. They chose Judas (called Barsabbas) and Silas, two men who were leaders among the brothers. 23 With them they sent the following letter:

The apostles and elders, your brothers,

To the Gentile believers in Antioch, Syria and Cilicia:

---

[a]14 Greek *Simeon*, a variant of *Simon*; that is, Peter [b]17 Amos 9:11,12
[c]17,18 Some manuscripts *things'— / 18known to the Lord for ages is his work*

15:8 *knows the heart:* See the note at 8:21.

15:11 *grace . . . saved:* Grace is undeserved kindness and favor. Paul makes the argument here and in many of his letters that all people—Jews or Gentiles alike—are saved by grace through faith, not by following certain laws or rituals. See also Gal 3:26-28; Rom 3:21-31; and the note at 2:21 (saved).

15:13 *James:* Jesus' brother, and one of the leaders of the church in Jerusalem. See the note at 12:17.

15:20 *abstain from food polluted by idols . . . sexual immorality . . . strangled animals . . . blood:* Some believers felt that eating food that had been offered to idols was wrong (see Exod 34:15-17). If they accepted such food, others might think they approved of the idol it was offered to. The leaders decided to tell people not to eat this food. See also 1 Cor 8:1-13.

"Sexual immorality" probably refers to the laws about the wrong kind of sexual relations, like those forbidden in Leviticus 18:6-23.

The Law of Moses said it was wrong to eat the meat of strangled animals because the meat would have kept all its blood. Before eating animals, the people would butcher them and drain the blood. The blood was not to be eaten (Lev 3:17; 7:26; 17:10-16; Deut 12:5-19, 23–24). See also the mini-article called "Blood," p. 180.

15:21 *Moses has been preached:* Referring to the Law of Moses. See the note at 7:20.

15:21 *Sabbath:* See the note at 13:14 (Sabbath).

15:22 *Antioch:* That is, Antioch in Syria. See the note at 6:5 (Antioch).

15:7 Acts 10:1-43. **15:8** Acts 2:4; 10:44-47. **15:16-18** Amos 9:11,12.

Greetings.

24We have heard that some went out from us without
our authorization and disturbed you, troubling your minds by
what they said. 25So we all agreed to choose some men and
send them to you with our dear friends Barnabas and Paul—
26men who have risked their lives for the name of our Lord
Jesus Christ. 27Therefore we are sending Judas and Silas to
confirm by word of mouth what we are writing. 28It seemed
good to the Holy Spirit and to us not to burden you with anything beyond the following requirements: 29You are to abstain
from food sacrificed to idols, from blood, from the meat of
strangled animals and from sexual immorality. You will do
well to avoid these things.

Farewell.

30The men were sent off and went down to Antioch, where
they gathered the church together and delivered the letter. 31The
people read it and were glad for its encouraging message. 32Judas
and Silas, who themselves were prophets, said much to encourage
and strengthen the brothers. 33After spending some time there,
they were sent off by the brothers with the blessing of peace to
return to those who had sent them.[a] 35But Paul and Barnabas
remained in Antioch, where they and many others taught and
preached the word of the Lord.

[a]33 Some manuscripts *them,* 34*but Silas decided to remain there*

15:22 *Judas (called Barsabbas) and Silas:* Judas Barsabbas may have been the brother of Joseph Barsabbas (1:23). But the name Barsabbas ("son of Sabbath") was fairly common among Jewish people. Judas and Silas were considered prophets (15:32; see the note at 11:28, Agabus). Like Paul, Silas was a Roman citizen (16:36,37). Silas went with Paul on his later journeys (Acts 15:37-40; 2 Cor 1:19; 1 Thes 1:1).

15:23 *Gentile believers in Antioch, Syria and Cilicia:* The letter was sent to the non-Jewish Christians in these areas. Antioch was the most important city in this region. See the note at 6:5 (Antioch) and the map on p. 2475.

15:28 *It seemed good to the Holy Spirit and to us:* See the note on p. 2100 (Holy Spirit). Priority was given to the Holy Spirit, but the agreement of the church was also essential.

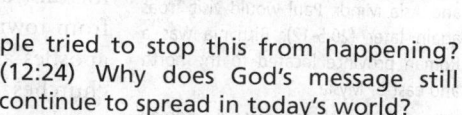

QUESTIONS ABOUT ACTS 9:32—15:35

1. What was important about Peter's vision and his meeting with Cornelius? (chapter 10) Peter says that he is certain that "God does not show favoritism" (10:34). What did that mean for the early church? What might it mean for Christ's followers today? Are all people treated the same in your community? In your church? Why or why not?

2. What happened to James and Peter? (12:1-17) How did the church respond? What happened next? What did Herod do? (12:18,19) What happened to him? (12:20-23) Why did God's message continue to spread, even though some people tried to stop this from happening? (12:24) Why does God's message still continue to spread in today's world?

3. What places did Barnabas and Saul (Paul) visit on their first missionary journey? (chapters 13 and 14) How were they received in the different places they visited? Describe at least one situation that was particularly interesting to you and tell why.

4. What major problem was discussed in Jerusalem? (15:1-21) What decision was made about the problem? (15:22-35) What effect did this decision have on the early church?

The Gospel Reaches Asia Minor, Greece, and Rome

The final section of Acts *focuses on Paul's mission to spread the faith. He takes two more journeys to preach the gospel. His travels take him to the important cities and countries that border the northern side of the Mediterranean Sea. On his return to Jerusalem, a mob is upset by Paul's teaching and begins to beat him up. When a Roman army commander arrests him, Paul demands his rights as a Roman citizen to be tried in court before being punished. Eventually, he is sent to Rome so the emperor can hear his case.*

PAUL'S SECOND JOURNEY

Disagreement Between Paul and Barnabas

36 Some time later Paul said to Barnabas, "Let us go back and
visit the brothers in all the towns where we preached the word of
the Lord and see how they are doing." 37 Barnabas wanted to take
John, also called Mark, with them, 38 but Paul did not think it wise
to take him, because he had deserted them in Pamphylia and had
not continued with them in the work. 39 They had such a sharp dis-
agreement that they parted company. Barnabas took Mark and
sailed for Cyprus, 40 but Paul chose Silas and left, commended by
the brothers to the grace of the Lord. 41 He went through Syria and
Cilicia, strengthening the churches.

Timothy Joins Paul and Silas

16 He came to Derbe and then to Lystra, where a disciple
named Timothy lived, whose mother was a Jewess and a believer,
but whose father was a Greek. 2 The brothers at Lystra and Iconium
spoke well of him. 3 Paul wanted to take him along on the journey,
so he circumcised him because of the Jews who lived in that area,
for they all knew that his father was a Greek. 4 As they traveled
from town to town, they delivered the decisions reached by the
apostles and elders in Jerusalem for the people to obey. 5 So the
churches were strengthened in the faith and grew daily in
numbers.

Paul's Vision of the Man of Macedonia

6 Paul and his companions traveled throughout the region of
Phrygia and Galatia, having been kept by the Holy Spirit from
preaching the word in the province of Asia. 7 When they came to
the border of Mysia, they tried to enter Bithynia, but the Spirit of
Jesus would not allow them to. 8 So they passed by Mysia and went
down to Troas. 9 During the night Paul had a vision of a man of
Macedonia standing and begging him, "Come over to Macedonia
and help us." 10 After Paul had seen the vision, we got ready at once

15:37 *John, also called Mark:* See the notes at 12:12 and 13:13 (John left them).

15:41 *Syria and Cilicia:* Syria was a Roman province north of Palestine on the northeastern coast of the Mediterranean Sea. Antioch and Damascus were its most important cities at this time. See the notes at 6:5 (Antioch); 9:2 (Damascus); and 6:9 (Cilicia).

16:1 *Timothy:* An important co-worker of Paul who is mentioned frequently in Paul's letters.

16:3 *circumcised . . . his father was a Greek:* Greeks did not circumcise their sons (see the note at 7:8). Even though Timothy's mother was Jewish, Timothy apparently hadn't been circumcised as an infant. Paul had Timothy circumcised in order to make Timothy acceptable to Jewish Christians, even though Paul had argued that circumcision was not necessary to be acceptable to God. See, for instance, Gal 2:1-5; 5:11.

16:6 *Phrygia and Galatia . . . Asia:* Phrygia was a region in Asia Minor that was divided between the Roman provinces of Asia and Galatia (see the map on p. 2476).

16:7,8 *Mysia . . . Bithynia . . . Troas:* Mysia was a small Roman province just north of the province of Asia. Troas in Mysia was a major seaport city on the narrow strip of sea that separated Macedonia in northern Greece and Asia Minor. Paul would visit Troas again later (20:5-12). Bithynia was a Roman province located to the north and east of Mysia.

16:9 *Macedonia:* A Roman province in northern Greece on the coast of the Aegean Sea and stretching northward to the Balkan Mountains. See the map on p. 2476. The Romans built a famous highway called the Egnatian Way, which ran east and west through the key cities of Macedonia, connecting the Adriatic and Aegean Seas. See the map on p. 2271. See also the note at 10:3,10 (vision).

15:38 Acts 13:13.

to leave for Macedonia, concluding that God had called us to
preach the gospel to them.

Lydia's Conversion in Philippi

11 From Troas we put out to sea and sailed straight for
Samothrace, and the next day on to Neapolis. 12 From there we
traveled to Philippi, a Roman colony and the leading city of that
district of Macedonia. And we stayed there several days.
13 On the Sabbath we went outside the city gate to the river,
where we expected to find a place of prayer. We sat down and
began to speak to the women who had gathered there. 14 One of
those listening was a woman named Lydia, a dealer in purple cloth
from the city of Thyatira, who was a worshiper of God. The Lord
opened her heart to respond to Paul's message. 15 When she and the
members of her household were baptized, she invited us to her
home. "If you consider me a believer in the Lord," she said, "come
and stay at my house." And she persuaded us.

Paul and Silas in Prison

16 Once when we were going to the place of prayer, we were
met by a slave girl who had a spirit by which she predicted the
future. She earned a great deal of money for her owners by fortune-
telling. 17 This girl followed Paul and the rest of us, shouting, "These
men are servants of the Most High God, who are telling you the
way to be saved." 18 She kept this up for many days. Finally Paul
became so troubled that he turned around and said to the spirit,
"In the name of Jesus Christ I command you to come out of her!"
At that moment the spirit left her.
19 When the owners of the slave girl realized that their hope
of making money was gone, they seized Paul and Silas and dragged
them into the marketplace to face the authorities. 20 They brought
them before the magistrates and said, "These men are Jews, and are
throwing our city into an uproar 21 by advocating customs unlawful for us Romans to accept or practice."
22 The crowd joined in the attack against Paul and Silas, and
the magistrates ordered them to be stripped and beaten. 23 After
they had been severely flogged, they were thrown into prison, and
the jailer was commanded to guard them carefully. 24 Upon receiving such orders, he put them in the inner cell and fastened their
feet in the stocks.
25 About midnight Paul and Silas were praying and singing
hymns to God, and the other prisoners were listening to them.
26 Suddenly there was such a violent earthquake that the foundations of the prison were shaken. At once all the prison doors flew
open, and everybody's chains came loose. 27 The jailer woke up, and
when he saw the prison doors open, he drew his sword and was
about to kill himself because he thought the prisoners had

16:10 *we got ready:* This is the first time the author of Acts uses the word "we." This may suggest that the information he begins to relate here is from personal experience. Or, it may suggest that the author is working from another person's first-hand account of Paul's travels.

16:11,12 *Samothrace . . . Neapolis . . . Philippi:* See the map on p. 2477. Philippi was named after Philip II, the father of Alexander the Great. Philip made the city into a fortress and the capital of his growing kingdom in the fourth century B.C. At the time of Paul, Philippi was a Roman colony and many Roman soldiers lived there after they retired.

16:13 *Sabbath . . . outside the city . . . place of prayer:* See the note at 13:14 (Sabbath). There was no synagogue in Philippi, perhaps because there were not enough heads of families to officially form one. See the mini-article called "Synagogues," p. 1857.

16:14 *Lydia . . . Thyatira:* Lydia was a business woman who came from Thyatira, which was in the Roman province of Asia (see the map on p. 2476). Thyatira was famous for the purple dye that was made there from the shells of sea snails. Lydia probably was not Jewish, but worshiped with Jews. The church in Philippi first met in her home (16:40).

16:16 *slave girl who had a spirit:* The Greek words translated here are *pythonic spirit.* A mythical serpent (Python) guarded the oracle at Delphi. Because of this, the term "pythonic" came to refer to persons who spoke by the power of this type of spirit.

16:21 *customs unlawful for us Romans:* The officials were probably charging Paul and Silas with encouraging people to practice a new religion, which was illegal (see the note at 18:13).

16:27 *drew his sword . . . to kill himself:* If a guard allowed a prisoner to escape, he was expected to give up his own life (see 12:19).

The jailer asked Paul and Barnabas, *"Sirs, what must I do to be saved?" They replied, "Believe in the Lord Jesus, and you will be saved—you and your household."*
Acts 16:30,31

16:30 *what must I do to be saved:* See the note at 2:21 and the mini-article called "Salvation," p. 2021.

16:33 *baptized:* See the mini-article called "Baptism," p. 1976, and the note at 1:5 (baptized).

escaped. 28But Paul shouted, "Don't harm yourself! We are all
here!"
29The jailer called for lights, rushed in and fell trembling
before Paul and Silas. 30He then brought them out and asked, "Sirs,
what must I do to be saved?"
31They replied, "Believe in the Lord Jesus, and you will be
saved—you and your household." 32Then they spoke the word of
the Lord to him and to all the others in his house. 33At that hour
of the night the jailer took them and washed their wounds; then
immediately he and all his family were baptized. 34The jailer
brought them into his house and set a meal before them; he was
filled with joy because he had come to believe in God—he and his
whole family.

The Arrest of Saint Paul, relief from the *Travellers* sarcophagus, second or third century. Paul suffered a lot and was even arrested because he preached the good news about Jesus Christ (see 2 Cor 6:3-10). When he and Silas were in Philippi, they were followed around by a slave girl who told fortunes and who was shouting things at them. Finally, when Paul had had enough, he ordered the spirit that was making the girl say these things to leave her. This upset her owners because they made a lot of money from her fortune-telling. They complained to the officials and had Paul and Silas arrested and thrown in jail (see 16:16-40).

[35]When it was daylight, the magistrates sent their officers to
the jailer with the order: "Release those men." [36]The jailer told
Paul, "The magistrates have ordered that you and Silas be released.
Now you can leave. Go in peace."
[37]But Paul said to the officers: "They beat us publicly without
a trial, even though we are Roman citizens, and threw us into
prison. And now do they want to get rid of us quietly? No! Let
them come themselves and escort us out."
[38]The officers reported this to the magistrates, and when
they heard that Paul and Silas were Roman citizens, they were
alarmed. [39]They came to appease them and escorted them from
the prison, requesting them to leave the city. [40]After Paul and Silas
came out of the prison, they went to Lydia's house, where they met
with the brothers and encouraged them. Then they left.

In Thessalonica

17 When they had passed through Amphipolis and Apollonia,
they came to Thessalonica, where there was a Jewish synagogue.
[2]As his custom was, Paul went into the synagogue, and on three
Sabbath days he reasoned with them from the Scriptures, [3]explain-
ing and proving that the Christ[a] had to suffer and rise from the
dead. "This Jesus I am proclaiming to you is the Christ,[a]" he said.
[4]Some of the Jews were persuaded and joined Paul and Silas, as did
a large number of God-fearing Greeks and not a few prominent
women.
[5]But the Jews were jealous; so they rounded up some bad
characters from the marketplace, formed a mob and started a riot
in the city. They rushed to Jason's house in search of Paul and Silas
in order to bring them out to the crowd.[b] [6]But when they did not
find them, they dragged Jason and some other brothers before the
city officials, shouting: "These men who have caused trouble all
over the world have now come here, [7]and Jason has welcomed
them into his house. They are all defying Caesar's decrees, saying
that there is another king, one called Jesus." [8]When they heard this,
the crowd and the city officials were thrown into turmoil. [9]Then
they made Jason and the others post bond and let them go.

In Berea

[10]As soon as it was night, the brothers sent Paul and Silas
away to Berea. On arriving there, they went to the Jewish synagogue. [11]Now the Bereans were of more noble character than the
Thessalonians, for they received the message with great eagerness
and examined the Scriptures every day to see if what Paul said was
true. [12]Many of the Jews believed, as did also a number of prominent Greek women and many Greek men.

---

[a]3 Or *Messiah* [b]5 Or *the assembly of the people*

16:37 *Roman citizens:* Only a small number of people living in the Roman empire were citizens, and they had special rights and privileges. For more, see the article called "The World of Jesus: Peoples, Powers, and Politics," p. 1821.

16:40 *Lydia:* See the note at 16:14.

17:1 *Amphipolis and Apollonia . . . Thessalonica:* Paul traveled through these Macedonian cities along the Egnatian Way (see the note at 16:9). Thessalonica was the provincial capital of Macedonia and had a population of nearly two hundred thousand, including a colony of Jewish people.

17:1 *synagogue:* See the note at 9:20.

17:2 *Sabbath days:* See the note at 13:14 (Sabbath).

17:3 *the Christ:* See the mini-article called "Messiah (Chosen One)," p. 1124.

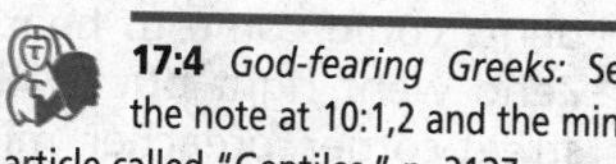

17:4 *God-fearing Greeks:* See the note at 10:1,2 and the mini-article called "Gentiles," p. 2127.

17:5 *Jason's house:* This may be the "Jason" who joined Paul in sending greetings to the church in Rome (Rom 16:21).

17:7 *defying Caesar's decrees:* Anyone who claimed to be a king, or said that anyone besides Caesar (the Roman emperor) was king, was breaking Roman law.

17:10 *Berea . . . synagogue:* Berea was about 50 miles southwest of Thessalonica in a different district of Macedonia. A Jewish group met regularly in Berea for study and worship. See the note at 9:20.

17:11 *the Scriptures:* That is, the Jewish Scriptures, which Christians call the Old Testament.

17:15 *Athens:* People settled in Athens as early as 3000 B.C. By about 440 B.C. it was the main center of Greece and the greatest cultural city in the Mediterranean world.

17:17 *marketplace:* It was common for someone to teach or lecture in the marketplace.

17:18 *Epicurean and Stoic philosophers:* The Epicureans were people who followed the teachings of the philosopher Epicurus. He taught that people ought to seek intellectual pleasure and avoid pain. For "Stoics," see the mini-article below. See also the article called "Religions and Philosophies in Bible Times," p. 1832.

[13]When the Jews in Thessalonica learned that Paul was preaching the word of God at Berea, they went there too, agitating the crowds and stirring them up. [14]The brothers immediately sent Paul to the coast, but Silas and Timothy stayed at Berea. [15]The men who escorted Paul brought him to Athens and then left with instructions for Silas and Timothy to join him as soon as possible.

In Athens

[16]While Paul was waiting for them in Athens, he was greatly distressed to see that the city was full of idols. [17]So he reasoned in the synagogue with the Jews and the God-fearing Greeks, as well as in the marketplace day by day with those who happened to be there. [18]A group of Epicurean and Stoic philosophers began to dispute with him. Some of them asked, "What is this babbler trying to say?" Others remarked, "He seems to be advocating foreign gods." They said this because Paul was preaching the good news about Jesus and the resurrection. [19]Then they took him and brought him

STOICS

The great thinker and teacher named Zeno of Citium lived from 332 to 262 B.C. Most teachers of his day rented a room where students could come to hear them teach. But Zeno went right out to the people, like a street-corner preacher might do today. In Athens, many beautiful columns stood in rows around the main city shops and public spaces. This area was called the Stoa. Because Zeno taught from this public area, he and his followers became known as "Stoics." Chrysippus of Soli (shown here) studied with Zeno's pupil Cleanthes of Assos and is considered one of the most important of the early Stoics.

The Stoics thought that the universe was a living being that had a god-like mind and purpose. They called this purpose "nature." They thought all humans had the ability and the responsibility to live according to nature's plan. This ability they called "conscience." If they lived by nature's plan, their lives would be filled with goodness and peace. If they didn't, fighting and destruction would happen. The Stoics believed that the only way people could control their lives was by controlling how they were affected by events in the world. By giving up the desire to control things that weren't in their power, Stoics sought to live without fear of the future.

Some Stoic ideas were adapted in Jewish writings, such as the noncanonical work, *The Wisdom of Solomon.* Tarsus, the apostle Paul's hometown (Acts 21:39), was a major center in Asia Minor for teaching Stoic ideas. When Paul gave a speech in the Stoa of Athens, he used some statements that would have been familiar to people who had studied Stoic teachings (Acts 17:16-34). In GALATIANS, Paul described what the Spirit of God does in the lives of people. These qualities that the Spirit produces were the same as qualities the Stoics thought would come if they lived according to nature. These include kindness, gentleness, patience, faithfulness, and self-control (Gal 5:22,23).

Athens. Athens is depicted here as it may have looked in the first century when Paul preached there. By that time it had been famous for over five hundred years as the home of many still-important ideas and people. Convicted of interfering with the religion of the city, Socrates, one of Athens' greatest philosophers, was sentenced to death in 399 B.C. Accepting this sentence, Socrates drank poison and died in the presence of his friends and disciples (top right). The plays of the great Greek dramatists were presented in the theater of Dionysus (top left). The Parthenon (bottom left, and top center in the drawing) was dedicated to the city's patron goddess, Athena. The agora (center of drawing) was the city's marketplace, as well as the political and social center of the city.

to a meeting of the Areopagus, where they said to him, "May we
know what this new teaching is that you are presenting? 20You are
bringing some strange ideas to our ears, and we want to know
what they mean." 21(All the Athenians and the foreigners who lived
there spent their time doing nothing but talking about and listening to the latest ideas.)

22Paul then stood up in the meeting of the Areopagus and
said: "Men of Athens! I see that in every way you are very religious.
23For as I walked around and looked carefully at your objects of

17:19 *a meeting of the Areopagus:* This was a council of powerful people from Athens who were in charge of the culture and morals of the city. They met on a small hill that was named for Ares, the Greek god of war. The Roman god of war was Mars, so sometimes the hill was also known as Mars Hill.

17:23 *TO AN UNKNOWN GOD:* The Greeks were afraid of offending some god that they did not know about, so they built altars to unknown gods.

17:28 *your own poets:* Paul quoted from two Greek poets in this verse: the Cretan poet Epimenides (sixth century B.C.) and the Stoic poet Aratus (third century B.C.) from Cilicia.

18:1 *Corinth:* This city was located on a piece of land separating the Aegean and the Adriatic Seas. Corinth was where many cultures met. It had theaters, marketplaces, temples, and a number of mystery religions. See also the Introduction to 1 CORINTHIANS, p. 2202.

18:2 *Aquila . . . Priscilla . . . Claudius:* Claudius threw out many of the Jews and Christians living in Rome because they were arguing with one another about who could be a part of God's people. Aquila and Priscilla were a Jewish Christian husband and wife who had to relocate because of this edict. This probably happened some time between A.D. 41 and 49. See also the note at 11:28 (Claudius).

18:3 *tentmaker:* Tents in Paul's day were often made from leather. Paul often talks in his letters about working to support himself (1 Cor 4:12; 1 Thes 2:9; 2 Thes 3:8).

18:7 *Titius Justus:* Probably a Gentile who had been going to the synagogue to worship.

18:8 *Crispus:* See 1 Cor 1:14. As ruler of the synagogue, Crispus was responsible for making arrangements and providing teachers for the meeting.

18:8 *Lord . . . baptized:* See the notes at 2:36 and 1:5 (baptized).

17:24,25 1 Kgs 8:27; Isa 42:5; Acts 7:48. **17:26** Gen 1:26-28; 2:7,8.

worship, I even found an altar with this inscription: TO AN
UNKNOWN GOD. Now what you worship as something unknown I
am going to proclaim to you.

24"The God who made the world and everything in it is the
Lord of heaven and earth and does not live in temples built by
hands. 25And he is not served by human hands, as if he needed
anything, because he himself gives all men life and breath and
everything else. 26From one man he made every nation of men,
that they should inhabit the whole earth; and he determined the
times set for them and the exact places where they should live.
27God did this so that men would seek him and perhaps reach out
for him and find him, though he is not far from each one of us.
28'For in him we live and move and have our being.' As some of
your own poets have said, 'We are his offspring.'

29"Therefore since we are God's offspring, we should not
think that the divine being is like gold or silver or stone—an image
made by man's design and skill. 30In the past God overlooked such
ignorance, but now he commands all people everywhere to repent.
31For he has set a day when he will judge the world with justice by
the man he has appointed. He has given proof of this to all men by
raising him from the dead."

32When they heard about the resurrection of the dead, some
of them sneered, but others said, "We want to hear you again on
this subject." 33At that, Paul left the Council. 34A few men became
followers of Paul and believed. Among them was Dionysius, a
member of the Areopagus, also a woman named Damaris, and a
number of others.

In Corinth

18 After this, Paul left Athens and went to Corinth. 2There he
met a Jew named Aquila, a native of Pontus, who had recently
come from Italy with his wife Priscilla, because Claudius had
ordered all the Jews to leave Rome. Paul went to see them, 3and
because he was a tentmaker as they were, he stayed and worked
with them. 4Every Sabbath he reasoned in the synagogue, trying to
persuade Jews and Greeks.

5When Silas and Timothy came from Macedonia, Paul
devoted himself exclusively to preaching, testifying to the Jews that
Jesus was the Christ.[a] 6But when the Jews opposed Paul and
became abusive, he shook out his clothes in protest and said to
them, "Your blood be on your own heads! I am clear of my
responsibility. From now on I will go to the Gentiles."

7Then Paul left the synagogue and went next door to the
house of Titius Justus, a worshiper of God. 8Crispus, the synagogue
ruler, and his entire household believed in the Lord; and

[a]5 Or *Messiah;* also in verse 28

many of the Corinthians who heard him believed and were
baptized.
9One night the Lord spoke to Paul in a vision: "Do not be
afraid; keep on speaking, do not be silent. 10For I am with you, and
no one is going to attack and harm you, because I have many people in this city." 11So Paul stayed for a year and a half, teaching
them the word of God.
12While Gallio was proconsul of Achaia, the Jews made a
united attack on Paul and brought him into court. 13"This man,"
they charged, "is persuading the people to worship God in ways
contrary to the law."
14Just as Paul was about to speak, Gallio said to the Jews, "If
you Jews were making a complaint about some misdemeanor or
serious crime, it would be reasonable for me to listen to you. 15But
since it involves questions about words and names and your own

18:12 *Gallio was proconsul of Achaia:* Gallio was the brother of the famous Roman Stoic philosopher Seneca. An ancient inscription found at Delphi shows that Gallio was the proconsul (ruler) of Achaia from A.D. 51 to 52.

18:13 *worship God . . . contrary to the law:* Paul did not get to defend himself, but later he argued that the good news about Christ was clearly based on the faith of his Jewish ancestors (24:14,15; 26:6,7). Therefore, his preaching was not a new religion but a new message based on the Jewish Scriptures and teachings.

Tentmaking in the Time of Paul. Paul was a tentmaker and practiced this trade in Corinth with Priscilla and Aquila. In biblical times, tents were mainly lived in, although they were also used as places to store things or to cover shrines. Tents were made from either cloth or animal skins (leather). The larger ones were constructed in sections that could be easily carried and set up. Fabric woven from goat hair was most common in the desert; wool or leather in other places. The leather for tents first had to be tanned by soaking the skins, scraping off the animal hairs, soaking the cleaned skins a second time (to tighten them), and then dried. The finished pieces of leather were then trimmed, cut into the appropriate shapes, and punctured so that they could be easily sewn together with thread.

law—settle the matter yourselves. I will not be a judge of such
things." [16]So he had them ejected from the court. [17]Then they all
turned on Sosthenes the synagogue ruler and beat him in front of
the court. But Gallio showed no concern whatever.

Priscilla, Aquila and Apollos

[18]Paul stayed on in Corinth for some time. Then he left the
brothers and sailed for Syria, accompanied by Priscilla and Aquila.
Before he sailed, he had his hair cut off at Cenchrea because of a
vow he had taken. [19]They arrived at Ephesus, where Paul left
Priscilla and Aquila. He himself went into the synagogue and reasoned with the Jews. [20]When they asked him to spend more time
with them, he declined. [21]But as he left, he promised, "I will come
back if it is God's will." Then he set sail from Ephesus. [22]When he
landed at Caesarea, he went up and greeted the church and then
went down to Antioch.

PAUL'S THIRD JOURNEY

After a long journey through Asia Minor, Macedonia, and Achaia, Paul returns to Antioch in Syria, probably to report how his mission has gone. He then heads back again to visit some of the same places he visited earlier and a few new places as well.

[23]After spending some time in Antioch, Paul set out from
there and traveled from place to place throughout the region of
Galatia and Phrygia, strengthening all the disciples.

[24]Meanwhile a Jew named Apollos, a native of Alexandria,
came to Ephesus. He was a learned man, with a thorough knowledge of the Scriptures. [25]He had been instructed in the way of the
Lord, and he spoke with great fervor[a] and taught about Jesus accurately, though he knew only the baptism of John. [26]He began to
speak boldly in the synagogue. When Priscilla and Aquila heard
him, they invited him to their home and explained to him the way
of God more adequately.

[27]When Apollos wanted to go to Achaia, the brothers
encouraged him and wrote to the disciples there to welcome him.
On arriving, he was a great help to those who by grace had
believed. [28]For he vigorously refuted the Jews in public debate,
proving from the Scriptures that Jesus was the Christ.

Paul in Ephesus

19 While Apollos was at Corinth, Paul took the road through
the interior and arrived at Ephesus. There he found some disciples

[a]25 Or *with fervor in the Spirit*

18:17 *Sosthenes the synagogue ruler:* See the note at 18:8 (Cyprus). It is not clear whether Sosthenes was beaten by Greeks in the crowd or by his own Jewish people.

18:18 *Priscilla and Aquila:* See the note at 18:2.

18:18 *had his hair cut off:* Paul probably had promised temporarily to be a "Nazirite," meaning that for the time of the vow he could not cut his hair or drink wine. See Numbers 6:18 and the mini-article called "Making Vows," p. 328.

18:18 *Cenchrea:* See the map on p. 2476.

18:19 *Ephesus:* Ephesus was the capital of the Roman province of Asia and a very important center for trading. For more about Ephesus, see the Introduction to EPHESIANS, p. 2260.

18:22 *Caesarea . . . Antioch:* See the notes at 8:40 and 6:5 (Antioch).

18:23 *Galatia and Phrygia:* See the note at 16:6.

18:24 *Apollos:* Apollos grew up in Alexandria, a major city in Egypt which had a large Jewish population. It is not surprising that Apollos knew the Jewish Scriptures well. See also 18:28; 1 Cor 1:12; 3:4–6.

18:25 *the baptism of John:* Referring to John the Baptist. See the note at 1:5 (baptized).

18:27 *Achaia:* Athens and Corinth were this region's most important cities. See the map on p. 2477.

18:27,28 *who by grace had believed . . . proving from the Scriptures:* For "grace" see the note at 15:11 and the mini-article called "Faith," p. 1932. For "Scriptures," see the note at 17:11 and the mini-article called "Inspiration of Scripture," p. 12.

2 and asked them, "Did you receive the Holy Spirit when[a] you
believed?"
They answered, "No, we have not even heard that there is a
Holy Spirit."
3 So Paul asked, "Then what baptism did you receive?"
"John's baptism," they replied.
4 Paul said, "John's baptism was a baptism of repentance. He
told the people to believe in the one coming after him, that is, in
Jesus." 5 On hearing this, they were baptized into[b] the name of the
Lord Jesus. 6 When Paul placed his hands on them, the Holy Spirit
came on them, and they spoke in tongues[c] and prophesied. 7 There
were about twelve men in all.
8 Paul entered the synagogue and spoke boldly there for three
months, arguing persuasively about the kingdom of God. 9 But
some of them became obstinate; they refused to believe and publicly maligned the Way. So Paul left them. He took the disciples
with him and had discussions daily in the lecture hall of Tyrannus.
10 This went on for two years, so that all the Jews and Greeks who
lived in the province of Asia heard the word of the Lord.
11 God did extraordinary miracles through Paul, 12 so that
even handkerchiefs and aprons that had touched him were taken
to the sick, and their illnesses were cured and the evil spirits left
them.
13 Some Jews who went around driving out evil spirits tried
to invoke the name of the Lord Jesus over those who were demon-
possessed. They would say, "In the name of Jesus, whom Paul
preaches, I command you to come out." 14 Seven sons of Sceva, a
Jewish chief priest, were doing this. 15 ⌞One day⌟ the evil spirit
answered them, "Jesus I know, and I know about Paul, but who are
you?" 16 Then the man who had the evil spirit jumped on them and
overpowered them all. He gave them such a beating that they ran
out of the house naked and bleeding.
17 When this became known to the Jews and Greeks living in
Ephesus, they were all seized with fear, and the name of the Lord
Jesus was held in high honor. 18 Many of those who believed now
came and openly confessed their evil deeds. 19 A number who had
practiced sorcery brought their scrolls together and burned them
publicly. When they calculated the value of the scrolls, the total
came to fifty thousand drachmas.[d] 20 In this way the word of the
Lord spread widely and grew in power.
21 After all this had happened, Paul decided to go to
Jerusalem, passing through Macedonia and Achaia. "After I have
been there," he said, "I must visit Rome also." 22 He sent two of his
helpers, Timothy and Erastus, to Macedonia, while he stayed in the
province of Asia a little longer.

---

[a]2 Or *after* [b]5 Or *in* [c]6 Or *other languages* [d]19 A drachma was a silver coin worth about a day's wages.

19:2 *Holy Spirit:* See the note on p. 2100.

19:3,4 *John's baptism:* See the note at 18:25.

19:6 *Holy Spirit came on them:* After being baptized in Jesus' name and through the laying on of hands, the Holy Spirit came to these new believers. Two gifts of the Spirit, prophecy and speaking in unknown languages (tongues), are mentioned here. See also Acts 2:4,11; 10:44–46; and the note at 8:17.

19:8 *kingdom of God:* This refers to God's rule, both in this life and in the next (see 1:3; 8:12; 28:21,23). See also Luke 10:9,11.

19:9 *the Way:* See the note at 9:2 (the Way).

19:9 *lecture hall of Tyrannus:* Tyrannus was a philosopher who probably lectured in this hall, which may have been a kind of school.

19:10 *Asia:* See the note at 16:6 and the map on p. 2476.

19:14 *sons of Sceva:* Sceva and his sons may have been related to the high priestly family in Jerusalem, but he was not the official high priest.

19:19 *practiced sorcery:* Some ancient papers found at Ephesus contained magical formulas and secret information. This has led some to conclude that Ephesus attracted people who practiced magic and witchcraft.

19:21 *Jerusalem . . . Macedonia and Achaia . . . Rome:* See the notes at 1:4 (Jerusalem); 16:9; 18:27; and 28:14. Paul had visited Achaia during his second missionary journey and was now going back to check on how the churches in those areas were doing before going to Jerusalem to report on his work to the apostles.

19:22 *Timothy and Erastus:* See the note at 16:1 (Timothy). Erastus is likely the person mentioned in Romans 16:23 as Corinth's director of public works. See also 2 Tim 4:20.

19:24 *silversmith named Demetrius . . . Artemis:* Demetrius created models of the temple of the goddess Artemis. Ephesus was famous all over Asia Minor as the center for worshiping Artemis. The temple of Artemis in Ephesus was a large, beautiful building that had 127 white marble columns. Inside the temple was an image of the goddess that was believed to have fallen from heaven (19:35).

19:29 *Gaius and Aristarchus:* A "Gaius" is mentioned in 20:4, but that may be a different person. Aristarchus is said to have traveled with Paul from Corinth to Jerusalem (20:3, 4) and sailed with him from Jerusalem to Rome (27:1, 2). See also Col 4:10 and Phlm 24.

The Riot in Ephesus

23About that time there arose a great disturbance about the
Way. 24A silversmith named Demetrius, who made silver shrines of
Artemis, brought in no little business for the craftsmen. 25He called
them together, along with the workmen in related trades, and said:
"Men, you know we receive a good income from this business.
26And you see and hear how this fellow Paul has convinced and led
astray large numbers of people here in Ephesus and in practically
the whole province of Asia. He says that man-made gods are no
gods at all. 27There is danger not only that our trade will lose its
good name, but also that the temple of the great goddess Artemis
will be discredited, and the goddess herself, who is worshiped
throughout the province of Asia and the world, will be robbed of
her divine majesty."

28When they heard this, they were furious and began shouting: "Great is Artemis of the Ephesians!" 29Soon the whole city was
in an uproar. The people seized Gaius and Aristarchus, Paul's trav-

Ephesus. Paul went to many cities on the Aegean Sea during his missionary journeys. After leaving Antioch he made his second visit to Ephesus, the greatest commercial city in the Roman province of Asia. Artemis was the patron goddess of Ephesus. Her temple was the largest building in the Greek world, making it one of the "Seven Wonders" of the ancient world. The column-lined Arcadian Way led to the Great Theater. It could seat twenty-five thousand people and may be the theater into which Paul's companions, Gaius and Aristarchus, were dragged. Paul upset the local silversmiths, who rioted in the marketplace because they felt their livelihood (selling miniature replicas of the temple) was being threatened by Paul's preaching of the gospel.

eling companions from Macedonia, and rushed as one man into
the theater. [30]Paul wanted to appear before the crowd, but the disciples would not let him. [31]Even some of the officials of the
province, friends of Paul, sent him a message begging him not to
venture into the theater.
[32]The assembly was in confusion: Some were shouting one
thing, some another. Most of the people did not even know why
they were there. [33]The Jews pushed Alexander to the front, and
some of the crowd shouted instructions to him. He motioned for
silence in order to make a defense before the people. [34]But when
they realized he was a Jew, they all shouted in unison for about two
hours: "Great is Artemis of the Ephesians!"
[35]The city clerk quieted the crowd and said: "Men of Ephesus, doesn't all the world know that the city of Ephesus is the
guardian of the temple of the great Artemis and of her image,
which fell from heaven? [36]Therefore, since these facts are undeni-
able, you ought to be quiet and not do anything rash. [37]You have
brought these men here, though they have neither robbed temples
nor blasphemed our goddess. [38]If, then, Demetrius and his fellow
craftsmen have a grievance against anybody, the courts are open
and there are proconsuls. They can press charges. [39]If there is anything further you want to bring up, it must be settled in a legal
assembly. [40]As it is, we are in danger of being charged with rioting
because of today's events. In that case we would not be able to
account for this commotion, since there is no reason for it." [41]After
he had said this, he dismissed the assembly.

Through Macedonia and Greece

20 When the uproar had ended, Paul sent for the disciples and,
after encouraging them, said good-by and set out for Macedonia.
[2]He traveled through that area, speaking many words of encouragement to the people, and finally arrived in Greece, [3]where he
stayed three months. Because the Jews made a plot against him just
as he was about to sail for Syria, he decided to go back through
Macedonia. [4]He was accompanied by Sopater son of Pyrrhus from
Berea, Aristarchus and Secundus from Thessalonica, Gaius from
Derbe, Timothy also, and Tychicus and Trophimus from the
province of Asia. [5]These men went on ahead and waited for us at
Troas. [6]But we sailed from Philippi after the Feast of Unleavened
Bread, and five days later joined the others at Troas, where we
stayed seven days.

Eutychus Raised From the Dead at Troas

[7]On the first day of the week we came together to break
bread. Paul spoke to the people and, because he intended to leave
the next day, kept on talking until midnight. [8]There were many
lamps in the upstairs room where we were meeting. [9]Seated in a

19:33 *Jews . . . Alexander:* The Jews who were against Paul probably wanted Alexander to make it clear to the Ephesian crowd that Paul was not a true Jew. They didn't want the blame that was being placed on Paul to be put on them too. They also might have seen this riot as an opportunity to get rid of Paul once and for all.

19:39 *a legal assembly:* A council that met regularly to deal with local arguments and to hear cases.

19:40 *being charged with rioting:* Since Ephesus was part of the Roman empire, it had to follow Roman laws. The Romans had strict rules against rioting. So the city clerk reminded the people that they might all get in trouble with the Roman authorities if they continued their shouting and complaining.

20:1,2 *Macedonia . . . Greece:* See the note at 16:9. Paul's visit to Greece probably refers to his three-month visit to Corinth.

20:4 *Sopater . . . Trophimus:* These men traveled with Paul and may have helped protect the money that they collected for the poor in Jerusalem. Three of them came from Macedonia, two from Asia, and two from Galatia.

Sopater could be the Sosipater mentioned in Romans 16:21. Regarding Aristarchus, see the note at 19:29. Secundus is not mentioned anywhere else in the Bible. Gaius from Derbe in Galatia may not be the same Gaius mentioned in 19:29, who was from Macedonia. Regarding Timothy, see the note at 16:1. Tychicus helped Paul with the churches in Asia (Eph 6:21, 22; Col 4:7-9; 2 Tim 4:12; Titus 3:12). Trophimus is mentioned again in 21:29 and 2 Timothy 4:20.

20:7 *On the first day of the week:* Sunday was the first day of the week. Since the Jewish day began at sunset, the meeting may have begun right after sunset on Saturday evening.

20:7 *came together to break bread:* See 20:11 and the note at 2:42.

20:13 *Assos:* See the map on p. 2477. Since the others had to sail the forty miles around the peninsula, they may have arrived in Assos at about the same time as Paul.

20:14,15 *Mitylene . . . Kios . . . Samos . . . Miletus:* Mitylene was a harbor on the southeast shore of the island of Lesbos. Kios was a large island off the coast of Asia. Paul decided not to go in to dock at Ephesus, because he would have lost time. So he headed directly for Samos and then Miletus (see the map on p. 2477).

20:16 *Pentecost:* See the note at 2:1. Paul spent Passover in Macedonia, probably at Philippi (20:5, 6). That meant he had fewer than fifty days to get from Macedonia to Jerusalem for the Pentecost celebration.

20:17 *Ephesus:* Ephesus was a day's journey north of Miletus. Even though Paul wanted to get to Jerusalem for Pentecost, he took time to talk with the church leaders from Ephesus.

20:22 *compelled by the Spirit . . . Jerusalem:* Jerusalem was the center of the Jewish religion and the place where the early church began. Paul knew that the Jewish leaders and the leaders of the church were probably still arguing with each other. He realized that going there might not be safe. Even so, he was driven by the Spirit to go. For more, see the mini-article called "Jerusalem," p. 574.

20:25 *the kingdom:* Referring to the kingdom of God. See the note at 19:8.

20:24 2 Tim 4:7.

window was a young man named Eutychus, who was sinking into
a deep sleep as Paul talked on and on. When he was sound asleep,
he fell to the ground from the third story and was picked up dead.
[10]Paul went down, threw himself on the young man and put his
arms around him. "Don't be alarmed," he said. "He's alive!" [11]Then
he went upstairs again and broke bread and ate. After talking until
daylight, he left. [12]The people took the young man home alive and
were greatly comforted.

Paul's Farewell to the Ephesian Elders

[13]We went on ahead to the ship and sailed for Assos, where
we were going to take Paul aboard. He had made this arrangement
because he was going there on foot. [14]When he met us at Assos, we
took him aboard and went on to Mitylene. [15]The next day we set
sail from there and arrived off Kios. The day after that we crossed
over to Samos, and on the following day arrived at Miletus. [16]Paul
had decided to sail past Ephesus to avoid spending time in the
province of Asia, for he was in a hurry to reach Jerusalem, if possible, by the day of Pentecost.
[17]From Miletus, Paul sent to Ephesus for the elders of the
church. [18]When they arrived, he said to them: "You know how I
lived the whole time I was with you, from the first day I came into
the province of Asia. [19]I served the Lord with great humility and
with tears, although I was severely tested by the plots of the Jews.
[20]You know that I have not hesitated to preach anything that
would be helpful to you but have taught you publicly and from
house to house. [21]I have declared to both Jews and Greeks that they
must turn to God in repentance and have faith in our Lord Jesus.
[22]"And now, compelled by the Spirit, I am going to Jerusalem, not knowing what will happen to me there. [23]I only know
that in every city the Holy Spirit warns me that prison and hardships are facing me. [24]However, I consider my life worth nothing to
me, if only I may finish the race and complete the task the Lord
Jesus has given me—the task of testifying to the gospel of God's
grace.
[25]"Now I know that none of you among whom I have gone
about preaching the kingdom will ever see me again. [26]Therefore,
I declare to you today that I am innocent of the blood of all men.
[27]For I have not hesitated to proclaim to you the whole will of
God. [28]Keep watch over yourselves and all the flock of which the
Holy Spirit has made you overseers.[a] Be shepherds of the church of
God,[b] which he bought with his own blood. [29]I know that after I
leave, savage wolves will come in among you and will not spare the
flock. [30]Even from your own number men will arise and distort the
truth in order to draw away disciples after them. [31]So be on your

[a]**28** Traditionally *bishops* [b]**28** Many manuscripts *of the Lord*

guard! Remember that for three years I never stopped warning
each of you night and day with tears.
32"Now I commit you to God and to the word of his grace,
which can build you up and give you an inheritance among all
those who are sanctified. 33I have not coveted anyone's silver or
gold or clothing. 34You yourselves know that these hands of mine
have supplied my own needs and the needs of my companions.
35In everything I did, I showed you that by this kind of hard work
we must help the weak, remembering the words the Lord Jesus
himself said: 'It is more blessed to give than to receive.' "
36When he had said this, he knelt down with all of them and
prayed. 37They all wept as they embraced him and kissed him.
38What grieved them most was his statement that they would
never see his face again. Then they accompanied him to the ship.

On to Jerusalem

21 After we had torn ourselves away from them, we put out to
sea and sailed straight to Cos. The next day we went to Rhodes and
from there to Patara. 2We found a ship crossing over to Phoenicia,
went on board and set sail. 3After sighting Cyprus and passing to
the south of it, we sailed on to Syria. We landed at Tyre, where our
ship was to unload its cargo. 4Finding the disciples there, we stayed
with them seven days. Through the Spirit they urged Paul not to
go on to Jerusalem. 5But when our time was up, we left and continued on our way. All the disciples and their wives and children
accompanied us out of the city, and there on the beach we knelt to
pray. 6After saying good-by to each other, we went aboard the ship,
and they returned home.
7We continued our voyage from Tyre and landed at Ptolemais, where we greeted the brothers and stayed with them for a
day. 8Leaving the next day, we reached Caesarea and stayed at the
house of Philip the evangelist, one of the Seven. 9He had four
unmarried daughters who prophesied.
10After we had been there a number of days, a prophet
named Agabus came down from Judea. 11Coming over to us, he
took Paul's belt, tied his own hands and feet with it and said, "The
Holy Spirit says, 'In this way the Jews of Jerusalem will bind the
owner of this belt and will hand him over to the Gentiles.' "
12When we heard this, we and the people there pleaded with
Paul not to go up to Jerusalem. 13Then Paul answered, "Why are
you weeping and breaking my heart? I am ready not only to be
bound, but also to die in Jerusalem for the name of the Lord
Jesus." 14When he would not be dissuaded, we gave up and said,
"The Lord's will be done."
15After this, we got ready and went up to Jerusalem. 16Some
of the disciples from Caesarea accompanied us and brought us to
the home of Mnason, where we were to stay. He was a man from
Cyprus and one of the early disciples.

20:34 *these hands of mine have supplied my own needs:* See the note at 18:3.

20:35 *It is more blessed to give:* This saying of Jesus is not recorded in any of the Gospels.

21:1 *we put out to sea:* See the note at 16:10.

21:1-3 *Cos . . . Tyre:* See the map on p. 2477. It took about a day to sail from Cos to Rhodes. Patara was another day's sailing from Rhodes. At Patara, Paul got on a ship that would sail across the Mediterranean to Phoenicia (see the note at 11:19). Tyre was one of the leading cities in Phoenicia, part of the Roman province of Syria.

21:7,8 *Ptolemais . . . Caesarea:* Originally Ptolemais was known as Acco. When the Greeks ruled the area, the city was named after the ruling family, the Ptolemies. Ptolemais came under Roman rule in 65 B.C. See the note at 8:40 (Caesarea).

21:8 *Philip the evangelist . . . Seven:* See 8:26-40 and the note at 8:5.

21:9 *prophesied:* See the note at 11:28 (Agabus) and the article called "Prophets and Prophecy," p. 935.

21:10 *prophet named Agabus:* See 11:28 and note (Agabus).

21:10 *Judea:* See the note at 15:1 (Judea).

21:11 *the Jews of Jerusalem . . . the Gentiles:* Agabus is referring to the Jewish religious authority and the Gentile political authorities.

21:16 *Mnason:* Nothing else is known of Mnason, but he must have had a house large enough to have a number of guests.

PAUL IN JERUSALEM

Paul returns to Jerusalem after his third missionary journey. As predicted by Agabus (21:10, 11), it isn't long before Paul is arrested and called to defend himself and his message.

Paul's Arrival at Jerusalem

17When we arrived at Jerusalem, the brothers received us warmly. 18The next day Paul and the rest of us went to see James, and all the elders were present. 19Paul greeted them and reported in detail what God had done among the Gentiles through his ministry.

20When they heard this, they praised God. Then they said to Paul: "You see, brother, how many thousands of Jews have believed, and all of them are zealous for the law. 21They have been informed that you teach all the Jews who live among the Gentiles to turn away from Moses, telling them not to circumcise their children or live according to our customs. 22What shall we do? They will certainly hear that you have come, 23so do what we tell you. There are four men with us who have made a vow. 24Take these men, join in their purification rites and pay their expenses, so that they can have their heads shaved. Then everybody will know there is no truth in these reports about you, but that you yourself are living in obedience to the law. 25As for the Gentile believers, we have written to them our decision that they should abstain from food sacrificed to idols, from blood, from the meat of strangled animals and from sexual immorality."

26The next day Paul took the men and purified himself along with them. Then he went to the temple to give notice of the date when the days of purification would end and the offering would be made for each of them.

Paul Arrested

27When the seven days were nearly over, some Jews from the province of Asia saw Paul at the temple. They stirred up the whole crowd and seized him, 28shouting, "Men of Israel, help us! This is the man who teaches all men everywhere against our people and our law and this place. And besides, he has brought Greeks into the temple area and defiled this holy place." 29(They had previously seen Trophimus the Ephesian in the city with Paul and assumed that Paul had brought him into the temple area.)

30The whole city was aroused, and the people came running from all directions. Seizing Paul, they dragged him from the temple, and immediately the gates were shut. 31While they were trying to kill him, news reached the commander of the Roman troops that the whole city of Jerusalem was in an uproar. 32He at once took some officers and soldiers and ran down to the crowd. When the rioters saw the commander and his soldiers, they stopped beating Paul.

21:18 *James:* The brother of Jesus. See the note at 12:17.

21:20 *zealous for the law:* See the note at 15:5 (Pharisees).

21:21 *Moses . . . circumcise their children:* See the notes at 7:20 and 7:8.

21:23 *four men with us who have made a vow:* They were evidently talking about the Nazirite vows (Num 6:5, 13-21). See also the note at 18:18 (had his hair cut off).

21:26 *when the days of purification would end and the offering would be made:* Part of the Nazirite vows mentioned in 21:23, 24.

21:27 *Jews from the province of Asia:* They were probably in Jerusalem for Pentecost. Paul had been persecuted by some Jews when he was in Asia. See 20:18,19 and the note at 16:6 (Asia).

21:28 *brought Greeks into the temple area and defiled this holy place:* See the note at 3:1 (temple). Certain Jewish laws said that non-Jews (Gentiles) were not allowed within the temple, except in a special area called the Court of the Gentiles.

21:29 *Trophimus the Ephesian:* See 20:4. Trophimus was a Gentile. Paul probably did not bring him into the forbidden area of the temple, because this would have put Trophimus's life in danger.

21:31 *commander:* The Greek word here is *chiliarch,* one who commanded one thousand soldiers (a regiment). His name, Claudius Lysias, is given in 23:26.

21:25 Acts 15:29.

33 The commander came up and arrested him and ordered
him to be bound with two chains. Then he asked who he was and
what he had done. 34 Some in the crowd shouted one thing and
some another, and since the commander could not get at the truth
because of the uproar, he ordered that Paul be taken into the barracks. 35 When Paul reached the steps, the violence of the mob was
so great he had to be carried by the soldiers. 36 The crowd that followed kept shouting, "Away with him!"

Paul Speaks to the Crowd

37 As the soldiers were about to take Paul into the barracks,
he asked the commander, "May I say something to you?"
"Do you speak Greek?" he replied. 38 "Aren't you the Egyptian
who started a revolt and led four thousand terrorists out into the
desert some time ago?"
39 Paul answered, "I am a Jew, from Tarsus in Cilicia, a citizen
of no ordinary city. Please let me speak to the people."
40 Having received the commander's permission, Paul stood
on the steps and motioned to the crowd. When they were all silent,
22 he said to them in Aramaic[a]: 1 "Brothers and fathers, listen
now to my defense." 2 When they heard him speak to them in Aramaic, they became very quiet.
Then Paul said: 3 "I am a Jew, born in Tarsus of Cilicia, but
brought up in this city. Under Gamaliel I was thoroughly trained
in the law of our fathers and was just as zealous for God as any of
you are today. 4 I persecuted the followers of this Way to their
death, arresting both men and women and throwing them into
prison, 5 as also the high priest and all the Council can testify. I
even obtained letters from them to their brothers in Damascus,
and went there to bring these people as prisoners to Jerusalem to
be punished.
6 "About noon as I came near Damascus, suddenly a bright
light from heaven flashed around me. 7 I fell to the ground and
heard a voice say to me, 'Saul! Saul! Why do you persecute me?'
8 " 'Who are you, Lord?' I asked.
" 'I am Jesus of Nazareth, whom you are persecuting,' he
replied. 9 My companions saw the light, but they did not understand the voice of him who was speaking to me.
10 " 'What shall I do, Lord?' I asked.
" 'Get up,' the Lord said, 'and go into Damascus. There you
will be told all that you have been assigned to do.' 11 My companions led me by the hand into Damascus, because the brilliance of
the light had blinded me.
12 "A man named Ananias came to see me. He was a devout
observer of the law and highly respected by all the Jews living

[a]**40** Or possibly *Hebrew*; also in 22:2

21:34 *the barracks:* This was in the Fortress of Antonia, which overlooked the temple area from the northwest. It was connected to the temple area by steps. Roman soldiers lived in the fortress in special barracks. See the map on p. 2474.

21:38 *the Egyptian who started a revolt:* The Jewish historian Josephus wrote about an Egyptian who was a false prophet. A few years earlier he had led a group of terrorists out to the Mount of Olives. The Romans soldiers killed hundreds of the terrorists, but their leader escaped.

21:39 *Tarsus in Cilicia:* See the notes at 9:11 and 6:9.

21:40 *Aramaic:* See the note at 6:1.

22:3,4 *Gamaliel . . . this Way:* See the notes at 5:34 and 9:2 (the Way).

22:5 *the high priest and all the Council:* See the notes at 5:17 and 5:21.

22:5 *Damascus:* See the note at 9:2 (Damascus).

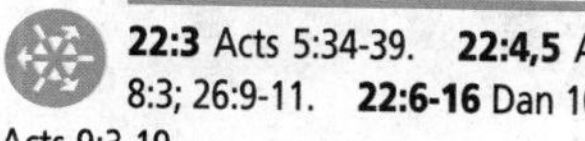

22:3 Acts 5:34-39. **22:4,5** Acts 8:3; 26:9-11. **22:6-16** Dan 10:7; Acts 9:3-19.

Ananias said to Paul, *"The God of our fathers has chosen you to know his will and to see the Righteous One and to hear words from his mouth. You will be his witness to all men of what you have seen and heard."*
Acts 22:14,15

22:14 *the Righteous One:* That is, Jesus.

22:16 *be baptized and wash your sins away:* See the note at 1:5 (baptized).

22:17 *I fell into a trance:* See the note at 10:3,10 (vision).

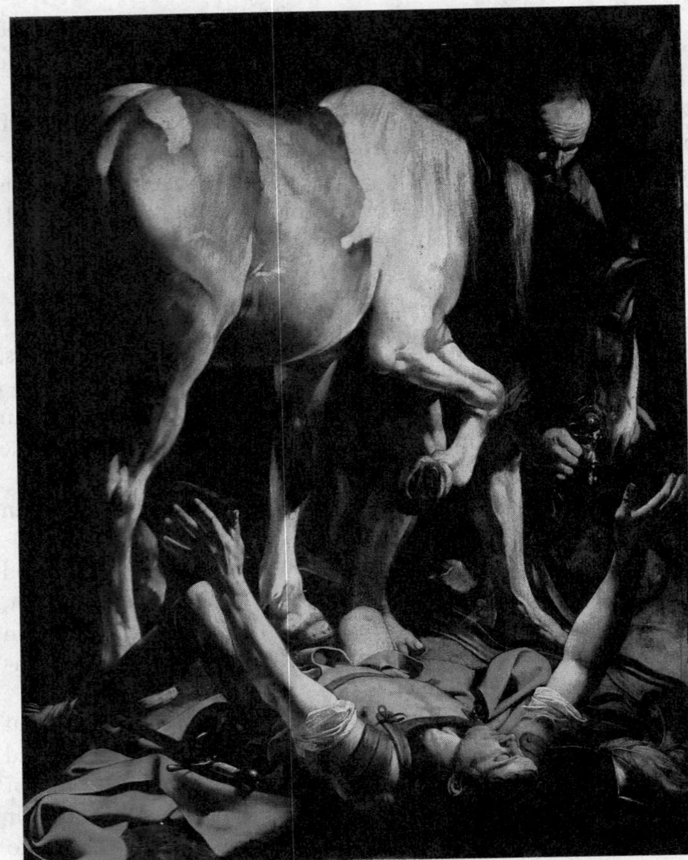

Conversion of Saint Paul, by Michelangelo Merisi da Caravaggio, early seventeenth century. Paul knew that telling personal stories could be a powerful way to let people know about what God can do to change people's lives. When Paul spoke to the crowds in Jerusalem, he spoke in Aramaic, the language of the people, rather than in the Greek he used when preaching to the Gentiles in Asia Minor and Greece. When the crowd heard him speak in Aramaic, "they became very quiet." Once he had their attention, he told them the story of how the Lord appeared to him on the road to Damascus. (See 22:1-21; see also 26:2-20, where Paul tells this same story to King Agrippa.)

there. 13He stood beside me and said, 'Brother Saul, receive your
sight!' And at that very moment I was able to see him.
14"Then he said: 'The God of our fathers has chosen you to
know his will and to see the Righteous One and to hear words
from his mouth. 15You will be his witness to all men of what you
have seen and heard. 16And now what are you waiting for? Get up,
be baptized and wash your sins away, calling on his name.'
17"When I returned to Jerusalem and was praying at the
temple, I fell into a trance 18and saw the Lord speaking. 'Quick!' he
said to me. 'Leave Jerusalem immediately, because they will not
accept your testimony about me.'

[19]“ ‘Lord,’ I replied, ‘these men know that I went from one
synagogue to another to imprison and beat those who believe in
you. [20]And when the blood of your martyr[a] Stephen was shed, I
stood there giving my approval and guarding the clothes of those
who were killing him.’
[21]“Then the Lord said to me, ‘Go; I will send you far away to
the Gentiles.’ ”

Paul the Roman Citizen

[22]The crowd listened to Paul until he said this. Then they raised
their voices and shouted, “Rid the earth of him! He's not fit to live!”
[23]As they were shouting and throwing off their cloaks and
flinging dust into the air, [24]the commander ordered Paul to be
taken into the barracks. He directed that he be flogged and questioned in order to find out why the people were shouting at him
like this. [25]As they stretched him out to flog him, Paul said to the
centurion standing there, “Is it legal for you to flog a Roman citizen who hasn't even been found guilty?”
[26]When the centurion heard this, he went to the commander
and reported it. “What are you going to do?” he asked. “This man
is a Roman citizen.”
[27]The commander went to Paul and asked, “Tell me, are you
a Roman citizen?”

“Yes, I am,” he answered.

[28]Then the commander said, “I had to pay a big price for my
citizenship.”

“But I was born a citizen,” Paul replied.

[29]Those who were about to question him withdrew immediately. The commander himself was alarmed when he realized that
he had put Paul, a Roman citizen, in chains.

Before the Sanhedrin

[30]The next day, since the commander wanted to find out
exactly why Paul was being accused by the Jews, he released him
and ordered the chief priests and all the Sanhedrin to assemble.
Then he brought Paul and had him stand before them.
23 Paul looked straight at the Sanhedrin and said, “My brothers,
I have fulfilled my duty to God in all good conscience to this day.”
[2]At this the high priest Ananias ordered those standing near Paul
to strike him on the mouth. [3]Then Paul said to him, “God will
strike you, you whitewashed wall! You sit there to judge me
according to the law, yet you yourself violate the law by commanding that I be struck!”
[4]Those who were standing near Paul said, “You dare to insult
God's high priest?”

[a]**20** Or *witness*

22:20 *your martyr Stephen:* See 7:54—8:1 and the notes at 6:5 (Stephen) and 7:58.

22:24 *the commander:* See the note at 21:31.

22:24 *the barracks:* See the note at 21:34.

22:25 *centurion:* See the note at 10:1 (Cornelius).

22:25 *Roman citizen:* As a Roman citizen Paul had certain rights, including the chance to argue his case directly to the Roman emperor. Only a small number of people in the Roman empire had the rights of a citizen, which included the privileges of voting, holding office, entering into a legal marriage, and holding property. Along with these privileges came the duties to pay taxes and serve in the army, if called to do so.

22:30 *chief priests and all the Sanhedrin:* See the notes at 4:5; 4:23; and 5:21. The Sanhedrin had the right to decide if someone had broken a Jewish law and to determine the punishment.

23:2 *the high priest Ananias:* Ananias, the son of Nedebaeus, served as high priest from A.D. 48 to 58, when he was removed from this position. He had a reputation for being cruel. Because of this and because he had been so friendly to the Roman authorities, he was killed by Jewish rebels at the beginning of the Jewish War of A.D. 66-70.

23:3 *whitewashed wall:* Someone who pretends to be good, but really isn't. See also Matt 23:27,28.

The Lord stood near Paul and said, "Take courage! As you have testified about me in Jerusalem, so you must also testify in Rome."
Acts 23:11

23:5 *it is written:* The law Paul is referring to is described in Exodus 22:28.

23:6 *Sadducees . . . Pharisees:* See the notes at 4:1 and 5:34. Paul knew his comment about the resurrection of the dead would start an argument between these two groups. See also Acts 26:4,5; Phil 3:5; and the mini-article called "Resurrection," p. 2210.

23:10 *commander:* See the note at 21:31.

23:10 *the barracks:* See the note at 21:34.

23:14 *chief priests and elders:* See the notes at 4:23 and 4:5.

23:15 *Sanhedrin:* See the note at 22:30.

23:16 *the son of Paul's sister:* Paul's nephew, whose name is not known.

23:17 *one of the centurions . . . commander:* See the notes at 10:1 (Cornelius) and 21:31.

23:23 *Caesarea:* See the note at 8:40. The Roman governor of the region lived in Caesarea.

23:8 Matt 22:23; Mark 12:18; Luke 20:27.

[5]Paul replied, "Brothers, I did not realize that he was the high
priest; for it is written: 'Do not speak evil about the ruler of your
people.'[a]"

[6]Then Paul, knowing that some of them were Sadducees and
the others Pharisees, called out in the Sanhedrin, "My brothers, I
am a Pharisee, the son of a Pharisee. I stand on trial because of my
hope in the resurrection of the dead." [7]When he said this, a dispute
broke out between the Pharisees and the Sadducees, and the
assembly was divided. [8](The Sadducees say that there is no resurrection, and that there are neither angels nor spirits, but the Pharisees acknowledge them all.)

[9]There was a great uproar, and some of the teachers of the
law who were Pharisees stood up and argued vigorously. "We find
nothing wrong with this man," they said. "What if a spirit or an
angel has spoken to him?" [10]The dispute became so violent that the
commander was afraid Paul would be torn to pieces by them. He
ordered the troops to go down and take him away from them by
force and bring him into the barracks.

[11]The following night the Lord stood near Paul and said,
"Take courage! As you have testified about me in Jerusalem, so you
must also testify in Rome."

The Plot to Kill Paul

[12]The next morning the Jews formed a conspiracy and
bound themselves with an oath not to eat or drink until they had
killed Paul. [13]More than forty men were involved in this plot.
[14]They went to the chief priests and elders and said, "We have
taken a solemn oath not to eat anything until we have killed Paul.
[15]Now then, you and the Sanhedrin petition the commander to
bring him before you on the pretext of wanting more accurate
information about his case. We are ready to kill him before he gets
here."

[16]But when the son of Paul's sister heard of this plot, he went
into the barracks and told Paul.

[17]Then Paul called one of the centurions and said, "Take this
young man to the commander; he has something to tell him." [18]So
he took him to the commander.

The centurion said, "Paul, the prisoner, sent for me and
asked me to bring this young man to you because he has something to tell you."

[19]The commander took the young man by the hand, drew
him aside and asked, "What is it you want to tell me?"

[20]He said: "The Jews have agreed to ask you to bring Paul
before the Sanhedrin tomorrow on the pretext of wanting more
accurate information about him. [21]Don't give in to them,

[a]5 Exodus 22:28

because more than forty of them are waiting in ambush for him.
They have taken an oath not to eat or drink until they have
killed him. They are ready now, waiting for your consent to their
request."
22 The commander dismissed the young man and cautioned
him, "Don't tell anyone that you have reported this to me."

PAUL IN CAESAREA

*Under a heavily armed military patrol,
Paul is taken to Caesarea, where the Roman governor
of the region can hear his case.*

Paul Transferred to Caesarea

23 Then he called two of his centurions and ordered them,
"Get ready a detachment of two hundred soldiers, seventy horsemen and two hundred spearmen[a] to go to Caesarea at nine
tonight. 24 Provide mounts for Paul so that he may be taken safely
to Governor Felix."
25 He wrote a letter as follows:

26 Claudius Lysias,

To His Excellency, Governor Felix:

Greetings.

27 This man was seized by the Jews and they were about
to kill him, but I came with my troops and rescued him, for I
had learned that he is a Roman citizen. 28 I wanted to know
why they were accusing him, so I brought him to their Sanhedrin. 29 I found that the accusation had to do with questions
about their law, but there was no charge against him that
deserved death or imprisonment. 30 When I was informed of a
plot to be carried out against the man, I sent him to you at
once. I also ordered his accusers to present to you their case
against him.

31 So the soldiers, carrying out their orders, took Paul with
them during the night and brought him as far as Antipatris. 32 The
next day they let the cavalry go on with him, while they returned
to the barracks. 33 When the cavalry arrived in Caesarea, they delivered the letter to the governor and handed Paul over to him. 34 The
governor read the letter and asked what province he was from.
Learning that he was from Cilicia, 35 he said, "I will hear your case
when your accusers get here." Then he ordered that Paul be kept
under guard in Herod's palace.

[a]**23** The meaning of the Greek for this word is uncertain.

23:24 *Governor Felix:* In A.D. 52, the emperor Claudius appointed Antonius Felix as governor of Judea. Felix knew something about Christianity (24:22) and liked talking to Paul, but he kept him in prison anyway (25:14). The bronze coin shown here was minted when Felix was governor (around A.D. 64). It displays a palm tree rather than the face of the ruler because this was less offensive to the Jewish population he ruled.

23:27 *Roman citizen:* See the note at 22:25 (Roman citizen).

23:29 *the accusation had to do with questions about their law:* The Romans allowed the Jewish people to decide cases that involved Jewish laws or customs, as long as they did not break any Roman law or cause a riot. Paul was a Roman citizen, so the commander saw it as his duty to protect Paul's rights.

23:31 *Antipatris:* This military post north of Jerusalem was rebuilt by Herod the Great and named after Herod's father Antipater.

23:35 *Herod's palace:* Herod the Great (73-4 B.C.) was appointed king of Judea by the Roman Senate and ruled from 40 B.C. until his death. He was famous for his extensive building projects. These included the building of whole cities like Sebaste and Caesarea as well as magnificent monuments and important buildings like the temple in Jerusalem. He built palaces for himself at Masada, Jericho, Herodium, and in Jerusalem. The one where Felix received Paul was in Caesarea.

The Trial Before Felix

24 Five days later the high priest Ananias went down to Caesarea with some of the elders and a lawyer named Tertullus, and
they brought their charges against Paul before the governor.
2When Paul was called in, Tertullus presented his case before Felix:
"We have enjoyed a long period of peace under you, and your
foresight has brought about reforms in this nation. 3Everywhere
and in every way, most excellent Felix, we acknowledge this with
profound gratitude. 4But in order not to weary you further, I
would request that you be kind enough to hear us briefly.

5"We have found this man to be a troublemaker, stirring up
riots among the Jews all over the world. He is a ringleader of the
Nazarene sect 6and even tried to desecrate the temple; so we seized
him. 8By[a] examining him yourself you will be able to learn the
truth about all these charges we are bringing against him."

9The Jews joined in the accusation, asserting that these
things were true.

10When the governor motioned for him to speak, Paul
replied: "I know that for a number of years you have been a judge
over this nation; so I gladly make my defense. 11You can easily ver-
ify that no more than twelve days ago I went up to Jerusalem to
worship. 12My accusers did not find me arguing with anyone at the
temple, or stirring up a crowd in the synagogues or anywhere else
in the city. 13And they cannot prove to you the charges they are
now making against me. 14However, I admit that I worship the
God of our fathers as a follower of the Way, which they call a sect.
I believe everything that agrees with the Law and that is written in
the Prophets, 15and I have the same hope in God as these men, that
there will be a resurrection of both the righteous and the wicked.
16So I strive always to keep my conscience clear before God and
man.

17"After an absence of several years, I came to Jerusalem to
bring my people gifts for the poor and to present offerings. 18I was
ceremonially clean when they found me in the temple courts
doing this. There was no crowd with me, nor was I involved in any
disturbance. 19But there are some Jews from the province of Asia,
who ought to be here before you and bring charges if they have
anything against me. 20Or these who are here should state what
crime they found in me when I stood before the Sanhedrin—
21unless it was this one thing I shouted as I stood in their presence:
'It is concerning the resurrection of the dead that I am on trial
before you today.' "

22Then Felix, who was well acquainted with the Way,
adjourned the proceedings. "When Lysias the commander comes,"

[a]**6-8** Some manuscripts *him and wanted to judge him according to our law. 7But the commander, Lysias, came and with the use of much force snatched him from our hands 8and ordered his accusers to come before you. By*

24:1 *the high priest Ananias . . . some of the elders:* See the notes at 23:2 and 4:5. This was a delegation of the Sanhedrin in Jerusalem.

24:1 *a lawyer named Tertullus:* Here "lawyer" means someone who was familiar with both Roman and Jewish law. Tertullus was probably a Jew who may have grown up outside of Palestine and who had been trained in Roman law.

24:5 *Nazarene sect:* Probably a term used to describe the followers of Jesus who came from Nazareth. Or, Tertullus could be saying that Paul was part of the Nazirite group who separated themselves and made special vows. See the notes at 18:18 (had his hair cut off) and 21:23.

24:14 *the Way:* Also in 24:22. See the note at 9:2 (the Way).

24:14 *the Law and . . . the Prophets:* When mentioned together, "the Law" (the first five books of the Jewish Scriptures) and "the Prophets" refer to all the Jewish Scriptures (Old Testament)—including "the Writings," the third category. See the chart called "Books of the Hebrew Scriptures," or "TANAK," p. 13.

24:21 *resurrection of the dead:* Paul recalls his earlier words in 23:6. See the note there.

24:24 *Drusilla:* She was Felix's third wife and the daughter of Herod Agrippa I (see the note at 12:1). She had married Azizus, the king of Emesa, when she was 15, but she left him to marry Felix.

24:17,18 Acts 21:17-28.
24:21 Acts 23:6.

he said, "I will decide your case." 23He ordered the centurion to keep Paul under guard but to give him some freedom and permit his friends to take care of his needs.

24Several days later Felix came with his wife Drusilla, who was a Jewess. He sent for Paul and listened to him as he spoke about faith in Christ Jesus. 25As Paul discoursed on righteousness, self-control and the judgment to come, Felix was afraid and said, "That's enough for now! You may leave. When I find it convenient, I will send for you." 26At the same time he was hoping that Paul would offer him a bribe, so he sent for him frequently and talked with him.

27When two years had passed, Felix was succeeded by Porcius Festus, but because Felix wanted to grant a favor to the Jews, he left Paul in prison.

The Trial Before Festus

25 Three days after arriving in the province, Festus went up from Caesarea to Jerusalem, 2where the chief priests and Jewish leaders appeared before him and presented the charges against Paul. 3They urgently requested Festus, as a favor to them, to have Paul transferred to Jerusalem, for they were preparing an ambush to kill him along the way. 4Festus answered, "Paul is being held at Caesarea, and I myself am going there soon. 5Let some of your leaders come with me and press charges against the man there, if he has done anything wrong."

6After spending eight or ten days with them, he went down to Caesarea, and the next day he convened the court and ordered that Paul be brought before him. 7When Paul appeared, the Jews who had come down from Jerusalem stood around him, bringing many serious charges against him, which they could not prove.

8Then Paul made his defense: "I have done nothing wrong against the law of the Jews or against the temple or against Caesar."

9Festus, wishing to do the Jews a favor, said to Paul, "Are you willing to go up to Jerusalem and stand trial before me there on these charges?"

10Paul answered: "I am now standing before Caesar's court, where I ought to be tried. I have not done any wrong to the Jews, as you yourself know very well. 11If, however, I am guilty of doing anything deserving death, I do not refuse to die. But if the charges brought against me by these Jews are not true, no one has the right to hand me over to them. I appeal to Caesar!"

12After Festus had conferred with his council, he declared: "You have appealed to Caesar. To Caesar you will go!"

Festus Consults King Agrippa

13A few days later King Agrippa and Bernice arrived at Caesarea to pay their respects to Festus. 14Since they were spending

24:27 *Felix was succeeded by Porcius Festus:* Although exact dates are uncertain, Porcius Festus was governor in Judea from A.D. 60 to 62. According to the Jewish historian Josephus, Festus got in trouble with the Jews for two things: (1) he tried to put down the Jewish terrorists known as *Sicarii,* and (2) he plotted with Herod Agrippa to take down a wall that blocked the king's view of temple rituals.

25:1 *Caesarea to Jerusalem:* See the notes at 8:40 and 20:22.

25:2 *the chief priests and Jewish leaders:* This refers to the Sanhedrin. See the note at 22:30.

25:11 *I appeal to Caesar:* Nero was the Roman emperor at this time (see the note at 27:24). As a Roman citizen, Paul had the right to have his case heard by the emperor or the emperor's representative in Rome. It was the highest court that could hear a case.

25:12 *his council:* The Roman governor had a group of advisers who were experts in the law.

25:13 *King Agrippa and Bernice:* This was Herod Agrippa II, son of Herod Agrippa I (see the note at 12:1). He was 17 when his father died in A.D. 44. When he was considered old enough, the Emperor Claudius allowed him to rule over areas north and east of the Sea of Galilee and parts of Perea (see the map on p. 2472). When the Jews revolted against the Romans in A.D. 66, Agrippa II was on the side of the Romans.

Bernice was the sister of Agrippa II. She married her uncle Herod of Chalcis when she was only 13. After he died, she went to live with her brother. Even after she married Polomon of Cilicia, she continued her incestuous relationship with Agrippa II.

Paul said, *"It is because of my hope in what God has promised our fathers that I am on trial today. This is the promise our twelve tribes are hoping to see fulfilled as they earnestly serve God day and night."*
Acts 26:6,7

25:14 *Felix:* See the note at 23:24.

25:23 *high ranking officers and the leading men of the city:* A number of Roman military units called regiments were stationed in Caesarea. All of their commanders would have been at the meeting (see also the note at 21:31). The leading men included both influential local Jews and Roman authorities.

26:4,5 Acts 23:6; Gal 1:14; Phil 3:5,6.

many days there, Festus discussed Paul's case with the king. He
said: "There is a man here whom Felix left as a prisoner. [15]When I
went to Jerusalem, the chief priests and elders of the Jews brought
charges against him and asked that he be condemned.
[16]"I told them that it is not the Roman custom to hand over
any man before he has faced his accusers and has had an opportunity to defend himself against their charges. [17]When they came
here with me, I did not delay the case, but convened the court the
next day and ordered the man to be brought in. [18]When his
accusers got up to speak, they did not charge him with any of the
crimes I had expected. [19]Instead, they had some points of dispute
with him about their own religion and about a dead man named
Jesus who Paul claimed was alive. [20]I was at a loss how to investigate such matters; so I asked if he would be willing to go to
Jerusalem and stand trial there on these charges. [21]When Paul
made his appeal to be held over for the Emperor's decision, I
ordered him held until I could send him to Caesar."
[22]Then Agrippa said to Festus, "I would like to hear this man
myself."

He replied, "Tomorrow you will hear him."

Paul Before Agrippa

[23]The next day Agrippa and Bernice came with great pomp
and entered the audience room with the high ranking officers and
the leading men of the city. At the command of Festus, Paul was
brought in. [24]Festus said: "King Agrippa, and all who are present
with us, you see this man! The whole Jewish community has peti-
tioned me about him in Jerusalem and here in Caesarea, shouting
that he ought not to live any longer. [25]I found he had done nothing deserving of death, but because he made his appeal to the
Emperor I decided to send him to Rome. [26]But I have nothing definite to write to His Majesty about him. Therefore I have brought
him before all of you, and especially before you, King Agrippa, so
that as a result of this investigation I may have something to write.
[27]For I think it is unreasonable to send on a prisoner without spec-
ifying the charges against him."

26 Then Agrippa said to Paul, "You have permission to speak for
yourself."

So Paul motioned with his hand and began his defense:
[2]"King Agrippa, I consider myself fortunate to stand before you
today as I make my defense against all the accusations of the Jews,
[3]and especially so because you are well acquainted with all the Jewish customs and controversies. Therefore, I beg you to listen to me
patiently.

[4]"The Jews all know the way I have lived ever since I was a
child, from the beginning of my life in my own country, and also
in Jerusalem. [5]They have known me for a long time and can testify, if they are willing, that according to the strictest sect of our religion, I lived as a Pharisee. [6]And now it is because of my hope in

what God has promised our fathers that I am on trial today. [7]This
is the promise our twelve tribes are hoping to see fulfilled as they
earnestly serve God day and night. O king, it is because of this
hope that the Jews are accusing me. [8]Why should any of you consider it incredible that God raises the dead?

[9]"I too was convinced that I ought to do all that was possible to oppose the name of Jesus of Nazareth. [10]And that is just
what I did in Jerusalem. On the authority of the chief priests I put
many of the saints in prison, and when they were put to death, I
cast my vote against them. [11]Many a time I went from one synagogue to another to have them punished, and I tried to force them
to blaspheme. In my obsession against them, I even went to foreign cities to persecute them.

[12]"On one of these journeys I was going to Damascus with
the authority and commission of the chief priests. [13]About noon,
O king, as I was on the road, I saw a light from heaven, brighter
than the sun, blazing around me and my companions. [14]We all fell
to the ground, and I heard a voice saying to me in Aramaic,[a] 'Saul,
Saul, why do you persecute me? It is hard for you to kick against
the goads.'

[15]"Then I asked, 'Who are you, Lord?'

" 'I am Jesus, whom you are persecuting,' the Lord replied.
[16]"Now get up and stand on your feet. I have appeared to you to
appoint you as a servant and as a witness of what you have seen of
me and what I will show you. [17]I will rescue you from your own
people and from the Gentiles. I am sending you to them [18]to open
their eyes and turn them from darkness to light, and from the
power of Satan to God, so that they may receive forgiveness of sins
and a place among those who are sanctified by faith in me.'

[19]"So then, King Agrippa, I was not disobedient to the vision
from heaven. [20]First to those in Damascus, then to those in
Jerusalem and in all Judea, and to the Gentiles also, I preached that
they should repent and turn to God and prove their repentance by
their deeds. [21]That is why the Jews seized me in the temple courts
and tried to kill me. [22]But I have had God's help to this very day, and
so I stand here and testify to small and great alike. I am saying nothing beyond what the prophets and Moses said would happen—
[23]that the Christ[b] would suffer and, as the first to rise from the dead,
would proclaim light to his own people and to the Gentiles."

[24]At this point Festus interrupted Paul's defense. "You are
out of your mind, Paul!" he shouted. "Your great learning is driving you insane."

[25]"I am not insane, most excellent Festus," Paul replied.
"What I am saying is true and reasonable. [26]The king is familiar
with these things, and I can speak freely to him. I am convinced
that none of this has escaped his notice, because it was not done in

[a]14 Or *Hebrew* [b]23 Or *Messiah*

26:7 *twelve tribes:* Meaning Israel. See the mini-article called "Israel," p. 264.

26:7 *the Jews:* Meaning the Jewish leaders. See 22:30 and the note there.

26:11 *I tried to force them to blaspheme:* Blasphemy is the sin of cursing God or slandering God's name. This can be done by attributing divine qualities to a mere mortal. Here Paul is probably saying that by provoking Jewish Christians to confess that Jesus is Lord he was guaranteeing that other Jews would take offense and demand that the Christians be stoned, the prescribed punishment for blasphemy.

26:14 *to kick against the goads:* A goad is a stick farmers use to poke their work animals to make them move. This proverb, taken from a play by Euripides, means to pointlessly resist something that ultimately can't be resisted.

26:18 *from darkness to light, and from the power of Satan to God:* In the Bible, darkness refers to places of pain and suffering (Ps 107:10) or confusion (Eccl 2:14). God's opponents are called the rulers of this dark world (Eph 6:12), who will be thrown "into the darkness" (Matt 22:13). Light is used in the Bible to describe God or God's word (1 John 1:5; Ps 119:105), and those people or things that reveal God's truth (Isa 49:6). For Satan, see the note at 5:3.

26:18 *forgiveness of sins:* See the note at 2:38 (forgiveness).

26:20 *Gentiles:* See the mini-article called "Gentiles," p. 2127.

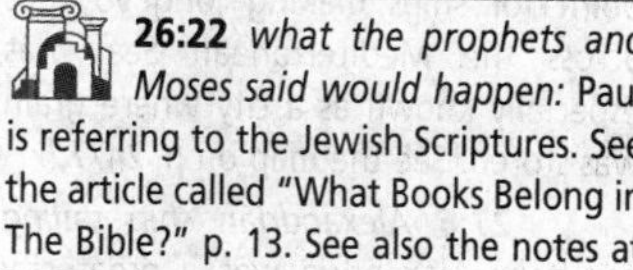

26:22 *what the prophets and Moses said would happen:* Paul is referring to the Jewish Scriptures. See the article called "What Books Belong in The Bible?" p. 13. See also the notes at 3:18 and 24:14.

26:23 *the Christ:* See the note at 2:36.

26:9-11 Acts 8:3; 9:2,13,14; 22:4,5. **26:12-16** Acts 9:3-7, 15,16. **26:20** Acts 9:20,28,29. **26:23** 1 Cor 15:20; Isa 42:6; 49:6.

26:27 *do you believe the prophets:* Paul was asking if Agrippa believed the writings of the prophets found in the Jewish Scriptures. See the note at 26:22.

26:32 *could have been set free:* Since Paul asked to have his case heard in front of the Roman emperor, he could not be set free.

27:1 *we would sail:* See the note at 16:10.

27:1 *a centurion named Julius:* This Roman officer is not mentioned anywhere else except here in ACTS.

27:2 *Adramyttium . . . Asia:* The ship that carried Paul had come from Adramyttium, a seaport on the west coast of the province of Asia near Troas and Assos (see the map on p. 2477). The ship was scheduled to stop at some ports along the coast of Asia.

27:2 *Aristarchus . . . Thessalonica:* See the note at 19:29. See also Colossians 4:10, which may indicate that he was with Paul in Rome. See the note at 17:1 (Thessalonica).

27:3,4 *Sidon . . . Cyprus:* Sidon was a port on the coast of Phoenicia about seventy miles north of Caesarea. See the note at 11:19, 20. The winds must have been from a westerly direction for Cyprus to give them protection. See the map on p. 2477.

27:5 *Cilicia and Pamphylia . . . Myra in Lycia:* See the note at 6:9. Paul grew up in Cilicia in the city of Tarsus. Myra was in Lycia, a province in southwest Asia. Myra, a favorite stopping point for ships making long voyages across the Mediterranean Sea, was especially known as a city where grain was stored. See the map on p. 2477.

27:6 *Alexandrian ship sailing for Italy:* Alexandria was a great city located on the northern coast of Egypt near the mouth of the Nile River. See the note at 18:24. Rome was in Italy, their final destination. See the map on p. 2477.

a corner. [27]King Agrippa, do you believe the prophets? I know you do."

[28]Then Agrippa said to Paul, "Do you think that in such a short time you can persuade me to be a Christian?"

[29]Paul replied, "Short time or long—I pray God that not only you but all who are listening to me today may become what I am, except for these chains."

[30]The king rose, and with him the governor and Bernice and those sitting with them. [31]They left the room, and while talking with one another, they said, "This man is not doing anything that deserves death or imprisonment."

[32]Agrippa said to Festus, "This man could have been set free if he had not appealed to Caesar."

PAUL BRINGS THE GOSPEL TO ROME

Paul is next sent to Rome so his case can be heard by the emperor. The journey was not an easy one.

Paul Sails for Rome

27 When it was decided that we would sail for Italy, Paul and some other prisoners were handed over to a centurion named Julius, who belonged to the Imperial Regiment. [2]We boarded a ship from Adramyttium about to sail for ports along the coast of the province of Asia, and we put out to sea. Aristarchus, a Macedonian from Thessalonica, was with us.

[3]The next day we landed at Sidon; and Julius, in kindness to Paul, allowed him to go to his friends so they might provide for his needs. [4]From there we put out to sea again and passed to the lee of Cyprus because the winds were against us. [5]When we had sailed across the open sea off the coast of Cilicia and Pamphylia, we landed at Myra in Lycia. [6]There the centurion found an Alexandrian ship sailing for Italy and put us on board. [7]We made slow headway for many days and had difficulty arriving off Cnidus. When the wind did not allow us to hold our course, we sailed to the lee of Crete, opposite Salmone. [8]We moved along the coast with difficulty and came to a place called Fair Havens, near the town of Lasea.

[9]Much time had been lost, and sailing had already become dangerous because by now it was after the Fast.[a] So Paul warned them, [10]"Men, I can see that our voyage is going to be disastrous and bring great loss to ship and cargo, and to our own lives also." [11]But the centurion, instead of listening to what Paul said, followed the advice of the pilot and of the owner of the ship. [12]Since the harbor was unsuitable to winter in, the majority decided that we should sail on, hoping to reach Phoenix and

[a]**9** That is, the Day of Atonement (Yom Kippur)

Sea Travel in Paul's Day. Ships in Paul's time were used almost exclusively for business and military purposes. However, passengers could travel on merchant ships if there was room after all the cargo was loaded. But because departures were unpredictable and shipwreck was always a danger, most people traveled long distances over land. In addition to its military fleet, Roman ships carrying goods, especially grain from Egypt, sailed the Mediterranean, stopping at ports along the way. Two of the three ships that carried Paul to Rome were carrying grain. These were very large, over one hundred feet long, and could also accommodate a large number of passengers.

winter there. This was a harbor in Crete, facing both southwest and northwest.

The Storm

[13]When a gentle south wind began to blow, they thought
they had obtained what they wanted; so they weighed anchor and
sailed along the shore of Crete. [14]Before very long, a wind of hur-
ricane force, called the "northeaster," swept down from the island.
[15]The ship was caught by the storm and could not head into the
wind; so we gave way to it and were driven along. [16]As we passed
to the lee of a small island called Cauda, we were hardly able to
make the lifeboat secure. [17]When the men had hoisted it aboard,
they passed ropes under the ship itself to hold it together. Fearing
that they would run aground on the sandbars of Syrtis, they lowered the sea anchor and let the ship be driven along. [18]We took
such a violent battering from the storm that the next day they
began to throw the cargo overboard. [19]On the third day, they threw
the ship's tackle overboard with their own hands. [20]When neither

27:7,8 *Cnidus . . . Lasea:* Cnidus was about 150 miles west of Myra. The westerly winds made it difficult to sail straight toward Achaia and on to Italy, so they had to go toward the eastern end of the island of Crete, which was a cape called Salmone. Then they sailed around the south side of Crete and put into port at Fair Havens. Lasea was about five miles from the port of Fair Havens. See the map on p. 2477.

27:9 *the Fast:* That is, the Jewish Day of Atonement, which took place near the end of September. See the chart called "Jewish Calendar and Festivals," p. 944. The sailing season was dangerous after the middle of September, and it stopped completely between the middle of November and the middle of March.

27:12 *Phoenix:* Phoenix, on the southern coast of Crete, was about eighty miles west of Fair Havens (see the map on p. 2477). Phoenix had a better harbor that gave more protection from winter storms.

27:14 *the "northeaster":* This was a hurricane-like wind (also called the Euraquillo) that came from the northeast and blew them away from the coast.

27:16 *Cauda:* Cauda is a small island about twenty-three miles south of Crete. They sailed along its south side to get some protection while they tightened up the ship to face the storm.

27:17 *passed ropes under the ship:* Most likely the ropes were run under the ship from side to side to keep the wooden boards it was made of from breaking apart.

27:17 *the sandbars of Syrtis:* This gulf was south of Italy and west of the province of Cyrenaica in Africa (see the map on p. 2477). The sandbars were most likely quicksand, which would swallow up a ship that was blown into it.

27:23 *an angel:* See the note at 5:19.

27:24 *Caesar:* The emperor was called Caesar. The Caesar at this time was Nero, who ruled from A.D. 54 to 68. He was the son of Claudius's fourth wife, Agrippina. See the note at 11:28 (Claudius). Nero's misuse of the empire's funds and his lack of interest in waging war made him increasingly unpopular with leading citizens and the Roman army. When a terrible fire destroyed much of Rome in A.D. 64, Nero put the blame on Christians. The apostles Peter and Paul are believed to have been executed in the persecution that followed.

sun nor stars appeared for many days and the storm continued
raging, we finally gave up all hope of being saved.
21After the men had gone a long time without food, Paul
stood up before them and said: "Men, you should have taken my
advice not to sail from Crete; then you would have spared yourselves this damage and loss. 22But now I urge you to keep up your
courage, because not one of you will be lost; only the ship will be
destroyed. 23Last night an angel of the God whose I am and whom
I serve stood beside me 24and said, 'Do not be afraid, Paul. You
must stand trial before Caesar; and God has graciously given you
the lives of all who sail with you.' 25So keep up your courage, men,
for I have faith in God that it will happen just as he told me.
26Nevertheless, we must run aground on some island."

Shipwreck, by Sister Clare, twentieth century. The description of Paul's journey to Rome in Acts 27 gives a clear picture of how dangerous sea travel was in the first century. But Paul was not afraid of the storm because an angel was sent by God to tell him that no one on Paul's ship would be harmed, even though the ship would be destroyed. The next day the ship hit a sandbar. The soldiers wanted to kill the prisoners, but the centurion wouldn't let them. People jumped overboard and everyone safely reached shore.

The Shipwreck

27 On the fourteenth night we were still being driven across
the Adriatic[a] Sea, when about midnight the sailors sensed they
were approaching land. 28 They took soundings and found that the
water was a hundred and twenty feet[b] deep. A short time later they
took soundings again and found it was ninety feet[c] deep. 29 Fearing
that we would be dashed against the rocks, they dropped four
anchors from the stern and prayed for daylight. 30 In an attempt to
escape from the ship, the sailors let the lifeboat down into the sea,
pretending they were going to lower some anchors from the bow.
31 Then Paul said to the centurion and the soldiers, "Unless these
men stay with the ship, you cannot be saved." 32 So the soldiers cut
the ropes that held the lifeboat and let it fall away.
33 Just before dawn Paul urged them all to eat. "For the last
fourteen days," he said, "you have been in constant suspense and
have gone without food—you haven't eaten anything. 34 Now I
urge you to take some food. You need it to survive. Not one of you
will lose a single hair from his head." 35 After he said this, he took
some bread and gave thanks to God in front of them all. Then he
broke it and began to eat. 36 They were all encouraged and ate some
food themselves. 37 Altogether there were 276 of us on board.
38 When they had eaten as much as they wanted, they lightened the
ship by throwing the grain into the sea.
39 When daylight came, they did not recognize the land, but
they saw a bay with a sandy beach, where they decided to run the
ship aground if they could. 40 Cutting loose the anchors, they left
them in the sea and at the same time untied the ropes that held
the rudders. Then they hoisted the foresail to the wind and made
for the beach. 41 But the ship struck a sandbar and ran aground.
The bow stuck fast and would not move, and the stern was broken
to pieces by the pounding of the surf.
42 The soldiers planned to kill the prisoners to prevent any of
them from swimming away and escaping. 43 But the centurion
wanted to spare Paul's life and kept them from carrying out their
plan. He ordered those who could swim to jump overboard first
and get to land. 44 The rest were to get there on planks or on pieces
of the ship. In this way everyone reached land in safety.

Ashore on Malta

28 Once safely on shore, we found out that the island was called
Malta. 2 The islanders showed us unusual kindness. They built a
fire and welcomed us all because it was raining and cold. 3 Paul
gathered a pile of brushwood and, as he put it on the fire, a viper,

[a]27 In ancient times the name referred to an area extending well south of Italy.
[b]28 Greek *twenty orguias* (about 37 meters) [c]28 Greek *fifteen orguias* (about 27 meters)

27:27 *Adriatic Sea:* This sea is part of the Mediterrean Sea, the large body of water separating Africa and Europe. Rome was located on the peninsula of Italy near the center of the Mediterranean, and at this time the Roman empire controlled all the lands surrounding the Mediterranean. Although trade and sea travel in the Mediterranean world began in the second millennium B.C., it was at its peak at the time of Paul. See the map on p. 2471.

27:28 *took soundings:* The sailors dropped a rope overboard with a weight tied to it in order to measure how deep the water was.

27:31 *the centurion:* Referring to Julius. See 27:1.

27:38 *lightened the ship by throwing the grain into the sea:* Some ships from this period could carry as many as three thousand large jars of grain. Less weight made the ship ride higher on the waves and allowed it to sail closer to shore.

28:1 *Malta:* The ship had sailed or drifted nearly 600 miles since it left Phoenix on Crete. When first under Roman control, Malta was governed by the governor of the large island of Sicily, which was about fifty-eight miles north of Malta. Later, the island had its own governor.

driven out by the heat, fastened itself on his hand. [4]When the
islanders saw the snake hanging from his hand, they said to each
other, "This man must be a murderer; for though he escaped from
the sea, Justice has not allowed him to live." [5]But Paul shook the
snake off into the fire and suffered no ill effects. [6]The people
expected him to swell up or suddenly fall dead, but after waiting a
long time and seeing nothing unusual happen to him, they
changed their minds and said he was a god.

[7]There was an estate nearby that belonged to Publius, the
chief official of the island. He welcomed us to his home and for
three days entertained us hospitably. [8]His father was sick in bed,
suffering from fever and dysentery. Paul went in to see him and,
after prayer, placed his hands on him and healed him. [9]When this
had happened, the rest of the sick on the island came and were
cured. [10]They honored us in many ways and when we were ready
to sail, they furnished us with the supplies we needed.

Arrival at Rome

[11]After three months we put out to sea in a ship that had win-
tered in the island. It was an Alexandrian ship with the figurehead of
the twin gods Castor and Pollux. [12]We put in at Syracuse and stayed
there three days. [13]From there we set sail and arrived at Rhegium. The
next day the south wind came up, and on the following day we
reached Puteoli. [14]There we found some brothers who invited us to
spend a week with them. And so we came to Rome. [15]The brothers
there had heard that we were coming, and they traveled as far as the
Forum of Appius and the Three Taverns to meet us. At the sight of
these men Paul thanked God and was encouraged. [16]When we got to
Rome, Paul was allowed to live by himself, with a soldier to guard him.

Paul Preaches at Rome Under Guard

[17]Three days later he called together the leaders of the Jews.
When they had assembled, Paul said to them: "My brothers,
although I have done nothing against our people or against the
customs of our ancestors, I was arrested in Jerusalem and handed
over to the Romans. [18]They examined me and wanted to release
me, because I was not guilty of any crime deserving death. [19]But
when the Jews objected, I was compelled to appeal to Caesar—not
that I had any charge to bring against my own people. [20]For this
reason I have asked to see you and talk with you. It is because of
the hope of Israel that I am bound with this chain."

[21]They replied, "We have not received any letters from Judea
concerning you, and none of the brothers who have come from
there has reported or said anything bad about you. [22]But we want
to hear what your views are, for we know that people everywhere
are talking against this sect."

[23]They arranged to meet Paul on a certain day, and came in

28:11 *After three months:* They had to wait until the weather was safe enough to sail again. See the note at 27:9.

28:11 *the twin gods Castor and Pollux:* Two gods that sailors looked to for protection at sea.

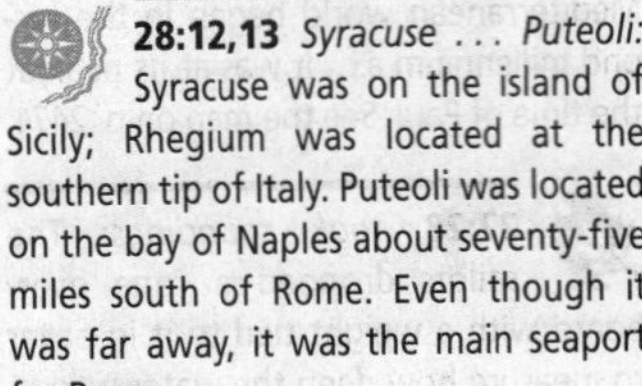

28:12,13 *Syracuse . . . Puteoli:* Syracuse was on the island of Sicily; Rhegium was located at the southern tip of Italy. Puteoli was located on the bay of Naples about seventy-five miles south of Rome. Even though it was far away, it was the main seaport for Rome.

28:14 *Rome:* Rome, the capital of the Roman empire, was built on a group of hills along the Tiber River. Jews had lived in Rome since the second century B.C. but didn't start to become a significant minority until the middle of the first century B.C. In Paul's day, Rome had at least thirteen Jewish synagogues and many shrines for various Roman gods. Although it is not known who first brought the good news about Jesus to Rome, there were probably a small number of Christians meeting there by the mid-40s. For more, see the map on p. 2471, the illustration on p. 2321, and the Introduction to ROMANS, p. 2173.

28:15 *The brothers:* Fellow Christians, followers of the Way. See the note at 9:2 (the Way).

28:15 *Forum of Appius and the Three Taverns:* The Forum of Appius was a transfer point for a canal that extended twenty miles farther south. The Three Taverns was a way station at an important intersection on the Appian Way about thirty miles south of Rome. See also the map on p. 2477.

28:21 *Judea:* The area where Jerusalem, the center of the Jewish religion, was located. By Paul's day the extensive network of Roman roads and improved sea travel significantly aided communication from one part of the Roman empire to the other.

28:19 Acts 25:11.

even larger numbers to the place where he was staying. From
morning till evening he explained and declared to them the kingdom of God and tried to convince them about Jesus from the Law
of Moses and from the Prophets. 24 Some were convinced by what
he said, but others would not believe. 25 They disagreed among
themselves and began to leave after Paul had made this final statement: "The Holy Spirit spoke the truth to your forefathers when
he said through Isaiah the prophet:

> 26 " 'Go to this people and say,
> "You will be ever hearing but never
> understanding;
> you will be ever seeing but never
> perceiving."
> 27 For this people's heart has become calloused;
> they hardly hear with their ears,
> and they have closed their eyes.
> Otherwise they might see with their eyes,
> hear with their ears,

28:22 *this sect:* Meaning the followers of Jesus of Nazareth.

28:23 *the kingdom of God:* See the note at 19:8.

28:23 *the Law of Moses . . . the Prophets:* See the note at 24:14.

28:25 *Holy Spirit:* See the note on p. 2100.

28:25 *Isaiah the prophet:* See the Introduction to ISAIAH, p. 1289.

28:26,27 Isa 6:9,10.

QUESTIONS ABOUT ACTS 15:36—28:31

1. What was Lydia's role in the community in Philippi? (16:13-15) Do you know anyone like Lydia? If so, what makes that person special?
2. What happened in the jail at Philippi? (16:16-40) How did the jailer react? What did Paul and Silas do? People today visit prisons for the purpose of spreading the good news about Jesus. Why is this important?
3. What was Paul's message to the people of Athens? (17:16-34) How did Paul get the people to listen to what he had to say? What were some of the different ways people responded to what Paul said? Have you shared your faith with others? If so, how did they respond?
4. What was the cause of the riot in Ephesus? (19:23-41) How was peace restored? What kinds of things cause riots in our world today? What needs to be done in order to restore peace? How can you be a "peacemaker" right where you are?
5. What did the prophet Agabus say, and what was Paul's answer? (21:10-13) Describe a situation in which you had to take a stand for something you believed in.
6. What happened to Paul when he returned to Jerusalem? (21:17—23:24) Who was trying to kill him, and why? Who helped him? Describe a time when you were helped, or when you helped someone else, during a time of trouble.
7. Describe Paul's imprisonment in Caesarea (23:25—26:32). Did he receive a fair trial there? Why or why not? Paul could have been set free if he hadn't appealed to Caesar. Besides his freedom, what would Paul and the rest of Jesus' followers have gained if the emperor had found him not guilty of starting a new kind of religion that was a threat to Rome?
8. Choose one scene from Paul's difficult trip to Rome, and describe what happened (27:1—28:16). How did Paul and the others respond to the situation?
9. What was Paul's life like in Rome? (28:16-31) Name people in today's world who are able to offer hope and encouragement to others, even though they are in difficult situations like being imprisoned, suffering from some kind of illness, or experiencing a tragedy.

28:28 *Gentiles:* See the mini-article called "Gentiles," p. 2127.

28:31 *kingdom of God:* See the note at 19:8.

understand with their hearts
and turn, and I would heal them.'[a]

[28]"Therefore I want you to know that God's salvation has
been sent to the Gentiles, and they will listen!"[b]
[30]For two whole years Paul stayed there in his own rented
house and welcomed all who came to see him. [31]Boldly and without hindrance he preached the kingdom of God and taught about
the Lord Jesus Christ.

---

[a]**27** Isaiah 6:9,10 [b]**28** Some manuscripts *listen!"* [29]*After he said this, the Jews left, arguing vigorously among themselves.*

LETTERS OF PAUL

THE LETTERS OF PAUL include some of the oldest writings in the New Testament. The dates of his earliest letters most likely fall in the period A.D. 50-60 and were written before the Gospels, ACTS, and other New Testament writings.

Paul studied the Jewish Scriptures and was a member of the Pharisees, a group devoted to teaching and living according to God's Law (Gal 1:14; Phil 3:5). In his letters, Paul admits that at one time he persecuted the followers of Jesus, the "church," because he believed they were questioning the authority of God's Law and living instead by Jesus' new teachings. But when God showed Paul who Jesus really was (Gal 1:15,16), Paul began to preach and teach the good news about Jesus. For more about Paul's background and how he became an apostle, see the mini-article called "Paul (Saul) of Tarsus," p. 2177.

Several themes are found throughout the Letters of Paul. For example, Paul taught that God sent Christ "as a sacrifice of atonement" (Rom 3:24-26). He also said that no one could please God or become acceptable to God by obeying the law (Gal 3:11; Rom 3:23); rather, people are justified "by faith in Jesus Christ" (Gal 2:16). Those who put their trust in Jesus benefit not only from the sacrifice he made, but they also share in the new life he received when he was raised from death (Rom 6:5-11). Paul told Christians to live according to God's Spirit, who gives gifts for serving others (Rom 12:6-21; 1 Cor 12,13; Gal 5:16-25). He looked forward to Christ's return (Phil 3:20; 4:5; 1 Thes 4:13-18), and so he encouraged Jesus' followers to live as if Jesus might return any day (1 Thes 5:1-8; 1 Cor 7:29-39).

The apostle Paul is named as the author of nearly half of the "books" in the New Testament. His name appears in the greeting of thirteen New Testament "letters," but some scholars today believe that he did not actually write all of them. All agree that Paul wrote ROMANS, 1 and 2 CORINTHIANS, GALATIANS, PHILIPPIANS, 1 THESSALONIANS, and PHILEMON. Three other letters include many of Paul's basic teachings but introduce ideas that are not found in the seven letters Paul most certainly wrote. This, along with differences in writing style and vocabulary, has led some scholars to present other theories about who may have written EPHESIANS, COLOSSIANS, and 2 THESSALONIANS. Finally, the three letters to early church leaders (1 and 2 TIMOTHY and TITUS) address issues of church leadership that some scholars feel did not become important until a generation or two after Paul's death when local churches had more members and the number of churches had increased. So, while these are traditionally seen as Paul's writings, some scholars believe they may have been written by persons very familiar with Paul's letters and teachings, and who wanted to apply what they had learned from Paul to new problems being faced by the church. For more, see the Introductions to each book.

Paul was certainly one of the most influential leaders in the early days of Christianity. He preached and taught in many places as he journeyed about the regions bordering the Mediterranean Sea. Some of his letters were written to churches and people he had already met in his travels and had taught the good news about Jesus Christ. Others were written to those he hoped to meet in the future. Paul's letters provide a picture of life among many groups of early Christians who struggled to understand what Jesus and his teachings meant for life in this world and the world to come. Although the New Testament writings of Paul were inspired by the Holy Spirit (see the mini-article called "Inspiration of Scripture," p. 12), Paul's teachings reflect the culture and society of his day. They also show his understanding of Jewish Scripture as well as his knowledge of Greek philosophy. Paul used everything he knew and all he had experienced to share the gospel of Christ Jesus. He was chosen by God to spread the gospel, "the power of God for the salvation of everyone who believes" (Rom 1:16).

ROMANS

What do people do in order to become acceptable to God? Read what Paul said to the Jewish and Gentile Christians in Rome about God's powerful way of saving people from their sin and accepting them as the people of God.

What makes Romans special?

In this letter, Paul provides his most detailed summary of the gospel of Jesus Christ. But Romans is more than a letter; it is also a well-organized essay. In the early church, Jewish Christians and Gentile Christians sometimes disagreed about what made a person acceptable to God and how the followers of Christ should live. In Romans, Paul boldly announces that the gospel is "the power of God for the salvation of everyone who believes: first for the Jew, then for the Gentile" (1:16).

Why was Romans written?

Paul wrote this letter about A.D. 55-56 to introduce himself to the followers of Christ at Rome, who likely included new Gentile Christians as well as Jewish Christians who had returned to Rome after being thrown out some years earlier (see below). These Christians, as well as Christians in other parts of the Mediterranean world, had more than one way of understanding the gospel. Jewish Christians in Rome and in Jerusalem continued to follow the Law of Moses, but Gentile Christians did not follow the law. So, who was right? What place, if any, did the Law of Moses have for Gentile Christians? And how did the people of Israel fit into God's plan for sharing the gospel?

Paul teaches in Romans that the gospel was based in the beginning on God's promise to Israel's ancestor Abraham, whose faith made him acceptable to God (4:13). The law, given later to Moses and the people of Israel, revealed how God's people were to live. Still later, God sent Jesus Christ to forgive sins and make people acceptable because of their faith, something which the law on its own could not do (3:21-26). This did not mean the law was useless or that God had forsaken the people who followed the law (Israel). But now, Paul says, only those who have faith in Jesus Christ can become acceptable to God.

What's the story behind the scene?

A group of believers who trusted in Jesus Christ as God's Messiah existed in Rome long before Paul planned his trip there. By A.D. 49 or 50, Jews who were not Jesus' followers and this new group of Jesus' followers were fighting so much that the Roman emperor Claudius made them all leave Rome (see Acts 18:1-4). Among the followers of Jesus who left were a married couple, Priscilla and Aquila, who later worked with Paul as tentmakers in Corinth and Ephesus (Acts 18:3; 1 Cor 16:19; Rom 16:3). Eventually, some of

Rome: Rome, the capital of the Roman empire in Paul's day, was a beautiful city located on the Tiber River and built on seven hills. It had many great buildings made of marble and was famous for its oval stadium (coliseum) the pantheon, great military arches, the Circus Maximus (a huge stadium that held 150,000 people), a theater that seated 40,000, and temples for the many Roman gods and goddesses. In Paul's day, Rome had at least thirteen synagogues as well as shrines for gods like Apollo, Mithra, and Isis. Although Romans was written before Paul had ever been to Rome, he eventually did see Rome when he was taken there as a prisoner. According to church tradition, the emperor Nero had Paul killed sometime after A.D. 64. See the map of Rome on p. 2475.

these followers returned to Rome, and Paul hoped to visit them on his way to bringing the gospel to Spain (15:28). But before he could make this trip, Paul wanted to take to Jerusalem the money he had collected from Gentile Christians in Macedonia and Achaia to give to the church in Jerusalem (15:25, 26). He hoped that his service would also be acceptable to the Jewish Christians in Jerusalem (15:30-32). The book of ACTS reports that Paul eventually got to Rome when he was taken there as a prisoner of the Roman emperor (Acts 27; 28). The Bible does not say whether or not he ever visited or preached the gospel in Spain.

HOW IS ROMANS CONSTRUCTED?

ROMANS is a letter written in the traditional Greek letter writing style of the first century A.D. Letter writers in Paul's day usually first identified who was sending the letter (1:1-6), then gave the names of the persons they were writing to (1:7). This was usually followed by a greeting. As in most of Paul's letters, a prayer of thanksgiving follows the greeting (1:8-10), and the letter closes with a final greeting and blessing (16:1-27).

The letter as a whole can be outlined in this way:

Paul introduces himself and the gospel (1:1-17)
Everyone is guilty before God (1:18—3:20)
How God accepts people (3:21—4:25)
Living the new life of faith (5:1—8:39)
God reaches out to the people of Israel (9:1—11:36)
Life in the body of Christ (12:1—15:13)
Paul's plans and personal greetings (15:14—16:27)

Paul Introduces Himself and the Gospel

Paul introduces himself to the followers of Christ at Rome by pointing out that he is an apostle called to preach the gospel. After offering a prayer of thanks for the Roman Christians, Paul proclaims the gospel as "the power of God for the salvation of everyone who believes" (1:16).

1 Paul, a servant of Christ Jesus, called to be an apostle and set
apart for the gospel of God— 2 the gospel he promised beforehand
through his prophets in the Holy Scriptures 3 regarding his Son,
who as to his human nature was a descendant of David, 4 and who
through the Spirit[a] of holiness was declared with power to be the
Son of God[b] by his resurrection from the dead: Jesus Christ our
Lord. 5 Through him and for his name's sake, we received grace and

[a]4 Or *who as to his spirit* [b]4 Or *was appointed to be the Son of God with power*

1:1 *Paul, a servant of Christ Jesus:* Paul was also known by his Jewish name, Saul (Acts 7:57—8:3; 9:1-30). Paul often described himself as a servant, which literally means "slave" of Christ. See also the mini-article called "Paul (Saul) of Tarsus," on p. 2177.

1:1 *apostle:* An apostle is a person chosen and sent by a leader to do a special job. Here "apostle" means someone chosen by God to spread the "gospel" (see the note at 1:9).

1:2 *prophets:* The prophets of Israel were special messengers who spoke for God. Paul quoted from many of the prophets' writings to show that God's plan was being fulfilled in Jesus Christ. See also the article called "Prophets and Prophecy," p. 935.

1:2 *the Holy Scriptures:* The Holy Scriptures here refers to the Jewish Scriptures, which Christians refer to as the Old Testament.

1:3,4 *his Son . . . Jesus Christ our Lord:* Paul proclaimed that Jesus was God's Son, which is what Jesus is often called in the Gospels (John 1:49; Mark 15:39). The Greek word for "lord" is *kyrios*, which emphasizes authority and power. "Christ" comes from the Greek word *christos*, which means the same thing as the Hebrew title "Messiah."

1:3 *descendant of David:* Paul wanted to emphasize the fact that Jesus was truly human, from the family of the great king David who lived about one thousand years before Jesus was born. The Jewish Scriptures say that the Christ would come from the family of David (Isa 11:1-10; 2 Sam 7:11-14), and both MATTHEW and LUKE list David as one of Jesus' ancestors (Matt 1:1-17; Luke 3:23-38).

1:4 *the Spirit of holiness . . . resurrection:* The Holy Spirit is the unseen power of God who carries out God's purposes in the world. Paul says that the Holy Spirit helped raise Jesus from death, proving that Jesus really is God's Son.

The apostles Peter and Paul, fourth century stone carving, artist unknown (Vatican Museum). Paul was originally an enemy of the first followers of Jesus. But after the Lord appeared to Paul on the road to Damascus, he became one of Christ's most energetic and effective apostles. Both Paul and Peter were important leaders in the early church and were put to death by the Romans because of their belief in Jesus.

apostleship to call people from among all the Gentiles to the obedience that comes from faith. [6]And you also are among those who
are called to belong to Jesus Christ.

[7]To all in Rome who are loved by God and called to be saints:

Grace and peace to you from God our Father and from the Lord Jesus Christ.

Paul's Longing to Visit Rome

[8]First, I thank my God through Jesus Christ for all of you,
because your faith is being reported all over the world. [9]God,
whom I serve with my whole heart in preaching the gospel of his
Son, is my witness how constantly I remember you [10]in my prayers
at all times; and I pray that now at last by God's will the way may
be opened for me to come to you.

[11]I long to see you so that I may impart to you some spiritual gift to make you strong— [12]that is, that you and I may be mutu-
ally encouraged by each other's faith. [13]I do not want you to be
unaware, brothers, that I planned many times to come to you (but
have been prevented from doing so until now) in order that I
might have a harvest among you, just as I have had among the
other Gentiles.

[14]I am obligated both to Greeks and non-Greeks, both to the
wise and the foolish. [15]That is why I am so eager to preach the
gospel also to you who are at Rome.

[16]I am not ashamed of the gospel, because it is the power of
God for the salvation of everyone who believes: first for the Jew,

1:5 *apostleship:* See the note at 1:1 (apostle).

1:7 *Rome:* See the note on p. 2173.

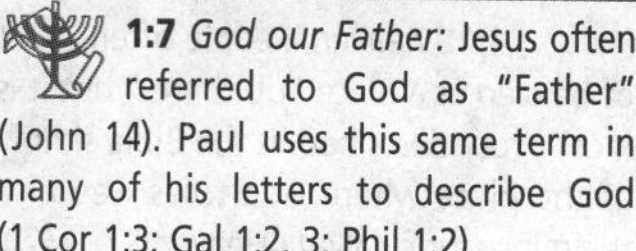

1:7 *God our Father:* Jesus often referred to God as "Father" (John 14). Paul uses this same term in many of his letters to describe God (1 Cor 1:3; Gal 1:2, 3; Phil 1:2).

1:8 *your faith is being reported all over the world:* Followers of Jesus everywhere in the lands surrounding the Mediterranean Sea had heard about the believers in Rome.

1:9 *gospel:* The word "gospel" comes from the old English word *godspel,* which means "good news"—an accurate translation of the Greek word here, *euangelion.* This gospel is both the message about Jesus and the message Jesus brings about God's Kingdom.

1:11 *spiritual gift:* See the note at 12:6.

1:16 *power of God for the salvation of everyone who believes:* This is a very important theme in all of Paul's letters, but especially in ROMANS. Here "salvation" points to how God freed humans from sin and the powers of evil. Salvation comes to those who have faith in Jesus as God's Son and as the Savior of the world. See also the mini-articles called "Salvation," p. 2021, "Eternal Life," p. 2072, and "Faith," p. 1932.

1:16 *Jew . . . Gentile:* See the note at 2:9,10 and the mini-article called "Gentiles," p. 2127.

1:13 Acts 19:21. **1:16** Mark 8:38.

then for the Gentile. [17]For in the gospel a righteousness from God
is revealed, a righteousness that is by faith from first to last,[a] just as
it is written: "The righteous will live by faith."[b]

Everyone Is Guilty before God

In this section of his letter, Paul explains that all people are guilty before God, whether they know God's law or not. Those who know the law cannot follow it perfectly, so following the law cannot be the way to gain God's approval. But God accepts and forgives because of what Jesus has done. Those who have faith in Jesus have God's approval.

God's Wrath Against Mankind

[18]The wrath of God is being revealed from heaven against all
the godlessness and wickedness of men who suppress the truth by
their wickedness, [19]since what may be known about God is plain to
them, because God has made it plain to them. [20]For since the creation of the world God's invisible qualities—his eternal power and
divine nature—have been clearly seen, being understood from
what has been made, so that men are without excuse.

[21]For although they knew God, they neither glorified him as
God nor gave thanks to him, but their thinking became futile and
their foolish hearts were darkened. [22]Although they claimed to be
wise, they became fools [23]and exchanged the glory of the immortal God for images made to look like mortal man and birds and
animals and reptiles.

[24]Therefore God gave them over in the sinful desires of their
hearts to sexual impurity for the degrading of their bodies with
one another. [25]They exchanged the truth of God for a lie, and worshiped and served created things rather than the Creator—who is
forever praised. Amen.

[26]Because of this, God gave them over to shameful lusts.
Even their women exchanged natural relations for unnatural ones.
[27]In the same way the men also abandoned natural relations with
women and were inflamed with lust for one another. Men committed indecent acts with other men, and received in themselves
the due penalty for their perversion.

[28]Furthermore, since they did not think it worthwhile to
retain the knowledge of God, he gave them over to a depraved
mind, to do what ought not to be done. [29]They have become filled
with every kind of wickedness, evil, greed and depravity. They are
full of envy, murder, strife, deceit and malice. They are gossips,
[30]slanderers, God-haters, insolent, arrogant and boastful; they
invent ways of doing evil; they disobey their parents; [31]they are

[a]17 Or *is from faith to faith* [b]17 Hab. 2:4

1:17 *righteousness . . . righteous:* To be "righteous" means to be in right standing or relationship with God.

1:18 *wrath of God:* God's justified anger toward sin.

1:18 *heaven:* People often think of heaven as a place "up there," but it is most often described in the Bible simply as the place where God rules. See also the mini-article called "Heaven," p. 1420.

1:19,20 *what may be known about God is plain:* Paul is saying here that everyone should be able to understand how God wants people to live by seeing how God has created the world.

1:21 *hearts were darkened:* In the Bible, as in the ancient world, "darkness" often represents confusion, punishment, and death (Deut 28:29; Isa 5:30). Since Jesus called himself "the light of the world," the "darkness" is a place for people who decide not to follow Jesus (John 8:12).

1:23 *images:* The Law of Moses forbids worshiping anything other than God, including making "images" or idols, such as statues of living things, to be objects of worship or devotion (Exod 20:3,4). In Paul's day, the Greeks, Romans, and many other peoples worshiped idols or built temples to gods. See also the chart called "Greek and Roman Gods and Goddesses," p. 2136.

1:24,25 *degrading of their bodies . . . worshiped and served created things:* Paul may be referring to people who engaged in sex as part of their religious ceremonies, as well as to those who worshiped objects from nature rather than worshiping God.

1:25 *Amen:* See the note at 11:36.

1:17 Hab 2:4; Gal 3:11; Heb 10:38. **1:21** Eph 4:17,18. **1:23** Deut 4:16-18.

senseless, faithless, heartless, ruthless. 32 Although they know God's
righteous decree that those who do such things deserve death, they
not only continue to do these very things but also approve of those
who practice them.

God's Righteous Judgment

2 You, therefore, have no excuse, you who pass judgment on
someone else, for at whatever point you judge the other, you are
condemning yourself, because you who pass judgment do the
same things. 2 Now we know that God's judgment against those
who do such things is based on truth. 3 So when you, a mere man,

2:1 *do the same things:* It is easy to judge others and accuse them of doing evil, but Paul reminds his readers that people are quick to notice in others the sins they themselves have committed.

2:2 *God's judgment . . . is based on truth:* See the mini-article called "Truth," p. 2087.

2:1 Matt 7:1; Luke 6:37.

PAUL (SAUL) OF TARSUS

Thirteen books, nearly half of the books in the New Testament, name Paul as their author, and another one (Acts) devotes more than half its pages to describing how Paul was chosen to be an apostle and how he preached the gospel throughout the Roman empire. Paul was born in Tarsus, which was a major center for Greek education and culture. But as a Jew, Paul also studied in Jerusalem with Gamaliel, a leading teacher of the Law of Moses (Acts 22:3). Paul, whose Jewish name was Saul, was part of a religious group called the Pharisees (Phil 3:5), who believed that people could serve God best by strictly obeying the Law of Moses.

Paul's strong beliefs as a Pharisee led him to persecute the followers of Jesus (Acts 8:1-3; 9:1,2). Paul did his best to try to destroy the movement that had become known as "the Way," but he was radically changed when the risen Christ appeared to him on the road to Damascus and chose him to be his follower and to spread the gospel to all people (Acts 9:1-18; Gal 1:11-17; 1 Cor 9:1). After three years in Damascus and Arabia (Gal 1:17, 18) and after meeting with the leaders of the church in Jerusalem (Gal 1:18—2:10), Paul set out to preach the gospel about Christ to the Gentiles.

From his letters and from Acts, we learn that Paul spent about twenty years preaching and helping to create new Christian churches in Asia Minor and Greece, where he worked in important cities such as Ephesus, Colosse, Thessalonica, Athens, and Corinth. As he preached and taught the gospel, he debated with philosophers (Acts 17) and worked with Jewish groups to show them that Jesus was the fulfillment of their hopes (Acts 18). He also faced persecution, was arrested, and tried to show the Roman officials that the followers of Christ were no threat to the Roman empire (Acts 24,25).

Paul believed that Jesus was sent to obey God and to die as a sacrifice for human sin (Rom 3:24,25). Jesus was seeking to bring all people—both Jews and Gentiles—together as members of God's new people. God also sent the Holy Spirit to guide and strengthen the followers of Jesus, so they could serve God by telling the gospel about Jesus and by loving one another. The Spirit, Paul said, produces love, joy, and peace (Gal 5), as well as the ability to do God's work in the world (1 Cor 12–14).

Paul was ready to accept death as a witness for Christ, knowing that God would raise him from the dead (Phil 1:20, 21; 2 Tim 4:6-8). Meanwhile, Paul expected Jesus to return to earth to "transform our lowly bodies so that they will be like his glorious body" (Phil 3:21). Then Christ Jesus would defeat human sin and death once and for all (1 Cor 15:50-57).

2:5 *righteous judgment will be revealed:* Many passages in Scripture talk about a future day when God will judge all people (see Ps 9; Eccl 3:17; Matt 25:31-46; John 3:18; Rev 20:11-15). Those who are faithful to God will receive rewards, and those who reject God's truth will be punished.

2:7 *eternal life:* By the time of Jesus, many Jewish people had come to believe in and hope for life after death. Some thought that life after death would be similar to life on earth. Paul talks of eternal life as beginning with being raised to new life with Christ (6:4-8). See also the mini-article called "Eternal Life," p. 2072.

2:9,10 *Jew . . . Gentile:* The Jews are descendants of Abraham and Sarah, and were also known as the people of Israel. Gentiles are people who are not Jewish. Paul argues that God accepts all people who have faith.

2:12 *the law:* Paul is referring to the Law of Moses, which told how God expected the people to live and worship and treat each other. Paul says that those who think God will accept them because they follow the law will be judged according to the law. See also the mini-article called "Law," p. 1160, and the article called "People of the Law: The Religion of Israel," p. 939.

2:14,15 *do by nature things required by the law:* Paul argues that even people who have never heard of the Law of Moses understand in their hearts (their consciences) what is right and wrong. In Paul's day, many people believed that the heart was the place where a person's true inner self, thoughts, and intentions came from.

2:6 Ps 62:12; Prov 24:12. **2:11** Deut 10:17; Gal 2:6; 3:26-29. **2:24** Isa 52:5.

pass judgment on them and yet do the same things, do you think you will escape God's judgment? 4Or do you show contempt for the riches of his kindness, tolerance and patience, not realizing that God's kindness leads you toward repentance?

5But because of your stubbornness and your unrepentant heart, you are storing up wrath against yourself for the day of God's wrath, when his righteous judgment will be revealed. 6God "will give to each person according to what he has done."[a] 7To those who by persistence in doing good seek glory, honor and immortality, he will give eternal life. 8But for those who are self-seeking and who reject the truth and follow evil, there will be wrath and anger. 9There will be trouble and distress for every human being who does evil: first for the Jew, then for the Gentile; 10but glory, honor and peace for everyone who does good: first for the Jew, then for the Gentile. 11For God does not show favoritism.

12All who sin apart from the law will also perish apart from the law, and all who sin under the law will be judged by the law. 13For it is not those who hear the law who are righteous in God's sight, but it is those who obey the law who will be declared righteous. 14(Indeed, when Gentiles, who do not have the law, do by nature things required by the law, they are a law for themselves, even though they do not have the law, 15since they show that the requirements of the law are written on their hearts, their consciences also bearing witness, and their thoughts now accusing, now even defending them.) 16This will take place on the day when God will judge men's secrets through Jesus Christ, as my gospel declares.

The Jews and the Law

17Now you, if you call yourself a Jew; if you rely on the law and brag about your relationship to God; 18if you know his will and approve of what is superior because you are instructed by the law; 19if you are convinced that you are a guide for the blind, a light for those who are in the dark, 20an instructor of the foolish, a teacher of infants, because you have in the law the embodiment of knowledge and truth— 21you, then, who teach others, do you not teach yourself? You who preach against stealing, do you steal? 22You who say that people should not commit adultery, do you commit adultery? You who abhor idols, do you rob temples? 23You who brag about the law, do you dishonor God by breaking the law? 24As it is written: "God's name is blasphemed among the Gentiles because of you."[b]

25Circumcision has value if you observe the law, but if you break the law, you have become as though you had not been circumcised. 26If those who are not circumcised keep the law's requirements, will they not be regarded as though they were circumcised? 27The one who is not circumcised physically and yet

[a]**6** Psalm 62:12; Prov. 24:12 [b]**24** Isaiah 52:5; Ezek. 36:22

obeys the law will condemn you who, even though you have the[a]
written code and circumcision, are a lawbreaker.
[28]A man is not a Jew if he is only one outwardly, nor is circumcision merely outward and physical. [29]No, a man is a Jew if he
is one inwardly; and circumcision is circumcision of the heart, by
the Spirit, not by the written code. Such a man's praise is not from
men, but from God.

God's Faithfulness

3 What advantage, then, is there in being a Jew, or what value is
there in circumcision? [2]Much in every way! First of all, they have
been entrusted with the very words of God.
[3]What if some did not have faith? Will their lack of faith nullify God's faithfulness? [4]Not at all! Let God be true, and every man
a liar. As it is written:

"So that you may be proved right when you speak
and prevail when you judge."[b]

[5]But if our unrighteousness brings out God's righteousness
more clearly, what shall we say? That God is unjust in bringing his
wrath on us? (I am using a human argument.) [6]Certainly not! If
that were so, how could God judge the world? [7]Someone might
argue, "If my falsehood enhances God's truthfulness and so
increases his glory, why am I still condemned as a sinner?" [8]Why
not say—as we are being slanderously reported as saying and as
some claim that we say—"Let us do evil that good may result"?
Their condemnation is deserved.

No One Is Righteous

[9]What shall we conclude then? Are we any better[c]? Not at all!
We have already made the charge that Jews and Gentiles alike are
all under sin. [10]As it is written:

"There is no one righteous, not even one;
11 there is no one who understands,
no one who seeks God.
12 All have turned away,
they have together become worthless;
there is no one who does good,
not even one."[d]
13 "Their throats are open graves;
their tongues practice deceit."[e]
"The poison of vipers is on their lips."[f]
14 "Their mouths are full of cursing and bitterness."[g]

[a]27 Or *who, by means of a* [b]4 Psalm 51:4 [c]9 Or *worse* [d]12 Psalms 14:1-3; 53:1-3; Eccles. 7:20 [e]13 Psalm 5:9 [f]13 Psalm 140:3 [g]14 Psalm 10:7

2:15 *requirements of the law:* Sin occurs when people rebel against God and disobey God's Word. According to the Jewish Scriptures, those who disobeyed God's Law can be forgiven by turning back to God. Paul says that forgiveness comes from Jesus, who died to take away sins (3:25, 26). Those who do not trust in God will be condemned, and may not share in the promise of eternal life.

2:25 *Circumcision:* The Law of Moses commanded all Jewish males to be circumcised (Gen 17:9-14). See the mini-article called "Circumcision," p. 2251. If someone chooses not to obey the law, circumcision cannot make that person a Jew (2:28).

3:2 *they have been entrusted with the very words of God:* The Bible tells how God chose Abraham and Sarah (Gen 12–22). Their descendants became known as the people of Israel (or Israelites) and later as Jews. God spoke to the people through the prophets. God also spoke through the stories and teachings passed on and collected in the Jewish Scriptures, which Christians call the Old Testament.

3:5 *wrath:* See the note at 1:18 (wrath of God).

3:8 *Let us do evil that good may result:* Some of Paul's opponents were saying that he was encouraging people to do evil and to disobey the Law of Moses just so God could show his love by forgiving them. These opponents wanted all the followers of Jesus to obey the laws and traditions that were part of the Law of Moses.

3:9 *Jews and Gentiles alike are all under sin:* Paul goes on to illustrate clearly that "no one is righteous" (2:11; see the note at 1:17); every person needs God's gift of salvation through Christ.

2:29 Deut 30:6. **3:4** Ps 51:4 (Septuagint). **3:10-12** Ps 14:1-3; 53:1-3. **3:13** Ps 5:9; 140:3. **3:14** Ps 10:7.

15 "Their feet are swift to shed blood;
16 ruin and misery mark their ways,
17 and the way of peace they do not know."[a]
18 "There is no fear of God before their eyes."[b]

19 Now we know that whatever the law says, it says to those
who are under the law, so that every mouth may be silenced and
the whole world held accountable to God. 20 Therefore no one will
be declared righteous in his sight by observing the law; rather,
through the law we become conscious of sin.

How God Accepts People

Paul makes it clear in this section that no one can be acceptable to God by following the law, since all fall short of this high goal. That is why God sent Jesus to forgive and free all who trust in him. Paul says in these verses that this is the only way to be acceptable to God.

Righteousness Through Faith

21 But now a righteousness from God, apart from law, has
been made known, to which the Law and the Prophets testify.
22 This righteousness from God comes through faith in Jesus Christ
to all who believe. There is no difference, 23 for all have sinned and
fall short of the glory of God, 24 and are justified freely by his grace
through the redemption that came by Christ Jesus. 25 God presented him as a sacrifice of atonement,[c] through faith in his blood. He
did this to demonstrate his justice, because in his forbearance he
had left the sins committed beforehand unpunished— 26 he did it
to demonstrate his justice at the present time, so as to be just and
the one who justifies those who have faith in Jesus.

27 Where, then, is boasting? It is excluded. On what principle?
On that of observing the law? No, but on that of faith. 28 For we
maintain that a man is justified by faith apart from observing the
law. 29 Is God the God of Jews only? Is he not the God of Gentiles
too? Yes, of Gentiles too, 30 since there is only one God, who will
justify the circumcised by faith and the uncircumcised through
that same faith. 31 Do we, then, nullify the law by this faith? Not at
all! Rather, we uphold the law.

Abraham Justified by Faith

4 What then shall we say that Abraham, our forefather, discovered in this matter? 2 If, in fact, Abraham was justified by works, he
had something to boast about—but not before God. 3 What does

[a] 17 Isaiah 59:7,8 [b] 18 Psalm 36:1 [c] 25 Or *as the one who would turn aside his wrath, taking away sin*

3:18 *no fear of God:* Meaning they do not have respect for God. See Ps 36:1.

3:22 *faith in Jesus Christ:* One of the major themes in Paul's writings. This is the way to be in a right relationship with God. See also Gal 3:26-29.

3:23 *all have sinned and fall short of the glory of God:* See the mini-article called "Sin," p. 2181. To "fall short of the glory of God" means that people cannot perfectly follow God's law or live according to all God's purposes. See Exod 40:34; Ps 143:2; Rom 5:2; 8:18.

3:24 *justified . . . grace . . . redemption:* These are key words in ROMANS and Paul's other letters. The Greek word translated here as "justified" means to be made acceptable to God. People are justified by believing in Christ and putting their faith and trust in him. God's "grace" is often defined as God's unmerited favor toward human beings. The "redemption" comes from the situation where a slave was released through the payment of a ransom. Paul uses the word in the context of Jesus' sacrificial death providing the ransom for our release from the slavery of sin and guilt.

3:25 *sacrifice of atonement:* The Greek word translated "atonement" is used to describe the top of ancient Israel's ark of the covenant. Each year on the Day of Atonement, the priests would sacrifice an animal and sprinkle its blood on the top of the ark to remove the sins of the Israelite people (Lev 16:14-16). Jesus gives his life as the perfect and final sacrifice. See also 1 Cor 1:30; Eph 1:7, 8; Heb 9:15; and the mini-article called "The Ark of the Covenant," p. 513.

3:31 *nullify the law:* Paul does not want to nullify or destroy the law, because the law shows what God expects. The problem comes when people make following the law more important than faith.

3:15-17 Isa 59:7,8. **3:20** Ps 143:2; Gal 2:16. **3:22** Gal 2:16. **3:30** Deut 6:4; Gal 3:20. **4:3** Gen 15:1-6; Gal 3:6; Heb 11:8-19.

the Scripture say? "Abraham believed God, and it was credited to
him as righteousness."[a]
4 Now when a man works, his wages are not credited to him
as a gift, but as an obligation. 5 However, to the man who does not
work but trusts God who justifies the wicked, his faith is credited
as righteousness. 6 David says the same thing when he speaks of the
blessedness of the man to whom God credits righteousness apart
from works:

7 "Blessed are they
whose transgressions are forgiven,
whose sins are covered.
8 Blessed is the man
whose sin the Lord will never count against him."[b]

---

[a]3 Gen. 15:6; also in verse 22 [b]8 Psalm 32:1,2

4:1-3 *Abraham . . . believed God:* See the mini-article called "Abraham," p. 2254. Abraham's righteousness, or right standing with God, was a result of his believing God.

4:6 *David:* See the note at 1:3. King David ruled Israel from around 1010 to 970 B.C., and was understood to be the author of many of the psalms. See also the mini-article called "David," p. 1028.

4:7,8 *Blessed are they . . . never count against him:* Paul is quoting Psalm 32:1,2, a psalm that tradition says King David wrote.

SIN

Sin is pictured in GENESIS as beginning with Adam and Eve, who disobeyed God by eating fruit from the tree of the knowledge of good and evil (Gen 2:16, 17; 3:1-6). The Jewish Scriptures, which Christians call the Old Testament, describe sin in a number of ways:

1. Sin is breaking the Law of Moses and failing to live as God intended (Exod 20:20; 32:31-34), or turning one's back on God to follow other gods (Ezek 44:10).

2. Sin is defying God or rebelling against God (Jer 2:22-24,29-37), with the result that a right relationship with God is broken.

3. Sins are acts of violence against others (Gen 6:11-13), or ways of secretly hurting or harming others (Ps 64:1-6).

4. Sin occurs when the people do not follow the Law of Moses by failing to offer correct sacrifices. This makes them unfit to come into God's presence (Lev 4; 5; Num 5:1-4).

5. Sinful people are proud of the wrongs they have done (Isa 2:12). The prophets understood this pride to come out of an evil human heart (Jer 17:9-11).

6. Sin is not living up to or reflecting God's glory. Humans are to reflect God's glory, since they were created in God's image (Gen 1:27; Ps 8:3-8). Sinful people do not live by the law or love others as God desires. This is why Paul says in Romans 3:23 that "all have sinned and fall short of the glory of God."

7. The sin of one person can have consequences for many others. For example, when the head of a family did wrong, all members were considered guilty (Josh 7; see also Exod 20:5). God was expected to punish the wicked, and the final punishment was to be death (Gen 2:17; Exod 21:15-17; Lev 24:10-17).

The New Testament brings a new message of hope. All people are descendants of Adam and are inheritors of sin that leads to death. But Jesus brings new life because he brings forgiveness. This new life includes being raised to life from the dead (1 Cor 15:22,23). God used Jesus' death to take away the power of sin (Rom 3:9) by having Jesus suffer the punishment for the sins of everyone (1 Cor 15:3; 2 Cor 5:21). He was sacrificed in order to forgive sins (Rom 3:25, 26; Heb 2:17; 9:25-28). Jesus paid the penalty for our sins, and God has a new covenant with people, which includes eternal life (Rom 6:23). Instead of continuing as slaves to sin, God's new people are now slaves to God (Rom 6:20-22).

4:9 *circumcised:* See the note at 2:25. Paul is arguing that Abraham was circumcised after God had accepted him because of his faith. That makes Abraham the father of those who have faith—those who are circumcised and those who are not (see 4:16).

4:16 *Abraham's offspring . . . father of us all:* See the note at 2:9,10 and the mini-article called "Abraham," p. 2254. No matter what nation a person comes from, that person can be a descendant of Abraham because of faith in God. See also Gal 3:26-29.

4:24 *raised Jesus our Lord from the dead:* Paul is referring to how Jesus rose to life three days after dying on a cross (Matt 28:1-10; Acts 2:22-24), which is sometimes called the "resurrection." See the mini-article called "Resurrection," p. 2210.

4:11 Gen 17:10. **4:13** Gen 12:1-3; 15:1-6; 17:4-6; 22:17, 18; Gal 3:29. **4:14** Gal 3:18. **4:16** Gal 3:7. **4:17** Gen 17:5; Ezek 37. **4:18** Gen 15:5. **4:19** Gen 17:17.

[9]Is this blessedness only for the circumcised, or also for the uncircumcised? We have been saying that Abraham's faith was credited to him as righteousness. [10]Under what circumstances was it credited? Was it after he was circumcised, or before? It was not after, but before! [11]And he received the sign of circumcision, a seal of the righteousness that he had by faith while he was still uncircumcised. So then, he is the father of all who believe but have not been circumcised, in order that righteousness might be credited to them. [12]And he is also the father of the circumcised who not only are circumcised but who also walk in the footsteps of the faith that our father Abraham had before he was circumcised.

[13]It was not through law that Abraham and his offspring received the promise that he would be heir of the world, but through the righteousness that comes by faith. [14]For if those who live by law are heirs, faith has no value and the promise is worthless, [15]because law brings wrath. And where there is no law there is no transgression.

[16]Therefore, the promise comes by faith, so that it may be by grace and may be guaranteed to all Abraham's offspring—not only to those who are of the law but also to those who are of the faith of Abraham. He is the father of us all. [17]As it is written: "I have made you a father of many nations."[a] He is our father in the sight of God, in whom he believed—the God who gives life to the dead and calls things that are not as though they were.

[18]Against all hope, Abraham in hope believed and so became the father of many nations, just as it had been said to him, "So shall your offspring be."[b] [19]Without weakening in his faith, he faced the fact that his body was as good as dead—since he was about a hundred years old—and that Sarah's womb was also dead. [20]Yet he did not waver through unbelief regarding the promise of

[a]17 Gen. 17:5 [b]18 Gen. 15:5

QUESTIONS ABOUT ROMANS 1:1—4:25

1. How does Paul describe himself at the beginning of his letter to the Romans? What is his task or special work?
2. How does Paul describe the "gospel"? (1:16,17) Have you heard this gospel before? If so, where? What difference does it make that this gospel exists?
3. Read 1:18—2:16. How do people "suppress the truth"? How does Paul describe God's judgment? (2:2-11) What does Paul say about the human conscience? What troubles you, if anything, about what Paul says? What gives you hope?
4. According to Paul, what does it mean to be a Jew? (2:25-29) Are Jews better off than Gentiles? Why or why not? (3:9-18)
5. What is the real purpose of the law? (3:19,20) If following the law is not the way to be saved or accepted by God, what is? (3:21-30) Does this mean that the law is useless or should be thrown out? Why or why not? (3:31)
6. What argument is Paul using in chapter 4 to prove what he has already said about the law, about being a Jew or Gentile, and about being acceptable to God?

God, but was strengthened in his faith and gave glory to God, [21]being fully persuaded that God had power to do what he had promised. [22]This is why "it was credited to him as righteousness." [23]The words "it was credited to him" were written not for him alone, [24]but also for us, to whom God will credit righteousness—for us who believe in him who raised Jesus our Lord from the dead. [25]He was delivered over to death for our sins and was raised to life for our justification.

Living the New Life of Faith

In the next four chapters of his letter, Paul explains what it means to live the new life of faith, which includes the promise that God's Holy Spirit will be present in the lives of Jesus' followers.

Peace and Joy

5 Therefore, since we have been justified through faith, we[a] have peace with God through our Lord Jesus Christ, [2]through whom we have gained access by faith into this grace in which we now stand. And we[a] rejoice in the hope of the glory of God. [3]Not only so, but we[a] also rejoice in our sufferings, because we know that suffering produces perseverance; [4]perseverance, character; and character, hope. [5]And hope does not disappoint us, because God has poured out his love into our hearts by the Holy Spirit, whom he has given us.

[6]You see, at just the right time, when we were still powerless, Christ died for the ungodly. [7]Very rarely will anyone die for a righteous man, though for a good man someone might possibly dare to die. [8]But God demonstrates his own love for us in this: While we were still sinners, Christ died for us.

[9]Since we have now been justified by his blood, how much more shall we be saved from God's wrath through him! [10]For if, when we were God's enemies, we were reconciled to him through the death of his Son, how much more, having been reconciled, shall we be saved through his life! [11]Not only is this so, but we also rejoice in God through our Lord Jesus Christ, through whom we have now received reconciliation.

Death Through Adam, Life Through Christ

[12]Therefore, just as sin entered the world through one man, and death through sin, and in this way death came to all men, because all sinned— [13]for before the law was given, sin was in the world. But sin is not taken into account when there is no law. [14]Nevertheless, death reigned from the time of Adam to the time of Moses, even over those who did not sin by breaking a command, as did Adam, who was a pattern of the one to come.

---

a1,2,3 Or *let us*

Therefore, since we have been justified through faith, we have peace with God through our Lord Jesus Christ.
Rom 5:1

4:25 *death for our sins . . . our justification:* See the notes at 3:24 and 3:25 (justified).

5:2 *grace:* Grace means God's undeserved kindness toward us.

5:5 *Holy Spirit:* See the note at 1:4. Paul taught that the Holy Spirit is present in the lives of Jesus' followers, helping them to live the new life based on faith (8:12-17; 1 Cor 2:1-11).

5:6-9 *Christ died for the ungodly . . . justified by his blood:* See the note at 3:25. For more about the sinfulness of humans, see 1:18 and 3:9-18. See also the mini-article called "Blood," p. 180.

5:12 *sin entered the world through one man, and death:* Adam, the first human created by God, sinned by disobeying God in the Garden of Eden (Gen 2:15-17; 3:1-24). Human beings had been created to live with God forever, but because of Adam's sin, all people sin and die. See also the mini-article called "Sin," p. 2181.

5:14 *from the time of Adam to the time of Moses:* God chose to give the Law to Moses many generations after the time of Adam. Paul wants to show that people were unfaithful to God even before God had given the Law to Moses. According to Paul, one of the chief functions of the law was to show people how sinful they are and how much they need God's forgiveness (see the note at 7:8).

4:22,23 Gen 15:6. **4:25** Isa 53:4,5. **5:12** Gen 3:6.

5:15,16 *the gift is not like the trespass:* The gift Paul is talking about here is the new life that God gives to those who trust in Jesus Christ, the one who brought forgiveness and justification, making people acceptable to God. Adam's sin brought condemnation and death.

5:17 *grace ... righteousness:* See the notes at 5:2 (grace) and 1:17 (righteousness).

5:20 *The law was added so that the trespass might increase:* See the note at 7:8.

5:21 *sin reigned . . . grace might reign:* Without the saving work of Jesus, sin would continue to reign in people's lives. But God's grace sent Jesus to forgive sin and to offer eternal life (see the note at 2:7).

6:2 *sin:* See the note at 2:12 and the mini-article called "Sin," p. 2181.

5:20 Rom 3:20; Gal 3:19.

[15]But the gift is not like the trespass. For if the many died by
the trespass of the one man, how much more did God's grace and
the gift that came by the grace of the one man, Jesus Christ, overflow to the many! [16]Again, the gift of God is not like the result of
the one man's sin: The judgment followed one sin and brought
condemnation, but the gift followed many trespasses and brought
justification. [17]For if, by the trespass of the one man, death reigned
through that one man, how much more will those who receive
God's abundant provision of grace and of the gift of righteousness
reign in life through the one man, Jesus Christ.

[18]Consequently, just as the result of one trespass was condemnation for all men, so also the result of one act of righteousness was justification that brings life for all men. [19]For just as
through the disobedience of the one man the many were made
sinners, so also through the obedience of the one man the many
will be made righteous.

[20]The law was added so that the trespass might increase. But
where sin increased, grace increased all the more, [21]so that, just as
sin reigned in death, so also grace might reign through righteousness to bring eternal life through Jesus Christ our Lord.

Dead to Sin, Alive in Christ

6 What shall we say, then? Shall we go on sinning so that grace
may increase? [2]By no means! We died to sin; how can we live in it

Serpent and Apple by Marti Shohet, cut paper, twentieth century. The Jewish Scriptures tell how Adam brought sin and death into the world when he rebelled against God's command and ate the fruit from the tree of the knowledge of good and evil (here shown as an apple; see Gen 3:1-8). In ROMANS Paul speaks about human sinfulness and compares Adam, the one who brought sin and death into the world, with Christ, the one who "justifies" people, making them acceptable to God, and gives them the gift of eternal life (Rom 5:12-21).

any longer? [3]Or don't you know that all of us who were baptized into Christ Jesus were baptized into his death? [4]We were therefore buried with him through baptism into death in order that, just as Christ was raised from the dead through the glory of the Father, we too may live a new life.

[5]If we have been united with him like this in his death, we will certainly also be united with him in his resurrection. [6]For we know that our old self was crucified with him so that the body of sin might be done away with,[a] that we should no longer be slaves to sin— [7]because anyone who has died has been freed from sin.

[8]Now if we died with Christ, we believe that we will also live with him. [9]For we know that since Christ was raised from the dead, he cannot die again; death no longer has mastery over him. [10]The death he died, he died to sin once for all; but the life he lives, he lives to God.

[11]In the same way, count yourselves dead to sin but alive to God in Christ Jesus. [12]Therefore do not let sin reign in your mortal body so that you obey its evil desires. [13]Do not offer the parts of your body to sin, as instruments of wickedness, but rather offer yourselves to God, as those who have been brought from death to life; and offer the parts of your body to him as instruments of righteousness. [14]For sin shall not be your master, because you are not under law, but under grace.

Slaves to Righteousness

[15]What then? Shall we sin because we are not under law but under grace? By no means! [16]Don't you know that when you offer yourselves to someone to obey him as slaves, you are slaves to the one whom you obey—whether you are slaves to sin, which leads to death, or to obedience, which leads to righteousness? [17]But thanks be to God that, though you used to be slaves to sin, you wholeheartedly obeyed the form of teaching to which you were entrusted. [18]You have been set free from sin and have become slaves to righteousness.

[19]I put this in human terms because you are weak in your natural selves. Just as you used to offer the parts of your body in slavery to impurity and to ever-increasing wickedness, so now offer them in slavery to righteousness leading to holiness. [20]When you were slaves to sin, you were free from the control of righteousness. [21]What benefit did you reap at that time from the things you are now ashamed of? Those things result in death! [22]But now that you have been set free from sin and have become slaves to God, the benefit you reap leads to holiness, and the result is eternal life. [23]For the wages of sin is death, but the gift of God is eternal life in[b] Christ Jesus our Lord.

6:3 *baptized:* Jesus would make people completely new inside and out by giving them the gift of the Holy Spirit. See also the mini-article called "Baptism," p. 1976. Paul explains being baptized as dying to sin and being raised to life, just as Jesus died and then was raised to life by God.

6:6-11 *our old self was crucified with him . . . count yourselves dead to sin:* Paul often talks about the old life of sin and the new life in Christ. Here he is saying that for those who are baptized and trust in Jesus, their old lives of sin died with Jesus when he was put to death on the cross (Luke 23:44-49; John 19:28-30). Those who are crucified with Christ will also be raised to life and live with him (Gal 2:20), which includes the gift of eternal life.

6:13 *offer yourselves to God:* Paul encourages the Roman believers to live the new life that God makes possible for them—not in order to get accepted by God by following the law, but as a way of giving thanks for what God in Christ has done for them. See the note at 2:12.

6:16 *slaves:* Slaves were common in Paul's society. They were expected to obey their masters without question. Paul is saying that those who have been baptized into Christ should no longer be slaves to the life of sin and obey their evil desires. Rather, they should be slaves who serve God. See the mini-article called "Slaves and Servants in the Time of Jesus," p. 2006. Paul reminds the Romans that until they trusted in Christ they were slaves to sin. But now that God has accepted them and shown them grace, they are to serve God.

6:23 *sin . . . eternal life:* When people sin, they rebel against God. See also the mini-articles called "Sin," p. 2181, and "Eternal Life," p. 2072.

6:4 Col 2:12.

[a]**6** Or *be rendered powerless* [b]**23** Or *through*

7:2 *by law:* Paul is likely teaching the traditional understanding of faithfulness in marriage, rather than a specific part of the Law of Moses.

7:4 *that you might belong to another:* Now that Christ has come, people can join themselves to him just as a husband and wife are joined in marriage. They are free to do this because the power of the law, which they had been "married to," is dead in their lives.

7:5 *the sinful nature:* The Greek here means "the flesh." This refers to a person's fallen human nature, which is controlled by sin rather than by the Holy Spirit.

7:6 *serve in the new way of the Spirit:* See the note at 1:4. Paul says that the new way of life God offers is life that is led by the Holy Spirit (Gal 5:16-26).

7:7 *Is the law sin:* See the note at 2:12. Some of Paul's opponents were saying that he was making the law into an evil or sinful thing. Paul wants to make it clear that this is not at all what he is saying. He goes on to explain the real function of God's law, which was given to show what sin was really like.

7:8 *apart from law, sin is dead:* Without the Law of Moses, no one would know what sin is. Hearing the law makes a person aware of what is sinful and "arouses" (7:5) or stimulates the fallen human nature to do wrong. This does not mean that the law causes sin. Rather, the law and its commands are holy and good and show just how evil sin really is (7:12,13).

7:14 *the law is spiritual; but I am unspiritual:* For Paul, the law was from God and expressed God's perfect will. But Paul was human and therefore imperfect and a slave to sin.

7:7 Exod 20:17; Deut 5:21. **7:11** Gen 3:13. **7:15** Gal 5:17.

An Illustration From Marriage

7 Do you not know, brothers—for I am speaking to men who
know the law—that the law has authority over a man only as long
as he lives? [2]For example, by law a married woman is bound to her
husband as long as he is alive, but if her husband dies, she is
released from the law of marriage. [3]So then, if she marries another man while her husband is still alive, she is called an adulteress.
But if her husband dies, she is released from that law and is not an
adulteress, even though she marries another man.
[4]So, my brothers, you also died to the law through the body
of Christ, that you might belong to another, to him who was raised
from the dead, in order that we might bear fruit to God. [5]For when
we were controlled by the sinful nature,[a] the sinful passions
aroused by the law were at work in our bodies, so that we bore
fruit for death. [6]But now, by dying to what once bound us, we have
been released from the law so that we serve in the new way of the
Spirit, and not in the old way of the written code.

Struggling With Sin

[7]What shall we say, then? Is the law sin? Certainly not!
Indeed I would not have known what sin was except through the
law. For I would not have known what coveting really was if the
law had not said, "Do not covet."[b] [8]But sin, seizing the opportunity afforded by the commandment, produced in me every kind of
covetous desire. For apart from law, sin is dead. [9]Once I was alive
apart from law; but when the commandment came, sin sprang to
life and I died. [10]I found that the very commandment that was
intended to bring life actually brought death. [11]For sin, seizing the
opportunity afforded by the commandment, deceived me, and
through the commandment put me to death. [12]So then, the law is
holy, and the commandment is holy, righteous and good.
[13]Did that which is good, then, become death to me? By no
means! But in order that sin might be recognized as sin, it produced death in me through what was good, so that through the
commandment sin might become utterly sinful.
[14]We know that the law is spiritual; but I am unspiritual, sold
as a slave to sin. [15]I do not understand what I do. For what I want
to do I do not do, but what I hate I do. [16]And if I do what I do not
want to do, I agree that the law is good. [17]As it is, it is no longer I
myself who do it, but it is sin living in me. [18]I know that nothing
good lives in me, that is, in my sinful nature.[c] For I have the desire
to do what is good, but I cannot carry it out. [19]For what I do is not
the good I want to do; no, the evil I do not want to do—this I keep
on doing. [20]Now if I do what I do not want to do, it is no longer I
who do it, but it is sin living in me that does it.

---

[a]**5** Or *the flesh*; also in verse 25 [b]**7** Exodus 20:17; Deut. 5:21 [c]**18** Or *my flesh*

21 So I find this law at work: When I want to do good, evil is
right there with me. 22 For in my inner being I delight in God's law;
23 but I see another law at work in the members of my body, waging war against the law of my mind and making me a prisoner of
the law of sin at work within my members. 24 What a wretched
man I am! Who will rescue me from this body of death? 25 Thanks
be to God—through Jesus Christ our Lord!
So then, I myself in my mind am a slave to God's law, but in
the sinful nature a slave to the law of sin.

Life Through the Spirit

8 Therefore, there is now no condemnation for those who are in
Christ Jesus,[a] 2 because through Christ Jesus the law of the Spirit of
life set me free from the law of sin and death. 3 For what the law was
powerless to do in that it was weakened by the sinful nature,[b] God
did by sending his own Son in the likeness of sinful man to be a sin
offering.[c] And so he condemned sin in sinful man,[d] 4 in order that the
righteous requirements of the law might be fully met in us, who do
not live according to the sinful nature but according to the Spirit.
5 Those who live according to the sinful nature have their
minds set on what that nature desires; but those who live in accordance with the Spirit have their minds set on what the Spirit
desires. 6 The mind of sinful man[e] is death, but the mind controlled
by the Spirit is life and peace; 7 the sinful mind[f] is hostile to God. It
does not submit to God's law, nor can it do so. 8 Those controlled
by the sinful nature cannot please God.
9 You, however, are controlled not by the sinful nature but by
the Spirit, if the Spirit of God lives in you. And if anyone does not
have the Spirit of Christ, he does not belong to Christ. 10 But if
Christ is in you, your body is dead because of sin, yet your spirit is
alive because of righteousness. 11 And if the Spirit of him who
raised Jesus from the dead is living in you, he who raised Christ
from the dead will also give life to your mortal bodies through his
Spirit, who lives in you.
12 Therefore, brothers, we have an obligation—but it is not to
the sinful nature, to live according to it. 13 For if you live according
to the sinful nature, you will die; but if by the Spirit you put to
death the misdeeds of the body, you will live, 14 because those who
are led by the Spirit of God are sons of God. 15 For you did not
receive a spirit that makes you a slave again to fear, but you
received the Spirit of sonship.[g] And by him we cry, "*Abba*,[h] Father."
16 The Spirit himself testifies with our spirit that we are God's
children. 17 Now if we are children, then we are heirs—heirs of God

[a]1 Some later manuscripts *Jesus, who do not live according to the sinful nature but according to the Spirit,* [b]3 Or *the flesh*; also in verses 4,5,8,9,12 and 13 [c]3 Or *man, for sin* [d]3 Or *in the flesh* [e]6 Or *mind set on the flesh* [f]7 Or *the mind set on the flesh* [g]15 Or *adoption* [h]15 Aramaic for *Father*

7:25 *slave to God's law . . . slave to the law of sin:* Paul summarizes this section by saying that he knew the Law of Moses was good, so he tried to serve it. However, his selfish desires made him want to rebel against the law and turn to sin. Since no one is free from these selfish desires, no one can follow God's law perfectly, even if they know it is the right thing to do. That's why Paul is so glad God sent Jesus to rescue everyone from this impossible situation.

8:2 *the Spirit of life:* See the notes at 1:4 and 5:5. Paul says God's Spirit works in the lives of Jesus' followers to help free them from the power of sin and live a life that pleases God. God strengthens and renews believers through the spirit.

8:3 *what the law was powerless to do . . . sending his own Son:* See the notes at 2:12 and 3:25.

8:5 *what the Spirit desires:* The things that are from God are pleasing to God. People who are controlled or led by the Holy Spirit want to keep their minds and actions focused on what the Spirit desires instead of on what the sinful nature desires (see the note at 7:5).

8:9 *Spirit of Christ:* This is the Holy Spirit. See the notes at 1:4 and 5:5. The Spirit is present in everyone who trusts in Jesus Christ.

8:11 *the Spirit of him who raised Jesus from the dead:* See the note at 4:24. The resurrection of Christ provides for and guarantees the resurrection of his followers.

8:14 *those who are led by the Spirit of God are sons of God:* This statement was especially directed to those who argued that a person could be a child of God simply by following the Law of Moses or by being born into a family descended from Abraham and Sarah.

8:15 *Abba, Father:* This shows the intimate relationship we can have with God.

8:11 1 Cor 3:16 **8:15** Mark 14:36; Gal 4:6. **8:15-17** Gal 4:5-7.

8:18 *present sufferings . . . glory that will be revealed:* Life on earth does cause suffering and pain, but God will give to all who trust Jesus a future that will be free of pain. This will happen when people receive eternal life. Paul offered hope concerning the future day when all God's children would live under God's care and love forever. Even other parts of creation are suffering and frustrated, waiting for the time when God will renew everything. Creation's groans are like those of a woman who is about to give birth (8:22).

8:23 *we wait eagerly for our adoption as sons, the redemption of our bodies:* God's people can put up with present suffering and difficulties because they know that God's Spirit is within them and continues to support and encourage them. This is how they can be sure they will be saved and why they wait patiently for it. One specific part of this hope is the promise of "the redemption of our bodies." In 1 Corinthians 15:35-57 Paul describes what people's bodies will be like when they are raised to life and taken to heaven.

8:26 *the Spirit himself intercedes for us:* Paul says that the Spirit's work includes interceding, or praying, for those who cannot find words to pray for themselves.

8:20 Gen 3:17-19. **8:23** 2 Cor 5:2-4.

and co-heirs with Christ, if indeed we share in his sufferings in
order that we may also share in his glory.

Future Glory

[18]I consider that our present sufferings are not worth comparing with the glory that will be revealed in us. [19]The creation
waits in eager expectation for the sons of God to be revealed. [20]For
the creation was subjected to frustration, not by its own choice,
but by the will of the one who subjected it, in hope [21]that[a] the creation itself will be liberated from its bondage to decay and brought
into the glorious freedom of the children of God.

[22]We know that the whole creation has been groaning as in
the pains of childbirth right up to the present time. [23]Not only so,
but we ourselves, who have the firstfruits of the Spirit, groan
inwardly as we wait eagerly for our adoption as sons, the redemption of our bodies. [24]For in this hope we were saved. But hope that
is seen is no hope at all. Who hopes for what he already has? [25]But
if we hope for what we do not yet have, we wait for it patiently.

[26]In the same way, the Spirit helps us in our weakness. We
do not know what we ought to pray for, but the Spirit himself
intercedes for us with groans that words cannot express. [27]And he
who searches our hearts knows the mind of the Spirit, because the
Spirit intercedes for the saints in accordance with God's will.

More Than Conquerors

[28]And we know that in all things God works for the good of
those who love him,[b] who[c] have been called according to his pur-

[a]20,21 Or *subjected it in hope. [21]For* [b]28 Some manuscripts *And we know that all things work together for good to those who love God* [c]28 Or *works together with those who love him to bring about what is good—with those who*

QUESTIONS ABOUT ROMANS 5:1—8:39

1. According to Paul, what is the relationship between suffering and having hope? (5:3-5) How do God's people have hope?
2. How did God show how much he loved us? (5:6-11)
3. How are Adam and Christ alike and different from each other? (5:12-21)
4. How is being baptized like dying? (6:1-11) Complete this sentence: "Death is . . ."
5. What does it mean to be a slave to sin? What does it mean to be a slave to God? (6:15-23)
6. Describe in your own words Paul's "struggle" with sin (7:7-25). Can you identify with this struggle? If so, how? What is the role of the law in this battle? What is the role of Christ?
7. Those who have the Spirit of Christ are no longer ruled by their desires. What does this mean? (8:1-17) How does God's Spirit help and provide hope for God's people? (8:18-27)
8. How does Paul answer his own question in 8:35? (8:36-39) What do you think of his answer?

pose. 29 For those God foreknew he also predestined to be conformed to the likeness of his Son, that he might be the firstborn
among many brothers. 30 And those he predestined, he also called;
those he called, he also justified; those he justified, he also glorified.
31 What, then, shall we say in response to this? If God is for us,
who can be against us? 32 He who did not spare his own Son, but gave
him up for us all—how will he not also, along with him, graciously
give us all things? 33 Who will bring any charge against those whom
God has chosen? It is God who justifies. 34 Who is he that condemns?
Christ Jesus, who died—more than that, who was raised to life—is at
the right hand of God and is also interceding for us. 35 Who shall separate us from the love of Christ? Shall trouble or hardship or persecution or famine or nakedness or danger or sword? 36 As it is written:

> "For your sake we face death all day long;
> we are considered as sheep to be slaughtered."[a]

37 No, in all these things we are more than conquerors through him
who loved us. 38 For I am convinced that neither death nor life, neither angels nor demons,[b] neither the present nor the future, nor
any powers, 39 neither height nor depth, nor anything else in all creation, will be able to separate us from the love of God that is in
Christ Jesus our Lord.

8:29 *God foreknew:* Before the creation of the world, God knew who would be Christ's followers (Eph 1:4).

8:29 *Son . . . firstborn among many brothers:* This refers to Jesus Christ. See the note at 1:3,4 and the mini-article called "Son of God," p. 2044. God the Father has given Christ the Son the highest position as "firstborn" in the family of God.

8:30 *justified:* See the note at 3:24.

8:34 *right hand of God:* The place of honor and power.

8:39 *Christ Jesus our Lord:* See the note at 1:3,4.

9:1 *my conscience confirms it in the Holy Spirit:* See the note at 1:4 (Spirit). See also the note at 2:14,15, where Paul describes the "conscience" in terms of the human heart. Here, Paul says the Holy Spirit acts as his teacher, speaking to his conscience and shaping his innermost thoughts and desires.

God Reaches Out to the People of Israel

Paul makes it clear in the next three chapters that God has not rejected the people of Israel, though many of them do not trust in Jesus Christ for salvation. Many Gentiles, on the other hand, have discovered that God accepts everyone who has faith. Now they, like the Jewish followers of Jesus, are included in God's people. Paul hopes that his own people (Israel) will believe the gospel about Jesus.

God's Sovereign Choice

9 I speak the truth in Christ—I am not lying, my conscience
confirms it in the Holy Spirit— 2 I have great sorrow and unceasing anguish in my heart. 3 For I could wish that I myself were
cursed and cut off from Christ for the sake of my brothers, those
of my own race, 4 the people of Israel. Theirs is the adoption as
sons; theirs the divine glory, the covenants, the receiving of the law,
the temple worship and the promises. 5 Theirs are the patriarchs,
and from them is traced the human ancestry of Christ, who is God
over all, forever praised![c] Amen.

9:3 *my own race:* Paul was born and raised a Jew. See the note at 1:1 (Paul) and the mini-article called "Paul (Saul) of Tarsus," p. 2177.

9:4 *people of Israel:* See the mini-article called "Israel," p. 264, and the note at 2:9,10. The covenant God made with the Israelites has two main parts: *(1)* God's promises to Abraham and his descendants (Gen 12:1-3); and *(2)* God's covenant with Moses at Mount Sinai expressed in the law (see the note at 2:12).

9:5 *patriarchs:* The famous ancestors of the people of Israel: Abraham, Isaac, Jacob and the twelve sons of Jacob.

8:36 Ps 44:22. **9:4** Exod 4:22.

---

[a] **36** Psalm 44:22 [b] **38** Or *nor heavenly rulers* [c] **5** Or *Christ, who is over all. God be forever praised!* Or *Christ. God who is over all be forever praised!*

[6]It is not as though God's word had failed. For not all who
are descended from Israel are Israel. [7]Nor because they are his
descendants are they all Abraham's children. On the contrary, "It is
through Isaac that your offspring will be reckoned."[a] [8]In other
words, it is not the natural children who are God's children, but it
is the children of the promise who are regarded as Abraham's offspring. [9]For this was how the promise was stated: "At the appointed time I will return, and Sarah will have a son."[b]
[10]Not only that, but Rebekah's children had one and the
same father, our father Isaac. [11]Yet, before the twins were born or
had done anything good or bad—in order that God's purpose in
election might stand: [12]not by works but by him who calls—she
was told, "The older will serve the younger."[c] [13]Just as it is written:
"Jacob I loved, but Esau I hated."[d]
[14]What then shall we say? Is God unjust? Not at all! [15]For he
says to Moses,

"I will have mercy on whom I have mercy,
and I will have compassion on whom I have
compassion."[e]

[16]It does not, therefore, depend on man's desire or effort, but on
God's mercy. [17]For the Scripture says to Pharaoh: "I raised you up
for this very purpose, that I might display my power in you and
that my name might be proclaimed in all the earth."[f] [18]Therefore
God has mercy on whom he wants to have mercy, and he hardens
whom he wants to harden.
[19]One of you will say to me: "Then why does God still blame
us? For who resists his will?" [20]But who are you, O man, to talk
back to God? "Shall what is formed say to him who formed it,
'Why did you make me like this?' "[g] [21]Does not the potter have the
right to make out of the same lump of clay some pottery for noble
purposes and some for common use?
[22]What if God, choosing to show his wrath and make his
power known, bore with great patience the objects of his wrath—
prepared for destruction? [23]What if he did this to make the riches
of his glory known to the objects of his mercy, whom he prepared
in advance for glory— [24]even us, whom he also called, not only
from the Jews but also from the Gentiles? [25]As he says in Hosea:

"I will call them 'my people' who are not my people;
and I will call her 'my loved one' who is not my
loved one,"[h]

[26]and,

"It will happen that in the very place where it was said
to them,

[a]7 Gen. 21:12 [b]9 Gen. 18:10,14 [c]12 Gen. 25:23 [d]13 Mal. 1:2,3 [e]15 Exodus 33:19 [f]17 Exodus 9:16 [g]20 Isaiah 29:16; 45:9 [h]25 Hosea 2:23

9:7-9 *the children of the promise who are regarded as Abraham's offspring:* See Gen 16; 21:8-21. Paul was talking about the fact that God's promises were made to the descendants of Abraham and Sarah's son Isaac. Abraham did have other children, such as Ishmael, his son with Sarah's slave Hagar.

9:10 *Rebekah's children . . . Isaac:* See the story of Jacob and Esau in Genesis 25:19-34; 27:1-40.

9:18 *Therefore God:* Paul emphasizes that God is the one who is in control of giving mercy or hardening people's hearts.

9:21 *potter . . . lump of clay:* Many of the household objects used by the Romans were made of pottery. These were less expensive and easier to produce than utensils made of metals. Pottery was used to create bowls, jars, and clay lamps. Some were simple in design, others were highly decorated.

9:24 *Jews . . . Gentiles:* See the note at 2:9, 10.

9:25 *Hosea:* Hosea was a prophet in Israel during the time Uzziah was king of Judah (783-746 B.C.) and Jeroboam II was king of Israel (786-746 B.C.). An important theme in HOSEA concerns Hosea's wife Gomer, who left him for another man. She is compared to the people of Israel, who left God to follow idols.

9:25,26 *not my people:* Paul is quoting from both Hosea 2:23 and 1:10. These prophecies speak to how God will invite people from all nations to be his children. See also Isa 2:2-4; 60:1-22; Mic 4:1-3; and Zech 8:20-23.

9:9 Gen 18:10. **9:13** Mal 1:2,3. **9:15** Exod 33:19. **9:17** Exod 9:16. **9:20** Isa 29:16; 45:9.

'You are not my people,'
they will be called 'sons of the living God.'"[a]

27 Isaiah cries out concerning Israel:

"Though the number of the Israelites be like the sand
by the sea,
only the remnant will be saved.
28 For the Lord will carry out
his sentence on earth with speed and finality."[b]

29 It is just as Isaiah said previously:

"Unless the Lord Almighty
had left us descendants,
we would have become like Sodom,
we would have been like Gomorrah."[c]

Israel's Unbelief

30 What then shall we say? That the Gentiles, who did not
pursue righteousness, have obtained it, a righteousness that is by
faith; 31 but Israel, who pursued a law of righteousness, has not
attained it. 32 Why not? Because they pursued it not by faith but as
if it were by works. They stumbled over the "stumbling stone." 33 As
it is written:

"See, I lay in Zion a stone that causes men to stumble
and a rock that makes them fall,
and the one who trusts in him will never be put
to shame."[d]

10 Brothers, my heart's desire and prayer to God for the
Israelites is that they may be saved. 2 For I can testify about them
that they are zealous for God, but their zeal is not based on knowledge. 3 Since they did not know the righteousness that comes from
God and sought to establish their own, they did not submit to
God's righteousness. 4 Christ is the end of the law so that there may
be righteousness for everyone who believes.
5 Moses describes in this way the righteousness that is by the
law: "The man who does these things will live by them."[e] 6 But the
righteousness that is by faith says: "Do not say in your heart, 'Who
will ascend into heaven?'[f]" (that is, to bring Christ down) 7 "or 'Who
will descend into the deep?'[g]" (that is, to bring Christ up from the
dead). 8 But what does it say? "The word is near you; it is in your
mouth and in your heart,"[h] that is, the word of faith we are proclaiming: 9 That if you confess with your mouth, "Jesus is Lord," and
believe in your heart that God raised him from the dead, you will
be saved. 10 For it is with your heart that you believe and are

[a]**26** Hosea 1:10 [b]**28** Isaiah 10:22,23 [c]**29** Isaiah 1:9 [d]**33** Isaiah 8:14; 28:16
[e]**5** Lev. 18:5 [f]**6** Deut. 30:12 [g]**7** Deut. 30:13 [h]**8** Deut. 30:14

9:27 *Isaiah:* Isaiah was a prophet in Judah from about 740 to 701 B.C. See also the Introduction to ISAIAH, p. 1289.

9:29 *Sodom . . . Gomorrah:* During Abraham's time, the Lord destroyed these two cities because the people were so sinful (Gen 18:16—19:29).

9:31 *law of righteousness:* See the note at 2:12.

9:32,33 *"stumbling stone":* Paul is referring to Jesus. See also Mark 12:10; 1 Pet 2:6-8.

9:33 *Zion:* Zion was the name of a hilltop fortress captured by King David, which became his royal city Jerusalem and was also considered the place where God lived among his people. See also the mini-article called "Zion," p. 1294.

10:3 *did not know the righteousness that comes from God and sought to establish their own:* See the notes at 2:12; 7:7; and 7:8. Some apparently believed that obeying the law was the only way to become acceptable to God.

10:6-9 *righteousness that is by faith:* Paul means that those who have faith in Christ realize that righteousness is something God gives to people, not something people can achieve on their own. The way to salvation is simple, sincere trust in Jesus as the risen Lord. See the notes at 1:4 and 1:16 (power of God) and the mini-article called "Lord (Title for Jesus)," p. 2106.

9:27,28 Isa 10:22,23. **9:29** Isa 1:9. **9:33** Isa 28:16. **10:5** Lev 18:5.

justified, and it is with your mouth that you confess and are saved.
11 As the Scripture says, "Anyone who trusts in him will never be put
to shame."[a] 12 For there is no difference between Jew and Gentile—
the same Lord is Lord of all and richly blesses all who call on him,
13 for, "Everyone who calls on the name of the Lord will be saved."[b]

14 How, then, can they call on the one they have not believed
in? And how can they believe in the one of whom they have not
heard? And how can they hear without someone preaching to
them? 15 And how can they preach unless they are sent? As it is written, "How beautiful are the feet of those who bring good news!"[c]

16 But not all the Israelites accepted the good news. For Isaiah
says, "Lord, who has believed our message?"[d] 17 Consequently, faith
comes from hearing the message, and the message is heard through
the word of Christ. 18 But I ask: Did they not hear? Of course they did:

> "Their voice has gone out into all the earth,
> their words to the ends of the world."[e]

19 Again I ask: Did Israel not understand? First, Moses says,

> "I will make you envious by those who are not a nation;
> I will make you angry by a nation that has no
> understanding."[f]

20 And Isaiah boldly says,

> "I was found by those who did not seek me;
> I revealed myself to those who did not ask for me."[g]

21 But concerning Israel he says,

> "All day long I have held out my hands
> to a disobedient and obstinate people."[h]

The Remnant of Israel

11 I ask then: Did God reject his people? By no means! I am an
Israelite myself, a descendant of Abraham, from the tribe of Benjamin. 2 God did not reject his people, whom he foreknew. Don't
you know what the Scripture says in the passage about Elijah—
how he appealed to God against Israel: 3 "Lord, they have killed
your prophets and torn down your altars; I am the only one left,
and they are trying to kill me"[i]? 4 And what was God's answer to
him? "I have reserved for myself seven thousand who have not
bowed the knee to Baal."[j] 5 So too, at the present time there is a
remnant chosen by grace. 6 And if by grace, then it is no longer by
works; if it were, grace would no longer be grace.[k]

[a] 11 Isaiah 28:16 [b] 13 Joel 2:32 [c] 15 Isaiah 52:7 [d] 16 Isaiah 53:1
[e] 18 Psalm 19:4 [f] 19 Deut. 32:21 [g] 20 Isaiah 65:1 [h] 21 Isaiah 65:2
[i] 3 1 Kings 19:10,14 [j] 4 1 Kings 19:18 [k] 6 Some manuscripts *by grace.*
But if by works, then it is no longer grace; if it were, work would no longer be work.

10:10 *with your heart . . . with your mouth:* Justification, or salvation (see the notes at 3:24 and 1:16, power of God), includes both inner belief and outer expression.

10:12 *no difference between Jew and Gentile:* See the note at 2:9,10.

10:15 *How beautiful are the feet of those who bring good news:* Joy and relief accompany those who bring good news. Paul quotes Isaiah 52:7, where the "good news" pertained to the release of the Jews from captivity in Babylon, but he applies the quotation to the preaching of the gospel of Christ.

10:18 *Their voice:* In Psalm 19:4, which Paul quotes, "their voice" refers to the heavens. Paul connects "their voice" to the message of those who preach the gospel, which the Israelites can't deny hearing.

10:19 *Moses:* See also the mini-article called "Moses," p. 2335.

10:19 *envious by those who are not a nation:* Paul is quoting Deuteronomy 32:21, where Moses stated that God would welcome other nations because some people of Israel had rebelled against God.

11:1 *I am an Israelite myself . . . tribe of Benjamin:* See the note at 1:1 (Paul). Israel's first king, Saul, was also from the tribe of Benjamin which took its name from the youngest son of Jacob (Israel).

11:2 *Elijah:* Over 800 years before Jesus was born, the prophet Elijah preached against worshiping other gods, especially the Canaanite god Baal. See also 1 Kgs 19:10-18 and the mini-article called "Elijah," p. 1816. As in the case of Elijah, in Paul's day there was a "remnant," a faithful minority of Jews who were saved by God's grace.

10:11 Isa 28:16. **10:13** Joel 2:32. **10:15** Isa 52:7. **10:16** Isa 53:1. **10:18** Ps 19:4. **10:20** Isa 65:1. **10:21** Isa 65:2. **11:1** Phil 3:5.

[7]What then? What Israel sought so earnestly it did not obtain, but the elect did. The others were hardened, [8]as it is written:

> "God gave them a spirit of stupor,
> eyes so that they could not see
> and ears so that they could not hear,
> to this very day."[a]

[9]And David says:

> "May their table become a snare and a trap,
> a stumbling block and a retribution for them.
> [10]May their eyes be darkened so they cannot see,
> and their backs be bent forever."[b]

Ingrafted Branches

[11]Again I ask: Did they stumble so as to fall beyond recovery? Not at all! Rather, because of their transgression, salvation has come to the Gentiles to make Israel envious. [12]But if their transgression means riches for the world, and their loss means riches for the Gentiles, how much greater riches will their fullness bring!

[13]I am talking to you Gentiles. Inasmuch as I am the apostle to the Gentiles, I make much of my ministry [14]in the hope that I may somehow arouse my own people to envy and save some of them. [15]For if their rejection is the reconciliation of the world, what will their acceptance be but life from the dead? [16]If the part of the dough offered as firstfruits is holy, then the whole batch is holy; if the root is holy, so are the branches.

[17]If some of the branches have been broken off, and you, though a wild olive shoot, have been grafted in among the others and now share in the nourishing sap from the olive root, [18]do not boast over those branches. If you do, consider this: You do not support the root, but the root supports you. [19]You will say then, "Branches were broken off so that I could be grafted in." [20]Granted. But they were broken off because of unbelief, and you stand by faith. Do not be arrogant, but be afraid. [21]For if God did not spare the natural branches, he will not spare you either.

[22]Consider therefore the kindness and sternness of God: sternness to those who fell, but kindness to you, provided that you continue in his kindness. Otherwise, you also will be cut off. [23]And if they do not persist in unbelief, they will be grafted in, for God is able to graft them in again. [24]After all, if you were cut out of an olive tree that is wild by nature, and contrary to nature were grafted into a cultivated olive tree, how much more readily will these, the natural branches, be grafted into their own olive tree!

[a]**8** Deut. 29:4; Isaiah 29:10 [b]**10** Psalm 69:22,23

11:7 *What Israel sought so earnestly it did not obtain:* All Jews desired right standing with God, but only the "elect," a faithful remnant, responded to Jesus as their Messiah.

11:9 *David:* See the note at 4:6.

11:12 *their transgression . . . their loss:* Referring to Israel's rejection of Jesus, God's Messiah. But Paul also has hope for "their fullness"—Israel's salvation through Christ.

11:13 *Gentiles . . . apostle:* See the notes at 2:9,10 and 1:1 (apostle).

11:16 *part of the dough . . . the root:* Paul uses two images to show that the holiness of the part leads to the holiness of the whole. See also Num 15:17-21. The first followers of Jesus among the people of Israel ("part of the dough"; "the root") make the Gentile believers ("the whole batch"; "the branches") holy and acceptable.

11:17 *wild olive shoot:* Since ancient times grafting has been done to improve the flavor and quality of fruit, normally by inserting a branch or shoot of a cultivated tree into a wild tree. Paul is saying that the Gentiles are like branches that are cut out of a wild tree and grafted into a cultivated tree. The people of Israel are God's cultivated olive tree, and the new "Gentile" branches have been grafted into the tree, which stands for the whole people of God.

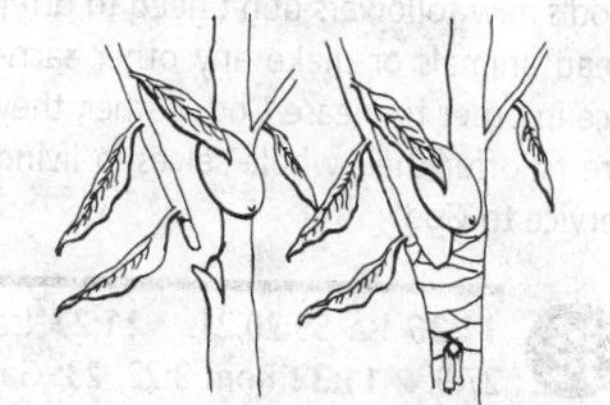

11:19 *Branches were broken off:* Paul is referring to those in Israel who did not follow Jesus. Paul warns that God can remove Gentiles who no longer have faith in Jesus (11:20-22).

11:25 *mystery . . . full number of the Gentiles has come in:* When Paul uses the word "mystery," he means that a previously hidden truth has now been made clear by God. Here the "mystery" is that God has invited Gentiles to be part of his people (see the note at 2:9,10), especially when some of the people of Israel stubbornly refused to accept Christ.

11:26 *all Israel will be saved:* It isn't certain exactly what Paul meant by this, but he seems to expect a great future response to Christ among his fellow Jews.

11:26,27 *Zion . . . covenant:* See the note at 9:33 (Zion). Paul is referring to the "new covenant" of Jeremiah 31:31-34. See the mini-article called "Covenants (Agreements)," p. 386.

11:28 *as far as election is concerned, they are loved on account of the patriarchs:* The people of Israel are also called the chosen people because God chose Abraham and his descendants to know God and to bring God's blessings to all nations (Gen 12:1-3). See the notes at 2:9,10; 3:2; 9:5.

11:36 *Amen:* In Hebrew this word means "truthful, reliable." It is also used as a way of saying, "yes, it is so." This is why it is often spoken at the end of a prayer.

12:1 *offer your bodies as living sacrifices:* Offering sacrifices was an important part of the Jewish religion as well as other religions of Paul's day. See also the mini-article called "Temple Offerings," p. 2027. But Paul says that God's new followers don't need to offer dead animals or make any other sacrifice in order to please God. Rather, they are to offer their whole selves in living service to God.

11:26 Isa 59:20,21. **11:27** Isa 27:9. **11:32** Rom 3:22, 23; Gal 3:22. **11:33** Isa 55:8. **11:34** Isa 40:13. **11:35** Job 41:11. **11:36** 1 Cor 8:6.

All Israel Will Be Saved

25 I do not want you to be ignorant of this mystery, brothers,
so that you may not be conceited: Israel has experienced a hardening in part until the full number of the Gentiles has come in.
26 And so all Israel will be saved, as it is written:

"The deliverer will come from Zion;
he will turn godlessness away from Jacob.
27 And this is[a] my covenant with them
when I take away their sins."[b]

28 As far as the gospel is concerned, they are enemies on your
account; but as far as election is concerned, they are loved on
account of the patriarchs, 29 for God's gifts and his call are irrevocable. 30 Just as you who were at one time disobedient to God have now
received mercy as a result of their disobedience, 31 so they too have
now become disobedient in order that they too may now[c] receive
mercy as a result of God's mercy to you. 32 For God has bound all
men over to disobedience so that he may have mercy on them all.

Doxology

33 Oh, the depth of the riches of the wisdom and[d]
knowledge of God!
How unsearchable his judgments,
and his paths beyond tracing out!
34 "Who has known the mind of the Lord?
Or who has been his counselor?"[e]
35 "Who has ever given to God,
that God should repay him?"[f]
36 For from him and through him and to him are all things.
To him be the glory forever! Amen.

Life in the Body of Christ

In the first eleven chapters of Romans *Paul has been focusing on the question, "Who is acceptable to God?" In the remaining chapters he describes how the followers of Christ (the body of Christ) should live, and he gives encouragement to the Roman Christians.*

Living Sacrifices

12 Therefore, I urge you, brothers, in view of God's mercy, to
offer your bodies as living sacrifices, holy and pleasing to God—
this is your spiritual[g] act of worship. 2 Do not conform any longer

[a]27 Or *will be* [b]27 Isaiah 59:20,21; 27:9; Jer. 31:33,34 [c]31 Some manuscripts do not have *now.* [d]33 Or *riches and the wisdom and the* [e]34 Isaiah 40:13 [f]35 Job 41:11 [g]1 Or *reasonable*

to the pattern of this world, but be transformed by the renewing of your mind. Then you will be able to test and approve what God's will is—his good, pleasing and perfect will.

[3]For by the grace given me I say to every one of you: Do not think of yourself more highly than you ought, but rather think of yourself with sober judgment, in accordance with the measure of faith God has given you. [4]Just as each of us has one body with many members, and these members do not all have the same function, [5]so in Christ we who are many form one body, and each member belongs to all the others. [6]We have different gifts, according to the grace given us. If a man's gift is prophesying, let him use it in proportion to his[a] faith. [7]If it is serving, let him serve; if it is teaching, let him teach; [8]if it is encouraging, let him encourage; if it is contributing to the needs of others, let him give generously; if it is leadership, let him govern diligently; if it is showing mercy, let him do it cheerfully.

Love

[9]Love must be sincere. Hate what is evil; cling to what is good. [10]Be devoted to one another in brotherly love. Honor one another above yourselves. [11]Never be lacking in zeal, but keep your spiritual fervor, serving the Lord. [12]Be joyful in hope, patient in affliction, faithful in prayer. [13]Share with God's people who are in need. Practice hospitality.

[14]Bless those who persecute you; bless and do not curse. [15]Rejoice with those who rejoice; mourn with those who mourn. [16]Live in harmony with one another. Do not be proud, but be willing to associate with people of low position.[b] Do not be conceited.

[17]Do not repay anyone evil for evil. Be careful to do what is right in the eyes of everybody. [18]If it is possible, as far as it depends on you, live at peace with everyone. [19]Do not take revenge, my friends, but leave room for God's wrath, for it is written: "It is mine to avenge; I will repay,"[c] says the Lord. [20]On the contrary:

"If your enemy is hungry, feed him;
if he is thirsty, give him something to drink.
In doing this, you will heap burning coals on his head."[d]

[21]Do not be overcome by evil, but overcome evil with good.

Submission to the Authorities

13 Everyone must submit himself to the governing authorities, for there is no authority except that which God has established. The authorities that exist have been established by God. [2]Consequently, he who rebels against the authority is rebelling against

---

[a]6 Or *in agreement with the* [b]16 Or *willing to do menial work*
[c]19 Deut. 32:35 [d]20 Prov. 25:21,22

12:2 *this world:* For Paul, the "world" stands for the present age, in which most of the things people put their trust in are against God. Paul knew such things were unreliable and would one day disappear (see 1 Cor 2:6-8).

12:5 *in Christ we who are many form one body:* This is another way Paul describes the whole group of Jesus' followers, the Christian church. See also 1 Cor 12:12-31.

12:6 *different gifts, according to the grace given us:* God's Spirit gives different gifts to the followers of Jesus. Some are listed in 12:6-8. "Prophesying" is the special ability to hear God's message and tell it to others. Other gifts mentioned are serving others, teaching, encouraging others, giving money in a generous way, and being a leader. See also 1 Cor 12:4-11 and the note at 5:2 (grace).

12:13 *Share with God's people who are in need. Practice hospitality:* Paul and other apostles in the early church were concerned about receiving offerings for the poor. Practicing hospitality, welcoming strangers into a home for a meal or rest, was customary among the Jewish people in Paul's day. Paul wanted all the followers of Jesus to continue this custom.

12:19 *God's wrath . . . it is written:* See the note at 1:18 (wrath of God). Paul means that "it is written" in the Jewish Scriptures (Old Testament).

13:1 *no authority except that which God has established:* Paul believed that God was in control of putting people in places of power. Those who opposed earthly rulers were opposing God.

12:4,5 1 Cor 12:12. **12:14** Matt 5:44; Luke 6:28. **12:16** Prov 3:7. **12:19** Deut 32:35; Lev 19:18. **12:20** Prov 25:21,22; Matt 5:44; Luke 6:27-36.

what God has instituted, and those who do so will bring judgment
on themselves. 3For rulers hold no terror for those who do right,
but for those who do wrong. Do you want to be free from fear of
the one in authority? Then do what is right and he will commend
you. 4For he is God's servant to do you good. But if you do wrong,
be afraid, for he does not bear the sword for nothing. He is God's
servant, an agent of wrath to bring punishment on the wrongdoer.
5Therefore, it is necessary to submit to the authorities, not only
because of possible punishment but also because of conscience.
6This is also why you pay taxes, for the authorities are God's
servants, who give their full time to governing. 7Give everyone
what you owe him: If you owe taxes, pay taxes; if revenue, then
revenue; if respect, then respect; if honor, then honor.

Love, for the Day Is Near

8Let no debt remain outstanding, except the continuing debt
to love one another, for he who loves his fellowman has fulfilled
the law. 9The commandments, "Do not commit adultery," "Do not
murder," "Do not steal," "Do not covet,"[a] and whatever other commandment there may be, are summed up in this one rule: "Love
your neighbor as yourself."[b] 10Love does no harm to its neighbor.
Therefore love is the fulfillment of the law.
11And do this, understanding the present time. The hour has
come for you to wake up from your slumber, because our salvation is nearer now than when we first believed. 12The night is nearly over; the day is almost here. So let us put aside the deeds of
darkness and put on the armor of light. 13Let us behave decently,
as in the daytime, not in orgies and drunkenness, not in sexual
immorality and debauchery, not in dissension and jealousy.
14Rather, clothe yourselves with the Lord Jesus Christ, and do not
think about how to gratify the desires of the sinful nature.[c]

The Weak and the Strong

14 Accept him whose faith is weak, without passing judgment
on disputable matters. 2One man's faith allows him to eat
everything, but another man, whose faith is weak, eats only vegetables. 3The man who eats everything must not look down on
him who does not, and the man who does not eat everything must
not condemn the man who does, for God has accepted him. 4Who
are you to judge someone else's servant? To his own master he
stands or falls. And he will stand, for the Lord is able to make him
stand.
5One man considers one day more sacred than another;
another man considers every day alike. Each one should be fully
convinced in his own mind. 6He who regards one day as special,

13:3,4 *rulers . . . God's servant to do you good:* Paul argued that the followers of Jesus should obey authorities because they are God's servants. If the early Christians started causing trouble and disobeying the government, the rulers might stop them from meeting together, or even kill them. This would stop the gospel from spreading throughout the Roman empire. Obeying the authorities meant paying taxes to support the government and the Roman military. This was difficult for the followers of Jesus when they saw that the taxes went to support emperors who did not believe in God or who even declared themselves to be gods.

13:11 *our salvation is nearer now than when we first believed:* Paul is talking about the second coming of Christ (see 8:23; 1 Pet 1:3-5). He believed the Lord's return was "near" (Phil 4:5). Paul challenged the Roman Christians to "wake up from [their] slumber" and live in faithful anticipation of Christ's return.

13:12 *night . . . day . . . darkness . . . light:* When Paul talks about the "night" he is referring to the present time before Jesus comes back to rule (see the note at 12:2). The "day" is the future time of complete salvation mentioned in 13:11. In the Bible, light is used to describe God (John 1:3,4; 1 John 1:5), God's Word (Ps 119:105), and those people or things that reveal God's truth (Isa 49:6). "Darkness" refers to confusion, destruction, and death (Ps 143:3; Isa 5:30) and to those who rebel against God (John 8:12). Here, Paul is referring to the things people do that are against God's commands (13:13).

14:1 *whose faith is weak:* This likely refers to Jewish believers in the church at Rome who had weak, or sensitive, consciences and held on to certain regulations of Judaism.

13:6,7 Matt 22:21; Mark 12:17; Luke 20:25. **13:8** Lev 19:18; Matt 22:37-39. **13:9** Exod 20:13-15, 17; Deut 5:17-19, 21; Lev 19:18. **14:1-6** Col 2:16.

[a]**9** Exodus 20:13-15,17; Deut. 5:17-19,21 [b]**9** Lev. 19:18 [c]**14** Or *the flesh*

does so to the Lord. He who eats meat, eats to the Lord, for he
gives thanks to God; and he who abstains, does so to the Lord and
gives thanks to God. [7]For none of us lives to himself alone and
none of us dies to himself alone. [8]If we live, we live to the Lord;
and if we die, we die to the Lord. So, whether we live or die, we
belong to the Lord.

[9]For this very reason, Christ died and returned to life so that
he might be the Lord of both the dead and the living. [10]You, then,
why do you judge your brother? Or why do you look down on
your brother? For we will all stand before God's judgment seat. [11]It
is written:

> " 'As surely as I live,' says the Lord,
> 'every knee will bow before me;
> every tongue will confess to God.' "[a]

[12]So then, each of us will give an account of himself to God.

[13]Therefore let us stop passing judgment on one another.
Instead, make up your mind not to put any stumbling block or
obstacle in your brother's way. [14]As one who is in the Lord Jesus, I
am fully convinced that no food[b] is unclean in itself. But if anyone
regards something as unclean, then for him it is unclean. [15]If your
brother is distressed because of what you eat, you are no longer
acting in love. Do not by your eating destroy your brother for
whom Christ died. [16]Do not allow what you consider good to be
spoken of as evil. [17]For the kingdom of God is not a matter of eating and drinking, but of righteousness, peace and joy in the Holy
Spirit, [18]because anyone who serves Christ in this way is pleasing to
God and approved by men.

[19]Let us therefore make every effort to do what leads to peace
and to mutual edification. [20]Do not destroy the work of God for
the sake of food. All food is clean, but it is wrong for a man to eat
anything that causes someone else to stumble. [21]It is better not to
eat meat or drink wine or to do anything else that will cause your
brother to fall.

[22]So whatever you believe about these things keep between
yourself and God. Blessed is the man who does not condemn himself by what he approves. [23]But the man who has doubts is condemned if he eats, because his eating is not from faith; and
everything that does not come from faith is sin.

15 We who are strong ought to bear with the failings of the
weak and not to please ourselves. [2]Each of us should please his
neighbor for his good, to build him up. [3]For even Christ did not
please himself but, as it is written: "The insults of those who insult
you have fallen on me."[c] [4]For everything that was written in the
past was written to teach us, so that through endurance and the
encouragement of the Scriptures we might have hope.

---

[a]**11** Isaiah 45:23 [b]**14** Or *that nothing* [c]**3** Psalm 69:9

14:2 *faith is weak . . . eats only vegetables:* Apparently some of the Christians in Rome believed that eating meat was wrong. Paul called them weak because they were still following certain customs or laws, as though that made them right with God. Paul said that God welcomes all people, regardless of their eating habits.

14:5 *one day more sacred than another:* Some of the Roman believers may have been observing the Jewish Sabbath day and celebrating certain festivals required by the Law of Moses. See the chart called "Jewish Calendar and Festivals," p. 944. Paul is saying that there will be differences among God's people, but all of Jesus' followers need to accept each other and not try to force their own rules on others.

14:9 *Lord of both the dead and the living:* See the note at 10:6-9 and the mini-article called "Lord (Title for Jesus)," p. 2106.

14:10 *we will all stand before God's judgment seat:* See the note at 2:5.

14:17 *Holy Spirit:* See the note at 1:4.

14:20 *All food is clean:* Rules about food were important to the people of Israel (Lev 11:1-45; Deut 14:4-21; 32:13,14). Although Paul believed that it does not matter what God's people eat, he knew that some still wanted to keep these rules, or other rules about not eating meat or drinking wine (14:21). Paul wanted to help the Christians in Rome respect each other's customs and to stop disagreements about food from causing division among them. See also the mini-article called "Purity (Clean and Unclean)," p. 2125.

14:23 *sin:* See the note at 2:15 (sin) and the mini-article called "Sin," p. 2181.

15:4 *Scriptures:* See the note at 10:11.

14:10 2 Cor 5:10. **14:11** Isa 45:23; Phil 2:10,11. **15:3** Ps 69:9.

15:6 *glorify:* In the simplest sense, people "glorify" God by giving praise for God's character and acts. But believers also bring glory to God by demonstrating God's presence and qualities in their own lives. See also 15:9.

15:8 *Christ has become a servant of the Jews:* See the notes at 9:4; 9:5; and 11:28. Paul repeats his belief that Jesus came to fulfill God's promise to send a chosen Messiah to the Jewish people.

15:9 *Gentiles:* See the notes at 2:9,10 and 11:17.

15:10 *Rejoice, O Gentiles, with his people:* See Deut 32:43. Paul is saying that the nations are invited to worship God and be part of God's new people.

15:12 *Isaiah . . . Root of Jesse:* See the note at 9:27 (Isaiah). "The Root of Jesse" is an expression for the Messiah. Jesse was King David's father. The Messiah was to come from the family of David (Isa 11:1-5; Matt 21:9).

15:13 *overflow with hope by the power of the Holy Spirit:* See the notes at 1:16 (power) and 1:4.

15:15 *grace:* "Grace" is God's undeserved kindness. Here, it includes God's enabling someone to fulfill a calling.

15:16 *priestly duty of proclaiming the gospel . . . an offering:* Jewish priests served God by making sure the rituals described in the Law of Moses were obeyed and by preparing special offerings and sacrifices. Paul says that he serves God by preaching the gospel (see the note at 1:9) to the Gentiles. The offering that Paul brings to God is the Gentiles who respond to the gospel. These Gentile believers are acceptable to God because they have been "sanctified," or made holy, by the Holy Spirit (see the note at 1:4).

15:9 2 Sam 22:50; Ps 18:49. **15:11** Ps 117:1. **15:12** Isa 11:10.

5 May the God who gives endurance and encouragement give
you a spirit of unity among yourselves as you follow Christ Jesus,
6 so that with one heart and mouth you may glorify the God and
Father of our Lord Jesus Christ.

7 Accept one another, then, just as Christ accepted you, in
order to bring praise to God. 8 For I tell you that Christ has become
a servant of the Jews[a] on behalf of God's truth, to confirm the
promises made to the patriarchs 9 so that the Gentiles may glorify
God for his mercy, as it is written:

> "Therefore I will praise you among the Gentiles;
> I will sing hymns to your name."[b]

10 Again, it says,

> "Rejoice, O Gentiles, with his people."[c]

11 And again,

> "Praise the Lord, all you Gentiles,
> and sing praises to him, all you peoples."[d]

12 And again, Isaiah says,

> "The Root of Jesse will spring up,
> one who will arise to rule over the nations;
> the Gentiles will hope in him."[e]

13 May the God of hope fill you with all joy and peace as you
trust in him, so that you may overflow with hope by the power of
the Holy Spirit.

Paul's Plans and Personal Greetings

Paul concludes his letter by telling the believers in Rome about his work as an apostle and his plans to come and visit them. Chapter 16 includes personal greetings to many people who are not mentioned anywhere else in the New Testament, so we know little or nothing about their lives.

Paul the Minister to the Gentiles

14 I myself am convinced, my brothers, that you yourselves
are full of goodness, complete in knowledge and competent to
instruct one another. 15 I have written you quite boldly on some
points, as if to remind you of them again, because of the grace
God gave me 16 to be a minister of Christ Jesus to the Gentiles with
the priestly duty of proclaiming the gospel of God, so that the

[a]8 Greek *circumcision* [b]9 2 Samuel 22:50; Psalm 18:49 [c]10 Deut. 32:43
[d]11 Psalm 117:1 [e]12 Isaiah 11:10

Gentiles might become an offering acceptable to God, sanctified
by the Holy Spirit.
[17]Therefore I glory in Christ Jesus in my service to God. [18]I
will not venture to speak of anything except what Christ has
accomplished through me in leading the Gentiles to obey God by
what I have said and done— [19]by the power of signs and miracles,
through the power of the Spirit. So from Jerusalem all the way
around to Illyricum, I have fully proclaimed the gospel of Christ.
[20]It has always been my ambition to preach the gospel where
Christ was not known, so that I would not be building on someone else's foundation. [21]Rather, as it is written:

> "Those who were not told about him will see,
> and those who have not heard will understand."[a]

[22]This is why I have often been hindered from coming to you.

Paul's Plan to Visit Rome

[23]But now that there is no more place for me to work in
these regions, and since I have been longing for many years to see
you, [24]I plan to do so when I go to Spain. I hope to visit you while
passing through and to have you assist me on my journey there,
after I have enjoyed your company for a while. [25]Now, however, I
am on my way to Jerusalem in the service of the saints there. [26]For
Macedonia and Achaia were pleased to make a contribution for the
poor among the saints in Jerusalem. [27]They were pleased to do it,
and indeed they owe it to them. For if the Gentiles have shared in
the Jews' spiritual blessings, they owe it to the Jews to share with
them their material blessings. [28]So after I have completed this task
and have made sure that they have received this fruit, I will go to
Spain and visit you on the way. [29]I know that when I come to you,
I will come in the full measure of the blessing of Christ.
[30]I urge you, brothers, by our Lord Jesus Christ and by the
love of the Spirit, to join me in my struggle by praying to God for
me. [31]Pray that I may be rescued from the unbelievers in Judea
and that my service in Jerusalem may be acceptable to the saints
there, [32]so that by God's will I may come to you with joy and
together with you be refreshed. [33]The God of peace be with you
all. Amen.

Personal Greetings

16 I commend to you our sister Phoebe, a servant[b] of the
church in Cenchrea. [2]I ask you to receive her in the Lord in a
way worthy of the saints and to give her any help she may need
from you, for she has been a great help to many people, including me.

[a]21 Isaiah 52:15 [b]1 Or *deaconess*

15:19 *Jerusalem . . . Illyricum:* Jerusalem was the capital city of Judea and the center for Israel's worship and government. See also the mini-article called "Jerusalem," p. 574. Illyricum was a Roman province on the eastern coast of the Adriatic Sea. See the map on p. 2472. The Bible does not say that Paul went to Illyricum, but he may have preached to some Illyrians while in Macedonia, who then took his message home with them.

15:24 *when I go to Spain:* The Bible does not say if Paul ever traveled to Spain. Some think that he may have gone to Spain after being released from house arrest in Rome (Acts 28). Others think Paul was put to death in Rome at that time. See the map on p. 2469.

15:25,26 *Jerusalem . . . Macedonia and Achaia:* See the note at 15:19. Macedonia, the land north of Greece, became part of the Roman empire in 168 B.C. (see the map on p. 2475). Achaia, after the Roman conquest in 146 B.C., referred to the central part of Greece. Athens and Corinth were in Achaia.

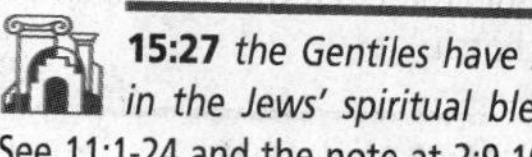

15:27 *the Gentiles have shared in the Jews' spiritual blessings:* See 11:1-24 and the note at 2:9,10.

15:29 *when I come to you:* That is, when Paul travels to Rome. See the note on p. 2173 (Rome).

15:31 *Judea . . . Jerusalem:* See the note at 15:19.

16:1 *Phoebe:* Phoebe is not mentioned anywhere else in the New Testament. The Greek word here translated as "servant" is sometimes translated as "deaconess." This mention of Phoebe is evidence that some women held leadership positions in the early church (see the chart called "Leaders of House Churches in the New Testament," p. 2326). Cenchrea was a seaport located seven miles southeast of Corinth. See the map on p. 2476.

15:22 Rom 1:13. **15:25,26** 1 Cor 16:1-4. **15:27** 1 Cor 9:11.

16:3 *Priscilla and Aquila:* This couple had lived previously in Rome, but were driven out along with other members of the Jewish community in about A.D. 49 (see the Introduction to ROMANS). They later worked as tentmakers with Paul. See also Acts 18:18-26; 1 Cor 16:19; and 2 Tim 4:19.

16:5,6 *Epenetus . . . Mary:* The New Testament does not mention Epenetus anywhere else, and it is not clear whether this Mary is the same person as any of the other Marys mentioned in the Gospels and ACTS.

16:7 *Andronicus and Junias:* These names are not mentioned anywhere else in the New Testament. "Junias" is most likely the name of a woman (perhaps Junia).

16:8-15 *Ampliatus . . . Olympas:* The Rufus in 16:13 may be the same Rufus mentioned in Mark 15:21. None of the rest of the many names in these verses are mentioned anywhere else in the New Testament. Tryphena, Tryphosa, Persis, Julia, and Olympas are women's names and are further evidence of the leadership roles that women held in the early church.

16:13 Mark 15:21.

3 Greet Priscilla[a] and Aquila, my fellow workers in Christ Jesus.
4 They risked their lives for me. Not only I but all the churches of the Gentiles are grateful to them.
5 Greet also the church that meets at their house.
Greet my dear friend Epenetus, who was the first convert to Christ in the province of Asia.
6 Greet Mary, who worked very hard for you.
7 Greet Andronicus and Junias, my relatives who have been in prison with me. They are outstanding among the apostles, and they were in Christ before I was.
8 Greet Ampliatus, whom I love in the Lord.
9 Greet Urbanus, our fellow worker in Christ, and my dear friend Stachys.
10 Greet Apelles, tested and approved in Christ.
Greet those who belong to the household of Aristobulus.
11 Greet Herodion, my relative.
Greet those in the household of Narcissus who are in the Lord.
12 Greet Tryphena and Tryphosa, those women who work hard in the Lord.
Greet my dear friend Persis, another woman who has worked very hard in the Lord.
13 Greet Rufus, chosen in the Lord, and his mother, who has been a mother to me, too.
14 Greet Asyncritus, Phlegon, Hermes, Patrobas, Hermas and the brothers with them.
15 Greet Philologus, Julia, Nereus and his sister, and Olympas and all the saints with them.

[a]3 Greek *Prisca*, a variant of *Priscilla*

QUESTIONS ABOUT ROMANS 9:1—16:27

1. In chapters 9–11, what points is Paul making about Israel (the Jewish people), Gentiles, and being saved?
2. How do people come to have faith in the Lord? (10:14-17) What does this mean for Christians today?
3. What does it mean to offer your body as a living sacrifice? (12:1) Paul compares the followers of Christ to one body. Each part of the body has special gifts. What are some of those gifts? (12:6-8) Which of these gifts do you have? What other gifts do you have that can be used to serve God?
4. Why did Paul encourage the followers of Christ in his day to obey their earthly rulers? (13:1-7) What about rulers who are opposed to God and God's people: Should they be obeyed and followed? Why or why not?
5. Paul offers lots of advice to the Roman Christians (13:8—15:13). How can this advice be helpful for people today? What piece of advice in this section was particularly meaningful to you? Why?
6. What request does Paul make of the believers in Rome? (15:30-32)
7. What have you learned from reading ROMANS? What questions, if any, has it raised for you?

16 Greet one another with a holy kiss.
All the churches of Christ send greetings.

17 I urge you, brothers, to watch out for those who cause divisions and put obstacles in your way that are contrary to the teaching you have learned. Keep away from them. 18 For such people are
not serving our Lord Christ, but their own appetites. By smooth
talk and flattery they deceive the minds of naive people. 19 Everyone
has heard about your obedience, so I am full of joy over you; but I
want you to be wise about what is good, and innocent about what
is evil.

20 The God of peace will soon crush Satan under your feet.
The grace of our Lord Jesus be with you.

21 Timothy, my fellow worker, sends his greetings to you, as
do Lucius, Jason and Sosipater, my relatives.

22 I, Tertius, who wrote down this letter, greet you in the
Lord.

23 Gaius, whose hospitality I and the whole church here
enjoy, sends you his greetings.

Erastus, who is the city's director of public works, and our
brother Quartus send you their greetings.[a]

25 Now to him who is able to establish you by my gospel and
the proclamation of Jesus Christ, according to the revelation of the
mystery hidden for long ages past, 26 but now revealed and made
known through the prophetic writings by the command of the
eternal God, so that all nations might believe and obey him— 27 to
the only wise God be glory forever through Jesus Christ! Amen.

---

[a]23 Some manuscripts *their greetings.* 24*May the grace of our Lord Jesus Christ be with all of you. Amen.*

16:20 *Satan . . . grace:* Satan means "adversary." See also the mini-article called "Satan," p. 963 and the note at 5:2 (grace).

16:21 *Timothy:* Timothy, the son of a Jewish Christian mother and a Gentile father, became one of the first Christian missionaries because of Paul (Acts 16:1-3).

16:21 *Lucius, Jason, and Sosipater:* A Lucius is mentioned in Acts 13:1 and the name Jason is mentioned in Acts 17:5-9, but it is not clear whether these are the same persons Paul is naming here. Sosipater may be a variation of the name Sopater, who is mentioned in Acts 20:4.

16:22 *Tertius:* The person who wrote down the words Paul dictated. A physical problem perhaps made it impossible for Paul to write down these words himself. See also 2 Cor 10:10; 12:7; Gal 4:13-16; 6:11.

16:23,24 *Gaius . . . Erastus . . . Quartus:* The name Gaius also occurs in Acts 19:29; 20:4; 1 Cor 1:14; and 3 John 1, but it is not the same person in each case. The name Quartus is not mentioned anywhere else in the New Testament. Erastus, a rather common name, is also found in Acts 19:22 and 2 Timothy 4:20, but it isn't known if these refer to the same person. The fact that Erastus was a city official shows that the good news of Jesus had reached not only the poor, but wealthy people as well.

16:25 *gospel . . . mystery:* See the notes at 1:1 (gospel) and 11:25 (mystery).

16:26 *prophetic writings:* See the note at 1:2 (prophets).

16:27 *Amen:* See the note at 11:36.

1 CORINTHIANS

Faith in Jesus Christ makes us friends with God and God's followers, wherever they live. Find out how Paul planted the seeds of faith among the people at Corinth, and see how his "faith-planting" also made his friendship with them grow and blossom.

WHAT MAKES 1 CORINTHIANS SPECIAL?

FIRST CORINTHIANS provides a clear idea of the kind of questions one early group of Jesus' followers faced. It also shows Paul's teaching on a number of issues. This letter is well-known for its chapters that discuss the gifts of the Holy Spirit and for Paul's teaching that love is the best gift of all (chapters 12–14). Chapter 15 includes Paul's encouraging words about how God has defeated death and promises eternal life and a "spiritual" body to all who have faith in Jesus.

WHY WAS 1 CORINTHIANS WRITTEN?

Paul had visited Corinth and spent time there teaching the gospel of Jesus Christ (see Acts 18:1-17). During this time he became close to the followers of Christ who lived in Corinth. He wrote to them because they were his friends and because he had heard about certain arguments and disputes among them. He was especially concerned about the way the Corinthian Christians were dividing themselves into different groups (1:10—4:21) and about their moral and ethical behavior (5:1—6:20). He also wrote to answer their questions about marriage (7:1-40) and about eating food offered to idols (8:1-13). They had earlier sent these questions to Paul in a letter (7:1). Finally, Paul wanted to let the Corinthian Christians know that he intended to return to Corinth and stay with them for a while (16:5-7).

WHAT'S THE STORY BEHIND THE SCENE?

Although this letter is called 1 CORINTHIANS, it is not the first one that Paul wrote to this church. We know this because he mentions in this letter that he had written one before (5:9). See also the Introduction to 2 CORINTHIANS.

The city of Corinth was located on a narrow strip of land that had a seaport to both the east and west. It was a very worldly city influenced by people of many cultures. People who lived in Corinth had a long tradition of devotion to the love goddess, Aphrodite. Paul's letter addresses some of the struggles the Corinthian Christians continued to face because of the many influences present in the city.

1:1 *Paul . . . an apostle . . . Sosthenes:* Paul was also known by his Jewish name, Saul (see Acts 7:57—8:3; 9:1-30). As a Pharisee, Paul had been a strict follower of the Law of Moses and tried to make trouble for the early followers of Christ (Gal 1:13; Phil 3:5,6). But he became an apostle of Jesus and devoted his life to preaching the gospel about Jesus. See also the mini-article called "Paul (Saul) of Tarsus," p. 2177.

"Apostle" is from the Greek word that means "someone sent to do a special job or to represent a major authority." In 1 CORINTHIANS, apostle means someone chosen by God to spread the message about Christ Jesus. Since Jesus appeared to Paul, this meant that he also was an apostle (9:1; see also Gal 1:15,16).

According to Acts 18:13-17, Sosthenes was one of the leaders of the Jewish people in Corinth. He was beaten by a crowd when the governor would not listen to the Jewish leaders' complaints about Paul's preaching. Paul reported that Sosthenes had become a follower of Jesus.

1:2 *Corinth:* A Greek city located on a three-and-a-half-mile-wide piece of land separating the Aegean and Adriatic Seas (see the map below). At the time of Paul, Corinth was a center where many cultures met, and it had a reputation for being a "wild" city with its theaters, marketplaces, and temples for a number of mystery religions. Corinth was also the center for Asclepius, a well-known god of healing, and for the worship of the love goddess Aphrodite.

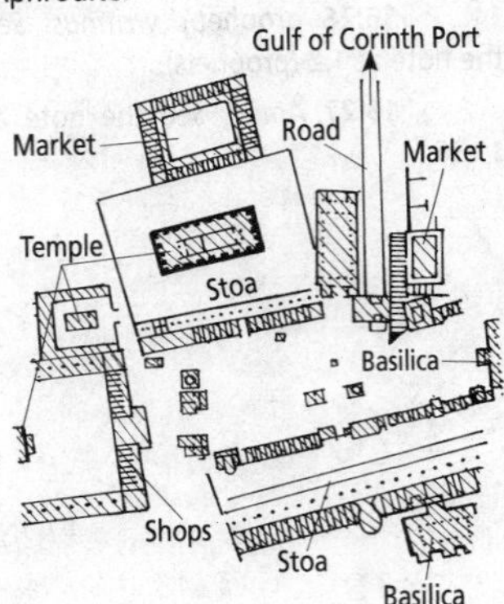

How is 1 Corinthians constructed?

The text of 1 Corinthians is probably one single letter, although some scholars believe it may combine more than one letter that Paul wrote to the believers at Corinth. Even so, it does begin with a greeting and ends with closing greetings in the style of other letters of that day. Most of the letter deals with the problems and questions the Corinthian Christians faced. Near the end of the letter, Paul does provide some personal information about his future plans. The letter can be outlined in the following way:

- **Greetings and a prayer of thanks (1:1-9)**
- **Be united by the cross of Christ (1:10—2:16)**
- **Trust the teaching of God's apostles (3:1—4:21)**
- **Instruction about moral and ethical situations (5:1—7:40)**
- **Honor God and not idols (8:1—11:1)**
- **Guidance for worship and the use of spiritual gifts (11:2—14:40)**
- **The meaning of Christ's victory over death (15:1-58)**
- **Future plans and final greetings (16:1-24)**

Greetings and a Prayer of Thanks

Paul greets the believers in the church at Corinth and prays that God will give them peace, since they are a church facing conflicts. Paul reminds them that God has given them many blessings and has chosen them to be partners with Jesus.

1 Paul, called to be an apostle of Christ Jesus by the will of God,
and our brother Sosthenes,
[2]To the church of God in Corinth, to those sanctified in
Christ Jesus and called to be holy, together with all those everywhere who call on the name of our Lord Jesus Christ—their Lord
and ours:
[3]Grace and peace to you from God our Father and the Lord
Jesus Christ.

Thanksgiving

[4]I always thank God for you because of his grace given you
in Christ Jesus. [5]For in him you have been enriched in every way—
in all your speaking and in all your knowledge— [6]because our testimony about Christ was confirmed in you. [7]Therefore you do not
lack any spiritual gift as you eagerly wait for our Lord Jesus Christ
to be revealed. [8]He will keep you strong to the end, so that you will
be blameless on the day of our Lord Jesus Christ. [9]God, who has
called you into fellowship with his Son Jesus Christ our Lord, is
faithful.

1:2 *Lord Jesus Christ:* See the note at 1:3.

1:3 *God our Father:* Jesus often referred to God as "Father" (see John 14, for example). Paul used this same term to describe God in many of his letters (Rom 1:7; Gal 1:2,3; Phil 1:2).

1:3 *Lord Jesus Christ:* The Greek word for "Lord" is *kyrios* and is used to address someone as "sir." When it is used for Jesus, it emphasizes his authority and power. See the mini-article called "Lord (Title for Jesus)," p. 2106. Jesus was a common name among Jewish men of this day, and was Greek for "Joshua." "Christ" is a title that comes from the Greek word *christos,* which means "Messiah" or "chosen one." See also the mini-article called "Messiah (Chosen One)," p. 1124.

1:7 *eagerly wait for our Lord Jesus Christ to be revealed:* Paul taught that Jesus would one day come back (15:20-28; see also Phil 3:20,21; 1 Thes 4:13-18). He said that the time was "near" (Phil 4:5). This day would also be the time when Jesus would save his followers. See also the mini-article called "Second Coming," p. 2277.

1:9 *Son:* Paul and others described Jesus as God's Son (Rom 1:4; see also Mark 1:10, 11; 15:39; John 1:14). "Son" was one of the titles used for the kings of Israel (Ps 2:7). Jesus refers to himself as God's Son in Luke 10:21,22 and in numerous places in John (see especially John 13–17). See also the mini-article called "Son of God," p. 2044.

1:2 Acts 18:1.

1:11 *Chloe's household:* This may refer to family members and slaves who lived in Chloe's house. It could also refer to those followers who met in her home for worship. Chloe is not mentioned anywhere else in the New Testament.

1:11,12 *quarrels among you . . . Apollos . . . Cephas:* The followers in Corinth apparently became divided because members were claiming different apostles as their true leaders. Some chose Paul, while others chose Apollos, who was famous for his ability to speak in public and to argue with those who opposed the gospel about Christ (Acts 18:24-28). Peter (Cephas) was one of Jesus' closest disciples from the very beginning (Matt 4:18-20; Mark 8:27-30).

1:13 *crucified . . . baptized:* It was Jesus who died on the cross (Luke 23:26-46), not Paul. Likewise, Paul baptized in the name of Jesus, not in his own name. So, Paul reminded the Corinthians that Jesus was to be the center of their faith.

1:14-16 *Crispus and Gaius . . . Stephanas:* Crispus is mentioned in Acts 18:8 as the leader of the synagogue in Corinth. Gaius is mentioned in Acts 19:29 and Romans 16:23,24. Stephanas and his family were the first people in Achaia who Paul convinced to become followers of Christ (16:15-17).

1:17,18 *gospel . . . message of the cross:* This message is the good news that Jesus died on the cross to defeat death and sin, and then was raised from death. "Those who are perishing" do not have faith in Jesus, but rely on human wisdom. To them the message about the cross is foolish.

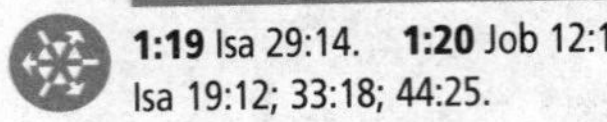

1:19 Isa 29:14. **1:20** Job 12:17; Isa 19:12; 33:18; 44:25.

Be United by the Cross of Christ

Paul addresses the problems caused by a lack of unity among the Corinthian Christians. They are dividing into groups, each claiming to follow different teachers or teachings. Paul reminds the Corinthians that Christ's death on the cross is the center of the gospel and that they should listen to God's Spirit rather than to earthly wisdom.

Divisions in the Church

10 I appeal to you, brothers, in the name of our Lord Jesus
Christ, that all of you agree with one another so that there may be
no divisions among you and that you may be perfectly united in
mind and thought. 11 My brothers, some from Chloe's household
have informed me that there are quarrels among you. 12 What I
mean is this: One of you says, "I follow Paul"; another, "I follow
Apollos"; another, "I follow Cephas[a]"; still another, "I follow
Christ."

13 Is Christ divided? Was Paul crucified for you? Were you
baptized into[b] the name of Paul? 14 I am thankful that I did not
baptize any of you except Crispus and Gaius, 15 so no one can say
that you were baptized into my name. 16 (Yes, I also baptized the
household of Stephanas; beyond that, I don't remember if I baptized anyone else.) 17 For Christ did not send me to baptize, but to
preach the gospel—not with words of human wisdom, lest the
cross of Christ be emptied of its power.

Christ the Wisdom and Power of God

18 For the message of the cross is foolishness to those who are
perishing, but to us who are being saved it is the power of God.
19 For it is written:

> "I will destroy the wisdom of the wise;
> the intelligence of the intelligent I will frustrate."[c]

20 Where is the wise man? Where is the scholar? Where is the
philosopher of this age? Has not God made foolish the wisdom of
the world? 21 For since in the wisdom of God the world through its
wisdom did not know him, God was pleased through the foolishness of what was preached to save those who believe. 22 Jews
demand miraculous signs and Greeks look for wisdom, 23 but we
preach Christ crucified: a stumbling block to Jews and foolishness
to Gentiles, 24 but to those whom God has called, both Jews and
Greeks, Christ the power of God and the wisdom of God. 25 For the
foolishness of God is wiser than man's wisdom, and the weakness
of God is stronger than man's strength.

[a]12 That is, Peter [b]13 Or *in*; also in verse 15 [c]19 Isaiah 29:14

26 Brothers, think of what you were when you were called.
Not many of you were wise by human standards; not many were
influential; not many were of noble birth. 27 But God chose the
foolish things of the world to shame the wise; God chose the weak
things of the world to shame the strong. 28 He chose the lowly
things of this world and the despised things—and the things that
are not—to nullify the things that are, 29 so that no one may boast
before him. 30 It is because of him that you are in Christ Jesus, who
has become for us wisdom from God—that is, our righteousness,
holiness and redemption. 31 Therefore, as it is written: "Let him
who boasts boast in the Lord."[a]

2 When I came to you, brothers, I did not come with eloquence
or superior wisdom as I proclaimed to you the testimony about
God.[b] 2 For I resolved to know nothing while I was with you except
Jesus Christ and him crucified. 3 I came to you in weakness and
fear, and with much trembling. 4 My message and my preaching
were not with wise and persuasive words, but with a demonstration of the Spirit's power, 5 so that your faith might not rest on
men's wisdom, but on God's power.

Wisdom From the Spirit

6 We do, however, speak a message of wisdom among the
mature, but not the wisdom of this age or of the rulers of this age,
who are coming to nothing. 7 No, we speak of God's secret wisdom,
a wisdom that has been hidden and that God destined for our
glory before time began. 8 None of the rulers of this age understood
it, for if they had, they would not have crucified the Lord of glory.
9 However, as it is written:

"No eye has seen,
    no ear has heard,
no mind has conceived
    what God has prepared for those who love him"[c]—

10 but God has revealed it to us by his Spirit.

The Spirit searches all things, even the deep things of God.
11 For who among men knows the thoughts of a man except the
man's spirit within him? In the same way no one knows the
thoughts of God except the Spirit of God. 12 We have not received
the spirit of the world but the Spirit who is from God, that we may
understand what God has freely given us. 13 This is what we speak,
not in words taught us by human wisdom but in words taught by
the Spirit, expressing spiritual truths in spiritual words.[d] 14 The
man without the Spirit does not accept the things that come from

[a] 31 Jer. 9:24 [b] 1 Some manuscripts *as I proclaimed to you God's mystery*
[c] 9 Isaiah 64:4 [d] 13 Or *Spirit, interpreting spiritual truths to spiritual men*

1:20-27 *wisdom of the world . . . foolish things:* For Paul, the "world" stands for those things that are against God (Rom 12:2; Gal 4:3; 6:14). God chose something that seemed to be a defeat—the cross of Christ—to be the instrument that brings new life to human beings. This seemed foolish to those who expected God to act in a more forceful way.

2:1 *testimony about God:* Paul says the good news is God's own plan, which human beings cannot understand on their own. The main part of this plan is that God provided the perfect sacrifice for human sins when Jesus died on the cross (see Rom 3:25,26).

2:4 *the Spirit's power:* See the note at 12:3.

2:7 *God's secret wisdom, a wisdom that has been hidden:* See the note at 2:1 and the mini-article called "Wisdom," p. 2206. According to Paul, this wisdom was a part of God's plan from the very beginning (see also Rom 16:25).

2:9 *what God has prepared:* Paul is quoting the prophet Isaiah (Isa 64:4). Isaiah saw that God was going to renew people in a way that no human could ever think up.

2:10 *his Spirit:* See the note at 12:3.

2:12 *the Spirit who is from God:* God's Spirit reveals the truth, which is not a truth the people of the world would otherwise understand or believe. See John 14:15-17; Acts 2:1-12; and Gal 5:22-25.

1:31 Jer 9:23,24. **2:3** Acts 18:9.

3:1 *worldly—mere infants in Christ:* See the note at 1:20-27.

3:3 *You are still worldly:* Paul was concerned that the Corinthians were not living like those who are led by God's Spirit. Though they had become followers of Christ, they continued to argue with each other and to go back to doing some of the "worldly" things they were doing before they heard Paul's message (5:1—6:20).

the Spirit of God, for they are foolishness to him, and he cannot
understand them, because they are spiritually discerned. [15]The
spiritual man makes judgments about all things, but he himself is
not subject to any man's judgment:

> [16]"For who has known the mind of the Lord
> that he may instruct him?"[a]

But we have the mind of Christ.

[a]16 Isaiah 40:13

WISDOM

According to PROVERBS, "The LORD gives wisdom, and from his mouth come knowledge and understanding" (Prov 2:6). This verse summarizes two important understandings of wisdom found in the Jewish Scriptures, which Christians call the Old Testament. First, true wisdom comes from God, and second, God's wisdom is based on the law that God gave to Moses and the people at Mount Sinai (Exod 19–34). This wisdom based on God's Law was what parents were to teach their children (Deut 5:16; 6:4-9).

The prophet Jeremiah warned that the people should not brag about their own wisdom or strength or wealth, but boast only that they understand and know the LORD (Jer 9:23,24). Jeremiah goes on to say that the wisdom God used to create the world will win out over the schemes of those who rely on their own wisdom and follow other gods (Jer 10:1-15).

Over the centuries God gave special wisdom to certain people. Chief among these was Solomon, who asked God for wisdom (1 Kgs 3:1-15; 10:1-10). Solomon's wisdom included legal wisdom, understanding of how people should treat one another, and knowledge about animals and plants. Many wise sayings in PROVERBS have traditionally been said to have been written by Solomon (Prov 1:1).

JOB mixes wise sayings about human behavior and God's will for his people with a story of the man who remained faithful to God in spite of difficulties and sufferings. ECCLESIASTES also includes many wisdom sayings. In the period that falls between the Old and New Testaments, Jewish wisdom writing continued to flourish. This is evidenced by a number of nonbiblical Greek texts such as *Wisdom of Solomon* and *Sirach*. (See the article called "What Books Belong in the Bible," p. 13.) Though the original Hebrew texts of these books have been lost, and they employ many styles of Greek rhetoric and philosophy, it is clear that they were addressed to an audience who highly prized Jewish religion and worship.

In the New Testament, Jesus is described as one whose wisdom is greater than that of Solomon (Matt 12:42). His wisdom is described as being so great that the people in his own hometown could not understand where he got it (Matt 13:54; Mark 6:2). The key to the "mystery of God" is Christ, "in whom are hidden all the treasures of wisdom and knowledge" (Col 2:2,3). Paul contrasted human wisdom, which is often foolishness, with the wisdom of God (1 Cor 1:18—2:16). God's mysterious wisdom is that God sent Jesus to die on a cross to forgive sins and to save those who believe this message about Jesus. To those who don't believe, this message seems foolish. People who think this way are using the world's wisdom and not the wisdom God gives.

Trust the Teaching of God's Apostles

Paul reminds the Corinthians of the work he and other apostles have done among them. Their message emphasizes the cross of Christ, but other teachers were making fun of Paul's teaching and trying to turn the people to another way of thinking.

On Divisions in the Church

3 Brothers, I could not address you as spiritual but as worldly—
mere infants in Christ. 2I gave you milk, not solid food, for you
were not yet ready for it. Indeed, you are still not ready. 3You are
still worldly. For since there is jealousy and quarreling among you,
are you not worldly? Are you not acting like mere men? 4For when
one says, "I follow Paul," and another, "I follow Apollos," are you
not mere men?
5What, after all, is Apollos? And what is Paul? Only servants,
through whom you came to believe—as the Lord has assigned to
each his task. 6I planted the seed, Apollos watered it, but God made
it grow. 7So neither he who plants nor he who waters is anything,
but only God, who makes things grow. 8The man who plants and
the man who waters have one purpose, and each will be rewarded
according to his own labor. 9For we are God's fellow workers; you
are God's field, God's building.
10By the grace God has given me, I laid a foundation as an
expert builder, and someone else is building on it. But each one
should be careful how he builds. 11For no one can lay any foundation
other than the one already laid, which is Jesus Christ. 12If any man
builds on this foundation using gold, silver, costly stones, wood, hay
or straw, 13his work will be shown for what it is, because the Day will
bring it to light. It will be revealed with fire, and the fire will test the
quality of each man's work. 14If what he has built survives, he will
receive his reward. 15If it is burned up, he will suffer loss; he himself
will be saved, but only as one escaping through the flames.
16Don't you know that you yourselves are God's temple and
that God's Spirit lives in you? 17If anyone destroys God's temple,
God will destroy him; for God's temple is sacred, and you are that
temple.
18Do not deceive yourselves. If any one of you thinks he is
wise by the standards of this age, he should become a "fool" so that
he may become wise. 19For the wisdom of this world is foolishness
in God's sight. As it is written: "He catches the wise in their craftiness"[a]; 20and again, "The Lord knows that the thoughts of the wise
are futile."[b] 21So then, no more boasting about men! All things are
yours, 22whether Paul or Apollos or Cephas[c] or the world or life or
death or the present or the future—all are yours, 23and you are of
Christ, and Christ is of God.

[a]**19** Job 5:13 [b]**20** Psalm 94:11 [c]**22** That is, Peter

Don't you know that you yourselves are God's temple and that God's Spirit lives in you? If anyone destroys God's temple, God will destroy him; for God's temple is sacred, and you are that temple.
1 Cor 3:16, 17

3:4 *Apollos:* See the note at 1:11,12.

3:6-10 *I planted the seed, Apollos watered it, but God made it grow:* Paul and Apollos had different jobs to do. Paul started the church in Corinth (planted the seed), and Apollos helped it grow (watered it). But the real foundation of this new "building" is Christ (1:10-17).

3:12,13 *the fire will test the quality of each man's work:* This refers to a time when God will examine how people have lived and whether they have been faithful. In the New Testament, the place of judgment for evildoers is often pictured as a place of fiery torture (Luke 16:23; Rev 20:14). Here Paul is talking about the kind of fire used to melt valuable metal. Wood, hay, or straw would burn up in such a fire. Gold, silver, and precious stones would not be burned at all. Paul is saying that his teaching will be tested by God's fire of judgment. If it has been a good teaching it will survive the fire. See also the mini-article called "Fire," p. 2383.

3:16 *you yourselves are God's temple:* The prophet Habakkuk describes the temple as the place where God is present with the people of Israel (Hab 2:20). According to Paul, God lives in the Corinthian Christians themselves, because God has given them the Holy Spirit. Now each of them is holy, because of God's presence.

2:16 Isa 40:13. **3:2** Heb 5:12,13. **3:6** Acts 18:4-11,24-28. **3:19** Job 5:12,13. **3:20** Ps 94:11.

4:1 *servants of Christ . . . secret things of God:* Paul often described himself as a servant, which literally means "slave" of Christ. See also the note at 2:7.

4:5 *wait till the Lord comes. He will bring to light what is hidden:* See the note at 1:7. When Jesus comes back, Paul says that he will reveal all of God's mysterious plans, which human minds have a hard time understanding.

4:6 *Apollos:* See the note at 1:11,12.

4:9 *God has put us apostles on display:* See the note at 1:1. Paul and other apostles had faced hunger, thirst, being laughed at, punishment, and being put in jail.

4:15 *I became your father through the gospel:* Paul saw himself as the Corinthians' father in the faith. See also Gal 4:19 and 1 Thes 2:7,8.

4:17 *Timothy:* Paul sent Timothy to carry on the teaching Paul had begun. Timothy was the son of a Jewish Christian mother and a Gentile father from Lystra. See also 2 Cor 1:1; 1 Thes 1:1; Phlm 1.

4:12 Acts 18:3.

Apostles of Christ

4 So then, men ought to regard us as servants of Christ and as those entrusted with the secret things of God. [2]Now it is required that those who have been given a trust must prove faithful. [3]I care very little if I am judged by you or by any human court; indeed, I do not even judge myself. [4]My conscience is clear, but that does not make me innocent. It is the Lord who judges me. [5]Therefore judge nothing before the appointed time; wait till the Lord comes. He will bring to light what is hidden in darkness and will expose the motives of men's hearts. At that time each will receive his praise from God.

[6]Now, brothers, I have applied these things to myself and Apollos for your benefit, so that you may learn from us the meaning of the saying, "Do not go beyond what is written." Then you will not take pride in one man over against another. [7]For who makes you different from anyone else? What do you have that you did not receive? And if you did receive it, why do you boast as though you did not?

[8]Already you have all you want! Already you have become rich! You have become kings—and that without us! How I wish that you really had become kings so that we might be kings with you! [9]For it seems to me that God has put us apostles on display at the end of the procession, like men condemned to die in the arena. We have been made a spectacle to the whole universe, to angels as well as to men. [10]We are fools for Christ, but you are so wise in Christ! We are weak, but you are strong! You are honored, we are dishonored! [11]To this very hour we go hungry and thirsty, we are in rags, we are brutally treated, we are homeless. [12]We work hard with our own hands. When we are cursed, we bless; when we are persecuted, we endure it; [13]when we are slandered, we answer kindly. Up to this moment we have become the scum of the earth, the refuse of the world.

QUESTIONS ABOUT 1 CORINTHIANS 1:1—4:21

1. Read the Introduction to 1 Corinthians. Why was Corinth a good place for the gospel about Christ to be preached and heard? What special challenges did it create for the person who wanted to preach the gospel?
2. What controversy or argument is taking place among the Christians at Corinth? (1:10-12; 3:1-4) What does Paul say about this? (1:13-17; 3:5-23)
3. Why does the message about Christ dying on a cross seem like foolishness to some people? (1:18-25) Why did God choose this "foolish" way to save people and make them wise, acceptable, and holy? (1:26-31)
4. How can God's people be a "temple"? (3:16,17)
5. How does Paul describe his life and the lives of other apostles? (4:9-13) Where do you think Paul got the strength to keep on preaching about Christ?
6. Who were the "arrogant" people? (4:18-21) What were they bragging about? Why did this cause problems for the rest of the church at Corinth?

14 I am not writing this to shame you, but to warn you, as my
dear children. 15 Even though you have ten thousand guardians in
Christ, you do not have many fathers, for in Christ Jesus I became
your father through the gospel. 16 Therefore I urge you to imitate
me. 17 For this reason I am sending to you Timothy, my son whom
I love, who is faithful in the Lord. He will remind you of my way
of life in Christ Jesus, which agrees with what I teach everywhere
in every church.

18 Some of you have become arrogant, as if I were not coming to you. 19 But I will come to you very soon, if the Lord is willing, and then I will find out not only how these arrogant people
are talking, but what power they have. 20 For the kingdom of
God is not a matter of talk but of power. 21 What do you prefer?
Shall I come to you with a whip, or in love and with a gentle
spirit?

Instruction about Moral and Ethical Situations

Paul gives instruction concerning moral and ethical situations he has heard the Corinthians are experiencing. His instruction on marriage is a direct answer to questions the Corinthians had asked about in a letter they sent to him (7:1).

Expel the Immoral Brother!

5 It is actually reported that there is sexual immorality among
you, and of a kind that does not occur even among pagans: A man
has his father's wife. 2 And you are proud! Shouldn't you rather
have been filled with grief and have put out of your fellowship the
man who did this? 3 Even though I am not physically present, I am
with you in spirit. And I have already passed judgment on the one
who did this, just as if I were present. 4 When you are assembled in
the name of our Lord Jesus and I am with you in spirit, and the
power of our Lord Jesus is present, 5 hand this man over to Satan,
so that the sinful nature[a] may be destroyed and his spirit saved on
the day of the Lord.

6 Your boasting is not good. Don't you know that a little yeast
works through the whole batch of dough? 7 Get rid of the old yeast
that you may be a new batch without yeast—as you really are. For
Christ, our Passover lamb, has been sacrificed. 8 Therefore let us
keep the Festival, not with the old yeast, the yeast of malice and
wickedness, but with bread without yeast, the bread of sincerity
and truth.

[a]5 Or *that his body*; or *that the flesh*

4:19 *how these arrogant people are talking:* This probably refers to those who are identified as the "super-apostles" in 2 Corinthians 12:11. These super-apostles claimed to have special wisdom that made them superior to Paul and the other apostles.

5:1,2 *pagans . . . you are proud:* Here "pagans" refers to Gentiles (non-Jews). Most Gentiles would have been unfamiliar with the Law of Moses. Some of the Corinthian Christians took Paul's message to mean that they didn't have to obey God's Law, and began doing immoral things.

5:6,7 *a little yeast . . . old yeast:* Yeast is a fungus that is mixed with water and flour to cause dough to rise. Paul means that a few bad examples can influence all the people in the Corinthian church to do evil things. Getting rid of old yeast refers to the Jewish practice of throwing out all dough containing yeast just before Passover each year (Exod 13:3-10).

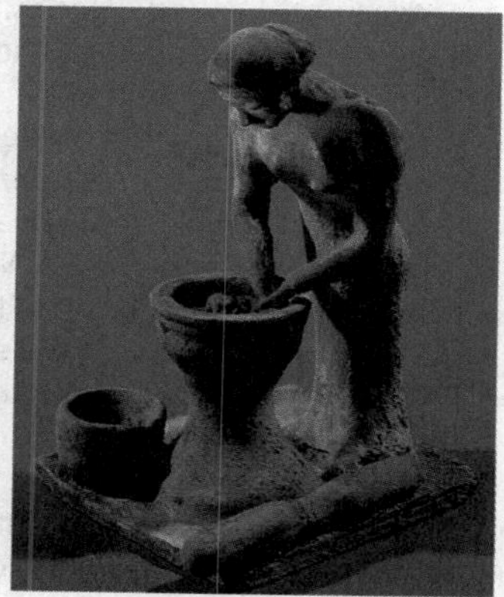

5:7 *Christ, our Passover lamb:* See the mini-article called "Passover and the Feast of Unleavened Bread," p. 2030. Paul compares Jesus' death with the sacrifice of the Passover lamb. Just as the blood of the lamb was used to save the Israelites from the angel of death, Jesus' death was a sacrifice that saved people from sin and death (Rom 3:25,26).

4:16 1 Cor 11:1; Phil 3:17. **5:1** Deut 22:30. **5:8** Exod 13:7; Deut 16:3.

5:9 *in my letter:* This refers to a letter that Paul wrote to the Christians at Corinth before he wrote the one he was presently writing. That first letter was not preserved.

5:13 Deut 13:5; 17:5-7.

[9]I have written you in my letter not to associate with sexually immoral people— [10]not at all meaning the people of this
world who are immoral, or the greedy and swindlers, or idolaters.
In that case you would have to leave this world. [11]But now I am
writing you that you must not associate with anyone who calls
himself a brother but is sexually immoral or greedy, an idolater
or a slanderer, a drunkard or a swindler. With such a man do not
even eat.
[12]What business is it of mine to judge those outside the
church? Are you not to judge those inside? [13]God will judge those
outside. "Expel the wicked man from among you."[a]

---

[a]13 Deut. 17:7; 19:19; 21:21; 22:21,24; 24:7

RESURRECTION

When people in ancient Israel died and were buried, it was believed that their souls went down and stayed in the dark underworld called "Hades." Some Hebrew prophets introduced the idea of someone coming back to life after being dead (Isa 26:19; Ezek 37). This helped the people of Judah, who were in exile in Babylon about 600 years before Jesus was born, to look forward to the future with hope. The prophet Daniel declared that the people will be raised from the dead. The wicked will be punished, but those who have obeyed God will awaken to everlasting life (Dan 12:2,3).

Other cultures in the ancient world had similar, but not identical, ideas about what happens to people after they die. Many Greeks, for instance, believed in the immortality of the soul, meaning that the soul would continue to exist even after the body died. But resurrection as it is often described in the New Testament is different because a person's whole being, including the body, is raised to life.

The disciples who saw Jesus after he had risen from death believed that God had accepted Jesus' death as a sacrifice for human sins. The Gospels report that the disciples actually saw Jesus after his resurrection (Matt 28; Luke 24; John 20,21). Paul describes how he met Christ risen from the dead, just as Peter and many others had (1 Cor 15:3-8). Adam's disobedience was the model for all human beings until Christ came. Now all God's people can be sure of life beyond the grave, since Christ continued to obey God even when it led to his being put to death (Phil 2:8). So, he was raised from death (Phil 2:9-11) and became the first of a whole new family of God (1 Cor 15:20-24) who would be raised from death.

Even though Jesus had told his followers that God would raise him from the dead, they did not believe him until he met them as the risen Christ and Lord. They were given his promise that they would always live with him (John 14:19,20) and that they would be accepted by God (Eph 2:5,6). The new family of God (Col 1:18) has confidence that sin and death will be completely overcome and that even now they are being changed by God and given new life (2 Cor 3:18; Phil 3:21). The climax will come when Christ comes back again as the one who defeats death and the powers of evil (1 Cor 15:23,24; 1 Thes 4:14). Christ's people will join with him in ruling over a brand new creation (Rev 20:4).

Lawsuits Among Believers

6 If any of you has a dispute with another, dare he take it before
the ungodly for judgment instead of before the saints? 2Do you not
know that the saints will judge the world? And if you are to judge
the world, are you not competent to judge trivial cases? 3Do you
not know that we will judge angels? How much more the things of
this life! 4Therefore, if you have disputes about such matters,
appoint as judges even men of little account in the church![a] 5I say
this to shame you. Is it possible that there is nobody among you
wise enough to judge a dispute between believers? 6But instead,
one brother goes to law against another—and this in front of
unbelievers!

7The very fact that you have lawsuits among you means you
have been completely defeated already. Why not rather be
wronged? Why not rather be cheated? 8Instead, you yourselves
cheat and do wrong, and you do this to your brothers.

9Do you not know that the wicked will not inherit the kingdom of God? Do not be deceived: Neither the sexually immoral
nor idolaters nor adulterers nor male prostitutes nor homosexual
offenders 10nor thieves nor the greedy nor drunkards nor slanderers nor swindlers will inherit the kingdom of God. 11And that is
what some of you were. But you were washed, you were sanctified,
you were justified in the name of the Lord Jesus Christ and by the
Spirit of our God.

Sexual Immorality

12"Everything is permissible for me"—but not everything is
beneficial. "Everything is permissible for me"—but I will not be
mastered by anything. 13"Food for the stomach and the stomach
for food"—but God will destroy them both. The body is not
meant for sexual immorality, but for the Lord, and the Lord for
the body. 14By his power God raised the Lord from the dead, and
he will raise us also. 15Do you not know that your bodies are members of Christ himself? Shall I then take the members of Christ and
unite them with a prostitute? Never! 16Do you not know that he
who unites himself with a prostitute is one with her in body? For
it is said, "The two will become one flesh."[b] 17But he who unites
himself with the Lord is one with him in spirit.

18Flee from sexual immorality. All other sins a man commits
are outside his body, but he who sins sexually sins against his own
body. 19Do you not know that your body is a temple of the Holy
Spirit, who is in you, whom you have received from God? You are
not your own; 20you were bought at a price. Therefore honor God
with your body.

---

[a]**4** Or *matters, do you appoint as judges men of little account in the church?*

[b]**16** Gen. 2:24

6:1 *ungodly . . . saints:* "Ungodly" here refers to worldly people who are judges for the state or government. "The saints" means the followers of Christ in Corinth.

6:11 *Lord Jesus Christ . . . Spirit:* See the notes at 1:3 (Lord Jesus Christ), and 12:3. This verse may refer to baptism, in which the followers of Christ are "washed," made holy, and become acceptable to God. See the mini-article called "Baptism," p. 1976.

6:12 *Everything is permissible:* See the note at 5:1,2. Though obeying the Law of Moses cannot "save" a person, doing so still provides an ethic that honors God and respects others. Paul is warning them that their outward behavior affects their spiritual lives.

6:13 *Food . . . stomach:* This may refer to the fact that some of the Corinthian Christians were eating food that had been offered to idols. See 8:1-13 for more.

6:14 *raise us:* See the note at 1:17,18. See also the mini-articles called "Eternal Life," p. 2072, and "Resurrection," p. 2210.

6:15 *bodies are members of Christ:* God's Spirit lives in Christ's true followers and makes them God's temple (3:16,17; 6:11). Since they are united with Jesus spiritually and physically, they should never pollute that purity.

6:19 *body . . . temple . . . . Spirit:* See the notes at 3:11; 6:13; 12:3.

6:20 *bought at a price:* God provided the perfect sacrifice for human sins when Jesus died on the cross (Rom 3:25,26). See also Heb 9:25-28.

6:16 Gen 2:24. **6:19** 1 Cor 3:16; 2 Cor 6:16.

7:1 *the matters you wrote about:* The Corinthians had sent a letter to Paul asking him a number of questions. The other questions are referred to in 7:25; 8:1; 12:1; and 16:1. The question in 7:1 has to do with sexual relations. Some of the Corinthians thought it was all right to have sexual relations outside of marriage, but Paul defended the Law of Moses, which called for married couples to be faithful to each other. Some other Corinthians said that not having sexual relations of any kind made them more spiritual than those who had sexual relations. Paul says that this is also not true. Then he goes on to give counsel concerning other issues related to marriage and singleness in this chapter.

7:5 *Satan:* See the mini-article called "Satan," p. 963.

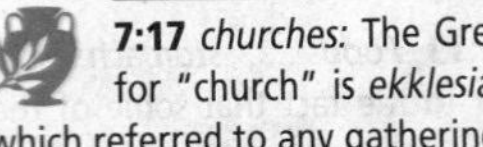

7:17 *churches:* The Greek word for "church" is *ekklesia*, a term which referred to any gathering of people. In the New Testament, "church" often refers to all the followers of Christ, but it can also refer to individual congregations, as it does in this verse. See also the mini-article called "Church," p. 2264.

7:18,19 *circumcised:* See the mini-article called "Circumcision," p. 2251. Some of the early Christians insisted that all males of God's new people (the church) be circumcised. Paul teaches here and in other letters that being circumcised should not be such a requirement. See also Rom 2:25-29; Gal 5:2-6.

7:10,11 Matt 5:32; 19:3-9; Mark 10:11,12; Luke 16:18.

Marriage

7 Now for the matters you wrote about: It is good for a man not
to marry.[a] 2But since there is so much immorality, each man
should have his own wife, and each woman her own husband.
3The husband should fulfill his marital duty to his wife, and likewise the wife to her husband. 4The wife's body does not belong to
her alone but also to her husband. In the same way, the husband's
body does not belong to him alone but also to his wife. 5Do not
deprive each other except by mutual consent and for a time, so
that you may devote yourselves to prayer. Then come together
again so that Satan will not tempt you because of your lack of self-
control. 6I say this as a concession, not as a command. 7I wish that
all men were as I am. But each man has his own gift from God;
one has this gift, another has that.

8Now to the unmarried and the widows I say: It is good for
them to stay unmarried, as I am. 9But if they cannot control themselves, they should marry, for it is better to marry than to burn
with passion.

10To the married I give this command (not I, but the Lord):
A wife must not separate from her husband. 11But if she does, she
must remain unmarried or else be reconciled to her husband. And
a husband must not divorce his wife.

12To the rest I say this (I, not the Lord): If any brother has a
wife who is not a believer and she is willing to live with him, he
must not divorce her. 13And if a woman has a husband who is not
a believer and he is willing to live with her, she must not divorce
him. 14For the unbelieving husband has been sanctified through
his wife, and the unbelieving wife has been sanctified through her
believing husband. Otherwise your children would be unclean, but
as it is, they are holy.

15But if the unbeliever leaves, let him do so. A believing man
or woman is not bound in such circumstances; God has called us
to live in peace. 16How do you know, wife, whether you will save
your husband? Or, how do you know, husband, whether you will
save your wife?

17Nevertheless, each one should retain the place in life that
the Lord assigned to him and to which God has called him. This is
the rule I lay down in all the churches. 18Was a man already circumcised when he was called? He should not become uncircumcised. Was a man uncircumcised when he was called? He should
not be circumcised. 19Circumcision is nothing and uncircumcision
is nothing. Keeping God's commands is what counts. 20Each one
should remain in the situation which he was in when God called
him. 21Were you a slave when you were called? Don't let it trouble
you—although if you can gain your freedom, do so. 22For he who

---

a1 Or "*It is good for a man not to have sexual relations with a woman.*"

was a slave when he was called by the Lord is the Lord's freedman; similarly, he who was a free man when he was called is Christ's slave. [23]You were bought at a price; do not become slaves of men. [24]Brothers, each man, as responsible to God, should remain in the situation God called him to.

[25]Now about virgins: I have no command from the Lord, but I give a judgment as one who by the Lord's mercy is trustworthy. [26]Because of the present crisis, I think that it is good for you to remain as you are. [27]Are you married? Do not seek a divorce. Are you unmarried? Do not look for a wife. [28]But if you do marry, you have not sinned; and if a virgin marries, she has not sinned. But those who marry will face many troubles in this life, and I want to spare you this.

[29]What I mean, brothers, is that the time is short. From now on those who have wives should live as if they had none; [30]those who mourn, as if they did not; those who are happy, as if they were not; those who buy something, as if it were not theirs to keep; [31]those who use the things of the world, as if not engrossed in them. For this world in its present form is passing away.

[32]I would like you to be free from concern. An unmarried man is concerned about the Lord's affairs—how he can please the Lord. [33]But a married man is concerned about the affairs of this world—how he can please his wife— [34]and his interests are divided. An unmarried woman or virgin is concerned about the Lord's affairs: Her aim is to be devoted to the Lord in both body and spirit. But a married woman is concerned about the affairs of this world—how she can please her husband. [35]I am saying this for your own good, not to restrict you, but that you may live in a right way in undivided devotion to the Lord.

[36]If anyone thinks he is acting improperly toward the virgin he is engaged to, and if she is getting along in years and he feels he ought to marry, he should do as he wants. He is not sinning. They should get married. [37]But the man who has settled the matter in his own mind, who is under no compulsion but has control over his own will, and who has made up his mind not to marry the virgin—this man also does the right thing. [38]So then, he who marries the virgin does right, but he who does not marry her does even better.[a]

[39]A woman is bound to her husband as long as he lives. But if her husband dies, she is free to marry anyone she wishes, but he must belong to the Lord. [40]In my judgment, she is happier if she stays as she is—and I think that I too have the Spirit of God.

---

[a]36-38 Or [36]*If anyone thinks he is not treating his daughter properly, and if she is getting along in years, and he feels she ought to marry, he should do as he wants. He is not sinning. He should let her get married.* [37]*But the man who has settled the matter in his own mind, who is under no compulsion but has control over his own will, and who has made up his mind to keep the virgin unmarried—this man also does the right thing.* [38]*So then, he who gives his virgin in marriage does right, but he who does not give her in marriage does even better.*

What I mean, brothers, is that the time is short . . . . For this world in its present form is passing away.
1 Cor 7:29,31

7:22,23 *Christ's slave . . . price:* Paul thought of himself and other followers of Christ as Christ's slaves or servants (Rom 1:1; Phil 1:1). All believers belong to the Lord because of the "price" that was paid for them. Among God's new people all are equal, whether they are "free" or "slaves" in the Roman system of government (Gal 3:26-29).

7:29 *the time is short:* See the note at 1:7.

7:40 *Spirit of God:* See the note at 12:3.

8:1 *Now about:* See the note at 7:1.

8:1 *food sacrificed to idols:* Many people in the ancient world made statues (idols) that represented the gods or goddesses they worshiped. Butchers usually had their meat dedicated to various idols so that their customers could take it to the pagan temples as offerings to the idols. Since the idols were not real, Paul says, the food offered to them was all right for Christians to eat. But some Christians felt that eating food which had been offered to idols was wrong. Others might think that they approved of the idol to which it had been offered.

8:5 *heaven:* Heaven is most often described in the Bible simply as the place where God lives and rules. Jesus often talks about how God's rule will be complete some time in the future. Living under God's rule will be the reward for those who are faithful. See also the mini-article called "Heaven," p. 1420.

8:6 *one Lord, Jesus Christ, through whom all things came:* Jesus was God's Son, but he was also fully present with God when God created the world (John 1:2,3).

8:7 *still so accustomed to idols:* Since the Gentiles in the Corinthian church had grown up believing that certain idols had life in them, many of them believed that eating food offered to idols would make them feel that they were betraying their trust in God. See also the note at 6:13.

8:10 *eating in an idol's temple:* Some Corinthian Christians may have been invited to feasts in the local temples. Food offered to the idols in these temples may have been served at these feasts. Paul reminded the followers that eating this food is not bad and does not mean they believe in the idol. But if a person with a weaker conscience sees the follower eating this food and eats it too, it may cause the weaker person to feel terribly guilty. Followers of Christ need to be careful not to do anything that will cause misunderstanding for others.

Honor God and Not Idols

The Corinthians wanted to know if it was all right to eat food that had been offered to idols. Paul answers this question and others about how Christians are to respond to idols. He makes the point that whatever Christians do should be done to honor God and show concern for others.

Food Sacrificed to Idols

8 Now about food sacrificed to idols: We know that we all possess knowledge.[a] Knowledge puffs up, but love builds up. [2]The
man who thinks he knows something does not yet know as he
ought to know. [3]But the man who loves God is known by God.
[4]So then, about eating food sacrificed to idols: We know that
an idol is nothing at all in the world and that there is no God but
one. [5]For even if there are so-called gods, whether in heaven or on
earth (as indeed there are many "gods" and many "lords"), [6]yet for
us there is but one God, the Father, from whom all things came
and for whom we live; and there is but one Lord, Jesus Christ,
through whom all things came and through whom we live.
[7]But not everyone knows this. Some people are still so accustomed to idols that when they eat such food they think of it as
having been sacrificed to an idol, and since their conscience is
weak, it is defiled. [8]But food does not bring us near to God; we are
no worse if we do not eat, and no better if we do.
[9]Be careful, however, that the exercise of your freedom does
not become a stumbling block to the weak. [10]For if anyone with a
weak conscience sees you who have this knowledge eating in an
idol's temple, won't he be emboldened to eat what has been sacrificed to idols? [11]So this weak brother, for whom Christ died, is
destroyed by your knowledge. [12]When you sin against your brothers in this way and wound their weak conscience, you sin against
Christ. [13]Therefore, if what I eat causes my brother to fall into sin,
I will never eat meat again, so that I will not cause him to fall.

The Rights of an Apostle

9 Am I not free? Am I not an apostle? Have I not seen Jesus our
Lord? Are you not the result of my work in the Lord? [2]Even though
I may not be an apostle to others, surely I am to you! For you are
the seal of my apostleship in the Lord.
[3]This is my defense to those who sit in judgment on me.
[4]Don't we have the right to food and drink? [5]Don't we have the
right to take a believing wife along with us, as do the other apostles and the Lord's brothers and Cephas[b]? [6]Or is it only I and Barnabas who must work for a living?
[7]Who serves as a soldier at his own expense? Who plants a

[a]1 Or *"We all possess knowledge," as you say* [b]5 That is, Peter

vineyard and does not eat of its grapes? Who tends a flock and does not drink of the milk? [8]Do I say this merely from a human point of view? Doesn't the Law say the same thing? [9]For it is written in the Law of Moses: "Do not muzzle an ox while it is treading out the grain."[a] Is it about oxen that God is concerned? [10]Surely he says this for us, doesn't he? Yes, this was written for us, because when the plowman plows and the thresher threshes, they ought to do so in the hope of sharing in the harvest. [11]If we have sown spiritual seed among you, is it too much if we reap a material harvest from you? [12]If others have this right of support from you, shouldn't we have it all the more?

But we did not use this right. On the contrary, we put up with anything rather than hinder the gospel of Christ. [13]Don't you know that those who work in the temple get their food from the temple, and those who serve at the altar share in what is offered on the altar? [14]In the same way, the Lord has commanded that those who preach the gospel should receive their living from the gospel.

[15]But I have not used any of these rights. And I am not writing this in the hope that you will do such things for me. I would rather die than have anyone deprive me of this boast. [16]Yet when I preach the gospel, I cannot boast, for I am compelled to preach. Woe to me if I do not preach the gospel! [17]If I preach voluntarily, I have a reward; if not voluntarily, I am simply discharging the trust committed to me. [18]What then is my reward? Just this: that in preaching the gospel I may offer it free of charge, and so not make use of my rights in preaching it.

[19]Though I am free and belong to no man, I make myself a slave to everyone, to win as many as possible. [20]To the Jews I became like a Jew, to win the Jews. To those under the law I became like one under the law (though I myself am not under the law), so as to win those under the law. [21]To those not having the law I became like one not having the law (though I am not free from God's law but am under Christ's law), so as to win those not having the law. [22]To the weak I became weak, to win the weak. I have become all things to all men so that by all possible means I might save some. [23]I do all this for the sake of the gospel, that I may share in its blessings.

[24]Do you not know that in a race all the runners run, but only one gets the prize? Run in such a way as to get the prize. [25]Everyone who competes in the games goes into strict training. They do it to get a crown that will not last; but we do it to get a crown that will last forever. [26]Therefore I do not run like a man running aimlessly; I do not fight like a man beating the air. [27]No, I beat my body and make it my slave so that after I have preached to others, I myself will not be disqualified for the prize.

---

a9 Deut. 25:4

9:2 *I may not be an apostle to others:* See the note at 1:1. Because Paul had not been with Jesus from the beginning, some thought he was not really an apostle. They questioned his authority.

9:4-6 *work for a living:* Paul argues that he and Barnabas (see Gal 2:1) have the right to be given food and drink and even to make a living by being preachers of the gospel, the way the other apostles do. According to Acts 18:3, Paul was a tentmaker.

9:8-12 *the Law ... sharing in the harvest:* Animals that were used to tread on grain to separate it from the chaff were free to eat the grain. As a leader of God's new people, Paul argued that he should be free to accept food and money.

9:13,14 *those who work in the temple:* Priests were free to take food from certain sacrifices in the temple (Lev 16:6). Paul argued that his work as a preacher of the gospel should be regarded in the same way.

9:25 *a crown:* Winners of athletic contests in ancient Corinth were awarded a crown made of fresh leaves. The leaves of this crown eventually died, but the crown that lasts forever is the reward the followers of Jesus will receive for being faithful. See also 2 Tim 4:8; 1 Pet 5:4; Rev 3:11.

9:8,9 Deut 25:4; 1 Tim 5:18. **9:11** Rom 15:27. **9:13** Deut 18:1. **9:14** Matt 10:10; Luke 10:7.

10:1 *our forefathers . . . passed through the sea:* Paul's ancestors were the people of Israel who escaped from slavery in Egypt. God saved them by opening a path through the sea (Exod 14:21-29).

10:2 *Moses:* See the mini-article called "Moses," p. 2335.

10:11 *written down as warnings for us:* This means the Jewish Scriptures, which Christians called the Old Testament.

10:16 *the cup . . . the bread:* At the Last Supper, Jesus used the bread and wine to show how his body would be broken and his blood poured out as a sacrifice to forgive sins (see 11:23-26).

10:3 Exod 16:35. **10:4** Exod 17:6; Num 20:11. **10:5** Num 14:29,30. **10:6** Num 11:4. **10:7** Exod 32:6. **10:9** Num 21:5,6. **10:10** Num 16:41-49. **10:16** Matt 26:26-28; Mark 14:22-24; Luke 22:19,20.

Warnings From Israel's History

10 For I do not want you to be ignorant of the fact, brothers,
that our forefathers were all under the cloud and that they all
passed through the sea. 2They were all baptized into Moses in the
cloud and in the sea. 3They all ate the same spiritual food 4and
drank the same spiritual drink; for they drank from the spiritual
rock that accompanied them, and that rock was Christ. 5Neverthe-
less, God was not pleased with most of them; their bodies were
scattered over the desert.

6Now these things occurred as examples[a] to keep us from setting our hearts on evil things as they did. 7Do not be idolaters, as
some of them were; as it is written: "The people sat down to eat and
drink and got up to indulge in pagan revelry."[b] 8We should not commit sexual immorality, as some of them did—and in one day twenty-
three thousand of them died. 9We should not test the Lord, as some
of them did—and were killed by snakes. 10And do not grumble, as
some of them did—and were killed by the destroying angel.

11These things happened to them as examples and were written down as warnings for us, on whom the fulfillment of the ages
has come. 12So, if you think you are standing firm, be careful that
you don't fall! 13No temptation has seized you except what is common to man. And God is faithful; he will not let you be tempted
beyond what you can bear. But when you are tempted, he will also
provide a way out so that you can stand up under it.

Idol Feasts and the Lord's Supper

14Therefore, my dear friends, flee from idolatry. 15I speak to
sensible people; judge for yourselves what I say. 16Is not the cup of
thanksgiving for which we give thanks a participation in the blood

[a]6 Or *types*; also in verse 11 [b]7 Exodus 32:6

QUESTIONS ABOUT 1 CORINTHIANS 5:1—11:1

1. Read what Paul had to say about "yeast" and "dough." (5:6-8) What does this saying have to do with the Christian group at Corinth?
2. Why did Paul suggest that the Corinthian Christians settle disputes among themselves rather than suing each other in court? (6:1-8) Should modern Christians consider following this advice? Why or why not?
3. Read 6:19,20. What is Paul saying here? How would life change if everyone followed Paul's advice?
4. Summarize Paul's key teachings about marriage. (7:1-40)
5. What does Paul say about food offered to idols? (8:1-13) In what other situations might Paul's advice apply?
6. How is living the Christian faith like a race or an athletic contest? (9:24-27)
7. Why does Paul talk to the Corinthian Christians about worshiping idols? (10:1-22) What idols exist in modern society?
8. What does Paul mean by his words in 10:33?

of Christ? And is not the bread that we break a participation in the
body of Christ? [17]Because there is one loaf, we, who are many, are
one body, for we all partake of the one loaf.
[18]Consider the people of Israel: Do not those who eat the
sacrifices participate in the altar? [19]Do I mean then that a sacrifice
offered to an idol is anything, or that an idol is anything? [20]No, but
the sacrifices of pagans are offered to demons, not to God, and I
do not want you to be participants with demons. [21]You cannot
drink the cup of the Lord and the cup of demons too; you cannot
have a part in both the Lord's table and the table of demons. [22]Are
we trying to arouse the Lord's jealousy? Are we stronger than he?

The Believer's Freedom

[23]"Everything is permissible"—but not everything is beneficial. "Everything is permissible"—but not everything is construc-
tive. [24]Nobody should seek his own good, but the good of others.
[25]Eat anything sold in the meat market without raising questions of conscience, [26]for, "The earth is the Lord's, and everything in it."[a]
[27]If some unbeliever invites you to a meal and you want to
go, eat whatever is put before you without raising questions of
conscience. [28]But if anyone says to you, "This has been offered in
sacrifice," then do not eat it, both for the sake of the man who told
you and for conscience' sake[b]— [29]the other man's conscience, I
mean, not yours. For why should my freedom be judged by another's conscience? [30]If I take part in the meal with thankfulness, why
am I denounced because of something I thank God for?
[31]So whether you eat or drink or whatever you do, do it all
for the glory of God. [32]Do not cause anyone to stumble, whether
Jews, Greeks or the church of God— [33]even as I try to please everybody in every way. For I am not seeking my own good but the
11 good of many, so that they may be saved. [1]Follow my example, as I follow the example of Christ.

Guidance for Worship and the Use of Spiritual Gifts

Paul gives instruction about how the Corinthians should worship and take part in the Lord's Supper. He also provides counsel about the use of spiritual gifts, which can help develop orderly worship that honors God and uplifts all of God's people.

Propriety in Worship

[2]I praise you for remembering me in everything and for
holding to the teachings,[c] just as I passed them on to you.

---

[a]26 Psalm 24:1 **[b]28** Some manuscripts *conscience' sake, for "the earth is the Lord's and everything in it"* **[c]2** Or *traditions*

10:19-21 *an idol . . . demons:* Some of the Corinthian Christians were probably invited to celebrations in local temples built to honor idols. Food and drink that had been offered to these gods may have been eaten at these celebrations. Paul warned that this food and drink is the same as food and drink that has been offered to demons. Those who took part in other religions by eating and drinking at these feasts dishonored the Lord.

10:23 *Everything is permissible:* See the notes at 6:12 and 5:1,2.

10:26 *The earth is the Lord's, and everything in it:* Paul is quoting Psalm 24:1 to say that all food comes from God and is all right to eat. See also Mark 7:15,16; Acts 10:1—11:18.

10:29 *why should my freedom be judged by another's conscience:* Although God's people are now free from having to keep the Law of Moses, they must take care to keep in mind how their actions may cause problems for others. Although idols have no real power, eating food that had been offered to idols may cause problems for Christians who used to worship other gods.

10:33—11:1 *I try to please everybody . . . I follow the example of Christ:* Paul believed that at times it was necessary to avoid doing things that might offend new followers of Christ (9:22,23). Jesus taught that his followers must be willing to be like servants to others (Mark 10:23-25).

10:20 Deut 32:17. **10:22** Deut 32:21. **11:1** 1 Cor 4:16; Phil 3:17.

The Last Supper by Sadao Watanabe, 1982. Paul reminded the Christians at Corinth about the meal Jesus shared with his disciples on the night he was betrayed. Paul also gave them instructions about the proper way to conduct themselves when gathering to celebrate the Lord's Supper (11:17-34).

3Now I want you to realize that the head of every man is
Christ, and the head of the woman is man, and the head of Christ
is God. 4Every man who prays or prophesies with his head covered
dishonors his head. 5And every woman who prays or prophesies
with her head uncovered dishonors her head—it is just as though
her head were shaved. 6If a woman does not cover her head, she
should have her hair cut off; and if it is a disgrace for a woman to
have her hair cut or shaved off, she should cover her head. 7A man
ought not to cover his head,[a] since he is the image and glory of
God; but the woman is the glory of man. 8For man did not come
from woman, but woman from man; 9neither was man created for
woman, but woman for man. 10For this reason, and because of the
angels, the woman ought to have a sign of authority on her head.
11In the Lord, however, woman is not independent of man,
nor is man independent of woman. 12For as woman came from
man, so also man is born of woman. But everything comes from
God. 13Judge for yourselves: Is it proper for a woman to pray to God
with her head uncovered? 14Does not the very nature of things
teach you that if a man has long hair, it is a disgrace to him, 15but
that if a woman has long hair, it is her glory? For long hair is given

[a]**4-7** Or *4Every man who prays or prophesies with long hair dishonors his head. 5And every woman who prays or prophesies with no covering* ⌞*of hair*⌟ *on her head dishonors her head—she is just like one of the "shorn women." 6If a woman has no covering, let her be for now with short hair, but since it is a disgrace for a woman to have her hair shorn or shaved, she should grow it again. 7A man ought not to have long hair*

11:3 *the head:* Paul later describes the followers of Jesus as the "body of Christ" (12:12). Jesus is the head of this body. Although Paul says in Galatians 3:28 that men and women are one in Christ, he also taught the Corinthian Christians what the Jewish Scriptures say about the first woman being formed from a man (Gen 1:26,27; 2:18-25).

11:10 *ought to have a sign of authority on her head:* Paul argues that whenever women pray or prophesy in public they should either keep their hair tied up on their head or cover it in some way, since unkempt hair was equated with adultery and prostitution in ancient Jewish culture. In 11:10, Paul is possibly arguing that a woman who prays and prophesies needs to cover her head as a sign to others and to the angels that she has the "authority" to do so and will not disrupt the worship service (see also Eph 3:10; 1 Tim 5:21).

11:17 *your meetings:* The problems that were dividing the Corinthians when they came together for worship included a misunderstanding of the Lord's Supper (11:20-34) and a disorderly use of spiritual gifts, which upset the worship gathering (12:1—14:40).

11:7 Gen 1:26,27. **11:8,9** Gen 2:18-23.

to her as a covering. [16]If anyone wants to be contentious about this,
we have no other practice—nor do the churches of God.

The Lord's Supper

[17]In the following directives I have no praise for you, for
your meetings do more harm than good. [18]In the first place, I hear
that when you come together as a church, there are divisions
among you, and to some extent I believe it. [19]No doubt there have
to be differences among you to show which of you have God's
approval. [20]When you come together, it is not the Lord's Supper
you eat, [21]for as you eat, each of you goes ahead without waiting
for anybody else. One remains hungry, another gets drunk. [22]Don't
you have homes to eat and drink in? Or do you despise the church
of God and humiliate those who have nothing? What shall I say to
you? Shall I praise you for this? Certainly not!

[23]For I received from the Lord what I also passed on to you:
The Lord Jesus, on the night he was betrayed, took bread, [24]and
when he had given thanks, he broke it and said, "This is my body,
which is for you; do this in remembrance of me." [25]In the same
way, after supper he took the cup, saying, "This cup is the new

11:20-22 *it is not the Lord's Supper you eat:* The arguments the Corinthians were having flaired up even when they gathered to share the bread and wine of the Lord's Supper. Some church members ate the bread and drank all the wine without waiting for the others. Some drank so much wine that they got drunk. This showed that they misunderstood what the Lord's Supper was all about. See the note at 10:16.

11:23 *on the night he was betrayed:* Paul's report of what Jesus said and did during his last Passover meal with his disciples is close to the one given in Luke 22:19,20. See the note at 10:16. By sharing in the Lord's Supper, the followers of Jesus remembered that they were united by his death until he returns. See the notes at 1:7 and 4:5.

11:25 Exod 24:6-8; Jer 31:31-34.

SPIRITUAL GIFTS

The Greek word *charisma* is translated as "spiritual gifts" in 1 Corinthians 12:1 and elsewhere. It emphasizes the kindness and generosity of God in giving special abilities and responsibilities to the followers of Christ, the Christian church. The gifts are intended to help them carry out their work, to reach out to those who might become members, and to strengthen the body of Christ by providing lives filled with joy, peace, and effective work and worship (1 Cor 12–14).

The spiritual gifts are of two general types: (1) something that God gives for the benefit of the community as a whole, and (2) some special ability given to an individual to carry out a job or meet a need in the life of the church. Paul told the Roman Christians that their right relationship with God and the new life they enjoyed were God's gift, or *charisma* (Rom 5:15-17; 6:23). He also said he longed to impart to the believers in Rome "some spiritual gift (*charisma*)" to strengthen them (Rom 1:11). The specific gifts Paul refers to in several of his letters include prophecy, speaking with wisdom and knowledge, serving and encouraging others, being generous, and taking leadership (Rom 12:4-8; 1 Cor 12:8). Paul explains that God chose some people for special leadership as apostles, prophets, and teachers (1 Cor 12:28). Others received the ability to work miracles or heal the sick, to help others to be leaders, to speak in different kinds of tongues, and to interpret what was being said in those tongues (1 Cor 12:7-11, 28; 14:1-25). But Paul said that the best gift of all was love (1 Cor 13).

Church leaders laid their hands on the ones chosen for a special task (Acts 6:1-6; 1 Tim 4:14). Paul compared the life of the church and all the duties within it with the human body. All the different parts receive from God's Spirit the ability to function for the spiritual health and growth of the whole body of Christ's followers (1 Cor 12:12-26).

covenant in my blood; do this, whenever you drink it, in remembrance of me." 26For whenever you eat this bread and drink this
cup, you proclaim the Lord's death until he comes.

27Therefore, whoever eats the bread or drinks the cup of the
Lord in an unworthy manner will be guilty of sinning against the
body and blood of the Lord. 28A man ought to examine himself
before he eats of the bread and drinks of the cup. 29For anyone
who eats and drinks without recognizing the body of the Lord eats
and drinks judgment on himself. 30That is why many among you
are weak and sick, and a number of you have fallen asleep. 31But if
we judged ourselves, we would not come under judgment. 32When
we are judged by the Lord, we are being disciplined so that we will
not be condemned with the world.

33So then, my brothers, when you come together to eat, wait
for each other. 34If anyone is hungry, he should eat at home, so that
when you meet together it may not result in judgment.

And when I come I will give further directions.

Spiritual Gifts

12 Now about spiritual gifts, brothers, I do not want you to be
ignorant. 2You know that when you were pagans, somehow or
other you were influenced and led astray to mute idols. 3Therefore
I tell you that no one who is speaking by the Spirit of God says,
"Jesus be cursed," and no one can say, "Jesus is Lord," except by the
Holy Spirit.

4There are different kinds of gifts, but the same Spirit. 5There
are different kinds of service, but the same Lord. 6There are different kinds of working, but the same God works all of them in
all men.

7Now to each one the manifestation of the Spirit is given for
the common good. 8To one there is given through the Spirit the
message of wisdom, to another the message of knowledge by
means of the same Spirit, 9to another faith by the same Spirit, to
another gifts of healing by that one Spirit, 10to another miraculous
powers, to another prophecy, to another distinguishing between
spirits, to another speaking in different kinds of tongues,[a] and to
still another the interpretation of tongues.[a] 11All these are the work
of one and the same Spirit, and he gives them to each one, just as
he determines.

One Body, Many Parts

12The body is a unit, though it is made up of many parts;
and though all its parts are many, they form one body. So it is with
Christ. 13For we were all baptized by[b] one Spirit into one body—

[a]**10** Or *languages*; also in verse 28 [b]**13** Or *with*; or *in*

11:29 *judgment on himself:* See the note at 11:20-22. Paul told the Corinthians to examine how they were celebrating the Lord's Supper. This examination should encourage them to see that they are the body of the Lord, and that they should not live or act in a way that dishonors the Lord (see 3:16, 17). The fact that some had become weak and died (fallen asleep) was one sign that they were not acting in a way that honored God (11:30).

12:1 *spiritual gifts:* See the mini-article called "Spiritual Gifts," p. 2219.

12:2 *led astray to mute idols:* Many of the Corinthian Christians had been followers of different gods before they became followers of Jesus. A number of temples or shrines to these idols were right in the city of Corinth. See the notes at 8:7 and 8:10.

12:3 *the Spirit of God:* This is the Holy Spirit, which is at work carrying out God's purposes in the world. The Spirit teaches and guides the people of God so that they can bear witness to the gospel and become the kind of people God wants them to be. Here, Paul also describes how the Spirit gives God's people special gifts. See also Rom 12:6-8 and the mini-article called "Holy Spirit," p. 2082.

12:10 *prophecy:* See also the article called "Prophets and Prophecy," p. 935.

12:10 *speaking in different kinds of tongues . . . interpretation of tongues:* To speak or interpret languages they had never learned. See Acts 2:1-12.

12:12 *one body:* Christ is the head of the body, which is made up of his followers.

12:13 *baptized by one Spirit:* The gift of the Holy Spirit was connected to baptism in Jesus' name (Acts 4:8; 13:3,9, 52; 19:5,6). This is what Paul meant when he says "we were all given the one Spirit to drink."

whether Jews or Greeks, slave or free—and we were all given the
one Spirit to drink.
14Now the body is not made up of one part but of many. 15If
the foot should say, "Because I am not a hand, I do not belong to
the body," it would not for that reason cease to be part of the body.
16And if the ear should say, "Because I am not an eye, I do not
belong to the body," it would not for that reason cease to be part
of the body. 17If the whole body were an eye, where would the
sense of hearing be? If the whole body were an ear, where would
the sense of smell be? 18But in fact God has arranged the parts in
the body, every one of them, just as he wanted them to be. 19If they
were all one part, where would the body be? 20As it is, there are
many parts, but one body.
21The eye cannot say to the hand, "I don't need you!" And the
head cannot say to the feet, "I don't need you!" 22On the contrary,
those parts of the body that seem to be weaker are indispensable,
23and the parts that we think are less honorable we treat with special honor. And the parts that are unpresentable are treated with
special modesty, 24while our presentable parts need no special treatment. But God has combined the members of the body and has
given greater honor to the parts that lacked it, 25so that there should
be no division in the body, but that its parts should have equal concern for each other. 26If one part suffers, every part suffers with it;
if one part is honored, every part rejoices with it.
27Now you are the body of Christ, and each one of you is a
part of it. 28And in the church God has appointed first of all apostles, second prophets, third teachers, then workers of miracles, also
those having gifts of healing, those able to help others, those with
gifts of administration, and those speaking in different kinds of
tongues. 29Are all apostles? Are all prophets? Are all teachers? Do all
work miracles? 30Do all have gifts of healing? Do all speak in
tongues[a]? Do all interpret? 31But eagerly desire[b] the greater gifts.

Love

And now I will show you the most excellent way.
13 If I speak in the tongues[c] of men and of angels, but have not
love, I am only a resounding gong or a clanging cymbal. 2If I have
the gift of prophecy and can fathom all mysteries and all knowledge, and if I have a faith that can move mountains, but have not
love, I am nothing. 3If I give all I possess to the poor and surrender my body to the flames,[d] but have not love, I gain nothing.
4Love is patient, love is kind. It does not envy, it does not
boast, it is not proud. 5It is not rude, it is not self-seeking, it is not
easily angered, it keeps no record of wrongs. 6Love does not delight

[a]30 Or *other languages* [b]31 Or *But you are eagerly desiring* [c]1 Or *languages*
[d]3 Some early manuscripts *body that I may boast*

12:27 *the body of Christ:* See the note at 12:12.

12:28 *God has appointed:* See the notes at 1:1 (apostle) and 12:10 (prophecy). Those who had the gift of teaching were able to explain the Scriptures and the gospel about Jesus in a way that people could understand. See the note at 12:10 (tongues).

13:1 *angels:* The word "angel" in English is based on the Greek word *angelos*, which means "messenger." See also the mini-article called "Angels," p. 88.

13:1 *gong or clanging cymbal:* The gong that is mentioned here may have been a musical instrument, or it may have been a large brass vase that was placed at the back of Greek theaters to make actor's voices more audible. The musical instrument-style cymbals were most likely either hand-held brass disks or small metal disks that were attached to the fingers.

13:2 *the gift of prophecy:* The act of telling God's truth about the present and future is to "prophesy." Prophecy is the message that is told.

13:4-7 *Love:* Of the several words for "love" in Greek, *storge* (love among family members) and *eros* (sexual love) do not occur in the New Testament. *Philia*, which means "friendly," does occur in the New Testament. But the special word for love used in these verses is the Greek word *agape*, which refers to God's love (John 3:16; Rom 5:5-8) and describes the kind of self-giving love God's followers are to show toward others (Mark 12:31; Rom 13:9; Lev 19:18). See also the mini-article called "Love," p. 2391.

12:28 Eph 4:11. **13:2** Matt 17:20; 21:21; Mark 11:23.

13:8-13 *Love:* See the note at 13:4-7.

13:8 *prophecies . . . tongues:* See the notes at 13:2 and 12:10 (tongues).

13:10-12 *perfection . . . know fully:* These phrases probably are a reference to that future day when Jesus will return. See the notes at 1:7 and 4:5.

13:12 *poor reflection as in a mirror:* The bronze mirrors used in the ancient world would not have given clear reflections. The mirror shown here is Egyptian and dates back to around 1200 B.C.

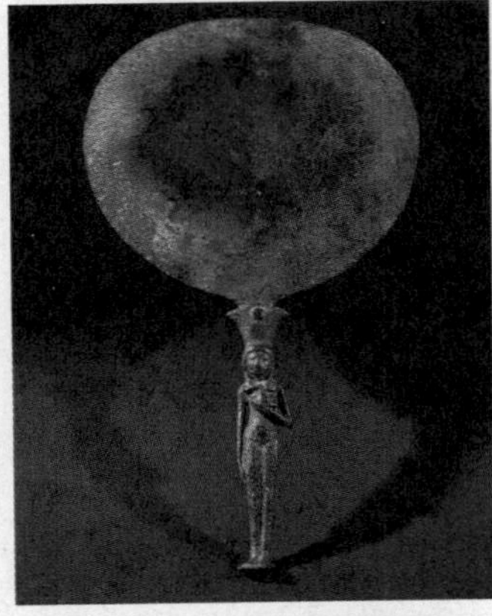

14:1 *spiritual gifts:* See the mini-article called "Spiritual Gifts," p. 2219, and the note at 12:3.

14:2-4 *speaks in a tongue does not speak to men but to God:* See the note at 12:10 (tongues). This gift of the Spirit helped the person who received it praise God. People who came into Christian worship where worshipers were speaking in other languages might have been amazed at this unusual ability. But they received no benefit because they could not understand the message.

Love by Robert Indiana, 1967. Every culture and every era has its own way of defining love. In one of the most frequently quoted passages from Paul's letters, the apostle gives a definition of love that is both inspiring and challenging to people who belong to the "body of Christ," the church. (See 13:1-13.)

in evil but rejoices with the truth. [7]It always protects, always trusts, always hopes, always perseveres.

[8]Love never fails. But where there are prophecies, they will cease; where there are tongues, they will be stilled; where there is knowledge, it will pass away. [9]For we know in part and we prophesy in part, [10]but when perfection comes, the imperfect disappears. [11]When I was a child, I talked like a child, I thought like a child, I reasoned like a child. When I became a man, I put childish ways behind me. [12]Now we see but a poor reflection as in a mirror; then we shall see face to face. Now I know in part; then I shall know fully, even as I am fully known.

[13]And now these three remain: faith, hope and love. But the greatest of these is love.

Gifts of Prophecy and Tongues

14 Follow the way of love and eagerly desire spiritual gifts, especially the gift of prophecy. [2]For anyone who speaks in a tongue[a] does not speak to men but to God. Indeed, no one understands him; he utters mysteries with his spirit.[b] [3]But everyone who proph-

[a]2 Or *another language*; also in verses 4,13,14,19,26 and 27   [b]2 Or *by the Spirit*

esies speaks to men for their strengthening, encouragement and
comfort. 4 He who speaks in a tongue edifies himself, but he who
prophesies edifies the church. 5 I would like every one of you to
speak in tongues,[a] but I would rather have you prophesy. He who
prophesies is greater than one who speaks in tongues,[a] unless he
interprets, so that the church may be edified.

6 Now, brothers, if I come to you and speak in tongues, what
good will I be to you, unless I bring you some revelation or knowledge or prophecy or word of instruction? 7 Even in the case of lifeless things that make sounds, such as the flute or harp, how will
anyone know what tune is being played unless there is a distinction in the notes? 8 Again, if the trumpet does not sound a clear
call, who will get ready for battle? 9 So it is with you. Unless you
speak intelligible words with your tongue, how will anyone know
what you are saying? You will just be speaking into the air.
10 Undoubtedly there are all sorts of languages in the world, yet
none of them is without meaning. 11 If then I do not grasp the
meaning of what someone is saying, I am a foreigner to the speaker, and he is a foreigner to me. 12 So it is with you. Since you are
eager to have spiritual gifts, try to excel in gifts that build up the
church.

13 For this reason anyone who speaks in a tongue should pray
that he may interpret what he says. 14 For if I pray in a tongue, my
spirit prays, but my mind is unfruitful. 15 So what shall I do? I will
pray with my spirit, but I will also pray with my mind; I will sing
with my spirit, but I will also sing with my mind. 16 If you are praising God with your spirit, how can one who finds himself among
those who do not understand[b] say "Amen" to your thanksgiving,
since he does not know what you are saying? 17 You may be giving
thanks well enough, but the other man is not edified.

18 I thank God that I speak in tongues more than all of you.
19 But in the church I would rather speak five intelligible words to
instruct others than ten thousand words in a tongue.

20 Brothers, stop thinking like children. In regard to evil be
infants, but in your thinking be adults. 21 In the Law it is written:

"Through men of strange tongues
and through the lips of foreigners
I will speak to this people,
but even then they will not listen to me,"[c]

says the Lord.

22 Tongues, then, are a sign, not for believers but for unbelievers; prophecy, however, is for believers, not for unbelievers.
23 So if the whole church comes together and everyone speaks in
tongues, and some who do not understand[d] or some unbelievers

[a] **5** Or *other languages*; also in verses 6,18,22,23 and 39 [b] **16** Or *among the inquirers* [c] **21** Isaiah 28:11,12 [d] **23** Or *some inquirers*

14:5 *I would rather have you prophesy:* See the notes at 13:2 and 12:10 (prophecy). Paul regarded prophecy as a gift that helped the whole body of Christ more than the gift of speaking in tongues.

14:8 *trumpet:* Besides being used in battle, horns were used at the temple in Jerusalem to call people to worship. Because Jews were offended by coins that had images of rulers, some coins used in Judea bore the image of the temple horns, even after the temple was destroyed by the Romans in A.D. 70.

14:15 *pray with my spirit . . . pray with my mind:* Praying with the spirit refers to praying in different languages that had not been learned. See the note at 12:10 (tongues). Praying with the mind refers to all sorts of ways people pray when they are aware of what they are saying.

14:21 Isa 28:11,12.

14:24,25 *he is a sinner and will be judged:* Sin is turning away from God and failing to live as God intended. See also the mini-article called "Sin," p. 2181. Prophecy that reveals God's true word can also make people realize that they have sinned and encourages them to tell, or confess, what is hidden in their hearts.

14:30 *if a revelation comes to someone:* In the Corinthian church, it apparently was common for different people to speak a message from God. The people had to respect each other and allow someone who had a prophecy to speak when the message came from the Spirit. Without this, many people might start speaking at the same time, which would cause confusion.

14:34 *women should remain silent in the churches:* Paul was not talking about a specific rule in the Law of Moses but about a "law" as commonly interpreted by tradition. See 11:5, which seems to assume that women do speak and pray during worship. See also the note at 11:10.

14:37 *prophet or spiritually gifted:* See the note at 12:10 (prophecy). A "spiritually gifted" person is someone who is led by God's Spirit or has been given some spiritual gift. See the mini-article called "Spiritual Gifts," p. 2219.

come in, will they not say that you are out of your mind? 24But if
an unbeliever or someone who does not understand[a] comes in
while everybody is prophesying, he will be convinced by all that he
is a sinner and will be judged by all, 25and the secrets of his heart
will be laid bare. So he will fall down and worship God, exclaim-
ing, "God is really among you!"

Orderly Worship

26What then shall we say, brothers? When you come together, everyone has a hymn, or a word of instruction, a revelation, a
tongue or an interpretation. All of these must be done for the
strengthening of the church. 27If anyone speaks in a tongue, two—
or at the most three—should speak, one at a time, and someone
must interpret. 28If there is no interpreter, the speaker should keep
quiet in the church and speak to himself and God.

29Two or three prophets should speak, and the others should
weigh carefully what is said. 30And if a revelation comes to someone who is sitting down, the first speaker should stop. 31For you
can all prophesy in turn so that everyone may be instructed and
encouraged. 32The spirits of prophets are subject to the control of
prophets. 33For God is not a God of disorder but of peace.

As in all the congregations of the saints, 34women should
remain silent in the churches. They are not allowed to speak, but
must be in submission, as the Law says. 35If they want to inquire
about something, they should ask their own husbands at home; for
it is disgraceful for a woman to speak in the church.

36Did the word of God originate with you? Or are you the
only people it has reached? 37If anybody thinks he is a prophet or
spiritually gifted, let him acknowledge that what I am writing to
you is the Lord's command. 38If he ignores this, he himself will be
ignored.[b]

[a]24 Or *or some inquirer* [b]38 Some manuscripts *If he is ignorant of this, let him be ignorant*

QUESTIONS ABOUT 1 CORINTHIANS 11:2—14:40

1. On what did Paul base his rules for worship in 11:2-16? What is your reaction to these rules? What do verses 11 and 12 tell you about how men and women should treat each other?
2. What did Paul teach about the Lord's Supper? Why did he have to offer this instruction? (11:17-34)
3. List the spiritual gifts described in chapter 12. What is the purpose of these gifts?
4. Why does Paul say that love is the greatest gift of the Spirit? (13:1-13)
5. What does Paul teach about the gift of speaking in tongues? About prophesying? (14:1-25)
6. What does Paul mean by "orderly worship"? How can worship be made more orderly? (14:26-40)

[39]Therefore, my brothers, be eager to prophesy, and do not
forbid speaking in tongues. [40]But everything should be done in a
fitting and orderly way.

The Meaning of Christ's Victory over Death

Paul gives his most detailed teaching about the Christian hope for life after death. God's people will be raised to new life, just as God raised Jesus from the dead. When this happens, earthly bodies will be changed into eternal bodies.

The Resurrection of Christ

15 Now, brothers, I want to remind you of the gospel I preached
to you, which you received and on which you have taken your
stand. [2]By this gospel you are saved, if you hold firmly to the word
I preached to you. Otherwise, you have believed in vain.
[3]For what I received I passed on to you as of first importance[a]: that Christ died for our sins according to the Scriptures,
[4]that he was buried, that he was raised on the third day according
to the Scriptures, [5]and that he appeared to Peter,[b] and then to the
Twelve. [6]After that, he appeared to more than five hundred of the
brothers at the same time, most of whom are still living, though
some have fallen asleep. [7]Then he appeared to James, then to all
the apostles, [8]and last of all he appeared to me also, as to one
abnormally born.
[9]For I am the least of the apostles and do not even deserve to
be called an apostle, because I persecuted the church of God. [10]But
by the grace of God I am what I am, and his grace to me was not
without effect. No, I worked harder than all of them—yet not I,
but the grace of God that was with me. [11]Whether, then, it was I or
they, this is what we preach, and this is what you believed.

The Resurrection of the Dead

[12]But if it is preached that Christ has been raised from the
dead, how can some of you say that there is no resurrection of the
dead? [13]If there is no resurrection of the dead, then not even Christ
has been raised. [14]And if Christ has not been raised, our preaching
is useless and so is your faith. [15]More than that, we are then found
to be false witnesses about God, for we have testified about God
that he raised Christ from the dead. But he did not raise him if in
fact the dead are not raised. [16]For if the dead are not raised, then
Christ has not been raised either. [17]And if Christ has not been
raised, your faith is futile; you are still in your sins. [18]Then those

[a]3 Or *you at the first* [b]5 Greek *Cephas*

14:39 *be eager to prophesy:* See the note at 13:2.

15:5,6 *Peter . . . the Twelve . . . five hundred:* See the note at 1:11,12. "The Twelve" refers to the close group of Christ's followers, also known as the disciples (Matt 10:2-4). It is not clear who the "five hundred followers" are.

15:7 *James . . . the apostles:* The James mentioned here is Jesus' brother (Mark 6:3; Gal 1:19; Acts 12:17; 15:13). See the note at 1:1.

15:9 *I persecuted the church of God:* Paul tried to destroy the followers of Christ before Christ chose him to preach the gospel (Gal 1:13-16; Acts 8:3; 9:1,2). "The church of God" here refers to all who follow Christ.

15:12 *some of you say that there is no resurrection of the dead:* Apparently some of the followers of Christ in Corinth did not believe that people who had died could be raised from death to eternal life. Some may have followed a philosophy which taught that the body of a dead person stays in the ground while the soul comes back to life apart from the body. This is called the "immortality of the soul." Paul's teachings about life after death are different from this view. See also the mini-article called "Resurrection," p. 2210.

15:17 *if Christ has not been raised, your faith is futile; you are still in your sins:* See 15:4-7, where Paul summarizes the good news about Jesus. Paul said that God's mysterious wisdom is that God sent Jesus to die on the cross to forgive sins (1 Cor 2:1,4). If God did not raise Jesus from death, Paul says, God's promise of forgiveness of sins could not be true.

15:3 Isa 53:5-12. **15:4** Ps 16:8-10; Matt 12:40; Acts 2:24-32. **15:5** Matt 28:16,17; Mark 16:14; Luke 24:34,36; John 20:9. **15:8** Acts 9:3-6.

15:21 *death came through a man:* Adam and Eve disobeyed God by eating fruit from the tree that gave the power to know the difference between right from wrong (Gen 3:17-19). This sin caused death to come into the world. But the forgiveness that Jesus brings will overcome sin and death.

15:24 *the end will come:* See the notes at 1:7; 3:12,13; 4:5.

15:29 *baptized for the dead:* See the note at 1:13. Some people were being baptized on behalf of friends or relatives who had died before being baptized into the Christian faith. Paul says that such baptizing is not necessary.

15:32 *fought wild beasts in Ephesus:* Paul was in Ephesus when he wrote to the Corinthians. See the map on p. 2476. It is not clear if Paul is talking about real wild animals or about human opponents who attacked his teachings. See Acts 19.

15:32 *Let us eat and drink:* Paul is quoting Isaiah 22:13. If people will not be raised from death, Paul says they might as well enjoy life and not worry about the future.

15:33 *Bad company corrupts good character:* Paul is quoting from a play called *Thais*, by Menander, one of the greatest Greek writers of the time.

15:34 *sinning:* See the note at 14:24,25.

15:35 *How are the dead raised:* This is likely another of the questions that the Corinthian Christians asked Paul (see the note at 7:1).

15:44 *spiritual body:* Paul teaches that those who are raised to life from death will have a completely new body. This is different from a popular belief in Paul's day which taught that death would release the soul from the body, which rotted away, while the soul lived forever.

15:25 Ps 110:1. **15:27** Ps 8:6.

also who have fallen asleep in Christ are lost. [19]If only for this life
we have hope in Christ, we are to be pitied more than all men.
[20]But Christ has indeed been raised from the dead, the firstfruits of those who have fallen asleep. [21]For since death came
through a man, the resurrection of the dead comes also through a
man. [22]For as in Adam all die, so in Christ all will be made alive.
[23]But each in his own turn: Christ, the firstfruits; then, when he
comes, those who belong to him. [24]Then the end will come, when
he hands over the kingdom to God the Father after he has destroyed
all dominion, authority and power. [25]For he must reign until he has
put all his enemies under his feet. [26]The last enemy to be destroyed
is death. [27]For he "has put everything under his feet."[a] Now when it
says that "everything" has been put under him, it is clear that this
does not include God himself, who put everything under Christ.
[28]When he has done this, then the Son himself will be made subject
to him who put everything under him, so that God may be all in all.
[29]Now if there is no resurrection, what will those do who are
baptized for the dead? If the dead are not raised at all, why are
people baptized for them? [30]And as for us, why do we endanger
ourselves every hour? [31]I die every day—I mean that, brothers—
just as surely as I glory over you in Christ Jesus our Lord. [32]If I
fought wild beasts in Ephesus for merely human reasons, what
have I gained? If the dead are not raised,

> "Let us eat and drink,
> for tomorrow we die."[b]

[33]Do not be misled: "Bad company corrupts good character."
[34]Come back to your senses as you ought, and stop sinning; for
there are some who are ignorant of God—I say this to your shame.

The Resurrection Body

[35]But someone may ask, "How are the dead raised? With
what kind of body will they come?" [36]How foolish! What you sow
does not come to life unless it dies. [37]When you sow, you do not
plant the body that will be, but just a seed, perhaps of wheat or of
something else. [38]But God gives it a body as he has determined,
and to each kind of seed he gives its own body. [39]All flesh is not
the same: Men have one kind of flesh, animals have another, birds
another and fish another. [40]There are also heavenly bodies and
there are earthly bodies; but the splendor of the heavenly bodies is
one kind, and the splendor of the earthly bodies is another. [41]The
sun has one kind of splendor, the moon another and the stars
another; and star differs from star in splendor.
[42]So will it be with the resurrection of the dead. The body
that is sown is perishable, it is raised imperishable; [43]it is sown in

---

[a]**27** Psalm 8:6 [b]**32** Isaiah 22:13

dishonor, it is raised in glory; it is sown in weakness, it is raised in
power; [44]it is sown a natural body, it is raised a spiritual body.
If there is a natural body, there is also a spiritual body. [45]So
it is written: "The first man Adam became a living being"[a]; the last
Adam, a life-giving spirit. [46]The spiritual did not come first, but
the natural, and after that the spiritual. [47]The first man was of the
dust of the earth, the second man from heaven. [48]As was the earthly man, so are those who are of the earth; and as is the man from
heaven, so also are those who are of heaven. [49]And just as we have
borne the likeness of the earthly man, so shall we[b] bear the likeness of the man from heaven.
[50]I declare to you, brothers, that flesh and blood cannot
inherit the kingdom of God, nor does the perishable inherit the
imperishable. [51]Listen, I tell you a mystery: We will not all sleep, but
we will all be changed— [52]in a flash, in the twinkling of an eye, at
the last trumpet. For the trumpet will sound, the dead will be raised
imperishable, and we will be changed. [53]For the perishable must
clothe itself with the imperishable, and the mortal with immortality. [54]When the perishable has been clothed with the imperishable,
and the mortal with immortality, then the saying that is written will
come true: "Death has been swallowed up in victory."[c]

[55]"Where, O death, is your victory?
Where, O death, is your sting?"[d]

[56]The sting of death is sin, and the power of sin is the law. [57]But
thanks be to God! He gives us the victory through our Lord Jesus
Christ.
[58]Therefore, my dear brothers, stand firm. Let nothing move
you. Always give yourselves fully to the work of the Lord, because
you know that your labor in the Lord is not in vain.

Future Plans and Final Greetings

Paul tells the Corinthians about the money he hopes to collect to help the followers in Jerusalem. He also hopes to come and see the Corinthians again soon. He closes by encouraging the Corinthians to welcome his friend Timothy and then sends greetings to many in Corinth.

The Collection for God's People

16 Now about the collection for God's people: Do what I told
the Galatian churches to do. [2]On the first day of every week, each
one of you should set aside a sum of money in keeping with his

[a]45 Gen. 2:7 [b]49 Some early manuscripts *so let us* [c]54 Isaiah 25:8
[d]55 Hosea 13:14

> *When the perishable has been clothed with the imperishable, and the mortal with immortality, then the saying that is written will come true: "Death has been swallowed up in victory."*
> 1 Cor 15:54

15:45-49 *first man Adam . . . last Adam:* See the note at 15:21. Paul calls Jesus the "last Adam," because he was the human who ended the curse of death brought on by the first Adam's sin. Those who have faith in Jesus now have human bodies that are like the first Adam, but they will have spiritual bodies like Jesus after they are raised from death.

15:51 *We will not all sleep, but we will all be changed:* Paul taught that when Jesus comes back, some people who are living will be transformed into heavenly, or spiritual, bodies (1 Thes 4:15-17).

15:52 *the trumpet will sound, the dead will be raised:* See Matt 24:31; John 5:25; 1 Thes 4:16; Rev 8:2—11:19.

15:54 *immortality:* See the mini-articles called "Eternal Life," p. 2072 and "Resurrection," p. 2210.

15:56 *the power of sin is the law:* Paul does not mean that the Law of Moses causes people to sin, but that because the law tells people what they shouldn't do, it actually makes people want to sin. See also Rom 7:7-12.

16:1 *the collection:* Paul was concerned about the Jewish Christians in Palestine and collected money to support the poor there (see Gal 2:1-10; 2 Cor 8:1-14; Rom 15:25,26).

15:45 Gen 2:7. **15:54** Isa 25:8. **15:55** Hos 13:14.

Do everything in love.
1 Cor 16:14

income, saving it up, so that when I come no collections will have
to be made. [3]Then, when I arrive, I will give letters of introduction
to the men you approve and send them with your gift to
Jerusalem. [4]If it seems advisable for me to go also, they will accompany me.

Personal Requests

[5]After I go through Macedonia, I will come to you—for I
will be going through Macedonia. [6]Perhaps I will stay with you
awhile, or even spend the winter, so that you can help me on my
journey, wherever I go. [7]I do not want to see you now and make
only a passing visit; I hope to spend some time with you, if the
Lord permits. [8]But I will stay on at Ephesus until Pentecost,
[9]because a great door for effective work has opened to me, and
there are many who oppose me.

[10]If Timothy comes, see to it that he has nothing to fear
while he is with you, for he is carrying on the work of the Lord,
just as I am. [11]No one, then, should refuse to accept him. Send him
on his way in peace so that he may return to me. I am expecting
him along with the brothers.

[12]Now about our brother Apollos: I strongly urged him to go
to you with the brothers. He was quite unwilling to go now, but he
will go when he has the opportunity.

[13]Be on your guard; stand firm in the faith; be men of
courage; be strong. [14]Do everything in love.

[15]You know that the household of Stephanas were the first
converts in Achaia, and they have devoted themselves to the service of the saints. I urge you, brothers, [16]to submit to such as these
and to everyone who joins in the work, and labors at it. [17]I was
glad when Stephanas, Fortunatus and Achaicus arrived, because
they have supplied what was lacking from you. [18]For they refreshed
my spirit and yours also. Such men deserve recognition.

16:5 *Macedonia:* Paul also visited and wrote letters to the cities of Thessalonica and Philippi, located in Macedonia. See the map on p. 2477.

16:8 *Ephesus . . . Pentecost:* See the note at 15:32 (Ephesus). Pentecost, also known as the Feast of Weeks, was one of the three Jewish pilgrimage festivals. See the chart called "Jewish Calendar and Festivals," p. 944.

16:10-12 *Timothy . . . Apollos:* See the notes at 4:17 and 1:11,12.

16:15 *Achaia:* Cities such as Athens and Corinth were in Achaia. See the map on p. 2476.

16:17 *Stephanas, Fortunatus and Achaicus:* For Stephanas, see the note at 1:14-16. Fortunatus and Achaicus are not mentioned anywhere else in the Bible.

16:5 Acts 19:21. **16:8** Lev 23:15-21; Deut 16:9-11. **16:8,9** Acts 19:8-10. **16:15** 1 Cor 1:16.

QUESTIONS ABOUT 1 CORINTHIANS 15:1—16:24

1. What is the message that Paul says has the power to "save"? (15:1-7) What would make this message "useless"? (15:12-15) Is the modern world skeptical about Jesus' rising from death? Why or why not? How can the church deal with this kind of skepticism?
2. How does Paul answer the Corinthians' questions in 15:35? What is your picture of life in God's perfect kingdom (heaven)? How can the hope of being raised to new life with Christ and living with God forever make a difference for people living today?
3. What passage from 1 Corinthians is still confusing or troubling to you? Why? What verse or verses in this letter were most comforting or satisfying for you? Why?

Final Greetings

19 The churches in the province of Asia send you greetings.
Aquila and Priscilla[a] greet you warmly in the Lord, and so does the
church that meets at their house. 20 All the brothers here send you
greetings. Greet one another with a holy kiss.
21 I, Paul, write this greeting in my own hand.
22 If anyone does not love the Lord—a curse be on him.
Come, O Lord[b]!
23 The grace of the Lord Jesus be with you.
24 My love to all of you in Christ Jesus. Amen.[c]

[a]**19** Greek *Prisca,* a variant of *Priscilla* [b]**22** In Aramaic the expression *Come, O Lord* is *Marana tha.* [c]**24** Some manuscripts do not have *Amen.*

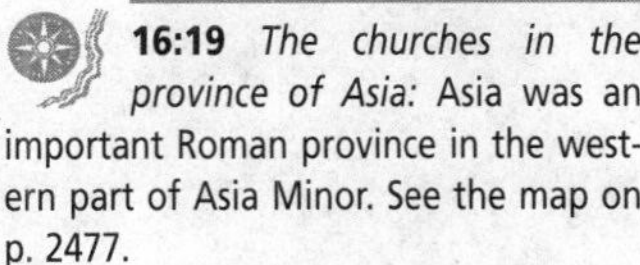

16:19 *The churches in the province of Asia:* Asia was an important Roman province in the western part of Asia Minor. See the map on p. 2477.

16:19 *Aquila and Priscilla:* This couple was driven out of Rome along with the rest of the Jewish community around A.D. 49 by the Emperor Claudius. They moved to Corinth (Acts 18:1-4) and later to Ephesus (Acts 18:18-26) where they worked as tentmakers with Paul. See also Rom 16:3; 2 Tim 4:19.

16:21 *write this greeting in my own hand:* Paul probably dictated the letter to someone who wrote it down for him. See Rom 16:22.

2 CORINTHIANS

What Paul said to the Corinthian Christians in earlier letters was true and meant to be helpful, but some took his words the wrong way. Read 2 Corinthians to discover how Paul pleads with them to "make room for us in your hearts."

What makes 2 Corinthians special?

This letter gives insights into Paul's personal relationship with the Corinthian Christians, especially how he tries to answer attacks that have been made against him. While many support him, some challenge his authority as an apostle. Others criticize him for the way he speaks and writes, and still others think he is unfriendly and too harsh in his comments. As Paul defends himself as an apostle of Christ he shares a number of important teachings about:

- forgiving others (2:5-17);
- God's new covenant that comes from the Holy Spirit and not from the law (3:1-18);
- how anyone who belongs to Christ is a new person (5:17-21);
- giving generously to help God's people in need (8:1-15; 9:1-15); and
- how God has changed Paul's own life (12:1-10).

Why was 2 Corinthians written?

Paul had lived and worked among the believers in Corinth. He had previously written to them in order to encourage them and to answer their questions (see the Introduction to 1 Corinthians). He also had promised to come and visit them (1 Cor 16:5, 6). At the beginning of 2 Corinthians, Paul writes to explain why he has changed his mind. He stayed away from Corinth so that he would not seem to be too hard and demanding (1:23), and because he wanted to see if they would follow his instructions about forgiving and comforting people who had sinned (2:5-11). Paul also wrote the letter in order to defend himself as a true apostle of Christ and to encourage the Corinthians to be generous in giving money to help Christians in other parts of the Roman world.

What's the story behind the scene?

Paul wrote a series of letters to the church in Corinth. These include an earlier letter mentioned in 1 Corinthians 5:9 and the letter we know as 1 Corinthians. He also mentions a letter he wrote when he was greatly distressed (2 Cor 2:3, 4). Many scholars believe that 2 Corinthians was originally two letters written by Paul—the first being made up of chapters 1–9, and the second, chapters 10–13—that circulated together and then were

1:1 *Paul . . . Timothy:* For more about Paul and his ministry to the Gentiles, see the note at 1 Corinthians 1:1 and the mini-article called "Paul (Saul) of Tarsus," p. 2177. One thing Paul did to help the Corinthians was to send Timothy to carry on the teaching Paul had begun (1 Cor 4:17; 16:10).

1:1 *Corinth . . . Achaia:* Formerly a powerful league of cities in ancient Greece, in Paul's day Achaia was the name of the Roman province in Greece just south of the province of Macedonia. Corinth and Athens were its most important cities. See the map on p. 2475.

Although Corinth has a history that goes back to the 8th century B.C., the Corinth Paul and his co-workers would have been familiar with dates to around 44 B.C. when Julius Caesar established a Roman colony there. (See Acts 18:1-17 for a description of Paul's visit to Corinth.) It was settled by veterans from the Roman army, and by 27 B.C. it was the thriving capital of Achaia. See the map of Corinth in the Introduction to 1 Corinthians, p. 2202.

eventually joined together. In addition, some scholars feel that 6:14—7:1 is a fragment of yet another letter, contending that this passage breaks the flow of thought from 6:11-13 to 7:2. Paul probably ministered in Corinth first in about A.D. 50-51 and wrote 1 CORINTHIANS around A.D. 53-54, while he was in Ephesus (1 Cor 16:8). The letter called 2 CORINTHIANS (or the two letters that form 2 CORINTHIANS) was written some time after that.

HOW IS 2 CORINTHIANS CONSTRUCTED?

Although 2 CORINTHIANS might not originally have been one single letter, its beginning and ending are typical of the greetings that people in Paul's day would use to open and close letters. The letter can be outlined in this way:

Greetings and prayers of thanks (1:1-11)

Paul wants to make peace with his opponents (1:12—7:16)

Paul encourages the Corinthians to be generous givers (8:1—9:15)

Paul defends himself as a true apostle of Christ (10:1—12:21)

A challenge and farewell (13:1-14)

For just as the sufferings of Christ flow over into our lives, so also through Christ our comfort overflows.
2 Cor 1:5

Greetings and Prayers of Thanks

Paul begins his letter with a formal introduction that names himself and Timothy as the ones sending the letter and God's people in Corinth and Achaia as the ones receiving it. This greeting is followed by Paul's prayers of thanks to God who has comforted Paul and others in times of great suffering.

1 Paul, an apostle of Christ Jesus by the will of God, and Timothy our brother,

To the church of God in Corinth, together with all the saints throughout Achaia:

2 Grace and peace to you from God our Father and the Lord Jesus Christ.

The God of All Comfort

3 Praise be to the God and Father of our Lord Jesus Christ,
the Father of compassion and the God of all comfort, 4 who comforts us in all our troubles, so that we can comfort those in any
trouble with the comfort we ourselves have received from God.
5 For just as the sufferings of Christ flow over into our lives, so also
through Christ our comfort overflows. 6 If we are distressed, it is
for your comfort and salvation; if we are comforted, it is for your
comfort, which produces in you patient endurance of the same
sufferings we suffer. 7 And our hope for you is firm, because we

1:1 *Paul . . . Timothy:* See the note at 1:1 (Paul).

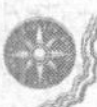

1:1 *Corinth . . . Achaia:* See the note at 1:1 (Corinth).

1:2 *God our Father and the Lord Jesus Christ:* See the notes at 1 Cor 1:3.

1:3 *comfort:* The "comfort" that God gave to Paul and to the Corinthians is the strength and hope that helped them face suffering, threats, and even death.

1:5 *the sufferings of Christ:* Jesus Christ faced suffering and death on the cross (Mark 8:31; Luke 9:22; 1 Pet 1:11; 4:13; Heb 2:9-11).

1:6 *salvation:* Here the word "salvation" points to what God has done and is still doing to free humans from sin and the powers of evil. "Being saved" also can refer to receiving "eternal life." See also the mini-articles called "Salvation," p. 2021 and "Eternal Life," p. 2072.

1:1 Acts 18:1.

know that just as you share in our sufferings, so also you share in
our comfort.
8 We do not want you to be uninformed, brothers, about the
hardships we suffered in the province of Asia. We were under great
pressure, far beyond our ability to endure, so that we despaired
even of life. 9 Indeed, in our hearts we felt the sentence of death.
But this happened that we might not rely on ourselves but on God,
who raises the dead. 10 He has delivered us from such a deadly peril,
and he will deliver us. On him we have set our hope that he will
continue to deliver us, 11 as you help us by your prayers. Then many
will give thanks on our[a] behalf for the gracious favor granted us in
answer to the prayers of many.

Paul Wants to Make Peace with His Opponents

Paul hopes that he can make peace with his opponents and encourage the Corinthians to forgive one another. Added to his personal comments are important teachings about God's new covenant that comes from the Holy Spirit and that makes a new person of anyone who belongs to Christ. Some scholars believe this section is "interrupted" by a possible fragment from another letter (6:14—7:1).

Paul's Change of Plans

12 Now this is our boast: Our conscience testifies that we have
conducted ourselves in the world, and especially in our relations
with you, in the holiness and sincerity that are from God. We have
done so not according to worldly wisdom but according to God's
grace. 13 For we do not write you anything you cannot read or
understand. And I hope that, 14 as you have understood us in part,
you will come to understand fully that you can boast of us just as
we will boast of you in the day of the Lord Jesus.
15 Because I was confident of this, I planned to visit you first
so that you might benefit twice. 16 I planned to visit you on my way
to Macedonia and to come back to you from Macedonia, and then
to have you send me on my way to Judea. 17 When I planned this,
did I do it lightly? Or do I make my plans in a worldly manner so
that in the same breath I say, "Yes, yes" and "No, no"?
18 But as surely as God is faithful, our message to you is not
"Yes" and "No." 19 For the Son of God, Jesus Christ, who was
preached among you by me and Silas[b] and Timothy, was not "Yes"
and "No," but in him it has always been "Yes." 20 For no matter how
many promises God has made, they are "Yes" in Christ. And so
through him the "Amen" is spoken by us to the glory of God.

[a]11 Many manuscripts *your* [b]19 Greek *Silvanus*, a variant of *Silas*

1:8 *hardships . . . Asia:* At the time of Paul, Asia was the name of a Roman province in the southwest part of what is now Turkey. See the map on p. 2476. Paul does not explain what kind of suffering he had experienced in Ephesus, but it probably included torture and the threat of death (see also Acts 20:17-19).

1:12 *worldly wisdom:* Paul is referring to human wisdom that does not believe God's wisdom or follow God's purposes. For Paul, "worldly" stood for all things that are against God (Rom 12:2; Gal 4:3). See also the mini-article called "Wisdom," p. 2206.

1:15 *I planned to visit you:* Paul had twice planned to visit the Corinthians (1 Cor 16:1-9) when he was taking a gift of money from other churches in Asia Minor and Greece. He decided not to visit them because he did not want to have to scold them for the way they were living (1:23,24).

1:16 *Macedonia . . . Judea:* Macedonia was the northern part of what is now Greece and became part of the Roman empire in 168 B.C. Paul also visited and wrote letters to the cities of Thessalonica and Philippi, located in Macedonia.

Judea was the area in southern Palestine where Jerusalem was located. The temple that was the center for the Jewish religion was located in Jerusalem. This is also where Jesus' apostles first began to teach the gospel about Jesus after he had been taken up to heaven (Acts 1, 2). Paul wanted to bring a money offering to the followers of Jesus in Jerusalem, because many of them were poor (see 1 Cor 16:1-3; Rom 15:25-28) and because the Jerusalem church was an important center for the whole early Christian church. See the map on p. 2476.

[21]Now it is God who makes both us and you stand firm in Christ.
He anointed us, [22]set his seal of ownership on us, and put his Spirit in our hearts as a deposit, guaranteeing what is to come.
[23]I call God as my witness that it was in order to spare you
that I did not return to Corinth. [24]Not that we lord it over your
faith, but we work with you for your joy, because it is by faith you
2 stand firm. [1]So I made up my mind that I would not make
another painful visit to you. [2]For if I grieve you, who is left to
make me glad but you whom I have grieved? [3]I wrote as I did so
that when I came I should not be distressed by those who ought to
make me rejoice. I had confidence in all of you, that you would all
share my joy. [4]For I wrote you out of great distress and anguish of
heart and with many tears, not to grieve you but to let you know
the depth of my love for you.

Forgiveness for the Sinner

[5]If anyone has caused grief, he has not so much grieved me
as he has grieved all of you, to some extent—not to put it too
severely. [6]The punishment inflicted on him by the majority is sufficient for him. [7]Now instead, you ought to forgive and comfort
him, so that he will not be overwhelmed by excessive sorrow. [8]I
urge you, therefore, to reaffirm your love for him. [9]The reason I
wrote you was to see if you would stand the test and be obedient
in everything. [10]If you forgive anyone, I also forgive him. And what
I have forgiven—if there was anything to forgive—I have forgiven
in the sight of Christ for your sake, [11]in order that Satan might not
outwit us. For we are not unaware of his schemes.

Ministers of the New Covenant

[12]Now when I went to Troas to preach the gospel of Christ
and found that the Lord had opened a door for me, [13]I still had no
peace of mind, because I did not find my brother Titus there. So I
said good-by to them and went on to Macedonia.
[14]But thanks be to God, who always leads us in triumphal
procession in Christ and through us spreads everywhere the fragrance of the knowledge of him. [15]For we are to God the aroma of
Christ among those who are being saved and those who are perishing. [16]To the one we are the smell of death; to the other, the fragrance of life. And who is equal to such a task? [17]Unlike so many,
we do not peddle the word of God for profit. On the contrary, in
Christ we speak before God with sincerity, like men sent from
God.
3 Are we beginning to commend ourselves again? Or do we
need, like some people, letters of recommendation to you or from
you? [2]You yourselves are our letter, written on our hearts, known
and read by everybody. [3]You show that you are a letter from Christ,

1:19 *Son of God:* The title, "Son," was given to the king God chose to rule over the people of Israel (Ps 2:6-8). By calling Jesus the Son of God, Paul is claiming that Jesus is the one God has chosen to rule over the new Israel. See also the mini-article called "Son of God," p. 2044.

1:19 *Silas and Timothy:* This probably refers to Silas who was said in Acts 15:32 to have the gift of being a prophet. Like Paul, Silas was a Roman citizen (Acts 16:37), and he went with Paul on his later journeys when Paul and Barnabas split up as a team (Acts 15:37-39). See also the note at 1:1 (Timothy).

1:22 *Spirit . . . hearts:* Paul is referring to the Holy Spirit. In 1 Corinthians 12–14, Paul describes how the Holy Spirit gives special gifts to individual followers in order to strengthen the church.

2:4 *I wrote . . . anguish:* Paul did not want to visit the Corinthians when he was angry with them and they were upset by his remarks.

2:6 *punishment:* Apparently one particular person had been attacking Paul and his teaching. Now Paul encourages the Corinthians to forgive this person.

2:12 *I went to Troas:* Troas was a major seaport city in Macedonia. See Acts 16:8; 20:5-12.

2:17 *for profit:* Although it was acceptable for those who preached the gospel to expect support from the churches who received them, preachers were not to take advantage of their hosts' generosity. See also 1 Cor 4:9-13; 9:11-18.

1:8 1 Cor 15:32. **1:16** Acts 19:21. **1:19** Acts 18:5. **2:12,13** Acts 20:1. **3:3** Exod 24:12; Jer 31:33; Ezek 11:19; 36:26.

3:6 *new covenant:* God's new covenant with his people was announced by the prophet Jeremiah (Jer 31:31-33). The new covenant is one given by God to bring the forgiveness of sins. According to Paul, the law brought death (Rom 3:20; 7:8-11). See also Rom 1:16, 17; 3:19-26.

3:7 *engraved in letters on stone . . . face of Moses:* See the mini-articles called "Law," p. 1160 and "Moses," p. 2335. When Moses came down from Mount Sinai with the Ten Commandments, his face was radiant with God's glory (Exod 34:29-35).

3:9 *condemns:* Paul means the law (see the note at 3:6).

3:15,16 *a veil covers their hearts:* Paul means that the people of Israel did not understand the true purpose of the Law of Moses. Paul says this veil can only be removed when people interpret the law by faith in Jesus as the Christ.

4:3 *perishing:* The "perishing" are those who do not have faith in Jesus. To them the message about Jesus and his death on the cross is foolish (1 Cor 1:18).

4:4 *god of this age . . . light of the gospel:* Paul is talking about Satan. Satan's temporary reign, as the god of this age, is contrasted with the eternal age to come when Christ returns and God's creation is perfected. See the mini-article called "Satan," p. 963 and the note at 1:12 (worldly). In the Bible, light is used to describe God or God's word (Ps 119:105; John 1:4, 5; 1 John 1:5), and those people or things that reveal God's truth (Isa 49:6). The followers of Jesus are sometimes called "sons of light" or "children of light" (John 12:36; Eph 5:8).

3:16 Exod 34:34. **3:17** Gal 5:1; John 8:36. **4:6** Gen 1:3; Isa 9:2; 60:2.

the result of our ministry, written not with ink but with the Spirit of the living God, not on tablets of stone but on tablets of
human hearts.
4Such confidence as this is ours through Christ before God.
5Not that we are competent in ourselves to claim anything for ourselves, but our competence comes from God. 6He has made us
competent as ministers of a new covenant—not of the letter but
of the Spirit; for the letter kills, but the Spirit gives life.

The Glory of the New Covenant

7Now if the ministry that brought death, which was engraved in letters on stone, came with glory, so that the Israelites
could not look steadily at the face of Moses because of its glory,
fading though it was, 8will not the ministry of the Spirit be even
more glorious? 9If the ministry that condemns men is glorious,
how much more glorious is the ministry that brings righteousness!
10For what was glorious has no glory now in comparison with the
surpassing glory. 11And if what was fading away came with glory,
how much greater is the glory of that which lasts!
12Therefore, since we have such a hope, we are very bold.
13We are not like Moses, who would put a veil over his face to keep
the Israelites from gazing at it while the radiance was fading away.
14But their minds were made dull, for to this day the same veil
remains when the old covenant is read. It has not been removed,
because only in Christ is it taken away. 15Even to this day when
Moses is read, a veil covers their hearts. 16But whenever anyone
turns to the Lord, the veil is taken away. 17Now the Lord is the
Spirit, and where the Spirit of the Lord is, there is freedom. 18And
we, who with unveiled faces all reflect[a] the Lord's glory, are being
transformed into his likeness with ever-increasing glory, which
comes from the Lord, who is the Spirit.

Treasures in Jars of Clay

4 Therefore, since through God's mercy we have this ministry,
we do not lose heart. 2Rather, we have renounced secret and
shameful ways; we do not use deception, nor do we distort the
word of God. On the contrary, by setting forth the truth plainly we
commend ourselves to every man's conscience in the sight of God.
3And even if our gospel is veiled, it is veiled to those who are perishing. 4The god of this age has blinded the minds of unbelievers,
so that they cannot see the light of the gospel of the glory of
Christ, who is the image of God. 5For we do not preach ourselves,
but Jesus Christ as Lord, and ourselves as your servants for Jesus'
sake. 6For God, who said, "Let light shine out of darkness,"[b] made

[a]**18** Or *contemplate* [b]**6** Gen. 1:3

his light shine in our hearts to give us the light of the knowledge
of the glory of God in the face of Christ.
7But we have this treasure in jars of clay to show that this all-
surpassing power is from God and not from us. 8We are hard
pressed on every side, but not crushed; perplexed, but not in
despair; 9persecuted, but not abandoned; struck down, but not
destroyed. 10We always carry around in our body the death of
Jesus, so that the life of Jesus may also be revealed in our body.
11For we who are alive are always being given over to death for
Jesus' sake, so that his life may be revealed in our mortal body. 12So
then, death is at work in us, but life is at work in you.
13It is written: "I believed; therefore I have spoken."[a] With
that same spirit of faith we also believe and therefore speak,
14because we know that the one who raised the Lord Jesus from the
dead will also raise us with Jesus and present us with you in his
presence. 15All this is for your benefit, so that the grace that is
reaching more and more people may cause thanksgiving to overflow to the glory of God.
16Therefore we do not lose heart. Though outwardly we are
wasting away, yet inwardly we are being renewed day by day. 17For
our light and momentary troubles are achieving for us an eternal
glory that far outweighs them all. 18So we fix our eyes not on what
is seen, but on what is unseen. For what is seen is temporary, but
what is unseen is eternal.

Our Heavenly Dwelling

5 Now we know that if the earthly tent we live in is destroyed,
we have a building from God, an eternal house in heaven, not built
by human hands. 2Meanwhile we groan, longing to be clothed with
our heavenly dwelling, 3because when we are clothed, we will not
be found naked. 4For while we are in this tent, we groan and are
burdened, because we do not wish to be unclothed but to be
clothed with our heavenly dwelling, so that what is mortal may be
swallowed up by life. 5Now it is God who has made us for this very
purpose and has given us the Spirit as a deposit, guaranteeing what
is to come.
6Therefore we are always confident and know that as long as
we are at home in the body we are away from the Lord. 7We live by
faith, not by sight. 8We are confident, I say, and would prefer to be
away from the body and at home with the Lord. 9So we make it
our goal to please him, whether we are at home in the body or
away from it. 10For we must all appear before the judgment seat of
Christ, that each one may receive what is due him for the things
done while in the body, whether good or bad.

[a]13 Psalm 116:10

4:7 *jars of clay:* In Paul's day, clay pottery jars were used to store many things. The first-century storage jar shown here is from Palestine.

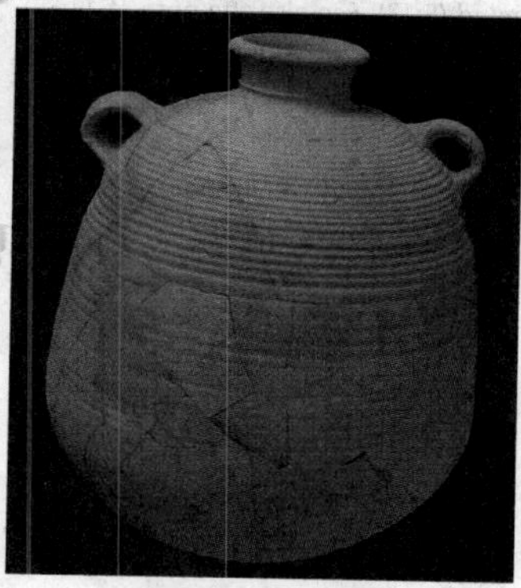

4:13,14 *faith . . . raised the Lord Jesus from the dead:* See the mini-article called "Faith," p. 1932. Paul is referring to how God raised Jesus to life three days after he died on the cross (Matt 28:1-10; Acts 2:22-24). See also the mini-article called "Resurrection," p. 2210.

4:17 *eternal glory:* Paul is referring to that future time when Jesus will give all who follow him new life and new spiritual bodies (1 Cor 15:45-57; Rom 8:18). See also the mini-article called "Eternal Life," p. 2072.

5:1 *the earthly tent we live in:* Paul compares our bodies to "tents" that we inhabit temporarily. God will provide a permanent new spiritual body after death (1 Cor 15).

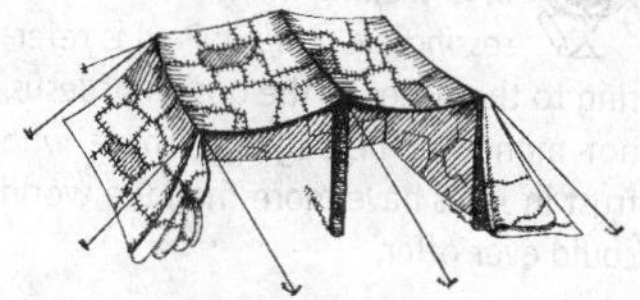

5:5 *Spirit:* See the note at 1:22.

4:13 Ps 116:10. **5:10** Rom 14:10.

5:12 *take pride in us:* Some in Corinth bragged about their own abilities and criticized Paul by telling people that he was out of his mind (5:13). See also the note at 11:5.

5:14 *one died for all:* Jesus died for everyone. Those who follow Jesus have died to sin, and have been given new life. See also Rom 5:6-8; 6:3-11.

5:16 *we once regarded Christ in this way:* Paul may be referring to the fact that, earlier in his life, he joined others who persecuted the followers of Jesus. See Phil 3:6; Acts 8:1-3; 9:1,2.

5:18 *God . . . reconciled us to himself through Christ:* Christ's death took away sin and made it possible for God and people to be at peace once again.

6:2 *salvation:* See the note at 1:6.

6:3-7 *we commend ourselves in every way:* Paul reminds the Corinthians that he and his co-workers have gone out of their way to work hard and not cause problems (1:22,23; 2:17; 1 Cor 9:1-23). See also the note at 1:8. Paul argues that what he has taught about Jesus is true, though some in Corinth have tried to convince the followers there that Paul's teaching is wrong (1 Cor 2:10-12; 2 Cor 10:1-13; 11:4-15; 12:11).

6:10 *making many rich . . . possessing everything:* Paul is referring to the riches of the gospel of Jesus, not money or belongings. Those who trust in Jesus have more than the world could ever offer.

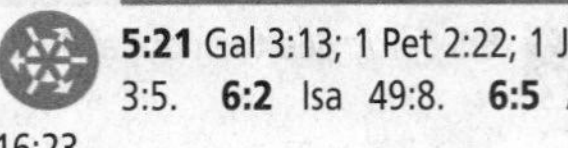

5:21 Gal 3:13; 1 Pet 2:22; 1 John 3:5. **6:2** Isa 49:8. **6:5** Acts 16:23.

The Ministry of Reconciliation

11 Since, then, we know what it is to fear the Lord, we try to persuade men. What we are is plain to God, and I hope it is also plain to
your conscience. 12 We are not trying to commend ourselves to you
again, but are giving you an opportunity to take pride in us, so that
you can answer those who take pride in what is seen rather than in
what is in the heart. 13 If we are out of our mind, it is for the sake of
God; if we are in our right mind, it is for you. 14 For Christ's love compels us, because we are convinced that one died for all, and therefore
all died. 15 And he died for all, that those who live should no longer live
for themselves but for him who died for them and was raised again.
16 So from now on we regard no one from a worldly point of
view. Though we once regarded Christ in this way, we do so no
longer. 17 Therefore, if anyone is in Christ, he is a new creation; the
old has gone, the new has come! 18 All this is from God, who reconciled us to himself through Christ and gave us the ministry of
reconciliation: 19 that God was reconciling the world to himself in
Christ, not counting men's sins against them. And he has committed to us the message of reconciliation. 20 We are therefore Christ's
ambassadors, as though God were making his appeal through us.
We implore you on Christ's behalf: Be reconciled to God. 21 God
made him who had no sin to be sin[a] for us, so that in him we
might become the righteousness of God.
6 As God's fellow workers we urge you not to receive God's grace
in vain. 2 For he says,

> "In the time of my favor I heard you,
> and in the day of salvation I helped you."[b]

I tell you, now is the time of God's favor, now is the day of salvation.

Paul's Hardships

3 We put no stumbling block in anyone's path, so that our
ministry will not be discredited. 4 Rather, as servants of God we commend ourselves in every way: in great endurance; in troubles, hardships and distresses; 5 in beatings, imprisonments and riots; in hard
work, sleepless nights and hunger; 6 in purity, understanding, patience
and kindness; in the Holy Spirit and in sincere love; 7 in truthful
speech and in the power of God; with weapons of righteousness in
the right hand and in the left; 8 through glory and dishonor, bad
report and good report; genuine, yet regarded as impostors; 9 known,
yet regarded as unknown; dying, and yet we live on; beaten, and yet
not killed; 10 sorrowful, yet always rejoicing; poor, yet making many
rich; having nothing, and yet possessing everything.
11 We have spoken freely to you, Corinthians, and opened
wide our hearts to you. 12 We are not withholding our affection

---

a21 Or *be a sin offering* b2 Isaiah 49:8

from you, but you are withholding yours from us. 13 As a fair
exchange—I speak as to my children—open wide your hearts also.

Do Not Be Yoked With Unbelievers

14 Do not be yoked together with unbelievers. For what do
righteousness and wickedness have in common? Or what fellowship can light have with darkness? 15 What harmony is there
between Christ and Belial[a]? What does a believer have in common
with an unbeliever? 16 What agreement is there between the temple
of God and idols? For we are the temple of the living God. As God
has said: "I will live with them and walk among them, and I will be
their God, and they will be my people."[b]

17 "Therefore come out from them
and be separate,
says the Lord.
Touch no unclean thing,
and I will receive you."[c]
18 "I will be a Father to you,
and you will be my sons and daughters,
says the Lord Almighty."[d]

7 Since we have these promises, dear friends, let us purify ourselves from everything that contaminates body and spirit, perfect-
ing holiness out of reverence for God.

Paul's Joy

2 Make room for us in your hearts. We have wronged no one,
we have corrupted no one, we have exploited no one. 3 I do not say

[a]15 Greek *Beliar*, a variant of *Belial* [b]16 Lev. 26:12; Jer. 32:38; Ezek. 37:27
[c]17 Isaiah 52:11; Ezek. 20:34,41 [d]18 2 Samuel 7:14; 7:8

6:14—7:1 *Do not . . . reverence for God:* Some scholars contend that this passage breaks the thought between 6:13 and 7:2 and that this section may be part of another letter.

6:14 *Do not be yoked together with unbelievers:* The Corinthian Christians had many temptations all around them. They likely had friends who were not followers of Christ and who expected the Corinthian Christians to keep living as they always had before they became part of the church (6:16).

6:15 *Belial:* Another name for Satan. See the mini-article called "Satan," p. 963.

6:16 *idols . . . we are the temple of the living God:* Some Corinthian Christians were probably invited to celebrations in local temples built to honor idols. Food and drink that had been offered to these gods may have been eaten at these celebrations. See also 1 Cor 8:1-12; 10:1-22. Paul said God's Spirit was present in every follower of Jesus, so each Christian's body is like the temple (1 Cor 3:16). Christ's followers should stay away from things like worshiping idols, which can make their lives unclean.

6:16 1 Cor 3:16; 6:19; Lev 26:12; Ezek 37:27. **6:17** Isa 52:11. **6:18** 2 Sam 7:14; 1 Chr 17:13; Isa 43:6; Jer 31:9.

QUESTIONS ABOUT 2 CORINTHIANS 1:1—7:16

1. What does Paul mean when he says that God's promises are "Yes" in Christ? (1:20)
2. What did Paul give as his reason for staying away from Corinth? (1:23—2:4) What apparently caused him to write a letter instead of making a personal visit? (2:5-11)
3. What does Paul mean when he says "the letter kills, but the Spirit gives life"? (3:5-17) What does this have to do with the "new covenant" Paul mentions?
4. Paul uses images like "jars of clay" and "tents" to describe Christ's followers (4:7—5:10). What does he mean by these statements? What other object or image might be used to describe Christ's followers?
5. Paul describes his suffering in 6:8-10. How is it possible for a follower of Christ to rejoice in times of suffering? How does Paul's view of life differ from how many people today think about happiness and wealth?
6. Read what Paul has to say about being hurt and made to feel sorry. (7:8-10) What is the difference between the sorrow that God causes and the sorrow caused by the world? (7:10)

7:5 *Macedonia . . . we were harassed at every turn:* See the note at 1:16. When Paul visited Philippi in Macedonia, he ran into opposition and was thrown in jail (Acts 16:16-40). He also faced trouble in Thessalonica, the capital of Macedonia (Acts 17:1-8). See also 2:13.

7:6 *Titus:* See 8:6. Paul was very grateful to hear from Titus that the Corinthians were concerned about Paul and were sorry for the way they had been acting.

7:8 *my letter:* There is no copy of this letter, which apparently criticized the way some of the Corinthian Christians had been acting. Some of the issues that Paul mentioned are probably similar to things he mentioned in 1 CORINTHIANS (1 Cor 5:1—6:20; 9:1-23; 10:1—11:34).

7:10 *salvation . . . worldly sorrow:* See the notes at 1:6 and 1:12.

8:1 *Macedonian churches:* These are the churches that Paul had started in Philippi, Thessalonica, and possibly, Berea (Acts 16:12—17:13). See the map on p. 2476.

8:2 *most severe trial:* The churches in Macedonia faced some kind of suffering and difficulty which Paul never completely describes. Paul mentions this in other letters (Phil 1:29,30; 1 Thes 1:6; 2:14; 3:3,4).

8:4 *sharing in this service to the saints:* Another way of translating the phrase that means "ministry to the saints," which refers to the original group of Jesus' followers in Jerusalem. These "saints" had little money to continue their work in Jerusalem, so Christians in other cities and lands were asked to support them. This special offering is mentioned elsewhere (1 Cor 16:1-3, 15; Rom 15:25, 26, 31; 2 Cor 9).

8:1-4 Rom 15:26.

this to condemn you; I have said before that you have such a place
in our hearts that we would live or die with you. 4I have great confidence in you; I take great pride in you. I am greatly encouraged;
in all our troubles my joy knows no bounds.
5For when we came into Macedonia, this body of ours had
no rest, but we were harassed at every turn—conflicts on the outside, fears within. 6But God, who comforts the downcast, comforted us by the coming of Titus, 7and not only by his coming but also
by the comfort you had given him. He told us about your longing
for me, your deep sorrow, your ardent concern for me, so that my
joy was greater than ever.
8Even if I caused you sorrow by my letter, I do not regret it.
Though I did regret it—I see that my letter hurt you, but only for
a little while— 9yet now I am happy, not because you were made
sorry, but because your sorrow led you to repentance. For you
became sorrowful as God intended and so were not harmed in any
way by us. 10Godly sorrow brings repentance that leads to salvation
and leaves no regret, but worldly sorrow brings death. 11See what
this godly sorrow has produced in you: what earnestness, what
eagerness to clear yourselves, what indignation, what alarm,
what longing, what concern, what readiness to see justice done. At
every point you have proved yourselves to be innocent in this matter. 12So even though I wrote to you, it was not on account of the
one who did the wrong or of the injured party, but rather that
before God you could see for yourselves how devoted to us you
are. 13By all this we are encouraged.
In addition to our own encouragement, we were especially
delighted to see how happy Titus was, because his spirit has been
refreshed by all of you. 14I had boasted to him about you, and you
have not embarrassed me. But just as everything we said to you
was true, so our boasting about you to Titus has proved to be true
as well. 15And his affection for you is all the greater when he
remembers that you were all obedient, receiving him with fear and
trembling. 16I am glad I can have complete confidence in you.

Paul Encourages the Corinthians to Be Generous Givers

Now that he has heard that the Corinthians are not angry with him, Paul brings up the issue of collecting money offerings. Their offerings would be part of a larger offering given by the churches in Macedonia. This offering was likely what Paul wanted to collect to bring to the suffering believers in Jerusalem.

Generosity Encouraged

8 And now, brothers, we want you to know about the grace that
God has given the Macedonian churches. 2Out of the most severe

trial, their overflowing joy and their extreme poverty welled up in rich generosity. [3]For I testify that they gave as much as they were able, and even beyond their ability. Entirely on their own, [4]they urgently pleaded with us for the privilege of sharing in this service to the saints. [5]And they did not do as we expected, but they gave themselves first to the Lord and then to us in keeping with God's will. [6]So we urged Titus, since he had earlier made a beginning, to bring also to completion this act of grace on your part. [7]But just as you excel in everything—in faith, in speech, in knowledge, in complete earnestness and in your love for us[a]—see that you also excel in this grace of giving.

[8]I am not commanding you, but I want to test the sincerity of your love by comparing it with the earnestness of others. [9]For you know the grace of our Lord Jesus Christ, that though he was rich, yet for your sakes he became poor, so that you through his poverty might become rich.

[10]And here is my advice about what is best for you in this matter: Last year you were the first not only to give but also to have the desire to do so. [11]Now finish the work, so that your eager willingness to do it may be matched by your completion of it, according to your means. [12]For if the willingness is there, the gift is acceptable according to what one has, not according to what he does not have.

[13]Our desire is not that others might be relieved while you are hard pressed, but that there might be equality. [14]At the present time your plenty will supply what they need, so that in turn their plenty will supply what you need. Then there will be equality, [15]as it is written: "He who gathered much did not have too much, and he who gathered little did not have too little."[b]

Titus Sent to Corinth

[16]I thank God, who put into the heart of Titus the same concern I have for you. [17]For Titus not only welcomed our appeal, but he is coming to you with much enthusiasm and on his own initiative. [18]And we are sending along with him the brother who is praised by all the churches for his service to the gospel. [19]What is more, he was chosen by the churches to accompany us as we carry the offering, which we administer in order to honor the Lord himself and to show our eagerness to help. [20]We want to avoid any criticism of the way we administer this liberal gift. [21]For we are taking pains to do what is right, not only in the eyes of the Lord but also in the eyes of men.

[22]In addition, we are sending with them our brother who has often proved to us in many ways that he is zealous, and now even more so because of his great confidence in you. [23]As for Titus, he

[a]7 Some manuscripts *in our love for you* [b]15 Exodus 16:18

For if the willingness is there, the gift is acceptable according to what one has, not according to what he does not have.
2 Cor 8:12

8:6 *Titus:* Titus was a Gentile Christian who worked closely with Paul and who had accompanied Paul on a trip to Jerusalem (Gal 2:1-3). See also 2:13 and the note at 7:6.

8:14 *your plenty will supply what they need:* The followers of Christ in Corinth were richer than some of the other churches, so Paul encouraged them to give more money.

8:15 *He who gathered much did not have too much:* Paul is quoting Exodus 16:17, 18, which describes how the Israelite people gathered God's gift of manna in the desert.

8:18 *the brother who is praised by all the churches:* This unnamed person was well-known for spreading the gospel about Jesus, and had a reputation for encouraging churches to give generously to the fund that Titus was collecting.

8:19 *churches:* The Greek word for "church" is *ekklesia*. It was used for any gathering of people. The church can refer to all the followers of Christ wherever they are, but it can also refer to a single congregation, as it does in this verse.

8:22 *we are sending with them our brother:* This follower is also unknown. Paul encouraged the Corinthians to treat Titus and the other two followers in a way that would confirm the Corinthians' good reputation.

8:21 Prov 3:4.

God loves a cheerful giver.
2 Cor 9:7

9:2 *Macedonians . . . Achaia:* See the notes at 1:1 (Achaia) and 1:16. Achaia was the central and southern part of Greece directly west across the Aegean Sea from Ephesus.

9:6 *sows . . . will also reap:* This folk saying was common among both Greek- and Hebrew-speaking people in Paul's day. It is like the idea expressed in Proverbs 11:24. See also Paul's words in Galatians 6:7-9.

9:12 *This service that you perform:* Refers to the money offering that the Corinthians were collecting.

9:13 *your confession of the gospel of Christ:* Paul says that the gospel of Jesus Christ is God's most generous gift to human beings.

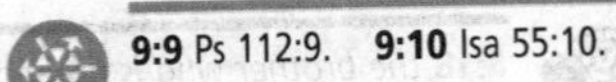

9:9 Ps 112:9. **9:10** Isa 55:10.

is my partner and fellow worker among you; as for our brothers,
they are representatives of the churches and an honor to Christ.
24 Therefore show these men the proof of your love and the reason
for our pride in you, so that the churches can see it.
9 There is no need for me to write to you about this service to
the saints. 2 For I know your eagerness to help, and I have been
boasting about it to the Macedonians, telling them that since last
year you in Achaia were ready to give; and your enthusiasm has
stirred most of them to action. 3 But I am sending the brothers in
order that our boasting about you in this matter should not prove
hollow, but that you may be ready, as I said you would be. 4 For if
any Macedonians come with me and find you unprepared, we—
not to say anything about you—would be ashamed of having been
so confident. 5 So I thought it necessary to urge the brothers to visit
you in advance and finish the arrangements for the generous gift
you had promised. Then it will be ready as a generous gift, not as
one grudgingly given.

Sowing Generously

6 Remember this: Whoever sows sparingly will also reap sparingly, and whoever sows generously will also reap generously.
7 Each man should give what he has decided in his heart to give,
not reluctantly or under compulsion, for God loves a cheerful
giver. 8 And God is able to make all grace abound to you, so that in
all things at all times, having all that you need, you will abound in
every good work. 9 As it is written:

"He has scattered abroad his gifts to the poor;
his righteousness endures forever."[a]

10 Now he who supplies seed to the sower and bread for food will
also supply and increase your store of seed and will enlarge the
harvest of your righteousness. 11 You will be made rich in every way
so that you can be generous on every occasion, and through us
your generosity will result in thanksgiving to God.
12 This service that you perform is not only supplying the
needs of God's people but is also overflowing in many expressions
of thanks to God. 13 Because of the service by which you have
proved yourselves, men will praise God for the obedience that
accompanies your confession of the gospel of Christ, and for your
generosity in sharing with them and with everyone else. 14 And in
their prayers for you their hearts will go out to you, because of the
surpassing grace God has given you. 15 Thanks be to God for his
indescribable gift!

[a] 9 Psalm 112:9

Paul Defends Himself as a True Apostle of Christ

Paul defends himself and his work against ongoing attacks made by his critics in the church at Corinth. He reminds the Corinthians that he has suffered for the sake of the gospel and has had visions from God. He speaks against the false apostles who have been bragging about their own visions, while mistreating the Corinthians.

Paul's Defense of His Ministry

10 By the meekness and gentleness of Christ, I appeal to you—
I, Paul, who am "timid" when face to face with you, but "bold"
when away! [2]I beg you that when I come I may not have to be as
bold as I expect to be toward some people who think that we live
by the standards of this world. [3]For though we live in the world, we
do not wage war as the world does. [4]The weapons we fight with
are not the weapons of the world. On the contrary, they have
divine power to demolish strongholds. [5]We demolish arguments
and every pretension that sets itself up against the knowledge of
God, and we take captive every thought to make it obedient to
Christ. [6]And we will be ready to punish every act of disobedience,
once your obedience is complete.
[7]You are looking only on the surface of things.[a] If anyone is
confident that he belongs to Christ, he should consider again that
we belong to Christ just as much as he. [8]For even if I boast somewhat freely about the authority the Lord gave us for building you
up rather than pulling you down, I will not be ashamed of it. [9]I do
not want to seem to be trying to frighten you with my letters. [10]For
some say, "His letters are weighty and forceful, but in person he is
unimpressive and his speaking amounts to nothing." [11]Such people
should realize that what we are in our letters when we are absent,
we will be in our actions when we are present.
[12]We do not dare to classify or compare ourselves with some
who commend themselves. When they measure themselves by
themselves and compare themselves with themselves, they are not
wise. [13]We, however, will not boast beyond proper limits, but will
confine our boasting to the field God has assigned to us, a field
that reaches even to you. [14]We are not going too far in our boasting, as would be the case if we had not come to you, for we did get
as far as you with the gospel of Christ. [15]Neither do we go beyond
our limits by boasting of work done by others.[b] Our hope is that,
as your faith continues to grow, our area of activity among you

---

[a]7 Or *Look at the obvious facts* [b]13-15 Or *[13]We, however, will not boast about things that cannot be measured, but we will boast according to the standard of measurement that the God of measure has assigned us—a measurement that relates even to you. [14] . . . [15]Neither do we boast about things that cannot be measured in regard to the work done by others.*

10:2 *think that we live by the standards of this world:* Some people claimed that Paul was nice when he was with them but nasty when he was away (10:1). Others claimed that Paul and his co-workers acted like the people of this world. For Paul, the "world" stood for the people and things that were opposed to God (Rom 12:2; Gal 4:3).

10:4 *divine power:* Paul is talking about the power of the Holy Spirit, which helps him and other apostles say and do things that convince people that the gospel about Jesus is true. See the note at 1:22.

10:10 *His letters are weighty and forceful:* At least one letter Paul wrote to the Corinthians had some harsh words that offended some of the followers. This may be the letter mentioned in 1 Corinthians 5:9 or the letter mentioned in 2 Corinthians 2:1-4. Some claimed that Paul was not a powerful speaker. In 1 Corinthians 2:3, Paul admits that when he first came to the Corinthians, he was weak and trembling with fear.

10:12 *measure themselves by themselves:* By only comparing themselves to each other, the false teachers overlook the Lord's standards, which are the only ones that truly matter (10:18).

10:15 *boasting of work done by others:* Apparently some of Paul's critics were also acting as if their message was their own rather than giving credit to Paul, or to the Spirit of God.

will greatly expand, [16]so that we can preach the gospel in the
regions beyond you. For we do not want to boast about work
already done in another man's territory. [17]But, "Let him who
boasts boast in the Lord."[a] [18]For it is not the one who commends
himself who is approved, but the one whom the Lord commends.

Paul and the False Apostles

11 I hope you will put up with a little of my foolishness; but you
are already doing that. [2]I am jealous for you with a godly jealousy.
I promised you to one husband, to Christ, so that I might present
you as a pure virgin to him. [3]But I am afraid that just as Eve was
deceived by the serpent's cunning, your minds may somehow be
led astray from your sincere and pure devotion to Christ. [4]For if
someone comes to you and preaches a Jesus other than the Jesus
we preached, or if you receive a different spirit from the one you
received, or a different gospel from the one you accepted, you put
up with it easily enough. [5]But I do not think I am in the least inferior to those "super-apostles." [6]I may not be a trained speaker, but
I do have knowledge. We have made this perfectly clear to you in
every way.

[7]Was it a sin for me to lower myself in order to elevate you
by preaching the gospel of God to you free of charge? [8]I robbed
other churches by receiving support from them so as to serve you.
[9]And when I was with you and needed something, I was not a burden to anyone, for the brothers who came from Macedonia supplied what I needed. I have kept myself from being a burden to
you in any way, and will continue to do so. [10]As surely as the truth
of Christ is in me, nobody in the regions of Achaia will stop this
boasting of mine. [11]Why? Because I do not love you? God knows I
do! [12]And I will keep on doing what I am doing in order to cut the
ground from under those who want an opportunity to be considered equal with us in the things they boast about.

[13]For such men are false apostles, deceitful workmen, mas-
querading as apostles of Christ. [14]And no wonder, for Satan himself masquerades as an angel of light. [15]It is not surprising, then, if
his servants masquerade as servants of righteousness. Their end
will be what their actions deserve.

Paul Boasts About His Sufferings

[16]I repeat: Let no one take me for a fool. But if you do, then
receive me just as you would a fool, so that I may do a little boasting. [17]In this self-confident boasting I am not talking as the Lord
would, but as a fool. [18]Since many are boasting in the way the
world does, I too will boast. [19]You gladly put up with fools since
you are so wise! [20]In fact, you even put up with anyone who

[a]17 Jer. 9:24

11:2 *present you as a pure virgin:* Paul may be suggesting that he is like a father who wants to protect his virgin daughter (the Corinthian Christians) until the time of her marriage to the most suitable husband (Christ). (See also Eph 5:23, 24; Phil 1:9-11; Rev 21:1, 2.)

11:5 *"super-apostles":* They were teaching a message different from the one Paul taught (11:4). The super-apostles apparently were convincing public speakers. They seem to have been asking for money to support their preaching and teaching (11:20).

These super-apostles may be the same ones that Paul talks about as "arrogant" in 1 Corinthians 4:19. There the super-apostles claimed to have special wisdom that was above Paul and the other apostles. This kind of wisdom showed up in Gnosticism, a term that describes a number of different religious movements and philosophies in the Greek world. Gnostics believed that the physical body and earthly world were evil while spiritual knowledge was good. They believed that people should try to reach God by following a certain set of spiritual truths. They looked down on the cross of Christ, because they believed God would not use such a physical thing to bring salvation to people. See also the article called, "Religions and Philosophies in Bible Times," p. 1832.

11:7 *preaching the gospel of God to you free of charge:* Paul did not ask to be paid while he was teaching and preaching among them (1 Cor 9:1-23). This meant that he had to rely on money gifts from other churches while he was in Corinth (11:8,9).

11:15 *his servants:* Servants of Satan, the false apostles mentioned in 11:13.

10:17 Jer 9:24; 1 Cor 1:31. **11:3** Gen 3:1-5,13. **11:9** Phil 4:15-18. **11:19** Phil 4:15-18.

enslaves you or exploits you or takes advantage of you or pushes
himself forward or slaps you in the face. 21 To my shame I admit
that we were too weak for that!

What anyone else dares to boast about—I am speaking as a
fool—I also dare to boast about. 22 Are they Hebrews? So am I. Are
they Israelites? So am I. Are they Abraham's descendants? So am I.
23 Are they servants of Christ? (I am out of my mind to talk like
this.) I am more. I have worked much harder, been in prison more
frequently, been flogged more severely, and been exposed to death
again and again. 24 Five times I received from the Jews the forty
lashes minus one. 25 Three times I was beaten with rods, once I was
stoned, three times I was shipwrecked, I spent a night and a day in
the open sea, 26 I have been constantly on the move. I have been in
danger from rivers, in danger from bandits, in danger from my
own countrymen, in danger from Gentiles; in danger in the city, in
danger in the country, in danger at sea; and in danger from false
brothers. 27 I have labored and toiled and have often gone without
sleep; I have known hunger and thirst and have often gone without food; I have been cold and naked. 28 Besides everything else, I
face daily the pressure of my concern for all the churches. 29 Who is
weak, and I do not feel weak? Who is led into sin, and I do not
inwardly burn?

11:22 *Hebrews . . . Abraham's descendants:* Like Paul, the false apostles were Jewish. Only those who follow Jesus Christ are the real people of God.

11:24,25 *forty lashes minus one . . . shipwrecked:* According to the Law of Moses, the maximum number of lashes a person could receive was forty (Deut 25:3). Acts 27 tells about one of Paul's shipwreck experiences.

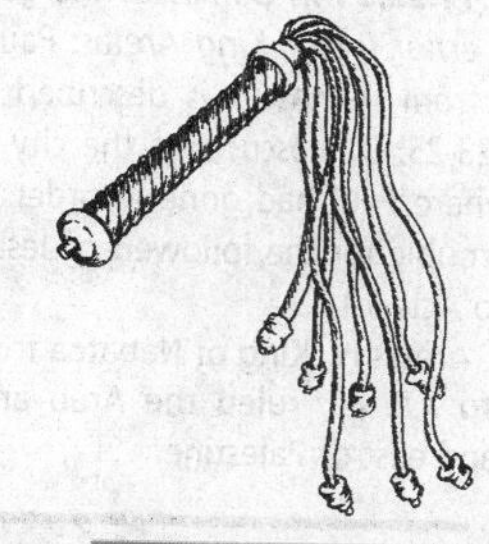

11:23 Acts 16:23. **11:26** Acts 9:23; 14:5.

PARADISE

The Hebrew word for "paradise" was borrowed from a Persian word which means a wooded park where everything is peaceful and beautiful. In Nehemiah 2:8, it is used for the king's forest, and in Song of Songs 4:13 and Ecclesiastes 2:5, it is a well-watered orchard or garden. Some of Israel's prophets had begun to say that the faithful who died would live again after dying (Dan 12:2, 3; Isa 26:19), and the term "paradise" eventually was used as the place where they would live after death. For some, "paradise" was thought of as being on the earth or in heaven. For others, it was a new Garden of Eden where the tree of life (see Gen 2:9) would grow forever. Still others believed paradise was where the faithful who had died would wait for the day of judgment.

A similar understanding of paradise can be found in various places in the New Testament. Jesus, for instance, promised the man who was crucified beside him that he would be with him in paradise that day (Luke 23:39-43). Another reference by Jesus to paradise can be inferred from the parable he told about a poor man, Lazarus, and a rich man. When the poor man in this story dies, he is described as being taken to a place of honor next to Abraham (Luke 16:19-22).

Paul teaches in 2 Corinthians 12:1-4 that when God was giving him a special message, he was "caught up to paradise." Paul was not sad at the prospect of dying, since he would be with Christ (Phil 1:23). In REVELATION, paradise is where the tree of life is (Rev 2:7; 22:1-5), and where God's people will be gathered when the powers of evil have been defeated and God's rule has taken over the whole of the creation. In this new paradise, God's people will share in the fruits of the tree of life (Rev 22:14). See also the mini-article called "Heaven," p. 1420.

[30]If I must boast, I will boast of the things that show my
weakness. [31]The God and Father of the Lord Jesus, who is to be
praised forever, knows that I am not lying. [32]In Damascus the governor under King Aretas had the city of the Damascenes guarded
in order to arrest me. [33]But I was lowered in a basket from a window in the wall and slipped through his hands.

Paul's Vision and His Thorn

12 I must go on boasting. Although there is nothing to be
gained, I will go on to visions and revelations from the Lord. [2]I
know a man in Christ who fourteen years ago was caught up to
the third heaven. Whether it was in the body or out of the body I
do not know—God knows. [3]And I know that this man—whether
in the body or apart from the body I do not know, but God
knows— [4]was caught up to paradise. He heard inexpressible
things, things that man is not permitted to tell. [5]I will boast about
a man like that, but I will not boast about myself, except about my
weaknesses. [6]Even if I should choose to boast, I would not be a
fool, because I would be speaking the truth. But I refrain, so no
one will think more of me than is warranted by what I do or say.
[7]To keep me from becoming conceited because of these sur-
passingly great revelations, there was given me a thorn in my flesh,
a messenger of Satan, to torment me. [8]Three times I pleaded with
the Lord to take it away from me. [9]But he said to me, "My grace is
sufficient for you, for my power is made perfect in weakness."
Therefore I will boast all the more gladly about my weaknesses, so
that Christ's power may rest on me. [10]That is why, for Christ's sake,
I delight in weaknesses, in insults, in hardships, in persecutions, in
difficulties. For when I am weak, then I am strong.

Paul's Concern for the Corinthians

[11]I have made a fool of myself, but you drove me to it. I
ought to have been commended by you, for I am not in the least
inferior to the "super-apostles," even though I am nothing. [12]The
things that mark an apostle—signs, wonders and miracles—were
done among you with great perseverance. [13]How were you inferi-
or to the other churches, except that I was never a burden to you?
Forgive me this wrong!
[14]Now I am ready to visit you for the third time, and I will
not be a burden to you, because what I want is not your possessions but you. After all, children should not have to save up for
their parents, but parents for their children. [15]So I will very gladly
spend for you everything I have and expend myself as well. If I love
you more, will you love me less? [16]Be that as it may, I have not been
a burden to you. Yet, crafty fellow that I am, I caught you by trickery! [17]Did I exploit you through any of the men I sent you? [18]I
urged Titus to go to you and I sent our brother with him. Titus

Therefore I will boast all the more gladly about my weaknesses, so that Christ's power may rest on me.
2 Cor 12:9

11:32,33 *In Damascus the governor under King Aretas:* Paul's escape from Damascus is described in Acts 9:23-25. Damascus was the city in Syria where Paul had gone in order to make trouble for the followers of Jesus. See also Acts 9:1-19.

Aretas IV, King of Nabatea from 9 B.C. to A.D. 40, ruled the Arab area north and east of Palestine.

12:2-4 *third heaven . . . paradise:* Paul begins to tell about his vision as if it happened to someone else, but he is really talking about himself (12:7). In Paul's day, people argued about just how many levels heaven had. The third was said to be where God dwells. See also the mini-articles called "Heaven," p. 1420 and "Paradise," p. 2243.

12:7 *thorn in my flesh:* It is not clear exactly what kind of suffering this was. Paul asked God to take this suffering away, but God allowed these difficulties so that Paul would continue to rely on the strength that God provides rather than relying on his own strength. Paul realized that God's grace and power was all he needed. That is why he was able to say, "when I am weak, then I am strong" (12:10).

12:11 *I have made a fool of myself:* Paul is embarrassed that he had to tell them about the great experiences God had given him, because they might think he was bragging.

12:11 *"super-apostles":* See the note at 11:5.

The Ecstasy of Saint Paul by Nicolas Poussin, around 1650. Paul tells the Corinthians about "a man in Christ who fourteen years ago was caught up to the third heaven . . . to paradise. He heard inexpressible things, things that man is not permitted to tell" (see 12:1-5). Most scholars believe that Paul was really speaking about his own experience in this passage. Nowhere else in his letters does Paul give any more information about this experience.

did not exploit you, did he? Did we not act in the same spirit and
follow the same course?
19 Have you been thinking all along that we have been
defending ourselves to you? We have been speaking in the sight of
God as those in Christ; and everything we do, dear friends, is for
your strengthening. 20 For I am afraid that when I come I may not
find you as I want you to be, and you may not find me as you want
me to be. I fear that there may be quarreling, jealousy, outbursts of
anger, factions, slander, gossip, arrogance and disorder. 21 I am
afraid that when I come again my God will humble me before you,
and I will be grieved over many who have sinned earlier and have
not repented of the impurity, sexual sin and debauchery in which
they have indulged.

12:12 *signs, wonders and miracles:* When Jesus chose his twelve apostles, he gave them power to drive out evil spirits, to heal diseases, and even to raise the dead to life (Matt 10:1, 8). Paul also identifies the ability to work miracles and the power to heal the sick as two of the special gifts the Holy Spirit gives to some of God's people (1 Cor 12:28, 29). Though he was not one of the original twelve apostles, Paul had the same powers they did (Acts 13:9-12; 19:11, 12; 28:3-6). See also the note at 1:1 (Paul).

12:13 *I was never a burden to you:* Paul reminded the Corinthians once again that, unlike the super-apostles, he didn't ask them to support him with money (11:7-10). Paul is concerned that the Corinthians missed out on a blessing when he didn't ask for money, and he thinks this made them take his teaching too lightly.

12:14 *visit you for the third time:* Paul first visited the Corinthians when he founded the church there (Acts 18:1-17). His second visit was the painful visit described in 2:1.

12:18 *Titus:* See the notes at 7:6 and 8:6. Paul reminded the Corinthians that Titus did not ask for money from them either.

12:20 *you may not find me as you want me to be:* Paul is afraid that when he visits the Corinthians, they will have bad arguments with Paul and among themselves because of him.

12:21 *grieved over many who have sinned earlier and have not repented:* Paul is also afraid that he will be ashamed and sad if some of the Corinthians have not given up old sins like sexual immorality (1 Cor 5).

> *Examine yourselves to see whether you are in the faith; test yourselves. Do you not realize that Christ Jesus is in you—unless, of course, you fail the test?*
> 2 Cor 13:5

13:2 *the second time . . . I will not spare those who sinned earlier:* See the notes at 12:14 and 12:20. The sins mentioned here are probably sins having to do with sexual immorality (1 Cor 5), worshiping idols (1 Cor 8; 2 Cor 6:14—7:1), and the disrespectful behavior some of the followers displayed when they took part in the Lord's Supper (1 Cor 11:17-34).

13:9 *whenever we are weak:* See the note at 12:7.

13:1 Deut 17:5-7; 19:15.

A Challenge and Farewell

Paul prepares the way for his planned visit by encouraging the Corinthians to take a close look at themselves to see if they are really being true to their faith in Christ. If they are, Paul will not have to criticize them when he arrives.

Final Warnings

13 This will be my third visit to you. "Every matter must be
established by the testimony of two or three witnesses."[a] 2I already
gave you a warning when I was with you the second time. I now
repeat it while absent: On my return I will not spare those who
sinned earlier or any of the others, 3since you are demanding proof
that Christ is speaking through me. He is not weak in dealing with
you, but is powerful among you. 4For to be sure, he was crucified
in weakness, yet he lives by God's power. Likewise, we are weak in
him, yet by God's power we will live with him to serve you.
5Examine yourselves to see whether you are in the faith; test
yourselves. Do you not realize that Christ Jesus is in you—unless,
of course, you fail the test? 6And I trust that you will discover that
we have not failed the test. 7Now we pray to God that you will not
do anything wrong. Not that people will see that we have stood the
test but that you will do what is right even though we may seem to
have failed. 8For we cannot do anything against the truth, but only
for the truth. 9We are glad whenever we are weak but you are

[a]1 Deut. 19:15

QUESTIONS ABOUT 2 CORINTHIANS 8:1—13:14

1. In chapters 8 and 9, Paul encourages the Corinthians to be generous givers. What was this offering of money to be used for? What does the saying about "sowing" in 9:6 have to do with giving, or with serving God in other ways?
2. What is the purpose of giving, whether it be money, time, or special abilities?
3. In chapter 10, Paul talks a lot about boasting. Who seems to be doing this boasting, and what are they boasting about? Is it ever right to boast? (10:17)
4. Who were the "super-apostles," and how were they affecting the church at Corinth? (11:1-21)
5. What has Paul's life been like as an apostle? (11:21-33) Why can he boast about how weak he is? (11:30—12:10) The world does not usually consider "weakness" to be a positive thing. How can weaknesses be turned into strengths?
6. Why is Paul worried about visiting the Corinthians? (12:14-21) What is his advice to them? (13:5-8)
7. Think about your own church or another one you are familiar with. In your opinion, what are its strengths and weaknesses? What can you do to communicate your concerns, encouragement, or thanks to those who are in charge?

strong; and our prayer is for your perfection. [10]This is why I write
these things when I am absent, that when I come I may not have
to be harsh in my use of authority—the authority the Lord gave
me for building you up, not for tearing you down.

Final Greetings

[11]Finally, brothers, good-by. Aim for perfection, listen to my
appeal, be of one mind, live in peace. And the God of love and
peace will be with you.
[12]Greet one another with a holy kiss. [13]All the saints send
their greetings.
[14]May the grace of the Lord Jesus Christ, and the love of
God, and the fellowship of the Holy Spirit be with you all.

13:12,13 *Greet one another with a holy kiss . . . saints send their greetings:* In the ancient Near East, public greetings with a kiss were a sign of friendship, respect, and love. (See also 1 Cor 16:20.)

Paul brought greetings from all the followers of Christ, or from all the followers in the place where he was writing this letter.

GALATIANS

What someone believes says a lot about who that person is. Find out why the apostle Paul had to defend himself and his message about Christ.

1:1 *Paul, an apostle:* An apostle is a person chosen and sent by a leader or a group to do a special job. In GALATIANS, "apostle" means someone chosen by God to spread the message about Jesus Christ. Paul claims that God, and not any human being, chose him to be an apostle. See also the mini-article called "Paul (Saul) of Tarsus," p. 2177.

1:2 *churches:* See the mini-article called "Church, p. 2264.

1:2 *Galatia:* Galatia is a province located in central Asia Minor which Paul is known to have visited on his missionary journeys (see Acts 13:1—14:23; 16:6; 18:23). The name of the province is a form of the word "Gauls," the name of a Celtic tribe who controlled much of this region from the third to the second century B.C.

WHAT MAKES GALATIANS SPECIAL?

GALATIANS is a very personal letter that provides help in understanding Paul's character and his strong beliefs. The letter also gives some clues that shed light on Paul's early life. Most of all, GALATIANS provides an inside view of a major controversy faced by the early Christian church. This controversy and Paul's response to it had a great effect on the way God's message about Jesus Christ was preached. Paul taught that God's message is that people become God's children by faith in Jesus Christ (3:26), not by following the Law of Moses. Further, Christ sets God's children free from the law (5:1), and the Holy Spirit leads them (5:16-18) and helps them to be loving, kind, and good (5:22,23).

WHY WAS GALATIANS WRITTEN?

Paul wrote this letter to the Galatians because he wanted them to know that he was a true apostle of Jesus Christ, and that the gospel he had given them about Jesus was the only true gospel (1:6-9). On an earlier visit Paul had brought the Galatians God's message, the gospel of Christ (1:7,8). In this letter he expresses his anger because he has learned that some people were telling the Galatian churches that they must obey the Law of Moses in order to be God's children. These false teachers claimed that they were following the rules kept by the leaders of the Christian church in Jerusalem, including Jesus' own brother, James (1:19; 2:12). But Paul tells the Galatians that the Jerusalem apostles accept him as an apostle, and that they agree with him that Gentiles (non-Jews) can be part of the new people of God without having to follow the Law of Moses and the traditions of the Jewish people.

WHAT'S THE STORY BEHIND THE SCENE?

Galatia was an area in northern central Asia Minor (modern-day Turkey). Many of the people who lived there were descended from a group of people called Gauls or Celts who settled in the region well before 200 B.C. At the time of Paul, the Romans ruled this region, which the Roman emperor Augustus named Galatia in 25 B.C. It is not clear exactly where or when Paul wrote GALATIANS.

HOW IS GALATIANS CONSTRUCTED?

GALATIANS is a letter, or "epistle," that begins with a brief greeting (1:1-5) and ends with a short blessing (6:18). Primarily, Paul uses the letter to present his case against the false teachers who are causing trouble for the Galatian believers, and to defend himself and his message about Christ. Notice these things in the following outline:

Paul defends his apostleship and his message (1:1—2:21)

Faith in Christ is the way to become God's children (3:1—4:31)

Christ gives freedom, and the Spirit guides (5:1—6:10)

Final warnings (6:11-18)

Paul Defends His Apostleship and His Message

Some in the Galatian churches were denying that God had chosen Paul to be a messenger of the gospel about Jesus Christ. In these chapters, Paul defends himself, saying that his message has come directly from Jesus Christ (1:12), and that God has chosen him to announce the message about Jesus to the Gentiles (1:15,16).

1 Paul, an apostle—sent not from men nor by man, but by Jesus
Christ and God the Father, who raised him from the dead—2and
all the brothers with me,

To the churches in Galatia:

3Grace and peace to you from God our Father and the Lord
Jesus Christ, 4who gave himself for our sins to rescue us from the
present evil age, according to the will of our God and Father, 5to
whom be glory for ever and ever. Amen.

No Other Gospel

6I am astonished that you are so quickly deserting the one
who called you by the grace of Christ and are turning to a different
gospel— 7which is really no gospel at all. Evidently some people
are throwing you into confusion and are trying to pervert the
gospel of Christ. 8But even if we or an angel from heaven should
preach a gospel other than the one we preached to you, let him be
eternally condemned! 9As we have already said, so now I say again:
If anybody is preaching to you a gospel other than what you
accepted, let him be eternally condemned!
10Am I now trying to win the approval of men, or of God?
Or am I trying to please men? If I were still trying to please men,
I would not be a servant of Christ.

Paul Called by God

11I want you to know, brothers, that the gospel I preached is
not something that man made up. 12I did not receive it from any

1:3 *God our Father and the Lord Jesus Christ:* Paul describes God as "Father" in many of his letters (1 Cor 1:3; Phil 1:2). See also the mini-articles called "Messiah (Chosen One)," p. 1124, and "Lord (Title for Jesus)," p. 2106.

1:4 *sins:* When people sin, they turn their backs on God and disobey God's commandments. See also the mini-article called "Sin," p. 2181.

1:5 *Amen:* Here used as an expression to mean, "Yes, it is true."

1:6 *turning to a different gospel:* The message has to do with the claim that a person must live according to the Law of Moses in order to be a true child of God (3:1-5,10,11; 5:1-6).

1:7 *some people are throwing you into confusion:* The trouble-makers insisted that Gentile (non-Jewish) believers must practice certain Jewish rites, including circumcision. They also claimed that Paul was not a true apostle, because he said that Gentiles didn't have to follow the Law of Moses or take part in Jewish ceremonies.

1:10 *Am I now trying to win the approval of men:* Paul was probably being accused of being a "people-pleaser" because he did not insist that Gentile males be circumcised. See the mini-article called "Circumcision," p. 2251.

1:12 *receive it:* How Paul became a follower of Jesus is described in Acts 9:1-18.

1:4 Rom 3:24-26.

man, nor was I taught it; rather, I received it by revelation from Jesus Christ.

13 For you have heard of my previous way of life in Judaism, how intensely I persecuted the church of God and tried to destroy it. 14 I was advancing in Judaism beyond many Jews of my own age and was extremely zealous for the traditions of my fathers. 15 But when God, who set me apart from birth[a] and called me by his grace, was pleased 16 to reveal his Son in me so that I might preach him among the Gentiles, I did not consult any man, 17 nor did I go up to Jerusalem to see those who were apostles before I was, but I went immediately into Arabia and later returned to Damascus.

18 Then after three years, I went up to Jerusalem to get acquainted with Peter[b] and stayed with him fifteen days. 19 I saw none of the other apostles—only James, the Lord's brother. 20 I assure you before God that what I am writing you is no lie. 21 Later I went to Syria and Cilicia. 22 I was personally unknown to the churches of Judea that are in Christ. 23 They only heard the report: "The man who formerly persecuted us is now preaching the faith he once tried to destroy." 24 And they praised God because of me.

Paul Accepted by the Apostles

2 Fourteen years later I went up again to Jerusalem, this time with Barnabas. I took Titus along also. 2 I went in response to a revelation and set before them the gospel that I preach among the Gentiles. But I did this privately to those who seemed to be leaders, for fear that I was running or had run my race in vain. 3 Yet not even Titus, who was with me, was compelled to be circumcised, even though he was a Greek. 4 ⌞This matter arose⌟ because some false brothers had infiltrated our ranks to spy on the freedom we have in Christ Jesus and to make us slaves. 5 We did not give in to them for a moment, so that the truth of the gospel might remain with you.

6 As for those who seemed to be important—whatever they were makes no difference to me; God does not judge by external appearance—those men added nothing to my message. 7 On the contrary, they saw that I had been entrusted with the task of preaching the gospel to the Gentiles,[c] just as Peter had been to the Jews.[d] 8 For God, who was at work in the ministry of Peter as an apostle to the Jews, was also at work in my ministry as an apostle to the Gentiles. 9 James, Peter[e] and John, those reputed to be pillars, gave me and Barnabas the right hand of fellowship when they recognized the grace given to me. They agreed that we should go to the Gentiles, and they to the Jews. 10 All they asked was that we should continue to remember the poor, the very thing I was eager to do.

---

[a]15 Or *from my mother's womb* [b]18 Greek *Cephas* [c]7 Greek *uncircumcised* [d]7 Greek *circumcised*; also in verses 8 and 9 [e]9 Greek *Cephas*; also in verses 11 and 14

1:13 *persecuted:* Paul had openly persecuted the followers of Jesus (Acts 8:1-3; 22:3-5; 26:9-11) because he believed they were traitors to Jewish traditions (Phil 3:4-6).

1:16 *Gentiles:* Non-Jews. See Acts 9:15; 13:44-48; and the mini-article called "Gentiles," p. 2127.

1:17 *Arabia . . . Damascus:* What Paul calls Arabia was probably Nabatea, south of Syria and east of the Jordan River.

Damascus was an important crossroads of culture and trade in Syria. Paul had his conversion experience on the road to Damascus. See the note at 1:1.

1:18 *Peter:* An apostle of Jesus and important leader in the early church (see Matt 16:13-20).

1:21 *Syria and Cilicia:* Paul was born in Tarsus in Cilicia (Acts 9:11; 22:3), a center of Greek culture.

1:22 *Judea:* The earliest churches began in Jerusalem, in Judea. See the mini-article called "Jerusalem," p. 574 and the map on p. 2473.

2:1 *Fourteen years later:* This visit is most likely the same one described in Acts 15:1-21.

2:1 *Barnabas . . . Titus:* Barnabas was from Cyprus and was a member of the Jewish tribe of Levi. See also Acts 9:27 and 13:1—14:28. Titus was a Gentile Christian who worked with Paul in Corinth (2 Cor 8:3-6) and in Ephesus, and also served in Crete (Titus 1:5).

2:9 *James, Peter and John:* James was Jesus' brother (1:19). For Peter, see the note at 1:18. John is probably the apostle John (Matt 4:21).

1:15,16 Acts 9:3-6; 22:6-10; 26:13-18. **1:18** Acts 9:26-30. **2:1** Acts 11:30; 15:2; Titus 1:5. **2:6** Deut 10:17.

Paul Opposes Peter

11When Peter came to Antioch, I opposed him to his face,
because he was clearly in the wrong. 12Before certain men came
from James, he used to eat with the Gentiles. But when they
arrived, he began to draw back and separate himself from the
Gentiles because he was afraid of those who belonged to the

2:12 *separate himself:* The law said not to eat certain foods or share meals with Gentiles. Peter had earlier agreed that these rules were not required of Gentile believers (Acts 11:1-18), but appears to have changed his position due to pressure.

CIRCUMCISION

"Circumcision" was the ceremony of cutting off the foreskin of a male's penis. This was a common rite among many people in the ancient Near East, though the reasons why are not clear.

Circumcision is first mentioned in the Bible in connection with God's promise to make Abraham's descendants a great nation and to give them a land they could call their own. In return, Abraham and his descendants were to obey God. To show that they were keeping their promise to God, every male descendant of Abraham was to be circumcised (Gen 17:1-14). Even non-Israelite men who wanted to be part of the Israelite people were to be circumcised (Gen 34:21-24). Circumcision became a requirement of the Law of Moses (Lev 12:3). The New Testament reports that both John the Baptist and Jesus were circumcised eight days after being born (Luke 1:59; 2:21).

The prophet Jeremiah warned that the outward practice of circumcision alone was not a true sign of being one of God's people since other nations also practiced circumcision. The important thing was to worship God. His strong words to the people of Judah were, "The whole house of Israel is uncircumcised in heart" (Jer 9:26). Later, he described a final and permanent renewal of the covenant with God that would be written on the people's hearts and minds (Jer 31:31-34). The writer of HEBREWS in the New Testament used Jeremiah's words to back up his message that the first covenant based on God's Law has been replaced by a new covenant brought by Christ (Heb 8).

The practice of circumcision caused arguments and division among early Christians. Some Jewish Christians who had lived according to the Law of Moses felt that they and any Gentile (non-Jewish) follower of Christ should obey all the Jewish laws and practice all the Jewish rituals, including circumcision (Acts 11:1, 2; 21:17-24). Others, especially the apostle Paul, challenged the belief that Gentiles had to be circumcised in order to be acceptable to God. Paul had been circumcised and was a strict follower of the Law of Moses (Phil 3:2-6). But he came to believe that Gentile men could be acceptable to God and become part of God's true people, even if they were not circumcised. Paul argued that being circumcised is worthwhile only if a person can obey the whole Law of Moses. If someone does not obey the whole law, circumcision cannot make that person a real Jew. Like Jeremiah, Paul believed true circumcision is something that happens in the heart (Rom 2:25-29). People are acceptable to God, not by doing everything the law requires, but because they have faith (Rom 3:28; Phil 3:7-9).

Paul also criticized the Jews who insisted that Gentile believers must practice the Jewish rites, such as circumcision (Gal 6:12-14; Phil 3:2). Paul said it was wrong for them to argue that being circumcised was the way to complete what God's Spirit started (Gal 3:1-3). In the end, Paul said simply, "Neither circumcision nor uncircumcision means anything; what counts is a new creation" (Gal 6:15).

circumcision group. [13]The other Jews joined him in his hypocrisy,
so that by their hypocrisy even Barnabas was led astray.
[14]When I saw that they were not acting in line with the truth
of the gospel, I said to Peter in front of them all, “You are a Jew, yet
you live like a Gentile and not like a Jew. How is it, then, that you
force Gentiles to follow Jewish customs?
[15]“We who are Jews by birth and not ‘Gentile sinners’ [16]know
that a man is not justified by observing the law, but by faith in
Jesus Christ. So we, too, have put our faith in Christ Jesus that we
may be justified by faith in Christ and not by observing the law,
because by observing the law no one will be justified.
[17]“If, while we seek to be justified in Christ, it becomes evident that we ourselves are sinners, does that mean that Christ
promotes sin? Absolutely not! [18]If I rebuild what I destroyed, I
prove that I am a lawbreaker. [19]For through the law I died to the
law so that I might live for God. [20]I have been crucified with
Christ and I no longer live, but Christ lives in me. The life I live in
the body, I live by faith in the Son of God, who loved me and gave
himself for me. [21]I do not set aside the grace of God, for if
righteousness could be gained through the law, Christ died for
nothing!”[a]

Faith in Christ Is the Way To Become God’s Children

Paul knows the Law of Moses and he uses this understanding to argue that following the Law of Moses doesn’t bring a person closer to God. What makes you a child of God is having faith in Jesus Christ. All who have this faith are children of Abraham, who was the father of the Jewish people and the first one to receive God’s promises.

Faith or Observance of the Law

3 You foolish Galatians! Who has bewitched you? Before your
very eyes Jesus Christ was clearly portrayed as crucified. [2]I would
like to learn just one thing from you: Did you receive the Spirit by
observing the law, or by believing what you heard? [3]Are you
so foolish? After beginning with the Spirit, are you now trying to
attain your goal by human effort? [4]Have you suffered so much for
nothing—if it really was for nothing? [5]Does God give you his
Spirit and work miracles among you because you observe the law,
or because you believe what you heard?
[6]Consider Abraham: “He believed God, and it was credited
to him as righteousness.”[b] [7]Understand, then, that those who
believe are children of Abraham. [8]The Scripture foresaw that God

[a]**21** Some interpreters end the quotation after verse 14. [b]**6** Gen. 15:6

2:15 *not ‘Gentile sinners’:* Paul describes Gentiles as sinners because they do not have the Law (Rom 2:14; 1 Cor 9:21).

2:16 *not by observing the law, because by observing the law no one will be justified:* This statement was at the heart of Paul’s message, the good news about Christ. The law here refers to the Law of Moses. See also the mini-article called “Law,” p. 1160.

2:19 *through the law I died:* Paul means that the Law of Moses shows people that they are sinners and cannot please God (2:17; see also Rom 3:20). When people discover this, they are then free to put their faith in Jesus. Faith in Jesus Christ gives new life, which is something the Law cannot give (Phil 3:8, 9).

2:20 *I have been crucified with Christ:* Though the cross was a symbol of death to the world, it meant new life to Paul. Christ’s death frees people from the “curse of the law” (3:13). Paul does not mean that he was literally crucified, but that his old life under the law became a new life based on faith in Christ.

3:2 *the Spirit:* Paul mentions the Holy Spirit many times in this letter. See also the mini-article called “Holy Spirit,” p. 2082.

3:3 *attain your goal by human effort:* Some Galatian Christians were apparently undergoing circumcision as a way of trying to finish what God’s Spirit started.

2:16 Ps 143:2; Rom 3:20,22.
3:6 Gen 15:6; Rom 4:3,9-14.

would justify the Gentiles by faith, and announced the gospel in
advance to Abraham: "All nations will be blessed through you."[a]
9 So those who have faith are blessed along with Abraham, the man
of faith.

10 All who rely on observing the law are under a curse, for it
is written: "Cursed is everyone who does not continue to do everything written in the Book of the Law."[b] 11 Clearly no one is justified
before God by the law, because, "The righteous will live by faith."[c]
12 The law is not based on faith; on the contrary, "The man who
does these things will live by them."[d] 13 Christ redeemed us from
the curse of the law by becoming a curse for us, for it is written:
"Cursed is everyone who is hung on a tree."[e] 14 He redeemed us in
order that the blessing given to Abraham might come to the Gentiles through Christ Jesus, so that by faith we might receive the
promise of the Spirit.

The Law and the Promise

15 Brothers, let me take an example from everyday life. Just as
no one can set aside or add to a human covenant that has been
duly established, so it is in this case. 16 The promises were spoken to
Abraham and to his seed. The Scripture does not say "and to
seeds," meaning many people, but "and to your seed,"[f] meaning
one person, who is Christ. 17 What I mean is this: The law, introduced 430 years later, does not set aside the covenant previously
established by God and thus do away with the promise. 18 For if the
inheritance depends on the law, then it no longer depends on a
promise; but God in his grace gave it to Abraham through a
promise.

19 What, then, was the purpose of the law? It was added
because of transgressions until the Seed to whom the promise
referred had come. The law was put into effect through angels by
a mediator. 20 A mediator, however, does not represent just one
party; but God is one.

21 Is the law, therefore, opposed to the promises of God?
Absolutely not! For if a law had been given that could impart life,
then righteousness would certainly have come by the law. 22 But the
Scripture declares that the whole world is a prisoner of sin, so that
what was promised, being given through faith in Jesus Christ,
might be given to those who believe.

23 Before this faith came, we were held prisoners by the law,
locked up until faith should be revealed. 24 So the law was put in
charge to lead us to Christ[g] that we might be justified by faith.
25 Now that faith has come, we are no longer under the supervision
of the law.

---

[a] 8 Gen. 12:3; 18:18; 22:18 [b] 10 Deut. 27:26 [c] 11 Hab. 2:4 [d] 12 Lev. 18:5
[e] 13 Deut. 21:23 [f] 16 Gen. 12:7; 13:15; 24:7 [g] 24 Or *charge until Christ came*

3:7 *children of Abraham:* God chose Abraham, and so it was believed that anyone who was a descendant of Abraham was also a child of God. Shown here are the souls of the righteous in Abraham's bosom from a twelfth-century Bible.

3:13 *the curse of the law:* Paul argues that God's Law is a curse because no one can follow it perfectly. Jesus took the place of all people and died under a curse, so that all who trust in him would be freed from the curse of the law.

3:16 *spoken to Abraham and to his seed:* The Greek word for "seed" means "descendant," and can mean one or many descendants. In this verse Paul uses it to mean "Christ."

3:17 *The law, introduced 430 years later:* God gave the Law to Moses and the Israelite people centuries after giving his promises to Abraham.

3:19 *purpose of the law:* See the note at 2:16.

3:19 *the Seed:* Meaning Jesus Christ. See the note at 3:16.

3:19 *law was put into effect through angels:* No Scripture passage says this directly, but it was believed according to Jewish tradition, that angels played a role in giving the law at Sinai (Deut 33:2).

3:10 Deut 27:26. **3:11** Hab 2:4. **3:12** Lev 18:4,5. **3:13** Deut 21:23. **3:17** Exod 12:40. **3:18** Rom 4:14.

3:27 *baptized:* Water is used in baptism to show how a person is made new and becomes part of God's family. See also the mini-article called "Baptism," p. 1976.

4:1 *heir is a child . . . slave:* Paul compares children to slaves because they had to obey their parents in everything until their parents decided they were old enough to be on their own.

Sons of God

[26]You are all sons of God through faith in Christ Jesus, [27]for
all of you who were baptized into Christ have clothed yourselves
with Christ. [28]There is neither Jew nor Greek, slave nor free, male
nor female, for you are all one in Christ Jesus. [29]If you belong to
Christ, then you are Abraham's seed, and heirs according to
the promise.

4 What I am saying is that as long as the heir is a child, he is
no different from a slave, although he owns the whole estate. [2]He
is subject to guardians and trustees until the time set by his father.
[3]So also, when we were children, we were in slavery under the basic
principles of the world. [4]But when the time had fully come, God
sent his Son, born of a woman, born under law, [5]to redeem those
under law, that we might receive the full rights of sons. [6]Because
you are sons, God sent the Spirit of his Son into our hearts, the
Spirit who calls out, "*Abba*,[a] Father." [7]So you are no longer a slave,
but a son; and since you are a son, God has made you also an heir.

[a]**6** Aramaic for *Father*

ABRAHAM

The list of the descendants of Noah's sons comes to an end (Gen 11:26) with Abram ("exalted father"). He later became known as Abraham ("father of many"). God told Abram (Gen 12:1-3) to move from his home in Ur of the Chaldeans (in southern Mesopotamia) to the land of Canaan (see the map on p. 2462). God promised that his family would become "a great nation" with a special relationship to God. And all nations would be blessed because of Abraham and his wife Sarah and their descendants (Gen 12:1-3; 15:1-21). So Abraham went with Sarah and his nephew Lot. After passing through places that would be important in the later history of Israel (Shechem and Bethel; Gen 12:4-9) and after a long stay in Egypt, they settled in the land of Canaan. Lot settled east of the Jordan River, and Abraham settled to the west, where he lived by the great trees of Mamre near Hebron (Gen 13).

God promised Abraham that he would have many descendants, even though he had no son (Gen 15). Finally, when Abraham was a hundred years old, Sarah bore him a son. This son was named Isaac, meaning "he laughs"—a pun on the fact that both Abraham and Sarah laughed at the idea that they would have a child in their old age (Gen 17:17-19; 18:9-15). Abraham trusted God's promise and the child was born. Isaac was circumcised as a sign of Abraham's special relationship with God (Gen 21:1-7). Abraham's trust in God continued even when God told him to kill Isaac as a sacrifice. But God spared Isaac and once again promised Abraham that his numerous descendants would be a blessing to all the nations of the earth (Gen 22:1-19).

In the New Testament, in addition to being called the "father" of all who have genuine faith (Rom 4:16,17), Abraham is frequently given as an example of human trust in the promises of God (Acts 7:2-8; Rom 4:1-25; Gal 3:1-29; Heb 6:13-15; 7:1-10; 11:8-19).

Paul's Concern for the Galatians

[8]Formerly, when you did not know God, you were slaves to those who by nature are not gods. [9]But now that you know God—or rather are known by God—how is it that you are turning back to those weak and miserable principles? Do you wish to be enslaved by them all over again? [10]You are observing special days and months and seasons and years! [11]I fear for you, that somehow I have wasted my efforts on you.

[12]I plead with you, brothers, become like me, for I became like you. You have done me no wrong. [13]As you know, it was because of an illness that I first preached the gospel to you. [14]Even though my illness was a trial to you, you did not treat me with contempt or scorn. Instead, you welcomed me as if I were an angel of God, as if I were Christ Jesus himself. [15]What has happened to all your joy? I can testify that, if you could have done so, you would have torn out your eyes and given them to me. [16]Have I now become your enemy by telling you the truth?

[17]Those people are zealous to win you over, but for no good. What they want is to alienate you ⌞from us⌟, so that you may be zealous for them. [18]It is fine to be zealous, provided the purpose is good, and to be so always and not just when I am with you. [19]My dear children, for whom I am again in the pains of childbirth until Christ is formed in you, [20]how I wish I could be with you now and change my tone, because I am perplexed about you!

Hagar and Sarah

[21]Tell me, you who want to be under the law, are you not aware of what the law says? [22]For it is written that Abraham had two sons, one by the slave woman and the other by the free woman. [23]His son by the slave woman was born in the ordinary way; but his son by the free woman was born as the result of a promise.

[24]These things may be taken figuratively, for the women represent two covenants. One covenant is from Mount Sinai and bears children who are to be slaves: This is Hagar. [25]Now Hagar stands for Mount Sinai in Arabia and corresponds to the present city of Jerusalem, because she is in slavery with her children. [26]But the Jerusalem that is above is free, and she is our mother. [27]For it is written:

"Be glad, O barren woman,
 who bears no children;
break forth and cry aloud,
 you who have no labor pains;
because more are the children of the desolate woman
 than of her who has a husband."[a]

[a]27 Isaiah 54:1

4:2 *subject to guardians and trustees:* A guardian was given the responsibility of taking care of a child up to age fourteen. A trustee watched over the finances of a young man until he was twenty-five. The carving shown here of a young child and his teacher is from a second century Roman stone coffin (sarcophagus).

4:6 *God sent the Spirit of his Son into our hearts:* In Bible times, the heart was considered the place where the human will was located. If Christ's Spirit is present in someone's heart, that person will have the power to live according to God's will.

4:6 *"Abba, Father":* The Greek word translated as "Father" is from the Aramaic word "Abba," which is like the English "Papa" or "Daddy."

4:9 *weak and miserable principles:* These powers may also be spirits that were believed to control human lives and were connected to the movements of the stars. These powers were "weak and miserable" when it came to giving people any help.

4:14,15 *my illness . . . your eyes:* Paul was sick when he first came to Galatia, which here sounds like it may have been some kind of eye disease.

4:22 *Abraham had two sons:* Because he didn't believe he could have a son by his wife Sarah, Abraham first had a son by Hagar, Sarah's slave. Hagar's son was named Ishmael (Gen 16:1-16). Later Sarah and Abraham had a child named Isaac. He was the child God had promised, and his descendants became the people of Israel. Anyone who follows the law in order to be saved is a slave like Hagar and her son. But those who have faith in Christ in order to be saved are like the descendants of Sarah, because she was the mother of the child born according to God's promise.

By faith we eagerly await through the Spirit the righteousness for which we hope.
Gal 5:5

4:29,30 *the son born in the ordinary way:* Paul is speaking of Ishmael (Gen 21:9,10). Paul is encouraging the Galatian Christians to quit relying on the law, which does not offer any inheritance.

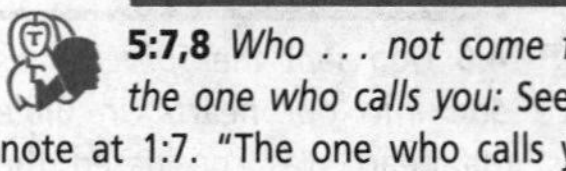

5:7,8 *Who . . . not come from the one who calls you:* See the note at 1:7. "The one who calls you" refers to God (1:6).

5:9 *A little yeast:* Yeast is a tiny yellowish fungus that is added to dough to make it rise. Paul means that one troublemaker or one small group can affect everyone in the Galatian churches.

5:11 *preaching circumcision:* Apparently the troublemakers were claiming that Paul approved of circumcision in order to become a believer, but he denies it.

5:12 *go the whole way and emasculate themselves:* See the mini-article called "Circumcision," p. 2251. Paul uses exaggeration to make his point.

5:9 1 Cor 5:6. **5:14** Lev 19:18; Matt 7:12; Mark 12:29-31.

[28]Now you, brothers, like Isaac, are children of promise. [29]At
that time the son born in the ordinary way persecuted the son
born by the power of the Spirit. It is the same now. [30]But what
does the Scripture say? "Get rid of the slave woman and her son,
for the slave woman's son will never share in the inheritance with
the free woman's son."[a] [31]Therefore, brothers, we are not children
of the slave woman, but of the free woman.

Christ Gives Freedom, and the Spirit Guides

Paul reminds the Galatians that Christ sets them free from the Law of Moses. Those who have faith in Christ are guided by the Holy Spirit who helps them live as children of God (5:22-26) and not to be controlled by evil desires (5:19-21).

Freedom in Christ

5 It is for freedom that Christ has set us free. Stand firm, then,
and do not let yourselves be burdened again by a yoke of slavery.
[2]Mark my words! I, Paul, tell you that if you let yourselves
be circumcised, Christ will be of no value to you at all. [3]Again I
declare to every man who lets himself be circumcised that he is
obligated to obey the whole law. [4]You who are trying to be justified
by law have been alienated from Christ; you have fallen away from
grace. [5]But by faith we eagerly await through the Spirit the righteousness for which we hope. [6]For in Christ Jesus neither circumcision nor uncircumcision has any value. The only thing that
counts is faith expressing itself through love.
[7]You were running a good race. Who cut in on you and kept
you from obeying the truth? [8]That kind of persuasion does not
come from the one who calls you. [9]"A little yeast works through the
whole batch of dough." [10]I am confident in the Lord that you will
take no other view. The one who is throwing you into confusion will
pay the penalty, whoever he may be. [11]Brothers, if I am still preaching circumcision, why am I still being persecuted? In that case the
offense of the cross has been abolished. [12]As for those agitators, I
wish they would go the whole way and emasculate themselves!
[13]You, my brothers, were called to be free. But do not use
your freedom to indulge the sinful nature[b]; rather, serve one
another in love. [14]The entire law is summed up in a single command: "Love your neighbor as yourself."[c] [15]If you keep on biting
and devouring each other, watch out or you will be destroyed by
each other.

[a]**30** Gen. 21:10 [b]**13** Or *the flesh*; also in verses 16, 17, 19 and 24
[c]**14** Lev. 19:18

Life by the Spirit

[16]So I say, live by the Spirit, and you will not gratify the
desires of the sinful nature. [17]For the sinful nature desires what is
contrary to the Spirit, and the Spirit what is contrary to the sinful
nature. They are in conflict with each other, so that you do not
do what you want. [18]But if you are led by the Spirit, you are not
under law.

[19]The acts of the sinful nature are obvious: sexual immorality, impurity and debauchery; [20]idolatry and witchcraft; hatred,
discord, jealousy, fits of rage, selfish ambition, dissensions, factions
[21]and envy; drunkenness, orgies, and the like. I warn you, as I did
before, that those who live like this will not inherit the kingdom
of God.

5:16 *live by the Spirit:* See the note at 3:2.

5:18 *not under law:* See the note at 2:16. Paul sounds as if he is saying that selfish desires and the Law of Moses are equally bad things. What he means is that evil selfish desires lead to death. And those who think that they can save themselves from death by following the Law of Moses are also wrong.

5:20 *idolatry and witchcraft:* At various points in their history, some Jewish people stopped worshiping the God of Israel and worshiped idols instead (Isa 44:1-20). Gentiles (including Greeks, Romans, and the Galatians) worshiped many different gods and goddesses. See the chart called "Greek and Roman Gods and Goddesses," p. 2136. Witchcraft here may refer to mixing potions or drugs to use for magical purposes.

5:21 *kingdom of God:* God's rule over people, both in this life and in the next.

5:17 Rom 7:15-23.

Decorative Ethiopian Crosses, various unknown artists, late nineteenth century. Because crucifixion was the most shameful form of execution in the Roman world, Christians did not use the cross as a symbol of their faith until centuries after Christ's death. Paul wrote to Christ's followers in Galatia, "May I never boast except in the cross of our Lord Jesus Christ" (see 6:14). Today, the cross is the most commonly recognized symbol of Christianity. For symbols that were more commonly used by the early church, see the illustration on p. 2130.

The fruit of the Spirit is love, joy, peace, patience, kindness, goodness, faithfulness, gentleness and self-control.
Gal 5:22,23

[22]But the fruit of the Spirit is love, joy, peace, patience, kindness, goodness, faithfulness, [23]gentleness and self-control. Against such things there is no law. [24]Those who belong to Christ Jesus have crucified the sinful nature with its passions and desires. [25]Since we live by the Spirit, let us keep in step with the Spirit. [26]Let us not become conceited, provoking and envying each other.

Doing Good to All

6 Brothers, if someone is caught in a sin, you who are spiritual should restore him gently. But watch yourself, or you also may be tempted. [2]Carry each other's burdens, and in this way you will fulfill the law of Christ. [3]If anyone thinks he is something when he is nothing, he deceives himself. [4]Each one should test his own actions. Then he can take pride in himself, without comparing himself to somebody else, [5]for each one should carry his own load.

[6]Anyone who receives instruction in the word must share all good things with his instructor.

[7]Do not be deceived: God cannot be mocked. A man reaps what he sows. [8]The one who sows to please his sinful nature, from that nature[a] will reap destruction; the one who sows to please the Spirit, from the Spirit will reap eternal life. [9]Let us not become weary in doing good, for at the proper time we will reap a harvest if we do not give up. [10]Therefore, as we have opportunity, let us do good to all people, especially to those who belong to the family of believers.

5:25 *we live by the Spirit:* See the note at 3:2. The Spirit leads to life. The law cannot give life. It can only make people aware of their sins.

6:1 *caught in a sin:* People sin when they turn their backs on God and disobey God's Law. See the mini-article called "Sin," p. 2181.

6:2 *the law of Christ:* The law of Christ is to love one another as Christ has loved human beings (John 13:34; 1 Cor 9:21; 1 John 2:7-11; 4:10-12). Followers of Christ love one another because they have been accepted by God and have received God's Spirit, not because they want to win God's approval.

a8 Or *his flesh, from the flesh*

QUESTIONS ABOUT GALATIANS

1. How were certain people trying to make the Galatians turn away from the gospel about Christ? (1:7; 3:1-14; 5:1-15; 6:12-15) Why was this a problem?
2. Both Peter and Paul were respected leaders in the early church. Describe in your own words the conflict Paul had with Peter. (2:11-21) What did Peter do that upset Paul? What did Paul say to correct Peter? How do leaders in churches today handle conflicts and differences of opinion?
3. What do you think Paul means when he says that "Christ redeemed us from the curse of the law"? (3:13) What does this mean for the way Christians are to live?
4. Paul says that "Christ has set us free." (5:1) In what ways are Christians free? What does this kind of freedom include? What, if anything, are its limits?
5. What does Paul mean when he says, "A man reaps what he sows"? (6:7) Think about your life a year from now . . . five years from now. How do the decisions you make today affect your future?
6. Compare the list in 5:19-21 with the list in 5:22,23. Where do the items in each list come from? What does Paul mean when he says that "we live by the Spirit"? (5:25)

Final Warnings

Paul concludes with some more strong words about the people who are trying to insist that the male Gentile Christians in Galatia be circumcised. He reminds the Galatians once more that the most important thing for a Christian is to die to sin and to be made a new person by faith in Christ.

Not Circumcision but a New Creation

11 See what large letters I use as I write to you with my own
hand!

12 Those who want to make a good impression outwardly are
trying to compel you to be circumcised. The only reason they do
this is to avoid being persecuted for the cross of Christ. 13 Not even
those who are circumcised obey the law, yet they want you to be
circumcised that they may boast about your flesh. 14 May I never
boast except in the cross of our Lord Jesus Christ, through which[a]
the world has been crucified to me, and I to the world. 15 Neither
circumcision nor uncircumcision means anything; what counts is
a new creation. 16 Peace and mercy to all who follow this rule, even
to the Israel of God.

17 Finally, let no one cause me trouble, for I bear on my body
the marks of Jesus.

18 The grace of our Lord Jesus Christ be with your spirit,
brothers. Amen.

---

a14 Or *whom*

6:8 *reap destruction . . . reap eternal life:* Many places in the New Testament talk about eternal life and eternal punishment (heaven and hell). See the mini-articles called "Eternal Life," p. 2072, "Heaven," p. 1420, and "Hell," p. 1944.

6:11 *See what large letters:* See the note at 4:14,15.

6:12 *compel you to be circumcised:* See the note at 1:7.

6:14 *the world has been crucified to me:* For Paul, the "world" stands for those people and things that are opposed to God and God's purposes.

6:17 *the marks:* In Greek, this word also means the kind of scars that were made to mark a slave or an animal, which are also called "brands." Paul says he is physically branded by scars that he received from those who persecuted him because of his belief in Jesus Christ. In 2 Corinthians 11:23-26 Paul describes how he had been beaten many times in the past. These beatings would have produced the scars he describes in this verse.

EPHESIANS

Why is being part of a team, a group, or a family so important? Read this letter to the Ephesians to find out how everyone who has faith in Christ Jesus is part of the same "body" and belongs to God's family.

1:1 *Paul, an apostle of Christ Jesus:* Paul was also known by his Jewish name, Saul (Acts 7:57—8:3; 9:1-30; 13:1-9). See also the mini-article called "Paul (Saul) of Tarsus," p. 2177.

In EPHESIANS, "apostle" means someone chosen by God to spread the message about Jesus Christ. The word "Christ" is from the Greek word *christos*, which means "Messiah" or "chosen one." For more, see the mini-article called "Messiah (Chosen One)," p. 1124.

1:1 *saints:* The Greek word translated here as "saints" means those who have been set apart as God's holy people.

1:1 *Ephesus:* Ephesus had once been a major seaport on the Aegean Sea, but by the time of Paul the harbor had filled in with muddy silt. Still, it was a beautiful city with the magnificent Temple of Artemis, where there was a famous meteorite that the goddess was supposed to have sent (Acts 19:35). Hundreds of prostitutes served at this temple, and local businesses sold all kinds of trinkets that honored Artemis (Acts 19:23-41). The city also had large theaters, a stadium for gladiator contests, and libraries. Paul worked in Ephesus for about three years (Acts 19:10; 20:31). A generation later, the author of REVELATION wrote that the Ephesian Christians had lost their love for Christ (Rev 2:1-7).

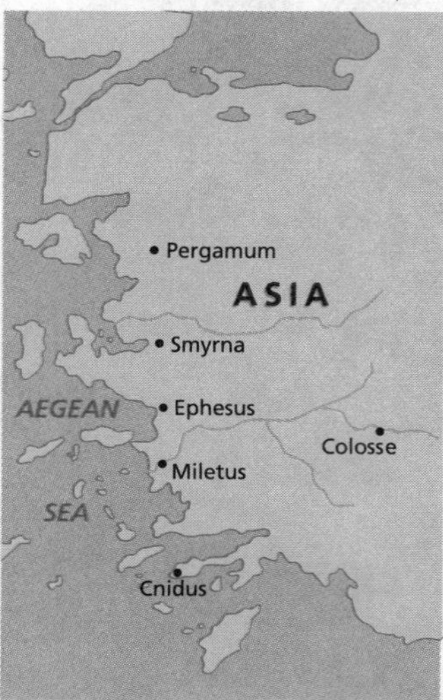

What makes Ephesians special?

This letter summarizes many of the important teachings found in the letters of the apostle Paul. It begins by describing how God raised Christ, who now rules beside God in heaven. Then the letter tells how Christ has brought both Gentiles and Jews together since he "has destroyed the barrier, the dividing wall of hostility" that separated them (2:14). Those who have faith in Jesus have been chosen by God's Spirit to be part of one body, which is the church. This body has "one Lord, one faith, one baptism" (4:5). Christ has chosen different people in the church to have different gifts as apostles, prophets, evangelists, pastors, and teachers (4:11). The last two and a half chapters of the letter offer practical instructions for living as God's people. This includes a description of the spiritual "armor" that God gives so the people of God can withstand the devil and the rulers of darkness (6:10-17).

Why was Ephesians written?

Many of Paul's letters give clues about why Paul wrote them. EPHESIANS, however, does not mention any particular questions or issues present among the members of the church in Ephesus. Without such a clue, it is hard to say exactly why the letter was written. However, Acts 19,20 may offer a clue. Those chapters tell about how Paul was effective at first when he told people in Ephesus about Jesus Christ. Later, the artisans who profited from producing idols related to the worship of Artemis, the favorite goddess in Ephesus, protested Paul's message. The local leader refused to punish Paul when a riot nearly broke out, but it seemed best for Paul to leave the city. Later, he met the leaders of the Ephesian church and gave them courage to face the problems they would meet. The biggest difficulty among the Ephesian followers was that some members were trying to split up the followers into different groups instead of following the message Paul had taught them. So Paul addresses the problem of unity within the church as one of the main concerns in EPHESIANS.

What's the story behind the scene?

Many ancient manuscripts say that this letter was addressed to "the saints in Ephesus." But some manuscripts do not name the Ephesians as the people who were to receive the letter. It may be that the letter was meant to be passed among a number of churches in Asia Minor. The Greek writing style and vocabulary used in EPHESIANS is somewhat different from those used in Paul's other letters. Also, Paul spent about three years in Ephesus trying to start a congregation (Acts 18:19-21; 19:1-20; 20:17-38), but the author and receivers of this letter (at least some of the receivers if this was intended to be a circular letter) don't seem to have met each other (1:15). Such things have led scholars to form different opinions about who wrote this letter and when it was written. But because of its similarities to Paul's writings, especially his letter to the Colossians, it has been linked with the apostle.

How is Ephesians constructed?

This letter has a brief greeting (1:1,2) and ending (6:21-24). In between are general teachings about the Christian faith and instructions for how the followers of Christ should live as God's people. The letter can be outlined in this way:

Greetings, blessings, and prayers (1:1-23)

Christ brings unity and peace to the people of God (2:1—3:21)

Living as the body of Christ, the children of light (4:1—6:24)

Greetings, Blessings, and Prayers

Paul identifies himself, greets the Ephesians, and praises God because Jesus Christ sacrificed his life's blood in order to bring about forgiveness of sins. Jesus also brought the good news about how people can be saved. Paul prays that the Holy Spirit will help the followers in Ephesus be wise and understand what it means to know God.

1 Paul, an apostle of Christ Jesus by the will of God,

To the saints in Ephesus,[a] the faithful[b] in Christ Jesus:

2 Grace and peace to you from God our Father and the Lord
Jesus Christ.

Spiritual Blessings in Christ

3 Praise be to the God and Father of our Lord Jesus Christ,
who has blessed us in the heavenly realms with every spiritual
blessing in Christ. 4 For he chose us in him before the creation of
the world to be holy and blameless in his sight. In love 5 he[c] predestined us to be adopted as his sons through Jesus Christ, in
accordance with his pleasure and will— 6 to the praise of his
glorious grace, which he has freely given us in the One he loves.
7 In him we have redemption through his blood, the forgiveness of
sins, in accordance with the riches of God's grace 8 that he lavished
on us with all wisdom and understanding. 9 And he[d] made known

[a] 1 Some early manuscripts do not have *in Ephesus.* [b] 1 Or *believers who are*
[c] 4,5 Or *sight in love.* 5 *He* [d] 8,9 Or *us. With all wisdom and understanding,* 9 *he*

1:2 *God our Father:* Jesus often referred to God as "Father" (see John 14, for example). Paul uses this same term in many of his letters to describe God (Rom 1:7; 1 Cor 1:3; Gal 1:2,3; Phil 1:2).

1:3 *Lord:* The Greek word for "lord" is *kyrios,* which may simply mean "master," or "sir." See also the mini-article called "Lord (Title for Jesus)," p. 2106.

1:3 *heavenly realms . . . spiritual blessing:* The spiritual blessings include forgiveness (1:7,8), wisdom and revelation (1:17), faith (2:8), and special gifts to be used to serve God and the church (4:11,12). See also 6:10-17.

When Paul says that Christ is in the heavenly realms, he is making it clear that Christ rules and is present in all things (1:20; 2:6; 4:10).

1:4 *chose us in him before the creation of the world:* When Christ chose people to be part of God's family, it was part of God's plan from the beginning.

1:6 *the One he loves:* Here, this refers to Jesus Christ.

1:7,8 *redemption through his blood, the forgiveness of sins:* The Greek word translated "redemption" has the meaning of paying a debt. Jesus bought forgiveness for all people by paying for it with his blood. See also Rom 3:24-26; 1 Cor 1:30; and Heb 9:15. Sin occurs when people turn away from God and disobey God's Law. Forgiveness removes the sin and allows people to turn back to God and become acceptable to God once again. See the mini-article called "Redeemer (Redemption)," p. 995.

1:1 Acts 18:19-21; 19:1.
1:7,8 Col 1:14.

1:9 *mystery:* The Greek word used here is *mysterion,* which means "secret." Many pagan mystery religions of the ancient world involved secret rites to welcome new members. In contrast, the good news about Jesus is not for a select few, but for everyone.

1:18 *the eyes of your heart may be enlightened:* In the Bible, light is used to describe God or God's Word (Ps 119:105; John 1:3,4; 1 John 1:5). The followers of Jesus are also called "children of light" (5:8).

1:22,23 *church . . . his body:* Christ is the head of the church, which is called the body of Christ (Rom 12:5; 1 Cor 12:27; Col 1:17,18).

2:1 *sins:* See the note at 1:7,8. Sin leads to separation from God, which in turn leads to death (Rom 5:12; 6:23).

2:2 *world . . . ruler:* Here, the "world" stands for all the forces that are against God. See also John 15:18,19. The devil, sometimes called Satan, is the ruler of these forces.

2:6 *raised us:* Paul may be talking about the new life that comes from being saved.

2:11 *Gentiles:* See the mini-article called "Gentiles," p. 2127.

2:11 *circumcision:* See the mini-article called "Circumcision," p. 2251.

1:20 Ps 110:1. **1:22** Ps 8:6; 1 Cor 15:27,28; Phil 3:20,21; Heb 2:8. **2:1-5** Col 2:13.

to us the mystery of his will according to his good pleasure, which
he purposed in Christ, 10 to be put into effect when the times will
have reached their fulfillment—to bring all things in heaven and
on earth together under one head, even Christ.
11 In him we were also chosen,[a] having been predestined
according to the plan of him who works out everything in con-
formity with the purpose of his will, 12 in order that we, who were
the first to hope in Christ, might be for the praise of his glory.
13 And you also were included in Christ when you heard the word
of truth, the gospel of your salvation. Having believed, you were
marked in him with a seal, the promised Holy Spirit, 14 who is a
deposit guaranteeing our inheritance until the redemption of
those who are God's possession—to the praise of his glory.

Thanksgiving and Prayer

15 For this reason, ever since I heard about your faith in the
Lord Jesus and your love for all the saints, 16 I have not stopped giving thanks for you, remembering you in my prayers. 17 I keep asking
that the God of our Lord Jesus Christ, the glorious Father, may give
you the Spirit[b] of wisdom and revelation, so that you may know him
better. 18 I pray also that the eyes of your heart may be enlightened in
order that you may know the hope to which he has called you, the
riches of his glorious inheritance in the saints, 19 and his incompara-
bly great power for us who believe. That power is like the working of
his mighty strength, 20 which he exerted in Christ when he raised
him from the dead and seated him at his right hand in the heavenly realms, 21 far above all rule and authority, power and dominion,
and every title that can be given, not only in the present age but also
in the one to come. 22 And God placed all things under his feet and
appointed him to be head over everything for the church, 23 which is
his body, the fullness of him who fills everything in every way.

Christ Brings Unity and Peace to the People of God

God saves all who have faith in Christ who breaks down the walls that separate Jews and Gentiles. All who believe in Jesus are united in one body. Paul describes his mission to bring the gospel to the Gentiles, and he prays that the power of Christ will be at work in the church to help its members "do immeasurably more than all we ask or imagine."

Made Alive in Christ

2 As for you, you were dead in your transgressions and sins, 2 in
which you used to live when you followed the ways of this world

[a]11 Or *were made heirs* [b]17 Or *a spirit*

and of the ruler of the kingdom of the air, the spirit who is now at
work in those who are disobedient. 3All of us also lived among
them at one time, gratifying the cravings of our sinful nature[a] and
following its desires and thoughts. Like the rest, we were by nature
objects of wrath. 4But because of his great love for us, God, who is
rich in mercy, 5made us alive with Christ even when we were dead
in transgressions—it is by grace you have been saved. 6And God
raised us up with Christ and seated us with him in the heavenly
realms in Christ Jesus, 7in order that in the coming ages he might
show the incomparable riches of his grace, expressed in his kindness to us in Christ Jesus. 8For it is by grace you have been saved,
through faith—and this not from yourselves, it is the gift of God—
9not by works, so that no one can boast. 10For we are God's work-
manship, created in Christ Jesus to do good works, which God
prepared in advance for us to do.

One in Christ

11Therefore, remember that formerly you who are Gentiles
by birth and called "uncircumcised" by those who call themselves
"the circumcision" (that done in the body by the hands of men)—
12remember that at that time you were separate from Christ,
excluded from citizenship in Israel and foreigners to the covenants
of the promise, without hope and without God in the world. 13But
now in Christ Jesus you who once were far away have been
brought near through the blood of Christ.

14For he himself is our peace, who has made the two one and
has destroyed the barrier, the dividing wall of hostility, 15by abolishing in his flesh the law with its commandments and regulations.
His purpose was to create in himself one new man out of the two,
thus making peace, 16and in this one body to reconcile both of
them to God through the cross, by which he put to death their
hostility. 17He came and preached peace to you who were far away
and peace to those who were near. 18For through him we both have
access to the Father by one Spirit.

19Consequently, you are no longer foreigners and aliens, but
fellow citizens with God's people and members of God's household, 20built on the foundation of the apostles and prophets, with
Christ Jesus himself as the chief cornerstone. 21In him the whole
building is joined together and rises to become a holy temple in
the Lord. 22And in him you too are being built together to become
a dwelling in which God lives by his Spirit.

Paul the Preacher to the Gentiles

3 For this reason I, Paul, the prisoner of Christ Jesus for the sake
of you Gentiles—

[a]3 Or *our flesh*

2:14 *has made the two one:* The "two" refers to Gentiles and Jews. Some Jews interpreted the Law of Moses to mean that they should have no contact with Gentiles. Christ gave his life to bring Jews and Gentiles together in God's family (2:15).

2:15 *abolishing . . . law:* Even though the law that God gave was holy, it could not save anyone. It could only point out sin (Rom 3:20; 7:7-12; Gal 3:12-14; 2:15,16).

2:16 *cross:* This refers to the way Jesus was put to death. See Matt 27:31-54 and the mini-article called "Crucifixion," p. 1914.

2:18 *Father . . . Spirit:* See the note at 1:2 and the mini-article called "Holy Spirit," p. 2082.

2:20 *apostles and prophets:* The apostles were those special messengers chosen to bring the good news to all people. The prophets may be those who spoke God's message to the people of Israel from 800 to 400 B.C. Or it may refer to those in the church who have received the gift of prophecy from the Holy Spirit (3:5; 4:11; see also 1 Cor 12:7-11).

2:21 *temple:* The temple was the central place of God's presence among the people of Israel (2 Chr 5:11—6:2; Hab 2:20). Paul says that those who have been given the Holy Spirit now form God's holy temple (1 Cor 3:16,17).

3:1 *prisoner:* This may refer to Paul's own imprisonment by Roman authorities. Or it may refer to how Christ has captured Paul's mind and heart so he could preach to the Gentiles (Acts 9:15,16).

2:9 Rom 3:27; 4:2; 1 Cor 1:29-31.
2:17 Isa 57:19.

3:4 *mystery of Christ:* See Col 1:26,27 and the note at 1:9.

3:6 *together:* By repeating this word, Paul emphasizes an important point of EPHESIANS: the coming unity of all things in Christ. (See 1:9,10.)

3:2 Acts 9:1-22; Rom 1:5; Gal 1:11-24.

[2]Surely you have heard about the administration of God's
grace that was given to me for you, [3]that is, the mystery made
known to me by revelation, as I have already written briefly. [4]In
reading this, then, you will be able to understand my insight into
the mystery of Christ, [5]which was not made known to men in other
generations as it has now been revealed by the Spirit to God's holy
apostles and prophets. [6]This mystery is that through the gospel the
Gentiles are heirs together with Israel, members together of one
body, and sharers together in the promise in Christ Jesus.

[7]I became a servant of this gospel by the gift of God's grace
given me through the working of his power. [8]Although I am less
than the least of all God's people, this grace was given me: to
preach to the Gentiles the unsearchable riches of Christ, [9]and to
make plain to everyone the administration of this mystery, which
for ages past was kept hidden in God, who created all things. [10]His
intent was that now, through the church, the manifold wisdom of
God should be made known to the rulers and authorities in the
heavenly realms, [11]according to his eternal purpose which he
accomplished in Christ Jesus our Lord. [12]In him and through faith
in him we may approach God with freedom and confidence. [13]I
ask you, therefore, not to be discouraged because of my sufferings
for you, which are your glory.

CHURCH

In the Bible, the Greek word translated as "church" (*ekklesia*) means an assembly or gathering of people who believe in the gospel of Christ Jesus. They have been shown God's purpose and have been chosen to do God's will in the world. The church belongs to Jesus the Lord, who is its "head" (Eph 1:22; Col 1:18). The Greek word for Lord is *kyrios*, so the church is also called *kyriakon*, which means "belonging to the Lord." *Kyriakon* is the basis of the English word "church."

The church is pictured in various ways in the New Testament. It is the obedient people of God in MATTHEW. Paul argues in ROMANS and GALATIANS that the church is a new people, and not the same as the chosen people of God who, in the Jewish Scriptures (Old Testament) were required to obey the Law of Moses. He also refers to the church as the "body of Christ" (1 Cor 12:27-31). In LUKE and ACTS the most important work of the followers of Christ is to reach out to the whole world (Acts 1:8), regardless of race or culture. The people who make up the church are described in 1 PETER as "a chosen people, a royal priesthood, a holy nation, a people belonging to God" (1 Pet 2:9; see also Exod 19:5,6). In JOHN the church is described as the flock belonging to the Good Shepherd (John 10:16) and as branches of Jesus, the true vine (John 15:1-16).

After the first generation of the apostles was gone, the church gradually became more structured in its organization, with clear leadership roles and rules for the behavior of its members clearly defined. Descriptions of this organization begin to appear in letters like EPHESIANS, 1 and 2 TIMOTHY, and TITUS, and in the writings of second-century church leaders known as the Apostolic Fathers.

A Prayer for the Ephesians

[14]For this reason I kneel before the Father, [15]from whom his whole family[a] in heaven and on earth derives its name. [16]I pray that out of his glorious riches he may strengthen you with power through his Spirit in your inner being, [17]so that Christ may dwell in your hearts through faith. And I pray that you, being rooted and established in love, [18]may have power, together with all the saints, to grasp how wide and long and high and deep is the love of Christ, [19]and to know this love that surpasses knowledge—that you may be filled to the measure of all the fullness of God.

[20]Now to him who is able to do immeasurably more than all we ask or imagine, according to his power that is at work within us, [21]to him be glory in the church and in Christ Jesus throughout all generations, for ever and ever! Amen.

Living as the Body of Christ, the Children of Light

Paul encourages the believers in Ephesus to live in unity and to serve the whole body of Christ, the church, by using the special gifts the Holy Spirit has given them. He also gives instruction about various relationships and for fighting evil as children of the light.

Unity in the Body of Christ

4 As a prisoner for the Lord, then, I urge you to live a life worthy of the calling you have received. [2]Be completely humble and gentle; be patient, bearing with one another in love. [3]Make every effort to keep the unity of the Spirit through the bond of peace. [4]There is one body and one Spirit— just as you were called to one hope when you were called— [5]one Lord, one faith, one baptism; [6]one God and Father of all, who is over all and through all and in all.

[7]But to each one of us grace has been given as Christ apportioned it. [8]This is why it[b] says:

> "When he ascended on high,
> he led captives in his train
> and gave gifts to men."[c]

[9](What does "he ascended" mean except that he also descended to the lower, earthly regions[d]? [10]He who descended is the very one who ascended higher than all the heavens, in order to fill the whole universe.) [11]It was he who gave some to be apostles, some to be prophets, some to be evangelists, and some to be pastors and

[a]**15** Or *whom all fatherhood* [b]**8** Or *God* [c]**8** Psalm 68:18 [d]**9** Or *the depths of the earth*

3:18 *grasp how wide . . . deep is the love of Christ:* This may refer to God's love or wisdom, or to the meaning of the cross. It may also refer directly to Christ's love.

4:1 *prisoner for the Lord:* See the note at 3:1.

4:4-6 *one body . . . one God and Father of all:* The body is the church (see the note at 1:22,23). EPHESIANS gives seven different examples of how the followers of Christ are unified. They are part of one body (2:16; 4:4), follow one Spirit (2:18), and share one hope (1:18). They claim one Lord (1:3; 4:5), one faith, and one baptism. See also the mini-article called "Baptism," p. 1976. The seventh way the followers of Christ are unified is by their worship of one God (4:6).

4:9,10 *ascended . . . descended:* Jesus was taken up to heaven forty days after God had raised him from death (Luke 24:50,51; Acts 1:3, 6-11; 2:33). According to 1 PETER, when Jesus was put to death he preached to the spirits being kept in prison (1 Pet 3:19), which may refer to the spirits of the dead who were imprisoned in the place of the dead.

4:11 *apostles . . . prophets:* See the note at 2:20. Here Christ is the one who chooses some people for special tasks. In other places in the New Testament, the Holy Spirit is identified as the one who gives out such gifts and abilities (1 Cor 12–14). In ROMANS, Paul says that God gives such gifts (Rom 12:4-8).

4:2 Col 3:12,13. **4:8** Ps 68:18.

teachers, [12]to prepare God's people for works of service, so that the body of Christ may be built up [13]until we all reach unity in the faith and in the knowledge of the Son of God and become mature, attaining to the whole measure of the fullness of Christ.

[14]Then we will no longer be infants, tossed back and forth by the waves, and blown here and there by every wind of teaching and by the cunning and craftiness of men in their deceitful scheming. [15]Instead, speaking the truth in love, we will in all things grow up into him who is the Head, that is, Christ. [16]From him the whole body, joined and held together by every supporting ligament, grows and builds itself up in love, as each part does its work.

Living as Children of Light

[17]So I tell you this, and insist on it in the Lord, that you must no longer live as the Gentiles do, in the futility of their thinking. [18]They are darkened in their understanding and separated from the life of God because of the ignorance that is in them due to the hardening of their hearts. [19]Having lost all sensitivity, they have given themselves over to sensuality so as to indulge in every kind of impurity, with a continual lust for more.

[20]You, however, did not come to know Christ that way. [21]Surely you heard of him and were taught in him in accordance with the truth that is in Jesus. [22]You were taught, with regard to your former way of life, to put off your old self, which is being corrupted by its deceitful desires; [23]to be made new in the attitude of your minds; [24]and to put on the new self, created to be like God in true righteousness and holiness.

[25]Therefore each of you must put off falsehood and speak truthfully to his neighbor, for we are all members of one body. [26]"In your anger do not sin"[a]: Do not let the sun go down while you are still angry, [27]and do not give the devil a foothold. [28]He who has been stealing must steal no longer, but must work, doing something useful with his own hands, that he may have something to share with those in need.

[29]Do not let any unwholesome talk come out of your mouths, but only what is helpful for building others up according to their needs, that it may benefit those who listen. [30]And do not grieve the Holy Spirit of God, with whom you were sealed for the day of redemption. [31]Get rid of all bitterness, rage and anger, brawling and slander, along with every form of malice. [32]Be kind and compassionate to one another, forgiving each other, just as in Christ God forgave you.

5 Be imitators of God, therefore, as dearly loved children [2]and live a life of love, just as Christ loved us and gave himself up for us as a fragrant offering and sacrifice to God.

---

[a]**26** Psalm 4:4

4:14 *cunning and craftiness of men:* Apparently some members of the church were spreading false teachings.

4:15 *him who is the Head, that is, Christ:* See the note at 1:22,23.

4:18 *darkened:* In the Bible, "dark" refers to places of pain (Ps 107:10) or confusion (Eccl 2:14). God's opponents are called the "powers of this dark world" (Eph 6:12), and those who do not do what God expects may be thrown "outside, into the darkness" (Matt 22:13), a place of everlasting torment.

4:25 *members of one body:* See the note at 1:22, 23.

4:27 *devil:* See the note at 2:2.

5:2 *gave himself up for us as a fragrant offering:* See the note at 1:7,8.

5:5 *idolater:* Those who worship false gods or statues representing false gods. Many people in Ephesus worshiped the goddess Artemis. Greed and immoral living also show a lack of trust in God, so those things are as bad as worshiping idols.

5:5 *the kingdom of Christ:* This is the only place in the New Testament that has the phrase, "kingdom of Christ." Like the similar terms "kingdom of God" (Mark 1:15; Luke 4:43) and "kingdom of heaven" (Matt 3:2), it means God's rule over people, both in this life and in the life to come. See also 1 Cor 15:24,25.

4:16 Col 2:19. **4:22** Col 3:9. **4:24** Gen 1:26; Col 3:10. **4:25** Zech 8:16. **4:26** Ps 4:4. **4:32** Col 3:13. **5:2** Exod 29:18; Ps 40:6.

[3]But among you there must not be even a hint of sexual
immorality, or of any kind of impurity, or of greed, because these
are improper for God's holy people. [4]Nor should there be obscen-
ity, foolish talk or coarse joking, which are out of place, but rather
thanksgiving. [5]For of this you can be sure: No immoral, impure or
greedy person—such a man is an idolater—has any inheritance in
the kingdom of Christ and of God.[a] [6]Let no one deceive you with
empty words, for because of such things God's wrath comes on
those who are disobedient. [7]Therefore do not be partners with
them.

[8]For you were once darkness, but now you are light in the
Lord. Live as children of light [9](for the fruit of the light consists in
all goodness, righteousness and truth) [10]and find out what pleases
the Lord. [11]Have nothing to do with the fruitless deeds of darkness,
but rather expose them. [12]For it is shameful even to mention what
the disobedient do in secret. [13]But everything exposed by the light
becomes visible, [14]for it is light that makes everything visible. This
is why it is said:

"Wake up, O sleeper,
rise from the dead,
and Christ will shine on you."

[15]Be very careful, then, how you live—not as unwise but as
wise, [16]making the most of every opportunity, because the days are
evil. [17]Therefore do not be foolish, but understand what the Lord's
will is. [18]Do not get drunk on wine, which leads to debauchery.
Instead, be filled with the Spirit. [19]Speak to one another with
psalms, hymns and spiritual songs. Sing and make music in your
heart to the Lord, [20]always giving thanks to God the Father for
everything, in the name of our Lord Jesus Christ.
[21]Submit to one another out of reverence for Christ.

Wives and Husbands

[22]Wives, submit to your husbands as to the Lord. [23]For the
husband is the head of the wife as Christ is the head of the church,
his body, of which he is the Savior. [24]Now as the church submits to
Christ, so also wives should submit to their husbands in everything.
[25]Husbands, love your wives, just as Christ loved the church
and gave himself up for her [26]to make her holy, cleansing[b] her by
the washing with water through the word, [27]and to present her to
himself as a radiant church, without stain or wrinkle or any other
blemish, but holy and blameless. [28]In this same way, husbands
ought to love their wives as their own bodies. He who loves his
wife loves himself. [29]After all, no one ever hated his own body, but
he feeds and cares for it, just as Christ does the church— [30]for we

[a]5 Or *kingdom of the Christ and God* [b]26 Or *having cleansed*

You were once darkness, but now you are light in the Lord. Live as children of light.
Eph 5:8

5:8 *once darkness . . . light:* See the notes at 4:18 and 1:18.

5:14 *Wake up . . . Christ will shine on you:* This phrase bears some resemblance to Isaiah 26:19 and 60:1. Some form of this quotation may have been used as an early Christian hymn or in a baptism ceremony.

5:18 *be filled with the Spirit:* See the mini-article called "Holy Spirit," p. 2082. Being filled with the Spirit meant God's people were to avoid being overcome by anger (4:26), unwholesome language (4:29; 5:4), cursing others (4:31), or being greedy and immoral (5:3) or drunk (5:18).

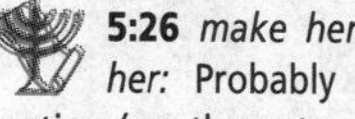

5:21-25 *Submit to one another out of reverence for Christ:* In Paul's day, people accepted certain levels of authority in households. Paul seems to be adding to this the idea of equality by telling Jesus' followers to "submit to one another." See also Col 3:19; 1 Pet 3:7; Gal 3:28,29.

5:26 *make her holy, cleansing her:* Probably a reference to baptism (see the note at 4:4-6).

5:28 *love:* The kind of love mentioned in this verse is the self-giving love that is commanded in Leviticus 19:18, repeated by Jesus (Matt 19:19; 22:39), and taught by Paul (Rom 13:9).

5:16 Col 4:5. **5:19, 20** Col 3:16, 17. **5:22** Col 3:18; 1 Pet 3:1. **5:25** Col 3:19; 1 Pet 3:7.

Two Soldiers Attacking, stone relief, first to third century A.D. Soldiers and their weapons were a familiar sight in all parts of the Roman empire. The Christians in Asia Minor would have been able to imagine the spiritual armor described by the author of EPHESIANS who told them, "Take up the shield of faith . . . Take the helmet of salvation and the sword of the Spirit, which is the word of God." (See 6:10-17.)

are members of his body. 31"For this reason a man will leave his
father and mother and be united to his wife, and the two will
become one flesh."[a] 32This is a profound mystery—but I am talking about Christ and the church. 33However, each one of you also
must love his wife as he loves himself, and the wife must respect
her husband.

Children and Parents

6 Children, obey your parents in the Lord, for this is right.
2"Honor your father and mother"—which is the first command-

6:1-4 *Children . . . Fathers:* Because children belong to the Lord, parents are to treat them with respect and teach them about the Lord. Paul also repeats one of the Ten Commandments (Exod 20:12; Deut 5:16) to remind Christians that the obedience that children are expected to give their parents is a path to one of God's promises.

5:31 Gen 2:24. **6:1-3** Col 3:20; Exod 20:12; Deut 5:16.

[a]**31** Gen. 2:24

ment with a promise— 3“that it may go well with you and that you
may enjoy long life on the earth.”[a]
4Fathers, do not exasperate your children; instead, bring
them up in the training and instruction of the Lord.

Slaves and Masters

5Slaves, obey your earthly masters with respect and fear, and
with sincerity of heart, just as you would obey Christ. 6Obey them
not only to win their favor when their eye is on you, but like slaves
of Christ, doing the will of God from your heart. 7Serve wholeheartedly, as if you were serving the Lord, not men, 8because you
know that the Lord will reward everyone for whatever good he
does, whether he is slave or free.
9And masters, treat your slaves in the same way. Do not
threaten them, since you know that he who is both their Master
and yours is in heaven, and there is no favoritism with him.

The Armor of God

10Finally, be strong in the Lord and in his mighty power.
11Put on the full armor of God so that you can take your stand
against the devil's schemes. 12For our struggle is not against flesh

[a]3 Deut. 5:16

6:5-9 *Slaves . . . masters:* See the mini-article called “Slaves and Servants in the Time of Jesus,” p. 2006. To show ownership, some masters forced their slaves to wear collars like the one shown here. The text says, “Return me to Apronilanus ... for I am a fugitive slave.” It would have been impossible for a slave wearing this collar to find work as a free person.

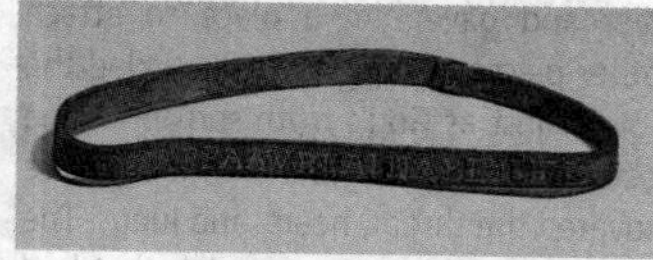

6:11 *devil's schemes:* The devil is also known as Satan, which means “God's opponent.” See also the mini-article called “Satan,” p. 963.

6:5-8 Col 3:22-25. **6:9** Deut 10:17; Col 3:25; 4:1.

QUESTIONS ABOUT EPHESIANS

1. Ephesians 1:4 states that “he chose us in him before the creation of the world.” What does this mean, and how is this possible? Why did Christ choose us? (1:5,6)
2. What is the “truth” that Christ has brought? (1:13) How does this truth differ from other kinds of truth?
3. Who belongs to God's family? (2:14-19) How does someone become part of God's family?
4. What seven things do the people of God share? (4:4-6) Choose one of these things and describe in your own words what it means.
5. List the things that are part of a Christian's “old self,” and list the “rules” for the “new self” (4:17—5:5). What is the hardest thing about trying to live this new life?
6. What do you think about the letter's description of how husbands and wives should relate to each other? (5:21-33) Why?
7. In your opinion, which of the following items is the most important thing in relationships—including relationships with spouses, siblings, and friends, and relationships with your boss and co-workers? Choose one and explain.
   - **a.** trust and loyalty
   - **b.** love
   - **c.** equality and fairness
   - **d.** openness and good communication
   - **e.** forgiveness
   - **f.** other . . .
8. Read the description of “the full armor of God” (6:10-17). Which pieces of *your* spiritual armor need shining, reinforcing, or sharpening? How can you get your armor in better condition?

and blood, but against the rulers, against the authorities, against
the powers of this dark world and against the spiritual forces of
evil in the heavenly realms. [13]Therefore put on the full armor of
God, so that when the day of evil comes, you may be able to stand
your ground, and after you have done everything, to stand. [14]Stand
firm then, with the belt of truth buckled around your waist, with
the breastplate of righteousness in place, [15]and with your feet fitted with the readiness that comes from the gospel of peace. [16]In
addition to all this, take up the shield of faith, with which you can
extinguish all the flaming arrows of the evil one. [17]Take the helmet
of salvation and the sword of the Spirit, which is the word of God.
[18]And pray in the Spirit on all occasions with all kinds of prayers
and requests. With this in mind, be alert and always keep on praying for all the saints.

[19]Pray also for me, that whenever I open my mouth, words
may be given me so that I will fearlessly make known the mystery
of the gospel, [20]for which I am an ambassador in chains. Pray that
I may declare it fearlessly, as I should.

Final Greetings

[21]Tychicus, the dear brother and faithful servant in the Lord,
will tell you everything, so that you also may know how I am and
what I am doing. [22]I am sending him to you for this very purpose,
that you may know how we are, and that he may encourage you.

[23]Peace to the brothers, and love with faith from God the
Father and the Lord Jesus Christ. [24]Grace to all who love our Lord
Jesus Christ with an undying love.

6:13 *when the day of evil comes:* Refers to a time of testing. This may be in the present (5:16) or some time in the future (1 Cor 3:10-15; Rev 2:10).

6:14-17 *belt . . . sword:* The belt referred to here was a broad belt made of leather or some other material that provided support for a soldier and gave him a place to attach other pieces of equipment. It circled the soldier just as God's truth surrounds the believer. The breastplate mentioned here covered the throat, heart, and lungs. The shoes of a soldier were sandals that had spikes on the bottom for good footing. The soldier's shield was a large rectangular piece of wood that was covered with canvas and animal hide. Just before a battle began, the shield was dipped in water. When flaming arrows hit the shield they would fizzle out. In the same way, faith is able to put out the flaming arrows of the evil one. The helmet was made of skin reinforced with metal, and the sword mentioned was most likely the short, straight sword of the Roman soldier. The sword is God's message, the only piece of equipment mentioned that is used for attack rather than defense (see also Heb 4:12).

6:16 *evil one:* See the note at 6:11.

6:18 *Spirit:* See the mini-article called "Holy Spirit," p. 2082.

6:19 *the mystery of the gospel:* See the note at 1:9. See also Rom 16:25, 26; 1 Cor 15:51-54; Col 1:26,27.

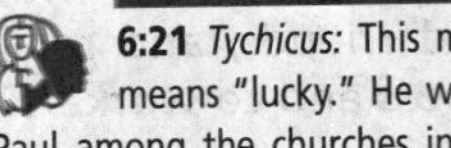

6:21 *Tychicus:* This man's name means "lucky." He worked with Paul among the churches in Asia (Acts 20:4; Col 4:7-9; 2 Tim 4:12; Titus 3:12).

6:23 *God the Father and the Lord Jesus Christ:* See the notes at 1:2 and 1:3 (Lord). See also the note at 1:1 (Paul).

6:14 Isa 11:5; 59:17. **6:15** Isa 52:7. **6:17** Isa 59:17.

PHILIPPIANS

God's messengers may be imprisoned, but the truth about Christ cannot be locked up. Read PHILIPPIANS to find out how the apostle Paul found courage during times of trouble.

WHAT MAKES PHILIPPIANS SPECIAL?

The apostle Paul wrote this letter to the Lord's followers at Philippi while he was in jail in a city he does not name. Even though he faced difficult times, Paul wanted to remind the Philippians to remain faithful to the gospel of Christ that Paul had first preached to them (Acts 16:12-40; Phil 4:15-17). Paul reminds the Philippians that they may have to face suffering, just as he has suffered (1:29,30; 2:17,18), but they should not be afraid of such suffering, since Christ gives believers the strength to face anything (4:13). Paul's strong words of faith in this short letter have given encouragement to Christians ever since it was first written.

WHY WAS PHILIPPIANS WRITTEN?

Paul wanted to thank the Philippians for helping him with their gifts and prayers (1:4,5; 4:10-19) and to tell them what had been happening to him since he was arrested by the Romans. Paul was also aware of problems among the followers in the church he had organized at Philippi some time earlier. For one thing, the Christians there were arguing about whether or not the new followers of Jesus needed to obey the Law of Moses (3:2-11).

WHAT'S THE STORY BEHIND THE SCENE?

ACTS reports that Philippi was the very first city Paul visited after he crossed over to southeastern Europe from Asia Minor (Acts 16:11,12). Philippi was an important city of Macedonia, located on the eastern end of the major highway called the Egnatian Way, which merchants and the Roman army used to carry goods and supplies between the eastern part of the empire and Rome in the west. Philippi was named after Philip II, the father of Alexander the Great. Philip made the city into a fortress and key city of his growing kingdom in the fourth century B.C.

PHILIPPIANS is considered one of Paul's "prison letters" (along with EPHESIANS, COLOSSIANS, and PHILEMON) because it was most likely written by Paul from jail. It is not known exactly how many times Paul was in jail or in how many different places. ACTS says that Paul was imprisoned in Caesarea (Acts 23:23—26:32) and was under house arrest in Rome (Acts 28:16-31). Some scholars believe that Paul was also imprisoned during the lengthy time he was in Ephesus (Acts 19:1—20:1). Paul may have written PHILIPPIANS from one of these cities or from some other city in the eastern Mediterranean, where Roman guards were stationed.

Philippi: At the time of Paul, Philippi was the center of a Roman colony. The city had theaters, baths, public squares for conducting business (called forums), and statues of Roman gods. Many Roman soldiers settled in Philippi after they retired. For more, see the mini-article called "Roman Empire," p. 2322.

Philippi was named after Philip II of Macedon, who was the father of Alexander the Great. Around 356 B.C., Philip conquered this unimportant settlement and the area surrounding it, because he was interested in the gold and silver mines in nearby Mount Pangaeus. Years later, Philippi became an important city after it was conquered by the Romans, who built the Egnatian Way, a road that connected Byzantium in the east with the seaports on the Adriatic in the west.

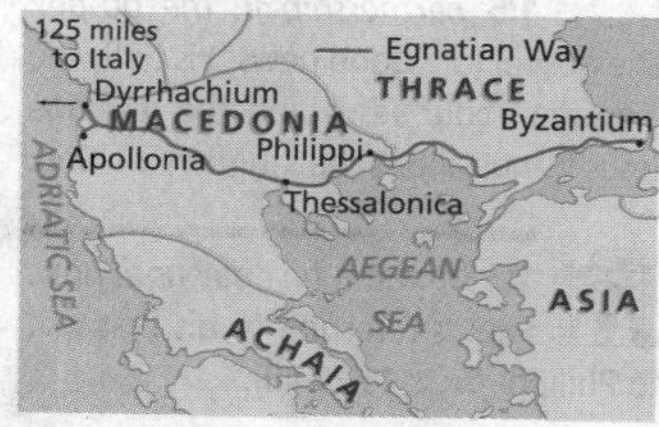

How is Philippians constructed?

Paul begins his letter with a Christian form of the words of greeting traditionally used in formal Greek letter writing, and he ends with a final greeting (4:21-23). As in many of Paul's letters, the introduction is followed by prayers of thanksgiving for the people to whom he is writing. In the rest of the letter Paul gives news about his present situation, gives instruction and encouragement to the Philippian Christians, and expresses his thanks for the help they had given him in the past.

PHILIPPIANS can be outlined in the following way:

Paul greets and gives thanks for the Philippians (1:1-11)

Living for Christ, God's humble servant (1:12—2:18)

Encouragement and instruction (2:19—4:9)

Final words of thanks and greeting (4:10-23)

Paul Greets and Gives Thanks for the Philippians

Paul begins with a formal greeting often used in Greek letter writing. As in many of his letters, he follows his greeting with a prayer of thanksgiving for those to whom he is writing.

1 Paul and Timothy, servants of Christ Jesus,

To all the saints in Christ Jesus at Philippi, together with the
overseers[a] and deacons:

2 Grace and peace to you from God our Father and the Lord
Jesus Christ.

Thanksgiving and Prayer

3 I thank my God every time I remember you. 4 In all my
prayers for all of you, I always pray with joy 5 because of your partnership in the gospel from the first day until now, 6 being confident
of this, that he who began a good work in you will carry it on to
completion until the day of Christ Jesus.

7 It is right for me to feel this way about all of you, since I
have you in my heart; for whether I am in chains or defending and
confirming the gospel, all of you share in God's grace with me.
8 God can testify how I long for all of you with the affection of
Christ Jesus.

9 And this is my prayer: that your love may abound more and

[a]1 Traditionally *bishops*

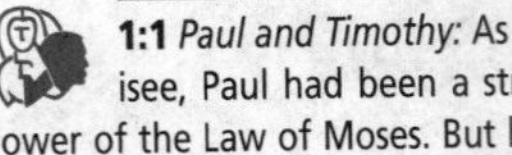

1:1 *Paul and Timothy:* As a Pharisee, Paul had been a strict follower of the Law of Moses. But here he identifies himself as a servant of Christ Jesus. For more, see the mini-article called "Paul (Saul) of Tarsus," p. 2177.

Timothy was the son of a Jewish Christian mother and a Gentile father from Lystra (Acts 16:1). He is named as Paul's co-worker in many of Paul's letters (1 Cor 4:17; 2 Cor 1:1; 1 Thes 1:1; Phlm 1).

1:1 *Christ Jesus:* The name *Jesus* was common among Jewish men of this day. The word "Christ" is a title that means "Messiah" or "chosen one." See also the mini-article called "Messiah (Chosen One)," p. 1124.

1:1 *overseers and deacons:* The overseers were the top leaders of each group of Jesus' followers in Philippi. The "deacons" helped meet the direct needs of the people in the churches by handling the distribution of food and money.

1:2 *God our Father . . . Lord:* Paul uses the term "Father" in many of his letters to describe God (Gal 1:2,3; 1 Cor 1:3; Rom 1:7). When it is used for Jesus, "Lord" emphasizes his authority and power. See also the mini-article called "Lord (Title for Jesus)," p. 2106.

1:5 *partnership in the gospel:* The gospel (or "good news") is both the message about Jesus and the message Jesus brings about the kingdom of God.

1:5 *from the first day until now:* Paul is referring to his first visit to Philippi (Acts 16:11-40).

1:6 *until the day of Christ Jesus:* In PHILIPPIANS, Paul mentions Jesus' return a number of times (1:10; 2:16; 3:20,21), and he expects it to be "near" (4:5). See also the mini-article called "Second Coming," p. 2277.

more in knowledge and depth of insight, [10]so that you may be able
to discern what is best and may be pure and blameless until the
day of Christ, [11]filled with the fruit of righteousness that comes
through Jesus Christ—to the glory and praise of God.

Living for Christ, God's Humble Servant

Even though Paul was in jail, he continued to share the gospel about Christ. Whether he lived or died or suffered, he would be with Christ. He encouraged the Philippian Christians to face suffering with the same hope. Paul reminds the recipients of his letter that Christ became a servant, and encourages them to follow his example and to "shine like stars" in the dark world.

Paul's Chains Advance the Gospel

[12]Now I want you to know, brothers, that what has happened
to me has really served to advance the gospel. [13]As a result, it has
become clear throughout the whole palace guard[a] and to everyone
else that I am in chains for Christ. [14]Because of my chains, most of
the brothers in the Lord have been encouraged to speak the word
of God more courageously and fearlessly.

[15]It is true that some preach Christ out of envy and rivalry,
but others out of goodwill. [16]The latter do so in love, knowing that
I am put here for the defense of the gospel. [17]The former preach
Christ out of selfish ambition, not sincerely, supposing that they
can stir up trouble for me while I am in chains.[b] [18]But what does
it matter? The important thing is that in every way, whether from
false motives or true, Christ is preached. And because of this I
rejoice.

Yes, and I will continue to rejoice, [19]for I know that through
your prayers and the help given by the Spirit of Jesus Christ, what
has happened to me will turn out for my deliverance.[c] [20]I eagerly
expect and hope that I will in no way be ashamed, but will have
sufficient courage so that now as always Christ will be exalted in
my body, whether by life or by death. [21]For to me, to live is Christ
and to die is gain. [22]If I am to go on living in the body, this will
mean fruitful labor for me. Yet what shall I choose? I do not know!
[23]I am torn between the two: I desire to depart and be with Christ,
which is better by far; [24]but it is more necessary for you that I
remain in the body. [25]Convinced of this, I know that I will remain,
and I will continue with all of you for your progress and joy in the
faith, [26]so that through my being with you again your joy in Christ
Jesus will overflow on account of me.

[a]**13** Or *whole palace* [b]**16,17** Some late manuscripts have verses 16 and 17 in reverse order. [c]**19** Or *salvation*

1:7 *I am in chains:* Paul may have been writing from some city in the eastern Mediterranean where Roman guards were stationed, or from Rome itself, where he was put under house arrest (Acts 28:16, 30, 31). The prison cell shown here is from the Roman period. It is located in Philippi and may even be part of the same prison where Paul was held captive (Acts 16:23,24).

1:10 *the day of Christ:* See the note at 1:6.

1:12 *gospel:* See the note at 1:5 (gospel).

1:13 *whole palace guard . . . in chains for Christ:* These men of the palace guard were special military guards assigned to protect the emperor in Rome or other high Roman officials who lived in certain cities outside of Rome. Paul probably told the guards about Jesus as they took their turns guarding him. See also the note at 1:7.

1:19 *the Spirit of Jesus Christ:* Paul mentions the Holy Spirit a number of times in this letter. The Spirit acts as a helper to keep Paul safe (1:19), as One who brings unity to the followers of Jesus (2:1), and as the One who leads the Lord's followers in true worship (3:3). See also the mini-article called "Holy Spirit," p. 2082.

1:23 *depart and be with Christ:* Paul believes that those who are faithful followers of Christ will be with Christ after they die. See also 2 Cor 5:1-9 and the mini-article called "Eternal Life," p. 2072.

1:13 Acts 28:30.

1:28 *those who oppose you:* Paul may be talking about those he later describes as "dogs" (3:2) who were trying to turn the people away from the gospel that Paul had taught them. Or, he may be referring to any group of people who made trouble for Christ's followers at Philippi.

1:30 *you are going through the same struggle you saw I had:* Paul was badly beaten and put in prison the first time he was in Philippi (Acts 16:16-40). Now he is in prison again. Regardless of the circumstances, Paul sees his suffering as an opportunity to serve Christ.

2:1 *the Spirit:* See the note at 1:19.

27 Whatever happens, conduct yourselves in a manner
worthy of the gospel of Christ. Then, whether I come and see you
or only hear about you in my absence, I will know that you stand
firm in one spirit, contending as one man for the faith of the
gospel 28 without being frightened in any way by those who oppose
you. This is a sign to them that they will be destroyed, but that you
will be saved—and that by God. 29 For it has been granted to you
on behalf of Christ not only to believe on him, but also to suffer
for him, 30 since you are going through the same struggle you saw
I had, and now hear that I still have.

Imitating Christ's Humility

2 If you have any encouragement from being united with Christ,
if any comfort from his love, if any fellowship with the Spirit, if
any tenderness and compassion, 2 then make my joy complete by
being like-minded, having the same love, being one in spirit and
purpose. 3 Do nothing out of selfish ambition or vain conceit, but
in humility consider others better than yourselves. 4 Each of you

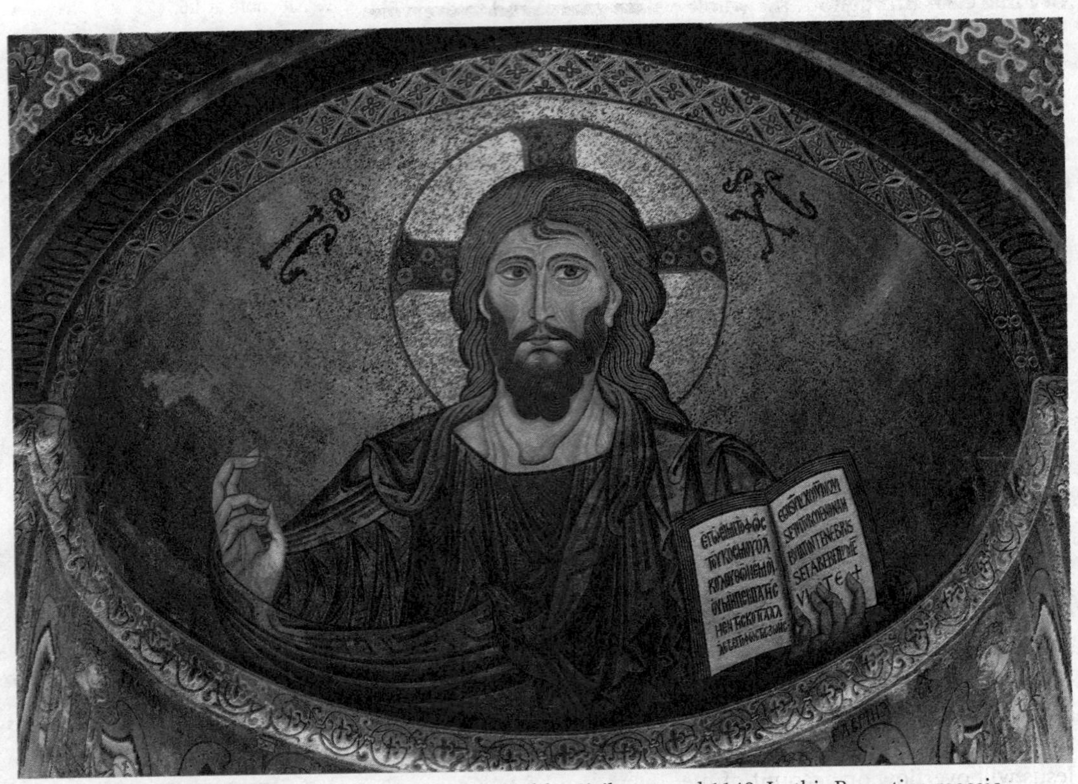

Christ Pantocrator, ceiling mosaic in cathedral in Cefalù, Sicily, around 1148. In this Byzantine mosaic Christ is shown as the "Ruler of All." His right hand is raised in a gesture of blessing and he holds a book in his left hand. The text says, "I am the light of the world." In PHILIPPIANS, Paul quotes an old hymn in which Christ is praised for both his greatness and his humility. "God exalted him to the highest place and gave him the name that is above every name." (See 2:6-11.)

should look not only to your own interests, but also to the interests of others.
[5]Your attitude should be the same as that of Christ Jesus:

[6]Who, being in very nature[a] God,
did not consider equality with God something to be grasped,
[7]but made himself nothing,
taking the very nature[b] of a servant,
being made in human likeness.
[8]And being found in appearance as a man,
he humbled himself
and became obedient to death—
even death on a cross!
[9]Therefore God exalted him to the highest place
and gave him the name that is above every name,
[10]that at the name of Jesus every knee should bow,
in heaven and on earth and under the earth,
[11]and every tongue confess that Jesus Christ is Lord,
to the glory of God the Father.

Shining as Stars

[12]Therefore, my dear friends, as you have always obeyed—not
only in my presence, but now much more in my absence—continue to work out your salvation with fear and trembling, [13]for it is God
who works in you to will and to act according to his good purpose.
[14]Do everything without complaining or arguing, [15]so that
you may become blameless and pure, children of God without

[a]6 Or *in the form of* [b]7 Or *the form*

Yeshua, name inscribed on stone coffin, around A.D. 100. Jesus' name in Hebrew was *Yeshua* (or Joshua), which means "The LORD (*Yahweh*) is salvation." Paul quotes an early Christian hymn when he writes, "At the name of Jesus every knee should bow, in heaven and on earth and under the earth, and every tongue confess that Jesus Christ is Lord." (See 2:10, 11.)

It is God who works in you to will and to act according to his good purpose.
Phil 2:13

2:6 *being in very nature God:* This same idea is expressed in John 1:1-18 and Colossians 1:15-20. The authors of the New Testament and the teachings of the early church leaders agreed that Jesus was truly God, but also truly human (2:7). See also the mini-article called "Son of God," p. 2044. Verses 6-11 are probably an early Christian hymn that the Philippians might have known.

2:7 *servant:* Paul means that Christ obeyed God as a servant obeys the master. For more, see the mini-article called "Slaves and Servants in the Time of Jesus," p. 2006.

2:8 *death on a cross:* Jesus was put to death on a cross, a Roman method of execution. See the mini-article called "Crucifixion," p. 1914.

2:11 *Jesus Christ is Lord:* When people said in public "Jesus is Lord," it showed that they believed that Jesus was truly God and that he was the master of their lives. See also the notes at 1:1 (Christ Jesus) and 1:2.

2:12 *work out your salvation:* Different words in the Bible are translated as "salvation," "save," and "savior." All of them point to what God has done and is still doing to free humans from sin and the powers of evil. See also the mini-articles called "Salvation," p. 2021 and "Eternal Life," p. 2072.

fault in a crooked and depraved generation, in which you shine
like stars in the universe 16as you hold out[a] the word of life—in
order that I may boast on the day of Christ that I did not run or
labor for nothing. 17But even if I am being poured out like a drink
offering on the sacrifice and service coming from your faith, I am
glad and rejoice with all of you. 18So you too should be glad and
rejoice with me.

Encouragement and Instruction

Paul tells the Philippian Christians that he is going to send two trusted friends, Timothy and Epaphroditus, to give them encouragement. He also warns them about following people who are insisting that new followers must live by the Law of Moses. He uses his own life as an example to show that faith in Christ is the most important thing, and to encourage them to live as God's children.

Timothy and Epaphroditus

19I hope in the Lord Jesus to send Timothy to you soon, that
I also may be cheered when I receive news about you. 20I have no
one else like him, who takes a genuine interest in your welfare.
21For everyone looks out for his own interests, not those of Jesus
Christ. 22But you know that Timothy has proved himself, because
as a son with his father he has served with me in the work of the
gospel. 23I hope, therefore, to send him as soon as I see how things
go with me. 24And I am confident in the Lord that I myself will
come soon.

25But I think it is necessary to send back to you Epaphroditus, my brother, fellow worker and fellow soldier, who is also your
messenger, whom you sent to take care of my needs. 26For he longs
for all of you and is distressed because you heard he was ill.
27Indeed he was ill, and almost died. But God had mercy on him,
and not on him only but also on me, to spare me sorrow upon sorrow. 28Therefore I am all the more eager to send him, so that when
you see him again you may be glad and I may have less anxiety.
29Welcome him in the Lord with great joy, and honor men like
him, 30because he almost died for the work of Christ, risking his
life to make up for the help you could not give me.

No Confidence in the Flesh

3 Finally, my brothers, rejoice in the Lord! It is no trouble for me
to write the same things to you again, and it is a safeguard for you.
2Watch out for those dogs, those men who do evil, those
mutilators of the flesh. 3For it is we who are the circumcision, we
who worship by the Spirit of God, who glory in Christ Jesus, and

[a]16 Or *hold on to*

2:15 *shine like stars:* Many of the biblical writers use "light" to describe God or God's Word (Ps 119:105; 1 John 1:5); and those people or things that reveal God's truth (Isa 49:6). The followers of Jesus are sometimes called "sons of light" or "children of light" (John 12:36; Eph 5:8) and "the light of the world" (Matt 5:14-16).

2:17 *offering . . . sacrifice:* The Law of Moses commanded the Jewish people to offer sacrifices to God. Here Paul says that faith in the Lord and lives of service are the sacrifices that God expects (2:17).

2:25 *Epaphroditus:* This follower of Christ had been sent to Paul with a gift from the Philippian Christians (4:18). He apparently stayed with Paul and worked beside him.

3:2 *Watch out for those dogs:* Refers to those who want to make all new followers of the Lord obey the Law of Moses, especially the law that says all boys and men need to be circumcised. See the notes at 3:3 (circumcised) and 3:18.

3:3 *circumcision:* The Law of Moses required all Jewish males who wanted to be part of God's chosen people of Israel to be circumcised when they were eight days old, or later when necessary (Gen 34:21-23; Lev 12:3). See also the mini-article called "Circumcision," p. 2251.

3:5 *the tribe of Benjamin, a Hebrew of Hebrews:* Paul reminded the Philippian Christians that he was from a Jewish family (the people of Israel). Israel had twelve tribes named for the sons of Jacob (Gen 49:1-28). Paul belonged to the tribe named for Jacob's youngest son, Benjamin (Rom 11:1). See also the mini-article called "Israel," p. 264.

2:10,11 Isa 45:23. **2:15** Deut 32:5.

who put no confidence in the flesh— 4though I myself have reasons for such confidence.

If anyone else thinks he has reasons to put confidence in the flesh, I have more: 5circumcised on the eighth day, of the people of Israel, of the tribe of Benjamin, a Hebrew of Hebrews; in regard to the law, a Pharisee; 6as for zeal, persecuting the church; as for legalistic righteousness, faultless.

7But whatever was to my profit I now consider loss for the sake of Christ. 8What is more, I consider everything a loss compared to the surpassing greatness of knowing Christ Jesus my Lord, for whose sake I have lost all things. I consider them rubbish, that I may gain Christ 9and be found in him, not having a righteousness of my own that comes from the law, but that which is through faith in

3:5 *in regard to the law, a Pharisee:* The name "Pharisee" may come from a word meaning "pure ones." They were especially strict about obeying the Law of Moses and opposed those who taught anything different.

3:9 *faith:* Paul believed that God accepted those who had faith in Christ rather than those who tried to gain God's favor by obeying the Law of Moses. See Gal 3:1-29.

3:5 Acts 23:6; 26:4,5. **3:6** Acts 8:1-3; 22:4; 26:9-11.

SECOND COMING

This term is used to refer to the future time Christ will return to judge people and establish the kingdom of God. The term "second coming" is not found in the New Testament, but Jesus says he will "come back" to take his disciples with him after preparing a place for them in heaven (John 14:1-3), and the author of HEBREWS says that Christ will come again "to bring salvation to those who are waiting for him" (Heb 9:28). A number of passages use the Greek word *parousia*, meaning "arrival" or "coming," to describe this future event (for example, 1 Cor 15:23; 1 Thes 3:13). In the Roman empire of the first century A.D., the term *parousia* was used to describe the public appearance of an emperor or king, whose visit would be greeted by loyal crowds.

ACTS reports that Jesus was taken up into heaven while his disciples watched, and two angels told them that Jesus "will come back in the same way you have seen him go" (Acts 1:9-11). A number of passages in the Gospels refer to a second coming of the Son of Man, a term for Jesus Christ. The appearance of the Son of Man will follow a time of suffering and distress (Matt 24:29-31; Mark 13:3-27). Though Jesus describes a number of signs that will happen before his return, the exact time is not known by the angels in heaven or the Son himself (Matt 24:36-44; Mark 13:32-37). The second coming of the Son of Man is often connected with a time of judgment when those who have done wrong will be punished and those who have done right will be rewarded (Matt 13:41-43; 16:27,28; 25:31-46; Luke 18:1-8; 21:34-36). SECOND PETER states that the Lord's return is linked to a day of judgment when the ungodly people will be destroyed and the present universe melted and replaced with a new heaven and earth (2 Pet 3:7-13; Rev 20:11—21:4; and the mini-article called "Day of the LORD," p. 1727).

In Paul's letters, the apostle describes the return of Christ as a time when Christ's people will be raised to life (1 Cor 15:23; 1 Thes 4:14-18) and Christ will destroy all powers and forces that oppose God, who will rule forever (1 Cor 15:24-28). In the meantime, Paul prayed that the followers of Christ would live in peace and holiness until Christ returns (1 Thes 5:23). The writer of JAMES probably echoed a belief common among many of the earliest Christians when he encouraged Jesus' followers to be patient, because "the Lord's coming is near" (Jas 5:7,8; see also 1 John 2:18; Rev 22:6-10,20). When Christ did not return as soon as the first Christians expected, some writers offered reasons why (John 21:20-23; 2 Pet 3:3-9). See also the mini-article called "End Times," p. 2295.

3:11 *resurrection from the dead:* Paul is talking about being raised to life from death. See the mini-articles called "Resurrection," p. 2210 and "Eternal Life," p. 2072.

3:12 *take hold of that for which Christ Jesus took hold of me:* Paul's final goal is the prize of being called to live with God in heaven (3:14).

3:18 *enemies of the cross of Christ:* These may be the same people Paul warns the Philippians about in 3:2. In addition to bragging about being circumcised, these people would only eat certain kinds of foods and probably went without eating to prove how much they loved God.

3:20 *our citizenship is in heaven . . . eagerly await a Savior:* In the Roman world, only a privileged few were able to become citizens. Paul wants to make it clear that it is much more important to be a citizen of the community whose Lord is in heaven. For more about Christ's return, see the note at 1:6.

4:2 *Euodia . . . Syntyche:* These women had Greek names. Euodia means "good journey" (or "success") and Syntyche means "with luck." Paul encourages these women who had helped him spread the gospel to stop arguing with each other.

4:3 *Clement:* This is the only place in the Bible where Clement is mentioned. He helped Paul spread the gospel in Philippi.

4:3 *book of life:* A book in which the names of God's people are written. See also Exod 32:32; Luke 10:20; Rev 3:5; 13:8.

4:5 *The Lord is near:* See the note at 1:6.

3:17 1 Cor 4:16; 11:1.

Christ—the righteousness that comes from God and is by faith. [10]I
want to know Christ and the power of his resurrection and the fellowship of sharing in his sufferings, becoming like him in his death,
[11]and so, somehow, to attain to the resurrection from the dead.

Pressing on Toward the Goal

[12]Not that I have already obtained all this, or have already
been made perfect, but I press on to take hold of that for which
Christ Jesus took hold of me. [13]Brothers, I do not consider myself
yet to have taken hold of it. But one thing I do: Forgetting what is
behind and straining toward what is ahead, [14]I press on toward the
goal to win the prize for which God has called me heavenward in
Christ Jesus.

[15]All of us who are mature should take such a view of things.
And if on some point you think differently, that too God will make
clear to you. [16]Only let us live up to what we have already attained.

[17]Join with others in following my example, brothers, and
take note of those who live according to the pattern we gave you.
[18]For, as I have often told you before and now say again even with
tears, many live as enemies of the cross of Christ. [19]Their destiny is
destruction, their god is their stomach, and their glory is in their
shame. Their mind is on earthly things. [20]But our citizenship is in
heaven. And we eagerly await a Savior from there, the Lord Jesus
Christ, [21]who, by the power that enables him to bring everything
under his control, will transform our lowly bodies so that they will
be like his glorious body.

4 Therefore, my brothers, you whom I love and long for, my joy
and crown, that is how you should stand firm in the Lord, dear
friends!

Exhortations

[2]I plead with Euodia and I plead with Syntyche to agree with
each other in the Lord. [3]Yes, and I ask you, loyal yokefellow,[a] help
these women who have contended at my side in the cause of the
gospel, along with Clement and the rest of my fellow workers,
whose names are in the book of life.

[4]Rejoice in the Lord always. I will say it again: Rejoice! [5]Let
your gentleness be evident to all. The Lord is near. [6]Do not be anxious about anything, but in everything, by prayer and petition,
with thanksgiving, present your requests to God. [7]And the peace
of God, which transcends all understanding, will guard your hearts
and your minds in Christ Jesus.

[8]Finally, brothers, whatever is true, whatever is noble, whatever is right, whatever is pure, whatever is lovely, whatever is
admirable—if anything is excellent or praiseworthy—think about

[a]3 Or *loyal Syzygus*

such things. 9 Whatever you have learned or received or heard from
me, or seen in me—put it into practice. And the God of peace will
be with you.

Final Words of Thanks and Greeting

Paul prays that God will take care of the needs of the Christians in Philippi in the same way they took care of Paul's needs in the past.

Thanks for Their Gifts

10 I rejoice greatly in the Lord that at last you have renewed
your concern for me. Indeed, you have been concerned, but you
had no opportunity to show it. 11 I am not saying this because I am
in need, for I have learned to be content whatever the circumstances. 12 I know what it is to be in need, and I know what it is to
have plenty. I have learned the secret of being content in any and
every situation, whether well fed or hungry, whether living in plenty or in want. 13 I can do everything through him who gives me
strength.
14 Yet it was good of you to share in my troubles. 15 Moreover,
as you Philippians know, in the early days of your acquaintance
with the gospel, when I set out from Macedonia, not one church
shared with me in the matter of giving and receiving, except you
only; 16 for even when I was in Thessalonica, you sent me aid again
and again when I was in need. 17 Not that I am looking for a gift,
but I am looking for what may be credited to your account. 18 I
have received full payment and even more; I am amply supplied,
now that I have received from Epaphroditus the gifts you sent.
They are a fragrant offering, an acceptable sacrifice, pleasing to

4:15 *Macedonia:* A region in the northern part of Greece. See the map on p. 2271. Paul is talking about his first visit to Philippi (Acts 16:12-40).

4:16 *Thessalonica:* The capital of Macedonia. The Egnatian Way enters Thessalonica from the east, and passes under the Arch of Galerius, which commemorates the Roman victory over the Persians in A.D. 298.

4:15,16 2 Cor 11:9. **4:16** Acts 17:1. **4:18** Exod 29:18.

QUESTIONS ABOUT PHILIPPIANS

1. What difference does it make knowing that Paul wrote his letter to the Philippians while he was a prisoner?
2. Paul describes choosing between living and dying as a difficult choice to make. (1:21-26) Why is this so? What do you live for? What would you be willing to die for?
3. Philippians 2:6-11 is probably a hymn that the early Christians sang as part of their worship. Summarize its key points. What hymns or songs are most meaningful to you? Why?
4. What does Paul mean when he refers to "sacrifice and service coming from your faith"? (2:17) What does it mean to be a servant of God?
5. What is the "prize" that Paul is running after? (3:12-14) How is the Christian life like a race?
6. Read Paul's instruction in 4:4-6. Of all the things he commands, which would be the easiest for you to do? Which would be the most difficult? Why?
7. Paul says "I have learned to be content whatever the circumstances." (4:11) Have there been times in your life when you had very little? When you've had a lot? What do you need to be equally satisfied in either circumstance?

4:22 *those who belong to Caesar's household:* May refer to some of the soldiers who guarded Paul (1:13).

God. 19And my God will meet all your needs according to his glorious riches in Christ Jesus.
20To our God and Father be glory for ever and ever. Amen.

Final Greetings

21Greet all the saints in Christ Jesus. The brothers who are
with me send greetings. 22All the saints send you greetings, especially those who belong to Caesar's household.
23The grace of the Lord Jesus Christ be with your spirit.
Amen.[a]

---

[a]**23** Some manuscripts do not have *Amen*.

COLOSSIANS

People are often searching for what is "real" in life. Read COLOSSIANS to find out about the real life that Christ brings.

WHAT MAKES COLOSSIANS SPECIAL?

The apostle Paul writes in his letters about the great change that is soon to come when Christ returns to conquer the powers of evil and to rule over all the world. But COLOSSIANS describes what Jesus Christ has already done. When Christ died on the cross, all the forces opposed to God were defeated (2:15, 20). This letter also includes a beautiful hymn that explains who Christ is (1:15-20). He is God's Son (1:15) and "the head of the body, the church" (1:18). The author goes on to say he is the key to God's mystery (2:2).

WHY WAS COLOSSIANS WRITTEN?

The apostle Paul, as the author of COLOSSIANS, wanted to encourage the Christians in Colosse to continue living in Christ Jesus (2:6) and not to be fooled by false teachings or tricked into following any of the many religious ideas and practices that were being taught in Asia Minor at that time (2:8, 16-23). The author also wanted to convince the Colossians to "live a life worthy of the Lord" (1:10). This meant that they were to leave behind the bad things that were part of their old life (3:1-9) and live as God's special people who are kind, humble, gentle, patient, forgiving, and loving (3:12-14). Paul's instruction also included some rules about how family members were to treat each other.

WHAT'S THE STORY BEHIND THE SCENE?

Colosse was a small inland city in Asia Minor, east of the major port city of Ephesus and close to the cities of Laodicea and Hierapolis (see the map, opposite). Colosse, Laodicea, and Hierapolis are mentioned in this letter. The writer of COLOSSIANS had never actually been to Colosse, but he was pleased to learn that the Christians there were strong in their faith (1:3-6; 2:6, 7). Instead, the Colossians had heard the gospel about Jesus from Epaphras, one of Paul's co-workers, who had once lived in Colosse (1:7; 4:12, 13).

HOW IS COLOSSIANS CONSTRUCTED?

COLOSSIANS is a letter that includes opening and concluding greetings that are similar to the ones found in several of Paul's letters. The opening greeting (1:1, 2) is nearly identical to the opening of EPHESIANS (Eph 1:1, 2). The letter can be outlined in this way:

Colosse: Colosse was located about 110 miles east of Ephesus, in the Lycus River valley, on an east-west trade route. It had been a prominent city for at least five hundred years before the time of Paul and was known for its wool and textile industry. But in Paul's day, Colosse was less important than the nearby cities of Hierapolis and Laodicea. Between A.D. 60 and 64, Colosse was completely destroyed by an earthquake.

Judging from this letter, the area around Colosse may have been a place where numerous religious traditions and philosophies were practiced, and sometimes blended. These included beliefs in astrology, called "the basic principles of this world" (2:8), as well as the worship of angels, and mystery cults that had strict rules for their members (2:16-23).

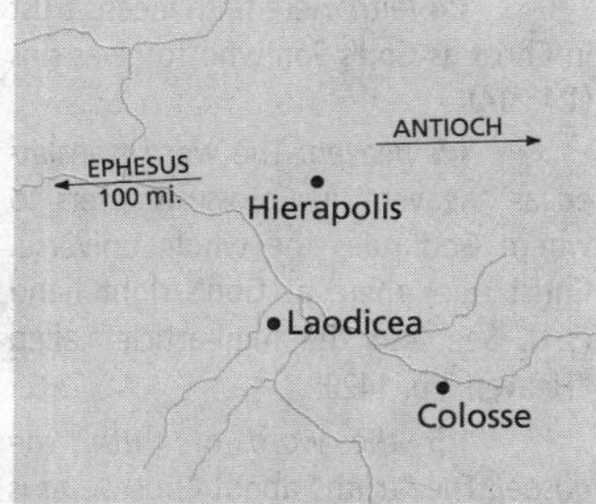

Paul, Timothy: Paul was also known by his Jewish name, Saul (Acts 7:57—8:3; 9:1-30). He had been a strict follower of the Law of Moses and persecuted the early followers of Jesus (Phil 3:5, 6). But the living Christ chose him to be an apostle and preach the gospel (Acts 9:1-19). See the mini-article called "Paul (Saul) of Tarsus," p. 2177.

Timothy was the son of a Jewish Christian mother and a Gentile father from Lystra (Acts 16:1). Paul guided him as a follower of Christ (1 Cor 4:17). He is named as Paul's co-worker in many of Paul's letters (2 Cor 1:1; 1 Thes 1:1; Phlm 1).

Greetings, prayers, and a hymn to Christ (1:1-23)
Paul teaches the truth about Christ (1:24—2:23)
Living the new life in Christ (3:1—4:6)
Farewell (4:7-18)

Greetings, Prayers, and a Hymn to Christ

Paul greets God's people in Colosse and gives thanks to God for all the good things he keeps hearing about the Colossian Christians. He prays that they will honor the Lord and stay deeply rooted in their faith in Christ. Verses 15-20 are probably an early Christian hymn that describes who Jesus is and what he has done.

1 Paul, an apostle of Christ Jesus by the will of God, and Timothy our brother,

[2]To the holy and faithful[a] brothers in Christ at Colosse:

Grace and peace to you from God our Father.[b]

Thanksgiving and Prayer

[3]We always thank God, the Father of our Lord Jesus Christ,
when we pray for you, [4]because we have heard of your faith in Christ
Jesus and of the love you have for all the saints— [5]the faith and love
that spring from the hope that is stored up for you in heaven and that
you have already heard about in the word of truth, the gospel [6]that
has come to you. All over the world this gospel is bearing fruit and
growing, just as it has been doing among you since the day you heard
it and understood God's grace in all its truth. [7]You learned it from
Epaphras, our dear fellow servant, who is a faithful minister of Christ
on our[c] behalf, [8]and who also told us of your love in the Spirit.
[9]For this reason, since the day we heard about you, we have
not stopped praying for you and asking God to fill you with the
knowledge of his will through all spiritual wisdom and understanding. [10]And we pray this in order that you may live a life worthy of the Lord and may please him in every way: bearing fruit in
every good work, growing in the knowledge of God, [11]being
strengthened with all power according to his glorious might so
that you may have great endurance and patience, and joyfully
[12]giving thanks to the Father, who has qualified you[d] to share in
the inheritance of the saints in the kingdom of light. [13]For he has

[a]2 Or *believing* [b]2 Some manuscripts *Father and the Lord Jesus Christ*
[c]7 Some manuscripts *your* [d]12 Some manuscripts *us*

1:1 *apostle of Christ Jesus:* Here "apostle" means someone chosen by God to spread the message about Jesus Christ. The word "Christ" is from the Greek word *christos*, which means "Messiah" or "chosen one." See also the mini-article called "Messiah (Chosen One)," p. 1124.

1:2 *holy and faithful brothers in Christ:* The term for God's people. The Greek word translated as "brothers" actually means members of a family—brothers and sisters.

1:3 *God, the Father of our Lord Jesus:* Jesus often referred to God as "Father" (John 14, for example). Paul uses this same term in many of his letters to describe God (Gal 1:2,3; 1 Cor 1:3; Phil 1:2; Rom 1:7). When it is used for Jesus, "Lord" emphasizes his authority and power.

1:4 *faith:* Here faith means trust in Christ as God's Son who forgives sins (1:13,14).

1:5 *heaven:* The word translated as "heaven" in COLOSSIANS refers to where God rules the whole universe. Christ rules there at God's right hand (3:1). See also the mini-article called "Heaven," p. 1420.

1:5 *the word of truth, the gospel:* The "truth" about Christ Jesus is the one that the Colossians heard from Epaphras and the one that Paul preaches. This message is the "gospel," the good news, which is both the message about Jesus Christ and the message Jesus brought about the kingdom of God. Paul also calls the gospel "the power of God for the salvation of everyone who believes" (Rom 1:16).

1:7 *Epaphras:* Paul's friend, Epaphras, was the one who brought the gospel to the Colossians. He was probably from Asia Minor (Col 4:12) and spent time in jail with Paul (Phlm 23,24). Epaphras was the one who had brought Paul the good reports about the love that God's Spirit gave the Colossian Christians.

1:8 *the Spirit:* Refers to the Holy Spirit, who gives special gifts to God's people. See also the mini-article called "Holy Spirit," p. 2082.

rescued us from the dominion of darkness and brought us into the
kingdom of the Son he loves, 14in whom we have redemption,[a] the
forgiveness of sins.

The Supremacy of Christ

15He is the image of the invisible God, the firstborn over all
creation. 16For by him all things were created: things in heaven and
on earth, visible and invisible, whether thrones or powers or rulers

---

[a]14 A few late manuscripts *redemption through his blood*

God Creating the World, illuminated page from a *Bible moralisée* around 1250. In the Middle Ages God was often depicted in art as a master builder who used the tools of his trade (here a compass) to create the world. The book of COLOSSIANS includes part of an early Christian hymn that celebrates Christ as co-creator of the universe. Christ is "the image of the invisible God, the firstborn over all creation. For by him all things were created . . . all things were created by him and for him" (see 1:15-20).

1:10 *Lord:* Meaning Christ (see the note at 1:3).

1:12,13 *kingdom of light . . . kingdom of the Son he loves:* In the Bible, light is used to describe God or God's Word (John 1:3,4; 1 John 1:5; Ps 119:105), and those people or things that reveal God's truth (Isa 49:6). The followers of Jesus are called "sons of light" and "children of light" (John 12:35,36,46; Eph 5:8).

The kingdom of God's Son is God's rule over people, both in this life and in the life to come (see also Eph 5:5). This phrase also expresses how Jesus will defeat Satan and the powers that oppose God. This victory means that those who trust in Christ have forgiveness and are free to love and serve God.

1:13 *dominion of darkness:* In the Bible, "darkness" refers to places of pain (Ps 107:10) or confusion (Eccl 2:14). God's opponents are called the rulers of darkness (Eph 6:12), and those who do not do what God expects may be thrown "outside, into the dark" (Matt 22:13), a place of everlasting torture. The name "Satan" means "God's opponent." The biblical writers understood Satan to be the leader of all the forces in the universe that oppose God. See also the mini-article called "Satan," p. 963.

1:14 *forgiveness of sins:* Sin occurs when people rebel against God and disobey God's Law. Forgiveness removes the sin as a barrier between them and God. According to the Jewish Scriptures (Old Testament), those who disobeyed God's Law could be forgiven by turning back to God and by making a sacrifice commanded by the Law of Moses (see the note at 1:20). Jesus died to take away sins (Rom 3:25,26; Eph 1:7, 8). See also the mini-article called "Sin," p. 2181.

1:15,16 *He is the image of the invisible God . . . all things were created:* When humans saw Christ Jesus, they saw what God was really like. Christ was present with God at the time God created the universe (John 1:1-3).

1:18 *head of the body, the church:* Christ is the head of the whole church, which Paul frequently called "the body of Christ" (Rom 12:5; 1 Cor 12:27; Eph 1:22,23). See also the mini-article called "Church," p. 2264.

1:18 *firstborn from among the dead:* After Jesus was put to death on a cross, God raised him from death (Matt 27:31—28:7; Acts 2:22-24, 32). See also 1 Cor 15:20,23 and the mini-article called "Resurrection," p. 2210.

1:20 *making peace through his blood, shed on the cross:* Jesus died on the cross in order to overcome death and to make it possible for all people to be made acceptable to God. The writer most likely is referring to what the priests did each year during the Jewish festival called the Day of Atonement (Yom Kippur). On this day the priests would sacrifice an animal and sprinkle its blood on the cover of the ark of the covenant to remove the sins of the people (Lev 16:14-16). Now God has made the sacrifice. See also Rom 3:25, 26; Eph 1:7, 8; Heb 9:15; 1 Cor 1:30.

1:23 *the gospel . . . I, Paul, have become a servant:* The Greek word for "servant" (*diakonos*) refers to a special helper or minister called a "deacon."

1:25 *I have become its servant:* Paul has been chosen to be a servant of the church by teaching the gospel.

1:26,27 *mystery:* The mystery is the gospel about what Jesus Christ has done to save people from sin and death (Rom 16:25,26). In EPHESIANS, Paul describes this mystery as God accepting the Gentiles and giving them a share of the same promises he gave to the Jews (Eph 3:3-6).

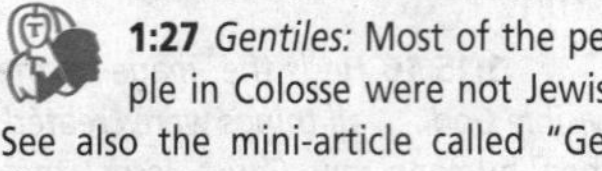

1:27 *Gentiles:* Most of the people in Colosse were not Jewish. See also the mini-article called "Gentiles," p. 2127.

1:20 Eph 2:16.

or authorities; all things were created by him and for him. [17]He is before all things, and in him all things hold together. [18]And he is the head of the body, the church; he is the beginning and the firstborn from among the dead, so that in everything he might have the supremacy. [19]For God was pleased to have all his fullness dwell in him, [20]and through him to reconcile to himself all things, whether things on earth or things in heaven, by making peace through his blood, shed on the cross.

[21]Once you were alienated from God and were enemies in your minds because of[a] your evil behavior. [22]But now he has reconciled you by Christ's physical body through death to present you holy in his sight, without blemish and free from accusation— [23]if you continue in your faith, established and firm, not moved from the hope held out in the gospel. This is the gospel that you heard and that has been proclaimed to every creature under heaven, and of which I, Paul, have become a servant.

Paul Teaches the Truth about Christ

Paul reminds the Colossians not to be fooled or misled by false teachers who were apparently trying to get them to follow certain rituals and observe certain feasts, or to worship the stars or angels. Paul claims that these false teachings no longer have control over the followers of Jesus who have "died" with Christ.

Paul's Labor for the Church

[24]Now I rejoice in what was suffered for you, and I fill up in my flesh what is still lacking in regard to Christ's afflictions, for the sake of his body, which is the church. [25]I have become its servant by the commission God gave me to present to you the word of God in its fullness— [26]the mystery that has been kept hidden for ages and generations, but is now disclosed to the saints. [27]To them God has chosen to make known among the Gentiles the glorious riches of this mystery, which is Christ in you, the hope of glory.

[28]We proclaim him, admonishing and teaching everyone with all wisdom, so that we may present everyone perfect in Christ. [29]To this end I labor, struggling with all his energy, which so powerfully works in me.

2 I want you to know how much I am struggling for you and for those at Laodicea, and for all who have not met me personally. [2]My purpose is that they may be encouraged in heart and united in love, so that they may have the full riches of complete understanding, in order that they may know the mystery of God, name-

[a]21 Or *minds, as shown by*

ly, Christ, [3]in whom are hidden all the treasures of wisdom and
knowledge. [4]I tell you this so that no one may deceive you by fine-
sounding arguments. [5]For though I am absent from you in body, I
am present with you in spirit and delight to see how orderly you
are and how firm your faith in Christ is.

Freedom From Human Regulations Through Life With Christ

[6]So then, just as you received Christ Jesus as Lord, continue
to live in him, [7]rooted and built up in him, strengthened in the
faith as you were taught, and overflowing with thankfulness.

[8]See to it that no one takes you captive through hollow and
deceptive philosophy, which depends on human tradition and the
basic principles of this world rather than on Christ.

[9]For in Christ all the fullness of the Deity lives in bodily
form, [10]and you have been given fullness in Christ, who is the head
over every power and authority. [11]In him you were also circumcised, in the putting off of the sinful nature,[a] not with a circumcision done by the hands of men but with the circumcision done by
Christ, [12]having been buried with him in baptism and raised with
him through your faith in the power of God, who raised him from
the dead.

[13]When you were dead in your sins and in the uncircumcision of your sinful nature,[b] God made you[c] alive with Christ. He
forgave us all our sins, [14]having canceled the written code, with its
regulations, that was against us and that stood opposed to us; he
took it away, nailing it to the cross. [15]And having disarmed the
powers and authorities, he made a public spectacle of them, tri-
umphing over them by the cross.[d]

[16]Therefore do not let anyone judge you by what you eat or
drink, or with regard to a religious festival, a New Moon celebration or a Sabbath day. [17]These are a shadow of the things that were
to come; the reality, however, is found in Christ. [18]Do not let anyone who delights in false humility and the worship of angels dis-
qualify you for the prize. Such a person goes into great detail about
what he has seen, and his unspiritual mind puffs him up with idle
notions. [19]He has lost connection with the Head, from whom the
whole body, supported and held together by its ligaments and
sinews, grows as God causes it to grow.

[20]Since you died with Christ to the basic principles of this
world, why, as though you still belonged to it, do you submit to its
rules: [21]"Do not handle! Do not taste! Do not touch!"? [22]These are
all destined to perish with use, because they are based on human
commands and teachings. [23]Such regulations indeed have an

[a]11 Or *the flesh in him* [b]13 Or *your flesh* [c]13 Some manuscripts *us* [d]15 Or *them*

2:3 *wisdom and knowledge:* See Prov 2:3-6; Isa 45:3; and the mini-article called "Wisdom," p. 2206.

2:8 *basic principles of this world:* Spirits and unseen forces were thought to control human lives. For Paul, the term "world" often referred to those who were opposed to God and God's plans (Rom 12:2).

2:11 *circumcision:* See the mini-article called "Circumcision," p. 2251.

2:12 *buried with him in baptism:* Being baptized is like dying to sin and being raised to life, just as Jesus died and then was raised to life by God (Rom 6:3-6). See also the mini-article called "Baptism," p. 1976.

2:13 *you were dead . . . God made you alive with Christ:* Paul means that sin leads to separation from God, which is worse than death.

Jesus defeated the power of evil and death when he died on the cross and was raised to life by God. He also promised forgiveness to those who had faith in him.

2:14 *the written code . . . cross:* The Law of Moses refers to the set of instructions that God gave to Moses and the people of Israel at Mount Sinai. When Jesus died on the cross, he removed the guilt that came from disobeying the Law of Moses.

2:16 *what you eat or drink:* Most likely this refers to Jewish Christians who were trying to convince the Colossians to follow the Jewish laws concerning food and religious celebrations.

2:18 *worship of angels:* The worship of angels may refer to some kind of mystery cult in which the participants worshiped certain heavenly beings or had visions of angels.

2:9,10 Col 1:16,19. **2:13** Eph 2:1-5. **2:14** Eph 2:15. **2:16** Rom 14:1-6.

appearance of wisdom, with their self-imposed worship, their false humility and their harsh treatment of the body, but they lack any value in restraining sensual indulgence.

Living the New Life in Christ

Paul encourages the Colossians to recognize what it means to be raised to new life with Christ. This new life will affect the way they live together as God's people. This section also includes instruction for family living and for the relationship between slaves and their masters.

Rules for Holy Living

3 Since, then, you have been raised with Christ, set your hearts
on things above, where Christ is seated at the right hand of God.
2 Set your minds on things above, not on earthly things. 3 For you
died, and your life is now hidden with Christ in God. 4 When
Christ, who is your[a] life, appears, then you also will appear with
him in glory.
5 Put to death, therefore, whatever belongs to your earthly
nature: sexual immorality, impurity, lust, evil desires and greed,
which is idolatry. 6 Because of these, the wrath of God is coming.[b]
7 You used to walk in these ways, in the life you once lived. 8 But
now you must rid yourselves of all such things as these: anger,
rage, malice, slander, and filthy language from your lips. 9 Do not
lie to each other, since you have taken off your old self with its
practices 10 and have put on the new self, which is being renewed in
knowledge in the image of its Creator. 11 Here there is no Greek or
Jew, circumcised or uncircumcised, barbarian, Scythian, slave or
free, but Christ is all, and is in all.
12 Therefore, as God's chosen people, holy and dearly loved,
clothe yourselves with compassion, kindness, humility, gentleness
and patience. 13 Bear with each other and forgive whatever griev-
ances you may have against one another. Forgive as the Lord forgave you. 14 And over all these virtues put on love, which binds
them all together in perfect unity.
15 Let the peace of Christ rule in your hearts, since as members of one body you were called to peace. And be thankful. 16 Let
the word of Christ dwell in you richly as you teach and admonish
one another with all wisdom, and as you sing psalms, hymns and
spiritual songs with gratitude in your hearts to God. 17 And whatever you do, whether in word or deed, do it all in the name of the
Lord Jesus, giving thanks to God the Father through him.

[a]4 Some manuscripts *our* [b]6 Some early manuscripts *coming on those who are disobedient*

3:1 *you have been raised with Christ:* See the note at 2:12.

3:1 *right hand:* The place of power and honor.

3:4 *When Christ . . . appears:* Paul often wrote in his letters about a day when Jesus would come back (1 Cor 1:8,9; 15:20-28; 1 Thes 4:13-18; Phil 1:6; 3:20,21). See also the mini-article called "Second Coming," p. 2277.

3:5 *sexual immorality . . . idolatry:* Those who have a new life in Christ are to avoid having sexual relations forbidden by the Law of Moses and impure sexual thoughts and desires.

3:9 *your old self:* The Colossians had been doing things that were opposed to the will of God and the new life that comes from Jesus. What they were doing may have been like what Paul criticized the Corinthians for doing (1 Cor 5; 6; 10; 11).

3:10 *Creator:* The writer may be referring to God, who created all things (Gen 1:1—2:4). "Creator" may also refer to Christ, who creates new persons by giving them the Holy Spirit (Rom 8:9; Phil 2:13).

3:11 *Greek or Jew . . . barbarian, Scythian:* See the note at 1:27 (Gentiles). For "Jews," see the mini-article called "Israel," p. 264. For circumcised, see the mini-article called "Circumcision," p. 2251.

Barbarians could not speak Greek and were considered in a lower class of society. Scythians, a people from the Caucasus region between the Black and Caspian Seas, often raided their southern neighbors, and were known for their cruelty. For more about the class structure of the Roman empire, see the article called "The World of Jesus: Peoples, Powers, and Politics," p. 1821, and the mini-article called "Slaves and Servants in the Time of Jesus," p. 2006.

3:1 Ps 110:1. **3:9** Eph 4:22. **3:10** Gen 1:26; 2:12,13; Eph 4:24; 2 Cor 5:17. **3:11** Gal 3:26-29. **3:12,13** Eph 4:2. **3:13** Eph 4:32. **3:14** 1 Cor 13. **3:16,17** Eph 5:19,20.

Rules for Christian Households

18 Wives, submit to your husbands, as is fitting in the Lord.
19 Husbands, love your wives and do not be harsh with them.
20 Children, obey your parents in everything, for this pleases
the Lord.
21 Fathers, do not embitter your children, or they will become
discouraged.
22 Slaves, obey your earthly masters in everything; and do it,
not only when their eye is on you and to win their favor, but with
sincerity of heart and reverence for the Lord. 23 Whatever you do,
work at it with all your heart, as working for the Lord, not for
men, 24 since you know that you will receive an inheritance from
the Lord as a reward. It is the Lord Christ you are serving. 25 Anyone who does wrong will be repaid for his wrong, and there is no
favoritism.
4 Masters, provide your slaves with what is right and fair,
because you know that you also have a Master in heaven.

3:18,19 *Wives . . . Husbands:* Just as wives are to honor their husbands and put them first, husbands are to love their wives as much as Christ loved the church. See also 1 Pet 3:7; Gal 3:28,29; Eph 5:22-25.

3:22—4:1 *Slaves . . . Masters:* See the note at 3:11. Paul argues that when slaves serve their masters they are really serving Christ, who will punish evil people, including evil slave owners.

3:22-25 Eph 6:5-8. **3:25** Deut 10:17. **4:1** Eph 6:9.

PRAYER

Prayer happens when people talk and listen to God, or when they praise God by speaking or singing. Prayers of confession are said in order to admit wrong actions or thoughts, and prayers of intercession are prayed to ask for God's help. Prayers are also spoken to give thanks to God for his blessings. People can pray to God when they are alone, as Jesus did at times (Matt 14:23), or they can pray in unison with other believers through words or through songs, or be led by one person who is speaking to God.

Psalms is a book of songs and prayers. It includes prayers of thanks (Ps 11; 18; 63; 103), prayers of praise to God (Ps 19; 104; 148), confession of wrongs that have been done (Ps 51), requests to be freed from one's enemies (Ps 59; 69), pleas to God to do what he has promised (Ps 89), praise to God for his law (Ps 119), and praise for what God has done for his people (Ps 136).

The prophets report how they experienced direct contact with God. For example, see Isaiah 6; Jeremiah 11:18-20; and 17:7-18. In Isaiah 66:22,23 all humanity is expected one day to join together in praising God.

Jesus is often seen at prayer in the Gospels (Mark 1:35-38; 6:46), but especially in the garden just before he was arrested by the authorities (Mark 14:36-39) and again on the cross (Mark 15:34), when he quoted the prayer from Psalm 22. Jesus gave a model of prayer for his followers to use that has come to be known as "The Lord's Prayer" (Luke 11:1-4; Matt 6:9-13). In John 17, Jesus prayed a long prayer of intercession for his disciples.

For Paul, prayer is possible because Christ has introduced his followers to God's undeserved kindness. God has accepted them because Christ sacrificed his life's blood for them (Rom 5:1-11). Having made peace between human beings and God, Jesus gave the Holy Spirit to help his followers to pray (Rom 8:26, 27; 1 Cor 2:10-13). In Paul's letter to the Ephesians, he includes a prayer that the Christians in Ephesus would grow in their understanding and knowledge of God and God's power (Eph 1:15-23). Above all, Paul encourages God's people to pray on all occasions (Eph 6:18; Phil 4:6; Col 4:2).

4:3 *message . . . mystery:* See the notes at 1:5 (word) and 1:26,27.

4:3 *for which I am in chains:* It is not known exactly how many times Paul was in jail or in how many different places. ACTS says that Paul was imprisoned in Caesarea (Acts 23:23—26:32), and was under house arrest in Rome (Acts 28:16-31). Some scholars believe that Paul was also imprisoned during the lengthy time he was in Ephesus (Acts 19:1—20:1).

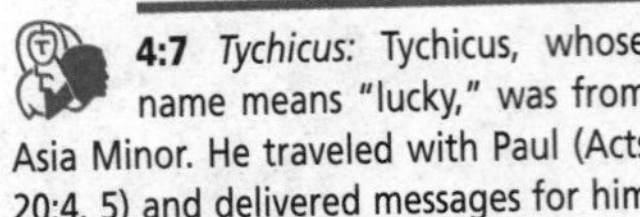

4:7 *Tychicus:* Tychicus, whose name means "lucky," was from Asia Minor. He traveled with Paul (Acts 20:4, 5) and delivered messages for him (Eph 6:21,22; 2 Tim 4:12; Titus 3:12).

4:9 *Onesimus:* Onesimus, whose name means "useful," had been a slave of Philemon (see PHILEMON).

4:5 Eph 5:16. **4:7,8** Eph 6:21, 22.

Further Instructions

[2]Devote yourselves to prayer, being watchful and thankful.
[3]And pray for us, too, that God may open a door for our message,
so that we may proclaim the mystery of Christ, for which I am in
chains. [4]Pray that I may proclaim it clearly, as I should. [5]Be wise in
the way you act toward outsiders; make the most of every opportunity. [6]Let your conversation be always full of grace, seasoned
with salt, so that you may know how to answer everyone.

Farewell

Paul explains how he will send his co-workers to share news about what has been happening to him. He also sends greetings from other followers who are with him and who the Colossian Christians know.

Final Greetings

[7]Tychicus will tell you all the news about me. He is a dear
brother, a faithful minister and fellow servant in the Lord. [8]I am
sending him to you for the express purpose that you may know
about our[a] circumstances and that he may encourage your hearts.
[9]He is coming with Onesimus, our faithful and dear brother, who
is one of you. They will tell you everything that is happening here.
[10]My fellow prisoner Aristarchus sends you his greetings, as
does Mark, the cousin of Barnabas. (You have received instruc-

[a]8 Some manuscripts *that he may know about your*

QUESTIONS ABOUT COLOSSIANS

1. What does Paul pray for concerning the Colossians? (1:9-12) What does it mean to "live a life worthy of the Lord"?
2. List the key points of the hymn in 1:15-20. Choose one point and describe what it means to you.
3. What is the message that Paul says had been kept secret for ages and ages, and why is it important to the Colossians? (1:24-28)
4. How is Paul's message different than the message that others are trying to teach the Colossians? (2:8-23) What messages in the world today pull people away from the new life that God offers in Christ Jesus?
5. Paul talks about dying with Christ (2:20) and being raised to life with Christ. (3:1) What does this mean?
6. Paul says those who trust in Christ are "new" people (3:10) and "God's chosen people." (3:12) What are some of the things God's people should not do? (3:5-9) What are the qualities God's people should begin to practice? (3:12-17)
7. Read again what Paul had to say about spreading the message and explaining the mystery about Christ. (4:2-6) What advice does he give about how to treat unbelievers? Which of Paul's points will help you most the next time you try to share your faith with someone?

tions about him; if he comes to you, welcome him.) [11]Jesus, who is
called Justus, also sends greetings. These are the only Jews among
my fellow workers for the kingdom of God, and they have proved
a comfort to me. [12]Epaphras, who is one of you and a servant of
Christ Jesus, sends greetings. He is always wrestling in prayer for
you, that you may stand firm in all the will of God, mature and
fully assured. [13]I vouch for him that he is working hard for you and
for those at Laodicea and Hierapolis. [14]Our dear friend Luke, the
doctor, and Demas send greetings. [15]Give my greetings to the
brothers at Laodicea, and to Nympha and the church in her house.
[16]After this letter has been read to you, see that it is also read
in the church of the Laodiceans and that you in turn read the letter from Laodicea.
[17]Tell Archippus: "See to it that you complete the work you
have received in the Lord."
[18]I, Paul, write this greeting in my own hand. Remember my
chains. Grace be with you.

4:10-17 *Aristarchus . . . Archippus:* Most of the people mentioned in these verses are mentioned elsewhere in the New Testament.

- Aristarchus (Acts 19:29; 20:4; 27:2; Phlm 24).
- Mark (also called John; Acts 12:12, 24, 25; 13:13; 15:36-39; 2 Tim 4:11).
- Epaphras (Col 1:7; Phlm 23).
- Luke (Phlm 24; 2 Tim 4:11).
- Demas (Phlm 24; 2 Tim 4:10).
- Archippus (Phlm 2)

Jesus (Justus) and Nympha are mentioned only here in COLOSSIANS.

4:13 *Laodicea and Hierapolis:* Laodicea was located about twelve miles west of Colosse. Hierapolis was a city famous for its dye and textile industry. It was located six miles away from Laodicea in the Upper Lycus Valley. See the map on p. 2281.

4:16 *read the letter from Laodicea:* This is the only place in the Bible that the letter to the church at Laodicea is mentioned.

4:18 *write this greeting in my own hand:* This seems to indicate that the letter was dictated to a secretary of some sort.

1 THESSALONIANS

What happens when we die? Find out what Paul says about this when he writes to his good friends in Thessalonica.

Paul's letters: FIRST THESSALONIANS may have been written as early as A.D. 43 and is most likely the earliest of Paul's letters. This papyrus fragment from the third century A.D. shows the beginning of 1 THESSALONIANS.

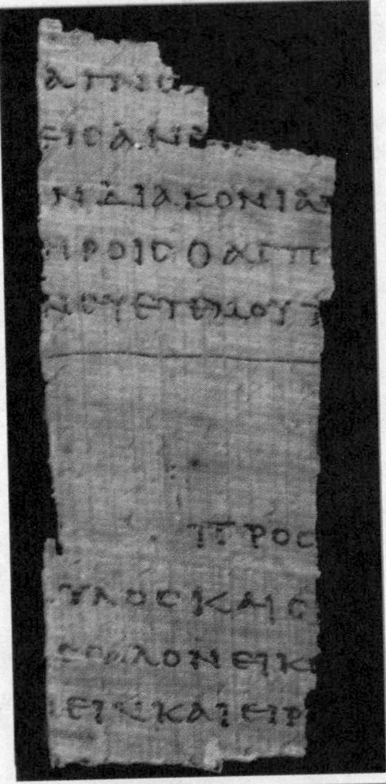

1:1 *Paul, Silas and Timothy:* See the mini-article called "Paul (Saul) of Tarsus," p. 2177. Timothy is named as Paul's co-worker in many of Paul's letters (1 Cor 16:10; 2 Cor 1:1; Phlm 1). Paul sent Timothy to help the Thessalonians settle some disputes (3:2-6). The apostles and church elders in Jerusalem sent Silas along with Paul to start new churches among the Gentiles (Acts 15:22). They were put in prison in Philippi (Acts 16:16-40) and later were attacked by a mob at Thessalonica (Acts 17:1-9).

1:1 *church:* See the mini-article called "Church," p. 2264.

1:1 *the Thessalonians:* Located in the Macedonian city of Thessalonica. See the note and the map at 2 Thes 1:1 (Thessalonica).

WHAT MAKES 1 THESSALONIANS SPECIAL?

This short letter provides a look at the relationship Paul had with the Thessalonian church. Much of the letter is devoted to his prayers and thanksgiving for their faith. He is like a pastor who is concerned for his congregation and thankful for the time he has spent with them. Paul repeatedly uses phrases like "You know" and "You remember," and then reminds the Thessalonians what they have learned from him. This makes it clear that he is writing to people who are already followers of Jesus Christ.

WHY WAS 1 THESSALONIANS WRITTEN?

Paul wanted to greet the Thessalonians and thank them for their faithfulness. He also wanted to let them know that he intended to come and see them again (3:11). Apparently some of the Thessalonian Christians had questions about what would happen to believers who had died before Christ came back again (sometimes called the "Second Coming"), so Paul included an answer to this question (4:13-18). He followed up this teaching by reminding them to be on the lookout for Christ's return at all times (5:1-11). As in most of his letters, Paul gives instruction about how to live in a way that pleases God (4:1-12).

WHAT'S THE STORY BEHIND THE SCENE?

ACTS describes the time of Paul's ministry among the Thessalonians (Acts 17:1-10). Just how long he stayed in Thessalonica is not clear, but Paul says in this letter that he worked long and hard to support himself (2:9) while starting the church in Thessalonica. This suggests that he must have stayed for at least several months.

Thessalonica, the capital of the Roman province of Macedonia in northern Greece, was located on a major east-west highway. Many of its people had worshiped idols before becoming Christians (1:9). But now they were faithful to the Lord, and because of them the Lord's message had spread everywhere in the region (1:7,8). This letter may be the oldest of Paul's letters found in the New Testament, and may even be the earliest of all the New Testament writings.

HOW IS 1 THESSALONIANS CONSTRUCTED?

The letter can be outlined in the following way:

The Thessalonians' faith and Paul's work (1:1—3:13)

Christian living and Christ's return (4:1—5:11)

Final greetings (5:12-28)

Serving with a ♡ like JESUS!

The Thessalonians' Faith and Paul's Work

Paul sends greetings to the followers of Christ at Thessalonica. He thanks them for becoming examples of faithfulness and love for all the followers throughout Greece. He praises them for turning away from idols and facing mistreatment because of their faith in Christ. Paul reminds them about how hard he worked when he was staying with them and giving them God's message. Although Paul's co-worker Timothy has given Paul good reports of their faith, Paul now hopes to visit them once again.

1 Paul, Silas[a] and Timothy,

To the church of the Thessalonians in God the Father and
the Lord Jesus Christ:

Grace and peace to you.[b]

Thanksgiving for the Thessalonians' Faith

[2]We always thank God for all of you, mentioning you in our
prayers. [3]We continually remember before our God and Father
your work produced by faith, your labor prompted by love, and
your endurance inspired by hope in our Lord Jesus Christ.
[4]For we know, brothers loved by God, that he has chosen
you, [5]because our gospel came to you not simply with words, but
also with power, with the Holy Spirit and with deep conviction.
You know how we lived among you for your sake. [6]You became
imitators of us and of the Lord; in spite of severe suffering, you
welcomed the message with the joy given by the Holy Spirit. [7]And
so you became a model to all the believers in Macedonia and
Achaia. [8]The Lord's message rang out from you not only in Macedonia and Achaia—your faith in God has become known everywhere. Therefore we do not need to say anything about it, [9]for they
themselves report what kind of reception you gave us. They tell
how you turned to God from idols to serve the living and true
God, [10]and to wait for his Son from heaven, whom he raised from
the dead—Jesus, who rescues us from the coming wrath.

Paul's Ministry in Thessalonica

2 You know, brothers, that our visit to you was not a failure. [2]We
had previously suffered and been insulted in Philippi, as you know,
but with the help of our God we dared to tell you his gospel in
spite of strong opposition. [3]For the appeal we make does not
spring from error or impure motives, nor are we trying to trick

[a]1 Greek *Silvanus*, a variant of *Silas* [b]1 Some early manuscripts *you from God our Father and the Lord Jesus Christ*

1:3 *faith:* See the mini-article called "Faith," p. 1932.

1:5 *gospel . . . Holy Spirit:* The "gospel" is both the message about Jesus and the message Jesus brings about the kingdom of God. Those who believe the gospel are part of God's new family of followers. See the note at 4:8 (Holy Spirit).

1:8 *Lord's message:* This refers to the gospel (see the note at 1:5).

1:9 *you turned to God from idols:* Most of the followers in the Thessalonian church were Gentile converts who likely had worshiped local gods or goddesses before turning to Jesus. See the chart called "Greek and Roman Gods and Goddesses," p. 2136.

1:10 *wait for his Son from heaven:* See also the mini-articles called "Son of God," p. 2044 and "Heaven," p. 1420.

1:10 *Jesus . . . rescues us from the coming wrath:* Paul often talked in his letters about a day when Jesus would come back (see 4:13-18; see also 1 Cor 15:20-28; Phil 1:10; 2:16; 3:20,21). Those who have faith in Christ will be saved (John 12:44-50), but those who reject God will experience God's punishment (Matt 13:47-50; 25:31-46; 1 Thes 5:1-11). See also the mini-articles called "Salvation," p. 2021 and "Second Coming," p. 2277.

2:2 *Philippi:* See the Introduction to PHILIPPIANS, p. 2271 and the map on p. 2298.

2:3 *nor are we trying to trick you:* Paul's message came straight from God, and his actions were honest and pure (2:9,10). Others may have taught another message to make money (2:5) or to get a reputation (2:6), but Paul did not (see also 2 Cor 2:17; 4:2).

1:6 Acts 17:5-9. **2:2** Acts 16:11—17:15.

2:6 *apostles:* An apostle is someone sent to do a special job or to represent a major authority. The twelve special disciples chosen by Jesus and the followers who saw Jesus after God raised him from death were apostles (Acts 1:2, 3). Since Jesus appeared to Paul (Acts 9:1-19), Paul also claimed to be an apostle (Gal 1:15,16; 1 Cor 9:1).

2:9 *we worked night and day:* Paul was a tentmaker (Acts 18:3) who probably made and repaired tents and other leather goods while in Thessalonica. See 1 Cor 9:1-18.

2:12 *calls you into his kingdom and glory:* Paul says that all those God has chosen will be glorified in the kingdom of God. See also 1 Cor 15:20-24,35-44.

2:13 *the word of God:* The "gospel." See the note at 1:5.

2:14 *God's churches in Judea:* See the mini-article called "Church," p. 2264. The Christian church began in Jerusalem in Judea (Acts 1,2). The earliest followers were Jewish, like Jesus and his twelve apostles. Many of these followers were treated badly (Acts 3–7).

When the Thessalonians listened to Paul's teachings and began to follow Jesus Christ, their own Jewish and Gentile neighbors persecuted them (see Acts 17:5).

2:14,15 *the Jews, who killed the Lord Jesus:* Paul is referring specifically to those Jewish leaders who rejected Jesus and his claim to be God's Son. They cooperated with the Roman authorities in seeing that he was executed. Each of the Gospels reports the arrest, trial, and death of Jesus (see, for example, Mark 14:43—15:41). It is not clear which prophets the author has in mind. See Acts 7:52; Jer 26:20-24.

2:15 Acts 9:23,29; 13:45,50; 14:2,5,19; 17:5,13; 18:12.

you. [4]On the contrary, we speak as men approved by God to be
entrusted with the gospel. We are not trying to please men but
God, who tests our hearts. [5]You know we never used flattery, nor
did we put on a mask to cover up greed—God is our witness. [6]We
were not looking for praise from men, not from you or anyone
else.

As apostles of Christ we could have been a burden to you,
[7]but we were gentle among you, like a mother caring for her little
children. [8]We loved you so much that we were delighted to share
with you not only the gospel of God but our lives as well, because
you had become so dear to us. [9]Surely you remember, brothers,
our toil and hardship; we worked night and day in order not to be
a burden to anyone while we preached the gospel of God to you.

[10]You are witnesses, and so is God, of how holy, righteous
and blameless we were among you who believed. [11]For you know
that we dealt with each of you as a father deals with his own children, [12]encouraging, comforting and urging you to live lives worthy of God, who calls you into his kingdom and glory.

[13]And we also thank God continually because, when you
received the word of God, which you heard from us, you accepted
it not as the word of men, but as it actually is, the word of God,
which is at work in you who believe. [14]For you, brothers, became
imitators of God's churches in Judea, which are in Christ Jesus:
You suffered from your own countrymen the same things those
churches suffered from the Jews, [15]who killed the Lord Jesus and
the prophets and also drove us out. They displease God and are
hostile to all men [16]in their effort to keep us from speaking to the
Gentiles so that they may be saved. In this way they always heap
up their sins to the limit. The wrath of God has come upon them
at last.[a]

Paul's Longing to See the Thessalonians

[17]But, brothers, when we were torn away from you for a
short time (in person, not in thought), out of our intense longing
we made every effort to see you. [18]For we wanted to come to you—
certainly I, Paul, did, again and again—but Satan stopped us. [19]For
what is our hope, our joy, or the crown in which we will glory in
the presence of our Lord Jesus when he comes? Is it not you?
[20]Indeed, you are our glory and joy.

3 So when we could stand it no longer, we thought it best to be
left by ourselves in Athens. [2]We sent Timothy, who is our brother
and God's fellow worker[b] in spreading the gospel of Christ, to
strengthen and encourage you in your faith, [3]so that no one would
be unsettled by these trials. You know quite well that we were destined for them. [4]In fact, when we were with you, we kept telling

[a]**16** Or *them fully* [b]**2** Some manuscripts *brother and fellow worker*; other manuscripts *brother and God's servant*

you that we would be persecuted. And it turned out that way, as
you well know. [5]For this reason, when I could stand it no longer, I
sent to find out about your faith. I was afraid that in some way the
tempter might have tempted you and our efforts might have been
useless.

Timothy's Encouraging Report

[6]But Timothy has just now come to us from you and has
brought good news about your faith and love. He has told us that
you always have pleasant memories of us and that you long to see
us, just as we also long to see you. [7]Therefore, brothers, in all our
distress and persecution we were encouraged about you because of
your faith. [8]For now we really live, since you are standing firm in
the Lord. [9]How can we thank God enough for you in return for all
the joy we have in the presence of our God because of you? [10]Night
and day we pray most earnestly that we may see you again and
supply what is lacking in your faith.

[11]Now may our God and Father himself and our Lord Jesus
clear the way for us to come to you. [12]May the Lord make your love
increase and overflow for each other and for everyone else, just as
ours does for you. [13]May he strengthen your hearts so that you will
be blameless and holy in the presence of our God and Father when
our Lord Jesus comes with all his holy ones.

Christian Living and Christ's Return

Paul reminds the Thessalonians that God wants them to be holy, which means treating one another with respect and avoiding immoral behavior. He then explains what will happen when Christ returns, a day Paul encourages the Thessalonians to be watching for at all times.

Living to Please God

4 Finally, brothers, we instructed you how to live in order to
please God, as in fact you are living. Now we ask you and urge you
in the Lord Jesus to do this more and more. [2]For you know what
instructions we gave you by the authority of the Lord Jesus.

[3]It is God's will that you should be sanctified: that you should
avoid sexual immorality; [4]that each of you should learn to control
his own body[a] in a way that is holy and honorable, [5]not in passionate lust like the heathen, who do not know God; [6]and that in this
matter no one should wrong his brother or take advantage of him.
The Lord will punish men for all such sins, as we have already told
you and warned you. [7]For God did not call us to be impure, but to

[a]**4** Or *learn to live with his own wife*; or *learn to acquire a wife*

2:16 *Gentiles:* Gentiles refers to those people who are not Jewish. Paul was chosen by God to bring the gospel to all people, but his special mission was to the Gentiles (Acts 9:15; 15:12; Gal 2:1-9). See also the mini-article called "Gentiles," p. 2127.

2:18 *Satan:* Satan means "adversary" and is also known as the devil ("accuser"; see Matt 4:1-11; John 13:2). See also the mini-article called "Satan," p. 963.

2:19 *crown:* Paul may be talking about the kind of crown that was given to winners of athletic contests in ancient Greece. These crowns were made of fresh leaves, and were symbols of honor and respect.

2:19 *Lord Jesus when he comes:* See the note at 1:10 (Jesus . . . rescue us).

3:1 *Athens:* See the map on p. 2298. The author of ACTS reports that Paul went to Athens after Jewish leaders persecuted him in Thessalonica and Berea (Acts 17:5-34).

3:2 *Timothy:* See the note at 1:1 (Paul . . . Timothy).

3:2 *the gospel of Christ:* See the note at 1:5.

3:5 *the tempter:* Referring to Satan. See the note at 2:18.

3:11 *our God and Father . . . Lord Jesus:* See the note at 2 Thes 1:1 (God our Father).

3:13 *when our Lord Jesus comes:* See the mini-article called "Second Coming," p. 2277.

4:3 *be sanctified . . . avoid sexual immorality:* To "be sanctified" means to be set apart or chosen to do what God wants. Holy living includes avoiding immoral sexual behavior (Acts 15:20,29; 21:25; 1 Cor 5:1; Gal 5:19). In Thessalonica, sexual intercourse was sometimes practiced as part of certain pagan ceremonies.

3:6 Acts 18:5.

live a holy life. [8]Therefore, he who rejects this instruction does not
reject man but God, who gives you his Holy Spirit.
[9]Now about brotherly love we do not need to write to you,
for you yourselves have been taught by God to love each other.
[10]And in fact, you do love all the brothers throughout Macedonia.
Yet we urge you, brothers, to do so more and more.

Make it your ambition to lead a quiet life, to mind your own business and to work with your hands, just as we told you.
1 Thes 4:11

4:8 *he who rejects this instruction:* The Thessalonian followers did not become God's children by keeping the rules set out in the Law of Moses, but the way they lived showed that they were part of God's people.

4:8 *Holy Spirit:* The Holy Spirit is the unseen power of God carrying out God's purposes in the world. For Paul, the Holy Spirit is present in the lives of Christ's followers to help them live in a way that pleases God. See also Rom 8:1-17; Gal 5:22-26. For more, see the mini-article called "Holy Spirit," p. 2082.

4:10 *Macedonia:* See the map on p. 2298.

The Second Coming of Christ, marble relief, Constantinople, fourth century A.D. Paul, like most Christians in the first decades after Jesus died and was resurrected, expected Jesus to return soon. In this letter Paul tries to comfort the Christians at Thessalonica who were worried about fellow believers who had already died. He tells them that when God brings Jesus back again, he will bring with him all who had faith in Jesus before they died. The living will be gathered together as well. From that time on, we will all "be with the Lord forever. Therefore encourage each other with these words." This sense of expectation is captured in this relief as the sheep (representing disciples of Christ) look up at the empty throne and await the day when Christ will return and rule all creation.

11Make it your ambition to lead a quiet life, to mind your
own business and to work with your hands, just as we told you,
12so that your daily life may win the respect of outsiders and so
that you will not be dependent on anybody.

END TIMES

Many biblical writers concerned themselves with thoughts about how the present world would come to an end and about how God would take complete control of the universe. These beliefs became important in Jewish writings before the time of Jesus. The prophet Daniel talked about God having appointed the "time of the end," when human plans and schemes would be replaced by the purposes of God and there would be a judgment of the dead (Dan 8:19). Habakkuk wrote that the LORD's time would come in the future, and those who lived by faith would be acceptable to him (Hab 2:3,4). See also the mini-article called "Day of the LORD," p. 1727.

These beliefs were also important in early Christian writings. Jesus tells the disciples about the time in the future when a great many terrible things will happen in the world and how the Son of Man (meaning Jesus himself) will return to gather his "elect" from all over the earth (Mark 13). In JOHN, Jesus' friend Martha speaks to Jesus about her belief that her brother Lazarus would rise again in the resurrection "at the last day" (John 11:24). Paul warns Christians about the terrible times that will come "in the last days" (2 Tim 3:1).

By the first century there were two very important beliefs about the "End Times" or "Last Days." First, that there would be a final conflict between the powers of good and evil. And second, that God's people would have to face hard times before the final age comes. These beliefs were influenced by some historical situations. First, the Judeans who returned from exile in Babylon hoped that their kingdom would be renewed and become as powerful as it was in the time of King David (see the mini-article called "Exile," p. 1541). This did not happen, and the people of Judea were ruled by a number of more powerful nations (Persians first, and later, Greeks and Romans). The one attempt to start a Jewish kingdom under the leadership of the Maccabees (168-63 B.C.) briefly succeeded but did not last.

Besides being forced to live through a period of political turmoil, the Judeans who returned after the exile had become familiar with the religious teachings of the Persians. The Persians taught that evil was not simply the result of human failings and selfishness but was also part of an unchanging battle between good and evil. They believed that all the evil that existed in the world was the work of hidden evil powers led by God's chief opponent, the leader of the evil powers. (In Hebrew, this leader is called "Satan." See the mini-article called "Satan," p. 963.) The Persians also believed the good forces would ultimately defeat the forces of evil. The nature of Satan as arch-enemy of God appears in later writings of the Jewish Scriptures (Zech 3) and is present throughout the New Testament (Mark 1:12,13; 3:22-26; Acts 26:12-18; Eph 6:10-13; Rev 20:1-3). See also the mini-article called "Apocalyptic Writing," p. 1656.

The Bible also teaches that God's purposes were revealed to the people of Israel in the Law of Moses. God judged the people according to how they obeyed the Law. Jesus followed God's purposes by calling the faithful people to obedience. They also believed that God would reward the faithful and punish the wicked. These beliefs are apparent in such Jewish writings as DANIEL and in others not included in the Jewish Scriptures, for example, *1 and 2 Enoch* and *Jubilees*. They also appear in the messages of Jesus and Paul, and in nearly all the books of the New Testament, but especially in REVELATION. The New Testament writers viewed the period that began with Christ's first coming and extending until he comes again as the "last days." Therefore, we are living in the last days.

4:15 *the coming of the Lord:* The Greek word that Paul uses here is *parousia*, which means "presence" or "arrival." It also was used throughout the Greek-speaking world to refer to a great event, such as when a king made a formal appearance before his people.

4:16 *heaven:* See the mini-article called "Heaven," p. 1420.

4:16 *the voice of the archangel:* The archangel here is probably Michael (Dan 10:13,20,21; Jude 9; Rev 12:7).

4:16 *the trumpet call of God:* Paul also mentions God's trumpet in 1 Corinthians 15:51,52. See also Zech 9:14; Isa 27:13; Joel 2:1,15.

4:16 *rise first:* Those who have died but had faith in Jesus will be given a new life with a new spiritual body (1 Cor 15:35-44,51,52). See the mini-article called "Resurrection," p. 2210.

5:2 Matt 24:42,43; Luke 12:35-40; 2 Pet 3:10; Rev 3:2,3. **5:8** Isa 59:17; Eph 6:13-17.

The Coming of the Lord

13 Brothers, we do not want you to be ignorant about those
who fall asleep, or to grieve like the rest of men, who have no
hope. 14 We believe that Jesus died and rose again and so we believe
that God will bring with Jesus those who have fallen asleep in him.
15 According to the Lord's own word, we tell you that we who are
still alive, who are left till the coming of the Lord, will certainly not
precede those who have fallen asleep. 16 For the Lord himself will
come down from heaven, with a loud command, with the voice of
the archangel and with the trumpet call of God, and the dead in
Christ will rise first. 17 After that, we who are still alive and are left
will be caught up together with them in the clouds to meet the
Lord in the air. And so we will be with the Lord forever. 18 Therefore encourage each other with these words.
5 Now, brothers, about times and dates we do not need to write
to you, 2 for you know very well that the day of the Lord will come
like a thief in the night. 3 While people are saying, "Peace and safety," destruction will come on them suddenly, as labor pains on a
pregnant woman, and they will not escape.
4 But you, brothers, are not in darkness so that this day
should surprise you like a thief. 5 You are all sons of the light and
sons of the day. We do not belong to the night or to the darkness.
6 So then, let us not be like others, who are asleep, but let us be alert
and self-controlled. 7 For those who sleep, sleep at night, and those
who get drunk, get drunk at night. 8 But since we belong to the day,
let us be self-controlled, putting on faith and love as a breastplate,
and the hope of salvation as a helmet. 9 For God did not appoint us

QUESTIONS ABOUT 1 THESSALONIANS

1. How had the Thessalonians been a model for other Christians in nearby cities? (1:7-9) How can Christians today be a model for others?
2. In 2:1-12 Paul describes his work in Thessalonica. What does he say was his motivation for preaching? What does he imply would be wrong motives for preaching the gospel?
3. Paul sent his friend Timothy to remind the Thessalonians of the message Paul had first taught them (3:1-6). Why is it important for Christians to be reminded often about the message about Christ? Have you had a good teacher tell you the message about Christ? If so, describe this person and how he or she taught this message.
4. What was a special concern for some of the Thessalonians? (4:13-15) What did Paul say to calm their fears?
5. How does Paul suggest the Thessalonian Christians prepare for the Lord's return? (5:1-11) How does he say they should live in the meantime? (5:12-22) Which of Paul's suggestions do you find most challenging right now? Why?
6. Some people consider 1 THESSALONIANS the "warmest" or "most affectionate" letter Paul wrote to a group of followers. Which of Paul's statements do you find the most encouraging? Why? Is there someone in your family, school, place of employment, or church who needs encouragement? What can you say to that person this week that will encourage him or her?

to suffer wrath but to receive salvation through our Lord Jesus
Christ. [10]He died for us so that, whether we are awake or asleep,
we may live together with him. [11]Therefore encourage one another and build each other up, just as in fact you are doing.

Final Greetings

Paul's warm greetings show how much he loved and appreciated the Thessalonian Christians. He prays that God will sanctify them until Christ returns again.

Final Instructions

[12]Now we ask you, brothers, to respect those who work hard
among you, who are over you in the Lord and who admonish you.
[13]Hold them in the highest regard in love because of their work.
Live in peace with each other. [14]And we urge you, brothers, warn
those who are idle, encourage the timid, help the weak, be patient
with everyone. [15]Make sure that nobody pays back wrong for
wrong, but always try to be kind to each other and to everyone
else.

[16]Be joyful always; [17]pray continually; [18]give thanks in all circumstances, for this is God's will for you in Christ Jesus.

[19]Do not put out the Spirit's fire; [20]do not treat prophecies
with contempt. [21]Test everything. Hold on to the good. [22]Avoid
every kind of evil.

[23]May God himself, the God of peace, sanctify you through
and through. May your whole spirit, soul and body be kept blameless at the coming of our Lord Jesus Christ. [24]The one who calls
you is faithful and he will do it.

[25]Brothers, pray for us. [26]Greet all the brothers with a holy
kiss. [27]I charge you before the Lord to have this letter read to all
the brothers.

[28]The grace of our Lord Jesus Christ be with you.

4:17 *caught up together . . . in the clouds:* Christ's followers who are still alive when Christ returns will be taken up to heaven in the same way that God took Jesus up to heaven (Acts 1:9).

5:5 *light . . . day . . . night . . . darkness:* In the Bible, light is used to describe God or God's Word (John 1:3,4; 1 John 1:5; Ps 119:105), and those people or things that reveal God's truth (Isa 49:6). The followers of Jesus are sometimes called "children of light" (Eph 5:8). "Darkness" and the night refer to pain, suffering (Ps 107:10), or confusion (Eccl 2:13,14). God's opponents are called the rulers of this "dark world" (Eph 6:12), and those who do not do what God expects risk being thrown "into the darkness" (Matt 22:13).

5:8 *hope of salvation:* See the note at 1:10 (Jesus . . . rescues).

5:9 *Lord Jesus Christ:* See the note at 2 Thes 1:1 (God our Father).

5:19,20 *Spirit's fire . . . prophecies:* Paul described the gifts of the Holy Spirit in 1 Corinthians 12–14. See the mini-article called "Spiritual Gifts," p. 2219, and the article called "Prophets and Prophecy," p. 935.

5:21 *Test everything:* Paul knew that Christians were not the only ones who claimed to have visions or special messages from God. It was important for Christians to test everything they heard to make sure it agreed with what Paul taught.

5:23 *peace . . . spirit, soul and body:* The kind of peace Paul talks about here includes more than just peace of mind or freedom from conflict. It includes a sense of well-being and the setting right of any disagreements among the members of God's people.

5:10 John 19:28-30; 3:16,17; Rom 3:25,26.

2 THESSALONIANS

Sometimes hearing or seeing something more than once can help us believe it or understand it better. Many of Paul's teachings from 1 THESSALONIANS are repeated and reinforced in this short letter.

WHAT MAKES 2 THESSALONIANS SPECIAL?

As in 1 THESSALONIANS, Paul thanks God that the Thessalonian Christians continue to grow in faith and love, in spite of the difficulties and suffering they are going through. He lets them know that they continue to be an example for other churches. The letter also gives further insight into the apostle's beliefs about the return of Christ and his teachings about how to prepare for this event.

WHY WAS 2 THESSALONIANS WRITTEN?

Some members of the Thessalonian church were upset because people were saying that Christ had already come back again, and that they had missed out on this event. But Paul tells them what will happen when Christ does return: the "man of lawlessness" and unbelievers will be punished (2:8,12), and those who are faithful to Christ will be saved (2:13). The Thessalonians are told to pray for the spread of the gospel (3:1-5), and they are warned to listen to Paul's teachings and avoid being lazy (3:6-13).

WHAT'S THE STORY BEHIND THE SCENE?

This letter was probably written shortly after 1 THESSALONIANS (see the Introduction to 1 THESSALONIANS). Even though the members of the Thessalonian church were good examples of faith and love, some of them were listening to some false teachings about Christ's return (2:1-5). Paul then explains more about the Lord's return and the Lord's victory over the "man of lawlessness." The author concludes by reminding them that the belief that Christ would return soon is no excuse to quit working.

HOW IS 2 THESSALONIANS CONSTRUCTED?

The letter can be outlined in the following way:

The truth about Christ's return (1:1—2:17)

Prayers and warnings (3:1-18)

1:1 *Paul, Silas and Timothy:* See the note at 1 Thes 1:1 (Paul).

1:1 *church:* See the mini-article called "Church," p. 2264.

1:1 *the Thessalonians:* People in the city of Thessalonica, a large and busy seaport city in northern Greece, located on the Thermaic Gulf (see the map below). Thessalonica was built in 316 B.C. by one of Alexander the Great's generals, who named the city for Alexander's wife, Thessalonike. The city was the capital of the Roman province of Macedonia and an important trade center located at the crossroads of the great highway called the Egnatian Way and a road that led north all the way to the Danube River. At the time of Paul it had a population of nearly 200,000, including a colony of Jewish people with their own synagogue (see Acts 17:1). The city was also a center for the worship of Greek and Egyptian gods and goddesses.

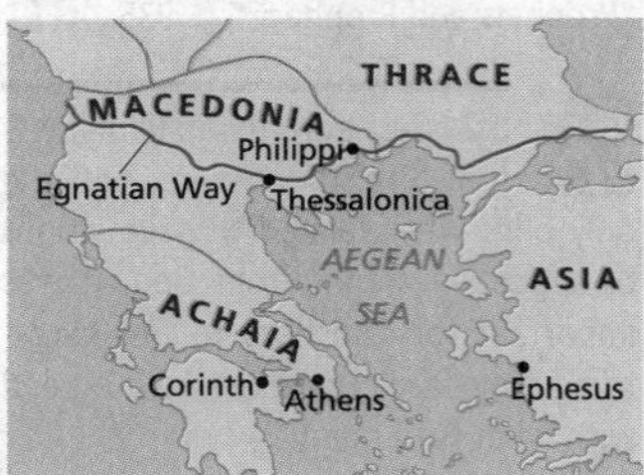

1:1 *God our Father . . . Lord Jesus Christ:* Jesus often referred to God as "Father" (see John 14, for example). Paul uses this same term in many of his letters to describe God (Rom 1:7; 1 Cor 1:3; Gal 1:2,3). The Greek word for "Lord" is *kyrios,* which may mean master. When it is used for Jesus, it emphasizes his authority and power. The word "Christ" is a title that means "Messiah" or "chosen one." See also the mini-articles called "Lord (Title for Jesus)," p. 2106 and "Messiah (Chosen One)," p. 1124.

The Truth about Christ's Return

Paul greets the Thessalonians and tells them he is pleased with their faith and love which has grown in spite of their suffering. God is using this suffering to get them ready for Christ's return when God will save them. Then he explains what will happen to the "man of lawlessness" who will try to fool people when the end is near. This section concludes with the repetition of the promise that God has chosen them to be saved.

1 Paul, Silas[a] and Timothy,

To the church of the Thessalonians in God our Father and
the Lord Jesus Christ:

2Grace and peace to you from God the Father and the Lord
Jesus Christ.

Thanksgiving and Prayer

3We ought always to thank God for you, brothers, and rightly so, because your faith is growing more and more, and the love
every one of you has for each other is increasing. 4Therefore,
among God's churches we boast about your perseverance and faith
in all the persecutions and trials you are enduring.
5All this is evidence that God's judgment is right, and as a
result you will be counted worthy of the kingdom of God, for
which you are suffering. 6God is just: He will pay back trouble to
those who trouble you 7and give relief to you who are troubled,
and to us as well. This will happen when the Lord Jesus is revealed
from heaven in blazing fire with his powerful angels. 8He will punish those who do not know God and do not obey the gospel of our
Lord Jesus. 9They will be punished with everlasting destruction
and shut out from the presence of the Lord and from the majesty
of his power 10on the day he comes to be glorified in his holy people and to be marveled at among all those who have believed. This
includes you, because you believed our testimony to you.
11With this in mind, we constantly pray for you, that our
God may count you worthy of his calling, and that by his power he
may fulfill every good purpose of yours and every act prompted
by your faith. 12We pray this so that the name of our Lord Jesus
may be glorified in you, and you in him, according to the grace of
our God and the Lord Jesus Christ.[b]

The Man of Lawlessness

2 Concerning the coming of our Lord Jesus Christ and our being
gathered to him, we ask you, brothers, 2not to become easily
unsettled or alarmed by some prophecy, report or letter supposed to

[a]1 Greek *Silvanus,* a variant of *Silas* [b]12 Or *God and Lord, Jesus Christ*

1:4 *among God's churches we boast about your perseverance and faith:* Probably refers to the churches in Achaia and Macedonia (1 Thes 1:7, 8). The Thessalonians have been patient and faithful in spite of the trouble and suffering they have experienced.

1:5 *worthy of the kingdom of God:* Paul is not saying that Christians must suffer in order to be part of this kingdom, but that those who follow Christ are likely to face suffering and opposition. See also Phil 1:28-30.

1:6 *pay back trouble to those who trouble you:* Apparently, the Thessalonians' own Gentile neighbors persecuted them when they listened to Paul's teachings and began to follow Jesus Christ.

1:7 *when the Lord Jesus is revealed . . . blazing fire . . . powerful angels:* See the note at 1 Thes 1:10 (Jesus rescues) and the mini-article called "Angels," p. 88. See also 1 Thes 4:16. Fire is often associated with God's appearances (Exod 3:2; 19:16-19; Ps 18:6-8; Ezek 1:4-28) or with the place of judgment where evildoers are punished. See the mini-articles called "Fire," p. 2383 and "Second Coming," p. 2277.

1:9 *everlasting destruction:* What will happen to those who do not follow Christ or live as God intends them to live. See also Rom 2:5-8; 5:21; Gal 6:8; 1Thes 5:3.

2:1 *our being gathered:* Paul describes how the followers of Jesus who have died and those still living will be taken up to be with Christ (1 Thes 4:13-17).

1:1 Acts 17:1. **1:9** Isa 2:10.

2:2 *saying . . . the day of the Lord has already come:* Some of the Thessalonians were uncertain about the meaning of Christ's return to earth because of confusion caused by some false teachers.

2:3 *man of lawlessness:* This person would be against God's Law and would even claim to be God (2:4). Satan may use this wicked person to work miracles that will fool people into thinking he is truly God (2:9). See also Dan 11:29-39; 1 John 2:18.

2:4 *God's temple:* The temple in Jerusalem was the center of Jewish worship until the Romans destroyed it in A.D. 70. Someone who sat in the temple and claimed to be God would have been guilty of a great sin against God.

2:7 *the one who now holds it back:* It is not clear who this "one" is. Some scholars think it may have been the Roman government, which kept order in the empire so that no group could try to destroy Christ's followers. Others think that this "one" may refer to the Holy Spirit, or to an angel like Michael (1 Thes 4:16), or the angel of the Abyss (Rev 20:1-3).

2:8 *overthrow with the breath of his mouth:* See Job 41:21; Rev 19:11-16.

2:9 *the lawless one . . . Satan:* See the note at 2:3. Satan will use the wicked one to fool people. See also the mini-article called "Satan," p. 963.

2:10 *those who are perishing:* The word "perish" points to those people who will die because they refuse to have faith in Jesus Christ.

2:10 *so be saved:* Being "saved" also can refer to receiving "eternal life." For more, see the mini-article called "Salvation," p. 2021.

2:4 Dan 11:36; Ezek 28:2. **2:8** Isa 11:4. **2:9** Matt 24:24.

have come from us, saying that the day of the Lord has already come.
3 Don't let anyone deceive you in any way, for ⸤that day will not come⸥
until the rebellion occurs and the man of lawlessness[a] is revealed, the
man doomed to destruction. 4 He will oppose and will exalt himself
over everything that is called God or is worshiped, so that he sets
himself up in God's temple, proclaiming himself to be God.

5 Don't you remember that when I was with you I used to tell
you these things? 6 And now you know what is holding him back, so
that he may be revealed at the proper time. 7 For the secret power of
lawlessness is already at work; but the one who now holds it back
will continue to do so till he is taken out of the way. 8 And then the
lawless one will be revealed, whom the Lord Jesus will overthrow
with the breath of his mouth and destroy by the splendor of his
coming. 9 The coming of the lawless one will be in accordance with
the work of Satan displayed in all kinds of counterfeit miracles, signs
and wonders, 10 and in every sort of evil that deceives those who are
perishing. They perish because they refused to love the truth and so
be saved. 11 For this reason God sends them a powerful delusion so
that they will believe the lie 12 and so that all will be condemned who
have not believed the truth but have delighted in wickedness.

Stand Firm

13 But we ought always to thank God for you, brothers loved
by the Lord, because from the beginning God chose you[b] to be
saved through the sanctifying work of the Spirit and through belief
in the truth. 14 He called you to this through our gospel, that you
might share in the glory of our Lord Jesus Christ. 15 So then, brothers, stand firm and hold to the teachings[c] we passed on to you,
whether by word of mouth or by letter.

16 May our Lord Jesus Christ himself and God our Father,
who loved us and by his grace gave us eternal encouragement and
good hope, 17 encourage your hearts and strengthen you in every
good deed and word.

Prayers and Warnings

Paul asks the Thessalonians to pray that he and his companions may be kept safe from evil people. In turn, he prays that God will continue to make them loving and patient. Finally, he warns them to stay away from people who do not work and people who refuse to obey what he has written in this letter.

Request for Prayer

3 Finally, brothers, pray for us that the message of the Lord may
spread rapidly and be honored, just as it was with you. 2 And pray

[a]3 Some manuscripts *sin* [b]13 Some manuscripts *because God chose you as his firstfruits* [c]15 Or *traditions*

that we may be delivered from wicked and evil men, for not everyone has faith. 3But the Lord is faithful, and he will strengthen and
protect you from the evil one. 4We have confidence in the Lord
that you are doing and will continue to do the things we command. 5May the Lord direct your hearts into God's love and
Christ's perseverance.

Warning Against Idleness

6In the name of the Lord Jesus Christ, we command you,
brothers, to keep away from every brother who is idle and does not
live according to the teaching[a] you received from us. 7For you
yourselves know how you ought to follow our example. We were
not idle when we were with you, 8nor did we eat anyone's food
without paying for it. On the contrary, we worked night and day,
laboring and toiling so that we would not be a burden to any of
you. 9We did this, not because we do not have the right to such
help, but in order to make ourselves a model for you to follow.
10For even when we were with you, we gave you this rule: "If a man
will not work, he shall not eat."

11We hear that some among you are idle. They are not busy;
they are busybodies. 12Such people we command and urge in the
Lord Jesus Christ to settle down and earn the bread they eat. 13And
as for you, brothers, never tire of doing what is right.

14If anyone does not obey our instruction in this letter, take
special note of him. Do not associate with him, in order that he
may feel ashamed. 15Yet do not regard him as an enemy, but warn
him as a brother.

[a]**6** Or *tradition*

2:13 *God chose you . . . sanctifying work of the Spirit:* A frequent theme in Paul's letters is that God chooses people to be part of his family. See the mini-articles called "Holy Spirit," p. 1964 and "Holiness," p. 1626. See also the note at 1 Thes 4:3.

2:16 *Lord Jesus Christ:* See the note at 1:1 (God our Father).

2:16 *gave us eternal encouragement:* The word "encouragement" used here comes from the same word that Jesus used as a name for the Holy Spirit, or "Counselor," in John 14:16.

3:1 *pray for us:* Paul often requests in his letters that readers pray for him (Rom 15:30; Phil 1:19; Col 4:3,4). See also the mini-article called "Prayer," p. 2289.

3:8 *we worked . . . laboring and toiling:* See the note at 1 Thes 2:9. See also Acts 18:3 and 1 Cor 9:1-18.

3:11 *some among you are idle:* Some church members probably took advantage of the kindness of others. It is also possible that some of them argued that they did not have to work, since Jesus was coming back soon anyway.

QUESTIONS ABOUT 2 THESSALONIANS

1. Why does Paul, in 2 THESSALONIANS, mention that he has been praying for the people he is writing to? (1:11,12) What is the value of prayer?
2. What does Paul mean by his statement that the Lord "will punish those who do not know God and do not obey the gospel of our Lord Jesus"? (1:8) What does it mean to know God? What does it mean to obey the gospel?
3. What false teaching was being spread in the Thessalonian church? (2:1,2) Why is this teaching dangerous or harmful?
4. Read 2:13-17. What does this passage teach about the importance of doing and saying the right thing? When in your life have you experienced God's encouragement? (2:16) How did this change the way you thought or the way you behaved toward others?
5. What advice does the author have for the Thessalonian Christians as they wait for Christ's return? (3:6-13) What are some of the hazards of idleness? What can you do to "never tire of doing what is right"?

3:17 *write this greeting in my own hand:* This seems to indicate that the letter was dictated to a secretary of some sort. Paul adds the final lines in his own handwriting (see Gal 6:11; Col 4:18).

Final Greetings

16Now may the Lord of peace himself give you peace at all
times and in every way. The Lord be with all of you.
17I, Paul, write this greeting in my own hand, which is the
distinguishing mark in all my letters. This is how I write.
18The grace of our Lord Jesus Christ be with you all.

1 TIMOTHY

Who gives you advice when you need it? Read this letter to find out what kind of advice Paul gave Timothy about being a leader in the church.

WHAT MAKES 1 TIMOTHY SPECIAL?

The books of 1 and 2 TIMOTHY and TITUS are often called the "Pastoral Letters" since they deal with the responsibilities of those who were in charge of some of the first Christian churches. Although this letter is addressed to Timothy personally, it actually served as a leadership manual for the early churches because it provided so many helpful standards and guidelines for organizing these new communities of faith.

WHY WAS 1 TIMOTHY WRITTEN?

This letter was written to give warnings about false teaching and to give instruction for all God's people. The letter also tells the church how its leaders are to be chosen, what titles are to be given to them, and what responsibilities they are to take on.

WHAT'S THE STORY BEHIND THE SCENE?

Timothy, the son of a Jewish Christian mother and a Gentile father from Lystra (Acts 16:1), was guided in his faith by Paul (1 Cor 4:17). He is named as Paul's co-worker in many of Paul's letters (2 Cor 1:1; 1 Thes 1:1; Phlm 1). Paul had great confidence in Timothy (1 Cor 16:10; 2 Cor 1:19; Phil 2:20-22), who served as his messenger and is often mentioned as a co-sender of many of Paul's letters (2 CORINTHIANS, 1 and 2 THESSALONIANS, PHILIPPIANS, PHILEMON). Timothy traveled and worked with Paul (Rom 16:21; Phil 2:19; Acts 16:1-3). Because of their shared faith, Timothy was like a son to Paul (1 Tim 1:2).

This letter may have been written toward the end of Paul's life, or, as some scholars believe, it may have been written in his name by one of his followers after Paul's death. It was not unusual in the ancient world for followers to honor their teacher by writing something in the teacher's name.

HOW IS 1 TIMOTHY CONSTRUCTED?

The letter can be outlined in the following way:

Instructions for church life (1:1—3:16)

Advice to Timothy and other church leaders (4:1—6:21)

Installing church leaders: 1 TIMOTHY has much to say about what kind of people were sought to serve in the early church as overseers (also called bishops), deacons, and elders. The installation of a new leader was done when other church leaders laid their hands on the chosen person's head (4:14). This practice is also described in the Old Testament (see Gen 48:13-20 and Num 27:23). In the New Testament, laying hands on a person's head was used in healing (Mark 1:41), giving a blessing (Mark 10:16), choosing someone for a special task (Acts 6:6; 1 Tim 5:22), or when passing on the gifts of the Holy Spirit (Acts 8:17; 19:6). In modern times, choosing someone for a special task in the church is often called "ordaining" or "commissioning."

Timothy, my son, I give you this instruction . . . so that . . . you may fight the good fight, holding on to faith and a good conscience.
1 Tim 1:18,19

Instructions for Church Life

This letter is addressed to Timothy, whom the apostle Paul considers his "son" in the faith. Paul then offers general instructions for life in the church, which include giving thanks, praying, and staying away from false teachings. Paul also gives instructions on how women are to dress and act and how church leaders should live. Most of Paul's letters include a section of thanksgiving near the beginning. In 1 TIMOTHY, this is replaced with warnings about false teachers.

1 Paul, an apostle of Christ Jesus by the command of God our
Savior and of Christ Jesus our hope,

2 To Timothy my true son in the faith:

Grace, mercy and peace from God the Father and Christ
Jesus our Lord.

Saint Timothy, stained glass window from the Abbey of Neuwiller, Alsace, France, twelfth century. Timothy, whose name means "honored by God," was a co-worker of Paul and accompanied the apostle on his missionary journeys to the Gentiles (non-Jews) in Asia Minor. Timothy was the son of a Gentile father and Jewish Christian mother. Paul considered him a "true son" and gave him advice so that he would be an effective and respected church leader.

1:1 *Paul, an apostle of Christ Jesus:* See the mini-article called "Paul (Saul) of Tarsus," p. 2177.

"Apostle" is from the Greek word that means "someone sent to do a special job or to represent an important authority." These apostles were sent by Jesus to preach the gospel throughout the world (Matt 28:18-20; Acts 1:8).

"Jesus" was a common name among Jewish men in the first century. "Christ" is a title that comes from the Greek word meaning "Messiah" or "chosen one." See also the mini-article called "Messiah (Chosen One)," p. 1124.

1:1 *God our Savior:* In 1 and 2 TIMOTHY and in TITUS the title of "Savior" refers to God (1 Tim 1:1; 2:3; 4:10; Titus 1:3; 2:10) as well as to Jesus (2 Tim 1:10; Titus 1:4; 2:13).

1:2 *Timothy:* See the Introduction on p. 2303.

1:2 *God the Father and Christ Jesus our Lord:* Jesus often referred to God as "Father" (see for example, John 14). Paul uses this same term in many of his letters to describe God (Rom 1:7; 1 Cor 1:3; Gal 1:2,3).

See also the note at 1:1 (Paul . . . Christ Jesus) and the mini-article called "Lord (Title for Jesus)," p. 2106.

1:3 *Macedonia . . . Ephesus:* Paul had preached the gospel in Macedonian cities like Thessalonica, Philippi, and Berea (Acts 16:6—17:14). At some point, he had asked Timothy to stay in Ephesus, a major city in Asia Minor. See the map on p. 2473.

1:2 Acts 16:1.

Warning Against False Teachers of the Law

3 As I urged you when I went into Macedonia, stay there in
Ephesus so that you may command certain men not to teach false
doctrines any longer 4 nor to devote themselves to myths and endless genealogies. These promote controversies rather than God's
work—which is by faith. 5 The goal of this command is love, which
comes from a pure heart and a good conscience and a sincere faith.
6 Some have wandered away from these and turned to meaningless
talk. 7 They want to be teachers of the law, but they do not know
what they are talking about or what they so confidently affirm.
8 We know that the law is good if one uses it properly. 9 We
also know that law[a] is made not for the righteous but for lawbreakers and rebels, the ungodly and sinful, the unholy and irreli-
gious; for those who kill their fathers or mothers, for murderers,
10 for adulterers and perverts, for slave traders and liars and perjurers—and for whatever else is contrary to the sound doctrine 11 that
conforms to the glorious gospel of the blessed God, which he
entrusted to me.

The Lord's Grace to Paul

12 I thank Christ Jesus our Lord, who has given me strength,
that he considered me faithful, appointing me to his service. 13 Even
though I was once a blasphemer and a persecutor and a violent
man, I was shown mercy because I acted in ignorance and unbelief. 14 The grace of our Lord was poured out on me abundantly,
along with the faith and love that are in Christ Jesus.
15 Here is a trustworthy saying that deserves full acceptance:
Christ Jesus came into the world to save sinners—of whom I am
the worst. 16 But for that very reason I was shown mercy so that in
me, the worst of sinners, Christ Jesus might display his unlimited
patience as an example for those who would believe on him and
receive eternal life. 17 Now to the King eternal, immortal, invisible,
the only God, be honor and glory for ever and ever. Amen.
18 Timothy, my son, I give you this instruction in keeping
with the prophecies once made about you, so that by following
them you may fight the good fight, 19 holding on to faith and a
good conscience. Some have rejected these and so have shipwrecked their faith. 20 Among them are Hymenaeus and Alexander,
whom I have handed over to Satan to be taught not to blaspheme.

Instructions on Worship

2 I urge, then, first of all, that requests, prayers, intercession and
thanksgiving be made for everyone— 2 for kings and all those in
authority, that we may live peaceful and quiet lives in all godliness
and holiness. 3 This is good, and pleases God our Savior, 4 who

[a] 9 Or *that the law*

1:3,4 *false doctrines . . . myths and endless genealogies:* The false doctrines mentioned here may have been the myths about the Greek and Roman gods and goddesses. The "genealogies" may refer to the lists of ancestors given in GENESIS. Myths about some of the people mentioned in the Jewish Scriptures were being taught as the truth in writings that circulated at this time. Still other groups believed that only people who received "special knowledge" could rise above the limitations of the body and material existence. See 4:7; see also 2 Tim 4:4.

1:7 *the law:* Certain teachers probably tried to convince some of Jesus' followers that they needed to obey all the dietary laws and rules about circumcision found in the Law of Moses in order to be true members of God's family. See also Rom 2:17-29; Gal 3:1-20.

1:18 *the prophecies once made about you:* This probably refers to Christian prophets mentioned in 4:14. Prophets often gave guidance about how God's people should live. See also the article called "Prophets and Prophecy," p. 935.

1:20 *Hymenaeus and Alexander:* Hymenaeus is mentioned in 2 Timothy 2:17 as someone who was claiming that Jesus had already returned. Alexander is mentioned in 2 Timothy 4:14. What he did to harm Paul is not clear.

1:20 *Satan:* See the mini-article called "Satan," p. 963.

2:1,2 *prayers . . . kings:* It was important for Christians to show respect to authorities so that they could avoid trouble. In this way, they could hope to gain respect for their beliefs, gain new members, and lessen the risk of being persecuted.

1:13 Acts 8:1-3; 9:1-19; Phil 3:5-11. **1:15** Luke 5:30-32; John 3:16; Rom 3:23,24.

wants all men to be saved and to come to a knowledge of the truth.
[5]For there is one God and one mediator between God and men,
the man Christ Jesus, [6]who gave himself as a ransom for all men—
the testimony given in its proper time. [7]And for this purpose I was
appointed a herald and an apostle—I am telling the truth, I am
not lying—and a teacher of the true faith to the Gentiles.

[8]I want men everywhere to lift up holy hands in prayer,
without anger or disputing.

[9]I also want women to dress modestly, with decency and
propriety, not with braided hair or gold or pearls or expensive
clothes, [10]but with good deeds, appropriate for women who profess to worship God.

[11]A woman should learn in quietness and full submission. [12]I
do not permit a woman to teach or to have authority over a man;
she must be silent. [13]For Adam was formed first, then Eve. [14]And
Adam was not the one deceived; it was the woman who was
deceived and became a sinner. [15]But women[a] will be saved[b]
through childbearing—if they continue in faith, love and holiness
with propriety.

Overseers and Deacons

3 Here is a trustworthy saying: If anyone sets his heart on being
an overseer,[c] he desires a noble task. [2]Now the overseer must be
above reproach, the husband of but one wife, temperate, self-
controlled, respectable, hospitable, able to teach, [3]not given to
drunkenness, not violent but gentle, not quarrelsome, not a lover
of money. [4]He must manage his own family well and see that his
children obey him with proper respect. [5](If anyone does not know
how to manage his own family, how can he take care of God's
church?) [6]He must not be a recent convert, or he may become conceited and fall under the same judgment as the devil. [7]He must
also have a good reputation with outsiders, so that he will not fall
into disgrace and into the devil's trap.

[8]Deacons, likewise, are to be men worthy of respect, sincere,
not indulging in much wine, and not pursuing dishonest gain.
[9]They must keep hold of the deep truths of the faith with a clear
conscience. [10]They must first be tested; and then if there is nothing
against them, let them serve as deacons.

[11]In the same way, their wives[d] are to be women worthy of
respect, not malicious talkers but temperate and trustworthy in
everything.

[12]A deacon must be the husband of but one wife and must
manage his children and his household well. [13]Those who have
served well gain an excellent standing and great assurance in their
faith in Christ Jesus.

[a]15 Greek *she* [b]15 Or *restored* [c]1 Traditionally *bishop*; also in verse 2
[d]11 Or *way, deaconesses*

2:7 *an apostle . . . Gentiles:* See the note at 1:1 (Paul). Paul's special mission was to the Gentiles (Acts 9:15; 15:12; Gal 2:1-9). See also the mini-article called "Gentiles," p. 2127.

2:7 *faith:* Paul often describes faith as trusting in Christ (Rom 3:27-31; Gal 2:16; Phil 3:9), but here "faith" is used more in the sense of a set of beliefs about right living. See also 1:14,19; 4:6; 6:12.

2:9 *women . . . gold or pearls:* See 3:11; 5:6-15. This suggests that there were people in Timothy's congregation who loved money and liked to show off their wealth (6:5-10,17).

3:1 *overseer:* This translates a Greek word *episkopos*, which means "overseer" or "bishop." In the early church an overseer was the chief leader of a local congregation.

3:6 *devil:* See the mini-article called "Satan," p. 963. See also Eph 2:2; 6:11-13; 1 Pet 5:8.

3:8 *Deacons:* This Greek word (*diakonos*) is most often translated as "deacons," which probably referred to special helpers in a congregation. They had the task of serving people and taking care of people's needs. Deacons were to be responsible and experienced followers.

3:15 *the church of the living God:* Here "church" refers to all the people who had become believers in Jesus Christ, rather than to any single local congregation. See the mini-article called "Church," p. 2264.

2:5,6 Rom 3:25,26; 5:6-8; Col 1:15-20; Eph 1:15-23. **2:7** 2 Tim 1:11. **2:9** 1 Pet 3:3. **2:13** Gen 2:7; 21,22. **2:14** Gen 3:1-6. **3:2-7** Titus 1:6-9.

[14]Although I hope to come to you soon, I am writing you
these instructions so that, [15]if I am delayed, you will know how
people ought to conduct themselves in God's household, which is
the church of the living God, the pillar and foundation of the
truth. [16]Beyond all question, the mystery of godliness is great:

He[a] appeared in a body,[b]
  was vindicated by the Spirit,
was seen by angels,
  was preached among the nations,
was believed on in the world,
  was taken up in glory.

Advice to Timothy and Other Church Leaders

The remainder of the letter includes personal advice to Timothy and general instructions for church leaders. It continues with more warnings about false teaching and the love of money, and ends with words of encouragement to "fight the good fight of the faith."

Instructions to Timothy

4 The Spirit clearly says that in later times some will abandon
the faith and follow deceiving spirits and things taught by demons.
[2]Such teachings come through hypocritical liars, whose consciences have been seared as with a hot iron. [3]They forbid people
to marry and order them to abstain from certain foods, which God
created to be received with thanksgiving by those who believe and
who know the truth. [4]For everything God created is good, and
nothing is to be rejected if it is received with thanksgiving,
[5]because it is consecrated by the word of God and prayer.
[6]If you point these things out to the brothers, you will be a
good minister of Christ Jesus, brought up in the truths of the faith
and of the good teaching that you have followed. [7]Have nothing to
do with godless myths and old wives' tales; rather, train yourself to
be godly. [8]For physical training is of some value, but godliness has
value for all things, holding promise for both the present life and
the life to come.
[9]This is a trustworthy saying that deserves full acceptance
[10](and for this we labor and strive), that we have put our hope in
the living God, who is the Savior of all men, and especially of those
who believe.
[11]Command and teach these things. [12]Don't let anyone look
down on you because you are young, but set an example for the

[a]16 Some manuscripts *God* [b]16 Or *in the flesh*

3:16 *Spirit . . . angels:* The Holy Spirit teaches and guides the people of God so that they can become the kind of people God wants them to be. See the mini-articles called "Holy Spirit," p. 2082, and "Angels," p. 88.

4:1 *later times . . . deceiving spirits . . . demons:* "Later times" refers to a time just before the end of the world, or to the time when God will judge the world. A number of New Testament passages say that false teachings will be spread during this time (2 Thes 2:1-12; 2 Tim 3:1-9; 2 Pet 3:3). See also the mini-article called "End Times," p. 2295. Deceiving spirits and demons are connected to the power of the devil, or Satan. See also Eph 6:11,12; 2 Thes 2:9-12; and the mini-article called "Satan," p. 963.

4:2,3 *Such teachings . . . forbid people to marry . . . certain foods:* Certain groups taught a very strict way of life called "asceticism." Ascetics abstained from sexual relations and limited their diet to certain foods or fasted (went without eating) for periods of time in order to prove how devoted they were to God. See also 1 Cor 7; Col 2:8-18.

4:7 *godless myths:* See the note at 1:3,4.

4:8 *physical training is of some value:* The source of this saying is not known. However, it seems to be related to the saying in 6:6.

4:10 *Savior:* See the note at 1:1 (God our Savior).

4:4 Rom 14:14; Acts 10:9-15; Mark 7:14-19.

4:14 *your gift . . . prophetic message:* The "gift" probably refers to Timothy's ability to teach and preach the gospel. This special gift was given to Timothy by the Holy Spirit. See the mini-article called "Spiritual Gifts," p. 2219.

"Prophetic message" here refers to a message given by a group of Christian prophets who had the special gift of receiving messages from God.

4:14 *laid their hands on you:* See the note on p. 2303.

5:1 *older man:* Refers to older men who were experienced church leaders. See the note at 5:17.

5:3 *widows:* Putting widows on the list (5:9,11) meant that the church took responsibility for taking care of their needs. The importance of taking care of widows in the early church is also described in Acts 6:1-6; 9:36,39; and James 1:27. Because of the church's limited resources, only certain widows could be put on the list—widows who had no other resource for support (such as family, see the note at 5:16). See also Exod 22:22; Deut 24:17,19-21; Isa 1:17; Jer 49:11.

5:11-14 *younger widows . . . marry:* Young widows were not to be put on the list of widows to receive special care. Once a widow was put on the list, she was expected to live a pure life (without sexual relations) and to perform certain duties that would strengthen the church. Paul advises young widows to find suitable new husbands rather than to be put on the list of widows to receive special care.

5:16 *widows in her family:* Christian family members were to take care of their relatives (5:8), including widows. The church was to help only those widows who didn't have family members to take care of their needs.

5:17 *elders:* This Greek word, *presbyteroi,* can also be translated "presbyters." This probably refers to all those who held a special office in the church, including overseers (bishops).

believers in speech, in life, in love, in faith and in purity. 13 Until I
come, devote yourself to the public reading of Scripture, to
preaching and to teaching. 14 Do not neglect your gift, which was
given you through a prophetic message when the body of elders
laid their hands on you.
15 Be diligent in these matters; give yourself wholly to them,
so that everyone may see your progress. 16 Watch your life and doctrine closely. Persevere in them, because if you do, you will save
both yourself and your hearers.

Advice About Widows, Elders and Slaves

5 Do not rebuke an older man harshly, but exhort him as if he
were your father. Treat younger men as brothers, 2 older women as
mothers, and younger women as sisters, with absolute purity.
3 Give proper recognition to those widows who are really in
need. 4 But if a widow has children or grandchildren, these should
learn first of all to put their religion into practice by caring for
their own family and so repaying their parents and grandparents,
for this is pleasing to God. 5 The widow who is really in need and
left all alone puts her hope in God and continues night and day to
pray and to ask God for help. 6 But the widow who lives for pleasure is dead even while she lives. 7 Give the people these instructions, too, so that no one may be open to blame. 8 If anyone does
not provide for his relatives, and especially for his immediate family, he has denied the faith and is worse than an unbeliever.
9 No widow may be put on the list of widows unless she is
over sixty, has been faithful to her husband,[a] 10 and is well known
for her good deeds, such as bringing up children, showing hospitality, washing the feet of the saints, helping those in trouble and
devoting herself to all kinds of good deeds.
11 As for younger widows, do not put them on such a list. For
when their sensual desires overcome their dedication to Christ,
they want to marry. 12 Thus they bring judgment on themselves,
because they have broken their first pledge. 13 Besides, they get into
the habit of being idle and going about from house to house. And
not only do they become idlers, but also gossips and busybodies,
saying things they ought not to. 14 So I counsel younger widows to
marry, to have children, to manage their homes and to give the
enemy no opportunity for slander. 15 Some have in fact already
turned away to follow Satan.
16 If any woman who is a believer has widows in her family, she
should help them and not let the church be burdened with them, so
that the church can help those widows who are really in need.
17 The elders who direct the affairs of the church well are
worthy of double honor, especially those whose work is preaching

[a]**9** Or *has had but one husband*

and teaching. [18]For the Scripture says, "Do not muzzle the ox while
it is treading out the grain,"[a] and "The worker deserves his wages."[b]
[19]Do not entertain an accusation against an elder unless it is
brought by two or three witnesses. [20]Those who sin are to be
rebuked publicly, so that the others may take warning.

[21]I charge you, in the sight of God and Christ Jesus and the
elect angels, to keep these instructions without partiality, and to
do nothing out of favoritism.

[22]Do not be hasty in the laying on of hands, and do not
share in the sins of others. Keep yourself pure.

[23]Stop drinking only water, and use a little wine because of
your stomach and your frequent illnesses.

[24]The sins of some men are obvious, reaching the place of
judgment ahead of them; the sins of others trail behind them. [25]In
the same way, good deeds are obvious, and even those that are not
cannot be hidden.

6 All who are under the yoke of slavery should consider their
masters worthy of full respect, so that God's name and our teaching may not be slandered. [2]Those who have believing masters are
not to show less respect for them because they are brothers.
Instead, they are to serve them even better, because those who benefit from their service are believers, and dear to them. These are
the things you are to teach and urge on them.

Love of Money

[3]If anyone teaches false doctrines and does not agree to the
sound instruction of our Lord Jesus Christ and to godly teaching,
[4]he is conceited and understands nothing. He has an unhealthy
interest in controversies and quarrels about words that result in
envy, strife, malicious talk, evil suspicions [5]and constant friction
between men of corrupt mind, who have been robbed of the truth
and who think that godliness is a means to financial gain.

[6]But godliness with contentment is great gain. [7]For we
brought nothing into the world, and we can take nothing out of it.
[8]But if we have food and clothing, we will be content with that.
[9]People who want to get rich fall into temptation and a trap and
into many foolish and harmful desires that plunge men into ruin
and destruction. [10]For the love of money is a root of all kinds of
evil. Some people, eager for money, have wandered from the faith
and pierced themselves with many griefs.

Paul's Charge to Timothy

[11]But you, man of God, flee from all this, and pursue righteousness, godliness, faith, love, endurance and gentleness. [12]Fight
the good fight of the faith. Take hold of the eternal life to which

[a]18 Deut. 25:4 [b]18 Luke 10:7

5:19,20 *elder . . . sin . . . rebuked publicly:* This teaching about how to correct those who have sinned is very similar to what Jesus taught his disciples (Matt 18:15-17). Since the elder's actions affected the whole group of followers, the elder's hearing and punishment should be public, in front of all the followers.

5:21 *angels:* See the note at 3:16.

5:22 *laying on of hands:* See the note on p. 2303.

6:1 *All under the yoke of slavery:* In some New Testament letters, slaves are encouraged to be loyal to their masters (Eph 6:5-8; Col 3:22-24), but see Gal 3:26-29. See also the mini-article called "Slaves and Servants in the Time of Jesus," p. 2006.

6:5 *financial gain:* Some false teachers wanted to make lots of money by teaching religion. But being part of the church does not include gaining wealth, and people who love money cause trouble (6:10).

In this relief from the second century A.D., a wealthy woman is shown being attended to by four servants.

6:12 *faith . . . eternal life:* See 1:16 and the note at 2:7 (faith).

5:18 Matt 10:10; 1 Cor 9:9. **5:19** Deut 17:5-7; 19:15; 2 Cor 13:1. **6:7** Eccl 5:10-15.

you were called when you made your good confession in the presence of many witnesses. 13 In the sight of God, who gives life to
everything, and of Christ Jesus, who while testifying before Pontius Pilate made the good confession, I charge you 14 to keep this
command without spot or blame until the appearing of our Lord
Jesus Christ, 15 which God will bring about in his own time—God,
the blessed and only Ruler, the King of kings and Lord of lords,
16 who alone is immortal and who lives in unapproachable light,
whom no one has seen or can see. To him be honor and might forever. Amen.

17 Command those who are rich in this present world not to
be arrogant nor to put their hope in wealth, which is so uncertain,
but to put their hope in God, who richly provides us with everything for our enjoyment. 18 Command them to do good, to be rich
in good deeds, and to be generous and willing to share. 19 In this
way they will lay up treasure for themselves as a firm foundation
for the coming age, so that they may take hold of the life that is
truly life.
20 Timothy, guard what has been entrusted to your care. Turn
away from godless chatter and the opposing ideas of what is falsely called knowledge, 21 which some have professed and in so doing
have wandered from the faith.

Grace be with you.

6:13 *Pontius Pilate:* Pontius Pilate was the Roman governor in charge of Judea from A.D. 26 to 36. Pilate said that Jesus was not guilty of anything, but the leaders of the Jewish people in Jerusalem insisted that Pilate have Jesus put to death (Luke 23:1-5; John 18:33-37).

6:14 *the appearing of our Lord Jesus Christ:* See the note at 4:1. Paul believed that Jesus was going to return to earth very soon, perhaps during his own lifetime (Phil 3:20; 4:5; 1 Thes 5:1-11). See also the mini-article called "Second Coming," p. 2277.

6:16 *lives in unapproachable light:* In the Bible, light is used to describe God or God's Word (Ps 119:105; John 1:3,4; 1 John 1:5), and those people or things that reveal God's truth (Isa 49:6). The followers of Jesus are also called "sons of light" (John 12:36). In the Jewish Scriptures (Old Testament), God brings light (Gen 1:3) and often is described as appearing in some kind of light (Exod 3:2,3; 13:20-22).

QUESTIONS ABOUT 1 TIMOTHY

1. This letter refers several times to the close relationship between the apostle Paul and his "son" Timothy (1:2,18; 3:14; 4:11; 6:11-14,20). How do you think sharing a common faith in God can strengthen a relationship? How can Christians help one another strengthen their individual relationships with God?
2. Paul gives Timothy much advice about how to deal with false teachers who are having a bad influence on the people of Timothy's church. What are some of these "false teachings" based on? (1:4; 4:3; 6:20) What, according to Paul, is "the truth"? (2:4-6; 4:16) What are some of the things he suggests followers of Christ do (and not do) in order to be faithful and have a clear conscience? (2:1; 4:7,16; 5:1-3; 6:11)
3. The book of 1 TIMOTHY is a kind of "Manual for Church Leaders." What does Paul say church leaders should be like, and what kind of behavior is expected of them? (3:1-13) Why do you think the standards are so high? (3:15; 4:16; 6:19) In your opinion, what are the five most important traits of a church leader?
4. Timothy seems to have been "young" for a church leader at this time. What special advice did Paul give Timothy about being a respected and effective leader? (4:12; 5:1, 2) How much does your own church encourage young people to be involved, to lead worship, and to serve?
5. Timothy's church seemed to have included both poor people (widows, 5:3-16) and rich people (6:17-19). How is each group to be treated? What is expected of each group?
6. What special warnings did Paul have for people who thought religion was supposed to make them rich? (6:3-10) How can religion make a person's life "rich"? Are you "content" with what you have? Why or why not?

2 TIMOTHY

Read this letter to find out why Paul tells Timothy to be a good soldier of Christ Jesus.

What makes 2 Timothy special?

This second letter to Timothy is more personal than the first one. Timothy is like a "dear son" to Paul, who always remembers Timothy in his prayers (1:2,3). Timothy's mother and grandmother are mentioned by name and Timothy is reminded to fan into flame the gift of God which is in him (1:6).

Why was 2 Timothy written?

The situation of the church changed throughout the first century A.D. Eventually, the leaders of the church were in danger of being put in jail by the Roman authorities. And within the church, people were coming up with new ideas that did not fit with the original message of the gospel concerning Jesus' death and resurrection. Paul tells Timothy to be a "good soldier" of Christ Jesus and to learn to endure suffering (2:1,3). He warns Timothy to run from those temptations that often catch young people (2:20-26; 3:1-9) and tells him to keep preaching God's message (4:2), and to be patient with the people in his care (4:3-5).

What's the story behind the scene?

Paul writes to his friend Timothy from prison (1:8,16,17), and as someone who expects to be put to death soon (4:6). Timothy was like a son to Paul (1 Tim 1:2; 2 Tim 1:2), because they had traveled and worked closely together (Rom 16:21; 1 Cor 16:10; Phil 2:19). Like 1 Timothy, this letter traditionally has been considered to be written by Paul toward the end of his life. However, some scholars believe the letter may have been written in Paul's name by one of his followers sometime after Paul's death. To write something in another person's name was considered to be a way of honoring that person and his work.

How is 2 Timothy constructed?

The letter can be outlined in the following way:

Encouragement and warnings for Timothy (1:1—2:26)
Courage and faithfulness to the end (3:1—4:8)
Final instructions and greetings (4:9-22)

Paul, an apostle . . . Timothy: Paul was also known by his Jewish name, Saul (Acts 7:57—8:3; 9:1-30). Paul had been a strict follower of the Law of Moses and persecuted the early followers of Jesus (Gal 1:13; Phil 3:5,6), but Jesus chose him to be his apostle and to preach the gospel (Acts 9:1-19). See also the mini-article called "Paul (Saul) of Tarsus," p. 2177.

"Apostle" is from the Greek word that means "someone sent to do a special job or to represent an important authority." In the New Testament it refers to the twelve special disciples chosen by Jesus and to the followers who saw Jesus after God had raised him from death (Luke 6:13; Acts 1:2,3). These apostles were sent by Jesus to preach the gospel throughout the world and to teach all people (Matt 28:18-20; Acts 1:8).

Timothy traveled with Paul (Acts 16:1-3) and is named as one of the apostle's co-workers in many of Paul's letters (2 Cor 1:1; 1 Thes 1:1; Phlm 1). This illuminated page from a fifteenth century Ethiopian manuscript was positioned opposite the first page of 2 Timothy. It was typical in Ethiopian manuscript painting to portray the apostle Paul with a high forehead (see figure below). For more, see the Introduction to 1 Timothy, p. 2303.

1:1,2 *Paul . . . Timothy:* See the note on p. 2311.

1:1 *the promise of life:* Refers to the promise of eternal life, which Jesus makes possible for Paul and others who trust in him. See also the mini-article called "Eternal Life," p. 2072.

1:2 *God the Father and Christ Jesus our Lord:* Jesus often referred to God as "Father" (see John 14). Paul uses this same term in many of his letters to describe God (Rom 1:7; 1 Cor 1:3; Gal 1:2,3).

The word "Christ" is a title that means "Messiah" or "Chosen One." See also the mini-articles called "Lord (Title for Jesus)," p. 2106, and "Messiah (Chosen One)," p. 1124.

1:3 *my forefathers:* Paul was Jewish, so his forefathers were the people of Israel.

1:5 *grandmother Lois . . . mother Eunice:* The book of Acts reports that Timothy's mother was a follower of Christ from a Jewish family (Acts 16:1).

1:6 *laying on of my hands:* Church leaders (elders) placed their hands on people who were being appointed to preach or teach. See 1 Tim 4:14.

1:8 *do not be ashamed . . . prisoner:* The Roman authorities in the provinces where Paul and Timothy had preached were beginning to arrest people who worshiped Jesus Christ. Some Roman emperors insisted on being worshiped by their subjects and even had temples built in their own honor. Titles that they sometimes gave themselves included "son of god," "lord," and "savior." Most Jews and Christians would have refused to participate in this kind of idolatry. Paul encourages Timothy to remain loyal to Christ, even though this could mean that Timothy might suffer.

1:2 Acts 16:1. **1:11** 1 Tim 2:7.

Encouragement and Warnings for Timothy

Paul claims to be an apostle of Christ and warmly greets Timothy who has been like Paul's own son. Paul reminds Timothy of how he came to be a follower of Christ and encourages him to join Paul in continuing to "testify about our Lord" no matter what happens. As a good follower of Christ Jesus, Timothy is instructed to teach the Lord's followers what Paul has taught him, and to stay away from worthless talk and temptations that capture young people.

1 Paul, an apostle of Christ Jesus by the will of God, according to
the promise of life that is in Christ Jesus,

2 To Timothy, my dear son:

Grace, mercy and peace from God the Father and Christ
Jesus our Lord.

Encouragement to Be Faithful

3 I thank God, whom I serve, as my forefathers did, with a
clear conscience, as night and day I constantly remember you in
my prayers. 4 Recalling your tears, I long to see you, so that I may
be filled with joy. 5 I have been reminded of your sincere faith,
which first lived in your grandmother Lois and in your mother
Eunice and, I am persuaded, now lives in you also. 6 For this reason
I remind you to fan into flame the gift of God, which is in you
through the laying on of my hands. 7 For God did not give us a
spirit of timidity, but a spirit of power, of love and of self-
discipline.
8 So do not be ashamed to testify about our Lord, or ashamed
of me his prisoner. But join with me in suffering for the gospel, by
the power of God, 9 who has saved us and called us to a holy life—
not because of anything we have done but because of his own purpose and grace. This grace was given us in Christ Jesus before the
beginning of time, 10 but it has now been revealed through the
appearing of our Savior, Christ Jesus, who has destroyed death and
has brought life and immortality to light through the gospel. 11 And
of this gospel I was appointed a herald and an apostle and a
teacher. 12 That is why I am suffering as I am. Yet I am not
ashamed, because I know whom I have believed, and am convinced that he is able to guard what I have entrusted to him for
that day.

13 What you heard from me, keep as the pattern of sound
teaching, with faith and love in Christ Jesus. 14 Guard the good
deposit that was entrusted to you—guard it with the help of the
Holy Spirit who lives in us.

15 You know that everyone in the province of Asia has deserted me, including Phygelus and Hermogenes.

Rekindle the Gift of God That Is within You by Gui-jie Zhang, contemporary. Paul gives the church leader Timothy words of advice and encouragement. "I remind you to fan into flame the gift of God, which is in you through the laying on of my hands. For God did not give us a spirit of timidity, but a spirit of power, of love and of self-discipline" (1:6,7).

16 May the Lord show mercy to the household of Onesiphorus, because he often refreshed me and was not ashamed of my
chains. 17 On the contrary, when he was in Rome, he searched hard
for me until he found me. 18 May the Lord grant that he will find
mercy from the Lord on that day! You know very well in how
many ways he helped me in Ephesus.
2 You then, my son, be strong in the grace that is in Christ Jesus.
2 And the things you have heard me say in the presence of many
witnesses entrust to reliable men who will also be qualified to teach
others. 3 Endure hardship with us like a good soldier of Christ Jesus.
4 No one serving as a soldier gets involved in civilian affairs—he
wants to please his commanding officer. 5 Similarly, if anyone competes as an athlete, he does not receive the victor's crown unless he
competes according to the rules. 6 The hardworking farmer should
be the first to receive a share of the crops. 7 Reflect on what I am saying, for the Lord will give you insight into all this.

Endure hardship with us like a good soldier of Christ Jesus.
2 Tim 2:3

1:8 *the gospel:* The gospel is both the message about Jesus and the message Jesus brings about the kingdom of God. Those who trust Jesus and believe the gospel will become part of God's new family of followers.

1:9 *saved us:* Being "saved" refers to what God has done and is still doing to free humans from sin and the powers of evil. See also the mini-article called "Salvation," p. 2021.

1:10 *brought life and immortality:* Being part of God's holy people is based on Jesus' resurrection and bringing the gospel and the promise of eternal life. See also Phil 2:6-11 and Col 1:15-20.

1:14 *good deposit . . . Holy Spirit:* The Holy Spirit teaches and guides the people of God so that they can become the kind of people God wants them to be. See the mini-article called "Holy Spirit," p. 2082. The "good deposit" is the true message about Christ that Timothy has received from Paul.

1:15 *everyone in . . . Asia has deserted me:* "Asia" refers to a province in the western section of what is now Turkey. See the map on p. 2475. Paul mentions the suffering he experienced in Ephesus (2 Cor 1:8), which probably included torture and the threat of death. See also Acts 20:17-19.

1:15 *Phygelus and Hermogenes:* This is the only time these names are mentioned in the New Testament, so it is not clear just how they opposed Paul.

1:16 *Onesiphorus:* Onesiphorus is mentioned only here and in 4:19. He apparently was in Ephesus at the same time as Timothy and Paul (1 Cor 16:8-10).

2:8 *descended from David:* A number of New Testament passages refer to the fact that Jesus was a descendant of David, Israel's greatest king (Matt 1:1-17; Luke 2:1-4; Rom 1:1-4). See also the mini-article called "David," p. 1028.

2:9 *chained like a criminal:* See the note at 1:8 (do not be ashamed).

2:9 *God's word:* Referring to the gospel message. See the note at 1:8 (gospel).

2:16-18 *godless chatter . . . the resurrection has already taken place:* One example of profane talk was the teaching of Hymenaeus and Philetus, who were saying that the dead had already been resurrected. They may have been teaching that new life in Christ was not physical, but only spiritual. This was not in agreement with Paul's teaching about how the dead will be raised to life (1 Thes 4:13-18) or his teaching that this new life included a brand new spiritual body (1 Cor 15:35-55). Hymenaeus is also mentioned in 1 Timothy 1:20, where Paul says that he was "handed over to Satan." This probably means that he was expelled from the church.

2:20 *articles . . . gold and silver . . . wood and clay:* Gold and silver dishes were used for special occasions, while dishes made of wood and clay were for everyday use. The decorated clay jug and bowls shown here are from Jerusalem, first century A.D.

2:11 Rom 6:8; Col 2:20; 3:1. **2:12** Rom 12:12; Matt 10:33; Luke 12:9. **2:19** John 10:14,15.

8 Remember Jesus Christ, raised from the dead, descended
from David. This is my gospel, 9 for which I am suffering even to
the point of being chained like a criminal. But God's word is not
chained. 10 Therefore I endure everything for the sake of the elect,
that they too may obtain the salvation that is in Christ Jesus, with
eternal glory.

11 Here is a trustworthy saying:

If we died with him,
we will also live with him;
12 if we endure,
we will also reign with him.
If we disown him,
he will also disown us;
13 if we are faithless,
he will remain faithful,
for he cannot disown himself.

A Workman Approved by God

14 Keep reminding them of these things. Warn them before
God against quarreling about words; it is of no value, and only
ruins those who listen. 15 Do your best to present yourself to God
as one approved, a workman who does not need to be ashamed
and who correctly handles the word of truth. 16 Avoid godless chatter, because those who indulge in it will become more and more
ungodly. 17 Their teaching will spread like gangrene. Among them
are Hymenaeus and Philetus, 18 who have wandered away from the
truth. They say that the resurrection has already taken place, and
they destroy the faith of some. 19 Nevertheless, God's solid foundation stands firm, sealed with this inscription: "The Lord knows
those who are his,"[a] and, "Everyone who confesses the name of the
Lord must turn away from wickedness."

20 In a large house there are articles not only of gold and silver, but also of wood and clay; some are for noble purposes and
some for ignoble. 21 If a man cleanses himself from the latter, he
will be an instrument for noble purposes, made holy, useful to the
Master and prepared to do any good work.

22 Flee the evil desires of youth, and pursue righteousness,
faith, love and peace, along with those who call on the Lord out of
a pure heart. 23 Don't have anything to do with foolish and stupid
arguments, because you know they produce quarrels. 24 And the
Lord's servant must not quarrel; instead, he must be kind to everyone, able to teach, not resentful. 25 Those who oppose him he must
gently instruct, in the hope that God will grant them repentance
leading them to a knowledge of the truth, 26 and that they will

[a] **19** Num. 16:5 (see Septuagint)

come to their senses and escape from the trap of the devil, who has
taken them captive to do his will.

Courage and Faithfulness to the End

Paul warns Timothy that some of Christ's followers will be fooled by false teachers who will be disobedient, sneaky, and reckless. In the end, their foolishness will be overcome by God's truth. Timothy is encouraged to be faithful to what he has been taught. This teaching includes an understanding of the Holy Scriptures, which are useful for teaching people and for showing them how to live. Since the followers of Christ will be tempted to turn from the truth, they need to remain faithful and to be willing to endure suffering.

Godlessness in the Last Days

3 But mark this: There will be terrible times in the last days.
[2]People will be lovers of themselves, lovers of money, boastful,
proud, abusive, disobedient to their parents, ungrateful, unholy,
[3]without love, unforgiving, slanderous, without self-control, brutal, not lovers of the good, [4]treacherous, rash, conceited, lovers of
pleasure rather than lovers of God— [5]having a form of godliness
but denying its power. Have nothing to do with them.
[6]They are the kind who worm their way into homes and gain
control over weak-willed women, who are loaded down with sins
and are swayed by all kinds of evil desires, [7]always learning but
never able to acknowledge the truth. [8]Just as Jannes and Jambres
opposed Moses, so also these men oppose the truth—men of
depraved minds, who, as far as the faith is concerned, are rejected.
[9]But they will not get very far because, as in the case of those men,
their folly will be clear to everyone.

Paul's Charge to Timothy

[10]You, however, know all about my teaching, my way of life,
my purpose, faith, patience, love, endurance, [11]persecutions, sufferings—what kinds of things happened to me in Antioch, Iconium
and Lystra, the persecutions I endured. Yet the Lord rescued me
from all of them. [12]In fact, everyone who wants to live a godly life
in Christ Jesus will be persecuted, [13]while evil men and impostors
will go from bad to worse, deceiving and being deceived. [14]But as
for you, continue in what you have learned and have become convinced of, because you know those from whom you learned it,
[15]and how from infancy you have known the holy Scriptures, which
are able to make you wise for salvation through faith in Christ
Jesus. [16]All Scripture is God-breathed and is useful for teaching,
rebuking, correcting and training in righteousness, [17]so that the
man of God may be thoroughly equipped for every good work.
4 In the presence of God and of Christ Jesus, who will judge the
living and the dead, and in view of his appearing and his kingdom,

2:21 *Master:* This could refer to the master of the house or to God or to both.

2:22 *evil desires of youth:* This could refer to a number of things such as false doctrines (4:3), lack of self control (3:3), and loving pleasure rather than loving God (3:4).

2:26 *devil:* The devil was the leader of the demons and evil forces that were against God and God's people. See also the mini-article called "Satan," p. 963.

3:1 *last days:* Refers to a time just before the end of the present age, or the time when God will judge the world. A number of New Testament passages say that false teachings would be common during this time. See also 2 Thes 3:1-12; 2 Pet 3:3; and the mini-article called "End Times," p. 2295.

3:6 *gain control over weak-willed women:* One strategy the false teachers used was to influence certain women in order to gain control of their families.

3:8 *Jannes and Jambres:* These names are not found in the Old Testament. But according to Jewish tradition these were the names of the two Egyptian magicians who opposed Moses. See Exod 7:11,22.

3:11 *persecutions, sufferings . . . Antioch, Iconium and Lystra:* This Antioch is the city in the region of Pisidia (Acts 13:14-52), where Paul and Barnabas preached the gospel with success. For more about Iconium and Lystra, see Acts 14:1-20.

3:15,16 *holy Scriptures . . . God-breathed:* This refers to the Jewish Scriptures (Old Testament). The writings included in the New Testament were not yet collected as Scripture at this time. See also the mini-article called "Inspiration of Scripture," p. 12.

4:1 *Christ Jesus, who will judge:* See the note at 3:1. See also Phil 3:20; 4:5; and the mini-article called "Second Coming," p. 2277.

I give you this charge: [2]Preach the Word; be prepared in season and
out of season; correct, rebuke and encourage—with great patience
and careful instruction. [3]For the time will come when men will not
put up with sound doctrine. Instead, to suit their own desires, they
will gather around them a great number of teachers to say what
their itching ears want to hear. [4]They will turn their ears away from
the truth and turn aside to myths. [5]But you, keep your head in all
situations, endure hardship, do the work of an evangelist, discharge all the duties of your ministry.
[6]For I am already being poured out like a drink offering, and
the time has come for my departure. [7]I have fought the good fight,
I have finished the race, I have kept the faith. [8]Now there is in store
for me the crown of righteousness, which the Lord, the righteous
Judge, will award to me on that day—and not only to me, but also
to all who have longed for his appearing.

4:4 *myths:* See the notes at 2:16-18 and 1 Tim 1:3,4.

4:6 *drink offering:* The water or wine offered by Jewish priests in the temple. Paul sees his life as being poured out as an offering to Christ. See Num 28:7; Phil 2:17.

4:8 *righteous Judge . . . that day:* See the notes at 3:1 and 4:1.

4:10 *Demas . . . Titus:* Demas is also mentioned in Colossians 4:14 and Philemon 24, but Crescens is not mentioned anywhere else in the Bible. Titus was one of Paul's most reliable helpers (2 Cor 7:5-7,13-16; 8:1-24; 12:14-18; Gal 2:1-3; Titus 1:4). See also the map on p. 2475.

4:11-13 *Luke . . . Carpus:* For Luke, see Introduction to ACTS, p. 2100. See also Col 4:14; Phlm 24. Mark may be John Mark, Paul's traveling companion (Acts 12:12,25; 13:13; 15:37-39). For Tychicus, see Acts 20:4; Eph 6:21,22; Col 4:7,8; Titus 3:12. Carpus is mentioned nowhere else in the Bible.

4:13 Acts 20:6.

Final Instructions and Greetings

Paul asks Timothy to come visit him in prison. He also makes some remarks and passes on instructions about a number of people that Timothy would know. The letter ends with a series of greetings.

Personal Remarks

[9]Do your best to come to me quickly, [10]for Demas, because
he loved this world, has deserted me and has gone to Thessalonica. Crescens has gone to Galatia, and Titus to Dalmatia. [11]Only
Luke is with me. Get Mark and bring him with you, because he is
helpful to me in my ministry. [12]I sent Tychicus to Ephesus. [13]When

QUESTIONS ABOUT 2 TIMOTHY

1. What three things does God's Spirit give? (1:7) Why would these things be important to a young leader of the church, like Timothy? How are they important for Christians living today?
2. In 2:3-7, three types of people are described as hard workers. What qualities did these different workers have that Paul wants Timothy to imitate? Which type of worker do you think best depicts the life of a Christian? Why?
3. Read the advice given to Timothy in 2:22-26. Why is this advice important to someone who is a leader in the church? In your opinion, what difficult temptations (desires) do Christians face today? Where do you find strength to face temptations?
4. In 3:1-5, Paul gives Timothy a brief description of how difficult the "last days" will be. What does Paul say people will be like at that time? How are the behavior and thoughts of the people described here different from the kinds of behavior and thoughts Christians are to practice?

you come, bring the cloak that I left with Carpus at Troas, and my
scrolls, especially the parchments.
14 Alexander the metalworker did me a great deal of harm.
The Lord will repay him for what he has done. 15 You too should be
on your guard against him, because he strongly opposed our message.
16 At my first defense, no one came to my support, but everyone deserted me. May it not be held against them. 17 But the Lord
stood at my side and gave me strength, so that through me the
message might be fully proclaimed and all the Gentiles might hear
it. And I was delivered from the lion's mouth. 18 The Lord will rescue me from every evil attack and will bring me safely to his heavenly kingdom. To him be glory for ever and ever. Amen.

Final Greetings

19 Greet Priscilla[a] and Aquila and the household of Onesiphorus. 20 Erastus stayed in Corinth, and I left Trophimus sick in
Miletus. 21 Do your best to get here before winter. Eubulus greets
you, and so do Pudens, Linus, Claudia and all the brothers.
22 The Lord be with your spirit. Grace be with you.

---

[a]19 Greek *Prisca,* a variant of *Priscilla*

4:13 *my scrolls, especially the parchments:* See the mini-article called "Scrolls," p. 1491.

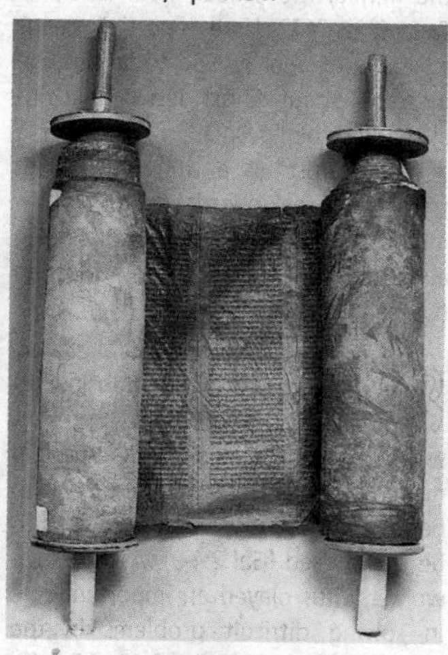

4:14 1 Tim 1:20; Ps 62:12; Rom 2:6. **4:19** Acts 18:2; 2 Tim 1:16, 17. **4:20** Acts 19:22; 20:4; 21:29; Rom 16:23.

TITUS

In a world that is full of different ideas and lifestyles, how do people discover the truth about God and being part of God's people? Read TITUS and find out.

WHAT MAKES TITUS SPECIAL?

Titus was a close friend of Paul who worked with him in Asia Minor and Greece and who was connected with the church in Corinth (see 2 Cor 2:13; 7:5-7,13-15; 8:6,16-24; 12:14-18; Gal 2:1-3). Titus apparently received this letter while he was still on the island of Crete, where Paul had left Titus to develop leaders for the churches in each town (Titus 1:5; see also Acts 14:23).

WHY WAS TITUS WRITTEN?

This letter was written to encourage Titus to continue teaching the truth about the faith and to instruct people how to live their lives as God wants. Apparently, some people in the churches on Crete were trying to deceive some of the believers by teaching false things (1:10-14; 3:9,10). The letter also provides instructions for church leaders and all the people of God.

WHAT'S THE STORY BEHIND THE SCENE?

TITUS focuses on instructions to church leaders (elders) about following correct beliefs and living in a proper way. Traditionally, it has been assumed that this was one of Paul's later letters, written after the events recorded in the book of ACTS. However, the letter's concern for how authority should be maintained within the churches has led some scholars to believe that the letter was written in Paul's name a number of years after the apostle died. Writing a letter in a person's name was considered a way of honoring that person's life and teachings and was a common practice in that age.

HOW IS TITUS CONSTRUCTED?

The letter may be outlined in the following way:

Church leaders and false teachers (1:1-16)

What to believe and how to live as God's people (2:1—3:15)

1:1 *Paul, a servant of God and an apostle of Jesus Christ:* See the mini-article called "Paul (Saul) of Tarsus," p. 2177. Here "apostle" means someone chosen by God to spread the message about Christ Jesus, which is also called the "gospel."

"Christ" is a title that comes from the Greek word *christos,* which means "Messiah" or "Chosen One." See also the mini-article called "Messiah (Chosen One)," p. 1124.

1:4 *Titus:* A Gentile (non-Jewish) Christian who was present when the church leaders in Jerusalem made a decision that Gentile men who became Christians were not required to be circumcised (Gal 2:1-9). As Paul's co-worker, Titus played an important role in solving difficult problems in the church at Corinth (2 Cor 2:13; 7:5-7,13-15; 8:6,16-24; 12:14-18).

1:4 *God the Father . . . Savior:* Jesus often referred to God as "Father" (see John 14, for example). Paul also uses this term in many of his letters to describe God (1 Cor 1:3; Gal 1:2,3; Phil 1:2).

1:5 *Crete:* Crete is a large island in the Mediterranean Sea southeast of Greece (see the map on p. 2475). Crete was the home of the Minoan culture that thrived between 2000 and 1100 B.C. The Minoans were a literate and wealthy society that traded with the Greeks and others in the Mediterranean world. At the height of their civilization the wealthy lived in palaces that included many "modern comforts" such as skylights, sophisticated drainage systems, and indoor pools for cooling the air on hot summer days. The book of ACTS tells of faithful Jews from Crete being in Jerusalem for Pentecost (Acts 2:11). Crete was one of the places where Paul's ship stopped when he was being taken as a prisoner to Rome (Acts 27:7-12). Apparently Paul and Titus visited Crete again after Paul's release from his first imprisonment in Rome.

Church Leaders and False Teachers

After a warm greeting Paul reminds Titus that his work is to appoint leaders for the churches of Crete. He tells Titus what qualities he should expect these leaders to have and reminds Titus of the importance of sticking to the true message. Paul also warns Titus about false teachers who apparently were upsetting families and causing trouble because of their teachings.

1 Paul, a servant of God and an apostle of Jesus Christ for the
faith of God's elect and the knowledge of the truth that leads to
godliness—[2]a faith and knowledge resting on the hope of eternal
life, which God, who does not lie, promised before the beginning
of time, [3]and at his appointed season he brought his word to light
through the preaching entrusted to me by the command of God
our Savior,

[4]To Titus, my true son in our common faith:

Grace and peace from God the Father and Christ Jesus our Savior.

Titus's Task on Crete

[5]The reason I left you in Crete was that you might straight-
en out what was left unfinished and appoint[a] elders in every town,
as I directed you. [6]An elder must be blameless, the husband of but
one wife, a man whose children believe and are not open to the
charge of being wild and disobedient. [7]Since an overseer[b] is
entrusted with God's work, he must be blameless—not overbear-
ing, not quick-tempered, not given to drunkenness, not violent,
not pursuing dishonest gain. [8]Rather he must be hospitable, one
who loves what is good, who is self-controlled, upright, holy and
disciplined. [9]He must hold firmly to the trustworthy message as it
has been taught, so that he can encourage others by sound doctrine and refute those who oppose it.
[10]For there are many rebellious people, mere talkers and
deceivers, especially those of the circumcision group. [11]They must
be silenced, because they are ruining whole households by teaching things they ought not to teach—and that for the sake of dishonest gain. [12]Even one of their own prophets has said, "Cretans
are always liars, evil brutes, lazy gluttons." [13]This testimony is true.
Therefore, rebuke them sharply, so that they will be sound in the
faith [14]and will pay no attention to Jewish myths or to the commands of those who reject the truth. [15]To the pure, all things are
pure, but to those who are corrupted and do not believe, nothing
is pure. In fact, both their minds and consciences are corrupted.

[a]5 Or *ordain* [b]7 Traditionally *bishop*

1:5 *appoint elders:* These elders were to teach the truth and help make decisions that concerned the local churches. See also the mini-article called "Church," p. 2264.

1:7 *an overseer:* This is a translation of the Greek word *episkopos,* which means "overseers" and can also be translated as "bishops." In the early church, an overseer was the chief leader of a local congregation. Later, overseers were put in charge of groups of churches in certain areas.

1:10 *deceivers . . . circumcision group:* The false teaching described here likely refers to Jewish members of the churches of Crete insisting that all the male followers of Jesus be circumcised. Paul and Titus had already settled this issue earlier when they met with other church leaders in Jerusalem (see Gal 2:1-10). These false teachers apparently tried to get money for themselves from other members by claiming that they had the truth (see also 1 Tim 6:5). Some false teachers tried to influence the women in order to control their whole families. (2 Tim 3:6,7)

1:12 *Cretans . . . gluttons:* This quote is from the Greek philosopher named Epimenides, who lived on Crete around 600 B.C.

1:14 *Jewish myths . . . commands:* Myths about some of the people mentioned in the genealogies in GENESIS were being taught as the truth in various Jewish writings of the time and in the writing of religious groups known as Gnostics. Gnosticism was a complex belief system that would become more developed in the centuries after TITUS was written. Gnostics believed they had "special knowledge" about God and the universe (see also 1 Tim 1:3,4; 4:7; 2 Tim 4:4). See also the article called "Religions and Philosophies in Bible Times," p. 1832.

1:4 2 Cor 8:23; Gal 2:3; 2 Tim 4:10. **1:6-9** 1 Tim 3:2-7.

2:3 *addicted to much wine:* Drinking moderate amounts of wine was acceptable and common in the ancient world, but being addicted to wine meant drinking too much or getting drunk. See also 1 Tim 3:8.

2:4 *younger women to love their husbands:* In Paul's day wives were to serve their husbands. Christian women who served their husbands and took care of their children were also serving Christ (Eph 5:21-25).

2:9 *slaves . . . masters:* Paul reminds Titus that slaves should respect their masters, and masters should take care of their slaves and treat them well (Eph 6:5-9). See also the mini-article called "Slaves and Servants in the Time of Jesus," p. 2006.

2:11 *salvation:* Here the word "salvation" points to what God has done and is still doing to free humans from sin and the powers of evil. See also the mini-article called "Salvation," p. 2021.

2:13 *glorious appearing of . . . Jesus Christ:* Paul often talked in his letters about a day when Jesus would come back (1 Cor 15:20-28; Phil 1:10; 2:16; 3:20,21). See also the mini-article called "Second Coming," p. 2277.

3:1 *be subject to rulers and authorities:* Paul may have been concerned that if the followers of Christ openly disobeyed and disrupted the government, government leaders would try to stop the believers from meeting together, or even kill them. If this happened, Christians would not be able to continue spreading the gospel throughout the Roman empire.

2:14 Exod 19:5; Deut 4:20; 7:6; 14:2; Ps 130:8; Rom 3:25,26; 1 Tim 2:5; Heb 9:14; 1 Pet 2:9.

[16]They claim to know God, but by their actions they deny him.
They are detestable, disobedient and unfit for doing anything
good.

What To Believe and How To Live as God's People

Titus is instructed to teach various church members how they are to live as God's people. Paul reminds Titus how God came in Christ to save God's people and wash them clean by the power of the Holy Spirit. The Spirit gives new birth and the promise of eternal life. The letter ends as Paul's letters often do with a number of personal greetings.

What Must Be Taught to Various Groups

2 You must teach what is in accord with sound doctrine. [2]Teach
the older men to be temperate, worthy of respect, self-controlled,
and sound in faith, in love and in endurance.
[3]Likewise, teach the older women to be reverent in the way
they live, not to be slanderers or addicted to much wine, but to
teach what is good. [4]Then they can train the younger women to
love their husbands and children, [5]to be self-controlled and pure,
to be busy at home, to be kind, and to be subject to their husbands, so that no one will malign the word of God.
[6]Similarly, encourage the young men to be self-controlled.
[7]In everything set them an example by doing what is good. In your
teaching show integrity, seriousness [8]and soundness of speech that
cannot be condemned, so that those who oppose you may be
ashamed because they have nothing bad to say about us.
[9]Teach slaves to be subject to their masters in everything, to
try to please them, not to talk back to them, [10]and not to steal from
them, but to show that they can be fully trusted, so that in every
way they will make the teaching about God our Savior attractive.
[11]For the grace of God that brings salvation has appeared to
all men. [12]It teaches us to say "No" to ungodliness and worldly passions, and to live self-controlled, upright and godly lives in this
present age, [13]while we wait for the blessed hope—the glorious
appearing of our great God and Savior, Jesus Christ, [14]who gave
himself for us to redeem us from all wickedness and to purify for
himself a people that are his very own, eager to do what is good.
[15]These, then, are the things you should teach. Encourage
and rebuke with all authority. Do not let anyone despise you.

Doing What Is Good

3 Remind the people to be subject to rulers and authorities, to be
obedient, to be ready to do whatever is good, [2]to slander no one, to

be peaceable and considerate, and to show true humility toward all men.

[3]At one time we too were foolish, disobedient, deceived and enslaved by all kinds of passions and pleasures. We lived in malice and envy, being hated and hating one another. [4]But when the kindness and love of God our Savior appeared, [5]he saved us, not because of righteous things we had done, but because of his mercy. He saved us through the washing of rebirth and renewal by the Holy Spirit, [6]whom he poured out on us generously through Jesus Christ our Savior, [7]so that, having been justified by his grace, we might become heirs having the hope of eternal life. [8]This is a trustworthy saying. And I want you to stress these things, so that those who have trusted in God may be careful to devote themselves to doing what is good. These things are excellent and profitable for everyone.

[9]But avoid foolish controversies and genealogies and arguments and quarrels about the law, because these are unprofitable and useless. [10]Warn a divisive person once, and then warn him

3:5 *washing of rebirth and renewal by the Holy Spirit:* This refers to the new birth. Paul likely had baptism in mind as well. Baptism doesn't, in itself, produce the new birth; but it is clearly a sign of it (see also Rom 6:3-5). See also the mini-articles called "Baptism," p. 1976, and "Holy Spirit," p. 2082.

3:9 *foolish controversies:* See the notes at 1:10 and 1:14.

3:10 Matt 18:15-17.

The Roman Empire. Coins circulated throughout the empire. As they were used, the images and inscriptions on the coins reminded the people of the emperor himself (the one here shows the first emperor, Augustus). The Arch of Titus (top left) was built to commemorate this general's conquest of Jerusalem in A.D. 70. Soldiers marched under arches like these when they returned from war. Celebrations of similar important events were held in the Forum (marketplace, top right), and games and entertainments were presented in the 50,000-seat Colisseum (bottom right), built during the reigns of three emperors—Vespasian (A.D. 69-79), Titus (A.D. 79-81), and Domitian (A.D. 81-96).

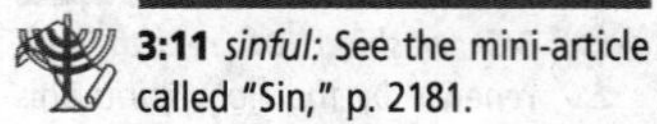

3:11 *sinful:* See the mini-article called "Sin," p. 2181.

a second time. After that, have nothing to do with him. 11 You may be
sure that such a man is warped and sinful; he is self-condemned.

Final Remarks

12 As soon as I send Artemas or Tychicus to you, do your best
to come to me at Nicopolis, because I have decided to winter there.

ROMAN EMPIRE

In 700 B.C., Rome was a small city in Italy that controlled only the area close around it. By 508 B.C. it had developed the form of government known as a republic in which the people chose the leaders they wanted to represent them. By the later second century B.C., Rome had conquered large parts of Greece and Asia Minor, as well as sections of North Africa, France, Spain, and many of the islands in the Mediterranean Sea. In 63 B.C., Roman troops led by the general Pompey (106-48 B.C.) took over Palestine. After Julius Caesar, the first Roman emperor, died in 44 B.C., his successor, Augustus, extended the empire to include Egypt, most of Asia Minor, England, and parts of Germany. See the map on p. 2471.

The top layer of Roman society was a group of 600 senators, who had to have a huge amount of money to hold this office. Below them were the knights, who needed considerably less money for their office. The population included citizens who had certain privileges and official protection, former slaves called "freedmen," and large numbers of slaves. The status of women was based on the social status of their fathers or husbands. Women from the upper classes enjoyed many legal rights and privileges not available to men or women of lower classes. Each region of the empire was ruled by a governor. Those governors who were appointed by the senate were called "proconsuls," and those chosen by the emperor were called "procurators."

Money to support the Roman government came from taxes. Taxes were placed on goods being transported, on inheritances, on farm products, and on personal property. Taxes were collected by tax collectors called "publicans," who signed a contract to bring in a specific amount of money each year.

Anyone who broke Roman laws could be called before the judges and forced to pay or be put in prison. They could even be put to death if what they did was considered to be a threat to the peace and order of the empire. Jesus' message about the coming kingdom of God was judged to be a political uprising, so Pilate, the procurator of the province of Judea, had him put to death.

In the early years after the time of Jesus, the Romans considered Christians to be one of the many Jewish sects. Jews were allowed to worship according to their ancient traditions, so Christians could also gather together in meetings without any interference from the Roman authorities. Later in the first century A.D., the Roman leaders no longer regarded Christianity as a protected official religion and began to persecute the followers of Christ. Even earlier, Emperor Nero, who ruled from A.D. 54 to 68, had sentenced some Christians to be killed as enemies of the empire. By the first part of the second century A.D., this kind of persecution became more widespread, especially when Christians refused to take part in ceremonies that honored the emperor as a god. Christians who suffered for their faith in this manner became known as "martyrs" (from the Greek word for "witness"). Roman persecution of Christians continued off and on until the time of Constantine the Great (emperor from A.D. 306 to 337). See also the article called "The World of Jesus: Peoples, Powers, and Politics," p. 1821.

13 Do everything you can to help Zenas the lawyer and Apollos on
their way and see that they have everything they need. 14 Our people must learn to devote themselves to doing what is good, in
order that they may provide for daily necessities and not live
unproductive lives.
15 Everyone with me sends you greetings. Greet those who
love us in the faith.

Grace be with you all.

3:12 *Artemas or Tychicus:* This is the only time Artemas is mentioned in the Bible. Tychicus was one of Paul's co-workers and someone Paul trusted to deliver messages and get information for him (Acts 20:4; Eph 6:21,22; Col 4:7,8; and 2 Tim 4:12).

3:12 *Nicopolis:* A port city on the western coast of Achaia. Travel by boat on the Mediterranean Sea was very dangerous during the winter months. This may be why Paul decided to stay in Nicopolis during the winter.

3:13 *Zenas . . . Apollos:* This is the only time Zenas is mentioned in the Bible. Apollos may be the same person mentioned in 1 Corinthians 3:1-9; 16:12; and in Acts 18:24.

QUESTIONS ABOUT TITUS

1. Titus begins with a short preface. (1:1-3) What does this preface say about Paul's role as an apostle? What does it teach about the relationship between faith, knowledge of truth, hope, and God's promises?
2. In 1:5-9 Paul decribes how the appointed (ordained) church leaders are to live. What is expected of elders? What is expected of overseers? Which seems to be held to a stricter standard? Why do you think this is so?
3. Compare the standards for church leaders given in Titus with those Paul gives in 1 Timothy 3:1-13. Taken together, what do these two letters have to say about how church leaders today should conduct themselves? What can church members do to help their leaders meet these standards?
4. In 1:13-15 Paul contrasts the attitudes of people who are "pure" and those who "do not believe." What does he say about each group? What do you think he means when he says, "To the pure, all things are pure"?
5. Compare the statements Paul makes in 2:11-14 and 3:4-7. What important thing did God do to show his kindness? For further reflection, read the mini-article called "Salvation," p. 2021. What does this article add to your understanding of these verses?
6. Why was Titus instructed to remind the people in his care to obey the government rulers and authorities? (3:1) What might have been the consequences if they were rebellious? What do you think of this advice? Compare Titus 3:1 to Acts 5:27-29. What do you make of the difference between these passages?
7. What was the most important thing you learned from reading Titus?

PHILEMON

Every society has laws and standards that it expects its people to live by. Read this short letter to find out what Paul had to say about God's love—how it can help the Lord's followers to do even more than what society expects of them.

What makes Philemon special?

This letter is typical of the kinds of letters people wrote in the Roman world. It is the shortest and most personal of Paul's letters. The way it is written suggests that Paul and Philemon were close friends. Most of the people mentioned in this letter, including Philemon's slave Onesimus, are also mentioned in COLOSSIANS (Col 1:7; 4:9-17).

Why was Philemon written?

Philemon was a wealthy man who probably lived in Colosse. Like many wealthy people in the Roman world, he owned slaves (see the mini-article called "Slaves and Servants in the Time of Jesus," p. 2006). But he was also a Christian who used his large house for church meetings (2). Paul is writing on behalf of Onesimus who had escaped from Philemon's household. Onesimus had become a follower of the Lord and a valuable friend to Paul. Paul is writing to say that he is sending Onesimus back to Philemon and to encourage Philemon to accept Onesimus as a "brother in the Lord."

What's the story behind the scene?

Paul may have written this letter while he was in prison in Ephesus, or he may have written it from Rome where he was forced to live in a house guarded by a soldier who made sure Paul did not go out and who could keep an eye on the kind of visitors he received (Acts 28:16-21).

Paul's concern is that Philemon treat his returning slave with kindness and love. He knew that Roman law allowed slave-owners to punish escaped slaves with death, and he does not question Philemon's right to own slaves. In fact, Paul seems to accept slavery as part of society in his day (1 Cor 7:20-22). In his letters he urged slaves to obey their masters. But more importantly, he urged masters to be kind to their slaves (Col 3:22—4:1). In GALATIANS, Paul says that slaves and free persons who have faith in Christ are equal with each other in God's family (Gal 3:26-28).

How is Philemon constructed?

The letter may be outlined in the following way:

Greetings and a prayer for Philemon (1-3)

Message to Philemon about his slave, Onesimus (4-22)

Final greetings and a prayer (23-25)

Paul and Philemon: Paul was also known by his Jewish name, Saul (see Acts 7:57—8:3; 9:1-30). Paul had been a strict follower of the Law of Moses and persecuted the early followers of Jesus (Gal 1:13; Phil 3:5,6), but Jesus chose him to be his apostle and to preach the gospel (Acts 9:1-19). Paul often described himself as a servant, which literally means "slave" of Christ. See also the mini-article called "Paul (Saul) of Tarsus," p. 2177.

Philemon was a wealthy Christian who owned slaves (15,16) and probably lived in Colosse in Asia Minor. His house was large enough to be a meeting place for Christians. Because Philemon had worked with Paul in the past, Paul considered him a dear friend (1). He was known to be a faithful follower of Jesus who loved God's people (5,7).

---

1 *Paul, a prisoner:* It is not clear where Paul was imprisoned when he wrote to Philemon. See the note about Paul above.

1 *Timothy:* Timothy is named as Paul's co-worker in many of Paul's letters (1 Cor 4:17; 16:10; 2 Cor 1:1,19; 1 Thes 1:1). See also Acts 16:1-3 and the Introduction to 1 TIMOTHY, on p. 2303.

2 *Apphia . . . Archippus:* Little is known about these two people, though both seem to have been involved in the church that met at Philemon's house. Archippus is also mentioned in Colossians 4:17.

---

2 *the church that meets in your home:* The Greek word translated as "church" is *ekklesia* and it originally referred to any gathering of people. In Paul's day Christians met in houses that were large enough for these kinds of gatherings. Here they came together for preaching, teaching, worship, sharing the Lord's Supper (Eucharist), and for social events. See also the mini-article called "Church," p. 2264.

Greetings and a Prayer for Philemon

Paul sends greetings to Philemon and others who are a part of the church that meets in Philemon's home. As in most of his letters, Paul follows the greeting by praying for Christ's blessing of peace.

[1]Paul, a prisoner of Christ Jesus, and Timothy our brother,

To Philemon our dear friend and fellow worker, [2]to Apphia
our sister, to Archippus our fellow soldier and to the church that
meets in your home:

[3]Grace to you and peace from God our Father and the Lord
Jesus Christ.

Message to Philemon about His Slave, Onesimus

Now Paul turns to the purpose of his letter. He tells Philemon that he is sending back to him the slave Onesimus who had run away from Philemon's household. Because Onesimus has helped Paul and has been like a son to him, Paul hopes Philemon will accept Onesimus back as a fellow brother in the Lord. Paul even offers to pay Philemon any money Onesimus may have taken from him.

Thanksgiving and Prayer

[4]I always thank my God as I remember you in my prayers,
[5]because I hear about your faith in the Lord Jesus and your love
for all the saints. [6]I pray that you may be active in sharing your
faith, so that you will have a full understanding of every good
thing we have in Christ. [7]Your love has given me great joy and
encouragement, because you, brother, have refreshed the hearts of
the saints.

Paul's Plea for Onesimus

[8]Therefore, although in Christ I could be bold and order you
to do what you ought to do, [9]yet I appeal to you on the basis of
love. I then, as Paul—an old man and now also a prisoner of
Christ Jesus— [10]I appeal to you for my son Onesimus,[a] who
became my son while I was in chains. [11]Formerly he was useless to
you, but now he has become useful both to you and to me.
[12]I am sending him—who is my very heart—back to you. [13]I
would have liked to keep him with me so that he could take your
place in helping me while I am in chains for the gospel. [14]But I did

[a]**10** *Onesimus* means *useful.*

3 *God our Father . . . Lord Jesus Christ:* Jesus often referred to God as "Father" (see John 14, for example). Paul uses this same term to describe God in many of his letters (1 Cor 1:3; Gal 1:1-3; Phil 1:2).

Jesus was a common name among Jewish men of this day. The Greek word for "Lord" is *kyrios* and was used to address someone as "sir." When it is used for Jesus, it emphasizes his authority and power. "Christ" is a title that comes from the Greek word *christos,* which means "Messiah" or "chosen one." See also the mini-articles called "Messiah (Chosen One)," p. 1124 and "Lord (Title for Jesus)," p. 2106.

10 *Onesimus:* In Greek, the name Onesimus means "useful." Onesimus was a slave who had run away from his master Philemon (15). He eventually ended up in the city where Paul was in prison or under house arrest. Verse 18 implies that Onesimus may have taken money or property from Philemon. Paul got to know Onesimus, although it is not clear whether Onesimus was also a prisoner. Paul feels especially fond of Onesimus because he had led Onesimus to Christ.

10 *became my son:* Paul is referring to Onesimus as his spiritual son.

11 *he was useless to you:* By using the word "useless," Paul is making a play on Onesimus's name which means "useful." Paul considers Onesimus "useful" because Onesimus has become a follower of the Lord and may be able to help him share the gospel (13).

13 *in chains for the gospel:* The gospel is both the message about Jesus and the message Jesus brings about the kingdom of God. To Paul, the gospel was "the power of God for the salvation of everyone who believes" (Rom 1:16).

10 Col 4:9.

14 *your consent . . . not forced:* Paul wanted Philemon to accept Onesimus back because he was a brother and follower of the Lord (16), not just because Paul was asking him to.

16 *slave:* Slavery was common in the Roman world of the first century. See the mini-article called "Slaves and Servants in the Time of Jesus," p. 2006.

19 *you owe me your very self:* This probably means that Paul was the one who first told Philemon about the gospel of God's love. When Philemon accepted this message by faith, he received new life in Christ.

LEADERS OF HOUSE CHURCHES IN THE NEW TESTAMENT

The Greek word for "church" (*ekklesia*) means "assembly" or "gathering." The first churches met in homes of Christians to pray, sing hymns, read the Scriptures, and share "love feasts" together. Although little is known about the individuals listed here, they are remembered as early followers of Christ who opened their homes for Christian fellowship or who led local groups of Christians.

LEADERS	CITY	SCRIPTURE PASSAGES
Phoebe	Cenchrea	Rom 16:1,2
Gaius	Corinth	Rom 16:23; 1 Cor 1:14
Priscilla and Aquila	Ephesus	Acts 18:1-26; Rom 16:3-5; 1 Cor 16:19
Philemon	Colosse	Phlm 1,2
Nympha	Laodicea	Col 4:15

not want to do anything without your consent, so that any favor
you do will be spontaneous and not forced. 15 Perhaps the reason
he was separated from you for a little while was that you might
have him back for good— 16 no longer as a slave, but better than a
slave, as a dear brother. He is very dear to me but even dearer to
you, both as a man and as a brother in the Lord.

17 So if you consider me a partner, welcome him as you
would welcome me. 18 If he has done you any wrong or owes you
anything, charge it to me. 19 I, Paul, am writing this with my own
hand. I will pay it back—not to mention that you owe me your

QUESTIONS ABOUT PHILEMON

1. Paul tells Philemon that he is "a prisoner of Christ Jesus" (1). What do you think this means? Can you think of other people who have been imprisoned because of their faith? How can Christians help people in this situation?
2. Everything we know about the wealthy Christian Philemon and his slave Onesimus is contained in this letter. What significant change has Onesimus experienced since leaving his master's household? (10) How did this change his relationship with Philemon? If Onesimus had intentionally run away from his master, Roman law would have allowed Philemon to punish him harshly, perhaps even putting him to death. What does Paul encourage Philemon to do instead? (12-20)
3. What does PHILEMON have to say about how Christians should treat one another? What can be learned from Paul's example and the actions he took on behalf of his friend and new fellow believer Onesimus?

very self. [20]I do wish, brother, that I may have some benefit from
you in the Lord; refresh my heart in Christ. [21]Confident of your
obedience, I write to you, knowing that you will do even more
than I ask.
[22]And one thing more: Prepare a guest room for me, because
I hope to be restored to you in answer to your prayers.

Final Greetings and a Prayer

Paul concludes by sending greetings from a number of the Lord's followers who were with him.

[23]Epaphras, my fellow prisoner in Christ Jesus, sends you
greetings. [24]And so do Mark, Aristarchus, Demas and Luke, my
fellow workers.
[25]The grace of the Lord Jesus Christ be with your spirit.

22 *Prepare a guest room for me:* Paul intended to visit Philemon soon. This may indicate that Paul was not imprisoned as far away as Rome, but may have been in Ephesus or some other city nearer to where Philemon lived.

23 *Epaphras:* He is also mentioned as a worker with Paul in Colossians 1:7; 4:12.

24 *Mark, Aristarchus, Demas and Luke:* These followers are all mentioned in Colossians 4:10-14. Mark (also called John) worked with both Paul and Barnabas and is mentioned several times in ACTS (Acts 12:12,25; 13:13; 15:36-39). Aristarchus was from Thessalonica in Greece, but traveled with Paul (Acts 19:29; 20:4,5), including his final journey to Rome (Acts 27:2). Demas is mentioned in 2 Timothy 4:10, where his actions are criticized.

Luke is mentioned in Colossians 4:14, where he is called a doctor, and in 2 Timothy 4:11. The books of LUKE and ACTS, have been traditionally considered his works (see the Introduction to LUKE, p. 1964).

25 *Lord Jesus Christ:* See the note at verse 3.

General Letters and Revelation

THE FINAL NINE BOOKS of the New Testament are written in a number of styles by different writers. The first eight (HEBREWS through JUDE) are often referred to as the General Letters. Some of these are clearly written in letter form, similar to the style of Paul's letters. These include JAMES, 1 and 2 PETER, 2 and 3 JOHN, and JUDE. HEBREWS is included in this group because it ends with personal greetings, though it reads more like a sermon or a series of sermons. 1 JOHN does not begin with the usual greeting found in a letter, but its advice for Christians is given in a personal way that sounds like one friend writing to another.

In order to point out the special nature of the early Christians, the eight General Letters include a number of warnings against following false teachers (2 Pet 2:1-3; 1 John 2:18-26; 4:1,2; Jude 3-13), as well as encouragement to live holy lives (Jas 2:14-26; 1 Pet 1:13-16; 2 Pet 1:5-11) and to love one another (Heb 13:1,2; 1 John 3:11-19; 2 John 5; 6). Christians are called God's chosen people (Heb 3:1; 1 Pet 2:9,10), but they are also warned that being chosen will not shield them from suffering or from having their faith tested (Heb 13:3; Jas 1:12; 1 Pet 1:5-7; 3:13-17; 4:12-14). The persecution of Christians at the hands of the Romans appears to have greatly increased in the late first century A.D. during the rule of Emperor Domitian. Because many of the General Letters deal with the suffering of the Christians who lived during this time, it is likely that they were written in the last few decades of the first century A.D. or perhaps a bit later.

This tension between Christians and their enemies is especially clear in REVELATION, the last book in this section. REVELATION records the visions of John of Patmos and includes a number of letters written to churches in Asia Minor (Rev 2; 3). REVELATION is an example of Apocalyptic writing which is based, in part, on earlier Jewish Apocalyptic writings such as DANIEL and EZEKIEL. Such writings describe the ongoing battle between God and the forces of evil, and they tell how God will achieve the final victory in the end. But, in the meantime, those who follow God may face suffering or even be killed by the enemies of God. Apocalyptic writings use a number of symbols and colorful images—such as the beasts in Revelation 13—to provide a message that God's people would understand but which would be confusing to their enemies. Another example of this "secret" type of imagery is the mention of the ancient city of Babylon (Rev 17:5—18:24). Christian readers in John's day knew that this was really a reference to Rome, which they had come to see as the great enemy of God and God's people.

Like many other apocalyptic writings, REVELATION has violent scenes of God's judgment, but the primary purpose of such books is to give hope and to encourage Christians to remain faithful in the midst of difficult times. The final chapters of the book provide a hopeful picture of the new heaven and new earth God will bring at the end of time. See also the mini-article called "Apocalyptic Writing," p. 1656.

HEBREWS

The Jewish people had a high priest who offered sacrifices in the temple so that the people would be forgiven. But how could the new Christians be forgiven and become friends with God? Read Hebrews to find out.

WHAT MAKES HEBREWS SPECIAL?

HEBREWS is a unique book about faith. It constantly uses the Jewish Scriptures (Old Testament) to help explain what the new Christian faith is all about. The writer used a style of Greek that is complex when compared to most of the other New Testament books. And he also made use of speech and debate tactics common in his day in order to prove his points.

HEBREWS is often referred to as a "letter," and it ends with final greetings (13:22-25). But it is really a teaching sermon that is carefully designed to answer some very basic questions about the Christian faith and to tell people how important Jesus really is.

WHY WAS HEBREWS WRITTEN?

Many religious people in the first century, both Jews and Gentiles, had questions about the religion of the early Christians. HEBREWS explains that Christianity is based in the Jewish religion but also tells how it is different. The main difference is Christ Jesus, who is the perfect high priest and who offered his own life as a perfect sacrifice for sin once for all time (9:23—10:18). By dying and returning from death he has opened the way for all people to come to God (4:14—5:10; 7:1—8:13).

The writer says that Jesus is greater than any of God's prophets or angels (1:1-14), and greater even than Moses and Joshua (2:1—4:14). The forgiveness and new life that Jesus offers come only by faith. And this faith makes his followers sure of what they hope for and gives them proof of what they cannot see (11:1). The writer praises God's faithful people of the past (11:2-40) who are part of the "cloud of witnesses" that surrounds Christians as they run the race of faith (12:1). But above all, Christians are to keep their eyes and minds focused on Jesus, who leads them in this race and makes their faith complete (12:2,3).

WHAT'S THE STORY BEHIND THE SCENE?

It is not clear who wrote HEBREWS or when it was written. The Greek style is different than the style of Paul's letters, and the complex thoughts concerning the identity and work of Jesus probably took a number of years to develop. So the letter was likely written after A.D. 60 and before A.D. 95 when parts of HEBREWS are quoted in a letter written by Clement of Rome. Many scholars believe that HEBREWS was written before

angels: The word "angel" in English is based on the Greek word *angelos*, which means "messenger." In the Bible angels are beings in a special relationship with God who carry out God's will. The author of HEBREWS states that God's Son (Christ) was also a messenger, but that because of his special relationship to God he is much greater than any angel, which is why all the angels worship him. See also the mini-article called "Angels," p. 88.

> *In these last days he has spoken to us by his Son, whom he appointed heir of all things, and through whom he made the universe.*
> Heb 1:2

1:1 *God spoke to our forefathers through the prophets:* This refers to the ancient Jewish prophets whose words are recorded in the Jewish Scriptures, which Christians call the Old Testament. These prophets interpreted the history of the Israelite people and preached messages from God concerning how they were to live and worship. See also the article called "Prophets and Prophecy," p. 935.

"Forefathers" here refers to the people of Israel, who were descendants of Abraham and Sarah. See also the mini-article called "Abraham," p. 2254. In HEBREWS, God's message often refers to the promises God made to Abraham and to the law God gave Moses and the people. Moses was also called a prophet, and Jesus is described in the New Testament as "a prophet" like Moses, whom God would send as the chosen Messiah (Acts 3:18-23; 7:37).

1:2 *Son:* This refers to Jesus Christ. He is the "Word" that was present with God at the beginning of creation (1:1-3; Col 1:15-17). He became a human being (John 1:14) but is like God in every way (Heb 1:3).

1:3 *his powerful word:* The "powerful word" that Christ uses to hold creation together is as mighty as the words God used to create the universe in the first place (Gen 1).

Jerusalem and the temple were destroyed by the Romans in A.D. 70, since the author writes as if the worship activities of the temple were still in place.

The exact identity of the letter's audience is also unclear. Hebrews 13:24 does mention followers from Italy, who may be sending greetings to friends at home. Some members of the audience have been persecuted, they were mistreated in public, and they had their property taken away (10:32-34). Some followers have quit meeting for worship, perhaps because Christ has not returned as soon as they expected (10:25). This suggests to some scholars that the audience was a second generation of Christians.

HOW IS HEBREWS CONSTRUCTED?

HEBREWS is a carefully organized speech or a sermon that makes its main points very clearly. The writer shifts back and forth between giving information and exhortation. The argument of the book is developed in five major themes. Each of these main themes is followed by sections that teach how God's people should live.

God chose Jesus to purify and renew the world (1:1-14)
Listen to the message that saves (2:1-4)

Jesus' way of saving God's people is greater than Moses' way (2:5—3:6)
Hold on to faith and enter the place of rest (3:7—4:13)

Jesus is the great high priest (4:14—5:10)
Turn away from deeds that bring death (5:11—6:12)

Jesus' sacrifice makes a new covenant (6:13—10:18)
Prepare for the Day of the Lord (10:19-39)

Faith has always been the way to please God (11:1-40)
Run the race of faith (12:1—13:25)

God Chose Jesus To Purify and Renew the World

The ancient prophets spoke God's message to his people, but now God has sent Jesus to tell God's message, wash away sins, and rule as King forever.

The Son Superior to Angels

1 In the past God spoke to our forefathers through the prophets
at many times and in various ways, 2 but in these last days he has
spoken to us by his Son, whom he appointed heir of all things, and
through whom he made the universe. 3 The Son is the radiance of
God's glory and the exact representation of his being, sustaining
all things by his powerful word. After he had provided purification
for sins, he sat down at the right hand of the Majesty in heaven.

4 So he became as much superior to the angels as the name he has
inherited is superior to theirs.
5 For to which of the angels did God ever say,

"You are my Son;
today I have become your Father"[a][b]?

Or again,

"I will be his Father,
and he will be my Son"[c]?

6 And again, when God brings his firstborn into the world, he
says,

"Let all God's angels worship him."[d]

7 In speaking of the angels he says,

"He makes his angels winds,
his servants flames of fire."[e]

8 But about the Son he says,

"Your throne, O God, will last for ever and ever,
and righteousness will be the scepter of your
kingdom.
9 You have loved righteousness and hated wickedness;
therefore God, your God, has set you above your
companions
by anointing you with the oil of joy."[f]

10 He also says,

"In the beginning, O Lord, you laid the foundations
of the earth,
and the heavens are the work of your hands.
11 They will perish, but you remain;
they will all wear out like a garment.
12 You will roll them up like a robe;
like a garment they will be changed.
But you remain the same,
and your years will never end."[g]

13 To which of the angels did God ever say,

"Sit at my right hand
until I make your enemies
a footstool for your feet"[h]?

14 Are not all angels ministering spirits sent to serve those who will
inherit salvation?

---

a5 Or *have begotten you* **b5** Psalm 2:7 **c5** 2 Samuel 7:14; 1 Chron. 17:13
d6 Deut. 32:43 (see Dead Sea Scrolls and Septuagint) **e7** Psalm 104:4
f9 Psalm 45:6,7 **g12** Psalm 102:25-27 **h13** Psalm 110:1

1:3 *purification for sins:* Those who need purification for sins are those who turn their backs on God and disobey God's Law. The Law of Moses stated that people who had sinned had become ritually unclean. People who were ritually unclean were required to go through a washing ceremony so they could once again be purified and take their place among God's people. But now, the writer says, Jesus has forgiven all sins.

1:3 *right hand of the Majesty in heaven:* Jesus now rules in heaven, sitting in a place of honor and power (at God's right hand).

1:4 *angels:* See the note on p. 2331. God has placed Jesus over all things, including the angels. See also Phil 2:9, 10; Eph 1:21.

1:5 *Father:* Jesus often referred to God as "Father" (John 14; see also Gal 1:2,3; 1 Cor 1:3; Phil 1:2). The relationship between God and the chosen one, whether an earthly king or Jesus, is that of Father and Son (Ps 2:7; 2 Sam 7:14; 1 Chr 17:13). The angels were not offered this close relationship.

1:6 *firstborn:* This is Christ. In the ancient world, firstborn sons had a place of honor and certain inheritance rights that the other children in a family did not have. In 12:23 "firstborn" refers to God's special people. Each believer, including women and girls, would be treated by God as firstborn sons.

1:14 *angels . . . serve those who will inherit salvation:* See the note on p. 2331. Angels help God's people until the time that God's rule becomes complete and everlasting.

Here the word "salvation" points to what God has done and is still doing to free humans from sin and the powers of evil. "Salvation" also can refer to receiving "eternal life," which in HEBREWS is also called the promised "rest" (4:1). See also the mini-article called "Salvation," p. 2021.

1:7 Ps 104:4. **1:8,9** Ps 45:6,7. **1:10-12** Ps 102:25-27. **1:13** Ps 110:1.

2:2 *message spoken by angels:* Acts 7:53 mentions that God's Law was "put into effect through angels." See also the note at 1:1. Those who did not follow the Law of Moses were to be punished.

2:3 *such a great salvation:* See the note at 1:14.

2:4 *wonders and various miracles:* The writer is referring to wonders like God helping the people of Israel pass through the Red Sea in order to escape from slavery in Egypt (Exod 14), and providing them with food called manna while they wandered in the desert (Num 11:4-9).

2:4 *Holy Spirit:* The Holy Spirit is the power of God carrying out God's purposes in the world. The Spirit teaches and guides the people of God so that they can become the kind of people God wants them to be. See also the mini-article called "Holy Spirit," p. 2082.

2:5 *angels:* See the note on p. 2331.

2:9 *lower than the angels:* The writer means that when Jesus was fully human, he became lower than the angels for a while. He humbly obeyed God and died on the cross (Phil 2:6-9). See also Ps 8:5.

2:9 *he might taste death for everyone:* Jesus was put to death on the cross (Mark 15:22-39; Acts 2:22-24; John 3:16). He died in order to defeat death and overcome sin and evil. Later, God raised Jesus from death and gave him a place of honor in heaven, where he rules with God (see Eph 1:19-22). For more about this ancient form of execution, see the mini-article called "Crucifixion," p. 1914.

2:10 *their salvation:* See the note at 1:14.

2:11 *made holy . . . same family:* The word "holy" here means "set apart" for God. See also the mini-article called "Holiness," p. 1626. The "family" here is God's family, which is made up of those who have faith in Christ.

LISTEN TO THE MESSAGE THAT SAVES

This first section of exhortation encourages believers to pay full attention to God's message.

Warning to Pay Attention

2 We must pay more careful attention, therefore, to what we
have heard, so that we do not drift away. [2]For if the message spoken by angels was binding, and every violation and disobedience
received its just punishment, [3]how shall we escape if we ignore
such a great salvation? This salvation, which was first announced
by the Lord, was confirmed to us by those who heard him. [4]God
also testified to it by signs, wonders and various miracles, and gifts
of the Holy Spirit distributed according to his will.

Jesus' Way of Saving God's People Is Greater Than Moses' Way

Jesus came to serve God as a faithful high priest and to sacrifice himself to forgive sins. Moses was a faithful servant, but Christ is God's Son, and now God has put him in charge of God's people.

Jesus Made Like His Brothers

[5]It is not to angels that he has subjected the world to come,
about which we are speaking. [6]But there is a place where someone
has testified:

"What is man that you are mindful of him,
 the son of man that you care for him?
[7]You made him a little[a] lower than the angels;
 you crowned him with glory and honor
8 and put everything under his feet."[b]

In putting everything under him, God left nothing that is not subject to him. Yet at present we do not see everything subject to him.
[9]But we see Jesus, who was made a little lower than the angels, now
crowned with glory and honor because he suffered death, so that
by the grace of God he might taste death for everyone.
[10]In bringing many sons to glory, it was fitting that God, for
whom and through whom everything exists, should make the
author of their salvation perfect through suffering. [11]Both the one
who makes men holy and those who are made holy are of the same
family. So Jesus is not ashamed to call them brothers. [12]He says,

"I will declare your name to my brothers;
 in the presence of the congregation I will sing your praises."[c]

[a]**7** Or *him for a little while;* also in verse 9 [b]**8** Psalm 8:4-6 [c]**12** Psalm 22:22

[13]And again,

"I will put my trust in him."[a]

And again he says,

"Here am I, and the children God has given me."[b]

[14]Since the children have flesh and blood, he too shared in
their humanity so that by his death he might destroy him who
holds the power of death—that is, the devil— [15]and free those who
all their lives were held in slavery by their fear of death. [16]For surely it is not angels he helps, but Abraham's descendants. [17]For this
reason he had to be made like his brothers in every way, in order
that he might become a merciful and faithful high priest in service

[a]13 Isaiah 8:17 [b]13 Isaiah 8:18

2:16 *Abraham's descendants:* See the note at 1:1.

2:17 *high priest:* The high priest of Israel entered into the Most Holy Place in the temple to offer animal sacrifices asking God to take away the sins of the people. This happened on the Day of Atonement (Lev 16:1-34; see also Exod 28:1-39). Like the high priest, in "service to God," Jesus offered a sacrifice for all people in order to forgive sins. But the sacrifice he brought was himself (see Rom 3:25,26).

2:13 Isa 8:17,18. **2:16** Isa 41:8,9.

MOSES

Moses was born in Egypt to Hebrew parents but later was adopted by Pharaoh's daughter (Exod 2:1-10). Growing up in Egypt, Moses saw how cruelly the Egyptians treated the Hebrew people. One day Moses killed an Egyptian guard and escaped to the land of Midian, where the LORD told him to go back to Egypt to free the Hebrew people from slavery (Exod 3:1—4:17). He did return to Egypt and warned Pharaoh that the LORD would send plagues on Egypt unless the Israelites were freed. Eventually, Moses led the people out of Egypt and through the Red Sea (Exod 5–15).

Moses was a great leader and a miracle-worker (Exod 15:22-25), but he had many other roles as well. He was the great "law-giver," chosen by the LORD to receive the Ten Commandments and other laws that were to guide the lives and worship of the Israelite people. These laws are described in detail in the books of EXODUS (20–40), LEVITICUS, NUMBERS, and DEUTERONOMY. Moses is also described as a prophet (Deut 34:10), who preached God's words of judgment and promise to the people (Deut 7:12-15).

Though Moses is not called a "priest," the LORD gave to him the directions for building Israel's tabernacle and the rules that were to govern Israel's worship and sacrifices. He also prayed to the LORD on behalf of the people (Num 14:11-20) and went to the tabernacle to meet the LORD (Exod 33:7-11).

Moses also decided legal cases, and he appointed judges to help him make decisions on the basis of God's laws (Exod 18:13-26). Moses acted as a military leader when Israel had to battle unfriendly people on their way to the promised land of Canaan (Num 21:21-35).

The LORD did not allow Moses to lead the people of Israel into the promised land because he had disobeyed God before the people (Num 20:1-12; Deut 3:23-29). However, Moses was able to look across the Jordan Valley from Mount Nebo and see the land that was to become the land of Israel (Deut 32:48-52).

The New Testament primarily refers to Moses' role as "law-giver" (Matt 19:7; John 1:17; 2 Cor 3:7-14), but he is also described as an example of faith (Heb 3:2; 11:23-28) and as a prophet (Acts 3:22,23).

See the chart on the next page for a list of key events and miracles in the life of Moses.

KEY EVENTS IN MOSES' LIFE

EVENTS	SCRIPTURE PASSAGES
Moses is born in Egypt	Exod 2:1-10
Moses kills an Egyptian and escapes to the land of Midian	Exod 2:11-15
Moses marries Zipporah, a Midianite	Exod 2:21, 22
God speaks to Moses from the burning bush	Exod 3:1—4:17
Moses and Aaron confront the Pharaoh of Egypt and the LORD brings about ten plagues	Exod 5:1—12:30
Moses leads the people of Israel out of Egypt and through the Red Sea	Exod 12:31-42; 13:17—14:31
The LORD makes the bitter waters at Marah drinkable	Exod 15:22-25
The LORD sends bread (manna) from heaven	Exod 16; Num 11:4-9
The LORD gives water from a rock	Exod 17:1-7; Num 20:1-13
Moses receives the Ten Commandments at Mount Sinai	Exod 20:1-17; Deut 5:1-21
Moses receives laws concerning community life matters	Exod 21:1—23:9; Num 30:1-16; 35:9—36:13; Deut 15:1-18; 16:18-20; 17:8-20; 19:1—25:16
Moses receives instructions about the tabernacle and other religious matters	Exod 25:1—31:18; 35:1—40:38; Lev 1–27; Num 19:1-22; 28:1—29:40; Deut 12:1—14:29; 15:19—16:17
The people demand an idol in the shape of a calf and Moses breaks the stones with the LORD's Commandments written on them	Exod 32:1-35; Deut 9:6-29
The LORD gives a second set of commandments	Exod 34:1-9; Deut 10:1-5
Moses' face shines from being in the LORD's presence on Mount Sinai	Exod 34:29-35
The LORD gives Moses instructions about making the tribe of Levi into priests to serve in the tabernacle	Num 3:5-13; 8:5-26; 18:1-32; Deut 10:8, 9
Korah, Dathan, and Abiram rebel against Moses' leadership	Num 16:1-40
Moses makes a bronze snake to heal the people bitten by poisonous snakes	Num 21:4-9
The LORD refuses to let Moses enter Canaan	Deut 3:23-29; 32:48-52
The LORD gives Moses the most important commandment	Deut 6:1-9
Moses blesses the tribes of Israel	Deut 33:1-29
Moses dies in Moab	Deut 34:1-8

to God, and that he might make atonement for[a] the sins of the people. [18]Because he himself suffered when he was tempted, he is able to help those who are being tempted.

We have come to share in Christ if we hold firmly till the end the confidence we had at first.
Heb 3:14

Jesus Greater Than Moses

3 Therefore, holy brothers, who share in the heavenly calling, fix your thoughts on Jesus, the apostle and high priest whom we confess. [2]He was faithful to the one who appointed him, just as Moses was faithful in all God's house. [3]Jesus has been found worthy of greater honor than Moses, just as the builder of a house has greater honor than the house itself. [4]For every house is built by someone, but God is the builder of everything. [5]Moses was faithful as a servant in all God's house, testifying to what would be said in the future. [6]But Christ is faithful as a son over God's house. And we are his house, if we hold on to our courage and the hope of which we boast.

HOLD ON TO FAITH AND ENTER THE PLACE OF REST

Next comes a warning about rebelling against God and a reminder to remain faithful in order to enter the place of rest.

Warning Against Unbelief

[7]So, as the Holy Spirit says:

"Today, if you hear his voice,
[8] do not harden your hearts
as you did in the rebellion,
during the time of testing in the desert,
[9]where your fathers tested and tried me
and for forty years saw what I did.
[10]That is why I was angry with that generation,
and I said, 'Their hearts are always going astray,
and they have not known my ways.'
[11]So I declared on oath in my anger,
'They shall never enter my rest.' "[b]

[12]See to it, brothers, that none of you has a sinful, unbelieving heart that turns away from the living God. [13]But encourage one another daily, as long as it is called Today, so that none of you may be hardened by sin's deceitfulness. [14]We have come to share in Christ if we hold firmly till the end the confidence we had at first. [15]As has just been said:

3:5 *Moses was faithful as a servant:* See the mini-article called "Moses," p. 2335.

3:6 *Christ:* "Christ" is from the Greek word *christos,* and has the same meaning as the Hebrew word *Messiah,* or "chosen one." Jesus is the one God chose to lead God's people.

3:7 *Holy Spirit:* See the note at 2:4 (Holy Spirit).

3:8 *do not harden your hearts . . . testing in the desert:* After escaping from Egypt, the people of Israel wandered for many years in the desert. They tested God by complaining and by disobeying God's commands (Exod 17:7; Deut 6:16; Num 14:21-23).

3:13 *sin's deceitfulness:* See the note at 1:3 (sins).

3:2 Num 12:7. **3:7-11** Ps 95:7-11. **3:15** Ps 95:7,8; Heb 3:7.

---

[a]17 Or *and that he might turn aside God's wrath, taking away* [b]11 Psalm 95:7-11

"Today, if you hear his voice,
do not harden your hearts
as you did in the rebellion."[a]

[16]Who were they who heard and rebelled? Were they not all those Moses led out of Egypt? [17]And with whom was he angry for forty years? Was it not with those who sinned, whose bodies fell in the desert? [18]And to whom did God swear that they would never enter his rest if not to those who disobeyed[b]? [19]So we see that they were not able to enter, because of their unbelief.

A Sabbath-Rest for the People of God

4 Therefore, since the promise of entering his rest still stands, let us be careful that none of you be found to have fallen short of it. [2]For we also have had the gospel preached to us, just as they did; but the message they heard was of no value to them, because those who heard did not combine it with faith.[c] [3]Now we who have believed enter that rest, just as God has said,

"So I declared on oath in my anger,
'They shall never enter my rest.'"[d]

And yet his work has been finished since the creation of the world. [4]For somewhere he has spoken about the seventh day in these words: "And on the seventh day God rested from all his work."[e] [5]And again in the passage above he says, "They shall never enter my rest."

[6]It still remains that some will enter that rest, and those who formerly had the gospel preached to them did not go in, because of their disobedience. [7]Therefore God again set a certain day, calling it Today, when a long time later he spoke through David, as was said before:

"Today, if you hear his voice,
do not harden your hearts."[f]

[8]For if Joshua had given them rest, God would not have spoken later about another day. [9]There remains, then, a Sabbath-rest for the people of God; [10]for anyone who enters God's rest also rests from his own work, just as God did from his. [11]Let us, therefore, make every effort to enter that rest, so that no one will fall by following their example of disobedience.

[12]For the word of God is living and active. Sharper than any double-edged sword, it penetrates even to dividing soul and spirit, joints and marrow; it judges the thoughts and attitudes of the heart. [13]Nothing in all creation is hidden from God's sight. Everything is uncovered and laid bare before the eyes of him to whom we must give account.

[a]**15** Psalm 95:7,8 [b]**18** Or *disbelieved* [c]**2** Many manuscripts *because they did not share in the faith of those who obeyed* [d]**3** Psalm 95:11; also in verse 5 [e]**4** Gen. 2:2 [f]**7** Psalm 95:7,8

3:16 *those Moses led out of Egypt:* See the note at 3:8. Because they disobeyed God and complained, most of the people who left Egypt were not allowed to enter the promised land of Canaan (Num 14:1-35).

4:1 *entering his rest:* The Israelite people who left Egypt were headed for Canaan, where they hoped to make their home in a land of plenty and peace. But the generation of Israelites that disobeyed God in the desert were not allowed to enter this place of rest (see the note at 3:16). God has provided a promised rest in heaven where those who have faith in Christ will live with God forever.

4:7 *David:* King David, who lived about 1000 years before Jesus was born, was considered by many to be Israel's greatest ruler. See also the mini-article called "David," p. 1028.

4:8 *Joshua:* Before Moses died Joshua was chosen to lead the people into Canaan (Deut 31:1-8). The Israelite people conquered much of the land and did experience some periods of peace (Josh 21:44; 22:4), but nothing like the promised "rest" still to come.

4:9 *Sabbath-rest:* The writer compares the new day of rest to the Jewish Sabbath. Sabbath means "rest" or to "stop working" and was a rule for all Jewish people (Exod 20:8-11; Deut 5:12-15).

4:11 *enter that rest:* See the note at 4:1. The writer warns that those who turn away from God and do not trust in Christ may miss receiving the eternal rest.

4:12 *double-edged sword:* God's powerful word can be a word of judgment "cutting" between good and evil. Nothing can be hidden from it, because it cuts right to our deepest thoughts and desires. See also Eph 6:17; Rev 1:16.

4:4 Gen 2:2; Exod 20:11. **4:7** Ps 95:7,8.

Jesus Is the Great High Priest

God chose Jesus Christ as the great high priest, whose suffering as a perfect sacrifice is able to save all who believe in him.

Jesus the Great High Priest

14Therefore, since we have a great high priest who has gone
through the heavens,[a] Jesus the Son of God, let us hold firmly to the
faith we profess. 15For we do not have a high priest who is unable to
sympathize with our weaknesses, but we have one who has been
tempted in every way, just as we are—yet was without sin. 16Let us
then approach the throne of grace with confidence, so that we may
receive mercy and find grace to help us in our time of need.
5 Every high priest is selected from among men and is appointed to
represent them in matters related to God, to offer gifts and sacrifices
for sins. 2He is able to deal gently with those who are ignorant and are
going astray, since he himself is subject to weakness. 3This is why he has
to offer sacrifices for his own sins, as well as for the sins of the people.
4No one takes this honor upon himself; he must be called by
God, just as Aaron was. 5So Christ also did not take upon himself the
glory of becoming a high priest. But God said to him,

> "You are my Son;
> today I have become your Father."[b][c]

6And he says in another place,

> "You are a priest forever,
> in the order of Melchizedek."[d]

7During the days of Jesus' life on earth, he offered up prayers
and petitions with loud cries and tears to the one who could save
him from death, and he was heard because of his reverent submission. 8Although he was a son, he learned obedience from what he
suffered 9and, once made perfect, he became the source of eternal
salvation for all who obey him 10and was designated by God to be
high priest in the order of Melchizedek.

TURN AWAY FROM DEEDS THAT BRING DEATH

Christ's followers are warned not to turn their backs on God's message, but to be mature in their faith and to live as people who have been saved.

Warning Against Falling Away

11We have much to say about this, but it is hard to explain
because you are slow to learn. 12In fact, though by this time you

[a]14 Or *gone into heaven* [b]5 Or *have begotten you* [c]5 Psalm 2:7 [d]6 Psalm 110:4

For the word of God is living and active. Sharper than any double-edged sword, it penetrates even to dividing soul and spirit, joints and marrow; it judges the thoughts and attitudes of the heart.
Heb 4:12

4:12 *heart:* In ancient times many people believed that a person's true inner self, thoughts, and intentions came from the heart.

4:14 *great high priest . . . Son of God:* See the note at 2:17 and the mini-article called "Son of God," p. 2044. See also John 17:1-5; Acts 1:6-11; Eph 1:19-22.

4:15 *was without sin:* See the note at 1:3 (sins). See also Luke 4:1-13.

5:1 *high priest . . . offer gifts and sacrifices for sins:* See the note at 2:17 and the mini-article called "Israel's Priests," p. 2344.

5:4 *Aaron:* God chose Aaron, Moses' brother, to be the first high priest (Exod 28:1—29:35).

5:6 *Melchizedek:* In the Old Testament, Melchizedek is described as a priest of God Most High and king of Salem (Gen 14:17-20). He blessed Abraham, promising him God's special favor. Melchizedek's death is not mentioned in GENESIS, so some Jewish teachers argued that Melchizedek would live forever (Ps 110:4). See also the note at 7:1-3.

5:9 *eternal salvation:* See the note at 1:14.

5:3 Lev 9:7. **5:5** Ps 2:7. **5:6** Ps 110:4. **5:7** Matt 26:36-46; 27:46; Mark 14:32-42; Luke 22:39-46. **5:12,13** 1 Cor 3:2.

ought to be teachers, you need someone to teach you the elementary truths of God's word all over again. You need milk, not solid
food! [13]Anyone who lives on milk, being still an infant, is not
acquainted with the teaching about righteousness. [14]But solid food
is for the mature, who by constant use have trained themselves to
distinguish good from evil.
6 Therefore let us leave the elementary teachings about Christ
and go on to maturity, not laying again the foundation of repentance from acts that lead to death,[a] and of faith in God, [2]instruc-
tion about baptisms, the laying on of hands, the resurrection of the
dead, and eternal judgment. [3]And God permitting, we will do so.
[4]It is impossible for those who have once been enlightened,
who have tasted the heavenly gift, who have shared in the Holy
Spirit, [5]who have tasted the goodness of the word of God and the
powers of the coming age, [6]if they fall away, to be brought back to
repentance, because[b] to their loss they are crucifying the Son of
God all over again and subjecting him to public disgrace.
[7]Land that drinks in the rain often falling on it and that produces a crop useful to those for whom it is farmed receives the blessing of God. [8]But land that produces thorns and thistles is worthless
and is in danger of being cursed. In the end it will be burned.
[9]Even though we speak like this, dear friends, we are confident of better things in your case—things that accompany salvation. [10]God is not unjust; he will not forget your work and the love
you have shown him as you have helped his people and continue
to help them. [11]We want each of you to show this same diligence to
the very end, in order to make your hope sure. [12]We do not want
you to become lazy, but to imitate those who through faith and
patience inherit what has been promised.

Jesus' Sacrifice Makes a New Covenant

This long section focuses on how God sent Jesus to make a new covenant with God's people that goes beyond the covenants God gave to Moses and the people of Israel. The old covenant was based on the law, but the new covenant is based on Christ's sacrifice to take away sins.

The Certainty of God's Promise

[13]When God made his promise to Abraham, since there was
no one greater for him to swear by, he swore by himself, [14]saying,
"I will surely bless you and give you many descendants."[c] [15]And so
after waiting patiently, Abraham received what was promised.

[a]1 Or *from useless rituals* [b]6 Or *repentance while* [c]14 Gen. 22:17

6:1 *elementary teachings about Christ:* The lessons the writer considered basic to the Christian faith are: "repentance from acts that lead to death"; salvation through "faith in God" (Eph 2:8-10); "baptisms," which is how someone becomes part of God's people (Acts 10:37, 38, 44-48; Eph 4:3-6); "laying on of hands," an action used to show that someone had been chosen by God for a special task; believing in the promise of "resurrection," to live with Jesus forever; expecting a time of "eternal judgment," when Jesus would return and the world's people would be judged (Matt 13:47-50; 25:31-46; Phil 1:10; 2:16; 3:20, 21; 1 Thes 4:13-18).

6:6 *crucifying the Son of God:* Those who abandon the message Jesus brought are like those who were actually responsible for crucifying him. See the note at 2:9 (taste death). See also the mini-article called "Crucifixion," p. 1914.

6:8 *burned:* Fields that produced only useless weeds or thorns were burned. The Crataegus thorn shown here is an example of the hardy thorn plants common in Palestine. Some thorn plants were placed in piles to create enclosures for farm animals or dried and used as fuel.

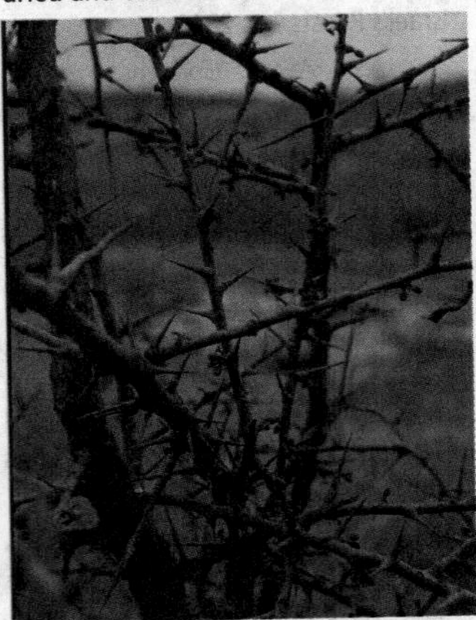

6:8 Gen 3:17,18. **6:14,15** Gen 12:2; 15:5; 22:16,17.

JESUS CLEARED THE WAY

[16]Men swear by someone greater than themselves, and the
oath confirms what is said and puts an end to all argument.
[17]Because God wanted to make the unchanging nature of his purpose very clear to the heirs of what was promised, he confirmed it
with an oath. [18]God did this so that, by two unchangeable things in
which it is impossible for God to lie, we who have fled to take hold
of the hope offered to us may be greatly encouraged. [19]We have
this hope as an anchor for the soul, firm and secure. It enters the
inner sanctuary behind the curtain, [20]where Jesus, who went before
us, has entered on our behalf. He has become a high priest forever,
in the order of Melchizedek.

Melchizedek the Priest

7 This Melchizedek was king of Salem and priest of God Most
High. He met Abraham returning from the defeat of the kings and
blessed him, [2]and Abraham gave him a tenth of everything. First,
his name means "king of righteousness"; then also, "king of Salem"
means "king of peace." [3]Without father or mother, without genealogy, without beginning of days or end of life, like the Son of God
he remains a priest forever.

[4]Just think how great he was: Even the patriarch Abraham
gave him a tenth of the plunder! [5]Now the law requires the descendants of Levi who become priests to collect a tenth from the people—
that is, their brothers—even though their brothers are descended
from Abraham. [6]This man, however, did not trace his descent from
Levi, yet he collected a tenth from Abraham and blessed him who
had the promises. [7]And without doubt the lesser person is blessed
by the greater. [8]In the one case, the tenth is collected by men who
die; but in the other case, by him who is declared to be living. [9]One
might even say that Levi, who collects the tenth, paid the tenth
through Abraham, [10]because when Melchizedek met Abraham, Levi
was still in the body of his ancestor.

Jesus Like Melchizedek

[11]If perfection could have been attained through the Levitical priesthood (for on the basis of it the law was given to the people), why was there still need for another priest to come—one in
the order of Melchizedek, not in the order of Aaron? [12]For when
there is a change of the priesthood, there must also be a change of
the law. [13]He of whom these things are said belonged to a different
tribe, and no one from that tribe has ever served at the altar. [14]For
it is clear that our Lord descended from Judah, and in regard to
that tribe Moses said nothing about priests. [15]And what we have
said is even more clear if another priest like Melchizedek appears,
[16]one who has become a priest not on the basis of a regulation as
to his ancestry but on the basis of the power of an indestructible
life. [17]For it is declared:

6:19 *this hope . . . curtain:* In the tabernacle that the ancient Israelites used for worship (Exod 25–27), a curtain separated the Holy Place from the Most Holy Place, which only the high priest could enter. The hope that "enters . . . behind the curtain" is the hope that Christians have because Jesus became the high priest, sacrificed himself for their sins, and entered heaven.

7:1-3 *Melchizedek . . . forever:* See the note at 5:6. Abraham showed how great he thought Melchizedek was by giving him one-tenth of the loot he had recovered in battle (Gen 14:18-20). The name Melchizedek here means "king of righteousness," and Salem means "peace." Both of these names draw attention to what Christ has done to bring justice and peace.

7:5 *descendants of Levi . . . collect a tenth:* According to the Law of Moses, the people of Israel were to give one-tenth of what they possessed to God. These gifts were given to the priests, who were descendants of Levi (Gen 35:23-26; Num 18:20-32).

7:6 *blessed him:* Melchizedek here is pronounced even greater than Abraham, because he gave Abraham his blessing (Gen 14:20).

7:9-11 *Aaron:* Aaron helped Moses lead the people of Israel out of slavery in Egypt. He became Israel's first high priest (Exod 28:1; Num 18:1-7).

7:14,15 *our Lord . . . Judah . . . like Melchizedek:* Jesus' earthly father, Joseph, came from the royal tribe of Judah (Gen 49:8-10; see also Matt 1:1-17). Melchizedek was not part of the priestly tribe of Levi either. The writer of HEBREWS says that Melchizedek and Jesus did not become high priests because of the Law of Moses. They became high priests because their lives can never end (7:16), unlike the priests from the tribe of Levi, who eventually die (7:8).

6:19 Lev 16:2. **6:20** Ps 110:4. **7:1,2** Gen 14:1,2,17-20. **7:17** Ps 110:4; Heb 5:6.

Abraham and Melchizedek, fifth century mosaic from Santa Maria Maggiore, Rome. In Genesis 14:17-24 Melchizedek is described as both a priest and the king of Salem (Jerusalem). He blesses Abraham, the ancestor of the people of Israel, and gives him bread and wine. The unknown artist of this mosaic shows Jesus looking on from heaven. The relationship between Jesus and Melchizedek was important to the writer of HEBREWS (see 7:1-28).

"You are a priest forever,
in the order of Melchizedek."[a]

[18]The former regulation is set aside because it was weak and
useless [19](for the law made nothing perfect), and a better hope is
introduced, by which we draw near to God.
[20]And it was not without an oath! Others became priests
without any oath, [21]but he became a priest with an oath when God
said to him:

a17 Psalm 110:4

7:22 *Jesus has become the guarantee of a better covenant:* God's new covenant is based on Jesus, who was sacrificed to forgive sins. This does not mean that the old covenant based on the Law of Moses is worthless (Matt 5:17; Rom 3:31). It means that trusting Jesus, the perfect high priest, is the way to be saved (Gal 3:1-14). See also the mini-article called "Covenants (Agreements)," p. 386.

7:19 Rom 3:20,21; Gal 2:16. **7:21** Ps 110:4.

"The Lord has sworn
and will not change his mind:
'You are a priest forever.' "[a]

22 Because of this oath, Jesus has become the guarantee of a better covenant.

23 Now there have been many of those priests, since death prevented them from continuing in office; 24 but because Jesus lives forever, he has a permanent priesthood. 25 Therefore he is able to save completely[b] those who come to God through him, because he always lives to intercede for them.

26 Such a high priest meets our need—one who is holy, blameless, pure, set apart from sinners, exalted above the heavens. 27 Unlike the other high priests, he does not need to offer sacrifices day after day, first for his own sins, and then for the sins of the people. He sacrificed for their sins once for all when he offered himself. 28 For the law appoints as high priests men who are weak; but the oath, which came after the law, appointed the Son, who has been made perfect forever.

The High Priest of a New Covenant

8 The point of what we are saying is this: We do have such a high priest, who sat down at the right hand of the throne of the Majesty in heaven, 2 and who serves in the sanctuary, the true tabernacle set up by the Lord, not by man.

3 Every high priest is appointed to offer both gifts and sacrifices, and so it was necessary for this one also to have something to offer. 4 If he were on earth, he would not be a priest, for there are already men who offer the gifts prescribed by the law. 5 They serve at a sanctuary that is a copy and shadow of what is in heaven. This is why Moses was warned when he was about to build the tabernacle: "See to it that you make everything according to the pattern shown you on the mountain."[c] 6 But the ministry Jesus has received is as superior to theirs as the covenant of which he is mediator is superior to the old one, and it is founded on better promises.

7 For if there had been nothing wrong with that first covenant, no place would have been sought for another. 8 But God found fault with the people and said[d]:

"The time is coming, declares the Lord,
when I will make a new covenant
with the house of Israel
and with the house of Judah.
9 It will not be like the covenant
I made with their forefathers
when I took them by the hand

[a] 21 Psalm 110:4 [b] 25 Or *forever* [c] 5 Exodus 25:40 [d] 8 Some manuscripts may be translated *fault and said to the people.*

7:26 *high priest . . . sinners:* See the notes at 2:17 and 1:3 (sins).

7:28 *the law appoints as high priests . . . appointed the Son:* Among other things, the Law of Moses describes the duties of the priests. God's promise to save humankind from sin was fulfilled by his Son Jesus. See also the note at 2:17.

8:1 *sat down at the right hand:* See the note at1:3 (right hand).

8:2 *true tabernacle:* See the note at 6:19. Though the Most Holy Place was in the tabernacle (and later in the temple), the writer says that the Most Holy Place is now in the "true tabernacle" (heaven). See also the note at 8:5.

8:5 *copy and shadow of what is in heaven:* God gave Moses the plan for building the first tabernacle (Exod 25:40). Israel's priests offered sacrifices at this tabernacle and later at the temple. But both the tabernacle and temple are imperfect when compared to the real place of worship in heaven.

8:6 *covenant:* See the note at 7:22. The same word in Greek means both "will" and "covenant." In the "first covenant" (8:7; see also Exod 19:1—20:17) God promised to protect and bless the people of Israel and to give them a land to call their own. In return, the people were commanded to follow the law, which included rules concerning correct worship (9:1) and instructions about how to live together in peace and justice. Above all, the people were to remain faithful to God alone. But the people were unable to live up to the first covenant, so God made a new covenant that was not written on stone tablets but directly on their hearts (Jer 31:31-34).

7:27 Lev 9:7; Heb 2:17. **8:1** Ps 110:1.

God said, *"I will be their God, and they will be my people."* Heb 8:10

to lead them out of Egypt,
because they did not remain faithful to my covenant,
and I turned away from them,
declares the Lord.
[10] This is the covenant I will make with the house of Israel
after that time, declares the Lord.
I will put my laws in their minds
and write them on their hearts.
I will be their God,
and they will be my people.

ISRAEL'S PRIESTS

The people of Israel were holy, or "set apart for God," and they were to obey God's commandments. In Exodus 19:6 God tells Moses to tell the Israelites, "You will be for me a kingdom of priests and a holy nation." The prophet Isaiah repeated this promise and challenge. He said to the people who mourned in Jerusalem, "You will be called priests of the LORD, you will be named ministers of our God" (Isa 61:6).

Even though all the people were like priests, God commanded that special priests be selected from the tribe of Levi (Num 1:49-51; 3:5-13) to serve first in the tabernacle, and then later in the temple that would be built in Jerusalem. These priests are described according to their duties: (1) the Levites, who did basic work in preparing sacrifices and cleaning the Holy Place; (2) the priests, who offered the sacrifices and performed various ritual acts; and (3) the high priest, who was in charge of the Holy Place, and who was the only one who could go into the inner part of the temple (Most Holy Place), the LORD's throne room on earth (Ps 28:2; 47:8).

The priests wore special robes, a golden crown with the words, "HOLY TO THE LORD," and a breastplate marked with the names of the twelve tribes of Israel (Exod 28). Israel's priests had two main purposes: (1) to keep contact with God in the holy place of worship (the tabernacle, and later the temple); and (2) to help the people become pure.

The Jewish people returned to Jerusalem from exile in Babylon beginning in 538 B.C. Soon after, the prophets told the people to rebuild the temple that the Babylonians had destroyed in 586 B.C. and once again worship God there (Hag 2:15-18; Zech 4:9; 8:9). In the second century B.C., the Syrian king, Antiochus IV, put a statue of a foreign god in the temple and tried to force Jews to offer sacrifices to it. The Jewish people were greatly offended by this and revolted until once again proper worship of God in the temple was restored.

Some of the priests helped lead the revolt that set up an independent Jewish nation. This nation existed from 165 to 63 B.C., when the Romans invaded and took over Palestine. Israel's priests then began to cooperate with the Romans, who let King Herod build a great new temple in Jerusalem. Israel's priesthood came to an end in A.D. 70 when the temple was destroyed by the Roman army during another Jewish rebellion. The temple has never been rebuilt.

Until this final destruction of the temple, it was the job of the priests to offer sacrifices to thank God and to gain God's forgiveness for the sins of the people. The New Testament says that Jesus offered himself on the cross (Mark 10:45) and that God sent Jesus as a sacrifice in order to set people free from their sins (Rom 3:25,26). In HEBREWS Jesus is seen as the great high priest, whose death on the cross was the full and final sacrifice for the sins of the world (Heb 4:14—5:10; 10:1-23).

[11]No longer will a man teach his neighbor,
or a man his brother, saying, 'Know the Lord,'
because they will all know me,
from the least of them to the greatest.
[12]For I will forgive their wickedness
and will remember their sins no more."[a]

[13]By calling this covenant "new," he has made the first one obsolete; and what is obsolete and aging will soon disappear.

Worship in the Earthly Tabernacle

9 Now the first covenant had regulations for worship and also
an earthly sanctuary. [2]A tabernacle was set up. In its first room
were the lampstand, the table and the consecrated bread; this was
called the Holy Place. [3]Behind the second curtain was a room
called the Most Holy Place, [4]which had the golden altar of incense
and the gold-covered ark of the covenant. This ark contained the
gold jar of manna, Aaron's staff that had budded, and the stone

[a]12 Jer. 31:31-34

8:13 *this covenant "new":* See the note at 7:22.

9:1 *first covenant:* This refers to the Law of Moses (see the note at 8:6).

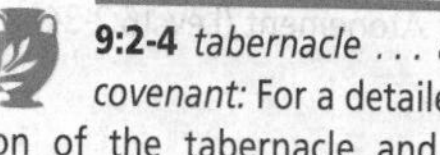

9:2-4 *tabernacle . . . ark of the covenant:* For a detailed description of the tabernacle and the holy objects in it, see Exodus 25–27; 30:1-6 and 36:8—38:31. See also the diagram below and the mini-article called "The Tabernacle," p. 2346.

9:4 *gold jar of manna:* See the note at 2:4 (wonders). See also Exod 16:33.

9:4 Deut 10:3-5.

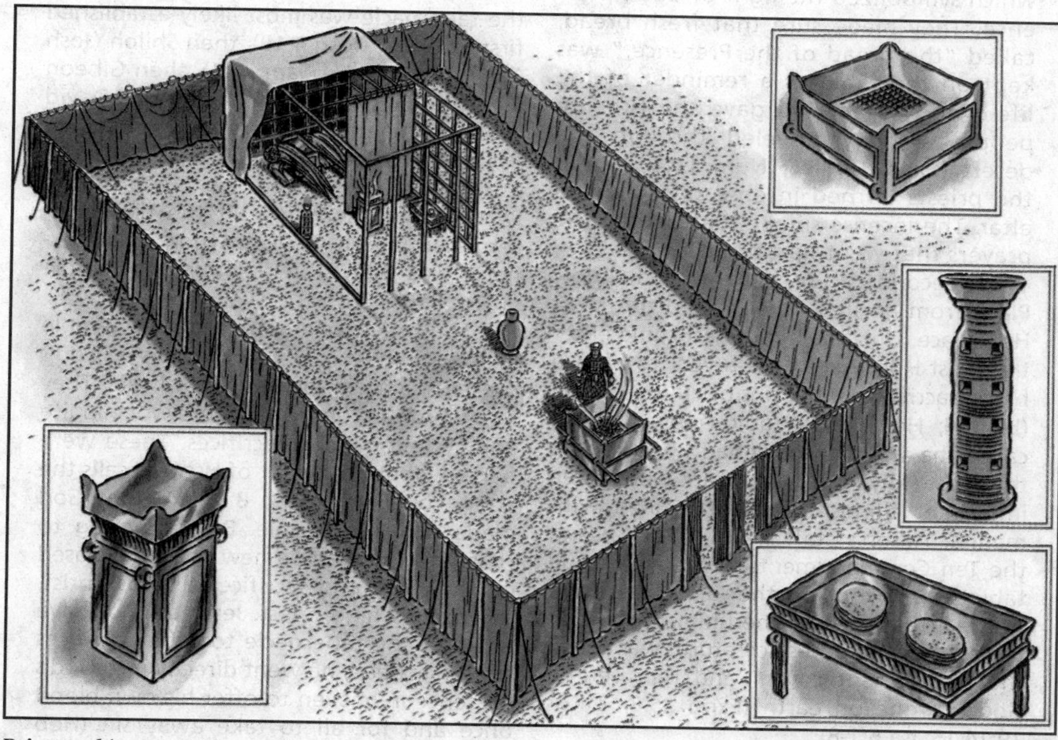

Priest making a sacrifice at the tabernacle. This cutaway view shows the layout of the tabernacle, and inset drawings show key furnishings in detail: (clockwise from top) the altar of burnt offering, lampstand, table with the bread of the Presence, and the altar of incense.

tablets of the covenant. 5 Above the ark were the cherubim of the Glory, overshadowing the atonement cover.[a] But we cannot discuss these things in detail now.

[a]5 Traditionally *the mercy seat*

9:6,7 *priests . . . high priest:* The priests offered sacrifices, kept the lampstand lit, and changed the bread of the Presence. The high priest could enter the Most Holy Place only on the Day of Atonement (Lev 16:2-34).

THE TABERNACLE

When God gave Moses the law at Mount Sinai, God also gave him instructions for making a tabernacle, also called the "Tent of Meeting" (Exod 25:1—27:21; 36:1—38:31). This sacred tent was to be Israel's place of worship, where the people would bring gifts and sacrifices to God. The people could gather in the first area of the tent, but only the priests could go beyond the first curtain into the Holy Place (see the diagram on p. 2345). There the priests tended the lampstand, which symbolized the light of God's presence. They made sure that fresh bread, called "the bread of the Presence," was kept on the table as a reminder of the life-giving bread God gave the Israelite people as they traveled through the desert (Exod 16:1-26; Num 11:4-9). And the priests burned incense on a golden altar. The incense smoke represented the prayers that went up to God.

A second curtain separated the Holy Place from an inner area called the Most Holy Place. Only the high priest could enter the Most Holy Place once a year to offer a blood sacrifice for the sins of all the people (Lev 16; Heb 9:7). A gold-covered chest, called the ark of the covenant, was kept in the Most Holy Place. In the ark were three important things: a gold jar filled with manna, Aaron's staff (Num 17:1-11), and the Ten Commandments written on stone tablets. On top of the ark were two winged creatures, or "cherubim." The lid of the ark between these creatures was called the "atonement cover" and represented God's throne on earth (Exod 25:8; 2 Kgs 19:14,15; Isa 6:1-8).

The outer court was 150 feet long and 75 feet wide, essentially a fence made from acacia wood and covered with curtains made from woven linen. The Holy Place, which contained the Most Holy Place, was about 15 feet square. This inner sanctuary was constructed of acacia wood overlaid with gold, and was covered with animal skins and fine linen. Bezalel and Oholiab were the craftsmen overseeing the project (Exod 31:1-11); and when the work was finished "the glory of the LORD filled the tabernacle" (Exod 40:34).

When the Israelites entered Canaan, the tabernacle was most likely established first at Gilgal (Josh 4:19), then Shiloh (Josh 18:1), then Nob (1 Sam 21:1), then Gibeon (1 Chr 16:39; 21:29). Although David brought the ark to a new tent he pitched for it in Jerusalem (2 Sam 6:17; 2 Chr 16:1), the tabernacle stayed at Gibeon until David's son Solomon built the temple in Jerusalem about 945 B.C., when the tabernacle was then stored within the temple (1 Kgs 8:4; 2 Chr 5:5).

The tabernacle and, later, the temple in Jerusalem were visible symbols of God's presence among the people of Israel. They also were the center of Israel's worship life and system of holy sacrifices. These were part of what the writer of HEBREWS calls the "new covenant" (Heb 8:7; 9:1) that God made with his people. But according to HEBREWS, God made a new covenant based on the work and sacrifice of Jesus Christ, the perfect high priest. Jesus did not have to enter the tabernacle to offer sacrifices for sin. Instead, he went directly into God's presence in heaven to offer his own blood once and for all to take away sin (Heb 9:11-28).

6 When everything had been arranged like this, the priests entered regularly into the outer room to carry on their ministry. 7 But only the high priest entered the inner room, and that only once a year, and never without blood, which he offered for himself and for the sins the people had committed in ignorance. 8 The Holy Spirit was showing by this that the way into the Most Holy Place had not yet been disclosed as long as the first tabernacle was still standing. 9 This is an illustration for the present time, indicating that the gifts and sacrifices being offered were not able to clear the conscience of the worshiper. 10 They are only a matter of food and drink and various ceremonial washings—external regulations applying until the time of the new order.

The Blood of Christ

11 When Christ came as high priest of the good things that are already here,[a] he went through the greater and more perfect tabernacle that is not man-made, that is to say, not a part of this creation. 12 He did not enter by means of the blood of goats and calves; but he entered the Most Holy Place once for all by his own blood, having obtained eternal redemption. 13 The blood of goats and bulls and the ashes of a heifer sprinkled on those who are ceremonially unclean sanctify them so that they are outwardly clean. 14 How much more, then, will the blood of Christ, who through the eternal Spirit offered himself unblemished to God, cleanse our consciences from acts that lead to death,[b] so that we may serve the living God!

15 For this reason Christ is the mediator of a new covenant, that those who are called may receive the promised eternal inheritance—now that he has died as a ransom to set them free from the sins committed under the first covenant.

16 In the case of a will,[c] it is necessary to prove the death of the one who made it, 17 because a will is in force only when somebody has died; it never takes effect while the one who made it is living. 18 This is why even the first covenant was not put into effect without blood. 19 When Moses had proclaimed every commandment of the law to all the people, he took the blood of calves, together with water, scarlet wool and branches of hyssop, and sprinkled the scroll and all the people. 20 He said, “This is the blood of the covenant, which God has commanded you to keep.”[d] 21 In the same way, he sprinkled with the blood both the tabernacle and everything used in its ceremonies. 22 In fact, the law requires that nearly everything be cleansed with blood, and without the shedding of blood there is no forgiveness.

23 It was necessary, then, for the copies of the heavenly things to be purified with these sacrifices, but the heavenly things themselves with better sacrifices than these. 24 For Christ did not enter a

[a] **11** Some early manuscripts *are to come* [b] **14** Or *from useless rituals*
[c] **16** Same Greek word as *covenant*; also in verse 17 [d] **20** Exodus 24:8

9:8 *Holy Spirit:* See the note at 2:4 (Holy Spirit).

9:10 *external regulations:* These refer to the rules in the Law of Moses that apply to proper eating and drinking, and to special cleansing ceremonies required to restore a person to ritual purity (Lev 11:1—15:32).

9:12 *obtained eternal redemption:* The author of HEBREWS refers several times to the sacrifice Christ made willingly to take away all sin. See also 1:3; 2:17; 9:25,26.

9:13 *sanctify them so that they are outwardly clean:* According to the Law of Moses, a number of things could make a person unclean (Lev 11–15; 16:15, 16; 17:10—18:30). See also the mini-article called "Purity (Clean and Unclean)," p. 2125. See also Num 19:9, 17-19.

9:14 *offered himself unblemished to God:* Jesus went directly into the presence of God in order to make the perfect sacrifice for the sins of humanity. His spiritual sacrifice changes people inside and lasts forever, while the sacrifices made by the priests were outward acts that had only a temporary effect.

9:15 *new covenant . . . first covenant:* See the notes at 7:22 and 8:6.

9:18 *not put into effect without blood:* In the Bible the power of life is understood to be present in blood, so blood was considered sacred. See Exod 24:4-8. See also the mini-article called "Blood," p. 180.

9:23 *copies of the heavenly things:* See the note at 8:5. The blood offerings described in 9:18-22 were physical acts that reminded the people of their relationship with God, but these acts were replaced by the offering Christ made to God.

9:5 Exod 25:18-22. **9:6** Num 18:2-6. **9:21** Lev 8:15. **9:22** Lev 4:1—6:30; 8:15; 17:11.

man-made sanctuary that was only a copy of the true one; he
entered heaven itself, now to appear for us in God's presence.
[25]Nor did he enter heaven to offer himself again and again, the way
the high priest enters the Most Holy Place every year with blood
that is not his own. [26]Then Christ would have had to suffer many
times since the creation of the world. But now he has appeared
once for all at the end of the ages to do away with sin by the sacrifice of himself. [27]Just as man is destined to die once, and after that
to face judgment, [28]so Christ was sacrificed once to take away the
sins of many people; and he will appear a second time, not to bear
sin, but to bring salvation to those who are waiting for him.

Christ's Sacrifice Once for All

10 The law is only a shadow of the good things that are coming—not the realities themselves. For this reason it can never, by
the same sacrifices repeated endlessly year after year, make perfect
those who draw near to worship. [2]If it could, would they not have
stopped being offered? For the worshipers would have been
cleansed once for all, and would no longer have felt guilty for their
sins. [3]But those sacrifices are an annual reminder of sins, [4]because
it is impossible for the blood of bulls and goats to take away sins.
[5]Therefore, when Christ came into the world, he said:

"Sacrifice and offering you did not desire,
but a body you prepared for me;
[6]with burnt offerings and sin offerings
you were not pleased.
[7]Then I said, 'Here I am—it is written about me
in the scroll—
I have come to do your will, O God.' "[a]

[8]First he said, "Sacrifices and offerings, burnt offerings and
sin offerings you did not desire, nor were you pleased with
them" (although the law required them to be made). [9]Then he
said, "Here I am, I have come to do your will." He sets aside the
first to establish the second. [10]And by that will, we have been
made holy through the sacrifice of the body of Jesus Christ once
for all.

[11]Day after day every priest stands and performs his religious
duties; again and again he offers the same sacrifices, which can
never take away sins. [12]But when this priest had offered for all time
one sacrifice for sins, he sat down at the right hand of God. [13]Since
that time he waits for his enemies to be made his footstool,
[14]because by one sacrifice he has made perfect forever those who
are being made holy.

[15]The Holy Spirit also testifies to us about this. First he says:

---

[a]7 Psalm 40:6-8 (see Septuagint)

9:25,26 *high priest . . . Christ:* See the notes at 2:17 and 7:22. Because Christ's sacrifice was the perfect sacrifice, it only had to be done once for all time.

9:27 *face judgment:* See the note at 10:27 and the mini-article called "Day of the LORD," p. 1727.

9:28 *he will appear a second time:* The New Testament says Jesus will return to earth (Phil 1:10; 2:16; 3:20, 21; 1 Thes 4:13-18). Those who follow Christ are to look forward to this day with hope, because Jesus will save them (1 Thes 5:1-11). See also the mini-article called "Second Coming," p. 2277.

10:3 *reminder of sins:* The Law of Moses cannot actually wash away sins or save; it can only remind people that they have sinned (see also Rom 3:20).

10:11 *priest stands and performs his religious duties:* See the mini-article called "Israel's Priests," p. 2344. See also Exod 29:38.

10:12 *right hand:* See the note at 1:3 (right hand).

10:14 *by one sacrifice:* See the notes at 2:17; 7:22; 9:25,26.

10:15 *Holy Spirit:* See the note at 2:4 (Holy Spirit).

9:28 Isa 53:12. **10:5-7** Ps 40:6-8; Amos 5:21,22. **10:8** Lev 4:1—6:30. **10:12,13** Ps 110:1; Phil 2:9-11.

[16]"This is the covenant I will make with them
after that time, says the Lord.
I will put my laws in their hearts,
and I will write them on their minds."[a]

[17]Then he adds:

"Their sins and lawless acts
I will remember no more."[b]

[18]And where these have been forgiven, there is no longer any sacrifice for sin.

Since we have a great priest over the house of God, let us draw near to God with a sincere heart in full assurance of faith.
Heb 10:21,22

PREPARE FOR THE DAY OF THE LORD

The believers are encouraged to keep their hearts pure and their consciences free from evil as they help each other prepare for the day when the Lord will return.

A Call to Persevere

[19]Therefore, brothers, since we have confidence to enter the
Most Holy Place by the blood of Jesus, [20]by a new and living way
opened for us through the curtain, that is, his body, [21]and since we
have a great priest over the house of God, [22]let us draw near to
God with a sincere heart in full assurance of faith, having our
hearts sprinkled to cleanse us from a guilty conscience and having
our bodies washed with pure water. [23]Let us hold unswervingly to
the hope we profess, for he who promised is faithful. [24]And let us
consider how we may spur one another on toward love and good
deeds. [25]Let us not give up meeting together, as some are in the
habit of doing, but let us encourage one another—and all the
more as you see the Day approaching.
[26]If we deliberately keep on sinning after we have received the
knowledge of the truth, no sacrifice for sins is left, [27]but only a fearful expectation of judgment and of raging fire that will consume the
enemies of God. [28]Anyone who rejected the law of Moses died without mercy on the testimony of two or three witnesses. [29]How much
more severely do you think a man deserves to be punished who has
trampled the Son of God under foot, who has treated as an unholy
thing the blood of the covenant that sanctified him, and who has
insulted the Spirit of grace? [30]For we know him who said, "It is mine
to avenge; I will repay,"[c] and again, "The Lord will judge his people."[d]
[31]It is a dreadful thing to fall into the hands of the living God.
[32]Remember those earlier days after you had received the
light, when you stood your ground in a great contest in the face of

10:17,18 *sins . . . have been forgiven:* See the note 1:3 (sins).

10:19 *Most Holy Place:* See the notes at 6:19; 8:2; 9:2-4.

10:21 *a great priest over the house of God:* See the notes at 2:17 and 9:14.

10:25 *as you see the Day approaching:* See the note at 9:28.

10:27 *expectation of judgment and of raging fire:* God's enemies sin by rejecting the gospel of Jesus even after they have heard it. They face God's terrible judgment, which includes a fiery punishment. In the New Testament, the place of judgment for evildoers is often pictured as a place of fiery torture (see Matt 5:22; Luke 16:23,24; Rev 20:14). See also the mini-articles called "Fire," p. 2383 and "Hell," p. 1944.

10:32 *the light:* In the Bible, light is used to describe God or God's word (Ps 119:105; 1 John 1:5), and those people or things that reveal God's truth (Isa 49:6). The followers of Jesus are also called "sons of light" (John 12:36).

10:16,17 Jer 31:33,34. **10:22** Lev 8:30; Ezek 36:25. **10:27** Isa 26:11. **10:28** Deut 17:4-7; 19:15. **10:29** Exod 24:8. **10:30** Deut 32:35,36.

a16 Jer. 31:33 **b17** Jer. 31:34 **c30** Deut. 32:35 **d30** Deut. 32:36; Psalm 135:14

PEOPLE OF FAITH

PERSON	DESCRIPTION	ACT OF FAITH	SCRIPTURE PASSAGES
Abel	Adam and Eve's second son, younger brother of Cain. Cain killed Abel when Abel offered a better sacrifice to the LORD.	Offered the best parts of a lamb as a sacrifice to the LORD.	Gen 4:1-16
Enoch	The Bible gives little information about him. Instead of saying he died, the Bible says that God "took him away."	He pleased God.	Gen 5:21-26
Noah	Son of Lamech and great-grandson of Enoch. His name sounds like the Hebrew word for "comfort."	Believed God's warning that God was going to destroy the evil people of the world in a flood. Built a large boat (ark) as God commanded to save his family and animals.	Gen 6:1—9:17
Abraham	A descendant of Noah's son Shem, husband of Sarah, and father of Isaac. He was named Abram, but God changed his name to Abraham, which sounds like the Hebrew for "father of many nations" (Gen 17:4, 5).	Left the security of his homeland when God called him to go to a new land where God would give him many descendants.	Gen 12:1-9; 17:1-8; see also Rom 4
Sarah	Wife of Abraham and mother of Isaac. Originally she was named Sarai but God changed her name to Sarah. Both names mean "princess" (Gen 17:15).	Was too old to have children, but she had faith that God would give her a child anyway.	Gen 18:1-15; 21:1-8
Isaac	Abraham and Sarah's son. Although Abraham had a son by his wife's slave Hagar, Isaac is called Abraham's "only son" because he was born as the result of God's promise to Abraham.	Gave a blessing to his sons Jacob and Esau.	Gen 27:1-40
Jacob	Son of Isaac and Rebekah and twin brother of Esau. His name was changed to Israel (Gen 32:22-28) which means "a man who struggles with God." The twelve tribes of Israel were named after his sons. God's promise to Abraham and Isaac was repeated to Jacob (Gen 28:13-15).	Blessed his grandsons Ephraim and Manasseh (Joseph's sons).	Gen 48:1-22

10:33,34 *insult and persecution . . . confiscation of your property:* At the time HEBREWS was written, some Christians were being viewed by their neighbors and by local officials with suspicion. For example, some Christians faced persecution from the Roman government when they chose not to pledge their loyalty to the emperor.

suffering. [33]Sometimes you were publicly exposed to insult and
persecution; at other times you stood side by side with those who
were so treated. [34]You sympathized with those in prison and joyfully accepted the confiscation of your property, because you knew
that you yourselves had better and lasting possessions.

[35]So do not throw away your confidence; it will be richly
rewarded. [36]You need to persevere so that when you have done the
will of God, you will receive what he has promised. [37]For in just a
very little while,

MENTIONED IN HEBREWS 11

PERSON	DESCRIPTION	ACT OF FAITH	SCRIPTURE PASSAGES
Joseph	Son of Jacob and Rachel. He was sold by his brothers to a passing caravan of traders and taken to Egypt where he later became an important official in the king's court.	Used his position in the Egyptian government to save his family during a time of famine in Canaan. Trusted that God would lead the people of Israel out of Egypt.	Gen 37–50; especially 50:22-25
Moses	A Hebrew born in Egypt, and adopted by the Egyptian royal household. The LORD appeared to him and commanded him to lead the Hebrew people out of slavery in Egypt; later the LORD gave him the law on Mount Sinai.	Refused to be considered the Pharaoh's grandson; led the Hebrew people out of Egypt; began the celebration of Passover according to the LORD's instructions.	Exod 1–15; 19–34
Rahab	A Canaanite prostitute who lived in Jericho before the Israelites conquered the city.	Helped two Israelite spies escape Jericho so they could make a report to their commanders.	Josh 2:1-3; 6:21-25
Gideon, Barak, Samson, and Jephthah	Leaders (also called "judges") of the tribes of Israel before Israel had a king.	Performed acts of heroism and helped the Israelites to gain control of the land (Canaan) promised to Abraham and his descendants.	Judg 4–16
David	A great warrior and Israel's greatest king. He made Jerusalem the capital of Israel and had the ark of the covenant brought there. He was the father of Solomon, a wise king who built the first temple in Jerusalem.	Killed the giant Goliath and helped the Israelites to conquer Canaan.	1 Sam 16:1; 1 Kgs 2:11; especially, 1 Sam 17
Samuel	Samuel was a prophet and the last judge of Israel. He anointed Saul and David to show that God had chosen them to be kings of Israel.	Led the people of Israel as a judge and prophet.	1 Sam 1:1—25:1

"He who is coming will come and will not delay.
38 But my righteous one[a] will live by faith.
And if he shrinks back,
I will not be pleased with him."[b]

39 But we are not of those who shrink back and are destroyed, but
of those who believe and are saved.

10:39 *saved:* See the note at 1:14.

10:37,38 Hab 2:3,4.

[a]**38** One early manuscript *But the righteous* [b]**38** Hab. 2:3,4

Faith Has Always Been the Way to Please God

Faith is the way to please God and receive God's promised reward, which is pictured as a place of "rest" or an eternal "city." This has been true since the time of creation and the days of Israel's earliest ancestors.

Now faith is being sure of what we hope for and certain of what we do not see.
Heb 11:1

By Faith

11 Now faith is being sure of what we hope for and certain of what we do not see. [2]This is what the ancients were commended for.

[3]By faith we understand that the universe was formed at God's command, so that what is seen was not made out of what was visible.

[4]By faith Abel offered God a better sacrifice than Cain did. By faith he was commended as a righteous man, when God spoke well of his offerings. And by faith he still speaks, even though he is dead.

[5]By faith Enoch was taken from this life, so that he did not experience death; he could not be found, because God had taken him away. For before he was taken, he was commended as one who pleased God. [6]And without faith it is impossible to please God, because anyone who comes to him must believe that he exists and that he rewards those who earnestly seek him.

[7]By faith Noah, when warned about things not yet seen, in holy fear built an ark to save his family. By his faith he condemned the world and became heir of the righteousness that comes by faith.

[8]By faith Abraham, when called to go to a place he would later receive as his inheritance, obeyed and went, even though he did not know where he was going. [9]By faith he made his home in the promised land like a stranger in a foreign country; he lived in tents, as did Isaac and Jacob, who were heirs with him of the same promise. [10]For he was looking forward to the city with foundations, whose architect and builder is God.

[11]By faith Abraham, even though he was past age—and Sarah herself was barren—was enabled to become a father because he[a] considered him faithful who had made the promise. [12]And so from this one man, and he as good as dead, came descendants as numerous as the stars in the sky and as countless as the sand on the seashore.

[13]All these people were still living by faith when they died. They did not receive the things promised; they only saw them and welcomed them from a distance. And they admitted that they were aliens and strangers on earth. [14]People who say such things show that they are looking for a country of their own. [15]If they had been thinking of the country they had left, they would have had oppor-

[a]**11** Or *By faith even Sarah, who was past age, was enabled to bear children because she*

11:1 *faith:* Here, faith means trusting in God rather than observing certain rituals or following a particular set of teachings. See also the mini-article called "Faith," p. 1932.

11:2 *the ancients:* Referring to people of ancient times, their forefathers (see the note at 1:1). In chapter 11, the writer says that some of the very earliest people who are mentioned in GENESIS pleased God because of their faith. So they are forever part of God's people. Most of these people lived before the law was given to Moses (see the note at 8:6).

11:10 *the city with foundations:* This is the promised place of rest (4:1) and the heavenly tabernacle (9:11) where Christ went to be with God. It is the heavenly place where those who are faithful to God will be with God forever. See also Rev 21:3; 21:10—22:5.

11:13 *the things promised . . . aliens and strangers:* This refers to, among other things, the place of heavenly rest (see the notes at 11:10 and 4:1). See also Gen 23:4; 1 Chr 29:15; Ps 39:12.

11:3 Gen 1:1; Ps 33:6,9; John 1:3. **11:4** Gen 4:3-10. **11:12** Gen 15:5; 22:17; 32:12. **11:5** Gen 5:21-24. **11:7** Gen 6:13-22. **11:8** Gen 12:1-5. **11:9** Gen 35:27. **11:11** Gen 21:2.

Noah's Ark and Moses in the Bullrushes, painted stone ceiling bosses, Norwich Cathedral, England. When a new ceiling was put on the cathedral in the fifteenth century, the "bosses" that helped hold the ceiling ribs in place were decorated with scenes from everyday life and from the Bible. In a similar way, the author of HEBREWS uses stories from the Jewish Scriptures (Old Testament) to teach his readers about faith. Both Noah, who built an ark as God commanded him to (11:7), and Moses' parents (11:23) are held up as examples of people who had faith.

tunity to return. [16]Instead, they were longing for a better country—a heavenly one. Therefore God is not ashamed to be called
their God, for he has prepared a city for them.
[17]By faith Abraham, when God tested him, offered Isaac as a
sacrifice. He who had received the promises was about to sacrifice
his one and only son, [18]even though God had said to him, "It is
through Isaac that your offspring[a] will be reckoned."[b] [19]Abraham
reasoned that God could raise the dead, and figuratively speaking,
he did receive Isaac back from death.
[20]By faith Isaac blessed Jacob and Esau in regard to their
future.
[21]By faith Jacob, when he was dying, blessed each of Joseph's
sons, and worshiped as he leaned on the top of his staff.
[22]By faith Joseph, when his end was near, spoke about the exodus of the Israelites from Egypt and gave instructions about his bones.
[23]By faith Moses' parents hid him for three months after he
was born, because they saw he was no ordinary child, and they
were not afraid of the king's edict.
[24]By faith Moses, when he had grown up, refused to be
known as the son of Pharaoh's daughter. [25]He chose to be mistreated along with the people of God rather than to enjoy the

11:17 *Abraham . . . sacrifice his one and only son:* God promised Abraham a son who would be the father of a great nation (Gen 15:4,5). Although Abraham had a son by a slave named Hagar, Abraham's son Isaac was considered his "only son" because he was born as the result of God's promise to Abraham. According to the writer of HEBREWS, Abraham was willing to sacrifice his only son (Gen 22:1-19) because he was sure God could raise people from death. See also Gen 21:12.

11:23 *the king's edict:* The king of Egypt ordered all Israelite baby boys to be killed (Exod 1:22) in order to reduce the growing Israelite population in Egypt (Exod 1:12—2:10).

11:20 Gen 25:19-34; 27:27-29, 39,40. **11:21** Gen 48:1-20. **11:22** Gen 50:24,25; Exod 13:19. **11:24** Exod 2:10-12.

[a]18 Greek *seed* **[b]18** Gen. 21:12

11:27 *saw him who is invisible:* God appeared to Moses in a burning bush (Exod 3:1-6). But because the God of Israel was considered a living God, he was not to be pictured or represented by any kind of a statue (Exod 20:2-6; Isa 45:20—46:7).

11:28 *Passover:* See the mini-article called "Passover and the Feast of Unleavened Bread," p. 2030.

11:29 *Red Sea:* In the Greek translation of the Scriptures (the Septuagint) made about 200 B.C., the name "Red Sea" was used for Hebrew name *yam suph,* which means "Sea of Reeds." The exact location of this body of water is not certain, but it may have been one of the marshes or freshwater lakes near the eastern part of the Nile River Delta, where the towns of Exodus 13:17—14:9 were located.

11:30 *Jericho:* At the time the Israelite people entered the promised land, Jericho was a key Canaanite city that guarded the Jordan River Valley. How the Israelites conquered this ancient city is described in Joshua 5:13—6:26.

11:35 *gain a better resurrection:* This refers to the promise that those who were faithful to God would be raised to new life, just as God raised Jesus from death. See also the mini-article called "Resurrection," p. 2210.

12:1 *great cloud of witnesses:* Those who have been faithful to God since the beginning of time, including those mentioned in Hebrews 11. This crowd was like the kind of crowd that filled the seats of an arena to watch an athletic contest.

11:29 Exod 14:21-31. **11:31** Josh 2:1-21; 6:22-25. **11:32** **a** Judg 6:1—8:32; **b** Judg 4:6—5:31; **c** Judg 13:2—16:31; **d** Judg 11:1—12:7; **e** 1 Sam 16:1—1 Kgs 2:11; **f** 1 Sam 1:1—25:1. **11:33** Dan 6:1-27. **11:34** Dan 3:1-30. **11:35** 1 Kgs 17:17-24; 2 Kgs 4:17-37. **11:36** 1 Kgs 22:26,27; 2 Chr 18:25,26; Jer 20:2; 37:15; 38:6. **11:37** 2 Chr 24:20,21.

pleasures of sin for a short time. [26]He regarded disgrace for the
sake of Christ as of greater value than the treasures of Egypt,
because he was looking ahead to his reward. [27]By faith he left
Egypt, not fearing the king's anger; he persevered because he saw
him who is invisible. [28]By faith he kept the Passover and the sprinkling of blood, so that the destroyer of the firstborn would not
touch the firstborn of Israel.

[29]By faith the people passed through the Red Sea[a] as on dry
land; but when the Egyptians tried to do so, they were drowned.

[30]By faith the walls of Jericho fell, after the people had
marched around them for seven days.

[31]By faith the prostitute Rahab, because she welcomed the
spies, was not killed with those who were disobedient.[b]

[32]And what more shall I say? I do not have time to tell about
Gideon, Barak, Samson, Jephthah, David, Samuel and the
prophets, [33]who through faith conquered kingdoms, administered
justice, and gained what was promised; who shut the mouths of
lions, [34]quenched the fury of the flames, and escaped the edge of
the sword; whose weakness was turned to strength; and who
became powerful in battle and routed foreign armies. [35]Women
received back their dead, raised to life again. Others were tortured
and refused to be released, so that they might gain a better resurrection. [36]Some faced jeers and flogging, while still others were
chained and put in prison. [37]They were stoned[c]; they were sawed in
two; they were put to death by the sword. They went about in
sheepskins and goatskins, destitute, persecuted and mistreated—
[38]the world was not worthy of them. They wandered in deserts and
mountains, and in caves and holes in the ground.

[39]These were all commended for their faith, yet none of
them received what had been promised. [40]God had planned something better for us so that only together with us would they be
made perfect.

RUN THE RACE OF FAITH

God's new people are surrounded by faithful witnesses from the past and present. This "great cloud of witnesses" is like a hometown crowd cheering on Christians as they run the race of faith. Christians are encouraged to keep their eyes on Jesus as they serve God and battle against sin. They are also told to help one another and obey their church leaders. The book ends with greetings and final prayers of encouragement.

God Disciplines His Sons

12 Therefore, since we are surrounded by such a great cloud of
witnesses, let us throw off everything that hinders and the sin that

[a]29 That is, Sea of Reeds [b]31 Or *unbelieving* [c]37 Some early manuscripts *stoned; they were put to the test;*

so easily entangles, and let us run with perseverance the race
marked out for us. [2]Let us fix our eyes on Jesus, the author and
perfecter of our faith, who for the joy set before him endured the
cross, scorning its shame, and sat down at the right hand of the
throne of God. [3]Consider him who endured such opposition from
sinful men, so that you will not grow weary and lose heart.
[4]In your struggle against sin, you have not yet resisted to the
point of shedding your blood. [5]And you have forgotten that word
of encouragement that addresses you as sons:

"My son, do not make light of the Lord's discipline,
and do not lose heart when he rebukes you,
[6]because the Lord disciplines those he loves,
and he punishes everyone he accepts as a son."[a]

[7]Endure hardship as discipline; God is treating you as sons.
For what son is not disciplined by his father? [8]If you are not disciplined (and everyone undergoes discipline), then you are illegitimate children and not true sons. [9]Moreover, we have all had
human fathers who disciplined us and we respected them for it.
How much more should we submit to the Father of our spirits and
live! [10]Our fathers disciplined us for a little while as they thought
best; but God disciplines us for our good, that we may share in his
holiness. [11]No discipline seems pleasant at the time, but painful.
Later on, however, it produces a harvest of righteousness and
peace for those who have been trained by it.
[12]Therefore, strengthen your feeble arms and weak knees.
[13]"Make level paths for your feet,"[b] so that the lame may not be
disabled, but rather healed.

Warning Against Refusing God

[14]Make every effort to live in peace with all men and to be
holy; without holiness no one will see the Lord. [15]See to it that no
one misses the grace of God and that no bitter root grows up to
cause trouble and defile many. [16]See that no one is sexually
immoral, or is godless like Esau, who for a single meal sold his
inheritance rights as the oldest son. [17]Afterward, as you know, when
he wanted to inherit this blessing, he was rejected. He could bring
about no change of mind, though he sought the blessing with tears.
[18]You have not come to a mountain that can be touched and
that is burning with fire; to darkness, gloom and storm; [19]to a
trumpet blast or to such a voice speaking words that those who
heard it begged that no further word be spoken to them, [20]because
they could not bear what was commanded: "If even an animal
touches the mountain, it must be stoned."[c] [21]The sight was so terrifying that Moses said, "I am trembling with fear."[d]

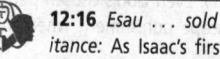

---

[a]6 Prov. 3:11,12 [b]13 Prov. 4:26 [c]20 Exodus 19:12,13 [d]21 Deut. 9:19

Let us fix our eyes on Jesus, the author and perfecter of our faith.
Heb 12:2

12:1 *sin . . . run . . . the race:* See the note at 1:3 (sins). The apostle Paul also compares the life of faith to running a race. He said the goal of the race is being invited to live with God in heaven (Phil 3:12-16). To reach this goal, Christians need to keep their eyes fixed on Jesus (12:2), their leader and the one who has already run this race and reached the goal.

12:2 *right hand of the throne of God:* See the note at 1:3 (right hand).

12:9 *the Father of our spirits:* This means God.

12:10 *share in his holiness:* "Holy" can mean "set apart" (or "chosen") by God in order to serve God. See also the mini-article called "Holiness," p. 1626.

12:16 *Esau . . . sold his inheritance:* As Isaac's firstborn son, Esau had certain inheritance privileges that were known as a "birthright." He sold this birthright to his younger brother Jacob for some stew that Jacob had made (Gen 25:27-34). The writer says that those who do not live godly lives are throwing away their rights as God's children, just as Esau threw away his birthright.

12:5,6 Job 5:17; Prov 3:11,12. **12:12** Isa 35:3. **12:13** Prov 4:26. **12:15** Deut 29:18. **12:17** Gen 27:30-40. **12:18,19** Exod 19:16-22; 20:18-21; Deut 4:11,12; 5:22-27. **12:20** Exod 19:12,13. **12:21** Deut 9:19.

22 But you have come to Mount Zion, to the heavenly
Jerusalem, the city of the living God. You have come to thousands
upon thousands of angels in joyful assembly, 23 to the church of
the firstborn, whose names are written in heaven. You have come
to God, the judge of all men, to the spirits of righteous men made
perfect, 24 to Jesus the mediator of a new covenant, and to the
sprinkled blood that speaks a better word than the blood of Abel.
25 See to it that you do not refuse him who speaks. If they did
not escape when they refused him who warned them on earth,
how much less will we, if we turn away from him who warns us
from heaven? 26 At that time his voice shook the earth, but now he
has promised, "Once more I will shake not only the earth but also
the heavens."[a] 27 The words "once more" indicate the removing of
what can be shaken—that is, created things—so that what cannot
be shaken may remain.
28 Therefore, since we are receiving a kingdom that cannot be
shaken, let us be thankful, and so worship God acceptably with
reverence and awe, 29 for our "God is a consuming fire."[b]

Concluding Exhortations

13 Keep on loving each other as brothers. 2 Do not forget to
entertain strangers, for by so doing some people have entertained
angels without knowing it. 3 Remember those in prison as if you
were their fellow prisoners, and those who are mistreated as if you
yourselves were suffering.

---

[a] **26** Haggai 2:6 [b] **29** Deut. 4:24

The Church of the Holy Sepulchre is thought to mark the place where Jesus was put to death and buried. In Jesus' day, this location would have been outside the outermost wall of Jerusalem (see 13:11-14).

12:22 *Mount Zion, to the heavenly Jerusalem:* Israel's King David conquered the Jebusite city of Jerusalem that included a high place known as Zion, or "Mount Zion" (2 Sam 5:6-10; 1 Chr 11:4-9). This fortress was also given the name, "City of David." Later, David's son Solomon built the temple on the site (1 Kgs 6–8). For more, see the mini-article called "Zion," p. 1294.

For "heavenly Jerusalem," see also the note at 11:10. The writer of REVELATION describes a new heaven and a new earth as the "new Jerusalem, coming down out of heaven from God" (Rev 21:1,2).

12:24 *new covenant:* See the notes at 7:22 and 8:6.

12:24 *blood of Abel:* See the chart called "People of Faith Mentioned in Hebrews 11," p. 2350. See also Gen 4:1-16.

12:25 *they did not escape:* The people of God often turned their backs on God and disobeyed the law, which God had given them at Mount Sinai (Exod 20:22). Even God's chosen people did not escape punishment when they disobeyed.

12:28 *kingdom that cannot be shaken:* This kingdom is God's heavenly kingdom, which cannot be destroyed because it is perfect and will last forever (7:22—8:13).

12:29 *God is a consuming fire:* See the note at 10:27. See also Deut 4:24.

13:3 *Remember those in prison:* See the note at 10:33, 34.

12:26 Hag 2:6. **13:2** Gen 18:1-8; 19:1-3.

[4]Marriage should be honored by all, and the marriage bed
kept pure, for God will judge the adulterer and all the sexually
immoral. [5]Keep your lives free from the love of money and be content with what you have, because God has said,

> "Never will I leave you;
> never will I forsake you."[a]

[6]So we say with confidence,

> "The Lord is my helper; I will not be afraid.
> What can man do to me?"[b]

[7]Remember your leaders, who spoke the word of God to
you. Consider the outcome of their way of life and imitate their
faith. [8]Jesus Christ is the same yesterday and today and forever.
[9]Do not be carried away by all kinds of strange teachings. It
is good for our hearts to be strengthened by grace, not by ceremonial foods, which are of no value to those who eat them. [10]We have
an altar from which those who minister at the tabernacle have no
right to eat.
[11]The high priest carries the blood of animals into the Most
Holy Place as a sin offering, but the bodies are burned outside the
camp. [12]And so Jesus also suffered outside the city gate to make the
people holy through his own blood. [13]Let us, then, go to him outside
the camp, bearing the disgrace he bore. [14]For here we do not have an
enduring city, but we are looking for the city that is to come.
[15]Through Jesus, therefore, let us continually offer to God a
sacrifice of praise—the fruit of lips that confess his name. [16]And

[a]**5** Deut. 31:6 [b]**6** Psalm 118:6,7

Jesus Christ is the same yesterday and today and forever.
Heb 13:8

13:9 *strange teachings . . . ceremonial foods:* The Law of Moses had rules about what could be eaten. The writer is saying that following these food rules is not as important as relying on God's grace. See also the notes at 9:10 and 9:13.

13:12 *Jesus also suffered outside the city gate:* Jesus was crucified at a place called "The Skull," which was outside Jerusalem's city walls (Luke 23:26-49). See the map on p. 2474.

13:14 *looking for the city that is to come:* See the notes at 11:10 and 12:22.

13:5 Deut 31:6,8; Jas 1:5. **13:6** Ps 118:6. **13:11** Exod 29:10-14; Lev 16:23-27.

QUESTIONS ABOUT HEBREWS

1. How does the first chapter of HEBREWS picture Jesus? List a number of things that describe who he is and what he does.
2. Read 2:14-18. What do you think it means that Christ shares in our humanity and that because Christ suffered "he is able to help those who are being tempted"?
3. What is the difference between the sacrifice that Jesus offers and the ones offered by the priests and high priests of Israel? (5:5-10; 7:20—8:6; 9:11,12,25-28)
4. Why does the writer say that "the law is only a shadow of the good things that are coming"? (10:1-18)
5. How did the ancestors of Israel please God? (11:1,2) What word would you use to describe your own faith in God? Why?
6. In 12:1-3, the writer compares the Christian life with a race that is being run in front of a great cloud of witnesses. How are these witnesses like the hometeam's crowd at a game? How is the Christian life like a race? Where do Christians get help to run this race?
7. What is the purpose of correction, or discipline, given by earthly parents or other authorities? Why does God correct his children? (12:7-11)
8. What kinds of service are pleasing to God? (13:1-7) In what particular way(s) can God's followers serve God and others?

do not forget to do good and to share with others, for with such
sacrifices God is pleased.
17 Obey your leaders and submit to their authority. They keep
watch over you as men who must give an account. Obey them so
that their work will be a joy, not a burden, for that would be of no
advantage to you.
18 Pray for us. We are sure that we have a clear conscience and
desire to live honorably in every way. 19 I particularly urge you to
pray so that I may be restored to you soon.
20 May the God of peace, who through the blood of the eternal covenant brought back from the dead our Lord Jesus, that
great Shepherd of the sheep, 21 equip you with everything good for
doing his will, and may he work in us what is pleasing to him,
through Jesus Christ, to whom be glory for ever and ever. Amen.

22 Brothers, I urge you to bear with my word of exhortation,
for I have written you only a short letter.
23 I want you to know that our brother Timothy has been
released. If he arrives soon, I will come with him to see you.
24 Greet all your leaders and all God's people. Those from
Italy send you their greetings.
25 Grace be with you all.

13:18 *Pray for us:* The unknown writer of HEBREWS may have been writing while in prison.

13:20 *the blood of the eternal covenant:* See the note at 9:18.

13:20,21 *our Lord Jesus, that great Shepherd:* The Greek word for "Lord" is *kyrios*. When it is used for Jesus, it emphasizes his authority and power. The word "Christ" means "Messiah" or "anointed one." See also the mini-articles called "Messiah (Chosen One)," p. 1124, and "Lord (Title for Jesus)," p. 2106. Jesus called himself the good shepherd (John 10:10-16).

13:23 *Timothy:* This Timothy may be the same person who was Paul's helper (Acts 16:1-3) and the church leader whose name appears on two New Testament letters (see Introductions to 1 and 2 TIMOTHY).

13:24 *Italy:* It is possible that the writer of HEBREWS was in Rome, the capital of the Roman empire. See the map on p. 2475.

JAMES

How can faith be "dead"?
The writer of JAMES gives advice about
how Christians can keep their faith alive.

What makes James special?

JAMES begins like a letter that is written to Christians scattered throughout the Roman empire (1:1), but it really is more like a short book of instructions on how God's people should live and treat others. The advice in the book is clear and to the point: If you are poor, don't despair! Don't give up when your faith is being tested. Don't get angry quickly. Don't favor the rich over the poor. Help others, and control your tongue and your desires. Rely on God's wisdom. Resist the devil. Don't brag about what you are going to do. If you are rich, use your money to help the poor. Be patient and kind, and pray for those who need God's help.

Why was James written?

For the writer of JAMES, faith means action! This letter says that the faith of a person who does not do kind deeds is as good as dead. The writer challenges God's people to obey "the royal law found in the Scripture"—to love others as much they love themselves (2:8).

What's the story behind the scene?

This letter is written to "the twelve tribes scattered among the nations" (1:1). This does not refer to the people of Israel but to Christians, who viewed themselves as heirs of the Jewish tradition. The author of the book calls himself James, which in Greek is *Iakobos*, a form of the Hebrew name "Jacob."

Church tradition has said that the book was written by James, the brother of Jesus. It is filled with teachings that are similar to the teachings of Jesus in the Gospels. However, some scholars believe the general language and style of the letter suggest that the writer was also familiar with the terms used by the broader Greek culture of the first century, and that this means the writer probably lived many years after James the brother of Jesus (Mark 6:3) or James the disciple (Matt 4:21).

How is James constructed?

After a brief greeting, the letter gives instruction about living as God's people. The letter can be outlined in the following way:

Ask for God's wisdom and be faithful (1:1-18)
Show that your faith is alive (1:19—2:26)
Watch what you say, and be wise (3:1—5:6)
Be patient, kind, and prayerful (5:7-20)

James: According to some early church traditions, the writer of JAMES was thought to be James the brother of Jesus and the leader of the Jerusalem church (Mark 6:3; Acts 15:13; Gal 1:19).

Lord Jesus Christ: The Greek word for "Lord" is *kyrios* , which can mean master or can be used to address someone as "sir." "Christ" is a title that comes from the Greek word *christos*, meaning "Messiah" or "chosen one." See also the mini-articles called "Lord (Title for Jesus)," p. 2106 and "Messiah (Chosen One)," p. 1124.

scattered among the nations: When Babylon defeated the Israelite people living in Judah in the sixth century B.C., many of them were scattered to countries outside their homeland. See the map on p. 931 and the mini-article called "Exile," p. 1541.

Ask for God's Wisdom and Be Faithful

The introduction to JAMES *follows typical Greek letter-writing style, which puts the writer's name first, then names the person or persons the letter is written to, and ends with a word of greeting. The writer encourages the readers to seek God's wisdom and remain faithful, even as they face testing and temptation.*

1 James, a servant of God and of the Lord Jesus Christ,

To the twelve tribes scattered among the nations:

Greetings.

Trials and Temptations

[2]Consider it pure joy, my brothers, whenever you face
trials of many kinds, [3]because you know that the testing of your
faith develops perseverance. [4]Perseverance must finish its work
so that you may be mature and complete, not lacking anything.
[5]If any of you lacks wisdom, he should ask God, who gives generously to all without finding fault, and it will be given to him.
[6]But when he asks, he must believe and not doubt, because
he who doubts is like a wave of the sea, blown and tossed by
the wind. [7]That man should not think he will receive anything
from the Lord; [8]he is a double-minded man, unstable in all
he does.

[9]The brother in humble circumstances ought to take
pride in his high position. [10]But the one who is rich should take
pride in his low position, because he will pass away like a wild
flower. [11]For the sun rises with scorching heat and withers the
plant; its blossom falls and its beauty is destroyed. In the same
way, the rich man will fade away even while he goes about his
business.

[12]Blessed is the man who perseveres under trial, because
when he has stood the test, he will receive the crown of life that
God has promised to those who love him.

[13]When tempted, no one should say, "God is tempting me."
For God cannot be tempted by evil, nor does he tempt anyone;
[14]but each one is tempted when, by his own evil desire, he is
dragged away and enticed. [15]Then, after desire has conceived, it
gives birth to sin; and sin, when it is full-grown, gives birth to
death.

[16]Don't be deceived, my dear brothers. [17]Every good and perfect gift is from above, coming down from the Father of the heavenly lights, who does not change like shifting shadows. [18]He chose
to give us birth through the word of truth, that we might be a kind
of firstfruits of all he created.

1:3 *faith:* In the Gospels and in Paul's letters, faith usually means trust in God and in God's promises. This is the meaning of faith in 1:3; 2:5; and 5:15. In other parts of JAMES, faith seems to refer to correct beliefs and actions (2:17,18,22,26).

1:5 *wisdom:* JAMES is a book full of wisdom and practical advice about how people with faith are to live. Much of this wisdom is similar to the kind of wisdom described in Proverbs 2:6,7, where the author of that book reminds the people of Israel that true wisdom comes from God, and that God's wisdom is based on the law that God gave to Moses and the people at Mount Sinai (Exod 19–34). In the Jewish community, wisdom was highly valued in the home and parents understood that they were to teach their children wisdom based on God's Law (Deut 6:1-9). See also the mini-article called "Wisdom," p. 2206.

1:10 *the one who is rich:* The writer is saying that poor Christians are actually better off than rich ones, because those without money and power need to depend on God. Rich people may be to tempted to ignore God and rely on their possessions and power.

1:12 *receive the crown of life:* In ancient times an athlete who won a contest was rewarded with a crown of fresh leaves or flowers as a sign of victory. See also 2 Tim 4:8 and 1 Pet 5:4.

1:15 *after desire has conceived, it gives birth to sin:* Selfish desires make people serve the law of sin (Rom 7:25), and "the wages of sin is death" (Rom 6:23). See also the mini-article called "Sin," p. 2181.

1:17 *the heavenly lights:* The sun, moon, and stars, which God created (Gen 1:14-19; Ps 136:7-9).

1:1 Matt 13:55; Mark 6:3; Gal 1:19. **1:10,11** Isa 40:6,7.

Show That Your Faith Is Alive

The writer encourages God's people to turn away from doing evil and to obey God's perfect law, which includes helping the needy, orphans, and widows. The people of God are not to give special attention to the rich, but are to love the poor and all others as much as they love themselves. In this way they will show that their faith is not dead, but is alive.

Listening and Doing

[19]My dear brothers, take note of this: Everyone should be
quick to listen, slow to speak and slow to become angry, [20]for
man's anger does not bring about the righteous life that God
desires. [21]Therefore, get rid of all moral filth and the evil that is so
prevalent and humbly accept the word planted in you, which can
save you.
[22]Do not merely listen to the word, and so deceive yourselves. Do what it says. [23]Anyone who listens to the word but does
not do what it says is like a man who looks at his face in a mirror
[24]and, after looking at himself, goes away and immediately forgets
what he looks like. [25]But the man who looks intently into the perfect law that gives freedom, and continues to do this, not forgetting
what he has heard, but doing it—he will be blessed in what he
does.
[26]If anyone considers himself religious and yet does not keep
a tight rein on his tongue, he deceives himself and his religion is
worthless. [27]Religion that God our Father accepts as pure and
faultless is this: to look after orphans and widows in their distress
and to keep oneself from being polluted by the world.

Favoritism Forbidden

2 My brothers, as believers in our glorious Lord Jesus Christ,
don't show favoritism. [2]Suppose a man comes into your meeting
wearing a gold ring and fine clothes, and a poor man in shabby
clothes also comes in. [3]If you show special attention to the man
wearing fine clothes and say, "Here's a good seat for you," but say
to the poor man, "You stand there" or "Sit on the floor by my feet,"
[4]have you not discriminated among yourselves and become judges
with evil thoughts?
[5]Listen, my dear brothers: Has not God chosen those who
are poor in the eyes of the world to be rich in faith and to inherit
the kingdom he promised those who love him? [6]But you have
insulted the poor. Is it not the rich who are exploiting you? Are
they not the ones who are dragging you into court? [7]Are they
not the ones who are slandering the noble name of him to whom
you belong?
[8]If you really keep the royal law found in Scripture, "Love

1:21 *the word planted in you, which can save you:* The "word" may refer to God's perfect law (1:25), or it may refer to the good news about Jesus, which is God's powerful way of saving all people who have faith (Rom 1:16). "Word" is a translation of the Greek word *logos.* In ancient Greek Stoic philosophy the term *logos* referred to the sense of reason planted in the human soul. See also the mini-article called "Stoics," p. 2144, and the article called "Religions and Philosophies in Bible Times," p. 1832.

The writer may have been borrowing this idea to explain how the message of God can save. That message is not simple human reason, but God's wisdom. See the note at 1:5 and the mini-article called "Salvation," p. 2021.

1:25 *perfect law that gives freedom:* This may refer to the commandment to "Love your neighbor as yourself" (2:8). Or it may refer to the will of God as revealed in the Jewish Scriptures (Old Testament) and in the life and teachings of Jesus Christ.

1:27 *Father:* Jesus often referred to God as "Father" (see John 14). This same term is also used to describe God in many of Paul's letters (Gal 1:1-3; 1 Cor 1:3; Phil 1:2).

2:3 *Here's a good seat:* The followers of Jesus in the early church may have been tempted to give special treatment to people who had power or riches, because these people could provide money or protection for the local church. But the writer warns Christians not to favor rich people while ignoring the poor. See also Luke 14:7-14.

2:8 *royal law . . . Love your neighbor as yourself:* This law, found in Leviticus 19:18, was emphasized by Jesus as well (Mark 12:28-31).

1:19 Eccl 7:8, 9. **1:27** Isa 1:17; Deut 14:29; 16:9-15; Ps 68:5.

2:11 *lawbreaker:* This refers to the Law of Moses, which the LORD gave to the people of Israel in the desert at Mount Sinai (see Exod 19–35). The law described how God expected the people to live, worship, and treat each other. See also the mini-article called "Law," p. 1160.

2:12 *law that gives freedom:* See the note at 1:25.

2:11a Exod 20:13, 14; Deut 5:17, 18; **b** Exod 20:13; Deut 5:17; Matt 5:21-30.

your neighbor as yourself,"[a] you are doing right. 9 But if you show
favoritism, you sin and are convicted by the law as lawbreakers.
10 For whoever keeps the whole law and yet stumbles at just one
point is guilty of breaking all of it. 11 For he who said, "Do not commit adultery,"[b] also said, "Do not murder."[c] If you do not commit
adultery but do commit murder, you have become a lawbreaker.
12 Speak and act as those who are going to be judged by the
law that gives freedom, 13 because judgment without mercy will be
shown to anyone who has not been merciful. Mercy triumphs over
judgment!

Faith and Deeds

14 What good is it, my brothers, if a man claims to have faith
but has no deeds? Can such faith save him? 15 Suppose a brother or

[a]8 Lev. 19:18 [b]11 Exodus 20:14; Deut. 5:18 [c]11 Exodus 20:13; Deut. 5:17

THE POOR

In the Bible, the "poor" refers to people whose lives are difficult (widows and orphans), people who have been displaced by war, and people who have nothing (Deut 15:11; Ps 82:3,4). "Poor" is also used to describe those who were considered to have little value, even to Israel's enemies (Jer 40:7; 52:15,16). The Law of Moses made it clear that God's people were to care for the needs of poor people, providing them with money, food, and clothing (Exod 22:22-27; Deut 16:9-15; 24:12-15).

The LORD God of Israel has special concern for the poor and homeless and changes their condition, as the story of Hannah and her prayer shows (1 Sam 2:7, 8). The prophet Amos reminded the people of Israel that they had abused the poor and robbed them of justice (Amos 5:11-13). He told the people that being just and fair was as important a part of their worship as their religious celebrations (Amos 5:21-24). He also warned that God would punish those who took advantage of the poor (Amos 8:4-12). God brought judgment on Israel's leaders, as well as on the people, because they failed to care for the poor (Ezek 22:23-29), and because they did not forgive the debts of the poor (Deut 15:1-11). Israel's wisdom writings proclaim that it is better to be righteous and poor than to be wealthy and wicked (Ps 37:16), and that the LORD will reward those who care for the poor (Prov 19:17).

The prophet Isaiah said that in the future God would "anoint" someone to preach good news to the poor (Isa 61:1-4). Jesus claimed that God had sent him to make this very promise come true (Luke 4:16-21). Jesus was friendly to people who were turned away by the religious leaders, and he invited them to be part of God's new people. He told the poor that God would bless them (Luke 6:20, 21), and that they would share in the new kingdom of God.

The one demand that the Jerusalem apostles made of Paul before he went out to bring the good news to the Gentiles is that he should "remember the poor" (Gal 2:10). Similarly, the Christians in Jerusalem put everything they had in one common fund so that the needs of the poor among them could be met (Acts 2:44,45; 4:32). See also the mini-article called "Justice," p. 1721.

Works of Mercy: Clothing the Naked, fresco by the school of Domenico Ghirlandaio, 1484-94. JAMES has much to say about how Christians are to live out their faith. "Suppose a brother or sister is without clothes and daily food. If one of you says to him, 'Go, I wish you well; keep warm and well fed,' but does nothing about his physical needs, what good is it?" (2:15,16). Besides feeding the hungry and clothing people who need clothes, Jesus describes four other acts of mercy that he wanted his disciples to perform: giving drink to the thirsty, welcoming strangers, taking care of sick people, and visiting people in jail. (See Matt 25:31-46.)

Someone will say, "You have faith; I have deeds." Show me your faith without deeds, and I will show you my faith by what I do.
Jas 2:18

sister is without clothes and daily food. 16 If one of you says to him,
"Go, I wish you well; keep warm and well fed," but does nothing
about his physical needs, what good is it? 17 In the same way, faith
by itself, if it is not accompanied by action, is dead.

18 But someone will say, "You have faith; I have deeds."

Show me your faith without deeds, and I will show you my
faith by what I do. 19 You believe that there is one God. Good! Even
the demons believe that—and shudder.

20 You foolish man, do you want evidence that faith without
deeds is useless[a]? 21 Was not our ancestor Abraham considered
righteous for what he did when he offered his son Isaac on the
altar? 22 You see that his faith and his actions were working together,
and his faith was made complete by what he did. 23 And the
scripture was fulfilled that says, "Abraham believed God, and it was
credited to him as righteousness,"[b] and he was called God's friend.
24 You see that a person is justified by what he does and not by faith
alone.

25 In the same way, was not even Rahab the prostitute considered
righteous for what she did when she gave lodging to the

[a]**20** Some early manuscripts *dead* [b]**23** Gen. 15:6

2:13 *judgment . . . will be shown:* The New Testament letters talk about a day when Jesus will come back (1 Cor 15:20-28; 1 Thes 4:13-18). This day was expected to be a time when God would judge the people of the world (Matt 13:47-50; 25:31-46). See also the mini-articles called "Second Coming," p. 2277 and "Day of the LORD," p. 1727.

2:14-18 *faith . . . no deeds:* See the note at 1:3. The author contrasts two kinds of faith: genuine faith which can be seen in deeds and actions, and a kind of "imitation faith" that never expresses itself in deeds and so cannot be considered real faith at all.

2:19 *demons:* Demons are evil spirits that work for the devil. See also Luke 4:31-34.

2:21 *Abraham . . . Isaac:* Abraham was considered the father of all the Israelite people. God promised that Abraham would have many descendants who would become a great nation (Gen 15:4, 5; 17:1-5). Abraham showed his faith by preparing to sacrifice Isaac as God had asked him to (Gen 22:1-8). At the last moment God stopped Abraham from killing his son and praised Abraham for being so faithful. For more, see the mini-article called "Abraham," p. 2254.

2:25 *Rahab:* Rahab was a Canaanite prostitute who helped two Israelite spies who had sneaked into Jericho before the Israelites came to defeat the city (Josh 2:1-21).

2:15,16 Luke 3:11; Matt 25:31-46. **2:23** Gen 15:6; Isa 41:8; Rom 4:1-3,11-14; Gal 3:6-9; Heb 11:8-12, 17,18.

spies and sent them off in a different direction? 26 As the body
without the spirit is dead, so faith without deeds is dead.

Watch What You Say, and Be Wise

Believers are warned to be careful to choose their words wisely, and not brag or say unkind things about others. They are also reminded to follow God's wisdom and to make sure that riches don't pull them away from living as God wants them to live.

Taming the Tongue

3 Not many of you should presume to be teachers, my brothers,
because you know that we who teach will be judged more strictly. 2 We all stumble in many ways. If anyone is never at fault in
what he says, he is a perfect man, able to keep his whole body in
check.

3 When we put bits into the mouths of horses to make them
obey us, we can turn the whole animal. 4 Or take ships as an example. Although they are so large and are driven by strong winds,
they are steered by a very small rudder wherever the pilot wants to
go. 5 Likewise the tongue is a small part of the body, but it makes
great boasts. Consider what a great forest is set on fire by a small
spark. 6 The tongue also is a fire, a world of evil among the parts of
the body. It corrupts the whole person, sets the whole course of his
life on fire, and is itself set on fire by hell.

7 All kinds of animals, birds, reptiles and creatures of the sea
are being tamed and have been tamed by man, 8 but no man can
tame the tongue. It is a restless evil, full of deadly poison.

9 With the tongue we praise our Lord and Father, and with it
we curse men, who have been made in God's likeness. 10 Out of the
same mouth come praise and cursing. My brothers, this should
not be. 11 Can both fresh water and salt[a] water flow from the same
spring? 12 My brothers, can a fig tree bear olives, or a grapevine bear
figs? Neither can a salt spring produce fresh water.

Two Kinds of Wisdom

13 Who is wise and understanding among you? Let him show
it by his good life, by deeds done in the humility that comes from
wisdom. 14 But if you harbor bitter envy and selfish ambition in
your hearts, do not boast about it or deny the truth. 15 Such "wisdom" does not come down from heaven but is earthly, unspiritual, of the devil. 16 For where you have envy and selfish ambition,
there you find disorder and every evil practice.

[a] 11 Greek *bitter* (see also verse 14)

3:1 *teachers:* Teaching is one of the special gifts that comes from the Holy Spirit (Rom 12:6, 7; 1 Cor 12:27-31). Teachers were given positions of honor in the early church. But they also had great responsibility, because what they said could influence many people.

3:3 *bits into the mouths of horses:* A bit, usually made of metal, is put into a horse's mouth and connected to leather straps called reins. The horse's rider pulls on the reins and moves the bit, which makes the horse turn the way the rider wants to go.

3:4 *rudder:* A rudder is a flat piece of wood or metal that is attached to the back of a boat. A rod connects the rudder with a steering wheel or lever. Turning or moving the lever or wheel turns the rudder, which changes the direction of the boat.

3:6 *hell:* For the word "hell," the author uses *gehenna*, the Greek form of the Hebrew word that means "Valley of Ben Hinnom," a place where the ancient Canaanites sacrificed children in fires built to honor the god Molech (2 Kgs 23:10; Jer 32:35). This valley later became a place where garbage was burning most of the time. In the New Testament, the place of judgment for evildoers is also pictured as a place of fiery torture (Luke 16:23,24; Rev 20:14). See the mini-articles called "Fire," p. 2383 and "Hell," p. 1944.

3:9 *Lord and Father:* See the notes at 1:1 (Lord Jesus Christ) and 1:27.

3:2 Prov 10:19-21; 11:9-13; 21:23. **3:6** Matt 15:11,18,19. **3:9** Gen 1:26.

17But the wisdom that comes from heaven is first of all pure;
then peace-loving, considerate, submissive, full of mercy and good
fruit, impartial and sincere. 18Peacemakers who sow in peace raise
a harvest of righteousness.

Submit Yourselves to God

4 What causes fights and quarrels among you? Don't they come
from your desires that battle within you? 2You want something but
don't get it. You kill and covet, but you cannot have what you
want. You quarrel and fight. You do not have, because you do not
ask God. 3When you ask, you do not receive, because you ask with
wrong motives, that you may spend what you get on your pleasures.

4You adulterous people, don't you know that friendship with
the world is hatred toward God? Anyone who chooses to be a
friend of the world becomes an enemy of God. 5Or do you think
Scripture says without reason that the spirit he caused to live in us
envies intensely?[a] 6But he gives us more grace. That is why Scripture says:

> "God opposes the proud
> but gives grace to the humble."[b]

7Submit yourselves, then, to God. Resist the devil, and he
will flee from you. 8Come near to God and he will come near to
you. Wash your hands, you sinners, and purify your hearts, you
double-minded. 9Grieve, mourn and wail. Change your laughter
to mourning and your joy to gloom. 10Humble yourselves before
the Lord, and he will lift you up.

11Brothers, do not slander one another. Anyone who speaks
against his brother or judges him speaks against the law and judges
it. When you judge the law, you are not keeping it, but sitting in
judgment on it. 12There is only one Lawgiver and Judge, the one
who is able to save and destroy. But you—who are you to judge
your neighbor?

Boasting About Tomorrow

13Now listen, you who say, "Today or tomorrow we will go to
this or that city, spend a year there, carry on business and make
money." 14Why, you do not even know what will happen tomorrow. What is your life? You are a mist that appears for a little while
and then vanishes. 15Instead, you ought to say, "If it is the Lord's
will, we will live and do this or that." 16As it is, you boast and brag.
All such boasting is evil. 17Anyone, then, who knows the good he
ought to do and doesn't do it, sins.

---

[a]5 Or *that God jealously longs for the spirit that he made to live in us*; or *that the Spirit he caused to live in us longs jealously* [b]6 Prov. 3:34

The wisdom that comes from heaven is first of all pure; then peace-loving, considerate, submissive, full of mercy and good fruit, impartial and sincere.
Jas 3:17

3:15 *wisdom . . . devil:* See the note at 1:5. Wisdom that does not come from above (from God) is here described as "earthly." Earthly wisdom that produces evil is said to be demonic or of the devil. The devil, also known as Satan, is the leader of the evil forces that are against God and God's people. See also the mini-article called "Satan," p. 963.

4:1 *desires that battle within you:* See the note at 1:15.

4:2 *you do not ask God:* Here the author is telling Christians to pray (ask God) in order to receive God's forgiveness and help. See also the mini-article called "Prayer," p. 2289.

4:4 *friendship with the world:* Here, the "world" refers to the evil people and forces that are against God and God's people. Describing the "world" as a source of evil may be related, in part, to a type of Greek philosophy that said the physical world was evil, and that only spiritual things were truly good or pure.

4:7 *devil:* See the note at 3:15.

4:11 *the law:* See the note at 2:11.

4:12 *one Lawgiver and Judge:* See the note at 2:13.

4:6 Prov 3:34. **4:13,14** Prov 27:1; Matt 6:31-34.

Warning to Rich Oppressors

5 Now listen, you rich people, weep and wail because of the misery that is coming upon you. 2Your wealth has rotted, and moths
have eaten your clothes. 3Your gold and silver are corroded. Their
corrosion will testify against you and eat your flesh like fire. You
have hoarded wealth in the last days. 4Look! The wages you failed
to pay the workmen who mowed your fields are crying out against
you. The cries of the harvesters have reached the ears of the Lord
Almighty. 5You have lived on earth in luxury and self-indulgence.
You have fattened yourselves in the day of slaughter.[a] 6You have
condemned and murdered innocent men, who were not opposing
you.

Be Patient, Kind, and Prayerful

Christians are told to be patient until the Lord returns, to avoid swearing or making oaths, and to pray for others, especially for sinners who have gone the wrong way.

Patience in Suffering

7Be patient, then, brothers, until the Lord's coming. See how
the farmer waits for the land to yield its valuable crop and how
patient he is for the autumn and spring rains. 8You too, be patient
and stand firm, because the Lord's coming is near. 9Don't grumble
against each other, brothers, or you will be judged. The Judge is
standing at the door!

10Brothers, as an example of patience in the face of suffering,
take the prophets who spoke in the name of the Lord. 11As you
know, we consider blessed those who have persevered. You have
heard of Job's perseverance and have seen what the Lord finally
brought about. The Lord is full of compassion and mercy.

12Above all, my brothers, do not swear—not by heaven or by
earth or by anything else. Let your "Yes" be yes, and your "No," no,
or you will be condemned.

The Prayer of Faith

13Is any one of you in trouble? He should pray. Is anyone
happy? Let him sing songs of praise. 14Is any one of you sick? He
should call the elders of the church to pray over him and anoint
him with oil in the name of the Lord. 15And the prayer offered in
faith will make the sick person well; the Lord will raise him up. If
he has sinned, he will be forgiven. 16Therefore confess your sins to

[a]5 Or *yourselves as in a day of feasting*

5:1 *rich people:* The writer is not warning against riches themselves, since money can be used to serve others. The warning is against those people who love money so much that they turn away from doing what God expects. It is the "love" of money that is the root of all kinds of evil (1 Tim 6:10). See also the note at 1:10.

5:4 *wages you failed to pay:* It was common for farmers to hire poor people to help with the planting and harvesting of crops. Both the Law of Moses and Jesus taught that it was important to pay these day-workers what they had earned (Lev 19:13; Deut 24:14, 15; Matt 20:1-16).

5:7 *until the Lord's coming:* Numerous passages in the New Testament tell about a time in the future when Jesus Christ (the Son of Man) will return to gather his people (Matt 24:29-31; Mark 13:24-27, 32-37; 1 Thes 4:13-18). See also the mini-article called "Second Coming," p. 2277.

5:9 *The Judge is standing at the door:* See the note at 2:13.

5:10 *the prophets:* "Prophets" here likely refers to ancient prophets of Israel who suffered because they spoke God's messages to the people. Jeremiah is an example of such a prophet (Jer 19:14—20:2). The prophets, whose writings are collected in the Jewish Scriptures (Old Testament), lived 400 to 800 years before Jesus was born. For more, see the article called "Prophets and Prophecy," p. 935.

5:11 *Job's perseverance:* The book of Job in the Old Testament tells the story of a wealthy man who lost his family and possessions and endured great physical suffering (Job 1:1—2:10). Though Job questioned why he was suffering, he continued to trust in God (Job 19:23-27; 42:1-6), and God helped him (Job 42:7-17). See also Ps 103:8.

5:2,3 Matt 6:19. **5:4** Deut 24:14,15. **5:12** Exod 20:7; Lev 19:12; Matt 5:34-37.

each other and pray for each other so that you may be healed. The
prayer of a righteous man is powerful and effective.
[17]Elijah was a man just like us. He prayed earnestly that it
would not rain, and it did not rain on the land for three and a half
years. [18]Again he prayed, and the heavens gave rain, and the earth
produced its crops.
[19]My brothers, if one of you should wander from the truth
and someone should bring him back, [20]remember this: Whoever
turns a sinner from the error of his way will save him from death
and cover over a multitude of sins.

5:14 *anoint him with oil:* Many ancient peoples used olive oil for healing. See Mark 6:13; 1 Cor 12:27, 28.

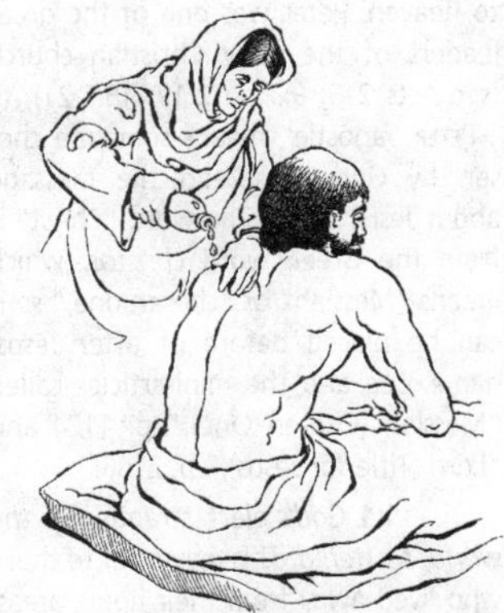

5:17 *Elijah:* Elijah was a prophet who warned Israel's King Ahab that God would cause a drought because Ahab allowed the people to worship Baal. See 1 Kgs 17:1—18:46 and the mini-article called "Elijah," p. 1816.

5:18 1 Kgs 18:42–45. **5:20** Prov 10:12; 1 Pet 4:8.

QUESTIONS ABOUT JAMES

1. Apparently the letter of JAMES was written to people who were having their faith tested (1:3). Name some ways the faith of the early Christians was tested. Does this kind of testing still occur today in the world? If so, where? What can be done to help those who are being tested or persecuted?
2. Read the advice JAMES gives about hearing and obeying (1:19-27). Which piece of advice do you find most challenging? Why?
3. The writer of JAMES was aware that the church included both rich and poor people (1:9-11; 2:1-9; 5:1-6). What does he say about how Christians are to treat rich people and poor people? What warnings does he give to rich people?
4. JAMES has much to say about how Christians are to speak to others (1:19; 3:1-12; 4:11-17). What are the dangers of speaking rashly or in anger? Of bragging? What are some positive ways in which Christians can speak out?
5. Read 2:14-26. Do you agree or disagree with the following statements? Why?
   a. It is possible to have faith without doing kind deeds.
   b. Faith that doesn't lead us to do good deeds is dead.
   c. Faith is trust in God and need not be proved by doing good deeds.
6. Compare the "wisdom that comes from heaven" with earthly wisdom (3:13-18). What are the results of each kind of wisdom? What can Christians do to receive the wisdom that comes from heaven?

1 PETER

First Peter 2:10 declares, "Once you were not a people, but now you are the people of God." Read this letter to discover the challenges and joys that are in store for people who follow Jesus.

1:1 *Peter, an apostle of Jesus Christ:* His real name was Simon, but he was also known as Peter, which means "the Rock." After Jesus went up to heaven, Peter was one of the great leaders of the early Christian church (see Acts 2–5; 9:32—12:19; 15:3-21). In 1 Peter "apostle" means someone chosen by God to spread the message about Jesus Christ. The word "Christ" is from the Greek word *christos,* which means "Messiah" or "chosen one," so it can be placed before or after Jesus' name. See also the mini-articles called "Messiah (Chosen One)," p. 1124 and "Lord (Title for Jesus)," p. 2106.

1:1 *God's elect, strangers in the world, scattered:* This may refer to those who lived away from their home areas. But it could also mean that the followers of Christ are like refugees or "strangers" because their lifestyle is different from non-believers who don't follow God (see Phil 3:20).

1:1 *Pontus, Galatia, Cappadocia, Asia, and Bithinia:* The five provinces mentioned in this letter, were located in the central or northern part of Asia Minor. Among the people who lived in these territories, some followed the Greek way of life and others followed the lifestyle of people to the east (in what is now Iran). A large number of Jews also lived in this region. See the map on p. 931. The apostle Paul traveled and preached in Galatia and parts of the province of Asia, but the Bible does not report that he went to the other provinces mentioned in 1 Peter. It may be that Peter went to these districts some time before Paul began preaching the gospel. See also the maps on pp. 2476 and 2477.

What makes 1 Peter special?

First Peter is written in the form of a letter, a form of communication frequently used in the Greek and Roman world. It begins and ends with formal greetings (1:1, 2; 5:12-14). The letter's main message (1:3—5:11) makes use of themes and styles that are found in many other New Testament writings. Like the Gospels, it tells of the importance of Jesus' death and God's raising him back to life. It also repeats Jesus' teachings concerning trust in God, and the importance of being humble and joyful even in times of suffering. Like Acts, it mentions the work of Peter, Silas, and Mark. It provides a picture of the early church, which met in private homes. First Peter encourages Christians to follow Christ's example, to live good lives, and tells Christians to expect suffering—themes that are also found in the letters of Paul.

Why was 1 Peter written?

The letter was written to Christians scattered over northern Asia Minor (1:1). The writer wants those who read the letter to realize that they may have to face suffering because of their faith (2:19-21; 3:13-15; 4:1,2, 12-19; 5:9-11). But because Jesus suffered and died to forgive their sins, Christians share the hope of being raised to new life. Other important themes presented in 1 Peter are:

1. God is at work in Jesus Christ to create a new people (1:3-25; 3:4-12);
2. God's new people (the church) are chosen to live a holy life and be a holy nation (1:13—2:17; 3:1-7; 4:1-11; 5:1-11);
3. God's new people should honor and respect the Roman emperor and Roman law (2:13-17), but should honor Christ and obey God above everything else (3:15-17), even if this means suffering or losing old friends (4:1-4); and
4. In baptism, Christians identify with the death and resurrection of Christ (3:21, 22).

What's the story behind the scene?

The letter has traditionally been connected to Jesus' disciple Peter (1:1), and includes greetings from those who worked closely with the apostle Paul: Silas and Mark (5:12, 13; Acts 15:37-40). Although written in a language more sophisticated than one would expect from a Galilean fisherman, (Mark 1:16, 17; 3:16), many scholars still affirm Peter's authorship contending that he received significant help from Silas in recording it (5:12). Because the letter mentions present and future suffering so much, some scholars believe 1 PETER was written after Peter's lifetime—during a time when the Roman authorities were changing their attitudes toward Christians. Until the reign of Emperor Domitian (A.D. 81-96), the Roman authorities did not persecute Christians, considering them to be part of the Jewish religion, which was protected by the Roman government. One exception to this was the Emperor Nero's persecution of Christians in Rome around A.D. 64. Those who hold to the traditional view believe that the apostle Peter wrote 1 PETER during this period. During the rule of Domitian, the Jewish and Christian movements clearly separated. The Romans began punishing Christians when they refused to offer sacrifices to the emperor, who had been officially declared to be a god. For more, see the mini-article called "Roman Empire," p. 2322.

FIRST PETER also appears to include parts of creeds or hymns that were used in Christian worship of the time (1:20; 2:21-25; 3:18-22). Looking at these closely can give modern readers a glimpse into the life of the early church.

How Is 1 Peter Constructed?

The bulk of this letter consists of teachings, hymns, and sayings that can be grouped as follows:

Chosen, protected, and saved (1:1-12)
Living as God's holy people (1:13—3:22)
Serving and suffering to the end (4:1—5:14)

Chosen, Protected, and Saved

God's people are facing trials, so this letter begins by reminding them that God has chosen them (1:2) and will protect them until the last day when Jesus Christ returns (1:7). In this way, they can be saved as God had always planned (1:5). By raising Jesus from death, God gives his people new life as well as the hope that will help them get through many hard trials.

1 Peter, an apostle of Jesus Christ,

To God's elect, strangers in the world, scattered throughout
Pontus, Galatia, Cappadocia, Asia and Bithynia, 2 who have been
chosen according to the foreknowledge of God the Father, through
the sanctifying work of the Spirit, for obedience to Jesus Christ
and sprinkling by his blood:

Grace and peace be yours in abundance.

Praise to God for a Living Hope

3 Praise be to the God and Father of our Lord Jesus Christ! In
his great mercy he has given us new birth into a living hope
through the resurrection of Jesus Christ from the dead, 4 and into
an inheritance that can never perish, spoil or fade—kept in

1:2 *God the Father . . . Spirit:* Jesus often referred to God as "Father" (see John 14, for example). This same term is also used to describe God in many of Paul's letters (1 Cor 1:3; Gal 1:1-3; Phil 1:2).

The Spirit here is the Holy Spirit, which makes God's people holy, set apart, in order that they can serve God. See also the mini-article called "Holy Spirit," p. 2082.

1:2 *sprinkling by his blood:* According to Exodus 24:3-8, Moses purified the people of Israel with the blood of bulls to show that the people would keep their covenant with God. For Christians, it is the blood of Jesus that seals the covenant between God and his people (see also Heb 9:18-22).

1:3 *Father of our Lord Jesus Christ . . . resurrection:* See the note at 1:2 (God the Father). See also the mini-article called "Lord (Title for Jesus)," p. 2106. God raised Jesus from death to life three days after he died on a cross (see Matt 28:1-10; Acts 2:22-24). See the mini-article called "Resurrection," p. 2210.

1:4 *an inheritance . . . kept in heaven:* Refers to eternal life, which God promises to those who trust in Jesus (see John 14:1-6; Col 3:1-4; 1 Thes 4:13-18; Heb 4:1-11). See also the mini-articles called "Eternal Life," p. 2072 and "Heaven," p. 1420.

1:5 *faith ... salvation ... revealed in the last time:* Here, faith means trust in God. Many New Testament letters talk about the time when Jesus will come back (1 Cor 15:20-28; Phil 1:10; 2:16; 3:20, 21; 1 Thes 4:13-18). See the mini-articles called "Day of the LORD," p. 1727 and "Second Coming," p. 2277. For "salvation" see the note at 1:9.

heaven for you, 5who through faith are shielded by God's power
until the coming of the salvation that is ready to be revealed in the
last time. 6In this you greatly rejoice, though now for a little while
you may have had to suffer grief in all kinds of trials. 7These have
come so that your faith—of greater worth than gold, which perishes even though refined by fire—may be proved genuine and
may result in praise, glory and honor when Jesus Christ is
revealed. 8Though you have not seen him, you love him; and even
though you do not see him now, you believe in him and are filled
with an inexpressible and glorious joy, 9for you are receiving the
goal of your faith, the salvation of your souls.
10Concerning this salvation, the prophets, who spoke of the

HOPE

In present-day society, the word "hope" often refers to wishful thinking or to the expectation that something positive is going to happen. This understanding of hope is certainly found in the Bible (see Luke 23:8, for example). In the Jewish Scriptures (Old Testament), Hebrew words translated as "hope" refer to "waiting with expectation," but also to "trusting and being full of confidence."

Often this kind of hope is used in connection with trust in God's saving help (Ps 71:5; Jer 14:8; 17:13). In some passages, God will watch over, that is, protect and bless, those who continue to place their trust in God alone (Ps 33:18). Trusting, or placing hope, in anyone or anything other than God leads to disaster (Exod 20:3-5; Ps 49:5-14; Isa 44:9-11). After the time of the exile in Babylon, Israel's prophets described Israel's hope for the future, not so much in terms of renewed political power, but in terms of renewed hearts and minds (Jer 29:10-14; 31:31-33).

In the centuries before Jesus, many Jewish people began to believe that Israel's hope for new life would be fully realized only when God defeated the people who opposed God's rule or oppressed God's people. At that time God would create a new kingdom for God's people. This kind of hope is especially important in a type of writing known as "apocalyptic" (see Dan 7–12; Zech 9–14; and the mini-article called "Apocalyptic Writing," p. 1656).

Hope is an important theme and idea in the New Testament, especially in the letters of Paul. For Paul, hope is closely connected to faith and love. The "hope of salvation" is a Christian's "helmet," while faith and love are like a "breastplate" (1 Thes 5:8). Paul thanks God for the Thessalonians' faith, love, and "endurance inspired by hope in our Lord Jesus Christ" (1 Thes 1:3). These three—faith, hope, and love—are combined and highlighted also in 1 Corinthians 13:13. Christians can hope, Paul says, because God raised Jesus to life, and all who have faith in Jesus will be raised to be with him forever (1 Thes 4:13-18). Jesus died on the cross to set people free from sin so that they could be accepted by God (Rom 3:25,26). Even so, those who have faith in this promise need hope so that they can continue to be faithful until the future time when their salvation is complete and they share in the glory of God (Rom 5:1-5; 8:23-25; Phil 3:10-14).

In the New Testament as in the Old Testament, one thing that sets apart God's people is their unique kind of hope (Heb 3:6; 6:11; 10:23), and it is their faith that makes them sure of what they hope for (Heb 11:1). So, faith creates hope, but hope, in turn, is needed to keep faith strong and to give Christ's followers courage to face trials and testing (1 Pet 1:3-9; 3:14-16).

Catacomb of Callistus I, near Rome, Italy, around A.D. 250. Catacombs are underground cemeteries that were built by Christians in the second through fifth centuries. Because they were burial places, Christians could gather there for worship with little fear of being bothered by the Roman authorities. Several hundred miles of catacombs still survive in the area outside of Rome. FIRST PETER is written to Christians who are facing the challenges of living in a world that was sometimes hostile to them. They are told that their "faith . . . may be proved genuine and may result in praise, glory and honor," and that the trials they must face will prove that their faith is of greater worth than gold. (See 1:5-7.)

grace that was to come to you, searched intently and with the
greatest care, 11trying to find out the time and circumstances to
which the Spirit of Christ in them was pointing when he predicted the sufferings of Christ and the glories that would follow. 12It
was revealed to them that they were not serving themselves but
you, when they spoke of the things that have now been told you by
those who have preached the gospel to you by the Holy Spirit sent
from heaven. Even angels long to look into these things.

Living as God's Holy People

God chooses a new people to live holy lives and to live as a nation of holy priests who will work as God's servants. They will probably suffer as they follow Christ, who suffered for them. They are told how to treat one another, as well as how they are to respond to old friends and to their surrounding culture which often does not accept their new life.

Be Holy

13Therefore, prepare your minds for action; be self-
controlled; set your hope fully on the grace to be given you when
Jesus Christ is revealed. 14As obedient children, do not conform to

1:7 *gold . . . refined by fire:* In a process called refining, gold is heated in order to burn away impurities. What is left after refining is very pure. The same is true for faith. When faith is tested and survives the "fires" of suffering and temptation, it is stronger and purer.

1:9 *salvation of your souls:* The word "salvation" points to what God has done and is still doing to free humans from sin. See the mini-article called "Salvation," p. 2021.

1:10 *prophets:* See the article called "Prophets and Prophecy," p. 935. The prophet Isaiah described a special servant who would suffer and then be given great honor (Isa 49:1-6; 50:4-7; 52:13—53:12). Early Christians identified Jesus Christ as the Messiah ("Christ") described by the prophets (Isa 9:6, 7; 11:1-9; Mic 5:2-5).

1:12 *angels:* The word "angel" in English is based on the Greek word *angelos,* which means "messenger." See also the mini-article called "Angels," p. 88.

1:13 *when Jesus Christ is revealed:* See the note at 1:5.

1:14 *obedient children . . . evil desires:* Christians are challenged to lead lives of self-discipline and obedience to God. By doing this their lives would contrast sharply with the lives of the people who live around them. Such holy living is sure to be a witness to others. "Evil desires" refers to past sinful desires and actions, and can include things like having wild parties and worshiping pagan gods and goddesses (see 4:1-4).

the evil desires you had when you lived in ignorance. 15 But just as
he who called you is holy, so be holy in all you do; 16 for it is written: "Be holy, because I am holy."[a]

17 Since you call on a Father who judges each man's work
impartially, live your lives as strangers here in reverent fear. 18 For
you know that it was not with perishable things such as silver or
gold that you were redeemed from the empty way of life handed
down to you from your forefathers, 19 but with the precious blood
of Christ, a lamb without blemish or defect. 20 He was chosen
before the creation of the world, but was revealed in these last
times for your sake. 21 Through him you believe in God, who raised
him from the dead and glorified him, and so your faith and hope
are in God.

22 Now that you have purified yourselves by obeying the truth
so that you have sincere love for your brothers, love one another
deeply, from the heart.[b] 23 For you have been born again, not of
perishable seed, but of imperishable, through the living and
enduring word of God. 24 For,

"All men are like grass,
and all their glory is like the flowers of the field;
the grass withers and the flowers fall,
25 but the word of the Lord stands forever."[c]

And this is the word that was preached to you.

2 Therefore, rid yourselves of all malice and all deceit, hypocrisy,
envy, and slander of every kind. 2 Like newborn babies, crave pure
spiritual milk, so that by it you may grow up in your salvation,
3 now that you have tasted that the Lord is good.

The Living Stone and a Chosen People

4 As you come to him, the living Stone—rejected by men but
chosen by God and precious to him— 5 you also, like living stones,
are being built into a spiritual house to be a holy priesthood, offering spiritual sacrifices acceptable to God through Jesus Christ. 6 For
in Scripture it says:

"See, I lay a stone in Zion,
a chosen and precious cornerstone,
and the one who trusts in him
will never be put to shame."[d]

7 Now to you who believe, this stone is precious. But to those who
do not believe,

"The stone the builders rejected
has become the capstone,[e]"[f]

8 and,

[a] 16 Lev. 11:44,45; 19:2 [b] 22 Some early manuscripts *from a pure heart*
[c] 25 Isaiah 40:6-8 [d] 6 Isaiah 28:16 [e] 7 Or *cornerstone* [f] 7 Psalm 118:22

1:19 *precious blood of Christ, a lamb:* Christ's death on the cross is described in the New Testament as a sacrifice to forgive sins (Rom 3:25, 26). He is also compared to the spotless lamb, whose blood has power to bring forgiveness (see Heb 9:23-28; 1 John 1:7).

2:2 *pure spiritual milk:* This is God's Word, which will help God's people grow in faith and show them how they can be saved. See also the mini-article called, "Inspiration of Scripture," p. 12.

2:4, 5 *the living Stone . . . living stones:* The prophet Isaiah compared the Messiah that God would put in Zion (Jerusalem) to a "precious cornerstone" (Isa 28:16). Cornerstones were large stones placed in the corner of a building's foundation. Later, Jesus compared himself to such a stone (Mark 12:1-12). See also Acts 4:8-12; Rom 9:30-33. Those who trust in Jesus as the cornerstone (2:6) will become living stones themselves. They are then built into a spiritual house, which is a temple or place of worship. See also 1 Cor 3:16, 17; Eph 2:19-22; Rev 3:12.

2:5 *holy priesthood, offering spiritual sacrifices acceptable to God:* The new people of God are not only God's temple, but the priests who serve in the temple. In ancient Israel, only descendants of the tribe of Levi could serve as priests (see the mini-article called "Israel's Priests," p. 2344). This text says that the new people of God will not offer animal sacrifices, but will instead offer sacrifices of praise to God and of love for one another.

2:6 *Zion:* Another name for Jerusalem and the high place where the temple was built in Jerusalem. See also the mini-article called "Zion," p. 1294.

1:16 Lev 11:44,45; 19:2; 20:7, 26. **1:20** John 1:1-14; Col 1:15-18. **1:24,25** Isa 40:6-8. **2:3** Ps 34:8. **2:6** Isa 28:16. **2:7** Ps 118:22.

"A stone that causes men to stumble
and a rock that makes them fall."[a]

They stumble because they disobey the message—which is also
what they were destined for.

9 But you are a chosen people, a royal priesthood, a holy
nation, a people belonging to God, that you may declare the
praises of him who called you out of darkness into his wonderful
light. 10 Once you were not a people, but now you are the people of
God; once you had not received mercy, but now you have received
mercy.

11 Dear friends, I urge you, as aliens and strangers in the
world, to abstain from sinful desires, which war against your soul.
12 Live such good lives among the pagans that, though they accuse
you of doing wrong, they may see your good deeds and glorify
God on the day he visits us.

Submission to Rulers and Masters

13 Submit yourselves for the Lord's sake to every authority
instituted among men: whether to the king, as the supreme authority, 14 or to governors, who are sent by him to punish those who do
wrong and to commend those who do right. 15 For it is God's will
that by doing good you should silence the ignorant talk of foolish
men. 16 Live as free men, but do not use your freedom as a cover-up
for evil; live as servants of God. 17 Show proper respect to everyone:
Love the brotherhood of believers, fear God, honor the king.

18 Slaves, submit yourselves to your masters with all respect,
not only to those who are good and considerate, but also to those
who are harsh. 19 For it is commendable if a man bears up under
the pain of unjust suffering because he is conscious of God. 20 But
how is it to your credit if you receive a beating for doing wrong
and endure it? But if you suffer for doing good and you endure it,
this is commendable before God. 21 To this you were called, because
Christ suffered for you, leaving you an example, that you should
follow in his steps.

22 "He committed no sin,
and no deceit was found in his mouth."[b]

23 When they hurled their insults at him, he did not retaliate; when
he suffered, he made no threats. Instead, he entrusted himself to
him who judges justly. 24 He himself bore our sins in his body on
the tree, so that we might die to sins and live for righteousness; by
his wounds you have been healed. 25 For you were like sheep going
astray, but now you have returned to the Shepherd and Overseer of
your souls.

[a] **8** Isaiah 8:14 [b] **22** Isaiah 53:9

2:9 *holy nation:* In EXODUS, God tells Moses to tell the people of Israel that they will be God's "holy nation" and serve him as "priests" (Exod 19:6). Though God chose the Israelites to be his special people in the past, God's new people is made up of all people who have faith (Rom 11:1-29; Gal 3:22-29). See also the note at 2:5.

2:13-17 *every authority . . . honor the king:* The Roman king would be the emperor, and his government protected the lives and property of law-abiding people and punished criminals. Christians could turn suspicion and fear concerning their worship practices into respect if they obeyed the local laws and were good neighbors. Nero, shown on this coin, was the Roman emperor from A.D. 54 to 68, and would have been the emperor who was in power at the time of Peter's death.

2:18 *Slaves . . . masters:* The early church included both slaves and slaveholders. The way slaves and masters behaved toward each other could affect how others viewed God. See also the mini-article called "Slaves and Servants in the Time of Jesus," p. 2006.

2:21 *follow in his steps:* Christians will suffer and be mistreated, but they are not to fight those who mistreat them, just as Jesus did not fight those who had put him to death.

2:9 Exod 19:5,6; Isa 43:20; Deut 4:20; 7:6; 14:2; Titus 2:14; Isa 43:21; Isa 9:2. **2:10** Hos 2:23. **2:8** Isa 8:14,15; Acts 4:8-12. **2:16** 1 Cor 7:22, 23; Gal 5:1. **2:23** Isa 53:7. **2:24,25** Isa 53:5,6; John 10:10-18; Heb 13:20.

3:1 *Wives . . . be submissive to your husbands:* Honoring God and living a pure life will convince a husband to believe in God faster than wearing fancy hairstyles or expensive clothes. (The bust shown here is of an upper class Roman woman.) See also 2:11-17; 3:8—4:11.

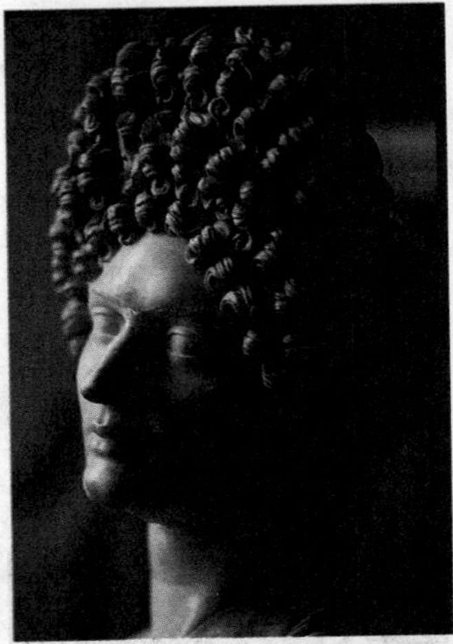

3:6 *Sarah:* Sarah faithfully followed Abraham when God called them to leave their homeland to go to Canaan (Gen 12–23). See also the mini-article called "Abraham," p. 2254.

3:7 *Husbands:* Christian husbands and wives share the gift of new life in Christ. See also Eph 5:25; Col 3:19.

3:18 *Christ died . . . made alive by the Spirit:* This verse is probably a very early Christian hymn that celebrates how Christ died to forgive sins, and God raised him to life again (see the notes at 1:3 and 1:19).

3:19 *preached to the spirits in prison:* Here, the "spirits" seem to be those who disobeyed God in the time of Noah and so were destroyed by God in the great flood (3:20). Christ's preaching to them upon his resurrection proved his power over the disobedient and over death.

3:1 Eph 5:22-25; Col 3:18,19. **3:3** 1 Tim 2:9. **3:14** Matt 5:10.

Wives and Husbands

3 Wives, in the same way be submissive to your husbands so
that, if any of them do not believe the word, they may be won over
without words by the behavior of their wives, [2]when they see the
purity and reverence of your lives. [3]Your beauty should not come
from outward adornment, such as braided hair and the wearing of
gold jewelry and fine clothes. [4]Instead, it should be that of your
inner self, the unfading beauty of a gentle and quiet spirit, which
is of great worth in God's sight. [5]For this is the way the holy
women of the past who put their hope in God used to make themselves beautiful. They were submissive to their own husbands, [6]like
Sarah, who obeyed Abraham and called him her master. You are
her daughters if you do what is right and do not give way to fear.
[7]Husbands, in the same way be considerate as you live with
your wives, and treat them with respect as the weaker partner and
as heirs with you of the gracious gift of life, so that nothing will
hinder your prayers.

Suffering for Doing Good

[8]Finally, all of you, live in harmony with one another; be
sympathetic, love as brothers, be compassionate and humble. [9]Do
not repay evil with evil or insult with insult, but with blessing,
because to this you were called so that you may inherit a blessing.
[10]For,

"Whoever would love life
 and see good days
must keep his tongue from evil
 and his lips from deceitful speech.
[11]He must turn from evil and do good;
 he must seek peace and pursue it.
[12]For the eyes of the Lord are on the righteous
 and his ears are attentive to their prayer,
but the face of the Lord is against those who do evil."[a]

[13]Who is going to harm you if you are eager to do good?
[14]But even if you should suffer for what is right, you are blessed.
"Do not fear what they fear[b]; do not be frightened."[c] [15]But in your
hearts set apart Christ as Lord. Always be prepared to give an
answer to everyone who asks you to give the reason for the hope
that you have. But do this with gentleness and respect, [16]keeping a
clear conscience, so that those who speak maliciously against your
good behavior in Christ may be ashamed of their slander. [17]It is
better, if it is God's will, to suffer for doing good than for doing
evil. [18]For Christ died for sins once for all, the righteous for the

[a]**12** Psalm 34:12-16 [b]**14** Or *not fear their threats* [c]**14** Isaiah 8:12

unrighteous, to bring you to God. He was put to death in the body
but made alive by the Spirit, 19 through whom[a] also he went and
preached to the spirits in prison 20 who disobeyed long ago when
God waited patiently in the days of Noah while the ark was being
built. In it only a few people, eight in all, were saved through water,
21 and this water symbolizes baptism that now saves you also—not
the removal of dirt from the body but the pledge[b] of a good conscience toward God. It saves you by the resurrection of Jesus
Christ, 22 who has gone into heaven and is at God's right hand—
with angels, authorities and powers in submission to him.

Serving and Suffering to the End

Being faithful to Christ means using God's gifts to serve others (4:10, 11). Christians are to be glad for the chance to suffer as Christ suffered, since this means they are obeying God. The elders of the churches are encouraged to be like shepherds watching over their sheep (the people of God) until Christ, the Chief Shepherd, returns.

Living for God

4 Therefore, since Christ suffered in his body, arm yourselves
also with the same attitude, because he who has suffered in his
body is done with sin. 2 As a result, he does not live the rest of his
earthly life for evil human desires, but rather for the will of God.
3 For you have spent enough time in the past doing what pagans
choose to do—living in debauchery, lust, drunkenness, orgies,
carousing and detestable idolatry. 4 They think it strange that you
do not plunge with them into the same flood of dissipation, and
they heap abuse on you. 5 But they will have to give account to him
who is ready to judge the living and the dead. 6 For this is the reason the gospel was preached even to those who are now dead, so
that they might be judged according to men in regard to the body,
but live according to God in regard to the spirit.

7 The end of all things is near. Therefore be clear minded and
self-controlled so that you can pray. 8 Above all, love each other
deeply, because love covers over a multitude of sins. 9 Offer hospitality to one another without grumbling. 10 Each one should use
whatever gift he has received to serve others, faithfully administering God's grace in its various forms. 11 If anyone speaks, he should
do it as one speaking the very words of God. If anyone serves, he
should do it with the strength God provides, so that in all things
God may be praised through Jesus Christ. To him be the glory and
the power for ever and ever. Amen.

[a] **18,19** Or *alive in the spirit, 19 through which* [b] **21** Or *response*

3:20 *Noah:* He was faithful to God when others were not (Gen 6:1—7:24). See also Ezek 14:14; Matt 24:37-39; Heb 11:7; 2 Pet 2:5.

3:21 *water symbolizes baptism:* God saved Noah and his family from the great flood, and used the flood to save them from the sinful world they lived in. As the flood waters symbolize baptism, so baptism now symbolizes salvation through Christ's death and resurrection. In 1 Corinthians 10:1, 2, God's saving of the Israelites at the Red Sea is also compared to baptism.

4:2 *evil human desires:* See the note at 1:14.

4:3 *what pagans choose to do . . . debauchery . . . idolatry:* The partying and drunkenness mentioned here is probably a reference to the kind of wild banquets held by many trade guilds and social clubs in Asia Minor. Some Christians may have joined these groups as a way of making business contacts and friends. The idolatry mentioned here might have been worship of statues representing Artemis, a fertility goddess (see Acts 19:23-29).

4:6 *gospel . . . dead:* The gospel is both the message about Jesus and the message Jesus brings about God's kingdom. The "dead" refers either to followers of Christ who have died, or to the people of Noah's day (3:19).

4:7 *The end of all things is near:* See the note at 1:5 and the mini-article called "End Times," p. 2295.

4:10 *whatever gift he has received:* In other New Testament writings this gifts is said to come from the Holy Spirit (Rom 12:3-8; 1 Cor 12:4-31).

4:8 Prov 10:12.

If you suffer as a Christian, do not be ashamed, but praise God that you bear that name.
1 Pet 4:16

4:12 *painful trial:* See the note at 1:7.

4:13 *when his glory is revealed:* See the notes at 1:5 and 4:7.

4:17 *time for judgment to begin:* See the note at 1:5.

5:1 *elders:* Most likely they were the leaders chosen to do special tasks in the church.

5:1 *witness of Christ's sufferings:* Peter, one of Jesus' original twelve apostles, was present when Jesus suffered prior to going to the cross.

5:2 *shepherds:* See also John 21:15-17 and the mini-article called "Shepherds," p. 1972.

5:4 *Chief Shepherd . . . crown of glory:* See also John 10:10-18 and Hebrews 13:20,21, which describe Jesus as the "good shepherd." In ancient times an athlete who had won a contest was awarded a crown of flowers as a sign of victory.

5:8 *the devil:* The leader of the evil forces that are against God and God's people. See also the mini-article called "Satan," p. 963.

5:10 *eternal glory:* See the mini-article called "Eternal Life," p. 2072.

4:18 Prov 11:31. **5:5** Prov 3:34. **5:6** Matt 23:12; Luke 14:11; 18:14.

Suffering for Being a Christian

12 Dear friends, do not be surprised at the painful trial you
are suffering, as though something strange were happening to you.
13 But rejoice that you participate in the sufferings of Christ, so that
you may be overjoyed when his glory is revealed. 14 If you are
insulted because of the name of Christ, you are blessed, for the
Spirit of glory and of God rests on you. 15 If you suffer, it should
not be as a murderer or thief or any other kind of criminal, or
even as a meddler. 16 However, if you suffer as a Christian, do not
be ashamed, but praise God that you bear that name. 17 For it is
time for judgment to begin with the family of God; and if it begins
with us, what will the outcome be for those who do not obey the
gospel of God? 18 And,

> "If it is hard for the righteous to be saved,
> what will become of the ungodly and the sinner?"[a]

19 So then, those who suffer according to God's will should
commit themselves to their faithful Creator and continue to do
good.

To Elders and Young Men

5 To the elders among you, I appeal as a fellow elder, a witness of
Christ's sufferings and one who also will share in the glory to be
revealed: 2 Be shepherds of God's flock that is under your care,
serving as overseers—not because you must, but because you are
willing, as God wants you to be; not greedy for money, but eager
to serve; 3 not lording it over those entrusted to you, but being
examples to the flock. 4 And when the Chief Shepherd appears, you
will receive the crown of glory that will never fade away.

5 Young men, in the same way be submissive to those who are
older. All of you, clothe yourselves with humility toward one
another, because,

> "God opposes the proud
> but gives grace to the humble."[b]

6 Humble yourselves, therefore, under God's mighty hand, that he
may lift you up in due time. 7 Cast all your anxiety on him because
he cares for you.

8 Be self-controlled and alert. Your enemy the devil prowls
around like a roaring lion looking for someone to devour. 9 Resist
him, standing firm in the faith, because you know that your brothers
throughout the world are undergoing the same kind of sufferings.

10 And the God of all grace, who called you to his eternal
glory in Christ, after you have suffered a little while, will himself

[a] **18** Prov. 11:31 [b] **5** Prov. 3:34

restore you and make you strong, firm and steadfast. [11]To him be
the power for ever and ever. Amen.

Final Greetings

[12]With the help of Silas,[a] whom I regard as a faithful brother,
I have written to you briefly, encouraging you and testifying that
this is the true grace of God. Stand fast in it.
[13]She who is in Babylon, chosen together with you, sends
you her greetings, and so does my son Mark. [14]Greet one another
with a kiss of love.

Peace to all of you who are in Christ.

---

[a]12 Greek *Silvanus,* a variant of *Silas*

5:12 *Silas:* "Silvanus" in Greek. Silas was a Christian prophet (Acts 15:32) and co-worker with Paul (Acts 15:22-41; 16:9—17:15; 2 Cor 1:19; 1 Thes 1:1; 2 Thes 1:1).

5:13 *Babylon:* Since Babylon was no longer a dominant world power in Peter's day, the city's name is being used here as a way of secretly referring to Rome. See the mini-article called "Babylon," p. 1363.

5:13 *Mark:* Mark went with Paul and Barnabas from the Syrian city of Antioch to Jerusalem in order to deliver money needed by the church there (Acts 11:27-30; 12:12,25; 13:13.) Later, Mark (John Mark) left Paul and worked with Barnabas (Acts 15:36-39).

5:14 *Greet one another with a kiss of love:* This phrase translates a Greek word that means "holy kiss."

QUESTIONS ABOUT 1 PETER

1. What does 1 PETER mean by saying that God has given his people "new birth into a living hope"? (1:3) How will this hope be tested? (1:6,7; 2:18-21; 4:1,12-19) Why are the Lord's followers to be glad for the chance to suffer? (4:13,14)
2. Many Christians in the early church suffered or were put to death because of their faith in Jesus Christ. Which of the following is worth dying for: family, country, friends, personal beliefs, or faith? Why?
3. How have God's people been rescued from the empty way of life they learned from their ancestors? (1:18; 4:3, 4) How are they to live instead?
4. A number of images are used in 2:1-12 to describe God's chosen people: living stones, royal priesthood, holy nation, aliens and strangers. What does each image tell you about what it means to be one of Christ's followers?
5. Describe the counsel 1 PETER gives to servants (2:18-21), wives (3:1-6), and husbands (3:7). What important instruction is given to all of God's people, no matter who they are? (3:8-15; 4:8-10)
6. What specific advice is given to church leaders? (5:1-4)
7. A number of times this letter mentions the importance of being obedient and humble (1:14-16; 3:8-12; 4:8-11; 5:5-7). What does being humble have to do with being one of God's people? Do you think that people who are humble can be successful in today's world? Why or why not?
8. How does the message of 1 PETER give you hope?

2 PETER

Christ Jesus came into the world to be its Savior and to choose a people to call his own. One day he will return to welcome his people into a glorious kingdom that will last forever. Read 2 PETER to see how Christians are to live in the meantime.

1:1 *Simon Peter:* Peter was a fisherman who became one of Jesus' first disciples and is named as one of the twelve apostles (Matt 4:18-22; 10:1-4). He was also one of the three disciples who saw Jesus' transfiguration and heard God call Jesus "my Son" on a mountaintop (Matt 17:1-13).

When Jesus called Simon to be his disciple, he gave him the name *Cephas* (Aramaic) or *Peter* (Greek), both of which mean "rock" (John 1:42). Later, when Jesus asked his disciples, "Who do you say I am?" Peter answered, "You are the Christ, the Son of the living God." Jesus replied, "Blessed are you . . . you are Peter, and on this rock I will build my church . . . I will give you the keys of the kingdom of heaven" (Matt 16:13-20). In Christian art, Peter is often shown holding a key (see below). After Jesus went up to heaven, Peter was one of the great leaders of the early Christian church (see Acts 2–5; 9:32—12:19; 15:3-21).

WHAT MAKES 2 PETER SPECIAL?

The book of 2 PETER is written in the form of a letter with a general greeting (1:1,2), but it is actually intended to be the farewell message, or last testament, of the apostle Peter. The writer offers some last words of instruction and warning to Christians, because he will soon leave his earthly body behind (1:13,14). In this way, 2 PETER is similar to some other farewell speeches found in the Bible (Mark 13; John 13–17; Acts 20:17-35; Josh 23; 24).

Though the letter is written as teaching and warning for the future (1:12-15; 3:1-13), its message also refers to ongoing problems affecting the faith of Christians. Parts of 2 PETER also appear to be very closely related to the letter of JUDE. These facts, and others listed under the heading "What's the story behind the scene," have caused a certain amount of uncertainty about who wrote 2 PETER and when it was written.

WHY WAS 2 PETER WRITTEN?

The writer warns Christians about false teachers and prophets who are trying to lead the believers away from the truth. When false teachers are at work, he says, Christians must stick to their faith and show others how to live right by living right themselves. The writer wants his readers to live in a way that pleases God (1:3) and to hold firmly to the truth they were given (1:12). He tells his readers that they must never forget that the Lord's return is certain, even though it has not happened as quickly as some expected (3:4). In the meantime, they are to wait with patience and obey God by living pure and spotless lives (3:14).

WHAT'S THE STORY BEHIND THE SCENE?

This letter claims the apostle Peter as its author (1:1). Peter was present on the mountain when Jesus' true glory was revealed (called the transfiguration; see 1:17, 18; Mark 9:2-8; Matt 17:1-9). Many scholars believe that this letter was written by a follower of Peter sometime after the great apostle died, as a way of honoring Peter and as a way of defending the teachings of the early apostles against new opponents. Consider the following clues observed by these scholars:

1. The style of the book more closely reflects the Greek culture of the second century A.D. than any other New Testament book. The apostle Peter was an uneducated

Galilean fisherman, who probably died around A.D. 65 in Rome.

2. The writer mentions Paul's letters as if they are being considered as Scripture for the Christian church at the time he was writing (3:15, 16). When other New Testament writings refer to the "Scriptures," they mean the Jewish Scriptures (Old Testament), which Jesus and his disciples used before the New Testament was written. Paul probably died about the same time as Peter, and it seems unlikely that Paul's letters, though known and respected, would have been regarded as Scripture until sometime after Paul's death.
3. Many New Testament letters looked forward to a time when Christ would soon return (Phil 3:20, 21; 1 Thes 4:13-18; Jas 5:9). But in 2 PETER, some false teachers are scoffing at the Christians who hope for the Lord's return, saying the church's first leaders have already died and "everything goes on as it has since the beginning of creation" (3:4). Peter was part of the first generation of church leaders. The writer emphasizes being patient about the Lord's return and not losing hope, since God isn't being slow about keeping his promise (3:9). This would not have been an important concern during Peter's lifetime.
4. A comparison of 2 PETER with JUDE may indicate that a large part of JUDE was borrowed by the author of 2 PETER who used it to support his own arguments (2 Pet 2:1—3:3; Jude 4-19). Since JUDE is thought to have been written after most of the other New Testament letters, 2 PETER would then have to have been written even later.

HOW IS 2 PETER CONSTRUCTED?

The letter begins with a brief greeting to a general Christian audience (1:1,2). It does not end with a closing set of greetings but rather with a challenge and a doxology (3:17, 18). The letter can therefore be outlined as follows:

Please God and hold firmly to the truth (1:1-21)

Watch out for false prophets and false teachers (2:1-22)

Be ready, because the Lord will return (3:1-18)

Please God and Hold Firmly to the Truth

The letter begins with a greeting to an unknown group of Christians. The writer tells them to live in a way that pleases God, improving their faith by adding goodness, knowledge, self-control, perseverance, godliness, kindness, and love (1:3,5-7). This is the writer's farewell message (1:14,15), so he wants his readers to remember the truth of his message after he is gone.

1 Simon Peter, a servant and apostle of Jesus Christ,

To those who through the righteousness of our God and
Savior Jesus Christ have received a faith as precious as ours:

Make every effort to add to your faith goodness; and to goodness, knowledge; and to knowledge, self-control; and to self-control, perseverance; and to perseverance, godliness; and to godliness, brotherly kindness; and to brotherly kindness, love.
2 Pet 1:5-7

1:1 *To those:* This letter may have been intended for followers of Christ in Asia Minor (see 1 Pet 1:1).

1:1 *God and Savior Jesus Christ:* Savior means "one who delivers." As Savior, Jesus Christ has the power to deliver all people from sin and death. The word "Christ" is from the Greek word *christos,* which means "Messiah" or "chosen one," so it can be placed before or after Jesus' name. See also the mini-article called "Messiah (Chosen One)," p. 1124.

1:2 *knowledge of God:* The writer prays that the readers will know more about God. The prophets and apostles have taught this knowledge (1:19; 3:1, 2), so the readers won't be fooled by false teachers.

1:4 *precious promises . . . escape the corruption . . . evil desires:* Becoming one with God's nature will help Jesus' followers escape their old evil desires and the corrupt influences of the world, which include greed, wild parties, worshiping idols, and sex outside of marriage (2:1-22; 1 Pet 4:1-4).

1:5-7 *add to your faith goodness . . . love:* In most New Testament writings, faith means trust in Christ, but here it means doing things that show that Jesus' followers are really one with God (1:4). This would set the followers apart from false teachers and the reckless, proud, and senseless people who will be destroyed by their own corrupt deeds (2:10-13).

SECOND PETER was written at a time when Christianity was competing with other popular religions and philosophies in the Roman world. Readers would have been familiar with the list of things mentioned in verses 5-7 because they were found in popular philosophies. But Christian growth and effectiveness (1:8, 9) was to be based on faith in Christ (1:8), and to result in love.

1:8 *Lord Jesus Christ:* The Greek word for "Lord," is *kyrios* and means "master" or "sir." When used for Jesus it emphasizes his authority and power. See also the note at 1:1 (Christ) and the mini-article called "Lord (Title for Jesus)," p. 2106.

1:11 *welcome into the eternal kingdom:* Christ will welcome those who are faithful to him into his heavenly kingdom (1 Cor 15:12-57; 1 Thes 4:13-18; 1 Pet 5:10,11). See also the mini-article called "Heaven," p. 1420.

2 Grace and peace be yours in abundance through the knowledge of God and of Jesus our Lord.

Making One's Calling and Election Sure

3 His divine power has given us everything we need for life
and godliness through our knowledge of him who called us by his
own glory and goodness. 4 Through these he has given us his very
great and precious promises, so that through them you may participate in the divine nature and escape the corruption in the
world caused by evil desires.
5 For this very reason, make every effort to add to your faith
goodness; and to goodness, knowledge; 6 and to knowledge, self-
control; and to self-control, perseverance; and to perseverance,
godliness; 7 and to godliness, brotherly kindness; and to brotherly
kindness, love. 8 For if you possess these qualities in increasing
measure, they will keep you from being ineffective and unproductive in your knowledge of our Lord Jesus Christ. 9 But if anyone
does not have them, he is nearsighted and blind, and has forgotten
that he has been cleansed from his past sins.
10 Therefore, my brothers, be all the more eager to make your
calling and election sure. For if you do these things, you will never
fall, 11 and you will receive a rich welcome into the eternal kingdom
of our Lord and Savior Jesus Christ.

Teacher and Pupils, scene sculpted on a gravestone, around A.D. 185. In the Greek and Roman world most children were taught by tutors, teachers who took on one or two pupils at a time. The qualities listed in 1:5-7 are ones that teachers knowledgeable in Greek philosophy would have taught their students. SECOND PETER uses similar language to encourage the followers of Christ to keep growing so that they can show that what they know about the Lord Jesus Christ has made their lives useful and meaningful (1:8).

Prophecy of Scripture

12So I will always remind you of these things, even though
you know them and are firmly established in the truth you now
have. 13I think it is right to refresh your memory as long as I live in
the tent of this body, 14because I know that I will soon put it aside,
as our Lord Jesus Christ has made clear to me. 15And I will make
every effort to see that after my departure you will always be able
to remember these things.

16We did not follow cleverly invented stories when we told
you about the power and coming of our Lord Jesus Christ, but we
were eyewitnesses of his majesty. 17For he received honor and glory
from God the Father when the voice came to him from the Majestic Glory, saying, "This is my Son, whom I love; with him I am well
pleased."[a] 18We ourselves heard this voice that came from heaven
when we were with him on the sacred mountain.

19And we have the word of the prophets made more certain,
and you will do well to pay attention to it, as to a light shining in
a dark place, until the day dawns and the morning star rises in
your hearts. 20Above all, you must understand that no prophecy of
Scripture came about by the prophet's own interpretation. 21For
prophecy never had its origin in the will of man, but men spoke
from God as they were carried along by the Holy Spirit.

1:12 *truth:* This refers to the truth about Jesus Christ that prophets and apostles have made known (3:1, 2).

1:13,14 *tent of this body . . . put it aside:* Describing the body as a "tent" follows the Greek idea that the physical body is a temporary building, which is left behind when a person dies (see also 2 Cor 5:1-5). Compare this to Paul's teaching in 1 Cor 15.

1:16 *coming of our Lord:* See the note at 1 Pet 1:5 and the mini-articles called "Day of the LORD," p. 1727 and "Second Coming," p. 2277.

1:19-21 *prophets . . . men spoke from God:* Just as the Jewish prophets spoke by the Holy Spirit, believers can understand what the Scriptures mean with God's help. See also the note at 1 Pet 1:10.

1:19 *until the day dawns and the morning star rises:* The coming of dawn refers to the new day that Christ will bring when he returns. The Greek word translated as "morning star" can also be translated "light-bringer." The New Testament describes Jesus as the true light (John 3:19-21) and the bright Morning Star (Rev 22:16). The author may have had Numbers 24:17 in mind when using this image to describe Jesus.

Watch Out for False Prophets and False Teachers

Christians are warned to be on guard against false prophets and false teachers who "introduce destructive heresies" (2:1). The Lord will be hard on these people, and their evil actions will be rewarded with evil (2:13).

False Teachers and Their Destruction

2 But there were also false prophets among the people, just as
there will be false teachers among you. They will secretly introduce destructive heresies, even denying the sovereign Lord who
bought them—bringing swift destruction on themselves. 2Many
will follow their shameful ways and will bring the way of truth
into disrepute. 3In their greed these teachers will exploit you
with stories they have made up. Their condemnation has long
been hanging over them, and their destruction has not been
sleeping.

4For if God did not spare angels when they sinned, but sent
them to hell,[b] putting them into gloomy dungeons[c] to be held for

2:1 *there were also false prophets:* The Jewish Scriptures (Old Testament) often mention false prophets, who encouraged the people of Israel to disobey God's commands (see 1 Kgs 18:1-39; Jer 14:13-16).

2:1 *sovereign Lord:* Meaning Jesus Christ, who died as a sacrifice to forgive the sins of all people (Rom 3:25, 26; Heb 2:14-18).

2:4 *angels when they sinned . . . hell:* This may refer to the angels who liked the human women on earth so much that they came down and had sex with them (Gen 6:1,2; Jude 6). See also the mini-article called "Hell," p. 1944.

[a]17 Matt. 17:5; Mark 9:7; Luke 9:35 [b]4 Greek *Tartarus* [c]4 Some manuscripts *into chains of darkness*

judgment; 5 if he did not spare the ancient world when he brought
the flood on its ungodly people, but protected Noah, a preacher of
righteousness, and seven others; 6 if he condemned the cities of
Sodom and Gomorrah by burning them to ashes, and made them
an example of what is going to happen to the ungodly; 7 and if he
rescued Lot, a righteous man, who was distressed by the filthy lives
of lawless men 8 (for that righteous man, living among them day
after day, was tormented in his righteous soul by the lawless deeds
he saw and heard)— 9 if this is so, then the Lord knows how to rescue godly men from trials and to hold the unrighteous for the day
of judgment, while continuing their punishment.[a] 10 This is especially true of those who follow the corrupt desire of the sinful
nature[b] and despise authority.

Bold and arrogant, these men are not afraid to slander celestial beings; 11 yet even angels, although they are stronger and more
powerful, do not bring slanderous accusations against such beings
in the presence of the Lord. 12 But these men blaspheme in matters
they do not understand. They are like brute beasts, creatures of
instinct, born only to be caught and destroyed, and like beasts they
too will perish.

13 They will be paid back with harm for the harm they have
done. Their idea of pleasure is to carouse in broad daylight. They
are blots and blemishes, reveling in their pleasures while they feast
with you.[c] 14 With eyes full of adultery, they never stop sinning;
they seduce the unstable; they are experts in greed—an accursed
brood! 15 They have left the straight way and wandered off to follow the way of Balaam son of Beor, who loved the wages of
wickedness. 16 But he was rebuked for his wrongdoing by a donkey—a beast without speech—who spoke with a man's voice and
restrained the prophet's madness.

17 These men are springs without water and mists driven by
a storm. Blackest darkness is reserved for them. 18 For they mouth
empty, boastful words and, by appealing to the lustful desires of
sinful human nature, they entice people who are just escaping
from those who live in error. 19 They promise them freedom, while
they themselves are slaves of depravity—for a man is a slave to
whatever has mastered him. 20 If they have escaped the corruption
of the world by knowing our Lord and Savior Jesus Christ and are
again entangled in it and overcome, they are worse off at the end
than they were at the beginning. 21 It would have been better for
them not to have known the way of righteousness, than to have
known it and then to turn their backs on the sacred command that
was passed on to them. 22 Of them the proverbs are true: "A dog
returns to its vomit,"[d] and, "A sow that is washed goes back to her
wallowing in the mud."

[a]9 Or *unrighteous for punishment until the day of judgment* [b]10 Or *the flesh*
[c]13 Some manuscripts *in their love feasts* [d]22 Prov. 26:11

2:6 *Sodom and Gomorrah:* Cities destroyed because the people there were so evil (Gen 19:24).

2:7 *Lot:* Lot went to live in the valley near Sodom after separating from his uncle Abraham (Gen 13:1-13; 19:1-16).

2:9 *day of judgment:* See the note at 1 Pet 1:5 and the mini-articles called "Day of the LORD," p. 1727 and "Second Coming," p. 2277.

2:10 *celestial beings:* This may refer to the angels (2:4).

2:13 *they feast with you:* This may refer to the "love feasts" (*agape* meals) celebrated by early Christians (Luke 22:14-20). Their shameful behavior showed that they misunderstood what the Lord's Supper was all about (see also 1 Cor 11:23-34).

2:15,16 *Balaam:* King Balak of Moab hired the prophet Balaam to curse the people of Israel (Num 22:4-35).

2:19 *They promise them freedom:* Some of the false teachers may have been twisting the truth about Christian freedom (3:16). The apostle Paul taught that Christians are free because of Christ, but this did not mean that they could use this freedom to do anything they felt like doing (see Gal 5:13). See also John 8:31-36; Rom 6:16.

2:20 *corruption of the world:* See the note at 1:4.

2:21 *sacred command:* This may refer to the commandment to love God and love one's neighbor (Mark 12:28-31) or to the Ten Commandments (Exod 20:1-17; Deut 5:1-21).

2:5 Gen 6:1—7:24. **2:22** Prov 26:11.

Be Ready, Because the Lord Will Return

The final chapter of this letter focuses on the day of Christ's return, which God has delayed in order to give more time for everyone to repent of their sins (3:9). Christians are not to be upset by people who scoff at them because this event has not already occurred. When the Lord returns he will bring a new heaven and earth (3:13).

The Day of the Lord

3 Dear friends, this is now my second letter to you. I have written both of them as reminders to stimulate you to wholesome
thinking. [2]I want you to recall the words spoken in the past by the
holy prophets and the command given by our Lord and Savior
through your apostles.
[3]First of all, you must understand that in the last days
scoffers will come, scoffing and following their own evil desires.

3:1 *my second letter:* The letter known as 1 PETER had already been passed around the churches. See the Introduction to 1 PETER, p. 2368.

3:2 *prophets . . . apostles:* See the note at 1:19-21. "Apostles" refers to the earliest followers of Jesus who were chosen to spread the message about Jesus. The "command given by our Lord and Savior" probably refers to the command to love (see the note at 2:21).

3:2 *Lord and Savior:* See the notes at 1:1 (God and Savior) and 1:8.

3:3 *the last days:* See the note at 1:16. See also Jude 18; 2 Tim 3:1-8.

FIRE

Fire is important in the Bible in at least four different ways:

(1) *Fire is one sign that God is present.* Examples of this in the Jewish Scriptures (Old Testament) are the burning bush from which God spoke to Moses (Exod 3:2); the pillar of fire that led Israel through the desert at night (Exod 13:21, 22); and God's appearance to Moses and the people on Mount Sinai (Exod 19:18; 24:17,18; Deut 4:11,35,36). In the New Testament, when Christ's followers were filled with the Holy Spirit on the day of Pentecost, what seemed to be tongues of fire came to rest on each of them (Acts 2:1-4). And when John sees Jesus in Revelation 1:14,15, "his eyes were like blazing fire" and "his feet were like bronze glowing in a furnace." The prophets of Israel expected God to appear surrounded by fire (Isa 4:5), to appear in fire (Isa 66:15), or to be seated on a throne surrounded by fire (Dan 7:9,10).

(2) *Fire was important in the worship of God in Israel's temple.* The flame that burned on the altar was a reminder that God was always present there (Lev 6:12,13). Fire was used to burn incense or to make offerings (Lev 6:14,15).

(3) *God would use fire to punish wicked people.* This was true at Sodom and Gomorrah (Gen 19:24,25) and when God punished Achan for taking items from the destroyed city of Jericho (Josh 7:15). Fire is a symbol of God's anger (Ps 79:5; 89:46), and God will use it to punish sin and evil in the future (Deut 32:22; Isa 50:10,11; 66:15,16; Amos 7:4). The evil powers will be destroyed by fire at the end of the age (Dan 7:11; Mal 4:1). Both John the Baptist and Jesus announce that the fire of judgment will fall on the earth and its wicked people (Matt 3:11,12; 13:37-42; Luke 17:29,30). God's final judgment of the evil world includes punishment by fire (2 Pet 3:7). This is pictured in detail in REVELATION (Rev 8:7; 9:18; 11:5; 14:9,10; 19:20; 20:9-15).

(4) *God will use fire to purify his people.* Often such purifying (or testing) is experienced by facing life's trials (Ps 66:12; Isa 43:2; 1 Pet 1:7). And God's judgment in the future will also purify God's people by fire (Zech 13:9; 1 Cor 3:12-15).

3:4 *since our fathers died:* This may refer to the apostles who were the very first generation of leaders in the church. The apostle Paul, for example, believed strongly that the Lord would return soon, perhaps in his own lifetime (Phil 4:5; 1 Thes 4:13-18).

The false teachers may have taught that God did not get directly involved in the lives of human beings and therefore Jesus would not return to change anything.

3:7 *reserved for fire . . . day of judgment:* See the note at 1 Pet 1:5 and the mini-articles called "Day of the LORD," p. 1727 and "Second Coming," p. 2277. See the note at 2:4.

3:9 *The Lord is not slow:* See the note at 3:4. See also Joel 2:12-14; Jonah 3:7-9; 4:2; Rom 2:4.

3:10 *day of the Lord . . . fire:* See the note at 1 Pet 1:5. See also Isa 66:15-18; Zeph 1:18; Mal 4:1; 1 Cor 3:12, 13; and the mini-article called "Fire," p. 2383.

3:13 *a new heaven and a new earth:* This idea can also be found in Isaiah 65:17; 66:22; and Revelation 21:1.

3:5 Gen 1:6-9. **3:6** Gen 6:17; 7:11,12. **3:8** Ps 90:4. **3:10** Matt 24:43; Luke 12:39; 1 Thes 5:2; Rev 16:15. **3:15** Rom 2:4; 2 Pet 3:9.

4They will say, "Where is this 'coming' he promised? Ever since our
fathers died, everything goes on as it has since the beginning of
creation." 5But they deliberately forget that long ago by God's word
the heavens existed and the earth was formed out of water and by
water. 6By these waters also the world of that time was deluged and
destroyed. 7By the same word the present heavens and earth are
reserved for fire, being kept for the day of judgment and destruction of ungodly men.

8But do not forget this one thing, dear friends: With the
Lord a day is like a thousand years, and a thousand years are like a
day. 9The Lord is not slow in keeping his promise, as some understand slowness. He is patient with you, not wanting anyone to perish, but everyone to come to repentance.

10But the day of the Lord will come like a thief. The heavens
will disappear with a roar; the elements will be destroyed by fire,
and the earth and everything in it will be laid bare.[a]

11Since everything will be destroyed in this way, what kind
of people ought you to be? You ought to live holy and godly lives
12as you look forward to the day of God and speed its coming.[b]
That day will bring about the destruction of the heavens by fire,
and the elements will melt in the heat. 13But in keeping with his
promise we are looking forward to a new heaven and a new earth,
the home of righteousness.

14So then, dear friends, since you are looking forward to this,
make every effort to be found spotless, blameless and at peace with
him. 15Bear in mind that our Lord's patience means salvation, just
as our dear brother Paul also wrote you with the wisdom that God
gave him. 16He writes the same way in all his letters, speaking in
them of these matters. His letters contain some things that are

[a]10 Some manuscripts *be burned up* [b]12 Or *as you wait eagerly for the day of God to come*

QUESTIONS ABOUT 2 PETER

1. How were the readers of 2 PETER encouraged to keep growing in their faith? (1:5-8) What is the purpose for growing in faith? (1:10,11)
2. What false teachings and immoral things did the followers of Christ face? (2:1-3, 10-22) What false teachings and immoral things are present in today's culture? Do these sorts of things go on where you live? If so, how are people, and churches in particular, dealing with these false and immoral things?
3. Why did some people make fun of their Christian neighbors who expected Jesus to return during their lifetime? (3:3,4) According to 2 PETER, why has God been patient about bringing the day of judgment? (3:8,9)
4. What will the day of the Lord's return be like? (3:10-13) Do you look forward to the day of the Lord's return? Why or why not?
5. How are Christ's followers to act as they wait for his return? (3:14-18)

hard to understand, which ignorant and unstable people distort, as they do the other Scriptures, to their own destruction.

[17]Therefore, dear friends, since you already know this, be on your guard so that you may not be carried away by the error of lawless men and fall from your secure position. [18]But grow in the grace and knowledge of our Lord and Savior Jesus Christ. To him be glory both now and forever! Amen.

3:15,16 *Paul . . . all his letters . . . Scriptures:* This mention of Paul in 2 PETER is early evidence that Paul's letters were read widely by the early church and considered to be Scripture on equal footing with the Jewish Scriptures. See also the Introduction to 2 PETER.

Those who were distorting what Paul taught may have used his teaching on freedom from the law (Rom 3:27-31; Gal 5:1) as an excuse to do anything they wanted (see the note at 2:19). Or they may have argued that Paul was wrong in teaching that the Lord would soon come back (Rom 13:11, 12; Phil 4:5; 1 Thes 4:15; and see the note at 3:4).

1 JOHN

Who are the children of God and who are the children of the devil? Read 1 JOHN and find out.

WHAT MAKES 1 JOHN SPECIAL?

Though 1 JOHN is called a letter, it does not have many of the features of a typical ancient Greek letter. For example, it does not have a formal greeting. Because it calls Jesus the "Word" and emphasizes that Christians should love one another, 1 JOHN has always been linked with the Gospel of John. See the Introduction to JOHN, p. 2041. The book also provides a look at how the early church dealt with disagreements between true followers of Jesus and those who had false ideas.

WHY WAS 1 JOHN WRITTEN?

FIRST JOHN and the other letters of JOHN seem to have been written to encourage the followers of Christ to remain faithful to the truth: Jesus, God's Son, was truly human and really shed his blood to take away sins (1:7). Some people were falsely claiming that Jesus only appeared to be a human being, but in fact he was a purely spiritual being. These teachers also believed that spiritual life was greater than moral life and spiritual knowledge was more important than moral rules. They taught that moral rules were only for those people who could not see beyond the physical level of life. For example, they believed that their spiritual rebirth made it impossible for them to sin, so they had no sins to confess (1:9,10).

Besides believing that "Jesus Christ has come in the flesh" (4:2) and is truly God's Son (2:22; 3:23), God's true children are those who also obey God and love one another (3:11-24). Only those who believe that Jesus Christ was truly both human and divine, and who love one another, really have eternal life.

WHAT'S THE STORY BEHIND THE SCENE?

The author was the apostle John (who also wrote the Gospel of JOHN). This book was probably written late in the first century, by A.D. 95. At that time the early church was trying to determine what made someone a true child of God. It was a time of many new religions. One trend among these new religions was toward Gnosticism, a movement which described the physical world as evil and the spiritual world as good. Gnostics believed that the goal of humans is to get special knowledge that would free them from the material, physical world. They claimed that this superior knowledge separated them from this corrupt world. But 1 JOHN shows that God made the world and sent Jesus to give God's children victory over the evil of the fallen world.

Light and darkness: Jesus called himself "the light of the world" (John 8:12). Because Jesus is one with God, then God is also "light." The Jewish Scriptures (Old Testament) refer to God as "light" (Ps 27:1; 139:11,12). In the Bible, light is used to describe God or God's word (Ps 119:105; John 1:3,4), and those people or things that reveal God's truth (Isa 49:6). The followers of Jesus are also called "children of light" (Eph 5:8) or "the light of the world" (Matt 5:14).

Darkness refers to places of pain and suffering (Ps 107:10) or confusion (Eccl 2:13,14). God's opponents are called the rulers of "this dark world" (Eph 6:12), and those who do not do what God expects may be thrown "outside, into the darkness" (Matt 22:13), a place of everlasting sadness. Here, those who live in the dark are lying and not living according to the truth (1:6).

The stained-glass window shown here, from the Church of St. Madeleine in Troyes, France, depicts God creating light on the first day of creation (Gen 1:3-5).

the evil one: FIRST JOHN uses this term to refer to the devil, whose name means "the accuser" (see 2:18). The devil is also known as Satan, meaning "adversary." The evil one is the leader of the forces in the world that are against God and God's people. God sent Jesus to defeat the devil and the powers of evil (see 3:7,8).

How is 1 John constructed?

The book does not have a formal opening greeting or closing greeting, though it was likely intended to be a letter (1:4). The book may be outlined in the following way:

Living in the light (1:1—2:17)

The devil's children and God's children (2:18—3:10)

Love that comes from God (3:11—4:21)

Faith that brings victory over the world (5:1-21)

Living in the Light

This letter begins by describing how God's Word came to earth in the flesh. The Word (Jesus Christ) was witnessed by people who actually saw, heard, and touched him. God's people are to live in the light by confessing their sins (1:8-10) and by following the example of Christ (2:5). True followers obey God by loving others with the kind of love that comes from Christ, who makes God's old message into a new commandment.

The Word of Life

1 That which was from the beginning, which we have heard, which
we have seen with our eyes, which we have looked at and our hands
have touched—this we proclaim concerning the Word of life. [2]The life
appeared; we have seen it and testify to it, and we proclaim to you the
eternal life, which was with the Father and has appeared to us. [3]We
proclaim to you what we have seen and heard, so that you also may
have fellowship with us. And our fellowship is with the Father and
with his Son, Jesus Christ. [4]We write this to make our[a] joy complete.

Walking in the Light

[5]This is the message we have heard from him and declare to
you: God is light; in him there is no darkness at all. [6]If we claim to
have fellowship with him yet walk in the darkness, we lie and do
not live by the truth. [7]But if we walk in the light, as he is in the
light, we have fellowship with one another, and the blood of Jesus,
his Son, purifies us from all[b] sin.

[8]If we claim to be without sin, we deceive ourselves and the
truth is not in us. [9]If we confess our sins, he is faithful and just and
will forgive us our sins and purify us from all unrighteousness. [10]If
we claim we have not sinned, we make him out to be a liar and his
word has no place in our lives.

2 My dear children, I write this to you so that you will not sin.
But if anybody does sin, we have one who speaks to the Father in

[a]4 Some manuscripts *your* [b]7 Or *every*

1:1 *the Word of life:* The Greek word translated here as "Word" also means "reason" or "purpose." Here the "Word" refers to Jesus Christ, who brings life. Jesus was truly God because he was present with God at the time of creation (John 1:2), but he also came as a human being who could be seen and touched and heard.

1:2 *eternal life:* "Eternal life" here refers to Christ Jesus himself, and to God's promise that those who have faith in Jesus will live forever with God. See also the mini-article called "Eternal Life," p. 2072.

1:2 *Father:* In the Gospel of John, Jesus often refers to God as his Father (3:35; 5:21-29; 15:1,16; 17:1-26). By calling God his Father, Jesus claims a special relationship with God.

1:3 *his Son, Jesus Christ:* By calling Jesus God's "Son," John shows how close Jesus was to God. The word "Christ" is a title that means "Messiah" or "chosen one."

1:6 *fellowship with him yet walk in the darkness:* Though Jesus died and was raised from death in order to defeat sin and death, his followers need to continue to confess their sins. This true teaching about Jesus is in contrast to the false teaching that Jesus was not really human and that his followers were free to live however they wished.

1:7 *blood of Jesus:* The New Testament teaches that God gave his Son as a sacrifice for sins (see Acts 2:23; Rom 3:25,26; Heb 2:16,17; 9:25,26). That Jesus actually shed blood means that he was truly human.

1:10 *If we claim we have not sinned:* Apparently some false teachers had been saying that it was not necessary for Jesus' followers to confess their sins. These persons may have taught that moral rules were only for those people who could not see beyond the physical level of life. They believed that their superior spiritual understanding made it impossible for them to sin, and so they had no sins to confess.

1:1,2 John 1:1-3,14.

our defense—Jesus Christ, the Righteous One. 2 He is the atoning
sacrifice for our sins, and not only for ours but also for[a] the sins of
the whole world.

3 We know that we have come to know him if we obey his
commands. 4 The man who says, "I know him," but does not do
what he commands is a liar, and the truth is not in him. 5 But if
anyone obeys his word, God's love[b] is truly made complete in him.
This is how we know we are in him: 6 Whoever claims to live in
him must walk as Jesus did.

7 Dear friends, I am not writing you a new command but an
old one, which you have had since the beginning. This old command is the message you have heard. 8 Yet I am writing you a new
command; its truth is seen in him and you, because the darkness
is passing and the true light is already shining.

9 Anyone who claims to be in the light but hates his brother
is still in the darkness. 10 Whoever loves his brother lives in the
light, and there is nothing in him[c] to make him stumble. 11 But
whoever hates his brother is in the darkness and walks around in
the darkness; he does not know where he is going, because the
darkness has blinded him.

12 I write to you, dear children,
because your sins have been forgiven on account of his name.
13 I write to you, fathers,
because you have known him who is from the beginning.
I write to you, young men,
because you have overcome the evil one.
I write to you, dear children,
because you have known the Father.
14 I write to you, fathers,
because you have known him who is from the beginning.
I write to you, young men,
because you are strong,
and the word of God lives in you,
and you have overcome the evil one.

Do Not Love the World

15 Do not love the world or anything in the world. If anyone
loves the world, the love of the Father is not in him. 16 For everything in the world—the cravings of sinful man, the lust of his eyes
and the boasting of what he has and does—comes not from the
Father but from the world. 17 The world and its desires pass away,
but the man who does the will of God lives forever.

[a]2 Or *He is the one who turns aside God's wrath, taking away our sins, and not only ours but also* [b]5 Or *word, love for God* [c]10 Or *it*

2:2 *He is the atoning sacrifice:* Jesus' death was a sacrifice that removes sins.

2:7 *command . . . an old one:* This is the command that Jesus gave his disciples in John 13:34,35. It builds on the old commandment from the Law of Moses: "Love your neighbor as yourself" (Lev 19:18).

2:13 *him who is from the beginning:* The Word, Jesus.

2:15 *world:* In the Gospel of John, "world" sometimes refers to the people who live in this world and to the evil forces that control it (John 8:23). In these verses, things like foolish pride and selfish desires are said to come from the world (2:16). This understanding of the world being the source of evil was not far from the philosophy of the false teachers (see the note at 1:10).

2:17 *lives forever:* See the note at 1:2 (eternal life). Those who continue to obey God will receive this promise.

2:18 *the last hour . . . many antichrists:* The "last hour" probably refers to the time when God will make the final judgment. False teachings will be widespread during this time (see also 2 Pet 3:3; 2 Thes 2:1-12; 2 Tim 3:1-9; 4:3,4). The Greek word translated "antichrist" is unique to 1, 2, and 3 John. Literally it means "against Christ." Although John warns against a coming great enemy of Christ, he warns readers to be alert to the false teachings of many lesser enemies of Christ, who have already appeared (1 John 2:18,22; 4:3; 2 John 7). See also 2 Thes 2:1-12 and Rev 12–14.

2:19 *They went out from us, but they did not really belong to us:* Christ's enemies, the antichrists (2:18), had been part of the church, but had left. They were denying that Jesus was truly Christ, God's chosen one (2:22). They also may have been claiming that it was impossible for them to sin (see the note at 1:10) and saying that Jesus did not really have a human body (4:2).

The Devil's Children and God's Children

The letter next turns to warnings about enemies of Christ, whose false beliefs make them the devil's children (3:10). Some of these enemies had once been part of the true followers of Christ, but now they have left. The true followers, God's children, are told not to let these enemies mislead them, but to listen only to the Holy Spirit who is their teacher and the life-giving power they need to keep them from sinning.

Warning Against Antichrists

[18]Dear children, this is the last hour; and as you have heard
that the antichrist is coming, even now many antichrists have
come. This is how we know it is the last hour. [19]They went out
from us, but they did not really belong to us. For if they had
belonged to us, they would have remained with us; but their going
showed that none of them belonged to us.

[20]But you have an anointing from the Holy One, and all of
you know the truth.[a] [21]I do not write to you because you do not
know the truth, but because you do know it and because no lie
comes from the truth. [22]Who is the liar? It is the man who denies
that Jesus is the Christ. Such a man is the antichrist—he denies the
Father and the Son. [23]No one who denies the Son has the Father;
whoever acknowledges the Son has the Father also.

[24]See that what you have heard from the beginning remains
in you. If it does, you also will remain in the Son and in the Father.
[25]And this is what he promised us—even eternal life.

[26]I am writing these things to you about those who are trying to lead you astray. [27]As for you, the anointing you received
from him remains in you, and you do not need anyone to teach
you. But as his anointing teaches you about all things and as that
anointing is real, not counterfeit—just as it has taught you, remain
in him.

Children of God

[28]And now, dear children, continue in him, so that when he
appears we may be confident and unashamed before him at his
coming.

[29]If you know that he is righteous, you know that everyone
who does what is right has been born of him.

3 How great is the love the Father has lavished on us, that we
should be called children of God! And that is what we are! The
reason the world does not know us is that it did not know him.
[2]Dear friends, now we are children of God, and what we will be
has not yet been made known. But we know that when he

2:20 *an anointing:* May refer to the ceremony of pouring olive oil on the followers of the Lord before they were baptized, or to the gift of the Holy Spirit which they were given at baptism (see 2:27).

2:20 *Holy One:* The word "holy" means to be set apart for the purpose of serving God. See also the mini-article called "Holiness," p. 1626.

2:21 *truth:* See the note at 1:6.

2:22 *Father and the Son:* See the notes at 1:2 (Father) and 1:3.

2:24 *remain in the Son:* To remain in the Son and in the Father means that true believers let God's message (truth) fill their thoughts and affect their actions. They also openly say that Jesus is the Son of God (4:15).

2:26 *those who are trying to lead you astray:* See the notes at 1:10 and 2:19.

2:27 *the anointing you received:* See the note at 2:20 (anointing). The anointing from the Spirit helps people to serve one another in the church and bring the gospel of Jesus to others (see 1 Cor 12:1-11). See also the mini-article called "Holy Spirit," p. 2082.

2:28 *dear children:* John uses the term "children" for all the true followers of Jesus, regardless of their age.

3:1 *the world does not know us:* See the note at 2:15.

3:2 *when he appears, we shall be like him:* See the mini-article called "Second Coming," p. 2277. See also Rom 8:28-30; 1 Cor 15:12-55.

2:23 John 14:7-13. **2:29** 1 John 3:7,9. **3:1** John 1:10-12.

[a]**20** Some manuscripts *and you know all things*

This is the message you heard from the beginning: We should love one another.
1 John 3:11

3:4 *breaks the law:* See the note at 1:7. To break God's law here may refer to breaking the Law of Moses as found in the Torah (Pentateuch), or it may refer to the lawless behavior the apostle Paul describes in Romans 1:18-32.

3:8 *the devil:* See the note on p. 2386 (the evil one).

3:9 *God's seed remains in him:* This may refer to the Holy Spirit who is in all who are God's children (2:27-29).

3:12 *Cain . . . murdered his brother:* See Gen 4:1-16.

3:15 *eternal life:* See the note at 1:2 (eternal life).

3:19 *the truth:* See the notes at 1:6 and 1:7.

3:23 *believe . . . love:* Faith is belief and trust in Jesus Christ as God's Son and as the Savior of the world. See the mini-article called "Faith," p. 1932. The importance of love can also be seen in the Gospel of JOHN (John 13:34,35; 15:12-17) where Jesus tells his disciples to love one another with the kind of love he has shown for them.

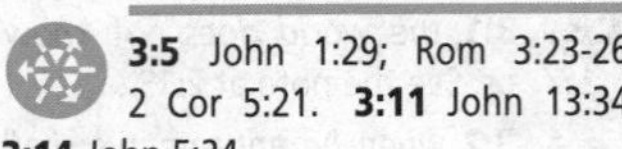

3:5 John 1:29; Rom 3:23-26; 2 Cor 5:21. **3:11** John 13:34. **3:14** John 5:24.

appears,[a] we shall be like him, for we shall see him as he is. 3 Everyone who has this hope in him purifies himself, just as he is pure.
4 Everyone who sins breaks the law; in fact, sin is lawlessness.
5 But you know that he appeared so that he might take away our
sins. And in him is no sin. 6 No one who lives in him keeps on sinning. No one who continues to sin has either seen him or known
him.
7 Dear children, do not let anyone lead you astray. He who
does what is right is righteous, just as he is righteous. 8 He who
does what is sinful is of the devil, because the devil has been sinning from the beginning. The reason the Son of God appeared was
to destroy the devil's work. 9 No one who is born of God will continue to sin, because God's seed remains in him; he cannot go on
sinning, because he has been born of God. 10 This is how we know
who the children of God are and who the children of the devil are:
Anyone who does not do what is right is not a child of God; nor is
anyone who does not love his brother.

Love that Comes from God

Christians know what God's love is because Jesus gave his life for them (3:16). They are to show this same love for others by helping them. Their love for each other shows that they follow the example of Christ and belong to the truth (3:19) and that they have been given new life (4:7).

Love One Another

11 This is the message you heard from the beginning: We
should love one another. 12 Do not be like Cain, who belonged to
the evil one and murdered his brother. And why did he murder
him? Because his own actions were evil and his brother's were
righteous. 13 Do not be surprised, my brothers, if the world hates
you. 14 We know that we have passed from death to life, because we
love our brothers. Anyone who does not love remains in death.
15 Anyone who hates his brother is a murderer, and you know that
no murderer has eternal life in him.
16 This is how we know what love is: Jesus Christ laid down
his life for us. And we ought to lay down our lives for our brothers. 17 If anyone has material possessions and sees his brother in
need but has no pity on him, how can the love of God be in him?
18 Dear children, let us not love with words or tongue but with
actions and in truth. 19 This then is how we know that we belong to
the truth, and how we set our hearts at rest in his presence 20 whenever our hearts condemn us. For God is greater than our hearts,
and he knows everything.

[a]2 Or *when it is made known*

21Dear friends, if our hearts do not condemn us, we have
confidence before God 22and receive from him anything we ask,
because we obey his commands and do what pleases him. 23And
this is his command: to believe in the name of his Son, Jesus
Christ, and to love one another as he commanded us. 24Those
who obey his commands live in him, and he in them. And this is
how we know that he lives in us: We know it by the Spirit he
gave us.

3:24 *live in him, and he in them:* See the note at 2:24.
3:24 *the Spirit:* See 2:27.

3:22 Matt 7:7-11; 21:22.

LOVE

In the Old Testament "love" has many meanings. As in the modern world, it describes the strong attraction and powerful feelings experienced by men and women in their relationships with one another (Gen 24:67; 29:20; Song 1–8). Other Old Testament stories describe love among family members (Gen 25:27,28; Ruth 1:1-18), between friends (2 Sam 1:26), and between slaves and their owners (Deut 15:16,17). Above all, the people of Israel are to love God (Deut 6:5), their neighbors, including friends and relatives (Lev 19:18), as well as strangers who are in the land (Deut 10:17-19).

Some prophets and poets compared God's love for his people with the love relationship between husband and wife. The deep love of a bride and groom in the SONG OF SONGS was understood by some to describe the deep love of God for his people. Hosea said that Israel's failure to obey God was like a woman who was unfaithful to her husband (Hos 2), but that God would act to rebuild this broken relationship (Hos 3). Hosea also describes God's love as being like the love of a parent for a child (Hos 11). Similarly, Isaiah compares the love of God for his people with that of a mother for her child (Isa 49).

In the Gospels, Jesus taught his followers to follow the commands to love God and love their neighbors as they love themselves (Mark 12:28-33; Matt 22:34-40). In LUKE, when Jesus was asked to explain what this meant, he answered by telling a story about a Samaritan who went out of his way to help a wounded stranger (Luke 10:29-37). In JOHN clear attention is given both to God's love for the world (John 3:16) and to the love that members of the community of Christ's followers are to have for each other (13:34,35). In Jesus' famous "Sermon on the Mount," Jesus tells his disciples that they are even to love their enemies, since this is what God does (Matt 5:43-48).

The apostle Paul says that it was because of love that God sent Christ to die for us (Rom 5:5-8), and that nothing can separate us from God's love (Rom 8:31-39). Paul also says God's Spirit is at work among his people to make God's love work in their lives (Gal 5:22). In his famous words about love, Paul says that love is not just a feeling, but a way of acting toward others, and requires a change of attitude (1 Cor 13). Love is to be the main guide for one's life (1 Cor 14:1; Rom 13:8-10).

In the New Testament, the most common Greek word for love is *agape*, which is self-giving love. Two other words are often translated into English as love. One is *eros*, meaning sexual desire. This term is not used anywhere in the New Testament. The other is *phileo*, meaning either friendship and family affection (Matt 10:37), or wanting a good reputation (Matt 6:5; Luke 20:46). But in both the Old and New Testaments, the kind of love that God calls his people to have is love that reaches out to help others, even one's enemies. This is what God has done in Christ, and what his people are to do in the world.

Test the Spirits

4 Dear friends, do not believe every spirit, but test the spirits to
see whether they are from God, because many false prophets have
gone out into the world. 2 This is how you can recognize the Spirit
of God: Every spirit that acknowledges that Jesus Christ has come
in the flesh is from God, 3 but every spirit that does not acknowledge Jesus is not from God. This is the spirit of the antichrist,
which you have heard is coming and even now is already in the
world.

4 You, dear children, are from God and have overcome them,
because the one who is in you is greater than the one who is in the
world. 5 They are from the world and therefore speak from the
viewpoint of the world, and the world listens to them. 6 We are
from God, and whoever knows God listens to us; but whoever is
not from God does not listen to us. This is how we recognize the
Spirit[a] of truth and the spirit of falsehood.

God's Love and Ours

7 Dear friends, let us love one another, for love comes from
God. Everyone who loves has been born of God and knows God.
8 Whoever does not love does not know God, because God is love.
9 This is how God showed his love among us: He sent his one and
only Son[b] into the world that we might live through him. 10 This is
love: not that we loved God, but that he loved us and sent his Son
as an atoning sacrifice for[c] our sins. 11 Dear friends, since God so
loved us, we also ought to love one another. 12 No one has ever seen
God; but if we love one another, God lives in us and his love is
made complete in us.

13 We know that we live in him and he in us, because he has
given us of his Spirit. 14 And we have seen and testify that the
Father has sent his Son to be the Savior of the world. 15 If anyone
acknowledges that Jesus is the Son of God, God lives in him and he
in God. 16 And so we know and rely on the love God has for us.

God is love. Whoever lives in love lives in God, and God in
him. 17 In this way, love is made complete among us so that we will
have confidence on the day of judgment, because in this world we
are like him. 18 There is no fear in love. But perfect love drives out
fear, because fear has to do with punishment. The one who fears is
not made perfect in love.

19 We love because he first loved us. 20 If anyone says, "I love
God," yet hates his brother, he is a liar. For anyone who does not
love his brother, whom he has seen, cannot love God, whom he has
not seen. 21 And he has given us this command: Whoever loves God
must also love his brother.

[a]6 Or *spirit* [b]9 Or *his only begotten Son* [c]10 Or *as the one who would turn aside his wrath, taking away*

This is love: not that we loved God, but that he loved us and sent his Son as an atoning sacrifice for our sins.
1 John 4:10

4:1,2 *false prophets . . . Christ has come in the flesh:* This likely refers to the false teachers who were denying that Jesus was truly a human being. Even though they claimed to have the Spirit of God, they really were one with the spirit of the antichrist (see the notes at 2:18 and 2:19).

4:4 *the one who is in the world:* See the note at 2:15.

4:10 *sent his Son as an atoning sacrifice for our sins:* See the note at 1:7.

4:16 *love God has for us:* See John 3:16 and the note at 1:7.

4:17 *the day of judgment:* See the mini-article called "Second Coming," p. 2277.

4:21 *Whoever loves God must also love his brother:* See Deut 6:5 and Lev 19:18. These commandments from the Law of Moses are the basis for Jesus' new commandment to love (Matt 22:34-40).

4:9 John 3:16. **4:12** John 1:18. **4:16** 1 John 2:24.

The Crucifixion, fifteenth century painted carving from Norwich Cathedral, England. When the soldier pierced Jesus' side as Jesus died on the cross, "blood and water" came out (John 19:34). FIRST JOHN reminds Jesus' followers of this so that they would not be taken in by false prophets who were claiming that Jesus was never really human (see 5:6).

For everyone born of God overcomes the world. This is the victory that has overcome the world, even our faith.
1 John 5:4

5:1 *Jesus is the Christ . . . his child:* See the notes at 1:3 and 2:28. Just as God has chosen Jesus, so Jesus has chosen his followers to be God's children.

5:4 *world . . . faith:* See the notes at 2:15 and 3:23.

5:3 John 14:15; 1 John 2:5,7.

Faith that Brings Victory over the World

Faith in Jesus as the Son of God is what gives God's children victory over the evil forces of the world (5:4,5). Those who have this faith have eternal life (5:11,13), and do not have to keep on sinning (5:18).

Faith in the Son of God

5 Everyone who believes that Jesus is the Christ is born of God,
and everyone who loves the father loves his child as well. [2]This is
how we know that we love the children of God: by loving God and
carrying out his commands. [3]This is love for God: to obey his
commands. And his commands are not burdensome, [4]for everyone born of God overcomes the world. This is the victory that has
overcome the world, even our faith. [5]Who is it that overcomes the
world? Only he who believes that Jesus is the Son of God.

[6]This is the one who came by water and blood—Jesus Christ.

He did not come by water only, but by water and blood. And it is the Spirit who testifies, because the Spirit is the truth. 7 For there are three that testify: 8 the[a] Spirit, the water and the blood; and the three are in agreement. 9 We accept man's testimony, but God's testimony is greater because it is the testimony of God, which he has given about his Son. 10 Anyone who believes in the Son of God has this testimony in his heart. Anyone who does not believe God has made him out to be a liar, because he has not believed the testimony God has given about his Son. 11 And this is the testimony: God has given us eternal life, and this life is in his Son. 12 He who has the Son has life; he who does not have the Son of God does not have life.

Concluding Remarks

13 I write these things to you who believe in the name of the Son of God so that you may know that you have eternal life. 14 This is the confidence we have in approaching God: that if we ask anything according to his will, he hears us. 15 And if we know that he hears us—whatever we ask—we know that we have what we asked of him.

16 If anyone sees his brother commit a sin that does not lead to death, he should pray and God will give him life. I refer to those whose sin does not lead to death. There is a sin that leads to death. I am not saying that he should pray about that. 17 All wrongdoing is sin, and there is sin that does not lead to death.

18 We know that anyone born of God does not continue to sin; the one who was born of God keeps him safe, and the evil one cannot harm him. 19 We know that we are children of God, and that the whole world is under the control of the evil one. 20 We know also that the Son of God has come and has given us understanding, so that we may know him who is true. And we are in him who is true—even in his Son Jesus Christ. He is the true God and eternal life.

21 Dear children, keep yourselves from idols.

---

[a] 7,8 Late manuscripts of the Vulgate *testify in heaven: the Father, the Word and the Holy Spirit, and these three are one.* [8] *And there are three that testify on earth: the* (not found in any Greek manuscript before the fourteenth century)

5:6 *the Spirit:* See the note at 2:27.

5:7,8 *three . . . the Spirit, the water and the blood:* Three "witnesses" testify that God's people really belong to God. The Spirit is God's power and the helper, which Jesus said he would send to his disciples after he was taken from them (John 16:5-15). Water is connected with baptism, which Jesus experienced when he was baptized by John the Baptist (Matt 3:13-17). Baptism also shows that God's new people have washed away the sins of the old way of life and have new life in Christ (Rom 6:3-5). Blood recalls the death of Jesus on the cross (John 19:34,35), as well as the Last Supper, when Jesus said that the cup of wine he shared with his disciples was his blood, which God uses to make his covenant to forgive sins (Matt 26:27,28).

5:21 *idols:* John knew that there were many different religions that did not follow the teachings of Christ. Many of the followers of these religions worshiped false gods, such as the gods and goddesses worshiped by the Greeks and Romans. Often statues (idols) intended to depict these gods were placed in temples where they could be worshiped and where offerings could be made in their honor. For more, see the chart called "Greek and Roman Gods and Goddesses," p. 2136.

5:11 John 3:36.

QUESTIONS ABOUT 1 JOHN

1. According to 1 JOHN, what does it mean to "walk in the light"? to live "in the darkness"? (1:5-10; 2:9-11)
2. This letter reveals a number of conflicts that were happening in the early church. What seems to have caused some of these conflicts? (1:8-10; 2:18-26; 4:1-3) What conflicts do you see happening in the church today? What can Christians do to resolve these conflicts?
3. Why is it important for Christians to show love for one another? (3:7-18; 4:7-18)
4. Who are God's children? (5:1) Who has eternal life? (5:11,12)
5. Choose one verse from 1 JOHN that you think is particularly helpful or meaningful and explain why.

2 JOHN

How should God's children respond to those who attack the truth about Jesus Christ? Read 2 John and find out.

What makes 2 John special?

The book of 2 John reads like a letter with standard greetings and conclusions. It encourages Christ's followers to love each other and to obey the truth.

Why was 2 John written?

Besides encouraging the believers, the letter warns them about the false teachers who were claiming that Jesus Christ did not actually come "in the flesh" (7). John says that the believers should not welcome these deceivers into their homes.

What's the story behind the scene?

The "chosen lady" (1) and the "chosen sister" (13) probably refer to two different groups of believers rather than to two individuals. See also the Introductions to 1 John and 3 John.

How is 2 John constructed?

This short book in the style of a letter may be outlined in the following way:

Greetings (1-3)

Obeying the truth and living in love (4-13)

Greetings

John sends greetings to a group of the Lord's followers, which he calls "the chosen lady and her children."

1 The elder,

To the chosen lady and her children, whom I love in the
truth—and not I only, but also all who know the truth— 2 because
of the truth, which lives in us and will be with us forever:

3 Grace, mercy and peace from God the Father and from
Jesus Christ, the Father's Son, will be with us in truth and love.

As you have heard from the beginning, his command is that you walk in love.
2 John 6

1 *elder:* John's way of identifying himself. An "elder" (or "presbyter") was not necessarily an older person, but someone who was respected by the group of Christ's followers and chosen to be a leader in the church. See also 1 Tim 5:17-19; 1 Pet 5:1-4.

1 *the chosen lady and her children:* This letter was most likely not written to a specific woman. The "chosen lady and her children" (1) and the "children of your chosen sister" (13) are probably poetic ways of referring to churches and their members in two different cities. The writer of 2 John (most likely John the apostle) may have used this expression to protect the churches mentioned in case the letter was intercepted by someone who didn't like Christians and might have made trouble for the sender or recipient. Some early churches, however, did meet in the homes of wealthy people who had become followers of Christ (Acts 16:14,15; 1 Cor 16:19; Col 4:15; Phlm 1,2; 2 John 4,5).

2 *the truth, which lives in us:* Here "truth" probably refers to the truth about God's love revealed in Jesus, God's Son, whose blood washes away sins (1 John 1:7). This true teaching about Jesus is in contrast to the false teaching that Jesus did not really have a human body (7). See also the mini-article called "Truth," p. 2087.

3 *God the Father . . . Jesus Christ . . . Son:* In John, Jesus often refers to God as his Father (John 3:35; 5:17-30; 15:1,16; 17:1-26). The word "Christ" is a title that means "Messiah" or "Chosen One," so it can be placed before or after Jesus' name. See also the mini-articles called "Messiah (Chosen One)," p. 1124 and "Son of God," p. 2044.

7 *deceivers:* These false teachers claimed that Jesus did not really have a human body, but belonged only to the spirit world. These false teachers may have been following a set of teachings (or philosophy) called Gnosticism, which taught that the whole physical universe is evil. They argued that if Jesus was God he couldn't have been human, since humans are part of the physical universe, and so the author calls them evil. They claimed that a superior spiritual understanding would separate them from the physical world.

8 *rewarded fully:* This refers to eternal life, which is promised to those who have faith in Jesus Christ and who obey God. See John 3:16; 1 John 2:24,25; 3:15; 4:17; 5:10-12.

9 *the teaching of Christ:* Which is the "truth" (see the note at 2).

9 *the Father and the Son:* See the note at 3.

10 *do not take him into your house:* Those who followed the truth about Jesus Christ were warned not to let the false teachers (deceivers) into their homes. Just accepting them into their homes was like accepting their false message. John feared that the false teachers might cause the believers to change what they believed about Christ (9).

13 *The children of your chosen sister:* This probably means the followers of Christ who are part of a church, which the writer here calls "chosen sister."

5 John 13:34; 15:12,17.

Obeying the Truth and Living in Love

The followers of Christ are to love each other and obey the truth about Jesus, who was truly human. They are also warned against following or welcoming the false teachers who were saying that Jesus did not really have a human body.

[4]It has given me great joy to find some of your children
walking in the truth, just as the Father commanded us. [5]And now,
dear lady, I am not writing you a new command but one we have
had from the beginning. I ask that we love one another. [6]And this
is love: that we walk in obedience to his commands. As you have
heard from the beginning, his command is that you walk in love.
[7]Many deceivers, who do not acknowledge Jesus Christ as
coming in the flesh, have gone out into the world. Any such person
is the deceiver and the antichrist. [8]Watch out that you do not lose
what you have worked for, but that you may be rewarded fully.
[9]Anyone who runs ahead and does not continue in the teaching of
Christ does not have God; whoever continues in the teaching has
both the Father and the Son. [10]If anyone comes to you and does
not bring this teaching, do not take him into your house or welcome him. [11]Anyone who welcomes him shares in his wicked
work.

[12]I have much to write to you, but I do not want to use paper
and ink. Instead, I hope to visit you and talk with you face to face,
so that our joy may be complete.

[13]The children of your chosen sister send their greetings.

QUESTIONS ABOUT 2 JOHN

1. What does 2 JOHN say about love? About truth?
2. What particular lie was being passed among the Christian churches? How were God's people supposed to act toward those who were spreading this lie? (7-10).
3. How do Christians today show love for God and for others?

3 JOHN

How should Christians support those who travel around telling the gospel? Read 3 JOHN and find out.

WHAT MAKES 3 JOHN SPECIAL?

Like 2 JOHN, this short book is in the style of a letter and has a standard greeting and conclusion. However, it is written to a specific person named Gaius. It was most likely written by the apostle John.

WHY WAS 3 JOHN WRITTEN?

John offers prayers and thanks for his friend Gaius, who has been welcoming the followers of the Lord who traveled to Gaius's area with the message about Jesus. One leader of Gaius's church group named Diotrephes has been refusing to welcome any of the Lord's followers and was urging others not to welcome them either. So Gaius is encouraged to keep showing hospitality to the traveling teachers, even if Diotrephes does not.

WHAT'S THE STORY BEHIND THE SCENE?

See the Introductions to 1 JOHN and 2 JOHN for background information on this short book.

HOW IS 3 JOHN CONSTRUCTED?

The book of 3 JOHN may be outlined in the following way:

Greetings (1-4)

Showing hospitality to traveling teachers (5-14)

Greetings

[1]The elder,

To my dear friend Gaius, whom I love in the truth.

[2]Dear friend, I pray that you may enjoy good health and that
all may go well with you, even as your soul is getting along well. [3]It
gave me great joy to have some brothers come and tell about your
faithfulness to the truth and how you continue to walk in the
truth. [4]I have no greater joy than to hear that my children are
walking in the truth.

1 *elder:* The writer, whom tradition identifies as the apostle John, refers to himself as "the elder." See the note at 2 John 1.

1 *Gaius:* A believer with a reputation for obeying the truth about Jesus Christ. John may have been the one who brought Gaius to trust in Christ. The writer praises Gaius because he has encouraged his church community to welcome traveling preachers and teachers who have come to his town and to provide hospitality for them. Gaius was a common name in the Roman world. Several men with this name are mentioned in the New Testament (Acts 19:29; Rom 16:23; 1 Cor 1:14). It is unlikely that any of these men are the same person as the man being addressed by John here.

3 *faithfulness to the truth:* Gaius was faithful to the truth about Jesus by trusting that Jesus was God's Son, the Christ (Messiah). This true teaching about Jesus is in contrast to the false teaching that Jesus did not have a truly human body and was not God's Son (see 1 John 2:18-23; 4:1-3; 2 John 7). See also the mini-article called "Truth," p. 2087.

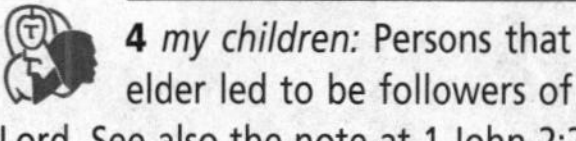

4 *my children:* Persons that the elder led to be followers of the Lord. See also the note at 1 John 2:28.

Dear friend, do not imitate what is evil but what is good. Anyone who does what is good is from God.
3 John 11

6 *send them on their way:* Probably to tell the gospel about Jesus (8).

9 *church:* The Greek word translated here as "church" is *ekklesia*, which originally referred to any kind of gathering of people. "Church" can refer to all the people of God who are followers of Jesus Christ, or it can refer to a local group of Christians known as a congregation. Here, the word means a local congregation. For more, see the mini-article called "Church," p. 2264.

9 *Diotrephes:* Diotrephes is not mentioned anywhere else in the Bible. He apparently was one of the leaders in the same church that Gaius belonged to. Diotrephes had attacked John by telling lies and saying terrible things about him, and refusing to welcome anyone who was associated with John (10).

12 *Demetrius:* A Christian that the elder praises for his truthful teaching about Christ. A different Demetrius is mentioned in Acts 19:23-41 as a silversmith who made idolatrous shrines out of silver.

11 1 John 3:11-18; 2 John 5,6.

Showing Hospitality to Traveling Teachers

John praises Gaius for helping the true followers of the Lord, and criticizes the church leader named Diotrephes, who has been refusing to welcome the Lord's followers and punishing other church members who do help. John hopes to see Gaius in person soon and sends greetings from Gaius's friends.

5Dear friend, you are faithful in what you are doing for the
brothers, even though they are strangers to you. 6They have told
the church about your love. You will do well to send them on their
way in a manner worthy of God. 7It was for the sake of the Name
that they went out, receiving no help from the pagans. 8We ought
therefore to show hospitality to such men so that we may work
together for the truth.

9I wrote to the church, but Diotrephes, who loves to be first,
will have nothing to do with us. 10So if I come, I will call attention
to what he is doing, gossiping maliciously about us. Not satisfied
with that, he refuses to welcome the brothers. He also stops those
who want to do so and puts them out of the church.

11Dear friend, do not imitate what is evil but what is good.
Anyone who does what is good is from God. Anyone who does
what is evil has not seen God. 12Demetrius is well spoken of by
everyone—and even by the truth itself. We also speak well of him,
and you know that our testimony is true.

13I have much to write you, but I do not want to do so with
pen and ink. 14I hope to see you soon, and we will talk face to face.

Peace to you. The friends here send their greetings. Greet the friends there by name.

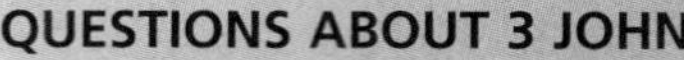

QUESTIONS ABOUT 3 JOHN

1. What seems to be the "truth" mentioned in this letter? (1-8,12) Who is attacking the truth in Gaius's church?
2. Based on this brief letter, how would you describe Gaius's church (congregation)?
3. What kinds of problems was Diotrephes causing in Gaius's church? (9,10) What problems have you observed happening when someone wants to be considered "the number one leader" in a church group?
4. Why is it important to encourage and welcome those who follow the Lord, especially those who teach and preach the truth?

JUDE

How should God's chosen people stand up for what they believe? Read JUDE *and find out.*

WHAT MAKES JUDE SPECIAL?

This letter gives a strong warning to Christians about false teachers and prophets who are trying to lead the believers away from the truth. The author uses a number of examples from the Jewish Scriptures (Old Testament) and even refers to two documents from Jewish literature that are not included in the Bible: *The Assumption of Moses* and *1 Enoch*. You may notice also that many verses of this letter are used in 2 PETER (compare 2 Peter 2 with Jude 4-18).

WHY WAS JUDE WRITTEN?

The writer of JUDE was worried about "godless" people who had secretly slipped into and claimed to be part of Christ's followers. These godless ones argued that they could live in an immoral way, because God was so kind and would always forgive them. They even denied that Jesus Christ was their only Lord (4). Readers of JUDE were encouraged to defend the faith against the teachings of godless people. And Christians themselves are to be faithful to Christ by living moral lives. This means avoiding sinful behavior, helping those who have doubts, and rescuing those who need to be saved.

WHAT'S THE STORY BEHIND THE SCENE?

The writer of this short book is identified as Jude, the traditional English form of the Greek name Judas and the Hebrew name Judah. "Judah" was the name of one of the sons of Jacob (Gen 29:35) and both King David and Jesus were members of the Israelite tribe that was named after him (Luke 3:33).

James and Jude (Judas) are named as Jesus' brothers in the Gospels (Matt 13:55; Mark 6:3). James was a leader of the early church in Jerusalem (see Acts 15:13; Gal 1:19). It is possible that Jude was also a leader in the early Jewish Christian church in Palestine.

It's not clear who the original readers of the letter were (1,2). They may have been early Jewish Christians who were familiar with the Jewish Scriptures, which Christians now call the Old Testament. Or, as some scholars have suggested, the letter may have been written after Jesus' brothers, James and Judas, had died. Such scholars propose that the style of the letter and the situation it describes seem to come from a time later than the first generation of Jesus' followers. These scholars believe that, for the most part, the kinds of false teachings the author is addressing in this letter were not big problems for the earlier followers of Jesus.

Keep yourselves in God's love as you wait for the mercy of our Lord Jesus Christ to bring you to eternal life.
Jude 21

Jude, a servant of Jesus Christ and a brother of James: Jude, or Judah, was a common Jewish name. In verse 1 Jude refers to himself as a servant of Jesus Christ. The word "Christ" is a title that means "Messiah" or "Chosen One." See also the mini-article called "Messiah (Chosen One)," p. 1124.

God the Father: See verse 1. In the Gospels, Jesus often referred to God as his Father (John 3:35; 5:20-30; 15:1,16; 17:1-26). The apostle Paul also used the term Father when referring to God in many of his letters (Gal 1:1-3; 1 Cor 1:3; Phil 1:2).

Salvation: See verse 3. The word "salvation" points to what God does in order to free humans from sin and the powers of evil. This salvation is given by the Holy Spirit who helps Jesus' followers keep themselves in God's love (20,21). See also the mini-article called "Salvation," p. 2021.

How is Jude constructed?

This letter may be outlined in the following way:

Greetings and a prayer (1,2)

Defending the faith against false teachers (3-25)

Greetings and a Prayer

The writer of this letter greets an unnamed group of Jesus' followers and prays that God will bless them.

[1]Jude, a servant of Jesus Christ and a brother of James,

To those who have been called, who are loved by God the Father and kept by[a] Jesus Christ:

[2]Mercy, peace and love be yours in abundance.

Defending the Faith against False Teachers

The writer encourages the believers to defend the true faith against those who are teaching false beliefs and living immoral lives. He compares these "godless" people to faithless people from Israel's past, and makes it clear that God will punish all ungodly people for the evil things they have done.

The Sin and Doom of Godless Men

[3]Dear friends, although I was very eager to write to you
about the salvation we share, I felt I had to write and urge you to
contend for the faith that was once for all entrusted to the saints.
[4]For certain men whose condemnation was written about[b] long
ago have secretly slipped in among you. They are godless men,
who change the grace of our God into a license for immorality and
deny Jesus Christ our only Sovereign and Lord.

[5]Though you already know all this, I want to remind you
that the Lord[c] delivered his people out of Egypt, but later
destroyed those who did not believe. [6]And the angels who did not
keep their positions of authority but abandoned their own
home—these he has kept in darkness, bound with everlasting
chains for judgment on the great Day. [7]In a similar way, Sodom
and Gomorrah and the surrounding towns gave themselves up to

[a]1 Or *for*; or *in* [b]4 Or *men who were marked out for condemnation* [c]5 Some early manuscripts *Jesus*

4 *condemnation was written about long ago:* A number of Bible passages warn that God will judge and destroy evil people (see, for example, Jer 14:13-16; Ps 94). See also 14-18.

4 *slipped in . . . godless men:* The godless people who secretly slipped in among the Christians were teaching false things about God's grace. The godless people described here apparently twisted this message and used it to excuse their immoral ways.

5 *I want to remind you:* God rescued the Hebrew people from slavery in Egypt. But because of their complaining and lack of faith, God did not allow them to enter the promised land of Canaan (Exod 12:51; Num 14:26-30).

6 *angels . . . bound with everlasting chains . . . great Day:* This short letter mentions angels several times. In verse 6, the angels mentioned may be the "sons of God" described in Genesis 6:1-4 (see also 2 Pet 2:4). The angels were punished because they abandoned their place in heaven to marry women on earth. They will stay bound until the day of judgment (Matt 13:47-50; 25:31-46; John 12:44-50; 2 Pet 3:10-14).

In verses 8 and 9, the writer speaks about how godless people reject all authority and insult angels ("slander celestial beings"). He also refers to an ancient Jewish story that describes a meeting between the archangel Michael and the devil. In verses 14 and 15, the writer quotes another ancient Jewish writing (*1 Enoch*) to warn his readers that thousands of holy angels will accompany the Lord when he comes to judge ungodly people. For more, see the mini-article called "Angels," p. 88.

7 *Sodom and Gomorrah:* God destroyed these cities because the people there were evil (Gen 19:1-24).

1 Matt 13:55; Mark 6:3. **9** Deut 34:6; Zech 3:2. **18** 2 Pet 3:3.

sexual immorality and perversion. They serve as an example of those who suffer the punishment of eternal fire.

[8]In the very same way, these dreamers pollute their own bodies, reject authority and slander celestial beings. [9]But even the archangel Michael, when he was disputing with the devil about the body of Moses, did not dare to bring a slanderous accusation against him, but said, "The Lord rebuke you!" [10]Yet these men speak abusively against whatever they do not understand; and what things they do understand by instinct, like unreasoning animals—these are the very things that destroy them.

[11]Woe to them! They have taken the way of Cain; they have rushed for profit into Balaam's error; they have been destroyed in Korah's rebellion.

[12]These men are blemishes at your love feasts, eating with you without the slightest qualm—shepherds who feed only themselves. They are clouds without rain, blown along by the wind; autumn trees, without fruit and uprooted—twice dead. [13]They are wild waves of the sea, foaming up their shame; wandering stars, for whom blackest darkness has been reserved forever.

[14]Enoch, the seventh from Adam, prophesied about these men: "See, the Lord is coming with thousands upon thousands of his holy ones [15]to judge everyone, and to convict all the ungodly of all the ungodly acts they have done in the ungodly way, and of all the harsh words ungodly sinners have spoken against him." [16]These men are grumblers and faultfinders; they follow their own evil desires; they boast about themselves and flatter others for their own advantage.

A Call to Persevere

[17]But, dear friends, remember what the apostles of our Lord Jesus Christ foretold. [18]They said to you, "In the last times there will be scoffers who will follow their own ungodly desires." [19]These are the men who divide you, who follow mere natural instincts and do not have the Spirit.

[20]But you, dear friends, build yourselves up in your most holy faith and pray in the Holy Spirit. [21]Keep yourselves in God's

9 *Michael . . . devil . . . Moses:* The story described here may have been part of a popular ancient Jewish book called *The Assumption of Moses*, which tells how Moses' body was taken up to heaven. See also Dan 10:13,21; 12:1; Rev 12:7. For more about Moses, see the mini-article called "Moses," p. 2335.

The devil is the opponent of God and God's people and the leader of the evil forces in the universe. See also the mini-article called "Satan," p. 963.

11 *way of Cain . . . Balaam's error . . . Korah's rebellion:* Cain was the first person to commit murder (Gen 4:1-16). Balaam was hired by Israel's enemy to put a curse on the people of Israel, but Balaam blessed them instead (Num 22:1—24:25). Korah led a rebellion against Moses and Aaron (Num 16:1-35; 26:9,10).

12 *love feasts:* Early Christians shared meals and celebrated the Lord's Supper (also known as Communion or Eucharist). See also 1 Cor 11:17-32.

14 *Enoch . . . seventh . . . Adam:* See Gen 5:18,21-24. Enoch truly loved God. In the centuries around the time of Christ, a number of prophetic writings written in Enoch's name were widely read in the Near East. The quotation in these verses is from a book known as *1 Enoch*.

19 *the Spirit:* See the mini-article called "Holy Spirit," p. 2082.

QUESTIONS ABOUT JUDE

1. How were the "godless men" described in this letter twisting the truth about God? (4)
2. The godless people used God's grace as an excuse to behave immorally. How would a "godly person" complete this sentence? "God treats us much better than we deserve, and so . . ."
3. What selfish and shameful actions spoiled the Christians' love feasts and celebrations of the Lord's Supper? (12) According to the writer, what will happen to those who do such shameful deeds? (13)
4. How can the Christians keep themselves "in God's love"? (21-23)

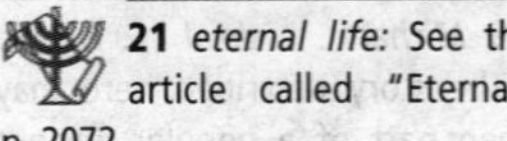

21 *eternal life:* See the mini-article called "Eternal Life," p. 2072.

25 *God our Savior . . . Jesus Christ our Lord:* The title Savior means "one who saves or rescues." For more about "Salvation," see the note on p. 2399. The Greek word for "Lord" is *kyrios,* which means "master" or "sir." When it is used for Jesus, it emphasizes his authority and power. See also the mini-article called "Lord (Title for Jesus)," p. 2106, and the note on p. 2399 (Jude . . . Jesus Christ).

love as you wait for the mercy of our Lord Jesus Christ to bring you to eternal life.
22Be merciful to those who doubt; 23snatch others from the
fire and save them; to others show mercy, mixed with fear—hating even the clothing stained by corrupted flesh.

Doxology

24To him who is able to keep you from falling and to present you before his glorious presence without fault and with great
joy— 25to the only God our Savior be glory, majesty, power and authority, through Jesus Christ our Lord, before all ages, now and forevermore! Amen.

REVELATION

War! Disasters! Famine! Armageddon!
REVELATION, the final book of the Bible,
shows how God brings about an end to evil
and prepares a new city of peace
for his chosen people.

WHAT MAKES REVELATION SPECIAL?

The word translated as "revelation" (1:1) comes from the Greek word *apokalypsis,* meaning a revealing or an unveiling. REVELATION belongs to a kind of writing called apocalyptic literature. Apocalyptic writings try to reveal the secrets of heaven to human beings, and are often about the way human history will end. Such writings usually divide the whole universe into two parts, one good and one evil. At the end of time, the good part of the universe, which God rules, will win a final victory over the evil part, which Satan has ruled. Having defeated evil, God will bring in a new creation, and everyone who has been faithful will live with God forever. Apocalyptic passages can be found in other books of the Bible such as Daniel 7–12 and Mark 13, but REVELATION is the only book of the Bible made up entirely of apocalyptic writing. See also the mini-article called "Apocalyptic Writing," p. 1656.

REVELATION excites the imagination. It features brilliant visions of a coming day of the Lord. These visions are expressed through many symbols, including numbers that have secret meaning and predictions about when God will bring the world to an end.

The author, traditionally understood to be the apostle John (Matt 10:2), knew the Jewish Scriptures (Old Testament) very well. Over half the verses in REVELATION are directly or indirectly based on Old Testament passages. This is important for understanding the meaning of the book.

WHY WAS REVELATION WRITTEN?

Around the end of the first century A.D., all people in the Roman empire were ordered to offer prayers and sacrifices to the Roman emperors, who had declared themselves gods. Those who refused were regarded as traitors to the empire, and could be put to death. Christians wondered whether their disobedience to Rome would mean the end of the church, and what would happen to the hope that God would rule on earth. The writer of REVELATION received a special message from God that answered these questions. He shared it with seven churches in the Roman province of Asia, but the message is really for all Christians. This message has three main parts:

1. Evil forces are at work in the world, and Christians may have to suffer and die;
2. Jesus is Lord, and he will conquer all people and powers—including the Roman empire—that oppose God; and

the Alpha and the Omega: This expression is used twice in REVELATION: in the beginning of the book (1:8) and toward the end of the book (21:6). The phrase represents the first and last letters of the Greek alphabet; the book also uses the phrase, "the First and the Last" (1:17; 2:8; 22:13). The prophet Isaiah uses a similar expression to describe the completeness and totality of God (Isa 44:6; 48:12).

priests to serve his God and Father: See 1:6. In JOHN, Jesus often calls God his Father (John 3:35; 5:17-27; 15:1,16; 17:1-26). For Jesus to call God his Father was to claim a special relationship with God and the authority to rule over God's people (see Ps 2:6-8).

Israelite men who were descendants of the tribe of Levi were expected to serve as priests at the tabernacle and later at the temple. Part of their work was to offer sacrifices and gifts to God on behalf of the whole people of Israel. See also the mini-article called "Israel's Priests," p. 2344. The book of 1 PETER refers to God's new people as "a holy priesthood" (1 Pet 2:5,9), who will offer sacrifices of holy living.

suffering: A key theme in REVELATION. Some Christians who refused to worship the Roman emperor were punished (1 Pet 4:12-19). Roman authorities sent John to Patmos because he preached God's message and the truth about Jesus (1:9). They were upset because John taught that Christ, not the Roman emperor, was the real king.

the tree of life: See 2:7. This tree is mentioned in Genesis 2:9, as growing in the Garden of Eden. Because of their rebellion, Adam and Eve were forbidden to eat the fruit of this tree (Gen 3:22-24). The tree of life is frequently represented in Jewish and Christian art, as in the plate shown here (Bernard Leach, 1923). It is also mentioned in 22:2,19, where trees bear fruit that give life, and leaves healing to the nations. See Ezek 28:13; 31:8.

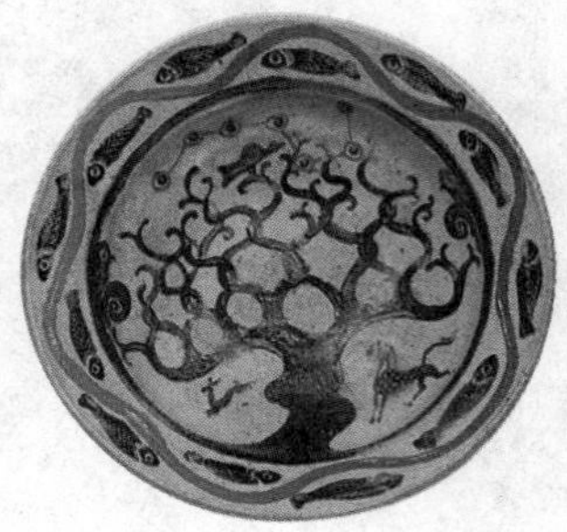

3. God has wonderful rewards for those who remain faithful to him, especially for those who lose their lives while serving him.

This was a powerful message of hope for those early Christians who had to suffer or die for their faith. In this book, they learned that, in spite of the cruel power of the Roman empire, Jesus (the Lamb of God) would win the final victory.

What's the Story Behind the Scene?

The exact identity of John, the writer of this book, is still debated today. Though the apostle John traditionally has been considered the author of REVELATION, John was a common name among Jews and Christians, and the author of the book never claims to be one of the twelve disciples. It may be easier to figure out when the book was written, though that is not certain either. Domitian, who ruled the Roman empire from A.D. 81 to 96, was the first Roman emperor who tried to make Christians worship the emperor as a god. The emperor Trajan later made a policy that also required everyone to worship the Roman emperors who had died. Since REVELATION seems to speak to Christians who are being persecuted for not worshiping the emperor, many scholars think the book was likely written sometime late in Domitian's reign or even later, when Trajan ruled. Other scholars, however, believe the book was written much earlier, just before the destruction of Jerusalem in A.D. 70, near the end of Nero's reign.

REVELATION uses many numbers as symbols, such as the number seven, which stands for completeness or perfection. Other kinds of symbols are also used. For example, the main symbol for the powers opposed to God is the city "Babylon." Christian readers knew that this really meant Rome, and they also knew that when the book says "the Lamb," the writer meant Jesus Christ.

How is Revelation Constructed?

This complicated book was written in a series of sections that show the struggle of the church against the enemies of God. This struggle begins in the story of seven earthly churches and ends with a vision of God's great victory and the completely new heaven and earth that God will bring in the future. REVELATION can be outlined in the following way:

John's prophecy and blessing (1:1-8)

Vision for the seven churches (1:9—3:22)

Vision of God and the Lamb (4:1—5:14)

Opening the seven seals (6:1—8:5)

The seven trumpets (8:6—11:19)

The opponents of God (12:1—13:18)

Visions of God's judgment and protection (14:1—16:21)

Victory over the enemies of God (17:1—20:15)

God makes all things new (21:1—22:6)

Final promises, blessings, and warnings (22:7-21)

NUMBERS IN THE BIBLE

Certain numbers had special meanings in the ancient world and to the writers of the Bible. This chart gives some key examples. Keep in mind, however, that sometimes these numbers represent actual quantities and are not intended to be understood symbolically.

ONE	**Monotheism, uniqueness, and unity.**
	"The LORD our God, the LORD is one." *Deut 6:4*
	"One Lord, one faith, one baptism." *Eph 4:5*
THREE	**Completeness or totality. Many ancient religions considered three a divine number.**
	Three men who visited Abraham at Mamre *Gen 18:1-15*
	Three annual pilgrimage festivals (Unleavened Bread, Harvest, Tabernacles) *Exod 23:14-19*
	Number of days and nights Jonah was inside the great fish *Jonah 1:17*
	Number of days between Jesus' death and resurrection *Mark 8:31; 1 Cor 15:4*
FOUR	**Totality of the created world. Most cultures speak of four winds or directions, and divide the year into four seasons.**
	Number of rivers flowing out of the Garden of Eden *Gen 2:10*
	Four living creatures of Ezekiel's vision *Ezek 1:4-28 (see also Rev 4:1-8)*
	Four horses and riders of John's vision *Rev 6:1-8*
SEVEN	**Completeness and perfection. Like three, seven was considered a sacred number to many cultures in the ancient world.**
	Number of days in the week based on Creation story *Gen 1:1—2:3*
	The "seventh" day is a holy day of rest (Sabbath) *Exod 20:8-11*
	The Israelites were to let the land rest every "seventh" year (Sabbath year) *Exod 23:10,11*
	Every fiftieth year (7 x 7 + 1) the Israelites were to celebrate a Year of Jubilee to mark a time of freedom and forgiveness *Lev 25:8-55*
	Temple furnishings and decorations were often arranged in seven parts *1 Kgs 7:17; Ezek 40:22,26*
	Number of times blood is to be sprinkled during sacrificial ceremonies *Lev 4:6,17; 14:7; Num 19:4*
	Number of several items mentioned in REVELATION (lampstands, stars, churches, seals, trumpets, bowls) *Rev 6–11; 15; 16*
	Number of times Jesus said to forgive (seventy-seven or seven x seventy) *Matt 18:21,22*
TEN	**Because ten is the sum of three and seven it sometimes represents complete perfection.**
	The number of times "God said" is repeated in the Hebrew text of the Creation story *Gen 1:1-31*
	The Ten Commandments *Exod 20:1-17; Deut 5:1-22*
TWELVE	**Also a number of completeness and perfection.**
	Number of Jacob's sons, and the number of tribes of Israel *Gen 35:23-26; 49:1-28*
	Number of gates to Jerusalem in Ezekiel's vision *Ezek 48:30-34 (see also Rev 21:11-21)*
	Number of Jesus' apostles *Matt 10:1-4; Mark 3:13-19; Luke 6:12-16; see also Acts 1:12-26*
FORTY	**A long, but limited period of time.**
	Number of days it rained during the great Flood *Gen 7:4,17,18*
	Number of days Moses stayed on Mount Sinai *Exod 24:17,18*
	Number of years the Israelites wandered in the desert *Num 14:33,34; Deut 2:7; 29:4-6*
	Number of days Jesus fasted in the desert *Matt 4:2; Mark 1:12,13; Luke 4:2*
	Number of years David and other favored kings ruled *2 Sam 5:4; 1 Kgs 11:41,42; 2 Chr 24:1*

John's Prophecy and Blessing

John tells how he received a message from an angel sent by Christ, who received it from God (1:1,2). He offers a blessing to all who read this prophecy and then introduces the main theme of the book: Jesus has conquered death, rules over all earthly powers, and will come again to judge all people.

Prologue

1 The revelation of Jesus Christ, which God gave him to show his
servants what must soon take place. He made it known by sending his
angel to his servant John, 2 who testifies to everything he saw—that is,
the word of God and the testimony of Jesus Christ. 3 Blessed is the one
who reads the words of this prophecy, and blessed are those who hear
it and take to heart what is written in it, because the time is near.

Greetings and Doxology

4 John,

To the seven churches in the province of Asia:

Grace and peace to you from him who is, and who was, and
who is to come, and from the seven spirits[a] before his throne, 5 and
from Jesus Christ, who is the faithful witness, the firstborn from
the dead, and the ruler of the kings of the earth.

To him who loves us and has freed us from our sins by his
blood, 6 and has made us to be a kingdom and priests to serve his God
and Father—to him be glory and power for ever and ever! Amen.

7 Look, he is coming with the clouds,
and every eye will see him,
even those who pierced him;
and all the peoples of the earth will mourn because
of him.
So shall it be! Amen.

8 "I am the Alpha and the Omega," says the Lord God, "who
is, and who was, and who is to come, the Almighty."

Vision for the Seven Churches

John tells about his vision of the risen Lord and gives the message he was told to write to all of the seven churches in the Roman province of Asia (1:9-20). Then he gives a separate message for each church (2:1—3:22).

One Like a Son of Man

9 I, John, your brother and companion in the suffering and
kingdom and patient endurance that are ours in Jesus, was on the

[a]4 Or *the sevenfold Spirit*

1:1 *Jesus Christ . . . angel:* "Christ" is the Greek translation of the Hebrew word "Messiah." It is a title that means "Chosen One." See also the mini-article called "Messiah (Chosen One)," p. 1124.

The word "angel" (Greek, *angelos*) means "messenger." See also the mini-article called "Angels," p. 88.

1:1 *his servant John:* Possibly the apostle John, son of Zebedee (Matt 10:2). John was well known by the churches he wrote to, since he didn't identify himself except by his first name. Apparently, the Romans sent John to the island of Patmos (1:9) as a punishment for preaching about Jesus among the churches of Asia. See the map on p. 2409.

1:3 *Blessed is the one who reads the words of this prophecy:* This is the first of seven different blessings in this book (see also 14:13; 16:15; 19:9; 20:6; 22:7; 22:14). The "prophecy" here refers to the contents of John's visions and the message he received from Jesus. See also the article called "Prophets and Prophecy," p. 935.

1:4 *seven churches in . . . Asia:* Here "Asia" refers to a province in the eastern part of the Roman empire. These seven churches represented the problems and the strengths present in all of the churches of Asia. See the map on p. 2409.

1:8 *the Alpha and the Omega:* See the note on p. 2403.

1:9 *island of Patmos:* A rocky, mountainous island in the Aegean Sea about thirty miles west of the province of Asia. The Romans sometimes used this isolated island as a penal colony.

1:4 Exod 3:14; Rev 4:5. **1:5** Isa 55:4; Ps 89:27; Rom 3:25,26; 1 Cor 15:20-28; 1 John 4:8-10. **1:6** Exod 19:6; Rev 5:10. **1:7** Dan 7:13; Zech 12:10; Matt 24:30; Mark 13:26; Luke 21:27; John 19:34,37; 1 Thes 4:17. **1:8** Exod 3:14; Rev 22:13.

The Angel, Seven Stars, and Eagle of Saint John, from the *Apocalypse of Saint John Lorvao,* Portuguese, twelfth century. "Because of the word of God and the testimony of Jesus" which John had preached, the Romans sent him to Patmos, an island in the Aegean Sea. While there he heard an angel with a loud voice that sounded like a trumpet telling him to write in a book what he was about to see. Once he had done this, he was to send his book to the "seven churches," represented here by seven stars. Since seven was a number that stood for completeness, John's book was really intended for all churches everywhere, not just for the seven named in 1:11. (See 1:9-20.)

island of Patmos because of the word of God and the testimony of
Jesus. [10]On the Lord's Day I was in the Spirit, and I heard behind
me a loud voice like a trumpet, [11]which said: "Write on a scroll
what you see and send it to the seven churches: to Ephesus, Smyrna, Pergamum, Thyatira, Sardis, Philadelphia and Laodicea."
[12]I turned around to see the voice that was speaking to me.
And when I turned I saw seven golden lampstands, [13]and among
the lampstands was someone "like a son of man,"[a] dressed in a robe reaching down to his feet and with a golden sash around his
chest. [14]His head and hair were white like wool, as white as snow,

[a]**13** Daniel 7:13

1:10 *the Lord's Day:* Sunday, the day when Jesus was raised from death, and when Christians gather for worship.

1:10 *I was in the Spirit:* The Holy Spirit took control of John, revealing many things to him in a vision or dream. See also the mini-article called "Holy Spirit," p. 2082.

1:11 *Ephesus . . . Laodicea:* Ephesus was the closest city to the island of Patmos and the capital of the Roman province of Asia. It was an important center for business, trade, and art. Its temple of the goddess Artemis, the largest Greek temple in ancient times, was one of the Seven Wonders of the ancient world. See the map on p. 2409.

1:12 *seven golden lampstands:* A golden lampstand with seven lamps, called a *menorah,* is shown below. It was kept in the tabernacle (see Exod 25:31-39; Zech 4:1-6). In this passage, the seven lampstands are the seven churches (1:20). Because the number seven stood for completeness (see the chart called "Numbers in the Bible," p. 2405), John's book was intended to be read to all churches, not just the seven named.

1:13 Dan 7:13; 10:5. **1:14** Dan 7:9. **1:14,15** Ezek 43:2; Dan 10:6.

1:16 *seven stars . . . sun shining:* The seven stars are the angels of the seven churches (1:20). See also Matt 17:1,2.

1:18 *the keys of death and Hades:* That is, power over death (John 5:28,29). See also the mini-article called "Hell," p. 1944.

2:2 *those who claim to be apostles:* Apparently some false teachers had become part of the church at Ephesus. The true followers had to work very hard (2:3) to overcome the influence of these false teachers.

2:6 *Nicolaitans:* They may have claimed to be followers of Nicolas from Antioch (Acts 6:5), and they may have eaten food that had been offered to idols or taken part in ceremonies that were part of serving and worshiping idols (see 1 Cor 8:7-13; 10:19-21; Rev 2:14,15).

2:8 *Smyrna:* About seventy years before REVELATION was written, the people of Smyrna built and dedicated a temple in honor of the Roman emperor Tiberius.

2:9 *I know . . . your poverty:* Some Christians at Smyrna were most likely poor immigrants from Galilee and Judea who had fled Palestine during the Jewish War of A.D. 66-74.

2:9 *those who say they are Jews and are not:* This may have been a group of local Jewish leaders who accused the Christians of causing trouble or of being disloyal to the Roman authorities.

2:11 *the second death:* The first death is physical death, and the "second death" is death of the soul or spirit and/or eternal punishment. See also 20:5,6,14; 21:8; and the mini-article called "Eternal Life," p. 2072.

1:17 Isa 44:6; 48:12; Rev 2:8; 22:13. **2:7** Gen 2:9; Ezek 28:13; 31:8; Rev 22:2.

and his eyes were like blazing fire. 15His feet were like bronze glowing in a furnace, and his voice was like the sound of rushing waters. 16In his right hand he held seven stars, and out of his mouth came a sharp double-edged sword. His face was like the sun shining in all its brilliance.

17When I saw him, I fell at his feet as though dead. Then he placed his right hand on me and said: "Do not be afraid. I am the First and the Last. 18I am the Living One; I was dead, and behold I am alive for ever and ever! And I hold the keys of death and Hades.

19"Write, therefore, what you have seen, what is now and what will take place later. 20The mystery of the seven stars that you saw in my right hand and of the seven golden lampstands is this: The seven stars are the angels[a] of the seven churches, and the seven lampstands are the seven churches.

To the Church in Ephesus

2 "To the angel[b] of the church in Ephesus write:

These are the words of him who holds the seven stars in his right hand and walks among the seven golden lampstands: 2I know your deeds, your hard work and your perseverance. I know that you cannot tolerate wicked men, that you have tested those who claim to be apostles but are not, and have found them false. 3You have persevered and have endured hardships for my name, and have not grown weary.

4Yet I hold this against you: You have forsaken your first love. 5Remember the height from which you have fallen! Repent and do the things you did at first. If you do not repent, I will come to you and remove your lampstand from its place. 6But you have this in your favor: You hate the practices of the Nicolaitans, which I also hate.

7He who has an ear, let him hear what the Spirit says to the churches. To him who overcomes, I will give the right to eat from the tree of life, which is in the paradise of God.

To the Church in Smyrna

8"To the angel of the church in Smyrna write:

These are the words of him who is the First and the Last, who died and came to life again. 9I know your afflictions and your poverty—yet you are rich! I know the slander of those who say they are Jews and are not, but are a synagogue of Satan. 10Do not be afraid of what you are about to suffer. I tell you, the devil will put some of you in prison to test you, and you will suffer persecution for ten days. Be faithful, even to the point of death, and I will give you the crown of life.

[a]20 Or *messengers* [b]1 Or *messenger*; also in verses 8, 12 and 18

The Seven Churches in Asia. Pictured (clockwise from left) are some important features of three of the cities of Asia Minor that John was told to write to: the Marble Hall in Sardis, a third century A.D. synagogue; the remains of the column-lined street of Smyrna's agora (marketplace); and a reconstruction of the altar to Zeus in Pergamum, one of the most beautiful Greek-style cities in the province of Asia. (See 2:1—3:22.)

11 He who has an ear, let him hear what the Spirit says to
the churches. He who overcomes will not be hurt at all by the
second death.

To the Church in Pergamum

12 "To the angel of the church in Pergamum write:

These are the words of him who has the sharp, double-
edged sword. 13 I know where you live—where Satan has his
throne. Yet you remain true to my name. You did not
renounce your faith in me, even in the days of Antipas, my
faithful witness, who was put to death in your city—where
Satan lives.
14 Nevertheless, I have a few things against you: You have
people there who hold to the teaching of Balaam, who taught
Balak to entice the Israelites to sin by eating food sacrificed to
idols and by committing sexual immorality. 15 Likewise you
also have those who hold to the teaching of the Nicolaitans.
16 Repent therefore! Otherwise, I will soon come to you and
will fight against them with the sword of my mouth.
17 He who has an ear, let him hear what the Spirit says to

2:12 *Pergamum:* A city famous for its large library and its many temples honoring various gods. On a hill overlooking the city stood a huge altar built to the god Zeus. Pergamum was also the center for the worship of Asclepios, the god of healing. See the chart called "Greek and Roman Gods and Goddesses, p. 2136.

2:13 *where Satan has his throne:* This may mean that the city is a center of emperor worship.

2:17 *a white stone:* The stone may be like a ticket that lets a person into God's banquet where the "hidden manna" is eaten.

2:12 Rev 1:16. **2:14** Num 22:5,7; Deut 23:4. **2:17** Exod 16:14,15; 16:33,34; Isa 62:2; 65:15; John 6:48-50.

the churches. To him who overcomes, I will give some of the hidden manna. I will also give him a white stone with a new name written on it, known only to him who receives it.

To the Church in Thyatira

18 "To the angel of the church in Thyatira write:

These are the words of the Son of God, whose eyes are like blazing fire and whose feet are like burnished bronze. 19 I know your deeds, your love and faith, your service and perseverance, and that you are now doing more than you did at first. 20 Nevertheless, I have this against you: You tolerate that woman Jezebel, who calls herself a prophetess. By her teaching she misleads my servants into sexual immorality and the eating of food sacrificed to idols. 21 I have given her time to repent of her immorality, but she is unwilling. 22 So I will cast her on a bed of suffering, and I will make those who commit adultery with her suffer intensely, unless they repent of her ways. 23 I will strike her children dead. Then all the churches will know that I am he who searches hearts and minds, and I will repay each of you according to your deeds. 24 Now I say to the rest of you in Thyatira, to you who do not hold to her teaching and have not learned Satan's so-called deep secrets (I will not impose any other burden on you): 25 Only hold on to what you have until I come.

26 To him who overcomes and does my will to the end, I will give authority over the nations—

27 'He will rule them with an iron scepter;
he will dash them to pieces like pottery'[a]—

just as I have received authority from my Father. 28 I will also give him the morning star. 29 He who has an ear, let him hear what the Spirit says to the churches.

To the Church in Sardis

3 "To the angel[b] of the church in Sardis write:

These are the words of him who holds the seven spirits[c] of God and the seven stars. I know your deeds; you have a reputation of being alive, but you are dead. 2 Wake up! Strengthen what remains and is about to die, for I have not found your deeds complete in the sight of my God. 3 Remember, therefore, what you have received and heard; obey it, and repent. But if you do not wake up, I will come like a thief, and you will not know at what time I will come to you.

4 Yet you have a few people in Sardis who have not soiled

2:18 *Thyatira:* This city was well known for making and trading cloth, dye, brass, leather, and pottery. See also Acts 16:14,15.

2:20 *Jezebel:* Probably a reference to Israel's evil Queen Jezebel (1 Kgs 18:1-14; 21:1-19; 2 Kgs 9:30-37).

2:20 *immorality . . . idols:* Business groups called guilds sometimes held banquets in temples to honor various gods. Christians who refused to participate in these feasts were often rejected by the business community. But participating in them was sinful and meant they were unfaithful to Christ.

2:26-28 *morning star:* A name for Christ (see 22:16). See also Num 24:17; 2 Pet 1:19.

3:1 *Sardis:* Especially known for its wool making, the city was damaged by a great earthquake in A.D. 17.

3:2,3 *Wake up . . . repent:* The Christians at Sardis were given two strong warnings: to be alert to what Christ has to reveal about himself and to turn away from their sins (repent). See Matt 24:43,44; Rev 16:15; and the mini-article called "Sin," p. 2181.

3:4 *dressed in white:* A traditional symbol of inner purity. See also Dan 7:9.

3:5 *the book of life:* The book where the names of God's people are recorded (Exod 32:32,33; Ps 69:28; Dan 12:1; Phil 4:3; Rev 20:12).

3:7 *Philadelphia:* The same earthquake that hit Sardis destroyed Philadelphia (see the note at 3:1), but Philadelphia was subsequently rebuilt. This prosperous city's key industries were farming, leather production, and textile manufacturing.

2:23 Ps 7:9; 62:12; Jer 17:10. **2:26-28** Ps 2:8,9. **3:1** Rev 1:20.

[a]27 Psalm 2:9 [b]1 Or *messenger*; also in verses 7 and 14 [c]1 Or *the sevenfold Spirit*

their clothes. They will walk with me, dressed in white, for
they are worthy. 5He who overcomes will, like them, be
dressed in white. I will never blot out his name from the book
of life, but will acknowledge his name before my Father and
his angels. 6He who has an ear, let him hear what the Spirit
says to the churches.

To the Church in Philadelphia

7"To the angel of the church in Philadelphia write:

These are the words of him who is holy and true, who
holds the key of David. What he opens no one can shut, and
what he shuts no one can open. 8I know your deeds. See, I
have placed before you an open door that no one can shut. I
know that you have little strength, yet you have kept my word
and have not denied my name. 9I will make those who are of
the synagogue of Satan, who claim to be Jews though they are
not, but are liars—I will make them come and fall down at
your feet and acknowledge that I have loved you. 10Since you
have kept my command to endure patiently, I will also keep
you from the hour of trial that is going to come upon the
whole world to test those who live on the earth.
11I am coming soon. Hold on to what you have, so that
no one will take your crown. 12Him who overcomes I will
make a pillar in the temple of my God. Never again will he
leave it. I will write on him the name of my God and the name
of the city of my God, the new Jerusalem, which is coming
down out of heaven from my God; and I will also write on
him my new name. 13He who has an ear, let him hear what the
Spirit says to the churches.

To the Church in Laodicea

14"To the angel of the church in Laodicea write:

These are the words of the Amen, the faithful and true
witness, the ruler of God's creation. 15I know your deeds, that

3:7 *the key of David:* The "key" stands for authority over David's kingdom. God promised David that one of his descendants would rule a kingdom that would last forever (2 Sam 7:10-16; Isa 9:6,7). Jesus is the descendant of David, the chosen one who fulfills these ancient prophecies.

3:9 *the synagogue of Satan:* This probably refers to members of the synagogue in Philadelphia who were against anyone who followed Jesus as the Lord's Messiah.

3:10 *hour of trial . . . test:* This refers to a time before Jesus will return to judge the world. Many Bible passages say that the time before Christ's return would be a time of trouble and testing for the followers of Christ (2 Tim 3:1-9; 2 Pet 3:3, 4; 1 John 2:18). See also the mini-article called "End Times," p. 2295.

3:14 *Laodicea:* This city was founded in the third century B.C. by Antiochus II of Syria who named the city for his wife Laodice. Laodicea was famous for banks, clothing and carpet making, black wool production, and for a medical center that produced an eye medicine used throughout the Roman empire.

3:14 *Amen:* Meaning "Trustworthy."

3:7 Isa 22:22; Job 12:14. **3:9** Isa 43:4; 49:23; 60:14. **3:12** Isa 62:2; 65:15; Rev 21:2. **3:14** Prov 8:22; Col 4:12,13.

QUESTIONS ABOUT REVELATION 1:1—3:22

1. Who was John, and why was he on the island of Patmos? (1:4,9) What happened to him while was there? (1:9-11)
2. Who spoke to him? (1:11-19)
3. John was told to write to seven churches in the province of Asia (1:9—3:22). What particular problems did each church face? What was the basic message John was instructed to give to each church?
4. Why was the Roman empire of the late first century and early second century A.D. a difficult place for Christians to live? What kind of messages do you think people who are facing persecution and suffering today need to hear? Why?

you are neither cold nor hot. I wish you were either one or the
other! 16 So, because you are lukewarm—neither hot nor
cold—I am about to spit you out of my mouth. 17 You say, 'I
am rich; I have acquired wealth and do not need a thing.' But
you do not realize that you are wretched, pitiful, poor, blind
and naked. 18 I counsel you to buy from me gold refined in the
fire, so you can become rich; and white clothes to wear, so you
can cover your shameful nakedness; and salve to put on your
eyes, so you can see.

19 Those whom I love I rebuke and discipline. So be
earnest, and repent. 20 Here I am! I stand at the door and
knock. If anyone hears my voice and opens the door, I will
come in and eat with him, and he with me.

21 To him who overcomes, I will give the right to sit with
me on my throne, just as I overcame and sat down with my

Behold I Stand at Your Door and Knock cut paper design by Gui-jie Zhang, twentieth century. Laodicea was the last of the seven churches John addressed. The Lord declared that the Christians there were "neither hot nor cold." They may have been wealthy, but they were also "pitiful, poor, blind and naked." This letter contains a very touching picture of the Lord's desire to be in a close relationship with his people: "Here I am!" the Lord says. "I stand at the door and knock. If anyone hears my voice and opens the door, I will come in and eat with him, and he with me" (3:20).

3:17 *I am rich:* In some ways this is the reverse of the message given to the poor Christians in Smyrna. See the note at 2:9 (poverty). Many Christians in the Laodicea church were rich and successful (see the note at 3:14). Yet because they did not live in a way that showed their faith, they were spiritually poor.

3:18 *buy from me gold . . . white clothes . . . salve:* The rich people of Laodicea probably had gold jewelry and expensive clothes. They were to trade their gold jewelry for pure gold, which may refer to the riches of the Holy Spirit, to the sacrifice of Christ who gave his life to bring them God's forgiveness (see 1 Pet 1:18,19), or to the rich spiritual life that comes by suffering for Christ.

For "white clothes," see the note at 3:4.

The salve they were to buy probably refers to the eye salve made in Laodicea. Just as that salve helped to heal physical eye diseases, the truth about Jesus would open the Laodiceans' eyes to spiritual life (3:19).

4:3 *jasper and carnelian . . . rainbow . . . emerald:* John's readers, who would have been familiar with the Jewish Scriptures, would have recognized in this description references to the gems in the breastpiece of the high priest of Israel (Exod 28:15-20) and the jewelry worn by the King of Tyre (Ezek 28:12-14). See also Ezek 1:26-28; 10:1. The rainbow here would have also reminded them of God's promise to Noah in Gen 9:16,17. See also the illustration on p. 2440.

3:19 Prov 3:12; Heb 12:6. **3:21** Matt 19:28; Luke 22:28-30.

Father on his throne. [22]He who has an ear, let him hear what
the Spirit says to the churches."

Vision of God and the Lamb

John's reports his vision of the One on the throne and the Lamb of God, who is Christ. Both are being praised by living creatures and by twenty-four elders.

The Throne in Heaven

4 After this I looked, and there before me was a door standing
open in heaven. And the voice I had first heard speaking to me like
a trumpet said, "Come up here, and I will show you what must
take place after this." [2]At once I was in the Spirit, and there before
me was a throne in heaven with someone sitting on it. [3]And the
one who sat there had the appearance of jasper and carnelian. A
rainbow, resembling an emerald, encircled the throne. [4]Surround-
ing the throne were twenty-four other thrones, and seated on them
were twenty-four elders. They were dressed in white and had
crowns of gold on their heads. [5]From the throne came flashes of
lightning, rumblings and peals of thunder. Before the throne,
seven lamps were blazing. These are the seven spirits[a] of God.
[6]Also before the throne there was what looked like a sea of glass,
clear as crystal.

In the center, around the throne, were four living creatures,
and they were covered with eyes, in front and in back. [7]The first living creature was like a lion, the second was like an ox, the third had
a face like a man, the fourth was like a flying eagle. [8]Each of the four
living creatures had six wings and was covered with eyes all around,
even under his wings. Day and night they never stop saying:

"Holy, holy, holy
is the Lord God Almighty,
who was, and is, and is to come."

[9]Whenever the living creatures give glory, honor and thanks to
him who sits on the throne and who lives for ever and ever, [10]the
twenty-four elders fall down before him who sits on the throne,
and worship him who lives for ever and ever. They lay their crowns
before the throne and say:

[11]"You are worthy, our Lord and God,
to receive glory and honor and power,
for you created all things,
and by your will they were created
and have their being."

---

[a]5 Or *the sevenfold Spirit*

Day and night they never stop saying: "Holy, holy, holy is the Lord God Almighty, who was, and is, and is to come."
Rev 4:8

4:4-10 *twenty-four other thrones . . . twenty-four elders:* The number of elders given here most likely represents the sum of the twelve tribes of Israel and the twelve apostles of Jesus. Together these symbolize all of God's chosen people. In most cultures of the ancient Near East, advisers usually stood before the enthroned ruler. Like Roman nobles who sat beside the emperor, these elders share some of the decision-making authority of their ruler (God). The council of elders is similar to the assembly of "gods" in Psalm 82.

4:6 *sea of glass:* Because it is clear as crystal, the sea may be a symbol for purity. It could also be meant to recall the vision that Moses had of God standing on something that looked like a "pavement made of sapphire." See also Exod 24:10.

4:6-9 *four living creatures:* These living creatures represent the people of God, in contrast to the four creatures in DANIEL who represent the evil empires that try to rule the world (Dan 7). The many eyes likely symbolize that they can see everything in every direction. The lion, ox, man, and eagle faces probably represent authority, strength, wisdom, and swiftness. These living creatures never stop praising God, echoing the words of the six-winged creatures in the prophet Isaiah's vision of the LORD (Isa 6:2,3; Ezek 1:22,23).

4:1 Rev 1:10. **4:5** Exod 19:16; Ezek 1:13; Zech 4:2; Rev 1:4; 8:5; 11:19; 16:18. **4:6,7** Ezek 1:5-10; 10:14. **4:8** Isa 6:2,3; Ezek 1:18; 10:12. **4:11** Gen 1; Eph 3:9; Rev 5:12.

The Scroll and the Lamb

5 Then I saw in the right hand of him who sat on the throne a
scroll with writing on both sides and sealed with seven seals. [2]And I
saw a mighty angel proclaiming in a loud voice, “Who is worthy to
break the seals and open the scroll?” [3]But no one in heaven or on
earth or under the earth could open the scroll or even look inside it.
[4]I wept and wept because no one was found who was worthy to
open the scroll or look inside. [5]Then one of the elders said to me,
“Do not weep! See, the Lion of the tribe of Judah, the Root of David,
has triumphed. He is able to open the scroll and its seven seals.”

[6]Then I saw a Lamb, looking as if it had been slain, standing
in the center of the throne, encircled by the four living creatures
and the elders. He had seven horns and seven eyes, which are the
seven spirits[a] of God sent out into all the earth. [7]He came and took
the scroll from the right hand of him who sat on the throne. [8]And

[a]**6** Or *the sevenfold Spirit*

Tetramorph. *Tetramorph* is a Greek word meaning “four forms.” The “four living creatures” described in 4:6-8 are similar to the creatures the prophet Ezekiel saw in a vision (Ezek 1:5-11). Over the centuries, these winged figures became associated with the four Gospel writers. From the fourth century A.D. on, they were commonly used in illuminated manuscripts and in mosaics and other elements of church architecture to represent Matthew (a man), Mark (a lion), Luke (an ox), and John (an eagle).

5:1 *scroll:* A roll of papyrus or parchment used for writing. Scrolls were sealed shut on the outside with one or more pieces of wax. See the mini-article called “Scrolls,” p. 1491.

5:2 *a mighty angel . . . Who is worthy:* See the note at 1:1 (angel). The scroll represents God’s plan for the future. To break the seals is to cause these events to happen. No human being is worthy to carry out this task, except Jesus the Lamb.

5:3 *under the earth:* See the note at 1:18.

5:5 *Lion of the tribe of Judah:* In Genesis 49:8,9 the tribe of Judah is called a “lion’s cub.” King David was from Judah. See the note at 3:7 (key). See also Isa 11:1,10.

5:6 *Lamb:* Though John may have expected to see Christ as a lion, he saw him instead as a lamb that showed signs of once being slaughtered (see John 1:29). This image is based, in part, on Isaiah 53:7, which talks about a servant of God who is silent like a lamb being led to the slaughter. Other New Testament passages describe Jesus as the lamb who was sacrificed for the sins of humanity (1 Cor 5:7; 1 Pet 1:19).

5:8 *four living creatures and the twenty-four elders:* See the notes at 4:4-10 (elders) and 4:6-9 (creatures). Because it was a custom in the Roman empire for subjects to bow down before the emperor, it would have been clear to John’s readers that he is saying the Lamb is superior to the earthly ruler Caesar.

5:8 *incense:* Incense was made of frankincense, other gums and spices, and salt, which together produced a sweet smell when burned. Sometimes incense is a symbol for the prayers of God’s people (Ps 141:2). See the chart called “Spices and Perfumes,” p. 1278.

5:1 Isa 29:11; Ezek 2:9,10. **5:6** Zech 4:10.

when he had taken it, the four living creatures and the twenty-four elders fell down before the Lamb. Each one had a harp and they were holding golden bowls full of incense, which are the prayers of the saints. 9 And they sang a new song:

"You are worthy to take the scroll
and to open its seals,
because you were slain,
and with your blood you purchased men for God
from every tribe and language and people and
nation.
10 You have made them to be a kingdom and priests to
serve our God,
and they will reign on the earth."

11 Then I looked and heard the voice of many angels, numbering thousands upon thousands, and ten thousand times ten thousand. They encircled the throne and the living creatures and the elders. 12 In a loud voice they sang:

"Worthy is the Lamb, who was slain,
to receive power and wealth and wisdom and strength
and honor and glory and praise!"

The Lamb of God, ceiling mosaic from the Church of San Vitale, Ravenna, Italy, sixth century. "The Lion of the tribe of Judah, the Root of David" in 5:5 becomes "a Lamb" in 5:6. This surprising transformation is typical of the reversals John uses in REVELATION. John shows that Jesus achieves victory through humility and self-sacrifice, not by flaunting his power the way worldly authorities do. Only the Lamb, Jesus, is worthy to open the scroll of the one sitting on the throne, because he was sacrificed so that people from every tribe and nation could be "purchased" for God. (See chapter 5.)

In a loud voice they sang: "Worthy is the Lamb, who was slain, to receive power and wealth and wisdom and strength and honor and glory and praise!"
Rev 5:12

5:9 *with your blood you purchased:* See the mini-article called "Redeemer (Redemption)," p. 995.

5:9,10 *from every tribe . . . and nation . . . to be a kingdom and priests:* God chose the Israelites to be his own people and to receive the Law of Moses (see the mini-articles called "Israel," p. 264, and "Israel's Priests," p. 2344. The "new song" given here declares that because of the sacrifice made by the Lamb (Christ), people from every nation will henceforth be welcome in God's kingdom, where they will share in God's authority. See Exod 19:6; Rev 1:6. The new people of God include not only the people of Israel but followers of Christ from every nation on earth.

5:9 Ps 33:3; 98:1; Isa 42:10. **5:11** Dan 7:10. **5:12** 1 Cor 1:24; 2 Cor 8:9; Eph 3:8; Phil 2:11; 4:19; 1 Chr 29:10-13.

13 Then I heard every creature in heaven and on earth and under the earth and on the sea, and all that is in them, singing:

"To him who sits on the throne and to the Lamb
be praise and honor and glory and power,
for ever and ever!"

14 The four living creatures said, "Amen," and the elders fell down and worshiped.

Opening the Seven Seals

The seven seals of the scroll describe God's plan for defeating the powers of evil. Two visions interrupt the opening of the scrolls: a vision of the 144,000 chosen from Israel (7:1-8) and a vision of a great multitude of people from every nation praising God (7:9-17).

The Seals

6 I watched as the Lamb opened the first of the seven seals. Then
I heard one of the four living creatures say in a voice like thunder,
"Come!" 2 I looked, and there before me was a white horse! Its rider
held a bow, and he was given a crown, and he rode out as a conqueror bent on conquest.

3 When the Lamb opened the second seal, I heard the second
living creature say, "Come!" 4 Then another horse came out, a fiery
red one. Its rider was given power to take peace from the earth and to make men slay each other. To him was given a large sword.

5 When the Lamb opened the third seal, I heard the third living creature say, "Come!" I looked, and there before me was a black
horse! Its rider was holding a pair of scales in his hand. 6 Then I
heard what sounded like a voice among the four living creatures, saying, "A quart[a] of wheat for a day's wages,[b] and three quarts of barley for a day's wages,[b] and do not damage the oil and the wine!"

7 When the Lamb opened the fourth seal, I heard the voice of
the fourth living creature say, "Come!" 8 I looked, and there before
me was a pale horse! Its rider was named Death, and Hades was following close behind him. They were given power over a fourth of the earth to kill by sword, famine and plague, and by the wild beasts of the earth.

9 When he opened the fifth seal, I saw under the altar the souls of those who had been slain because of the word of God and
the testimony they had maintained. 10 They called out in a loud voice, "How long, Sovereign Lord, holy and true, until you judge
the inhabitants of the earth and avenge our blood?" 11 Then each
of them was given a white robe, and they were told to wait a little

[a]6 Greek *a choinix* (probably about a liter) [b]6 Greek *a denarius*

5:14 *"Amen":* Here used as an expression to mean, "Yes, it is true."

6:1 *Lamb . . . seven seals:* See the notes at 5:6 and 5:1. The opening of the seals shows that what has been predicted is now going to happen.

6:2 *white horse:* This horse and the rider carrying a bow symbolize military victory. The Parthians, who lived on the eastern borders of the Roman empire, used a bow and arrow as their main weapon. This verse could be suggesting that Parthians might successfully invade the Roman empire. The crown is a symbol of victory and authority.

The horses that come out when the scroll is unsealed (6:1-8) are similar to the horses mentioned in Zechariah's eighth vision (Zech 6:1-6; see also Zech 1:7,8).

6:4 *horse . . . a fiery red one:* This horse symbolizes fierce and bloody war, including revolution.

6:5 *black horse . . . pair of scales:* The black horse probably is meant to symbolize famine. (See the note at 6:6; see also Zech 6:2,6.) Black was associated with death because the world of the dead (Hades) was thought to be a land of darkness. See the note at 1:18.

6:6 *quart of wheat . . . oil and the wine:* At this time, a "day's wage" could have bought eight to sixteen times the amount of grain mentioned in this verse. However, during famines the prices for basic foods (wheat and barley) could increase drastically. This vision shows a time when basic food items will be scarce while less essential items (olive oil and wine) will be plentiful. The instruction not to ruin the olive trees and vineyards may mean that this great famine will not continue so long that all earth's people will be destroyed.

6:4 Zech 1:8; 6:2. **6:8** Ezek 14:21.

The Four Horseman of the Apocalypse, a woodcut by Albrecht Dürer, around 1500. The opening of the seven seals begins God's judgment on those who persecuted his followers. When the first four seals are opened different colored horses come out, each one bringing a different punishment for God's enemies. The first horse is white, the second red, the third black, and the fourth pale. They bring war, famine, plague, and death to the world. When the fifth seal is broken the souls of everyone who was killed for speaking God's message are revealed and given a white robe. (See chapter 6.)

longer, until the number of their fellow servants and brothers who
were to be killed as they had been was completed.
12 I watched as he opened the sixth seal. There was a great
earthquake. The sun turned black like sackcloth made of goat hair,
the whole moon turned blood red, 13 and the stars in the sky fell to
earth, as late figs drop from a fig tree when shaken by a strong
wind. 14 The sky receded like a scroll, rolling up, and every mountain and island was removed from its place.
15 Then the kings of the earth, the princes, the generals, the
rich, the mighty, and every slave and every free man hid in caves
and among the rocks of the mountains. 16 They called to the

6:8 *pale horse . . . Death . . . Hades:* The pale-colored horse is meant to suggest death. This verse gives a picture of dead bodies scattered about as the result of war and the famine and disease that would follow. Wild animals are eating the decaying bodies. Hades is the kingdom of death (see the note at 1:18).

6:9,10 *souls . . . testimony:* These martyrs are asking God when he will judge and punish the people who killed them. Christians living at the time of John's vision would have had Christian friends or neighbors who were put in prison, tortured, or killed because they refused to worship the emperor.

6:11 *white robe . . . wait a little longer:* See the note at 3:4. Those who died (martyrs) would live in peace after death. More will die before the final victory.

6:13 *figs:* Figs are sweet fruits that grow on bushy trees. Fig trees can grow as high as thirty feet. Throughout the Mediterranean world they were an important source of food. The fig tree, like the grapevine, is a symbol of peace and plenty (Mic 4:4).

6:14 *scroll:* See the note at 5:1.

6:12 Rev 11:13; 16:18; Isa 13:10; Joel 2:10,31; 3:15; Matt 24:29; Mark 13:24,25; Luke 21:25. **6:13,14** Isa 34:4. **6:14** Rev 16:20. **6:15** Isa 2:19, 21. **6:16** Hos 10:8; Luke 23:30.

mountains and the rocks, "Fall on us and hide us from the face of
him who sits on the throne and from the wrath of the Lamb! 17For
the great day of their wrath has come, and who can stand?"

144,000 Sealed

7 After this I saw four angels standing at the four corners of the
earth, holding back the four winds of the earth to prevent any
wind from blowing on the land or on the sea or on any tree. 2Then
I saw another angel coming up from the east, having the seal of the
living God. He called out in a loud voice to the four angels who
had been given power to harm the land and the sea: 3"Do not
harm the land or the sea or the trees until we put a seal on the
foreheads of the servants of our God." 4Then I heard the number
of those who were sealed: 144,000 from all the tribes of Israel.

5From the tribe of Judah 12,000 were sealed,
from the tribe of Reuben 12,000,
from the tribe of Gad 12,000,
6from the tribe of Asher 12,000,
from the tribe of Naphtali 12,000,
from the tribe of Manasseh 12,000,
7from the tribe of Simeon 12,000,
from the tribe of Levi 12,000,
from the tribe of Issachar 12,000,
8from the tribe of Zebulun 12,000,
from the tribe of Joseph 12,000,
from the tribe of Benjamin 12,000.

The Great Multitude in White Robes

9After this I looked and there before me was a great multitude that no one could count, from every nation, tribe, people and
language, standing before the throne and in front of the Lamb.
They were wearing white robes and were holding palm branches in
their hands. 10And they cried out in a loud voice:

"Salvation belongs to our God,
who sits on the throne,
and to the Lamb."

11All the angels were standing around the throne and around the
elders and the four living creatures. They fell down on their faces
before the throne and worshiped God, 12saying:

"Amen!
Praise and glory
and wisdom and thanks and honor
and power and strength
be to our God for ever and ever.
Amen!"

6:16 *him who sits on the throne . . . wrath of the Lamb:* Meaning God and Christ (see the note at 5:6).

6:17 *the great day of their wrath:* The day when God will judge the world (see the note at 3:10).

7:1 *four angels:* See the note at 1:1 (angel). These angels have the power to harm the earth. However, they also will protect God's people so they can survive and be part of God's new creation.

7:2 *seal of the living God:* This seal may have been like the design on a king's signet ring, used to put the king's special mark on official papers or to mark the king's personal property. It is a sign of ownership.

7:4 *144,000:* This is a symbolic number for the twelve tribes of Israel multiplied by twelve and then by one thousand. Among other things, the number twelve was considered a symbol of completeness. So this group represents the complete people of God. The actual number is more than John could count (7:9). See the chart called "Numbers in the Bible," p. 2405.

7:5-8 *Judah . . . Benjamin:* These verses list the names of the tribes of Israel (see the mini-article called "Israel," p. 264). In this list, Manasseh (named after one of Joseph's sons) has replaced Dan, mostly likely because the tribe of Dan had sinned against the Lord by worshiping idols (Judg 18; 1 Kgs 12:28-33).

7:9 *white robes . . . palm branches:* See the note at 3:4 (white). Palm branches were symbols of victory.

7:11 *the elders and the four living creatures:* See the notes at 4:4-10 (elders) and 4:6–9 (creatures).

7:12 *Amen:* See the notes at 3:14 and 5:14.

6:17 Joel 2:11; Mal 3:2. **7:1** Jer 49:36; Dan 7:2; Zech 6:5. **7:3** Ezek 9:4-6.

Angels Restraining the Winds, an illuminated page from Beatus' *Commentary on the Apocalypse,* Spanish, around 1175. Before the last of the seven seals is opened, four angels hold back the winds as a fifth angel descends from the sun. The four angels prevent anything from harming the earth until 144,000 "servants of our God" have their foreheads marked by the fifth angel. The number 144,000 represents the entire people of God: twelve thousand from each of the twelve tribes of Israel. (See 7:1-8.)

13Then one of the elders asked me, "These in white robes—
who are they, and where did they come from?"
14I answered, "Sir, you know."
And he said, "These are they who have come out of the great
tribulation; they have washed their robes and made them white in
the blood of the Lamb. 15Therefore,

"they are before the throne of God
and serve him day and night in his temple;
and he who sits on the throne will spread his tent over
them.

7:14 *washed their robes ... blood of the Lamb:* Meaning that Christ has forgiven them. See also the note at 5:6. The clean robes show that their lives have been made pure.

7:14 Dan 12:1; Matt 24:21; Mark 13:19.

> One of the elders said to John: *"The Lamb at the center of the throne will be their shepherd; he will lead them to springs of living water. And God will wipe away every tear from their eyes."*
> Rev 7:17

7:17 *the Lamb . . . will be their shepherd:* See the note at 5:6. In the Bible, God and Jesus are pictured as shepherds (see Ps 23:1; Ezek 34:11-31; John 10:7-16).

8:2 *trumpets:* The trumpets given to the seven angels represent a series of judgments against those who disobeyed God. Trumpets were used to gather God's people for the great Jewish festivals (Num 10:3,10; 29:1) or to proclaim that a new king had begun to rule (1 Kgs 1:34,39; 2 Kgs 9:13; see also 1 Thes 4:16).

8:6 *seven angels:* This probably refers to a specific group of angels who were above the others, according to some Jewish traditions.

8:8 *huge mountain, all ablaze, was thrown into the sea:* REVELATION was likely written after the eruption in A.D. 79 of Mount Vesuvius, a volcano that buried the city of Pompeii and destroyed many ships in the city's harbor. Details of this disaster surely would have reached the cities of Asia Minor. Volcanos, like earthquakes, were often seen as punishment from the gods in the ancient world.

7:16 Isa 49:10; Ps 121:5,6; Rev 21:3-7; 22:14. **7:17** Ps 23:2; Isa 25:8; 49:10; Rev 21:6. **8:3** Exod 30:1,3; Amos 9:1. **8:4** Ps 141:2. **8:5** Exod 19:16; Lev 16:12; Ezek 10:2; Rev 11:19; 16:18. **8:7** Exod 9:23-25; Ezek 38:22. **8:10** Isa 14:12.

16 Never again will they hunger;
never again will they thirst.
The sun will not beat upon them,
nor any scorching heat.
17 For the Lamb at the center of the throne will be
their shepherd;
he will lead them to springs of living water.
And God will wipe away every tear from their
eyes."

The Seventh Seal and the Golden Censer

8 When he opened the seventh seal, there was silence in heaven
for about half an hour.
2 And I saw the seven angels who stand before God, and to
them were given seven trumpets.
3 Another angel, who had a golden censer, came and stood at
the altar. He was given much incense to offer, with the prayers of
all the saints, on the golden altar before the throne. 4 The smoke of
the incense, together with the prayers of the saints, went up before
God from the angel's hand. 5 Then the angel took the censer, filled
it with fire from the altar, and hurled it on the earth; and there
came peals of thunder, rumblings, flashes of lightning and an
earthquake.

The Seven Trumpets

In John's vision the angels blow trumpets, which announce the beginning of several severe punishments. The first four angels send punishments on nature, and the last three send punishments directly on the people who are enemies of God. Some of these punishments are like the plagues God sent upon Egypt many centuries earlier (Exod 7–10). The faithful followers who received the special mark from God are protected from these punishments.

The Trumpets

6 Then the seven angels who had the seven trumpets prepared to sound them.
7 The first angel sounded his trumpet, and there came hail
and fire mixed with blood, and it was hurled down upon the earth.
A third of the earth was burned up, a third of the trees were
burned up, and all the green grass was burned up.
8 The second angel sounded his trumpet, and something like
a huge mountain, all ablaze, was thrown into the sea. A third of the
sea turned into blood, 9 a third of the living creatures in the sea
died, and a third of the ships were destroyed.
10 The third angel sounded his trumpet, and a great star, blazing like a torch, fell from the sky on a third of the rivers and on

the springs of water— [11]the name of the star is Wormwood.[a] A third of the waters turned bitter, and many people died from the waters that had become bitter.

[12]The fourth angel sounded his trumpet, and a third of the sun was struck, a third of the moon, and a third of the stars, so that a third of them turned dark. A third of the day was without light, and also a third of the night.

[13]As I watched, I heard an eagle that was flying in midair call out in a loud voice: "Woe! Woe! Woe to the inhabitants of the earth, because of the trumpet blasts about to be sounded by the other three angels!"

9 The fifth angel sounded his trumpet, and I saw a star that had fallen from the sky to the earth. The star was given the key to the shaft of the Abyss. [2]When he opened the Abyss, smoke rose from it like the smoke from a gigantic furnace. The sun and sky were darkened by the smoke from the Abyss. [3]And out of the smoke locusts came down upon the earth and were given power like that of scorpions of the earth. [4]They were told not to harm the grass of the earth or any plant or tree, but only those people who did not have the seal of God on their foreheads. [5]They were not given power to kill them, but only to torture them for five months. And the agony they suffered was like that of the sting of a scorpion when it strikes a man. [6]During those days men will seek death, but will not find it; they will long to die, but death will elude them.

[7]The locusts looked like horses prepared for battle. On their heads they wore something like crowns of gold, and their faces resembled human faces. [8]Their hair was like women's hair, and their teeth were like lions' teeth. [9]They had breastplates like breastplates of iron, and the sound of their wings was like the thundering of many horses and chariots rushing into battle. [10]They had tails and stings like scorpions, and in their tails they had power to torment people for five months. [11]They had as king over them the angel of the Abyss, whose name in Hebrew is Abaddon, and in Greek, Apollyon.[b]

[12]The first woe is past; two other woes are yet to come.

[13]The sixth angel sounded his trumpet, and I heard a voice coming from the horns[c] of the golden altar that is before God. [14]It said to the sixth angel who had the trumpet, "Release the four angels who are bound at the great river Euphrates." [15]And the four angels who had been kept ready for this very hour and day and month and year were released to kill a third of mankind. [16]The number of the mounted troops was two hundred million. I heard their number.

[17]The horses and riders I saw in my vision looked like this: Their breastplates were fiery red, dark blue, and yellow as sulfur.

[a]11 That is, Bitterness [b]11 *Abaddon* and *Apollyon* mean *Destroyer.* [c]13 That is, projections

8:11 *Wormwood:* The word translated as "Wormwood" sounds like the name of a tree that grew in Palestine. Its leaves were used to make medicine, and its roots contained a bitter juice. At Marah, Moses made bitter water fit to drink when he threw a piece of wood into it (Exod 15:22-25). Here the reverse is happening. See also Jer 9:15.

8:12 *turned dark:* This punishment sounds like what happens during an eclipse of the sun or moon. Here it means that the light of God is being taken from many on earth.

9:1 *star that had fallen . . . Abyss:* The fifth angel symbolizes plagues that spread over the peoples of the earth. In the ancient world, people often thought of stars as living beings, such as angels. The Abyss here refers to the underworld, a place in the depths of the earth where the evil and the disobedient spirits waited to be judged. See also the mini-article called "Hell," p. 1944.

9:3-10 *locusts . . . stings like scorpions:* In the Bible locusts are frequently used as a symbol of God's anger and punishment. See the mini-article called "Locusts," p. 1708. But these locusts have stinging tails like scorpions. The stinging locusts hurt only those who do not have God's seal on their foreheads (See 7:1-4).

9:14 *great river Euphrates:* This river marked the eastern boundary of the land God promised to give Abraham (see Gen 15:18; Deut 11:24; Josh 1:4). At the time of John's vision, the Euphrates was at the eastern boundary of the Roman empire (see the map on p. 2471). Across the river lived the Parthians, who were fierce warriors.

8:12 Isa 13:10; Ezek 32:7; Joel 2:10,31; 3:15. **9:2** Gen 19:28. **9:3** Exod 10:12-15. **9:4** Ezek 9:4. **9:6** Job 3:21; Jer 8:3. **9:7** Joel 2:4. **9:8** Joel 1:6. **9:9** Joel 2:5. **9:13** Exod 30:1-3; Rev 1:10; 4:1.

The heads of the horses resembled the heads of lions, and out of
their mouths came fire, smoke and sulfur. 18 A third of mankind
was killed by the three plagues of fire, smoke and sulfur that came
out of their mouths. 19 The power of the horses was in their
mouths and in their tails; for their tails were like snakes, having
heads with which they inflict injury.
20 The rest of mankind that were not killed by these plagues
still did not repent of the work of their hands; they did not stop
worshiping demons, and idols of gold, silver, bronze, stone and
wood—idols that cannot see or hear or walk. 21 Nor did they repent
of their murders, their magic arts, their sexual immorality or their
thefts.

The Angel and the Little Scroll

10 Then I saw another mighty angel coming down from heaven.
He was robed in a cloud, with a rainbow above his head; his face
was like the sun, and his legs were like fiery pillars. 2 He was holding a little scroll, which lay open in his hand. He planted his right
foot on the sea and his left foot on the land, 3 and he gave a loud
shout like the roar of a lion. When he shouted, the voices of the
seven thunders spoke. 4 And when the seven thunders spoke, I was
about to write; but I heard a voice from heaven say, "Seal up what
the seven thunders have said and do not write it down."
5 Then the angel I had seen standing on the sea and on the
land raised his right hand to heaven. 6 And he swore by him who
lives for ever and ever, who created the heavens and all that is in
them, the earth and all that is in it, and the sea and all that is in it,
and said, "There will be no more delay! 7 But in the days when the
seventh angel is about to sound his trumpet, the mystery of God
will be accomplished, just as he announced to his servants the
prophets."
8 Then the voice that I had heard from heaven spoke to me
once more: "Go, take the scroll that lies open in the hand of the
angel who is standing on the sea and on the land."
9 So I went to the angel and asked him to give me the little
scroll. He said to me, "Take it and eat it. It will turn your stomach
sour, but in your mouth it will be as sweet as honey." 10 I took the
little scroll from the angel's hand and ate it. It tasted as sweet as
honey in my mouth, but when I had eaten it, my stomach turned
sour. 11 Then I was told, "You must prophesy again about many
peoples, nations, languages and kings."

The Two Witnesses

11 I was given a reed like a measuring rod and was told, "Go
and measure the temple of God and the altar, and count the worshipers there. 2 But exclude the outer court; do not measure it,
because it has been given to the Gentiles. They will trample on the

9:20 *idols of gold, silver, bronze, stone and wood:* Even these horrible experiences did not convince some to stop worshiping idols. Those who followed false gods and worshiped images disobeyed the living God (Exod 20:4-6). Christians in John's day faced pressure to worship idols and the Roman emperor. See the Introduction to REVELATION, p. 2403.

9:21 *their magic arts:* Magic, forbidden by the Law of Moses (Lev 19:26), was practiced by some people living in the Roman empire. See also Acts 8:9-11 and the article called "Miracles, Magic, and Medicine," p. 1838.

10:1 *mighty angel:* See the note at 1:1 (angel). Before the seventh trumpet sounds, two visions show how God continues to speak to his people.

10:2 *little scroll:* See the note at 5:1.

10:7 *mystery . . . prophets:* This refers to the prophets of ancient Israel who spoke God's messages of hope and judgment. The "mystery" probably refers to what God promised to do by raising Christ from death. See Rom 1:2-4; 16:25; see also the note at 1:3.

11:1 *a reed like a measuring rod:* Refers to a giant reed surveyors used for measuring. This reed grows in swampy areas and can reach a height of twenty feet.

11:1 *measure the temple of God:* For more about the temple, see the article called "People of the Law: The Religion of Israel," p. 939. Here the temple may refer to all of God's true followers, who, like the courtyard, will be trampled by the heathen who don't know God (11:2). John is to measure the people of God to see if they are being faithful to God. See 1 Cor 3:16; 2 Cor 6:16; 1 Pet 2:5; Eph 2:21.

9:20 Ps 115:4-7; 135:15-17; Dan 5:23. **10:5-7** Exod 20:11; Deut 32:40; Dan 12:7; Amos 3:7. **10:8-10** Ezek 2:8—3:3. **11:1** Ezek 40:3; Zech 2:1,2. **11:2** Luke 21:24.

holy city for 42 months. 3And I will give power to my two witnesses, and they will prophesy for 1,260 days, clothed in sackcloth."
4These are the two olive trees and the two lampstands that stand
before the Lord of the earth. 5If anyone tries to harm them, fire
comes from their mouths and devours their enemies. This is how
anyone who wants to harm them must die. 6These men have
power to shut up the sky so that it will not rain during the time
they are prophesying; and they have power to turn the waters into
blood and to strike the earth with every kind of plague as often as
they want.

7Now when they have finished their testimony, the beast that
comes up from the Abyss will attack them, and overpower and kill
them. 8Their bodies will lie in the street of the great city, which is
figuratively called Sodom and Egypt, where also their Lord was
crucified. 9For three and a half days men from every people, tribe,
language and nation will gaze on their bodies and refuse them
burial. 10The inhabitants of the earth will gloat over them and will
celebrate by sending each other gifts, because these two prophets
had tormented those who live on the earth.

11But after the three and a half days a breath of life from God
entered them, and they stood on their feet, and terror struck those
who saw them. 12Then they heard a loud voice from heaven saying
to them, "Come up here." And they went up to heaven in a cloud,
while their enemies looked on.

13At that very hour there was a severe earthquake and a tenth
of the city collapsed. Seven thousand people were killed in the
earthquake, and the survivors were terrified and gave glory to the
God of heaven.

14The second woe has passed; the third woe is coming soon.

The Seventh Trumpet

15The seventh angel sounded his trumpet, and there were
loud voices in heaven, which said:

"The kingdom of the world has become the kingdom of
our Lord and of his Christ,
and he will reign for ever and ever."

16And the twenty-four elders, who were seated on their thrones
before God, fell on their faces and worshiped God, 17saying:

"We give thanks to you, Lord God Almighty,
the One who is and who was,
because you have taken your great power
and have begun to reign.
18The nations were angry;
and your wrath has come.
The time has come for judging the dead,
and for rewarding your servants the prophets

11:2 *42 months:* In 167 B.C., a ruler named Antiochus IV Epiphanes set up pagan images in the temple and commanded the Jewish people to worship them. The images stayed there three and a half years until the Jewish people led by the Maccabees reclaimed and purified the temple.

11:3 *two witnesses:* The identity of these two is not clear. The reference to olive trees in 11:4 is like that of Zechariah's vision (Zech 4:3,11-14), which mentions the two "anointed to serve the Lord" whom God will use to renew the temple and God's people. The powers mentioned in 11:5,6 sound like the punishment of enemies carried out by Elijah (1 Kgs 17:1; 2 Kgs 1:10) and Moses (Exod 7:17-19).

11:3 *sackcloth:* A rough dark cloth worn in times of trouble to show sorrow.

11:7 *beast that comes up from the Abyss:* See the note at 9:1. The beast is the enemy of God's people (see also 13:11-18).

11:8 *great city . . . Sodom and Egypt:* The "great city" is Jerusalem. It had once been the city where God was present in the temple. Now, in John's vision, it has become a symbol of evil and opposition to God like the immoral city Sodom (see Gen 18:16—19:29) and Israel's ancient oppressor Egypt (see Exod 1).

11:14 *second woe:* The first woe (9:12) was the destruction that happened after the fifth angel blew his trumpet. The beast killing the Lord's two witnesses is the second woe.

11:16 *twenty-four elders:* See the note at 4:4-10.

11:18 *judging the dead:* See the notes at 3:10 and 6:17.

11:5 1 Kgs 18:38. **11:6** 1 Kgs 17:1; Exod 7:17-19; 1 Sam 4:8. **11:7** Dan 7:7,21; Rev 13:5-7; 17:8. **11:8** Isa 1:9,10. **11:11** Ezek 37:1-10. **1:12** 2 Kgs 2:11; Luke 24:50,51; Acts 1:6-11. **11:13** Ezek 38:19,20; Rev 6:12; 16:18. **11:15** Exod 15:18; Dan 2:44; 7:14,27. **11:18** Ps 2:5; 110:5; 115:13.

and your saints and those who reverence your name,
both small and great—
and for destroying those who destroy the earth."

[19]Then God's temple in heaven was opened, and within his
temple was seen the ark of his covenant. And there came flashes of
lightning, rumblings, peals of thunder, an earthquake and a great
hailstorm.

A loud voice in heaven said, *"Now have come the salvation and the power and the kingdom of our God, and the authority of his Christ."* Rev 12:10

The Opponents of God

John describes a battle between God's forces and the forces of evil, pictured as a dragon and two beasts. For a time the dragon and beasts are allowed to fight against God's people, to rule over people, and to work miracles that fool people into worshiping the image of the beast.

The Woman and the Dragon

12 A great and wondrous sign appeared in heaven: a woman
clothed with the sun, with the moon under her feet and a crown of
twelve stars on her head. [2]She was pregnant and cried out in pain
as she was about to give birth. [3]Then another sign appeared in
heaven: an enormous red dragon with seven heads and ten horns
and seven crowns on his heads. [4]His tail swept a third of the stars
out of the sky and flung them to the earth. The dragon stood in
front of the woman who was about to give birth, so that he might
devour her child the moment it was born. [5]She gave birth to a son,
a male child, who will rule all the nations with an iron scepter. And
her child was snatched up to God and to his throne. [6]The woman
fled into the desert to a place prepared for her by God, where she
might be taken care of for 1,260 days.

[7]And there was war in heaven. Michael and his angels fought
against the dragon, and the dragon and his angels fought back.
[8]But he was not strong enough, and they lost their place in heav-
en. [9]The great dragon was hurled down—that ancient serpent
called the devil, or Satan, who leads the whole world astray. He was
hurled to the earth, and his angels with him.

[10]Then I heard a loud voice in heaven say:

"Now have come the salvation and the power and the
kingdom of our God,
and the authority of his Christ.
For the accuser of our brothers,
who accuses them before our God day and night,
has been hurled down.
[11]They overcame him
by the blood of the Lamb
and by the word of their testimony;
they did not love their lives so much

11:19 *ark of his covenant:* See the mini-article called "The Ark of the Covenant," p. 513. The ark of the covenant was the symbol of God's presence with his people.

12:1-6 *a woman . . . a place prepared for her by God:* The woman in these verses probably is a symbol for Israel (12:5) or the whole people of God (12:6).

12:3,4 *red dragon with seven heads and ten horns . . . devour her child:* The dragon is identified in 12:9 as the devil, God's chief opponent. See the mini-article called "Satan," p. 963. The seven heads and ten horns may refer to the series of men who struggled to gain control of the Roman empire, or to Rome itself, which was built on seven hills. The stars swept from the sky may symbolize the Roman emperors' claims to be gods. The newborn child that the dragon wanted to devour is Jesus.

12:6 *1,260 days:* This equals three and a half years (see the note at 11:2).

12:7 *Michael and his angels:* Michael was a chief angel who was the special protector of Israel, and would save the people of Israel from destruction in the last days (Dan 12:1). Michael will also protect God's new people, the church. (See also Dan 10:13,20,21; Jude 9.)

11:19 Rev 8:5; 16:18,21. **12:3** Dan 7:7. **12:4** Dan 8:10. **12:5** Isa 66:7; Ps 2:9; Acts 1:6-11; Heb 1:3,4. **12:9** Gen 3:1; Luke 10:18. **12:10** Job 1:9-11; Zech 3:1.

as to shrink from death.
[12]Therefore rejoice, you heavens
and you who dwell in them!
But woe to the earth and the sea,
because the devil has gone down to you!
He is filled with fury,
because he knows that his time is short."

[13]When the dragon saw that he had been hurled to the earth,
he pursued the woman who had given birth to the male child.

12:9 *the devil, or Satan:* See the note at 12:3,4.

12:10 *Christ:* "Christ" is based on the Greek word *Christos,* and like the Hebrew word *Messiah* means "Chosen One." For more, see the mini-article called "Messiah (Chosen One)," p. 1124.

12:11 *the Lamb:* See the note at 5:6. The death of Christ on the cross, and Christ's resurrection, defeated Satan.

Archangel Michael surrounded by saints, a Byzantine relief icon, tenth or eleventh century. The Christians who first read REVELATION would have been familiar with the reptile-like monsters called dragons from the myths of the ancient Near East. But John used the dragon nine times in REVELATION to represent God's enemy, Satan. REVELATION includes a vision of the day when the archangel Michael will lead the other angels in the battle against the dragon and its angels. Michael and his angels will win, and Satan and his angels will be thrown out of heaven. (See 12:7-9.)

14The woman was given the two wings of a great eagle, so that she
might fly to the place prepared for her in the desert, where she
would be taken care of for a time, times and half a time, out of the
serpent's reach. 15Then from his mouth the serpent spewed water
like a river, to overtake the woman and sweep her away with the
torrent. 16But the earth helped the woman by opening its mouth
and swallowing the river that the dragon had spewed out of his
mouth. 17Then the dragon was enraged at the woman and went off
to make war against the rest of her offspring—those who obey God's
13 commandments and hold to the testimony of Jesus. 1And the
dragon[a] stood on the shore of the sea.

The Beast out of the Sea

And I saw a beast coming out of the sea. He had ten horns
and seven heads, with ten crowns on his horns, and on each head a
blasphemous name. 2The beast I saw resembled a leopard, but had
feet like those of a bear and a mouth like that of a lion. The dragon
gave the beast his power and his throne and great authority. 3One of
the heads of the beast seemed to have had a fatal wound, but the
fatal wound had been healed. The whole world was astonished and
followed the beast. 4Men worshiped the dragon because he had
given authority to the beast, and they also worshiped the beast and
asked, "Who is like the beast? Who can make war against him?"

5The beast was given a mouth to utter proud words and
blasphemies and to exercise his authority for forty-two months.
6He opened his mouth to blaspheme God, and to slander his name
and his dwelling place and those who live in heaven. 7He was given
power to make war against the saints and to conquer them. And he
was given authority over every tribe, people, language and nation.
8All inhabitants of the earth will worship the beast—all whose
names have not been written in the book of life belonging to the
Lamb that was slain from the creation of the world.[b]

9He who has an ear, let him hear.

10If anyone is to go into captivity,
  into captivity he will go.
If anyone is to be killed[c] with the sword,
  with the sword he will be killed.

This calls for patient endurance and faithfulness on the part of the
saints.

[a]1 Some late manuscripts *And I* [b]8 Or *written from the creation of the world in the book of life belonging to the Lamb that was slain* [c]10 Some manuscripts *anyone kills*

12:14 *a time, times and half a time:* Three and a half years. See the notes at 11:2 and 12:6.

12:15 *serpent . . . river:* The flood of water symbolizes the troubles that the forces of evil would pour out upon people.

13:1 *beast coming out of the sea:* This may symbolize the Roman empire, whose armies came across the sea to attack parts of Asia Minor. The heads, horns, and crowns likely refer to the series of Roman emperors, whose names became an insult to God because they insisted on being worshiped as if they were gods. The beast (Rome and its emperors) received power from the dragon (Satan, 13:4).

13:3 *One of the heads:* May refer to how the Roman emperors struggled to gain and keep power.

13:5 *forty-two months:* The length of time the empire was to last was one-half the sacred number of seven, since 42 months equals three and a half years. See the note at 11:2.

13:6,7 *blaspheme God . . . make war against the saints:* In A.D. 70, the Romans destroyed the Jewish temple, which was considered the place where God was present among his people. By blaspheming (cursing) God, the beast was also cursing all those who fought and died to remain faithful to God. The Roman emperors and local leaders punished and imprisoned Christians who refused to take part in emperor worship.

13:11 *another beast:* This probably refers to a particular leader who forced people, especially Christians, to worship the Roman emperor.

12:14 Dan 7:25; 12:7. **13:1** Dan 7:3; Rev 17:3,7-12. **13:2** Dan 7:4-6. **13:5,6** Dan 7:8,25; 11:36; 12:7. **13:7** Dan 7:21. **13:8** Ps 69:28. **13:10** Jer 15:2; 43:11.

The Beast out of the Earth

11 Then I saw another beast, coming out of the earth. He had
two horns like a lamb, but he spoke like a dragon. 12 He exercised
all the authority of the first beast on his behalf, and made the earth
and its inhabitants worship the first beast, whose fatal wound had
been healed. 13 And he performed great and miraculous signs, even
causing fire to come down from heaven to earth in full view of
men. 14 Because of the signs he was given power to do on behalf of
the first beast, he deceived the inhabitants of the earth. He ordered
them to set up an image in honor of the beast who was wounded
by the sword and yet lived. 15 He was given power to give breath to
the image of the first beast, so that it could speak and cause all
who refused to worship the image to be killed. 16 He also forced
everyone, small and great, rich and poor, free and slave, to receive
a mark on his right hand or on his forehead, 17 so that no one could
buy or sell unless he had the mark, which is the name of the beast
or the number of his name.

18 This calls for wisdom. If anyone has insight, let him calculate the number of the beast, for it is man's number. His number
is 666.

13:16,17 *a mark . . . name of the beast or the number of his name:* This may refer to some sort of mark that showed a person took part in ceremonies worshiping the emperor. It may also refer to the Roman coins that had the image of the emperor on them. Christians who refused to use the coins could be forced to give up their businesses. See also the note at 2:20.

13:18 *His number is 666:* The number of the beast is the number of incompleteness and imperfection, since six is the sacred number seven minus one. Repeating it three times (666) emphasizes just how imperfect the number is. In both Greek and Hebrew, letters of the alphabet also were used as numbers. Some scholars believe this number stood for the Roman emperor Nero.

QUESTIONS ABOUT REVELATION 4:1—13:18

1. In John's vision, what was happening at the "throne"? (chapters 4,5) Who are the twenty-four elders? (4:4,10)
2. Who is the Lamb? (5:6-13) What is the scroll with the seven seals? (5:1-5; 6:1—8:1) What animals are connected with the opening of the first four seals? What does each represent?
3. Who does John see when the fifth seal is opened? (6:9-11) What happens when the sixth seal is opened? (6:12—7:17) Who are the 144,000 who are marked on their foreheads? (7:4-8)
4. What happens when each of the first six angels blows his trumpet? (8:2—9:21) What is revealed when the seventh and last trumpet is sounded? (10:1-11)
5. Describe the two witnesses (11:1-6). What is their task? What happens to them? (11:7-13)
6. What happens when the seventh trumpet is sounded? (11:15-19) Who are the woman and the dragon? (12:1-6) After fighting in heaven with the archangel Michael, what does the dragon do next? (12:13-17) What do you think this battle represents?
7. Who is the beast that comes up from the sea? (13:1-4) From where did it get its power? How long was the beast allowed to rule? (13:5) What is significant about this amount of time? What was the second beast able to do? (13:11-18)
8. Chapters 4 through 13 are filled with many images and symbols. How do you think the original readers interpreted their meanings? What, if anything, do these passages have to say to us today?

14:1 *Mount Zion:* Where the temple in Jerusalem had been. See the mini-article called "Zion," p. 1294.

14:1 *Lamb . . . 144,000 . . . his Father's name:* See the notes at 5:6; 7:4 (144,000); and the note on p. 2404 (priests . . . Father).

14:3 *four living creatures:* See the note at 4:6-9.

14:4 *firstfruits:* This phrase could also be translated "the most precious people." The special people who have been redeemed by Christ are the first of many who will share in the new life of God's people.

14:8 *Babylon the Great:* Babylon was one of the splendid and powerful empires of the ancient world. Because it oppressed the people of Judah, looting and destroying the temple in Jerusalem (587 B.C.), John uses it as a symbol for Rome. Because Rome was evil and caused other nations to be immoral, the second angel announces that it will fall. See the mini-article called "Babylon," p. 1363.

14:10 *wine of God's fury . . . burning sulfur:* To drink the wine of God's fury means to receive God's punishment. Fire and burning are often connected with God's judgment of those who reject him. Sulfur is a mineral that gives off a very strong odor when burned.

14:14 *sickle:* A knife with a long curved blade used to cut down stalks of grain and other crops.

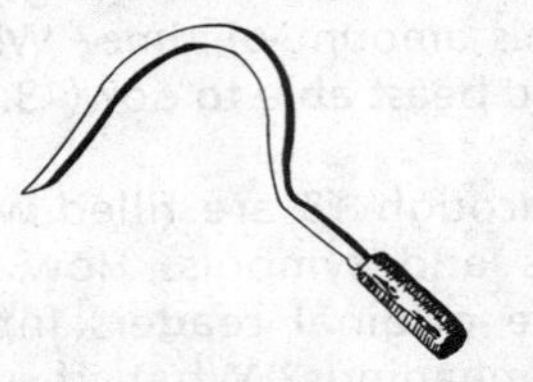

14:1 Ezek 9:4; Rev 7:3. **14:5** Zeph 3:13. **14:8** Isa 21:9; Jer 51:8; Rev 18:2. **14:10** Isa 51:17; Gen 19:24; Ezek 38:22. **14:11** Isa 34:10.

Visions of God's Judgment and Protection

This section begins with a vision of the Lamb and continues with a description of how God will judge everyone. Those who worship the beast will face God's anger and punishment. Seven angels empty seven bowls of God's anger on the earth.

The Lamb and the 144,000

14 Then I looked, and there before me was the Lamb, standing
on Mount Zion, and with him 144,000 who had his name and his
Father's name written on their foreheads. 2And I heard a sound from
heaven like the roar of rushing waters and like a loud peal of thunder. The sound I heard was like that of harpists playing their harps.
3And they sang a new song before the throne and before the four living creatures and the elders. No one could learn the song except the
144,000 who had been redeemed from the earth. 4These are those
who did not defile themselves with women, for they kept themselves pure. They follow the Lamb wherever he goes. They were
purchased from among men and offered as firstfruits to God and
the Lamb. 5No lie was found in their mouths; they are blameless.

The Three Angels

6Then I saw another angel flying in midair, and he had the
eternal gospel to proclaim to those who live on the earth—to every
nation, tribe, language and people. 7He said in a loud voice, "Fear
God and give him glory, because the hour of his judgment has
come. Worship him who made the heavens, the earth, the sea and
the springs of water."
8A second angel followed and said, "Fallen! Fallen is Babylon
the Great, which made all the nations drink the maddening wine
of her adulteries."
9A third angel followed them and said in a loud voice: "If
anyone worships the beast and his image and receives his mark on
the forehead or on the hand, 10he, too, will drink of the wine of
God's fury, which has been poured full strength into the cup of his
wrath. He will be tormented with burning sulfur in the presence of
the holy angels and of the Lamb. 11And the smoke of their torment
rises for ever and ever. There is no rest day or night for those who
worship the beast and his image, or for anyone who receives the
mark of his name." 12This calls for patient endurance on the part
of the saints who obey God's commandments and remain faithful
to Jesus.
13Then I heard a voice from heaven say, "Write: Blessed are
the dead who die in the Lord from now on."
"Yes," says the Spirit, "they will rest from their labor, for their
deeds will follow them."

The Harvest of the Earth

[14]I looked, and there before me was a white cloud, and seated on the cloud was one "like a son of man"[a] with a crown of gold
on his head and a sharp sickle in his hand. [15]Then another angel
came out of the temple and called in a loud voice to him who was
sitting on the cloud, "Take your sickle and reap, because the time
to reap has come, for the harvest of the earth is ripe." [16]So he who
was seated on the cloud swung his sickle over the earth, and the
earth was harvested.

[17]Another angel came out of the temple in heaven, and he
too had a sharp sickle. [18]Still another angel, who had charge of the
fire, came from the altar and called in a loud voice to him who had
the sharp sickle, "Take your sharp sickle and gather the clusters of
grapes from the earth's vine, because its grapes are ripe." [19]The
angel swung his sickle on the earth, gathered its grapes and threw
them into the great winepress of God's wrath. [20]They were trampled in the winepress outside the city, and blood flowed out of the
press, rising as high as the horses' bridles for a distance of 1,600
stadia.[b]

Seven Angels With Seven Plagues

15 I saw in heaven another great and marvelous sign: seven
angels with the seven last plagues—last, because with them God's
wrath is completed. [2]And I saw what looked like a sea of glass
mixed with fire and, standing beside the sea, those who had been
victorious over the beast and his image and over the number of his
name. They held harps given them by God [3]and sang the song of
Moses the servant of God and the song of the Lamb:

"Great and marvelous are your deeds,
  Lord God Almighty.
Just and true are your ways,
  King of the ages.
[4]Who will not fear you, O Lord,
  and bring glory to your name?
For you alone are holy.
All nations will come
  and worship before you,
for your righteous acts have been revealed."

[5]After this I looked and in heaven the temple, that is, the
tabernacle of the Testimony, was opened. [6]Out of the temple came
the seven angels with the seven plagues. They were dressed in
clean, shining linen and wore golden sashes around their chests.
[7]Then one of the four living creatures gave to the seven angels
seven golden bowls filled with the wrath of God, who lives for ever

[a]14 Daniel 7:13 [b]20 That is, about 180 miles (about 300 kilometers)

14:18,19 *grapes . . . winepress of God's wrath:* The prophets of Israel spoke of God's people as a vineyard where grapes are grown (Isa 5). They also compare God's judgment on the people for their disobedience to the harvesting of grapes (Joel 3:13). Similar images are used here to describe what will happen to all people who reject God. In the ancient world, wine was made by putting ripe grapes in a press and stomping on them to extract the juice. Those who rejected God would be crushed just like grapes in a winepress. See also the mini-article called "Wine," p. 2047.

15:1 *seven last plagues:* The seven bowls of God's anger are described in 16:1-21.

15:2 *sea of glass mixed with fire:* Like the Red Sea in Exodus, the glass sea symbolizes the boundary set by God to protect God's people from their enemies (Exod 14).

15:3 *Moses:* The great leader who led the Israelite people out of slavery in Egypt and received God's Law for the people. See the mini-article called "Moses," p. 2335. Moses helped save the people of Israel. Jesus Christ, the Lamb, is the Savior of all people.

15:5 *tabernacle of the Testimony:* The ancient people of Israel were commanded to create a tent that would be the place where God would live among them. They carried this tent (called the tabernacle or Tent of Meeting) with them as they wandered in the desert after leaving Egypt (Num 17:7; 18:4). The real tabernacle of God's presence is here seen in heaven (see also Heb 8:1-5).

15:7 *four living creatures:* See the note at 4:6-9.

14:14 Dan 7:13. **14:15** Joel 3:13. **14:20** Isa 63:3; Lam 1:15; Rev 19:15. **15:3** Exod 15:1; Deut 32:4; Ps 145:17. **15:4** Jer 10:7; Ps 86:9. **15:5** Exod 38:21-31.

and ever. 8And the temple was filled with smoke from the glory of God and from his power, and no one could enter the temple until the seven plagues of the seven angels were completed.

The Seven Bowls of God's Wrath

16 Then I heard a loud voice from the temple saying to the seven angels, "Go, pour out the seven bowls of God's wrath on the earth."

2The first angel went and poured out his bowl on the land, and ugly and painful sores broke out on the people who had the mark of the beast and worshiped his image.

3The second angel poured out his bowl on the sea, and it turned into blood like that of a dead man, and every living thing in the sea died.

4The third angel poured out his bowl on the rivers and springs of water, and they became blood. 5Then I heard the angel in charge of the waters say:

"You are just in these judgments,
you who are and who were, the Holy One,
because you have so judged;
6for they have shed the blood of your saints and prophets,
and you have given them blood to drink as they deserve."

7And I heard the altar respond:

"Yes, Lord God Almighty,
true and just are your judgments."

8The fourth angel poured out his bowl on the sun, and the sun was given power to scorch people with fire. 9They were seared by the intense heat and they cursed the name of God, who had control over these plagues, but they refused to repent and glorify him.

10The fifth angel poured out his bowl on the throne of the beast, and his kingdom was plunged into darkness. Men gnawed their tongues in agony 11and cursed the God of heaven because of their pains and their sores, but they refused to repent of what they had done.

12The sixth angel poured out his bowl on the great river Euphrates, and its water was dried up to prepare the way for the kings from the East. 13Then I saw three evil[a] spirits that looked like frogs; they came out of the mouth of the dragon, out of the mouth of the beast and out of the mouth of the false prophet. 14They are spirits of demons performing miraculous signs, and they go out to

[a]13 Greek *unclean*

16:2 *mark of the beast:* See the notes at 7:2 and 13:16,17.

16:6 *shed the blood of your saints:* A way of saying, "They murdered, so now they will die."

16:10 *the throne of the beast:* See the note at 13:1.

16:12 *great river Euphrates:* See the note at 9:14.

16:13 *three evil spirits . . . beast . . . false prophet:* Three evil spirits appear. One that looks like a frog comes from the dragon (Satan; see the note at 12:3,4). Frogs were thought to represent the ability to trick people by lying. See also Exod 8:2-14. A second evil spirit came out of the mouth of the beast (the Roman empire; see the note at 13:1). A third came out of the mouth of the false prophet (see the note at 13:11).

15:8 Exod 40:34; 1 Kgs 8:10,11; 2 Chr 5:11-14; Isa 6:4. **16:2** Exod 9:10; Rev 13:14,15. **16:3,4** Exod 7:17-21; Ps 78:44. **16:6** Isa 49:26. **16:7** Ps 19:9; 119:137. **16:10** Exod 10:21. **16:12** Isa 11:15; Jer 50:38. **16:15** Matt 24:43,44; Luke 12:39,40; Rev 3:3. **16:16** Zech 12:11. **16:18** Rev 8:5; 11:13,19. **16:19** Isa 51:17; Rev 14:10. **16:20** Rev 6:14. **16:21** Exod 9:23,24; Rev 11:19. **17:1** Jer 51:13. **17:2** Isa 23:17; Jer 51:7. **17:4** Jer 51:7.

the kings of the whole world, to gather them for the battle on the
great day of God Almighty.
15“Behold, I come like a thief! Blessed is he who stays awake
and keeps his clothes with him, so that he may not go naked and
be shamefully exposed.”
16Then they gathered the kings together to the place that in
Hebrew is called Armageddon.
17The seventh angel poured out his bowl into the air, and out
of the temple came a loud voice from the throne, saying, “It is
done!” 18Then there came flashes of lightning, rumblings, peals of
thunder and a severe earthquake. No earthquake like it has ever
occurred since man has been on earth, so tremendous was the
quake. 19The great city split into three parts, and the cities of the
nations collapsed. God remembered Babylon the Great and gave
her the cup filled with the wine of the fury of his wrath. 20Every
island fled away and the mountains could not be found. 21From
the sky huge hailstones of about a hundred pounds each fell upon
men. And they cursed God on account of the plague of hail,
because the plague was so terrible.

Victory Over the Enemies of God

God will defeat his enemies, Babylon (the Roman empire), and Satan. This vision of God's judgment is interrupted by another brief vision. In it John sees the fulfillment of God's purpose for his people, the wedding supper of the Lamb (chapter 19).

The Woman on the Beast

17 One of the seven angels who had the seven bowls came and
said to me, “Come, I will show you the punishment of the great
prostitute, who sits on many waters. 2With her the kings of the
earth committed adultery and the inhabitants of the earth were
intoxicated with the wine of her adulteries.”
3Then the angel carried me away in the Spirit into a desert.
There I saw a woman sitting on a scarlet beast that was covered
with blasphemous names and had seven heads and ten horns. 4The
woman was dressed in purple and scarlet, and was glittering with
gold, precious stones and pearls. She held a golden cup in her
hand, filled with abominable things and the filth of her adulteries.
5This title was written on her forehead:

MYSTERY
BABYLON THE GREAT
THE MOTHER OF PROSTITUTES
AND OF THE ABOMINATIONS OF THE EARTH.

6I saw that the woman was drunk with the blood of the saints, the
blood of those who bore testimony to Jesus.

16:16 *Armageddon:* The Hebrew form of the name would be "Har Megiddo," meaning "Hill of Megiddo," where many battles were fought in ancient times (Judg 5:19; 2 Kgs 23:29, 30). Pictured here is the site (Tell-el-Mutesellim) archaeologists believe to be the location of ancient Megiddo.

16:19 *Babylon:* See the note at 14:8.

17:1 *great prostitute:* This unflattering image refers to the empire's capital, the city of Rome, with its evil way of life and its shameless pride. The other nations and rulers that Rome has taken over are like those who have practiced immorality with the prostitute (17:2). For more, see the mini-article called "Prostitution in the Bible," p. 1688.

17:3 *woman sitting on a scarlet beast:* For "beast," see the note at 13:1. The woman is likely meant to be a symbol for Rome (17:18), the same woman who is called a prostitute in 17:1.

17:4 *dressed in purple and scarlet:* Purple was a color that symbolized royalty (see Judg 8:26; Dan 5:7). Scarlet was considered a dramatic color, but here it may also be connected with the blood of God's people (17:6).

17:6 *drunk with the blood of the saints:* Certain Roman leaders were responsible for putting many Christians to death. A Roman history writer named Tacitus, in his *Annals,* described the emperor Nero's persecution of Christians in the A.D. 60s.

An angel shouted:
"Fallen! Fallen is Babylon the Great! She has become a home for demons and a haunt for every evil spirit, a haunt for every unclean and detestable bird."
Rev 18:2

17:7 *beast . . . seven heads and ten horns:* See the note at 13:1.

17:8 *book of life:* See the note at 3:5.

17:9-11 *seven:* Ancient Rome was built on seven hills. The "seven heads" stand for the emperors (here called "kings") of Rome. Which seven emperors John means is not clear.

17:12,13 *ten:* This may refer to ten more Roman emperors who give power to the beast (Satan). Or it may refer to ten world rulers who give power to the Roman Empire.

17:14 *Lamb:* See the note at 5:6. The worldly kings (17:12,13) will fight against the Lamb, meaning that they will persecute Jesus' followers and the church (see 19:11-21).

17:16 *will hate the prostitute:* The nations that support Rome will eventually turn against it and defeat it.

18:1 *angel:* See the mini-article called "Angels," p. 88.

18:2 *demons:* Evil spirits that follow and work for Satan. See the note at 12:3,4.

18:3 *drunk the maddening wine:* Wine here is used to symbolize how Rome's authority and attitudes attracted people, and how Rome used this attraction to control the world. Just as someone can become intoxicated and lose good judgment from drinking too much wine, so people could be fooled by Rome's military power and wealth.

When I saw her, I was greatly astonished. [7]Then the angel
said to me: "Why are you astonished? I will explain to you the mystery of the woman and of the beast she rides, which has the seven
heads and ten horns. [8]The beast, which you saw, once was, now is
not, and will come up out of the Abyss and go to his destruction.
The inhabitants of the earth whose names have not been written
in the book of life from the creation of the world will be astonished when they see the beast, because he once was, now is not,
and yet will come.
[9]"This calls for a mind with wisdom. The seven heads are
seven hills on which the woman sits. [10]They are also seven kings.
Five have fallen, one is, the other has not yet come; but when he
does come, he must remain for a little while. [11]The beast who once
was, and now is not, is an eighth king. He belongs to the seven and
is going to his destruction.
[12]"The ten horns you saw are ten kings who have not yet
received a kingdom, but who for one hour will receive authority
as kings along with the beast. [13]They have one purpose and will
give their power and authority to the beast. [14]They will make war
against the Lamb, but the Lamb will overcome them because he is
Lord of lords and King of kings—and with him will be his called,
chosen and faithful followers."
[15]Then the angel said to me, "The waters you saw, where the
prostitute sits, are peoples, multitudes, nations and languages.
[16]The beast and the ten horns you saw will hate the prostitute.
They will bring her to ruin and leave her naked; they will eat her
flesh and burn her with fire. [17]For God has put it into their hearts
to accomplish his purpose by agreeing to give the beast their
power to rule, until God's words are fulfilled. [18]The woman you
saw is the great city that rules over the kings of the earth."

The Fall of Babylon

18 After this I saw another angel coming down from heaven. He
had great authority, and the earth was illuminated by his splendor.
[2]With a mighty voice he shouted:

"Fallen! Fallen is Babylon the Great!
She has become a home for demons
and a haunt for every evil[a] spirit,
a haunt for every unclean and detestable bird.
[3]For all the nations have drunk
the maddening wine of her adulteries.
The kings of the earth committed adultery with her,
and the merchants of the earth grew rich from her
excessive luxuries."

[a]2 Greek *unclean*

The Burning of Babylon, an illuminated manuscript, eleventh century. John uses the name "Babylon" as a way of talking about the great world power of his day, the Roman empire. He calls it "The Mother of Prostitutes and of the Abominations of the Earth" (17:5). In John's vision, it is destroyed by fire when the seventh angel empties his bowl. (See chapter 18.)

4 Then I heard another voice from heaven say:
"Come out of her, my people,
so that you will not share in her sins,
so that you will not receive any of her plagues;
5 for her sins are piled up to heaven,
and God has remembered her crimes.
6 Give back to her as she has given;
pay her back double for what she has done.
Mix her a double portion from her own cup.
7 Give her as much torture and grief
as the glory and luxury she gave herself.
In her heart she boasts,
'I sit as queen; I am not a widow,

17:8 Dan 7:7; Rev 11:7; Ps 69:28. **17:12** Dan 7:20-24. **18:2** Isa 21:9; 13:21; Jer 50:39; 51:8; Rev 14:8. **18:3** Isa 23:17; Jer 3:2; 25:15,16; 51:7; Hos 4:10; Rev 17:2. **18:4** Isa 48:20; Jer 50:8; 51:6,45. **18:5** Gen 18:20,21; Jer 51:9. **18:6** Ps 137:8; Isa 40:2; Jer 50:29. **18:7,8** Isa 47:7-9; Ezek 28:2-8.

and I will never mourn.'
8 Therefore in one day her plagues will overtake her:
death, mourning and famine.
She will be consumed by fire,
for mighty is the Lord God who judges her.

9 "When the kings of the earth who committed adultery with
her and shared her luxury see the smoke of her burning, they will
weep and mourn over her. 10 Terrified at her torment, they will
stand far off and cry:

" 'Woe! Woe, O great city,
O Babylon, city of power!
In one hour your doom has come!'

11 "The merchants of the earth will weep and mourn over her
because no one buys their cargoes any more— 12 cargoes of gold,
silver, precious stones and pearls; fine linen, purple, silk and scarlet cloth; every sort of citron wood, and articles of every kind
made of ivory, costly wood, bronze, iron and marble; 13 cargoes of
cinnamon and spice, of incense, myrrh and frankincense, of wine
and olive oil, of fine flour and wheat; cattle and sheep; horses and
carriages; and bodies and souls of men.
14 "They will say, 'The fruit you longed for is gone from you.
All your riches and splendor have vanished, never to be recovered.'
15 The merchants who sold these things and gained their wealth
from her will stand far off, terrified at her torment. They will weep
and mourn 16 and cry out:

" 'Woe! Woe, O great city,
dressed in fine linen, purple and scarlet,
and glittering with gold, precious stones and
pearls!
17 In one hour such great wealth has been brought to
ruin!'

"Every sea captain, and all who travel by ship, the sailors,
and all who earn their living from the sea, will stand far off.
18 When they see the smoke of her burning, they will exclaim, 'Was
there ever a city like this great city?' 19 They will throw dust on their
heads, and with weeping and mourning cry out:

" 'Woe! Woe, O great city,
where all who had ships on the sea
became rich through her wealth!
In one hour she has been brought to ruin!
20 Rejoice over her, O heaven!
Rejoice, saints and apostles and prophets!
God has judged her for the way she treated you.' "

21 Then a mighty angel picked up a boulder the size of a large
millstone and threw it into the sea, and said:

18:11 *merchants ... mourn over her:* The Roman empire controlled the seaports and highways throughout the Mediterranean world. The merchants had to follow Roman laws and pay taxes to Rome. In return, the empire protected them and provided a huge market for their goods.

18:13 *myrrh and frankincense:* Myrrh is a dark-red gum with a strong smell that was crushed into powder and used to make expensive perfumes. Frankincense comes from a white gummy substance produced by certain trees in India and northern Arabia. It was pounded into a valuable powder that was burned to make a sweet smell.

18:13 *bodies and souls of men:* The Romans took people from the many lands they had captured and made them slaves. They brought many of these slaves to Rome to serve in the homes of wealthy leaders and in the court of the emperor. In the late first century, slaves made up nearly half the population of Rome. "Bodies" here may refer to people who were made to fight and die in arenas to entertain the Roman leaders and crowds. See also the mini-article called "Slaves and Servants in the Time of Jesus," p. 2006.

18:16 *purple and scarlet:* See the note at 17:4.

18:20 *apostles and prophets:* Here "apostles" means those chosen by God to spread the message about Jesus Christ. The apostles included the twelve closest followers of Jesus named in the Gospels and other important teachers, such as Paul. For "prophets," see the note at 10:7.

18:9,10 Ezek 26:16,17. **18:11** Ezek 27:25-27,31,36. **18:12,13** Ezek 27:12,13,22. **18:15** Ezek 27:31, 36; Rev 18:11. **18:17** Isa 23:14; Ezek 27:26-30. **18:18** Ezek 27:32. **18:19** Ezek 27:28-34. **18:20** Deut 32:43; Jer 51:48. **18:21** Jer 51:63,64; Ezek 26:21.

"With such violence
the great city of Babylon will be thrown down,
never to be found again.
22 The music of harpists and musicians, flute players and
trumpeters,
will never be heard in you again.
No workman of any trade
will ever be found in you again.
The sound of a millstone
will never be heard in you again.
23 The light of a lamp
will never shine in you again.
The voice of bridegroom and bride
will never be heard in you again.
Your merchants were the world's great men.
By your magic spell all the nations were led
astray.
24 In her was found the blood of prophets and of the
saints,
and of all who have been killed on the earth."

Hallelujah!

19 After this I heard what sounded like the roar of a great multitude in heaven shouting:

"Hallelujah!
Salvation and glory and power belong to our God,
2 for true and just are his judgments.
He has condemned the great prostitute
who corrupted the earth by her adulteries.
He has avenged on her the blood of his servants."

3 And again they shouted:

"Hallelujah!
The smoke from her goes up for ever and ever."

4 The twenty-four elders and the four living creatures fell down and worshiped God, who was seated on the throne. And they cried:

"Amen, Hallelujah!"

5 Then a voice came from the throne, saying:

"Praise our God,
all you his servants,
you who fear him,
both small and great!"

6 Then I heard what sounded like a great multitude, like the roar of rushing waters and like loud peals of thunder, shouting:

A great multitude in heaven was shouting, *"Hallelujah! Salvation and glory and power belong to our God, for true and just are his judgments."*
Rev 19:1,2

18:21 *large millstone:* Millstones were used to grind grain. Just as a large stone would quickly sink if thrown into the sea, so Rome's end would be violent and sudden.

18:23 *your magic spell:* Meaning Babylon's (Rome's) evil use of authority. See the notes at 9:21 and 18:3.

18:24 *blood of prophets and of the saints:* See the note at 17:6. See also Jer 51:49.

19:1 *Hallelujah:* A Greek form of the Hebrew phrase that means "Praise *Yahweh.*" This phrase is repeated throughout the chapter (see 19:3,4,6).

19:1 *Salvation:* The word "salvation" points to what God has done and is still doing to free humans from sin and the powers of evil. "Salvation" can also refer to receiving "eternal life." See also the mini-articles called "Salvation," p. 2021, and "Eternal Life," p. 2072.

19:2 *great prostitute:* See the note at 17:1.

19:4 *twenty-four elders and the four living creatures:* See the notes at 4:4-10 and 4:6-9.

18:22 Isa 24:8; Ezek 26:13. **18:22,23** Jer 7:34; 25:10. **19:2** Deut 32:43; 2 Kgs 9:7. **19:3** Isa 34:10; Jer 51:25,58-64. **19:5** Ps 115:13. **19:6** Ps 93:1; 97:1; 99:1; Ezek 1:24.

Then the angel said to me, "Write: 'Blessed are those who are invited to the wedding supper of the Lamb!'" And he added, "These are the true words of God."
Rev 19:9

19:7 *wedding of the Lamb . . . his bride:* This is the celebration when Christ (the Lamb) and his people (the bride) will be united. It also signals that God is about to defeat Satan for all time. Israel's prophets used the idea of marriage as a way to describe the relationship between God and the people of Israel (see Isa 54:1-8; Ezek 16:7,8; Hos 2:19,20). In the New Testament, the church is pictured as the bride of Christ (Eph 5:23-32).

19:11 *white horse, whose rider is called Faithful and True:* See the note at 6:2. The rider is Christ, who appears as a military leader going to war. The many crowns he wears symbolize his authority (19:12). In John's day it was not unusual for a king to wear several crowns, one for each country he ruled.

19:13 *robe dipped in blood . . . Word of God:* The blood is Christ's who won a victory over sin and death by shedding his blood on the cross (see Rom 3:24-26; Rev 5:6,9; 7:14; 12:11). Jesus is the "Word of God" (see John 1:1-3,14; Heb 4:12).

19:14 *fine linen, white and clean:* See the note at 3:4.

19:15 *treads the winepress:* See the note at 14:18,19.

19:19,20 *beast . . . false prophet:* See the notes at 13:1; 13:11; and 16:13.

19:20 *fiery lake of burning sulfur:* See the notes at 14:10 and 9:1.

19:9 Matt 22:2,3. **19:11** Ps 96:13; Isa 11:4; Ezek 1:1-3. **19:12** Dan 10:6. **19:15** Ps 2:9; Isa 63:3; Joel 3:13; Rev 1:16; 14:20. **19:17,18** Ezek 39:17-20. **19:20** Rev 13:1-18.

"Hallelujah!
For our Lord God Almighty reigns.
7 Let us rejoice and be glad
and give him glory!
For the wedding of the Lamb has come,
and his bride has made herself ready.
8 Fine linen, bright and clean,
was given her to wear."
(Fine linen stands for the righteous acts of the saints.)

9 Then the angel said to me, "Write: 'Blessed are those who
are invited to the wedding supper of the Lamb!'" And he added,
"These are the true words of God."
10 At this I fell at his feet to worship him. But he said to me,
"Do not do it! I am a fellow servant with you and with your brothers who hold to the testimony of Jesus. Worship God! For the testimony of Jesus is the spirit of prophecy."

The Rider on the White Horse

11 I saw heaven standing open and there before me was a
white horse, whose rider is called Faithful and True. With justice
he judges and makes war. 12 His eyes are like blazing fire, and on
his head are many crowns. He has a name written on him that no
one knows but he himself. 13 He is dressed in a robe dipped in
blood, and his name is the Word of God. 14 The armies of heaven
were following him, riding on white horses and dressed in fine
linen, white and clean. 15 Out of his mouth comes a sharp sword
with which to strike down the nations. "He will rule them with an
iron scepter."[a] He treads the winepress of the fury of the wrath of
God Almighty. 16 On his robe and on his thigh he has this name
written:

KING OF KINGS AND LORD OF LORDS.

17 And I saw an angel standing in the sun, who cried in a loud
voice to all the birds flying in midair, "Come, gather together for
the great supper of God, 18 so that you may eat the flesh of kings,
generals, and mighty men, of horses and their riders, and the flesh
of all people, free and slave, small and great."
19 Then I saw the beast and the kings of the earth and their
armies gathered together to make war against the rider on the
horse and his army. 20 But the beast was captured, and with him the
false prophet who had performed the miraculous signs on his
behalf. With these signs he had deluded those who had received
the mark of the beast and worshiped his image. The two of them
were thrown alive into the fiery lake of burning sulfur. 21 The rest of

[a]15 Psalm 2:9

them were killed with the sword that came out of the mouth of the
rider on the horse, and all the birds gorged themselves on their
flesh.

The Thousand Years

20 And I saw an angel coming down out of heaven, having the
key to the Abyss and holding in his hand a great chain. [2]He seized
the dragon, that ancient serpent, who is the devil, or Satan, and
bound him for a thousand years. [3]He threw him into the Abyss,
and locked and sealed it over him, to keep him from deceiving the
nations anymore until the thousand years were ended. After that,
he must be set free for a short time.
[4]I saw thrones on which were seated those who had been
given authority to judge. And I saw the souls of those who had
been beheaded because of their testimony for Jesus and because of
the word of God. They had not worshiped the beast or his image
and had not received his mark on their foreheads or their hands.
They came to life and reigned with Christ a thousand years. [5](The
rest of the dead did not come to life until the thousand years were
ended.) This is the first resurrection. [6]Blessed and holy are those
who have part in the first resurrection. The second death has no
power over them, but they will be priests of God and of Christ and
will reign with him for a thousand years.

Satan's Doom

[7]When the thousand years are over, Satan will be released from
his prison [8]and will go out to deceive the nations in the four corners
of the earth—Gog and Magog—to gather them for battle. In number
they are like the sand on the seashore. [9]They marched across the
breadth of the earth and surrounded the camp of God's people, the
city he loves. But fire came down from heaven and devoured them.
[10]And the devil, who deceived them, was thrown into the lake of
burning sulfur, where the beast and the false prophet had been
thrown. They will be tormented day and night for ever and ever.

The Dead Are Judged

[11]Then I saw a great white throne and him who was seated
on it. Earth and sky fled from his presence, and there was no place
for them. [12]And I saw the dead, great and small, standing before
the throne, and books were opened. Another book was opened,
which is the book of life. The dead were judged according to what
they had done as recorded in the books. [13]The sea gave up the dead
that were in it, and death and Hades gave up the dead that were in
them, and each person was judged according to what he had done.
[14]Then death and Hades were thrown into the lake of fire. The lake
of fire is the second death. [15]If anyone's name was not found written in the book of life, he was thrown into the lake of fire.

20:1 *the key to the Abyss:* See the note at 9:1.

20:2 *bound him for a thousand years:* See the note at 12:3,4. The thousand years of peace or calm begin when Satan is imprisoned in the Abyss. This number likely is meant to symbolize the fact that the final victory will not come immediately, or even during the lifetime of John's readers. The thousand years are measured in God's time, not human time (see Ps 90:4; 2 Pet 3:8).

20:4 *thrones . . . souls of those who had been beheaded:* See the note at 4:4-10 (thrones). Christians who were put to death because they preached God's message about Jesus and refused to take part in emperor worship are known as martyrs. These martyrs will be raised to life and rule with God.

20:6 *The second death:* See the note at 2:11.

20:8 *Gog and Magog:* The prophet Ezekiel tells of a wicked ruler named Gog from the land of Magog who would one day attack the people of Israel from the north (Ezek 38:2-16). However, in this verse Gog and Magog represent all the worldly powers that are against God and God's people.

20:10 *lake of burning sulfur:* See the notes at 9:1 and 14:10. This is the second and final time that the devil and those who followed him are thrown into the Abyss and lake of burning sulfur.

20:10 *beast and the false prophet:* See the notes at 13:1; 13:11; and 16:13.

20:12 *book of life . . . dead were judged:* See the notes at 3:5 and 3:10. Other New Testament passages talk about how God will judge the world and its people at the end of time (see Matt 13:49,50; 25:31-46).

20:14 *second death:* See the note at 2:11.

20:2 Gen 3:1. **20:4** Dan 7:9, 22; Rev 6:9. **20:8** Ezek 7:2; 38:2,9,15. **20:11,12** Dan 7:9,10.

God Makes All Things New

God has defeated the devil and death. John's vision now describes God bringing a new heaven and earth as well as a new city, which represents a renewal of the whole creation. God and the Lamb will live among the faithful people in a place where hunger, sorrow, and death will be wiped out forever. Through the middle of the city's main street, a river of life will flow. On each side of the river, trees will produce fruit all year round.

The New Jerusalem

21 Then I saw a new heaven and a new earth, for the first heav-
en and the first earth had passed away, and there was no longer any
sea. 2 I saw the Holy City, the new Jerusalem, coming down out of
heaven from God, prepared as a bride beautifully dressed for her
husband. 3 And I heard a loud voice from the throne saying, "Now
the dwelling of God is with men, and he will live with them. They
will be his people, and God himself will be with them and be their
God. 4 He will wipe every tear from their eyes. There will be no
more death or mourning or crying or pain, for the old order of
things has passed away."
5 He who was seated on the throne said, "I am making everything new!" Then he said, "Write this down, for these words are
trustworthy and true."
6 He said to me: "It is done. I am the Alpha and the Omega,
the Beginning and the End. To him who is thirsty I will give to
drink without cost from the spring of the water of life. 7 He who
overcomes will inherit all this, and I will be his God and he will be
my son. 8 But the cowardly, the unbelieving, the vile, the murderers,
the sexually immoral, those who practice magic arts, the idolaters
and all liars—their place will be in the fiery lake of burning sulfur.
This is the second death."
9 One of the seven angels who had the seven bowls full of
the seven last plagues came and said to me, "Come, I will show
you the bride, the wife of the Lamb." 10 And he carried me away in
the Spirit to a mountain great and high, and showed me the Holy
City, Jerusalem, coming down out of heaven from God. 11 It shone
with the glory of God, and its brilliance was like that of a very
precious jewel, like a jasper, clear as crystal. 12 It had a great, high
wall with twelve gates, and with twelve angels at the gates. On the
gates were written the names of the twelve tribes of Israel. 13 There
were three gates on the east, three on the north, three on the south
and three on the west. 14 The wall of the city had twelve foundations, and on them were the names of the twelve apostles of the
Lamb.
15 The angel who talked with me had a measuring rod of gold
to measure the city, its gates and its walls. 16 The city was laid out
like a square, as long as it was wide. He measured the city with the

---

21:1 *new heaven and a new earth:* In this vision, the first earth, which had become filled with evil, war, sickness, and pollution, is gone. In its place will be a new earth.

21:2 *new Jerusalem . . . as a bride:* Jerusalem was the center of the religious life of the people of Israel and the place where they had built the LORD's temple. See the mini-article called "Jerusalem," p. 574. That it was the "Holy City" meant that it was set apart for God's use in the world. God was said to live in the temple. John sees the new Jerusalem as "coming down" from God, which shows how God comes down to live among his chosen people. The city is also described as a bride who is ready to meet her husband (God). Note that 21:3,4 mentions no temple. The new Jerusalem has no temple because in the new heaven and earth God will live openly among the people (21:3,22).

21:5 *He who was seated on the throne:* Meaning God (see 4:2).

21:6 *the Alpha and the Omega, the Beginning and the End:* See the note on p. 2403.

21:8 *fiery lake of burning sulfur . . . second death:* See the notes at 14:10 and 2:11.

21:9 *bride, the wife of the Lamb:* See the notes at 19:7 (bride) and 5:6.

21:10 *Spirit . . . Holy City, Jerusalem:* See the notes at 1:10 (Spirit) and 21:2.

21:11,18-21 *jasper . . . pure gold:* The original meaning of the ancient terms used to describe these precious and semiprecious stones is not clear. The stones mentioned in these verses all have different colors.

21:1 Isa 65:17; 66:22; 2 Pet 3:13. **21:2** Isa 52:1; Rev 3:12; Isa 61:10. **21:3** Ezek 37:27; Lev 26:11,12. **21:4** Isa 25:8; 35:10; 65:19. **21:6** Isa 55:1; John 4:10-14; Rev 1:8; 22:13. **21:7** 2 Sam 7:14; Ps 89:26,27. **21:10** Ezek 40:1,2. **21:12,13** Ezek 48:30-35. **21:15** Ezek 40:3.

The Heavenly Jerusalem, a tapestry from the *Apocalypse of Angers* by Nicolas Bataille, around 1380. From the top of a very high mountain, an angel showed John the Holy City of Jerusalem coming down from God in heaven. It was made of pure gold and built on twelve foundation stones, each one a precious stone. This holy city did not have a temple. "The Lord God Almighty and the Lamb are its temple. The city does not need the sun or the moon to shine on it, for the glory of God gives it light, and the Lamb is its lamp." (See 21:9-27.)

rod and found it to be 12,000 stadia[a] in length, and as wide and
high as it is long. [17]He measured its wall and it was 144 cubits[b]
thick,[c] by man's measurement, which the angel was using. [18]The
wall was made of jasper, and the city of pure gold, as pure as glass.
[19]The foundations of the city walls were decorated with every kind
of precious stone. The first foundation was jasper, the second sapphire, the third chalcedony, the fourth emerald, [20]the fifth sardonyx, the sixth carnelian, the seventh chrysolite, the eighth beryl,
the ninth topaz, the tenth chrysoprase, the eleventh jacinth, and
the twelfth amethyst.[d] [21]The twelve gates were twelve pearls, each
gate made of a single pearl. The great street of the city was of pure
gold, like transparent glass.
[22]I did not see a temple in the city, because the Lord God
Almighty and the Lamb are its temple. [23]The city does not need
the sun or the moon to shine on it, for the glory of God gives it

[a]**16** That is, about 1,400 miles (about 2,200 kilometers) [b]**17** That is, about 200 feet (about 65 meters) [c]**17** Or *high* [d]**20** The precise identification of some of these precious stones is uncertain.

21:12-14 *twelve tribes . . . twelve apostles:* See the notes at 7:5-8 and 18:20. The Holy City brings together the people of Israel and the Christian church—all who put their trust in God.

21:22,23 *temple . . . glory of God:* See the note at 21:2. In ancient Israel only priests could enter the holiest parts of the temple. In the new Jerusalem, all the people will praise and worship God face to face.

21:18-21 Isa 54:11,12. **21:23** Isa 60:19,20.

21:25 *no day will its gates ever be shut . . . no night:* This symbolizes how God mercifully welcomes all whose names are in the book of life. The gates don't need to be closed, since no evil thing or person can enter (21:27). The never-ending light is evidence that the powers of darkness (evil) have been defeated forever.

21:24 Isa 60:3. **21:25,26** Isa 60:11; Zech 14:7. **21:27** Isa 52:1; Ezek 44:9. **22:2** Gen 2:9; Ezek 47:12.

light, and the Lamb is its lamp. [24]The nations will walk by its light,
and the kings of the earth will bring their splendor into it. [25]On no
day will its gates ever be shut, for there will be no night there.
[26]The glory and honor of the nations will be brought into it.
[27]Nothing impure will ever enter it, nor will anyone who does what
is shameful or deceitful, but only those whose names are written in
the Lamb's book of life.

The River of Life

22 Then the angel showed me the river of the water of life, as
clear as crystal, flowing from the throne of God and of the Lamb
[2]down the middle of the great street of the city. On each side of

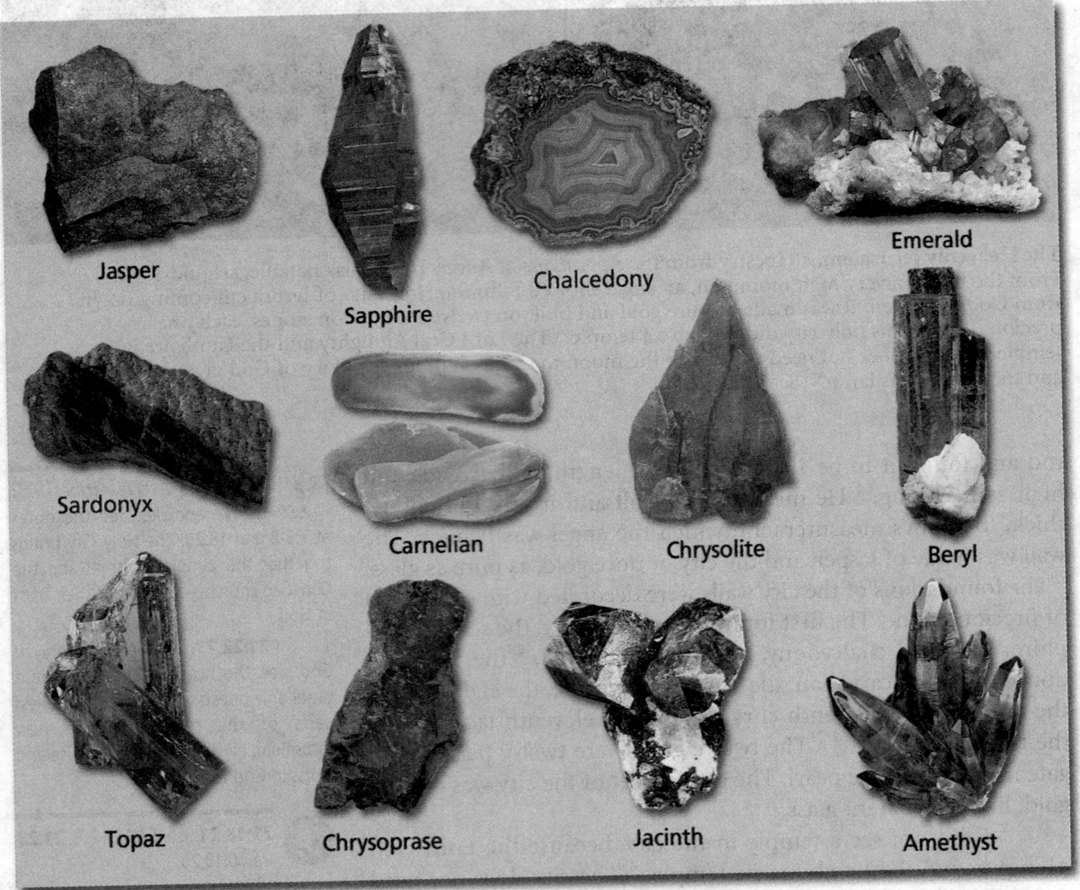

The Foundation Stones of the New Jerusalem. When John is given a vision of the new Jerusalem, he sees that many of the precious stones that will be used for the foundation of the new Jerusalem are also ones that were used on the breastpieces of the Jewish high priests (see Exod 39:8-14). Most precious stones (gems) are small and imperfect in some way. The brilliance and beauty of the new Jerusalem can be imagined by picturing the twelve foundation stones, each one being over seven hundred square feet and made from a single precious gem. (See 21:18-21.)

the river stood the tree of life, bearing twelve crops of fruit, yielding its fruit every month. And the leaves of the tree are for the
healing of the nations. [3]No longer will there be any curse. The
throne of God and of the Lamb will be in the city, and his servants
will serve him. [4]They will see his face, and his name will be on
their foreheads. [5]There will be no more night. They will not need
the light of a lamp or the light of the sun, for the Lord God will
give them light. And they will reign for ever and ever.
[6]The angel said to me, "These words are trustworthy and
true. The Lord, the God of the spirits of the prophets, sent his
angel to show his servants the things that must soon take place."

Final Promises, Blessings, and Warnings

John's vision gives a reminder that Jesus will come soon and bless those who are faithful. Christians must keep their lives clean ("wash their robes") and avoid doing evil deeds. John also warns that anyone who adds to or takes away from the message of his vision will not be allowed to enter the holy city.

Jesus Is Coming

[7]"Behold, I am coming soon! Blessed is he who keeps the
words of the prophecy in this book."

[8]I, John, am the one who heard and saw these things. And
when I had heard and seen them, I fell down to worship at the feet
of the angel who had been showing them to me. [9]But he said to
me, "Do not do it! I am a fellow servant with you and with your
brothers the prophets and of all who keep the words of this book.
Worship God!"
[10]Then he told me, "Do not seal up the words of the prophecy of this book, because the time is near. [11]Let him who does
wrong continue to do wrong; let him who is vile continue to be
vile; let him who does right continue to do right; and let him who
is holy continue to be holy."

[12]"Behold, I am coming soon! My reward is with me, and I
will give to everyone according to what he has done. [13]I am the
Alpha and the Omega, the First and the Last, the Beginning and
the End.
[14]"Blessed are those who wash their robes, that they may
have the right to the tree of life and may go through the gates into
the city. [15]Outside are the dogs, those who practice magic arts, the
sexually immoral, the murderers, the idolaters and everyone who
loves and practices falsehood.

22:1 *river:* The river in the new Jerusalem is like the life-giving rivers God created to flow in the Garden of Eden (Gen 2:10-14). See also Ezek 47:1-12; Zech 14:8.

22:3 *curse:* When Adam and Eve ate from the tree of the knowledge of good and evil (Gen 2:17; 3:6), God cursed them and sent them out of the garden so they could never eat fruit from the other tree, the one that would let them live forever (Gen 3:22). In the new Jerusalem, God's people are again able to eat fruit from the tree of life, because the curse of sin has been taken away forever. See also the note on p. 2404 (tree of life).

22:3 *the Lamb:* See the note at 5:6.

22:6 *prophets:* See the note at 1:3.

22:7 *I am coming soon:* This phrase is repeated three times in the final verses (see also 22:12,20). It is both a promise and a warning. Many New Testament passages talk about a last day when Jesus will return (1 Cor 15:20-28; Phil 1:10; 2:16; 3:20,21; 1 Thes 4:13-18). Other passages compare Christ's sudden return to the unexpected break-in of a thief (Matt 24:42,43; Luke 12:35-40; 2 Pet 3:10; and Rev 3:2,3). The message is that followers of Christ always need to be ready for Christ's return. See also the mini-articles called "End Times," p. 2295, and "Second Coming," p. 2277.

22:8 *John:* See the Introduction to REVELATION, p. 2403, and the note at 1:1 (John).

22:13 *the Alpha and the Omega:* See the note on p. 2403.

22:14 *wash their robes . . . tree of life:* See the notes at 7:14 and 22:3.

22:3 Zech 14:10,11 (compare Gen 3:17). **22:5** Isa 60:19; Dan 7:18. **22:11** Dan 12:10. **22:12** Ps 28:4; Isa 40:10; 62:11; Jer 17:10. **22:13** Isa 44:6; 48:12; Rev 1:8,17; 2:8. **22:14** Gen 2:9; 3:22.

22:16 *Root and the Offspring of David, and the bright Morning Star:* See the notes at 3:7; 5:5; and 2:26-28.

22:17 *Spirit and the bride:* See the note at 1:10 (Spirit). "The bride" here refers to the new Jerusalem (the new people of God). See also Matt 22:1-10; Eph 5:22-32.

22:17 *let him who hears:* REVELATION was intended to be read in services of worship.

22:19 *tree of life . . . holy city:* See the notes on p. 2404 (tree of life) and at 21:2 (new Jerusalem).

22:16 Isa 11:1,10. **22:17** Isa 55:1. **22:18,19** Deut 4:2; 12:32.

16"I, Jesus, have sent my angel to give you[a] this testimony for
the churches. I am the Root and the Offspring of David, and the
bright Morning Star."

17The Spirit and the bride say, "Come!" And let him who
hears say, "Come!" Whoever is thirsty, let him come; and whoever
wishes, let him take the free gift of the water of life.

18I warn everyone who hears the words of the prophecy of
this book: If anyone adds anything to them, God will add to him
the plagues described in this book. 19And if anyone takes words
away from this book of prophecy, God will take away from him his
share in the tree of life and in the holy city, which are described in
this book.

20He who testifies to these things says, "Yes, I am coming
soon."

Amen. Come, Lord Jesus.

21The grace of the Lord Jesus be with God's people. Amen.

[a]16 The Greek is plural.

QUESTIONS ABOUT REVELATION 14:1—22:21

1. What messages were given by the three angels? (14:6-13) What effect might these messages have had on early Christians living in a society that was often hostile to the Christian faith?
2. What or who are the "grapes" mentioned in 14:14-20? What happened to the grapes?
3. What was in the seven bowls of wrath? (16:1-21)
4. Who or what is the "prostitute"? What is the prostitute's connection to the beast? (17:1-18)
5. What does Babylon stand for? (18:1-24) Why do kings and merchants mourn when Babylon falls? (18:9-18)
6. What is the wedding day of the Lamb? Who is the Lamb's bride? (19:7-9) Who is invited to the Lamb's wedding supper?
7. In the end, what happens to the beast and the dragon? (19:19—20:15)
8. Describe the new heaven and new earth (21:1-8). What is the new Jerusalem? (21:9—22:5) How is the new Jerusalem like the Garden of Eden? (Gen 1,2)
9. How would you summarize the basic message of REVELATION? What did you find most meaningful about the book? What new questions does it raise?

HELPS FOR THE READER

TABLE OF WEIGHTS AND MEASURES

The figures of the table are calculated on the basis of a shekel equaling 11.5 grams, a cubit equaling 18 inches and an ephah equaling 22 liters. The quart referred to is either a dry quart (slightly larger than a liter) or a liquid quart (slightly smaller than a liter), whichever is applicable. The ton referred to in the footnotes is the American ton of 2,000 pounds.

This table is based upon the best available information, but it is not intended to be mathematically precise; like the measurement equivalents in the footnotes, it merely gives approximate amounts and distances. Weights and measures differed somewhat at various times and places in the ancient world. There is uncertainty particularly about the ephah and the bath; further discoveries may shed more light on these units of capacity.

		BIBLICAL UNIT	APPROXIMATE AMERICAN EQUIVALENT	APPROXIMATE METRIC UNIT
WEIGHTS	talent	(60 minas)	75 pounds	34 kilograms
	mina	(50 shekels)	1 1/4 pounds	0.6 kilogram
	shekel	(2 bekas)	2/5 ounce	11.5 grams
	pim	(2/3 shekel)	1/3 ounce	7.6 grams
	beka	(10 gerahs)	1/5 ounce	5.5 grams
	gerah		1/50 ounce	0.6 gram
LENGTH	cubit		18 inches	0.5 meter
	span		9 inches	23 centimeters
	handbreadth		3 inches	8 centimeters
CAPACITY				
Dry Measure	cor [homer]	(10 ephahs)	6 bushels	220 liters
	lethek	(5 ephahs)	3 bushels	110 liters
	ephah	(10 omers)	3/5 bushel	22 liters
	seah	(1/3 ephah)	7 quarts	7.3 liters
	omer	(1/10 ephah)	2 quarts	2 liters
	cab	(1/18 ephah)	1 quart	1 liter
Liquid Measure	bath	(1 ephah)	6 gallons	22 liters
	hin	(1/6 bath)	4 quarts	4 liters
	log	(1/72 bath)	1/3 quart	0.3 liter

A MOMENT WITH SCRIPTURE

Many people have found that taking a moment each morning to read the Bible and pray is a wonderful way to prepare themselves for whatever the day has to offer. This daily Bible reading plan is designed to introduce you to many of the important stories and key themes that have made God's Word such a source of comfort and strength for people who turn to it regularly for guidance.

Most of the passages selected can be easily read in less than five minutes. Before reading the passage for the day, ask God to clear your mind and open your heart to receive God's Word. Some Bible readers have found it helpful to keep a journal of the insights they gain while reading the Scriptures. Many have found that taking time to thank God and to remember others in prayer further enriches their devotional experience.

JANUARY

1 The Story of Creation
❑ Gen 1:1—2:3
2 John the Baptist Prepares the Way
❑ Mark 1:1-8
3 Jesus Is Baptized and Tempted
❑ Matt 3:13—4:11
4 The Garden of Eden
❑ Gen 2:4-25
5 Jesus Begins His Work in Galilee
❑ Luke 4:14-30
6 The Trouble with Sin
❑ Gen 3:1-24
7 Warnings about False Prophets
❑ Matt 7:15-23
8 A Man with Evil Spirits
❑ Mark 1:21-28
9 The First Murder
❑ Gen 4:1-16
10 Jesus Turns Water into Wine
❑ John 2:1-11
11 God Warns Noah about a Coming Flood
❑ Gen 6:1-22
12 The Flood Comes
❑ Gen 7:1-24
13 Jesus and Nicodemus
❑ John 3:1-21
14 The Floodwaters Dry Up
❑ Gen 8:1-19
15 God's Promise to Noah
❑ Gen 9:1-17
16 Jesus Heals a Paralytic
❑ Mark 2:1-12
17 Jesus Chooses Twelve to Be His Disciples
❑ Matt 9:9-13; 10:1-4
18 A Promise to Abraham and Sarah
❑ Gen 17:1-27
19 Jesus and Beelzebub
❑ Mark 3:20-30
20 The LORD Tests Abraham
❑ Gen 22:1-19
21 Jesus and the Samaritan Woman
❑ John 4:4-26
22 Jacob's Name Is Changed to Israel
❑ Gen 32:22-32
23 Jesus Heals a Centurion's Servant
❑ Luke 7:1-10
24 Joseph and His Brothers
❑ Gen 37:1-11
25 Jesus Raises a Widow's Son to Life
❑ Luke 7:11-17
26 A Parable about a Shrewd Manager
❑ Luke 16:1-15
27 Jesus Heals an Invalid
❑ John 5:1-15
28 Joseph Is Taken to Egypt
❑ Gen 37:12-36
29 A Storm on the Sea of Galilee
❑ Mark 4:35-41
30 Joseph Interprets the King's Dreams
❑ Gen 41:1-40
31 Another Demon-possessed Man
❑ Mark 5:1-20

FEBRUARY

1 Joseph Is Put in Charge of Egypt
❑ Gen 41:41-57
2 A Dead Girl and a Sick Woman
❑ Mark 5:21-43
3 Joseph's Brothers Go to Egypt
❑ Gen 42:1-24
4 Wisdom and Folly
❑ Prov 9:1-18
5 Joseph's Brothers Return to Egypt
❑ Gen 43:1-34
6 The Death of John the Baptist
❑ Mark 6:14-29
7 Joseph Sends for Jacob
❑ Gen 45:1-28
8 Salt and Light
❑ Matt 5:13-16
9 Jesus Feeds the Five Thousand
❑ John 6:1-15
10 Jacob and His Family Go to Egypt
❑ Gen 46:1-7, 28-34
11 The People of Israel Suffer in Egypt
❑ Exod 1:1-22
12 Jesus Walks on Water
❑ Matt 14:22-33
13 Moses Escapes from Egypt
❑ Exod 2:1-25
14 Love Never Fails
❑ 1 Cor 13:1-13

15 Jesus Challenges the Pharisees and Teachers of the Law
❑ Mark 7:1-13
16 God Speaks to Moses
❑ Exod 3:1-22
17 Moses Performs Miracles
❑ Exod 4:1-23, 27-31
18 What Really Makes People Unclean
❑ Mark 7:14-23
19 The LORD Promises to Free the People of Israel
❑ Exod 5:1—6:12
20 A Canaanite Woman's Faith
❑ Matt 15:21-28
21 The People of Israel Leave Egypt
❑ Exod 12:31-42
22 Jesus Heals a Deaf and Mute Man
❑ Mark 7:31-37
23 The Israelites Cross the Red Sea
❑ Exod 14:1-31
24 Jesus Speaks about His Suffering and Death
❑ Luke 9:21-27
25 Songs of Deliverance
❑ Exod 15:1-21
26 The Transfiguration
❑ Luke 9:28-36
27 Jesus Teaches about Anger and Revenge
❑ Matt 5:21-26, 38-42
28 The Ten Commandments
❑ Exod 20:1-17
29 Jesus Heals a Boy
❑ Mark 9:14-29

March

1 Women Who Helped Jesus
❑ Luke 8:1-3; 10:38-42
2 Manna and Quail from Heaven
❑ Exod 16:1-36
3 True Humility
❑ Phil 2:1-11
4 The Work of the Seventy-two Followers
❑ Luke 10:1-12, 17-20
5 A Promise and a Warning
❑ Exod 23:20-33
6 Humility and Being a Disciple of Christ
❑ Mark 9:33-41
7 The Year of Jubilee
❑ Lev 25:8-34
8 Being a Follower of Jesus
❑ Matt 18:2-9; 19:13-15
9 Help the Poor
❑ Lev 25:35-43
10 The Request of James and John
❑ Mark 10:35-45
11 Jesus Heals Ten Men with Leprosy
❑ Luke 17:11-19
12 A Blessing for the People
❑ Num 6:22-27
13 Jesus Answers the Rich Ruler
❑ Luke 18:18-30
14 The People Grumble about Being Hungry
❑ Num 11:4-15
15 Jesus Heals Blind Bartimaeus
❑ Mark 10:46-52
16 Twelve Men Are Sent to Explore Canaan
❑ Num 13:1-24
17 Jesus Helps a Woman Caught in Adultery
❑ John 8:2-11
18 The Twelve Spies Report Back
❑ Num 13:26-33
19 The Death of Jesus' Friend Lazarus
❑ John 11:1-16
20 The LORD Provides Water from a Rock
❑ Num 20:1-13
21 Jesus Brings Lazarus to Life
❑ John 11:17-44
22 King Balak of Moab and the Prophet Balaam
❑ Num 22:2-21
23 Jesus Calls Out to Zacchaeus
❑ Luke 19:1-10
24 Balaam and His Donkey
❑ Num 22:22-35
25 Jesus Enters Jerusalem
❑ Luke 19:28-44
26 Balaam's First Two Oracles
❑ Num 23:1-26
27 Jesus in the Temple
❑ Mark 11:15-19
28 Balaam's Final Oracles
❑ Num 23:27—24:25
29 A Question about Jesus' Authority
❑ Mark 11:27-33
30 Love the LORD Your God
❑ Deut 6:1-9
31 A Question about Paying Taxes
❑ Matt 22:15-22

April

1 Christ Is God's Power and Wisdom
❑ 1 Cor 1:18-31
2 Worship Only the LORD
❑ Deut 6:10-25
3 Life in the Future World
❑ Matt 22:23-33
4 God's Spirit Brings Wisdom and Blessings
❑ 1 Cor 2:1-16
5 The Greatest Commandment
❑ Matt 22:34-40
6 The LORD Cares
❑ Deut 8:1-20
7 A Widow's Offering
❑ Mark 12:41-44
8 Remembering How God Rescued His People
❑ Deut 16:1-8
9 Jesus Talks about Signs of the End of the Age
❑ Matt 24:1-14
10 Firstfruits and Tithes
❑ Deut 26:1-11

11 A Time of Suffering before the Son of Man Appears
❑ Matt 24:15-31

12 Choose Life
❑ Deut 30:1-20

13 No One Knows the Day or Time
❑ Matt 24:36-44

14 The Song of Moses
❑ Deut 32:1-43

15 Putting God First
❑ Matt 6:19-34

16 Jesus Is Honored and Betrayed
❑ Matt 26:1-16

17 Joshua Becomes Israel's Leader
❑ Josh 1:1-9

18 The Last Supper (part 1)
❑ Matt 26:17-25

19 The Last Supper (part 2)
❑ Matt 26:26-35

20 The Bread of Life
❑ John 6:25-40

21 Jesus Washes the Feet of His Disciples
❑ John 13:1-17

22 Jesus Is the True Vine
❑ John 15:1-17

23 Jesus Prays in Gethsemane
❑ Matthew 26:36-46

24 The People of Israel Cross the Jordan River
❑ Josh 3:1-17

25 Jesus Prays for His Disciples
❑ John 17:1-19

26 Jesus Prays for All Believers
❑ John 17:20-26

27 The Fall of Jericho
❑ Josh 5:13—6:21

28 We Will Worship and Obey the LORD
❑ Josh 24:1-27

29 Jesus Is Arrested
❑ Matt 26:47-56

30 Israel's Disobedience and Defeat
❑ Judg 2:6-19

MAY

1 Jesus Is Questioned by the Sanhedrin
❑ Matt 26:57-68

2 Deborah and Barak
❑ Judg 4:1-24

3 Peter Disowns Jesus
❑ Matt 26:69-75

4 Deborah's Song
❑ Judg 5:1-31

5 Jesus and Pontius Pilate
❑ Matt 27:1-14

6 Gideon Will Defeat the Midianites
❑ Judg 6:11-24

7 Jesus Is Sentenced to Die
❑ Matt 27:15-26

8 Gideon Needs Proof from the LORD
❑ Judg 6:33-40

9 Jesus Is Crucified
❑ Matt 27:27-44

10 Delilah Tricks Samson
❑ Judg 16:1-22

11 The Death of Jesus
❑ Matt 27:45-56

12 Jesus Is the Great High Priest
❑ Heb 4:14—5:10

13 Jesus Is Buried
❑ Matt 27:57-66

14 Samson's Strength Returns
❑ Judg 16:23-31

15 Jesus Is Alive
❑ Matt 28:1-10

16 The Resurrection of Christ
❑ 1 Cor 15:1-11

17 Jesus Appears to Two Disciples
❑ Luke 24:13-35

18 The Resurrection of God's People
❑ 1 Cor 15:12-34

19 Jesus and Thomas
❑ John 20:24-29

20 What Our Bodies Will Be Like
❑ 1 Cor 15:35-58

21 Jesus Questions Peter
❑ John 21:15-19

22 Ruth and Naomi
❑ Ruth 1:1-22

23 Ruth Meets Boaz
❑ Ruth 2:1-23

24 Boaz Promises to Take Care of Ruth
❑ Ruth 3:1-18

25 Ruth and Boaz Are Married
❑ Ruth 4:11-22

26 The Great Commission
❑ Matt 28:16-20

27 Jesus Is Taken Up into Heaven
❑ Acts 1:1-11

28 From Death to Life
❑ Eph 2:1-10

29 Someone to Take the Place of Judas
❑ Acts 1:12-26

30 The Prophet Samuel Is Born
❑ 1 Sam 1:1-20

31 The Holy Spirit Is Promised to Jesus' Disciples
❑ John 14:15-31

JUNE

1 A Parable about a Farmer
❑ Luke 8:4-15

2 Hannah's Song
❑ 1 Sam 2:1-10

3 The Work of the Holy Spirit
❑ John 16:1-16

4 The LORD Speaks to Samuel
❑ 1 Sam 3:1-18

5 The Philistines Capture the Ark of the LORD's Covenant
❑ 1 Sam 4:1-11

6 The Coming of the Holy Spirit
❑ Acts 2:1-13

7 God Punishes the Philistines
❑ 1 Sam 5:1-12

8 The Good Samaritan
❑ Luke 10:25-37

9 Peter Speaks to the Crowd
❑ Acts 2:14-41

10 The Ark of the LORD's Covenant Is Returned
❑ 1 Sam 6:1-18

11 Jesus Warns about Judging Others
❑ Matt 7:1-6

12 Peter and John Heal a Crippled Beggar
❑ Acts 3:1-10

13 Israel Demands a King
❑ 1 Sam 8:1-22

14 Saul Is Chosen to Be Israel's First King
❑ 1 Sam 10:17-27

15 Peter Speaks in the Temple
❑ Acts 3:11-26

16 Samuel's Farewell Speech
❑ 1 Sam 12:1-25

17 A Parable about the Rich Fool
❑ Luke 12:13-21

18 Life Among the Lord's Followers
❑ Acts 2:42-47; 4:32-37

19 King Saul Disobeys the LORD
❑ 1 Sam 13:1-15

20 David Is Chosen to Be King
❑ 1 Sam 16:1-13

21 Peter Condemns Ananias and Sapphira
❑ Acts 5:1-11

22 David Kills Goliath
❑ 1 Sam 17:41-54

23 Celebrate the Return of the Lost Sheep
❑ Luke 15:1-10

24 Trouble for the Apostles
❑ Acts 5:17-42

25 A Parable of the Lost Son
❑ Luke 15:11-32

26 King Saul Tries to Kill David
❑ 1 Sam 18:6-16

27 Seven Leaders for the Church
❑ Acts 6:1-7

28 David Lets the King Live
❑ 1 Sam 24:1-22

29 King Saul Dies in Battle
❑ 1 Sam 31:1-13

30 Stephen Is Arrested
❑ Acts 6:8-15

JULY

1 Parables about God's Kingdom
❑ Luke 13:18-30

2 David Mourns the Death of Saul
❑ 2 Sam 1:17-27

3 Stephen's Speech to the Sanhedrin (part 1)
❑ Acts 7:1-19

4 Stephen's Speech to the Sanhedrin (part 2)
❑ Acts 7:20-53

5 David Makes Jerusalem the Capital City
❑ 2 Sam 5:1-12

6 The Death of Stephen
❑ Acts 7:54—8:3

7 King David Brings the Ark to Jerusalem
❑ 2 Sam 6:1-19

8 God's Promise to King David
❑ 2 Sam 7:1-17

9 Philip and the Ethiopian Eunuch
❑ Acts 8:26-40

10 A Parable about a Widow and a Judge
❑ Luke 18:1-8

11 King David and Bathsheba
❑ 2 Sam 11:1-27

12 Saul Becomes a Follower of the Lord
❑ Acts 9:1-19

13 How Paul Became an Apostle
❑ Gal 1:11—2:10

14 The Prophet Nathan Confronts King David
❑ 2 Sam 12:1-14

15 Saul Begins Telling People about Jesus
❑ Acts 9:20-31

16 The LORD Gives King Solomon Wisdom
❑ 1 Kgs 3:1-15

17 King Solomon's Wise Ruling
❑ 1 Kgs 3:16-28

18 Peter Brings Tabitha (Dorcas) Back to Life
❑ Acts 9:36-43

19 God's Blessings
❑ Matt 5:1-12

20 Peter and Cornelius (part 1)
❑ Acts 10:1-26

21 Peter and Cornelius (part 2)
❑ Acts 10:27-48

22 The Ark of the LORD's Covenant Is Brought to the Temple
❑ 1 Kgs 8:1-21

23 The LORD Warns King Solomon about Disobedience
❑ 1 Kgs 9:1-9

24 The Church in Antioch
❑ Acts 11:19-30

25 How to Be a Guest
❑ Luke 14:7-14

26 King Solomon Disobeys the LORD
❑ 1 Kgs 11:1-13

27 Peter Is Rescued
❑ Acts 12:6-19

28 The Northern Tribes Rebel
❑ 1 Kgs 12:1-20

29 Elijah Helps a Widow
❑ 1 Kgs 17:7-16

30 Paul and Barnabas in Lystra
❑ Acts 14:8-20

31 Elijah Brings a Boy Back to Life
❑ 1 Kgs 17:17-24

AUGUST

1 Seeing God's Blessings
❑ Matt 7:7-12

2 The Church Council Meets in Jerusalem
❑ Acts 15:1-21

3 The LORD Speaks to Elijah
❑ 1 Kgs 19:9-18
4 Elisha Heals Naaman
❑ 2 Kgs 5:1-18
5 Lydia Becomes a Follower of the Lord
❑ Acts 16:11-15
6 Samaria Is Destroyed
❑ 2 Kgs 17:1-23
7 Josiah's Religious Reforms
❑ 2 Kgs 23:4-20
8 Paul and Silas in Prison (part 1)
❑ Acts 16:16-24
9 Paul and Silas in Prison (part 2)
❑ Acts 16:25-40
10 A Parable of the Talents
❑ Matt 25:14-30
11 The Babylonians Destroy Jerusalem
❑ 2 Kgs 25:1-21
12 Paul in Athens
❑ Acts 17:16-34
13 Cyrus of Persia Lets the Exiles Return Home
❑ Ezra 1:1-11
14 Rebuilding the Jerusalem Temple Begins
❑ Ezra 3:7-13
15 Trouble for Paul in Ephesus
❑ Acts 19:23-41
16 Christ's Love for His Followers
❑ Eph 3:14-21
17 Living as Children of Light
❑ Eph 5:6-20
18 Nehemiah Prays for Jerusalem
❑ Neh 1:1-11
19 Lazarus and the Rich Man
❑ Luke 16:19-31
20 Paul Says Farewell to the Church Elders of Ephesus
❑ Acts 20:13-38
21 Nehemiah Goes to Jerusalem
❑ Neh 2:1-10
22 The People Pray at the Rebuilt Walls of Jerusalem
❑ Neh 9:5-37
23 Paul Visits James
❑ Acts 21:17-26
24 Paul Asks a Friend to Show Kindness
❑ Phlm 1-25
25 Paul Is Tried by the Sanhedrin
❑ Acts 22:30—23:11
26 The Wonderful Name of the LORD
❑ Ps 8
27 The Parable of the Great Banquet
❑ Luke 14:15-24
28 A Plot to Kill Paul
❑ Acts 23:12-22
29 In Praise of the Law of the LORD
❑ Ps 119:1-16
30 The LORD's Word Is a Lamp
❑ Ps 119:97-112
31 Paul Asks to Be Tried by the Roman Emperor
❑ Acts 25:1-12

SEPTEMBER

1 There Is Still Hope
❑ Lam 3:1-24
2 Jesus Teaches His Disciples to Pray
❑ Matt 6:5-15
3 Paul Is Taken to Rome
❑ Acts 27:1-12
4 Suffering and Praise (part 1)
❑ Ps 22:1-22
5 Suffering and Praise (part 2)
❑ Ps 22:23-31
6 Paul Faces a Storm at Sea
❑ Acts 27:13-38
7 The Law of the LORD Is Perfect
❑ Ps 19:1-14
8 Paul Is Shipwrecked near Malta
❑ Acts 27:39—28:10
9 Jeremiah's Temple Sermon
❑ Jer 7:1-15
10 Paul in Rome
❑ Acts 28:17-31
11 Living by the Power of the Holy Spirit
❑ Rom 8:1-17
12 Sing a New Song to the LORD
❑ Ps 96:1-13
13 A Wonderful Future for God's People
❑ Rom 8:18-30
14 God's Love Is Sure
❑ Rom 8:31-39
15 The Parable about Tenants of a Vineyard
❑ Luke 20:9-19
16 Hope for a Return Home
❑ Jer 23:1-8
17 Living Sacrifices
❑ Rom 12:1-8
18 Nations Will Serve the LORD
❑ Zeph 3:8-13
19 Rules for Christian Living
❑ Rom 12:9-21
20 God's People Are Never in Need
❑ Ps 23:1-6
21 Putting Others First
❑ Rom 13:8-10; 15:1-6
22 A Prayer for Forgiveness
❑ Ps 39:1-13
23 Spiritual Gifts for God's People
❑ 1 Cor 12:1-11
24 False Priests Have Disobeyed the LORD
❑ Mal 2:1-17
25 The Body of Christ in the World
❑ 1 Cor 12:12-31
26 The Day of Judgment
❑ Mal 4:1-6
27 The Parable of the Ten Virgins
❑ Matt 25:1-13
28 Faith in the Lord
❑ 2 Cor 4:16—5:10
29 Bringing People to God
❑ 2 Cor 5:11—6:10
30 Don't Worship Idols
❑ Jer 2:22-28

October

1 Jerusalem Will Be at Peace
❑ Zech 8:1-17
2 What People Desire and What God's Spirit Offers
❑ Gal 5:16-26
3 The LORD Is a Strong Shield
❑ Ps 28:1-9
4 Help Each Other
❑ Gal 6:1-10
5 Judgment on Jerusalem and Judah
❑ Isa 3:1-15
6 Israel's Sin Is Like a Crack in a Wall
❑ Isa 30:8-18
7 The Old Life and the New Life
❑ Eph 4:17-24
8 Habakkuk Praises the LORD's Power
❑ Hab 3:1-15
9 Pressing on Toward the Goal
❑ Phil 3:12-21
10 Always Be Glad because of the Lord
❑ Phil 4:4-9
11 God Is a Mighty Fortress
❑ Ps 46:1-11
12 The Power of Prayer
❑ 1 Tim 2:1-8
13 The LORD Commissions Isaiah
❑ Isa 6:1-13
14 False Teaching and True Wealth
❑ 1 Tim 6:3-10
15 Obey the LORD
❑ Ps 1:1-6
16 Love and Giving
❑ Matt 5:43—6:4
17 Fighting the Good Fight of the Faith
❑ 1 Tim 6:11-19
18 Daniel in the Den of Lions
❑ Dan 6:1-24
19 A Good Soldier of Christ Jesus
❑ 2 Tim 2:1-13
20 God's Love for Israel
❑ Hos 11:1-11
21 How to Be an Approved Worker
❑ 2 Tim 2:14-26
22 The Fierce Anger of the LORD
❑ Nah 1:1-6
23 Warning against Showing Favoritism
❑ Jas 2:1-13
24 A Glorious New Temple
❑ Hag 2:1-9
25 Taming the Tongue
❑ Jas 3:1-12
26 It's Wise to Be Honest
❑ Prov 11:1-11
27 Be Patient and Kind
❑ Jas 5:7-20
28 All Creation Praises the LORD
❑ Ps 148:1-14
29 A New Commandment
❑ 1 John 2:7-17
30 God Is Love
❑ 1 John 4:1-21
31 The Fight against Evil
❑ Eph 6:10-20

November

1 Powerful Leaders Are Condemned
❑ Mic 2:1-11
2 See that Justice Is Done
❑ Mic 6:6-8
3 A Reason for Hope
❑ 1 Pet 1:3-12
4 Ezekiel Condemns Israel's Leaders
❑ Ezek 11:1-13
5 The LORD Is the Good Shepherd
❑ Ezek 34:1-16
6 The Living Stone and a Chosen People
❑ 1 Pet 2:1-10
7 Dry Bones Live Again
❑ Ezek 37:1-14
8 The River Flowing from the New Temple
❑ Ezek 47:1-12
9 Suffering for Doing Right
❑ 1 Pet 3:8-22
10 God's Love Never Fails
❑ Ps 136:1-26
11 Helping Christian Elders to Do Their Best
❑ 1 Pet 5:1-11
12 Wise Sayings about Foolishness
❑ Prov 18:1-19
13 Living As the Lord's Followers
❑ 2 Pet 1:3-15
14 Jeremiah's Letter to the Exiles in Babylon
❑ Jer 29:1-14
15 A New Covenant with Israel and Judah
❑ Jer 31:31-37
16 A Great Cloud of Witnesses
❑ Heb 12:1-13
17 Trust the LORD
❑ Isa 40:21-31
18 The LORD's People Are Coming Home
❑ Isa 60:1-9
19 A New Day for Jerusalem
❑ Isa 65:17-25
20 God's Kindness and the New Life
❑ Titus 2:11-15
21 Everything Has Its Time
❑ Eccl 3:1-8
22 Being Kind and Doing Good
❑ Titus 3:1-11
23 Choose Good and Not Evil
❑ Amos 5:3-17
24 Visions of Coming Punishment
❑ Amos 7:1-9
25 The New Heaven and the New Earth
❑ Rev 21:1-8
26 The LORD Is Merciful
❑ Jer 3:11-20
27 The New Jerusalem (part 1)
❑ Rev 21:9-21
28 The New Jerusalem (part 2)
❑ Rev 21:22—22:6

29 A Prayer for Help
❑ Ps 88:1-18

30 Jesus Is the Light of the World
❑ John 8:12-20; 12:44-50

December

1 The Coming of the Lord
❑ 1 Thes 4:13—5:11

2 Facing Discouragement
❑ Ps 42:1-11

3 Jesus Is the Way to the Father
❑ John 14:1-14

4 The Scroll and the Lamb
❑ Rev 5:1-14

5 God's Son Gives Life
❑ 1 John 5:6-12

6 Job Loses Everything
❑ Job 1:1-22

7 Job Curses His Own Life
❑ Job 3:20-26

8 Job Complains to God
❑ Job 10:1-22

9 Job Asks God for Help
❑ Job 17:1-16

10 Job Recalls His Innocence
❑ Job 31:16-40

11 The Son's Authority
❑ John 5:19-30

12 What It Means to Be Acceptable to God
❑ Rom 5:1-11

13 The LORD Questions Job
❑ Job 38:1-30

14 The LORD Controls All of Nature
❑ Job 38:31-41

15 Job Answers the LORD Almighty
❑ Job 40:1-14

16 The Mighty Leviathan
❑ Job 41:1-17

17 A Happy Ending for Job
❑ Job 42:1-17

18 The Person and Work of Christ
❑ Col 1:9-23

19 Christ Brings Spiritual Blessings
❑ Eph 1:3-14

20 The LORD Will Work Wonders
❑ Joel 2:18-24

21 An Angel Tells about the Birth of Jesus
❑ Luke 1:26-38

22 Mary and Elizabeth Rejoice in God's Goodness
❑ Luke 1:39-56

23 Encouragement for God's People
❑ Isa 40:1-11

24 Jesus Is the Word of Life
❑ John 1:1-18

25 The Birth of Jesus
❑ Luke 2:1-20

26 The Visit of the Magi
❑ Matt 2:1-12

27 Jonah Runs from the LORD
❑ Jonah 1:1-17

28 Jonah Prays
❑ Jonah 2:1-10

29 Jonah Goes to Nineveh
❑ Jonah 3:1-10

30 Jonah Complains to the LORD
❑ Jonah 4:1-11

31 The Boy Jesus in the Temple
❑ Luke 2:41-52

HOW TO LOOK UP A SCRIPTURE REFERENCE

Here's a helpful hint for those who are unfamiliar with looking up Bible passages. Like many books, the Bible is divided into units (here called "books" of the Bible); and each book is divided into chapters. However, unlike most books, chapters are divided into much smaller units called "verses" (usually consisting of a sentence or two). Both chapters and verses are numbered. This provides a very convenient and useful system for identifying specific verses in the Bible. References to Bible passages will be listed in the following way.

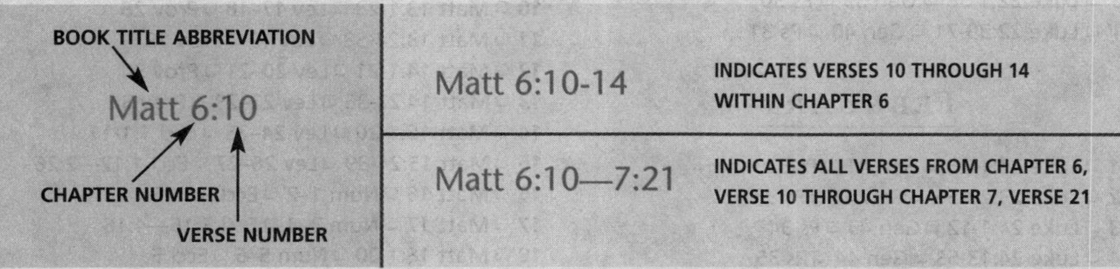

The more you look up Scripture references, the sooner you will become familiar with the abbreviations used and this system of notation. In the meantime, the "Alphabetical Listing with Abbreviations" located immediately after the "Contents" page will help you become familiar with any abbreviations you don't recognize.

READ THROUGH THE BIBLE IN A YEAR

Have you ever read the entire Bible all the way through? If you set aside just twenty or thirty minutes a day, you can do just that in one year. By following this reading plan you will read part of the Old and New Testaments each day. When the reading plan directs you to a new book of the Bible, be sure to read the Introduction to that book so that you will be alert to its key themes, characters, and passages. Begin today and discover the riches of God's Word!

JANUARY

1 ❑ Luke 5:27-39 ❑ Gen 1–2 ❑ Ps 1
2 ❑ Luke 6:1-26 ❑ Gen 3–5 ❑ Ps 2
3 ❑ Luke 6:27-49 ❑ Gen 6–7 ❑ Ps 3
4 ❑ Luke 1:1-17 ❑ Gen 8–10 ❑ Ps 4
5 ❑ Luke 7:18-50 ❑ Gen 11 ❑ Ps 5
6 ❑ Luke 8:1-25 ❑ Gen 12 ❑ Ps 6
7 ❑ Luke 8:26-56 ❑ Gen 13–14 ❑ Ps 7
8 ❑ Luke 9:1-27 ❑ Gen 15 ❑ Ps 8
9 ❑ Luke 9:28-62 ❑ Gen 16 ❑ Ps 9
10 ❑ Luke 10:1-24 ❑ Gen 17 ❑ Ps 10
11 ❑ Luke 10:25-42 ❑ Gen 18 ❑ Ps 11
12 ❑ Luke 11:1-28 ❑ Gen 19 ❑ Ps 12
13 ❑ Luke 11:29-54 ❑ Gen 20 ❑ Ps 13
14 ❑ Luke 12:1-34 ❑ Gen 21 ❑ Ps 14
15 ❑ Luke 12:35-59 ❑ Gen 22 ❑ Ps 15
16 ❑ Luke 13:1-17 ❑ Gen 23 ❑ Ps 16
17 ❑ Luke 13:18-35 ❑ Gen 24 ❑ Ps 17
18 ❑ Luke 14:1-24 ❑ Gen 25 ❑ Ps 18
19 ❑ Luke 14:25-35 ❑ Gen 26 ❑ Ps 19
20 ❑ Luke 15 ❑ Gen 27:1-45 ❑ Ps 20
21 ❑ Luke 16 ❑ Gen 27:46—28:22 ❑ Ps 21
22 ❑ Luke 17 ❑ Gen 29:1-30 ❑ Ps 22
23 ❑ Luke 18:1-17 ❑ Gen 29:31—30:43 ❑ Ps 23
24 ❑ Luke 18:18-43 ❑ Gen 31 ❑ Ps 24
25 ❑ Luke 19:1-27 ❑ Gen 32–33 ❑ Ps 25
26 ❑ Luke 19:28-48 ❑ Gen 34 ❑ Ps 26
27 ❑ Luke 20:1-26 ❑ Gen 35–36 ❑ Ps 27
28 ❑ Luke 20:27-47 ❑ Gen 37 ❑ Ps 28
29 ❑ Luke 21 ❑ Gen 38 ❑ Ps 29
30 ❑ Luke 22:1-38 ❑ Gen 39 ❑ Ps 30
31 ❑ Luke 22:39-71 ❑ Gen 40 ❑ Ps 31

FEBRUARY

1 ❑ Luke 23:1-25 ❑ Gen 41 ❑ Ps 32
2 ❑ Luke 23:26-56 ❑ Gen 42 ❑ Ps 33
3 ❑ Luke 24:1-12 ❑ Gen 43 ❑ Ps 34
4 ❑ Luke 24:13-53 ❑ Gen 44 ❑ Ps 35
5 ❑ Heb 1 ❑ Gen 45:1—46:27 ❑ Ps 36
6 ❑ Heb 2 ❑ Gen 46:28—47:31 ❑ Ps 37
7 ❑ Heb 3:1—4:13 ❑ Gen 48 ❑ Ps 38
8 ❑ Heb 4:14—6:12 ❑ Gen 49–50 ❑ Ps 39
9 ❑ Heb 6:13-20 ❑ Exod 1–2 ❑ Ps 40
10 ❑ Heb 7 ❑ Exod 3–4 ❑ Ps 41
11 ❑ Heb 8 ❑ Exod 5:1—6:27 ❑ Prov 1
12 ❑ Heb 9:1-22 ❑ Exod 6:28—8:32 ❑ Prov 2
13 ❑ Heb 9:23—10:18 ❑ Exod 9–10 ❑ Prov 3
14 ❑ Heb 10:19-39 ❑ Exod 11–12 ❑ Prov 4
15 ❑ Heb 11:1-22 ❑ Exod 13–14 ❑ Prov 5
16 ❑ Heb 11:23-40 ❑ Exod 15 ❑ Prov 6:1—7:5
17 ❑ Heb 12 ❑ Exod 16–17 ❑ Prov 7:6-27
18 ❑ Heb 13 ❑ Exod 18–19 ❑ Prov 8
19 ❑ Matt 1 ❑ Exod 20–21 ❑ Prov 9
20 ❑ Matt 2 ❑ Exod 22–23 ❑ Prov 10
21 ❑ Matt 3 ❑ Exod 24 ❑ Prov 11
22 ❑ Matt 4 ❑ Exod 25–27 ❑ Prov 12
23 ❑ Matt 5:1-20 ❑ Exod 28–29 ❑ Prov 13
24 ❑ Matt 5:21-48 ❑ Exod 30–32 ❑ Prov 14
25 ❑ Matt 6:1-18 ❑ Exod 33–34 ❑ Prov 15
26 ❑ Matt 6:19-34 ❑ Exod 35–36 ❑ Prov 16
27 ❑ Matt 7 ❑ Exod 37–38 ❑ Prov 17
28 ❑ Matt 8:1-13 ❑ Exod 39–40 ❑ Prov 18

MARCH

1 ❑ Matt 8:14-34 ❑ Lev 1–2 ❑ Prov 19
2 ❑ Matt 9:1-17 ❑ Lev 3–4 ❑ Prov 20
3 ❑ Matt 9:18-38 ❑ Lev 5–6 ❑ Prov 21
4 ❑ Matt 10:1-25 ❑ Lev 7–8 ❑ Prov 22
5 ❑ Matt 10:26-42 ❑ Lev 9–10 ❑ Prov 23
6 ❑ Matt 11:1-19 ❑ Lev 11–12 ❑ Prov 24
7 ❑ Matt 11:20-30 ❑ Lev 13 ❑ Prov 25
8 ❑ Matt 12:1-21 ❑ Lev 14 ❑ Prov 26
9 ❑ Matt 12:22-50 ❑ Lev 15–16 ❑ Prov 27
10 ❑ Matt 13:1-23 ❑ Lev 17–18 ❑ Prov 28
11 ❑ Matt 13:24-58 ❑ Lev 19 ❑ Prov 29
12 ❑ Matt 14:1-21 ❑ Lev 20–21 ❑ Prov 30
13 ❑ Matt 14:22-36 ❑ Lev 22–23 ❑ Prov 31
14 ❑ Matt 15:1-20 ❑ Lev 24–25 ❑ Eccl 1:1-11
15 ❑ Matt 15:21-39 ❑ Lev 26–27 ❑ Eccl 1:12—2:26
16 ❑ Matt 16 ❑ Num 1–2 ❑ Eccl 3:1-15
17 ❑ Matt 17 ❑ Num 3–4 ❑ Eccl 3:16—4:16
18 ❑ Matt 18:1-20 ❑ Num 5–6 ❑ Eccl 5
19 ❑ Matt 18:21-35 ❑ Num 7–8 ❑ Eccl 6
20 ❑ Matt 19:1-15 ❑ Num 9–10 ❑ Eccl 7
21 ❑ Matt 19:16-30 ❑ Num 11–12 ❑ Eccl 8
22 ❑ Matt 20:1-16 ❑ Num 13–14 ❑ Eccl 9:1-12
23 ❑ Matt 20:17-34 ❑ Num 15–16 ❑ Eccl 9:13—10:20

24 ❑ Matt 21:1-27 ❑ Num 17–18 ❑ Eccl 11
25 ❑ Matt 21:28-46 ❑ Num 19–20 ❑ Eccl 12
26 ❑ Matt 22:1-22 ❑ Num 21 ❑ Song 1:1—2:13
27 ❑ Matt 22:23-46 ❑ Num 22 ❑ Song 2:14—3:11
28 ❑ Matt 23:1-12 ❑ Num 23:1-26 ❑ Song 4:1—5:1
29 ❑ Matt 23:13-39 ❑ Num 23:27—24:25 ❑ Song 5:2—6:3
30 ❑ Matt 24:1-35 ❑ Num 25–27 ❑ Song 6:4—8:4
31 ❑ Matt 24:36-51 ❑ Num 28–29 ❑ Song 8:5-14

April

1 ❑ Matt 25:1-30 ❑ Num 30–31 ❑ Job 1
2 ❑ Matt 25:31-46 ❑ Num 32–34 ❑ Job 2
3 ❑ Matt 26:1-30 ❑ Num 35–36 ❑ Job 3
4 ❑ Matt 26:31-46 ❑ Deut 1–2 ❑ Job 4
5 ❑ Matt 26:47-75 ❑ Deut 3–4 ❑ Job 5
6 ❑ Matt 27:1-31 ❑ Deut 5–6 ❑ Job 6
7 ❑ Matt 27:32-66 ❑ Deut 7–8 ❑ Job 7
8 ❑ Matt 28 ❑ Deut 9–10 ❑ Job 8
9 ❑ Acts 1 ❑ Deut 11–12 ❑ Job 9
10 ❑ Acts 2:1-13 ❑ Deut 13–14 ❑ Job 10
11 ❑ Acts 2:14-47 ❑ Deut 15–16 ❑ Job 11
12 ❑ Acts 3 ❑ Deut 17–18 ❑ Job 12
13 ❑ Acts 4:1-22 ❑ Deut 19–20 ❑ Job 13
14 ❑ Acts 4:23-37 ❑ Deut 21–22 ❑ Job 14
15 ❑ Acts 5:1-16 ❑ Deut 23–24 ❑ Job 15
16 ❑ Acts 5:17-42 ❑ Deut 25–27 ❑ Job 16
17 ❑ Acts 6 ❑ Deut 28 ❑ Job 17
18 ❑ Acts 7:1-22 ❑ Deut 29–30 ❑ Job 18
19 ❑ Acts 7:23—8:1a ❑ Deut 31–32 ❑ Job 19
20 ❑ Acts 8:1b-25 ❑ Deut 33–34 ❑ Job 20
21 ❑ Acts 8:26-40 ❑ Josh 1–2 ❑ Job 21
22 ❑ Acts 9:1-31 ❑ Josh 3:1—4:24 ❑ Job 22
23 ❑ Acts 9:32-43 ❑ Josh 5:1—6:27 ❑ Job 23
24 ❑ Acts 10:1-33 ❑ Josh 7–8 ❑ Job 24
25 ❑ Acts 10:34-48 ❑ Josh 9–10 ❑ Job 25
26 ❑ Acts 11:1-18 ❑ Josh 11–12 ❑ Job 26
27 ❑ Acts 11:19-30 ❑ Josh 13–14 ❑ Job 27
28 ❑ Acts 12 ❑ Josh 15–17 ❑ Job 28
29 ❑ Acts 13:1-25 ❑ Josh 18–19 ❑ Job 29
30 ❑ Acts 13:26-52 ❑ Josh 20–21 ❑ Job 30

May

1 ❑ Acts 14 ❑ Josh 22 ❑ Job 31
2 ❑ Acts 15:1-21 ❑ Josh 23–24 ❑ Job 32
3 ❑ Acts 15:22-41 ❑ Judg 1 ❑ Job 33
4 ❑ Acts 16:1-15 ❑ Judg 2–3 ❑ Job 34
5 ❑ Acts 16:16-40 ❑ Judg 4–5 ❑ Job 35
6 ❑ Acts 17:1-15 ❑ Judg 6 ❑ Job 36
7 ❑ Acts 17:16-34 ❑ Judg 7–8 ❑ Job 37
8 ❑ Acts 18 ❑ Judg 9 ❑ Job 38
9 ❑ Acts 19:1-22 ❑ Judg 10:1—11:33 ❑ Job 39
10 ❑ Acts 19:23-41 ❑ Judg 11:34—12:15 ❑ Job 40
11 ❑ Acts 20:1-12 ❑ Judg 13 ❑ Job 41
12 ❑ Acts 20:13-38 ❑ Judg 14–15 ❑ Job 42
13 ❑ Acts 21:1-36 ❑ Judg 16 ❑ Ps 42
14 ❑ Acts 21:37—22:29 ❑ Judg 17–18 ❑ Ps 43
15 ❑ Acts 22:30—23:22 ❑ Judg 19 ❑ Ps 44
16 ❑ Acts 23:23—24:9 ❑ Judg 20 ❑ Ps 45
17 ❑ Acts 24:10-27 ❑ Judg 21 ❑ Ps 46
18 ❑ Acts 25 ❑ Ruth 1–2 ❑ Ps 47
19 ❑ Acts 26:1-18 ❑ Ruth 3–4 ❑ Ps 48
20 ❑ Acts 26:19-32 ❑ 1 Sam 1:1—2:11 ❑ Ps 49
21 ❑ Acts 27:1-12 ❑ 1 Sam 2:12-36 ❑ Ps 50
22 ❑ Acts 27:13-44 ❑ 1 Sam 3 ❑ Ps 51
23 ❑ Acts 28:1-16 ❑ 1 Sam 4–5 ❑ Ps 52
24 ❑ Acts 28:17-31 ❑ 1 Sam 6–7 ❑ Ps 53
25 ❑ Rom 1:1-17 ❑ 1 Sam 8 ❑ Ps 54
26 ❑ Rom 1:18-32 ❑ 1 Sam 9:1—10:16 ❑ Ps 55
27 ❑ Rom 2:1—3:8 ❑ 1 Sam 10:17—11:15 ❑ Ps 56
28 ❑ Rom 3:9-31 ❑ 1 Sam 12 ❑ Ps 57
29 ❑ Rom 4 ❑ 1 Sam 13 ❑ Ps 58
30 ❑ Rom 5 ❑ 1 Sam 14 ❑ Ps 59
31 ❑ Rom 6 ❑ 1 Sam 15 ❑ Ps 60

June

1 ❑ Rom 7 ❑ 1 Sam 16 ❑ Ps 61
2 ❑ Rom 8 ❑ 1 Sam 17 ❑ Ps 62
3 ❑ Rom 9:1-29 ❑ 1 Sam 18 ❑ Ps 63
4 ❑ Rom 9:30—10:21 ❑ 1 Sam 19 ❑ Ps 64
5 ❑ Rom 11:1-24 ❑ 1 Sam 20 ❑ Ps 65
6 ❑ Rom 11:25-36 ❑ 1 Sam 21–22 ❑ Ps 66
7 ❑ Rom 12 ❑ 1 Sam 23–24 ❑ Ps 67
8 ❑ Rom 13 ❑ 1 Sam 25 ❑ Ps 68
9 ❑ Rom 14 ❑ 1 Sam 26 ❑ Ps 69
10 ❑ Rom 15:1-13 ❑ 1 Sam 27–28 ❑ Ps 70
11 ❑ Rom 15:14-33 ❑ 1 Sam 29–31 ❑ Ps 71
12 ❑ Rom 16 ❑ 2 Sam 1 ❑ Ps 72
13 ❑ Mark 1:1-20 ❑ 2 Sam 2:1—3:5 ❑ Dan 1
14 ❑ Mark 1:21-45 ❑ 2 Sam 3:6-39 ❑ Dan 2:1-23
15 ❑ Mark 2 ❑ 2 Sam 4–5 ❑ Dan 2:24-49
16 ❑ Mark 3:1-19 ❑ 2 Sam 6 ❑ Dan 3
17 ❑ Mark 3:20-35 ❑ 2 Sam 7–8 ❑ Dan 4
18 ❑ Mark 4:1-20 ❑ 2 Sam 9–10 ❑ Dan 5
19 ❑ Mark 4:21-41 ❑ 2 Sam 11–12 ❑ Dan 6
20 ❑ Mark 5:1-20 ❑ 2 Sam 13 ❑ Dan 7
21 ❑ Mark 5:21-43 ❑ 2 Sam 14 ❑ Dan 8
22 ❑ Mark 6:1-29 ❑ 2 Sam 15 ❑ Dan 9
23 ❑ Mark 6:30-56 ❑ 2 Sam 16 ❑ Dan 10:1—11:1
24 ❑ Mark 7:1-23 ❑ 2 Sam 17 ❑ Dan 11:2-19
25 ❑ Mark 7:24-37 ❑ 2 Sam 18 ❑ Dan 11:20-45

26 ❑ Mark 8:1-21 ❑ 2 Sam 19 ❑ Dan 12
27 ❑ Mark 8:22—9:1 ❑ 2 Sam 20–21 ❑ Hos 1:1—2:1
28 ❑ Mark 9:2-50 ❑ 2 Sam 22 ❑ Hos 2:2-23
29 ❑ Mark 10:1-31 ❑ 2 Sam 23 ❑ Hos 3
30 ❑ Mark 10:32-52 ❑ 2 Sam 24 ❑ Hos 4:1-9

July

1 ❑ Mark 11:1-11 ❑ 1 Kgs 1 ❑ Hos 4:10-19
2 ❑ Mark 11:12-33 ❑ 1 Kgs 2 ❑ Hos 5
3 ❑ Mark 12:1-27 ❑ 1 Kgs 3 ❑ Hos 6:1—7:2
4 ❑ Mark 12:28-44 ❑ 1 Kgs 4–5 ❑ Hos 7:3-16
5 ❑ Mark 13:1-13 ❑ 1 Kgs 6 ❑ Hos 8
6 ❑ Mark 13:14-37 ❑ 1 Kgs 7 ❑ Hos 9
7 ❑ Mark 14:1-31 ❑ 1 Kgs 8 ❑ Hos 10
8 ❑ Mark 14:32-72 ❑ 1 Kgs 9 ❑ Hos 11:1-11
9 ❑ Mark 15:1-20 ❑ 1 Kgs 10 ❑ Hos 11:12—12:14
10 ❑ Mark 15:21-47 ❑ 1 Kgs 11 ❑ Hos 13
11 ❑ Mark 16 ❑ 1 Kgs 12 ❑ Hos 14
12 ❑ 1 Cor 1:1-17 ❑ 1 Kgs 13 ❑ Joel 1
13 ❑ 1 Cor 1:18-31 ❑ 1 Kgs 14 ❑ Joel 2:1-11
14 ❑ 1 Cor 2 ❑ 1 Kgs 15:1-32 ❑ Joel 2:12-32
15 ❑ 1 Cor 3 ❑ 1 Kgs 15:33—16:34 ❑ Joel 3
16 ❑ 1 Cor 4 ❑ 1 Kgs 17 ❑ Amos 1
17 ❑ 1 Cor 5 ❑ 1 Kgs 18 ❑ Amos 2:1—3:2
18 ❑ 1 Cor 6 ❑ 1 Kgs 19 ❑ Amos 3:3—4:3
19 ❑ 1 Cor 7:1-24 ❑ 1 Kgs 20 ❑ Amos 4:4-13
20 ❑ 1 Cor 7:25-40 ❑ 1 Kgs 21 ❑ Amos 5
21 ❑ 1 Cor 8 ❑ 1 Kgs 22 ❑ Amos 6
22 ❑ 1 Cor 9 ❑ 2 Kgs 1–2 ❑ Amos 7
23 ❑ 1 Cor 10 ❑ 2 Kgs 3 ❑ Amos 8
24 ❑ 1 Cor 11:1-16 ❑ 2 Kgs 4 ❑ Amos 9
25 ❑ 1 Cor 11:17-34 ❑ 2 Kgs 5 ❑ Obad
26 ❑ 1 Cor 12 ❑ 2 Kgs 6:1—7:2 ❑ Jonah 1
27 ❑ 1 Cor 13 ❑ 2 Kgs 7:3-20 ❑ Jonah 2
28 ❑ 1 Cor 14:1-25 ❑ 2 Kgs 8 ❑ Jonah 3
29 ❑ 1 Cor 14:26-40 ❑ 2 Kgs 9 ❑ Jonah 4
30 ❑ 1 Cor 15:1-34 ❑ 2 Kgs 10 ❑ Mic 1
31 ❑ 1 Cor 15:35-58 ❑ 2 Kgs 11 ❑ Mic 2

August

1 ❑ 1 Cor 16 ❑ 2 Kgs 12–13 ❑ Mic 3
2 ❑ 2 Cor 1:1—2:4 ❑ 2 Kgs 14 ❑ Mic 4
3 ❑ 2 Cor 2:5—3:18 ❑ 2 Kgs 15–16 ❑ Mic 5
4 ❑ 2 Cor 4:1—5:10 ❑ 2 Kgs 17 ❑ Mic 6
5 ❑ 2 Cor 5:11—6:13 ❑ 2 Kgs 18 ❑ Mic 7
6 ❑ 2 Cor 6:14—7:16 ❑ 2 Kgs 19 ❑ Nah 1
7 ❑ 2 Cor 8 ❑ 2 Kgs 20–21 ❑ Nah 2
8 ❑ 2 Cor 9 ❑ 2 Kgs 22:1—23:35 ❑ Nah 3
9 ❑ 2 Cor 10 ❑ 2 Kgs 23:36—24:20 ❑ Hab 1
10 ❑ 2 Cor 11 ❑ 2 Kgs 25 ❑ Hab 2
11 ❑ 2 Cor 12 ❑ 1 Chr 1–2 ❑ Hab 3
12 ❑ 2 Cor 13 ❑ 1 Chr 3–4 ❑ Zeph 1
13 ❑ John 1:1-18 ❑ 1 Chr 5–6 ❑ Zeph 2
14 ❑ John 1:19-34 ❑ 1 Chr 7–8 ❑ Zeph 3
15 ❑ John 1:35-51 ❑ 1 Chr 9 ❑ Hag 1–2
16 ❑ John 2 ❑ 1 Chr 10–11 ❑ Zech 1
17 ❑ John 3:1-21 ❑ 1 Chr 12 ❑ Zech 2
18 ❑ John 3:22-36 ❑ 1 Chr 13–14 ❑ Zech 3
19 ❑ John 4:1-26 ❑ 1 Chr 15:1—16:6 ❑ Zech 4
20 ❑ John 4:27-42 ❑ 1 Chr 16:7-43 ❑ Zech 5
21 ❑ John 4:43-54 ❑ 1 Chr 17 ❑ Zech 6
22 ❑ John 5:1-15 ❑ 1 Chr 18–19 ❑ Zech 7
23 ❑ John 5:16-47 ❑ 1 Chr 20:1—22:1 ❑ Zech 8
24 ❑ John 6:1-24 ❑ 1 Chr 22:2—23:32 ❑ Zech 9
25 ❑ John 6:25-59 ❑ 1 Chr 24 ❑ Zech 10
26 ❑ John 6:60-71 ❑ 1 Chr 25–26 ❑ Zech 11
27 ❑ John 7:1-24 ❑ 1 Chr 27–28 ❑ Zech 12
28 ❑ John 7:25-52 ❑ 1 Chr 29 ❑ Zech 13
29 ❑ John 7:53—8:30 ❑ 2 Chr 1–2 ❑ Zech 14
30 ❑ John 8:31-47 ❑ 2 Chr 3:1—5:1 ❑ Mal 1:1—2:9
31 ❑ John 8:48-59 ❑ 2 Chr 5:2-14 ❑ Mal 2:10-16

September

1 ❑ John 9:1-23 ❑ 2 Chr 6 ❑ Mal 2:17—3:18
2 ❑ John 9:24-41 ❑ 2 Chr 7 ❑ Mal 4
3 ❑ John 10:1-21 ❑ 2 Chr 8 ❑ Ps 73
4 ❑ John 10:22-42 ❑ 2 Chr 9 ❑ Ps 74
5 ❑ John 11:1-27 ❑ 2 Chr 10–11 ❑ Ps 75
6 ❑ John 11:28-57 ❑ 2 Chr 12–13 ❑ Ps 76
7 ❑ John 12:1-26 ❑ 2 Chr 14–15 ❑ Ps 77
8 ❑ John 12:27-50 ❑ 2 Chr 16–17 ❑ Ps 78:1-20
9 ❑ John 13:1-20 ❑ 2 Chr 18 ❑ Ps 78:21-37
10 ❑ John 13:21-38 ❑ 2 Chr 19 ❑ Ps 78:38-55
11 ❑ John 14:1-14 ❑ 2 Chr 20:1—21:3 ❑ Ps 78:56-72
12 ❑ John 14:15-31 ❑ 2 Chr 21:4—22:12 ❑ Ps 79
13 ❑ John 15:1—16:4 ❑ 2 Chr 23 ❑ Ps 80
14 ❑ John 16:5-33 ❑ 2 Chr 24 ❑ Ps 81
15 ❑ John 17 ❑ 2 Chr 25 ❑ Ps 82
16 ❑ John 18:1-18 ❑ 2 Chr 26 ❑ Ps 83
17 ❑ John 18:19-40 ❑ 2 Chr 27–28 ❑ Ps 84
18 ❑ John 19:1-16a ❑ 2 Chr 29 ❑ Ps 85
19 ❑ John 19:16b-42 ❑ 2 Chr 30 ❑ Ps 86
20 ❑ John 20:1-18 ❑ 2 Chr 31 ❑ Ps 87
21 ❑ John 20:19-31 ❑ 2 Chr 32 ❑ Ps 88
22 ❑ John 21 ❑ 2 Chr 33 ❑ Ps 89:1-18
23 ❑ 1 John 1 ❑ 2 Chr 34 ❑ Ps 89:19-37
24 ❑ 1 John 2 ❑ 2 Chr 35 ❑ Ps 89:38-52
25 ❑ 1 John 3 ❑ 2 Chr 36 ❑ Ps 90
26 ❑ 1 John 4 ❑ Ezra 1–2 ❑ Ps 91

27 ❑ 1 John 5 ❑ Ezra 3–4 ❑ Ps 92
28 ❑ 2 John ❑ Ezra 5–6 ❑ Ps 93
29 ❑ 3 John ❑ Ezra 7–8 ❑ Ps 94
30 ❑ Jude ❑ Ezra 9–10 ❑ Ps 95

October

1 ❑ Rev 1 ❑ Neh 1–2 ❑ Ps 96
2 ❑ Rev 2 ❑ Neh 3 ❑ Ps 97
3 ❑ Rev 3 ❑ Neh 4 ❑ Ps 98
4 ❑ Rev 4 ❑ Neh 5:1—7:3 ❑ Ps 99
5 ❑ Rev 5 ❑ Neh 7:4—8:12 ❑ Ps 100
6 ❑ Rev 6 ❑ Neh 8:13—9:37 ❑ Ps 101
7 ❑ Rev 7 ❑ Neh 9:38—10:39 ❑ Ps 102
8 ❑ Rev 8 ❑ Neh 11 ❑ Ps 103
9 ❑ Rev 9 ❑ Neh 12 ❑ Ps 104:1-23
10 ❑ Rev 10 ❑ Neh 13 ❑ Ps 104:24-35
11 ❑ Rev 11 ❑ Esth 1 ❑ Ps 105:1-25
12 ❑ Rev 12 ❑ Esth 2 ❑ Ps 105:26-45
13 ❑ Rev 13 ❑ Esth 3–4 ❑ Ps 106:1-23
14 ❑ Rev 14 ❑ Esth 5–6 ❑ Ps 106:24-48
15 ❑ Rev 15 ❑ Esth 7–8 ❑ Ps 107:1-22
16 ❑ Rev 16 ❑ Esth 9-10 ❑ Ps 107:23-43
17 ❑ Rev 17 ❑ Isa 1–2 ❑ Ps 108
18 ❑ Rev 18 ❑ Isa 3–4 ❑ Ps 109:1-20
19 ❑ Rev 19 ❑ Isa 5–6 ❑ Ps 109:21-31
20 ❑ Rev 20 ❑ Isa 7–8 ❑ Ps 110
21 ❑ Rev 21–22 ❑ Isa 9–10 ❑ Ps 111
22 ❑ 1 Thes 1 ❑ Isa 11–13 ❑ Ps 112
23 ❑ 1 Thes 2:1-16 ❑ Isa 14–16 ❑ Ps 113
24 ❑ 1 Thes 2:17—3:13 ❑ Isa 17–19 ❑ Ps 114
25 ❑ 1 Thes 4 ❑ Isa 20–22 ❑ Ps 115
26 ❑ 1 Thes 5 ❑ Isa 23–24 ❑ Ps 116
27 ❑ 2 Thes 1 ❑ Isa 25–26 ❑ Ps 117
28 ❑ 2 Thes 2 ❑ Isa 27–28 ❑ Ps 118
29 ❑ 2 Thes 3 ❑ Isa 29–30 ❑ Ps 119:1-32
30 ❑ 1 Tim 1 ❑ Isa 31–33 ❑ Ps 119:33-64
31 ❑ 1 Tim 2 ❑ Isa 34–35 ❑ Ps 119:65-96

November

1 ❑ 1 Tim 3 ❑ Isa 36–37 ❑ Ps 119:97-120
2 ❑ 1 Tim 4 ❑ Isa 38–39 ❑ Ps 119:121-144
3 ❑ 1 Tim 5 ❑ Jer 1–2 ❑ Ps 119:145-176
4 ❑ 1 Tim 6 ❑ Jer 3–4 ❑ Ps 120
5 ❑ 2 Tim 1 ❑ Jer 5–6 ❑ Ps 121
6 ❑ 2 Tim 2 ❑ Jer 7–8 ❑ Ps 122
7 ❑ 2 Tim 3 ❑ Jer 9–10 ❑ Ps 123
8 ❑ 2 Tim 4 ❑ Jer 11–12 ❑ Ps 124
9 ❑ Titus 1 ❑ Jer 13–14 ❑ Ps 125
10 ❑ Titus 2 ❑ Jer 15–16 ❑ Ps 126
11 ❑ Titus 3 ❑ Jer 17–18 ❑ Ps 127
12 ❑ Phlm ❑ Jer 19–20 ❑ Ps 128
13 ❑ Jas 1 ❑ Jer 21–22 ❑ Ps 129
14 ❑ Jas 2 ❑ Jer 23–24 ❑ Ps 130
15 ❑ Jas 3 ❑ Jer 25–26 ❑ Ps 131
16 ❑ Jas 4 ❑ Jer 27–28 ❑ Ps 132
17 ❑ Jas 5 ❑ Jer 29–30 ❑ Ps 133
18 ❑ 1 Pet 1 ❑ Jer 31–32 ❑ Ps 134
19 ❑ 1 Pet 2 ❑ Jer 33–34 ❑ Ps 135
20 ❑ 1 Pet 3 ❑ Jer 35–36 ❑ Ps 136
21 ❑ 1 Pet 4 ❑ Jer 37–38 ❑ Ps 137
22 ❑ 1 Pet 5 ❑ Jer 39–40 ❑ Ps 138
23 ❑ 2 Pet 1 ❑ Jer 41–42 ❑ Ps 139
24 ❑ 2 Pet 2 ❑ Jer 43–44 ❑ Ps 140
25 ❑ 2 Pet 3 ❑ Jer 45–46 ❑ Ps 141
26 ❑ Gal 1 ❑ Jer 47–48 ❑ Ps 142
27 ❑ Gal 2 ❑ Jer 49–50 ❑ Ps 143
28 ❑ Gal 3:1-14 ❑ Jer 51–52 ❑ Ps 144
29 ❑ Gal 3:15—4:20 ❑ Lam 1–2 ❑ Ps 145
30 ❑ Gal 4:21-31 ❑ Lam 3–4 ❑ Ps 146

December

1 ❑ Gal 5:1-15 ❑ Lam 5 ❑ Ps 147
2 ❑ Gal 5:16-26 ❑ Ezek 1 ❑ Ps 148
3 ❑ Gal 6 ❑ Ezek 2–3 ❑ Ps 149
4 ❑ Eph 1 ❑ Ezek 4–5 ❑ Ps 150
5 ❑ Eph 2 ❑ Ezek 6–7 ❑ Isa 40
6 ❑ Eph 3 ❑ Ezek 8–9 ❑ Isa 41
7 ❑ Eph 4:1-16 ❑ Ezek 10–11 ❑ Isa 42
8 ❑ Eph 4:17-32 ❑ Ezek 12–13 ❑ Isa 43
9 ❑ Eph 5:1-21 ❑ Ezek 14–15 ❑ Isa 44
10 ❑ Eph 5:22-33 ❑ Ezek 16 ❑ Isa 45
11 ❑ Eph 6 ❑ Ezek 17 ❑ Isa 46
12 ❑ Phil 1:1-11 ❑ Ezek 18 ❑ Isa 47
13 ❑ Phil 1:12-30 ❑ Ezek 19 ❑ Isa 48
14 ❑ Phil 2:1-11 ❑ Ezek 20 ❑ Isa 49
15 ❑ Phil 2:12-30 ❑ Ezek 21–22 ❑ Isa 50
16 ❑ Phil 3 ❑ Ezek 23 ❑ Isa 51
17 ❑ Phil 4 ❑ Ezek 24 ❑ Isa 52
18 ❑ Col 1:1-23 ❑ Ezek 25–26 ❑ Isa 53
19 ❑ Col 1:24—2:19 ❑ Ezek 27–28 ❑ Isa 54
20 ❑ Col 2:20—3:17 ❑ Ezek 29–30 ❑ Isa 55
21 ❑ Col 3:18—4:18 ❑ Ezek 31–32 ❑ Isa 56
22 ❑ Luke 1:1-25 ❑ Ezek 33 ❑ Isa 57
23 ❑ Luke 1:26-56 ❑ Ezek 34 ❑ Isa 58
24 ❑ Luke 1:57-80 ❑ Ezek 35–36 ❑ Isa 59
25 ❑ Luke 2:1-20 ❑ Ezek 37 ❑ Isa 60
26 ❑ Luke 2:21-52 ❑ Ezek 38–39 ❑ Isa 61
27 ❑ Luke 3:1-20 ❑ Ezek 40–41 ❑ Isa 62
28 ❑ Luke 3:21-38 ❑ Ezek 42–43 ❑ Isa 63
29 ❑ Luke 4:1-30 ❑ Ezek 44–45 ❑ Isa 64
30 ❑ Luke 4:31-44 ❑ Ezek 46–47 ❑ Isa 65
31 ❑ Luke 5:1-26 ❑ Ezek 48 ❑ Isa 66

THE BEGINNINGS: EVENTS IN PREHISTORY	THE ANCESTORS OF THE ISRAELITES 1900 TO 1700 B.C.	THE ISRAELITES IN EGYPT AND THE DESERT 1700 TO 1250 B.C.
Creation. Adam and Eve in the Garden. Cain and Abel. Noah and the Flood. The Tower of Babel. *In the beginning God created the heavens and the earth.* (Gen 1:1)	**Beginning around 1900 B.C.** Abraham comes to Palestine. Isaac is born to Abraham. Jacob is born to Isaac. Jacob has twelve sons, who become the ancestors of the twelve tribes of Israel. The most prominent of these sons is Joseph, who becomes advisor to the Pharaoh of Egypt. *He took him outside and said, "Look up at the heavens and count the stars . . . So shall your offspring be."* (Gen 15:5)	**1700-1290 B.C.** The descendants of Jacob are enslaved in Egypt. **1290 B.C.** Moses leads the Israelites out of Egypt. **1290-1250 B.C.** The Israelites wander in the desert. During this time Moses receives God's Law on Mount Sinai. *Afterward Moses and Aaron went to Pharaoh and said, "This is what the LORD, the God of Israel, says: 'Let my people go, so that they may hold a festival to me in the desert.'"* (Exod 5:1)

ARCHAEOLOGICAL AGES

Archaeologists classify ancient civilizations according to a series of technological "Ages." By naming an Age by the common technology and objects of an ancient civilization, archaeologists describe how advanced that civilization was.

AGE	TECHNOLOGY	APPROXIMATE TIME PERIOD
Stone Age	Making and using stone tools	2,000,000 to 6000 B.C.
Pottery Age (Late Stone Age)	Making and using clay pottery	6000 to 5000 B.C.
Copper Age	Making and using cast copper utensils	5000 to 3000 B.C.
Bronze Age	Making and using bronze (cast copper and tin) tools	3000 to 1200 B.C.
Iron Age	Making and using iron tools	1200 to 300 B.C.

THE CONQUEST AND SETTLEMENT OF CANAAN 1250 TO 1030 B.C.	THE UNITED ISRAELITE KINGDOM 1030 TO 931 B.C.	THE TWO ISRAELITE KINGDOMS 931 TO 687 B.C.		
	KINGS	*KINGS* **JUDAH** (SOUTHERN KINGDOM)	*PROPHETS*	*KINGS* **ISRAEL** (NORTHERN KINGDOM)
1250 B.C. Joshua leads the first stage of the invasion of Canaan.	**1030-1010 B.C.** Saul	**931-913 B.C. Rehoboam**		**931-910 B.C. Jeroboam**
	1010-970 B.C. David	**913-911 B.C. Abijah**		**910-909 B.C. Nadab**
Israel remains a loose confederation of tribes, and leadership is exercised by heroic figures known as the Judges.	**970-931 B.C.** Solomon	**911-870 B.C. Asa**		**909-886 B.C. Baasha**
				886-885 B.C. Elah
	David said, *"Is not my house right with God? Has he not made with me an everlasting covenant, arranged and secured in every part?"* (2 Sam 23:5)			**7 days IN 885 B.C. Zimri**
				885-874 B.C. Omri
The LORD said to Joshua, son of Nun, Moses' aide: "Moses my servant is dead. Now then, you and all these people, get ready to cross the Jordan River into the land I am about to give to them—to the Israelites." (Josh 1:1, 2)		**870-848 B.C. Jehoshaphat**	Elijah	**874-853 B.C. Ahab**
				853-852 B.C. Ahaziah
				852-841 B.C. Joram
		848-841 B.C. Jehoram		**841-814 B.C. Jehu**
		841 B.C. Ahaziah	Elisha	
		841-835 B.C. Queen Athaliah		
		835-796 B.C. Joash		**814-798 B.C. Jehoahaz**
		796-781 B.C. Amaziah		**798-783 B.C. Jehoash**
				783-743 B.C. Jeroboam II
		781-740 B.C. Azariah (Uzziah)	Jonah Amos	**6 mo. in 743 B.C. Zechariah** **1 mo. in 743 B.C. Shallum**
				743-738 B.C. Menahem
		740-736 B.C. Jotham	Hosea	**738-737 B.C. Pekahiah**
		736-716 B.C. Ahaz	Micah Isaiah	**737-732 B.C. Pekah** **732-723 B.C. Hoshea**
		716-687 B.C. Hezekiah		**722 B.C.** ***FALL OF SAMARIA***

THE LAST YEARS OF THE KINGDOM OF JUDAH 687 TO 586 B.C.

Kings	*Prophets*
687-642 B.C. **Manasseh**	
642-640 B.C. **Amon**	
640-609 B.C. **Josiah**	**Zephaniah**
3 MO. IN 609 B.C. **Jehoahaz**	**Nahum**
609-598 B.C. **Jehoiakim**	**Jeremiah**
3 MO. IN 598 B.C. **Jehoiachin**	**Habakkuk**
598-587 B.C. **Zedekiah**	**Ezekiel**

JULY 587 OR 586 B.C.
FALL OF JERUSALEM

The Babylonians broke up the bronze pillars . . .
that were at the temple of the LORD
and they carried the bronze to Babylon . . .
So Judah went into captivity,
away from her land.
(2 Kgs 25:13-21)

THE EXILE AND THE RESTORATION 586 TO 443 B.C.

	Prophets
586 B.C. The Judeans taken into exile in Babylon after the fall of Jerusalem.	
539 B.C. Persian rule begins.	
538 B.C. Edict of Cyrus allows Jews to return.	**Haggai** **Zechariah**
520 B.C. Foundations of new temple are laid.	**Obadiah** **Daniel**
445-443 B.C. The walls of Jerusalem are restored.	**Malachi** **Joel?**

This is what Cyrus king of Persia says:
"The LORD, the God of heaven, has given me
all the kingdoms of the earth and he has
appointed me to build a temple for him
at Jerusalem in Judah."
(Ezra 1:2)

A WORD ABOUT DATES

The initials B.C. have traditionally been an abbreviation for "Before Christ." Based on information presented in LUKE, then, Jesus was born at least four years before the years known as A.D. began. (A.D. stands for the Latin phrase "in the year of our Lord.") Christian dating was actually not introduced until A.D. 526 by a monk named Dionysius Exiguus. He was given the job of creating a calendar for the feasts of the church. He fixed the birth of Jesus in the Roman year 754, which was selected as the first year of the Christian era beginning on January 1. Dionysius apparently misjudged Herod's reign by about five years.

The initials B.C.E. (Before the Common Era) and C.E. (in the Common Era) are sometimes used in place of the traditional B.C. and A.D.

All dates in this timeline are approximate.

THE TIME BETWEEN THE TESTAMENTS 333 TO 4 B.C.

333 B.C.
Alexander the Great establishes Greek rule in Palestine.

323-198 B.C.
The Ptolemies, descendants of one of Alexander's generals who had been given the position of ruler over Egypt, rule Palestine.

198-166 B.C.
The Seleucids, descendants of one of Alexander's generals who had acquired the rule of Syria, rule Palestine.

166-63 B.C.
Jewish revolt under Judas Maccabeus reestablishes Jewish independence. Judas' family and descendants, the Hasmoneans, rule Palestine.

63 B.C.
The Roman general Pompey takes Jerusalem.

37-4 B.C.
Puppet kings appointed by Rome rule Palestine. One of these is Herod the Great.

"Then the sovereignty, power and greatness
of the kingdoms under the whole heaven
will be handed over to the saints,
the people of the Most High.
His kingdom will be an everlasting kingdom,
and all rulers will worship and obey him."
(Dan 7:27)

THE TIME OF THE NEW TESTAMENT 6 B.C. TO A.D. 70

Birth of Jesus.

Ministry of John the Baptist; baptism of Jesus and beginning of his public ministry.

around A.D. 32
Death and resurrection of Jesus.

A.D. 37
Conversion of Paul (Saul of Tarsus).

A.D. 41-65
Ministry of Paul.

A.D. 65
Final imprisonment of Paul.

A.D. 70
Herod's temple destroyed.

When Jesus spoke again to the people,
he said,
"I am the light of the world.
Whoever follows me will never walk
in darkness, but will have
the light of life."
(John 8:12)

The Ancient Near East, 1800 to 1400 B.C.

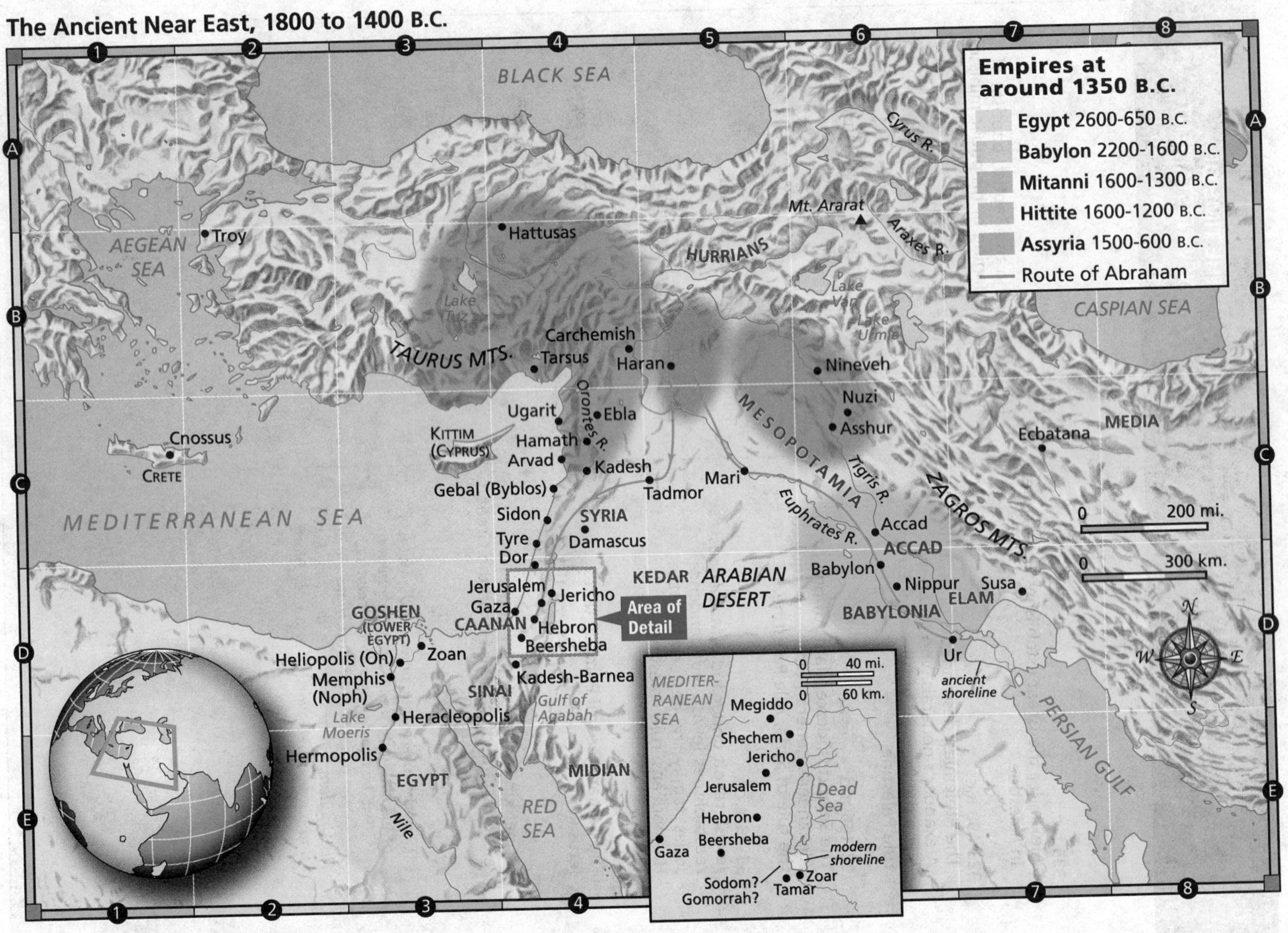

Empires at around 1350 B.C.
Egypt 2600-650 B.C.
Babylon 2200-1600 B.C.
Mitanni 1600-1300 B.C.
Hittite 1600-1200 B.C.
Assyria 1500-600 B.C.
Route of Abraham
BLACK SEA
CASPIAN SEA
AEGEAN SEA
MEDITERRANEAN SEA
RED SEA
PERSIAN GULF
Troy
Cnossus
CRETE
Hattusas
Lake Tuz
TAURUS MTS.
Tarsus
Carchemish
Haran
HURRIANS
Mt. Ararat
Araxes R.
Cyrus R.
Lake Van
Lake Urmia
Nineveh
Nuzi
Asshur
Tigris R.
MEDIA
Ecbatana
ZAGROS MTS.
MESOPOTAMIA
Euphrates R.
Mari
Accad
ACCAD
Babylon
BABYLONIA
Nippur
ELAM
Susa
Ur
ancient shoreline
0 200 mi.
0 300 km.
KITTIM (CYPRUS)
Ugarit
Ebla
Orontes R.
Hamath
Arvad
Kadesh
Tadmor
Gebal (Byblos)
Sidon
Tyre
Dor
SYRIA
Damascus
KEDAR
ARABIAN DESERT
Area of Detail
Jerusalem
Jericho
Gaza
CAANAN
Hebron
Beersheba
Kadesh-Barnea
SINAI
Gulf of Aqabah
MIDIAN
GOSHEN (LOWER EGYPT)
Zoan
Heliopolis (On)
Memphis (Noph)
Heracleopolis
Lake Moeris
Hermopolis
EGYPT
Nile
MEDITERRANEAN SEA
0 40 mi.
0 60 km.
Megiddo
Shechem
Jericho
Jerusalem
Dead Sea
Hebron
Beersheba
Gaza
modern shoreline
Sodom?
Gomorrah?
Zoar
Tamar
A B C D E
1 2 3 4 5 6 7 8

Egypt and Sinai, 1400 to 1200 B.C.

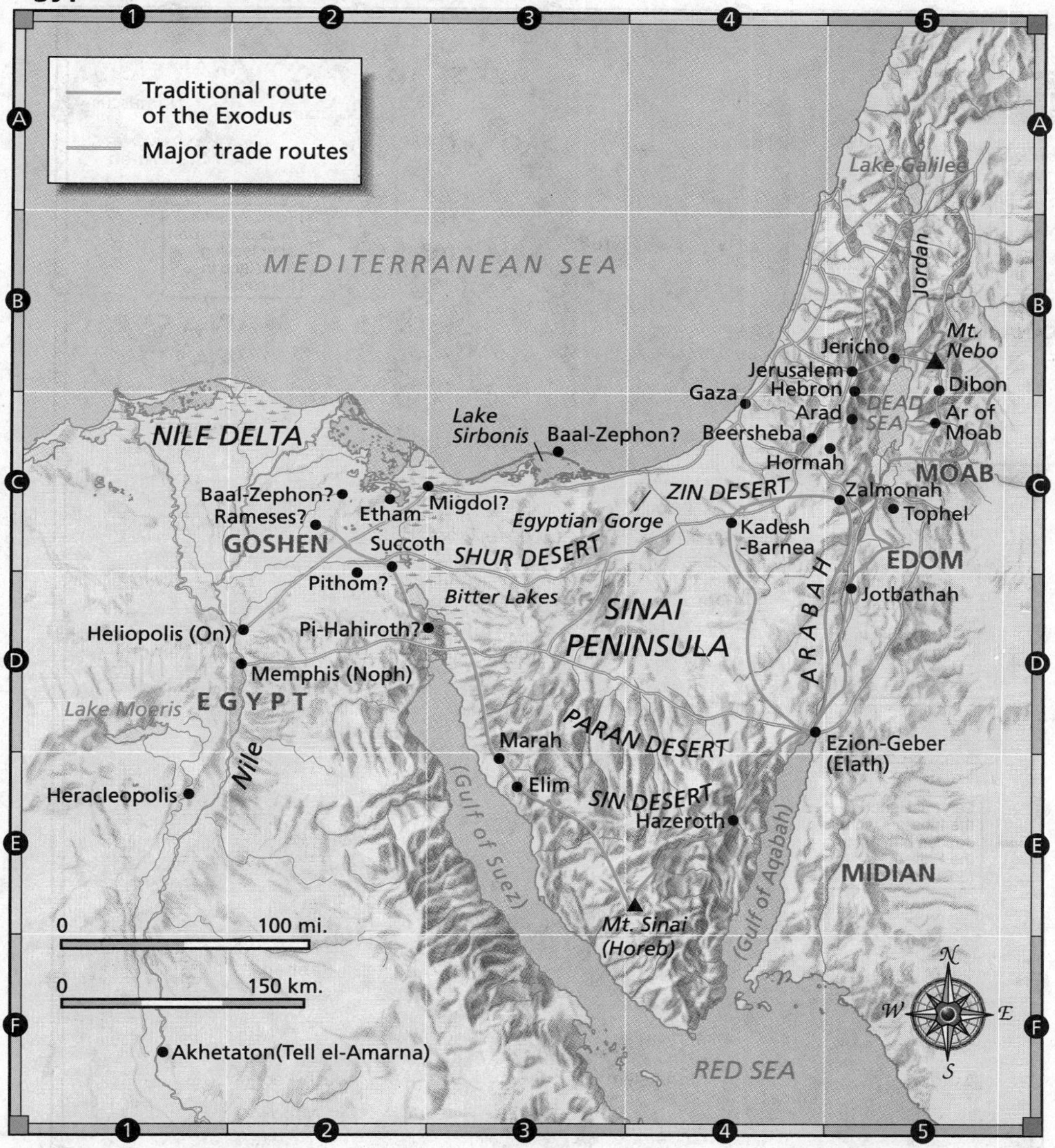

Traditional route of the Exodus
Major trade routes

MEDITERRANEAN SEA
Lake Galilee
Jordan
Mt. Nebo
Jericho
Jerusalem
Hebron
Gaza
DEAD SEA
Dibon
Arad
Ar of Moab
Beersheba
Hormah
MOAB
NILE DELTA
Lake Sirbonis
Baal-Zephon?
Baal-Zephon?
Migdol?
Etham
Rameses?
GOSHEN
Succoth
ZIN DESERT
Egyptian Gorge
Zalmonah
Tophel
Kadesh -Barnea
SHUR DESERT
EDOM
Pithom?
Bitter Lakes
SINAI PENINSULA
ARABAH
Jotbathah
Heliopolis (On)
Pi-Hahiroth?
Memphis (Noph)
EGYPT
Lake Moeris
Nile
PARAN DESERT
Marah
Ezion-Geber (Elath)
Elim
Heracleopolis
SIN DESERT
Hazeroth
(Gulf of Suez)
(Gulf of Aqabah)
MIDIAN
Mt. Sinai (Horeb)
0 100 mi.
0 150 km.
N E S W
Akhetaton(Tell el-Amarna)
RED SEA

1 2 3 4 5
A B C D E F

Division of Canaan, 1200 to 1030 B.C.

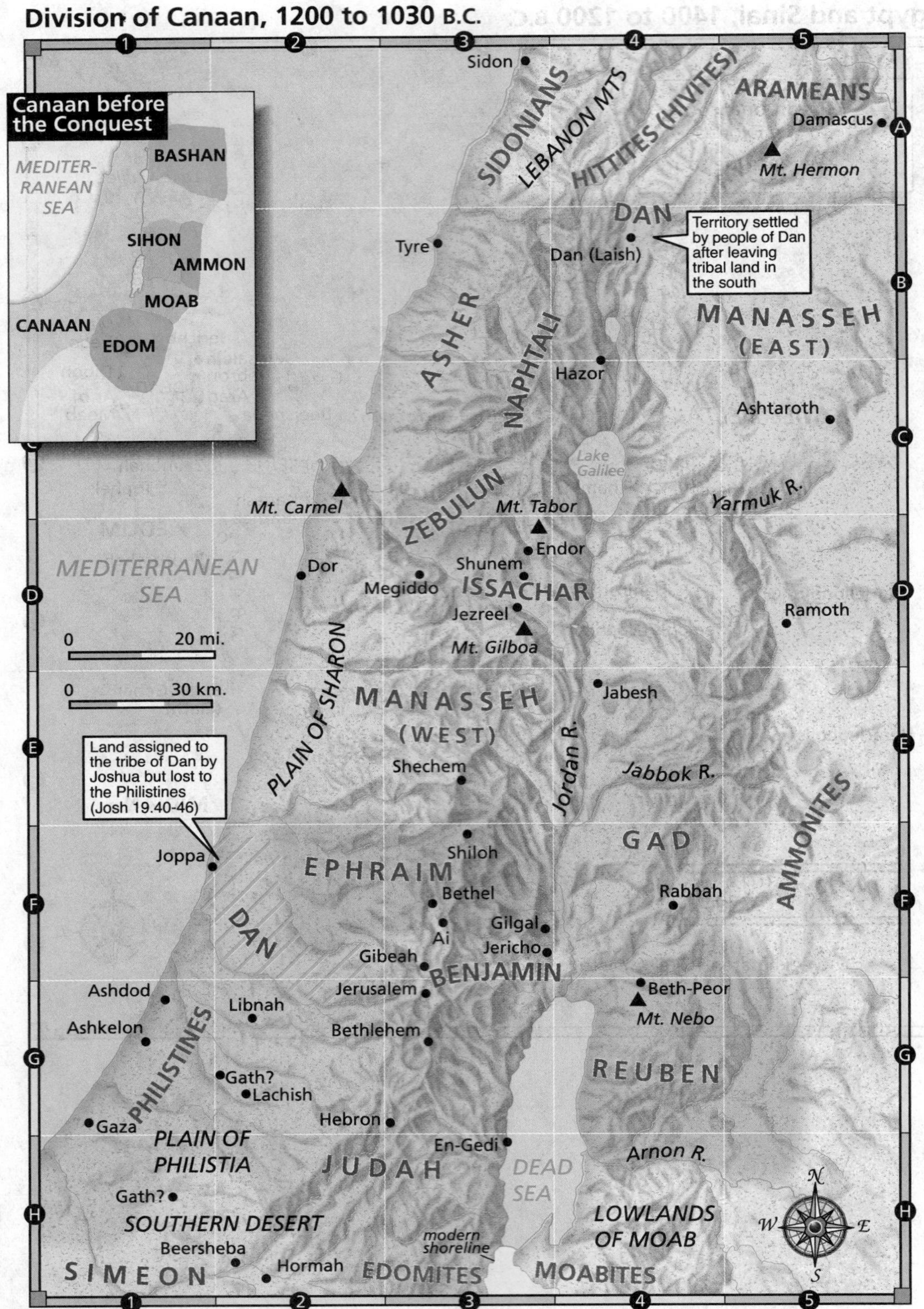

Canaan before the Conquest
BASHAN
MEDITERRANEAN SEA
SIHON
AMMON
MOAB
CANAAN
EDOM
Sidon
SIDONIANS
LEBANON MTS
HITTITES (HIVITES)
ARAMEANS
Damascus
Mt. Hermon
DAN
Dan (Laish)
Territory settled by people of Dan after leaving tribal land in the south
Tyre
ASHER
NAPHTALI
MANASSEH (EAST)
Hazor
Ashtaroth
Lake Galilee
Yarmuk R.
Mt. Carmel
ZEBULUN
Mt. Tabor
Endor
Shunem
Dor
Megiddo
ISSACHAR
Jezreel
Mt. Gilboa
Ramoth
MEDITERRANEAN SEA
0 20 mi.
0 30 km.
PLAIN OF SHARON
MANASSEH (WEST)
Jabesh
Jordan R.
Jabbok R.
Shechem
Land assigned to the tribe of Dan by Joshua but lost to the Philistines (Josh 19.40-46)
AMMONITES
Shiloh
GAD
Joppa
EPHRAIM
Bethel
Rabbah
DAN
Gilgal
Ai
Jericho
Gibeah
BENJAMIN
Ashdod
Jerusalem
Beth-Peor
Libnah
Mt. Nebo
Ashkelon
Bethlehem
PHILISTINES
Gath?
Lachish
REUBEN
Hebron
Gaza
PLAIN OF PHILISTIA
En-Gedi
Arnon R.
JUDAH
DEAD SEA
Gath?
SOUTHERN DESERT
LOWLANDS OF MOAB
modern shoreline
Beersheba
Hormah
SIMEON
EDOMITES
MOABITES
N
W
E
S
A
B
C
D
E
F
G
H
1
2
3
4
5

United Israelite Kingdom, Israel in the Time of Kings Saul, David and Solomon, 1000 to 924 B.C.

Jerusalem in Old Testament Times, The Growth of David's City, 960 to 44 B.C.

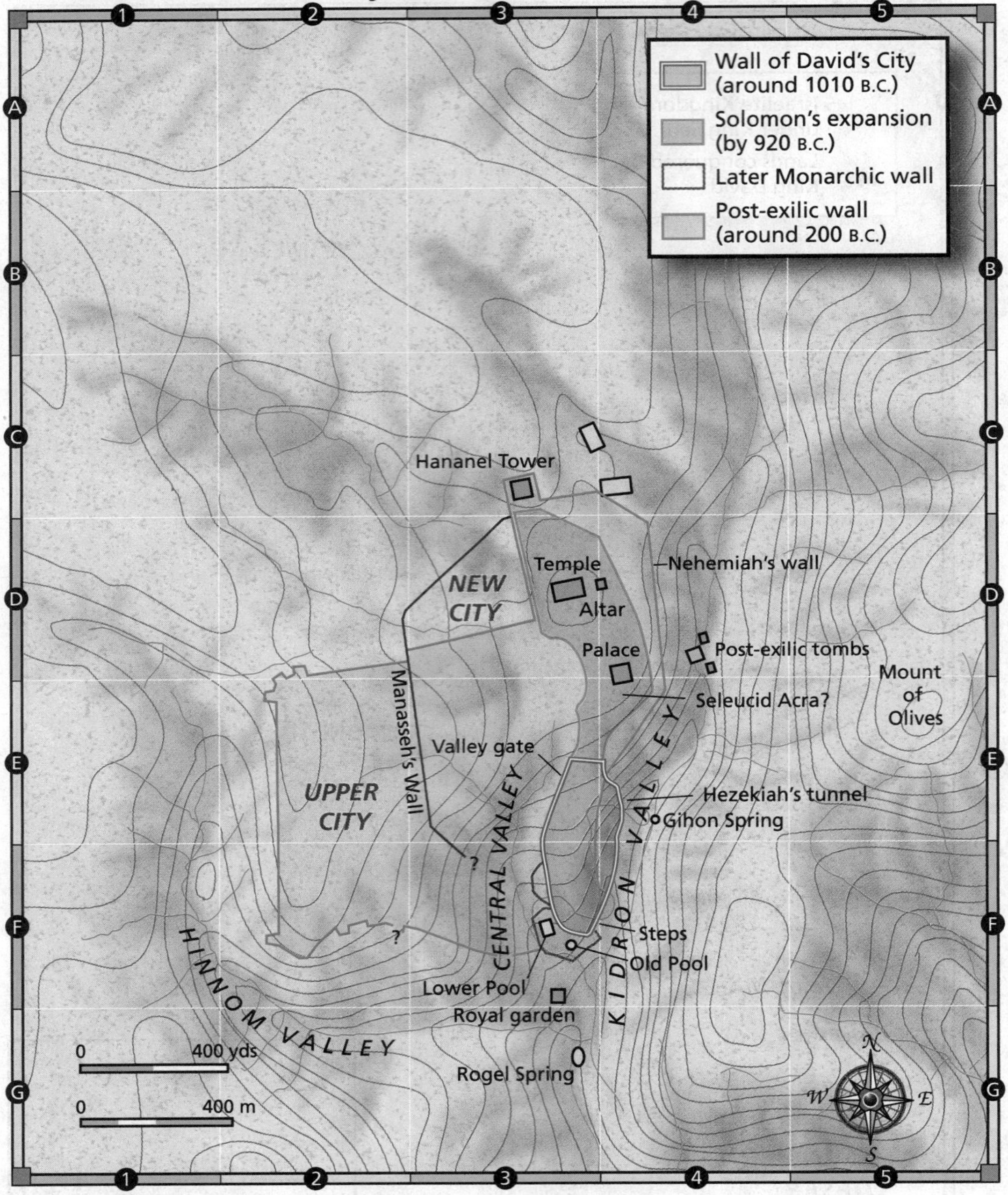

Wall of David's City (around 1010 B.C.)
Solomon's expansion (by 920 B.C.)
Later Monarchic wall
Post-exilic wall (around 200 B.C.)

Hananel Tower
Temple
Altar
Nehemiah's wall
NEW CITY
Palace
Post-exilic tombs
Mount of Olives
Seleucid Acra?
Manasseh's Wall
Valley gate
UPPER CITY
CENTRAL VALLEY
KIDRON VALLEY
Hezekiah's tunnel
Gihon Spring
Steps
Old Pool
Lower Pool
Royal garden
HINNOM VALLEY
Rogel Spring
0 400 yds
0 400 m
N E S W

The Kingdoms of Israel and Judah, 924 to 722 B.C.

Sidon
PHOENICIA
LEBANON MTS.
ARAM
(SYRIA)
Damascus
Zarephath
Mt. Hermon
Tyre
Leontes R.
MEDITERRANEAN SEA
Kedesh
Hazor
BASHAN
GALILEE
Lake Galilee
Mt. Carmel
Edrei
Yarmuk R.
Shunem
Megiddo
Jezreel
Ramoth
Mt. Gilboa
GILEAD
ISRAEL
Samaria
Succoth
Penuel
Shechem
Mahanaim
Jabbok R.
AMMON
Shiloh
Joppa
Jordan R.
Rabbah
Bethel
Geba
Gilgal
Ekron
Jericho
Jerusalem
Ashdod (Azotus)
Heshbon
Libnah
Ashkelon
Bethlehem
PHILISTIA
Gath?
Lachish
Hebron
Gaza
Dead Sea
Arnon R.
JUDAH
Gath?
Besor Gorge
Beersheba
modern shoreline
Kir-Hareseth
0
30 mi.
0
40 km.
EDOM
MOAB
Zered R.
N
W
E
S

Assyrian and Babylonian Kingdoms, 9th to 6th Centuries B.C.

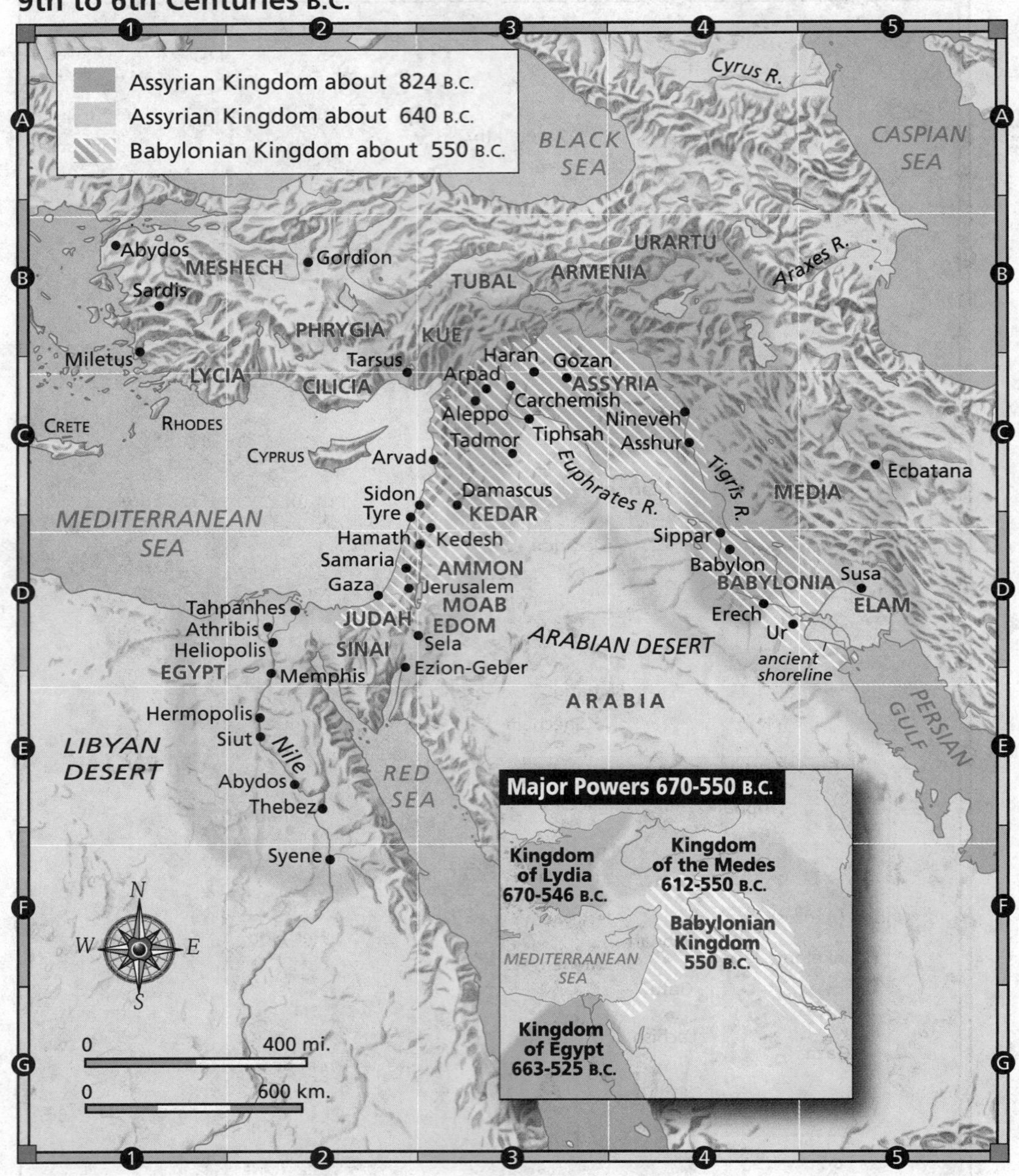

Assyrian Kingdom about 824 B.C.
Assyrian Kingdom about 640 B.C.
Babylonian Kingdom about 550 B.C.
BLACK SEA
CASPIAN SEA
Cyrus R.
Araxes R.
URARTU
ARMENIA
TUBAL
Abydos
MESHECH
Gordion
Sardis
PHRYGIA
KUE
Miletus
LYCIA
CILICIA
Tarsus
Haran
Gozan
Arpad
ASSYRIA
Carchemish
Aleppo
Nineveh
Tiphsah
Tadmor
Asshur
CRETE
RHODES
CYPRUS
Arvad
Euphrates R.
Tigris R.
Ecbatana
MEDIA
Sidon
Damascus
Tyre
KEDAR
MEDITERRANEAN SEA
Hamath
Kedesh
Sippar
Samaria
AMMON
Babylon
Gaza
Jerusalem
BABYLONIA
Susa
Tahpanhes
MOAB
ELAM
JUDAH
Erech
Athribis
EDOM
Ur
Heliopolis
SINAI
Sela
ARABIAN DESERT
EGYPT
Memphis
Ezion-Geber
ancient shoreline
ARABIA
PERSIAN GULF
Hermopolis
Siut
LIBYAN DESERT
Nile
RED SEA
Abydos
Thebez
Syene
N
W
E
S
0
400 mi.
0
600 km.
Major Powers 670-550 B.C.
Kingdom of Lydia 670-546 B.C.
Kingdom of the Medes 612-550 B.C.
Babylonian Kingdom 550 B.C.
MEDITERRANEAN SEA
Kingdom of Egypt 663-525 B.C.

Persian Kingdom, 550 to 330 B.C.

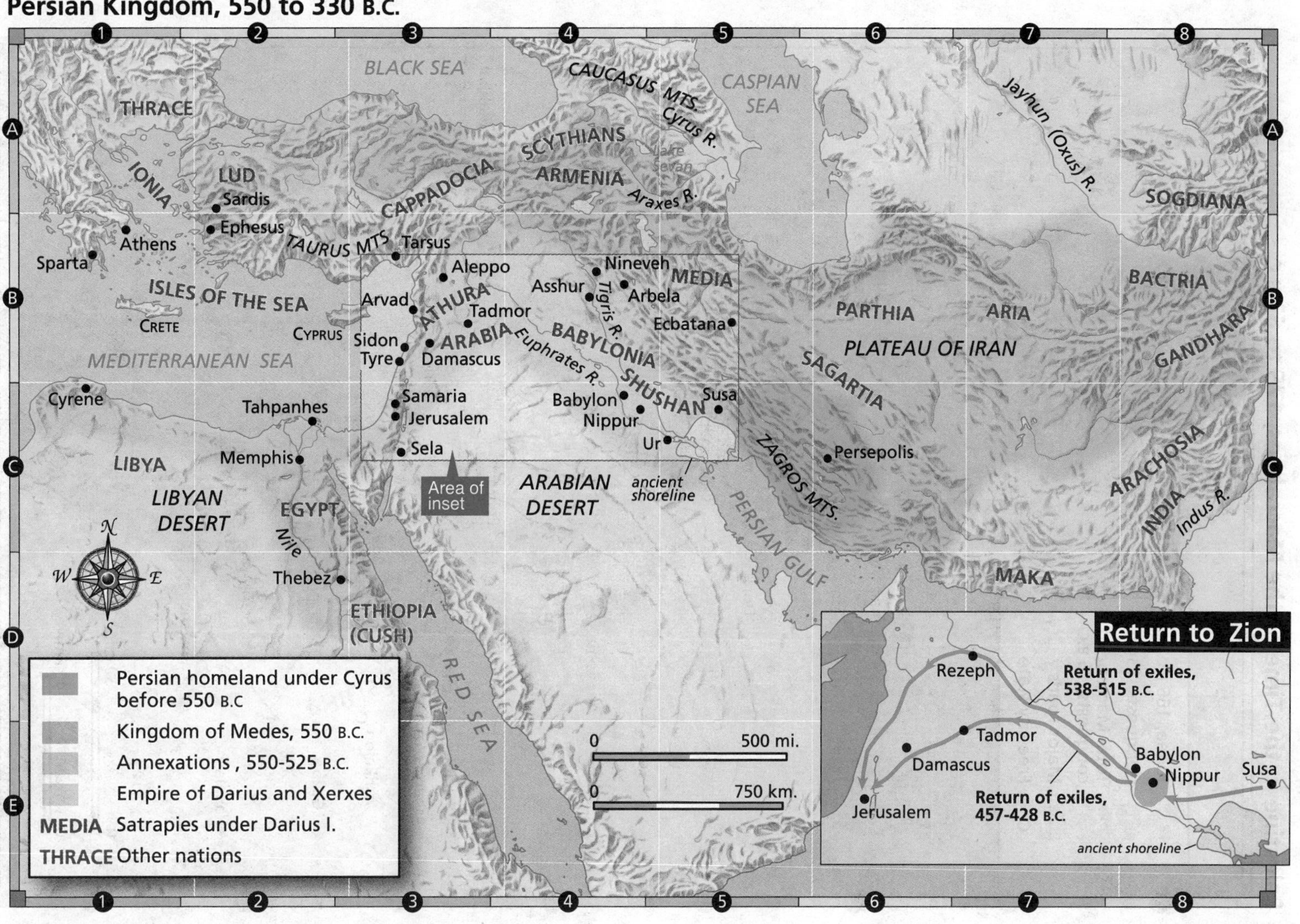

BLACK SEA
CASPIAN SEA
MEDITERRANEAN SEA
RED SEA
PERSIAN GULF
THRACE
IONIA
LUD
CAPPADOCIA
SCYTHIANS
ARMENIA
CAUCASUS MTS.
TAURUS MTS
ISLES OF THE SEA
CYPRUS
CRETE
ATHURA
ARABIA
BABYLONIA
SHUSHAN
MEDIA
ARABIAN DESERT
LIBYAN DESERT
LIBYA
EGYPT
ETHIOPIA (CUSH)
PARTHIA
PLATEAU OF IRAN
SAGARTIA
ZAGROS MTS.
ARIA
BACTRIA
SOGDIANA
GANDHARA
ARACHOSIA
INDIA
MAKA
Jayhun (Oxus) R.
Cyrus R.
Lake Sevan
Araxes R.
Tigris R.
Euphrates R.
Indus R.
Nile
Sparta
Athens
Sardis
Ephesus
Tarsus
Arvad
Sidon
Tyre
Aleppo
Tadmor
Damascus
Samaria
Jerusalem
Sela
Asshur
Nineveh
Arbela
Ecbatana
Babylon
Nippur
Susa
Ur
Persepolis
Tahpanhes
Memphis
Thebez
Cyrene
ancient shoreline
Area of inset
0 500 mi.
0 750 km.
N E S W
Persian homeland under Cyrus before 550 B.C
Kingdom of Medes, 550 B.C.
Annexations , 550-525 B.C.
Empire of Darius and Xerxes
MEDIA Satrapies under Darius I.
THRACE Other nations
Return to Zion
Return of exiles, 538-515 B.C.
Return of exiles, 457-428 B.C.
Rezeph
Tadmor
Damascus
Jerusalem
Babylon
Nippur
Susa
ancient shoreline

Palestine in the Time of the Maccabees, 175 to 63 B.C.

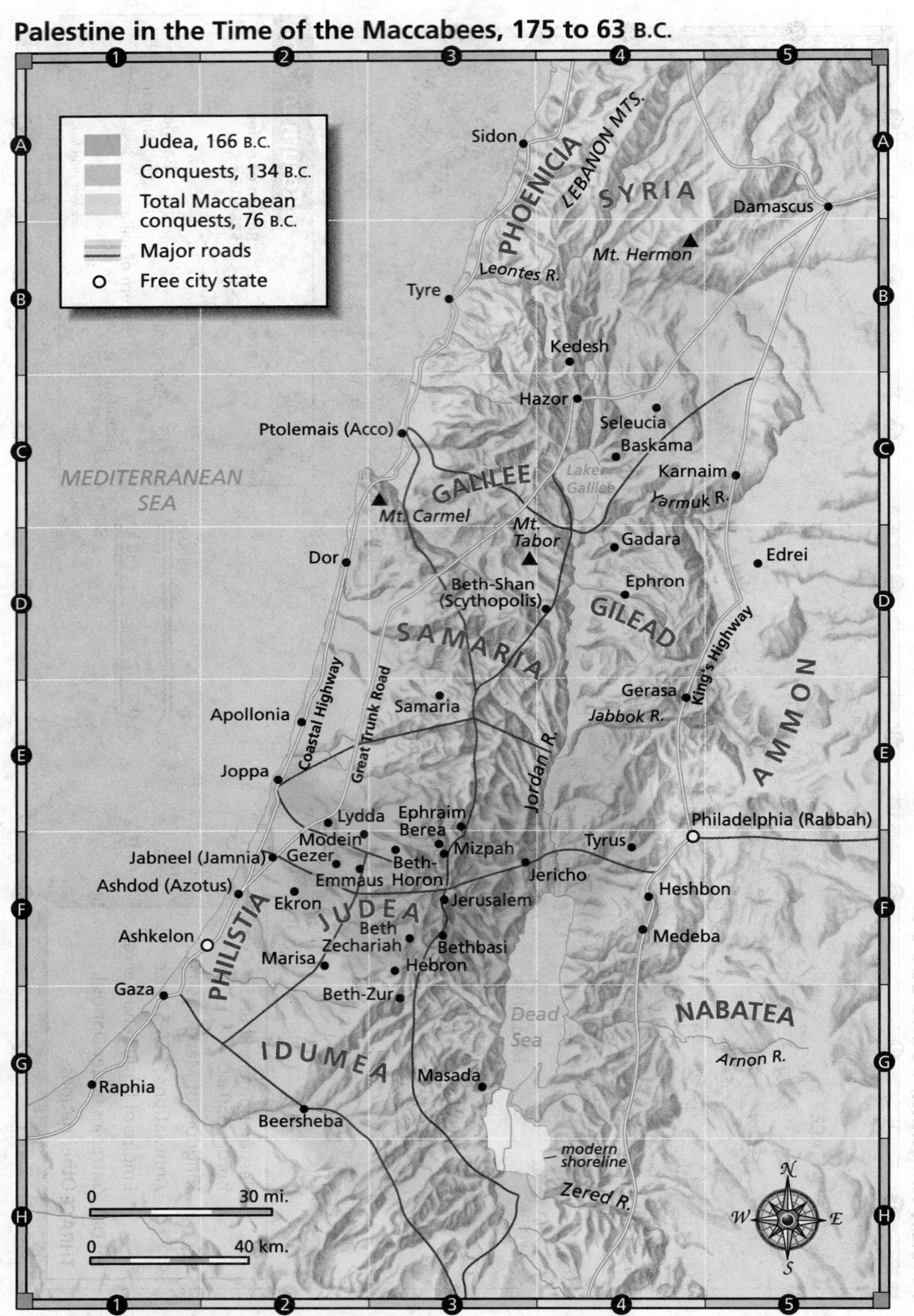

Judea, 166 B.C.
Conquests, 134 B.C.
Total Maccabean conquests, 76 B.C.
Major roads
Free city state
MEDITERRANEAN SEA
PHOENICIA
LEBANON MTS.
SYRIA
Sidon
Damascus
Mt. Hermon
Leontes R.
Tyre
Kedesh
Hazor
Seleucia
Ptolemais (Acco)
Baskama
Karnaim
Lake Galilee
GALILEE
Yarmuk R.
Mt. Carmel
Mt. Tabor
Gadara
Dor
Edrei
Ephron
Beth-Shan (Scythopolis)
GILEAD
SAMARIA
King's Highway
Coastal Highway
Great Trunk Road
AMMON
Gerasa
Samaria
Jabbok R.
Apollonia
Jordan R.
Joppa
Lydda
Ephraim
Berea
Philadelphia (Rabbah)
Modein
Tyrus
Jabneel (Jamnia)
Gezer
Mizpah
Beth-Horon
Emmaus
Jericho
Ashdod (Azotus)
Ekron
Jerusalem
Heshbon
JUDEA
Beth Zechariah
Ashkelon
Bethbasi
Medeba
PHILISTIA
Marisa
Hebron
Gaza
Beth-Zur
Dead Sea
NABATEA
IDUMEA
Arnon R.
Raphia
Masada
Beersheba
modern shoreline
Zered R.
0 30 mi.
0 40 km.
N
W
E
S

Growth of the Roman Empire, 27 B.C to A.D. 180

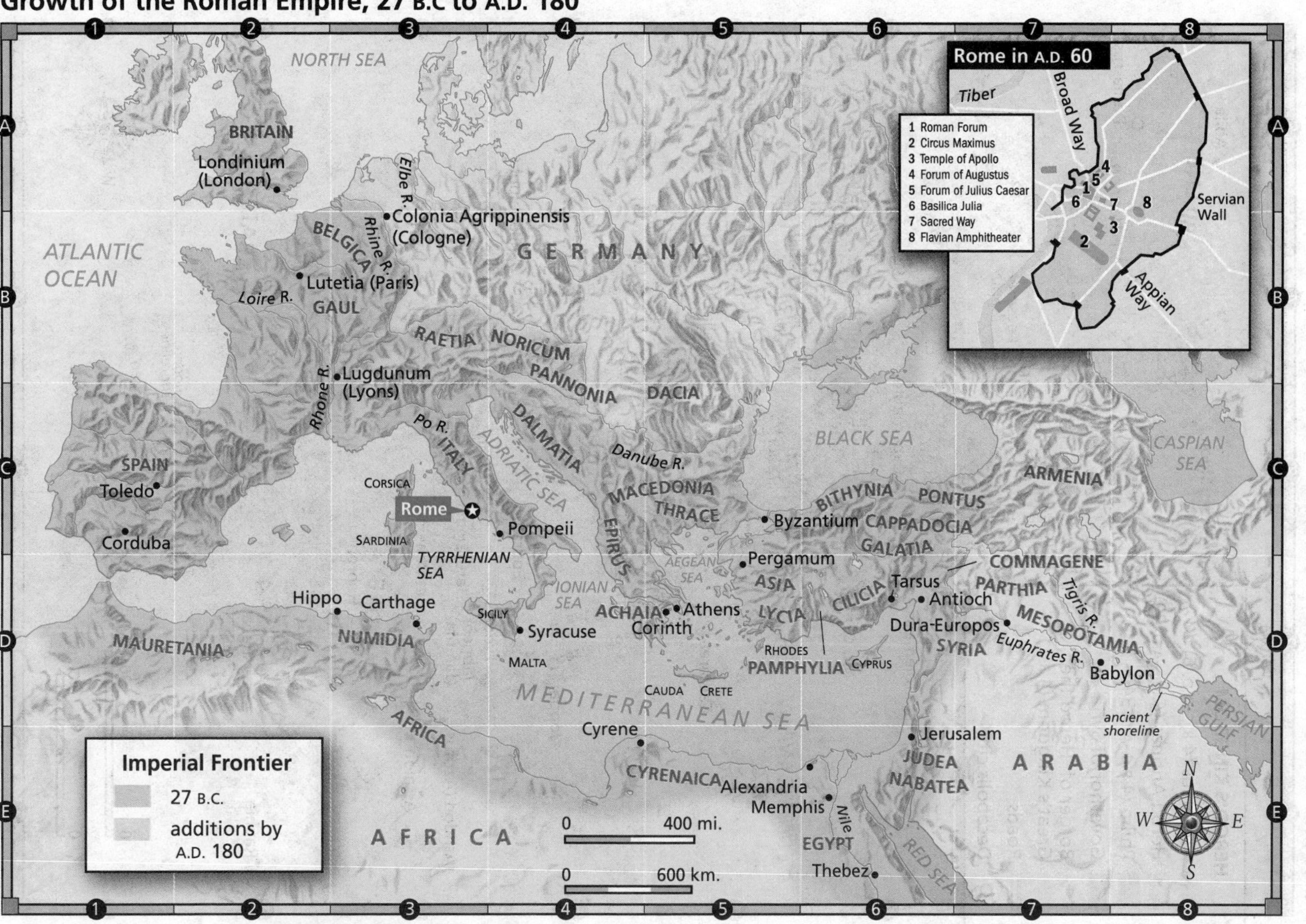

Palestine Under the Herods, 4 B.C to A.D. 44

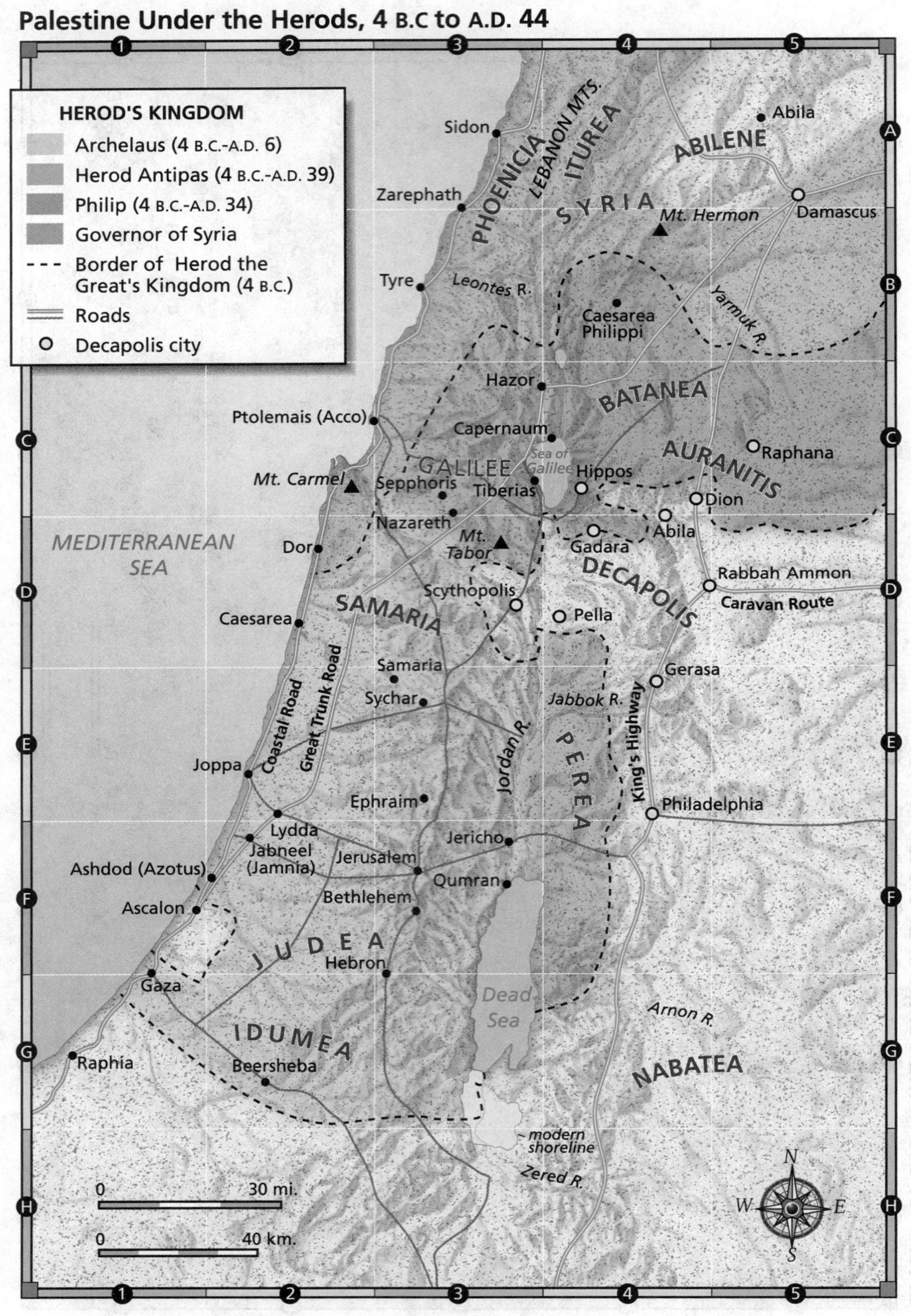

HERODS KINGDOM
Archelaus (4 B.C.-A.D. 6)
Herod Antipas (4 B.C.-A.D. 39)
Philip (4 B.C.-A.D. 34)
Governor of Syria
Border of Herod the Great's Kingdom (4 B.C.)
Roads
Decapolis city
Sidon
Abila
PHOENICIA
LEBANON MTS.
ITUREA
ABILENE
Zarephath
SYRIA
Mt. Hermon
Damascus
Tyre
Leontes R.
Caesarea Philippi
Yarmuk R.
Hazor
BATANEA
Ptolemais (Acco)
Capernaum
AURANITIS
Raphana
GALILEE
Sea of Galilee
Hippos
Mt. Carmel
Sepphoris
Tiberias
Dion
Nazareth
Abila
MEDITERRANEAN SEA
Dor
Mt. Tabor
Gadara
DECAPOLIS
Rabbah Ammon
Scythopolis
Caravan Route
SAMARIA
Pella
Caesarea
Samaria
Gerasa
Sychar
Jabbok R.
Coastal Road
Great Trunk Road
Jordan R.
PEREA
King's Highway
Joppa
Ephraim
Philadelphia
Lydda
Jericho
Jabneel (Jamnia)
Jerusalem
Ashdod (Azotus)
Qumran
Ascalon
Bethlehem
JUDEA
Hebron
Gaza
Dead Sea
Arnon R.
IDUMEA
Raphia
Beersheba
NABATEA
modern shoreline
Zered R.
0 30 mi.
0 40 km.
N
W
E
S
1 2 3 4 5
A B C D E F G H

Palestine in the Time of Jesus, A.D. 6 to 30

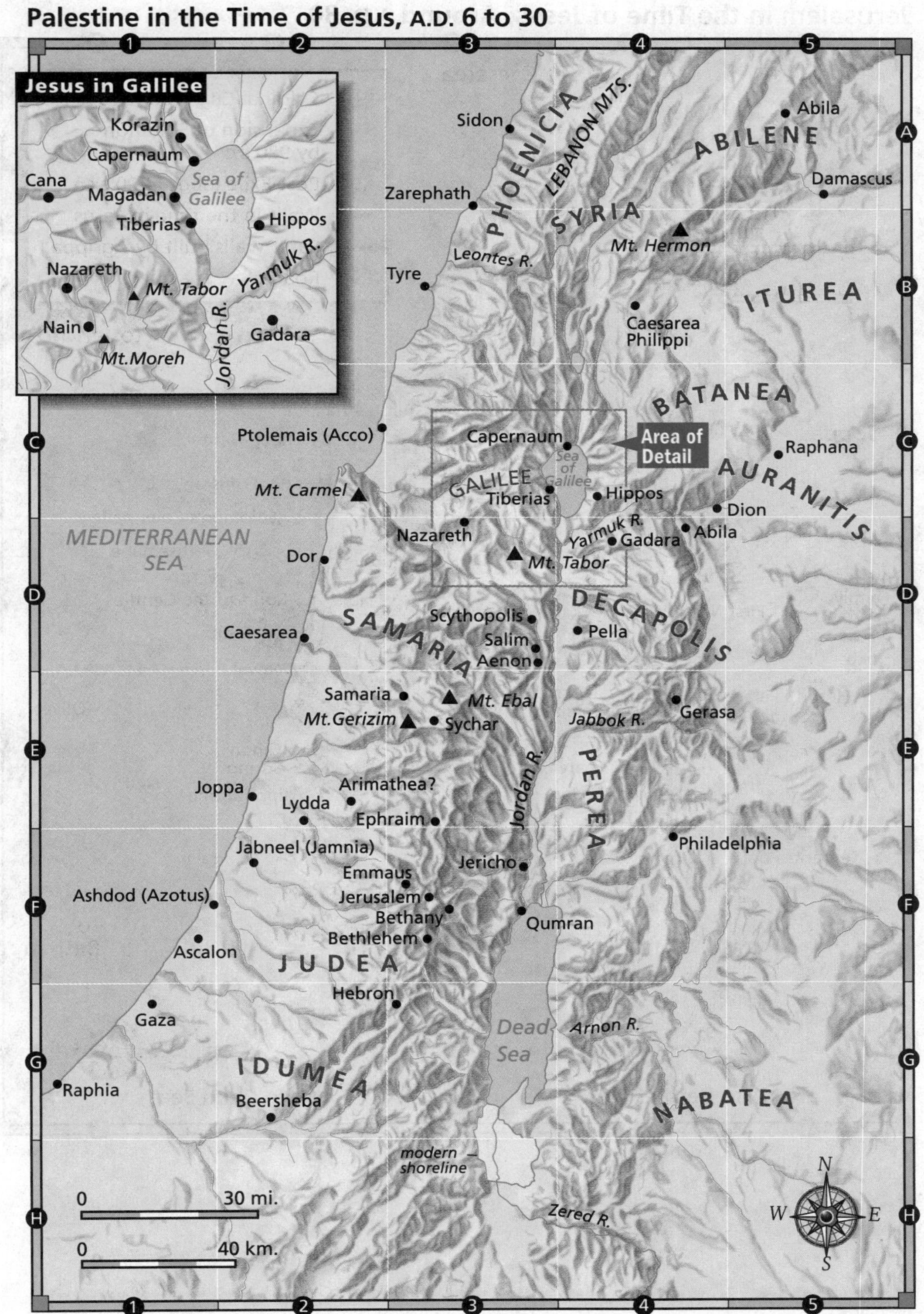

Jesus in Galilee
Korazin
Capernaum
Sea of Galilee
Cana
Magadan
Tiberias
Hippos
Nazareth
Yarmuk R.
Mt. Tabor
Jordan R.
Nain
Gadara
Mt.Moreh
Sidon
PHOENICIA
LEBANON MTS.
Abila
ABILENE
Damascus
Zarephath
SYRIA
Mt. Hermon
Leontes R.
Tyre
ITUREA
Caesarea Philippi
BATANEA
Ptolemais (Acco)
Area of Detail
Raphana
AURANITIS
Mt. Carmel
GALILEE
Dion
MEDITERRANEAN SEA
Dor
DECAPOLIS
SAMARIA
Scythopolis
Caesarea
Salim
Pella
Aenon
Samaria
Mt. Ebal
Gerasa
Mt.Gerizim
Sychar
Jabbok R.
PEREA
Joppa
Arimathea?
Lydda
Ephraim
Philadelphia
Jabneel (Jamnia)
Jericho
Emmaus
Ashdod (Azotus)
Jerusalem
Bethany
Qumran
Bethlehem
Ascalon
JUDEA
Hebron
Gaza
Dead Sea
Arnon R.
IDUMEA
Raphia
Beersheba
NABATEA
modern shoreline
0 30 mi.
0 40 km.
Zered R.
N
W
E
S

Jerusalem in the Time of Jesus, Around A.D. 30

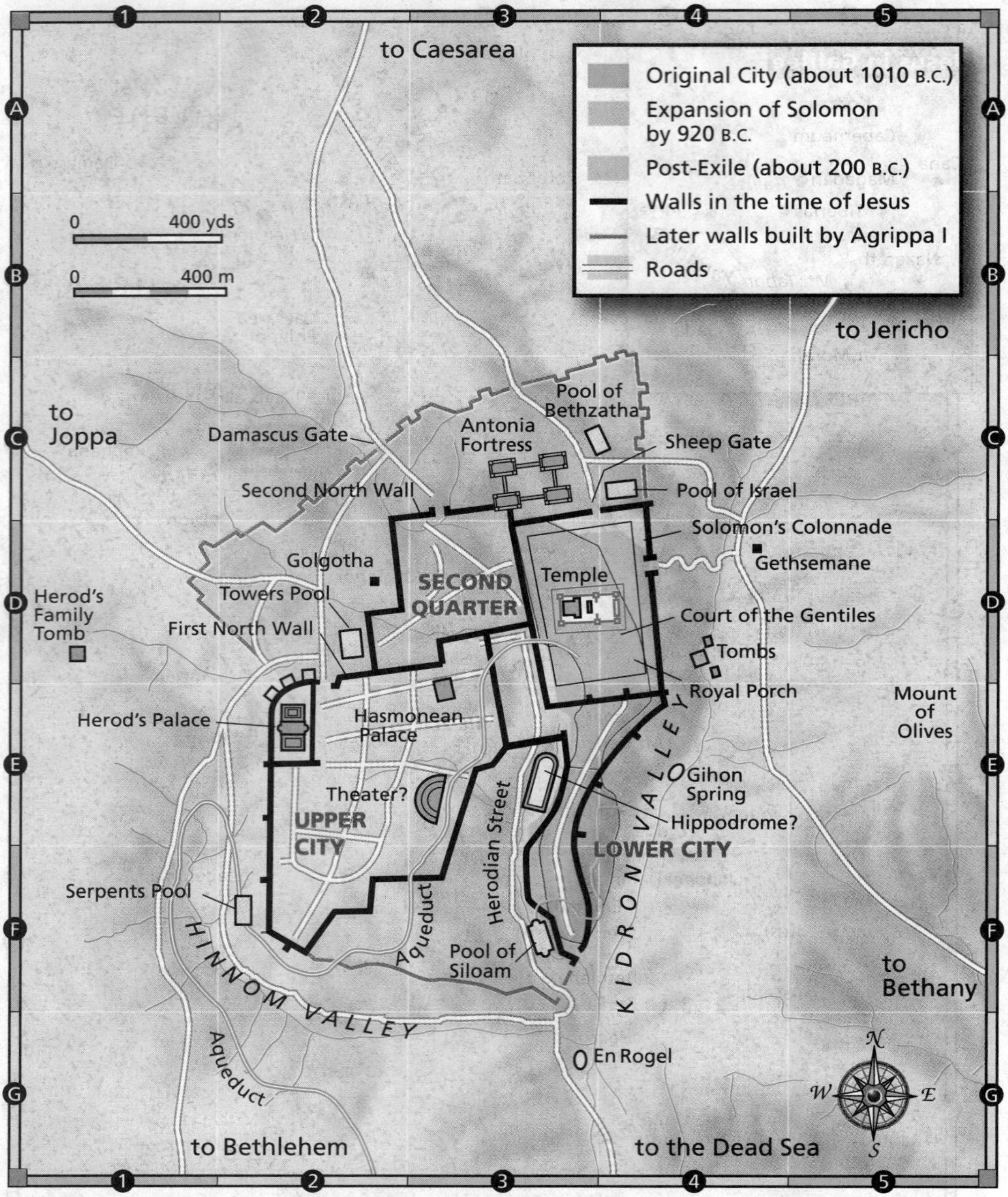

Original City (about 1010 B.C.)
Expansion of Solomon by 920 B.C.
Post-Exile (about 200 B.C.)
Walls in the time of Jesus
Later walls built by Agrippa I
Roads

0 400 yds
0 400 m

to Caesarea
to Jericho
to Joppa
to Bethany
to Bethlehem
to the Dead Sea

Pool of Bethzatha
Antonia Fortress
Damascus Gate
Sheep Gate
Second North Wall
Pool of Israel
Solomon's Colonnade
Gethsemane
Golgotha
SECOND QUARTER
Temple
Herod's Family Tomb
Towers Pool
First North Wall
Court of the Gentiles
Tombs
Royal Porch
Mount of Olives
Herod's Palace
Hasmonean Palace
Theater?
UPPER CITY
Herodian Street
Gihon Spring
Hippodrome?
LOWER CITY
KIDRON VALLEY
Serpents Pool
Aqueduct
Pool of Siloam
HINNOM VALLEY
Aqueduct
En Rogel

N E S W

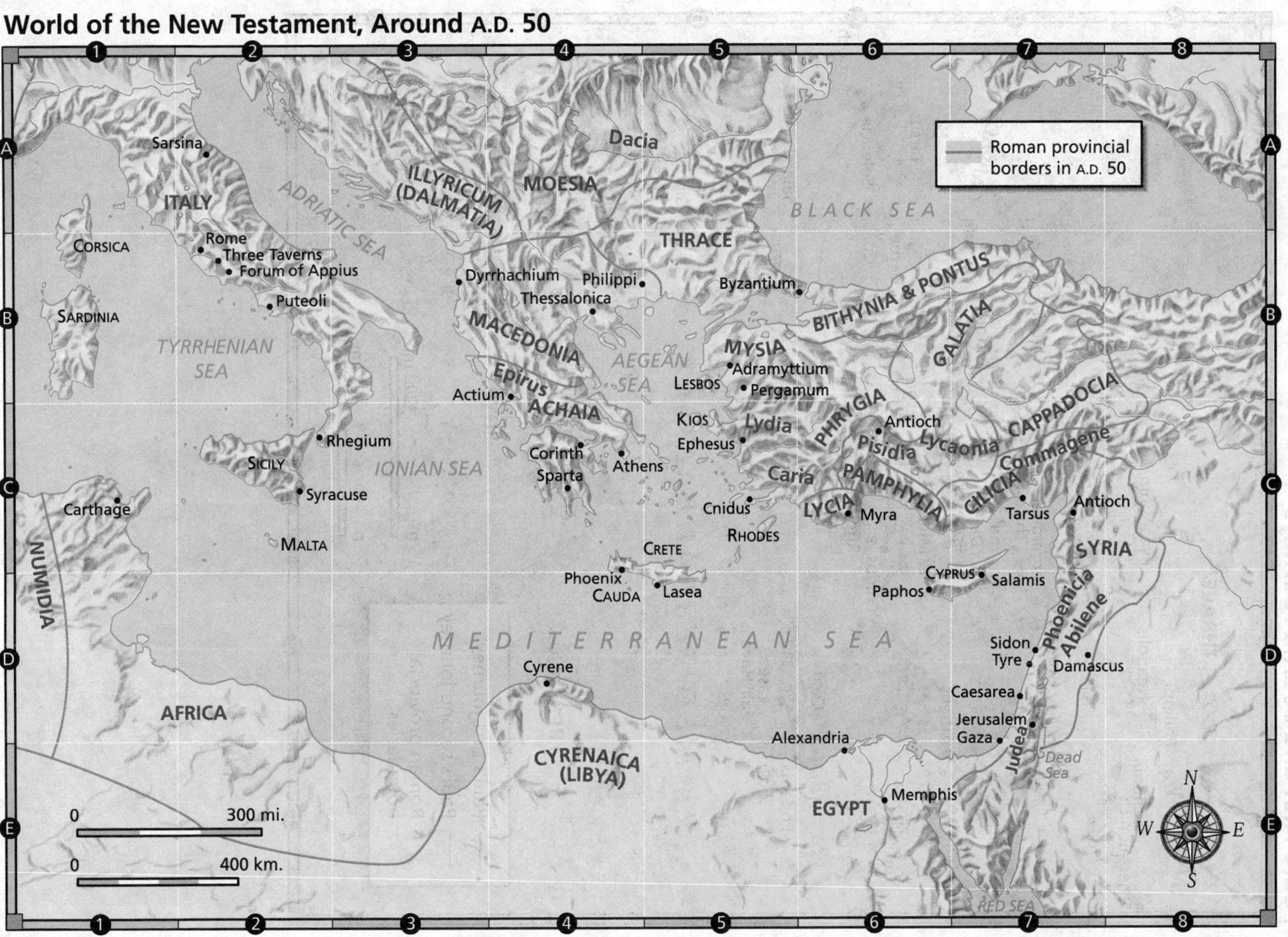
World of the New Testament, Around A.D. 50
Roman provincial borders in A.D. 50
BLACK SEA
ADRIATIC SEA
TYRRHENIAN SEA
AEGEAN SEA
IONIAN SEA
MEDITERRANEAN SEA
Dead Sea
RED SEA
Dacia
MOESIA
ILLYRICUM (DALMATIA)
THRACE
ITALY
MACEDONIA
Epirus
ACHAIA
MYSIA
BITHYNIA & PONTUS
GALATIA
PHRYGIA
Lydia
Caria
LYCIA
Pisidia
Lycaonia
PAMPHYLIA
CAPPADOCIA
Commagene
CILICIA
SYRIA
Phoenicia
Abilene
Judea
NUMIDIA
AFRICA
CYRENAICA (LIBYA)
EGYPT
Sarsina
Rome
Three Taverns
Forum of Appius
Puteoli
CORSICA
SARDINIA
SICILY
Rhegium
Syracuse
MALTA
Carthage
Dyrrhachium
Philippi
Thessalonica
Actium
Corinth
Sparta
Athens
Byzantium
LESBOS
Adramyttium
Pergamum
KIOS
Ephesus
Antioch
Cnidus
RHODES
Myra
Tarsus
Antioch
CRETE
Phoenix
CAUDA
Lasea
CYPRUS
Salamis
Paphos
Sidon
Tyre
Damascus
Caesarea
Jerusalem
Gaza
Cyrene
Alexandria
Memphis
0
300 mi.
0
400 km.
N
S
E
W

Paul's First and Second Journeys

BLACK SEA
THRACE
MACEDONIA
Philippi
Neapolis
Apollonia
Thessalonica
Byzantium
Berea
SAMOTHRACE
BITHYNIA
MYSIA
Troas
AEGEAN SEA
ASIA
GALATIA
Pergamum
Thyatira
Sardis
Smyrna
ACHAIA
LYDIA
PHRYGIA
CAPPADOCIA
Antioch
Iconium
Corinth
Cenchrea
Athens
Ephesus
Colosse
Lystra
Miletus
Sparta
Perga
Attalia
PAMPHYLIA
Derbe
Tarsus
CILICIA
Cnidus
LYCIA
Rhodes
RHODES
Patara
Myra
Seleucia
Antioch
CRETE
Phoenix
CAUDA
Lasea
Fair Havens
CYPRUS
Salamis
Paphos
SYRIA
MEDITERRANEAN SEA
Sidon
Tyre
PHOENICIA
ABILENE
Caesarea
Jerusalem
JUDEA
Alexandria
CYRENAICA
EGYPT
RED SEA

Paul's first journey
Paul's second journey
Roman provincial boundaries

0 200 mi.
0 300 km.

N W E S

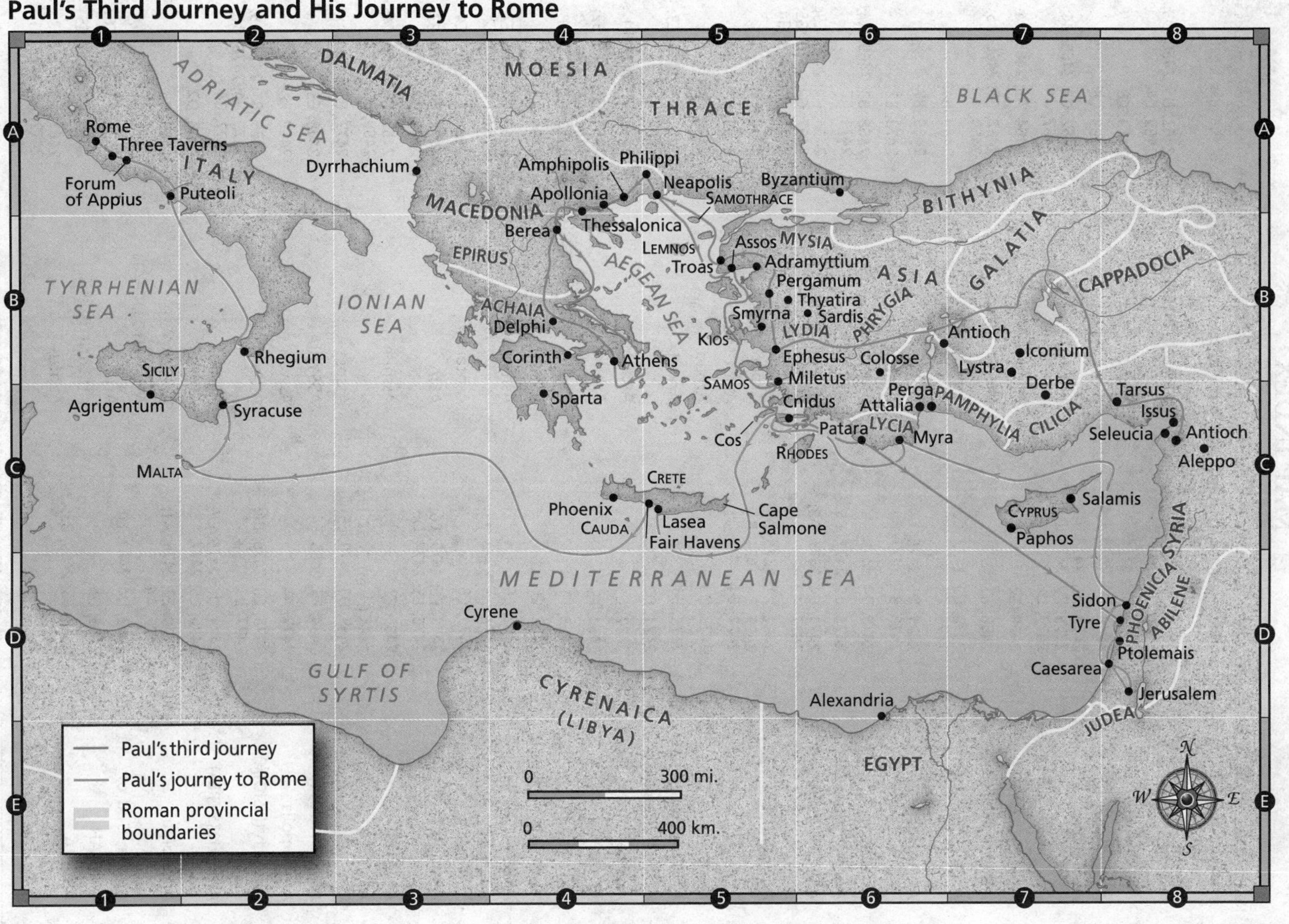
Paul's Third Journey and His Journey to Rome
DALMATIA
MOESIA
THRACE
BLACK SEA
ADRIATIC SEA
Rome
Three Taverns
Forum of Appius
Puteoli
ITALY
Dyrrhachium
Amphipolis
Philippi
Neapolis
Apollonia
Byzantium
SAMOTHRACE
MACEDONIA
Thessalonica
Berea
BITHYNIA
GALATIA
CAPPADOCIA
LEMNOS
Assos
MYSIA
EPIRUS
Troas
Adramyttium
AEGEAN SEA
ASIA
Pergamum
Thyatira
TYRRHENIAN SEA
IONIAN SEA
ACHAIA
Delphi
Smyrna
Sardis
PHRYGIA
KIOS
LYDIA
Antioch
Iconium
Rhegium
Corinth
Athens
Ephesus
Colosse
Lystra
SICILY
SAMOS
Miletus
Derbe
Sparta
Perga
PAMPHYLIA
Tarsus
Agrigentum
Syracuse
Cnidus
Attalia
CILICIA
Issus
Cos
Patara
LYCIA
Myra
Seleucia
Antioch
RHODES
Aleppo
MALTA
CRETE
Salamis
Phoenix
CAUDA
Lasea
Fair Havens
Cape Salmone
CYPRUS
Paphos
SYRIA
MEDITERRANEAN SEA
PHOENICIA
ABILENE
Sidon
Tyre
Cyrene
Ptolemais
Caesarea
GULF OF SYRTIS
CYRENAICA (LIBYA)
Alexandria
Jerusalem
JUDEA
EGYPT
Paul's third journey
Paul's journey to Rome
Roman provincial boundaries
0
300 mi.
0
400 km.
N
W
E
S

MAP INDEX

Regions, nations, mountain ranges, and large bodies of water are listed in CAPITAL letters. The labels for these features may stretch out across the maps. Where this occurs, the coordinates given will direct you to the beginning of the map label.

A

L

M

U

Y

Z

OTHER MAPS

INDEX OF MINI-ARTICLES

INDEX OF CHARTS

CREDITS

Cover *top to bottom* The Andromeda Galaxy:Tony Hallas/Science Photo Library/Photo Researchers. Tower of Babel: © Erich Lessing/Art Resource, NY. Abraham and the Three Angels: © Erich Lessing/Art Resource, NY. Elijah and Elisha: Master Stonecarver Simon Verity; photo by Martha Cooper. The Mystical Lamb, detail: © Scala/Art Resource, NY.

9,10 Illustrations by Hal Just, © ABS. **17** © Bettmann/CORBIS. **20** Le Nouveau Testament, 1664, Antoine Cellier, Charenton, France. From the collection of the American Bible Society. **21** Datafoto and Christian History Institute. **22** New Testament: A Pictorial Archive from Nineteenth Century Sources, edited by Don Rice, © 1986 by Dover Publications, Inc. **24** Engraving in John Foxe's Acts and Monuments of Martyrs, 1684 edition: image in public domain. From the collection of the American Bible Society. **27** © Zev Radovan, Jerusalem. **31** *top* © The Israel Museum, Jerusalem. *bottom* Courtesy of the Leon Levy Expedition to Ashkelon/Carl Andrews, Photographer. **39** Tony Hallas/Science Photo Library/Photo Researchers. **43** Glasgow University Library, Department of Special Collections. **48** Sadao Watanabe, Japan, "Noah's Ark," from Biblical Prints of Sadao Watanabe, published by Shinkyo Shuppansha, Tokyo. **51** Illustrations by Gregor Goethals, © ABS. **55,64** © Erich Lessing/Art Resource, NY. **68** © 1997 David Sailors. **71** © Zev Radovan, Jerusalem. **72** *top right* © David Harris, Jerusalem. *left* Illustration by Gregor Goethals, © ABS. **75** © Russian Ethnographical Museum, from the collection of the Russian Ethnographical Museum, St. Petersburg, Russia, (Cat. No. 6396-52). **86** Zeev Raban (1890-1970), Jacob's Ladder, gouache on paper, 1963, Amir Doron collection, Jerusalem, from the exhibition Raban Remembered: Jerusalem's Forgotten Master, Yeshiva University Museum, New York, 1982-83. **98** © Erich Lessing/Art Resource NY. **104** Detail from "Story of Joseph," © 1986 by John August Swanson, Serigraph 23 1/2" by 15 1/2", www.JohnAugustSwanson.com. **110** © Erich Lessing/Art Resource, NY. **113** © Cameraphoto Arte, Venice/Art Resource, NY. **125** Illustration by Hal Just, © ABS. **127** Staatliche Museen Kassel, Germany. **133** Map by Collin Kellogg, © ABS. **138** © The Jewish Museum of New York/Art Resource, NY. **140** The Granger Collection, New York. **143** Illustration by Hal Just, © ABS. **147** Collection of Lee and Ed Kogan. Photograph courtesy of the American Folk Art Museum. **148** Illustration by Gregor Goethals, © ABS. **153** By permission of the British Library, OR. 1404 f. 5v. **156** Illustration by Gregor Goethals, © ABS. **159** From Images from the Bible: The Words of Elie Wiesel, The Paintings of Shalom of Safed, Copyright © 1980 by Shalom of Safed. Published by The Overlook Press, Woodstock, NY 12498. **160** Illustration by Kate McKeon, © ABS. **161** From The Copenhagen Haggadah, Royal Danish Library and the Jewish Community, Copenhagen. **163** Lucy D'Souza, Bangalore, India. "Miriam-Prophetess and Sister," from The Bible through Asian Eyes, by M. Takenaka and R. O'Grady. **165** Illustration by Gregor Goethals, © ABS. **166** Domstiftsarchiv Merseburg. **173** By permission of the British Library, MS. 10546 f. 25v. **182** Cliché Bibliothèque nationale de France, Paris. **187** Illustration by Hal Just, © ABS. **194** "The Golden Calf" by Ora

Lerman, oil on canvas, 45 x 60 inches, © 1987. 213 © Erich Lessing/Art Resource, NY. 214, 227 Illustration by Gregor Goethals, © ABS. 222 Jewish National & University Library, Jerusalem. 238 The Day of Atonement, 1919, by Jacob Kramer/Leeds Museums and Galleries (City Art Gallery) UK/Bridgeman Art Library. 239 Illustration by Hal Just, © ABS. 243 Illustration by Kate McKeon, © ABS. 250 The Kiddush at the Sabbath Meal, 196, by Dora Holzhandler, Private Collection/Bridgeman Art Library. 251,252 Illustrations by Kate McKeon, © ABS. 254 By permission of the British Library, ADD.MS.11639, f. 114r. 269 © David Harris, Jerusalem. 274 © Sonia Halliday Photographs, photo by Jane Taylor. 286 *top* © Scala/Art Resource, NY. bottom © Boltin Picture Library. 293 Sadao Watanabe, Japan. "Grapes of Canaan," from Biblical Prints of Sadao Watanabe, published by Shinkyo Shuppansha, Tokyo. 301 © Richard L. Carlton, The National Audubon Society Collection/Photo Researchers. 305 © Erich Lessing/Art Resource, NY. 307 © Art Resource, NY. 312 © Russian Ethnographical Museum, from the collection of the Russian Ethnographical Museum, St. Petersburg, Russia, (Cat. No. 6396-51). 322 Gloria Ortiz Hernandez, The Daughters of Zelophehad, 20 x 20 x 3 inches, 1999, mixed media on board, © ABS. 328 Jephthah's Vow; his return from defeating the Ammonites to greet his daughter, 1886 (detail) by Edwin Long/Russell-Cotes Art Gallery and Museum, Bournemouth, UK/Bridgeman Art Library. 342 Photo by Hugh Witzmann, O.S.B. Used with permission of the Liturgical Press and The Bible Today, Collegeville, Minnesota. 353 From The Copenhagen Haggadah, Royal Danish Library and the Jewish Community, Copenhagen. 356 Illustration by Hal Just, © ABS. 360 © Erich Lessing/Art Resource, NY. 363 Laziz Hamani/Editions Assouline, Paris. 373 Boundary stone from the time of Nebuchadnezzar, 1140 BC, British Museum, London, UK/Bridgeman Art Library. 377 Illustration by Kate McKeon, © ABS. 380 Illustration by Hal Just, © ABS. 381 Illustration by Kate McKeon, © ABS. 393 © The Jewish Museum of New York/Art Resource, NY. 401 © Scala/Art Resource, NY. 411 *clockwise from center* Map by Joe LeMonier, © ABS. *right top and bottom* Illustrations by Kate McKeon, © ABS. *left* Illustration by Theresa Heidel, © ABS. 413 © Scala/Art Resource, NY. 415 © The Jewish Museum of New York/Art Resource, NY. 417 Illustration by Kate McKeon, © ABS. 418 Reproduced by permission of Hodde and Stoughton Limited. 422 © David Harris, Jerusalem. 428 © Sonia Halliday and Laura Lushington. 434 Illustration by Gregor Goethals, © ABS. 443 Map by Collin Kellogg, © ABS. 449 © Erich Lessing/Art Resource, NY. 461 The Granger Collection, New York. 468 R. Koiso/Japan Bible Society. 482 Benjamin Shelton Fund. Courtesy, Museum of Fine Arts, Boston. 483 Illustration by Theresa Heidel, © ABS. 485 © Scala/Art Resource, NY. 497 Map by Collin Kellogg, © ABS. 499 "Story of Ruth," © 1991 by John August Swanson, Serigraph 21 1/4" x 27 3/4", www.JohnAugustSwanson.com. 502 Illustration by Gregor Goethals, © ABS. 509 © Sonia Halliday and Laura Lushington. 513 Illustration by Hal Just, © ABS. 516 © Ronald Sheridan/Ancient Art & Architecture Collection. 517 Map by Collin Kellogg, © ABS. 518 © Zev Radovan, Jerusalem. 523 Karl-Heinz Raach, © 1999. 528 © 1998 Richard T. Nowitz. 529 Illustration by Kate McKeon, © ABS. 536 © The Jewish Museum of New York/Art Resource, NY. 537 Illustration by Kate McKeon, © ABS. 540 Illustration by Esben Hanefelt Kristensen from Bibelen: Udvalgte fortaellinger, © The Danish Bible Society. 542 Leslie Xuereb/SuperStock. 551 MS. M. 638, f.33, © The

Pierpont Morgan Library/Art Resource, NY. **563** © David Harris, Jerusalem. **567** © Erich Lessing/Art Resource, NY. **570** Illustration by Kate McKeon, © ABS. **575** ***left*** © Baron Wolman. ***center*** © The Israel Museum, Jerusalem. Photo: David Harris. ***right*** Photograph by Bencini Raffaello, Florence, Italy, © American Bible Society Archives. **576** AKG London. **585** Gui-jie Zhang. **598** Lyman Allyn Art Museum, New London, Connecticut. **608** From The Copenhagen Haggadah, Royal Danish Library and the Jewish Community, Copenhagen. **617** © Zev Radovan, Jerusalem. **626** Emmanuil and Janet Snitkovsky. Chassidic Art Institute, Brooklyn, NY. **632** Scala/Art Resource, NY. **642** Manuscript is property of Staatsbibliothek Zu Berlin, Preussischer Kulturbesitz, Orientabtellung, Tafel 105 (Hs. Or. 3542), photo by Malcolm Varon, N.Y.C. © 1999. **658, 661** © Erich Lessing/Art Resource, NY. **663** Sister Genevieve, Bangalore, India. "A Still, Small Voice," from The Bible through Asian Eyes, by M. Takenaka and R. O'Grady. **664** Master Stonecarver Simon Verity; photo by Martha Cooper. **667** © Zev Radovan, Jerusalem. **669** King Ahab's Coveting: Ahab and Jezebel, 1879, by Thomas Matthews Rooke Russell-Cotes Art Gallery and Museum, Bournemouth, UK/Bridgeman Art Library. **679, 682** Erich Lessing/Art Resource, NY. **685** The Granger Collection, New York. **710** ***left*** Louvre © Photo RMN - Chuzeville. ***center*** Illustration by Kate McKeon, © ABS. ***right*** © Giraudon/Art Resource, NY. **718** Austrian National Library, Vienna (Codex # 1191, fol. 145v). **719** © Fred Maroon, Photo Researchers. **725** © Ronald Sheridan/Ancient Art & Architecture Collection. **730** Illustration by Hal Just, © ABS. **736** Part of the Window Series located at the Synagogue of the Hadassah-Hebrew University Medical Center, Jerusalem, Israel, reproduced with the consent of Hadassah on specified terms, © 1999 Artist Rights Society (ARS), New York, ADAGP, Paris. **763** Model of the City of Jerusalem during the First Temple Period by the Bible Lands Museum, Jerusalem. Photo used by permission. **772** ***All photos*** © Zev Radovan, Jerusalem, ***except for bottom right*** © Erich Lessing/Art Resource, NY. **790** Mary Evans Picture Library. **795** From The Doré Bible Illustrations, © 1974 by Dover Publications, Inc. **798** Mary Evans Picture Library. **806** © Zev Radovan, Jerusalem. **810** © Erich Lessing/Art Resource, NY. **831** © Zev Radovan, Jerusalem. **849** Cliché Bibliothèque nationale de France, Paris. **854** Licensed by the Trustees of the British Museum, © The British Museum. **858** © Paolo Koch, The National Audubon Society Collection/Photo Researchers. **860** ***left*** © Werner Forman/Art Resource, NY. ***top right*** © Giraudon/Art Resource, NY. ***bottom right*** © Ronald Sheridan/Ancient Art & Architecture Collection. **862** Illustration by Hal Just, © ABS. **863** Illustration by Kate McKeon, © ABS. **865** © Scala/Art Resource, NY. **877** Illustration by Hal Just, © ABS. **881** From The Doré Bible Illustrations, © 1974 by Dover Publications, Inc. **881** Illustration by Kate McKeon, © ABS. **888** © The Israel Museum, Jerusalem. **897** Illustration by Hal Just, © ABS. **906** Illustration by Hal Just, © ABS. ***photo inset*** © Zev Radovan, Jerusalem. **908** Licensed by the Trustees of the British Museum, © The British Museum. **909** ***top*** Miniature from MS 288, fol. 278, photograph by Ferdinand Reiss/EMB-Service for Publishers. ***bottom*** Illustration by Kate McKeon, © ABS. **911** From My First Book of Jewish Holidays by Maida Silverman, illustrated by Barbara Garrison. Copyright © 1994 by Barbara Garrison. Used by permission of Dial Books for Young Readers, a division of Penguin Putnam Inc. **912** © Zev Radovan, Jerusalem. **916** © The Jewish Museum of New York/Art

Resource, NY. 917 Hanging of Haman and his Sons, Universitätsbibliothek Leipzig, Leipzig Mahzor, Ms Vollers 1102, Bd. 1, f. 51v. 919 Jewish Museum, New York/SuperStock. 920 *all photos* © Erich Lessing/Art Resource, NY. 922 *clockwise from top left* © Erich Lessing/Art Resource, NY. *top right* Patrick Landmann/Gamma Liaison. *bottom right* Photograph by Bencini Raffaello, Florence, Italy, © American Bible Society Archives. *center* © The Stock Market/Michele Burgess, 1994. *bottom left* © 1993 Carol Sailors. 924 *top* © David Harris, Jerusalem. *bottom* © Erich Lessing/Art Resource, NY. 927 © Erich Lessing/Art Resource, NY. 928 Map by Collin Kellogg, © ABS. 930 The Granger Collection, New York. 931 Map by Collin Kellogg, © ABS. 932 © Erich Lessing/Art Resource, NY. 933 *center* © John C. Trever. *bottom left* © The Israel Museum, Jerusalem. Photo: David Harris. *bottom right* © Jeff Greenberg/Visuals Unlimited. 936 Grec 139 f. 136v The Penitence of David, with David and Nathan, from a psalter, 10th century/Bibliothèque nationale de France/Bridgeman Art Library. 937 Woodcut print by Sally Barton Elliott, 1973. 942 Illustration by Laszlo Kubinyi, © ABS. 944, 945 Illustrations of scroll, stone tablets, ram's horn, candlesticks by Steve Morrell, © ABS. Illustration of barley by Gregor Goethals, © ABS. Illustration of loaves of bread by Theresa Heidel, © ABS. Illustration of priest with scapegoat by Hal Just, © ABS. Illustration of shelter by Kate McKeon, © ABS. 946 © Scala/Art Resource, NY. 953 Illustration by Hal Just, © ABS. *photo inset* © The Stock Market/M. Mastrorillo. 955 James L. Stanfield/National Geographic Society Image Collection. 957 © Scala/Art Resource, NY. 958 Illustration by Hal Just, © ABS. 964 Private Collection/Bridgeman Art Library, London/New York. 974 © Mary M. Thacher, The National Audubon Society Collection/Photo Researchers. 975 Collection of Camille O. and William H. Cosby, Jr. 994, 1000 Illustrations by Hal Just, © ABS. 1006 Illustration by Troy Yulfo, © ABS. 1015 Illustrations to the Book of Job, III, 45, pl.13, © The Pierpont Morgan Library/Art Resource, NY. 1021 Illustrations to the Book of Job, III, 45, pl.15, © The Pierpont Morgan Library, /Art Resource, NY. 1025 © 1991 Richard T. Nowitz. 1033 M. 730, F. 9, © The Pierpont Morgan Library/Art Resource, NY. 1036, 1039 © Erich Lessing/Art Resource, NY. 1043 © David Harris, Jerusalem. 1044 The Bodleian Library, University of Oxford, MS. Ashmole 1511, fol. 75v (detail). 1050 George Tooker, Girl Praying, 1977, egg tempera on gesso panel, 17 x 15 inches, collection unknown, courtesy DC Moore Gallery, NYC. 1071 © Scala/Art Resource, NY. 1074 Illustration by Hal Just, © ABS. 1076 From The Bible in Word and Art, 1988 edition published by Arch Cape Press, distributed by Crown Publishers, Inc., NY, © 1988 by Weiss Verlag, GmbH Dreieich, Federal Republic of Germany. 1083 Barnes Foundation, Merion, Pennsylvania/SuperStock. 1088 Illustration by Theresa Heidel, © ABS. 1093 © 1989 Richard T. Nowitz. 1103 Siegfried Wilheim/Bruce Coleman Inc. 1106 © Erich Lessing/Art Resource, NY 1108 *top* B. Anthony Stewart/National Geographic Society Image Collection. 1111 Israelites passing through the Wilderness by William West (1801-61) Bristol City Museum and Art Gallery, UK/Bridgeman Art Library. 1118 Illustration by Theresa Heidel, © ABS. 1121 Collection of Irina Rapoport. 1129 © David Harris, Jerusalem. 1132 © Scala/Art Resource, NY. 1139 Illustration by Theresa Heidel, © ABS. 1141 From the HUC Skirball Cultural Center, Museum Collection, Los Angeles, CA. Photography by John Reed Forsman. 1149 Illustration by Kate McKeon, © ABS. 1150 Cott Vesp A I f.30v King David with his court musicians, English (Canterbury), c. 730 Vespasian Psalter, (c.730)/British Library, London, UK/Bridgeman Art Library. **1156** © Zev Radovan, Jerusalem. **1157** © The Jewish Museum of New York/Art Resource, NY. **1159** Calligraphy by Karen Silver, © ABS. **1169** "The Prière" by François Cauvin. **1171** Illustration by Hal Just, © ABS. **1176** Illustration by Kate McKeon, © ABS. **1179** Photo by Werner Braun. **1180** © Tate Gallery, London/Art Resource, NY. **1190** Illustration by Hal Just, © ABS. *left photo inset* © Erich Lessing/Art Resource, NY. *center photo inset* © Zev Radovan, Jerusalem. *right photo inset* © Erich Lessing/Art Resource, NY. **1196** Illustration by Kate McKeon, © ABS. **1200** Illustration by Hal Just, © ABS. **1201** © 1991 Richard T. Nowitz. **1203** Illustration by Kate McKeon, © ABS. **1222** © Paolo Koch, The National Audubon Society Collection/Photo Researchers. **1237** The Metropolitan Museum of Art, Rogers Fund, 1906. (06.1083, 06.1085), Photograph © 1993 The Metropolitan Museum of Art. **1238** © Erich Lessing/Art Resource, NY. **1251** The Jewish Museum of New York/Superstock. **1255** "A Time to Weep and A Time to Sow, A Time to Embrace," Details from Ecclesiastes, © 1989 by John August Swanson, serigraph 22 1/2" x 28 1/4", www.JohnAugustSwanson.com. **1259** Still Life: An Allegory of the Vanities of Human Life, c. 1640 by Harmen van Steenwyck/National Gallery, London, UK Bridgeman Art Library. **1266** © The Jewish Museum of New York/Art Resource NY. **1270** Illustration by Gregor Goethals, © ABS. **1275** © Meinrad Craighead 1997, from Sacred Marriage, Nicholas Ayo, Continuum Publishers, 1997, page 243. **1276** *top* Illustration by Theresa Heidel, © ABS. *bottom* Illustration by Kate McKeon, © ABS. **1277** Illustration by Theresa Heidel, © ABS. **1292** © Sonia Halliday Photographs. **1301** © 1991 Richard T. Nowitz. **1305** Reuven Rubin, "Isaiah's Lips Being Sealed," colored lithograph from *The Prophets*, 1973. The Rubin Museum Collection, Tel-Aviv, Israel. **1311** Map by Collin Kellogg, © ABS. **1314** The Heard Museum, Phoenix, Arizona, courtesy Mrs. C. Terry Saul. **1318** Illustration by Gregor Goethals, © ABS. **1321** Map by Collin Kellogg, © ABS. **1326** Illustration by Hal Just, © ABS. *photo inset* © Louis Goldman, Photo Researchers. **1339** © Scala/Art Resource, NY. **1358** © Erich Lessing/Art Resource, NY. **1362** *clockwise from top left* Illustration by Laszlo Kubinyi, © ABS. *top center, right* © Erich Lessing/Art Resource, NY. *bottom right* Illustration by Laszlo Kubinyi, © ABS. *bottom left* © Erich Lessing/Art Resource, NY. **1368** Lu Hsu Chia, Singapore. "Mount Up with Wings," from The Bible through Asian Eyes, by M. Takenaka and R. O'Grady. **1377** © David Harris, Jerusalem. **1378** Mary Evans Picture Library. **1381** © Erich Lessing/Art Resource, NY. **1384** Courtesy, The Chaim Gross Studio Museum, New York. **1402** Illustration by Theresa Heidel, © ABS. **1408** Courtesy, The Chaim Gross Studio Museum, New York. **1417** The Peaceable Kingdom, c. 1840-45 by Edward Hicks, Brooklyn Museum of Art, New York, USA/Bridgeman Art Library. **1419** Illustration by Kate McKeon, © ABS. **1427** © Scala/Art Resource, NY. **1438** Illustration by Hal Just, © ABS. **1445** Illustration by Theresa Heidel, © ABS. **1447** The LuEsther T. Mertz Library of the New York Botanical Garden, Bronx, New York. **1466** © Zev Radovan, Jerusalem. **1467** Illustration by Hal Just, © ABS. **1483** Illustration by Gregor Goethals, © ABS. **1491** Illustration by Hal Just, © ABS. **1503** Collection of Mr. Shlomo Moussaieff. **1509** The J. Paul Getty Museum, Los Angeles, Master of Jean de Mandeville (illuminator) and Peter Comestor (author) and Guiart des Moulins (translator and author), Bible Historiale (Volume 2), about 1360-1370, detail, tempera on parchment bound between wood boards covered with eighteenth-century green morocco. Size: 13 3/4 x 10 1/4 in., 35 x 26 cm. **1528** © David Harris, Jerusalem. **1529** © Erich Lessing/Art Resource, NY. **1546** © The Jewish Museum of New York/Art Resource, NY. **1547** Illustration by Theresa Heidel, © ABS. **1551** Illustration by Hal Just, © ABS. **1555** © Scala/Art Resource, NY. **1563** Duke University Collection. **1567** © Art Resource, NY. **1579** Photograph courtesy of Dean and Chapter of Canterbury. © Sonia Halliday and Laura Lushington. **1603** *clockwise from top left* Map by Joe LeMonier, © ABS. *top right* American Museum of Natural History. *bottom right* © Erich Lessing/Art Resource, NY. *bottom left* Illustration by Kate McKeon, © ABS. **1615** © Zev Radovan, Jerusalem. **1627** © The Jewish Museum of New York/Art Resource, NY. **1633** Ezekiel's Vision of the Restored Temple, adapted from the Good News Study Bible, © British and Foreign Bible Society, 1997. **1645** © The Jewish Museum of New York/Art Resource, NY. **1648** *clockwise from top left* © Garo Nalbandian. *top right* © Zev Radovan, Jerusalem. *bottom right* © Erich Lessing/Art Resource, NY. *bottom left* Illustration by Hal Just, © ABS. **1661** MS. M. 644, f. 248v, © The Pierpont Morgan Library/Art Resource, NY. **1667** © Art Resource, NY. **1670** © Alinari/SEAT/Art Resource, NY. **1673** Archives/Photo Researchers. **1686** *Plaque with Seated Prophet from a Reliquary Shrine: Osea (Hosea)*, c. 1185. Weland Workshop, Germany, 12th century. Champlevé enamel, niello, gilt copper, 8.95 x 5.75 cm. © The Cleveland Museum of Art, 2003, Purchase from the J. H. Wade Fund, 1950.574.4. **1700** Illustration by Theresa Heidel, © ABS. **1707** Illustration by Gregor Goethals, © ABS. **1709** © David Harris, Jerusalem. **1717** Map by Collin Kellogg, © ABS. **1718** M. 81, f. 68, © The Pierpont Morgan Library/Art Resource, NY. **1730** Illustration by Kate McKeon, © ABS. **1732** Illustration by Hal Just, © ABS. *photo inset* © David Harris, Jerusalem. **1734** Illustration by Hal Just, © ABS. **1738** Annie Griffiths-Belt/National Geographic Society Image Collection. **1743** © Scala/Art Resource, NY. **1746** Illustrations by Gregor Goethals, © ABS. **1750** Map by Collin Kellogg, © ABS. **1755** Gai Muo-Seng, China. "World Peace," from The Bible through Asian Eyes, by M. Takenaka and R. O'Grady. **1765** © Erich Lessing/Art Resource, NY. **1766** Illustration by Kate McKeon, © ABS. **1773, 1783** Illustrations by Gregor Goethals, © ABS. **1790** From The Bible in Word and Art, 1988 edition published by Arch Cape Press, distributed by Crown Publishers, Inc., NY, © 1988 by Weiss Verlag, GmbH Dreieich, Federal Republic of Germany. **1794** The LuEsther T. Mertz Library of the New York Botanical Garden, Bronx, New York. **1797** Private Collection/Mark Ari/SuperStock. **1799** From The Doré Bible Illustrations, © 1974 by Dover Publications, Inc. **1810, 1811** Illustrations by Kate McKeon, © ABS. **1817** Michel Schwartz. **1821** © Erich Lessing/Art Resource, NY. **1823** © North Wind Picture Archives. **1826, 1827, 1828** Illustrations by Hal Just, © ABS. **1829** Illustrations by Hal Just, © ABS. *top left photo inset* © Joyce Photographics, The National Audubon Society Collection/Photo Researchers, NY. *top right* photo inset © 1997 Richard T. Nowitz. **1834** Statuette of the goddess Isis and the child Horus, Egyptian, Late Period (c. 664-332 bc) Louvre, Paris, France/Peter Willi/Bridgeman Art Library. **1835** © Erich Lessing/Art Resource, NY. **1836** © Vanni/Art Resource, NY. **1841** © Erich Lessing/Art Resource, NY.**1847** Photograph by Gregor Goethals. **1850** By permission of the British Library, OR. 607 f. 14v. **1856** Illustration by Gregor Goethals, © ABS. **1858** *clockwise from top left* © David Harris, Jerusalem. *top center* © 1997 David Sailors. *right* Map by Joe LeMonier, ©

ABS. *bottom left* © 1997 David Sailors. **1859** © Scala/Art Resource, NY. **1863, 1864** Illustrations by Gregor Goethals, © ABS. **1867** R. Koiso/Japan Bible Society. **1878** Illustration by Gregor Goethals, © ABS. **1880** Photograph by Gregor Goethals. **1881** Worcester Art Museum, Worcester, Massachusetts. **1890** Illustration by Gregor Goethals, © ABS. **1891** Illustration by Hal Just, © ABS. **1892, 1894** Illustrations by Gregor Goethals, © ABS. **1895** The Minneapolis Institute of Arts. **1897** Courtesy of Cecilia Ross. Reprined by permission of Harold Ober Associates Incorporated. **1899** Illustration by Gregor Goethals, © ABS. **1902** *top left and bottom right* Yale University Art Gallery, Dura-Europos Archive. *top right* Photograph by Gregor Goethals. *bottom left* Illustration by Gregor Goethals, © ABS. **1905** Gui-jie Zhang. **1906, 1908** Illustrations by Gregor Goethals, © ABS. **1913** S.M.A. Fathers. **1914** Illustration by Hal Just, © ABS. **1920** © Scala/Art Resource, NY. **1923** Illustration by Hal Just, © ABS. *photo inset* © David Harris, Jerusalem. **1924** Illustration by Hal Just, © ABS. **1929** Hessische Landes- und Hochschulbibliothek Darmstadt, Hs 1640, fol. 117r (Hitda-Codex). **1931** © Erich Lessing/Art Resource, NY. **1934** Ernesto Cardenal. **1940** © Scala/Art Resource, NY. **1948** © Sonia Halliday Photographs, photo by F. H. C. Birch. **1949** © Art Resource, NY. **1952** Reprinted from Imaging the Word, Volume 1, page 64. © 1994 by United Church Press.**1953** Armenian Gospel Iconography: The Tradition of the Glajor Gospel, Department of Special Collections, Young Research Library, UCLA. **1954** Illustration by Gregor Goethals, © ABS. **1959** © Boltin Picture Library. **1962** © Scala/Art Resource, NY. **1968** © Giraudon/Art Resource, NY. **1971** © David Harris, Jerusalem. **1970** © Erich Lessing/Art Resource, NY. **1972, 1975** Illustrations by Hal Just, © ABS. **1977** © Giraudon/Art Resource, NY. **1980** Illustration by Hal Just, © ABS. **1981** *center* Map by Joe LeMonier, © ABS. *top center* Illustration by Theresa Heidel, © ABS. *top right* © Sonia Halliday Photographs, photo by Jane Taylor. *bottom right, center* Illustrations by Theresa Heidel, © ABS. *far left* © Gil Yarom, Israel. *near left* Photographer: Shalom Zisso, The Israel Department of Antiquities, The Yigal Allon Museum. **1983** © Scala/Art Resource, NY. **1985** Illustration by Hal Just, © ABS. **1994** Illustration by Theresa Heidel, © ABS. **1999** Illustration by Hal Just, © ABS. *top left photo inset* Collection of the Israel Antiquities Authority, courtesy of the G. Barkay, Ketef Hinnom Expedition. *top right photo inset* Photograph by Bencini Raffaello, Florence, Italy, © American Bible Society Archives. **2000** Vincent Van Gogh, Stichting Kröller-Müller Museum. **2005** Illustration by Theresa Heidel, © ABS. **2008** © Erich Lessing/Art Resource, NY. **2012** Illustration by Gregor Goethals, © ABS. **2013** © Scala/Art Resource, NY. **2015** © Vanni/Art Resource, NY. **2017** Photo copyright Julia Hedgecoe, from Stories in Stone: The Medieval Roof Carvings of Norwich Cathedral, Herbert Press, A & C Black, London; Thames & Hudson, N. Y. **2031** Illustration by Hal Just, © ABS. *photo inset* © The Jewish Museum of New York/Art Resource, NY. **2032** By permission of the British Library, OR. 481, f. 104v. **2034** Illustration by Hal Just, © ABS. **3035** © Smithsonian American Art Museum, Washington DC/Art Resource, NY. **2038** Karl Schmidt-Rottluff, *Way to Emmaus*, 1918, Philadelphia Museum of Art: Gift of Dr. George J. Roth. **2046** Illustration by Hal Just, © ABS. **2051** Hatigammana Uttarananda, Sri Lanka. "Woman at the Well," from The Bible through Asian Eyes, by M. Takenaka and R. O'Grady. **2057** Samuel H. Kress Collection, © 1997 Board of Trustees, National Gallery of Art, Washington. **2059** Illustration by Hal

Just, © ABS. **2064** The Saint Louis Art Museum: bequest of Curt Valentin. **2068** S.M.A. Fathers. **2069** © G. Dagli Orti, Paris. **2074** © Erich Lessing/Art Resource, NY. **2079** Jyoti Sahi, Bangalore, India. "Washing the Feet," from The Bible through Asian Eyes, by M. Takenaka and R. O'Grady. **2083** © Zev Radovan, Jerusalem. **2089** © Erich Lessing/Art Resource, NY. **2092** Illustration by Gregor Goethals, © ABS. **2093** SuperStock. **2095** Illustration by Gregor Goethals, © ABS. **2097** Michael Smither, Taranaki, New Zealand, "Doubting Thomas," from The Bible through Asian Eyes, by M. Takenaka and R. O'Grady. **2100** Illustration by Gregor Goethals, © ABS. **2104** © Giraudon/Art Resource, NY. **2116** © Erich Lessing/Art Resource, NY. **2119** Illustration by Kate McKeon, © ABS. **2120** ***top*** © Ronald Sheridan/Ancient Art & Archtecture Collection. ***bottom*** William Curtsinger/National Geographic Society Image Collection. **2122** © Erich Lessing/Art Resource, NY. **2130** Illustrations by Hal Just, © ABS. ***top right photo inset*** © David Harris, Jerusalem. **2142, 2144** © Erich Lessing/Art Resource, NY. **2145** ***top left*** Courtesy Greek National Tourist Organization. ***top right*** The Metropolitan Museum of Art, Catharine Lorillard Wolfe Collection, Wolfe Fund, 1931. (31.45). Photograph © 1995 The Metropolitan Museum of Art. ***bottom center*** Illustration by Laszlo Kubinyi, © ABS. ***bottom left*** © The Stock Market/David Ball. **2147** Illustration by Hal Just, © ABS. **2150** ***top left and right*** John M. Lundquist. ***bottom center*** Illustration by Laszlo Kubinyi, © ABS. **2156** © Scala/Art Resource, NY. **2159** © Zev Radovan, Jerusalem. **2165** Illustration by Kate McKeon, © ABS. **2166** Sister Clare, Bagalore, India, "Shipwreck," from The Bible through Asian Eyes, by M. Takenaka and R. O'Grady. **2176** © Erich Lessing/Art Resource, NY. **2184** Marti Shohet. **2190** © Zev Radovan, Jerusalem. **2193, 2202** Illustrations by Kate McKeon, © ABS. **2209** © Erich Lessing/Art Resource, NY. **2215** Illustration by Theresa Heidel, © ABS. **2218** Sadao Watanabe, Japan. "The Last Supper," from The Bible through Asian Eyes, by M. Takenaka and R. O'Grady. **2222** ***top*** Robert Indiana, Love. 1967. Screenprint, printed in color, composition: 33 15/16 x 33 15/16. The Museum of Modern Art, New York. Riva Castleman Fund. Photograph © 1999 The Museum of Modern Art, New York. ***bottom*** © Erich Lessing/Art Resource, NY. **2223** © Zev Radovan, Jerusalem. **2235** ***top*** © Zev Radovan, Jerusalem. ***bottom*** Illustration by Hal Just, © ABS. **2243** Illustration by Kate McKeon, © ABS. **2245** © Erich Lessing/Art Resource, NY. **2253** © Giraudon/Art Resource, NY. **2255** © Erich Lessing/Art Resource, NY. **2257** S.M.A. Fathers. **2260** Map by Collin Kellogg, © ABS. **2263** Illustration by Hal Just © ABS. **2268** © Erich Lessing/Art Resource, NY. **2269** © Photothèque des Musées de Ville de Paris/Pierrain. **2271** Map by Collin Kellogg, © ABS. **2273** © Zev Radovan, Jerusalem. **2274** © Scala/Art Resource, NY. **2275** © Erich Lessing/Art Resource, NY. **2279** © Robert Frerck/Odyssey/Chicago. **2281** Map by Collin Kellogg, © ABS. **2283** "God Creating the World," from Bible Moralisée, Codex # 2554, Austrian National Library, Vienna. **2290** Reproduced by kind permission of the Trustees of the Chester Beatty Library, Dublin. **2294** © Werner Forman/Art Resource, NY. **2298** Map by Collin Kellogg, © ABS. **2303** Illustration by Hal Just, © ABS. **2304** © Giraudon/Art Resource, NY. **2307** © Borromeo/Art Resource, NY. **2309** © Erich Lessing/Art Resource, NY. **2311** Photo by Malcolm Varon, N.Y.C., © 1993. Courtesy Institute of Ethiopian Studies. **2313** Gui-jie Zhang, courtesy of Mission Interpretation and Promotion, Congregational Ministries Division, Presbyterian Church (USA). **2314, 2317** © Zev

Radovan, Jerusalem. **2321** ***clockwise from top left*** Richard T. Nowitz/National Geographic Society Image Collection. ***center*** Licensed by the Trustees of the British Museum, © The British Museum. ***top right*** Charles Phelphs/National Geographic Society Image Collection. ***bottom right*** © The Stock Market/Lance Nelson. ***bottom left*** Coin bearing the portrait of Emperor Gaius Julius Ceasar Octavianus Augustus (63 bc-14 ad), Roman, 1st century ad (gold)/Museo Archeologico Nazionale, Naples, Italy/Bridgeman Art Library. **2340** © Zev Radovan, Jerusalem. **2342** © Scala/Art Resource, NY. **2345** Illustration by Hal Just, © ABS. **2353** Photos copyright Julia Hedgecoe, from Stories in Stone: The Medieval Roof Carvings of Norwich Cathedral, Herbert Press, A & C Black, London; Thames & Hudson, N.Y. **2356** © Dave Bartruff/The Image Works. **2363** © Scala/Art Resource, NY. **2364** Illustration by Kate McKeon, © ABS. **2367** Illustration by Hal Just, © ABS. **2371** © Scala/Art Resource, NY. **2373** Gold coin of the Roman Emperor Nero (ad 54-68) Private Collection/Bridgeman Art Library. **2374** © John Ross/Art Resource, NY. **2378, 2380** © Erich Lessing/Art Resource, NY. **2386** The Bridgeman Art Library International Ltd/London/New York. **2393** Photo copyright Julia Hedgecoe, from Stories in Stone: The Medieval Roof Carvings of Norwich Cathedral, Herbert Press, A & C Black, London; Thames & Hudson, N.Y. **2403** Illustration by Gregor Goethals, © ABS. **2404** Plate showing Tree of Life, by Bernard Leach, 1923, Victoria & Albert Museum, London, UK/Bridgeman Art Library. **2407** ***top*** © Giraudon/Art Resource, NY. ***bottom*** © The Jewish Museum of New York/Art Resource, NY. **2409** ***clockwise from top left*** © Vanni/Art Resource, NY. ***top right*** © The Stock Market/Oddo and Sinibaldi. ***bottom right*** © Bildarchiv Preussischer Kulturbesitz, Berlin, photograph by Reinhard Saczewski. ***bottom left*** Map by Joe LeMonier, © ABS. **2412** Gui-jie Zhang. **2414** Illustration by Gregor Goethals, © ABS. **2415** © Scala/Art Resource, NY. **2417** © Foto Marburg/Art Resource, NY. **2419** Reproduced by courtesy of the Director and University Librarian, the John Rylands University Library of Manchester. **2425** © Cameraphoto Arte, Venice/Art Resource, NY. **2428** Illustration by Kate McKeon, © ABS. **2431** © Zev Radovan, Jerusalem. **2433** © Werner Forman/Art Resource, NY. **2439** © Giraudon/Art Resource, NY. **2440** Jasper © Biophoto Associates/Photo Researchers. Sapphire, chalcedony, emerald © Jeff Scovil. Sardonyx © E. R. Degginger. Carnelian, chrysolite, beryl, topaz © Jeff Scovil. Chryosprase © A. J. Copley/Visuals Unlimited. Jacinth, amethyst © Jeff Scovil. **2462 - 2477** Maps by Joe LeMonier, © ABS.

Sharing God's Word with the World

This Bible represents a legacy of translating God's Word into the language of the people—into languages that will bring the Scriptures to life in the hearts of readers and hearers. The American Bible Society works with scholars from many countries to faithfully translate the Scriptures into languages and formats that speak clearly to both mind and heart. We encourage people everywhere to engage with the inspired Word of God—to embody its message and to experience a relationship with God through its reading.

To this end the American Bible Society, a not-for-profit Christian organization, offers programs to churches, other Bible-centered organizations, and individuals that connect people with God's living Word, and support the work of more than 100 other Bible Societies worldwide. Since our founding in 1816, people have generously supported the American Bible Society in its global mission to translate, publish, and provide Scriptures that are easily understood and affordable. In many areas of the world, and even within the United States, the cost of a Bible often represents a hardship for many who thirst for God's Word. Thanks to the faithful support of many individuals, churches, and ministry partners, the American Bible Society continues to respond to the Scripture needs of the underserved and under engaged through effective programs and ministry partnerships.

We invite you to participate with us as we share God's Word with the world. To find how, please contact us at:

American Bible Society
1865 Broadway
New York, New York 10023-7505
www.americanbible.org
1-888-227-8262